HOLY BIBLE

HOLY BIBLE

NEW INTERNATIONAL VERSION

ZONDERVAN®

www.Zondervan.com

Library of Congress Catalog Card Number 2015946797

Printed in China

24 25 26 27 28 29 30 31 32 /DSC/ 20 19 18 17 16 15 14 13 12 11

Table of Contents

Old Testament

New Testament

Abbreviations of Books of the Bible

The Old Testament

Book	Abbreviation	Book	Abbreviation
Genesis	Gen.	Ecclesiastes	Eccl.
Exodus	Ex.	Song of Songs	Song
Leviticus	Lev.	Isaiah	Is.
Numbers	Num.	Jeremiah	Jer.
Deuteronomy	Deut.	Lamentations	Lam.
Joshua	Josh.	Ezekiel	Ezek.
Judges	Judg.	Daniel	Dan.
Ruth	Ruth	Hosea	Hos.
1 Samuel	1 Sam.	Joel	Joel
2 Samuel	2 Sam.	Amos	Amos
1 Kings	1 Kin.	Obadiah	Obad.
2 Kings	2 Kin.	Jonah	Jon.
1 Chronicles	1 Chr.	Micah	Mic.
2 Chronicles	2 Chr.	Nahum	Nah.
Ezra	Ezra	Habakkuk	Hab.
Nehemiah	Neh.	Zephaniah	Zeph.
Esther	Esth.	Haggai	Hag.
Job	Job	Zechariah	Zech.
Psalms	Ps.	Malachi	Mal.
Proverbs	Prov.		

The New Testament

Book	Abbreviation	Book	Abbreviation
Matthew	Matt.	1 Timothy	1 Tim.
Mark	Mark	2 Timothy	2 Tim.
Luke	Luke	Titus	Titus
John	John	Philemon	Philem.
Acts	Acts	Hebrews	Heb.
Romans	Rom.	James	James
1 Corinthians	1 Cor.	1 Peter	1 Pet.
2 Corinthians	2 Cor.	2 Peter	2 Pet.
Galatians	Gal.	1 John	1 John
Ephesians	Eph.	2 John	2 John
Philippians	Phil.	3 John	3 John
Colossians	Col.	Jude	Jude
1 Thessalonians	1 Thess.	Revelation	Rev.
2 Thessalonians	2 Thess.		

Introduction to This Study Bible

This basic study Bible is designed to provide a foundation for Bible study. It is intended for both beginning and experienced students of the Scriptures who want a Bible that contains the key features of a study Bible in a convenient, compact, and concise form.

Features include:

- The full text of the New International Version of the Bible. The New International Version is the world's most-read and most-trusted modern-English Bible translation—easy to understand, yet rich with the detail found in the original languages. The NIV is the result of over 50 years of work by the Committee on Bible Translation, overseeing the efforts of many contributing scholars. Their calling is to ensure that the NIV remains at the forefront of accessibility, relevance, and authority.
- Concise study notes are trusted, time-tested, and application-oriented, providing succinct comments on passages of Scripture.
- Theological notes draw attention to important doctrinal content in the Bible. These notes are signified by a bold Roman heading followed by a dash. They are indexed in the back of the Bible both by title and by location.
- In-text subject headings help to organize and illuminate Bible reading and study.
- Book introductions give background information about each of the Bible's 66 books.
- Cross-references direct attention to other passages for further study of words and concepts in Scripture. Conceptual cross-references are indicated by square brackets.
- A concordance provides an alphabetical listing of important passages by key words.

Preface to the New International Version

Preface

The goal of the New International Version (NIV) is to enable English-speaking people from around the world to read and hear God's eternal Word in their own language. Our work as translators is motivated by our conviction that the Bible is God's Word in written form. We believe that the Bible contains the divine answer to the deepest needs of humanity, sheds unique light on our path in a dark world and sets forth the way to our eternal well-being. Out of these deep convictions, we have sought to recreate as far as possible the experience of the original audience—blending transparency to the original text with accessibility for the millions of English speakers around the world. We have prioritized accuracy, clarity and literary quality with the goal of creating a translation suitable for public and private reading, evangelism, teaching, preaching, memorizing and liturgical use. We have also sought to preserve a measure of continuity with the long tradition of translating the Scriptures into English.

The complete NIV Bible was first published in 1978. It was a completely new translation made by over a hundred scholars working directly from the best available Hebrew, Aramaic and Greek texts. The translators came from the United States, Great Britain, Canada, Australia and New Zealand, giving the translation an international scope. They were from many denominations and churches—including Anglican, Assemblies of God, Baptist, Brethren, Christian Reformed, Church of Christ, Evangelical Covenant, Evangelical Free, Lutheran, Mennonite, Methodist, Nazarene, Presbyterian, Wesleyan and others. This breadth of denominational and theological perspective helped to safeguard the translation from sectarian bias. For these reasons, and by the grace of God, the NIV has gained a wide readership in all parts of the English-speaking world.

The work of translating the Bible is never finished. As good as they are, English translations must be regularly updated so that they will continue to communicate accurately the meaning of God's Word. Updates are needed in order to reflect the latest developments in our understanding of the biblical world and its languages and to keep pace with changes in English usage. Recognizing, then, that the NIV would retain its ability to communicate God's Word accurately only if it were regularly updated, the original translators established the Committee on Bible Translation (CBT). The Committee is a self-perpetuating group of biblical scholars charged with keeping abreast of advances in biblical scholarship and changes in English and issuing periodic updates to the NIV. The CBT is an independent, self-governing body and has sole responsibility for the NIV text. The Committee mirrors the original group of translators in its diverse international and denominational makeup and in its unifying commitment to the Bible as God's inspired Word.

In obedience to its mandate, the Committee has issued periodic updates to the NIV. An initial revision was released in 1984. A more thorough revision process was completed in 2005, resulting in the separately published TNIV. The updated NIV you now have in your hands builds on both the original NIV and the TNIV and represents the latest effort of the Committee to articulate God's unchanging Word in the way the original authors might have said it had they been speaking in English to the global English-speaking audience today.

Translation Philosophy

The Committee's translating work has been governed by three widely accepted principles about the way people use words and about the way we understand them.

First, the meaning of words is determined by the way that users of the language actually use them at any given time. For the biblical languages, therefore, the Committee utilizes the best and most recent scholarship on the way Hebrew, Aramaic and Greek words were being used in biblical times. At the same time, the Committee carefully studies the state of modern English. Good translation is like good communication: one must know the target audience so that the appropriate choices can be made about which English words to use to represent the original words of Scripture. From its inception, the NIV has had as its target the general English-speaking population all over the world, the "International" in its title reflecting this concern. The aim of the Committee is to put the Scriptures into natural English that will communicate effectively with the broadest possible audience of English speakers.

Modern technology has enhanced the Committee's ability to choose the right English words to convey the meaning of the original text. The field of computational linguistics harnesses the power of computers to provide broadly applicable and current data about the state of the language. Translators can now access huge databases of modern English to better understand the current meaning and usage of key words. The Committee utilized this resource in preparing the 2011 edition of the NIV. An area of especially rapid and significant change in English is the way certain nouns and pronouns are used to refer to human beings. The Committee therefore requested experts in computational linguistics at Collins Dictionaries to pose some key questions about this usage to its database of English—the largest in the world, with over 4.4 billion words, gathered from several English-speaking countries and including both spoken and written English. (The Collins Study, called "The Development and Use of Gender Language in Contemporary English," can be accessed at *http://www.thenivbible.com/about-the-niv/about-the-2011-edition/.*) The study revealed that the most popular words to describe the human race in modern U.S. English were "humanity," "man" and "mankind." The Committee then used this data in the updated NIV, choosing from among these three words (and occasionally others also) depending on the context.

A related issue creates a larger problem for modern translations: the move away from using the third-person masculine singular pronouns—"he/him/his"—to refer to men and women equally. This usage does persist in some forms of English, and this revision therefore occasionally uses these pronouns in a generic sense. But the tendency, recognized in day-to-day usage and confirmed by the Collins study, is away from the generic use of "he," "him" and "his." In recognition of this shift in language and in an effort to translate into the natural English that people are actually using, this revision of the NIV generally uses other constructions when the biblical text is plainly addressed to men and women equally. The reader will encounter especially frequently a "they," "their" or "them" to express a generic singular idea. Thus, for instance, Mark 8:36 reads: "What good is it for someone to gain the whole world, yet forfeit their soul?" This generic use of the "distributive" or "singular" "they/them/their" has been used for many centuries by respected writers of English and has now become established as standard English, spoken and written, all over the world.

A second linguistic principle that feeds into the Committee's translation work is that meaning is found not in individual words, as vital as they are, but in larger clusters: phrases, clauses, sentences, discourses. Translation is not, as many people think, a matter of word substitution: English word *x* in place of Hebrew word *y*. Translators must first determine the meaning of the words of the biblical languages in the context of the passage and then select English words that accurately communicate that meaning to modern listeners and readers. This means that accurate translation will not always reflect the exact structure of the original language. To be sure, there is debate over the degree to which translators should try to preserve the "form" of the original text in English. From the beginning, the NIV has taken a mediating position on this issue. The manual produced when the translation that became the NIV was first being planned states: "If the Greek or Hebrew syntax has a good parallel in modern English, it should be used. But if there is no good parallel, the English syntax appropriate to the meaning of the original is to be chosen." It is fine, in other words, to carry over the form of the biblical languages into English—but not at the expense of natural expression. The principle that meaning resides in larger clusters of words means that the Committee has not insisted on a "word-for-word" approach to translation. We certainly believe that every word of Scripture is inspired by God and therefore to be carefully studied to determine what God is saying to us. It is for this reason that the Committee labors over every single word of the original texts, working hard to determine how each of those words contributes to what the text is saying. Ultimately, however, it is how these individual words function in combination with other words that determines meaning.

A third linguistic principle guiding the Committee in its translation work is the recognition that words have a spectrum of meaning. It is popular to define a word by using another word, or "gloss," to substitute for it. This substitute word is then sometimes called the "literal" meaning of a word. In fact, however, words have a range of possible meanings. Those meanings will vary depending on the context, and words in one language will usually not occupy the same semantic range as words in another language. The Committee therefore studies each original word of Scripture in its context to identify its meaning in a particular verse and then chooses an appropriate English word (or phrase) to represent it. It is impossible, then, to translate any given Hebrew, Aramaic or Greek word with the same English word all the time. The Committee does try to translate related occurrences of a word in the original languages with the same English word in order to preserve the connection for the English reader. But the Committee generally privileges clear natural meaning over a concern with consistency in rendering particular words.

Textual Basis

For the Old Testament the standard Hebrew text, the Masoretic Text as published in the latest edition of *Biblia Hebraica*, has been used throughout. The Masoretic Text tradition contains marginal notations that offer variant readings. These have sometimes been followed instead of the text itself. Because such instances involve variants within the Masoretic tradition, they have not been indicated in the textual notes. In a few cases, words in the basic consonantal text have been divided differently than in the Masoretic Text. Such cases are usually indicated in the textual footnotes. The Dead Sea Scrolls contain biblical texts that represent an earlier stage of the transmission of the Hebrew text. They have been consulted, as have been the Samaritan Pentateuch and the ancient scribal traditions concerning deliberate textual changes. The translators also consulted the more important early versions. Readings from these versions, the Dead Sea Scrolls and the scribal traditions were occasionally followed where the Masoretic Text seemed doubtful and where accepted principles of textual criticism showed that one or more of these textual witnesses appeared to provide the correct reading. In rare cases, the translators have emended the Hebrew text where it appears to have become corrupted at an even earlier stage of its transmission. These departures from the Masoretic Text are also indicated in the textual footnotes. Sometimes the vowel indicators (which are later additions to the basic consonantal text) found in the Masoretic Text did not, in the judgment of the translators, represent the correct vowels for the original text. Accordingly, some words have been read with a different set of vowels. These instances are usually not indicated in the footnotes.

The Greek text used in translating the New Testament has been an eclectic one, based on the latest editions of the Nestle-Aland/United Bible Societies' Greek New Testament. The translators have made their choices among the variant readings in accordance with widely accepted principles of New Testament textual criticism. Footnotes call attention to places where uncertainty remains.

The New Testament authors, writing in Greek, often quote the Old Testament from its ancient Greek version, the Septuagint. This is one reason why some of the Old Testament quotations in the NIV New Testament are not identical to the corresponding passages in the NIV Old Testament. Such quotations in the New Testament are indicated with the footnote "(see Septuagint)."

Footnotes and Formatting

Footnotes in this version are of several kinds, most of which need no explanation. Those giving alternative translations begin with "Or" and generally introduce the alternative with the last word preceding it in the text, except when it is a single-word alternative. When poetry is quoted in a footnote a slash mark indicates a line division.

It should be noted that references to diseases, minerals, flora and fauna, architectural details, clothing, jewelry, musical instruments and other articles cannot always be identified with precision. Also, linear measurements and measures of capacity can only be approximated (see the Table of Weights and Measures). Although *Selah*, used mainly in the Psalms, is probably a musical term, its meaning is uncertain. Since it may interrupt reading and distract the reader, this word has not been kept in the English text, but every occurrence has been signaled by a footnote.

As an aid to the reader, sectional headings have been inserted. They are not to be regarded as part of the biblical text and are not intended for oral reading. It is the Committee's hope that these headings may prove more helpful to the reader than the traditional chapter divisions, which were introduced long after the Bible was written.

Sometimes the chapter and/or verse numbering in English translations of the Old Testament differs from that found in published Hebrew texts. This is particularly the case in the Psalms, where the traditional titles are included in the Hebrew verse numbering. Such differences are indicated in the footnotes at the bottom of the page. In the New Testament, verse numbers that marked off portions of the traditional English text not supported by the best Greek manuscripts now appear in brackets, with a footnote indicating the text that has been omitted (see, for example, Matthew 17:[21]).

Mark 16:9–20 and John 7:53—8:11, although long accorded virtually equal status with the rest of the Gospels in which they stand, have a questionable standing in the textual history of the New Testament, as noted in the bracketed annotations with which they are set off. A different typeface has been chosen for these passages to indicate their uncertain status.

Basic formatting of the text, such as lining the poetry, paragraphing (both prose and poetry), setting up of (administrative-like) lists, indenting letters and lengthy prayers within narratives and the insertion of sectional headings, has been the work of the Committee. However, the choice between single-column and double-column formats has been left to the publishers. Also the issuing of "red-letter" editions is a publisher's choice—one that the Committee does not endorse.

The Committee has again been reminded that every human effort is flawed—including this revision of the NIV. We trust, however, that many will find in it an improved representation of the Word of God, through which they hear his call to faith in our Lord Jesus Christ and to service in his kingdom. We offer this version of the Bible to him in whose name and for whose glory it has been made.

THE COMMITTEE ON
BIBLE TRANSLATION

THE OLD TESTAMENT

GENESIS

▶ **AUTHOR:** Nowhere in the Book of Genesis is the author named. Although the events of the book end 300 years before Moses was born, the rest of the Bible and most of church historians attribute the authorship of Genesis to Moses. Both the Old and New Testaments have many references to Moses as its author (Ex. 7:14; Lev. 1:1–2; Num. 33:2; Deut. 1:1; Dan. 9:11–13; Mal. 4:4; Matt. 8:4; Mark 12:26; Luke 16:29; John 7:19; Acts 26:22; Rom. 10:19). Both early Jewish and Christian writers name Moses as the author.

▶ **TIME:** c. 4000–1804 B.C. ▶ **KEY VERSE:** Gen. 3:15

▶ **THEME:** After the initial story of the world's creation, Genesis (beginnings) covers two basic subjects: God and man. God creates man. Man disobeys God and alienates himself from God. Genesis is the story then of the subsequent interactions between God and man that bring them back together into a right relationship. As such, the book points to the beginnings of the way of change, of restoration, and of a new way of life. Genesis sets the tone for the rest of the Bible with clear teaching on following God's call, believing in His promises, and being obedient to His commands. The main characters who dominate the story are the patriarchs: Abraham, Isaac, Jacob, and Joseph.

The Beginning

1 In the beginning[a] God created the
heavens and the earth.[b] 2 Now the
earth was formless and empty,[c] darkness was over the surface of the deep,
and the Spirit of God[d] was hovering
over the waters.

3 And God said,[e] "Let there be light," and
there was light.[f] 4 God saw that the
light was good, and he separated the
light from the darkness. 5 God called
the light "day," and the darkness he
called "night."[g] And there was evening, and there was morning—the
first day.
6 And God said, "Let there be a vault[h] between the waters to separate water
from water." 7 So God made the vault
and separated the water under the
vault from the water above it.[i] And it
was so. 8 God called the vault "sky."
And there was evening, and there was
morning—the second day.
9 And God said, "Let the water under the
sky be gathered to one place,[j] and let
dry ground appear." And it was so.
10 God called the dry ground "land,"

1:1 Creation—Biblical revelation begins with a simple, strong, and sublime affirmation. Instead of arguing the existence of God, it declares that the very existence of the universe depends on the creative power of God. The world we live in was created by God and belongs to Him. His absolute ownership requires our faithful stewardship of all things.

1:1 *In the beginning.* No information is given to us about what happened before the creation of the physical universe, though John 1:1 speaks of this time. It is possible that the rise, rebellion, and judgment of Satan transpired before the events of this chapter. ***God.*** This standard Hebrew term for deity *Elohim* is in the form called the plural of majesty or plural of intensity. In contrast to the ordinary plural (gods), this plural means "the fullness of deity" or "God very God." Furthermore, the use of the plural allows for the later revelation of the Trinity (see 11:7; Matt. 28:19; John 1:1–3).

1:3 *Let there be light.* These words express a principal theme of the Bible: God bringing light into darkness (see Is. 9:1–2). Here, God produced physical light. The New Testament records God sending His Son to be the light of the world (John 8:12), bringing release from the spiritual darkness of bondage to sin. In the end, there will no longer be any darkness at all and we will be face to face with the source of light (Rev. 21:23).

1:7 *separated the water.* The description of upper and lower waters is somewhat mysterious; it has been theorized that this is simply a reference to the division between the water of the seas and rivers on the surface of the earth and the water vapor which is part of the atmosphere.

1:1 [a] Jn 1:1-2 [b] Job 38:4; Ps 90:2; Isa 42:5; 44:24; 45:12, 18; Ac 17:24; Heb 11:3; Rev 4:11 **1:2** [c] Jer 4:23 [d] Ps 104:30 **1:3** [e] Ps 33:6, 9; 148:5; Heb 11:3 [f] 2Co 4:6* **1:5** [g] Ps 74:16 **1:6** [h] Jer 10:12 **1:7** [i] Job 38:8-11, 16; Ps 148:4 **1:9** [j] Job 38:8-11; Ps 104:6-9; Pr 8:29; Jer 5:22; 2Pe 3:5

and the gathered waters he called
"seas." And God saw that it was good.
[11]Then God said, "Let the land produce vegetation:[k] seed-bearing plants
and trees on the land that bear fruit
with seed in it, according to their various kinds." And it was so. [12]The land
produced vegetation: plants bearing
seed according to their kinds and trees
bearing fruit with seed in it according
to their kinds. And God saw that it was
good. [13]And there was evening, and
there was morning—the third day.
[14]And God said, "Let there be lights[l] in the
vault of the sky to separate the day
from the night, and let them serve as
signs[m] to mark sacred times,[n] and days
and years, [15]and let them be lights in
the vault of the sky to give light on the
earth." And it was so. [16]God made two
great lights—the greater light to govern[o] the day and the lesser light to govern[p] the night. He also made the stars.[q]
[17]God set them in the vault of the sky
to give light on the earth, [18]to govern
the day and the night,[r] and to separate light from darkness. And God
saw that it was good. [19]And there was
evening, and there was morning—the
fourth day.
[20]And God said, "Let the water teem with
living creatures, and let birds fly
above the earth across the vault of
the sky." [21]So God created the great
creatures of the sea and every living
thing with which the water teems and
that moves about in it,[s] according to
their kinds, and every winged bird according to its kind. And God saw that
it was good. [22]God blessed them and
said, "Be fruitful and increase in number and fill the water in the seas, and
let the birds increase on the earth."[t]
[23]And there was evening, and there
was morning—the fifth day.
[24]And God said, "Let the land produce
living creatures according to their
kinds: the livestock, the creatures that
move along the ground, and the wild
animals, each according to its kind."
And it was so. [25]God made the wild
animals[u] according to their kinds, the
livestock according to their kinds, and
all the creatures that move along the
ground according to their kinds. And
God saw that it was good.
[26]Then God said, "Let us[v] make
mankind in our image,[w] in our likeness, so that they may rule[x] over the
fish in the sea and the birds in the sky,
over the livestock and all the wild animals,[a] and over all the creatures that
move along the ground."

[27]So God created mankind in his own
image,[y]
in the image of God he created them;
male and female[z] he created them.

[28]God blessed them and said to
them, "Be fruitful and increase in
number; fill the earth[a] and subdue it.
Rule over the fish in the sea and the
birds in the sky and over every living
creature that moves on the ground."
[29]Then God said, "I give you every

a *26* Probable reading of the original Hebrew text (see Syriac); Masoretic Text *the earth*

1:11 – 12 *seed . . . kinds.* God not only created plant life; He also set in motion the process that makes plant life reproduce.

1:14 *for signs to mark sacred times.* Some have mistakenly viewed these words as a biblical basis for astrology. The signs in this case relate to phases of the moon and the relative positions of stars that mark the passage of time from the vantage point of earth. The two words form a pair that may be translated *seasonal signs.*

1:16 *He also made the stars.* This is a remarkable statement. In the ancient Middle East, other religions worshipped, deified, and mystified the stars. Israel's neighbors revered the stars and looked to them for guidance. In contrast, the biblical creation story gives the stars only the barest mention, as though the writer shrugged and said, *And, oh, yes, He also made the stars.* Such a statement showed great contempt for ancient Babylonian astrology (Ps. 29; 93).

1:24 *living creatures.* This expression contains the word sometimes used for the soul, but the word can also mean "life," "being," "living thing," or "person," depending on the context. The same phrase is used for man in 2:7.

1:26 *in our image.* Since God is spirit (John 4:24), there can be no "image" or "likeness" of Him in the normal sense of these words. The traditional view of this passage is that God's image in man is in specific moral, ethical, and intellectual abilities. A more recent view, based on a possible interpretation of Hebrew grammar and the knowledge of the Middle East, interprets the phrase as meaning "Let Us make man *as* our image." In ancient times an emperor might command statues of himself to be placed in remote parts of his empire. These symbols would declare that these areas were under his power and reign. So God placed humankind as living symbols of Himself on earth to represent His reign. This interpretation fits well with the command that follows—to reign over all that God has made.

1:28 *fill the earth and subdue it.* The word translated *subdue* means "bring into bondage." This harsh term is used elsewhere of military conquest (Zech. 9:15) and of God subduing our iniquities (Mic. 7:19). Since this direction was given before the fall, it appears that the need to subdue the earth is not because of sin but because God left part of the arranging and ordering of the creation as work for mankind to do. Whatever the case, subdue does not

1:11 [k] Ps 65:9-13; 104:14 **1:14** [l] Ps 74:16 [m] Jer 10:2 [n] Ps 104:19 **1:16** [o] Ps 136:8 [p] Ps 136:9 [q] Job 38:7, 31-32; Ps 8:3; Isa 40:26 **1:18** [r] Jer 33:20, 25 **1:21** [s] Ps 104:25-26 **1:22** [t] ver 28; Ge 8:17 **1:25** [u] Jer 27:5 **1:26** [v] Ps 100:3 [w] Ge 9:6; Jas 3:9 [x] Ps 8:6-8 **1:27** [y] 1Co 11:7 [z] Ge 5:2; Mt 19:4*; Mk 10:6* **1:28** [a] Ge 9:1, 7; Lev 26:9

seed-bearing plant on the face of the whole earth and every tree that has fruit with seed in it. They will be yours for food.[b] 30And to all the beasts of the earth and all the birds in the sky and all the creatures that move along the ground—everything that has the breath of life in it—I give every green plant for food.[c]" And it was so.

31God saw all that he had made,[d] and it was very good.[e] And there was evening, and there was morning—the sixth day.

2 Thus the heavens and the earth were completed in all their vast array.

2By the seventh day God had finished the work he had been doing; so on the seventh day he rested from all his work.[f] 3Then God blessed the seventh day and made it holy,[g] because on it he rested from all the work of creating that he had done.

Adam and Eve

4This is the account of the heavens and the earth when they were created, when the LORD God made the earth and the heavens.

5Now no shrub had yet appeared on the earth[a] and no plant had yet sprung up,[h] for the LORD God had not sent rain on the earth[i] and there was no one to work the ground, 6but streams[b] came up from the earth and watered the whole surface of the ground. 7Then the LORD God formed a man[c] from the dust[j] of the ground[k] and breathed into his nostrils the breath[l] of life,[m] and the man became a living being.[n]

8Now the LORD God had planted a garden in the east, in Eden;[o] and there he put the man he had formed. 9The LORD God made all kinds of trees grow out of the ground—trees that were pleasing to the eye and good for food. In the middle of the garden were the tree of life[p] and the tree of the knowledge of good and evil.[q]

10A river watering the garden flowed from Eden; from there it was separated into four headwaters. 11The name of the first is the Pishon; it winds through the entire land of Havilah, where there is gold. 12(The gold of that land is good; aromatic resin[d] and onyx are also there.) 13The name of the second river is the Gihon; it winds through the entire land of Cush.[e] 14The name of the third river is the Tigris;[r] it runs along the east side of Ashur. And the fourth river is the Euphrates.

15The LORD God took the man and put him in the Garden of Eden to work it and take care of it. 16And the LORD God commanded the man, "You are free to eat from any tree in the garden; 17but you must not eat from the tree of the knowledge of good and evil, for when you eat from it you will certainly die."[s]

---

[a] 5 Or *land*; also in verse 6 [b] 6 Or *mist*
[c] 7 The Hebrew for *man (adam)* sounds like and may be related to the Hebrew for *ground (adamah)*; it is also the name *Adam* (see verse 20).
[d] 12 Or *good; pearls* [e] 13 Possibly southeast Mesopotamia

---

mean "destroy" or "ruin." It does mean to "act as managers who have the authority to run everything as God planned." This command applies equally to male and female.

2:2 *on the seventh day he rested.* God did not rest because of fatigue, but because of His accomplishment. God is never weary (Is. 40:28–29). The verb translated "rested" is related to the word for Sabbath, which means "rest." God's rest on the seventh day showed that He was satisfied with the work He had done.

2:4 *the LORD God.* This is a significant term. The word translated *God* is the same word as in 1:1. The word translated LORD is the proper name of God, Yahweh (or Jehovah; see Ex. 3:14–15). The God of chapter 1 and the LORD God of chapter 2 are one and the same.

2:6 *streams.* The precise meaning of this word is uncertain. Obviously it refers to some manner of irrigation before the Lord brought the cycles of rain into being.

2:7 *the breath of life.* Although God created light with a mere word (1:3), He created man by fashioning a body out of mud and clay, transforming the clay into something new, and then breathing life into it. This "breath of life" is something which only God can bestow. Medical knowledge enables doctors to keep a human body "alive," keeping the heart pumping and the vital organs functioning, but it does not enable them to keep or to call back the breath of life. Some have speculated that the "breath of life" is the human soul, but later on, animals are also described as having the "breath of life" in their nostrils (7:22), which would seem to indicate that this is simply a reference to the miracle of living, breathing flesh.

2:15–17 The First Covenant—In biblical times the purpose of a covenant was to establish an agreement between two persons or groups. The elements of a covenant included a promise on the part of one person and the conditions that needed to be fulfilled, on the part of the other person, in order for the promises to be carried out by both parties to the covenant. The Edenic Covenant is the first covenant mentioned in the Bible. God gave Adam a place in His creation and charged him with the responsibility of caring for the garden. The only condition in the covenant was that Adam could not allow himself to eat of the fruit of the tree of the knowledge of good and evil or he would die. This covenant was terminated by Adam's disobedience which also resulted in man's spiritual and physical death. God then established a new covenant with Adam in Genesis 3:14–21.

2:17 *will certainly die.* These emphatic words are made of two forms of the verb meaning "to die." The point is not that the guilty person would drop dead

1:29 [b] Ps 104:14 **1:30** [c] Ps 104:14,27; 145:15
1:31 [d] Ps 104:24 [e] 1Ti 4:4 **2:2** [f] Ex 20:11; 31:17; Heb 4:4*
2:3 [g] Lev 23:3; Isa 58:13 **2:5** [h] Ge 1:11 [i] Ps 65:9-10
2:7 [j] Ge 3:19 [k] Ps 103:14 [l] Job 33:4 [m] Ac 17:25 [n] 1Co 15:45*
2:8 [o] Ge 3:23,24; Isa 51:3 **2:9** [p] Ge 3:22,24; Rev 2:7; 22:2,14,19 [q] Eze 47:12 **2:14** [r] Da 10:4 **2:17** [s] Dt 30:15,19; Ro 5:12; 6:23; Jas 1:15

18The LORD God said, "It is not good for
the man to be alone. I will make a helper
suitable for him."[t]
19Now the LORD God had formed out of
the ground all the wild animals[u] and all
the birds in the sky. He brought them to
the man to see what he would name them;
and whatever the man called each living
creature,[v] that was its name. 20So the man
gave names to all the livestock, the birds in
the sky and all the wild animals.
But for Adam[a] no suitable helper was
found. 21So the LORD God caused the man
to fall into a deep sleep; and while he was
sleeping, he took one of the man's ribs[b] and
then closed up the place with flesh. 22Then
the LORD God made a woman from the
rib[c][w] he had taken out of the man, and he
brought her to the man.
23The man said,

"This is now bone of my bones
and flesh of my flesh;[x]
she shall be called 'woman,'
for she was taken out of man."

24That is why a man leaves his father and
mother and is united[y] to his wife, and they
become one flesh.[z]
25Adam and his wife were both naked,[a]
and they felt no shame.

The Fall

3 Now the serpent[b] was more crafty than
any of the wild animals the LORD God
had made. He said to the woman, "Did God
really say, 'You must not eat from any tree
in the garden'?"
2The woman said to the serpent, "We
may eat fruit from the trees in the garden,
3but God did say, 'You must not eat fruit
from the tree that is in the middle of the
garden, and you must not touch it, or you
will die.'"
4"You will not certainly die," the serpent said to the woman.[c] 5"For God knows
that when you eat from it your eyes will be
opened, and you will be like God,[d] knowing good and evil."
6When the woman saw that the fruit of
the tree was good for food and pleasing
to the eye, and also desirable[e] for gaining
wisdom, she took some and ate it. She also
gave some to her husband, who was with
her, and he ate it.[f] 7Then the eyes of both of
them were opened, and they realized they
were naked; so they sewed fig leaves together and made coverings for themselves.

---

a 20 Or *the man* *b* 21 Or *took part of the man's side* *c* 22 Or *part*

---

on the instant, but that death would surely happen—there is no escape (Heb. 9:27).

2:18 *It is not good.* Until this point, everything in creation was very good.

2:19 *to see what he would name them.* In giving each animal its name, Adam demonstrated his right as God's agent (1:26–28), the one set in place as lord of the created order.

2:20 *suitable helper.* Some have felt that calling the woman man's helper indicates that she is inferior in value, but this is far from true. In fact, the term "help" is used to describe God Himself, when He comes to our aid. The word "helper" indicates role, not value or position. The helper Adam needed was not merely a servant or a slave, nor another man exactly like himself. He needed a complement, equal in value and with the same intelligence, personality, spirituality, and ethical and moral sense; but with different qualities and a different role, a helper who could join with him in his work of subduing the earth.

2:21 *he took one of the man's ribs.* God's use of Adam's rib was fitting. He might have started over with dust and clay. But by using a part of Adam himself, the identification of Adam with his partner would be ensured. As Martin Luther observed, God might have taken a bone from a toe, and thus signified that Adam was to rule over her; or He might have taken a bone from his head to indicate her rule over him. But by taking a bone from his side, God implied equality and mutual respect.

2:24 *one flesh.* This phrase suggests both a physical, sexual bonding and a lifelong relationship. They are still separate persons, but together they are as one (Eph. 5:31). In the New Testament, Jesus refers to this text as the foundation of the biblical view of marriage (Matt. 19:5). A married couple functions as "we," rather than "me and you." They are a new unit, separate from the family units they each came from. This does not mean that they will no longer relate to their extended families, but that their "one flesh" is a unit distinct from either family.

3:1 *the serpent.* With no introduction, Satan appears in the garden of Eden. This is the first clue in Scripture of creation outside the one Adam and Eve experienced. It is interesting to note that Eve expressed no surprise at the serpent speaking to her in intelligible language.

3:3 *You must not eat . . . and you must not touch it.* Some interpreters suggest that the woman was already sinning by adding to the word of God, for these words were not part of God's instructions in 2:17. Scripture, however, always refers to the eating of the fruit as the sin, and never comments on Eve's addition. Her words reflected the original command well enough, and indeed they would have ensured that the command would be kept.

3:5 *you will be like God.* God's fullness of knowledge was only one of the superiorities that set Him apart from the woman. But the serpent combined all of God's superiority over the woman into this one audacious appeal to her pride.

3:6–7 Sin's Consequences—At first Adam's sin does not appear to be all that significant. All he did was take a bite of some fruit. But Scripture takes it very seriously. Adam's sin was one of disobedience and rebellion. God told Adam not to eat the fruit of the "tree of the knowledge of good and evil" under

2:18 [t] 1Co 11:9 **2:19** [u] Ps 8:7 [v] Ge 1:24 **2:22** [w] 1Co 11:8, 9, 12 **2:23** [x] Ge 29:14; Eph 5:28-30 **2:24** [y] Mal 2:15 [z] Mt 19:5*; Mk 10:7-8*; 1Co 6:16*; Eph 5:31* **2:25** [a] Ge 3:7, 10-11 **3:1** [b] 2Co 11:3; Rev 12:9; 20:2 **3:4** [c] Jn 8:44; 2Co 11:3 **3:5** [d] Isa 14:14; Eze 28:2 **3:6** [e] Jas 1:14-15; 1Jn 2:16 [f] 1Ti 2:14

8Then the man and his wife heard the
sound of the LORD God as he was walking[g] in the garden in the cool of the day,
and they hid[h] from the LORD God among
the trees of the garden. 9But the LORD God
called to the man, "Where are you?"
10He answered, "I heard you in the garden, and I was afraid because I was naked;
so I hid."
11And he said, "Who told you that you
were naked? Have you eaten from the tree
that I commanded you not to eat from?"
12The man said, "The woman you put
here with me—she gave me some fruit
from the tree, and I ate it."
13Then the LORD God said to the woman,
"What is this you have done?"
The woman said, "The serpent deceived
me,[i] and I ate."
14So the LORD God said to the serpent,
"Because you have done this,

"Cursed[j] are you above all livestock
and all wild animals!
You will crawl on your belly
and you will eat dust[k]
all the days of your life.
15 And I will put enmity
between you and the woman,
and between your offspring[a][l] and
hers;[m]
he will crush[b] your head,[n]
and you will strike his heel."

16To the woman he said,

"I will make your pains in childbearing
very severe;
with painful labor you will give birth
to children.
Your desire will be for your husband,
and he will rule over you.[o]"

17To Adam he said, "Because you listened to your wife and ate fruit from the
tree about which I commanded you, 'You
must not eat from it,'

"Cursed[p] is the ground because of you;
through painful toil you will eat food
from it
all the days of your life.[q]
18 It will produce thorns and thistles for
you,
and you will eat the plants of the
field.[r]
19 By the sweat of your brow
you will eat your food[s]
until you return to the ground,
since from it you were taken;
for dust you are
and to dust you will return."[t]

20Adam[c] named his wife Eve,[d] because
she would become the mother of all the
living.
21The LORD God made garments of skin
for Adam and his wife and clothed them.

[a] 15 Or *seed* [b] 15 Or *strike* [c] 20 Or *The man*
[d] 20 *Eve* probably means *living*.

---

penalty of death (2:17). That action of eating the fruit changed Adam's whole nature as well as his relationship with God. Adam became a sinner and as such he died. His spiritual death was immediate, the physical death progressive. Adam, who began the human race, then became the source of sin for the world. We are all sinners by nature because Adam sinned (Rom. 5:12–14). We inherit sin from Adam in our natures in the same way we inherit many of our physical characteristics from our parents. Sin is a universal part of our spiritual inheritance.

3:14–21 The Covenant with Adam—The Adamic Covenant is the second covenant God made with man. It sets forth conditions that will be in effect until the curse of death is lifted (Is. 11:6–10; Rom. 8:18–23). In Christ's death and resurrection we have the beginning (firstfruits) of the lifting of the curse. The ultimate lifting of the curse will happen as Christ establishes his final reign on earth.

3:14 *to the serpent.* The Lord turned first to the serpent and brought judgment upon him. God did not excuse the woman because she was deceived, but He did bring the harsher judgment on the one who had deceived her.

3:15 Christ—This passage is sometimes referred to as the "preaching of Messiah in the garden of Eden," because it introduces the One who will deliver mankind from the power of the Tempter. The seed of the serpent, those of the human race who choose evil and thus give themselves into the control of the Evil One, would hate and destroy the Seed of the woman, who was Jesus Christ. But in that very act, Evil condemned itself. Jesus rose triumphant from the grave, having paid the blood atonement for the sin of the world and conquered death forever. Thus the Seed of woman crushed the head of the serpent.

3:16 *pains in child bearing.* The woman's joy in conceiving and bearing children would be affected by the pain of it. ***desire . . . rule.*** The word *desire* can also mean "an attempt to usurp authority or control" as in 4:7. The last two lines of this verse could be paraphrased, "You will now have a tendency to try to dominate your husband and he will have the tendency to act as a tyrant." Each strives for control and neither lives in the best interest of the other (Phil. 2:3–4). The antidote is in the restoration of mutual respect and dignity through Jesus Christ (Eph. 5:21–23).

3:17–19 *Cursed is the ground . . . By the sweat of your brow.* Humans sometimes tend to look upon work itself as a curse, but it is important to remember that work in itself is part of the "very good" creation. The curse on the ground simply means that work is now painful and tiresome toil instead of the pure satisfaction that it was designed to be. ***to dust you will return.*** The word of God was sure: God had stated that they would certainly die (2:17). Now they were served notice concerning the process of aging and decay that was already at work (5:5; 6:3).

3:8 [g] Dt 23:14 [h] Job 31:33; Ps 139:7-12; Jer 23:24 **3:13** [i] 2Co 11:3; 1Ti 2:14 **3:14** [j] Dt 28:15-20 [k] Isa 65:25; Mic 7:17 **3:15** [l] Jn 8:44; Ac 13:10; 1Jn 3:8 [m] Isa 7:14; Mt 1:23; Rev 12:17 [n] Ro 16:20; Heb 2:14 **3:16** [o] 1Co 11:3; Eph 5:22 **3:17** [p] Ge 5:29; Ro 8:20-22 [q] Job 5:7; 14:1; Ecc 2:23 **3:18** [r] Ps 104:14 **3:19** [s] 2Th 3:10 [t] Ge 2:7; Ps 90:3; 104:29; Ecc 12:7

22 And the LORD God said, "The man has now become like one of us, knowing good and evil. He must not be allowed to reach out his hand and take also from the tree of life[u] and eat, and live forever." 23 So the LORD God banished him from the Garden of Eden[v] to work the ground[w] from which he had been taken. 24 After he drove the man out, he placed on the east side[a] of the Garden of Eden cherubim[x] and a flaming sword[y] flashing back and forth to guard the way to the tree of life.[z]

Cain and Abel

4 Adam[b] made love to his wife Eve, and she became pregnant and gave birth to Cain.[c] She said, "With the help of the LORD I have brought forth[d] a man." 2 Later she gave birth to his brother Abel.[a]

Now Abel kept flocks, and Cain worked the soil. 3 In the course of time Cain brought some of the fruits of the soil as an offering to the LORD.[b] 4 And Abel also brought an offering—fat portions[c] from some of the firstborn of his flock.[d] The LORD looked with favor on Abel and his offering,[e] 5 but on Cain and his offering he did not look with favor. So Cain was very angry, and his face was downcast.

6 Then the LORD said to Cain, "Why are you angry? Why is your face downcast? 7 If you do what is right, will you not be accepted? But if you do not do what is right, sin is crouching at your door;[f] it desires to have you, but you must rule over it.[g]"

8 Now Cain said to his brother Abel, "Let's go out to the field."[e] While they were in the field, Cain attacked his brother Abel and killed him.[h]

9 Then the LORD said to Cain, "Where is your brother Abel?"

"I don't know," he replied. "Am I my brother's keeper?"

10 The LORD said, "What have you done? Listen! Your brother's blood cries out to me from the ground.[i] 11 Now you are under a curse and driven from the ground, which opened its mouth to receive your brother's blood from your hand. 12 When you work the ground, it will no longer yield its crops for you. You will be a restless wanderer on the earth."

13 Cain said to the LORD, "My punishment is more than I can bear. 14 Today you are driving me from the land, and I will be hidden from your presence;[j] I will be a restless wanderer on the earth, and whoever finds me will kill me."[k]

15 But the LORD said to him, "Not so[f]; anyone who kills Cain[l] will suffer vengeance seven times over.[m]" Then the LORD put a mark on Cain so that no one who found him would kill him. 16 So Cain went out from the LORD's presence and lived in the land of Nod,[g] east of Eden.[n]

17 Cain made love to his wife, and she became pregnant and gave birth to Enoch. Cain was then building a city, and he named it after his son[o] Enoch. 18 To Enoch was born Irad, and Irad was the father of Mehujael, and Mehujael was the father of Methushael, and Methushael was the father of Lamech.

19 Lamech married two women, one

---

[a] 24 Or *placed in front* [b] 1 Or *The man*
[c] 1 *Cain* sounds like the Hebrew for *brought forth* or *acquired.* [d] 1 Or *have acquired*
[e] 8 Samaritan Pentateuch, Septuagint, Vulgate and Syriac; Masoretic Text does not have *"Let's go out to the field."* [f] 15 Septuagint, Vulgate and Syriac; Hebrew *Very well* [g] 16 *Nod* means *wandering* (see verses 12 and 14).

3:22 *tree of life.* Adam and Eve apparently had free access to this tree before the fall, and by continuing to eat its fruit they would live forever. The penalty for sin was not instant death, but banishment from this tree and eventual death and decay. One day this tree will be planted anew and its fruit will be for the healing of the nations (Rev. 22:2).

4:3 *Cain brought ... an offering.* Genesis does not explain how the practice of sacrificial worship began, but it is clear that Adam and Eve's two sons understood the custom. Some people assume that Cain's offering was unsuitable because it was not a blood offering, and blood is required for the forgiveness of sins (Heb. 9:22). But nothing in this chapter indicates that Cain and Abel were coming to God for forgiveness. Their sacrifices were acts of worship, and as such a bloodless offering was not necessarily inappropriate (see Lev. 6:14–23). Apparently the deficiency was in Cain's heart, not in the actual offering. Abel's offering was "better" than Cain's because of his faith in the Lord (Heb. 11:4).

4:8 *killed him.* The murder was stunning in its lack of precedent, its suddenness, and its finality. Jesus spoke of this ghastly event as a historical fact (Matt. 23:35).

4:17 *Cain made love to his wife.* The identity of Cain's wife has long been a source of puzzlement and argument to the readers and critics of the Book of Genesis. Some have postulated that God created other humans outside of the garden of Eden, but the Scriptures give no such indication, and in fact Adam refers to his wife as "the mother of all living" (3:20). It makes the most sense to assume that Cain married one of his sisters. While this idea seems repugnant to us today, it must be remembered that Adam and Eve's children had a near perfect gene pool, and there would not have been any genetic complications with close intermarrying. God's strict prohibition against siblings and other close relatives marrying did not come until much later (Lev. 18); even Abraham's wife Sarah was his half sister. ***Enoch.*** The fact that Cain named a city after his son indicates the rapid and dramatic increase in population.

3:22 [u] Rev 22:14 **3:23** [v] Ge 2:8 [w] Ge 4:2
3:24 [x] Ex 25:18-22 [y] Ps 104:4 [z] Ge 2:9 **4:2** [a] Lk 11:51
4:3 [b] Nu 18:12 **4:4** [c] Lev 3:16 [d] Ex 13:2, 12 [e] Heb 11:4
4:7 [f] Nu 32:23 [g] Ro 6:16 **4:8** [h] Mt 23:35; 1Jn 3:12
4:10 [i] Ge 9:5; Nu 35:33; Heb 12:24; Rev 6:9-10
4:14 [j] 2Ki 17:18; Ps 51:11; 139:7-12; Jer 7:15; 52:3 [k] Ge 9:6; Nu 35:19, 21, 27, 33 **4:15** [l] Eze 9:4, 6 [m] ver 24; Ps 79:12
4:16 [n] Ge 2:8 **4:17** [o] Ps 49:11

named Adah and the other Zillah. 20 Adah
gave birth to Jabal; he was the father of
those who live in tents and raise livestock.
21 His brother's name was Jubal; he was the
father of all who play stringed instruments
and pipes. 22 Zillah also had a son, Tubal-
Cain, who forged all kinds of tools out of[a]
bronze and iron. Tubal-Cain's sister was
Naamah.
23 Lamech said to his wives,

"Adah and Zillah, listen to me;
wives of Lamech, hear my words.
I have killed[p] a man for wounding me,
a young man for injuring me.
24 If Cain is avenged[q] seven times,[r]
then Lamech seventy-seven times."

25 Adam made love to his wife again, and
she gave birth to a son and named him
Seth,[b][s] saying, "God has granted me another child in place of Abel, since Cain killed
him."[t] 26 Seth also had a son, and he named
him Enosh.
At that time people began to call on[c] the
name of the LORD.[u]

From Adam to Noah

5 This is the written account of Adam's
family line.

When God created mankind, he made
them in the likeness of God.[v] 2 He created
them male and female[w] and blessed them.
And he named them "Mankind"[d] when
they were created.
3 When Adam had lived 130 years, he had
a son in his own likeness, in his own image;[x] and he named him Seth. 4 After Seth
was born, Adam lived 800 years and had
other sons and daughters. 5 Altogether,
Adam lived a total of 930 years, and then
he died.[y]
6 When Seth had lived 105 years, he became the father[e] of Enosh. 7 After he became the father of Enosh, Seth lived 807
years and had other sons and daughters.
8 Altogether, Seth lived a total of 912 years,
and then he died.
9 When Enosh had lived 90 years, he became the father of Kenan. 10 After he became the father of Kenan, Enosh lived 815
years and had other sons and daughters.
11 Altogether, Enosh lived a total of 905
years, and then he died.
12 When Kenan had lived 70 years, he became the father of Mahalalel. 13 After he became the father of Mahalalel, Kenan lived
840 years and had other sons and daughters. 14 Altogether, Kenan lived a total of 910
years, and then he died.
15 When Mahalalel had lived 65 years, he
became the father of Jared. 16 After he became the father of Jared, Mahalalel lived
830 years and had other sons and daughters. 17 Altogether, Mahalalel lived a total of
895 years, and then he died.
18 When Jared had lived 162 years, he
became the father of Enoch.[z] 19 After he
became the father of Enoch, Jared lived
800 years and had other sons and daughters. 20 Altogether, Jared lived a total of 962
years, and then he died.
21 When Enoch had lived 65 years, he became the father of Methuselah. 22 After he
became the father of Methuselah, Enoch
walked faithfully with God[a] 300 years and
had other sons and daughters. 23 Altogether, Enoch lived a total of 365 years. 24 Enoch
walked faithfully with God;[b] then he was
no more, because God took him away.[c]
25 When Methuselah had lived 187 years,
he became the father of Lamech. 26 After
he became the father of Lamech, Methuselah lived 782 years and had other sons and
daughters. 27 Altogether, Methuselah lived
a total of 969 years, and then he died.

a 22 Or *who instructed all who work in* *b* 25 *Seth* probably means *granted.* *c* 26 Or *to proclaim* *d* 2 Hebrew *adam* *e* 6 *Father* may mean *ancestor*; also in verses 7-26.

4:25 *Seth.* While it is certain that Adam and Eve had other daughters, and possibly other sons as well, the death of righteous Abel and the banishment of their firstborn, Cain, had left them with no one to carry on their line for good and for the promise of the Messiah. Seth is specifically mentioned among Adam and Eve's children because it would be through his descendants that the Messiah would come. His name is related to a Hebrew verb meaning "to place" or "to set" for he was appointed to take this special place in the plan of God.
4:26 *people began to call on the name of the LORD.* These words can hardly mean that only now did people begin to pray to God. Rather, the verb *call* means "to make proclamation." That is, this is the beginning of preaching, of witnessing, and testifying in the name of the Lord (12:8).
5:3 *130 years.* The long lives of the people of the early chapters of Genesis have led to considerable speculation. One suggestion is that these ages were possible because of tremendously different climate and environmental conditions that were in effect before the flood.
5:5 *and then he died.* God created humans for eternity; if Adam and Eve had not disobeyed, they would have lived forever. There is a profound sadness in Adam's death, for it reminds us of Adam's mortality—and hence our own.
5:21 – 24 *because God took him.* Only Enoch and Elijah were taken by God without experiencing death (2 Kin. 2:11). This was both a testimony of Enoch's deep faith in God (Heb. 11:5 – 6) and a strong reminder at the beginning of biblical history that for God's people, there is life in God's presence after our physical bodies have died.

4:23 [p] Ex 20:13; Lev 19:18 **4:24** [q] Dt 32:35 [r] ver 15 **4:25** [s] Ge 5:3 [t] ver 8 **4:26** [u] Ge 12:8; 1Ki 18:24; Ps 116:17; Joel 2:32; Zep 3:9; Ac 2:21; 1Co 1:2 **5:1** [v] Ge 1:27; Eph 4:24; Col 3:10 **5:2** [w] Ge 1:27; Mt 19:4; Mk 10:6; Gal 3:28 **5:3** [x] Ge 1:26; 1Co 15:49 **5:5** [y] Ge 3:19 **5:18** [z] Jude 1:14 **5:22** [a] ver 24; Ge 6:9; 17:1; 48:15; Mic 6:8; Mal 2:6 **5:24** [b] ver 22 [c] 2Ki 2:1, 11; Heb 11:5

28When Lamech had lived 182 years, he had a son. 29He named him Noah[a] and said, "He will comfort us in the labor and painful toil of our hands caused by the ground the LORD has cursed.[d]" 30After Noah was born, Lamech lived 595 years and had other sons and daughters. 31Altogether, Lamech lived a total of 777 years, and then he died.

32After Noah was 500 years old, he became the father of Shem, Ham and Japheth.

Wickedness in the World

6 When human beings began to increase in number on the earth[e] and daughters were born to them, 2the sons of God saw that the daughters of humans were beautiful, and they married any of them they chose. 3Then the LORD said, "My Spirit will not contend with[b] humans forever,[f] for they are mortal[c];[g] their days will be a hundred and twenty years."

4The Nephilim[h] were on the earth in those days—and also afterward—when the sons of God went to the daughters of humans and had children by them. They were the heroes of old, men of renown.

5The LORD saw how great the wickedness of the human race had become on the earth, and that every inclination of the thoughts of the human heart was only evil all the time.[i] 6The LORD regretted[j] that he had made human beings on the earth, and his heart was deeply troubled. 7So the LORD said, "I will wipe from the face of the earth the human race I have created—and with them the animals, the birds and the creatures that move along the ground—for I regret that I have made them." 8But Noah found favor in the eyes of the LORD.[k]

Noah and the Flood

9This is the account of Noah and his family.

Noah was a righteous man, blameless among the people of his time,[l] and he walked faithfully with God.[m] 10Noah had three sons: Shem, Ham and Japheth.[n]

11Now the earth was corrupt in God's sight and was full of violence.[o] 12God saw how corrupt the earth had become, for all the people on earth had corrupted their ways.[p] 13So God said to Noah, "I am going to put an end to all people, for the earth is filled with violence because of them. I am surely going to destroy both them and the earth.[q] 14So make yourself an ark of cypress[d] wood;[r] make rooms in it and coat it with pitch[s] inside and out. 15This is how you are to build it: The ark is to be three hundred cubits long, fifty cubits wide and thirty cubits high.[e] 16Make a roof for it, leaving

[a] *29 Noah* sounds like the Hebrew for *comfort.*
[b] *3* Or *My spirit will not remain in* [c] *3* Or *corrupt*
[d] *14* The meaning of the Hebrew for this word is uncertain. [e] *15* That is, about 450 feet long, 75 feet wide and 45 feet high or about 135 meters long, 23 meters wide and 14 meters high

6:2 *sons of God ... daughters of humans.* This passage is very difficult to interpret. Some believe that the "sons of God" were the men of the righteous line of Seth, while the "daughters of humans" were Cain's offspring. This does not account for the fact that their offspring were giants, men of extraordinary size and talents; it is also problematic in that it assumes that Cain's descendants were universally more sinful than Seth's descendants. Since Noah was the only descendant of Seth who was considered righteous, this is obviously not accurate. A second view is that the "sons of God" were angelic beings. The phrase "sons of God" is used elsewhere in Scripture to refer to angelic beings (Job 1:6), but it seems impossible since angels in heaven do not marry (Matt. 22:30). It may be, however, that these "sons of God" were some of the rebellious angels who had joined Satan (Jude 6; 2 Pet. 2:4); they took on human form (as Satan was apparently able to take on the form of a snake), and out of perverted lust, seduced human women. The problem with this theory is that verse 4 says that these unions produced children. Nothing in the rest of Scripture would indicate that angels reproduce, or that a spirit being could mate with a human being. Nor is there any reference to half-man/half-spirit beings. Whichever view one settles on, it is clear that what happened here was corrupt and one of the reasons for the flood.

6:11 *corrupt.* The verb translated *corrupt* has the idea of being ruined, spoiled, or destroyed. Sinful people were bringing ruin to the world that belonged to the living God (Ps. 24:1).

6:11–13 Disobedience—In the beginning, God pronounced His creative work good. But with the entrance of sin and decadence on the scene, the world became corrupt in His sight. It was not merely that some individuals or groups had corrupted their ways, but a matter of pervasive perversity. Because sin is repugnant to His holiness, God declared His purpose of destroying both mankind and the earth he had polluted. Defying God's will affects our environment as well as ourselves. Judgment for disobedience is only averted through repentance and fresh submission to God.

6:14 *ark.* The word *ark* simply means "box," the same word is used for the box in which the baby Moses was placed in the Nile (Ex. 2:3), and for the gold-covered chest which contained the stone tablets of the Covenant (Ex. 25:10). We usually picture Noah's ark as a huge ship, with curved bow and stern, but it was very likely more like a large box. It was not designed for navigation, but simply to stay safely afloat.

6:15 *cubits.* A cubit was supposed to be the measurement of a man's forearm, from the tip of the bent elbow to the fingertips. This is naturally a somewhat imprecise measurement, but it is generally considered to equal about 18 inches. Hence the ark was about 450 feet long, 75 feet wide, and 45 feet high.

5:29 [d] Ge 3:17; Ro 8:20 **6:1** [e] Ge 1:28 **6:3** [f] Isa 57:16 [g] Ps 78:39 **6:4** [h] Nu 13:33 **6:5** [i] Ge 8:21; Ps 14:1-3 **6:6** [j] 1Sa 15:11,35; Isa 63:10 **6:8** [k] Ge 19:19; Ex 33:12,13,17; Lk 1:30; Ac 7:46 **6:9** [l] Ge 7:1; Eze 14:14,20; Heb 11:7; 2Pe 2:5 [m] Ge 5:22 **6:10** [n] Ge 5:32 **6:11** [o] Eze 7:23; 8:17 **6:12** [p] Ps 14:1-3 **6:13** [q] ver 17; Eze 7:2-3 **6:14** [r] Heb 11:7; 1Pe 3:20 [s] Ex 2:3

below the roof an opening one cubit[a] high
all around.[b] Put a door in the side of the ark
and make lower, middle and upper decks.
17I am going to bring floodwaters on the
earth to destroy all life under the heavens,
every creature that has the breath of life in
it. Everything on earth will perish.[t] 18But I
will establish my covenant with you,[u] and
you will enter the ark[v]—you and your sons
and your wife and your sons' wives with
you. 19You are to bring into the ark two of
all living creatures, male and female, to
keep them alive with you. 20Two[w] of every
kind of bird, of every kind of animal and
of every kind of creature that moves along
the ground will come to you to be kept
alive. 21You are to take every kind of food
that is to be eaten and store it away as food
for you and for them."

22Noah did everything just as God commanded him.[x]

7 The LORD then said to Noah, "Go into
the ark, you and your whole family,[y] because I have found you righteous[z] in this
generation. 2Take with you seven pairs of
every kind of clean[a] animal, a male and its
mate, and one pair of every kind of unclean
animal, a male and its mate, 3and also seven
pairs of every kind of bird, male and female,
to keep their various kinds alive throughout
the earth. 4Seven days from now I will send
rain on the earth for forty days and forty
nights, and I will wipe from the face of the
earth every living creature I have made."

5And Noah did all that the LORD commanded him.[b]

6Noah was six hundred years old when
the floodwaters came on the earth. 7And
Noah and his sons and his wife and his
sons' wives entered the ark to escape the
waters of the flood. 8Pairs of clean and unclean animals, of birds and of all creatures
that move along the ground, 9male and female, came to Noah and entered the ark,
as God had commanded Noah. 10And after
the seven days the floodwaters came on the
earth.

11In the six hundredth year of Noah's
life, on the seventeenth day of the second
month—on that day all the springs of the
great deep[c] burst forth, and the floodgates of the heavens[d] were opened. 12And
rain fell on the earth forty days and forty
nights.[e]

13On that very day Noah and his sons,
Shem, Ham and Japheth, together with
his wife and the wives of his three sons,
entered the ark. 14They had with them every wild animal according to its kind, all
livestock according to their kinds, every
creature that moves along the ground according to its kind and every bird according
to its kind, everything with wings. 15Pairs
of all creatures that have the breath of life
in them came to Noah and entered the ark.[f]
16The animals going in were male and female of every living thing, as God had commanded Noah. Then the LORD shut him in.

17For forty days[g] the flood kept coming
on the earth, and as the waters increased
they lifted the ark high above the earth.
18The waters rose and increased greatly
on the earth, and the ark floated on the
surface of the water. 19They rose greatly
on the earth, and all the high mountains
under the entire heavens were covered.[h]
20The waters rose and covered the mountains to a depth of more than fifteen cubits.[c,d] 21Every living thing that moved
on land perished—birds, livestock, wild

[a] *16* That is, about 18 inches or about 45 centimeters [b] *16* The meaning of the Hebrew for this clause is uncertain. [c] *20* That is, about 23 feet or about 6.8 meters [d] *20* Or *rose more than fifteen cubits, and the mountains were covered*

6:17 *I am going to bring.* The Hebrew text places significant emphasis on the personal role of God in the ensuing storm.

6:18–19 *covenant.* This is the first time the word *covenant* is used in the Bible. The details of this covenant were given after the flood (9:9). Here, in the midst of judgment, the Lord stooped down to meet the needs of His servant (Ps. 40:1; 113:6) and to enter into a binding oath with him.

7:9 *came to Noah and entered the ark*. The gathering and cooperation of the animals must have been arranged by God. It appears that after Noah and his wife and sons entered the ark, the animals followed of their own accord.

7:11 *springs of the great deep ... floodgates of the heavens.* Until this time, no rain had fallen on the earth, but it was watered by a mist (2:5–6). This description of the first rain portrays a thundering, catastrophic event, accompanied by violent upheaval of the earth's crust and geysers of water bursting from the depths. The violence and the amount of water involved are more than enough to account for many peculiarities of the earth's surface, such as the formation of the Grand Canyon. The flood also explains the enormous quantity of fossilized remains of plants, animals, and shellfish that are buried in layers of rock over the entire surface of the earth and even on the tops of mountains.

7:16 *shut him in.* The Lord who had drawn them now closed the door on them. That shut door was a symbol of closure, safety, and God's deliverance.

7:19 *the high mountains under the entire heavens were covered.* This explicit declaration, accompanied by the assertion in verse 21 that every living thing died, makes it clear that this was no localized event, but in actuality a worldwide catastrophic flood (see 8:5). Jesus affirmed the historicity of the "days of Noah" when he compared them to the end days (Matt. 24:37–38; Luke 17:26–27). Peter similarly used the story of Noah and the flood as a pattern for the final judgment (1 Pet. 3:20; 2 Pet. 2:5; 3:5–6).

6:17 [t] Ge 7:4,21-23; 2Pe 2:5 **6:18** [u] Ge 9:9-16 [v] Ge 7:1,7, 13 **6:20** [w] Ge 7:15 **6:22** [x] Ge 7:5,9,16 **7:1** [y] Mt 24:38 [z] Ge 6:9; Eze 14:14 **7:2** [a] ver 8; Ge 8:20; Lev 10:10; 11:1-47 **7:5** [b] Ge 6:22 **7:11** [c] Eze 26:19 [d] Ge 8:2 **7:12** [e] ver 4 **7:15** [f] Ge 6:19 **7:17** [g] ver 4 **7:19** [h] Ps 104:6

animals, all the creatures that swarm over the earth, and all mankind.[i] 22Everything on dry land that had the breath of life[j] in its nostrils died. 23Every living thing on the face of the earth was wiped out; people and animals and the creatures that move along the ground and the birds were wiped from the earth.[k] Only Noah was left, and those with him in the ark.[l]

24The waters flooded the earth for a hundred and fifty days.[m]

8 But God remembered[n] Noah and all the wild animals and the livestock that were with him in the ark, and he sent a wind over the earth,[o] and the waters receded. 2Now the springs of the deep and the floodgates of the heavens[p] had been closed, and the rain had stopped falling from the sky. 3The water receded steadily from the earth. At the end of the hundred and fifty days the water had gone down, 4and on the seventeenth day of the seventh month the ark came to rest on the mountains of Ararat. 5The waters continued to recede until the tenth month, and on the first day of the tenth month the tops of the mountains became visible.

6After forty days Noah opened a window he had made in the ark 7and sent out a raven, and it kept flying back and forth until the water had dried up from the earth. 8Then he sent out a dove to see if the water had receded from the surface of the ground. 9But the dove could find nowhere to perch because there was water over all the surface of the earth; so it returned to Noah in the ark. He reached out his hand and took the dove and brought it back to himself in the ark. 10He waited seven more days and again sent out the dove from the ark. 11When the dove returned to him in the evening, there in its beak was a freshly plucked olive leaf! Then Noah knew that the water had receded from the earth. 12He waited seven more days and sent the dove out again, but this time it did not return to him.

13By the first day of the first month of Noah's six hundred and first year, the water had dried up from the earth. Noah then removed the covering from the ark and saw that the surface of the ground was dry. 14By the twenty-seventh day of the second month the earth was completely dry.

15Then God said to Noah, 16"Come out of the ark, you and your wife and your sons and their wives.[q] 17Bring out every kind of living creature that is with you—the birds, the animals, and all the creatures that move along the ground—so they can multiply on the earth and be fruitful and increase in number on it."[r]

18So Noah came out, together with his sons and his wife and his sons' wives. 19All the animals and all the creatures that move along the ground and all the birds—everything that moves on land—came out of the ark, one kind after another.

20Then Noah built an altar to the LORD[s] and, taking some of all the clean animals and clean[t] birds, he sacrificed burnt offerings[u] on it. 21The LORD smelled the pleasing aroma[v] and said in his heart: "Never again will I curse the ground[w] because of humans, even though[a] every inclination of the human heart is evil from childhood.[x] And never again will I destroy all living creatures,[y] as I have done.

22"As long as the earth endures,
seedtime and harvest,
cold and heat,
summer and winter,
day and night
will never cease."[z]

God's Covenant With Noah

9 Then God blessed Noah and his sons, saying to them, "Be fruitful and increase in number and fill the earth.[a] 2The fear and dread of you will fall on all the beasts of the earth, and on all the birds in the sky, on every creature that moves along the ground, and on all the fish in the sea; they are given into your hands. 3Everything that lives and moves about will be food for you.[b] Just as I gave you the green plants, I now give you everything.

[a] 21 Or *humans, for*

8:14 ***the earth was dry.*** After more than a full year, the waters had returned to their place (7:11). As in the beginning, God brought the waters of earth into their place (1:9–13). The flood began in Noah's 600th year, in the 2nd month, on day 17 (7:11) and ended in Noah's 601st year, in the 2nd month, on day 27 (8:14).

8:20 ***an altar.*** This is the first mention of sacrificial worship since the days of Cain and Abel (4:3–5); yet we may assume that the principle of sacrificial worship was perpetuated through the line of faithful people (ch. 5).

8:22 ***as the earth endures.*** The words of this verse are a poem of powerful effect. These words might easily have become a song of faith, the response of the people of God to the promise He made (v. 21). Later in Israel's history, the prophets recalled God's great promise to Noah (Is. 54:9–10).

9:1–19 God's Promise to Noah—Only when we think of God as Creator, as well as Redeemer, can we begin to understand His covenant of redemption as being related to the covenant of creation (Gen. 1:26–30; 2:15–17). God doesn't abandon His creation. On the contrary, though evil has corrupted it, He graciously (for it is undeserved) establishes a

7:21 [i] Ge 6:7, 13 **7:22** [j] Ge 1:30 **7:23** [k] Mt 24:39; Lk 17:27; 1Pe 3:20; 2Pe 2:5 [l] Heb 11:7 **7:24** [m] Ge 8:3
8:1 [n] Ge 9:15; 19:29; Ex 2:24; 1Sa 1:11, 19 [o] Ex 14:21
8:2 [p] Ge 7:11 **8:16** [q] Ge 7:13 **8:17** [r] Ge 1:22
8:20 [s] Ge 12:7-8; 13:18; 22:9 [t] Ge 7:8; Lev 11:1-47 [u] Ge 22:2, 13; Ex 10:25 **8:21** [v] Lev 1:9, 13; 2Co 2:15 [w] Ge 3:17 [x] Ge 6:5; Ps 51:5; Jer 17:9 [y] Ge 9:11, 15; Isa 54:9
8:22 [z] Ge 1:14; Jer 33:20, 25 **9:1** [a] Ge 1:22
9:3 [b] Ge 1:29

4“But you must not eat meat that has its
lifeblood still in it.[c] 5And for your lifeblood
I will surely demand an accounting. I will
demand an accounting from every animal.[d] And from each human being, too, I
will demand an accounting for the life of
another human being.[e]

6“Whoever sheds human blood,
by humans shall their blood be shed;[f]
for in the image of God[g]
has God made mankind.

7As for you, be fruitful and increase in
number; multiply on the earth and increase
upon it.”[h]
8Then God said to Noah and to his sons
with him: 9“I now establish my covenant
with you[i] and with your descendants after you 10and with every living creature
that was with you—the birds, the livestock and all the wild animals, all those
that came out of the ark with you—every
living creature on earth. 11I establish my
covenant[j] with you: Never again will all
life be destroyed by the waters of a flood;
never again will there be a flood to destroy
the earth.[k]”
12And God said, “This is the sign of the
covenant[l] I am making between me and
you and every living creature with you, a
covenant for all generations to come: 13I
have set my rainbow in the clouds, and it
will be the sign of the covenant between
me and the earth. 14Whenever I bring
clouds over the earth and the rainbow appears in the clouds, 15I will remember my
covenant[m] between me and you and all living creatures of every kind. Never again
will the waters become a flood to destroy
all life. 16Whenever the rainbow appears
in the clouds, I will see it and remember
the everlasting covenant[n] between God
and all living creatures of every kind on
the earth.”
17So God said to Noah, “This is the sign
of the covenant[o] I have established between me and all life on the earth.”

The Sons of Noah

18The sons of Noah who came out of the
ark were Shem, Ham and Japheth. (Ham
was the father of Canaan.)[p] 19These were
the three sons of Noah, and from them
came the people who were scattered over
the whole earth.[q]
20Noah, a man of the soil, proceeded[a] to
plant a vineyard. 21When he drank some
of its wine, he became drunk and lay uncovered inside his tent. 22Ham, the father
of Canaan, saw his father naked and told
his two brothers outside. 23But Shem and
Japheth took a garment and laid it across
their shoulders; then they walked in backward and covered their father's naked
body. Their faces were turned the other
way so that they would not see their father
naked.
24When Noah awoke from his wine and
found out what his youngest son had done
to him, 25he said,

“Cursed be Canaan![r]
The lowest of slaves
will he be to his brothers.[s]”

26He also said,

“Praise be to the LORD, the God of
Shem!
May Canaan be the slave of Shem.
27May God extend Japheth's[b] territory;
may Japheth live in the tents of Shem,
and may Canaan be the slave of
Japheth.”

28After the flood Noah lived 350 years.
29Noah lived a total of 950 years, and then
he died.

The Table of Nations

10 This is the account[t] of Shem, Ham
and Japheth, Noah's sons, who themselves had sons after the flood.

[a] 20 Or *soil, was the first* [b] 27 *Japheth* sounds like the Hebrew for *extend.*

covenantal relationship with Noah's descendants as well as with every beast of the earth. This note of universality is given further expression by Hosea (2:18) and Jonah (4:11). When Paul encourages Roman believers about struggles in this life, he reminds them that they are not alone, but assures them that the whole creation also groans and suffers, eagerly anticipating that final redemption from the curse of sin. The promise given here is to never destroy the earth again by flood (v. 11). The rainbow is then a testimony of the existence of this promise.

9:4 *lifeblood.* This restriction gets more attention in Leviticus (see Lev. 17:11–12). Blood represents the animal's life. It may be used in sacrifice, for all life belongs to the Lord.

9:6 *image of God.* Sin did not destroy man as the image of God. God values human life more highly than animal life because only humankind possesses God's image.

9:9 *covenant.* This is the second occurrence in Genesis of the important concept of covenant (6:18). God promised that He would establish His covenant with Noah and here He accomplished this great work.

9:26–27 *Shem.* Shem was given precedence over his brothers. Eber and Abram were descended from Shem (11:10–30), so Shem's blessing is ultimately a blessing on Israel.

9:29 *and then he died.* Noah's death was the end of an era. Only he and his family spanned two worlds, that of the earth before and after the flood. His long

9:4 [c] Lev 3:17; 17:10-14; Dt 12:16, 23-25; 1Sa 14:33 **9:5** [d] Ex 21:28-32 [e] Ge 4:10 **9:6** [f] Ge 4:14; Ex 21:12, 14; Lev 24:17; Mt 26:52 [g] Ge 1:26 **9:7** [h] Ge 1:22 **9:9** [i] Ge 6:18 **9:11** [j] ver 16; Isa 24:5 [k] Ge 8:21; Isa 54:9 **9:12** [l] ver 17; Ge 17:11 **9:15** [m] Ex 2:24; Lev 26:42, 45; Dt 7:9; Eze 16:60 **9:16** [n] ver 11; Ge 17:7, 13, 19; 2Sa 7:13, 23:5 **9:17** [o] ver 12; Ge 17:11 **9:18** [p] ver 25-27; Ge 10:6, 15 **9:19** [q] Ge 10:32 **9:25** [r] ver 18 [s] Ge 25:23; Jos 9:23 **10:1** [t] Ge 2:4

The Japhethites

2The sons[a] of Japheth:
Gomer,[u] Magog,[v] Madai, Javan, Tubal,[w] Meshek and Tiras.
3The sons of Gomer:
Ashkenaz,[x] Riphath and Togarmah.[y]
4The sons of Javan:
Elishah, Tarshish,[z] the Kittites and the Rodanites.[b] 5(From these the maritime peoples spread out into their territories by their clans within their nations, each with its own language.)

The Hamites

6The sons of Ham:
Cush, Egypt, Put and Canaan.[a]
7The sons of Cush:
Seba, Havilah, Sabtah, Raamah and Sabteka.
The sons of Raamah:
Sheba and Dedan.

8Cush was the father[c] of Nimrod, who
became a mighty warrior on the earth. 9He
was a mighty hunter before the LORD; that
is why it is said, "Like Nimrod, a mighty
hunter before the LORD." 10The first centers of his kingdom were Babylon,[b] Uruk,
Akkad and Kalneh, in[d] Shinar.[ec] 11From
that land he went to Assyria,[d] where he
built Nineveh,[e] Rehoboth Ir,[f] Calah 12and
Resen, which is between Nineveh and Calah—which is the great city.

13Egypt was the father of
the Ludites, Anamites, Lehabites, Naphtuhites, 14Pathrusites, Kasluhites (from whom the Philistines[f] came) and Caphtorites.
15Canaan[g] was the father of
Sidon[h] his firstborn,[g] and of the Hittites,[i] 16Jebusites,[j] Amorites, Girgashites, 17Hivites, Arkites, Sinites, 18Arvadites, Zemarites and Hamathites.

Later the Canaanite[k] clans scattered
19and the borders of Canaan[l] reached from
Sidon[m] toward Gerar as far as Gaza, and
then toward Sodom, Gomorrah, Admah
and Zeboyim, as far as Lasha.
20These are the sons of Ham by their
clans and languages, in their territories
and nations.

The Semites

21Sons were also born to Shem, whose
older brother was[h] Japheth; Shem was the
ancestor of all the sons of Eber.[n]

22The sons of Shem:
Elam,[o] Ashur, Arphaxad,[p] Lud and Aram.
23The sons of Aram:
Uz,[q] Hul, Gether and Meshek.[i]
24Arphaxad was the father of[j] Shelah, and Shelah the father of Eber.[r]
25Two sons were born to Eber:
One was named Peleg,[k] because in his time the earth was divided; his brother was named Joktan.
26Joktan was the father of
Almodad, Sheleph, Hazarmaveth,
Jerah, 27Hadoram, Uzal, Diklah,
28Obal, Abimael, Sheba, 29Ophir,
Havilah and Jobab. All these were sons of Joktan.

30The region where they lived stretched
from Mesha toward Sephar, in the eastern
hill country.
31These are the sons of Shem by their
clans and languages, in their territories
and nations.

---

[a] 2 *Sons* may mean *descendants* or *successors* or *nations*; also in verses 3, 4, 6, 7, 20-23, 29 and 31. [b] 4 Some manuscripts of the Masoretic Text and Samaritan Pentateuch (see also Septuagint and 1 Chron. 1:7); most manuscripts of the Masoretic Text *Dodanites* [c] 8 *Father* may mean *ancestor* or *predecessor* or *founder*; also in verses 13, 15, 24 and 26. [d] 10 Or *Uruk and Akkad—all of them in* [e] 10 That is, Babylonia [f] 11 Or *Nineveh with its city squares* [g] 15 Or *of the Sidonians, the foremost* [h] 21 Or *Shem, the older brother of* [i] 23 See Septuagint and 1 Chron. 1:17; Hebrew *Mash.* [j] 24 Hebrew; Septuagint *father of Cainan, and Cainan was the father of* [k] 25 *Peleg* means *division.*

---

life (950 years) gave him opportunity to transmit to his many descendants the dramatic story that he had lived out with his family. Peoples in places and cultures the world over have memories and stories of a great flood in antiquity. The details differ, but the stories remain.

10:2 *The sons of Japheth.* The listing of Japheth's descendants is briefer than the others. Among the persons and peoples mentioned is Javan, an ancient name for the Greek people. It is thought that many of Japheth's descendants migrated to Europe.

10:6 *The sons of Ham.* Cush is the ancient name for Ethiopia; Mizraim is a name for Egypt.

10:7–11 *Nimrod.* Like Lamech the descendant of Cain, Nimrod's infamy was proverbial. His territory was in the lands of the east, the fabled ancient cities of Mesopotamia. The prophet Micah would later use the name Nimrod to describe the region of Assyria, which would come under God's judgment (Mic. 5:5–6).

10:21–24 *Eber.* This is the name that gives rise to the term *Hebrew*, which is first used of Abram in 14:13. Eber descended from Shem, the one of Noah's sons who was appointed to carry on the messianic line. Abram was a direct descendant of Eber.

10:2 [u] Eze 38:6 [v] Eze 38:2; Rev 20:8 [w] Isa 66:19 **10:3** [x] Jer 51:27 [y] Eze 27:14; 38:6 **10:4** [z] Eze 27:12, 25; Jnh 1:3 **10:6** [a] ver 15; Ge 9:18 **10:10** [b] Ge 11:9 [c] Ge 11:2 **10:11** [d] Ps 83:8; Mic 5:6 [e] Jnh 1:2; 4:11; Na 1:1 **10:14** [f] Ge 21:32, 34; 26:1, 8 **10:15** [g] ver 6; Ge 9:18 [h] Eze 28:21 [i] Ge 23:3, 20 **10:16** [j] 1Ch 11:4 **10:18** [k] Ge 12:6; Ex 13:11 **10:19** [l] Ge 11:31; 13:12; 17:8 [m] ver 15 **10:21** [n] ver 24; Nu 24:24 **10:22** [o] Jer 49:34 [p] Lk 3:36 **10:23** [q] Job 1:1 **10:24** [r] ver 21

32 These are the clans of Noah's sons,[s]
according to their lines of descent, within their nations. From these the nations
spread out over the earth[t] after the flood.

The Tower of Babel

11 Now the whole world had one language and a common speech. 2 As
people moved eastward,[a] they found a
plain in Shinar[bu] and settled there.
3 They said to each other, "Come, let's
make bricks[v] and bake them thoroughly."
They used brick instead of stone, and tar[w]
for mortar. 4 Then they said, "Come, let us
build ourselves a city, with a tower that
reaches to the heavens,[x] so that we may
make a name[y] for ourselves; otherwise we
will be scattered over the face of the whole
earth."[z]
5 But the LORD came down[a] to see the city
and the tower the people were building.
6 The LORD said, "If as one people speaking the same language they have begun to
do this, then nothing they plan to do will
be impossible for them. 7 Come, let us[b] go
down and confuse their language so they
will not understand each other."[c]
8 So the LORD scattered them from there
over all the earth,[d] and they stopped building the city. 9 That is why it was called Babel[ce]—because there the LORD confused
the language of the whole world. From
there the LORD scattered them over the face
of the whole earth.

From Shem to Abram

10 This is the account of Shem's family
line.

Two years after the flood, when Shem
was 100 years old, he became the father[d]
of Arphaxad. 11 And after he became the
father of Arphaxad, Shem lived 500 years
and had other sons and daughters.
12 When Arphaxad had lived 35 years, he
became the father of Shelah.[f] 13 And after
he became the father of Shelah, Arphaxad lived 403 years and had other sons and
daughters.[e]
14 When Shelah had lived 30 years, he
became the father of Eber. 15 And after he
became the father of Eber, Shelah lived 403
years and had other sons and daughters.
16 When Eber had lived 34 years, he became the father of Peleg. 17 And after he
became the father of Peleg, Eber lived 430
years and had other sons and daughters.
18 When Peleg had lived 30 years, he
became the father of Reu. 19 And after he
became the father of Reu, Peleg lived 209
years and had other sons and daughters.
20 When Reu had lived 32 years, he became the father of Serug.[g] 21 And after he
became the father of Serug, Reu lived 207
years and had other sons and daughters.
22 When Serug had lived 30 years, he became the father of Nahor. 23 And after he
became the father of Nahor, Serug lived
200 years and had other sons and daughters.
24 When Nahor had lived 29 years, he became the father of Terah.[h] 25 And after he
became the father of Terah, Nahor lived
119 years and had other sons and daughters.

---

a 2 Or *from the east*; or *in the east* *b* 2 That is, Babylonia *c* 9 That is, Babylon; *Babel* sounds like the Hebrew for *confused*. *d* 10 *Father* may mean *ancestor*; also in verses 11-25.
e *12,13* Hebrew; Septuagint (see also Luke 3:35, 36 and note at Gen. 10:24) *35 years, he became the father of Cainan. 13And after he became the father of Cainan, Arphaxad lived 430 years and had other sons and daughters, and then he died. When Cainan had lived 130 years, he became the father of Shelah. And after he became the father of Shelah, Cainan lived 330 years and had other sons and daughters*

10:32 *the clans of Noah's sons.* Although not every ancient people group is listed in this "Table of the Nations," its clear teaching is that all the varied peoples of the earth, no matter of what land or language, are descended from Noah.

11:2 *a plain in Shinar.* This is the region of ancient Babylon in Mesopotamia (10:10).

11:4 Pride—God divided the human race into different language groups because they had refused to obey His command to fill the earth, and had become united for an evil purpose. This does not mean that God wants the world to remain divided. Christ came to reconcile the world to God (2 Cor. 5:19), and when we are in Christ we are not only reconciled to God, but to one another (Eph. 2:11–19). The unity God destroyed by judgment at Babel was restored by grace on the day of Pentecost. On that day people from different nations came together to hear the gospel in their own languages.

11:7 *let us go down.* The plural "us" in this passage is similar to the language of 1:26–28. The plural pronoun emphasizes the majesty of the speaker.

11:9 *Babel.* There is a pun in this name that no Hebrew reader would miss. The verb for *confuse* sounds similar to the name of the city. ***confused . . . scattered.*** Because of their pride and arrogance, God scattered the peoples of the earth and confused their language, but one day peoples of all languages and cultures will unite to celebrate the grace of God's risen Son, lifting their voices together in praise of the Lamb (Rev. 5:8–14).

11:10–25 *Shem's family line.* This genealogy shows that Abram was a descendant of Noah through Shem, just as Noah was a descendant of Adam through Seth. It is interesting to note that while the people mentioned in this genealogy lived to be very old, they did not reach the great ages of the peoples before the flood. Instead, their lives appear to be growing progressively shorter.

10:32 [s] ver 1 [t] Ge 9:19 **11:2** [u] Ge 10:10 **11:3** [v] Ex 1:14 [w] Ge 14:10 **11:4** [x] Dt 1:28; 9:1 [y] Ge 6:4 [z] Dt 4:27 **11:5** [a] ver 7; Ge 18:21; Ex 3:8; 19:11, 18, 20 **11:7** [b] Ge 1:26 [c] Ge 42:23 **11:8** [d] Ge 9:19; Lk 1:51 **11:9** [e] Ge 10:10 **11:12** [f] Lk 3:35 **11:20** [g] Lk 3:35 **11:24** [h] Lk 3:34

26 After Terah had lived 70 years, he became the father of Abram,[i] Nahor[j] and Haran.

Abram's Family

27 This is the account of Terah's family
line.

Terah became the father of Abram, Nahor and Haran. And Haran became the father of Lot.[k] 28 While his father Terah was
still alive, Haran died in Ur of the Chaldeans,[l] in the land of his birth. 29 Abram and
Nahor both married. The name of Abram's
wife was Sarai,[m] and the name of Nahor's
wife was Milkah;[n] she was the daughter of
Haran, the father of both Milkah and Is-
kah. 30 Now Sarai was childless because
she was not able to conceive.[o]
31 Terah took his son Abram, his grandson Lot son of Haran, and his daughter-in-
law Sarai, the wife of his son Abram, and
together they set out from Ur of the Chaldeans[p] to go to Canaan.[q] But when they came
to Harran, they settled there.
32 Terah lived 205 years, and he died in
Harran.

The Call of Abram

12 The LORD had said to Abram, "Go
from your country, your people and
your father's household to the land I will
show you.[r]

2 "I will make you into a great nation,[s]
    and I will bless you;[t]
I will make your name great,
    and you will be a blessing.[a]
3 I will bless those who bless you,
    and whoever curses you I will curse;[u]
and all peoples on earth
    will be blessed through you.[v]"[b]

4 So Abram went, as the LORD had told
him; and Lot went with him. Abram was
seventy-five years old when he set out from
Harran.[w] 5 He took his wife Sarai, his nephew Lot, all the possessions they had accumulated and the people[x] they had acquired
in Harran, and they set out for the land of
Canaan, and they arrived there.
6 Abram traveled through the land[y] as
far as the site of the great tree of Moreh[z]
at Shechem. At that time the Canaanites[a]
were in the land. 7 The LORD appeared to
Abram[b] and said, "To your offspring[c] I will
give this land."[c] So he built an altar there to
the LORD,[d] who had appeared to him.
8 From there he went on toward the hills
east of Bethel[e] and pitched his tent, with
Bethel on the west and Ai on the east.
There he built an altar to the LORD and
called on the name of the LORD.
9 Then Abram set out and continued toward the Negev.[f]

Abram in Egypt

10 Now there was a famine in the land,
and Abram went down to Egypt to live
there for a while because the famine was
severe. 11 As he was about to enter Egypt,
he said to his wife Sarai, "I know what a
beautiful woman you are. 12 When the

---

[a] 2 Or *be seen as blessed* [b] 3 Or *earth / will use your name in blessings* (see 48:20) [c] 7 Or *seed*

11:28 ***Ur of the Chaldeans.*** For generations, scholars have believed this to be the famous Ur located near the ancient delta in the Persian Gulf where the Tigris and Euphrates Rivers flow together. More recently, some scholars have noted the tablets at Ebla that speak of an Ur in the region of north Syria and suggest that this is the city of Haran's death.

11:29 ***Sarai.*** The name Sarai means "princess," implying a person of noble birth. Later we learn that Sarai was Abram's half sister (20:12).

12:1 ***LORD.*** Even though the name Yahweh (translated LORD) is not explained until Exodus 3:14–15, it is used here to make it clear to the readers that this was the same God who later formed the nation of Israel, and who was the creator (2:4).

12:1–3 God's Covenant with Abram — The covenant with Abram is the first covenant that pertains to the rule of God. It is unconditional, and depends only on God who obligates Himself in grace, indicated by the unconditional declaration, "I will." The Abrahamic covenant is also the basis of other covenants and it promises blessings in three areas: (1) *national*—"I will make you into a great nation," (2) *personal*—"I will make your name great," and (3) *universal*—"all the peoples on earth will be blessed through you." The Abrahamic Covenant is an important link in all that God began to do, has done throughout history, and will continue to do until the consummation of history. God blesses Abram and all his descendants through the Messiah, who is Abram's progeny and provides salvation for the entire world.

12:2–3 ***I will bless you.*** There are seven elements in God's promise to Abram. The number seven is often used in Scripture to suggest fullness and completeness.

12:7 ***To your offspring.*** The land of Canaan was a gift to the descendants of Abram. God owned the land (Ps. 24:1); it was His to do with as He pleased. The people of Canaan had lost their right to occupy the land due to their awful depravity (see 15:16). Thus God declared that this land would become the land of Israel (15:18–21; 17:6–8).

12:8 ***called on the name of the LORD.*** This was not a private prayer but a public proclamation. Abram was telling others about the Lord.

12:11 ***beautiful woman.*** Sarai's physical beauty was remarkable considering her age. She was ten years younger than Abram, or about 65 (12:4; 17:17).

11:26 [i] Lk 3:34 [j] Jos 24:2 **11:27** [k] ver 31; Ge 12:4; 14:12; 19:1; 2Pe 2:7 **11:28** [l] ver 31; Ge 15:7 **11:29** [m] Ge 17:15 [n] Ge 22:20 **11:30** [o] Ge 16:1; 18:11 **11:31** [p] Ge 15:7; Ne 9:7; Ac 7:4 [q] Ge 10:19 **12:1** [r] Ac 7:3*; Heb 11:8 **12:2** [s] Ge 15:5; 17:2, 4; 18:18; 22:17; Dt 26:5 [t] Ge 24:1, 35 **12:3** [u] Ge 27:29; Ex 23:22; Nu 24:9 [v] Ge 18:18; 22:18; 26:4; Ac 3:25; Gal 3:8* **12:4** [w] Ge 11:31 **12:5** [x] Ge 14:14; 17:23 **12:6** [y] Heb 11:9 [z] Ge 35:4; Dt 11:30 [a] Ge 10:18 **12:7** [b] Ge 17:1; 18:1; Ex 6:3 [c] Ge 13:15, 17; 15:18; 17:8; Ps 105:9-11 [d] Ge 13:4 **12:8** [e] Ge 13:3 **12:9** [f] Ge 13:1, 3

Egyptians see you, they will say, 'This is his wife.' Then they will kill me but will let you live. 13Say you are my sister,[g] so that I will be treated well for your sake and my life will be spared because of you."

14When Abram came to Egypt, the Egyptians saw that Sarai was a very beautiful woman. 15And when Pharaoh's officials saw her, they praised her to Pharaoh, and she was taken into his palace. 16He treated Abram well for her sake, and Abram acquired sheep and cattle, male and female donkeys, male and female servants, and camels.

17But the LORD inflicted serious diseases on Pharaoh and his household[h] because of Abram's wife Sarai. 18So Pharaoh summoned Abram. "What have you done to me?"[i] he said. "Why didn't you tell me she was your wife? 19Why did you say, 'She is my sister,' so that I took her to be my wife? Now then, here is your wife. Take her and go!" 20Then Pharaoh gave orders about Abram to his men, and they sent him on his way, with his wife and everything he had.

Abram and Lot Separate

13 So Abram went up from Egypt to the Negev,[j] with his wife and everything he had, and Lot went with him. 2Abram had become very wealthy in livestock and in silver and gold.

3From the Negev he went from place to place until he came to Bethel,[k] to the place between Bethel and Ai where his tent had been earlier 4and where he had first built an altar.[l] There Abram called on the name of the LORD.

5Now Lot, who was moving about with Abram, also had flocks and herds and tents. 6But the land could not support them while they stayed together, for their possessions were so great that they were not able to stay together.[m] 7And quarreling[n] arose between Abram's herders and Lot's. The Canaanites and Perizzites were also living in the land[o] at that time.

8So Abram said to Lot, "Let's not have any quarreling between you and me,[p] or between your herders and mine, for we are close relatives.[q] 9Is not the whole land before you? Let's part company. If you go to the left, I'll go to the right; if you go to the right, I'll go to the left."

10Lot looked around and saw that the whole plain of the Jordan toward Zoar[r] was well watered, like the garden of the LORD,[s] like the land of Egypt. (This was before the LORD destroyed Sodom and Gomorrah.)[t] 11So Lot chose for himself the whole plain of the Jordan and set out toward the east. The two men parted company: 12Abram lived in the land of Canaan, while Lot lived among the cities of the plain[u] and pitched his tents near Sodom.[v] 13Now the people of Sodom were wicked and were sinning greatly against the LORD.[w]

14The LORD said to Abram after Lot had parted from him, "Look around from where you are, to the north and south, to the east and west.[x] 15All the land that you see I will give to you and your offspring[a] forever.[y] 16I will make your offspring like the dust of the earth, so that if anyone could count the dust, then your offspring could be counted. 17Go, walk through the length and breadth of the land,[z] for I am giving it to you."

18So Abram went to live near the great trees of Mamre[a] at Hebron,[b] where he pitched his tents. There he built an altar to the LORD.[c]

Abram Rescues Lot

14 At the time when Amraphel was king of Shinar,[b][d] Arioch king of Ellasar, Kedorlaomer king of Elam and Tidal king of Goyim, 2these kings went to war against Bera king of Sodom, Birsha king of Gomorrah, Shinab king of Admah, Shemeber king of Zeboyim,[e] and the king of Bela (that is, Zoar).[f] 3All these latter kings joined forces in the Valley of Siddim (that is, the Dead Sea Valley[g]). 4For twelve years they had been subject to Kedorlaomer, but in the thirteenth year they rebelled.

5In the fourteenth year, Kedorlaomer and the kings allied with him went out and defeated the Rephaites[h] in Ashteroth

---

[a] *15* Or *seed;* also in verse 16 [b] *1* That is, Babylonia; also in verse 9

12:13 ***my sister.*** Sarai *was* Abram's half sister, the daughter of his father but not of his mother (20:12).
12:17 ***the LORD inflicted ... Pharaoh.*** This is the first example of the cursing and blessing element of God's promise (see 12:2–3).
13:7 ***The Canaanites and Perizzites.*** As in 12:6, the point of this phrase is that the land was already populated; Abram and Lot did not come into an empty region but had to compete for land for their rapidly growing herds and flocks.
13:14–17 This section forms part of the set of texts that set the stage for the Abrahamic covenant (see the list at 15:1–21). This section builds on 12:1–3,7, the passage in which God first gave His great promise to Abram.
14:3 ***the Valley of Siddim.*** This valley is most likely submerged under the waters of the Dead Sea today.

12:13 [g] Ge 20:2; 26:7 **12:17** [h] 1Ch 16:21 **12:18** [i] Ge 20:9; 26:10 **13:1** [j] Ge 12:9 **13:3** [k] Ge 12:8 **13:4** [l] Ge 12:7 **13:6** [m] Ge 36:7 **13:7** [n] Ge 26:20,21 [o] Ge 12:6 **13:8** [p] Pr 15:18; 20:3 [q] Ps 133:1 **13:10** [r] Ge 19:22,30 [s] Ge 2:8-10; Isa 51:3 [t] Ge 14:8; 19:17-29 **13:12** [u] Ge 19:17,25,29 [v] Ge 14:12 **13:13** [w] Ge 18:20; Eze 16:49-50; 2Pe 2:8 **13:14** [x] Ge 28:14; Dt 3:27 **13:15** [y] Ge 12:7; Gal 3:16* **13:17** [z] ver 15; Nu 13:17-25 **13:18** [a] Ge 14:13,24; 18:1 [b] Ge 35:27 [c] Ge 8:20 **14:1** [d] Ge 10:10 **14:2** [e] Ge 10:19 [f] Ge 13:10 **14:3** [g] Nu 34:3,12; Dt 3:17; Jos 3:16; 15:2,5 **14:5** [h] Ge 15:20; Dt 2:11,20

Karnaim, the Zuzites in Ham, the Emites[i]
in Shaveh Kiriathaim 6and the Horites[j] in
the hill country of Seir,[k] as far as El Paran[l]
near the desert. 7Then they turned back
and went to En Mishpat (that is, Kadesh),
and they conquered the whole territory of
the Amalekites, as well as the Amorites
who were living in Hazezon Tamar.[m]
8Then the king of Sodom, the king of
Gomorrah,[n] the king of Admah, the king
of Zeboyim[o] and the king of Bela (that is,
Zoar) marched out and drew up their battle lines in the Valley of Siddim 9against
Kedorlaomer king of Elam, Tidal king of
Goyim, Amraphel king of Shinar and Arioch king of Ellasar—four kings against
five. 10Now the Valley of Siddim was full of
tar pits, and when the kings of Sodom and
Gomorrah fled, some of the men fell into
them and the rest fled to the hills.[p] 11The
four kings seized all the goods of Sodom
and Gomorrah and all their food; then
they went away. 12They also carried off
Abram's nephew Lot and his possessions,
since he was living in Sodom.
13A man who had escaped came and
reported this to Abram the Hebrew. Now
Abram was living near the great trees of
Mamre[q] the Amorite, a brother[a] of Eshkol and Aner, all of whom were allied with
Abram. 14When Abram heard that his relative had been taken captive, he called out
the 318 trained men born in his household[r]
and went in pursuit as far as Dan.[s] 15Dur-
ing the night Abram divided his men to
attack them and he routed them, pursuing
them as far as Hobah, north of Damascus.
16He recovered all the goods and brought
back his relative Lot and his possessions,
together with the women and the other
people.
17After Abram returned from defeating
Kedorlaomer and the kings allied with
him, the king of Sodom came out to meet
him in the Valley of Shaveh (that is, the
King's Valley).[t]
18Then Melchizedek[u] king of Salem[v]
brought out bread and wine. He was
priest of God Most High, 19and he blessed
Abram,[w] saying,

"Blessed be Abram by God Most High,
Creator of heaven and earth.[x]
20And praise be to God Most High,[y]
who delivered your enemies into your
hand."

Then Abram gave him a tenth of everything.[z]
21The king of Sodom said to Abram,
"Give me the people and keep the goods
for yourself."
22But Abram said to the king of Sodom,
"With raised hand[a] I have sworn an oath to
the LORD, God Most High, Creator of heav-
en and earth,[b] 23that I will accept nothing
belonging to you,[c] not even a thread or the
strap of a sandal, so that you will never be
able to say, 'I made Abram rich.' 24I will accept nothing but what my men have eaten
and the share that belongs to the men who
went with me—to Aner, Eshkol and Mamre. Let them have their share."

The LORD's Covenant With Abram

15 After this, the word of the LORD came
to Abram[d] in a vision:

"Do not be afraid,[e] Abram.
I am your shield,[b][f]
your very great reward.[c]"

2But Abram said, "Sovereign LORD, what
can you give me since I remain childless[g]

[a] 13 Or *a relative*; or *an ally* [b] 1 Or *sovereign*
[c] 1 Or *shield; / your reward will be very great*

14:14 *318 trained men.* The fact that Abram could find this many fighting men from among his own servants is an indication of the great wealth and honor that the Lord had given him (12:2–3).

14:18 *Melchizedek.* This name means "My King is Righteous." Melchizedek was a contemporary of Abram who worshipped the living God. He is described as the "king of Salem," an older shorter name for Jerusalem. The word is based on the root from which the word *shalom* (peace) comes. Melchizedek is a mysterious figure, apparently appearing from nowhere, and with no explanation of his family or background. He is a priest of God Most High, even though there is no indication that he is of Abram's family or even a descendant of Shem. The writer of Hebrews compares Melchizedek with another priest, the Lord Jesus Christ (see Heb. 5:9; Ps. 110:4).

14:20 *praise be to God Most High.* When we bless God, we acknowledge Him as the source of all our blessings (Ps. 103:1–2). ***gave him a tenth.*** This is the first mention of tithing in the Bible. Even though there is no record of tithing as a command until much later (Deut. 14:22), the concept of a tenth belonging to God was apparently known. Abram's gift indicates that he considered Melchizedek a true priest of the living God; in giving this gift Abram was giving to the Lord.

14:22 *the LORD, God Most High.* Abraham identified Yahweh, translated here as "the LORD," with the most high God for whom Melchizedek was priest. This is a clear statement that he and Melchizedek worshipped the same God.

15:1–21 This section is one of the texts that present the Abrahamic covenant (see 17:1–22; 18:1–15; 22:15–18; 26:23–24; 35:9–15; compare also 12:1–3, 7; 13:14–17).

15:2 *Eliezer of Damascus.* This man had the honor of being Abram's heir because Abram and Sarai had

14:5 [i] Dt 2:10 **14:6** [j] Dt 2:12, 22 [k] Dt 2:1, 5, 22 [l] Ge 21:21; Nu 10:12 **14:7** [m] 2Ch 20:2 **14:8** [n] Ge 13:10; 19:17-29 [o] Dt 29:23 **14:10** [p] Ge 19:17, 30 **14:13** [q] ver 24; Ge 13:18 **14:14** [r] Ge 15:3 [s] Dt 34:1; Jdg 18:29 **14:17** [t] 2Sa 18:18 **14:18** [u] Ps 110:4; Heb 5:6 [v] Ps 76:2; Heb 7:2 **14:19** [w] Heb 7:6 [x] ver 22 **14:20** [y] Ge 24:27 [z] Ge 28:22; Dt 26:12; Heb 7:4 **14:22** [a] Ex 6:8; Da 12:7; Rev 10:5-6 [b] ver 19 **14:23** [c] 2Ki 5:16 **15:1** [d] Da 10:1 [e] Ge 21:17; 26:24; 46:3; 2Ki 6:16; Ps 27:1; Isa 41:10, 13-14 [f] Dt 33:29; 2Sa 22:3, 31; Ps 3:3 **15:2** [g] Ac 7:5

and the one who will inherit[a] my estate is
Eliezer of Damascus?" 3And Abram said,
"You have given me no children; so a servant[h] in my household will be my heir."
4Then the word of the LORD came to him:
"This man will not be your heir, but a son
who is your own flesh and blood will be
your heir.[i]" 5He took him outside and said,
"Look up at the sky and count the stars[j]—if
indeed you can count them." Then he said
to him, "So shall your offspring[b] be."[k]
6Abram believed the LORD, and he credited it to him as righteousness.[l]
7He also said to him, "I am the LORD, who
brought you out of Ur of the Chaldeans to
give you this land to take possession of it."
8But Abram said, "Sovereign LORD, how
can I know[m] that I will gain possession
of it?"
9So the LORD said to him, "Bring me a
heifer, a goat and a ram, each three years
old, along with a dove and a young pigeon."
10Abram brought all these to him, cut
them in two and arranged the halves opposite each other;[n] the birds, however, he
did not cut in half.[o] 11Then birds of prey
came down on the carcasses, but Abram
drove them away.
12As the sun was setting, Abram fell into
a deep sleep,[p] and a thick and dreadful
darkness came over him. 13Then the LORD
said to him, "Know for certain that for four
hundred years[q] your descendants will be
strangers in a country not their own and
that they will be enslaved[r] and mistreated
there. 14But I will punish the nation they
serve as slaves, and afterward they will
come out[s] with great possessions.[t] 15You,
however, will go to your ancestors in peace
and be buried at a good old age.[u] 16In the
fourth generation your descendants will
come back here, for the sin of the Amorites[v]
has not yet reached its full measure."
17When the sun had set and darkness
had fallen, a smoking firepot with a blazing torch appeared and passed between
the pieces.[w] 18On that day the LORD made
a covenant with Abram and said, "To your
descendants I give this land,[x] from the
Wadi[c] of Egypt[y] to the great river, the Euphrates— 19the land of the Kenites, Kenizzites, Kadmonites, 20Hittites, Perizzites,
Rephaites, 21Amorites, Canaanites, Girgashites and Jebusites."

Hagar and Ishmael

16 Now Sarai, Abram's wife, had borne
him no children.[z] But she had an
Egyptian slave[a] named Hagar; 2so she
said to Abram, "The LORD has kept me
from having children. Go, sleep with my

---

[a] 2 The meaning of the Hebrew for this phrase is uncertain. [b] 5 Or *seed* [c] 18 Or *river*

---

no child of their own. Some have wondered if Eliezer is also the unnamed servant of Abraham who went on the quest for a wife for Isaac (24:2 – 5).

15:6 *Abram believed.* Almost ten years had passed since the original promises were given. As Abram grew older and still had no children, it was natural for him to wonder how the promises could be fulfilled. In answer to Abram's questions, God, who had revealed Himself in word, and who had faithfully protected him and sustained him, again pledged His word of promise. Abram believed and his faith was accounted to him as righteousness. Some have thought that in Old Testament times people were saved by their good deeds rather than by faith, but this idea is mistaken. Abram was not saved because of righteous living or obedience, but by believing in God and so being declared righteous by Him. The only valid work is the work of faith (John 6:28 – 29; James 2:2).

15:9 *Bring me.* Abram prepared the sacrifice, but God enacted the sign (v. 17). This emphasizes the unilateral, unconditional nature of the covenant.

15:12 *dreadful darkness.* These two words give great emphasis to the meaning "an overwhelmingly dark terror." This kind of reaction to the indescribable holiness of the Lord (Is. 6:3; 40:25) is natural—Abram was about to experience the presence of the Almighty. This was a moment of profound dread and holy awe.

15:13 *four hundred years.* Moses wrote down the story of Abram's life from the vantage point of the generation who fulfilled this prophecy (Ex. 12:40 – 42).

15:17 *between the pieces.* This last element has profound implications. In solemn agreements between equals (parity treaties), both parties would pass between the bloody pieces of slain animals and birds. The symbol would be evident to all: "May I become like this if I do not keep my part of the agreement." But Abram was not to walk this grisly pathway. Only God made the journey in the symbols of smoke and fire. The fulfillment of the promise of God to Abram, the Abrahamic covenant, is as sure as the ongoing life of the Lord.

15:18 *this land.* God's promise to Abram included his descendants and the Promised One, the Seed of Genesis 3:15. But the promise also included the land of Canaan. God removed the people of Israel from the land of Canaan several times, but He never revoked His everlasting promise 17:8). The promise will be fulfilled in its fullness when Jesus Christ returns (Is. 9:1 – 7). ***the Wadi of Egypt.*** The "Wadi of Egypt" may refer to the Nile, or it may be what is called today the Wadi el Arish, a smaller watercourse at the natural boundary of Egypt and the land of Israel. ***the great river, the Euphrates.*** This is the northern arm of the Euphrates in Syria.

15:20 *Rephaites.* A people of unusually tall stature; they are also referred to in 2 Samuel 21:15 – 22 (see Num. 13:33; Deut. 2:11; 3:11).

16:2 *Go, sleep with my slave.* This seems to have been an accepted practice in the ancient middle east.

15:3 [h] Ge 24:2,34 **15:4** [i] Gal 4:28 **15:5** [j] Ps 147:4; Jer 33:22 [k] Ge 12:2; 22:17; Ex 32:13; Ro 4:18*; Heb 11:12 **15:6** [l] Ps 106:31; Ro 4:3*, 20-24*; Gal 3:6*; Jas 2:23* **15:8** [m] Lk 1:18 **15:10** [n] ver 17; Jer 34:18 [o] Lev 1:17 **15:12** [p] Ge 2:21 **15:13** [q] ver 16; Ex 12:40; Ac 7:6, 17 [r] Ex 1:11 **15:14** [s] Ac 7:7* [t] Ex 12:32-38 **15:15** [u] Ge 25:8 **15:16** [v] 1Ki 21:26 **15:17** [w] ver 10 **15:18** [x] Ge 12:7 [y] Nu 34:5 **16:1** [z] Ge 11:30; Gal 4:24-25 [a] Ge 21:9

slave; perhaps I can build a family through
her."[b]
Abram agreed to what Sarai said. 3So
after Abram had been living in Canaan[c]
ten years, Sarai his wife took her Egyptian
slave Hagar and gave her to her husband
to be his wife. 4He slept with Hagar, and
she conceived.
When she knew she was pregnant, she
began to despise her mistress. 5Then Sarai said to Abram, "You are responsible for
the wrong I am suffering. I put my slave in
your arms, and now that she knows she is
pregnant, she despises me. May the LORD
judge between you and me."[d]
6"Your slave is in your hands," Abram
said. "Do with her whatever you think
best." Then Sarai mistreated Hagar; so she
fled from her.
7The angel of the LORD[e] found Hagar
near a spring in the desert; it was the
spring that is beside the road to Shur.[f] 8And
he said, "Hagar, slave of Sarai, where have
you come from, and where are you going?"
"I'm running away from my mistress Sarai," she answered.
9Then the angel of the LORD told her, "Go
back to your mistress and submit to her."
10The angel added, "I will increase your
descendants so much that they will be too
numerous to count."[g]
11The angel of the LORD also said to her:

"You are now pregnant
and you will give birth to a son.
You shall name him Ishmael,*[a]*
for the LORD has heard of your
misery.[h]
12He will be a wild donkey of a man;
his hand will be against everyone
and everyone's hand against him,
and he will live in hostility
toward*[b]* all his brothers.[i]"

13She gave this name to the LORD who
spoke to her: "You are the God who sees
me," for she said, "I have now seen[c] the One
who sees me."[j] 14That is why the well was
called Beer Lahai Roi*[d]*; it is still there, between Kadesh and Bered.
15So Hagar bore Abram a son,[k] and
Abram gave the name Ishmael to the son
she had borne. 16Abram was eighty-six
years old when Hagar bore him Ishmael.

The Covenant of Circumcision

17 When Abram was ninety-nine years
old, the LORD appeared to him and
said, "I am God Almighty*[e]*;[l] walk before me
faithfully and be blameless.[m] 2Then I will
make my covenant between me and you[n]
and will greatly increase your numbers."
3Abram fell facedown, and God said
to him, 4"As for me, this is my covenant
with you:[o] You will be the father of many
nations.[p] 5No longer will you be called
Abram*[f]*; your name will be Abraham,*[g]*[q]
for I have made you a father of many nations.[r] 6I will make you very fruitful;[s] I will
make nations of you, and kings will come
from you.[t] 7I will establish my covenant as
an everlasting covenant between me and
you and your descendants after you for the
generations to come, to be your God[u] and
the God of your descendants after you.[v]
8The whole land of Canaan,[w] where you
now reside as a foreigner,[x] I will give as
an everlasting possession to you and your
descendants after you;[y] and I will be their
God."
9Then God said to Abraham, "As for you,
you must keep my covenant, you and your
descendants after you for the generations
to come. 10This is my covenant with you
and your descendants after you, the covenant you are to keep: Every male among

a *11 Ishmael* means *God hears.* *b* *12* Or *live to the east / of* *c* *13* Or *seen the back of*
d *14 Beer Lahai Roi* means *well of the Living One who sees me.* *e* *1* Hebrew *El-Shaddai*
f *5 Abram* means *exalted father.* *g* *5 Abraham* probably means *father of many.*

If a woman was unable to bear children, she might use her servant as a surrogate mother, and adopt the child as her own.

16:11 *Ishmael.* The name Ishmael uses the divine name El, and means "God hears."

17:4 *covenant.* While the peoples who descended directly from Abram (the nation of Israel, the Midianites, Ishmaelites, and Edomites) were certainly numerous, Abram was "father of many" in a much broader sense yet. The message of the New Testament reveals that God's promise to Abram is to be fulfilled in the community of faith in every nation. The promise was so certain that his name was changed to Abraham, as an everlasting reminder of God's gracious covenant. Furthermore, the emphatic "as for Me" underscores the identity of the all-sufficient God who takes the initiative for establishing the covenantal relationship. This relationship is both spiritual and personal, anticipating the divine pledge, "and I will be their God." The wonder of it all is that we who believe in Jesus Christ are part of that "multitude of nations" who share in the faith of Abraham "who is the father of us all."

17:5 *Abram ... Abraham.* This name change is significant. Abram means "exalted Father." Abraham means "Father of Many"—a direct reflection of his new role.

17:8 *the land ... an everlasting possession.* The promise clearly included the Israelite people *and* the land of Canaan. The two are linked in the language of the covenant in chapter 15. Even though God removed Israel more than once from

16:2 [b] Ge 30:3-4,9-10 **16:3** [c] Ge 12:5 **16:5** [d] Ge 31:53
16:7 [e] Ge 21:17; 22:11, 15; 31:11 [f] Ge 20:1
16:10 [g] Ge 13:16; 17:20 **16:11** [h] Ex 2:24; 3:7,9
16:12 [i] Ge 25:18 **16:13** [j] Ge 32:30 **16:15** [k] Gal 4:22
17:1 [l] Ge 28:3; Ex 6:3 [m] Dt 18:13 **17:2** [n] Ge 15:18
17:4 [o] Ge 15:18 [p] ver 16; Ge 12:2; 35:11; 48:19
17:5 [q] ver 15; Ne 9:7 [r] Ro 4:17* **17:6** [s] Ge 35:11 [t] Mt 1:6
17:7 [u] Ex 29:45, 46 [v] Ro 9:8; Gal 3:16 **17:8** [w] Ps 105:9, 11
[x] Ge 23:4; 28:4; Ex 6:4 [y] Ge 12:7

you shall be circumcised.[z] 11You are to
undergo circumcision,[a] and it will be the
sign of the covenant[b] between me and you.
12For the generations to come every male
among you who is eight days old must be
circumcised,[c] including those born in your
household or bought with money from a
foreigner—those who are not your offspring. 13Whether born in your household
or bought with your money, they must be
circumcised. My covenant in your flesh is
to be an everlasting covenant. 14Any uncircumcised male, who has not been circumcised in the flesh, will be cut off from his
people;[d] he has broken my covenant."

15God also said to Abraham, "As for Sarai your wife, you are no longer to call her
Sarai; her name will be Sarah. 16I will bless
her and will surely give you a son by her.[e] I
will bless her so that she will be the mother of nations;[f] kings of peoples will come
from her."

17Abraham fell facedown; he laughed[g]
and said to himself, "Will a son be born to a
man a hundred years old? Will Sarah bear
a child at the age of ninety?" 18And Abraham said to God, "If only Ishmael might
live under your blessing!"

19Then God said, "Yes, but your wife Sarah will bear you a son,[h] and you will call
him Isaac.[a] I will establish my covenant
with him[i] as an everlasting covenant for his
descendants after him. 20And as for Ishmael, I have heard you: I will surely bless him;
I will make him fruitful and will greatly
increase his numbers.[j] He will be the father
of twelve rulers,[k] and I will make him into
a great nation.[l] 21But my covenant I will establish with Isaac, whom Sarah will bear
to you by this time next year."[m] 22When he
had finished speaking with Abraham, God
went up from him.

23On that very day Abraham took his son
Ishmael and all those born in his household
or bought with his money, every male in
his household, and circumcised them, as
God told him. 24Abraham was ninety-nine
years old when he was circumcised,[n] 25and
his son Ishmael was thirteen; 26Abraham
and his son Ishmael were both circumcised on that very day. 27And every male
in Abraham's household, including those
born in his household or bought from a foreigner, was circumcised with him.

The Three Visitors

18 The LORD appeared to Abraham near
the great trees of Mamre[o] while he
was sitting at the entrance to his tent in the
heat of the day. 2Abraham looked up and
saw three men[p] standing nearby. When he
saw them, he hurried from the entrance of
his tent to meet them and bowed low to the
ground.

3He said, "If I have found favor in your
eyes, my lord,[b] do not pass your servant
by. 4Let a little water be brought, and then
you may all wash your feet[q] and rest under this tree. 5Let me get you something to
eat,[r] so you can be refreshed and then go
on your way—now that you have come to
your servant."

"Very well," they answered, "do as you
say."

6So Abraham hurried into the tent to
Sarah. "Quick," he said, "get three seahs[c]
of the finest flour and knead it and bake
some bread."

7Then he ran to the herd and selected a
choice, tender calf and gave it to a servant,
who hurried to prepare it. 8He then brought
some curds and milk and the calf that had
been prepared, and set these before them.[s]
While they ate, he stood near them under
a tree.

9"Where is your wife Sarah?" they asked
him.

"There, in the tent," he said.

10Then one of them said, "I will surely
return to you about this time next year, and
Sarah your wife will have a son."[t]

---

[a] *19 Isaac* means *he laughs.* [b] *3* Or *eyes, Lord*
[c] *6* That is, probably about 36 pounds or about 16 kilograms

---

the land, He promised them ultimate possession of Canaan.

17:13 *circumcised.* Circumcision in and of itself did not make people acceptable to God. It was meant as a tangible symbol of God's covenant in their lives, as an outward sign standing for the inward reality of a thorough commitment to God. In the New Testament, the apostle Paul speaks of having a "circumcised heart," pointing to the fact that a circumcised body means nothing if the heart is not in accord (Rom. 2:25–29).

17:15 *Sarai ... Sarah.* Both names come from the same root, meaning "Princess." No explanation is given for the change in Sarah's name, but like the name change from Abram to Abraham (vv. 4–5) the new name accompanied a new relationship with God.

17:19 *Isaac.* The name Isaac means "laughter" (see 21:1–6).

18:1 *the LORD appeared.* This was the fifth time the Lord appeared to Abraham since he came into the land of Canaan (12:7; 13:14–17; 15:1–21; 17:1–22).

18:2–3 *three men.* Verse 1 states that the Lord appeared to Abraham, then the next verse refers to "three men." It seems clear from verses 1, 13 and 17 that one of the three was the Lord Himself, and from 19:1 on the other two are referred to as angels. Apparently all three were in human form, and were able to eat the meal that Abraham had prepared. Many have speculated that this was an appearance of the pre-incarnate Christ.

17:10 [z] ver 23; Ge 21:4; Jn 7:22; Ac 7:8; Ro 4:11 **17:11** [a] Ex 12:48; Dt 10:16 [b] Ro 4:11 **17:12** [c] Lev 12:3; Lk 2:21 **17:14** [d] Ex 4:24-26 **17:16** [e] Ge 18:10 [f] Ge 35:11; Gal 4:31 **17:17** [g] Ge 18:12; 21:6 **17:19** [h] Ge 18:14; 21:2 [i] Ge 26:3 **17:20** [j] Ge 16:10 [k] Ge 25:12-16 [l] Ge 21:18 **17:21** [m] Ge 21:2 **17:24** [n] Ro 4:11 **18:1** [o] Ge 13:18; 14:13 **18:2** [p] ver 16, 22; Ge 32:24; Jos 5:13; Jdg 13:6-11; Heb 13:2 **18:4** [q] Ge 19:2; 43:24 **18:5** [r] Jdg 13:15 **18:8** [s] Ge 19:3 **18:10** [t] Ro 9:9*

Now Sarah was listening at the entrance
to the tent, which was behind him. 11 Abraham and Sarah were already very old,[u]
and Sarah was past the age of childbearing.[v] 12 So Sarah laughed[w] to herself as she
thought, "After I am worn out and my lord[x]
is old, will I now have this pleasure?"
13 Then the LORD said to Abraham, "Why
did Sarah laugh and say, 'Will I really have
a child, now that I am old?' 14 Is anything
too hard for the LORD?[y] I will return to you
at the appointed time next year, and Sarah
will have a son."
15 Sarah was afraid, so she lied and said,
"I did not laugh."
But he said, "Yes, you did laugh."

Abraham Pleads for Sodom

16 When the men got up to leave, they
looked down toward Sodom, and Abraham walked along with them to see them
on their way. 17 Then the LORD said, "Shall
I hide from Abraham[z] what I am about to
do?[a] 18 Abraham will surely become a great
and powerful nation,[b] and all nations on
earth will be blessed through him.[a] 19 For
I have chosen him, so that he will direct
his children[c] and his household after him
to keep the way of the LORD[d] by doing what
is right and just, so that the LORD will bring
about for Abraham what he has promised
him."
20 Then the LORD said, "The outcry
against Sodom and Gomorrah is so great
and their sin so grievous 21 that I will go
down[e] and see if what they have done is as
bad as the outcry that has reached me. If
not, I will know."
22 The men turned away and went toward
Sodom,[f] but Abraham remained standing
before the LORD.[b] 23 Then Abraham approached him and said: "Will you sweep
away the righteous with the wicked?[g]
24 What if there are fifty righteous people in
the city? Will you really sweep it away and
not spare[c] the place for the sake of the fifty
righteous people in it?[h] 25 Far be it from you
to do such a thing—to kill the righteous
with the wicked, treating the righteous and
the wicked alike. Far be it from you! Will
not the Judge of all the earth do right?"[i]
26 The LORD said, "If I find fifty righteous
people in the city of Sodom, I will spare the
whole place for their sake.[j]"
27 Then Abraham spoke up again: "Now
that I have been so bold as to speak to the
Lord, though I am nothing but dust and
ashes,[k] 28 what if the number of the righteous is five less than fifty? Will you destroy the whole city for lack of five people?"
"If I find forty-five there," he said, "I will
not destroy it."
29 Once again he spoke to him, "What if
only forty are found there?"
He said, "For the sake of forty, I will not
do it."
30 Then he said, "May the Lord not be angry, but let me speak. What if only thirty
can be found there?"
He answered, "I will not do it if I find
thirty there."
31 Abraham said, "Now that I have been
so bold as to speak to the Lord, what if only
twenty can be found there?"
He said, "For the sake of twenty, I will
not destroy it."
32 Then he said, "May the Lord not be angry, but let me speak just once more.[l] What
if only ten can be found there?"
He answered, "For the sake of ten,[m] I will
not destroy it."
33 When the LORD had finished speaking
with Abraham, he left, and Abraham returned home.

Sodom and Gomorrah Destroyed

19 The two angels arrived at Sodom[n]
in the evening, and Lot was sitting
in the gateway of the city.[o] When he saw
them, he got up to meet them and bowed
down with his face to the ground. 2 "My
lords," he said, "please turn aside to your
servant's house. You can wash your feet[p]
and spend the night and then go on your
way early in the morning."
"No," they answered, "we will spend the
night in the square."
3 But he insisted so strongly that they did
go with him and entered his house. He prepared a meal for them, baking bread without yeast, and they ate.[q] 4 Before they had
gone to bed, all the men from every part of
the city of Sodom—both young and old—
surrounded the house. 5 They called to Lot,
"Where are the men who came to you tonight? Bring them out to us so that we can
have sex with them."[r]

---

[a] 18 Or *will use his name in blessings* (see 48:20)
[b] 22 Masoretic Text; an ancient Hebrew scribal tradition *but the LORD remained standing before Abraham*
[c] 24 Or *forgive*; also in verse 26

18:19 *For I have chosen him.* The language speaks of the intimate relationship which motivates the Lord to accomplish His purpose in Abraham (22:12). ***right and just.*** One idea in two words—"genuine righteousness".

19:2 *My lords.* This is a greeting of respect for special visitors.

19:5 *sex with them.* God has declared that homosexual activity is "detestable" (Lev. 18:22).

18:11 [u] Ge 17:17 [v] Ro 4:19 **18:12** [w] Ge 17:17; 21:6 [x] 1Pe 3:6 **18:14** [y] Jer 32:17, 27; Zec 8:6; Mt 19:26; Lk 1:37; Ro 4:21 **18:17** [z] Am 3:7 [a] Ge 19:24 **18:18** [b] Gal 3:8* **18:19** [c] Dt 4:9-10; 6:7 [d] Jos 24:15; Eph 6:4 **18:21** [e] Ge 11:5 **18:22** [f] Ge 19:1 **18:23** [g] Nu 16:22 **18:24** [h] Jer 5:1 **18:25** [i] Job 8:3, 20; Ps 58:11; 94:2; Isa 3:10-11; Ro 3:6 **18:26** [j] Jer 5:1 **18:27** [k] Ge 2:7; 3:19; Job 30:19; 42:6 **18:32** [l] Jdg 6:39 [m] Jer 5:1 **19:1** [n] Ge 18:22 [o] Ge 18:1 **19:2** [p] Ge 18:4; Lk 7:44 **19:3** [q] Ge 18:6 **19:5** [r] Jdg 19:22; Isa 3:9; Ro 1:24-27

6 Lot went outside to meet them[s] and shut
the door behind him 7 and said, "No, my
friends. Don't do this wicked thing. 8 Look,
I have two daughters who have never slept
with a man. Let me bring them out to you,
and you can do what you like with them.
But don't do anything to these men, for
they have come under the protection of my
roof."[t]
9 "Get out of our way," they replied. "This
fellow came here as a foreigner, and now
he wants to play the judge![u] We'll treat
you worse than them." They kept bringing pressure on Lot and moved forward to
break down the door.
10 But the men inside reached out and
pulled Lot back into the house and shut
the door. 11 Then they struck the men who
were at the door of the house, young and
old, with blindness[v] so that they could not
find the door.
12 The two men said to Lot, "Do you have
anyone else here—sons-in-law, sons or
daughters, or anyone else in the city who
belongs to you?[w] Get them out of here, 13 because we are going to destroy this place.
The outcry to the LORD against its people
is so great that he has sent us to destroy it."[x]
14 So Lot went out and spoke to his sons-
in-law, who were pledged to marry[a] his
daughters. He said, "Hurry and get out
of this place, because the LORD is about
to destroy the city![y]" But his sons-in-law
thought he was joking.[z]
15 With the coming of dawn, the angels
urged Lot, saying, "Hurry! Take your wife
and your two daughters who are here, or
you will be swept away[a] when the city is
punished.[b]"
16 When he hesitated, the men grasped
his hand and the hands of his wife and of
his two daughters and led them safely out
of the city, for the LORD was merciful to
them. 17 As soon as they had brought them
out, one of them said, "Flee for your lives![c]
Don't look back,[d] and don't stop anywhere
in the plain! Flee to the mountains or you
will be swept away!"
18 But Lot said to them, "No, my lords,[b]
please! 19 Your[c] servant has found favor
in your[c] eyes, and you[c] have shown great
kindness to me in sparing my life. But I
can't flee to the mountains; this disaster
will overtake me, and I'll die. 20 Look, here
is a town near enough to run to, and it is
small. Let me flee to it—it is very small,
isn't it? Then my life will be spared."
21 He said to him, "Very well, I will grant
this request too; I will not overthrow the
town you speak of. 22 But flee there quickly, because I cannot do anything until you
reach it." (That is why the town was called
Zoar.[d])
23 By the time Lot reached Zoar, the sun
had risen over the land. 24 Then the LORD
rained down burning sulfur on Sodom
and Gomorrah[e]—from the LORD out of the
heavens.[f] 25 Thus he overthrew those cities
and the entire plain, destroying all those
living in the cities—and also the vegetation in the land.[g] 26 But Lot's wife looked
back,[h] and she became a pillar of salt.[i]
27 Early the next morning Abraham got
up and returned to the place where he had
stood before the LORD.[j] 28 He looked down
toward Sodom and Gomorrah, toward all
the land of the plain, and he saw dense
smoke rising from the land, like smoke
from a furnace.[k]
29 So when God destroyed the cities of
the plain, he remembered Abraham, and
he brought Lot out of the catastrophe[l] that
overthrew the cities where Lot had lived.

Lot and His Daughters

30 Lot and his two daughters left Zoar and
settled in the mountains,[m] for he was afraid
to stay in Zoar. He and his two daughters
lived in a cave. 31 One day the older daughter said to the younger, "Our father is old,
and there is no man around here to give
us children—as is the custom all over the
earth. 32 Let's get our father to drink wine
and then sleep with him and preserve our
family line through our father."
33 That night they got their father to

a 14 Or *were married to* *b* 18 Or *No, Lord*; or *No, my lord* *c* 19 The Hebrew is singular. *d* 22 *Zoar* means *small.*

19:16 *the LORD was merciful to them.* This is the whole point of the story. God could have destroyed the city of Sodom with no word to Lot or Abraham (18:17). But because of His mercy, God's angels grabbed Lot and his family and brought them forcibly to safety. In this passage, Lot appears weak, indecisive, and unsure of whether he really wants to be rescued. However, the New Testament speaks a good word for Lot's character, calling him a "righteous man" and telling us that he was grieved by the sin he saw in Sodom and Gomorrah (2 Pet. 2:6–8).

19:22 *Zoar.* This name means "Insignificant in Size."

19:23–26 *burning sulfur.* This may be simply a supernatural judgment on the cities, but some have also theorized that the burning sulfur which "rained" down on them may have been from a volcanic eruption. In any case, it is clear that the destruction was a judgment from God, and that it was under His control.

19:26 *pillar of salt.* Near the Dead Sea, which is believed to now cover the site of Sodom and Gomorrah, there are numerous rock salt formations, including pillars about the size of a human. Jesus referred to the fate of Lot's wife as a historical fact (Luke 17:32).

19:6 [s] Jdg 19:23 **19:8** [t] Jdg 19:24 **19:9** [u] Ex 2:14; Ac 7:27 **19:11** [v] Dt 28:28-29; 2Ki 6:18; Ac 13:11 **19:12** [w] Ge 7:1 **19:13** [x] 1Ch 21:15 **19:14** [y] Nu 16:21 [z] Ex 9:21; Lk 17:28 **19:15** [a] Nu 16:26 [b] Rev 18:4 **19:17** [c] Jer 48:6 [d] ver 26 **19:24** [e] Dt 29:23; Isa 1:9; 13:19 [f] Lk 17:29; 2Pe 2:6; Jude 7 **19:25** [g] Ps 107:34; Eze 16:48 **19:26** [h] ver 17 [i] Lk 17:32 **19:27** [j] Ge 18:22 **19:28** [k] Rev 9:2; 18:9 **19:29** [l] 2Pe 2:7 **19:30** [m] ver 19

drink wine, and the older daughter went in and slept with him. He was not aware of it when she lay down or when she got up.

34 The next day the older daughter said to the younger, "Last night I slept with my father. Let's get him to drink wine again tonight, and you go in and sleep with him so we can preserve our family line through our father." 35 So they got their father to drink wine that night also, and the younger daughter went in and slept with him. Again he was not aware of it when she lay down or when she got up.

36 So both of Lot's daughters became pregnant by their father. 37 The older daughter had a son, and she named him Moab[a]; he is the father of the Moabites[n] of today. 38 The younger daughter also had a son, and she named him Ben-Ammi[b]; he is the father of the Ammonites[c][o] of today.

Abraham and Abimelek

20 Now Abraham moved on from there[p] into the region of the Negev and lived between Kadesh and Shur. For a while he stayed in Gerar,[q] 2 and there Abraham said of his wife Sarah, "She is my sister.[r]" Then Abimelek king of Gerar sent for Sarah and took her.[s]

3 But God came to Abimelek in a dream[t] one night and said to him, "You are as good as dead because of the woman you have taken; she is a married woman."[u]

4 Now Abimelek had not gone near her, so he said, "Lord, will you destroy an innocent nation?[v] 5 Did he not say to me, 'She is my sister,' and didn't she also say, 'He is my brother'? I have done this with a clear conscience and clean hands."

6 Then God said to him in the dream, "Yes, I know you did this with a clear conscience, and so I have kept[w] you from sinning against me. That is why I did not let you touch her. 7 Now return the man's wife, for he is a prophet, and he will pray for you[x] and you will live. But if you do not return her, you may be sure that you and all who belong to you will die."

8 Early the next morning Abimelek summoned all his officials, and when he told them all that had happened, they were very much afraid. 9 Then Abimelek called Abraham in and said, "What have you done to us? How have I wronged you that you have brought such great guilt upon me and my kingdom? You have done things to me that should never be done.[y]" 10 And Abimelek asked Abraham, "What was your reason for doing this?"

11 Abraham replied, "I said to myself, 'There is surely no fear of God[z] in this place, and they will kill me because of my wife.'[a] 12 Besides, she really is my sister, the daughter of my father though not of my mother; and she became my wife. 13 And when God had me wander from my father's household, I said to her, 'This is how you can show your love to me: Everywhere we go, say of me, "He is my brother."'"

14 Then Abimelek brought sheep and cattle and male and female slaves and gave them to Abraham,[b] and he returned Sarah his wife to him. 15 And Abimelek said, "My land is before you; live wherever you like."[c]

16 To Sarah he said, "I am giving your brother a thousand shekels[d] of silver. This is to cover the offense against you before all who are with you; you are completely vindicated."

17 Then Abraham prayed to God,[d] and God healed Abimelek, his wife and his female slaves so they could have children again, 18 for the LORD had kept all the women in Abimelek's household from conceiving because of Abraham's wife Sarah.[e]

The Birth of Isaac

21 Now the LORD was gracious to Sarah[f] as he had said, and the LORD did for Sarah what he had promised.[g] 2 Sarah became pregnant and bore a son[h] to Abra-

[a] 37 *Moab* sounds like the Hebrew for *from father.*
[b] 38 *Ben-Ammi* means *son of my father's people.*
[c] 38 Hebrew *Bene-Ammon* [d] *16* That is, about 25 pounds or about 12 kilograms

19:36–38 *Moab ... Ben-Ammi.* The shameful act of incest led to the births of two sons whose descendants (the Moabites and the Ammonites) would greatly trouble Israel.

20:2 *She is my sister.* The complete truth told in such a way as to deceive or mislead is still a falsehood. Abraham's words were true: "She is my sister," but the message he intended to convey was false: "She is not married to me." His intent was deceit and the consequences he reaped were the same as if he had directly lied. A man speaks the real truth when he speaks the truth in his heart (Ps. 15:2).

20:3 *God came ... in a dream.* Presumably, Abimelech was a pagan king. Yet God warned him of the wrong he was about to commit. This is another instance of the protective care that the Lord gives His people (31:24; Num. 22:12–20).

20:12 *Besides, she really is my sister.* Later the law would prohibit the marriage of people so closely related, but in the early years of the earth it was apparently acceptable for half siblings to marry (see note on 4:17).

21:1 *Now the LORD was gracious to Sarah as he had said.* The Bible stresses that the Lord causes conceptions; that children are a gift of the Lord (Ps. 127:3). The verb *was gracious* is an extraordinary choice here, indicating that the Lord entered directly into the affairs of His people.

19:37 [n] Dt 2:9 **19:38** [o] Dt 2:19 **20:1** [p] Ge 18:1 [q] Ge 26:1, 6, 17 **20:2** [r] ver 12; Ge 12:13; 26:7 [s] Ge 12:15 **20:3** [t] Job 33:15; Mt 27:19 [u] Ps 105:14 **20:4** [v] Ge 18:25 **20:6** [w] 1Sa 25:26, 34 **20:7** [x] ver 17; 1Sa 7:5; Job 42:8 **20:9** [y] Ge 12:18; 26:10; 34:7 **20:11** [z] Ge 42:18; Ps 36:1 [a] Ge 12:12; 26:7 **20:14** [b] Ge 12:16 **20:15** [c] Ge 13:9 **20:17** [d] Job 42:9 **20:18** [e] Ge 12:17 **21:1** [f] 1Sa 2:21 [g] Ge 8:1; 17:16, 21; Gal 4:23 **21:2** [h] Ge 17:19

ham in his old age,[i] at the very time God had
promised him. **3**Abraham gave the name
Isaac[a][j] to the son Sarah bore him. **4**When
his son Isaac was eight days old, Abraham
circumcised him,[k] as God commanded him.
5Abraham was a hundred years old when
his son Isaac was born to him.
6Sarah said, "God has brought me laughter,[l] and everyone who hears about this will
laugh with me." **7**And she added, "Who
would have said to Abraham that Sarah
would nurse children? Yet I have borne him
a son in his old age."

Hagar and Ishmael Sent Away

8The child grew and was weaned, and on
the day Isaac was weaned Abraham held
a great feast. **9**But Sarah saw that the son
whom Hagar the Egyptian had borne to
Abraham[m] was mocking,[n] **10**and she said
to Abraham, "Get rid of that slave woman and her son, for that woman's son will
never share in the inheritance with my son
Isaac."[o]
11The matter distressed Abraham greatly because it concerned his son.[p] **12**But
God said to him, "Do not be so distressed
about the boy and your slave woman. Listen to whatever Sarah tells you, because it
is through Isaac that your offspring[b] will
be reckoned.[q] **13**I will make the son of the
slave into a nation[r] also, because he is your
offspring."
14Early the next morning Abraham took
some food and a skin of water and gave
them to Hagar. He set them on her shoulders and then sent her off with the boy. She
went on her way and wandered in the Desert of Beersheba.[s]
15When the water in the skin was gone,
she put the boy under one of the bushes.
16Then she went off and sat down about a
bowshot away, for she thought, "I cannot
watch the boy die." And as she sat there,
she[c] began to sob.
17God heard the boy crying,[t] and the angel of God called to Hagar from heaven and
said to her, "What is the matter, Hagar? Do
not be afraid; God has heard the boy crying as he lies there. **18**Lift the boy up and
take him by the hand, for I will make him
into a great nation.[u]"
19Then God opened her eyes[v] and she
saw a well of water. So she went and filled
the skin with water and gave the boy a
drink.
20God was with the boy[w] as he grew up.
He lived in the desert and became an archer.
21While he was living in the Desert of Paran,
his mother got a wife for him[x] from Egypt.

The Treaty at Beersheba

22At that time Abimelek and Phicol the
commander of his forces said to Abraham,
"God is with you in everything you do.
23Now swear[y] to me here before God that
you will not deal falsely with me or my
children or my descendants. Show to me
and the country where you now reside as a
foreigner the same kindness I have shown
to you."
24Abraham said, "I swear it."
25Then Abraham complained to Abimelek about a well of water that Abimelek's
servants had seized.[z] **26**But Abimelek said,
"I don't know who has done this. You did
not tell me, and I heard about it only today."
27So Abraham brought sheep and cattle
and gave them to Abimelek, and the two
men made a treaty.[a] **28**Abraham set apart
seven ewe lambs from the flock, **29**and
Abimelek asked Abraham, "What is the
meaning of these seven ewe lambs you
have set apart by themselves?"
30He replied, "Accept these seven lambs
from my hand as a witness[b] that I dug this
well."

---

[a] *3* Isaac *means* he laughs. [b] *12* Or *seed*
[c] *16* Hebrew; Septuagint *the child*

21:3 ***Isaac.*** Isaac means "He (God) Is Laughing (Now)." At one time Abraham and Sarah had both laughed at the improbability of having a son in their old age (17:17; 18:12); now with the birth of the promised child their laughter took on a happier meaning.

21:12 ***listen to whatever Sarah tells you.*** As painful as the situation was, God confirmed that Sarah was right that Ishmael would have to leave. Only Isaac was the child of promise, the one through whom the covenant would be fulfilled. This complicated situation was part of the price Abraham had to pay for trying to bring about God's promises in his own time. Nevertheless, God is merciful and He did not abandon Hagar and Ishmael.

21:17 ***God heard.*** What wonderful words these are! There is no pain of His people that He does not see or hear about (Is. 40:27–28; Heb. 2:10,18; 4:15). Even though Ishmael was not the son of promise, God still had His hand on his life.

21:23 ***kindness.*** This exceedingly important term, sometimes translated *loyal love* or *loving-kindness* is often used in the Psalms to describe God's character (Ps. 100:5). Here we see its proper context in a binding relationship. The term basically describes covenant loyalty (24:12).

21:27 ***treaty.*** This is a binding agreement between two equals, similar to today's business contracts.

21:28–31 ***seven ewe lambs ... Beersheba.*** The Hebrew number seven is similar in sound to the verb meaning "to swear" (v. 24). Thus Beersheba would be the well where they swore and the well of the seven ewe lambs.

21:2 [i] Gal 4:22; Heb 11:11 **21:3** [j] Ge 17:19 **21:4** [k] Ge 17:10, 12; Ac 7:8 **21:6** [l] Ge 17:17; Isa 54:1 **21:9** [m] Ge 16:15 [n] Gal 4:29 **21:10** [o] Gal 4:30* **21:11** [p] Ge 17:18 **21:12** [q] Ro 9:7*; Heb 11:18* **21:13** [r] ver 18 **21:14** [s] ver 31, 32 **21:17** [t] Ex 3:7 **21:18** [u] ver 13 **21:19** [v] Nu 22:31 **21:20** [w] Ge 26:3, 24; 28:15; 39:2, 21, 23 **21:21** [x] Ge 24:4, 38 **21:23** [y] ver 31; Jos 2:12 **21:25** [z] Ge 26:15, 18, 20-22 **21:27** [a] Ge 26:28, 31 **21:30** [b] Ge 31:44, 47, 48, 50, 52

31So that place was called Beersheba,[a,c]
because the two men swore an oath there.
32After the treaty had been made at Beersheba, Abimelek and Phicol the commander of his forces returned to the land of
the Philistines. 33Abraham planted a tamarisk tree in Beersheba, and there he called
on the name of the LORD,[d] the Eternal God.[e]
34And Abraham stayed in the land of the
Philistines for a long time.

Abraham Tested

22 Some time later God tested[f] Abraham. He said to him, "Abraham!"
"Here I am," he replied.
2Then God said, "Take your son[g], your
only son, whom you love—Isaac—and
go to the region of Moriah.[h] Sacrifice him
there as a burnt offering on a mountain I
will show you."
3Early the next morning Abraham
got up and loaded his donkey. He took
with him two of his servants and his son
Isaac. When he had cut enough wood for
the burnt offering, he set out for the place
God had told him about. 4On the third day
Abraham looked up and saw the place in
the distance. 5He said to his servants, "Stay
here with the donkey while I and the boy go
over there. We will worship and then we
will come back to you."
6Abraham took the wood for the burnt
offering and placed it on his son Isaac,[i] and
he himself carried the fire and the knife.
As the two of them went on together, 7Isaac
spoke up and said to his father Abraham,
"Father?"
"Yes, my son?" Abraham replied.
"The fire and wood are here," Isaac said,
"but where is the lamb[j] for the burnt offering?"
8Abraham answered, "God himself will
provide the lamb for the burnt offering, my
son." And the two of them went on together.
9When they reached the place God had
told him about, Abraham built an altar
there and arranged the wood on it. He
bound his son Isaac and laid him on the altar,[k] on top of the wood. 10Then he reached
out his hand and took the knife to slay his
son. 11But the angel of the LORD called out
to him from heaven, "Abraham! Abraham!"
"Here I am," he replied.
12"Do not lay a hand on the boy," he said.
"Do not do anything to him. Now I know
that you fear God,[l] because you have not
withheld from me your son, your only son.[m]"
13Abraham looked up and there in a
thicket he saw a ram[b] caught by its horns.
He went over and took the ram and sacrificed it as a burnt offering instead of his
son.[n] 14So Abraham called that place The
LORD Will Provide. And to this day it is
said, "On the mountain of the LORD it will
be provided.[o]"
15The angel of the LORD called to Abraham from heaven a second time 16and said,
"I swear by myself,[p] declares the LORD,
that because you have done this and have
not withheld your son, your only son, 17I
will surely bless you and make your descendants[q] as numerous as the stars in
the sky[r] and as the sand on the seashore.[s]
Your descendants will take possession of
the cities of their enemies,[t] 18and through
your offspring[c] all nations on earth will be
blessed,[d,u] because you have obeyed me."[v]

---

[a] *31 Beersheba* can mean *well of seven* and *well of the oath.* [b] *13* Many manuscripts of the Masoretic Text, Samaritan Pentateuch, Septuagint and Syriac; most manuscripts of the Masoretic Text *a ram behind him* [c] *18* Or *seed* [d] *18* Or *and all nations on earth will use the name of your offspring in blessings* (see 48:20)

21:34 ***the land of the Philistines.*** The name Palestine comes from the word for Philistine.

22:5 ***worship and . . . come back to you.*** Abraham's comment to his servants is a significant avowal of his faith in God. Even though he was going to sacrifice his son, he was confident that they both would return.

22:8 ***God himself will provide.*** Abraham's faith in God's promise is shown in his response to a very real and terrible test. Many times this is seen as a test of the quality of Abraham's love for God—who would he choose, God or his son? However, there is no sign that Abraham made this mistake. He knew beyond a shadow of doubt that Isaac was given to him directly by God, the son of promise. Therefore it was right that he should love his son of promise as a gift from God. God's covenant said that a great nation would descend from Isaac, therefore it would be so. Abraham's test was not "whom do you love most?" but "do you really believe Me?" The answer was a resounding, "Yes!" Abraham carried his faith to the knife edge on his son's flesh. God had promised, and it would be so, even if Isaac had to be raised from the dead to make His words come to pass (Heb. 11:17–19).

22:9 ***bound his son Isaac.*** Surely Isaac could have struggled or run away at this point, but there is no evidence that he did so. Apparently Isaac's faith and trust both in God and in his father was sufficient to stand the test.

22:14 ***The LORD Will Provide.*** As God provided a ram to take the place of Abraham's son, so one day He would provide His own Son to take our place. Some believe that Mount Moriah later became part of the city of Jerusalem, and was the site of Solomon's temple.

22:17 ***bless . . . make your descendants numerous.*** In the Hebrew, this is stated by doubling the verbs, a Hebrew idiom that powerfully emphasizes the certainty of the action.

22:18 ***offspring.*** Here this is a grand play on words. Some translations use the word "seed" as it relates to

21:31 [c] Ge 26:33 **21:33** [d] Ge 4:26 [e] Dt 33:27
22:1 [f] Dt 8:2, 16; Heb 11:17; Jas 1:12-13 **22:2** [g] ver 12, 16; Jn 3:16; Heb 11:17; 1Jn 4:9 [h] 2Ch 3:1 **22:6** [i] Jn 19:17
22:7 [j] Lev 1:10 **22:9** [k] Heb 11:17-19; Jas 2:21
22:12 [l] 1Sa 15:22; Jas 2:21-22 [m] ver 2; Jn 3:16
22:13 [n] Ro 8:32 **22:14** [o] ver 8 **22:16** [p] Lk 1:73; Heb 6:13 **22:17** [q] Heb 6:14* [r] Ge 15:5 [s] Ge 26:24; 32:12 [t] Ge 24:60 **22:18** [u] Ge 12:2, 3; Ac 3:25*; Gal 3:8* [v] ver 10

19Then Abraham returned to his servants, and they set off together for Beersheba. And Abraham stayed in Beersheba.

Nahor's Sons

20Some time later Abraham was told,
"Milkah is also a mother; she has borne
sons to your brother Nahor:[w] 21Uz the firstborn, Buz his brother, Kemuel (the father
of Aram), 22Kesed, Hazo, Pildash, Jidlaph
and Bethuel." 23Bethuel became the father
of Rebekah.[x] Milkah bore these eight sons
to Abraham's brother Nahor. 24His concubine, whose name was Reumah, also had
sons: Tebah, Gaham, Tahash and Maakah.

The Death of Sarah

23 Sarah lived to be a hundred and
twenty-seven years old. 2She died at
Kiriath Arba[y] (that is, Hebron)[z] in the land
of Canaan, and Abraham went to mourn
for Sarah and to weep over her.
3Then Abraham rose from beside his
dead wife and spoke to the Hittites.[a] He
said, 4"I am a foreigner and stranger[a]
among you. Sell me some property for a
burial site here so I can bury my dead."
5The Hittites replied to Abraham, 6"Sir,
listen to us. You are a mighty prince[b]
among us. Bury your dead in the choicest
of our tombs. None of us will refuse you his
tomb for burying your dead."
7Then Abraham rose and bowed down
before the people of the land, the Hittites.
8He said to them, "If you are willing to let
me bury my dead, then listen to me and intercede with Ephron son of Zohar[c] on my
behalf 9so he will sell me the cave of Machpelah, which belongs to him and is at the
end of his field. Ask him to sell it to me for
the full price as a burial site among you."
10Ephron the Hittite was sitting among
his people and he replied to Abraham in
the hearing of all the Hittites who had
come to the gate[d] of his city. 11"No, my
lord," he said. "Listen to me; I give[b e] you
the field, and I give[b] you the cave that is
in it. I give[b] it to you in the presence of my
people. Bury your dead."
12Again Abraham bowed down before
the people of the land 13and he said to
Ephron in their hearing, "Listen to me, if
you will. I will pay the price of the field.
Accept it from me so I can bury my dead
there."
14Ephron answered Abraham, 15"Listen
to me, my lord; the land is worth four hundred shekels[c] of silver,[f] but what is that between you and me? Bury your dead."
16Abraham agreed to Ephron's terms
and weighed out for him the price he had
named in the hearing of the Hittites: four
hundred shekels of silver,[g] according to the
weight current among the merchants.
17So Ephron's field in Machpelah near
Mamre[h]—both the field and the cave in
it, and all the trees within the borders of
the field—was deeded 18to Abraham as his
property in the presence of all the Hittites
who had come to the gate of the city. 19Af-
terward Abraham buried his wife Sarah
in the cave in the field of Machpelah near
Mamre (which is at Hebron) in the land of
Canaan. 20So the field and the cave in it
were deeded[i] to Abraham by the Hittites as
a burial site.

Isaac and Rebekah

24 Abraham was now very old, and the
LORD had blessed him in every way.[j]
2He said to the senior servant in his household, the one in charge of all that he had,[k]
"Put your hand under my thigh.[l] 3I want
you to swear by the LORD, the God of heav-
en and the God of earth,[m] that you will not
get a wife for my son[n] from the daughters
of the Canaanites,[o] among whom I am living, 4but will go to my country and my own
relatives[p] and get a wife for my son Isaac."
5The servant asked him, "What if the
woman is unwilling to come back with me

[a] *3* Or *the descendants of Heth*; also in verses 5, 7, 10, 16, 18 and 20 [b] *11* Or *sell* [c] *15* That is, about 10 pounds or about 4.6 kilograms

---

"offspring," which is a poetic image in this instance. The seed was Isaac, and by extension the Jewish nation. Specifically the Seed, in terms of God's promise of salvation, was one descendant of Abraham: Jesus the Messiah.

23:13 *I will pay the price of the field.* Abraham would not have been offering "money" as we think of it today; minted coins were not invented until at least 650 B.C. Instead, trading was done by barter, or with precious metals by weight.

23:15 *What is that between you and me?* The dialogue in this chapter gives a wonderfully detailed example of the bargaining process of the day. Abraham clearly understood Ephron's generous statement as a politely phrased way of setting his price.

23:20 *field . . . cave . . . were deeded to Abraham.* It is interesting to note that the only piece of the Promised Land that Abraham ever personally possessed was this field and cave to bury his wife.

24:2 *the senior servant.* Some have thought that this might be Eliezer of Damascus, the one who had been named as Abraham's heir before the births of Ishmael and Isaac.

24:3 *the daughters of the Canaanites.* This was not an issue of racism, as is sometimes thought—it was theological. The Canaanite peoples worshipped the false gods Baal and Asherah (Deut. 7:3).

22:20 [w] Ge 11:29 **22:23** [x] Ge 24:15 **23:2** [y] Jos 14:15 [z] ver 19; Ge 13:18 **23:4** [a] Ge 17:8; 1Ch 29:15; Ps 105:12; Heb 11:9, 13 **23:6** [b] Ge 14:14-16; 24:35 **23:8** [c] Ge 25:9 **23:10** [d] Ge 34:20-24; Ru 4:4 **23:11** [e] 2Sa 24:23 **23:15** [f] Eze 45:12 **23:16** [g] Jer 32:9; Zec 11:12 **23:17** [h] Ge 25:9; 49:30-32; 50:13; Ac 7:16 **23:20** [i] Jer 32:10 **24:1** [j] ver 35 **24:2** [k] Ge 39:4-6 [l] ver 9; Ge 47:29 **24:3** [m] Ge 14:19 [n] Ge 28:1; Dt 7:3 [o] Ge 10:15-19 **24:4** [p] Ge 12:1; 28:2

to this land? Shall I then take your son back to the country you came from?"

6"Make sure that you do not take my son back there," Abraham said. 7"The LORD, the God of heaven, who brought me out of my father's household and my native land and who spoke to me and promised me on oath, saying, 'To your offspring[a][q] I will give this land'[r]—he will send his angel before you[s] so that you can get a wife for my son from there. 8If the woman is unwilling to come back with you, then you will be released from this oath of mine. Only do not take my son back there." 9So the servant put his hand under the thigh[t] of his master Abraham and swore an oath to him concerning this matter.

10Then the servant left, taking with him ten of his master's camels loaded with all kinds of good things from his master. He set out for Aram Naharaim[b] and made his way to the town of Nahor. 11He had the camels kneel down near the well[u] outside the town; it was toward evening, the time the women go out to draw water.[v]

12Then he prayed, "LORD, God of my master Abraham,[w] make me successful today, and show kindness to my master Abraham. 13See, I am standing beside this spring, and the daughters of the townspeople are coming out to draw water. 14May it be that when I say to a young woman, 'Please let down your jar that I may have a drink,' and she says, 'Drink, and I'll water your camels too'—let her be the one you have chosen for your servant Isaac. By this I will know[x] that you have shown kindness to my master."

15Before he had finished praying,[y] Rebekah[z] came out with her jar on her shoulder. She was the daughter of Bethuel son of Milkah,[a] who was the wife of Abraham's brother Nahor.[b] 16The woman was very beautiful,[c] a virgin; no man had ever slept with her. She went down to the spring, filled her jar and came up again.

17The servant hurried to meet her and said, "Please give me a little water from your jar."

18"Drink,[d] my lord," she said, and quickly lowered the jar to her hands and gave him a drink.

19After she had given him a drink, she said, "I'll draw water for your camels too,[e] until they have had enough to drink." 20So she quickly emptied her jar into the trough, ran back to the well to draw more water, and drew enough for all his camels. 21Without saying a word, the man watched her closely to learn whether or not the LORD had made his journey successful.[f]

22When the camels had finished drinking, the man took out a gold nose ring[g] weighing a beka[c] and two gold bracelets weighing ten shekels.[d] 23Then he asked, "Whose daughter are you? Please tell me, is there room in your father's house for us to spend the night?"

24She answered him, "I am the daughter of Bethuel, the son that Milkah bore to Nahor.[h]" 25And she added, "We have plenty of straw and fodder, as well as room for you to spend the night."

26Then the man bowed down and worshiped the LORD,[i] 27saying, "Praise be to the LORD,[j] the God of my master Abraham, who has not abandoned his kindness and faithfulness[k] to my master. As for me, the LORD has led me on the journey[l] to the house of my master's relatives."[m]

28The young woman ran and told her mother's household about these things. 29Now Rebekah had a brother named Laban,[n] and he hurried out to the man at the spring. 30As soon as he had seen the nose ring, and the bracelets on his sister's arms, and had heard Rebekah tell what the man said to her, he went out to the man and found him standing by the camels near the spring. 31"Come, you who are blessed by the LORD,"[o] he said. "Why are you standing out here? I have prepared the house and a place for the camels."

32So the man went to the house, and the camels were unloaded. Straw and fodder were brought for the camels, and water for him and his men to wash their feet.[p] 33Then food was set before him, but he said, "I will not eat until I have told you what I have to say."

"Then tell us," Laban said.

---

[a] 7 Or *seed* [b] *10* That is, Northwest Mesopotamia [c] *22* That is, about 1/5 ounce or about 5.7 grams [d] *22* That is, about 4 ounces or about 115 grams

---

24:12 *LORD, God of my master Abraham.* This language does not mean that the servant himself did not believe in God. The servant was making his appeal on the basis of God's covenant loyalty to Abraham.

24:15 Providence—Abraham sent his servant to choose Isaac's bride, confident that his servant would be led by the Lord and that in God's providence he would make the right choice. The servant prayed for very specific guidance, and God sent him Rebekah. He was impressed not only with her physical beauty, but also with her kind, generous, and hospitable character. His decision was confirmed when her parents gave their consent and she agreed to return with him. Today we must remember to seek the Lord's guidance and trust in His providence just as Abraham's servant, Rebekah, and her family did.

24:7 [q] Gal 3:16* [r] Ge 12:7; 13:15 [s] Ex 23:20, 23 **24:9** [t] ver 2 **24:11** [u] Ex 2:15 [v] ver 13; 1Sa 9:11 **24:12** [w] ver 27, 42, 48; Ge 26:24; Ex 3:6, 15, 16 **24:14** [x] Jdg 6:17, 37 **24:15** [y] ver 45 [z] Ge 22:23 [a] Ge 22:20 [b] Ge 11:29 **24:16** [c] Ge 26:7 **24:18** [d] ver 14 **24:19** [e] ver 14 **24:21** [f] ver 12 **24:22** [g] ver 47 **24:24** [h] ver 15 **24:26** [i] ver 48, 52; Ex 4:31 **24:27** [j] Ex 18:10; Ru 4:14; 1Sa 25:32 [k] ver 49; Ge 32:10; Ps 98:3 [l] ver 21 [m] ver 12, 48 **24:29** [n] ver 4; Ge 29:5, 12, 13 **24:31** [o] Ge 26:29; Ru 3:10; Ps 115:15 **24:32** [p] Ge 43:24; Jdg 19:21

34 So he said, "I am Abraham's servant.
35 The LORD has blessed my master abundantly,[q] and he has become wealthy. He
has given him sheep and cattle, silver and
gold, male and female servants, and camels and donkeys.[r] 36 My master's wife Sarah
has borne him a son in her old age,[s] and he
has given him everything he owns.[t] 37 And
my master made me swear an oath, and
said, 'You must not get a wife for my son
from the daughters of the Canaanites, in
whose land I live,[u] 38 but go to my father's
family and to my own clan, and get a wife
for my son.'[v]

39 "Then I asked my master, 'What if the
woman will not come back with me?'[w]

40 "He replied, 'The LORD, before whom I
have walked faithfully, will send his angel
with you[x] and make your journey a success, so that you can get a wife for my son
from my own clan and from my father's
family. 41 You will be released from my oath
if, when you go to my clan, they refuse to
give her to you—then you will be released
from my oath.'[y]

42 "When I came to the spring today, I
said, 'LORD, God of my master Abraham,
if you will, please grant success[z] to the
journey on which I have come. 43 See, I am
standing beside this spring.[a] If a young
woman comes out to draw water and I say
to her, "Please let me drink a little water
from your jar,"[b] 44 and if she says to me,
"Drink, and I'll draw water for your camels
too," let her be the one the LORD has chosen
for my master's son.'

45 "Before I finished praying in my heart,[c]
Rebekah came out, with her jar on her
shoulder.[d] She went down to the spring and
drew water, and I said to her, 'Please give
me a drink.'[e]

46 "She quickly lowered her jar from her
shoulder and said, 'Drink, and I'll water
your camels too.'[f] So I drank, and she watered the camels also.

47 "I asked her, 'Whose daughter are
you?'[g]

"She said, 'The daughter of Bethuel son of Nahor, whom Milkah bore to him.'[h]

"Then I put the ring in her nose and
the bracelets on her arms,[i] 48 and I bowed
down and worshiped the LORD.[j] I praised
the LORD, the God of my master Abraham,
who had led me on the right road to get the
granddaughter of my master's brother for
his son.[k] 49 Now if you will show kindness
and faithfulness[l] to my master, tell me; and
if not, tell me, so I may know which way
to turn."

50 Laban and Bethuel answered, "This is
from the LORD;[m] we can say nothing to you
one way or the other.[n] 51 Here is Rebekah;
take her and go, and let her become the
wife of your master's son, as the LORD has
directed."

52 When Abraham's servant heard what
they said, he bowed down to the ground before the LORD.[o] 53 Then the servant brought
out gold and silver jewelry and articles of
clothing and gave them to Rebekah; he also
gave costly gifts[p] to her brother and to her
mother. 54 Then he and the men who were
with him ate and drank and spent the night
there.

When they got up the next morning, he said, "Send me on my way[q] to my master."

55 But her brother and her mother replied,
"Let the young woman remain with us ten
days or so; then you[a] may go."

56 But he said to them, "Do not detain me,
now that the LORD has granted success to
my journey. Send me on my way so I may
go to my master."

57 Then they said, "Let's call the young
woman and ask her about it." 58 So they
called Rebekah and asked her, "Will you
go with this man?"

"I will go," she said.

59 So they sent their sister Rebekah on
her way, along with her nurse[r] and Abraham's servant and his men. 60 And they
blessed Rebekah and said to her,

"Our sister, may you increase
 to thousands upon thousands;[s]
may your offspring possess
 the cities of their enemies."[t]

61 Then Rebekah and her attendants got
ready and mounted the camels and went
back with the man. So the servant took Rebekah and left.

62 Now Isaac had come from Beer Lahai
Roi,[u] for he was living in the Negev.[v] 63 He
went out to the field one evening to meditate,[b][w] and as he looked up, he saw camels approaching. 64 Rebekah also looked
up and saw Isaac. She got down from her
camel 65 and asked the servant, "Who is
that man in the field coming to meet us?"

---

[a] *55* Or *she* [b] *63* The meaning of the Hebrew for this word is uncertain.

24:50 *This is from the LORD.* It appears that the family of Bethuel and Laban also worshipped the living God, or at least acknowledged Him along with other gods (see 31:19; Josh. 24:2).

24:60 *they blessed Rebekah.* These words are not mere sentiment, nor are they a magical charm, but a prayer for God's blessing on her life. ***cities.*** The possession of the cities of one's enemies meant power over them (22:17).

24:35 [q] ver 1 [r] Ge 13:2 **24:36** [s] Ge 21:2, 10 [t] Ge 25:5 **24:37** [u] ver 3 **24:38** [v] ver 4 **24:39** [w] ver 5 **24:40** [x] ver 7 **24:41** [y] ver 8 **24:42** [z] ver 12 **24:43** [a] ver 13 [b] ver 14 **24:45** [c] 1Sa 1:13 [d] ver 15 [e] ver 17 **24:46** [f] ver 18-19 **24:47** [g] ver 23 [h] ver 24 [i] Eze 16:11-12 **24:48** [j] ver 26 [k] ver 27 **24:49** [l] Ge 47:29; Jos 2:14 **24:50** [m] Ps 118:23 [n] Ge 31:7, 24, 29, 42 **24:52** [o] ver 26 **24:53** [p] ver 10, 22 **24:54** [q] ver 56, 59 **24:59** [r] Ge 35:8 **24:60** [s] Ge 17:16 [t] Ge 22:17 **24:62** [u] Ge 16:14; 25:11 [v] Ge 20:1 **24:63** [w] Ps 1:2; 77:12; 119:15, 27, 48, 97, 148; 143:5; 145:5

"He is my master," the servant answered.
So she took her veil and covered herself.
66Then the servant told Isaac all he had
done. 67Isaac brought her into the tent of
his mother Sarah, and he married Rebekah.[x] So she became his wife, and he loved
her;[y] and Isaac was comforted after his
mother's death.[z]

The Death of Abraham

25 Abraham had taken another wife,
whose name was Keturah. 2She bore
him Zimran, Jokshan, Medan, Midian, Ishbak and Shuah.[a] 3Jokshan was the father of
Sheba and Dedan; the descendants of Dedan were the Ashurites, the Letushites and
the Leummites. 4The sons of Midian were
Ephah, Epher, Hanok, Abida and Eldaah.
All these were descendants of Keturah.
5Abraham left everything he owned to
Isaac.[b] 6But while he was still living, he
gave gifts to the sons of his concubines[c]
and sent them away from his son Isaac[d] to
the land of the east.
7Abraham lived a hundred and seventy-five years. 8Then Abraham breathed
his last and died at a good old age,[e] an old
man and full of years; and he was gathered
to his people.[f] 9His sons Isaac and Ishmael
buried him[g] in the cave of Machpelah near
Mamre, in the field of Ephron son of Zohar the Hittite,[h] 10the field Abraham had
bought from the Hittites.[a][i] There Abraham was buried with his wife Sarah. 11Af-
ter Abraham's death, God blessed his son
Isaac, who then lived near Beer Lahai Roi.[j]

Ishmael's Sons

12This is the account of the family line
of Abraham's son Ishmael, whom Sarah's
slave, Hagar[k] the Egyptian, bore to Abraham.[l]
13These are the names of the sons of Ishmael, listed in the order of their birth: Nebaioth the firstborn of Ishmael, Kedar, Adbeel,
Mibsam, 14Mishma, Dumah, Massa, 15Ha-
dad, Tema, Jetur, Naphish and Kedemah.
16These were the sons of Ishmael, and these
are the names of the twelve tribal rulers[m]
according to their settlements and camps.
17Ishmael lived a hundred and thirty-seven
years. He breathed his last and died, and he
was gathered to his people.[n] 18His descendants settled in the area from Havilah to
Shur, near the eastern border of Egypt, as
you go toward Ashur. And they lived in hostility toward[b] all the tribes related to them.[o]

Jacob and Esau

19This is the account of the family line of
Abraham's son Isaac.
Abraham became the father of Isaac,
20and Isaac was forty years old[p] when he
married Rebekah[q] daughter of Bethuel the
Aramean from Paddan Aram[c] and sister of
Laban[r] the Aramean.
21Isaac prayed to the LORD on behalf of
his wife, because she was childless. The
LORD answered his prayer,[s] and his wife
Rebekah became pregnant. 22The babies
jostled each other within her, and she said,
"Why is this happening to me?" So she
went to inquire of the LORD.[t]
23The LORD said to her,

"Two nations[u] are in your womb,
and two peoples from within you will
be separated;
one people will be stronger than the
other,
and the older will serve the
younger.[v]"

24When the time came for her to give

---

[a] 10 Or *the descendants of Heth* [b] 18 Or *lived to the east of* [c] 20 That is, Northwest Mesopotamia

---

24:67 *he loved her.* The love of Isaac for Rebekah is a wonderful fulfillment and illustration of God's original purpose for marriage. Realizing it was not good for man to be alone (Gen. 2:18), the Creator graciously created Eve, a helper for Adam. God Himself then performed history's first wedding. Isaac and Rebekah serve not only as a lovely example of godly marriage, but also as a beautiful picture of the love between Christ and the church in the New Testament. Rebekah, like the church, loved her bridegroom without first seeing him (compare Gen. 24:58 with 1 Pet. 1:8). Like the church, Rebekah was prayed for by her bridegroom (Gen. 24:63; Rom. 8:34). Isaac, having previously been presented for offering on Mt. Moriah (Gen. 22:1–14), was content to await the arrival of his bride. He was an early portrayal of the Son of God who now awaits the arrival of His bride in heaven (Heb. 10:12–14).

25:1 *taken another wife.* In 1 Chronicles 1:32, Keturah is described as Abraham's concubine. It is not really known exactly what position she had in Abraham's household, or when the relationship began. Her sons had a status similar to that of Ishmael, Abraham's son by Hagar (ch. 16), but without Ishmael's particular blessing (16:10–16).

25:2 *Midian.* This son was the father of the Midianites, some of whom later bought Joseph from his brothers (37:28,36).

25:11 *God blessed.* God blessed Isaac because He had already established "an everlasting covenant" with him (17:19; Heb. 11:17). Later God renewed the covenant with Isaac personally (26:2–5).

25:21 *prayed.* The Hebrew verb here indicates that Isaac prayed passionately for his wife. For examples of passionate prayer, see Ex. 8:30; 2 Sam. 21:14; 24:25.

24:67 [x] Ge 25:20 [y] Ge 29:18,20 [z] Ge 23:1-2
25:2 [a] 1Ch 1:32,33 **25:5** [b] Ge 24:36 **25:6** [c] Ge 22:24 [d] Ge 21:10,14 **25:8** [e] Ge 15:15 [f] ver 17; Ge 35:29; 49:29, 33 **25:9** [g] Ge 35:29 [h] Ge 50:13 **25:10** [i] Ge 23:16
25:11 [j] Ge 16:14 **25:12** [k] Ge 16:1 [l] Ge 16:15
25:16 [m] Ge 17:20 **25:17** [n] ver 8 **25:18** [o] Ge 16:12
25:20 [p] ver 26; Ge 26:34 [q] Ge 24:67 [r] Ge 24:29
25:21 [s] 1Ch 5:20; 2Ch 33:13; Ezr 8:23; Ps 127:3; Ro 9:10
25:22 [t] 1Sa 9:9; 10:22 **25:23** [u] Ge 17:4 [v] Ge 27:29,40; Mal 1:3; Ro 9:11-12*

birth, there were twin boys in her womb.
25The first to come out was red, and his
whole body was like a hairy garment;[w] so
they named him Esau.[a] 26After this, his
brother came out, with his hand grasping Esau's heel;[x] so he was named Jacob.[b][y]
Isaac was sixty years old when Rebekah
gave birth to them.
27The boys grew up, and Esau became a
skillful hunter, a man of the open country,[z]
while Jacob was content to stay at home
among the tents. 28Isaac, who had a taste
for wild game,[a] loved Esau, but Rebekah
loved Jacob.[b]
29Once when Jacob was cooking some
stew, Esau came in from the open country,
famished. 30He said to Jacob, "Quick, let
me have some of that red stew! I'm famished!" (That is why he was also called
Edom.[c])
31Jacob replied, "First sell me your birthright."
32"Look, I am about to die," Esau said.
"What good is the birthright to me?"
33But Jacob said, "Swear to me first." So
he swore an oath to him, selling his birthright[c] to Jacob.
34Then Jacob gave Esau some bread and
some lentil stew. He ate and drank, and
then got up and left.
So Esau despised his birthright.

Isaac and Abimelek

26 Now there was a famine in the
land[d]—besides the previous famine in Abraham's time—and Isaac went to
Abimelek king of the Philistines in Gerar.[e]
2The LORD appeared[f] to Isaac and said,
"Do not go down to Egypt; live in the land
where I tell you to live.[g] 3Stay in this land
for a while,[h] and I will be with you and
will bless you.[i] For to you and your descendants I will give all these lands[j] and will
confirm the oath I swore to your father
Abraham. 4I will make your descendants
as numerous as the stars in the sky[k] and
will give them all these lands, and through
your offspring[d] all nations on earth will be
blessed,[e][l] 5because Abraham obeyed me[m]
and did everything I required of him, keeping my commands, my decrees and my instructions." 6So Isaac stayed in Gerar.
7When the men of that place asked him
about his wife, he said, "She is my sister,[n]"
because he was afraid to say, "She is my
wife." He thought, "The men of this place
might kill me on account of Rebekah, because she is beautiful."
8When Isaac had been there a long time,
Abimelek king of the Philistines looked
down from a window and saw Isaac caress-
ing his wife Rebekah. 9So Abimelek summoned Isaac and said, "She is really your
wife! Why did you say, 'She is my sister'?"
Isaac answered him, "Because I thought
I might lose my life on account of her."
10Then Abimelek said, "What is this you
have done to us?[o] One of the men might
well have slept with your wife, and you
would have brought guilt upon us."
11So Abimelek gave orders to all the people: "Anyone who harms[p] this man or his
wife shall surely be put to death."
12Isaac planted crops in that land and the
same year reaped a hundredfold, because
the LORD blessed him.[q] 13The man became
rich, and his wealth continued to grow until he became very wealthy.[r] 14He had so
many flocks and herds and servants[s] that
the Philistines envied him.[t] 15So all the
wells[u] that his father's servants had dug in
the time of his father Abraham, the Philistines stopped up,[v] filling them with earth.
16Then Abimelek said to Isaac, "Move
away from us; you have become too powerful for us.[w]"
17So Isaac moved away from there and
encamped in the Valley of Gerar, where he
settled. 18Isaac reopened the wells[x] that had

---

[a] *25 Esau* may mean *hairy*. [b] *26 Jacob* means *he grasps the heel*, a Hebrew idiom for *he deceives*.. [c] *30 Edom* means *red*. [d] *4* Or *seed* [e] *4* Or *and all nations on earth will use the name of your offspring in blessings* (see 48:20)

25:25 *Esau.* This name sounds like the Hebrew word that means "hairy."
25:26 *Jacob.* The Hebrew word that means "heel" sounds similar to the name Jacob. The name may mean either "He Who Grasps at the Heel (of Another)" or "He (the Lord) Is at His Heels (Is His Protector)."
25:30 *Edom.* This name means "red." The nickname is here connected to the red stew for which he traded his birthright; many have speculated that Esau may have had ruddy skin, or even red hair since the name stuck and even became the name of his land and the nation of his descendants (36:8).
26:1 *Philistines.* The Philistines are thought to have come to the coastland of Canaan following their defeat by the Egyptians around 1200 B.C. The Egyptians called them the "Sea Peoples"; they were apparently Greek peoples who migrated eastward (see 1 Sam. 4:1; 2 Sam. 5:17).
26:3 *bless you.* The Lord fulfilled His promise to Abraham concerning Isaac (17:19). He established His everlasting covenant with Isaac, just as He had with Abraham.
26:7 *sister.* Rebekah was Isaac's close relative, but she was not his sister (she was his first cousin once removed). Isaac was even more deceitful than his father Abraham (20:2,12).
26:12–13 *blessed.* God's special work for Abraham was extended to the son.

25:25 [w] Ge 27:11 **25:26** [x] Hos 12:3 [y] Ge 27:36 **25:27** [z] Ge 27:3,5 **25:28** [a] Ge 27:19 [b] Ge 27:6 **25:33** [c] Ge 27:36; Heb 12:16 **26:1** [d] Ge 12:10 [e] Ge 20:1 **26:2** [f] Ge 12:7; 17:1; 18:1 [g] Ge 12:1 **26:3** [h] Ge 20:1; 28:15 [i] Ge 12:2; 22:16-18 [j] Ge 12:7; 13:15; 15:18 **26:4** [k] Ge 15:5; 22:17; Ex 32:13 [l] Ge 12:3; 22:18; Gal 3:8 **26:5** [m] Ge 22:16 **26:7** [n] Ge 12:13; 20:2, 12; Pr 29:25 **26:10** [o] Ge 20:9 **26:11** [p] Ps 105:15 **26:12** [q] ver 3; Job 42:12 **26:13** [r] Pr 10:22 **26:14** [s] Ge 24:36 [t] Ge 37:11 **26:15** [u] Ge 21:30 [v] Ge 21:25 **26:16** [w] Ex 1:9 **26:18** [x] Ge 21:30

been dug in the time of his father Abraham,
which the Philistines had stopped up after
Abraham died, and he gave them the same
names his father had given them.
19Isaac’s servants dug in the valley and
discovered a well of fresh water there.
20But the herders of Gerar quarreled
with those of Isaac and said, “The water
is ours!”[y] So he named the well Esek,[a]
because they disputed with him. 21Then
they dug another well, but they quarreled
over that one also; so he named it Sitnah.[b]
22He moved on from there and dug another well, and no one quarreled over it.
He named it Rehoboth,[c] saying, “Now the
LORD has given us room and we will flourish[z] in the land.”
23From there he went up to Beersheba.
24That night the LORD appeared to him and
said, “I am the God of your father Abraham.[a] Do not be afraid,[b] for I am with you;
I will bless you and will increase the number of your descendants[c] for the sake of my
servant Abraham.”[d]
25Isaac built an altar[e] there and called on
the name of the LORD. There he pitched his
tent, and there his servants dug a well.
26Meanwhile, Abimelek had come to him
from Gerar, with Ahuzzath his personal
adviser and Phicol the commander of his
forces.[f] 27Isaac asked them, “Why have you
come to me, since you were hostile to me
and sent me away?[g]”
28They answered, “We saw clearly that
the LORD was with you;[h] so we said, ‘There
ought to be a sworn agreement between
us’—between us and you. Let us make a
treaty with you 29that you will do us no
harm, just as we did not harm you but always treated you well and sent you away
peacefully. And now you are blessed by the
LORD.”[i]
30Isaac then made a feast[j] for them, and
they ate and drank. 31Early the next morning the men swore an oath[k] to each other.
Then Isaac sent them on their way, and
they went away peacefully.
32That day Isaac’s servants came and
told him about the well they had dug. They
said, “We’ve found water!” 33He called it
Shibah,[d] and to this day the name of the
town has been Beersheba.[e][l]

Jacob Takes Esau’s Blessing

34When Esau was forty years old,[m] he
married Judith daughter of Beeri the Hittite, and also Basemath daughter of Elon
the Hittite.[n] 35They were a source of grief
to Isaac and Rebekah.[o]
27 When Isaac was old and his eyes
were so weak that he could no lon-
ger see,[p] he called for Esau his older son[q]
and said to him, “My son.”
“Here I am,” he answered.
2Isaac said, “I am now an old man and
don’t know the day of my death.[r] 3Now
then, get your equipment—your quiver
and bow—and go out to the open country[s]
to hunt some wild game for me. 4Prepare
me the kind of tasty food I like and bring
it to me to eat, so that I may give you my
blessing[t] before I die.”
5Now Rebekah was listening as Isaac
spoke to his son Esau. When Esau left for
the open country to hunt game and bring
it back, 6Rebekah said to her son Jacob,[u]
“Look, I overheard your father say to your
brother Esau, 7‘Bring me some game and
prepare me some tasty food to eat, so that
I may give you my blessing in the presence
of the LORD before I die.’ 8Now, my son, listen carefully and do what I tell you:[v] 9Go
out to the flock and bring me two choice
young goats, so I can prepare some tasty
food for your father, just the way he likes
it. 10Then take it to your father to eat, so
that he may give you his blessing before
he dies.”
11Jacob said to Rebekah his mother, “But
my brother Esau is a hairy man[w] while I
have smooth skin. 12What if my father
touches me?[x] I would appear to be tricking
him and would bring down a curse on myself rather than a blessing.”
13His mother said to him, “My son, let the
curse fall on me.[y] Just do what I say;[z] go
and get them for me.”
14So he went and got them and brought
them to his mother, and she prepared some
tasty food, just the way his father liked it.

---

[a] 20 *Esek* means *dispute.* [b] 21 *Sitnah* means *opposition.* [c] 22 *Rehoboth* means *room.*
[d] 33 *Shibah* can mean *oath* or *seven.*
[e] 33 *Beersheba* can mean *well of the oath* and *well of seven.*

26:25 called on the name of the LORD. Isaac followed the practice of his father (12:8). At this altar Isaac not only prayed to the Lord, he also affirmed the reality of the living God in this special land (12:8; 21:33).

26:34 Hittite. Because the Hittite’s believed in many different gods, Esau’s marriages were unacceptable for one belonging to God’s covenant family.

27:8 listen carefully ... do what I tell you. Rebekah certainly appears calculating and devious in this passage, but God had told her before they were even born that the younger son would have precedence over the older (25:23). He had not, however, told her to make sure that it happened, and the results of her deception were family strife and the loss of her younger son.

26:20 [y] Ge 21:25 **26:22** [z] Ge 17:6; Ex 1:7
26:24 [a] Ge 24:12; Ex 3:6 [b] Ge 15:1 [c] ver 4 [d] Ge 17:7
26:25 [e] Ge 12:7, 8; 13:4, 18; Ps 116:17 **26:26** [f] Ge 21:22
26:27 [g] ver 16 **26:28** [h] Ge 21:22 **26:29** [i] Ge 24:31; Ps 115:15 **26:30** [j] Ge 19:3 **26:31** [k] Ge 21:31
26:33 [l] Ge 21:14 **26:34** [m] Ge 25:20 [n] Ge 28:9; 36:2
26:35 [o] Ge 27:46 **27:1** [p] Ge 48:10; 1Sa 3:2 [q] Ge 25:25
27:2 [r] Ge 47:29 **27:3** [s] Ge 25:27 **27:4** [t] ver 10, 25, 31; Ge 49:28; Dt 33:1; Heb 11:20 **27:6** [u] Ge 25:28
27:8 [v] ver 13, 43 **27:11** [w] Ge 25:25 **27:12** [x] ver 22
27:13 [y] Mt 27:25 [z] ver 8

15Then Rebekah took the best clothes[a] of
Esau her older son, which she had in the
house, and put them on her younger son
Jacob. 16She also covered his hands and
the smooth part of his neck with the goatskins. 17Then she handed to her son Jacob
the tasty food and the bread she had made.
18He went to his father and said, "My father."
"Yes, my son," he answered. "Who is it?"
19Jacob said to his father, "I am Esau
your firstborn. I have done as you told me.
Please sit up and eat some of my game, so
that you may give me your blessing."[b]
20Isaac asked his son, "How did you find
it so quickly, my son?"
"The LORD your God gave me success,[c]"
he replied.
21Then Isaac said to Jacob, "Come near
so I can touch you,[d] my son, to know whether you really are my son Esau or not."
22Jacob went close to his father Isaac,
who touched him and said, "The voice is
the voice of Jacob, but the hands are the
hands of Esau." 23He did not recognize
him, for his hands were hairy like those of
his brother Esau;[e] so he proceeded to bless
him. 24"Are you really my son Esau?" he
asked.
"I am," he replied.
25Then he said, "My son, bring me some
of your game to eat, so that I may give you
my blessing."[f]
Jacob brought it to him and he ate; and
he brought some wine and he drank.
26Then his father Isaac said to him, "Come
here, my son, and kiss me."
27So he went to him and kissed him[g].
When Isaac caught the smell of his
clothes,[h] he blessed him and said,

"Ah, the smell of my son
is like the smell of a field
that the LORD has blessed.[i]
28May God give you heaven's
dew[j]
and earth's richness[k]—
an abundance of grain and new
wine.[l]
29May nations serve you
and peoples bow down to you.[m]
Be lord over your brothers,
and may the sons of your mother bow
down to you.[n]
May those who curse you be cursed
and those who bless you be blessed.[o]"

30After Isaac finished blessing him, and
Jacob had scarcely left his father's presence, his brother Esau came in from hunting. 31He too prepared some tasty food and
brought it to his father. Then he said to him,
"My father, please sit up and eat some of
my game, so that you may give me your
blessing."[p]
32His father Isaac asked him, "Who are
you?"[q]
"I am your son," he answered, "your
firstborn, Esau."
33Isaac trembled violently and said,
"Who was it, then, that hunted game and
brought it to me? I ate it just before you
came and I blessed him—and indeed he
will be blessed![r]"
34When Esau heard his father's words,
he burst out with a loud and bitter cry[s] and
said to his father, "Bless me—me too, my
father!"
35But he said, "Your brother came deceitfully[t] and took your blessing."
36Esau said, "Isn't he rightly named Jacob[a]?[u] This is the second time he has taken
advantage of me: He took my birthright,[v]
and now he's taken my blessing!" Then he
asked, "Haven't you reserved any blessing
for me?"
37Isaac answered Esau, "I have made
him lord over you and have made all his
relatives his servants, and I have sustained
him with grain and new wine.[w] So what
can I possibly do for you, my son?"
38Esau said to his father, "Do you have
only one blessing, my father? Bless me too,
my father!" Then Esau wept aloud.[x]
39His father Isaac answered him,

"Your dwelling will be
away from the earth's richness,
away from the dew[y] of heaven
above.
40You will live by the sword
and you will serve[z] your
brother.[a]
But when you grow restless,
you will throw his yoke
from off your neck.[b]"

[a] *36 Jacob* means *he grasps the heel,* a Hebrew idiom for *he takes advantage of* or *he deceives.*

27:18–29 Falsehood—Jacob may have felt justified in deceiving his father, since Esau had already sold him the birthright. Esau had clearly demonstrated his contempt of the position (including the spiritual responsibility) which was his by right, while Jacob valued and desired it. However, lofty purposes and aspirations cannot justify deceit and trickery. We must be content to leave the fulfillment of God's promises in His hand and wait for His time.

27:29 *peoples bow down to you.* Isaac predicted that Jacob's descendants would obtain supremacy over other peoples. Jesus, as the King of kings, and a descendant of Jacob, ultimately fulfilled this prediction (1 Tim. 6:14–16).

27:15 [a] ver 27 **27:19** [b] ver 4 **27:20** [c] Ge 24:12 **27:21** [d] ver 12 **27:23** [e] ver 16 **27:25** [f] ver 4 **27:27** [g] Heb 11:20 [h] SS 4:11 [i] Ps 65:9-13 **27:28** [j] Dt 33:13 [k] ver 39 [l] Ge 45:18; Nu 18:12; Dt 33:28 **27:29** [m] Isa 45:14, 23; 49:7, 23 [n] Ge 9:25; 25:23; 37:7 [o] Ge 12:3; Nu 24:9; Zep 2:8 **27:31** [p] ver 4 **27:32** [q] ver 18 **27:33** [r] ver 29; Ge 28:3, 4; Ro 11:29 **27:34** [s] Heb 12:17 **27:35** [t] Jer 9:4; 12:6 **27:36** [u] Ge 25:26 [v] Ge 25:33 **27:37** [w] ver 28 **27:38** [x] Heb 12:17 **27:39** [y] ver 28 **27:40** [z] 2Sa 8:14 [a] Ge 25:23 [b] 2Ki 8:20-22

41 Esau held a grudge[c] against Jacob[d]
because of the blessing his father had giv-
en him. He said to himself, "The days of
mourning[e] for my father are near; then I
will kill my brother Jacob."[f]
42 When Rebekah was told what her older
son Esau had said, she sent for her younger son Jacob and said to him, "Your brother Esau is planning to avenge himself by
killing you. 43 Now then, my son, do what I
say:[g] Flee at once to my brother Laban[h] in
Harran.[i] 44 Stay with him for a while[j] until your brother's fury subsides. 45 When
your brother is no longer angry with you
and forgets what you did to him,[k] I'll send
word for you to come back from there. Why
should I lose both of you in one day?"
46 Then Rebekah said to Isaac, "I'm disgusted with living because of these Hittite
women. If Jacob takes a wife from among
the women of this land, from Hittite women
like these, my life will not be worth living."[l]

28 So Isaac called for Jacob and blessed
him. Then he commanded him: "Do
not marry a Canaanite woman.[m] 2 Go at
once to Paddan Aram,[a] to the house of your
mother's father Bethuel.[n] Take a wife for
yourself there, from among the daughters
of Laban, your mother's brother. 3 May God
Almighty[b][o] bless you and make you fruitful[p] and increase your numbers until you
become a community of peoples. 4 May he
give you and your descendants the blessing
given to Abraham,[q] so that you may take
possession of the land where you now reside as a foreigner,[r] the land God gave to
Abraham." 5 Then Isaac sent Jacob on his
way, and he went to Paddan Aram,[s] to Laban son of Bethuel the Aramean, the brother of Rebekah,[t] who was the mother of Jacob and Esau.
6 Now Esau learned that Isaac had
blessed Jacob and had sent him to Paddan
Aram to take a wife from there, and that
when he blessed him he commanded him,
"Do not marry a Canaanite woman,"[u] 7 and
that Jacob had obeyed his father and mother and had gone to Paddan Aram. 8 Esau
then realized how displeasing the Canaanite women[v] were to his father Isaac;[w] 9 so he
went to Ishmael and married Mahalath, the
sister of Nebaioth[x] and daughter of Ishmael
son of Abraham, in addition to the wives he
already had.[y]

Jacob's Dream at Bethel

10 Jacob left Beersheba and set out for
Harran.[z] 11 When he reached a certain
place, he stopped for the night because the
sun had set. Taking one of the stones there,
he put it under his head and lay down to
sleep. 12 He had a dream[a] in which he saw
a stairway resting on the earth, with its
top reaching to heaven, and the angels of
God were ascending and descending on
it.[b] 13 There above it[c] stood the LORD,[c] and
he said: "I am the LORD, the God of your
father Abraham and the God of Isaac.[d] I
will give you and your descendants the
land[e] on which you are lying. 14 Your descendants will be like the dust of the earth,
and you[f] will spread out to the west and to
the east, to the north and to the south.[g] All
peoples on earth will be blessed through
you and your offspring.[d][h] 15 I am with you[i]
and will watch over you[j] wherever you go,
and I will bring you back to this land. I will
not leave you[k] until I have done what I have
promised you."[l]
16 When Jacob awoke from his sleep, he
thought, "Surely the LORD is in this place,
and I was not aware of it." 17 He was afraid
and said, "How awesome is this place![m]
This is none other than the house of God;
this is the gate of heaven."
18 Early the next morning Jacob took the
stone he had placed under his head and set
it up as a pillar[n] and poured oil on top of it.[o]
19 He called that place Bethel,[e] though the
city used to be called Luz.[p]

---

[a] *2* That is, Northwest Mesopotamia; also in verses 5, 6 and 7 [b] *3* Hebrew *El-Shaddai*
[c] *13* Or *There beside him* [d] *14* Or *will use your name and the name of your offspring in blessings* (see 48:20) [e] *19* *Bethel* means *house of God.*

27:46 *Hittite women.* Intermarrying with the pagan women of Canaan was dangerous because they would bring their pagan gods and pagan worship into their new homes.

28:2 *Paddan Aram.* This is a region of Haran in northern Aram (Syria) near the Euphrates River.

28:3 *God Almighty.* This Hebrew name, *El Shaddai* is used by or in the hearing of Abraham, Isaac, and Jacob (35:11). God later identified Himself to Moses with this same name (Ex. 6:3).

28:9 *Mahalath.* This daughter of Ishmael is probably the same woman as Basemath (36:3). Her name means "dance."

28:10–15 Jacob's Dream—The ladder of Jacob's dream reminds us of Jesus' words about the angels "ascending and descending upon the Son of Man" (John 1:51), vividly depicting Himself as the Way into the heavenlies. Certainly Jacob did not deserve such grace after cheating his brother out of the blessings of Isaac. Indeed, he was already suffering by being banished from the fellowship of his family. Nevertheless, God mercifully confirmed the covenant promises made to Abraham and Isaac concerning the land and the descendants. His words, "I am with you, and will watch over you" speak of God's personal presence for

27:41 [c] Ge 37:4 [d] Ge 32:11 [e] Ge 50:4, 10 [f] Ob 1:10
27:43 [g] ver 8 [h] Ge 24:29 [i] Ge 11:31 **27:44** [j] Ge 31:38, 41
27:45 [k] ver 35 **27:46** [l] Ge 26:35 **28:1** [m] Ge 24:3
28:2 [n] Ge 25:20 **28:3** [o] Ge 17:1 [p] Ge 17:6
28:4 [q] Ge 12:2, 3 [r] Ge 17:8 **28:5** [s] Hos 12:12 [t] Ge 24:29
28:6 [u] ver 1 **28:8** [v] Ge 24:3 [w] Ge 26:35
28:9 [x] Ge 25:13 [y] Ge 26:34 **28:10** [z] Ge 11:31
28:12 [a] Ge 20:3 [b] Jn 1:51 **28:13** [c] Ge 12:7; 35:7, 9; 48:3
[d] Ge 26:24 [e] Ge 13:15; 35:12 **28:14** [f] Ge 26:4 [g] Ge 13:14
[h] Ge 12:3; 18:18; 22:18; Gal 3:8 **28:15** [i] Ge 26:3; 48:21
[j] Nu 6:24; Ps 121:5, 7-8 [k] Dt 31:6, 8 [l] Nu 23:19
28:17 [m] Ex 3:5; Jos 5:15 **28:18** [n] Ge 35:14 [o] Lev 8:11
28:19 [p] Jdg 1:23, 26

20Then Jacob made a vow,[q] saying, "If God will be with me and will watch over me[r] on this journey I am taking and will give me food to eat and clothes to wear 21so that I return safely[s] to my father's household, then the LORD[a] will be my God[t] 22and[b] this stone that I have set up as a pillar will be God's house,[u] and of all that you give me I will give you a tenth.[v]"

Jacob Arrives in Paddan Aram

29 Then Jacob continued on his journey and came to the land of the eastern peoples.[w] 2There he saw a well in the open country, with three flocks of sheep lying near it because the flocks were watered from that well. The stone over the mouth of the well was large. 3When all the flocks were gathered there, the shepherds would roll the stone away from the well's mouth and water the sheep. Then they would return the stone to its place over the mouth of the well.

4Jacob asked the shepherds, "My brothers, where are you from?"

"We're from Harran,[x]" they replied.

5He said to them, "Do you know Laban, Nahor's grandson?"

"Yes, we know him," they answered.

6Then Jacob asked them, "Is he well?"

"Yes, he is," they said, "and here comes his daughter Rachel with the sheep."

7"Look," he said, "the sun is still high; it is not time for the flocks to be gathered. Water the sheep and take them back to pasture."

8"We can't," they replied, "until all the flocks are gathered and the stone has been rolled away from the mouth of the well. Then we will water the sheep."

9While he was still talking with them, Rachel came with her father's sheep,[y] for she was a shepherd. 10When Jacob saw Rachel daughter of his uncle Laban, and Laban's sheep, he went over and rolled the stone away from the mouth of the well and watered his uncle's sheep.[z] 11Then Jacob kissed Rachel and began to weep aloud.[a] 12He had told Rachel that he was a relative[b] of her father and a son of Rebekah. So she ran and told her father.[c]

13As soon as Laban[d] heard the news about Jacob, his sister's son, he hurried to meet him. He embraced him and kissed him and brought him to his home, and there Jacob told him all these things. 14Then Laban said to him, "You are my own flesh and blood."[e]

Jacob Marries Leah and Rachel

After Jacob had stayed with him for a whole month, 15Laban said to him, "Just because you are a relative of mine, should you work for me for nothing? Tell me what your wages should be."

16Now Laban had two daughters; the name of the older was Leah, and the name of the younger was Rachel. 17Leah had weak[c] eyes, but Rachel had a lovely figure and was beautiful. 18Jacob was in love with Rachel and said, "I'll work for you seven years in return for your younger daughter Rachel."[f]

19Laban said, "It's better that I give her to you than to some other man. Stay here with me." 20So Jacob served seven years to get Rachel, but they seemed like only a few days to him because of his love for her.[g]

21Then Jacob said to Laban, "Give me my wife. My time is completed, and I want to make love to her.[h]"

22So Laban brought together all the people of the place and gave a feast.[i] 23But when evening came, he took his daughter Leah and brought her to Jacob, and Jacob made love to her. 24And Laban gave his servant Zilpah to his daughter as her attendant.

25When morning came, there was Leah! So Jacob said to Laban, "What is this you have done to me?[j] I served you for Rachel, didn't I? Why have you deceived me?[k]"

26Laban replied, "It is not our custom here to give the younger daughter in marriage before the older one. 27Finish this daughter's bridal week;[l] then we will give you the younger one also, in return for another seven years of work."

[a] 20,21 Or *Since God . . . father's household, the* LORD [b] 21,22 Or *household, and the* LORD *will be my God,* [22]*then* [c] 17 Or *delicate*

---

protection and guidance, anticipating Jacob's return to the land, so that all the promises might be fulfilled. Surely the grace of God goes far beyond our small expectations.

28:22 *a tenth.* Jacob promised to give a tenth of his possessions to God. Abraham had given the same proportion to Melchizedek, the priest of the most high God. Later the Mosaic law required giving a tenth to God (Deut. 14:22).

29:6 *Rachel.* This name is a term of endearment meaning "Ewe Lamb."

29:21 – 25 Deception — Many times we see God's prohibitions as mere taboos. We somehow imagine that God says no just because He can, instead of acknowledging both His goodwill towards us, and His wisdom. God does not merely prohibit lying because He can, it is because it is destructive. Jacob learned through experience that trickery and deceit bring complicated and painful consequences. False dealing destroys trust in a relationship, and once trust has been broken it is difficult, if not impossible, to entirely restore it.

28:20 [q] Ge 31:13; Jdg 11:30; 2Sa 15:8 [r] ver 15
28:21 [s] Jdg 11:31 [t] Dt 26:17 **28:22** [u] Ge 35:7, 14
[v] Ge 14:20; Lev 27:30 **29:1** [w] Jdg 6:3, 33
29:4 [x] Ge 28:10 **29:9** [y] Ex 2:16 **29:10** [z] Ex 2:17
29:11 [a] Ge 33:4 **29:12** [b] Ge 13:8; 14:14, 16 [c] Ge 24:28
29:13 [d] Ge 24:29 **29:14** [e] Ge 2:23; Jdg 9:2; 2Sa 19:12-13
29:18 [f] Hos 12:12 **29:20** [g] SS 8:7; Hos 12:12
29:21 [h] Jdg 15:1 **29:22** [i] Jdg 14:10; Jn 2:1-2
29:25 [j] Ge 12:18 [k] Ge 27:36 **29:27** [l] Jdg 14:12

28 And Jacob did so. He finished the week with Leah, and then Laban gave him his daughter Rachel to be his wife. 29 Laban gave his servant Bilhah[m] to his daughter Rachel as her attendant.[n] 30 Jacob made love to Rachel also, and his love for Rachel was greater than his love for Leah.[o] And he worked for Laban another seven years.[p]

Jacob's Children

31 When the LORD saw that Leah was not loved,[q] he enabled her to conceive,[r] but Rachel remained childless. 32 Leah became pregnant and gave birth to a son. She named him Reuben,[a] for she said, "It is because the LORD has seen my misery.[s] Surely my husband will love me now."

33 She conceived again, and when she gave birth to a son she said, "Because the LORD heard that I am not loved, he gave me this one too." So she named him Simeon.[b][t]

34 Again she conceived, and when she gave birth to a son she said, "Now at last my husband will become attached to me,[u] because I have borne him three sons." So he was named Levi.[c][v]

35 She conceived again, and when she gave birth to a son she said, "This time I will praise the LORD." So she named him Judah.[d][w] Then she stopped having children.

30 When Rachel saw that she was not bearing Jacob any children,[x] she became jealous of her sister.[y] So she said to Jacob, "Give me children, or I'll die!"

2 Jacob became angry with her and said, "Am I in the place of God, who has kept you from having children?"[z]

3 Then she said, "Here is Bilhah, my servant. Sleep with her so that she can bear children for me and I too can build a family through her."[a]

4 So she gave him her servant Bilhah as a wife.[b] Jacob slept with her,[c] 5 and she became pregnant and bore him a son. 6 Then Rachel said, "God has vindicated me;[d] he has listened to my plea and given me a son." Because of this she named him Dan.[e][e]

7 Rachel's servant Bilhah conceived again and bore Jacob a second son. 8 Then Rachel said, "I have had a great struggle with my sister, and I have won."[f] So she named him Naphtali.[f][g]

9 When Leah saw that she had stopped having children, she took her servant Zilpah and gave her to Jacob as a wife.[h] 10 Leah's servant Zilpah bore Jacob a son. 11 Then Leah said, "What good fortune!"[g] So she named him Gad.[h][i]

12 Leah's servant Zilpah bore Jacob a second son. 13 Then Leah said, "How happy I am! The women will call me[j] happy."[k] So she named him Asher.[i][l]

14 During wheat harvest, Reuben went out into the fields and found some mandrake plants,[m] which he brought to his mother Leah. Rachel said to Leah, "Please give me some of your son's mandrakes."

15 But she said to her, "Wasn't it enough[n] that you took away my husband? Will you take my son's mandrakes too?"

"Very well," Rachel said, "he can sleep with you tonight in return for your son's mandrakes."

16 So when Jacob came in from the fields that evening, Leah went out to meet him. "You must sleep with me," she said. "I have hired you with my son's mandrakes." So he slept with her that night.

17 God listened to Leah,[o] and she became pregnant and bore Jacob a fifth son. 18 Then Leah said, "God has rewarded me for giving my servant to my husband." So she named him Issachar.[j][p]

19 Leah conceived again and bore Jacob a sixth son. 20 Then Leah said, "God has presented me with a precious gift. This time my husband will treat me with honor, because I have borne him six sons." So she named him Zebulun.[k][q]

21 Some time later she gave birth to a daughter and named her Dinah.

22 Then God remembered Rachel;[r] he listened to her and enabled her to conceive.[s] 23 She became pregnant and gave birth to a son[t] and said, "God has taken away my

---

[a] 32 *Reuben* sounds like the Hebrew for *he has seen my misery*; the name means *see, a son.*
[b] 33 *Simeon* probably means *one who hears.*
[c] 34 *Levi* sounds like and may be derived from the Hebrew for *attached.* [d] 35 *Judah* sounds like and may be derived from the Hebrew for *praise.*
[e] 6 *Dan* here means *he has vindicated.*
[f] 8 *Naphtali* means *my struggle.* [g] 11 Or "*A troop is coming!*" [h] 11 *Gad* can mean *good fortune* or *a troop.* [i] 13 *Asher* means *happy.*
[j] 18 *Issachar* sounds like the Hebrew for *reward.*
[k] 20 *Zebulun* probably means *honor.*

29:31 *not loved.* God was kind to Leah in her predicament. Even though she was the unloved wife, it was through her son Judah that the messianic line was carried out.

30:14 *mandrakes.* This is a plant which was regarded as an aid to conception. Its aroma was associated with lovemaking (Song 7:13).

30:22 *remembered ... listened to her ... enabled.* These three verbs emphasize conception as a gift from God.

29:29 [m] Ge 30:3 [n] Ge 16:1 **29:30** [o] ver 16 [p] Ge 31:41
29:31 [q] Dt 21:15-17 [r] Ge 11:30; 30:1; Ps 127:3
29:32 [s] Ge 16:11; 31:42; Ex 4:31; Dt 26:7; Ps 25:18
29:33 [t] Ge 34:25; 49:5 **29:34** [u] Ge 30:20; 1Sa 1:2-4
[v] Ge 49:5-7 **29:35** [w] Ge 49:8; Mt 1:2-3 **30:1** [x] Ge 29:31; 1Sa 1:5-6 [y] Lev 18:18 **30:2** [z] Ge 16:2; 20:18; 29:31
30:3 [a] Ge 16:2 **30:4** [b] ver 9, 18 [c] Ge 16:3-4
30:6 [d] Ps 35:24; 43:1; La 3:59 [e] Ge 49:16-17
30:8 [f] Hos 12:3-4 [g] Ge 49:21 **30:9** [h] ver 4
30:11 [i] Ge 49:19 **30:13** [j] Ps 127:3 [k] Pr 31:28; Lk 1:48
[l] Ge 49:20 **30:14** [m] SS 7:13 **30:15** [n] Nu 16:9, 13
30:17 [o] Ge 25:21 **30:18** [p] Ge 49:14 **30:20** [q] Ge 35:23; 49:13; Mt 4:13 **30:22** [r] Ge 8:1; 1Sa 1:19-20 [s] Ge 29:31
30:23 [t] ver 6

disgrace."[u] 24She named him Joseph,[a][v]
and said, "May the LORD add to me another son."[w]

Jacob's Flocks Increase

25After Rachel gave birth to Joseph, Jacob said to Laban, "Send me on my way[x] so
I can go back to my own homeland. 26Give
me my wives and children, for whom I have
served you,[y] and I will be on my way. You
know how much work I've done for you."

27But Laban said to him, "If I have found
favor in your eyes, please stay. I have
learned by divination that the LORD has
blessed me because of you."[z] 28He added,
"Name your wages,[a] and I will pay them."

29Jacob said to him, "You know how I
have worked for you[b] and how your livestock has fared under my care.[c] 30The little
you had before I came has increased greatly, and the LORD has blessed you wherever
I have been. But now, when may I do something for my own household?[d]"

31"What shall I give you?" he asked.

"Don't give me anything," Jacob replied.
"But if you will do this one thing for me, I
will go on tending your flocks and watching over them: 32Let me go through all your
flocks today and remove from them every
speckled or spotted sheep, every dark-colored lamb and every spotted or speckled
goat.[e] They will be my wages. 33And my
honesty will testify for me in the future,
whenever you check on the wages you
have paid me. Any goat in my possession
that is not speckled or spotted, or any lamb
that is not dark-colored, will be considered
stolen."

34"Agreed," said Laban. "Let it be as you
have said." 35That same day he removed
all the male goats that were streaked or
spotted, and all the speckled or spotted female goats (all that had white on them) and
all the dark-colored lambs, and he placed
them in the care of his sons.[f] 36Then he put
a three-day journey between himself and
Jacob, while Jacob continued to tend the
rest of Laban's flocks.

37Jacob, however, took fresh-cut branches from poplar, almond and plane trees and
made white stripes on them by peeling the
bark and exposing the white inner wood of
the branches. 38Then he placed the peeled
branches in all the watering troughs, so
that they would be directly in front of the
flocks when they came to drink. When
the flocks were in heat and came to drink,
39they mated in front of the branches.
And they bore young that were streaked
or speckled or spotted. 40Jacob set apart
the young of the flock by themselves, but
made the rest face the streaked and dark-
colored animals that belonged to Laban.
Thus he made separate flocks for himself
and did not put them with Laban's animals.
41Whenever the stronger females were in
heat, Jacob would place the branches in
the troughs in front of the animals so they
would mate near the branches, 42but if the
animals were weak, he would not place
them there. So the weak animals went to
Laban and the strong ones to Jacob. 43In
this way the man grew exceedingly prosperous and came to own large flocks, and
female and male servants, and camels and
donkeys.[g]

Jacob Flees From Laban

31 Jacob heard that Laban's sons were
saying, "Jacob has taken everything
our father owned and has gained all this
wealth from what belonged to our father."
2And Jacob noticed that Laban's attitude
toward him was not what it had been.

3Then the LORD said to Jacob, "Go back[h]
to the land of your fathers and to your relatives, and I will be with you."[i]

4So Jacob sent word to Rachel and Leah
to come out to the fields where his flocks
were. 5He said to them, "I see that your
father's attitude toward me is not what it
was before, but the God of my father has
been with me.[j] 6You know that I've worked
for your father with all my strength,[k] 7yet
your father has cheated me by changing
my wages ten times.[l] However, God has
not allowed him to harm me.[m] 8If he said,
'The speckled ones will be your wages,'

[a] *24 Joseph* means *may he add.*

30:25 *own homeland.* Even though Jacob had lived for twenty years with Laban's family, he had not adopted that place as his own. He never forgot that promise and covenant of God were for the land of Canaan, and he knew that he must return.

30:27 *blessed.* God had promised to bless others through Abraham's descendants (12:2–3). Now God blessed Laban through Jacob.

30:37 *fresh-cut branches from poplar.* Just what significance these sticks hold is unknown. Some have theorized that they were simply symbols of Jacob's faith in God. Whatever the case, God blessed Jacob by causing Laban's stock to give birth to speckled and spotted young.

31:7 *cheated me.* Jacob had surely lived up to his name, deceiving his old father and tricking his brother out of the birthright. But in Laban he met his match, and tasted some of his own medicine. The consequences of dishonesty reach both ways. Because of his own trickery, Jacob had to flee from his home. He apparently never saw his mother again, and his relationship with his father and his only brother was broken. Lying not only harms the liar, but it also affects

30:23 [u] Isa 4:1; Lk 1:25 **30:24** [v] Ge 35:24; 37:2; 39:1; 49:22-26 [w] Ge 35:17 **30:25** [x] Ge 24:54 **30:26** [y] Ge 29:20, 30; Hos 12:12 **30:27** [z] Ge 26:24; 39:3, 5 **30:28** [a] Ge 29:15 **30:29** [b] Ge 31:6 [c] Ge 31:38-40 **30:30** [d] 1Ti 5:8 **30:32** [e] Ge 31:8, 12 **30:35** [f] Ge 31:1 **30:43** [g] ver 30; Ge 12:16; 13:2; 24:35; 26:13-14 **31:3** [h] ver 13; Ge 32:9 [i] Ge 21:22; 26:3; 28:15 **31:5** [j] Ge 21:22; 26:3 **31:6** [k] Ge 30:29 **31:7** [l] ver 41; Job 19:3 [m] ver 52; Ps 37:28; 105:14

then all the flocks gave birth to speckled young; and if he said, 'The streaked ones will be your wages,'[n] then all the flocks bore streaked young. 9So God has taken away your father's livestock and has given them to me.[o]

10"In breeding season I once had a dream in which I looked up and saw that the male goats mating with the flock were streaked, speckled or spotted. 11The angel of God[p] said to me in the dream, 'Jacob.' I answered, 'Here I am.' 12And he said, 'Look up and see that all the male goats mating with the flock are streaked, speckled or spotted, for I have seen all that Laban has been doing to you.[q] 13I am the God of Bethel,[r] where you anointed a pillar and where you made a vow to me. Now leave this land at once and go back to your native land.[s]' "

14Then Rachel and Leah replied, "Do we still have any share in the inheritance of our father's estate? 15Does he not regard us as foreigners? Not only has he sold us, but he has used up what was paid for us.[t] 16Surely all the wealth that God took away from our father belongs to us and our children. So do whatever God has told you."

17Then Jacob put his children and his wives on camels, 18and he drove all his livestock ahead of him, along with all the goods he had accumulated in Paddan Aram,[a] to go to his father Isaac[u] in the land of Canaan.[v]

19When Laban had gone to shear his sheep, Rachel stole her father's household gods.[w] 20Moreover, Jacob deceived[x] Laban the Aramean by not telling him he was running away.[y] 21So he fled with all he had, crossed the Euphrates River, and headed for the hill country of Gilead.[z]

Laban Pursues Jacob

22On the third day Laban was told that Jacob had fled. 23Taking his relatives with him, he pursued Jacob for seven days and caught up with him in the hill country of Gilead. 24Then God came to Laban the Aramean in a dream at night and said to him,[a] "Be careful not to say anything to Jacob, either good or bad."[b]

25Jacob had pitched his tent in the hill country of Gilead when Laban overtook him, and Laban and his relatives camped there too. 26Then Laban said to Jacob, "What have you done? You've deceived me,[c] and you've carried off my daughters like captives in war.[d] 27Why did you run off secretly and deceive me? Why didn't you tell me, so I could send you away with joy and singing to the music of timbrels[e] and harps?[f] 28You didn't even let me kiss my grandchildren and my daughters goodbye.[g] You have done a foolish thing. 29I have the power to harm you;[h] but last night the God of your father[i] said to me, 'Be careful not to say anything to Jacob, either good or bad.' 30Now you have gone off because you longed to return to your father's household. But why did you steal my gods?[j]"

31Jacob answered Laban, "I was afraid, because I thought you would take your daughters away from me by force. 32But if you find anyone who has your gods, that person shall not live.[k] In the presence of our relatives, see for yourself whether there is anything of yours here with me; and if so, take it." Now Jacob did not know that Rachel had stolen the gods.

33So Laban went into Jacob's tent and into Leah's tent and into the tent of the two female servants, but he found nothing. After he came out of Leah's tent, he entered Rachel's tent. 34Now Rachel had taken the household gods and put them inside her camel's saddle and was sitting on them. Laban searched[l] through everything in the tent but found nothing.

35Rachel said to her father, "Don't be angry, my lord, that I cannot stand up in your presence;[m] I'm having my period." So he searched but could not find the household gods.

36Jacob was angry and took Laban to task. "What is my crime?" he asked Laban. "How have I wronged you that you hunt me down? 37Now that you have searched through all my goods, what have you found that belongs to your household? Put it here in front of your relatives[n] and mine, and let them judge between the two of us.

38"I have been with you for twenty years now. Your sheep and goats have not miscarried, nor have I eaten rams from your flocks. 39I did not bring you animals torn by wild beasts; I bore the loss myself. And you demanded payment from me for whatever was stolen by day or night.[o] 40This

[a] *18* That is, Northwest Mesopotamia

those he lies to. Because of Laban's trickery, Jacob was saddled with an unloved wife, quarreling sons, and consistent domestic strife.

31:19 ***gods.*** Laban's family may have been polytheistic (believing in many gods), as Abraham's father Terah evidently was (Josh. 24:1 – 3). Considering the evidence of verses 25 – 50 it seems likely that they worshipped Yahweh along with other "lesser gods." In this culture, the possession of the idols was the right of the principal heir. Rachel probably did not steal the idols in order to worship them, but because they represented ownership of her father's property.

31:8 [n] Ge 30:32 **31:9** [o] ver 1, 16; Ge 30:42 **31:11** [p] Ge 16:7; 48:16 **31:12** [q] Ex 3:7 **31:13** [r] Ge 28:10-22 [s] ver 3; Ge 32:9 **31:15** [t] Ge 29:20 **31:18** [u] Ge 35:27 [v] Ge 10:19 **31:19** [w] ver 30, 32, 34-35; Ge 35:2; Jdg 17:5; 1Sa 19:13; Hos 3:4 **31:20** [x] Ge 27:36 [y] ver 27 **31:21** [z] Ge 37:25 **31:24** [a] Ge 20:3; Job 33:15 [b] Ge 24:50 **31:26** [c] Ge 27:36 [d] 1Sa 30:2-3 **31:27** [e] Ex 15:20 [f] Ge 4:21 **31:28** [g] ver 55 **31:29** [h] ver 7 [i] ver 53 **31:30** [j] ver 19; Jdg 18:24 **31:32** [k] Ge 44:9 **31:34** [l] ver 37; Ge 44:12 **31:35** [m] Ex 20:12; Lev 19:3, 32 **31:37** [n] ver 23 **31:39** [o] Ex 22:13

was my situation: The heat consumed me in the daytime and the cold at night, and sleep fled from my eyes. 41It was like this for the twenty years I was in your household. I worked for you fourteen years for your two daughters[p] and six years for your flocks, and you changed my wages ten times.[q] 42If the God of my father,[r] the God of Abraham and the Fear of Isaac,[s] had not been with me,[t] you would surely have sent me away empty-handed. But God has seen my hardship and the toil of my hands,[u] and last night he rebuked you."

43Laban answered Jacob, "The women are my daughters, the children are my children, and the flocks are my flocks. All you see is mine. Yet what can I do today about these daughters of mine, or about the children they have borne? 44Come now, let's make a covenant,[v] you and I, and let it serve as a witness between us."[w]

45So Jacob took a stone and set it up as a pillar.[x] 46He said to his relatives, "Gather some stones." So they took stones and piled them in a heap, and they ate there by the heap. 47Laban called it Jegar Sahadutha, and Jacob called it Galeed.[a]

48Laban said, "This heap is a witness between you and me today." That is why it was called Galeed. 49It was also called Mizpah,[b][y] because he said, "May the LORD keep watch between you and me when we are away from each other. 50If you mistreat my daughters or if you take any wives besides my daughters, even though no one is with us, remember that God is a witness[z] between you and me."

51Laban also said to Jacob, "Here is this heap, and here is this pillar[a] I have set up between you and me. 52This heap is a witness, and this pillar is a witness,[b] that I will not go past this heap to your side to harm you and that you will not go past this heap and pillar to my side to harm me.[c] 53May the God of Abraham[d] and the God of Nahor, the God of their father, judge between us."[e]

So Jacob took an oath[f] in the name of the Fear of his father Isaac.[g] 54He offered a sacrifice there in the hill country and invited his relatives to a meal. After they had eaten, they spent the night there.

55Early the next morning Laban kissed his grandchildren and his daughters[h] and blessed them. Then he left and returned home.[c][i]

Jacob Prepares to Meet Esau

32 [d]Jacob also went on his way, and the angels of God[j] met him. 2When Jacob saw them, he said, "This is the camp of God!"[k] So he named that place Mahanaim.[e][l]

3Jacob sent messengers ahead of him to his brother Esau[m] in the land of Seir, the country of Edom.[n] 4He instructed them: "This is what you are to say to my lord Esau: 'Your servant Jacob says, I have been staying with Laban and have remained there till now. 5I have cattle and donkeys, sheep and goats, male and female servants.[o] Now I am sending this message to my lord, that I may find favor in your eyes.[p]'"

6When the messengers returned to Jacob, they said, "We went to your brother Esau, and now he is coming to meet you, and four hundred men are with him."[q]

7In great fear[r] and distress Jacob divided the people who were with him into two groups,[f] and the flocks and herds and camels as well. 8He thought, "If Esau comes and attacks one group,[g] the group[g] that is left may escape."

9Then Jacob prayed, "O God of my father Abraham, God of my father Isaac,[s] LORD, you who said to me, 'Go back to your country and your relatives, and I will make you prosper,'[t] 10I am unworthy of all the kindness and faithfulness[u] you have shown your servant. I had only my staff when I crossed this Jordan, but now I have become two camps. 11Save me, I pray, from the hand of my brother Esau, for I am afraid he will come and attack me,[v] and also the mothers with their children.[w] 12But you have said, 'I will surely make you prosper and will make your descendants like the sand[x] of the sea, which cannot be counted.[y]'"

---

[a] 47 The Aramaic *Jegar Sahadutha* and the Hebrew *Galeed* both mean *witness heap.*
[b] 49 *Mizpah* means *watchtower.*
[c] 55 In Hebrew texts this verse (31:55) is numbered 32:1.
[d] In Hebrew texts 32:1-32 is numbered 32:2-33.
[e] 2 *Mahanaim* means *two camps.*
[f] 7 Or *camps*
[g] 8 Or *camp*

31:44 *covenant.* This instance of a covenant was an agreement between two equals.

31:49 *Mizpah.* This name means "Outlook Point," a place to keep watch. God above had His eyes on both men to make them keep their covenant.

31:53 *The God of Abraham.* The wording in Laban's oath suggests that Abraham, Nahor, and their father Terah all worshipped the same One True God. Joshua records the fact that Terah at least worshipped other gods as well (Josh. 24:1 – 3). It is possible that they were henotheistic—worshipping God not as the only God but as the most important and powerful among many.

32:11 *Save me, I pray.* Jacob did not pray in generalities. He named his concerns openly, and concluded with another appeal to God's promises. Christians today can likewise base their prayers on God's proven character and His promises in the Bible.

31:41 [p]Ge 29:30 [q]ver 7 **31:42** [r]ver 5; Ex 3:15; 1Ch 12:17 [s]ver 53; Isa 8:13 [t]Ps 124:1-2 [u]Ge 29:32 **31:44** [v]Ge 21:27; 26:28 [w]Jos 24:27 **31:45** [x]Ge 28:18 **31:49** [y]Jdg 11:29; 1Sa 7:5-6 **31:50** [z]Jer 29:23; 42:5 **31:51** [a]Ge 28:18 **31:52** [b]Ge 21:30 [c]ver 7; Ge 26:29 **31:53** [d]Ge 28:13 [e]Ge 16:5 [f]Ge 21:23,27 [g]ver 42 **31:55** [h]ver 28 [i]Ge 18:33; 30:25 **32:1** [j]Ge 16:11; 2Ki 6:16-17; Ps 34:7; 91:11; Heb 1:14 **32:2** [k]Ge 28:17 [l]2Sa 2:8,29 **32:3** [m]Ge 27:41-42 [n]Ge 25:30; 36:8,9 **32:5** [o]Ge 12:16; 30:43 [p]Ge 33:8,10,15 **32:6** [q]Ge 33:1 **32:7** [r]ver 11 **32:9** [s]Ge 28:13; 31:42 [t]Ge 31:13 **32:10** [u]Ge 24:27 **32:11** [v]Ps 59:2 [w]Ge 27:41 **32:12** [x]Ge 22:17 [y]Ge 28:13-15; Hos 1:10; Ro 9:27

13He spent the night there, and from what he had with him he selected a gift[z] for his brother Esau: 14two hundred female goats and twenty male goats, two hundred ewes and twenty rams, 15thirty female camels with their young, forty cows and ten bulls, and twenty female donkeys and ten male donkeys. 16He put them in the care of his servants, each herd by itself, and said to his servants, "Go ahead of me, and keep some space between the herds."

17He instructed the one in the lead: "When my brother Esau meets you and asks, 'Who do you belong to, and where are you going, and who owns all these animals in front of you?' 18then you are to say, 'They belong to your servant[a] Jacob. They are a gift sent to my lord Esau, and he is coming behind us.'"

19He also instructed the second, the third and all the others who followed the herds: "You are to say the same thing to Esau when you meet him. 20And be sure to say, 'Your servant Jacob is coming behind us.'" For he thought, "I will pacify him with these gifts I am sending on ahead; later, when I see him, perhaps he will receive me."[b] 21So Jacob's gifts went on ahead of him, but he himself spent the night in the camp.

Jacob Wrestles With God

22That night Jacob got up and took his two wives, his two female servants and his eleven sons and crossed the ford of the Jabbok.[c] 23After he had sent them across the stream, he sent over all his possessions. 24So Jacob was left alone, and a man[d] wrestled with him till daybreak. 25When the man saw that he could not overpower him, he touched the socket of Jacob's hip[e] so that his hip was wrenched as he wrestled with the man. 26Then the man said, "Let me go, for it is daybreak."

But Jacob replied, "I will not let you go unless you bless me."[f]

27The man asked him, "What is your name?"

"Jacob," he answered.

28Then the man said, "Your name will no longer be Jacob, but Israel,[a][g] because you have struggled with God and with humans and have overcome."

29Jacob said, "Please tell me your name."[h]

But he replied, "Why do you ask my name?"[i] Then he blessed[j] him there.

30So Jacob called the place Peniel,[b] saying, "It is because I saw God face to face,[k] and yet my life was spared."

31The sun rose above him as he passed Peniel,[c] and he was limping because of his hip. 32Therefore to this day the Israelites do not eat the tendon attached to the socket of the hip, because the socket of Jacob's hip was touched near the tendon.

Jacob Meets Esau

33 Jacob looked up and there was Esau, coming with his four hundred men;[l] so he divided the children among Leah, Rachel and the two female servants. 2He put the female servants and their children in front, Leah and her children next, and Rachel and Joseph in the rear. 3He himself went on ahead and bowed down to the ground[m] seven times as he approached his brother.

4But Esau ran to meet Jacob and embraced him; he threw his arms around his neck and kissed him. And they wept.[n] 5Then Esau looked up and saw the women and children. "Who are these with you?" he asked.

Jacob answered, "They are the children God has graciously given your servant.[o]"

6Then the female servants and their children approached and bowed down. 7Next, Leah and her children came and bowed down. Last of all came Joseph and Rachel, and they too bowed down.

8Esau asked, "What's the meaning of all these flocks and herds I met?"[p]

"To find favor in your eyes, my lord,"[q] he said.

9But Esau said, "I already have plenty, my brother. Keep what you have for yourself."

10"No, please!" said Jacob. "If I have found favor in your eyes, accept this gift from me. For to see your face is like seeing the face of God,[r] now that you have received me favorably.[s] 11Please accept the

[a] 28 *Israel* probably means *he struggles with God.* [b] 30 *Peniel* means *face of God.* [c] 31 Hebrew *Penuel,* a variant of *Peniel*

32:24 *a man wrestled with him.* Some believe that the Man who wrestled with Jacob was the pre-incarnate Jesus Christ. Others believe the Man was the Angel of God (21:17; 31:11). In any case, Jacob wrestled with a manifestation of God (vv. 28–30), and because of God's mercy he survived.

32:28 *Israel.* Before Jacob wrestled with the angel, his name, "One Who Supplants," described a man who was deceitful in character. Afterwards he was given the new status of a champion, "One Who Strives (or Prevails) with God," or "Prince with God."

32:30 *God face to face.* The dramatic name ("Face of God") given to the location shows the awesome nature of the encounter. Here God's messenger in human form was the same as God Himself, a fact which Jacob recognized to his amazement. In Hebrew thought, the penalty for seeing God face to face was death (Ex. 33:20), yet Jacob had passed through such an experience and had survived.

32:13 [z] Ge 43:11, 15, 25, 26; Pr 18:16 **32:18** [a] Ge 18:3 **32:20** [b] Ge 33:10; Pr 21:14 **32:22** [c] Dt 2:37; 3:16; Jos 12:2 **32:24** [d] Ge 18:2 **32:25** [e] ver 32 **32:26** [f] Hos 12:4 **32:28** [g] Ge 17:5; 35:10; 1Ki 18:31 **32:29** [h] Jdg 13:17 [i] Jdg 13:18 [j] Ge 35:9 **32:30** [k] Ge 16:13; Ex 24:11; Nu 12:8; Jdg 6:22; 13:22 **33:1** [l] Ge 32:6 **33:3** [m] Ge 18:2; 42:6 **33:4** [n] Ge 45:14-15 **33:5** [o] Ge 48:9; Ps 127:3; Isa 8:18 **33:8** [p] Ge 32:14-16 [q] Ge 24:9; 32:5 **33:10** [r] Ge 16:13 [s] Ge 32:20

present[t] that was brought to you, for God has been gracious to me[u] and I have all I need." And because Jacob insisted, Esau accepted it.

12Then Esau said, "Let us be on our way; I'll accompany you."

13But Jacob said to him, "My lord knows that the children are tender and that I must care for the ewes and cows that are nursing their young. If they are driven hard just one day, all the animals will die. **14**So let my lord go on ahead of his servant, while I move along slowly at the pace of the flocks and herds before me and the pace of the children, until I come to my lord in Seir.[v]"

15Esau said, "Then let me leave some of my men with you."

"But why do that?" Jacob asked. "Just let me find favor in the eyes of my lord."[w]

16So that day Esau started on his way back to Seir. **17**Jacob, however, went to Sukkoth,[x] where he built a place for himself and made shelters for his livestock. That is why the place is called Sukkoth.[a]

18After Jacob came from Paddan Aram,[b][y] he arrived safely at the city of Shechem[z] in Canaan and camped within sight of the city. **19**For a hundred pieces of silver,[c] he bought from the sons of Hamor, the father of Shechem,[a] the plot of ground[b] where he pitched his tent. **20**There he set up an altar and called it El Elohe Israel.[d]

Dinah and the Shechemites

34 Now Dinah,[c] the daughter Leah had borne to Jacob, went out to visit the women of the land. **2**When Shechem son of Hamor the Hivite, the ruler of that area, saw her, he took her and raped her. **3**His heart was drawn to Dinah daughter of Jacob; he loved the young woman and spoke tenderly to her. **4**And Shechem said to his father Hamor, "Get me this girl as my wife."

5When Jacob heard that his daughter Dinah had been defiled, his sons were in the fields with his livestock; so he did nothing about it until they came home.

6Then Shechem's father Hamor went out to talk with Jacob.[d] **7**Meanwhile, Jacob's sons had come in from the fields as soon as they heard what had happened. They were shocked and furious, because Shechem had done an outrageous thing in[e] Israel[e] by sleeping with Jacob's daughter—a thing that should not be done.[f]

8But Hamor said to them, "My son Shechem has his heart set on your daughter. Please give her to him as his wife. **9**Intermarry with us; give us your daughters and take our daughters for yourselves. **10**You can settle among us;[g] the land is open to you.[h] Live in it, trade[f] in it,[i] and acquire property in it."

11Then Shechem said to Dinah's father and brothers, "Let me find favor in your eyes, and I will give you whatever you ask. **12**Make the price for the bride[j] and the gift I am to bring as great as you like, and I'll pay whatever you ask me. Only give me the young woman as my wife."

13Because their sister Dinah had been defiled, Jacob's sons replied deceitfully as they spoke to Shechem and his father Hamor. **14**They said to them, "We can't do such a thing; we can't give our sister to a man who is not circumcised.[k] That would be a disgrace to us. **15**We will enter into an agreement with you on one condition only: that you become like us by circumcising all your males.[l] **16**Then we will give you our daughters and take your daughters for ourselves. We'll settle among you and become one people with you. **17**But if you will not agree to be circumcised, we'll take our sister and go."

18Their proposal seemed good to Hamor and his son Shechem. **19**The young man, who was the most honored of all his father's family, lost no time in doing what they said, because he was delighted with Jacob's daughter.[m] **20**So Hamor and his son Shechem went to the gate of their city[n] to speak to the men of their city. **21**"These men are friendly toward us," they said. "Let them live in our land and trade in it; the land has plenty of room for them. We can marry their daughters and they can marry ours. **22**But the men will agree to live with us as one people only on the condition that our males be circumcised, as they themselves are. **23**Won't their livestock, their property and all their other animals become ours? So let us agree to their terms, and they will settle among us."

24All the men who went out of the city gate[o] agreed with Hamor and his son Shechem, and every male in the city was circumcised.

---

[a] 17 *Sukkoth* means *shelters*. [b] 18 That is, Northwest Mesopotamia [c] 19 Hebrew *hundred kesitahs*; a kesitah was a unit of money of unknown weight and value. [d] 20 *El Elohe Israel* can mean *El is the God of Israel* or *mighty is the God of Israel*. [e] 7 Or *against* [f] 10 Or *move about freely*; also in verse 21

33:11 ***Please accept the present.*** Before, Jacob had done all he could to take Esau's blessing (25:29–34; 27:1–45). Now a wiser man, Jacob wanted to bless his brother with what God had given him.

33:20 ***There he set up an altar.*** The name Jacob gave this altar reflected his mature faith in "God, the God of Israel." The God of Jacob's fathers was now Jacob's personal God, for He had fulfilled His promises and protected him (28:13–15).

33:11 [t] 1Sa 25:27 [u] Ge 30:43 **33:14** [v] Ge 32:3 **33:15** [w] Ge 34:11; 47:25; Ru 2:13 **33:17** [x] Jos 13:27; Jdg 8:5,6,8,14-16; Ps 60:6 **33:18** [y] Ge 25:20; 28:2 [z] Jos 24:1; Jdg 9:1 **33:19** [a] Jos 24:32 [b] Jn 4:5 **34:1** [c] Ge 30:21 **34:6** [d] Jdg 14:2-5 **34:7** [e] Dt 22:21; Jdg 20:6; 2Sa 13:12 [f] Jos 7:15 **34:10** [g] Ge 47:6,27 [h] Ge 13:9; 20:15 [i] Ge 42:34 **34:12** [j] Ex 22:16; Dt 22:29; 1Sa 18:25 **34:14** [k] Ge 17:14; Jdg 14:3 **34:15** [l] Ex 12:48 **34:19** [m] ver 3 **34:20** [n] Ru 4:1; 2Sa 15:2 **34:24** [o] Ge 23:10

25Three days later, while all of them were still in pain, two of Jacob's sons, Simeon and Levi, Dinah's brothers, took their swords[p] and attacked the unsuspecting city, killing every male.[q] 26They put Hamor and his son Shechem to the sword and took Dinah from Shechem's house and left. 27The sons of Jacob came upon the dead bodies and looted the city where[a] their sister had been defiled. 28They seized their flocks and herds and donkeys and everything else of theirs in the city and out in the fields. 29They carried off all their wealth and all their women and children, taking as plunder everything in the houses.

30Then Jacob said to Simeon and Levi, "You have brought trouble on me by making me obnoxious[r] to the Canaanites and Perizzites, the people living in this land.[s] We are few in number,[t] and if they join forces against me and attack me, I and my household will be destroyed."

31But they replied, "Should he have treated our sister like a prostitute?"

Jacob Returns to Bethel

35 Then God said to Jacob, "Go up to Bethel[u] and settle there, and build an altar there to God, who appeared to you when you were fleeing from your brother Esau."[v]

2So Jacob said to his household[w] and to all who were with him, "Get rid of the foreign gods[x] you have with you, and purify yourselves and change your clothes.[y] 3Then come, let us go up to Bethel, where I will build an altar to God, who answered me in the day of my distress[z] and who has been with me wherever I have gone.[a]" 4So they gave Jacob all the foreign gods they had and the rings in their ears, and Jacob buried them under the oak at Shechem.[b] 5Then they set out, and the terror of God[c] fell on the towns all around them so that no one pursued them.

6Jacob and all the people with him came to Luz[d] (that is, Bethel) in the land of Canaan. 7There he built an altar, and he called the place El Bethel,[b] because it was there that God revealed himself to him[e] when he was fleeing from his brother.

8Now Deborah, Rebekah's nurse,[f] died and was buried under the oak outside Bethel. So it was named Allon Bakuth.[c]

9After Jacob returned from Paddan Aram,[d] God appeared to him again and blessed him.[g] 10God said to him, "Your name is Jacob,[e] but you will no longer be called Jacob; your name will be Israel.[f]"[h] So he named him Israel.

11And God said to him, "I am God Almighty[g];[i] be fruitful and increase in number. A nation[j] and a community of nations will come from you, and kings will be among your descendants.[k] 12The land I gave to Abraham and Isaac I also give to you, and I will give this land to your descendants after you.[l]"[m] 13Then God went up from him[n] at the place where he had talked with him.

14Jacob set up a stone pillar at the place where God had talked with him, and he poured out a drink offering on it; he also poured oil on it.[o] 15Jacob called the place where God had talked with him Bethel.[h][p]

The Deaths of Rachel and Isaac

16Then they moved on from Bethel. While they were still some distance from Ephrath, Rachel began to give birth and had great difficulty. 17And as she was having great difficulty in childbirth, the midwife said to her, "Don't despair, for you have another son."[q] 18As she breathed her

---

[a] 27 Or *because* [b] 7 *El Bethel* means *God of Bethel.* [c] 8 *Allon Bakuth* means *oak of weeping.* [d] 9 That is, Northwest Mesopotamia; also in verse 26 [e] 10 *Jacob* means *he grasps the heel*, a Hebrew idiom for *he deceives.* [f] 10 *Israel* probably means *he struggles with God.* [g] 11 Hebrew *El-Shaddai* [h] 15 *Bethel* means *house of God.*

34:25 *killing every male.* Jacob's sons were correct that God did not want them to intermarry with the pagan Canaanite families. According to later Levitical law, they were even correct that rape was punishable by death. However, their treacherous pretended friendship and the massacre of all the men of Shechem, along with their greedy looting of all the Shechemites goods, was clearly not a justifiable execution of justice, and God condemned their violence and anger (49:5–7).

35:2 *foreign gods.* Jacob's command included the idols that Rachel had stolen (31:22–35) as well as any idols among his servants. These were not gods Jacob himself had been worshipping, but he had apparently been allowing others in his household to do so.

35:10–12 *your name will be Israel.* The renewal of God's covenant with Jacob was introduced by confirming Jacob's change of name to Israel, the one who "struggled with God and ... overcome." The promises made to Abraham and Isaac were once again repeated, underscoring the continuity of the covenant. Furthermore, a rather significant phrase is added, "be fruitful and increase in number," which incorporated the creation ordinance, thus exhibiting the continuity with the covenant of creation. The covenant Lord is the God of creation and of redemption.

35:16 *Ephrath.* This is an alternative name for the region around Bethlehem (v. 19; 48:7; Ruth 1:2; Mic. 5:2). The King of Glory would one day be born near the birthplace of Benjamin (Matt. 2:1).

34:25 [p] Ge 49:5 [q] Ge 49:7 **34:30** [r] Ex 5:21; 1Sa 13:4 [s] Ge 13:7 [t] Ge 46:27; 1Ch 16:19; Ps 105:12 **35:1** [u] Ge 28:19 [v] Ge 27:43 **35:2** [w] Ge 18:19; Jos 24:15 [x] Ge 31:19 [y] Ex 19:10, 14 **35:3** [z] Ge 32:7 [a] Ge 28:15, 20-22; 31:3, 42 **35:4** [b] Jos 24:25-26 **35:5** [c] Ex 15:16; 23:27; Jos 2:9 **35:6** [d] Ge 28:19; 48:3 **35:7** [e] Ge 28:13 **35:8** [f] Ge 24:59 **35:9** [g] Ge 32:29 **35:10** [h] Ge 17:5 **35:11** [i] Ge 17:1; Ex 6:3 [j] Ge 28:3; 48:4 [k] Ge 17:6 **35:12** [l] Ge 13:15; 28:13 [m] Ge 12:7; 26:3 **35:13** [n] Ge 17:22 **35:14** [o] Ge 28:18 **35:15** [p] Ge 28:19 **35:17** [q] Ge 30:24

last—for she was dying—she named her
son Ben-Oni.[a] But his father named him
Benjamin.[b]
19 So Rachel died and was buried on
the way to Ephrath (that is, Bethlehem[r]).
20 Over her tomb Jacob set up a pillar, and
to this day that pillar marks Rachel's tomb.[s]
21 Israel moved on again and pitched his
tent beyond Migdal Eder. 22 While Israel
was living in that region, Reuben went in
and slept with his father's concubine[t] Bilhah,[u] and Israel heard of it.

Jacob had twelve sons:
23 The sons of Leah:
Reuben the firstborn[v] of Jacob,
Simeon, Levi, Judah,[w] Issachar and
Zebulun.[x]
24 The sons of Rachel:
Joseph[y] and Benjamin.[z]
25 The sons of Rachel's servant Bilhah:
Dan and Naphtali.[a]
26 The sons of Leah's servant Zilpah:
Gad[b] and Asher.[c]
These were the sons of Jacob, who were
born to him in Paddan Aram.

27 Jacob came home to his father Isaac
in Mamre,[d] near Kiriath Arba[e] (that is,
Hebron), where Abraham and Isaac had
stayed. 28 Isaac lived a hundred and eighty
years.[f] 29 Then he breathed his last and died
and was gathered to his people,[g] old and
full of years.[h] And his sons Esau and Jacob
buried him.[i]

Esau's Descendants

36 This is the account of the family line
of Esau (that is, Edom).[j]
2 Esau took his wives from the wom-
en of Canaan:[k] Adah daughter of Elon
the Hittite,[l] and Oholibamah daughter of Anah[m] and granddaughter of
Zibeon the Hivite— 3 also Basemath
daughter of Ishmael and sister of Nebaioth.
4 Adah bore Eliphaz to Esau, Basemath bore Reuel,[n] 5 and Oholibamah
bore Jeush, Jalam and Korah. These
were the sons of Esau, who were born
to him in Canaan.
6 Esau took his wives and sons and
daughters and all the members of his
household, as well as his livestock
and all his other animals and all the
goods he had acquired in Canaan,[o]
and moved to a land some distance
from his brother Jacob. 7 Their possessions were too great for them to
remain together; the land where they
were staying could not support them
both because of their livestock.[p] 8 So
Esau[q] (that is, Edom) settled in the hill
country of Seir.[r]

9 This is the account of the family line of
Esau the father of the Edomites in the hill
country of Seir.

10 These are the names of Esau's sons:
Eliphaz, the son of Esau's wife
Adah, and Reuel, the son of Esau's
wife Basemath.
11 The sons of Eliphaz:[s]
Teman,[t] Omar, Zepho, Gatam and
Kenaz.
12 Esau's son Eliphaz also had a con-
cubine named Timna, who bore him
Amalek.[u] These were grandsons of
Esau's wife Adah.[v]
13 The sons of Reuel:
Nahath, Zerah, Shammah and
Mizzah. These were grandsons of
Esau's wife Basemath.
14 The sons of Esau's wife Oholibamah
daughter of Anah and granddaughter
of Zibeon, whom she bore to Esau:
Jeush, Jalam and Korah.

15 These were the chiefs[w] among Esau's
descendants:
The sons of Eliphaz the firstborn of
Esau:
Chiefs Teman,[x] Omar, Zepho, Kenaz, 16 Korah,[c] Gatam and Amalek.
These were the chiefs descended
from Eliphaz in Edom; they were
grandsons of Adah.[y]
17 The sons of Esau's son Reuel:[z]
Chiefs Nahath, Zerah, Shammah
and Mizzah. These were the chiefs
descended from Reuel in Edom; they
were grandsons of Esau's wife Basemath.
18 The sons of Esau's wife Oholibamah:
Chiefs Jeush, Jalam and Korah.
These were the chiefs descended from Esau's wife Oholibamah
daughter of Anah.

[a] *18 Ben-Oni* means *son of my trouble.*
[b] *18 Benjamin* means *son of my right hand.*
[c] *16* Masoretic Text; Samaritan Pentateuch (also verse 11 and 1 Chron. 1:36) does not have *Korah*.

35:27 *Jacob came home to his father Isaac.* After more than 20 years of exile Jacob finally visited his father. Sadly, his mother Rebekah was probably dead since she is not mentioned.

36:12 *Amalek.* Esau's grandson Amalek founded a people that later would trouble the Israelites (Num. 14:39–45).

35:19 [r] Ge 48:7; Ru 1:1, 19; Mic 5:2; Mt 2:16 **35:20** [s] 1Sa 10:2 **35:22** [t] Ge 49:4; 1Ch 5:1 [u] Ge 29:29; Lev 18:8 **35:23** [v] Ge 46:8 [w] Ge 29:35 [x] Ge 30:20 **35:24** [y] Ge 30:24 [z] ver 18 **35:25** [a] Ge 30:8 **35:26** [b] Ge 30:11 [c] Ge 30:13 **35:27** [d] Ge 13:18; 18:1 [e] Jos 14:15 **35:28** [f] Ge 25:7, 20 **35:29** [g] Ge 25:8; 49:33 [h] Ge 15:15 [i] Ge 25:9 **36:1** [j] Ge 25:30 **36:2** [k] Ge 28:8-9 [l] Ge 26:34 [m] ver 25 **36:4** [n] 1Ch 1:35 **36:6** [o] Ge 12:5 **36:7** [p] Ge 13:6; 17:8; 28:4 **36:8** [q] Dt 2:4 [r] Ge 32:3 **36:11** [s] ver 15-16; Job 2:11 [t] Am 1:12; Hab 3:3 **36:12** [u] Ex 17:8, 16; Nu 24:20; 1Sa 15:2 [v] ver 16 **36:15** [w] Ex 15:15 [x] Job 2:11 **36:16** [y] ver 12 **36:17** [z] 1Ch 1:37

19These were the sons of Esau (that is,
Edom),[a] and these were their chiefs.

20These were the sons of Seir the Horite,[b]
who were living in the region:
Lotan, Shobal, Zibeon, Anah, 21Di-
shon, Ezer and Dishan. These sons
of Seir in Edom were Horite chiefs.
22The sons of Lotan:
Hori and Homam.[a] Timna was Lotan's sister.
23The sons of Shobal:
Alvan, Manahath, Ebal, Shepho and Onam.
24The sons of Zibeon:
Aiah and Anah. This is the Anah who discovered the hot springs[b] in the desert while he was grazing the donkeys of his father Zibeon.
25The children of Anah:
Dishon and Oholibamah daughter of Anah.
26The sons of Dishon[c]:
Hemdan, Eshban, Ithran and Keran.
27The sons of Ezer:
Bilhan, Zaavan and Akan.
28The sons of Dishan:
Uz and Aran.
29These were the Horite chiefs:
Lotan, Shobal, Zibeon, Anah, 30Di-
shon, Ezer and Dishan. These were the Horite chiefs, according to their divisions, in the land of Seir.

The Rulers of Edom

31These were the kings who reigned in Edom before any Israelite king[c] reigned:
32Bela son of Beor became king of Edom. His city was named Dinhabah.
33When Bela died, Jobab son of Zerah from Bozrah[d] succeeded him as king.
34When Jobab died, Husham from the land of the Temanites[e] succeeded him as king.
35When Husham died, Hadad son of Bedad, who defeated Midian in the country of Moab,[f] succeeded him as king. His city was named Avith.
36When Hadad died, Samlah from Masrekah succeeded him as king.
37When Samlah died, Shaul from Rehoboth on the river succeeded him as king.
38When Shaul died, Baal-Hanan son of Akbor succeeded him as king.
39When Baal-Hanan son of Akbor died, Hadad[d] succeeded him as king. His city was named Pau, and his wife's name was Mehetabel daughter of Matred, the daughter of Me-Zahab.

40These were the chiefs descended from Esau, by name, according to their clans and regions:
Timna, Alvah, Jetheth, 41Oholiba-
mah, Elah, Pinon, 42Kenaz, Teman,
Mibzar, 43Magdiel and Iram. These
were the chiefs of Edom, according to their settlements in the land they occupied.

This is the family line of Esau, the father of the Edomites.

Joseph's Dreams

37 Jacob lived in the land where his father had stayed,[g] the land of Canaan.[h]

2This is the account of Jacob's family line.

Joseph, a young man of seventeen, was tending the flocks[i] with his brothers, the sons of Bilhah[j] and the sons of Zilpah,[k] his father's wives, and he brought their father a bad report[l] about them.

3Now Israel loved Joseph more than any
of his other sons,[m] because he had been
born to him in his old age;[n] and he made an
ornate[e] robe[o] for him. 4When his brothers
saw that their father loved him more than any of them, they hated him[p] and could not speak a kind word to him.

---

[a] 22 Hebrew *Hemam*, a variant of *Homam* (see 1 Chron. 1:39) [b] 24 Vulgate; Syriac *discovered water;* the meaning of the Hebrew for this word is uncertain. [c] 26 Hebrew *Dishan*, a variant of *Dishon* [d] 39 Many manuscripts of the Masoretic Text, Samaritan Pentateuch and Syriac (see also 1 Chron. 1:50); most manuscripts of the Masoretic Text *Hadar* [e] 3 The meaning of the Hebrew for this word is uncertain; also in verses 23 and 32.

36:40–43 *Esau, the father of the Edomites.* Although Esau was not the heir of God's everlasting covenant with the family of Abraham, God still blessed his family and made them into a nation.

37:1 *where his father had stayed.* The Lord had promised that this land would become a permanent possession of Abraham's family (12:7). To the third generation, that promise was still not realized. Jacob and his family were still aliens in the land.

37:2 *a bad report.* Since Joseph in general demonstrated his integrity (see ch. 39), he was probably not slandering his brothers, but accurately reporting some negligence on their part.

37:3 *ornate robe.* The Hebrew phrase may simply mean a garment with long sleeves. The robe was certainly distinctive in some way, and probably costly.

37:4 *hated him.* Because fallen and unregenerate man hates God, he displays hatred in his relations with others. The hatred of Joseph's brothers is attributed primarily to the love which Jacob had for his youngest son. As a result of their hatred the brothers were not able to speak kindly to Joseph, and the hatred led to a plot to kill him. Jesus remarked that the world's hatred of His people is a reflection of hatred

36:19 [a] Ge 25:30 **36:20** [b] Ge 14:6; Dt 2:12,22; 1Ch 1:38 **36:31** [c] Ge 17:6; 1Ch 1:43 **36:33** [d] Jer 49:13,22 **36:34** [e] Eze 25:13 **36:35** [f] Ge 19:37; Nu 22:1; Dt 1:5; Ru 1:1,6 **37:1** [g] Ge 17:8 [h] Ge 10:19 **37:2** [i] Ps 78:71 [j] Ge 35:25 [k] Ge 35:26 [l] 1Sa 2:24 **37:3** [m] Ge 25:28 [n] Ge 44:20 [o] 2Sa 13:18-19 **37:4** [p] Ge 27:41; 49:22-23; Ac 7:9

5Joseph had a dream,[q] and when he
told it to his brothers, they hated him all
the more. 6He said to them, "Listen to this
dream I had: 7We were binding sheaves of
grain out in the field when suddenly my
sheaf rose and stood upright, while your
sheaves gathered around mine and bowed
down to it."[r]
8His brothers said to him, "Do you intend to reign over us? Will you actually
rule us?"[s] And they hated him all the more
because of his dream and what he had said.
9Then he had another dream, and he told
it to his brothers. "Listen," he said, "I had
another dream, and this time the sun and
moon and eleven stars were bowing down
to me."
10When he told his father as well as his
brothers,[t] his father rebuked him and said,
"What is this dream you had? Will your
mother and I and your brothers actually
come and bow down to the ground before
you?"[u] 11His brothers were jealous of him,[v]
but his father kept the matter in mind.[w]

Joseph Sold by His Brothers

12Now his brothers had gone to graze
their father's flocks near Shechem, 13and
Israel said to Joseph, "As you know, your
brothers are grazing the flocks near Shechem. Come, I am going to send you to
them."
"Very well," he replied.
14So he said to him, "Go and see if all
is well with your brothers and with the
flocks, and bring word back to me." Then
he sent him off from the Valley of Hebron.[x]
When Joseph arrived at Shechem, 15a
man found him wandering around in the
fields and asked him, "What are you looking for?"
16He replied, "I'm looking for my brothers. Can you tell me where they are grazing
their flocks?"
17"They have moved on from here," the
man answered. "I heard them say, 'Let's go
to Dothan.[y]'"
So Joseph went after his brothers and
found them near Dothan. 18But they saw
him in the distance, and before he reached
them, they plotted to kill him.[z]
19"Here comes that dreamer!" they said
to each other. 20"Come now, let's kill him
and throw him into one of these cisterns[a]
and say that a ferocious animal devoured
him. Then we'll see what comes of his
dreams."[b]
21When Reuben heard this, he tried to
rescue him from their hands. "Let's not
take his life," he said.[c] 22"Don't shed any
blood. Throw him into this cistern here
in the wilderness, but don't lay a hand on
him." Reuben said this to rescue him from
them and take him back to his father.
23So when Joseph came to his brothers,
they stripped him of his robe—the ornate
robe he was wearing— 24and they took
him and threw him into the cistern.[d] The
cistern was empty; there was no water in it.
25As they sat down to eat their meal, they
looked up and saw a caravan of Ishmaelites
coming from Gilead. Their camels were
loaded with spices, balm and myrrh,[e] and
they were on their way to take them down
to Egypt.[f]
26Judah said to his brothers, "What will
we gain if we kill our brother and cover
up his blood?[g] 27Come, let's sell him to the
Ishmaelites and not lay our hands on him;
after all, he is our brother,[h] our own flesh
and blood." His brothers agreed.
28So when the Midianite[i] merchants
came by, his brothers pulled Joseph up out
of the cistern and sold him for twenty shekels[a] of silver to the Ishmaelites, who took
him to Egypt.[j]
29When Reuben returned to the cistern
and saw that Joseph was not there, he tore
his clothes.[k] 30He went back to his brothers
and said, "The boy isn't there! Where can
I turn now?"[l]
31Then they got Joseph's robe,[m] slaughtered a goat and dipped the robe in the
blood. 32They took the ornate robe back to
their father and said, "We found this. Examine it to see whether it is your son's robe."

a 28 That is, about 8 ounces or about 230 grams

against Himself (John 15:18). Love is the leading characteristic of the godly as hatred is the mark of the worldly person.

37:17 *Dothan.* This is about ten miles north of Shechem, near Mount Gilboa.

37:21 *Let's not take his life.* Reuben, as the firstborn son and principal heir, had the most to lose if Joseph's dreams came true. Yet Reuben intervened to spare Joseph's life. This was something of a contrast with his earlier wicked actions (35:22).

37:25 *Ishmaelites.* The Ishmaelites of this passage were wandering traders. The name (referring to descendants of Ishmael, the son of Abraham and Hagar) is loosely equivalent with the name Midianite (Midian was another son of Abraham, by Keturah). Probably the families of the two half brothers had a strong alliance and were so closely associated that the names became interchangeable (v. 28).

37:28 *twenty shekels of silver.* The standard price for a slave in later Israelite law was 30 shekels of silver.

37:29 *tore his clothes.* Tearing one's clothes was a common expression of grief and dismay. Reuben's grief was genuine feeling for his younger brother mixed with fear that he, the oldest brother, would be blamed.

37:5 [q] Ge 20:3; 28:12 **37:7** [r] Ge 42:6, 9; 43:26, 28; 44:14; 50:18 **37:8** [s] Ge 49:26 **37:10** [t] ver 5 [u] ver 7; Ge 27:29 **37:11** [v] Ac 7:9 [w] Lk 2:19, 51 **37:14** [x] Ge 13:18; 35:27 **37:17** [y] 2Ki 6:13 **37:18** [z] 1Sa 19:1; Mk 14:1; Ac 23:12 **37:20** [a] Jer 38:6, 9 [b] Ge 50:20 **37:21** [c] Ge 42:22 **37:24** [d] Jer 41:7 **37:25** [e] Ge 43:11 [f] ver 28 **37:26** [g] ver 20; Ge 4:10 **37:27** [h] Ge 42:21 **37:28** [i] Ge 25:2; Jdg 6:1-3 [j] Ge 45:4-5; Ps 105:17; Ac 7:9 **37:29** [k] ver 34; Ge 44:13; Job 1:20 **37:30** [l] ver 22; Ge 42:13, 36 **37:31** [m] ver 3, 23

33He recognized it and said, "It is my
son's robe! Some ferocious animal[n] has devoured him. Joseph has surely been torn
to pieces."[o]
34Then Jacob tore his clothes,[p] put on
sackcloth[q] and mourned for his son many
days.[r] 35All his sons and daughters came to
comfort him, but he refused to be comforted. "No," he said, "I will continue to mourn
until I join my son in the grave.[s]" So his father wept for him.
36Meanwhile, the Midianites[a] sold Joseph in Egypt to Potiphar, one of Pharaoh's
officials, the captain of the guard.[t]

Judah and Tamar

38 At that time, Judah left his brothers
and went down to stay with a man of
Adullam named Hirah. 2There Judah met
the daughter of a Canaanite man named
Shua.[u] He married her and made love to
her; 3she became pregnant and gave birth
to a son, who was named Er.[v] 4She conceived again and gave birth to a son and
named him Onan. 5She gave birth to still
another son and named him Shelah. It was
at Kezib that she gave birth to him.
6Judah got a wife for Er, his firstborn,
and her name was Tamar. 7But Er, Judah's
firstborn, was wicked in the LORD's sight;
so the LORD put him to death.[w]
8Then Judah said to Onan, "Sleep with
your brother's wife and fulfill your duty
to her as a brother-in-law to raise up offspring for your brother."[x] 9But Onan knew
that the child would not be his; so whenever
he slept with his brother's wife, he spilled
his semen on the ground to keep from providing offspring for his brother. 10What he
did was wicked in the LORD's sight; so the
LORD put him to death also.[y]
11Judah then said to his daughter-in-law
Tamar, "Live as a widow in your father's
household until my son Shelah grows up."[z]
For he thought, "He may die too, just like
his brothers." So Tamar went to live in her
father's household.
12After a long time Judah's wife, the
daughter of Shua, died. When Judah had
recovered from his grief, he went up to
Timnah,[a] to the men who were shearing his
sheep, and his friend Hirah the Adullamite
went with him.
13When Tamar was told, "Your father-
in-law is on his way to Timnah to shear his
sheep," 14she took off her widow's clothes,
covered herself with a veil to disguise herself, and then sat down at the entrance to
Enaim, which is on the road to Timnah.
For she saw that, though Shelah[b] had now
grown up, she had not been given to him as
his wife.
15When Judah saw her, he thought
she was a prostitute, for she had covered
her face. 16Not realizing that she was his
daughter-in-law,[c] he went over to her by the
roadside and said, "Come now, let me sleep
with you."
"And what will you give me to sleep with
you?" she asked.
17"I'll send you a young goat[d] from my
flock," he said.
"Will you give me something as a pledge[e]
until you send it?" she asked.
18He said, "What pledge should I give
you?"
"Your seal[f] and its cord, and the staff in
your hand," she answered. So he gave them to
her and slept with her, and she became pregnant by him. 19After she left, she took off her
veil and put on her widow's clothes[g] again.
20Meanwhile Judah sent the young goat
by his friend the Adullamite in order to get
his pledge back from the woman, but he did
not find her. 21He asked the men who lived
there, "Where is the shrine prostitute[h] who
was beside the road at Enaim?"

---

[a] *36* Samaritan Pentateuch, Septuagint, Vulgate and Syriac (see also verse 28); Masoretic Text *Medanites*

38:1 – 30 At first glance it appears that the story of Judah and Tamar is an intrusion into the story of Joseph, but it is here for a reason. It provides a stunning contrast between the morals of Judah and Joseph. It illustrates the further disintegration of Jacob's family. If this process continued, Jacob's family, the family of promise, would become like the people of Canaan.

38:8 ***your brother's wife.*** In order to maintain the family line and the name of the deceased, it was the custom in ancient times for the dead man's brother to marry the widow and father a child that would carry on the man's family. This is called *levirate* marriage, from the Latin word meaning "husband's brother." The custom became part of the Mosaic law (Deut. 25:5 – 10; Ruth 4:1 – 12).

38:15 – 18 Fornication—God designed sexual relations to be enjoyed exclusively within the framework of marriage: one man, for one woman, mutually committed for life. Outside of this framework, all sexual relations are sin. This is not because God wants to deprive His people of pleasure, but because He wants to protect them from the painful and destructive consequences of sin. Sexual union is not only a union of the body, but of the whole person (1 Cor. 6:15 – 20). Illicit sexual relations defile the temple of God, breed both physical and social disease, and serve as a source for many other sins.

38:18 ***seal.*** This was an ancient means of identification. The seal was distinctively etched in stone, metal, or ivory. To confirm a business transaction, or make an order official, the sealt was pressed into soft clay, leaving its distinctive impression. Basically, Judah gave Tamar the equivalent of a modern credit card.

37:33 [n] ver 20 [o] Ge 44:20,28 **37:34** [p] ver 29 [q] 2Sa 3:31 [r] Ge 50:3, 10, 11 **37:35** [s] Ge 42:38; 44:22, 29, 31 **37:36** [t] Ge 39:1 **38:2** [u] 1Ch 2:3 **38:3** [v] ver 6; Ge 46:12; Nu 26:19 **38:7** [w] ver 10; Ge 46:12; 1Ch 2:3 **38:8** [x] Dt 25:5-6; Mt 22:24-28 **38:10** [y] Ge 46:12; Dt 25:7-10 **38:11** [z] Ru 1:13 **38:12** [a] ver 14; Jos 15:10, 57 **38:14** [b] ver 11 **38:16** [c] Lev 18:15; 20:12 **38:17** [d] Eze 16:33 [e] ver 20 **38:18** [f] ver 25 **38:19** [g] ver 14 **38:21** [h] Lev 19:29; Hos 4:14

"There hasn't been any shrine prostitute
here," they said.
22So he went back to Judah and said, "I
didn't find her. Besides, the men who lived
there said, 'There hasn't been any shrine
prostitute here.'"
23Then Judah said, "Let her keep what
she has, or we will become a laughingstock. After all, I did send her this young
goat, but you didn't find her."
24About three months later Judah was
told, "Your daughter-in-law Tamar is guilty
of prostitution, and as a result she is now
pregnant."
Judah said, "Bring her out and have her
burned to death!"[i]
25As she was being brought out, she
sent a message to her father-in-law. "I am
pregnant by the man who owns these," she
said. And she added, "See if you recognize
whose seal and cord and staff these are."[j]
26Judah recognized them and said, "She
is more righteous than I,[k] since I wouldn't
give her to my son Shelah.[l]" And he did not
sleep with her again.
27When the time came for her to give
birth, there were twin boys in her womb.[m]
28As she was giving birth, one of them put
out his hand; so the midwife took a scarlet thread and tied it on his wrist and said,
"This one came out first." 29But when he
drew back his hand, his brother came out,
and she said, "So this is how you have
broken out!" And he was named Perez.[a][n]
30Then his brother, who had the scarlet
thread on his wrist, came out. And he was
named Zerah.[b][o]

Joseph and Potiphar's Wife

39 Now Joseph had been taken down
to Egypt. Potiphar, an Egyptian who
was one of Pharaoh's officials, the captain
of the guard,[p] bought him from the Ishmaelites who had taken him there.[q]
2The LORD was with Joseph[r] so that he
prospered, and he lived in the house of his
Egyptian master. 3When his master saw
that the LORD was with him[s] and that the
LORD gave him success in everything he
did,[t] 4Joseph found favor in his eyes and
became his attendant. Potiphar put him in
charge of his household, and he entrusted
to his care everything he owned.[u] 5From
the time he put him in charge of his household and of all that he owned, the LORD
blessed the household of the Egyptian because of Joseph.[v] The blessing of the LORD
was on everything Potiphar had, both in
the house and in the field. 6So Potiphar left
everything he had in Joseph's care; with
Joseph in charge, he did not concern himself with anything except the food he ate.
Now Joseph was well-built and handsome,[w] 7and after a while his master's wife
took notice of Joseph and said, "Come to
bed with me!"[x]
8But he refused.[y] "With me in charge,"
he told her, "my master does not concern
himself with anything in the house; everything he owns he has entrusted to my care.
9No one is greater in this house than I am.[z]
My master has withheld nothing from me
except you, because you are his wife. How
then could I do such a wicked thing and sin
against God?"[a] 10And though she spoke to
Joseph day after day, he refused to go to
bed with her or even be with her.
11One day he went into the house to attend to his duties, and none of the household servants was inside. 12She caught him
by his cloak[b] and said, "Come to bed with
me!" But he left his cloak in her hand and
ran out of the house.
13When she saw that he had left his
cloak in her hand and had run out of the
house, 14she called her household servants.
"Look," she said to them, "this Hebrew has
been brought to us to make sport of us!
He came in here to sleep with me, but I
screamed.[c] 15When he heard me scream for
help, he left his cloak beside me and ran out
of the house."
16She kept his cloak beside her until
his master came home. 17Then she told
him this story:[d] "That Hebrew slave you
brought us came to me to make sport of
me. 18But as soon as I screamed for help,

---

a 29 *Perez* means *breaking out.* *b* 30 *Zerah* can mean *scarlet* or *brightness.*

38:26 *She is more righteous than I.* Judah, one of the heirs of the everlasting covenant with the living God, was put to shame by a Canaanite woman. To his credit, Judah confessed his sins.

38:29 *Perez.* Perez was in the lineage of David, and eventually Jesus the Messiah (Ruth 4:18; Matt. 1:3).

39:2 *The LORD was with Joseph.* This key phrase of this section is repeated (vv. 21, 23). This phrase indicates that God cared for, protected, and blessed Joseph.

39:4 *found favor.* Joseph's life illustrates the principle that one who is faithful in little will be given charge over much (Matt. 25:21; 1 Cor. 4:2).

39:5 *the LORD blessed the house of the Egyptian.* God blessed Potiphar's house because of Joseph, just as He had blessed Laban because of Jacob.

39:9 *sin against God.* Joseph rejected the solicitation to sin, regarding it both as a wicked act of treachery against his master, and as a defiling and rebellious act before a holy God. Because Joseph's conscience was bound by God and His truth, he was able to resist this evil suggestion more than once. Pleasing God was more important to Joseph than engaging in the pleasures of sin for a season. His fear and reverence of God was the directing power of his life.

38:24 [i] Lev 21:9; Dt 22:21,22 **38:25** [j] ver 18
38:26 [k] 1Sa 24:17 [l] ver 11 **38:27** [m] Ge 25:24
38:29 [n] Ge 46:12; Nu 26:20,21; Ru 4:12,18; 1Ch 2:4; Mt 1:3
38:30 [o] 1Ch 2:4 **39:1** [p] Ge 37:36 [q] Ge 37:25; Ps 105:17
39:2 [r] Ge 21:20,22; Ac 7:9 **39:3** [s] Ge 21:22; 26:28 [t] Ps 1:3
39:4 [u] ver 8,22; Ge 24:2 **39:5** [v] Ge 26:24; 30:27
39:6 [w] 1Sa 16:12 **39:7** [x] 2Sa 13:11; Pr 7:15-18
39:8 [y] Pr 6:23-24 **39:9** [z] Ge 41:33,40 [a] Ge 20:6; 42:18; 2Sa 12:13 **39:12** [b] Pr 7:13 **39:14** [c] Dt 22:24, 27 **39:17** [d] Ex 23:1,7; Ps 101:5

he left his cloak beside me and ran out of the house."

19When his master heard the story his wife told him, saying, "This is how your slave treated me," he burned with anger.[e] 20Joseph's master took him and put him in prison,[f] the place where the king's prisoners were confined.

But while Joseph was there in the prison, 21the LORD was with him; he showed him kindness and granted him favor in the eyes of the prison warden.[g] 22So the warden put Joseph in charge of all those held in the prison, and he was made responsible for all that was done there.[h] 23The warden paid no attention to anything under Joseph's care, because the LORD was with Joseph and gave him success in whatever he did.[i]

The Cupbearer and the Baker

40 Some time later, the cupbearer[j] and the baker of the king of Egypt offended their master, the king of Egypt. 2Pharaoh was angry[k] with his two officials, the chief cupbearer and the chief baker, 3and put them in custody in the house of the captain of the guard,[l] in the same prison where Joseph was confined. 4The captain of the guard assigned them to Joseph,[m] and he attended them.

After they had been in custody for some time, 5each of the two men—the cupbearer and the baker of the king of Egypt, who were being held in prison—had a dream the same night, and each dream had a meaning of its own.[n]

6When Joseph came to them the next morning, he saw that they were dejected. 7So he asked Pharaoh's officials who were in custody with him in his master's house, "Why do you look so sad today?"[o]

8"We both had dreams," they answered, "but there is no one to interpret them."[p]

Then Joseph said to them, "Do not interpretations belong to God?[q] Tell me your dreams."

9So the chief cupbearer told Joseph his dream. He said to him, "In my dream I saw a vine in front of me, 10and on the vine were three branches. As soon as it budded, it blossomed, and its clusters ripened into grapes. 11Pharaoh's cup was in my hand, and I took the grapes, squeezed them into Pharaoh's cup and put the cup in his hand."

12"This is what it means,[r]" Joseph said to him. "The three branches are three days. 13Within three days Pharaoh will lift up your head and restore you to your position, and you will put Pharaoh's cup in his hand, just as you used to do when you were his cupbearer. 14But when all goes well with you, remember me[s] and show me kindness;[t] mention me to Pharaoh and get me out of this prison. 15I was forcibly carried off from the land of the Hebrews,[u] and even here I have done nothing to deserve being put in a dungeon."

16When the chief baker saw that Joseph had given a favorable interpretation, he said to Joseph, "I too had a dream: On my head were three baskets of bread.[a] 17In the top basket were all kinds of baked goods for Pharaoh, but the birds were eating them out of the basket on my head."

18"This is what it means," Joseph said. "The three baskets are three days.[v] 19Within three days Pharaoh will lift off your head[w] and impale your body on a pole. And the birds will eat away your flesh."

20Now the third day was Pharaoh's birthday,[x] and he gave a feast for all his officials.[y] He lifted up the heads of the chief cupbearer and the chief baker in the presence of his officials: 21He restored the chief cupbearer to his position, so that he once again put the cup into Pharaoh's hand[z]— 22but he impaled the chief baker,[a] just as Joseph had said to them in his interpretation.[b]

23The chief cupbearer, however, did not remember Joseph; he forgot him.[c]

Pharaoh's Dreams

41 When two full years had passed, Pharaoh had a dream:[d] He was standing by the Nile, 2when out of the river there came up seven cows, sleek and fat,[e] and they grazed among the reeds.[f] 3After them, seven other cows, ugly and gaunt, came up out of the Nile and stood beside

[a] 16 Or *three wicker baskets*

39:20 *in prison.* Surprisingly, Potiphar did not simply kill Joseph outright. It is possible that knowledge of Joseph's character (or his own wife's character) caused him to suspect that the story was not wholly true.

39:21 *kindness.* This word can be translated *loyal love* (Ps. 13:5). God faithfully kept His promises by staying with His people (12:1–3; 50:24).

39:23 *gave him success.* Because of God's blessing, everything Joseph did prospered (Ps. 1:1–3).

40:8 *interpretations belong to God?* Joseph not only announced his faith, he then quickly acted upon it. Joseph had received dreams and visions as a younger man, and he had understood their meaning (37:5–11).

40:22 *he impaled the chief baker.* Pharaoh was clearly a ruthless ruler who rewarded those who served him well, but destroyed those he perceived as threats.

39:19 [e] Pr 6:34 **39:20** [f] Ge 40:3; Ps 105:18
39:21 [g] Ex 3:21 **39:22** [h] ver 4 **39:23** [i] ver 3
40:1 [j] Ne 1:11 **40:2** [k] Pr 16:14, 15 **40:3** [l] Ge 39:20
40:4 [m] Ge 39:4 **40:5** [n] Ge 41:11 **40:7** [o] Ne 2:2
40:8 [p] Ge 41:8, 15 [q] Ge 41:16; Da 2:22, 28, 47
40:12 [r] Ge 41:12, 15, 25; Da 2:36; 4:19 **40:14** [s] Lk 23:42
[t] Jos 2:12; 1Sa 20:14, 42; 1Ki 2:7 **40:15** [u] Ge 37:26-28
40:18 [v] ver 12 **40:19** [w] ver 13 **40:20** [x] Mt 14:6-10
[y] Mk 6:21 **40:21** [z] ver 13 **40:22** [a] ver 19 [b] Ps 105:19
40:23 [c] Job 19:14; Ecc 9:15 **41:1** [d] Ge 20:3
41:2 [e] ver 26 [f] Isa 19:6

those on the riverbank. 4And the cows that were ugly and gaunt ate up the seven sleek, fat cows. Then Pharaoh woke up.

5He fell asleep again and had a second dream: Seven heads of grain, healthy and good, were growing on a single stalk. 6After them, seven other heads of grain sprouted—thin and scorched by the east wind. 7The thin heads of grain swallowed up the seven healthy, full heads. Then Pharaoh woke up; it had been a dream.

8In the morning his mind was troubled,[g] so he sent for all the magicians[h] and wise men of Egypt. Pharaoh told them his dreams, but no one could interpret them for him.

9Then the chief cupbearer said to Pharaoh, "Today I am reminded of my shortcomings. 10Pharaoh was once angry with his servants,[i] and he imprisoned me and the chief baker in the house of the captain of the guard.[j] 11Each of us had a dream the same night, and each dream had a meaning of its own.[k] 12Now a young Hebrew was there with us, a servant of the captain of the guard. We told him our dreams, and he interpreted them for us, giving each man the interpretation of his dream.[l] 13And things turned out exactly as he interpreted them to us: I was restored to my position, and the other man was impaled.[m]"

14So Pharaoh sent for Joseph, and he was quickly brought from the dungeon.[n] When he had shaved and changed his clothes, he came before Pharaoh.

15Pharaoh said to Joseph, "I had a dream, and no one can interpret it. But I have heard it said of you that when you hear a dream you can interpret it."[o]

16"I cannot do it," Joseph replied to Pharaoh, "but God will give Pharaoh the answer he desires."[p]

17Then Pharaoh said to Joseph, "In my dream I was standing on the bank of the Nile, 18when out of the river there came up seven cows, fat and sleek, and they grazed among the reeds. 19After them, seven other cows came up—scrawny and very ugly and lean. I had never seen such ugly cows in all the land of Egypt. 20The lean, ugly cows ate up the seven fat cows that came up first. 21But even after they ate them, no one could tell that they had done so; they looked just as ugly as before. Then I woke up.

22"In my dream I saw seven heads of grain, full and good, growing on a single stalk. 23After them, seven other heads sprouted—withered and thin and scorched by the east wind. 24The thin heads of grain swallowed up the seven good heads. I told this to the magicians, but none of them could explain it to me.[q]"

25Then Joseph said to Pharaoh, "The dreams of Pharaoh are one and the same. God has revealed to Pharaoh what he is about to do.[r] 26The seven good cows[s] are seven years, and the seven good heads of grain are seven years; it is one and the same dream. 27The seven lean, ugly cows that came up afterward are seven years, and so are the seven worthless heads of grain scorched by the east wind: They are seven years of famine.[t]

28"It is just as I said to Pharaoh: God has shown Pharaoh what he is about to do. 29Seven years of great abundance[u] are coming throughout the land of Egypt, 30but seven years of famine[v] will follow them. Then all the abundance in Egypt will be forgotten, and the famine will ravage the land.[w] 31The abundance in the land will not be remembered, because the famine that follows it will be so severe. 32The reason the dream was given to Pharaoh in two forms is that the matter has been firmly decided[x] by God, and God will do it soon.

33"And now let Pharaoh look for a discerning and wise man[y] and put him in charge of the land of Egypt. 34Let Pharaoh appoint commissioners over the land to take a fifth[z] of the harvest of Egypt during the seven years of abundance.[a] 35They should collect all the food of these good years that are coming and store up the grain under the authority of Pharaoh, to be kept in the cities for food.[b] 36This food should be held in reserve for the country, to be used during the seven years of famine that will come upon Egypt,[c] so that the country may not be ruined by the famine."

37The plan seemed good to Pharaoh and

41:8 ***magicians.*** The Hebrew term is related to the word for *stylus*, a writing instrument. Thus the magicians were associated in some manner with writing and knowledge, no doubt of the occult. ***wise men.*** These were a class of scholars associated with the courts of the ancient Middle East. They were either functionaries of pagan religions, or merely observers and interpreters of life.

41:14 ***shaved.*** Egyptian men not only shaved their faces, but their entire bodies and heads. Egyptian officials scorned the "hairy" Canaanites, including the Hebrews (43:32). While he lived in Egypt Joseph apparently adopted the dress and manner of the Egyptians.

41:16 ***God.*** Joseph praised the power of the living God in the pagan court of Pharaoh. He would not take any credit to himself, nor did he try to use the situation to plead for his own release.

41:32 ***God, and God.*** Joseph made it clear that he was speaking about the one God, not the numerous false gods that filled the Egyptian court, or Pharaoh himself who was believed to be a god (22:1; 42:18).

41:8 [g] Da 2:1, 3; 4:5, 19 [h] Ex 7:11, 22; Da 1:20; 2:2, 27; 4:7 **41:10** [i] Ge 40:2 [j] Ge 39:20 **41:11** [k] Ge 40:5 **41:12** [l] Ge 40:12 **41:13** [m] Ge 40:22 **41:14** [n] Ps 105:20; Da 2:25 **41:15** [o] Da 5:16 **41:16** [p] Ge 40:8; Da 2:30; Ac 3:12; 2Co 3:5 **41:24** [q] ver 8 **41:25** [r] Da 2:45 **41:26** [s] ver 2 **41:27** [t] Ge 12:10; 2Ki 8:1 **41:29** [u] ver 47 **41:30** [v] ver 54; Ge 47:13 [w] ver 56 **41:32** [x] Nu 23:19; Isa 46:10-11 **41:33** [y] ver 39 **41:34** [z] 1Sa 8:15 [a] ver 48 **41:35** [b] ver 48 **41:36** [c] ver 56

to all his officials.[d] 38So Pharaoh asked them, "Can we find anyone like this man, one in whom is the spirit of God[a]?"[e]

39Then Pharaoh said to Joseph, "Since God has made all this known to you, there is no one so discerning and wise as you. 40You shall be in charge of my palace, and all my people are to submit to your orders.[f] Only with respect to the throne will I be greater than you."

Joseph in Charge of Egypt

41So Pharaoh said to Joseph, "I hereby put you in charge of the whole land of Egypt."[g] 42Then Pharaoh took his signet ring[h] from his finger and put it on Joseph's finger. He dressed him in robes of fine linen and put a gold chain around his neck.[i] 43He had him ride in a chariot as his second-in-command,[b] and people shouted before him, "Make way[c]!"[j] Thus he put him in charge of the whole land of Egypt.

44Then Pharaoh said to Joseph, "I am Pharaoh, but without your word no one will lift hand or foot in all Egypt."[k] 45Pharaoh gave Joseph the name Zaphenath-Paneah and gave him Asenath daughter of Potiphera, priest of On,[d] to be his wife.[l] And Joseph went throughout the land of Egypt.

46Joseph was thirty years old[m] when he entered the service[n] of Pharaoh king of Egypt. And Joseph went out from Pharaoh's presence and traveled throughout Egypt. 47During the seven years of abundance the land produced plentifully. 48Joseph collected all the food produced in those seven years of abundance in Egypt and stored it in the cities. In each city he put the food grown in the fields surrounding it. 49Joseph stored up huge quantities of grain, like the sand of the sea; it was so much that he stopped keeping records because it was beyond measure.

50Before the years of famine came, two sons were born to Joseph by Asenath daughter of Potiphera, priest of On.[o] 51Joseph named his firstborn[p] Manasseh[e] and said, "It is because God has made me forget all my trouble and all my father's household." 52The second son he named Ephraim[f][q] and said, "It is because God has made me fruitful[r] in the land of my suffering."

53The seven years of abundance in Egypt came to an end, 54and the seven years of famine began,[s] just as Joseph had said. There was famine in all the other lands, but in the whole land of Egypt there was food. 55When all Egypt began to feel the famine,[t] the people cried to Pharaoh for food. Then Pharaoh told all the Egyptians, "Go to Joseph and do what he tells you."[u]

56When the famine had spread over the whole country, Joseph opened all the storehouses and sold grain to the Egyptians, for the famine[v] was severe throughout Egypt. 57And all the world came to Egypt to buy grain from Joseph,[w] because the famine was severe everywhere.

Joseph's Brothers Go to Egypt

42 When Jacob learned that there was grain in Egypt,[x] he said to his sons, "Why do you just keep looking at each other?" 2He continued, "I have heard that there is grain in Egypt. Go down there and buy some for us, so that we may live and not die."[y]

3Then ten of Joseph's brothers went down to buy grain from Egypt. 4But Jacob did not send Benjamin, Joseph's brother, with the others, because he was afraid that harm might come to him.[z] 5So Israel's sons were among those who went to buy grain,[a] for there was famine in the land of Canaan also.[b]

6Now Joseph was the governor of the

---

[a] 38 Or *of the gods* [b] 43 Or *in the chariot of his second-in-command;* or *in his second chariot* [c] 43 Or *Bow down* [d] 45 That is, Heliopolis; also in verse 50 [e] 51 *Manasseh* sounds like and may be derived from the Hebrew for *forget.* [f] 52 *Ephraim* sounds like the Hebrew for *twice fruitful.*

41:38 ***in whom is the Spirit of God.*** Even if he did not follow God himself, Pharaoh was at least acknowledging that Joseph was extraordinarily wise, and that the power of his God was obvious in his life.

41:39 ***discerning and wise.*** Joseph is an illustration of the instructions Paul gave Colosse: "Be wise in the way you act toward outsiders" (Col. 4:5). Pharaoh recognized that Joseph's wisdom was not the ordinary powers of a clever man, but something unique and outside of himself. Joseph was wise because he listened to God, not just because of his extraordinary intelligence and perspicacity. God's wisdom is moral. It discerns between good and evil. It is seen through prudence in secular affairs and comes through personal experience with the Lord.

41:45 ***Zaphenath-Paneah.*** This Egyptian name probably means something like "The God Speaks and Lives." ***Asenath.*** This name means "Belonging to (the Goddess) Neith." ***Potiphera.*** This name means "He Whom Ra (the sun god) Gave." Even though his father-in-law was the priest of a pagan god, Joseph and Asenath's sons were worshippers of the Lord, not Ra.

42:4 ***Benjamin.*** Jacob still played favorites, but this time there is no mention of jealousy among the other brothers as there had been before (37:8).

41:37 [d] Ge 45:16 **41:38** [e] Nu 27:18; Job 32:8; Da 4:8-9, 18; 5:11, 14 **41:40** [f] Ps 105:21-22; Ac 7:10 **41:41** [g] Ge 42:6; Da 6:3 **41:42** [h] Est 3:10 [i] Da 5:7, 16, 29 **41:43** [j] Est 6:9 **41:44** [k] Ps 105:22 **41:45** [l] ver 50; Ge 46:20, 27 **41:46** [m] Ge 37:2 [n] 1Sa 16:21; Da 1:19 **41:50** [o] Ge 46:20; 48:5 **41:51** [p] Ge 48:14, 18, 20 **41:52** [q] Ge 48:1, 5; 50:23 [r] Ge 17:6; 28:3; 49:22 **41:54** [s] ver 30; Ps 105:11; Ac 7:11 **41:55** [t] Dt 32:24 [u] ver 41 **41:56** [v] Ge 12:10 **41:57** [w] Ge 42:5; 47:15 **42:1** [x] Ac 7:12 **42:2** [y] Ge 43:8 **42:4** [z] ver 38 **42:5** [a] Ge 41:57 [b] Ge 12:10; Ac 7:11

land,[c] the person who sold grain to all its
people. So when Joseph's brothers arrived,
they bowed down to him with their faces
to the ground.[d] 7 As soon as Joseph saw his
brothers, he recognized them, but he pretended to be a stranger and spoke harshly
to them.[e] "Where do you come from?" he
asked.

"From the land of Canaan," they replied,
"to buy food."

8 Although Joseph recognized his brothers, they did not recognize him.[f] 9 Then he
remembered his dreams[g] about them and
said to them, "You are spies! You have
come to see where our land is unprotected."

10 "No, my lord," they answered. "Your
servants have come to buy food. 11 We are
all the sons of one man. Your servants are
honest men, not spies."

12 "No!" he said to them. "You have come
to see where our land is unprotected."

13 But they replied, "Your servants were
twelve brothers, the sons of one man, who
lives in the land of Canaan. The youngest is
now with our father, and one is no more."[h]

14 Joseph said to them, "It is just as I told
you: You are spies! 15 And this is how you
will be tested: As surely as Pharaoh lives,[i]
you will not leave this place unless your
youngest brother comes here. 16 Send one
of your number to get your brother; the rest
of you will be kept in prison, so that your
words may be tested to see if you are telling
the truth.[j] If you are not, then as surely as
Pharaoh lives, you are spies!" 17 And he put
them all in custody[k] for three days.

18 On the third day, Joseph said to them,
"Do this and you will live, for I fear God:[l]
19 If you are honest men, let one of your
brothers stay here in prison, while the rest
of you go and take grain back for your
starving households. 20 But you must bring
your youngest brother to me,[m] so that your
words may be verified and that you may
not die." This they proceeded to do.

21 They said to one another, "Surely we
are being punished because of our brother.[n] We saw how distressed he was when
he pleaded with us for his life, but we would
not listen; that's why this distress[o] has
come on us."

22 Reuben replied, "Didn't I tell you not to
sin against the boy?[p] But you wouldn't listen! Now we must give an accounting[q] for
his blood."[r] 23 They did not realize that Joseph could understand them, since he was
using an interpreter.

24 He turned away from them and began
to weep, but then came back and spoke to
them again. He had Simeon taken from
them and bound before their eyes.[s]

25 Joseph gave orders to fill their bags
with grain,[t] to put each man's silver back
in his sack,[u] and to give them provisions
for their journey.[v] After this was done for
them, 26 they loaded their grain on their
donkeys and left.

27 At the place where they stopped for
the night one of them opened his sack to
get feed for his donkey, and he saw his silver in the mouth of his sack.[w] 28 "My silver
has been returned," he said to his brothers.
"Here it is in my sack."

Their hearts sank and they turned to
each other trembling and said, "What is
this that God has done to us?"[x]

29 When they came to their father Jacob in the land of Canaan, they told him
all that had happened to them. They said,
30 "The man who is lord over the land spoke
harshly to us[y] and treated us as though we
were spying on the land. 31 But we said to
him, 'We are honest men; we are not spies.[z]
32 We were twelve brothers, sons of one father. One is no more, and the youngest is
now with our father in Canaan.'

33 "Then the man who is lord over the
land said to us, 'This is how I will know
whether you are honest men: Leave one of
your brothers here with me, and take food
for your starving households and go.[a] 34 But
bring your youngest brother to me so I will
know that you are not spies but honest
men. Then I will give your brother back to
you, and you can trade[a] in the land.[b]'"

35 As they were emptying their sacks,
there in each man's sack was his pouch
of silver! When they and their father saw
the money pouches, they were frightened.[c]
36 Their father Jacob said to them, "You
have deprived me of my children. Joseph
is no more and Simeon is no more, and now
you want to take Benjamin.[d] Everything is
against me!"

---

[a] *34* Or *move about freely*

42:6 ***bowed down to him.*** God fulfilled the dreams He gave to Joseph at the age of 17 (37:5 – 11).

42:9 ***You are spies.*** Joseph set out to learn whether his brothers had changed for the better. Would they betray each other when under pressure?

42:18 ***I fear God.*** Joseph gave his brothers a clue about who he was.

42:22 ***Didn't I tell you.*** Joseph's brothers were fearful because they knew they were guilty before God and that they deserved any punishment that God might choose to send. They must have been troubled by feelings of guilt for years, and even though they did not realize who Joseph really was, they immediately attributed their troubles to their guilt.

42:25 ***silver.*** This refers to a certain weight of raw silver. Coins had not yet been invented at this time.

42:6 [c] Ge 41:41 [d] Ge 37:7-10 **42:7** [e] ver 30 **42:8** [f] Ge 37:2 **42:9** [g] Ge 37:7 **42:13** [h] Ge 37:30, 33; 44:20 **42:15** [i] 1Sa 17:55 **42:16** [j] ver 11 **42:17** [k] Ge 40:4 **42:18** [l] Ge 20:11; Lev 25:43 **42:20** [m] ver 15, 34; Ge 43:5; 44:23 **42:21** [n] Ge 37:26-28 [o] Hos 5:15 **42:22** [p] Ge 37:21-22 [q] Ge 9:5 [r] 1Ki 2:32; 2Ch 24:22; Ps 9:12 **42:24** [s] ver 13; Ge 43:14, 23; 45:14-15 **42:25** [t] Ge 43:2 [u] Ge 44:1, 8 [v] Ro 12:17, 20-21 **42:27** [w] Ge 43:21-22 **42:28** [x] Ge 43:23 **42:30** [y] ver 7 **42:31** [z] ver 11 **42:33** [a] ver 19, 20 **42:34** [b] Ge 34:10 **42:35** [c] Ge 43:12, 15, 18 **42:36** [d] Ge 43:14

37Then Reuben said to his father, "You
may put both of my sons to death if I do not
bring him back to you. Entrust him to my
care, and I will bring him back."
38But Jacob said, "My son will not go
down there with you; his brother is dead[e]
and he is the only one left. If harm comes
to him[f] on the journey you are taking, you
will bring my gray head down to the grave[g]
in sorrow.[h]"

The Second Journey to Egypt

43 Now the famine was still severe in
the land.[i] 2So when they had eaten
all the grain they had brought from Egypt,
their father said to them, "Go back and buy
us a little more food."
3But Judah said to him, "The man
warned us solemnly, 'You will not see my
face again unless your brother is with you.'[j]
4If you will send our brother along with
us, we will go down and buy food for you.
5But if you will not send him, we will not go
down, because the man said to us, 'You will
not see my face again unless your brother
is with you.[k]'"
6Israel asked, "Why did you bring this
trouble on me by telling the man you had
another brother?"
7They replied, "The man questioned us
closely about ourselves and our family. 'Is
your father still living?'[l] he asked us. 'Do
you have another brother?'[m] We simply
answered his questions. How were we to
know he would say, 'Bring your brother
down here'?"
8Then Judah said to Israel his father,
"Send the boy along with me and we will
go at once, so that we and you and our
children may live and not die.[n] 9I myself
will guarantee his safety; you can hold me
personally responsible for him. If I do not
bring him back to you and set him here before you, I will bear the blame before you
all my life.[o] 10As it is, if we had not delayed,
we could have gone and returned twice."
11Then their father Israel said to them,
"If it must be, then do this: Put some of the
best products of the land in your bags and
take them down to the man as a gift[p]—a
little balm[q] and a little honey, some spices[r] and myrrh, some pistachio nuts and
almonds. 12Take double the amount of silver with you, for you must return the silver
that was put back into the mouths of your
sacks.[s] Perhaps it was a mistake. 13Take
your brother also and go back to the man
at once. 14And may God Almighty[a][t] grant
you mercy before the man so that he will
let your other brother and Benjamin come
back with you.[u] As for me, if I am bereaved,
I am bereaved."[v]
15So the men took the gifts and double
the amount of silver, and Benjamin also.
They hurried[w] down to Egypt and presented themselves[x] to Joseph. 16When Joseph
saw Benjamin with them, he said to the
steward of his house,[y] "Take these men to
my house, slaughter an animal and prepare
a meal;[z] they are to eat with me at noon."
17The man did as Joseph told him and
took the men to Joseph's house. 18Now the
men were frightened[a] when they were tak-
en to his house. They thought, "We were
brought here because of the silver that was
put back into our sacks the first time. He
wants to attack us and overpower us and
seize us as slaves and take our donkeys."
19So they went up to Joseph's steward
and spoke to him at the entrance to the
house. 20"We beg your pardon, our lord,"
they said, "we came down here the first
time to buy food.[b] 21But at the place where
we stopped for the night we opened our
sacks and each of us found his silver—the
exact weight—in the mouth of his sack.
So we have brought it back with us.[c] 22We
have also brought additional silver with us
to buy food. We don't know who put our
silver in our sacks."
23"It's all right," he said. "Don't be afraid.
Your God, the God of your father, has giv-
en you treasure in your sacks;[d] I received
your silver." Then he brought Simeon out
to them.[e]
24The steward took the men into Joseph's
house,[f] gave them water to wash their feet[g]
and provided fodder for their donkeys.
25They prepared their gifts for Joseph's arrival at noon, because they had heard that
they were to eat there.
26When Joseph came home, they presented to him the gifts[h] they had brought
into the house, and they bowed down before him to the ground.[i] 27He asked them
how they were, and then he said, "How is
your aged father you told me about? Is he
still living?"[j]

---

[a] 14 Hebrew *El-Shaddai*

43:8 ***Send the boy along with me.*** Judah promised that he would keep Benjamin safe. Judah had changed tremendously (38:1). Instead of leaving the family, he protected his brother and was concerned about his father's welfare.

43:23 ***Your God, the God of your father.*** Surprisingly, the steward expressed his own faith in the God of Joseph and Jacob.

43:26 ***bowed.*** For the second time (42:6) the brothers of Joseph bowed down to him, just as his dreams had predicted (37:5–11).

42:38 [e] Ge 37:33 [f] ver 4 [g] Ge 37:35 [h] Ge 44:29, 34 **43:1** [i] Ge 12:10; 41:56-57 **43:3** [j] Ge 42:15; 44:23 **43:5** [k] Ge 42:15; 2Sa 3:13 **43:7** [l] ver 27 [m] Ge 42:13 **43:8** [n] Ge 42:2; Ps 33:18-19 **43:9** [o] Ge 42:37; 44:32; Phm 1:18-19 **43:11** [p] Ge 32:20; Pr 18:16 [q] Ge 37:25; Jer 8:22 [r] 1Ki 10:2 **43:12** [s] Ge 42:25 **43:14** [t] Ge 17:1; 28:3; 35:11 [u] Ge 42:24 [v] Est 4:16 **43:15** [w] Ge 45:9, 13 [x] Ge 47:2, 7 **43:16** [y] Ge 44:1, 4, 12 [z] ver 31; Lk 15:23 **43:18** [a] Ge 42:35 **43:20** [b] Ge 42:3 **43:21** [c] ver 15; Ge 42:27, 35 **43:23** [d] Ge 42:28 [e] Ge 42:24 **43:24** [f] ver 16 [g] Ge 18:4; 24:32 **43:26** [h] Mt 2:11 [i] Ge 37:7, 10 **43:27** [j] ver 7

28 They replied, "Your servant our father is still alive and well." And they bowed down, prostrating themselves before him.[k]

29 As he looked about and saw his brother Benjamin, his own mother's son, he asked, "Is this your youngest brother, the one you told me about?"[l] And he said, "God be gracious to you,[m] my son." 30 Deeply moved[n] at the sight of his brother, Joseph hurried out and looked for a place to weep. He went into his private room and wept[o] there.

31 After he had washed his face, he came out and, controlling himself,[p] said, "Serve the food."

32 They served him by himself, the brothers by themselves, and the Egyptians who ate with him by themselves, because Egyptians could not eat with Hebrews,[q] for that is detestable to Egyptians.[r] 33 The men had been seated before him in the order of their ages, from the firstborn to the youngest; and they looked at each other in astonishment. 34 When portions were served to them from Joseph's table, Benjamin's portion was five times as much as anyone else's.[s] So they feasted and drank freely with him.

A Silver Cup in a Sack

44 Now Joseph gave these instructions to the steward of his house: "Fill the men's sacks with as much food as they can carry, and put each man's silver in the mouth of his sack.[t] 2 Then put my cup, the silver one, in the mouth of the youngest one's sack, along with the silver for his grain." And he did as Joseph said.

3 As morning dawned, the men were sent on their way with their donkeys. 4 They had not gone far from the city when Joseph said to his steward, "Go after those men at once, and when you catch up with them, say to them, 'Why have you repaid good with evil?[u] 5 Isn't this the cup my master drinks from and also uses for divination?[v] This is a wicked thing you have done.'"

6 When he caught up with them, he repeated these words to them. 7 But they said to him, "Why does my lord say such things? Far be it from your servants to do anything like that! 8 We even brought back to you from the land of Canaan the silver we found inside the mouths of our sacks.[w] So why would we steal silver or gold from your master's house? 9 If any of your servants is found to have it, he will die;[x] and the rest of us will become my lord's slaves."

10 "Very well, then," he said, "let it be as you say. Whoever is found to have it will become my slave; the rest of you will be free from blame."

11 Each of them quickly lowered his sack to the ground and opened it. 12 Then the steward proceeded to search, beginning with the oldest and ending with the youngest. And the cup was found in Benjamin's sack.[y] 13 At this, they tore their clothes.[z] Then they all loaded their donkeys and returned to the city.

14 Joseph was still in the house when Judah and his brothers came in, and they threw themselves to the ground before him.[a] 15 Joseph said to them, "What is this you have done? Don't you know that a man like me can find things out by divination?[b]"

16 "What can we say to my lord?" Judah replied. "What can we say? How can we prove our innocence? God has uncovered your servants' guilt. We are now my lord's slaves[c]—we ourselves and the one who was found to have the cup.[d]"

17 But Joseph said, "Far be it from me to do such a thing! Only the man who was found to have the cup will become my slave. The rest of you, go back to your father in peace."

18 Then Judah went up to him and said: "Pardon your servant, my lord, let me speak a word to my lord. Do not be angry[e] with your servant, though you are equal to Pharaoh himself. 19 My lord asked his servants, 'Do you have a father or a brother?'[f] 20 And we answered, 'We have an aged father, and there is a young son born to him in his old age.[g] His brother is dead,[h] and he is the only one of his mother's sons left, and his father loves him.'[i]

21 "Then you said to your servants, 'Bring him down to me so I can see him for myself.'[j] 22 And we said to my lord, 'The boy cannot leave his father; if he leaves him, his father will die.'[k] 23 But you told your

---

43:32 ***detestable.*** This word can indicate the strongest revulsion, something that might cause physical illness (46:34). The Egyptians (who carefully shaved their entire bodies) may have been repulsed by the "hairy" Hebrews.

44:15 ***can find things out by divination.*** This curious verse is not very clear in meaning. Clearly a God-fearing man like Joseph who knew that only God can interpret dreams and visions (40:8) would not have been one to dabble with the occult. He may just have been trying to frighten his brothers by appearing to know things supernaturally (this would certainly have been backed up by his uncanny knowledge of their birth order in 43:33).

44:17 ***go back to your father in peace.*** Joseph was testing his brothers again, to see if they had changed in their attitude to the son of their father's favorite wife. Would they leave Benjamin a slave in Egypt as they had Joseph?

43:28 [k] Ge 37:7 **43:29** [l] Ge 42:13 [m] Nu 6:25; Ps 67:1 **43:30** [n] Jn 11:33, 38 [o] Ge 42:24; 45:2, 14, 15; 46:29 **43:31** [p] Ge 45:1 **43:32** [q] Gal 2:12 [r] Ge 46:34; Ex 8:26 **43:34** [s] Ge 37:3; 45:22 **44:1** [t] Ge 42:25 **44:4** [u] Ps 35:12 **44:5** [v] Ge 30:27; Dt 18:10-14 **44:8** [w] Ge 42:25; 43:21 **44:9** [x] Ge 31:32 **44:12** [y] ver 2 **44:13** [z] Ge 37:29; Nu 14:6; 2Sa 1:11 **44:14** [a] Ge 37:7, 10 **44:15** [b] ver 5; Ge 30:27 **44:16** [c] ver 9; Ge 43:18 [d] ver 2 **44:18** [e] Ge 18:30; Ex 32:22 **44:19** [f] Ge 43:7 **44:20** [g] Ge 37:3 [h] Ge 37:33 [i] Ge 42:13 **44:21** [j] Ge 42:15 **44:22** [k] Ge 37:35

servants, 'Unless your youngest brother comes down with you, you will not see my face again.'[l] 24 When we went back to your servant my father, we told him what my lord had said.

25 "Then our father said, 'Go back and buy a little more food.'[m] 26 But we said, 'We cannot go down. Only if our youngest brother is with us will we go. We cannot see the man's face unless our youngest brother is with us.'

27 "Your servant my father said to us, 'You know that my wife bore me two sons.[n] 28 One of them went away from me, and I said, "He has surely been torn to pieces."[o] And I have not seen him since. 29 If you take this one from me too and harm comes to him, you will bring my gray head down to the grave in misery.'[p]

30 "So now, if the boy is not with us when I go back to your servant my father, and if my father, whose life is closely bound up with the boy's life,[q] 31 sees that the boy isn't there, he will die. Your servants will bring the gray head of our father down to the grave in sorrow. 32 Your servant guaranteed the boy's safety to my father. I said, 'If I do not bring him back to you, I will bear the blame before you, my father, all my life!'[r]

33 "Now then, please let your servant remain here as my lord's slave[s] in place of the boy,[t] and let the boy return with his brothers. 34 How can I go back to my father if the boy is not with me? No! Do not let me see the misery that would come on my father."[u]

Joseph Makes Himself Known

45 Then Joseph could no longer control himself[v] before all his attendants, and he cried out, "Have everyone leave my presence!" So there was no one with Joseph when he made himself known to his brothers. 2 And he wept[w] so loudly that the Egyptians heard him, and Pharaoh's household heard about it.[x]

3 Joseph said to his brothers, "I am Joseph! Is my father still living?"[y] But his brothers were not able to answer him,[z] because they were terrified at his presence.

4 Then Joseph said to his brothers, "Come close to me." When they had done so, he said, "I am your brother Joseph, the one you sold into Egypt![a] 5 And now, do not be distressed[b] and do not be angry with yourselves for selling me here,[c] because it was to save lives that God sent me ahead of you.[d] 6 For two years now there has been famine in the land, and for the next five years there will be no plowing and reaping. 7 But God sent me ahead of you to preserve for you a remnant[e] on earth and to save your lives by a great deliverance.[a][f]

8 "So then, it was not you who sent me here, but God. He made me father[g] to Pharaoh, lord of his entire household and ruler of all Egypt.[h] 9 Now hurry back to my father and say to him, 'This is what your son Joseph says: God has made me lord of all Egypt. Come down to me; don't delay.[i] 10 You shall live in the region of Goshen[j] and be near me—you, your children and grandchildren, your flocks and herds, and all you have. 11 I will provide for you there,[k] because five years of famine are still to come. Otherwise you and your household and all who belong to you will become destitute.'

12 "You can see for yourselves, and so can my brother Benjamin, that it is really I who am speaking to you. 13 Tell my father about all the honor accorded me in Egypt and about everything you have seen. And bring my father down here quickly."

14 Then he threw his arms around his brother Benjamin and wept, and Benjamin embraced him, weeping. 15 And he kissed[m] all his brothers and wept over them. Afterward his brothers talked with him.[n]

16 When the news reached Pharaoh's palace that Joseph's brothers had come,[o] Pharaoh and all his officials were pleased. 17 Pharaoh said to Joseph, "Tell your brothers, 'Do this: Load your animals and return

[a] 7 Or *save you as a great band of survivors*

45:1–4 Real Love—A profound comparison can be made between the life of Joseph and the life of Christ. Both Joseph and Jesus were persecuted unjustly (Gen. 37:11–28; Matt. 26:59). Both were lost to their brothers for a while (Gen. 45:1–15; Rom. 10:1–4). Both later forgave and restored their repentant brothers (Gen. 45;1–15; Zech. 8:1–8).

45:3 *I am Joseph.* Joseph must have said this in Hebrew, finally dropping the ruse of the interpreter (42:23).

45:5 *God sent me.* God often permits the wicked to carry out their evil plans in order to fulfill some larger purpose He has for the objects of their violence and cruelty. Since it is not possible for us to see the whole picture from God's perspective, we must exercise faith and believe that the God of all the earth will do right and that all things do work together for good to those who love God, who are called according to His purpose. Joseph was able to freely forgive his brothers partly because he recognized that their sin had been turned by God into something good.

45:10 *You shall live in the region of Goshen.* This was God's plan, He had told Abraham that his descendants would live in a foreign land (15:13–16).

44:23 [l] Ge 43:5 **44:25** [m] Ge 43:2 **44:27** [n] Ge 46:19 **44:28** [o] Ge 37:33 **44:29** [p] Ge 42:38 **44:30** [q] 1Sa 18:1 **44:32** [r] Ge 43:9 **44:33** [s] Ge 43:18 [t] Jn 15:13 **44:34** [u] Est 8:6 **45:1** [v] Ge 43:31 **45:2** [w] Ge 29:11 [x] ver 16; Ge 46:29 **45:3** [y] Ac 7:13 [z] ver 15 **45:4** [a] Ge 37:28 **45:5** [b] Ge 42:21 [c] Ge 42:22 [d] ver 7-8; Ge 50:20; Ps 105:17 **45:7** [e] 2Ki 19:4, 30, 31; Isa 10:20, 21; Mic 4:7; Zep 2:7 [f] Ex 15:2; Est 4:14; Isa 25:9 **45:8** [g] Jdg 17:10 [h] Ge 41:41 **45:9** [i] Ge 43:10 **45:10** [j] Ge 46:28, 34; 47:1 **45:11** [k] Ge 47:12 **45:13** [l] Ac 7:14 **45:15** [m] Lk 15:20 [n] ver 3 **45:16** [o] Ac 7:13

to the land of Canaan, 18and bring your father and your families back to me. I will give you the best of the land of Egypt[p] and you can enjoy the fat of the land.'[q]

19"You are also directed to tell them, 'Do this: Take some carts[r] from Egypt for your children and your wives, and get your father and come. 20Never mind about your belongings, because the best of all Egypt will be yours.'"

21So the sons of Israel did this. Joseph gave them carts, as Pharaoh had commanded, and he also gave them provisions for their journey.[s] 22To each of them he gave new clothing, but to Benjamin he gave three hundred shekels[a] of silver and five sets of clothes.[t] 23And this is what he sent to his father: ten donkeys loaded with the best things of Egypt, and ten female donkeys loaded with grain and bread and other provisions for his journey. 24Then he sent his brothers away, and as they were leaving he said to them, "Don't quarrel on the way!"[u]

25So they went up out of Egypt and came to their father Jacob in the land of Canaan. 26They told him, "Joseph is still alive! In fact, he is ruler of all Egypt." Jacob was stunned; he did not believe them.[v] 27But when they told him everything Joseph had said to them, and when he saw the carts[w] Joseph had sent to carry him back, the spirit of their father Jacob revived. 28And Israel said, "I'm convinced! My son Joseph is still alive. I will go and see him before I die."

Jacob Goes to Egypt

46 So Israel set out with all that was his, and when he reached Beersheba,[x] he offered sacrifices to the God of his father Isaac.[y]

2And God spoke to Israel in a vision at night[z] and said, "Jacob! Jacob!"

"Here I am,"[a] he replied.

3"I am God, the God of your father,"[b] he said. "Do not be afraid to go down to Egypt, for I will make you into a great nation[c] there.[d] 4I will go down to Egypt with you, and I will surely bring you back again.[e] And Joseph's own hand will close your eyes.[f]"

5Then Jacob left Beersheba, and Israel's sons took their father Jacob and their children and their wives in the carts[g] that Pharaoh had sent to transport him. 6So Jacob and all his offspring went to Egypt,[h] taking with them their livestock and the possessions they had acquired in Canaan. 7Jacob brought with him to Egypt his sons and grandsons and his daughters and granddaughters—all his offspring.[i]

8These are the names of the sons of Israel[j] (Jacob and his descendants) who went to Egypt:

Reuben the firstborn of Jacob.
9The sons of Reuben:[k]
Hanok, Pallu, Hezron and Karmi.
10The sons of Simeon:[l]
Jemuel,[m] Jamin, Ohad, Jakin, Zohar and Shaul the son of a Canaanite woman.
11The sons of Levi:[n]
Gershon, Kohath and Merari.
12The sons of Judah:[o]
Er, Onan, Shelah, Perez and Zerah (but Er and Onan had died in the land of Canaan).
The sons of Perez:[p]
Hezron and Hamul.
13The sons of Issachar:[q]
Tola, Puah,[b][r] Jashub[c] and Shimron.
14The sons of Zebulun:[s]
Sered, Elon and Jahleel.

15These were the sons Leah bore to Jacob in Paddan Aram,[d] besides his daughter Dinah. These sons and daughters of his were thirty-three in all.

16The sons of Gad:[t]
Zephon,[e][u] Haggi, Shuni, Ezbon, Eri, Arodi and Areli.
17The sons of Asher:[v]
Imnah, Ishvah, Ishvi and Beriah.
Their sister was Serah.
The sons of Beriah:
Heber and Malkiel.

[a] 22 That is, about 7 1/2 pounds or about 3.5 kilograms [b] *13* Samaritan Pentateuch and Syriac (see also 1 Chron. 7:1); Masoretic Text *Puvah* [c] *13* Samaritan Pentateuch and some Septuagint manuscripts (see also Num. 26:24 and 1 Chron. 7:1); Masoretic Text *Iob* [d] *15* That is, Northwest Mesopotamia [e] *16* Samaritan Pentateuch and Septuagint (see also Num. 26:15); Masoretic Text *Ziphion*

46:1 *Israel set out.* Jacob's journey to Egypt began a four-hundred-year sojourn away from the promised land of Canaan. Jacob entered Egypt with his twelve sons and their families; Jacob's descendants would leave Egypt as a small nation.
46:2 *Israel ... Jacob.* The fact that these names are used interchangeably indicates that the earlier negative connotations of the name Jacob had faded (31:11; 32:28; 35:10).
46:11 *Gershon, Kohath and Merari.* These sons of Levi became the founders of the Levitical families (Ex. 6:16–19). Aaron and Moses descended from Kohath (Ex. 6:20–25).

45:18 p Ge 27:28; 46:34; 47:6, 11, 27; Nu 18:12, 29 q Ps 37:19 **45:19** r Ge 46:5 **45:21** s Ge 42:25 **45:22** t Ge 37:3; 43:34 **45:24** u Ge 42:21-22 **45:26** v Ge 44:28 **45:27** w ver 19 **46:1** x Ge 21:14; 28:10 y Ge 26:24; 28:13; 31:42 **46:2** z Ge 15:1; Job 33:14-15 a Ge 22:1; 31:11 **46:3** b Ge 28:13 c Ge 12:2; Dt 26:5 d Ex 1:7 **46:4** e Ge 28:15; 48:21; Ex 3:8 f Ge 50:1, 24 **46:5** g Ge 45:19 **46:6** h Dt 26:5; Jos 24:4; Ps 105:23; Isa 52:4; Ac 7:15 **46:7** i Ge 45:10 **46:8** j Ex 1:1; Nu 26:4 **46:9** k 1Ch 5:3 **46:10** l Ge 29:33; Nu 26:14 m Ex 6:15 **46:11** n Ge 29:34; Nu 3:17 **46:12** o Ge 29:35 p 1Ch 2:5, Mt 1:3 **46:13** q Ge 30:18 r 1Ch 7:1 **46:14** s Ge 30:20 **46:16** t Ge 30:11 u Nu 26:15 **46:17** v Ge 30:13; 1Ch 7:30-31

18 These were the children born to Jacob
by Zilpah,[w] whom Laban had given to his
daughter Leah[x]—sixteen in all.

19 The sons of Jacob's wife Rachel:
Joseph and Benjamin.[y] 20 In Egypt,
Manasseh[z] and Ephraim[a] were born
to Joseph by Asenath daughter of
Potiphera, priest of On.[a]
21 The sons of Benjamin:[b]
Bela, Beker, Ashbel, Gera, Naaman,
Ehi, Rosh, Muppim, Huppim and
Ard.

22 These were the sons of Rachel who
were born to Jacob—fourteen in all.

23 The son of Dan:
Hushim.
24 The sons of Naphtali:
Jahziel, Guni, Jezer and Shillem.

25 These were the sons born to Jacob
by Bilhah,[c] whom Laban had given to his
daughter Rachel[d]—seven in all.

26 All those who went to Egypt with Jacob—those who were his direct descendants, not counting his sons' wives—
numbered sixty-six persons.[e] 27 With the
two sons[b] who had been born to Joseph
in Egypt, the members of Jacob's family,
which went to Egypt, were seventy[c] in all.[f]

28 Now Jacob sent Judah ahead of him to
Joseph to get directions to Goshen.[g] When
they arrived in the region of Goshen, 29 Joseph had his chariot made ready and went
to Goshen to meet his father Israel. As soon
as Joseph appeared before him, he threw
his arms around his father[d] and wept for
a long time.[h]

30 Israel said to Joseph, "Now I am ready
to die, since I have seen for myself that you
are still alive."

31 Then Joseph said to his brothers and
to his father's household, "I will go up and
speak to Pharaoh and will say to him, 'My
brothers and my father's household, who
were living in the land of Canaan, have
come to me.[i] 32 The men are shepherds;
they tend livestock, and they have brought
along their flocks and herds and everything they own.' 33 When Pharaoh calls
you in and asks, 'What is your occupation?'[j] 34 you should answer, 'Your servants
have tended livestock from our boyhood
on, just as our fathers did.' Then you will
be allowed to settle in the region of Goshen,[k] for all shepherds are detestable to
the Egyptians.[l]"

47 Joseph went and told Pharaoh, "My
father and brothers, with their flocks
and herds and everything they own, have
come from the land of Canaan and are now
in Goshen."[m] 2 He chose five of his brothers
and presented them before Pharaoh.

3 Pharaoh asked the brothers, "What is
your occupation?"[n]

"Your servants are shepherds," they replied to Pharaoh, "just as our fathers were."
4 They also said to him, "We have come to
live here for a while,[o] because the famine
is severe in Canaan[p] and your servants'
flocks have no pasture. So now, please let
your servants settle in Goshen."[q]

5 Pharaoh said to Joseph, "Your father
and your brothers have come to you, 6 and
the land of Egypt is before you; settle your
father and your brothers in the best part
of the land.[r] Let them live in Goshen. And
if you know of any among them with special ability,[s] put them in charge of my own
livestock."

7 Then Joseph brought his father Jacob in
and presented him before Pharaoh. After
Jacob blessed[e] Pharaoh,[t] 8 Pharaoh asked
him, "How old are you?"

---

[a] 20 That is, Heliopolis [b] 27 Hebrew; Septuagint *the nine children* [c] 27 Hebrew (see also Exodus 1:5 and note); Septuagint (see also Acts 7:14) *seventy-five* [d] 29 Hebrew *around him* [e] 7 Or *greeted*

46:26–27 *sixty-six ... seventy.* When Joseph, his two sons, and Jacob himself are added, the number of males in Jacob's family equals seventy.

46:34 *all shepherds are detestable to the Egyptians.* God used the racial and ethnic prejudice of the Egyptians as a way of preserving the ethnic and spiritual identity of His own people. Jacob's family was already intermarrying with the Canaanites (ch. 38) and was in danger of losing its identity as the people of God.

47:5–6 *Pharaoh.* There is some uncertainty concerning the identity of this Pharaoh. Many believe he was Amenhotep I of the eleventh dynasty. Prior to his reign Egypt had suffered political and economic chaos for 200 years. Irrigation and building projects fell into ruin, and civil war raged. But Pharaoh Amenhotep was able to reunite Egypt, rebuilding the country and developing world trade. One of the reasons for his success no doubt stemmed from the fact that he was a generous man as we are told here. Not only was he generous to his own people, but he was kind to Israel. God had already promised to bless those who blessed the descendants of Abraham (Gen. 12:3). The lesson is clear. If a pagan king can experience God's blessing for his generosity, how much more can born-again believers know the riches of heaven for their generosity? Solomon reminds us of this principle: "A generous person will prosper" (Prov. 11:25).

47:8 *How old are you?* Pharaoh's question suggests that the long ages of the patriarchal family were truly exceptional, even for this period. Jacob's final 147 years (47:28) were fewer than the 175 years of Abraham (25:7) and the 180 years of Isaac (35:28), but still a significant age.

46:18 [w] Ge 30:10 [x] Ge 29:24 **46:19** [y] Ge 44:27 **46:20** [z] Ge 41:51 [a] Ge 41:52 **46:21** [b] Nu 26:38-41; 1Ch 7:6-12; 8:1 **46:25** [c] Ge 30:8 [d] Ge 29:29 **46:26** [e] ver 5-7; Ex 1:5; Dt 10:22 **46:27** [f] Ac 7:14 **46:28** [g] Ge 45:10 **46:29** [h] Ge 45:14-15; Lk 15:20 **46:31** [i] Ge 47:1 **46:33** [j] Ge 47:3 **46:34** [k] Ge 45:10 [l] Ge 43:32; Ex 8:26 **47:1** [m] Ge 46:31 **47:3** [n] Ge 46:33 **47:4** [o] Ge 15:13; Dt 26:5 [p] Ge 43:1 [q] Ge 46:34 **47:6** [r] Ge 45:18 [s] Ex 18:21,25 **47:7** [t] ver 10; 2Sa 14:22

9And Jacob said to Pharaoh, "The years
of my pilgrimage are a hundred and thirty.[u] My years have been few and difficult,[v]
and they do not equal the years of the pilgrimage of my fathers.[w]" 10Then Jacob
blessed[a] Pharaoh[x] and went out from his
presence.
11So Joseph settled his father and his
brothers in Egypt and gave them property
in the best part of the land, the district of
Rameses,[y] as Pharaoh directed. 12Joseph
also provided his father and his brothers
and all his father's household with food,
according to the number of their children.[z]

Joseph and the Famine

13There was no food, however, in the
whole region because the famine was severe; both Egypt and Canaan wasted away
because of the famine.[a] 14Joseph collected
all the money that was to be found in Egypt
and Canaan in payment for the grain they
were buying, and he brought it to Pharaoh's palace.[b] 15When the money of the
people of Egypt and Canaan was gone, all
Egypt came to Joseph and said, "Give us
food. Why should we die before your eyes?[c]
Our money is all gone."
16"Then bring your livestock," said Joseph. "I will sell you food in exchange for
your livestock, since your money is gone."
17So they brought their livestock to Joseph,
and he gave them food in exchange for
their horses,[d] their sheep and goats, their
cattle and donkeys. And he brought them
through that year with food in exchange
for all their livestock.
18When that year was over, they came to
him the following year and said, "We cannot hide from our lord the fact that since
our money is gone and our livestock belongs to you, there is nothing left for our
lord except our bodies and our land. 19Why
should we perish before your eyes—we
and our land as well? Buy us and our land
in exchange for food, and we with our land
will be in bondage to Pharaoh. Give us seed
so that we may live and not die, and that
the land may not become desolate."
20So Joseph bought all the land in Egypt
for Pharaoh. The Egyptians, one and all,
sold their fields, because the famine was
too severe for them. The land became
Pharaoh's, 21and Joseph reduced the people to servitude,[b] from one end of Egypt
to the other. 22However, he did not buy the
land of the priests, because they received
a regular allotment from Pharaoh and had
food enough from the allotment[e] Pharaoh
gave them. That is why they did not sell
their land.
23Joseph said to the people, "Now that I
have bought you and your land today for
Pharaoh, here is seed for you so you can
plant the ground. 24But when the crop
comes in, give a fifth[f] of it to Pharaoh. The
other four-fifths you may keep as seed for
the fields and as food for yourselves and
your households and your children."
25"You have saved our lives," they said.
"May we find favor in the eyes of our lord;[g]
we will be in bondage to Pharaoh."
26So Joseph established it as a law concerning land in Egypt—still in force today—that a fifth of the produce belongs to
Pharaoh. It was only the land of the priests
that did not become Pharaoh's.[h]
27Now the Israelites settled in Egypt in
the region of Goshen. They acquired property there and were fruitful and increased
greatly in number.[i]
28Jacob lived in Egypt[j] seventeen years,
and the years of his life were a hundred
and forty-seven. 29When the time drew
near for Israel to die,[k] he called for his son
Joseph and said to him, "If I have found favor in your eyes, put your hand under my
thigh[l] and promise that you will show me
kindness and faithfulness.[m] Do not bury
me in Egypt, 30but when I rest with my fathers, carry me out of Egypt and bury me
where they are buried."[n]
"I will do as you say," he said.
31"Swear to me,"[o] he said. Then Joseph
swore to him,[p] and Israel worshiped as he
leaned on the top of his staff.[c][q]

Manasseh and Ephraim

48 Some time later Joseph was told,
"Your father is ill." So he took his
two sons Manasseh and Ephraim[r] along
with him. 2When Jacob was told, "Your son
Joseph has come to you," Israel rallied his
strength and sat up on the bed.
3Jacob said to Joseph, "God Almighty[d]
appeared to me at Luz[s] in the land of Canaan, and there he blessed me[t] 4and said
to me, 'I am going to make you fruitful and

[a] 10 Or *said farewell to* [b] 21 Samaritan Pentateuch and Septuagint (see also Vulgate); Masoretic Text *and he moved the people into the cities* [c] 31 Or *Israel bowed down at the head of his bed* [d] 3 Hebrew *El-Shaddai*

47:20 *the land.* Pharaoh's ownership of all the land of Egypt would one day lead to gross abuses of power (see the Book of Exodus).

47:29 *kindness and faithfulness.* In other words, "demonstrate to me the utmost covenant loyalty." Jacob showed his vigorous faith in God's promises by asking to be buried in the land promised to his descendants.

47:9 [u] Ge 25:7 [v] Heb 11:9, 13 [w] Ge 35:28 **47:10** [x] ver 7 **47:11** [y] Ex 1:11; 12:37 **47:12** [z] Ge 45:11 **47:13** [a] Ge 41:30; Ac 7:11 **47:14** [b] Ge 41:56 **47:15** [c] ver 19; Ex 16:3 **47:17** [d] Ex 14:9 **47:22** [e] Dt 14:28-29; Ezr 7:24 **47:24** [f] Ge 41:34 **47:25** [g] Ge 32:5 **47:26** [h] ver 22 **47:27** [i] Ge 17:6; 46:3; Ex 1:7 **47:28** [j] Ps 105:23 **47:29** [k] Dt 31:14 [l] Ge 24:2 [m] Ge 24:49 **47:30** [n] Ge 49:29-32; 50:5, 13; Ac 7:15-16 **47:31** [o] Ge 21:23 [p] Ge 24:3 [q] Heb 11:21 *fn*; 1Ki 1:47 **48:1** [r] Ge 41:52 **48:3** [s] Ge 28:19 [t] Ge 28:13; 35:9-12

increase your numbers.[u] I will make you a community of peoples, and I will give this land as an everlasting possession to your descendants after you.'
[5]"Now then, your two sons born to you
in Egypt[v] before I came to you here will be
reckoned as mine; Ephraim and Manasseh
will be mine,[w] just as Reuben and Simeon
are mine. [6]Any children born to you after
them will be yours; in the territory they
inherit they will be reckoned under the
names of their brothers. [7]As I was returning from Paddan,[a] to my sorrow Rachel
died in the land of Canaan while we were
still on the way, a little distance from Ephrath. So I buried her there beside the road
to Ephrath" (that is, Bethlehem).[x]
[8]When Israel saw the sons of Joseph, he
asked, "Who are these?"
[9]"They are the sons God has given me
here,"[y] Joseph said to his father.
Then Israel said, "Bring them to me so I
may bless[z] them."
[10]Now Israel's eyes were failing because
of old age, and he could hardly see.[a] So Joseph brought his sons close to him, and his
father kissed them[b] and embraced them.
[11]Israel said to Joseph, "I never expected
to see your face again, and now God has
allowed me to see your children too."[c]
[12]Then Joseph removed them from Israel's knees and bowed down with his face
to the ground. [13]And Joseph took both of
them, Ephraim on his right toward Israel's
left hand and Manasseh on his left toward
Israel's right hand,[d] and brought them close
to him. [14]But Israel reached out his right
hand and put it on Ephraim's head, though
he was the younger, and crossing his arms,
he put his left hand on Manasseh's head,
even though Manasseh was the firstborn.[e]
[15]Then he blessed[f] Joseph and said,

"May the God before whom my fathers
Abraham and Isaac walked
faithfully,
the God who has been my shepherd[g]
all my life to this day,
[16]the Angel who has delivered me from
all harm
—may he bless these boys.[h]
May they be called by my name
and the names of my fathers
Abraham and Isaac,[i]
and may they increase greatly
on the earth."

[17]When Joseph saw his father placing
his right hand on Ephraim's head[j] he was
displeased; so he took hold of his father's
hand to move it from Ephraim's head to
Manasseh's head. [18]Joseph said to him,
"No, my father, this one is the firstborn;
put your right hand on his head."
[19]But his father refused and said, "I
know, my son, I know. He too will become
a people, and he too will become great.[k]
Nevertheless, his younger brother will be
greater than he,[l] and his descendants will
become a group of nations." [20]He blessed
them that day and said,

"In your[b] name will Israel pronounce
this blessing:
'May God make you like Ephraim[m]
and Manasseh.[n]'"

So he put Ephraim ahead of Manasseh.
[21]Then Israel said to Joseph, "I am about
to die, but God will be with you[c][o] and take
you[c] back to the land of your[c] fathers.[p]
[22]And to you I give one more ridge of land[d][q]
than to your brothers,[r] the ridge I took from
the Amorites with my sword and my bow."

Jacob Blesses His Sons

49 Then Jacob called for his sons and
said: "Gather around so I can tell you
what will happen to you in days to come.[s]

[2]"Assemble and listen, sons of Jacob;
listen to your father Israel.[t]

[3]"Reuben, you are my firstborn,[u]
my might, the first sign of my
strength,[v]
excelling in honor, excelling in power.
[4]Turbulent as the waters,[w] you will no
longer excel,
for you went up onto your father's bed,
onto my couch and defiled it.[x]

[5]"Simeon and Levi are brothers—
their swords[e] are weapons of
violence.[y]

---

[a] *7* That is, Northwest Mesopotamia [b] *20* The Hebrew is singular. [c] *21* The Hebrew is plural. [d] *22* The Hebrew for *ridge of land* is identical with the place name Shechem.
[e] *5* The meaning of the Hebrew for this word is uncertain.

48:5–7 *Ephraim and Manasseh.* As firstborn, Reuben should have received a double portion of the inheritance, but he had forfeited his birthright by his sins (35:22). By adopting Ephraim and Manasseh as his own sons, Jacob gave the double portion to Joseph.
48:22 *one more ridge of land.* Jacob promised Joseph that he would one day return to the land of Canaan. The promise was fulfilled after Joseph's death (50:24–26).
49:5–7 *Simeon and Levi.* This prophecy was fulfilled when the Israelites settled in the promised land. Simeon's allotment was scattered within the larger portion of the tribe of Judah, and Levi's allotment was scattered cities throughout the land (Josh. 21).

48:4 [u] Ge 17:6 **48:5** [v] Ge 41:50-52; 46:20 [w] 1Ch 5:1; Jos 14:4 **48:7** [x] Ge 35:19 **48:9** [y] Ge 33:5 [z] Ge 27:4 **48:10** [a] Ge 27:1 [b] Ge 27:27 **48:11** [c] Ge 50:23; Ps 128:6 **48:13** [d] Ps 110:1 **48:14** [e] Ge 41:51 **48:15** [f] Ge 17:1 [g] Ge 49:24 **48:16** [h] Heb 11:21 [i] Ge 28:13 **48:17** [j] ver 14 **48:19** [k] Ge 17:20 [l] Ge 25:23 **48:20** [m] Nu 2:18 [n] Nu 2:20; Ru 4:11 **48:21** [o] Ge 26:3; 46:4 [p] Ge 28:13; 50:24 **48:22** [q] Jos 24:32; Jn 4:5 [r] Ge 37:8 **49:1** [s] Nu 24:14; Jer 23:20 **49:2** [t] Ps 34:11 **49:3** [u] Ge 29:32 [v] Dt 21:17; Ps 78:51 **49:4** [w] Isa 57:20 [x] Ge 35:22; Dt 27:20 **49:5** [y] Ge 34:25; Pr 4:17

6 Let me not enter their council,
let me not join their assembly,[z]
for they have killed men in their anger[a]
and hamstrung oxen as they pleased.
7 Cursed be their anger, so fierce,
and their fury, so cruel!
I will scatter them in Jacob
and disperse them in Israel.[b]

8 "Judah,[a] your brothers will praise you;
your hand will be on the neck of your enemies;
your father's sons will bow down to you.[c]
9 You are a lion's[d] cub, Judah;[e]
you return from the prey, my son.
Like a lion he crouches and lies down,
like a lioness—who dares to rouse him?
10 The scepter will not depart from Judah,[f]
nor the ruler's staff from between his feet,[b]
until he to whom it belongs[c] shall come
and the obedience of the nations shall be his.[g]
11 He will tether his donkey to a vine,
his colt to the choicest branch;
he will wash his garments in wine,
his robes in the blood of grapes.
12 His eyes will be darker than wine,
his teeth whiter than milk.[d]

13 "Zebulun[h] will live by the seashore
and become a haven for ships;
his border will extend toward Sidon.

14 "Issachar[i] is a rawboned[e] donkey
lying down among the sheep pens.[f]
15 When he sees how good is his resting place
and how pleasant is his land,
he will bend his shoulder to the burden
and submit to forced labor.

16 "Dan[g][j] will provide justice for his people
as one of the tribes of Israel.
17 Dan[k] will be a snake by the roadside,
a viper along the path,
that bites the horse's heels
so that its rider tumbles backward.

18 "I look for your deliverance, LORD.[l]

19 "Gad[h][m] will be attacked by a band of raiders,
but he will attack them at their heels.

20 "Asher's[n] food will be rich;
he will provide delicacies fit for a king.

21 "Naphtali[o] is a doe set free
that bears beautiful fawns.[i]

22 "Joseph[p] is a fruitful vine,
a fruitful vine near a spring,
whose branches climb over a wall.[j]
23 With bitterness archers attacked him;
they shot at him with hostility.[q]
24 But his bow remained steady,
his strong arms[r] stayed[k] limber,
because of the hand of the Mighty One of Jacob,[s]
because of the Shepherd, the Rock of Israel,[t]
25 because of your father's God,[u] who helps you,
because of the Almighty,[l] who blesses you
with blessings of the skies above,
blessings of the deep springs below,[v]
blessings of the breast and womb.
26 Your father's blessings are greater
than the blessings of the ancient mountains,
than[m] the bounty of the age-old hills.
Let all these rest on the head of Joseph,
on the brow of the prince among[n] his brothers.[w]

27 "Benjamin[x] is a ravenous wolf;
in the morning he devours the prey,
in the evening he divides the plunder."

28 All these are the twelve tribes of Israel, and this is what their father said to

[a] 8 *Judah* sounds like and may be derived from the Hebrew for *praise.* [b] 10 Or *from his descendants* [c] 10 Or *to whom tribute belongs*; the meaning of the Hebrew for this phrase is uncertain. [d] 12 Or *will be dull from wine, / his teeth white from milk* [e] 14 Or *strong* [f] 14 Or *the campfires*; or *the saddlebags* [g] 16 *Dan* here means *he provides justice.* [h] 19 *Gad* sounds like the Hebrew for *attack* and also for *band of raiders.* [i] 21 Or *free; / he utters beautiful words* [j] 22 Or *Joseph is a wild colt, / a wild colt near a spring, / a wild donkey on a terraced hill* [k] 23,24 Or *archers will attack . . . will shoot . . . will remain . . . will stay* [l] 25 Hebrew *Shaddai* [m] 26 Or *of my progenitors, / as great as* [n] 26 Or *of the one separated from*

49:10 ***scepter.*** With these words, Jacob predicted that a royal line would rise from Judah's descendants. In this context, "he to whom it belongs" is a reference to the coming Messiah.
49:11–12 ***wine . . . blood.*** The imagery in this verse describes the warfare that the Messiah will wage to establish His reign (Ps. 2; 110; Rev. 19:11–21).
49:24 ***Shepherd.*** The image of God as a shepherd occurs many times in Scripture. This term would have had great significance for a family of shepherds. God shepherded and cared for their families just as they shepherded and cared for their own flocks. God is the one Good Shepherd (Ps. 23; John 10).
49:28 ***the twelve tribes of Israel.*** Jacob's blessings are prophecies about the destiny of each tribe. Some of the blessings are obscure, but the blessings on Judah and Joseph are clear prophecies from God about their destinies (compare Moses' blessing of the tribes of Israel, Deut. 33).

49:6 [z] Pr 1:15; Eph 5:11 [a] Ge 34:26 **49:7** [b] Jos 19:1, 9; 21:1-42 **49:8** [c] Dt 33:7; 1Ch 5:2 **49:9** [d] Nu 24:9; Eze 19:5; Mic 5:8 [e] Rev 5:5 **49:10** [f] Nu 24:17, 19; Ps 60:7 [g] Ps 2:9; Isa 42:1, 4 **49:13** [h] Ge 30:20; Dt 33:18-19; Jos 19:10-11 **49:14** [i] Ge 30:18 **49:16** [j] Ge 30:6; Dt 33:22; Jdg 18:26-27 **49:17** [k] Jdg 18:27 **49:18** [l] Ps 119:166, 174 **49:19** [m] Ge 30:11; Dt 33:20; 1Ch 5:18 **49:20** [n] Ge 30:13; Dt 33:24 **49:21** [o] Ge 30:8; Dt 33:23 **49:22** [p] Ge 30:24; Dt 33:13-17 **49:23** [q] Ge 37:24 **49:24** [r] Ps 18:34 [s] Ps 132:2, 5; Isa 1:24; 41:10 [t] Isa 28:16 **49:25** [u] Ge 28:13 [v] Ge 27:28 **49:26** [w] Dt 33:15-16 **49:27** [x] Ge 35:18; Jdg 20:12-13

them when he blessed them, giving each the blessing appropriate to him.

The Death of Jacob

29Then he gave them these instructions:[y] "I am about to be gathered to my people.[z] Bury me with my fathers[a] in the cave in the field of Ephron the Hittite, 30the cave in the field of Machpelah,[b] near Mamre in Canaan, which Abraham bought along with the field[c] as a burial place from Ephron the Hittite. 31There Abraham[d] and his wife Sarah[e] were buried, there Isaac and his wife Rebekah[f] were buried, and there I buried Leah. 32The field and the cave in it were bought from the Hittites.[a]"

33When Jacob had finished giving instructions to his sons, he drew his feet up into the bed, breathed his last and was gathered to his people.[g]

50 Joseph threw himself on his father and wept over him and kissed him.[h] 2Then Joseph directed the physicians in his service to embalm his father Israel. So the physicians embalmed him,[i] 3taking a full forty days, for that was the time required for embalming. And the Egyptians mourned for him seventy days.[j]

4When the days of mourning had passed, Joseph said to Pharaoh's court, "If I have found favor in your eyes, speak to Pharaoh for me. Tell him, 5'My father made me swear an oath[k] and said, "I am about to die; bury me in the tomb I dug for myself[l] in the land of Canaan."[m] Now let me go up and bury my father; then I will return.'"

6Pharaoh said, "Go up and bury your father, as he made you swear to do."

7So Joseph went up to bury his father. All Pharaoh's officials accompanied him—the dignitaries of his court and all the dignitaries of Egypt— 8besides all the members of Joseph's household and his brothers and those belonging to his father's household. Only their children and their flocks and herds were left in Goshen. 9Chariots and horsemen[b] also went up with him. It was a very large company.

10When they reached the threshing floor of Atad, near the Jordan, they lamented loudly and bitterly;[n] and there Joseph observed a seven-day period[o] of mourning for his father. 11When the Canaanites who lived there saw the mourning at the threshing floor of Atad, they said, "The Egyptians are holding a solemn ceremony of mourning." That is why that place near the Jordan is called Abel Mizraim.[c]

12So Jacob's sons did as he had commanded them: 13They carried him to the land of Canaan and buried him in the cave in the field of Machpelah, near Mamre, which Abraham had bought along with the field[p] as a burial place from Ephron the Hittite. 14After burying his father, Joseph returned to Egypt, together with his brothers and all the others who had gone with him to bury his father.

Joseph Reassures His Brothers

15When Joseph's brothers saw that their father was dead, they said, "What if Joseph holds a grudge against us and pays us back for all the wrongs we did to him?"[q] 16So they sent word to Joseph, saying, "Your father left these instructions before he died: 17'This is what you are to say to Joseph: I ask you to forgive your brothers the sins and the wrongs they committed in treating you so badly.' Now please forgive the sins of the servants of the God of your father." When their message came to him, Joseph wept.

18His brothers then came and threw themselves down before him.[r] "We are your slaves,"[s] they said.

19But Joseph said to them, "Don't be afraid. Am I in the place of God?[t] 20You intended to harm me,[u] but God intended[v] it for good[w] to accomplish what is now being done, the saving of many lives.[x] 21So then, don't be afraid. I will provide for you and your children.[y]" And he reassured them and spoke kindly to them.

The Death of Joseph

22Joseph stayed in Egypt, along with all his father's family. He lived a hundred and

---

[a] 32 Or *the descendants of Heth* [b] 9 Or *charioteers* [c] 11 *Abel Mizraim* means *mourning of the Egyptians.*

50:5–6 *swear.* Bound by an oath, Joseph requested leave to bury his father in Canaan in a place ready for his remains. It seems today that we do not take vows as seriously as Joseph took his promise to his father, and everything from casual promises to solemn marriage vows are broken with little remorse. Honoring vows, both in small matters and significant, honors God because He asks us to put away lying and speak truth (Eph. 4:25). Broken vows result in broken hearts and ruined relationships, blasted memories, ineffective lives and testimonies. Even a foolish or wrong vow cannot be lightly set aside, but must be repented of before God. We must learn to promise wisely, and honor our promises faithfully.

50:20 *God intended it for good.* God transformed the evil of a group of men into an exceedingly great work. Joseph not only saved the lives of numerous people in the ancient world, he also testified to the power and goodness of the living God.

49:29 [y] Ge 50:16 [z] Ge 25:8 [a] Ge 15:15; 47:30; 50:13 **49:30** [b] Ge 23:9 [c] Ge 23:20 **49:31** [d] Ge 25:9 [e] Ge 23:19 [f] Ge 35:29 **49:33** [g] ver 29; Ge 25:8; Ac 7:15 **50:1** [h] Ge 46:4 **50:2** [i] ver 26; 2Ch 16:14 **50:3** [j] Ge 37:34; Nu 20:29; Dt 34:8 **50:5** [k] Ge 47:31 [l] 2Ch 16:14; Isa 22:16 [m] Ge 47:31 **50:10** [n] 2Sa 1:17; Ac 8:2 [o] 1Sa 31:13; Job 2:13 **50:13** [p] Ge 23:20; Ac 7:16 **50:15** [q] Ge 37:28; 42:21-22 **50:18** [r] Ge 37:7 [s] Ge 43:18 **50:19** [t] Ro 12:19; Heb 10:30 **50:20** [u] Ge 37:20 [v] Mic 4:11-12 [w] Ro 8:28 [x] Ge 45:5 **50:21** [y] Ge 45:11; 47:12

ten years[z] 23and saw the third generation[a] of Ephraim's children. Also the children of Makir[b] son of Manasseh were placed at birth on Joseph's knees.[a]

24Then Joseph said to his brothers, "I am about to die.[c] But God will surely come to your aid[d] and take you up out of this land to the land[e] he promised on oath to Abraham, Isaac and Jacob."[f] 25And Joseph made the Israelites swear an oath and said, "God will surely come to your aid, and then you must carry my bones up from this place."[g]

26So Joseph died at the age of a hundred and ten. And after they embalmed him,[h] he was placed in a coffin in Egypt.

---

a 23 That is, were counted as his

50:24 ***to Abraham, Isaac and Jacob.*** This phrase is the standard way of referring to God's covenant with Abraham's family (50:24; Ex. 2:24; 3:16). The recital of the three names reaffirms the certainty of the promise and God's commitment to fulfill it.

50:25 ***carry my bones.*** Hundreds of years later, Moses would keep the Israelites' oath by taking Joseph's bones with the people into the wilderness (Ex. 13:19). Finally, Joshua would bury the bones of Joseph at Shechem (Josh. 24:32).

50:22 [z] Ge 25:7; Jos 24:29 **50:23** [a] Job 42:16 [b] Nu 32:39, 40 **50:24** [c] Ge 48:21 [d] Ex 3:16-17 [e] Ge 15:14 [f] Ge 12:7; 26:3; 28:13; 35:12 **50:25** [g] Ge 47:29-30; Ex 13:19; Jos 24:32; Heb 11:22 **50:26** [h] ver 2

EXODUS

▶ **AUTHOR:** Exodus has been attributed to Moses since the time of Joshua (cf. 20:25; Josh. 8:30–32), and there is a great deal of both internal and external evidence that supports Moses as the author. The claims in Joshua are backed by similar testimony from Malachi (4:4), the disciples (John 1:45), Paul (Rom. 10:5), and Christ (Mark 7:10; 12:26; Luke 20:37; John 5:46–47; 7:19,22–23). Portions of the book itself claim the authorship of Moses (ch. 15; 17:8–14; 20:1–17; 24:4,7,12; 31:18; 34:1–27). The author of Exodus must have been a man familiar with the customs and climate of Egypt. Its consistency of style points to a single author and its ancient literary devices support its antiquity.

▶ **TIME:** c. 1875–1445 B.C. ▶ **KEY VERSE:** Ex. 19:5–6

▶ **THEME:** The main character of Exodus is clearly Moses. God gives him the job of leading the exodus from Egypt. Moses also takes on the job of establishing, at God's direction, the essential elements of the Jewish patterns of life and worship. He is simultaneously God's designated representative of the people to God and God's messenger and representative to the people. The critical events in Exodus are the Passover and the giving of the Ten Commandments. The remainder of the Old Testament continually refers back to God's deliverance of Israel from Egypt and the law as delivered at Sinai. In these events God's identity and purpose is revealed. There are many signs and wonders of His power. Aspects of His nature and His expectations of the people also become increasingly clear.

The Israelites Oppressed

1 These are the names of the sons of Israel[a] who went to Egypt with Jacob, each
with his family: 2Reuben, Simeon, Levi and
Judah; 3Issachar, Zebulun and Benjamin;
4Dan and Naphtali; Gad and Asher. 5The
descendants of Jacob numbered seventy[a]
in all;[b] Joseph was already in Egypt.
6Now Joseph and all his brothers and
all that generation died,[c] 7but the Israelites
were exceedingly fruitful; they multiplied
greatly, increased in numbers[d] and became
so numerous that the land was filled with
them.
8Then a new king, to whom Joseph
meant nothing, came to power in Egypt.
9"Look," he said to his people, "the Israelites have become far too numerous[e] for us.
10Come, we must deal shrewdly[f] with them
or they will become even more numerous
and, if war breaks out, will join our enemies, fight against us and leave the country."[g]
11So they put slave masters[h] over them to
oppress them with forced labor,[i] and they
built Pithom and Rameses[j] as store cities[k]

[a] 5 Masoretic Text (see also Gen. 46:27); Dead Sea Scrolls and Septuagint (see also Acts 7:14 and note at Gen. 46:27) *seventy-five*

1:1 ***Israel.*** Originally, Israel was called Jacob. His twelve sons became the founders of the twelve tribes of the nation Israel.
1:2–4 The sons are listed according to their mothers and their ages. Reuben, Simeon, Levi, Judah, Issachar, and Zebulun were all sons of Leah. Benjamin was the son of Rachel. Dan and Naphtali were sons of Bilhah, the maid of Rachel. Gad and Asher were sons of Zilpah, the maid of Leah (for each son's birth, see Gen. 29:31–35; 35:16–20,23–26).
1:8 ***a new king.*** This king did not remember Joseph, his privileged position in the older pharaoh's administration, his administrative skill that saved the Egyptians from starvation, and his enrichment of the pharaoh's treasury. This pharaoh was probably one of the Hyksos kings who descended from foreign invaders. Ethnically they were a minority in Egypt, and they may have perceived the growing numbers of Hebrews as a personal challenge.
1:11–22 ***to oppress them.*** Long before the sons of Israel came to Egypt, Abraham received a remarkable revelation from the Lord (Gen. 15:13–16): his descendants would be strangers in a foreign land and would be enslaved and oppressed for four hundred years.

1:1 [a] Ge 46:8 **1:5** [b] Ge 46:26 **1:6** [c] Ge 50:26 **1:7** [d] Ge 46:3; Dt 26:5; Ac 7:17 **1:9** [e] Ps 105:24-25 **1:10** [f] Ps 83:3 [g] Ac 7:17-19 **1:11** [h] Ex 3:7 [i] Ge 15:13; Ex 2:11; 5:4; 6:6-7 [j] Ge 47:11 [k] 1Ki 9:19; 2Ch 8:4

for Pharaoh. 12But the more they were
oppressed, the more they multiplied and
spread; so the Egyptians came to dread
the Israelites 13and worked them ruthlessly.[l] 14They made their lives bitter with
harsh labor in brick and mortar and with
all kinds of work in the fields; in all their
harsh labor the Egyptians worked them
ruthlessly.[m]
15The king of Egypt said to the Hebrew
midwives, whose names were Shiphrah
and Puah, 16"When you are helping the
Hebrew women during childbirth on the
delivery stool, if you see that the baby is a
boy, kill him; but if it is a girl, let her live."
17The midwives, however, feared[n] God and
did not do what the king of Egypt had told
them to do;[o] they let the boys live. 18Then
the king of Egypt summoned the midwives
and asked them, "Why have you done this?
Why have you let the boys live?"
19The midwives answered Pharaoh, "Hebrew women are not like Egyptian women;
they are vigorous and give birth before the
midwives arrive."[p]
20So God was kind to the midwives[q] and
the people increased and became even
more numerous. 21And because the midwives feared God, he gave them families[r]
of their own.
22Then Pharaoh gave this order to all his
people: "Every Hebrew boy that is born you
must throw into the Nile, but let every girl
live."[s]

The Birth of Moses

2 Now a man of the tribe of Levi married a Levite woman,[t] 2and she became
pregnant and gave birth to a son. When she
saw that he was a fine child, she hid him for
three months.[u] 3But when she could hide
him no longer, she got a papyrus basket[a]
for him and coated it with tar and pitch.
Then she placed the child in it and put it
among the reeds along the bank of the
Nile. 4His sister[v] stood at a distance to see
what would happen to him.
5Then Pharaoh's daughter went down to
the Nile to bathe, and her attendants were
walking along the riverbank.[w] She saw
the basket among the reeds and sent her
female slave to get it. 6She opened it and
saw the baby. He was crying, and she felt
sorry for him. "This is one of the Hebrew
babies," she said.
7Then his sister asked Pharaoh's daughter, "Shall I go and get one of the Hebrew
women to nurse the baby for you?"
8"Yes, go," she answered. So the girl
went and got the baby's mother. 9Phar-
aoh's daughter said to her, "Take this baby
and nurse him for me, and I will pay you."
So the woman took the baby and nursed
him. 10When the child grew older, she took
him to Pharaoh's daughter and he became
her son. She named him Moses,[b] saying, "I
drew him out of the water."

Moses Flees to Midian

11One day, after Moses had grown up, he
went out to where his own people[x] were and
watched them at their hard labor. He saw
an Egyptian beating a Hebrew, one of his

[a] *3* The Hebrew can also mean *ark*, as in Gen. 6:14.
[b] *10 Moses* sounds like the Hebrew for *draw out*.

"In all their distress he too was distressed" (Is. 63:9). At the point when Israel's afflictions became unbearable they cried for help, and God responded in faithfulness to His promise.

1:11 *Pithom and Rameses.* These storage cities are mentioned according to the names by which they were known in later times. The Pharaoh Rameses (whose name presumably relates to the name of one of these cities) was not yet in power.

1:15 *king of Egypt.* This king was probably not the Hyksos king alluded to in verses 8–14. This king, perhaps Thutmose I (c. 1539–1514 B.C.), ruled Egypt when Moses was born (2:1–10). ***Hebrew midwives.*** The names of these women (Shiphrah—"beautiful one," and Puah—"splendid one") are preserved in this account because they were godly women with a courageous faith. At the same time, the names of the pharaohs—the "important" people of the day—are omitted.

1:17 *feared.* The Hebrew term for "fear" is the word regularly used for piety, obedience, and the true worship of God (20:20; Gen. 22:12).

2:2 *gave birth to a son.* This was not their first child, both Miriam and Aaron were older than Moses (v. 4; 7:7).

2:6 *one of the Hebrew babies.* A Hebrew baby would have been circumcised on the eighth day. Although circumcision was practiced in Egypt, it was not done to infants. Upon unwrapping the infant's clothing, the women would have seen his special mark.

2:10 *I drew him out.* In Hebrew, the name Moses means "he who draws out." In this manner, Moses' name can refer the reader to the living God, who is the true Deliverer, and also to Moses, who was used by God to deliver the Israelites from the Red Sea (chs. 14–15). The one who was drawn out of water would be the means of drawing the Israelite nation out of water.

2:11 *after Moses had grown.* The years of Moses' experience in the pharaoh's court are not detailed. Yet Stephen, the New Testament martyr, reported the long-held and surely accurate tradition: "Moses was educated in all the wisdom of the Egyptians and was powerful in speech and action" (Acts 7:22). The training Moses received was the best education the world had to offer at the time. He would have learned three languages: Egyptian, Akkadian, and Hebrew. When Moses came into the presence of Pharaoh to demand freedom for his people, he was no "uneducated slave," but had received an education on a par with the king's.

1:13 [l] Dt 4:20 **1:14** [m] Ex 2:23; 6:9; Nu 20:15; Ps 81:6; Ac 7:19 **1:17** [n] ver 21; Pr 16:6 [o] Da 3:16-18; Ac 4:18-20; 5:29 **1:19** [p] Jos 2:4-6; 2Sa 17:20 **1:20** [q] ver 12; Pr 11:18; Isa 3:10 **1:21** [r] 1Sa 2:35; 2Sa 7:11,27-29; 1Ki 11:38 **1:22** [s] Ac 7:19 **2:1** [t] Ex 6:20; Nu 26:59 **2:2** [u] Ac 7:20; Heb 11:23 **2:4** [v] Ex 15:20; Nu 26:59 **2:5** [w] Ex 7:15; 8:20 **2:11** [x] Ac 7:23; Heb 11:24-26

own people. [12]Looking this way and that and seeing no one, he killed the Egyptian and hid him in the sand. [13]The next day he went out and saw two Hebrews fighting. He asked the one in the wrong, "Why are you hitting your fellow Hebrew?"[y]

[14]The man said, "Who made you ruler and judge over us?[z] Are you thinking of killing me as you killed the Egyptian?" Then Moses was afraid and thought, "What I did must have become known."

[15]When Pharaoh heard of this, he tried to kill Moses, but Moses fled from Pharaoh and went to live in Midian,[a] where he sat down by a well. [16]Now a priest of Midian[b] had seven daughters, and they came to draw water[c] and fill the troughs to water their father's flock. [17]Some shepherds came along and drove them away, but Moses got up and came to their rescue and watered their flock.[d]

[18]When the girls returned to Reuel[e] their father, he asked them, "Why have you returned so early today?"

[19]They answered, "An Egyptian rescued us from the shepherds. He even drew water for us and watered the flock."

[20]"And where is he?" Reuel asked his daughters. "Why did you leave him? Invite him to have something to eat."[f]

[21]Moses agreed to stay with the man, who gave his daughter Zipporah[g] to Moses in marriage. [22]Zipporah gave birth to a son, and Moses named him Gershom,[*a*] saying, "I have become a foreigner[h] in a foreign land."

[23]During that long period,[i] the king of Egypt died. The Israelites groaned in their slavery and cried out, and their cry[j] for help because of their slavery went up to God. [24]God heard their groaning and he remembered his covenant[k] with Abraham, with Isaac and with Jacob. [25]So God looked on the Israelites and was concerned[l] about them.

Moses and the Burning Bush

3 Now Moses was tending the flock of Jethro[m] his father-in-law, the priest of Midian, and he led the flock to the far side of the wilderness and came to Horeb,[n] the mountain[o] of God. [2]There the angel of the LORD[p] appeared to him in flames of fire from within a bush.[q] Moses saw that though the bush was on fire it did not burn up. [3]So Moses thought, "I will go over and see this strange sight—why the bush does not burn up."

[4]When the LORD saw that he had gone over to look, God called to him from within the bush, "Moses! Moses!"

And Moses said, "Here I am."

[5]"Do not come any closer," God said. "Take off your sandals, for the place where you are standing is holy ground."[r] [6]Then he said, "I am the God of your father,[*b*] the God of Abraham, the God of Isaac and the God of Jacob."[s] At this, Moses hid his face, because he was afraid to look at God.

[7]The LORD said, "I have indeed seen the misery of my people in Egypt. I have heard them crying out because of their slave drivers, and I am concerned[t] about their suffering. [8]So I have come down[u] to rescue them from the hand of the Egyptians and to bring them up out of that land into a good and spacious land, a land flowing with milk and honey[v]—the home of the Canaanites, Hittites, Amorites, Perizzites, Hivites and Jebusites.[w] [9]And now the cry of the Israelites has reached me, and I have seen the way the Egyptians are oppressing[x] them. [10]So now, go. I am sending you to Pharaoh to bring my people the Israelites out of Egypt."[y]

---

a *22 Gershom* sounds like the Hebrew for *a foreigner there.* *b* *6* Masoretic Text; Samaritan Pentateuch (see Acts 7:32) *fathers*

2:15 *Midian.* This is the region of the Sinai Peninsula and Arabian deserts where the seminomadic Midianites lived (for the Abrahamic origin of this people group, see Gen. 25:1).
2:16 *a priest of Midian.* This man appears to have been a foreigner who had come to worship the true and living God.
2:18 *Reuel.* Reuel is also called Jethro (4:18).
2:19 *An Egyptian.* Moses apparently still dressed and spoke as an Egyptian, rather than as a Hebrew.
2:22 *Gershom.* Gershom means "a stranger there." Moses was doubly removed from his land. He and his people, the Israelites, were strangers in Egypt, and now he was estranged even from his people.
2:23 *the king of Egypt died.* The death of Pharaoh (likely Thutmose III, who died about 1447 B.C.) meant that Moses could return to Egypt (4:19).
3:1 *Horeb.* This alternate name for Mount Sinai means "desolate place." Yet because of God's appearance on the mountain, this desolate place would become holy. Usually the site of this mountain is identified as Jebel el-Musa, a mountain in the southern Sinai Peninsula.
3:2 *angel.* The word *angel* simply means "messenger" (Mal. 1:1). In the Old Testament, the term "the Angel of the Lord" is used numerous times, and is identified with God as well as being distinguished from Him. In this passage, having mentioned that the Angel of the Lord appeared to Moses, it is immediately established that it was the Lord Himself (v. 4).
3:6 *the God of your father.* God identified Himself as the God worshipped by Abraham, Isaac, and Jacob. In announcing these names, the Lord was assuring Moses that the covenant He had made with them was still intact.

2:13 [y] Ac 7:26 **2:14** [z] Ac 7:27* **2:15** [a] Ac 7:29; Heb 11:27 **2:16** [b] Ex 3:1 [c] Ge 24:11 **2:17** [d] Ge 29:10 **2:18** [e] Nu 10:29 **2:20** [f] Ge 31:54 **2:21** [g] Ex 18:2 **2:22** [h] Ex 18:3-4; Heb 11:13 **2:23** [i] Ac 7:30 [j] Ex 3:7,9; Dt 26:7; Jas 5:4 **2:24** [k] Ex 6:5; Ps 105:10,42 **2:25** [l] Ex 3:7; 4:31 **3:1** [m] Ex 2:18 [n] 1Ki 19:8 [o] Ex 18:5 **3:2** [p] Ge 16:7 [q] Dt 33:16; Mk 12:26; Ac 7:30 **3:5** [r] Ge 28:17; Jos 5:15; Ac 7:33* **3:6** [s] Ex 4:5; Mt 22:32*; Mk 12:26*; Lk 20:37*; Ac 7:32* **3:7** [t] Ex 2:25 **3:8** [u] Ge 50:24 [v] ver 17; Ex 13:5; Dt 1:25 [w] Ge 15:18-21 **3:9** [x] Ex 1:14; 2:23 **3:10** [y] Mic 6:4

11 But Moses said to God, "Who am I[z] that
I should go to Pharaoh and bring the Israelites out of Egypt?"
12 And God said, "I will be with you.[a] And
this will be the sign to you that it is I who
have sent you: When you have brought the
people out of Egypt, you[a] will worship God
on this mountain."
13 Moses said to God, "Suppose I go to the
Israelites and say to them, 'The God of your
fathers has sent me to you,' and they ask
me, 'What is his name?' Then what shall
I tell them?"
14 God said to Moses, "I AM WHO I AM.[b]
This is what you are to say to the Israelites:
'I AM[b] has sent me to you.'"
15 God also said to Moses, "Say to the
Israelites, 'The LORD,[c] the God of your fathers—the God of Abraham, the God of
Isaac and the God of Jacob—has sent me
to you.'

"This is my name[c] forever,
the name you shall call me
from generation to generation.

16 "Go, assemble the elders[d] of Israel and
say to them, 'The LORD, the God of your
fathers—the God of Abraham, Isaac and
Jacob—appeared to me and said: I have
watched over you and have seen what has
been done to you in Egypt. 17 And I have
promised to bring you up out of your misery in Egypt[e] into the land of the Canaanites, Hittites, Amorites, Perizzites, Hivites
and Jebusites—a land flowing with milk
and honey.'
18 "The elders of Israel will listen[f] to you.
Then you and the elders are to go to the
king of Egypt and say to him, 'The LORD,
the God of the Hebrews, has met with us.
Let us take a three-day journey into the
wilderness to offer sacrifices[g] to the LORD
our God.' 19 But I know that the king of
Egypt will not let you go unless a mighty
hand[h] compels him. 20 So I will stretch out
my hand[i] and strike the Egyptians with
all the wonders[j] that I will perform among
them. After that, he will let you go.[k]
21 "And I will make the Egyptians favorably disposed[l] toward this people, so
that when you leave you will not go empty-handed.[m] 22 Every woman is to ask her
neighbor and any woman living in her
house for articles of silver and gold[n] and for
clothing, which you will put on your sons
and daughters. And so you will plunder[o]
the Egyptians."

Signs for Moses

4 Moses answered, "What if they do not
believe me or listen[p] to me and say, 'The
LORD did not appear to you'?"
2 Then the LORD said to him, "What is
that in your hand?"
"A staff,"[q] he replied.
3 The LORD said, "Throw it on the
ground."
Moses threw it on the ground and it became a snake, and he ran from it. 4 Then
the LORD said to him, "Reach out your hand
and take it by the tail." So Moses reached
out and took hold of the snake and it turned
back into a staff in his hand. 5 "This," said
the LORD, "is so that they may believe[r] that
the LORD, the God of their fathers—the
God of Abraham, the God of Isaac and the
God of Jacob—has appeared to you."
6 Then the LORD said, "Put your hand inside your cloak." So Moses put his hand
into his cloak, and when he took it out, the
skin was leprous[d]—it had become as white
as snow.[s]
7 "Now put it back into your cloak," he
said. So Moses put his hand back into his
cloak, and when he took it out, it was restored,[t] like the rest of his flesh.
8 Then the LORD said, "If they do not believe you or pay attention to the first sign,
they may believe the second. 9 But if they
do not believe these two signs or listen to
you, take some water from the Nile and
pour it on the dry ground. The water you
take from the river will become blood[u] on
the ground."
10 Moses said to the LORD, "Pardon your
servant, Lord. I have never been eloquent,
neither in the past nor since you have spoken to your servant. I am slow of speech
and tongue."[v]

---

a 12 The Hebrew is plural. *b 14* Or *I WILL BE WHAT I WILL BE* *c 15* The Hebrew for *LORD* sounds like and may be related to the Hebrew for *I AM* in verse 14. *d 6* The Hebrew word for *leprous* was used for various diseases affecting the skin.

3:14 *I AM WHO I AM.* The One who spoke to Moses declared Himself to be the Eternal One—uncaused and independent. Only the Creator of all things can call Himself the *I AM* in the absolute sense; all other creatures are in debt to Him for their existence. But in addition, God the Creator declares His relationship with the people of Israel. The future tense of the Hebrew verb related to God's name is used in verse 12: The I AM *will be* with His people. Thus God declares His covenantal relationship with Israel by His name.

3:15 *The LORD.* LORD in capital letters is the form translators have chosen to represent the Hebrew name YHWH (also transliterated Yahweh, or Jehovah). The Hebrew word meaning "I Am" used in verse 14 is very similar.

4:6–7 *leprous.* The term *leprosy* included a wide variety of skin diseases.

3:11 [z] Ex 6:12,30; 1Sa 18:18 **3:12** [a] Ge 31:3; Jos 1:5; Ro 8:31 **3:14** [b] Ex 6:2-3; Jn 8:58; Heb 13:8 **3:15** [c] Ps 135:13; Hos 12:5 **3:16** [d] Ex 4:29 **3:17** [e] Ge 15:16; Jos 24:11 **3:18** [f] Ex 4:1,8,31 [g] Ex 5:1,3 **3:19** [h] Ex 4:21; 5:2 **3:20** [i] Ex 6:1,6; 9:15 [j] Dt 6:22; Ne 9:10; Ac 7:36 [k] Ex 12:31-33 **3:21** [l] Ex 12:36 [m] Ps 105:37 **3:22** [n] Ex 11:2 [o] Eze 39:10 **4:1** [p] Ex 3:18; 6:30 **4:2** [q] ver 17,20 **4:5** [r] Ex 19:9 **4:6** [s] Nu 12:10; 2Ki 5:1,27 **4:7** [t] Nu 12:13-15; Dt 32:39; 2Ki 5:14; Mt 8:3 **4:9** [u] Ex 7:17-21 **4:10** [v] Ex 6:12; Jer 1:6

11The LORD said to him, "Who gave human beings their mouths? Who makes
them deaf or mute? Who gives them sight
or makes them blind?[w] Is it not I, the LORD?
12Now go; I will help you speak and will
teach you what to say."[x]
13But Moses said, "Pardon your servant,
Lord. Please send someone else."
14Then the LORD's anger burned against
Moses and he said, "What about your brother, Aaron the Levite? I know he can speak
well. He is already on his way to meet[y] you,
and he will be glad to see you. **15**You shall
speak to him and put words in his mouth;[z]
I will help both of you speak and will teach
you what to do. **16**He will speak to the people for you, and it will be as if he were your
mouth[a] and as if you were God to him. **17**But
take this staff[b] in your hand so you can perform the signs[c] with it."

Moses Returns to Egypt

18Then Moses went back to Jethro his father-in-law and said to him, "Let me return
to my own people in Egypt to see if any of
them are still alive."
Jethro said, "Go, and I wish you well."
19Now the LORD had said to Moses in
Midian, "Go back to Egypt, for all those
who wanted to kill[d] you are dead."[e] **20**So
Moses took his wife and sons, put them on
a donkey and started back to Egypt. And
he took the staff[f] of God in his hand.
21The LORD said to Moses, "When you
return to Egypt, see that you perform before Pharaoh all the wonders[g] I have given
you the power to do. But I will harden his
heart[h] so that he will not let the people go.
22Then say to Pharaoh, 'This is what the
LORD says: Israel is my firstborn son,[i] **23**and
I told you, "Let my son go,[j] so he may worship me." But you refused to let him go; so
I will kill your firstborn son.' "[k]
24At a lodging place on the way, the
LORD met Moses[a] and was about to kill[l]
him. **25**But Zipporah took a flint knife, cut
off her son's foreskin[m] and touched Moses' feet with it.[b] "Surely you are a bridegroom of blood to me," she said. **26**So the
LORD let him alone. (At that time she said
"bridegroom of blood," referring to circumcision.)
27The LORD said to Aaron, "Go into the
wilderness to meet Moses." So he met Moses at the mountain[n] of God and kissed[o]
him. **28**Then Moses told Aaron everything
the LORD had sent him to say,[p] and also
about all the signs he had commanded him
to perform.
29Moses and Aaron brought together all
the elders[q] of the Israelites, **30**and Aaron
told them everything the LORD had said to
Moses. He also performed the signs before
the people, **31**and they believed.[r] And when
they heard that the LORD was concerned[s]
about them and had seen their misery, they
bowed down and worshiped.

Bricks Without Straw

5 Afterward Moses and Aaron went to
Pharaoh and said, "This is what the
LORD, the God of Israel, says: 'Let my people go, so that they may hold a festival[t] to
me in the wilderness.' "
2Pharaoh said, "Who is the LORD,[u] that I
should obey him and let Israel go? I do not
know the LORD and I will not let Israel go."[v]
3Then they said, "The God of the Hebrews has met with us. Now let us take a

---

a *24* Hebrew *him* b *25* The meaning of the Hebrew for this clause is uncertain.

4:19 *who wanted to kill you.* God promised Abraham that those who persecuted Israel would be judged (Gen. 12:3), and it is clear from history that God fulfilled His promise. In Exodus 14, the Egyptians attempted to destroy the Israelites by driving them into the Red Sea, but instead were drowned themselves. Those who threw Daniel to the lions were devoured by those same beasts (Dan. 6). Haman plotted to destroy all the Jews in Persia, and ended up signing his own death warrant (Esth. 7). "The LORD preserves all who love Him" (Ps. 145:20).

4:21 *Pharaoh.* This Pharaoh was most likely Amenhotep II (c. 1447–1421). ***I will harden his heart.*** Some interpret these words to mean that God would confirm what Pharaoh had stubbornly determined to do. In the first five plagues, the hardening was attributed to Pharaoh (7:13,22; 8:15,19,32; 9:7). Then for the sixth plague, God hardened a heart that had already rejected Him (9:12). Others insist that God had determined Pharaoh's negative response to Moses long before Pharaoh could harden his heart. These interpreters point to this verse and to 9:16, in which God says that He raised up Pharaoh for the purpose of demonstrating His power.

4:24 *was about to kill him.* The precise meaning of this passage is unclear. Apparently someone in Moses' family was not circumcised, despite God's command. It is possible that Moses had kept one of his sons uncircumcised in order to please his Midianite family. (The Midianites practiced adult male circumcision at the time of marriage, rather than infant circumcision as the Hebrews did). Moses' neglect of the sign of God's covenant was very serious, especially for the future leader of God's people.

5:2 *Who is the LORD.* Later these words would haunt Pharaoh (12:31–32). Meanwhile, Pharaoh believed himself to be a god in his own right, and certainly felt no need to cave in to the demands of a god who claimed to be the champion of his slave labor force.

4:11 [w] Ps 94:9; Mt 11:5 **4:12** [x] Isa 50:4; Jer 1:9; Mt 10:19-20; Mk 13:11; Lk 12:12; 21:14-15 **4:14** [y] ver 27 **4:15** [z] Nu 23:5, 12, 16 **4:16** [a] Ex 7:1-2 **4:17** [b] ver 2 [c] Ex 7:9-21 **4:19** [d] Ex 2:15 [e] Ex 2:23 **4:20** [f] Ex 17:9; Nu 20:8-9, 11 **4:21** [g] Ex 3:19, 20 [h] Ex 7:3, 13; 9:12, 35; 14:4, 8; Dt 2:30; Isa 63:17; Jn 12:40; Ro 9:18 **4:22** [i] Isa 63:16; 64:8; Jer 31:9; Hos 11:1; Ro 9:4 **4:23** [j] Ex 5:1; 7:16 [k] Ex 11:5; 12:12, 29 **4:24** [l] Nu 22:22 **4:25** [m] Ge 17:14; Jos 5:2, 3 **4:27** [n] Ex 3:1 [o] ver 14 **4:28** [p] ver 8-9, 16 **4:29** [q] Ex 3:16 **4:31** [r] ver 8; Ex 3:18 [s] Ex 2:25 **5:1** [t] Ex 3:18 **5:2** [u] 2Ki 18:35; Job 21:15 [v] Ex 3:19

three-day journey into the wilderness to
offer sacrifices to the LORD our God, or he
may strike us with plagues[w] or with the
sword."
4But the king of Egypt said, "Moses and
Aaron, why are you taking the people away
from their labor?[x] Get back to your work!"
5Then Pharaoh said, "Look, the people of
the land are now numerous,[y] and you are
stopping them from working."
6That same day Pharaoh gave this order
to the slave drivers and overseers in charge
of the people: 7"You are no longer to supply
the people with straw for making bricks;
let them go and gather their own straw.
8But require them to make the same number of bricks as before; don't reduce the
quota. They are lazy; that is why they are
crying out, 'Let us go and sacrifice to our
God.' 9Make the work harder for the people so that they keep working and pay no
attention to lies."
10Then the slave drivers and the overseers went out and said to the people, "This
is what Pharaoh says: 'I will not give you
any more straw. 11Go and get your own
straw wherever you can find it, but your
work will not be reduced at all.'" 12So the
people scattered all over Egypt to gather
stubble to use for straw. 13The slave drivers kept pressing them, saying, "Complete
the work required of you for each day, just
as when you had straw." 14And Pharaoh's
slave drivers beat the Israelite overseers
they had appointed,[z] demanding, "Why
haven't you met your quota of bricks yesterday or today, as before?"
15Then the Israelite overseers went and
appealed to Pharaoh: "Why have you treated your servants this way? 16Your servants
are given no straw, yet we are told, 'Make
bricks!' Your servants are being beaten,
but the fault is with your own people."
17Pharaoh said, "Lazy, that's what you
are—lazy![a] That is why you keep saying, 'Let us go and sacrifice to the LORD.'
18Now get to work. You will not be given
any straw, yet you must produce your full
quota of bricks."
19The Israelite overseers realized they
were in trouble when they were told, "You
are not to reduce the number of bricks required of you for each day." 20When they
left Pharaoh, they found Moses and Aaron waiting to meet them, 21and they said,
"May the LORD look on you and judge you!
You have made us obnoxious[b] to Pharaoh
and his officials and have put a sword in
their hand to kill us."[c]

God Promises Deliverance

22Moses returned to the LORD and said,
"Why, Lord, why have you brought trouble
on this people?[d] Is this why you sent me?
23Ever since I went to Pharaoh to speak in
your name, he has brought trouble on this
people, and you have not rescued[e] your
people at all."

6 Then the LORD said to Moses, "Now you
will see what I will do to Pharaoh: Because of my mighty hand[f] he will let them
go;[g] because of my mighty hand he will
drive them out of his country."[h]
2God also said to Moses, "I am the LORD.
3I appeared to Abraham, to Isaac and to Jacob as God Almighty,[a][i] but by my name[j] the
LORD[b][k] I did not make myself fully known
to them. 4I also established my covenant[l]
with them to give them the land of Canaan,
where they resided as foreigners.[m] 5More-
over, I have heard the groaning[n] of the Israelites, whom the Egyptians are enslaving,
and I have remembered my covenant.
6"Therefore, say to the Israelites: 'I am
the LORD, and I will bring you out from under the yoke of the Egyptians. I will free
you from being slaves to them, and I will
redeem[o] you with an outstretched arm[p]
and with mighty acts of judgment. 7I will
take you as my own people, and I will be
your God.[q] Then you will know[r] that I am
the LORD your God, who brought you out
from under the yoke of the Egyptians.
8And I will bring you to the land[s] I swore
with uplifted hand[t] to give to Abraham, to
Isaac and to Jacob.[u] I will give it to you as a
possession. I am the LORD.'"
9Moses reported this to the Israelites, but
they did not listen to him because of their
discouragement and harsh labor.

---

[a] 3 Hebrew *El-Shaddai* [b] 3 See note at 3:15.

5:7–9 *let them go and gather their own straw.* It is easy to rationalize our cruel treatment of others when it is in our selfish interest to do so. We often hear "Pharaoh's reasoning" about minority peoples or people on welfare today. Of course laziness and discontent is a genuine problem for some who are on welfare, or who feel oppressed (just as it is for some who were born into wealth and privilege), but too often we turn off the concern we should have for the poor and oppressed with the comfortable conviction that somehow they deserve their problems. If we continue in this attitude, we may be sure that God will judge our sin. God cares deeply for the weak, the poor, and the downtrodden; if we are genuine disciples we will share His concern.

5:23 *speak in your name.* It seems that Moses expected Pharaoh to cave in as soon as he heard the use of the Lord's name Yahweh (3:13–15; 5:1). Yet God had warned Moses that Pharaoh would do the opposite (3:19; 4:21).

6:4 *my covenant.* This is a reference to the Abrahamic covenant celebrated in Genesis (Gen. 12:1–3,7; 15:12–21; 17:1–16; 22:15–18).

5:3 [w] Ex 3:18 **5:4** [x] Ex 1:11 **5:5** [y] Ex 1:7, 9
5:14 [z] Isa 10:24 **5:17** [a] ver 8 **5:21** [b] Ge 34:30 [c] Ex 14:11
5:22 [d] Nu 11:11 **5:23** [e] Jer 4:10 **6:1** [f] Ex 3:19 [g] Ex 3:20
[h] Ex 12:31, 33, 39 **6:3** [i] Ge 17:1 [j] Ps 68:4; 83:18; Isa 52:6
[k] Ex 3:14 **6:4** [l] Ge 15:18 [m] Ge 28:4, 13 **6:5** [n] Ex 2:23
6:6 [o] Dt 7:8; 1Ch 17:21 [p] Dt 26:8 **6:7** [q] Dt 4:20; 2Sa 7:24
[r] Ex 16:12; Isa 41:20 **6:8** [s] Ge 15:18; 26:3 [t] Ge 14:22
[u] Ps 136:21-22

10 Then the LORD said to Moses, 11 "Go,
tell Pharaoh king of Egypt to let the Israelites go out of his country."
12 But Moses said to the LORD, "If the Israelites will not listen to me, why would
Pharaoh listen to me, since I speak with
faltering lips[a]?"[v]

Family Record of Moses and Aaron

13 Now the LORD spoke to Moses and Aaron about the Israelites and Pharaoh king of
Egypt, and he commanded them to bring
the Israelites out of Egypt.
14 These were the heads of their families[b]:[w]

The sons of Reuben the firstborn
son of Israel were Hanok and Pallu,
Hezron and Karmi. These were the
clans of Reuben.
15 The sons of Simeon[x] were Jemuel,
Jamin, Ohad, Jakin, Zohar and Shaul
the son of a Canaanite woman. These
were the clans of Simeon.
16 These were the names of the sons
of Levi according to their records: Gershon,[y] Kohath and Merari.[z] Levi lived
137 years.
17 The sons of Gershon, by clans,
were Libni and Shimei.[a]
18 The sons of Kohath were Amram,
Izhar, Hebron and Uzziel.[b] Kohath
lived 133 years.
19 The sons of Merari were Mahli
and Mushi.[c]
These were the clans of Levi according to their records.
20 Amram married his father's sister
Jochebed, who bore him Aaron and
Moses.[d] Amram lived 137 years.
21 The sons of Izhar[e] were Korah,
Nepheg and Zikri.
22 The sons of Uzziel were Mishael,
Elzaphan[f] and Sithri.
23 Aaron married Elisheba, daughter of Amminadab[g] and sister of Nahshon, and she bore him Nadab and
Abihu,[h] Eleazar[i] and Ithamar.[j]
24 The sons of Korah[k] were Assir, Elkanah and Abiasaph. These were the
Korahite clans.
25 Eleazar son of Aaron married one
of the daughters of Putiel, and she bore
him Phinehas.[l]

These were the heads of the Levite
families, clan by clan.
26 It was this Aaron and Moses to whom
the LORD said, "Bring the Israelites out of
Egypt by their divisions."[m] 27 They were
the ones who spoke to Pharaoh king of
Egypt about bringing the Israelites out of
Egypt—this same Moses and Aaron.

Aaron to Speak for Moses

28 Now when the LORD spoke to Moses in
Egypt, 29 he said to him, "I am the LORD.[n]
Tell Pharaoh king of Egypt everything I
tell you."
30 But Moses said to the LORD, "Since I
speak with faltering lips,[o] why would Pharaoh listen to me?"
7 Then the LORD said to Moses, "See,
I have made you like God[p] to Pharaoh, and your brother Aaron will be your
prophet. 2 You are to say everything I command you, and your brother Aaron is to
tell Pharaoh to let the Israelites go out of
his country. 3 But I will harden Pharaoh's
heart,[q] and though I multiply my signs and
wonders in Egypt, 4 he will not listen[r] to
you. Then I will lay my hand on Egypt and
with mighty acts of judgment[s] I will bring
out my divisions, my people the Israelites.
5 And the Egyptians will know that I am the
LORD[t] when I stretch out my hand[u] against
Egypt and bring the Israelites out of it."
6 Moses and Aaron did just as the LORD
commanded[v] them. 7 Moses was eighty
years old[w] and Aaron eighty-three when
they spoke to Pharaoh.

Aaron's Staff Becomes a Snake

8 The LORD said to Moses and Aaron,
9 "When Pharaoh says to you, 'Perform a
miracle,[x]' then say to Aaron, 'Take your
staff and throw it down before Pharaoh,'
and it will become a snake."[y]

a *12* Hebrew *I am uncircumcised of lips*; also in verse 30 *b* *14* The Hebrew for *families* here and in verse 25 refers to units larger than clans.

6:14–27 *their families.* The family history of Moses, Aaron, and Miriam is important because all of Israel's future priests would come from this family.
7:1 *your prophet.* As Moses was the prophet of the Lord, so Aaron became Moses' prophet. Aaron would speak for Moses, for a prophet was the "mouth" of the one who sent him.
7:3 *I will harden Pharaoh's heart.* It was a part of God's plan that Pharaoh would be inflexibly stubborn, thus setting the scene for God to deliver His people by powerful signs and wonders.
7:7 *eighty . . . eighty-three.* These men had already lived as long as the average lifetime of our day before their principal life work had begun. Moses and Aaron each lived another forty years as leaders of the nation of Israel.

7:9–10 Miracles—A miracle could be defined as the temporary suspension of some natural law (like turning a staff into a snake), or the manipulation of natural forces (such as weather) over which humans

6:12 [v] ver 30; Ex 4:10; Jer 1:6 **6:14** [w] Ge 46:9
6:15 [x] Ge 46:10; 1Ch 4:24 **6:16** [y] Ge 46:11 [z] Nu 3:17
6:17 [a] 1Ch 6:17 **6:18** [b] 1Ch 6:2, 18 **6:19** [c] Nu 3:20, 33; 1Ch 6:19; 23:21 **6:20** [d] Ex 2:1-2; Nu 26:59
6:21 [e] 1Ch 6:38 **6:22** [f] Lev 10:4; Nu 3:30
6:23 [g] Ru 4:19, 20 [h] Lev 10:1 [i] Nu 3:2, 32 [j] Nu 26:60
6:24 [k] Nu 26:11 **6:25** [l] Nu 25:7, 11; Jos 24:33; Ps 106:30
6:26 [m] Ex 7:4; 12:17, 41, 51 **6:29** [n] ver 11; Ex 7:2
6:30 [o] ver 12; Ex 4:10 **7:1** [p] Ex 4:16 **7:3** [q] Ex 4:21; 11:9
7:4 [r] Ex 11:9 [s] Ex 3:20; 6:6 **7:5** [t] ver 17; Ex 8:19, 22 [u] Ex 3:20 **7:6** [v] ver 2 **7:7** [w] Dt 31:2; 34:7; Ac 7:23, 30
7:9 [x] Isa 7:11; Jn 2:18 [y] Ex 4:2-5

10 So Moses and Aaron went to Pharaoh and did just as the LORD commanded. Aaron threw his staff down in front of
Pharaoh and his officials, and it became
a snake. 11 Pharaoh then summoned wise
men and sorcerers, and the Egyptian magicians[z] also did the same things by their
secret arts:[a] 12 Each one threw down his
staff and it became a snake. But Aaron's
staff swallowed up their staffs. 13 Yet Pharaoh's heart[b] became hard and he would not
listen to them, just as the LORD had said.

The Plague of Blood

14 Then the LORD said to Moses, "Pharaoh's heart is unyielding;[c] he refuses to
let the people go. 15 Go to Pharaoh in the
morning as he goes out to the river. Confront him on the bank of the Nile, and take
in your hand the staff that was changed
into a snake. 16 Then say to him, 'The LORD,
the God of the Hebrews, has sent me to say
to you: Let my people go, so that they may
worship[d] me in the wilderness. But until
now you have not listened. 17 This is what
the LORD says: By this you will know that
I am the LORD:[e] With the staff that is in my
hand I will strike the water of the Nile, and
it will be changed into blood.[f] 18 The fish in
the Nile will die, and the river will stink;
the Egyptians will not be able to drink its
water.'"[g]
19 The LORD said to Moses, "Tell Aaron, 'Take your staff and stretch out your
hand[h] over the waters of Egypt—over the
streams and canals, over the ponds and
all the reservoirs—and they will turn to
blood.' Blood will be everywhere in Egypt,
even in vessels[a] of wood and stone."
20 Moses and Aaron did just as the LORD
had commanded. He raised his staff in the
presence of Pharaoh and his officials and
struck the water of the Nile,[i] and all the
water was changed into blood.[j] 21 The fish
in the Nile died, and the river smelled so
bad that the Egyptians could not drink its
water. Blood was everywhere in Egypt.
22 But the Egyptian magicians did the
same things by their secret arts,[k] and
Pharaoh's heart became hard; he would
not listen to Moses and Aaron, just as the
LORD had said. 23 Instead, he turned and
went into his palace, and did not take even
this to heart. 24 And all the Egyptians dug
along the Nile to get drinking water, because they could not drink the water of the
river.

The Plague of Frogs

25 Seven days passed after the LORD
8[b] struck the Nile. 1 Then the LORD said to
Moses, "Go to Pharaoh and say to him,
'This is what the LORD says: Let my people
go, so that they may worship[l] me. 2 If you
refuse to let them go, I will send a plague
of frogs on your whole country. 3 The Nile
will teem with frogs. They will come up
into your palace and your bedroom and
onto your bed, into the houses of your officials and on your people,[m] and into your
ovens and kneading troughs. 4 The frogs
will come up on you and your people and
all your officials.'"
5 Then the LORD said to Moses, "Tell Aaron, 'Stretch out your hand with your staff[n]
over the streams and canals and ponds,
and make frogs come up on the land of
Egypt.'"
6 So Aaron stretched out his hand over
the waters of Egypt, and the frogs[o] came up
and covered the land. 7 But the magicians
did the same things by their secret arts;[p]
they also made frogs come up on the land
of Egypt.

---

[a] *19* Or *even on their idols* [b] In Hebrew texts 8:1-4 is numbered 7:26-29, and 8:5-32 is numbered 8:1-28.

---

ordinarily have no jurisdiction. We tend to look for miracles only for their immediate results (healing, retribution, etc.), but in the Bible miracles are always for a "sign." The focus isn't on the actual miracle, but on the supernatural as a sign of God's working in the situation. This is clearly seen in the miracles of Jesus. If His purpose had just been physical healing, He would have set up a clinic and systematically healed everyone. Instead, His miracles were for a sign, to let people know who and what He was (John 20:30–31).

7:11 ***wise men ... sorcerers ... magicians.*** The king's wise men were his counselors, men of learning and insight. In ancient times, the "wise men" of a court were often associated with occult practices. The power of these men may have been in trickery and slight-of-hand illusions, or demonic power. Later the royal courts of Israel had wise men (1 Kin. 4:34; Prov. 25:1), but the black arts of sorcery, divination, and astrology were forbidden (Deut. 18:9–14).

7:12 ***his staff ... snake.*** The text does not say whether this was a genuine transformation or a trick of Pharaoh's evil sorcerers. Whatever the case, their serpents were no match for the serpent of God's sign.

7:15 ***to the river ... the bank of the Nile.*** Pharaoh went to the waters of the Nile not to bathe but to be empowered. Pharaoh's bath in the Nile was a sacred Egyptian rite connected to his claim of divinity. The plague on the waters of the Nile was a direct attack on the Egyptian religion.

7:23 ***turned and went into his palace.*** Pharaoh showed his utter disdain for the revelation of God's power and his complete lack of concern for the suffering of his own people.

8:7 ***the magicians ... by their secret arts.*** We do not know how or in what quantities the magicians produced frogs, but doing so hardly helped the situation. Clearly the power they had was not strong enough to counteract the plagues God sent.

7:11 [z] Ge 41:8; 2Ti 3:8 [a] ver 22; Ex 8:7, 18 **7:13** [b] Ex 4:21 **7:14** [c] Ex 8:15, 32; 10:1, 20, 27 **7:16** [d] Ex 3:18; 5:1, 3 **7:17** [e] Ex 5:2 [f] Ex 4:9; Rev 11:6; 16:4 **7:18** [g] ver 21, 24 **7:19** [h] Ex 8:5-6, 16; 9:22; 10:12, 21; 14:21 **7:20** [i] Ex 17:5 [j] Ps 78:44; 105:29 **7:22** [k] ver 11 **8:1** [l] Ex 3:12, 18; 4:23 **8:3** [m] Ex 10:6 **8:5** [n] Ex 7:19 **8:6** [o] Ps 78:45; 105:30 **8:7** [p] Ex 7:11

8 Pharaoh summoned Moses and Aar-
on and said, "Pray[q] to the LORD to take the
frogs away from me and my people, and I
will let your people go to offer sacrifices[r]
to the LORD."
9 Moses said to Pharaoh, "I leave to you the
honor of setting the time for me to pray for
you and your officials and your people that
you and your houses may be rid of the frogs,
except for those that remain in the Nile."
10 "Tomorrow," Pharaoh said.
Moses replied, "It will be as you say, so
that you may know there is no one like the
LORD our God.[s] 11 The frogs will leave you
and your houses, your officials and your
people; they will remain only in the Nile."
12 After Moses and Aaron left Pharaoh,
Moses cried out to the LORD about the
frogs he had brought on Pharaoh. 13 And
the LORD did what Moses asked. The frogs
died in the houses, in the courtyards and
in the fields. 14 They were piled into heaps,
and the land reeked of them. 15 But when
Pharaoh saw that there was relief, he hardened his heart[t] and would not listen to Moses and Aaron, just as the LORD had said.

The Plague of Gnats

16 Then the LORD said to Moses, "Tell
Aaron, 'Stretch out your staff and strike
the dust of the ground,' and throughout the
land of Egypt the dust will become gnats."
17 They did this, and when Aaron stretched
out his hand with the staff and struck the
dust of the ground, gnats[u] came on people
and animals. All the dust throughout the
land of Egypt became gnats. 18 But when
the magicians[v] tried to produce gnats by
their secret arts,[w] they could not.
Since the gnats were on people and animals everywhere, 19 the magicians said to
Pharaoh, "This is the finger[x] of God." But
Pharaoh's heart was hard and he would not
listen, just as the LORD had said.

The Plague of Flies

20 Then the LORD said to Moses, "Get up
early in the morning[y] and confront Pharaoh as he goes to the river and say to him,
'This is what the LORD says: Let my people
go, so that they may worship[z] me. 21 If you
do not let my people go, I will send swarms
of flies on you and your officials, on your
people and into your houses. The houses of
the Egyptians will be full of flies; even the
ground will be covered with them.
22 "'But on that day I will deal differently
with the land of Goshen, where my people
live;[a] no swarms of flies will be there, so
that you will know[b] that I, the LORD, am
in this land. 23 I will make a distinction*[a]*
between my people and your people. This
sign will occur tomorrow.'"
24 And the LORD did this. Dense swarms
of flies poured into Pharaoh's palace and
into the houses of his officials; throughout
Egypt the land was ruined by the flies.[c]
25 Then Pharaoh summoned[d] Moses and
Aaron and said, "Go, sacrifice to your God
here in the land."
26 But Moses said, "That would not be
right. The sacrifices we offer the LORD our
God would be detestable to the Egyptians.[e]
And if we offer sacrifices that are detestable in their eyes, will they not stone us?
27 We must take a three-day journey into
the wilderness to offer sacrifices[f] to the
LORD our God, as he commands us."
28 Pharaoh said, "I will let you go to offer
sacrifices to the LORD your God in the wilderness, but you must not go very far. Now
pray[g] for me."
29 Moses answered, "As soon as I leave
you, I will pray to the LORD, and tomorrow
the flies will leave Pharaoh and his officials and his people. Only let Pharaoh be
sure that he does not act deceitfully[h] again
by not letting the people go to offer sacrifices to the LORD."
30 Then Moses left Pharaoh and prayed
to the LORD,[i] 31 and the LORD did what Moses asked. The flies left Pharaoh and his
officials and his people; not a fly remained.
32 But this time also Pharaoh hardened his
heart[j] and would not let the people go.

---

a 23 Septuagint and Vulgate; Hebrew *will put a deliverance*

8:8 *summoned Moses and Aaron.* Note that Pharaoh did not turn to his magicians to relieve the land of the frogs.

8:15 Instability—The action of this Egyptian pharaoh is a case study in instability. He gave permission for the people to go and then changed his mind more than once. He alternated between denying the power of God and actually admitting his sin. Pharaoh was a rebel against God, tossed about by his own lack of integrity. Believers can take warning from Pharaoh's behavior. The apostle James informs us that a double-minded man is unstable in all his ways (James 1:8). But stability isn't something we achieve by sheer willpower. Real integrity and stability comes from the security of our relationship with God.

8:18 the magicians . . . secret arts . . . they could not. Perhaps the lack of announcement meant they had no time to prepare. The magicians could not duplicate God's work; further proof that this was no trick, but the hand of God.

8:26 *detestable to the Egyptians.* Moses employed the ethnic and cultural sensibilities of the Egyptians to free the Israelites (Gen. 43:32; 46:34). The sacrificial animals of Israel would include sheep, something the Egyptians regarded as detestable.

8:8 [q] ver 28; Ex 9:28; 10:17 [r] ver 25 **8:10** [s] Ex 9:14; Dt 4:35; 33:26; 2Sa 7:22; 1Ch 17:20; Ps 86:8; Isa 46:9; Jer 10:6 **8:15** [t] Ex 7:14 **8:17** [u] Ps 105:31 **8:18** [v] Ex 9:11; Da 5:8 [w] Ex 7:11 **8:19** [x] Ex 7:5; 10:7; Ps 8:3; Lk 11:20 **8:20** [y] Ex 7:15; 9:13 [z] ver 1; Ex 3:18 **8:22** [a] Ex 9:4, 6, 26; 10:23; 11:7 [b] Ex 7:5; 9:29 **8:24** [c] Ps 78:45; 105:31 **8:25** [d] ver 8; Ex 9:27 **8:26** [e] Ge 43:32; 46:34 **8:27** [f] Ex 3:18 **8:28** [g] ver 8; Ex 9:28; 1Ki 13:6 **8:29** [h] ver 15 **8:30** [i] ver 12 **8:32** [j] ver 8, 15; Ex 4:21

The Plague on Livestock

9 Then the LORD said to Moses, "Go to Pharaoh and say to him, 'This is what the LORD, the God of the Hebrews, says: "Let my people go, so that they may worship[k] me." 2If you refuse to let them go and continue to hold them back, 3the hand[l] of the LORD will bring a terrible plague on your livestock in the field—on your horses, donkeys and camels and on your cattle, sheep and goats. 4But the LORD will make a distinction between the livestock of Israel and that of Egypt,[m] so that no animal belonging to the Israelites will die.'"

5The LORD set a time and said, "Tomorrow the LORD will do this in the land." 6And the next day the LORD did it: All the livestock[n] of the Egyptians died,[o] but not one animal belonging to the Israelites died. 7Pharaoh investigated and found that not even one of the animals of the Israelites had died. Yet his heart was unyielding and he would not let the people go.[p]

The Plague of Boils

8Then the LORD said to Moses and Aaron, "Take handfuls of soot from a furnace and have Moses toss it into the air in the presence of Pharaoh. 9It will become fine dust over the whole land of Egypt, and festering boils[q] will break out on people and animals throughout the land."

10So they took soot from a furnace and stood before Pharaoh. Moses tossed it into the air, and festering boils broke out on people and animals. 11The magicians[r] could not stand before Moses because of the boils that were on them and on all the Egyptians. 12But the LORD hardened Pharaoh's heart[s] and he would not listen to Moses and Aaron, just as the LORD had said to Moses.

The Plague of Hail

13Then the LORD said to Moses, "Get up early in the morning, confront Pharaoh and say to him, 'This is what the LORD, the God of the Hebrews, says: Let my people go, so that they may worship[t] me, 14or this time I will send the full force of my plagues against you and against your officials and your people, so you may know[u] that there is no one like[v] me in all the earth. 15For by now I could have stretched out my hand and struck you and your people[w] with a plague that would have wiped you off the earth. 16But I have raised you up[a] for this very purpose,[x] that I might show you my power[y] and that my name might be proclaimed in all the earth. 17You still set yourself against my people and will not let them go. 18Therefore, at this time tomorrow I will send the worst hailstorm[z] that has ever fallen on Egypt, from the day it was founded till now.[a] 19Give an order now to bring your livestock and everything you have in the field to a place of shelter, because the hail will fall on every person and animal that has not been brought in and is still out in the field, and they will die.'"

20Those officials of Pharaoh who feared[b] the word of the LORD hurried to bring their slaves and their livestock inside. 21But those who ignored the word of the LORD left their slaves and livestock in the field.

22Then the LORD said to Moses, "Stretch out your hand toward the sky so that hail will fall all over Egypt—on people and animals and on everything growing in the fields of Egypt." 23When Moses stretched out his staff toward the sky, the LORD sent thunder[c] and hail,[d] and lightning flashed down to the ground. So the LORD rained hail on the land of Egypt; 24hail fell and lightning flashed back and forth. It was the worst storm in all the land of Egypt since it had become a nation. 25Throughout Egypt hail struck everything in the fields—both people and animals; it beat down everything growing in the fields and stripped every tree.[e] 26The only place it did not hail was the land of Goshen,[f] where the Israelites were.[g]

27Then Pharaoh summoned Moses and Aaron. "This time I have sinned,"[h] he said to them. "The LORD is in the right,[i] and I

a 16 Or *have spared you*

9:11 ***the boils that were on them.*** The reference to the hapless magicians is almost humorous. Not only were they powerless, but they also suffered from the plague.

9:16 ***I have raised you up for this very purpose.*** God used Pharaoh's stubbornness and disobedience to demonstrate His power. Pharaoh was not only an evil ruler in a powerful state; he was an evil man, ungodly, and unrighteous. Pharaoh set himself up as a god who maintained the stability of his kingdom. The Lord's judgment on him was an appropriate response to this fraud.

9:17 ***set yourself against.*** Pharaoh was behaving like the king of Tyre (Ezek. 28:1–10) and Satan, whom the king of Tyre emulated (Ezek. 28:11–19).

9:19 ***bring your livestock.*** The fact that God was judging Pharaoh does not mean that He was unmerciful. The Lord could have destroyed Pharaoh and his people in a moment (v. 15), but instead He warned them of the calamities about to befall them. Apparently some of the Egyptians took the word of the Lord seriously.

9:27 ***I have sinned.*** This was a stunning admission for such a proud man. Sadly, these words of

9:1 [k] Ex 8:1 **9:3** [l] Ex 7:4 **9:4** [m] ver 26; Ex 8:22 **9:6** [n] ver 19-21; Ex 11:5 [o] Ps 78:48-50 **9:7** [p] Ex 7:14; 8:32 **9:9** [q] Dt 28:27, 35; Rev 16:2 **9:11** [r] Ex 8:18 **9:12** [s] Ex 4:21 **9:13** [t] Ex 8:20 **9:14** [u] Ex 8:10 [v] 2Sa 7:22; 1Ch 17:20; Ps 86:8; Isa 46:9; Jer 10:6 **9:15** [w] Ex 3:20 **9:16** [x] Pr 16:4 [y] Ro 9:17* **9:18** [z] ver 23 [a] ver 24 **9:20** [b] Pr 13:13 **9:23** [c] Ps 18:13 [d] Jos 10:11; Ps 78:47; 105:32; Isa 30:30; Eze 38:22; Rev 8:7; 16:21 **9:25** [e] Ps 105:32-33 **9:26** [f] ver 4 [g] Ex 8:22; 10:23; 11:7; 12:13 **9:27** [h] Ex 10:16 [i] 2Ch 12:6; Ps 129:4; La 1:18

and my people are in the wrong. 28Pray[j] to the LORD, for we have had enough thunder and hail. I will let you go;[k] you don't have to stay any longer."

29Moses replied, "When I have gone out of the city, I will spread out my hands[l] in prayer to the LORD. The thunder will stop and there will be no more hail, so you may know that the earth[m] is the LORD's. 30But I know that you and your officials still do not fear the LORD God."

31(The flax and barley[n] were destroyed, since the barley had headed and the flax was in bloom. 32The wheat and spelt, however, were not destroyed, because they ripen later.)

33Then Moses left Pharaoh and went out of the city. He spread out his hands toward the LORD; the thunder and hail stopped, and the rain no longer poured down on the land. 34When Pharaoh saw that the rain and hail and thunder had stopped, he sinned again: He and his officials hardened their hearts. 35So Pharaoh's heart[o] was hard and he would not let the Israelites go, just as the LORD had said through Moses.

The Plague of Locusts

10 Then the LORD said to Moses, "Go to Pharaoh, for I have hardened his heart[p] and the hearts of his officials so that I may perform these signs[q] of mine among them 2that you may tell your children[r] and grandchildren how I dealt harshly with the Egyptians and how I performed my signs among them, and that you may know that I am the LORD."

3So Moses and Aaron went to Pharaoh and said to him, "This is what the LORD, the God of the Hebrews, says: 'How long will you refuse to humble[s] yourself before me? Let my people go, so that they may worship me. 4If you refuse to let them go, I will bring locusts[t] into your country tomorrow. 5They will cover the face of the ground so that it cannot be seen. They will devour what little you have left[u] after the hail, including every tree that is growing in your fields. 6They will fill your houses and those of all your officials and all the Egyptians—something neither your parents nor your ancestors have ever seen from the day they settled in this land till now.'" Then Moses turned and left Pharaoh.

7Pharaoh's officials said to him, "How long will this man be a snare[v] to us? Let the people go, so that they may worship the LORD their God. Do you not yet realize that Egypt is ruined?"[w]

8Then Moses and Aaron were brought back to Pharaoh. "Go, worship[x] the LORD your God," he said. "But tell me who will be going."

9Moses answered, "We will go with our young and our old, with our sons and our daughters, and with our flocks and herds, because we are to celebrate a festival to the LORD."

10Pharaoh said, "The LORD be with you—if I let you go, along with your women and children! Clearly you are bent on evil.[a] 11No! Have only the men go and worship the LORD, since that's what you have been asking for." Then Moses and Aaron were driven out of Pharaoh's presence.

12And the LORD said to Moses, "Stretch out your hand[y] over Egypt so that locusts swarm over the land and devour everything growing in the fields, everything left by the hail."

13So Moses stretched out his staff over Egypt, and the LORD made an east wind blow across the land all that day and all that night. By morning the wind had brought the locusts;[z] 14they invaded all Egypt and settled down in every area of the country in great numbers. Never before had there been such a plague of locusts,[a] nor will there ever be again. 15They covered all the ground until it was black. They devoured[b] all that was left after the hail—everything growing in the fields and the fruit on the trees. Nothing green remained on tree or plant in all the land of Egypt.

16Pharaoh quickly summoned Moses and Aaron and said, "I have sinned[c] against the LORD your God and against you. 17Now

[a] 10 Or *Be careful, trouble is in store for you!*

---

contrition would not hold. Pharaoh repeated them later (10:16–17), only to take them back in the end.

10:1 *I have hardened his heart.* Three verbs are used in Exodus to describe God's hardening of Pharaoh's heart. Usually the verb meaning "to make hard" is used (4:21). In 7:3 the verb "to make stiff" is used. Here the Hebrew verb that means "to make heavy" or "to make insensitive" is used.

10:3 *refuse to humble yourself.* Pharaoh's pride was his undoing. He believed himself to be a god and paraded himself like one. God resists the proud but gives grace to the humble (Ps. 18:27; 1 Pet. 5:5).

10:12–16 Repentance — In Exodus 9 and 10 there are two vivid examples of "foxhole religion" recorded for us. This kind of "faith" freely acknowledges the person and power of God during a terrible crisis, and then promptly forgets all about Him when the danger passes. Just like little children, we want to avert punishment by saying, "I'm sorry, I'm sorry!" and then go about our business as usual. God is not interested in empty "I've sinned" confessions. Only true repentance from the heart is acceptable to God.

9:28 [j] Ex 10:17 [k] Ex 8:8 **9:29** [l] 1Ki 8:22,38; Ps 143:6; Isa 1:15 [m] Ex 19:5; Ps 24:1; 1Co 10:26 **9:31** [n] Ru 1:22; 2:23 **9:35** [o] Ex 4:21 **10:1** [p] Ex 4:21 [q] Ex 7:3 **10:2** [r] Ex 12:26-27; 13:8,14; Dt 4:9; Ps 44:1; 78:4,5; Joel 1:3 **10:3** [s] 1Ki 21:29; Jas 4:10; 1Pe 5:6 **10:4** [t] Rev 9:3 **10:5** [u] Ex 9:32; Joel 1:4 **10:7** [v] Ex 23:33; Jos 23:13; 1Sa 18:21; Ecc 7:26 [w] Ex 8:19 **10:8** [x] Ex 8:8 **10:12** [y] Ex 7:19 **10:13** [z] Ps 105:34 **10:14** [a] Ps 78:46; Joel 2:1-11,25 **10:15** [b] ver 5; Ps 105:34-35 **10:16** [c] Ex 9:27

forgive my sin once more and pray[d] to the LORD your God to take this deadly plague away from me."

18Moses then left Pharaoh and prayed to the LORD.[e] 19And the LORD changed the wind to a very strong west wind, which caught up the locusts and carried them into the Red Sea.[a] Not a locust was left anywhere in Egypt. 20But the LORD hardened Pharaoh's heart,[f] and he would not let the Israelites go.

The Plague of Darkness

21Then the LORD said to Moses, "Stretch out your hand toward the sky so that darkness[g] spreads over Egypt—darkness that can be felt." 22So Moses stretched out his hand toward the sky, and total darkness[h] covered all Egypt for three days. 23No one could see anyone else or move about for three days. Yet all the Israelites had light in the places where they lived.[i]

24Then Pharaoh summoned Moses and said, "Go, worship the LORD. Even your women and children[j] may go with you; only leave your flocks and herds behind."

25But Moses said, "You must allow us to have sacrifices and burnt offerings to present to the LORD our God. 26Our livestock too must go with us; not a hoof is to be left behind. We have to use some of them in worshiping the LORD our God, and until we get there we will not know what we are to use to worship the LORD."

27But the LORD hardened Pharaoh's heart,[k] and he was not willing to let them go. 28Pharaoh said to Moses, "Get out of my sight! Make sure you do not appear before me again! The day you see my face you will die."

29"Just as you say," Moses replied. "I will never appear[l] before you again."

The Plague on the Firstborn

11 Now the LORD had said to Moses, "I will bring one more plague on Pharaoh and on Egypt. After that, he will let you go from here, and when he does, he will drive you out completely. 2Tell the people that men and women alike are to ask their neighbors for articles of silver and gold."[m] 3(The LORD made the Egyptians favorably disposed toward the people, and Moses himself was highly regarded[n] in Egypt by Pharaoh's officials and by the people.)

4So Moses said, "This is what the LORD says: 'About midnight[o] I will go throughout Egypt. 5Every firstborn[p] son in Egypt will die, from the firstborn son of Pharaoh, who sits on the throne, to the firstborn son of the female slave, who is at her hand mill, and all the firstborn of the cattle as well. 6There will be loud wailing[q] throughout Egypt—worse than there has ever been or ever will be again. 7But among the Israelites not a dog will bark at any person or animal.' Then you will know that the LORD makes a distinction[r] between Egypt and Israel. 8All these officials of yours will come to me, bowing down before me and saying, 'Go,[s] you and all the people who follow you!' After that I will leave." Then Moses, hot with anger, left Pharaoh.

9The LORD had said to Moses, "Pharaoh will refuse to listen[t] to you—so that my wonders may be multiplied in Egypt." 10Moses and Aaron performed all these wonders before Pharaoh, but the LORD hardened Pharaoh's heart,[u] and he would not let the Israelites go out of his country.

[a] 19 Or *the Sea of Reeds*

10:20 *But the LORD hardened Pharaoh's heart.* See 3:19; 4:21; 5:2; 7:3,13–14.

10:22 *total darkness.* This calamity was another direct attack on the Egyptian religious system. They worshipped many gods, but none so much as the sun. An enshrouding darkness that lasted three days was a clear statement that their gods, their Pharaoh with his supposed control of nature, and all Pharaoh's counselors were, in reality, helpless before the God of Israel.

10:27 *But the LORD hardened Pharaoh's heart.* See 3:19; 4:21; 5:2; 7:3,13–14.

11:3 *favorably.* After all that had happened, we might suppose that the Egyptians would have universally hated the Hebrews. Instead, most of the people felt positively towards them, even Pharaoh's own servants.

11:7 *a distinction between Egypt and Israel.* The institution of the Passover accentuated this great distinction. The Lord in His mercy protected His people even as He executed judgment on those who opposed Him.

11:9–10 *wonders.* We tend to think that if God would only send a miracle, people would have to believe. Sadly, history shows that this is not true. Often those individuals who have seen God's mightiest miracles have responded by displaying a total lack of faith. Pharaoh had all the proof one could want of who God was, and did not believe. The Pharisees saw a man raised from the dead, and wanted to kill both the man and his healer (John 11:53; 12:9–11). God desires us to believe His word by faith, and not be dependent on supernatural and external signs and wonders. Miracles are signs, just as the creation itself is a sign of God's power and authority (Rom. 1:19–20), but a person whose heart is hardened toward God will not be any more impressed with a miracle than with a sunset.

10:17 [d] Ex 8:8 **10:18** [e] Ex 8:30 **10:20** [f] Ex 4:21; 11:10
10:21 [g] Dt 28:29 **10:22** [h] Ps 105:28; Rev 16:10
10:23 [i] Ex 8:22 **10:24** [j] ver 8-10 **10:27** [k] ver 20; Ex 4:21
10:29 [l] Heb 11:27 **11:2** [m] Ex 3:21,22 **11:3** [n] Dt 34:11
11:4 [o] Ex 12:29 **11:5** [p] Ex 4:23; Ps 78:51 **11:6** [q] Ex 12:30
11:7 [r] Ex 8:22 **11:8** [s] Ex 12:31-33 **11:9** [t] Ex 7:4
11:10 [u] Ex 4:21; 10:20,27

The Passover and the Festival of Unleavened Bread

12 The LORD said to Moses and Aaron in Egypt, 2“This month is to be for you the first month,[v] the first month of your year. 3Tell the whole community of Israel that on the tenth day of this month each man is to take a lamb[a] for his family, one for each household. 4If any household is too small for a whole lamb, they must share one with their nearest neighbor, having taken into account the number of people there are. You are to determine the amount of lamb needed in accordance with what each person will eat. 5The animals you choose must be year-old males without defect,[w] and you may take them from the sheep or the goats. 6Take care of them until the fourteenth day of the month,[x] when all the members of the community of Israel must slaughter them at twilight.[y] 7Then they are to take some of the blood and put it on the sides and tops of the doorframes of the houses where they eat the lambs. 8That same night[z] they are to eat the meat roasted[a] over the fire, along with bitter herbs,[b] and bread made without yeast.[c] 9Do not eat the meat raw or boiled in water, but roast it over a fire—with the head, legs and internal organs. 10Do not leave any of it till morning;[d] if some is left till morning, you must burn it. 11This is how you are to eat it: with your cloak tucked into your belt, your sandals on your feet and your staff in your hand. Eat it in haste;[e] it is the LORD’s Passover.[f]

12“On that same night I will pass through[g] Egypt and strike down every firstborn of both people and animals, and I will bring judgment on all the gods[h] of Egypt. I am the LORD.[i] 13The blood will be a sign for you on the houses where you are, and when I see the blood, I will pass over you. No destructive plague will touch you when I strike Egypt.

14“This is a day you are to commemorate;[j] for the generations to come you shall celebrate it as a festival to the LORD—a lasting ordinance.[k] 15For seven days you are to eat bread made without yeast.[l] On the first day remove the yeast from your houses, for whoever eats anything with yeast in it from the first day through the seventh must be cut off[m] from Israel. 16On the first day hold a sacred assembly, and another one on the seventh day. Do no work at all on these days, except to prepare food for everyone to eat; that is all you may do.

17“Celebrate the Festival of Unleavened Bread, because it was on this very day that I brought your divisions out of Egypt.[n] Celebrate this day as a lasting ordinance for the generations to come. 18In the first month[o] you are to eat bread made without yeast, from the evening of the fourteenth day until the evening of the twenty-first day. 19For seven days no yeast is to be found in your houses. And anyone, whether foreigner or native-born, who eats anything with yeast in it must be cut off from the community of Israel. 20Eat nothing made with yeast. Wherever you live, you must eat unleavened bread.”

21Then Moses summoned all the elders of Israel and said to them, “Go at once and select the animals for your families and slaughter the Passover[p] lamb. 22Take a bunch of hyssop, dip it into the blood in the basin and put some of the blood[q] on the top and on both sides of the doorframe. None of you shall go out of the door of your house until morning. 23When the LORD goes through the land to strike down the Egyptians, he will see the blood[r] on the top and

---

[a] 3 The Hebrew word can mean *lamb* or *kid*; also in verse 4.

12:1 – 14 The Passover—There was only one Passover. The Passover feast has always been one of the primary elements of Jewish religious tradition and is their way of remembering the “pass over” by the Lord, sparing the people of a visit by “the destroyer” (v. 23). By celebrating it, Jews remember one of the key elements of their history. It points to their national identity and to their deliverance as a community of faith. One could say that it was a defining moment of their faith. For the Christian, the event clearly foreshadows the cross of Christ. He is our Passover Lamb who delivers us from death by taking it all on Himself. The parallels between Exodus 12 and the Christian communion service are noteworthy (1 Cor. 11:23 – 26).

12:2 *the first month.* This month, called Abib in 13:4 corresponds to April/May and is also called Nisan. The Hebrew people began to mark time in relation to the time of their departure from Egypt.

12:5 *without defect.* Sacrifice was not a way to get rid of unwanted animals. Only the very best lambs were suitable. The Passover lamb sacrificed for the Israelites was meant as a picture of the coming death of the perfect, sinless Savior, Jesus Christ.

12:8 *bitter herbs . . . bread made without yeast.* The Passover meal is full of symbolism, the unleavened bread reminded them that the first Passover was eaten in haste, ready for flight. The bitter herbs were a reminder of the bitterness of the slavery from which they were rescued.

12:12 *I will pass through . . . I will bring.* The repetition of the pronoun *I* emphasizes that God did this, not an angel or some other agent.

12:13 *sign.* The term “sign” can mean a reminder, memorial, or symbol, as it does here, or a miracle that points to the power of God.

12:2 [v] Ex 13:4; Dt 16:1 **12:5** [w] Lev 22:18-21; Heb 9:14 **12:6** [x] Lev 23:5; Nu 9:1-3, 5, 11 [y] Ex 16:12; Dt 16:4, 6 **12:8** [z] Ex 34:25; Nu 9:12 [a] Dt 16:7 [b] Nu 9:11 [c] Dt 16:3-4; 1Co 5:8 **12:10** [d] Ex 23:18; 34:25 **12:11** [e] Dt 16:3 [f] ver 13, 21, 27, 43; Dt 16:1 **12:12** [g] Ex 11:4; Am 5:17 [h] Nu 33:4 [i] Ex 6:2 **12:14** [j] Ex 13:9 [k] ver 17, 24; Ex 13:5, 10; 2Ki 23:21 **12:15** [l] Ex 13:6-7; 23:15; 34:18; Lev 23:6; Dt 16:3 [m] Ge 17:14; Nu 9:13 **12:17** [n] ver 41; Ex 13:3 **12:18** [o] ver 2; Lev 23:5-8; Nu 28:16-25 **12:21** [p] ver 11; Mk 14:12-16 **12:22** [q] ver 7; Heb 11:28 **12:23** [r] Rev 7:3

sides of the doorframe and will pass over[s]
that doorway, and he will not permit the
destroyer[t] to enter your houses and strike
you down.
24 "Obey these instructions as a lasting
ordinance for you and your descendants.
25 When you enter the land that the LORD
will give you as he promised, observe this
ceremony. 26 And when your children[u] ask
you, 'What does this ceremony mean to
you?' 27 then tell them, 'It is the Passover[v]
sacrifice to the LORD, who passed over the
houses of the Israelites in Egypt and spared
our homes when he struck down the Egyptians.'" Then the people bowed down and
worshiped.[w] 28 The Israelites did just what
the LORD commanded Moses and Aaron.
29 At midnight[x] the LORD struck down all
the firstborn[y] in Egypt, from the firstborn
of Pharaoh, who sat on the throne, to the
firstborn of the prisoner, who was in the
dungeon, and the firstborn of all the livestock[z] as well. 30 Pharaoh and all his officials and all the Egyptians got up during
the night, and there was loud wailing[a] in
Egypt, for there was not a house without
someone dead.

The Exodus

31 During the night Pharaoh summoned
Moses and Aaron and said, "Up! Leave my
people, you and the Israelites! Go, worship[b]
the LORD as you have requested. 32 Take
your flocks and herds,[c] as you have said,
and go. And also bless me."
33 The Egyptians urged the people to hurry and leave[d] the country. "For otherwise,"
they said, "we will all die!" 34 So the people took their dough before the yeast was
added, and carried it on their shoulders in
kneading troughs wrapped in clothing.
35 The Israelites did as Moses instructed
and asked the Egyptians for articles of
silver and gold[e] and for clothing. 36 The
LORD had made the Egyptians favorably
disposed toward the people, and they gave
them what they asked for; so they plundered[f] the Egyptians.
37 The Israelites journeyed from Rameses to Sukkoth.[g] There were about six
hundred thousand men[h] on foot, besides
women and children. 38 Many other people[i]
went up with them, and also large droves
of livestock, both flocks and herds. 39 With
the dough the Israelites had brought from
Egypt, they baked loaves of unleavened
bread. The dough was without yeast because they had been driven out[j] of Egypt
and did not have time to prepare food for
themselves.
40 Now the length of time the Israelite people lived in Egypt[a] was 430 years.[k]
41 At the end of the 430 years, to the very
day, all the LORD's divisions[l] left Egypt.[m]
42 Because the LORD kept vigil that night to
bring them out of Egypt, on this night all
the Israelites are to keep vigil to honor the
LORD for the generations to come.[n]

Passover Restrictions

43 The LORD said to Moses and Aaron,
"These are the regulations for the Passover meal:[o]

---

[a] *40* Masoretic Text; Samaritan Pentateuch and Septuagint *Egypt and Canaan*

12:29–33 *the LORD struck down all the firstborn.* In the Passover we have a summary of God's eternal plan of salvation. Jesus, the final sacrifice, was killed at the time of the Passover feast; His blood provides salvation from eternal death. Note some similarities between the first and final Passover: (1) the blood of an innocent sacrifice must be shed, (2) the sacrifice must be blameless, and (3) the shed blood must be applied by faith.

12:29 *the firstborn of all the livestock.* Though not nearly as awful as the death of firstborn children, the death of the livestock was a blow to the Egyptians economically. These deaths were also attacks on the power of their gods (v. 12).

12:32 *And also bless me.* At last Pharaoh capitulated (10:9,26). The death of his son—and the deaths of firstborn sons everywhere—must have shattered him to the core of his being.

12:36 *plundered the Egyptians.* Newly freed slaves do not usually make their escape with their masters pushing the family silver into their hands. Far from wanting to keep the Israelites in bondage, the rest of Egypt couldn't wait to get rid of them.

12:37 *Rameses.* The reference to Rameses most likely relates to the store city Rameses, mentioned in 1:11, perhaps Tel el-Maskhuta further to the east. ***six hundred thousand men.*** This number of men would indicate a total population of perhaps three million men, women, and children (Num. 1:46).

12:38 *many other people.* Apparently a number of Egyptians and perhaps other non-Hebrews joined the flight out of Egypt. Some of these people later caused trouble when things did not go as smoothly as expected (Num. 11:4).

12:39 *unleavened bread.* The symbolism in this has to do with the haste of their departure, not (as some have supposed) that there is something evil in leaven itself. If leaven were intrinsically evil, the Israelites would have been forbidden to eat leaven at any time. In the New Testament, leaven is often used as a symbolic way of speaking about sin, but again, leaven in and of itself is not evil.

12:40 *430 years.* If the exodus took place around 1446 B.C., Jacob's arrival in Egypt would have been around 1876 B.C.

12:23 [s] ver 13 [t] 1Co 10:10; Heb 11:28 **12:26** [u] Ex 10:2; 13:8, 14-15; Jos 4:6 **12:27** [v] ver 11 [w] Ex 4:31 **12:29** [x] Ex 11:4 [y] Ex 4:23; Ps 78:51 [z] Ex 9:6 **12:30** [a] Ex 11:6 **12:31** [b] Ex 8:8 **12:32** [c] Ex 10:9, 26 **12:33** [d] Ps 105:38 **12:35** [e] Ex 3:22 **12:36** [f] Ex 3:22 **12:37** [g] Nu 33:3-5 [h] Ex 38:26; Nu 1:46; 11:13, 21 **12:38** [i] Nu 11:4 **12:39** [j] ver 31-33; Ex 6:1; 11:1 **12:40** [k] Ge 15:13; Ac 7:6; Gal 3:17 **12:41** [l] ver 17; Ex 6:26 [m] Ex 3:10 **12:42** [n] Ex 13:10; Dt 16:1, 6 **12:43** [o] ver 11

“No foreigner[p] may eat it. 44Any slave
you have bought may eat it after you have
circumcised[q] him, 45but a temporary resident or a hired worker[r] may not eat it.
46“It must be eaten inside the house; take
none of the meat outside the house. Do not
break any of the bones.[s] 47The whole community of Israel must celebrate it.
48“A foreigner residing among you who
wants to celebrate the LORD’s Passover
must have all the males in his household
circumcised; then he may take part like
one born in the land.[t] No uncircumcised
male may eat it. 49The same law applies
both to the native-born and to the foreigner[u] residing among you.”

50All the Israelites did just what the LORD
had commanded Moses and Aaron. 51And
on that very day the LORD brought the Israelites out of Egypt by their divisions.[v]

Consecration of the Firstborn

13 The LORD said to Moses, 2“Consecrate
to me every firstborn male.[w] The first
offspring of every womb among the Israelites belongs to me, whether human or
animal.”
3Then Moses said to the people, “Commemorate this day, the day you came out
of Egypt, out of the land of slavery, because
the LORD brought you out of it with a mighty
hand.[x] Eat nothing containing yeast.[y] 4To-
day, in the month of Aviv,[z] you are leaving.
5When the LORD brings you into the land
of the Canaanites, Hittites, Amorites, Hivites and Jebusites[a]—the land he swore to
your ancestors to give you, a land flowing
with milk and honey—you are to observe
this ceremony[b] in this month: 6For seven
days eat bread made without yeast and
on the seventh day hold a festival[c] to the
LORD. 7Eat unleavened bread during those
seven days; nothing with yeast in it is to
be seen among you, nor shall any yeast be
seen anywhere within your borders. 8On
that day tell your son,[d] ‘I do this because of
what the LORD did for me when I came out
of Egypt.’ 9This observance will be for you
like a sign on your hand and a reminder
on your forehead[e] that this law of the LORD
is to be on your lips. For the LORD brought
you out of Egypt with his mighty hand.
10You must keep this ordinance[f] at the appointed time year after year.
11“After the LORD brings you into the
land of the Canaanites and gives it to you,
as he promised on oath to you and your ancestors, 12you are to give over to the LORD
the first offspring of every womb. All the
firstborn males of your livestock belong
to the LORD.[g] 13Redeem with a lamb every
firstborn donkey, but if you do not redeem
it, break its neck.[h] Redeem every firstborn
among your sons.[i]
14“In days to come, when your son[j] asks
you, ‘What does this mean?’ say to him,
‘With a mighty hand the LORD brought us
out of Egypt, out of the land of slavery.[k]
15When Pharaoh stubbornly refused to let
us go, the LORD killed the firstborn of both
people and animals in Egypt. This is why
I sacrifice to the LORD the first male offspring of every womb and redeem each of
my firstborn sons.’[l] 16And it will be like a
sign on your hand and a symbol on your
forehead[m] that the LORD brought us out of
Egypt with his mighty hand.”

Crossing the Sea

17When Pharaoh let the people go, God
did not lead them on the road through the
Philistine country, though that was shorter. For God said, “If they face war, they
might change their minds and return to
Egypt.”[n] 18So God led[o] the people around
by the desert road toward the Red Sea.[a]
The Israelites went up out of Egypt ready
for battle.[p]

a 18 Or *the Sea of Reeds*

12:46 *Do not break any of the bones.* Not breaking the bones of the lamb foreshadowed Jesus' death. None of the Savior's bones were broken, even though He suffered a horrible death (Ps. 34:20; John 19:33–36).

13:1–22 *Consecrate to me.* Before the dramatic story of the crossing of the Red Sea there is a record of foundational institutions that the Lord gave to Israel. These are: (1) the consecration of the firstborn (vv. 1–2); (2) the Feast of Unleavened Bread (vv. 3–10); and (3) the law concerning the firstborn (vv. 11–16). This is followed by the Lord's command to the Israelites to travel in an unexpected direction (vv. 17–22).

13:9 *sign.* A similar commandment is found in Deuteronomy 6:8. Jews would fasten a small box containing passages of Scripture to their foreheads or arms during prayer, to serve as a memorial. The physical symbol was designed to be a reminder of the inner reality of making God's law the guiding rule of all we do.

13:13 *firstborn donkey.* Donkeys were unclean animals, and could not be used as a sacrifice. Instead they were redeemed with a lamb. Similarly, a firstborn son was redeemed. God would never allow human sacrifice. Later the Lord claimed the Levites for Himself in exchange for the firstborn sons of the people (Num. 3:40–51).

13:18 *desert road.* The route the Israelites traveled from Egypt to Canaan has been disputed. The traditional route has the people moving in a southerly

12:43 [p] ver 48; Nu 9:14 **12:44** [q] Ge 17:12-13
12:45 [r] Lev 22:10 **12:46** [s] Nu 9:12; Jn 19:36*
12:48 [t] Nu 9:14 **12:49** [u] Nu 15:15-16, 29; Gal 3:28
12:51 [v] ver 41; Ex 6:26 **13:2** [w] ver 12, 13, 15; Ex 22:29; Nu 3:13; Dt 15:19; Lk 2:23* **13:3** [x] Ex 3:20; 6:1 [y] Ex 12:19
13:4 [z] Ex 12:2 **13:5** [a] Ex 3:8 [b] Ex 12:25-26
13:6 [c] Ex 12:15-20 **13:8** [d] ver 14; Ex 10:2; Ps 78:5-6
13:9 [e] ver 16; Dt 6:8; 11:18 **13:10** [f] Ex 12:24-25
13:12 [g] Lev 27:26; Lk 2:23* **13:13** [h] Ex 34:20 [i] Nu 18:15
13:14 [j] Ex 10:2; 12:26-27; Dt 6:20 [k] ver 3, 9
13:15 [l] Ex 12:29 **13:16** [m] ver 9 **13:17** [n] Ex 14:11; Nu 14:1-4; Dt 17:16 **13:18** [o] Ps 136:16 [p] Jos 1:14

19Moses took the bones of Joseph[q] with
him because Joseph had made the Israelites swear an oath. He had said, "God
will surely come to your aid, and then you
must carry my bones up with you from this
place."[a][r]
20After leaving Sukkoth they camped at
Etham on the edge of the desert.[s] 21By day
the LORD went ahead of them in a pillar of
cloud[t] to guide them on their way and by
night in a pillar of fire to give them light,
so that they could travel by day or night.
22Neither the pillar of cloud by day nor the
pillar of fire by night left its place in front
of the people.

14 Then the LORD said to Moses, 2"Tell
the Israelites to turn back and encamp near Pi Hahiroth, between Migdol[u]
and the sea. They are to encamp by the sea,
directly opposite Baal Zephon. 3Pharaoh
will think, 'The Israelites are wandering
around the land in confusion, hemmed in
by the desert.' 4And I will harden Pharaoh's heart,[v] and he will pursue them. But
I will gain glory[w] for myself through Pharaoh and all his army, and the Egyptians
will know that I am the LORD."[x] So the Israelites did this.
5When the king of Egypt was told that
the people had fled, Pharaoh and his officials changed their minds about them and
said, "What have we done? We have let the
Israelites go and have lost their services!"
6So he had his chariot made ready and took
his army with him. 7He took six hundred
of the best chariots, along with all the other chariots of Egypt, with officers over all
of them. 8The LORD hardened the heart[y] of
Pharaoh king of Egypt, so that he pursued
the Israelites, who were marching out boldly.[z] 9The Egyptians—all Pharaoh's horses
and chariots, horsemen[b] and troops—pursued the Israelites and overtook[a] them as
they camped by the sea near Pi Hahiroth,
opposite Baal Zephon.
10As Pharaoh approached, the Israelites
looked up, and there were the Egyptians,
marching after them. They were terrified
and cried[b] out to the LORD. 11They said
to Moses, "Was it because there were no
graves in Egypt that you brought us to the
desert to die?[c] What have you done to us
by bringing us out of Egypt? 12Didn't we
say to you in Egypt, 'Leave us alone; let us
serve the Egyptians'? It would have been
better for us to serve the Egyptians than to
die in the desert!"
13Moses answered the people, "Do not
be afraid.[d] Stand firm and you will see[e]
the deliverance the LORD will bring you today. The Egyptians you see today you will
never see[f] again. 14The LORD will fight[g] for
you; you need only to be still."[h]
15Then the LORD said to Moses, "Why are
you crying out to me? Tell the Israelites to
move on. 16Raise your staff[i] and stretch out
your hand over the sea to divide the water[j]
so that the Israelites can go through the sea
on dry ground. 17I will harden the hearts of
the Egyptians so that they will go in after
them.[k] And I will gain glory through Pharaoh and all his army, through his chariots
and his horsemen. 18The Egyptians will
know that I am the LORD when I gain glory through Pharaoh, his chariots and his
horsemen."
19Then the angel of God, who had been
traveling in front of Israel's army, withdrew and went behind them. The pillar of
cloud[l] also moved from in front and stood
behind them, 20coming between the armies
of Egypt and Israel. Throughout the night
the cloud brought darkness to the one side
and light to the other side; so neither went
near the other all night long.
21Then Moses stretched out his hand over
the sea, and all that night the LORD drove
the sea back with a strong east wind[m] and
turned it into dry land. The waters were

---

a *19* See Gen. 50:25. *b* *9* Or *charioteers*; also in verses 17, 18, 23, 26 and 28

---

direction along the western shore of the Sinai Peninsula until they reached Mount Sinai in the far south central region of the peninsula. ***Red Sea.*** This translation comes from the Septuagint (the Greek translation of the Old Testament); the Hebrew phrase means "Sea of Reeds." This phrase may refer to the ancient northern extension of the Red Sea. Many believe that it was one of the marshy lakes of the region.

13:19 ***the bones of Joseph.*** The story of the last wish of Joseph and his death is found in Genesis 50:22–26.

14:11–12 ***What have you done.*** This marks the first of ten episodes of Israel's unbelief, beginning at the Red Sea, and concluding at Kadesh Barnea (Num. 14:22). Because of these ten events an entire generation was prevented from entering the Promised Land. The New Testament book of Hebrews recalls these events, using the Promised Land as a picture of heaven and warning that disobedience and unbelief will still keep people out of the final land of "rest" (Heb. 4).

14:13 ***the deliverance the LORD will bring.*** The Hebrew word for salvation comes from a term that has to do with room or space. The people were under great pressure, squeezed between the waters before them and the armies of Pharaoh behind them. Salvation relieved the pressure in a most dramatic way.

14:19 ***angel of God.*** The term "angel of God" is an alternative expression for the angel of the Lord. The pillar of cloud is later strongly associated with the Lord Himself (33:9–11).

13:19 [q] Jos 24:32; Ac 7:16 [r] Ge 50:24-25 **13:20** [s] Nu 33:6 **13:21** [t] Ex 14:19, 24; 33:9-10; Nu 9:16; Dt 1:33; Ne 9:12, 19; Ps 78:14; 99:7; 105:39; Isa 4:5; 1Co 10:1 **14:2** [u] Nu 33:7; Jer 44:1 **14:4** [v] Ex 4:21 [w] Ro 9:17, 22-23 [x] Ex 7:5 **14:8** [y] ver 4; Ex 11:10 [z] Nu 33:3; Ac 13:17 **14:9** [a] Ex 15:9 **14:10** [b] Jos 24:7; Ne 9:9; Ps 34:17 **14:11** [c] Ps 106:7-8 **14:13** [d] Ge 15:1 [e] 2Ch 20:17; Isa 41:10, 13-14 [f] ver 30 **14:14** [g] ver 25; Ex 15:3; Dt 1:30; 3:22; 2Ch 20:29 [h] Ps 37:7; 46:10; Isa 30:15 **14:16** [i] Ex 4:17; Nu 20:8-9, 11 [j] Isa 10:26 **14:17** [k] ver 4 **14:19** [l] Ex 13:21 **14:21** [m] Ex 15:8

divided,[n] 22and the Israelites went through
the sea on dry ground,[o] with a wall of water
on their right and on their left.
23The Egyptians pursued them, and all
Pharaoh's horses and chariots and horsemen followed them into the sea. 24During
the last watch of the night the LORD looked
down from the pillar of fire and cloud[p] at
the Egyptian army and threw it into confusion. 25He jammed[a] the wheels of their
chariots so that they had difficulty driving.
And the Egyptians said, "Let's get away
from the Israelites! The LORD is fighting[q]
for them against Egypt."
26Then the LORD said to Moses, "Stretch
out your hand over the sea so that the waters may flow back over the Egyptians
and their chariots and horsemen." 27Mo-
ses stretched out his hand over the sea,
and at daybreak the sea went back to its
place.[r] The Egyptians were fleeing toward[b]
it, and the LORD swept them into the sea.[s]
28The water flowed back and covered the
chariots and horsemen—the entire army
of Pharaoh that had followed the Israelites
into the sea. Not one of them survived.
29But the Israelites went through the sea
on dry ground,[t] with a wall of water on
their right and on their left. 30That day the
LORD saved[u] Israel from the hands of the
Egyptians, and Israel saw the Egyptians
lying dead on the shore. 31And when the
Israelites saw the mighty hand of the LORD
displayed against the Egyptians, the people feared the LORD and put their trust[v] in
him and in Moses his servant.

The Song of Moses and Miriam

15 Then Moses and the Israelites sang this song[w] to the LORD:

"I will sing[x] to the LORD,
for he is highly exalted.
Both horse and driver
he has hurled into the sea.

2 "The LORD is my strength[y] and my defense[c];
he has become my salvation.[z]
He is my God,[a] and I will praise him,
my father's God, and I will exalt[b] him.
3 The LORD is a warrior;[c]
the LORD is his name.[d]
4 Pharaoh's chariots and his army[e]
he has hurled into the sea.
The best of Pharaoh's officers
are drowned in the Red Sea.[d]
5 The deep waters have covered them;
they sank to the depths like a stone.[f]
6 Your right hand,[g] LORD,
was majestic in power.
Your right hand, LORD,
shattered the enemy.

7 "In the greatness of your majesty
you threw down those who opposed you.
You unleashed your burning anger;[h]
it consumed them like stubble.
8 By the blast of your nostrils[i]
the waters piled up.[j]
The surging waters stood up like a wall;[k]
the deep waters congealed in the heart of the sea.
9 The enemy boasted,
'I will pursue,[l] I will overtake them.
I will divide the spoils;[m]
I will gorge myself on them.
I will draw my sword
and my hand will destroy them.'
10 But you blew with your breath,
and the sea covered them.
They sank like lead
in the mighty waters.[n]
11 Who among the gods
is like you,[o] LORD?
Who is like you—
majestic in holiness,[p]
awesome in glory,[q]
working wonders?

[a] *25* See Samaritan Pentateuch, Septuagint and Syriac; Masoretic Text *removed* [b] *27* Or *from* [c] *2* Or *song* [d] *4* Or *the Sea of Reeds*; also in verse 22

14:25 *the LORD is fighting for them.* This was the confession the Lord demanded; word spread widely that the Lord fought for the Israelites.
14:31 *the people . . . put their trust in him.* Similar wording is used of Abraham's saving faith in Genesis 15:6 (see also Rom. 4). The people were transformed spiritually even as they were delivered physically.
15:2 *my father's God.* The Israelites had worshipped, believed, and obeyed. Today, Christians are part of Abraham's line because they also believe, obey, and worship the same God (Gal. 3:6–7). Many faithful believers have preceded us.
15:3 *the LORD is his name.* Other supposed gods had secret names that only guilds of priests knew. By knowing a god's secret name, a priest supposedly had special access to that god. But the living God had made His name known to all, and salvation is found in His name alone.
15:11 *Who among the gods is like you.* Many times, the Bible uses the language of incomparability to describe the true God. In a world in which there are many supposed gods, the Lord is unique. He alone is God. He is not just better than other gods; there *are* no other gods. No person, god, or thing can be compared to the one true God (Ps. 96:4; Is. 40:25–26; Mic. 7:18).

14:21 [n] Ps 74:13; 114:5; Isa 63:12 **14:22** [o] Ex 15:19; Ne 9:11; Ps 66:6; Heb 11:29 **14:24** [p] Ex 13:21 **14:25** [q] ver 14 **14:27** [r] Jos 4:18 [s] Ex 15:1,21; Ps 78:53; 106:11 **14:29** [t] ver 22 **14:30** [u] Ps 106:8, 10, 21 **14:31** [v] Ps 106:12; Jn 2:11 **15:1** [w] Rev 15:3 [x] Ps 106:12 **15:2** [y] Ps 59:17 [z] Ps 18:2, 46; Isa 12:2; Hab 3:18 [a] Ge 28:21 [b] Ex 3:6, 15-16; Isa 25:1 **15:3** [c] Ex 14:14; Ps 24:8; Rev 19:11 [d] Ex 6:2-3, 7-8; Ps 83:18 **15:4** [e] Ex 14:6-7 **15:5** [f] ver 10; Ne 9:11 **15:6** [g] Ps 118:15 **15:7** [h] Ps 78:49-50 **15:8** [i] Ex 14:21 [j] Ps 78:13 [k] Ex 14:22 **15:9** [l] Ex 14:5-9 [m] Jdg 5:30; Isa 53:12 **15:10** [n] ver 5; Ex 14:27-28 **15:11** [o] Ex 8:10; Dt 3:24; Ps 77:13 [p] Isa 6:3; Rev 4:8 [q] Ps 8:1

12 "You stretch out your right hand,
and the earth swallows your enemies.
13 In your unfailing love you will lead[r]
the people you have redeemed.
In your strength you will guide them
to your holy dwelling.[s]
14 The nations will hear and tremble;[t]
anguish will grip the people of
Philistia.
15 The chiefs[u] of Edom will be terrified,
the leaders of Moab will be seized
with trembling,[v]
the people[a] of Canaan will melt[w] away;
16 terror[x] and dread will fall on them.
By the power of your arm
they will be as still as a stone[y]—
until your people pass by, LORD,
until the people you bought[bz] pass by.
17 You will bring them in and plant[a] them
on the mountain[b] of your
inheritance—
the place, LORD, you made for your
dwelling,
the sanctuary, Lord, your hands
established.

18 "The LORD reigns
for ever and ever."

19When Pharaoh's horses, chariots and
horsemen[c] went into the sea,[c] the LORD
brought the waters of the sea back over
them, but the Israelites walked through
the sea on dry ground.[d] 20Then Miriam[e]
the prophet,[f] Aaron's sister, took a timbrel
in her hand, and all the women followed
her, with timbrels and dancing.[g] 21Miriam
sang to them:

"Sing to the LORD,
for he is highly exalted.
Both horse and driver
he has hurled into the sea."[h]

The Waters of Marah and Elim

22Then Moses led Israel from the Red
Sea and they went into the Desert of Shur.
For three days they traveled in the desert
without finding water. 23When they came
to Marah, they could not drink its water because it was bitter. (That is why the place
is called Marah.[di]) 24So the people grumbled[j] against Moses, saying, "What are we
to drink?"
25Then Moses cried out[k] to the LORD, and
the LORD showed him a piece of wood. He
threw it into the water, and the water became fit to drink.
There the LORD issued a ruling and instruction for them and put them to the
test.[l] 26He said, "If you listen carefully to
the LORD your God and do what is right in
his eyes, if you pay attention to his commands and keep all his decrees,[m] I will not
bring on you any of the diseases[n] I brought
on the Egyptians, for I am the LORD, who
heals[o] you."
27Then they came to Elim, where there
were twelve springs and seventy palm
trees, and they camped[p] there near the water.

Manna and Quail

16 The whole Israelite community set out
from Elim and came to the Desert of
Sin,[q] which is between Elim and Sinai, on
the fifteenth day of the second month after
they had come out of Egypt. 2In the desert
the whole community grumbled[r] against
Moses and Aaron. 3The Israelites said to
them, "If only we had died by the LORD's
hand in Egypt![s] There we sat around pots
of meat and ate all the food[t] we wanted, but
you have brought us out into this desert to
starve this entire assembly to death."
4Then the LORD said to Moses, "I will
rain down bread from heaven[u] for you. The
people are to go out each day and gather
enough for that day. In this way I will test

---

a *15* Or *rulers* *b* *16* Or *created* *c* *19* Or *charioteers* *d* *23* *Marah* means *bitter.*

15:18 *The LORD reigns for ever and ever.* Ultimately, the salvation of Israel from Egypt points to the coming reign of the living God on earth over His redeemed people.

This victory song ends with the assertion of the eternal rule of the Lord, promising the kingdom of God rather than the conquering of neighboring lands. Its emphasis is spiritual, not material. Now that deliverance from slavery in Egypt had been accomplished, the Hebrews would be formed by God into a nation which was designed to be a witness to the rest of the world of God's character and authority.

15:20 *Miriam the prophet.* Although there is no record of women serving as priests in ancient Israel, women did serve as prophetesses (Deborah, Judg. 4:4; the wife of Isaiah, Is. 8:3; Huldah, 2 Kin. 22:14). As a prophetess, Miriam spoke authoritatively from God. However, it is apparent that neither she nor Aaron had the level of intimacy with God that Moses had.

15:24 *grumbled.* The people's recent deliverance from the Egyptian armies makes this complaint seem fickle and a true test of God's mercy. We are like the Israelites far too often, turning from praise to complaint at a moment's notice.

15:27 *Elim.* Elim means "place of trees." The wells and palms of this oasis would have been a welcome relief from the barren wasteland.

16:1 *Desert of Sin.* The location of this wasteland is uncertain; its position between Elim and Sinai depends on the location of Mount Sinai. (The name Sin has nothing to do with the English word "sin").

15:13 [r] Ne 9:12; Ps 77:20 [s] Ps 78:54 **15:14** [t] Dt 2:25 **15:15** [u] Ge 36:15 [v] Nu 22:3 [w] Jos 5:1 **15:16** [x] Ex 23:27; Jos 2:9 [y] 1Sa 25:37 [z] Ps 74:2 **15:17** [a] Ps 44:2 [b] Ps 78:54, 68 **15:19** [c] Ex 14:28 [d] Ex 14:22 **15:20** [e] Nu 26:59 [f] Jdg 4:4 [g] Jdg 11:34; 1Sa 18:6; Ps 30:11; 150:4 **15:21** [h] ver 1; Ex 14:27 **15:23** [i] Nu 33:8 **15:24** [j] Ex 14:12; 16:2 **15:25** [k] Ex 14:10 [l] Jdg 3:4 **15:26** [m] Dt 7:12 [n] Dt 28:27, 58-60 [o] Ex 23:25-26 **15:27** [p] Nu 33:9 **16:1** [q] Nu 33:11, 12 **16:2** [r] Ex 14:11; 15:24; 1Co 10:10 **16:3** [s] Ex 17:3 [t] Nu 11:4, 34 **16:4** [u] Dt 8:3; Jn 6:31*

them and see whether they will follow my
instructions. 5On the sixth day they are to
prepare what they bring in, and that is to be
twice[v] as much as they gather on the other days."
6So Moses and Aaron said to all the Israelites, "In the evening you will know
that it was the LORD who brought you out
of Egypt,[w] 7and in the morning you will
see the glory[x] of the LORD, because he has
heard your grumbling[y] against him. Who
are we, that you should grumble against
us?"[z] 8Moses also said, "You will know that
it was the LORD when he gives you meat
to eat in the evening and all the bread you
want in the morning, because he has heard
your grumbling against him. Who are we?
You are not grumbling against us, but
against the LORD."[a]
9Then Moses told Aaron, "Say to the entire Israelite community, 'Come before the
LORD, for he has heard your grumbling.'"
10While Aaron was speaking to the
whole Israelite community, they looked toward the desert, and there was the glory[b]
of the LORD appearing in the cloud.[c]
11The LORD said to Moses, 12"I have
heard the grumbling[d] of the Israelites. Tell
them, 'At twilight you will eat meat, and in
the morning you will be filled with bread.
Then you will know that I am the LORD
your God.'"
13That evening quail[e] came and covered
the camp, and in the morning there was a
layer of dew[f] around the camp. 14When the
dew was gone, thin flakes like frost[g] on
the ground appeared on the desert floor.
15When the Israelites saw it, they said to
each other, "What is it?" For they did not
know what it was.
Moses said to them, "It is the bread[h] the
LORD has given you to eat. 16This is what
the LORD has commanded: 'Everyone is
to gather as much as they need. Take an
omer[a][i] for each person you have in your
tent.'"
17The Israelites did as they were told;
some gathered much, some little. 18And
when they measured it by the omer, the
one who gathered much did not have too
much, and the one who gathered little did
not have too little.[j] Everyone had gathered
just as much as they needed.
19Then Moses said to them, "No one is to
keep any of it until morning."[k]
20However, some of them paid no attention to Moses; they kept part of it until morning, but it was full of maggots and
began to smell. So Moses was angry with
them.
21Each morning everyone gathered as
much as they needed, and when the sun
grew hot, it melted away. 22On the sixth
day, they gathered twice[l] as much—two
omers[b] for each person—and the leaders
of the community[m] came and reported this
to Moses. 23He said to them, "This is what
the LORD commanded: 'Tomorrow is to be
a day of sabbath rest, a holy sabbath[n] to the
LORD. So bake what you want to bake and
boil what you want to boil. Save whatever
is left and keep it until morning.'"
24So they saved it until morning, as Moses commanded, and it did not stink or get
maggots in it. 25"Eat it today," Moses said,
"because today is a sabbath to the LORD.
You will not find any of it on the ground
today. 26Six days you are to gather it, but
on the seventh day, the Sabbath,[o] there will
not be any."
27Nevertheless, some of the people went
out on the seventh day to gather it, but they
found none. 28Then the LORD said to Moses, "How long will you[c] refuse to keep my
commands[p] and my instructions? 29Bear in
mind that the LORD has given you the Sabbath; that is why on the sixth day he gives

---

[a] *16* That is, possibly about 3 pounds or about 1.4 kilograms; also in verses 18, 32, 33 and 36
[b] *22* That is, possibly about 6 pounds or about 2.8 kilograms
[c] *28* The Hebrew is plural.

16:5 *twice as much.* Gathering extra food on the sixth day would allow for the Sabbath rest (v. 25).

16:10 *the glory of the LORD.* This is one of the grand appearances of God recorded in Exodus. We do not know exactly what the people saw in the cloud, but the sight certainly made them aware of God's majestic and somewhat ominous presence (Ps. 97:2 – 5).

16:14 *thin flakes like frost on the ground.* There have been many attempts to explain manna as a naturally occurring substance that still might be found in the desert, suggesting that it was some kind of plant or animal secretion. However, it is clear from the wording of these verses that this was not so. The description of the manna was necessary precisely because it was *not* a naturally occurring substance, or something they had ever seen before (Num. 11:1 – 15).

16:15 – 18 God's Provision—It is easy to think we trust in God and believe He will supply all of our needs when we have food, shelter, and clothing. It is more difficult when the food is low, the clothing has disappeared, and there is no money to pay the rent. Sometimes God allows us to be in this kind of position so that we will have to learn to consciously rely on His providence. When we really place our lives in His hands, we will experience a depth of relationship which is worth far more than all the security in the world.

16:19 *No one is to keep any of it.* The Israelites' daily dependence on manna was an act of faith in God's provision.

16:26 *Six days . . . the Sabbath.* The characteristics of manna were a built-in reminder of the importance of the Sabbath day in the life of the people of Israel.

16:5 [v] ver 22 **16:6** [w] Ex 6:6 **16:7** [x] ver 10; Isa 35:2; 40:5 [y] ver 12; Nu 14:2, 27, 28 [z] Nu 16:11 **16:8** [a] 1Sa 8:7; Ro 13:2 **16:10** [b] ver 7; Nu 16:19 [c] Ex 13:21; 1Ki 8:10 **16:12** [d] ver 7 **16:13** [e] Nu 11:31; Ps 78:27-28; 105:40 [f] Nu 11:9 **16:14** [g] ver 31; Nu 11:7-9; Ps 105:40 **16:15** [h] ver 4; Jn 6:31 **16:16** [i] ver 32, 36 **16:18** [j] 2Co 8:15* **16:19** [k] ver 23; Ex 12:10; 23:18 **16:22** [l] ver 5 [m] Ex 34:31 **16:23** [n] Ge 2:3; Ex 20:8; 23:12; Lev 23:3 **6:26** [o] Ex 20:9-10 **16:28** [p] 2Ki 17:14; Ps 78:10; 106:13

you bread for two days. Everyone is to stay
where they are on the seventh day; no one
is to go out." 30So the people rested on the
seventh day.
31The people of Israel called the bread
manna.[a][q] It was white like coriander seed
and tasted like wafers made with honey.
32Moses said, "This is what the LORD has
commanded: 'Take an omer of manna
and keep it for the generations to come, so
they can see the bread I gave you to eat in
the wilderness when I brought you out of
Egypt.'"
33So Moses said to Aaron, "Take a jar
and put an omer of manna[r] in it. Then place
it before the LORD to be kept for the generations to come."
34As the LORD commanded Moses, Aaron put the manna with the tablets of the
covenant law,[s] so that it might be preserved. 35The Israelites ate manna[t] forty
years,[u] until they came to a land that was
settled; they ate manna until they reached
the border of Canaan.[v]
36(An omer is one-tenth of an ephah.)

Water From the Rock

17 The whole Israelite community set
out from the Desert of Sin,[w] traveling
from place to place as the LORD commanded. They camped at Rephidim, but there
was no water[x] for the people to drink. 2So
they quarreled with Moses and said, "Give
us water[y] to drink."
Moses replied, "Why do you quarrel with
me? Why do you put the LORD to the test?"[z]
3But the people were thirsty for water
there, and they grumbled[a] against Moses.
They said, "Why did you bring us up out
of Egypt to make us and our children and
livestock die of thirst?"
4Then Moses cried out to the LORD,
"What am I to do with these people? They
are almost ready to stone[b] me."
5The LORD answered Moses, "Go out in
front of the people. Take with you some of
the elders of Israel and take in your hand
the staff with which you struck the Nile,[c]
and go. 6I will stand there before you by the
rock at Horeb. Strike the rock, and water[d]
will come out of it for the people to drink."
So Moses did this in the sight of the elders
of Israel. 7And he called the place Massah[b]
and Meribah[c][e] because the Israelites quarreled and because they tested the LORD saying, "Is the LORD among us or not?"

The Amalekites Defeated

8The Amalekites[f] came and attacked the
Israelites at Rephidim. 9Moses said to Joshua, "Choose some of our men and go out
to fight the Amalekites. Tomorrow I will
stand on top of the hill with the staff[g] of
God in my hands."
10So Joshua fought the Amalekites as
Moses had ordered, and Moses, Aaron and
Hur[h] went to the top of the hill. 11As long
as Moses held up his hands, the Israelites
were winning,[i] but whenever he lowered
his hands, the Amalekites were winning.
12When Moses' hands grew tired, they took
a stone and put it under him and he sat on
it. Aaron and Hur held his hands up—one
on one side, one on the other—so that his
hands remained steady till sunset. 13So
Joshua overcame the Amalekite army with
the sword.
14Then the LORD said to Moses, "Write[j]
this on a scroll as something to be remembered and make sure that Joshua hears it,
because I will completely blot out the name
of Amalek[k] from under heaven."
15Moses built an altar and called it The
LORD is my Banner. 16He said, "Because
hands were lifted up against[d] the throne of
the LORD,[e] the LORD will be at war against
the Amalekites from generation to generation."

---

[a] *31 Manna* sounds like the Hebrew for *What is it?* (see verse 15). [b] *7 Massah* means *testing.* [c] *7 Meribah* means *quarreling.* [d] *16* Or *to* [e] *16* The meaning of the Hebrew for this clause is uncertain.

16:31 *coriander seed ... honey.* Apparently the manna was very tasty. It must also have been very nutritious since it was the staple of the Israelites for a full generation.

16:32 *keep it for the generations.* This pot of manna was not only a reminder of God's miraculous provision, but a miracle in itself since it did not spoil as did the extra manna Israelites gathered for themselves.

17:7 *Is the LORD among us.* The people had seen God's power in the plagues, the exodus, the crossing of the Red Sea, and the provision of manna. Every day they saw the pillar of His presence. We can wonder at their lack of faith until we look at our own weakness.

17:8 *Amalekites.* The people of Amalek were descendants of Esau, and thus relatives of the Hebrews (Gen. 36:12). Their attack on Israel was unprovoked. The Israelites—and the Lord—regarded this attack as particularly heinous (vv. 14–16).

17:14 *Write this.* Some people allege that the first five books of the Old Testament were not actually written down until centuries after Moses' death. Others concede that Moses may have written certain small sections, such as the one to which this verse seems to refer (24:4). However, strong tradition supports the assertion that Moses really wrote all of the first five books (except for the account of his own death); ancient Jews, including Jesus, referred to this portion of the Scripture as "the books of Moses."

16:31 [q] Nu 11:7-9 **16:33** [r] Heb 9:4 **16:34** [s] Ex 25:16, 21, 22; 40:20; Nu 17:4, 10 **16:35** [t] Jn 6:31, 49 [u] Ne 9:21 [v] Jos 5:12 **17:1** [w] Ex 16:1 [x] Nu 33:14 **17:2** [y] Nu 20:2 [z] Dt 6:16; Ps 78:18, 41; 1Co 10:9 **17:3** [a] Ex 15:24; 16:2-3 **17:4** [b] Nu 14:10; 1Sa 30:6 **17:5** [c] Ex 7:20 **17:6** [d] Nu 20:11; Ps 114:8; 1Co 10:4 **17:7** [e] Nu 20:13, 24; Ps 81:7 **17:8** [f] Ge 36:12; Dt 25:17-19 **17:9** [g] Ex 4:17 **17:10** [h] Ex 24:14 **17:11** [i] Jas 5:16 **17:14** [j] Ex 24:4; 34:27; Nu 33:2 [k] 1Sa 15:3; 30:17-18

Jethro Visits Moses

18 Now Jethro, the priest of Midian[l] and
father-in-law of Moses, heard of everything God had done for Moses and for
his people Israel, and how the LORD had
brought Israel out of Egypt.
2 After Moses had sent away his wife
Zipporah,[m] his father-in-law Jethro received her 3 and her two sons.[n] One son was
named Gershom,[a] for Moses said, "I have
become a foreigner in a foreign land";[o]
4 and the other was named Eliezer,[b][p] for he
said, "My father's God was my helper; he
saved me from the sword of Pharaoh."
5 Jethro, Moses' father-in-law, together
with Moses' sons and wife, came to him in
the wilderness, where he was camped near
the mountain[q] of God. 6 Jethro had sent
word to him, "I, your father-in-law Jethro,
am coming to you with your wife and her
two sons."
7 So Moses went out to meet his father-
in-law and bowed down[r] and kissed[s] him.
They greeted each other and then went
into the tent. 8 Moses told his father-in-
law about everything the LORD had done
to Pharaoh and the Egyptians for Israel's
sake and about all the hardships they had
met along the way and how the LORD had
saved[t] them.
9 Jethro was delighted to hear about all
the good things the LORD had done for
Israel in rescuing them from the hand of
the Egyptians. 10 He said, "Praise be to the
LORD,[u] who rescued you from the hand of
the Egyptians and of Pharaoh, and who
rescued the people from the hand of the
Egyptians. 11 Now I know that the LORD is
greater than all other gods,[v] for he did this
to those who had treated Israel arrogantly."[w] 12 Then Jethro, Moses' father-in-law,
brought a burnt offering and other sacrifices to God, and Aaron came with all the
elders of Israel to eat a meal with Moses'
father-in-law in the presence[x] of God.
13 The next day Moses took his seat to
serve as judge for the people, and they
stood around him from morning till evening. 14 When his father-in-law saw all that
Moses was doing for the people, he said,
"What is this you are doing for the people?
Why do you alone sit as judge, while all
these people stand around you from morning till evening?"
15 Moses answered him, "Because the
people come to me to seek God's will.[y]
16 Whenever they have a dispute, it is
brought to me, and I decide between the
parties and inform them of God's decrees
and instructions."[z]
17 Moses' father-in-law replied, "What
you are doing is not good. 18 You and these
people who come to you will only wear
yourselves out. The work is too heavy for
you; you cannot handle it alone.[a] 19 Listen
now to me and I will give you some advice,
and may God be with you.[b] You must be
the people's representative before God and
bring their disputes[c] to him. 20 Teach them
his decrees and instructions,[d] and show
them the way they are to live[e] and how
they are to behave.[f] 21 But select capable
men[g] from all the people—men who fear
God, trustworthy men who hate dishonest gain[h]—and appoint them as officials[i]
over thousands, hundreds, fifties and tens.
22 Have them serve as judges for the people at all times, but have them bring every
difficult case[j] to you; the simple cases they
can decide themselves. That will make
your load lighter, because they will share[k]
it with you. 23 If you do this and God so
commands, you will be able to stand the
strain, and all these people will go home
satisfied."
24 Moses listened to his father-in-law and
did everything he said. 25 He chose capable
men from all Israel and made them leaders of the people, officials over thousands,
hundreds, fifties and tens.[l] 26 They served
as judges for the people at all times. The
difficult cases they brought to Moses, but
the simple ones they decided themselves.[m]
27 Then Moses sent his father-in-law on
his way, and Jethro returned to his own
country.[n]

---

[a] *3 Gershom* sounds like the Hebrew for *a foreigner there.* [b] *4 Eliezer* means *my God is helper.*

18:6 *her two sons.* Zipporah's two sons stayed with Moses and became part of the families of Israel. However, the subsequent history of the family of Gershom involved a return to idols and inappropriate priesthood (Judg. 18:30).

18:7 *bowed down and kissed him.* The ancient Middle Eastern acts of bowing and kissing were not acts of worship, but signs of respect and reminders of obligations between two people.

18:11 *Now I know that the LORD is greater.* Jethro's words imply that he had once regarded the Lord as one among many gods, or perhaps as the principal deity over the lesser. Here he declares full faith in God as the supreme Deity.

18:21 *dishonest gain.* Jethro's five qualifications for judges are similar to the qualifications for elders in the New Testament (1 Tim. 3:1 – 13). In particular, the men recommended by Jethro were to be God-fearing and haters of dishonesty. As such they would not be susceptible to bribery, and justice would not be perverted. God takes no bribes (Deut. 10:17), so neither must a judge. A bribe blinds the eyes. Human justice must reflect divine justice, which is impartial (Rom. 2:11).

18:1 [l] Ex 2:16; 3:1 **18:2** [m] Ex 2:21; 4:25 **18:3** [n] Ex 4:20; Ac 7:29 [o] Ex 2:22 **18:4** [p] 1Ch 23:15 **18:5** [q] Ex 3:1 **18:7** [r] Ge 43:28 [s] Ge 29:13 **18:8** [t] Ex 15:6, 16; Ps 81:7 **18:10** [u] Ge 14:20; Ps 68:19-20 **18:11** [v] Ex 12:12; 15:11; 2Ch 2:5 [w] Lk 1:51 **18:12** [x] Dt 12:7 **18:15** [y] Nu 9:6, 8; Dt 17:8-13 **18:16** [z] Lev 24:12 **18:18** [a] Nu 11:11, 14, 17 **18:19** [b] Ex 3:12 [c] Nu 27:5 **18:20** [d] Dt 5:1 [e] Ps 143:8 [f] Dt 1:18 **18:21** [g] Ac 6:3 [h] Dt 16:19; Ps 15:5; Eze 18:8 [i] Dt 1:13, 15; 2Ch 19:5-10 **18:22** [j] Dt 1:17-18 [k] Nu 11:17 **18:25** [l] Dt 1:13-15 **18:26** [m] ver 22 **18:27** [n] Nu 10:29-30

At Mount Sinai

19 On the first day of the third month after the Israelites left Egypt—on that very day—they came to the Desert of Sinai. 2After they set out from Rephidim,[o] they entered the Desert of Sinai, and Israel camped there in the desert in front of the mountain.[p]

3Then Moses went up to God, and the LORD called[q] to him from the mountain and said, "This is what you are to say to the descendants of Jacob and what you are to tell the people of Israel: 4'You yourselves have seen what I did to Egypt,[r] and how I carried you on eagles' wings[s] and brought you to myself. 5Now if you obey me fully[t] and keep my covenant,[u] then out of all nations you will be my treasured possession.[v] Although the whole earth[w] is mine, 6you[a] will be for me a kingdom of priests[x] and a holy nation.'[y] These are the words you are to speak to the Israelites."

7So Moses went back and summoned the elders of the people and set before them all the words the LORD had commanded him to speak. 8The people all responded together, "We will do everything the LORD has said."[z] So Moses brought their answer back to the LORD.

9The LORD said to Moses, "I am going to come to you in a dense cloud,[a] so that the people will hear me speaking[b] with you and will always put their trust in you." Then Moses told the LORD what the people had said.

10And the LORD said to Moses, "Go to the people and consecrate[c] them today and tomorrow. Have them wash their clothes[d] 11and be ready by the third day,[e] because on that day the LORD will come down on Mount Sinai in the sight of all the people. 12Put limits for the people around the mountain and tell them, 'Be careful that you do not approach the mountain or touch the foot of it. Whoever touches the mountain is to be put to death. 13They are to be stoned[f] or shot with arrows; not a hand is to be laid on them. No person or animal shall be permitted to live.' Only when the ram's horn sounds a long blast may they approach the mountain."

14After Moses had gone down the mountain to the people, he consecrated them, and they washed their clothes. 15Then he said to the people, "Prepare yourselves for the third day. Abstain from sexual relations."

16On the morning of the third day there was thunder and lightning, with a thick cloud over the mountain, and a very loud trumpet blast.[g] Everyone in the camp trembled.[h] 17Then Moses led the people out of the camp to meet with God, and they stood at the foot of the mountain. 18Mount Sinai was covered with smoke,[i] because the LORD descended on it in fire.[j] The smoke billowed up from it like smoke from a furnace,[k] and the whole mountain[b] trembled[l] violently. 19As the sound of the trumpet grew louder and louder, Moses spoke and the voice[m] of God answered[n] him.[c]

20The LORD descended to the top of Mount Sinai and called Moses to the top of the mountain. So Moses went up 21and the LORD said to him, "Go down and warn the people so they do not force their way through to see[o] the LORD and many of them perish. 22Even the priests, who approach[p] the LORD, must consecrate themselves, or the LORD will break out against them."[q]

---

[a] 5,6 Or *possession, for the whole earth is mine.* 6*You* [b] 18 Most Hebrew manuscripts; a few Hebrew manuscripts and Septuagint *and all the people* [c] 19 Or *and God answered him with thunder*

19:5 – 8 God Gives His Covenant—The covenant with Moses is the second covenant that pertains to the rule of God. It is different than the Abrahamic covenant in that it is conditional. It is introduced by the conditional formula "if you obey me fully … you will be my treasured possession." This covenant was given to the nation Israel so that those who believed God's promises given to Abraham in the Abrahamic Covenant (Gen. 12:1 – 3) would know how they should live. The Mosaic Covenant in its entirety governs three areas of their lives: (1) the commandments governed their personal lives (Ex. 20:1 – 26); (2) the law governed their social lives particularly as they related to one another (Ex. 21:1 – 24:11); and (3) the ordinances governed their religious lives so that the people would know how to approach God (Ex. 24:12 – 31:18). The Mosaic Covenant did not replace the Abrahamic Covenant. It was added alongside the Abrahamic Covenant so that the people of Israel would know how to live until the Messiah comes and makes the complete and perfect sacrifice. The Mosaic Covenant was never given so that by keeping it people could be saved, but so that they might realize that they cannot do what God wants, even when God writes it down on stone tablets. The law was given that man might realize that he is helpless and that his only hope is to receive the righteousness of God by faith in Jesus (Gal. 3:17 – 24).

19:16 *a very loud trumpet blast.* Amazingly, one of the heavenly visitors played the trumpet rather than someone in the camp of Israel (compare Is. 27:13; 1 Cor. 15:52; 1 Thess. 4:16). No wonder they trembled (20:18 – 19).

19:18 *the LORD descended.* Even though we know God is everywhere, language such as this gives us a greater appreciation of His merciful grace.

19:2 [o] Ex 17:1 [p] Ex 3:1 **19:3** [q] Ex 3:4; Ac 7:38 **19:4** [r] Dt 29:2 [s] Isa 63:9 **19:5** [t] Ex 15:26 [u] Dt 5:2 [v] Dt 14:2; Ps 135:4 [w] Ex 9:29; Dt 10:14 **19:6** [x] 1Pe 2:5 [y] Dt 7:6; 26:19; Isa 62:12 **19:8** [z] Ex 24:3,7; Dt 5:27 **19:9** [a] ver 16; Ex 24:15-16 [b] Dt 4:12,36 **19:10** [c] Lev 11:44; Heb 10:22 [d] Ge 35:2 **19:11** [e] ver 16 **19:13** [f] Heb 12:20* **19:16** [g] Heb 12:18-19; Rev 4:1 [h] Heb 12:21 **19:18** [i] Ps 104:32 [j] Ex 3:2; 24:17; Dt 4:11; 2Ch 7:1; Ps 18:8; Heb 12:18 [k] Ge 19:28 [l] Jdg 5:5; Ps 68:8; Jer 4:24 **19:19** [m] Ne 9:13 [n] Ps 81:7 **19:21** [o] Ex 3:5; 1Sa 6:19 **19:22** [p] Lev 10:3 [q] 2Sa 6:7

23 Moses said to the LORD, "The people
cannot come up Mount Sinai, because you
yourself warned us, 'Put limits[r] around the
mountain and set it apart as holy.'"
24 The LORD replied, "Go down and bring
Aaron[s] up with you. But the priests and the
people must not force their way through to
come up to the LORD, or he will break out
against them."
25 So Moses went down to the people and
told them.

The Ten Commandments

20 And God spoke all these words:

2 "I am the LORD your God, who
brought you out of Egypt, out of
the land of slavery.[t]
3 "You shall have no other gods before[a] me.[u]
4 "You shall not make for yourself an
image[v] in the form of anything
in heaven above or on the earth
beneath or in the waters below.
5 You shall not bow down to them
or worship[w] them; for I, the LORD
your God, am a jealous God,[x] punishing the children for the sin of
the parents to the third and fourth
generation[y] of those who hate me,
6 but showing love to a thousand[z]
generations of those who love me
and keep my commandments.
7 "You shall not misuse the name of the
LORD your God, for the LORD will
not hold anyone guiltless who
misuses his name.[a]
8 "Remember the Sabbath[b] day by keeping it holy. 9 Six days you shall labor and do all your work,[c] 10 but
the seventh day is a sabbath to
the LORD your God. On it you
shall not do any work, neither
you, nor your son or daughter, nor
your male or female servant, nor
your animals, nor any foreigner
residing in your towns. 11 For in
six days the LORD made the heavens and the earth, the sea, and
all that is in them, but he rested[d]
on the seventh day. Therefore the
LORD blessed the Sabbath day and
made it holy.

[a] 3 Or *besides*

20:1 *And God spoke.* The following words of God are known as the law of Moses, but this is only because they were delivered to the people from God through Moses, not because Moses invented them.

20:1–17 The Ten Commandments—The first four Commandments (20:1–11) lay out the basics of the relationship with God. God is not a mere abstraction or figment of imagination. He is the God who spoke dramatically to the patriarchs and continues to speak to us. Our responsibility is to have a relationship with Him whereby we explicitly recognize Him, listen to what He says and then obey. What He wants isn't all that complicated. He is the Creator and Master of the world, as we know it. Any view of God that makes Him less, falls short of what is required to make the relationship between God and man work. For example if God is not the creator and sustainer of the world, then the perspective of Genesis 1:28 and our responsibility as stewards of His creation don't make much sense.

The last six Commandments (20:12–17) give us the basics for living—with our families, our neighbors and our communities. Disregarding and disobeying any of these commands leads to the breakdown and possible destruction of those relationships. The relationship between a parent and a child can only go downhill if the basic respect for the parent has not been created and maintained. Adultery clearly has enormous potential to destroy a marriage because it creates distrust where trust should be. Trust is one of the foundational blocks of the marriage relationship. While many would like to say that these Commandments are limiting, confining and outdated, in reality, they provide the basis for a society to function harmoniously. Only when a culture places limits on itself, is it able to prosper. Followed correctly, these Commandments provide safety and freedom, the same way a fish functions best within the confines of water. In the water it lives and prospers. On land it dies.

20:3 *no other gods.* God is not to be viewed as one god among many, or even as the highest among many. He is the one and only.

20:4 *not make ... an image.* This command has often been misunderstood as a prohibition against all kinds of art. In fact, God used many likenesses of created things to beautify His tabernacle, including carved images and woven pictures. The prohibition was not against art, but against attempting to "picture" God. Any statue, icon, painting, or image of any sort which is meant to be a representation of God can only detract from His glory. God does not want His people to worship a picture of "what He might look like," He wants all our worship for Himself alone.

20:5 *a jealous God.* In other words, He has a zeal for the truth that He alone is God, and He is jealous of any rivals.

20:6 *showing love to a thousand generations.* The contrasting of the phrases "third and fourth generation" (v. 5) with "thousands" demonstrates that God's mercy is greater than His wrath. The lingering effects of righteousness will last far longer than the lingering effects of wrath.

20:7 *misuse.* Using God's name in vain is trivializing His name by regarding it as insignificant, trying to advance evil purposes by coaxing God to violate His character and purposes, or even simply using it thoughtlessly, without any attempt to realize of whom we are speaking.

20:8–11 *Remember the Sabbath day.* The word Sabbath means "rest." The command to rest and remember the Lord on the seventh day goes back to the pattern set at the time of creation (Gen. 2:2–3).

19:23 [r] ver 12 **19:24** [s] Ex 24:1,9 **20:2** [t] Ex 13:3 **20:3** [u] Dt 6:14; Jer 35:15 **20:4** [v] Lev 26:1; Dt 4:15-19,23; 27:15 **20:5** [w] Isa 44:15, 17, 19 [x] Ex 34:14; Dt 4:24 [y] Nu 14:18; Jer 32:18 **20:6** [z] Dt 7:9 **20:7** [a] Lev 19:12; Mt 5:33 **20:8** [b] Ex 31:13-16; Lev 26:2 **20:9** [c] Ex 34:21; Lk 13:14 **20:11** [d] Ge 2:2

12 "Honor your father and your mother,[e]
so that you may live long in the
land the LORD your God is giving
you.
13 "You shall not murder.[f]
14 "You shall not commit adultery.[g]
15 "You shall not steal.[h]
16 "You shall not give false testimony
against your neighbor.[i]
17 "You shall not covet[j] your neighbor's
house. You shall not covet your
neighbor's wife, or his male or
female servant, his ox or donkey,
or anything that belongs to your
neighbor."

18 When the people saw the thunder and
lightning and heard the trumpet[k] and saw
the mountain in smoke, they trembled with
fear. They stayed at a distance 19 and said
to Moses, "Speak to us yourself and we will
listen. But do not have God speak to us or
we will die."[l]

20 Moses said to the people, "Do not be
afraid. God has come to test you, so that
the fear[m] of God will be with you to keep
you from sinning."[n]

21 The people remained at a distance,
while Moses approached the thick darkness[o] where God was.

Idols and Altars

22 Then the LORD said to Moses, "Tell the
Israelites this: 'You have seen for yourselves that I have spoken to you from heav-
en:[p] 23 Do not make any gods to be alongside me;[q] do not make for yourselves gods
of silver or gods of gold.[r]

24 "'Make an altar of earth for me and
sacrifice on it your burnt offerings and fellowship offerings, your sheep and goats
and your cattle. Wherever I cause my
name[s] to be honored, I will come to you
and bless[t] you. 25 If you make an altar of
stones for me, do not build it with dressed
stones, for you will defile it if you use a
tool[u] on it. 26 And do not go up to my altar
on steps, or your private parts may be exposed.'

21 "These are the laws[v] you are to set
before them:

Hebrew Servants

2 "If you buy a Hebrew servant, he is
to serve you for six years. But in the seventh year, he shall go free,[w] without paying anything. 3 If he comes alone, he is to
go free alone; but if he has a wife when he
comes, she is to go with him. 4 If his master
gives him a wife and she bears him sons
or daughters, the woman and her children
shall belong to her master, and only the
man shall go free.

5 "But if the servant declares, 'I love my
master and my wife and children and do
not want to go free,'[x] 6 then his master must
take him before the judges.[a][y] He shall take
him to the door or the doorpost and pierce
his ear with an awl. Then he will be his servant for life.[z]

7 "If a man sells his daughter as a servant,
she is not to go free as male servants do.
8 If she does not please the master who has
selected her for himself,[b] he must let her be
redeemed. He has no right to sell her to foreigners, because he has broken faith with
her. 9 If he selects her for his son, he must
grant her the rights of a daughter. 10 If he
marries another woman, he must not deprive the first one of her food, clothing and
marital rights.[a] 11 If he does not provide her
with these three things, she is to go free,
without any payment of money.

Personal Injuries

12 "Anyone who strikes a person with a
fatal blow is to be put to death.[b] 13 However,

[a] 6 Or *before God* [b] 8 Or *master so that he does not choose her*

20:12 *Honor your father and your mother.* The term "honor" means "to treat with significance." Many times we equate "honor" with "obey," but in fact the two are not synonyms. Adult children or children of ungodly parents can find ways to honor when they cannot in good conscience obey.
20:14 *adultery.* God regards the sanctity of marriage as a sacred trust similar to the sanctity of life (v. 13). The marriage relationship is a symbol of God's faithfulness to us.
20:16 *false testimony.* This command is an essential foundation for a just and effective judicial system.
20:20 *fear of God.* God did not want His people to live in terror of Him, as though He were an irrational, uncontrolled, violent force, ready to be unleashed on innocent people without provocation. Rather, God wanted His people to respect the obvious hazards of wanton sin. Appropriate fear of God in this sense would make them circumspect, reverent, obedient, and worshipful, so that they might not sin.
20:26 *your private parts.* The pagan worship of the Canaanites involved sexually perverse acts. Nothing obscene or unseemly was permitted in the pure worship of the living God.
21:1 *the laws.* Also translated "ordinances," this word describes God's response to a specific action, something like an umpire's call. The judgments of God set forth here are responses to specific situations; the Ten Commandments are more general laws, a code for living rather than a response to a certain problem.

20:12 [e] Mt 15:4*; Mk 7:10*; Eph 6:2 **20:13** [f] Mt 5:21*; Ro 13:9* **20:14** [g] Mt 19:18* **20:15** [h] Lev 19:11, 13; Mt 19:18* **20:16** [i] Ex 23:1, 7; Mt 19:18* **20:17** [j] Ro 7:7*; 13:9*; Eph 5:3 **20:18** [k] Ex 19:16-19; Heb 12:18-19 **20:19** [l] Dt 5:5, 23-27; Gal 3:19 **20:20** [m] Dt 4:10; Isa 8:13 [n] Pr 16:6 **20:21** [o] Dt 5:22 **20:22** [p] Ne 9:13 **20:23** [q] ver 3 [r] Ex 32:4, 8, 31 **20:24** [s] Dt 12:5; 16:6, 11; 2Ch 6:6 [t] Ge 12:2 **20:25** [u] Dt 27:5-6 **21:1** [v] Dt 4:14 **21:2** [w] Jer 34:8, 14 **21:5** [x] Dt 15:16 **21:6** [y] Ex 22:8-9 [z] Ne 5:5 **21:10** [a] 1Co 7:3-5 **21:12** [b] Ge 9:6; Mt 26:52

if it is not done intentionally, but God lets it happen, they are to flee to a place[c] I will designate. 14But if anyone schemes and kills someone deliberately,[d] that person is to be taken from my altar and put to death.[e]

15"Anyone who attacks[a] their father or mother is to be put to death.

16"Anyone who kidnaps someone is to be put to death,[f] whether the victim has been sold[g] or is still in the kidnapper's possession.

17"Anyone who curses their father or mother is to be put to death.[h]

18"If people quarrel and one person hits another with a stone or with their fist[b] and the victim does not die but is confined to bed, 19the one who struck the blow will not be held liable if the other can get up and walk around outside with a staff; however, the guilty party must pay the injured person for any loss of time and see that the victim is completely healed.

20"Anyone who beats their male or female slave with a rod must be punished if the slave dies as a direct result, 21but they are not to be punished if the slave recovers after a day or two, since the slave is their property.[i]

22"If people are fighting and hit a pregnant woman and she gives birth prematurely[c] but there is no serious injury, the offender must be fined whatever the woman's husband demands[j] and the court allows. 23But if there is serious injury, you are to take life for life,[k] 24eye for eye, tooth for tooth,[l] hand for hand, foot for foot, 25burn for burn, wound for wound, bruise for bruise.

26"An owner who hits a male or female slave in the eye and destroys it must let the slave go free to compensate for the eye. 27And an owner who knocks out the tooth of a male or female slave must let the slave go free to compensate for the tooth.

28"If a bull gores a man or woman to death, the bull is to be stoned to death,[m] and its meat must not be eaten. But the owner of the bull will not be held responsible. 29If, however, the bull has had the habit of goring and the owner has been warned but has not kept it penned up and it kills a man or woman, the bull is to be stoned and its owner also is to be put to death. 30However, if payment is demanded, the owner may redeem his life by the payment of whatever is demanded.[n] 31This law also applies if the bull gores a son or daughter. 32If the bull gores a male or female slave, the owner must pay thirty shekels[d][o] of silver to the master of the slave, and the bull is to be stoned to death.

33"If anyone uncovers a pit or digs one and fails to cover it and an ox or a donkey falls into it, 34the one who opened the pit must pay the owner for the loss and take the dead animal in exchange.

35"If anyone's bull injures someone else's bull and it dies, the two parties are to sell the live one and divide both the money and the dead animal equally. 36However, if it was known that the bull had the habit of goring, yet the owner did not keep it penned up, the owner must pay, animal for animal, and take the dead animal in exchange.

Protection of Property

22 [e] "Whoever steals an ox or a sheep and slaughters it or sells it must pay back[p] five head of cattle for the ox and four sheep for the sheep.

2"If a thief is caught breaking in[q] at night and is struck a fatal blow, the defender is not guilty of bloodshed;[r] 3but if it happens after sunrise, the defender is guilty of bloodshed.

"Anyone who steals must certainly make restitution, but if they have nothing, they must be sold[s] to pay for their theft. 4If the stolen animal is found alive in their possession—whether ox or donkey or sheep—they must pay back double.[t]

5"If anyone grazes their livestock in a field or vineyard and lets them stray and they graze in someone else's field, the offender must make restitution from the best of their own field or vineyard.

6"If a fire breaks out and spreads into thornbushes so that it burns shocks of grain or standing grain or the whole field, the one who started the fire must make restitution.

7"If anyone gives a neighbor silver or goods for safekeeping and they are stolen from the neighbor's house, the thief, if caught, must pay back double.[u] 8But if the thief is not found, the owner of the

---

[a] 15 Or *kills* [b] 18 Or *with a tool* [c] 22 Or *she has a miscarriage* [d] 32 That is, about 12 ounces or about 345 grams [e] In Hebrew texts 22:1 is numbered 21:37, and 22:2-31 is numbered 22:1-30.

21:24 *eye for eye, tooth for tooth.* Here we encounter the best known statement of the "law of retaliation." The idea here is not to foster revenge, but to curtail it. The natural, sinful human response is "a head for an eye, a jaw for a tooth, an arm for a hand." This law says "*no more than* eye for eye, tooth for tooth."

22:1 – 4 *after sunrise.* There is a difference between struggling with an intruder at the moment when he is caught red-handed, and hunting him up in order to

21:13 [c] Nu 35:10-34; Dt 19:2-13; Jos 20:9; 1Sa 24:4, 10, 18 **21:14** [d] Heb 10:26 [e] Dt 19:11-12; 1Ki 2:28-34 **21:16** [f] Ex 22:4; Dt 24:7 [g] Ge 37:28 **21:17** [h] Lev 20:9-10; Mt 15:4*; Mk 7:10* **21:21** [i] Lev 25:44-46 **21:22** [j] ver 30; Dt 22:18-19 **21:23** [k] Lev 24:19; Dt 19:21 **21:24** [l] Mt 5:38* **21:28** [m] ver 32; Ge 9:5 **21:30** [n] ver 22; Nu 35:31 **21:32** [o] Zec 11:12-13; Mt 26:15; 27:3,9 **22:1** [p] 2Sa 12:6; Pr 6:31; Lk 19:8 **22:2** [q] Mt 6:19-20; 24:43 [r] Nu 35:27 **22:3** [s] Ex 21:2; Mt 18:25 **22:4** [t] Ge 43:12 **22:7** [u] ver 4

house must appear before the judges,[v] and they must[a] determine whether the owner of the house has laid hands on the other person's property. 9In all cases of illegal possession of an ox, a donkey, a sheep, a garment, or any other lost property about which somebody says, 'This is mine,' both parties are to bring their cases before the judges.[b][w] The one whom the judges declare[c] guilty must pay back double to the other.

10"If anyone gives a donkey, an ox, a sheep or any other animal to their neighbor for safekeeping and it dies or is injured or is taken away while no one is looking, 11the issue between them will be settled by the taking of an oath[x] before the LORD that the neighbor did not lay hands on the other person's property. The owner is to accept this, and no restitution is required. 12But if the animal was stolen from the neighbor, restitution must be made to the owner. 13If it was torn to pieces by a wild animal, the neighbor shall bring in the remains as evidence and shall not be required to pay for the torn animal.[y]

14"If anyone borrows an animal from their neighbor and it is injured or dies while the owner is not present, they must make restitution. 15But if the owner is with the animal, the borrower will not have to pay. If the animal was hired, the money paid for the hire covers the loss.

Social Responsibility

16"If a man seduces a virgin[z] who is not pledged to be married and sleeps with her, he must pay the bride-price, and she shall be his wife. 17If her father absolutely refuses to give her to him, he must still pay the bride-price for virgins.

18"Do not allow a sorceress[a] to live.

19"Anyone who has sexual relations with an animal[b] is to be put to death.

20"Whoever sacrifices to any god other than the LORD must be destroyed.[d][c]

21"Do not mistreat or oppress a foreigner,[d] for you were foreigners[e] in Egypt.

22"Do not take advantage of the widow or the fatherless.[f] 23If you do and they cry out[g] to me, I will certainly hear their cry.[h] 24My anger will be aroused, and I will kill you with the sword; your wives will become widows and your children fatherless.[i]

25"If you lend money to one of my people among you who is needy, do not treat it like a business deal; charge no interest.[j] 26If you take your neighbor's cloak as a pledge,[k] return it by sunset, 27because that cloak is the only covering your neighbor has. What else can they sleep in? When they cry out to me, I will hear, for I am compassionate.[l]

28"Do not blaspheme God[e][m] or curse the ruler of your people.[n]

29"Do not hold back offerings[o] from your granaries or your vats.[f]

"You must give me the firstborn of your sons.[p] 30Do the same with your cattle and your sheep.[q] Let them stay with their mothers for seven days, but give them to me on the eighth day.[r]

31"You are to be my holy people.[s] So do not eat the meat of an animal torn by wild beasts;[t] throw it to the dogs.

Laws of Justice and Mercy

23 "Do not spread false reports.[u] Do not help a guilty person by being a malicious witness.[v]

2"Do not follow the crowd in doing wrong. When you give testimony in a lawsuit, do not pervert justice[w] by siding with the crowd, 3and do not show favoritism to a poor person in a lawsuit.

4"If you come across your enemy's ox or donkey wandering off, be sure to return it.[x] 5If you see the donkey[y] of someone who hates you fallen down under its load, do not leave it there; be sure you help them with it.

6"Do not deny justice[z] to your poor people in their lawsuits. 7Have nothing to do with a false charge[a] and do not put an innocent or honest person to death, for I will not acquit the guilty.

8"Do not accept a bribe,[b] for a bribe blinds those who see and twists the words of the innocent.

---

[a] 8 Or *before God, and he will* [b] 9 Or *before God* [c] 9 Or *whom God declares* [d] 20 The Hebrew term refers to the irrevocable giving over of things or persons to the LORD, often by totally destroying them. [e] 28 Or *Do not revile the judges* [f] 29 The meaning of the Hebrew for this phrase is uncertain.

---

kill him later on. The law made a distinction between self-defense and murder as retaliation.

22:18 *Do not allow a sorceress to live.* The Bible does not record any executions of sorcerers or sorceresses, but it does recount the deadly consequences of false worship (ch. 32; Num. 25).

23:1 *false reports.* Malicious talk is everywhere condemned in Scripture (see James 3:1 – 12).

23:3 *show favoritism to a poor person.* God's support of the poor did not overrule His justice. Here God anticipated that some would use poverty as an excuse for greedy, even criminal activity.

22:8 [v] Ex 21:6; Dt 17:8-9; 19:17 **22:9** [w] ver 28; Dt 25:1 **22:11** [x] Heb 6:16 **22:13** [y] Ge 31:39 **22:16** [z] Dt 22:28 **22:18** [a] Lev 20:27; Dt 18:11; 1Sa 28:3 **22:19** [b] Lev 18:23; Dt 27:21 **22:20** [c] Dt 17:2-5 **22:21** [d] Lev 19:33 [e] Dt 10:19 **22:22** [f] Dt 24:6, 10, 12, 17 **22:23** [g] Lk 18:7 [h] Dt 15:9; Ps 18:6 **22:24** [i] Ps 69:24; 109:9 **22:25** [j] Lev 25:35-37; Dt 23:20; Ps 15:5 **22:26** [k] Dt 24:6 **22:27** [l] Ex 34:6 **22:28** [m] Lev 24:11, 16 [n] Ecc 10:20; Ac 23:5* **22:29** [o] Ex 23:15, 16, 19 [p] Ex 13:2 **22:30** [q] Ex 13:12; Dt 15:19 [r] Lev 22:27 **22:31** [s] Lev 19:2 [t] Eze 4:14 **23:1** [u] Ex 20:16; Ps 101:5 [v] Ps 35:11; Ac 6:11 **23:2** [w] Dt 16:19 **23:4** [x] Dt 22:1-3 **23:5** [y] Dt 22:4 **23:6** [z] ver 2 **23:7** [a] Eph 4:25 **23:8** [b] Dt 10:17; 16:19; Pr 15:27

9"Do not oppress a foreigner;[c] you yourselves know how it feels to be foreigners,
because you were foreigners in Egypt.

Sabbath Laws

10"For six years you are to sow your
fields and harvest the crops, 11but during
the seventh year let the land lie unplowed
and unused. Then the poor among your
people may get food from it, and the wild
animals may eat what is left. Do the same
with your vineyard and your olive grove.
12"Six days do your work,[d] but on the
seventh day do not work, so that your ox
and your donkey may rest, and so that the
slave born in your household and the foreigner living among you may be refreshed.
13"Be careful[e] to do everything I have
said to you. Do not invoke the names of
other gods; do not let them be heard on
your lips.

The Three Annual Festivals

14"Three times[f] a year you are to celebrate a festival to me.
15"Celebrate the Festival of Unleavened
Bread;[g] for seven days eat bread made
without yeast, as I commanded you. Do
this at the appointed time in the month
of Aviv, for in that month you came out of
Egypt.
"No one is to appear before me empty-
handed.[h]
16"Celebrate the Festival of Harvest with
the firstfruits[i] of the crops you sow in your
field.
"Celebrate the Festival of Ingathering
at the end of the year, when you gather in
your crops from the field.[j]
17"Three times[k] a year all the men are to
appear before the Sovereign LORD.
18"Do not offer the blood of a sacrifice to
me along with anything containing yeast.[l]
"The fat of my festival offerings must not
be kept until morning.[m]
19"Bring the best of the firstfruits[n] of
your soil to the house of the LORD your God.
"Do not cook a young goat in its mother's milk.[o]

God's Angel to Prepare the Way

20"See, I am sending an angel[p] ahead
of you to guard you along the way and to
bring you to the place I have prepared.[q]
21Pay attention to him and listen[r] to what
he says. Do not rebel against him; he will
not forgive your rebellion,[s] since my Name
is in him. 22If you listen carefully to what
he says and do all that I say, I will be an
enemy[t] to your enemies and will oppose
those who oppose you. 23My angel will go
ahead of you and bring you into the land of
the Amorites, Hittites, Perizzites, Canaanites, Hivites and Jebusites,[u] and I will wipe
them out. 24Do not bow down before their
gods or worship[v] them or follow their practices.[w] You must demolish[x] them and break
their sacred stones to pieces. 25Worship the
LORD your God,[y] and his blessing[z] will be
on your food and water. I will take away
sickness[a] from among you, 26and none will
miscarry or be barren[b] in your land. I will
give you a full life span.[c]
27"I will send my terror[d] ahead of you
and throw into confusion[e] every nation
you encounter. I will make all your enemies
turn their backs and run. 28I will send the
hornet[f] ahead of you to drive the Hivites,
Canaanites and Hittites out of your way.
29But I will not drive them out in a single
year, because the land would become desolate and the wild animals[g] too numerous
for you. 30Little by little I will drive them
out before you, until you have increased
enough to take possession of the land.
31"I will establish your borders from the
Red Sea[a] to the Mediterranean Sea,[b] and
from the desert to the Euphrates River.[h] I
will give into your hands the people who
live in the land, and you will drive them
out[i] before you. 32Do not make a covenant[j]
with them or with their gods. 33Do not let
them live in your land or they will cause
you to sin against me, because the worship
of their gods will certainly be a snare[k] to
you."

---

[a] 31 Or *the Sea of Reeds* [b] 31 Hebrew *to the Sea of the Philistines*

23:11 *unplowed and unused.* Letting the land rest allowed the poor to glean any produce that might grow during the fallow year. It also gave the land time to rejuvenate for greater productivity in subsequent years. The year of rest was an act of faith, for the Israelites would have to trust God to meet their needs.

23:17 *Sovereign LORD.* Here two names for God emphasize God's sovereignty.

23:20 *angel.* The statement "my Name is in him" (v. 21) shows that this messenger is the Angel of the Lord, who is none other than God Himself; with the promise of His presence and protection comes the warning "listen to what he says," for the Lord is a holy God who cannot dwell in the presence of sin. Obedience is the evidence of reality of the covenant relationship. The Angel of the Lord "encamps around those who fear him" (Ps. 34:7).

23:26 *miscarry or be barren.* God reminded His people that He was the one who controlled reproduction — not the fertility cults of the pagan Canaanites.

23:9 [c] Ex 22:21 **23:12** [d] Ex 20:9 **23:13** [e] 1Ti 4:16
23:14 [f] Ex 34:23,24 **23:15** [g] Ex 12:17 [h] Ex 34:20
23:16 [i] Ex 34:22 [j] Dt 16:13 **23:17** [k] Dt 16:16
23:18 [l] Ex 34:25 [m] Dt 16:4 **23:19** [n] Ex 22:29; Dt 26:2,10 [o] Dt 14:21 **23:20** [p] Ex 14:19; 32:34 [q] Ex 15:17
23:21 [r] Nu 14:11; Dt 18:19 [s] Ps 78:8,40,56
23:22 [t] Ge 12:3; Dt 30:7 **23:23** [u] ver 20; Jos 24:8,11
23:24 [v] Ex 20:5 [w] Dt 12:30-31 [x] Ex 34:13; Nu 33:52
23:25 [y] Dt 6:13; Mt 4:10 [z] Dt 7:12-15; 28:1-14 [a] Ex 15:26
23:26 [b] Dt 7:14; Mal 3:11 [c] Job 5:26 **23:27** [d] Ex 15:14; Dt 2:25 [e] Dt 7:23 **23:28** [f] Dt 7:20; Jos 24:12
23:29 [g] Dt 7:22 **23:31** [h] Ge 15:18 [i] Jos 21:44; 24:12,18
23:32 [j] Ex 34:12; Dt 7:2 **23:33** [k] Dt 7:16; Ps 106:36

The Covenant Confirmed

24 Then the LORD said to Moses, "Come up to the LORD, you and Aaron, Nadab and Abihu,[l] and seventy of the elders[m] of Israel. You are to worship at a distance, 2but Moses alone is to approach the LORD; the others must not come near. And the people may not come up with him."

3When Moses went and told the people all the LORD's words and laws, they responded with one voice, "Everything the LORD has said we will do."[n] 4Moses then wrote[o] down everything the LORD had said.

He got up early the next morning and built an altar at the foot of the mountain and set up twelve stone pillars[p] representing the twelve tribes of Israel. 5Then he sent young Israelite men, and they offered burnt offerings and sacrificed young bulls as fellowship offerings to the LORD. 6Moses took half of the blood[q] and put it in bowls, and the other half he splashed against the altar. 7Then he took the Book of the Covenant[r] and read it to the people. They responded, "We will do everything the LORD has said; we will obey."

8Moses then took the blood, sprinkled it on the people and said, "This is the blood of the covenant[s] that the LORD has made with you in accordance with all these words."

9Moses and Aaron, Nadab and Abihu, and the seventy elders[t] of Israel went up 10and saw[u] the God of Israel. Under his feet was something like a pavement made of lapis lazuli,[v] as bright blue as the sky.[w] 11But God did not raise his hand against these leaders of the Israelites; they saw[x] God, and they ate and drank.

12The LORD said to Moses, "Come up to me on the mountain and stay here, and I will give you the tablets of stone[y] with the law and commandments I have written for their instruction."

13Then Moses set out with Joshua[z] his aide, and Moses went up on the mountain[a] of God. 14He said to the elders, "Wait here for us until we come back to you. Aaron and Hur are with you, and anyone involved in a dispute can go to them."

15When Moses went up on the mountain, the cloud[b] covered it, 16and the glory[c] of the LORD settled on Mount Sinai. For six days the cloud covered the mountain, and on the seventh day the LORD called to Moses from within the cloud.[d] 17To the Israelites the glory of the LORD looked like a consuming fire[e] on top of the mountain. 18Then Moses entered the cloud as he went on up the mountain. And he stayed on the mountain forty[f] days and forty nights.[g]

Offerings for the Tabernacle

25 The LORD said to Moses, 2"Tell the Israelites to bring me an offering. You are to receive the offering for me from everyone whose heart prompts[h] them to give. 3These are the offerings you are to receive from them: gold, silver and bronze; 4blue, purple and scarlet yarn and fine linen; goat hair; 5ram skins dyed red and another type of durable leather[a]; acacia wood; 6olive oil[i] for the light; spices for the anointing oil and for the fragrant incense; 7and onyx stones and other gems to be mounted on the ephod[j] and breastpiece.[k]

8"Then have them make a sanctuary[l] for me, and I will dwell[m] among them. 9Make this tabernacle and all its furnishings exactly like the pattern[n] I will show you.

The Ark

10"Have them make an ark[b][o] of acacia wood—two and a half cubits long, a cubit

[a] *5* Possibly the hides of large aquatic mammals
[b] *10* That is, a chest

24:6 ***blood.*** This blood anticipated the death of the coming Messiah, Jesus. His blood could do what the blood of bulls and goats could never accomplish; His death opened the way for direct communication with God (12:7; Rom. 3:23–26; Heb. 10:4,10).

24:8 ***the blood of the covenant.*** Just as their houses were protected from the Passover by the sign of blood (ch. 12), now the people were brought into a covenant relationship with the Lord with a sign of blood. This is a picture of our own relationship with God, brought about by the blood of Jesus (1 Pet. 1:2).

24:9–17 ***God of Israel.*** This vision of God was a great privilege. The elders of the people saw God standing on a structure resembling a transparent sapphire platform, which emphasized His grandeur. Blue was one of the colors favored by some members of ancient Near Eastern royalty. God's glory is the manifestation of all His divine characteristics, including power and holiness, which for Israel were represented by the billowing consuming fire (Heb. 12:29).

24:12 ***Come up to me.*** Only Moses could draw near to God at that time. Today, we are all called to draw near to God through Jesus (see Heb. 4:14–16).

25:2 ***everyone whose heart prompts them to give.*** God does not need the gifts of His people, but He desires us to give to Him as an expression of true worship.

25:9 ***the pattern.*** The language of these verses suggests that there is a heavenly pattern that the earthly tabernacle was designed to resemble (see v. 40; 26:30; 27:8; Acts 7:44; Heb. 8:5).

25:10 ***ark.*** In contrast to the idolatry of Israel's neighbors, the shrine of the living God had no likeness or idol of any sort (20:2–6). ***cubit.*** This measurement

24:1 [l] Ex 6:23; Lev 10:1-2 [m] Nu 11:16 **24:3** [n] Ex 19:8; Dt 5:27 **24:4** [o] Dt 31:9 [p] Ge 28:18 **24:6** [q] Heb 9:18 **24:7** [r] Heb 9:19 **24:8** [s] Heb 9:20*; 1Pe 1:2 **24:9** [t] ver 1 **24:10** [u] Mt 17:2; Jn 1:18; 6:46 [v] Eze 1:26 [w] Rev 4:3 **24:11** [x] Ge 32:30; Ex 19:21 **24:12** [y] Ex 32:15-16 **24:13** [z] Ex 17:9 [a] Ex 3:1 **24:15** [b] Ex 19:9 **24:16** [c] Ex 16:10 [d] Ps 99:7 **24:17** [e] Ex 3:2; Dt 4:36; Heb 12:18,29 **24:18** [f] Dt 9:9 [g] Ex 34:28 **25:2** [h] Ex 35:21; 1Ch 29:5,7,9; Ezr 2:68; 2Co 8:11-12; 9:7 **25:6** [i] Ex 27:20; 30:22-32 **25:7** [j] Ex 28:4,6-14 [k] Ex 28:15-30 **25:8** [l] Ex 36:1-5; Heb 9:1-2 [m] Ex 29:45; 1Ki 6:13; 2Co 6:16; Rev 21:3 **25:9** [n] ver 40; Ac 7:44; Heb 8:5 **25:10** [o] Dt 10:1-5; Heb 9:4

and a half wide, and a cubit and a half
high.[a] 11Overlay it with pure gold, both
inside and out, and make a gold molding
around it. 12Cast four gold rings for it and
fasten them to its four feet, with two rings
on one side and two rings on the other.
13Then make poles of acacia wood and
overlay them with gold. 14Insert the poles
into the rings on the sides of the ark to carry it. 15The poles are to remain in the rings
of this ark; they are not to be removed.[p]
16Then put in the ark the tablets of the covenant law,[q] which I will give you.
17"Make an atonement cover[r] of pure
gold—two and a half cubits long and a cubit and a half wide. 18And make two cherubim out of hammered gold at the ends of
the cover. 19Make one cherub on one end
and the second cherub on the other; make
the cherubim of one piece with the cover, at
the two ends. 20The cherubim are to have
their wings spread upward, overshadowing[s] the cover with them. The cherubim are
to face each other, looking toward the cover. 21Place the cover on top of the ark[t] and
put in the ark the tablets of the covenant
law[u] that I will give you. 22There, above
the cover between the two cherubim[v] that
are over the ark of the covenant law, I will
meet[w] with you and give you all my commands for the Israelites.

The Table

23"Make a table[x] of acacia wood—two
cubits long, a cubit wide and a cubit and
a half high.[b] 24Overlay it with pure gold
and make a gold molding around it. 25Also
make around it a rim a handbreadth[c]
wide and put a gold molding on the rim.
26Make four gold rings for the table and
fasten them to the four corners, where the
four legs are. 27The rings are to be close
to the rim to hold the poles used in carrying the table. 28Make the poles of acacia wood, overlay them with gold and
carry the table with them. 29And make
its plates and dishes of pure gold, as well
as its pitchers and bowls for the pouring
out of offerings.[y] 30Put the bread of the
Presence[z] on this table to be before me at
all times.

The Lampstand

31"Make a lampstand[a] of pure gold.
Hammer out its base and shaft, and make
its flowerlike cups, buds and blossoms
of one piece with them. 32Six branches
are to extend from the sides of the lampstand—three on one side and three on
the other. 33Three cups shaped like almond flowers with buds and blossoms
are to be on one branch, three on the next
branch, and the same for all six branches extending from the lampstand. 34And
on the lampstand there are to be four cups
shaped like almond flowers with buds and
blossoms. 35One bud shall be under the
first pair of branches extending from the
lampstand, a second bud under the second pair, and a third bud under the third
pair—six branches in all. 36The buds
and branches shall all be of one piece
with the lampstand, hammered out of pure
gold.
37"Then make its seven lamps[b] and set
them up on it so that they light the space
in front of it. 38Its wick trimmers and trays
are to be of pure gold. 39A talent[d] of pure
gold is to be used for the lampstand and
all these accessories. 40See that you make
them according to the pattern[c] shown you
on the mountain.

[a] *10* That is, about 3 3/4 feet long and 2 1/4 feet wide and high or about 1.1 meters long and 68 centimeters wide and high; similarly in verse 17
[b] *23* That is, about 3 feet long, 1 1/2 feet wide and 2 1/4 feet high or about 90 centimeters long, 45 centimeters wide and 68 centimeters high
[c] *25* That is, about 3 inches or about 7.5 centimeters
[d] *39* That is, about 75 pounds or about 34 kilograms

was represented by the length of a man's arm from elbow to extended middle finger. The commonly accepted estimate for the cubit is eighteen inches. Therefore, the ark was about four feet long and two and one quarter feet wide and high.

25:17 ***atonement cover.*** This English phrase translates a Hebrew noun derived from the verb meaning "atone for," "to cover over," or "to make propitiation." The atonement cover was the lid of the ark, the place where God's spirit rested.

25: 22 ***I will meet with you.*** God dwells with His people in the space-time reality in which He created them, and communicates with them in the language with which He endowed them. He is not aloof and He is not silent. His words are an extension of Himself and reflect His nature. They are altogether pure and without blemish, and they are fully authoritative. At the same time, His words reach out to man and are rooted in love, issued from the mercy seat. He speaks them Himself or has them spoken by His authority. He preserves them. He writes them or has them written under His superintendence. God is the ultimate Author of His own Word. This Word is and remains His living and abiding Voice.

25:29 ***pure gold.*** All of the implements for making bread were also to be costly and wonderfully designed to physically represent their holiness. They were "set apart" to God.

25:30 ***the bread of the Presence.*** Twelve loaves representing the twelve tribes of Israel were placed in two rows with six loaves in each row (Lev. 24:5–9). It was called the bread of the presence because it was placed symbolically before the face of God.

25:39 ***talent.*** A talent weighed about 75 pounds.

25:15 [p] 1Ki 8:8 **25:16** [q] Dt 31:26; Heb 9:4
25:17 [r] Ro 3:25 **25:20** [s] 1Ki 8:7; 1Ch 28:18; Heb 9:5
25:21 [t] Ex 26:34 [u] ver 16 **25:22** [v] Nu 7:89; 1Sa 4:4; 2Sa 6:2; 2Ki 19:15; Ps 80:1; Isa 37:16 [w] Ex 29:42-43
25:23 [x] Heb 9:2 **25:29** [y] Nu 4:7 **25:30** [z] Lev 24:5-9
25:31 [a] 1Ki 7:49; Zec 4:2; Heb 9:2; Rev 1:12
25:37 [b] Ex 27:21; Lev 24:3-4; Nu 8:2 **25:40** [c] Ex 26:30; Nu 8:4; Ac 7:44; Heb 8:5*

The Tabernacle

26 "Make the tabernacle with ten curtains of finely twisted linen and blue, purple and scarlet yarn, with cherubim woven into them by a skilled worker. 2All the curtains are to be the same size—twenty-eight cubits long and four cubits wide.[a] 3Join five of the curtains together, and do the same with the other five. 4Make loops of blue material along the edge of the end curtain in one set, and do the same with the end curtain in the other set. 5Make fifty loops on one curtain and fifty loops on the end curtain of the other set, with the loops opposite each other. 6Then make fifty gold clasps and use them to fasten the curtains together so that the tabernacle is a unit.

7"Make curtains of goat hair for the tent over the tabernacle—eleven altogether. 8All eleven curtains are to be the same size—thirty cubits long and four cubits wide.[b] 9Join five of the curtains together into one set and the other six into another set. Fold the sixth curtain double at the front of the tent. 10Make fifty loops along the edge of the end curtain in one set and also along the edge of the end curtain in the other set. 11Then make fifty bronze clasps and put them in the loops to fasten the tent together as a unit. 12As for the additional length of the tent curtains, the half curtain that is left over is to hang down at the rear of the tabernacle. 13The tent curtains will be a cubit[c] longer on both sides; what is left will hang over the sides of the tabernacle so as to cover it. 14Make for the tent a covering of ram skins dyed red, and over that a covering of the other durable leather.[d][d]

15"Make upright frames of acacia wood for the tabernacle. 16Each frame is to be ten cubits long and a cubit and a half wide,[e] 17with two projections set parallel to each other. Make all the frames of the tabernacle in this way. 18Make twenty frames for the south side of the tabernacle 19and make forty silver bases to go under them—two bases for each frame, one under each projection. 20For the other side, the north side of the tabernacle, make twenty frames 21and forty silver bases—two under each frame. 22Make six frames for the far end, that is, the west end of the tabernacle, 23and make two frames for the corners at the far end. 24At these two corners they must be double from the bottom all the way to the top and fitted into a single ring; both shall be like that. 25So there will be eight frames and sixteen silver bases—two under each frame.

26"Also make crossbars of acacia wood: five for the frames on one side of the tabernacle, 27five for those on the other side, and five for the frames on the west, at the far end of the tabernacle. 28The center crossbar is to extend from end to end at the middle of the frames. 29Overlay the frames with gold and make gold rings to hold the crossbars. Also overlay the crossbars with gold.

30"Set up the tabernacle according to the plan[e] shown you on the mountain.

31"Make a curtain[f] of blue, purple and scarlet yarn and finely twisted linen, with cherubim[g] woven into it by a skilled worker. 32Hang it with gold hooks on four posts of acacia wood overlaid with gold and standing on four silver bases. 33Hang the curtain from the clasps and place the ark of the covenant law behind the curtain.[h] The curtain will separate the Holy Place from the Most Holy Place.[i] 34Put the atonement cover[j] on the ark of the covenant law in the Most Holy Place. 35Place the table[k] outside the curtain on the north side of the tabernacle and put the lampstand[l] opposite it on the south side.

36"For the entrance to the tent make a curtain of blue, purple and scarlet yarn and finely twisted linen—the work of an embroiderer. 37Make gold hooks for this curtain and five posts of acacia wood overlaid with gold. And cast five bronze bases for them.

The Altar of Burnt Offering

27 "Build an altar[m] of acacia wood, three cubits[f] high; it is to be square, five cubits long and five cubits wide.[g] 2Make a horn[n] at each of the four corners, so that the horns and the altar are of one piece, and overlay the altar with bronze. 3Make all its utensils of bronze—its pots to remove the ashes, and its shovels, sprinkling bowls, meat forks and firepans. 4Make a grating for it, a bronze network, and make a bronze ring at each of the four corners of the network. 5Put it under the ledge of the altar so that it is halfway up the altar. 6Make poles of acacia wood for the altar and overlay them with bronze. 7The poles

---

[a] *2* That is, about 42 feet long and 6 feet wide or about 13 meters long and 1.8 meters wide
[b] *8* That is, about 45 feet long and 6 feet wide or about 13.5 meters long and 1.8 meters wide
[c] *13* That is, about 18 inches or about 45 centimeters
[d] *14* Possibly the hides of large aquatic mammals (see 25:5)
[e] *16* That is, about 15 feet long and 2 1/4 feet wide or about 4.5 meters long and 68 centimeters wide
[f] *1* That is, about 4 1/2 feet or about 1.4 meters
[g] *1* That is, about 7 1/2 feet or about 2.3 meters long and wide

---

26:1 ***tabernacle.*** The word tabernacle simply means "tent."

26:14 [d] Ex 36:19; Nu 4:25 **26:30** [e] Ex 25:9,40; Ac 7:44; Heb 8:5 **26:31** [f] 2Ch 3:14; Mt 27:51; Heb 9:3 [g] Ex 36:35 **26:33** [h] Ex 40:3,21; Lev 16:2 [i] Heb 9:2-3 **26:34** [j] Ex 25:21; 40:20; Heb 9:5 **26:35** [k] Heb 9:2 [l] Ex 40:22,24 **27:1** [m] Eze 43:13 **27:2** [n] Ps 118:27

are to be inserted into the rings so they will
be on two sides of the altar when it is carried. 8Make the altar hollow, out of boards.
It is to be made just as you were shown[o] on
the mountain.

The Courtyard

9"Make a courtyard for the tabernacle.
The south side shall be a hundred cubits[a]
long and is to have curtains of finely twisted linen, 10with twenty posts and twenty
bronze bases and with silver hooks and
bands on the posts. 11The north side shall
also be a hundred cubits long and is to have
curtains, with twenty posts and twenty
bronze bases and with silver hooks and
bands on the posts.
12"The west end of the courtyard shall be
fifty cubits[b] wide and have curtains, with
ten posts and ten bases. 13On the east end,
toward the sunrise, the courtyard shall
also be fifty cubits wide. 14Curtains fifteen
cubits[c] long are to be on one side of the entrance, with three posts and three bases,
15and curtains fifteen cubits long are to
be on the other side, with three posts and
three bases.
16"For the entrance to the courtyard, provide a curtain twenty cubits[d] long, of blue,
purple and scarlet yarn and finely twisted
linen—the work of an embroiderer—with
four posts and four bases. 17All the posts
around the courtyard are to have silver
bands and hooks, and bronze bases. 18The
courtyard shall be a hundred cubits long
and fifty cubits wide,[e] with curtains of
finely twisted linen five cubits[f] high, and
with bronze bases. 19All the other articles
used in the service of the tabernacle, whatever their function, including all the tent
pegs for it and those for the courtyard, are
to be of bronze.

Oil for the Lampstand

20"Command the Israelites to bring you
clear oil of pressed olives for the light so that
the lamps may be kept burning. 21In the tent
of meeting,[p] outside the curtain that shields
the ark of the covenant law,[q] Aaron and his
sons are to keep the lamps[r] burning before
the LORD from evening till morning. This is
to be a lasting ordinance[s] among the Israelites for the generations to come.

The Priestly Garments

28 "Have Aaron[t] your brother brought
to you from among the Israelites,
along with his sons Nadab and Abihu, Eleazar and Ithamar, so they may serve me as
priests.[u] 2Make sacred garments[v] for your
brother Aaron to give him dignity and hon-
or. 3Tell all the skilled workers[w] to whom
I have given wisdom[x] in such matters that
they are to make garments for Aaron, for his
consecration, so he may serve me as priest.
4These are the garments they are to make:
a breastpiece,[y] an ephod, a robe,[z] a woven
tunic,[a] a turban and a sash. They are to
make these sacred garments for your brother Aaron and his sons, so they may serve
me as priests. 5Have them use gold, and
blue, purple and scarlet yarn, and fine linen.

The Ephod

6"Make the ephod of gold, and of blue,
purple and scarlet yarn, and of finely
twisted linen—the work of skilled hands.
7It is to have two shoulder pieces attached
to two of its corners, so it can be fastened.
8Its skillfully woven waistband is to be like
it—of one piece with the ephod and made
with gold, and with blue, purple and scarlet yarn, and with finely twisted linen.
9"Take two onyx stones and engrave on
them the names of the sons of Israel 10in
the order of their birth—six names on one
stone and the remaining six on the other.
11Engrave the names of the sons of Israel on the two stones the way a gem cutter
engraves a seal. Then mount the stones in
gold filigree settings 12and fasten them on
the shoulder pieces of the ephod as memorial stones for the sons of Israel. Aaron is
to bear the names on his shoulders as a

---

[a] *9* That is, about 150 feet or about 45 meters; also in verse 11 [b] *12* That is, about 75 feet or about 23 meters; also in verse 13 [c] *14* That is, about 23 feet or about 6.8 meters; also in verse 15
[d] *16* That is, about 30 feet or about 9 meters
[e] *18* That is, about 150 feet long and 75 feet wide or about 45 meters long and 23 meters wide
[f] *18* That is, about 7 1/2 feet or about 2.3 meters

27:9–18 ***courtyard for the tabernacle.*** The courtyard separated the ceremonies of worship from common areas. It was arranged to keep people and stray animals from wandering into the tabernacle. Entering the tent could only be a deliberate act.
27:20 ***clear oil of pressed olives.*** All that was used in the tabernacle and sacrifices must be pure and without blemish in order to honor God's holiness. ***the lamp may be kept burning.*** The oil for the lampstand was the gift of the children of Israel. It had to be pure oil, as a symbol of our need to call upon the Lord from a pure heart (2 Tim. 2:22). The lamps were to burn continuously, a reminder of the perpetual need of the sinner for the light of God's word, "a lamp for my feet, a light on my path" (Ps. 119:105).

28:3 ***all the skilled workers.*** This expression literally means "those who are wise at heart." The same expression is used of the skillful women who did the weaving (35:25).
28:5–14 ***ephod.*** The ephod has been described as a cape or vest made of fine linen with brilliant colors. Its two main sections covered the chest and back, with seams at the shoulders and a band at the waist.

27:8 [o] Ex 25:9,40 **27:21** [p] Ex 28:43 [q] Ex 26:31,33 [r] Ex 25:37; 30:8; 1Sa 3:3; 2Ch 13:11 [s] Ex 29:9; Lev 3:17; 16:34; Nu 18:23; 19:21 **28:1** [t] Heb 5:4 [u] Nu 18:1-7; Heb 5:1 **28:2** [v] Ex 29:5,29; 31:10; 39:1; Lev 8:7-9,30 **28:3** [w] Ex 31:6; 36:1 [x] Ex 31:3 **28:4** [y] ver 15-30 [z] ver 31-35 [a] ver 39

memorial before the LORD. 13Make gold filigree settings 14and two braided chains of pure gold, like a rope, and attach the chains to the settings.

The Breastpiece

15"Fashion a breastpiece for making decisions—the work of skilled hands. Make it like the ephod: of gold, and of blue, purple and scarlet yarn, and of finely twisted linen. 16It is to be square—a span[a] long and a span wide—and folded double. 17Then mount four rows of precious stones on it. The first row shall be carnelian, chrysolite and beryl; 18the second row shall be turquoise, lapis lazuli and emerald; 19the third row shall be jacinth, agate and amethyst; 20the fourth row shall be topaz, onyx and jasper.[b] Mount them in gold filigree settings. 21There are to be twelve stones, one for each of the names of the sons of Israel, each engraved like a seal with the name of one of the twelve tribes.

22"For the breastpiece make braided chains of pure gold, like a rope. 23Make two gold rings for it and fasten them to two corners of the breastpiece. 24Fasten the two gold chains to the rings at the corners of the breastpiece, 25and the other ends of the chains to the two settings, attaching them to the shoulder pieces of the ephod at the front. 26Make two gold rings and attach them to the other two corners of the breastpiece on the inside edge next to the ephod. 27Make two more gold rings and attach them to the bottom of the shoulder pieces on the front of the ephod, close to the seam just above the waistband of the ephod. 28The rings of the breastpiece are to be tied to the rings of the ephod with blue cord, connecting it to the waistband, so that the breastpiece will not swing out from the ephod.

29"Whenever Aaron enters the Holy Place,[b] he will bear the names of the sons of Israel over his heart on the breastpiece of decision as a continuing memorial before the LORD. 30Also put the Urim and the Thummim[c] in the breastpiece, so they may be over Aaron's heart whenever he enters the presence of the LORD. Thus Aaron will always bear the means of making decisions for the Israelites over his heart before the LORD.

Other Priestly Garments

31"Make the robe of the ephod entirely of blue cloth, 32with an opening for the head in its center. There shall be a woven edge like a collar[c] around this opening, so that it will not tear. 33Make pomegranates of blue, purple and scarlet yarn around the hem of the robe, with gold bells between them. 34The gold bells and the pomegranates are to alternate around the hem of the robe. 35Aaron must wear it when he ministers. The sound of the bells will be heard when he enters the Holy Place before the LORD and when he comes out, so that he will not die.

36"Make a plate of pure gold and engrave on it as on a seal: HOLY TO THE LORD.[d] 37Fasten a blue cord to it to attach it to the turban; it is to be on the front of the turban. 38It will be on Aaron's forehead, and he will bear the guilt[e] involved in the sacred gifts the Israelites consecrate, whatever their gifts may be. It will be on Aaron's forehead continually so that they will be acceptable to the LORD.

39"Weave the tunic of fine linen and make the turban of fine linen. The sash is to be the work of an embroiderer. 40Make tunics, sashes and caps for Aaron's sons[f] to give them dignity and honor. 41After you put these clothes on your brother Aaron and his sons, anoint[g] and ordain them. Consecrate them so they may serve me as priests.[h]

42"Make linen undergarments[i] as a covering for the body, reaching from the waist to the thigh. 43Aaron and his sons must wear them whenever they enter the tent of meeting[j] or approach the altar to minister in the Holy Place, so that they will not incur guilt and die.[k]

"This is to be a lasting ordinance[l] for Aaron and his descendants.

Consecration of the Priests

29 "This is what you are to do to consecrate them, so they may serve me as priests: Take a young bull and two rams

[a] *16* That is, about 9 inches or about 23 centimeters
[b] *20* The precise identification of some of these precious stones is uncertain.
[c] *32* The meaning of the Hebrew for this word is uncertain.

28:16 *span.* The span was determined as the length from the tip of the thumb to the tip of the small finger on an outstretched hand. It is generally estimated as nine inches, or half a cubit.

28:30 *the Urim and the Thummim.* These translated Hebrew words mean "Lights" and "Perfections." Together their names may mean "perfect knowledge" or a similar idea. It is not known exactly what the Urim and Thummim were, or how they were used. Some have suggested that they were two stones used for the casting of lots.

28:42 *undergarments.* The command to wear undergarments protected the modesty of the priests. Given the sexually preoccupied worship of Israel's neighbors, this provision was decidedly countercultural.

29:1–9 *consecrate them.* The outward purification process was used to symbolize the inward purity which was demanded of the priests of Israel, the

28:29 [b] ver 12 **28:30** [c] Lev 8:8; Nu 27:21; Dt 33:8; Ezr 2:63; Ne 7:65 **28:36** [d] Zec 14:20 **28:38** [e] Lev 10:17; 22:9, 16; Nu 18:1; Heb 9:28; 1Pe 2:24 **28:40** [f] ver 4; Ex 39:41 **28:41** [g] Ex 29:7; Lev 10:7 [h] Ex 29:7-9; 30:30; 40:15; Lev 8:1-36; Heb 7:28 **28:42** [i] Lev 6:10; 16:4, 23; Eze 44:18 **28:43** [j] Ex 27:21 [k] Ex 20:26 [l] Lev 17:7

without defect. 2And from the finest wheat
flour make round loaves without yeast,
thick loaves without yeast and with olive
oil mixed in, and thin loaves without yeast
and brushed with olive oil.[m] 3Put them in
a basket and present them along with the
bull and the two rams. 4Then bring Aaron
and his sons to the entrance to the tent of
meeting and wash them with water.[n] 5Take
the garments[o] and dress Aaron with the
tunic, the robe of the ephod, the ephod itself and the breastpiece. Fasten the ephod
on him by its skillfully woven waistband.[p]
6Put the turban on his head and attach the
sacred emblem[q] to the turban. 7Take the
anointing oil[r] and anoint him by pouring it
on his head. 8Bring his sons and dress them
in tunics 9and fasten caps on them. Then tie
sashes on Aaron and his sons.[a][s] The priesthood is theirs by a lasting ordinance.[t]

"Then you shall ordain Aaron and his
sons.

10"Bring the bull to the front of the tent of
meeting, and Aaron and his sons shall lay
their hands on its head. 11Slaughter it in the
LORD's presence at the entrance to the tent
of meeting. 12Take some of the bull's blood
and put it on the horns[u] of the altar with
your finger, and pour out the rest of it at the
base of the altar. 13Then take all the fat[v] on
the internal organs, the long lobe of the liver, and both kidneys with the fat on them,
and burn them on the altar. 14But burn the
bull's flesh and its hide and its intestines
outside the camp.[w] It is a sin offering.[b]

15"Take one of the rams, and Aaron
and his sons shall lay their hands on its
head. 16Slaughter it and take the blood and
splash it against the sides of the altar. 17Cut
the ram into pieces and wash the internal
organs and the legs, putting them with the
head and the other pieces. 18Then burn the
entire ram on the altar. It is a burnt offering to the LORD, a pleasing aroma,[x] a food
offering presented to the LORD.

19"Take the other ram,[y] and Aaron and
his sons shall lay their hands on its head.
20Slaughter it, take some of its blood and put
it on the lobes of the right ears of Aaron and
his sons, on the thumbs of their right hands,
and on the big toes of their right feet. Then
splash blood against the sides of the altar.
21And take some blood[z] from the altar and
some of the anointing oil[a] and sprinkle it on
Aaron and his garments and on his sons
and their garments. Then he and his sons
and their garments will be consecrated.[b]

22"Take from this ram the fat, the fat tail,
the fat on the internal organs, the long lobe
of the liver, both kidneys with the fat on
them, and the right thigh. (This is the ram
for the ordination.) 23From the basket of
bread made without yeast, which is before
the LORD, take one round loaf, one thick
loaf with olive oil mixed in, and one thin
loaf. 24Put all these in the hands of Aaron
and his sons and have them wave them before the LORD as a wave offering.[c] 25Then
take them from their hands and burn them
on the altar along with the burnt offering
for a pleasing aroma to the LORD, a food
offering presented to the LORD. 26After you
take the breast of the ram for Aaron's ordination, wave it before the LORD as a wave
offering, and it will be your share.[d]

27"Consecrate those parts of the ordination ram that belong to Aaron and his
sons:[e] the breast that was waved and the
thigh that was presented. 28This is always
to be the perpetual share from the Israelites for Aaron and his sons. It is the contribution the Israelites are to make to the
LORD from their fellowship offerings.[f]

29"Aaron's sacred garments will belong
to his descendants so that they can be
anointed and ordained in them.[g] 30The son[h]
who succeeds him as priest and comes to
the tent of meeting to minister in the Holy
Place is to wear them seven days.

31"Take the ram for the ordination and
cook the meat in a sacred place. 32At the
entrance to the tent of meeting, Aaron and
his sons are to eat the meat of the ram and
the bread[i] that is in the basket. 33They are
to eat these offerings by which atonement
was made for their ordination and consecration. But no one else may eat[j] them,
because they are sacred. 34And if any of the

---

[a] 9 Hebrew; Septuagint *on them* [b] *14* Or *purification offering*; also in verse 36

---

intermediaries between the people and their holy God. Obviously the priests were not perfectly pure; it was only God's gracious act of accepting blood sacrifices that allowed the priests to stand in His presence on behalf of the people. The outward washings of the priests showed that they were doing everything possible to live their lives in the way they had been commanded by God. Likewise, in the New Testament era, the only reason that Christians can stand before God as believer-priests is because God graciously accepts Christ's sacrifice on behalf of our sins.

29:9 ***ordain.*** The verb translated *ordain* in this verse literally means "to fill one's hand." A king was handed a rod as the symbol of his political power; so the hand of the priest was filled with spiritual power.

29:18 ***burnt offering.*** Aaron and his sons needed to offer sacrifices for themselves as much as for their fellow Israelites (Heb. 5:1 – 4).

29:24 ***wave offering.*** This offering made it clear that everything was owed to God, but some was received back as God's gift (Lev. 7:30; 10:14).

29:2 [m] Lev 2:1, 4; 6:19-23 **29:4** [n] Ex 40:12; Heb 10:22 **29:5** [o] Ex 28:2; Lev 8:7 [p] Ex 28:8 **29:6** [q] Lev 8:9 **29:7** [r] Ex 30:25, 30, 31; Lev 8:12; 21:10; Nu 35:25; Ps 133:2 **29:9** [s] Ex 28:40 [t] Ex 40:15; Nu 3:10; 18:7; 25:13; Dt 18:5 **29:12** [u] Ex 27:2 **29:13** [v] Lev 3:3, 5, 9 **29:14** [w] Lev 4:11-12, 21; Heb 13:11 **29:18** [x] Ge 8:21 **29:19** [y] ver 3 **29:21** [z] Heb 9:22 [a] Ex 30:25, 31 [b] ver 1 **29:24** [c] Lev 7:30 **29:26** [d] Lev 7:31-34 **29:27** [e] Lev 7:31, 34; Dt 18:3 **29:28** [f] Lev 10:15 **29:29** [g] Nu 20:26, 28 **29:30** [h] Nu 20:28 **29:32** [i] Mt 12:4 **29:33** [j] Lev 10:14; 22:10, 13

meat of the ordination ram or any bread is
left over till morning,[k] burn it up. It must
not be eaten, because it is sacred.
35"Do for Aaron and his sons everything
I have commanded you, taking seven days
to ordain them. 36Sacrifice a bull each day[l]
as a sin offering to make atonement. Purify
the altar by making atonement for it, and
anoint it to consecrate[m] it. 37For seven days
make atonement for the altar and consecrate it. Then the altar will be most holy,
and whatever touches it will be holy.[n]
38"This is what you are to offer on the altar regularly each day:[o] two lambs a year
old. 39Offer one in the morning and the other at twilight.[p] 40With the first lamb offer a
tenth of an ephah[a] of the finest flour mixed
with a quarter of a hin[b] of oil from pressed
olives, and a quarter of a hin of wine as a
drink offering. 41Sacrifice the other lamb
at twilight with the same grain offering
and its drink offering as in the morning—a
pleasing aroma, a food offering presented
to the LORD.
42"For the generations to come[q] this
burnt offering is to be made regularly at
the entrance to the tent of meeting, before
the LORD. There I will meet you and speak
to you;[r] 43there also I will meet with the Israelites, and the place will be consecrated
by my glory.[s]
44"So I will consecrate the tent of meeting and the altar and will consecrate Aaron and his sons to serve me as priests.[t]
45Then I will dwell[u] among the Israelites
and be their God.[v] 46They will know that I
am the LORD their God, who brought them
out of Egypt so that I might dwell among
them. I am the LORD their God.[w]

The Altar of Incense

30 "Make an altar[x] of acacia wood for
burning incense.[y] 2It is to be square,
a cubit long and a cubit wide, and two cubits high[c]—its horns[z] of one piece with
it. 3Overlay the top and all the sides and
the horns with pure gold, and make a gold
molding around it. 4Make two gold rings
for the altar below the molding—two on
each of the opposite sides—to hold the
poles used to carry it. 5Make the poles of
acacia wood and overlay them with gold.
6Put the altar in front of the curtain that
shields the ark of the covenant law—before the atonement cover[a] that is over the
tablets of the covenant law—where I will
meet with you.
7"Aaron must burn fragrant incense[b] on
the altar every morning when he tends the
lamps. 8He must burn incense again when
he lights the lamps at twilight so incense
will burn regularly before the LORD for the
generations to come. 9Do not offer on this
altar any other incense[c] or any burnt offering or grain offering, and do not pour a
drink offering on it. 10Once a year Aaron
shall make atonement[d] on its horns. This
annual atonement must be made with the
blood of the atoning sin offering[d] for the
generations to come. It is most holy to the
LORD."

Atonement Money

11Then the LORD said to Moses, 12"When
you take a census[e] of the Israelites to count
them, each one must pay the LORD a ransom[f] for his life at the time he is counted.
Then no plague[g] will come on them when
you number them. 13Each one who crosses over to those already counted is to give

---

[a] *40* That is, probably about 3 1/2 pounds or about 1.6 kilograms [b] *40* That is, probably about 1 quart or about 1 liter [c] *2* That is, about 1 1/2 feet long and wide and 3 feet high or about 45 centimeters long and wide and 90 centimeters high [d] *10* Or *purification offering*

29:40 *ephah ... hin.* One tenth of an ephah was about two quarts; one fourth of a hin was about one quart.

29:45 *dwell among the Israelites.* Man is God's special creation, created in His image and likeness. A part of that image and likeness is the uniqueness of personality that allows communion with God. He did not create a race of robots but rather endowed man with a will so that he might choose fellowship with God. In Israel, fellowship with God centered in the tabernacle and especially in the mercy seat which symbolized His presence. Today, believers have fellowship with God through the indwelling of the Holy Spirit. In eternity He will dwell in the midst of His people more fully than ever before.

30:7 *fragrant incense.* Burning incense was a privilege restricted to those who were allowed to approach God.

30:9 *other incense.* The incense offered to God was to be made from a special recipe consecrated to be used only in the worship at the tabernacle. No other incense was acceptable.

30:10 *atonement.* The sacrificial blood of the sin offering (Lev. 16:18) was applied to the incense altar to indicate that even this article needed cleansing to preserve its ideal holiness because of man's willful or accidental sin. The Hebrew word for "atonement" involves the covering or canceling of sin, resulting in the offender being reconciled to God. Without blood being shed there can be no forgiveness (Heb. 9:22). The atonement made annually for this small altar is a reminder that everything in God's service must be holy to the Lord (Zech. 14:20).

30:12 *ransom.* The idea is to pay a price for one's life. The Israelites had to acknowledge that their lives

29:34 [k] Ex 12:10 **29:36** [l] Heb 10:11 [m] Ex 40:10 **29:37** [n] Ex 30:28-29; 40:10; Mt 23:19 **29:38** [o] Nu 28:3-8; 1Ch 16:40; Da 12:11 **29:39** [p] Eze 46:13-15 **29:42** [q] Ex 30:8 [r] Ex 25:22 **29:43** [s] 1Ki 8:11 **29:44** [t] Lev 21:15 **29:45** [u] Ex 25:8; Lev 26:12; Zec 2:10; Jn 14:17 [v] 2Co 6:16; Rev 21:3 **29:46** [w] Ex 20:2 **30:1** [x] Ex 37:25 [y] Rev 8:3 **30:2** [z] Ex 27:2 **30:6** [a] Ex 25:22; 26:34 **30:7** [b] ver 34-35; Ex 27:21; 1Sa 2:28 **30:9** [c] Lev 10:1 **30:10** [d] Lev 16:18-19, 30 **30:12** [e] Ex 38:25; Nu 1:2, 49; 2Sa 24:1 [f] Nu 31:50; Mt 20:28 [g] 2Sa 24:13

a half shekel,[a] according to the sanctuary shekel,[h] which weighs twenty gerahs. This half shekel is an offering to the LORD. 14All who cross over, those twenty years old or more, are to give an offering to the LORD. 15The rich are not to give more than a half shekel and the poor are not to give less[i] when you make the offering to the LORD to atone for your lives. 16Receive the atonement money from the Israelites and use it for the service of the tent of meeting.[j] It will be a memorial for the Israelites before the LORD, making atonement for your lives."

Basin for Washing

17Then the LORD said to Moses, 18"Make a bronze basin,[k] with its bronze stand, for washing. Place it between the tent of meeting and the altar, and put water in it. 19Aaron and his sons are to wash their hands and feet[l] with water[m] from it. 20Whenever they enter the tent of meeting, they shall wash with water so that they will not die. Also, when they approach the altar to minister by presenting a food offering to the LORD, 21they shall wash their hands and feet so that they will not die. This is to be a lasting ordinance[n] for Aaron and his descendants for the generations to come."

Anointing Oil

22Then the LORD said to Moses, 23"Take the following fine spices: 500 shekels[b] of liquid myrrh,[o] half as much (that is, 250 shekels) of fragrant cinnamon, 250 shekels[c] of fragrant calamus, 24500 shekels of cassia[p]—all according to the sanctuary shekel—and a hin[d] of olive oil. 25Make these into a sacred anointing oil, a fragrant blend, the work of a perfumer.[q] It will be the sacred anointing oil.[r] 26Then use it to anoint[s] the tent of meeting, the ark of the covenant law, 27the table and all its articles, the lampstand and its accessories, the altar of incense, 28the altar of burnt offering and all its utensils, and the basin with its stand. 29You shall consecrate them so they will be most holy, and whatever touches them will be holy.[t]

30"Anoint Aaron and his sons and consecrate[u] them so they may serve me as priests. 31Say to the Israelites, 'This is to be my sacred anointing oil for the generations to come. 32Do not pour it on anyone else's body and do not make any other oil using the same formula. It is sacred, and you are to consider it sacred.[v] 33Whoever makes perfume like it and puts it on anyone other than a priest must be cut off[w] from their people.'"

Incense

34Then the LORD said to Moses, "Take fragrant spices—gum resin, onycha and galbanum—and pure frankincense, all in equal amounts, 35and make a fragrant blend of incense, the work of a perfumer.[x] It is to be salted and pure and sacred. 36Grind some of it to powder and place it in front of the ark of the covenant law in the tent of meeting, where I will meet with you. It shall be most holy[y] to you. 37Do not make any incense with this formula for yourselves; consider it holy[z] to the LORD. 38Whoever makes incense like it to enjoy its fragrance must be cut off[a] from their people."

Bezalel and Oholiab

31 Then the LORD said to Moses, 2"See, I have chosen Bezalel[b] son of Uri, the son of Hur, of the tribe of Judah, 3and I have filled him with the Spirit of God, with wisdom, with understanding, with knowledge and with all kinds of skills[c]—4to make artistic designs for work in gold, silver and bronze, 5to cut and set stones, to work in wood, and to engage in all kinds of crafts. 6Moreover, I have appointed Oholiab son of Ahisamak, of the tribe of Dan, to help him. Also I have given ability to all the skilled workers to make everything I have commanded you: 7the tent of meeting,[d] the ark of the covenant law[e] with the atonement cover[f] on it, and all the other furnishings of the tent— 8the table[g] and its articles, the pure gold lampstand[h] and all its accessories, the altar of incense, 9the altar of burnt offering and all its utensils, the basin with its stand— 10and also the woven garments[i], both the sacred garments for Aaron the priest and the garments for his sons when they serve as priests, 11and

---

[a] *13* That is, about 1/5 ounce or about 5.8 grams; also in verse 15 [b] *23* That is, about 12 1/2 pounds or about 5.8 kilograms; also in verse 24
[c] *23* That is, about 6 1/4 pounds or about 2.9 kilograms [d] *24* That is, probably about 1 gallon or about 3.8 liters

---

were from God and governed by Him by giving Him an offering of money.

30:19 ***wash their hands and feet.*** The continual washing was symbolic of the need to be cleansed from sin regularly.

31:3 ***filled him with the Spirit of God.*** We often think of the "filling of the Spirit" only in connection with Acts 2, but passages such as this one help us to see the continuity of God's work among His people through the ages. In this case, the Spirit empowered uniquely gifted people to design and build a tabernacle befitting a holy and magnificent God.

30:13 [h] Nu 3:47; Mt 17:24 **30:15** [i] Pr 22:2; Eph 6:9 **30:16** [j] Ex 38:25-28 **30:18** [k] Ex 38:8; 40:7,30 **30:19** [l] Ex 40:31-32; Isa 52:11 [m] Ps 26:6 **30:21** [n] Ex 27:21; 28:43 **30:23** [o] Ge 37:25 **30:24** [p] Ps 45:8 **30:25** [q] Ex 37:29 [r] Ex 40:9 **30:26** [s] Ex 40:9; Lev 8:10; Nu 7:1 **30:29** [t] Ex 29:37 **30:30** [u] Ex 29:7; Lev 8:2,12,30 **30:32** [v] ver 25,37 **30:33** [w] ver 38; Ge 17:14 **30:35** [x] ver 25 **30:36** [y] ver 32; Ex 29:37; Lev 2:3 **30:37** [z] ver 32 **30:38** [a] ver 33 **31:2** [b] Ex 36:1,2; 1Ch 2:20 **31:3** [c] 1Ki 7:14 **31:7** [d] Ex 36:8-38 [e] Ex 37:1-5 [f] Ex 37:6 **31:8** [g] Ex 37:10-16 [h] Ex 37:17-24 **31:10** [i] Ex 28:2; 39:1,41

the anointing oil[j] and fragrant incense for the Holy Place. They are to make them just as I commanded you."

The Sabbath

12Then the LORD said to Moses, 13"Say to the Israelites, 'You must observe my Sabbaths.[k] This will be a sign[l] between me and you for the generations to come, so you may know that I am the LORD, who makes you holy.[m]

14" 'Observe the Sabbath, because it is holy to you. Anyone who desecrates it is to be put to death;[n] those who do any work on that day must be cut off from their people. 15For six days work[o] is to be done, but the seventh day is a day of sabbath rest,[p] holy to the LORD. Whoever does any work on the Sabbath day is to be put to death. 16The Israelites are to observe the Sabbath, celebrating it for the generations to come as a lasting covenant. 17It will be a sign[q] between me and the Israelites forever, for in six days the LORD made the heavens and the earth, and on the seventh day he rested and was refreshed.[r]' "

18When the LORD finished speaking to Moses on Mount Sinai, he gave him the two tablets of the covenant law, the tablets of stone[s] inscribed by the finger of God.[t]

The Golden Calf

32 When the people saw that Moses was so long in coming down from the mountain,[u] they gathered around Aaron and said, "Come, make us gods[a] who will go before us. As for this fellow Moses who brought us up out of Egypt, we don't know what has happened to him."[v]

2Aaron answered them, "Take off the gold earrings[w] that your wives, your sons and your daughters are wearing, and bring them to me." 3So all the people took off their earrings and brought them to Aaron. 4He took what they handed him and made it into an idol cast in the shape of a calf,[x] fashioning it with a tool. Then they said, "These are your gods,[b] Israel, who brought you up out of Egypt."

5When Aaron saw this, he built an altar in front of the calf and announced, "Tomorrow there will be a festival[y] to the LORD." 6So the next day the people rose early and sacrificed burnt offerings and presented fellowship offerings.[z] Afterward they sat down to eat and drink and got up to indulge in revelry.[a]

7Then the LORD said to Moses, "Go down, because your people, whom you brought up out of Egypt,[b] have become corrupt.[c] 8They have been quick to turn away from what I commanded them and have made themselves an idol[d] cast in the shape of a calf. They have bowed down to it and sacrificed[e] to it and have said, 'These are your gods, Israel, who brought you up out of Egypt.'[f]

9"I have seen these people," the LORD said to Moses, "and they are a stiff-necked[g] people. 10Now leave me alone so that my anger may burn against them and that I may destroy them. Then I will make you into a great nation."[h]

11But Moses sought the favor[i] of the LORD his God. "LORD," he said, "why should your anger burn against your people, whom you brought out of Egypt with great power and a mighty hand?[j] 12Why should the Egyptians say, 'It was with evil intent that he brought them out, to kill them in the mountains and to wipe them off the face of the earth'?[k] Turn from your fierce anger; relent and do not bring disaster on your people. 13Remember[l] your servants Abraham, Isaac and Israel, to whom you swore by your own self:[m] 'I will make your descendants as numerous as the stars[n] in the sky and I will give your descendants all this land[o] I promised them, and it will be their inheritance forever.' "

[a] *1* Or *a god*; also in verses 23 and 31 [b] *4* Or *This is your god*; also in verse 8

31:18 *the finger of God.* This verse underscores the divine origin of the law. Scholars of religion have long spoken of Israel's religious ideas as its unique contribution to civilization, much as the Greeks developed philosophy and the Romans displayed a genius for organization and empire-building. Yet such a comparison misses the point of Scripture. The Bible speaks not of the genius of Israel, but of the finger of God. The Ten Commandments were not the product of man, but the revelation of the Lord.

32:1–35 The Golden Calf—The story of the Israelites' worship of the golden calf reveals both the unfaithfulness of the Israelites and God's great mercy. Even though the people had so quickly broken their promise to obey Him, God forgave their sin and began again with them

32:2–3 *gold earrings.* These were part of the treasure from Egypt that should have been used for building the tabernacle (35:20–29).

32:4 *cast in the shape of a calf.* This was an ominous worship symbol. Not only were the cow and the bull worshipped in Egypt, but the bull was a familiar embodiment of Baal seen in Canaan. It appears that the worship of the Lord had been blended with the symbols of Baal and other fertility gods. In this one scene, the people broke the first three of God's commandments.

31:11 [j] Ex 30:22-32 **31:13** [k] Ex 20:8; Lev 19:3,30 [l] Eze 20:12,20 [m] Lev 11:44 **31:14** [n] Nu 15:32-36 **31:15** [o] Ex 20:8-11 [p] Ge 2:3; Ex 16:23 **31:17** [q] ver 13 [r] Ge 2:2-3 **31:18** [s] Ex 24:12 [t] Ex 32:15-16; 34:1,28; Dt 4:13; 5:22 **32:1** [u] Ex 24:18; Dt 9:9-12 [v] Ac 7:40* **32:2** [w] Ex 35:22 **32:4** [x] Dt 9:16; Ne 9:18; Ps 106:19; Ac 7:41 **32:5** [y] Lev 23:2,37; 2Ki 10:20 **32:6** [z] Nu 25:2; Ac 7:41 [a] ver 17-19; 1Co 10:7* **32:7** [b] ver 4,11 [c] Ge 6:11-12; Dt 9:12 **32:8** [d] Ex 20:4 [e] Ex 22:20 [f] 1Ki 12:28 **32:9** [g] Ex 33:3,5; 34:9; Isa 48:4; Ac 7:51 **32:10** [h] Nu 14:12; Dt 9:14 **32:11** [i] Dt 9:18 [j] Dt 9:26 **32:12** [k] Nu 14:13-16; Dt 9:28 **32:13** [l] Ex 2:24 [m] Ge 22:16; Heb 6:13 [n] Ge 15:5; 26:4 [o] Ge 12:7

14Then the LORD relented[p] and did not
bring on his people the disaster he had
threatened.
15Moses turned and went down the
mountain with the two tablets of the covenant law[q] in his hands.[r] They were inscribed on both sides, front and back.
16The tablets were the work of God; the
writing was the writing of God, engraved
on the tablets.[s]
17When Joshua heard the noise of the
people shouting, he said to Moses, "There
is the sound of war in the camp."
18Moses replied:

"It is not the sound of victory,
it is not the sound of defeat;
it is the sound of singing that I hear."

19When Moses approached the camp and
saw the calf[t] and the dancing, his anger
burned and he threw the tablets out of his
hands, breaking them to pieces[u] at the foot
of the mountain. 20And he took the calf the
people had made and burned it in the fire;
then he ground it to powder, scattered it on
the water[v] and made the Israelites drink it.
21He said to Aaron, "What did these people do to you, that you led them into such
great sin?"
22"Do not be angry, my lord," Aaron answered. "You know how prone these people are to evil.[w] 23They said to me, 'Make
us gods who will go before us. As for this
fellow Moses who brought us up out of
Egypt, we don't know what has happened
to him.'[x] 24So I told them, 'Whoever has any
gold jewelry, take it off.' Then they gave me
the gold, and I threw it into the fire, and out
came this calf!"[y]
25Moses saw that the people were running wild and that Aaron had let them get
out of control and so become a laughingstock to their enemies. 26So he stood at the
entrance to the camp and said, "Whoever
is for the LORD, come to me." And all the
Levites rallied to him.
27Then he said to them, "This is what
the LORD, the God of Israel, says: 'Each
man strap a sword to his side. Go back
and forth through the camp from one end
to the other, each killing his brother and
friend and neighbor.'"[z] 28The Levites did
as Moses commanded, and that day about
three thousand of the people died. 29Then
Moses said, "You have been set apart to the
LORD today, for you were against your own
sons and brothers, and he has blessed you
this day."
30The next day Moses said to the people,
"You have committed a great sin.[a] But now
I will go up to the LORD; perhaps I can make
atonement[b] for your sin."
31So Moses went back to the LORD and
said, "Oh, what a great sin these people
have committed![c] They have made themselves gods of gold.[d] 32But now, please forgive their sin—but if not, then blot me[e] out
of the book[f] you have written."
33The LORD replied to Moses, "Whoever has sinned against me I will blot out[g] of
my book. 34Now go, lead the people to the
place[h] I spoke of, and my angel[i] will go before you. However, when the time comes
for me to punish,[j] I will punish them for
their sin."
35And the LORD struck the people with a
plague because of what they did with the
calf[k] Aaron had made.

33 Then the LORD said to Moses, "Leave
this place, you and the people you
brought up out of Egypt, and go up to
the land I promised on oath to Abraham,
Isaac and Jacob, saying, 'I will give it to
your descendants.'[l] 2I will send an angel[m]
before you and drive out the Canaanites,
Amorites, Hittites, Perizzites, Hivites and
Jebusites.[n] 3Go up to the land flowing with
milk and honey.[o] But I will not go with you,
because you are a stiff-necked[p] people and
I might destroy[q] you on the way."
4When the people heard these distressing words, they began to mourn[r] and no

---

32:14 *the LORD relented.* Here is a wonderful example of the interaction of faithful intercessory prayer and the purpose of the Lord. He uses our prayer combined with His own determination to make His will come to pass.

32:25–26 *were running wild.* Obedience to God is many times just the opposite of "what everybody else is doing." Humans are very prone to giving in to peer pressure at the crucial moment. We often care more about what those around us think than about what God thinks. Aaron and the other Levites fell into this trap initially, but when Moses gave them another chance to say where their loyalties really lay, they chose the path of obedience. Even though almost "everybody was doing it," they were willing to say, "No, this is wrong. We were wrong." The Levites were not innocent, but God blessed them for their repentance and their obedience.

32:27–28 *his brother . . . friend . . . neighbor.* This terrible massacre is hard for us to reconcile with our feelings, but we must realize that sin is loathsome, and deserving of death. The Levites were used by God to execute His judgment in this instance, but they were not given general authority to kill sinners.

32:32–33 *blot me out of the book.* Like Paul many centuries later, Moses could almost wish himself to be cursed, if by being so he could secure the salvation of his people (Rom. 9:3).

32:34 *the time comes.* This may refer to the day of the Lord, proclaimed by later prophets (Joel 2; Zeph. 1).

32:14 [p] 2Sa 24:16; Ps 106:45 **32:15** [q] Ex 31:18 [r] Dt 9:15
32:16 [s] Ex 31:18 **32:19** [t] Dt 9:16 [u] Dt 9:17
32:20 [v] Dt 9:21 **32:22** [w] Dt 9:24 **32:23** [x] ver 1
32:24 [y] ver 4 **32:27** [z] Nu 25:3,5; Dt 33:9
32:30 [a] 1Sa 12:20 [b] Lev 1:4; Nu 25:13 **32:31** [c] Dt 9:18
[d] Ex 20:23 **32:32** [e] Ro 9:3 [f] Ps 69:28; Da 12:1; Php 4:3;
Rev 3:5; 21:27 **32:33** [g] Dt 29:20; Ps 9:5 **32:34** [h] Ex 3:17
[i] Ex 23:20 [j] Dt 32:35; Ps 99:8; Ro 2:5-6 **32:35** [k] ver 4
33:1 [l] Ge 12:7 **33:2** [m] Ex 32:34 [n] Ex 23:27-31; Jos 24:11
33:3 [o] Ex 3:8 [p] Ex 32:9 [q] Ex 32:10 **33:4** [r] Nu 14:39

one put on any ornaments. 5For the LORD
had said to Moses, "Tell the Israelites, 'You
are a stiff-necked people. If I were to go
with you even for a moment, I might destroy you. Now take off your ornaments
and I will decide what to do with you.'" 6So
the Israelites stripped off their ornaments
at Mount Horeb.

The Tent of Meeting

7Now Moses used to take a tent and pitch
it outside the camp some distance away,
calling it the "tent of meeting."[s] Anyone inquiring of the LORD would go to the tent of
meeting outside the camp. 8And whenever
Moses went out to the tent, all the people
rose and stood at the entrances to their
tents,[t] watching Moses until he entered the
tent. 9As Moses went into the tent, the pillar of cloud[u] would come down and stay at
the entrance, while the LORD spoke[v] with
Moses. 10Whenever the people saw the pillar of cloud standing at the entrance to the
tent, they all stood and worshiped, each
at the entrance to their tent. 11The LORD
would speak to Moses face to face,[w] as one
speaks to a friend. Then Moses would return to the camp, but his young aide Joshua
son of Nun did not leave the tent.

Moses and the Glory of the LORD

12Moses said to the LORD, "You have
been telling me, 'Lead these people,'[x] but
you have not let me know whom you will
send with me. You have said, 'I know you
by name[y] and you have found favor with
me.' 13If you are pleased with me, teach me
your ways[z] so I may know you and continue to find favor with you. Remember that
this nation is your people."[a]
14The LORD replied, "My Presence[b] will
go with you, and I will give you rest."[c]
15Then Moses said to him, "If your Presence does not go with us, do not send us
up from here. 16How will anyone know
that you are pleased with me and with
your people unless you go with us?[d] What
else will distinguish me and your people
from all the other people on the face of the
earth?"[e]
17And the LORD said to Moses, "I will do
the very thing you have asked, because I
am pleased with you and I know you by
name."
18Then Moses said, "Now show me your
glory."
19And the LORD said, "I will cause all
my goodness to pass in front of you, and I
will proclaim my name, the LORD, in your
presence. I will have mercy on whom I will
have mercy, and I will have compassion on
whom I will have compassion.[f] 20But," he
said, "you cannot see my face, for no one
may see[g] me and live."
21Then the LORD said, "There is a place
near me where you may stand on a rock.
22When my glory passes by, I will put you
in a cleft in the rock and cover you with my
hand[h] until I have passed by. 23Then I will
remove my hand and you will see my back;
but my face must not be seen."

The New Stone Tablets

34 The LORD said to Moses, "Chisel out
two stone tablets like the first ones,
and I will write on them the words that
were on the first tablets,[i] which you broke.[j]
2Be ready in the morning, and then come
up on Mount Sinai.[k] Present yourself to me
there on top of the mountain. 3No one is to
come with you or be seen anywhere on the
mountain;[l] not even the flocks and herds
may graze in front of the mountain."
4So Moses chiseled out two stone tablets
like the first ones and went up Mount Sinai
early in the morning, as the LORD had commanded him; and he carried the two stone
tablets in his hands. 5Then the LORD came
down in the cloud and stood there with him
and proclaimed his name, the LORD.[m] 6And
he passed in front of Moses, proclaiming,

33:5 *stiff-necked.* Contrary to popular belief, God did not choose the Hebrew people because of their righteousness or willingness to serve Him (Deut. 9:7). In fact, one of Israel's besetting sins was obstinacy (vv. 3,5), and God saw them as a rebellious and stiff-necked people. The opposite of being obstinate is to have a "circumcised heart" (Deut. 10:16). Such a heart is inclined to obey the Word of God. God's presence with His people was in response to His covenantal promise: if they obeyed Him they would be His "special treasure" (Ex. 19:5).

33:6 *stripped off their ornaments.* These ornaments were probably associated with the idolatrous worship of the golden calf. Their removal was a mark of genuine repentance and renewal.

33:8 *all the people rose ... and stood.* In contrast to their former wickedness, the people now responded reverently to the living God.

33:11 *his young aide Joshua.* The word translated *aide* here conveys the sense of a minister, one who does spiritual service.

33:17 *I know you by name.* God's grace was accompanied by His intimate knowledge of and care for Moses.

33:22 – 23 *my hand.* The use of words such as hand, back, and face is a way of describing God, who is Spirit, in terms familiar to humans.

34:6 *compassionate and gracious ... abounding in love and faithfulness.* God is overwhelmingly gracious. John's description of the coming of Jesus echoes this passage, describing the Messiah as "full of grace and truth" (John 1:14,17). To see Jesus is to see the Father (John 1:18).

33:7 [s] Ex 29:42-43 **33:8** [t] Nu 16:27 **33:9** [u] Ex 13:21 [v] Ex 31:18; Ps 99:7 **33:11** [w] Nu 12:8; Dt 34:10 **33:12** [x] Ex 3:10 [y] ver 17; Jn 10:14-15; 2Ti 2:19 **33:13** [z] Ps 25:4; 86:11; 119:33 [a] Ex 34:9; Dt 9:26,29 **33:14** [b] Isa 63:9 [c] Jos 21:44; 22:4 **33:16** [d] Nu 14:14 [e] Ex 34:10 **33:19** [f] Ro 9:15* **33:20** [g] Ge 32:30; Isa 6:5 **33:22** [h] Ps 91:4 **34:1** [i] Dt 10:2,4 [j] Ex 32:19 **34:2** [k] Ex 19:11 **34:3** [l] Ex 19:12-13,21 **34:5** [m] Ex 33:19

"The LORD, the LORD, the compassionate[n]
and gracious God, slow to anger,[o] abounding in love[p] and faithfulness,[q] 7maintaining
love to thousands,[r] and forgiving wickedness, rebellion and sin.[s] Yet he does not
leave the guilty unpunished;[t] he punishes
the children and their children for the sin
of the parents to the third and fourth generation."
8Moses bowed to the ground at once
and worshiped. 9"Lord," he said, "if I have
found favor in your eyes, then let the Lord
go with us.[u] Although this is a stiff-necked
people, forgive our wickedness and our sin,
and take us as your inheritance."[v]
10Then the LORD said: "I am making a
covenant[w] with you. Before all your people I will do wonders never before done
in any nation in all the world.[x] The people
you live among will see how awesome is
the work that I, the LORD, will do for you.
11Obey what I command you today. I will
drive out before you the Amorites, Canaanites, Hittites, Perizzites, Hivites and Jebusites.[y] 12Be careful not to make a treaty
with those who live in the land where you
are going, or they will be a snare[z] among
you. 13Break down their altars, smash their
sacred stones and cut down their Asherah
poles.[a][a] 14Do not worship any other god,[b]
for the LORD, whose name is Jealous, is a
jealous God.[c]
15"Be careful not to make a treaty with
those who live in the land; for when they
prostitute[d] themselves to their gods and
sacrifice to them, they will invite you and
you will eat their sacrifices.[e] 16And when
you choose some of their daughters as
wives[f] for your sons and those daughters
prostitute themselves to their gods,[g] they
will lead your sons to do the same.
17"Do not make any idols.[h]
18"Celebrate the Festival of Unleavened
Bread.[i] For seven days eat bread made without yeast,[j] as I commanded you. Do this at
the appointed time in the month of Aviv,[k] for
in that month you came out of Egypt.
19"The first offspring[l] of every womb
belongs to me, including all the firstborn
males of your livestock, whether from herd
or flock. 20Redeem the firstborn donkey
with a lamb, but if you do not redeem it,
break its neck.[m] Redeem all your firstborn
sons.
"No one is to appear before me empty-
handed.[n]
21"Six days you shall labor, but on the
seventh day you shall rest;[o] even during the
plowing season and harvest you must rest.
22"Celebrate the Festival of Weeks with
the firstfruits of the wheat harvest, and the
Festival of Ingathering[p] at the turn of the
year.[b] 23Three times[q] a year all your men
are to appear before the Sovereign LORD,
the God of Israel. 24I will drive out nations[r]
before you and enlarge your territory, and
no one will covet your land when you go up
three times each year to appear before the
LORD your God.
25"Do not offer the blood of a sacrifice to
me along with anything containing yeast,[s]
and do not let any of the sacrifice from the
Passover Festival remain until morning.[t]
26"Bring the best of the firstfruits of your
soil to the house of the LORD your God.
"Do not cook a young goat in its mother's milk."[u]
27Then the LORD said to Moses, "Write[v]
down these words, for in accordance with
these words I have made a covenant with
you and with Israel." 28Moses was there
with the LORD forty days and forty nights[w]
without eating bread or drinking water.
And he wrote on the tablets[x] the words of
the covenant—the Ten Commandments.[y]

The Radiant Face of Moses

29When Moses came down from Mount
Sinai with the two tablets of the covenant
law in his hands,[z] he was not aware that
his face was radiant[a] because he had spo-

a 13 That is, wooden symbols of the goddess Asherah *b 22* That is, in the autumn

34:7 *forgiving wickedness.* God is a God of unlimited grace, mercy, and forgiveness. But man is not automatically forgiven — He will by no means leave the guilty unpunished. We receive forgiveness from God only when we repent and seek reconciliation with Him. The second covenant with Israel (34:10) included relief from the judgment of the people's sins to allow them to be taught their need and seek forgiveness.

34:15 *prostitute themselves.* This is probably more than a figure of speech. Unfaithfulness to the Lord was often manifested in sexual rites with temple prostitutes (male and female), acts of supposed union with Baal, Asherah, and other pagan deities.

34:16 *their daughters as wives for your sons.* The quickest way for the Israelites to become corrupted with the false worship of the Canaanites would have been to marry into it.

34:28 *forty days and forty nights.* A person can survive without food for weeks, but no one can go entirely without water for more than three or four days. This fact has been used to cast doubt on the truth of this passage, but we must recall that there is no reason to think that God could not keep His servant hydrated in any way He chose.

34:6 [n] Ps 86:15 [o] Nu 14:18; Ro 2:4 [p] Ne 9:17; Ps 103:8; Joel 2:13 [q] Ps 108:4 **34:7** [r] Ex 20:6 [s] Ps 103:3; 130:4, 8; Da 9:9; 1Jn 1:9 [t] Job 10:14; Na 1:3 **34:9** [u] Ex 33:15 [v] Ps 33:12 **34:10** [w] Dt 5:2-3 [x] Ex 33:16; Dt 4:32 **34:11** [y] Ex 33:2 **34:12** [z] Ex 23:32-33 **34:13** [a] Ex 23:24; Dt 12:3; 2Ki 18:4 **34:14** [b] Ex 20:3 [c] Ex 20:5; Dt 4:24 **34:15** [d] Jdg 2:17 [e] Nu 25:2; 1Co 8:4 **34:16** [f] Dt 7:3 [g] 1Ki 11:4 **34:17** [h] Ex 32:8 **34:18** [i] Ex 12:17 [j] Ex 12:15 [k] Ex 12:2 **34:19** [l] Ex 13:2 **34:20** [m] Ex 13:13, 15 [n] Ex 23:15; Dt 16:16 **34:21** [o] Ex 20:9; Lk 13:14 **34:22** [p] Ex 23:16 **34:23** [q] Ex 23:14 **34:24** [r] Ex 23:28; 33:2; Ps 78:55 **34:25** [s] Ex 23:18 [t] Ex 12:8, 10 **34:26** [u] Ex 23:19 **34:27** [v] Ex 17:14; 24:4 **34:28** [w] Ge 7:4; Ex 24:18; Mt 4:2 [x] ver 1; Ex 31:18 [y] Dt 4:13; 10:4 **34:29** [z] Ex 32:15 [a] Ps 34:5; Mt 17:2; 2Co 3:7, 13

ken with the LORD. 30When Aaron and all
the Israelites saw Moses, his face was radiant, and they were afraid to come near
him. 31But Moses called to them; so Aaron
and all the leaders of the community came
back to him, and he spoke to them. 32After-
ward all the Israelites came near him, and
he gave them all the commands[b] the LORD
had given him on Mount Sinai.
33When Moses finished speaking to
them, he put a veil[c] over his face. 34But
whenever he entered the LORD's presence
to speak with him, he removed the veil until he came out. And when he came out and
told the Israelites what he had been commanded, 35they saw that his face was radiant. Then Moses would put the veil back
over his face until he went in to speak with
the LORD.

Sabbath Regulations

35 Moses assembled the whole Israelite
community and said to them, "These
are the things the LORD has commanded[d]
you to do: 2For six days, work is to be done,
but the seventh day shall be your holy day,
a day of sabbath[e] rest to the LORD. Whoever does any work on it is to be put to death.
3Do not light a fire in any of your dwellings
on the Sabbath day.[f]"

Materials for the Tabernacle

4Moses said to the whole Israelite community, "This is what the LORD has commanded: 5From what you have, take an
offering for the LORD. Everyone who is
willing is to bring to the LORD an offering
of gold, silver and bronze; 6blue, purple and
scarlet yarn and fine linen; goat hair; 7ram
skins dyed red and another type of durable leather[a]; acacia wood; 8olive oil for the
light; spices for the anointing oil and for
the fragrant incense; 9and onyx stones and
other gems to be mounted on the ephod and
breastpiece.
10"All who are skilled among you are
to come and make everything the LORD
has commanded:[g] 11the tabernacle[h] with
its tent and its covering, clasps, frames,
crossbars, posts and bases; 12the ark[i] with
its poles and the atonement cover and the
curtain that shields it; 13the table[j] with its
poles and all its articles and the bread of
the Presence; 14the lampstand[k] that is for
light with its accessories, lamps and oil
for the light; 15the altar[l] of incense with its
poles, the anointing oil[m] and the fragrant
incense;[n] the curtain for the doorway at
the entrance to the tabernacle; 16the altar[o]
of burnt offering with its bronze grating,
its poles and all its utensils; the bronze
basin with its stand; 17the curtains of the
courtyard with its posts and bases, and the
curtain for the entrance to the courtyard;[p]
18the tent pegs for the tabernacle and for
the courtyard, and their ropes; 19the woven garments worn for ministering in the
sanctuary—both the sacred garments[q] for
Aaron the priest and the garments for his
sons when they serve as priests."
20Then the whole Israelite community
withdrew from Moses' presence, 21and everyone who was willing and whose heart
moved them came and brought an offering to the LORD for the work on the tent
of meeting, for all its service, and for the
sacred garments. 22All who were willing,
men and women alike, came and brought
gold jewelry of all kinds: brooches, earrings, rings and ornaments. They all presented their gold as a wave offering to the
LORD. 23Everyone who had blue, purple
or scarlet yarn[r] or fine linen, or goat hair,
ram skins dyed red or the other durable
leather brought them. 24Those presenting
an offering of silver or bronze brought it
as an offering to the LORD, and everyone
who had acacia wood for any part of the
work brought it. 25Every skilled woman[s]
spun with her hands and brought what she
had spun—blue, purple or scarlet yarn or
fine linen. 26And all the women who were
willing and had the skill spun the goat hair.
27The leaders[t] brought onyx stones and
other gems to be mounted on the ephod and
breastpiece. 28They also brought spices
and olive oil for the light and for the anointing oil and for the fragrant incense.[u] 29All
the Israelite men and women who were
willing[v] brought to the LORD freewill offerings[w] for all the work the LORD through
Moses had commanded them to do.

Bezalel and Oholiab

30Then Moses said to the Israelites, "See,
the LORD has chosen Bezalel son of Uri, the
son of Hur, of the tribe of Judah, 31and he
has filled him with the Spirit of God, with
wisdom, with understanding, with knowledge and with all kinds of skills[x]— 32to
make artistic designs for work in gold,

[a] 7 Possibly the hides of large aquatic mammals; also in verse 23

34:33 *a veil over his face.* Paul taught that Moses wore the veil because the glow faded, a sign of imperfect glory (2 Cor. 3:7,13).
35:31 – 35 *Spirit of God.* The work of the Holy Spirit is often thought to have begun at Pentecost (Acts 2), but in fact the Holy Spirit of God was at work long before that time. The Old Testament shows that He was active in creation (Gen. 1:2; Job 33:4). The Spirit came upon men for prophetic utterance (1 Sam. 10:10) and

34:32 [b] Ex 24:3 **34:33** [c] 2Co 3:13 **35:1** [d] Ex 34:32
35:2 [e] Ex 20:9-10; 34:21; Lev 23:3 **35:3** [f] Ex 16:23
35:10 [g] Ex 31:6 **35:11** [h] Ex 26:1-37 **35:12** [i] Ex 25:10-22
35:13 [j] Ex 25:23-30; Lev 24:5-6 **35:14** [k] Ex 25:31
35:15 [l] Ex 30:1-6 [m] Ex 30:25 [n] Ex 30:34-38
35:16 [o] Ex 27:1-8 **35:17** [p] Ex 27:9 **35:19** [q] Ex 28:2; 31:10; 39:1 **35:23** [r] 1Ch 29:8 **35:25** [s] Ex 28:3
35:27 [t] 1Ch 29:6; Ezr 2:68 **35:28** [u] Ex 25:6
35:29 [v] ver 21; 1Ch 29:9 [w] ver 4-9; Ex 25:1-7; 36:3; 2Ki 12:4
35:31 [x] ver 35; 2Ch 2:7,14

silver and bronze, [33]to cut and set stones, to work in wood and to engage in all kinds of artistic crafts. [34]And he has given both him and Oholiab[y] son of Ahisamak, of the tribe of Dan, the ability to teach[z] others. [35]He has filled them with skill to do all kinds of work[a] as engravers, designers, embroiderers in blue, purple and scarlet yarn and fine linen, and weavers—all of them skilled workers and designers. **36** [1]So Bezalel, Oholiab and every skilled person[b] to whom the LORD has given skill and ability to know how to carry out all the work of constructing the sanctuary[c] are to do the work just as the LORD has commanded."

[2]Then Moses summoned Bezalel[d] and Oholiab[e] and every skilled person to whom the LORD had given ability and who was willing[f] to come and do the work. [3]They received from Moses all the offerings[g] the Israelites had brought to carry out the work of constructing the sanctuary. And the people continued to bring freewill offerings morning after morning. [4]So all the skilled workers who were doing all the work on the sanctuary left what they were doing [5]and said to Moses, "The people are bringing more than enough[h] for doing the work the LORD commanded to be done."

[6]Then Moses gave an order and they sent this word throughout the camp: "No man or woman is to make anything else as an offering for the sanctuary." And so the people were restrained from bringing more, [7]because what they already had was more[i] than enough to do all the work.

The Tabernacle

[8]All those who were skilled among the workers made the tabernacle with ten curtains of finely twisted linen and blue, purple and scarlet yarn, with cherubim woven into them by expert hands. [9]All the curtains were the same size—twenty-eight cubits long and four cubits wide.[a] [10]They joined five of the curtains together and did the same with the other five. [11]Then they made loops of blue material along the edge of the end curtain in one set, and the same was done with the end curtain in the other set. [12]They also made fifty loops on one curtain and fifty loops on the end curtain of the other set, with the loops opposite each other. [13]Then they made fifty gold clasps and used them to fasten the two sets of curtains together so that the tabernacle was a unit.[j]

[14]They made curtains of goat hair for the tent over the tabernacle—eleven altogether. [15]All eleven curtains were the same size—thirty cubits long and four cubits wide.[b] [16]They joined five of the curtains into one set and the other six into another set. [17]Then they made fifty loops along the edge of the end curtain in one set and also along the edge of the end curtain in the other set. [18]They made fifty bronze clasps to fasten the tent together as a unit.[k] [19]Then they made for the tent a covering of ram skins dyed red, and over that a covering of the other durable leather.[c]

[20]They made upright frames of acacia wood for the tabernacle. [21]Each frame was ten cubits long and a cubit and a half wide,[d] [22]with two projections set parallel to each other. They made all the frames of the tabernacle in this way. [23]They made twenty frames for the south side of the tabernacle [24]and made forty silver bases to go under them—two bases for each frame, one under each projection. [25]For the other side, the north side of the tabernacle, they made twenty frames [26]and forty silver bases—two under each frame. [27]They made six frames for the far end, that is, the west end of the tabernacle, [28]and two frames were made for the corners of the tabernacle at the far end. [29]At these two corners the frames were double from the bottom all the way to the top and fitted into a single ring; both were made alike. [30]So there were eight frames and sixteen silver bases—two under each frame.

[31]They also made crossbars of acacia wood: five for the frames on one side of the tabernacle, [32]five for those on the other side, and five for the frames on the west, at the far end of the tabernacle. [33]They made the center crossbar so that it extended from end to end at the middle of the frames. [34]They overlaid the frames with gold and made gold rings to hold the crossbars. They also overlaid the crossbars with gold.

---

[a] *9* That is, about 42 feet long and 6 feet wide or about 13 meters long and 1.8 meters wide
[b] *15* That is, about 45 feet long and 6 feet wide or about 14 meters long and 1.8 meters wide
[c] *19* Possibly the hides of large aquatic mammals (see 35:7)
[d] *21* That is, about 15 feet long and 2 1/4 feet wide or about 4.5 meters long and 68 centimeters wide

---

for all divine revelation (2 Sam. 23:2). Men were endowed for special functions by the power of the Holy Spirit (Ex. 31:3; Judg. 11:29; 13:25; 14:6). Bezalel is a good example of a man indwelt by the Spirit of God in the Old Testament (37:1–9).

36:8–37:29 Servant—Not only ability was required for service in building the tabernacle. God also wanted willing hearts (36:2). Even if we do not feel that we are particularly good at anything, we must remember that every talent we possess, no matter how small, is a gift from God. He gives us these gifts so that we will have something to give back to Him. We should look at ourselves, not saying, "I don't have any great skill, I'll just sit and watch," but rather, "Here's what I have—where shall I start?"

35:34 [y] Ex 31:6 [z] 2Ch 2:14 **35:35** [a] ver 31; Ex 31:3, 6; 1Ki 7:14 **36:1** [b] Ex 28:3 [c] Ex 25:8 **36:2** [d] Ex 31:2 [e] Ex 31:6 [f] Ex 25:2; 35:21, 26; 1Ch 29:5 **36:3** [g] Ex 35:29 **36:5** [h] 2Ch 24:14; 31:10; 2Co 8:2-3 **36:7** [i] 1Ki 7:47 **36:13** [j] ver 18 **36:18** [k] ver 13

[35]They made the curtain[l] of blue, purple
and scarlet yarn and finely twisted linen,
with cherubim woven into it by a skilled
worker. [36]They made four posts of acacia
wood for it and overlaid them with gold.
They made gold hooks for them and cast
their four silver bases. [37]For the entrance
to the tent they made a curtain of blue,
purple and scarlet yarn and finely twisted linen—the work of an embroiderer;[m]
[38]and they made five posts with hooks for
them. They overlaid the tops of the posts
and their bands with gold and made their
five bases of bronze.

The Ark

37 Bezalel[n] made the ark[o] of acacia
wood—two and a half cubits long,
a cubit and a half wide, and a cubit and a
half high.[a] [2]He overlaid it with pure gold,[p]
both inside and out, and made a gold molding around it. [3]He cast four gold rings for
it and fastened them to its four feet, with
two rings on one side and two rings on the
other. [4]Then he made poles of acacia wood
and overlaid them with gold. [5]And he inserted the poles into the rings on the sides
of the ark to carry it.

[6]He made the atonement cover[q] of pure
gold—two and a half cubits long and a
cubit and a half wide. [7]Then he made two
cherubim[r] out of hammered gold at the
ends of the cover. [8]He made one cherub
on one end and the second cherub on the
other; at the two ends he made them of
one piece with the cover. [9]The cherubim
had their wings spread upward, overshadowing[s] the cover with them. The cherubim faced each other, looking toward the
cover.[t]

The Table

[10]They[b] made the table[u] of acacia
wood—two cubits long, a cubit wide and
a cubit and a half high.[c] [11]Then they overlaid it with pure gold[v] and made a gold
molding around it. [12]They also made
around it a rim a handbreadth[d] wide and
put a gold molding on the rim. [13]They
cast four gold rings for the table and fastened them to the four corners, where
the four legs were. [14]The rings[w] were put
close to the rim to hold the poles used in
carrying the table. [15]The poles for carrying the table were made of acacia wood
and were overlaid with gold. [16]And they
made from pure gold the articles for the table—its plates and dishes and bowls and
its pitchers for the pouring out of drink offerings.

The Lampstand

[17]They made the lampstand[x] of pure
gold. They hammered out its base and
shaft, and made its flowerlike cups, buds
and blossoms of one piece with them.
[18]Six branches extended from the sides
of the lampstand—three on one side and
three on the other. [19]Three cups shaped
like almond flowers with buds and blossoms were on one branch, three on the
next branch and the same for all six
branches extending from the lampstand.
[20]And on the lampstand were four cups
shaped like almond flowers with buds
and blossoms. [21]One bud was under the
first pair of branches extending from the
lampstand, a second bud under the second pair, and a third bud under the third
pair—six branches in all. [22]The buds and
the branches were all of one piece with
the lampstand, hammered out of pure
gold.[y]

[23]They made its seven lamps,[z] as well as
its wick trimmers and trays, of pure gold.
[24]They made the lampstand and all its accessories from one talent[e] of pure gold.

The Altar of Incense

[25]They made the altar of incense[a] out of
acacia wood. It was square, a cubit long
and a cubit wide and two cubits high[f]—its
horns[b] of one piece with it. [26]They overlaid
the top and all the sides and the horns with
pure gold, and made a gold molding around
it. [27]They made two gold rings[c] below the
molding—two on each of the opposite
sides—to hold the poles used to carry it.
[28]They made the poles of acacia wood and
overlaid them with gold.[d]

[29]They also made the sacred anointing
oil[e] and the pure, fragrant incense[f]—the
work of a perfumer.

---

[a] *1* That is, about 3 3/4 feet long and 2 1/4 feet wide and high or about 1.1 meters long and 68 centimeters wide and high; similarly in verse 6
[b] *10* Or *He*; also in verses 11-29
[c] *10* That is, about 3 feet long, 1 1/2 feet wide and 2 1/4 feet high or about 90 centimeters long, 45 centimeters wide and 68 centimeters high
[d] *12* That is, about 3 inches or about 7.5 centimeters
[e] *24* That is, about 75 pounds or about 34 kilograms
[f] *25* That is, about 1 1/2 feet long and wide and 3 feet high or about 45 centimeters long and wide and 90 centimeters high

---

37:1–9 *Bezalel.* Bezalel carefully reproduced the pattern given to Moses (25:10–22). Obviously this pattern wasn't just a "design suggestion" from God. Each detail had to be just like the plan because each part was a symbol or reminder of their relationship with God, His character, and His holiness.

36:35 [l] Ex 39:38; Mt 27:51; Lk 23:45; Heb 9:3
36:37 [m] Ex 27:16 **37:1** [n] Ex 31:2 [o] Ex 30:6; 39:35; Dt 10:3
37:2 [p] ver 11,26 **37:6** [q] Ex 26:34; 31:7; Heb 9:5
37:7 [r] Eze 41:18 **37:9** [s] Heb 9:5 [t] Dt 10:3
37:10 [u] Heb 9:2 **37:11** [v] ver 2 **37:14** [w] ver 27
37:17 [x] Heb 9:2; Rev 1:12 **37:22** [y] ver 17; Nu 8:4
37:23 [z] Ex 40:4,25 **37:25** [a] Ex 30:34-36; Lk 1:11; Heb 9:4; Rev 8:3 [b] Ex 27:2; Rev 9:13 **37:27** [c] ver 14
37:28 [d] Ex 25:13 **37:29** [e] Ex 31:11 [f] Ex 30:1,25; 39:38

The Altar of Burnt Offering

38 They[a] built the altar of burnt offering of acacia wood, three cubits[b] high; it was square, five cubits long and five cubits wide.[c] 2They made a horn at each of the four corners, so that the horns and the altar were of one piece, and they overlaid the altar with bronze.[g] 3They made all its utensils[h] of bronze—its pots, shovels, sprinkling bowls, meat forks and firepans. 4They made a grating for the altar, a bronze network, to be under its ledge, halfway up the altar. 5They cast bronze rings to hold the poles for the four corners of the bronze grating. 6They made the poles of acacia wood and overlaid them with bronze. 7They inserted the poles into the rings so they would be on the sides of the altar for carrying it. They made it hollow, out of boards.

The Basin for Washing

8They made the bronze basin[i] and its bronze stand from the mirrors of the women[j] who served at the entrance to the tent of meeting.

The Courtyard

9Next they made the courtyard. The south side was a hundred cubits[d] long and had curtains of finely twisted linen, 10with twenty posts and twenty bronze bases, and with silver hooks and bands on the posts. 11The north side was also a hundred cubits long and had twenty posts and twenty bronze bases, with silver hooks and bands on the posts.

12The west end was fifty cubits[e] wide and had curtains, with ten posts and ten bases, with silver hooks and bands on the posts. 13The east end, toward the sunrise, was also fifty cubits wide. 14Curtains fifteen cubits[f] long were on one side of the entrance, with three posts and three bases, 15and curtains fifteen cubits long were on the other side of the entrance to the courtyard, with three posts and three bases. 16All the curtains around the courtyard were of finely twisted linen. 17The bases for the posts were bronze. The hooks and bands on the posts were silver, and their tops were overlaid with silver; so all the posts of the courtyard had silver bands.

18The curtain for the entrance to the courtyard was made of blue, purple and scarlet yarn and finely twisted linen—the work of an embroiderer. It was twenty cubits[g] long and, like the curtains of the courtyard, five cubits[h] high, 19with four posts and four bronze bases. Their hooks and bands were silver, and their tops were overlaid with silver. 20All the tent pegs[k] of the tabernacle and of the surrounding courtyard were bronze.

The Materials Used

21These are the amounts of the materials used for the tabernacle, the tabernacle of the covenant law,[l] which were recorded at Moses' command by the Levites under the direction of Ithamar[m] son of Aaron, the priest. 22(Bezalel[n] son of Uri, the son of Hur, of the tribe of Judah, made everything the LORD commanded Moses; 23with him was Oholiab[o] son of Ahisamak, of the tribe of Dan—an engraver and designer, and an embroiderer in blue, purple and scarlet yarn and fine linen.) 24The total amount of the gold from the wave offering used for all the work on the sanctuary[p] was 29 talents and 730 shekels,[i] according to the sanctuary shekel.[q]

25The silver obtained from those of the community who were counted in the census[r] was 100 talents[j] and 1,775 shekels,[k] according to the sanctuary shekel— 26one beka per person,[s] that is, half a shekel,[l] according to the sanctuary shekel,[t] from

[a] *1* Or *He*; also in verses 2-9 [b] *1* That is, about 4 1/2 feet or about 1.4 meters [c] *1* That is, about 7 1/2 feet or about 2.3 meters long and wide
[d] *9* That is, about 150 feet or about 45 meters
[e] *12* That is, about 75 feet or about 23 meters
[f] *14* That is, about 22 feet or about 6.8 meters
[g] *18* That is, about 30 feet or about 9 meters
[h] *18* That is, about 7 1/2 feet or about 2.3 meters
[i] *24* The weight of the gold was a little over a ton or about 1 metric ton. [j] *25* That is, about 3 3/4 tons or about 3.4 metric tons; also in verse 27
[k] *25* That is, about 44 pounds or about 20 kilograms; also in verse 28 [l] *26* That is, about 1/5 ounce or about 5.7 grams

38:22–23 Responsibility—No higher tribute can be paid than "Well done—you've finished." Bezalel and his assistant, Aholiab, were called, Spirit-endowed, and commissioned for one work and one work alone. Neither of these individuals ever became celebrities, but God does not measure our effectiveness in His kingdom work by how many times we make the headlines in the local media. God cares about whether we obey Him faithfully, not whether other people approve of us. It is easy to make verbal commitments that sound really good, but God isn't looking for fine words. He complimented Bezalel and Aholiab on finishing their assignment, not on their fine start or their good intentions (39:43).

38:24 *total amount of the gold.* The weight of all the gold used in the work may have been about a ton. The talent weighed about 75 pounds, and equaled 3,000 shekels.

38:25 *the silver.* The quantity of silver was enormous, about 7,000 pounds.

38:26 *one beka per person.* The census of Numbers 14:6 puts the number of men over the age of 20 at 603,550.

38:2 [g] 2Ch 1:5 **38:3** [h] Ex 31:9 **38:8** [i] Ex 30:18; 40:7 [j] Dt 23:17; 1Sa 2:22; 1Ki 14:24 **38:20** [k] Ex 35:18 **38:21** [l] Nu 1:50, 53; 8:24; 9:15; 10:11; 17:7; 1Ch 23:32; 2Ch 24:6; Ac 7:44; Rev 15:5 [m] Nu 4:28, 33 **38:22** [n] Ex 31:2 **38:23** [o] Ex 31:6 **38:24** [p] Ex 30:16 [q] Ex 30:13; Lev 27:25; Nu 3:47; 18:16 **38:25** [r] Ex 30:12 **38:26** [s] Ex 30:12 [t] Ex 30:13

everyone who had crossed over to those counted, twenty years old or more,[u] a total of 603,550 men.[v] 27The 100 talents of silver were used to cast the bases[w] for the sanctuary and for the curtain—100 bases from the 100 talents, one talent for each base. 28They used the 1,775 shekels to make the hooks for the posts, to overlay the tops of the posts, and to make their bands.

29The bronze from the wave offering was 70 talents and 2,400 shekels.[a] 30They used it to make the bases for the entrance to the tent of meeting, the bronze altar with its bronze grating and all its utensils, 31the bases for the surrounding courtyard and those for its entrance and all the tent pegs for the tabernacle and those for the surrounding courtyard.

The Priestly Garments

39 From the blue, purple and scarlet yarn[x] they made woven garments for ministering in the sanctuary.[y] They also made sacred garments[z] for Aaron, as the LORD commanded Moses.

The Ephod

2They[b] made the ephod of gold, and of blue, purple and scarlet yarn, and of finely twisted linen. 3They hammered out thin sheets of gold and cut strands to be worked into the blue, purple and scarlet yarn and fine linen—the work of skilled hands. 4They made shoulder pieces for the ephod, which were attached to two of its corners, so it could be fastened. 5Its skillfully woven waistband was like it—of one piece with the ephod and made with gold, and with blue, purple and scarlet yarn, and with finely twisted linen, as the LORD commanded Moses.

6They mounted the onyx stones in gold filigree settings and engraved them like a seal with the names of the sons of Israel. 7Then they fastened them on the shoulder pieces of the ephod as memorial[a] stones for the sons of Israel, as the LORD commanded Moses.

The Breastpiece

8They fashioned the breastpiece[b]—the work of a skilled craftsman. They made it like the ephod: of gold, and of blue, purple and scarlet yarn, and of finely twisted linen. 9It was square—a span[c] long and a span wide—and folded double. 10Then they mounted four rows of precious stones on it. The first row was carnelian, chrysolite and beryl; 11the second row was turquoise, lapis lazuli and emerald; 12the third row was jacinth, agate and amethyst; 13the fourth row was topaz, onyx and jasper.[d] They were mounted in gold filigree settings. 14There were twelve stones, one for each of the names of the sons of Israel, each engraved like a seal with the name of one of the twelve tribes.[c]

15For the breastpiece they made braided chains of pure gold, like a rope. 16They made two gold filigree settings and two gold rings, and fastened the rings to two of the corners of the breastpiece. 17They fastened the two gold chains to the rings at the corners of the breastpiece, 18and the other ends of the chains to the two settings, attaching them to the shoulder pieces of the ephod at the front. 19They made two gold rings and attached them to the other two corners of the breastpiece on the inside edge next to the ephod. 20Then they made two more gold rings and attached them to the bottom of the shoulder pieces on the front of the ephod, close to the seam just above the waistband of the ephod. 21They tied the rings of the breastpiece to the rings of the ephod with blue cord, connecting it to the waistband so that the breastpiece would not swing out from the ephod—as the LORD commanded Moses.

Other Priestly Garments

22They made the robe of the ephod entirely of blue cloth—the work of a weaver— 23with an opening in the center of the robe like the opening of a collar,[e] and a band around this opening, so that it would not tear. 24They made pomegranates of blue, purple and scarlet yarn and finely twisted linen around the hem of the robe. 25And they made bells of pure gold and attached them around the hem between the pomegranates. 26The bells and pomegranates alternated around the hem of the robe to be worn for ministering, as the LORD commanded Moses.

27For Aaron and his sons, they made tunics of fine linen[d]—the work of a weaver— 28and the turban[e] of fine linen, the linen caps and the undergarments of finely twisted linen. 29The sash was made of finely twisted linen and blue, purple and scarlet yarn—the work of an embroiderer—as the LORD commanded Moses.

---

a 29 The weight of the bronze was about 2 1/2 tons or about 2.4 metric tons. *b* 2 Or *He*; also in verses 7, 8 and 22 *c* 9 That is, about 9 inches or about 23 centimeters *d* 13 The precise identification of some of these precious stones is uncertain. *e* 23 The meaning of the Hebrew for this word is uncertain.

38:27–28 *the sanctuary.* Although the tabernacle was a tent, it was not a makeshift dwelling. It was a glorious shrine that symbolized the presence of the living God in the midst of the people.

38:29 *bronze.* About 5,000 pounds of bronze were used.

38:26 [u] Ex 30:14 [v] Ex 12:37; Nu 1:46 **38:27** [w] Ex 26:19
39:1 [x] Ex 35:23 [y] Ex 35:19 [z] ver 41; Ex 28:2
39:7 [a] Lev 24:7; Jos 4:7 **39:8** [b] Lev 8:8
39:14 [c] Rev 21:12 **39:27** [d] Lev 6:10
39:28 [e] Ex 28:4

30They made the plate, the sacred emblem, out of pure gold and engraved on it,
like an inscription on a seal: HOLY TO THE
LORD. 31Then they fastened a blue cord to it
to attach it to the turban, as the LORD commanded Moses.

Moses Inspects the Tabernacle

32So all the work on the tabernacle, the
tent of meeting, was completed. The Israelites did everything just as the LORD
commanded Moses.[f] 33Then they brought
the tabernacle to Moses: the tent and all
its furnishings, its clasps, frames, crossbars, posts and bases; 34the covering
of ram skins dyed red and the covering of
another durable leather[a] and the shielding curtain; 35the ark of the covenant
law[g] with its poles and the atonement
cover; 36the table with all its articles and
the bread of the Presence; 37the pure
gold lampstand[h] with its row of lamps
and all its accessories, and the olive oil for
the light; 38the gold altar,[i] the anointing
oil, the fragrant incense, and the curtain[j]
for the entrance to the tent; 39the bronze
altar with its bronze grating, its poles and
all its utensils; the basin with its stand;
40the curtains of the courtyard with its
posts and bases, and the curtain for the
entrance to the courtyard;[k] the ropes
and tent pegs for the courtyard; all the
furnishings for the tabernacle, the tent of
meeting; 41and the woven garments worn
for ministering in the sanctuary, both the
sacred garments for Aaron the priest and
the garments for his sons when serving as
priests.

42The Israelites had done all the work
just as the LORD had commanded Moses.[l]
43Moses inspected the work and saw that
they had done it just as the LORD had commanded. So Moses blessed[m] them.

Setting Up the Tabernacle

40 Then the LORD said to Moses: 2"Set
up the tabernacle, the tent of meeting,[n] on the first day of the first month.[o]
3Place the ark[p] of the covenant law in it and
shield the ark with the curtain. 4Bring in
the table and set out what belongs on it.[q]
Then bring in the lampstand[r] and set up
its lamps. 5Place the gold altar[s] of incense
in front of the ark of the covenant law and
put the curtain at the entrance to the tabernacle.

6"Place the altar of burnt offering in
front of the entrance to the tabernacle, the
tent of meeting; 7place the basin[t] between
the tent of meeting and the altar and put
water in it. 8Set up the courtyard around it
and put the curtain at the entrance to the
courtyard.

9"Take the anointing oil and anoint[u] the
tabernacle and everything in it; consecrate
it and all its furnishings, and it will be holy.
10Then anoint the altar of burnt offering
and all its utensils; consecrate[v] the altar,
and it will be most holy. 11Anoint the basin
and its stand and consecrate them.

12"Bring Aaron and his sons to the entrance to the tent of meeting and wash
them with water.[w] 13Then dress Aaron in
the sacred garments,[x] anoint him and consecrate[y] him so he may serve me as priest.
14Bring his sons and dress them in tunics.
15Anoint them just as you anointed their father, so they may serve me as priests. Their
anointing will be to a priesthood that will
continue throughout their generations.[z]"
16Moses did everything just as the LORD
commanded him.

17So the tabernacle[a] was set up on the
first day of the first month[b] in the second
year. 18When Moses set up the tabernacle, he put the bases in place, erected the
frames, inserted the crossbars and set up
the posts. 19Then he spread the tent over
the tabernacle and put the covering over
the tent, as the LORD commanded him.

20He took the tablets of the covenant law[c]
and placed them in the ark, attached the
poles to the ark and put the atonement cover over it. 21Then he brought the ark into
the tabernacle and hung the shielding curtain[d] and shielded the ark of the covenant
law, as the LORD commanded him.

22Moses placed the table[e] in the tent of
meeting on the north side of the tabernacle outside the curtain 23and set out the
bread[f] on it before the LORD, as the LORD
commanded him.

---

a *34* Possibly the hides of large aquatic mammals

39:32–43 *the Israelites did.* Because it was so important in God's plan for His people, both in the wilderness and today, the tabernacle had to be constructed in exact accordance with the divine pattern. It was the place where His glory would actually dwell and where they could meet Him. Because they had done just as the Lord had commanded, "Moses blessed them." A mood of celebration pervades these verses. One can sense the pride of accomplishment coupled with the reverence for all of these holy objects.

40:2 *first month.* This was the month of Abib, also called Nisan (12:2; 13:4). The tabernacle was completed nine months after the arrival of the people at Mount Sinai (19:1) and two weeks before the second celebration of the Passover (v. 17).

39:32 [f] ver 42-43; Ex 25:9 **39:35** [g] Ex 30:6
39:37 [h] Ex 25:31 **39:38** [i] Ex 30:1-10 [j] Ex 36:35
39:40 [k] Ex 27:9-19 **39:42** [l] Ex 25:9 **39:43** [m] Lev 9:22, 23; Nu 6:23-27; 2Sa 6:18; 1Ki 8:14, 55; 2Ch 30:27
40:2 [n] Nu 1:1 [o] ver 17; Ex 12:2 **40:3** [p] ver 21; Nu 4:5; Ex 26:33 **40:4** [q] Ex 25:30 [r] ver 22-25; Ex 26:35
40:5 [s] ver 26; Ex 30:1 **40:7** [t] ver 30; Ex 30:18
40:9 [u] Ex 30:26; Lev 8:10 **40:10** [v] Ex 29:36
40:12 [w] Lev 8:1-13 **40:13** [x] Ex 28:41 [y] Lev 8:12
40:15 [z] Ex 29:9; Nu 25:13 **40:17** [a] Nu 7:1 [b] ver 2
40:20 [c] Ex 16:34; 25:16; Dt 10:5; 1Ki 8:9; Heb 9:4
40:21 [d] Ex 26:33 **40:22** [e] Ex 26:35 **40:23** [f] ver 4

24He placed the lampstand[g] in the tent
of meeting opposite the table on the south
side of the tabernacle 25and set up the
lamps[h] before the LORD, as the LORD commanded him.
26Moses placed the gold altar[i] in the tent
of meeting in front of the curtain 27and
burned fragrant incense on it, as the LORD
commanded[j] him.
28Then he put up the curtain[k] at the entrance to the tabernacle. 29He set the altar
of burnt offering near the entrance to the
tabernacle, the tent of meeting, and offered
on it burnt offerings and grain offerings,[l]
as the LORD commanded him.
30He placed the basin[m] between the tent
of meeting and the altar and put water in it
for washing, 31and Moses and Aaron and
his sons used it to wash their hands and
feet. 32They washed whenever they entered
the tent of meeting or approached the altar,[n] as the LORD commanded Moses.
33Then Moses set up the courtyard[o]
around the tabernacle and altar and put up
the curtain[p] at the entrance to the courtyard. And so Moses finished the work.

The Glory of the LORD

34Then the cloud[q] covered the tent of
meeting, and the glory of the LORD filled
the tabernacle. 35Moses could not enter the
tent of meeting because the cloud had settled on it, and the glory of the LORD filled
the tabernacle.[r]
36In all the travels of the Israelites,
whenever the cloud lifted from above the
tabernacle, they would set out;[s] 37but if the
cloud did not lift, they did not set out—until the day it lifted. 38So the cloud[t] of the
LORD was over the tabernacle by day,
and fire was in the cloud by night, in the
sight of all the Israelites during all their
travels.

40:34 ***cloud ... glory.*** When the Lord came near in 19:20, the people were terrified, but this time they were overjoyed. The glory of the Lord filling the tabernacle demonstrated His presence with the Israelites, His significance to them, and His awe-inspiring wonder.

40:35 ***the cloud had settled on it.*** God is not "far away in heaven," occasionally looking at the earth. He lives among His people, and He desires to communicate with them (John 1:14).

40:38 ***the cloud of the LORD.*** The Book of Exodus ends with the picture of the gracious God hovering protectively over His people. He allowed His presence to be felt and seen.

40:24 [g] Ex 26:35 **40:25** [h] ver 4; Ex 25:37 **40:26** [i] ver 5; Ex 30:6 **40:27** [j] Ex 30:7 **40:28** [k] Ex 26:36 **40:29** [l] ver 6; Ex 29:38-42 **40:30** [m] ver 7 **40:32** [n] Ex 30:20 **40:33** [o] Ex 27:9 [p] ver 8 **40:34** [q] Nu 9:15-23; 1Ki 8:12 **40:35** [r] 1Ki 8:11; 2Ch 5:13-14 **40:36** [s] Nu 9:17-23; 10:13; Ne 9:19 **40:38** [t] Ex 13:21; Nu 9:15; 1Co 10:1

LEVITICUS

▶ **AUTHOR:** Moses is declared to be the author of Leviticus fifty-six times within the book. External evidence supporting the authorship of Moses includes 1) A uniform ancient testimony. 2) Parallels found in the Ras Shamra Tablets dating from 1400 B.C. 3) The testimony of Christ (Matt. 8:2–4 and Lev. 14:1–4; Matt. 12:4 and Lev. 24:9; Luke 2:22).

▶ **TIME:** c. 1405 B.C. ▶ **KEY VERSE:** Lev. 20:7–8

▶ **THEME:** Leviticus is God's guidebook for His newly redeemed people. It shows them how to worship and live holy lives. The instructions for the sacrificial system point to a holy God and what he requires from people who would serve him. The laws of holiness and sanctification provide basic instructions for living in a community. Together the two groups of laws are a framework for relationship between God and man. Blessings result from obedience to these laws and discipline is the result of disobedience.

The Burnt Offering

1 The LORD called to Moses[a] and spoke to
him from the tent of meeting.[b] He said,
2"Speak to the Israelites and say to them:
'When anyone among you brings an offering to the LORD, bring as your offering an
animal from either the herd or the flock.[c]
3" 'If the offering is a burnt offering from
the herd, you are to offer a male without
defect.[d] You must present it at the entrance
to the tent[e] of meeting so that it will be acceptable to the LORD. 4You are to lay your
hand on the head[f] of the burnt offering, and
it will be accepted on your behalf to make
atonement[g] for you. 5You are to slaughter[h]
the young bull before the LORD, and then
Aaron's sons the priests shall bring the
blood and splash it against the sides of the
altar[i] at the entrance to the tent of meeting.
6You are to skin[j] the burnt offering and cut
it into pieces. 7The sons of Aaron the priest
are to put fire on the altar and arrange
wood[k] on the fire. 8Then Aaron's sons the
priests shall arrange the pieces, including
the head and the fat,[l] on the wood that is
burning on the altar. 9You are to wash the
internal organs and the legs with water,
and the priest is to burn all of it on the altar.[m] It is a burnt offering, a food offering,
an aroma pleasing to the LORD.[n]
10" 'If the offering is a burnt offering
from the flock, from either the sheep or
the goats,[o] you are to offer a male without
defect. 11You are to slaughter it at the north

1:1–17 ***offering to the LORD.*** Leviticus continues the Exodus narrative of the dedication of the tabernacle by indicating how the liberated Israelites are to worship their God. This book deals with the voluntary sacrifices for thanksgiving, communion, or cleansing from sin. These offerings from the herd or flock represented the labor and financial investment of the owner, and were a continual reminder that a price always has to be paid for sin.

1:3 ***burnt offering.*** The "burnt offering" was the only offering that was entirely consumed on the altar. It foreshadows the total sacrifice of Christ on the cross, as well as representing wholehearted, unreserved worship where nothing is withheld or left over. It reminds us that nothing must be held back for ourselves; it all belongs to Him. ***male without defect.*** Offering a perfect animal was a real sacrifice, not just "something they didn't really need or want." These perfect animals were valuable for breeding or for sale. The principle still holds. God's people are to offer their best, of their own free will, and with joy.

1:4 ***you are to lay your hand on the head of the burnt offering.*** Each worshipper brought his or her own offering and laid his own hand on the animal's head. No one could send another to act on his behalf. In the same way, no one today can send someone else to accept Christ's atonement for him; we must each come to Christ ourselves, acknowledging our own sin before Him.

1:9 ***aroma pleasing to the LORD.*** Never does Scripture represent God as eating the offerings brought to Him, as the pagan gods were thought to do. When a sacrifice was done in faith with a free will, it was accepted by the Lord as desirable, or sweet.

1:1 [a] Ex 19:3; 25:22 [b] Nu 7:89 **1:2** [c] Lev 22:18-19 **1:3** [d] Ex 12:5; Dt 15:21; Heb 9:14; 1Pe 1:19 [e] Lev 17:9 **1:4** [f] Ex 29:10, 15; Lev 3:2 [g] 2Ch 29:23-24 **1:5** [h] Lev 3:2, 8 [i] Heb 12:24; 1Pe 1:2 **1:6** [j] Lev 7:8 **1:7** [k] Lev 6:12 **1:8** [l] ver 12 **1:9** [m] Ex 29:18 [n] ver 13; Ge 8:21; Nu 15:8-10; Eph 5:2 **1:10** [o] ver 3; Ex 12:5

side of the altar before the LORD, and Aaron's sons the priests shall splash its blood against the sides of the altar.[p] 12You are to cut it into pieces, and the priest shall arrange them, including the head and the fat, on the wood that is burning on the altar. 13You are to wash the internal organs and the legs with water, and the priest is to bring all of them and burn them on the altar. It is a burnt offering, a food offering, an aroma pleasing to the LORD.

14" 'If the offering to the LORD is a burnt offering of birds, you are to offer a dove or a young pigeon.[q] 15The priest shall bring it to the altar, wring off the head and burn it on the altar; its blood shall be drained out on the side of the altar.[r] 16He is to remove the crop and the feathers[a] and throw them down east of the altar where the ashes[s] are. 17He shall tear it open by the wings, not dividing it completely,[t] and then the priest shall burn it on the wood[u] that is burning on the altar. It is a burnt offering, a food offering, an aroma pleasing to the LORD.

The Grain Offering

2 " 'When anyone brings a grain offering[v] to the LORD, their offering is to be of the finest flour. They are to pour olive oil[w] on it, put incense on it 2and take it to Aaron's sons the priests. The priest shall take a handful of the flour[x] and oil, together with all the incense,[y] and burn this as a memorial[b] portion[z] on the altar, a food offering, an aroma pleasing to the LORD. 3The rest of the grain offering belongs to Aaron and his sons;[a] it is a most holy part of the food offerings presented to the LORD.

4" 'If you bring a grain offering baked in an oven, it is to consist of the finest flour: either thick loaves made without yeast and with olive oil mixed in or thin loaves made without yeast and brushed with olive oil.[b] 5If your grain offering is prepared on a griddle, it is to be made of the finest flour mixed with oil, and without yeast. 6Crumble it and pour oil on it; it is a grain offering. 7If your grain offering is cooked in a pan,[c] it is to be made of the finest flour and some olive oil. 8Bring the grain offering made of these things to the LORD; present it to the priest, who shall take it to the altar. 9He shall take out the memorial portion[d] from the grain offering and burn it on the altar as a food offering, an aroma pleasing to the LORD.[e] 10The rest of the grain offering belongs to Aaron and his sons;[f] it is a most holy part of the food offerings presented to the LORD.

11" 'Every grain offering you bring to the LORD must be made without yeast,[g] for you are not to burn any yeast or honey in a food offering presented to the LORD. 12You may bring them to the LORD as an offering of the firstfruits,[h] but they are not to be offered on the altar as a pleasing aroma. 13Season all your grain offerings with salt. Do not leave the salt of the covenant[i] of your God out of your grain offerings; add salt to all your offerings.

14" 'If you bring a grain offering of firstfruits[j] to the LORD, offer crushed heads of new grain roasted in the fire. 15Put oil and incense on it; it is a grain offering. 16The priest shall burn the memorial portion[k] of the crushed grain and the oil, together with all the incense, as a food offering presented to the LORD.

The Fellowship Offering

3 " 'If your offering is a fellowship offering,[l] and you offer an animal from the

a 16 Or *crop with its contents*; the meaning of the Hebrew for this word is uncertain. *b* 2 Or *representative*; also in verses 9 and 16

2:1 *oil ... incense.* Olive oil was a primary part of the diet and a prominent symbol of blessing and prosperity. Incense, from South Arabia and East Africa, was an imported luxury that would have to be bought with money. By including incense, as well as the animals and grain they could raise on their land, every aspect of Israel's wealth was made a part of the offerings to God.

2:3 *belongs to Aaron and his sons.* A significant portion of the priest's daily food came from this part of the grain offering. Only the consecrated priests were allowed to eat it, and only within the tabernacle.

2:8–9 *priest.* There were always two individuals involved when the ancient Hebrew brought his sacrifice to God. One was the offerer himself and the other was the officiating priest, who was the "bridge builder" between men and God. Jesus, as a better priest and a better sacrifice, once for all time bridged the gap between God and man, and through Him we can have direct access to God, to confess our sins and receive forgiveness.

2:11 *yeast.* Yeast and honey were prohibited because both cause fermentation, which represents corruption.

2:13 *salt of the covenant of your God.* Salt was to be used in every grain offering. This was a reminder of the covenant that God had made with Israel at Sinai, and was a symbol of faithfulness to God and His covenant. There is an old saying, "he has eaten my salt," which means that you have taken someone into your home, given them shelter, food, and hospitality. The idea of the "salt" of God's covenant was a well understood concept.

3:1 *fellowship offering.* The Hebrew word for "fellowship" means "wholeness, completeness, soundness, health." When a person possesses all of these attributes, he is at peace. The fellowship offerings were a time of celebrating and enjoying the gift of

1:11 [p] ver 5 **1:14** [q] Ge 15:9; Lev 5:7; Lk 2:24 **1:15** [r] Lev 5:9 **1:16** [s] Lev 6:10 **1:17** [t] Ge 15:10 [u] Lev 5:8 **2:1** [v] Lev 6:14-18 [w] Nu 15:4 **2:2** [x] Lev 5:11 [y] Lev 6:15; Isa 66:3 [z] ver 9, 16; Lev 5:12; 6:15; 24:7; Ac 10:4 **2:3** [a] ver 10; Lev 6:16; 10:12, 13 **2:4** [b] Ex 29:2 **2:7** [c] Lev 7:9 **2:9** [d] ver 2 [e] Ex 29:18; Lev 6:15 **2:10** [f] ver 3 **2:11** [g] Ex 23:18; 34:25; Lev 6:16 **2:12** [h] Lev 7:13; 23:10 **2:13** [i] Nu 18:19; Eze 43:24 **2:14** [j] Lev 23:10 **2:16** [k] ver 2 **3:1** [l] Lev 7:11-34

herd, whether male or female, you are to present before the LORD an animal without defect.[m] 2 You are to lay your hand on the head[n] of your offering and slaughter it[o] at the entrance to the tent of meeting. Then Aaron's sons the priests shall splash the blood against the sides of the altar. 3 From the fellowship offering you are to bring a food offering to the LORD: the internal organs and all the fat[p] that is connected to them, 4 both kidneys with the fat on them near the loins, and the long lobe of the liver, which you will remove with the kidneys. 5 Then Aaron's sons[q] are to burn it on the altar on top of the burnt offering[r] that is lying on the burning wood; it is a food offering, an aroma pleasing to the LORD.

6 " 'If you offer an animal from the flock as a fellowship offering[s] to the LORD, you are to offer a male or female without defect. 7 If you offer a lamb, you are to present it before the LORD,[t] 8 lay your hand on its head and slaughter it[u] in front of the tent of meeting. Then Aaron's sons shall splash its blood against the sides of the altar. 9 From the fellowship offering you are to bring a food offering to the LORD: its fat, the entire fat tail cut off close to the backbone, the internal organs and all the fat that is connected to them, 10 both kidneys with the fat on them near the loins, and the long lobe of the liver, which you will remove with the kidneys. 11 The priest shall burn them on the altar[v] as a food offering[w] presented to the LORD.

12 " 'If your offering is a goat, you are to present it before the LORD, 13 lay your hand on its head and slaughter it in front of the tent of meeting. Then Aaron's sons shall splash[x] its blood against the sides of the altar. 14 From what you offer you are to present this food offering to the LORD: the internal organs and all the fat that is connected to them, 15 both kidneys with the fat on them near the loins, and the long lobe of the liver, which you will remove with the kidneys. 16 The priest shall burn them on the altar as a food offering, a pleasing aroma. All the fat is the LORD's.[y]

17 " 'This is a lasting ordinance for the generations to come,[z] wherever you live: You must not eat any fat or any blood.[a] ' "

The Sin Offering

4 The LORD said to Moses, 2 "Say to the Israelites: 'When anyone sins unintentionally[b] and does what is forbidden in any of the LORD's commands—

3 " 'If the anointed priest sins, bringing guilt on the people, he must bring to the LORD a young bull[c] without defect as a sin offering[a][d] for the sin he has committed. 4 He is to present the bull at the entrance to the tent of meeting before the LORD.[e] He is to lay his hand on its head and slaughter it there before the LORD. 5 Then the anointed priest shall take some of the bull's blood[f] and carry it into the tent of meeting. 6 He is to dip his finger into the blood and sprinkle some of it seven times before the LORD, in front of the curtain of the sanctuary. 7 The priest shall then put some of the blood on the horns of the altar of fragrant incense that is before the LORD in the tent of meeting. The rest of the bull's blood he shall pour out at the base of the altar[g] of burnt offering[h] at the entrance to the tent of meeting. 8 He shall remove all the fat[i] from the bull of the sin offering—all the fat that is connected to the internal organs, 9 both kidneys with the fat on them near the loins, and the long lobe of the liver, which he will remove with the kidneys[j]— 10 just as the fat is removed from the ox[b] sacrificed as a fellowship offering. Then the priest shall burn them on the altar of burnt offering. 11 But the hide of the bull and all its flesh,

---

a 3 Or *purification offering*; here and throughout this chapter *b* 10 The Hebrew word can refer to either male or female.

---

peace with God. Yet it was only after Christ's death and resurrection, when He became our perfect fellowship offering (Col. 1:20) that we could really have perfect peace with God. The sacrifices had to be made over and over, but Christ's death was once, for all time.

3:3–4 *both kidneys with the fat on them ... the long lobe of the liver.* The fat was one of the most prized portions of the meat, and the kidneys were considered the seat of the emotions. The liver was an essential organ for telling the future in the pagan cultures surrounding Israel. Giving all of these things to God symbolized giving Him the best, giving Him the hopes, dreams, and desires of life; recognizing that He alone has control of the future, and that He will reveal it in His own way, at His own time.

3:5 *on top of the burnt offering.* The fellowship offering normally followed the burnt offering, which was entirely consumed on the altar. Being reconciled to God through the burnt offering, the worshiper was in a position to fellowship with God. Repentance and reconciliation must always come before genuine fellowship.

3:9 *the entire fat tail.* The tail of the Palestinian broad-tailed sheep is almost entirely fat and can weigh more than 16 pounds. This explains its special mention in the regulations for offering the fat of the sheep.

4:11–12 *the hide of the bull and all its flesh.* Burning the whole bull ensured that the priest did not profit in any way from his own sin or the

3:1 [m] Lev 1:3; 22:21 **3:2** [n] Ex 29:10, 15 [o] Lev 1:5 **3:3** [p] Ex 29:13 **3:5** [q] Lev 7:29-34 [r] Ex 29:13, 38-42 **3:6** [s] ver 1 **3:7** [t] Lev 17:8-9 **3:8** [u] ver 2; Lev 1:5 **3:11** [v] ver 5 [w] ver 16; Lev 21:6, 17 **3:13** [x] Ex 24:6 **3:16** [y] 1Sa 2:16 **3:17** [z] Lev 6:18; 17:7 [a] Ge 9:4; Lev 7:25-26; 17:10-16; Dt 12:16; Ac 15:20 **4:2** [b] Lev 5:15-18; Ps 19:12; Heb 9:7 **4:3** [c] ver 14; Ps 66:15 [d] Lev 9:2-22; Heb 9:13-14 **4:4** [e] Lev 1:3 **4:5** [f] Lev 16:14 **4:7** [g] ver 34; Lev 8:15 [h] ver 18, 30; Lev 5:9; 9:9; 16:18 **4:8** [i] Lev 3:3-5 **4:9** [j] Lev 3:4

as well as the head and legs, the internal organs and the intestines[k]— 12that is, all the rest of the bull—he must take outside the camp[l] to a place ceremonially clean,[m] where the ashes are thrown, and burn it there in a wood fire on the ash heap.

13" 'If the whole Israelite community sins unintentionally[n] and does what is forbidden in any of the LORD's commands, even though the community is unaware of the matter, when they realize their guilt 14and the sin they committed becomes known, the assembly must bring a young bull[o] as a sin offering[p] and present it before the tent of meeting. 15The elders of the community are to lay their hands on the bull's head[q] before the LORD, and the bull shall be slaughtered before the LORD. 16Then the anointed priest is to take some of the bull's blood[r] into the tent of meeting. 17He shall dip his finger into the blood and sprinkle it before the LORD[s] seven times in front of the curtain. 18He is to put some of the blood on the horns of the altar that is before the LORD[t] in the tent of meeting. The rest of the blood he shall pour out at the base of the altar of burnt offering at the entrance to the tent of meeting. 19He shall remove all the fat[u] from it and burn it on the altar, 20and do with this bull just as he did with the bull for the sin offering. In this way the priest will make atonement[v] for the community, and they will be forgiven.[w] 21Then he shall take the bull outside the camp and burn it as he burned the first bull. This is the sin offering for the community.[x]

22" 'When a leader[y] sins unintentionally[z] and does what is forbidden in any of the commands of the LORD his God, when he realizes his guilt 23and the sin he has committed becomes known, he must bring as his offering a male goat without defect. 24He is to lay his hand on the goat's head and slaughter it at the place where the burnt offering is slaughtered before the LORD. It is a sin offering. 25Then the priest shall take some of the blood of the sin offering with his finger and put it on the horns of the altar of burnt offering and pour out the rest of the blood at the base of the altar.[a] 26He shall burn all the fat on the altar as he burned the fat of the fellowship offering. In this way the priest will make atonement for the leader's sin, and he will be forgiven.[b]

27" 'If any member of the community sins unintentionally[c] and does what is forbidden in any of the LORD's commands, when they realize their guilt 28and the sin they have committed becomes known, they must bring as their offering[d] for the sin they committed a female goat[e] without defect. 29They are to lay their hand on the head[f] of the sin offering[g] and slaughter it at the place of the burnt offering. 30Then the priest is to take some of the blood with his finger and put it on the horns of the altar of burnt offering[h] and pour out the rest of the blood at the base of the altar. 31They shall remove all the fat, just as the fat is removed from the fellowship offering, and the priest shall burn it on the altar as an aroma pleasing to the LORD.[i] In this way the priest will make atonement for them, and they will be forgiven.

32" 'If someone brings a lamb as their sin offering, they are to bring a female without defect.[j] 33They are to lay their hand on its head and slaughter it for a sin offering at the place where the burnt offering is slaughtered.[k] 34Then the priest shall take some of the blood of the sin offering with his finger and put it on the horns of the altar of burnt offering and pour out the rest of the blood at the base of the altar.[l] 35They shall remove all the fat, just as the fat is removed from the lamb of the fellowship offering, and the priest shall burn it on the altar[m] on top of the food offerings presented to the LORD. In this way the priest will make atonement for them for the sin they have committed, and they will be forgiven.

5 " 'If anyone sins because they do not speak up when they hear a public charge to testify[n] regarding something they have seen or learned about, they will be held responsible.[o]

2" 'If anyone becomes aware that they are guilty—if they unwittingly touch anything ceremonially unclean (whether the carcass of an unclean animal, wild or domestic, or of any unclean creature that moves along the ground)[p] and they are unaware that

---

atonement for his sin. Carrying it outside the camp was another way of symbolizing the seriousness and pollution of sin.

4:13–21 ***the community.*** Interestingly, not only individuals bring a sin offering to God, but the whole congregation as well. We are used to thinking of individuals coming under conviction and repenting, but how can a whole community come to this way of thinking? A congregation or community can begin to realize that they have misrepresented God, or fallen short of their God-given responsibilities, and together repent and ask for forgiveness, even though the members repenting may not have been the actual people who made the bad decisions that created the problem. Groups need to turn around and redirect their actions, just as much as individuals do, and this is one of the ways that God changes whole societies.

4:11 [k] Ex 29:14; Lev 9:11; Nu 19:5 **4:12** [l] Heb 13:11 [m] Lev 6:11 **4:13** [n] ver 2; Lev 5:2-4, 17; Nu 15:24-26 **4:14** [o] ver 3 [p] ver 23, 28 **4:15** [q] Lev 1:4; 8:14, 22; Nu 8:10 **4:16** [r] ver 5 **4:17** [s] ver 6 **4:18** [t] ver 7 **4:19** [u] ver 8 **4:20** [v] Heb 10:10-12 [w] Nu 15:25 **4:21** [x] Lev 16:5, 15 **4:22** [y] Nu 31:13 [z] ver 2 **4:25** [a] ver 7, 18, 30, 34; Lev 9:9 **4:26** [b] Lev 5:10 **4:27** [c] ver 2; Nu 15:27 **4:28** [d] ver 23 [e] ver 3 **4:29** [f] ver 4, 24 [g] Lev 1:4 **4:30** [h] ver 7 **4:31** [i] Ge 8:21 **4:32** [j] ver 28 **4:33** [k] ver 29 **4:34** [l] ver 7 **4:35** [m] ver 26, 31 **5:1** [n] Pr 29:24 [o] ver 17 **5:2** [p] Lev 11:11, 24-40; Dt 14:8

they have become unclean, but then they come to realize their guilt; 3or if they touch human uncleanness[q] (anything that would make them unclean) even though they are unaware of it, but then they learn of it and realize their guilt; 4or if anyone thoughtlessly takes an oath[r] to do anything, whether good or evil (in any matter one might carelessly swear about) even though they are unaware of it, but then they learn of it and realize their guilt— 5when anyone becomes aware that they are guilty in any of these matters, they must confess[s] in what way they have sinned. 6As a penalty for the sin they have committed, they must bring to the LORD a female lamb or goat from the flock as a sin offering[a];[t] and the priest shall make atonement for them for their sin.

7" 'Anyone who cannot afford[u] a lamb is to bring two doves or two young pigeons to the LORD as a penalty for their sin—one for a sin offering and the other for a burnt offering. 8They are to bring them to the priest, who shall first offer the one for the sin offering. He is to wring its head from its neck,[v] not dividing it completely,[w] 9and is to splash some of the blood of the sin offering against the side of the altar; the rest of the blood must be drained out at the base of the altar.[x] It is a sin offering. 10The priest shall then offer the other as a burnt offering in the prescribed way[y] and make atonement for them for the sin they have committed, and they will be forgiven.[z]

11" 'If, however, they cannot afford two doves or two young pigeons, they are to bring as an offering for their sin a tenth of an ephah[b] of the finest flour[a] for a sin offering. They must not put olive oil or incense on it, because it is a sin offering. 12They are to bring it to the priest, who shall take a handful of it as a memorial[c] portion and burn it on the altar on top of the food offerings presented to the LORD. It is a sin offering. 13In this way the priest will make atonement[b] for them for any of these sins they have committed, and they will be forgiven. The rest of the offering will belong to the priest,[c] as in the case of the grain offering.' "

The Guilt Offering

14The LORD said to Moses: 15"When anyone is unfaithful to the LORD by sinning unintentionally in regard to any of the LORD's holy things, they are to bring to the LORD as a penalty[d] a ram[e] from the flock, one without defect and of the proper value in silver, according to the sanctuary shekel.[d][f] It is a guilt offering. 16They must make restitution[g] for what they have failed to do in regard to the holy things, pay an additional penalty of a fifth of its value[h] and give it all to the priest. The priest will make atonement for them with the ram as a guilt offering, and they will be forgiven.

17"If anyone sins and does what is forbidden in any of the LORD's commands, even though they do not know it,[i] they are guilty

[a] 6 Or *purification offering*; here and throughout this chapter [b] *11* That is, probably about 3 1/2 pounds or about 1.6 kilograms [c] *12* Or *representative* [d] *15* That is, about 2/5 ounce or about 12 grams

---

5:3 *human uncleanness.* Body fluids, a person's waste, and contact with a corpse were all causes of uncleanness. The ancient Israelites knew nothing about microbiology, but God, who knows everything, gave them laws that prevented disease and made them distinct from their neighbors.

5:4 *oath . . . even though they are unaware.* Certainly a person would know when he makes a vow, but he might not be immediately aware of how rash his vow is, or that the long term consequences are undesirable. Whether the vow was made with good intentions, but not carried out, or made with wicked intentions, but not carried out, the person who made the vow is still responsible to repent of his foolishness when he becomes aware of it.

5:7 *two doves.* Part of the purification offering was burned on the altar, and part was not burned. When offering birds, the worshipper brought two in order to accomplish this.

5:11 *a tenth of an ephah.* This was approximately two quarts.

5:13 *the rest . . . will belong to the priest.* Part of the offering was burned on the altar, as was part of the animal sacrifices. The rest belonged to the priests, as did the remainder of the animal sacrifices brought by ordinary citizens, except for their burnt offerings.

5:15 *unfaithful to the LORD by sinning unintentionally . . . guilt offering.* This refers both to the objective responsibility of a sinner for his or her actions and the subjective feeling of guilt experienced by the sinner. The offering righted the wrong of the offense and cleared the conscience of the sinner.

5:15 – 6:7 *if anyone sins.* The guilt offering covers both offenses against God (5:15 – 19) and against people (6:1 – 7). The offense may be unintentional, or quite deliberate, but regardless of the motive, such actions make the perpetrator guilty. The quickest way to mend relationships with God and with fellow human beings is to honestly admit our guilt and wrongdoing, pay back or repair where we can, and ask forgiveness of those we have sinned against. This responsibility cannot be sidestepped.

5:17 *though they do not know it, they are guilty.* Ignorance does not make an offense harmless. The offender was still guilty and bore responsibility for his sin. He might also be troubled in conscience, though he might never learn the exact nature of his offense. This raises the concept that a person can be aware of a break in his fellowship with God, without being sure what caused this break.

5:3 [q] Nu 19:11-16 **5:4** [r] Nu 30:6,8 **5:5** [s] Lev 16:21; 26:40; Nu 5:7; Pr 28:13 **5:6** [t] Lev 4:28 **5:7** [u] Lev 12:8; 14:21 **5:8** [v] Lev 1:15 [w] Lev 1:17 **5:9** [x] Lev 4:7,18 **5:10** [y] Lev 1:14-17 [z] Lev 4:26 **5:11** [a] Lev 2:1 **5:13** [b] Lev 4:26 [c] Lev 2:3 **5:15** [d] Lev 22:14 [e] Nu 5:8 [f] Ex 30:13 **5:16** [g] Lev 6:4 [h] Lev 22:14; Nu 5:7 **5:17** [i] ver 15; Lev 4:2

and will be held responsible. 18They are to
bring to the priest as a guilt offering a ram
from the flock, one without defect and of
the proper value. In this way the priest will
make atonement for them for the wrong
they have committed unintentionally, and
they will be forgiven.[j] 19It is a guilt offering; they have been guilty of[a] wrongdoing
against the LORD."

6 [b] The LORD said to Moses: 2"If anyone
sins and is unfaithful to the LORD[k] by
deceiving a neighbor[l] about something
entrusted to them or left in their care[m] or
about something stolen, or if they cheat
their neighbor, 3or if they find lost property and lie about it,[n] or if they swear falsely
about any such sin that people may commit— 4when they sin in any of these ways
and realize their guilt, they must return[o]
what they have stolen or taken by extortion, or what was entrusted to them, or the
lost property they found, 5or whatever it
was they swore falsely about. They must
make restitution[p] in full, add a fifth of the
value to it and give it all to the owner on
the day they present their guilt offering.[q]
6And as a penalty they must bring to the
priest, that is, to the LORD, their guilt offering,[r] a ram from the flock, one without
defect and of the proper value. 7In this way
the priest will make atonement[s] for them
before the LORD, and they will be forgiven
for any of the things they did that made
them guilty."

The Burnt Offering

8The LORD said to Moses: 9"Give Aaron and his sons this command: 'These are
the regulations for the burnt offering: The
burnt offering is to remain on the altar
hearth throughout the night, till morning,
and the fire must be kept burning on the altar. 10The priest shall then put on his linen
clothes, with linen undergarments next to
his body,[t] and shall remove the ashes of the
burnt offering that the fire has consumed
on the altar and place them beside the altar.
11Then he is to take off these clothes and
put on others, and carry the ashes outside
the camp to a place that is ceremonially
clean.[u] 12The fire on the altar must be kept
burning; it must not go out. Every morning
the priest is to add firewood and arrange
the burnt offering on the fire and burn the
fat of the fellowship offerings on it. 13The
fire must be kept burning on the altar continuously; it must not go out.

The Grain Offering

14" 'These are the regulations for the
grain offering:[v] Aaron's sons are to bring
it before the LORD, in front of the altar.
15The priest is to take a handful of the finest flour and some olive oil, together with
all the incense on the grain offering,[w] and
burn the memorial[c] portion[x] on the altar
as an aroma pleasing to the LORD. 16Aaron
and his sons[y] shall eat the rest[z] of it, but it is
to be eaten without yeast[a] in the sanctuary
area;[b] they are to eat it in the courtyard of
the tent of meeting. 17It must not be baked
with yeast; I have given it as their share of
the food offerings presented to me. Like
the sin offering[d] and the guilt offering, it is
most holy.[c] 18Any male descendant of Aaron may eat it.[d] For all generations to come it
is his perpetual share of the food offerings
presented to the LORD. Whatever touches
them will become holy.[e][e]' "

---

[a] 19 Or *offering; atonement has been made for their* [b] In Hebrew texts 6:1-7 is numbered 5:20-26, and 6:8-30 is numbered 6:1-23 [c] 15 Or *representative* [d] 17 Or *purification offering*; also in verses 25 and 30 [e] 18 Or *Whoever touches them must be holy*; similarly in verse 27

5:18 the wrong they have committed unintentionally. This was not a sin of rebellion, but one for which the offender earnestly desired to atone, though he did not know what it was.

5:19 they have been guilty of wrongdoing against the LORD. The fact that the priest declared him forgiven, and the peace of conscience that the worshipper had, declares that he was indeed guilty of some trespass; it was not his imagination. It is possible for a Christian to have an overactive conscience that keeps the believer in a constant state of anxiety about unknown sins. It is good to remember that God knows all about this, and if we confess our feelings of guilt, He will either show us our true guilt and grant us forgiveness and a clear conscience, or show us the error in our thinking regarding what He expects from us.

6:5–6 restitution. Restitution and a one fifth fine were evidence of genuine repentance. Then the offender could bring the ram for the guilt offering and be forgiven for the sin of swearing falsely in God's name. Jesus preserved this order for the person who remembered at the altar that he had offended his brother (Matt. 5:23).

6:10 undergarments. These were linen trousers that prevented immodest exposure as the priest ascended and descended the altar ramp. This modesty communicated to the Israelites that human sexuality could not influence God. That idea was a central feature of Baal worship, which continually tempted the Israelites. The priests of Baal would use obscene gestures and actions in the pagan worship of their depraved god.

6:13 fire must be kept burning. There are at least three reasons the priests are instructed to keep the fire burning. The original fire on the altar came from God, perpetual fire symbolized perpetual worship, and perpetual fire was a reminder of the continual need for atonement and reconciliation with God.

5:18 [j] ver 15 **6:2** [k] Nu 5:6; Ac 5:4; Col 3:9 [l] Pr 24:28 [m] Ex 22:7 **6:3** [n] Dt 22:1-3 **6:4** [o] Lk 19:8 **6:5** [p] Nu 5:7 [q] Lev 5:15 **6:6** [r] Lev 5:15 **6:7** [s] Lev 4:26 **6:10** [t] Ex 28:39-42, 43; 39:28 **6:11** [u] Lev 4:12 **6:14** [v] Lev 2:1; 15:4 **6:15** [w] Lev 2:9 [x] Lev 2:2 **6:16** [y] Lev 2:3 [z] Eze 44:29 [a] Lev 2:11 [b] Lev 10:13 **6:17** [c] ver 29; Ex 40:10; Nu 18:9, 10 **6:18** [d] ver 29; Nu 18:9-10 [e] ver 27

19 The LORD also said to Moses, 20 "This is the offering Aaron and his sons are to bring to the LORD on the day he[a] is anointed: a tenth of an ephah[b][f] of the finest flour as a regular grain offering,[g] half of it in the morning and half in the evening. 21 It must be prepared with oil on a griddle;[h] bring it well-mixed and present the grain offering broken[c] in pieces as an aroma pleasing to the LORD. 22 The son who is to succeed him as anointed priest shall prepare it. It is the LORD's perpetual share and is to be burned completely. 23 Every grain offering of a priest shall be burned completely; it must not be eaten."

The Sin Offering

24 The LORD said to Moses, 25 "Say to Aaron and his sons: 'These are the regulations for the sin offering: The sin offering is to be slaughtered before the LORD[i] in the place[j] the burnt offering is slaughtered; it is most holy. 26 The priest who offers it shall eat it; it is to be eaten in the sanctuary area,[k] in the courtyard[l] of the tent of meeting. 27 Whatever touches any of the flesh will become holy,[m] and if any of the blood is spattered on a garment, you must wash it in the sanctuary area. 28 The clay pot[n] the meat is cooked in must be broken; but if it is cooked in a bronze pot, the pot is to be scoured and rinsed with water. 29 Any male in a priest's family may eat it;[o] it is most holy.[p] 30 But any sin offering whose blood is brought into the tent of meeting to make atonement in the Holy Place[q] must not be eaten; it must be burned up.[r]

The Guilt Offering

7 " 'These are the regulations for the guilt offering,[s] which is most holy: 2 The guilt offering is to be slaughtered in the place where the burnt offering is slaughtered, and its blood is to be splashed against the sides of the altar. 3 All its fat[t] shall be offered: the fat tail and the fat that covers the internal organs, 4 both kidneys with the fat on them near the loins, and the long lobe of the liver, which is to be removed with the kidneys. 5 The priest shall burn them on the altar as a food offering presented to the LORD. It is a guilt offering. 6 Any male in a priest's family may eat it,[u] but it must be eaten in the sanctuary area; it is most holy.[v]

7 " 'The same law applies to both the sin offering[d] and the guilt offering: They belong to the priest[w] who makes atonement with them. 8 The priest who offers a burnt offering for anyone may keep its hide for himself. 9 Every grain offering baked in an oven or cooked in a pan or on a griddle[x] belongs to the priest who offers it, 10 and every grain offering, whether mixed with olive oil or dry, belongs equally to all the sons of Aaron.

The Fellowship Offering

11 " 'These are the regulations for the fellowship offering anyone may present to the LORD:

12 " 'If they offer it as an expression of thankfulness, then along with this thank offering[y] they are to offer thick loaves made without yeast and with olive oil mixed in, thin loaves[z] made without yeast and brushed with oil, and thick loaves of the finest flour well-kneaded and with oil mixed in. 13 Along with their fellowship offering of thanksgiving they are to present an offering with thick loaves of bread made with yeast.[a] 14 They are to bring one of each kind as an offering, a contribution to the LORD; it belongs to the priest who splashes the blood of the fellowship offering against the altar. 15 The meat of their fellowship offering of thanksgiving must be eaten on the day it is offered; they must leave none of it till morning.[b]

16 " 'If, however, their offering is the result of a vow or is a freewill offering, the sacrifice shall be eaten on the day they offer it, but anything left over may be eaten on the next day.[c] 17 Any meat of the sacrifice left over till the third day must be burned up. 18 If any meat of the fellowship offering is eaten on the third day, the one who of-

[a] *20* Or *each* [b] *20* That is, probably about 3 1/2 pounds or about 1.6 kilograms [c] *21* The meaning of the Hebrew for this word is uncertain.
[d] *7* Or *purification offering*; also in verse 37

6:20 *half of it in the morning . . . half in the evening.* The idea of a morning and evening appointment with God is ancient. It is a precious privilege, open to every believer because Jesus opened the door into the presence of God when He died on the cross for our sins.

6:22 *perpetual share.* This grain offering and the burnt offering were sacrificed daily—with some interruptions, most notably during the exile—until the destruction of the temple in A.D. 70. Even in the periods of Judah's worst apostasy, the evidence suggests that the daily offerings continued, though often for incorrect or inadequate reasons (Is. 1:10–17; Jer. 7:8–15; Mic. 6:6–8).

7:1–7 *guilt offering.* The guilt or trespass offering was "most holy," showing how seriously and carefully God considers the acts of reparation made by His people. The priest was to eat it in a holy place. It was his to eat, as part of God's provision for him, but he was to remember where it came from. The price of atonement has never been cheap in God's eyes, even when it was as incomplete as the offering of a goat or lamb.

6:20 [f] Ex 16:36 [g] Ex 29:2 **6:21** [h] Lev 2:5 **6:25** [i] Lev 1:3 [j] Lev 1:5,11 **6:26** [k] ver 16 [l] Lev 10:17-18 **6:27** [m] Ex 29:37 **6:28** [n] Lev 11:33; 15:12 **6:29** [o] ver 18 [p] ver 17 **6:30** [q] Lev 4:18 [r] Lev 4:12 **7:1** [s] Lev 5:14-6:7 **7:3** [t] Ex 29:13; Lev 3:4,9 **7:6** [u] Lev 6:18; Nu 18:9-10 [v] Lev 2:3 **7:7** [w] Lev 6:17,26; 1Co 9:13 **7:9** [x] Lev 2:5 **7:12** [y] ver 13,15 [z] Lev 2:4; Nu 6:15 **7:13** [a] Lev 23:17; Am 4:5 **7:15** [b] Lev 22:30 **7:16** [c] Lev 19:5-8

fered it will not be accepted.[d] It will not be reckoned[e] to their credit, for it has become impure; the person who eats any of it will be held responsible.

19"'Meat that touches anything ceremonially unclean must not be eaten; it must be burned up. As for other meat, anyone ceremonially clean may eat it. 20But if anyone who is unclean eats any meat of the fellowship offering belonging to the LORD, they must be cut off from their people.[f] 21Anyone who touches something unclean[g]—whether human uncleanness or an unclean animal or any unclean creature that moves along the ground[a]—and then eats any of the meat of the fellowship offering belonging to the LORD must be cut off from their people.'"

Eating Fat and Blood Forbidden

22The LORD said to Moses, 23"Say to the Israelites: 'Do not eat any of the fat of cattle, sheep or goats.[h] 24The fat of an animal found dead or torn by wild animals[i] may be used for any other purpose, but you must not eat it. 25Anyone who eats the fat of an animal from which a food offering may be[b] presented to the LORD must be cut off from their people. 26And wherever you live, you must not eat the blood[j] of any bird or animal. 27Anyone who eats blood[k] must be cut off from their people.'"

The Priests' Share

28The LORD said to Moses, 29"Say to the Israelites: 'Anyone who brings a fellowship offering to the LORD is to bring part of it as their sacrifice to the LORD. 30With their own hands they are to present the food offering to the LORD; they are to bring the fat, together with the breast, and wave the breast before the LORD as a wave offering.[l] 31The priest shall burn the fat on the altar, but the breast belongs to Aaron and his sons.[m] 32You are to give the right thigh of your fellowship offerings to the priest as a contribution.[n] 33The son of Aaron who offers the blood and the fat of the fellowship offering shall have the right thigh as his share. 34From the fellowship offerings of the Israelites, I have taken the breast that is waved and the thigh[o] that is presented and have given them to Aaron the priest and his sons[p] as their perpetual share from the Israelites.'"

35This is the portion of the food offerings presented to the LORD that were allotted to Aaron and his sons on the day they were presented to serve the LORD as priests. 36On the day they were anointed,[q] the LORD commanded that the Israelites give this to them as their perpetual share for the generations to come.

37These, then, are the regulations for the burnt offering,[r] the grain offering,[s] the sin offering, the guilt offering, the ordination offering[t] and the fellowship offering, 38which the LORD gave Moses at Mount Sinai in the Desert of Sinai on the day he commanded the Israelites to bring their offerings to the LORD.[u]

The Ordination of Aaron and His Sons

8 The LORD said to Moses, 2"Bring Aaron and his sons, their garments, the anointing oil,[v] the bull for the sin offering,[c] the two rams and the basket containing bread made without yeast,[w] 3and gather the entire assembly[x] at the entrance to the tent of meeting." 4Moses did as the LORD commanded him, and the assembly gathered at the entrance to the tent of meeting.

5Moses said to the assembly, "This is what the LORD has commanded to be done." 6Then Moses brought Aaron and his sons forward and washed them with water.[y] 7He put the tunic on Aaron, tied the sash around him, clothed him with the robe and put the ephod on him. He also fastened the ephod with a decorative waistband, which he tied around him.[z] 8He placed the breastpiece on him and put the Urim and Thummim[a] in the breastpiece. 9Then he placed

[a] *21* A few Hebrew manuscripts, Samaritan Pentateuch, Syriac and Targum (see 5:2); most Hebrew manuscripts *any unclean, detestable thing*
[b] *25* Or *offering is* [c] *2* Or *purification offering*; also in verse 14

7:34 *the breast that is waved and the thigh that is presented.* This present was a contribution to the officiating priest as his portion of the fellowship offerings for thanksgiving. The offering was waved before the Lord as an acknowledgment that He is the giver of all gifts.

8:6–13 Purification—Moses carried out the Lord's command (Ex. 29:4) by purifying Aaron and his sons for the priesthood. The purification process began with an outward washing of water which symbolized an inward purity. The believer today also shows his inward reality (his acceptance of Christ and the presence of the Holy Spirit) with his outward actions. These acts of obedience do not create the inward reality, but they confirm it.

8:8 *the Urim and the Thummim.* These were the sacred lots used to determine the will of God. What they looked like and how they were used is not known. Apparently, the high priest phrased questions so the answers would be yes, or no, depending on how the lots came up.

7:18 [d] Lev 19:7 [e] Nu 18:27 **7:20** [f] Lev 22:3-7
7:21 [g] Lev 5:2; 11:24, 28 **7:23** [h] Lev 3:17; 17:13-14
7:24 [i] Ex 22:31 **7:26** [j] Ge 9:4 **7:27** [k] Lev 17:10-24; Ac 15:20, 29 **7:30** [l] Ex 29:24; Nu 6:20 **7:31** [m] ver 34
7:32 [n] ver 34; Lev 9:21; Nu 6:20 **7:34** [o] Lev 10:15 [p] Ex 29:27; Nu 18:18-19 **7:36** [q] Ex 40:13, 15; Lev 8:12, 30
7:37 [r] Lev 6:9 [s] Lev 6:14 [t] ver 1, 11 **7:38** [u] Lev 1:2
8:2 [v] Ex 30:23-25, 30 [w] Ex 29:2-3 **8:3** [x] Nu 8:9
8:6 [y] Ex 29:4; 30:19; Ps 26:6; Ac 22:16; 1Co 6:11; Eph 5:26
8:7 [z] Ex 28:4 **8:8** [a] Ex 28:30

the turban on Aaron's head and set the gold plate, the sacred emblem,[b] on the front of it, as the LORD commanded Moses.

10Then Moses took the anointing oil[c] and anointed[d] the tabernacle and everything in it, and so consecrated them. 11He sprinkled some of the oil on the altar seven times, anointing the altar and all its utensils and the basin with its stand, to consecrate them.[e] 12He poured some of the anointing oil on Aaron's head and anointed[f] him to consecrate him.[g] 13Then he brought Aaron's sons forward, put tunics on them, tied sashes around them and fastened caps on them, as the LORD commanded Moses.

14He then presented the bull[h] for the sin offering,[i] and Aaron and his sons laid their hands on its head. 15Moses slaughtered the bull and took some of the blood, and with his finger he put it on all the horns of the altar[j] to purify the altar.[k] He poured out the rest of the blood at the base of the altar. So he consecrated it to make atonement for it.[l] 16Moses also took all the fat around the internal organs, the long lobe of the liver, and both kidneys and their fat, and burned it on the altar. 17But the bull with its hide and its flesh and its intestines[m] he burned up outside the camp,[n] as the LORD commanded Moses.

18He then presented the ram[o] for the burnt offering, and Aaron and his sons laid their hands on its head. 19Then Moses slaughtered the ram and splashed the blood against the sides of the altar. 20He cut the ram into pieces and burned the head, the pieces and the fat. 21He washed the internal organs and the legs with water and burned the whole ram on the altar. It was a burnt offering, a pleasing aroma, a food offering presented to the LORD, as the LORD commanded Moses.

22He then presented the other ram, the ram for the ordination,[p] and Aaron and his sons laid their hands on its head. 23Moses slaughtered the ram and took some of its blood and put it on the lobe of Aaron's right ear, on the thumb of his right hand and on the big toe of his right foot. 24Moses also brought Aaron's sons forward and put some of the blood on the lobes of their right ears, on the thumbs of their right hands and on the big toes of their right feet. Then he splashed blood against the sides of the altar.[q] 25After that, he took the fat, the fat tail, all the fat around the internal organs, the long lobe of the liver, both kidneys and their fat and the right thigh. 26And from the basket of bread made without yeast, which was before the LORD, he took one thick loaf, one thick loaf with olive oil mixed in, and one thin loaf, and he put these on the fat portions and on the right thigh. 27He put all these in the hands of Aaron and his sons, and they waved them before the LORD as a wave offering. 28Then Moses took them from their hands and burned them on the altar on top of the burnt offering as an ordination offering, a pleasing aroma, a food offering presented to the LORD. 29Moses also took the breast, which was his share of the ordination ram,[r] and waved it before the LORD as a wave offering, as the LORD commanded Moses.

30Then Moses took some of the anointing oil and some of the blood from the altar and sprinkled them on Aaron and his garments[s] and on his sons and their garments. So he consecrated[t] Aaron and his garments and his sons and their garments.

31Moses then said to Aaron and his sons, "Cook the meat at the entrance to the tent of meeting and eat it there with the bread from the basket of ordination offerings, as I was commanded: 'Aaron and his sons are to eat it.' 32Then burn up the rest of the meat and the bread. 33Do not leave the entrance to the tent of meeting for seven days, until the days of your ordination are completed, for your ordination will last seven days. 34What has been done today was commanded by the LORD[u] to make atonement for you. 35You must stay at the entrance to the tent of meeting day and night for seven days and do what the LORD requires,[v] so you will not die; for that is what I have been commanded."

36So Aaron and his sons did everything the LORD commanded through Moses.

The Priests Begin Their Ministry

9 On the eighth day[w] Moses summoned Aaron and his sons and the elders of Israel. 2He said to Aaron, "Take a bull calf for your sin offering[a] and a ram for your burnt offering, both without defect, and present them before the LORD. 3Then say to the Israelites: 'Take a male goat for a sin offering, a calf and a lamb—both a year old and

[a] 2 Or *purification offering*; here and throughout this chapter

8:12 *anointed him.* The high priests of Israel, beginning here with Aaron, were anointed, as were the kings of Israel (1 Sam. 10:1; 16:13) and at least one of the prophets (1 Kin. 19:16). Jesus combines in His person the offices of High Priest, King, and Prophet, so He is *the* Anointed One, which is the meaning of the names Messiah (Hebrew) and Christ (Greek).

8:35 *so you will not die.* This statement was a reminder that it is dangerous to approach God carelessly, without reverence, or ignore His instructions. Two of Aaron's sons failed to heed this warning and died (ch. 10).

8:9 [b] Ex 28:36 **8:10** [c] ver 2 [d] Ex 30:26 **8:11** [e] Ex 30:29 **8:12** [f] Lev 21:10, 12 [g] Ex 30:30 **8:14** [h] Lev 4:3 [i] Ps 66:15; Eze 43:19 **8:15** [j] Lev 4:7 [k] Heb 9:22 [l] Eze 43:20 **8:17** [m] Lev 4:11 [n] Lev 4:12 **8:18** [o] ver 2 **8:22** [p] ver 2 **8:24** [q] Heb 9:18-22 **8:29** [r] Lev 7:31-34 **8:30** [s] Ex 28:2 [t] Nu 3:3 **8:34** [u] Heb 7:16 **8:35** [v] Nu 3:7; 9:19; Dt 11:1; 1Ki 2:3; Eze 48:11 **9:1** [w] Eze 43:27

without defect—for a burnt offering, 4and
an ox[a] and a ram for a fellowship offering
to sacrifice before the LORD, together with
a grain offering mixed with olive oil. For
today the LORD will appear to you.[x]'"
5They took the things Moses commanded
to the front of the tent of meeting, and the
entire assembly came near and stood before
the LORD. 6Then Moses said, "This is what
the LORD has commanded you to do, so that
the glory of the LORD[y] may appear to you."
7Moses said to Aaron, "Come to the altar and sacrifice your sin offering and your
burnt offering and make atonement for yourself and the people; sacrifice the offering
that is for the people and make atonement
for them, as the LORD has commanded.[z]"
8So Aaron came to the altar and slaughtered the calf as a sin offering[a] for himself.
9His sons brought the blood to him,[b] and
he dipped his finger into the blood and put
it on the horns of the altar; the rest of the
blood he poured out at the base of the altar.[c] 10On the altar he burned the fat, the
kidneys and the long lobe of the liver from
the sin offering, as the LORD commanded
Moses; 11the flesh and the hide[d] he burned
up outside the camp.[e]
12Then he slaughtered the burnt offering. His sons handed him the blood, and
he splashed it against the sides of the altar.
13They handed him the burnt offering piece
by piece, including the head, and he burned
them on the altar.[f] 14He washed the internal
organs and the legs and burned them on top
of the burnt offering on the altar.
15Aaron then brought the offering that
was for the people.[g] He took the goat for
the people's sin offering and slaughtered it
and offered it for a sin offering as he did
with the first one.
16He brought the burnt offering and offered it in the prescribed way.[h] 17He also
brought the grain offering, took a handful
of it and burned it on the altar in addition
to the morning's burnt offering.[i]
18He slaughtered the ox and the ram
as the fellowship offering for the people.[j] His sons handed him the blood, and
he splashed it against the sides of the altar. 19But the fat portions of the ox and
the ram—the fat tail, the layer of fat, the
kidneys and the long lobe of the liver—
20these they laid on the breasts, and then
Aaron burned the fat on the altar. 21Aaron
waved the breasts and the right thigh before the LORD as a wave offering,[k] as Moses commanded.
22Then Aaron lifted his hands toward the
people and blessed them.[l] And having sacrificed the sin offering, the burnt offering and
the fellowship offering, he stepped down.
23Moses and Aaron then went into the
tent of meeting. When they came out, they
blessed the people; and the glory of the
LORD[m] appeared to all the people. 24Fire[n]
came out from the presence of the LORD
and consumed the burnt offering and the
fat portions on the altar. And when all the
people saw it, they shouted for joy and fell
facedown.[o]

The Death of Nadab and Abihu

10 Aaron's sons Nadab and Abihu[p]
took their censers, put fire in them[q]
and added incense; and they offered unauthorized fire before the LORD, contrary
to his command.[r] 2So fire came out from
the presence of the LORD and consumed
them,[s] and they died before the LORD. 3Mo-
ses then said to Aaron, "This is what the
LORD spoke of when he said:

"'Among those who approach me[t]
  I will be proved holy;[u]
in the sight of all the people
  I will be honored.[v]'"

Aaron remained silent.

---

a 4 The Hebrew word can refer to either male or female; also in verses 18 and 19.

9:4 *the LORD will appear to you.* The purpose of all worship is to fellowship with God. The sacrifices were not an end in themselves; they allowed the worshiper to meet with God without being destroyed. The Israelites looked forward and we look back to Christ's atonement, which made the way for us to come freely into God's presence.

9:15 *the goat for the people's sin offering.* This goat was offered for atonement of the people as a general acknowledgment that they would always need to make things right with God before they could worship Him, and is referred to again in ch. 16. The bull for the sin offering (4:14) was for a specific sin, rather than dealing with sin nature (that is, our ability to sin).

9:22 *Aaron ... blessed them.* The ultimate function of the priests was to bless the people. The purpose of the priest's sacrifices was to cleanse the priests so they could bless the people, and the purpose of the people's sacrifices was to cleanse the people to receive this blessing from God.

10:1–2 *unauthorized fire.* Aaron and his sons served the Lord as high priests in the worship of the tabernacle. They had been properly appointed, purified, clothed, anointed, and ordained. Initially they did everything that the Lord commanded through Moses. But when Nadab and Abihu disobeyed God in the very performance of their duties, the Lord swiftly punished them with a consuming fire. Being blessed with a thriving ministry is no excuse to go off and do things our own way. God doesn't take such actions lightly, and neither should we.

10:3 *Among those who approach me ... I will be honored.* Although this passage refers specifically

9:4 [x] Ex 29:43 **9:6** [y] ver 23; Ex 24:16 **9:7** [z] Heb 5:1, 3; 7:27 **9:8** [a] Lev 4:1-12 **9:9** [b] ver 12, 18 [c] Lev 4:7 **9:11** [d] Lev 4:11 [e] Lev 4:12; 8:17 **9:13** [f] Lev 1:8 **9:15** [g] Lev 4:27-31 **9:16** [h] Lev 1:1-13 **9:17** [i] Lev 2:1-2; 3:5 **9:18** [j] Lev 3:1-11 **9:21** [k] Ex 29:24, 26; Lev 7:30-34 **9:22** [l] Nu 6:23; Dt 21:5; Lk 24:50 **9:23** [m] ver 6 **9:24** [n] Jdg 6:21; 2Ch 7:1 [o] 1Ki 18:39 **10:1** [p] Ex 24:1; Nu 3:2-4; 26:61 [q] Lev 16:12 [r] Ex 30:9 **10:2** [s] Nu 3:4; 16:35; 26:61 **10:3** [t] Ex 19:22 [u] Ex 30:29; Lev 21:6; Eze 28:22 [v] Isa 49:3

4 Moses summoned Mishael and Elzaphan,[w] sons of Aaron's uncle Uzziel,[x] and said to them, "Come here; carry your cousins outside the camp,[y] away from the front of the sanctuary." 5 So they came and carried them, still in their tunics,[z] outside the camp, as Moses ordered.

6 Then Moses said to Aaron and his sons Eleazar and Ithamar, "Do not let your hair become unkempt[a][a] and do not tear your clothes, or you will die and the LORD will be angry with the whole community.[b] But your relatives, all the Israelites, may mourn for those the LORD has destroyed by fire. 7 Do not leave the entrance to the tent of meeting or you will die, because the LORD's anointing oil[c] is on you." So they did as Moses said.

8 Then the LORD said to Aaron, 9 "You and your sons are not to drink wine[d] or other fermented drink[e] whenever you go into the tent of meeting, or you will die. This is a lasting ordinance for the generations to come, 10 so that you can distinguish between the holy and the common, between the unclean and the clean,[f] 11 and so you can teach[g] the Israelites all the decrees the LORD has given them through Moses.[h]"

12 Moses said to Aaron and his remaining sons, Eleazar and Ithamar, "Take the grain offering left over from the food offerings prepared without yeast and presented to the LORD and eat it beside the altar,[i] for it is most holy. 13 Eat it in the sanctuary area, because it is your share and your sons' share of the food offerings presented to the LORD; for so I have been commanded. 14 But you and your sons and your daughters may eat the breast that was waved and the thigh that was presented. Eat them in a ceremonially clean place;[j] they have been given to you and your children as your share of the Israelites' fellowship offerings. 15 The thigh[k] that was presented and the breast that was waved must be brought with the fat portions of the food offerings, to be waved before the LORD as a wave offering. This will be the perpetual share for you and your children, as the LORD has commanded."

16 When Moses inquired about the goat of the sin offering[b][l] and found that it had been burned up, he was angry with Eleazar and Ithamar, Aaron's remaining sons, and asked, 17 "Why didn't you eat the sin offering[m] in the sanctuary area? It is most holy; it was given to you to take away the guilt of the community by making atonement for them before the LORD. 18 Since its blood was not taken into the Holy Place,[n] you should have eaten the goat in the sanctuary area, as I commanded."

19 Aaron replied to Moses, "Today they sacrificed their sin offering and their burnt offering[o] before the LORD, but such things as this have happened to me. Would the LORD have been pleased if I had eaten the sin offering today?" 20 When Moses heard this, he was satisfied.

Clean and Unclean Food

11 The LORD said to Moses and Aaron, 2 "Say to the Israelites: 'Of all the animals that live on land, these are the ones you may eat:[p] 3 You may eat any animal that has a divided hoof and that chews the cud.

4 " 'There are some that only chew the cud or only have a divided hoof, but you must not eat them. The camel, though it chews the cud, does not have a divided hoof; it is ceremonially unclean for you. 5 The hyrax, though it chews the cud, does not have a divided hoof; it is unclean for you. 6 The rabbit, though it chews the cud, does not have a divided hoof; it is unclean for you. 7 And the pig,[q] though it has a divided hoof, does not chew the cud; it is unclean for you. 8 You must not eat their meat or touch their carcasses; they are unclean for you.[r]

[a] 6 Or *Do not uncover your heads* [b] 16 Or *purification offering*; also in verses 17 and 19

---

to the priests of Israel, it is still a good concept for all believers. We are close to God, we remember that He is holy, that He paid a great price to redeem us, and it is our purpose to glorify Him.

11:3 *chews the cud.* Ruminants, like cows, sheep, goats, deer, and antelope, eat only plants, mainly grasses and grains. No meat-eating animal chews the cud.

11:4 *The camel.* Some of Israel's neighbors considered the camel a great delicacy.

11:5–6 *hyrax ... rabbit.* The hyrax, or coney, lives in colonies among the rocks. It is about the size of the rabbit, and like the rabbit, appears to chew constantly, but it is not a true ruminant, nor does it have a hoof.

11:7 *the pig.* The pig is the best known of the unclean animals. We know now that pigs can pass some diseases to humans, and that inadequately cooked meat is one way these diseases are transferred. Pigs were sacrificed to pagan deities, and God was carefully steering His people away from these corrupted cultures.

11:8 *You must not eat ... or touch their carcasses.* In the case of these unclean animals, eating their meat or touching their dead bodies caused the Israelite to be unclean, or ritually impure. However, touching a live animal did not make the Israelites unclean, and they were allowed to use camels and donkeys as beasts of burden.

10:4 [w] Ex 6:22 [x] Ex 6:18 [y] Ac 5:6,9,10 **10:5** [z] Lev 8:13 **10:6** [a] Lev 21:10 [b] Nu 1:53; 16:22; Jos 7:1; 22:18; 2Sa 24:1 **10:7** [c] Ex 28:41; Lev 21:12 **10:9** [d] Hos 4:11 [e] Pr 20:1; Isa 28:7; Eze 44:21; Lk 1:15; Eph 5:18; 1Ti 3:3; Titus 1:7 **10:10** [f] Lev 11:47; 20:25; Eze 22:26 **10:11** [g] Mal 2:7 [h] Dt 24:8 **10:12** [i] Lev 6:14-18; 21:22 **10:14** [j] Ex 29:24, 26-27; Lev 7:31,34; Nu 18:11 **10:15** [k] Lev 7:34 **10:16** [l] Lev 9:3 **10:17** [m] Lev 6:24-30 **10:18** [n] Lev 6:26, 30 **10:19** [o] Lev 9:12 **11:2** [p] Ac 10:12-14 **11:7** [q] Isa 65:4; 66:3, 17 **11:8** [r] Isa 52:11; Heb 9:10

9“‘Of all the creatures living in the water of the seas and the streams you may
eat any that have fins and scales. 10But all
creatures in the seas or streams that do not
have fins and scales—whether among all
the swarming things or among all the other living creatures in the water—you are to
regard as unclean.[s] 11And since you are to
regard them as unclean, you must not eat
their meat; you must regard their carcasses
as unclean. 12Anything living in the water
that does not have fins and scales is to be
regarded as unclean by you.

13“‘These are the birds you are to regard
as unclean and not eat because they are
unclean: the eagle,[a] the vulture, the black
vulture, 14the red kite, any kind of black
kite, 15any kind of raven, 16the horned
owl, the screech owl, the gull, any kind of
hawk, 17the little owl, the cormorant, the
great owl, 18the white owl, the desert owl,
the osprey, 19the stork, any kind of heron,
the hoopoe and the bat.

20“‘All flying insects that walk on all
fours are to be regarded as unclean by
you.[t] 21There are, however, some flying insects that walk on all fours that you may
eat: those that have jointed legs for hopping
on the ground. 22Of these you may eat any
kind of locust,[u] katydid, cricket or grasshopper. 23But all other flying insects that
have four legs you are to regard as unclean.

24“‘You will make yourselves unclean by
these; whoever touches their carcasses will
be unclean till evening. 25Whoever picks
up one of their carcasses must wash their
clothes,[v] and they will be unclean till evening.[w]

26“‘Every animal that does not have a divided hoof or that does not chew the cud
is unclean for you; whoever touches the
carcass of any of them will be unclean.
27Of all the animals that walk on all fours,
those that walk on their paws are unclean
for you; whoever touches their carcasses
will be unclean till evening. 28Anyone who
picks up their carcasses must wash their
clothes, and they will be unclean till evening. These animals are unclean for you.

29“‘Of the animals that move along the
ground, these are unclean for you: the wea-
sel, the rat,[x] any kind of great lizard, 30the
gecko, the monitor lizard, the wall lizard,
the skink and the chameleon. 31Of all those
that move along the ground, these are unclean for you. Whoever touches them when
they are dead will be unclean till evening.
32When one of them dies and falls on something, that article, whatever its use, will be
unclean, whether it is made of wood, cloth,
hide or sackcloth.[y] Put it in water; it will
be unclean till evening, and then it will be
clean. 33If one of them falls into a clay pot,
everything in it will be unclean, and you
must break the pot.[z] 34Any food you are
allowed to eat that has come into contact
with water from any such pot is unclean,
and any liquid that is drunk from such
a pot is unclean. 35Anything that one of
their carcasses falls on becomes unclean;
an oven or cooking pot must be broken up.
They are unclean, and you are to regard
them as unclean. 36A spring, however, or a
cistern for collecting water remains clean,
but anyone who touches one of these carcasses is unclean. 37If a carcass falls on
any seeds that are to be planted, they remain clean. 38But if water has been put on
the seed and a carcass falls on it, it is unclean for you.

39“‘If an animal that you are allowed to
eat dies, anyone who touches its carcass
will be unclean till evening. 40Anyone who
eats some of its carcass must wash their
clothes, and they will be unclean till evening.[a] Anyone who picks up the carcass
must wash their clothes, and they will be
unclean till evening.

41“‘Every creature that moves along the
ground is to be regarded as unclean; it is
not to be eaten. 42You are not to eat any
creature that moves along the ground,
whether it moves on its belly or walks on
all fours or on many feet; it is unclean. 43Do
not defile yourselves by any of these creatures.[b] Do not make yourselves unclean
by means of them or be made unclean by
them. 44I am the LORD your God;[c] consecrate yourselves[d] and be holy,[e] because I
am holy.[f] Do not make yourselves unclean
by any creature that moves along the
ground. 45I am the LORD, who brought you

[a] *13* The precise identification of some of the birds, insects and animals in this chapter is uncertain.

11:11–12 *unclean.* The phrasing is careful, deliberate, and repetitive to remove any possibility of finding any exception anywhere.

11:20 *walk on all fours.* This phrase is an idiom for crawling on the ground, as insects do on their six legs. Many insects move about in filth and eat refuse.

11:21 *jointed legs.* The joints are the enlarged third legs of locusts and grasshoppers that enable them to leap. Locusts and grasshoppers do not live in filth or eat dung; they eat only plants.

11:44–45 *be holy.* Our Lord calls us to personal holiness, and holy living can only come from a life which spends time with the Lord, meditating on who He is, seeking His power to be like Him. We will make mistakes and sin all of our lives, which God never does; when He asks us to be holy because He is holy, it is a goal that we grow toward. Even though we never finish, we still overcome many, many areas of sin, and this growth shows others that we serve a holy God, because they see His characteristics in us.

11:10 [s] Lev 7:18 **11:20** [t] Ac 10:14 **11:22** [u] Mt 3:4; Mk 1:6 **11:25** [v] Lev 14:8, 47; 15:5 [w] ver 40; Nu 31:24 **11:29** [x] Isa 66:17 **11:32** [y] Lev 15:12 **11:33** [z] Lev 6:28; 15:12 **11:40** [a] Lev 17:15; 22:8; Eze 44:31 **11:43** [b] Lev 20:25 **11:44** [c] Ex 6:2, 7; Isa 43:3; 51:15 [d] Lev 20:7 [e] Ex 19:6 [f] Lev 19:2; Ps 99:3; Eph 1:4; 1Th 4:7; 1Pe 1:15, 16*

up out of Egypt[g] to be your God;[h] therefore be holy, because I am holy.[i]

46“ ‘These are the regulations concerning animals, birds, every living thing that moves about in the water and every creature that moves along the ground. 47You must distinguish between the unclean and the clean, between living creatures that may be eaten and those that may not be eaten.[j]’ ”

Purification After Childbirth

12 The LORD said to Moses, 2“Say to the Israelites: ‘A woman who becomes pregnant and gives birth to a son will be ceremonially unclean for seven days, just as she is unclean during her monthly period.[k] 3On the eighth day the boy is to be circumcised.[l] 4Then the woman must wait thirty-three days to be purified from her bleeding. She must not touch anything sacred or go to the sanctuary until the days of her purification are over. 5If she gives birth to a daughter, for two weeks the woman will be unclean, as during her period. Then she must wait sixty-six days to be purified from her bleeding.

6“ ‘When the days of her purification for a son or daughter are over,[m] she is to bring to the priest at the entrance to the tent of meeting a year-old lamb[n] for a burnt offering and a young pigeon or a dove for a sin offering.[a][o] 7He shall offer them before the LORD to make atonement for her, and then she will be ceremonially clean from her flow of blood.

“ ‘These are the regulations for the woman who gives birth to a boy or a girl. 8But if she cannot afford a lamb, she is to bring two doves or two young pigeons,[p] one for a burnt offering and the other for a sin offering.[q] In this way the priest will make atonement for her, and she will be clean.[r]’ ”

Regulations About Defiling Skin Diseases

13 The LORD said to Moses and Aaron, 2“When anyone has a swelling[s] or a rash or a shiny spot[t] on their skin that may be a defiling skin disease,[b][u] they must be brought to Aaron the priest[v] or to one of his sons[c] who is a priest. 3The priest is to examine the sore on the skin, and if the hair in the sore has turned white and the sore appears to be more than skin deep, it is a defiling skin disease. When the priest examines that person, he shall pronounce them ceremonially unclean.[w] 4If the shiny spot[x] on the skin is white but does not appear to be more than skin deep and the hair in it has not turned white, the priest is to isolate the affected person for seven days.[y] 5On the seventh day[z] the priest is to examine them,[a] and if he sees that the sore is unchanged and has not spread in the skin, he is to isolate them for another seven days. 6On the seventh day the priest is to examine them again, and if the sore has faded and has not spread in the skin, the priest shall pronounce them clean;[b] it is only a rash. They must wash their clothes,[c] and they will be clean.[d] 7But if the rash does spread in their skin after they have shown themselves to the priest to be pronounced clean, they must appear before the priest again.[e] 8The priest is to examine that person, and if the rash has spread in the skin, he shall pronounce them unclean; it is a defiling skin disease.

9“When anyone has a defiling skin disease, they must be brought to the priest. 10The priest is to examine them, and if there is a white swelling in the skin that

[a] 6 Or *purification offering*; also in verse 8
[b] 2 The Hebrew word for *defiling skin disease*, traditionally translated “leprosy,” was used for various diseases affecting the skin; here and throughout verses 3-46. [c] 2 Or *descendants*

12:2 *pregnant and gives birth to a son ... unclean.* The child did not cause the mother to be unclean. God had ordained and blessed childbirth from the beginning, even before the sin in the garden (Gen. 1:28). It was the blood and other fluids in childbirth that made the mother ritually unclean for a period of time, just as other bodily fluids caused people to be unclean.

12:4 *thirty-three days to be purified from her bleeding.* There is a practical as well as a ceremonial aspect to these instructions. The eighth day marked the end of the mother's uncleanness with regard to everyday objects and activities; she would no longer make them unclean by touching them. But her personal uncleanness continued. This corresponds with the medical characteristics of childbirth, and the need for special care and rest for the mother. (There is no reason given why this period is double with the birth of a female child.)

12:8 *if she cannot afford a lamb.* Mary, following the birth of Jesus and the days of her purification, went to the temple in Jerusalem and offered a pair of doves because she was poor. ***be clean.*** The law of purification after childbirth demonstrates that all aspects of human existence are touched by sin. Childbirth itself is not sinful, and having children was one of the good commands that the Lord gave Adam and Eve in the garden. Yet pain in childbirth was one of the curses of the fall, and this time of purification can be viewed as a reminder that humans are still dealing with a sin nature that needs God's mercy and purification.

11:45 [g] Lev 25:38, 55; Ex 6:7; 20:2 [h] Ge 17:7 [i] Ex 19:6; 1Pe 1:16* **11:47** [j] Lev 10:10 **12:2** [k] Lev 15:19; 18:19 **12:3** [l] Ge 17:12; Lk 1:59; 2:21 **12:6** [m] Lk 2:22 [n] Ex 29:38; Lev 23:12; Nu 6:12, 14; 7:15 [o] Lev 5:7 **12:8** [p] Ge 15:9; Lev 14:22 [q] Lev 5:7; Lk 2:22-24* [r] Lev 4:26 **13:2** [s] ver 10, 19, 28, 43 [t] ver 4, 38, 39; Lev 14:56 [u] ver 3, 9, 15; Ex 4:6; Lev 14:3, 32; Nu 5:2; Dt 24:8 [v] Dt 24:8 **13:3** [w] ver 8, 11, 20, 30; Lev 21:1; Nu 9:6 **13:4** [x] ver 2 [y] ver 5, 21, 26, 33, 46; Lev 14:38; Nu 12:14, 15; Dt 24:9 **13:5** [z] Lev 14:9 [a] ver 27, 32, 34, 51 **13:6** [b] ver 13, 17, 23, 28, 34; Mt 8:3; Lk 5:12-14 [c] Lev 11:25 [d] Lev 11:25; 14:8, 9, 20, 48; 15:8; Nu 8:7 **13:7** [e] Lk 5:14

has turned the hair white and if there is
raw flesh in the swelling, 11it is a chronic skin disease[f] and the priest shall pronounce them unclean. He is not to isolate
them, because they are already unclean.
12"If the disease breaks out all over
their skin and, so far as the priest can
see, it covers all the skin of the affected
person from head to foot, 13the priest is to
examine them, and if the disease has covered their whole body, he shall pronounce
them clean. Since it has all turned white,
they are clean. 14But whenever raw flesh
appears on them, they will be unclean.
15When the priest sees the raw flesh, he
shall pronounce them unclean. The raw
flesh is unclean; they have a defiling disease.[g] 16If the raw flesh changes and turns
white, they must go to the priest. 17The
priest is to examine them, and if the sores
have turned white, the priest shall pronounce the affected person clean;[h] then
they will be clean.
18"When someone has a boil[i] on their
skin and it heals, 19and in the place where
the boil was, a white swelling or reddish-
white[j] spot[k] appears, they must present
themselves to the priest. 20The priest is
to examine it, and if it appears to be more
than skin deep and the hair in it has turned
white, the priest shall pronounce that person unclean. It is a defiling skin disease[l]
that has broken out where the boil was.
21But if, when the priest examines it, there
is no white hair in it and it is not more than
skin deep and has faded, then the priest
is to isolate them for seven days. 22If it is
spreading in the skin, the priest shall pronounce them unclean; it is a defiling disease. 23But if the spot is unchanged and
has not spread, it is only a scar from the
boil, and the priest shall pronounce them
clean.[m]
24"When someone has a burn on their
skin and a reddish-white or white spot appears in the raw flesh of the burn, 25the
priest is to examine the spot, and if the
hair in it has turned white, and it appears
to be more than skin deep, it is a defiling
disease that has broken out in the burn.
The priest shall pronounce them unclean;
it is a defiling skin disease.[n] 26But if the
priest examines it and there is no white
hair in the spot and if it is not more than
skin deep and has faded, then the priest is
to isolate them for seven days.[o] 27On the
seventh day the priest is to examine that
person,[p] and if it is spreading in the skin,
the priest shall pronounce them unclean; it
is a defiling skin disease. 28If, however, the
spot is unchanged and has not spread in
the skin but has faded, it is a swelling from
the burn, and the priest shall pronounce
them clean; it is only a scar from the burn.[q]
29"If a man or woman has a sore on their
head[r] or chin, 30the priest is to examine the
sore, and if it appears to be more than skin
deep and the hair in it is yellow and thin,
the priest shall pronounce them unclean;
it is a defiling skin disease on the head or
chin. 31But if, when the priest examines
the sore, it does not seem to be more than
skin deep and there is no black hair in it,
then the priest is to isolate the affected
person for seven days.[s] 32On the seventh
day the priest is to examine the sore,[t] and
if it has not spread and there is no yellow
hair in it and it does not appear to be more
than skin deep, 33then the man or woman
must shave themselves, except for the affected area, and the priest is to keep them
isolated another seven days. 34On the seventh day the priest is to examine the sore,[u]
and if it has not spread in the skin and appears to be no more than skin deep, the
priest shall pronounce them clean. They
must wash their clothes, and they will be
clean.[v] 35But if the sore does spread in the
skin after they are pronounced clean, 36the
priest is to examine them, and if he finds
that the sore has spread in the skin, he
does not need to look for yellow hair; they
are unclean.[w] 37If, however, the sore is unchanged so far as the priest can see, and
if black hair has grown in it, the affected
person is healed. They are clean, and the
priest shall pronounce them clean.
38"When a man or woman has white
spots on the skin, 39the priest is to examine them, and if the spots are dull white, it
is a harmless rash that has broken out on
the skin; they are clean.
40"A man who has lost his hair and is
bald[x] is clean. 41If he has lost his hair from
the front of his scalp and has a bald forehead, he is clean. 42But if he has a reddish-
white sore on his bald head or forehead, it
is a defiling disease breaking out on his
head or forehead. 43The priest is to examine him, and if the swollen sore on his head
or forehead is reddish-white like a defiling
skin disease, 44the man is diseased and is
unclean. The priest shall pronounce him
unclean because of the sore on his head.
45"Anyone with such a defiling disease
must wear torn clothes,[y] let their hair be

13:11 ***is not to isolate them.*** Isolation, or quarantine, was for the purpose of protecting the community until a diagnosis was reached. In this case, the patient was already diagnosed as "unclean," which meant he had to live outside the camp (v. 46).

13:45–46 ***torn clothes ... hair be unkempt.*** These actions were signs of mourning, for chronic skin diseases isolated the patients from life and

13:11 [f] Ex 4:6; Lev 14:8; Nu 12:10; Mt 8:2 **13:15** [g] ver 2 **13:17** [h] ver 6 **13:18** [i] Ex 9:9 **13:19** [j] ver 24, 42; Lev 14:37 [k] ver 2 **13:20** [l] ver 2 **13:23** [m] ver 6 **13:25** [n] ver 11 **13:26** [o] ver 4 **13:27** [p] ver 5 **13:28** [q] ver 2 **13:29** [r] ver 43, 44 **13:31** [s] ver 4 **13:32** [t] ver 5 **13:34** [u] ver 5 [v] Lev 11:25 **13:36** [w] ver 30 **13:40** [x] Lev 21:5; 2Ki 2:23; Isa 3:24; 15:2; 22:12; Eze 27:31; 29:18; Am 8:10; Mic 1:16 **13:45** [y] Lev 10:6

unkempt,[a] cover the lower part of their
face[z] and cry out, 'Unclean! Unclean!'[a] 46As
long as they have the disease they remain
unclean. They must live alone; they must
live outside the camp.[b]

Regulations About Defiling Molds

47"As for any fabric that is spoiled with a
defiling mold—any woolen or linen clothing, 48any woven or knitted material of lin-
en or wool, any leather or anything made
of leather— 49if the affected area in the
fabric, the leather, the woven or knitted
material, or any leather article, is greenish
or reddish, it is a defiling mold and must
be shown to the priest.[c] 50The priest is to
examine the affected area[d] and isolate the
article for seven days. 51On the seventh day
he is to examine it,[e] and if the mold has
spread in the fabric, the woven or knitted
material, or the leather, whatever its use,
it is a persistent defiling mold; the article
is unclean.[f] 52He must burn the fabric, the
woven or knitted material of wool or linen,
or any leather article that has been spoiled;
because the defiling mold is persistent, the
article must be burned.[g]

53"But if, when the priest examines it,
the mold has not spread in the fabric, the
woven or knitted material, or the leather
article, 54he shall order that the spoiled
article be washed. Then he is to isolate it
for another seven days. 55After the article
has been washed, the priest is to examine
it again, and if the mold has not changed its
appearance, even though it has not spread,
it is unclean. Burn it, no matter which side
of the fabric has been spoiled. 56If, when
the priest examines it, the mold has faded
after the article has been washed, he is to
tear the spoiled part out of the fabric, the
leather, or the woven or knitted material.
57But if it reappears in the fabric, in the
woven or knitted material, or in the leather article, it is a spreading mold; whatever
has the mold must be burned. 58Any fabric,
woven or knitted material, or any leather
article that has been washed and is rid of
the mold, must be washed again. Then it
will be clean."

59These are the regulations concerning
defiling molds in woolen or linen clothing,
woven or knitted material, or any leather
article, for pronouncing them clean or unclean.

Cleansing From Defiling Skin Diseases

14 The LORD said to Moses, 2"These are
the regulations for any diseased person at the time of their ceremonial cleansing, when they are brought to the priest:[h]
3The priest is to go outside the camp and
examine them.[i] If they have been healed
of their defiling skin disease,[b] 4the priest
shall order that two live clean birds and
some cedar wood, scarlet yarn and hyssop
be brought for the person to be cleansed.[j]
5Then the priest shall order that one of the
birds be killed over fresh water in a clay
pot. 6He is then to take the live bird and dip
it, together with the cedar wood, the scarlet
yarn and the hyssop, into the blood of the
bird that was killed over the fresh water.[k]
7Seven times he shall sprinkle[l] the one to
be cleansed of the defiling disease, and
then pronounce them clean. After that, he
is to release the live bird in the open fields.

---

[a] 45 Or *clothes, uncover their head* [b] 3 The Hebrew word for *defiling skin disease*, traditionally translated "leprosy," was used for various diseases affecting the skin; also in verses 7, 32, 54 and 57.

---

family as if they had died. It is easy to see how leprosy became a metaphor for sin. Like serious skin diseases, sin is dangerous and ultimately fatal, often difficult to diagnose, and incurable without God's intervention.

13:47 ***defiling mold.*** This would include any mold, mildew, or other fungus growths on clothing.

13:50–58 ***priest is to examine the affected area.*** The procedures for diagnosing a problem with a garment were similar to those for diagnosing human skin ailments. The fact that a garment was considered worth saving after a piece had been torn out of it was an economic consideration, reflecting the value of cloth.

14:1–9 ***cleansing.*** It is likely that the sprigs of hyssop were tied to the cedar with the scarlet thread. With that in one hand and the living bird in the other, the priest would dip them all in the blood and water mixture in the pottery bowl and shake them over the head of the person to be cleansed. It may seem like a rather messy procedure, but being purified from sin has never been a tidy process. In the end, it took Christ's death on the cross to cleanse His followers. The bird which was released is a reminder of the real freedom and joy that any forgiven sinner experiences.

14:2 ***they are brought to the priest.*** The priest was responsible for the diagnosis, and he was the one who administered the sacrifices and rituals that celebrated the return of the person to the community of Israel. Jesus was aware of these laws when he touched the leper and healed him, and then directed the leper to show himself to the priest (Matt. 8:4).

14:4 ***cedar wood, scarlet yarn and hyssop.*** Cedar is both durable and resistant to decay, scarlet is a reminder of blood, and hyssop is an aromatic herb used for flavor, fragrance, and medicine. Each of these items would have been a reminder of the blood that cleansed, the decay that was stopped, and the sweetness of good health.

14:5 ***fresh water.*** This is literally "living water," water from a spring or stream rather than water from a cistern, vessel, or pool. Living water symbolizes life. Jesus told the woman at the well to ask for living water (John 4:7–14).

13:45 [z] Eze 24:17,22; Mic 3:7 [a] Lev 5:2; La 4:15; Lk 17:12
13:46 [b] Nu 5:1-4; 12:14; 2Ki 7:3; 15:5; Lk 17:12
13:49 [c] Mk 1:44 **13:50** [d] Eze 44:23 **13:51** [e] ver 5
[f] Lev 14:44 **13:52** [g] ver 55,57 **14:2** [h] Mt 8:2-4;
Mk 1:40-44; Lk 5:12-14; 17:14 **14:3** [i] Lev 13:46
14:4 [j] ver 6,49,51,52; Nu 19:6; Ps 51:7 **14:6** [k] ver 4
14:7 [l] 2Ki 5:10,14; Isa 52:15; Eze 36:25

8“The person to be cleansed must wash
their clothes,[m] shave off all their hair and
bathe with water;[n] then they will be ceremonially clean.[o] After this they may come
into the camp,[p] but they must stay outside
their tent for seven days. 9On the seventh
day they must shave off all their hair; they
must shave their head, their beard, their
eyebrows and the rest of their hair. They
must wash their clothes and bathe themselves with water, and they will be clean.

10“On the eighth day[q] they must bring
two male lambs and one ewe lamb a
year old, each without defect, along with
three-tenths of an ephah[a] of the finest flour
mixed with olive oil for a grain offering,[r]
and one log[b] of oil.[s] 11The priest who pronounces them clean shall present both the
one to be cleansed and their offerings before the LORD at the entrance to the tent of
meeting.

12“Then the priest is to take one of the
male lambs and offer it as a guilt offering,[t]
along with the log of oil; he shall wave
them before the LORD as a wave offering.[u]
13He is to slaughter the lamb in the sanctuary area[v] where the sin offering[c] and the
burnt offering are slaughtered. Like the
sin offering, the guilt offering belongs to
the priest;[w] it is most holy. 14The priest is
to take some of the blood of the guilt offering and put it on the lobe of the right ear
of the one to be cleansed, on the thumb of
their right hand and on the big toe of their
right foot.[x] 15The priest shall then take
some of the log of oil, pour it in the palm of
his own left hand, 16dip his right forefinger
into the oil in his palm, and with his finger
sprinkle some of it before the LORD seven
times. 17The priest is to put some of the oil
remaining in his palm on the lobe of the
right ear of the one to be cleansed, on the
thumb of their right hand and on the big
toe of their right foot, on top of the blood
of the guilt offering. 18The rest of the oil in
his palm the priest shall put on the head of
the one to be cleansed and make atonement
for them before the LORD.

19“Then the priest is to sacrifice the sin
offering and make atonement for the one
to be cleansed from their uncleanness. After that, the priest shall slaughter the burnt
offering 20and offer it on the altar, together
with the grain offering, and make atonement for them, and they will be clean.[y]

21“If, however, they are poor[z] and cannot afford these,[a] they must take one male
lamb as a guilt offering to be waved to
make atonement for them, together with a
tenth of an ephah[d] of the finest flour mixed
with olive oil for a grain offering, a log of
oil, 22and two doves or two young pigeons,[b]
such as they can afford, one for a sin offering and the other for a burnt offering.

23“On the eighth day they must bring
them for their cleansing to the priest at the
entrance to the tent of meeting, before the
LORD.[c] 24The priest is to take the lamb for
the guilt offering,[d] together with the log
of oil,[e] and wave them before the LORD as
a wave offering.[f] 25He shall slaughter the
lamb for the guilt offering and take some of
its blood and put it on the lobe of the right
ear of the one to be cleansed, on the thumb
of their right hand and on the big toe of
their right foot.[g] 26The priest is to pour
some of the oil into the palm of his own
left hand,[h] 27and with his right forefinger
sprinkle some of the oil from his palm sev-
en times before the LORD. 28Some of the oil
in his palm he is to put on the same places
he put the blood of the guilt offering—on
the lobe of the right ear of the one to be
cleansed, on the thumb of their right hand
and on the big toe of their right foot. 29The
rest of the oil in his palm the priest shall
put on the head of the one to be cleansed,
to make atonement for them before the
LORD.[i] 30Then he shall sacrifice the doves
or the young pigeons, such as the person
can afford,[j] 31one as a sin offering and the
other as a burnt offering,[k] together with the
grain offering. In this way the priest will
make atonement before the LORD on behalf
of the one to be cleansed.[l]”

32These are the regulations for anyone

---

[a] *10* That is, probably about 11 pounds or about 5 kilograms [b] *10* That is, about 1/3 quart or about 0.3 liter; also in verses 12, 15, 21 and 24 [c] *13* Or *purification offering*; also in verses 19, 22 and 31 [d] *21* That is, probably about 3 1/2 pounds or about 1.6 kilograms

---

14:9–32 *shave ... wash.* What is termed leprosy was apparently a number of skin diseases which were infectious, and thus were an apt picture of sin, which also corrupts the flesh, and is spread through social contact. The picture of isolating, analyzing, and finally cleansing these skin diseases is similar to the process of recognizing, repenting, and being forgiven for sin. Blood is necessary in both cases, and in both cases the touch of the Holy Spirit, symbolized by oil, is present.

14:10 *the eighth day.* The eighth day was the day of circumcision for a newborn male, and the cleansed person was starting again, almost like being born again into the community.

14:21–32 *if ... they are poor.* God's legislation for Israel showed special concern for the poor. In these sacrifices the poor Israelite still had to bring a lamb for the guilt offering, but for the sin offering or burnt offering he was allowed to bring doves or pigeons. The grain offering was reduced from three-tenths to one-tenth of an ephah of fine flour.

14:8 [m] Lev 11:25; 13:6 [n] ver 9 [o] ver 20 [p] Nu 5:2, 3; 12:14, 15; 2Ch 26:21 **14:10** [q] Mt 8:4; Mk 1:44; Lk 5:14 [r] Lev 2:1 [s] ver 12, 15, 21, 24 **14:12** [t] Lev 5:18; 6:6-7 [u] Ex 29:24 **14:13** [v] Ex 29:11 [w] Lev 6:24-30; 7:7 **14:14** [x] Ex 29:20; Lev 8:23 **14:20** [y] ver 8 **14:21** [z] Lev 5:7; 12:8 [a] ver 22, 32 **14:22** [b] Lev 5:7 **14:23** [c] ver 10, 11 **14:24** [d] Nu 6:14 [e] ver 10 [f] ver 12 **14:25** [g] ver 14; Ex 29:20 **14:26** [h] ver 15 **4:29** [i] ver 18 **14:30** [j] Lev 5:7 **14:31** [k] ver 22; Lev 5:7; 15:15, 30 [l] ver 18, 19

who has a defiling skin disease[m] and who cannot afford the regular offerings[n] for their cleansing.

Cleansing From Defiling Molds

[33]The LORD said to Moses and Aaron,
[34]"When you enter the land of Canaan,[o] which I am giving you as your possession,[p] and I put a spreading mold in a house in that land,
[35]the owner of the house must go and tell the priest, 'I have seen something that looks like a defiling mold in my house.'
[36]The priest is to order the house to be emptied before he goes in to examine the mold, so that nothing in the house will be pronounced unclean. After this the priest is to go in and inspect the house.
[37]He is to examine the mold on the walls, and if it has greenish or reddish[q] depressions that appear to be deeper than the surface of the wall,
[38]the priest shall go out the doorway of the house and close it up for seven days.[r]
[39]On the seventh day[s] the priest shall return to inspect the house. If the mold has spread on the walls,
[40]he is to order that the contaminated stones be torn out and thrown into an unclean place outside the town.[t]
[41]He must have all the inside walls of the house scraped and the material that is scraped off dumped into an unclean place outside the town.
[42]Then they are to take other stones to replace these and take new clay and plaster the house.

[43]"If the defiling mold reappears in the house after the stones have been torn out and the house scraped and plastered,
[44]the priest is to go and examine it and, if the mold has spread in the house, it is a persistent defiling mold; the house is unclean.[u]
[45]It must be torn down—its stones, timbers and all the plaster—and taken out of the town to an unclean place.

[46]"Anyone who goes into the house while it is closed up will be unclean till evening.[v]
[47]Anyone who sleeps or eats in the house must wash their clothes.[w]

[48]"But if the priest comes to examine it and the mold has not spread after the house has been plastered, he shall pronounce the house clean,[x] because the defiling mold is gone.
[49]To purify the house he is to take two birds and some cedar wood, scarlet yarn and hyssop.[y]
[50]He shall kill one of the birds over fresh water in a clay pot.[z]
[51]Then he is to take the cedar wood, the hyssop,[a] the scarlet yarn and the live bird, dip them into the blood of the dead bird and the fresh water, and sprinkle the house seven times.[b]
[52]He shall purify the house with the bird's blood, the fresh water, the live bird, the cedar wood, the hyssop and the scarlet yarn.
[53]Then he is to release the live bird in the open fields[c] outside the town. In this way he will make atonement for the house, and it will be clean.[d]"

[54]These are the regulations for any defiling skin disease,[e] for a sore,
[55]for defiling molds[f] in fabric or in a house,
[56]and for a swelling, a rash or a shiny spot,[g]
[57]to determine when something is clean or unclean.

These are the regulations for defiling skin diseases and defiling molds.[h]

Discharges Causing Uncleanness

15 The LORD said to Moses and Aaron,
[2]"Speak to the Israelites and say to them: 'When any man has an unusual bodily discharge,[i] such a discharge is unclean.
[3]Whether it continues flowing from his body or is blocked, it will make him unclean. This is how his discharge will bring about uncleanness:

[4]" 'Any bed the man with a discharge lies on will be unclean, and anything he sits on will be unclean.
[5]Anyone who touches his bed must wash their clothes[j] and bathe with water,[k] and they will be unclean till evening.[l]
[6]Whoever sits on anything that the man with a discharge sat on must wash their clothes and bathe with water, and they will be unclean till evening.

[7]" 'Whoever touches the man[m] who has a discharge[n] must wash their clothes and bathe with water, and they will be unclean till evening.

[8]" 'If the man with the discharge spits[o] on anyone who is clean, they must wash their clothes and bathe with water, and they will be unclean till evening.

[9]" 'Everything the man sits on when riding will be unclean,
[10]and whoever touches any of the things that were under him will be unclean till evening; whoever picks up those things[p] must wash their clothes and bathe with water, and they will be unclean till evening.

[11]" 'Anyone the man with a discharge touches without rinsing his hands with water must wash their clothes and bathe with water, and they will be unclean till evening.

14:34 ***spreading mold in a house.*** This is the same term used of serious skin diseases in chapter 13. All of these conditions were harmful, whether on human skin, clothing, or the wall of a house.

14:54–57 ***the regulations for any defiling skin disease.*** The uncleanness of leprosy required action. If it could not be removed, the thing that carried the uncleanness had to be removed from among God's people. In the same way, the uncleanness of sin requires action, but God has provided an infinitely stronger remedy through the blood of Christ.

14:32 [m] Lev 13:2 [n] ver 21 **14:34** [o] Ge 12:5; Ex 6:4; Nu 13:2 [p] Ge 17:8; 48:4; Nu 27:12; 32:22; Dt 3:27; 7:1; 32:49 **14:37** [q] Lev 13:19 **14:38** [r] Lev 13:4 **14:39** [s] Lev 13:5 **14:40** [t] ver 45 **14:44** [u] Lev 13:51 **14:46** [v] Lev 11:24 **14:47** [w] Lev 11:25 **14:48** [x] Lev 13:6 **14:49** [y] ver 4; 1Ki 4:33; ver 4 **14:50** [z] ver 5 **14:51** [a] ver 6; Ps 51:7 [b] ver 4,7 **14:53** [c] ver 7 [d] ver 20 **14:54** [e] Lev 13:2,30 **14:55** [f] Lev 13:47-52 **14:56** [g] Lev 13:2 **14:57** [h] Lev 10:10 **15:2** [i] ver 16,32; Lev 22:4; Nu 5:2; 2Sa 3:29; Mt 9:20 **15:5** [j] Lev 11:25 [k] Lev 14:8 [l] Lev 11:24 **15:7** [m] ver 19; Lev 22:5 [n] ver 16; Lev 22:4 **15:8** [o] Nu 12:14 **15:10** [p] Nu 19:10

12“‘A clay pot[q] that the man touches must
be broken, and any wooden article[r] is to be
rinsed with water.
13“‘When a man is cleansed from his discharge, he is to count off seven days[s] for
his ceremonial cleansing; he must wash his
clothes and bathe himself with fresh water, and he will be clean.[t] 14On the eighth
day he must take two doves or two young
pigeons[u] and come before the LORD to the
entrance to the tent of meeting and give
them to the priest. 15The priest is to sacrifice them, the one for a sin offering[a][v] and
the other for a burnt offering.[w] In this way
he will make atonement before the LORD
for the man because of his discharge.[x]
16“‘When a man has an emission of semen,[y] he must bathe his whole body with
water, and he will be unclean till evening.[z]
17Any clothing or leather that has semen
on it must be washed with water, and it will
be unclean till evening. 18When a man has
sexual relations with a woman and there is
an emission of semen,[a] both of them must
bathe with water, and they will be unclean
till evening.
19“‘When a woman has her regular flow
of blood, the impurity of her monthly period[b] will last seven days, and anyone who
touches her will be unclean till evening.
20“‘Anything she lies on during her period will be unclean, and anything she sits
on will be unclean. 21Anyone who touches
her bed will be unclean; they must wash
their clothes and bathe with water, and
they will be unclean till evening.[c] 22Any-
one who touches anything she sits on will
be unclean; they must wash their clothes
and bathe with water, and they will be unclean till evening. 23Whether it is the bed or
anything she was sitting on, when anyone
touches it, they will be unclean till evening.
24“‘If a man has sexual relations with her
and her monthly flow[d] touches him, he will
be unclean for seven days; any bed he lies
on will be unclean.
25“‘When a woman has a discharge of
blood for many days at a time other than
her monthly period[e] or has a discharge
that continues beyond her period, she
will be unclean as long as she has the discharge, just as in the days of her period.
26Any bed she lies on while her discharge
continues will be unclean, as is her bed
during her monthly period, and anything
she sits on will be unclean, as during her
period. 27Anyone who touches them will be
unclean; they must wash their clothes and
bathe with water, and they will be unclean
till evening.
28“‘When she is cleansed from her discharge, she must count off seven days, and
after that she will be ceremonially clean.
29On the eighth day she must take two
doves or two young pigeons[f] and bring
them to the priest at the entrance to the
tent of meeting. 30The priest is to sacrifice
one for a sin offering and the other for a
burnt offering. In this way he will make
atonement for her before the LORD for the
uncleanness of her discharge.[g]
31“‘You must keep the Israelites separate from things that make them unclean,
so they will not die in their uncleanness
for defiling my dwelling place,[b][h] which is
among them.’”
32These are the regulations for a man
with a discharge, for anyone made unclean
by an emission of semen,[i] 33for a woman in
her monthly period, for a man or a woman
with a discharge, and for a man who has
sexual relations with a woman who is ceremonially unclean.[j]

The Day of Atonement

16 The LORD spoke to Moses after the
death of the two sons of Aaron who
died when they approached the LORD.[k]

---

a 15 Or *purification offering*; also in verse 30
b 31 Or *my tabernacle*

15:18 *bathe with water ... unclean.* God's plan from the beginning includes sexual intercourse between a man and his wife, this is not sinful in God's eyes. The uncleanness and requirements of washing were a ritual cleansing, a reminder of the holiness of God, not a prohibition of intimate relationships.
15:19 *woman ... regular flow of blood.* There are rules for cleansing, but no sacrifice was required. Menstruation was not regarded as sinful.
15:25–27 *blood for many days.* If a woman had a flow of blood at any time other than her normal monthly period, or if this was unusually long, her uncleanness continued the whole time and passed to all she touched. The woman with a hemorrhage who touched Jesus secretly (Luke 8:43–48) was in this situation.
15:28–30 *cleansed from her discharge.* The woman was to bring the smallest allowable sacrifice for the atonement of sins she may have committed during the period of her uncleanness.
15:31–33 *separate from things that make them unclean.* Hygiene and health were important by-products, but the focus of these regulations concerning uncleanness was on keeping God's tabernacle undefiled. Ceremonial laws in regard to natural impurity seem strange to us, because these ceremonies were made obsolete by the perfect sacrifice of Christ. But in the Old Testament one form of blasphemy was the defilement of sanctuary worship by certain forms of ceremonial impurity.

15:12 [q] Lev 6:28 [r] Lev 11:32 **15:13** [s] Lev 8:33 [t] ver 5 **15:14** [u] Lev 14:22 **15:15** [v] Lev 5:7 [w] Lev 14:31 [x] Lev 14:18, 19 **15:16** [y] ver 2; Lev 22:4; Dt 23:10 [z] ver 5; Dt 23:11 **15:18** [a] 1Sa 21:4 **15:19** [b] ver 24; Lev 12:2 **15:21** [c] ver 27 **15:24** [d] ver 19; Lev 12:2; 18:19; 20:18; Eze 18:6 **15:25** [e] Mt 9:20; Mk 5:25; Lk 8:43 **15:29** [f] Lev 14:22 **15:30** [g] Lev 5:10; 14:20, 31; 18:19; 2Sa 11:4; Mk 5:25; Lk 8:43 **15:31** [h] Lev 20:3; Nu 5:3; 19:13, 20; 2Sa 15:25; 2Ki 21:7; Ps 33:14; 74:7; 76:2; Eze 5:11; 23:38 **15:32** [i] ver 2 **15:33** [j] ver 19, 24, 25 **16:1** [k] Lev 10:1

2 The LORD said to Moses: "Tell your brother
Aaron that he is not to come whenever he
chooses[l] into the Most Holy Place[m] behind
the curtain in front of the atonement cover
on the ark, or else he will die. For I will appear[n] in the cloud[o] over the atonement cover.
3 "This is how Aaron is to enter the Most
Holy Place:[p] He must first bring a young
bull for a sin offering[a] and a ram for a burnt
offering. 4 He is to put on the sacred linen
tunic, with linen undergarments next to his
body; he is to tie the linen sash around him
and put on the linen turban.[q] These are sacred garments;[r] so he must bathe himself
with water[s] before he puts them on. 5 From
the Israelite community[t] he is to take two
male goats[u] for a sin offering and a ram for
a burnt offering.
6 "Aaron is to offer the bull for his own sin
offering to make atonement for himself and
his household.[v] 7 Then he is to take the two
goats and present them before the LORD at
the entrance to the tent of meeting. 8 He is
to cast lots for the two goats—one lot for
the LORD and the other for the scapegoat.[b]
9 Aaron shall bring the goat whose lot falls
to the LORD and sacrifice it for a sin offering.
10 But the goat chosen by lot as the scapegoat
shall be presented alive before the LORD to
be used for making atonement[w] by sending
it into the wilderness as a scapegoat.
11 "Aaron shall bring the bull for his own
sin offering to make atonement for himself
and his household,[x] and he is to slaughter
the bull for his own sin offering. 12 He is to
take a censer full of burning coals[y] from
the altar before the LORD and two handfuls of finely ground fragrant incense[z] and
take them behind the curtain. 13 He is to
put the incense on the fire before the LORD,
and the smoke of the incense will conceal
the atonement cover above the tablets of
the covenant law, so that he will not die.[a]
14 He is to take some of the bull's blood[b] and
with his finger sprinkle it on the front of
the atonement cover; then he shall sprinkle some of it with his finger seven times
before the atonement cover.[c]
15 "He shall then slaughter the goat for
the sin offering for the people[d] and take
its blood behind the curtain[e] and do with
it as he did with the bull's blood: He shall
sprinkle it on the atonement cover and in
front of it. 16 In this way he will make atonement[f] for the Most Holy Place because of
the uncleanness and rebellion of the Israelites, whatever their sins have been. He
is to do the same for the tent of meeting,
which is among them in the midst of their
uncleanness. 17 No one is to be in the tent
of meeting from the time Aaron goes in to
make atonement in the Most Holy Place until he comes out, having made atonement
for himself, his household and the whole
community of Israel.
18 "Then he shall come out to the altar[g]
that is before the LORD and make atonement
for it. He shall take some of the bull's blood
and some of the goat's blood and put it on all
the horns of the altar.[h] 19 He shall sprinkle
some of the blood on it with his finger seven
times to cleanse it and to consecrate it from
the uncleanness of the Israelites.[i]
20 "When Aaron has finished making
atonement for the Most Holy Place, the tent
of meeting and the altar, he shall bring forward the live goat. 21 He is to lay both hands
on the head of the live goat and confess[j]
over it all the wickedness and rebellion
of the Israelites—all their sins—and put
them on the goat's head. He shall send the
goat away into the wilderness in the care
of someone appointed for the task. 22 The
goat will carry on itself all their sins[k] to a
remote place; and the man shall release it
in the wilderness.

---

[a] 3 Or *purification offering*; here and throughout this chapter [b] 8 The meaning of the Hebrew for this word is uncertain; also in verses 10 and 26.

16:2 *come whenever he chooses.* This refers to the arrogant attitude in which Aaron's sons had approached to offer unauthorized sacrifice. God is Holy, and must not be approached carelessly. After Christ opened the way for all believers to approach God at any time, it is perhaps easy to forget that we still approach with reverence and awe. It was because of the terrible price of the cross that we have this privilege, not because God has suddenly become casual.

16:6 *for his own sin offering.* After atoning for himself the high priest could offer the sacrifice to atone for the people. The author of Hebrews places great emphasis on this point in discussing the superior priesthood of Jesus, who did not have to offer a sacrifice for Himself before He could be the sacrifice of atonement, one time for all people (Heb. 7:26; 9:11–28; 10:19–22).

16:15–19 *the goat . . . for the people.* Aaron offered the goat for the people, and the other actions involved in this sacrifice made it clear that the sins of the people had a defiling effect on the tabernacle. If not removed, the sins would have caused the ministry to be ineffective in atoning for the people.

16:21 *He is to lay both hands on the head of the live goat.* Sending the goat into the wilderness was a public ceremony. Everyone could see Aaron symbolically placing the sins of the people on the goat's head. All of the ways that people could offend God were placed on the head of the goat, which took them away from the camp, away from the people, away from God.

16:22 *goat will carry on itself.* This is the origin of the common expression "scapegoat." The goat was not guilty of the sins, but he bore them anyway, allowing the guilty to escape the consequences of their

16:2 [l] Ex 30:10; Heb 9:7 [m] Heb 9:25; 10:19 [n] Ex 25:22 [o] Ex 40:34 **16:3** [p] Heb 9:24,25 **16:4** [q] Ex 28:39 [r] Ex 28:42 [s] ver 24; Heb 10:22 **16:5** [t] Lev 4:13-21 [u] 2Ch 29:23 **16:6** [v] Lev 9:7; Heb 5:3; 7:27; 9:7,12 **16:10** [w] Isa 53:4-10; Ro 3:25; 1Jn 2:2 **16:11** [x] Heb 7:27; 9:7 **16:12** [y] Lev 10:1 [z] Ex 30:34-38 **16:13** [a] Ex 28:43; Lev 22:9 **16:14** [b] Lev 4:5; Heb 9:7,13,25 [c] Lev 4:6 **16:15** [d] Heb 9:7,12 [e] Heb 9:3 **16:16** [f] Ex 29:36 **16:18** [g] Lev 4:7 [h] Lev 4:25 **16:19** [i] Eze 43:20 **16:21** [j] Lev 5:5 **16:22** [k] Isa 53:12

23"Then Aaron is to go into the tent of
meeting and take off the linen garments
he put on before he entered the Most Holy
Place, and he is to leave them there.[l] 24He
shall bathe himself with water in the sanctuary area and put on his regular garments.[m] Then he shall come out and sacrifice the burnt offering for himself and
the burnt offering for the people, to make
atonement for himself and for the people.
25He shall also burn the fat of the sin offering on the altar.
26"The man who releases the goat as
a scapegoat must wash his clothes[n] and
bathe himself with water; afterward he
may come into the camp. 27The bull and
the goat for the sin offerings, whose blood
was brought into the Most Holy Place to
make atonement, must be taken outside
the camp;[o] their hides, flesh and intestines
are to be burned up. 28The man who burns
them must wash his clothes and bathe himself with water; afterward he may come
into the camp.
29"This is to be a lasting ordinance for
you: On the tenth day of the seventh month
you must deny yourselves[a][p] and not do
any work—whether native-born or a foreigner residing among you— 30because on
this day atonement will be made for you,
to cleanse you. Then, before the LORD, you
will be clean from all your sins.[q] 31It is a
day of sabbath rest, and you must deny
yourselves;[r] it is a lasting ordinance. 32The
priest who is anointed and ordained to succeed his father as high priest is to make
atonement. He is to put on the sacred linen
garments[s] 33and make atonement for the
Most Holy Place, for the tent of meeting
and the altar, and for the priests and all the
members of the community.[t]
34"This is to be a lasting ordinance for
you: Atonement is to be made once a year[u]
for all the sins of the Israelites."
And it was done, as the LORD commanded Moses.

Eating Blood Forbidden

17 The LORD said to Moses, 2"Speak to
Aaron and his sons and to all the Israelites and say to them: 'This is what the
LORD has commanded: 3Any Israelite who
sacrifices an ox,[b] a lamb or a goat in the
camp or outside of it 4instead of bringing
it to the entrance to the tent of meeting to
present it as an offering to the LORD in front
of the tabernacle of the LORD[v]—that person
shall be considered guilty of bloodshed;
they have shed blood and must be cut off
from their people.[w] 5This is so the Israelites
will bring to the LORD the sacrifices they
are now making in the open fields. They
must bring them to the priest, that is, to the
LORD, at the entrance to the tent of meeting
and sacrifice them as fellowship offerings.
6The priest is to splash the blood against
the altar of the LORD[x] at the entrance to the
tent of meeting and burn the fat as an aroma pleasing to the LORD.[y] 7They must no
longer offer any of their sacrifices to the
goat idols[c][z] to whom they prostitute themselves.[a] This is to be a lasting ordinance for
them and for the generations to come.'

[a] 29 Or *must fast*; also in verse 31 [b] 3 The Hebrew word can refer to either male or female. [c] 7 Or *the demons*

---

sins. In Jesus' bearing the sins of the human race, and in His death outside the city (outside the camp), He fulfilled this annual ritual of the Day of Atonement. Not only was Jesus the perfect High Priest, He was the perfect Sacrifice.

16:29 ***the seventh month.*** The Day of Atonement fell between mid-September and mid-October.

16:29–34 The Day of Atonement—This whole process of animal sacrifice seems foreign to us. There is no enjoyment in seeing an animal killed. Special underwear and extra washings do not fit our religious experience. It is easy for us to wonder why this was necessary. What is the big deal anyway? The primary reason we have trouble with this is that we have such a superficial understanding of sin and God's attitude toward it. We tend to think of sin as a kind of correctable mistake, easily taken care of. Why be so upset about it? The Day of Atonement pointed the Israelites to the seriousness of sin. They were able to see that sin was an affront to God that had to be dealt with. It is like cancer. If it is not treated, death is the ultimate consequence. At its core, sin is rebellion against God. This ceremony stood as a permanent reminder of these truths. It pointed to God's holiness, to the drastic measures needed to deal with sin. Our souls are to be cleansed thoroughly and the sacrifices on the Day of Atonement accomplished this cleansing for the Israelite community. As such it was the most important day in the Jewish religious calendar.

17:5 ***sacrifices ... in the open fields.*** Such sacrifices were strictly forbidden. All sacrifices were to be clearly and unequivocally made to God alone, and in His way.

17:7 ***goat idols ... prostitute themselves.*** Pagan deities in the form of goats, like satyrs, were a part of the cultures surrounding the Israelites. Israel's worship of other gods, and God's attitude toward it was likened to the way a husband would feel if his wife became a prostitute. This was a picture of betrayal that the Israelites could understand. ***lasting ordinance.*** Because this was a permanent rule, it becomes clear that it was not an injunction against slaughtering animals for meat, but referred to sacrifices. When Israel's worship was centered in Jerusalem, some families lived more than a hundred miles from the temple. They could not have traveled so far to kill animals for meat, although they did make the journey for sacrifices.

16:23 [l] Eze 42:14; 44:19 **16:24** [m] ver 3-5
16:26 [n] Lev 11:25 **16:27** [o] Lev 4:12,21; Heb 13:11
16:29 [p] Lev 23:27,32; Nu 29:7; Isa 58:3 **16:30** [q] Jer 33:8; Eph 5:26 **16:31** [r] Isa 58:3,5 **16:32** [s] ver 4; Nu 20:26,28
16:33 [t] ver 11,16-18 **16:34** [u] Heb 9:7,25
17:4 [v] Dt 12:5-21 [w] Ge 17:14 **17:6** [x] Lev 3:2 [y] Nu 18:17
17:7 [z] Ex 22:20; 2Ch 11:15 [a] Ex 32:8; 34:15; Dt 32:17; 1Co 10:20

8“Say to them: ‘Any Israelite or any foreigner residing among them who offers a burnt offering or sacrifice 9and does not bring it to the entrance to the tent of meeting[b] to sacrifice it to the LORD must be cut off from the people of Israel.

10“ ‘I will set my face against any Israelite or any foreigner residing among them who eats blood,[c] and I will cut them off from the people. 11For the life of a creature is in the blood,[d] and I have given it to you to make atonement for yourselves on the altar; it is the blood that makes atonement for one’s life.[a][e] 12Therefore I say to the Israelites, “None of you may eat blood, nor may any foreigner residing among you eat blood.”

13“ ‘Any Israelite or any foreigner residing among you who hunts any animal or bird that may be eaten must drain out the blood and cover it with earth,[f] 14because the life of every creature is its blood. That is why I have said to the Israelites, “You must not eat the blood of any creature, because the life of every creature is its blood; anyone who eats it must be cut off.”[g]

15“ ‘Anyone, whether native-born or foreigner, who eats anything found dead or torn by wild animals[h] must wash their clothes and bathe with water, and they will be ceremonially unclean till evening; then they will be clean. 16But if they do not wash their clothes and bathe themselves, they will be held responsible.’ ”

Unlawful Sexual Relations

18 The LORD said to Moses, 2“Speak to the Israelites and say to them: ‘I am the LORD your God.[i] 3You must not do as they do in Egypt, where you used to live, and you must not do as they do in the land of Canaan, where I am bringing you. Do not follow their practices.[j] 4You must obey my laws and be careful to follow my decrees. I am the LORD your God.[k] 5Keep my decrees and laws, for the person who obeys them will live by them.[l] I am the LORD.

6“ ‘No one is to approach any close relative to have sexual relations. I am the LORD.

7“ ‘Do not dishonor your father[m] by having sexual relations with your mother.[n] She is your mother; do not have relations with her.

8“ ‘Do not have sexual relations with your father’s wife;[o] that would dishonor your father.[p]

9“ ‘Do not have sexual relations with your sister,[q] either your father’s daughter or your mother’s daughter, whether she was born in the same home or elsewhere.

10“ ‘Do not have sexual relations with your son’s daughter or your daughter’s daughter; that would dishonor you.

11“ ‘Do not have sexual relations with the daughter of your father’s wife, born to your father; she is your sister.

12“ ‘Do not have sexual relations with your father’s sister;[r] she is your father’s close relative.

13“ ‘Do not have sexual relations with your mother’s sister, because she is your mother’s close relative.

14“ ‘Do not dishonor your father’s brother by approaching his wife to have sexual relations; she is your aunt.[s]

15“ ‘Do not have sexual relations with your daughter-in-law.[t] She is your son’s wife; do not have relations with her.

16“ ‘Do not have sexual relations with your brother’s wife;[u] that would dishonor your brother.

---

[a] 11 Or *atonement by the life in the blood*

17:10 *eats blood.* Eating blood was forbidden in the strongest possible terms.

17:13 *cover it with earth.* Blood was to be treated respectfully, and covering it with earth was a token of burial.

18:2 *the LORD.* This is the translation of the name for God, sometimes called Yahweh, the name by which God revealed Himself to Moses (Ex. 6:2–8). In using this name, God was basing His claim to the Israelites' devotion on His willingness to reveal Himself to them, to redeem them and to be their God.

18:4 *my laws . . . my decrees.* "Laws" refers to judicial decisions involving situations that might not be addressed in the statutes. "Decrees" are ordinances, laws and acts of a permanent nature.

18:5 *the person who obeys them will live.* God gave the law as a means of life on all levels—physical, moral, spiritual, and relational.

18:6 *No one . . . any close relative . . . sexual relations.* This term covers cases such as incest between father and daughter and between brother and full sister, even though they are absent from the following list.

18:7 *dishonor your father . . . do not have relations.* The point of this passage is that committing incest with the wife of one's father is symbolically to uncover the father's nakedness too, because the two are one flesh through marriage.

18:8 *father's wife.* Even if your father's wife is not your mother, it is still wrong to have sexual relations with her. In Israel at that time multiple wives or concubines were still part of society, as well as a second wife coming into the family through death or divorce of the first wife.

18:9 *your sister.* Though this may seem redundant, God wanted to make it abundantly clear that a sister who did not share the same pair of parents as her brother was still off limits. This would cover husbands of multiple wives and illegitimate children. Sexual sin is serious with long reaching consequences, and it is clearly forbidden within the family.

17:9 [b] ver 4 **17:10** [c] Ge 9:4; Lev 3:17; Dt 12:16, 23; 1Sa 14:33 **17:11** [d] ver 14; Ge 9:4 [e] Heb 9:22 **17:13** [f] Lev 7:26; Dt 12:16 **17:14** [g] ver 11; Ge 9:4 **17:15** [h] Ex 22:31; Dt 14:21 **18:2** [i] Ex 6:7; Lev 11:44; Eze 20:5 **18:3** [j] ver 24-30; Ex 23:24; Lev 20:23 **18:4** [k] ver 2 **18:5** [l] Eze 20:11; Ro 10:5*; Gal 3:12* **18:7** [m] Lev 20:11 [n] Eze 22:10 **18:8** [o] 1Co 5:1 [p] Lev 20:11 **18:9** [q] Lev 20:17 **18:12** [r] Lev 20:19 **18:14** [s] Lev 20:20 **18:15** [t] Lev 20:12 **18:16** [u] Lev 20:21

17“ ‘Do not have sexual relations with
both a woman and her daughter.[v] Do not
have sexual relations with either her son’s
daughter or her daughter’s daughter; they
are her close relatives. That is wickedness.
18“ ‘Do not take your wife’s sister as a rival wife and have sexual relations with her
while your wife is living.
19“ ‘Do not approach a woman to have
sexual relations during the uncleanness of
her monthly period.[w]
20“ ‘Do not have sexual relations with
your neighbor’s wife[x] and defile yourself
with her.
21“ ‘Do not give any of your children[y] to be
sacrificed to Molek,[z] for you must not profane the name of your God.[a] I am the LORD.
22“ ‘Do not have sexual relations with a
man as one does with a woman;[b] that is
detestable.
23“ ‘Do not have sexual relations with an
animal and defile yourself with it. A woman must not present herself to an animal
to have sexual relations with it; that is a
perversion.[c]
24“ ‘Do not defile yourselves in any of
these ways, because this is how the nations that I am going to drive out before
you[d] became defiled.[e] 25Even the land was
defiled; so I punished it for its sin,[f] and the
land vomited out its inhabitants.[g] 26But you
must keep my decrees and my laws. The
native-born and the foreigners residing
among you must not do any of these detestable things, 27for all these things were
done by the people who lived in the land
before you, and the land became defiled.
28And if you defile the land, it will vomit
you out as it vomited out the nations that
were before you.
29“ ‘Everyone who does any of these detestable things—such persons must be cut
off from their people. 30Keep my requirements[h] and do not follow any of the detestable customs that were practiced before
you came and do not defile yourselves with
them. I am the LORD your God.[i]’ ”

Various Laws

19 The LORD said to Moses, 2“Speak to
the entire assembly of Israel and say
to them: ‘Be holy because I, the LORD your
God, am holy.[j]
3“ ‘Each of you must respect your mother
and father,[k] and you must observe my Sabbaths. I am the LORD your God.[l]
4“ ‘Do not turn to idols or make metal
gods for yourselves.[m] I am the LORD your
God.
5“ ‘When you sacrifice a fellowship offering to the LORD, sacrifice it in such a way
that it will be accepted on your behalf. 6It
shall be eaten on the day you sacrifice it
or on the next day; anything left over until
the third day must be burned up. 7If any of
it is eaten on the third day, it is impure and
will not be accepted. 8Whoever eats it will
be held responsible because they have desecrated what is holy to the LORD; they must
be cut off from their people.
9“ ‘When you reap the harvest of your
land, do not reap to the very edges of your
field or gather the gleanings of your harvest.[n] 10Do not go over your vineyard a second time or pick up the grapes that have
fallen. Leave them for the poor and the foreigner. I am the LORD your God.
11“ ‘Do not steal.[o]
“ ‘Do not lie.[p]
“ ‘Do not deceive one another.
12“ ‘Do not swear falsely by my name[q]
and so profane the name of your God. I am
the LORD.
13“ ‘Do not defraud or rob your neighbor.[r]
“ ‘Do not hold back the wages of a hired
worker overnight.[s]

18:20 ***with your neighbor’s wife.*** Adultery is forbidden in Exodus 20:14 and its penalty is given in Leviticus 20:10.

18:21 ***your children . . . to Molek.*** God forbids child sacrifice right along with incest. This is destructive behavior with far-reaching consequences, and all followers of the Lord will abhor it as God does.

18:22 ***sexual relations with a man.*** Homosexuality here is labeled as, something detestable to God both ritually (as a part of the Canaanite religion) and morally. To abominate something is to be repulsed by it, and when God is repulsed, it is a clear message that homosexuality is not part of His plan for human relationships.

18:23 ***an animal.*** Bestiality is labeled a perversion, something out of the natural order and a defilement. It, too, was a feature of some of the religions of Israel’s neighbors.

18:24–30 ***defile.*** The land had become so defiled by the perverted practices of the Canaanites that it was vomiting them out. For that reason, the land would be available to Israel to settle. The Israelites, however, needed to be careful to live as God’s holy people, or the land would vomit them out as well.

19:3 ***observe my Sabbaths.*** The weekly Sabbath was an acknowledgment that not everything depended on the Israelites’ efforts. It was an acknowledgment of God’s lordship and His grace.

19:5 ***fellowship offering.*** The fellowship offering was a free will offering.

19:10 ***for the poor and the foreigner.*** Providing for the poor and the alien who could not own land was a priority in ancient Israel. The generosity of God’s people was rooted in God’s generosity toward the Israelites.

18:17 [v] Lev 20:14 **18:19** [w] Lev 15:24; 20:18 **18:20** [x] Ex 20:14; Lev 20:10; Mt 5:27,28; 1Co 6:9; Heb 13:4 **18:21** [y] Dt 12:31 [z] Lev 20:2-5 [a] Lev 19:12; 21:6; Eze 36:20 **18:22** [b] Lev 20:13; Dt 23:18; Ro 1:27 **18:23** [c] Ex 22:19; Lev 20:15; Dt 27:21 **18:24** [d] ver 3,27,30 [e] Dt 18:12 **18:25** [f] Lev 20:23; Dt 9:5; 18:12 [g] ver 28; Lev 20:22 **18:30** [h] Dt 11:1 [i] ver 2 **19:2** [j] 1Pe 1:16*; Lev 11:44 **19:3** [k] Ex 20:12 [l] Lev 11:44 **19:4** [m] Ex 20:4,23; 34:17; Lev 26:1; Ps 96:5; 115:4-7 **19:9** [n] Lev 23:10,22; Dt 24:19-22 **19:11** [o] Ex 20:15 [p] Eph 4:25 **19:12** [q] Ex 20:7; Mt 5:33 **19:13** [r] Ex 22:15,25-27 [s] Dt 24:15; Jas 5:4

14 “ ‘Do not curse the deaf or put a stumbling block in front of the blind,[t] but fear
your God. I am the LORD.
15 “ ‘Do not pervert justice;[u] do not show
partiality[v] to the poor or favoritism to the
great, but judge your neighbor fairly.
16 “ ‘Do not go about spreading slander[w]
among your people.
“ ‘Do not do anything that endangers
your neighbor’s life.[x] I am the LORD.
17 “ ‘Do not hate a fellow Israelite in your
heart.[y] Rebuke your neighbor frankly[z] so
you will not share in their guilt.
18 “ ‘Do not seek revenge[a] or bear a
grudge[b] against anyone among your people, but love your neighbor as yourself.[c] I
am the LORD.
19 “ ‘Keep my decrees.
“ ‘Do not mate different kinds of animals.
“ ‘Do not plant your field with two kinds
of seed.[d]
“ ‘Do not wear clothing woven of two
kinds of material.[e]
20 “ ‘If a man sleeps with a female slave
who is promised to another man but who
has not been ransomed or given her freedom, there must be due punishment.[a] Yet
they are not to be put to death, because she
had not been freed. 21 The man, however,
must bring a ram to the entrance to the tent
of meeting for a guilt offering to the LORD.[f]
22 With the ram of the guilt offering the
priest is to make atonement for him before
the LORD for the sin he has committed, and
his sin will be forgiven.
23 “ ‘When you enter the land and plant
any kind of fruit tree, regard its fruit as forbidden.[b] For three years you are to consider it forbidden[b]; it must not be eaten. 24 In
the fourth year all its fruit will be holy,[g] an
offering of praise to the LORD. 25 But in the
fifth year you may eat its fruit. In this way
your harvest will be increased. I am the
LORD your God.
26 “ ‘Do not eat any meat with the blood
still in it.[h]
“ ‘Do not practice divination or seek
omens.[i]
27 “ ‘Do not cut the hair at the sides of your
head or clip off the edges of your beard.[j]
28 “ ‘Do not cut your bodies for the dead
or put tattoo marks on yourselves. I am the
LORD.
29 “ ‘Do not degrade your daughter by
making her a prostitute,[k] or the land will
turn to prostitution and be filled with wickedness.
30 “ ‘Observe my Sabbaths and have reverence for my sanctuary. I am the LORD.[l]
31 “ ‘Do not turn to mediums or seek out
spiritists,[m] for you will be defiled by them.
I am the LORD your God.
32 “ ‘Stand up in the presence of the aged,
show respect for the elderly[n] and revere
your God. I am the LORD.
33 “ ‘When a foreigner resides among you
in your land, do not mistreat them. 34 The
foreigner residing among you must be
treated as your native-born.[o] Love them as
yourself, for you were foreigners in Egypt.[p]
I am the LORD your God.

---

a 20 Or *be an inquiry*   *b* 23 Hebrew *uncircumcised*

19:16 ***slander.*** A slanderer is one who is not only a gossip, but one who is actively seeking to destroy another’s reputation.

19:17 ***hate ... in your heart.*** Jesus addressed this principle in the Sermon on the Mount (Matt. 5:21–24).

19:18 ***seek revenge.*** Vengeance belongs to God (Deut. 32:35); His vengeance is entirely just. It is easy for human vengeance to be carried out too zealously, leaving the by-products of bitterness and hatred. Instead, we are to do good to those who hate us and pray for those who persecute us (Matt. 5:44). ***love.*** The word “love” is first found in Genesis 22:2, where God told Abraham to offer up his son whom he loved as a burnt sacrifice upon Mount Moriah, and the first mention of love in the New Testament is God proclaiming that Jesus is His beloved Son (Matt. 3:17). Family love is something people find easy to understand. Even if it is not very strong in one’s nuclear family, the longing for love shows us that we understand what it is to be. To take this love one step further, that a parent would allow a child to die for the good of others, stretches the concept of love. And yet it is that very love that caused God to send His Son to die for the whole world.

19:20 ***a female slave.*** The slave woman had a low social standing and few rights, and may not have had the freedom to cry out when approached sexually. Therefore, she remained guiltless. Because she was a slave, the man escaped death, but remained guilty before God. Atonement was necessary for him to receive forgiveness.

19:26 ***divination.*** God, and not a demon or impersonal force, is all powerful and directs the future. Practicing divination reveals a lack of trust in God to bring the best in the future in His timing.

19:27–28 ***beard ... cut your bodies ... tattoo marks.*** The human body was designed by God to be beautiful. Disfiguring the body for the dead, or as a sign of mourning, is dishonoring to God. Some disfiguring was a part of pagan religions, and was forbidden to God’s people for any reason.

19:29 ***making her a prostitute.*** Sexual relations are sacred. Forcing a daughter to violate that sanctity defiled her against her will.

19:31 ***mediums ... spiritists.*** In principle this is no different than divination. Its practice involves consulting the spirits of the dead, or other spirits, both of which are strictly forbidden. It demonstrates lack of faith and rebellion against God and His ways.

19:14 [t] Dt 27:18 **19:15** [u] Ex 23:2,6 [v] Dt 1:17 **19:16** [w] Ps 15:3; Eze 22:9 [x] Ex 23:7 **19:17** [y] 1Jn 2:9; 3:15 [z] Mt 18:15; Lk 17:3 **19:18** [a] Ro 12:19 [b] Ps 103:9 [c] Mt 5:43*; 19:16*; 22:39*; Mk 12:31*; Lk 10:27*; Jn 13:34; Ro 13:9*; Gal 5:14*; Jas 2:8* **19:19** [d] Dt 22:9 [e] Dt 22:11 **19:21** [f] Lev 5:15 **19:24** [g] Pr 3:9 **19:26** [h] Lev 17:10 [i] Dt 18:10 **19:27** [j] Lev 21:5 **19:29** [k] Dt 23:18 **19:30** [l] Lev 26:2 **19:31** [m] Lev 20:6; Isa 8:19 **19:32** [n] 1Ti 5:1 **19:34** [o] Ex 12:48 [p] Dt 10:19

35 " 'Do not use dishonest standards when measuring length, weight or quantity. 36 Use honest scales and honest weights, an honest ephah[a] and an honest hin.[b][q] I am the LORD your God, who brought you out of Egypt.

37 " 'Keep all my decrees and all my laws and follow them. I am the LORD.' "

Punishments for Sin

20 The LORD said to Moses, 2 "Say to the Israelites: 'Any Israelite or any foreigner residing in Israel who sacrifices any of his children to Molek is to be put to death. The members of the community are to stone him. 3 I myself will set my face against him and will cut him off from his people; for by sacrificing his children to Molek, he has defiled my sanctuary[r] and profaned my holy name.[s] 4 If the members of the community close their eyes when that man sacrifices one of his children to Molek and if they fail to put him to death,[t] 5 I myself will set my face against him and his family and will cut them off from their people together with all who follow him in prostituting themselves to Molek.

6 " 'I will set my face against anyone who turns to mediums and spiritists to prostitute themselves by following them, and I will cut them off from their people.[u]

7 " 'Consecrate yourselves and be holy,[v] because I am the LORD your God. 8 Keep my decrees and follow them. I am the LORD, who makes you holy.[w]

9 " 'Anyone who curses their father or mother[x] is to be put to death.[y] Because they have cursed their father or mother, their blood will be on their own head.[z]

10 " 'If a man commits adultery with another man's wife[a]—with the wife of his neighbor—both the adulterer and the adulteress are to be put to death.

11 " 'If a man has sexual relations with his father's wife, he has dishonored his father.[b] Both the man and the woman are to be put to death; their blood will be on their own heads.

12 " 'If a man has sexual relations with his daughter-in-law,[c] both of them are to be put to death. What they have done is a perversion; their blood will be on their own heads.

13 " 'If a man has sexual relations with a man as one does with a woman, both of them have done what is detestable.[d] They are to be put to death; their blood will be on their own heads.

14 " 'If a man marries both a woman and her mother,[e] it is wicked. Both he and they must be burned in the fire, so that no wickedness will be among you.[f]

15 " 'If a man has sexual relations with an animal,[g] he is to be put to death, and you must kill the animal.

16 " 'If a woman approaches an animal to have sexual relations with it, kill both the woman and the animal. They are to be put to death; their blood will be on their own heads.

17 " 'If a man marries his sister[h], the daughter of either his father or his mother, and they have sexual relations, it is a disgrace. They are to be publicly removed from their people. He has dishonored his sister and will be held responsible.

18 " 'If a man has sexual relations with a woman during her monthly period,[i] he has exposed the source of her flow, and she has also uncovered it. Both of them are to be cut off from their people.

19 " 'Do not have sexual relations with the sister of either your mother or your father,[j] for that would dishonor a close relative; both of you would be held responsible.

20 " 'If a man has sexual relations with his aunt,[k] he has dishonored his uncle. They will be held responsible; they will die childless.

21 " 'If a man marries his brother's wife,[l] it is an act of impurity; he has dishonored his brother. They will be childless.

22 " 'Keep all my decrees and laws and follow them, so that the land[m] where I am

---

[a] *36* An ephah was a dry measure having the capacity of about 3/5 of a bushel or about 22 liters.
[b] *36* A hin was a liquid measure having the capacity of about 1 gallon or about 3.8 liters.

19:35–36 *dishonest standards when measuring.* Injustice in legal transactions or in business are equally wrong. God is just and generous, and His people are to be the same.

20:2–5 *sacrifices any of his children to Molek ... put to death ... stone him.* The penalty for child sacrifice, whether carried out by an alien or a citizen of Israel, was death, either carried out by the justice system or by God Himself. Children are a trust and blessing from God, and killing them in a pagan ritual is a wickedness that God will not overlook.

20:8 *who makes you holy.* To be sanctified is to be "set apart." The worshiper was set apart to God, from all other allegiances.

20:9 *their blood will be on their own head.* This statement assured the executioners that they were not guilty of shedding the offender's blood.

20:21 *marries his brother's wife.* It may be assumed that this passage refers to marrying his brother's wife while his brother is still living. Deuteronomy 25:5–10 gives a fairly detailed directive for a brother marrying his brother's childless widow and giving the firstborn the name of the dead brother, so that his family line will be maintained.

19:36 [q] Dt 25:13-15 **20:3** [r] Lev 15:31 [s] Lev 18:21 **20:4** [t] Dt 17:2-5 **20:6** [u] Lev 19:31 **20:7** [v] Eph 1:4; 1Pe 1:16* **20:8** [w] Ex 31:13 **20:9** [x] Dt 27:16 [y] Ex 21:17; Mt 15:4*; Mk 7:10* [z] ver 11; 2Sa 1:16 **20:10** [a] Ex 20:14; Dt 5:18; 22:22 **20:11** [b] Lev 18:7; Dt 27:23 **20:12** [c] Lev 18:15 **20:13** [d] Lev 18:22 **20:14** [e] Lev 18:17 [f] Dt 27:23 **20:15** [g] Lev 18:23 **20:17** [h] Lev 18:9 **20:18** [i] Lev 15:24; 18:19 **20:19** [j] Lev 18:12-13 **20:20** [k] Lev 18:14 **20:21** [l] Lev 18:16 **20:22** [m] Lev 18:25-28

bringing you to live may not vomit you out. 23You must not live according to the customs of the nations[n] I am going to drive out before you.[o] Because they did all these things, I abhorred them. 24But I said to you, "You will possess their land; I will give it to you as an inheritance, a land flowing with milk and honey."[p] I am the LORD your God, who has set you apart from the nations.[q]

25" 'You must therefore make a distinction between clean and unclean animals and between unclean and clean birds.[r] Do not defile yourselves by any animal or bird or anything that moves along the ground—those that I have set apart as unclean for you. 26You are to be holy to me because I, the LORD, am holy,[s] and I have set you apart from the nations to be my own.

27" 'A man or woman who is a medium or spiritist among you must be put to death.[t] You are to stone them; their blood will be on their own heads.' "

Rules for Priests

21 The LORD said to Moses, "Speak to the priests, the sons of Aaron, and say to them: 'A priest must not make himself ceremonially unclean for any of his people who die,[u] 2except for a close relative, such as his mother or father, his son or daughter, his brother, 3or an unmarried sister who is dependent on him since she has no husband—for her he may make himself unclean. 4He must not make himself unclean for people related to him by marriage,[a] and so defile himself.

5" 'Priests must not shave their heads or shave off the edges of their beards[v] or cut their bodies.[w] 6They must be holy to their God and must not profane the name of their God.[x] Because they present the food offerings to the LORD,[y] the food of their God, they are to be holy.

7" 'They must not marry women defiled by prostitution or divorced from their husbands,[z] because priests are holy to their God.[a] 8Regard them as holy,[b] because they offer up the food of your God. Consider them holy, because I the LORD am holy—I who make you holy.

9" 'If a priest's daughter defiles herself by becoming a prostitute, she disgraces her father; she must be burned in the fire.[c]

10" 'The high priest, the one among his brothers who has had the anointing oil poured on his head and who has been ordained to wear the priestly garments,[d] must not let his hair become unkempt[b] or tear his clothes.[e] 11He must not enter a place where there is a dead body.[f] He must not make himself unclean,[g] even for his father or mother, 12nor leave the sanctuary of his God or desecrate it, because he has been dedicated by the anointing oil[h] of his God. I am the LORD.

13" 'The woman he marries must be a virgin.[i] 14He must not marry a widow, a divorced woman, or a woman defiled by prostitution, but only a virgin from his own people, 15so that he will not defile his offspring among his people. I am the LORD, who makes him holy.' "

16The LORD said to Moses, 17"Say to Aaron: 'For the generations to come none of your descendants who has a defect may come near to offer the food of his God.[j] 18No man who has any defect[k] may come near: no man who is blind or lame, disfigured or deformed; 19no man with a crippled foot or hand, 20or who is a hunchback or a dwarf, or who has any eye defect, or who has festering or running sores or damaged testicles.[l] 21No descendant of Aaron the priest who has any defect is to come near to present the food offerings to the LORD. He has a defect; he must not come near to offer the food of his God. 22He may eat the most holy food of his God,[m] as well as the holy food; 23yet because of his defect, he must not go near the curtain or approach the altar, and so desecrate my sanctuary. I am the LORD, who makes them holy.' "

24So Moses told this to Aaron and his sons and to all the Israelites.

22 The LORD said to Moses, 2"Tell Aaron and his sons to treat with respect the sacred offerings the Israelites consecrate to me, so they will not profane my holy name. I am the LORD.

3"Say to them: 'For the generations to come, if any of your descendants is ceremonially unclean and yet comes near the sacred offerings that the Israelites consecrate to the LORD, that person must be cut off from my presence.[n] I am the LORD.

---

[a] 4 Or *unclean as a leader among his people*
[b] 10 Or *not uncover his head*

21:5 *not shave their heads . . . cut their bodies.* These were pagan customs, and all Israel was forbidden to observe them (19:27).

21:9 *defiles herself by becoming a prostitute.* Prostitution, the ultimate promiscuity, was the opposite of holiness, the ultimate faithfulness. The daughter was to reflect her father's holiness to God.

21:22 *He may eat.* Physical defect did not imply a moral defect. The person afflicted was to receive his food as the other priests did, from the sacrifices.

22:3 *your descendants.* In the Hebrew, this statement makes the restriction as broad as possible in any one generation, and as broad as possible through all time. ***cut off from my presence.*** The individual was not executed or banished from the community, but was permanently barred from ministering as a priest.

20:23 [n] Lev 18:3 [o] Lev 18:24,27,30 **20:24** [p] Ex 3:8; 13:5; 33:3 [q] Ex 33:16 **20:25** [r] Lev 11:1-47; Dt 14:3-21 **20:26** [s] Lev 19:2 **20:27** [t] Lev 19:31 **21:1** [u] Eze 44:25 **21:5** [v] Eze 44:20 [w] Lev 19:28; Dt 14:1 **21:6** [x] Lev 18:21 [y] Lev 3:11 **21:7** [z] ver 13, 14 [a] Eze 44:22 **21:8** [b] ver 6 **21:9** [c] Ge 38:24; Lev 19:29 **21:10** [d] Lev 16:32 [e] Lev 10:6 **21:11** [f] Nu 19:11, 13, 14 [g] Lev 19:28 **21:12** [h] Ex 29:6-7; Lev 10:7 **21:13** [i] Eze 44:22 **21:17** [j] ver 6 **21:18** [k] Lev 22:19-25 **21:20** [l] Dt 23:1; Isa 56:3 **21:22** [m] 1Co 9:13 **22:3** [n] Lev 7:20, 21; Nu 19:13

4“‘If a descendant of Aaron has a defiling skin disease[a] or a bodily discharge,[o]
he may not eat the sacred offerings until
he is cleansed. He will also be unclean if
he touches something defiled by a corpse[p]
or by anyone who has an emission of semen, 5or if he touches any crawling thing[q]
that makes him unclean, or any person[r]
who makes him unclean, whatever the uncleanness may be. 6The one who touches
any such thing will be unclean till evening.
He must not eat any of the sacred offerings
unless he has bathed himself with water.
7When the sun goes down, he will be clean,
and after that he may eat the sacred offerings, for they are his food.[s] 8He must not eat
anything found dead[t] or torn by wild animals,[u] and so become unclean[v] through it.
I am the LORD.

9“‘The priests are to perform my service
in such a way that they do not become guilty
and die[w] for treating it with contempt. I am
the LORD, who makes them holy.

10“‘No one outside a priest’s family may
eat the sacred offering, nor may the guest
of a priest or his hired worker eat it. 11But
if a priest buys a slave with money, or if
slaves are born in his household, they may
eat his food.[x] 12If a priest’s daughter marries anyone other than a priest, she may not
eat any of the sacred contributions. 13But if
a priest’s daughter becomes a widow or is
divorced, yet has no children, and she returns to live in her father’s household as in
her youth, she may eat her father’s food. No
unauthorized person, however, may eat it.

14“‘Anyone who eats a sacred offering by
mistake must make restitution to the priest
for the offering and add a fifth of the value[y] to it. 15The priests must not desecrate
the sacred offerings the Israelites present
to the LORD[z] 16by allowing them to eat the
sacred offerings and so bring upon them
guilt requiring payment.[a] I am the LORD,
who makes them holy.’”

Unacceptable Sacrifices

17The LORD said to Moses, 18“Speak to
Aaron and his sons and to all the Israelites
and say to them: ‘If any of you—whether an Israelite or a foreigner residing in
Israel—presents a gift[b] for a burnt offering to the LORD, either to fulfill a vow or
as a freewill offering, 19you must present
a male without defect[c] from the cattle,
sheep or goats in order that it may be accepted on your behalf. 20Do not bring anything with a defect,[d] because it will not be
accepted on your behalf. 21When anyone
brings from the herd or flock a fellowship
offering[e] to the LORD to fulfill a special
vow or as a freewill offering, it must be
without defect or blemish to be acceptable. 22Do not offer to the LORD the blind,
the injured or the maimed, or anything
with warts or festering or running sores.
Do not place any of these on the altar as
a food offering presented to the LORD.
23You may, however, present as a freewill
offering an ox[b] or a sheep that is deformed
or stunted, but it will not be accepted in
fulfillment of a vow. 24You must not offer
to the LORD an animal whose testicles are
bruised, crushed, torn or cut.[f] You must
not do this in your own land, 25and you
must not accept such animals from the
hand of a foreigner and offer them as the
food of your God.[g] They will not be accepted on your behalf, because they are
deformed and have defects.’”

26The LORD said to Moses, 27“When a
calf, a lamb or a goat is born, it is to remain with its mother for seven days.[h] From
the eighth day on, it will be acceptable as
a food offering presented to the LORD.
28Do not slaughter a cow or a sheep and its
young on the same day.[i]

29“When you sacrifice a thank offering[j]
to the LORD, sacrifice it in such a way that
it will be accepted on your behalf. 30It must
be eaten that same day; leave none of it till
morning.[k] I am the LORD.

31“Keep[l] my commands and follow them.
I am the LORD. 32Do not profane my holy

---

a 4 The Hebrew word for *defiling skin disease*, traditionally translated “leprosy,” was used for various diseases affecting the skin. *b* 23 The Hebrew word can refer to either male or female.

22:7 *they are his food.* The sacrifices brought by the Israelites were a major part of the daily provisions of the priests.

22:8 *found dead or torn by wild animals.* An ordinary Israelite was unclean until evening if he ate such animals (17:15 – 16), but a priest was not to eat them at all.

22:11 *buys a slave ... they may eat.* Strangers, guests, and hired servants were forbidden to eat of the holy gifts, but slaves and their children were considered as a part of the priest’s family, and could eat of the consecrated food.

22:10 *foreigner residing in Israel.* Resident aliens in Israel were permitted to worship God with the Israelites, and were subject to the same regulations about sacrifices.

22:21 *it must be without defect ... to be acceptable.* This is a very clear directive, yet the prophet Malachi addressed the problem of defective sacrifices in his day (Mal. 1:7 – 14). God called that “despising” His name.

22:31 *commands.* As Christians, it is important to understand the relationship between grace and law. A focus on the law without grace leads to rule

22:4 [o] Lev 14:1-32; 15:2-15 [p] Lev 11:24-28, 39
22:5 [q] Lev 11:24-28, 43 [r] Lev 15:7 **22:7** [s] Nu 18:11
22:8 [t] Lev 11:39 [u] Ex 22:31; Lev 17:15 [v] Lev 11:40
22:9 [w] ver 16; Ex 28:43 **22:11** [x] Ge 17:13; Ex 12:44
22:14 [y] Lev 5:15 **22:15** [z] Nu 18:32 **22:16** [a] ver 9
22:18 [b] Lev 1:2 **22:19** [c] Lev 1:3 **22:20** [d] Dt 15:21; 17:1; Mal 1:8, 14; Heb 9:14; 1Pe 1:19 **22:21** [e] Lev 3:6; Nu 15:3, 8
22:24 [f] Lev 21:20 **22:25** [g] Lev 21:6 **22:27** [h] Ex 22:30
22:28 [i] Dt 22:6, 7 **22:29** [j] Lev 7:12; Ps 107:22
22:30 [k] Lev 7:15 **22:31** [l] Dt 4:2, 40; Ps 105:45

name,[m] for I must be acknowledged as holy by the Israelites.[n] I am the LORD, who made you holy 33and who brought you out of Egypt to be your God.[o] I am the LORD."

The Appointed Festivals

23 The LORD said to Moses, 2"Speak to the Israelites and say to them: 'These are my appointed festivals,[p] the appointed festivals of the LORD, which you are to proclaim as sacred assemblies.[q]

The Sabbath

3" 'There are six days when you may work,[r] but the seventh day is a day of sabbath rest,[s] a day of sacred assembly. You are not to do any work; wherever you live, it is a sabbath to the LORD.

The Passover and the Festival of Unleavened Bread

4" 'These are the LORD's appointed festivals, the sacred assemblies you are to proclaim at their appointed times: 5The LORD's Passover begins at twilight on the fourteenth day of the first month.[t] 6On the fifteenth day of that month the LORD's Festival of Unleavened Bread begins; for seven days you must eat bread made without yeast. 7On the first day hold a sacred assembly[u] and do no regular work. 8For seven days present a food offering to the LORD. And on the seventh day hold a sacred assembly and do no regular work.' "

Offering the Firstfruits

9The LORD said to Moses, 10"Speak to the Israelites and say to them: 'When you enter the land I am going to give you and you reap its harvest, bring to the priest a sheaf[v] of the first grain you harvest. 11He is to wave the sheaf before the LORD[w] so it will be accepted on your behalf; the priest is to wave it on the day after the Sabbath. 12On the day you wave the sheaf, you must sacrifice as a burnt offering to the LORD a lamb a year old without defect, 13together with its grain offering[x] of two-tenths of an ephah[a] of the finest flour mixed with olive oil—a food offering presented to the LORD, a pleasing aroma—and its drink offering of a quarter of a hin[b] of wine. 14You must not eat any bread, or roasted or new grain, until the very day you bring this offering to your God.[y] This is to be a lasting ordinance for the generations to come,[z] wherever you live.

The Festival of Weeks

15" 'From the day after the Sabbath, the day you brought the sheaf of the wave offering, count off seven full weeks. 16Count off fifty days up to the day after the seventh Sabbath,[a] and then present an offering of new grain to the LORD. 17From wherever you live, bring two loaves made of two-tenths of an ephah of the finest flour, baked with yeast, as a wave offering of firstfruits[b] to the LORD. 18Present with this bread seven male lambs, each a year old and without defect, one young bull and two rams. They will be a burnt offering to the LORD, together with their grain offerings and drink offerings—a food offering, an aroma pleasing to the LORD. 19Then sacrifice one male goat for a sin offering[c] and two lambs, each a year old, for a fellowship offering. 20The priest is to wave the two lambs before the LORD as a wave offering, together with the bread of the firstfruits. They are a sacred offering to the LORD for the priest. 21On that same day you are to proclaim a sacred assembly[c] and do no regular work.[d] This is to be a lasting ordinance for the generations to come, wherever you live.

[a] *13* That is, probably about 7 pounds or about 3.2 kilograms; also in verse 17 [b] *13* That is, about 1 quart or about 1 liter [c] *19* Or *purification offering*

---

oriented life, where our actions may be decent enough, but our heart is hard toward God. But if the focus is only on grace, we may be without the guidelines necessary to keep us from just doing what is right in our own eyes. Certain directives are given to us because even when we are born again, we are not all wise. The best way to balance all of this is to consider the whole counsel of God by reading and seeking to understand the whole Bible.

23:3 ***six days when you may work.*** Work was given to the human race in the garden of Eden. It is one of the ways humans bear the image of God, and is not a curse on the race. Even after the fall it remains God's good gift. ***a day of sabbath rest . . . wherever you live.*** The regular seventh day of rest is for our refreshment, and a day of solemn, joyful worship. It was not to be observed only in the sanctuary, it was to be celebrated in every household. The writer of Hebrews (ch. 4) calls belief in the saving work of Jesus, "entering His rest," and compares that to the Sabbath rest.

23:5 ***fourteenth day of the first month.*** This month would fall between mid-March and mid-April. The Passover celebrated Israel's exodus from Egypt (Ex. 12:1 – 28).

23:6 – 8 ***Festival of Unleavened Bread.*** This festival immediately followed Passover, and later in Israel's history, it involved pilgrimages to the central sanctuary; first in Shiloh, and later in Jerusalem.

23:10 ***sheaf of the first grain.*** This bundle of the first harvested barley belonged to God as a special offering, acknowledging God's provision for the harvest.

22:32 [m] Lev 18:21 [n] Lev 10:3 **22:33** [o] Lev 11:45
23:2 [p] ver 4,37,44; Nu 29:39 [q] ver 21,27 **23:3** [r] Ex 20:9 [s] Ex 20:10; 31:13-17; Lev 19:3; Dt 5:13; Heb 4:9, 10
23:5 [t] Ex 12:18-19; Nu 28:16-17; Dt 16:1-8 **23:7** [u] ver 3,8
23:10 [v] Ex 23:16, 19; 34:26 **23:11** [w] Ex 29:24
23:13 [x] Lev 2:14-16; 6:20 **23:14** [y] Ex 34:26 [z] Nu 15:21
23:16 [a] Nu 28:26; Ac 2:1 **23:17** [b] Ex 34:22; Lev 2:12
23:21 [c] ver 2 [d] ver 3

22“ ‘When you reap the harvest[e] of your
land, do not reap to the very edges of your
field or gather the gleanings of your harvest.[f] Leave them for the poor and for the
foreigner residing among you. I am the
LORD your God.’ ”

The Festival of Trumpets

23The LORD said to Moses, 24“Say to the
Israelites: ‘On the first day of the seventh
month you are to have a day of sabbath
rest, a sacred assembly commemorated with trumpet blasts.[g] 25Do no regular
work,[h] but present a food offering to the
LORD.’ ”

The Day of Atonement

26The LORD said to Moses, 27“The tenth
day of this seventh month[i] is the Day of
Atonement.[j] Hold a sacred assembly[k] and
deny yourselves,[a] and present a food offering to the LORD. 28Do not do any work
on that day, because it is the Day of Atonement, when atonement is made for you before the LORD your God. 29Those who do
not deny themselves on that day must be
cut off from their people.[l] 30I will destroy
from among their people[m] anyone who
does any work on that day. 31You shall do
no work at all. This is to be a lasting ordinance for the generations to come, wherever you live. 32It is a day of sabbath rest for
you, and you must deny yourselves. From
the evening of the ninth day of the month
until the following evening you are to observe your sabbath.”

The Festival of Tabernacles

33The LORD said to Moses, 34“Say to the
Israelites: ‘On the fifteenth day of the seventh month the LORD’s Festival of Tabernacles[n] begins, and it lasts for seven days.
35The first day is a sacred assembly; do
no regular work. 36For seven days present food offerings to the LORD, and on the
eighth day hold a sacred assembly[o] and
present a food offering to the LORD. It is
the closing special assembly; do no regular work.
37(“ ‘These are the LORD’s appointed festivals, which you are to proclaim as sacred
assemblies for bringing food offerings to
the LORD—the burnt offerings and grain
offerings, sacrifices and drink offerings[p]
required for each day. 38These offerings
are in addition to those for the LORD’s Sabbaths[q] and[b] in addition to your gifts and
whatever you have vowed and all the freewill offerings you give to the LORD.)
39“ ‘So beginning with the fifteenth day
of the seventh month, after you have gathered the crops of the land, celebrate the festival to the LORD for seven days;[r] the first
day is a day of sabbath rest, and the eighth
day also is a day of sabbath rest. 40On the
first day you are to take branches from
luxuriant trees—from palms, willows and
other leafy trees[s]—and rejoice before the
LORD your God for seven days. 41Celebrate
this as a festival to the LORD for seven days
each year. This is to be a lasting ordinance
for the generations to come; celebrate it in
the seventh month. 42Live in temporary
shelters[t] for seven days: All native-born
Israelites are to live in such shelters 43so
your descendants will know[u] that I had the
Israelites live in temporary shelters when I
brought them out of Egypt. I am the LORD
your God.’ ”
44So Moses announced to the Israelites
the appointed festivals of the LORD.

Olive Oil and Bread Set Before the LORD

24 The LORD said to Moses, 2“Command
the Israelites to bring you clear oil
of pressed olives for the light so that the
lamps may be kept burning continually.
3Outside the curtain that shields the ark
of the covenant law in the tent of meeting, Aaron is to tend the lamps before the
LORD from evening till morning, continually. This is to be a lasting ordinance for
the generations to come. 4The lamps on the
pure gold lampstand[v] before the LORD must
be tended continually.

---

[a] 27 Or *and fast;* similarly in verses 29 and 32
[b] 38 Or *These festivals are in addition to the LORD’s Sabbaths, and these offerings are*

23:24 *the seventh month.* This holiday falls in mid-September. It was a reminder of God’s goodness, which was expressed in the covenant, and asked God to continue to remember that covenant.

23:26–32 Atonement—The Day of Atonement was a time to set aside all the thoughts and actions that typically fill the day and consider one’s relationship with God. This was to be a time of humbleness, which would preclude any self-righteousness or merely comparing oneself with others. It was a time to remember that even people who want to follow God need to have their lives realigned with Him. Christians regularly take time to think of these things as they remember the Lord’s death until He comes again, with the bread and the cup of communion.

23:27 *Day of Atonement.* The day was not given this name in chapter 16, but this was the day of all days, when complete atonement was made for all Israel.

23:40 *branches from luxurious trees.* The leafy tree is thought to be the myrtle.

23:22 [e] Lev 19:9 [f] Lev 19:10; Dt 24:19-21; Ru 2:15 **23:24** [g] Lev 25:9; Nu 10:9, 10; 29:1 **23:25** [h] ver 21 **23:27** [i] Lev 16:29 [j] Ex 30:10 [k] Nu 29:7 **23:29** [l] Ge 17:14; Nu 5:2 **23:30** [m] Lev 20:3 **23:34** [n] Ex 23:16; Dt 16:13; Ezr 3:4; Ne 8:14; Zec 14:16; Jn 7:2 **23:36** [o] 2Ch 7:9; Ne 8:18; Jn 7:37 **23:37** [p] ver 2, 4 **23:38** [q] Eze 45:17 **23:39** [r] Ex 23:16; Dt 16:13 **23:40** [s] Ne 8:14-17 **23:42** [t] Ne 8:14-16 **23:43** [u] Dt 31:13; Ps 78:5 **24:4** [v] Ex 25:31; 31:8

5"Take the finest flour and bake twelve loaves of bread,[w] using two-tenths of an ephah[a] for each loaf. 6Arrange them in two stacks, six in each stack, on the table of pure gold[x] before the LORD. 7By each stack put some pure incense as a memorial[b] portion[y] to represent the bread and to be a food offering presented to the LORD. 8This bread is to be set out before the LORD regularly,[z] Sabbath after Sabbath,[a] on behalf of the Israelites, as a lasting covenant. 9It belongs to Aaron and his sons,[b] who are to eat it in the sanctuary area, because it is a most holy part of their perpetual share of the food offerings presented to the LORD."

A Blasphemer Put to Death

10Now the son of an Israelite mother and an Egyptian father went out among the Israelites, and a fight broke out in the camp between him and an Israelite. 11The son of the Israelite woman blasphemed the Name[c] with a curse; so they brought him to Moses. (His mother's name was Shelomith, the daughter of Dibri the Danite.) 12They put him in custody until the will of the LORD should be made clear to them.[d]

13Then the LORD said to Moses: 14"Take the blasphemer outside the camp. All those who heard him are to lay their hands on his head, and the entire assembly is to stone him.[e] 15Say to the Israelites: 'Anyone who curses their God[f] will be held responsible; 16anyone who blasphemes the name of the LORD is to be put to death.[g] The entire assembly must stone them. Whether foreigner or native-born, when they blaspheme the Name they are to be put to death.

17" 'Anyone who takes the life of a human being is to be put to death.[h] 18Anyone who takes the life of someone's animal must make restitution[i]—life for life. 19Anyone who injures their neighbor is to be injured in the same manner: 20fracture for fracture, eye for eye, tooth for tooth.[j] The one who has inflicted the injury must suffer the same injury. 21Whoever kills an animal must make restitution, but whoever kills a human being is to be put to death.[k] 22You are to have the same law for the foreigner[l] and the native-born.[m] I am the LORD your God.' "

23Then Moses spoke to the Israelites, and they took the blasphemer outside the camp and stoned him. The Israelites did as the LORD commanded Moses.

The Sabbath Year

25 The LORD said to Moses at Mount Sinai, 2"Speak to the Israelites and say to them: 'When you enter the land I am going to give you, the land itself must observe a sabbath to the LORD. 3For six years sow your fields, and for six years prune your vineyards and gather their crops.[n] 4But in the seventh year the land is to have a year of sabbath rest, a sabbath to the LORD. Do not sow your fields or prune your vineyards. 5Do not reap what grows of itself or harvest the grapes of your untended vines. The land is to have a year of rest. 6Whatever the land yields during the sabbath year[o] will be food for you—for yourself, your male and female servants, and the hired worker and temporary resident who live among you, 7as well as for your livestock and the wild animals in your land. Whatever the land produces may be eaten.

The Year of Jubilee

8" 'Count off seven sabbath years—seven times seven years—so that the seven sabbath years amount to a period of forty-nine years. 9Then have the trumpet[p] sounded everywhere on the tenth day of the seventh month; on the Day of Atonement sound the trumpet throughout your land. 10Consecrate the fiftieth year and proclaim liberty[q] throughout the land to all its inhabitants. It shall be a jubilee[r] for you; each of you is to return to your family property and to your own clan. 11The fiftieth year shall be a jubilee for you; do not sow and do not reap what grows of itself or harvest the untended vines. 12For it is a ju-

[a] 5 That is, probably about 7 pounds or about 3.2 kilograms [b] 7 Or *representative*

24:19–20 *eye for eye.* This law is also found in Exodus 21:23–25. Its purpose is not to require the injured party to inflict equal bodily harm on the one who had injured him, but to restrict him from inflicting greater harm than he received.

24:22 *the same law.* These laws are repeated here in order to answer the question of whether these laws apply to non-Israelites. The answer is yes, they also apply to the stranger in the land.

25:5 *Do not reap.* Reaping and gathering for storage and selling were not permitted. However, harvesting for daily needs was allowed.

25:10 *return.* This word could also be translated "liberty." It meant specifically that all debts were cancelled, all Israelites who had sold themselves into slavery were freed, and all the land reverted to its original owners, from the time the land was divided by Joshua. The same phrase occurs in Isaiah 61:1, the passage Jesus read in the synagogue in Nazareth at the beginning of His earthly ministry. Jesus declares liberty to all who have lost their inheritance and become slaves to sin.

25:11 *jubilee.* The fiftieth, or jubilee year, followed a Sabbath year of rest, so this meant that there were two years of rest in a row for the land.

24:5 [w] Ex 25:30 **24:6** [x] Ex 25:23-30; 1Ki 7:48 **24:7** [y] Lev 2:2 **24:8** [z] Nu 4:7; 1Ch 9:32; 2Ch 2:4 [a] Mt 12:5 **24:9** [b] Lev 8:31; Mt 12:4; Mk 2:26; Lk 6:4 **24:11** [c] Ex 3:15 **24:12** [d] Ex 18:16; Nu 15:34 **24:14** [e] Lev 20:27; Dt 13:9; 17:5,7; 21:21 **24:15** [f] Ex 22:28 **24:16** [g] 1Ki 21:10, 13; Mt 26:66 **24:17** [h] Ge 9:6; Ex 21:12; Nu 35:30-31; Dt 27:24 **24:18** [i] ver 21 **24:20** [j] Ex 21:24; Mt 5:38* **24:21** [k] ver 17 **24:22** [l] Ex 12:49 [m] Nu 9:14; 15:16 **25:3** [n] Ex 23:10 **25:6** [o] ver 20 **25:9** [p] Lev 23:24 **25:10** [q] Isa 61:1; Jer 34:8, 15, 17; Lk 4:19 [r] Nu 36:4

bilee and is to be holy for you; eat only what
is taken directly from the fields.
13"'In this Year of Jubilee[s] everyone is to
return to their own property.
14"'If you sell land to any of your own
people or buy land from them, do not take
advantage of each other.[t] 15You are to buy
from your own people on the basis of the
number of years[u] since the Jubilee. And
they are to sell to you on the basis of the
number of years left for harvesting crops.
16When the years are many, you are to increase the price, and when the years are
few, you are to decrease the price,[v] because
what is really being sold to you is the number of crops. 17Do not take advantage of
each other,[w] but fear your God.[x] I am the
LORD your God.[y]
18"'Follow my decrees and be careful
to obey my laws, and you will live safely
in the land.[z] 19Then the land will yield its
fruit,[a] and you will eat your fill and live
there in safety. 20You may ask, "What will
we eat in the seventh year[b] if we do not
plant or harvest our crops?" 21I will send
you such a blessing[c] in the sixth year that
the land will yield enough for three years.
22While you plant during the eighth year,
you will eat from the old crop and will continue to eat from it until the harvest of the
ninth year comes in.[d]
23"'The land must not be sold permanently, because the land is mine[e] and you
reside in my land as foreigners[f] and strangers. 24Throughout the land that you hold
as a possession, you must provide for the
redemption of the land.
25"'If one of your fellow Israelites becomes poor and sells some of their property, their nearest relative[g] is to come and
redeem[h] what they have sold. 26If, however,
there is no one to redeem it for them but
later on they prosper and acquire sufficient
means to redeem it themselves, 27they are
to determine the value for the years since
they sold it and refund the balance to the
one to whom they sold it; they can then go
back to their own property. 28But if they do
not acquire the means to repay, what was
sold will remain in the possession of the
buyer until the Year of Jubilee. It will be
returned in the Jubilee, and they can then
go back to their property.[i]
29"'Anyone who sells a house in a walled
city retains the right of redemption a full
year after its sale. During that time the seller may redeem it. 30If it is not redeemed before a full year has passed, the house in the
walled city shall belong permanently to the
buyer and the buyer's descendants. It is not
to be returned in the Jubilee. 31But houses
in villages without walls around them are
to be considered as belonging to the open
country. They can be redeemed, and they
are to be returned in the Jubilee.
32"'The Levites always have the right to
redeem their houses in the Levitical towns,[j]
which they possess. 33So the property of
the Levites is redeemable—that is, a house
sold in any town they hold—and is to be returned in the Jubilee, because the houses in
the towns of the Levites are their property
among the Israelites. 34But the pastureland
belonging to their towns must not be sold;
it is their permanent possession.[k]
35"'If any of your fellow Israelites become poor[l] and are unable to support
themselves among you, help them[m] as you
would a foreigner and stranger, so they can
continue to live among you. 36Do not take
interest[n] or any profit from them, but fear
your God, so that they may continue to live
among you. 37You must not lend them money at interest or sell them food at a profit.
38I am the LORD your God, who brought
you out of Egypt to give you the land of
Canaan and to be your God.[o]
39"'If any of your fellow Israelites become poor and sell themselves to you, do
not make them work as slaves.[p] 40They are
to be treated as hired workers or temporary residents among you; they are to work
for you until the Year of Jubilee. 41Then
they and their children are to be released,
and they will go back to their own clans
and to the property[q] of their ancestors.
42Because the Israelites are my servants,
whom I brought out of Egypt, they must not
be sold as slaves. 43Do not rule over them
ruthlessly,[r] but fear your God.
44"'Your male and female slaves are to
come from the nations around you; from
them you may buy slaves. 45You may also
buy some of the temporary residents living among you and members of their clans
born in your country, and they will become

25:17 *fear your God.* Fear of God includes respect of man, who is God's highest creation. A deep respect of the life of man, who is created in God's image and likeness, is stressed in Scriptures. This text prohibits taking advantage of or oppressing others, and for the Christian there is the added reminder that we are not to injure those "for whom Christ died" (1 Cor. 8:11).

25:23 *foreigners and strangers.* The principle governing all of these laws was that the land did not belong to Israel; it belonged to God.

25:44–46 *slaves for life.* The fact that God made laws to govern the current practices of slavery does not mean that He approved of slavery. He made laws about divorce, too, but He also said that He hates divorce.

25:13 [s] ver 10 **25:14** [t] Lev 19:13; 1Sa 12:3,4
25:15 [u] Lev 27:18,23 **25:16** [v] ver 27,51,52
25:17 [w] Pr 22:22; Jer 7:5,6; 1Th 4:6 [x] Lev 19:14 [y] Lev 19:32
25:18 [z] Lev 26:4,5; Dt 12:10; Ps 4:8; Jer 23:6
25:19 [a] Lev 26:4 **25:20** [b] ver 4 **25:21** [c] Dt 28:8,12; Hag 2:19; Mal 3:10 **25:22** [d] Lev 26:10 **25:23** [e] Ex 19:5 [f] Ge 23:4; 1Ch 29:15; Ps 39:12; Heb 11:13; 1Pe 2:11
25:25 [g] Ru 2:20; Jer 32:7 [h] Lev 27:13,19,31; Ru 4:4
25:28 [i] ver 10 **25:32** [j] Nu 35:1-8; Jos 21:2
25:34 [k] Nu 35:2-5 **25:35** [l] Dt 24:14,15 [m] Dt 15:8; Ps 37:21,26; Lk 6:35 **25:36** [n] Ex 22:25; Dt 23:19-20
25:38 [o] Ge 17:7; Lev 11:45 **25:39** [p] Ex 21:2; Dt 15:12; 1Ki 9:22 **25:41** [q] ver 28 **25:43** [r] Ex 1:13; Eze 34:4; Col 4:1

your property. 46You can bequeath them to
your children as inherited property and
can make them slaves for life, but you
must not rule over your fellow Israelites
ruthlessly.
47“ ‘If a foreigner residing among you becomes rich and any of your fellow Israelites become poor and sell themselves to the
foreigner or to a member of the foreigner’s
clan, 48they retain the right of redemption
after they have sold themselves. One of
their relatives[s] may redeem them: 49An uncle or a cousin or any blood relative in their
clan may redeem them. Or if they prosper,[t]
they may redeem themselves. 50They and
their buyer are to count the time from the
year they sold themselves up to the Year of
Jubilee. The price for their release is to be
based on the rate paid to a hired worker[u]
for that number of years. 51If many years
remain, they must pay for their redemption
a larger share of the price paid for them.
52If only a few years remain until the Year
of Jubilee, they are to compute that and pay
for their redemption accordingly. 53They
are to be treated as workers hired from
year to year; you must see to it that those
to whom they owe service do not rule over
them ruthlessly.
54“ ‘Even if someone is not redeemed in
any of these ways, they and their children
are to be released in the Year of Jubilee,
55for the Israelites belong to me as servants.
They are my servants, whom I brought out
of Egypt. I am the LORD your God.

Reward for Obedience

26 “ ‘Do not make idols[v] or set up an image or a sacred stone[w] for yourselves,
and do not place a carved stone[x] in your
land to bow down before it. I am the LORD
your God.
2“ ‘Observe my Sabbaths and have reverence for my sanctuary.[y] I am the LORD.
3“ ‘If you follow my decrees and are careful to obey[z] my commands, 4I will send
you rain[a] in its season, and the ground will
yield its crops and the trees their fruit.[b]
5Your threshing will continue until grape
harvest and the grape harvest will continue until planting, and you will eat all the
food you want[c] and live in safety in your
land.[d]
6“ ‘I will grant peace in the land,[e] and you
will lie down[f] and no one will make you
afraid.[g] I will remove wild beasts[h] from the
land, and the sword will not pass through
your country. 7You will pursue your enemies, and they will fall by the sword before
you. 8Five of you will chase a hundred, and
a hundred of you will chase ten thousand,
and your enemies will fall by the sword before you.[i]
9“ ‘I will look on you with favor and
make you fruitful and increase your numbers,[j] and I will keep my covenant[k] with
you. 10You will still be eating last year’s
harvest when you will have to move it out
to make room for the new.[l] 11I will put my
dwelling place[a][m] among you, and I will not
abhor you. 12I will walk[n] among you and be
your God, and you will be my people.[o] 13I
am the LORD your God, who brought you
out of Egypt so that you would no longer
be slaves to the Egyptians; I broke the bars
of your yoke[p] and enabled you to walk with
heads held high.

Punishment for Disobedience

14“ ‘But if you will not listen to me and carry out all these commands,[q] 15and if you reject my decrees and abhor my laws and fail
to carry out all my commands and so violate
my covenant, 16then I will do this to you: I
will bring on you sudden terror, wasting

[a] *11 Or my tabernacle*

26:1 *sacred stone.* A sacred pillar was a stone or wooden column erected to represent a pagan god or goddess. It was not a likeness, but a symbol. Together, the four terms used in this verse cover all the possibilities for pagan images.
26:4–5 *rain in its season ... threshing ... grape harvest ... planting.* Not only will God provide the rain when needed, He would provide abundant harvests. The grain harvest was finished by early to mid-June, and the grape harvest began about two months later. Having two months to thresh the grain indicated a large harvest. Likewise sowing could not occur until after the first rains softened the ground, usually in mid-October. A two month grape harvest would be a bumper crop. This is the first of the three blessings from God.
26:6–10 *peace in the land.* Neither animal nor human adversaries would be successful against Israel. This is the second of the three blessings from God.
26:11–13 *I will walk among you.* The third blessing was the promise of His presence within Israel, actively walking among them and looking out for their welfare.
26:12–13 *be your God.* The image in these verses is a dramatic one, reminding the Israelites that God would be their intimate associate continually. He would walk with them, support them in times of difficulty and danger, and abundantly provide for both their physical and spiritual needs. To be God’s people meant that the Israelites had to obey God’s laws scrupulously, to be holy as God is holy, and to be a witness of God among the pagan nations.
26:14–15 *not listen to me and carry out all these commands.* As with the blessings, the curses are presented in an “if-then” format.
26:16–17 *terror ... wasting diseases and fever.*

25:48 [s] Ne 5:5 **25:49** [t] ver 26 **25:50** [u] Job 7:1; Isa 16:14; 21:16 **26:1** [v] Ex 20:4; Lev 19:4; Dt 5:8 [w] Ex 23:24 [x] Nu 33:52 **26:2** [y] Lev 19:30 **26:3** [z] Dt 7:12; 11:13,22; 28:1,9 **26:4** [a] Dt 11:14 [b] Ps 67:6 **26:5** [c] Dt 11:15; Joel 2:19,26; Am 9:13 [d] Lev 25:18 **26:6** [e] Ps 29:11; 85:8; 147:14 [f] Ps 4:8 [g] Zep 3:13 [h] ver 22 **26:8** [i] Dt 32:30; Jos 23:10 **26:9** [j] Ge 17:6; Ne 9:23 [k] Ge 17:7 **26:10** [l] Lev 25:22 **26:11** [m] Ex 25:8; Ps 76:2; Eze 37:27 **26:12** [n] Ge 3:8 [o] 2Co 6:16* **26:13** [p] Eze 34:27 **26:14** [q] Dt 28:15-68; Mal 2:2

diseases and fever[r] that will destroy your
sight and sap your strength.[s] You will plant
seed in vain, because your enemies will eat
it.[t] 17 I will set my face[u] against you so that
you will be defeated by your enemies; those
who hate you will rule over you,[v] and you
will flee even when no one is pursuing you.[w]

18 " 'If after all this you will not listen to
me, I will punish you for your sins seven
times over.[x] 19 I will break down your stubborn pride[y] and make the sky above you
like iron and the ground beneath you like
bronze.[z] 20 Your strength will be spent in
vain,[a] because your soil will not yield its
crops, nor will the trees of your land yield
their fruit.[b]

21 " 'If you remain hostile toward me and
refuse to listen to me, I will multiply your
afflictions seven times over,[c] as your sins
deserve. 22 I will send wild animals[d] against
you, and they will rob you of your children,
destroy your cattle and make you so few in
number that your roads will be deserted.

23 " 'If in spite of these things you do not
accept my correction[e] but continue to be
hostile toward me, 24 I myself will be hostile toward you and will afflict you for your
sins seven times over. 25 And I will bring the
sword on you to avenge the breaking of the
covenant. When you withdraw into your
cities, I will send a plague[f] among you, and
you will be given into enemy hands. 26 When
I cut off your supply of bread,[g] ten women
will be able to bake your bread in one oven,
and they will dole out the bread by weight.
You will eat, but you will not be satisfied.

27 " 'If in spite of this you still do not listen to me but continue to be hostile toward
me, 28 then in my anger I will be hostile toward you, and I myself will punish you for
your sins seven times over. 29 You will eat
the flesh of your sons and the flesh of your
daughters.[h] 30 I will destroy your high places,[i] cut down your incense altars[j] and pile
your dead bodies[a] on the lifeless forms of
your idols,[k] and I will abhor you. 31 I will
turn your cities into ruins and lay waste
your sanctuaries,[l] and I will take no delight
in the pleasing aroma of your offerings. 32 I
myself will lay waste the land,[m] so that your
enemies who live there will be appalled. 33 I
will scatter you among the nations[n] and will
draw out my sword and pursue you. Your
land will be laid waste, and your cities will
lie in ruins. 34 Then the land will enjoy its
sabbath years all the time that it lies desolate and you are in the country of your enemies;[o] then the land will rest and enjoy its
sabbaths. 35 All the time that it lies desolate,
the land will have the rest it did not have
during the sabbaths you lived in it.

36 " 'As for those of you who are left, I will
make their hearts so fearful in the lands
of their enemies that the sound of a windblown leaf will put them to flight.[p] They will
run as though fleeing from the sword, and
they will fall, even though no one is pursuing them. 37 They will stumble over one
another as though fleeing from the sword,
even though no one is pursuing them. So
you will not be able to stand before your
enemies.[q] 38 You will perish among the nations; the land of your enemies will devour
you.[r] 39 Those of you who are left will waste

[a] 30 Or *your funeral offerings*

Fear, illness, poor harvest, and enemies in the land would be God's first attempts to draw Israel back to Himself.

26:18–20 *sky above you like iron.* The second series of curses were characterized as "seven times more." Rain was essential to the whole nation, both the fall and spring rains.

26:19 *stubborn pride.* Stubborn pride will often cause a person or nation to trust in its own strength and accomplishments rather than to submit to God and give Him the honor and glory. The punishment for this pride was drought—skies like iron, with not even a hint of rain. This can be true on a personal level as well as a national level if one forgets that it is God who has given the position of significance. Then the iron heavens make it seem as if prayers are not heard, and the parched spirit cries out for God's touch again.

26:21–22 *multiply your afflictions seven times over.* The third series of curses are again increased "seven times," so that the land is plagued with wild beasts that attack both their children and their domestic animals.

26:23–26 *the sword ... plague ... enemy hands ... eat but not be satisfied.* The fourth series of curses are also increased "seven times." When enemies invaded the land, the people living in unwalled villages fled to walled cities, and if the city was besieged, the overcrowding created prime conditions for epidemics and famine.

26:29 *eat the flesh of your sons ... daughters.* The fifth and final curse, "seven times for your sins," was cannibalism. This actually happened centuries later during a siege of Samaria, and later still in Jerusalem (2 Kin. 6:28–29; Lam. 2:20; 4:10).

26:30 *high places ... idols.* The high places and images or incense altars were dedicated to the worship of pagan gods.

26:33 *scatter.* This threat was fulfilled in the Babylonian exile of 587–536 B.C.

26:36–37 *hearts so fearful.* Survivors would not enjoy relief or peace of mind after escaping the disasters. They would still be timid, even when no one pursued them.

26:38–39 *perish among the nations.* Having been exiled to foreign lands, the people were not to think they were beyond God's punitive reach.

26:16 [r] Dt 28:22,35 [s] 1Sa 2:33 [t] Job 31:8
26:17 [u] Lev 17:10 [v] Ps 106:41 [w] ver 36,37; Dt 28:7,25; Ps 53:5 **26:18** [x] ver 21 **26:19** [y] Isa 25:11 [z] Dt 28:23
26:20 [a] Ps 127:1; Isa 17:11 [b] Dt 11:17 **26:21** [c] ver 18
26:22 [d] Dt 32:24 **26:23** [e] Jer 2:30; 5:3
26:25 [f] Nu 14:12; Eze 5:17 **26:26** [g] Ps 105:16; Isa 3:1; Mic 6:14 **26:29** [h] Dt 28:53 **26:30** [i] 2Ch 34:3; Eze 6:3 [j] Eze 6:6 [k] Eze 6:13 **26:31** [l] Ps 74:3-7 **26:32** [m] Jer 9:11
26:33 [n] Dt 4:27; Eze 12:15; 20:23; Zec 7:14
26:34 [o] ver 43; 2Ch 36:21 **26:36** [p] Eze 21:7
26:37 [q] Jos 7:12 **26:38** [r] Dt 4:26

away in the lands of their enemies because
of their sins; also because of their ancestors' sins they will waste away.[s]
40"'But if they will confess their sins
and the sins of their ancestors[t]—their unfaithfulness and their hostility toward me,
41which made me hostile toward them so
that I sent them into the land of their enemies—then when their uncircumcised
hearts[u] are humbled and they pay for their
sin, 42I will remember my covenant with Jacob[v] and my covenant with Isaac[w] and my
covenant with Abraham, and I will remember the land. 43For the land will be deserted
by them and will enjoy its sabbaths while
it lies desolate without them. They will pay
for their sins because they rejected my laws
and abhorred my decrees. 44Yet in spite of
this, when they are in the land of their enemies, I will not reject them or abhor[x] them
so as to destroy them completely,[y] breaking
my covenant[z] with them. I am the LORD their
God. 45But for their sake I will remember[a]
the covenant with their ancestors whom I
brought out of Egypt[b] in the sight of the nations to be their God. I am the LORD.'"
46These are the decrees, the laws and
the regulations that the LORD established
at Mount Sinai between himself and the Israelites through Moses.[c]

Redeeming What Is the LORD's

27 The LORD said to Moses, 2"Speak
to the Israelites and say to them: 'If
anyone makes a special vow[d] to dedicate a
person to the LORD by giving the equivalent
value, 3set the value of a male between the
ages of twenty and sixty at fifty shekels[a] of
silver, according to the sanctuary shekel[b];[e]
4for a female, set her value at thirty shekels[c]; 5for a person between the ages of five
and twenty, set the value of a male at twenty shekels[d] and of a female at ten shekels[e];
6for a person between one month and five
years, set the value of a male at five shekels[f][f] of silver and that of a female at three
shekels[g] of silver; 7for a person sixty years
old or more, set the value of a male at fifteen shekels[h] and of a female at ten shekels. 8If anyone making the vow is too poor
to pay[g] the specified amount, the person
being dedicated is to be presented to the
priest, who will set the value[h] according to
what the one making the vow can afford.
9"'If what they vowed is an animal that is
acceptable as an offering to the LORD, such
an animal given to the LORD becomes holy.
10They must not exchange it or substitute
a good one for a bad one, or a bad one for
a good one;[i] if they should substitute one
animal for another, both it and the substitute become holy. 11If what they vowed is a
ceremonially unclean animal—one that is
not acceptable as an offering to the LORD—
the animal must be presented to the priest,
12who will judge its quality as good or bad.
Whatever value the priest then sets, that is
what it will be. 13If the owner wishes to redeem[j] the animal, a fifth must be added to
its value.
14"'If anyone dedicates their house as
something holy to the LORD, the priest will
judge its quality as good or bad. Whatever
value the priest then sets, so it will remain.
15If the one who dedicates their house
wishes to redeem it,[k] they must add a fifth
to its value, and the house will again become theirs.
16"'If anyone dedicates to the LORD part
of their family land, its value is to be set
according to the amount of seed required
for it—fifty shekels of silver to a homer[i] of

---

a 3 That is, about 1 1/4 pounds or about 575 grams; also in verse 16 *b* 3 That is, about 2/5 ounce or about 12 grams; also in verse 25 *c* 4 That is, about 12 ounces or about 345 grams *d* 5 That is, about 8 ounces or about 230 grams *e* 5 That is, about 4 ounces or about 115 grams; also in verse 7 *f* 6 That is, about 2 ounces or about 58 grams *g* 6 That is, about 1 1/4 ounces or about 35 grams *h* 7 That is, about 6 ounces or about 175 grams *i* 16 That is, probably about 300 pounds or about 135 kilograms

---

26:42 *my covenant.* God's covenant with the patriarchs took precedence over the covenant at Sinai (Gal. 3:15–18). Even when Israel violated the Sinai covenant, God honored the patriarchal covenant.
26:44–45 *I will not reject them ... remember the covenant.* Ultimately, God's character is grace, mercy, love and redemption. On that basis, God would remember the covenant and redeem them because He is God.
27:2–8 *special vow ... equivalent value.* While people could dedicate themselves or their children to the Lord (1 Sam. 1:11, 22) only the Levites were allowed to serve God as priests. Therefore, those others vowed in service to the Lord had to be redeemed, and the value of his service was given to the sanctuary.
27:8 *too poor.* Fifty shekels might have represented about four years' earnings. If a person was too poor to pay this price, the priest set a price that the person could pay.
27:14–24 *dedicates.* Consecrating or dedicating property to the Lord, and then buying it back with cash if one wants to use it for oneself is a curious idea to modern people. We tend to consider dedication of something to God as using it in a way that pleases Him, and the line between "God's" and "mine" may be very fuzzy. We are familiar with offering praises or tithes to God as worship, but think of the way we handle property as "good" or "poor" stewardship. A passage like this reminds us that we are not to be casual in worship. Are we offering it to God or not? Is it His, or do we want it back at no cost to ourselves?
27:16 *homer of barley.* A homer was a donkey load.

26:39 [s] Eze 4:17 **26:40** [t] Jer 3:12-15; Lk 15:18; 1Jn 1:9 **26:41** [u] Eze 44:7, 9; Ac 7:51 **26:42** [v] Ge 22:15-18; 28:15 [w] Ge 26:5 **26:44** [x] Ro 11:2 [y] Dt 4:31; Jer 30:11 [z] Jer 33:26 **26:45** [a] Ge 17:7 [b] Ex 6:8; Lev 25:38 **26:46** [c] Lev 7:38; 27:34 **27:2** [d] Nu 6:2 **27:3** [e] Ex 30:13; Nu 3:47; 18:16 **27:6** [f] Nu 18:16 **27:8** [g] Lev 5:11 [h] ver 12, 14 **27:10** [i] ver 33 **27:13** [j] ver 15, 19; Lev 25:25 **27:15** [k] ver 13, 20

barley seed. 17If they dedicate a field during the Year of Jubilee, the value that has been set remains. 18But if they dedicate a field after the Jubilee, the priest will determine the value according to the number of years that remain[l] until the next Year of Jubilee, and its set value will be reduced. 19If the one who dedicates the field wishes to redeem it, they must add a fifth to its value, and the field will again become theirs. 20If, however, they do not redeem the field, or if they have sold it to someone else, it can never be redeemed. 21When the field is released in the Jubilee,[m] it will become holy, like a field devoted to the LORD;[n] it will become priestly property.

22" 'If anyone dedicates to the LORD a field they have bought, which is not part of their family land, 23the priest will determine its value up to the Year of Jubilee, and the owner must pay its value on that day as something holy to the LORD. 24In the Year of Jubilee the field will revert to the person from whom it was bought,[o] the one whose land it was. 25Every value is to be set according to the sanctuary shekel,[p] twenty gerahs[q] to the shekel.

26" 'No one, however, may dedicate the firstborn of an animal, since the firstborn already belongs to the LORD;[r] whether an ox[a] or a sheep, it is the LORD's. 27If it is one of the unclean animals,[s] it may be bought back at its set value, adding a fifth of the value to it. If it is not redeemed, it is to be sold at its set value.

28" 'But nothing that a person owns and devotes[b][t] to the LORD—whether a human being or an animal or family land—may be sold or redeemed; everything so devoted is most holy to the LORD.

29" 'No person devoted to destruction[c] may be ransomed; they are to be put to death.

30" 'A tithe[u] of everything from the land, whether grain from the soil or fruit from the trees, belongs to the LORD; it is holy to the LORD. 31Whoever would redeem any of their tithe must add a fifth of the value to it. 32Every tithe of the herd and flock—every tenth animal that passes under the shepherd's rod[v]—will be holy to the LORD. 33No one may pick out the good from the bad or make any substitution.[w] If anyone does make a substitution, both the animal and its substitute become holy and cannot be redeemed.' "

34These are the commands the LORD gave Moses at Mount Sinai for the Israelites.[x]

---

[a] *26* The Hebrew word can refer to either male or female. [b] *28* The Hebrew term refers to the irrevocable giving over of things or persons to the LORD. [c] *29* The Hebrew term refers to the irrevocable giving over of things or persons to the LORD, often by totally destroying them.

27:28 *devotes to the LORD.* Devoting a possession was a stronger act than dedication. Nothing devoted could be redeemed; persons devoted (under the ban) were to be put to death. No private citizen would have had the power to put himself or anyone else "under the ban."

27:31 *redeem any of their tithe.* For a person living a distance from the sanctuary, it may have been more practical to redeem the tithe than to bring the crops to the sanctuary.

27:32 *under the shepherd's rod.* Sheep and goats were inspected when they passed under the rod that the shepherd placed across the entrance to the fold. This was a time to determine if the animals were under any distress from disease or injury, and was also the time that some of them were set aside for the Lord.

27:18 [l] Lev 25:15 **27:21** [m] Lev 25:10 [n] ver 28; Nu 18:14; Eze 44:29 **27:24** [o] Lev 25:28 **27:25** [p] Ex 30:13; Nu 18:16 [q] Nu 3:47; Eze 45:12 **27:26** [r] Ex 13:2, 12 **27:27** [s] ver 11 **27:28** [t] Nu 18:14; Jos 6:17-19 **27:30** [u] Ge 28:22; 2Ch 31:6; Mal 3:8 **27:32** [v] Jer 33:13; Eze 20:37 **27:33** [w] ver 10 **27:34** [x] Lev 26:46; Dt 4:5

NUMBERS

▶ **AUTHOR:** The Jews, Samaritans, and the early church testify to Moses' authorship. Several New Testament passages attribute events cited from Numbers to Moses (John 3:14; Acts 7; 13; 1 Cor. 10:1 – 11; Heb. 3 – 4), and there are more than eighty claims within Numbers that state that the Lord spoke to Moses (1:1). Numbers 33:2 says that Moses recorded their journeys at the Lord's command. As an eyewitness who kept detailed records, and the central character of the events in the book, no one was better qualified to write this book than Moses.

▶ **TIME:** c. 1114 – 1405 B.C. ▶ **KEY VERSE:** Num. 14:22 – 23

▶ **THEME:** At Sinai, this newly resurrected nation of Israel receives its laws, its system of sacrifices and its national charter. The people then should have been ready to take the next step into the Promised Land, but they aren't. Numbers largely has Israel in a holding pattern. While the book records further steps taken in organizing the nation, its central narrative is that of the refusal of the people to go into Canaan. But God still doesn't give up on His people. He continues to discipline them in an effort to have a new generation ready to fulfill His plan. In this context Numbers points to God's sovereignty, His patience, and His desire to bless His people.

The Census

1 The LORD spoke to Moses in the tent of meeting[a] in the Desert of Sinai[b] on the first day of the second month[c] of the second year after the Israelites came out of Egypt. He said: 2"Take a census[d] of the whole Israelite community by their clans and families, listing every man by name, one by one. 3You and Aaron are to count according to their divisions all the men in Israel who are twenty years old or more[e] and able to serve in the army. 4One man from each tribe, each of them the head of his family,[f] is to help you.[g] 5These are the names of the men who are to assist you:

from Reuben,[h] Elizur son of Shedeur;
6 from Simeon, Shelumiel son of Zurishaddai;
7 from Judah,[i] Nahshon son of Amminadab;[j]
8 from Issachar,[k] Nethanel son of Zuar;
9 from Zebulun,[l] Eliab son of Helon;
10 from the sons of Joseph:
from Ephraim,[m] Elishama son of Ammihud;
from Manasseh, Gamaliel son of Pedahzur;
11 from Benjamin, Abidan son of Gideoni;
12 from Dan,[n] Ahiezer son of Ammishaddai;
13 from Asher,[o] Pagiel son of Okran;
14 from Gad, Eliasaph son of Deuel;[p]
15 from Naphtali,[q] Ahira son of Enan."

16These were the men appointed from the community, the leaders[r] of their ancestral tribes. They were the heads of the clans of Israel.[s]

17Moses and Aaron took these men whose names had been specified, 18and they called the whole community together on the first day of the second month.[t] The people registered their ancestry[u] by their clans and families, and the men twenty years old or more were listed by name, one by one, 19as the LORD commanded Moses. And so he counted them in the Desert of Sinai:

20 From the descendants of Reuben[v] the firstborn son of Israel:
All the men twenty years old or more who were able to serve in the army were listed by name, one

---

1:1 ***Desert of Sinai.*** The setting of the book of Numbers is the desert. Not only did the Israelites live in the desert, but they as a nation were traveling through a time of spiritual emptiness. They were starting all over in their relationship with God after a time of slavery. The empty desert kept them dependent, and kept them from being distracted with the normal affairs of caring for land and animals.

1:1 [a] Ex 40:2 [b] Ex 19:1 [c] Ex 40:17 **1:2** [d] Ex 30:11-16; Nu 26:2 **1:3** [e] Ex 30:14 **1:4** [f] ver 16 [g] Ex 18:21; Dt 1:15 **1:5** [h] Ge 29:32; Dt 33:6; Rev 7:5 **1:7** [i] Ge 29:35; Ps 78:68 [j] Ru 4:20; 1Ch 2:10; Lk 3:32 **1:8** [k] Ge 30:18 **1:9** [l] ver 30 **1:10** [m] ver 32 **1:12** [n] ver 38 **1:13** [o] ver 40 **1:14** [p] Nu 2:14 **1:15** [q] ver 42 **1:16** [r] Ex 18:25 [s] ver 4; Ex 18:21; Nu 7:2 **1:18** [t] ver 1 [u] Ezr 2:59; Heb 7:3 **1:20** [v] Nu 26:5-11; Rev 7:5

by one, according to the records of their clans and families. 21The number from the tribe of Reuben was 46,500.

22 From the descendants of Simeon:[w]
All the men twenty years old or more who were able to serve in the army were counted and listed by name, one by one, according to the records of their clans and families. 23The number from the tribe of Simeon was 59,300.

24 From the descendants of Gad:[x]
All the men twenty years old or more who were able to serve in the army were listed by name, according to the records of their clans and families. 25The number from the tribe of Gad was 45,650.

26 From the descendants of Judah:[y]
All the men twenty years old or more who were able to serve in the army were listed by name, according to the records of their clans and families. 27The number from the tribe of Judah was 74,600.

28 From the descendants of Issachar:[z]
All the men twenty years old or more who were able to serve in the army were listed by name, according to the records of their clans and families. 29The number from the tribe of Issachar was 54,400.

30 From the descendants of Zebulun:[a]
All the men twenty years old or more who were able to serve in the army were listed by name, according to the records of their clans and families. 31The number from the tribe of Zebulun was 57,400.

32 From the sons of Joseph:
From the descendants of Ephraim:[b]
All the men twenty years old or more who were able to serve in the army were listed by name, according to the records of their clans and families. 33The number from the tribe of Ephraim was 40,500.

34 From the descendants of Manasseh:[c]
All the men twenty years old or more who were able to serve in the army were listed by name, according to the records of their clans and families. 35The number from the tribe of Manasseh was 32,200.

36 From the descendants of Benjamin:[d]
All the men twenty years old or more who were able to serve in the army were listed by name, according to the records of their clans and families. 37The number from the tribe of Benjamin was 35,400.

38 From the descendants of Dan:[e]
All the men twenty years old or more who were able to serve in the army were listed by name, according to the records of their clans and families. 39The number from the tribe of Dan was 62,700.

40 From the descendants of Asher:[f]
All the men twenty years old or more who were able to serve in the army were listed by name, according to the records of their clans and families. 41The number from the tribe of Asher was 41,500.

42 From the descendants of Naphtali:[g]
All the men twenty years old or more who were able to serve in the army were listed by name, according to the records of their clans and families. 43The number from the tribe of Naphtali was 53,400.

44These were the men counted by Moses
and Aaron[h] and the twelve leaders of Israel, each one representing his family. 45All
the Israelites twenty years old or more who
were able to serve in Israel's army were
counted according to their families. 46The
total number was 603,550.[i]
47The ancestral tribe of the Levites,[j]
however, was not counted[k] along with
the others. 48The LORD had said to Moses:
49"You must not count the tribe of Levi or
include them in the census of the other Israelites. 50Instead, appoint the Levites to be
in charge of the tabernacle of the covenant
law[l]—over all its furnishings and everything belonging to it. They are to carry the
tabernacle and all its furnishings; they are
to take care of it and encamp around it.
51Whenever the tabernacle is to move, the
Levites are to take it down, and whenever
the tabernacle is to be set up, the Levites
shall do it.[m] Anyone else who approaches it
is to be put to death. 52The Israelites are to
set up their tents by divisions, each of them
in their own camp under their standard.[n]
53The Levites, however, are to set up their
tents around the tabernacle of the covenant

1:44–46 ***the men counted.*** The number of able-bodied men who were at least twenty years old would indicate a population of between two and five million, including the women, children, and older or infirm men who were not counted in this census.

1:50 ***the tabernacle.*** The term *tabernacle* points to the temporary and portable nature of the tent.

1:22 [w] Nu 26:12-14; Rev 7:7 **1:24** [x] Ge 30:11; Nu 26:15-18; Rev 7:5 **1:26** [y] Ge 29:35; Nu 26:19-22; Mt 1:2; Rev 7:5 **1:28** [z] Nu 26:23-25; Rev 7:7 **1:30** [a] Nu 26:26-27; Rev 7:8 **1:32** [b] Nu 26:35-37 **1:34** [c] Nu 26:28-34; Rev 7:6 **1:36** [d] Nu 26:38-41; 2Ch 17:17; Rev 7:8 **1:38** [e] Ge 30:6; Nu 26:42-43 **1:40** [f] Nu 26:44-47; Rev 7:6 **1:42** [g] Nu 26:48-50; Rev 7:6 **1:44** [h] Nu 26:64 **1:46** [i] Ex 12:37; 38:26; Nu 2:32; 26:51 **1:47** [j] Nu 2:33; 26:57 [k] Nu 4:3,49 **1:50** [l] Ex 38:21; Ac 7:44 **1:51** [m] Nu 3:38; 4:1-33 **1:52** [n] Nu 2:2; Ps 20:5

law so that my wrath will not fall[o] on the Israelite community. The Levites are to be responsible for the care of the tabernacle of the covenant law.[p]"

54The Israelites did all this just as the LORD commanded Moses.

The Arrangement of the Tribal Camps

2 The LORD said to Moses and Aaron: 2"The Israelites are to camp around the tent of meeting some distance from it, each of them under their standard[q] and holding the banners of their family."

3On the east, toward the sunrise, the divisions of the camp of Judah are to encamp under their standard. The leader of the people of Judah is Nahshon son of Amminadab.[r] 4His division numbers 74,600.

5The tribe of Issachar will camp next to them. The leader of the people of Issachar is Nethanel son of Zuar.[s] 6His division numbers 54,400.

7The tribe of Zebulun will be next. The leader of the people of Zebulun is Eliab son of Helon.[t] 8His division numbers 57,400.

9All the men assigned to the camp of Judah, according to their divisions, number 186,400. They will set out first.[u]

10On the south will be the divisions of the camp of Reuben under their standard. The leader of the people of Reuben is Elizur son of Shedeur.[v] 11His division numbers 46,500.

12The tribe of Simeon will camp next to them. The leader of the people of Simeon is Shelumiel son of Zurishaddai.[w] 13His division numbers 59,300.

14The tribe of Gad will be next. The leader of the people of Gad is Eliasaph son of Deuel.[a][x] 15His division numbers 45,650.

16All the men assigned to the camp of Reuben,[y] according to their divisions, number 151,450. They will set out second.

17Then the tent of meeting and the camp of the Levites[z] will set out in the middle of the camps. They will set out in the same order as they encamp, each in their own place under their standard.

18On the west will be the divisions of the camp of Ephraim[a] under their standard. The leader of the people of Ephraim is Elishama son of Ammihud.[b] 19His division numbers 40,500.

20The tribe of Manasseh will be next to them. The leader of the people of Manasseh is Gamaliel son of Pedahzur.[c] 21His division numbers 32,200.

22The tribe of Benjamin will be next. The leader of the people of Benjamin is Abidan son of Gideoni.[d] 23His division numbers 35,400.

24All the men assigned to the camp of Ephraim,[e] according to their divisions, number 108,100. They will set out third.[f]

25On the north will be the divisions of the camp of Dan under their standard. The leader of the people of Dan is Ahiezer son of Ammishaddai.[g] 26His division numbers 62,700.

27The tribe of Asher will camp next to them. The leader of the people of Asher is Pagiel son of Okran.[h] 28His division numbers 41,500.

29The tribe of Naphtali will be next. The leader of the people of Naphtali is Ahira son of Enan.[i] 30His division numbers 53,400.

31All the men assigned to the camp of Dan number 157,600. They will set out last,[j] under their standards.

32These are the Israelites, counted according to their families. All the men in the camps, by their divisions, number 603,550.[k] 33The Levites, however, were not counted[l] along with the other Israelites, as the LORD commanded Moses.

34So the Israelites did everything the LORD commanded Moses; that is the way they encamped under their standards, and that is the way they set out, each of them with their clan and family.

a 14 Many manuscripts of the Masoretic Text, Samaritan Pentateuch and Vulgate (see also 1:14); most manuscripts of the Masoretic Text *Reuel*

2:1–2 under their standard. A person's identity was not only derived from his or her tribe, but also from his or her place in relation to the tabernacle. This is a chapter on design and order; it speaks to the importance of knowing one's duties in relation to the holy and living God.

2:3–9 on the east side, toward the sunrise. The east side was the favored side, facing the rising sun. The Israelites were not a seafaring people; in effect they turned their backs to the sea, so the word for "back" could mean "west" or "the sea."

2:17 tent of meeting . . . the Levites will set out in the middle. In the line of march the tabernacle was in a central position—a symbol not only of Israel's protection of the holy objects, but also of the presence of God among His people.

1:53 [o] Lev 10:6; Nu 16:46; 18:5 [p] Nu 18:2-4
2:2 [q] Nu 1:52; Ps 74:4; Isa 31:9 **2:3** [r] Nu 10:14; Ru 4:20; 1Ch 2:10 **2:5** [s] Nu 1:8 **2:7** [t] Nu 1:9 **2:9** [u] Nu 10:14
2:10 [v] Nu 1:5 **2:12** [w] Nu 1:6 **2:14** [x] Nu 1:14
2:16 [y] Nu 10:18 **2:17** [z] Nu 1:53; 10:21 **2:18** [a] Ge 48:20; Jer 31:18-20 [b] Nu 1:10 **2:20** [c] Nu 1:10 **2:22** [d] Nu 1:11; Ps 68:27 **2:24** [e] Nu 10:22 [f] Ps 80:2 **2:25** [g] Nu 1:12
2:27 [h] Nu 1:13 **2:29** [i] Nu 1:15 **2:31** [j] Nu 10:25
2:32 [k] Ex 38:26; Nu 1:46 **2:33** [l] Nu 1:47; 26:57-62

The Levites

3 This is the account of the family of
Aaron and Moses[m] at the time the LORD
spoke to Moses at Mount Sinai.
2The names of the sons of Aaron were
Nadab the firstborn and Abihu, Eleazar
and Ithamar.[n] 3Those were the names of
Aaron's sons, the anointed priests,[o] who
were ordained to serve as priests. 4Nadab
and Abihu, however, died before the LORD[p]
when they made an offering with unauthorized fire before him in the Desert of
Sinai.[q] They had no sons, so Eleazar and
Ithamar served as priests during the lifetime of their father Aaron.[r]
5The LORD said to Moses, 6"Bring the
tribe of Levi[s] and present them to Aaron the priest to assist him.[t] 7They are to
perform duties for him and for the whole
community at the tent of meeting by doing
the work[u] of the tabernacle. 8They are to
take care of all the furnishings of the tent
of meeting, fulfilling the obligations of the
Israelites by doing the work of the tabernacle. 9Give the Levites to Aaron and his
sons;[v] they are the Israelites who are to be
given wholly to him.[a] 10Appoint Aaron and
his sons to serve as priests;[w] anyone else
who approaches the sanctuary is to be put
to death."[x]
11The LORD also said to Moses, 12"I have
taken the Levites[y] from among the Israelites in place of the first male offspring[z]
of every Israelite woman. The Levites are
mine,[a] 13for all the firstborn are mine.[b]
When I struck down all the firstborn in
Egypt, I set apart for myself every firstborn
in Israel, whether human or animal. They
are to be mine. I am the LORD."
14The LORD said to Moses in the Desert of
Sinai, 15"Count[c] the Levites by their families and clans. Count every male a month
old or more."[d] 16So Moses counted them,
as he was commanded by the word of the
LORD.
17These were the names of the sons of
Levi:[e]
Gershon, Kohath and Merari.[f]
18These were the names of the Gershonite clans:
Libni and Shimei.[g]
19The Kohathite clans:
Amram, Izhar, Hebron and Uzziel.[h]
20The Merarite clans:[i]
Mahli and Mushi.[j]
These were the Levite clans, according
to their families.

21To Gershon belonged the clans of the
Libnites and Shimeites;[k] these were the
Gershonite clans. 22The number of all
the males a month old or more who were
counted was 7,500. 23The Gershonite clans
were to camp on the west, behind the tabernacle. 24The leader of the families of the
Gershonites was Eliasaph son of Lael. 25At
the tent of meeting the Gershonites were
responsible for the care of the tabernacle[l]
and tent, its coverings,[m] the curtain at the
entrance[n] to the tent of meeting, 26the curtains of the courtyard[o], the curtain at the
entrance to the courtyard surrounding the
tabernacle and altar, and the ropes[p]—and
everything related to their use.

27To Kohath belonged the clans of the
Amramites, Izharites, Hebronites and Uzzielites;[q] these were the Kohathite clans.
28The number of all the males a month old
or more was 8,600.[b] The Kohathites were
responsible for the care of the sanctuary.
29The Kohathite clans were to camp on the
south side[r] of the tabernacle. 30The leader
of the families of the Kohathite clans was
Elizaphan son of Uzziel. 31They were responsible for the care of the ark,[s] the table,[t]
the lampstand,[u] the altars,[v] the articles of
the sanctuary used in ministering, the curtain,[w] and everything related to their use.[x]
32The chief leader of the Levites was Eleazar son of Aaron, the priest. He was appointed over those who were responsible
for the care of the sanctuary.

33To Merari belonged the clans of the
Mahlites and the Mushites;[y] these were
the Merarite clans. 34The number of all
the males a month old or more who were
counted was 6,200. 35The leader of the families of the Merarite clans was Zuriel son
of Abihail; they were to camp on the north
side of the tabernacle.[z] 36The Merarites

[a] 9 Most manuscripts of the Masoretic Text; some manuscripts of the Masoretic Text, Samaritan Pentateuch and Septuagint (see also 8:16) *to me*
[b] 28 Hebrew; some Septuagint manuscripts *8,300*

3:1–10 *family of Aaron.* The priests had privileged access to God. In the New Covenant this is no longer confined only to a particular group of God's people. All Christians comprise God's new temple and constitute "a holy priesthood, offering spiritual sacrifices acceptable to God through Jesus Christ" (1 Pet. 2:5).
3:5–10 *Aaron and his sons.* The Levites could care for the holy things, but only the priests, who ministered in the tabernacle, drew near to God. Only the high priest entered the Most Holy Place.
3:11–13 *I set apart for myself.* God is directly involved in redemption. When God redeemed and saved His people, it was by His own person.

3:1 [m] Ex 6:27 **3:2** [n] Ex 6:23; Nu 26:60 **3:3** [o] Ex 28:41 **3:4** [p] Lev 10:2 [q] Lev 10:1 [r] 1Ch 24:1 **3:6** [s] Dt 10:8; 31:9; 1Ch 15:2 [t] Nu 8:6-22; 18:1-7; 2Ch 29:11 **3:7** [u] Lev 8:35; Nu 1:50 **3:9** [v] Nu 8:19; 18:6 **3:10** [w] Ex 29:9 [x] Nu 1:51 **3:12** [y] Mal 2:4 [z] ver 41; Nu 8:16, 18 [a] Ex 13:2 **3:13** [b] Ex 13:12 **3:15** [c] ver 39 [d] Nu 26:62 **3:17** [e] Ge 46:11 [f] Ex 6:16 **3:18** [g] Ex 6:17 **3:19** [h] Ex 6:18 **3:20** [i] Ge 46:11 [j] Ex 6:19 **3:21** [k] Ex 6:17 **3:25** [l] Ex 25:9 [m] Ex 26:14 [n] Ex 26:36; Nu 4:25 **3:26** [o] Ex 27:9 [p] Ex 35:18 **3:27** [q] 1Ch 26:23 **3:29** [r] Nu 1:53 **3:31** [s] Ex 25:10-22 [t] Ex 25:23 [u] Ex 25:31 [v] Ex 27:1; 30:1 [w] Ex 26:33 [x] Nu 4:15 **3:33** [y] Ex 6:19 **3:35** [z] Nu 1:53; 2:25

were appointed[a] to take care of the frames of the tabernacle, its crossbars, posts, bases, all its equipment, and everything related to their use, 37 as well as the posts of the surrounding courtyard with their bases, tent pegs and ropes.

38 Moses and Aaron and his sons were to camp to the east[b] of the tabernacle, toward the sunrise, in front of the tent of meeting.[c] They were responsible for the care of the sanctuary[d] on behalf of the Israelites. Anyone else who approached the sanctuary was to be put to death.[e]

39 The total number of Levites counted at the LORD's command by Moses and Aaron according to their clans, including every male a month old or more, was 22,000.[f]

40 The LORD said to Moses, "Count all the firstborn Israelite males who are a month old or more[g] and make a list of their names. 41 Take the Levites for me in place of all the firstborn of the Israelites,[h] and the livestock of the Levites in place of all the firstborn of the livestock of the Israelites. I am the LORD."

42 So Moses counted all the firstborn of the Israelites, as the LORD commanded him. 43 The total number of firstborn males a month old or more, listed by name, was 22,273.[i]

44 The LORD also said to Moses, 45 "Take the Levites in place of all the firstborn of Israel, and the livestock of the Levites in place of their livestock. The Levites are to be mine. I am the LORD. 46 To redeem[j] the 273 firstborn Israelites who exceed the number of the Levites, 47 collect five shekels[a][k] for each one, according to the sanctuary shekel,[l] which weighs twenty gerahs.[m] 48 Give the money for the redemption of the additional Israelites to Aaron and his sons."

49 So Moses collected the redemption money from those who exceeded the number redeemed by the Levites. 50 From the firstborn of the Israelites he collected silver weighing 1,365 shekels,[b][n] according to the sanctuary shekel. 51 Moses gave the redemption money to Aaron and his sons, as he was commanded by the word of the LORD.

The Kohathites

4 The LORD said to Moses and Aaron: 2 "Take a census[o] of the Kohathite branch of the Levites by their clans and families. 3 Count all the men from thirty to fifty years of age[p] who come to serve in the work at the tent of meeting.

4 "This is the work of the Kohathites at the tent of meeting: the care of the most holy things.[q] 5 When the camp is to move, Aaron and his sons are to go in and take down the shielding curtain[r] and put it over the ark of the covenant law.[s] 6 Then they are to cover the curtain with a durable leather,[c] spread a cloth of solid blue over that and put the poles[t] in place.

7 "Over the table of the Presence[u] they are to spread a blue cloth and put on it the plates, dishes and bowls, and the jars for drink offerings; the bread that is continually there[v] is to remain on it. 8 They are to spread a scarlet cloth over them, cover that with the durable leather and put the poles in place.

9 "They are to take a blue cloth and cover the lampstand that is for light, together with its lamps, its wick trimmers and trays,[w] and all its jars for the olive oil used to supply it. 10 Then they are to wrap it and all its accessories in a covering of the durable leather and put it on a carrying frame.

11 "Over the gold altar[x] they are to spread a blue cloth and cover that with the durable leather and put the poles in place.

12 "They are to take all the articles used for ministering in the sanctuary, wrap them in a blue cloth, cover that with the durable leather and put them on a carrying frame.

---

a *47* That is, about 2 ounces or about 58 grams
b *50* That is, about 35 pounds or about 16 kilograms
c *6* Possibly the hides of large aquatic mammals; also in verses 8, 10, 11, 12, 14 and 25

3:38 *care of the sanctuary.* Caring for the sanctuary was committed to a particular group of people, and no one else was to intrude on that task. Believers, as part of the body of Christ, also have certain duties. These roles are not rigid, but they are definite, planned, and created by God for the good of the whole church. The teamwork of the whole body creates a harmonious whole, and if one fails in his duty, the whole team suffers (1 Cor. 12).

3:40–42 *Count all the firstborn.* When God passed over the homes of the Hebrew families who had obeyed His commands in the Passover (Ex. 12:23–51), He declared the surviving firstborn Hebrew children—and also the firstborn of animals—to be His. The animals were sacrificed, the firstborn were redeemed (paid for), at first by the Levites who took the place of all the other firstborn, and then by a set sum of money for those that numbered more than the Levites. It is a clear statement of fact that people belong to God.

4:3 *from thirty to fifty years of age.* According to 8:24, the Levites were to be twenty-five years old, which seems like a contradiction to this passage. It is possible that the difference reflects a time of apprenticeship.

3:36 [a] Nu 4:32 **3:38** [b] Nu 2:3 [c] Nu 1:53 [d] ver 7; Nu 18:5 [e] ver 10; Nu 1:51 **3:39** [f] Nu 26:62 **3:40** [g] ver 15 **3:41** [h] ver 12 **3:43** [i] ver 39 **3:46** [j] Ex 13:13; Nu 18:15 **3:47** [k] Lev 27:6 [l] Ex 30:13 [m] Lev 27:25 **3:50** [n] ver 46-48 **4:2** [o] Ex 30:12 **4:3** [p] ver 23; Nu 8:25; 1Ch 23:3, 24, 27; Ezr 3:8 **4:4** [q] ver 19 **4:5** [r] Ex 26:31, 33 [s] Ex 25:10, 16 **4:6** [t] Ex 25:13-15; 1Ki 8:7; 2Ch 5:8 **4:7** [u] Ex 25:23, 29; Lev 24:6 [v] Ex 25:30 **4:9** [w] Ex 25:31, 37, 38 **4:11** [x] Ex 30:1

13 “They are to remove the ashes from the bronze altar[y] and spread a purple cloth over it. 14 Then they are to place on it all the utensils used for ministering at the altar, including the firepans, meat forks,[z] shovels and sprinkling bowls.[a] Over it they are to spread a covering of the durable leather and put the poles[b] in place.

15 “After Aaron and his sons have finished covering the holy furnishings and all the holy articles, and when the camp is ready to move, only then are the Kohathites to come and do the carrying.[c] But they must not touch the holy things or they will die.[d] The Kohathites are to carry those things that are in the tent of meeting.

16 “Eleazar[e] son of Aaron, the priest, is to have charge of the oil for the light,[f] the fragrant incense, the regular grain offering[g] and the anointing oil. He is to be in charge of the entire tabernacle and everything in it, including its holy furnishings and articles.”

17 The LORD said to Moses and Aaron, 18 “See that the Kohathite tribal clans are not destroyed from among the Levites. 19 So that they may live and not die when they come near the most holy things,[h] do this for them: Aaron and his sons are to go into the sanctuary and assign to each man his work and what he is to carry. 20 But the Kohathites must not go in to look[i] at the holy things, even for a moment, or they will die.”

The Gershonites

21 The LORD said to Moses, 22 “Take a census also of the Gershonites by their families and clans. 23 Count all the men from thirty to fifty years of age[j] who come to serve in the work at the tent of meeting.

24 “This is the service of the Gershonite clans in their carrying and their other work: 25 They are to carry the curtains of the tabernacle,[k] that is, the tent of meeting,[l] its covering[m] and its outer covering of durable leather, the curtains for the entrance to the tent of meeting, 26 the curtains of the courtyard surrounding the tabernacle and altar, the curtain for the entrance to the courtyard, the ropes and all the equipment used in the service of the tent. The Gershonites are to do all that needs to be done with these things. 27 All their service, whether carrying or doing other work, is to be done under the direction of Aaron and his sons. You shall assign to them as their responsibility all they are to carry. 28 This is the service of the Gershonite clans[n] at the tent of meeting. Their duties are to be under the direction of Ithamar son of Aaron, the priest.

The Merarites

29 “Count the Merarites by their clans and families.[o] 30 Count all the men from thirty to fifty years of age who come to serve in the work at the tent of meeting. 31 As part of all their service at the tent, they are to carry the frames of the tabernacle, its crossbars, posts and bases,[p] 32 as well as the posts of the surrounding courtyard with their bases, tent pegs, ropes, all their equipment and everything related to their use. Assign to each man the specific things he is to carry. 33 This is the service of the Merarite clans as they work at the tent of meeting under the direction of Ithamar son of Aaron, the priest.”

The Numbering of the Levite Clans

34 Moses, Aaron and the leaders of the community counted the Kohathites[q] by their clans and families. 35 All the men from thirty to fifty years of age who came to serve in the work at the tent of meeting, 36 counted by clans, were 2,750. 37 This was the total of all those in the Kohathite clans[r] who served at the tent of meeting. Moses and Aaron counted them according to the LORD’s command through Moses.

38 The Gershonites[s] were counted by their clans and families. 39 All the men from thirty to fifty years of age who came to serve in the work at the tent of meeting, 40 counted by their clans and families, were 2,630. 41 This was the total of those in the Gershonite clans who served at the tent of meeting. Moses and Aaron counted them according to the LORD’s command.

42 The Merarites were counted by their clans and families. 43 All the men from thirty to fifty years of age who came to serve in the work at the tent of meeting, 44 counted by their clans, were 3,200. 45 This was the total of those in the Merarite clans.[t] Moses and Aaron counted them according to the LORD’s command through Moses.

4:16 *Eleazar ... is to have charge.* God made arrangements for the priest to approach Him in the way He prescribed. If the priests did not do their job, no one else could do it for them. It was a big responsibility, and the well-being of the whole nation depended upon their faithfulness.

4:21 – 28 *come to serve.* There are various tasks given to us in the kingdom of God which appear to be of minor importance. Daily faithfulness in the little things is the best preparation for greater trusts. Mary, the mother of Jesus is an example of this. Her response to the angel when she was told that she would be the mother of Jesus was, “I am the Lord’s servant ...” (Luke 1:38). She had found favor in the way she conducted her daily life, and God chose her for a unique and blessed role.

4:13 [y] Ex 27:1-8 **4:14** [z] 2Ch 4:16 [a] Jer 52:18 [b] Ex 27:6
4:15 [c] Nu 7:9 [d] Nu 1:51; 2Sa 6:6,7 **4:16** [e] Lev 10:6
[f] Ex 25:6 [g] Ex 29:41; Lev 6:14-23 **4:19** [h] ver 15
4:20 [i] Ex 19:21; 1Sa 6:19 **4:23** [j] ver 3; 1Ch 23:3,24,27
4:25 [k] Ex 27:10-18; Nu 3:26 [l] Nu 3:25 [m] Ex 26:14
4:28 [n] Nu 7:7 **4:29** [o] Ge 46:11 **4:31** [p] Nu 3:36
4:34 [q] ver 2 **4:37** [r] Nu 3:27 **4:38** [s] Ge 46:11
4:45 [t] ver 29

46So Moses, Aaron and the leaders of Israel counted all the Levites by their clans
and families. 47All the men from thirty to
fifty years of age[u] who came to do the work
of serving and carrying the tent of meeting
48numbered 8,580.[v] 49At the LORD's command through Moses, each was assigned
his work and told what to carry.
Thus they were counted,[w] as the LORD
commanded Moses.

The Purity of the Camp

5 The LORD said to Moses, 2"Command
the Israelites to send away from the
camp anyone who has a defiling skin disease[a][x] or a discharge[y] of any kind, or who
is ceremonially unclean[z] because of a dead
body. 3Send away male and female alike;
send them outside the camp so they will
not defile their camp, where I dwell among
them.[a]" 4The Israelites did so; they sent
them outside the camp. They did just as
the LORD had instructed Moses.

Restitution for Wrongs

5The LORD said to Moses, 6"Say to the Israelites: 'Any man or woman who wrongs
another in any way[b] and so is unfaithful[b] to
the LORD is guilty[c] 7and must confess[d] the
sin they have committed. They must make
full restitution[e] for the wrong they have
done, add a fifth of the value to it and give
it all to the person they have wronged. 8But
if that person has no close relative to whom
restitution can be made for the wrong, the
restitution belongs to the LORD and must be
given to the priest, along with the ram with
which atonement is made for the wrongdoer.[f] 9All the sacred contributions the Israelites bring to a priest will belong to him.[g]
10Sacred things belong to their owners, but
what they give to the priest will belong to
the priest.[h]'"

The Test for an Unfaithful Wife

11Then the LORD said to Moses, 12"Speak
to the Israelites and say to them: 'If a man's
wife goes astray[i] and is unfaithful to him
13so that another man has sexual relations
with her,[j] and this is hidden from her husband and her impurity is undetected (since
there is no witness against her and she has
not been caught in the act), 14and if feelings
of jealousy[k] come over her husband and he
suspects his wife and she is impure—or if
he is jealous and suspects her even though
she is not impure— 15then he is to take his
wife to the priest. He must also take an
offering of a tenth of an ephah[c][l] of barley
flour[m] on her behalf. He must not pour olive oil on it or put incense on it, because it
is a grain offering for jealousy, a reminder-
offering[n] to draw attention to wrongdoing.
16"'The priest shall bring her and have
her stand before the LORD. 17Then he shall
take some holy water in a clay jar and put
some dust from the tabernacle floor into
the water. 18After the priest has had the
woman stand before the LORD, he shall
loosen her hair[o] and place in her hands the
reminder-offering, the grain offering for
jealousy, while he himself holds the bitter
water that brings a curse. 19Then the priest
shall put the woman under oath and say
to her, "If no other man has had sexual
relations with you and you have not gone
astray[p] and become impure while married to your husband, may this bitter water that brings a curse not harm you. 20But
if you have gone astray[q] while married to

[a] 2 The Hebrew word for *defiling skin disease,* traditionally translated "leprosy," was used for various diseases affecting the skin. [b] 6 Or *woman who commits any wrong common to mankind* [c] 15 That is, probably about 3 1/2 pounds or about 1.6 kilograms

5:3 *not defile their camp . . . I dwell.* Ritual purity was important because God wanted the Israelites to remember that He lived among them. They needed to think of Him walking around in the camp and live in such a way that there was not something offensive for God to discover.

5:6 *unfaithful to the LORD.* Not only did God deal with ritual impurity, He was also concerned about how the people treated each other. To label sin as "acting unfaithfully" kept the real issue right in front. When we mistreat our fellow citizens, God cares, and He takes it personally. He made us; He made them. We each belong to Him, and we are not to wrong other people.

5:12 *wife goes astray.* The wife belonged to her husband. If she was unfaithful, she could be stoned. If she was not guilty, and he acted on his unsubstantiated suspicions, he would be guilty of murder. The woman had a serious responsibility to her husband because the reliability of family lines depended upon her faithfulness. It is obvious if a woman is pregnant, but it is not obvious who the father is. By bringing the whole sorry problem to God, the Israelites could be sure of justice.

5:15 *take his wife to the priest.* Determining if a woman had been unfaithful to her husband, when she had not been caught in wrongdoing, was more difficult than detecting skin diseases. But because God was in the camp, the issue could be resolved by the priest, in the presence of God. Again, it reminded the Israelites that nothing was hidden from God.

5:18 *bitter water that brings a curse.* This was not a magic potion, but dust from the floor of the tabernacle and holy water. The woman held in her own hands the grain offering for jealousy. These things reminded everyone that they were standing in the presence of God, and that it was He who would determine if the woman bore any guilt.

4:47 [u] ver 3 **4:48** [v] Nu 3:39 **4:49** [w] Nu 1:47 **5:2** [x] Lev 13:46 [y] Lev 15:2; Mt 9:20 [z] Lev 13:3; Nu 9:6-10 **5:3** [a] Lev 26:12; Nu 35:34; 2Co 6:16 **5:6** [b] Lev 6:2 [c] Lev 5:14-6:7 **5:7** [d] Lev 5:5; 26:40; Jos 7:19; Lk 19:8 [e] Lev 6:5 **5:8** [f] Lev 6:6, 7; 7:7 **5:9** [g] Lev 6:17; 7:6-14 **5:10** [h] Lev 10:13 **5:12** [i] Ex 20:14 **5:13** [j] Lev 18:20; 20:10 **5:14** [k] Pr 6:34; SS 8:6 **5:15** [l] Ex 16:36 [m] Lev 6:20 [n] Eze 29:16 **5:18** [o] Lev 10:6; 1Co 11:6 **5:19** [p] ver 12, 29 **5:20** [q] ver 12

your husband and you have made yourself impure by having sexual relations with a man other than your husband"— **21**here the priest is to put the woman under this curse[r]—"may the LORD cause you to become a curse[a] among your people when he makes your womb miscarry and your abdomen swell. **22**May this water[s] that brings a curse[t] enter your body so that your abdomen swells or your womb miscarries."

"'Then the woman is to say, "Amen. So be it.[u]"

23"'The priest is to write these curses on a scroll[v] and then wash them off into the bitter water. **24**He shall make the woman drink the bitter water that brings a curse, and this water that brings a curse and causes bitter suffering will enter her. **25**The priest is to take from her hands the grain offering for jealousy, wave it before the LORD[w] and bring it to the altar. **26**The priest is then to take a handful of the grain offering as a memorial[b] offering and burn it on the altar; after that, he is to have the woman drink the water. **27**If she has made herself impure and been unfaithful to her husband, this will be the result: When she is made to drink the water that brings a curse and causes bitter suffering, it will enter her, her abdomen will swell and her womb will miscarry, and she will become a curse.[x] **28**If, however, the woman has not made herself impure, but is clean, she will be cleared of guilt and will be able to have children.

29"'This, then, is the law of jealousy when a woman goes astray[y] and makes herself impure while married to her husband, **30**or when feelings of jealousy come over a man because he suspects his wife. The priest is to have her stand before the LORD and is to apply this entire law to her. **31**The husband will be innocent of any wrongdoing, but the woman will bear the consequences[z] of her sin.'"

The Nazirite

6 The LORD said to Moses, **2**"Speak to the Israelites and say to them: 'If a man or woman wants to make a special vow[a], a vow of dedication to the LORD as a Nazirite,[b] **3**they must abstain from wine[c] and other fermented drink and must not drink vinegar[d] made from wine or other fermented drink. They must not drink grape juice or eat grapes or raisins. **4**As long as they remain under their Nazirite vow, they must not eat anything that comes from the grapevine, not even the seeds or skins.

5"'During the entire period of their Nazirite vow, no razor[e] may be used on their head.[f] They must be holy until the period of their dedication to the LORD is over; they must let their hair grow long.

6"'Throughout the period of their dedication to the LORD, the Nazirite must not go near a dead body.[g] **7**Even if their own father or mother or brother or sister dies, they must not make themselves ceremonially unclean[h] on account of them, because the symbol of their dedication to God is on their head. **8**Throughout the period of their dedication, they are consecrated to the LORD.

9"'If someone dies suddenly in the Nazirite's presence, thus defiling the hair that symbolizes their dedication,[i] they must shave their head on the seventh day—the day of their cleansing.[j] **10**Then on the eighth day they must bring two doves or two young pigeons[k] to the priest at the entrance to the tent of meeting. **11**The priest is to offer one as a sin offering[c] and the other as a burnt offering[l] to make atonement[m] for the Nazirite because they sinned by being in the presence of the dead body. That same day they are to consecrate their head again. **12**They must rededicate themselves to the LORD for the same period of dedication and must bring a year-old male lamb as a guilt offering. The previous days do not count, because they became defiled during their period of dedication.

---

[a] *21* That is, may he cause your name to be used in cursing (see Jer. 29:22); or, may others see that you are cursed; similarly in verse 27. [b] *26* Or *representative* [c] *11* Or *purification offering;* also in verses 14 and 16

5:21 ***your abdomen swells or your womb miscarries.*** These words speak symbolically of a miscarriage (of an illegitimate child) if the woman was pregnant, and the inability to conceive again. In the biblical world, a woman who was unable to bear children was regarded as being under a curse; in this case it would have been true.

5:31 ***woman will bear the consequences.*** Throughout the Bible God compares idolatry with marital unfaithfulness, so it is clear that this is a subject that touches close to the heart of every man and woman. God is faithful to His people, and they are to be true to Him. In the same way, as a daily picture of this faithfulness, the husband and wife are to be true and faithful to each other. The law recognizes the volatility of unfaithfulness, provides a limit to unjust accusations, and underlines the seriousness of the moral lapse that comes with adultery. A guilty woman would indeed bear her guilt, but a faithful woman would be exonerated.

6:1–8 Self-Denial—To serve God by abstaining from legitimate things is the Christian's privilege today as well. It is not that God is looking for sacrifice, but He is looking for a willing heart that will lay aside the good to spend time on the best.

5:21 [r] Jos 6:26; 1Sa 14:24; Ne 10:29 **5:22** [s] Ps 109:18 [t] ver 18 [u] Dt 27:15 **5:23** [v] Jer 45:1 **5:25** [w] Lev 8:27 **5:27** [x] Isa 43:28; 65:15; Jer 26:6; 29:18; 42:18; 44:12, 22; Zec 8:13 **5:29** [y] ver 19 **5:31** [z] Lev 5:1; 20:17 **6:2** [a] Ge 28:20; Ac 21:23 [b] Jdg 13:5; 16:17; Am 2:11, 12 **6:3** [c] Lk 1:15 [d] Ru 2:14; Ps 69:21; Pr 10:26 **6:5** [e] Ps 52:2; 57:4; 59:7; Isa 7:20; Eze 5:1 [f] 1Sa 1:11 **6:6** [g] Lev 21:1-3; Nu 19:11-22 **6:7** [h] Nu 9:6 **6:9** [i] ver 18 [j] Lev 14:9 **6:10** [k] Lev 5:7; 14:22 **6:11** [l] Ge 8:20 [m] Ex 29:36

13“‘Now this is the law of the Nazirite
when the period of their dedication is over.[n]
They are to be brought to the entrance to
the tent of meeting. 14There they are to present their offerings to the LORD: a year-old
male lamb without defect for a burnt offering, a year-old ewe lamb without defect for
a sin offering,[o] a ram without defect for a
fellowship offering, 15together with their
grain offerings and drink offerings,[p] and
a basket of bread made with the finest flour
and without yeast—thick loaves with olive
oil mixed in, and thin loaves brushed with
olive oil.[q]
16“‘The priest is to present all these before the LORD and make the sin offering
and the burnt offering. 17He is to present
the basket of unleavened bread and is to
sacrifice the ram as a fellowship offering
to the LORD, together with its grain offering
and drink offering.
18“‘Then at the entrance to the tent of
meeting, the Nazirite must shave off the
hair that symbolizes their dedication.[r]
They are to take the hair and put it in the
fire that is under the sacrifice of the fellowship offering.
19“‘After the Nazirite has shaved off the
hair that symbolizes their dedication, the
priest is to place in their hands a boiled
shoulder of the ram, and one thick loaf and
one thin loaf from the basket, both made
without yeast. 20The priest shall then wave
these before the LORD as a wave offering;
they are holy and belong to the priest, together with the breast that was waved and
the thigh that was presented. After that,
the Nazirite may drink wine.[s]
21“‘This is the law of the Nazirite who
vows offerings to the LORD in accordance
with their dedication, in addition to whatever else they can afford. They must fulfill
the vows they have made, according to the
law of the Nazirite.’”

The Priestly Blessing

22The LORD said to Moses, 23“Tell Aaron
and his sons, ‘This is how you are to bless[t]
the Israelites. Say to them:

24“‘“The LORD bless you[u]
and keep you;[v]
25the LORD make his face shine on you[w]
and be gracious to you;[x]
26the LORD turn his face[y] toward you
and give you peace.[z]”’

27“So they will put my name[a] on the Israelites, and I will bless them.”

Offerings at the Dedication of the Tabernacle

7 When Moses finished setting up the
tabernacle,[b] he anointed and consecrated it and all its furnishings.[c] He also
anointed and consecrated the altar and all
its utensils.[d] 2Then the leaders of Israel,[e]
the heads of families who were the tribal
leaders in charge of those who were counted, made offerings. 3They brought as their
gifts before the LORD six covered carts and
twelve oxen—an ox from each leader and a
cart from every two. These they presented
before the tabernacle.
4The LORD said to Moses, 5“Accept these
from them, that they may be used in the
work at the tent of meeting. Give them to
the Levites as each man’s work requires.”
6So Moses took the carts and oxen and
gave them to the Levites. 7He gave two
carts and four oxen to the Gershonites,[f]
as their work required, 8and he gave four
carts and eight oxen to the Merarites,[g] as
their work required. They were all under
the direction of Ithamar son of Aaron, the
priest. 9But Moses did not give any to the
Kohathites, because they were to carry on
their shoulders[h] the holy things, for which
they were responsible.
10When the altar was anointed,[i] the leaders brought their offerings for its dedication[j] and presented them before the altar.
11For the LORD had said to Moses, “Each
day one leader is to bring his offering for
the dedication of the altar.”

12The one who brought his offering on the
first day was Nahshon son of Amminadab
of the tribe of Judah.

6:21 *the law of the Nazirite.* Not to be confused with a Nazarene (one from Nazareth), the Nazirite vows were practiced both in the Old and New Testament. It is likely that John the Baptist was a Nazirite, probably all of his life.

6:23 *bless the Israelites.* This special blessing shows the love and mercy of God toward His chosen people. God's keeping power, His shining personal presence, His eye contact, and His own peace would be a blessing that would mark the Israelites as belonging to God Himself, and they would be called with His name.

7:1 *when Moses finished setting up the tabernacle.* This phrasing places the events of this chapter before the taking of the census in chapters 1–4. The tabernacle was completed on the first day of the first month of the second year. The census began one month later.

7:1–11 *brought as their gifts.* The tabernacle from the beginning to the end was constructed and furnished by willing hearts and hands. God wants us to give to His work because we are eager to, not because we are required. Jesus directed, “Give, and it will be given to you. A good measure, pressed down, shaken together and running over, will be poured into your lap.” (Luke 6:38). We can never outgive God.

6:13 [n] Ac 21:26 **6:14** [o] Lev 14:10; Nu 15:27 **6:15** [p] Nu 15:1-7 [q] Ex 29:2; Lev 2:4 **6:18** [r] ver 9; Ac 21:24 **6:20** [s] Ecc 9:7 **6:23** [t] Dt 21:5; 1Ch 23:13 **6:24** [u] Dt 28:3-6; Ps 28:9 [v] 1Sa 2:9; Ps 17:8 **6:25** [w] Job 29:24; Ps 31:16; 80:3; 119:135 [x] Ge 43:29; Ps 25:16; 86:16 **6:26** [y] Ps 4:6; 44:3 [z] Ps 29:11; 37:11, 37; Jn 14:27 **6:27** [a] Dt 28:10; 2Sa 7:23; 2Ch 7:14; Ne 9:10; Jer 25:29 **7:1** [b] Ex 40:17 [c] Ex 40:9 [d] ver 84, 88; Ex 40:10 **7:2** [e] Nu 1:5-16 **7:7** [f] Nu 4:24-26, 28 **7:8** [g] Nu 4:31-33 **7:9** [h] Nu 4:15 **7:10** [i] ver 1 [j] 2Ch 7:9

13His offering was one silver plate
weighing a hundred and thirty shekels[a] and one silver sprinkling bowl
weighing seventy shekels,[b] both according to the sanctuary shekel,[k] each
filled with the finest flour mixed with
olive oil as a grain offering;[l] 14one
gold dish weighing ten shekels,[c] filled
with incense;[m] 15one young bull,[n] one
ram and one male lamb a year old for
a burnt offering;[o] 16one male goat for
a sin offering[d];[p] 17and two oxen, five
rams, five male goats and five male
lambs a year old to be sacrificed as
a fellowship offering.[q] This was the
offering of Nahshon son of Amminadab.[r]

18On the second day Nethanel son of Zuar,[s]
the leader of Issachar, brought his offering.

19The offering he brought was one silver plate weighing a hundred and thirty shekels and one silver sprinkling
bowl weighing seventy shekels, both
according to the sanctuary shekel,
each filled with the finest flour mixed
with olive oil as a grain offering; 20one
gold dish[t] weighing ten shekels, filled
with incense; 21one young bull, one
ram and one male lamb a year old for
a burnt offering; 22one male goat for
a sin offering; 23and two oxen, five
rams, five male goats and five male
lambs a year old to be sacrificed as a
fellowship offering. This was the offering of Nethanel son of Zuar.

24On the third day, Eliab son of Helon,[u] the
leader of the people of Zebulun, brought
his offering.

25His offering was one silver plate
weighing a hundred and thirty shekels
and one silver sprinkling bowl weighing seventy shekels, both according
to the sanctuary shekel, each filled
with the finest flour mixed with olive
oil as a grain offering; 26one gold dish
weighing ten shekels, filled with incense; 27one young bull, one ram and
one male lamb a year old for a burnt
offering; 28one male goat for a sin offering; 29and two oxen, five rams, five
male goats and five male lambs a year
old to be sacrificed as a fellowship offering. This was the offering of Eliab
son of Helon.

30On the fourth day Elizur son of Shedeur,[v]
the leader of the people of Reuben, brought
his offering.

31His offering was one silver plate
weighing a hundred and thirty shekels
and one silver sprinkling bowl weighing seventy shekels, both according
to the sanctuary shekel, each filled
with the finest flour mixed with olive
oil as a grain offering; 32one gold dish
weighing ten shekels, filled with incense; 33one young bull, one ram and
one male lamb a year old for a burnt
offering; 34one male goat for a sin offering; 35and two oxen, five rams, five
male goats and five male lambs a year
old to be sacrificed as a fellowship offering. This was the offering of Elizur
son of Shedeur.

36On the fifth day Shelumiel son of Zurishaddai,[w] the leader of the people of Simeon, brought his offering.

37His offering was one silver plate
weighing a hundred and thirty shekels
and one silver sprinkling bowl weighing seventy shekels, both according
to the sanctuary shekel, each filled
with the finest flour mixed with olive
oil as a grain offering; 38one gold dish
weighing ten shekels, filled with incense; 39one young bull, one ram and
one male lamb a year old for a burnt
offering; 40one male goat for a sin offering; 41and two oxen, five rams, five
male goats and five male lambs a year
old to be sacrificed as a fellowship offering. This was the offering of Shelumiel son of Zurishaddai.

42On the sixth day Eliasaph son of Deuel,[x]
the leader of the people of Gad, brought his
offering.

43His offering was one silver plate
weighing a hundred and thirty shekels
and one silver sprinkling bowl weighing seventy shekels, both according
to the sanctuary shekel, each filled
with the finest flour mixed with olive
oil as a grain offering; 44one gold dish
weighing ten shekels, filled with incense; 45one young bull, one ram and
one male lamb a year old for a burnt
offering; 46one male goat for a sin offering; 47and two oxen, five rams, five
male goats and five male lambs a year
old to be sacrificed as a fellowship offering. This was the offering of Eliasaph son of Deuel.

48On the seventh day Elishama son of Ammihud,[y] the leader of the people of Ephraim, brought his offering.

---

[a] *13* That is, about 3 1/4 pounds or about 1.5 kilograms; also elsewhere in this chapter
[b] *13* That is, about 1 3/4 pounds or about 800 grams; also elsewhere in this chapter
[c] *14* That is, about 4 ounces or about 115 grams; also elsewhere in this chapter
[d] *16* Or *purification offering*; also elsewhere in this chapter

7:13 [k] Ex 30:13; Nu 3:47 [l] Lev 2:1 **7:14** [m] Ex 30:34
7:15 [n] Ex 24:5; 29:3; Nu 28:11 [o] Lev 1:3
7:16 [p] Lev 4:3,23 **7:17** [q] Lev 3:1 [r] Nu 1:7
7:18 [s] Nu 1:8 **7:20** [t] ver 14 **7:24** [u] Nu 1:9
7:30 [v] Nu 1:5 **7:36** [w] Nu 1:6 **7:42** [x] Nu 1:14
7:48 [y] Nu 1:10

[49]His offering was one silver plate
weighing a hundred and thirty shekels
and one silver sprinkling bowl weighing seventy shekels, both according
to the sanctuary shekel, each filled
with the finest flour mixed with olive
oil as a grain offering; [50]one gold dish
weighing ten shekels, filled with incense; [51]one young bull, one ram and
one male lamb a year old for a burnt
offering; [52]one male goat for a sin offering; [53]and two oxen, five rams, five
male goats and five male lambs a year
old to be sacrificed as a fellowship offering. This was the offering of Elishama son of Ammihud.[z]

[54]On the eighth day Gamaliel son of Pedahzur,[a] the leader of the people of Manasseh, brought his offering.

[55]His offering was one silver plate
weighing a hundred and thirty shekels
and one silver sprinkling bowl weighing seventy shekels, both according
to the sanctuary shekel, each filled
with the finest flour mixed with olive
oil as a grain offering; [56]one gold dish
weighing ten shekels, filled with incense; [57]one young bull, one ram and
one male lamb a year old for a burnt
offering; [58]one male goat for a sin offering; [59]and two oxen, five rams, five
male goats and five male lambs a year
old to be sacrificed as a fellowship offering. This was the offering of Gamaliel son of Pedahzur.

[60]On the ninth day Abidan son of Gideoni,[b] the leader of the people of Benjamin,
brought his offering.

[61]His offering was one silver plate
weighing a hundred and thirty shekels
and one silver sprinkling bowl weighing seventy shekels, both according
to the sanctuary shekel, each filled
with the finest flour mixed with olive
oil as a grain offering; [62]one gold dish
weighing ten shekels, filled with incense; [63]one young bull, one ram and
one male lamb a year old for a burnt
offering; [64]one male goat for a sin offering; [65]and two oxen, five rams, five
male goats and five male lambs a year
old to be sacrificed as a fellowship offering. This was the offering of Abidan son of Gideoni.

[66]On the tenth day Ahiezer son of Ammishaddai,[c] the leader of the people of Dan,
brought his offering.

[67]His offering was one silver plate
weighing a hundred and thirty shekels
and one silver sprinkling bowl weighing seventy shekels, both according
to the sanctuary shekel, each filled
with the finest flour mixed with olive
oil as a grain offering; [68]one gold dish
weighing ten shekels, filled with incense; [69]one young bull, one ram and
one male lamb a year old for a burnt
offering; [70]one male goat for a sin offering; [71]and two oxen, five rams, five
male goats and five male lambs a year
old to be sacrificed as a fellowship offering. This was the offering of Ahiezer son of Ammishaddai.

[72]On the eleventh day Pagiel son of Okran,[d] the leader of the people of Asher,
brought his offering.

[73]His offering was one silver plate
weighing a hundred and thirty shekels
and one silver sprinkling bowl weighing seventy shekels, both according
to the sanctuary shekel, each filled
with the finest flour mixed with olive
oil as a grain offering; [74]one gold dish
weighing ten shekels, filled with incense; [75]one young bull, one ram and
one male lamb a year old for a burnt
offering; [76]one male goat for a sin offering; [77]and two oxen, five rams, five
male goats and five male lambs a year
old to be sacrificed as a fellowship offering. This was the offering of Pagiel
son of Okran.

[78]On the twelfth day Ahira son of Enan,[e]
the leader of the people of Naphtali,
brought his offering.

[79]His offering was one silver plate
weighing a hundred and thirty shekels
and one silver sprinkling bowl weighing seventy shekels, both according
to the sanctuary shekel, each filled
with the finest flour mixed with olive
oil as a grain offering; [80]one gold dish
weighing ten shekels, filled with incense; [81]one young bull, one ram and
one male lamb a year old for a burnt
offering; [82]one male goat for a sin offering; [83]and two oxen, five rams, five
male goats and five male lambs a year
old to be sacrificed as a fellowship offering. This was the offering of Ahira
son of Enan.

[84]These were the offerings of the Israelite leaders for the dedication of the altar
when it was anointed:[f] twelve silver plates,
twelve silver sprinkling bowls[g] and twelve
gold dishes.[h] [85]Each silver plate weighed
a hundred and thirty shekels, and each
sprinkling bowl seventy shekels. Altogether, the silver dishes weighed two thousand
four hundred shekels,[a] according to the
sanctuary shekel. [86]The twelve gold dishes filled with incense weighed ten shekels
each, according to the sanctuary shek-

[a] *85* That is, about 60 pounds or about 28 kilograms

7:53 [z] Nu 1:10 **7:54** [a] Nu 1:10; 2:20
7:60 [b] Nu 1:11 **7:66** [c] Nu 1:12; 2:25 **7:72** [d] Nu 1:13

7:78 [e] Nu 1:15; 2:29 **7:84** [f] ver 1, 10 [g] Nu 4:14
[h] ver 14

el. Altogether, the gold dishes weighed a
hundred and twenty shekels.[a] 87The total
number of animals for the burnt offering
came to twelve young bulls, twelve rams
and twelve male lambs a year old, together with their grain offering. Twelve male
goats were used for the sin offering. 88The
total number of animals for the sacrifice
of the fellowship offering came to twenty-
four oxen, sixty rams, sixty male goats and
sixty male lambs a year old. These were
the offerings for the dedication of the altar
after it was anointed.[i]
89When Moses entered the tent of meeting to speak with the LORD,[j] he heard the
voice speaking to him from between the
two cherubim above the atonement cover[k]
on the ark of the covenant law. In this way
the LORD spoke to him.

Setting Up the Lamps

8 The LORD said to Moses, 2"Speak to
Aaron and say to him, 'When you set
up the lamps, see that all seven light up the
area in front of the lampstand.[l]' "
3Aaron did so; he set up the lamps so that
they faced forward on the lampstand, just
as the LORD commanded Moses. 4This is
how the lampstand was made: It was made
of hammered gold[m]—from its base to its
blossoms. The lampstand was made exactly like the pattern[n] the LORD had shown
Moses.

The Setting Apart of the Levites

5The LORD said to Moses: 6"Take the
Levites from among all the Israelites and
make them ceremonially clean.[o] 7To purify
them, do this: Sprinkle the water of cleansing[p] on them; then have them shave their
whole bodies[q] and wash their clothes.[r] And
so they will purify themselves. 8Have them
take a young bull with its grain offering of
the finest flour mixed with olive oil;[s] then
you are to take a second young bull for a
sin offering.[b] 9Bring the Levites to the front
of the tent of meeting[t] and assemble the
whole Israelite community.[u] 10You are to
bring the Levites before the LORD, and the
Israelites are to lay their hands on them.[v]
11Aaron is to present the Levites before the
LORD as a wave offering[w] from the Israelites, so that they may be ready to do the
work of the LORD.
12"Then the Levites are to lay their hands
on the heads of the bulls,[x] using one for a
sin offering to the LORD and the other for a
burnt offering, to make atonement[y] for the
Levites. 13Have the Levites stand in front
of Aaron and his sons and then present
them as a wave offering to the LORD. 14In
this way you are to set the Levites apart
from the other Israelites, and the Levites
will be mine.[z]
15"After you have purified the Levites
and presented them as a wave offering,[a]
they are to come to do their work at the tent
of meeting. 16They are the Israelites who
are to be given wholly to me. I have taken
them as my own in place of the firstborn,
the first male offspring[b] from every Israelite woman. 17Every firstborn male in Israel,
whether human or animal,[c] is mine. When
I struck down all the firstborn in Egypt, I
set them apart for myself.[d] 18And I have
taken the Levites in place of all the firstborn sons in Israel.[e] 19From among all the
Israelites, I have given the Levites as gifts
to Aaron and his sons[f] to do the work at the
tent of meeting on behalf of the Israelites[g]
and to make atonement for them[h] so that no
plague will strike the Israelites when they
go near the sanctuary."
20Moses, Aaron and the whole Israelite
community did with the Levites just as the
LORD commanded Moses. 21The Levites purified themselves and washed their clothes.[i]
Then Aaron presented them as a wave offering before the LORD and made atonement for them to purify them.[j] 22After that,
the Levites came to do their work at the tent

[a] 86 That is, about 3 pounds or about 1.4 kilograms
[b] 8 Or *purification offering*; also in verse 12

7:89 *heard the voice.* The tabernacle is referred to as the "tent of meeting," because it was here that the Lord communicated with His people. Moses knew that it was the Lord he was hearing, and he took that word very seriously. The Word of God is still something that God's people can hear, usually through the Bible, sometimes in creation (Rom. 1), and sometimes through the work of the Holy Spirit. This is usually a strong impression that God wants you to pay attention to something, wait, change a decision, or pray. The leading of the Holy Spirit will never contradict Scripture, so it is exceedingly important for believers to maintain a familiarity with the Bible, so they can know God and hear Him.

8:10–12 *lay their hands on.* The sons of Israel who laid their hands on the Levites in this ancient symbol of dedication were showing their support for and agreement with the special role that the Levites had been set aside for. This would be an event that everyone could look back on and remember as an important, solemn time of dedication and asking for God's blessing.

8:16 *given wholly to me.* The Hebrew words for this phrase are an emphatic doubling: "given, given."

8:19 *no plague.* God's holiness would not bear an improper approach. But in His mercy He provided the protective hedge of the Levites, to keep the Israelites from coming near the sanctuary in an unauthorized way, and thus causing a plague.

7:88 [i] ver 1, 10 **7:89** [j] Ex 25:21, 22; 33:9, 11 [k] Ps 80:1; 99:1 **8:2** [l] Ex 25:37; Lev 24:2, 4 **8:4** [m] Ex 25:18, 36; 25:18 [n] Ex 25:9 **8:6** [o] Lev 22:2; Isa 1:16; 52:11 **8:7** [p] Nu 19:9, 17 [q] Lev 14:9; Dt 21:12 [r] Lev 14:8 **8:8** [s] Lev 2:1; Nu 15:8-10 **8:9** [t] Ex 40:12 [u] Lev 8:3 **8:10** [v] Ac 6:6 **8:11** [w] Lev 7:30 **8:12** [x] Ex 29:10 [y] Ex 29:36 **8:14** [z] Nu 3:12 **8:15** [a] Ex 29:24 **8:16** [b] Nu 3:12 **8:17** [c] Ex 4:23 [d] Ex 13:2; Lk 2:23 **8:18** [e] Nu 3:12 **8:19** [f] Nu 3:9 [g] Nu 1:53 [h] Nu 16:46 **8:21** [i] ver 7 [j] ver 12

of meeting under the supervision of Aaron and his sons. They did with the Levites just as the LORD commanded Moses.

23 The LORD said to Moses, 24 "This applies to the Levites: Men twenty-five years old or more[k] shall come to take part in the work at the tent of meeting,[l] 25 but at the age of fifty, they must retire from their regular service and work no longer. 26 They may assist their brothers in performing their duties at the tent of meeting, but they themselves must not do the work. This, then, is how you are to assign the responsibilities of the Levites."

The Passover

9 The LORD spoke to Moses in the Desert of Sinai in the first month[m] of the second year after they came out of Egypt.[n] He said, 2 "Have the Israelites celebrate the Passover at the appointed time. 3 Celebrate it at the appointed time, at twilight on the fourteenth day of this month, in accordance with all its rules and regulations.[o]"

4 So Moses told the Israelites to celebrate the Passover, 5 and they did so in the Desert of Sinai at twilight on the fourteenth day of the first month.[p] The Israelites did everything just as the LORD commanded Moses. 6 But some of them could not celebrate the Passover on that day because they were ceremonially unclean[q] on account of a dead body. So they came to Moses and Aaron[r] that same day 7 and said to Moses, "We have become unclean because of a dead body, but why should we be kept from presenting the LORD's offering with the other Israelites at the appointed time?"

8 Moses answered them, "Wait until I find out what the LORD commands concerning you."[s]

9 Then the LORD said to Moses, 10 "Tell the Israelites: 'When any of you or your descendants are unclean because of a dead body or are away on a journey, they are still to celebrate[t] the LORD's Passover, 11 but they are to do it on the fourteenth day of the second month at twilight. They are to eat the lamb, together with unleavened bread and bitter herbs.[u] 12 They must not leave any of it till morning[v] or break any of its bones.[w] When they celebrate the Passover, they must follow all the regulations. 13 But if anyone who is ceremonially clean and not on a journey fails to celebrate the Passover, they must be cut off from their people[x] for not presenting the LORD's offering at the appointed time. They will bear the consequences of their sin.

14 " 'A foreigner[y] residing among you is also to celebrate the LORD's Passover in accordance with its rules and regulations. You must have the same regulations for both the foreigner and the native-born.' "

The Cloud Above the Tabernacle

15 On the day the tabernacle, the tent of the covenant law, was set up, the cloud[z] covered it. From evening till morning the cloud above the tabernacle looked like fire.[a] 16 That is how it continued to be; the cloud covered it, and at night it looked like fire. 17 Whenever the cloud lifted from above the tent, the Israelites set out; wherever the cloud settled, the Israelites encamped.[b] 18 At the LORD's command the Israelites set out, and at his command they encamped. As long as the cloud stayed over the tabernacle, they remained in camp. 19 When the cloud remained over the tabernacle a long time, the Israelites obeyed the LORD's order and did not set out. 20 Sometimes the cloud was over the tabernacle only a few days; at the LORD's command they would encamp, and then at his command they would set out. 21 Sometimes the cloud stayed only from evening till morning, and when it lifted in the morning, they set out. Whether by day or by night, whenever the cloud lifted, they set out. 22 Whether the cloud stayed over the tabernacle for two days or a month or a year, the Israelites would remain in camp and not set out; but when it lifted, they would set out. 23 At

---

8:24 *twenty-five years old.* According to 4:3, the Levites were to be thirty years old, which seems like a contradiction to this passage. It is possible that the difference reflects a time of apprenticeship.

9:1 *the first month of the second year.* This phrasing places the events of this chapter before the taking of the census. (See note for 7:1).

9:1–5 *celebrate the Passover.* When the first Passover was celebrated in Egypt, the command was given to commemorate it throughout Israel's generations (Ex. 12:14). This would be the second time that the Israelites had observed this special commemorative event. Passover had greater significance than any Israelite of that day could imagine, however wonderful the exodus events were. Redemption from Egypt was a picture of greater redemption yet to be, when the blood of Christ would speak of better things than the blood applied to the doors in Egypt. Christ is now our eternal Passover (1 Cor. 5:7).

9:12 *or break any of its bones.* It is fitting to remember that when the Savior was crucified as our "Passover Lamb," none of His bones were broken (John 19:36).

9:15–23 *the cloud.* The cloud was a dramatic symbol of the active presence of God with His people, hovering over them in protection, moving ahead of them for direction, and coming near at night as fire for comfort in the darkness.

8:24 [k] 1Ch 23:3 [l] Ex 38:21; Nu 4:3 **9:1** [m] Ex 40:2 [n] Nu 1:1
9:3 [o] Ex 12:2-11,43-49; Lev 23:5-8; Dt 16:1-8
9:5 [p] Ex 12:1-13; Jos 5:10 **9:6** [q] Lev 5:3 [r] Ex 18:15; Nu 27:2
9:8 [s] Ex 18:15; Nu 27:5,21; Ps 85:8 **9:10** [t] 2Ch 30:2
9:11 [u] Ex 12:8 **9:12** [v] Ex 12:10,43 [w] Ex 12:46; Jn 19:36*
9:13 [x] Ge 17:14; Ex 12:15 **9:14** [y] Ex 12:48,49
9:15 [z] Ex 40:34 [a] Ex 13:21 **9:17** [b] Ex 40:36-38; Nu 10:11, 12; 1Co 10:1

the LORD's command they encamped, and
at the LORD's command they set out. They
obeyed the LORD's order, in accordance
with his command through Moses.

The Silver Trumpets

10 The LORD said to Moses: 2"Make two
trumpets[c] of hammered silver, and
use them for calling the community[d] together and for having the camps set out.
3When both are sounded, the whole community is to assemble before you at the entrance to the tent of meeting. 4If only one
is sounded, the leaders[e]—the heads of the
clans of Israel—are to assemble before
you. 5When a trumpet blast is sounded,
the tribes camping on the east are to set
out.[f] 6At the sounding of a second blast,
the camps on the south are to set out.[g] The
blast will be the signal for setting out. 7To
gather the assembly, blow the trumpets,[h]
but not with the signal for setting out.[i]
8"The sons of Aaron, the priests, are to
blow the trumpets. This is to be a lasting
ordinance for you and the generations to
come.[j] 9When you go into battle in your
own land against an enemy who is oppressing you,[k] sound a blast on the trumpets.
Then you will be remembered[l] by the LORD
your God and rescued from your enemies.[m]
10Also at your times of rejoicing—your appointed festivals and New Moon feasts[n]—
you are to sound the trumpets[o] over your
burnt offerings and fellowship offerings,
and they will be a memorial for you before
your God. I am the LORD your God."

The Israelites Leave Sinai

11On the twentieth day of the second
month of the second year,[p] the cloud lifted[q] from above the tabernacle of the covenant law. 12Then the Israelites set out
from the Desert of Sinai and traveled from
place to place until the cloud came to rest
in the Desert of Paran. 13They set out, this
first time, at the LORD's command through
Moses.[r]
14The divisions of the camp of Judah
went first, under their standard.[s] Nahshon
son of Amminadab[t] was in command.
15Nethanel son of Zuar was over the division of the tribe of Issachar, 16and Eliab son
of Helon was over the division of the tribe
of Zebulun. 17Then the tabernacle was tak-
en down, and the Gershonites and Merarites, who carried it, set out.[u]
18The divisions of the camp of Reuben
went next, under their standard.[v] Elizur
son of Shedeur was in command. 19Shelu-
miel son of Zurishaddai was over the division of the tribe of Simeon, 20and Eliasaph
son of Deuel was over the division of the
tribe of Gad. 21Then the Kohathites set out,
carrying the holy things.[w] The tabernacle
was to be set up before they arrived.[x]
22The divisions of the camp of Ephraim[y]
went next, under their standard. Elishama
son of Ammihud was in command. 23Ga-
maliel son of Pedahzur was over the division of the tribe of Manasseh, 24and Abidan son of Gideoni was over the division
of the tribe of Benjamin.
25Finally, as the rear guard[z] for all the
units, the divisions of the camp of Dan set
out under their standard. Ahiezer son of
Ammishaddai was in command. 26Pagiel
son of Okran was over the division of the
tribe of Asher, 27and Ahira son of Enan
was over the division of the tribe of Naphtali. 28This was the order of march for the
Israelite divisions as they set out.
29Now Moses said to Hobab[a] son of Reuel[b] the Midianite, Moses' father-in-law,[c]
"We are setting out for the place about
which the LORD said, 'I will give it to you.'[d]
Come with us and we will treat you well,
for the LORD has promised good things to
Israel."
30He answered, "No, I will not go;[e] I am
going back to my own land and my own
people."
31But Moses said, "Please do not leave
us. You know where we should camp in the
wilderness, and you can be our eyes.[f] 32If
you come with us, we will share with you[g]
whatever good things the LORD gives us.[h]"
33So they set out[i] from the mountain of
the LORD and traveled for three days. The
ark of the covenant of the LORD[j] went before them during those three days to find
them a place to rest. 34The cloud of the

9:23 *At the LORD's command.* Like the children of Israel, our existence often seems to us like a desert. Most often we want to *move*, to *do*, to know. Without waiting and following God's directions, His Word, His plan, we miss His best, and lessons are lost or delayed. How blessed to wait for God's direction, to obey Him in both stops and starts in all of life! No words spoken, no money spent, no job taken, no engagement ring given or received, without knowing we will be keeping God's charge.

10:2 *two trumpets of hammered silver.* The two silver trumpets were different from the curved ram's horn trumpets (Lev. 25:9). Made of hammered silver, these instruments were straight with a flaring bell, like the post horns of medieval Europe. Since they did not have valves, they would have been played like a bugle.

10:29 *Reuel.* Also called Jethro (Ex. 3:1), Reuel was the priest of Midian who befriended Moses and gave his daughter Zipporah to him as his wife.

10:2 [c] Ne 12:35; Ps 47:5 [d] Jer 4:5, 19; 6:1; Hos 5:8; Joel 2:1, 15; Am 3:6 **10:4** [e] Ex 18:21; Nu 1:16; 7:2 **10:5** [f] ver 14 **10:6** [g] ver 18 **10:7** [h] Eze 33:3; Joel 2:1 [i] 1Co 14:8 **10:8** [j] Nu 31:6 **10:9** [k] Jdg 2:18; 6:9; 1Sa 10:18; Ps 106:42 [l] Ge 8:1 [m] Ps 106:4 **10:10** [n] Ps 81:3 [o] Lev 23:24 **10:11** [p] Ex 40:17 [q] Nu 9:17 **10:13** [r] Dt 1:6 **10:14** [s] Nu 2:3-9 [t] Nu 1:7 **10:17** [u] Nu 4:21-32 **10:18** [v] Nu 2:10-16 **10:21** [w] Nu 4:20 [x] ver 17 **10:22** [y] Nu 2:24 **10:25** [z] Nu 2:31; Jos 6:9 **10:29** [a] Jdg 4:11 [b] Ex 2:18 [c] Ex 3:1 [d] Ge 12:7 **10:30** [e] Mt 21:29 **10:31** [f] Job 29:15 **10:32** [g] Dt 10:18 [h] Ps 22:27-31; 67:5-7 **10:33** [i] ver 12; Dt 1:33 [j] Jos 3:3

LORD was over them by day when they set out from the camp.[k]

35Whenever the ark set out, Moses said,

“Rise up, LORD!
May your enemies be scattered;[l]
may your foes flee before you.[m]”

36Whenever it came to rest, he said,

“Return,[n] LORD,
to the countless thousands of Israel.[o]”

Fire From the LORD

11 Now the people complained about their hardships in the hearing of the LORD, and when he heard them his anger was aroused. Then fire from the LORD burned among them[p] and consumed some of the outskirts of the camp. 2When the people cried out to Moses, he prayed to the LORD[q] and the fire died down. 3So that place was called Taberah,[a][r] because fire from the LORD had burned among them.

Quail From the LORD

4The rabble with them began to crave other food,[s] and again the Israelites started wailing[t] and said, “If only we had meat to eat! 5We remember the fish we ate in Egypt at no cost—also the cucumbers, melons, leeks, onions and garlic.[u] 6But now we have lost our appetite; we never see anything but this manna!”

7The manna was like coriander seed[v] and looked like resin.[w] 8The people went around gathering it, and then ground it in a hand mill or crushed it in a mortar. They cooked it in a pot or made it into loaves. And it tasted like something made with olive oil. 9When the dew[x] settled on the camp at night, the manna also came down.

10Moses heard the people of every family wailing at the entrance to their tents. The LORD became exceedingly angry, and Moses was troubled. 11He asked the LORD, “Why have you brought this trouble on your servant? What have I done to displease you that you put the burden of all these people on me?[y] 12Did I conceive all these people? Did I give them birth? Why do you tell me to carry them in my arms, as a nurse carries an infant,[z] to the land you promised on oath to their ancestors?[a] 13Where can I get meat for all these people?[b] They keep wailing to me, ‘Give us meat to eat!’ 14I cannot carry all these people by myself; the burden is too heavy for me.[c] 15If this is how you are going to treat me, please go ahead and kill me[d]—if I have found favor in your eyes—and do not let me face my own ruin.”

16The LORD said to Moses: “Bring me seventy of Israel’s elders who are known to you as leaders and officials among the people. Have them come to the tent of meeting, that they may stand there with you. 17I will come down and speak with you there, and I will take some of the power of the Spirit that is on you and put it on them.[e] They will share the burden of the people with you so that you will not have to carry it alone.[f]

18“Tell the people: ‘Consecrate yourselves[g] in preparation for tomorrow, when you will eat meat. The LORD heard you when you wailed,[h] “If only we had meat to eat! We were better off in Egypt!”[i] Now the LORD will give you meat, and you will eat it. 19You will not eat it for just one day, or two days, or five, ten or twenty days, 20but for a whole month—until it comes out of your nostrils and you loathe it[j]—because you have rejected the LORD,[k] who is among you, and have wailed before him, saying, “Why did we ever leave Egypt?” ’ ”

21But Moses said, “Here I am among six hundred thousand men[l] on foot, and you say, ‘I will give them meat to eat for a whole month!’ 22Would they have enough if flocks and herds were slaughtered for them? Would they have enough if all the fish in the sea were caught for them?”[m]

23The LORD answered Moses, “Is the LORD’s arm too short?[n] Now you will see whether or not what I say will come true for you.[o]”

24So Moses went out and told the people what the LORD had said. He brought together seventy of their elders and had them stand around the tent. 25Then the LORD came down in the cloud[p] and spoke

---

[a] 3 *Taberah* means *burning.*

11:1 *complained.* Murmuring and complaining demonstrated a lack of trust in God’s plan, provision, and judgment. Such attitudes are no more pleasing to God now than they were then, although He does not discipline complainers with fire from heaven.

11:4 *rabble.* The presence of a rabble indicates that there were people in the camp who had escaped from slavery or poverty in Egypt, but were not Israelites. They seem to have been the instigators of dissatisfaction, who made discomfort an excuse to agitate rebellion against God. God’s people have always had the responsibility to keep their ears tuned to God’s voice instead of the voices of the unbelievers around them.

11:10 *wailing.* Instead of thankfulness, the Israelites complained against what they had been given and asked for more. This is a serious sin (Ps. 78:17), and in response God chastened them. We ought to learn from the example of the Israelites in the wilderness and make thankfulness our lifestyle (Phil. 4:4).

10:34 [k] Nu 9:15-23 **10:35** [l] Ps 68:1 [m] Dt 7:10; 32:41; Ps 68:2; Isa 17:12-14 **10:36** [n] Isa 63:17 [o] Dt 1:10 **11:1** [p] Lev 10:2 **11:2** [q] Nu 21:7 **11:3** [r] Dt 9:22 **11:4** [s] Ex 12:38 [t] Ps 78:18; 1Co 10:6 **11:5** [u] Ex 16:3 **11:7** [v] Ex 16:31 [w] Ge 2:12 **11:9** [x] Ex 16:13 **11:11** [y] Ex 5:22 **11:12** [z] Isa 40:11; 49:23 [a] Ex 13:5 **11:13** [b] Jn 6:5-9 **11:14** [c] Ex 18:18 **11:15** [d] Ex 32:32; 1Ki 19:4; Jnh 4:3 **11:17** [e] ver 25, 29; 1Sa 10:6; 2Ki 2:9, 15; Joel 2:28 [f] Ex 18:18 **11:18** [g] Ex 19:10 [h] Ex 16:7 [i] ver 5; Ac 7:39 **11:20** [j] Ps 78:29; 106:14, 15 [k] Jos 24:27; 1Sa 10:19 **11:21** [l] Ex 12:37 **11:22** [m] Mt 15:33 **11:23** [n] Isa 50:2; 59:1 [o] Nu 23:19; Eze 12:25; 24:14

with him,[q] and he took some of the power of the Spirit[r] that was on him and put it on the seventy elders.[s] When the Spirit rested on them, they prophesied[t]—but did not do so again.

26 However, two men, whose names were Eldad and Medad, had remained in the camp. They were listed among the elders, but did not go out to the tent. Yet the Spirit also rested on them, and they prophesied in the camp. 27 A young man ran and told Moses, "Eldad and Medad are prophesying in the camp."

28 Joshua son of Nun, who had been Moses' aide[u] since youth, spoke up and said, "Moses, my lord, stop them!"[v]

29 But Moses replied, "Are you jealous for my sake? I wish that all the LORD's people were prophets[w] and that the LORD would put his Spirit on them!" 30 Then Moses and the elders of Israel returned to the camp.

31 Now a wind went out from the LORD and drove quail[x] in from the sea. It scattered them up to two cubits[a] deep all around the camp, as far as a day's walk in any direction. 32 All that day and night and all the next day the people went out and gathered quail. No one gathered less than ten homers.[b] Then they spread them out all around the camp. 33 But while the meat was still between their teeth[y] and before it could be consumed, the anger of the LORD burned against the people, and he struck them with a severe plague.[z] 34 Therefore the place was named Kibroth Hattaavah,[c][a] because there they buried the people who had craved other food.

35 From Kibroth Hattaavah the people traveled to Hazeroth[b] and stayed there.

Miriam and Aaron Oppose Moses

12 Miriam and Aaron began to talk against Moses because of his Cushite wife,[c] for he had married a Cushite. 2 "Has the LORD spoken only through Moses?" they asked. "Hasn't he also spoken through us?"[d] And the LORD heard this.[e]

3 (Now Moses was a very humble man,[f] more humble than anyone else on the face of the earth.)

4 At once the LORD said to Moses, Aaron and Miriam, "Come out to the tent of meeting, all three of you." So the three of them went out. 5 Then the LORD came down in a pillar of cloud;[g] he stood at the entrance to the tent and summoned Aaron and Miriam. When the two of them stepped forward, 6 he said, "Listen to my words:

"When there is a prophet among you,
I, the LORD, reveal myself to them in visions,[h]
I speak to them in dreams.[i]
7 But this is not true of my servant Moses;[j]
he is faithful in all my house.[k]
8 With him I speak face to face,
clearly and not in riddles;[l]
he sees the form of the LORD.[m]
Why then were you not afraid
to speak against my servant Moses?"

9 The anger of the LORD burned against them, and he left them.[n]

10 When the cloud lifted from above the tent, Miriam's skin was leprous[d]—it became as white as snow.[o] Aaron turned toward her and saw that she had a defiling skin disease,[p] 11 and he said to Moses, "Please, my lord, I ask you not to hold against us the sin we have so foolishly committed.[q] 12 Do not let her be like a stillborn infant coming from its mother's womb with its flesh half eaten away."

13 So Moses cried out to the LORD, "Please, God, heal her![r]"

14 The LORD replied to Moses, "If her father had spit in her face,[s] would she not have been in disgrace for seven days? Confine her outside the camp[t] for seven days; after that she can be brought back." 15 So Miriam was confined outside the camp for seven days, and the people did not move on till she was brought back.

16 After that, the people left Hazeroth[u] and encamped in the Desert of Paran.

---

[a] *31* That is, about 3 feet or about 90 centimeters
[b] *32* That is, possibly about 1 3/4 tons or about 1.6 metric tons
[c] *34 Kibroth Hattaavah* means *graves of craving.*
[d] *10* The Hebrew for *leprous* was used for various diseases affecting the skin.

11:26 *Eldad . . . Medad.* These two men prophesied, even though they had not joined the other elders at the tabernacle. They were not obedient, but neither were they presumptuous, and the Lord showed that He still wanted them as leaders.

11:34 *Kibroth Hattaavah.* The place was called "Graves of Craving," for the greedy people buried there.

11:35 *Hazeroth.* This place of rest is called "Enclosures."

12:5 *the LORD came down.* The language of this verse is more directly physical than usual. God came down, stood, and then called Aaron and Miriam forward. God's presence had been in the camp, but this was apparently distinctly more direct.

12:8 *face to face, clearly.* These verses speak of the completely intimate relationship that God had with Moses.

12:16 *the Desert of Paran.* Paran had been the destination of the people since they set out from Mount Sinai. The journey had been marred by discontent, complaining, and rebellion.

11:25 [p] Nu 12:5 [q] ver 17 [r] 1Sa 10:6 [s] Ac 2:17 [t] 1Sa 10:10 **11:28** [u] Ex 33:11; Jos 1:1 [v] Mk 9:38-40 **11:29** [w] 1Co 14:5 **11:31** [x] Ex 16:13; Ps 78:26-28 **11:33** [y] Ps 78:30 [z] Ps 106:15 **11:34** [a] Dt 9:22 **11:35** [b] Nu 33:17 **12:1** [c] Ex 2:21 **12:2** [d] Nu 16:3 [e] Nu 11:1 **12:3** [f] Mt 11:29 **12:5** [g] Nu 11:25 **12:6** [h] Ge 15:1; 46:2 [i] Ge 31:10; 1Ki 3:5; Heb 1:1 **12:7** [j] Jos 1:1-2; Ps 105:26 [k] Heb 3:2,5 **12:8** [l] Dt 34:10 [m] Ex 20:4; Ps 17:15 **12:9** [n] Ge 17:22 **12:10** [o] Ex 4:6; Dt 24:9 [p] 2Ki 5:1,27 **12:11** [q] 2Sa 19:19; 24:10 **12:13** [r] Isa 30:26; Jer 17:14 **12:14** [s] Dt 25:9; Job 17:6; 30:9-10; Isa 50:6 [t] Lev 13:46; Nu 5:2-3 **12:16** [u] Nu 11:35

Exploring Canaan

13 The LORD said to Moses, 2“Send some
men to explore[v] the land of Canaan,
which I am giving to the Israelites. From
each ancestral tribe send one of its leaders.”
3So at the LORD’s command Moses sent
them out from the Desert of Paran. All of
them were leaders of the Israelites. 4These
are their names:

from the tribe of Reuben, Shammua son of Zakkur;
5from the tribe of Simeon, Shaphat son of Hori;
6from the tribe of Judah, Caleb son of Jephunneh;[w]
7from the tribe of Issachar, Igal son of Joseph;
8from the tribe of Ephraim, Hoshea son of Nun;
9from the tribe of Benjamin, Palti son of Raphu;
10from the tribe of Zebulun, Gaddiel son of Sodi;
11from the tribe of Manasseh (a tribe of Joseph), Gaddi son of Susi;
12from the tribe of Dan, Ammiel son of Gemalli;
13from the tribe of Asher, Sethur son of Michael;
14from the tribe of Naphtali, Nahbi son of Vophsi;
15from the tribe of Gad, Geuel son of Maki.

16These are the names of the men Moses
sent to explore the land. (Moses gave Hoshea son of Nun[x] the name Joshua.)[y]
17When Moses sent them to explore Canaan, he said, “Go up through the Negev[z]
and on into the hill country.[a] 18See what
the land is like and whether the people
who live there are strong or weak, few or
many. 19What kind of land do they live in?
Is it good or bad? What kind of towns do
they live in? Are they unwalled or fortified? 20How is the soil? Is it fertile or poor?
Are there trees in it or not? Do your best to
bring back some of the fruit of the land.[b]”
(It was the season for the first ripe grapes.)
21So they went up and explored the land
from the Desert of Zin[c] as far as Rehob,[d]
toward Lebo Hamath.[e] 22They went up
through the Negev and came to Hebron,
where Ahiman, Sheshai and Talmai,[f] the
descendants of Anak,[g] lived. (Hebron had
been built seven years before Zoan in
Egypt.)[h] 23When they reached the Valley
of Eshkol,[a] they cut off a branch bearing a
single cluster of grapes. Two of them carried it on a pole between them, along with
some pomegranates and figs. 24That place
was called the Valley of Eshkol because of
the cluster of grapes the Israelites cut off
there. 25At the end of forty days they returned from exploring the land.

Report on the Exploration

26They came back to Moses and Aaron
and the whole Israelite community at Kadesh in the Desert of Paran. There they
reported to them[i] and to the whole assembly and showed them the fruit of the land.
27They gave Moses this account: “We went
into the land to which you sent us, and it
does flow with milk and honey![j] Here is its
fruit.[k] 28But the people who live there are
powerful, and the cities are fortified and
very large.[l] We even saw descendants of
Anak there. 29The Amalekites live in the
Negev; the Hittites, Jebusites and Amorites
live in the hill country; and the Canaanites
live near the sea and along the Jordan.”
30Then Caleb silenced the people before
Moses and said, “We should go up and take
possession of the land, for we can certainly do it.”
31But the men who had gone up with him
said, “We can’t attack those people; they
are stronger than we are.”[m] 32And they
spread among the Israelites a bad report[n]
about the land they had explored. They
said, “The land we explored devours[o] those
living in it. All the people we saw there are
of great size.[p] 33We saw the Nephilim[q]
there (the descendants of Anak[r] come from
the Nephilim). We seemed like grasshoppers in our own eyes, and we looked the
same to them.”

The People Rebel

14 That night all the members of the
community raised their voices and
wept aloud. 2All the Israelites grumbled
against Moses and Aaron, and the whole
assembly said to them, “If only we had died
in Egypt! Or in this wilderness![s] 3Why is

[a] *23 Eshkol* means *cluster*; also in verse 24.

13:16 ***Joshua.*** Hoshea means “salvation.” Joshua means “the Lord saves.” Moses may have changed Hoshea’s name to emphasize that it was the Lord, not any particular leader, that they were dependent on. Jesus is another form of the name Joshua.

13:27 ***flow with milk and honey.*** This phrase brought visions of pleasure and plenty to the Israelites. Canaan was a good land, a land with pasture for sheep and goats, with orchards and vineyards. The orchards and beekeeping went hand in hand, and thriving orchards meant honey. This was a land that was already developed and prospering.

14:3 ***wives and our children will be taken as plunder.*** Not only did the Israelites complain against

13:2 [v] Dt 1:22 **13:6** [w] ver 30; Nu 14:6, 24; 34:19; Jdg 1:12-15 **13:16** [x] ver 8 [y] Dt 32:44 **13:17** [z] Ge 12:9 [a] Jdg 1:9 **13:20** [b] Dt 1:25 **13:21** [c] Nu 20:1; 27:14; 33:36; Jos 15:1 [d] Jos 19:28 [e] Jos 13:5 **13:22** [f] Jos 15:14 [g] Jos 15:13 [h] Ps 78:12, 43; Isa 19:11, 13 **13:26** [i] Nu 32:8 **13:27** [j] Ex 3:8 [k] Dt 1:25 **13:28** [l] Dt 1:28; 9:1, 2 **13:31** [m] Dt 1:28; 9:1; Jos 14:8 **13:32** [n] Nu 14:36, 37 [o] Eze 36:13, 14 [p] Am 2:9 **13:33** [q] Ge 6:4 [r] Dt 1:28 **14:2** [s] Nu 11:1

the LORD bringing us to this land only to
let us fall by the sword? Our wives and children will be taken as plunder. Wouldn't it
be better for us to go back to Egypt?" 4And
they said to each other, "We should choose
a leader and go back to Egypt.[t]"
5Then Moses and Aaron fell facedown[u]
in front of the whole Israelite assembly
gathered there. 6Joshua son of Nun and
Caleb son of Jephunneh, who were among
those who had explored the land, tore their
clothes 7and said to the entire Israelite assembly, "The land we passed through and
explored is exceedingly good.[v] 8If the LORD
is pleased with us,[w] he will lead us into that
land, a land flowing with milk and honey,[x]
and will give it to us. 9Only do not rebel[y]
against the LORD. And do not be afraid of
the people of the land,[z] because we will devour them. Their protection is gone, but the
LORD is with us. Do not be afraid of them."
10But the whole assembly talked about
stoning[a] them. Then the glory of the LORD[b]
appeared at the tent of meeting to all the
Israelites. 11The LORD said to Moses, "How
long will these people treat me with contempt? How long will they refuse to believe
in me,[c] in spite of all the signs I have performed among them? 12I will strike them
down with a plague and destroy them, but
I will make you into a nation[d] greater and
stronger than they."
13Moses said to the LORD, "Then the
Egyptians will hear about it! By your power you brought these people up from among
them.[e] 14And they will tell the inhabitants
of this land about it. They have already
heard[f] that you, LORD, are with these people and that you, LORD, have been seen face
to face, that your cloud stays over them,
and that you go before them in a pillar of
cloud by day and a pillar of fire by night.[g]
15If you put all these people to death, leaving none alive, the nations who have heard
this report about you will say, 16'The LORD
was not able to bring these people into
the land he promised them on oath, so he
slaughtered them in the wilderness.'[h]
17"Now may the Lord's strength be displayed, just as you have declared: 18'The
LORD is slow to anger, abounding in love
and forgiving sin and rebellion.[i] Yet he
does not leave the guilty unpunished; he
punishes the children for the sin of the
parents to the third and fourth generation.'[j]
19In accordance with your great love, forgive[k] the sin of these people,[l] just as you
have pardoned them from the time they left
Egypt until now."[m]
20The LORD replied, "I have forgiven
them,[n] as you asked. 21Nevertheless, as
surely as I live[o] and as surely as the glory
of the LORD fills the whole earth,[p] 22not one
of those who saw my glory and the signs I
performed in Egypt and in the wilderness
but who disobeyed me and tested me ten
times[q]— 23not one of them will ever see the
land I promised on oath[r] to their ancestors.
No one who has treated me with contempt
will ever see it.[s] 24But because my servant
Caleb has a different spirit and follows me
wholeheartedly,[t] I will bring him into the
land he went to, and his descendants will
inherit it.[u] 25Since the Amalekites and the
Canaanites are living in the valleys, turn[v]
back tomorrow and set out toward the desert along the route to the Red Sea.[a]"
26The LORD said to Moses and Aaron:
27"How long will this wicked community grumble against me? I have heard the
complaints of these grumbling Israelites.[w]
28So tell them, 'As surely as I live,[x] declares
the LORD, I will do to you the very thing
I heard you say: 29In this wilderness your
bodies will fall[y]—every one of you twenty
years old or more[z] who was counted in the
census and who has grumbled against me.
30Not one of you will enter the land I swore

[a] 25 Or *the Sea of Reeds*

Moses and Aaron, they dishonored God, saying that He would heartlessly bring them to a place where they would die along with their wives and children.

14:11 ***How long.*** This chapter records perhaps the saddest and most far reaching event in the history of Israel, surpassed only by the crucifixion of their own Messiah. The miracles performed in the exodus did not convince the Israelites of God's trustworthiness, and the miracles of Christ did not convince the leaders of the day that He was the promised Messiah (Matt. 16:1–4).

14:19 ***forgive them.*** This passage records the divine testing of Moses. God was not speaking lightly when He offered to smite the Israelites and start over with another group, new descendants from Moses. But Moses needed to know his own heart about the Israelites. As frustrating as they had been, they were still a living history of the mighty hand of God, and Moses did not want the story of their rescue to end with annihilation in the wilderness. Moses' response was what God wanted to hear, and in passionately and humbly asking for their pardon, Moses had no room for bitterness toward the people who were so difficult to lead.

14:23 ***not one of them will ever see the land.*** God pardoned those who turned against Him, but there was a price to pay. They would not see the land that they had complained was impossible to possess. There is often a lifelong consequence to sin, even with forgiveness.

14:4 [t] Ne 9:17 **14:5** [u] Nu 16:4, 22, 45 **14:7** [v] Nu 13:27; Dt 1:25 **14:8** [w] Dt 10:15 [x] Nu 13:27 **14:9** [y] Dt 1:26; 9:7, 23, 24 [z] Dt 1:21; 7:18; 20:1 **14:10** [a] Ex 17:4 [b] Lev 9:23 **14:11** [c] Ps 78:22; 106:24 **14:12** [d] Ex 32:10 **14:13** [e] Ex 32:11-14; Ps 106:23 **14:14** [f] Ex 15:14 [g] Ex 13:21 **14:16** [h] Jos 7:7 **14:18** [i] Ex 34:6; Ps 145:8; Jnh 4:2 [j] Ex 20:5 **14:19** [k] Ex 34:9 [l] Ps 106:45 [m] Ps 78:38 **14:20** [n] Ps 106:23; Mic 7:18-20 **14:21** [o] Dt 32:40; Isa 49:18 [p] Ps 72:19; Isa 6:3; Hab 2:14 **14:22** [q] Ex 14:11; 32:1; 1Co 10:5 **14:23** [r] Nu 32:11 [s] Heb 3:18 **14:24** [t] ver 6-9; Jos 14:8, 14 [u] Nu 32:12 **14:25** [v] Dt 1:40 **14:27** [w] Ex 16:12 **14:28** [x] ver 21 **14:29** [y] Nu 26:65 [z] Nu 1:45

with uplifted hand to make your home, except Caleb son of Jephunneh and Joshua
son of Nun. 31 As for your children that you
said would be taken as plunder, I will bring
them in to enjoy the land you have rejected.[a] 32 But as for you, your bodies will fall[b]
in this wilderness. 33 Your children will
be shepherds here for forty years, suffering for your unfaithfulness, until the last
of your bodies lies in the wilderness. 34 For
forty years—one year for each of the forty
days you explored the land[c]—you will suffer for your sins and know what it is like to
have me against you.' 35 I, the LORD, have
spoken, and I will surely do these things[d]
to this whole wicked community, which
has banded together against me. They will
meet their end in this wilderness; here they
will die."

36 So the men Moses had sent[e] to explore the land, who returned and made the
whole community grumble against him by
spreading a bad report[f] about it— 37 these
men who were responsible for spreading
the bad report[g] about the land were struck
down and died of a plague[h] before the
LORD. 38 Of the men who went to explore
the land, only Joshua son of Nun and Caleb son of Jephunneh survived.[i]

39 When Moses reported this to all the
Israelites, they mourned[j] bitterly. 40 Early
the next morning they set out for the highest point in the hill country, saying, "Now
we are ready to go up to the land the LORD
promised. Surely we have sinned![k]"

41 But Moses said, "Why are you disobeying the LORD's command? This will not succeed![l] 42 Do not go up, because the LORD is
not with you. You will be defeated by your
enemies,[m] 43 for the Amalekites and the
Canaanites will face you there. Because
you have turned away from the LORD, he
will not be with you and you will fall by
the sword."

44 Nevertheless, in their presumption
they went up[n] toward the highest point in
the hill country, though neither Moses nor
the ark of the LORD's covenant moved from
the camp.[o] 45 Then the Amalekites and the
Canaanites who lived in that hill country
came down and attacked them and beat
them down all the way to Hormah.[p]

Supplementary Offerings

15 The LORD said to Moses, 2 "Speak to
the Israelites and say to them: 'After
you enter the land I am giving you[q] as a
home 3 and you present to the LORD food
offerings from the herd or the flock,[r] as
an aroma pleasing to the LORD[s]—whether
burnt offerings[t] or sacrifices, for special
vows or freewill offerings[u] or festival offerings[v]— 4 then the person who brings an
offering shall present to the LORD a grain
offering[w] of a tenth of an ephah[a] of the finest flour mixed with a quarter of a hin[b] of
olive oil. 5 With each lamb for the burnt offering or the sacrifice, prepare a quarter of
a hin of wine[x] as a drink offering.

6 " 'With a ram[y] prepare a grain offering[z]
of two-tenths of an ephah[c] of the finest
flour mixed with a third of a hin[d] of olive
oil,[a] 7 and a third of a hin of wine as a drink
offering. Offer it as an aroma pleasing to
the LORD.

8 " 'When you prepare a young bull as
a burnt offering or sacrifice, for a special vow or a fellowship offering[b] to the
LORD, 9 bring with the bull a grain offering
of three-tenths of an ephah[e][c] of the finest
flour mixed with half a hin[f] of olive oil,
10 and also bring half a hin of wine as a
drink offering. This will be a food offering,
an aroma pleasing to the LORD. 11 Each bull
or ram, each lamb or young goat, is to be
prepared in this manner. 12 Do this for each
one, for as many as you prepare.

13 " 'Everyone who is native-born[d] must
do these things in this way when they present a food offering as an aroma pleasing
to the LORD. 14 For the generations to come,
whenever a foreigner or anyone else living
among you presents a food offering as an
aroma pleasing to the LORD, they must do
exactly as you do. 15 The community is to
have the same rules for you and for the foreigner residing among you; this is a last-

---

[a] *4* That is, probably about 3 1/2 pounds or about 1.6 kilograms [b] *4* That is, about 1 quart or about 1 liter; also in verse 5 [c] *6* That is, probably about 7 pounds or about 3.2 kilograms [d] *6* That is, about 1 1/3 quarts or about 1.3 liters; also in verse 7 [e] *9* That is, probably about 11 pounds or about 5 kilograms [f] *9* That is, about 2 quarts or about 1.9 liters; also in verse 10

14:45 *Hormah.* The name of this place is very apt; it means "utter destruction."

15:2 *After you enter the land.* These words may seem inappropriate following God's punishment for disobedience. But His overall purpose had not changed, and the children would enter the land the parents had rejected.

15:5 *wine.* The wine was poured out on the altar in an accompaniment to the burnt offering. It was another way of giving freely back to God that which the worshipper valued. Paul refers to himself as being poured out like a drink offering (2 Tim. 4:6). There is a sense of being finished, emptied of himself, and physically spent, as he does his final work. In the same way, the wine was emptied for God; it was used up. It was not waved, nor was a portion saved for the priests.

14:31 [a] Ps 106:24 **14:32** [b] 1Co 10:5 **14:34** [c] Nu 13:25 **14:35** [d] Nu 23:19 **14:36** [e] Nu 13:4-16 [f] Nu 13:32 **14:37** [g] 1Co 10:10 [h] Nu 16:49 **14:38** [i] Jos 14:6 **14:39** [j] Ex 33:4 **14:40** [k] Dt 1:41 **14:41** [l] 2Ch 24:20 **14:42** [m] Dt 1:42 **14:44** [n] Dt 1:43 [o] Nu 31:6 **14:45** [p] Nu 21:3; Dt 1:44; Jdg 1:17 **15:2** [q] Lev 23:10 **15:3** [r] Lev 1:2 [s] ver 24; Ge 8:21; Ex 29:18 [t] Nu 28:19,27 [u] Lev 22:18,21; Ezr 1:4 [v] Lev 23:1-44 **15:4** [w] Lev 2:1; 6:14 **15:5** [x] Nu 28:7,14 **15:6** [y] Lev 5:15 [z] Nu 28:12 [a] Eze 46:14 **15:8** [b] Lev 1:3; 3:1 **15:9** [c] Lev 14:10 **15:13** [d] Lev 16:29

ing ordinance for the generations to come.[e] You and the foreigner shall be the same before the LORD: 16The same laws and regulations will apply both to you and to the foreigner residing among you.[f]'"

17The LORD said to Moses, 18"Speak to the Israelites and say to them: 'When you enter the land to which I am taking you 19and you eat the food of the land,[g] present a portion as an offering to the LORD. 20Present a loaf from the first of your ground meal[h] and present it as an offering from the threshing floor.[i] 21Throughout the generations to come you are to give this offering to the LORD from the first of your ground meal.[j]

Offerings for Unintentional Sins

22" 'Now if you as a community unintentionally fail to keep any of these commands the LORD gave Moses[k]— 23any of the LORD's commands to you through him, from the day the LORD gave them and continuing through the generations to come— 24and if this is done unintentionally without the community being aware of it,[l] then the whole community is to offer a young bull for a burnt offering[m] as an aroma pleasing to the LORD, along with its prescribed grain offering and drink offering, and a male goat for a sin offering.[a][n] 25The priest is to make atonement for the whole Israelite community, and they will be forgiven,[o] for it was not intentional and they have presented to the LORD for their wrong a food offering and a sin offering. 26The whole Israelite community and the foreigners residing among them will be forgiven, because all the people were involved in the unintentional wrong.[p]

27" 'But if just one person sins unintentionally,[q] that person must bring a year-old female goat for a sin offering. 28The priest is to make atonement before the LORD for the one who erred by sinning unintentionally, and when atonement has been made, that person will be forgiven.[r] 29One and the same law applies to everyone who sins unintentionally, whether a native-born Israelite or a foreigner residing among you.

30" 'But anyone who sins defiantly,[s] whether native-born or foreigner,[t] blasphemes the LORD and must be cut off from the people of Israel. 31Because they have despised the LORD's word and broken his commands,[u] they must surely be cut off; their guilt remains on them.[v]'"

The Sabbath-Breaker Put to Death

32While the Israelites were in the wilderness, a man was found gathering wood on the Sabbath day.[w] 33Those who found him gathering wood brought him to Moses and Aaron and the whole assembly, 34and they kept him in custody, because it was not clear what should be done to him.[x] 35Then the LORD said to Moses, "The man must die.[y] The whole assembly must stone him outside the camp.[z]" 36So the assembly took him outside the camp and stoned him to death, as the LORD commanded Moses.

Tassels on Garments

37The LORD said to Moses, 38"Speak to the Israelites and say to them: 'Throughout the generations to come you are to make tassels on the corners of your garments,[a] with a blue cord on each tassel. 39You will have these tassels to look at and so you will remember[b] all the commands of the LORD, that you may obey them and not prostitute yourselves by chasing after the lusts of your own hearts and eyes. 40Then you will remember to obey all my commands and will be consecrated to your God.[c] 41I am the LORD your God, who brought you out of Egypt to be your God. I am the LORD your God.'"

Korah, Dathan and Abiram

16 Korah[d] son of Izhar, the son of Kohath, the son of Levi, and certain Reubenites—Dathan and Abiram, sons of Eliab,[e] and On son of Peleth—became insolent[b] 2and rose up against Moses. With them were 250 Israelite men, well-known

---

a 24 Or *purification offering*; also in verses 25 and 27 *b* 1 Or *Peleth—took men*

15:19 – 21 *a portion as an offering.* By holding up the very first produce from a harvest, or the first cake made from the first grain of the season, the worshiper thanked God as the giver of all good gifts.

15:30 – 31 *defiantly.* Moses spoke of unfaithfulness when he reminded the people of their presumption at Kadesh (Deut. 1:43). Their presumption was overstepping the limits of what God allowed, and doing it defiantly. If they had trusted God, they would have been happy to do things His way. Christians need to be on guard, lest they too be guilty of presumptuous sin. Consider the words of David, "Keep your servant also from willful sins" (Ps. 19:13).

15:39 *prostitute yourselves.* Prostitution of the heart is unfaithfulness to God, in the same way that prostitution is unfaithfulness to the sanctity of marriage.

16:1 *Korah.* Korah was already set aside in a special position; he was a Levite. His sin was greater than jealousy of his cousins, the priests. He had set himself against God, and led others to do the same.

16:1 – 3 *became insolent and rose up.* Churches,

15:15 [e] ver 29; Nu 9:14 **15:16** [f] Nu 9:14 **15:19** [g] Jos 5:11, 12 **15:20** [h] Ex 34:26; Lev 23:14; Dt 26:2, 10 [i] Lev 2:14 **15:21** [j] Ro 11:16 **15:22** [k] Lev 4:2 **15:24** [l] Lev 5:15 [m] Lev 4:14 [n] Lev 4:3 **15:25** [o] Lev 4:20; Ro 3:25; Heb 2:17 **15:26** [p] ver 24 **15:27** [q] Lev 4:27 **15:28** [r] Lev 4:35 **15:30** [s] Nu 14:40-44; Dt 1:43; 17:13; Ps 19:13 [t] ver 14 **15:31** [u] 2Sa 12:9; Ps 119:126; Pr 13:13 [v] Lev 5:1; Eze 18:20 **15:32** [w] Ex 31:14, 15; 35:2, 3 **15:34** [x] Nu 9:8 **15:35** [y] Ex 31:14, 15; Dt 21:21 [z] Lev 20:2; 24:14; Ac 7:58 **15:38** [a] Dt 22:12; Mt 23:5 **15:39** [b] Dt 4:23; 6:12; Ps 73:27 **15:40** [c] Lev 11:44; Ro 12:1; Col 1:22; 1Pe 1:15 **16:1** [d] Jude 1:11 [e] Nu 26:8; Dt 11:6

community leaders who had been appointed members of the council.[f] **3**They came as a group to oppose Moses and Aaron[g] and said to them, "You have gone too far! The whole community is holy,[h] every one of them, and the LORD is with them.[i] Why then do you set yourselves above the LORD's assembly?"[j]

4When Moses heard this, he fell facedown.[k] **5**Then he said to Korah and all his followers: "In the morning the LORD will show who belongs to him and who is holy,[l] and he will have that person come near him. The man he chooses[m] he will cause to come near him. **6**You, Korah, and all your followers are to do this: Take censers **7**and tomorrow put burning coals and incense in them before the LORD. The man the LORD chooses will be the one who is holy. You Levites have gone too far!"

8Moses also said to Korah, "Now listen, you Levites! **9**Isn't it enough for you that the God of Israel has separated you from the rest of the Israelite community and brought you near himself to do the work at the LORD's tabernacle and to stand before the community and minister to them?[n] **10**He has brought you and all your fellow Levites near himself, but now you are trying to get the priesthood too.[o] **11**It is against the LORD that you and all your followers have banded together. Who is Aaron that you should grumble[p] against him?[q]"

12Then Moses summoned Dathan and Abiram, the sons of Eliab. But they said, "We will not come! **13**Isn't it enough that you have brought us up out of a land flowing with milk and honey to kill us in the wilderness?[r] And now you also want to lord it over us![s] **14**Moreover, you haven't brought us into a land flowing with milk and honey[t] or given us an inheritance of fields and vineyards.[u] Do you want to treat these men like slaves[a]?[v] No, we will not come!"

15Then Moses became very angry and said to the LORD, "Do not accept their offering. I have not taken so much as a donkey[w] from them, nor have I wronged any of them."

16Moses said to Korah, "You and all your followers are to appear before the LORD tomorrow—you and they and Aaron.[x] **17**Each man is to take his censer and put incense in it—250 censers in all—and present it before the LORD. You and Aaron are to present your censers also." **18**So each of them took his censer, put burning coals and incense in it, and stood with Moses and Aaron at the entrance to the tent of meeting. **19**When Korah had gathered all his followers in opposition to them[y] at the entrance to the tent of meeting, the glory of the LORD[z] appeared to the entire assembly. **20**The LORD said to Moses and Aaron, **21**"Separate yourselves from this assembly so I can put an end to them at once."[a]

22But Moses and Aaron fell facedown[b] and cried out, "O God, the God who gives breath to all living things,[c] will you be angry with the entire assembly when only one man sins?"[d]

23Then the LORD said to Moses, **24**"Say to the assembly, 'Move away from the tents of Korah, Dathan and Abiram.'"

25Moses got up and went to Dathan and Abiram, and the elders of Israel followed him. **26**He warned the assembly, "Move back from the tents of these wicked men![e] Do not touch anything belonging to them, or you will be swept away[f] because of all their sins." **27**So they moved away from the tents of Korah, Dathan and Abiram. Dathan and Abiram had come out and were standing with their wives, children and little ones at the entrances to their tents.

28Then Moses said, "This is how you will know that the LORD has sent me[g] to do all these things and that it was not my idea: **29**If these men die a natural death and suffer the fate of all mankind, then the LORD has not sent me.[h] **30**But if the LORD brings about something totally new, and the earth opens its mouth and swallows them, with everything that belongs to them, and they go down alive into the realm of the dead,[i] then you will know that these men have treated the LORD with contempt."

31As soon as he finished saying all this, the ground under them split apart[j] **32**and the earth opened its mouth and swallowed them[k] and their households, and all those associated with Korah, together with their possessions. **33**They went down alive into

[a] 14 Or *to deceive these men*; Hebrew *Will you gouge out the eyes of these men*

organizations, marriages, and homes can all be affected by complaining, by rebelling against those whom God has appointed to lead. Great blessing and joy and guidance come from turning such feelings over to God and obeying Him and those whom He has designated.

16:24 ***Move away.*** The Lord was giving the people a chance to show to whom they really had allegiance: God, or Korah and his followers.

16:32 ***all those associated with Korah.*** The whole families of Dathan and Abiram were swallowed up, but some of Korah's descendants did not follow him, and were not destroyed. Some of them contributed a considerable number of psalms (see Ps. 42). God is always merciful, even when dealing with the flagrant troublemakers.

16:2 [f] Nu 1:16; 26:9 **16:3** [g] ver 7; Ps 106:16 [h] Ex 19:6 [i] Nu 14:14 [j] Nu 12:2 **16:4** [k] Nu 14:5 **16:5** [l] Lev 10:3; 2Ti 2:19* [m] Nu 17:5; Ps 65:4 **16:9** [n] Nu 3:6; Dt 10:8 **16:10** [o] Nu 3:10; 18:7 **16:11** [p] 1Co 10:10 [q] Ex 16:7 **16:13** [r] Nu 14:2 [s] Ac 7:27,35 **16:14** [t] Lev 20:24 [u] Ex 22:5; 23:11; Nu 20:5 [v] Jdg 16:21; 1Sa 11:2 **16:15** [w] 1Sa 12:3 **16:16** [x] ver 6 **16:19** [y] ver 42 [z] Ex 16:7; Nu 14:10; 20:6 **16:21** [a] Ex 32:10 **16:22** [b] Nu 14:5 [c] Nu 27:16; Job 12:10; Heb 12:9 [d] Ge 18:23 **16:26** [e] Isa 52:11 [f] Ge 19:15 **16:28** [g] Ex 3:12; Jn 5:36; 6:38 **16:29** [h] Ecc 3:19 **16:30** [i] ver 33; Ps 55:15 **16:31** [j] Mic 1:3-4 **16:32** [k] Nu 26:11; Dt 11:6; Ps 106:17

the realm of the dead, with everything they owned; the earth closed over them, and they perished and were gone from the community. 34At their cries, all the Israelites around them fled, shouting, "The earth is going to swallow us too!"

35And fire came out from the LORD[l] and consumed[m] the 250 men who were offering the incense.

36The LORD said to Moses, 37"Tell Eleazar son of Aaron, the priest, to remove the censers from the charred remains and scatter the coals some distance away, for the censers are holy— 38the censers of the men who sinned at the cost of their lives.[n] Hammer the censers into sheets to overlay the altar, for they were presented before the LORD and have become holy. Let them be a sign[o] to the Israelites."

39So Eleazar the priest collected the bronze censers brought by those who had been burned to death, and he had them hammered out to overlay the altar, 40as the LORD directed him through Moses. This was to remind the Israelites that no one except a descendant of Aaron should come to burn incense[p] before the LORD,[q] or he would become like Korah and his followers.[r]

41The next day the whole Israelite community grumbled against Moses and Aaron. "You have killed the LORD's people," they said.

42But when the assembly gathered in opposition[s] to Moses and Aaron and turned toward the tent of meeting, suddenly the cloud covered it and the glory of the LORD appeared. 43Then Moses and Aaron went to the front of the tent of meeting, 44and the LORD said to Moses, 45"Get away from this assembly so I can put an end to them at once." And they fell facedown.

46Then Moses said to Aaron, "Take your censer and put incense in it, along with burning coals from the altar, and hurry to the assembly[t] to make atonement[u] for them. Wrath has come out from the LORD; the plague[v] has started." 47So Aaron did as Moses said, and ran into the midst of the assembly. The plague had already started among the people,[w] but Aaron offered the incense and made atonement for them. 48He stood between the living and the dead, and the plague stopped.[x] 49But 14,700 people died from the plague, in addition to those who had died because of Korah.[y] 50Then Aaron returned to Moses at the entrance to the tent of meeting, for the plague had stopped.[a]

The Budding of Aaron's Staff

17 [b] The LORD said to Moses, 2"Speak to the Israelites and get twelve staffs from them, one from the leader of each of their ancestral tribes. Write the name of each man on his staff. 3On the staff of Levi write Aaron's name,[z] for there must be one staff for the head of each ancestral tribe. 4Place them in the tent of meeting in front of the ark of the covenant law,[a] where I meet with you.[b] 5The staff belonging to the man I choose[c] will sprout, and I will rid myself of this constant grumbling against you by the Israelites."

6So Moses spoke to the Israelites, and their leaders gave him twelve staffs, one for the leader of each of their ancestral tribes, and Aaron's staff was among them. 7Moses placed the staffs before the LORD in the tent of the covenant law.[d]

8The next day Moses entered the tent and saw that Aaron's staff, which represented the tribe of Levi, had not only sprouted but had budded, blossomed and produced almonds.[e] 9Then Moses brought out all the staffs from the LORD's presence to all the Israelites. They looked at them, and each of the leaders took his own staff.

10The LORD said to Moses, "Put back Aaron's staff in front of the ark of the covenant law, to be kept as a sign to the rebellious.[f] This will put an end to their grumbling against me, so that they will not die." 11Moses did just as the LORD commanded him.

12The Israelites said to Moses, "We will

---

[a] *50* In Hebrew texts 16:36-50 is numbered 17:1-15.
[b] In Hebrew texts 17:1-13 is numbered 17:16-28.

16:37 *remove the censers.* Just as He spared the relatives of Korah who were not in rebellion, so, also, did He save the censers. They were holy because they had been dedicated to God, but they would not be used as incense burners again.

16:41 *grumbled against Moses and Aaron.* Incredibly, even after watching the dramatic destruction of the rebels, the congregation blamed the very leaders who had pleaded for the Lord to spare the rest of the congregation (v. 20). Obviously the people still strongly identified with Korah and his followers, and did not comprehend what they had just witnessed. Witnessing the destructiveness of sin does not always make people wake up and change their ways.

16:48 *he stood between the living and the dead.* Aaron stood between the living and the dead to stop the plague—just like the Savior, who stands in the gap between life and death.

17:12 *we will die.* The Israelites were overshadowed by despondency. Aware of God's righteous judgments against their constant grumbling, they were gripped by fear. They knew they were guilty, they knew that God would punish them, and the warm light of peace had left their lives. When this happens,

16:35 [l] Nu 11:1-3; 26:10 [m] Lev 10:2 **16:38** [n] Pr 20:2 [o] Nu 26:10; Eze 14:8; 2Pe 2:6 **16:40** [p] Ex 30:7-10; Nu 1:51 [q] 2Ch 26:18 [r] Nu 3:10 **16:42** [s] ver 19; Nu 20:6 **16:46** [t] Lev 10:6 [u] Nu 18:5; 25:13; Dt 9:22 [v] Nu 8:19; Ps 106:29 **16:47** [w] Nu 25:6-8 **16:48** [x] Nu 25:8; Ps 106:30 **16:49** [y] ver 32 **17:3** [z] Nu 1:3 **17:4** [a] ver 7 [b] Ex 25:22 **17:5** [c] Nu 16:5 **17:7** [d] Ex 38:21; Ac 7:44 **17:8** [e] Eze 17:24; Heb 9:4 **17:10** [f] Dt 9:24

die! We are lost, we are all lost![g] 13Anyone who even comes near the tabernacle of the LORD will die.[h] Are we all going to die?"

Duties of Priests and Levites

18 The LORD said to Aaron, "You, your sons and your family are to bear the responsibility for offenses connected with the sanctuary,[i] and you and your sons alone are to bear the responsibility for offenses connected with the priesthood. 2Bring your fellow Levites from your ancestral tribe to join you and assist you when you and your sons minister[j] before the tent of the covenant law. 3They are to be responsible to you and are to perform all the duties of the tent,[k] but they must not go near the furnishings of the sanctuary or the altar. Otherwise both they and you will die.[l] 4They are to join you and be responsible for the care of the tent of meeting—all the work at the tent—and no one else may come near where you are.

5"You are to be responsible for the care of the sanctuary and the altar,[m] so that my wrath will not fall on the Israelites again. 6I myself have selected your fellow Levites from among the Israelites as a gift to you,[n] dedicated to the LORD to do the work at the tent of meeting. 7But only you and your sons may serve as priests in connection with everything at the altar and inside the curtain.[o] I am giving you the service of the priesthood as a gift.[p] Anyone else who comes near the sanctuary is to be put to death.[q]"

Offerings for Priests and Levites

8Then the LORD said to Aaron, "I myself have put you in charge of the offerings presented to me; all the holy offerings the Israelites give me I give to you and your sons as your portion, your perpetual share.[r] 9You are to have the part of the most holy offerings that is kept from the fire. From all the gifts they bring me as most holy offerings, whether grain[s] or sin[a][t] or guilt offerings,[u] that part belongs to you and your sons. 10Eat it as something most holy; every male shall eat it.[v] You must regard it as holy.

11"This also is yours: whatever is set aside from the gifts of all the wave offerings[w] of the Israelites. I give this to you and your sons and daughters as your perpetual share. Everyone in your household who is ceremonially clean[x] may eat it.

12"I give you all the finest olive oil and all the finest new wine and grain they give the LORD as the firstfruits of their harvest.[y] 13All the land's firstfruits that they bring to the LORD will be yours.[z] Everyone in your household who is ceremonially clean may eat it.

14"Everything in Israel that is devoted[b] to the LORD[a] is yours. 15The first offspring of every womb, both human and animal, that is offered to the LORD is yours.[b] But you must redeem[c] every firstborn son and every firstborn male of unclean animals.[d] 16When they are a month old, you must redeem them at the redemption price set at five shekels[c][e] of silver, according to the sanctuary shekel,[f] which weighs twenty gerahs.

17"But you must not redeem the firstborn of a cow, a sheep or a goat; they are holy.[g] Splash their blood[h] against the altar and burn their fat as a food offering, an aroma pleasing to the LORD. 18Their meat is to be yours, just as the breast of the wave offering[i] and the right thigh are yours. 19Whatever is set aside from the holy offerings the Israelites present to the LORD I give to you and your sons and daughters as your perpetual share. It is an everlasting covenant of salt[j] before the LORD for both you and your offspring."

20The LORD said to Aaron, "You will have no inheritance in their land, nor will you have any share among them;[k] I am your share and your inheritance[l] among the Israelites.

21"I give to the Levites all the tithes[m] in Israel as their inheritance[n] in return for the work they do while serving at the tent of

[a] *9* Or *purification* [b] *14* The Hebrew term refers to the irrevocable giving over of things or persons to the LORD. [c] *16* That is, about 2 ounces or about 58 grams

---

let us remember that there is still one way back into the sunshine. Repentance leads to the happy experience of the remission of sins and peace with God (Luke 24:47).

17:13 *Are we all going to die?* Finally the people realized that God had revealed His will through His miraculous actions among them. They suddenly saw their presumption and God's opinion of it.

18:1 *bear responsibility for offenses connected to the sanctuary . . . priesthood.* The priests stood as intermediaries between God and man. If the people had no advocate before the Lord, they would die in their offenses. The priests had a formidable responsibility, for if they did not do their job, the whole community suffered.

18:19 *as your perpetual share.* The priests lived off the produce of the land as God provided for them through the gifts of His people. Instead of inheriting land, God was their inheritance. They would be well supplied as long as the people were faithful, and this would be a good incentive to the priests to be responsible.

17:12 [g] Isa 6:5 **17:13** [h] Nu 1:51 **18:1** [i] Ex 28:38 **18:2** [j] Nu 3:10 **18:3** [k] Nu 1:51 [l] ver 7; Nu 4:15 **18:5** [m] Nu 16:46 **18:6** [n] Nu 3:9 **18:7** [o] Heb 9:3,6 [p] ver 20; Ex 29:9 [q] Nu 3:10 **18:8** [r] Lev 6:16; 7:6,31-34,36 **18:9** [s] Lev 2:1 [t] Lev 6:25 [u] Lev 5:15; 7:7 **18:10** [v] Lev 6:16 **18:11** [w] Ex 29:26 [x] Lev 22:1-16 **18:12** [y] Ex 23:19; Ne 10:35 **18:13** [z] Ex 22:29; 23:19 **18:14** [a] Lev 27:28 **18:15** [b] Ex 13:2 [c] Nu 3:46 [d] Ex 13:13 **18:16** [e] Lev 27:6 [f] Ex 30:13 **18:17** [g] Dt 15:19 [h] Lev 3:2 **18:18** [i] Lev 7:30 **18:19** [j] Lev 2:13; 2Ch 13:5 **18:20** [k] Dt 12:12 [l] Dt 10:9; 14:27; 18:1-2; Jos 13:33; Eze 44:28 **18:21** [m] Dt 14:22; Mal 3:8 [n] Lev 27:30-33; Heb 7:5

meeting. 22From now on the Israelites must not go near the tent of meeting, or they will bear the consequences of their sin and will die.[o] 23It is the Levites who are to do the work at the tent of meeting and bear the responsibility for any offenses they commit against it. This is a lasting ordinance for the generations to come. They will receive no inheritance[p] among the Israelites. 24Instead, I give to the Levites as their inheritance the tithes that the Israelites present as an offering to the LORD. That is why I said concerning them: 'They will have no inheritance among the Israelites.' "

25The LORD said to Moses, 26"Speak to the Levites and say to them: 'When you receive from the Israelites the tithe I give you[q] as your inheritance, you must present a tenth of that tithe as the LORD's offering.[r] 27Your offering will be reckoned to you as grain from the threshing floor or juice from the winepress. 28In this way you also will present an offering to the LORD from all the tithes[s] you receive from the Israelites. From these tithes you must give the LORD's portion to Aaron the priest. 29You must present as the LORD's portion the best and holiest part of everything given to you.'

30"Say to the Levites: 'When you present the best part, it will be reckoned to you as the product of the threshing floor or the winepress.[t] 31You and your households may eat the rest of it anywhere, for it is your wages for your work at the tent of meeting. 32By presenting the best part[u] of it you will not be guilty in this matter; then you will not defile the holy offerings[v] of the Israelites, and you will not die.' "

The Water of Cleansing

19 The LORD said to Moses and Aaron: 2"This is a requirement of the law that the LORD has commanded: Tell the Israelites to bring you a red heifer[w] without defect or blemish[x] and that has never been under a yoke.[y] 3Give it to Eleazar[z] the priest; it is to be taken outside the camp[a] and slaughtered in his presence. 4Then Eleazar the priest is to take some of its blood on his finger and sprinkle[b] it seven times toward the front of the tent of meeting. 5While he watches, the heifer is to be burned—its hide, flesh, blood and intestines.[c] 6The priest is to take some cedar wood, hyssop[d] and scarlet wool[e] and throw them onto the burning heifer. 7After that, the priest must wash his clothes and bathe himself with water.[f] He may then come into the camp, but he will be ceremonially unclean till evening. 8The man who burns it must also wash his clothes and bathe with water, and he too will be unclean till evening.

9"A man who is clean shall gather up the ashes of the heifer[g] and put them in a ceremonially clean place outside the camp. They are to be kept by the Israelite community for use in the water of cleansing;[h] it is for purification from sin. 10The man who gathers up the ashes of the heifer must also wash his clothes, and he too will be unclean till evening. This will be a lasting ordinance both for the Israelites and for the foreigners residing among them.

11"Whoever touches a human corpse[i] will be unclean for seven days.[j] 12They must purify themselves with the water on the third day and on the seventh day;[k] then they will be clean. But if they do not purify themselves on the third and seventh days, they will not be clean. 13If they fail to purify themselves after touching a human corpse,[l] they defile the LORD's tabernacle.[m] They must be cut off from Israel.[n] Because the water of cleansing has not been sprinkled on them, they are unclean;[o] their uncleanness remains on them.

14"This is the law that applies when a person dies in a tent: Anyone who enters the tent and anyone who is in it will be unclean for seven days, 15and every open container without a lid fastened on it will be unclean.

16"Anyone out in the open who touches someone who has been killed with a sword or someone who has died a natural death,[p] or anyone who touches a human bone or a grave,[q] will be unclean for seven days.

17"For the unclean person, put some ashes[r] from the burned purification offering into a jar and pour fresh water over them. 18Then a man who is ceremonially clean is to take some hyssop,[s] dip it in the water and sprinkle the tent and all the furnishings and the people who were there. He must

---

19:2 *red heifer.* The animal sacrificed for making the waters of purification was different than sacrifices for sins or thanksgivings. It was a female, not a male, its color was specified, it was killed outside the camp, and cedar and hyssop, used in purification ceremonies, were added to the burning heifer.

19:9 *the water of cleansing.* It is not that this water was "magic," but it was prepared in obedience to God's commands, and was an outward symbol of the inner work that God does to remove impurity. It is important to recognize that the rituals and celebrations were designed by God to create an awareness in His people of their spiritual needs, and ultimately to prepare them for Christ. All of the washings and sacrifices were still powerless to change hearts. That is a spiritual work done by God alone.

18:22 [o] Lev 22:9; Nu 1:51 **18:23** [p] ver 20
18:26 [q] ver 21 [r] Ne 10:38 **18:28** [s] Mal 3:8
18:30 [t] ver 27 **18:32** [u] Lev 22:15 [v] Lev 19:8
19:2 [w] Ge 15:9; Heb 9:13 [x] Lev 22:19-25 [y] Dt 21:3; 1Sa 6:7
19:3 [z] Nu 3:4 [a] Lev 4:12, 21; Heb 13:11 **19:4** [b] Lev 4:17
19:5 [c] Ex 29:14 **19:6** [d] ver 18; Ps 51:7 [e] Lev 14:4
19:7 [f] Lev 11:25; 16:26, 28; 22:6 **19:9** [g] Heb 9:13 [h] ver 13; Nu 8:7 **19:11** [i] Lev 21:1; Nu 5:2 [j] Nu 31:19
19:12 [k] ver 19; Nu 31:19 **19:13** [l] Lev 20:3 [m] Lev 15:31; 2Ch 36:14 [n] Lev 7:20; 22:3 [o] Hag 2:13 **19:16** [p] Nu 31:19
[q] Mt 23:27 **19:17** [r] ver 9 **19:18** [s] ver 6

also sprinkle anyone who has touched a human bone or a grave or anyone who has been killed or anyone who has died a natural death. 19The man who is clean is to sprinkle those who are unclean on the third and seventh days, and on the seventh day he is to purify them.[t] Those who are being cleansed must wash their clothes and bathe with water, and that evening they will be clean. 20But if those who are unclean do not purify themselves, they must be cut off from the community, because they have defiled the sanctuary of the LORD. The water of cleansing has not been sprinkled on them, and they are unclean. 21This is a lasting ordinance for them.

"The man who sprinkles the water of cleansing must also wash his clothes, and anyone who touches the water of cleansing will be unclean till evening. 22Anything that an unclean[u] person touches becomes unclean, and anyone who touches it becomes unclean till evening."

Water From the Rock

20 In the first month the whole Israelite community arrived at the Desert of Zin,[v] and they stayed at Kadesh.[w] There Miriam[x] died and was buried.

2Now there was no water for the community,[y] and the people gathered in opposition[z] to Moses and Aaron. 3They quarreled[a] with Moses and said, "If only we had died when our brothers fell dead before the LORD![b] 4Why did you bring the LORD's community into this wilderness, that we and our livestock should die here?[c] 5Why did you bring us up out of Egypt to this terrible place? It has no grain or figs, grapevines or pomegranates.[d] And there is no water to drink!"

6Moses and Aaron went from the assembly to the entrance to the tent of meeting and fell facedown,[e] and the glory of the LORD[f] appeared to them. 7The LORD said to Moses, 8"Take the staff,[g] and you and your brother Aaron gather the assembly together. Speak to that rock before their eyes and it will pour out its water.[h] You will bring water out of the rock for the community so they and their livestock can drink."

9So Moses took the staff from the LORD's presence,[i] just as he commanded him. 10He and Aaron gathered the assembly together in front of the rock and Moses said to them, "Listen, you rebels, must we bring you water out of this rock?"[j] 11Then Moses raised his arm and struck the rock twice with his staff. Water[k] gushed out, and the community and their livestock drank.

12But the LORD said to Moses and Aaron, "Because you did not trust in me enough to honor me as holy[l] in the sight of the Israelites, you will not bring this community into the land I give them."[m]

13These were the waters of Meribah,[a][n] where the Israelites quarreled[o] with the LORD and where he was proved holy among them.

Edom Denies Israel Passage

14Moses sent messengers from Kadesh[p] to the king of Edom,[q] saying:

"This is what your brother Israel says: You know[r] about all the hard-

[a] *13 Meribah* means *quarreling.*

19:20 *does not purify themselves.* The issues of uncleanness were so serious that the one who applied the waters of purification became unclean also. Refusing to accept the need for cleansing was not just the act of an uncouth person who didn't care about germs. Every time someone dies, it is a reminder that death came into the world through sin (Rom. 5:12–14). The ritual for cleansing was a way of addressing the fact that it was sin that made this happen: the world is not the way God created it to be, and humans are in continual need of being reconciled to their Creator.

20:1 *in the first month.* No year is associated with this month; most likely it is the fortieth year, the end of the sojourn in the wilderness.

20:2 *no water.* Having no water was the subject of the first crisis that the Israelites had on their journey out of Egypt (Ex. 17). The same problem, forty years later, provokes the same ingratitude and anger from the people.

20:11 *struck the rock twice.* The first time God brought water from the rock, He asked Moses to strike it. This time He asked Moses to speak to it. In his anger at the Israelites' attitude, Moses spoke roughly to the Israelites and struck the rock. Even Moses could mess things up by responding in anger.

20:11,23–24 *because both of you rebelled.* Up to this point, Moses' obedience had been impeccable. It may seem that his anger was so understandable that God was overly harsh in His discipline of Moses. But Moses was the only representative of God to the people. It was only with Moses that God had spoken face to face, and Moses had a grave responsibility to only communicate what God actually said. Moses' attitude was displeasing to God, and his actions went beyond what God had directed. Anger and presumption are still two quick ways to break our fellowship with God.

20:13 *Meribah.* This is the same name that was given 40 years earlier to the location of the first water crisis (Ex. 17:7). The word means "contention."

20:14 *your brother Israel.* The Edomites were descendants of Jacob's brother Esau. Because of this relationship, Moses had a special basis of appeal, and for the same reason, the Israelites were not to fight the Edomites.

19:19 [t] Eze 36:25; Heb 10:22 **19:22** [u] Lev 5:2; Hag 2:13, 14 **20:1** [v] Nu 13:21 [w] Nu 33:36 [x] Ex 15:20 **20:2** [y] Ex 17:1 [z] Nu 16:19 **20:3** [a] Ex 17:2 [b] Nu 14:2; 16:31-35 **20:4** [c] Ex 14:11; 17:3; Nu 14:3; 16:13 **20:5** [d] Nu 16:14 **20:6** [e] Nu 14:5 [f] Nu 16:19 **20:8** [g] Ex 4:17, 20 [h] Ex 17:6; Isa 43:20 **20:9** [i] Nu 17:10 **20:10** [j] Ps 106:32, 33 **20:11** [k] Ex 17:6; Dt 8:15; Ps 78:16; Isa 48:2; 1Co 10:4 **20:12** [l] Nu 27:14 [m] ver 24; Dt 1:37; 3:27 **20:13** [n] Ex 17:7 [o] Dt 33:8; Ps 95:8; 106:32 **20:14** [p] Jdg 11:16-17 [q] Dt 2:4 [r] Jos 2:11; 9:9

ships that have come on us. 15 Our ancestors went down into Egypt,[s] and we lived there many years.[t] The Egyptians mistreated[u] us and our ancestors, 16 but when we cried out to the LORD, he heard our cry[v] and sent an angel[w] and brought us out of Egypt.

"Now we are here at Kadesh, a town on the edge of your territory. 17 Please let us pass through your country. We will not go through any field or vineyard, or drink water from any well. We will travel along the King's Highway and not turn to the right or to the left until we have passed through your territory.[x]"

18 But Edom answered:

"You may not pass through here; if you try, we will march out and attack you with the sword."

19 The Israelites replied:

"We will go along the main road, and if we or our livestock[y] drink any of your water, we will pay for it.[z] We only want to pass through on foot—nothing else."

20 Again they answered:

"You may not pass through."

Then Edom came out against them with a large and powerful army. 21 Since Edom refused to let them go through their territory, Israel turned away from them.[a]

The Death of Aaron

22 The whole Israelite community set out from Kadesh and came to Mount Hor.[b] 23 At Mount Hor, near the border of Edom,[c] the LORD said to Moses and Aaron, 24 "Aaron will be gathered to his people.[d] He will not enter the land I give the Israelites, because both of you rebelled against my command[e] at the waters of Meribah. 25 Get Aaron and his son Eleazar and take them up Mount Hor.[f] 26 Remove Aaron's garments and put them on his son Eleazar, for Aaron will be gathered to his people;[g] he will die there."

27 Moses did as the LORD commanded: They went up Mount Hor in the sight of the whole community. 28 Moses removed Aaron's garments and put them on his son Eleazar.[h] And Aaron died there[i] on top of the mountain. Then Moses and Eleazar came down from the mountain, 29 and when the whole community learned that Aaron had died, all the Israelites mourned for him[j] thirty days.

Arad Destroyed

21 When the Canaanite king of Arad,[k] who lived in the Negev,[l] heard that Israel was coming along the road to Atharim, he attacked the Israelites and captured some of them. 2 Then Israel made this vow to the LORD: "If you will deliver these people into our hands, we will totally destroy[*a*] their cities." 3 The LORD listened to Israel's plea and gave the Canaanites over to them. They completely destroyed them and their towns; so the place was named Hormah.[*b*]

The Bronze Snake

4 They traveled from Mount Hor[m] along the route to the Red Sea,[*c*] to go around Edom. But the people grew impatient on the way;[n] 5 they spoke against God[o] and against Moses, and said, "Why have you brought us up out of Egypt to die in the wilderness?[p] There is no bread! There is no water! And we detest this miserable food!"[q]

6 Then the LORD sent venomous snakes[r] among them; they bit the people and many Israelites died.[s] 7 The people came to Moses[t] and said, "We sinned when we spoke against the LORD and against you. Pray that the LORD[u] will take the snakes away from us." So Moses prayed[v] for the people.

8 The LORD said to Moses, "Make a snake and put it up on a pole;[w] anyone who is bitten can look at it and live." 9 So Moses made a bronze snake[x] and put it up on a pole. Then when anyone was bitten by a snake and looked at the bronze snake, they lived.[y]

---

a *2* The Hebrew term refers to the irrevocable giving over of things or persons to the LORD, often by totally destroying them; also in verse 3.
b *3 Hormah* means *destruction.* *c* *4* Or *the Sea of Reeds*

21:5 ***detest this miserable food.*** As the psalmist later observed, "How often they rebelled against him in the wilderness and grieved him in the wasteland!" (Ps. 78:40). In their contempt of the food, the people were actually spurning God who had given them this food. It is a sharp reminder to believers to do all things without grumbling (Phil. 2:14) so the glory of the Lord will be evident to those who are watching.

21:8 ***snake . . . anyone who is bitten can look at it and live.*** Jesus pointed to this stunning image in His dialogue with Nicodemus (John 3:14–15). Jesus was nailed to the cross, and those who look at it—who realize, "the cross is the price for *my* sins"—will receive eternal life. Each Israelite who looked at the bronze snake knew that the snake bites were the penalty for his own sinful attitudes. In both cases, only God has the cure.

20:15 [s] Ge 46:6 [t] Ge 15:13; Ex 12:40 [u] Ex 1:11; Dt 26:6
20:16 [v] Ex 2:23; 3:7 [w] Ex 14:19 **20:17** [x] Nu 21:22
20:19 [y] Ex 12:38 [z] Dt 2:6,28 **20:21** [a] Dt 2:8; Jdg 11:18
20:22 [b] Nu 33:37 **20:23** [c] Nu 33:37 **20:24** [d] Ge 25:8 [e] ver 10 **20:25** [f] Nu 33:38 **20:26** [g] ver 24
20:28 [h] Ex 29:29 [i] Nu 33:38; Dt 10:6; 32:50
20:29 [j] Dt 34:8 **21:1** [k] Nu 33:40; Jos 12:14 [l] Jdg 1:9,16
21:4 [m] Nu 20:22 [n] Dt 2:8; Jdg 11:18 **21:5** [o] Ps 78:19 [p] Nu 14:2,3 [q] Nu 11:6 **21:6** [r] Dt 8:15; Jer 8:17 [s] 1Co 10:9
21:7 [t] Ps 78:34; Hos 5:15 [u] Ex 8:8; Ac 8:24 [v] Nu 11:2
21:8 [w] Jn 3:14 **21:9** [x] 2Ki 18:4 [y] Jn 3:14-15

The Journey to Moab

10The Israelites moved on and camped
at Oboth.[z] 11Then they set out from Oboth
and camped in Iye Abarim, in the wilderness that faces Moab[a] toward the sunrise.
12From there they moved on and camped in
the Zered Valley.[b] 13They set out from there
and camped alongside the Arnon[c], which is
in the wilderness extending into Amorite
territory. The Arnon is the border of Moab,
between Moab and the Amorites. 14That is
why the Book of the Wars of the LORD says:

"... Zahab[a] in Suphah and the ravines,
the Arnon 15and[b] the slopes of the ravines
that lead to the settlement of Ar[d]
and lie along the border of Moab."

16From there they continued on to Beer,[e]
the well where the LORD said to Moses,
"Gather the people together and I will give
them water."

17Then Israel sang this song:[f]

"Spring up, O well!
Sing about it,
18 about the well that the princes dug,
that the nobles of the people sank—
the nobles with scepters and staffs."

Then they went from the wilderness to
Mattanah, 19from Mattanah to Nahaliel,
from Nahaliel to Bamoth, 20and from Bamoth to the valley in Moab where the top of
Pisgah overlooks the wasteland.

Defeat of Sihon and Og

21Israel sent messengers to say to Sihon[g]
king of the Amorites:

22"Let us pass through your country. We will not turn aside into any
field or vineyard, or drink water from
any well. We will travel along the
King's Highway until we have passed
through your territory.[h]"

23But Sihon would not let Israel pass
through his territory.[i] He mustered his
entire army and marched out into the wilderness against Israel. When he reached
Jahaz,[j] he fought with Israel. 24Israel, however, put him to the sword[k] and took over
his land from the Arnon to the Jabbok, but
only as far as the Ammonites,[l] because
their border was fortified. 25Israel captured
all the cities of the Amorites[m] and occupied them, including Heshbon and all its
surrounding settlements. 26Heshbon was
the city of Sihon[n] king of the Amorites,
who had fought against the former king of
Moab and had taken from him all his land
as far as the Arnon.

27That is why the poets say:

"Come to Heshbon and let it be rebuilt;
let Sihon's city be restored.

28 "Fire went out from Heshbon,
a blaze from the city of Sihon.[o]
It consumed Ar[p] of Moab,
the citizens of Arnon's heights.[q]
29 Woe to you, Moab![r]
You are destroyed, people of Chemosh![s]
He has given up his sons as fugitives[t]
and his daughters as captives[u]
to Sihon king of the Amorites.

30 "But we have overthrown them;
Heshbon's dominion has been destroyed all the way to Dibon.[v]
We have demolished them as far as Nophah,
which extends to Medeba."

31So Israel settled in the land of the Amorites.

32After Moses had sent spies to Jazer,[w]
the Israelites captured its surrounding settlements and drove out the Amorites who
were there. 33Then they turned and went
up along the road toward Bashan[x],[y] and
Og king of Bashan and his whole army
marched out to meet them in battle at Edrei.[z]

34The LORD said to Moses, "Do not be
afraid of him, for I have delivered him into
your hands, along with his whole army and

a 14 Septuagint; Hebrew *Waheb* *b* 14,15 Or "*I have been given from Suphah and the ravines / of the Arnon* 15*to*

21:21 *king of the Amorites.* The Amorites were one of the peoples that God had commissioned Israel to destroy (Ex. 33:2; 34:11).

21:21–24 Saying No to God—A stubborn "no" to an innocent and reasonable request can produce a counter-reaction. It is not that it is wrong to ever say "no," but the key fault on the part of the Amorites was a hard hearted refusal to consider a request that would cost them nothing to grant. With God's wisdom, we need to consider our words carefully, and "If it is possible, as far as it depends on you, live at peace with everyone" (Rom. 12:18).

21:27–32 *people of Chemosh.* This song begins with a recital of the earlier victory of the Amorites over the people of Moab and their god Chemosh. After defeating Sihon and the Amorites, Israel became a formidable threat to Moab. The Amorites were pointing out that the Moabites' god did not help them. Now that the Amorites had been defeated, it was clear that the God of Israel was greater than the gods of both the Moabites and the Amorites.

21:10 [z] Nu 33:43 **21:11** [a] Nu 33:44 **21:12** [b] Dt 2:13, 14 **21:13** [c] Nu 22:36; Jdg 11:13, 18 **21:15** [d] ver 28; Dt 2:9, 18 **21:16** [e] Jdg 9:21 **21:17** [f] Ex 15:1 **21:21** [g] Dt 1:4; 2:26-27; Jdg 11:19-21 **21:22** [h] Nu 20:17 **21:23** [i] Nu 20:21 [j] Dt 2:32; Jdg 11:20 **21:24** [k] Dt 2:33; Ps 135:10-11; Am 2:9 [l] Dt 2:37 **21:25** [m] Nu 13:29; Jdg 10:11; Am 2:10 **21:26** [n] Dt 29:7; Ps 135:11 **21:28** [o] Jer 48:45 [p] ver 15 [q] Nu 22:41; Isa 15:2 **21:29** [r] Isa 25:10; Jer 48:46 [s] Jdg 11:24; 1Ki 11:7, 33; 2Ki 23:13; Jer 48:7, 46 [t] Isa 15:5 [u] Isa 16:2 **21:30** [v] Nu 32:3; Isa 15:2; Jer 48:18, 22 **21:32** [w] Nu 32:1, 3, 35; Jer 48:32 **21:33** [x] Dt 3:3 [y] Dt 3:4 [z] Dt 1:4; 3:1, 10; Jos 13:12, 31

his land. Do to him what you did to Sihon
king of the Amorites, who reigned in Heshbon.[a]"
35 So they struck him down, together
with his sons and his whole army, leaving
them no survivors. And they took possession of his land.

Balak Summons Balaam

22 Then the Israelites traveled to the
plains of Moab and camped along
the Jordan across from Jericho.[b]
2 Now Balak son of Zippor[c] saw all that
Israel had done to the Amorites, 3 and
Moab was terrified because there were so
many people. Indeed, Moab was filled with
dread[d] because of the Israelites.
4 The Moabites said to the elders of Midian, "This horde is going to lick up everything around us, as an ox licks up the grass
of the field."

So Balak son of Zippor, who was king
of Moab at that time, 5 sent messengers to
summon Balaam son of Beor,[e] who was at
Pethor, near the Euphrates River, in his native land. Balak said:

> "A people has come out of Egypt;
> they cover the face of the land and
> have settled next to me. 6 Now come
> and put a curse[f] on these people, be-
> cause they are too powerful for me.
> Perhaps then I will be able to defeat
> them and drive them out of the land.
> For I know that whoever you bless
> is blessed, and whoever you curse is
> cursed."

7 The elders of Moab and Midian left, taking with them the fee for divination.[g] When
they came to Balaam, they told him what
Balak had said.
8 "Spend the night here," Balaam said to
them, "and I will report back to you with
the answer the LORD gives me.[h]" So the Moabite officials stayed with him.
9 God came to Balaam[i] and asked,[j] "Who
are these men with you?"
10 Balaam said to God, "Balak son of Zippor, king of Moab, sent me this message:
11 'A people that has come out of Egypt
covers the face of the land. Now come and
put a curse on them for me. Perhaps then
I will be able to fight them and drive them
away.'"
12 But God said to Balaam, "Do not go
with them. You must not put a curse on
those people, because they are blessed.[k]"
13 The next morning Balaam got up and
said to Balak's officials, "Go back to your
own country, for the LORD has refused to let
me go with you."
14 So the Moabite officials returned to
Balak and said, "Balaam refused to come
with us."
15 Then Balak sent other officials, more
numerous and more distinguished than the
first. 16 They came to Balaam and said:

> "This is what Balak son of Zippor
> says: Do not let anything keep you
> from coming to me, 17 because I will
> reward you handsomely[l] and do what-
> ever you say. Come and put a curse[m]
> on these people for me."

18 But Balaam answered them, "Even if
Balak gave me all the silver and gold in
his palace, I could not do anything great
or small to go beyond the command of the
LORD my God.[n] 19 Now spend the night here
so that I can find out what else the LORD
will tell me.[o]"
20 That night God came to Balaam[p] and
said, "Since these men have come to summon you, go with them, but do only what
I tell you."[q]

Balaam's Donkey

21 Balaam got up in the morning, saddled
his donkey and went with the Moabite officials. 22 But God was very angry[r] when he
went, and the angel of the LORD[s] stood in
the road to oppose him. Balaam was riding
on his donkey, and his two servants were
with him. 23 When the donkey saw the angel of the LORD standing in the road with a
drawn sword[t] in his hand, it turned off the
road into a field. Balaam beat it[u] to get it
back on the road.

22:5 *Balaam.* Balak hired Balaam to destroy Israel by spiritual means. He thought that Balaam could cause Israel's "gods" to stop protecting them.
22:6 *whoever you curse is cursed.* The reality is that God's blessing on Israel could not be tampered with. It is important to remember that the Creator God is the source of all blessing and that no evil can stand against God's blessing and protection.
22:8 *the LORD gives me.* Balaam speaks of the Lord as if he were intimate with Him. No doubt he had heard of the Lord, and no doubt the Lord did give him the words to say when Balaam looked at the Israelites. But Balaam did not give the Lord God any greater place in his own life than he gave to pagan gods, as is evidenced by his subsequent actions.
22:18 *the LORD my God.* This is not a confession of faith on Balaam's part, but a bold and false claim to be a medium of Israel's "god." Balaam was motivated by greed, not by a desire to please the Lord (2 Pet. 2:15; Jude 11).
22:22 *God was very angry when he went.* God had given Balaam permission to go, after he asked the second time, and yet God was angry. This is a little puzzling, but if we remember that God is not

21:34 [a] Dt 3:2 **22:1** [b] Nu 33:48 **22:2** [c] Jdg 11:25 **22:3** [d] Ex 15:15 **22:5** [e] Dt 23:4; Jos 13:22; 24:9; Ne 13:2; Mic 6:5; 2Pe 2:15 **22:6** [f] ver 12, 17; Nu 23:7, 11, 13 **22:7** [g] Nu 23:23; 24:1 **22:8** [h] ver 19 **22:9** [i] Ge 20:3 [j] ver 20 **22:12** [k] Ge 12:2; 22:17; Nu 23:20 **22:17** [l] ver 37; Nu 24:11 [m] ver 6 **22:18** [n] ver 38; Nu 23:12, 26; 24:13; 1Ki 22:14; 2Ch 18:13; Jer 42:4 **22:19** [o] ver 8 **22:20** [p] Ge 20:3 [q] ver 35, 38; Nu 23:5, 12, 16, 26; 24:13; 2Ch 18:13 **22:22** [r] Ex 4:14 [s] Ge 16:7; Ex 23:20; Jdg 13:3, 6, 13 **22:23** [t] Jos 5:13 [u] ver 25, 27

24 Then the angel of the LORD stood in a narrow path through the vineyards, with walls on both sides. 25 When the donkey saw the angel of the LORD, it pressed close to the wall, crushing Balaam's foot against it. So he beat the donkey again.

26 Then the angel of the LORD moved on ahead and stood in a narrow place where there was no room to turn, either to the right or to the left. 27 When the donkey saw the angel of the LORD, it lay down under Balaam, and he was angry[v] and beat it with his staff. 28 Then the LORD opened the donkey's mouth,[w] and it said to Balaam, "What have I done to you to make you beat me these three times?[x]"

29 Balaam answered the donkey, "You have made a fool of me! If only I had a sword in my hand, I would kill you right now.[y]"

30 The donkey said to Balaam, "Am I not your own donkey, which you have always ridden, to this day? Have I been in the habit of doing this to you?"

"No," he said.

31 Then the LORD opened Balaam's eyes,[z] and he saw the angel of the LORD standing in the road with his sword drawn. So he bowed low and fell facedown.

32 The angel of the LORD asked him, "Why have you beaten your donkey these three times? I have come here to oppose you because your path is a reckless one before me.[*a*] 33 The donkey saw me and turned away from me these three times. If it had not turned away, I would certainly have killed you by now,[a] but I would have spared it."

34 Balaam said to the angel of the LORD, "I have sinned.[b] I did not realize you were standing in the road to oppose me. Now if you are displeased, I will go back."

35 The angel of the LORD said to Balaam, "Go with the men, but speak only what I tell you." So Balaam went with Balak's officials.

36 When Balak heard that Balaam was coming, he went out to meet him at the Moabite town on the Arnon[c] border, at the edge of his territory. 37 Balak said to Balaam, "Did I not send you an urgent summons? Why didn't you come to me? Am I really not able to reward you?"

38 "Well, I have come to you now," Balaam replied. "But I can't say whatever I please. I must speak only what God puts in my mouth."[d]

39 Then Balaam went with Balak to Kiriath Huzoth. 40 Balak sacrificed cattle and sheep,[e] and gave some to Balaam and the officials who were with him. 41 The next morning Balak took Balaam up to Bamoth Baal,[f] and from there he could see the outskirts of the Israelite camp.[g]

Balaam's First Message

23 Balaam said, "Build me seven altars here, and prepare seven bulls and seven rams[h] for me." 2 Balak did as Balaam said, and the two of them offered a bull and a ram on each altar.[i]

3 Then Balaam said to Balak, "Stay here beside your offering while I go aside. Perhaps the LORD will come to meet with me.[j] Whatever he reveals to me I will tell you." Then he went off to a barren height.

4 God met with him,[k] and Balaam said, "I have prepared seven altars, and on each altar I have offered a bull and a ram."

5 The LORD put a word in Balaam's mouth[l] and said, "Go back to Balak and give him this word."[m]

6 So he went back to him and found him standing beside his offering, with all the Moabite officials.[n] 7 Then Balaam[o] spoke his message:[p]

"Balak brought me from Aram,
the king of Moab from the eastern mountains.
'Come,' he said, 'curse Jacob for me;
come, denounce Israel.'[q]
8 How can I curse
those whom God has not cursed?[r]

a 32 The meaning of the Hebrew for this clause is uncertain.

---

whimsical, it makes sense. God had already told Balaam "no," and when Balak's leaders came to him again, Balaam came to God again, saying in essence, "but now there is a lot of money and power available, so let me run this by you again...." He was treating the Lord as if He were any little demon god, who is appealed to by money and divination rituals. Balaam did not comprehend that he was dealing with the real powerful, awesome, and almighty God, until he encountered the angel with his drawn sword. God had a plan, and He was going to use Balaam to sabotage Balak's plans in a way that would definitely communicate to Balak exactly who the Israelites' God was, and what His plan was for His people. But Balaam needed to understand that it was the Lord who was in charge, not Balaam and his divination methods.

23:5 *the LORD put a word in Balaam's mouth.* Even though Balaam was not a true servant of God, the words that Balaam spoke were truly God's blessing.

23:7–10 *spoke his message.* The words that Balaam spoke, however unwillingly, certainly affirmed God's providence for the nation Israel. It is curious how the Lord used a mercenary and devious diviner to clearly speak the blessing on Israel, but that too was a part of God's providence. Balaam was claiming to speak for the Lord; the Lord would make sure that Balaam indeed spoke for Him.

22:27 [v] Nu 11:1; Jas 1:19 **22:28** [w] 2Pe 2:16 [x] ver 32 **22:29** [y] Dt 25:4; Pr 12:10; 27:23-27; Mt 15:19 **22:31** [z] Ge 21:19 **22:33** [a] ver 29 **22:34** [b] Ge 39:9; Nu 14:40; 1Sa 15:24, 30; 2Sa 12:13; 24:10; Job 33:27; Ps 51:4 **22:36** [c] Nu 21:13 **22:38** [d] Nu 23:5, 16, 26 **22:40** [e] Nu 23:1, 14, 29; Eze 45:23 **22:41** [f] Nu 21:28 [g] Nu 23:13 **23:1** [h] Nu 22:40 **23:2** [i] ver 14, 30 **23:3** [j] ver 15 **23:4** [k] ver 16 **23:5** [l] Dt 18:18; Jer 1:9 [m] Nu 22:20 **23:6** [n] ver 17 **23:7** [o] Nu 22:5 [p] ver 18; Nu 24:3, 21 [q] Nu 22:6; Dt 23:4 **23:8** [r] Nu 22:12

How can I denounce
those whom the LORD has not
denounced?
9 From the rocky peaks I see them,
from the heights I view them.
I see a people who live apart
and do not consider themselves one
of the nations.[s]
10 Who can count the dust of Jacob[t]
or number even a fourth of Israel?
Let me die the death of the righteous,[u]
and may my final end be like theirs![v]"

11 Balak said to Balaam, "What have you
done to me? I brought you to curse my enemies, but you have done nothing but bless
them!"[w]
12 He answered, "Must I not speak what
the LORD puts in my mouth?"[x]

Balaam's Second Message

13 Then Balak said to him, "Come with
me to another place where you can see
them; you will not see them all but only the
outskirts of their camp. And from there,
curse them for me." 14 So he took him to the
field of Zophim on the top of Pisgah, and
there he built seven altars and offered a
bull and a ram on each altar.[y]
15 Balaam said to Balak, "Stay here beside your offering while I meet with him
over there."
16 The LORD met with Balaam and put a
word in his mouth[z] and said, "Go back to
Balak and give him this word."
17 So he went to him and found him
standing beside his offering, with the Moabite officials. Balak asked him, "What did
the LORD say?"
18 Then he spoke his message:

"Arise, Balak, and listen;
hear me, son of Zippor.
19 God is not human,[a] that he should lie,
not a human being, that he should
change his mind.[b]
Does he speak and then not act?
Does he promise and not fulfill?
20 I have received a command to bless;
he has blessed,[c] and I cannot change it.[d]

21 "No misfortune is seen in Jacob,[e]
no misery observed[a] in Israel.[f]
The LORD their God is with them;[g]
the shout of the King[h] is among
them.
22 God brought them out of Egypt;[i]
they have the strength of a wild ox.[j]
23 There is no divination against[b] Jacob,
no evil omens[k] against[b] Israel.
It will now be said of Jacob
and of Israel, 'See what God has
done!'
24 The people rise like a lioness;[l]
they rouse themselves like a lion[m]
that does not rest till it devours its prey
and drinks the blood of its victims."

25 Then Balak said to Balaam, "Neither
curse them at all nor bless them at all!"
26 Balaam answered, "Did I not tell you I
must do whatever the LORD says?"

Balaam's Third Message

27 Then Balak said to Balaam, "Come, let
me take you to another place.[n] Perhaps it
will please God to let you curse them for
me from there." 28 And Balak took Balaam
to the top of Peor,[o] overlooking the wasteland.
29 Balaam said, "Build me seven altars
here, and prepare seven bulls and seven
rams for me." 30 Balak did as Balaam had
said, and offered a bull and a ram on each
altar.

24 Now when Balaam saw that it pleased
the LORD to bless Israel, he did not
resort to divination[p] as at other times, but
turned his face toward the wilderness.[q]
2 When Balaam looked out and saw Israel
encamped tribe by tribe, the Spirit of God
came on him[r] 3 and he spoke his message:

"The prophecy of Balaam son of Beor,
the prophecy of one whose eye sees
clearly,
4 the prophecy of one who hears the
words of God,[s]
who sees a vision from the
Almighty,[c][t]
who falls prostrate, and whose eyes
are opened:

5 "How beautiful are your tents, Jacob,
your dwelling places, Israel!

6 "Like valleys they spread out,
like gardens beside a river,
like aloes[u] planted by the LORD,
like cedars beside the waters.[v]
7 Water will flow from their buckets;
their seed will have abundant water.

"Their king will be greater than Agag;[w]
their kingdom will be exalted.[x]

8 "God brought them out of Egypt;
they have the strength of a wild ox.

---

[a] *21* Or *He has not looked on Jacob's offenses / or on the wrongs found* [b] *23* Or *in* [c] *4* Hebrew *Shaddai*; also in verse 16

23:9 [s] Ex 33:16; Dt 32:8; 33:28 **23:10** [t] Ge 13:16 [u] Ps 116:15; Isa 57:1 [v] Ps 37:37 **23:11** [w] Nu 24:10; Ne 13:2 **23:12** [x] Nu 22:20, 38 **23:14** [y] ver 2 **23:16** [z] Nu 22:38 **23:19** [a] Isa 55:9; Hos 11:9 [b] 1Sa 15:29; Mal 3:6; Titus 1:2; Jas 1:17 **23:20** [c] Ge 22:17; Nu 22:12 [d] Isa 43:13 **23:21** [e] Ps 32:2, 5; Ro 4:7-8 [f] Isa 40:2; Jer 50:20 [g] Ex 29:45, 46; Ps 145:18 [h] Dt 33:5; Ps 89:15-18

23:22 [i] Nu 24:8 [j] Dt 33:17; Job 39:9 **23:23** [k] Nu 24:1; Jos 13:22 **23:24** [l] Na 2:11 [m] Ge 49:9 **23:27** [n] ver 13 **23:28** [o] Ps 106:28 **24:1** [p] Nu 23:23 [q] Nu 23:28 **24:2** [r] Nu 11:25, 26; 1Sa 10:10; 19:20; 2Ch 15:1 **24:4** [s] Nu 22:20 [t] Ge 15:1 **24:6** [u] Ps 45:8 [v] Ps 1:3; 104:16 **24:7** [w] 2Sa 15:8 [x] 2Sa 5:12; 1Ch 14:2; Ps 145:11-13

They devour hostile nations
and break their bones in pieces;[y]
with their arrows they pierce them.[z]
9 Like a lion they crouch and lie down,
like a lioness[a]—who dares to rouse
them?

"May those who bless you be blessed
and those who curse you be cursed!"[b]

10 Then Balak's anger burned against
Balaam. He struck his hands together[c] and
said to him, "I summoned you to curse my
enemies, but you have blessed them[d] these
three times.[e] 11 Now leave at once and go
home! I said I would reward you hand-
somely,[f] but the LORD has kept you from
being rewarded."
12 Balaam answered Balak, "Did I not tell
the messengers you sent me,[g] 13 'Even if Balak gave me all the silver and gold in his
palace, I could not do anything of my own
accord, good or bad, to go beyond the command of the LORD[h]—and I must say only
what the LORD says'?[i] 14 Now I am going
back to my people, but come, let me warn
you of what this people will do to your people in days to come."[j]

Balaam's Fourth Message

15 Then he spoke his message:

"The prophecy of Balaam son of Beor,
the prophecy of one whose eye sees
clearly,
16 the prophecy of one who hears the
words of God,
who has knowledge from the Most
High,
who sees a vision from the Almighty,
who falls prostrate, and whose eyes
are opened:

17 "I see him, but not now;
I behold him, but not near.[k]
A star will come out of Jacob;[l]
a scepter will rise out of Israel.[m]
He will crush the foreheads of Moab,[n]
the skulls[a] of[b] all the people of Sheth.[c]
18 Edom[o] will be conquered;
Seir, his enemy, will be conquered,
but Israel will grow strong.
19 A ruler will come out of Jacob[p]
and destroy the survivors of the city."

Balaam's Fifth Message

20 Then Balaam saw Amalek[q] and spoke
his message:

"Amalek was first among the nations,
but their end will be utter destruction."

Balaam's Sixth Message

21 Then he saw the Kenites[r] and spoke his
message:

"Your dwelling place is secure,
your nest is set in a rock;
22 yet you Kenites will be destroyed
when Ashur[s] takes you captive."

Balaam's Seventh Message

23 Then he spoke his message:

"Alas! Who can live when God does
this?[d]
24 Ships will come from the shores of
Cyprus;[t]
they will subdue Ashur and Eber,[u]
but they too will come to ruin.[v]"

25 Then Balaam[w] got up and returned
home, and Balak went his own way.

Moab Seduces Israel

25 While Israel was staying in Shittim,[x]
the men began to indulge in sexual
immorality[y] with Moabite women,[z] 2 who

[a] *17* Samaritan Pentateuch (see also Jer. 48:45); the meaning of the word in the Masoretic Text is uncertain. [b] *17* Or possibly *Moab, / batter* [c] *17* Or *all the noisy boasters* [d] *23* Masoretic Text; with a different word division of the Hebrew *The people from the islands will gather from the north.*

24:17–19 *I see him, but not now; . . . a star will come out of Jacob.* This poetic language clearly refers to the Messiah. The pagan Balaam had a vision of the coming of the Hebrew Messiah, the Lord Jesus Christ. He was visible from afar, He was like a star, radiant and beautiful. And He is the victor over His enemies, including Moab—the nation that hired Balaam to curse Israel.

24:19 *ruler.* At this point Balaam should have repented of his involvement with Balak. It was clear that the Lord God was in control, not Balaam, and that the Lord's curses were not for hire. This should be a great encouragement to believers in our day, because we can trust in a God who has promised to bless those who trust in Him. Our God will not change His mind and forget those who have put their faith in Him.

24:22 *when Ashur takes you captive.* Ashur is Assyria. This nation did take the rebellious Northern Kingdom of Israel captive in 772 B.C.

25:1–3 *indulge in sexual immorality.* Right on the edge of the promised land the Israelites had shown unfaithfulness to God again. It was not just that they had illicit sex with women outside their nation. They had participated in the licentious worship of the Baal of Peor. Worshipping idols on the side is not just a little slip, like eating between meals. They had enough information to know how seriously offended God would be, and they just did not care. Such behavior is always likened to adultery, and this was something that God rebuked His people for repeatedly (Is. 1:21; Jer. 3:1; Ezek. 16; Hos. 2:5).

25:1 *Moabite women.* What the men of Moab could not do, the women were able to accomplish.

24:8 [y] Ps 2:9; Jer 50:17 [z] Ps 45:5 **24:9** [a] Ge 49:9; Nu 23:24 [b] Ge 12:3 **24:10** [c] Eze 21:14 [d] Nu 23:11 [e] Ne 13:2 **24:11** [f] Nu 22:17 **24:12** [g] Nu 22:18 **24:13** [h] Nu 22:18 [i] Nu 22:20 **24:14** [j] Ge 49:1; Nu 31:8, 16; Da 2:28; Mic 6:5 **24:17** [k] Rev 1:7 [l] Mt 2:2 [m] Ge 49:10 [n] Nu 21:29; Isa 15:1-16:14 **24:18** [o] Am 9:12 **24:19** [p] Ge 49:10; Mic 5:2 **24:20** [q] Ex 17:14 **24:21** [r] Ge 15:19 **24:22** [s] Ge 10:22 **24:24** [t] Ge 10:4 [u] Ge 10:21 [v] ver 20 **24:25** [w] Nu 31:8 **25:1** [x] Jos 2:1; Mic 6:5 [y] 1Co 10:8; Rev 2:14 [z] Nu 31:16

invited them to the sacrifices[a] to their
gods.[b] The people ate the sacrificial meal
and bowed down before these gods. 3So Israel yoked themselves to the Baal of Peor.[c]
And the LORD's anger burned against them.
4The LORD said to Moses, "Take all the
leaders of these people, kill them and expose them in broad daylight before the
LORD,[d] so that the LORD's fierce anger[e] may
turn away from Israel."
5So Moses said to Israel's judges, "Each
of you must put to death[f] those of your people who have yoked themselves to the Baal
of Peor."
6Then an Israelite man brought into the
camp a Midianite woman right before the
eyes of Moses and the whole assembly of
Israel while they were weeping at the entrance to the tent of meeting. 7When Phinehas son of Eleazar, the son of Aaron, the
priest, saw this, he left the assembly, took
a spear in his hand 8and followed the Israelite into the tent. He drove the spear
into both of them, right through the Israelite man and into the woman's stomach.
Then the plague against the Israelites
was stopped;[g] 9but those who died in the
plague[h] numbered 24,000.[i]
10The LORD said to Moses, 11"Phinehas
son of Eleazar, the son of Aaron, the priest,
has turned my anger away from the Israelites.[j] Since he was as zealous for my honor[k]
among them as I am, I did not put an end to
them in my zeal. 12Therefore tell him I am
making my covenant of peace[l] with him.
13He and his descendants will have a covenant of a lasting priesthood,[m] because he
was zealous for the honor of his God and
made atonement[n] for the Israelites."
14The name of the Israelite who was
killed with the Midianite woman was Zimri son of Salu, the leader of a Simeonite
family. 15And the name of the Midianite
woman who was put to death was Kozbi[o]
daughter of Zur, a tribal chief of a Midianite family.[p]
16The LORD said to Moses, 17"Treat the
Midianites[q] as enemies and kill them.
18They treated you as enemies when they
deceived you in the Peor incident[r] involving their sister Kozbi, the daughter of a
Midianite leader, the woman who was
killed when the plague came as a result of
that incident."

The Second Census

26 After the plague the LORD said to
Moses and Eleazar son of Aaron, the
priest, 2"Take a census[s] of the whole Israelite community by families—all those twenty years old or more who are able to serve
in the army[t] of Israel." 3So on the plains of
Moab[u] by the Jordan across from Jericho,[v]
Moses and Eleazar the priest spoke with
them and said, 4"Take a census of the men
twenty years old or more, as the LORD commanded Moses."

These were the Israelites who came out of Egypt:

5The descendants of Reuben, the firstborn
son of Israel, were:
through Hanok,[w] the Hanokite clan;
through Pallu,[x] the Palluite clan;
6through Hezron, the Hezronite clan;
through Karmi, the Karmite clan.
7These were the clans of Reuben; those
numbered were 43,730.
8The son of Pallu was Eliab, 9and the
sons of Eliab[y] were Nemuel, Dathan and
Abiram. The same Dathan and Abiram
were the community[z] officials who rebelled
against Moses and Aaron and were among
Korah's followers when they rebelled
against the LORD.[a] 10The earth opened its
mouth and swallowed them along with
Korah, whose followers died when the fire
devoured the 250 men. And they served as
a warning sign.[b] 11The line of Korah,[c] however, did not die out.[d]

12The descendants of Simeon by their clans
were:
through Nemuel, the Nemuelite clan;
through Jamin,[e] the Jaminite clan;
through Jakin, the Jakinite clan;
13through Zerah,[f] the Zerahite clan;
through Shaul, the Shaulite clan.

They trapped the Israelite men in sexual immorality and false worship. The principle instigator of this sorry affair was none other than Balaam (31:16). Perhaps the most sobering aspect is the fact that the Moabites were descendants of Lot, through his daughter's incestuous relationship with her father, after their long sojourn in Sodom (Gen. 19). Sexual perversion had a long history in this group.

25:4 – 5 *the LORD's fierce anger.* This was the most serious challenge to God's authority yet. The people had been seduced into joining the worship of Baal. And it was Baal worship that they had been sent to Canaan to eliminate.

25:7 *Phinehas son of Eleazar.* For this decisive and courageous act, Phineas is praised, not only in this book, but in Psalm 106:30 – 31. In the psalm, it says that this act was "credited to him as righteousness."

26:2 *Take a census of the whole Israelite community.* The plague is over, the old generation has all died. This is a new beginning and a new census. Despite all the people who had died in the wilderness, the total population was not significantly different than the first census.

25:2 [a] Ex 34:15 [b] Ex 20:5; Dt 32:38; 1Co 10:20 **25:3** [c] Ps 106:28; Hos 9:10 **25:4** [d] Dt 4:3 [e] Dt 13:17 **25:5** [f] Ex 32:27 **25:8** [g] Nu 16:46-48; Ps 106:30 **25:9** [h] Nu 14:37; 1Co 10:8 [i] Nu 31:16 **25:11** [j] Ps 106:30 [k] Ex 20:5; Dt 32:16, 21; Ps 78:58 **25:12** [l] Isa 54:10; Eze 34:25; Mal 2:4, 5 **25:13** [m] Ex 29:9 [n] Nu 16:46 **25:15** [o] ver 18 [p] Nu 31:8; Jos 13:21 **25:17** [q] Nu 31:1-3 **25:18** [r] Nu 31:16 **26:2** [s] Ex 30:11-16; 38:25-26; Nu 1:2 [t] Nu 1:3 **26:3** [u] Nu 33:48 [v] Nu 22:1 **26:5** [w] Ge 46:9 [x] 1Ch 5:3 **26:9** [y] Nu 16:1 [z] Nu 1:16 [a] Nu 16:2 **26:10** [b] Nu 16:35, 38 **26:11** [c] Ex 6:24 [d] Nu 16:33; Dt 24:16 **26:12** [e] 1Ch 4:24 **26:13** [f] Ge 46:10

14These were the clans of Simeon; those numbered were 22,200.[g]

15The descendants of Gad by their clans were:
through Zephon,[h] the Zephonite clan;
through Haggi, the Haggite clan;
through Shuni, the Shunite clan;
16through Ozni, the Oznite clan;
through Eri, the Erite clan;
17through Arodi,[a] the Arodite clan;
through Areli, the Arelite clan.
18These were the clans of Gad;[i] those numbered were 40,500.

19Er and Onan were sons of Judah, but they died[j] in Canaan.
20The descendants of Judah by their clans were:
through Shelah,[k] the Shelanite clan;
through Perez, the Perezite clan;
through Zerah, the Zerahite clan.[l]
21The descendants of Perez were:
through Hezron,[m] the Hezronite clan;
through Hamul, the Hamulite clan.
22These were the clans of Judah;[n] those numbered were 76,500.

23The descendants of Issachar by their clans were:
through Tola,[o] the Tolaite clan;
through Puah, the Puite[b] clan;
24through Jashub,[p] the Jashubite clan;
through Shimron, the Shimronite clan.
25These were the clans of Issachar;[q] those numbered were 64,300.

26The descendants of Zebulun by their clans were:
through Sered, the Seredite clan;
through Elon, the Elonite clan;
through Jahleel, the Jahleelite clan.
27These were the clans of Zebulun;[r] those numbered were 60,500.

28The descendants of Joseph by their clans through Manasseh and Ephraim were:

29The descendants of Manasseh:
through Makir,[s] the Makirite clan (Makir was the father of Gilead[t]);
through Gilead, the Gileadite clan.
30These were the descendants of Gilead:
through Iezer,[u] the Iezerite clan;
through Helek, the Helekite clan;
31through Asriel, the Asrielite clan;
through Shechem, the Shechemite clan;
32through Shemida, the Shemidaite clan;
through Hepher, the Hepherite clan.
33(Zelophehad[v] son of Hepher had no sons; he had only daughters, whose names were Mahlah, Noah, Hoglah, Milkah and Tirzah.)[w]
34These were the clans of Manasseh; those numbered were 52,700.[x]

35These were the descendants of Ephraim by their clans:
through Shuthelah, the Shuthelahite clan;
through Beker, the Bekerite clan;
through Tahan, the Tahanite clan.
36These were the descendants of Shuthelah:
through Eran, the Eranite clan.
37These were the clans of Ephraim;[y] those numbered were 32,500.

These were the descendants of Joseph by their clans.

38The descendants of Benjamin[z] by their clans were:
through Bela, the Belaite clan;
through Ashbel, the Ashbelite clan;
through Ahiram, the Ahiramite clan;
39through Shupham,[c] the Shuphamite clan;
through Hupham, the Huphamite clan.
40The descendants of Bela through Ard[a] and Naaman were:
through Ard,[d] the Ardite clan;
through Naaman, the Naamite clan.
41These were the clans of Benjamin;[b] those numbered were 45,600.

42These were the descendants of Dan by their clans:
through Shuham,[c] the Shuhamite clan.
These were the clans of Dan: 43All of them were Shuhamite clans; and those numbered were 64,400.

44The descendants of Asher by their clans were:
through Imnah, the Imnite clan;
through Ishvi, the Ishvite clan;
through Beriah, the Beriite clan;
45and through the descendants of Beriah:
through Heber, the Heberite clan;
through Malkiel, the Malkielite clan.

---

[a] *17* Samaritan Pentateuch and Syriac (see also Gen. 46:16); Masoretic Text *Arod* [b] *23* Samaritan Pentateuch, Septuagint, Vulgate and Syriac (see also 1 Chron. 7:1); Masoretic Text *through Puvah, the Punite* [c] *39* A few manuscripts of the Masoretic Text, Samaritan Pentateuch, Vulgate and Syriac (see also Septuagint); most manuscripts of the Masoretic Text *Shephupham*
[d] *40* Samaritan Pentateuch and Vulgate (see also Septuagint); Masoretic Text does not have *through Ard.*

26:14 [g] Nu 1:23 **26:15** [h] Ge 46:16 **26:18** [i] Nu 1:25; Jos 13:24-28 **26:19** [j] Ge 38:2-10; 46:12 **26:20** [k] 1Ch 2:3 [l] Jos 7:17 **26:21** [m] Ru 4:19; 1Ch 2:9 **26:22** [n] Nu 1:27 **26:23** [o] Ge 46:13; 1Ch 7:1 **26:24** [p] Ge 46:13 **26:25** [q] Nu 1:29 **26:27** [r] Nu 1:31

26:29 [s] Jos 17:1 [t] Jdg 11:1 **26:30** [u] Jos 17:2; Jdg 6:11 **26:33** [v] Nu 27:1 [w] Nu 36:11 **26:34** [x] Nu 1:35 **26:37** [y] Nu 1:33 **26:38** [z] Ge 46:21; 1Ch 7:6 **26:40** [a] Ge 46:21; 1Ch 8:3 **26:41** [b] Nu 1:37 **26:42** [c] Ge 46:23

46 (Asher had a daughter named Serah.)
47 These were the clans of Asher;[d] those
numbered were 53,400.

48 The descendants of Naphtali[e] by their
clans were:
through Jahzeel, the Jahzeelite clan;
through Guni, the Gunite clan;
49 through Jezer, the Jezerite clan;
through Shillem, the Shillemite clan.
50 These were the clans of Naphtali;[f] those
numbered were 45,400.

51 The total number of the men of Israel was
601,730.[g]

52 The LORD said to Moses, 53 "The land
is to be allotted to them as an inheritance
based on the number of names.[h] 54 To a
larger group give a larger inheritance, and
to a smaller group a smaller one; each is
to receive its inheritance according to the
number[i] of those listed. 55 Be sure that the
land is distributed by lot.[j] What each group
inherits will be according to the names for
its ancestral tribe. 56 Each inheritance is to
be distributed by lot among the larger and
smaller groups."

57 These were the Levites[k] who were counted by their clans:
through Gershon, the Gershonite clan;
through Kohath, the Kohathite clan;
through Merari, the Merarite clan.
58 These also were Levite clans:
the Libnite clan,
the Hebronite clan,
the Mahlite clan,
the Mushite clan,
the Korahite clan.
(Kohath was the forefather of Amram;[l]
59 the name of Amram's wife was Jochebed,[m] a descendant of Levi, who was
born to the Levites[a] in Egypt. To Amram she bore Aaron, Moses[n] and their
sister Miriam. 60 Aaron was the father
of Nadab and Abihu, Eleazar and Ithamar.[o] 61 But Nadab and Abihu[p] died
when they made an offering before the
LORD with unauthorized fire.)[q]

62 All the male Levites a month old or more
numbered 23,000.[r] They were not counted[s] along with the other Israelites because
they received no inheritance[t] among
them.[u]

63 These are the ones counted by Moses
and Eleazar the priest when they counted
the Israelites on the plains of Moab[v] by the
Jordan across from Jericho. 64 Not one of
them was among those counted[w] by Moses
and Aaron the priest when they counted
the Israelites in the Desert of Sinai. 65 For
the LORD had told those Israelites they
would surely die in the wilderness,[x] and
not one of them was left except Caleb son
of Jephunneh and Joshua son of Nun.[y]

Zelophehad's Daughters

27 The daughters of Zelophehad[z] son of
Hepher,[a] the son of Gilead, the son
of Makir,[b] the son of Manasseh, belonged
to the clans of Manasseh son of Joseph.
The names of the daughters were Mahlah, Noah, Hoglah, Milkah and Tirzah.
They came forward 2 and stood before Moses, Eleazar the priest, the leaders and the
whole assembly at the entrance to the tent
of meeting and said, 3 "Our father died in
the wilderness.[c] He was not among Korah's
followers, who banded together against the
LORD,[d] but he died for his own sin and left
no sons.[e] 4 Why should our father's name
disappear from his clan because he had no
son? Give us property among our father's
relatives."

5 So Moses brought their case[f] before the
LORD,[g] 6 and the LORD said to him, 7 "What
Zelophehad's daughters are saying is right.
You must certainly give them property as
an inheritance[h] among their father's relatives and give their father's inheritance to
them.[i]

8 "Say to the Israelites, 'If a man dies and
leaves no son, give his inheritance to his
daughter. 9 If he has no daughter, give his
inheritance to his brothers. 10 If he has no
brothers, give his inheritance to his father's brothers. 11 If his father had no brothers, give his inheritance to the nearest relative in his clan, that he may possess it. This
is to have the force of law[j] for the Israelites,
as the LORD commanded Moses.' "

[a] 59 Or *Jochebed, a daughter of Levi, who was born to Levi*

26:51 *the total number of men.* The totals of the twelve tribes are very similar. Some had increased, some had decreased. The final figure shows a slight decrease, from 603,550 to 601,730.

27:1–5 *The daughters of Zelophehad.* In ancient Israel, women did not inherit land. Yet because their case made sense, Moses took the issue to the Lord.

27:7 *saying is right.* Justice was done to women regarding inheritance because Moses took the case to God, and His truth was used as the foundation for the decree. Only as we base our decisions in life on God's truth, as expressed in the Bible and in Jesus Himself, will we be acting in truth. Any other way can bring injustice and decisions regretted because they spring from error.

26:47 [d] Nu 1:41 **26:48** [e] Ge 46:24; 1Ch 7:13 **26:50** [f] Nu 1:43 **26:51** [g] Ex 12:37; 38:26; Nu 1:46; 11:21 **26:53** [h] Jos 11:23; 14:1; Eze 45:8 **26:54** [i] Nu 33:54 **26:55** [j] Nu 34:14 **26:57** [k] Ge 46:11; Ex 6:16-19 **26:58** [l] Ex 6:20 **26:59** [m] Ex 2:1 [n] Ex 6:20 **26:60** [o] Nu 3:2 **26:61** [p] Lev 10:1-2 [q] Nu 3:4 **26:62** [r] Nu 3:39 [s] Nu 1:47 [t] Nu 18:23 [u] Nu 2:33; Dt 10:9 **26:63** [v] ver 3 **26:64** [w] Nu 14:29; Dt 2:14-15; Heb 3:17 **26:65** [x] Nu 14:28; 1Co 10:5 [y] Jos 14:6-10 **27:1** [z] Nu 26:33 [a] Jos 17:2,3 [b] Nu 36:1 **27:3** [c] Nu 26:65 [d] Nu 16:2 [e] Nu 26:33 **27:5** [f] Ex 18:19 [g] Nu 9:8 **27:7** [h] Job 42:15 [i] Jos 17:4 **27:11** [j] Nu 35:29

Joshua to Succeed Moses

12 Then the LORD said to Moses, "Go up this mountain in the Abarim Range[k] and see the land[l] I have given the Israelites. 13 After you have seen it, you too will be gathered to your people,[m] as your brother Aaron[n] was, 14 for when the community rebelled at the waters in the Desert of Zin, both of you disobeyed my command to honor me as holy[o] before their eyes." (These were the waters of Meribah[p] Kadesh, in the Desert of Zin.)

15 Moses said to the LORD, 16 "May the LORD, the God who gives breath to all living things,[q] appoint someone over this community 17 to go out and come in before them, one who will lead them out and bring them in, so the LORD's people will not be like sheep without a shepherd."[r]

18 So the LORD said to Moses, "Take Joshua son of Nun, a man in whom is the spirit of leadership,[a][s] and lay your hand on him.[t] 19 Have him stand before Eleazar the priest and the entire assembly and commission him[u] in their presence.[v] 20 Give him some of your authority so the whole Israelite community will obey him.[w] 21 He is to stand before Eleazar the priest, who will obtain decisions for him by inquiring[x] of the Urim[y] before the LORD. At his command he and the entire community of the Israelites will go out, and at his command they will come in."

22 Moses did as the LORD commanded him. He took Joshua and had him stand before Eleazar the priest and the whole assembly. 23 Then he laid his hands on him and commissioned him, as the LORD instructed through Moses.

Daily Offerings

28 The LORD said to Moses, 2 "Give this command to the Israelites and say to them: 'Make sure that you present to me at the appointed time my food[z] offerings, as an aroma pleasing to me.' 3 Say to them: 'This is the food offering you are to present to the LORD: two lambs a year old without defect, as a regular burnt offering each day.[a] 4 Offer one lamb in the morning and the other at twilight, 5 together with a grain offering of a tenth of an ephah[b] of the finest flour mixed with a quarter of a hin[c] of oil[b] from pressed olives. 6 This is the regular burnt offering instituted at Mount Sinai[c] as a pleasing aroma, a food offering presented to the LORD. 7 The accompanying drink offering[d] is to be a quarter of a hin of fermented drink with each lamb. Pour out the drink offering to the LORD at the sanctuary.[e] 8 Offer the second lamb at twilight, along with the same kind of grain offering and drink offering that you offer in the morning. This is a food offering, an aroma pleasing to the LORD.[f]

Sabbath Offerings

9 " 'On the Sabbath[g] day, make an offering of two lambs a year old without defect, together with its drink offering and a grain offering of two-tenths of an ephah[d][h] of the finest flour mixed with olive oil. 10 This is the burnt offering for every Sabbath, in addition to the regular burnt offering[i] and its drink offering.

Monthly Offerings

11 " 'On the first of every month,[j] present to the LORD a burnt offering of two young bulls, one ram and seven male lambs a year old, all without defect.[k] 12 With each bull there is to be a grain offering[l] of three-tenths of an ephah[e][m] of the finest flour mixed with oil; with the ram, a grain offering of two-tenths of an ephah of the finest flour mixed with oil; 13 and with each lamb, a grain offering[n] of a tenth of an ephah of the finest flour mixed with oil. This is for a burnt offering, a pleasing aroma, a food offering presented to the LORD. 14 With each bull there is to be a drink offering[o] of half a hin[f] of wine; with the ram, a third of a hin[g]; and with each lamb, a quarter of a hin. This is the monthly burnt offering to be made at each new moon[p] during the year. 15 Besides the regular burnt offering[q] with its drink offering, one male goat is to be presented to the LORD as a sin offering.[h][r]

---

a 18 Or *the Spirit* *b* 5 That is, probably about 3 1/2 pounds or about 1.6 kilograms; also in verses 13, 21 and 29 *c* 5 That is, about 1 quart or about 1 liter; also in verses 7 and 14 *d* 9 That is, probably about 7 pounds or about 3.2 kilograms; also in verses 12, 20 and 28 *e* 12 That is, probably about 11 pounds or about 5 kilograms; also in verses 20 and 28 *f* 14 That is, about 2 quarts or about 1.9 liters *g* 14 That is, about 1 1/3 quarts or about 1.3 liters *h* 15 Or *purification offering*; also in verse 22

27:18 Holy Spirit—Joshua was "a man in whom is the spirit." In the Old Testament, only a few people had the Holy Spirit. It was not until after Jesus' resurrection that the Holy Spirit indwelt every believer. The way that God speaks to the heart of man, apart from the written Word, has generally been through the quiet voice of the Holy Spirit. Joshua apparently was a man led by the voice of the Spirit of God. He is not pictured as seeing visions or being led by angels, yet his leadership was effective and faithful.

27:12 [k] Nu 33:47; Jer 22:20 [l] Dt 3:23-27; 32:48-52
27:13 [m] Nu 31:2 [n] Nu 20:28 **27:14** [o] Nu 20:12 [p] Ex 17:7; Dt 32:51; Ps 106:32 **27:16** [q] Nu 16:22 **27:17** [r] Dt 31:2; 1Ki 22:17; Eze 34:5; Zec 10:2; Mt 9:36; Mk 6:34
27:18 [s] Ge 41:38; Nu 11:25-29 [t] ver 23; Dt 34:9
27:19 [u] Dt 3:28; 31:14, 23 [v] Dt 31:7 **27:20** [w] Jos 1:16, 17
27:21 [x] Jos 9:14 [y] Ex 28:30 **28:2** [z] Lev 3:11
28:3 [a] Ex 29:38 **28:5** [b] Lev 2:1; Nu 15:4 **28:6** [c] Ex 19:3
28:7 [d] Ex 29:41 [e] Lev 3:7 **28:8** [f] Lev 1:9
28:9 [g] Ex 20:10 [h] Lev 23:13 **28:10** [i] ver 3
28:11 [j] Nu 10:10 [k] Lev 1:3 **28:12** [l] Nu 15:6 [m] Nu 15:9
28:13 [n] Lev 6:14 **28:14** [o] Nu 15:7 [p] Ezr 3:5
28:15 [q] ver 3, 23, 24 [r] Lev 4:3

The Passover

16"'On the fourteenth day of the first month the LORD's Passover[s] is to be held. 17On the fifteenth day of this month there is to be a festival; for seven days[t] eat bread made without yeast.[u] 18On the first day hold a sacred assembly and do no regular work.[v] 19Present to the LORD a food offering consisting of a burnt offering of two young bulls, one ram and seven male lambs a year old, all without defect. 20With each bull offer a grain offering of three-tenths of an ephah[w] of the finest flour mixed with oil; with the ram, two-tenths; 21and with each of the seven lambs, one-tenth. 22Include one male goat as a sin offering[x] to make atonement for you.[y] 23Offer these in addition to the regular morning burnt offering. 24In this way present the food offering every day for seven days as an aroma pleasing to the LORD; it is to be offered in addition to the regular burnt offering and its drink offering. 25On the seventh day hold a sacred assembly and do no regular work.

The Festival of Weeks

26"'On the day of firstfruits,[z] when you present to the LORD an offering of new grain during the Festival of Weeks,[a] hold a sacred assembly and do no regular work.[b] 27Present a burnt offering of two young bulls, one ram and seven male lambs a year old as an aroma pleasing to the LORD. 28With each bull there is to be a grain offering of three-tenths of an ephah of the finest flour mixed with oil; with the ram, two-tenths; 29and with each of the seven lambs, one-tenth.[c] 30Include one male goat to make atonement for you. 31Offer these together with their drink offerings, in addition to the regular burnt offering[d] and its grain offering. Be sure the animals are without defect.

The Festival of Trumpets

29 "'On the first day of the seventh month hold a sacred assembly and do no regular work.[e] It is a day for you to sound the trumpets. 2As an aroma pleasing to the LORD,[f] offer a burnt offering of one young bull, one ram and seven male lambs a year old, all without defect.[g] 3With the bull offer a grain offering of three-tenths of an ephah[a] of the finest flour mixed with olive oil; with the ram, two-tenths[b]; 4and with each of the seven lambs, one-tenth.[c] 5Include one male goat[h] as a sin offering[d] to make atonement for you. 6These are in addition to the monthly[i] and daily burnt offerings[j] with their grain offerings and drink offerings as specified. They are food offerings presented to the LORD, a pleasing aroma.

The Day of Atonement

7"'On the tenth day of this seventh month hold a sacred assembly. You must deny yourselves[e][k] and do no work.[l] 8Present as an aroma pleasing to the LORD a burnt offering of one young bull, one ram and seven male lambs a year old, all without defect. 9With the bull offer a grain offering[m] of three-tenths of an ephah of the finest flour mixed with oil; with the ram, two-tenths; 10and with each of the seven lambs, one-tenth.[n] 11Include one male goat as a sin offering, in addition to the sin offering for atonement and the regular burnt offering[o] with its grain offering, and their drink offerings.

The Festival of Tabernacles

12"'On the fifteenth day of the seventh[p] month,[q] hold a sacred assembly and do no regular work. Celebrate a festival to the LORD for seven days. 13Present as an aroma pleasing to the LORD a food offering

---

[a] *3* That is, probably about 11 pounds or about 5 kilograms; also in verses 9 and 14 [b] *3* That is, probably about 7 pounds or about 3.2 kilograms; also in verses 9 and 14 [c] *4* That is, probably about 3 1/2 pounds or about 1.6 kilograms; also in verses 10 and 15 [d] *5* Or *purification offering*; also elsewhere in this chapter [e] *7* Or *must fast*

28:26 *Festival of Weeks.* The Festival of Weeks occurred 50 days after Passover and the Festival of Unleavened Bread.

29:1 – 40 *sacred assembly.* This chapter regulates offerings to the Lord during the three sacred festivals of the seventh month: the Festival of Trumpets, the Day of Atonement, and the Festival of Tabernacles. The Festival of Trumpets marked the beginning of Israel's civil year. It was a day of preparation for the next two celebrations. The Day of Atonement was a solemn day on which sins were confessed and special sacrifices made for the holy place, the priests, and the people. The Festival of Tabernacles was a time of rejoicing.

29:1 *a day for you to sound the trumpets.* The celebration of the Festival of Trumpets involved blowing ram's horns. Later this festival became identified with the New Year festival.

29:11 *offering for atonement.* The Day of Atonement, or Yom Kippur, was regarded as the most holy day of all. Leviticus 16 describes it as a day of fasting, rather than feasting.

29:12 *festival to the LORD for seven days.* The celebration of the Festival of Tabernacles, or Succoth, included both sacrifices and eight days of "no work." In later years Israelites lived in tents or booths during this celebration, to commemorate the years that their ancestors lived in tents in the desert.

28:16 [s] Ex 12:6, 18; Lev 23:5; Dt 16:1 **28:17** [t] Ex 12:19 [u] Ex 23:15; 34:18; Lev 23:6; Dt 16:3-8 **28:18** [v] Ex 12:16; Lev 23:7 **28:20** [w] Lev 14:10 **28:22** [x] Ro 8:3 [y] Nu 15:28 **28:26** [z] Ex 34:22 [a] Ex 23:16 [b] ver 18; Dt 16:10 **28:29** [c] ver 13 **28:31** [d] ver 3, 19 **29:1** [e] Lev 23:24 **29:2** [f] Nu 28:2 [g] Nu 28:3 **29:5** [h] Nu 28:15 **29:6** [i] Nu 28:11 [j] Nu 28:3 **29:7** [k] Ac 27:9 [l] Ex 31:15; Lev 16:29; 23:26-32 **29:9** [m] ver 3, 18 **29:10** [n] Nu 28:13 **29:11** [o] Lev 16:3; Nu 28:3 **29:12** [p] 1Ki 8:2 [q] Lev 23:24

consisting of a burnt offering of thirteen young bulls, two rams and fourteen male lambs a year old, all without defect. 14With each of the thirteen bulls offer a grain offering[r] of three-tenths of an ephah of the finest flour mixed with oil; with each of the two rams, two-tenths; 15and with each of the fourteen lambs, one-tenth. 16Include one male goat as a sin offering, in addition to the regular burnt offering with its grain offering and drink offering.[s]

17" 'On the second day[t] offer twelve young bulls, two rams and fourteen male lambs a year old, all without defect.[u] 18With the bulls, rams and lambs, offer their grain offerings[v] and drink offerings[w] according to the number specified.[x] 19Include one male goat as a sin offering,[y] in addition to the regular burnt offering with its grain offering, and their drink offerings.

20" 'On the third day offer eleven bulls, two rams and fourteen male lambs a year old, all without defect.[z] 21With the bulls, rams and lambs, offer their grain offerings and drink offerings according to the number specified.[a] 22Include one male goat as a sin offering, in addition to the regular burnt offering with its grain offering and drink offering.

23" 'On the fourth day offer ten bulls, two rams and fourteen male lambs a year old, all without defect. 24With the bulls, rams and lambs, offer their grain offerings and drink offerings according to the number specified. 25Include one male goat as a sin offering, in addition to the regular burnt offering with its grain offering and drink offering.

26" 'On the fifth day offer nine bulls, two rams and fourteen male lambs a year old, all without defect. 27With the bulls, rams and lambs, offer their grain offerings and drink offerings according to the number specified. 28Include one male goat as a sin offering, in addition to the regular burnt offering with its grain offering and drink offering.

29" 'On the sixth day offer eight bulls, two rams and fourteen male lambs a year old, all without defect. 30With the bulls, rams and lambs, offer their grain offerings and drink offerings according to the number specified. 31Include one male goat as a sin offering, in addition to the regular burnt offering with its grain offering and drink offering.

32" 'On the seventh day offer seven bulls, two rams and fourteen male lambs a year old, all without defect. 33With the bulls, rams and lambs, offer their grain offerings and drink offerings according to the number specified. 34Include one male goat as a sin offering, in addition to the regular burnt offering with its grain offering and drink offering.

35" 'On the eighth day hold a closing special assembly[b] and do no regular work. 36Present as an aroma pleasing to the LORD[c] a food offering consisting of a burnt offering of one bull, one ram and seven male lambs a year old,[d] all without defect. 37With the bull, the ram and the lambs, offer their grain offerings and drink offerings according to the number specified. 38Include one male goat as a sin offering, in addition to the regular burnt offering with its grain offering and drink offering.

39" 'In addition to what you vow[e] and your freewill offerings, offer these to the LORD at your appointed festivals:[f] your burnt offerings,[g] grain offerings, drink offerings and fellowship offerings.' "

40Moses told the Israelites all that the LORD commanded him.[a]

Vows

30 [b] Moses said to the heads of the tribes of Israel:[h] "This is what the LORD commands: 2When a man makes a vow to the LORD or takes an oath to obligate himself by a pledge, he must not break his word but must do everything he said.[i]

3"When a young woman still living in her father's household makes a vow to the LORD or obligates herself by a pledge 4and her father hears about her vow or pledge but says nothing to her, then all her vows and every pledge by which she obligated herself will stand.[j] 5But if her father forbids her when he hears about it, none of her vows or the pledges by which she obligated herself will stand; the LORD will release her because her father has forbidden her.

6"If she marries after she makes a vow[k] or after her lips utter a rash promise by which she obligates herself 7and her husband hears about it but says nothing to her, then her vows or the pledges by which she obligated herself will stand. 8But if her husband[l] forbids her when he hears about it, he nullifies the vow that obligates her or the

---

a *40* In Hebrew texts this verse (29:40) is numbered 30:1. *b* In Hebrew texts 30:1-16 is numbered 30:2-17.

30:2 ***When a man makes a vow.*** The key issue is clear: One who makes a vow shall not break his word. Vows that are made to the Lord must be carried out.

30:3 ***When a young woman.*** In Israelite culture, an unmarried woman was under the protection of her father. If she made a vow, she might bring her father into an obligation that he did not want to fulfill, or could not fulfill. The same was true of a married woman (v.6). Her vows would involve her husband, so the husband or father had to agree to the vow.

29:14 [r] ver 3 **29:16** [s] ver 6 **29:17** [t] Lev 23:36 [u] Nu 28:3 **29:18** [v] ver 9 [w] Nu 28:7 [x] Nu 15:4-12 **29:19** [y] Nu 28:15 **29:20** [z] ver 17 **29:21** [a] ver 18 **29:35** [b] Lev 23:36 **29:36** [c] Lev 1:9 [d] ver 2 **29:39** [e] Nu 6:2 [f] Lev 23:2 [g] Lev 1:3; 1Ch 23:31; 2Ch 31:3 **30:1** [h] Nu 1:4 **30:2** [i] Dt 23:21-23; Jdg 11:35; Job 22:27; Ps 22:25; 50:14; 116:14; Pr 20:25; Ecc 5:4,5; Jnh 1:16 **30:4** [j] ver 7 **30:6** [k] Lev 5:4 **30:8** [l] Ge 3:16

rash promise by which she obligates herself, and the LORD will release her.

9“Any vow or obligation taken by a widow or divorced woman will be binding on her.

10“If a woman living with her husband makes a vow or obligates herself by a pledge under oath 11and her husband hears about it but says nothing to her and does not forbid her, then all her vows or the pledges by which she obligated herself will stand. 12But if her husband nullifies them when he hears about them, then none of the vows or pledges that came from her lips will stand.[m] Her husband has nullified them, and the LORD will release her. 13Her husband may confirm or nullify any vow she makes or any sworn pledge to deny herself.[a] 14But if her husband says nothing to her about it from day to day, then he confirms all her vows or the pledges binding on her. He confirms them by saying nothing to her when he hears about them. 15If, however, he nullifies them some time after he hears about them, then he must bear the consequences of her wrongdoing.”

16These are the regulations the LORD gave Moses concerning relationships between a man and his wife, and between a father and his young daughter still living at home.

Vengeance on the Midianites

31 The LORD said to Moses, 2“Take vengeance on the Midianites[n] for the Israelites. After that, you will be gathered to your people.[o]”

3So Moses said to the people, “Arm some of your men to go to war against the Midianites so that they may carry out the LORD’s vengeance[p] on them. 4Send into battle a thousand men from each of the tribes of Israel.” 5So twelve thousand men armed for battle, a thousand from each tribe, were supplied from the clans of Israel. 6Moses sent them into battle, a thousand from each tribe, along with Phinehas son of Eleazar, the priest, who took with him articles from the sanctuary[q] and the trumpets[r] for signaling.

7They fought against Midian, as the LORD commanded Moses, and killed every man.[s] 8Among their victims were Evi, Rekem, Zur, Hur and Reba[t]—the five kings of Midian.[u] They also killed Balaam son of Beor with the sword.[v] 9The Israelites captured the Midianite women and children and took all the Midianite herds, flocks and goods as plunder. 10They burned all the towns where the Midianites had settled, as well as all their camps.[w] 11They took all the plunder and spoils, including the people and animals,[x] 12and brought the captives, spoils and plunder to Moses and Eleazar the priest and the Israelite assembly[y] at their camp on the plains of Moab, by the Jordan across from Jericho.

13Moses, Eleazar the priest and all the leaders of the community went to meet them outside the camp. 14Moses was angry with the officers of the army[z]—the commanders of thousands and commanders of hundreds—who returned from the battle.

15“Have you allowed all the women to live?” he asked them. 16“They were the ones who followed Balaam’s advice[a] and enticed the Israelites to be unfaithful to the LORD in the Peor incident,[b] so that a plague struck the LORD’s people. 17Now kill all the boys. And kill every woman who has slept with a man,[c] 18but save for yourselves every girl who has never slept with a man.

19“Anyone who has killed someone or touched someone who was killed[d] must stay outside the camp seven days. On the third and seventh days you must purify yourselves[e] and your captives. 20Purify every garment[f] as well as everything made of leather, goat hair or wood.”

21Then Eleazar the priest said to the soldiers who had gone into battle, “This is what is required by the law that the LORD gave Moses: 22Gold, silver, bronze, iron,[g] tin, lead 23and anything else that can withstand fire must be put through the fire,[h] and then it will be clean. But it must also be purified with the water of cleansing.[i] And whatever cannot withstand fire must be put through that water. 24On the seventh day wash your clothes and you will be clean.[j] Then you may come into the camp.”

---

[a] 13 Or *to fast*

31:2 *Midianites.* The Midianites were descendants of Abraham and his wife Keturah, but were not part of the covenant that God had with Abraham, Isaac, and Jacob.

31:7 – 16 Unfaithfulness—Moses was ordered to campaign against the Midianites because of their wicked involvement in the seduction of Israel (25:17 – 18). He was angry with the officers of the army because they had not carried out the Lord’s directive concerning the women who had caused Israel to act unfaithfully toward the Lord. There was no excuse for the officers’ unfaithfulness. The plague that followed the seduction of Israel should have been enough to make them aware of the great responsibility they had to obey God’s directives.

30:12 [m] Eph 5:22; Col 3:18 **31:2** [n] Ge 25:2 [o] Nu 20:26; 27:13 **31:3** [p] Jdg 11:36; 1Sa 24:12; 2Sa 4:8; 22:48; Ps 94:1; 149:7 **31:6** [q] Nu 14:44 [r] Nu 10:9 **31:7** [s] Dt 20:13; Jdg 21:11; 1Ki 11:15,16 **31:8** [t] Jos 13:21 [u] Nu 25:15 [v] Jos 13:22 **31:10** [w] Ge 25:16; 1Ch 6:54; Ps 69:25; Eze 25:4 **31:11** [x] Dt 20:14 **31:12** [y] Nu 27:2 **31:14** [z] ver 48; Ex 18:21; Dt 1:15 **31:16** [a] 2Pe 2:15; Rev 2:14 [b] Nu 25:1-9 **31:17** [c] Dt 7:2; 20:16-18; Jdg 21:11 **31:19** [d] Nu 19:16 [e] Nu 19:12 **31:20** [f] Nu 19:19 **31:22** [g] Jos 6:19; 22:8 **31:23** [h] 1Co 3:13 [i] Nu 19:9,17 **31:24** [j] Lev 11:25

Dividing the Spoils

25 The LORD said to Moses, 26 "You and Eleazar the priest and the family heads of the community are to count all the people[k] and animals that were captured. 27 Divide[l] the spoils equally between the soldiers who took part in the battle and the rest of the community. 28 From the soldiers who fought in the battle, set apart as tribute for the LORD[m] one out of every five hundred, whether people, cattle, donkeys or sheep. 29 Take this tribute from their half share and give it to Eleazar the priest as the LORD's part. 30 From the Israelites' half, select one out of every fifty, whether people, cattle, donkeys, sheep or other animals. Give them to the Levites, who are responsible for the care of the LORD's tabernacle.[n]" 31 So Moses and Eleazar the priest did as the LORD commanded Moses.

32 The plunder remaining from the spoils that the soldiers took was 675,000 sheep, 33 72,000 cattle, 34 61,000 donkeys 35 and 32,000 women who had never slept with a man.

36 The half share of those who fought in the battle was:

337,500 sheep, 37 of which the tribute for the LORD[o] was 675;
38 36,000 cattle, of which the tribute for the LORD was 72;
39 30,500 donkeys, of which the tribute for the LORD was 61;
40 16,000 people, of whom the tribute for the LORD was 32.

41 Moses gave the tribute to Eleazar the priest as the LORD's part,[p] as the LORD commanded Moses.

42 The half belonging to the Israelites, which Moses set apart from that of the fighting men— 43 the community's half—was 337,500 sheep, 44 36,000 cattle, 45 30,500 donkeys 46 and 16,000 people. 47 From the Israelites' half, Moses selected one out of every fifty people and animals, as the LORD commanded him, and gave them to the Levites, who were responsible for the care of the LORD's tabernacle.

48 Then the officers who were over the units of the army—the commanders of thousands and commanders of hundreds—went to Moses 49 and said to him, "Your servants have counted the soldiers under our command, and not one is missing.[q] 50 So we have brought as an offering to the LORD the gold articles each of us acquired—armlets, bracelets, signet rings, earrings and necklaces—to make atonement for ourselves[r] before the LORD."

51 Moses and Eleazar the priest accepted from them the gold—all the crafted articles. 52 All the gold from the commanders of thousands and commanders of hundreds that Moses and Eleazar presented as a gift to the LORD weighed 16,750 shekels.[a] 53 Each soldier had taken plunder[s] for himself. 54 Moses and Eleazar the priest accepted the gold from the commanders of thousands and commanders of hundreds and brought it into the tent of meeting as a memorial[t] for the Israelites before the LORD.

The Transjordan Tribes

32 The Reubenites and Gadites, who had very large herds and flocks, saw that the lands of Jazer[u] and Gilead were suitable for livestock.[v] 2 So they came to Moses and Eleazar the priest and to the leaders of the community, and said, 3 "Ataroth,[w] Dibon, Jazer, Nimrah,[x] Heshbon, Elealeh,[y] Sebam, Nebo and Beon[z]— 4 the land the LORD subdued[a] before the people of Israel—are suitable for livestock,[b] and your servants have livestock. 5 If we have found favor in your eyes," they said, "let this land be given to your servants as our possession. Do not make us cross the Jordan."

6 Moses said to the Gadites and Reubenites, "Should your fellow Israelites go to war while you sit here? 7 Why do you discourage the Israelites from crossing over into the land the LORD has given them?[c] 8 This is what your fathers did when I sent them from Kadesh Barnea to look over the land.[d] 9 After they went up to the Valley of Eshkol[e] and viewed the land, they discouraged the Israelites from entering the land the LORD had given them. 10 The LORD's anger was aroused[f] that day and he swore this

[a] *52* That is, about 420 pounds or about 190 kilograms

31:27 ***divide the spoils.*** The division of the plunder among those who had gone to war and those who had not, set a standard for future battles. The proportion that was regarded as the Lord's also became a standard.

31:52 ***16,750 shekels.*** The officers' gift was over 400 pounds of gold.

32:5 ***If we have found favor.*** Although an inheritance on the east side of the Jordan was not part of God's promise, the respectful request of the Reubenites and Gadites was granted, because they came humbly, not rebelliously.

32:8–13 ***This is what your fathers did.*** To discourage obedience of God's orders and so prevent His people from entering upon the full enjoyment of the promises is a serious sin. Let us never forget that without an obedient faith, it is impossible to please God (Heb. 11:6).

31:26 [k] Nu 1:19 **31:27** [l] Jos 22:8; 1Sa 30:24
31:28 [m] Nu 18:21 **31:30** [n] Nu 3:7; 18:3
31:37 [o] ver 38-41 **31:41** [p] Nu 5:9; 18:8
31:49 [q] Jer 23:4 **31:50** [r] Ex 30:16 **31:53** [s] Dt 20:14
31:54 [t] Ex 28:12 **32:1** [u] Nu 21:32 [v] Ex 12:38
32:3 [w] ver 34 [x] ver 36 [y] ver 37; Isa 15:4; 16:9; Jer 48:34 [z] ver 38; Jos 13:17; Eze 25:9 **32:4** [a] Nu 21:34 [b] Ex 12:38
32:7 [c] Nu 13:27-14:4 **32:8** [d] Nu 13:3,26; Dt 1:19-25
32:9 [e] Nu 13:23; Dt 1:24 **32:10** [f] Nu 11:1

oath: 11‘Because they have not followed me wholeheartedly, not one of those who were twenty years old or more[g] when they came up out of Egypt will see the land I promised on oath[h] to Abraham, Isaac and Jacob[i]— 12not one except Caleb son of Jephunneh the Kenizzite and Joshua son of Nun, for they followed the LORD wholeheartedly.’[j] 13The LORD’s anger burned against Israel[k] and he made them wander in the wilderness forty years, until the whole generation of those who had done evil in his sight was gone.[l]

14“And here you are, a brood of sinners, standing in the place of your fathers and making the LORD even more angry with Israel.[m] 15If you turn away from following him, he will again leave all this people in the wilderness, and you will be the cause of their destruction.[n]”

16Then they came up to him and said, “We would like to build pens here for our livestock[o] and cities for our women and children. 17But we will arm ourselves for battle[a] and go ahead of the Israelites[p] until we have brought them to their place.[q] Meanwhile our women and children will live in fortified cities, for protection from the inhabitants of the land. 18We will not return to our homes until each of the Israelites has received their inheritance.[r] 19We will not receive any inheritance with them on the other side of the Jordan, because our inheritance has come to us on the east side of the Jordan.”[s]

20Then Moses said to them, “If you will do this—if you will arm yourselves before the LORD for battle[t] 21and if all of you who are armed cross over the Jordan before the LORD until he has driven his enemies out before him— 22then when the land is subdued before the LORD, you may return[u] and be free from your obligation to the LORD and to Israel. And this land will be your possession before the LORD.[v]

23“But if you fail to do this, you will be sinning against the LORD; and you may be sure that your sin will find you out.[w] 24Build cities for your women and children, and pens for your flocks,[x] but do what you have promised.[y]”

25The Gadites and Reubenites said to Moses, “We your servants will do as our lord commands. 26Our children and wives, our flocks and herds will remain here in the cities of Gilead.[z] 27But your servants, every man who is armed for battle, will cross over to fight before the LORD, just as our lord says.”

28Then Moses gave orders about them[a] to Eleazar the priest and Joshua son of Nun and to the family heads of the Israelite tribes. 29He said to them, “If the Gadites and Reubenites, every man armed for battle, cross over the Jordan with you before the LORD, then when the land is subdued before you, you must give them the land of Gilead as their possession. 30But if they do not cross over with you armed, they must accept their possession with you in Canaan.”

31The Gadites and Reubenites answered, “Your servants will do what the LORD has said.[b] 32We will cross over before the LORD into Canaan armed, but the property we inherit will be on this side of the Jordan.”

33Then Moses gave to the Gadites,[c] the Reubenites and the half-tribe of Manasseh son of Joseph the kingdom of Sihon king of the Amorites[d] and the kingdom of Og king of Bashan—the whole land with its cities and the territory around them.[e]

34The Gadites built up Dibon, Ataroth, Aroer,[f] 35Atroth Shophan, Jazer,[g] Jogbehah, 36Beth Nimrah[h] and Beth Haran as fortified cities, and built pens for their flocks. 37And the Reubenites rebuilt Heshbon, Elealeh and Kiriathaim, 38as well as Nebo[i] and Baal Meon (these names were changed) and Sibmah. They gave names to the cities they rebuilt.

39The descendants of Makir[j] son of Manasseh went to Gilead, captured it and drove out the Amorites who were there. 40So Moses gave Gilead to the Makirites,[k] the descendants of Manasseh, and they settled there. 41Jair, a descendant of Manasseh, captured their settlements and called them Havvoth Jair.[b][l] 42And Nobah captured Kenath and its surrounding settlements and called it Nobah after himself.[m]

Stages in Israel’s Journey

33 Here are the stages in the journey of the Israelites when they came out of Egypt[n] by divisions under the leadership of Moses and Aaron.[o] 2At the LORD’s

[a] 17 Septuagint; Hebrew *will be quick to arm ourselves* [b] 41 Or *them the settlements of Jair*

32:31 ***Your servants will do.*** Reuben and Gad gladly affirmed their allegiance to the Lord and their consideration of the remainder of the community of Israel. The benevolence of Reuben and Gad is a beautiful picture of the mutual ties between God’s people. Truly, we are one body.

32:11 [g] Ex 30:14 [h] Nu 14:23 [i] Nu 14:28-30 **32:12** [j] Nu 14:24, 30; Dt 1:36; Ps 63:8 **32:13** [k] Ex 4:14 [l] Nu 14:28-35; 26:64, 65 **32:14** [m] ver 10; Dt 1:34; Ps 78:59

32:15 [n] Dt 30:17-18; 2Ch 7:20 **32:16** [o] Ex 12:38; Dt 3:19 **32:17** [p] Jos 4:12, 13 [q] Nu 22:4; Dt 3:20 **32:18** [r] Jos 22:1-4 **32:19** [s] Jos 12:1 **32:20** [t] Dt 3:18 **32:22** [u] Jos 22:4 [v] Dt 3:18-20 **32:23** [w] Ge 4:7; 44:16; Isa 59:12 **32:24** [x] ver 1, 16 [y] Nu 30:2 **32:26** [z] Jos 1:14 **32:28** [a] Dt 3:18-20; Jos 1:13 **32:31** [b] ver 29 **32:33** [c] Jos 13:24-28; 1Sa 13:7 [d] Dt 2:26 [e] Nu 21:24; Jos 12:6 **32:34** [f] Dt 2:36; Jdg 11:26 **32:35** [g] ver 3 **32:36** [h] ver 3 **32:38** [i] ver 3; Isa 15:2; Jer 48:1, 22 **32:39** [j] Ge 50:23 **32:40** [k] Dt 3:15; Jos 17:1 **32:41** [l] Dt 3:14; Jos 13:30; Jdg 10:4; 1Ch 2:23 **32:42** [m] 2Sa 18:18; Ps 49:11 **33:1** [n] Mic 6:4 [o] Ps 77:20

command Moses recorded the stages in
their journey. This is their journey by stages:

3 The Israelites set out from Rameses on the fifteenth day of the first
month, the day after the Passover.[p]
They marched out defiantly[q] in full
view of all the Egyptians, 4 who were
burying all their firstborn, whom the
LORD had struck down among them;
for the LORD had brought judgment on
their gods.[r]
5 The Israelites left Rameses and
camped at Sukkoth.[s]
6 They left Sukkoth and camped at
Etham, on the edge of the desert.[t]
7 They left Etham, turned back to Pi
Hahiroth, to the east of Baal Zephon,[u]
and camped near Migdol.[v]
8 They left Pi Hahiroth[a] and passed
through the sea[w] into the desert, and
when they had traveled for three days
in the Desert of Etham, they camped
at Marah.[x]
9 They left Marah and went to Elim,
where there were twelve springs and
seventy palm trees, and they camped[y]
there.
10 They left Elim and camped by the
Red Sea.[b]
11 They left the Red Sea and camped
in the Desert of Sin.[z]
12 They left the Desert of Sin and
camped at Dophkah.
13 They left Dophkah and camped at
Alush.
14 They left Alush and camped at
Rephidim, where there was no water
for the people to drink.
15 They left Rephidim[a] and camped
in the Desert of Sinai.[b]
16 They left the Desert of Sinai and
camped at Kibroth Hattaavah.[c]
17 They left Kibroth Hattaavah and
camped at Hazeroth.[d]
18 They left Hazeroth and camped at
Rithmah.
19 They left Rithmah and camped at
Rimmon Perez.
20 They left Rimmon Perez and
camped at Libnah.[e]
21 They left Libnah and camped at
Rissah.
22 They left Rissah and camped at
Kehelathah.
23 They left Kehelathah and camped
at Mount Shepher.
24 They left Mount Shepher and
camped at Haradah.
25 They left Haradah and camped at
Makheloth.
26 They left Makheloth and camped
at Tahath.
27 They left Tahath and camped at
Terah.
28 They left Terah and camped at
Mithkah.
29 They left Mithkah and camped at
Hashmonah.
30 They left Hashmonah and camped
at Moseroth.[f]
31 They left Moseroth and camped at
Bene Jaakan.
32 They left Bene Jaakan and
camped at Hor Haggidgad.
33 They left Hor Haggidgad and
camped at Jotbathah.[g]
34 They left Jotbathah and camped
at Abronah.
35 They left Abronah and camped at
Ezion Geber.[h]
36 They left Ezion Geber and camped
at Kadesh, in the Desert of Zin.[i]
37 They left Kadesh and camped at
Mount Hor,[j] on the border of Edom.[k]
38 At the LORD's command Aaron the
priest went up Mount Hor, where he
died[l] on the first day of the fifth month
of the fortieth year after the Israelites
came out of Egypt.[m] 39 Aaron was a
hundred and twenty-three years old
when he died on Mount Hor.
40 The Canaanite king of Arad,[n] who
lived in the Negev of Canaan, heard
that the Israelites were coming.
41 They left Mount Hor and camped
at Zalmonah.
42 They left Zalmonah and camped
at Punon.
43 They left Punon and camped at
Oboth.[o]
44 They left Oboth and camped at Iye
Abarim, on the border of Moab.[p]
45 They left Iye Abarim and camped
at Dibon Gad.
46 They left Dibon Gad and camped
at Almon Diblathaim.
47 They left Almon Diblathaim and
camped in the mountains of Abarim,[q]
near Nebo.
48 They left the mountains of Abarim and camped on the plains of Moab
by the Jordan across from Jericho.[r]
49 There on the plains of Moab they
camped along the Jordan from Beth
Jeshimoth to Abel Shittim.[s]

a 8 Many manuscripts of the Masoretic Text, Samaritan Pentateuch and Vulgate; most manuscripts of the Masoretic Text *left from before Hahiroth* *b* 10 Or *the Sea of Reeds*; also in verse 11

33:3 [p] Ex 13:4 [q] Ex 14:8 **33:4** [r] Ex 12:12 **33:5** [s] Ex 12:37 **33:6** [t] Ex 13:20 **33:7** [u] Ex 14:9 [v] Ex 14:2 **33:8** [w] Ex 14:22 [x] Ex 15:23 **33:9** [y] Ex 15:27 **33:11** [z] Ex 16:1 **33:15** [a] Ex 17:1 [b] Ex 19:1 **33:16** [c] Nu 11:34 **33:17** [d] Nu 11:35 **33:20** [e] Jos 10:29

33:30 [f] Dt 10:6 **33:33** [g] Dt 10:7 **33:35** [h] Dt 2:8; 1Ki 9:26; 22:48 **33:36** [i] Nu 20:1 **33:37** [j] Nu 20:22 [k] Nu 20:16; 21:4 **33:38** [l] Dt 10:6 [m] Nu 20:25-28 **33:40** [n] Nu 21:1 **33:43** [o] Nu 21:10 **33:44** [p] Nu 21:11 **33:47** [q] Nu 27:12 **33:48** [r] Nu 22:1 **33:49** [s] Nu 25:1

50 On the plains of Moab by the Jordan
across from Jericho the LORD said to Moses, 51 "Speak to the Israelites and say to
them: 'When you cross the Jordan into Canaan,[t] 52 drive out all the inhabitants of the
land before you. Destroy all their carved
images and their cast idols, and demolish
all their high places.[u] 53 Take possession of
the land and settle in it, for I have given
you the land to possess.[v] 54 Distribute the
land by lot, according to your clans.[w] To a
larger group give a larger inheritance, and
to a smaller group a smaller one. Whatever
falls to them by lot will be theirs. Distribute
it according to your ancestral tribes.

55 " 'But if you do not drive out the inhabitants of the land, those you allow to remain
will become barbs in your eyes and thorns[x]
in your sides. They will give you trouble in
the land where you will live. 56 And then I
will do to you what I plan to do to them.' "

Boundaries of Canaan

34 The LORD said to Moses, 2 "Command
the Israelites and say to them: 'When
you enter Canaan, the land that will be allotted to you as an inheritance[y] is to have
these boundaries:[z]

3 " 'Your southern side will include some
of the Desert of Zin[a] along the border of
Edom. Your southern boundary will start
in the east from the southern end of the
Dead Sea,[b] 4 cross south of Scorpion Pass,[c]
continue on to Zin and go south of Kadesh
Barnea.[d] Then it will go to Hazar Addar
and over to Azmon, 5 where it will turn, join
the Wadi of Egypt[e] and end at the Mediterranean Sea.

6 " 'Your western boundary will be the
coast of the Mediterranean Sea. This will
be your boundary on the west.

7 " 'For your northern boundary,[f] run a
line from the Mediterranean Sea to Mount
Hor 8 and from Mount Hor to Lebo Hamath.[g]
Then the boundary will go to Zedad, 9 con-
tinue to Ziphron and end at Hazar Enan.
This will be your boundary on the north.

10 " 'For your eastern boundary, run a
line from Hazar Enan to Shepham. 11 The
boundary will go down from Shepham to
Riblah[h] on the east side of Ain and continue along the slopes east of the Sea of Galilee.[a][i] 12 Then the boundary will go down
along the Jordan and end at the Dead Sea.

" 'This will be your land, with its boundaries on every side.' "

13 Moses commanded the Israelites: "Assign this land by lot as an inheritance.[j]
The LORD has ordered that it be given to
the nine and a half tribes, 14 because the
families of the tribe of Reuben, the tribe of
Gad and the half-tribe of Manasseh have
received their inheritance.[k] 15 These two
and a half tribes have received their inheritance east of the Jordan across from Jericho, toward the sunrise."

16 The LORD said to Moses, 17 "These are
the names of the men who are to assign the
land for you as an inheritance: Eleazar the
priest and Joshua[l] son of Nun. 18 And appoint one leader from each tribe to help[m]
assign the land. 19 These are their names:

Caleb[n] son of Jephunneh,
from the tribe of Judah;[o]
20 Shemuel son of Ammihud,
from the tribe of Simeon;[p]
21 Elidad son of Kislon,
from the tribe of Benjamin;[q]
22 Bukki son of Jogli,
the leader from the tribe of Dan;
23 Hanniel son of Ephod,
the leader from the tribe of Manasseh son of Joseph;
24 Kemuel son of Shiphtan,
the leader from the tribe of Ephraim
son of Joseph;
25 Elizaphan son of Parnak,
the leader from the tribe of Zebulun;
26 Paltiel son of Azzan,
the leader from the tribe of Issachar;
27 Ahihud son of Shelomi,
the leader from the tribe of Asher;[r]
28 Pedahel son of Ammihud,
the leader from the tribe of Naphtali."

29 These are the men the LORD commanded to assign the inheritance to the Israelites
in the land of Canaan.

---

[a] 11 Hebrew *Kinnereth*

33:53 *for I have given you the land to possess.* It was God's land, and He had transferred it from the Canaanites to the Israelites. Though the land was promised to the nation as a gift, it did not come into the possession of the people without their involvement. Israel had to drive out the inhabitants, destroy their high places, their figures, stones, and molten images. Still, the land was God's gracious gift to His people. In spite of all of our striving, we have only what we receive from the hand of the Lord.

33:55–56 *But if you do not.* If the idolatrous Canaanites were allowed to live among God's people, they would be a constant enticement to sin. If the Israelites fell into the same sin as the Canaanites, their punishment would be the same.

34:1–12 *Canaan, the land ... is to have these boundaries.* Chapter 34 serves as a detailed display of the grandeur of the land that God was about to give to His people.

34:16–29 *These are the names of the men.* The listing of the men serves several purposes. It gives

33:51 [t] Jos 3:17 **33:52** [u] Ex 23:24; 34:13; Lev 26:1; Dt 7:2, 5; 12:3; Jos 11:12; Ps 106:34-36 **33:53** [v] Dt 11:31; Jos 21:43 **33:54** [w] Nu 26:54 **33:55** [x] Jos 23:13; Jdg 2:3; Ps 106:36 **34:2** [y] Ge 17:8; Dt 1:7-8; Ps 78:54-55 [z] Eze 47:15 **34:3** [a] Jos 15:1-3 [b] Ge 14:3 **34:4** [c] Jos 15:3 [d] Nu 32:8 **34:5** [e] Ge 15:18; Jos 15:4 **34:7** [f] Eze 47:15-17 **34:8** [g] Nu 13:21; Jos 13:5 **34:11** [h] 2Ki 23:33; Jer 39:5 [i] Dt 3:17; Jos 11:2; 13:27 **34:13** [j] Jos 14:1-5 **34:14** [k] Nu 32:33; Jos 14:3 **34:17** [l] Jos 14:1 **34:18** [m] Nu 1:4, 16 **34:19** [n] Nu 26:65 [o] Ge 29:35; Dt 33:7 **34:20** [p] Ge 49:5 **34:21** [q] Ge 49:27; Ps 68:27 **34:27** [r] Nu 1:40

Towns for the Levites

35 On the plains of Moab by the Jordan across from Jericho, the LORD said to Moses, 2“Command the Israelites to give the Levites towns to live in[s] from the inheritance the Israelites will possess. And give them pasturelands around the towns. 3Then they will have towns to live in and pasturelands for the cattle they own and all their other animals.

4“The pasturelands around the towns that you give the Levites will extend a thousand cubits[a] from the town wall. 5Outside the town, measure two thousand cubits[b] on the east side, two thousand on the south side, two thousand on the west and two thousand on the north, with the town in the center. They will have this area as pastureland for the towns.

Cities of Refuge

6“Six of the towns you give the Levites will be cities of refuge, to which a person who has killed someone may flee.[t] In addition, give them forty-two other towns. 7In all you must give the Levites forty-eight towns, together with their pasturelands. 8The towns you give the Levites from the land the Israelites possess are to be given in proportion to the inheritance of each tribe: Take many towns from a tribe that has many, but few from one that has few.”[u]

9Then the LORD said to Moses: 10“Speak to the Israelites and say to them: ‘When you cross the Jordan into Canaan,[v] 11select some towns to be your cities of refuge, to which a person who has killed someone[w] accidentally[x] may flee. 12They will be places of refuge from the avenger,[y] so that anyone accused of murder may not die before they stand trial before the assembly. 13These six towns you give will be your cities of refuge. 14Give three on this side of the Jordan and three in Canaan as cities of refuge. 15These six towns will be a place of refuge for Israelites and for foreigners residing among them, so that anyone who has killed another accidentally can flee there.

16“ ‘If anyone strikes someone a fatal blow with an iron object, that person is a murderer; the murderer is to be put to death.[z] 17Or if anyone is holding a stone and strikes someone a fatal blow with it, that person is a murderer; the murderer is to be put to death. 18Or if anyone is holding a wooden object and strikes someone a fatal blow with it, that person is a murderer; the murderer is to be put to death. 19The avenger of blood shall put the murderer to death; when the avenger comes upon the murderer, the avenger shall put the murderer to death.[a] 20If anyone with malice aforethought shoves another or throws something at them intentionally[b] so that they die 21or if out of enmity one person hits another with their fist so that the other dies, that person is to be put to death; that person is a murderer. The avenger of blood shall put the murderer to death when they meet.

22“ ‘But if without enmity someone suddenly pushes another or throws something at them unintentionally[c] 23or, without seeing them, drops on them a stone heavy enough to kill them, and they die, then since that other person was not an enemy and no harm was intended, 24the assembly[d] must judge between the accused and the avenger of blood according to these regulations. 25The assembly must protect the one accused of murder from the avenger of blood and send the accused back to the city of refuge to which they fled. The accused must stay there until the death of the high priest, who was anointed with the holy oil.[e]

26“ ‘But if the accused ever goes outside the limits of the city of refuge to which they fled 27and the avenger of blood finds them outside the city, the avenger of blood may kill the accused without being guilty of murder. 28The accused must stay in the city of refuge until the death of the high priest; only after the death of the high priest may they return to their own property.

29“ ‘This is to have the force of law[f] for you throughout the generations to come, wherever you live.

30“ ‘Anyone who kills a person is to be put to death as a murderer only on the testimony of witnesses. But no one is to be put to death on the testimony of only one witness.[g]

---

[a] 4 That is, about 1,500 feet or about 450 meters
[b] 5 That is, about 3,000 feet or about 900 meters

---

authenticity to the record, it memorializes these individuals in the history of Israel, and it serves as a legal arrangement so that the transfer of the land to the tribes would be done in order.

35:29–34 *force of law.* The practice of blood vengeance was common in the ancient Near East. Divine law was formulated to control and limit blood vengeance in Israel (vv. 9–34). God's Word differed significantly from the surrounding cultures. The difference of practice was due to Israel's unique view of man created in God's image. These directives regarding blood vengeance are referred to here as a "force of law," coming from a word meaning "to engrave." The Word of God was written, given to govern and direct their conduct wherever they lived. We can be truly grateful that the revelation of God comes to us in a permanently accessible form.

35:30–34 *who kills a person.* The people were not to confuse accidental manslaughter with premeditated murder.

35:2 [s] Lev 25:32-34; Jos 14:3,4 **35:6** [t] Jos 20:7-9; 21:3, 13 **35:8** [u] Nu 26:54; 33:54; Jos 21:1-42 **35:10** [v] Jos 20:2 **35:11** [w] ver 22-25 [x] Ex 21:13; Dt 19:1-13 **35:12** [y] Dt 19:6; Jos 20:3 **35:16** [z] Ex 21:12; Lev 24:17 **35:19** [a] ver 21 **35:20** [b] Ge 4:8; Ex 21:14; Dt 19:11; 2Sa 3:27; 20:10 **35:22** [c] ver 11; Ex 21:13 **35:24** [d] ver 12; Jos 20:6 **35:25** [e] Ex 29:7 **35:29** [f] Nu 27:11 **35:30** [g] ver 16; Dt 17:6; 19:15; Mt 18:16; Jn 7:51; 2Co 13:1; Heb 10:28

31“ ‘Do not accept a ransom for the life of a murderer, who deserves to die. They are to be put to death.

32“ ‘Do not accept a ransom for anyone who has fled to a city of refuge and so allow them to go back and live on their own land before the death of the high priest.

33“ ‘Do not pollute the land where you are. Bloodshed pollutes the land,[h] and atonement cannot be made for the land on which blood has been shed, except by the blood of the one who shed it. 34Do not defile the land[i] where you live and where I dwell,[j] for I, the LORD, dwell among the Israelites.’ ”

Inheritance of Zelophehad’s Daughters

36 The family heads of the clan of Gilead[k] son of Makir, the son of Manasseh, who were from the clans of the descendants of Joseph, came and spoke before Moses and the leaders,[l] the heads of the Israelite families. 2They said, “When the LORD commanded my lord to give the land as an inheritance to the Israelites by lot, he ordered you to give the inheritance of our brother Zelophehad[m] to his daughters. 3Now suppose they marry men from other Israelite tribes; then their inheritance will be taken from our ancestral inheritance and added to that of the tribe they marry into. And so part of the inheritance allotted to us will be taken away. 4When the Year of Jubilee[n] for the Israelites comes, their inheritance will be added to that of the tribe into which they marry, and their property will be taken from the tribal inheritance of our ancestors.”

5Then at the LORD’s command Moses gave this order to the Israelites: “What the tribe of the descendants of Joseph is saying is right. 6This is what the LORD commands for Zelophehad’s daughters: They may marry anyone they please as long as they marry within their father’s tribal clan. 7No inheritance[o] in Israel is to pass from one tribe to another, for every Israelite shall keep the tribal inheritance of their ancestors. 8Every daughter who inherits land in any Israelite tribe must marry someone in her father’s tribal clan,[p] so that every Israelite will possess the inheritance of their ancestors. 9No inheritance may pass from one tribe to another, for each Israelite tribe is to keep the land it inherits.”

10So Zelophehad’s daughters did as the LORD commanded Moses. 11Zelophehad’s daughters—Mahlah, Tirzah, Hoglah, Milkah and Noah[q]—married their cousins on their father’s side. 12They married within the clans of the descendants of Manasseh son of Joseph, and their inheritance remained in their father’s tribe and clan.

13These are the commands and regulations the LORD gave through Moses[r] to the Israelites on the plains of Moab by the Jordan across from Jericho.[s]

36:5 – 13 ***within their father’s tribal clan.*** This beautiful example of concern for fair treatment of Zelophehad’s daughters, consideration for the well-being of the tribe, and obedience to Moses’ decision is a happy ending to this book that is so full of hard heartedness and disobedience.

35:33 [h] Ge 9:6; Ps 106:38; Mic 4:11 **35:34** [i] Lev 18:24,25 [j] Ex 29:45 **36:1** [k] Nu 26:29 [l] Nu 27:2 **36:2** [m] Nu 26:33; 27:1,7 **36:4** [n] Lev 25:10 **36:7** [o] 1Ki 21:3 **36:8** [p] 1Ch 23:22 **36:11** [q] Nu 26:33; 27:1 **36:13** [r] Lev 26:46; 27:34 [s] Nu 22:1

DEUTERONOMY

▶ **AUTHOR:** Numerous external and internal evidences support the authorship of Moses. The Old Testament attributes Deuteronomy to Moses (Josh. 1:7; Judg. 3:4; 1 Kin. 2:3; 2 Kin. 14:6; Ezra 3:2; Neh. 1:7; Ps. 103:7; Dan. 9:11; Mal. 4:4), and there is evidence from Joshua and 1 Samuel to indicate that these laws existed in the form of codified written statutes that influenced the Israelites in Canaan. Christ quoted Deuteronomy when He was being tempted (Matt. 4:4,7,10) and attributed it to Moses (Matt. 19:7–9; Mark 7:10; Luke 20:28; John 5:45–47) as do the more than eighty citations of Deuteronomy in the New Testament. Internally, the book includes about forty claims to Moses as the author (31:24–26; 1:1–5; 4:44–46; 29:1; 31:9). The political and geographic details of Deuteronomy indicate a firsthand knowledge of the events.

▶ **TIME:** c. 1405 B.C. ▶ **KEY VERSE:** Deut. 30:19–20

▶ **THEME:** Deuteronomy is a series of addresses that Moses gives to the nation of Israel just before it enters the Promised Land. In many ways it can be seen as the coach's speech given to a team just before it takes the field. The book reviews and reiterates what has been taught in the previous books of Moses in the same way that a coach's last instructions contain a review of the basic game plan and what has been covered in practice. The purpose of that speech is to focus on what to do and then create the motivation to carry it out. For the Israelites much of the previous instruction was somewhat hypothetical. Many of the laws assumed the occupation of the land. Now, as they stand looking over the Jordan River, they're within reach of moving from the hypothetical to the real and practical. God has renewed His marvelous covenant with them. Now is the time to live up to its requirements.

The Command to Leave Horeb

1 These are the words Moses spoke to
all Israel in the wilderness east of the
Jordan—that is, in the Arabah—opposite
Suph, between Paran and Tophel, Laban,
Hazeroth and Dizahab. 2(It takes eleven
days to go from Horeb[a] to Kadesh Barnea[b]
by the Mount Seir road.)
3In the fortieth year,[c] on the first day of
the eleventh month, Moses proclaimed[d] to
the Israelites all that the LORD had commanded him concerning them. 4This was
after he had defeated Sihon[e] king of the
Amorites, who reigned in Heshbon,[f] and
at Edrei had defeated Og[g] king of Bashan,
who reigned in Ashtaroth.
5East of the Jordan in the territory of
Moab, Moses began to expound this law,
saying:

6The LORD our God said to us[h] at Horeb,[i] "You have stayed long enough at this
mountain. 7Break camp and advance into
the hill country of the Amorites; go to all
the neighboring peoples in the Arabah,
in the mountains, in the western foothills,
in the Negev[j] and along the coast, to the
land of the Canaanites and to Lebanon,[k] as
far as the great river, the Euphrates. 8See,
I have given you this land. Go in and take
possession of the land the LORD swore[l] he
would give to your fathers—to Abraham,
Isaac and Jacob—and to their descendants
after them."

The Appointment of Leaders

9At that time I said to you, "You are too
heavy a burden for me to carry alone.[m]
10The LORD your God has increased your
numbers so that today you are as numerous[n] as the stars in the sky.[o] 11May the
LORD, the God of your ancestors, increase
you a thousand times and bless you as he

1:2 ***eleven days to go.*** A journey that might have taken Israel less than two weeks to complete lasted forty years because of unbelief and disobedience (Num. 13–14).

1:5 ***law.*** The Hebrew word translated "law" basically means "instruction."

1:2 [a] Ex 3:1 [b] Nu 13:26; Dt 9:23 **1:3** [c] Nu 33:38 [d] Dt 4:1-2 **1:4** [e] Nu 21:21-26 [f] Nu 21:25 [g] Nu 21:33-35; Jos 13:12 **1:6** [h] Nu 10:13 [i] Ex 3:1 **1:7** [j] Jos 10:40 [k] Dt 11:24 **1:8** [l] Ge 12:7; 15:18; 17:7-8; 26:4; 28:13 **1:9** [m] Ex 18:18 **1:10** [n] Ge 15:5 [o] Dt 10:22; 28:62

has promised![p] 12But how can I bear your
problems and your burdens and your disputes all by myself? 13Choose some wise,
understanding and respected men[q] from
each of your tribes, and I will set them
over you."
14You answered me, "What you propose
to do is good."
15So I took[r] the leading men of your
tribes, wise and respected men, and appointed them to have authority over you—
as commanders of thousands, of hundreds,
of fifties and of tens and as tribal officials.
16And I charged your judges at that time,
"Hear the disputes between your people
and judge fairly,[s] whether the case is between two Israelites or between an Israelite
and a foreigner residing among you.[t] 17Do
not show partiality[u] in judging; hear both
small and great alike. Do not be afraid
of anyone,[v] for judgment belongs to God.
Bring me any case too hard for you, and I
will hear it."[w] 18And at that time I told you
everything you were to do.

Spies Sent Out

19Then, as the LORD our God commanded
us, we set out from Horeb and went toward
the hill country of the Amorites through
all that vast and dreadful wilderness[x] that
you have seen, and so we reached Kadesh
Barnea.[y] 20Then I said to you, "You have
reached the hill country of the Amorites,
which the LORD our God is giving us. 21See,
the LORD your God has given you the land.
Go up and take possession of it as the LORD,
the God of your ancestors, told you. Do not
be afraid;[z] do not be discouraged."
22Then all of you came to me and said,
"Let us send men ahead to spy out the land
for us and bring back a report about the
route we are to take and the towns we will
come to."
23The idea seemed good to me; so I selected[a] twelve of you, one man from each
tribe. 24They left and went up into the
hill country, and came to the Valley of
Eshkol[b] and explored it. 25Taking with
them some of the fruit of the land, they
brought it down to us and reported,[c] "It is
a good land that the LORD our God is giving us."

Rebellion Against the LORD

26But you were unwilling to go up;[d] you
rebelled against the command of the LORD
your God. 27You grumbled[e] in your tents
and said, "The LORD hates us; so he brought
us out of Egypt to deliver us into the hands
of the Amorites to destroy us. 28Where can
we go? Our brothers have made our hearts
melt in fear. They say, 'The people are
stronger and taller[f] than we are; the cities
are large, with walls up to the sky. We even
saw the Anakites[g] there.'"
29Then I said to you, "Do not be terrified;
do not be afraid of them. 30The LORD your
God, who is going before you, will fight[h] for
you, as he did for you in Egypt, before your
very eyes, 31and in the wilderness. There
you saw how the LORD your God carried[i]
you, as a father carries his son, all the way
you went until you reached this place."
32In spite of this, you did not trust[j] in
the LORD your God, 33who went ahead of
you on your journey, in fire by night and
in a cloud by day,[k] to search[l] out places for
you to camp and to show you the way you
should go.
34When the LORD heard what you said,
he was angry and solemnly swore:[m] 35"No
one from this evil generation shall see the
good land[n] I swore to give your ancestors,
36except Caleb son of Jephunneh. He will
see it, and I will give him and his descendants the land he set his feet on, because he
followed the LORD wholeheartedly.[o]"
37Because of you the LORD became angry[p] with me also and said, "You shall
not enter[q] it, either. 38But your assistant,
Joshua[r] son of Nun, will enter it. Encourage[s] him, because he will lead[t] Israel to inherit it. 39And the little ones that you said
would be taken captive,[u] your children who

1:13 ***wise, understanding.*** The qualities of the leaders reflect the attributes of God. Wisdom is the ability to judge fairly and understand and make wise use of facts. Discernment or understanding is the ability to find the hidden or obscure aspects of a situation.

1:20 ***Amorites.*** The Amorites were one of the groups Israel encountered in their approach to the promised land. This term is often a general designation for the Canaanites.

1:26–28 ***you grumbled.*** An attitude of complaining and criticism toward the circumstances in our lives keeps us from seeing God's hand in the situation. Our situation may indeed be difficult, but God has promised that He will never leave us nor forsake us. Paul said that he had learned how to be content in every circumstance. He made it a habit to give thanks in all things, and knew how to be contented with little, and how to be contented with much. He knew that he could do anything through Christ, who gives us strength (Phil. 4:13).

1:28 ***the Anakites.*** The Anakites were an ancient people known for their great size (Num. 13:28).

1:39 ***the little ones that you said will be taken captive.*** The most outrageous of Israel's complaints

1:11 [p] Ge 22:17; Ex 32:13 **1:13** [q] Ex 18:21
1:15 [r] Ex 18:25 **1:16** [s] Dt 16:18; Jn 7:24 [t] Lev 24:22
1:17 [u] Lev 19:15; Dt 16:19; Pr 24:23; Jas 2:1 [v] 2Ch 19:6
[w] Ex 18:26 **1:19** [x] Dt 8:15; Jer 2:2,6 [y] ver 2; Nu 13:26
1:21 [z] Jos 1:6,9,18 **1:23** [a] Nu 13:1-3
1:24 [b] Nu 13:21-25 **1:25** [c] Nu 13:27 **1:26** [d] Nu 14:1-4
1:27 [e] Dt 9:28; Ps 106:25 **1:28** [f] Nu 13:32 [g] Nu 13:33;
Dt 9:1-3 **1:30** [h] Ex 14:14; Dt 3:22; Ne 4:20
1:31 [i] Dt 32:10-12; Isa 46:3-4; 63:9; Hos 11:3; Ac 13:18
1:32 [j] Ps 106:24; Jude 1:5 **1:33** [k] Ex 13:21; Ps 78:14
[l] Nu 10:33 **1:34** [m] Nu 14:23,28-30 **1:35** [n] Ps 95:11
1:36 [o] Nu 14:24; Jos 14:9 **1:37** [p] Dt 3:26; 4:21 [q] Nu 20:12
1:38 [r] Nu 14:30 [s] Dt 31:7 [t] Dt 3:28 **1:39** [u] Nu 14:3

do not yet know[v] good from bad—they will
enter the land. I will give it to them and
they will take possession of it. 40 But as for
you, turn around and set out toward the
desert along the route to the Red Sea.[a][w]"
41 Then you replied, "We have sinned
against the LORD. We will go up and fight,
as the LORD our God commanded us." So
every one of you put on his weapons, thinking it easy to go up into the hill country.
42 But the LORD said to me, "Tell them,
'Do not go up and fight, because I will not
be with you. You will be defeated by your
enemies.'"[x]
43 So I told you, but you would not listen.
You rebelled against the LORD's command
and in your arrogance you marched up into
the hill country. 44 The Amorites who lived
in those hills came out against you; they
chased you like a swarm of bees[y] and beat
you down from Seir all the way to Hormah.
45 You came back and wept before the LORD,
but he paid no attention to your weeping
and turned a deaf ear to you. 46 And so you
stayed in Kadesh[z] many days—all the time
you spent there.

Wanderings in the Wilderness

2 Then we turned back and set out toward the wilderness along the route to
the Red Sea,[a][a] as the LORD had directed me.
For a long time we made our way around
the hill country of Seir.
2 Then the LORD said to me, 3 "You have
made your way around this hill country
long enough; now turn north. 4 Give the
people these orders:[b] 'You are about to pass
through the territory of your relatives the
descendants of Esau, who live in Seir. They
will be afraid of you, but be very careful.
5 Do not provoke them to war, for I will not
give you any of their land, not even enough
to put your foot on. I have given Esau the
hill country of Seir as his own.[c] 6 You are to
pay them in silver for the food you eat and
the water you drink.'"
7 The LORD your God has blessed you in
all the work of your hands. He has watched[d]
over your journey through this vast wilderness. These forty years the LORD your God
has been with you, and you have not lacked
anything.
8 So we went on past our relatives the
descendants of Esau, who live in Seir. We
turned from the Arabah road, which comes
up from Elath and Ezion Geber,[e] and traveled along the desert road of Moab.[f]
9 Then the LORD said to me, "Do not harass the Moabites or provoke them to war,
for I will not give you any part of their land.
I have given Ar[g] to the descendants of Lot[h]
as a possession."
10 (The Emites[i] used to live there—a people strong and numerous, and as tall as the
Anakites.[j] 11 Like the Anakites, they too
were considered Rephaites, but the Moabites called them Emites. 12 Horites used
to live in Seir, but the descendants of Esau
drove them out. They destroyed the Horites
from before them and settled in their place,
just as Israel did[k] in the land the LORD gave
them as their possession.)
13 And the LORD said, "Now get up and
cross the Zered Valley." So we crossed the
valley.
14 Thirty-eight years passed from the
time we left Kadesh Barnea[l] until we
crossed the Zered Valley. By then, that
entire generation[m] of fighting men had
perished from the camp, as the LORD had
sworn to them.[n] 15 The LORD's hand was
against them until he had completely eliminated[o] them from the camp.
16 Now when the last of these fighting
men among the people had died, 17 the LORD
said to me, 18 "Today you are to pass by the
region of Moab at Ar. 19 When you come
to the Ammonites,[p] do not harass them or
provoke them to war, for I will not give you
possession of any land belonging to the
Ammonites. I have given it as a possession
to the descendants of Lot.[q]"
20 (That too was considered a land of the
Rephaites, who used to live there; but the

[a] *40,1* Or *the Sea of Reeds*

against God was that He had wanted their children to die (Num. 14:31). But the Lord demonstrated His love and faithfulness to His people by protecting those younger than 20 so that they could inherit the land.

1:44 *Hormah.* This name means "destruction," and probably refers to a site south of the Amorite hill country by Kadesh Barnea that was later called by that name.

2:7 *God has blessed.* The Israelites could not have survived forty years in the wilderness without the miraculous provision of God. That care has been an inspiration and encouragement to God's people throughout history. Those who receive God's bounty with a thankful heart find that it is enough, no matter how difficult the circumstances, and those who complain never recognize His blessing at all.

2:8 *We turned ... and traveled.* The Israelites turned away from the way of the Red Sea, on which these cities were located and turned to the desert of Moab, which was the area east of Moab (Num. 33:44).

2:9 *Ar.* Ar is a synonym for the region of Moab. The Moabites were related to the Israelites through Lot (Gen. 19:37).

2:13 *Zered.* The brook of Zered was east of the Dead Sea at the border between Edom and Moab.

2:15 *hand.* The term "hand" suggests God's personal involvement both in acts of deliverance (Ex. 15:6) and in chastisement.

1:39 [v] Isa 7:15-16 **1:40** [w] Nu 14:25 **1:42** [x] Nu 14:41-43 **1:44** [y] Ps 118:12 **1:46** [z] Nu 20:1; Jdg 11:17 **2:1** [a] Nu 21:4 **2:4** [b] Nu 20:14-21 **2:5** [c] Ge 36:8; Jos 24:4 **2:7** [d] Dt 8:2-4 **2:8** [e] 1Ki 9:26 [f] Jdg 11:18 **2:9** [g] Nu 21:15 [h] Ge 19:36-38 **2:10** [i] Ge 14:5 [j] Nu 13:22,33 **2:12** [k] ver 22 **2:14** [l] Nu 13:26 [m] Nu 14:29-35 [n] Dt 1:34-35 **2:15** [o] Ps 106:26 **2:19** [p] Ge 19:38 [q] ver 9

Ammonites called them Zamzummites.
21 They were a people strong and numerous,
and as tall as the Anakites.[r] The LORD destroyed them from before the Ammonites,
who drove them out and settled in their
place. 22 The LORD had done the same for
the descendants of Esau, who lived in Seir,[s]
when he destroyed the Horites from before
them. They drove them out and have lived
in their place to this day. 23 And as for the
Avvites[t] who lived in villages as far as Gaza,
the Caphtorites[u] coming out from Caphtor[a][v]
destroyed them and settled in their place.)

Defeat of Sihon King of Heshbon

24 "Set out now and cross the Arnon
Gorge.[w] See, I have given into your hand
Sihon the Amorite, king of Heshbon, and
his country. Begin to take possession of it
and engage him in battle. 25 This very day I
will begin to put the terror[x] and fear[y] of you
on all the nations under heaven. They will
hear reports of you and will tremble[z] and
be in anguish because of you."

26 From the Desert of Kedemoth I sent
messengers to Sihon king of Heshbon offering peace and saying, 27 "Let us pass
through your country. We will stay on the
main road; we will not turn aside to the right
or to the left.[a] 28 Sell us food to eat and water to drink for their price in silver. Only let
us pass through on foot[b]— 29 as the descendants of Esau, who live in Seir, and the Moabites, who live in Ar, did for us—until we
cross the Jordan into the land the LORD our
God is giving us." 30 But Sihon king of Heshbon refused to let us pass through. For the
LORD[c] your God had made his spirit stubborn[d] and his heart obstinate in order to give
him into your hands, as he has now done.

31 The LORD said to me, "See, I have begun to deliver Sihon and his country over
to you. Now begin to conquer and possess
his land."[e]

32 When Sihon and all his army came out
to meet us in battle[f] at Jahaz, 33 the LORD
our God delivered him over to us and we
struck him down,[g] together with his sons
and his whole army. 34 At that time we took
all his towns and completely destroyed[b][h]
them—men, women and children. We left
no survivors. 35 But the livestock and the
plunder from the towns we had captured
we carried off for ourselves. 36 From Aroer[i]
on the rim of the Arnon Gorge, and from
the town in the gorge, even as far as Gilead, not one town was too strong for us. The
LORD our God gave[j] us all of them. 37 But in
accordance with the command of the LORD
our God,[k] you did not encroach on any of
the land of the Ammonites,[l] neither the
land along the course of the Jabbok[m] nor
that around the towns in the hills.

Defeat of Og King of Bashan

3 Next we turned and went up along the
road toward Bashan, and Og king of
Bashan with his whole army marched out
to meet us in battle at Edrei.[n] 2 The LORD
said to me, "Do not be afraid[o] of him, for I
have delivered him into your hands, along
with his whole army and his land. Do to
him what you did to Sihon king of the Amorites, who reigned in Heshbon."

3 So the LORD our God also gave into our
hands Og king of Bashan and all his army.
We struck them down, leaving no survivors.[p] 4 At that time we took all his cities.
There was not one of the sixty cities that
we did not take from them—the whole region of Argob, Og's kingdom in Bashan.[q]
5 All these cities were fortified with high
walls and with gates and bars, and there
were also a great many unwalled villages. 6 We completely destroyed[b] them, as
we had done with Sihon king of Heshbon,
destroying[b][r] every city—men, women and

---

a 23 That is, Crete *b* 34,6 The Hebrew term refers to the irrevocable giving over of things or persons to the LORD, often by totally destroying them.

2:23 *Avvites ... Gaza ... Caphtorites ... Caphtor.* The Avvites lived in villages between the Jordan and the Mediterranean coast. Gaza was a Philistine city on the Mediterranean coast. The Caphtorites were a group of tribes that came by sea to the coasts of Canaan and Egypt. Caphtor is possibly the same as Crete (Gen. 10:14).

2:24 *Arnon Gorge.* The Arnon Gorge was the traditional border between Moab and Ammon.

2:26 *Desert of Kedemoth.* This desert within the territory of Sihon was located on its eastern border, east of the Dead Sea.

2:32 *Jahaz.* Jahaz was located north of Kedemoth (Is. 15:4).

2:34–35 *completely destroyed.* By the law of the ban, every living thing, human and animal, was to be put to death. Sometimes, as in this case, the Lord permitted the Israelites to take livestock and property as spoil, and sometimes the Lord permitted the women and children to be spared. Canaanite idolatry had reached such abominable levels that the Lord was not willing to put up with it any longer. He intended to put an end to it, and also to prevent the Israelites from being corrupted by the Canaanites.

2:36–37 *Aroer ... Gilead ... Jabbok.* Aroer was a city on the northern bank of the river Arnon at the border between Sihon and Moab. Gilead was the northern boundary of Sihon. Jabbok was the river Jacob crossed on his way back to Canaan (Gen. 32:22).

3:1 *Bashan ... Og.* Bashan was the region east of the Sea of Galilee. The territory of Og may have extended south of the river Yarmuk into Gilead.

2:21 [r] ver 10 **2:22** [s] Ge 36:8 **2:23** [t] Jos 13:3 [u] Ge 10:14 [v] Am 9:7 **2:24** [w] Nu 21:13-14; Jdg 11:13, 18 **2:25** [x] Dt 11:25 [y] Jos 2:9, 11 [z] Ex 15:14-16 **2:27** [a] Nu 21:21-22 **2:28** [b] Nu 20:19 **2:30** [c] Jos 11:20 [d] Ex 4:21; Nu 21:23; Ro 9:18 **2:31** [e] Dt 1:8 **2:32** [f] Nu 21:23 **2:33** [g] Dt 29:7 **2:34** [h] Dt 3:6; 7:2 **2:36** [i] Dt 3:12; 4:48; Jos 13:9 [j] Ps 44:3 **2:37** [k] ver 18-19 [l] Nu 21:24 [m] Ge 32:22; Dt 3:16 **3:1** [n] Nu 21:33 **3:2** [o] Nu 21:34 **3:3** [p] Nu 21:35 **3:4** [q] 1Ki 4:13 **3:6** [r] Dt 2:24, 34

children. 7But all the livestock and the plunder from their cities we carried off for ourselves.

8So at that time we took from these two kings of the Amorites the territory east of the Jordan, from the Arnon Gorge as far as Mount Hermon. 9(Hermon is called Sirion[s] by the Sidonians; the Amorites call it Senir.)[t] 10We took all the towns on the plateau, and all Gilead, and all Bashan as far as Salekah[u] and Edrei, towns of Og's kingdom in Bashan. 11(Og king of Bashan was the last of the Rephaites.[v] His bed was decorated with iron and was more than nine cubits long and four cubits wide.[a] It is still in Rabbah[w] of the Ammonites.)

Division of the Land

12Of the land that we took over at that time, I gave the Reubenites and the Gadites the territory north of Aroer[x] by the Arnon Gorge, including half the hill country of Gilead, together with its towns. 13The rest of Gilead and also all of Bashan, the kingdom of Og, I gave to the half-tribe of Manasseh. (The whole region of Argob in Bashan used to be known as a land of the Rephaites. 14Jair,[y] a descendant of Manasseh, took the whole region of Argob as far as the border of the Geshurites and the Maakathites; it was named after him, so that to this day Bashan is called Havvoth Jair.[b]) 15And I gave Gilead to Makir.[z] 16But to the Reubenites and the Gadites I gave the territory extending from Gilead down to the Arnon Gorge (the middle of the gorge being the border) and out to the Jabbok River,[a] which is the border of the Ammonites. 17Its western border was the Jordan in the Arabah, from Kinnereth[b] to the Sea of the Arabah (that is, the Dead Sea[c]), below the slopes of Pisgah.

18I commanded you at that time: "The LORD your God has given you this land to take possession of it. But all your able-bodied men, armed for battle, must cross over ahead of the other Israelites.[d] 19However, your wives, your children and your livestock (I know you have much livestock) may stay in the towns I have given you, 20until the LORD gives rest to your fellow Israelites as he has to you, and they too have taken over the land that the LORD your God is giving them across the Jordan. After that, each of you may go back to the possession I have given you."

Moses Forbidden to Cross the Jordan

21At that time I commanded Joshua: "You have seen with your own eyes all that the LORD your God has done to these two kings. The LORD will do the same to all the kingdoms over there where you are going. 22Do not be afraid[e] of them; the LORD your God himself will fight[f] for you."

23At that time I pleaded with the LORD: 24"Sovereign LORD, you have begun to show to your servant your greatness[g] and your strong hand. For what god[h] is there in heaven or on earth who can do the deeds and mighty works[i] you do?[j] 25Let me go over and see the good land[k] beyond the Jordan—that fine hill country and Lebanon."

26But because of you the LORD was angry[l] with me and would not listen to me. "That is enough," the LORD said. "Do not speak to me anymore about this matter. 27Go up to the top of Pisgah and look west and north and south and east. Look at the

[a] *11* That is, about 14 feet long and 6 feet wide or about 4 meters long and 1.8 meters wide
[b] *14* Or *called the settlements of Jair*

3:8 *Mount Hermon.* Mount Hermon is in the mountain range in the north between Canaan and Lebanon.
3:9–11 *Sidonians.* The Sidonians were Phoenicians, a well-known ancient seafaring people.
3:10 *Salekah.* Salekah was a city located at the eastern border of Bashan.
3:11 *bed.* "Bed" could also be translated *sarcophagus,* that is, *stone coffin.* ***Rabbah.*** Rabbah was on the site of Amman, the capital of modern Jordan. ***cubits.*** The ordinary cubit is about eighteen inches. Nine cubits is about thirteen feet, and four cubits is about six feet.
3:14 *Geshurites . . . Maakathites.* The Geshurites lived east of the Sea of Galilee and south of Mount Hermon. The Maakathites were descended from Abraham's brother Nahor.
3:17 *Kinnereth.* Kinnereth is another name for the Sea of Galilee.
3:23–25 *pleaded with the LORD.* Moses was a man of prayer and a man of God. He had repeatedly interceded with God for the rebellious Israelites, and God had answered those prayers. Yet this request of Moses to enter the promised land was answered with a decided "no," and with the command not to mention the matter again. We usually don't know why God says "no," to things that seem not only reasonable, but right and good to us. It is hard to give thanks for the answer we did not want, but we must learn that "no" can also be the hand of our loving Heavenly Father. Most of the time we won't see, this side of heaven, how grateful we ought to be for the "no" of God.
3:24 *Sovereign LORD.* The Hebrew word for "Lord," or "Master" is followed by the personal name of God (Yahweh, here translated "GOD"). The respect and humbleness in calling God "Master," the long companionship revealed in calling God by the covenant name, and the pleading, just to see the Promised Land, poignantly speak of Moses' longing.

3:9 [s] Dt 4:48; Ps 29:6 [t] 1Ch 5:23 **3:10** [u] Jos 13:11 **3:11** [v] Ge 14:5 [w] 2Sa 12:26; Jer 49:2 **3:12** [x] Nu 32:32-38; Dt 2:36; Jos 13:8-13 **3:14** [y] Nu 32:41; 1Ch 2:22 **3:15** [z] Nu 32:39-40 **3:16** [a] Nu 21:24 **3:17** [b] Nu 34:11; Jos 13:27 [c] Ge 14:3; Jos 12:3 **3:18** [d] Nu 32:17 **3:22** [e] Dt 1:29 [f] Ex 14:14; Dt 20:4 **3:24** [g] Dt 11:2 [h] Ex 15:11; Ps 86:8 [i] Ps 71:16, 19 [j] 2Sa 7:22 **3:25** [k] Dt 4:22 **3:26** [l] Dt 1:37; 31:2

land with your own eyes, since you are not going to cross this Jordan.[m] **28**But commission[n] Joshua, and encourage and strengthen him, for he will lead this people across[o] and will cause them to inherit the land that you will see." **29**So we stayed in the valley near Beth Peor.[p]

Obedience Commanded

4 Now, Israel, hear the decrees and laws I am about to teach you. Follow them so that you may live[q] and may go in and take possession of the land the LORD, the God of your ancestors, is giving you. **2**Do not add[r] to what I command you and do not subtract from it, but keep the commands of the LORD your God that I give you.

3You saw with your own eyes what the LORD did at Baal Peor.[s] The LORD your God destroyed from among you everyone who followed the Baal of Peor, **4**but all of you who held fast to the LORD your God are still alive today.

5See, I have taught you decrees and laws as the LORD my God commanded me, so that you may follow them in the land you are entering to take possession of it. **6**Observe them carefully, for this will show your wisdom[t] and understanding to the nations, who will hear about all these decrees and say, "Surely this great nation is a wise and understanding people."[u] **7**What other nation is so great[v] as to have their gods near[w] them the way the LORD our God is near us whenever we pray to him? **8**And what other nation is so great as to have such righteous decrees and laws as this body of laws I am setting before you today?

9Only be careful,[x] and watch yourselves closely so that you do not forget the things your eyes have seen or let them fade from your heart as long as you live. Teach[y] them to your children[z] and to their children after them. **10**Remember the day you stood before the LORD your God at Horeb,[a] when he said to me, "Assemble the people before me to hear my words so that they may learn to revere me as long as they live in the land and may teach them to their children." **11**You came near and stood at the foot of the mountain while it blazed with fire[b] to the very heavens, with black clouds and deep darkness. **12**Then the LORD spoke[c] to you out of the fire. You heard the sound of words but saw no form; there was only a voice. **13**He declared to you his covenant,[d] the Ten Commandments,[e] which he commanded you to follow and then wrote them on two stone tablets. **14**And the LORD directed me at that time to teach you the decrees and laws you are to follow in the land that you are crossing the Jordan to possess.

Idolatry Forbidden

15You saw no form[f] of any kind the day the LORD spoke to you at Horeb out of the fire. Therefore watch yourselves very carefully,[g] **16**so that you do not become corrupt and make for yourselves an idol,[h] an image of any shape, whether formed like a man or a woman, **17**or like any animal on earth or any bird that flies in the air, **18**or like any creature that moves along the ground or any fish in the waters below. **19**And when you look up to the sky and see the sun,[i] the moon and the stars—all the heavenly array[j]—do not be enticed into bowing down to them and worshiping things the LORD your God has apportioned to all the nations under heaven. **20**But as for you, the LORD took you and brought you out of the iron-smelting furnace,[k] out of Egypt, to be the people of his inheritance,[l] as you now are.

3:29 ***Beth Peor.*** This was a pagan site dedicated to Baal of Peor (Num. 25:3–5) and was the scene of Israel's first disastrous encounter with the sexually centered worship of Baal (4:3).

4:1 ***hear.*** The exhortation to listen includes an encouragement to obey (4:9; 5:1; 6:3–4).

4:6 ***to the nations.*** By living in obedience to God, Israel would become a countercultural force, showing the way of God in both society and government.

4:9 ***your children.*** One of the purposes of the family is to pass on from generation to generation the acts of God among men. In times where the written record did not exist, or where people could not read, the wonderful acts of God were repeated in stories and conversations. With the Bible readily available, we don't have to rely on our memories alone to recall the things that God has done, but we are still responsible to make these things known to our children. It is also important to tell our children about the times that the Lord has answered our prayers, convicted our conscience, and blessed us with His peace. The best role model a child can have is a parent whose heart is centered on the Lord.

4:12 ***heard . . . but saw no form.*** The Lord revealed His glory to the Israelites, but they saw no visual image other than darkness and fire. They did hear God's voice, however (v. 15). This verse reminds us that God is Spirit (John 4:24).

4:15–19 ***You saw no form.*** There was no way of describing or giving shape with any image to the experience of God's presence at Sinai (Ex. 20:18). Since Israel had not seen the form of God, they could not represent Him in any way. Although people were created in the likeness of God (Gen. 1:26–27), no image created in human likeness could represent God, nor could any animal or the majestic heavenly bodies. The Israelites could know God's creation, His power, and His character, but they would have to be satisfied to know Him without any visual image.

3:27 [m] Nu 27:12 **3:28** [n] Nu 27:18-23 [o] Dt 31:3, 23 **3:29** [p] Dt 4:46; 34:6 **4:1** [q] Dt 5:33; 8:1; 16:20; 30:15-20; Eze 20:11; Ro 10:5 **4:2** [r] Dt 12:32; Jos 1:7; Rev 22:18-19 **4:3** [s] Nu 25:1-9; Ps 106:28 **4:6** [t] Dt 30:19-20; Ps 19:7; Pr 1:7 [u] Job 28:28 **4:7** [v] 2Sa 7:23 [w] Ps 46:1; Isa 55:6 **4:9** [x] Pr 4:23 [y] Ge 18:19; Eph 6:4 [z] Ps 78:5-6 **4:10** [a] Ex 19:9, 16 **4:11** [b] Ex 19:18; Heb 12:18-19 **4:12** [c] Ex 20:22; Dt 5:4, 22 **4:13** [d] Dt 9:9, 11 [e] Ex 24:12; 31:18; 34:28 **4:15** [f] Isa 40:18 [g] Jos 23:11 **4:16** [h] Ex 20:4-5; 32:7; Dt 5:8; Ro 1:23 **4:19** [i] Dt 17:3; Job 31:26 [j] 2Ki 17:16; 21:3; Ro 1:25 **4:20** [k] 1Ki 8:51; Jer 11:4 [l] Ex 19:5; Dt 9:29

21The LORD was angry with me[m] because
of you, and he solemnly swore that I would
not cross the Jordan and enter the good land
the LORD your God is giving you as your inheritance. 22I will die in this land; I will not
cross the Jordan; but you are about to cross
over and take possession of that good land.[n]
23Be careful not to forget the covenant[o] of
the LORD your God that he made with you;
do not make for yourselves an idol[p] in the
form of anything the LORD your God has
forbidden. 24For the LORD your God is a
consuming fire,[q] a jealous God.
25After you have had children and
grandchildren and have lived in the land
a long time—if you then become corrupt
and make any kind of idol, doing evil[r] in
the eyes of the LORD your God and arousing his anger, 26I call the heavens and the
earth as witnesses against you[s] this day
that you will quickly perish from the land
that you are crossing the Jordan to possess. You will not live there long but will
certainly be destroyed. 27The LORD will
scatter[t] you among the peoples, and only a
few of you will survive among the nations
to which the LORD will drive you. 28There
you will worship man-made gods[u] of wood
and stone, which cannot see or hear or eat
or smell.[v] 29But if from there you seek[w] the
LORD your God, you will find him if you
seek him with all your heart[x] and with all
your soul.[y] 30When you are in distress and
all these things have happened to you, then
in later days[z] you will return to the LORD
your God and obey him. 31For the LORD
your God is a merciful[a] God; he will not
abandon or destroy you or forget the covenant with your ancestors, which he confirmed to them by oath.

The LORD Is God

32Ask[b] now about the former days, long
before your time, from the day God created human beings on the earth;[c] ask from
one end of the heavens to the other.[d] Has
anything so great as this ever happened,
or has anything like it ever been heard of?
33Has any other people heard the voice of
God[a] speaking out of fire, as you have, and
lived?[e] 34Has any god ever tried to take for
himself one nation out of another nation,[f]
by testings, by signs[g] and wonders,[h] by
war, by a mighty hand and an outstretched
arm,[i] or by great and awesome deeds,[j] like
all the things the LORD your God did for
you in Egypt before your very eyes?
35You were shown these things so that
you might know that the LORD is God; besides him there is no other.[k] 36From heaven
he made you hear his voice[l] to discipline
you. On earth he showed you his great fire,
and you heard his words from out of the
fire. 37Because he loved[m] your ancestors
and chose their descendants after them, he
brought you out of Egypt by his Presence
and his great strength,[n] 38to drive out before you nations greater and stronger than
you and to bring you into their land to give
it to you for your inheritance,[o] as it is today.
39Acknowledge and take to heart this
day that the LORD is God in heaven above
and on the earth below. There is no other.[p] 40Keep[q] his decrees and commands,
which I am giving you today, so that it may
go well[r] with you and your children after
you and that you may live long[s] in the land
the LORD your God gives you for all time.

Cities of Refuge

41Then Moses set aside three cities east
of the Jordan, 42to which anyone who had
killed a person could flee if they had unintentionally killed a neighbor without
malice aforethought. They could flee into
one of these cities and save their life. 43The
cities were these: Bezer in the wilderness
plateau, for the Reubenites; Ramoth in Gilead, for the Gadites; and Golan in Bashan,
for the Manassites.

Introduction to the Law

44This is the law Moses set before the
Israelites. 45These are the stipulations,

---

[a] 33 Or *of a god*

4:24 *a consuming fire ... jealous.* God is free to destroy disobedient and rebellious people. Israel had witnessed His righteous anger during the wilderness journey as well as in Canaan (Heb. 12:19; Num. 16). "Jealous" means that God will tolerate no rivalry or unfaithfulness. This word can also be translated *zealous*. God is zealous for His holiness.

4:26 *the heavens and the earth.* All creation would act as God's witness against a rebellious and obstinate people. God's invisible attributes, His eternal power and divine nature are all clearly seen in creation (Rom. 1:20), so that man is without excuse. The creation belongs to God just as much as man does, and God uses it for His eternal purposes, one of which is to stand as a witness to the disobedient.

4:27 *scatter you among the peoples.* This is a prophetic warning of the exiles that would take place in 722 and 586 B.C.

4:40 *that it may go well with you.* The promise of blessing in the land was conditional—it required obedience.

4:21 [m] Nu 20:12; Dt 1:37 **4:22** [n] Dt 3:25 **4:23** [o] ver 9, 16 [p] Ex 20:4 **4:24** [q] Ex 24:17; Dt 9:3; Heb 12:29 **4:25** [r] 2Ki 17:2, 17 **4:26** [s] Dt 30:18-19; Isa 1:2; Mic 6:2 **4:27** [t] Lev 26:33; Dt 28:36, 64; Ne 1:8 **4:28** [u] Dt 28:36, 64; 1Sa 26:19; Jer 16:13 [v] Ps 115:4-8; 135:15-18 **4:29** [w] 2Ch 15:4; Isa 55:6 [x] Jer 29:13 [y] Dt 30:1-3, 10 **4:30** [z] Dt 31:29; Jer 23:20; Hos 3:5 **4:31** [a] 2Ch 30:9; Ne 9:31; Ps 116:5; Jnh 4:2 **4:32** [b] Dt 32:7; Job 8:8 [c] Ge 1:27 [d] Mt 24:31 **4:33** [e] Ex 20:22; Dt 5:24-26 **4:34** [f] Ex 6:6 [g] Ex 7:3 [h] Dt 7:19; 26:8 [i] Ex 13:3 [j] Dt 34:12 **4:35** [k] Dt 32:39; 1Sa 2:2; Isa 45:5, 18 **4:36** [l] Ex 19:9, 19 **4:37** [m] Dt 10:15 [n] Ex 13:3, 9, 14 **4:38** [o] Dt 7:1; 9:5 **4:39** [p] ver 35; Jos 2:11 **4:40** [q] Lev 22:31; Dt 5:33 [r] Dt 5:16 [s] Dt 6:3, 18; Eph 6:2-3

decrees and laws Moses gave them when
they came out of Egypt 46and were in the
valley near Beth Peor east of the Jordan,
in the land of Sihon[t] king of the Amorites,
who reigned in Heshbon and was defeated
by Moses and the Israelites as they came
out of Egypt. 47They took possession of his
land and the land of Og king of Bashan,
the two Amorite kings east of the Jordan.
48This land extended from Aroer[u] on the
rim of the Arnon Gorge to Mount Sirion[a][v]
(that is, Hermon), 49and included all the Arabah east of the Jordan, as far as the Dead
Sea,[b] below the slopes of Pisgah.

The Ten Commandments

5 Moses summoned all Israel and said:
Hear, Israel, the decrees and laws I declare in your hearing today. Learn them
and be sure to follow them. 2The LORD our
God made a covenant[w] with us at Horeb. 3It
was not with our ancestors[c] that the LORD
made this covenant, but with us, with all
of us who are alive here today.[x] 4The LORD
spoke[y] to you face to face out of the fire on
the mountain. 5(At that time I stood between[z] the LORD and you to declare to you
the word of the LORD, because you were
afraid[a] of the fire and did not go up the
mountain.) And he said:

6"I am the LORD your God, who brought you out of Egypt, out of the land of slavery.

7"You shall have no other gods before[d] me.

8"You shall not make for yourself an image in the form of anything in heaven above or on the earth beneath or in the waters below.
9You shall not bow down to them
or worship them; for I, the LORD
your God, am a jealous God, punishing the children for the sin of
the parents to the third and fourth
generation of those who hate me,[b]
10but showing love to a thousand
generations of those who love me
and keep my commandments.[c]

11"You shall not misuse the name of the LORD your God, for the LORD will not hold anyone guiltless who misuses his name.[d]

12"Observe the Sabbath day by keeping
it holy,[e] as the LORD your God has
commanded you. 13Six days you
shall labor and do all your work,
14but the seventh day[f] is a sabbath
to the LORD your God. On it you
shall not do any work, neither
you, nor your son or daughter,
nor your male or female servant,
nor your ox, your donkey or any
of your animals, nor any foreigner residing in your towns, so that
your male and female servants
may rest, as you do. 15Remember
that you were slaves in Egypt and
that the LORD your God brought
you out of there with a mighty
hand and an outstretched arm.[g]
Therefore the LORD your God has
commanded you to observe the
Sabbath day.

16"Honor your father and your mother,[h] as the LORD your God has commanded you, so that you may live long[i] and that it may go well with you in the land the LORD your God is giving you.

17"You shall not murder.[j]

18"You shall not commit adultery.[k]

19"You shall not steal.

20"You shall not give false testimony against your neighbor.

21"You shall not covet your neighbor's wife. You shall not set your desire on your neighbor's house or land, his male or female servant, his ox or donkey, or anything that belongs to your neighbor."[l]

22These are the commandments the
LORD proclaimed in a loud voice to your

---

[a] 48 Syriac (see also 3:9); Hebrew *Siyon*
[b] 49 Hebrew *the Sea of the Arabah*
[c] 3 Or *not only with our parents*
[d] 7 Or *besides*

5:6–21 Commandments—The Ten Commandments are the basis for holy living, not just a list of rules, but an explanation of what God expects of us. Loving God comes first. Setting aside a day to focus on God is essential for maintaining this relationship. The way we feel about God will affect the way we feel about people, and this will have a direct effect on how we treat others. Even though these three ideas summarize the Commandments, it is also essential to examine each individual command and think about how it applies to our lives. It is not easy to faithfully obey these simple statements.

5:11 *misuse.* Misusing the name of the Lord refers to the abuse, blasphemy, cursing, or manipulation of the Lord's name. .

5:12 *the Sabbath.* The primary significance of the Sabbath was that it belonged to the Lord.

5:18 *adultery.* Adultery was a betrayal not only of a commitment, but of a relationship. Anyone who treated marriage lightly would also treat his or her relationship with God lightly.

5:21 *covet.* This command deals specifically with an attitude, rather than an action. Covetousness is self-centered dissatisfaction, which does not reflect loving concern for the well-being of others. Loving God and loving others are closely connected (Matt. 22:37–39).

5:22 *wrote them on two stone tablets . . . gave*

4:46 [t] Nu 21:26; Dt 3:29 **4:48** [u] Dt 2:36 [v] Dt 3:9
5:2 [w] Ex 19:5 **5:3** [x] Heb 8:9 **5:4** [y] Dt 4:12, 33, 36
5:5 [z] Gal 3:19 [a] Ex 20:18, 21 **5:9** [b] Ex 34:7
5:10 [c] Jer 32:18 **5:11** [d] Lev 19:12; Mt 5:33-37
5:12 [e] Ex 20:8 **5:14** [f] Ge 2:2; Heb 4:4 **5:15** [g] Dt 4:34
5:16 [h] Ex 20:12; Lev 19:3; Dt 27:16; Eph 6:2-3*; Col 3:20
[i] Dt 4:40 **5:17** [j] Mt 5:21-22* **5:18** [k] Mt 5:27-30;
Lk 18:20*; Jas 2:11* **5:21** [l] Ro 7:7*; 13:9*

whole assembly there on the mountain
from out of the fire, the cloud and the deep
darkness; and he added nothing more.
Then he wrote them on two stone tablets[m]
and gave them to me.
23 When you heard the voice out of the
darkness, while the mountain was ablaze
with fire, all the leaders of your tribes and
your elders came to me. 24 And you said,
"The LORD our God has shown us his glory and his majesty, and we have heard his
voice from the fire. Today we have seen that
a person can live even if God speaks with
them.[n] 25 But now, why should we die? This
great fire will consume us, and we will die
if we hear the voice of the LORD our God any
longer.[o] 26 For what mortal has ever heard
the voice of the living God speaking out of
fire, as we have, and survived?[p] 27 Go near
and listen to all that the LORD our God says.
Then tell us whatever the LORD our God tells
you. We will listen and obey."
28 The LORD heard you when you spoke to
me, and the LORD said to me, "I have heard
what this people said to you. Everything
they said was good.[q] 29 Oh, that their hearts
would be inclined to fear me[r] and keep all
my commands[s] always, so that it might go
well with them and their children forever![t]
30 "Go, tell them to return to their tents.
31 But you stay here[u] with me so that I may
give you all the commands, decrees and
laws you are to teach them to follow in the
land I am giving them to possess."
32 So be careful to do what the LORD your
God has commanded you; do not turn aside
to the right or to the left.[v] 33 Walk in obedience to all that the LORD your God has
commanded you,[w] so that you may live and
prosper and prolong your days[x] in the land
that you will possess.

Love the LORD Your God

6 These are the commands, decrees and
laws the LORD your God directed me to
teach you to observe in the land that you
are crossing the Jordan to possess, 2 so that
you, your children and their children after
them may fear[y] the LORD your God as long
as you live by keeping all his decrees and
commands that I give you, and so that you
may enjoy long life. 3 Hear, Israel, and be
careful to obey so that it may go well with
you and that you may increase greatly[z] in a
land flowing with milk and honey,[a] just as
the LORD, the God of your ancestors, promised you.
4 Hear, O Israel: The LORD our God, the
LORD is one.[a][b] 5 Love[c] the LORD your God
with all your heart and with all your soul
and with all your strength.[d] 6 These com-

[a] 4 Or *The LORD our God is one LORD*; or *The LORD is our God, the LORD is one*; or *The LORD is our God, the LORD alone*

them. The two tablets were two complete copies of the law. Usually two copies were made of ancient Middle Eastern treaties. One was retained by each of the contracting parties. But God gave both copies to Moses, signifying that God Himself would be with the Israelites. God and the Israelites kept their copies in the same place because they lived together.

5:25–26 *why should we die ... LORD our God.* The Israelites' fear was an important part of understanding their sin and need for help in meeting the requirements of God. The living God is powerful, great, and holy, and He wants us to be like Him, so each sinner needs to realize the need for God's mercy.

5:29 *their hearts.* The people were impressed with what they saw and heard, but their hearts were unchanged.

6:2 *fear.* The fear of the Lord includes awe for His greatness and holiness, love for Him, and submission to His will. Initially, the fear of God may involve fright, knowing that God has the right to punish us for our sins. But when we look at his holiness and love, there is a joy in knowing God, who not only sees us for who we really are, but helps us to be who He wants us to be.

6:3 *God of your ancestors.* God was their God, generation after generation, and He expected them to follow Him, from generation to generation as well.

6:4 *Hear, O Israel.* This verse is the celebrated Shema, the basic confession of faith in Judaism (Matt. 22:37; Mark 12:29; Luke 10:27). The first word, "hear," is the Hebrew word *shema.* The people are to hear and respond properly to God. He is their God, and He alone is the Lord.

6:4–9 Passing on the Faith—In the days leading up to the end of Moses' leadership, he laid out the essentials of raising a family to follow God. Moses knew that these instructions were a foundational element in Israel's future. The only way the Israelites could maintain the land they were going to possess was to make sure that the faith would be passed on to each succeeding generation. Nothing has changed. Today we need to heed the same instructions.

In a family's life the teaching of God is to be a constant, daily effort. God is to be made a part of everyday life. It is the responsibility of a parent to be constantly looking for opportunities to teach children about God's instructions for living. God's instructions should be like clothing. They should be put on the minute we get up and kept on all day. They are to be our constant companions. Sharing our faith should be a natural part of daily communication with our children. We should also remember that these instructions come in the text subsequent to the command to love God with all of our heart and soul and strength. How else can we love Him better than by obeying and following Him and teaching our children to do the same?

6:5 *Love.* Moses repeatedly exhorted the Israelites to respond to God's love with devotion. God

5:22 [m] Ex 24:12; 31:18; Dt 4:13 **5:24** [n] Ex 19:19 **5:25** [o] Dt 18:16 **5:26** [p] Dt 4:33 **5:28** [q] Dt 18:17 **5:29** [r] Ps 81:8, 13 [s] Dt 11:1; Isa 48:18 [t] Dt 4:1, 40 **5:31** [u] Ex 24:12 **5:32** [v] Dt 17:11, 20; 28:14; Jos 1:7; 23:6; Pr 4:27 **5:33** [w] Jer 7:23 [x] Dt 4:40 **6:2** [y] Ex 20:20; Dt 10:12-13 **6:3** [z] Dt 5:33 [a] Ex 3:8 **6:4** [b] Mk 12:29*; 1Co 8:4 **6:5** [c] Mt 22:37*; Mk 12:30*; Lk 10:27* [d] Dt 10:12

mandments that I give you today are to be
on your hearts.[e] 7Impress them on your
children. Talk about them when you sit at
home and when you walk along the road,
when you lie down and when you get up.[f]
8Tie them as symbols on your hands and
bind them on your foreheads.[g] 9Write them
on the doorframes of your houses and on
your gates.[h]

10When the LORD your God brings you
into the land he swore to your fathers, to
Abraham, Isaac and Jacob, to give you—a
land with large, flourishing cities you did
not build,[i] 11houses filled with all kinds of
good things you did not provide, wells you
did not dig, and vineyards and olive groves
you did not plant—then when you eat and
are satisfied,[j] 12be careful that you do not
forget the LORD, who brought you out of
Egypt, out of the land of slavery.

13Fear the LORD[k] your God, serve him
only[l] and take your oaths in his name. 14Do
not follow other gods, the gods of the peoples around you; 15for the LORD your God[m],
who is among you, is a jealous God and his
anger will burn against you, and he will
destroy you from the face of the land. 16Do
not put the LORD your God to the test[n] as
you did at Massah. 17Be sure to keep the
commands of the LORD your God and the
stipulations and decrees he has given you.[o]
18Do what is right and good in the LORD's
sight, so that it may go well[p] with you and
you may go in and take over the good land
the LORD promised on oath to your ancestors, 19thrusting out all your enemies before you, as the LORD said.

20In the future, when your son asks
you,[q] "What is the meaning of the stipulations, decrees and laws the LORD our
God has commanded you?" 21tell him:
"We were slaves of Pharaoh in Egypt, but
the LORD brought us out of Egypt with a
mighty hand. 22Before our eyes the LORD
sent signs and wonders—great and terrible—on Egypt and Pharaoh and his whole
household. 23But he brought us out from
there to bring us in and give us the land he
promised on oath to our ancestors. 24The
LORD commanded us to obey all these decrees and to fear the LORD our God,[r] so that
we might always prosper and be kept alive,
as is the case today.[s] 25And if we are careful to obey all this law before the LORD our
God, as he has commanded us, that will be
our righteousness.[t]"

Driving Out the Nations

7 When the LORD your God brings you
into the land you are entering to possess
and drives out before you many nations[u]—
the Hittites, Girgashites, Amorites, Canaanites, Perizzites, Hivites and Jebusites,
seven nations larger and stronger than
you— 2and when the LORD your God has
delivered them over to you and you have
defeated them, then you must destroy them
totally.[a] Make no treaty[v] with them, and
show them no mercy.[w] 3Do not intermarry
with them.[x] Do not give your daughters to
their sons or take their daughters for your
sons, 4for they will turn your children away
from following me to serve other gods, and
the LORD's anger will burn against you and
will quickly destroy[y] you. 5This is what you
are to do to them: Break down their altars,
smash their sacred stones, cut down their
Asherah poles[b] and burn their idols in the

---

[a] 2 The Hebrew term refers to the irrevocable giving over of things or persons to the LORD, often by totally destroying them; also in verse 26.
[b] 5 That is, wooden symbols of the goddess Asherah; here and elsewhere in Deuteronomy

---

commanded His people to choose Him with all their being, and in the process to deny all other supposed deities.

6:8–9 ***hands ... foreheads ... doorframes ... gates.*** In later years the Jews interpreted these instructions by wearing phylacteries (boxes containing Scripture) when they prayed. They attached a small vessel called a mezuzah, which contained these verses, to the doorpost. The purpose of this whole passage is to emphasize that God's ways are to be a part of our conversations, our homes, and every activity. They are to be as close to us and as visible as our hand or our forehead.

6:20–24 ***your son asks.*** The answer to the Israelite child's question would include four components: we were slaves in Egypt, the Lord brought us out with a mighty hand, He gave us land, and we have a challenge to responsible action. This is a powerful teaching tool, and one that applies to all Christians. We are to teach our children that we were slaves to sin, the Lord Jesus brought us out with a mighty hand, He has given us a Kingdom, and we have a challenge to responsible action.

7:1 ***Hittites, Girgashites, Amorites, Canaanites, Perizzites, Hivites and Jebusites.*** The Hittites came originally from Asia Minor (Gen. 23:10). The Girgashites are an unknown people (Gen. 10:16; 1 Chr. 1:14). The Amorites were the native population of Canaan that had settled in the mountains. The Canaanites were the native population that had settled in the coastland, the Perizzites were the native population that had settled in the hill country, and the Hivites were the native population that had settled south of the Lebanon mountains. The Jebusites (perhaps an offshoot of the Hittites) were the native population settled near what later became Jerusalem.

7:2 ***treaty.*** Treaty refers to any covenant with the Canaanite nations that might undermine God's covenant with Israel.

6:6 [e] Dt 11:18 **6:7** [f] Dt 4:9; 11:19; Eph 6:4 **6:8** [g] Ex 13:9, 16; Dt 11:18 **6:9** [h] Dt 11:20 **6:10** [i] Jos 24:13 **6:11** [j] Dt 8:10 **6:13** [k] Dt 10:20 [l] Mt 4:10*; Lk 4:8* **6:15** [m] Dt 4:24 **6:16** [n] Ex 17:7; Mt 4:7*; Lk 4:12* **6:17** [o] Dt 11:22; Ps 119:4 **6:18** [p] Dt 4:40 **6:20** [q] Ex 13:14 **6:24** [r] Dt 10:12; Jer 32:39 [s] Ps 41:2 **6:25** [t] Dt 24:13, Ro 10:3, 5 **7:1** [u] Dt 31:3; Ac 13:19 **7:2** [v] Ex 23:32 [w] Dt 13:8 **7:3** [x] Ex 34:15-16; Ezr 9:2 **7:4** [y] Dt 6:15

fire.[z] 6For you are a people holy[a] to the
LORD your God.[b] The LORD your God has
chosen[c] you out of all the peoples on the
face of the earth to be his people, his treasured possession.
7The LORD did not set his affection on
you and choose you because you were
more numerous than other peoples, for
you were the fewest of all peoples.[d] 8But it
was because the LORD loved[e] you and kept
the oath he swore[f] to your ancestors that he
brought you out with a mighty hand and
redeemed you from the land of slavery,[g]
from the power of Pharaoh king of Egypt.
9Know therefore that the LORD your God is
God;[h] he is the faithful God,[i] keeping his
covenant of love[j] to a thousand generations
of those who love him and keep his commandments. 10But

those who hate him he will repay to
their face by destruction;
he will not be slow to repay to their
face those who hate him.

11Therefore, take care to follow the commands, decrees and laws I give you today.
12If you pay attention to these laws and
are careful to follow them, then the LORD
your God will keep his covenant of love
with you, as he swore to your ancestors.[k]
13He will love you and bless you[l] and increase your numbers. He will bless the
fruit of your womb, the crops of your
land—your grain, new wine and olive oil—
the calves of your herds and the lambs of
your flocks in the land he swore to your ancestors to give you.[m] 14You will be blessed
more than any other people; none of your
men or women will be childless, nor will
any of your livestock be without young.[n]
15The LORD will keep you free from every
disease.[o] He will not inflict on you the horrible diseases you knew in Egypt, but he
will inflict them on all who hate you. 16You
must destroy all the peoples the LORD your
God gives over to you. Do not look on them
with pity[p] and do not serve their gods, for
that will be a snare[q] to you.
17You may say to yourselves, "These nations are stronger than we are. How can we
drive them out?[r]" 18But do not be afraid[s] of
them; remember well what the LORD your
God did to Pharaoh and to all Egypt.[t] 19You
saw with your own eyes the great trials, the
signs and wonders, the mighty hand and
outstretched arm, with which the LORD
your God brought you out. The LORD your
God will do the same to all the peoples you
now fear.[u] 20Moreover, the LORD your God
will send the hornet[v] among them until
even the survivors who hide from you have
perished. 21Do not be terrified by them, for
the LORD your God, who is among you,[w]
is a great and awesome God.[x] 22The LORD
your God will drive out those nations before you, little by little.[y] You will not be
allowed to eliminate them all at once, or
the wild animals will multiply around you.
23But the LORD your God will deliver them
over to you, throwing them into great confusion until they are destroyed. 24He will
give their kings into your hand, and you
will wipe out their names from under heav-
en. No one will be able to stand up against
you;[z] you will destroy them. 25The images
of their gods you are to burn[a] in the fire. Do
not covet[b] the silver and gold on them, and
do not take it for yourselves, or you will be
ensnared[c] by it, for it is detestable[d] to the
LORD your God. 26Do not bring a detestable
thing into your house or you, like it, will be
set apart for destruction.[e] Regard it as vile
and utterly detest it, for it is set apart for
destruction.

Do Not Forget the LORD

8 Be careful to follow every command I
am giving you today, so that you may
live[f] and increase and may enter and possess the land the LORD promised on oath to
your ancestors. 2Remember how the LORD
your God led[g] you all the way in the wilderness these forty years, to humble and
test you in order to know what was in your
heart, whether or not you would keep his
commands. 3He humbled you, causing you
to hunger and then feeding you with manna,[h] which neither you nor your ancestors
had known, to teach you that man does not
live on bread alone but on every word that
comes from the mouth of the LORD.[i] 4Your

7:22 *little by little.* God's plan was that the land would be conquered in two stages. The first was a broad, rapid conquest under Joshua, and the second was a gradual, area by area conquest.

8:3 *man does not live on bread alone.* Humans have a spiritual nature that can be satisfied only by the spiritual nutrients of God's Word. Jesus used these words to rebuke Satan when Jesus was tempted in the wilderness (Matt. 4:4; Luke 4:1–4). ***comes from the mouth of the LORD.*** The Bible is valuable because it is the word of God. It is inspired by God not only in the sense that it is relating true events, but because God knows the kinds of things that people need to know to follow Him in a world of sin, uncertainty, and death. God's word is man's only wisdom and hope. When people study it, rely on it, and apply it, the word will prove to be both wise and right. For God is as good as His every word, and God's every word is as good as the One from whom it comes.

7:5 [z] Ex 23:24; Dt 12:2-3 **7:6** [a] Ex 19:5-6; 1Pe 2:9 [b] Ps 50:5; Jer 2:3 [c] Dt 14:2 **7:7** [d] Dt 10:22 **7:8** [e] Dt 10:15 [f] Ex 32:13 [g] Ex 13:14 **7:9** [h] Dt 4:35 [i] 1Co 1:9; 2Ti 2:13 [j] Ne 1:5; Da 9:4 **7:12** [k] Lev 26:3-13; Dt 28:1-14; Ps 105:8-9 **7:13** [l] Jn 14:21 [m] Dt 28:4 **7:14** [n] Ex 23:26 **7:15** [o] Ex 15:26 **7:16** [p] ver 2; Ex 23:33 [q] Jdg 8:27 **7:17** [r] Nu 33:53 **7:18** [s] Dt 31:6 [t] Ps 105:5 **7:19** [u] Dt 4:34 **7:20** [v] Ex 23:28; Jos 24:12 **7:21** [w] Jos 3:10 [x] Dt 10:17; Ne 9:32 **7:22** [y] Ex 23:28-30 **7:24** [z] Jos 23:9 **7:25** [a] Ex 32:20; 1Ch 14:12 [b] Jos 7:21 [c] Jdg 8:27 [d] Dt 17:1 **7:26** [e] Lev 27:28-29 **8:1** [f] Dt 4:1 **8:2** [g] Am 2:10 **8:3** [h] Ex 16:12, 14, 35 [i] Ex 16:2-3; Mt 4:4*; Lk 4:4*

clothes did not wear out and your feet did not swell during these forty years.[j] 5Know then in your heart that as a man disciplines his son, so the LORD your God disciplines you.[k]

6Observe the commands of the LORD your God, walking in obedience to him and revering him.[l] 7For the LORD your God is bringing you into a good land—a land with brooks, streams, and deep springs gushing out into the valleys and hills;[m] 8a land with wheat and barley, vines and fig trees, pomegranates, olive oil and honey; 9a land where bread will not be scarce and you will lack nothing; a land where the rocks are iron and you can dig copper out of the hills.

10When you have eaten and are satisfied,[n] praise the LORD your God for the good land he has given you. 11Be careful that you do not forget the LORD your God, failing to observe his commands, his laws and his decrees that I am giving you this day. 12Otherwise, when you eat and are satisfied, when you build fine houses and settle down,[o] 13and when your herds and flocks grow large and your silver and gold increase and all you have is multiplied, 14then your heart will become proud and you will forget[p] the LORD your God, who brought you out of Egypt, out of the land of slavery. 15He led you through the vast and dreadful wilderness,[q] that thirsty and waterless land, with its venomous snakes[r] and scorpions. He brought you water out of hard rock.[s] 16He gave you manna to eat in the wilderness, something your ancestors had never known,[t] to humble and test you so that in the end it might go well with you. 17You may say to yourself,[u] "My power and the strength of my hands have produced this wealth for me." 18But remember the LORD your God, for it is he who gives you the ability to produce wealth,[v] and so confirms his covenant, which he swore to your ancestors, as it is today.

19If you ever forget the LORD your God and follow other gods and worship and bow down to them, I testify against you today that you will surely be destroyed.[w] 20Like the nations the LORD destroyed before you, so you will be destroyed for not obeying the LORD your God.

Not Because of Israel's Righteousness

9 Hear, Israel: You are now about to cross the Jordan to go in and dispossess nations greater and stronger than you,[x] with large cities that have walls up to the sky.[y] 2The people are strong and tall—Anakites! You know about them and have heard it said: "Who can stand up against the Anakites?"[z] 3But be assured today that the LORD your God is the one who goes across ahead of you[a] like a devouring fire.[b] He will destroy them; he will subdue them before you. And you will drive them out and annihilate them quickly,[c] as the LORD has promised you.

4After the LORD your God has driven them out before you, do not say to yourself,[d] "The LORD has brought me here to take possession of this land because of my righteousness." No, it is on account of the wickedness of these nations[e] that the LORD is going to drive them out before you. 5It is not because of your righteousness or your integrity[f] that you are going in to take possession of their land; but on account of the wickedness of these nations, the LORD your God will drive them out before you, to accomplish what he swore[g] to your fathers, to Abraham, Isaac and Jacob. 6Understand, then, that it is not because of your righteousness that the LORD your God is giving you this good land to possess, for you are a stiff-necked people.[h]

The Golden Calf

7Remember this and never forget how you aroused the anger of the LORD your God in the wilderness. From the day you left Egypt until you arrived here, you have been rebellious against the LORD. 8At Horeb you aroused the LORD's wrath so that he was angry enough to destroy you.[i] 9When I went up on the mountain to receive the tablets of stone, the tablets of the covenant that the LORD had made with

---

8:16 ***test you so that ... it might go well with you.*** Through the whole experience in Egypt and the wilderness, the Lord was leading His children into decisions that would bring out their true nature. Difficult as the tests were, the Lord knew what was necessary to reveal to the Israelites not only His character, but theirs as well.

8:17 ***My power.*** Moses warned the people that prosperity and wealth often lead to an exaltation of self and a rejection of God.

9:4–6 ***to take possession of this land.*** The conquest of Canaan was both a judgment on the wickedness of the native population and a promise fulfilled to Abraham, Isaac, and Jacob (Gen. 15:18–21). The land was a gift of grace, not a gift given because of the merits of the Israelites.

9:7 ***never forget.*** In addition to remembering the grace of God, the people also had to remember how vulnerable they were to apostasy (1:6—3:29).

9:9 ***drank no water.*** A person cannot go more than approximately three days without water and survive. God supernaturally preserved Moses during the forty days.

8:4 [j] Dt 29:5; Ne 9:21 **8:5** [k] 2Sa 7:14; Pr 3:11-12; Heb 12:5-11; Rev 3:19 **8:6** [l] Dt 5:33 **8:7** [m] Dt 11:9-12 **8:10** [n] Dt 6:10-12 **8:12** [o] Hos 13:6 **8:14** [p] Ps 106:21 **8:15** [q] Jer 2:6 [r] Nu 21:6 [s] Nu 20:11; Ps 78:15; 114:8 **8:16** [t] Ex 16:15 **8:17** [u] Dt 9:4, 7, 24 **8:18** [v] Pr 10:22; Hos 2:8 **8:19** [w] Dt 4:26; 30:18 **9:1** [x] Dt 4:38; 11:23, 31 [y] Dt 1:28 **9:2** [z] Nu 13:22, 28, 32-33 **9:3** [a] Dt 31:3; Jos 3:11 [b] Dt 4:24; Heb 12:29 [c] Ex 23:31; Dt 7:23-24 **9:4** [d] Dt 8:17 [e] Lev 18:21, 24-30; Dt 18:9-14 **9:5** [f] Titus 3:5 [g] Ge 12:7; 13:15; 15:7; 17:8; 26:4 **9:6** [h] ver 13; Ex 32:9; Dt 31:27 **9:8** [i] Ex 32:7-10; Ps 106:19

you, I stayed on the mountain forty days
and forty nights; I ate no bread and drank
no water.[j] 10The LORD gave me two stone
tablets inscribed by the finger of God.[k]
On them were all the commandments the
LORD proclaimed to you on the mountain
out of the fire, on the day of the assembly.
11At the end of the forty days and forty
nights, the LORD gave me the two stone tablets, the tablets of the covenant. 12Then the
LORD told me, "Go down from here at once,
because your people whom you brought
out of Egypt have become corrupt.[l] They
have turned away quickly[m] from what I
commanded them and have made an idol
for themselves."
13And the LORD said to me, "I have seen
this people[n], and they are a stiff-necked
people indeed! 14Let me alone,[o] so that I
may destroy them and blot out[p] their name
from under heaven. And I will make you
into a nation stronger and more numerous
than they."
15So I turned and went down from the
mountain while it was ablaze with fire.
And the two tablets of the covenant were
in my hands.[q] 16When I looked, I saw that
you had sinned against the LORD your God;
you had made for yourselves an idol cast in
the shape of a calf.[r] You had turned aside
quickly from the way that the LORD had
commanded you. 17So I took the two tablets
and threw them out of my hands, breaking
them to pieces before your eyes.
18Then once again I fell[s] prostrate before
the LORD for forty days and forty nights; I
ate no bread and drank no water, because
of all the sin you had committed, doing
what was evil in the LORD's sight and so
arousing his anger. 19I feared the anger
and wrath of the LORD, for he was angry
enough with you to destroy you.[t] But again
the LORD listened to me.[u] 20And the LORD
was angry enough with Aaron to destroy
him, but at that time I prayed for Aaron too.
21Also I took that sinful thing of yours, the
calf you had made, and burned it in the fire.
Then I crushed it and ground it to powder
as fine as dust and threw the dust into a
stream that flowed down the mountain.[v]
22You also made the LORD angry at Taberah,[w] at Massah[x] and at Kibroth Hattaavah.[y]
23And when the LORD sent you out from
Kadesh Barnea, he said, "Go up and take
possession of the land I have given you."
But you rebelled against the command of
the LORD your God. You did not trust[z] him
or obey him. 24You have been rebellious
against the LORD ever since I have known
you.[a]
25I lay prostrate before the LORD those
forty days and forty nights because the
LORD had said he would destroy you.[b] 26I
prayed to the LORD and said, "Sovereign
LORD, do not destroy your people, your
own inheritance that you redeemed by
your great power and brought out of Egypt
with a mighty hand.[c] 27Remember your
servants Abraham, Isaac and Jacob. Overlook the stubbornness of this people, their
wickedness and their sin. 28Otherwise, the
country from which you brought us will
say, 'Because the LORD was not able to take
them into the land he had promised them,
and because he hated them, he brought
them out to put them to death in the wilderness.'[d] 29But they are your people, your
inheritance[e] that you brought out by your
great power and your outstretched arm.[f]"

Tablets Like the First Ones

10 At that time the LORD said to me,
"Chisel out two stone tablets[g] like the
first ones and come up to me on the mountain. Also make a wooden ark.[a] 2I will
write on the tablets the words that were on
the first tablets, which you broke. Then you
are to put them in the ark."[h]
3So I made the ark out of acacia wood[i]
and chiseled[j] out two stone tablets like the
first ones, and I went up on the mountain
with the two tablets in my hands. 4The
LORD wrote on these tablets what he had

[a] *1* That is, a chest

9:10 *finger of God.* The Ten Commandments were written on stone by the hand of God. This visual picture of God writing His words is so personal. There is another time that God writes on tablets, and that is on the tablet of the human heart (2 Cor. 3:3). This, too, is intensely personal and life changing. In the end, His followers can only put the words of the stone tablets into effect after the Spirit of the Living God has written on their hearts.

9:19 *the LORD listened to me.* For Moses' prayer, see verses 26–29. Daniel's prayer for the nation resembled Moses' intercession (Dan. 9:3–23).

9:26–29 *I prayed.* Moses took God's judgment seriously. Nevertheless he asked God for what he felt was important. He appealed to God's faithfulness, mercy, and honor. It is always all right to beseech the Lord for what seems right to us from our point of view, but as we pray, we remember that God knows more than we do, and we can trust Him to take the best course of action.

10:3 *acacia wood.* The acacia or shittim tree is still found in the Sinai peninsula, but in smaller numbers than when the Israelites passed through. Some varieties produce an attractive, highly figured hardwood.

9:9 [j] Ex 24:12, 15, 18; 34:28 **9:10** [k] Ex 31:18; Dt 4:13 **9:12** [l] Ex 32:7-8; Dt 31:29 [m] Jdg 2:17 **9:13** [n] ver 6; Ex 32:9; Dt 10:16 **9:14** [o] Ex 32:10 [p] Nu 14:12; Dt 29:20 **9:15** [q] Ex 19:18; 32:15 **9:16** [r] Ex 32:19 **9:18** [s] Ex 34:28 **9:19** [t] Ex 32:10-11, 14 [u] Dt 10:10 **9:21** [v] Ex 32:20 **9:22** [w] Nu 11:3 [x] Ex 17:7 [y] Nu 11:34 **9:23** [z] Ps 106:24 **9:24** [a] ver 7; Dt 31:27 **9:25** [b] ver 18 **9:26** [c] Ex 32:11 **9:28** [d] Ex 32:12; Nu 14:16 **9:29** [e] Dt 4:20; 1Ki 8:51 [f] Dt 4:34; Ne 1:10 **10:1** [g] Ex 25:10; 34:1-2 **10:2** [h] Ex 25:16, 21; Dt 4:13 **10:3** [i] Ex 25:5, 10; 37:1-9 [j] Ex 34:4

written before, the Ten Commandments he had proclaimed[k] to you on the mountain, out of the fire, on the day of the assembly. And the LORD gave them to me. 5Then I came back down the mountain[l] and put the tablets in the ark[m] I had made, as the LORD commanded me, and they are there now.[n]

6(The Israelites traveled from the wells of Bene Jaakan to Moserah.[o] There Aaron died and was buried, and Eleazar his son succeeded him as priest.[p] 7From there they traveled to Gudgodah and on to Jotbathah, a land with streams of water.[q] 8At that time the LORD set apart the tribe of Levi[r] to carry the ark of the covenant of the LORD, to stand before the LORD to minister[s] and to pronounce blessings[t] in his name, as they still do today. 9That is why the Levites have no share or inheritance among their fellow Israelites; the LORD is their inheritance,[u] as the LORD your God told them.)

10Now I had stayed on the mountain forty days and forty nights, as I did the first time, and the LORD listened to me at this time also. It was not his will to destroy you.[v] 11"Go," the LORD said to me, "and lead the people on their way, so that they may enter and possess the land I swore to their ancestors to give them."

Fear the LORD

12And now, Israel, what does the LORD your God ask of you[w] but to fear the LORD your God, to walk in obedience to him, to love him,[x] to serve the LORD your God with all your heart[y] and with all your soul, 13and to observe the LORD's commands and decrees that I am giving you today for your own good?

14To the LORD your God belong the heavens, even the highest heavens,[z] the earth and everything in it.[a] 15Yet the LORD set his affection on your ancestors and loved[b] them, and he chose you, their descendants, above all the nations—as it is today. 16Circumcise[c] your hearts, therefore, and do not be stiff-necked[d] any longer. 17For the LORD your God is God of gods[e] and Lord of lords, the great God, mighty and awesome, who shows no partiality[f] and accepts no bribes. 18He defends the cause of the fatherless and the widow,[g] and loves the foreigner residing among you, giving them food and clothing. 19And you are to love those who are foreigners, for you yourselves were foreigners in Egypt.[h] 20Fear the LORD your God and serve him.[i] Hold fast[j] to him and take your oaths in his name.[k] 21He is the one you praise;[l] he is your God, who performed for you those great and awesome wonders[m] you saw with your own eyes. 22Your ancestors who went down into Egypt were seventy in all,[n] and now the LORD your God has made you as numerous as the stars in the sky.[o]

Love and Obey the LORD

11 Love[p] the LORD your God and keep his requirements, his decrees, his laws and his commands always.[q] 2Remember today that your children were not the ones who saw and experienced the discipline of the LORD your God:[r] his majesty, his mighty hand, his outstretched arm; 3the signs he performed and the things he did in the heart of Egypt, both to Pharaoh king of Egypt and to his whole country; 4what he did to the Egyptian army, to its horses and chariots, how he overwhelmed them with the waters of the Red Sea[a][s] as they were pursuing you, and how the LORD brought lasting ruin on them. 5It was not your children who saw what he did for you in the wilderness until you arrived at this place, 6and what he did[t] to Dathan and Abiram, sons of Eliab the Reubenite, when the earth opened its mouth right in the middle of all Israel and swallowed them up with their households, their tents and every living thing that belonged to them. 7But it was your own eyes that saw all these great things the LORD has done.

8Observe therefore all the commands I am giving you today, so that you may have the strength to go in and take over the land that you are crossing the Jordan to possess,[u] 9and so that you may live long[v] in the land the LORD swore[w] to your ancestors to give to them and their descendants, a land flowing with milk and honey.[x] 10The land you are

[a] 4 Or *the Sea of Reeds*

10:19 ***love those who are foreigners.*** God's good provision for their own needs should have motivated the Israelites to love the stranger among them. To love and provide for the disadvantaged was in fact following God's example.

11:1 ***keep his requirements.*** Loving God is in response to His love for us. We are directed to love God, but God first demonstrates His love for us. He rescued the Israelites from slavery to the Egyptians; He rescues us from slavery to sin (Rom. 6:20). Our first response is to return this love He has shown us. Our second response is to keep His commandments, to do the things He says to do. Love oils the wheels of obedience and makes obedience a blessing, not a burden.

11:9–12 ***not like the land of Egypt.*** Agriculture in Egypt depended on irrigation, the annual flooding of the Nile.

10:4 [k] Ex 20:1 **10:5** [l] Ex 34:29 [m] Ex 40:20 [n] 1Ki 8:9 **10:6** [o] Nu 33:30-31,38 [p] Nu 20:25-28 **10:7** [q] Nu 33:32-34 **10:8** [r] Nu 3:6 [s] Dt 18:5 [t] Dt 21:5 **10:9** [u] Nu 18:20; Dt 18:1-2; Eze 44:28 **10:10** [v] Ex 33:17; 34:28; Dt 9:18-19,25 **10:12** [w] Mic 6:8 [x] Dt 5:33; 6:13; Mt 22:37 [y] Dt 6:5 **10:14** [z] 1Ki 8:27 [a] Ex 19:5 **10:15** [b] Dt 4:37 **10:16** [c] Jer 4:4 [d] Dt 9:6 **10:17** [e] Jos 22:22; Da 2:47 [f] Ac 10:34; Ro 2:11; Eph 6:9 **10:18** [g] Ps 68:5 **10:19** [h] Lev 19:34 **10:20** [i] Mt 4:10 [j] Dt 11:22 [k] Ps 63:11 **10:21** [l] Ex 15:2; Jer 17:14 [m] Ps 106:21-22 **10:22** [n] Ge 46:26-27 [o] Ge 15:5; Dt 1:10 **11:1** [p] Dt 10:12 [q] Zec 3:7 **11:2** [r] Dt 5:24; 8:5 **11:4** [s] Ex 14:27 **11:6** [t] Nu 16:1-35 **11:8** [u] Jos 1:7 **11:9** [v] Dt 4:40; Pr 10:27 [w] Dt 9:5 [x] Ex 3:8

entering to take over is not like the land of
Egypt, from which you have come, where
you planted your seed and irrigated it by
foot as in a vegetable garden. 11But the land
you are crossing the Jordan to take possession of is a land of mountains and valleys
that drinks rain from heaven.[y] 12It is a land
the LORD your God cares for; the eyes[z] of the
LORD your God are continually on it from
the beginning of the year to its end.
13So if you faithfully obey[a] the commands I am giving you today—to love[b] the
LORD your God and to serve him with all
your heart and with all your soul— 14then
I will send rain[c] on your land in its season,
both autumn and spring rains,[d] so that
you may gather in your grain, new wine
and olive oil. 15I will provide grass[e] in the
fields for your cattle, and you will eat and
be satisfied.[f]
16Be careful, or you will be enticed to
turn away and worship other gods and
bow down to them.[g] 17Then the LORD's
anger[h] will burn against you, and he will
shut up[i] the heavens so that it will not rain
and the ground will yield no produce, and
you will soon perish[j] from the good land
the LORD is giving you. 18Fix these words
of mine in your hearts and minds; tie them
as symbols on your hands and bind them
on your foreheads.[k] 19Teach them to your
children,[l] talking about them when you sit
at home and when you walk along the road,
when you lie down and when you get up.[m]
20Write them on the doorframes of your
houses and on your gates,[n] 21so that your
days and the days of your children may be
many[o] in the land the LORD swore to give
your ancestors, as many as the days that
the heavens are above the earth.[p]
22If you carefully observe[q] all these commands I am giving you to follow—to love
the LORD your God, to walk in obedience
to him and to hold fast[r] to him— 23then the
LORD will drive out all these nations before
you, and you will dispossess nations larger and stronger than you.[s] 24Every place
where you set your foot will be yours:[t] Your
territory will extend from the desert to Lebanon, and from the Euphrates River to the
Mediterranean Sea. 25No one will be able to
stand against you. The LORD your God, as
he promised you, will put the terror and fear
of you on the whole land, wherever you go.[u]
26See, I am setting before you today a
blessing and a curse[v]— 27the blessing[w] if
you obey the commands of the LORD your
God that I am giving you today; 28the curse
if you disobey[x] the commands of the LORD
your God and turn from the way that I command you today by following other gods,
which you have not known. 29When the
LORD your God has brought you into the
land you are entering to possess, you are to
proclaim on Mount Gerizim the blessings,
and on Mount Ebal the curses.[y] 30As you
know, these mountains are across the Jordan, westward, toward the setting sun, near
the great trees of Moreh,[z] in the territory of
those Canaanites living in the Arabah in the
vicinity of Gilgal.[a] 31You are about to cross
the Jordan to enter and take possession[b] of
the land the LORD your God is giving you.
When you have taken it over and are living
there, 32be sure that you obey all the decrees
and laws I am setting before you today.

The One Place of Worship

12 These are the decrees and laws you
must be careful to follow in the land
that the LORD, the God of your ancestors,
has given you to possess—as long as you
live in the land.[c] 2Destroy completely all
the places on the high mountains, on the
hills and under every spreading tree,[d]
where the nations you are dispossessing
worship their gods. 3Break down their altars, smash[e] their sacred stones and burn
their Asherah poles in the fire; cut down
the idols of their gods and wipe out their
names from those places.
4You must not worship the LORD your
God in their way. 5But you are to seek the
place the LORD your God will choose from
among all your tribes to put his Name there
for his dwelling.[f] To that place you must go;
6there bring your burnt offerings and sacrifices, your tithes[g] and special gifts, what

---

11:14 *autumn ... spring rains.* The autumn rain encouraged the sprouting of seed and new growth. The spring rain brought crops to maturity.

12:1–4 *altars . . . sacred stones.* The sacred pillars were monuments dedicated to one of the gods. They represented the power of fertility. The poles refer to the altars dedicated to the goddess Asherah, who was frequently associated with Baal.

12:5 *seek.* Whatever one seeks is the object of one's desire and devotion. Once they were settled in the land, the different tribes would be spread out, but they would still find God in their midst, in the place that God chose. This place was to be the object of their desire, God Himself the object of their devotion.

12:6 *sacrifices.* The Hebrew word for sacrifice always designates the offering of an animal. The contribution of the hand was one which the priest lifted up to signify that it was a gift to the Lord (Ex. 29:27; Lev. 7:34). The priest took his share and the worshipper and his family ate the rest. A votive offering was made in the fulfillment of a vow (Lev. 7:16; Num. 6:21). A freewill offering was voluntary (Ex. 35:27–29; Lev. 7:16).

11:11 [y] Dt 8:7 **11:12** [z] 1Ki 9:3 **11:13** [a] Dt 6:17 [b] Dt 10:12 **11:14** [c] Lev 26:4; Dt 28:12 [d] Joel 2:23; Jas 5:7 **11:15** [e] Ps 104:14 [f] Dt 6:11 **11:16** [g] Dt 8:19; 29:18; Job 31:9,27 **11:17** [h] Dt 6:15 [i] 1Ki 8:35; 2Ch 6:26 [j] Dt 4:26 **11:18** [k] Dt 6:6-8 **11:19** [l] Dt 6:7 [m] Dt 4:9-10 **11:20** [n] Dt 6:9 **11:21** [o] Pr 3:2; 4:10 [p] Ps 72:5 **11:22** [q] Dt 6:17 [r] Dt 10:20 **11:23** [s] Dt 4:38; 9:1 **11:24** [t] Ge 15:18; Ex 23:31; Jos 1:3; 14:9 **11:25** [u] Ex 23:27; Dt 7:24 **11:26** [v] Dt 30:1, 15, 19 **11:27** [w] Dt 28:1-14 **11:28** [x] Dt 28:15 **11:29** [y] Dt 27:12-13; Jos 8:33 **11:30** [z] Ge 12:6 [a] Jos 4:19 **11:31** [b] Dt 9:1; Jos 1:11 **12:1** [c] Dt 4:9-10; 1Ki 8:40 **12:2** [d] 2Ki 16:4; 17:10 **12:3** [e] Nu 33:52; Dt 7:5; Jdg 2:2 **12:5** [f] ver 11, 13; 2Ch 7:12, 16 **12:6** [g] Dt 14:22-23

you have vowed to give and your freewill
offerings, and the firstborn of your herds
and flocks. 7There, in the presence of the
LORD your God, you and your families shall
eat and shall rejoice[h] in everything you
have put your hand to, because the LORD
your God has blessed you.
8You are not to do as we do here today,
everyone doing as they see fit, 9since you
have not yet reached the resting place and
the inheritance the LORD your God is giving you. 10But you will cross the Jordan
and settle in the land the LORD your God is
giving[i] you as an inheritance, and he will
give you rest from all your enemies around
you so that you will live in safety. 11Then
to the place the LORD your God will choose
as a dwelling for his Name[j]—there you
are to bring everything I command you:
your burnt offerings and sacrifices, your
tithes and special gifts, and all the choice
possessions you have vowed to the LORD.
12And there rejoice[k] before the LORD your
God—you, your sons and daughters, your
male and female servants, and the Levites
from your towns who have no allotment or
inheritance[l] of their own. 13Be careful not
to sacrifice your burnt offerings anywhere
you please. 14Offer them only at the place
the LORD will choose[m] in one of your tribes,
and there observe everything I command
you.
15Nevertheless, you may slaughter your
animals in any of your towns and eat as
much of the meat as you want, as if it were
gazelle or deer,[n] according to the blessing
the LORD your God gives you. Both the ceremonially unclean and the clean may eat
it. 16But you must not eat the blood;[o] pour
it out on the ground like water.[p] 17You must
not eat in your own towns the tithe of your
grain and new wine and olive oil, or the
firstborn of your herds and flocks, or whatever you have vowed to give, or your freewill offerings or special gifts. 18Instead,
you are to eat[q] them in the presence of
the LORD your God at the place the LORD
your God will choose[r]—you, your sons and
daughters, your male and female servants,
and the Levites from your towns—and you
are to rejoice[s] before the LORD your God in
everything you put your hand to. 19Be careful not to neglect the Levites[t] as long as you
live in your land.
20When the LORD your God has enlarged
your territory[u] as he promised[v] you, and
you crave meat and say, "I would like some
meat," then you may eat as much of it as
you want. 21If the place where the LORD
your God chooses to put his Name is too
far away from you, you may slaughter animals from the herds and flocks the LORD
has given you, as I have commanded you,
and in your own towns you may eat as
much of them as you want. 22Eat them as
you would gazelle or deer.[w] Both the ceremonially unclean and the clean may eat.
23But be sure you do not eat the blood,[x] because the blood is the life, and you must
not eat the life with the meat. 24You must
not eat the blood; pour it out on the ground
like water. 25Do not eat it, so that it may go
well[y] with you and your children after you,
because you will be doing what is right[z] in
the eyes of the LORD.
26But take your consecrated things and
whatever you have vowed to give,[a] and go
to the place the LORD will choose. 27Pre-
sent your burnt offerings[b] on the altar of
the LORD your God, both the meat and the
blood. The blood of your sacrifices must be
poured beside the altar of the LORD your
God, but you may eat the meat. 28Be careful to obey all these regulations I am giving
you, so that it may always go well[c] with you
and your children after you, because you
will be doing what is good and right in the
eyes of the LORD your God.
29The LORD your God will cut off[d] before you the nations you are about to invade and dispossess. But when you have
driven them out and settled in their land,
30and after they have been destroyed before you, be careful not to be ensnared by
inquiring about their gods, saying, "How
do these nations serve their gods? We will

12:7 *eat ... rejoice.* The communal offerings were to be eaten and enjoyed by those who offered them. It was a time of celebration before the Lord.

12:8 *doing as they see fit.* In the wilderness the people did not develop a common focus on the Lord. Moses challenged the new generation to act with common faithfulness and obedience.

12:17 *eat in your own towns.* Aspects of God's worship were designed for community celebration, and were not to be done in the privacy of the home.

12:30–31 *be careful not to be ensnared.* For forty years the basic sin which kept Israel out of Canaan was unbelief. However, once they settled in the promised land, the sin that eventually drove them out was idolatry. Idolatry is not only bowing down to a stone or wood image of a god; idolatry takes place every time our trust for our well-being is placed on something that is not the one true God. In the end, idolatry is the ultimate form of unbelief. It mocks God, because it imitates the dependence that people should have on Him, choosing a powerless placebo for the living God. The Lord would remove the temptation of the Canaanite nations, but the Israelites must not become curious and imitate the practices of the vanquished peoples. Calling it a snare was a warning that the temptation to copy would be hidden, a trick, something that would catch them unaware.

12:7 [h] ver 12, 18; Lev 23:40; Dt 14:26 **12:10** [i] Dt 11:31 **12:11** [j] ver 5; Dt 15:20; 16:2 **12:12** [k] ver 7 [l] Dt 10:9; 14:29 **12:14** [m] ver 11 **12:15** [n] ver 20-23; Dt 14:5; 15:22 **12:16** [o] Ge 9:4; Lev 7:26; 17:10-12 [p] Dt 15:23 **12:18** [q] Dt 14:23 [r] ver 5 [s] ver 7, 12 **12:19** [t] Dt 14:27 **12:20** [u] Dt 19:8 [v] Ge 15:18; Dt 11:24 **12:22** [w] ver 15 **12:23** [x] ver 16; Ge 9:4; Lev 17:11, 14 **12:25** [y] Dt 4:40; Isa 3:10 [z] Ex 15:26; Dt 13:18; 1Ki 11:38 **12:26** [a] ver 17; Nu 5:9-10 **12:27** [b] Lev 1:5, 9, 13 **12:28** [c] ver 25; Dt 4:40 **12:29** [d] Jos 23:4

do the same.” 31You must not worship the
LORD your God in their way, because in
worshiping their gods, they do all kinds
of detestable things the LORD hates.[e] They
even burn their sons[f] and daughters in the
fire as sacrifices to their gods.
32See that you do all I command you; do
not add[g] to it or take away from it.[a]

Worshiping Other Gods

13[b] If a prophet,[h] or one who foretells by
dreams, appears among you and announces to you a sign or wonder, 2and if
the sign or wonder spoken of takes place,
and the prophet says, “Let us follow other
gods”[i] (gods you have not known) “and let
us worship them,” 3you must not listen to
the words of that prophet or dreamer. The
LORD your God is testing[j] you to find out
whether you love him with all your heart
and with all your soul. 4It is the LORD your
God you must follow,[k] and him you must
revere. Keep his commands and obey him;
serve him and hold fast[l] to him. 5That
prophet or dreamer must be put to death
for inciting rebellion against the LORD
your God, who brought you out of Egypt
and redeemed you from the land of slavery. That prophet or dreamer tried to turn
you from the way the LORD your God commanded you to follow. You must purge the
evil[m] from among you.
6If your very own brother, or your son
or daughter, or the wife you love, or your
closest friend secretly entices[n] you, saying, “Let us go and worship other gods”
(gods that neither you nor your ancestors
have known, 7gods of the peoples around
you, whether near or far, from one end
of the land to the other), 8do not yield[o]
to them or listen to them. Show them no
pity. Do not spare them or shield them.
9You must certainly put them to death.[p]
Your hand must be the first in putting
them to death, and then the hands of all
the people. 10Stone them to death, because they tried to turn you away from the
LORD your God, who brought you out of
Egypt, out of the land of slavery. 11Then
all Israel will hear and be afraid,[q] and no
one among you will do such an evil thing
again.
12If you hear it said about one of the
towns the LORD your God is giving you
to live in 13that troublemakers[r] have aris-
en among you and have led the people of
their town astray, saying, “Let us go and
worship other gods” (gods you have not
known), 14then you must inquire, probe
and investigate it thoroughly. And if it is
true and it has been proved that this detestable thing has been done among you,
15you must certainly put to the sword all
who live in that town. You must destroy
it completely,[c] both its people and its livestock. 16You are to gather all the plunder
of the town into the middle of the public
square and completely burn the town and
all its plunder as a whole burnt offering
to the LORD your God.[s] That town is to remain a ruin[t] forever, never to be rebuilt,
17and none of the condemned things[c] are
to be found in your hands. Then the LORD
will turn from his fierce anger,[u] will show
you mercy, and will have compassion[v] on
you. He will increase your numbers,[w] as
he promised[x] on oath to your ancestors—
18because you obey the LORD your God by
keeping all his commands that I am giving you today and doing what is right[y] in
his eyes.

[a] *32* In Hebrew texts this verse (12:32) is numbered 13:1. [b] In Hebrew texts 13:1-18 is numbered 13:2-19. [c] *15,17* The Hebrew term refers to the irrevocable giving over of things or persons to the LORD, often by totally destroying them.

13:1–2 *a prophet, or one who foretells by dreams.* Both prophecy and dreams were legitimate forms of revelation.

13:3 *testing you.* The revelation of God through Moses was the test of any sign or message. When the message deviated from God's prior revelation, Israel had to discern false teaching.

13:5 *purge the evil.* Discipline, punishment, and testing were God's means of keeping His people pure.

13:9 *your hand must be the first.* The relative or friend who brought the charge would lead in the capital punishment of the one who suggested idolatrous practices. With unforgettable words, Jesus emphasized the severity of this offense. Such a person should not have been born (Matt. 18:6–7).

13:13 *worship other gods.* Falling away from the truth is apostasy. Sometimes this can be fairly subtle, and that is why the word “seduced” is used with this concept. God clearly lays out a test that will always separate the truth from the lie. If someone says, “let us go after other gods…” we know that the speaker is not from God. Our hope is in Christ alone. People do not recognize that they are going after “other gods” because they do not know the one true God. This is why it is so important to faithfully study the Bible, for in it all of the character and actions of God are revealed. We will not be fooled by the counterfeit if we are familiar with the genuine.

13:17–18 *turn from his fierce anger, will show you mercy, and will have compassion on you.* This seemingly harsh judgment of evil was an act of obedience. God required the punishment of evildoers so that immoral practices would not spread throughout the land. God would bless the Israelites, and bless the land, but not while the evil practices were still going on.

12:31 [e] Dt 9:5 [f] Dt 18:10; Jer 32:35 **12:32** [g] Dt 4:2; Jos 1:7; Rev 22:18-19 **13:1** [h] Mt 24:24; Mk 13:22; 2Th 2:9 **13:2** [i] ver 6, 13 **13:3** [j] Dt 8:2, 16 **13:4** [k] 2Ki 23:3; 2Ch 34:31 [l] Dt 10:20 **13:5** [m] Dt 17:7, 12; 1Co 5:13 **13:6** [n] Dt 17:2-7; 29:18 **13:8** [o] Pr 1:10 **13:9** [p] Dt 17:5, 7 **13:11** [q] Dt 19:20 **13:13** [r] ver 2, 6; 1Jn 2:19 **13:16** [s] Jos 6:24 [t] Jos 8:28; Jer 49:2 **13:17** [u] Nu 25:4 [v] Dt 30:3 [w] Dt 7:13 [x] Ge 22:17; 26:4, 24; 28:14 **13:18** [y] Dt 12:25, 28

Clean and Unclean Food

14 You are the children[z] of the LORD your
God. Do not cut yourselves or shave
the front of your heads for the dead, 2 for
you are a people holy to the LORD your
God.[a] Out of all the peoples on the face of
the earth, the LORD has chosen you to be
his treasured possession.[b]

3 Do not eat any detestable thing.[c] 4 These
are the animals you may eat:[d] the ox, the
sheep, the goat, 5 the deer, the gazelle, the
roe deer, the wild goat, the ibex, the antelope and the mountain sheep.[a] 6 You may
eat any animal that has a divided hoof and
that chews the cud. 7 However, of those that
chew the cud or that have a divided hoof
you may not eat the camel, the rabbit or the
hyrax. Although they chew the cud, they
do not have a divided hoof; they are ceremonially unclean for you. 8 The pig is also
unclean; although it has a divided hoof, it
does not chew the cud. You are not to eat
their meat or touch their carcasses.[e]

9 Of all the creatures living in the water,
you may eat any that has fins and scales.
10 But anything that does not have fins and
scales you may not eat; for you it is unclean.

11 You may eat any clean bird. 12 But these
you may not eat: the eagle, the vulture, the
black vulture, 13 the red kite, the black kite,
any kind of falcon, 14 any kind of raven,
15 the horned owl, the screech owl, the gull,
any kind of hawk, 16 the little owl, the great
owl, the white owl, 17 the desert owl, the osprey, the cormorant, 18 the stork, any kind
of heron, the hoopoe and the bat.

19 All flying insects are unclean to you;
do not eat them. 20 But any winged creature
that is clean you may eat.

21 Do not eat anything you find already
dead.[f] You may give it to the foreigner residing in any of your towns, and they may
eat it, or you may sell it to any other foreigner. But you are a people holy to the
LORD your God.[g]

Do not cook a young goat in its mother's milk.[h]

Tithes

22 Be sure to set aside a tenth[i] of all that
your fields produce each year. 23 Eat the
tithe of your grain, new wine and olive oil,
and the firstborn of your herds and flocks
in the presence of the LORD your God at the
place he will choose as a dwelling for his
Name,[j] so that you may learn[k] to revere the
LORD your God always. 24 But if that place
is too distant and you have been blessed by
the LORD your God and cannot carry your
tithe (because the place where the LORD
will choose to put his Name is so far away),
25 then exchange your tithe for silver, and
take the silver with you and go to the place
the LORD your God will choose. 26 Use the
silver to buy whatever you like: cattle,
sheep, wine or other fermented drink, or
anything you wish. Then you and your
household shall eat there in the presence
of the LORD your God and rejoice.[l] 27 And
do not neglect the Levites[m] living in your
towns, for they have no allotment or inheritance of their own.[n]

28 At the end of every three years, bring
all the tithes of that year's produce and
store it in your towns,[o] 29 so that the Levites
(who have no allotment[p] or inheritance of
their own) and the foreigners,[q] the fatherless and the widows who live in your towns
may come and eat and be satisfied, and so
that the LORD your God may bless[r] you in
all the work of your hands.

---

a 5 The precise identification of some of the birds and animals in this chapter is uncertain.

14:2 God's Plan and Israel—The modern-day student of the Bible may well ask why so much of Scripture is taken up with the history of a single nation. Certainly many Christians wonder why one nation should be called "God's chosen people." The answer to this question is bound up in God's purpose for Israel. When God promised Abraham that he would become the father of a great nation, He also promised that He would bless all peoples through that nation (Gen. 12:1–3). Therefore Israel was to be a channel of blessing as well as a recipient. Even their deliverance from Egypt was at least partially designed to show other nations that Israel's God was the only true God (Ex. 7:5; 14:18; Josh. 2:9–11). It was further prophesied by Isaiah that the Messiah would bring salvation to the Gentiles (Is. 49:6) The Psalms contain many invitations to other nations to come and worship the Lord in Israel (Ps. 2:10–12; 117:1). Ruth the Moabitess is an example of a foreigner who believed in Israel's God.

It is clear that God's promise to Abraham to bless the whole world through him is still being fulfilled. The life, ministry and death of Jesus Christ and the existence and influence of the church today, all came about through God's choice of Israel. All those the church wins to Christ, whether Jew or Gentile, enter into these great blessings channeled through Israel.

14:21 ***not cook . . . in its mother's milk.*** Unlike the Canaanites who boiled young goats alive in the milk of their mothers as a sacrifice to fertility gods, Israel was to practice a more humane method of animal sacrifice.

14:22–29 ***tithe of your grain.*** The tithe was to be enjoyed in the presence of the Lord, unless the people had come from a great distance. Then they could exchange it for silver and purchase food and drink with it in Jerusalem.

14:25 ***silver.*** Uncoined silver was the currency of the day. Coins were not struck until the Persian era.

14:1 [z] Lev 19:28; 21:5; Jer 16:6; 41:5; Ro 8:14; 9:8; Gal 3:26
14:2 [a] Lev 20:26 [b] Dt 7:6; 26:18-19 **14:3** [c] Eze 4:14
14:4 [d] Lev 11:2-45; Ac 10:14 **14:8** [e] Lev 11:26-27
14:21 [f] Lev 17:15; 22:8 [g] ver 2 [h] Ex 23:19; 34:26
14:22 [i] Lev 27:30; Dt 12:6, 17; Ne 10:37 **14:23** [j] Dt 12:5
[k] Dt 4:10 **14:26** [l] Dt 12:7-8 **14:27** [m] Dt 12:19
[n] Nu 18:20 **14:28** [o] Dt 26:12 **14:29** [p] ver 27 [q] Dt 26:12
[r] Dt 15:10; Mal 3:10

The Year for Canceling Debts

15 At the end of every seven years you
must cancel debts.[s] 2This is how it is
to be done: Every creditor shall cancel any
loan they have made to a fellow Israelite.
They shall not require payment from anyone among their own people, because the
LORD's time for canceling debts has been
proclaimed. 3You may require payment
from a foreigner,[t] but you must cancel any
debt your fellow Israelite owes you. 4How-
ever, there need be no poor people among
you, for in the land the LORD your God is
giving you to possess as your inheritance,
he will richly bless[u] you, 5if only you fully
obey the LORD your God and are careful
to follow[v] all these commands I am giving
you today. 6For the LORD your God will
bless you as he has promised, and you will
lend to many nations but will borrow from
none. You will rule over many nations but
none will rule over you.[w]

7If anyone is poor among your fellow
Israelites in any of the towns of the land
the LORD your God is giving you, do not be
hardhearted or tightfisted[x] toward them.
8Rather, be openhanded[y] and freely lend
them whatever they need. 9Be careful not
to harbor this wicked thought: "The seventh year, the year for canceling debts,[z] is
near," so that you do not show ill will[a] toward the needy among your fellow Israelites and give them nothing. They may then
appeal to the LORD against you, and you
will be found guilty of sin.[b] 10Give generously to them and do so without a grudging heart;[c] then because of this the LORD
your God will bless[d] you in all your work
and in everything you put your hand to.
11There will always be poor people in the
land. Therefore I command you to be openhanded toward your fellow Israelites who
are poor and needy in your land.[e]

Freeing Servants

12If any of your people—Hebrew men or
women—sell themselves to you and serve
you six years, in the seventh year you
must let them go free.[f] 13And when you release them, do not send them away empty-handed. 14Supply them liberally from
your flock, your threshing floor and your
winepress. Give to them as the LORD your
God has blessed you. 15Remember that you
were slaves[g] in Egypt and the LORD your
God redeemed you.[h] That is why I give you
this command today.

16But if your servant says to you, "I do
not want to leave you," because he loves
you and your family and is well off with
you, 17then take an awl and push it through
his earlobe into the door, and he will become your servant for life. Do the same for
your female servant.

18Do not consider it a hardship to set
your servant free, because their service to
you these six years has been worth twice
as much as that of a hired hand. And the
LORD your God will bless you in everything
you do.

The Firstborn Animals

19Set apart for the LORD your God every
firstborn male[i] of your herds and flocks.
Do not put the firstborn of your cows to
work, and do not shear the firstborn of
your sheep. 20Each year you and your family are to eat them in the presence of the
LORD your God at the place he will choose.[j]
21If an animal has a defect, is lame or blind,
or has any serious flaw, you must not sacrifice it to the LORD your God.[k] 22You are to
eat it in your own towns. Both the ceremonially unclean and the clean may eat it, as
if it were gazelle or deer.[l] 23But you must
not eat the blood; pour it out on the ground
like water.[m]

The Passover

16 Observe the month of Aviv[n] and celebrate the Passover of the LORD your
God, because in the month of Aviv he
brought you out of Egypt by night. 2Sacri-
fice as the Passover to the LORD your God
an animal from your flock or herd at the
place the LORD will choose as a dwelling

15:1 *every seven years.* God taught His people to think in cycles of holy time: six days of work, the seventh to rest; six years of business, the seventh of giving freedom to the poor; six years of agricultural cultivation, and the seventh to let the land lie fallow (Ex. 23:10–13; Lev. 25:1–7).

15:7 *do not be hardened.* The people's attitude toward the poor should have been a reflection of their gratitude for God's gifts to them.

15:7–15 *poor.* Israel's uniqueness in the ancient world is seen in the laws which connect a right relationship with God and worship of Him with interpersonal relationships. If you love God, you will also treat others well. God is intensely interested in the poor, and it is the responsibility of His people to imitate His concern. The story of the Good Samaritan (Luke 10:30–37) is both the simplest and the most profound picture of how this concern works out in real life.

15:19 *Do not put ... to work, and do not shear.* The owners of firstborn male livestock could not profit from the firstborn because they belonged to the Lord.

16:1 *Passover.* Passover was observed on the fourteenth of Aviv, or Nisan, which corresponds to our March-April (Ex. 12:1–21; Lev. 23:5–8; Num. 28:16–25).

15:1 [s] Dt 31:10 **15:3** [t] Dt 23:20 **15:4** [u] Dt 28:8 **15:5** [v] Dt 28:1 **15:6** [w] Dt 28:12-13, 44 **15:7** [x] 1Jn 3:17 **15:8** [y] Mt 5:42; Lk 6:34 **15:9** [z] ver 1 [a] Mt 20:15 [b] Dt 24:15 **15:10** [c] 2Co 9:5 [d] Dt 14:29; 24:19 **15:11** [e] Mt 26:11; Mk 14:7; Jn 12:8 **15:12** [f] Ex 21:2; Lev 25:39; Jer 34:14 **15:15** [g] Dt 5:15 [h] Dt 16:12 **15:19** [i] Ex 13:2 **15:20** [j] Dt 12:5-7, 17, 18; 14:23 **15:21** [k] Lev 22:19-25 **15:22** [l] Dt 12:15, 22 **15:23** [m] Dt 12:16 **16:1** [n] Ex 12:2; 13:4

for his Name.[o] 3Do not eat it with bread made with yeast, but for seven days eat unleavened bread, the bread of affliction,[p] because you left Egypt in haste[q]—so that all the days of your life you may remember the time of your departure from Egypt.[r] 4Let no yeast be found in your possession in all your land for seven days. Do not let any of the meat you sacrifice on the evening of the first day remain until morning.[s]

5You must not sacrifice the Passover in any town the LORD your God gives you 6except in the place he will choose as a dwelling for his Name. There you must sacrifice the Passover in the evening, when the sun goes down, on the anniversary[a][t] of your departure from Egypt. 7Roast[u] it and eat it at the place the LORD your God will choose. Then in the morning return to your tents. 8For six days eat unleavened bread and on the seventh day hold an assembly[v] to the LORD your God and do no work.

The Festival of Weeks

9Count off seven weeks[w] from the time you begin to put the sickle to the standing grain.[x] 10Then celebrate the Festival of Weeks to the LORD your God by giving a freewill offering in proportion to the blessings the LORD your God has given you. 11And rejoice[y] before the LORD your God at the place he will choose as a dwelling for his Name—you, your sons and daughters, your male and female servants, the Levites[z] in your towns, and the foreigners, the fatherless and the widows living among you. 12Remember that you were slaves in Egypt,[a] and follow carefully these decrees.

The Festival of Tabernacles

13Celebrate the Festival of Tabernacles for seven days after you have gathered the produce of your threshing floor[b] and your winepress.[c] 14Be joyful[d] at your festival—you, your sons and daughters, your male and female servants, and the Levites, the foreigners, the fatherless and the widows who live in your towns. 15For seven days celebrate the festival to the LORD your God at the place the LORD will choose. For the LORD your God will bless you in all your harvest and in all the work of your hands, and your joy[e] will be complete.

16Three times a year all your men must appear before the LORD your God at the place he will choose: at the Festival of Unleavened Bread, the Festival of Weeks and the Festival of Tabernacles.[f] No one should appear before the LORD empty-handed:[g] 17Each of you must bring a gift in proportion to the way the LORD your God has blessed you.

Judges

18Appoint judges[h] and officials for each of your tribes in every town the LORD your God is giving you, and they shall judge the people fairly. 19Do not pervert justice[i] or show partiality.[j] Do not accept a bribe,[k] for a bribe blinds the eyes of the wise and twists the words of the innocent. 20Follow justice and justice alone, so that you may live and possess the land the LORD your God is giving you.

Worshiping Other Gods

21Do not set up any wooden Asherah pole[l] beside the altar you build to the LORD your God,[m] 22and do not erect a sacred stone,[n] for these the LORD your God hates.

17 Do not sacrifice to the LORD your God an ox or a sheep that has any defect[o] or flaw in it, for that would be detestable to him.[p]

2If a man or woman living among you in one of the towns the LORD gives you is found doing evil in the eyes of the LORD your God in violation of his covenant,[q] 3and contrary to my command[r] has worshiped other gods, bowing down to them or to the sun[s] or the moon or the stars in the sky, 4and this has been brought to your attention, then you must investigate

[a] 6 Or *down, at the time of day*

16:6 *the sun goes down.* The twilight sacrifice was in commemoration of the exodus, which occurred at night.

16:9 *sickle to the standing grain.* This took place on the second day of the Passover.

16:13–15 *Festival of Tabernacles.* The harvest festival was a time to celebrate God's goodness, and to remember how He cared for them when they lived in tents in the wilderness. Today this celebration is called Succoth, from the Hebrew word for booths.

16:19 *not pervert justice.* The foundation for a just and honest application of law in human society is God Himself. God entrusts rule to men who function in His place in dispensing justice. To pervert this justice with favoritism or bribes is to malign the character of God, and that is a sin that God always deals with sooner or later.

17:2 *doing evil.* The Hebrew verb for doing evil is used elsewhere to indicate the crossing of a border or stream. Here the word is used to indicate "crossing over" the boundaries that God had set for His people.

17:4–6 *investigate it thoroughly.* An investigation, rather than gossip, determined the truth of any

16:2 [o] Dt 12:5,26 **16:3** [p] Ex 12:8,39; 34:18 [q] Ex 12:11,15,19 [r] Ex 13:3,6-7 **16:4** [s] Ex 12:10; 34:25 **16:6** [t] Ex 12:6; Dt 12:5 **16:7** [u] Ex 12:8; 2Ch 35:13 **16:8** [v] Ex 12:16; 13:6; Lev 23:8 **16:9** [w] Ex 34:22; Lev 23:15 [x] Ex 23:16; Nu 28:26 **16:11** [y] Dt 12:7 [z] Dt 12:12 **16:12** [a] Dt 15:15 **16:13** [b] Lev 23:34 [c] Ex 23:16 **16:14** [d] ver 11 **16:15** [e] Lev 23:39 **16:16** [f] Ex 23:14,16 [g] Ex 34:20 **16:18** [h] Dt 1:16 **16:19** [i] Ex 23:2,8 [j] Lev 19:15; Dt 1:17 [k] Ecc 7:7 **16:21** [l] Dt 7:5 [m] Ex 34:13; 2Ki 17:16; 21:3; 2Ch 33:3 **16:22** [n] Lev 26:1 **17:1** [o] Mal 1:8,13 [p] Dt 15:21 **17:2** [q] Dt 13:6-11 **17:3** [r] Jer 7:22-23 [s] Job 31:26

it thoroughly. If it is true and it has been proved that this detestable thing has been done in Israel,[t] **5**take the man or woman who has done this evil deed to your city gate and stone that person to death.[u] **6**On the testimony of two or three witnesses a person is to be put to death, but no one is to be put to death on the testimony of only one witness.[v] **7**The hands of the witnesses must be the first in putting that person to death, and then the hands of all the people. You must purge the evil[w] from among you.

Law Courts

8If cases come before your courts that are too difficult for you to judge—whether bloodshed, lawsuits or assaults[x]—take them to the place the LORD your God will choose.[y] **9**Go to the Levitical priests and to the judge who is in office at that time. Inquire of them and they will give you the verdict.[z] **10**You must act according to the decisions they give you at the place the LORD will choose. Be careful to do everything they instruct you to do. **11**Act according to whatever they teach you and the decisions they give you. Do not turn aside from what they tell you, to the right or to the left.[a] **12**Anyone who shows contempt[b] for the judge or for the priest who stands ministering there to the LORD your God is to be put to death. You must purge the evil from Israel. **13**All the people will hear and be afraid, and will not be contemptuous again.[c]

The King

14When you enter the land the LORD your God is giving you and have taken possession of it and settled in it, and you say, "Let us set a king over us like all the nations around us,"[d] **15**be sure to appoint over you a king the LORD your God chooses. He must be from among your fellow Israelites.[e] Do not place a foreigner over you, one who is not an Israelite. **16**The king, moreover, must not acquire great numbers of horses for himself[f] or make the people return to Egypt[g] to get more of them,[h] for the LORD has told you, "You are not to go back that way again."[i] **17**He must not take many wives,[j] or his heart will be led astray. He must not accumulate large amounts of silver and gold.

18When he takes the throne of his kingdom, he is to write[k] for himself on a scroll a copy of this law, taken from that of the Levitical priests. **19**It is to be with him, and he is to read it all the days of his life[l] so that he may learn to revere the LORD his God and follow carefully all the words of this law and these decrees **20**and not consider himself better than his fellow Israelites and turn from the law[m] to the right or to the left.[n] Then he and his descendants will reign a long time over his kingdom in Israel.

Offerings for Priests and Levites

18 The Levitical priests—indeed, the whole tribe of Levi—are to have no allotment or inheritance with Israel. They shall live on the food offerings presented to the LORD, for that is their inheritance.[o] **2**They shall have no inheritance among their fellow Israelites; the LORD is their inheritance, as he promised them.

3This is the share due the priests from the people who sacrifice a bull or a sheep: the shoulder, the internal organs and the meat from the head.[p] **4**You are to give them the firstfruits of your grain, new wine and olive oil, and the first wool from the shearing of your sheep,[q] **5**for the LORD your God has chosen them[r] and their descendants out of all your tribes to stand and minister[s] in the LORD's name always.

6If a Levite moves from one of your towns anywhere in Israel where he is living, and comes in all earnestness to the place the LORD will choose,[t] **7**he may minister in the name of the LORD his God like all his fellow Levites who serve there in the presence of the LORD. **8**He is to share equally in their benefits, even though he has received money from the sale of family possessions.[u]

---

report of idolatry. There must be two or three witnesses for a person to be condemned to death.

17:7 *hands of the witnesses ... first.* The witnesses participated in the stoning of the guilty because they were responsible for the person's condemnation. Jesus' words about throwing the "first stone" referred to this practice (John 8:7).

17:8 *too difficult for you to judge.* This refers to cases of manslaughter or murder—that is, accidental or intentional homicide.

17:12 *shows contempt.* It is presumptuous to ask for judgment and then to refuse to follow the verdict of the priests. It is both asking them to take the weight of the decision and then willfully disregarding that decision.

17:13 *hear.* To hear is to respond and obey.

17:14 *a king.* The regulations that follow anticipate the request that the Israelites would make for a king. At the time of Moses the Israelites were unique among nations. God Himself ruled them through appointed leaders, but there was no king.

17:4 [t] Dt 13:12-14 **17:5** [u] Lev 24:14 **17:6** [v] Nu 35:30; Dt 19:15; Jos 7:25; Mt 18:16; Jn 8:17; 2Co 13:1; 1Ti 5:19; Heb 10:28 **17:7** [w] Dt 13:5, 9 **17:8** [x] 2Ch 19:10 [y] Dt 12:5; Hag 2:11 **17:9** [z] Dt 19:17; Eze 44:24 **17:11** [a] Dt 25:1 **17:12** [b] Nu 15:30 **17:13** [c] Dt 13:11; 19:20 **17:14** [d] Dt 11:31; 1Sa 8:5, 19-20 **17:15** [e] Jer 30:21 **17:16** [f] 1Ki 4:26; 10:26 [g] Isa 31:1; Hos 11:5 [h] 1Ki 10:28; Eze 17:15 [i] Ex 13:17 **17:17** [j] 1Ki 11:3 **17:18** [k] Dt 31:22, 24 **17:19** [l] Jos 1:8 **17:20** [m] 1Ki 15:5 [n] Dt 5:32 **18:1** [o] Dt 10:9; 1Co 9:13 **18:3** [p] Lev 7:28-34 **18:4** [q] Ex 22:29; Nu 18:12 **18:5** [r] Ex 28:1 [s] Dt 10:8 **18:6** [t] Nu 35:2-3 **18:8** [u] 2Ch 31:4; Ne 12:44, 47

Occult Practices

9When you enter the land the LORD your God is giving you, do not learn to imitate[v] the detestable ways of the nations there. 10Let no one be found among you who sacrifices their son or daughter in the fire, who practices divination[w] or sorcery, interprets omens, engages in witchcraft,[x] 11or casts spells, or who is a medium or spiritist or who consults the dead. 12Anyone who does these things is detestable to the LORD; because of these same detestable practices the LORD your God will drive out those nations before you.[y] 13You must be blameless before the LORD your God.

The Prophet

14The nations you will dispossess listen to those who practice sorcery or divination. But as for you, the LORD your God has not permitted you to do so. 15The LORD your God will raise up for you a prophet like me from among you, from your fellow Israelites.[z] You must listen to him. 16For this is what you asked of the LORD your God at Horeb on the day of the assembly when you said, "Let us not hear the voice of the LORD our God nor see this great fire anymore, or we will die."[a]

17The LORD said to me: "What they say is good. 18I will raise up for them a prophet like you from among their fellow Israelites, and I will put my words[b] in his mouth. He will tell them everything I command him.[c] 19I myself will call to account[d] anyone who does not listen to my words that the prophet speaks in my name. 20But a prophet who presumes to speak in my name anything I have not commanded, or a prophet who speaks in the name of other gods,[e] is to be put to death."[f]

21You may say to yourselves, "How can we know when a message has not been spoken by the LORD?" 22If what a prophet proclaims in the name of the LORD does not take place or come true, that is a message the LORD has not spoken.[g] That prophet has spoken presumptuously,[h] so do not be alarmed.

Cities of Refuge

19 When the LORD your God has destroyed the nations whose land he is giving you, and when you have driven them out and settled in their towns and houses,[i] 2then set aside for yourselves three cities in the land the LORD your God is giving you to possess. 3Determine the distances involved and divide into three parts the land the LORD your God is giving you as an inheritance, so that a person who kills someone may flee for refuge to one of these cities.

4This is the rule concerning anyone who kills a person and flees there for safety—anyone who kills a neighbor unintentionally, without malice aforethought. 5For instance, a man may go into the forest with his neighbor to cut wood, and as he swings his ax to fell a tree, the head may fly off and hit his neighbor and kill him. That man may flee to one of these cities and save his life. 6Otherwise, the avenger of blood[j] might pursue him in a rage, overtake him if the distance is too great, and kill him even though he is not deserving of death, since he did it to his neighbor without malice aforethought. 7This is why I command you to set aside for yourselves three cities.

8If the LORD your God enlarges your territory, as he promised on oath to your ancestors, and gives you the whole land he promised them, 9because you carefully follow all these laws I command you today—to love the LORD your God and to walk always in obedience to him[k]—then you are to set aside three more cities. 10Do this so that innocent blood will not be shed in your land, which the LORD your God is giving you as your inheritance, and so that you will not be guilty of bloodshed.[l]

11But if out of hate someone lies in wait, assaults and kills a neighbor,[m] and then

---

18:10–12 *sacrifices their son or daughter in the fire ... witchcraft.* Each of the activities that the Lord forbids in this passage come under the category of occult activities. Passing through the fire was sacrificing a son or daughter to learn about the future or seek favor with a supposed deity. Divination, witchcraft, sorcery, casting spells and interpreting omens, mediums, spiritists, and necromancers (those who call up the dead) are all part of the demonic realm, an attempt to bypass God in foretelling and controlling the future. These activities are detestable to God and should be to His followers as well.

18:15 *raise up for you a prophet.* A true prophet came from the Lord; no one could become a true prophet by self-will or desire.

18:22 *do not be alarmed.* These words of warning for discerning a false prophet were also words of comfort. If the prophet did not come from God, there was no need to become anxious about whatever he might predict.

19:3–4 *divide into three parts.* The cities of refuge were intertribal cities. Anyone from any tribe could flee to the city that was closest to him.

19:6 *avenger of blood.* The avenger was possibly a relative commissioned by the elders of the city to execute justice. This Hebrew word is sometimes translated *kinsman redeemer,* and in this verse means "protector of family rights." This individual also stood up for the family to redeem property and persons. The glory of Israel was that its Avenger and Kinsman Redeemer was God Himself (Is. 41:14).

19:9–13 *follow all these.* The people of Israel

18:9 [v] Dt 12:29-31 **18:10** [w] Dt 12:31 [x] Lev 19:31
18:12 [y] Lev 18:24; Dt 9:4 **18:15** [z] Jn 1:21; Ac 3:22*; 7:37*
18:16 [a] Ex 20:19; Dt 5:23-27 **18:18** [b] Isa 51:16; Jn 17:8 [c] Jn 4:25-26; 8:28; 12:49-50 **18:19** [d] Ac 3:23*
18:20 [e] Jer 14:14 [f] Dt 13:1-5 **18:22** [g] Jer 28:9 [h] ver 20
19:1 [i] Dt 12:29 **19:6** [j] Nu 35:12 **19:9** [k] Jos 20:7-8
19:10 [l] Nu 35:33; Dt 21:1-9 **19:11** [m] Nu 35:16

flees to one of these cities, 12the killer shall
be sent for by the town elders, be brought
back from the city, and be handed over
to the avenger of blood to die. 13Show no
pity.[n] You must purge from Israel the guilt
of shedding innocent blood,[o] so that it may
go well with you.

14Do not move your neighbor's boundary
stone set up by your predecessors in the inheritance you receive in the land the LORD
your God is giving you to possess.[p]

Witnesses

15One witness is not enough to convict
anyone accused of any crime or offense
they may have committed. A matter must
be established by the testimony of two or
three witnesses.[q]

16If a malicious witness[r] takes the stand
to accuse someone of a crime, 17the two
people involved in the dispute must stand
in the presence of the LORD before the
priests and the judges[s] who are in office
at the time. 18The judges must make a
thorough investigation, and if the witness
proves to be a liar, giving false testimony
against a fellow Israelite, 19then do to the
false witness as that witness intended to do
to the other party.[t] You must purge the evil
from among you. 20The rest of the people
will hear of this and be afraid,[u] and never again will such an evil thing be done
among you. 21Show no pity:[v] life for life,
eye for eye, tooth for tooth, hand for hand,
foot for foot.[w]

Going to War

20 When you go to war against your enemies and see horses and chariots
and an army greater than yours,[x] do not
be afraid[y] of them,[z] because the LORD your
God, who brought you up out of Egypt,
will be with you. 2When you are about to
go into battle, the priest shall come forward and address the army. 3He shall say:
"Hear, Israel: Today you are going into battle against your enemies. Do not be fainthearted[a] or afraid; do not panic or be terrified by them. 4For the LORD your God is
the one who goes with you to fight[b] for you
against your enemies to give you victory."

5The officers shall say to the army: "Has
anyone built a new house and not yet begun to live in[c] it? Let him go home, or he
may die in battle and someone else may begin to live in it. 6Has anyone planted a vineyard and not begun to enjoy it? Let him go
home, or he may die in battle and someone
else enjoy it. 7Has anyone become pledged
to a woman and not married her? Let him
go home, or he may die in battle and someone else marry her.[d]" 8Then the officers
shall add, "Is anyone afraid or fainthearted? Let him go home so that his fellow soldiers will not become disheartened too."[e]
9When the officers have finished speaking
to the army, they shall appoint commanders over it.

10When you march up to attack a city,
make its people an offer of peace.[f] 11If they
accept and open their gates, all the people
in it shall be subject to forced labor[g] and
shall work for you. 12If they refuse to make
peace and they engage you in battle, lay
siege to that city. 13When the LORD your
God delivers it into your hand, put to the
sword all the men in it.[h] 14As for the wom-
en, the children, the livestock[i] and everything else in the city, you may take these as
plunder for yourselves. And you may use
the plunder the LORD your God gives you
from your enemies. 15This is how you are
to treat all the cities that are at a distance
from you and do not belong to the nations
nearby.

16However, in the cities of the nations
the LORD your God is giving you as an inheritance, do not leave alive anything that

---

were about to enter a land where they would be exposed to ideas and practices in the name of religion that God says are an abomination. The temptation to imitate would be great, but they must not do so. The believer is not different from his world for the sake of difference, but because he must not imitate the things that are inconsistent with a life of fellowship with a holy and just God. Copying the ways of the ungodly not only grieves the Lord, but it mars the picture He is making of Himself in the lives of those who follow Him.

19:14 ***move your neighbor's boundary.*** Removing a landmark was far more than moving a stone. It was changing a property line and in effect cheating some family out of the inheritance of land that God had given them.

19:15 ***by the testimony of two or three witnesses.*** Requiring two or three witnesses was a safeguard against the dangerous lies of an individual.

19:21 ***life for life, eye for eye.*** The law of retribution established the principal that the punishment should not exceed the crime.

20:5–7 ***built a new house ... planted a vineyard ... pledged to a woman.*** Each of these activities represents a time of planning and preparation that has not yet been fulfilled. The Lord graciously acknowledges that it is right for people to have a chance to enjoy the fruits of their labor before they risk their lives for the nation.

20:8 ***afraid or fainthearted.*** Unlike the previous situations, the fearful and fainthearted endanger their fellow soldiers. The number of warriors was not as important as the army's belief that God was fighting for them.

19:13 [n] Dt 7:2 [o] 1Ki 2:31 **19:14** [p] Dt 27:17; Pr 22:28; Hos 5:10 **19:15** [q] Nu 35:30; Dt 17:6; Mt 18:16*; Jn 8:17; 2Co 13:1*; 1Ti 5:19; Heb 10:28 **19:16** [r] Ex 23:1; Ps 27:12 **19:17** [s] Dt 17:9 **19:19** [t] Pr 19:5, 9 **19:20** [u] Dt 17:13; 21:21 **19:21** [v] ver 13 [w] Ex 21:24; Lev 24:20; Mt 5:38* **20:1** [x] Ps 20:7; Isa 31:1 [y] Dt 31:6, 8 [z] 2Ch 32:7-8 **20:3** [a] Jos 23:10 **20:4** [b] Dt 1:30; 3:22; Jos 23:10 **20:5** [c] Ne 12:27 **20:7** [d] Dt 24:5 **20:8** [e] Jdg 7:3 **20:10** [f] Lk 14:31-32 **20:11** [g] 1Ki 9:21 **20:13** [h] Nu 31:7 **20:14** [i] Jos 8:2; 22:8

breathes.[j] 17Completely destroy[a] them—the Hittites, Amorites, Canaanites, Perizzites, Hivites and Jebusites—as the LORD your God has commanded you. 18Otherwise, they will teach you to follow all the detestable things they do in worshiping their gods,[k] and you will sin[l] against the LORD your God.

19When you lay siege to a city for a long time, fighting against it to capture it, do not destroy its trees by putting an ax to them, because you can eat their fruit. Do not cut them down. Are the trees people, that you should besiege them?[b] 20However, you may cut down trees that you know are not fruit trees and use them to build siege works until the city at war with you falls.

Atonement for an Unsolved Murder

21 If someone is found slain, lying in a field in the land the LORD your God is giving you to possess, and it is not known who the killer was, 2your elders and judges shall go out and measure the distance from the body to the neighboring towns. 3Then the elders of the town nearest the body shall take a heifer that has never been worked and has never worn a yoke 4and lead it down to a valley that has not been plowed or planted and where there is a flowing stream. There in the valley they are to break the heifer's neck. 5The Levitical priests shall step forward, for the LORD your God has chosen them to minister and to pronounce blessings[m] in the name of the LORD and to decide all cases of dispute and assault.[n] 6Then all the elders of the town nearest the body shall wash their hands[o] over the heifer whose neck was broken in the valley, 7and they shall declare: "Our hands did not shed this blood, nor did our eyes see it done. 8Accept this atonement for your people Israel, whom you have redeemed, LORD, and do not hold your people guilty of the blood of an innocent person." Then the bloodshed will be atoned for,[p] 9and you will have purged[q] from yourselves the guilt of shedding innocent blood, since you have done what is right in the eyes of the LORD.

Marrying a Captive Woman

10When you go to war against your enemies and the LORD your God delivers them into your hands[r] and you take captives, 11if you notice among the captives a beautiful woman and are attracted to her, you may take her as your wife. 12Bring her into your home and have her shave her head,[s] trim her nails 13and put aside the clothes she was wearing when captured. After she has lived in your house and mourned her father and mother for a full month,[t] then you may go to her and be her husband and she shall be your wife. 14If you are not pleased with her, let her go wherever she wishes. You must not sell her or treat her as a slave, since you have dishonored her.[u]

The Right of the Firstborn

15If a man has two wives, and he loves one but not the other, and both bear him sons but the firstborn is the son of the wife he does not love,[v] 16when he wills his property to his sons, he must not give the rights of the firstborn to the son of the wife he loves in preference to his actual firstborn, the son of the wife he does not love.[w] 17He must acknowledge the son of his unloved wife as the firstborn by giving him a double share of all he has. That son is the first sign of his father's strength.[x] The right of the firstborn belongs to him.[y]

A Rebellious Son

18If someone has a stubborn and rebellious son who does not obey his father and mother[z] and will not listen to them when

a 17 The Hebrew term refers to the irrevocable giving over of things or persons to the LORD, often by totally destroying them. *b* 19 Or *down to use in the siege, for the fruit trees are for the benefit of people.*

20:17 *Completely destroy.* This was not just a symbolic war; the entire Canaanite population was to be destroyed.

20:18 *they will teach you.* The principle concern of the Lord was for the welfare of His people. The Canaanite population in the land was like a deadly tumor eating away at the body. If the tumor was cut out, the body could live. No one could thrive in that land as a follower of God as long as the Canaanites were there.

21:1–9 *someone is found slain.* Although the people were innocent of the act and of any knowledge of the actual death of this individual, the elders must still ask the Lord for forgiveness for the shedding of innocent blood. An honest attempt must be made to find justice and to say, "We know this was wrong." God is teaching His people about an active social conscience in this passage. When we know that an innocent party has been wronged we are not to turn our backs and say that we are not involved. Even the simple act of publicly saying that such action is not pleasing to God is effective in reminding those who hear that God sees all and will judge the perpetrators of sin at some point.

21:15 *two wives.* Polygamy was commonly practiced in the cultures of the ancient Middle East and was assumed in the law of Moses. It is apparently something that God allowed, as He did divorce, (Matt. 19:3–9), but from the beginning it was not that way.

21:16 *firstborn.* A father was expected to show consideration for the firstborn child, regardless of his attitude toward the child's mother.

20:16 [j] Ex 23:31-33; Nu 21:2-3; Dt 7:2; Jos 11:14
20:18 [k] Ex 34:16; Dt 7:4; 12:30-31 [l] Ex 23:33
21:5 [m] 1Ch 23:13 [n] Dt 17:8-11 **21:6** [o] Mt 27:24
21:8 [p] Nu 35:33-34 **21:9** [q] Dt 19:13 **21:10** [r] Jos 21:44
21:12 [s] Lev 14:9; Nu 6:9 **21:13** [t] Ps 45:10
21:14 [u] Ge 34:2 **21:15** [v] Ge 29:33 **21:16** [w] 1Ch 26:10
21:17 [x] Ge 49:3 [y] Ge 25:31 **21:18** [z] Pr 1:8; Isa 30:1; Eph 6:1-3

they discipline him, 19his father and mother shall take hold of him and bring him to
the elders at the gate of his town. 20They
shall say to the elders, "This son of ours is
stubborn and rebellious. He will not obey
us. He is a glutton and a drunkard." 21Then
all the men of his town are to stone him
to death. You must purge the evil[a] from
among you. All Israel will hear of it and
be afraid.[b]

Various Laws

22If someone guilty of a capital offense[c]
is put to death and their body is exposed
on a pole, 23you must not leave the body
hanging on the pole overnight.[d] Be sure to
bury it that same day, because anyone who
is hung on a pole is under God's curse.[e] You
must not desecrate[f] the land the LORD your
God is giving you as an inheritance.

22 If you see your fellow Israelite's ox
or sheep straying, do not ignore it
but be sure to take it back to its owner.[g] 2If
they do not live near you or if you do not
know who owns it, take it home with you
and keep it until they come looking for it.
Then give it back. 3Do the same if you find
their donkey or cloak or anything else they
have lost. Do not ignore it.

4If you see your fellow Israelite's donkey[h]
or ox fallen on the road, do not ignore it.
Help the owner get it to its feet.

5A woman must not wear men's clothing,
nor a man wear women's clothing, for the
LORD your God detests anyone who does
this.

6If you come across a bird's nest beside
the road, either in a tree or on the ground,
and the mother is sitting on the young or on
the eggs, do not take the mother with the
young.[i] 7You may take the young, but be
sure to let the mother go, so that it may go
well with you and you may have a long life.[j]

8When you build a new house, make a
parapet around your roof so that you may
not bring the guilt of bloodshed on your
house if someone falls from the roof.

9Do not plant two kinds of seed in your
vineyard;[k] if you do, not only the crops you
plant but also the fruit of the vineyard will
be defiled.[*a*]

10Do not plow with an ox and a donkey
yoked together.[l]

11Do not wear clothes of wool and linen
woven together.[m]

12Make tassels on the four corners of the
cloak you wear.[n]

Marriage Violations

13If a man takes a wife and, after sleeping with her[o], dislikes her 14and slanders
her and gives her a bad name, saying,
"I married this woman, but when I approached her, I did not find proof of her
virginity," 15then the young woman's father and mother shall bring to the town elders at the gate proof that she was a virgin.
16Her father will say to the elders, "I gave
my daughter in marriage to this man, but
he dislikes her. 17Now he has slandered her
and said, 'I did not find your daughter to be
a virgin.' But here is the proof of my daughter's virginity." Then her parents shall display the cloth before the elders of the town,
18and the elders[p] shall take the man and
punish him. 19They shall fine him a hundred shekels[*b*] of silver and give them to the
young woman's father, because this man
has given an Israelite virgin a bad name.
She shall continue to be his wife; he must
not divorce her as long as he lives.

20If, however, the charge is true and no
proof of the young woman's virginity can
be found, 21she shall be brought to the door
of her father's house and there the men of
her town shall stone her to death. She has
done an outrageous thing[q] in Israel by
being promiscuous while still in her father's house. You must purge the evil from
among you.

22If a man is found sleeping with another
man's wife, both the man who slept with
her and the woman must die.[r] You must
purge the evil from Israel.

23If a man happens to meet in a town a

---

a 9 Or *be forfeited to the sanctuary* *b* 19 That is, about 2 1/2 pounds or about 1.2 kilograms

---

21:22 *exposed on a pole.* The guilty person was not executed by hanging, but after the person was stoned the corpse was impaled for public viewing as an example.

22:1–4 Kindness. In the same way that God cares for us, we are to care for others. If we see a kindness that we can do for another, we are to do it cheerfully and willingly. Receiving an act of kindness is heartwarming; doing such an act is a great joy.

22:8 *parapet.* The parapet was a low wall around the edge of the roof. The rooftop was used as an extra room, and if the home owner did not provide safety measures, he would be responsible for any accidents.

22:11 *wool and linen woven together.* These restrictions were a reminder that the Hebrews were not a mixed people. They were separated to God and they were not to mix with other nations, nor were they to mix two kinds of animals, grain, or fabric. It was part of the concept of purity that governed every aspect of life.

22:14 *gives her a bad name.* Charging her indicated a public accusation. Virginity was highly regarded, for if the legitimacy of children was disputable, inheritance rights and positions in family would also be disputed. It is easy to determine the mother of a child, for pregnancy is obvious, but determining the

21:21 [a] Dt 19:19; 1Co 5:13* [b] Dt 13:11 **21:22** [c] Dt 22:26; Mk 14:64; Ac 23:29 **21:23** [d] Jos 8:29; 10:27; Jn 19:31 [e] Gal 3:13* [f] Lev 18:25; Nu 35:34 **22:1** [g] Ex 23:4-5 **22:4** [h] Ex 23:5 **22:6** [i] Lev 22:28 **22:7** [j] Dt 4:40 **22:9** [k] Lev 19:19 **22:10** [l] 2Co 6:14 **22:11** [m] Lev 19:19 **22:12** [n] Nu 15:37-41; Mt 23:5 **22:13** [o] Dt 24:1 **22:18** [p] Ex 18:21 **22:21** [q] Ge 34:7; Dt 13:5; 23:17-18; Jdg 20:6; 2Sa 13:12 **22:22** [r] Lev 20:10; Jn 8:5

virgin pledged to be married and he sleeps
with her, 24you shall take both of them to the
gate of that town and stone them to death—
the young woman because she was in a town
and did not scream for help, and the man because he violated another man's wife. You
must purge the evil from among you.[s]
25But if out in the country a man happens to meet a young woman pledged to be
married and rapes her, only the man who
has done this shall die. 26Do nothing to the
woman; she has committed no sin deserving death. This case is like that of someone
who attacks and murders a neighbor, 27for
the man found the young woman out in the
country, and though the betrothed woman
screamed, there was no one to rescue her.
28If a man happens to meet a virgin who
is not pledged to be married and rapes her
and they are discovered,[t] 29he shall pay her
father fifty shekels[a] of silver. He must marry the young woman, for he has violated
her. He can never divorce her as long as
he lives.
30A man is not to marry his father's wife;
he must not dishonor his father's bed.[b][u]

Exclusion From the Assembly

23[c] No one who has been emasculated
by crushing or cutting may enter the
assembly of the LORD.
2No one born of a forbidden marriage[d]
nor any of their descendants may enter the
assembly of the LORD, not even in the tenth
generation.
3No Ammonite or Moabite or any of
their descendants may enter the assembly
of the LORD, not even in the tenth generation.[v] 4For they did not come to meet you
with bread and water on your way when
you came out of Egypt, and they hired Balaam[w] son of Beor from Pethor in Aram
Naharaim[e] to pronounce a curse on you.
5However, the LORD your God would not
listen to Balaam but turned the curse[x] into
a blessing for you, because the LORD your
God loves you. 6Do not seek a treaty of
friendship with them as long as you live.[y]
7Do not despise an Edomite, for the
Edomites are related to you.[z] Do not despise an Egyptian, because you resided as
foreigners in their country.[a] 8The third generation of children born to them may enter
the assembly of the LORD.

Uncleanness in the Camp

9When you are encamped against your
enemies, keep away from everything impure. 10If one of your men is unclean because of a nocturnal emission, he is to go
outside the camp and stay there.[b] 11But as
evening approaches he is to wash himself,
and at sunset he may return to the camp.
12Designate a place outside the camp
where you can go to relieve yourself. 13As
part of your equipment have something to
dig with, and when you relieve yourself, dig
a hole and cover up your excrement. 14For
the LORD your God moves[c] about in your
camp to protect you and to deliver your enemies to you. Your camp must be holy,[d] so
that he will not see among you anything
indecent and turn away from you.

Miscellaneous Laws

15If a slave has taken refuge with you, do
not hand them over to their master.[e] 16Let
them live among you wherever they like
and in whatever town they choose. Do not
oppress[f] them.
17No Israelite man[g] or woman is to become a shrine prostitute.[h] 18You must not
bring the earnings of a female prostitute
or of a male prostitute[f] into the house of the
LORD your God to pay any vow, because the
LORD your God detests them both.
19Do not charge a fellow Israelite interest, whether on money or food or anything
else that may earn interest.[i] 20You may
charge a foreigner interest, but not a fellow
Israelite, so that the LORD your God may
bless[j] you in everything you put your hand
to in the land you are entering to possess.
21If you make a vow to the LORD your God,
do not be slow to pay it, for the LORD your

[a] *29* That is, about 1 1/4 pounds or about 575 grams [b] *30* In Hebrew texts this verse (22:30) is numbered 23:1. [c] In Hebrew texts 23:1-25 is numbered 23:2-26. [d] *2* Or *one of illegitimate birth* [e] *4* That is, Northwest Mesopotamia [f] *18* Hebrew *of a dog*

father of the child was a matter of trust that the wife was faithful to marriage vows.

23:1 *emasculated.* An emasculated man had had all or part of the sexual organs removed. This was done to men who were put in charge of harems to prevent sexual relations with the women. It was also a pagan practice. Genital mutilation was prohibited in Israel.

23:17 *shrine prostitute.* The cult prostitute was used for the worship of the Canaanite gods and goddesses of fertility. They believed that having intimate relations with the cult prostitutes (either male or female) would bring fertility to their families, fields, and herds. This debased system of worship was one of the reasons God had decided to utterly destroy this group of people.

23:18 *earnings of a female prostitute or a male prostitute.* God did not need or want money earned by such practices that He called abominations.

23:21 *vow.* A vow was purely voluntary, and not necessary for the development of godliness. But if a vow was made, it must be kept.

22:24 [s] ver 21-22; 1Co 5:13* **22:28** [t] Ex 22:16 **22:30** [u] Lev 18:8; 20:11; Dt 27:20; 1Co 5:1 **23:3** [v] Ne 13:2 **23:4** [w] Nu 22:5-6; 23:7; 2Pe 2:15 **23:5** [x] Pr 26:2 **23:6** [y] Ezr 9:12 **23:7** [z] Ge 25:26; Ob 1:10, 12 [a] Ex 22:21; 23:9; Lev 19:34; Dt 10:19 **23:10** [b] Lev 15:16 **23:14** [c] Lev 26:12 [d] Ex 3:5 **23:15** [e] 1Sa 30:15 **23:16** [f] Ex 22:21 **23:17** [g] Ge 19:25; 2Ki 23:7 [h] Lev 19:29; Dt 22:21 **23:19** [i] Ex 22:25; Lev 25:35-37 **23:20** [j] Dt 15:10; 28:12

God will certainly demand it of you and you
will be guilty of sin.[k] 22But if you refrain
from making a vow, you will not be guilty.
23Whatever your lips utter you must be sure
to do, because you made your vow freely to
the LORD your God with your own mouth.
24If you enter your neighbor's vineyard,
you may eat all the grapes you want, but do
not put any in your basket. 25If you enter
your neighbor's grainfield, you may pick
kernels with your hands, but you must not
put a sickle to their standing grain.[l]

24 If a man marries a woman who becomes displeasing to him[m] because
he finds something indecent about her, and
he writes her a certificate of divorce,[n] gives
it to her and sends her from his house, 2and
if after she leaves his house she becomes
the wife of another man, 3and her second
husband dislikes her and writes her a certificate of divorce, gives it to her and sends
her from his house, or if he dies, 4then her
first husband, who divorced her, is not allowed to marry her again after she has
been defiled. That would be detestable in
the eyes of the LORD. Do not bring sin upon
the land the LORD[o] your God is giving you
as an inheritance.
5If a man has recently married, he must
not be sent to war or have any other duty
laid on him. For one year he is to be free
to stay at home and bring happiness to the
wife he has married.[p]
6Do not take a pair of millstones—not
even the upper one—as security for a debt,
because that would be taking a person's
livelihood as security.
7If someone is caught kidnapping a fellow Israelite and treating or selling them as
a slave, the kidnapper must die.[q] You must
purge the evil from among you.
8In cases of defiling skin diseases,[a] be
very careful to do exactly as the Levitical priests instruct you. You must follow
carefully what I have commanded them.[r]
9Remember what the LORD your God did
to Miriam along the way after you came
out of Egypt.[s]
10When you make a loan of any kind to
your neighbor, do not go into their house
to get what is offered to you as a pledge.
11Stay outside and let the neighbor to
whom you are making the loan bring the
pledge out to you. 12If the neighbor is poor,
do not go to sleep with their pledge in your
possession. 13Return their cloak by sunset[t]
so that your neighbor may sleep in it. Then
they will thank you, and it will be regarded
as a righteous act in the sight of the LORD
your God.[u]
14Do not take advantage of a hired worker who is poor and needy, whether that
worker is a fellow Israelite or a foreigner residing in one of your towns.[v] 15Pay
them their wages each day before sunset,
because they are poor[w] and are counting
on it.[x] Otherwise they may cry to the LORD
against you, and you will be guilty of sin.[y]
16Parents are not to be put to death for
their children, nor children put to death for
their parents; each will die for their own sin.[z]
17Do not deprive the foreigner or the fatherless of justice,[a] or take the cloak of the
widow as a pledge. 18Remember that you
were slaves in Egypt and the LORD your
God redeemed you from there. That is why
I command you to do this.
19When you are harvesting in your field
and you overlook a sheaf, do not go back
to get it.[b] Leave it for the foreigner, the fatherless and the widow, so that the LORD
your God may bless[c] you in all the work
of your hands. 20When you beat the olives
from your trees, do not go over the branches a second time.[d] Leave what remains for
the foreigner, the fatherless and the widow. 21When you harvest the grapes in your
vineyard, do not go over the vines again.
Leave what remains for the foreigner, the
fatherless and the widow. 22Remember
that you were slaves in Egypt. That is why
I command you to do this.[e]

[a] 8 The Hebrew word for *defiling skin diseases*, traditionally translated "leprosy," was used for various diseases affecting the skin.

24:1–4 *a certificate of divorce.* Marriage was instituted by God (Gen. 2:24). It was intended to be a union of one man and one woman for life. And yet, the Mosaic law allowed divorce, even though God said through His prophet Malachi (Mal. 2:16) that He hates divorce. When the Pharisees were asking Jesus about divorce, Jesus explained that it had not been so designed in the beginning, but "because of your hardness of heart" Moses had allowed it. Then Jesus raised the standard set by Moses, saying that those whom God had joined, no man should separate. With the death and resurrection of Christ, all believers receive the Holy Spirit, and it is at this point that hard hearts are changed.

24:4 *defiled.* Returning to her first husband after an intervening marriage might have placed the woman in the same position as an unfaithful wife.

24:6 *millstones.* A pair of millstones was used for grinding grain into flour. The flour was ground between two stones, and to deprive a household of the use of one of the stones was to deprive them of the necessities of daily life.

24:8 *defiling skin disease.* Often these words are translated as leprosy, but the disease known today as leprosy, Hansen's disease, is different from the diseases described here.

23:21 [k] Nu 30:1-2; Ecc 5:4-5; Mt 5:33 **23:25** [l] Mt 12:1; Mk 2:23; Lk 6:1 **24:1** [m] Dt 22:13 [n] Mt 5:31*; 19:7-9; Mk 10:4-5 **24:4** [o] Jer 3:1 **24:5** [p] Dt 20:7 **24:7** [q] Ex 21:16 **24:8** [r] Lev 13:1-46; 14:2 **24:9** [s] Nu 12:10 **24:13** [t] Ex 22:26 [u] Dt 6:25; Da 4:27 **24:14** [v] Lev 25:35-43; Dt 15:12-18 **24:15** [w] Jer 22:13 [x] Lev 19:13 [y] Dt 15:9; Jas 5:4 **24:16** [z] 2Ki 14:6; 2Ch 25:4; Jer 31:29-30; Eze 18:20 **24:17** [a] Dt 1:17; 10:17-18; 16:19 **24:19** [b] Lev 19:9; 23:22 [c] Pr 19:17 **24:20** [d] Lev 19:10 **24:22** [e] ver 18

25 When people have a dispute, they are to take it to court and the judges will decide the case,[f] acquitting the innocent and condemning the guilty.[g] 2If the guilty person deserves to be beaten,[h] the judge shall make them lie down and have them flogged in his presence with the number of lashes the crime deserves, 3but the judge must not impose more than forty lashes.[i] If the guilty party is flogged more than that, your fellow Israelite will be degraded in your eyes.[j]

4Do not muzzle an ox while it is treading out the grain.[k]

5If brothers are living together and one of them dies without a son, his widow must not marry outside the family. Her husband's brother shall take her and marry her and fulfill the duty of a brother-in-law to her.[l] 6The first son she bears shall carry on the name of the dead brother so that his name will not be blotted out from Israel.[m]

7However, if a man does not want to marry his brother's wife, she shall go to the elders at the town gate and say, "My husband's brother refuses to carry on his brother's name in Israel. He will not fulfill the duty of a brother-in-law to me."[n] 8Then the elders of his town shall summon him and talk to him. If he persists in saying, "I do not want to marry her," 9his brother's widow shall go up to him in the presence of the elders, take off one of his sandals,[o] spit in his face and say, "This is what is done to the man who will not build up his brother's family line." 10That man's line shall be known in Israel as The Family of the Unsandaled.

11If two men are fighting and the wife of one of them comes to rescue her husband from his assailant, and she reaches out and seizes him by his private parts, 12you shall cut off her hand. Show her no pity.[p]

13Do not have two differing weights in your bag—one heavy, one light.[q] 14Do not have two differing measures in your house—one large, one small. 15You must have accurate and honest weights and measures, so that you may live long[r] in the land the LORD your God is giving you. 16For the LORD your God detests anyone who does these things, anyone who deals dishonestly.[s]

17Remember what the Amalekites[t] did to you along the way when you came out of Egypt. 18When you were weary and worn out, they met you on your journey and attacked all who were lagging behind; they had no fear of God.[u] 19When the LORD your God gives you rest from all the enemies around you in the land he is giving you to possess as an inheritance, you shall blot out the name of Amalek[v] from under heaven. Do not forget!

Firstfruits and Tithes

26 When you have entered the land the LORD your God is giving you as an inheritance and have taken possession of it and settled in it, 2take some of the firstfruits[w] of all that you produce from the soil of the land the LORD your God is giving you and put them in a basket. Then go to the place the LORD your God will choose as a dwelling for his Name[x] 3and say to the priest in office at the time, "I declare today to the LORD your God that I have come to the land the LORD swore to our ancestors to give us." 4The priest shall take the basket from your hands and set it down in front of the altar of the LORD your God. 5Then you shall declare before the LORD your God: "My father was a wandering Aramean,[y] and he went down into Egypt with a few people[z] and lived there and became a great nation, powerful and numerous. 6But the Egyptians mistreated us and made us suffer,[a] subjecting us to harsh labor. 7Then we cried out to the LORD, the God of our ancestors, and the LORD heard our voice[b] and saw[c] our misery, toil and oppression. 8So the LORD brought us out of Egypt with a mighty hand and an outstretched arm, with great terror and with signs and wonders.[d] 9He brought us to this place and gave

---

25:3 ***forty lashes.*** Later Jewish law restricted the number to forty minus one (2 Cor. 11:24) to make sure that the authorities remained within the set limits.
25:4 ***not muzzle an ox.*** Muzzling kept the animal from eating while it worked. Later the apostle Paul used this law as a principle for providing a living for those who spend their lives preaching the gospel (1 Tim. 5:18).
25:5 ***dies without a son.*** The firstborn son of the marriage would be acknowledged as the legal son of the dead brother. Taking a brother's widow as a second wife provided her with care, and preserved the name, position, and inheritance of the dead brother.
25:7–10 ***does not want to marry.*** Legally the brother-in-law was bound to keep the family name alive. His unwillingness to do so was a public issue, involving the elders of the community. The removal of the sandal was a sign of giving up of one's rights, and spitting was a strong act of public contempt.
25:19 ***blot out the name.*** The Amalekites would in effect come under the same ban as the Canaanite nations. The fact that they did not fear God made them a stumbling block to any nation that was following God.
26:5 ***Aramean.*** This is a reference to Jacob, whose parents' ancestral home was in Aramea (Gen. 24:1–10).
26:8 ***mighty hand ... outstretched arm.*** God with His own hand demonstrated His power to the

25:1 [f] Dt 19:17 [g] Dt 1:16-17 **25:2** [h] Lk 12:47-48 **25:3** [i] 2Co 11:24 [j] Job 18:3 **25:4** [k] Pr 12:10; 1Co 9:9*; 1Ti 5:18* **25:5** [l] Mt 22:24; Mk 12:19; Lk 20:28 **25:6** [m] Ge 38:9; Ru 4:5, 10 **25:7** [n] Ru 4:1-2, 5-6 **25:9** [o] Ru 4:7-8, 11 **25:12** [p] Dt 19:13 **25:13** [q] Lev 19:35-37; Pr 11:1; Eze 45:10; Mic 6:11 **25:15** [r] Ex 20:12 **25:16** [s] Pr 11:1 **25:17** [t] Ex 17:8 **25:18** [u] Ps 36:1; Ro 3:18 **25:19** [v] 1Sa 15:2-3 **26:2** [w] Ex 22:29; 23:16, 19; Nu 18:13; Pr 3:9 [x] Dt 12:5 **26:5** [y] Hos 12:12 [z] Ge 43:1-2; 45:7, 11; 46:27; Dt 10:22 **26:6** [a] Ex 1:11, 14 **26:7** [b] Ex 2:23-25 [c] Ex 3:9 **26:8** [d] Dt 4:34

us this land, a land flowing with milk and
honey;[e] 10and now I bring the firstfruits
of the soil that you, LORD, have given me."
Place the basket before the LORD your God
and bow down before him. 11Then you and
the Levites[f] and the foreigners residing
among you shall rejoice[g] in all the good
things the LORD your God has given to you
and your household.
12When you have finished setting aside
a tenth[h] of all your produce in the third
year, the year of the tithe,[i] you shall give it
to the Levite, the foreigner, the fatherless
and the widow, so that they may eat in your
towns and be satisfied. 13Then say to the
LORD your God: "I have removed from my
house the sacred portion and have given
it to the Levite, the foreigner, the fatherless and the widow, according to all you
commanded. I have not turned aside from
your commands nor have I forgotten any of
them.[j] 14I have not eaten any of the sacred
portion while I was in mourning, nor have
I removed any of it while I was unclean,[k]
nor have I offered any of it to the dead. I
have obeyed the LORD my God; I have done
everything you commanded me. 15Look
down from heaven,[l] your holy dwelling
place, and bless your people Israel and the
land you have given us as you promised on
oath to our ancestors, a land flowing with
milk and honey."

Follow the LORD's Commands

16The LORD your God commands you
this day to follow these decrees and laws;
carefully observe them with all your heart
and with all your soul.[m] 17You have declared this day that the LORD is your God
and that you will walk in obedience to him,
that you will keep his decrees, commands
and laws—that you will listen to him.
18And the LORD has declared this day that
you are his people, his treasured possession[n] as he promised, and that you are to
keep all his commands. 19He has declared
that he will set you in praise, fame and hon-
or high above all the nations[o] he has made
and that you will be a people holy[p] to the
LORD your God, as he promised.

The Altar on Mount Ebal

27 Moses and the elders of Israel commanded the people: "Keep all these
commands that I give you today. 2When
you have crossed the Jordan into the land
the LORD your God is giving you, set up
some large stones and coat them with plaster.[q] 3Write on them all the words of this
law when you have crossed over to enter
the land the LORD your God is giving you,
a land flowing with milk and honey,[r] just as
the LORD, the God of your ancestors, promised you. 4And when you have crossed the
Jordan, set up these stones on Mount Ebal,[s]
as I command you today, and coat them
with plaster. 5Build there an altar[t] to the
LORD your God, an altar of stones. Do not
use any iron tool[u] on them. 6Build the altar
of the LORD your God with fieldstones and
offer burnt offerings on it to the LORD your
God. 7Sacrifice fellowship offerings there,
eating them and rejoicing in the presence
of the LORD your God. 8And you shall write
very clearly all the words of this law on
these stones you have set up."

Curses From Mount Ebal

9Then Moses and the Levitical priests
said to all Israel, "Be silent, Israel, and listen! You have now become the people of the
LORD your God.[v] 10Obey the LORD your God
and follow his commands and decrees that
I give you today."
11On the same day Moses commanded
the people:
12When you have crossed the Jordan,
these tribes shall stand on Mount Gerizim[w]
to bless the people: Simeon, Levi, Judah,
Issachar, Joseph and Benjamin.[x] 13And
these tribes shall stand on Mount Ebal to
pronounce curses: Reuben, Gad, Asher,
Zebulun, Dan and Naphtali.

Egyptians and delivered the Israelites. The idea of God rescuing His people with His mighty arm is repeated in Isaiah 62 and 63.

26:10 *I bring.* When the worshipper made a statement of what he was doing, (see v. 13) he was taking responsibility for the items he was presenting to the Lord, not just blindly following a set form.

26:15 *your holy dwelling place.* People direct their prayers to heaven, acknowledging at the same time that God is everywhere (Is. 66:1–2). Heaven most often refers to the dwelling place of God and the holy angels. Heaven is the place from which Christ came when He came to earth and He returned there after He was resurrected (Acts 1:11). One day He will come from heaven back to earth (Matt. 24:30) and Heaven will ultimately be the home of all believers (1 Pet. 1:4). Heaven is the place where the will of God is perfectly done, so it is a place of hope and inspiration.

26:16 *with all your heart and with all your soul.* This is a regular emphasis in Deuteronomy. God wants obedience, but He wants it to be the obedience of the engaged heart and mind.

27:7 *fellowship offerings.* Many of the sacrifices had to do with sin, repentance, and making things right with God. This particular sacrifice was a time to be thankful and to rejoice in the good care of God.

27:11–13 *Mount Gerizim ... Mount Ebal.* Mount Gerizim, the mountain of blessing, is usually covered with vegetation. Mount Ebal, the mountain of cursing, is a barren peak. The visual contrast made a memorable object lesson.

26:9 [e] Ex 3:8 **26:11** [f] Dt 12:7 [g] Dt 16:11
26:12 [h] Lev 27:30 [i] Nu 18:24; Dt 14:28-29; Heb 7:5, 9
26:13 [j] Ps 119:141, 153, 176 **26:14** [k] Lev 7:20; Hos 9:4
26:15 [l] Isa 63:15; Zec 2:13 **26:16** [m] Dt 4:29
26:18 [n] Ex 6:7; 19:5; Dt 7:6; 14:2; 28:9 **26:19** [o] Dt 4:7-8; 28:1, 13, 44 [p] Ex 19:6; Dt 7:6; 1Pe 2:9 **27:2** [q] Jos 8:31
27:3 [r] Dt 26:9 **27:4** [s] Dt 11:29 **27:5** [t] Jos 8:31
[u] Ex 20:25 **27:9** [v] Dt 26:18 **27:12** [w] Dt 11:29 [x] Jos 8:35

[14]The Levites shall recite to all the people of Israel in a loud voice:

[15]"Cursed is anyone who makes an idol[y]—a thing detestable to the LORD, the work of skilled hands—and sets it up in secret."
Then all the people shall say, "Amen!"

[16]"Cursed is anyone who dishonors their father or mother."[z]
Then all the people shall say, "Amen!"

[17]"Cursed is anyone who moves their neighbor's boundary stone."[a]
Then all the people shall say, "Amen!"

[18]"Cursed is anyone who leads the blind astray on the road."[b]
Then all the people shall say, "Amen!"

[19]"Cursed is anyone who withholds justice from the foreigner,[c] the fatherless or the widow."[d]
Then all the people shall say, "Amen!"

[20]"Cursed is anyone who sleeps with his father's wife, for he dishonors his father's bed."[e]
Then all the people shall say, "Amen!"

[21]"Cursed is anyone who has sexual relations with any animal."[f]
Then all the people shall say, "Amen!"

[22]"Cursed is anyone who sleeps with his sister, the daughter of his father or the daughter of his mother."[g]
Then all the people shall say, "Amen!"

[23]"Cursed is anyone who sleeps with his mother-in-law."[h]
Then all the people shall say, "Amen!"

[24]"Cursed is anyone who kills[i] their neighbor secretly."
Then all the people shall say, "Amen!"

[25]"Cursed is anyone who accepts a bribe to kill an innocent person."[j]
Then all the people shall say, "Amen!"

[26]"Cursed is anyone who does not uphold the words of this law by carrying them out."[k]
Then all the people shall say, "Amen!"

Blessings for Obedience

28 If you fully obey the LORD your God and carefully follow all his commands[l] I give you today, the LORD your God will set you high above all the nations on earth.[m] [2]All these blessings will come on you[n] and accompany you if you obey the LORD your God:

[3]You will be blessed[o] in the city and blessed in the country.[p]

[4]The fruit of your womb will be blessed, and the crops of your land and the young of your livestock—the calves of your herds and the lambs of your flocks.[q]

[5]Your basket and your kneading trough will be blessed.

[6]You will be blessed when you come in and blessed when you go out.[r]

[7]The LORD will grant that the enemies who rise up against you will be defeated before you. They will come at you from one direction but flee from you in seven.[s]

[8]The LORD will send a blessing on your barns and on everything you put your hand to. The LORD your God will bless you in the land he is giving you.

[9]The LORD will establish you as his holy people,[t] as he promised you on oath, if you keep the commands of the LORD your God and walk in obedience to him. [10]Then all the peoples on earth will see that you are called by the name[u] of the LORD, and they will fear you. [11]The LORD will grant you abundant prosperity—in the fruit of your womb, the young of your livestock and the crops of your ground—in the land he swore to your ancestors to give you.[v]

[12]The LORD will open the heavens, the storehouse of his bounty, to send rain[w] on your land in season and to bless all the work of your hands. You will lend to many nations but will borrow from none.[x] [13]The LORD will make you the head, not the tail. If you pay attention to the commands of the LORD your God that I give you this day and carefully follow them, you will always be at

27:26 uphold all the words of this law by carrying them out. All of the actions listed in the curses are contrary to the law, as explained in the Book of Leviticus.

28:1–9 *fully obey.* This passage repeatedly emphasizes the Israelites' responsibility to obey. God had already saved them from slavery, made them His people, promised to be their God, and to give them a land to dwell in. But the blessings would only come with Israel's obedience. Sadly, Israel failed again and again to follow God. It was only after Christ that the followers of God could have the new Spirit which enabled them to obey from the heart (Rom. 7).

27:15 [y] Ex 20:4; 34:17; Lev 19:4; 26:1; Dt 4:16,23; 5:8; Isa 44:9 **27:16** [z] Ex 20:12; 21:17; Lev 19:3; 20:9 **27:17** [a] Dt 19:14; Pr 22:28 **27:18** [b] Lev 19:14 **27:19** [c] Ex 22:21; Dt 24:19 [d] Dt 10:18 **27:20** [e] Lev 18:7; Dt 22:30 **27:21** [f] Lev 18:23 **27:22** [g] Lev 18:9; 20:17 **27:23** [h] Lev 20:14 **27:24** [i] Lev 24:17; Nu 35:31 **27:25** [j] Ex 23:7-8; Dt 10:17; Eze 22:12 **27:26** [k] Jer 11:3; Gal 3:10* **28:1** [l] Ex 15:26; Lev 26:3; Dt 7:12-26 [m] Dt 26:19 **28:2** [n] Zec 1:6 **28:3** [o] Ps 128:1,4 [p] Ge 39:5 **28:4** [q] Ge 49:25; Pr 10:22 **28:6** [r] Ps 121:8 **28:7** [s] Lev 26:8, 17 **28:9** [t] Ex 19:6; Dt 7:6 **28:10** [u] 2Ch 7:14 **28:11** [v] Dt 30:9; Pr 10:22 **28:12** [w] Lev 26:4 [x] Dt 15:3,6

the top, never at the bottom. 14Do not turn
aside from any of the commands I give you
today, to the right or to the left,[y] following
other gods and serving them.

Curses for Disobedience

15However, if you do not obey[z] the LORD
your God and do not carefully follow all his
commands and decrees I am giving you today, all these curses will come on you and
overtake you:[a]

> 16You will be cursed in the city and
> cursed in the country.
> 17Your basket and your kneading
> trough will be cursed.
> 18The fruit of your womb will be
> cursed, and the crops of your land, and
> the calves of your herds and the lambs
> of your flocks.
> 19You will be cursed when you come
> in and cursed when you go out.

20The LORD will send on you curses,[b]
confusion and rebuke[c] in everything you
put your hand to, until you are destroyed
and come to sudden ruin[d] because of the
evil you have done in forsaking him.[α] 21The
LORD will plague you with diseases until he
has destroyed you from the land you are
entering to possess.[e] 22The LORD will strike
you with wasting disease, with fever and
inflammation, with scorching heat and
drought,[f] with blight and mildew, which
will plague you until you perish.[g] 23The sky
over your head will be bronze, the ground
beneath you iron.[h] 24The LORD will turn the
rain of your country into dust and powder;
it will come down from the skies until you
are destroyed.
25The LORD will cause you to be defeated before your enemies. You will come at
them from one direction but flee from them
in seven,[i] and you will become a thing of
horror to all the kingdoms on earth.[j] 26Your
carcasses will be food for all the birds and
the wild animals, and there will be no one
to frighten them away.[k] 27The LORD will afflict you with the boils of Egypt[l] and with
tumors, festering sores and the itch, from
which you cannot be cured. 28The LORD
will afflict you with madness, blindness
and confusion of mind. 29At midday you
will grope[m] about like a blind person in
the dark. You will be unsuccessful in everything you do; day after day you will be
oppressed and robbed, with no one to rescue you.
30You will be pledged to be married to a
woman, but another will take her and rape
her.[n] You will build a house, but you will
not live in it.[o] You will plant a vineyard, but
you will not even begin to enjoy its fruit.[p]
31Your ox will be slaughtered before your
eyes, but you will eat none of it. Your donkey will be forcibly taken from you and
will not be returned. Your sheep will be
given to your enemies, and no one will rescue them. 32Your sons and daughters will
be given to another nation,[q] and you will
wear out your eyes watching for them day
after day, powerless to lift a hand. 33A people that you do not know will eat what your
land and labor produce, and you will have
nothing but cruel oppression all your days.[r]
34The sights you see will drive you mad.
35The LORD will afflict your knees and legs
with painful boils[s] that cannot be cured,
spreading from the soles of your feet to the
top of your head.
36The LORD will drive you and the king[t]
you set over you to a nation unknown to
you or your ancestors.[u] There you will worship other gods, gods of wood and stone.[v]
37You will become a thing of horror, a byword and an object of ridicule among all
the peoples where the LORD will drive you.[w]

[α] 20 Hebrew *me*

28:15–19 Disobedience—The price of disobedience is always more than one can imagine in the beginning. It is not only the loss of peace or blessing, great as that may be, but there is also the loss of all that might have been. In God's plan the obedience is for the benefit of the follower of God, for the benefit of those who are watching and are influenced by this follower, and for the kingdom of God. If the follower disobeys, he may see how his actions affect himself, but he cannot know what other blessings are lost in the wider sphere of his own influence. It is a terrible thing to find oneself in the position of working against God.

28:20–57 *curses, confusion, and rebuke.* Disobedience brings suffering, and this suffering often spills over onto other people, even into future generations. The suffering is a wake-up call, something that is meant to remind the disobedient that they are living against God, and that they need to repent, turn to God, and ask for help. The problem is, that often the disobedient have a skewed idea of who God is and what He desires, so they blame God and become more rebellious. There is another kind of suffering as well. This is the suffering of the innocent, as in the case of Job, where God allowed Satan to test him to show Satan that Job really loved God and was not merely faithful because God had blessed him.

28:30 *married to a woman ... build a house ... plant a vineyard.* Each of these momentous events of life were reasons to be excused from service in the army (20:5–7), yet if the Israelites were disobedient, life itself would prevent them from realizing the fruits of their labors.

28:14 [y] Dt 5:32 **28:15** [z] Lev 26:14 [a] Jos 23:15; Da 9:11; Mal 2:2 **28:20** [b] Mal 2:2 [c] Isa 51:20; 66:15 [d] Dt 4:26 **28:21** [e] Lev 26:25; Jer 24:10 **28:22** [f] Lev 26:16 [g] Am 4:9 **28:23** [h] Lev 26:19 **28:25** [i] Isa 30:17 [j] Jer 15:4; 24:9; Eze 23:46 **28:26** [k] Jer 7:33; 16:4; 34:20 **28:27** [l] ver 60-61; 1Sa 5:6 **28:29** [m] Job 5:14; Isa 59:10 **28:30** [n] Job 31:10; Jer 8:10 [o] Am 5:11 [p] Jer 12:13 **28:32** [q] ver 41 **28:33** [r] Jer 5:15-17 **28:35** [s] ver 27 **28:36** [t] 2Ki 17:4, 6; 24:12, 14; 25:7, 11 [u] Jer 16:13 [v] Dt 4:28 **28:37** [w] Jer 24:9

38You will sow much seed in the field but you will harvest little,[x] because locusts will devour[y] it. 39You will plant vineyards and cultivate them but you will not drink the wine or gather the grapes, because worms will eat them.[z] 40You will have olive trees throughout your country but you will not use the oil, because the olives will drop off.[a] 41You will have sons and daughters but you will not keep them, because they will go into captivity.[b] 42Swarms of locusts will take over all your trees and the crops of your land.

43The foreigners who reside among you will rise above you higher and higher, but you will sink lower and lower.[c] 44They will lend to you, but you will not lend to them.[d] They will be the head, but you will be the tail.[e]

45All these curses will come on you. They will pursue you and overtake you until you are destroyed,[f] because you did not obey the LORD your God and observe the commands and decrees he gave you. 46They will be a sign and a wonder to you and your descendants forever.[g] 47Because you did not serve[h] the LORD your God joyfully and gladly[i] in the time of prosperity, 48therefore in hunger and thirst, in nakedness and dire poverty, you will serve the enemies the LORD sends against you. He will put an iron yoke[j] on your neck until he has destroyed you.

49The LORD will bring a nation against you from far away, from the ends of the earth,[k] like an eagle[l] swooping down, a nation whose language you will not understand, 50a fierce-looking nation without respect for the old[m] or pity for the young. 51They will devour the young of your livestock and the crops of your land until you are destroyed. They will leave you no grain, new wine or olive oil, nor any calves of your herds or lambs of your flocks until you are ruined.[n] 52They will lay siege to all the cities throughout your land until the high fortified walls in which you trust fall down. They will besiege all the cities throughout the land the LORD your God is giving you.[o]

53Because of the suffering your enemy will inflict on you during the siege, you will eat the fruit of the womb, the flesh of the sons and daughters the LORD your God has given you.[p] 54Even the most gentle and sensitive man among you will have no compassion on his own brother or the wife he loves or his surviving children, 55and he will not give to one of them any of the flesh of his children that he is eating. It will be all he has left because of the suffering your enemy will inflict on you during the siege of all your cities. 56The most gentle and sensitive[q] woman among you—so sensitive and gentle that she would not venture to touch the ground with the sole of her foot—will begrudge the husband she loves and her own son or daughter 57the afterbirth from her womb and the children she bears. For in her dire need she intends to eat them secretly because of the suffering your enemy will inflict on you during the siege of your cities.

58If you do not carefully follow all the words of this law, which are written in this book, and do not revere[r] this glorious and awesome name[s]—the LORD your God— 59the LORD will send fearful plagues on you and your descendants, harsh and prolonged disasters, and severe and lingering illnesses. 60He will bring on you all the diseases of Egypt[t] that you dreaded, and they will cling to you. 61The LORD will also bring on you every kind of sickness and disaster not recorded in this Book of the Law, until you are destroyed.[u] 62You who were as numerous as the stars in the sky[v] will be left but few in number, because you did not obey the LORD your God. 63Just as it pleased[w] the LORD to make you prosper and increase in number, so it will please[x] him to ruin and destroy you. You will be uprooted[y] from the land you are entering to possess.

64Then the LORD will scatter[z] you among all nations,[a] from one end of the earth to the other. There you will worship other gods—gods of wood and stone, which neither you nor your ancestors have known. 65Among those nations you will find no repose, no resting place for the sole of your foot. There the LORD will give you an anxious mind, eyes weary with longing, and a despairing heart.[b] 66You will live in constant suspense, filled with dread both night and day, never sure of your life. 67In the morning you will say, "If only it were evening!" and in the evening, "If only it were morning!"—because of the terror that will fill your hearts and the sights that your eyes will see.[c] 68The LORD will send you back in ships to Egypt on a journey I said you should never make again. There you will offer yourselves for sale to your enemies as male and female slaves, but no one will buy you.

28:52–57 ***lay siege to all the cities throughout your land.*** Moses forewarned the people of the terrible stresses of sieges (2 Kin. 6:24–31; Lam. 2:20; 4:10). The horrors of hunger and deprivation would lead people to behave in ways that they otherwise could never imagine.

28:38 [x] Mic 6:15; Hag 1:6,9 [y] Joel 1:4 **28:39** [z] Isa 5:10; 17:10-11 **28:40** [a] Mic 6:15 **28:41** [b] ver 32

28:43 [c] ver 13 **28:44** [d] ver 12 [e] ver 13 **28:45** [f] ver 15 **28:46** [g] Isa 8:18; Eze 14:8 **28:47** [h] Dt 32:15 [i] Ne 9:35 **28:48** [j] Jer 28:13-14 **28:49** [k] Jer 5:15; 6:22 [l] La 4:19; Hos 8:1 **28:50** [m] Isa 47:6 **28:51** [n] ver 33 **28:52** [o] Jer 10:18; Zep 1:14-16, 17 **28:53** [p] Lev 26:29; 2Ki 6:28-29; Jer 19:9; La 2:20; 4:10 **28:56** [q] ver 54 **28:58** [r] Mal 1:14 [s] Ex 6:3 **28:60** [t] ver 27 **28:61** [u] Dt 4:25-26 **28:62** [v] Dt 4:27; 10:22; Ne 9:23 **28:63** [w] Jer 32:41 [x] Pr 1:26 [y] Jer 12:14; 45:4 **28:64** [z] Lev 26:33; Dt 4:27 [a] Ne 1:8 **28:65** [b] Lev 26:16, 36 **28:67** [c] ver 34; Job 7:4

Renewal of the Covenant

29[a] These are the terms of the covenant
the LORD commanded Moses to
make with the Israelites in Moab, in addition to the covenant he had made with them
at Horeb.[d]
2Moses summoned all the Israelites and
said to them:

Your eyes have seen all that the LORD
did in Egypt to Pharaoh, to all his officials
and to all his land.[e] 3With your own eyes
you saw those great trials, those signs and
great wonders.[f] 4But to this day the LORD
has not given you a mind that understands
or eyes that see or ears that hear.[g] 5Yet the
LORD says, "During the forty years that
I led you through the wilderness, your
clothes did not wear out, nor did the sandals on your feet.[h] 6You ate no bread and
drank no wine or other fermented drink. I
did this so that you might know that I am
the LORD your God."[i]
7When you reached this place, Sihon[j]
king of Heshbon and Og king of Bashan
came out to fight against us, but we defeated them.[k] 8We took their land and gave it as
an inheritance to the Reubenites, the Gadites and the half-tribe of Manasseh.[l]
9Carefully follow[m] the terms of this covenant, so that you may prosper in everything you do.[n] 10All of you are standing
today in the presence of the LORD your
God—your leaders and chief men, your
elders and officials, and all the other men
of Israel, 11together with your children and
your wives, and the foreigners living in
your camps who chop your wood and carry
your water.[o] 12You are standing here in order to enter into a covenant with the LORD
your God, a covenant the LORD is making
with you this day and sealing with an oath,
13to confirm you this day as his people,[p]
that he may be your God[q] as he promised
you and as he swore to your fathers, Abraham, Isaac and Jacob. 14I am making this
covenant,[r] with its oath, not only with you
15who are standing here with us today in
the presence of the LORD our God but also
with those who are not here today.[s]
16You yourselves know how we lived
in Egypt and how we passed through
the countries on the way here. 17You saw
among them their detestable images and
idols of wood and stone, of silver and gold.[t]
18Make sure there is no man or woman,
clan or tribe among you today whose heart
turns away from the LORD our God to go
and worship the gods of those nations;
make sure there is no root among you that
produces such bitter poison.[u]
19When such a person hears the words
of this oath and they invoke a blessing on
themselves, thinking, "I will be safe, even
though I persist in going my own way," they
will bring disaster on the watered land as
well as the dry. 20The LORD will never be
willing to forgive them; his wrath and zeal[v]
will burn[w] against them. All the curses
written in this book will fall on them, and
the LORD will blot[x] out their names from
under heaven. 21The LORD will single them
out from all the tribes of Israel for disaster,
according to all the curses of the covenant
written in this Book of the Law.
22Your children who follow you in later generations and foreigners who come
from distant lands will see the calamities
that have fallen on the land and the diseases with which the LORD has afflicted it.[y]
23The whole land will be a burning waste[z]
of salt[a] and sulfur—nothing planted, nothing sprouting, no vegetation growing on it.
It will be like the destruction of Sodom and
Gomorrah,[b] Admah and Zeboyim, which
the LORD overthrew in fierce anger. 24All
the nations will ask: "Why has the LORD
done this to this land?[c] Why this fierce,
burning anger?"

[a] In Hebrew texts 29:1 is numbered 28:69, and 29:2-29 is numbered 29:1-28.

29:9–13 ***follow the terms of this covenant.*** The members of the covenant community included all adults, children, and strangers who had joined the Israelites, as well as those yet to be born.
29:10–15 The Covenant Renewed—As Israel reached the plains of Moab, anticipating their entrance into the Promised Land, it was important for the people to review and renew their covenantal relationship with God. So Moses summoned the people together and challenged them to keep the covenant that God had established with their forefathers. The essential terms of the covenant gave Israel the Promised Land and prosperity in their possession of it, but only on the condition of their obedience and willingness to walk in God's ways.
29:18 ***heart turns away.*** To be in the position of once having known the way of the Lord, and then to have turned and followed a path of disobedience and rebellion is a miserable position. It is the cause of great heartache for the faithful ones who see it happening. The backslider becomes more and more hardened against God, and it will ultimately affect a wider and wider group of people. There is no security or safety while persisting in a course of flagrant and continuous rebellion. ***root among you that produces such bitter poison.*** Tolerance for idolatry and pagan practices would always corrupt the community, and therefore the covenant relationship with God.
29:24–28 ***Why has the LORD done this.*** The lesson of faithless Israel would become known among

29:1 [d] Dt 5:2-3 **29:2** [e] Ex 19:4 **29:3** [f] Dt 4:34; 7:19 **29:4** [g] Isa 6:10; Ac 28:26-27; Ro 11:8*; Eph 4:18 **29:5** [h] Dt 8:4 **29:6** [i] Dt 8:3 **29:7** [j] Dt 2:32; 3:1 [k] Nu 21:21-24, 33-35 **29:8** [l] Nu 32:33; Dt 3:12-13 **29:9** [m] Dt 4:6; Jos 1:7 [n] 1Ki 2:3 **29:11** [o] Jos 9:21, 23, 27 **29:13** [p] Dt 28:9 [q] Ge 17:7; Ex 6:7 **29:14** [r] Jer 31:31 **29:15** [s] Ac 2:39 **29:17** [t] Dt 28:36 **29:18** [u] Dt 11:16; Heb 12:15 **29:20** [v] Eze 23:25 [w] Ps 74:1; 79:5 [x] Ex 32:33; Dt 9:14 **29:22** [y] Jer 19:8 **29:23** [z] Isa 34:9 [a] Jer 17:6 [b] Ge 19:24, 25; Zep 2:9 **29:24** [c] 1Ki 9:8; Jer 22:8-9

25And the answer will be: "It is because
this people abandoned the covenant of the
LORD, the God of their ancestors, the covenant he made with them when he brought
them out of Egypt. 26They went off and worshiped other gods and bowed down to them,
gods they did not know, gods he had not
given them. 27Therefore the LORD's anger
burned against this land, so that he brought
on it all the curses written in this book.[d] 28In
furious anger and in great wrath the LORD
uprooted[e] them from their land and thrust
them into another land, as it is now."

29The secret things belong to the LORD
our God, but the things revealed belong to
us and to our children forever, that we may
follow all the words of this law.

Prosperity After Turning to the LORD

30 When all these blessings and curses[f] I
have set before you come on you and
you take them to heart wherever the LORD
your God disperses you among the nations,[g]
2and when you and your children return[h] to
the LORD your God and obey him with all
your heart and with all your soul according to everything I command you today,
3then the LORD your God will restore your
fortunes[a][i] and have compassion on you and
gather[j] you again from all the nations where
he scattered you.[k] 4Even if you have been
banished to the most distant land under
the heavens, from there the LORD your God
will gather you and bring you back.[l] 5He
will bring[m] you to the land that belonged
to your ancestors, and you will take possession of it. He will make you more prosperous and numerous than your ancestors.
6The LORD your God will circumcise your
hearts and the hearts of your descendants,[n]
so that you may love him with all your heart
and with all your soul, and live. 7The LORD
your God will put all these curses on your
enemies who hate and persecute you.[o] 8You
will again obey the LORD and follow all his
commands I am giving you today. 9Then the
LORD your God will make you most prosperous in all the work of your hands and in
the fruit of your womb, the young of your
livestock and the crops of your land.[p] The
LORD will again delight in you and make
you prosperous, just as he delighted in your
ancestors, 10if you obey the LORD your God
and keep his commands and decrees that
are written in this Book of the Law and turn
to the LORD your God with all your heart
and with all your soul.[q]

The Offer of Life or Death

11Now what I am commanding you today
is not too difficult for you or beyond your
reach.[r] 12It is not up in heaven, so that you
have to ask, "Who will ascend into heaven
to get it and proclaim it to us so we may obey
it?"[s] 13Nor is it beyond the sea, so that you
have to ask, "Who will cross the sea to get
it and proclaim it to us so we may obey it?"
14No, the word is very near you; it is in your
mouth and in your heart so you may obey it.

[a] 3 Or *will bring you back from captivity*

---

the nations, even as the deliverance of Israel was to be known by them.

29:29 Revelation—Revelation may be defined as that process by which God gives to us truths that we would not otherwise know. The details of the creation story in Genesis 1 and 2 are an example of general revelation. In that man was not created until the sixth day, there was no human to even write about creation until after it happened. God revealed the creation facts to Moses. All created things have an innate knowledge of their Creator through creation itself.

We know God spoke to the human authors of our Bible. We are not sure exactly how it happened, but Scripture gives some examples of specific revelation. God's call to Samuel was in an audible voice he mistook for Eli's (1 Sam. 3). Often God spoke through angels such as when Gabriel was sent to tell Mary she would give birth to the Messiah (Luke 1:26–37). On other occasions it appears that God spoke directly to an individual, as he did to Noah (Gen. 6) and Moses through the burning bush (Ex. 3). On still other occasions God communicated through dreams or visions as he did with the wise men (Matt. 2:12) and Peter (Acts 10).

One of the most important ways God reveals Himself to people in Scripture is through encounters where God takes on human form called a theophany or Christophany. In Genesis 32 Jacob wrestled with God, and in Joshua 5 Joshua encounters a commander of the Lord's that most Bible students take to be a pre-incarnate Christ.

30:1 *When all these . . . come on you.* God had allowed Moses to foresee Israel's future apostasy and God's dispersal of the people among the nations. Hundreds of years later, these verses must have been both sad and encouraging to the Israelites as they saw the time of their dispersal.

30:6 *circumcise your hearts.* God's intentions for His people have always been for the whole person to respond to Him. Outward symbols, such as circumcision, were always intended to be the mark of an inner reality, the heart that was tender to the Lord.

30:10 *this Book of the law.* A reference to the Book of Deuteronomy. ***all your heart . . . all your soul.*** An open heart in the presence God through the law creates a dynamic of "life" and "blessing" (v. 19).

30:11 *not too difficult for you.* This is not a task that is hard to understand.

30:12–13 *not up in heaven . . . beyond the sea.* Obeying God's law is entirely within the reach of the average person.

30:14 *very near you.* The revelation of God, unlike

29:27 [d] Da 9:11, 13, 14 **29:28** [e] 1Ki 14:15; 2Ch 7:20; Ps 52:5; Pr 2:22 **30:1** [f] ver 15, 19; Dt 11:26 [g] Lev 26:40-45; Dt 28:64; 29:28; 1Ki 8:47 **30:2** [h] Dt 4:30; Ne 1:9 **30:3** [i] Ps 126:4 [j] Ps 147:2; Jer 32:37; Eze 34:13 [k] Jer 29:14 **30:4** [l] Ne 1:8-9; Isa 43:6 **30:5** [m] Jer 29:14 **30:6** [n] Dt 10:16; Jer 32:39 **30:7** [o] Dt 7:15 **30:9** [p] Dt 28:11; Jer 31:28; 32:41 **30:10** [q] Dt 4:29 **30:11** [r] Isa 45:19, 23 **30:12** [s] Ro 10:6*

15See, I set before you today life and prosperity, death and destruction.[t] 16For I command you today to love the LORD your God, to walk in obedience to him, and to keep his commands, decrees and laws; then you will live and increase, and the LORD your God will bless you in the land you are entering to possess.

17But if your heart turns away and you are not obedient, and if you are drawn away to bow down to other gods and worship them, 18I declare to you this day that you will certainly be destroyed.[u] You will not live long in the land you are crossing the Jordan to enter and possess.

19This day I call the heavens and the earth as witnesses against you[v] that I have set before you life and death, blessings and curses.[w] Now choose life, so that you and your children may live 20and that you may love[x] the LORD your God, listen to his voice, and hold fast to him. For the LORD is your life,[y] and he will give you many years in the land he swore to give to your fathers, Abraham, Isaac and Jacob.

Joshua to Succeed Moses

31 Then Moses went out and spoke these words to all Israel: 2"I am now a hundred and twenty years old[z] and I am no longer able to lead you.[a] The LORD has said to me, 'You shall not cross the Jordan.'[b] 3The LORD your God himself will cross[c] over ahead of you.[d] He will destroy these nations before you, and you will take possession of their land. Joshua also will cross[e] over ahead of you, as the LORD said. 4And the LORD will do to them what he did to Sihon and Og, the kings of the Amorites, whom he destroyed along with their land. 5The LORD will deliver[f] them to you, and you must do to them all that I have commanded you. 6Be strong and courageous.[g] Do not be afraid or terrified[h] because of them, for the LORD your God goes with you;[i] he will never leave you[j] nor forsake[k] you."

7Then Moses summoned Joshua and said[l] to him in the presence of all Israel, "Be strong and courageous, for you must go with this people into the land that the LORD swore to their ancestors to give them, and you must divide it among them as their inheritance. 8The LORD himself goes before you and will be with you;[m] he will never leave you nor forsake you. Do not be afraid; do not be discouraged."

Public Reading of the Law

9So Moses wrote down this law and gave it to the Levitical priests, who carried[n] the ark of the covenant of the LORD, and to all the elders of Israel. 10Then Moses commanded them: "At the end of every seven years, in the year for canceling debts,[o] during the Festival of Tabernacles,[p] 11when all Israel comes to appear[q] before the LORD your God at the place he will choose, you shall read this law[r] before them in their hearing. 12Assemble the people—men, women and children, and the foreigners residing in your towns—so they can listen and learn[s] to fear the LORD your God and follow carefully all the words of this law. 13Their children,[t] who do not know this law, must hear it and learn to fear the LORD your God as long as you live in the land you are crossing the Jordan to possess."

Israel's Rebellion Predicted

14The LORD said to Moses, "Now the day of your death[u] is near. Call Joshua and present yourselves at the tent of meeting, where I will commission him." So Moses and Joshua came and presented themselves at the tent of meeting.

---

any other book, makes the truth of immediate importance to the reader.

30:18 ***this day.*** Moses establishes here the best pattern for the preaching of the Word of God. Responses to God should not be delayed. Assuming that there will be a later day to respond to Him is dangerous thinking.

30:19 ***life and death.*** Biblical teaching is remarkable for the clarity with which it presents the great issues that demand decision. Either we love the Lord and walk in His ways, or we turn from Him to worship idols. We can choose life or death, blessing or cursing. God takes no pleasure in the misery of sinners, but urges us to choose life for our good and the good of unborn generations. The Lord has spoken, and we cannot plead ignorance. ***and your children.*** The present generation's choice always determines the direction of future generations.

31:2–3 ***You shall not cross the Jordan.*** Moses spoke regretfully of God's refusal to permit him to enter the promised land, yet he continued to make the most important point of all. The leadership of God Himself would not cease with Moses' death.

31:12–13 Obeying God—Because the Israelites had no Bibles, they had to come together to listen to God's word as read by a priest from a scroll. The laws were to be read to the whole assembly including women and children. No doubt memorization was important as a way of impressing the laws on the minds and hearts of the people. But it was not the end. The expected end result of hearing was obedience. Obedience to the Word of God is the only way that the child of God can please God in the new life. "Do not merely listen to the word, and so deceive yourselves." (James 1:22).

30:15 [t] Dt 11:26 **30:18** [u] Dt 8:19 **30:19** [v] Dt 4:26 [w] ver 1 **30:20** [x] Dt 6:5; 10:20 [y] Ps 27:1; Jn 11:25
31:2 [z] Dt 34:7 [a] Nu 27:17; 1Ki 3:7 [b] Dt 3:23,26
31:3 [c] Nu 27:18 [d] Dt 9:3 [e] Dt 3:28 **31:5** [f] Dt 7:2
31:6 [g] Jos 10:25; 1Ch 22:13 [h] Dt 7:18 [i] Dt 1:29; 20:4 [j] Jos 1:5 [k] Heb 13:5* **31:7** [l] Dt 1:38; 3:28
31:8 [m] Ex 13:21; 33:14 **31:9** [n] ver 25; Nu 4:15; Jos 3:3
31:10 [o] Dt 15:1 [p] Lev 23:34 **31:11** [q] Dt 16:16 [r] Jos 8:34-35; 2Ki 23:2 **31:12** [s] Dt 4:10 **31:13** [t] Dt 11:2; Ps 78:6-7 **31:14** [u] Nu 27:13; Dt 32:49-50

15Then the LORD appeared at the tent in
a pillar of cloud, and the cloud stood over
the entrance to the tent.[v] 16And the LORD
said to Moses: "You are going to rest with
your ancestors, and these people will soon
prostitute[w] themselves to the foreign gods
of the land they are entering. They will forsake[x] me and break the covenant I made
with them. 17And in that day I will become
angry[y] with them and forsake[z] them; I will
hide[a] my face from them, and they will be
destroyed. Many disasters and calamities
will come on them, and in that day they
will ask, 'Have not these disasters come on
us because our God is not with us?'[b] 18And
I will certainly hide my face in that day because of all their wickedness in turning to
other gods.

19"Now write down this song and teach
it to the Israelites and have them sing it,
so that it may be a witness for me against
them. 20When I have brought them into
the land flowing with milk and honey, the
land I promised on oath to their ancestors,[c]
and when they eat their fill and thrive, they
will turn to other gods[d] and worship them,
rejecting me and breaking my covenant.[e]
21And when many disasters and calamities come on them,[f] this song will testify
against them, because it will not be forgotten by their descendants. I know what they
are disposed to do,[g] even before I bring
them into the land I promised them on
oath." 22So Moses wrote[h] down this song
that day and taught it to the Israelites.

23The LORD gave this command[i] to Joshua son of Nun: "Be strong and courageous,[j]
for you will bring the Israelites into the
land I promised them on oath, and I myself
will be with you."

24After Moses finished writing in a book
the words of this law from beginning to end,
25he gave this command to the Levites who
carried the ark of the covenant of the LORD:
26"Take this Book of the Law and place it
beside the ark of the covenant of the LORD
your God. There it will remain as a witness
against you.[k] 27For I know how rebellious
and stiff-necked[l] you are. If you have been
rebellious against the LORD while I am still
alive and with you, how much more will
you rebel after I die! 28Assemble before me
all the elders of your tribes and all your officials, so that I can speak these words in
their hearing and call the heavens and the
earth to testify against them.[m] 29For I know
that after my death you are sure to become
utterly corrupt[n] and to turn from the way
I have commanded you. In days to come,
disaster[o] will fall on you because you will
do evil in the sight of the LORD and arouse
his anger by what your hands have made."

The Song of Moses

30And Moses recited the words of this
song from beginning to end in the hearing
of the whole assembly of Israel:

32 Listen, you heavens,[p] and I will speak;
hear, you earth, the words of my mouth.
2Let my teaching fall like rain
and my words descend like dew,[q]
like showers[r] on new grass,
like abundant rain on tender plants.

3I will proclaim the name of the LORD.[s]
Oh, praise the greatness[t] of our God!
4He is the Rock,[u] his works are perfect,[v]
and all his ways are just.
A faithful God[w] who does no wrong,
upright and just is he.

5They are corrupt and not his children;
to their shame they are a warped and crooked generation.[x]
6Is this the way you repay[y] the LORD,
you foolish and unwise people?[z]
Is he not your Father,[a] your Creator,[a]
who made you and formed you?[b]

7Remember the days of old;
consider the generations long past.
Ask your father and he will tell you,
your elders, and they will explain to you.[c]

[a] 6 Or *Father, who bought you*

31:16 *prostitute.* This expression speaks both of spiritual adultery and physical acts of sexual immorality that were performed in association with the worship of Baal and Asherah, the gods of Canaan.

31:22 *So Moses wrote.* Psalm 90 is also attributed to Moses, and perhaps Psalm 91. Both Psalms are logical meditations for these last chapters of Deuteronomy.

32:7 Remembering the Works of God—The Bible's revelation of God's work in the past provides an informative and exciting panorama of centuries of divine activity toward man.

First, it gives man an education in truths unknowable apart from divine revelation. For example, the creation of man described in Genesis 1 and 2 answers man's most basic questions: "Who am I?" and "Where did I come from?" The only way we can get this information is from God Himself.

Second, the Bible sets forth a significant body of historical evidence for the truth and validity of the Christian faith. These evidences include fulfilled prophecy, the miracles of Christ, and Christ's death and resurrection. The believer's faith is thus grounded in historical events and is much more than just "a leap in the dark."

31:15 [v] Ex 33:9 **31:16** [w] Jdg 2:12 [x] Jdg 10:6, 13 **31:17** [y] Jdg 2:14, 20 [z] Jdg 6:13; 2Ch 15:2 [a] Dt 32:20; Isa 1:15; 8:17 [b] Nu 14:42 **31:20** [c] Dt 6:10-12 [d] Dt 32:15-17 [e] ver 16 **31:21** [f] ver 17 [g] Hos 5:3 **31:22** [h] ver 19 **31:23** [i] ver 7 [j] Jos 1:6 **31:26** [k] ver 19 **31:27** [l] Ex 32:9; Dt 9:6, 24 **31:28** [m] Dt 4:26; 30:19; 32:1 **31:29** [n] Dt 32:5; Jdg 2:19 [o] Dt 28:15 **32:1** [p] Isa 1:2 **32:2** [q] Isa 55:11 [r] Ps 72:6 **32:3** [s] Ex 33:19 [t] Dt 3:24 **32:4** [u] ver 15, 18, 30 [v] 2Sa 22:31 [w] Dt 7:9 **32:5** [x] Dt 31:29 **32:6** [y] Ps 116:12 [z] Ps 74:2 [a] Dt 1:31; Isa 63:16 [b] ver 15 **32:7** [c] Ex 13:14

8 When the Most High gave the nations
their inheritance,
when he divided all mankind,[d]
he set up boundaries for the peoples
according to the number of the sons
of Israel.[a]
9 For the LORD's portion[e] is his people,
Jacob his allotted inheritance.[f]

10 In a desert[g] land he found him,
in a barren and howling waste.
He shielded him and cared for him;
he guarded him as the apple of his
eye,[h]
11 like an eagle that stirs up its nest
and hovers over its young,[i]
that spreads its wings to catch them
and carries them aloft.
12 The LORD alone led him;
no foreign god was with him.[j]

13 He made him ride on the heights[k] of the
land
and fed him with the fruit of the
fields.
He nourished him with honey from the
rock,
and with oil[l] from the flinty crag,
14 with curds and milk from herd and
flock
and with fattened lambs and
goats,
with choice rams of Bashan
and the finest kernels of wheat.[m]
You drank the foaming blood of the
grape.[n]

15 Jeshurun[b] grew fat[o] and kicked;
filled with food, they became heavy
and sleek.
They abandoned[p] the God who made
them
and rejected the Rock[q] their Savior.
16 They made him jealous[r] with their
foreign gods
and angered[s] him with their
detestable idols.
17 They sacrificed to false gods, which are
not God—
gods they had not known,[t]
gods that recently appeared,[u]
gods your ancestors did not fear.
18 You deserted the Rock, who fathered
you;
you forgot[v] the God who gave you
birth.

19 The LORD saw this and rejected them[w]
because he was angered by his sons
and daughters.[x]
20 "I will hide my face[y] from them," he
said,
"and see what their end will be;
for they are a perverse generation,[z]
children who are unfaithful.
21 They made me jealous[a] by what is no
god
and angered me with their worthless
idols.[b]
I will make them envious by those who
are not a people;
I will make them angry by a nation
that has no understanding.[c]
22 For a fire will be kindled by my wrath,
one that burns down to the realm of
the dead below.[d]
It will devour the earth and its harvests
and set afire the foundations of the
mountains.

23 "I will heap calamities[e] on them
and spend my arrows[f] against them.

---

[a] 8 Masoretic Text; Dead Sea Scrolls (see also Septuagint) *sons of God* [b] 15 *Jeshurun* means *the upright one*, that is, Israel.

Third, the Bible records examples to help present-day Christians. Israel's failures and the consequences that resulted are used by the New Testament writers as lessons. Believers are urged to avoid grumbling, as Israel did (1 Cor. 10:10–11), and the deviant behavior of Sodom and Gomorrah (2 Pet. 2: 4–9). Paul is said to be a living example for believers to follow (1 Cor. 4:16; 11:1), as is Jesus' humility in the midst of suffering (1 Pet. 2:21).

Fourth, the Bible provides encouragement for Christians in their life and witness. If God could use an adulterer and murderer like David, then God can surely use a struggling Christian today if that person has David's passion for the Lord. Likewise, if God saved Saul of Tarsus, the chief enemy of the early church (Acts 9:1–31), he can certainly save the people with whom Christians daily share their faith.

32:12 *The LORD alone.* Deuteronomy is an extended argument against idolatry and paganism. Clearly the Israelites had no reason to abandon the God of grace and love, who had given them all they needed.

32:15 *Jeshurun.* Jeshurun, a pet name for Israel, means "uprightness." This part of the song contrasts what Israel should have been (upright) and what they became (rebellious). ***They abandoned the God who made them.*** A nation or a person who has forsaken God is godless. Because God is the source of blessing, peace, joy, wisdom, and comfort, they have also forsaken all of these attributes. One would think that that would be enough to drive people back to God. But persistence in willful disobedience and willful ignorance of God's ways creates a kind of blindness and deafness that makes people unwilling to turn back. At this point God sometimes hides His face, and they experience greater misfortunes.

32:17 *false gods.* Scripture makes it clear that the false gods do not exist as such. It is important to remember this, especially in this era of multiculturalism, when many voices protest the exclusiveness of Christianity.

32:8 [d] Ge 11:8; Ac 17:26 **32:9** [e] Jer 10:16 [f] 1Ki 8:51,53 **32:10** [g] Jer 2:6 [h] Ps 17:8; Zec 2:8 **32:11** [i] Ex 19:4 **32:12** [j] ver 39 **32:13** [k] Isa 58:14 [l] Job 29:6 **32:14** [m] Ps 81:16; 147:14 [n] Ge 49:11 **32:15** [o] Dt 31:20 [p] ver 6; Isa 1:4,28 [q] ver 4 **32:16** [r] 1Co 10:22 [s] Ps 78:58 **32:17** [t] Dt 28:64 [u] Jdg 5:8 **32:18** [v] Isa 17:10 **32:19** [w] Jer 44:21-23 [x] Ps 106:40 **32:20** [y] Dt 31:17,29 [z] ver 5 **32:21** [a] 1Co 10:22 [b] 1Ki 16:13,26 [c] Ro 10:19* **32:22** [d] Ps 18:7-8; Jer 15:14; La 4:11 **32:23** [e] Dt 29:21 [f] Ps 7:13; Eze 5:16

[24]I will send wasting famine against
them,
consuming pestilence[g] and deadly
plague;[h]
I will send against them the fangs of
wild beasts,[i]
the venom of vipers[j] that glide in the
dust.
[25]In the street the sword will make them
childless;
in their homes terror will reign.[k]
The young men and young women will
perish,
the infants and those with gray hair.[l]
[26]I said I would scatter[m] them
and erase their name from human
memory,[n]
[27]but I dreaded the taunt of the enemy,
lest the adversary misunderstand
and say, 'Our hand has triumphed;
the LORD has not done all this.'"[o]

[28]They are a nation without sense,
there is no discernment in them.
[29]If only they were wise and would
understand this[p]
and discern what their end will be!
[30]How could one man chase a
thousand,
or two put ten thousand to flight,[q]
unless their Rock had sold them,
unless the LORD had given them up?[r]
[31]For their rock is not like our Rock,
as even our enemies concede.
[32]Their vine comes from the vine of
Sodom
and from the fields of Gomorrah.
Their grapes are filled with poison,
and their clusters with bitterness.
[33]Their wine is the venom of serpents,
the deadly poison of cobras.[s]

[34]"Have I not kept this in reserve
and sealed it in my vaults?[t]
[35]It is mine to avenge; I will repay.[u]
In due time their foot will slip;[v]
their day of disaster is near
and their doom rushes upon them.[w]"

[36]The LORD will vindicate his people
and relent concerning his servants[x]
when he sees their strength is gone
and no one is left, slave or free.[a]
[37]He will say: "Now where are their gods,
the rock they took refuge in,[y]
[38]the gods who ate the fat of their
sacrifices
and drank the wine of their drink
offerings?
Let them rise up to help you!
Let them give you shelter!

[39]"See now that I myself am he![z]
There is no god besides me.[a]
I put to death and I bring to life,[b]
I have wounded and I will heal,[c]
and no one can deliver out of my
hand.[d]
[40]I lift my hand to heaven and solemnly
swear:
As surely as I live forever,
[41]when I sharpen my flashing sword[e]
and my hand grasps it in judgment,
I will take vengeance on my
adversaries
and repay those who hate me.[f]
[42]I will make my arrows drunk with
blood,[g]
while my sword devours flesh:[h]
the blood of the slain and the captives,
the heads of the enemy leaders."

[a] 36 Or *and they are without a ruler or leader*

32:29 *discern what their end will be.* In this great prophetic song Moses longs for the nation of Israel to turn to God and repent of its wickedness. As history proved, there was continual need for Israel to repent and turn back to God. They did abandon their covenant with God, but God did not abandon them, although He let them reap the consequences of their disobedience. Moses was not the last prophet to long for their repentance, and we can only guess at the heavenly joy Moses felt on the Mount of Transfiguration, seeing Jesus the Christ, who would finally redeem the people (Mark 9).

32:35 *It is mine to avenge.* Only God who is completely just can judge and make right all the wrongs committed (Rom. 12:19–20).

32:36 *relent concerning his servants.* God will discern between the righteous and the wicked (Mal. 3:16).

32:39 God's Sovereignty—In his final words to the Israelites, Moses reminds them where they came from. Their history could not be written without God being in the central position. Their future, likewise, was intimately tied to God. To think otherwise would be folly (32:28–29). The basic point is that no matter how you want to look at it, God is in charge. That was the most basic fact in the Israelites' situation. God's sovereignty is also the central fact in ours. It is not always easy to affirm it. We would much rather see *ourselves* as the central controlling force in our lives. Most of us simply don't like being told what to do or how to live. The problem is that the whole history of man teaches us that when God's laws are not followed, disaster ensues. When we put ourselves in charge, sooner or later we pay the price.

A whole generation of Israelites failed to understand God's sovereignty. As a result, they died in the desert, never having arrived at the Promised Land. While it is true that they lived out their lives, they surely missed out on what could have been. That fact is the basic backdrop for Moses' last words to the new generation, as they approached the Promised Land. We dare not ignore the lesson.

32:24 [g] Dt 28:22 [h] Ps 91:6 [i] Lev 26:22 [j] Am 5:18-19 **32:25** [k] Eze 7:15 [l] 2Ch 36:17; La 2:21 **32:26** [m] Dt 4:27 [n] Ps 34:16 **32:27** [o] Isa 10:13 **32:29** [p] Dt 5:29; Ps 81:13 **32:30** [q] Lev 26:8 [r] Ps 44:12 **32:33** [s] Ps 58:4 **32:34** [t] Jer 2:22; Hos 13:12 **32:35** [u] Ro 12:19*; Heb 10:30* [v] Jer 23:12 [w] Eze 7:8-9 **32:36** [x] Dt 30:1-3; Ps 135:14; Joel 2:14 **32:37** [y] Jdg 10:14; Jer 2:28 **32:39** [z] Isa 41:4 [a] Isa 45:5 [b] 1Sa 2:6; Ps 68:20 [c] Hos 6:1 [d] Ps 50:22 **32:41** [e] Isa 34:6; 66:16; Eze 21:9-10 [f] Jer 50:29 **32:42** [g] ver 23 [h] Jer 46:10, 14

43 Rejoice,[i] you nations, with his people,[a,b]
for he will avenge the blood of his servants;[j]
he will take vengeance on his enemies
and make atonement for his land and people.[k]

44 Moses came with Joshua[c] [l] son of Nun
and spoke all the words of this song in
the hearing of the people. 45 When Moses
finished reciting all these words to all Israel, 46 he said to them, "Take to heart all
the words I have solemnly declared to you
this day,[m] so that you may command your
children to obey carefully all the words of
this law. 47 They are not just idle words for
you—they are your life.[n] By them you will
live long in the land you are crossing the
Jordan to possess."

Moses to Die on Mount Nebo

48 On that same day the LORD told Moses, 49 "Go up into the Abarim[o] Range to
Mount Nebo in Moab, across from Jericho,
and view Canaan, the land I am giving the
Israelites as their own possession. 50 There
on the mountain that you have climbed you
will die[p] and be gathered to your people,
just as your brother Aaron died on Mount
Hor and was gathered to his people. 51 This
is because both of you broke faith with me
in the presence of the Israelites at the waters of Meribah Kadesh in the Desert of
Zin[q] and because you did not uphold my
holiness among the Israelites.[r] 52 Therefore,
you will see the land only from a distance;[s]
you will not enter[t] the land I am giving to
the people of Israel."

Moses Blesses the Tribes

33 This is the blessing that Moses the
man of God[u] pronounced on the Israelites before his death. 2 He said:

"The LORD came from Sinai[v]
and dawned over them from Seir;[w]
he shone forth from Mount Paran.[x]
He came with[d] myriads of holy ones[y]
from the south, from his mountain slopes.[e]
3 Surely it is you who love[z] the people;
all the holy ones are in your hand.[a]
At your feet they all bow down,[b]
and from you receive instruction,
4 the law that Moses gave us,[c]
the possession of the assembly of Jacob.[d]
5 He was king over Jeshurun[f]
when the leaders of the people assembled,
along with the tribes of Israel.

6 "Let Reuben live and not die,
nor[g] his people be few."

7 And this he said about Judah:[e]

"Hear, LORD, the cry of Judah;
bring him to his people.
With his own hands he defends his cause.
Oh, be his help against his foes!"

8 About Levi he said:

"Your Thummim and Urim[f] belong
to your faithful servant.
You tested him at Massah;
you contended with him at the waters of Meribah.[g]
9 He said of his father and mother,[h]
'I have no regard for them.'
He did not recognize his brothers
or acknowledge his own children,
but he watched over your word
and guarded your covenant.[i]
10 He teaches your precepts to Jacob
and your law to Israel.[j]
He offers incense before you
and whole burnt offerings on your altar.[k]
11 Bless all his skills, LORD,
and be pleased with the work of his hands.[l]

[a] 43 Or *Make his people rejoice, you nations* [b] 43 Masoretic Text; Dead Sea Scrolls (see also Septuagint) *people, / and let all the angels worship him, /* [c] 44 Hebrew *Hoshea,* a variant of *Joshua* [d] 2 Or *from* [e] 2 The meaning of the Hebrew for this phrase is uncertain. [f] 5 *Jeshurun* means *the upright one,* that is, Israel; also in verse 26. [g] 6 Or *but let*

32:43 *Rejoice, you nations.* The Gentiles are invited here to join in worship of the living God. All through history there have been a few who accepted this invitation (such as Ruth), and it was fulfilled in Christ (Rom. 15).

33:1 *Moses the man of God.* In spite of his failure at the waters of Meribah Kadesh, Moses is noted here and throughout the Bible as "the man of God."

33:4 *the law that Moses gave us.* God chose Israel alone to receive His instructions, yet the law was ultimately for His whole creation, as Jesus demonstrated when He broke down the wall between Jew and Gentile (Rom. 3–7).

33:9–10 *he watched over your word.* The Levites were keepers of God's word, even when it meant drawing their swords against their own brothers (Ex. 32:25–29). This is a degree of testing that most believers will never experience, but Jesus promised that the world would hate His followers, and they would experience opposition even from their own families (Matt. 10:22). It is not easy to be a follower of God in a world of sin and death, but the Christian may be assured that as he walks in obedience to God's truth, God "always leads us as captives in Christ's triumphal procession" (2 Cor. 2:14).

32:43 [i] Ro 15:10* [j] 2Ki 9:7 [k] Ps 65:3; 85:1; Rev 19:2 **32:44** [l] Nu 13:8, 16 **32:46** [m] Eze 40:4 **32:47** [n] Dt 30:20 **32:49** [o] Nu 27:12 **32:50** [p] Ge 25:8 **32:51** [q] Nu 20:11-13 [r] Nu 27:14 **32:52** [s] Dt 34:1-3 [t] Dt 1:37 **33:1** [u] Jos 14:6 **33:2** [v] Ex 19:18; Ps 68:8 [w] Jdg 5:4 [x] Hab 3:3 [y] Da 7:10; Ac 7:53; Rev 5:11 **33:3** [z] Hos 11:1 [a] Dt 14:2 [b] Lk 10:39 **33:4** [c] Jn 1:17 [d] Ps 119:111 **33:7** [e] Ge 49:10 **33:8** [f] Ex 28:30 [g] Ex 17:7 **33:9** [h] Ex 32:26-29 [i] Mal 2:5 **33:10** [j] Lev 10:11; Dt 31:9-13 [k] Ps 51:19 **33:11** [l] 2Sa 24:23

Strike down those who rise against
him,
his foes till they rise no more."

12 About Benjamin he said:

"Let the beloved of the LORD rest secure
in him,[m]
for he shields him all day long,
and the one the LORD loves rests
between his shoulders.[n]"

13 About Joseph[o] he said:

"May the LORD bless his land
with the precious dew from heaven
above
and with the deep waters that lie
below;[p]
14 with the best the sun brings forth
and the finest the moon can yield;
15 with the choicest gifts of the ancient
mountains[q]
and the fruitfulness of the everlasting
hills;
16 with the best gifts of the earth and its
fullness
and the favor of him who dwelt in the
burning bush.[r]
Let all these rest on the head of
Joseph,
on the brow of the prince among[a] his
brothers.
17 In majesty he is like a firstborn bull;
his horns are the horns of a
wild ox.[s]
With them he will gore[t] the nations,
even those at the ends of the earth.
Such are the ten thousands of
Ephraim;
such are the thousands of
Manasseh."

18 About Zebulun[u] he said:

"Rejoice, Zebulun, in your going out,
and you, Issachar, in your tents.
19 They will summon peoples to the
mountain[v]
and there offer the sacrifices of the
righteous;[w]
they will feast on the abundance of the
seas,[x]
on the treasures hidden in the sand."

20 About Gad[y] he said:

"Blessed is he who enlarges Gad's
domain!
Gad lives there like a lion,
tearing at arm or head.
21 He chose the best land for himself;[z]
the leader's portion was kept for
him.
When the heads of the people
assembled,
he carried out the LORD's righteous
will,[a]
and his judgments concerning
Israel."

22 About Dan[b] he said:

"Dan is a lion's cub,
springing out of Bashan."

23 About Naphtali he said:

"Naphtali is abounding with the favor
of the LORD
and is full of his blessing;
he will inherit southward to the
lake."

24 About Asher[c] he said:

"Most blessed of sons is Asher;
let him be favored by his brothers,
and let him bathe his feet in oil.[d]
25 The bolts of your gates will be iron and
bronze,
and your strength will equal your
days.[e]
26 "There is no one like the God of
Jeshurun,[f]
who rides across the heavens to help
you[g]
and on the clouds in his majesty.
27 The eternal God is your refuge,[h]
and underneath are the everlasting
arms.
He will drive out your enemies before
you,[i]
saying, 'Destroy them!'[j]
28 So Israel will live in safety;[k]
Jacob will dwell[b] secure
in a land of grain and new wine,
where the heavens drop dew.[l]
29 Blessed are you, Israel![m]
Who is like you,[n]
a people saved by the LORD?[o]
He is your shield and helper[p]
and your glorious sword.
Your enemies will cower before you,
and you will tread on their
heights.[q]"

[a] 16 Or *of the one separated from*
[b] 28 Septuagint; Hebrew *Jacob's spring is*

33:22 ***lion's cub.*** This may refer to the small size of the tribe of Dan. Though Dan's land inheritance was close to Judah by the coastal plains, the tribe would not be able to keep their inheritance because of the hostility of the Philistines. Therefore, the Danites would one day migrate to the region of Bashan, south of Mount Hermon (Judg. 18).

33:12 [m] Dt 12:10 [n] Ex 28:12 **33:13** [o] Ge 49:25 [p] Ge 27:28 **33:15** [q] Hab 3:6 **33:16** [r] Ex 3:2 **33:17** [s] Nu 23:22 [t] 1Ki 22:11; Ps 44:5 **33:18** [u] Ge 49:13-15 **33:19** [v] Ex 15:17; Isa 2:3 [w] Ps 4:5 [x] Isa 60:5, 11 **33:20** [y] Ge 49:19 **33:21** [z] Nu 32:1-5, 31-32 [a] Jos 4:12; 22:1-3 **33:22** [b] Ge 49:16 **33:24** [c] Ge 49:21 [d] Ge 49:20; Job 29:6 **33:25** [e] Dt 4:40, 32:47 **33:26** [f] Ex 15:11 [g] Ps 104:3 **33:27** [h] Ps 90:1 [i] Jos 24:18 [j] Dt 7:2 **33:28** [k] Nu 23:9; Jer 23:6 [l] Ge 27:28 **33:29** [m] Ps 144:15 [n] Ps 18:44 [o] 2Sa 7:23 [p] Ps 115:9-11 [q] Dt 32:13

The Death of Moses

34 Then Moses climbed Mount Nebo
from the plains of Moab to the top
of Pisgah, across from Jericho.[r] There the
LORD showed[s] him the whole land—from
Gilead to Dan, 2all of Naphtali, the territory
of Ephraim and Manasseh, all the land of
Judah as far as the Mediterranean Sea,[t] 3the
Negev and the whole region from the Valley
of Jericho, the City of Palms,[u] as far as Zoar.
4Then the LORD said to him, "This is the land
I promised on oath[v] to Abraham, Isaac and
Jacob when I said, 'I will give it[w] to your descendants.' I have let you see it with your
eyes, but you will not cross[x] over into it."
5And Moses the servant of the LORD[y]
died[z] there in Moab, as the LORD had said.
6He buried him[a] in Moab, in the valley opposite Beth Peor,[a] but to this day no one
knows where his grave is.[b] 7Moses was a
hundred and twenty years old[c] when he
died, yet his eyes were not weak[d] nor his
strength gone. 8The Israelites grieved for
Moses in the plains of Moab thirty days,
until the time of weeping and mourning[e]
was over.
9Now Joshua son of Nun was filled with
the spirit[b] of wisdom[f] because Moses had
laid his hands on him.[g] So the Israelites
listened to him and did what the LORD had
commanded Moses.
10Since then, no prophet has risen in Israel like Moses,[h] whom the LORD knew face
to face,[i] 11who did all those signs and wonders[j] the LORD sent him to do in Egypt—to
Pharaoh and to all his officials[k] and to his
whole land. 12For no one has ever shown
the mighty power or performed the awesome deeds that Moses did in the sight of
all Israel.

---

[a] 6 Or *He was buried* [b] 9 Or *Spirit*

34:1–2 *Moab . . . Jericho . . . Mediterranean Sea.* Moab was where Moses had given Israel an explanation of the law and led them in a covenant renewal. Jericho was the first city in Canaan to be conquered.
34:6 *no one knows where his grave is.* If his burial place had been known, some people would have been tempted to make it a shrine and possibly have begun to worship there.
34:9 *Joshua . . . filled with the spirit of wisdom.* Joshua was the leader chosen to succeed Moses, and God filled him with the spirit of wisdom. But there was another, a prophet like Moses, who would be greater even than Moses. That other was the Lord Jesus Christ (Acts 3:19–26).

34:1 [r] Dt 32:49 [s] Dt 32:52 **34:2** [t] Dt 11:24 **34:3** [u] Jdg 1:16; 3:13; 2Ch 28:15 **34:4** [v] Ge 28:13 [w] Ge 12:7 [x] Dt 3:27 **34:5** [y] Nu 12:7 [z] Dt 32:50; Jos 1:1-2 **34:6** [a] Dt 3:29 [b] Jude 1:9 **34:7** [c] Dt 31:2 [d] Ge 27:1 **34:8** [e] Ge 50:3, 10; 2Sa 11:27 **34:9** [f] Ge 41:38; Isa 11:2; Da 6:3 [g] Nu 27:18, 23 **34:10** [h] Dt 18:15, 18 [i] Ex 33:11; Nu 12:6, 8; Dt 5:4 **34:11** [j] Dt 4:34 [k] Dt 7:19

JOSHUA

▶ **AUTHOR:** Jewish tradition seems correct in assigning the authorship of this book to Joshua himself. The unity of style and organization suggest a single authorship for the majority of the book, with the exception of three small portions that may have been added after Joshua's death: Othniel's capture of Kiriath Sepher (15:13 – 19); Dan's migration to the north (19:47); and Joshua's death and burial (24:29 – 33). However, Joshua 24:26 makes this clear statement: "Then Joshua wrote these words in the Book of the Law of God."

▶ **TIME:** c. 1405 – 1398 B.C. ▶ **KEY VERSE:** Josh. 11:23

▶ **THEME:** In the Book of Joshua, the Israelites are commanded to destroy everything and everybody so that they can take full possession of the land. The transition of leadership is from Moses to Joshua. A nomadic people attach themselves to given tracts of land, and a nation is formed from a wandering tribe as the conquest is completed in 21:43 – 45. We also see how a failure to carry out God's plan completely lays a foundation for future problems.

Joshua Installed as Leader

1 After the death of Moses the servant of
the LORD,[a] the LORD said to Joshua[b] son
of Nun, Moses' aide: 2"Moses my servant is
dead. Now then, you and all these people,
get ready to cross the Jordan River[c] into the
land I am about to give to them—to the Israelites. 3I will give you every place where
you set your foot,[d] as I promised Moses.
4Your territory will extend from the desert
to Lebanon, and from the great river, the
Euphrates[e]—all the Hittite country—to
the Mediterranean Sea in the west.[f] 5No
one will be able to stand against you[g] all
the days of your life. As I was with[h] Moses, so I will be with you; I will never leave
you nor forsake[i] you. 6Be strong and courageous, because you will lead these people
to inherit the land I swore to their ancestors[j] to give them.
7"Be strong and very courageous. Be
careful to obey all the law my servant Moses gave you; do not turn from it to the right
or to the left,[k] that you may be successful
wherever you go.[l] 8Keep this Book of the
Law always on your lips; meditate on it
day and night, so that you may be careful
to do everything written in it. Then you
will be prosperous and successful.[m] 9Have
I not commanded you? Be strong and courageous. Do not be afraid;[n] do not be discouraged, for the LORD your God will be
with you wherever you go."[o]
10So Joshua ordered the officers of the

1:1 ***the servant of the LORD.*** In the Hebrew Scripture this is a special title given only to Moses, Joshua (24:29; Judg. 2:8), David (Ps. 18:title; 36:title), and the Messiah (Is. 42:19). ***the LORD said to Joshua.*** God spoke directly to Joshua encouraging him and urging him to obey all the law. True success cannot occur apart from knowing God personally and doing His will.

1:7 – 8 Perseverance—A successful mission in the service of the Lord is dependent upon courage, meditation and obedience. Keeping God's words in our hearts molds our character and guides our footsteps.

1:8 Meditating upon God's Word—Helping people become prosperous and successful is big business. Late night infomercials point to a plethora of techniques for getting rich. Everyone wants to be wealthy. Everyone wants to be successful. These kinds of feelings are particularly strong when starting a new endeavor as Joshua was. At the very beginning of Joshua's leadership of Israel, God lays out for Joshua His key to success, meditating on God's word. Meditate upon the Word of God by rehearsing it in thought over and over in order to understand its implications for the situations of life. The meditation process results in changed thinking, because God's thoughts can literally become our thoughts. Then we are more likely to do what God wants of us. As we live in sync with God's plan for our lives, it follows that we will be more successful and prosperous than if we ignore His teachings.

People spend a large part of their lives in obtaining an education and working at a career in order to be prosperous and successful. Scripture points to itself as the primary means toward that end.

1:1 [a] Nu 12:7; Dt 34:5 [b] Ex 24:13; Dt 1:38 **1:2** [c] ver 11 **1:3** [d] Dt 11:24 **1:4** [e] Ge 15:18 [f] Nu 34:2-12 **1:5** [g] Dt 7:24 [h] Jos 3:7; 6:27 [i] Dt 31:6-8 **1:6** [j] Dt 31:23 **1:7** [k] Dt 5:32; 28:14 [l] Jos 11:15 **1:8** [m] Dt 29:9; Ps 1:1-3 **1:9** [n] Ps 27:1 [o] ver 7; Dt 31:7-8; Jer 1:8

people: 11“Go through the camp and tell the people, ‘Get your provisions ready. Three days from now you will cross the Jordan here to go in and take possession[p] of the land the LORD your God is giving you for your own.’ ”

12But to the Reubenites, the Gadites and the half-tribe of Manasseh,[q] Joshua said, 13“Remember the command that Moses the servant of the LORD gave you after he said, ‘The LORD your God will give you rest[r] by giving you this land.’ 14Your wives, your children and your livestock may stay in the land that Moses gave you east of the Jordan, but all your fighting men, ready for battle, must cross over ahead of your fellow Israelites. You are to help them 15until the LORD gives them rest, as he has done for you, and until they too have taken possession of the land the LORD your God is giving them. After that, you may go back and occupy your own land, which Moses the servant of the LORD gave you east of the Jordan toward the sunrise.”[s]

16Then they answered Joshua, “Whatever you have commanded us we will do, and wherever you send us we will go. 17Just as we fully obeyed Moses, so we will obey you.[t] Only may the LORD your God be with you as he was with Moses. 18Whoever rebels against your word and does not obey it, whatever you may command them, will be put to death. Only be strong and courageous!”

Rahab and the Spies

2 Then Joshua son of Nun secretly sent two spies[u] from Shittim.[v] “Go, look over the land,” he said, “especially Jericho.” So they went and entered the house of a prostitute named Rahab[w] and stayed there.

2The king of Jericho was told, “Look, some of the Israelites have come here tonight to spy out the land.” 3So the king of Jericho sent this message to Rahab: “Bring out the men who came to you and entered your house, because they have come to spy out the whole land.”

4But the woman had taken the two men and hidden them.[x] She said, “Yes, the men came to me, but I did not know where they had come from. 5At dusk, when it was time to close the city gate, they left. I don’t know which way they went. Go after them quickly. You may catch up with them.” 6(But she had taken them up to the roof and hidden them under the stalks of flax[y] she had laid out on the roof.)[z] 7So the men set out in pursuit of the spies on the road that leads to the fords of the Jordan, and as soon as the pursuers had gone out, the gate was shut.

8Before the spies lay down for the night, she went up on the roof 9and said to them, “I know that the LORD has given you this land and that a great fear[a] of you has fallen on us, so that all who live in this country are melting in fear because of you. 10We have heard how the LORD dried up[b] the water of the Red Sea[a] for you when you came out of Egypt,[c] and what you did to Sihon and Og,[d] the two kings of the Amorites east of the Jordan, whom you completely destroyed.[b] 11When we heard of it, our hearts melted in fear and everyone’s courage failed because of you,[e] for the LORD your God is God in heaven above and on the earth[f] below.

12“Now then, please swear to me by the LORD that you will show kindness to my family, because I have shown kindness to you. Give me a sure sign[g] 13that you will spare the lives of my father and mother, my brothers and sisters, and all who belong to them—and that you will save us from death.”

14“Our lives for your lives!” the men assured her. “If you don’t tell what we are doing, we will treat you kindly and faithfully[h] when the LORD gives us the land.”

15So she let them down by a rope through the window,[i] for the house she lived in was part of the city wall. 16She said to them, “Go to the hills so the pursuers will not find you. Hide yourselves there three days[j] until they return, and then go on your way.”[k]

---

[a] *10* Or *the Sea of Reeds* [b] *10* The Hebrew term refers to the irrevocable giving over of things or persons to the LORD, often by totally destroying them.

1:18 *be strong and courageous.* Joshua’s task was not an easy one, for not only must he deal with the ungodly inhabitants of the Promised Land, he must also provide leadership for his own fearful and complaining people.

2:1 *Rahab.* Rahab was a Canaanite prostitute, yet out of all the populace of Jericho, only she reached out to the living God, and He in turn saved her (6:25).

2:4–6 *I did not know where they had come from.* Rahab lied to the men searching for the Israelite spies, and Joshua praised her, as did the apostle James and the writer of Hebrews (Heb. 11:31; James 2:25). Throughout both the Old and the New Testament, the commands of God forbid lying, the prophets condemn it and godly people avoid doing it. Scripture does not address Rahab’s sin, but it does praise her for her faith in God. Christians have struggled for centuries over whether lying to save an innocent person’s life is acceptable. There does not seem to be a clear-cut answer, but Rahab did her best with the knowledge she had to protect the Israelite men.

2:16 *Go to the hills.* The pursuers had gone down to the Jordan River (v. 7), logically supposing that the spies would be returning to their camp on the eastern side of the river. The only hills near Jericho are to the west, in the opposite direction from the Israelite camp, and further into the land of Canaan.

1:11 [p] Joel 3:2 **1:12** [q] Nu 32:20-22 **1:13** [r] Dt 3:18-20 **1:15** [s] Jos 22:1-4 **1:17** [t] ver 5,9 **2:1** [u] Jas 2:25 [v] Nu 25:1; Jos 3:1 [w] Heb 11:31 **2:4** [x] 2Sa 17:19-20 **2:6** [y] Jas 2:25 [z] Ex 1:17, 19; 2Sa 17:19 **2:9** [a] Ge 35:5; Ex 23:27; Dt 2:25 **2:10** [b] Ex 14:21 [c] Nu 23:22 [d] Nu 21:21, 24, 34-35 **2:11** [e] Ex 15:14; Jos 5:1; 7:5; Ps 22:14; Isa 13:7 [f] Dt 4:39 **2:12** [g] ver 18 **2:14** [h] Jdg 1:24; Mt 5:7 **2:15** [i] Ac 9:25 **2:16** [j] Jas 2:25 [k] Heb 11:31

17Now the men had said to her, "This oath[l] you made us swear will not be binding on us 18unless, when we enter the land, you have tied this scarlet cord in the window through which you let us down, and unless you have brought your father and mother, your brothers and all your family[m] into your house. 19If any of them go outside your house into the street, their blood will be on their own heads;[n] we will not be responsible. As for those who are in the house with you, their blood will be on our head[o] if a hand is laid on them. 20But if you tell what we are doing, we will be released from the oath you made us swear."

21"Agreed," she replied. "Let it be as you say."

So she sent them away, and they departed. And she tied the scarlet cord in the window.

22When they left, they went into the hills and stayed there three days, until the pursuers had searched all along the road and returned without finding them. 23Then the two men started back. They went down out of the hills, forded the river and came to Joshua son of Nun and told him everything that had happened to them. 24They said to Joshua, "The LORD has surely given the whole land into our hands;[p] all the people are melting in fear because of us."

Crossing the Jordan

3 Early in the morning Joshua and all the Israelites set out from Shittim[q] and went to the Jordan, where they camped before crossing over. 2After three days the officers went throughout the camp,[r] 3giving orders to the people: "When you see the ark of the covenant[s] of the LORD your God, and the Levitical priests[t] carrying it, you are to move out from your positions and follow it. 4Then you will know which way to go, since you have never been this way before. But keep a distance of about two thousand cubits[a] between you and the ark; do not go near it."

5Joshua told the people, "Consecrate yourselves,[u] for tomorrow the LORD will do amazing things among you."

6Joshua said to the priests, "Take up the ark of the covenant and pass on ahead of the people." So they took it up and went ahead of them.

7And the LORD said to Joshua, "Today I will begin to exalt you[v] in the eyes of all Israel, so they may know that I am with you as I was with Moses.[w] 8Tell the priests[x] who carry the ark of the covenant: 'When you reach the edge of the Jordan's waters, go and stand in the river.'"

9Joshua said to the Israelites, "Come here and listen to the words of the LORD your God. 10This is how you will know that the living God[y] is among you and that he will certainly drive out before you the Canaanites, Hittites, Hivites, Perizzites, Girgashites, Amorites and Jebusites.[z] 11See, the ark of the covenant of the Lord of all the earth[a] will go into the Jordan ahead of you. 12Now then, choose twelve men[b] from the tribes of Israel, one from each tribe. 13And as soon as the priests who carry the ark of the LORD—the Lord of all the earth[c]—set foot in the Jordan, its waters flowing downstream[d] will be cut off and stand up in a heap.[e]"

14So when the people broke camp to cross the Jordan, the priests carrying the ark of the covenant[f] went ahead[g] of them. 15Now the Jordan is at flood stage[h] all during harvest. Yet as soon as the priests who carried the ark reached the Jordan and their feet touched the water's edge, 16the water from upstream stopped flowing.[i] It piled up in a heap a great distance away, at a town called Adam in the vicinity of Zarethan,[j] while the water flowing down[k] to the Sea of the Arabah[l] (that is, the Dead Sea[m]) was completely cut off. So the people crossed over opposite Jericho. 17The priests who carried the ark of the covenant of the LORD stopped in the middle of the Jordan and stood on dry ground, while all Israel passed by until the whole nation had completed the crossing on dry ground.[n]

[a] *4* That is, about 3,000 feet or about 900 meters

3:4 *two thousand cubits.* Two thousand cubits was more than half a mile. God was serious about the people showing due respect for the ark of the covenant.

3:9 Inspiration—God conveyed His message by means of words spoken by a specific, chosen person. He descended to the human level and through humanity spoke His word of absolute truth.

3:13 *Lord of all the earth.* The term "Adonai," translated "Lord," means "master." It refers to the fact that God is indeed the Sovereign of the entire universe.

3:15 *Jordan is at flood stage.* God did not merely slow the great river to a trickle during a time of drought; he stopped the waters when the river was high. This is significant because it makes the point that a great miracle was involved.

3:16 *Adam.* Adam was a city about 18 miles north of Jericho. The Sea of Arabah is another name for the Dead Sea, into which the Jordan flows from the north. The Dead Sea is the lowest place on earth, 1,286 feet below sea level. The sea has no outlet and loses its water by evaporation, making the concentration of salt and other minerals so high that nothing can live in it.

2:17 [l] Ge 24:8 **2:18** [m] ver 12; Jos 6:23 **2:19** [n] Eze 33:4 [o] Mt 27:25 **2:24** [p] ver 9; Jos 6:2 **3:1** [q] Jos 2:1 **3:2** [r] Jos 1:11 **3:3** [s] Nu 10:33 [t] Dt 31:9 **3:5** [u] Ex 19:10, 14; Lev 20:7; Jos 7:13; 1Sa 16:5; Joel 2:16 **3:7** [v] Jos 4:14; 1Ch 29:25 [w] Jos 1:5 **3:8** [x] ver 3 **3:10** [y] Dt 5:26; 1Sa 17:26, 36; 2Ki 19:4, 16; Hos 1:10; Mt 16:16; 1Th 1:9 [z] Ex 33:2; Dt 7:1 **3:11** [a] ver 13; Job 41:11; Zec 6:5 **3:12** [b] Jos 4:2, 4 **3:13** [c] ver 11 [d] ver 16 [e] Ex 15:8; Ps 78:13 **3:14** [f] Ps 132:8 [g] Ac 7:44-45 **3:15** [h] Jos 4:18; 1Ch 12:15 **3:16** [i] Ps 66:6; 74:15 [j] 1Ki 4:12; 7:46 [k] ver 13 [l] Dt 1:1 [m] Ge 14:3 **3:17** [n] Ex 14:22, 29

4 When the whole nation had finished crossing the Jordan,[o] the LORD said to Joshua, 2“Choose twelve men[p] from among the people, one from each tribe, 3and tell them to take up twelve stones[q] from the middle of the Jordan, from right where the priests are standing, and carry them over with you and put them down at the place where you stay tonight.[r]”

4So Joshua called together the twelve men he had appointed from the Israelites, one from each tribe, 5and said to them, “Go over before the ark of the LORD your God into the middle of the Jordan. Each of you is to take up a stone on his shoulder, according to the number of the tribes of the Israelites, 6to serve as a sign among you. In the future, when your children ask you, ‘What do these stones mean?’[s] 7tell them that the flow of the Jordan was cut off[t] before the ark of the covenant of the LORD. When it crossed the Jordan, the waters of the Jordan were cut off. These stones are to be a memorial[u] to the people of Israel forever.”

8So the Israelites did as Joshua commanded them. They took twelve stones from the middle of the Jordan, according to the number of the tribes of the Israelites, as the LORD had told Joshua;[v] and they carried them over with them to their camp, where they put them down. 9Joshua set up the twelve stones[w] that had been[a] in the middle of the Jordan at the spot where the priests who carried the ark of the covenant had stood. And they are there to this day.

10Now the priests who carried the ark remained standing in the middle of the Jordan until everything the LORD had commanded Joshua was done by the people, just as Moses had directed Joshua. The people hurried over, 11and as soon as all of them had crossed, the ark of the LORD and the priests came to the other side while the people watched. 12The men of Reuben, Gad and the half-tribe of Manasseh crossed over, ready for battle, in front of the Israelites,[x] as Moses had directed them. 13About forty thousand armed for battle crossed over before the LORD to the plains of Jericho for war.

14That day the LORD exalted[y] Joshua in the sight of all Israel; and they stood in awe of him all the days of his life, just as they had stood in awe of Moses.

15Then the LORD said to Joshua, 16“Command the priests carrying the ark of the covenant law[z] to come up out of the Jordan.”

17So Joshua commanded the priests, “Come up out of the Jordan.”

18And the priests came up out of the river carrying the ark of the covenant of the LORD. No sooner had they set their feet on the dry ground than the waters of the Jordan returned to their place and ran at flood stage[a] as before.

19On the tenth day of the first month the people went up from the Jordan and camped at Gilgal[b] on the eastern border of Jericho. 20And Joshua set up at Gilgal the twelve stones[c] they had taken out of the Jordan. 21He said to the Israelites, “In the future when your descendants ask their parents, ‘What do these stones mean?’[d] 22tell them, ‘Israel crossed the Jordan on dry ground.’[e] 23For the LORD your God dried up the Jordan before you until you had crossed over. The LORD your God did to the Jordan what he had done to the Red Sea[b] when he dried it up before us until we had crossed over.[f] 24He did this so that all the peoples of the earth might know[g] that the hand of the LORD is powerful[h] and so that you might always fear the LORD your God.[i]”

5 Now when all the Amorite kings west of the Jordan and all the Canaanite kings along the coast[j] heard how the LORD had dried up the Jordan before the Israelites until they[c] had crossed over, their hearts melted in fear[k] and they no longer had the courage to face the Israelites.

Circumcision and Passover at Gilgal

2At that time the LORD said to Joshua, “Make flint knives[l] and circumcise the Israelites again.” 3So Joshua made flint

[a] 9 Or *Joshua also set up twelve stones*
[b] 23 Or *the Sea of Reeds*
[c] 1 Another textual tradition *we*

4:10 *The people hurried over.* This is a flashback, 3:17 and 4:1 have already told of the crossing over. The purpose is to look back and reflect upon the people's obedience.

4:14 *the LORD exalted Joshua.* God is once again proclaiming Joshua as the man He has chosen to take Moses' place as leader of His people.

4:16 *the covenant law.* The ark contained the two stone tablets on which the Ten Commandments were written, reminding people of God's covenant and His law.

4:21–24 Fear of God—The Scriptures are full of stories of the acts God performed that built up the respect of the people for Him. The awesome things God did were told to each new generation to develop respect for who God is. This miracle was performed not only for the purpose of getting the Israelites across the Jordan. It was also a sign to all peoples of the power of God.

5:2 *circumcise the Israelites again.* The generation that left Egypt had been circumcised. However, that generation had died in the wilderness and for some reason they had neglected to circumcise their children, the generation which would enter the Promised Land.

4:1 [o] Dt 27:2 **4:2** [p] Jos 3:12 **4:3** [q] ver 20 [r] ver 19
4:6 [s] ver 21; Ex 12:26; 13:14 **4:7** [t] Jos 3:13 [u] Ex 12:14
4:8 [v] ver 20 **4:9** [w] Ge 28:18; Jos 24:26; 1Sa 7:12
4:12 [x] Nu 32:27 **4:14** [y] Jos 3:7 **4:16** [z] Ex 25:22
4:18 [a] Jos 3:15 **4:19** [b] Jos 5:9 **4:20** [c] ver 3,8
4:21 [d] ver 6 **4:22** [e] Jos 3:17 **4:23** [f] Ex 14:21
4:24 [g] 1Ki 8:42-43; 2Ki 19:19; Ps 106:8; Jer 10:7 [h] Ex 15:16; 1Ch 29:12; Ps 89:13 [i] Ex 14:31 **5:1** [j] Nu 13:29 [k] Jos 2:9-11
5:2 [l] Ex 4:25

knives and circumcised the Israelites at Gibeath Haaraloth.[a]

4 Now this is why he did so: All those who came out of Egypt—all the men of military age—died in the wilderness on the way after leaving Egypt.[m] 5 All the people that came out had been circumcised, but all the people born in the wilderness during the journey from Egypt had not. 6 The Israelites had moved about in the wilderness forty years[n] until all the men who were of military age when they left Egypt had died, since they had not obeyed the LORD. For the LORD had sworn to them that they would not see the land he had solemnly promised their ancestors to give us,[o] a land flowing with milk and honey.[p] 7 So he raised up their sons in their place, and these were the ones Joshua circumcised. They were still uncircumcised because they had not been circumcised on the way. 8 And after the whole nation had been circumcised, they remained where they were in camp until they were healed.[q]

9 Then the LORD said to Joshua, "Today I have rolled away the reproach of Egypt from you." So the place has been called Gilgal[b] to this day.

10 On the evening of the fourteenth day of the month,[r] while camped at Gilgal on the plains of Jericho, the Israelites celebrated the Passover. 11 The day after the Passover, that very day, they ate some of the produce of the land:[s] unleavened bread and roasted grain.[t] 12 The manna stopped the day after[c] they ate this food from the land; there was no longer any manna for the Israelites, but that year they ate the produce of Canaan.[u]

The Fall of Jericho

13 Now when Joshua was near Jericho, he looked up and saw a man[v] standing in front of him with a drawn sword[w] in his hand. Joshua went up to him and asked, "Are you for us or for our enemies?"

14 "Neither," he replied, "but as commander of the army of the LORD I have now come." Then Joshua fell facedown[x] to the ground in reverence, and asked him, "What message does my Lord[d] have for his servant?"

15 The commander of the LORD's army replied, "Take off your sandals, for the place where you are standing is holy."[y] And Joshua did so.

6 Now the gates of Jericho[z] were securely barred because of the Israelites. No one went out and no one came in.

2 Then the LORD said to Joshua, "See, I have delivered[a] Jericho into your hands, along with its king and its fighting men. 3 March around the city once with all the armed men. Do this for six days. 4 Have seven priests carry trumpets of rams' horns in front of the ark. On the seventh day, march around the city seven times, with the priests blowing the trumpets.[b] 5 When you hear them sound a long blast[c] on the trumpets, have the whole army give a loud shout;[d] then the wall of the city will collapse and the army will go up, everyone straight in."

6 So Joshua son of Nun called the priests and said to them, "Take up the ark of the covenant of the LORD and have seven priests carry trumpets in front of it." 7 And he ordered the army, "Advance[e]! March around the city, with an armed guard going ahead of the ark of the LORD."

8 When Joshua had spoken to the people, the seven priests carrying the seven trumpets before the LORD went forward, blowing their trumpets, and the ark of the LORD's covenant followed them. 9 The armed guard marched ahead of the priests who blew the trumpets, and the rear guard[f] followed the ark. All this time the trumpets were sounding. 10 But Joshua had commanded the army, "Do not give a war cry, do not raise your voices, do not say a word until the day I tell you to shout. Then shout![g]" 11 So he had the ark of the LORD carried around the city, circling it once. Then the army returned to camp and spent the night there.

---

[a] *3 Gibeath Haaraloth* means *the hill of foreskins.*
[b] *9 Gilgal* sounds like the Hebrew for *roll.*
[c] *12* Or *the day*   [d] *14* Or *lord*

5:6 *milk and honey.* The land God had promised to Israel was no wilderness, but a land that was fertile for both crops and cattle, and ready to provide for them and supply all their needs.

5:15 *Take off your sandals.* The command for Joshua to remove his sandal was practically identical to the command Moses received at the burning bush (Ex. 3:1–6). Joshua was confronted with the living God, just as Moses had been (Ex. 33:9–11).

6:3 *around the city once.* The city of Jericho measured less than half a mile in circumference, so the march would have been completed quickly.

6:6–21 Zeal—Crossing the Jordan marked the beginning step in the fulfillment of God's promise to give His people the land of Canaan. Immediately the task of conquering Jericho loomed before them. The Lord appeared to Joshua reminding him that God Himself was in charge and the presence of the Holy One assured victory (v. 2). The plan for Jericho's capture was a test of Israel's zeal for the Lord and seems to have been designed to instill the lesson that submission to God's directives was key to victory. How different Israel's history would have been if they had continued to carry out God's plans fully and zealously! God calls us to the same level of obedience today.

5:4 [m] Dt 2:14 **5:6** [n] Dt 2:7 [o] Nu 14:23, 29-35; Dt 2:14 [p] Ex 3:8 **5:8** [q] Ge 34:25 **5:10** [r] Ex 12:6 **5:11** [s] Nu 15:19 [t] Lev 23:14 **5:12** [u] Ex 16:35 **5:13** [v] Ge 18:2; 32:24 [w] Nu 22:23 **5:14** [x] Ge 17:3 **5:15** [y] Ex 3:5; Ac 7:33 **6:1** [z] Jos 24:11 **6:2** [a] Dt 7:24; Jos 2:9, 24; 8:1 **6:4** [b] Lev 25:9; Nu 10:8 **6:5** [c] Ex 19:13 [d] ver 20; 1Sa 4:5; Ps 42:4; Isa 42:13 **6:7** [e] Ex 14:15 **6:9** [f] ver 13; Isa 52:12 **6:10** [g] ver 20

12 Joshua got up early the next morning
and the priests took up the ark of the LORD.
13 The seven priests carrying the seven
trumpets went forward, marching before
the ark of the LORD and blowing the trumpets. The armed men went ahead of them
and the rear guard followed the ark of
the LORD, while the trumpets kept sounding. 14 So on the second day they marched
around the city once and returned to the
camp. They did this for six days.

15 On the seventh day, they got up at daybreak and marched around the city seven
times in the same manner, except that on
that day they circled the city seven times.[h]
16 The seventh time around, when the
priests sounded the trumpet blast, Joshua commanded the army, "Shout! For the
LORD has given you the city! 17 The city
and all that is in it are to be devoted[a][i] to
the LORD. Only Rahab the prostitute and
all who are with her in her house shall
be spared, because she hid[j] the spies we
sent. 18 But keep away from the devoted
things,[k] so that you will not bring about
your own destruction by taking any of
them. Otherwise you will make the camp
of Israel liable to destruction[l] and bring
trouble[m] on it. 19 All the silver and gold
and the articles of bronze and iron[n] are
sacred to the LORD and must go into his
treasury."

20 When the trumpets sounded,[o] the army
shouted, and at the sound of the trumpet,
when the men gave a loud shout,[p] the wall
collapsed; so everyone charged straight in,
and they took the city.[q] 21 They devoted the
city to the LORD and destroyed[r] with the
sword every living thing in it—men and
women, young and old, cattle, sheep and
donkeys.

22 Joshua said to the two men who had
spied out the land, "Go into the prostitute's house and bring her out and all who
belong to her, in accordance with your
oath to her.[s]" 23 So the young men who had
done the spying went in and brought out
Rahab, her father and mother, her brothers and sisters and all who belonged to
her.[t] They brought out her entire family
and put them in a place outside the camp
of Israel.

24 Then they burned the whole city and
everything in it, but they put the silver and
gold and the articles of bronze and iron[u]
into the treasury of the LORD's house. 25 But
Joshua spared Rahab the prostitute,[v] with
her family and all who belonged to her, because she hid the men Joshua had sent as
spies to Jericho[w]—and she lives among the
Israelites to this day.

26 At that time Joshua pronounced this
solemn oath: "Cursed before the LORD is
the one who undertakes to rebuild this city,
Jericho:

"At the cost of his firstborn son
he will lay its foundations;
at the cost of his youngest
he will set up its gates."[x]

27 So the LORD was with Joshua,[y] and his
fame spread[z] throughout the land.

Achan's Sin

7 But the Israelites were unfaithful in
regard to the devoted things[b];[a] Achan
son of Karmi, the son of Zimri,[c] the son of
Zerah,[b] of the tribe of Judah, took some of
them. So the LORD's anger burned against
Israel.

2 Now Joshua sent men from Jericho to
Ai, which is near Beth Aven[c] to the east of
Bethel, and told them, "Go up and spy out
the region." So the men went up and spied
out Ai.

3 When they returned to Joshua, they
said, "Not all the army will have to go
up against Ai. Send two or three thousand men to take it and do not weary the
whole army, for only a few people live
there." 4 So about three thousand went up;
but they were routed by the men of Ai,[d]
5 who killed about thirty-six of them. They
chased the Israelites from the city gate as
far as the stone quarries and struck them
down on the slopes. At this the hearts of
the people melted in fear[e] and became like
water.

6 Then Joshua tore his clothes[f] and fell
facedown to the ground before the ark of

---

[a] *17* The Hebrew term refers to the irrevocable giving over of things or persons to the LORD, often by totally destroying them; also in verses 18 and 21.
[b] *1* The Hebrew term refers to the irrevocable giving over of things or persons to the LORD, often by totally destroying them; also in verses 11, 12, 13 and 15.
[c] *1* See Septuagint and 1 Chron. 2:6; Hebrew *Zabdi*; also in verses 17 and 18.

6:26 *Cursed before the LORD.* Joshua's curse found dramatic fulfillment many centuries later when Hiel of Bethel laid its foundation and rebuilt its gates at great personal cost (1 Kin. 16:34).

7:6–9 Suffering—Joshua's prayer was one of despair. Why had God allowed their defeat? Whenever tragedy strikes it is hard to understand why God allowed it to happen to us. In this case it is clearly explained. Achan had greedily taken what was banned by God. Through his sin the whole camp was guilty of deception and thievery. There are other reasons, not related to sin, for God's permission of tragedy. Sometimes people suffer in order to fulfill a sovereign purpose not immediately apparent.

6:15 [h] 1Ki 18:44 **6:17** [i] Lev 27:28; Dt 20:17 [j] Jos 2:4
6:18 [k] Jos 7:1 [l] Jos 7:12 [m] Jos 7:25, 26 **6:19** [n] ver 24;
Nu 31:22 **6:20** [o] Jdg 6:34; Jer 4:21; Am 2:2 [p] ver 5
[q] Heb 11:30 **6:21** [r] Dt 20:16 **6:22** [s] Jos 2:14; Heb 11:31
6:23 [t] Jos 2:13 **6:24** [u] ver 19 **6:25** [v] Heb 11:31
[w] Jos 2:6 **6:26** [x] 1Ki 16:34 **6:27** [y] Ge 39:2; Jos 1:5
[z] Jos 9:1 **7:1** [a] Jos 6:18 [b] Jos 22:20 **7:2** [c] Jos 18:12;
1Sa 13:5; 14:23 **7:4** [d] Lev 26:17; Dt 28:25
7:5 [e] Lev 26:36; Jos 2:9, 11; Eze 21:7; Na 2:10
7:6 [f] Ge 37:29

the LORD, remaining there till evening. The
elders of Israel did the same, and sprinkled
dust[g] on their heads. 7And Joshua said,
"Alas, Sovereign LORD, why did you ever
bring this people across the Jordan to deliver us into the hands of the Amorites to
destroy us?[h] If only we had been content
to stay on the other side of the Jordan!
8Pardon your servant, Lord. What can I
say, now that Israel has been routed by its
enemies? 9The Canaanites and the other
people of the country will hear about this
and they will surround us and wipe out our
name from the earth.[i] What then will you
do for your own great name?"

10The LORD said to Joshua, "Stand up!
What are you doing down on your face?
11Israel has sinned; they have violated
my covenant,[j] which I commanded them
to keep. They have taken some of the devoted things; they have stolen, they have
lied,[k] they have put them with their own
possessions. 12That is why the Israelites
cannot stand against their enemies;[l] they
turn their backs and run because they have
been made liable to destruction.[m] I will not
be with you anymore unless you destroy
whatever among you is devoted to destruction.

13"Go, consecrate the people. Tell them,
'Consecrate yourselves[n] in preparation
for tomorrow; for this is what the LORD,
the God of Israel, says: There are devoted things among you, Israel. You cannot
stand against your enemies until you remove them.

14"'In the morning, present yourselves
tribe by tribe. The tribe the LORD chooses[o] shall come forward clan by clan; the
clan the LORD chooses shall come forward family by family; and the family the
LORD chooses shall come forward man by
man. 15Whoever is caught with the devoted things shall be destroyed by fire, along
with all that belongs to him.[p] He has violated the covenant[q] of the LORD and has done
an outrageous thing in Israel!'"[r]

16Early the next morning Joshua had
Israel come forward by tribes, and Judah
was chosen. 17The clans of Judah came
forward, and the Zerahites were chosen.[s]
He had the clan of the Zerahites come forward by families, and Zimri was chosen.
18Joshua had his family come forward man
by man, and Achan son of Karmi, the son
of Zimri, the son of Zerah, of the tribe of
Judah, was chosen.

19Then Joshua said to Achan, "My son,
give glory[t] to the LORD, the God of Israel,
and honor him. Tell[u] me what you have
done; do not hide it from me."

20Achan replied, "It is true! I have sinned
against the LORD, the God of Israel. This
is what I have done: 21When I saw in the
plunder a beautiful robe from Babylonia,[a]
two hundred shekels[b] of silver and a bar
of gold weighing fifty shekels,[c] I coveted[v]
them and took them. They are hidden in
the ground inside my tent, with the silver
underneath."

22So Joshua sent messengers, and they
ran to the tent, and there it was, hidden in
his tent, with the silver underneath. 23They
took the things from the tent, brought them
to Joshua and all the Israelites and spread
them out before the LORD.

24Then Joshua, together with all Israel,
took Achan son of Zerah, the silver, the
robe, the gold bar, his sons and daughters,
his cattle, donkeys and sheep, his tent and
all that he had, to the Valley of Achor.[w]
25Joshua said, "Why have you brought this
trouble[x] on us? The LORD will bring trouble
on you today."

Then all Israel stoned him,[y] and after
they had stoned the rest, they burned them.
26Over Achan they heaped up a large pile
of rocks, which remains to this day. Then
the LORD turned from his fierce anger.[z]
Therefore that place has been called the
Valley of Achor[d][a] ever since.

---

[a] 21 Hebrew *Shinar* [b] 21 That is, about 5 pounds or about 2.3 kilograms [c] 21 That is, about 1 1/4 pounds or about 575 grams [d] 26 *Achor* means *trouble.*

7:9 *your own great name.* Joshua is aware that there is an even larger issue at stake: God's reputation.

7:10–15 *Israel has sinned.* God had consistent standards for both Israel and the Canaanites. He had ordered Israel to destroy Canaan because of their sin. He could not allow Israel to accommodate sin and corruption, even that of only one man.

7:13 *until you remove.* The relationship between obedience and blessing is well illustrated here. Israel would have no further successes until the sin had been uncovered.

7:19 give glory to the LORD ... Tell me what you have done. We too dishonor the Lord when we hide our sins, and we honor Him when we confess them.

7:25 stoned him, and after they stoned the rest. Achan and all that he had were brought out and stoned. This seems like a severe punishment and one that is hard to understand. But it illustrated God's firm insistence on holiness. God could not tolerate the sin Achan had committed and He had to deal with him. It is a sobering thought for us, to remember that often our sins do not affect only ourselves, they also cause others to stumble and fall. We deserve punishment as severe as Achan's, but Jesus Christ took over our penalty and through His blood we can be reconciled to God.

7:6 [g] 1Sa 4:12; 2Sa 13:19; Ne 9:1; Job 2:12; La 2:10; Rev 18:19 **7:7** [h] Ex 5:22 **7:9** [i] Ex 32:12; Dt 9:28 **7:11** [j] Jos 6:17-19 [k] Ac 5:1-2 **7:12** [l] Nu 14:45; Jdg 2:14 [m] Jos 6:18 **7:13** [n] Jos 3:5; 6:18 **7:14** [o] Pr 16:33 **7:15** [p] 1Sa 14:39 [q] ver 11 [r] Ge 34:7 **7:17** [s] Nu 26:20 **7:19** [t] 1Sa 6:5; Jer 13:16; Jn 9:24* [u] 1Sa 14:43 **7:21** [v] Dt 7:25; Eph 5:5; 1Ti 6:10 **7:24** [w] ver 26; Jos 15:7 **7:25** [x] Jos 6:18 [y] Dt 17:5 **7:26** [z] Nu 25:4; Dt 13:17 [a] ver 24; Isa 65:10; Hos 2:15

Ai Destroyed

8 Then the LORD said to Joshua, "Do not be afraid;[b] do not be discouraged.[c] Take the whole army[d] with you, and go up and attack Ai. For I have delivered[e] into your hands the king of Ai, his people, his city and his land. 2You shall do to Ai and its king as you did to Jericho and its king, except that you may carry off their plunder and livestock for yourselves.[f] Set an ambush behind the city."

3So Joshua and the whole army moved out to attack Ai. He chose thirty thousand of his best fighting men and sent them out at night 4with these orders: "Listen carefully. You are to set an ambush behind the city. Don't go very far from it. All of you be on the alert. 5I and all those with me will advance on the city, and when the men come out against us, as they did before, we will flee from them. 6They will pursue us until we have lured them away from the city, for they will say, 'They are running away from us as they did before.' So when we flee from them, 7you are to rise up from ambush and take the city. The LORD your God will give it into your hand.[g] 8When you have taken the city, set it on fire.[h] Do what the LORD has commanded.[i] See to it; you have my orders."

9Then Joshua sent them off, and they went to the place of ambush[j] and lay in wait between Bethel and Ai, to the west of Ai—but Joshua spent that night with the people.

10Early the next morning[k] Joshua mustered his army, and he and the leaders of Israel[l] marched before them to Ai. 11The entire force that was with him marched up and approached the city and arrived in front of it. They set up camp north of Ai, with the valley between them and the city. 12Joshua had taken about five thousand men and set them in ambush between Bethel and Ai, to the west of the city. 13So the soldiers took up their positions—with the main camp to the north of the city and the ambush to the west of it. That night Joshua went into the valley.

14When the king of Ai saw this, he and all the men of the city hurried out early in the morning to meet Israel in battle at a certain place overlooking the Arabah.[m] But he did not know[n] that an ambush had been set against him behind the city. 15Joshua and all Israel let themselves be driven back[o] before them, and they fled toward the wilderness.[p] 16All the men of Ai were called to pursue them, and they pursued Joshua and were lured away[q] from the city. 17Not a man remained in Ai or Bethel who did not go after Israel. They left the city open and went in pursuit of Israel.

18Then the LORD said to Joshua, "Hold out toward Ai the javelin[r] that is in your hand,[s] for into your hand I will deliver the city." So Joshua held out toward the city the javelin that was in his hand.[t] 19As soon as he did this, the men in the ambush rose quickly[u] from their position and rushed forward. They entered the city and captured it and quickly set it on fire.[v]

20The men of Ai looked back and saw the smoke of the city rising up into the sky,[w] but they had no chance to escape in any direction; the Israelites who had been fleeing toward the wilderness had turned back against their pursuers. 21For when Joshua and all Israel saw that the ambush had taken the city and that smoke was going up from it, they turned around and attacked the men of Ai. 22Those in the ambush also came out of the city against them, so that they were caught in the middle, with Israelites on both sides. Israel cut them down, leaving them neither survivors nor fugitives.[x] 23But they took the king of Ai alive[y] and brought him to Joshua.

24When Israel had finished killing all the men of Ai in the fields and in the wilderness where they had chased them, and when every one of them had been put to the sword, all the Israelites returned to Ai and killed those who were in it. 25Twelve thousand men and women fell that day—all the people of Ai.[z] 26For Joshua did not draw back the hand that held out his javelin until he had destroyed[aa] all who lived in Ai.[b] 27But Israel did carry off for themselves the livestock and plunder of this city, as the LORD had instructed Joshua.[c]

---

a 26 The Hebrew term refers to the irrevocable giving over of things or persons to the LORD, often by totally destroying them.

8:1 *Do not be afraid; do not be discouraged.* The sins of Achan had broken the special relationship God had established with His people, but God had not abandoned them.

8:7 the LORD your God will give it into your hand. Israel was completely dependent on God for their success.

8:12–17 Wisdom—The name Ai means "ruin" or "heap." Unlike Jericho, Ai was not a walled city, to Israel it was just a rubble heap. It looked so easy, especially after their resounding victory at Jericho, that they set out to attack without asking for the Lord's direction. In facing tasks that seem well within our powers, we also often forget to ask for the Lord's help. Wisdom in the believer's life demands persistence in depending on the Lord's strength and direction in little problems as well as the big ones.

8:1 [b] Dt 31:6 [c] Dt 1:21; 7:18; Jos 1:9 [d] Jos 10:7 [e] Jos 6:2
8:2 [f] ver 27; Dt 20:14 **8:7** [g] Jdg 7:7; 1Sa 23:4
8:8 [h] Jdg 20:29-38 [i] ver 19 **8:9** [j] 2Ch 13:13
8:10 [k] Ge 22:3 [l] Jos 7:6 **8:14** [m] Dt 1:1 [n] Jdg 20:34
8:15 [o] Jdg 20:36 [p] Jos 15:61; 16:1; 18:12 **8:16** [q] Jdg 20:31
8:18 [r] Job 41:26; Ps 35:3 [s] Ex 4:2; 14:16; 17:9-12 [t] ver 26
8:19 [u] Jdg 20:33 [v] ver 8 **8:20** [w] Jdg 20:40
8:22 [x] Dt 7:2; Jos 10:1 **8:23** [y] 1Sa 15:8
8:25 [z] Dt 20:16-18 **8:26** [a] Nu 21:2 [b] Ex 17:12
8:27 [c] ver 2

28 So Joshua burned[d] Ai[a][e] and made it a permanent heap of ruins,[f] a desolate place to this day.[g] 29 He impaled the body of the king of Ai on a pole and left it there until evening. At sunset,[h] Joshua ordered them to take the body from the pole and throw it down at the entrance of the city gate. And they raised a large pile of rocks[i] over it, which remains to this day.

The Covenant Renewed at Mount Ebal

30 Then Joshua built on Mount Ebal[j] an altar[k] to the LORD, the God of Israel, 31 as Moses the servant of the LORD had commanded the Israelites. He built it according to what is written in the Book of the Law of Moses—an altar of uncut stones, on which no iron tool[l] had been used. On it they offered to the LORD burnt offerings and sacrificed fellowship offerings.[m] 32 There, in the presence of the Israelites, Joshua wrote on stones a copy of the law of Moses.[n] 33 All the Israelites, with their elders, officials and judges, were standing on both sides of the ark of the covenant of the LORD, facing the Levitical[o] priests who carried it. Both the foreigners living among them and the native-born[p] were there. Half of the people stood in front of Mount Gerizim and half of them in front of Mount Ebal,[q] as Moses the servant of the LORD had formerly commanded when he gave instructions to bless the people of Israel.

34 Afterward, Joshua read all the words of the law—the blessings and the curses—just as it is written in the Book of the Law.[r] 35 There was not a word of all that Moses had commanded that Joshua did not read to the whole assembly of Israel, including the women and children, and the foreigners who lived among them.[s]

The Gibeonite Deception

9 Now when all the kings west of the Jordan heard about these things—the kings in the hill country, in the western foothills, and along the entire coast of the Mediterranean Sea[t] as far as Lebanon (the kings of the Hittites, Amorites, Canaanites, Perizzites, Hivites and Jebusites)[u]—2 they came together to wage war against Joshua and Israel.

3 However, when the people of Gibeon[v] heard what Joshua had done to Jericho and Ai, 4 they resorted to a ruse: They went as a delegation whose donkeys were loaded[b] with worn-out sacks and old wineskins, cracked and mended. 5 They put worn and patched sandals on their feet and wore old clothes. All the bread of their food supply was dry and moldy. 6 Then they went to Joshua in the camp at Gilgal[w] and said to him and the Israelites, "We have come from a distant country; make a treaty with us."

7 The Israelites said to the Hivites,[x] "But perhaps you live near us, so how can we make a treaty[y] with you?"

8 "We are your servants,[z]" they said to Joshua.

But Joshua asked, "Who are you and where do you come from?"

9 They answered: "Your servants have come from a very distant country[a] because of the fame of the LORD your God. For we have heard reports[b] of him: all that he did in Egypt, 10 and all that he did to the two kings of the Amorites east of the Jordan—Sihon king of Heshbon, and Og king of Bashan,[c] who reigned in Ashtaroth.[d] 11 And our elders and all those living in our country said to us, 'Take provisions for your journey; go and meet them and say to them, "We are your servants; make a treaty with us."' 12 This bread of ours was warm when we packed it at home on the day we left to come to you. But now see how dry and moldy it is. 13 And these wineskins that we filled were new, but see how cracked they are. And our clothes and sandals are worn out by the very long journey."

14 The Israelites sampled their provisions but did not inquire[e] of the LORD. 15 Then Joshua made a treaty of peace[f] with them to let them live, and the leaders of the assembly ratified it by oath.

16 Three days after they made the treaty with the Gibeonites, the Israelites heard that they were neighbors, living near them. 17 So the Israelites set out and on the third day came to their cities: Gibeon, Kephirah, Beeroth[g] and Kiriath Jearim.[h] 18 But the Israelites did not attack them, because the leaders of the assembly had sworn an oath[i] to them by the LORD, the God of Israel.

---

[a] 28 *Ai* means *the ruin.* [b] 4 Most Hebrew manuscripts; some Hebrew manuscripts, Vulgate and Syriac (see also Septuagint) *They prepared provisions and loaded their donkeys*

9:3 *Gibeon.* Gibeon was relatively close to Ai, and about five miles northwest of Jerusalem.

9:6 *We have come from a distant country.* Israel was allowed to make treaties with cities that were far away (Ex. 34:11–12; Deut. 20:10–18). If the Gibeonites had been telling the truth, a treaty with them would have been permissible.

9:14 *did not inquire of the LORD.* Significantly, the Israelites did not ask God's advice about making peace with the Gibeonites, contrary to God's explicit instructions to Joshua (Num. 27:21).

9:18 Questioning—The congregation rose up and

8:28 [d] Nu 31:10 [e] Jos 7:2; Jer 49:3 [f] Dt 13:16; Jos 10:1 [g] Ge 35:20 **8:29** [h] Dt 21:23; Jn 19:31 [i] 2Sa 18:17 **8:30** [j] Dt 11:29 [k] Ex 20:24 **8:31** [l] Ex 20:25 [m] Dt 27:6-7 **8:32** [n] Dt 27:8 **8:33** [o] Dt 31:12 [p] Lev 16:29 [q] Dt 11:29; 27:11-14 **8:34** [r] Dt 28:61; 31:11; Jos 1:8 **8:35** [s] Ex 12:38; Dt 31:12 **9:1** [t] Nu 34:6 [u] Ex 3:17; Jos 3:10 **9:3** [v] ver 17; Jos 10:2; 2Sa 2:12; 2Ch 1:3; Isa 28:21 **9:6** [w] Jos 5:10 **9:7** [x] ver 1; Jos 11:19 [y] Ex 23:32; Dt 7:2 **9:8** [z] Dt 20:11; 2Ki 10:5 **9:9** [a] Dt 20:15 [b] ver 24; Jos 2:9 **9:10** [c] Nu 21:33 [d] Nu 21:24,35 **9:14** [e] Nu 27:21 **9:15** [f] Ex 23:32; Jos 11:19; 2Sa 21:2 **9:17** [g] Jos 18:25 [h] 1Sa 7:1-2 **9:18** [i] Ps 15:4

The whole assembly grumbled[j] against the leaders, 19but all the leaders answered, "We have given them our oath by the LORD, the God of Israel, and we cannot touch them now. 20This is what we will do to them: We will let them live, so that God's wrath will not fall on us for breaking the oath we swore to them." 21They continued, "Let them live,[k] but let them be woodcutters and water carriers[l] in the service of the whole assembly." So the leaders' promise to them was kept.

22Then Joshua summoned the Gibeonites and said, "Why did you deceive us by saying, 'We live a long way[m] from you,' while actually you live near[n] us? 23You are now under a curse:[o] You will never be released from service as woodcutters and water carriers for the house of my God."

24They answered Joshua, "Your servants were clearly told[p] how the LORD your God had commanded his servant Moses to give you the whole land and to wipe out all its inhabitants from before you. So we feared for our lives because of you, and that is why we did this. 25We are now in your hands.[q] Do to us whatever seems good and right to you."

26So Joshua saved them from the Israelites, and they did not kill them. 27That day he made the Gibeonites woodcutters and water carriers for the assembly, to provide for the needs of the altar of the LORD at the place the LORD would choose.[r] And that is what they are to this day.

The Sun Stands Still

10 Now Adoni-Zedek king of Jerusalem[s] heard that Joshua had taken Ai[t] and totally destroyed[a][u] it, doing to Ai and its king as he had done to Jericho and its king, and that the people of Gibeon had made a treaty of peace[v] with Israel and had become their allies. 2He and his people were very much alarmed at this, because Gibeon was an important city, like one of the royal cities; it was larger than Ai, and all its men were good fighters. 3So Adoni-Zedek king of Jerusalem appealed to Hoham king of Hebron,[w] Piram king of Jarmuth, Japhia king of Lachish[x] and Debir king of Eglon. 4"Come up and help me attack Gibeon," he said, "because it has made peace[y] with Joshua and the Israelites."

5Then the five kings of the Amorites[z]—the kings of Jerusalem, Hebron, Jarmuth, Lachish and Eglon—joined forces. They moved up with all their troops and took up positions against Gibeon and attacked it.

6The Gibeonites then sent word to Joshua in the camp at Gilgal: "Do not abandon your servants. Come up to us quickly and save us! Help us, because all the Amorite kings from the hill country have joined forces against us."

7So Joshua marched up from Gilgal with his entire army,[a] including all the best fighting men. 8The LORD said to Joshua, "Do not be afraid[b] of them; I have given them into your hand. Not one of them will be able to withstand you."

9After an all-night march from Gilgal, Joshua took them by surprise. 10The LORD threw them into confusion before Israel,[c] so Joshua and the Israelites defeated them completely at Gibeon. Israel pursued them along the road going up to Beth Horon[d] and cut them down all the way to Azekah[e] and Makkedah. 11As they fled before Israel on the road down from Beth Horon to Azekah, the LORD hurled large hailstones[f] down on them, and more of them died from the hail than were killed by the swords of the Israelites.

12On the day the LORD gave the Amorites[g] over to Israel, Joshua said to the LORD in the presence of Israel:

"Sun, stand still over Gibeon,
  and you, moon, over the Valley of
    Aijalon.[h]"
13So the sun stood still,[i]
  and the moon stopped,
  till the nation avenged itself on[b] its
    enemies,

as it is written in the Book of Jashar.[j]

---

a 1 The Hebrew term refers to the irrevocable giving over of things or persons to the LORD, often by totally destroying them; also in verses 28, 35, 37, 39 and 40. *b 13* Or *nation triumphed over*

---

complained to their leaders about making the treaty with Gibeon because they knew the leaders had not consulted the Lord. There is a time to confront leaders, specifically when they sin or when they act in their own wisdom without asking for God's direction. When the leaders appear to be traveling down the wrong path, the people can always ask respectfully, "Have you consulted the Lord about this? Did you get an answer?"

9:20 *the oath we swore.* Oath taking and swearing was serious business. To take an oath was to give a sacred and unbreakable promise to do a certain thing. Because of the unbreakable nature of an oath, the covenant the Israelites made with the Gibeonites could not be revoked, even though it was obtained under false pretenses.

10:10 *the LORD threw them into confusion.* Despite Joshua's presence with his warriors, it was God who gave the victory, and God who received the credit.

10:13 *the Book of Jashar.* This piece of literature is mentioned again in 2 Samuel 1:18, confirming what is said here. Nothing else is known of the Book of Jashar; it is not part of the Bible, and no known portion of it has survived.

9:18 [j] Ex 15:24 **9:21** [k] ver 15 [l] Dt 29:11 **9:22** [m] ver 6 [n] ver 16 **9:23** [o] Ge 9:25 **9:24** [p] ver 9 **9:25** [q] Ge 16:6 **9:27** [r] Dt 12:5 **10:1** [s] Jdg 1:7 [t] Jos 8:1 [u] Dt 20:16; Jos 8:22 [v] Jos 9:15 **10:3** [w] Ge 13:18 [x] 2Ch 11:9; 25:27; Ne 11:30; Isa 36:2; 37:8; Jer 34:7; Mic 1:13 **10:4** [y] Jos 9:15 **10:5** [z] Nu 13:29 **10:7** [a] Jos 8:1 **10:8** [b] Dt 3:2; Jos 1:9 **10:10** [c] Dt 7:23 [d] Jos 16:3, 5 [e] Jos 15:35 **10:11** [f] Ps 18:12; Isa 28:2, 17 **10:12** [g] Am 2:9 [h] Jdg 1:35; 12:12 **10:13** [i] Hab 3:11 [j] 2Sa 1:18

The sun stopped[k] in the middle of the sky and delayed going down about a full day. 14There has never been a day like it before or since, a day when the LORD listened to a human being. Surely the LORD was fighting[l] for Israel!

15Then Joshua returned with all Israel to the camp at Gilgal.[m]

Five Amorite Kings Killed

16Now the five kings had fled and hidden in the cave at Makkedah. 17When Joshua was told that the five kings had been found hiding in the cave at Makkedah, 18he said, "Roll large rocks up to the mouth of the cave, and post some men there to guard it. 19But don't stop; pursue your enemies! Attack them from the rear and don't let them reach their cities, for the LORD your God has given them into your hand."

20So Joshua and the Israelites defeated them completely,[n] but a few survivors managed to reach their fortified cities. 21The whole army then returned safely to Joshua in the camp at Makkedah, and no one uttered a word against the Israelites.

22Joshua said, "Open the mouth of the cave and bring those five kings out to me." 23So they brought the five kings out of the cave—the kings of Jerusalem, Hebron, Jarmuth, Lachish and Eglon. 24When they had brought these kings to Joshua, he summoned all the men of Israel and said to the army commanders who had come with him, "Come here and put your feet[o] on the necks of these kings." So they came forward and placed their feet[p] on their necks.

25Joshua said to them, "Do not be afraid; do not be discouraged. Be strong and courageous.[q] This is what the LORD will do to all the enemies you are going to fight." 26Then Joshua put the kings to death and exposed their bodies on five poles, and they were left hanging on the poles until evening.

27At sunset[r] Joshua gave the order and they took them down from the poles and threw them into the cave where they had been hiding. At the mouth of the cave they placed large rocks, which are there to this day.

Southern Cities Conquered

28That day Joshua took Makkedah. He put the city and its king to the sword and totally destroyed everyone in it. He left no survivors.[s] And he did to the king of Makkedah as he had done to the king of Jericho.[t]

29Then Joshua and all Israel with him moved on from Makkedah to Libnah and attacked it. 30The LORD also gave that city and its king into Israel's hand. The city and everyone in it Joshua put to the sword. He left no survivors there. And he did to its king as he had done to the king of Jericho.

31Then Joshua and all Israel with him moved on from Libnah to Lachish; he took up positions against it and attacked it. 32The LORD gave Lachish into Israel's hands, and Joshua took it on the second day. The city and everyone in it he put to the sword, just as he had done to Libnah. 33Meanwhile, Horam king of Gezer[u] had come up to help Lachish, but Joshua defeated him and his army—until no survivors were left.

34Then Joshua and all Israel with him moved on from Lachish to Eglon; they took up positions against it and attacked it. 35They captured it that same day and put it to the sword and totally destroyed everyone in it, just as they had done to Lachish.

36Then Joshua and all Israel with him went up from Eglon to Hebron[v] and attacked it. 37They took the city and put it to the sword, together with its king, its villages and everyone in it. They left no survivors. Just as at Eglon, they totally destroyed it and everyone in it.

38Then Joshua and all Israel with him turned around and attacked Debir.[w] 39They took the city, its king and its villages, and put them to the sword. Everyone in it they totally destroyed. They left no survivors. They did to Debir and its king as they had done to Libnah and its king and to Hebron.

10:14 *the LORD listened to a human being.* Any person can gain God's attention in prayer. God may answer our pleas by saying no, but we can be certain that He always listens and answers. This incident was remembered as being like no other because God said "Yes" to a request which He otherwise always answers "No": He actually stopped time to allow the Israelites to finish the battle.

10:24 *put your feet on the necks of these kings.* Putting one's foot on a slain enemy was a declaration of victory. In Psalm 110:1 the Lord said, "I [will] make your enemies a footstool" (see also Ps. 8:6). God also speaks of placing Jesus' enemies under His feet (1 Cor. 15:25–27). Ancient sculptures show Assyrian kings doing this to their vanquished enemies.

10:25 *be strong and courageous.* Joshua encourages the people with the same words God used to encourage him (1:6,9; 10:8). God's words, written for us in the Bible are the best form of encouragement we could have.

10:30 *the LORD.* Here again we are reminded that the Lord was Israel's warrior. As He fought for them, we too can trust Him fully to fight for us. Indeed, He fought the ultimate fight for us on the cross, to set us free from death forever. We can also trust Him to be with us in the day-to-day fight against evil and sin.

10:28–43 Fervor—All of Israel was zealous to do just as the Lord commanded, and the success they experienced was attributed to the Lord. But how can such destruction be regarded as honoring to God? The Bible gives reasons for the wiping out of these peoples, and these reasons are in accord with the tenor of the whole Bible. The Canaanites were guilty

10:13 [k] Isa 38:8 **10:14** [l] ver 42; Ex 14:14; Dt 1:30; Ps 106:43; 136:24 **10:15** [m] ver 43 **10:20** [n] Dt 20:16 **10:24** [o] Mal 4:3 [p] Ps 110:1 **10:25** [q] Dt 31:6 **10:27** [r] Dt 21:23; Jos 8:9,29 **10:28** [s] Dt 20:16 [t] Jos 6:21 **10:33** [u] Jos 16:3, 10; Jdg 1:29; 1Ki 9:15 **10:36** [v] Jos 14:13; 15:13; Jdg 1:10 **10:38** [w] Jos 15:15; Jdg 1:11

40So Joshua subdued the whole region,
including the hill country, the Negev,[x]
the western foothills and the mountain
slopes,[y] together with all their kings.[z] He
left no survivors. He totally destroyed all
who breathed, just as the LORD, the God
of Israel, had commanded.[a] 41Joshua subdued them from Kadesh Barnea[b] to Gaza[c]
and from the whole region of Goshen[d] to
Gibeon. 42All these kings and their lands
Joshua conquered in one campaign, because the LORD, the God of Israel, fought[e]
for Israel.
43Then Joshua returned with all Israel to
the camp at Gilgal.[f]

Northern Kings Defeated

11 When Jabin[g] king of Hazor[h] heard
of this, he sent word to Jobab king
of Madon, to the kings of Shimron[i] and
Akshaph, 2and to the northern kings who
were in the mountains, in the Arabah[j]
south of Kinnereth,[k] in the western foothills and in Naphoth Dor[l] on the west; 3to
the Canaanites in the east and west; to the
Amorites, Hittites, Perizzites and Jebusites
in the hill country; and to the Hivites[m] below Hermon in the region of Mizpah.[n]
4They came out with all their troops and
a large number of horses and chariots—a
huge army, as numerous as the sand on the
seashore.[o] 5All these kings joined forces[p]
and made camp together at the Waters of
Merom to fight against Israel.
6The LORD said to Joshua, "Do not be
afraid of them, because by this time tomorrow I will hand[q] all of them, slain, over to
Israel. You are to hamstring[r] their horses
and burn their chariots."
7So Joshua and his whole army came
against them suddenly at the Waters of
Merom and attacked them, 8and the LORD
gave them into the hand of Israel. They defeated them and pursued them all the way
to Greater Sidon, to Misrephoth Maim,[s] and
to the Valley of Mizpah on the east, until no
survivors were left. 9Joshua did to them as
the LORD had directed: He hamstrung their
horses and burned their chariots.
10At that time Joshua turned back and
captured Hazor and put its king to the
sword. (Hazor had been the head of all
these kingdoms.) 11Everyone in it they put
to the sword. They totally destroyed[α] them,
not sparing anyone that breathed,[t] and he
burned Hazor itself.
12Joshua took all these royal cities and
their kings and put them to the sword. He
totally destroyed them, as Moses the servant of the LORD had commanded.[u] 13Yet
Israel did not burn any of the cities built on
their mounds—except Hazor, which Joshua burned. 14The Israelites carried off for
themselves all the plunder and livestock of
these cities, but all the people they put to
the sword until they completely destroyed
them, not sparing anyone that breathed.[v]
15As the LORD commanded his servant
Moses, so Moses commanded Joshua, and
Joshua did it; he left nothing undone of all
that the LORD commanded Moses.[w]
16So Joshua took this entire land: the hill
country, all the Negev, the whole region of
Goshen, the western foothills,[x] the Arabah
and the mountains of Israel with their foothills, 17from Mount Halak, which rises toward Seir, to Baal Gad in the Valley of Lebanon[y] below Mount Hermon. He captured all
their kings and put them to death.[z] 18Joshua
waged war against all these kings for a long
time. 19Except for the Hivites living in Gibeon,[a] not one city made a treaty of peace with
the Israelites, who took them all in battle.

[α] *11* The Hebrew term refers to the irrevocable giving over of things or persons to the LORD, often by totally destroying them; also in verses 12, 20 and 21.

---

of extreme wickedness (Deut. 7:2–11; 20:16–18). God is completely holy, and He therefore cannot tolerate sin. Sin must be judged. He is also patient. For many years the Canaanite sin did not justify annihilation. But that time did arrive, and it came in the time of Joshua. Israel was a tool in the hand of God to judge the wickedness of those nations. Leviticus 18 is a gruesome list of their evil actions, including incest, adultery, child sacrifice, homosexuality, and bestiality. The Canaanites brought God's judgment on themselves by their own sins. Canaan was not destroyed without plenty of warning. God is never unjust. They were a thoroughly debased society, hostile to all God's ways (Deut. 9:4–5). The most sobering reflection is that now, today, many of those wicked sins listed in Leviticus 18 are present in our society. God's judgment in the last day will be complete indeed.

11:4 *large number of horses and chariots.* In this time in history, horses were used for pulling chariots which accompanied the infantry and carried a rider with a bow or a supply of spears. The enemy of Israel came well armed and with many soldiers to fight—but it made no difference. Again God defeated Israel's enemy. God limited the size of the Israelite army so they would not be depending on military strength, but rather on Him.

11:8 *Greater Sidon, to Misrephoth Maim.* Great Sidon was a Phoenician city on the Mediterranean coast, and Misrephoth was south of it. The defeat of the Canaanites described here shows them fleeing in all directions.

11:16–12:24 Zeal—Joshua and the people served as the instruments of divine justice and fulfilled the word spoken to Moses concerning the gift of the

10:40 [x] Ge 12:9; Jos 12:8 [y] Dt 1:7 [z] Dt 7:24 [a] Dt 20:16-17
10:41 [b] Ge 14:7 [c] Ge 10:19 [d] Jos 11:16; 15:51
10:42 [e] ver 14 **10:43** [f] ver 15; Jos 5:9 **11:1** [g] Jdg 4:2, 7, 23 [h] ver 10; 1Sa 12:9 [i] Jos 19:15 **11:2** [j] Jos 12:3
[k] Nu 34:11 [l] Jos 17:11; Jdg 1:27; 1Ki 4:11 **11:3** [m] Dt 7:1; Jdg 3:3, 5; 1Ki 9:20 [n] Ge 31:49; Jos 15:38; 18:26
11:4 [o] Jdg 7:12; 1Sa 13:5 **11:5** [p] Jdg 5:19
11:6 [q] Jos 10:8 [r] 2Sa 8:4 **11:8** [s] Jos 13:6
11:11 [t] Dt 20:16-17 **11:12** [u] Nu 33:50-52; Dt 7:2
11:14 [v] Nu 31:11-12 **11:15** [w] Ex 34:11; Jos 1:7
11:16 [x] Jos 10:41 **11:17** [y] Jos 12:7 [z] Dt 7:24
11:19 [a] Jos 9:3

[20]For it was the LORD himself who hardened their hearts[b] to wage war against Israel, so that he might destroy them totally, exterminating them without mercy, as the LORD had commanded Moses.[c]

[21]At that time Joshua went and destroyed the Anakites[d] from the hill country: from Hebron, Debir and Anab, from all the hill country of Judah, and from all the hill country of Israel. Joshua totally destroyed them and their towns. [22]No Anakites were left in Israelite territory; only in Gaza, Gath[e] and Ashdod[f] did any survive.

[23]So Joshua took the entire land,[g] just as the LORD had directed Moses, and he gave it as an inheritance[h] to Israel according to their tribal divisions.[i] Then the land had rest from war.[j]

List of Defeated Kings

12 These are the kings of the land whom the Israelites had defeated and whose territory they took over east of the Jordan, from the Arnon Gorge to Mount Hermon,[k] including all the eastern side of the Arabah:

[2]Sihon king of the Amorites, who reigned in Heshbon.
He ruled from Aroer on the rim of the Arnon Gorge—from the middle of the gorge—to the Jabbok River, which is the border of the Ammonites. This included half of Gilead.[l]
[3]He also ruled over the eastern Arabah from the Sea of Galilee[a][m] to the Sea of the Arabah (that is, the Dead Sea), to Beth Jeshimoth,[n] and then southward below the slopes of Pisgah.

[4]And the territory of Og king of Bashan,[o] one of the last of the Rephaites, who reigned in Ashtaroth[p] and Edrei.
[5]He ruled over Mount Hermon, Salekah,[q] all of Bashan to the border of the people of Geshur[r] and Maakah,[s] and half of Gilead to the border of Sihon king of Heshbon.

[6]Moses, the servant of the LORD, and the Israelites conquered them. And Moses the servant of the LORD gave their land to the Reubenites, the Gadites and the half-tribe of Manasseh to be their possession.[t]

[7]Here is a list of the kings of the land that
Joshua and the Israelites conquered on the west side of the Jordan, from Baal Gad in the Valley of Lebanon[u] to Mount Halak, which rises toward Seir. Joshua gave their lands as an inheritance to the tribes of Israel according to their tribal divisions.
[8]The lands included the hill country, the western foothills, the Arabah, the mountain slopes, the wilderness and the Negev.[v] These were the lands of the Hittites, Amorites, Canaanites, Perizzites, Hivites and Jebusites. These were the kings:

[9]the king of Jericho[w] one
the king of Ai[x] (near Bethel) one
[10]the king of Jerusalem[y] one
the king of Hebron one
[11]the king of Jarmuth one
the king of Lachish one
[12]the king of Eglon one
the king of Gezer[z] one
[13]the king of Debir one
the king of Geder one
[14]the king of Hormah one
the king of Arad[a] one
[15]the king of Libnah one
the king of Adullam one
[16]the king of Makkedah one
the king of Bethel[b] one
[17]the king of Tappuah one
the king of Hepher[c] one
[18]the king of Aphek[d] one
the king of Lasharon one
[19]the king of Madon one
the king of Hazor one
[20]the king of Shimron Meron one
the king of Akshaph[e] one
[21]the king of Taanach one
the king of Megiddo one
[22]the king of Kedesh[f] one
the king of Jokneam in Carmel[g] one
[23]the king of Dor (in Naphoth Dor[h]) one
the king of Goyim in Gilgal one
[24]the king of Tirzah one
thirty-one kings in all.[i]

Land Still to Be Taken

13 When Joshua had grown old,[j] the LORD said to him, "You are now very old, and there are still very large areas of land to be taken over.

a 3 Hebrew *Kinnereth*

land of Canaan. The list of the defeated kings who had banded together against Israel bears testimony to the zeal of Israel for God and the obedience and faithfulness of Joshua. As Christians we can eagerly anticipate the final outcome of world history, when the "kingdom of the world has become the kingdom of our Lord and of his Messiah" (Rev. 11:15).

11:20 ***hardened their hearts.*** The people whose hearts God hardened were not good people, but people already committed to doing evil.

11:20 [b] Ex 14:17; Ro 9:18 [c] Dt 7:16; Jdg 14:4 **11:21** [d] Nu 13:22, 33; Dt 9:2 **11:22** [e] 1Sa 17:4; 1Ki 2:39; 1Ch 8:13 [f] 1Sa 5:1; Isa 20:1 **11:23** [g] Jos 21:43-45 [h] Dt 1:38; 12:9-10; 25:19 [i] Nu 26:53 [j] Jos 14:15 **12:1** [k] Dt 3:8 **12:2** [l] Dt 2:36 **12:3** [m] Jos 11:2 [n] Jos 13:20 **12:4** [o] Nu 21:21, 33; Dt 3:11 [p] Dt 1:4 **12:5** [q] Dt 3:10 [r] 1Sa 27:8 [s] Dt 3:14 **12:6** [t] Nu 32:29, 33; Jos 13:8 **12:7** [u] Jos 11:17 **12:8** [v] Jos 11:16 **12:9** [w] Jos 6:2 [x] Jos 8:29 **12:10** [y] Jos 10:23 **12:12** [z] Jos 10:33 **12:14** [a] Nu 21:1 **12:16** [b] Jos 7:2 **12:17** [c] 1Ki 4:10 **12:18** [d] Jos 13:4 **12:20** [e] Jos 11:1 **12:22** [f] Jos 19:37; 20:7; 21:32 [g] 1Sa 15:12 **12:23** [h] Jos 11:2 **12:24** [i] Ps 135:11; Dt 7:24 **13:1** [j] Ge 24:1; Jos 14:10

2"This is the land that remains: all the regions of the Philistines and Geshurites, 3from the Shihor River[k] on the east of Egypt to the territory of Ekron[l] on the north, all of it counted as Canaanite though held by the five Philistine rulers[m] in Gaza, Ashdod, Ashkelon, Gath and Ekron; the territory of the Avvites[n] 4on the south; all the land of the Canaanites, from Arah of the Sidonians as far as Aphek[o] and the border of the Amorites;[p] 5the area of Byblos;[q] and all Lebanon[r] to the east, from Baal Gad below Mount Hermon to Lebo Hamath.

6"As for all the inhabitants of the mountain regions from Lebanon to Misrephoth Maim,[s] that is, all the Sidonians, I myself will drive them out before the Israelites. Be sure to allocate this land to Israel for an inheritance, as I have instructed you,[t] 7and divide it as an inheritance[u] among the nine tribes and half of the tribe of Manasseh."

Division of the Land East of the Jordan

8The other half of Manasseh,[a] the Reubenites and the Gadites had received the inheritance that Moses had given them east of the Jordan, as he, the servant of the LORD, had assigned[v] it to them.

9It extended from Aroer[w] on the rim of the Arnon Gorge, and from the town in the middle of the gorge, and included the whole plateau[x] of Medeba as far as Dibon,[y] 10and all the towns of Sihon king of the Amorites, who ruled in Heshbon, out to the border of the Ammonites.[z] 11It also included Gilead, the territory of the people of Geshur and Maakah, all of Mount Hermon and all Bashan as far as Salekah[a]— 12that is, the whole kingdom of Og in Bashan,[b] who had reigned in Ashtaroth[c] and Edrei. (He was the last of the Rephaites.[d]) Moses had defeated them and taken over their land. 13But the Israelites did not drive out the people of Geshur[e] and Maakah,[f] so they continue to live among the Israelites to this day.

14But to the tribe of Levi he gave no inheritance, since the food offerings presented to the LORD, the God of Israel, are their inheritance, as he promised them.[g]

15This is what Moses had given to the tribe of Reuben, according to its clans:

16The territory from Aroer[h] on the rim of the Arnon Gorge, and from the town in the middle of the gorge, and the whole plateau past Medeba[i] 17to Heshbon and all its towns on the plateau, including Dibon,[j] Bamoth Baal, Beth Baal Meon,[k] 18Jahaz,[l] Kedemoth, Mephaath,[m] 19Kiriathaim,[n] Sibmah, Zereth Shahar on the hill in the valley, 20Beth Peor,[o] the slopes of Pisgah, and Beth Jeshimoth— 21all the towns on the plateau and the entire realm of Sihon king of the Amorites, who ruled at Heshbon. Moses had defeated him and the Midianite chiefs,[p] Evi, Rekem, Zur, Hur and Reba[q]—princes allied with Sihon—who lived in that country. 22In addition to those slain in battle, the Israelites had put to the sword Balaam son of Beor,[r] who practiced divination. 23The boundary of the Reubenites was the bank of the Jordan. These towns and their villages were the inheritance of the Reubenites, according to their clans.

24This is what Moses had given to the tribe of Gad, according to its clans:

25The territory of Jazer,[s] all the towns of Gilead and half the Ammonite country as far as Aroer, near Rabbah; 26and from Heshbon[t] to Ramath Mizpah and Betonim, and from Mahanaim to the territory of Debir;[u] 27and in the valley, Beth Haram, Beth Nimrah, Sukkoth[v] and Zaphon with the rest of the realm of Sihon king of Heshbon (the east side of the Jordan, the territory up to the end of the Sea of Galilee[b][w]). 28These towns and their villages were the inheritance of the Gadites,[x] according to their clans.

29This is what Moses had given to the half-tribe of Manasseh, that is, to half the family of the descendants of Manasseh, according to its clans:

---

[a] 8 Hebrew *With it* (that is, with the other half of Manasseh) [b] 27 Hebrew *Kinnereth*

13:14 *to the tribe of Levi he gave no inheritance.* Originally, the tribe of Levi was sentenced to be landless because of Levi's violent behavior (Gen. 49:5–7). But later the Levites showed their faithfulness to the Lord (Ex. 32:25–28) and were promised a blessing (Deut. 33:8–11). Instead of land, the sacrifices of God would be their privileged inheritance.

13:22 *Balaam son of Beor.* Balaam was a pagan fortune-teller who had been hired by Balak, king of Moab, to curse the Israelites in the wilderness (Num. 22–24).

13:3 [k] Jer 2:18 [l] Jdg 1:18 [m] Jdg 3:3 [n] Dt 2:23 **13:4** [o] Jos 12:18; 19:30 [p] Am 2:10 **13:5** [q] 1Ki 5:18; Ps 83:7; Eze 27:9 [r] Jos 12:7 **13:6** [s] Jos 11:8 [t] Nu 33:54 **13:7** [u] Jos 11:23; Ps 78:55 **13:8** [v] Jos 12:6 **13:9** [w] ver 16; Jdg 11:26 [x] Jer 48:8,21 [y] Nu 21:30 **13:10** [z] Nu 21:24 **13:11** [a] Jos 12:5 **13:12** [b] Dt 3:11 [c] Jos 12:4 [d] Ge 14:5 **13:13** [e] Jos 12:5 [f] Dt 3:14 **13:14** [g] ver 33; Dt 18:1-2 **13:16** [h] ver 9; Jos 12:2 [i] Nu 21:30 **13:17** [j] Nu 32:3 [k] 1Ch 5:8 **13:18** [l] Nu 21:23 [m] Jer 48:21 **13:19** [n] Nu 32:37 **13:20** [o] Dt 3:29 **13:21** [p] Nu 25:15 [q] Nu 31:8 **13:22** [r] Nu 22:5; 31:8 **13:25** [s] Nu 21:32; Jos 21:39 **13:26** [t] Nu 21:25; Jer 49:3 [u] Jos 10:3 **13:27** [v] Ge 33:17 [w] Nu 34:11 **13:28** [x] Nu 32:33

30The territory extending from Mahanaim[y] and including all of Bashan, the
entire realm of Og king of Bashan—
all the settlements of Jair[z] in Bashan,
sixty towns, 31half of Gilead, and Ashtaroth and Edrei (the royal cities of Og
in Bashan). This was for the descendants of Makir[a] son of Manasseh—for
half of the sons of Makir, according to
their clans.

32This is the inheritance Moses had
given when he was in the plains of Moab
across the Jordan east of Jericho. 33But to
the tribe of Levi, Moses had given no inheritance; the LORD, the God of Israel, is their
inheritance,[b] as he promised them.[c]

Division of the Land West of the Jordan

14 Now these are the areas the Israelites
received as an inheritance in the land
of Canaan, which Eleazar the priest, Joshua son of Nun and the heads of the tribal clans of Israel allotted to them.[d] 2Their
inheritances were assigned by lot[e] to the
nine and a half tribes, as the LORD had
commanded through Moses. 3Moses had
granted the two and a half tribes their inheritance east of the Jordan[f] but had not
granted the Levites an inheritance among
the rest,[g] 4for Joseph's descendants had
become two tribes—Manasseh and Ephraim.[h] The Levites received no share of the
land but only towns to live in, with pasturelands for their flocks and herds. 5So the Israelites divided the land, just as the LORD
had commanded Moses.[i]

Allotment for Caleb

6Now the people of Judah approached
Joshua at Gilgal, and Caleb son of Jephunneh[j] the Kenizzite said to him, "You know
what the LORD said to Moses the man of
God at Kadesh Barnea[k] about you and
me. 7I was forty years old when Moses the
servant of the LORD sent me from Kadesh
Barnea to explore the land.[l] And I brought
him back a report according to my convictions,[m] 8but my fellow Israelites who went
up with me made the hearts of the people
melt in fear.[n] I, however, followed the LORD
my God wholeheartedly.[o] 9So on that day
Moses swore to me, 'The land on which
your feet have walked will be your inheritance and that of your children[p] forever,
because you have followed the LORD my
God wholeheartedly.'[a]

10"Now then, just as the LORD promised,[q]
he has kept me alive for forty-five years
since the time he said this to Moses, while
Israel moved about in the wilderness. So
here I am today, eighty-five years old! 11I
am still as strong[r] today as the day Moses
sent me out; I'm just as vigorous to go out
to battle now as I was then. 12Now give me
this hill country that the LORD promised me
that day. You yourself heard then that the
Anakites[s] were there and their cities were
large and fortified,[t] but, the LORD helping
me, I will drive them out just as he said."

13Then Joshua blessed[u] Caleb son of
Jephunneh and gave him Hebron[v] as his
inheritance.[w] 14So Hebron has belonged
to Caleb son of Jephunneh the Kenizzite
ever since, because he followed the LORD,
the God of Israel, wholeheartedly. 15(Hebron used to be called Kiriath Arba[x] after
Arba,[y] who was the greatest man among
the Anakites.)

Then the land had rest[z] from war.

Allotment for Judah

15 The allotment for the tribe of Judah,
according to its clans, extended down
to the territory of Edom,[a] to the Desert of
Zin[b] in the extreme south.

2Their southern boundary started
from the bay at the southern end of the
Dead Sea, 3crossed south of Scorpion

[a] *9* Deut. 1:36

14:6 *Caleb ... the Kenizzite.* The Kenizzites were a non-Israelite group descended from Esau through Kenaz (Gen. 15:19; 36:11,15,42). It seems that Caleb, one of the most faithful to God of his time, was just a generation removed from a non-Israelite family. Although the Jews are indeed God's chosen people, He loves and honors anyone who obeys His commands.

14:10–11 Thankfulness—God's Word is as dependable as its author. His promise to Caleb waited forty-five years for fulfillment, but His blessing was sure. Caleb's view of all God's goodness to him resounded with thankfulness. Being silently thankful is important—God knows our hearts—but thankfulness should also be expressed with words of praise and glorification for the Giver of all good things.

14:14 *he followed the LORD.* Caleb's wholehearted devotion to God was never a question, even in the wilderness. In the Bible, people are sometimes rewarded in this life for their faithfulness to God, but not always (Heb. 11:32–40). The believer's ultimate blessing will come in eternity. Those who set their hope on that promise will lose nothing, whatever they suffer in this life.

15:1–12 *the allotment for the tribe.* The boundaries of Judah in southern Canaan are described in detail. These details may at first seem uninteresting, but they serve to underline the fact that this passage is talking about real people, in a real place, in a real time in history.

13:30 [y] Ge 32:2 [z] Nu 32:41 **13:31** [a] Ge 50:23
13:33 [b] Nu 18:20 [c] ver 14; Jos 18:7 **14:1** [d] Nu 34:17-18
14:2 [e] Nu 26:55 **14:3** [f] Nu 32:33 [g] Jos 13:14
14:4 [h] Ge 41:52; 48:5 **14:5** [i] Nu 34:13; 35:2; Jos 21:2
14:6 [j] Nu 13:6; 14:30 [k] Nu 13:26 **14:7** [l] Nu 13:17
[m] Nu 13:30; 14:6-9 **14:8** [n] Nu 13:31 [o] Nu 14:24
14:9 [p] Nu 14:24; Dt 1:36 **14:10** [q] Nu 14:30
14:11 [r] Dt 34:7 **14:12** [s] Nu 13:33 [t] Nu 13:28
14:13 [u] Jos 22:6,7 [v] Jos 10:36 [w] Jdg 1:20; 1Ch 6:56
14:15 [x] Ge 23:2 [y] Jos 15:13 [z] Jos 11:23 **15:1** [a] Nu 34:3
[b] Nu 33:36

Pass,[c] continued on to Zin and went over to the south of Kadesh Barnea. Then it ran past Hezron up to Addar and curved around to Karka. 4It then passed along to Azmon[d] and joined the Wadi of Egypt,[e] ending at the Mediterranean Sea. This is their[a] southern boundary.

5The eastern boundary[f] is the Dead Sea as far as the mouth of the Jordan.

The northern boundary[g] started from the bay of the sea at the mouth of the Jordan, 6went up to Beth Hoglah[h] and continued north of Beth Arabah to the Stone of Bohan[i] son of Reuben. 7The boundary then went up to Debir from the Valley of Achor[j] and turned north to Gilgal, which faces the Pass of Adummim south of the gorge. It continued along to the waters of En Shemesh and came out at En Rogel.[k] 8Then it ran up the Valley of Ben Hinnom along the southern slope of the Jebusite[l] city (that is, Jerusalem). From there it climbed to the top of the hill west of the Hinnom Valley at the northern end of the Valley of Rephaim. 9From the hilltop the boundary headed toward the spring of the waters of Nephtoah,[m] came out at the towns of Mount Ephron and went down toward Baalah[n] (that is, Kiriath Jearim). 10Then it curved westward from Baalah to Mount Seir, ran along the northern slope of Mount Jearim (that is, Kesalon), continued down to Beth Shemesh and crossed to Timnah.[o] 11It went to the northern slope of Ekron, turned toward Shikkeron, passed along to Mount Baalah and reached Jabneel.[p] The boundary ended at the sea.

12The western boundary is the coastline of the Mediterranean Sea.[q]

These are the boundaries around the people of Judah by their clans.

13In accordance with the LORD's command to him, Joshua gave to Caleb son of Jephunneh a portion in Judah—Kiriath Arba, that is, Hebron. (Arba was the forefather of Anak.)[r] 14From Hebron Caleb drove out the three Anakites[s]—Sheshai, Ahiman and Talmai,[t] the sons of Anak.[u] 15From there he marched against the people living in Debir (formerly called Kiriath Sepher). 16And Caleb said, "I will give my daughter Aksah[v] in marriage to the man who attacks and captures Kiriath Sepher." 17Othniel[w] son of Kenaz, Caleb's brother, took it; so Caleb gave his daughter Aksah to him in marriage.

18One day when she came to Othniel, she urged him[b] to ask her father for a field. When she got off her donkey, Caleb asked her, "What can I do for you?"

19She replied, "Do me a special favor. Since you have given me land in the Negev, give me also springs of water." So Caleb gave her the upper and lower springs.

20This is the inheritance of the tribe of Judah, according to its clans:

21The southernmost towns of the tribe of Judah in the Negev toward the boundary of Edom were:

Kabzeel, Eder,[x] Jagur, 22Kinah, Dimonah, Adadah, 23Kedesh, Hazor, Ithnan, 24Ziph,[y] Telem, Bealoth, 25Hazor Hadattah, Kerioth Hezron (that is, Hazor), 26Amam, Shema, Moladah,[z] 27Hazar Gaddah, Heshmon, Beth Pelet, 28Hazar Shual, Beersheba,[a] Biziothiah, 29Baalah,[b] Iyim, Ezem, 30Eltolad,[c] Kesil, Hormah, 31Ziklag,[d] Madmannah, Sansannah, 32Lebaoth, Shilhim, Ain and Rimmon[e]—a total of twenty-nine towns and their villages.

33In the western foothills:

Eshtaol,[f] Zorah, Ashnah, 34Zanoah,[g] En Gannim, Tappuah, Enam, 35Jarmuth,[h] Adullam,[i] Sokoh, Azekah, 36Shaaraim, Adithaim and Gederah[j] (or Gederothaim)[c]—fourteen towns and their villages.

37Zenan, Hadashah, Migdal Gad, 38Dilean, Mizpah, Joktheel,[k] 39Lachish,[l] Bozkath,[m] Eglon, 40Kabbon, Lahmas, Kitlish, 41Gederoth, Beth Dagon, Naamah and Makkedah[n]—sixteen towns and their villages.

42Libnah, Ether, Ashan,[o] 43Iphtah, Ashnah, Nezib, 44Keilah, Akzib[p] and Mareshah[q]—nine towns and their villages.

---

[a] *4* Septuagint; Hebrew *your* [b] *18* Hebrew and some Septuagint manuscripts; other Septuagint manuscripts (see also note at Judges 1:14) *Othniel, he urged her* [c] *36* Or *Gederah and Gederothaim*

15:13 Word of God—Caleb was not afraid to face the giants of Hebron because he knew God would be with him. In the same way, we as Christians need not fear the "giants" we face in spiritual battle. God will be with us also. His resources are more than sufficient to overcome the hosts of darkness which confront us in this world (1 John 4:4).

15:3 [c] Nu 34:4 **15:4** [d] Nu 34:5 [e] Ge 15:18 **15:5** [f] Nu 34:10 [g] Jos 18:15-19 **15:6** [h] Jos 18:19,21 [i] Jos 18:17 **15:7** [j] Jos 7:24 [k] 2Sa 17:17; 1Ki 1:9

15:8 [l] ver 63; Jos 18:16,28; Jdg 1:21; 19:10 **15:9** [m] Jos 18:15 [n] 1Ch 13:6 **15:10** [o] Ge 38:12; Jdg 14:1 **15:11** [p] Jos 19:33 **15:12** [q] Nu 34:6 **15:13** [r] Jos 14:13-15 **15:14** [s] Nu 13:33 [t] Nu 13:22 [u] Jdg 1:10,20 **15:16** [v] Jdg 1:12 **15:17** [w] Jdg 3:9,11 **15:21** [x] Ge 35:21 **15:24** [y] 1Sa 23:14 **15:26** [z] 1Ch 4:28 **15:28** [a] Ge 21:31 **15:29** [b] ver 9 **15:30** [c] Jos 19:4 **15:31** [d] 1Sa 27:6 **15:32** [e] Jdg 20:45 **15:33** [f] Jdg 13:25; 16:31 **15:34** [g] 1Ch 4:18; Ne 3:13 **15:35** [h] Jos 10:3 [i] 1Sa 22:1 **15:36** [j] 1Ch 12:4 **15:38** [k] 2Ki 14:7 **15:39** [l] Jos 10:3; 2Ki 14:19 [m] 2Ki 22:1 **15:41** [n] Jos 10:10 **15:42** [o] 1Sa 30:30 **15:44** [p] Jdg 1:31 [q] Mic 1:15

45Ekron, with its surrounding settlements and villages; 46west of Ekron,
all that were in the vicinity of Ashdod,
together with their villages; 47Ash-
dod,[r] its surrounding settlements and
villages; and Gaza, its settlements and
villages, as far as the Wadi of Egypt[s]
and the coastline of the Mediterranean Sea.[t]

48In the hill country:

Shamir, Jattir,[u] Sokoh, 49Dan-
nah, Kiriath Sannah (that is, Debir[v]),
50Anab, Eshtemoh,[w] Anim, 51Goshen,[x]
Holon and Giloh—eleven towns and
their villages.

52Arab, Dumah,[y] Eshan, 53Janim,
Beth Tappuah, Aphekah, 54Humtah,
Kiriath Arba (that is, Hebron) and
Zior—nine towns and their villages.

55Maon, Carmel,[z] Ziph, Juttah,
56Jezreel,[a] Jokdeam, Zanoah, 57Kain,
Gibeah[b] and Timnah—ten towns and
their villages.

58Halhul, Beth Zur,[c] Gedor, 59Ma-
arath, Beth Anoth and Eltekon—six
towns and their villages.[a]

60Kiriath Baal (that is, Kiriath Jearim[d]) and Rabbah[e]—two towns and
their villages.

61In the wilderness:

Beth Arabah, Middin, Sekakah,
62Nibshan, the City of Salt and En
Gedi[f]—six towns and their villages.

63Judah could not[g] dislodge the Jebusites[h], who were living in Jerusalem; to this
day the Jebusites live there with the people
of Judah.

Allotment for Ephraim and Manasseh

16 The allotment for Joseph began at the Jordan, east of the
springs of Jericho, and went up from
there through the desert[i] into the hill
country of Bethel. 2It went on from
Bethel (that is, Luz[j]),[b] crossed over
to the territory of the Arkites in Ataroth, 3descended westward to the
territory of the Japhletites as far as
the region of Lower Beth Horon[k] and
on to Gezer,[l] ending at the Mediterranean Sea.

4So Manasseh and Ephraim, the descendants of Joseph, received their inheritance.[m]

5This was the territory of Ephraim, according to its clans:

The boundary of their inheritance
went from Ataroth Addar[n] in the east
to Upper Beth Horon 6and continued
to the Mediterranean Sea. From Mikmethath[o] on the north it curved eastward to Taanath Shiloh, passing by it
to Janoah on the east. 7Then it went
down from Janoah to Ataroth[p] and
Naarah, touched Jericho and came out
at the Jordan. 8From Tappuah the border went west to the Kanah Ravine[q]
and ended at the Mediterranean Sea.
This was the inheritance of the tribe
of the Ephraimites, according to its
clans. 9It also included all the towns
and their villages that were set aside
for the Ephraimites within the inheritance of the Manassites.

10They did not dislodge the Canaanites
living in Gezer; to this day the Canaanites
live among the people of Ephraim but are
required to do forced labor.[r]

17 This was the allotment for the tribe of
Manasseh as Joseph's firstborn,[s] that
is, for Makir,[t] Manasseh's firstborn. Makir was the ancestor of the Gileadites, who
had received Gilead and Bashan because
the Makirites were great soldiers. 2So this
allotment was for the rest of the people of
Manasseh—the clans of Abiezer,[u] Helek,
Asriel, Shechem, Hepher and Shemida.
These are the other male descendants of
Manasseh son of Joseph by their clans.

3Now Zelophehad son of Hepher,[v] the
son of Gilead, the son of Makir, the son of
Manasseh, had no sons but only daugh-
ters,[w] whose names were Mahlah, Noah,
Hoglah, Milkah and Tirzah. 4They went to
Eleazar the priest, Joshua son of Nun, and

[a] *59* The Septuagint adds another district of eleven towns, including Tekoa and Ephrathah (Bethlehem). [b] *2* Septuagint; Hebrew *Bethel to Luz*

15:63 *with the people of Judah.* Judges 1:21 repeats this verse almost verbatim, except that it says Benjamin, not Judah, failed to drive the Jebusites out of Jerusalem. Jerusalem sat astride the boundary between Judah and Benjamin. In the early period, Jerusalem did not belong strictly to either tribe. The tribe of Judah later captured the city from the Jebusites (Judg. 1:8), and from then on it was considered a city of Judah.

17:3–6 *Zelophehad ... had no sons but only daughters.* This account serves to show again the theme of the Book of Joshua—that God is faithful to keep His promises. Joshua also was faithful to carry out the commands of God concerning His promise through Moses for the daughters of Zelophehad (Num. 26:33; 27:1–11).

15:47 [r] Jos 11:22 [s] ver 4 [t] Nu 34:6 **15:48** [u] 1Sa 30:27 **15:49** [v] Jos 10:3 **15:50** [w] Jos 21:14 **15:51** [x] Jos 10:41; 11:16 **15:52** [y] Ge 25:14 **15:55** [z] Jos 12:22

15:56 [a] Jos 17:16 **15:57** [b] Jos 18:28; Jdg 19:12 **15:58** [c] 1Ch 2:45 **15:60** [d] Jos 18:14 [e] Dt 3:11 **15:62** [f] 1Sa 23:29 **15:63** [g] Jdg 1:21 [h] 2Sa 5:6 **16:1** [i] Jos 8:15; 18:12 **16:2** [j] Jos 18:13 **16:3** [k] 2Ch 8:5 [l] Jos 10:33; 1Ki 9:15 **16:4** [m] Jos 17:14 **16:5** [n] Jos 18:13 **16:6** [o] Jos 17:7 **16:7** [p] 1Ch 7:28 **16:8** [q] Jos 17:9 **16:10** [r] Jos 17:13; Jdg 1:28-29; 1Ki 9:16 **17:1** [s] Ge 41:51 [t] Ge 50:23 **17:2** [u] Nu 26:30; 1Ch 7:18 **17:3** [v] Nu 27:1 [w] Nu 26:33

the leaders and said, "The LORD commanded Moses to give us an inheritance among
our relatives." So Joshua gave them an inheritance along with the brothers of their
father, according to the LORD's command.[x]
5Manasseh's share consisted of ten tracts
of land besides Gilead and Bashan east
of the Jordan, 6because the daughters of
the tribe of Manasseh received an inheritance among the sons. The land of Gilead
belonged to the rest of the descendants of
Manasseh.

7The territory of Manasseh extended from Asher to Mikmethath[y] east of
Shechem.[z] The boundary ran southward from there to include the people
living at En Tappuah. 8(Manasseh had
the land of Tappuah, but Tappuah[a] itself, on the boundary of Manasseh,
belonged to the Ephraimites.) 9Then
the boundary continued south to the
Kanah Ravine.[b] There were towns belonging to Ephraim lying among the
towns of Manasseh, but the boundary
of Manasseh was the northern side of
the ravine and ended at the Mediterranean Sea. 10On the south the land
belonged to Ephraim, on the north to
Manasseh. The territory of Manasseh
reached the Mediterranean Sea and
bordered Asher on the north and Issachar[c] on the east.

11Within Issachar and Asher, Manasseh also had Beth Shan,[d] Ibleam
and the people of Dor,[e] Endor,[f] Taanach and Megiddo,[g] together with
their surrounding settlements (the
third in the list is Naphoth[a]).

12Yet the Manassites were not able[h] to occupy these towns, for the Canaanites were
determined to live in that region. 13Howev-
er, when the Israelites grew stronger, they
subjected the Canaanites to forced labor
but did not drive them out completely.[i]

14The people of Joseph said to Joshua,
"Why have you given us only one allotment and one portion for an inheritance?
We are a numerous people, and the LORD
has blessed us abundantly."[j]

15"If you are so numerous," Joshua answered, "and if the hill country of Ephraim
is too small for you, go up into the forest
and clear land for yourselves there in the
land of the Perizzites and Rephaites.[k]"

16The people of Joseph replied, "The hill
country is not enough for us, and all the
Canaanites who live in the plain have char-
iots fitted with iron,[l] both those in Beth
Shan and its settlements and those in the
Valley of Jezreel."

17But Joshua said to the tribes of Joseph—to Ephraim and Manasseh—"You
are numerous and very powerful. You will
have not only one allotment 18but the forested hill country as well. Clear it, and its
farthest limits will be yours; though the
Canaanites have chariots fitted with iron[m]
and though they are strong, you can drive
them out."

Division of the Rest of the Land

18 The whole assembly of the Israelites
gathered at Shiloh[n] and set up the
tent of meeting[o] there. The country was
brought under their control, 2but there
were still seven Israelite tribes who had not
yet received their inheritance.

3So Joshua said to the Israelites: "How
long will you wait before you begin to take
possession of the land that the LORD, the
God of your ancestors, has given you? 4Ap-
point three men from each tribe. I will send
them out to make a survey of the land and
to write a description of it, according to the
inheritance of each.[p] Then they will return
to me. 5You are to divide the land into seven
parts. Judah is to remain in its territory on
the south[q] and the tribes of Joseph in their
territory on the north.[r] 6After you have
written descriptions of the seven parts of
the land, bring them here to me and I will
cast lots[s] for you in the presence of the
LORD our God. 7The Levites, however, do
not get a portion among you, because the
priestly service of the LORD is their inheritance.[t] And Gad, Reuben and the half-tribe
of Manasseh have already received their
inheritance on the east side of the Jordan.
Moses the servant of the LORD gave it to
them.[u]"

8As the men started on their way to map

---

a 11 That is, Naphoth Dor

18:1 *Shiloh.* Shiloh was about 15 miles northwest of Jericho. Here the Israelites set up the tent of meeting (Ex. 26). This remained an important religious center for several hundred years (Judg. 18:31; 1 Sam. 1:9) until the taking of Jerusalem in David's day.

18:3 Unfaithfulness—The seven tribes yet to be settled seemed to have little desire to receive their inheritance and were rebuked for their half-heartedness. They had easily defeated the Canaanites, but they had not followed up on their victories and taken possession of all the land. This laziness was disobedience to God and showed lack of faith in His promises. In our own lives it is fatally easy to begin a work that God sets before us, and then slack off in our faithfulness before it is finished. The believer's inheritance is reserved in heaven, and cannot be bought by any work of our own. However, God requests holiness of living on our part, and His commands must be obeyed.

17:4 [x] Nu 27:5-7 **17:7** [y] Jos 16:6 [z] Ge 12:6; Jos 21:21 **17:8** [a] Jos 16:8 **17:9** [b] Jos 16:8 **17:10** [c] Ge 30:18 **17:11** [d] 1Sa 31:10; 1Ki 4:12; 1Ch 7:29 [e] Jos 11:2 [f] 1Sa 28:7; Ps 83:10 [g] 1Ki 9:15 **17:12** [h] Jdg 1:27 **17:13** [i] Jos 16:10 **17:14** [j] Nu 26:28-37 **17:15** [k] Ge 14:5 **17:16** [l] Jdg 1:19; 4:3,13 **17:18** [m] ver 16 **18:1** [n] Jos 19:51; 21:2; Jdg 18:31; 21:12,19; 1Sa 1:3; 4:3; Jer 7:12; 26:6 [o] Ex 27:21 **18:4** [p] Mic 2:5 **18:5** [q] Jos 15:1 [r] Jos 16:1-4 **18:6** [s] Jos 14:2 **18:7** [t] Jos 13:33 [u] Jos 13:8

out the land, Joshua instructed them, "Go and make a survey of the land and write a description of it. Then return to me, and I will cast lots for you here at Shiloh[v] in the presence of the LORD." 9So the men left and went through the land. They wrote its description on a scroll, town by town, in seven parts, and returned to Joshua in the camp at Shiloh. 10Joshua then cast lots[w] for them in Shiloh in the presence[x] of the LORD, and there he distributed the land to the Israelites according to their tribal divisions.[y]

Allotment for Benjamin

11The first lot came up for the tribe of Benjamin according to its clans. Their allotted territory lay between the tribes of Judah and Joseph:

12On the north side their boundary began at the Jordan, passed the northern slope of Jericho and headed west into the hill country, coming out at the wilderness[z] of Beth Aven.[a] 13From there it crossed to the south slope of Luz[b] (that is, Bethel[c]) and went down to Ataroth Addar[d] on the hill south of Lower Beth Horon.

14From the hill facing Beth Horon[e] on the south the boundary turned south along the western side and came out at Kiriath Baal (that is, Kiriath Jearim), a town of the people of Judah. This was the western side.

15The southern side began at the outskirts of Kiriath Jearim on the west, and the boundary came out at the spring of the waters of Nephtoah.[f] 16The boundary went down to the foot of the hill facing the Valley of Ben Hinnom, north of the Valley of Rephaim. It continued down the Hinnom Valley[g] along the southern slope of the Jebusite city and so to En Rogel.[h] 17It then curved north, went to En Shemesh, continued to Geliloth, which faces the Pass of Adummim, and ran down to the Stone of Bohan[i] son of Reuben. 18It continued to the northern slope of Beth Arabah[a][j] and on down into the Arabah. 19It then went to the northern slope of Beth Hoglah and came out at the northern bay of the Dead Sea,[k] at the mouth of the Jordan in the south. This was the southern boundary.

20The Jordan formed the boundary on the eastern side.

These were the boundaries that marked out the inheritance of the clans of Benjamin on all sides.[l]

21The tribe of Benjamin, according to its clans, had the following towns:

Jericho, Beth Hoglah, Emek Keziz, 22Beth Arabah, Zemaraim, Bethel,[m] 23Avvim, Parah, Ophrah, 24Kephar Ammoni, Ophni and Geba[n]—twelve towns and their villages.

25Gibeon,[o] Ramah,[p] Beeroth,[q] 26Mizpah,[r] Kephirah, Mozah, 27Rekem, Irpeel, Taralah, 28Zelah,[s] Haeleph, the Jebusite city[t] (that is, Jerusalem[u]), Gibeah[v] and Kiriath—fourteen towns and their villages.

This was the inheritance of Benjamin for its clans.

Allotment for Simeon

19 The second lot came out for the tribe of Simeon according to its clans. Their inheritance lay within the territory of Judah.[w] 2It included:

Beersheba[x] (or Sheba),[b] Moladah, 3Hazar Shual, Balah, Ezem, 4Eltolad, Bethul, Hormah, 5Ziklag, Beth Markaboth, Hazar Susah, 6Beth Lebaoth and Sharuhen—thirteen towns and their villages;

7Ain, Rimmon, Ether and Ashan[y]—four towns and their villages— 8and all the villages around these towns as far as Baalath Beer (Ramah in the Negev).[z]

This was the inheritance of the tribe of the Simeonites, according to its clans. 9The inheritance of the Simeonites was taken from the share of Judah,[a] because Judah's portion was more than they needed. So the Simeonites received their inheritance within the territory of Judah.[b]

Allotment for Zebulun

10The third lot came up for Zebulun[c] according to its clans:

The boundary of their inheritance went as far as Sarid. 11Going west it ran to Maralah, touched Dabbesheth, and extended to the ravine near Jokneam.[d] 12It turned east from Sarid toward the sunrise to the territory of Kisloth Tabor and went on to Daberath and up to Japhia. 13Then it continued eastward to Gath Hepher and Eth Kazin; it came out at Rimmon[e] and turned toward Neah. 14There the boundary went around on the north to Hannathon and ended at the Valley

[a] 18 Septuagint; Hebrew *slope facing the Arabah*
[b] 2 Or *Beersheba, Sheba*; 1 Chron. 4:28 does not have *Sheba*.

18:8 [v] ver 1 **18:10** [w] Nu 34:13 [x] ver 1; Jer 7:12 [y] Nu 33:54; Jos 19:51 **18:12** [z] Jos 16:1 [a] Jos 7:2 **18:13** [b] Ge 28:19 [c] Jdg 1:23 [d] Jos 16:5 **18:14** [e] Jos 10:10 **18:15** [f] Jos 15:9 **18:16** [g] Jos 15:8; 2Ki 23:10 [h] Jos 15:7 **18:17** [i] Jos 15:6 **18:18** [j] Jos 15:6 **18:19** [k] Ge 14:3 **18:20** [l] Jos 21:4, 17; 1Sa 9:1 **18:22** [m] Jos 16:1

18:24 [n] Isa 10:29 **18:25** [o] Jos 9:3 [p] Jdg 4:5 [q] Jos 9:17 **18:26** [r] Jos 11:3 **18:28** [s] 2Sa 21:14 [t] Jos 15:8 [u] Jos 10:1 [v] Jos 15:57 **19:1** [w] ver 9; Ge 49:7 **19:2** [x] Ge 21:14; 1Ki 19:3 **19:7** [y] Jos 15:42 **19:8** [z] Jos 10:40 **19:9** [a] Ge 49:7 [b] Eze 48:24 **19:10** [c] Jos 21:7, 34 **19:11** [d] Jos 12:22 **19:13** [e] Jos 15:32

of Iphtah El. 15Included were Kattath,
Nahalal, Shimron, Idalah and Bethlehem.[f] There were twelve towns and
their villages.
16These towns and their villages were the
inheritance of Zebulun,[g] according to its
clans.[h]

Allotment for Issachar

17The fourth lot came out for Issachar[i] according to its clans. 18Their territory included:
Jezreel,[j] Kesulloth, Shunem,[k]
19Hapharaim, Shion, Anaharath,
20Rabbith, Kishion, Ebez, 21Remeth,
En Gannim, En Haddah and Beth Paz-
zez. 22The boundary touched Tabor,[l]
Shahazumah and Beth Shemesh,[m]
and ended at the Jordan. There were
sixteen towns and their villages.
23These towns and their villages were the
inheritance of the tribe of Issachar,[n] according to its clans.[o]

Allotment for Asher

24The fifth lot came out for the tribe of Asher[p] according to its clans. 25Their territory
included:
Helkath, Hali, Beten, Akshaph, 26Al-
lammelek, Amad and Mishal. On the
west the boundary touched Carmel[q]
and Shihor Libnath. 27It then turned
east toward Beth Dagon, touched Zebulun[r] and the Valley of Iphtah El, and
went north to Beth Emek and Neiel,
passing Kabul[s] on the left. 28It went
to Abdon,[a] Rehob,[t] Hammon[u] and Kanah, as far as Greater Sidon.[v] 29The
boundary then turned back toward
Ramah[w] and went to the fortified city
of Tyre,[x] turned toward Hosah and
came out at the Mediterranean Sea
in the region of Akzib,[y] 30Ummah,
Aphek and Rehob. There were twenty-two towns and their villages.
31These towns and their villages were the
inheritance of the tribe of Asher,[z] according to its clans.

Allotment for Naphtali

32The sixth lot came out for Naphtali according to its clans:
33Their boundary went from He-
leph and the large tree in Zaanannim,
passing Adami Nekeb and Jabneel to
Lakkum and ending at the Jordan.
34The boundary ran west through Az-
noth Tabor and came out at Hukkok.
It touched Zebulun on the south, Asher on the west and the Jordan[b] on the
east. 35The fortified towns were Zid-
dim, Zer, Hammath, Rakkath, Kinnereth,[a] 36Adamah, Ramah,[b] Hazor,[c]
37Kedesh, Edrei,[d] En Hazor, 38Iron,
Migdal El, Horem, Beth Anath and
Beth Shemesh. There were nineteen
towns and their villages.
39These towns and their villages were the
inheritance of the tribe of Naphtali, according to its clans.[e]

Allotment for Dan

40The seventh lot came out for the tribe of
Dan according to its clans. 41The territory
of their inheritance included:
Zorah, Eshtaol, Ir Shemesh, 42Sha-
alabbin, Aijalon,[f] Ithlah, 43Elon, Timnah,[g] Ekron, 44Eltekeh, Gibbethon,
Baalath, 45Jehud, Bene Berak, Gath
Rimmon,[h] 46Me Jarkon and Rakkon,
with the area facing Joppa.[i]
47(When the territory of the Danites was
lost to them,[j] they went up and attacked Leshem[k], took it, put it to the sword and occupied it. They settled in Leshem and named
it Dan after their ancestor.)[l]
48These towns and their villages were the
inheritance of the tribe of Dan,[m] according
to its clans.

Allotment for Joshua

49When they had finished dividing the
land into its allotted portions, the Israelites gave Joshua son of Nun an inheritance
among them, 50as the LORD had commanded. They gave him the town he asked
for—Timnath Serah[c][n] in the hill country
of Ephraim. And he built up the town and
settled there.
51These are the territories that Eleazar
the priest, Joshua son of Nun and the heads
of the tribal clans of Israel assigned by lot
at Shiloh in the presence of the LORD at the
entrance to the tent of meeting. And so they
finished dividing the land.[o]

---

[a] *28* Some Hebrew manuscripts (see also 21:30); most Hebrew manuscripts *Ebron*
[b] *34* Septuagint; Hebrew *west, and Judah, the Jordan,* [c] *50* Also known as *Timnath Heres* (see Judges 2:9)

19:50 Commandments—The account of the distribution of the land began with the recognition of Caleb's faithfulness to God. The conclusion recognizes Joshua as one who also believed God. Joshua's extreme service and faithfulness was rewarded by the Lord's command. When we delight to obey the word of the Lord, He also delights in giving us the desires of our hearts (Ps. 37:4).

19:15 [f] Ge 35:19 **19:16** [g] ver 10; Jos 21:7 [h] Eze 48:26
19:17 [i] Ge 30:18 **19:18** [j] Jos 15:56 [k] 1Sa 28:4; 2Ki 4:8

19:22 [l] Jdg 4:6, 12; Ps 89:12 [m] Jos 15:10
19:23 [n] Jos 17:10 [o] Ge 49:15; Eze 48:25 **19:24** [p] Jos 17:7
19:26 [q] Jos 12:22 **19:27** [r] ver 10 [s] 1Ki 9:13
19:28 [t] Jdg 1:31 [u] 1Ch 6:76 [v] Ge 10:19; Jos 11:8
19:29 [w] Jos 18:25 [x] 2Sa 5:11; 24:7; Isa 23:1; Jer 25:22; Eze 26:2 [y] Jdg 1:31 **19:31** [z] Ge 30:13; Eze 48:2
19:35 [a] Jos 11:2 **19:36** [b] Jos 18:25 [c] Jos 11:1
19:37 [d] Nu 21:33 **19:39** [e] Dt 33:23; Eze 48:3
19:42 [f] Jdg 1:35 **19:43** [g] Ge 38:12 **19:45** [h] Jos 21:24; 1Ch 6:69 **19:46** [i] 2Ch 2:16; Jnh 1:3 **19:47** [j] Jdg 18:1 [k] Jdg 18:7, 14 [l] Jdg 18:27, 29 **19:48** [m] Ge 30:6
19:50 [n] Jos 24:30 **19:51** [o] Jos 14:1; 18:10; Ac 13:19

Cities of Refuge

20 Then the LORD said to Joshua: 2"Tell the Israelites to designate the cities of refuge, as I instructed you through Moses, 3so that anyone who kills a person accidentally and unintentionally[p] may flee there and find protection from the avenger of blood.[q] 4When they flee to one of these cities, they are to stand in the entrance of the city gate[r] and state their case before the elders[s] of that city. Then the elders are to admit the fugitive into their city and provide a place to live among them. 5If the avenger of blood comes in pursuit, the elders must not surrender the fugitive, because the fugitive killed their neighbor unintentionally and without malice aforethought. 6They are to stay in that city until they have stood trial before the assembly[t] and until the death of the high priest who is serving at that time. Then they may go back to their own home in the town from which they fled."

7So they set apart Kedesh[u] in Galilee in the hill country of Naphtali, Shechem[v] in the hill country of Ephraim, and Kiriath Arba (that is, Hebron[w]) in the hill country of Judah.[x] 8East of the Jordan (on the other side from Jericho) they designated Bezer[y] in the wilderness on the plateau in the tribe of Reuben, Ramoth in Gilead[z] in the tribe of Gad, and Golan in Bashan in the tribe of Manasseh. 9Any of the Israelites or any foreigner residing among them who killed someone accidentally could flee to these designated cities and not be killed by the avenger of blood prior to standing trial before the assembly.[a]

Towns for the Levites

21 Now the family heads of the Levites approached Eleazar the priest, Joshua son of Nun, and the heads of the other tribal families of Israel[b] 2at Shiloh[c] in Canaan and said to them, "The LORD commanded through Moses that you give us towns to live in, with pasturelands for our livestock."[d] 3So, as the LORD had commanded, the Israelites gave the Levites the following towns and pasturelands out of their own inheritance:

4The first lot came out for the Kohathites, according to their clans. The Levites who were descendants of Aaron the priest were allotted thirteen towns from the tribes of Judah, Simeon and Benjamin.[e] 5The rest of Kohath's descendants were allotted ten towns from the clans of the tribes of Ephraim, Dan and half of Manasseh.[f]

6The descendants of Gershon were allotted thirteen towns from the clans of the tribes of Issachar,[g] Asher, Naphtali and the half-tribe of Manasseh in Bashan.

7The descendants of Merari,[h] according to their clans, received twelve towns from the tribes of Reuben, Gad and Zebulun.[i]

8So the Israelites allotted to the Levites these towns and their pasturelands, as the LORD had commanded through Moses.

9From the tribes of Judah and Simeon they allotted the following towns by name 10(these towns were assigned to the descendants of Aaron who were from the Kohathite clans of the Levites, because the first lot fell to them):

11They gave them Kiriath Arba (that is, Hebron[j]), with its surrounding pastureland, in the hill country of Judah. (Arba was the forefather of Anak.) 12But the fields and villages around the city they had given to Caleb son of Jephunneh as his possession.

13So to the descendants of Aaron the priest they gave Hebron (a city of refuge for one accused of murder), Libnah,[k] 14Jattir,[l] Eshtemoa,[m] 15Holon,[n] Debir, 16Ain, Juttah[o] and Beth Shemesh,[p] together with their pasturelands—nine towns from these two tribes.

17And from the tribe of Benjamin they gave them Gibeon, Geba,[q] 18Anathoth and Almon, together with their pasturelands—four towns.

19The total number of towns for the priests, the descendants of Aaron, came to thirteen, together with their pasturelands.

20The rest of the Kohathite clans of the Levites were allotted towns from the tribe of Ephraim:

21In the hill country of Ephraim they were given Shechem[r] (a city of refuge for one accused of murder) and Gezer,

---

20:3 *accidentally.* God's laws made allowance for motive and intent, just as modern criminal codes distinguish unintentional killing from murder. The avenger of blood was a close relative who was the "protector of family rights." (Ruth 3:13 and 4:1 translate the word used here for "avenger of blood" as "guardian-redeemer.") God did not give license to take revenge however. He has clearly reserved that task for Himself alone (Deut. 32:35; Is. 34:8; Rom. 12:19). God's provision of these cities of refuge put a limit on private acts of vengeance.

20:7–8 *set apart.* The cities of refuge were evenly distributed so that none was more than a day's journey from any part of Israel's land.

21:4–8 *lot.* Even though this seems as if it was done by chance, we know God was in control of every aspect of the inheritance process.

20:3 [p] Lev 4:2 [q] Nu 35:12 **20:4** [r] Ru 4:1; Jer 38:7 [s] Jos 7:6 **20:6** [t] Nu 35:12 **20:7** [u] Jos 21:32; 1Ch 6:76 [v] Ge 12:6 [w] Jos 10:36; 21:11 [x] Lk 1:39 **20:8** [y] Jos 21:36; 1Ch 6:78 [z] Jos 12:2 **20:9** [a] Ex 21:13; Nu 35:15 **21:1** [b] Jos 14:1 **21:2** [c] Jos 18:1 [d] Nu 35:2-3 **21:4** [e] ver 19 **21:5** [f] ver 26 **21:6** [g] Ge 30:18 **21:7** [h] Ex 6:16 [i] Jos 19:10 **21:11** [j] Jos 15:13; 1Ch 6:55 **21:13** [k] Jos 15:42; 1Ch 6:57 **21:14** [l] Jos 15:48 [m] Jos 15:50 **21:15** [n] Jos 15:51 **21:16** [o] Jos 15:55 [p] Jos 15:10 **21:17** [q] Jos 18:24 **21:21** [r] Jos 17:7; 20:7

22Kibzaim and Beth Horon,[s] together
with their pasturelands—four towns.[t]
23Also from the tribe of Dan they
received Eltekeh, Gibbethon, 24Aija-
lon and Gath Rimmon,[u] together with
their pasturelands—four towns.
25From half the tribe of Manasseh they received Taanach and Gath
Rimmon, together with their pasturelands—two towns.
26All these ten towns and their pasturelands were given to the rest of the Kohathite clans.

27The Levite clans of the Gershonites were
given:
from the half-tribe of Manasseh,
Golan in Bashan[v] (a city of refuge for
one accused of murder[w]) and Be Esh-
terah, together with their pasturelands—two towns;
28from the tribe of Issachar,[x]
Kishion, Daberath, 29Jarmuth and En
Gannim, together with their pasturelands—four towns;
30from the tribe of Asher,[y]
Mishal, Abdon, 31Helkath and Rehob,
together with their pasturelands—
four towns;
32from the tribe of Naphtali,
Kedesh[z] in Galilee (a city of refuge for
one accused of murder[a]), Hammoth
Dor and Kartan, together with their
pasturelands—three towns.
33The total number of towns of the Gershonite[b] clans came to thirteen, together
with their pasturelands.

34The Merarite clans (the rest of the Levites) were given:
from the tribe of Zebulun,[c]
Jokneam, Kartah, 35Dimnah and
Nahalal, together with their pasturelands—four towns;
36from the tribe of Reuben,
Bezer,[d] Jahaz, 37Kedemoth and Mephaath, together with their pasturelands—four towns;
38from the tribe of Gad,
Ramoth[e] in Gilead (a city of refuge for
one accused of murder), Mahanaim,[f]
39Heshbon and Jazer, together with
their pasturelands—four towns in all.
40The total number of towns allotted to the
Merarite clans, who were the rest of the Levites, came to twelve.

41The towns of the Levites in the territory held by the Israelites were forty-eight
in all, together with their pasturelands.[g]
42Each of these towns had pasturelands
surrounding it; this was true for all these
towns.

43So the LORD gave Israel all the land
he had sworn to give their ancestors,[h]
and they took possession[i] of it and settled
there.[j] 44The LORD gave them rest[k] on every
side, just as he had sworn to their ancestors. Not one of their enemies[l] withstood
them; the LORD gave all their enemies[m] into
their hands.[n] 45Not one of all the LORD's
good promises[o] to Israel failed; every one
was fulfilled.

Eastern Tribes Return Home

22 Then Joshua summoned the Reubenites, the Gadites and the half-tribe of
Manasseh 2and said to them, "You have
done all that Moses the servant of the LORD
commanded,[p] and you have obeyed me in
everything I commanded. 3For a long time
now—to this very day—you have not deserted your fellow Israelites but have carried out the mission the LORD your God
gave you. 4Now that the LORD your God
has given them rest as he promised, return
to your homes[q] in the land that Moses the
servant of the LORD gave you on the other
side of the Jordan.[r] 5But be very careful to
keep the commandment[s] and the law that
Moses the servant of the LORD gave you: to
love the LORD your God, to walk in obedience to him, to keep his commands,[t] to hold
fast to him and to serve him with all your
heart and with all your soul.[u]"
6Then Joshua blessed[v] them and sent
them away, and they went to their homes.
7(To the half-tribe of Manasseh Moses had
given land in Bashan,[w] and to the other half
of the tribe Joshua gave land on the west
side[x] of the Jordan along with their fellow
Israelites.) When Joshua sent them home,
he blessed them, 8saying, "Return to your
homes with your great wealth—with large
herds of livestock,[y] with silver, gold, bronze
and iron, and a great quantity of clothing—
and divide[z] the plunder[a] from your enemies
with your fellow Israelites."
9So the Reubenites, the Gadites and the
half-tribe of Manasseh left the Israelites at
Shiloh in Canaan to return to Gilead,[b] their

21:43–45 *he had sworn.* Again we see the nature of our God—not only did He keep every promise, He also guaranteed that His people would have rest.

22:5 Perseverance—Past victories do not lessen the responsibility for present faithfulness. Joshua impressed upon the people, especially the tribes of Reuben, Gad and Manasseh (because they would be living in isolation from the rest of Israel), the urgent need to continue to zealously serve God. Our zeal for the Lord cannot cease because a crisis has passed. There is no certificate of discharge from the army of Christ.

21:22 [s] Jos 10:10 [t] 1Sa 1:1 **21:24** [u] Jos 19:45
21:27 [v] Jos 12:5 [w] Nu 35:6 **21:28** [x] Ge 30:18
21:30 [y] Jos 17:7 **21:32** [z] Jos 12:22 [a] Nu 35:6; Jos 20:7
21:33 [b] ver 6 **21:34** [c] Jos 19:10; 1Ch 6:77
21:36 [d] Jos 20:8 **21:38** [e] Dt 4:43 [f] Ge 32:2
21:41 [g] Nu 35:7 **21:43** [h] Dt 34:4 [i] Dt 11:31 [j] Dt 17:14
21:44 [k] Ex 33:14; Jos 1:13 [l] Dt 6:19 [m] Ex 23:31 [n] Dt 7:24; 21:10 **21:45** [o] Jos 23:14; Ne 9:8 **22:2** [p] Nu 32:25
22:4 [q] Nu 32:22; Dt 3:20 [r] Nu 32:18; Jos 1:13-15
22:5 [s] Isa 43:22 [t] Dt 5:29 [u] Dt 6:6, 17 **22:6** [v] Ex 39:43
22:7 [w] Nu 32:33; Jos 12:5 [x] Jos 17:2, 5 **22:8** [y] Dt 20:14 [z] Nu 31:27 [a] Ge 49:27; 1Sa 30:16; Isa 9:3
22:9 [b] Nu 32:26, 29

own land, which they had acquired in accordance with the command of the LORD
through Moses.
10When they came to Geliloth near the
Jordan in the land of Canaan, the Reubenites, the Gadites and the half-tribe of Manasseh built an imposing altar there by the
Jordan. 11And when the Israelites heard
that they had built the altar on the border
of Canaan at Geliloth near the Jordan on
the Israelite side, 12the whole assembly
of Israel gathered at Shiloh[c] to go to war
against them.
13So the Israelites sent Phinehas[d] son
of Eleazar,[e] the priest, to the land of Gilead—to Reuben, Gad and the half-tribe of
Manasseh. 14With him they sent ten of the
chief men, one from each of the tribes of
Israel, each the head of a family division
among the Israelite clans.[f]
15When they went to Gilead—to Reuben, Gad and the half-tribe of Manasseh—
they said to them: 16"The whole assembly
of the LORD says: 'How could you break
faith[g] with the God of Israel like this?
How could you turn away from the LORD
and build yourselves an altar in rebellion[h]
against him now? 17Was not the sin of Peor[i]
enough for us? Up to this very day we have
not cleansed ourselves from that sin, even
though a plague fell on the community of
the LORD! 18And are you now turning away
from the LORD?
"'If you rebel against the LORD today, tomorrow he will be angry with the whole
community[j] of Israel. 19If the land you
possess is defiled, come over to the LORD's
land, where the LORD's tabernacle stands,
and share the land with us. But do not rebel
against the LORD or against us by building
an altar for yourselves, other than the altar
of the LORD our God. 20When Achan son of
Zerah was unfaithful in regard to the devoted things,[a][k] did not wrath[l] come on the
whole community of Israel? He was not the
only one who died for his sin.'"[m]
21Then Reuben, Gad and the half-tribe of
Manasseh replied to the heads of the clans
of Israel: 22"The Mighty One, God, the
LORD! The Mighty One, God,[n] the LORD![o]
He knows![p] And let Israel know! If this
has been in rebellion or disobedience to
the LORD, do not spare us this day. 23If we
have built our own altar to turn away from
the LORD and to offer burnt offerings and
grain offerings,[q] or to sacrifice fellowship
offerings on it, may the LORD himself call
us to account.[r]
24"No! We did it for fear that some day
your descendants might say to ours, 'What
do you have to do with the LORD, the God
of Israel? 25The LORD has made the Jordan
a boundary between us and you—you Reubenites and Gadites! You have no share in
the LORD.' So your descendants might
cause ours to stop fearing the LORD.
26"That is why we said, 'Let us get ready
and build an altar—but not for burnt offerings or sacrifices.' 27On the contrary, it is to
be a witness[s] between us and you and the
generations that follow, that we will worship the LORD at his sanctuary with our
burnt offerings, sacrifices and fellowship
offerings.[t] Then in the future your descendants will not be able to say to ours, 'You
have no share in the LORD.'
28"And we said, 'If they ever say this to
us, or to our descendants, we will answer:
Look at the replica of the LORD's altar,
which our ancestors built, not for burnt
offerings and sacrifices, but as a witness
between us and you.'
29"Far be it from us to rebel[u] against the
LORD and turn away from him today by
building an altar for burnt offerings, grain
offerings and sacrifices, other than the altar of the LORD our God that stands before
his tabernacle.[v]"
30When Phinehas the priest and the leaders of the community—the heads of the
clans of the Israelites—heard what Reuben, Gad and Manasseh had to say, they
were pleased. 31And Phinehas son of Eleazar, the priest, said to Reuben, Gad and
Manasseh, "Today we know that the LORD
is with us,[w] because you have not been

[a] *20* The Hebrew term refers to the irrevocable giving over of things or persons to the LORD, often by totally destroying them.

22:11–12 *had built the altar.* The Bible does not reveal why this altar was built until the events have developed into a full blown crisis. God had commanded Israel not to offer burnt offerings or sacrifices at any location except the tabernacle (Lev. 17:8–9) and not to worship other gods (Deut. 13:12–15). The punishment for violating both laws was death. This was why Israel gathered together to go to war against the three apparently erring tribes.

22:16–18 *break faith.* This is sometimes translated "trespass" and is the same word used to describe Achan's sin (7:1). No one can sin in isolation. If the tribes east of the Jordan were indeed sinning, then the entire nation would feel the effects, as in the case of Achan.

22:23–28 *We did it for fear.* The tribes to the east of the Jordan were afraid that geographical distance would isolate them and in time cause the Israelites west of the Jordan to reject them. Thus they built the altar to help prevent the existing unity from being lost. The eastern tribes were careful to label the altar for what it really was—a replica to serve as a witness for future generations.

22:30–31 Prudence—Jumping to conclusions can bring one to the brink of disaster. While their

22:12 [c] Jos 18:1 **22:13** [d] Nu 25:7 [e] Nu 3:32; Jos 24:33
22:14 [f] Nu 1:4 **22:16** [g] Dt 13:14 [h] Dt 12:13-14
22:17 [i] Nu 25:1-9 **22:18** [j] Lev 10:6; Nu 16:22
22:20 [k] Jos 7:1 [l] Ps 7:11 [m] Jos 7:5 **22:22** [n] Dt 10:17
[o] Ps 50:1 [p] 1Ki 8:39; Job 10:7; Ps 44:21; Jer 17:10
22:23 [q] Jer 41:5 [r] Dt 12:11; 18:19; 1Sa 20:16
22:27 [s] Ge 21:30; Jos 24:27 [t] Dt 12:6 **22:29** [u] Jos 24:16
[v] Dt 12:13-14 **22:31** [w] Lev 26:11-12; 2Ch 15:2

unfaithful to the LORD in this matter. Now you have rescued the Israelites from the LORD's hand."

32 Then Phinehas son of Eleazar, the priest, and the leaders returned to Canaan from their meeting with the Reubenites and Gadites in Gilead and reported to the Israelites. 33 They were glad to hear the report and praised God.[x] And they talked no more about going to war against them to devastate the country where the Reubenites and the Gadites lived.

34 And the Reubenites and the Gadites gave the altar this name: A Witness[y] Between Us—that the LORD is God.

Joshua's Farewell to the Leaders

23 After a long time had passed and the LORD had given Israel rest[z] from all their enemies around them, Joshua, by then a very old man,[a] 2 summoned all Israel—their elders,[b] leaders, judges and officials[c]—and said to them: "I am very old. 3 You yourselves have seen everything the LORD your God has done to all these nations for your sake; it was the LORD your God who fought for you.[d] 4 Remember how I have allotted[e] as an inheritance for your tribes all the land of the nations that remain—the nations I conquered—between the Jordan and the Mediterranean Sea[f] in the west. 5 The LORD your God himself will push them out for your sake. He will drive them out before you, and you will take possession of their land, as the LORD your God promised you.[g]

6 "Be very strong; be careful to obey all that is written in the Book of the Law of Moses, without turning aside to the right or to the left.[h] 7 Do not associate with these nations that remain among you; do not invoke the names of their gods or swear[i] by them. You must not serve them or bow down[j] to them. 8 But you are to hold fast to the LORD[k] your God, as you have until now.

9 "The LORD has driven out before you great and powerful nations;[l] to this day no one has been able to withstand you.[m] 10 One of you routs a thousand,[n] because the LORD your God fights for you,[o] just as he promised. 11 So be very careful to love the LORD[p] your God.

12 "But if you turn away and ally yourselves with the survivors of these nations that remain among you and if you intermarry with them[q] and associate with them,[r] 13 then you may be sure that the LORD your God will no longer drive out these nations before you. Instead, they will become snares[s] and traps for you, whips on your backs and thorns in your eyes,[t] until you perish from this good land, which the LORD your God has given you.

14 "Now I am about to go the way of all the earth.[u] You know with all your heart and soul that not one of all the good promises the LORD your God gave you has failed. Every promise has been fulfilled; not one has failed.[v] 15 But just as all the good things the LORD your God has promised you have come to you, so he will bring on you all the evil things he has threatened, until the LORD your God has destroyed you from this good land he has given you.[w] 16 If you violate the covenant of the LORD your God, which he commanded you, and go and serve other gods and bow down to them, the LORD's anger will burn against you, and you will quickly perish from the good land he has given you.[x]"

The Covenant Renewed at Shechem

24 Then Joshua assembled all the tribes of Israel at Shechem. He summoned

---

motives were good (maintaining purity), they did not stop to find out what was really going on. This incident provides us with a good example of the importance of communicating before we act. Even when we are dealing with a case of serious sin (as the western tribes thought they were), the first reaction should be to try and persuade the sinner to repent and return to the Lord.

23:3 *who fought for you.* This is a reminder that the land belonged to the Lord and that He gave it to Israel.

23:10 *One of you routs a thousand.* The power seen in God's people was so dramatic it had to be miraculous.

23:11 Duty—Certain outlines of duty are imposed on all mankind (Mic. 6:8). We know that one man's specific duty may differ from another's, but all share a single common requirement: all must give account before God of what they have done or left undone. The church cannot decide how well each person is performing; there is no "spiritual commitment meter" to give an exact rating of each person's fulfillment of duty. Each person is responsible to maintain his or her own spiritual life.

23:12–13 *intermarry with them.* Years later, Solomon ignored this command and proved how destructive the sin of being unequally yoked could be (1 Kin. 3:1; 11:1–8; 2 Cor. 6:14).

23:16 *perish from the good land.* This warning saw its most dramatic fulfillment when Judah was carried into Babylon because of its repeated rebellion against God (2 Kin. 25). The saddest thing is that Israel's rebellion began almost immediately. God lovingly gave them every good thing, but when they disobeyed, they had to be punished.

24:1 *Shechem.* Shechem was a site of ancient religious significance and covenant making going back to Abraham's day (Gen. 12:6; 33:18–20).

22:33 [x] 1Ch 29:20; Da 2:19; Lk 2:28 **22:34** [y] Ge 21:30
23:1 [z] Dt 12:9; Jos 21:44 [a] Jos 13:1 **23:2** [b] Jos 7:6 [c] Jos 24:1 **23:3** [d] Ex 14:14 **23:4** [e] Jos 19:51 [f] Nu 34:6
23:5 [g] Ex 23:30; Nu 33:53 **23:6** [h] Dt 5:32; Jos 1:7
23:7 [i] Ex 23:13; Ps 16:4; Jer 5:7 [j] Ex 20:5 **23:8** [k] Dt 10:20
23:9 [l] Dt 11:23 [m] Dt 7:24 **23:10** [n] Lev 26:8 [o] Ex 14:14; Dt 3:22 **23:11** [p] Jos 22:5 **23:12** [q] Dt 7:3 [r] Ex 34:16; Ps 106:34-35 **23:13** [s] Ex 23:33 [t] Nu 33:55
23:14 [u] 1Ki 2:2 [v] Jos 21:45 **23:15** [w] Lev 26:17; Dt 28:15
23:16 [x] Dt 4:25-26

the elders, leaders, judges and officials of
Israel,[y] and they presented themselves before God.
2Joshua said to all the people, "This is
what the LORD, the God of Israel, says:
'Long ago your ancestors, including Terah
the father of Abraham and Nahor, lived beyond the Euphrates River and worshiped
other gods.[z] **3**But I took your father Abraham from the land beyond the Euphrates
and led him throughout Canaan[a] and gave
him many descendants.[b] I gave him Isaac,[c]
4and to Isaac I gave Jacob and Esau.[d] I assigned the hill country of Seir[e] to Esau, but
Jacob and his family went down to Egypt.[f]
5" 'Then I sent Moses and Aaron,[g] and I
afflicted the Egyptians by what I did there,
and I brought you out. **6**When I brought
your people out of Egypt, you came to the
sea, and the Egyptians pursued them with
chariots and horsemen[a][h] as far as the Red
Sea.[b] **7**But they cried to the LORD for help,
and he put darkness[i] between you and the
Egyptians; he brought the sea over them
and covered them.[j] You saw with your own
eyes what I did to the Egyptians. Then you
lived in the wilderness for a long time.[k]
8" 'I brought you to the land of the Amorites who lived east of the Jordan. They
fought against you, but I gave them into
your hands. I destroyed them from before
you, and you took possession of their land.[l]
9When Balak son of Zippor,[m] the king of
Moab, prepared to fight against Israel, he
sent for Balaam son of Beor to put a curse
on you.[n] **10**But I would not listen to Balaam,
so he blessed you[o] again and again, and I
delivered you out of his hand.
11" 'Then you crossed the Jordan[p] and
came to Jericho.[q] The citizens of Jericho
fought against you, as did also the Amorites, Perizzites, Canaanites, Hittites, Girgashites, Hivites and Jebusites, but I gave
them into your hands.[r] **12**I sent the hornet[s]
ahead of you, which drove them out before
you—also the two Amorite kings. You did
not do it with your own sword and bow.
13So I gave you a land on which you did
not toil and cities you did not build; and you
live in them and eat from vineyards and olive groves that you did not plant.'[t]
14"Now fear the LORD and serve him
with all faithfulness.[u] Throw away the
gods[v] your ancestors worshiped beyond
the Euphrates River and in Egypt,[w] and
serve the LORD. **15**But if serving the LORD
seems undesirable to you, then choose for
yourselves this day whom you will serve,
whether the gods your ancestors served
beyond the Euphrates, or the gods of the
Amorites,[x] in whose land you are living.
But as for me and my household, we will
serve the LORD."[y]
16Then the people answered, "Far be it
from us to forsake the LORD to serve other gods! **17**It was the LORD our God himself
who brought us and our parents up out of
Egypt, from that land of slavery, and performed those great signs before our eyes.
He protected us on our entire journey and
among all the nations through which we
traveled. **18**And the LORD drove out before
us all the nations, including the Amorites,
who lived in the land. We too will serve the
LORD, because he is our God."
19Joshua said to the people, "You are not
able to serve the LORD. He is a holy God;[z] he
is a jealous God.[a] He will not forgive your
rebellion[b] and your sins. **20**If you forsake
the LORD[c] and serve foreign gods, he will
turn[d] and bring disaster on you and make
an end of you,[e] after he has been good to
you."
21But the people said to Joshua, "No! We
will serve the LORD."
22Then Joshua said, "You are witnesses
against yourselves that you have chosen[f] to
serve the LORD."
"Yes, we are witnesses," they replied.
23"Now then," said Joshua, "throw away
the foreign gods[g] that are among you and
yield your hearts[h] to the LORD, the God of
Israel."
24And the people said to Joshua, "We will
serve the LORD our God and obey him."[i]
25On that day Joshua made a covenant[j]
for the people, and there at Shechem he
reaffirmed for them decrees and laws.[k]
26And Joshua recorded these things in the
Book of the Law of God.[l] Then he took a
large stone[m] and set it up there under the
oak near the holy place of the LORD.
27"See!" he said to all the people. "This
stone will be a witness[n] against us. It has
heard all the words the LORD has said to us.
It will be a witness against you if you are
untrue to your God."

---

a 6 Or *charioteers* *b* 6 Or *the Sea of Reeds*

24:13 ***a land on which you did not toil.*** This fulfills the promise given to Moses in Deuteronomy 6:10–11. The land was a gift from God to His people. In a similar sense, He has given us another gift for which we did not labor. The gift of salvation, through Jesus Christ, cannot be bought or paid for; it is graciously given from a loving God to those who will accept it.

24:15 ***as for me and my household.*** Joshua's famous words show the stand we must take—on the side of the living God.

24:1 [y] Jos 23:2 **24:2** [z] Ge 11:32 **24:3** [a] Ge 12:1 [b] Ge 15:5 [c] Ge 21:3 **24:4** [d] Ge 25:26 [e] Dt 2:5 [f] Ge 46:5-6 **24:5** [g] Ex 3:10 **24:6** [h] Ex 14:9 **24:7** [i] Ex 14:20 [j] Ex 14:28 [k] Dt 1:46 **24:8** [l] Nu 21:31 **24:9** [m] Nu 22:2 [n] Nu 22:6 **24:10** [o] Nu 23:11; Dt 23:5 **24:11** [p] Jos 3:16-17 [q] Jos 6:1 [r] Ex 23:23; Dt 7:1 **24:12** [s] Ex 23:28; Dt 7:20; Ps 44:3, 6-7 **24:13** [t] Dt 6:10-11 **24:14** [u] Dt 10:12; 18:13; 1Sa 12:24; 2Co 1:12 [v] ver 23 [w] Eze 23:3 **24:15** [x] Jdg 6:10; Ru 1:15 [y] Ru 1:16; 1Ki 18:21 **24:19** [z] Lev 19:2; 20:26 [a] Ex 20:5 [b] Ex 23:21 **24:20** [c] 1Ch 28:9, 20 [d] Ac 7:42 [e] Jos 23:15 **24:22** [f] Ps 119:30, 173 **24:23** [g] ver 14 [h] 1Ki 8:58, Ps 119:36; 141:4 **24:24** [i] Ex 19:8; 24:3, 7; Dt 5:27 **24:25** [j] Ex 24:8 [k] Ex 15:25 **24:26** [l] Dt 31:24 [m] Ge 28:18 **24:27** [n] Jos 22:27

28Then Joshua dismissed the people,
each to their own inheritance.

Buried in the Promised Land

29After these things, Joshua son of Nun,
the servant of the LORD, died at the age of
a hundred and ten.[o] 30And they buried him
in the land of his inheritance, at Timnath
Serah[a][p] in the hill country of Ephraim,
north of Mount Gaash.

31Israel served the LORD throughout
the lifetime of Joshua and of the elders[q]
who outlived him and who had experienced everything the LORD had done for
Israel.

32And Joseph's bones, which the Israelites had brought up from Egypt,[r] were
buried at Shechem in the tract of land[s] that
Jacob bought for a hundred pieces of silver[b] from the sons of Hamor, the father of
Shechem. This became the inheritance of
Joseph's descendants.

33And Eleazar son of Aaron[t] died and
was buried at Gibeah, which had been allotted to his son Phinehas[u] in the hill country of Ephraim.

[a] *30* Also known as *Timnath Heres* (see Judges 2:9)
[b] *32* Hebrew *hundred kesitahs;* a kesitah was a unit of money of unknown weight and value.

24:32 *Joseph's bones.* The brief account of the transfer of Joseph's body to Canaan from Egypt notes the fulfillment of Joseph's prophecy hundreds of years before (Gen. 50:24–25).

24:29 [o] Jdg 2:8 **24:30** [p] Jos 19:50 **24:31** [q] Jdg 2:7
24:32 [r] Ge 50:25; Ex 13:19 [s] Ge 33:19; Jn 4:5; Ac 7:16
24:33 [t] Jos 22:13 [u] Ex 6:25

JUDGES

▶ **AUTHOR:** Although the author of Judges is anonymous, Jewish tradition contained in the Talmud attributes Judges to Samuel. Samuel lived during the time the book could have been written, and he was a principal character in the transition to the next phase. He would have been aware of the events that occur in the book. Samuel certainly was the crucial link between the period of the judges and the period of the kings. His prophetic ministry clearly fits the moral commentary of Judges, and the consistent style and orderly scheme of the book points to a single compiler.

▶ **TIME:** c. 1380 – 1045 B.C. ▶ **KEY VERSES:** Judg. 2:20 – 21

▶ **THEME:** During the Book of Judges, the land wasn't fully conquered. There was political chaos. The Israelites appeared to live mostly in the land between the cities of the Philistines, who dominate them much of the time. Two common phrases occur in the book: The first is the Israelites "did evil in the eyes of the LORD." The second is "everyone did as they saw fit." In the midst of this situation God raises up judges, who in addition to playing the role of adjudicator, also provide leadership in pulling the tribes together to fight the unconquered nations. Most are reluctant. Nevertheless, God is able to use them and demonstrate His power through these individuals.

Israel Fights the Remaining Canaanites

1 After the death[a] of Joshua, the Israelites
asked the LORD, "Who of us is to go up
first[b] to fight against the Canaanites?[c]"
2The LORD answered, "Judah[d] shall go
up; I have given the land into their hands.[e]"
3The men of Judah then said to the Simeonites their fellow Israelites, "Come up
with us into the territory allotted to us, to
fight against the Canaanites. We in turn
will go with you into yours." So the Simeonites[f] went with them.
4When Judah attacked, the LORD gave
the Canaanites and Perizzites[g] into their
hands, and they struck down ten thousand men at Bezek.[h] 5It was there that they
found Adoni-Bezek and fought against
him, putting to rout the Canaanites and
Perizzites. 6Adoni-Bezek fled, but they
chased him and caught him, and cut off
his thumbs and big toes.
7Then Adoni-Bezek said, "Seventy kings
with their thumbs and big toes cut off have
picked up scraps under my table. Now God
has paid me back[i] for what I did to them."
They brought him to Jerusalem, and he
died there.
8The men of Judah attacked Jerusalem[j]
also and took it. They put the city to the
sword and set it on fire.
9After that, Judah went down to fight
against the Canaanites living in the hill
country,[k] the Negev[l] and the western foothills. 10They advanced against the Canaanites living in Hebron[m] (formerly called
Kiriath Arba[n]) and defeated Sheshai, Ahiman and Talmai.[o] 11From there they advanced against the people living in Debir[p]
(formerly called Kiriath Sepher).

1:1 ***After the death of Joshua.*** Judges begins as the Book of Joshua does, with reference to the death of the previous leader. Yet no new leader was commissioned to lead Israel after Joshua. The tribe of Judah was designated to lead in the fight against the Canaanites, the first hint of the fulfillment of Jacob's prophecy (Gen. 49:8 – 12).
1:3 ***Judah ... Simeonites.*** History bound the tribes of Judah and Simeon together. They were descended from the same mother (Gen. 29:33 – 35), and Simeon had inherited land in Judah's territory (Josh. 19:1,9).
1:6 – 7 ***thumbs and big toes.*** To cut off a warrior's thumbs and big toes would prevent him from ever engaging in battle again, besides subjecting him to pain and humiliation.
1:8 ***Jerusalem.*** Jerusalem was captured and burned, but not settled. The complete conquest and settlement of Jerusalem was not accomplished until David's day (2 Sam. 5:6 – 10).
1:10 ***Hebron.*** Hebron, about 20 miles southwest of

1:1 [a] Jos 24:29 [b] Nu 27:21 [c] ver 27; Jdg 3:1-6
1:2 [d] Ge 49:8 [e] ver 4; Jdg 3:28 **1:3** [f] ver 17
1:4 [g] Ge 13:7; Jos 3:10 [h] 1Sa 11:8 **1:7** [i] Lev 24:19
1:8 [j] ver 21; Jos 15:63 **1:9** [k] Nu 13:17 [l] Nu 21:1
1:10 [m] Ge 13:18 [n] Ge 35:27 [o] Jos 15:14 **1:11** [p] Jos 15:15

12 And Caleb said, "I will give my daughter Aksah in marriage to the man who attacks and captures Kiriath Sepher." 13 Othniel son of Kenaz, Caleb's younger brother, took it; so Caleb gave his daughter Aksah to him in marriage.

14 One day when she came to Othniel, she urged him[a] to ask her father for a field. When she got off her donkey, Caleb asked her, "What can I do for you?"

15 She replied, "Do me a special favor. Since you have given me land in the Negev, give me also springs of water." So Caleb gave her the upper and lower springs.

16 The descendants of Moses' father-in-law,[q] the Kenite,[r] went up from the City of Palms[b][s] with the people of Judah to live among the inhabitants of the Desert of Judah in the Negev near Arad.[t]

17 Then the men of Judah went with the Simeonites[u] their fellow Israelites and attacked the Canaanites living in Zephath, and they totally destroyed[c] the city. Therefore it was called Hormah.[d][v] 18 Judah also took[e] Gaza,[w] Ashkelon and Ekron—each city with its territory.

19 The LORD was with[x] the men of Judah. They took possession of the hill country, but they were unable to drive the people from the plains, because they had chariots fitted with iron.[y] 20 As Moses had promised, Hebron[z] was given to Caleb, who drove from it the three sons of Anak.[a] 21 The Benjamites, however, did not drive out[b] the Jebusites, who were living in Jerusalem;[c] to this day the Jebusites live there with the Benjamites.

22 Now the tribes of Joseph attacked Bethel, and the LORD was with them. 23 When they sent men to spy out Bethel (formerly called Luz),[d] 24 the spies saw a man coming out of the city and they said to him, "Show us how to get into the city and we will see that you are treated well."[e] 25 So he showed them, and they put the city to the sword but spared[f] the man and his whole family. 26 He then went to the land of the Hittites, where he built a city and called it Luz, which is its name to this day.

27 But Manasseh did not drive out the people of Beth Shan or Taanach or Dor or Ibleam[g] or Megiddo and their surrounding settlements, for the Canaanites[h] were determined to live in that land. 28 When Israel became strong, they pressed the Canaanites into forced labor but never drove them out completely. 29 Nor did Ephraim drive out the Canaanites living in Gezer,[i] but the Canaanites continued to live there among them.[j] 30 Neither did Zebulun drive out the Canaanites living in Kitron or Nahalol, so these Canaanites lived among them, but Zebulun did subject them to forced labor. 31 Nor did Asher drive out those living in Akko or Sidon or Ahlab or Akzib[k] or Helbah or Aphek or Rehob. 32 The Asherites lived among the Canaanite inhabitants of the land because they did not drive them out. 33 Neither did Naphtali drive out those living in Beth Shemesh or Beth Anath[l]; but the Naphtalites too lived among the Canaanite inhabitants of the land, and those living in Beth Shemesh and Beth Anath became forced laborers for them. 34 The Amorites[m] confined the Danites to the hill country, not allowing them to come down into the plain. 35 And the Amorites were determined also to hold out in Mount Heres, Aijalon[n] and Shaalbim, but when the power of the tribes of Joseph increased, they too were pressed into forced labor. 36 The boundary of the Amorites was from Scorpion Pass[o] to Sela and beyond.

The Angel of the LORD at Bokim

2 The angel of the LORD[p] went up from Gilgal to Bokim[q] and said, "I brought you up out of Egypt[r] and led you into the land I swore to give to your ancestors.[s] I said, 'I will never break my covenant with

---

[a] *14* Hebrew; Septuagint and Vulgate *Othniel, he urged her* [b] *16* That is, Jericho [c] *17* The Hebrew term refers to the irrevocable giving over of things or persons to the LORD, often by totally destroying them. [d] *17 Hormah* means *destruction.* [e] *18* Hebrew; Septuagint *Judah did not take*

Jerusalem, was where Abraham settled and built an altar (Gen. 13:18).

1:16 *the Kenite.* The Kenites were Midianites, descendants of Abraham's son by Keturah (Gen. 25:1–4).

1:18 *Gaza, Ashkelon and Ekron.* Israel was not able to hold these cities for long. By Samson's day, all three were in Philistine hands again (14:19; 16:1; 1 Sam. 5:10).

1:21 Unfaithfulness—This verse duplicates Joshua 15:63 almost exactly, except that in Joshua the tribe of Judah is held responsible. Jerusalem lay on the border between Judah and Benjamin; either or both tribes were responsible for driving out the Canaanites. Their failure to do so was not because the task was too hard, but because they did not really take God's commands and promises seriously. Jerusalem was not claimed for Israel until David came, a man who trusted the Lord for his victories and obeyed His word. Victories for the Lord are won only through faith.

1:22 *Bethel.* Bethel means "house of God." It was a site with an honored history, beginning with Abraham's first sacrifice to God (Gen. 13:3–4) and Jacob's revelation from God there (Gen. 31:13).

2:1 *the angel of the LORD.* The angel of the Lord

1:16 [q] Nu 10:29 [r] Ge 15:19; Jdg 4:11 [s] Dt 34:3; Jdg 3:13 [t] Nu 21:1 **1:17** [u] ver 3 [v] Nu 21:3 **1:18** [w] Jos 11:22 **1:19** [x] ver 2 [y] Jos 17:16 **1:20** [z] Jos 14:9; 15:13-14 [a] ver 10; Jos 14:13 **1:21** [b] Jos 15:63 [c] ver 8 **1:23** [d] Ge 28:19 **1:24** [e] Jos 2:12, 14 **1:25** [f] Jos 6:25 **1:27** [g] Jos 17:11 [h] ver 1 **1:29** [i] 1Ki 9:16 [j] Jos 16:10 **1:31** [k] Jdg 10:6 **1:33** [l] Jos 19:38 **1:34** [m] Ex 3:17 **1:35** [n] Jos 19:42 **1:36** [o] Jos 15:3 **2:1** [p] Jdg 6:11 [q] ver 5 [r] Ex 20:2 [s] Ge 17:8 [t] Lev 26:42-44; Dt 7:9

you,[t] 2and you shall not make a covenant
with the people of this land,[u] but you shall
break down their altars.[v]' Yet you have disobeyed me. Why have you done this? 3And I
have also said, 'I will not drive them out before you;[w] they will become traps[x] for you,
and their gods will become snares[y] to you.'"
4When the angel of the LORD had spoken
these things to all the Israelites, the people
wept aloud, 5and they called that place Bokim.[a] There they offered sacrifices to the
LORD.

Disobedience and Defeat

6After Joshua had dismissed the Israelites, they went to take possession of the
land, each to their own inheritance. 7The
people served the LORD throughout the lifetime of Joshua and of the elders who outlived him and who had seen all the great
things the LORD had done for Israel.
8Joshua son of Nun, the servant of the
LORD, died at the age of a hundred and
ten. 9And they buried him in the land of
his inheritance, at Timnath Heres[b][z] in the
hill country of Ephraim, north of Mount
Gaash.
10After that whole generation had been
gathered to their ancestors, another generation grew up who knew neither the LORD
nor what he had done for Israel.[a] 11Then the
Israelites did evil in the eyes of the LORD[b]
and served the Baals.[c] 12They forsook the
LORD, the God of their ancestors, who had
brought them out of Egypt. They followed
and worshiped various gods[d] of the peoples
around them.[e] They aroused the LORD's anger 13because they forsook him and served
Baal and the Ashtoreths.[f] 14In his anger[g]
against Israel the LORD gave them into the
hands[h] of raiders who plundered them. He
sold them[i] into the hands of their enemies
all around, whom they were no longer able
to resist.[j] 15Whenever Israel went out to
fight, the hand of the LORD was against
them to defeat them, just as he had sworn
to them. They were in great distress.
16Then the LORD raised up judges,[c][k] who
saved[l] them out of the hands of these raiders. 17Yet they would not listen to their
judges but prostituted[m] themselves to other gods and worshiped them. They quickly
turned from the ways of their ancestors,
who had been obedient to the LORD's commands.[n] 18Whenever the LORD raised up
a judge for them, he was with the judge
and saved them out of the hands of their
enemies as long as the judge lived; for the
LORD relented[o] because of their groaning[p]
under those who oppressed and afflicted
them. 19But when the judge died, the people
returned to ways even more corrupt[q] than
those of their ancestors, following other
gods and serving and worshiping them.[r]
They refused to give up their evil practices
and stubborn ways.
20Therefore the LORD was very angry[s]
with Israel and said, "Because this nation has violated the covenant I ordained
for their ancestors and has not listened
to me, 21I will no longer drive out[t] before
them any of the nations Joshua left when
he died. 22I will use them to test[u] Israel and
see whether they will keep the way of the
LORD and walk in it as their ancestors did."
23The LORD had allowed those nations to
remain; he did not drive them out at once
by giving them into the hands of Joshua.
3 These are the nations the LORD left to
test[v] all those Israelites who had not
experienced any of the wars in Canaan
2(he did this only to teach warfare to the

a 5 *Bokim* means *weepers.* *b* 9 Also known as *Timnath Serah* (see Joshua 19:50 and 24:30)
c 16 Or *leaders*; similarly in verses 17-19

---

appears as God's representative here, speaking authoritatively to the people about their covenant disobedience.

2:2 ***you shall not make a covenant.*** God's commands to make no covenants with pagan nations and to tear down their altars are found in Exodus 23:32; 34:13; Deuteronomy 12:3.

2:8–10 ***Joshua ... died.*** Most likely the reference to Joshua's death in 1:1 is placed chronologically, and this subsequent passage has been inserted by the author out of sequence. It is a "flashback" that leads into the second major section of the book, emphasizing the spiritual downfall of the nation after their leader was gone.

2:13 ***Ashtoreths.*** Ashtoreth was a female fertility goddess and a goddess of love and war, closely associated with Baal (10:6; 1 Sam. 7:4; 12:10).

2:15 ***as he had sworn.*** God had promised to deliver Israel into the hands of its enemies if the people forsook Him (Deut. 28:25; Josh. 23:13).

2:18 **Pity**—God is compassionate toward His people at all times. But God had given notice to His people (Deut. 28) that if they disobeyed Him, and did not live according to the covenant, then He would have to discipline them. However, if they did live according to the covenant, then He would bless them as a nation. Throughout Judges the pattern occurred that when the people forgot God another nation would come down upon them as an act of judgment from God. When the nation turned to God, He also would turn and "hear" and "pity" them and bring deliverance. God had not forgotten them when they were in trouble, but He wanted that trouble to cause them to turn to Him.

3:1 ***test all those Israelites.*** The idea of testing implies difficulty and adversity; elsewhere the same word refers to God's testing of Abraham (Gen. 22:1)

2:2 [u] Ex 23:32; 34:12; Dt 7:2 [v] Ex 34:13 **2:3** [w] Jos 23:13 [x] Nu 33:55 [y] Dt 7:16; Jdg 3:6; Ps 106:36 **2:9** [z] Jos 19:50 **2:10** [a] Ex 5:2; 1Sa 2:12; 1Ch 28:9; Gal 4:8 **2:11** [b] Jdg 3:12; 4:1; 6:1; 10:6 [c] Jdg 3:7; 8:33 **2:12** [d] Ps 106:36 [e] Dt 31:16; Jdg 10:6 **2:13** [f] Jdg 10:6 **2:14** [g] Dt 31:17 [h] Ps 106:41 [i] Dt 32:30; Jdg 3:8 [j] Dt 28:25 **2:16** [k] Ac 13:20 [l] Ps 106:43 **2:17** [m] Ex 34:15 [n] ver 7 **2:18** [o] Dt 32:36; Jos 1:5 [p] Ps 106:44 **2:19** [q] Jdg 3:12 [r] Jdg 4:1; 8:33 **2:20** [s] ver 14; Jos 23:16 **2:21** [t] Jos 23:13 **2:22** [u] Dt 8:2, 16; Jdg 3:1, 14 **3:1** [v] Jdg 2:21-22

descendants of the Israelites who had not
had previous battle experience): 3the five[w]
rulers of the Philistines, all the Canaanites,
the Sidonians, and the Hivites living in the
Lebanon mountains from Mount Baal Hermon to Lebo Hamath. 4They were left to
test[x] the Israelites to see whether they would
obey the LORD's commands, which he had
given their ancestors through Moses.
5The Israelites lived[y] among the Canaanites, Hittites, Amorites, Perizzites, Hivites
and Jebusites. 6They took their daughters
in marriage and gave their own daughters
to their sons, and served their gods.[z]

Othniel

7The Israelites did evil in the eyes of the
LORD; they forgot the LORD[a] their God and
served the Baals and the Asherahs.[b] 8The
anger of the LORD burned against Israel so that he sold[c] them into the hands of
Cushan-Rishathaim king of Aram Naharaim,[*a*] to whom the Israelites were subject
for eight years. 9But when they cried out[d]
to the LORD, he raised up for them a deliverer, Othniel[e] son of Kenaz, Caleb's younger
brother, who saved them. 10The Spirit of
the LORD came on him,[f] so that he became
Israel's judge[*b*] and went to war. The LORD
gave Cushan-Rishathaim king of Aram
into the hands of Othniel, who overpowered him. 11So the land had peace for forty
years, until Othniel son of Kenaz died.

Ehud

12Again the Israelites did evil in the eyes
of the LORD,[g] and because they did this evil
the LORD gave Eglon king of Moab[h] power
over Israel. 13Getting the Ammonites and
Amalekites to join him, Eglon came and
attacked Israel, and they took possession
of the City of Palms.[*c*][i] 14The Israelites were
subject to Eglon king of Moab for eighteen
years.
15Again the Israelites cried out to the
LORD, and he gave them a deliverer[j]—
Ehud, a left-handed man, the son of Gera
the Benjamite. The Israelites sent him with
tribute to Eglon king of Moab. 16Now Ehud
had made a double-edged sword about a
cubit[*d*] long, which he strapped to his right
thigh under his clothing. 17He presented
the tribute to Eglon king of Moab, who was
a very fat man.[k] 18After Ehud had presented the tribute, he sent on their way those
who had carried it. 19But on reaching the
stone images near Gilgal he himself went
back to Eglon and said, "Your Majesty, I
have a secret message for you."
The king said to his attendants, "Leave
us!" And they all left.
20Ehud then approached him while he
was sitting alone in the upper room of his
palace[*e*] and said, "I have a message from
God for you." As the king rose from his
seat, 21Ehud reached with his left hand,
drew the sword from his right thigh and
plunged it into the king's belly. 22Even
the handle sank in after the blade, and
his bowels discharged. Ehud did not pull
the sword out, and the fat closed in over
it. 23Then Ehud went out to the porch[*f*]; he
shut the doors of the upper room behind
him and locked them.
24After he had gone, the servants came
and found the doors of the upper room
locked. They said, "He must be relieving
himself[l] in the inner room of the palace."
25They waited to the point of embarrassment,[m] but when he did not open the doors
of the room, they took a key and unlocked
them. There they saw their lord fallen to
the floor, dead.
26While they waited, Ehud got away. He
passed by the stone images and escaped to
Seirah. 27When he arrived there, he blew
a trumpet[n] in the hill country of Ephraim, and the Israelites went down with him
from the hills, with him leading them.
28"Follow me," he ordered, "for the LORD
has given Moab, your enemy, into your
hands.[o]" So they followed him down and
took possession of the fords of the Jordan[p]
that led to Moab; they allowed no one to

a *8* That is, Northwest Mesopotamia *b* *10* Or *leader* *c* *13* That is, Jericho *d* *16* That is, about 18 inches or about 45 centimeters *e* *20* The meaning of the Hebrew for this word is uncertain; also in verse 24. *f* *23* The meaning of the Hebrew for this word is uncertain.

and Hezekiah (2 Chr. 32:31). Here God was testing Israel to refine it.

3:8 *Cushan-Rishathaim.* This name means "Cushan of Double Wickedness." This may not have been his actual name, but instead a name pinned on him by the author of Judges for ridicule.

3:9 *Othniel.* Othniel was the hero who captured the city of Kiriath Sepher (1:13; Josh. 15:17). He was from Judah and was Caleb's near kinsman.

3:12 *Moab.* Moab was a plateau southeast of the Dead Sea. It was populated by nomadic herders and farmers in small agrarian settlements but had no large cities. It sat on either side of the King's Highway, an important north-south trade route. The ancestor of the Moabites was the offspring of Lot's incestuous relationship with his older daughter (Gen. 19:37), so the Moabites and Israelites were distantly related. The Bible frequently mentions conflict between the two peoples, and particularly the trouble caused by the Israelite tendency to embrace Moab's false gods.

3:20 *upper room.* In ancient cities, a small room was often built onto the flat roof of a house, providing a cool, private place away from the cooking fires and general living areas.

3:3 [w] Jos 13:3 **3:4** [x] Dt 8:2; Jdg 2:22 **3:5** [y] Ps 106:35 **3:6** [z] Ex 34:16; Dt 7:3-4 **3:7** [a] Dt 4:9 [b] Ex 34:13; Jdg 2:11, 13 **3:8** [c] Jdg 2:14 **3:9** [d] ver 15; Jdg 6:6, 7; 10:10; Ps 106:44 [e] Jdg 1:13 **3:10** [f] Nu 11:25, 29; 24:2; Jdg 6:34; 11:29; 13:25; 14:6, 19; 1Sa 11:6 **3:12** [g] Jdg 2:11, 14 [h] 1Sa 12:9 **3:13** [i] Jdg 1:16 **3:15** [j] ver 9; Ps 78:34; 107:13 **3:17** [k] ver 12 **3:24** [l] 1Sa 24:3 **3:25** [m] 2Ki 2:17; 8:11 **3:27** [n] Jdg 6:34; 1Sa 13:3 **3:28** [o] Jdg 7:9, 15 [p] Jos 2:7; Jdg 7:24; 12:5

cross over. 29At that time they struck down
about ten thousand Moabites, all vigorous
and strong; not one escaped. 30That day
Moab was made subject to Israel, and the
land had peace[q] for eighty years.

Shamgar

31After Ehud came Shamgar son of
Anath,[r] who struck down six hundred[s]
Philistines with an oxgoad. He too saved
Israel.

Deborah

4 Again the Israelites did evil[t] in the eyes
of the LORD, now that Ehud was dead.
2So the LORD sold them into the hands of
Jabin king of Canaan, who reigned in Hazor.[u] Sisera,[v] the commander of his army,
was based in Harosheth Haggoyim. 3Be-
cause he had nine hundred chariots fitted
with iron[w] and had cruelly oppressed[x] the
Israelites for twenty years, they cried to the
LORD for help.

4Now Deborah, a prophet, the wife of
Lappidoth, was leading[a] Israel at that time.
5She held court under the Palm of Deborah between Ramah and Bethel[y] in the
hill country of Ephraim, and the Israelites
went up to her to have their disputes decided. 6She sent for Barak son of Abinoam[z]
from Kedesh in Naphtali and said to him,
"The LORD, the God of Israel, commands
you: 'Go, take with you ten thousand men
of Naphtali and Zebulun and lead them
up to Mount Tabor. 7I will lead Sisera, the
commander of Jabin's army, with his chariots and his troops to the Kishon River[a] and
give him into your hands.'"

8Barak said to her, "If you go with me,
I will go; but if you don't go with me, I
won't go."

9"Certainly I will go with you," said Deborah. "But because of the course you are
taking, the honor will not be yours, for the
LORD will deliver Sisera into the hands of
a woman." So Deborah went with Barak to
Kedesh.[b] 10There Barak summoned[c] Zebulun and Naphtali, and ten thousand men
went up under his command. Deborah also
went up with him.

11Now Heber the Kenite had left the other Kenites,[d] the descendants of Hobab,[e]
Moses' brother-in-law,[b] and pitched his
tent by the great tree in Zaanannim[f] near
Kedesh.

12When they told Sisera that Barak son
of Abinoam had gone up to Mount Tabor,
13Sisera summoned from Harosheth Haggoyim to the Kishon River all his men and
his nine hundred chariots fitted with iron.[g]

14Then Deborah said to Barak, "Go! This
is the day the LORD has given Sisera into
your hands. Has not the LORD gone ahead[h]
of you?" So Barak went down Mount Tabor,
with ten thousand men following him. 15At
Barak's advance, the LORD routed[i] Sisera
and all his chariots and army by the sword,
and Sisera got down from his chariot and
fled on foot.

16Barak pursued the chariots and army
as far as Harosheth Haggoyim, and all Sisera's troops fell by the sword; not a man
was left.[j] 17Sisera, meanwhile, fled on foot
to the tent of Jael, the wife of Heber the
Kenite, because there was an alliance between Jabin king of Hazor and the family
of Heber the Kenite.

18Jael went out to meet Sisera and said to
him, "Come, my lord, come right in. Don't
be afraid." So he entered her tent, and she
covered him with a blanket.

19"I'm thirsty," he said. "Please give me
some water." She opened a skin of milk,[k]
gave him a drink, and covered him up.

20"Stand in the doorway of the tent," he
told her. "If someone comes by and asks
you, 'Is anyone in there?' say 'No.'"

21But Jael, Heber's wife, picked up a tent
peg and a hammer and went quietly to him
while he lay fast asleep, exhausted. She
drove the peg through his temple into the
ground, and he died.[l]

22Just then Barak came by in pursuit
of Sisera, and Jael went out to meet him.
"Come," she said, "I will show you the man
you're looking for." So he went in with
her, and there lay Sisera with the tent peg
through his temple—dead.

---

[a] 4 Traditionally *judging* [b] 11 Or *father-in-law*

4:2 *Jabin king of Canaan, who reigned in Hazor.* Years earlier, Joshua had defeated a king of Hazor named Jabin (Josh. 11:1–15). Probably Jabin was a title rather than a proper name.

4:4 *Deborah.* Deborah is shown in the best light of all the judges in the book. She is called a prophetess (v. 4), and many sought out her decisions (v. 5). For this reason, she is called "a mother in Israel" (5:7). She is probably included among the leaders in Israel (5:2), and she instructed Barak in the strategy of the battle (4:9,14). She was also a prominent author of the victory song (5:1) and gave her name to a place in Israel, the palm tree of Deborah (v. 5).

4:9 *the honor will not be yours.* Barak clearly respected Deborah as the Lord's spokesperson, and wanted her to be nearby so that he could receive instructions from the Lord. It is not clear whether Deborah's response was a rebuke, or just a statement, but it seems that part of the reason Israel was judged by a woman was because the men were not listening that closely to God, or willing to take the responsibility. Whatever his stage of spiritual growth was at the time, Barak did obey the Lord and is listed in the Book of Hebrews as a man of great faith (Heb. 11:32).

3:30 [q] ver 11 **3:31** [r] Jdg 5:6 [s] Jos 23:10 **4:1** [t] Jdg 2:19
4:2 [u] Jos 11:1 [v] ver 13, 16; 1Sa 12:9; Ps 83:9
4:3 [w] Jdg 1:19 [x] Ps 106:42 **4:5** [y] Ge 35:8
4:6 [z] Heb 11:32 **4:7** [a] Ps 83:9 **4:9** [b] ver 21; Jdg 2:14
4:10 [c] ver 14; Jdg 5:15, 18 **4:11** [d] Jdg 1:16 [e] Nu 10:29
[f] Jos 19:33 **4:13** [g] ver 3 **4:14** [h] Dt 9:3; 2Sa 5:24; Ps 68:7
4:15 [i] Jos 10:10; Ps 83:9-10 **4:16** [j] Ps 83:9
4:19 [k] Jdg 5:25 **4:21** [l] Jdg 5:26

23On that day God subdued[m] Jabin king
of Canaan before the Israelites. 24And the
hand of the Israelites pressed harder and
harder against Jabin king of Canaan until
they destroyed him.

The Song of Deborah

5 On that day Deborah and Barak son of Abinoam sang this song:[n]

2 "When the princes in Israel take the lead,
when the people willingly offer[o] themselves—
praise the LORD![p]

3 "Hear this, you kings! Listen, you rulers!
I, even I, will sing to[a] the LORD;
I will praise the LORD, the God of Israel, in song.[q]

4 "When you, LORD, went out from Seir,[r]
when you marched from the land of Edom,
the earth shook, the heavens poured,
the clouds poured down water.[s]
5 The mountains quaked[t] before the LORD, the One of Sinai,
before the LORD, the God of Israel.

6 "In the days of Shamgar son of Anath,[u]
in the days of Jael,[v] the highways[w] were abandoned;
travelers took to winding paths.
7 Villagers in Israel would not fight;
they held back until I, Deborah, arose,
until I arose, a mother in Israel.
8 God chose new leaders[x]
when war came to the city gates,
but not a shield or spear was seen
among forty thousand in Israel.
9 My heart is with Israel's princes,
with the willing volunteers[y] among the people.
Praise the LORD!

10 "You who ride on white donkeys,[z]
sitting on your saddle blankets,
and you who walk along the road,
consider 11the voice of the singers[b] at the watering places.
They recite the victories[a] of the LORD,
the victories of his villagers in Israel.

"Then the people of the LORD
went down to the city gates.[b]
12 'Wake up,[c] wake up, Deborah!
Wake up, wake up, break out in song!
Arise, Barak!
Take captive your captives,[d] son of Abinoam.'

13 "The remnant of the nobles came down;
the people of the LORD came down to me against the mighty.
14 Some came from Ephraim, whose roots were in Amalek;[e]
Benjamin was with the people who followed you.
From Makir captains came down,
from Zebulun those who bear a commander's[b] staff.
15 The princes of Issachar were with Deborah;[f]
yes, Issachar was with Barak,
sent under his command into the valley.
In the districts of Reuben
there was much searching of heart.
16 Why did you stay among the sheep pens[c]
to hear the whistling for the flocks?[g]
In the districts of Reuben
there was much searching of heart.
17 Gilead stayed beyond the Jordan.
And Dan, why did he linger by the ships?
Asher remained on the coast[h]
and stayed in his coves.
18 The people of Zebulun risked their very lives;
so did Naphtali on the terraced fields.[i]

19 "Kings came[j], they fought,
the kings of Canaan fought.
At Taanach, by the waters of Megiddo,[k]
they took no plunder of silver.[l]
20 From the heavens[m] the stars fought,
from their courses they fought against Sisera.

[a] *3* Or *of* [b] *11,14* The meaning of the Hebrew for this word is uncertain. [c] *16* Or *the campfires*; or *the saddlebags*

5:2 *when the princes in Israel take the lead.* The phrase literally means "the long-haired ones who let their hair hang loose." The precise meaning of the phrase is obscure, but it may mean that loosed locks or flowing hair were signs of great strength or leadership.

5:2–3 Praise—Deborah did not attribute their success to herself or to Barak, or even to Jael, but to the Lord. He was the one to whom all praise and thanksgiving were directed in the celebration of their victory.

5:7 *a mother in Israel.* This phrase occurs twice in the Old Testament, here and in 2 Samuel 20:19. The title is given to Deborah as one of honor, respect, and prominence.

5:10 *ride on white donkeys ... walk along the road.* This verse calls all classes of society to bear witness to the mighty acts of God, from the ruling classes, those riding on white donkeys, to the lowest classes, those who walk on the road.

5:17 *linger by the ships.* The reference to Dan remaining "in ships" probably reflects the location of their original inheritance, which was along the south-central coastal plain where they would have had access to the sea (Josh. 19:40–46). Later they

4:23 [m] Ne 9:24; Ps 18:47 **5:1** [n] Ex 15:1 **5:2** [o] 2Ch 17:16; Ps 110:3 [p] ver 9 **5:3** [q] Ps 27:6 **5:4** [r] Dt 33:2 [s] Ps 68:8 **5:5** [t] Ex 19:18; Ps 68:8; 97:5; Isa 64:3 **5:6** [u] Jdg 3:31 [v] Jdg 4:17 [w] Isa 33:8 **5:8** [x] Dt 32:17 **5:9** [y] ver 2 **5:10** [z] Jdg 10:4; 12:14 **5:11** [a] 1Sa 12:7; Mic 6:5 [b] ver 8 **5:12** [c] Ps 57:8 [d] Ps 68:18; Eph 4:8 **5:14** [e] Jdg 3:13 **5:15** [f] Jdg 4:10 **5:16** [g] Nu 32:1 **5:17** [h] Jos 19:29 **5:18** [i] Jdg 4:6, 10 **5:19** [j] Jos 11:5; Jdg 4:13 [k] Jdg 1:27 [l] ver 30 **5:20** [m] Jos 10:11

21 The river Kishon[n] swept them away,
the age-old river, the river Kishon.
March on, my soul; be strong!
22 Then thundered the horses' hooves—
galloping, galloping go his mighty steeds.
23 'Curse Meroz,' said the angel of the LORD.
'Curse its people bitterly,
because they did not come to help the LORD,
to help the LORD against the mighty.'

24 "Most blessed of women be Jael,[o]
the wife of Heber the Kenite,
most blessed of tent-dwelling women.
25 He asked for water, and she gave him milk;[p]
in a bowl fit for nobles she brought him curdled milk.
26 Her hand reached for the tent peg,
her right hand for the workman's hammer.
She struck Sisera, she crushed his head,
she shattered and pierced his temple.[q]
27 At her feet he sank,
he fell; there he lay.
At her feet he sank, he fell;
where he sank, there he fell—dead.

28 "Through the window peered Sisera's mother;
behind the lattice she cried out,[r]
'Why is his chariot so long in coming?
Why is the clatter of his chariots delayed?'
29 The wisest of her ladies answer her;
indeed, she keeps saying to herself,
30 'Are they not finding and dividing the spoils:[s]
a woman or two for each man,
colorful garments as plunder for Sisera,
colorful garments embroidered,
highly embroidered garments for my neck—
all this as plunder?'

31 "So may all your enemies perish, LORD!
But may all who love you be like the sun[t]
when it rises in its strength."

Then the land had peace[u] forty years.

Gideon

6 The Israelites did evil in the eyes of the
LORD,[v] and for seven years he gave them
into the hands of the Midianites.[w] 2 Because
the power of Midian was so oppressive,[x] the
Israelites prepared shelters for themselves
in mountain clefts, caves and strongholds.[y]
3 Whenever the Israelites planted their
crops, the Midianites, Amalekites[z] and
other eastern peoples invaded the country. 4 They camped on the land and ruined
the crops[a] all the way to Gaza and did not
spare a living thing for Israel, neither sheep
nor cattle nor donkeys. 5 They came up with
their livestock and their tents like swarms of
locusts.[b] It was impossible to count them or
their camels;[c] they invaded the land to ravage it. 6 Midian so impoverished the Israelites that they cried out[d] to the LORD for help.
7 When the Israelites cried out to the
LORD because of Midian, 8 he sent them a
prophet, who said, "This is what the LORD,
the God of Israel, says: I brought you up out
of Egypt,[e] out of the land of slavery. 9 I rescued you from the hand of the Egyptians.
And I delivered you from the hand of all
your oppressors; I drove them out before
you and gave you their land.[f] 10 I said to you,
'I am the LORD your God; do not worship[g]
the gods of the Amorites,[h] in whose land
you live.' But you have not listened to me."
11 The angel of the LORD[i] came and sat
down under the oak in Ophrah that belonged to Joash the Abiezrite,[j] where his
son Gideon[k] was threshing wheat in a
winepress to keep it from the Midianites.
12 When the angel of the LORD appeared to
Gideon, he said, "The LORD is with you,[l]
mighty warrior."

---

migrated northward, having been forced out of their territory (1:34; 18:1; Josh. 19:47).

5:26 *Sisera.* The poem describes Sisera's death using graphic, emotive language, which it repeats several times to make the point. Sisera's death was probably a bloodier affair than the prose account indicates.

6:1 *Midianites.* Midian was located in the Arabian Peninsula, southeast of Israel and east of the Sinai Peninsula. The Midianites were descendants of Abraham through his wife Keturah (Gen. 25:1–2), so they were distantly related to the Israelites. Midianites bought Joseph from his brothers (Gen. 37:25–36), welcomed Moses in the wilderness (Ex. 2:15–21), and hired Balaam to curse Israel (Num. 22:7). Generally speaking, Israel counted Midian among its foes. In this account, the Midianites were menacing Israel, burning, looting, and leaving many near starvation (6:4–5).

6:3 *Amalekites.* The Amalekites were a nomadic people who lived in the Sinai desert and the Negev, the desert south of Israel. They were descendants of Esau (Gen. 36:12) and they joined the Midianites against Israel.

6:11–16 Doubt—Doubt, at first thought, appears to be an innocuous sin, so harmless that it affects only the attitude of the one who doubts. But doubt is much more serious than this. Doubt of God's Word, planted by the arch deceiver, was at the root of that first sin committed in the garden of Eden. Doubt of God's goodness and truth arose before desire for the forbidden fruit led to disobedience. Doubt of God and doubt of God's Word cause men to make decisions based on human reckonings. Doubts undispelled lead to sin and defeat.

6:11 *oak.* This is actually a terebinth tree, but it is sometimes called an oak. The terebinth is a large

5:21 [n] Jdg 4:7 **5:24** [o] Jdg 4:17 **5:25** [p] Jdg 4:19 **5:26** [q] Jdg 4:21 **5:28** [r] Pr 7:6 **5:30** [s] Ex 15:9; 1Sa 30:24 **5:31** [t] 2Sa 23:4; Ps 19:4; 89:36 [u] Jdg 3:11 **6:1** [v] Jdg 2:11 [w] Nu 25:15-18; 31:1-3 **6:2** [x] 1Sa 13:6; Isa 8:21 [y] Heb 11:38 **6:3** [z] Jdg 3:13 **6:4** [a] Lev 26:16, Dt 28:30,51 **6:5** [b] Jdg 7:12 [c] Jdg 8:10 **6:6** [d] Jdg 3:9 **6:8** [e] Jdg 2:1 **6:9** [f] Ps 44:2 **6:10** [g] 2Ki 17:35 [h] Jer 10:2 **6:11** [i] Ge 16:7 [j] Jos 17:2 [k] Heb 11:32 **6:12** [l] Jos 1:5; Jdg 13:3; Lk 1:11,28

13 “Pardon me, my lord,” Gideon replied,
“but if the LORD is with us, why has all this
happened to us? Where are all his wonders
that our ancestors told[m] us about when they
said, ‘Did not the LORD bring us up out of
Egypt?’ But now the LORD has abandoned[n]
us and given us into the hand of Midian.”
14 The LORD turned to him and said, “Go
in the strength you have[o] and save Israel
out of Midian’s hand. Am I not sending
you?”
15 “Pardon me, my lord,” Gideon replied,
“but how can I save Israel? My clan is the
weakest in Manasseh, and I am the least
in my family.[p]”
16 The LORD answered, “I will be with
you[q], and you will strike down all the Midianites, leaving none alive.”
17 Gideon replied, “If now I have found
favor in your eyes, give me a sign[r] that it
is really you talking to me. 18 Please do not
go away until I come back and bring my
offering and set it before you.”
And the LORD said, “I will wait until you
return.”
19 Gideon went inside, prepared a young
goat, and from an ephah[a] of flour he made
bread without yeast. Putting the meat in a
basket and its broth in a pot, he brought
them out and offered them to him under
the oak.[s]
20 The angel of God said to him, “Take
the meat and the unleavened bread, place
them on this rock,[t] and pour out the broth.”
And Gideon did so. 21 Then the angel of the
LORD touched the meat and the unleavened
bread[u] with the tip of the staff that was in
his hand. Fire flared from the rock, consuming the meat and the bread. And the angel
of the LORD disappeared. 22 When Gideon
realized[v] that it was the angel of the LORD,
he exclaimed, “Alas, Sovereign LORD! I have
seen the angel of the LORD face to face!”[w]
23 But the LORD said to him, “Peace! Do
not be afraid.[x] You are not going to die.”
24 So Gideon built an altar to the LORD
there and called[y] it The LORD Is Peace. To
this day it stands in Ophrah[z] of the Abiezrites.
25 That same night the LORD said to him,
“Take the second bull from your father’s
herd, the one seven years old.[b] Tear down
your father’s altar to Baal and cut down
the Asherah pole[c][a] beside it. 26 Then build a
proper kind of[d] altar to the LORD your God
on the top of this height. Using the wood of
the Asherah pole that you cut down, offer
the second[e] bull as a burnt offering.”
27 So Gideon took ten of his servants and
did as the LORD told him. But because he
was afraid of his family and the townspeople, he did it at night rather than in the
daytime.
28 In the morning when the people of the
town got up, there was Baal’s altar,[b] demolished, with the Asherah pole beside it cut
down and the second bull sacrificed on the
newly built altar!
29 They asked each other, “Who did this?”
When they carefully investigated, they
were told, “Gideon son of Joash did it.”
30 The people of the town demanded of
Joash, “Bring out your son. He must die,
because he has broken down Baal’s altar
and cut down the Asherah pole beside it.”
31 But Joash replied to the hostile crowd
around him, “Are you going to plead Baal’s
cause? Are you trying to save him? Whoever fights for him shall be put to death
by morning! If Baal really is a god, he

[a] *19* That is, probably about 36 pounds or about 16 kilograms [b] *25* Or *Take a full-grown, mature bull from your father’s herd* [c] *25* That is, a wooden symbol of the goddess Asherah; also in verses 26, 28 and 30 [d] *26* Or *build with layers of stone an* [e] *26* Or *full-grown*; also in verse 28

---

tree with a thick trunk and heavy branches. Botanically speaking, it is not an oak tree, but it has a similar majestic appearance. winepress. A winepress was a square or circular pit carved into rock, in which grapes were crushed. Wheat was usually separated on open threshing floors so the wind could carry away the chaff in the winnowing process. The fact that Gideon was forced to thresh wheat hidden inside a winepress—despite the fact that he had access to a threshing floor (v. 37)—is yet another illustration of the desperate state the Israelites were in.

6:13 *my lord ... the LORD.* “My lord” was a polite form of address, but “the LORD” is the personal name of God (Yahweh).

6:15 *I am the least in my family.* Gideon’s objection is reminiscent of the words spoken by Moses (Ex. 3:11) and Jeremiah (Jer. 1:6).

6:16 *I will be with you.* This was the same great promise that God had given to Moses and Joshua previously (Ex. 3:12; Josh. 1:5–9). This should have greatly encouraged Gideon, but he still had doubts. Often we are quick to judge those who doubt God even when they have firsthand evidence of His mighty works. But we all fail to trust God fully at times. God accomplished His will despite Gideon’s weakness, and He can do the same through us.

6:22 *Gideon realized.* When the angel of the Lord vanished, then Gideon realized who it was and feared for his life. This reaction of fear appears to have been rooted in the knowledge that anyone who gazed upon God would die (Ex. 33:20).

6:24 *To this day.* This expression lends authenticity to the account. It is the author’s way of declaring to later generations that they could verify the story by going and seeing this altar themselves.

6:25 *Asherah pole.* Asherah was the Canaanite fertility goddess. Sacred wooden poles or groves were erected at places where she was worshiped.

6:26 *the wood of the Asherah pole.* Gideon’s sacrifice was to be a bold statement of the superiority

6:13 [m] Ps 44:1 [n] 2Ch 15:2 **6:14** [o] Heb 11:34
6:15 [p] Ex 3:11; 1Sa 9:21 **6:16** [q] Ex 3:12; Jos 1:5
6:17 [r] ver 36-37; Ge 24:14; Isa 38:7-8 **6:19** [s] Ge 18:7-8
6:20 [t] Jdg 13:19 **6:21** [u] Lev 9:24 **6:22** [v] Jdg 13:16, 21
[w] Ge 32:30; Ex 33:20; Jdg 13:22 **6:23** [x] Da 10:19
6:24 [y] Ge 22:14 [z] Jdg 8:32 **6:25** [a] Ex 34:13; Dt 7:5
6:28 [b] 1Ki 16:32

can defend himself when someone breaks down his altar." 32So because Gideon broke down Baal's altar, they gave him the name Jerub-Baal[a][c] that day, saying, "Let Baal contend with him."

33Now all the Midianites, Amalekites and other eastern peoples[d] joined forces and crossed over the Jordan and camped in the Valley of Jezreel.[e] 34Then the Spirit of the LORD came on[f] Gideon, and he blew a trumpet,[g] summoning the Abiezrites to follow him. 35He sent messengers throughout Manasseh, calling them to arms, and also into Asher, Zebulun and Naphtali,[h] so that they too went up to meet them.

36Gideon said to God, "If you will save[i] Israel by my hand as you have promised— 37look, I will place a wool fleece on the threshing floor.[j] If there is dew only on the fleece and all the ground is dry, then I will know[k] that you will save Israel by my hand, as you said." 38And that is what happened. Gideon rose early the next day; he squeezed the fleece and wrung out the dew—a bowlful of water.

39Then Gideon said to God, "Do not be angry with me. Let me make just one more request.[l] Allow me one more test with the fleece, but this time make the fleece dry and let the ground be covered with dew." 40That night God did so. Only the fleece was dry; all the ground was covered with dew.

Gideon Defeats the Midianites

7 Early in the morning, Jerub-Baal[m] (that is, Gideon) and all his men camped at the spring of Harod. The camp of Midian was north of them in the valley near the hill of Moreh.[n] 2The LORD said to Gideon, "You have too many men. I cannot deliver Midian into their hands, or Israel would boast against me, 'My own strength[o] has saved me.' 3Now announce to the army, 'Anyone who trembles with fear may turn back and leave Mount Gilead.[p]'" So twenty-two thousand men left, while ten thousand remained.

4But the LORD said to Gideon, "There are still too many[q] men. Take them down to the water, and I will thin them out for you there. If I say, 'This one shall go with you,' he shall go; but if I say, 'This one shall not go with you,' he shall not go."

5So Gideon took the men down to the water. There the LORD told him, "Separate those who lap the water with their tongues as a dog laps from those who kneel down to drink." 6Three hundred of them drank from cupped hands, lapping like dogs. All the rest got down on their knees to drink.

7The LORD said to Gideon, "With the three hundred men that lapped I will save you and give the Midianites into your hands. Let all the others go home."[r] 8So Gideon sent the rest of the Israelites home but kept the three hundred, who took over the provisions and trumpets of the others.

Now the camp of Midian lay below him in the valley. 9During that night the LORD said to Gideon, "Get up, go down against the camp, because I am going to give it into your hands.[s] 10If you are afraid to attack, go down to the camp with your servant Purah 11and listen to what they are saying. Afterward, you will be encouraged to attack the camp." So he and Purah his servant went down to the outposts of the camp. 12The Midianites, the Amalekites[t] and all the other eastern peoples had settled in the valley, thick as locusts.[u] Their camels[v] could no more be counted than the sand on the seashore.[w]

13Gideon arrived just as a man was telling a friend his dream. "I had a dream," he was saying. "A round loaf of barley bread came tumbling into the Midianite camp. It struck the tent with such force that the tent overturned and collapsed."

14His friend responded, "This can be nothing other than the sword of Gideon son of Joash, the Israelite. God has given the Midianites and the whole camp into his hands."

[a] *32 Jerub-Baal* probably means *let Baal contend.*

---

of the Lord over the false gods His people were worshiping.

6:36–40 Prayer—Gideon had already received an unmistakable message from God, and he had been assured that God would lead him to victory. His prayer and request for a sign were the result of his lack of faith, but in spite of Gideon's wavering, God kindly accommodated his requests. Many people have relied on Gideon's example as a way of seeking guidance from the Lord. Occasionally God has chosen to answer such requests, even as He did for Gideon, because He is compassionate and makes allowances for our weakness, but putting out a fleece is not the action of faith. Isaiah modeled a proper response to God's clearly revealed will: he said, "Here am I. Send me!" (Is. 6:8). So too did the disciples, who dropped their nets immediately and followed Jesus (Mark 1:18).

6:39 *Let me make just one more request.* Gideon's desire to test God's sign could have been a violation of the law which prohibited people from testing God (Deut. 6:16). Gideon himself was aware that he was doing something unwise, if not sinful, since he asked God not to be angry with him.

7:3 *trembles with fear.* Mosaic law allowed military exemptions for several classes of people, including those who had just built a home, those who had just planted a vineyard, those engaged to be married, and those who were fearful (Deut. 20:5–8).

7:4–5 *There are still too many men.* God reduced Gideon's army to emphasize who was really bringing victory.

6:32 [c] Jdg 7:1; 8:29,35; 1Sa 12:11 **6:33** [d] ver 3 [e] Jos 17:16 **6:34** [f] Jdg 3:10; 1Ch 12:18; 2Ch 24:20 [g] Jdg 3:27 **6:35** [h] Jdg 4:6 **6:36** [i] ver 14 **6:37** [j] Ex 4:3-7 [k] Ge 24:14 **6:39** [l] Ge 18:32 **7:1** [m] Jdg 6:32 [n] Ge 12:6 **7:2** [o] Dt 8:17; 2Co 4:7 **7:3** [p] Dt 20:8 **7:4** [q] 1Sa 14:6 **7:7** [r] 1Sa 14:6 **7:9** [s] Jos 2:24; 10:8; 11:6 **7:12** [t] Jdg 8:10 [u] Jdg 6:5 [v] Jer 49:29 [w] Jos 11:4

15When Gideon heard the dream and its
interpretation, he bowed down and worshiped.[x] He returned to the camp of Israel and called out, "Get up! The LORD has
given the Midianite camp into your hands."
16Dividing the three hundred men[y] into
three companies,[z] he placed trumpets and
empty jars in the hands of all of them, with
torches inside.

17"Watch me," he told them. "Follow my
lead. When I get to the edge of the camp,
do exactly as I do. 18When I and all who
are with me blow our trumpets,[a] then from
all around the camp blow yours and shout,
'For the LORD and for Gideon.'"

19Gideon and the hundred men with him
reached the edge of the camp at the beginning of the middle watch, just after they
had changed the guard. They blew their
trumpets and broke the jars that were in
their hands. 20The three companies blew
the trumpets and smashed the jars. Grasping the torches in their left hands and holding in their right hands the trumpets they
were to blow, they shouted, "A sword[b] for
the LORD and for Gideon!" 21While each
man held his position around the camp, all
the Midianites ran, crying out as they fled.[c]

22When the three hundred trumpets
sounded,[d] the LORD caused the men
throughout the camp to turn on each other[e]
with their swords. The army fled to Beth
Shittah toward Zererah as far as the border of Abel Meholah[f] near Tabbath. 23Is-
raelites from Naphtali, Asher and all Manasseh were called out,[g] and they pursued
the Midianites. 24Gideon sent messengers
throughout the hill country of Ephraim,
saying, "Come down against the Midianites and seize the waters of the Jordan[h]
ahead of them as far as Beth Barah."

So all the men of Ephraim were called
out and they seized the waters of the Jordan as far as Beth Barah. 25They also captured two of the Midianite leaders, Oreb
and Zeeb[i]. They killed Oreb at the rock of
Oreb,[j] and Zeeb at the winepress of Zeeb.
They pursued the Midianites and brought
the heads of Oreb and Zeeb to Gideon, who
was by the Jordan.[k]

Zebah and Zalmunna

8 Now the Ephraimites asked Gideon,
"Why have you treated us like this?
Why didn't you call us when you went to
fight Midian?"[l] And they challenged him
vigorously.[m]

2But he answered them, "What have I
accomplished compared to you? Aren't the
gleanings of Ephraim's grapes better than
the full grape harvest of Abiezer? 3God
gave Oreb and Zeeb,[n] the Midianite leaders, into your hands. What was I able to
do compared to you?" At this, their resentment against him subsided.

4Gideon and his three hundred men, exhausted yet keeping up the pursuit, came
to the Jordan[o] and crossed it. 5He said
to the men of Sukkoth,[p] "Give my troops
some bread; they are worn out, and I am
still pursuing Zebah and Zalmunna,[q] the
kings of Midian."

6But the officials of Sukkoth said, "Do
you already have the hands of Zebah and
Zalmunna in your possession? Why should
we give bread[r] to your troops?"[s]

7Then Gideon replied, "Just for that,
when the LORD has given Zebah and Zalmunna[t] into my hand, I will tear your flesh
with desert thorns and briers."

8From there he went up to Peniel[a][u] and
made the same request of them, but they
answered as the men of Sukkoth had. 9So
he said to the men of Peniel, "When I return
in triumph, I will tear down this tower."[v]

10Now Zebah and Zalmunna were in
Karkor with a force of about fifteen thousand men, all that were left of the armies of
the eastern peoples; a hundred and twenty
thousand swordsmen had fallen.[w] 11Gide-
on went up by the route of the nomads east
of Nobah[x] and Jogbehah[y] and attacked the
unsuspecting army. 12Zebah and Zalmunna, the two kings of Midian, fled, but he
pursued them and captured them, routing
their entire army.

13Gideon son of Joash then returned
from the battle by the Pass of Heres. 14He
caught a young man of Sukkoth and questioned him, and the young man wrote down
for him the names of the seventy-seven officials of Sukkoth, the elders of the town.
15Then Gideon came and said to the men of
Sukkoth, "Here are Zebah and Zalmunna,
about whom you taunted me by saying, 'Do

[a] 8 Hebrew *Penuel*, a variant of *Peniel*; also in verses 9 and 17

7:19 *middle watch.* According to Jewish tradition, the hours between sunset and sunrise were divided into three watches, which would put the time of this attack at roughly 10:00 P.M.

8:5 *Sukkoth.* Sukkoth was east of the Jordan, near the Jabbok River.

8:14 *he wrote down for him the ... officials of Sukkoth.* Literacy in early civilizations was at first limited to the educated elite, as in Mesopotamia and Egypt. Their writing systems were complex and only a tiny portion of the population could read and write. However, the spread of alphabetic systems vastly simplified the task of reading and writing. Hundreds of potsherds from throughout Palestine have simple inscriptions on them, indicating that some degree of literacy had become widely accessible by Gideon's day.

7:15 [x] 1Sa 15:31 **7:16** [y] Ge 14:15 [z] 2Sa 18:2 **7:18** [a] Jdg 3:27 **7:20** [b] ver 14 **7:21** [c] 2Ki 7:7 **7:22** [d] Jos 6:20 [e] 1Sa 14:20; 2Ch 20:23 [f] 1Ki 4:12; 19:16 **7:23** [g] Jdg 6:35 **7:24** [h] Jdg 3:28 **7:25** [i] Jdg 8:3; Ps 83:11 [j] Isa 10:26 [k] Jdg 8:4 **8:1** [l] Jdg 12:1 [m] 2Sa 19:41 **8:3** [n] Jdg 7:25; Pr 15:1 **8:4** [o] Jdg 7:25 **8:5** [p] Ge 33:17 [q] Ps 83:11 **8:6** [r] 1Sa 25:11 [s] ver 15 **8:7** [t] Jdg 7:15 **8:8** [u] Ge 32:30; 1Ki 12:25 **8:9** [v] ver 17 **8:10** [w] Jdg 6:5; 7:12; Isa 9:4 **8:11** [x] Nu 32:42 [y] Nu 32:35

you already have the hands of Zebah and
Zalmunna in your possession? Why should
we give bread to your exhausted men?[z]'"
16He took the elders of the town and taught
the men of Sukkoth a lesson[a] by punishing
them with desert thorns and briers. 17He
also pulled down the tower of Peniel and
killed the men of the town.[b]
18Then he asked Zebah and Zalmunna,
"What kind of men did you kill at Tabor?[c]"
"Men like you," they answered, "each
one with the bearing of a prince."
19Gideon replied, "Those were my brothers, the sons of my own mother. As surely
as the LORD lives, if you had spared their
lives, I would not kill you." 20Turning to
Jether, his oldest son, he said, "Kill them!"
But Jether did not draw his sword, because
he was only a boy and was afraid.
21Zebah and Zalmunna said, "Come,
do it yourself. 'As is the man, so is his
strength.'" So Gideon stepped forward and
killed them, and took the ornaments[d] off
their camels' necks.

Gideon's Ephod

22The Israelites said to Gideon, "Rule
over us—you, your son and your grandson—because you have saved us from the
hand of Midian."
23But Gideon told them, "I will not rule
over you, nor will my son rule over you.
The LORD will rule[e] over you." 24And he
said, "I do have one request, that each of
you give me an earring from your share of
the plunder." (It was the custom of the Ishmaelites[f] to wear gold earrings.)
25They answered, "We'll be glad to give
them." So they spread out a garment, and
each of them threw a ring from his plunder onto it. 26The weight of the gold rings
he asked for came to seventeen hundred
shekels,[a] not counting the ornaments, the
pendants and the purple garments worn by
the kings of Midian or the chains that were
on their camels' necks. 27Gideon made the
gold into an ephod,[g] which he placed in
Ophrah, his town. All Israel prostituted
themselves by worshiping it there, and it
became a snare[h] to Gideon and his family.

Gideon's Death

28Thus Midian was subdued before the
Israelites and did not raise its head again.
During Gideon's lifetime, the land had
peace[i] forty years.
29Jerub-Baal[j] son of Joash went back
home to live. 30He had seventy sons[k] of his
own, for he had many wives. 31His concubine, who lived in Shechem, also bore him
a son, whom he named Abimelek.[l] 32Gide-
on son of Joash died at a good old age[m] and
was buried in the tomb of his father Joash
in Ophrah of the Abiezrites.
33No sooner had Gideon died than the Israelites again prostituted themselves to the
Baals.[n] They set up Baal-Berith[o] as their
god[p] 34and did not remember[q] the LORD
their God, who had rescued them from the
hands of all their enemies on every side.
35They also failed to show any loyalty to
the family of Jerub-Baal (that is, Gideon)
in spite of all the good things he had done
for them.[r]

Abimelek

9 Abimelek[s] son of Jerub-Baal went to his
mother's brothers in Shechem and said
to them and to all his mother's clan, 2"Ask
all the citizens of Shechem, 'Which is better for you: to have all seventy of Jerub-Baal's sons rule over you, or just one man?'
Remember, I am your flesh and blood.[t]"

a *26* That is, about 43 pounds or about 20 kilograms

8:22–23 Self-Denial—In the initial flush of victory Gideon was offered hereditary rulership over Israel, which he wisely rejected. God the Lord was Judge with ultimate authority, and He would rule over the people. Gideon knew his place before God. In the same way, we are taught not to think more highly of ourselves than we ought, but "soberly in accordance with the faith God has distributed to each of [us]" (Rom. 12:3).

8:22 *Rule over us.* This request, while understandable from a human perspective, failed to acknowledge that it was God, not Gideon, who had delivered the people.

8:23 *The LORD will rule over you.* The word order of the Hebrew makes it clear that God's claim was exclusive; it might be paraphrased, "It is the Lord, and no one else, who shall rule over you." This statement is widely assumed to indicate that God intended that Israel should never have a king, but that He would be their only King. However, God had promised Abraham that he would count kings among his descendants (Gen. 17:6). The problem was not in the concept of having a king, but in their motivation. They wanted to have a visible, human leader, rather than trusting in God's leadership. The role of a true king would be to lead the people in devotion to God's rule.

8:27 *ephod.* The original ephod was an ornate ceremonial garment worn by the high priest (Ex. 29:5). Gideon's motivation for making this golden ephod is unclear, but his imitation of the sacred objects devoted to the worship of God ended up distracting the people and undermining the true worship of God.

8:31 *Abimelek.* This name means "my father is king." Some think that Gideon did become a king in practice if not in name, for he gave his son a royal name and acted as a leader of the people (vv. 24–27).

9:1–57 Conspiracy—The seeds of Abimelek's violent grab for power were sown in Israel's persistent

8:15 [z] ver 6 **8:16** [a] ver 7 **8:17** [b] ver 9
8:18 [c] Jos 19:22; Jdg 4:6 **8:21** [d] ver 26; Ps 83:11
8:23 [e] Ex 16:8; 1Sa 8:7; 10:19; 12:12 **8:24** [f] Ge 25:13
8:27 [g] Jdg 17:5; 18:14 [h] Dt 7:16; Ps 106:39
8:28 [i] Jdg 5:31 **8:29** [j] Jdg 7:1 **8:30** [k] Jdg 9:2, 5, 18, 24
8:31 [l] Jdg 9:1 **8:32** [m] Ge 25:8 **8:33** [n] Jdg 2:11, 13, 19
[o] Jdg 9:4 [p] Jdg 9:27, 46 **8:34** [q] Jdg 3:7; Dt 4:9; Ps 78:11, 42 **8:35** [r] Jdg 9:16 **9:1** [s] Jdg 8:31 **9:2** [t] Ge 29:14; Jdg 8:30

3When the brothers repeated all this to the citizens of Shechem, they were inclined to follow Abimelek, for they said, "He is related to us." 4They gave him seventy shekels[a] of silver from the temple of Baal-Berith,[u] and Abimelek used it to hire reckless scoundrels,[v] who became his followers. 5He went to his father's home in Ophrah and on one stone murdered his seventy brothers,[w] the sons of Jerub-Baal. But Jotham, the youngest son of Jerub-Baal, escaped by hiding.[x] 6Then all the citizens of Shechem and Beth Millo gathered beside the great tree at the pillar in Shechem to crown Abimelek king.

7When Jotham was told about this, he climbed up on the top of Mount Gerizim[y] and shouted to them, "Listen to me, citizens of Shechem, so that God may listen to you. 8One day the trees went out to anoint a king for themselves. They said to the olive tree, 'Be our king.'

9"But the olive tree answered, 'Should I give up my oil, by which both gods and humans are honored, to hold sway over the trees?'

10"Next, the trees said to the fig tree, 'Come and be our king.'

11"But the fig tree replied, 'Should I give up my fruit, so good and sweet, to hold sway over the trees?'

12"Then the trees said to the vine, 'Come and be our king.'

13"But the vine answered, 'Should I give up my wine,[z] which cheers both gods and humans, to hold sway over the trees?'

14"Finally all the trees said to the thornbush, 'Come and be our king.'

15"The thornbush said to the trees, 'If you really want to anoint me king over you, come and take refuge in my shade;[a] but if not, then let fire come out[b] of the thornbush and consume the cedars of Lebanon!'[c]

16"Have you acted honorably and in good faith by making Abimelek king? Have you been fair to Jerub-Baal and his family? Have you treated him as he deserves? 17Remember that my father fought for you and risked his life to rescue you from the hand of Midian. 18But today you have revolted against my father's family. You have murdered his seventy sons[d] on a single stone and have made Abimelek, the son of his female slave, king over the citizens of Shechem because he is related to you. 19So have you acted honorably and in good faith toward Jerub-Baal and his family today? If you have, may Abimelek be your joy, and may you be his, too! 20But if you have not, let fire come out[e] from Abimelek and consume you, the citizens of Shechem and Beth Millo, and let fire come out from you, the citizens of Shechem and Beth Millo, and consume Abimelek!"

21Then Jotham fled, escaping to Beer, and he lived there because he was afraid of his brother Abimelek.

22After Abimelek had governed Israel three years, 23God stirred up animosity[f] between Abimelek and the citizens of Shechem so that they acted treacherously against Abimelek. 24God did this in order that the crime against Jerub-Baal's seventy sons, the shedding[g] of their blood, might be avenged[h] on their brother Abimelek and on the citizens of Shechem, who had helped him[i] murder his brothers. 25In opposition to him these citizens of Shechem set men on the hilltops to ambush and rob everyone who passed by, and this was reported to Abimelek.

26Now Gaal son of Ebed moved with his clan into Shechem, and its citizens put their confidence in him. 27After they had gone out into the fields and gathered the grapes and trodden[j] them, they held a festival in the temple of their god.[k] While they were eating and drinking, they cursed Abimelek. 28Then Gaal son of Ebed said, "Who[l] is Abimelek, and why should we Shechemites be subject to him? Isn't he Jerub-Baal's son, and isn't Zebul his deputy? Serve the family of Hamor,[m] Shechem's father! Why should we serve Abimelek? 29If only this people were under my command![n] Then I would get rid of him. I would say to Abimelek, 'Call out your whole army!'"[b]

30When Zebul the governor of the city heard what Gaal son of Ebed said, he was very angry. 31Under cover he sent mes-

[a] *4* That is, about 1 3/4 pounds or about 800 grams
[b] *29* Septuagint; Hebrew *him." Then he said to Abimelek, "Call out your whole army!"*

infidelity to God, which led to another rejection of the Lord (8:22,24–27,33–35).

9:6 *the great tree at the pillar.* Sadly, this coronation took place at the same tree where Jacob had put away his foreign gods many years before (Gen. 35:4), and where Joshua had commemorated his covenant with God (Josh. 24:26).

9:14–15 Pride—The pomp and ceremony that goes with royalty is a source of pride not only for the king but also for his subjects. The idea of having a man from their own tribe ruling the entire nation appealed to the pride of the men of Shechem. Pride led them to surrender their freedom and submit to the rule of man rather than God. It is the cause of many kinds of injustice in society: social, economic, and political. It often leads to war and violence, as it did in this case. Within a brief period of time after Abimelek was anointed king they realized their mistake. The prophecy of Jotham was fulfilled, since fire did come out of the bramble (from Abimelek) to consume the men of Shechem. Pride led to their destruction.

9:4 [u] Jdg 8:33 [v] Jdg 11:3; 2Ch 13:7 **9:5** [w] ver 2; Jdg 8:30 [x] 2Ki 11:2 **9:7** [y] Dt 11:29; 27:12; Jn 4:20 **9:13** [z] Ecc 2:3 **9:15** [a] Isa 30:2 [b] ver 20 [c] Isa 2:13 **9:18** [d] ver 5-6; Jdg 8:30 **9:20** [e] ver 15 **9:23** [f] 1Sa 16:14,23; 18:10; 1Ki 22:22; Isa 19:14; 33:1 **9:24** [g] Nu 35:33; 1Ki 2:32 [h] ver 56-57 [i] Dt 27:25 **9:27** [j] Am 9:13 [k] Jdg 8:33 **9:28** [l] 1Sa 25:10; 1Ki 12:16 [m] Ge 34:2,6 **9:29** [n] 2Sa 15:4

sengers to Abimelek, saying, "Gaal son of Ebed and his clan have come to Shechem and are stirring up the city against you. **32**Now then, during the night you and your men should come and lie in wait[o] in the fields. **33**In the morning at sunrise, advance against the city. When Gaal and his men come out against you, seize the opportunity to attack them.[p]"

34So Abimelek and all his troops set out by night and took up concealed positions near Shechem in four companies. **35**Now Gaal son of Ebed had gone out and was standing at the entrance of the city gate just as Abimelek and his troops came out from their hiding place.[q]

36When Gaal saw them, he said to Zebul, "Look, people are coming down from the tops of the mountains!"

Zebul replied, "You mistake the shadows of the mountains for men."

37But Gaal spoke up again: "Look, people are coming down from the central hill,[a] and a company is coming from the direction of the diviners' tree."

38Then Zebul said to him, "Where is your big talk now, you who said, 'Who is Abimelek that we should be subject to him?' Aren't these the men you ridiculed?[r] Go out and fight them!"

39So Gaal led out[b] the citizens of Shechem and fought Abimelek. **40**Abimelek chased him all the way to the entrance of the gate, and many were killed as they fled. **41**Then Abimelek stayed in Arumah, and Zebul drove Gaal and his clan out of Shechem.

42The next day the people of Shechem went out to the fields, and this was reported to Abimelek. **43**So he took his men, divided them into three companies[s] and set an ambush in the fields. When he saw the people coming out of the city, he rose to attack them. **44**Abimelek and the companies with him rushed forward to a position at the entrance of the city gate. Then two companies attacked those in the fields and struck them down. **45**All that day Abimelek pressed his attack against the city until he had captured it and killed its people. Then he destroyed the city[t] and scattered salt[u] over it.

46On hearing this, the citizens in the tower of Shechem went into the stronghold of the temple[v] of El-Berith. **47**When Abimelek heard that they had assembled there, **48**he and all his men went up Mount Zalmon.[w] He took an ax and cut off some branches, which he lifted to his shoulders. He ordered the men with him, "Quick! Do what you have seen me do!" **49**So all the men cut branches and followed Abimelek. They piled them against the stronghold and set it on fire with the people still inside. So all the people in the tower of Shechem, about a thousand men and women, also died.

50Next Abimelek went to Thebez[x] and besieged it and captured it. **51**Inside the city, however, was a strong tower, to which all the men and women—all the people of the city—had fled. They had locked themselves in and climbed up on the tower roof. **52**Abimelek went to the tower and attacked it. But as he approached the entrance to the tower to set it on fire, **53**a woman dropped an upper millstone on his head and cracked his skull.[y]

54Hurriedly he called to his armor-bearer, "Draw your sword and kill me,[z] so that they can't say, 'A woman killed him.'" So his servant ran him through, and he died. **55**When the Israelites saw that Abimelek was dead, they went home.

56Thus God repaid the wickedness that Abimelek had done to his father by murdering his seventy brothers. **57**God also made the people of Shechem pay for all their wickedness.[a] The curse of Jotham son of Jerub-Baal came on them.

Tola

10 After the time of Abimelek, a man of Issachar[b] named Tola son of Puah,[c] the son of Dodo, rose to save[d] Israel. He lived in Shamir, in the hill country of Ephraim. **2**He led[c] Israel twenty-three years; then he died, and was buried in Shamir.

Jair

3He was followed by Jair of Gilead, who led Israel twenty-two years. **4**He had thirty sons, who rode thirty donkeys. They controlled thirty towns in Gilead, which to this day are called Havvoth Jair.[de] **5**When Jair died, he was buried in Kamon.

---

[a] 37 The Hebrew for this phrase means *the navel of the earth.* [b] 39 Or *Gaal went out in the sight of* [c] 2 Traditionally *judged;* also in verse 3 [d] 4 Or *called the settlements of Jair*

9:37 *the diviners' tree.* This appears to have had some association with occult or magical practices, and this particular tree was certainly an important landmark (Gen. 35:4; Josh. 24:26).

9:45 *scattered salt over it.* Spreading salt on the land turned the area into a barren desert. Salt will kill most vegetation, and it takes a long time for the land to become good again.

9:56 *God repaid the wickedness that Abimelek had done.* Abimelek was not a true king; he had established his reign through murder and in no way sought to lead the people to the Lord. God did not allow this kind of rebellion to pass unnoticed.

9:32 [o] Jos 8:2 **9:33** [p] 1Sa 10:7 **9:35** [q] Ps 32:7; Jer 49:10 **9:38** [r] ver 28-29 **9:43** [s] Jdg 7:16 **9:45** [t] ver 20; 2Ki 3:25 [u] Dt 29:23 **9:46** [v] Jdg 8:33 **9:48** [w] Ps 68:14 **9:50** [x] 2Sa 11:21 **9:53** [y] 2Sa 11:21 **9:54** [z] 1Sa 31:4; 2Sa 1:9 **9:57** [a] ver 20 **10:1** [b] Ge 30:18 [c] Ge 46:13 [d] Jdg 2:16; 6:14 **10:4** [e] Nu 32:41

Jephthah

6 Again the Israelites did evil in the eyes of the LORD.[f] They served the Baals and the Ashtoreths,[g] and the gods of Aram, the gods of Sidon, the gods of Moab, the gods of the Ammonites and the gods of the Philistines.[h] And because the Israelites forsook the LORD[i] and no longer served him, 7 he became angry[j] with them. He sold them[k] into the hands of the Philistines and the Ammonites, 8 who that year shattered and crushed them. For eighteen years they oppressed all the Israelites on the east side of the Jordan in Gilead, the land of the Amorites. 9 The Ammonites also crossed the Jordan to fight against Judah, Benjamin and Ephraim; Israel was in great distress. 10 Then the Israelites cried out to the LORD, "We have sinned against you, forsaking our God and serving the Baals."[l]

11 The LORD replied, "When the Egyptians,[m] the Amorites, the Ammonites,[n] the Philistines,[o] 12 the Sidonians, the Amalekites and the Maonites[a] oppressed you[p] and you cried to me for help, did I not save you from their hands? 13 But you have forsaken me and served other gods, so I will no longer save you. 14 Go and cry out to the gods you have chosen. Let them save you when you are in trouble![q]"

15 But the Israelites said to the LORD, "We have sinned. Do with us whatever you think best,[r] but please rescue us now." 16 Then they got rid of the foreign gods among them and served the LORD.[s] And he could bear Israel's misery[t] no longer.[u]

17 When the Ammonites were called to arms and camped in Gilead, the Israelites assembled and camped at Mizpah.[v] 18 The leaders of the people of Gilead said to each other, "Whoever will take the lead in attacking the Ammonites will be head[w] over all who live in Gilead."

11 Jephthah[x] the Gileadite was a mighty warrior.[y] His father was Gilead; his mother was a prostitute. 2 Gilead's wife also bore him sons, and when they were grown up, they drove Jephthah away. "You are not going to get any inheritance in our family," they said, "because you are the son of another woman." 3 So Jephthah fled from his brothers and settled in the land of Tob,[z] where a gang of scoundrels[a] gathered around him and followed him.

4 Some time later, when the Ammonites[b] were fighting against Israel, 5 the elders of Gilead went to get Jephthah from the land of Tob. 6 "Come," they said, "be our commander, so we can fight the Ammonites."

7 Jephthah said to them, "Didn't you hate me and drive me from my father's house?[c] Why do you come to me now, when you're in trouble?"

8 The elders of Gilead said to him, "Nevertheless, we are turning to you now; come with us to fight the Ammonites, and you will be head[d] over all of us who live in Gilead."

9 Jephthah answered, "Suppose you take me back to fight the Ammonites and the LORD gives them to me—will I really be your head?"

10 The elders of Gilead replied, "The LORD is our witness;[e] we will certainly do as you say." 11 So Jephthah went with the elders of Gilead, and the people made him head and commander over them. And he repeated all his words before the LORD in Mizpah.[f]

12 Then Jephthah sent messengers to the

a 12 Hebrew; some Septuagint manuscripts *Midianites*

10:6–18 Mercy—A lengthy introduction precedes the story of Jephthah. These verses repeat the themes of apostasy and God's unfailing mercy. A new theme here is the emphasis on Israel's confession and repentance (vv. 10,15–16).

10:6 *Baals and the Ashtoreths, the gods of Aram ... Sidon ... Moab ... Ammonites ... Philistines.* This list demonstrates the extent of Israel's idolatry. Not only did the people worship the major Canaanite gods (Baal and Asherah), but they also absorbed the religions of other groups.

10:7–8 Suffering—Here and elsewhere the Book of Judges underscores the consequences of disobedience. Those consequences are always tragic. The Israelites were never oppressed because they did not have a big enough military, or a strong enough leader, or because God could not protect them. They were oppressed by God's permission because of their disobedience and sin. Defeat and miserable suffering do loom large whenever believers retreat from their exclusive commitment to God. They become their own worst enemy.

10:14 *the gods you have chosen.* This is a response of confrontation. When Israel cried out to God, He reminded them again of their faithless ways.

10:16 *he could bear Israel's misery no longer.* Not only is God a God of great justice, He is a God of great mercy and compassion. Despite their constant sinning and backsliding, God still loved the Israelites and shared their misery, much as parents are moved by their children's suffering.

11:8 *come with us to fight.* This is almost the same phrase that the Israelites used when they asked Samuel for a king (1 Sam. 8:20).

11:11 *words before the LORD.* Jephthah's "words before the LORD" are a strange mixture of faith and foolishness. While Jephthah did acknowledge God, his self-interest and foolishness often overruled his faith. The Book of Hebrews has a more positive view of him. Jephthah is one of those listed "who through faith conquered kingdoms, administered justice, and gained what was promised ..." (Heb. 11:32–33).

10:6 [f] Jdg 2:11 [g] Jdg 2:13 [h] Jdg 2:12 [i] Dt 32:15
10:7 [j] Dt 31:17 [k] Dt 32:30; Jdg 2:14; 1Sa 12:9
10:10 [l] 1Sa 12:10 **10:11** [m] Ex 14:30 [n] Nu 21:21; Jdg 3:13 [o] Jdg 3:31 **10:12** [p] Ps 106:42 **10:14** [q] Dt 32:37
10:15 [r] 1Sa 3:18; 2Sa 15:26 **10:16** [s] Jos 24:23; Jer 18:8 [t] Isa 63:9 [u] Dt 32:36; Ps 106:44-45 **10:17** [v] Ge 31:49; Jdg 11:29 **10:18** [w] Jdg 11:8,9 **11:1** [x] Heb 11:32 [y] Jdg 6:12 **11:3** [z] 2Sa 10:6,8 [a] Jdg 9:4 **11:4** [b] Jdg 10:9
11:7 [c] Ge 26:27 **11:8** [d] Jdg 10:18 **11:10** [e] Ge 31:50; Jer 42:5 **11:11** [f] Jos 11:3; Jdg 10:17; 20:1; 1Sa 10:17

Ammonite king with the question: "What
do you have against me that you have attacked my country?"
13 The king of the Ammonites answered
Jephthah's messengers, "When Israel came
up out of Egypt, they took away my land
from the Arnon to the Jabbok,[g] all the way
to the Jordan. Now give it back peaceably."
14 Jephthah sent back messengers to the
Ammonite king, 15 saying:

"This is what Jephthah says: Israel
did not take the land of Moab[h] or the
land of the Ammonites.[i] 16 But when
they came up out of Egypt, Israel
went through the wilderness to the
Red Sea[a][j] and on to Kadesh.[k] 17 Then
Israel sent messengers[l] to the king of
Edom, saying, 'Give us permission
to go through your country,'[m] but the
king of Edom would not listen. They
sent also to the king of Moab, and he
refused.[n] So Israel stayed at Kadesh.
18 "Next they traveled through the
wilderness, skirted the lands of Edom[o]
and Moab, passed along the eastern
side[p] of the country of Moab, and
camped on the other side of the Arnon.[q] They did not enter the territory
of Moab, for the Arnon was its border.
19 "Then Israel sent messengers to
Sihon king of the Amorites, who ruled
in Heshbon, and said to him, 'Let us
pass through your country to our own
place.'[r] 20 Sihon, however, did not trust
Israel[b] to pass through his territory. He
mustered all his troops and encamped
at Jahaz and fought with Israel.[s]
21 "Then the LORD, the God of Israel, gave Sihon and his whole army
into Israel's hands, and they defeated
them. Israel took over all the land of
the Amorites who lived in that country, 22 capturing all of it from the Arnon to the Jabbok and from the desert
to the Jordan.[t]
23 "Now since the LORD, the God of
Israel, has driven the Amorites out before his people Israel, what right have
you to take it over? 24 Will you not
take what your god Chemosh[u] gives
you? Likewise, whatever the LORD
our God has given us, we will possess. 25 Are you any better than Balak
son of Zippor,[v] king of Moab? Did he
ever quarrel with Israel or fight with
them?[w] 26 For three hundred years Israel occupied[x] Heshbon, Aroer, the
surrounding settlements and all the
towns along the Arnon. Why didn't
you retake them during that time? 27 I
have not wronged you, but you are doing me wrong by waging war against
me. Let the LORD, the Judge,[y] decide[z]
the dispute this day between the Israelites and the Ammonites."

28 The king of Ammon, however, paid no attention to the message Jephthah sent him.
29 Then the Spirit[a] of the LORD came on
Jephthah. He crossed Gilead and Manasseh, passed through Mizpah of Gilead, and
from there he advanced against the Ammonites. 30 And Jephthah made a vow[b] to
the LORD: "If you give the Ammonites into
my hands, 31 whatever comes out of the
door of my house to meet me when I return in triumph from the Ammonites will
be the LORD's, and I will sacrifice it as a
burnt offering."
32 Then Jephthah went over to fight the

[a] *16 Or the Sea of Reeds* [b] *20 Or however, would not make an agreement for Israel*

11:21 *the LORD, the God of Israel.* Israel was not merely an aggressor, but the recipient of the Lord's generosity. The Ammonites had brought their misfortune on themselves by hindering Israel's advance into the Promised Land. Israel would not have taken Ammonite land, since God had expressly commanded them not to (Deut. 2:19). The Ammonites were only indirectly affected by Israel's expansion (Num. 21:25–26). In addition, the Ammonites never really had true claim to the land to begin with; it was in fact the land of the Amorites (vv. 19–22). The limits of the Amorite land in verse 22 are precisely what the Ammonites claimed as theirs in verse 13 (Num. 21:24 also rebuts the Ammonites' claim). Israel had occupied the land in dispute for at least three hundred years, long enough to make a legitimate claim on it (v. 26).

11:24 *what your god Chemosh gives you.* Usually the worship of Chemosh is associated with Moab, elsewhere the Ammonites' god was called Molech. However, Ammon and Moab lived side by side, and apparently shared culture and religion as well as their common descent from Lot (Gen. 19:37–38) Jephthah's comment was a derisive jab at the ineffectiveness of their gods.

11:27 *the LORD, the Judge.* God is the ultimate source of all justice. He has the right to judge every man and woman. With His divine authority and power, God always judges with justice, while at the same time He is loving, compassionate, and perfect. **Strife** — Given the depravity of the human heart it is only expected that nation will declare war on nation. We also deal with "wars" and strife in our interpersonal relationships. When we are faced with unjust attacks, we can only do as Jephthah did and trust God to judge rightly between the two sides of the dispute.

11:31 *whatever comes out of the doors of my house.* Some have interpreted Jephthah's vow as a clear intention to offer a human sacrifice. The phrase "to meet me," coupled with coming out of the house seems to refer more appropriately to a human than an animal. Undoubtedly Jephthah knew that human

11:13 [g] Ge 32:22; Nu 21:24 **11:15** [h] Dt 2:9 [i] Dt 2:19 **11:16** [j] Nu 14:25; Dt 1:40 [k] Nu 20:1 **11:17** [l] Nu 20:14 [m] Nu 20:18, 21 [n] Jos 24:9 **11:18** [o] Nu 21:4 [p] Dt 2:8 [q] Nu 21:13 **11:19** [r] Nu 21:21-22; Dt 2:26-27 **11:20** [s] Nu 21:23; Dt 2:32 **11:22** [t] Dt 2:36 **11:24** [u] Nu 21:29; Jos 3:10; 1Ki 11:7 **11:25** [v] Nu 22:2 [w] Jos 24:9 **11:26** [x] Nu 21:25 **11:27** [y] Ge 18:25 [z] Ge 16:5; 31:53; 1Sa 24:12, 15 **11:29** [a] Nu 11:25; Jdg 3:10; 6:34; 14:6, 19; 15:14; 1Sa 11:6; 16:13; Isa 11:2 **11:30** [b] Ge 28:20

Ammonites, and the LORD gave them into
his hands. 33He devastated twenty towns
from Aroer to the vicinity of Minnith,[c] as
far as Abel Keramim. Thus Israel subdued
Ammon.
34When Jephthah returned to his home
in Mizpah, who should come out to meet
him but his daughter, dancing to the sound
of timbrels![d] She was an only child. Except for her he had neither son nor daughter. 35When he saw her, he tore his clothes
and cried, "Oh no, my daughter! You have
brought me down and I am devastated. I
have made a vow to the LORD that I cannot
break.[e]"
36"My father," she replied, "you have giv-
en your word to the LORD. Do to me just
as you promised,[f] now that the LORD has
avenged you of your enemies,[g] the Ammonites. 37But grant me this one request,"
she said. "Give me two months to roam the
hills and weep with my friends, because I
will never marry."
38"You may go," he said. And he let her
go for two months. She and her friends
went into the hills and wept because
she would never marry. 39After the two
months, she returned to her father, and he
did to her as he had vowed. And she was
a virgin.
From this comes the Israelite tradition
40that each year the young women of Israel go out for four days to commemorate the
daughter of Jephthah the Gileadite.

Jephthah and Ephraim

12 The Ephraimite forces were called
out, and they crossed over to Zaphon.
They said to Jephthah, "Why did you go to
fight the Ammonites without calling us to
go with you?[h] We're going to burn down
your house over your head."
2Jephthah answered, "I and my people
were engaged in a great struggle with the
Ammonites, and although I called, you
didn't save me out of their hands. 3When
I saw that you wouldn't help, I took my life
in my hands[i] and crossed over to fight the
Ammonites, and the LORD gave me the victory over them. Now why have you come
up today to fight me?"
4Jephthah then called together the men
of Gilead and fought against Ephraim.
The Gileadites struck them down because
the Ephraimites had said, "You Gileadites
are renegades from Ephraim and Manasseh." 5The Gileadites captured the fords
of the Jordan[j] leading to Ephraim, and
whenever a survivor of Ephraim said, "Let
me cross over," the men of Gilead asked
him, "Are you an Ephraimite?" If he replied, "No," 6they said, "All right, say
'Shibboleth.'" If he said, "Sibboleth," because he could not pronounce the word
correctly, they seized him and killed
him at the fords of the Jordan. Forty-two
thousand Ephraimites were killed at that
time.

---

sacrifice was strictly forbidden in Israel (Lev. 18:21; 20:2; Deut. 12:31; 18:10; Jer. 19:5 Ezek. 20:30–31; 23:37–39), but his foolishness and lack of faith impelled him to make a reckless vow in order to try to manipulate God.

11:35 *I have made a vow ... that I cannot break.* Did Jephthah have to follow through on his vow? Ordinarily the answer would be yes. Vows were made only to God, and they were solemn pledges that had to be kept (Deut. 23:21–23; Ps. 15:4; Eccl. 5:4–5). But if Jephthah intended his vow to include human sacrifice, he was vowing to sin, an action which could hardly please the Lord.

11:39 *he did to her as he had vowed.* The text does not explicitly say that he killed his daughter, and some believe that instead he "sacrificed" her by dedicating her to a life of virginity. Human sacrifice was contrary to the law of Moses (Lev. 18:21; 20:2–5; Deut. 12:31; 18:10). Until the wicked reigns of Ahaz and Manasseh centuries later (2 Kin. 16:3; 21:6), there is no record of human sacrifice in Israel, even by those who followed Baal. The great respect that Jephthah had for God would surely have prevented him from making such a perverse offering. The several references to her virginity seem to support the idea of lifelong celibacy, and the Bible provides evidence that such devoted service for women did exist at the central sanctuary (Ex. 38:8; 1 Sam. 2:22; Luke 2:36–37). Jephthah's vow in verse 31 could be translated "shall be the LORD's, *or* I will offer it up as a burnt offering." Thus his vow could be interpreted that if a person came out first, he would dedicate that person to the Lord, or if an animal came out first, he would offer the animal as a burnt sacrifice. As is frequently the case in the Book of Judges, we are given the bare facts of a puzzling story and no comment about what God thought of it.

12:2 Strife—Gilead and Ephraim grew so hostile that they came to blows, brother fighting against brother. Instead of putting their energy into fighting their common enemy, they were fighting each other. In the same way, today, Christians often react with hurt feelings, pride, and resentment, and prefer to fight against flesh and blood rather than against principalities and powers. The constant infighting Christians indulge in is often a reason for the rest of the world to pass the church off as much ado about nothing.

12:4 *You ... are renegades from Ephraim.* This insult may have its roots in the division of the nation into eastern and western groups (5:17; Josh. 1:12–15). Despite the emphasis in Joshua on the unity of all the tribes (Josh. 1:12–15; 22:1–34), the practical reality in the period of the judges was dramatically different.

12:6 *Shibboleth ... Sibboleth.* This is the only significant reference to the linguistic differences which apparently existed between the tribes. Today the English word *shibboleth* means an otherwise minor difference that becomes a sticking point because it distinguishes one side from the other.

11:33 [c] Eze 27:17 **11:34** [d] Ex 15:20; Jer 31:4
11:35 [e] Nu 30:2; Ecc 5:2, 4, 5 **11:36** [f] Lk 1:38 [g] 2Sa 18:19
12:1 [h] Jdg 8:1 **12:3** [i] 1Sa 19:5; 28:21; Job 13:14
12:5 [j] Jos 22:11; Jdg 3:28

7Jephthah led[a] Israel six years. Then
Jephthah the Gileadite died and was buried in a town in Gilead.

Ibzan, Elon and Abdon

8After him, Ibzan of Bethlehem led Israel. 9He had thirty sons and thirty daughters. He gave his daughters away in marriage to those outside his clan, and for his
sons he brought in thirty young women as
wives from outside his clan. Ibzan led Israel seven years. 10Then Ibzan died and was
buried in Bethlehem.
11After him, Elon the Zebulunite led Israel ten years. 12Then Elon died and was
buried in Aijalon in the land of Zebulun.
13After him, Abdon son of Hillel, from
Pirathon, led Israel. 14He had forty sons
and thirty grandsons,[k] who rode on seventy donkeys.[l] He led Israel eight years.
15Then Abdon son of Hillel died and was
buried at Pirathon in Ephraim, in the hill
country of the Amalekites.[m]

The Birth of Samson

13 Again the Israelites did evil in the
eyes of the LORD, so the LORD delivered them into the hands of the Philistines[n]
for forty years.
2A certain man of Zorah,[o] named Manoah, from the clan of the Danites, had a wife
who was childless, unable to give birth.
3The angel of the LORD[p] appeared to her[q]
and said, "You are barren and childless,
but you are going to become pregnant and
give birth to a son.[r] 4Now see to it that you
drink no wine or other fermented drink
and that you do not eat anything unclean.[s]
5You will become pregnant and have a son
whose head is never to be touched by a razor[t] because the boy is to be a Nazirite,[u]
dedicated to God from the womb. He will
take the lead[v] in delivering Israel from the
hands of the Philistines."
6Then the woman went to her husband
and told him, "A man of God[w] came to me.
He looked like an angel of God,[x] very awesome. I didn't ask him where he came from,
and he didn't tell me his name. 7But he said
to me, 'You will become pregnant and have
a son. Now then, drink no wine or other
fermented drink and do not eat anything
unclean, because the boy will be a Nazirite
of God from the womb until the day of his
death.'"
8Then Manoah prayed to the LORD: "Pardon your servant, Lord. I beg you to let the
man of God you sent to us come again to
teach us how to bring up the boy who is to
be born."
9God heard Manoah, and the angel of
God came again to the woman while she
was out in the field; but her husband Manoah was not with her. 10The woman hurried
to tell her husband, "He's here! The man
who appeared to me the other day!"
11Manoah got up and followed his wife.
When he came to the man, he said, "Are
you the man who talked to my wife?"
"I am," he said.
12So Manoah asked him, "When your
words are fulfilled, what is to be the rule
that governs the boy's life and work?"
13The angel of the LORD answered, "Your
wife must do all that I have told her. 14She
must not eat anything that comes from the
grapevine, nor drink any wine or other fermented drink[y] nor eat anything unclean.[z]
She must do everything I have commanded her."
15Manoah said to the angel of the LORD,
"We would like you to stay until we prepare
a young goat[a] for you."
16The angel of the LORD replied, "Even
though you detain me, I will not eat any
of your food. But if you prepare a burnt
offering,[b] offer it to the LORD." (Manoah
did not realize that it was the angel of the
LORD.)
17Then Manoah inquired of the angel
of the LORD, "What is your name,[c] so that
we may honor you when your word comes
true?"

[a] 7 Traditionally *judged*; also in verses 8-14

13:1—16:31 Samson—The last of the judges lived at the beginning of the eleventh century B.C. He was unusual among the judges in many ways. He did not lead an army, but carried on his campaign against the Philistines singlehanded. He is mentioned in Hebrews 11:32 in the list of judges who accomplished great things through faith. The Book of Judges, in contrast, paints a darker picture. His checkered history of heroism and moral failure resembles Israel's troubles during the time of the judges.

13:3 *The angel of the LORD.* The angel of the Lord made a supernatural appearance, described here as "very awesome." Manoah's wife recognized him as "a Man of God." The essential character of the angel, embodied in his name, was not revealed to them (vv. 17–18). It seems that the angel of the Lord was God Himself, in a form they could perceive (13:21–22; Gen. 22:11; Ex. 3:14–15).

13:5 *Nazirite.* The regulations of the Nazirite vows are found in Numbers 6:1–21. Samson's Nazirite service was remarkable in three ways. First, he did not take his vow voluntarily; it was his before birth. Second, his service was to be lifelong, not temporary. Third, he eventually broke every one of its stipulations.

13:6 *man of God.* This was a term used to describe the prophets (Deut. 33:1; 1 Kin. 17:18). At first Samson's mother may have thought she was talking to a prophet, but His radiant appearance convinced her otherwise.

12:14 [k] Jdg 10:4 [l] Jdg 5:10 **12:15** [m] Jdg 5:14
13:1 [n] Jdg 2:11; 1Sa 12:9 **13:2** [o] Jos 15:33; 19:41
13:3 [p] ver 6, 8; Jdg 6:12 [q] ver 10 [r] Lk 1:13 **13:4** [s] ver 14; Nu 6:2-4; Lk 1:15 **13:5** [t] Nu 6:5, 1Sa 1:11 [u] Nu 6:2, 13 [v] 1Sa 7:13 **13:6** [w] ver 8; 1Sa 2:27; 9:6 [x] ver 17-18; Mt 28:3
13:14 [y] Nu 6:4 [z] ver 4 **13:15** [a] ver 3; Jdg 6:19
13:16 [b] Jdg 6:20 **13:17** [c] Ge 32:29

18 He replied, "Why do you ask my
name?[d] It is beyond understanding.[a]"
19 Then Manoah took a young goat, together with the grain offering, and sacrificed it
on a rock[e] to the LORD. And the LORD did an
amazing thing while Manoah and his wife
watched: 20 As the flame[f] blazed up from
the altar toward heaven, the angel of the
LORD ascended in the flame. Seeing this,
Manoah and his wife fell with their faces to
the ground.[g] 21 When the angel of the LORD
did not show himself again to Manoah and
his wife, Manoah realized[h] that it was the
angel of the LORD.

22 "We are doomed[i] to die!" he said to his
wife. "We have seen[j] God!"

23 But his wife answered, "If the LORD
had meant to kill us, he would not have
accepted a burnt offering and grain offering from our hands, nor shown us all these
things or now told us this."[k]

24 The woman gave birth to a boy and
named him Samson.[l] He grew[m] and the
LORD blessed him,[n] 25 and the Spirit of the
LORD began to stir[o] him while he was in Mahaneh Dan,[p] between Zorah and Eshtaol.

Samson's Marriage

14 Samson went down to Timnah[q] and
saw there a young Philistine woman.
2 When he returned, he said to his father
and mother, "I have seen a Philistine woman in Timnah; now get her for me as my
wife."[r]

3 His father and mother replied, "Isn't
there an acceptable woman among your
relatives or among all our people?[s] Must
you go to the uncircumcised[t] Philistines to
get a wife?[u]"

But Samson said to his father, "Get her
for me. She's the right one for me." 4 (His
parents did not know that this was from
the LORD, who was seeking an occasion to
confront the Philistines;[v] for at that time
they were ruling over Israel.)[w]

5 Samson went down to Timnah together with his father and mother. As they approached the vineyards of Timnah, suddenly a young lion came roaring toward
him. 6 The Spirit of the LORD came powerfully upon him[x] so that he tore the lion
apart with his bare hands as he might have
torn a young goat. But he told neither his
father nor his mother what he had done.
7 Then he went down and talked with the
woman, and he liked her.

8 Some time later, when he went back to
marry her, he turned aside to look at the
lion's carcass, and in it he saw a swarm of
bees and some honey. 9 He scooped out the
honey with his hands and ate as he went
along. When he rejoined his parents, he
gave them some, and they too ate it. But he
did not tell them that he had taken the honey from the lion's carcass.

10 Now his father went down to see the
woman. And there Samson held a feast, as
was customary for young men. 11 When the

a 18 Or *is wonderful*

13:21–22 *the angel of the LORD.* Manoah's reaction is similar to the reaction Gideon had when he recognized the angel of the Lord (6:22).

13:25 *the Spirit of the LORD began to stir him.* The Hebrew word translated *stir* can also mean *impel.* The Spirit of the Lord was pushing Samson toward doing the work that God wanted him to do.

14:2 *get her for me as my wife.* Such marriages with foreigners were prohibited for Israelites (Ex. 34:16; Deut. 7:3).

14:3 She's the right one for me. Samson's words reveal his self-centered attitude. Instead of seeking to serve God, he was seeking to please himself. Samson's comment here foreshadows the author's summary of the entire period of the judges (17:6; 18:1; 19:1; 21:25).

Unfaithfulness—The beginning of Samson's downfall was his disobedience to the Lord in his marriage. The theme of marriage within the covenant is common in the Old Testament. From earliest times the people of God were told not to contract marriages with unbelievers (Gen. 6:2). When the covenant was renewed prior to the people's entry into Canaanite territory, Joshua warned them not to intermarry; to do so would be evidence of their failure to cling to the Lord (Josh. 23:8,12). It is a tragic picture of the decadence of this period to see Samson's unfaithfulness to the Lord in taking a pagan wife. The New Covenant believer remains under the same divine command to marry only in the Lord (1 Cor. 7:39; 2 Cor. 6:14).

14:4 *this was from the LORD.* God would use Samson's defiant wish as a way of defeating the Philistines and providing relief for His people.

14:6 *The Spirit of the LORD came powerfully upon him.* The Old Testament speaks numerous times of God's Spirit coming mightily upon individuals, usually to empower them physically for great feats of strength (3:10; 6:34; 11:29). The Spirit empowered others for the important task of speaking God's word (Gen. 41:38; Num. 24:2; 1 Sam. 10:6; 19:20). It appears that the work of the Holy Spirit in the Old Testament was primarily a special anointing to accomplish a certain task, and was different from the indwelling Presence that believers enjoy today. Saul (1 Sam. 10:10; 16:23) and David (1 Sam. 16:13; Ps. 51:11) were both filled with the Holy Spirit when they were anointed as king, but this presence seems to have been directly linked to their obedience.

14:8–9 *the lion's carcass.* Touching the dead lion violated Samson's Nazirite vow (13:5).

14:10 *feast.* The word translated *feast* denotes a banquet with considerable drinking. The passage does not say so, but it is not unlikely that this occasioned another violation of Samson's Nazirite vow (13:5).

13:18 [d] Isa 9:6 **13:19** [e] Jdg 6:20 **13:20** [f] Lev 9:24 [g] 1Ch 21:16; Eze 1:28; Mt 17:6 **13:21** [h] ver 16; Jdg 6:22 **13:22** [i] Dt 5:26 [j] Ge 32:30; Jdg 6:22 **13:23** [k] Ps 25:14 **13:24** [l] Heb 11:32 [m] 1Sa 3:19 [n] Lk 1:80 **13:25** [o] Jdg 3:10 [p] Jdg 18:12 **14:1** [q] Ge 38:12 **14:2** [r] Ge 21:21; 34:4 **14:3** [s] Ge 24:4 [t] Dt 7:3 [u] Ex 34:16 **14:4** [v] Jos 11:20 [w] Jdg 13:1 **14:6** [x] Jdg 3:10; 13:25

people saw him, they chose thirty men to
be his companions.
12“Let me tell you a riddle,[y]” Samson said
to them. “If you can give me the answer
within the seven days of the feast,[z] I will
give you thirty linen garments and thirty
sets of clothes.[a] 13If you can’t tell me the
answer, you must give me thirty linen garments and thirty sets of clothes.”
“Tell us your riddle,” they said. “Let’s
hear it.”
14He replied,

“Out of the eater, something to eat;
out of the strong, something sweet.”

For three days they could not give the answer.
15On the fourth[a] day, they said to Samson’s wife, “Coax[b] your husband into explaining the riddle for us, or we will burn
you and your father’s household to death.[c]
Did you invite us here to steal our property?”
16Then Samson’s wife threw herself on
him, sobbing, “You hate me! You don’t really love me.[d] You’ve given my people a riddle, but you haven’t told me the answer.”
“I haven’t even explained it to my father
or mother,” he replied, “so why should I explain it to you?” 17She cried the whole seven
days[e] of the feast. So on the seventh day he
finally told her, because she continued to
press him. She in turn explained the riddle
to her people.
18Before sunset on the seventh day the
men of the town said to him,

“What is sweeter than honey?
What is stronger than a lion?”[f]

Samson said to them,

“If you had not plowed with my heifer,
you would not have solved my riddle.”

19Then the Spirit of the LORD came powerfully upon him.[g] He went down to Ashkelon, struck down thirty of their men,
stripped them of everything and gave their
clothes to those who had explained the riddle. Burning with anger,[h] he returned to his
father’s home. 20And Samson’s wife was
given to one of his companions[i] who had
attended him at the feast.

Samson’s Vengeance on the Philistines

15 Later on, at the time of wheat harvest,
Samson took a young goat[j] and went
to visit his wife. He said, “I’m going to my
wife’s room.” But her father would not let
him go in.
2“I was so sure you hated her,” he said,
“that I gave her to your companion.[k] Isn’t
her younger sister more attractive? Take
her instead.”
3Samson said to them, “This time I
have a right to get even with the Philistines; I will really harm them.” 4So he
went out and caught three hundred foxes and tied them tail to tail in pairs. He
then fastened a torch to every pair of tails,
5lit the torches and let the foxes loose in
the standing grain of the Philistines. He
burned up the shocks and standing grain,
together with the vineyards and olive
groves.
6When the Philistines asked, “Who did
this?” they were told, “Samson, the Tim-
nite’s son-in-law, because his wife was giv-
en to his companion.”
So the Philistines went up and burned
her and her father to death.[l] 7Samson said
to them, “Since you’ve acted like this, I
swear that I won’t stop until I get my revenge on you.” 8He attacked them vicious-
ly and slaughtered many of them. Then he
went down and stayed in a cave in the rock
of Etam.
9The Philistines went up and camped
in Judah, spreading out near Lehi.[m] 10The
people of Judah asked, “Why have you
come to fight us?”
“We have come to take Samson prisoner,” they answered, “to do to him as he did
to us.”
11Then three thousand men from Judah
went down to the cave in the rock of Etam
and said to Samson, “Don’t you realize that
the Philistines are rulers over us?[n] What
have you done to us?”
He answered, “I merely did to them what
they did to me.”
12They said to him, “We’ve come to tie
you up and hand you over to the Philistines.”
Samson said, “Swear to me that you
won’t kill me yourselves.”
13“Agreed,” they answered. “We will
only tie you up and hand you over to them.
We will not kill you.” So they bound him
with two new ropes and led him up from
the rock. 14As he approached Lehi, the Philistines came toward him shouting. The
Spirit of the LORD came powerfully upon
him.[o] The ropes on his arms became like
charred flax, and the bindings dropped

---

[a] *15* Some Septuagint manuscripts and Syriac; Hebrew *seventh*

15:1 *the time of wheat harvest.* This would have been late May or early June. The wheat harvest was associated with the second of the three great festivals in Israel, the Festival of Weeks, also known as Pentecost (Lev. 23:15–22; Deut. 16:9–12).

15:13 *two new ropes.* Ropes were made of leather, hair, or plant fibers; one common fiber was flax (Josh. 2:6). Being new, these ropes were the strongest possible.

14:12 [y] 1Ki 10:1; Eze 17:2 [z] Ge 29:27 [a] Ge 45:22; 2Ki 5:5 **14:15** [b] Jdg 16:5; Ecc 7:26 [c] Jdg 15:6 **14:16** [d] Jdg 16:15 **14:17** [e] Est 1:5 **14:18** [f] ver 14 **14:19** [g] Nu 11:25; Jdg 3:10; 6:34; 11:29; 13:25; 15:14; 1Sa 11:6; 16:13; 1Ki 18:46; 2Ch 24:20; Isa 11:2 [h] 1Sa 11:6 **14:20** [i] Jdg 15:2, 6; Jn 3:29 **15:1** [j] Ge 38:17 **15:2** [k] Jdg 14:20 **15:6** [l] Jdg 14:15 **15:9** [m] ver 14, 17, 19 **15:11** [n] Jdg 13:1; 14:4; Ps 106:40-42 **15:14** [o] Jdg 3:10; 14:19; 1Sa 11:6

from his hands. 15 Finding a fresh jawbone
of a donkey, he grabbed it and struck down
a thousand men.[p]
16 Then Samson said,

"With a donkey's jawbone
I have made donkeys of them.[a]
With a donkey's jawbone
I have killed a thousand men."

17 When he finished speaking, he threw
away the jawbone; and the place was called
Ramath Lehi.[b]
18 Because he was very thirsty, he cried
out to the LORD,[q] "You have given your
servant this great victory. Must I now die
of thirst and fall into the hands of the uncircumcised?" 19 Then God opened up the
hollow place in Lehi, and water came out
of it. When Samson drank, his strength returned and he revived.[r] So the spring was
called En Hakkore,[c] and it is still there in
Lehi.
20 Samson led[d] Israel for twenty years[s] in
the days of the Philistines.

Samson and Delilah

16 One day Samson went to Gaza, where
he saw a prostitute. He went in to
spend the night with her. 2 The people of
Gaza were told, "Samson is here!" So they
surrounded the place and lay in wait for
him all night at the city gate.[t] They made
no move during the night, saying, "At dawn
we'll kill him."
3 But Samson lay there only until the middle of the night. Then he got up and took
hold of the doors of the city gate, together with the two posts, and tore them loose,
bar and all. He lifted them to his shoulders
and carried them to the top of the hill that
faces Hebron.[u]
4 Some time later, he fell in love[v] with a
woman in the Valley of Sorek whose name
was Delilah. 5 The rulers of the Philistines[w]
went to her and said, "See if you can lure[x]
him into showing you the secret of his
great strength and how we can overpower
him so we may tie him up and subdue him.
Each one of us will give you eleven hundred shekels[e] of silver."[y]
6 So Delilah said to Samson, "Tell me the
secret of your great strength and how you
can be tied up and subdued."
7 Samson answered her, "If anyone ties
me with seven fresh bowstrings that have
not been dried, I'll become as weak as any
other man."
8 Then the rulers of the Philistines
brought her seven fresh bowstrings that
had not been dried, and she tied him with
them. 9 With men hidden in the room,[z] she
called to him, "Samson, the Philistines are
upon you!" But he snapped the bowstrings
as easily as a piece of string snaps when it
comes close to a flame. So the secret of his
strength was not discovered.
10 Then Delilah said to Samson, "You
have made a fool of me;[a] you lied to me.
Come now, tell me how you can be tied."
11 He said, "If anyone ties me securely
with new ropes[b] that have never been used,
I'll become as weak as any other man."
12 So Delilah took new ropes and tied him
with them. Then, with men hidden in the
room, she called to him, "Samson, the Philistines are upon you!" But he snapped the
ropes off his arms as if they were threads.
13 Delilah then said to Samson, "All this
time you have been making a fool of me
and lying to me. Tell me how you can be
tied."
He replied, "If you weave the seven
braids of my head into the fabric on the
loom and tighten it with the pin, I'll become as weak as any other man." So while
he was sleeping, Delilah took the seven
braids of his head, wove them into the fabric 14 and[f] tightened it with the pin.
Again she called to him, "Samson, the
Philistines are upon you!"[c] He awoke from
his sleep and pulled up the pin and the
loom, with the fabric.
15 Then she said to him, "How can you
say, 'I love you,'[d] when you won't confide in
me? This is the third time[e] you have made a
fool of me and haven't told me the secret of
your great strength.[f]" 16 With such nagging
she prodded him day after day until he was
sick to death of it.

[a] 16 Or *made a heap or two*; the Hebrew for *donkey* sounds like the Hebrew for *heap*. [b] 17 *Ramath Lehi* means *jawbone hill*. [c] 19 *En Hakkore* means *caller's spring*. [d] 20 Traditionally *judged* [e] 5 That is, about 28 pounds or about 13 kilograms [f] 13,14 Some Septuagint manuscripts; Hebrew *replied, "I can if you weave the seven braids of my head into the fabric on the loom."* 14 *So she*

15:15 *a fresh jawbone.* A fresh jawbone would have been tough, resilient, and virtually unbreakable.
15:18 *cried out to the LORD.* This is the first record of Samson calling on the Lord.
16:2 *at the city gate.* The gates of this time in history were at least two stories high, with guard rooms on either side of a narrow opening. The Philistines waited in the recesses of the gate, hoping to trap Samson.
16:3 *carried them to the top of the hill.* Given the large size of the doors of a city gate, Samson's feat was astounding. Hebron is 40 miles east of Gaza. Samson's trip would have taken the better part of a day.
16:16 *prodded him.* Delilah pestered him just as his wife had done earlier (14:17). Samson's foolishness prevented him from learning the lesson of his earlier experience.

15:15 [p] Lev 26:8; Jos 23:10; Jdg 3:31 **15:18** [q] Jdg 16:28 **15:19** [r] Ge 45:27; Isa 40:29 **15:20** [s] Jdg 13:1; 16:31; Heb 11:32 **16:2** [t] 1Sa 23:26; Ps 118:10-12; Ac 9:24 **16:3** [u] Jos 10:36 **16:4** [v] Ge 24:67 **16:5** [w] Jos 13:3 [x] Ex 10:7; Jdg 14:15 [y] ver 18 **16:9** [z] ver 12 **16:10** [a] ver 13 **16:11** [b] Jdg 15:13 **16:14** [c] ver 9, 20 **16:15** [d] Jdg 14:16 [e] Nu 24:10 [f] ver 5

17 So he told her everything.[g] “No razor
has ever been used on my head,” he said,
“because I have been a Nazirite[h] dedicated
to God from my mother’s womb. If my head
were shaved, my strength would leave me,
and I would become as weak as any other
man.”
18 When Delilah saw that he had told her
everything, she sent word to the rulers of
the Philistines[i], “Come back once more; he
has told me everything.” So the rulers of
the Philistines returned with the silver in
their hands. 19 After putting him to sleep on
her lap, she called for someone to shave off
the seven braids of his hair, and so began
to subdue him.[a] And his strength left him.[j]
20 Then she called, “Samson, the Philistines are upon you!”
He awoke from his sleep and thought,
“I’ll go out as before and shake myself
free.” But he did not know that the LORD
had left him.[k]
21 Then the Philistines[l] seized him,
gouged out his eyes[m] and took him down
to Gaza. Binding him with bronze shackles, they set him to grinding grain[n] in the
prison. 22 But the hair on his head began to
grow again after it had been shaved.

The Death of Samson

23 Now the rulers of the Philistines assembled to offer a great sacrifice to Dagon[o]
their god and to celebrate, saying, “Our god
has delivered Samson, our enemy, into our
hands.”
24 When the people saw him, they praised
their god,[p] saying,

“Our god has delivered our enemy
into our hands,[q]
the one who laid waste our land
and multiplied our slain.”

25 While they were in high spirits,[r] they
shouted, “Bring out Samson to entertain
us.” So they called Samson out of the prison, and he performed for them.
When they stood him among the pillars,
26 Samson said to the servant who held
his hand, “Put me where I can feel the pillars that support the temple, so that I may
lean against them.” 27 Now the temple was
crowded with men and women; all the rulers of the Philistines were there, and on
the roof[s] were about three thousand men
and women watching Samson perform.
28 Then Samson prayed to the LORD,[t] “Sovereign LORD, remember me. Please, God,
strengthen me just once more, and let me
with one blow get revenge[u] on the Philistines for my two eyes.” 29 Then Samson
reached toward the two central pillars on
which the temple stood. Bracing himself
against them, his right hand on the one and
his left hand on the other, 30 Samson said,
“Let me die with the Philistines!” Then he
pushed with all his might, and down came
the temple on the rulers and all the people
in it. Thus he killed many more when he
died than while he lived.
31 Then his brothers and his father’s
whole family went down to get him. They
brought him back and buried him between
Zorah and Eshtaol in the tomb of Manoah[v] his father. He had led[b][w] Israel twenty
years.[x]

Micah’s Idols

17 Now a man named Micah[y] from the
hill country of Ephraim 2 said to his
mother, “The eleven hundred shekels[c] of

[a] 19 Hebrew; some Septuagint manuscripts *and he began to weaken* [b] 31 Traditionally *judged*
[c] 2 That is, about 28 pounds or about 13 kilograms

16:19 *And his strength left him.* When he broke the final stipulation of the Nazirite vow by allowing his hair to be cut, the Lord left him and he was captured.

16:20 *he did not know.* This is one of the few editorial comments by the author.

16:23 *Dagon.* Dagon was the principal Philistine god. A Philistine temple for Dagon was at Beth Shan, in northern Israel, in the days of Saul (1 Sam. 31:9–10; 1 Chr. 10:10), and it was in another such temple that the Philistines stored the ark of the covenant for a time (1 Sam. 5:1–7). Dagon was once commonly thought to be a fish god, but modern excavations have shown that he was a god of grain. In fact, one of the Hebrew words for grain is *dagan.*

16:24 *Our god has delivered our enemy into our hands.* The Philistines viewed their success over Samson as a triumph for their god (Judg. 16:23–24). In reality it was the Lord who had delivered Samson into their hands, for "the LORD had left him" (v. 20).

16:30 Zeal—The famous lament of David over Saul and Jonathan, "How the mighty have fallen!" (2 Sam. 1:19,27), could also be applied to Samson. He came from a godly home, but often was overcome by evil passion, pride, and violence. Yet at death his zeal for the Lord brought about a great victory over the Philistines and their god Dagon, and he is listed in Hebrews as a man of faith (Heb. 11:32). The plan and purpose of God overruled Samson's folly and the Philistines' arrogance.

16:31 *He had led Israel twenty years.* The story of the judges concludes with final editorial comments. Samson, the last judge, had been empowered by God's Spirit, just as the first had been. Despite the manifold failings of the judges themselves, God had delivered Israel and caused other nations to bow before Him. Samson's life is ultimately a story about God's faithfulness in spite of human weakness.

17:1—21:25 Conclusion—The Book of Judges closes with two appendices (chs. 17–18; 19–21). They seem to be unrelated to the material preceding

16:17 [g] Mic 7:5 [h] Nu 6:2, 5; Jdg 13:5 **16:18** [i] Jos 13:3; 1Sa 5:8 **16:19** [j] Pr 7:26-27 **16:20** [k] Nu 14:42; Jos 7:12; 1Sa 16:14; 18:12; 28:15 **16:21** [l] Jer 47:1 [m] Nu 16:14 [n] Job 31:10; Isa 47:2 **16:23** [o] 1Sa 5:2; 1Ch 10:10 **16:24** [p] Da 5:4 [q] 1Sa 31:9; 1Ch 10:9 **16:25** [r] Jdg 9:27; Ru 3:7; Est 1:10 **16:27** [s] Dt 22:8; Jos 2:8 **16:28** [t] Jdg 15:18 [u] Jer 15:15 **16:31** [v] Jdg 13:2 [w] Ru 1:1; 1Sa 4:18 [x] Jdg 15:20 **17:1** [y] Jdg 18:2, 13

silver that were taken from you and about
which I heard you utter a curse—I have
that silver with me; I took it."
Then his mother said, "The LORD bless
you,[z] my son!"
3When he returned the eleven hundred
shekels of silver to his mother, she said, "I
solemnly consecrate my silver to the LORD
for my son to make an image overlaid with
silver.[a] I will give it back to you."
4So after he returned the silver to his
mother, she took two hundred shekels[a] of
silver and gave them to a silversmith, who
used them to make the idol.[b] And it was put
in Micah's house.
5Now this man Micah had a shrine,[c] and
he made an ephod[d] and some household
gods[e] and installed[f] one of his sons as his
priest.[g] 6In those days Israel had no king;[h]
everyone did as they saw fit.[i]
7A young Levite from Bethlehem in Judah,[j] who had been living within the clan of
Judah, 8left that town in search of some other place to stay. On his way[b] he came to Micah's house in the hill country of Ephraim.
9Micah asked him, "Where are you
from?"
"I'm a Levite from Bethlehem in Judah,"
he said, "and I'm looking for a place to
stay."
10Then Micah said to him, "Live with
me and be my father and priest,[k] and I'll
give you ten shekels[c] of silver a year, your
clothes and your food." 11So the Levite
agreed to live with him, and the young
man became like one of his sons to him.
12Then Micah installed[l] the Levite, and the
young man became his priest and lived in
his house. 13And Micah said, "Now I know
that the LORD will be good to me, since this
Levite has become my priest."

The Danites Settle in Laish

18 In those days Israel had no king.[m]
And in those days the tribe of the
Danites was seeking a place of their own
where they might settle, because they had
not yet come into an inheritance among
the tribes of Israel.[n] 2So the Danites[o] sent
five of their leading men from Zorah and
Eshtaol to spy out the land and explore it.
These men represented all the Danites.
They told them, "Go, explore the land."[p]
So they entered the hill country of Ephraim and came to the house of Micah,[q] where
they spent the night. 3When they were near
Micah's house, they recognized the voice of
the young Levite; so they turned in there
and asked him, "Who brought you here?
What are you doing in this place? Why are
you here?"
4He told them what Micah had done for
him, and said, "He has hired me and I am
his priest.[r]"
5Then they said to him, "Please inquire
of God[s] to learn whether our journey will
be successful."
6The priest answered them, "Go in
peace[t]. Your journey has the LORD's approval."
7So the five men left and came to Laish,[u]
where they saw that the people were living
in safety, like the Sidonians, at peace and
secure. And since their land lacked nothing, they were prosperous.[d] Also, they
lived a long way from the Sidonians[v] and
had no relationship with anyone else.[e]
8When they returned to Zorah and Eshtaol, their fellow Danites asked them, "How
did you find things?"
9They answered, "Come on, let's attack
them! We have seen the land, and it is very
good. Aren't you going to do something?
Don't hesitate to go there and take it over.[w]

---

[a] 4 That is, about 5 pounds or about 2.3 kilograms
[b] 8 Or *To carry on his profession* [c] 10 That is, about 4 ounces or about 115 grams [d] 7 The meaning of the Hebrew for this clause is uncertain.
[e] 7 Hebrew; some Septuagint manuscripts *with the Arameans*

---

them, and to each other. While chapters 2–16 describe foreign threats to Israel, these last chapters show an internal breakdown of Israel's worship and unity. Furthermore, the events of these chapters appear to have taken place early in the period of the judges. These chapters may have been written independently of the book's earlier chapters, but there is a certain logic to placing them at the end of the book. The structure highlights the theme of the disintegration of Israel, with the last chapters emphasizing that "everyone did as they saw fit" (17:6; 21:25).

17:3 *I solemnly consecrate my silver to the LORD.* Micah's mother approved of his action, claiming that these images would be offered on the Lord's behalf. • Today the temptation to mix elements of true worship of God with practices unacceptable to Him remains with us, even though it is in different ways.

17:5 *shrine.* This is literally "a house of God." This was a perversion of the true sanctuary where all worship was to take place. At this time the true "house of God" was at Shiloh (18:31). Micah further violated the law by appointing his own son as his private priest. Micah sinned because his son had not descended from Aaron, nor was he even a Levite (Ex. 28:1; 40:12–15; Num. 16:39–40; 17:8).

17:6 *as they saw fit.* This editorial comment is echoed in the last verse of the book (21:25). The author suggests that times were so bad that people did whatever they wanted, not what was right in the Lord's eyes (14:3). We may infer that a king who focused Israel's attention on the Lord would have prevented the outbreaks of sin and oppression so prevalent during the time of the judges.

17:2 [z] Ru 2:20; 1Sa 15:13; 2Sa 2:5 **17:3** [a] Ex 20:4,23; 34:17; Lev 19:4 **17:4** [b] Ex 32:4; Isa 17:8 **17:5** [c] Isa 44:13; Eze 8:10 [d] Jdg 8:27 [e] Ge 31:19; Jdg 18:14 [f] Nu 16:10 [g] Ex 29:9; Jdg 18:24 **17:6** [h] Jdg 18:1; 19:1; 21:25 [i] Dt 12:8 **17:7** [j] Jdg 19:1; Ru 1:1-2; Mic 5:2; Mt 2:1 **17:10** [k] Jdg 18:19 **17:12** [l] Nu 16:10 **18:1** [m] Jdg 17:6; 19:1 [n] Jos 19:47 **18:2** [o] Jdg 13:25 [p] Jos 2:1 [q] Jdg 17:1 **18:4** [r] Jdg 17:12 **18:5** [s] 1Ki 22:5 **18:6** [t] 1Ki 22:6 **18:7** [u] Jos 19:47 [v] ver 28 **18:9** [w] Nu 13:30; 1Ki 22:3

10When you get there, you will find an unsuspecting people and a spacious land that
God has put into your hands, a land that
lacks nothing[x] whatever.[y]"
11Then six hundred men[z] of the Danites,[a]
armed for battle, set out from Zorah and
Eshtaol. 12On their way they set up camp
near Kiriath Jearim in Judah. This is why
the place west of Kiriath Jearim is called
Mahaneh Dan[a][b] to this day. 13From there
they went on to the hill country of Ephraim
and came to Micah's house.
14Then the five men who had spied out
the land of Laish said to their fellow Danites, "Do you know that one of these houses
has an ephod, some household gods and an
image overlaid with silver?[c] Now you know
what to do." 15So they turned in there and
went to the house of the young Levite at
Micah's place and greeted him. 16The six
hundred Danites,[d] armed for battle, stood
at the entrance of the gate. 17The five men
who had spied out the land went inside and
took the idol, the ephod and the household
gods[e] while the priest and the six hundred
armed men stood at the entrance of the gate.
18When the five men went into Micah's
house and took[f] the idol, the ephod and the
household gods, the priest said to them,
"What are you doing?"
19They answered him, "Be quiet![g] Don't
say a word. Come with us, and be our father
and priest.[h] Isn't it better that you serve a
tribe and clan in Israel as priest rather than
just one man's household?" 20The priest was
very pleased. He took the ephod, the household gods and the idol and went along with
the people. 21Putting their little children,
their livestock and their possessions in front
of them, they turned away and left.
22When they had gone some distance
from Micah's house, the men who lived
near Micah were called together and overtook the Danites. 23As they shouted after
them, the Danites turned and said to Micah, "What's the matter with you that you
called out your men to fight?"
24He replied, "You took the gods I made,
and my priest, and went away. What else
do I have? How can you ask, 'What's the
matter with you?'"
25The Danites answered, "Don't argue
with us, or some of the men may get angry and attack you, and you and your family will lose your lives." 26So the Danites
went their way, and Micah, seeing that they
were too strong for him,[i] turned around
and went back home.
27Then they took what Micah had made,
and his priest, and went on to Laish,
against a people at peace and secure.[j] They
attacked them with the sword and burned
down their city.[k] 28There was no one to
rescue them because they lived a long way
from Sidon[l] and had no relationship with
anyone else. The city was in a valley near
Beth Rehob.[m]
The Danites rebuilt the city and settled
there. 29They named it Dan[n] after their
ancestor Dan, who was born to Israel—
though the city used to be called Laish.[o]
30There the Danites set up for themselves
the idol, and Jonathan son of Gershom,[p] the
son of Moses,[b] and his sons were priests for
the tribe of Dan until the time of the captivity of the land. 31They continued to use the
idol Micah had made, all the time the house
of God[q] was in Shiloh.[r]

A Levite and His Concubine

19 In those days Israel had no king.
Now a Levite who lived in a remote
area in the hill country of Ephraim[s] took
a concubine from Bethlehem in Judah.[t]
2But she was unfaithful to him. She left

---

[a] *12 Mahaneh Dan* means *Dan's camp.*
[b] *30* Many Hebrew manuscripts, some Septuagint manuscripts and Vulgate; many other Hebrew manuscripts and some other Septuagint manuscripts *Manasseh*

17:10 *be my father and priest.* To be called father was a title of honor. Micah wanted the Levite to be his priest, since his background would lend legitimacy to his service. Micah thought this would bring him God's favor (v. 13).
18:1 *Danites.* The Danites were looking for a place to settle because they had been unable to settle effectively in their allotted territory. Compare their allotment in Joshua 19:41–47 and their failure to capture it all (1:34–35). It seems clear that this story is not placed chronologically, but refers back to the first chapters of Judges. The Danites' migration in search of new land probably would have come soon after the events of 1:34, not some three centuries or more later.
18:7 *Sidonians.* Sidon was a port city northwest of Israel, in what today is Lebanon.
18:19 *be our father and priest.* The Levite's cynical acceptance of this opportunity for greater prestige indicates further how debased conditions had become. Those who had been divinely appointed to minister before the Lord were selling false spiritual services to the highest bidder.
18:31 *all the time that the house of God was in Shiloh.* The true worship of God in the appointed place was available all this time—the Danites just did not want to bother with it.
19:1 *a concubine.* A concubine was a female servant regarded as a part of the family, often chosen to bear children. Several of the patriarchs had children with concubines: Abraham with Hagar (Gen. 16); Jacob with Bilhah and Zilpah (Gen. 30:4–13).

18:10 [x] ver 7,27; Dt 8:9 [y] 1Ch 4:40 **18:11** [z] ver 16,17 [a] Jdg 13:2 **18:12** [b] Jdg 13:25 **18:14** [c] Ge 31:19; Jdg 17:5 **18:16** [d] ver 11 **18:17** [e] Ge 31:19; Mic 5:13 **18:18** [f] Isa 46:2; Jer 43:11; Hos 10:5 **18:19** [g] Job 21:5; 29:9; 40:4; Mic 7:16 [h] Jdg 17:10 **18:26** [i] Ps 18:17; 35:10 **18:27** [j] ver 7,10 [k] Ge 49:17; Jos 19:47 **18:28** [l] ver 7 [m] Nu 13:21; 2Sa 10:6 **18:29** [n] Ge 14:14 [o] Jos 19:47; 1Ki 15:20 **18:30** [p] Ex 2:22; Jdg 17:3,5 **18:31** [q] Jdg 19:18 [r] Jos 18:1; Jer 7:14 **19:1** [s] Jdg 18:1 [t] Ru 1:1

him and went back to her parents' home
in Bethlehem, Judah. After she had been
there four months, 3her husband went to
her to persuade her to return. He had with
him his servant and two donkeys. She took
him into her parents' home, and when her
father saw him, he gladly welcomed him.
4His father-in-law, the woman's father, prevailed on him to stay; so he remained with
him three days, eating and drinking,[u] and
sleeping there.
5On the fourth day they got up early and
he prepared to leave, but the woman's father said to his son-in-law, "Refresh yourself[v] with something to eat; then you can
go." 6So the two of them sat down to eat and
drink together. Afterward the woman's father said, "Please stay tonight and enjoy
yourself.[w]" 7And when the man got up to
go, his father-in-law persuaded him, so he
stayed there that night. 8On the morning of
the fifth day, when he rose to go, the woman's father said, "Refresh yourself. Wait till
afternoon!" So the two of them ate together.
9Then when the man, with his concubine
and his servant, got up to leave, his father-
in-law, the woman's father, said, "Now look,
it's almost evening. Spend the night here;
the day is nearly over. Stay and enjoy yourself. Early tomorrow morning you can get
up and be on your way home." 10But, unwilling to stay another night, the man left and
went toward Jebus[x] (that is, Jerusalem), with
his two saddled donkeys and his concubine.
11When they were near Jebus and the
day was almost gone, the servant said to
his master, "Come, let's stop at this city of
the Jebusites[y] and spend the night."
12His master replied, "No. We won't go
into any city whose people are not Israelites. We will go on to Gibeah." 13He added,
"Come, let's try to reach Gibeah or Ramah[z]
and spend the night in one of those places." 14So they went on, and the sun set as
they neared Gibeah in Benjamin.[a] 15There
they stopped to spend the night. They went
and sat in the city square,[b] but no one took
them in for the night.
16That evening[c] an old man from the hill
country of Ephraim,[d] who was living in
Gibeah (the inhabitants of the place were
Benjamites), came in from his work in the
fields. 17When he looked and saw the traveler in the city square, the old man asked,
"Where are you going? Where did you
come from?"[e]
18He answered, "We are on our way from
Bethlehem in Judah to a remote area in the
hill country of Ephraim where I live. I have
been to Bethlehem in Judah and now I am
going to the house of the LORD.[a][f] No one
has taken me in for the night. 19We have
both straw and fodder[g] for our donkeys
and bread and wine[h] for ourselves your
servants—me, the woman and the young
man with us. We don't need anything."
20"You are welcome at my house," the
old man said. "Let me supply whatever you need. Only don't spend the night
in the square." 21So he took him into his
house and fed his donkeys. After they had
washed their feet, they had something to
eat and drink.[i]
22While they were enjoying themselves,[j]
some of the wicked men[k] of the city surrounded the house. Pounding on the door,
they shouted to the old man who owned
the house, "Bring out the man who came to
your house so we can have sex with him.[l]"
23The owner of the house went outside[m]
and said to them, "No, my friends, don't be
so vile. Since this man is my guest, don't
do this outrageous thing.[n] 24Look, here is
my virgin daughter,[o] and his concubine. I
will bring them out to you now, and you
can use them and do to them whatever you
wish. But as for this man, don't do such an
outrageous thing."
25But the men would not listen to him.
So the man took his concubine and sent
her outside to them, and they raped her
and abused her[p] throughout the night, and
at dawn they let her go. 26At daybreak the
woman went back to the house where her
master was staying, fell down at the door
and lay there until daylight.
27When her master got up in the morning and opened the door of the house and
stepped out to continue on his way, there

a 18 Hebrew, Vulgate, Syriac and Targum; Septuagint *going home*

19:10 ***Jebus (that is, Jerusalem).*** The city of Jerusalem was at this time in the hands of the Jebusites, and it is called a "city whose people are not Israelites" in v. 12 (see Josh. 15:63).

19:22 ***wicked men.*** Literally "sons of Belial," this is a phrase describing wicked or worthless people. The name Belial came to designate Satan, as it is used in 2 Corinthians 6:15. ***so we can have sex with him.*** This same expression is found in Genesis 19:5, where the men of Sodom wanted to force homosexual relations on Lot's guests.

19:22–26 ***men of the city.*** This section closely resembles Genesis 19:4–9; indeed, the author may have written this story to make the comparison with Sodom unmistakable, as if to say, "Things were as bad as they were in the days of Sodom and Gomorrah."

19:22–30 Perversion—For a man to be raped by a group of town ruffians would be a terrible humiliation; the fact that offering the concubine and the virgin daughter could be considered a solution clearly illustrates the level of perversion and depravity to which the people had sunk. Women were no longer considered the companions and helpers that they

19:4 [u] Ex 32:6 **19:5** [v] ver 8; Ge 18:5 **19:6** [w] ver 9,22; Jdg 16:25 **19:10** [x] Ge 10:16; Jos 15:8; 1Ch 11:4-5 **19:11** [y] Jos 3:10 **19:13** [z] Jos 18:25 **19:14** [a] 1Sa 10:26; Isa 10:29 **19:15** [b] Ge 19:2 **19:16** [c] Ps 104:23 [d] ver 1 **19:17** [e] Ge 29:4 **19:18** [f] Jdg 18:31 **19:19** [g] Ge 24:25 [h] Ge 14:18 **19:21** [i] Ge 24:32-33; Lk 7:44 **19:22** [j] Jdg 16:25 [k] Dt 13:13 [l] Ge 19:4-5; Jdg 20:5; Ro 1:26-27 **19:23** [m] Ge 19:6 [n] Ge 34:7; Lev 19:29; Dt 22:21; Jdg 20:6; 2Sa 13:12; Ro 1:27 **19:24** [o] Ge 19:8; Dt 21:14 **19:25** [p] 1Sa 31:4

lay his concubine, fallen in the doorway of the house, with her hands on the threshold. 28He said to her, "Get up; let's go." But there was no answer. Then the man put her on his donkey and set out for home.

29When he reached home, he took a knife[q] and cut up his concubine, limb by limb, into twelve parts and sent them into all the areas of Israel.[r] 30Everyone who saw it was saying to one another, "Such a thing has never been seen or done, not since the day the Israelites came up out of Egypt.[s] Just imagine! We must do something! So speak up![t]"

The Israelites Punish the Benjamites

20 Then all Israel[u] from Dan to Beersheba[v] and from the land of Gilead came together as one[w] and assembled[x] before the LORD in Mizpah. 2The leaders of all the people of the tribes of Israel took their places in the assembly of God's people, four hundred thousand men[y] armed with swords. 3(The Benjamites heard that the Israelites had gone up to Mizpah.) Then the Israelites said, "Tell us how this awful thing happened."

4So the Levite, the husband of the murdered woman, said, "I and my concubine came to Gibeah[z] in Benjamin to spend the night.[a] 5During the night the men of Gibeah came after me and surrounded the house, intending to kill me.[b] They raped my concubine, and she died.[c] 6I took my concubine, cut her into pieces and sent one piece to each region of Israel's inheritance,[d] because they committed this lewd and outrageous act[e] in Israel. 7Now, all you Israelites, speak up and tell me what you have decided to do.[f]"

8All the men rose up together as one, saying, "None of us will go home. No, not one of us will return to his house. 9But now this is what we'll do to Gibeah: We'll go up against it in the order decided by casting lots.[g] 10We'll take ten men out of every hundred from all the tribes of Israel, and a hundred from a thousand, and a thousand from ten thousand, to get provisions for the army. Then, when the army arrives at Gibeah[a] in Benjamin, it can give them what they deserve for this outrageous act done in Israel." 11So all the Israelites got together and united as one against the city.[h]

12The tribes of Israel sent messengers throughout the tribe of Benjamin, saying, "What about this awful crime that was committed among you? 13Now turn those wicked men[i] of Gibeah over to us so that we may put them to death and purge the evil from Israel.[j]"

But the Benjamites would not listen to their fellow Israelites. 14From their towns they came together at Gibeah to fight against the Israelites. 15At once the Benjamites mobilized twenty-six thousand swordsmen from their towns, in addition to seven hundred able young men from those living in Gibeah. 16Among all these soldiers there were seven hundred select troops who were left-handed,[k] each of whom could sling a stone at a hair and not miss.

17Israel, apart from Benjamin, mustered four hundred thousand swordsmen, all of them fit for battle.

18The Israelites went up to Bethel[b] and inquired of God.[l] They said, "Who of us is to go up first to fight[m] against the Benjamites?"

The LORD replied, "Judah shall go first."

19The next morning the Israelites got up and pitched camp near Gibeah. 20The Israelites went out to fight the Benjamites and took up battle positions against them at Gibeah. 21The Benjamites came out of

[a] *10* One Hebrew manuscript; most Hebrew manuscripts *Geba*, a variant of *Gibeah*
[b] *18* Or *to the house of God*; also in verse 26

---

were created to be (Gen. 2:22–24), but as property, to be misused or disposed of at will. The author offers no comment upon the horror perpetrated here, merely stating the cold facts and leaving a strong impression of the heartless and conscienceless state of the people.

19:30 *Such a thing has never been seen or done.* This phrase is ambiguous. It is uncertain whether they were horrified by discovering the dismembered body or by learning about the cruel rape and murder.

20:1 *from Dan to Beersheba.* This is a common expression for the full extent of the land of Israel from north to south.

20:1–2,8 Unity—Both individually and corporately the Israelites of this period were functioning as a law unto themselves. "everyone did as they saw fit" (21:25). One notable exception to this was the response to the loathsome rape and killing of a concubine in the Benjamite territory of Gibeah (19:11–30). The result of this outrageous covenant violation was that all Israel gathered together as one man, and decided that they would not rest until the crime was punished. The people were shocked into unity against sin. It is still true that crises in life often serve to bring people together to work for a common cause or fight against a common enemy. While this can be a good result of difficult times, it is important that God's people be united in serving Him in peace as well as crisis.

20:9 *by casting lots.* God's role is not mentioned here, but one can assume that the people were using lots to seek His will. To their credit, the Israelite tribes were united together as one man, a quality notably absent up to this point in the Book of Judges (v. 11).

20:18 *Judah shall go first.* The book begins and ends with Judah in this prominent position (1:1–2). This is no accident, since the end of the book points

19:29 [q] Ge 22:6 [r] Jdg 20:6; 1Sa 11:7 **19:30** [s] Hos 9:9 [t] Jdg 20:7; Pr 13:10 **20:1** [u] Jdg 21:5 [v] 1Sa 3:20; 2Sa 3:10; 1Ki 4:25 [w] 1Sa 11:7 [x] 1Sa 7:5 **20:2** [y] Jdg 8:10 **20:4** [z] Jos 15:57 [a] Jdg 19:15 **20:5** [b] Jdg 19:22 [c] Jdg 19:25-26 **20:6** [d] Jdg 19:29 [e] Jos 7:15; Jdg 19:23 **20:7** [f] Jdg 19:30 **20:9** [g] Lev 16:8 **20:11** [h] ver 1 **20:13** [i] Dt 13:13; Jdg 19:22 [j] Dt 17:12 **20:16** [k] Jdg 3:15; 1Ch 12:2 **20:18** [l] ver 26-27; Nu 27:21 [m] ver 23,28

Gibeah and cut down twenty-two thousand
Israelites[n] on the battlefield that day. 22But
the Israelites encouraged one another and
again took up their positions where they
had stationed themselves the first day.
23The Israelites went up and wept before
the LORD until evening,[o] and they inquired
of the LORD. They said, "Shall we go up
again to fight[p] against the Benjamites, our
fellow Israelites?"
The LORD answered, "Go up against
them."
24Then the Israelites drew near to Benjamin the second day. 25This time, when the
Benjamites came out from Gibeah to oppose them, they cut down another eighteen
thousand Israelites,[q] all of them armed
with swords.
26Then all the Israelites, the whole army,
went up to Bethel, and there they sat weeping before the LORD.[r] They fasted that day
until evening and presented burnt offerings and fellowship offerings to the LORD.[s]
27And the Israelites inquired of the LORD.
(In those days the ark of the covenant of
God[t] was there, 28with Phinehas son of Eleazar,[u] the son of Aaron, ministering before
it.)[v] They asked, "Shall we go up again to
fight against the Benjamites, our fellow Israelites, or not?"
The LORD responded, "Go, for tomorrow
I will give them into your hands.[w]"
29Then Israel set an ambush[x] around
Gibeah. 30They went up against the Benjamites on the third day and took up positions
against Gibeah as they had done before.
31The Benjamites came out to meet them
and were drawn away[y] from the city. They
began to inflict casualties on the Israelites
as before, so that about thirty men fell in
the open field and on the roads—the one
leading to Bethel and the other to Gibeah.
32While the Benjamites were saying, "We
are defeating them as before,"[z] the Israelites were saying, "Let's retreat and draw
them away from the city to the roads."
33All the men of Israel moved from their
places and took up positions at Baal Tamar,
and the Israelite ambush charged out of its
place[a] on the west[a] of Gibeah.[b] 34Then ten
thousand of Israel's able young men made a
frontal attack on Gibeah. The fighting was
so heavy that the Benjamites did not realize[b] how near disaster was.[c] 35The LORD
defeated Benjamin[d] before Israel, and on
that day the Israelites struck down 25,100
Benjamites, all armed with swords. 36Then
the Benjamites saw that they were beaten.
Now the men of Israel had given way[e] before Benjamin, because they relied on the
ambush they had set near Gibeah. 37Those
who had been in ambush made a sudden
dash into Gibeah, spread out and put the
whole city to the sword.[f] 38The Israelites
had arranged with the ambush that they
should send up a great cloud of smoke[g]
from the city, 39and then the Israelites
would counterattack.
The Benjamites had begun to inflict casualties on the Israelites (about thirty),
and they said, "We are defeating them as
in the first battle."[h] 40But when the column
of smoke began to rise from the city, the
Benjamites turned and saw the whole city
going up in smoke.[i] 41Then the Israelites
counterattacked, and the Benjamites were
terrified, because they realized that disaster
had come on them. 42So they fled before the
Israelites in the direction of the wilderness,
but they could not escape the battle. And
the Israelites who came out of the towns
cut them down there. 43They surrounded
the Benjamites, chased them and easily[c]
overran them in the vicinity of Gibeah on
the east. 44Eighteen thousand Benjamites
fell, all of them valiant fighters.[j] 45As they
turned and fled toward the wilderness to the
rock of Rimmon,[k] the Israelites cut down five
thousand men along the roads. They kept
pressing after the Benjamites as far as Gi-
dom and struck down two thousand more.
46On that day twenty-five thousand Benjamite swordsmen fell, all of them valiant fighters. 47But six hundred of them turned and
fled into the wilderness to the rock of Rimmon, where they stayed four months. 48The
men of Israel went back to Benjamin and
put all the towns to the sword, including the
animals and everything else they found. All
the towns they came across they set on fire.[l]

---

[a] *33* Some Septuagint manuscripts and Vulgate; the meaning of the Hebrew for this word is uncertain. [b] *33* Hebrew *Geba,* a variant of *Gibeah* [c] *43* The meaning of the Hebrew for this word is uncertain.

---

toward the monarchy, whose true expression would come out of Judah.

20:23 ***Go up against them.*** The Lord graciously answered the Israelites twice when they called upon Him (v. 18).

20:26 ***went up to Bethel, and there they sat weeping.*** The Israelites suffered a second major defeat (v. 25). The result drove them to fasting and sacrificing at Bethel, something done very rarely in this period.

20:28 ***Phinehas.*** Phinehas was the grandson of Aaron who had stopped the plague at Peor (Num. 25:6–11). The fact that he was still alive shows that the organization of the Book of Judges is not strictly chronological. The author may have placed this account at the end of the book to make the point even more strongly about the spiritual deterioration of the nation.

20:48 ***put all the towns to the sword.*** The spiritual decay of Israel had resulted in the destruction of its own people with a vengeance once reserved for pagan people.

20:21 [n] ver 25 **20:23** [o] Jos 7:6 [p] ver 18 **20:25** [q] ver 21 **20:26** [r] ver 23 [s] Jdg 21:4 **20:27** [t] Jos 18:1 **20:28** [u] Jos 24:33 [v] Dt 18:5 [w] Jdg 7:9 **20:29** [x] Jos 8:2,4 **20:31** [y] Jos 8:16 **20:32** [z] ver 39 **20:33** [a] Jos 8:19 **20:34** [b] Jos 8:14 [c] Isa 47:11 **20:35** [d] 1Sa 9:21 **20:36** [e] Jos 8:15 **20:37** [f] Jos 8:19 **20:38** [g] Jos 8:20 **20:39** [h] ver 32 **20:40** [i] Jos 8:20 **20:44** [j] Ps 76:5 **20:45** [k] Jos 15:32; Jdg 21:13 **20:48** [l] Jdg 21:23

Wives for the Benjamites

21 The men of Israel had taken an oath[m]
at Mizpah:[n] "Not one of us will give[o]
his daughter in marriage to a Benjamite."
2The people went to Bethel,[a] where they
sat before God until evening, raising their
voices and weeping bitterly. 3"LORD, God of
Israel," they cried, "why has this happened
to Israel? Why should one tribe be missing
from Israel today?"
4Early the next day the people built an
altar and presented burnt offerings and fellowship offerings.[p]
5Then the Israelites asked, "Who from
all the tribes of Israel[q] has failed to assemble before the LORD?" For they had taken a
solemn oath that anyone who failed to assemble before the LORD at Mizpah was to
be put to death.
6Now the Israelites grieved for the tribe
of Benjamin, their fellow Israelites. "Today
one tribe is cut off from Israel," they said.
7"How can we provide wives for those who
are left, since we have taken an oath[r] by the
LORD not to give them any of our daughters
in marriage?" 8Then they asked, "Which
one of the tribes of Israel failed to assemble
before the LORD at Mizpah?" They discovered that no one from Jabesh Gilead[s] had
come to the camp for the assembly. 9For
when they counted the people, they found
that none of the people of Jabesh Gilead
were there.
10So the assembly sent twelve thousand fighting men with instructions to
go to Jabesh Gilead and put to the sword
those living there, including the women
and children. 11"This is what you are to
do," they said. "Kill every male and every
woman who is not a virgin.[t]" 12They found
among the people living in Jabesh Gilead
four hundred young women who had never
slept with a man, and they took them to the
camp at Shiloh[u] in Canaan.
13Then the whole assembly sent an offer of peace[v] to the Benjamites at the rock
of Rimmon.[w] 14So the Benjamites returned
at that time and were given the women of
Jabesh Gilead who had been spared. But
there were not enough for all of them.
15The people grieved for Benjamin,[x]
because the LORD had made a gap in the
tribes of Israel. 16And the elders of the assembly said, "With the women of Benjamin
destroyed, how shall we provide wives for
the men who are left? 17The Benjamite survivors must have heirs," they said, "so that
a tribe of Israel will not be wiped out. 18We
can't give them our daughters as wives,
since we Israelites have taken this oath:
'Cursed be anyone who gives[y] a wife to a
Benjamite.' 19But look, there is the annual
festival of the LORD in Shiloh,[z] which lies
north of Bethel, east of the road that goes
from Bethel to Shechem, and south of Le-
bonah."
20So they instructed the Benjamites, saying, "Go and hide in the vineyards 21and
watch. When the young women of Shiloh
come out to join in the dancing,[a] rush from
the vineyards and each of you seize one of
them to be your wife. Then return to the
land of Benjamin. 22When their fathers
or brothers complain to us, we will say to
them, 'Do us the favor of helping them, because we did not get wives for them during
the war. You will not be guilty of breaking
your oath because you did not give[b] your
daughters to them.'"
23So that is what the Benjamites did.
While the young women were dancing,
each man caught one and carried her off
to be his wife. Then they returned to their
inheritance and rebuilt the towns and settled in them.[c]
24At that time the Israelites left that place
and went home to their tribes and clans,
each to his own inheritance.
25In those days Israel had no king; everyone did as they saw fit.[d]

---

[a] 2 Or *to the house of God*

21:6 Repentance—In the midst of this terrible account of great sin within the nation of Israel, we find that the people realized that it was important that none of the tribes should perish. The example set by the nation of Israel is important for believers today. The people of Israel felt sorry for their brothers after the brothers had been disciplined for their great sin. Restoration and continuance of fellowship are important for people who have fallen into sin (2 Cor. 2:6–8; Gal. 6:1–2).

21:11 ***Kill.*** This phrase, sometimes translated "utterly destroy," is found numerous times in the Book of Joshua in regard to the conquest of the Canaanites. However, there is no hint that God supported the bloodbath at Jabesh Gilead.

21:19 ***festival of the LORD.*** Because of the dancing association, some believe that the yearly feast mentioned here was the Passover. Others believe that it was the Festival of Tabernacles, celebrated in the fall, since vineyards are mentioned (vv. 20–21). The grape harvest came in the early fall.

21:23 ***each man caught one and carried her off to be his wife.*** No justification is given for this peculiar abduction except for the supposed needs of the Benjamites. This interesting episode was a way for the rest of Israel to sidestep their oath (v. 1), and try to preserve the tribe of Benjamin.

21:25 ***everyone did what they saw fit.*** This statement sums up the whole Book of Judges. What happened was governed by whatever people happened to feel like, rather than by listening to God, and the stories at the end of the book clearly illustrate the results of this mindset.

21:1 [m] Jos 9:18 [n] Jdg 20:1 [o] ver 7, 18 **21:4** [p] Jdg 20:26; 2Sa 24:25 **21:5** [q] Jdg 5:23; 20:1 **21:7** [r] ver 1 **21:8** [s] 1Sa 11:1; 31:11 **21:11** [t] Nu 31:17-18 **21:12** [u] Jos 18:1 **21:13** [v] Dt 20:10 [w] Jdg 20:47 **21:15** [x] ver 6 **21:18** [y] ver 1 **21:19** [z] Jos 18:1; Jdg 18:31; 1Sa 1:3 **21:21** [a] Ex 15:20; Jdg 11:34 **21:22** [b] ver 1, 18 **21:23** [c] Jdg 20:48 **21:25** [d] Dt 12:8; Jdg 17:6; 18:1; 19:1

RUTH

▶ **AUTHOR:** The Book of Ruth provides a cameo to the other side of the biblical story—the godly remnant who remain true to the laws of God. Although the author of Ruth is not given anywhere in the book, the anonymity should not detract from its spiritual value or literary beauty. Tradition has attributed the writing of Ruth to Samuel, but this is difficult to reconcile with the mention of David when Samuel died before David was installed as king.

▶ **TIME:** During the Judges ▶ **KEY VERSE:** Ruth 1:16

▶ **THEME:** Ruth is a simple yet intriguing short story. Throughout the story, the characters develop and eventually exhibit wisdom, loyalty, and obedience to God and the customs of the day. We see an interesting romance bloom out of most unusual circumstances. It provides a platform for some profound understanding of God's covenant plans with His people, Israel. We see the details of His plan unfold in the lives of a widow, her foreign born daughter-in-law, and a distant relative. We also see the lineage of David and Christ established and blessed.

Naomi Loses Her Husband and Sons

1 In the days when the judges ruled,[a][a]
there was a famine in the land.[b] So a
man from Bethlehem in Judah, together
with his wife and two sons, went to live for
a while in the country of Moab.[c] 2The man's
name was Elimelek, his wife's name was
Naomi, and the names of his two sons were
Mahlon and Kilion. They were Ephrathites
from Bethlehem,[d] Judah. And they went to
Moab and lived there.
3Now Elimelek, Naomi's husband, died,
and she was left with her two sons. 4They
married Moabite women, one named Orpah and the other Ruth.[e] After they had
lived there about ten years, 5both Mahlon and Kilion also died, and Naomi
was left without her two sons and her
husband.

Naomi and Ruth Return to Bethlehem

6When Naomi heard in Moab that
the LORD had come to the aid of his people[f] by providing food[g] for them, she
and her daughters-in-law prepared to
return home from there. 7With her two
daughters-in-law she left the place where
she had been living and set out on the road
that would take them back to the land of
Judah.
8Then Naomi said to her two daughters-in-law, "Go back, each of you, to your mother's home. May the LORD show you kindness,[h] as you have shown kindness to your
dead husbands[i] and to me. 9May the LORD
grant that each of you will find rest[j] in the
home of another husband."
Then she kissed them goodbye and they
wept aloud 10and said to her, "We will go
back with you to your people."
11But Naomi said, "Return home, my
daughters. Why would you come with me?
Am I going to have any more sons, who
could become your husbands?[k] 12Return
home, my daughters; I am too old to have
another husband. Even if I thought there
was still hope for me—even if I had a husband tonight and then gave birth to sons—
13would you wait until they grew up?
Would you remain unmarried for them?
No, my daughters. It is more bitter for me
than for you, because the LORD's hand has
turned against me![l]"

[a] 1 Traditionally *judged*

1:4 ***Ruth.*** The name Ruth means "friend" or "compassionate friend." Throughout the account of her life it is easy to see that this name fittingly described Ruth's character.

1:8 ***kindness.*** The Hebrew word translated "kindness" is often used to describe God. It can also be interpreted as "loyal love."

1:13 ***turned against me.*** Naomi felt that the Lord was disciplining her. To be a widow in such a time and also without children was very difficult indeed.

1:1 [a] Jdg 2:16-18 [b] Ge 12:10; Ps 105:16 [c] Jdg 3:30 **1:2** [d] Ge 35:19 **1:4** [e] Mt 1:5 **1:6** [f] Ex 4:31; Jer 29:10; Zep 2:7 [g] Ps 132:15; Mt 6:11 **1:8** [h] Ru 2:20; 2Ti 1:16 [i] ver 5 **1:9** [j] Ru 3:1 **1:11** [k] Ge 38:11; Dt 25:5 **1:13** [l] Jdg 2:15; Job 4:5; 19:21; Ps 32:4

14At this they wept aloud again. Then
Orpah kissed her mother-in-law[m] goodbye,
but Ruth clung to her.[n]
15"Look," said Naomi, "your sister-in-law
is going back to her people and her gods.[o]
Go back with her."
16But Ruth replied, "Don't urge me to
leave you[p] or to turn back from you. Where
you go I will go, and where you stay I will
stay. Your people will be my people and
your God my God.[q] 17Where you die I will
die, and there I will be buried. May the
LORD deal with me, be it ever so severely,[r] if
even death separates you and me." 18When
Naomi realized that Ruth was determined
to go with her, she stopped urging her.[s]
19So the two women went on until they
came to Bethlehem. When they arrived in
Bethlehem, the whole town was stirred[t] because of them, and the women exclaimed,
"Can this be Naomi?"
20"Don't call me Naomi,[a]" she told them.
"Call me Mara,[b] because the Almighty[c][u]
has made my life very bitter.[v] 21I went
away full, but the LORD has brought me
back empty.[w] Why call me Naomi? The
LORD has afflicted[d] me; the Almighty has
brought misfortune upon me."
22So Naomi returned from Moab accompanied by Ruth the Moabite, her daughter-
in-law, arriving in Bethlehem as the barley
harvest[x] was beginning.[y]

Ruth Meets Boaz in the Grain Field

2 Now Naomi had a relative[z] on her husband's side, a man of standing from the
clan of Elimelek,[a] whose name was Boaz.[b]
2And Ruth the Moabite said to Naomi,
"Let me go to the fields and pick up the left-
over grain[c] behind anyone in whose eyes I
find favor."
Naomi said to her, "Go ahead, my daughter." 3So she went out, entered a field and
began to glean behind the harvesters. As
it turned out, she was working in a field
belonging to Boaz, who was from the clan
of Elimelek.
4Just then Boaz arrived from Bethlehem
and greeted the harvesters, "The LORD be
with you![d]"
"The LORD bless you![e]" they answered.
5Boaz asked the overseer of his harvesters, "Who does that young woman belong to?"
6The overseer replied, "She is the Moabite[f] who came back from Moab with Naomi.
7She said, 'Please let me glean and gather
among the sheaves behind the harvesters.'
She came into the field and has remained
here from morning till now, except for a
short rest in the shelter."
8So Boaz said to Ruth, "My daughter, listen to me. Don't go and glean in another
field and don't go away from here. Stay here
with the women who work for me. 9Watch
the field where the men are harvesting, and
follow along after the women. I have told the
men not to lay a hand on you. And whenever
you are thirsty, go and get a drink from the
water jars the men have filled."
10At this, she bowed down with her face
to the ground.[g] She asked him, "Why have
I found such favor in your eyes that you notice me[h]—a foreigner?[i]"
11Boaz replied, "I've been told all about
what you have done for your mother-in-
law[j] since the death of your husband—how
you left your father and mother and your
homeland and came to live with a people
you did not know before.[k] 12May the LORD
repay you for what you have done. May you
be richly rewarded by the LORD,[l] the God of
Israel, under whose wings[m] you have come
to take refuge.[n]"
13"May I continue to find favor in your
eyes, my lord," she said. "You have put me
at ease by speaking kindly to your servant—though I do not have the standing
of one of your servants."
14At mealtime Boaz said to her, "Come
over here. Have some bread and dip it in
the wine vinegar."

---

[a] 20 *Naomi* means *pleasant.* [b] 20 *Mara* means *bitter.* [c] 20 Hebrew *Shaddai*; also in verse 21
[d] 21 Or *has testified against*

1:14 Perseverance—When we sacrifice what would seem to be our best interest for another's welfare, God may unexpectedly use it to uplift and reward us. Ruth's desire to stay with Naomi not only lightened Naomi's lot, but it also brought Ruth into the Messiah's ancestral line.

1:16–17 *your God my God.* Ruth is casting her lot with Naomi, turning her back on all she has known. Most important she is turning away from the many gods of Moab to the One True God of Israel.

1:22 *Moabite.* God extended His protection to Ruth even though she was a foreigner and a member of a nation which had been the enemy of God and Israel (Num. 22–25).

2:1 *Boaz.* As a relative of Naomi's husband Elimelek, as well as a man of both wealth and good character, Boaz was the ideal person to stand up for the rights of the two widows. In the ancient Middle East, a woman without a husband or father was a woman unprotected and with no way to make a living.

2:2 *pick up.* The law of Moses allowed the poor to glean in the fields of the farmers (Lev. 23:22), picking up the loose grain that fell from the sheaves as the reapers gathered them up.

2:14–16 *Come over here. Have some bread.* Boaz not only let Ruth glean, he also amply provided her with food. He went beyond the letter of the law, demonstrating God's compassion and the concern that each believer ought to show for others.

1:14 [m] Ru 2:11 [n] Pr 17:17; 18:24 **1:15** [o] Jos 24:14; Jdg 11:24 **1:16** [p] 2Ki 2:2 [q] Ru 2:11, 12 **1:17** [r] 1Sa 3:17; 25:22; 2Sa 19:13; 2Ki 6:31 **1:18** [s] Ac 21:14 **1:19** [t] Mt 21:10 **1:20** [u] Ex 6:3 [v] ver 13; Job 6:4 **1:21** [w] Job 1:21 **1:22** [x] Ex 9:31; Ru 2:23 [y] 2Sa 21:9 **2:1** [z] Ru 3:2, 12 [a] Ru 1:2 [b] Ru 4:21 **2:2** [c] ver 7; Lev 19:9; 23:22; Dt 24:19 **2:4** [d] Jdg 6:12; Lk 1:28; 2Th 3:16 [e] Ps 129:7-8 **2:6** [f] Ru 1:22 **2:10** [g] 1Sa 25:23 [h] Ps 41:1 [i] Dt 15:3 **2:11** [j] Ru 1:14 [k] Ru 1:16-17 **2:12** [l] 1Sa 24:19 [m] Ps 17:8; 36:7; 57:1; 61:4; 63:7; 91:4 [n] Ru 1:16

When she sat down with the harvesters, he offered her some roasted grain. She ate all she wanted and had some left over.[o] 15As she got up to glean, Boaz gave orders to his men, "Let her gather among the sheaves and don't reprimand her. 16Even pull out some stalks for her from the bundles and leave them for her to pick up, and don't rebuke her."

17So Ruth gleaned in the field until evening. Then she threshed the barley she had gathered, and it amounted to about an ephah.[a] 18She carried it back to town, and her mother-in-law saw how much she had gathered. Ruth also brought out and gave her what she had left over[p] after she had eaten enough.

19Her mother-in-law asked her, "Where did you glean today? Where did you work? Blessed be the man who took notice of you![q]"

Then Ruth told her mother-in-law about the one at whose place she had been working. "The name of the man I worked with today is Boaz," she said.

20"The LORD bless him!" Naomi said to her daughter-in-law. "He has not stopped showing his kindness[r] to the living and the dead." She added, "That man is our close relative; he is one of our guardian-redeemers.[bs]"

21Then Ruth the Moabite said, "He even said to me, 'Stay with my workers until they finish harvesting all my grain.'"

22Naomi said to Ruth her daughter-in-law, "It will be good for you, my daughter, to go with the women who work for him, because in someone else's field you might be harmed."

23So Ruth stayed close to the women of Boaz to glean until the barley and wheat harvests[t] were finished. And she lived with her mother-in-law.

Ruth and Boaz at the Threshing Floor

3 One day Ruth's mother-in-law Naomi said to her, "My daughter, I must find a home[cu] for you, where you will be well provided for. 2Now Boaz, with whose women you have worked, is a relative[v] of ours. Tonight he will be winnowing barley on the threshing floor. 3Wash, put on perfume,[w] and get dressed in your best clothes. Then go down to the threshing floor, but don't let him know you are there until he has finished eating and drinking. 4When he lies down, note the place where he is lying. Then go and uncover his feet and lie down. He will tell you what to do."

5"I will do whatever you say,"[x] Ruth answered. 6So she went down to the threshing floor and did everything her mother-in-law told her to do.

7When Boaz had finished eating and drinking and was in good spirits,[y] he went over to lie down at the far end of the grain pile. Ruth approached quietly, uncovered his feet and lay down. 8In the middle of the night something startled the man; he turned—and there was a woman lying at his feet!

9"Who are you?" he asked.

"I am your servant Ruth," she said. "Spread the corner of your garment[z] over me, since you are a guardian-redeemer[da] of our family."

10"The LORD bless you, my daughter," he replied. "This kindness is greater than that which you showed earlier: You have not run after the younger men, whether rich or poor. 11And now, my daughter, don't be afraid. I will do for you all you ask. All the people of my town know that you are a woman of noble character.[b] 12Although it is true that I am a guardian-redeemer of our family,[c] there is another who is more closely related than[d] I. 13Stay here for the night, and in the morning if he wants to do his duty as your guardian-redeemer,[e] good; let him redeem you. But if he is not willing, as surely as the LORD lives[f] I will do it. Lie here until morning."

14So she lay at his feet until morning, but got up before anyone could be recognized; and he said, "No one must know that a woman came to the threshing floor."[g]

---

a *17* That is, probably about 30 pounds or about 13 kilograms *b* *20* The Hebrew word for *guardian-redeemer* is a legal term for one who has the obligation to redeem a relative in serious difficulty (see Lev. 25:25-55). *c* *1* Hebrew *find rest* (see 1:9) *d* *9* The Hebrew word for *guardian-redeemer* is a legal term for one who has the obligation to redeem a relative in serious difficulty (see Lev. 25:25-55); also in verses 12 and 13.

3:4 ***uncover his feet.*** By uncovering Boaz's feet in this manner Ruth was showing her submission to him while also asking him to be her protector.

3:9 ***guardian-redeemer.*** Ruth reminded Boaz that he was a close relative of her dead husband, and in keeping with the law a close relative was required to be a "guardian-redeemer." This meant that if a man was slain, his guardian-redeemer had to avenge his death. If a man was sold into slavery, his guardian-redeemer paid the price to release him. If a man died childless, his guardian-redeemer had the responsibility to marry his wife and father a child to bear his name (Deut. 15:5 – 10). Ruth was placing herself so that Boaz would know that she was willing for him to redeem her.

3:12 ***closer related than I.*** Boaz remembers that there is yet a closer relative; that relative would have the responsibility and the right to redeem Ruth first. If, however, he did not wish to or was unable to, Boaz would be free to do it himself.

2:14 [o] ver 18 **2:18** [p] ver 14 **2:19** [q] ver 10; Ps 41:1 **2:20** [r] Ru 3:10; 2Sa 2:5; Pr 17:17 [s] Ru 3:9, 12; 4:1, 14 **2:23** [t] Dt 16:9 **3:1** [u] Ru 1:9 **3:2** [v] Dt 25:5-10; Ru 2:1 **3:3** [w] 2Sa 14:2 **3:5** [x] Eph 6:1; Col 3:20 **3:7** [y] Jdg 19:6, 9, 22; 2Sa 13:28; 1Ki 21:7; Est 1:10 **3:9** [z] Eze 16:8 [a] ver 12; Ru 2:20 **3:11** [b] Pr 12:4; 31:10 **3:12** [c] ver 9 [d] Ru 4:1 **3:13** [e] Dt 25:5; Ru 4:5; Mt 22:24 [f] Jdg 8:19; Jer 4:2 **3:14** [g] Ro 14:16; 2Co 8:21

15He also said, "Bring me the shawl you
are wearing and hold it out." When she did
so, he poured into it six measures of barley and placed the bundle on her. Then he[a]
went back to town.
16When Ruth came to her mother-in-law,
Naomi asked, "How did it go, my daughter?"
Then she told her everything Boaz
had done for her 17and added, "He gave
me these six measures of barley, saying,
'Don't go back to your mother-in-law empty-handed.'"
18Then Naomi said, "Wait, my daughter,
until you find out what happens. For the
man will not rest until the matter is settled
today."[h]

Boaz Marries Ruth

4 Meanwhile Boaz went up to the town
gate and sat down there just as the
guardian-redeemer[b] he had mentioned[i]
came along. Boaz said, "Come over here,
my friend, and sit down." So he went over
and sat down.
2Boaz took ten of the elders[j] of the town
and said, "Sit here," and they did so. 3Then
he said to the guardian-redeemer, "Naomi,
who has come back from Moab, is selling
the piece of land that belonged to our relative Elimelek. 4I thought I should bring the
matter to your attention and suggest that
you buy it in the presence of these seated
here and in the presence of the elders of my
people. If you will redeem it, do so. But if
you[c] will not, tell me, so I will know. For no
one has the right to do it except you,[k] and I
am next in line."
"I will redeem it," he said.
5Then Boaz said, "On the day you buy
the land from Naomi, you also acquire
Ruth the Moabite, the[d] dead man's widow,
in order to maintain the name of the dead
with his property."[l]
6At this, the guardian-redeemer said,
"Then I cannot redeem[m] it because I might
endanger my own estate. You redeem it
yourself. I cannot do it."
7(Now in earlier times in Israel, for the
redemption and transfer of property to become final, one party took off his sandal
and gave it to the other. This was the method of legalizing transactions in Israel.)[n]
8So the guardian-redeemer said to Boaz,
"Buy it yourself." And he removed his sandal.
9Then Boaz announced to the elders and
all the people, "Today you are witnesses that I have bought from Naomi all the
property of Elimelek, Kilion and Mahlon.
10I have also acquired Ruth the Moabite,
Mahlon's widow, as my wife, in order to
maintain the name of the dead with his
property, so that his name will not disappear from among his family or from his
hometown.[o] Today you are witnesses!"
11Then the elders and all the people at
the gate said, "We are witnesses.[p] May the
LORD make the woman who is coming into
your home like Rachel and Leah,[q] who together built up the family of Israel. May
you have standing in Ephrathah[r] and be
famous in Bethlehem. 12Through the offspring the LORD gives you by this young
woman, may your family be like that of Perez,[s] whom Tamar bore to Judah."

Naomi Gains a Son

13So Boaz took Ruth and she became his
wife. When he made love to her, the LORD
enabled her to conceive,[t] and she gave birth
to a son. 14The women[u] said to Naomi:
"Praise be to the LORD, who this day has
not left you without a guardian-redeemer.
May he become famous throughout Israel!
15He will renew your life and sustain you
in your old age. For your daughter-in-law,
who loves you and who is better to you than
seven sons,[v] has given him birth."
16Then Naomi took the child in her arms

---

[a] *15* Most Hebrew manuscripts; many Hebrew manuscripts, Vulgate and Syriac *she* [b] *1* The Hebrew word for *guardian-redeemer* is a legal term for one who has the obligation to redeem a relative in serious difficulty (see Lev. 25:25-55); also in verses 3, 6, 8 and 14. [c] *4* Many Hebrew manuscripts, Septuagint, Vulgate and Syriac; most Hebrew manuscripts *he* [d] *5* Vulgate and Syriac; Hebrew (see also Septuagint) *Naomi and from Ruth the Moabite, you acquire the*

4:1–2 *the town gate.* The gate of the city was the place where the men congregated and where the officials of a city were to be found. Legal business was typically carried on here where the elders of the city were present to be witnesses.

4:11 *like Rachel and Leah.* The people blessed Ruth and asked the Lord to bless her as He had the founding mothers of the twelve tribes of Israel. Even though she was a Moabitess, Ruth was accepted.

4:14–15 *who loves you ... is better to you than seven sons.* Ruth, although not knowing the outcome, sowed kindness by staying with Naomi. Because of this she also reaped what she had sown: abundant blessing. She became the great-grandmother of King David, and had a place in the genealogy of Christ Jesus. Boaz, as the guardian-redeemer had to sacrifice his name—the son that was born would bear the family name of Mahlon—but he was also abundantly blessed. Boaz received the admiration of the people (4:11), the beautiful and faithful Ruth became his wife and together they became ancestors of the great Redeemer, Jesus Christ. This story of Boaz's redemption of the foreign woman points to the wonderful redemption of Jesus for all those who believe in Him.

3:18 [h] Ps 37:3-5 **4:1** [i] Ru 3:12 **4:2** [j] 1Ki 21:8; Pr 31:23 **4:4** [k] Lev 25:25; Jer 32:7-8 **4:5** [l] Ge 38:8; Dt 25:5-6; Ru 3:13; Mt 22:24 **4:6** [m] Lev 25:25; Ru 3:13 **4:7** [n] Dt 25:7-9 **4:10** [o] Dt 25:6 **4:11** [p] Dt 25:9 [q] Ps 127:3; 128:3 [r] Ge 35:16 **4:12** [s] ver 18; Ge 38:29 **4:13** [t] Ge 29:31; 33:5; Ru 3:11 **4:14** [u] Lk 1:58 **4:15** [v] Ru 1:16-17; 2:11-12; 1Sa 1:8

and cared for him. 17The women living
there said, "Naomi has a son!" And they
named him Obed. He was the father of Jesse,[w] the father of David.

The Genealogy of David

18This, then, is the family line of Perez[x]:

Perez was the father of Hezron,
19 Hezron the father of Ram,
Ram the father of Amminadab,[y]
20 Amminadab the father of Nahshon,
Nahshon the father of Salmon,[a]
21 Salmon the father of Boaz,[z]
Boaz the father of Obed,
22 Obed the father of Jesse,
and Jesse the father of David.

[a] *20* A few Hebrew manuscripts, some Septuagint manuscripts and Vulgate (see also verse 21 and Septuagint of 1 Chron. 2:11); most Hebrew manuscripts *Salma*

4:17 [w] ver 22; 1Sa 16:1, 18; 1Ch 2:12, 13 **4:18** [x] Mt 1:3-6

4:19 [y] Ex 6:23 **4:21** [z] Ru 2:1

1 SAMUEL

▶ **AUTHOR:** The author of 1 and 2 Samuel is anonymous. Samuel may have written the first portion of the book, but his death recorded in 1 Samuel 25:1 makes it clear that he did not write all of 1 or 2 Samuel. It is very possible that a single compiler, perhaps a member of the prophetic school mentioned in 1 Chronicles 29:29, used the various writings referenced as the chronicles of "Nathan the prophet," "Gad the seer" and "Samuel the seer."

▶ **TIME:** c. 1105 – 1011 B.C. ▶ **KEY VERSE:** 1 Sam. 13:14

▶ **THEME:** First Samuel tells the story of three characters: Samuel, Saul, and David. Saul's story begins the line of Israel's monarchy. His story ends with the end of 1 Samuel. David's starts in 1 Samuel, goes through 2 Samuel and ends in the first few chapters of 1 Kings. All three of the main characters in this book make mistakes that cost them dearly. Samuel has problems with his own sons. The result is the end of the rule of judges. Saul seems to be a classic study in what a poor self-image can do to a person. David's early violence prevents him from being able to build the temple later on when he is king.

The Birth of Samuel

1 There was a certain man from Ramathaim, a Zuphite[a] from the hill country[a]
of Ephraim, whose name was Elkanah[b]
son of Jeroham, the son of Elihu, the son
of Tohu, the son of Zuph, an Ephraimite.
2He had two wives;[c] one was called Hannah and the other Peninnah. Peninnah had
children, but Hannah had none.
3Year after year[d] this man went up from
his town to worship[e] and sacrifice to the
LORD Almighty at Shiloh,[f] where Hophni
and Phinehas, the two sons of Eli, were
priests of the LORD. 4Whenever the day
came for Elkanah to sacrifice,[g] he would
give portions of the meat to his wife Peninnah and to all her sons and daughters.
5But to Hannah he gave a double portion
because he loved her, and the LORD had
closed her womb.[h] 6Because the LORD had
closed Hannah's womb, her rival kept provoking her in order to irritate her.[i] 7This
went on year after year. Whenever Hannah went up to the house of the LORD, her rival provoked her till she wept and would not
eat. 8Her husband Elkanah would say to
her, "Hannah, why are you weeping? Why don't you eat? Why are you downhearted? Don't I mean more to you than ten sons?[j]"
9Once when they had finished eating and drinking in Shiloh, Hannah stood up. Now Eli the priest was sitting on his chair
by the doorpost of the LORD's house.[k] 10In
her deep anguish[l] Hannah prayed to the
LORD, weeping bitterly. 11And she made a
vow, saying, "LORD Almighty, if you will only look on your servant's misery and remember[m] me, and not forget your servant but give her a son, then I will give him to the LORD for all the days of his life, and no razor[n] will ever be used on his head."

[a] *1* See Septuagint and 1 Chron. 6:26-27,33-35; or *from Ramathaim Zuphim.*

1:1 ***Elkanah.*** Elkanah was a Levite (1 Chr. 6:26) who lived in a village about five miles north of Jerusalem. He is referred to as an Ephraimite because he lived in the territory of Ephraim.
1:3 ***LORD Almighty.*** The term "LORD Almighty" refers to God as the One who commands the angelic armies of heaven (1 Kin. 22:19; Rev. 19:14) and the armies of Israel (17:45). ***Shiloh.*** Shiloh, located twenty miles north of Jerusalem, was the religious center for the nation at this time and the location of the tabernacle (Josh. 18:1).
1:9 ***Eli.*** Eli, Israel's high priest and judge, was from the family of Ithamar, Aaron's fourth son (1 Chr. 24:1 – 3). The last high priest mentioned before him was Phinehas, the son of Eleazar (Judg. 20:28). It is not known why or how the office of high priest passed from the house of Eleazar to that of Ithamar.
1:11 ***vow.*** Hannah vowed that the child she would bear would be a servant to the Lord all of his life. Can a parent really make a vow that the child will carry out? Hannah surely both taught Samuel and prayed for

1:1 [a] Jos 17:17-18 [b] 1Ch 6:27, 34 **1:2** [c] Dt 21:15-17; Lk 2:36 **1:3** [d] ver 21; Ex 23:14; 34:23; Lk 2:41 [e] Dt 12:5-7 [f] Jos 18:1 **1:4** [g] Dt 12:17-18 **1:5** [h] Ge 16:1; 30:2 **1:6** [i] Job 24:21 **1:8** [j] Ru 4:15 **1:9** [k] 1Sa 3:3 **1:10** [l] Job 7:11 **1:11** [m] Ge 8:1; 28:20; 29:32 [n] Nu 6:1-21; Jdg 13:5

12 As she kept on praying to the LORD, Eli
observed her mouth. 13 Hannah was praying in her heart, and her lips were moving
but her voice was not heard. Eli thought
she was drunk 14 and said to her, "How long
are you going to stay drunk? Put away your
wine."
15 "Not so, my lord," Hannah replied, "I
am a woman who is deeply troubled. I have
not been drinking wine or beer; I was pouring[o] out my soul to the LORD. 16 Do not take
your servant for a wicked woman; I have
been praying here out of my great anguish
and grief."
17 Eli answered, "Go in peace,[p] and may
the God of Israel grant you what you have
asked of him.[q]"
18 She said, "May your servant find favor
in your eyes.[r]" Then she went her way and
ate something, and her face was no longer
downcast.[s]
19 Early the next morning they arose
and worshiped before the LORD and then
went back to their home at Ramah. Elkanah made love to his wife Hannah, and the
LORD remembered[t] her. 20 So in the course
of time Hannah became pregnant and gave
birth to a son. She named[u] him Samuel,[a]
saying, "Because I asked the LORD for him."

Hannah Dedicates Samuel

21 When her husband Elkanah went up
with all his family to offer the annual[v] sacrifice to the LORD and to fulfill his vow,[w]
22 Hannah did not go. She said to her husband, "After the boy is weaned, I will take
him and present[x] him before the LORD, and
he will live there always."[b]
23 "Do what seems best to you," her husband Elkanah told her. "Stay here until
you have weaned him; only may the LORD
make good[y] his[c] word." So the woman
stayed at home and nursed her son until
she had weaned him.
24 After he was weaned, she took the boy
with her, young as he was, along with a
three-year-old bull,[d][z] an ephah[e] of flour
and a skin of wine, and brought him to the
house of the LORD at Shiloh. 25 When the
bull had been sacrificed, they brought the
boy to Eli, 26 and she said to him, "Pardon
me, my lord. As surely as you live, I am the
woman who stood here beside you praying
to the LORD. 27 I prayed[a] for this child, and
the LORD has granted me what I asked of
him. 28 So now I give him to the LORD. For
his whole life[b] he will be given over to the
LORD." And he worshiped the LORD there.

Hannah's Prayer

2 Then Hannah prayed and said:[c]

"My heart rejoices[d] in the LORD;
in the LORD my horn[f][e] is lifted high.
My mouth boasts over my enemies,
for I delight in your deliverance.

2 "There is no one holy[f] like the LORD;
there is no one besides you;
there is no Rock[g] like our God.

[a] *20 Samuel* sounds like the Hebrew for *heard by God.* [b] *22* Masoretic Text; Dead Sea Scrolls *always. I have dedicated him as a Nazirite—all the days of his life."* [c] *23* Masoretic Text; Dead Sea Scrolls, Septuagint and Syriac *your* [d] *24* Dead Sea Scrolls, Septuagint and Syriac; Masoretic Text *with three bulls* [e] *24* That is, probably about 36 pounds or about 16 kilograms [f] *1 Horn* here symbolizes strength; also in verse 10.

him, but it was Samuel who said "yes" to the Lord and to the promise his mother had made. Every single relationship with the Lord is between that individual and the Lord. No one is a follower of God just because his parents are. But there is much that parents can do to encourage and teach their children about loving and serving the Lord, and a heartfelt enthusiastic example is the very best incentive that a parent can provide. ***no razor will ever be used on his head.*** The Nazirite vow involved a designated period of time (usually a few weeks or months) during which there was a commitment to refrain completely from wine, from cutting the hair, and touching any dead body. Hannah promised that her son would be a Nazirite for life.

1:17 Petition—The Lord went to great lengths to ensure that Scripture records all the instances in which God heard and answered prayer; unlike the gods of Israel's surrounding nations. In the contest on Mount Carmel, Elijah's prayers were answered while the prayers of the prophets of Baal went nowhere (1 Kin. 18). The psalmist says, "But God has surely listened and has heard my prayer" (Ps. 66:19).

Petitions are requests that we pray by faith (James 1:6), in the name of Jesus (John 14:13). If we pray in this manner, we are assured that God hears us (1 John 5:14–15). We should pray for ourselves, asking for cleansing (1 John 1:9), and wisdom (James 1:5), spiritual leaders (Col. 4:3), sick believers (James 5:14), rulers (1 Tim. 2:1–3), and even for our enemies (Matt. 5:44).

1:22 *After the boy is weaned.* Hebrew children were normally weaned when they were two or three years old.

1:23 *Do what seems best to you.* According to law, Elkanah could have declared Hannah's vow a rash promise and prohibited her from fulfilling it (Num. 30:10–15). When he told her to "do what seems best to you" he was validating her promise to God.

2:1–10 Prayer—Hannah's prayer is one of praise to God. We often think of prayer as supplication or intercession, but this is a prayer of rejoicing in the Lord, His salvation, His power to raise up and to shatter, His justice and His strength. To pray like this requires focusing on who God is, thoughtful recollection of His attributes, and thanksgiving for His work in our lives.

1:15 [o] Ps 42:4; 62:8; La 2:19 **1:17** [p] Jdg 18:6; 1Sa 25:35; 2Ki 5:19; Mk 5:34 [q] Ps 20:3-5 **1:18** [r] Ru 2:13 [s] Ecc 9:7; Ro 15:13 **1:19** [t] Ge 4:1; 30:22 **1:20** [u] Ge 41:51-52; Ex 2:10, 22; Mt 1:21 **1:21** [v] ver 3 [w] Dt 12:11 **1:22** [x] ver 11, 28; Lk 2:22 **1:23** [y] ver 17; Nu 30:7 **1:24** [z] Nu 15:8-10; Dt 12:5; Jos 18:1 **1:27** [a] ver 11-13; Ps 66:19-20 **1:28** [b] ver 11, 22; Ge 24:26, 52 **2:1** [c] Lk 1:46-55 [d] Ps 9:14; 13:5 [e] Ps 89:17, 24; 92:10; Isa 12:2-3 **2:2** [f] Ex 15:11; Lev 19:2 [g] Dt 32:30-31; 2Sa 22:2, 32

3 "Do not keep talking so proudly
or let your mouth speak such
arrogance,[h]
for the LORD is a God who knows,
and by him deeds[i] are weighed.[j]

4 "The bows of the warriors are broken,[k]
but those who stumbled are armed
with strength.
5 Those who were full hire themselves
out for food,
but those who were hungry are
hungry no more.
She who was barren[l] has borne seven
children,
but she who has had many sons pines
away.

6 "The LORD brings death and makes
alive;[m]
he brings down to the grave and
raises up.[n]
7 The LORD sends poverty and wealth;[o]
he humbles and he exalts.[p]
8 He raises[q] the poor from the dust
and lifts the needy from the ash
heap;
he seats them with princes
and has them inherit a throne of
honor.[r]

"For the foundations[s] of the earth are
the LORD's;
on them he has set the world.
9 He will guard the feet[t] of his faithful
servants,
but the wicked will be silenced in the
place of darkness.[u]

"It is not by strength[v] that one prevails;
10 those who oppose the LORD will be
broken.[w]
The Most High will thunder[x] from
heaven;
the LORD will judge[y] the ends of the
earth.

"He will give strength[z] to his king
and exalt the horn[a] of his anointed."

11 Then Elkanah went home to Ramah,
but the boy ministered[b] before the LORD
under Eli the priest.

Eli's Wicked Sons

12 Eli's sons were scoundrels; they had
no regard[c] for the LORD. 13 Now it was the
practice of the priests that, whenever any
of the people offered a sacrifice, the priest's
servant would come with a three-pronged
fork in his hand while the meat[d] was being
boiled 14 and would plunge the fork into the
pan or kettle or caldron or pot. Whatever
the fork brought up the priest would take
for himself. This is how they treated all the
Israelites who came to Shiloh. 15 But even
before the fat was burned, the priest's servant would come and say to the person who
was sacrificing, "Give the priest some meat
to roast; he won't accept boiled meat from
you, but only raw."
16 If the person said to him, "Let the fat
be burned first, and then take whatever
you want," the servant would answer, "No,
hand it over now; if you don't, I'll take it
by force."
17 This sin of the young men was very
great in the LORD's sight, for they[a] were
treating the LORD's offering with contempt.[e]
18 But Samuel was ministering[f] before
the LORD—a boy wearing a linen ephod.[g]
19 Each year his mother made him a little
robe and took it to him when she went up
with her husband to offer the annual[h] sacrifice. 20 Eli would bless Elkanah and his
wife, saying, "May the LORD give you children by this woman to take the place of the
one she prayed[i] for and gave to[b] the LORD."
Then they would go home. 21 And the LORD
was gracious to Hannah;[j] she gave birth to
three sons and two daughters. Meanwhile,
the boy Samuel grew[k] up in the presence
of the LORD.
22 Now Eli, who was very old, heard
about everything his sons were doing to
all Israel and how they slept with the women[l] who served at the entrance to the tent
of meeting. 23 So he said to them, "Why
do you do such things? I hear from all the
people about these wicked deeds of yours.
24 No, my sons; the report I hear spreading
among the LORD's people is not good. 25 If
one person sins against another, God[c] may
mediate for the offender; but if anyone sins
against the LORD, who will[m] intercede[n] for
them?" His sons, however, did not listen to
their father's rebuke, for it was the LORD's
will to put them to death.
26 And the boy Samuel continued to
grow[o] in stature and in favor with the LORD
and with people.

---

[a] 17 Dead Sea Scrolls and Septuagint; Masoretic Text *people* [b] 20 Dead Sea Scrolls; Masoretic Text *and asked from* [c] 25 Or *the judges*

2:13–15 ***take for himself.*** The priests' rightful share of a sacrifice was the breast and the right thigh of the animal (Lev. 7:34). Eli's sons sinned by taking any part they wanted and demanding the meat immediately, before the fat consecrated to God had been burned on the altar.

2:3 [h] Pr 8:13 [i] 1Sa 16:7; 1Ki 8:39 [j] Pr 16:2; 24:11-12 **2:4** [k] Ps 37:15 **2:5** [l] Ps 113:9; Jer 15:9 **2:6** [m] Dt 32:39 [n] Isa 26:19 **2:7** [o] Dt 8:18 [p] Job 5:11; Ps 75:7 **2:8** [q] Ps 113:7-8 [r] Job 36:7 [s] Job 38:4 **2:9** [t] Ps 91:12 [u] Mt 8:12 [v] Ps 33:16-17 **2:10** [w] Ps 2:9 [x] Ps 18:13 [y] Ps 96:13 [z] Ps 21:1 [a] Ps 89:24 **2:11** [b] ver 18; 1Sa 3:1 **2:12** [c] Jer 2:8; 9:6 **2:13** [d] Lev 7:29-34 **2:17** [e] Mal 2:7-9 **2:18** [f] ver 11; 1Sa 3:1 [g] ver 28 **2:19** [h] 1Sa 1:3 **2:20** [i] 1Sa 1:11,27-28; Lk 2:34 **2:21** [j] Ge 21:1 [k] ver 26; Jdg 13:24; 1Sa 3:19; Lk 2:40 **2:22** [l] Ex 38:8 **2:25** [m] Nu 15:30; Jos 11:20 [n] Dt 1:17; 1Sa 3:14; Heb 10:26 **2:26** [o] ver 21; Lk 2:52

Prophecy Against the House of Eli

27Now a man of God[p] came to Eli and said to him, "This is what the LORD says: 'Did I not clearly reveal myself to your ancestor's family when they were in Egypt under Pharaoh? 28I chose[q] your ancestor out of all the tribes of Israel to be my priest, to go up to my altar, to burn incense, and to wear an ephod[r] in my presence. I also gave your ancestor's family all the food offerings presented by the Israelites. 29Why do you[a] scorn my sacrifice and offering[s] that I prescribed for my dwelling?[t] Why do you honor your sons more than me by fattening yourselves on the choice parts of every offering made by my people Israel?'

30"Therefore the LORD, the God of Israel, declares: 'I promised that members of your family would minister before me forever.[u]' But now the LORD declares: 'Far be it from me! Those who honor me I will honor,[v] but those who despise[w] me will be disdained. 31The time is coming when I will cut short your strength and the strength of your priestly house, so that no one in it will reach old age,[x] 32and you will see distress in my dwelling. Although good will be done to Israel, no one in your family line will ever reach old age.[y] 33Every one of you that I do not cut off from serving at my altar I will spare only to destroy your sight and sap your strength, and all your descendants will die in the prime of life.

34"'And what happens to your two sons, Hophni and Phinehas, will be a sign to you—they will both die[z] on the same day.[a] 35I will raise up for myself a faithful priest,[b] who will do according to what is in my heart and mind. I will firmly establish his priestly house, and they will minister before my anointed[c] one always. 36Then everyone left in your family line will come and bow down before him for a piece of silver and a loaf of bread and plead, "Appoint me to some priestly office so I can have food to eat.[d]"'"

The LORD Calls Samuel

3 The boy Samuel ministered[e] before the LORD under Eli. In those days the word of the LORD was rare;[f] there were not many visions.[g]

2One night Eli, whose eyes[h] were becoming so weak that he could barely see, was lying down in his usual place. 3The lamp[i] of God had not yet gone out, and Samuel was lying down in the house of the LORD, where the ark of God was. 4Then the LORD called Samuel.

Samuel answered, "Here I am.[j]" 5And he ran to Eli and said, "Here I am; you called me."

But Eli said, "I did not call; go back and lie down." So he went and lay down.

6Again the LORD called, "Samuel!" And Samuel got up and went to Eli and said, "Here I am; you called me."

"My son," Eli said, "I did not call; go back and lie down."

7Now Samuel did not yet know the LORD: The word of the LORD had not yet been revealed[k] to him.

8A third time the LORD called, "Samuel!" And Samuel got up and went to Eli and said, "Here I am; you called me."

Then Eli realized that the LORD was calling the boy. 9So Eli told Samuel, "Go and lie down, and if he calls you, say, 'Speak, LORD, for your servant is listening.'" So Samuel went and lay down in his place.

10The LORD came and stood there, calling as at the other times, "Samuel! Samuel!"

Then Samuel said, "Speak, for your servant is listening."

11And the LORD said to Samuel: "See, I am about to do something in Israel that will make the ears of everyone who hears about it tingle.[l] 12At that time I will carry out against Eli everything[m] I spoke against his

[a] 29 The Hebrew is plural.

2:30 Godlessness—Whenever a priesthood or church or nation falls into apostasy, the people who should have been served suffer. Eli failed his people far more than his disgraceful sons did, because the Israelites trusted Eli's integrity and his discernment. He should have restrained his sons, and he did not. The price of disobedience is always high, and the spiritual cost to a community that has lost trust in one whom they thought was close to God is greater than most people are willing to calculate.

2:31–34 *no one in your family line will ever reach old age.* The judgment was partially fulfilled in the massacre of the priests of Nob (22:11–19), and was ultimately fulfilled when the priesthood was transferred to the family of Zadok in the time of Solomon (1 Kin. 2:26–27,35).

2:35 *faithful priest.* This term refers to Zadok, who was faithful to God and to the line of David (1 Kin. 1:7–8; 2:26–27,35).

3:14 *shall not be atoned for.* Eli and his sons were guilty of presumptuous sin (Num. 15:30–31). For such sin, there was no atoning sacrifice.

3:1–19 Listening for God's Call—Samuel heard God's call in an audible voice. That experience is not a common one in the history of those who follow after God. While most of us get a sense of a call by some other means, Samuel's experience does help us to understand what our attitude and response should be.

Samuel's attitude was one of readiness and eager response with a desire to listen. It is that attitude of listening that was foundational to Samuel's whole

2:27 [p] Ex 4:14-16; 1Ki 13:1 **2:28** [q] Ex 28:1 [r] Lev 8:7-8 **2:29** [s] ver 12-17 [t] Dt 12:5; Mt 10:37 **2:30** [u] Ex 29:9 [v] Ps 50:23; 91:15 [w] Mal 2:9 **2:31** [x] 1Sa 4:11-18; 22:16-20 **2:32** [y] 1Ki 2:26-27; Zec 8:4 **2:34** [z] 1Sa 4:11 [a] 1Ki 13:3 **2:35** [b] 1Sa 12:3; 1Ki 2:35 [c] 1Sa 16:13; 2Sa 7:11,27; 1Ki 11:38 **2:36** [d] 1Ki 2:27 **3:1** [e] 1Sa 2:11 [f] Ps 74:9 [g] Am 8:11 **3:2** [h] 1Sa 4:15 **3:3** [i] Lev 24:1-4 **3:4** [j] Isa 6:8 **3:7** [k] Ac 19:12 **3:11** [l] 2Ki 21:12; Jer 19:3 **3:12** [m] 1Sa 2:27-36

family—from beginning to end. 13For I told
him that I would judge his family forever
because of the sin he knew about; his sons
blasphemed God,[a] and he failed to restrain[n]
them. 14Therefore I swore to the house of
Eli, 'The guilt of Eli's house will never be
atoned[o] for by sacrifice or offering.'"
15Samuel lay down until morning and
then opened the doors of the house of the
LORD. He was afraid to tell Eli the vision,
16but Eli called him and said, "Samuel, my
son."
Samuel answered, "Here I am."
17"What was it he said to you?" Eli asked.
"Do not hide it from me. May God deal with
you, be it ever so severely,[p] if you hide from
me anything he told you." 18So Samuel told
him everything, hiding nothing from him.
Then Eli said, "He is the LORD; let him do
what is good in his eyes."[q]
19The LORD was with[r] Samuel as he
grew[s] up, and he let none[t] of Samuel's
words fall to the ground. 20And all Israel
from Dan to Beersheba[u] recognized that
Samuel was attested as a prophet of the
LORD. 21The LORD continued to appear at
Shiloh, and there he revealed[v] himself to
Samuel through his word.
4 And Samuel's word came to all Israel.

The Philistines Capture the Ark

Now the Israelites went out to fight
against the Philistines. The Israelites
camped at Ebenezer,[w] and the Philistines
at Aphek.[x] 2The Philistines deployed their
forces to meet Israel, and as the battle
spread, Israel was defeated by the Philistines, who killed about four thousand of
them on the battlefield. 3When the soldiers returned to camp, the elders of Israel asked, "Why[y] did the LORD bring defeat
on us today before the Philistines? Let us
bring the ark[z] of the LORD's covenant from
Shiloh, so that he may go with us and save
us from the hand of our enemies."
4So the people sent men to Shiloh, and
they brought back the ark of the covenant
of the LORD Almighty, who is enthroned
between the cherubim.[a] And Eli's two sons,
Hophni and Phinehas, were there with the
ark of the covenant of God.
5When the ark of the LORD's covenant
came into the camp, all Israel raised such
a great shout[b] that the ground shook.
6Hearing the uproar, the Philistines asked,
"What's all this shouting in the Hebrew
camp?"
When they learned that the ark of the
LORD had come into the camp, 7the Philistines were afraid.[c] "A god has[b] come
into the camp," they said. "Oh no! Nothing like this has happened before. 8We're
doomed! Who will deliver us from the hand
of these mighty gods? They are the gods
who struck the Egyptians with all kinds of
plagues in the wilderness. 9Be strong, Philistines! Be men, or you will be subject to
the Hebrews, as they[d] have been to you. Be
men, and fight!"
10So the Philistines fought, and the Israelites were defeated[e] and every man fled
to his tent. The slaughter was very great;
Israel lost thirty thousand foot soldiers.
11The ark of God was captured, and Eli's
two sons, Hophni and Phinehas, died.[f]

Death of Eli

12That same day a Benjamite ran from
the battle line and went to Shiloh with his
clothes torn and dust[g] on his head. 13When
he arrived, there was Eli[h] sitting on his
chair by the side of the road, watching, because his heart feared for the ark of God.
When the man entered the town and told
what had happened, the whole town sent
up a cry.
14Eli heard the outcry and asked, "What
is the meaning of this uproar?"
The man hurried over to Eli, 15who was
ninety-eight years old and whose eyes[i] had

a *13* An ancient Hebrew scribal tradition (see also Septuagint); Masoretic Text *sons made themselves contemptible* *b* 7 Or "*Gods have* (see Septuagint)

---

life and ministry. Throughout his life we see him listening to God's word and following God's direction. He listened for the general will of God and also had an ear for the more specific directions that God gave him. Sometimes he raised questions about why he was doing a particular thing, but the word from God was paramount. He listened for it and responded to it.

3:20 ***from Dan to Beersheba.*** This expression denotes the whole territory of Israel, from its most northern point to its most southern (Judg. 20:1).

4:1 ***the Philistines.*** Abraham and Isaac had contact with the Philistines as early as the twentieth century B.C. With their aggressive invasions and fortress cities, the Philistines established strong political and military control of the southern coastal plain of Palestine. They had iron weapons, and were a significant threat to the Israelites.

4:4 ***who is enthroned between the cherubim.*** Cherubim are angels generally regarded as guardians of God's holiness (Gen. 3:24; Ps. 80:1; Ezek. 10:9).

4:6–7 ***the ark of the LORD had come into the camp, the Philistines were afraid.*** Apparently the Philistines viewed the ark as some sort of idol.

4:11 ***the ark of God was captured.*** The loss of the ark, symbolic of God's presence among His people, was a great tragedy for Israel—even worse than the loss of life. The ark probably never returned to Shiloh.

3:13 [n] 1Sa 2:12, 17, 22, 29-31 **3:14** [o] Lev 15:30-31; 1Sa 2:25; Isa 22:14 **3:17** [p] Ru 1:17; 2Sa 3:35 **3:18** [q] Job 2:10; Isa 39:8 **3:19** [r] Ge 21:22; 39:2 [s] 1Sa 2:21 [t] 1Sa 9:6 **3:20** [u] Jdg 20:1 **3:21** [v] ver 10 **4:1** [w] 1Sa 7:12 [x] Jos 12:18; 1Sa 29:1 **4:3** [y] Jos 7:7 [z] Nu 10:35; Jos 6:7 **4:4** [a] Ex 25:22; 2Sa 6:2 **4:5** [b] Jos 6:5, 10 **4:7** [c] Ex 15:14 **4:9** [d] Jdg 13:1; 1Co 16:13 **4:10** [e] ver 2; Dt 28:25; 2Sa 18:17; 2Ki 14:12 **4:11** [f] 1Sa 2:34; Ps 78:61, 64 **4:12** [g] Jos 7:6; 2Sa 1:2; 15:32; Ne 9:1; Job 2:12 **4:13** [h] ver 18; 1Sa 1:9 **4:15** [i] 1Sa 3:2

failed so that he could not see. 16 He told Eli, "I have just come from the battle line; I fled from it this very day."

Eli asked, "What happened, my son?"

17 The man who brought the news replied, "Israel fled before the Philistines, and the army has suffered heavy losses. Also your two sons, Hophni and Phinehas, are dead, and the ark of God has been captured."

18 When he mentioned the ark of God, Eli fell backward off his chair by the side of the gate. His neck was broken and he died, for he was an old man, and he was heavy. He had led[a][j] Israel forty years.

19 His daughter-in-law, the wife of Phinehas, was pregnant and near the time of delivery. When she heard the news that the ark of God had been captured and that her father-in-law and her husband were dead, she went into labor and gave birth, but was overcome by her labor pains. 20 As she was dying, the women attending her said, "Don't despair; you have given birth to a son." But she did not respond or pay any attention.

21 She named the boy Ichabod,[b][k] saying, "The Glory[l] has departed from Israel"—because of the capture of the ark of God and the deaths of her father-in-law and her husband. 22 She said, "The Glory has departed from Israel, for the ark of God has been captured."

The Ark in Ashdod and Ekron

5 After the Philistines had captured the ark of God, they took it from Ebenezer[m] to Ashdod.[n] 2 Then they carried the ark into Dagon's temple and set it beside Dagon.[o] 3 When the people of Ashdod rose early the next day, there was Dagon, fallen[p] on his face on the ground before the ark of the LORD! They took Dagon and put him back in his place. 4 But the following morning when they rose, there was Dagon, fallen on his face on the ground before the ark of the LORD! His head and hands had been broken[q] off and were lying on the threshold; only his body remained. 5 That is why to this day neither the priests of Dagon nor any others who enter Dagon's temple at Ashdod step on the threshold.[r]

6 The LORD's hand[s] was heavy on the people of Ashdod and its vicinity; he brought devastation[t] on them and afflicted them with tumors.[c][u] 7 When the people of Ashdod saw what was happening, they said, "The ark of the god of Israel must not stay here with us, because his hand is heavy on us and on Dagon our god." 8 So they called together all the rulers of the Philistines and asked them, "What shall we do with the ark of the god of Israel?"

They answered, "Have the ark of the god of Israel moved to Gath.[v]" So they moved the ark of the God of Israel.

9 But after they had moved it, the LORD's hand was against that city, throwing it into a great panic.[w] He afflicted the people of the city, both young and old, with an outbreak of tumors.[d] 10 So they sent the ark of God to Ekron.

As the ark of God was entering Ekron, the people of Ekron cried out, "They have brought the ark of the god of Israel around to us to kill us and our people." 11 So they called together all the rulers[x] of the Philistines and said, "Send the ark of the god of Israel away; let it go back to its own place, or it[e] will kill us and our people." For death had filled the city with panic; God's hand was very heavy on it. 12 Those who did not die were afflicted with tumors, and the outcry of the city went up to heaven.

The Ark Returned to Israel

6 When the ark of the LORD had been in Philistine territory seven months, 2 the Philistines called for the priests and the diviners[y] and said, "What shall we do with the ark of the LORD? Tell us how we should send it back to its place."

3 They answered, "If you return the ark of the god of Israel, do not send it back to him without a gift;[z] by all means send a guilt offering[a] to him. Then you will be healed, and you will know why his hand[b] has not been lifted from you."

4 The Philistines asked, "What guilt offering should we send to him?"

---

[a] 18 Traditionally *judged* [b] 21 *Ichabod* means *no glory.* [c] 6 Hebrew; Septuagint and Vulgate *tumors. And rats appeared in their land, and there was death and destruction throughout the city* [d] 9 Or *with tumors in the groin* (see Septuagint) [e] 11 Or *he*

4:21 *Ichabod.* The name Ichabod, meaning "No Glory," reflected Israel's circumstances. The loss of the ark meant the absence of God's glory in Israel.

5:2 *Dagon.* This god appears to be a Philistine adaptation of the Canaanite god Baal. Philistia was in an important grain producing area, and the worship of Dagon was thought to ensure a good crop.

5:6–7 Idolatry—The residents of Ashdod made one fatal mistake. They tried to place a false god alongside the true God. These ancient Philistines are not the only ones who have tried this sort of idolatry. People are quick to recognize that there is "something" about the Living God, and they want Him. But they want to have God with qualifiers—"God and my career track," "God and my dedication to entertainment," "God and my secret sin," "God and my own way." But God will not share the throne of any man's heart. It has to be God, and God alone.

4:18 [j] ver 13 **4:21** [k] Ge 35:18 [l] Ps 26:8; Jer 2:11 **5:1** [m] 1Sa 4:1; 7:12 [n] Jos 13:3 **5:2** [o] Jdg 16:23 **5:3** [p] Isa 19:1; 46:7 **5:4** [q] Eze 6:6; Mic 1:7 **5:5** [r] Zep 1:9 **5:6** [s] ver 7; Ex 9:3; Ps 32:4; Ac 13:11 [t] ver 11; Ps 78:66 [u] Dt 28:27; 1Sa 6:5 **5:8** [v] ver 11 **5:9** [w] ver 6, 11; Dt 2:15; 1Sa 7:13; Ps 78:66 **5:11** [x] ver 6, 8-9 **6:2** [y] Ge 41:8; Ex 7:11; Isa 2:6 **6:3** [z] Ex 23:15; Dt 16:16 [a] Lev 5:15 [b] ver 9

They replied, "Five gold tumors and five gold rats, according to the number[c] of the Philistine rulers, because the same plague has struck both you and your rulers. 5Make models of the tumors[d] and of the rats that are destroying the country, and give glory[e] to Israel's god. Perhaps he will lift his hand from you and your gods and your land. 6Why do you harden[f] your hearts as the Egyptians and Pharaoh did? When Israel's god dealt harshly with them, did they[g] not send the Israelites out so they could go on their way?

7"Now then, get a new cart[h] ready, with two cows that have calved and have never been yoked.[i] Hitch the cows to the cart, but take their calves away and pen them up. 8Take the ark of the LORD and put it on the cart, and in a chest beside it put the gold objects you are sending back to him as a guilt offering. Send it on its way, 9but keep watching it. If it goes up to its own territory, toward Beth Shemesh,[j] then the LORD has brought this great disaster on us. But if it does not, then we will know that it was not his hand that struck us but that it happened to us by chance."

10So they did this. They took two such cows and hitched them to the cart and penned up their calves. 11They placed the ark of the LORD on the cart and along with it the chest containing the gold rats and the models of the tumors. 12Then the cows went straight up toward Beth Shemesh, keeping on the road and lowing all the way; they did not turn to the right or to the left. The rulers of the Philistines followed them as far as the border of Beth Shemesh.

13Now the people of Beth Shemesh were harvesting their wheat in the valley, and when they looked up and saw the ark, they rejoiced at the sight. 14The cart came to the field of Joshua of Beth Shemesh, and there it stopped beside a large rock. The people chopped up the wood of the cart and sacrificed the cows as a burnt offering[k] to the LORD. 15The Levites[l] took down the ark of the LORD, together with the chest containing the gold objects, and placed them on the large rock. On that day the people of Beth Shemesh offered burnt offerings and made sacrifices to the LORD. 16The five rulers of the Philistines saw all this and then returned that same day to Ekron.

17These are the gold tumors the Philistines sent as a guilt offering to the LORD—one each[m] for Ashdod, Gaza, Ashkelon, Gath and Ekron. 18And the number of the gold rats was according to the number of Philistine towns belonging to the five rulers—the fortified towns with their country villages. The large rock on which the Levites set the ark of the LORD is a witness to this day in the field of Joshua of Beth Shemesh.

19But God struck down[n] some of the inhabitants of Beth Shemesh, putting seventy[a] of them to death because they looked[o] into the ark of the LORD. The people mourned because of the heavy blow the LORD had dealt them. 20And the people of Beth Shemesh asked, "Who can stand[p] in the presence of the LORD, this holy[q] God? To whom will the ark go up from here?"

21Then they sent messengers to the people of Kiriath Jearim,[r] saying, "The Philistines have returned the ark of the LORD. Come down and take it up to your town."

7 1So the men of Kiriath Jearim came and took up the ark of the LORD. They brought it to Abinadab's[s] house on the hill and consecrated Eleazar his son to guard the ark of the LORD. 2The ark remained at Kiriath Jearim a long time—twenty years in all.

Samuel Subdues the Philistines at Mizpah

Then all the people of Israel turned back to the LORD. 3So Samuel said to all the Israelites, "If you are returning[t] to the LORD with all your hearts, then rid[u] yourselves of the foreign gods and the Ashtoreths[v] and commit[w] yourselves to the LORD and serve him only,[x] and he will deliver you out of the hand of the Philistines." 4So the Israelites

[a] *19* A few Hebrew manuscripts; most Hebrew manuscripts and Septuagint *50,070*

6:8 *Send it on its way.* This seemed like a good test to the Philistines. The natural inclination of the cows would be to return home to their calves. If the cows went against their normal instincts, it would show that God was causing them to walk away from their calves.

6:14 *sacrificed the cows as a burnt offering.* The law required that sacrifices be offered only at the central sanctuary (Deut. 12:4–14). Apparently the people felt that special circumstances required an immediate offering of thanksgiving.

6:19 Presumption—The Israelites who looked into the ark were glad to have it back. Perhaps they thought that the Philistines had looked inside it, and certainly they had more right than the Philistines to gaze upon the holy objects contained in the ark. Their reasons may have seemed good at the moment, but they were ignoring God's specific commands and treating His holiness as unimportant. In the same way today, we can end up trivializing who God is. We can speak frivolously of the things of God, calling Him the "Man upstairs," or being "Sunday Christians." We can presume on our relationship with God without remembering what it cost Jesus to obtain it for us.

7:2 *twenty years.* It was probably twenty years before Samuel called the assembly at Mizpah (v. 5). The

6:4 [c] ver 17-18; Jos 13:3; Jdg 3:3 **6:5** [d] 1Sa 5:6-11 [e] Jos 7:19; Isa 42:12; Jn 9:24; Rev 14:7 **6:6** [f] Ex 7:13; 8:15; 9:34; 14:17 [g] Ex 12:31,33 **6:7** [h] 2Sa 6:3 [i] Nu 19:2 **6:9** [j] ver 3; Jos 15:10; 21:16 **6:14** [k] 2Sa 24:22; 1Ki 19:21 **6:15** [l] Jos 3:3 **6:17** [m] ver 4 **6:19** [n] 2Sa 6:7 [o] Ex 19:21; Nu 4:5,15,20 **6:20** [p] 2Sa 6:9; Mal 3:2; Rev 6:17 [q] Lev 11:45 **6:21** [r] Jos 9:17; 15:9,60; 1Ch 13:5-6 **7:1** [s] 2Sa 6:3 **7:3** [t] Dt 30:10; Isa 55:7; Hos 6:1 [u] Ge 35:2; Jos 24:14 [v] Jdg 2:12-13; 1Sa 31:10 [w] Joel 2:12 [x] Dt 6:13; Mt 4:10; Lk 4:8

put away their Baals and Ashtoreths, and served the LORD only.

5Then Samuel said, "Assemble all Israel at Mizpah,[y] and I will intercede with the LORD for you." 6When they had assembled at Mizpah, they drew water and poured[z] it out before the LORD. On that day they fasted and there they confessed, "We have sinned against the LORD." Now Samuel was serving as leader[a][a] of Israel at Mizpah.

7When the Philistines heard that Israel had assembled at Mizpah, the rulers of the Philistines came up to attack them. When the Israelites heard of it, they were afraid[b] because of the Philistines. 8They said to Samuel, "Do not stop crying[c] out to the LORD our God for us, that he may rescue us from the hand of the Philistines." 9Then Samuel[d] took a suckling lamb and sacrificed it as a whole burnt offering to the LORD. He cried out to the LORD on Israel's behalf, and the LORD answered him.[e]

10While Samuel was sacrificing the burnt offering, the Philistines drew near to engage Israel in battle. But that day the LORD thundered[f] with loud thunder against the Philistines and threw them into such a panic[g] that they were routed before the Israelites. 11The men of Israel rushed out of Mizpah and pursued the Philistines, slaughtering them along the way to a point below Beth Kar.

12Then Samuel took a stone[h] and set it up between Mizpah and Shen. He named it Ebenezer,[b] saying, "Thus far the LORD has helped us."

13So the Philistines were subdued[i] and they stopped invading Israel's territory. Throughout Samuel's lifetime, the hand of the LORD was against the Philistines. 14The towns from Ekron to Gath that the Philistines had captured from Israel were restored to Israel, and Israel delivered the neighboring territory from the hands of the Philistines. And there was peace between Israel and the Amorites.

15Samuel[j] continued as Israel's leader all the days of his life. 16From year to year he went on a circuit from Bethel to Gilgal to Mizpah, judging Israel in all those places. 17But he always went back to Ramah,[k] where his home was, and there he also held court for Israel. And he built an altar[l] there to the LORD.

Israel Asks for a King

8 When Samuel grew old, he appointed[m] his sons as Israel's leaders.[c] 2The name of his firstborn was Joel and the name of his second was Abijah, and they served at Beersheba.[n] 3But his sons did not follow his ways. They turned aside after dishonest gain and accepted bribes[o] and perverted justice.

4So all the elders of Israel gathered together and came to Samuel at Ramah.[p] 5They said to him, "You are old, and your sons do not follow your ways; now appoint a king[q] to lead[d] us, such as all the other nations have."

6But when they said, "Give us a king to lead us," this displeased[r] Samuel; so he prayed to the LORD. 7And the LORD told him: "Listen to all that the people are saying to you; it is not you they have rejected, but they have rejected me as their king.[s] 8As they have done from the day I brought them up out of Egypt until this day, forsaking me and serving other gods, so they are doing to you. 9Now listen to them; but warn them solemnly and let them know[t] what the king who will reign over them will claim as his rights."

10Samuel told all the words of the LORD to the people who were asking him for a king. 11He said, "This is what the king who will reign over you will claim as his

a 6 Traditionally *judge*; also in verse 15
b 12 *Ebenezer* means *stone of help.*
c 1 Traditionally *judges*
d 5 Traditionally *judge*; also in verses 6 and 20

---

ark remained at Kiriath Jearim until David brought it to Jerusalem in the first year of his reign over all Israel.

7:6 *poured it out.* The pouring of water was symbolic of repentance (Lam. 2:19).

7:12 *Ebenezer.* The name Ebenezer means "stone of help." Samuel followed Joshua's practice of commemorating the victories of God for His people with stone markers. Some old gospel hymns refer to an "Ebenezer," meaning a particular notation of something special God has done.

7:14 *Amorites.* This name may refer to the original inhabitants of Canaan (Gen. 15:16).

7:17 *Ramah.* Samuel was back in the town where he was born.

8:5 *appoint a king.* The reasons given for wanting a king were Samuel's age and his sons' unreliability. This is a sad commentary on Samuel's failure to raise his sons to honor and obey the Lord, particularly considering the example of Eli's sons. But this was not really a reason to ask for a king. The Israelite judges had always been appointed by God, rather than gaining their position by inheritance. There was no reason to think that God would not appoint someone to succeed Samuel.

8:7 *they have rejected me.* This actually fulfilled the prophecy in Deuteronomy 17:14–20. God knew long ago that the Israelites would chose to be like the other nations and have a king, instead of being ruled more directly by God through judges. He warned them of the pitfalls of having a king, and set out some guidelines for the kings to follow.

7:5 [y] Jdg 20:1 **7:6** [z] Ps 62:8; La 2:19 [a] Jdg 10:10; Ne 9:1; Ps 106:6 **7:7** [b] 1Sa 17:11 **7:8** [c] 1Sa 12:19,23; Isa 37:4; Jer 15:1 **7:9** [d] Ps 99:6 [e] Jer 15:1 **7:10** [f] 1Sa 2:10; 2Sa 22:14-15 [g] Jos 10:10 **7:12** [h] Ge 35:14; Jos 4:9 **7:13** [i] Jdg 13:1,5; 1Sa 13:5 **7:15** [j] ver 6; 1Sa 12:11 **7:17** [k] 1Sa 1:19; 8:4 [l] Jdg 21:4 **8:1** [m] Dt 16:18-19 **8:2** [n] Ge 22:19; 1Ki 19:3; Am 5:4-5 **8:3** [o] Ex 23:8; Dt 16:19; Ps 15:5 **8:4** [p] 1Sa 7:17 **8:5** [q] Dt 17:14-20 **8:6** [r] 1Sa 15:11 **8:7** [s] Ex 16:8; 1Sa 10:19 **8:9** [t] ver 11-18; 1Sa 10:25

rights: He will take[u] your sons and make
them serve with his chariots and horses,
and they will run in front of his chariots.[v]
12 Some he will assign to be commanders[w]
of thousands and commanders of fifties,
and others to plow his ground and reap his
harvest, and still others to make weapons
of war and equipment for his chariots. 13 He
will take your daughters to be perfumers
and cooks and bakers. 14 He will take the
best of your[x] fields and vineyards[y] and olive groves and give them to his attendants.
15 He will take a tenth of your grain and of
your vintage and give it to his officials and
attendants. 16 Your male and female servants and the best of your cattle[a] and donkeys he will take for his own use. 17 He will
take a tenth of your flocks, and you yourselves will become his slaves. 18 When that
day comes, you will cry out for relief from
the king you have chosen, but the LORD will
not answer[z] you in that day."

19 But the people refused[a] to listen to
Samuel. "No!" they said. "We want a king
over us. 20 Then we will be like all the other
nations,[b] with a king to lead us and to go
out before us and fight our battles."

21 When Samuel heard all that the people
said, he repeated[c] it before the LORD. 22 The
LORD answered, "Listen[d] to them and give
them a king."

Then Samuel said to the Israelites, "Everyone go back to your own town."

Samuel Anoints Saul

9 There was a Benjamite, a man of standing, whose name was Kish[e] son of Abiel, the son of Zeror, the son of Bekorath,
the son of Aphiah of Benjamin. 2 Kish had
a son named Saul, as handsome a young
man as could be found[f] anywhere in Israel,
and he was a head taller[g] than anyone else.

3 Now the donkeys belonging to Saul's
father Kish were lost, and Kish said to his
son Saul, "Take one of the servants with
you and go and look for the donkeys."
4 So he passed through the hill[h] country
of Ephraim and through the area around
Shalisha,[i] but they did not find them. They
went on into the district of Shaalim, but the
donkeys were not there. Then he passed
through the territory of Benjamin, but they
did not find them.

5 When they reached the district of Zuph,[j]
Saul said to the servant who was with him,
"Come, let's go back, or my father will stop
thinking about the donkeys and start worrying[k] about us."

6 But the servant replied, "Look, in this
town there is a man of God;[l] he is highly
respected, and everything[m] he says comes
true. Let's go there now. Perhaps he will tell
us what way to take."

7 Saul said to his servant, "If we go, what
can we give the man? The food in our sacks
is gone. We have no gift[n] to take to the man
of God. What do we have?"

8 The servant answered him again.
"Look," he said, "I have a quarter of a shekel[b] of silver. I will give it to the man of God
so that he will tell us what way to take."
9 (Formerly in Israel, if someone went to inquire of God, they would say, "Come, let
us go to the seer," because the prophet of
today used to be called a seer.)[o]

10 "Good," Saul said to his servant.
"Come, let's go." So they set out for the
town where the man of God was.

11 As they were going up the hill to the
town, they met some young women coming
out to draw[p] water, and they asked them,
"Is the seer here?"

12 "He is," they answered. "He's ahead of
you. Hurry now; he has just come to our
town today, for the people have a sacrifice[q]
at the high place.[r] 13 As soon as you enter
the town, you will find him before he goes
up to the high place to eat. The people will
not begin eating until he comes, because he
must bless the sacrifice; afterward, those
who are invited will eat. Go up now; you
should find him about this time."

14 They went up to the town, and as they
were entering it, there was Samuel, coming toward them on his way up to the high
place.

15 Now the day before Saul came, the
LORD had revealed this to Samuel: 16 "About
this time tomorrow I will send you a man
from the land of Benjamin. Anoint[s] him
ruler over my people Israel; he will deliver[t] them from the hand of the Philistines.
I have looked on my people, for their cry
has reached me."

[a] *16* Septuagint; Hebrew *young men* [b] *8* That is, about 1/10 ounce or about 3 grams

8:20 *and fight our battles.* The Israelites were looking for human leadership on the battlefield, instead of recognizing that God would lead them in battle, and win (Ex. 15:3; Judg. 7).

9:12 *the high place.* A hill that was used for worship was called "a high place." The Canaanites were known for building their places for worship on hills, and the Israelites apparently used similar sites for worship after the ark was taken from the tabernacle at Shiloh. They believed that the presence of the Lord had departed from the tabernacle, and it was apparently at that point that Shiloh ceased to be a gathering center for the nation.

8:11 [u] 1Sa 10:25; 14:52 [v] Dt 17:16; 2Sa 15:1
8:12 [w] 1Sa 22:7 **8:14** [x] Eze 46:18 [y] 1Ki 21:7, 15
8:18 [z] Pr 1:28; Isa 1:15; Mic 3:4 **8:19** [a] Isa 66:4; Jer 44:16
8:20 [b] ver 5 **8:21** [c] Jdg 11:11 **8:22** [d] ver 7
9:1 [e] 1Sa 14:51; 1Ch 8:33; 9:39 **9:2** [f] 1Sa 10:24
[g] 1Sa 10:23 **9:4** [h] Jos 24:33 [i] 2Ki 4:42 **9:5** [j] 1Sa 1:1
[k] 1Sa 10:2 **9:6** [l] Dt 33:1; 1Ki 13:1 [m] 1Sa 3:19
9:7 [n] 1Ki 14:3; 2Ki 5:5, 15; 8:8 **9:9** [o] 2Sa 24:11; 2Ki 17:13;
1Ch 9:22; 26:28; 29:29; Isa 30:10; Am 7:12
9:11 [p] Ge 24:11, 13 **9:12** [q] Nu 28:11-15; 1Sa 7:17
[r] Ge 31:54; 1Sa 10:5; 1Ki 3:2 **9:16** [s] 1Sa 10:1 [t] Ex 3:7-9

17 When Samuel caught sight of Saul, the
LORD said to him, "This[u] is the man I spoke
to you about; he will govern my people."
18 Saul approached Samuel in the gateway and asked, "Would you please tell me
where the seer's house is?"
19 "I am the seer," Samuel replied. "Go up
ahead of me to the high place, for today you
are to eat with me, and in the morning I
will send you on your way and will tell you
all that is in your heart. 20 As for the donkeys[v] you lost three days ago, do not worry
about them; they have been found. And to
whom is all the desire[w] of Israel turned, if
not to you and your whole family line?"
21 Saul answered, "But am I not a Benjamite, from the smallest tribe[x] of Israel,
and is not my clan the least of all the clans
of the tribe of Benjamin?[y] Why do you say
such a thing to me?"
22 Then Samuel brought Saul and his servant into the hall and seated them at the
head of those who were invited—about
thirty in number. 23 Samuel said to the
cook, "Bring the piece of meat I gave you,
the one I told you to lay aside."
24 So the cook took up the thigh[z] with
what was on it and set it in front of Saul.
Samuel said, "Here is what has been kept
for you. Eat, because it was set aside for
you for this occasion from the time I said, 'I
have invited guests.'" And Saul dined with
Samuel that day.
25 After they came down from the high
place to the town, Samuel talked with Saul
on the roof[a] of his house. 26 They rose about
daybreak, and Samuel called to Saul on
the roof, "Get ready, and I will send you on
your way." When Saul got ready, he and
Samuel went outside together. 27 As they
were going down to the edge of the town,
Samuel said to Saul, "Tell the servant to go
on ahead of us"—and the servant did so—
"but you stay here for a while, so that I may
give you a message from God."
10 Then Samuel took a flask[b] of olive
oil and poured it on Saul's head and
kissed him, saying, "Has not the LORD
anointed[c] you ruler over his inheritance?[a][d]
2 When you leave me today, you will meet
two men near Rachel's tomb,[e] at Zelzah on
the border of Benjamin. They will say to
you, 'The donkeys[f] you set out to look for
have been found. And now your father has
stopped thinking about them and is worried[g] about you. He is asking, "What shall
I do about my son?"'
3 "Then you will go on from there until
you reach the great tree of Tabor. Three
men going up to worship God at Bethel[h]
will meet you there. One will be carrying
three young goats, another three loaves of
bread, and another a skin of wine. 4 They
will greet you and offer you two loaves of
bread, which you will accept from them.
5 "After that you will go to Gibeah of God,
where there is a Philistine outpost.[i] As you
approach the town, you will meet a procession of prophets coming down from the
high place[j] with lyres, timbrels, pipes and
harps[k] being played before them, and they
will be prophesying.[l] 6 The Spirit[m] of the
LORD will come powerfully upon you, and
you will prophesy with them; and you will
be changed into a different person. 7 Once
these signs are fulfilled, do whatever[n] your
hand finds to do, for God is with[o] you.
8 "Go down ahead of me to Gilgal.[p] I will
surely come down to you to sacrifice burnt
offerings and fellowship offerings, but you
must wait seven days until I come to you
and tell you what you are to do."

Saul Made King

9 As Saul turned to leave Samuel, God
changed[q] Saul's heart, and all these signs
were fulfilled that day. 10 When he and his
servant arrived at Gibeah, a procession of
prophets met him; the Spirit of God came

---

[a] *1* Hebrew; Septuagint and Vulgate *over his people Israel? You will reign over the LORD's people and save them from the power of their enemies round about. And this will be a sign to you that the LORD has anointed you ruler over his inheritance:*

9:20 Providence—God, in His providence, is directing our lives according to His plan and purpose. Searching for livestock or having a vehicle break down are normal nuisances, something we can handle, but seldom think about as being the providence of God. Yet if we realize that God has His hand on all of our circumstances, everything that changes our plans puts us into a position to meet, pray for, help, or witness to someone else who would not normally come our way.

9:21 ***the smallest tribe.*** Benjamin was the second smallest tribe at the first census following the exodus (Num. 1:36–37). The tribe was reduced to six hundred fighting men during the punishment of Benjamin for the atrocity at Gibeah (Judg. 19–20).

9:24 ***the thigh.*** Giving Saul the thigh was intended to honor him in the presence of the other guests.

10:1 ***the LORD anointed you.*** The anointing of a ruler was a religious act. That is why David had such high regard for Saul, refusing to lift a hand against "the LORD's anointed." ***his inheritance.*** The land of Israel was God's gift to His people, but it would return to God's direct control if the people did not manage it according to God's laws (Deut. 27–30).

10:4 ***two loaves of bread.*** The bread that the strangers would offer to Saul would have been bread prepared for use in the worship of God. Giving the bread to Saul was a sacred act, as well as a sign for Saul.

10:9 ***God changed Saul's heart.*** God's Spirit prepared Saul for the kingship. It probably was not

9:17 [u] 1Sa 16:12 **9:20** [v] ver 3 [w] 1Sa 8:5; 12:13
9:21 [x] 1Sa 15:17 [y] Jdg 20:35,46 **9:24** [z] Lev 7:32-34;
Nu 18:18 **9:25** [a] Dt 22:8; Ac 10:9 **10:1** [b] 1Sa 16:13;
2Ki 9:1,3,6 [c] Ps 2:12 [d] Dt 32:9; Ps 78:62,71
10:2 [e] Ge 35:20 [f] 1Sa 9:4 [g] 1Sa 9:5 **10:3** [h] Ge 28:22;
35:7-8 **10:5** [i] 1Sa 13:3 [j] 1Sa 9:12 [k] 2Ki 3:15 [l] 1Sa 19:20;
1Co 14:1 **10:6** [m] ver 10; Nu 11:25; 1Sa 19:23-24
10:7 [n] Ecc 9:10 [o] Jos 1:5; Jdg 6:12; Heb 13:5
10:8 [p] 1Sa 11:14-15 **10:9** [q] ver 6

powerfully upon him, and he joined in their prophesying.[r] 11When all those who had formerly known him saw him prophesying with the prophets, they asked each other, "What is this[s] that has happened to the son of Kish? Is Saul also among the prophets?"[t]

12A man who lived there answered, "And who is their father?" So it became a saying: "Is Saul also among the prophets?" 13After Saul stopped prophesying, he went to the high place.

14Now Saul's uncle[u] asked him and his servant, "Where have you been?"

"Looking for the donkeys," he said. "But when we saw they were not to be found, we went to Samuel."

15Saul's uncle said, "Tell me what Samuel said to you."

16Saul replied, "He assured us that the donkeys[v] had been found." But he did not tell his uncle what Samuel had said about the kingship.

17Samuel summoned the people of Israel to the LORD at Mizpah[w] 18and said to them, "This is what the LORD, the God of Israel, says: 'I brought Israel up out of Egypt, and I delivered you from the power of Egypt and all the kingdoms that oppressed[x] you.' 19But you have now rejected your God, who saves you out of all your disasters and calamities. And you have said, 'No, appoint a king[y] over us.' So now present[z] yourselves before the LORD by your tribes and clans."

20When Samuel had all Israel come forward by tribes, the tribe of Benjamin was taken by lot. 21Then he brought forward the tribe of Benjamin, clan by clan, and Matri's clan was taken. Finally Saul son of Kish was taken. But when they looked for him, he was not to be found. 22So they inquired[a] further of the LORD, "Has the man come here yet?"

And the LORD said, "Yes, he has hidden himself among the supplies."

23They ran and brought him out, and as he stood among the people he was a head taller[b] than any of the others. 24Samuel said to all the people, "Do you see the man the LORD has chosen?[c] There is no one like him among all the people."

Then the people shouted, "Long live[d] the king!"

25Samuel explained to the people the rights and duties[e] of kingship. He wrote them down on a scroll and deposited it before the LORD. Then Samuel dismissed the people to go to their own homes.

26Saul also went to his home in Gibeah,[f] accompanied by valiant men whose hearts God had touched. 27But some scoundrels[g] said, "How can this fellow save us?" They despised him and brought him no gifts.[h] But Saul kept silent.

Saul Rescues the City of Jabesh

11 Nahash[a][i] the Ammonite went up and besieged Jabesh Gilead.[j] And all the men of Jabesh said to him, "Make a treaty[k] with us, and we will be subject to you."

2But Nahash the Ammonite replied, "I will make a treaty with you only on the condition that I gouge[l] out the right eye of every one of you and so bring disgrace[m] on all Israel."

3The elders of Jabesh said to him, "Give us seven days so we can send messengers throughout Israel; if no one comes to rescue us, we will surrender to you."

---

[a] *1* Masoretic Text; Dead Sea Scrolls *gifts. Now Nahash king of the Ammonites oppressed the Gadites and Reubenites severely. He gouged out all their right eyes and struck terror and dread in Israel. Not a man remained among the Israelites beyond the Jordan whose right eye was not gouged out by Nahash king of the Ammonites, except that seven thousand men fled from the Ammonites and entered Jabesh Gilead. About a month later,* [1]*Nahash*

---

spiritual regeneration in the way it is understood in New Testament times. Saul wanted to worship God, but he continually struggled with wanting to do things his own way.

10:19 Unfaithfulness—This was not the first time that the Israelites had been unfaithful. Sometimes they could see what God was doing and respond with thanksgiving, and sometimes they seemed to forget everything about Him and go headlong into the very sins He had warned them would bring nothing but disaster. Believers today have the incredible gift of the Holy Spirit to direct them and remind them of the ways of God. It is hard to imagine what it would be like to follow God without the help of the Holy Spirit, the comforter, the helper (John 14:25–26). It is important to remember that for humanity, unfaithfulness is our middle name, and to thank God for His mercy and grace which provided a way for us to belong to Him.

10:20 *was taken by lot.* Even though Samuel already knew that Saul was to be the king, the designation of Saul as Israel's first monarch was made by casting lots. The lots were cast like dice, and God's will was determined by asking yes and no questions. They believed that God controlled all events, including the lots when they were used to seek God.

10:24 *the man the LORD has chosen.* Long ago, before they crossed the Jordan, the Lord had told Moses that the Israelites would want a king. At that time the Lord laid out guidelines for the king, and one of them was that the king must be an Israelite chosen by the Lord (Deut. 17:14–20).

11:1 *Ammonite.* The Ammonites, who were descendants of Lot, occupied the fringes of the desert east of the territories of Gad and Manasseh.

10:10 [r] ver 5-6; 1Sa 19:20 **10:11** [s] Mt 13:54; Jn 7:15 [t] 1Sa 19:24 **10:14** [u] 1Sa 14:50 **10:16** [v] 1Sa 9:20 **10:17** [w] Jdg 20:1; 1Sa 7:5 **10:18** [x] Jdg 6:8-9 **10:19** [y] 1Sa 8:5-7; 12:12 [z] Jos 7:14; 24:1 **10:22** [a] 1Sa 23:2, 4, 9-11 **10:23** [b] 1Sa 9:2 **10:24** [c] Dt 17:15; 2Sa 21:6 [d] 1Ki 1:25, 34, 39 **10:25** [e] Dt 17:14-20; 1Sa 8:11-18 **10:26** [f] 1Sa 11:4 **10:27** [g] Dt 13:13 [h] 1Ki 10:25; 2Ch 17:5 **11:1** [i] 1Sa 12:12 [j] Jdg 21:8 [k] 1Ki 20:34; Eze 17:13 **11:2** [l] Nu 16:14 [m] 1Sa 17:26

4When the messengers came to Gibeah[n]
of Saul and reported these terms to the people, they all wept[o] aloud. 5Just then Saul
was returning from the fields, behind his
oxen, and he asked, "What is wrong with
everyone? Why are they weeping?" Then
they repeated to him what the men of Jabesh had said.
6When Saul heard their words, the Spirit[p] of God came powerfully upon him, and
he burned with anger. 7He took a pair of
oxen, cut them into pieces, and sent the
pieces by messengers throughout Israel,[q]
proclaiming, "This is what will be done
to the oxen of anyone[r] who does not follow Saul and Samuel." Then the terror of
the LORD fell on the people, and they came
out together as one. 8When Saul mustered[s]
them at Bezek,[t] the men of Israel numbered
three hundred thousand and those of Judah thirty thousand.
9They told the messengers who had
come, "Say to the men of Jabesh Gilead,
'By the time the sun is hot tomorrow, you
will be rescued.'" When the messengers
went and reported this to the men of Jabesh, they were elated. 10They said to the
Ammonites, "Tomorrow we will surrender[u] to you, and you can do to us whatever
you like."
11The next day Saul separated his men
into three divisions;[v] during the last watch
of the night they broke into the camp of the
Ammonites and slaughtered them until the
heat of the day. Those who survived were
scattered, so that no two of them were left
together.

Saul Confirmed as King

12The people then said to Samuel, "Who[w]
was it that asked, 'Shall Saul reign over
us?' Turn these men over to us so that we
may put them to death."
13But Saul said, "No one will be put to
death today,[x] for this day the LORD has rescued[y] Israel."
14Then Samuel said to the people, "Come,
let us go to Gilgal[z] and there renew the
kingship.[a]" 15So all the people went to Gilgal[b] and made Saul king in the presence of
the LORD. There they sacrificed fellowship
offerings before the LORD, and Saul and all
the Israelites held a great celebration.

Samuel's Farewell Speech

12 Samuel said to all Israel, "I have listened[c] to everything you said to me
and have set a king[d] over you. 2Now you
have a king as your leader.[e] As for me, I
am old and gray, and my sons are here with
you. I have been your leader from my youth
until this day. 3Here I stand. Testify against
me in the presence of the LORD and his
anointed.[f] Whose ox have I taken? Whose
donkey[g] have I taken? Whom have I cheated? Whom have I oppressed? From whose
hand have I accepted a bribe[h] to make me
shut my eyes? If I have done[i] any of these
things, I will make it right."
4"You have not cheated or oppressed us,"
they replied. "You have not taken anything
from anyone's hand."
5Samuel said to them, "The LORD is witness against you, and also his anointed is
witness this day, that you have not found
anything[j] in my hand.[k]"
"He is witness," they said.
6Then Samuel said to the people, "It is the
LORD who appointed Moses and Aaron and
brought[l] your ancestors up out of Egypt.
7Now then, stand here, because I am going
to confront[m] you with evidence before the
LORD as to all the righteous acts performed
by the LORD for you and your ancestors.
8"After Jacob entered Egypt, they cried[n]
to the LORD for help, and the LORD sent[o]
Moses and Aaron, who brought your ancestors out of Egypt and settled them in
this place.
9"But they forgot[p] the LORD their God;
so he sold them into the hand of Sisera,[q]
the commander of the army of Hazor, and
into the hands of the Philistines[r] and the
king of Moab,[s] who fought against them.
10They cried out to the LORD and said, 'We
have sinned; we have forsaken[t] the LORD
and served the Baals and the Ashtoreths.[u]
But now deliver us from the hands of our
enemies, and we will serve you.' 11Then
the LORD sent Jerub-Baal,[a][v] Barak,[b][w] Jephthah[x] and Samuel,[c] and he delivered you
from the hands of your enemies all around
you, so that you lived in safety.

[a] *11* Also called *Gideon* [b] *11* Some Septuagint manuscripts and Syriac; Hebrew *Bedan* [c] *11* Hebrew; some Septuagint manuscripts and Syriac *Samson*

11:5 *from the fields.* Saul had been appointed king, but he did not assume governmental authority at once. He continued farming until he could answer Israel's expectations of him by delivering them from their enemies. This pattern was more in the style of the judges of Israel.

11:11 *last watch.* The Israelites divided the night into three watches: nine to twelve, twelve to three, and three to six in the morning.

12:9 *they forgot the LORD their God.* Samuel recounted the nation's apostasy and subsequent divine discipline. Israel was having problems because they had stopped obeying God. It was not because either God or Samuel was inadequate.

11:4 [n] 1Sa 10:5,26; 15:34 [o] Jdg 2:4; 1Sa 30:4
11:6 [p] Jdg 3:10; 6:34; 13:25; 14:6; 1Sa 10:10; 16:13
11:7 [q] Jdg 19:29 [r] Jdg 21:5 **11:8** [s] Jdg 20:2 [t] Jdg 1:4
11:10 [u] ver 3 **11:11** [v] Jdg 7:16 **11:12** [w] 1Sa 10:27; Lk 19:27 **11:13** [x] 2Sa 19:22 [y] Ex 14:13; 1Sa 19:5
11:14 [z] 1Sa 10:8 [a] 1Sa 10:25 **11:15** [b] 1Sa 10:8, 17
12:1 [c] 1Sa 8:7 [d] 1Sa 10:24; 11:15 **12:2** [e] 1Sa 8:5
12:3 [f] 1Sa 10:1; 24:6; 2Sa 1:14 [g] Nu 16:15 [h] Dt 16:19 [i] Ac 20:33 **12:5** [j] Ac 23:9; 24:20 [k] Ex 22:4
12:6 [l] Ex 6:26; Mic 6:4 **12:7** [m] Isa 1:18; Mic 6:1-5
12:8 [n] Ex 2:23 [o] Ex 3:10; 4:16 **12:9** [p] Jdg 3:7 [q] Jdg 4:2 [r] Jdg 10:7; 13:1 [s] Jdg 3:12 **12:10** [t] Jdg 10:10, 15 [u] Jdg 2:13 **12:11** [v] Jdg 6:14, 32 [w] Jdg 4:6 [x] Jdg 11:1

12 “But when you saw that Nahash[y] king[z] of the Ammonites was moving against you, you said to me, ‘No, we want a king to rule[a] over us’—even though the LORD your God was your king. 13 Now here is the king[b] you have chosen, the one you asked[c] for; see, the LORD has set a king over you. 14 If you fear[d] the LORD and serve and obey him and do not rebel against his commands, and if both you and the king who reigns over you follow the LORD your God—good! 15 But if you do not obey the LORD, and if you rebel against[e] his commands, his hand will be against you, as it was against your ancestors.

16 “Now then, stand still and see[f] this great thing the LORD is about to do before your eyes! 17 Is it not wheat harvest[g] now? I will call[h] on the LORD to send thunder and rain.[i] And you will realize what an evil[j] thing you did in the eyes of the LORD when you asked for a king.”

18 Then Samuel called on the LORD, and that same day the LORD sent thunder and rain. So all the people stood in awe[k] of the LORD and of Samuel.

19 The people all said to Samuel, “Pray[l] to the LORD your God for your servants so that we will not die, for we have added to all our other sins the evil of asking for a king.”

20 “Do not be afraid,” Samuel replied. “You have done all this evil; yet do not turn away from the LORD, but serve the LORD with all your heart. 21 Do not turn away after useless[m] idols.[n] They can do you no good, nor can they rescue you, because they are useless. 22 For the sake[o] of his great name[p] the LORD will not reject[q] his people, because the LORD was pleased to make[r] you his own. 23 As for me, far be it from me that I should sin against the LORD by failing to pray[s] for you. And I will teach[t] you the way that is good and right. 24 But be sure to fear[u] the LORD and serve him faithfully with all your heart; consider[v] what great[w] things he has done for you. 25 Yet if you persist[x] in doing evil, both you and your king will perish.”[y]

Samuel Rebukes Saul

13 Saul was thirty[a] years old when he became king, and he reigned over Israel forty-[b] two years.

2 Saul chose three thousand men from Israel; two thousand were with him at Mikmash and in the hill country of Bethel, and a thousand were with Jonathan at Gibeah[z] in Benjamin. The rest of the men he sent back to their homes.

3 Jonathan attacked the Philistine outpost[a] at Geba, and the Philistines heard about it. Then Saul had the trumpet blown throughout the land and said, “Let the Hebrews hear!” 4 So all Israel heard the news: “Saul has attacked the Philistine outpost, and now Israel has become obnoxious[b] to the Philistines.” And the people were summoned to join Saul at Gilgal.

5 The Philistines assembled to fight Israel, with three thousand[c] chariots, six thousand charioteers, and soldiers as numerous as the sand[c] on the seashore. They went up and camped at Mikmash, east of Beth Aven. 6 When the Israelites saw that their situation was critical and that their army was hard pressed, they hid in caves and thickets, among the rocks, and in pits and cisterns.[d] 7 Some Hebrews even crossed the Jordan to the land of Gad[e] and Gilead.

Saul remained at Gilgal, and all the troops with him were quaking with fear. 8 He waited seven[f] days, the time set by Samuel; but Samuel did not come to Gilgal, and Saul’s men began to scatter. 9 So he said, “Bring me the burnt offering and the fellowship offerings.” And Saul offered[g] up the burnt offering. 10 Just as he finished making the offering, Samuel[h] arrived, and Saul went out to greet him.

---

[a] *1* A few late manuscripts of the Septuagint; Hebrew does not have *thirty*. [b] *1* Probable reading of the original Hebrew text (see Acts 13:21); Masoretic Text does not have *forty-*.
[c] *5* Some Septuagint manuscripts and Syriac; Hebrew *thirty thousand*

12:17 *wheat harvest.* The season for harvesting wheat in Israel is the months of May and June. ***thunder and rain.*** The land of Israel receives its rainfall during the winter season. For rain to fall during the wheat harvest would be both unusual and detrimental to the harvest.

12:22 *his people.* God’s desire to raise up a people for His great name’s sake is not based on pride, but on love. He is pleased to show His goodness to the world, and He is willing to reach out to us in spite of our rebellion and foolishness. The whole history of the human race is littered with mankind’s failure to acknowledge and follow the living God who created us. But even if we are faithless, God will remain faithful (2 Tim. 2:13), and that is our great comfort. We cannot even be faithful without His help, but “If God is for us, who can be against us?” (Rom. 8:31).

13:8–9 Presumption—We will never know what would have happened if Saul had waited for Samuel. Whenever we assume we “know better” and take action on our own authority, we cannot know what would have happened if we had followed God’s way. Some of the snarls that are the result of stubborn rebellion are often too difficult for us to set right. This is why we must pay such careful attention not only to the direct commandments in the Bible, but to the spirit behind them.

12:12 [y] 1Sa 11:1 [z] 1Sa 8:5 [a] Jdg 8:23; 1Sa 8:6, 19
12:13 [b] 1Sa 8:5; Hos 13:11 [c] 1Sa 10:24 **12:14** [d] Jos 24:14
12:15 [e] ver 9; Jos 24:20; Isa 1:20 **12:16** [f] Ex 14:13
12:17 [g] 1Sa 7:9-10 [h] Jas 5:18 [i] Pr 26:1 [j] 1Sa 8:6-7
12:18 [k] Ex 14:31 **12:19** [l] ver 23; Ex 9:28; Jas 5:18; 1Jn 5:16
12:21 [m] Isa 41:24, 29; Jer 16:19; Hab 2:18 [n] Dt 11:16
12:22 [o] Ps 106:8 [p] Jos 7:9 [q] 1Ki 6:13 [r] Dt 7:7; 1Pe 2:9
12:23 [s] Ro 1:9-10; Col 1:9; 2Ti 1:3 [t] 1Ki 8:36; Ps 34:11; Pr 4:11 **12:24** [u] Ecc 12:13 [v] Isa 5:12 [w] Dt 10:21
12:25 [x] 1Sa 31:1-5 [y] Jos 24:20 **13:2** [z] 1Sa 10:26
13:3 [a] 1Sa 10:5 **13:4** [b] Ge 34:30 **13:5** [c] Jos 11:4
13:6 [d] Jdg 6:2 **13:7** [e] Nu 32:33 **13:8** [f] 1Sa 10:8
13:9 [g] 2Sa 24:25; 1Ki 3:4 **13:10** [h] 1Sa 15:13

11“What have you done?” asked Samuel.

Saul replied, “When I saw that the men were scattering, and that you did not come at the set time, and that the Philistines were assembling at Mikmash,[i] 12I thought, ‘Now the Philistines will come down against me at Gilgal, and I have not sought the LORD’s favor.[j]’ So I felt compelled to offer the burnt offering.”

13“You have done a foolish thing,[k]” Samuel said. “You have not kept[l] the command the LORD your God gave you; if you had, he would have established your kingdom over Israel for all time. 14But now your kingdom[m] will not endure; the LORD has sought out a man after his own heart[n] and appointed[o] him ruler of his people, because you have not kept the LORD’s command.”

15Then Samuel left Gilgal[a] and went up to Gibeah[p] in Benjamin, and Saul counted the men who were with him. They numbered about six hundred.

Israel Without Weapons

16Saul and his son Jonathan and the men with them were staying in Gibeah[b] in Benjamin, while the Philistines camped at Mikmash. 17Raiding[q] parties went out from the Philistine camp in three detachments. One turned toward Ophrah[r] in the vicinity of Shual, 18another toward Beth Horon,[s] and the third toward the borderland overlooking the Valley of Zeboyim[t] facing the wilderness.

19Not a blacksmith[u] could be found in the whole land of Israel, because the Philistines had said, “Otherwise the Hebrews will make swords or spears!” 20So all Israel went down to the Philistines to have their plow points, mattocks, axes and sickles[c] sharpened. 21The price was two-thirds of a shekel[d] for sharpening plow points and mattocks, and a third of a shekel[e] for sharpening forks and axes and for repointing goads.

22So on the day of the battle not a soldier with Saul and Jonathan[v] had a sword or spear[w] in his hand; only Saul and his son Jonathan had them.

Jonathan Attacks the Philistines

23Now a detachment of Philistines had gone out to the pass[x] at Mikmash.

14 1One day Jonathan son of Saul said to his young armor-bearer, “Come, let’s go over to the Philistine outpost on the other side.” But he did not tell his father.

2Saul was staying on the outskirts of Gibeah[y] under a pomegranate tree in Migron.[z] With him were about six hundred men, 3among whom was Ahijah, who was wearing an ephod. He was a son of Ichabod’s[a] brother Ahitub[b] son of Phinehas, the son of Eli,[c] the LORD’s priest in Shiloh. No one was aware that Jonathan had left.

4On each side of the pass[d] that Jonathan intended to cross to reach the Philistine outpost was a cliff; one was called Bozez and the other Seneh. 5One cliff stood to the north toward Mikmash, the other to the south toward Geba.

6Jonathan said to his young armor-bearer, “Come, let’s go over to the outpost of those uncircumcised[e] men. Perhaps the LORD will act in our behalf. Nothing[f] can hinder the LORD from saving, whether by many[g] or by few.[h]”

7“Do all that you have in mind,” his armor-bearer said. “Go ahead; I am with you heart and soul.”

8Jonathan said, “Come on, then; we will cross over toward them and let them see us. 9If they say to us, ‘Wait there until we come to you,’ we will stay where we are and not go up to them. 10But if they say, ‘Come up to us,’ we will climb up, because that will be our sign[i] that the LORD has given them into our hands.”

11So both of them showed themselves to the Philistine outpost. “Look!” said the Philistines. “The Hebrews are crawling out of the holes they were hiding[j] in.” 12The men of the outpost shouted to Jonathan and his armor-bearer, “Come up to us and we’ll teach you a lesson.[k]”

So Jonathan said to his armor-bearer, “Climb up after me; the LORD has given them into the hand[l] of Israel.”

13Jonathan climbed up, using his hands and feet, with his armor-bearer right behind him. The Philistines fell before Jonathan, and his armor-bearer followed and killed behind him. 14In that first attack Jonathan and his armor-bearer killed some twenty men in an area of about half an acre.

---

[a] *15* Hebrew; Septuagint *Gilgal and went his way; the rest of the people went after Saul to meet the army, and they went out of Gilgal*
[b] *16* Two Hebrew manuscripts; most Hebrew manuscripts *Geba,* a variant of *Gibeah*
[c] *20* Septuagint; Hebrew *plow points*
[d] *21* That is, about 1/4 ounce or about 8 grams
[e] *21* That is, about 1/8 ounce or about 4 grams

13:19 ***Not a blacksmith.*** The Canaanites and Philistines learned how to forge iron from the Hittites. Although they were not great in numerical strength, the Philistines were able to dominate Israel because of their superior weaponry. By the end of David’s reign, the Israelites had also acquired iron technology.

13:22 ***not a soldier . . . had a sword or spear.*** The weapons available to the Israelite soldiers would have included slings, bows and arrows, and numerous instruments made of bronze.

14:14 ***about half an acre.*** This can also be translated

13:11 [i] ver 2,5,16,23 **13:12** [j] Jer 26:19 **13:13** [k] 2Ch 16:9 [l] 1Sa 15:23,24 **13:14** [m] 1Sa 15:28 [n] Ac 7:46; 13:22 [o] 2Sa 6:21 **13:15** [p] 1Sa 14:2 **13:17** [q] 1Sa 14:15 [r] Jos 18:23 **13:18** [s] Jos 18:13-14 [t] Ne 11:34 **13:19** [u] 2Ki 24:14; Jer 24:1 **13:22** [v] 1Ch 9:39 [w] Jdg 5:8 **13:23** [x] 1Sa 14:4 **14:2** [y] 1Sa 13:15 [z] Isa 10:28 **14:3** [a] 1Sa 4:21 [b] 1Sa 22:11,20 [c] 1Sa 2:28 **14:4** [d] 1Sa 13:23 **14:6** [e] 1Sa 17:26,36; Jer 9:26 [f] Heb 11:34 [g] Jdg 7:4 [h] 1Sa 17:46-47 **14:10** [i] Ge 24:14; Jdg 6:36-37 **14:11** [j] 1Sa 13:6 **14:12** [k] 1Sa 17:43-44 [l] 2Sa 5:24

Israel Routs the Philistines

15Then panic[m] struck the whole army—
those in the camp and field, and those in
the outposts and raiding[n] parties—and the
ground shook. It was a panic sent by God.[a]
16Saul's lookouts[o] at Gibeah in Benjamin
saw the army melting away in all directions.
17Then Saul said to the men who were with
him, "Muster the forces and see who has left
us." When they did, it was Jonathan and his
armor-bearer who were not there.
18Saul said to Ahijah, "Bring[p] the ark
of God." (At that time it was with the Israelites.)[b] 19While Saul was talking to the
priest, the tumult in the Philistine camp increased more and more. So Saul said to the
priest,[q] "Withdraw your hand."
20Then Saul and all his men assembled
and went to the battle. They found the Philistines in total confusion, striking[r] each
other with their swords. 21Those Hebrews
who had previously been with the Philistines and had gone up with them to their
camp went[s] over to the Israelites who were
with Saul and Jonathan. 22When all the Israelites who had hidden[t] in the hill country
of Ephraim heard that the Philistines were
on the run, they joined the battle in hot pursuit. 23So on that day the LORD saved[u] Israel,
and the battle moved on beyond Beth Aven.[v]

Jonathan Eats Honey

24Now the Israelites were in distress that
day, because Saul had bound the people
under an oath,[w] saying, "Cursed be anyone who eats food before evening comes,
before I have avenged myself on my enemies!" So none of the troops tasted food.
25The entire army entered the woods,
and there was honey on the ground.
26When they went into the woods, they saw
the honey oozing out; yet no one put his
hand to his mouth, because they feared the
oath. 27But Jonathan had not heard that his
father had bound the people with the oath,
so he reached out the end of the staff that
was in his hand and dipped it into the honeycomb.[x] He raised his hand to his mouth,
and his eyes brightened.[c] 28Then one of the
soldiers told him, "Your father bound the
army under a strict oath, saying, 'Cursed
be anyone who eats food today!' That is
why the men are faint."
29Jonathan said, "My father has made
trouble[y] for the country. See how my eyes
brightened when I tasted a little of this honey. 30How much better it would have been if
the men had eaten today some of the plunder they took from their enemies. Would
not the slaughter of the Philistines have
been even greater?"
31That day, after the Israelites had struck
down the Philistines from Mikmash to
Aijalon,[z] they were exhausted. 32They
pounced on the plunder[a] and, taking sheep,
cattle and calves, they butchered them on
the ground and ate them, together with
the blood.[b] 33Then someone said to Saul,
"Look, the men are sinning against the
LORD by eating meat that has blood in it."
"You have broken faith," he said. "Roll
a large stone over here at once." 34Then
he said, "Go out among the men and tell
them, 'Each of you bring me your cattle
and sheep, and slaughter them here and
eat them. Do not sin against the LORD by
eating meat with blood still in it.'"
So everyone brought his ox that night
and slaughtered it there. 35Then Saul built
an altar[c] to the LORD; it was the first time
he had done this.
36Saul said, "Let us go down and pursue
the Philistines by night and plunder them
till dawn, and let us not leave one of them
alive."
"Do whatever seems best to you," they
replied.
But the priest said, "Let us inquire of God
here."
37So Saul asked God, "Shall I go down
and pursue the Philistines? Will you give
them into Israel's hand?" But God did not
answer[d] him that day.

---

[a] *15* Or *a terrible panic* [b] *18* Hebrew; Septuagint *"Bring the ephod." (At that time he wore the ephod before the Israelites.)* [c] *27* Or *his strength was renewed*; similarly in verse 29

"half a yoke of land." A yoke of land was the area a pair of oxen could plow in one day.

14:24 *had bound the people under an oath.* This was not only an oath, but an oath with a curse. Yet food would have helped the soldiers fight with better stamina. Keeping the oath was a matter of loyalty to Saul as he avenged his enemies. But the enemies were not Saul's personal enemies, they were the enemies of the whole nation, and the power in the vengeance came from God, not Saul. Saul should have focused the faith of the people on God, not on himself. This oath is an example of poor leadership, foolish vows, and misplaced loyalties. It is easy to get into trouble with an impulsive vow. It may sound very noble and wise in the heat of the moment, but it doesn't turn out to be practical. The kinds of vows that will never get us in trouble are the vows that echo the things that Scripture teaches. Such vows as determining to raise our children for the Lord, promising to stay away from habits that control us, or commitment to pray for certain people will never leave us entangled in promises that we should not have made.

14:32 *pounced on.* If the soldiers had not been fasting as they fought, they might have had the self-control to properly bleed the animals before they began eating.

14:37 *God did not answer him.* God's silence was taken by Saul as evidence of sin in the camp.

14:15 [m] Ge 35:5; 2Ki 7:5-7 [n] 1Sa 13:17 **14:16** [o] 2Sa 18:24 **14:18** [p] 1Sa 30:7 **14:19** [q] Nu 27:21 **14:20** [r] Jdg 7:22; 2Ch 20:23 **14:21** [s] 1Sa 29:4 **14:22** [t] 1Sa 13:6 **14:23** [u] Ex 14:30; Ps 44:6-7 [v] 1Sa 13:5 **14:24** [w] Jos 6:26 **14:27** [x] ver 43; 1Sa 30:12 **14:29** [y] Jos 7:25; 1Ki 18:18 **14:31** [z] Jos 10:12 **14:32** [a] 1Sa 15:19 [b] Ge 9:4; Lev 3:17; 7:26; 17:10-14; 19:26; Dt 12:16,23-24 **14:35** [c] 1Sa 7:17 **14:37** [d] 1Sa 10:22; 28:6,15

38Saul therefore said, "Come here, all
you who are leaders of the army, and let
us find out what sin has been committed[e]
today. 39As surely as the LORD who rescues
Israel lives,[f] even if the guilt lies with my
son Jonathan, he must die." But not one of
them said a word.
40Saul then said to all the Israelites, "You
stand over there; I and Jonathan my son
will stand over here."
"Do what seems best to you," they replied.
41Then Saul prayed to the LORD, the God
of Israel, "Why have you not answered
your servant today? If the fault is in me or
my son Jonathan, respond with Urim, but if
the men of Israel are at fault,[a] respond with
Thummim." Jonathan and Saul were tak-
en by lot, and the men were cleared. 42Saul
said, "Cast the lot between me and Jonathan my son." And Jonathan was taken.
43Then Saul said to Jonathan, "Tell me
what you have done."[g]
So Jonathan told him, "I tasted a little
honey[h] with the end of my staff. And now
I must die!"
44Saul said, "May God deal with me, be
it ever so severely,[i] if you do not die, Jonathan.[j]"
45But the men said to Saul, "Should Jonathan die—he who has brought about this
great deliverance in Israel? Never! As surely as the LORD lives, not a hair[k] of his head
will fall to the ground, for he did this today
with God's help." So the men rescued[l] Jonathan, and he was not put to death.
46Then Saul stopped pursuing the Philistines, and they withdrew to their own land.
47After Saul had assumed rule over Israel, he fought against their enemies on every side: Moab, the Ammonites,[m] Edom, the
kings[b] of Zobah,[n] and the Philistines. Wherever he turned, he inflicted punishment on
them.[c] 48He fought valiantly and defeated
the Amalekites,[o] delivering Israel from the
hands of those who had plundered them.

Saul's Family

49Saul's sons were Jonathan, Ishvi and
Malki-Shua.[p] The name of his older daughter was Merab, and that of the younger was
Michal.[q] 50His wife's name was Ahinoam
daughter of Ahimaaz. The name of the
commander of Saul's army was Abner son
of Ner, and Ner was Saul's uncle. 51Saul's
father Kish[r] and Abner's father Ner were
sons of Abiel.
52All the days of Saul there was bitter
war with the Philistines, and whenever
Saul saw a mighty or brave man, he took[s]
him into his service.

The LORD Rejects Saul as King

15 Samuel said to Saul, "I am the one the
LORD sent to anoint[t] you king over his
people Israel; so listen now to the message
from the LORD. 2This is what the LORD Almighty says: 'I will punish the Amalekites[u] for what they did to Israel when they
waylaid them as they came up from Egypt.
3Now go, attack the Amalekites and totally[v] destroy[d] all that belongs to them. Do not
spare them; put to death men and women,
children and infants, cattle and sheep,
camels and donkeys.'"
4So Saul summoned the men and mustered them at Telaim—two hundred thousand foot soldiers and ten thousand from
Judah. 5Saul went to the city of Amalek
and set an ambush in the ravine. 6Then he
said to the Kenites,[w] "Go away, leave the
Amalekites so that I do not destroy you
along with them; for you showed kindness
to all the Israelites when they came up out
of Egypt." So the Kenites moved away from
the Amalekites.
7Then Saul attacked the Amalekites[x] all
the way from Havilah to Shur,[y] near the
eastern border of Egypt. 8He took Agag
king of the Amalekites alive,[z] and all his
people he totally destroyed with the sword.
9But Saul and the army spared[a] Agag and

[a] *41* Septuagint; Hebrew does not have *"Why . . . at fault.* [b] *47* Masoretic Text; Dead Sea Scrolls and Septuagint *king* [c] *47* Hebrew; Septuagint *he was victorious* [d] *3* The Hebrew term refers to the irrevocable giving over of things or persons to the LORD, often by totally destroying them; also in verses 8, 9, 15, 18, 20 and 21.

14:39 *he must die.* This was Saul's second foolish oath. Saul is not the only one who found himself in trouble because of an impulsive oath. Jephthah made a tragic vow (Judg. 11:29–40), John the Baptist was beheaded because of Herod's thoughtless oath (Matt. 14:7–9), and a group of Jews bound themselves together with a curse, promising not to eat or drink until they had killed Paul (Acts 23:12). Jesus taught his followers not to swear to foolish vows, but to let their yes be yes, and their no be no (Matt. 5:37; James 5:12).

14:47 *Moab, the Ammonites.* The Moabites and Ammonites were descendants of Lot (Gen. 19:30–38). They occupied regions east of the Jordan and Dead Sea. ***Edom.*** The Edomites were descendants of Esau (Gen. 36:8) who ruled over a region southeast of the Dead Sea. ***Zobah.*** This was the Aramean kingdom in the Bekaa valley. ***Philistines.*** The Philistines lived on the coastal plain west of the hill country.

14:48 *Amalekites.* These nomadic desert tribesmen lived south of the hill country.

15:6 *Kenites.* The Kenites were a nomadic offshoot of the Midianites (Num. 10:29). They had been loosely associated with the Israelites since Moses' marriage to the daughter of Jethro, a Kenite (Judg. 1:16; 4:11).

14:38 [e] Jos 7:11; 1Sa 10:19 **14:39** [f] 2Sa 12:5
14:43 [g] Jos 7:19 [h] ver 27 **14:44** [i] Ru 1:17 [j] ver 39
14:45 [k] 1Ki 1:52; Lk 21:18; Ac 27:34 [l] 2Sa 14:11
14:47 [m] 1Sa 11:1-13 [n] ver 52; 2Sa 10:6
14:48 [o] 1Sa 15:2,7 **14:49** [p] 1Sa 31:2; 1Ch 8:33
[q] 1Sa 18:17-20 **14:51** [r] 1Sa 9:1 **14:52** [s] 1Sa 8:11
15:1 [t] 1Sa 9:16 **15:2** [u] Ex 17:8-14; Nu 24:20; Dt 25:17-19
15:3 [v] Nu 24:20; Dt 20:16-18; Jos 6:17; 1Sa 22:19
15:6 [w] Ex 18:10, 19; Nu 10:29-32; 24:22; Jdg 1:16; 4:1
15:7 [x] 1Sa 14:48 [y] Ge 16:7; 25:17-18; Ex 15:22
15:8 [z] 1Sa 30:1 **15:9** [a] ver 3, 15

the best of the sheep and cattle, the fat
calves[a] and lambs—everything that was
good. These they were unwilling to destroy completely, but everything that was
despised and weak they totally destroyed.
10Then the word of the LORD came to
Samuel: 11"I regret[b] that I have made Saul
king, because he has turned[c] away from
me and has not carried out my instructions."[d] Samuel was angry,[e] and he cried
out to the LORD all that night.
12Early in the morning Samuel got up
and went to meet Saul, but he was told,
"Saul has gone to Carmel.[f] There he has
set up a monument in his own honor and
has turned and gone on down to Gilgal."
13When Samuel reached him, Saul said,
"The LORD bless you! I have carried out the
LORD's instructions."
14But Samuel said, "What then is this
bleating of sheep in my ears? What is this
lowing of cattle that I hear?"
15Saul answered, "The soldiers brought
them from the Amalekites; they spared
the best of the sheep and cattle to sacrifice
to the LORD your God, but we totally destroyed the rest."
16"Enough!" Samuel said to Saul. "Let
me tell you what the LORD said to me last
night."
"Tell me," Saul replied.
17Samuel said, "Although you were once
small[g] in your own eyes, did you not become the head of the tribes of Israel? The
LORD anointed you king over Israel. 18And
he sent you on a mission, saying, 'Go and
completely destroy those wicked people,
the Amalekites; wage war against them
until you have wiped them out.' 19Why
did you not obey the LORD? Why did you
pounce on the plunder[h] and do evil in the
eyes of the LORD?"
20"But I did obey[i] the LORD," Saul said. "I
went on the mission the LORD assigned me.
I completely destroyed the Amalekites and
brought back Agag their king. 21The soldiers took sheep and cattle from the plunder, the best of what was devoted to God,
in order to sacrifice them to the LORD your
God at Gilgal."
22But Samuel replied:

"Does the LORD delight in burnt
offerings and sacrifices
as much as in obeying the LORD?
To obey is better than sacrifice,[j]
and to heed is better than the fat of rams.
23For rebellion is like the sin of divination,[k]
and arrogance like the evil of idolatry.
Because you have rejected[l] the word of
the LORD,
he has rejected you as king."

24Then Saul said to Samuel, "I have
sinned.[m] I violated the LORD's command
and your instructions. I was afraid[n] of the
men and so I gave in to them. 25Now I beg
you, forgive[o] my sin and come back with
me, so that I may worship the LORD."
26But Samuel said to him, "I will not go
back with you. You have rejected[p] the word
of the LORD, and the LORD has rejected you
as king over Israel!"
27As Samuel turned to leave, Saul caught
hold of the hem of his robe, and it tore.[q]
28Samuel said to him, "The LORD has torn[r]
the kingdom of Israel from you today and
has given it to one of your neighbors—to
one better than you. 29He who is the Glory
of Israel does not lie[s] or change[t] his mind;
for he is not a human being, that he should
change his mind."
30Saul replied, "I have sinned. But please
honor[u] me before the elders of my people
and before Israel; come back with me, so
that I may worship the LORD your God."
31So Samuel went back with Saul, and Saul
worshiped the LORD.
32Then Samuel said, "Bring me Agag
king of the Amalekites."
Agag came to him in chains.[b] And he
thought, "Surely the bitterness of death is
past."
33But Samuel said,

"As your sword has made women childless,
so will your mother be childless
among women."[v]

And Samuel put Agag to death before the
LORD at Gilgal.

---

[a] 9 Or *the grown bulls*; the meaning of the Hebrew for this phrase is uncertain. [b] *32* The meaning of the Hebrew for this phrase is uncertain.

15:22 Obedience—If we love God we are commanded to keep His commandments (John 14:15). The problem is, we sometimes fool ourselves. Saul thought he was doing something good for God. He was partially obeying. He killed a lot of the Amalekites, and instead of killing the animals, he sacrificed them. They would still be dead, and it would honor God, too. But He was not pleased. Saul did what was "right in his own eyes" but this was not obedience.

15:23 *divination.* Divination, witchcraft, idolatry, and other occult activities are an attempt to manipulate spiritual powers for our own ends. In his rebellion Saul was treating God as if He were a moody, cranky pagan god, who could be thwarted, and then appeased by sacrifices. ***he has rejected you.*** Saul was rejected because he was still treating God as a force to be used. He was sorry he got caught, but he still thought he was right and could give a quick sacrifice and go on with the plan.

15:11 [b] Ge 6:6; 2Sa 24:16 [c] Jos 22:16 [d] 1Sa 13:13; 1Ki 9:6-7 [e] ver 35 **15:12** [f] Jos 15:55 **15:17** [g] 1Sa 9:21 **15:19** [h] 1Sa 14:32 **15:20** [i] ver 13 **15:22** [j] Ps 40:6-8; 51:16; Isa 1:11-15; Jer 7:22; Hos 6:6; Mic 6:6-8; Mt 12:7; Mk 12:33; Heb 10:6-9 **15:23** [k] Dt 18:10 [l] 1Sa 13:13 **15:24** [m] 2Sa 12:13 [n] Pr 29:25; Isa 51:12-13 **15:25** [o] Ex 10:17 **15:26** [p] 1Sa 13:14 **15:27** [q] 1Ki 11:11, 31 **15:28** [r] 1Sa 28:17; 1Ki 11:31 **15:29** [s] 1Ch 29:11; Titus 1:2 [t] Nu 23:19; Eze 24:14 **15:30** [u] Isa 29:13; Jn 5:44; 12:43 **15:33** [v] Ge 9:6; Jdg 1:7

34Then Samuel left for Ramah,[w] but
Saul went up to his home in Gibeah[x] of
Saul. 35Until the day Samuel[y] died, he did
not go to see Saul again, though Samuel
mourned[z] for him. And the LORD regretted
that he had made Saul king over Israel.

Samuel Anoints David

16 The LORD said to Samuel, "How long
will you mourn[a] for Saul, since I have
rejected[b] him as king over Israel? Fill your
horn with oil[c] and be on your way; I am
sending you to Jesse[d] of Bethlehem. I have
chosen[e] one of his sons to be king."
2But Samuel said, "How can I go? If Saul
hears about it, he will kill me."
The LORD said, "Take a heifer with you
and say, 'I have come to sacrifice to the
LORD.' 3Invite Jesse to the sacrifice, and
I will show[f] you what to do. You are to
anoint[g] for me the one I indicate."
4Samuel did what the LORD said. When
he arrived at Bethlehem,[h] the elders of the
town trembled when they met him. They
asked, "Do you come in peace?[i]"
5Samuel replied, "Yes, in peace; I have
come to sacrifice to the LORD. Consecrate[j]
yourselves and come to the sacrifice with
me." Then he consecrated Jesse and his
sons and invited them to the sacrifice.
6When they arrived, Samuel saw Eliab[k]
and thought, "Surely the LORD's anointed
stands here before the LORD."
7But the LORD said to Samuel, "Do not
consider his appearance or his height, for I
have rejected him. The LORD does not look
at the things people look at. People look
at the outward appearance,[l] but the LORD
looks at the heart."[m]
8Then Jesse called Abinadab[n] and had
him pass in front of Samuel. But Samuel
said, "The LORD has not chosen this one either." 9Jesse then had Shammah pass by,
but Samuel said, "Nor has the LORD chosen
this one." 10Jesse had seven of his sons pass
before Samuel, but Samuel said to him,
"The LORD has not chosen these." 11So he
asked Jesse, "Are these all[o] the sons you
have?"
"There is still the youngest," Jesse answered. "He is tending the sheep."
Samuel said, "Send for him; we will not
sit down until he arrives."
12So he[p] sent for him and had him
brought in. He was glowing with health
and had a fine appearance and handsome[q]
features.
Then the LORD said, "Rise and anoint
him; this is the one."
13So Samuel took the horn of oil and
anointed him in the presence of his brothers, and from that day on the Spirit of the
LORD[r] came powerfully upon David.[s] Samuel then went to Ramah.

David in Saul's Service

14Now the Spirit of the LORD had departed[t] from Saul, and an evil[a] spirit[u] from the
LORD tormented him.
15Saul's attendants said to him, "See,
an evil spirit from God is tormenting you.
16Let our lord command his servants here
to search for someone who can play the
lyre.[v] He will play when the evil spirit from
God comes on you, and you will feel better."
17So Saul said to his attendants, "Find
someone who plays well and bring him
to me."
18One of the servants answered, "I have
seen a son of Jesse of Bethlehem who
knows how to play the lyre. He is a brave
man and a warrior. He speaks well and is
a fine-looking man. And the LORD is with[w]
him."

---

[a] *14* Or *and a harmful*; similarly in verses 15, 16 and 23

15:35 ***see.*** God was through with Saul as king, and so was Samuel.

16:2 ***I have come to sacrifice to the LORD.*** At this time Shiloh was still the designated central location for sacrifices (Deut. 12:4–14). But with the disruptions of the priesthood, the ark located at Kiriath Jearim (7:2), and the general belief that God had removed His presence from Shiloh, it would not be surprising if the sacrificial system had been interrupted as well. In any case, God did direct Samuel to make this sacrifice at Bethlehem.

16:7 God—Our Creator knows His human creatures intimately, and He is able to discern our thoughts and purposes before we ourselves are aware of them. He always looks beyond appearance and stature to the heart.

16:12 ***anoint him.*** David was anointed with olive oil. This religious ritual consecrated him to the kingship, although he did not take the role of king for many years. The heart God saw in David is the one He wants to see in all of us. It has purposefulness, intelligence, and willingness to obey. If our heart is centered on God, He can use us to extend His kingdom.

16:14 ***departed from Saul.*** After the Spirit of God came upon David, Saul was no longer empowered by the Spirit to serve as king. In Old Testament times the Holy Spirit came upon people selectively, usually a king, prophet, or judge. It was only after the resurrection of Jesus that the Holy Spirit came to indwell all believers (John 16:5–11; Acts 2:4).

16:15 ***evil spirit from God.*** This affliction is understood in various ways. Perhaps the spirit was a demon that God allowed to harass Saul, in the same way that God allowed Satan to tempt Job (Job 1:8–12). Perhaps Saul had a spirit of discontent in his heart,

15:34 [w] 1Sa 7:17 [x] 1Sa 11:4 **15:35** [y] 1Sa 19:24 [z] 1Sa 16:1 **16:1** [a] 1Sa 15:35 [b] 1Sa 15:23 [c] 2Ki 9:1 [d] Ru 4:17; 1Sa 9:16 [e] Ps 78:70; Ac 13:22 **16:3** [f] Ex 4:15 [g] Dt 17:15; 1Sa 9:16 **16:4** [h] Ge 48:7; Lk 2:4 [i] 1Ki 2:13; 2Ki 9:17 **16:5** [j] Ex 19:10, 22 **16:6** [k] 1Sa 17:13 **16:7** [l] Ps 147:10 [m] 1Ki 8:39; 1Ch 28:9; Isa 55:8 **16:8** [n] 1Sa 17:13 **16:11** [o] 1Sa 17:12 **16:12** [p] 1Sa 9:17 [q] Ge 39:6; 1Sa 17:42 **16:13** [r] Nu 27:18; Jdg 11:29 [s] 1Sa 10:1, 6, 9-10; 11:6 **16:14** [t] Jdg 16:20 [u] Jdg 9:23; 1Sa 18:10 **16:16** [v] ver 23; 1Sa 18:10; 19:9; 2Ki 3:15 **16:18** [w] 1Sa 3:19; 17:32-37

19Then Saul sent messengers to Jesse
and said, "Send me your son David, who
is with the sheep." 20So Jesse took a donkey loaded with bread,[x] a skin of wine and
a young goat and sent them with his son
David to Saul.
21David came to Saul and entered his
service.[y] Saul liked him very much, and
David became one of his armor-bearers.
22Then Saul sent word to Jesse, saying,
"Allow David to remain in my service, for I
am pleased with him."
23Whenever the spirit from God came
on Saul, David would take up his lyre and
play. Then relief would come to Saul; he
would feel better, and the evil spirit[z] would
leave him.

David and Goliath

17 Now the Philistines gathered their
forces for war and assembled[a] at Sokoh in Judah. They pitched camp at Ephes
Dammim, between Sokoh[b] and Azekah.
2Saul and the Israelites assembled and
camped in the Valley of Elah[c] and drew
up their battle line to meet the Philistines.
3The Philistines occupied one hill and the
Israelites another, with the valley between
them.
4A champion named Goliath,[d] who
was from Gath, came out of the Philistine camp. His height was six cubits and a
span.[a] 5He had a bronze helmet on his head
and wore a coat of scale armor of bronze
weighing five thousand shekels[b]; 6on his
legs he wore bronze greaves, and a bronze
javelin[e] was slung on his back. 7His spear
shaft was like a weaver's rod,[f] and its iron
point weighed six hundred shekels.[c] His
shield bearer[g] went ahead of him.
8Goliath stood and shouted to the ranks
of Israel, "Why do you come out and line
up for battle? Am I not a Philistine, and
are you not the servants of Saul? Choose[h]
a man and have him come down to me. 9If
he is able to fight and kill me, we will become your subjects; but if I overcome him
and kill him, you will become our subjects
and serve us." 10Then the Philistine said,
"This day I defy[i] the armies of Israel! Give
me a man and let us fight each other." 11On
hearing the Philistine's words, Saul and all
the Israelites were dismayed and terrified.
12Now David was the son of an Ephrathite named Jesse,[j] who was from Bethlehem[k] in Judah. Jesse had eight[l] sons, and
in Saul's time he was very old. 13Jesse's
three oldest sons had followed Saul to the
war: The firstborn was Eliab;[m] the second, Abinadab; and the third, Shammah.[n]
14David was the youngest. The three oldest
followed Saul, 15but David went back and
forth from Saul to tend his father's sheep[o]
at Bethlehem.
16For forty days the Philistine came forward every morning and evening and took
his stand.
17Now Jesse said to his son David, "Take
this ephah[d] of roasted grain[p] and these ten
loaves of bread for your brothers and hurry

[a] *4* That is, about 9 feet 9 inches or about 3 meters
[b] *5* That is, about 125 pounds or about 58 kilograms
[c] *7* That is, about 15 pounds or about 6.9 kilograms
[d] *17* That is, probably about 36 pounds or about 16 kilograms

caused by the absence of the Holy Spirit. Perhaps pride, that same sin that caused Satan to fall, was allowed to grow in Saul's heart and dominate his thoughts and actions. Scripture is clear that God is always holy, just, and righteous, so this spirit was something that God allowed to come upon Saul, but it was not a part of God.

16:21 *David came to Saul.* David played for Saul, and was his armor-bearer. It is unclear exactly how much time David spent with Saul. Probably David at this time continued to come and go from Saul's household to his father's.

17:1 *the Philistines gathered their forces for war.* The Philistine and Israelite armies were gathered in the Valley of Elah, about 15 miles west of David's hometown of Bethlehem. The Philistines were camped on a hill, south of the valley, between the cities of Azekah and Sokoh.

17:2 *Valley of Elah.* The valley is an east-west valley, leading from the hill country of Judah toward the lowlands of the Philistines. It had a steep ravine that extended the length of the valley, making it unfit for the Philistines' chariots. Probably the ravine prevented a full-scale assault by the Philistines, causing the long delay before engaging in battle.

17:4 *champion.* The champion was a warrior who would fight in single combat as a stand-in for the entire army. The most likely person to take on this champion would be Saul, who, when he was chosen king, stood head and shoulders above his countrymen. ***six cubits and a span.*** The cubit was about 18 inches, and a span was 9 inches. Goliath stood approximately nine feet, nine inches tall.

17:5 *bronze helmet.* Ordinary troops had leather helmets. ***coat of scale armor.*** Goliath's coat of scale armor was made of overlapping plates of bronze sewn on leather. ***five thousand shekels.*** The coat of armor weighed about 125 pounds.

17:7 *six hundred shekels.* The spear was a weapon designed for hand-to-hand combat, like a long sword. The head of Goliath's spear weighed about 17 pounds. ***shield bearer.*** The soldier carried a small round shield, usually worn on the left arm. The shield-carrier bore the much larger, oblong shield.

17:12 *Ephrathite.* Ephrath was the early name for Bethlehem.

17:17 *Take . . . for your brothers.* In ancient times, soldiers usually lived off the land they conquered or depended on personal supplies that they or someone else brought from home.

16:20 [x] 1Sa 10:27; Pr 18:16 **16:21** [y] Ge 41:46; Pr 22:29
16:23 [z] ver 14-16 **17:1** [a] 1Sa 13:5 [b] Jos 15:35; 2Ch 28:18
17:2 [c] 1Sa 21:9 **17:4** [d] Jos 11:21-22; 2Sa 21:19
17:6 [e] ver 45 **17:7** [f] 2Sa 21:19 [g] ver 41 **17:8** [h] 1Sa 8:17
17:10 [i] ver 26, 45; 2Sa 21:21 **17:12** [j] Ru 4:17; 1Ch 2:13-15
[k] Ge 35:19 [l] 1Sa 16:11 **17:13** [m] 1Sa 16:6 [n] 1Sa 16:9
17:15 [o] 1Sa 16:19 **17:17** [p] 1Sa 25:18

to their camp. 18Take along these ten chees-
es to the commander of their unit. See how
your brothers[q] are and bring back some assurance[a] from them. 19They are with Saul
and all the men of Israel in the Valley of
Elah, fighting against the Philistines."
20Early in the morning David left the
flock in the care of a shepherd, loaded
up and set out, as Jesse had directed. He
reached the camp as the army was going
out to its battle positions, shouting the war
cry. 21Israel and the Philistines were drawing up their lines facing each other. 22David
left his things with the keeper of supplies,
ran to the battle lines and asked his brothers how they were. 23As he was talking with
them, Goliath, the Philistine champion from
Gath, stepped out from his lines and shouted his usual[r] defiance, and David heard it.
24Whenever the Israelites saw the man, they
all fled from him in great fear.
25Now the Israelites had been saying,
"Do you see how this man keeps coming
out? He comes out to defy Israel. The king
will give great wealth to the man who kills
him. He will also give him his daughter[s] in
marriage and will exempt his family from
taxes in Israel."
26David asked the men standing near
him, "What will be done for the man who
kills this Philistine and removes this disgrace[t] from Israel? Who is this uncircumcised[u] Philistine that he should defy[v] the
armies of the living[w] God?"
27They repeated to him what they had
been saying and told him, "This is what
will be done for the man who kills him."
28When Eliab, David's oldest brother, heard him speaking with the men, he
burned with anger[x] at him and asked,
"Why have you come down here? And with
whom did you leave those few sheep in the
wilderness? I know how conceited you are
and how wicked your heart is; you came
down only to watch the battle."
29"Now what have I done?" said David.
"Can't I even speak?" 30He then turned
away to someone else and brought up the
same matter, and the men answered him as
before. 31What David said was overheard
and reported to Saul, and Saul sent for him.
32David said to Saul, "Let no one lose
heart[y] on account of this Philistine; your
servant will go and fight him."
33Saul replied,[z] "You are not able to go
out against this Philistine and fight him;
you are only a young man, and he has been
a warrior from his youth."
34But David said to Saul, "Your servant has been keeping his father's sheep.
When a lion[a] or a bear came and carried
off a sheep from the flock, 35I went after
it, struck it and rescued the sheep from its
mouth. When it turned on me, I seized it
by its hair, struck it and killed it. 36Your
servant has killed both the lion and the
bear; this uncircumcised Philistine will be
like one of them, because he has defied the
armies of the living God. 37The LORD who
rescued[b] me from the paw of the lion[c] and
the paw of the bear will rescue me from the
hand of this Philistine."
Saul said to David, "Go, and the LORD be
with[d] you."
38Then Saul dressed David in his own
tunic. He put a coat of armor on him and
a bronze helmet on his head. 39David fastened on his sword over the tunic and tried
walking around, because he was not used
to them.
"I cannot go in these," he said to Saul,
"because I am not used to them." So he
took them off. 40Then he took his staff in
his hand, chose five smooth stones from
the stream, put them in the pouch of his
shepherd's bag and, with his sling in his
hand, approached the Philistine.
41Meanwhile, the Philistine, with his
shield bearer in front of him, kept coming
closer to David. 42He looked David over
and saw that he was little more than a boy,
glowing with health and handsome,[e] and he
despised[f] him. 43He said to David, "Am I a
dog,[g] that you come at me with sticks?" And
the Philistine cursed David by his gods.
44"Come here," he said, "and I'll give your
flesh to the birds and the wild animals![h]"
45David said to the Philistine, "You come
against me with sword and spear and javelin, but I come against you in the name[i]
of the LORD Almighty, the God of the armies of Israel, whom you have defied.[j]

---

[a] 18 Or *some token*; or *some pledge of spoils*

17:39–40 Wisdom—David had embarked on a risky venture. It might seem smart to meet Goliath with the best armor, but David had wisdom enough to know that if he was going to attack the giant, it would have to be on his own terms. The years of solitary shepherding had given David the time to practice with his sling, and the opportunity to know that it was the Lord who gave him the strength and the will to kill the predators that threatened his flock. The insight and practices gained through difficult experiences blossom as wisdom. We can look back on these times with thankfulness because that is how God has equipped us for the next task.

17:40 *sling.* A sling was the typical equipment of the shepherd. It was a hollow pocket of leather attached to two cords. Putting a stone in the pouch, the slinger would whirl it around his head to build up momentum. Releasing one of the cords would hurl the stone at its target. It takes skill and practice to be expert with a sling. Slingers were a regular part of armies in the ancient Middle East.

17:18 [q] Ge 37:14 **17:23** [r] ver 8-10 **17:25** [s] Jos 15:16; 1Sa 18:17 **17:26** [t] 1Sa 11:2 [u] 1Sa 14:6 [v] ver 10 [w] Dt 5:26 **17:28** [x] Ge 37:4, 8, 11; Pr 18:19; Mt 10:36 **17:32** [y] Dt 20:3; 1Sa 16:18 **17:33** [z] Nu 13:31 **17:34** [a] Jer 49:19; Am 3:12 **17:37** [b] 2Co 1:10 [c] 2Ti 4:17 [d] 1Sa 20:13; 1Ch 22:11, 16 **17:42** [e] 1Sa 16:12 [f] Ps 123:3-4; Pr 16:18 **17:43** [g] 1Sa 24:14; 2Sa 3:8; 9:8; 2Ki 8:13 **17:44** [h] 1Ki 20:10-11 **17:45** [i] 2Sa 22:33, 35; 2Ch 32:8; Ps 124:8; Heb 11:32-34 [j] ver 10

46This day the LORD will deliver you into
my hands, and I'll strike you down and
cut off your head. This very day I will give
the carcasses[k] of the Philistine army to the
birds and the wild animals, and the whole
world[l] will know that there is a God in Israel.[m] 47All those gathered here will know
that it is not by sword[n] or spear that the
LORD saves;[o] for the battle[p] is the LORD's,
and he will give all of you into our hands."

48As the Philistine moved closer to attack him, David ran quickly toward the
battle line to meet him. 49Reaching into his
bag and taking out a stone, he slung it and
struck the Philistine on the forehead. The
stone sank into his forehead, and he fell
facedown on the ground.

50So David triumphed over the Philistine
with a sling[q] and a stone; without a sword
in his hand he struck down the Philistine
and killed him.

51David ran and stood over him. He took
hold of the Philistine's sword and drew it
from the sheath. After he killed him, he cut[r]
off his head with the sword.[s]

When the Philistines saw that their hero
was dead, they turned and ran. 52Then the
men of Israel and Judah surged forward
with a shout and pursued the Philistines
to the entrance of Gath[a] and to the gates
of Ekron.[t] Their dead were strewn along
the Shaaraim[u] road to Gath and Ekron.
53When the Israelites returned from chasing the Philistines, they plundered their
camp.

54David took the Philistine's head and
brought it to Jerusalem; he put the Philistine's weapons in his own tent.

55As Saul watched David[v] going out to
meet the Philistine, he said to Abner, commander of the army, "Abner, whose son is
that young man?"

Abner replied, "As surely as you live,
Your Majesty, I don't know."

56The king said, "Find out whose son this
young man is."

57As soon as David returned from killing
the Philistine, Abner took him and brought
him before Saul, with David still holding
the Philistine's head.

58"Whose son are you, young man?"
Saul asked him.

David said, "I am the son of your servant
Jesse[w] of Bethlehem."

Saul's Growing Fear of David

18 After David had finished talking with
Saul, Jonathan became one in spirit
with David, and he loved[x] him as himself.[y]
2From that day Saul kept David with him
and did not let him return home to his
family. 3And Jonathan made a covenant[z]
with David because he loved him as himself. 4Jonathan took off the robe[a] he was
wearing and gave it to David, along with
his tunic, and even his sword, his bow and
his belt.

5Whatever mission Saul sent him on, David was so successful that Saul gave him a
high rank in the army. This pleased all the
troops, and Saul's officers as well.

6When the men were returning home
after David had killed the Philistine, the
women came out from all the towns of Israel to meet King Saul with singing and
dancing,[b] with joyful songs and with timbrels[c] and lyres. 7As they danced, they
sang:[d]

"Saul has slain his thousands,
 and David his tens[e] of thousands."

8Saul was very angry; this refrain displeased him greatly. "They have credited
David with tens of thousands," he thought,
"but me with only thousands. What more
can he get but the kingdom?[f]" 9And from
that time on Saul kept a close eye on David.

10The next day an evil[b] spirit[g] from God
came forcefully on Saul. He was prophesying in his house, while David was playing the lyre, as he usually[h] did. Saul had a
spear in his hand 11and he hurled it, saying
to himself,[i] "I'll pin David to the wall." But
David eluded[j] him twice.

12Saul was afraid[k] of David, because the
LORD[l] was with[m] David but had departed
from Saul. 13So he sent David away from
him and gave him command over a thousand men, and David led[n] the troops in
their campaigns.[o] 14In everything he did he
had great success,[p] because the LORD was
with[q] him. 15When Saul saw how successful he was, he was afraid of him. 16But all
Israel and Judah loved David, because he
led them in their campaigns.[r]

[a] 52 Some Septuagint manuscripts; Hebrew *of a valley* [b] 10 Or *a harmful*

17:55 *whose son is that young man?* How does this question fit with the fact that David had been serving as a musician in Saul's court and as Saul's armor-bearer, and that Saul "liked him very much" (16:18–23)? Possibly in Saul's unstable mental condition he did not recall David, or perhaps he did not know his name, even if he did recognize him. David was not at court full time until after he had killed Goliath. It would not be unusual for the king to know nothing personal about a servant, even a servant he appreciated.

18:16 *he led them in their campaigns.* David's military activities elevated him to prominence before the people.

17:46 [k] Dt 28:26 [l] Jos 4:24; 1Ki 8:43; Isa 52:10 [m] 1Ki 18:36; 2Ki 19:19; Isa 37:20 **17:47** [n] Hos 1:7; Zec 4:6 [o] 1Sa 14:6; 2Ch 14:11 [p] 2Ch 20:15; Ps 44:6-7 **17:50** [q] 2Sa 23:21 **17:51** [r] Heb 11:34 [s] 1Sa 21:9 **17:52** [t] Jos 15:11 [u] Jos 15:36 **17:55** [v] 1Sa 16:21 **17:58** [w] ver 12 **18:1** [x] 2Sa 1:26 [y] Ge 44:30 **18:3** [z] 1Sa 20:8, 16, 17, 42 **18:4** [a] Ge 41:42 **18:6** [b] Ex 15:20 [c] Jdg 11:34; Ps 68:25 **18:7** [d] Ex 15:21 [e] 1Sa 21:11; 29:5 **18:8** [f] 1Sa 15:8 **18:10** [g] 1Sa 16:14 [h] 1Sa 19:7 **18:11** [i] 1Sa 20:7, 33 [j] 1Sa 19:10 **18:12** [k] ver 15, 29 [l] 1Sa 16:13 [m] 1Sa 28:15 **18:13** [n] ver 16; Nu 27:17 [o] 2Sa 5:2 **18:14** [p] Ge 39:3 [q] Ge 39:2, 23; Jos 6:27; 1Sa 16:18 **18:16** [r] ver 5

17 Saul said to David, "Here is my older
daughter[s] Merab. I will give her to you in
marriage; only serve me bravely and fight
the battles[t] of the LORD." For Saul said to
himself,[u] "I will not raise a hand against
him. Let the Philistines do that!"
18 But David said to Saul, "Who am I,[v] and
what is my family or my clan in Israel, that
I should become the king's son-in-law?[w]"
19 So[a] when the time came for Merab,[x] Saul's
daughter, to be given to David, she was giv-
en in marriage to Adriel of Meholah.[y]
20 Now Saul's daughter Michal[z] was in
love with David, and when they told Saul
about it, he was pleased. 21 "I will give her
to him," he thought, "so that she may be a
snare[a] to him and so that the hand of the
Philistines may be against him." So Saul
said to David, "Now you have a second opportunity to become my son-in-law."
22 Then Saul ordered his attendants:
"Speak to David privately and say, 'Look,
the king likes you, and his attendants all
love you; now become his son-in-law.'"
23 They repeated these words to David.
But David said, "Do you think it is a small
matter to become the king's son-in-law?
I'm only a poor man and little known."
24 When Saul's servants told him what
David had said, 25 Saul replied, "Say to David, 'The king wants no other price[b] for the
bride than a hundred Philistine foreskins,
to take revenge on his enemies.'" Saul's
plan[c] was to have David fall by the hands
of the Philistines.
26 When the attendants told David these
things, he was pleased to become the
king's son-in-law. So before the allotted
time elapsed, 27 David took his men with
him and went out and killed two hundred
Philistines and brought back their foreskins. They counted out the full number to
the king so that David might become the
king's son-in-law. Then Saul gave him his
daughter Michal[d] in marriage.
28 When Saul realized that the LORD was
with David and that his daughter Michal
loved David, 29 Saul became still more
afraid of him, and he remained his enemy
the rest of his days.
30 The Philistine commanders continued
to go out to battle, and as often as they did,
David met with more success[e] than the rest
of Saul's officers, and his name became
well known.

Saul Tries to Kill David

19 Saul told his son Jonathan[f] and all the
attendants to kill[g] David. But Jonathan had taken a great liking to David 2 and
warned him, "My father Saul is looking for a
chance to kill you. Be on your guard tomorrow morning; go into hiding and stay there.
3 I will go out and stand with my father in the
field where you are. I'll speak[h] to him about
you and will tell you what I find out."
4 Jonathan spoke[i] well of David to Saul
his father and said to him, "Let not the king
do wrong[j] to his servant David; he has not
wronged you, and what he has done has
benefited you greatly. 5 He took his life in
his hands when he killed the Philistine.
The LORD won a great victory[k] for all Israel, and you saw it and were glad. Why then
would you do wrong to an innocent[l] man
like David by killing him for no reason?"
6 Saul listened to Jonathan and took this
oath: "As surely as the LORD lives, David
will not be put to death."
7 So Jonathan called David and told him
the whole conversation. He brought him to
Saul, and David was with Saul as before.[m]
8 Once more war broke out, and David
went out and fought the Philistines. He
struck them with such force that they fled
before him.
9 But an evil[b] spirit[n] from the LORD came
on Saul as he was sitting in his house with
his spear in his hand. While David was
playing the lyre, 10 Saul tried to pin him to
the wall with his spear, but David eluded[o]
him as Saul drove the spear into the wall.
That night David made good his escape.
11 Saul sent men to David's house to
watch[p] it and to kill him in the morning.
But Michal, David's wife, warned him, "If
you don't run for your life tonight, tomorrow you'll be killed." 12 So Michal let David

---

[a] 19 Or *However,* [b] 9 Or *But a harmful*

18:25 *price of the bride.* A sum of money, about fifty shekels (Deut. 22:29), was paid by the bridegroom to the father of the bride as economic compensation for the loss of a daughter.

18:30 Wisdom — David was popular, he had even been privately anointed to be the next king, and Saul had just thrown a spear at him. Yet David did nothing to take justice in his own hands. He remained calm and loyal. It is clear that David decided very early in the time after he was anointed that if he became king, it would have to be totally by the hand of God. He would do nothing to destroy the man that God had previously anointed king. Historically we can see what a very wise choice this was, but it must have been very difficult for David to choose the path of wisdom when he could have raised the power of the people to his side so easily.

19:11 *tomorrow you'll be killed.* The story of David's escape is alluded to in the title of Psalm 59.

19:12 *Michal let David down through a window.* Saul had imagined that Michal would be loyal to him and a snare to David. But she loved David, and her loyalty was to her husband.

18:17 [s] 1Sa 17:25 [t] Nu 21:14; 1Sa 25:28 [u] ver 25
18:18 [v] 1Sa 9:21; 2Sa 7:18 [w] ver 23 **18:19** [x] 2Sa 21:8
[y] Jdg 7:22 **18:20** [z] ver 28 **18:21** [a] ver 17, 26
18:25 [b] Ge 34:12; Ex 22:17; 1Sa 14:24 [c] ver 17
18:27 [d] ver 13; 2Sa 3:14 **18:30** [e] ver 5; 2Sa 11:1
19:1 [f] 1Sa 18:1 [g] 1Sa 18:9 **19:3** [h] 1Sa 20:12
19:4 [i] 1Sa 20:32; Pr 31:8, 9; Jer 18:20 [j] Ge 42:22; Pr 17:13
19:5 [k] 1Sa 11:13; 17:49-50; 1Ch 11:14 [l] Dt 19:10-13;
1Sa 20:32; Mt 27:4 **19:7** [m] 1Sa 16:21; 18:2, 13
19:9 [n] 1Sa 16:14; 18:10-11 **19:10** [o] 1Sa 18:11
19:11 [p] Ps 59 Title

down through a window,[q] and he fled and
escaped. 13Then Michal took an idol and
laid it on the bed, covering it with a garment
and putting some goats' hair at the head.
14When Saul sent the men to capture David, Michal said,[r] "He is ill."
15Then Saul sent the men back to see David and told them, "Bring him up to me in
his bed so that I may kill him." 16But when
the men entered, there was the idol in the
bed, and at the head was some goats' hair.
17Saul said to Michal, "Why did you deceive me like this and send my enemy away
so that he escaped?"
Michal told him, "He said to me, 'Let me
get away. Why should I kill you?'"
18When David had fled and made his
escape, he went to Samuel at Ramah[s] and
told him all that Saul had done to him.
Then he and Samuel went to Naioth and
stayed there. 19Word came to Saul: "David
is in Naioth at Ramah"; 20so he sent men to
capture him. But when they saw a group of
prophets[t] prophesying, with Samuel standing there as their leader, the Spirit of God
came on[u] Saul's men, and they also prophesied.[v] 21Saul was told about it, and he sent
more men, and they prophesied too. Saul
sent men a third time, and they also prophesied. 22Finally, he himself left for Ramah
and went to the great cistern at Seku. And
he asked, "Where are Samuel and David?"
"Over in Naioth at Ramah," they said.
23So Saul went to Naioth at Ramah. But
the Spirit of God came even on him, and he
walked along prophesying[w] until he came
to Naioth. 24He stripped[x] off his garments,
and he too prophesied in Samuel's presence. He lay naked all that day and all that
night. This is why people say, "Is Saul also
among the prophets?"[y]

David and Jonathan

20 Then David fled from Naioth at
Ramah and went to Jonathan and
asked, "What have I done? What is my
crime? How have I wronged[z] your father,
that he is trying to kill me?"
2"Never!" Jonathan replied. "You are
not going to die! Look, my father doesn't
do anything, great or small, without letting
me know. Why would he hide this from
me? It isn't so!"
3But David took an oath[a] and said, "Your
father knows very well that I have found favor in your eyes, and he has said to himself,
'Jonathan must not know this or he will be
grieved.' Yet as surely as the LORD lives and
as you live, there is only a step between me
and death."
4Jonathan said to David, "Whatever you
want me to do, I'll do for you."
5So David said, "Look, tomorrow is the
New Moon feast,[b] and I am supposed to
dine with the king; but let me go and hide[c]
in the field until the evening of the day after tomorrow. 6If your father misses me at
all, tell him, 'David earnestly asked my
permission to hurry to Bethlehem,[d] his
hometown, because an annual[e] sacrifice
is being made there for his whole clan.' 7If
he says, 'Very well,' then your servant is
safe. But if he loses his temper,[f] you can be
sure that he is determined to harm me. 8As
for you, show kindness to your servant,
for you have brought him into a covenant[g]
with you before the LORD. If I am guilty,
then kill[h] me yourself! Why hand me over
to your father?"
9"Never!" Jonathan said. "If I had the
least inkling that my father was determined to harm you, wouldn't I tell you?"
10David asked, "Who will tell me if your
father answers you harshly?"
11"Come," Jonathan said, "let's go out
into the field." So they went there together.
12Then Jonathan said to David, "I swear
by the LORD, the God of Israel, that I will
surely sound out my father by this time the
day after tomorrow! If he is favorably disposed toward you, will I not send you word
and let you know? 13But if my father intends to harm you, may the LORD deal with
Jonathan, be it ever so severely,[i] if I do not
let you know and send you away in peace.
May the LORD be with[j] you as he has been
with my father. 14But show me unfailing
kindness like the LORD's kindness as long
as I live, so that I may not be killed, 15and
do not ever cut off your kindness from my
family[k]—not even when the LORD has cut
off every one of David's enemies from the
face of the earth."
16So Jonathan made a covenant[l] with
the house of David, saying, "May the LORD
call David's enemies to account." 17And

20:5 *tomorrow is the New Moon.* The first day of the month, the New Moon, was observed as a religious feast (Num. 10:10; 28:11–15). It was celebrated with a sacrificial meal and rest from work.

20:6 *annual sacrifice.* Apparently Jesse's family gathered for a special time of worship during the New Moon celebration.

20:16 *May the LORD call David's enemies to account.* Jonathan prayed that the Lord would hold David's enemies accountable.

20:16–17 Love—The love and loyalty displayed by Jonathan to David is unparalleled among human relationships in the Bible. He was a living example of the New Testament phrase, "does not seek its own" (1 Cor. 13:5). In protecting David from the murderous plots of Saul, Jonathan was in reality closing the door

19:12 [q] Jos 2:15; Ac 9:25 **19:14** [r] Jos 2:4
19:18 [s] 1Sa 7:17 **19:20** [t] ver 11, 14; Jn 7:32, 45 [u] Nu 11:25
[v] 1Sa 10:5; Joel 2:28 **19:23** [w] 1Sa 10:13
19:24 [x] 2Sa 6:20; Isa 20:2; Mic 1:8 [y] 1Sa 10:11
20:1 [z] 1Sa 24:9 **20:3** [a] Dt 6:13 **20:5** [b] Nu 10:10; 28:11
[c] 1Sa 19:2 **20:6** [d] 1Sa 17:58 [e] Dt 12:5 **20:7** [f] 1Sa 25:17
20:8 [g] 1Sa 18:3; 23:18 [h] 2Sa 14:32 **20:13** [i] Ru 1:17;
1Sa 3:17 [j] Jos 1:5; 1Sa 17:37; 18:12; 1Ch 22:11, 16
20:15 [k] 2Sa 9:7 **20:16** [l] 1Sa 25:22

Jonathan had David reaffirm his oath[m] out
of love for him, because he loved him as he
loved himself.
18 Then Jonathan said to David, "Tomorrow is the New Moon feast. You will be
missed, because your seat will be empty.[n]
19 The day after tomorrow, toward evening,
go to the place where you hid[o] when this
trouble began, and wait by the stone Ezel.
20 I will shoot three arrows to the side of
it, as though I were shooting at a target.
21 Then I will send a boy and say, 'Go, find
the arrows.' If I say to him, 'Look, the arrows are on this side of you; bring them
here,' then come, because, as surely as the
LORD lives, you are safe; there is no danger. 22 But if I say to the boy, 'Look, the arrows are beyond[p] you,' then you must go,
because the LORD has sent you away. 23 And
about the matter you and I discussed—remember, the LORD is witness[q] between you
and me forever."
24 So David hid in the field, and when the
New Moon feast came, the king sat down
to eat. 25 He sat in his customary place by
the wall, opposite Jonathan,[a] and Abner
sat next to Saul, but David's place was
empty.[r] 26 Saul said nothing that day, for
he thought, "Something must have happened to David to make him ceremonially unclean—surely he is unclean.[s]" 27 But
the next day, the second day of the month,
David's place was empty again. Then Saul
said to his son Jonathan, "Why hasn't the
son of Jesse come to the meal, either yesterday or today?"
28 Jonathan answered, "David earnestly
asked me for permission[t] to go to Bethlehem. 29 He said, 'Let me go, because our
family is observing a sacrifice in the town
and my brother has ordered me to be there.
If I have found favor in your eyes, let me get
away to see my brothers.' That is why he
has not come to the king's table."
30 Saul's anger flared up at Jonathan and
he said to him, "You son of a perverse and
rebellious woman! Don't I know that you
have sided with the son of Jesse to your
own shame and to the shame of the mother who bore you? 31 As long as the son of
Jesse lives on this earth, neither you nor
your kingdom will be established. Now
send someone to bring him to me, for he
must die!"
32 "Why[u] should he be put to death?
What[v] has he done?" Jonathan asked his
father. 33 But Saul hurled his spear at him
to kill him. Then Jonathan knew that his
father intended[w] to kill David.
34 Jonathan got up from the table in fierce
anger; on that second day of the feast he
did not eat, because he was grieved at his
father's shameful treatment of David.
35 In the morning Jonathan went out to
the field for his meeting with David. He had
a small boy with him, 36 and he said to the
boy, "Run and find the arrows I shoot." As
the boy ran, he shot an arrow beyond him.
37 When the boy came to the place where
Jonathan's arrow had fallen, Jonathan
called out after him, "Isn't the arrow beyond[x] you?" 38 Then he shouted, "Hurry! Go
quickly! Don't stop!" The boy picked up the
arrow and returned to his master. 39 (The
boy knew nothing about all this; only Jonathan and David knew.) 40 Then Jonathan
gave his weapons to the boy and said, "Go,
carry them back to town."
41 After the boy had gone, David got up
from the south side of the stone and bowed
down before Jonathan three times, with his
face to the ground. Then they kissed each
other and wept together—but David wept
the most.
42 Jonathan said to David, "Go in peace,[y]
for we have sworn friendship[z] with each
other in the name of the LORD, saying, 'The
LORD is witness between you and me, and
between your descendants and my descendants forever.'" Then David left, and Jonathan went back to the town.[b]

David at Nob

21 [c] David went to Nob,[a] to Ahimelek the
priest. Ahimelek trembled[b] when he
met him, and asked, "Why are you alone?
Why is no one with you?"
2 David answered Ahimelek the priest,
"The king sent me on a mission and said
to me, 'No one is to know anything about

[a] 25 Septuagint; Hebrew *wall. Jonathan arose*
[b] 42 In Hebrew texts this sentence (20:42b) is numbered 21:1. [c] In Hebrew texts 21:1-15 is numbered 21:2-16.

---

to his own possible reign over Israel after his father's death. Jonathan knew this, but his faithfulness to David continued until his death on a battlefield (1 Sam. 31:2).

20:30 ***to the shame of the mother who bore you.*** This was a way of saying that Jonathan shamed his mother who conceived him by maintaining loyalty to David. It was a slur on Jonathan, and a slur on his mother.

20:31 Justice—If David had been taking matters into his own hands, and making moves to secure the kingdom for himself, perhaps Saul would have been justified in seeking David's life. But Saul could charge David with no wrongdoing. Saul was enraged at David, at Jonathan, and in rebellion against God. Because he was driven by anger, Saul could no longer see the injustice in his own thinking.

21:1 ***Nob.*** Nob was a Levitical community in Benjamin where the tabernacle was located after it was in Shiloh. ***Ahimelek.*** Ahimelek, the great-grandson of Eli, was serving as high priest.

20:17 [m] 1Sa 18:3 **20:18** [n] ver 5,25 **20:19** [o] 1Sa 19:2 **20:22** [p] ver 37 **20:23** [q] ver 14-15; Ge 31:50 **20:25** [r] ver 18 **20:26** [s] Lev 7:20-21; 15:5; 1Sa 16:5 **20:28** [t] ver 6 **20:32** [u] 1Sa 19:4; Mt 27:23 [v] Ge 31:36; Lk 23:22 **20:33** [w] ver 7; 1Sa 18:11, 17 **20:37** [x] ver 22 **20:42** [y] ver 22; 1Sa 1:17 [z] 2Sa 1:26; Pr 18:24 **21:1** [a] 1Sa 14:3; 22:9, 19; Ne 11:32; Isa 10:32 [b] 1Sa 16:4

the mission I am sending you on.' As for
my men, I have told them to meet me at a
certain place. 3Now then, what do you have
on hand? Give me five loaves of bread, or
whatever you can find."
4But the priest answered David, "I don't
have any ordinary bread[c] on hand; however,
there is some consecrated[d] bread here—
provided the men have kept[e] themselves
from women."
5David replied, "Indeed women have
been kept from us, as usual whenever[a] I
set out. The men's bodies are holy[f] even on
missions that are not holy. How much more
so today!" 6So the priest gave him the consecrated
bread,[g] since there was no bread
there except the bread of the Presence that
had been removed from before the LORD
and replaced by hot bread on the day it was
taken away.
7Now one of Saul's servants was there
that day, detained before the LORD; he
was Doeg[h] the Edomite,[i] Saul's chief shepherd.
8David asked Ahimelek, "Don't you have
a spear or a sword here? I haven't brought
my sword or any other weapon, because
the king's mission was urgent."
9The priest replied, "The sword[j] of Goliath
the Philistine, whom you killed in the
Valley of Elah,[k] is here; it is wrapped in a
cloth behind the ephod. If you want it, take
it; there is no sword here but that one."

David said, "There is none like it; give
it to me."

David at Gath

10That day David fled from Saul and
went[l] to Achish king of Gath. 11But the servants
of Achish said to him, "Isn't this David,
the king of the land? Isn't he the one
they sing about in their dances:

"'Saul has slain his thousands,
and David his tens of thousands'?"[m]

12David took these words to heart and
was very much afraid of Achish king of
Gath. 13So he pretended to be insane[n] in
their presence; and while he was in their
hands he acted like a madman, making
marks on the doors of the gate and letting
saliva run down his beard.
14Achish said to his servants, "Look at
the man! He is insane! Why bring him to
me? 15Am I so short of madmen that you
have to bring this fellow here to carry on
like this in front of me? Must this man
come into my house?"

David at Adullam and Mizpah

22 David left Gath and escaped to the
cave[o] of Adullam. When his brothers
and his father's household heard about
it, they went down to him there. 2All those
who were in distress or in debt or discontented
gathered[p] around him, and he became
their commander. About four hundred
men were with him.
3From there David went to Mizpah in
Moab and said to the king of Moab, "Would
you let my father and mother come and
stay with you until I learn what God will
do for me?" 4So he left them with the king
of Moab, and they stayed with him as long
as David was in the stronghold.
5But the prophet Gad[q] said to David, "Do
not stay in the stronghold. Go into the land
of Judah." So David left and went to the forest
of Hereth.

Saul Kills the Priests of Nob

6Now Saul heard that David and his men
had been discovered. And Saul was seated,[r]
spear in hand, under the tamarisk[s] tree
on the hill at Gibeah, with all his officials
standing at his side. 7He said to them, "Listen,
men of Benjamin! Will the son of Jesse

---

[a] 5 Or *from us in the past few days since*

21:4 ***ordinary bread.*** Ahimelek explained that the only bread available was holy bread, sometimes called the "showbread," which had been displayed before the Lord in the tabernacle (Ex. 25:30; Lev. 24:5–9). According to God's law, this bread could be eaten only by priests.

21:6 ***gave him the consecrated bread.*** This was the bread that had been displayed before the Lord for a week, and was removed for fresh bread. In giving the bread to David, Ahimelek broke the Law, yet in his compassion he kept the spirit of the Law. Jesus referred to this incident when He explained to the Pharisees that it was all right to pick grain to eat on the Sabbath (Matt. 12:2–4).

21:7 ***detained before the LORD.*** Apparently Doeg, although he was not an Israelite, was at the tabernacle under a spiritual vow.

21:10 ***Gath.*** Gath was, one of the five major cities of the Philistines (6:17).

21:12–13 ***Achish king of Gath.*** These verses provide the background for Psalms 34 and 56. In Psalm 34 Achish is referred to as Abimelek, which was apparently a dynastic title used by the Philistine rulers (Gen. 26:1).

22:1 ***cave of Adullam.*** The cave near the city of Adullam was about ten miles southeast of Gath and sixteen miles southwest of Jerusalem. It was here that David composed Psalm 142, and possibly Psalm 57.

22:2 ***All those who were in distress . . . debt.*** The men who gathered around David were not so much taking sides with him as escaping Saul. The sense of desolation in Psalm 142:4 reflects David's feeling of being all alone. ***became their commander.*** Nevertheless, David organized them, governed them, and made them into a loyal and obedient unit.

21:4 [c] Lev 24:8-9 [d] Ex 25:30; Mt 12:4 [e] Ex 19:15 **21:5** [f] 1Th 4:4 **21:6** [g] Lev 24:8-9; Mt 12:3-4; Mk 2:25-28; Lk 6:1-5 **21:7** [h] 1Sa 22:9, 22 [i] 1Sa 14:47; Ps 52 Title **21:9** [j] 1Sa 17:51 [k] 1Sa 17:2 **21:10** [l] 1Sa 27:2 **21:11** [m] 1Sa 18:7; 29:5; Ps 56 Title **21:13** [n] Ps 34 Title **22:1** [o] 2Sa 23:13; Ps 57 Title; 142 Title **22:2** [p] 1Sa 23:13; 25:13; 2Sa 15:20 **22:5** [q] 2Sa 24:11; 1Ch 21:9; 29:29; 2Ch 29:25 **22:6** [r] Jdg 4:5 [s] Ge 21:33

give all of you fields and vineyards? Will he make all of you commanders[t] of thousands and commanders of hundreds? 8 Is that why you have all conspired against me? No one tells me when my son makes a covenant[u] with the son of Jesse. None of you is concerned[v] about me or tells me that my son has incited my servant to lie in wait for me, as he does today."

9 But Doeg[w] the Edomite, who was standing with Saul's officials, said, "I saw the son of Jesse come to Ahimelek son of Ahitub at Nob.[x] 10 Ahimelek inquired[y] of the LORD for him; he also gave him provisions[z] and the sword of Goliath the Philistine."

11 Then the king sent for the priest Ahimelek son of Ahitub and all the men of his family, who were the priests at Nob, and they all came to the king. 12 Saul said, "Listen now, son of Ahitub."

"Yes, my lord," he answered.

13 Saul said to him, "Why have you conspired[a] against me, you and the son of Jesse, giving him bread and a sword and inquiring of God for him, so that he has rebelled against me and lies in wait for me, as he does today?"

14 Ahimelek answered the king, "Who[b] of all your servants is as loyal as David, the king's son-in-law, captain of your bodyguard and highly respected in your household? 15 Was that day the first time I inquired of God for him? Of course not! Let not the king accuse your servant or any of his father's family, for your servant knows nothing at all about this whole affair."

16 But the king said, "You will surely die, Ahimelek, you and your whole family."

17 Then the king ordered the guards at his side: "Turn and kill the priests of the LORD, because they too have sided with David. They knew he was fleeing, yet they did not tell me."

But the king's officials were unwilling[c] to raise a hand to strike the priests of the LORD.

18 The king then ordered Doeg, "You turn and strike down the priests." So Doeg the Edomite turned and struck them down. That day he killed eighty-five men who wore the linen ephod.[d] 19 He also put to the sword[e] Nob, the town of the priests, with its men and women, its children and infants, and its cattle, donkeys and sheep.

20 But one son of Ahimelek son of Ahitub, named Abiathar,[f] escaped and fled to join David.[g] 21 He told David that Saul had killed the priests of the LORD. 22 Then David said to Abiathar, "That day, when Doeg[h] the Edomite was there, I knew he would be sure to tell Saul. I am responsible for the death of your whole family. 23 Stay with me; don't be afraid. The man who wants to kill you[i] is trying to kill me too. You will be safe with me."

David Saves Keilah

23 When David was told, "Look, the Philistines are fighting against Keilah[j] and are looting the threshing floors," 2 he inquired[k] of the LORD, saying, "Shall I go and attack these Philistines?"

The LORD answered him, "Go, attack the Philistines and save Keilah."

3 But David's men said to him, "Here in Judah we are afraid. How much more, then, if we go to Keilah against the Philistine forces!"

4 Once again David inquired of the LORD, and the LORD answered him, "Go down to Keilah, for I am going to give the Philistines into your hand.[l]" 5 So David and his men went to Keilah, fought the Philistines and carried off their livestock. He inflicted heavy losses on the Philistines and saved the people of Keilah. 6 (Now Abiathar[m] son of Ahimelek had brought the ephod down with him when he fled to David at Keilah.)

Saul Pursues David

7 Saul was told that David had gone to Keilah, and he said, "God has delivered him into my hands, for David has imprisoned himself by entering a town with gates and bars." 8 And Saul called up all his forces for battle, to go down to Keilah to besiege David and his men.

9 When David learned that Saul was plotting against him, he said to Abiathar[n] the priest, "Bring the ephod." 10 David said, "LORD, God of Israel, your servant has heard definitely that Saul plans to come to Keilah and destroy the town on account of me. 11 Will the citizens of Keilah surrender me to him? Will Saul come down, as your servant has heard? LORD, God of Israel, tell your servant."

And the LORD said, "He will."

12 Again David asked, "Will the citizens of Keilah surrender[o] me and my men to Saul?"

And the LORD said, "They will."

13 So David and his men,[p] about six hundred in number, left Keilah and kept mov-

---

22:18 *Doeg.* Only Doeg, who was a descendant of Esau, but not an Israelite, was willing to kill the priests of the living God.

22:22 *I am responsible for the death.* David felt responsible for the death of the priests and their families because he knew that he was jeopardizing them by receiving help from them. He knew Doeg would betray him, and he felt that he should have done something to prevent this or to warn the priests.

22:7 [t] 1Sa 8:14 **22:8** [u] 1Sa 18:3; 20:16 [v] 1Sa 23:21 **22:9** [w] 1Sa 21:7; Ps 52 Title [x] 1Sa 21:1 **22:10** [y] Nu 27:21; 1Sa 10:22 [z] 1Sa 21:6 **22:13** [a] ver 8 **22:14** [b] 1Sa 19:4 **22:17** [c] Ex 1:17 **22:18** [d] 1Sa 2:18, 31 **22:19** [e] 1Sa 15:3 **22:20** [f] 1Sa 23:6, 9; 30:7; 1Ki 2:22, 26, 27 [g] 1Sa 2:32 **22:22** [h] 1Sa 21:7 **22:23** [i] 1Ki 2:26 **23:1** [j] Jos 15:44 **23:2** [k] ver 4, 12; 1Sa 30:8; 2Sa 5:19, 23 **23:4** [l] Jos 8:7; Jdg 7:7 **23:6** [m] 1Sa 22:20 **23:9** [n] ver 6; 1Sa 22:20; 30:7 **23:12** [o] ver 20 **23:13** [p] 1Sa 22:2; 25:13

ing from place to place. When Saul was told that David had escaped from Keilah, he did not go there.

14 David stayed in the wilderness strongholds and in the hills of the Desert of Ziph.[q] Day after day Saul searched[r] for him, but God did not[s] give David into his hands.

15 While David was at Horesh in the Desert of Ziph, he learned that[a] Saul had come out to take his life. 16 And Saul's son Jonathan went to David at Horesh and helped him find strength[t] in God. 17 "Don't be afraid," he said. "My father Saul will not lay a hand on you. You will be king[u] over Israel, and I will be second to you. Even my father Saul knows this." 18 The two of them made a covenant[v] before the LORD. Then Jonathan went home, but David remained at Horesh.

19 The Ziphites[w] went up to Saul at Gibeah and said, "Is not David hiding among us[x] in the strongholds at Horesh, on the hill of Hakilah,[y] south of Jeshimon? 20 Now, Your Majesty, come down whenever it pleases you to do so, and we will be responsible for giving[z] him into your hands."

21 Saul replied, "The LORD bless you for your concern[a] for me. 22 Go and get more information. Find out where David usually goes and who has seen him there. They tell me he is very crafty. 23 Find out about all the hiding places he uses and come back to me with definite information. Then I will go with you; if he is in the area, I will track him down among all the clans of Judah."

24 So they set out and went to Ziph ahead of Saul. Now David and his men were in the Desert of Maon,[b] in the Arabah south of Jeshimon. 25 Saul and his men began the search, and when David was told about it, he went down to the rock and stayed in the Desert of Maon. When Saul heard this, he went into the Desert of Maon in pursuit of David.

26 Saul[c] was going along one side of the mountain, and David and his men were on the other side, hurrying to get away from Saul. As Saul and his forces were closing in on David and his men to capture them, 27 a messenger came to Saul, saying, "Come quickly! The Philistines are raiding the land." 28 Then Saul broke off his pursuit of David and went to meet the Philistines. That is why they call this place Sela Hammahlekoth.[b] 29 And David went up from there and lived in the strongholds of En Gedi.[cd]

David Spares Saul's Life

24 [d] After Saul returned from pursuing the Philistines, he was told, "David is in the Desert of En Gedi.[e]" 2 So Saul took three thousand able young men from all Israel and set out to look[f] for David and his men near the Crags of the Wild Goats.

3 He came to the sheep pens along the way; a cave[g] was there, and Saul went in to relieve[h] himself. David and his men were far back in the cave. 4 The men said, "This is the day the LORD spoke[i] of when he said[e] to you, 'I will give your enemy into your hands for you to deal with as you wish.'"[j] Then David crept up unnoticed and cut off a corner of Saul's robe.

5 Afterward, David was conscience-stricken[k] for having cut off a corner of his robe. 6 He said to his men, "The LORD forbid that I should do such a thing to my master, the LORD's anointed,[l] or lay my hand on him; for he is the anointed of the LORD." 7 With these words David sharply rebuked his men and did not allow them to attack Saul. And Saul left the cave and went his way.

---

[a] 15 Or *he was afraid because* [b] 28 *Sela Hammahlekoth* means *rock of parting.* [c] 29 In Hebrew texts this verse (23:29) is numbered 24:1. [d] In Hebrew texts 24:1-22 is numbered 24:2-23. [e] 4 Or *"Today the LORD is saying*

23:14 *Desert of Ziph.* This barren region about four miles southeast of Hebron had many caves and ravines in which David and his men could hide.

23:16–18 *strength in God.* Visiting David was risky, for Saul considered David his enemy. Jonathan was treading a narrow line between following his own convictions and obeying his father. He had a fervent love for God, and encouraged David to continue in his obedient walk with the Lord at a time when David must have been feeling very discouraged and alone.

23:17–18 Love—Love "rejoices with the truth" (1 Cor. 13:6). Jonathan had the happy faculty of delighting in the Lord's plan. He is never seen comparing his role with David's role, but he continually encouraged David to live up to the great responsibility that God had given him. Jonathan was the kind of friend that we all need and seldom find. If we want to put love into action, we can look at Jonathan and rejoice with our friends over the great favor God has shown them, encourage them to remain faithful to their calling, and remind them that we will be "next to them," if not in fact, then in prayer.

23:19 *Jeshimon.* Jeshimon is the barren wilderness of Judah.

23:19–29 *Is not David hiding among us.* The background for Psalm 54 is David's narrow escape from being captured by Saul.

24:3 *sheep pens.* At night shepherds in the wild area would gather their sheep into a protective rock enclosure. A low stone wall would keep the sheep from wandering, and the shepherd would position himself at the entrance to keep guard. Often a cave with a wall built across its mouth served as a sheep pen.

23:14 [q] Jos 15:24,55 [r] Ps 54:3-4 [s] Ps 32:7 **23:16** [t] 1Sa 30:6 **23:17** [u] 1Sa 20:31; 24:20 **23:18** [v] 1Sa 18:3; 20:16,42; 2Sa 9:1; 21:7 **23:19** [w] 1Sa 26:1 [x] Ps 54 Title [y] 1Sa 26:3 **23:20** [z] ver 12 **23:21** [a] 1Sa 22:8 **23:24** [b] Jos 15:55; 1Sa 25:2 **23:26** [c] Ps 17:9 **23:29** [d] 2Ch 20:2 **24:1** [e] 1Sa 23:28-29 **24:2** [f] 1Sa 26:2 **24:3** [g] Ps 57 Title; 142 Title [h] Jdg 3:24 **24:4** [i] 1Sa 25:28-30 [j] 1Sa 23:17; 26:8 **24:5** [k] 2Sa 24:10 **24:6** [l] 1Sa 26:11

8Then David went out of the cave and called out to Saul, "My lord the king!" When Saul looked behind him, David bowed down and prostrated himself with his face to the ground.[m] 9He said to Saul, "Why do you listen when men say, 'David is bent on harming you'? 10This day you have seen with your own eyes how the LORD delivered you into my hands in the cave. Some urged me to kill you, but I spared you; I said, 'I will not lay my hand on my lord, because he is the LORD's anointed.' 11See, my father, look at this piece of your robe in my hand! I cut off the corner of your robe but did not kill you. See that there is nothing in my hand to indicate that I am guilty[n] of wrongdoing or rebellion. I have not wronged you, but you are hunting[o] me down to take my life. 12May the LORD judge[p] between you and me. And may the LORD avenge[q] the wrongs you have done to me, but my hand will not touch you. 13As the old saying goes, 'From evildoers come evil deeds,[r]' so my hand will not touch you.

14"Against whom has the king of Israel come out? Who are you pursuing? A dead dog?[s] A flea?[t] 15May the LORD be our judge[u] and decide between us. May he consider my cause and uphold[v] it; may he vindicate[w] me by delivering[x] me from your hand."

16When David finished saying this, Saul asked, "Is that your voice,[y] David my son?" And he wept aloud. 17"You are more righteous than I,"[z] he said. "You have treated me well,[a] but I have treated you badly. 18You have just now told me about the good you did to me; the LORD delivered[b] me into your hands, but you did not kill me. 19When a man finds his enemy, does he let him get away unharmed? May the LORD reward you well for the way you treated me today. 20I know that you will surely be king[c] and that the kingdom[d] of Israel will be established in your hands. 21Now swear[e] to me by the LORD that you will not kill off my descendants or wipe out my name from my father's family.[f]"

22So David gave his oath to Saul. Then Saul returned home, but David and his men went up to the stronghold.[g]

David, Nabal and Abigail

25 Now Samuel died,[h] and all Israel assembled and mourned[i] for him; and they buried him at his home in Ramah.[j] Then David moved down into the Desert of Paran.[a]

2A certain man in Maon,[k] who had property there at Carmel, was very wealthy. He had a thousand goats and three thousand sheep, which he was shearing in Carmel. 3His name was Nabal and his wife's name was Abigail.[l] She was an intelligent and beautiful woman, but her husband was surly and mean in his dealings—he was a Calebite.[m]

4While David was in the wilderness, he heard that Nabal was shearing sheep. 5So he sent ten young men and said to them, "Go up to Nabal at Carmel and greet him in my name. 6Say to him: 'Long life to you! Good health[n] to you and your household! And good health to all that is yours![o]

7" 'Now I hear that it is sheep-shearing time. When your shepherds were with us, we did not mistreat[p] them, and the whole time they were at Carmel nothing of theirs was missing. 8Ask your own servants and they will tell you. Therefore be favorable toward my men, since we come at a festive time. Please give your servants and your son David whatever[q] you can find for them.' "

9When David's men arrived, they gave Nabal this message in David's name. Then they waited.

10Nabal answered David's servants, "Who[r] is this David? Who is this son of Jesse? Many servants are breaking away from their masters these days. 11Why should I take my bread[s] and water, and the meat I

---

[a] *1* Hebrew and some Septuagint manuscripts; other Septuagint manuscripts *Maon*

24:10–12 Mercy—David does not say the words, "I forgive you," in this passage, but he speaks as one who has forgiven Saul for his foolish and violent acts against himself. A big part of forgiving an unrepentant individual is deliberately putting the whole situation in God's hands, knowing that it is only God who can judge rightly. God will vindicate the innocent, and punish the guilty, if necessary.

24:12 *my hand will not touch you.* David knew that the Lord had anointed him to be the king to succeed Saul, and Saul knew it too. Saul, probably thinking of how he himself would have responded, was sure that David would seize power and oust him with trickery and violence. David had to prove to Saul that he was not going to harm him, and the only way to do this was to turn down every opportunity he had to kill the king. It was God's job, and His alone, to arrange the transfer of power from Saul to David.

24:22 *David gave his oath to Saul.* David agreed to Saul's requests, and he kept his promise (2 Sam. 9:1–13; 21:1–14), as Saul knew he would. However, David had no great confidence in the lasting value of Saul's expressions of remorse, so David remained in hiding.

25:2 *Maon.* Located in the Judean hill country, Maon was about eight miles south of Hebron. ***Carmel.*** Carmel was located on the edge of the Judean wilderness, about a mile north of Maon. he was ***shearing.*** Like the times of harvest, sheep shearing was a festive occasion.

24:8 [m] 1Sa 25:23-24 **24:11** [n] Ps 7:3 [o] 1Sa 23:14, 23; 26:20 **24:12** [p] Ge 16:5; 31:53; Job 5:8 [q] Jdg 11:27; 1Sa 26:10 **24:13** [r] Mt 7:20 **24:14** [s] 1Sa 17:43; 2Sa 9:8 [t] 1Sa 26:20 **24:15** [u] ver 12 [v] Ps 35:1, 23; Mic 7:9 [w] Ps 43:1 [x] Ps 119:134, 154 **24:16** [y] 1Sa 26:17 **24:17** [z] Ge 38:26; 1Sa 26:21 [a] Mt 5:44 **24:18** [b] 1Sa 26:23 **24:20** [c] 1Sa 23:17 [d] 1Sa 13:14 **24:21** [e] Ge 21:23; 2Sa 21:1-9 [f] 1Sa 20:14-15 **24:22** [g] 1Sa 23:29 **25:1** [h] 1Sa 28:3 [i] Nu 20:29; Dt 34:8 [j] Ge 21:21; 2Ch 33:20 **25:2** [k] Jos 15:55; 1Sa 23:24 **25:3** [l] Pr 31:10 [m] Jos 15:13 **25:6** [n] Ps 122:7; Lk 10:5 [o] 1Ch 12:18 **25:7** [p] ver 15 **25:8** [q] Ne 8:10 **25:10** [r] Jdg 9:28 **25:11** [s] Jdg 8:6

have slaughtered for my shearers, and give
it to men coming from who knows where?"
12 David's men turned around and went
back. When they arrived, they reported every word. 13 David said to his men, "Each of
you strap on your sword!" So they did, and
David strapped his on as well. About four
hundred men went[t] up with David, while
two hundred stayed with the supplies.[u]
14 One of the servants told Abigail, Nabal's wife, "David sent messengers from
the wilderness to give our master his greetings,[v] but he hurled insults at them. 15 Yet
these men were very good to us. They did
not mistreat[w] us, and the whole time we
were out in the fields near them nothing
was missing.[x] 16 Night and day they were
a wall[y] around us the whole time we were
herding our sheep near them. 17 Now think
it over and see what you can do, because
disaster is hanging over our master and his
whole household. He is such a wicked[z] man
that no one can talk to him."
18 Abigail acted quickly. She took two
hundred loaves of bread, two skins of wine,
five dressed sheep, five seahs[*a*] of roasted
grain, a hundred cakes of raisins[a] and two
hundred cakes of pressed figs, and loaded
them on donkeys.[b] 19 Then she told her servants, "Go on ahead;[c] I'll follow you." But
she did not tell her husband Nabal.
20 As she came riding her donkey into a
mountain ravine, there were David and his
men descending toward her, and she met
them. 21 David had just said, "It's been useless—all my watching over this fellow's
property in the wilderness so that nothing
of his was missing. He has paid[d] me back
evil for good. 22 May God deal with David,[*b*]
be it ever so severely,[e] if by morning I leave
alive one male[f] of all who belong to him!"
23 When Abigail saw David, she quickly
got off her donkey and bowed down before
David with her face to the ground.[g] 24 She
fell at his feet and said: "Pardon your servant, my lord, and let me speak to you; hear
what your servant has to say. 25 Please pay
no attention, my lord, to that wicked man
Nabal. He is just like his name—his name
means Fool,[h] and folly goes with him. And
as for me, your servant, I did not see the
men my lord sent. 26 And now, my lord, as
surely as the LORD your God lives and as
you live, since the LORD has kept you from
bloodshed[i] and from avenging[j] yourself
with your own hands, may your enemies
and all who are intent on harming my lord
be like Nabal.[k] 27 And let this gift,[l] which
your servant has brought to my lord, be
given to the men who follow you.
28 "Please forgive[m] your servant's presumption. The LORD your God will certainly make a lasting[n] dynasty for my lord, because you fight the LORD's battles,[o] and no
wrongdoing[p] will be found in you as long
as you live. 29 Even though someone is pursuing you to take your life, the life of my
lord will be bound securely in the bundle
of the living by the LORD your God, but the
lives of your enemies he will hurl[q] away
as from the pocket of a sling. 30 When the
LORD has fulfilled for my lord every good
thing he promised concerning him and has
appointed him ruler[r] over Israel, 31 my lord
will not have on his conscience the staggering burden of needless bloodshed or
of having avenged himself. And when the
LORD your God has brought my lord success, remember[s] your servant."
32 David said to Abigail, "Praise[t] be to the
LORD, the God of Israel, who has sent you
today to meet me. 33 May you be blessed for
your good judgment and for keeping me
from bloodshed[u] this day and from avenging myself with my own hands. 34 Otherwise, as surely as the LORD, the God of Israel, lives, who has kept me from harming
you, if you had not come quickly to meet
me, not one male belonging to Nabal would
have been left alive by daybreak."

---

a 18 That is, probably about 60 pounds or about 27 kilograms   *b* 22 Some Septuagint manuscripts; Hebrew *with David's enemies*

25:21 ***paid me back evil for good.*** Saul had returned David evil for good, and David refrained from retaliation. But Nabal's insult did not meet with such forbearance. David's fierce response is actually a response of the natural man, and as such gives an even better understanding of the force of David's commitment to restrain his natural response to Saul for the sake of his Lord.

25:29 ***bound securely in the bundle of the living by the LORD your God.*** This metaphor reflects the custom of binding valuables in a bundle to protect them from injury. The point here is that God cares for His own as a man cares for his valuable treasure.

25:30–31 Prudence—Abigail's courageous and gracious intervention saved not only her own household, but all that David had worked so hard to maintain during the years he was a fugitive. It takes more strength of character to restrain oneself than to lash out and return sting for sting. But the bitterness of grief that follows a vicious tongue or a vicious deed is a far heavier burden than suffering an injustice.

25:33 ***be blessed for your good judgment and for keeping me.*** David responds to the wisdom of Abigail's entreaty, and he also shows that he knows she came to him without regard to personal risk. Abigail laid out the facts and David responded to her godly counsel because he was accustomed to listening to the Lord, and recognized that she was representing God's point of view.

25:13 [t] 1Sa 23:13 [u] 1Sa 30:24 **25:14** [v] 1Sa 13:10 **25:15** [w] ver 7 [x] ver 21 **25:16** [y] Ex 14:22; Job 1:10 **25:17** [z] 1Sa 20:7 **25:18** [a] 1Ch 12:40 [b] 2Sa 16:1 **25:19** [c] Ge 32:20 **25:21** [d] Ps 109:5 **25:22** [e] 1Sa 3:17; 20:13 [f] 1Ki 14:10; 21:21; 2Ki 9:8 **25:23** [g] 1Sa 20:41 **25:25** [h] Pr 14:16 **25:26** [i] ver 33 [j] Heb 10:30 [k] 2Sa 18:32 **25:27** [l] Ge 33:11, 1Sa 30:26 **25:28** [m] ver 24 [n] 2Sa 7:11, 26 [o] 1Sa 18:17 [p] 1Sa 24:11 **25:29** [q] Jer 10:18 **25:30** [r] 1Sa 13:14 **25:31** [s] Ge 40:14 **25:32** [t] Ge 24:27; Ex 18:10; Lk 1:68 **25:33** [u] ver 26

35Then David accepted from her hand
what she had brought him and said, "Go
home in peace. I have heard your words
and granted[v] your request."
36When Abigail went to Nabal, he was
in the house holding a banquet like that of
a king. He was in high[w] spirits and very
drunk.[x] So she told[y] him nothing at all until daybreak. 37Then in the morning, when
Nabal was sober, his wife told him all these
things, and his heart failed him and he became like a stone. 38About ten days later,
the LORD struck[z] Nabal and he died.
39When David heard that Nabal was
dead, he said, "Praise be to the LORD, who
has upheld my cause against Nabal for
treating me with contempt. He has kept
his servant from doing wrong and has
brought Nabal's wrongdoing down on his
own head."
Then David sent word to Abigail, asking
her to become his wife. 40His servants went
to Carmel and said to Abigail, "David has
sent us to you to take you to become his wife."
41She bowed down with her face to the
ground and said, "I am your servant and
am ready to serve you and wash the feet of
my lord's servants." 42Abigail[a] quickly got
on a donkey and, attended by her five female servants, went with David's messengers and became his wife. 43David had also
married Ahinoam[b] of Jezreel, and they
both were his wives.[c] 44But Saul had given
his daughter Michal, David's wife, to Paltiel[ad] son of Laish, who was from Gallim.[e]

David Again Spares Saul's Life

26 The Ziphites[f] went to Saul at Gibeah
and said, "Is not David hiding[g] on the
hill of Hakilah, which faces Jeshimon?"
2So Saul went down to the Desert of
Ziph, with his three thousand select Israelite troops, to search[h] there for David. 3Saul
made his camp beside the road on the hill of
Hakilah facing Jeshimon, but David stayed
in the wilderness. When he saw that Saul
had followed him there, 4he sent out scouts
and learned that Saul had definitely arrived.
5Then David set out and went to the
place where Saul had camped. He saw
where Saul and Abner[i] son of Ner, the commander of the army, had lain down. Saul
was lying inside the camp, with the army
encamped around him.
6David then asked Ahimelek the Hittite
and Abishai son of Zeruiah,[j] Joab's brother, "Who will go down into the camp with
me to Saul?"
"I'll go with you," said Abishai.
7So David and Abishai went to the army
by night, and there was Saul, lying asleep
inside the camp with his spear stuck in the
ground near his head. Abner and the soldiers were lying around him.
8Abishai said to David, "Today God has
delivered your enemy into your hands. Now
let me pin him to the ground with one thrust
of the spear; I won't strike him twice."
9But David said to Abishai, "Don't destroy him! Who can lay a hand on the
LORD's anointed[k] and be guiltless?[l] 10As
surely as the LORD lives," he said, "the LORD
himself will strike[m] him, or his time[n] will
come and he will die,[o] or he will go into battle and perish. 11But the LORD forbid that I
should lay a hand on the LORD's anointed.
Now get the spear and water jug that are
near his head, and let's go."
12So David took the spear and water jug
near Saul's head, and they left. No one saw
or knew about it, nor did anyone wake up.
They were all sleeping, because the LORD
had put them into a deep sleep.[p]
13Then David crossed over to the other side and stood on top of the hill some
distance away; there was a wide space between them. 14He called out to the army
and to Abner son of Ner, "Aren't you going
to answer me, Abner?"
Abner replied, "Who are you who calls
to the king?"
15David said, "You're a man, aren't you?
And who is like you in Israel? Why didn't
you guard your lord the king? Someone
came to destroy your lord the king. 16What
you have done is not good. As surely as the
LORD lives, you and your men must die, because you did not guard your master, the

---

a 44 Hebrew *Palti,* a variant of *Paltiel*

25:39 ***the LORD . . . has brought Nabal's wrongdoing down on his own head.*** David was very thankful that the Lord had kept him from taking revenge on Nabal, for that would have been evil. But David was also thankful that the Lord, in His justice, had seen fit to punish Nabal. For David this would have been a reminder of his situation with Saul. David was not to touch the Lord's anointed, and the Lord would indeed at some point deal with Saul for trying to take David's life.

26:2 ***Ziph.*** Ziph was four miles southeast of Hebron, which would have been about 4 or 5 miles from Maon, where Nabal lived.

26:6 ***Abishai.*** Abishai was David's nephew (1 Chr. 2:16).

26:10 ***the LORD himself will strike him, or . . . he will die.*** David had just been reminded that the Lord could and would deal with his enemies, which strengthened him for his next encounter with Saul. David had not trusted in the value of Saul's expressions of remorse, but it must have been discouraging even so, to be faced with the same relentless pursuit, the same dogged determination to kill him, even though David repeatedly said he would not stretch out his hand against Saul, the king who had been anointed by God.

25:35 [v] Ge 19:21; 1Sa 20:42; 2Ki 5:19 **25:36** [w] 2Sa 13:23 [x] Pr 20:1; Isa 5:11,22; Hos 4:11 [y] ver 19 **25:38** [z] 1Sa 26:10; 2Sa 6:7 **25:42** [a] Ge 24:61-67 **25:43** [b] Jos 15:56 [c] 1Sa 27:3; 30:5 **25:44** [d] 2Sa 3:15 [e] Isa 10:30 **26:1** [f] 1Sa 23:19 [g] Ps 54 Title **26:2** [h] 1Sa 13:2; 24:2 **26:5** [i] 1Sa 14:50; 17:55 **26:6** [j] Jdg 7:10-11; 1Ch 2:16 **26:9** [k] 2Sa 1:14 [l] 1Sa 24:5 **26:10** [m] 1Sa 25:38; Ro 12:19 [n] Ge 47:29; Dt 31:14; Ps 37:13 [o] 1Sa 31:6; 2Sa 1:1 **26:12** [p] Ge 2:21; 15:12

LORD's anointed. Look around you. Where
are the king's spear and water jug that
were near his head?"
17 Saul recognized David's voice and
said, "Is that your voice,[q] David my son?"
David replied, "Yes it is, my lord the king."
18 And he added, "Why is my lord pursuing
his servant? What have I done, and what
wrong[r] am I guilty of? 19 Now let my lord
the king listen to his servant's words. If the
LORD has incited you against me, then may
he accept an offering.[s] If, however, people
have done it, may they be cursed before the
LORD! They have driven me today from my
share in the LORD's inheritance[t] and have
said, 'Go, serve other gods.' 20 Now do not
let my blood fall to the ground far from the
presence of the LORD. The king of Israel has
come out to look for a flea[u]—as one hunts a
partridge in the mountains."
21 Then Saul said, "I have sinned.[v] Come
back, David my son. Because you considered my life precious[w] today, I will not try
to harm you again. Surely I have acted like
a fool and have been terribly wrong."
22 "Here is the king's spear," David answered. "Let one of your young men come
over and get it. 23 The LORD rewards[x] everyone for their righteousness[y] and faithfulness. The LORD delivered you into my
hands today, but I would not lay a hand on
the LORD's anointed. 24 As surely as I valued
your life today, so may the LORD value my
life and deliver[z] me from all trouble."
25 Then Saul said to David, "May you be
blessed, David my son; you will do great
things and surely triumph."
So David went on his way, and Saul returned home.

David Among the Philistines

27 But David thought to himself, "One
of these days I will be destroyed by
the hand of Saul. The best thing I can do
is to escape to the land of the Philistines.
Then Saul will give up searching for me
anywhere in Israel, and I will slip out of
his hand."
2 So David and the six hundred men[a] with
him left and went[b] over to Achish[c] son of
Maok king of Gath. 3 David and his men
settled in Gath with Achish. Each man had
his family with him, and David had his two
wives:[d] Ahinoam of Jezreel and Abigail of
Carmel, the widow of Nabal. 4 When Saul
was told that David had fled to Gath, he no
longer searched for him.
5 Then David said to Achish, "If I have
found favor in your eyes, let a place be assigned to me in one of the country towns,
that I may live there. Why should your servant live in the royal city with you?"
6 So on that day Achish gave him Ziklag,[e]
and it has belonged to the kings of Judah
ever since. 7 David lived[f] in Philistine territory a year and four months.
8 Now David and his men went up and
raided the Geshurites,[g] the Girzites and
the Amalekites.[h] (From ancient times
these peoples had lived in the land extending to Shur[i] and Egypt.) 9 Whenever David
attacked an area, he did not leave a man
or woman alive,[j] but took sheep and cattle,
donkeys and camels, and clothes. Then he
returned to Achish.
10 When Achish asked, "Where did
you go raiding today?" David would say,
"Against the Negev of Judah" or "Against
the Negev of Jerahmeel[k]" or "Against the
Negev of the Kenites.[l]" 11 He did not leave a
man or woman alive to be brought to Gath,
for he thought, "They might inform on us
and say, 'This is what David did.'" And
such was his practice as long as he lived in
Philistine territory. 12 Achish trusted David
and said to himself, "He has become so obnoxious to his people, the Israelites, that he
will be my servant for life."

26:19 ***If the LORD has incited you.*** David knew that God could bring adverse events into someone's life to turn him to the Lord. If Saul was pursuing David because God wanted him to, God would accept a sin offering from David. But if men had stirred up Saul to kill David, that would be wicked injustice. In that case, David had no hesitation in asking God to curse them. For in driving David out of his homeland, he was effectively cut off from the inheritance of the Lord, which would include the land, the blessings on the land and people, and the special ways God had ordained for worship and sacrifice.

26:20 ***partridge.*** A partridge was known to flee for safety by running rather than fighting. David was reminding Saul that he was not fighting against the king.

26:23 Righteousness—One mark of a righteous person is that he can walk away from a situation where he has a golden chance to get in the last kick. And as he walks away, he says, "Father, forgive him, for he does not know what he is doing." David never lost sight of the fact that this business of being king was God's plan, not his own.

27:5 ***let a place be assigned to me.*** David was probably wanting more independence of movement in his own city and freedom from daily involvement with Achish's household and religious practices. This request was also a good way to find out how much Achish trusted him. If Achish was willing for David to live independently, he was not likely to be treating David as a spy or enemy.

27:10 ***the Negev of Judah.*** The Negev was a dry pastoral region, south of Hebron.

27:12 ***he will be my servant for life.*** It seems that David was double dealing with Achish in a way that was dishonest, and indeed he was. But Achish was not David's friend. He was the sworn enemy of

26:17 [q] 1Sa 24:16 **26:18** [r] 1Sa 24:9, 11-14
26:19 [s] 2Sa 16:11 [t] 2Sa 14:16 **26:20** [u] 1Sa 24:14
26:21 [v] Ex 9:27; 1Sa 15:24 [w] 1Sa 24:17 **26:23** [x] Ps 62:12
[y] Ps 7:8; 18:20, 24 **26:24** [z] Ps 54:7 **27:2** [a] 1Sa 25:13
[b] 1Sa 21:10 [c] 1Ki 2:39 **27:3** [d] 1Sa 25:43; 30:3
27:6 [e] Jos 15:31; 19:5; Ne 11:28 **27:7** [f] 1Sa 29:3
27:8 [g] Jos 13:2, 13 [h] Ex 17:8; 1Sa 15:7-8 [i] Ex 15:22
27:9 [j] 1Sa 15:3 **27:10** [k] 1Sa 30:29; 1Ch 2:9, 25 [l] Jdg 1:16

28 In those days the Philistines gathered[m] their forces to fight against
Israel. Achish said to David, "You must
understand that you and your men will accompany me in the army."
2David said, "Then you will see for yourself what your servant can do."
Achish replied, "Very well, I will make
you my bodyguard for life."

Saul and the Medium at Endor

3Now Samuel was dead,[n] and all Israel
had mourned for him and buried him in his
own town of Ramah.[o] Saul had expelled
the mediums and spiritists[p] from the land.
4The Philistines assembled and came
and set up camp at Shunem,[q] while Saul
gathered all Israel and set up camp at Gilboa.[r] 5When Saul saw the Philistine army,
he was afraid; terror filled his heart. 6He
inquired[s] of the LORD, but the LORD did not
answer him by dreams[t] or Urim[u] or prophets. 7Saul then said to his attendants, "Find
me a woman who is a medium,[v] so I may go
and inquire of her."
"There is one in Endor,[w]" they said.
8So Saul disguised[x] himself, putting on other clothes, and at night he and two men went
to the woman. "Consult[y] a spirit for me," he
said, "and bring up for me the one I name."
9But the woman said to him, "Surely you
know what Saul has done. He has cut off[z]
the mediums and spiritists from the land.
Why have you set a trap for my life to bring
about my death?"
10Saul swore to her by the LORD, "As
surely as the LORD lives, you will not be
punished for this."
11Then the woman asked, "Whom shall I
bring up for you?"
"Bring up Samuel," he said.
12When the woman saw Samuel, she
cried out at the top of her voice and said
to Saul, "Why have you deceived me? You
are Saul!"
13The king said to her, "Don't be afraid.
What do you see?"
The woman said, "I see a ghostly figure[a]
coming up out of the earth."
14"What does he look like?" he asked.
"An old man wearing a robe[a] is coming
up," she said.
Then Saul knew it was Samuel, and he
bowed down and prostrated himself with
his face to the ground.
15Samuel said to Saul, "Why have you
disturbed me by bringing me up?"
"I am in great distress," Saul said. "The
Philistines are fighting against me, and
God has departed[b] from me. He no lon-

---

a *13* Or *see spirits;* or *see gods*

David's people and all that David held dear. Achish intended to use David's military expertise for his own ends. This account does not say what God, whose very character is truth, thought about David's strategy. It is clear that God continued to protect and bless David during this very vulnerable time, and the raiding that David had done was continuing the commission the Lord had given the Israelites when they first came into the land.

28:2 ***you will see for yourself what your servant can do.*** In this case, David is purposely ambiguous. He states that his prowess is well known, without saying that he commits this skill to Achish. David could not refuse Achish's offer without risking his life. He trusted the Lord to rescue him from this compromising situation.

28:3 ***Samuel was dead.*** No one could go to Samuel for advice or direction from the Lord. ***mediums and spiritists.*** The term *mediums* refers to necromancers, those who presume to communicate with the dead. *Spiritist* is a general term for those who have contact with spirits. In keeping with God's law, persons associated with necromancy and spiritism had been expelled from the land (Ex. 22:18; Lev. 19:31; Deut. 18:9–14).

28:6 ***He inquired of the LORD.*** It sounds as if Saul was desperate to hear from the Lord. But he had never said, "Whatever You want, Lord, I will do it." Saul knew that he had been rejected by God as king, and if he wanted to repent, Saul could have admitted to God that he was not fit to be king, and asked God to turn the kingdom over to the man of His choice. But Saul wanted to be king, and to hear from God, and have David ejected, and have the Philistines leave him alone, none of which was possible for a man who had decided to deliberately disobey the Lord.

28:7–11 Unfaithfulness—It started with disobeying God's directions about fighting with the Amalekites, and it ended with a medium. Saul apparently never saw himself as a rebel. He knew that the Lord had rejected him, but he thought that it was unjust. Rejecting God is the beginning of a downward spiral, and finally the man who had hounded the mediums from the land, was asking one for guidance because he had no hope of hearing from God.

28:10 ***Saul swore to her by the LORD.*** While engaging in a practice that was essentially a denial of God's control of everything, Saul swore in God's name that he would protect the woman.

28:12 ***When the woman saw Samuel.*** The appearance of Samuel has been interpreted in various ways. Some think that a demon impersonated Samuel, and others think that Saul was tricked into believing it was Samuel. It seems best to follow the early view that this was a genuine appearance of Samuel, which God Himself brought about. Several points favor this interpretation. The medium herself was surprised and frightened by his appearance. Saul identified the figure as Samuel. The message Samuel spoke was clearly from God. The text says the figure was Samuel. There is no inherent difficulty with God bringing back the spirit of Samuel from heaven and allowing him to appear to Saul—in spite of the woman's evil profession.

28:1 [m] 1Sa 29:1 **28:3** [n] 1Sa 25:1 [o] 1Sa 7:17 [p] Ex 22:18; Lev 19:31; 20:27; Dt 18:10-11; 1Sa 15:23 **28:4** [q] Jos 19:18; 2Ki 4:8 [r] 1Sa 31:1,3 **28:6** [s] 1Sa 14:37; 1Ch 10:13-14; Pr 1:28 [t] Nu 12:6 [u] Ex 28:30; Nu 27:21 **28:7** [v] Ac 16:16 [w] Jos 17:11 **28:8** [x] 2Ch 18:29; 35:22 [y] Dt 18:10-11; 1Ch 10:13; Isa 8:19 **28:9** [z] ver 3 **28:14** [a] 1Sa 15:27; 24:8 **28:15** [b] ver 6; 1Sa 18:12

ger answers me, either by prophets or by
dreams. So I have called on you to tell me
what to do."
16Samuel said, "Why do you consult me,
now that the LORD has departed from you
and become your enemy? 17The LORD has
done what he predicted through me. The
LORD has torn[c] the kingdom out of your
hands and given it to one of your neighbors—to David. 18Because you did not
obey[d] the LORD or carry out his fierce
wrath[e] against the Amalekites, the LORD
has done this to you today. 19The LORD will
deliver both Israel and you into the hands
of the Philistines, and tomorrow you and
your sons[f] will be with me. The LORD will
also give the army of Israel into the hands
of the Philistines."
20Immediately Saul fell full length on the
ground, filled with fear because of Samuel's
words. His strength was gone, for he had
eaten nothing all that day and all that night.
21When the woman came to Saul and
saw that he was greatly shaken, she said,
"Look, your servant has obeyed you. I took
my life[g] in my hands and did what you told
me to do. 22Now please listen to your servant and let me give you some food so you
may eat and have the strength to go on
your way."
23He refused[h] and said, "I will not eat."
But his men joined the woman in urging him, and he listened to them. He got
up from the ground and sat on the couch.
24The woman had a fattened calf at the
house, which she butchered at once. She
took some flour, kneaded it and baked
bread without yeast. 25Then she set it before Saul and his men, and they ate. That
same night they got up and left.

Achish Sends David Back to Ziklag

29 The Philistines gathered[i] all their
forces at Aphek,[j] and Israel camped
by the spring in Jezreel.[k] 2As the Philistine
rulers marched with their units of hundreds and thousands, David and his men
were marching at the rear[l] with Achish.
3The commanders of the Philistines asked,
"What about these Hebrews?"
Achish replied, "Is this not David, who
was an officer of Saul king of Israel? He
has already been with me for over a year,[m]
and from the day he left Saul until now, I
have found no fault in him."
4But the Philistine commanders were
angry with Achish and said, "Send[n] the
man back, that he may return to the place
you assigned him. He must not go with us
into battle, or he will turn[o] against us during the fighting. How better could he regain his master's favor than by taking the
heads of our own men? 5Isn't this the David
they sang about in their dances:

"'Saul has slain his thousands,
and David his tens of thousands'?"[p]

6So Achish called David and said to him,
"As surely as the LORD lives, you have been
reliable, and I would be pleased to have you
serve with me in the army. From the day[q]
you came to me until today, I have found no
fault in you, but the rulers[r] don't approve
of you. 7Now turn back and go in peace; do
nothing to displease the Philistine rulers."
8"But what have I done?" asked David.
"What have you found against your servant from the day I came to you until now?
Why can't I go and fight against the enemies of my lord the king?"
9Achish answered, "I know that you
have been as pleasing in my eyes as an
angel[s] of God; nevertheless, the Philistine
commanders[t] have said, 'He must not go
up with us into battle.' 10Now get up early, along with your master's servants who
have come with you, and leave[u] in the
morning as soon as it is light."
11So David and his men got up early in
the morning to go back to the land of the
Philistines, and the Philistines went up to
Jezreel.

David Destroys the Amalekites

30 David and his men reached Ziklag[v]
on the third day. Now the Amalekites[w] had raided the Negev and Ziklag.
They had attacked Ziklag and burned it,
2and had taken captive the women and

28:19 ***with me.*** The words "with me" refer to the grave. This text is not intended to provide a final answer concerning Saul's spiritual status. At the very least, it does indicate the reality of life after death.

29:6 ***you have been reliable.*** David had not been honest with Achish, but he had not turned his hand against Achish personally.

29:7 ***turn back and go in peace.*** This was the God-orchestrated escape from a compromising situation that David was confident God would provide. ***go in peace.*** This farewell was more than a courtesy. Achish was releasing David from any further obligation that he had incurred when Achish had made David his vassal in Ziklag.

29:9–10 Prudence—Achish saw David as an angel of God. There must have been something in the way that David conducted himself that showed even a pagan Philistine that David belonged to the God of Israel, and that this was a good place to be. David was being very careful in how he dealt with the Philistine. He could not endanger the people who depended on him, nor be unfaithful to his Lord. Only God can help us when we have to live in such a difficult situation.

30:1 ***Amalekites.*** The Amalekites were a nomadic people who roamed the dry land south of the hill country. For their attack on the Israelites after the

28:17 [c] 1Sa 15:28 **28:18** [d] 1Sa 15:20 [e] 1Ki 20:42
28:19 [f] 1Sa 31:2 **28:21** [g] Jdg 12:3; 1Sa 19:5; Job 13:14
28:23 [h] 2Ki 5:13 **29:1** [i] 1Sa 28:1 [j] Jos 12:18; 1Sa 4:1
[k] 2Ki 9:30 **29:2** [l] 1Sa 28:2 **29:3** [m] 1Sa 27:7; Da 6:5
29:4 [n] 1Ch 12:19 [o] 1Sa 14:21 **29:5** [p] 1Sa 18:7; 21:11
29:6 [q] 1Sa 27:8-12 [r] ver 3 **29:9** [s] 2Sa 14:17, 20; 19:27
[t] ver 4 **29:10** [u] 1Ch 12:19 **30:1** [v] 1Sa 29:4, 11
[w] 1Sa 15:7; 27:8

everyone else in it, both young and old.
They killed none of them, but carried them
off as they went on their way.
3When David and his men reached Ziklag, they found it destroyed by fire and
their wives and sons and daughters tak-
en captive. 4So David and his men wept
aloud until they had no strength left to
weep. 5David's two wives[x] had been captured—Ahinoam of Jezreel and Abigail,
the widow of Nabal of Carmel. 6David was
greatly distressed because the men were
talking of stoning[y] him; each one was bitter in spirit because of his sons and daughters. But David found strength[z] in the LORD
his God.
7Then David said to Abiathar[a] the
priest, the son of Ahimelek, "Bring me
the ephod.[b]" Abiathar brought it to him,
8and David inquired[c] of the LORD, "Shall I
pursue this raiding party? Will I overtake
them?"
"Pursue them," he answered. "You will
certainly overtake them and succeed[d] in
the rescue."
9David and the six hundred men[e] with
him came to the Besor Valley, where some
stayed behind. 10Two hundred of them
were too exhausted[f] to cross the valley, but
David and the other four hundred continued the pursuit.
11They found an Egyptian in a field and
brought him to David. They gave him water to drink and food to eat— 12part of a
cake of pressed figs and two cakes of raisins. He ate and was revived,[g] for he had
not eaten any food or drunk any water for
three days and three nights.
13David asked him, "Who do you belong
to? Where do you come from?"
He said, "I am an Egyptian, the slave of
an Amalekite. My master abandoned me
when I became ill three days ago. 14We
raided the Negev of the Kerethites,[h] some
territory belonging to Judah and the Negev
of Caleb.[i] And we burned[j] Ziklag."
15David asked him, "Can you lead me
down to this raiding party?"
He answered, "Swear to me before God
that you will not kill me or hand me over
to my master, and I will take you down to
them."
16He led David down, and there they
were, scattered over the countryside, eating, drinking and reveling[k] because of the
great amount of plunder[l] they had taken
from the land of the Philistines and from
Judah. 17David fought[m] them from dusk
until the evening of the next day, and
none of them got away, except four hundred young men who rode off on camels
and fled.[n] 18David recovered[o] everything
the Amalekites had taken, including his
two wives. 19Nothing was missing: young
or old, boy or girl, plunder or anything else
they had taken. David brought everything
back. 20He took all the flocks and herds,
and his men drove them ahead of the other livestock, saying, "This is David's plunder."
21Then David came to the two hundred
men who had been too exhausted[p] to follow
him and who were left behind at the Besor
Valley. They came out to meet David and
the men with him. As David and his men
approached, he asked them how they were.
22But all the evil men and troublemakers
among David's followers said, "Because
they did not go out with us, we will not
share with them the plunder we recovered.
However, each man may take his wife and
children and go."
23David replied, "No, my brothers, you
must not do that with what the LORD has
given us. He has protected us and delivered
into our hands the raiding party that came
against us. 24Who will listen to what you
say? The share of the man who stayed with
the supplies is to be the same as that of him
who went down to the battle. All will share
alike.[q]" 25David made this a statute and ordinance for Israel from that day to this.
26When David reached Ziklag, he sent
some of the plunder to the elders of Judah,
who were his friends, saying, "Here is a gift
for you from the plunder of the LORD's enemies."
27David sent it to those who were in Bethel,[r] Ramoth[s] Negev and Jattir;[t] 28to those in
Aroer,[u] Siphmoth, Eshtemoa[v] 29and Rakal;
to those in the towns of the Jerahmeelites[w]
and the Kenites;[x] 30to those in Hormah,[y]
Bor Ashan,[z] Athak 31and Hebron;[a] and to
those in all the other places where he and
his men had roamed.

---

exodus from Egypt (Ex. 17:8–13), they were placed under divine judgment (Deut. 25:19).

30:7 ***ephod.*** The Urim and Thumim were attached to the ephod. The Lord could be consulted by the means of the Urim and Thummim, but the Bible does not say how this worked.

30:10 ***too exhausted.*** The weariness of David's men was due to the fact that they had traveled about 80 miles from Aphek to Ziklag (29:1; 30:1), only to set off immediately in pursuit of the Amalekites.

30:26 ***sent some of the plunder to the elders of Judah.*** This goodwill gesture helped David reestablish his relationships among the leaders of Judah after his stay in Philistine territory.

30:31 ***Hebron.*** Hebron was a Levitical city, and a city of refuge, and it was soon to become David's capital (2 Sam. 5:3).

30:5 [x] 1Sa 25:43; 2Sa 2:2 **30:6** [y] Ex 17:4; Jn 8:59 [z] Ps 27:14; 56:3-4, 11; Ro 4:20 **30:7** [a] 1Sa 22:20 [b] 1Sa 23:9 **30:8** [c] 1Sa 23:2 [d] ver 18 **30:9** [e] 1Sa 27:2 **30:10** [f] ver 9, 21 **30:12** [g] Jdg 15:19 **30:14** [h] 2Sa 8:18; 1Ki 1:38, 44; Eze 25:16; Zep 2:5 [i] ver 16; Jos 14:13; 15:13 [j] ver 1 **30:16** [k] Lk 12:19 [l] ver 14 **30:17** [m] 1Sa 11:11 [n] 1Sa 15:3 **30:18** [o] Ge 14:16 **30:21** [p] ver 10 **30:24** [q] Nu 31:27; Jos 22:8 **30:27** [r] Jos 7:2 [s] Jos 19:8 [t] Jos 15:48 **30:28** [u] Jos 13:16 [v] Jos 15:50 **30:29** [w] 1Sa 27:10 [x] Jdg 1:16; 1Sa 15:6 **30:30** [y] Nu 14:45; Jdg 1:17 [z] Jos 15:42 **30:31** [a] Jos 14:13; 2Sa 2:1, 4

Saul Takes His Life

31 Now the Philistines fought against
Israel; the Israelites fled before them,
and many fell dead on Mount Gilboa.[b] 2The
Philistines were in hot pursuit of Saul and
his sons, and they killed his sons Jonathan,
Abinadab and Malki-Shua. 3The fighting
grew fierce around Saul, and when the archers overtook him, they wounded[c] him
critically.

4Saul said to his armor-bearer, "Draw
your sword and run me through,[d] or these
uncircumcised[e] fellows will come and run
me through and abuse me."

But his armor-bearer was terrified and
would not do it; so Saul took his own sword
and fell on it. 5When the armor-bearer saw
that Saul was dead, he too fell on his sword
and died with him. 6So Saul and his three
sons and his armor-bearer and all his men
died together that same day.

7When the Israelites along the valley and
those across the Jordan saw that the Israelite army had fled and that Saul and his
sons had died, they abandoned their towns
and fled. And the Philistines came and occupied them.

8The next day, when the Philistines
came to strip the dead, they found Saul
and his three sons fallen on Mount Gilboa. 9They cut off his head and stripped
off his armor, and they sent messengers
throughout the land of the Philistines to
proclaim the news[f] in the temple of their
idols and among their people.[g] 10They put
his armor in the temple of the Ashtoreths[h]
and fastened his body to the wall of Beth
Shan.[i]

11When the people of Jabesh Gilead[j] heard what the Philistines had done
to Saul, 12all their valiant men marched
through the night to Beth Shan. They took
down the bodies of Saul and his sons from
the wall of Beth Shan and went to Jabesh,
where they burned[k] them. 13Then they took
their bones[l] and buried them under a tamarisk[m] tree at Jabesh, and they fasted[n] seven
days.[o]

31:2 *Saul and his sons.* Saul's fourth son, Ish-Bosheth, was apparently not present at this battle, since Abner promoted him to king after Saul's death (2 Sam. 2:8–10).

31:6 *all his men.* This does not refer to the whole army, but rather to men who were particularly associated with Saul, such as his royal body guards.

31:11 *people of Jabesh Gilead.* The inhabitants of this town had been delivered from the threats of Nahash the Ammonite by Saul in his first military campaign as king of Israel (11:1–11).

31:13 *and they fasted seven days.* In ancient Israel, fasting was a way of expressing sorrow in mourning. With their fasting, the men of Jabesh showed their respect for Israel's first king.

31:1 [b] 1Sa 28:4; 1Ch 10:1-12 **31:3** [c] 2Sa 1:6 **31:4** [d] Jdg 9:54; 2Sa 1:6, 10 [e] 1Sa 14:6 **31:9** [f] 2Sa 1:20 [g] Jdg 16:24 **31:10** [h] Jdg 2:12-13; 1Sa 7:3 [i] Jos 17:11; 2Sa 21:12 **31:11** [j] 1Sa 11:1 **31:12** [k] 2Sa 2:4-7; 2Ch 16:14; Am 6:10 **31:13** [l] 2Sa 21:12-14 [m] 1Sa 22:6 [n] 2Sa 1:12 [o] Ge 50:10

2 SAMUEL

▶ **AUTHOR:** No author is mentioned anywhere in this book. Although the traditional view is that Samuel wrote 2 Samuel, it was probably compiled by one man who combined the written chronicles of "Nathan the prophet" and "Gad the seer" (1 Chr. 29:29). In addition to these written sources, the compiler evidently used another source called the "Book of Jasher" (1:18).

▶ **TIME:** c. 1011 – 971 B.C. ▶ **KEY VERSES:** 2 Sam. 7:12 – 13

▶ **THEME:** Second Samuel begins with Saul's death and David's ascension to the throne of Judah. A few years later he becomes the king of all of Israel. During his reign there were many problems, most of which can be traced back to David's own behavior. He abuses power and plays favorites with his sons. The result is much personal sorrow and the seeds of discord that follow in succeeding generations. Second Samuel gives us a full picture of a king, a poet, a soldier, and a sinner who yearns after God's own heart and follows where He leads.

David Hears of Saul's Death

1 After the death[a] of Saul, David returned from striking down[b] the Amalekites and stayed in Ziklag two days. 2On
the third day a man[c] arrived from Saul's
camp with his clothes torn and dust on his
head.[d] When he came to David, he fell to
the ground to pay him honor.

3"Where have you come from?" David
asked him.

He answered, "I have escaped from the
Israelite camp."

4"What happened?" David asked.
"Tell me."

"The men fled from the battle," he replied. "Many of them fell and died. And
Saul and his son Jonathan are dead."

5Then David said to the young man who
brought him the report, "How do you know
that Saul and his son Jonathan are dead?"

6"I happened to be on Mount Gilboa,[e]"
the young man said, "and there was Saul,
leaning on his spear, with the chariots
and their drivers in hot pursuit. 7When he
turned around and saw me, he called out to
me, and I said, 'What can I do?'

8"He asked me, 'Who are you?'

"'An Amalekite,[f]' I answered.

9"Then he said to me, 'Stand here by me
and kill me! I'm in the throes of death, but
I'm still alive.'

10"So I stood beside him and killed him,
because I knew that after he had fallen he
could not survive. And I took the crown[g]
that was on his head and the band on his
arm and have brought them here to my
lord."

11Then David and all the men with him
took hold of their clothes and tore[h] them.
12They mourned and wept and fasted till
evening for Saul and his son Jonathan, and
for the army of the LORD and for the nation of Israel, because they had fallen by
the sword.

13David said to the young man who
brought him the report, "Where are you
from?"

"I am the son of a foreigner, an Amalekite,[i]" he answered.

14David asked him, "Why weren't you
afraid to lift your hand to destroy the
LORD's anointed?[j]"

1:2 *clothes torn and dust on his head.* Dust or ashes on the head, torn clothing, and sackcloth were all signs of mourning.

1:12 *fasted.* Spiritual fasting is abstaining from food to devote time and energy to prayer. Sometimes people plan a time of fasting, and sometimes it just comes upon them because overwhelming spiritual needs supersede all thought of food. This was a time of true calamity for Israel, even though it solved a problem for David. He was personally very grieved, for he had known the man Saul as he could have been, and he had lost Jonathan, the best friend he would ever have. His future as king seemed assured, but the task of uniting the nation would be very difficult.

1:14 *the LORD's anointed.* David's use of the phrase "the LORD's anointed" indicates that even though Saul was his enemy, David honored the position that Saul had as God's representative. David repeatedly refused to harm Saul because of this (1 Sam. 24:6; 26:9).

1:1 [a] 1Sa 31:6 [b] 1Sa 30:17 **1:2** [c] 2Sa 4:10 [d] 1Sa 4:12 **1:6** [e] 1Sa 28:4; 31:2-4 **1:8** [f] 1Sa 15:2; 30:13, 17 **1:10** [g] Jdg 9:54; 2Ki 11:12 **1:11** [h] Ge 37:29; 2Sa 3:31; 13:31 **1:13** [i] ver 8 **1:14** [j] 1Sa 24:6; 26:9

15Then David called one of his men and
said, "Go, strike him down!"[k] So he struck
him down, and he died.[l] 16For David had said
to him, "Your blood be on your own head.[m]
Your own mouth testified against you when
you said, 'I killed the LORD's anointed.'"

David's Lament for Saul and Jonathan

17David took up this lament[n] concerning
Saul and his son Jonathan, 18and he ordered that the people of Judah be taught
this lament of the bow (it is written in the
Book of Jashar):[o]

19"A gazelle[a] lies slain on your heights,
Israel.
How the mighty have fallen![p]

20"Tell it not in Gath,[q]
proclaim it not in the streets of
Ashkelon,
lest the daughters of the Philistines[r] be
glad,
lest the daughters of the
uncircumcised rejoice.[s]

21"Mountains of Gilboa,[t]
may you have neither dew nor rain,
may no showers fall on your terraced
fields.[b][u]
For there the shield of the mighty was
despised,
the shield of Saul—no longer rubbed
with oil.[v]

22"From the blood[w] of the slain,
from the flesh of the mighty,
the bow[x] of Jonathan did not turn back,
the sword of Saul did not return
unsatisfied.
23Saul and Jonathan—
in life they were loved and admired,
and in death they were not parted.
They were swifter than eagles,[y]
they were stronger than lions.[z]

24"Daughters of Israel,
weep for Saul,
who clothed you in scarlet and finery,
who adorned your garments with
ornaments of gold.

25"How the mighty have fallen in battle!
Jonathan lies slain on your heights.
26I grieve for you, Jonathan my brother;[a]
you were very dear to me.
Your love for me was wonderful,[b]
more wonderful than that of women.

27"How the mighty have fallen!
The weapons of war have perished!"[c]

David Anointed King Over Judah

2 In the course of time, David inquired[d]
of the LORD. "Shall I go up to one of the
towns of Judah?" he asked.
The LORD said, "Go up."
David asked, "Where shall I go?"
"To Hebron,"[e] the LORD answered.
2So David went up there with his two
wives,[f] Ahinoam of Jezreel and Abigail,[g]
the widow of Nabal of Carmel. 3David also
took the men who were with him,[h] each
with his family, and they settled in Hebron
and its towns. 4Then the men of Judah
came to Hebron,[i] and there they anointed[j]
David king over the tribe of Judah.
When David was told that it was the men
from Jabesh Gilead[k] who had buried Saul,
5he sent messengers to them to say to them,
"The LORD bless[l] you for showing this kindness to Saul your master by burying him.
6May the LORD now show you kindness
and faithfulness,[m] and I too will show you
the same favor because you have done this.
7Now then, be strong and brave, for Saul
your master is dead, and the people of Judah have anointed me king over them."

War Between the Houses of David and Saul

8Meanwhile, Abner[n] son of Ner, the commander of Saul's army, had taken Ish-Bosheth son of Saul and brought him over to
Mahanaim.[o] 9He made him king over Gilead,[p] Ashuri[q] and Jezreel, and also over
Ephraim, Benjamin and all Israel.[r]
10Ish-Bosheth son of Saul was forty years
old when he became king over Israel, and he
reigned two years. The tribe of Judah, however, remained loyal to David. 11The length
of time David was king in Hebron over Judah was seven years and six months.[s]
12Abner son of Ner, together with the
men of Ish-Bosheth son of Saul, left Mahanaim and went to Gibeon.[t] 13Joab[u] son of
Zeruiah and David's men went out and met

---

[a] 19 *Gazelle* here symbolizes a human dignitary.
[b] 21 Or / *nor fields that yield grain for offerings*

1:15 *struck him.* The Amalekite had probably been hoping for a reward from David. His story was a lie (1 Sam. 31), and this lie cost him his life. David's execution of the Amalekite was a strong testimony to those under his command that he had no part in Saul's death and did not reward it in any way.

2:5 *kindness.* David was grateful to the men who had shown kindness to Saul. This acknowledgement was not an act of politeness, but came from David's own heart of compassion. Saul repeatedly demonstrated that he considered himself above correction, but David was careful to maintain an attitude of kindness and humility.

1:15 [k] 2Sa 4:12 [l] 2Sa 4:10 **1:16** [m] Lev 20:9; 2Sa 3:28-29; 1Ki 2:32; Mt 27:24-25; Ac 18:6 **1:17** [n] 2Ch 35:25 **1:18** [o] Jos 10:13; 1Sa 31:3 **1:19** [p] ver 27 **1:20** [q] Mic 1:10 [r] 1Sa 31:8 [s] Ex 15:20; 1Sa 18:6 **1:21** [t] ver 6; 1Sa 31:1 [u] Eze 31:15 [v] Isa 21:5 **1:22** [w] Isa 34:3,7 [x] Dt 32:42; 1Sa 18:4 **1:23** [y] Dt 28:49; Jer 4:13 [z] Jdg 14:18 **1:26** [a] 1Sa 20:42 [b] 1Sa 18:1 **1:27** [c] ver 19,25; 1Sa 2:4 **2:1** [d] 1Sa 23:2,11-12 [e] Ge 13:18; 1Sa 30:31 **2:2** [f] 1Sa 25:43; 30:5 [g] 1Sa 25:42 **2:3** [h] 1Sa 27:2; 30:9 **2:4** [i] 1Sa 30:31 [j] 1Sa 2:35; 2Sa 5:3-5 [k] 1Sa 31:11-13 **2:5** [l] 1Sa 23:21 **2:6** [m] Ex 34:6; 1Ti 1:16 **2:8** [n] 1Sa 14:50 [o] Ge 32:2 **2:9** [p] Nu 32:26 [q] Jdg 1:32 [r] 1Ch 12:29 **2:11** [s] 2Sa 5:5 **2:12** [t] Jos 18:25 **2:13** [u] 2Sa 8:16; 1Ch 2:16; 11:6

them at the pool of Gibeon. One group sat
down on one side of the pool and one group
on the other side.
14 Then Abner said to Joab, "Let's have
some of the young men get up and fight
hand to hand in front of us."
"All right, let them do it," Joab said.
15 So they stood up and were counted
off—twelve men for Benjamin and Ish-Bosheth son of Saul, and twelve for David.
16 Then each man grabbed his opponent by
the head and thrust his dagger into his opponent's side, and they fell down together.
So that place in Gibeon was called Helkath
Hazzurim.[a]
17 The battle that day was very fierce, and
Abner and the Israelites were defeated[v] by
David's men.
18 The three sons of Zeruiah[w] were there:
Joab,[x] Abishai[y] and Asahel.[z] Now Asahel
was as fleet-footed as a wild gazelle.[a] 19 He
chased Abner, turning neither to the right
nor to the left as he pursued him. 20 Abner
looked behind him and asked, "Is that you,
Asahel?"
"It is," he answered.
21 Then Abner said to him, "Turn aside to
the right or to the left; take on one of the
young men and strip him of his weapons."
But Asahel would not stop chasing him.
22 Again Abner warned Asahel, "Stop
chasing me! Why should I strike you
down? How could I look your brother Joab
in the face?"[b]
23 But Asahel refused to give up the pursuit; so Abner thrust the butt of his spear
into Asahel's stomach,[c] and the spear came
out through his back. He fell there and died
on the spot. And every man stopped when
he came to the place where Asahel had fall-
en and died.[d]
24 But Joab and Abishai pursued Abner,
and as the sun was setting, they came to
the hill of Ammah, near Giah on the way
to the wasteland of Gibeon. 25 Then the men
of Benjamin rallied behind Abner. They
formed themselves into a group and took
their stand on top of a hill.
26 Abner called out to Joab, "Must the
sword devour[e] forever? Don't you realize
that this will end in bitterness? How long
before you order your men to stop pursuing
their fellow Israelites?"
27 Joab answered, "As surely as God lives,
if you had not spoken, the men would have
continued pursuing them until morning."
28 So Joab[f] blew the trumpet,[g] and all the
troops came to a halt; they no longer pursued Israel, nor did they fight anymore.
29 All that night Abner and his men
marched through the Arabah. They
crossed the Jordan, continued through the
morning hours[b] and came to Mahanaim.[h]
30 Then Joab stopped pursuing Abner
and assembled the whole army. Besides Asahel, nineteen of David's men were found
missing. 31 But David's men had killed
three hundred and sixty Benjamites who
were with Abner. 32 They took Asahel and
buried him in his father's tomb[i] at Bethlehem. Then Joab and his men marched all
night and arrived at Hebron by daybreak.

3

The war between the house of Saul and
the house of David lasted a long time.[j]
David grew stronger and stronger,[k] while
the house of Saul grew weaker and weaker.[l]
2 Sons were born to David in Hebron:
His firstborn was Amnon the son of
Ahinoam[m] of Jezreel;
3 his second, Kileab the son of Abigail[n] the widow of Nabal of Carmel;
the third, Absalom[o] the son of Maakah daughter of Talmai king of Geshur;[p]
4 the fourth, Adonijah[q] the son of
Haggith;
the fifth, Shephatiah the son of Abital;
5 and the sixth, Ithream the son of David's wife Eglah.
These were born to David in Hebron.

---

[a] 16 *Helkath Hazzurim* means *field of daggers* or *field of hostilities.* [b] 29 See Septuagint; the meaning of the Hebrew for this phrase is uncertain.

2:18 *Joab, Abishai and Asahel.* The three brothers were David's nephews, children of his sister Zeruiah (1 Chr. 2:13–16).

2:19 *He chased Abner.* Asahel did not have a personal grudge against Abner. This was a military move. If Abner, the chief military leader, was dead, Ish-Bosheth's power base would dissolve.

3:1 Strife—Finally David was in a position to push to establish his kingdom. It was still a contest of power and loyalty. An important question had to be settled: Is the king chosen by God? Or is the one who seizes the power the king? David knew he had to establish himself both politically and militarily, but he wanted to show, even in battle, that he trusted God to establish his kingdom.

3:2 *Sons were born to David.* David began his reign in Judah with two wives, Ahinoam and Abigail. His wife Michal, the daughter of Saul, had been given to another when David fled from Saul. In Hebron David married four more wives, in spite of the warning from Moses that a king should not "take many wives" (Deut. 17:17).

3:3 *Kileab.* Kileab is also called Daniel (1 Chr. 3:1).

3:5 *born to David in Hebron.* These six sons, each from a different mother, constituted the royal family during David's reign over the house of Judah. The dynastic lists in Chronicles include four sons of David by Bathsheba (1 Chr. 3:5) and nine other sons whose mothers are not named (1 Chr. 3:6–8).

2:17 [v] 2Sa 3:1 **2:18** [w] 2Sa 3:39 [x] 2Sa 3:30 [y] 1Sa 26:6 [z] 1Ch 2:16 [a] 1Ch 12:8 **2:22** [b] 2Sa 3:27 **2:23** [c] 2Sa 3:27; 4:6 [d] 2Sa 20:12 **2:26** [e] Dt 32:42; Jer 46:10, 14 **2:28** [f] 2Sa 18:16 [g] Jdg 3:27 **2:29** [h] ver 8 **2:32** [i] Ge 49:29 **3:1** [j] 1Ki 14:30 [k] 2Sa 5:10 [l] 2Sa 2:17 **3:2** [m] 1Sa 25:43; 1Ch 3:1-3 **3:3** [n] 1Sa 25:42 [o] 2Sa 13:1, 28 [p] 1Sa 27:8; 2Sa 13:37; 14:32; 15:8 **3:4** [q] 1Ki 1:5, 11

Abner Goes Over to David

6During the war between the house of
Saul and the house of David, Abner had
been strengthening his own position in the
house of Saul. 7Now Saul had had a concubine[r] named Rizpah[s] daughter of Aiah.
And Ish-Bosheth said to Abner, "Why did
you sleep with my father's concubine?"

8Abner was very angry because of what
Ish-Bosheth said. So he answered, "Am I
a dog's head[t]—on Judah's side? This very
day I am loyal to the house of your father Saul and to his family and friends. I
haven't handed you over to David. Yet now
you accuse me of an offense involving this
woman! 9May God deal with Abner, be
it ever so severely, if I do not do for David what the LORD promised[u] him on oath
10and transfer the kingdom from the house
of Saul and establish David's throne over
Israel and Judah from Dan to Beersheba."[v]
11Ish-Bosheth did not dare to say another
word to Abner, because he was afraid of
him.

12Then Abner sent messengers on his
behalf to say to David, "Whose land is it?
Make an agreement with me, and I will
help you bring all Israel over to you."

13"Good," said David. "I will make an
agreement with you. But I demand one
thing of you: Do not come into my presence unless you bring Michal daughter of
Saul when you come to see me."[w] 14Then
David sent messengers to Ish-Bosheth
son of Saul, demanding, "Give me my
wife Michal,[x] whom I betrothed to myself
for the price of a hundred Philistine foreskins."

15So Ish-Bosheth gave orders and had
her taken away from her husband[y] Paltiel[z]
son of Laish. 16Her husband, however, went
with her, weeping behind her all the way
to Bahurim.[a] Then Abner said to him, "Go
back home!" So he went back.

17Abner conferred with the elders[b] of
Israel and said, "For some time you have
wanted to make David your king. 18Now
do it! For the LORD promised David, 'By my
servant David I will rescue my people Israel from the hand of the Philistines[c] and
from the hand of all their enemies.[d]'"

19Abner also spoke to the Benjamites in
person. Then he went to Hebron to tell David everything that Israel and the whole
tribe of Benjamin[e] wanted to do. 20When
Abner, who had twenty men with him,
came to David at Hebron, David prepared
a feast for him and his men. 21Then Abner
said to David, "Let me go at once and assemble all Israel for my lord the king, so
that they may make a covenant[f] with you,
and that you may rule over all that your
heart desires."[g] So David sent Abner away,
and he went in peace.

Joab Murders Abner

22Just then David's men and Joab returned from a raid and brought with them
a great deal of plunder. But Abner was no
longer with David in Hebron, because David had sent him away, and he had gone
in peace. 23When Joab and all the soldiers
with him arrived, he was told that Abner
son of Ner had come to the king and that
the king had sent him away and that he had
gone in peace.

24So Joab went to the king and said,
"What have you done? Look, Abner came
to you. Why did you let him go? Now he
is gone! 25You know Abner son of Ner;
he came to deceive you and observe your
movements and find out everything you
are doing."

26Joab then left David and sent messengers after Abner, and they brought him
back from the cistern at Sirah. But David
did not know it. 27Now when Abner[h] returned to Hebron, Joab took him aside into
an inner chamber, as if to speak with him
privately. And there, to avenge the blood of
his brother Asahel, Joab stabbed him in the
stomach, and he died.[i]

28Later, when David heard about this,
he said, "I and my kingdom are forever innocent[j] before the LORD concerning
the blood of Abner son of Ner. 29May his

3:7 ***sleep with my father's concubine.*** The royal harem was the property of the king's successor. Taking a king's concubine was tantamount to claiming the throne.

3:8 ***dog's head.*** In the ancient Middle East dogs were scavengers, living off dead animals and garbage, and were viewed with contempt. ***Judah's side.*** The tribe of Judah was the enemy of Ish-Bosheth. In essence Abner was saying, "Do you think I am the scum of the enemy?"

3:13 ***Michal.*** David's first wife, Michal (1 Sam. 18:17–27) was left in Gibeah when David fled from Saul's court (1 Sam. 19:11–27). Saul then gave his daughter Michal, perhaps out of spite, to a man named Paltiel (1 Sam. 25:44). This request of David's was certainly in line with his rights as a husband who had given a proper dowry for his bride, and it was also a political statement. He was asserting his power over the house of Saul. (See note for 3:7.)

3:16 ***Her husband . . . went with her.*** Michal's husband wept. Nothing is said of Michal's feelings, or of David's. A king did not leave his wife with another man, for that was in the same category as another man taking the king's concubines. How he, or anyone else felt about it, had no bearing on the situation. (See note for 3:7.)

3:22 ***gone in peace.*** The words "gone in peace" are repeated (v. 21), to emphasize that the hostilities between David and Abner had been resolved.

3:7 [r] 2Sa 16:21-22 [s] 2Sa 21:8-11 **3:8** [t] 1Sa 24:14; 2Sa 9:8; 16:9 **3:9** [u] 1Sa 15:28; 1Ki 19:2 **3:10** [v] Jdg 20:1; 1Sa 3:20 **3:13** [w] Ge 43:5; 1Sa 18:20 **3:14** [x] 1Sa 18:27 **3:15** [y] Dt 24:1-4 [z] 1Sa 25:44 **3:16** [a] 2Sa 16:5; 19:16 **3:17** [b] Jdg 11:11 **3:18** [c] 1Sa 9:16 [d] 1Sa 15:28; 2Sa 8:6 **3:19** [e] 1Sa 10:20-21; 1Ch 12:2, 16, 29 **3:21** [f] ver 10, 12 [g] 1Ki 11:37 **3:27** [h] 2Sa 2:8 [i] 2Sa 2:22; 20:9-10; 1Ki 2:5 **3:28** [j] ver 37; Dt 21:9

blood[k] fall on the head of Joab and on his
whole family![l] May Joab's family never be
without someone who has a running sore[m]
or leprosy[a] or who leans on a crutch or who
falls by the sword or who lacks food."
30(Joab and his brother Abishai murdered Abner because he had killed their
brother Asahel in the battle at Gibeon.)
31Then David said to Joab and all the
people with him, "Tear your clothes and
put on sackcloth[n] and walk in mourning[o]
in front of Abner." King David himself
walked behind the bier. 32They buried Abner in Hebron, and the king wept[p] aloud
at Abner's tomb. All the people wept also.
33The king sang this lament[q] for Abner:

"Should Abner have died as the lawless
die?
34 Your hands were not bound,
your feet were not fettered.
You fell as one falls before the wicked."

And all the people wept over him again.
35Then they all came and urged David
to eat something while it was still day; but
David took an oath, saying, "May God deal
with me, be it ever so severely,[r] if I taste
bread[s] or anything else before the sun sets!"
36All the people took note and were
pleased; indeed, everything the king did
pleased them. 37So on that day all the people
there and all Israel knew that the king had
no part[t] in the murder of Abner son of Ner.
38Then the king said to his men, "Do you
not realize that a commander and a great
man has fallen[u] in Israel this day? 39And
today, though I am the anointed king, I am
weak, and these sons of Zeruiah[v] are too
strong for me.[w] May the LORD repay[x] the
evildoer according to his evil deeds!"

Ish-Bosheth Murdered

4 When Ish-Bosheth son of Saul heard
that Abner[y] had died in Hebron, he lost
courage, and all Israel became alarmed.
2Now Saul's son had two men who were
leaders of raiding bands. One was named
Baanah and the other Rekab; they were
sons of Rimmon the Beerothite from the
tribe of Benjamin—Beeroth[z] is considered
part of Benjamin, 3because the people of
Beeroth fled to Gittaim[a] and have resided
there as foreigners to this day.
4(Jonathan[b] son of Saul had a son who
was lame in both feet. He was five years old
when the news[c] about Saul and Jonathan
came from Jezreel. His nurse picked him
up and fled, but as she hurried to leave, he
fell and became disabled.[d] His name was
Mephibosheth.)[e]
5Now Rekab and Baanah, the sons of
Rimmon the Beerothite, set out for the
house of Ish-Bosheth,[f] and they arrived
there in the heat of the day while he was
taking his noonday rest. 6They went into
the inner part of the house as if to get some
wheat, and they stabbed[g] him in the stomach. Then Rekab and his brother Baanah
slipped away.
7They had gone into the house while he
was lying on the bed in his bedroom. After
they stabbed and killed him, they cut off
his head. Taking it with them, they traveled all night by way of the Arabah. 8They
brought the head of Ish-Bosheth to David
at Hebron and said to the king, "Here is the
head of Ish-Bosheth son of Saul,[h] your enemy, who tried to kill you. This day the LORD
has avenged my lord the king against Saul
and his offspring."
9David answered Rekab and his brother Baanah, the sons of Rimmon the Beerothite, "As surely as the LORD lives, who
has delivered[i] me out of every trouble,
10when someone told me, 'Saul is dead,'
and thought he was bringing good news,
I seized him and put him to death in Ziklag.[j] That was the reward I gave him for
his news! 11How much more—when wicked men have killed an innocent man in his
own house and on his own bed—should I
not now demand his blood[k] from your hand
and rid the earth of you!"
12So David gave an order to his men, and
they killed them.[l] They cut off their hands
and feet and hung the bodies by the pool
in Hebron. But they took the head of Ish-
Bosheth and buried it in Abner's tomb at
Hebron.

---

[a] 29 The Hebrew for *leprosy* was used for various diseases affecting the skin.

4:9–12 Strife—Once again David was faced with the question: Who was going to establish his kingdom? In David's mind the answer could only be "God." David wanted to meet his adversary honestly on the field of battle or over a flag of truce, but he would have nothing to do with murder. There was another compelling reason for David to conduct himself honorably. David was closely associated with Ish-Bosheth as the brother of his wife and of his best friend, and he did not find it easy to be at war with him.

4:8–10 *brought the head of Ish-Bosheth to David.* Ish-Bosheth was Jonathan's brother. Whether or not they looked alike, David had no desire to have the head of his beloved friend's brother brought to him as a prize. Once again, greed for a reward overcame prudence, and the plotters lost their lives on their own testimony.

4:11 *innocent man.* Ish-Bosheth had accepted what he considered to be his rightful role as the next king after his father, Saul. Apparently, even in David's mind, Ish-Bosheth's supposition was reasonable.

3:29 [k] Lev 20:9 [l] 1Ki 2:31-33 [m] Lev 15:2 **3:31** [n] 2Sa 1:2, 11; Ps 30:11; Isa 20:2 [o] Ge 37:34 **3:32** [p] Nu 14:1; Pr 24:17 **3:33** [q] 2Sa 1:17 **3:35** [r] Ru 1:17; 1Sa 3:17 [s] 1Sa 31:13; 2Sa 1:12; 12:17; Jer 16:7 **3:37** [t] ver 28 **3:38** [u] 2Sa 1:19 **3:39** [v] 2Sa 2:18 [w] 2Sa 19:5-7 [x] 1Ki 2:5-6, 33-34; Ps 41:10; 101:8 **4:1** [y] 2Sa 3:27; Ezr 4:4 **4:2** [z] Jos 9:17; 18:25 **4:3** [a] Ne 11:33 **4:4** [b] 1Sa 18:1 [c] 1Sa 31:1-4 [d] Lev 21:18 [e] 2Sa 9:3, 6; 1Ch 8:34; 9:40 **4:5** [f] 2Sa 2:8 **4:6** [g] 2Sa 2:23 **4:8** [h] 1Sa 24:4; 25:29 **4:9** [i] Ge 48:16; 1Ki 1:29 **4:10** [j] 2Sa 1:2-16 **4:11** [k] Ge 9:5; Ps 9:12 **4:12** [l] 2Sa 1:15

David Becomes King Over Israel

5 All the tribes of Israel[m] came to David at Hebron and said, "We are your own flesh and blood.[n] 2In the past, while Saul was king over us, you were the one who led Israel on their military campaigns.[o] And the LORD said to you, 'You will shepherd[p] my people Israel, and you will become their ruler.[q]'"

3When all the elders of Israel had come to King David at Hebron, the king made a covenant[r] with them at Hebron before the LORD, and they anointed[s] David king over Israel.

4David was thirty years old[t] when he became king, and he reigned[u] forty[v] years. 5In Hebron he reigned over Judah seven years and six months,[w] and in Jerusalem he reigned over all Israel and Judah thirty-three years.

David Conquers Jerusalem

6The king and his men marched to Jerusalem[x] to attack the Jebusites,[y] who lived there. The Jebusites said to David, "You will not get in here; even the blind and the lame can ward you off." They thought, "David cannot get in here." 7Nevertheless, David captured the fortress of Zion—which is the City of David.[z]

8On that day David had said, "Anyone who conquers the Jebusites will have to use the water shaft to reach those 'lame and blind' who are David's enemies.[a]" That is why they say, "The 'blind and lame' will not enter the palace."

9David then took up residence in the fortress and called it the City of David. He built up the area around it, from the terraces[b][a] inward. 10And he became more and more powerful,[b] because the LORD God Almighty was with him.

11Now Hiram[c] king of Tyre sent envoys to David, along with cedar logs and carpenters and stonemasons, and they built a palace for David. 12Then David knew that the LORD had established him as king over Israel and had exalted his kingdom for the sake of his people Israel.

13After he left Hebron, David took more concubines and wives[d] in Jerusalem, and more sons and daughters were born to him. 14These are the names of the children born to him there:[e] Shammua, Shobab, Nathan, Solomon, 15Ibhar, Elishua, Nepheg, Japhia, 16Elishama, Eliada and Eliphelet.

David Defeats the Philistines

17When the Philistines heard that David had been anointed king over Israel, they went up in full force to search for him, but David heard about it and went down to the stronghold.[f] 18Now the Philistines had come and spread out in the Valley of Rephaim;[g] 19so David inquired[h] of the LORD, "Shall I go and attack the Philistines? Will you deliver them into my hands?"

The LORD answered him, "Go, for I will surely deliver the Philistines into your hands."

20So David went to Baal Perazim, and there he defeated them. He said, "As waters break out, the LORD has broken out against my enemies before me." So that place was called Baal Perazim.[c][i] 21The Philistines

---

[a] 8 Or *are hated by David* [b] 9 Or *the Millo*
[c] 20 *Baal Perazim* means *the lord who breaks out.*

5:3 *anointed David king over Israel.* This was the third time that David was anointed as king. The first time was in anticipation of his rule (1 Sam. 16:13), the second time was acknowledgment of his rule over Judah (2:4), and the third time acknowledged his rule over the entire nation.

5:6 *marched to Jerusalem.* The city of Jerusalem was strategically located on a hill, just south of Mount Moriah, with steep cliffs on all sides except the north, making it a natural fortress. It was near the border of Judah and Benjamin. Jerusalem became the site of the temple, and the place, more than any other place on earth, which was identified with the Jewish people. It was there that Jesus was crucified, and it is there that He will come again (Zech. 14:4). ***the blind and the lame.*** Jerusalem was so strategically situated that the blind and the lame would be enough to defeat David.

5:7 *Zion.* The word Zion originally applied to the Jebusite stronghold, which became the City of David after its capture. As the city expanded to the north, encompassing Mount Moriah, the temple mount came to be called Zion (Ps. 78:68–69). Eventually the term was used as a synonym for Jerusalem (Is. 40:9).

5:8 *water shaft.* The water tunnel extended about 230 feet up from the Gihon spring to the top of the hill where the Jebusite fortress was situated (2 Chr. 32:30). The tunnel gave the city a secure water supply in the event of a siege.

5:11 *cedar logs.* Most buildings in Israel were made of stone. The use of cedar added elegance to David's palace.

5:13 *took more concubines and wives.* These marriages probably reflect David's involvement in international treaties and alliances which were sealed with the marriage of a king's daughter to the other participant in the treaty. Concubines, wives who did not have the legal rights of a true marriage, were a part of a royal harem. The status of kings in ancient times was often measured in part by the size of their harem. But Israel's kings had been warned not to acquire many wives (Deut. 17:17).

5:18 *Valley of Rephaim.* This valley extends southwest from Jerusalem toward the coastal plain, and is a strategic approach to the city.

5:21 *abandoned their idols.* The Philistines would have regarded their gods as being defeated by the God of Israel.

5:1 [m] 2Sa 19:43 [n] 1Ch 11:1 **5:2** [o] 1Sa 18:5, 13, 16 [p] 1Sa 16:1; 2Sa 7:7 [q] 1Sa 25:30 **5:3** [r] 2Sa 3:21 [s] 2Sa 2:4 **5:4** [t] Lk 3:23 [u] 1Ki 2:11; 1Ch 3:4 [v] 1Ch 26:31; 29:27 **5:5** [w] 2Sa 2:11; 1Ch 3:4 **5:6** [x] Jdg 1:8 [y] Jos 15:8 **5:7** [z] 2Sa 6:12, 16; 1Ki 2:10 **5:9** [a] ver 7; 1Ki 9:15, 24 **5:10** [b] 2Sa 3:1 **5:11** [c] 1Ki 5:1, 18; 1Ch 14:1 **5:13** [d] Dt 17:17; 1Ch 3:9 **5:14** [e] 1Ch 3:5 **5:17** [f] 2Sa 23:14; 1Ch 11:16 **5:18** [g] Jos 15:8; 17:15; 18:16 **5:19** [h] 1Sa 23:2; 2Sa 2:1 **5:20** [i] Isa 28:21

abandoned their idols there, and David and
his men carried them off.[j]
22 Once more the Philistines came up
and spread out in the Valley of Rephaim;
23 so David inquired of the LORD, and he
answered, "Do not go straight up, but circle around behind them and attack them
in front of the poplar trees. 24 As soon as
you hear the sound[k] of marching in the tops
of the poplar trees, move quickly, because
that will mean the LORD has gone out in
front[l] of you to strike the Philistine army."
25 So David did as the LORD commanded
him, and he struck down the Philistines all
the way from Gibeon[am] to Gezer.[n]

The Ark Brought to Jerusalem

6 David again brought together all the
able young men of Israel—thirty thousand. 2 He and all his men went to Baalah[bo]
in Judah to bring up from there the ark[p]
of God, which is called by the Name,[cq]
the name of the LORD Almighty, who is
enthroned[r] between the cherubim[s] on the
ark. 3 They set the ark of God on a new cart[t]
and brought it from the house of Abinadab,
which was on the hill. Uzzah and Ahio,
sons of Abinadab, were guiding the new
cart 4 with the ark of God on it,[d] and Ahio
was walking in front of it. 5 David and all
Israel were celebrating with all their might
before the LORD, with castanets,[e] harps,
lyres, timbrels, sistrums and cymbals.[u]
6 When they came to the threshing floor
of Nakon, Uzzah reached out and took hold
of[v] the ark of God, because the oxen stumbled. 7 The LORD's anger burned against
Uzzah because of his irreverent act;[w] therefore God struck him down,[x] and he died
there beside the ark of God.
8 Then David was angry because the
LORD's wrath[y] had broken out against Uzzah, and to this day that place is called Perez Uzzah.[fz]
9 David was afraid of the LORD that day
and said, "How[a] can the ark of the LORD
ever come to me?" 10 He was not willing
to take the ark of the LORD to be with him
in the City of David. Instead, he took it to
the house of Obed-Edom[b] the Gittite. 11 The
ark of the LORD remained in the house of
Obed-Edom the Gittite for three months,
and the LORD blessed him and his entire
household.[c]
12 Now King David[d] was told, "The LORD
has blessed the household of Obed-Edom
and everything he has, because of the ark
of God." So David went to bring up the ark
of God from the house of Obed-Edom to the
City of David with rejoicing. 13 When those
who were carrying the ark of the LORD had
taken six steps, he sacrificed[e] a bull and a
fattened calf. 14 Wearing a linen ephod,[f] David was dancing[g] before the LORD with all

---

a 25 Septuagint (see also 1 Chron. 14:16); Hebrew *Geba* *b* 2 That is, Kiriath Jearim (see 1 Chron. 13:6) *c* 2 Hebrew; Septuagint and Vulgate do not have *the Name.* *d* 3,4 Dead Sea Scrolls and some Septuagint manuscripts; Masoretic Text *cart* *4and they brought it with the ark of God from the house of Abinadab, which was on the hill*
e 5 Masoretic Text; Dead Sea Scrolls and Septuagint (see also 1 Chron. 13:8) *songs*
f 8 *Perez Uzzah* means *outbreak against Uzzah.*

6:2 *Baalah in Judah.* The name means "Masters of Judah," and the city was also called Baale and Kiriath Jearim. It was here that the ark had been left after it was returned by the Philistines in the days when Samuel was a young man and there was no king (1 Sam. 7:1–2). ***cherubim.*** Cherubim are angelic beings generally regarded as guardians of God's holiness (Ex. 25:22).

6:3 *set the ark of God on a new cart.* The law was specific that the ark was to be carried by the sons of Kohath, not by a cart or any other vehicle (Ex. 25:14–15; Num. 7:8–9).

6:6–8 Respect for the Ark—It is easy to understand David's anger at God. Uzzah's death seems quite unnecessary. It looks like his motives were in fact good ones. Reading about this event elicits fear and questioning. Why? We can't see how the punishment fits the crime. This seems incredibly arbitrary. How can we possibly understand the mystery that's involved here? Why such tragedy in the midst of this celebration?

The instructions on handling the ark are found in Numbers 4:15,19–20. There it says if you touch the holy things you die. We still don't understand why, but obviously there was more to the ark than anybody could imagine and no human could control it or use it. It was God's, made to be representative of His holiness and glory. God placed such power in the ark that a human would be overwhelmed by it.

We have such a poor sense of the holiness of God that we only see this event from our perspective. Fear and awe must be a part of a healthy relationship with God. While God is love, He is also to be feared.

6:6 *threshing floor.* A threshing floor was a place for processing grain, separating kernels from the chaff (Ruth 3:2).

6:7 *because of his irreverent act.* God had warned His people that not even the Kohathites of the tribe of Levi could touch the holy objects of the tabernacle. All of the holy objects were to be covered by the priests before the sons of Kohath came to carry them so they would not "touch any holy thing, lest they die" (Num. 4:15).

6:10 *Obed-Edom.* Obed-Edom was a Levite of the family of Korah, and later one of the doorkeepers for the tabernacle (1 Chr. 15:18,24; 26:4–8). ***the Gittite.*** He was called the Gittite because he was from the Levitical city of Gath Rimmon (Josh. 21:24).

6:14 *linen ephod.* The linen ephod was a short sleeveless garment worn by priests (1 Sam. 2:18). David wore it to honor the Lord because of his worshipful activities that day (v. 13).

5:21 [j] Dt 7:5; 1Ch 14:12; Isa 46:2 **5:24** [k] 2Ki 7:6 [l] Jdg 4:14
5:25 [m] Isa 28:21 [n] 1Ch 14:16 **6:2** [o] Jos 15:9 [p] 1Sa 4:4; 7:1
[q] Lev 24:16; Isa 63:14 [r] Ps 99:1 [s] Ex 25:22; 1Ch 13:5-6
6:3 [t] Nu 7:4-9; 1Sa 6:7 **6:5** [u] 1Sa 18:6-7; Ezr 3:10; Ps 150:5
6:6 [v] Nu 4:15, 19-20; 1Ch 13:9 **6:7** [w] 1Ch 15:13-15
[x] Ex 19:22; 1Sa 6:19 **6:8** [y] Ps 7:11 [z] Ge 38:29
6:9 [a] Ps 119:120 **6:10** [b] 1Ch 13:13; 26:4-5
6:11 [c] Ge 30:27; 39:5 **6:12** [d] 1Ki 8:1; 1Ch 15:25
6:13 [e] 1Ki 8:5,62 **6:14** [f] Ex 19:6; 1Sa 2:18 [g] Ex 15:20

his might, 15while he and all Israel were
bringing up the ark of the LORD with shouts
and the sound of trumpets.[h]
16As the ark of the LORD was entering
the City of David,[i] Michal daughter of Saul
watched from a window. And when she saw
King David leaping and dancing before the
LORD, she despised him in her heart.
17They brought the ark of the LORD and
set it in its place inside the tent that David
had pitched for it,[j] and David sacrificed
burnt offerings[k] and fellowship offerings
before the LORD. 18After he had finished
sacrificing[l] the burnt offerings and fellowship offerings, he blessed the people in
the name of the LORD Almighty. 19Then he
gave a loaf of bread, a cake of dates and a
cake of raisins[m] to each person in the whole
crowd of Israelites, both men and women.[n]
And all the people went to their homes.
20When David returned home to bless
his household, Michal daughter of Saul
came out to meet him and said, "How the
king of Israel has distinguished himself today, going around half-naked[o] in full view
of the slave girls of his servants as any vul-
gar fellow would!"
21David said to Michal, "It was before
the LORD, who chose me rather than your
father or anyone from his house when he
appointed[p] me ruler over the LORD's people
Israel—I will celebrate before the LORD. 22I
will become even more undignified than
this, and I will be humiliated in my own
eyes. But by these slave girls you spoke of,
I will be held in honor."
23And Michal daughter of Saul had no
children to the day of her death.

God's Promise to David

7 After the king was settled in his palace[q] and the LORD had given him rest
from all his enemies around him, 2he said
to Nathan the prophet, "Here I am, living
in a house[r] of cedar, while the ark of God
remains in a tent."[s]
3Nathan replied to the king, "Whatever
you have in mind, go ahead and do it, for
the LORD is with you."
4But that night the word of the LORD
came to Nathan, saying:

5"Go and tell my servant David,
'This is what the LORD says: Are you[t]
the one to build me a house to dwell
in?[u] 6I have not dwelt in a house from
the day I brought the Israelites up out
of Egypt to this day. I have been moving from place to place with a tent[v]
as my dwelling.[w] 7Wherever I have
moved with all the Israelites,[x] did I
ever say to any of their rulers whom
I commanded to shepherd[y] my people
Israel, "Why have you not built me a
house of cedar?[z]"'
8"Now then, tell my servant David, 'This is what the LORD Almighty
says: I took you from the pasture,
from tending the flock,[a] and appointed you ruler[b] over my people Israel.[c]
9I have been with you wherever you
have gone,[d] and I have cut off all your
enemies from before you.[e] Now I will
make your name great, like the names
of the greatest men on earth. 10And I
will provide a place for my people Israel and will plant[f] them so that they can
have a home of their own and no longer be disturbed. Wicked[g] people will
not oppress them anymore,[h] as they
did at the beginning 11and have done
ever since the time I appointed leaders[a][i] over my people Israel. I will also
give you rest from all your enemies.[j]
"'The LORD declares to you that the
LORD himself will establish[k] a house[l]
for you: 12When your days are over

[a] 11 Traditionally *judges*

6:17 *the tent that David had pitched for it.* There are no descriptive details of this tent. It is not clear exactly what happened to the ark after it was moved from Shiloh to Nob (1 Sam. 5; 21:1–5). At the time that David bought the threshing floor from Araunah (2 Sam. 24:21–25), the tabernacle of the Lord, which Moses had made in the wilderness, and the altar of burnt offering were in the high place of Gibeon (1 Chr. 21:29), which was about six miles northwest of Jerusalem.
6:18–19 *fellowship offerings.* A distinctive feature of the fellowship offering was that a portion of it would be eaten by the worshiper as a fellowship meal before the Lord.
6:20–23 *half-naked.* The love and respect that Michal once had for David was gone. She ridiculed his enthusiasm as he worshiped the Lord, and for David that was not an attitude he could overlook. It is difficult to comprehend the complexities of a marriage where multiple wives and concubines are a part of the picture, and the wife is viewed as chattel before she is viewed as a person. As in so many places in the Bible, the picture is drawn, but without comment on what God thought. Jesus clarifies this a little when He comments on the hardness of hearts, and says, "it was not this way from the beginning" (Matt. 19:8).
7:2 *Nathan.* Nathan was a personal advisor to David. As a prophet, he spoke for God, advising David on religious matters. He also chronicled the reigns of David and Solomon (1 Chr. 29:29).
7:4–17 The Covenant with David—The Davidic covenant contains God's promise to Israel and to David. God promised Israel that Palestine would always be their place (v. 10). He also promised that David would have an unending dynasty and an everlasting kingdom. This promise is fulfilled in Christ.

6:15 [h] Ps 47:5; 98:6 **6:16** [i] 2Sa 5:7 **6:17** [j] 1Ch 15:1; 2Ch 1:4 [k] Lev 1:1-17; 1Ki 8:62-64 **6:18** [l] 1Ki 8:22 **6:19** [m] Hos 3:1 [n] Ne 8:10 **6:20** [o] ver 14, 16 **6:21** [p] 1Sa 13:14; 15:28 **7:1** [q] 1Ch 17:1 **7:2** [r] 2Sa 5:11 [s] Ex 26:1; Ac 7:45-46 **7:5** [t] 1Ki 8:19; 1Ch 22:8 [u] 1Ki 5:3-5 **7:6** [v] Ex 40:18, 34 [w] 1Ki 8:16 **7:7** [x] Dt 23:14 [y] 2Sa 5:2 [z] Lev 26:11-12 **7:8** [a] 1Sa 16:11 [b] 2Sa 6:21 [c] Ps 78:70-72; 2Co 6:18* **7:9** [d] 2Sa 5:10 [e] Ps 18:37-42 **7:10** [f] Ex 15:17; Isa 5:1-7 [g] Ps 89:22-23 [h] Isa 60:18 **7:11** [i] Jdg 2:16; 1Sa 12:9-11 [j] ver 1 [k] 1Sa 25:28 [l] ver 27

and you rest[m] with your ancestors,
I will raise up your offspring to succeed you, your own flesh and blood,[n]
and I will establish his kingdom. 13He
is the one who will build a house for
my Name,[o] and I will establish the
throne of his kingdom forever.[p] 14I will
be his father, and he will be my son.[q]
When he does wrong, I will punish
him with a rod[r] wielded by men, with
floggings inflicted by human hands.
15But my love will never be taken
away from him, as I took it away from
Saul,[s] whom I removed from before
you. 16Your house and your kingdom
will endure forever before me[*a*]; your
throne[t] will be established forever.[u]' "

17Nathan reported to David all the words
of this entire revelation.

David's Prayer

18Then King David went in and sat before the LORD, and he said:

"Who am I,[v] Sovereign LORD, and
what is my family, that you have
brought me this far? 19And as if this
were not enough in your sight, Sovereign LORD, you have also spoken
about the future of the house of your
servant—and this decree,[w] Sovereign
LORD, is for a mere human![*b*]

20"What more can David say to you?
For you know[x] your servant,[y] Sovereign LORD. 21For the sake of your
word and according to your will, you
have done this great thing and made it
known to your servant.

22"How great[z] you are,[a] Sovereign
LORD! There is no one like you, and
there is no God[b] but you, as we have
heard with our own ears.[c] 23And who
is like your people Israel[d]—the one
nation on earth that God went out to
redeem as a people for himself, and to
make a name for himself, and to perform great and awesome wonders[e]
by driving out nations and their gods
from before your people, whom you
redeemed[f] from Egypt?[*c*] 24You have
established your people Israel as your
very own[g] forever, and you, LORD,
have become their God.[h]

25"And now, LORD God, keep forever
the promise you have made concerning your servant and his house. Do
as you promised, 26so that your name
will be great forever. Then people will
say, 'The LORD Almighty is God over
Israel!' And the house of your servant
David will be established in your sight.

27"LORD Almighty, God of Israel,
you have revealed this to your servant,
saying, 'I will build a house for you.'
So your servant has found courage to
pray this prayer to you. 28Sovereign
LORD, you are God! Your covenant is
trustworthy,[i] and you have promised
these good things to your servant.
29Now be pleased to bless the house
of your servant, that it may continue
forever in your sight; for you, Sovereign LORD, have spoken, and with your
blessing[j] the house of your servant will
be blessed forever."

David's Victories

8 In the course of time, David defeated
the Philistines and subdued them, and
he took Metheg Ammah from the control
of the Philistines.

2David also defeated the Moabites.[k] He
made them lie down on the ground and
measured them off with a length of cord.
Every two lengths of them were put to
death, and the third length was allowed to
live. So the Moabites became subject to David and brought him tribute.

---

a *16* Some Hebrew manuscripts and Septuagint; most Hebrew manuscripts *you* *b* *19* Or *for the human race* *c* *23* See Septuagint and 1 Chron. 17:21; Hebrew *wonders for your land and before your people, whom you redeemed from Egypt, from the nations and their gods.*

Both Matthew and Luke, in their Gospels, trace Jesus' ancestry back to David.

7:13 ***the throne of his kingdom forever.*** This is not to say that Solomon would rule forever. Rather, the right to rule, represented by the image of the throne, would always belong to his descendants. Further, there would always be a male heir who would be able to rule. Ultimately this promise is fulfilled in Christ (Matt. 1).

7:19 ***the future of the house of your servant.*** God extended the promise concerning David's dynasty far into the future. All of human history leads inevitably to the rule of Christ on earth. This is its destiny, its prophetic fulfillment, the final meaning of all history.

7:27 ***prayer.*** David was a king for God, not for himself. It is not likely that he was totally without pride in his position, but he did not seem to be a man who was full of himself. His purpose in wanting to build the temple was to glorify God whom he loved, not to glorify himself. David's prayer of worship and thanksgiving is an intimate key that shows how he was able to keep himself both willing and trusting as he followed God.

7:28 ***you are God ... Your covenant is trustworthy.*** This is David's theme, throughout his life, and this is why he was a man after God's heart (1 Sam. 13:14).

8:2 ***Moabites.*** The Moabites were descendants of the incestuous relationship between Lot and his older daughter (Gen. 19:36–37).

7:12 [m] 1Ki 2:1 [n] Ps 132:11-12 **7:13** [o] 1Ki 5:5; 8:19,29 [p] Isa 9:7 **7:14** [q] Ps 89:26; Heb 1:5* [r] Ps 89:30-33 **7:15** [s] 1Sa 15:23,28 **7:16** [t] Ps 89:36-37 [u] ver 13 **7:18** [v] Ex 3:11; 1Sa 18:18 **7:19** [w] Isa 55:8-9 **7:20** [x] Jn 21:17 [y] 1Sa 16:7 **7:22** [z] Ps 48:1; 86:10; Jer 10:6 [a] Dt 3:24 [b] Ex 15:11 [c] Ex 10:2; Ps 44:1 **7:23** [d] Dt 4:32-38 [e] Dt 10:21 [f] Dt 9:26; 15:15 **7:24** [g] Dt 26:18 [h] Ex 6:6-7; Ps 48:14 **7:28** [i] Ex 34:6; Jn 17:17 **7:29** [j] Nu 6:23-27 **8:2** [k] Ge 19:37; Nu 24:17

[3]Moreover, David defeated Hadadezer[l]
son of Rehob, king of Zobah,[m] when he
went to restore his monument at[a] the Euphrates River. [4]David captured a thousand
of his chariots, seven thousand charioteers[b] and twenty thousand foot soldiers.
He hamstrung[n] all but a hundred of the
chariot horses.
[5]When the Arameans of Damascus[o]
came to help Hadadezer king of Zobah,
David struck down twenty-two thousand
of them. [6]He put garrisons in the Aramean
kingdom of Damascus, and the Arameans
became subject to him and brought tribute.
The LORD gave David victory wherever he
went.[p]
[7]David took the gold shields[q] that belonged to the officers of Hadadezer and
brought them to Jerusalem. [8]From Tebah[c]
and Berothai,[r] towns that belonged to Hadadezer, King David took a great quantity
of bronze.
[9]When Tou[d] king of Hamath[s] heard
that David had defeated the entire army
of Hadadezer, [10]he sent his son Joram[e] to
King David to greet him and congratulate
him on his victory in battle over Hadadezer, who had been at war with Tou. Joram
brought with him articles of silver, of gold
and of bronze.
[11]King David dedicated[t] these articles to
the LORD, as he had done with the silver
and gold from all the nations he had subdued: [12]Edom[f] and Moab,[u] the Ammonites[v]
and the Philistines,[w] and Amalek.[x] He also
dedicated the plunder taken from Hadadezer son of Rehob, king of Zobah.
[13]And David became famous[y] after he returned from striking down eighteen thousand Edomites[g] in the Valley of Salt.[z]
[14]He put garrisons throughout Edom,
and all the Edomites[a] became subject to
David.[b] The LORD gave David victory wherever he went.[c]

David's Officials

[15]David reigned over all Israel, doing
what was just and right for all his people.
[16]Joab[d] son of Zeruiah was over the army;
Jehoshaphat[e] son of Ahilud was recorder;
[17]Zadok[f] son of Ahitub and Ahimelek son
of Abiathar were priests; Seraiah was secretary;[g] [18]Benaiah[h] son of Jehoiada was
over the Kerethites[i] and Pelethites; and
David's sons were priests.[h]

David and Mephibosheth

9 David asked, "Is there anyone still left
of the house of Saul to whom I can show
kindness for Jonathan's sake?"[j]
[2]Now there was a servant of Saul's
household named Ziba.[k] They summoned
him to appear before David, and the king
said to him, "Are you Ziba?"
"At your service," he replied.
[3]The king asked, "Is there no one still
alive from the house of Saul to whom I can
show God's kindness?"
Ziba answered the king, "There is still a
son of Jonathan;[l] he is lame[m] in both feet."
[4]"Where is he?" the king asked.
Ziba answered, "He is at the house of
Makir[n] son of Ammiel in Lo Debar."
[5]So King David had him brought from
Lo Debar, from the house of Makir son of
Ammiel.

[a] 3 Or *his control along* [b] 4 Septuagint (see also Dead Sea Scrolls and 1 Chron. 18:4); Masoretic Text *captured seventeen hundred of his charioteers* [c] 8 See some Septuagint manuscripts (see also 1 Chron. 18:8); Hebrew *Betah.* [d] 9 Hebrew *Toi,* a variant of *Tou;* also in verse 10 [e] 10 A variant of *Hadoram* [f] 12 Some Hebrew manuscripts, Septuagint and Syriac (see also 1 Chron. 18:11); most Hebrew manuscripts *Aram* [g] 13 A few Hebrew manuscripts, Septuagint and Syriac (see also 1 Chron. 18:12); most Hebrew manuscripts *Aram* (that is, Arameans) [h] 18 Or *were chief officials* (see Septuagint and Targum; see also 1 Chron. 18:17)

8:4 *hamstrung.* David disabled the horses by cutting the back sinews of the hind legs to prevent them from being used for military activity (Josh. 11:6,9).
8:5 *Damascus.* Damascus was located at an oasis near the foot of the Anti-Lebanon mountains and was one of the most strategically located cities of the ancient world. Damascus lay at the crossroads of the two main international highways: the Via Maris, leading south and west to Egypt, and the King's Highway, leading from the east side of the Jordan south to Arabia.
8:8 *Berothai.* This city was about 30 miles northwest of Damascus.
8:15 *David reigned over all Israel.* As a result of David's conquests, the sovereignty of Israel extended from the Gulf of Aqaba and the River of Egypt to the Euphrates River — the very region God had promised Abraham (Gen. 15:18).
9:1 – 13 *kindness.* David wrote in Psalm 23:5, "You prepare a table before me in the presence of my enemies." And that is just what David did for Mephibosheth, for the sake of his father Jonathan. Jonathan and David had been separated by the hostility that Saul had for David, and as far as Mephibosheth would have understood, David was an enemy to the house of Saul. But the bond of love and friendship that David and Jonathan had was greater than the hostility of Saul, and David was faithful to honor those bonds.
9:4 *Makir son of Ammiel.* Makir was a man, apparently of wealth and position, who extended hospitality to David during Absalom's revolt (17:27 – 29). He showed himself to be a man of kindness who was willing to help someone in need, even if it might not be politically expedient.

8:3 [l] 2Sa 10:16,19 [m] 1Sa 14:47 **8:4** [n] Jos 11:9
8:5 [o] 1Ki 11:24 **8:6** [p] ver 14; 2Sa 3:18; 7:9
8:7 [q] 1Ki 10:16 **8:8** [r] Eze 47:16 **8:9** [s] 1Ki 8:65; 2Ch 8:4
8:11 [t] 1Ki 7:51; 1Ch 26:26 **8:12** [u] ver 2 [v] 2Sa 10:14
[w] 2Sa 5:25 [x] 1Sa 27:8 **8:13** [y] 2Sa 7:9 [z] 2Ki 14:7; 1Ch 18:12
8:14 [a] Nu 24:17-18 [b] Ge 27:29,37-40 [c] ver 6
8:16 [d] 2Sa 19:13; 1Ch 11:6 [e] 2Sa 20:24; 1Ki 4:3
8:17 [f] 2Sa 15:24,29; 1Ch 16:39; 24:3 [g] 1Ki 4:3; 2Ki 12:10
8:18 [h] 2Sa 20:23; 1Ki 1:8,38; 1Ch 18:17 [i] 1Sa 30:14
9:1 [j] 1Sa 20:14-17,42 **9:2** [k] 2Sa 16:1-4; 19:17,26,29
9:3 [l] 1Sa 20:14 [m] 2Sa 4:4 **9:4** [n] 2Sa 17:27-29

6When Mephibosheth son of Jonathan,
the son of Saul, came to David, he bowed
down to pay him honor.[o]

David said, "Mephibosheth!"

"At your service," he replied.

7"Don't be afraid," David said to him,
"for I will surely show you kindness for the
sake of your father Jonathan. I will restore
to you all the land that belonged to your
grandfather Saul, and you will always eat
at my table.[p]"

8Mephibosheth bowed down and said,
"What is your servant, that you should notice a dead dog[q] like me?"

9Then the king summoned Ziba, Saul's
steward, and said to him, "I have given
your master's grandson everything that
belonged to Saul and his family. 10You and
your sons and your servants are to farm the
land for him and bring in the crops, so that
your master's grandson[r] may be provided
for. And Mephibosheth, grandson of your
master, will always eat at my table." (Now
Ziba had fifteen sons and twenty servants.)

11Then Ziba said to the king, "Your servant will do whatever my lord the king
commands his servant to do." So Mephibosheth ate at David's[a] table like one of the
king's sons.[s]

12Mephibosheth had a young son named
Mika, and all the members of Ziba's household were servants of Mephibosheth.[t]
13And Mephibosheth lived in Jerusalem,
because he always ate at the king's table;
he was lame in both feet.

David Defeats the Ammonites

10 In the course of time, the king of the
Ammonites died, and his son Hanun
succeeded him as king. 2David thought, "I
will show kindness to Hanun son of Nahash,[u] just as his father showed kindness
to me." So David sent a delegation to express his sympathy to Hanun concerning
his father.

When David's men came to the land of
the Ammonites, 3the Ammonite commanders said to Hanun their lord, "Do you think
David is honoring your father by sending
envoys to you to express sympathy? Hasn't
David sent them to you only to explore the
city and spy it out and overthrow it?" 4So
Hanun seized David's envoys, shaved off
half of each man's beard,[v] cut off their
garments at the buttocks,[w] and sent them
away.

5When David was told about this, he sent
messengers to meet the men, for they were
greatly humiliated. The king said, "Stay at
Jericho till your beards have grown, and
then come back."

6When the Ammonites realized that they
had become obnoxious[x] to David, they hired
twenty thousand Aramean[y] foot soldiers
from Beth Rehob[z] and Zobah, as well as the
king of Maakah[a] with a thousand men, and
also twelve thousand men from Tob.

7On hearing this, David sent Joab out
with the entire army of fighting men. 8The
Ammonites came out and drew up in battle
formation at the entrance of their city gate,
while the Arameans of Zobah and Rehob
and the men of Tob and Maakah were by
themselves in the open country.

9Joab saw that there were battle lines in
front of him and behind him; so he selected
some of the best troops in Israel and deployed them against the Arameans. 10He
put the rest of the men under the command
of Abishai his brother and deployed them
against the Ammonites. 11Joab said, "If the
Arameans are too strong for me, then you
are to come to my rescue; but if the Ammonites are too strong for you, then I will
come to rescue you. 12Be strong,[b] and let us
fight bravely for our people and the cities
of our God. The LORD will do what is good
in his sight."[c]

---

[a] *11* Septuagint; Hebrew *my*

9:11 ***like one of the king's sons.*** David kept his promise to Jonathan. The two young men had vowed that the Lord would be between them, and between their descendants forever (1 Sam. 20:42). It was a way of saying that the Lord would always be in their relationships with each other, keeping them loyal, kind, honest, and willing to bear each other's burdens. Now Jonathan's son was provided for as one of David's sons.

10:1 ***the king of the Ammonites.*** The king of Ammon was probably the same Nahash who was defeated by Saul at Jabesh Gilead (1 Sam. 11:1 – 11).

10:2 ***as his father showed kindness to me.*** The occasion of Nahash's kindness is not recorded. One possibility is that Nahash, an enemy of Saul, had given aid to David during his war with Ish-Bosheth (2:8 — 4:12).

10:6 ***Beth Rehob and Zobah.*** These two Aramean city-states were located north of Israel. ***Maakah.*** The small Aramean kingdom east of the Jordan was part of the territory assigned to the half-tribe of Manasseh (Josh. 12:5; 13:11). ***Tob.*** Tob was also an area east of the Jordan, but not a part of Israel. (Judg. 11:3).

10:8 ***entrance of their city gate.*** Some cities had multiple gates. If attackers broke through one gate, they would find another gate in front of them. The Ammonites fought near the entrance of the city so they could retreat behind the city gates if the battle turned against them. The mercenary soldiers were in more exposed positions in the field.

10:10 ***Abishai.*** Abishai was one of David's mighty men (23:18). He was a brave warrior (1 Sam. 26:6 – 9) and a successful commander (1 Chr. 18:12 – 13), but was impetuous and perhaps even bloodthirsty (16:9; 19:21). He had played a part in the murder of Abner.

9:6 [o] 2Sa 16:4; 19:24-30 **9:7** [p] ver 1, 3; 2Sa 12:8; 19:28; 1Ki 2:7; 2Ki 25:29 **9:8** [q] 2Sa 16:9 **9:10** [r] ver 7, 11, 13; 2Sa 19:28 **9:11** [s] Job 36:7; Ps 113:8 **9:12** [t] 1Ch 8:34 **10:2** [u] 1Sa 11:1 **10:4** [v] Lev 19:27; Isa 15:2; Jer 48:37 [w] Isa 20:4 **10:6** [x] Ge 34:30 [y] 2Sa 8:5 [z] Jdg 18:28 [a] Dt 3:14 **10:12** [b] Dt 31:6; 1Co 16:13; Eph 6:10 [c] Jdg 10:15; 1Sa 3:18; Ne 4:14

13 Then Joab and the troops with him advanced to fight the Arameans, and they fled before him. 14 When the Ammonites realized that the Arameans were fleeing, they fled before Abishai and went inside the city. So Joab returned from fighting the Ammonites and came to Jerusalem.

15 After the Arameans saw that they had been routed by Israel, they regrouped. 16 Hadadezer had Arameans brought from beyond the Euphrates River; they went to Helam, with Shobak the commander of Hadadezer's army leading them.

17 When David was told of this, he gathered all Israel, crossed the Jordan and went to Helam. The Arameans formed their battle lines to meet David and fought against him. 18 But they fled before Israel, and David killed seven hundred of their charioteers and forty thousand of their foot soldiers.[a] He also struck down Shobak the commander of their army, and he died there. 19 When all the kings who were vassals of Hadadezer saw that they had been routed by Israel, they made peace with the Israelites and became subject[d] to them.

So the Arameans[e] were afraid to help the Ammonites anymore.

David and Bathsheba

11 In the spring,[f] at the time when kings go off to war, David sent Joab[g] out with the king's men and the whole Israelite army.[h] They destroyed the Ammonites and besieged Rabbah.[i] But David remained in Jerusalem.

2 One evening David got up from his bed and walked around on the roof[j] of the palace. From the roof he saw[k] a woman bathing. The woman was very beautiful, 3 and David sent someone to find out about her. The man said, "She is Bathsheba,[l] the daughter of Eliam[m] and the wife of Uriah[n] the Hittite." 4 Then David sent messengers to get her.[o] She came to him, and he slept[p] with her. (Now she was purifying herself from her monthly uncleanness.)[q] Then she went back home. 5 The woman conceived and sent word to David, saying, "I am pregnant."

6 So David sent this word to Joab: "Send me Uriah[r] the Hittite." And Joab sent him to David. 7 When Uriah came to him, David asked him how Joab was, how the soldiers were and how the war was going. 8 Then David said to Uriah, "Go down to your house and wash your feet."[s] So Uriah left the palace, and a gift from the king was sent after him. 9 But Uriah slept at the entrance to the palace with all his master's servants and did not go down to his house.

10 David was told, "Uriah did not go home." So he asked Uriah, "Haven't you just come from a military campaign? Why didn't you go home?"

11 Uriah said to David, "The ark[t] and Israel and Judah are staying in tents,[b] and my commander Joab and my lord's men are camped in the open country. How could I go to my house to eat and drink and make love to my wife? As surely as you live, I will not do such a thing!"

12 Then David said to him, "Stay here one more day, and tomorrow I will send you back." So Uriah remained in Jerusalem that day and the next. 13 At David's invitation, he ate and drank with him, and David made him drunk. But in the evening Uriah went out to sleep on his mat among his master's servants; he did not go home.

14 In the morning David wrote a letter[u] to Joab and sent it with Uriah. 15 In it he wrote, "Put Uriah out in front where the fighting is fiercest. Then withdraw from him so he will be struck down[v] and die.[w]"

16 So while Joab had the city under siege, he put Uriah at a place where he knew the strongest defenders were. 17 When the men of the city came out and fought against Joab, some of the men in David's army fell; moreover, Uriah the Hittite died.

18 Joab sent David a full account of the battle. 19 He instructed the messenger: "When you have finished giving the king this account of the battle, 20 the king's anger may flare up, and he may ask you, 'Why did you get so close to the city to fight? Didn't you know they would shoot arrows from the wall? 21 Who killed Abimelek[x] son of Jerub-Besheth[c]? Didn't a woman drop an upper millstone on him from the wall,[y] so that he died in Thebez? Why

---

[a] *18* Some Septuagint manuscripts (see also 1 Chron. 19:18); Hebrew *horsemen* [b] *11* Or *staying at Sukkoth* [c] *21* Also known as *Jerub-Baal* (that is, Gideon)

11:1 *In the spring, at the time when kings go off to war.* Spring was a good time to mount a campaign. They could be assured of good weather and an abundance of food along the way.

11:2 *From the roof he saw a woman bathing.* She was probably in the enclosed courtyard of her home, a place of privacy, not visible from the street.

11:5 *The woman conceived.* The law commanded both parties in an adulterous relationship to be put to death (Lev. 20:10). In practice, a woman who became pregnant might be forced to bear the shame and guilt alone (John 8:1–11).

11:21 *Didn't a woman.* The story referred to here is recorded in Judges 9:50–55. For a soldier to die at the hand of a woman was at best shameful, if not a point of ridicule (Judg. 4:17–24). It seems that Joab was letting David know that he knew David's real reasons for wanting Uriah dead.

10:19 [d] 2Sa 8:6 [e] 1Ki 11:25; 2Ki 5:1 **11:1** [f] 1Ki 20:22,26 [g] 2Sa 2:18 [h] 1Ch 20:1 [i] 2Sa 12:26-28 **11:2** [j] Dt 22:8; Jos 2:8 [k] Mt 5:28 **11:3** [l] 1Ch 3:5 [m] 2Sa 23:34 [n] 2Sa 23:39 **11:4** [o] Lev 20:10; Ps 51 Title; Jas 1:14-15 [p] Dt 22:22 [q] Lev 15:25-30; 18:19 **11:6** [r] 1Ch 11:41 **11:8** [s] Ge 18:4; 43:24; Lk 7:44 **11:11** [t] 2Sa 7:2 **11:14** [u] 1Ki 21:8 **11:15** [v] 2Sa 12:9 [w] 2Sa 12:12 **11:21** [x] Jdg 8:31 [y] Jdg 9:50-54

did you get so close to the wall?' If he asks
you this, then say to him, 'Moreover, your
servant Uriah the Hittite is dead.'"
22The messenger set out, and when he
arrived he told David everything Joab
had sent him to say. 23The messenger said
to David, "The men overpowered us and
came out against us in the open, but we
drove them back to the entrance of the city
gate. 24Then the archers shot arrows at
your servants from the wall, and some of
the king's men died. Moreover, your servant Uriah the Hittite is dead."
25David told the messenger, "Say this to
Joab: 'Don't let this upset you; the sword
devours one as well as another. Press the
attack against the city and destroy it.' Say
this to encourage Joab."
26When Uriah's wife heard that her husband was dead, she mourned for him. 27Af-
ter the time of mourning was over, David
had her brought to his house, and she became his wife and bore him a son. But the
thing David had done displeased[z] the LORD.

Nathan Rebukes David

12 The LORD sent Nathan[a] to David.[b]
When he came to him,[c] he said,
"There were two men in a certain town,
one rich and the other poor. 2The rich man
had a very large number of sheep and cattle, 3but the poor man had nothing except
one little ewe lamb he had bought. He
raised it, and it grew up with him and his
children. It shared his food, drank from his
cup and even slept in his arms. It was like a
daughter to him.
4"Now a traveler came to the rich man,
but the rich man refrained from taking one
of his own sheep or cattle to prepare a meal
for the traveler who had come to him. Instead, he took the ewe lamb that belonged
to the poor man and prepared it for the one
who had come to him."
5David[d] burned with anger against the
man and said to Nathan, "As surely as
the LORD lives, the man who did this must
die! 6He must pay for that lamb four times
over,[e] because he did such a thing and had
no pity."
7Then Nathan said to David, "You are
the man! This is what the LORD, the God
of Israel, says: 'I anointed[f] you[g] king over
Israel, and I delivered you from the hand of
Saul. 8I gave your master's house to you,[h]
and your master's wives into your arms. I
gave you all Israel and Judah. And if all
this had been too little, I would have given
you even more. 9Why did you despise[i] the
word of the LORD by doing what is evil in
his eyes? You struck down[j] Uriah the Hittite with the sword and took his wife to be
your own. You killed him with the sword
of the Ammonites. 10Now, therefore, the
sword[k] will never depart from your house,
because you despised me and took the wife
of Uriah the Hittite to be your own.'
11"This is what the LORD says: 'Out of
your own household I am going to bring
calamity on you.[l] Before your very eyes I
will take your wives and give them to one
who is close to you, and he will sleep with
your wives in broad daylight. 12You did it
in secret,[m] but I will do this thing in broad
daylight[n] before all Israel.'"
13Then David said to Nathan, "I have
sinned[o] against the LORD."
Nathan replied, "The LORD has tak-
en away[p] your sin.[q] You are not going to
die.[r] 14But because by doing this you have
shown utter contempt for[a] the LORD,[s] the
son born to you will die."
15After Nathan had gone home, the LORD
struck[t] the child that Uriah's wife had
borne to David, and he became ill. 16David
pleaded with God for the child. He fasted
and spent the nights lying[u] in sackcloth[b]
on the ground. 17The elders of his household stood beside him to get him up from
the ground, but he refused, and he would
not eat any food with them.[v]
18On the seventh day the child died. David's attendants were afraid to tell him that
the child was dead, for they thought, "While
the child was still living, he wouldn't listen
to us when we spoke to him. How can we

a 14 An ancient Hebrew scribal tradition; Masoretic Text *for the enemies of* *b 16* Dead Sea Scrolls and Septuagint; Masoretic Text does not have *in sackcloth.*

12:7 *You are the man.* It took courage and a strong commitment to the Lord for Nathan to speak these words to the king. Nathan's rebuke was centered on who the Lord is, and what the Lord expects of His servants. It was the word of the Lord that convicted David, not the force of Nathan's character or rhetoric.
12:9 *despise the word of the LORD.* David had broken the commandments about coveting, adultery, and murder (Ex. 20:13 – 17). The word despised, in this context, means "to think lightly of."
12:13 *I have sinned against the LORD.* David did not attempt to rationalize his sin or make an excuse for himself. A fuller expression of David's confession is found in Psalm 51. ***You are not going to die.*** David deserved death (Lev. 20:10; Num. 35:31 – 33), but God's grace is able to circumvent His own plan for punishment.

12:14 Adultery—Adultery is forbidden in the Ten Commandments (Ex. 20:14), and it is not difficult to think of a long list of the messy problems that accompany adultery. But adultery is not just a problem involving other people. It is also a problem with God. It is a direct and deliberate disobedience

11:27 [z] 2Sa 12:9; Ps 51:4-5 **12:1** [a] 2Sa 7:2; 1Ki 20:35-41 [b] Ps 51 Title [c] 2Sa 14:4 **12:5** [d] 1Ki 20:40 **12:6** [e] Ex 22:1; Lk 19:8 **12:7** [f] 1Sa 16:13 [g] 1Ki 20:42 **12:8** [h] 2Sa 9:7 **12:9** [i] Nu 15:31; 1Sa 15:19 [j] 2Sa 11:15 **12:10** [k] 2Sa 13:28; 18:14-15; 1Ki 2:25 **12:11** [l] Dt 28:30; 2Sa 16:21-22 **12:12** [m] 2Sa 11:4-15 [n] 2Sa 16:22 **12:13** [o] Ge 13:13; Nu 22:34; 1Sa 15:24; 2Sa 24:10 [p] Ps 32:1-5; 51:1,9; 103:12; Zec 3:4,9 [q] Pr 28:13; Mic 7:18-19 [r] Lev 20:10; 24:17 **12:14** [s] Isa 52:5; Ro 2:24 **12:15** [t] 1Sa 25:38 **12:16** [u] 2Sa 13:31; Ps 5:7 **12:17** [v] 2Sa 3:35

now tell him the child is dead? He may do
something desperate."
19David noticed that his attendants were
whispering among themselves, and he
realized the child was dead. "Is the child
dead?" he asked.
"Yes," they replied, "he is dead."
20Then David got up from the ground.
After he had washed,[w] put on lotions and
changed his clothes,[x] he went into the
house of the LORD and worshiped. Then he
went to his own house, and at his request
they served him food, and he ate.
21His attendants asked him, "Why are
you acting this way? While the child was
alive, you fasted and wept,[y] but now that
the child is dead, you get up and eat!"
22He answered, "While the child was
still alive, I fasted and wept. I thought,
'Who knows?[z] The LORD may be gracious
to me and let the child live.'[a] 23But now that
he is dead, why should I go on fasting? Can
I bring him back again? I will go to him,[b]
but he will not return to me."[c]
24Then David comforted his wife Bathsheba,[d] and he went to her and made love
to her. She gave birth to a son, and they
named him Solomon.[e] The LORD loved him;
25and because the LORD loved him, he sent
word through Nathan the prophet to name
him Jedidiah.[a][f]
26Meanwhile Joab fought against Rabbah[g] of the Ammonites and captured the
royal citadel. 27Joab then sent messengers
to David, saying, "I have fought against
Rabbah and taken its water supply. 28Now
muster the rest of the troops and besiege
the city and capture it. Otherwise I will
take the city, and it will be named after me."
29So David mustered the entire army
and went to Rabbah, and attacked and
captured it. 30David took the crown[h] from
their king's[b] head, and it was placed on his
own head. It weighed a talent[c] of gold, and
it was set with precious stones. David took
a great quantity of plunder from the city
31and brought out the people who were
there, consigning them to labor with saws
and with iron picks and axes, and he made
them work at brickmaking.[d] David did this
to all the Ammonite[i] towns. Then he and
his entire army returned to Jerusalem.

Amnon and Tamar

13 In the course of time, Amnon[j] son of
David fell in love with Tamar,[k] the
beautiful sister of Absalom[l] son of David.
2Amnon became so obsessed with his
sister Tamar that he made himself ill. She
was a virgin, and it seemed impossible for
him to do anything to her.
3Now Amnon had an adviser named
Jonadab son of Shimeah,[m] David's brother. Jonadab was a very shrewd man. 4He
asked Amnon, "Why do you, the king's
son, look so haggard morning after morning? Won't you tell me?"
Amnon said to him, "I'm in love with Tamar, my brother Absalom's sister."
5"Go to bed and pretend to be ill," Jonadab said. "When your father comes to
see you, say to him, 'I would like my sister
Tamar to come and give me something to
eat. Let her prepare the food in my sight so
I may watch her and then eat it from her
hand.'"
6So Amnon lay down and pretended
to be ill. When the king came to see him,
Amnon said to him, "I would like my sister Tamar to come and make some special
bread in my sight, so I may eat from her
hand."
7David sent word to Tamar at the palace: "Go to the house of your brother Amnon and prepare some food for him." 8So

[a] 25 *Jedidiah* means *loved by the LORD.*
[b] 30 Or *from Milkom's* (that is, Molek's)
[c] 30 That is, about 75 pounds or about 34 kilograms
[d] 31 The meaning of the Hebrew for this clause is uncertain.

of a nonnegotiable command. This kind of disobedience is also a choice to stop listening to God in other areas—not because He won't communicate, but because we won't. We don't want to ask for help because we don't want to hear Him say, "And what about the affair with ____?" Adultery is more expensive than we can calculate.

12:24 *Solomon.* The name Solomon is related to the Hebrew word for *peace.*

12:25 *Jedidiah.* The name Jedidiah means "Beloved of the LORD." The Hebrew name is related to David's name, meaning "beloved." This name, coming from the prophet Nathan, surely must have comforted David and Bathsheba with assurance of God's forgiveness.

12:30 *a talent of gold.* The crown weighed about 75 pounds.

13:1 Temptation—Not all temptation is equal. Some kinds of temptations are easily squelched, and others must be fought with vigilance and every ounce of energy that we have. The battle begins in the mind, and one of the first steps in combating temptation is to make up one's mind that the answer must be "no." Once we begin thinking of how nice it would be to give in, the temptation has a foothold that can grow into full blown sin. God always provides a way out, but we have to want to take that way (1 Cor. 10:13).

13:4 *I'm in love with ... my brother Absalom's sister.* Such relationships are clearly forbidden in the law (Lev. 18:9,29; 20:17). The lust that he conceived in his heart gave birth to sin, and that sin, when accomplished, brought death (James 1:15). Amnon did die, but even worse, his heart was hardened so that he did not care what he had done to Tamar. For her, the price of his wickedness was very high.

12:20 [w] Mt 6:17 [x] Job 1:20 **12:21** [y] Jdg 20:26 **12:22** [z] Jnh 3:9 [a] Isa 38:1-5 **12:23** [b] Ge 37:35 [c] 1Sa 31:13; 2Sa 13:39; Job 7:10; 10:21 **12:24** [d] 1Ki 1:11 [e] 1Ki 1:10; 1Ch 22:9; 28:5; Mt 1:6 **12:25** [f] Ne 13:26 **12:26** [g] Dt 3:11; 1Ch 20:1-3 **12:30** [h] 1Ch 20:2; Est 8:15; Ps 21:3; 132:18 **12:31** [i] 1Sa 14:47 **13:1** [j] 2Sa 3:2 [k] 2Sa 14:27; 1Ch 3:9 [l] 2Sa 3:3 **13:3** [m] 1Sa 16:9

Tamar went to the house of her brother
Amnon, who was lying down. She took
some dough, kneaded it, made the bread
in his sight and baked it. 9Then she took
the pan and served him the bread, but he
refused to eat.
"Send everyone out of here,"[n] Amnon
said. So everyone left him. 10Then Amnon said to Tamar, "Bring the food here
into my bedroom so I may eat from your
hand." And Tamar took the bread she had
prepared and brought it to her brother Amnon in his bedroom. 11But when she took
it to him to eat, he grabbed[o] her and said,
"Come to bed with me, my sister."[p]
12"No, my brother!" she said to him.
"Don't force me! Such a thing should not be
done in Israel![q] Don't do this wicked thing.[r]
13What about me?[s] Where could I get rid
of my disgrace? And what about you? You
would be like one of the wicked fools in Israel. Please speak to the king; he will not
keep me from being married to you." 14But
he refused to listen to her, and since he was
stronger than she, he raped her.[t]
15Then Amnon hated her with intense
hatred. In fact, he hated her more than he
had loved her. Amnon said to her, "Get up
and get out!"
16"No!" she said to him. "Sending me
away would be a greater wrong than what
you have already done to me."
But he refused to listen to her. 17He called
his personal servant and said, "Get this
woman out of my sight and bolt the door
after her." 18So his servant put her out and
bolted the door after her. She was wearing
an ornate[a] robe,[u] for this was the kind of
garment the virgin daughters of the king
wore. 19Tamar put ashes[v] on her head and
tore the ornate robe she was wearing. She
put her hands on her head and went away,
weeping aloud as she went.
20Her brother Absalom said to her, "Has
that Amnon, your brother, been with you?
Be quiet for now, my sister; he is your
brother. Don't take this thing to heart."
And Tamar lived in her brother Absalom's
house, a desolate woman.
21When King David heard all this, he
was furious.[w] 22And Absalom never said
a word to Amnon, either good or bad;[x] he
hated[y] Amnon because he had disgraced
his sister Tamar.

Absalom Kills Amnon

23Two years later, when Absalom's
sheepshearers[z] were at Baal Hazor near
the border of Ephraim, he invited all the
king's sons to come there. 24Absalom went
to the king and said, "Your servant has had
shearers come. Will the king and his attendants please join me?"
25"No, my son," the king replied. "All of us
should not go; we would only be a burden to
you." Although Absalom urged him, he still
refused to go but gave him his blessing.
26Then Absalom said, "If not, please let
my brother Amnon come with us."
The king asked him, "Why should he go
with you?" 27But Absalom urged him, so he
sent with him Amnon and the rest of the
king's sons.
28Absalom[a] ordered his men, "Listen!
When Amnon is in high[b] spirits from
drinking wine and I say to you, 'Strike Amnon down,' then kill him. Don't be afraid.
Haven't I given you this order? Be strong
and brave.[c]" 29So Absalom's men did to
Amnon what Absalom had ordered. Then
all the king's sons got up, mounted their
mules and fled.
30While they were on their way, the report came to David: "Absalom has struck
down all the king's sons; not one of them is
left." 31The king stood up, tore[d] his clothes

a *18* The meaning of the Hebrew for this word is uncertain; also in verse 19.

13:17 ***Get this woman out.*** It is difficult to translate the contempt which Amnon had for Tamar. His order to his servant suggests the words and tone used when asking a servant to dump trash. If she had not been his sister, Amnon would have been forced to marry her (Deut. 22:28–29).

13:19 ***ashes on her head ... tore the ornate robe ... put her hands on her head.*** All of these gestures, as well as her public weeping, were traditional signs of mourning. Amnon had wantonly destroyed her, and there was nothing anyone could do to set her life right. Women who have been raped often feel abandoned by society, and the very people who should have protected them are oblivious to their need for comfort. Rape is a private crime, and yet it is also a very public menace. It is difficult to redress the wrongs caused by rape without subjecting the victim to more publicity than is comfortable for someone who has already been severely traumatized.

13:21 ***furious.*** David was angry, but he took no steps to discipline his son. Perhaps he felt he could not enforce exile on his son (Lev. 18:9,29; 20:17), when the Lord had forgiven him in a similar circumstance. The big difference between David and Amnon was that David acknowledged his sin and was remorseful and repentant.

13:23 ***Ephraim.*** This does not refer to the tribal area, but to a city about 13 miles north of Jerusalem (John 11:54).

13:29 ***mules.*** The mule, the offspring of a donkey and a horse, combines the size and strength of a horse with the surefootedness and endurance of a donkey. Although the Israelites were forbidden to breed such hybrids (Lev. 19:19), mules were imported into Israel. They were the preferred mount of royalty during this period. (18:9; 1 Kin. 1:33).

13:9 [n] Ge 45:1 **13:11** [o] Ge 39:12 [p] Ge 38:16
13:12 [q] Lev 20:17; Jdg 20:6 [r] Ge 34:7; Jdg 19:23
13:13 [s] Ge 20:12; Lev 18:9; Dt 22:21, 23-24
13:14 [t] Ge 34:2; Dt 22:25; Eze 22:11 **13:18** [u] Ge 37:23; Jdg 5:30 **13:19** [v] Jos 7:6; 1Sa 4:12; 2Sa 1:2; Est 4:1; Da 9:3
13:21 [w] Ge 34:7 **13:22** [x] Ge 31:24 [y] Lev 19:17-18; 1Jn 2:9-11 **13:23** [z] 1Sa 25:7 **13:28** [a] 2Sa 3:3
[b] Jdg 19:6, 9, 22; Ru 3:7; 1Sa 25:36 [c] 2Sa 12:10
13:31 [d] Nu 14:6; 2Sa 1:11; 12:16

and lay down on the ground; and all his
attendants stood by with their clothes torn.
32 But Jonadab son of Shimeah, David's
brother, said, "My lord should not think that
they killed all the princes; only Amnon is
dead. This has been Absalom's express intention ever since the day Amnon raped his
sister Tamar. 33 My lord the king should not
be concerned about the report that all the
king's sons are dead. Only Amnon is dead."
34 Meanwhile, Absalom had fled.
Now the man standing watch looked up
and saw many people on the road west of
him, coming down the side of the hill. The
watchman went and told the king, "I see
men in the direction of Horonaim, on the
side of the hill."[a]
35 Jonadab said to the king, "See, the
king's sons have come; it has happened just
as your servant said."
36 As he finished speaking, the king's
sons came in, wailing loudly. The king, too,
and all his attendants wept very bitterly.
37 Absalom fled and went to Talmai[e] son
of Ammihud, the king of Geshur. But King
David mourned many days for his son.
38 After Absalom fled and went to Geshur, he stayed there three years. 39 And
King David longed to go to Absalom,[f] for he
was consoled[g] concerning Amnon's death.

Absalom Returns to Jerusalem

14 Joab[h] son of Zeruiah knew that the
king's heart longed for Absalom.
2 So Joab sent someone to Tekoa[i] and had
a wise woman[j] brought from there. He
said to her, "Pretend you are in mourning.
Dress in mourning clothes, and don't use
any cosmetic lotions.[k] Act like a woman
who has spent many days grieving for the
dead. 3 Then go to the king and speak these
words to him." And Joab[l] put the words in
her mouth.
4 When the woman from Tekoa went[b]
to the king, she fell with her face to the
ground to pay him honor, and she said,
"Help me, Your Majesty!"
5 The king asked her, "What is troubling
you?"
She said, "I am a widow; my husband is
dead. 6 I your servant had two sons. They
got into a fight with each other in the field,
and no one was there to separate them.
One struck the other and killed him. 7 Now
the whole clan has risen up against your
servant; they say, 'Hand over the one who
struck his brother down, so that we may
put him to death[m] for the life of his brother
whom he killed; then we will get rid of the
heir[n] as well.' They would put out the only
burning coal I have left,[o] leaving my husband neither name nor descendant on the
face of the earth."
8 The king said to the woman, "Go home,[p]
and I will issue an order in your behalf."
9 But the woman from Tekoa said to him,
"Let my lord the king pardon[q] me and my
family,[r] and let the king and his throne be
without guilt.[s]"
10 The king replied, "If anyone says anything to you, bring them to me, and they
will not bother you again."
11 She said, "Then let the king invoke
the LORD his God to prevent the avenger[t]
of blood from adding to the destruction, so
that my son will not be destroyed."
"As surely as the LORD lives," he said,
"not one hair[u] of your son's head will fall
to the ground.[v]"
12 Then the woman said, "Let your servant speak a word to my lord the king."
"Speak," he replied.
13 The woman said, "Why then have you
devised a thing like this against the people
of God? When the king says this, does he
not convict himself,[w] for the king has not
brought back his banished son?[x] 14 Like water[y] spilled on the ground, which cannot be
recovered, so we must die.[z] But that is not
what God desires; rather, he devises ways
so that a banished person[a] does not remain
banished from him.
15 "And now I have come to say this to my

---

[a] *34* Septuagint; Hebrew does not have this sentence. [b] *4* Many Hebrew manuscripts, Septuagint, Vulgate and Syriac; most Hebrew manuscripts *spoke*

13:37 *Talmai.* Talmai was Absalom's grandfather, the father of David's wife Maakah (3:3). He ruled as king of the territory of Geshur, northeast of the Sea of Galilee.

14:7 *put out the only burning coal I have left.* The woman used a graphic picture of the extinction of her family. The demise of a family name and the end of a surviving remnant or family line were crucial matters to the Hebrew people.

14:11 *avenger of blood.* The Hebrew phrase, "avenger of blood" or "redeemer of blood" is closely related to the term "guardian-redeemer." The guardian-redeemer is the protector of family rights. Here, the protector of the family would be expected to bring vengeance on one who had taken the life of a family member. Cities of refuge had been established under Moses for protection from a blood avenger in cases where the killing was accidental (Num. 35:9–34).

14:14 Restoration — The wise woman from Tekoa spoke compellingly of Absalom's (the banished one's) need to make things right with God. David, whose heart was leaning toward his son, was touched, and he brought Absalom back. But no restoration took place. Neither Absalom nor David discussed how they had failed to seek justice according to law in the case of Amnon and Tamar. Restoration is only possible if

13:37 [e] ver 34; 2Sa 3:3; 14:23,32 **13:39** [f] 2Sa 14:13 [g] 2Sa 12:19-23 **14:1** [h] 2Sa 2:18 **14:2** [i] 2Ch 11:6; Ne 3:5; Jer 6:1; Am 1:1 [j] 2Sa 20:16 [k] Ru 3:3; 2Sa 12:20; Isa 1:6 **14:3** [l] ver 19 **14:7** [m] Nu 35:19 [n] Mt 21:38 [o] Dt 19:10-13 **14:8** [p] 1Sa 25:35 **14:9** [q] 1Sa 25:24 [r] Mt 27:25 [s] 1Sa 25:28; 1Ki 2:33 **14:11** [t] Nu 35:12, 21 [u] Mt 10:30 [v] 1Sa 14:45 **14:13** [w] 2Sa 12:7; 1Ki 20:40 [x] 2Sa 13:38-39 **14:14** [y] Job 14:11; Ps 58:7; Isa 19:5 [z] Job 10:8; 17:13; 30:23; Ps 22:15; Heb 9:27 [a] Nu 35:15,25-28; Job 34:15

lord the king because the people have made me afraid. Your servant thought, 'I will speak to the king; perhaps he will grant his servant's request.
16Perhaps the king will agree to deliver his servant from the hand of the man who is trying to cut off both me and my son from God's inheritance.'[b]
17"And now your servant says, 'May the word of my lord the king secure my inheritance, for my lord the king is like an angel[c] of God in discerning[d] good and evil. May the LORD your God be with you.'"
18Then the king said to the woman, "Don't keep from me the answer to what I am going to ask you."

"Let my lord the king speak," the woman said.
19The king asked, "Isn't the hand of Joab[e] with you in all this?"

The woman answered, "As surely as you live, my lord the king, no one can turn to the right or to the left from anything my lord the king says. Yes, it was your servant Joab who instructed me to do this and who put all these words into the mouth of your servant.
20Your servant Joab did this to change the present situation. My lord has wisdom[f] like that of an angel of God—he knows everything that happens in the land.[g]"
21The king said to Joab, "Very well, I will do it. Go, bring back the young man Absalom."
22Joab fell with his face to the ground to pay him honor, and he blessed the king.[h] Joab said, "Today your servant knows that he has found favor in your eyes, my lord the king, because the king has granted his servant's request."
23Then Joab went to Geshur and brought Absalom back to Jerusalem.
24But the king said, "He must go to his own house; he must not see my face." So Absalom went to his own house and did not see the face of the king.
25In all Israel there was not a man so highly praised for his handsome appearance as Absalom. From the top of his head to the sole of his foot there was no blemish in him.
26Whenever he cut the hair of his head[i]—he used to cut his hair once a year because it became too heavy for him—he would weigh it, and its weight was two hundred shekels[a] by the royal standard.
27Three sons[j] and a daughter were born to Absalom. His daughter's name was Tamar,[k] and she became a beautiful woman.
28Absalom lived two years in Jerusalem without seeing the king's face.
29Then Absalom sent for Joab in order to send him to the king, but Joab refused to come to him. So he sent a second time, but he refused to come.
30Then he said to his servants, "Look, Joab's field is next to mine, and he has barley[l] there. Go and set it on fire." So Absalom's servants set the field on fire.
31Then Joab did go to Absalom's house, and he said to him, "Why have your servants set my field on fire?[m]"
32Absalom said to Joab, "Look, I sent word to you and said, 'Come here so I can send you to the king to ask, "Why have I come from Geshur?[n] It would be better for me if I were still there!"' Now then, I want to see the king's face, and if I am guilty of anything, let him put me to death."[o]

[a] *26* That is, about 5 pounds or about 2.3 kilograms

---

we are willing to look sin in the face and acknowledge the need to repent before God and turn to new and righteous ways.

It is difficult to know exactly what the woman is saying to David, because she is speaking with double meanings. On the surface is her made-up story, which is supposed to speak allegorically to David. In this instance she is referring to the fact that because "her son" did not kill "his brother" in premeditated murder, he should have found safety in a city of refuge. Absalom, however, did kill his brother in premeditated murder. The mitigating factor is that Amnon should have been banished for his rape of Tamar, and the king, Tamar's first protector, had done nothing. Absalom was the next in line as near relative of Tamar, so there was some justice in his desire to bring Amnon to account.

14:19 ***hand of Joab.*** The exact extent of the game Joab was playing is not explained. Joab had been a difficult force in David's life (13:37–39). Joab had killed Abner in a way that David considered unjust, and it was Joab who arranged Uriah's death for David. These factors, and the fact that Joab was in some way sponsoring Absalom's return, made the relationship between David and Joab uneasy. The old trust was gone.

14:24 ***he must not see my face.*** Absalom was allowed to return, but his position was not restored. There were issues of justice that had not been settled. One was David's apparent indifference to the sin of Amnon, and the other was whether Amnon's death was an act of justice or an act of murder. It never pays to let matters of justice remain undecided for a long period of time. It creates bitterness and disrespect for the authorities whose job it is to decide matters of justice, and the people involved become set in their attitudes in a way that makes repentance and restitution virtually impossible.

14:26 ***two hundred shekels.*** The weight of Absalom's hair was about 5 pounds.

14:27 ***Three sons.*** Apparently Absalom's sons did not live to maturity. When he set up a pillar in Jerusalem to memorialize his name, he said it was because he had no son.

14:32 ***Come here.*** Apparently Joab did not sponsor Absalom to the extent of acting as a go-between with his father. Absalom responded with the attitude of a superior to an inferior, not what one might expect from the king's son to his father's highest ranking officer. It seems from the fearless and high handed way

14:16 [b] Ex 34:9; 1Sa 26:19 **14:17** [c] ver 20; 1Sa 29:9; 2Sa 19:27 [d] 1Ki 3:9; Da 2:21 **14:19** [e] ver 3
14:20 [f] 1Ki 3:12, 28; Isa 28:6 [g] ver 17; 2Sa 18:13; 19:27
14:22 [h] Ge 47:7 **14:26** [i] 2Sa 18:9; Eze 44:20
14:27 [j] 2Sa 18:18 [k] 2Sa 13:1 **14:30** [l] Ex 9:31
14:31 [m] Jdg 15:5 **14:32** [n] 2Sa 3:3 [o] 1Sa 20:8

33So Joab went to the king and told him
this. Then the king summoned Absalom,
and he came in and bowed down with his
face to the ground before the king. And the
king kissed[p] Absalom.

Absalom's Conspiracy

15 In the course of time,[q] Absalom provided himself with a chariot[r] and
horses and with fifty men to run ahead of
him. 2He would get up early and stand by
the side of the road leading to the city gate.[s]
Whenever anyone came with a complaint
to be placed before the king for a decision,
Absalom would call out to him, "What
town are you from?" He would answer,
"Your servant is from one of the tribes of
Israel." 3Then Absalom would say to him,
"Look, your claims are valid and proper,
but there is no representative of the king to
hear you."[t] 4And Absalom would add, "If
only I were appointed judge in the land![u]
Then everyone who has a complaint or
case could come to me and I would see that
they receive justice."
5Also, whenever anyone approached
him to bow down before him, Absalom
would reach out his hand, take hold of him
and kiss him. 6Absalom behaved in this
way toward all the Israelites who came to
the king asking for justice, and so he stole
the hearts[v] of the people of Israel.
7At the end of four[a] years, Absalom said
to the king, "Let me go to Hebron and fulfill a vow I made to the LORD. 8While your
servant was living at Geshur[w] in Aram, I
made this vow:[x] 'If the LORD takes me back
to Jerusalem, I will worship the LORD in
Hebron.[b]'"
9The king said to him, "Go in peace." So
he went to Hebron.
10Then Absalom sent secret messengers
throughout the tribes of Israel to say, "As
soon as you hear the sound of the trumpets,[y] then say, 'Absalom is king in Hebron.'" 11Two hundred men from Jerusalem had accompanied Absalom. They had
been invited as guests and went quite inno-
cently, knowing nothing about the matter.
12While Absalom was offering sacrifices,
he also sent for Ahithophel[z] the Gilonite,
David's counselor,[a] to come from Giloh,[b]
his hometown. And so the conspiracy
gained strength, and Absalom's following
kept on increasing.[c]

David Flees

13A messenger came and told David,
"The hearts of the people of Israel are with
Absalom."
14Then David said to all his officials who
were with him in Jerusalem, "Come! We
must flee,[d] or none of us will escape from
Absalom.[e] We must leave immediately, or he
will move quickly to overtake us and bring
ruin on us and put the city to the sword."
15The king's officials answered him,
"Your servants are ready to do whatever
our lord the king chooses."
16The king set out, with his entire household following him; but he left ten concubines[f] to take care of the palace. 17So the
king set out, with all the people following
him, and they halted at the edge of the city.
18All his men marched past him, along with
all the Kerethites[g] and Pelethites; and all the
six hundred Gittites who had accompanied
him from Gath marched before the king.
19The king said to Ittai[h] the Gittite, "Why
should you come along with us? Go back
and stay with King Absalom. You are a
foreigner,[i] an exile from your homeland.
20You came only yesterday. And today shall
I make you wander[j] about with us, when I do
not know where I am going? Go back, and
take your people with you. May the LORD
show you kindness and faithfulness."[c][k]

a 7 Some Septuagint manuscripts, Syriac and Josephus; Hebrew *forty* *b* 8 Some Septuagint manuscripts; Hebrew does not have *in Hebron.* *c* 20 Septuagint; Hebrew *May kindness and faithfulness be with you*

---

in which he answered Joab that Absalom was already seeing himself as his father's successor.

15:4 *I would see that they receive justice.* Administration of justice, the proper relationship between people in society according to God's standard of righteousness, was a major concern of the Old Testament rulers and prophets (8:15; 1 Kin. 3:28; Is. 1:17; Amos 5:24). Absalom is playing on the people's emotions, and perhaps justifying himself in his actions against Amnon as well.

15:13 *The hearts of the people of Israel.* When David's power in Judah was confined to Hebron (ch. 2) he was resented by the supporters of Saul in the rest of the country. Old suspicions and resentments can be stoked again by a person who knows how to use people to his own advantage—a disreputable quality in which Absalom excelled.

15:15 *Your servants are ready.* The loyalty of David's servants must have been a real encouragement in a time of such disloyalty from David's own family.

15:18 *Kerethites ... Pelethites.* The Kerethites and Pelethites were elite units of David's army. These trusted troops of David were not Israelites, but mercenaries from a variety of nations, possibly Crete and Philistia. They had been with David for years, owed him their loyalty, and would defend him and his family to the death. ***Gittites.*** The Gittites were probably Philistine mercenary soldiers who were among David's original followers from Gath (1 Sam. 22:1–2).

15:19–21 Righteousness—Making the choice to stand with the right man, even when it looked like he

14:33 [p] Ge 33:4; Lk 15:20 **15:1** [q] 2Sa 12:11 [r] 1Sa 8:11; 1Ki 1:5 **15:2** [s] Ge 23:10; 2Sa 19:8 **15:3** [t] Pr 12:2 **15:4** [u] Jdg 9:29 **15:6** [v] Ro 16:18 **15:8** [w] 2Sa 3:3; 13:37-38 [x] Ge 28:20 **15:10** [y] 1Ki 1:34, 39; 2Ki 9:13 **15:12** [z] ver 31, 34; 2Sa 16:15, 23; 1Ch 27:33 [a] Job 19:14; Ps 41:9; 55:13; Jer 9:4 [b] Jos 15:51 [c] Ps 3:1 **15:14** [d] 2Sa 12:11; 1Ki 2:26; Ps 3 Title; 132:1 [e] 2Sa 19:9 **15:16** [f] 2Sa 16:21-22; 20:3 **15:18** [g] 1Sa 30:14; 2Sa 8:18; 20:7, 23; 1Ki 1:38, 44; 1Ch 18:17 **15:19** [h] 2Sa 18:2 [i] Ge 31:15 **15:20** [j] 1Sa 23:13 [k] 2Sa 2:6

21But Ittai replied to the king, "As surely
as the LORD lives, and as my lord the king
lives, wherever my lord the king may be,
whether it means life or death, there will
your servant be."[l]
22David said to Ittai, "Go ahead, march
on." So Ittai the Gittite marched on with
all his men and the families that were with
him.
23The whole countryside wept aloud as
all the people passed by. The king also
crossed the Kidron Valley,[m] and all the
people moved on toward the wilderness.
24Zadok[n] was there, too, and all the Levites who were with him were carrying the
ark[o] of the covenant of God. They set down
the ark of God, and Abiathar[p] offered sacrifices until all the people had finished
leaving the city.
25Then the king said to Zadok, "Take the
ark of God back into the city. If I find favor
in the LORD's eyes, he will bring me back
and let me see it and his dwelling place[q]
again. 26But if he says, 'I am not pleased
with you,' then I am ready; let him do to me
whatever seems good to him.[r]"
27The king also said to Zadok the priest,
"Do you understand?[s] Go back to the city
with my blessing. Take your son Ahimaaz with you, and also Abiathar's son Jonathan.[t] You and Abiathar return with your
two sons. 28I will wait at the fords[u] in the
wilderness until word comes from you
to inform me." 29So Zadok and Abiathar
took the ark of God back to Jerusalem and
stayed there.
30But David continued up the Mount of
Olives, weeping[v] as he went; his head[w] was
covered and he was barefoot. All the people with him covered their heads too and
were weeping as they went up. 31Now David had been told, "Ahithophel[x] is among
the conspirators with Absalom." So David
prayed, "LORD, turn Ahithophel's counsel
into foolishness."
32When David arrived at the summit,
where people used to worship God, Hushai
the Arkite[y] was there to meet him, his robe
torn and dust[z] on his head. 33David said to
him, "If you go with me, you will be a burden[a] to me. 34But if you return to the city
and say to Absalom, 'Your Majesty, I will
be your servant; I was your father's servant
in the past, but now I will be your servant,'[b]
then you can help me by frustrating Ahithophel's advice. 35Won't the priests Zadok
and Abiathar be there with you? Tell them
anything you hear in the king's palace.[c]
36Their two sons, Ahimaaz son of Zadok
and Jonathan[d] son of Abiathar, are there
with them. Send them to me with anything
you hear."
37So Hushai,[e] David's confidant, arrived
at Jerusalem as Absalom[f] was entering the
city.

David and Ziba

16 When David had gone a short distance beyond the summit, there was
Ziba,[g] the steward of Mephibosheth, waiting to meet him. He had a string of donkeys saddled and loaded with two hundred
loaves of bread, a hundred cakes of raisins,
a hundred cakes of figs and a skin of wine.[h]
2The king asked Ziba, "Why have you
brought these?"

Ziba answered, "The donkeys are for the
king's household to ride on, the bread and
fruit are for the men to eat, and the wine is
to refresh[i] those who become exhausted in
the wilderness."
3The king then asked, "Where is your
master's grandson?"[j]

Ziba said to him, "He is staying in Jerusalem, because he thinks, 'Today the Israelites will restore to me my grandfather's
kingdom.'"
4Then the king said to Ziba, "All that belonged to Mephibosheth is now yours."

"I humbly bow," Ziba said. "May I find
favor in your eyes, my lord the king."

---

might spend the rest of his life in exile was not practical, but it was right. We will all have to make choices to tell the truth, stand up for honorable actions, or support someone who is right but not powerful. Taking the right path does not mean it will be easy, but when we are on the right path, God is with us even "through the darkest valley" (Ps. 23:4).

15:21 *whether it means life or death.* David rewarded Ittai's loyalty when he made Ittai commander of a third of the army (18:2).

15:23 *Kidron Valley.* The Kidron Valley separates Jerusalem and the Mount of Olives. ***toward the wilderness.*** "Toward the wilderness" refers to traveling the road leading through the wilderness of Judah to Jericho and down to the fords of the Jordan.

15:25 *he will bring me back.* David committed the entire situation to the care and will of the Lord.

15:31 *Ahithophel.* Ahithophel was Bathsheba's grandfather (11:3; 23:34). A wise counselor (16:23), he had been in David's service (v. 12) but had switched his allegiance to Absalom. David's prayer was for his enemy to be confused. The name Ahithophel may mean "Brother of Folly."

15:34 *frustrating . . . advice.* David had committed the entire situation to the care and will of the Lord, but he was acting wisely to protect himself and to provide a source of information as well as an inside confederate to confound the enemy.

16:1 *Ziba.* A longtime servant of both Saul and Mephibosheth, Ziba was expressing his loyalty to King David.

15:21 [l] Ru 1:16-17; Pr 17:17 **15:23** [m] 2Ch 29:16
15:24 [n] 2Sa 8:17 [o] Nu 4:15 [p] 1Sa 22:20 **15:25** [q] Ex 15:13; Ps 43:3; Jer 25:30 **15:26** [r] 1Sa 3:18; 2Sa 22:20; 1Ki 10:9
15:27 [s] 1Sa 9:9 [t] 2Sa 17:17 **15:28** [u] 2Sa 17:16
15:30 [v] 2Sa 19:4; Ps 126:6 [w] Est 6:12; Isa 20:2-4
15:31 [x] ver 12; 2Sa 16:23; 17:14,23 **15:32** [y] Jos 16:2 [z] 2Sa 1:2 **15:33** [a] 2Sa 19:35 **15:34** [b] 2Sa 16:19
15:35 [c] 2Sa 17:15-16 **15:36** [d] ver 27; 2Sa 17:17
15:37 [e] 2Sa 16:16-17; 1Ch 27:33 [f] 2Sa 16:15
16:1 [g] 2Sa 9:1-13 [h] 1Sa 25:18 **16:2** [i] 2Sa 17:27-29
16:3 [j] 2Sa 9:9-10; 19:26-27

Shimei Curses David

5As King David approached Bahurim,[k] a man from the same clan as Saul's family came out from there. His name was Shimei[l] son of Gera, and he cursed[m] as he came out. 6He pelted David and all the king's officials with stones, though all the troops and the special guard were on David's right and left. 7As he cursed, Shimei said, "Get out, get out, you murderer, you scoundrel! 8The LORD has repaid you for all the blood you shed in the household of Saul, in whose place you have reigned.[n] The LORD has given the kingdom into the hands of your son Absalom. You have come to ruin because you are a murderer!"

9Then Abishai[o] son of Zeruiah said to the king, "Why should this dead dog curse my lord the king? Let me go over and cut off his head."[p]

10But the king said, "What does this have to do with you, you sons of Zeruiah?[q] If he is cursing because the LORD said to him, 'Curse David,' who can ask, 'Why do you do this?' "[r]

11David then said to Abishai and all his officials, "My son,[s] my own flesh and blood, is trying to kill me. How much more, then, this Benjamite! Leave him alone; let him curse, for the LORD has told him to.[t] 12It may be that the LORD will look upon my misery[u] and restore to me his covenant blessing[v] instead of his curse today.[w]"

13So David and his men continued along the road while Shimei was going along the hillside opposite him, cursing as he went and throwing stones at him and showering him with dirt. 14The king and all the people with him arrived at their destination exhausted.[x] And there he refreshed himself.

The Advice of Ahithophel and Hushai

15Meanwhile, Absalom[y] and all the men of Israel came to Jerusalem, and Ahithophel[z] was with him. 16Then Hushai[a] the Arkite, David's confidant, went to Absalom and said to him, "Long live the king! Long live the king!"

17Absalom said to Hushai, "So this is the love you show your friend? If he's your friend, why didn't you go with him?"[b]

18Hushai said to Absalom, "No, the one chosen by the LORD, by these people, and by all the men of Israel—his I will be, and I will remain with him. 19Furthermore, whom should I serve? Should I not serve the son? Just as I served your father, so I will serve you."[c]

20Absalom said to Ahithophel, "Give us your advice. What should we do?"

21Ahithophel answered, "Sleep with your father's concubines whom he left to take care of the palace. Then all Israel will hear that you have made yourself obnoxious to your father, and the hands of everyone with you will be more resolute." 22So they pitched a tent for Absalom on the roof, and he slept with his father's concubines in the sight of all Israel.[d]

23Now in those days the advice[e] Ahithophel gave was like that of one who inquires of God. That was how both David[f] and Absalom regarded all of Ahithophel's advice.

17 Ahithophel said to Absalom, "I would[a] choose twelve thousand men and set out tonight in pursuit of David. 2I would attack him while he is weary and weak.[g] I would strike him with terror, and then all the people with him will flee. I would strike down only the king[h] 3and bring all the people back to you. The death of the man you seek will mean the return of all; all the people will be unharmed." 4This plan seemed good to Absalom and to all the elders of Israel.

5But Absalom said, "Summon also Hushai[i] the Arkite, so we can hear what he has to say as well." 6When Hushai came to

[a] *1* Or *Let me*

16:5 ***Bahurim.*** Bahurim was near Jerusalem, east of the Mount of Olives (3:16). ***cursed.*** These were not simple insults or the words of someone with a foul mouth. Shimei was asking God to destroy David (Num. 22:6).

16:6 ***pelted ... with stones.*** Throwing stones is a gesture of contempt, as if the fleeing king were merely a stray dog. Stones can also be deadly, as is shown by the fact that stoning was a normal means of capital punishment among the Hebrews (1 Kin. 21:13).

16:9–13 Forbearance—David was more aware of his failure as a father than his dignity as a king. David knew that both Moses and Saul had been disciplined by God, and he certainly did not rule out the idea that both Absalom's rebellion and Shimei's cursing might be part of a lesson that God had for him. He was willing to endure both while he waited to see how God would work things out.

16:10 ***What does this have to do with you.*** This idiom means that David did not share the feelings and views of Abishai.

16:21–22 ***concubines.*** In ancient times taking over a king's harem was a recognized means of claiming the throne. Once Absalom violated David's concubines, he was set on a course of sure and final alienation from his father. Putting his tent on the roof was a public and insolent act.

17:2 ***I would strike down only the king.*** In a battle, it is a little rash to promise to kill only one person. Ahithophel was suggesting that David's companions and troops would switch their loyalty to Absalom if David were killed.

16:5 [k] 2Sa 3:16 [l] 2Sa 19:16-23; 1Ki 2:8-9, 36, 44 [m] Ex 22:28
16:8 [n] 2Sa 21:9 **16:9** [o] 2Sa 9:8 [p] Ex 22:28; Lk 9:54
16:10 [q] 2Sa 19:22 [r] Ro 9:20 **16:11** [s] 2Sa 12:11 [t] Ge 45:5
16:12 [u] Ps 4:1; 25:18 [v] Dt 23:5; Ro 8:28 [w] Ps 109:28
16:14 [x] 2Sa 17:2 **16:15** [y] 2Sa 15:37 [z] 2Sa 15:12
16:16 [a] 2Sa 15:37 **16:17** [b] 2Sa 19:25 **16:19** [c] 2Sa 15:34
16:22 [d] 2Sa 12:11-12; 15:16 **16:23** [e] 2Sa 17:14, 23
[f] 2Sa 15:12 **17:2** [g] 2Sa 16:14 [h] 1Ki 22:31; Zec 13:7
17:5 [i] 2Sa 15:32

him, Absalom said, "Ahithophel has given
this advice. Should we do what he says? If
not, give us your opinion."
7Hushai replied to Absalom, "The advice
Ahithophel has given is not good this time.
8You know your father and his men; they
are fighters, and as fierce as a wild bear
robbed of her cubs.[j] Besides, your father is
an experienced fighter;[k] he will not spend
the night with the troops. 9Even now, he is
hidden in a cave or some other place.[l] If he
should attack your troops first,[a] whoever
hears about it will say, 'There has been a
slaughter among the troops who follow
Absalom.' 10Then even the bravest soldier,
whose heart is like the heart of a lion,[m] will
melt[n] with fear, for all Israel knows that
your father is a fighter and that those with
him are brave.[o]
11"So I advise you: Let all Israel, from
Dan to Beersheba[p]—as numerous as the
sand[q] on the seashore—be gathered to
you, with you yourself leading them into
battle. 12Then we will attack him wherever
he may be found, and we will fall on him
as dew settles on the ground. Neither he
nor any of his men will be left alive. 13If he
withdraws into a city, then all Israel will
bring ropes to that city, and we will drag it
down to the valley[r] until not so much as a
pebble is left."
14Absalom and all the men of Israel said,
"The advice[s] of Hushai the Arkite is better
than that of Ahithophel."[t] For the LORD had
determined to frustrate[u] the good advice of
Ahithophel in order to bring disaster[v] on
Absalom.[w]
15Hushai told Zadok and Abiathar, the
priests, "Ahithophel has advised Absalom
and the elders of Israel to do such and such,
but I have advised them to do so and so.
16Now send a message at once and tell David, 'Do not spend the night at the fords in
the wilderness;[x] cross over without fail, or
the king and all the people with him will be
swallowed up.[y]'"
17Jonathan[z] and Ahimaaz were staying at En Rogel.[a] A female servant was
to go and inform them, and they were to
go and tell King David, for they could not
risk being seen entering the city. 18But a
young man saw them and told Absalom.
So the two of them left at once and went
to the house of a man in Bahurim.[b] He had
a well in his courtyard, and they climbed
down into it. 19His wife took a covering and
spread it out over the opening of the well
and scattered grain over it. No one knew
anything about it.[c]
20When Absalom's men came to the
woman[d] at the house, they asked, "Where
are Ahimaaz and Jonathan?"
The woman answered them, "They
crossed over the brook."[b] The men
searched but found no one, so they returned to Jerusalem.
21After they had gone, the two climbed
out of the well and went to inform King David. They said to him, "Set out and cross
the river at once; Ahithophel has advised
such and such against you." 22So David
and all the people with him set out and
crossed the Jordan. By daybreak, no one
was left who had not crossed the Jordan.
23When Ahithophel saw that his advice[e]
had not been followed, he saddled his donkey and set out for his house in his hometown. He put his house in order[f] and then
hanged himself. So he died and was buried
in his father's tomb.

Absalom's Death

24David went to Mahanaim,[g] and Absalom crossed the Jordan with all the men of
Israel. 25Absalom had appointed Amasa[h]
over the army in place of Joab. Amasa was
the son of Jether,[c][i] an Ishmaelite[d] who had
married Abigail,[e] the daughter of Nahash
and sister of Zeruiah the mother of Joab.
26The Israelites and Absalom camped in
the land of Gilead.
27When David came to Mahanaim, Shobi son of Nahash[j] from Rabbah[k] of the
Ammonites, and Makir[l] son of Ammiel
from Lo Debar, and Barzillai[m] the Gileadite[n] from Rogelim 28brought bedding and
bowls and articles of pottery. They also

[a] 9 Or *When some of the men fall at the first attack* [b] 20 Or *"They passed by the sheep pen toward the water."* [c] 25 Hebrew *Ithra,* a variant of *Jether* [d] 25 Some Septuagint manuscripts (see also 1 Chron. 2:17); Hebrew and other Septuagint manuscripts *Israelite* [e] 25 Hebrew *Abigal,* a variant of *Abigail*

17:8 ***bear robbed of her cubs.*** There is no more dangerous foe in the woods than a mother bear who believes her cubs to be in danger.

17:22 ***crossed the Jordan.*** Although the Jordan was not a large river, crossing it provided a barrier between him and his enemies. The tribal allotments included land on both sides of the Jordan, but there was always an emotional understanding that the "real" land of Israel was west of the Jordan. David was truly an exile.

17:27 ***Shobi ... Barzillai.*** The gifts of these three men showed a real understanding of the material needs of the exiles, and this act of kindness must have been very encouraging to them. ***Makir.*** Jonathan's son Mephibosheth was living with Makir when David found him (9:4).

17:8 [j] Hos 13:8 [k] 1Sa 16:18 **17:9** [l] Jer 41:9 **17:10** [m] 1Ch 12:8 [n] Jos 2:9,11; Eze 21:15 [o] 2Sa 23:8; 1Ch 11:11 **17:11** [p] Jdg 20:1 [q] Ge 12:2; 22:17; Jos 11:4 **17:13** [r] Mic 1:6 **17:14** [s] 2Sa 16:23 [t] 2Sa 15:12 [u] 2Sa 15:34; Ne 4:15 [v] Ps 9:16 [w] 2Ch 10:8 **17:16** [x] 2Sa 15:28 [y] 2Sa 15:35 **17:17** [z] 2Sa 15:27,36 [a] Jos 15:7; 18:16 **17:18** [b] 2Sa 3:16; 16:5 **17:19** [c] Jos 2:6 **17:20** [d] Ex 1:19; Jos 2:3-5; 1Sa 19:12-17 **17:23** [e] 2Sa 15:12; 16:23 [f] 2Ki 20:1; Mt 27:5 **17:24** [g] Ge 32:2; 2Sa 2:8 **17:25** [h] 2Sa 19:13; 20:4,9-12; 1Ki 2:5,32; 1Ch 12:18 [i] 1Ch 2:13-17 **17:27** [j] 1Sa 11:1 [k] Dt 3:11; 2Sa 10:1-2; 12:26, 29 [l] 2Sa 9:4 [m] 2Sa 19:31-39; 1Ki 2:7 [n] 2Sa 19:31; Ezr 2:61

brought wheat and barley, flour and roasted grain, beans and lentils,[a] 29honey and
curds, sheep, and cheese from cows' milk
for David and his people to eat.[o] For they
said, "The people have become exhausted
and hungry and thirsty in the wilderness.[p]"

18 David mustered the men who were
with him and appointed over them
commanders of thousands and commanders of hundreds. 2David sent out his
troops,[q] a third under the command of
Joab, a third under Joab's brother Abishai[r]
son of Zeruiah, and a third under Ittai[s] the
Gittite. The king told the troops, "I myself
will surely march out with you."

3But the men said, "You must not go out;
if we are forced to flee, they won't care
about us. Even if half of us die, they won't
care; but you are worth ten[t] thousand of
us.[b] It would be better now for you to give
us support from the city."[u]

4The king answered, "I will do whatever
seems best to you."

So the king stood beside the gate while
all his men marched out in units of hundreds and of thousands. 5The king commanded Joab, Abishai and Ittai, "Be gentle
with the young man Absalom for my sake."
And all the troops heard the king giving
orders concerning Absalom to each of the
commanders.

6David's army marched out of the city
to fight Israel, and the battle took place
in the forest[v] of Ephraim. 7There Israel's
troops were routed by David's men, and
the casualties that day were great—twenty thousand men. 8The battle spread out
over the whole countryside, and the forest
swallowed up more men that day than the
sword.

9Now Absalom happened to meet David's men. He was riding his mule, and as
the mule went under the thick branches of
a large oak, Absalom's hair[w] got caught
in the tree. He was left hanging in midair,
while the mule he was riding kept on going.

10When one of the men saw what had
happened, he told Joab, "I just saw Absalom hanging in an oak tree."

11Joab said to the man who had told him
this, "What! You saw him? Why didn't you
strike[x] him to the ground right there? Then
I would have had to give you ten shekels[c] of
silver and a warrior's belt.[y]"

12But the man replied, "Even if a thousand shekels[d] were weighed out into my
hands, I would not lay a hand on the king's
son. In our hearing the king commanded you and Abishai and Ittai, 'Protect the
young man Absalom for my sake.[e]' 13And
if I had put my life in jeopardy[f]—and nothing is hidden from the king[z]—you would
have kept your distance from me."

14Joab[a] said, "I'm not going to wait like
this for you." So he took three javelins in
his hand and plunged them into Absalom's
heart while Absalom was still alive in the
oak tree. 15And ten of Joab's armor-bearers surrounded Absalom, struck him and
killed him.[b]

16Then Joab[c] sounded the trumpet, and
the troops stopped pursuing Israel, for
Joab halted them. 17They took Absalom,
threw him into a big pit in the forest and
piled up[d] a large heap of rocks[e] over him.
Meanwhile, all the Israelites fled to their
homes.

18During his lifetime Absalom had taken
a pillar and erected it in the King's Valley[f]
as a monument[g] to himself, for he thought,
"I have no son[h] to carry on the memory of
my name." He named the pillar after himself, and it is called Absalom's Monument
to this day.

David Mourns

19Now Ahimaaz[i] son of Zadok said, "Let
me run and take the news to the king that
the LORD has vindicated him by delivering
him from the hand of his enemies.[j]"

20"You are not the one to take the news
today," Joab told him. "You may take the
news another time, but you must not do so
today, because the king's son is dead."

21Then Joab said to a Cushite, "Go, tell
the king what you have seen." The Cushite
bowed down before Joab and ran off.

22Ahimaaz son of Zadok again said to
Joab, "Come what may, please let me run
behind the Cushite."

---

[a] *28* Most Septuagint manuscripts and Syriac; Hebrew *lentils, and roasted grain*
[b] *3* Two Hebrew manuscripts, some Septuagint manuscripts and Vulgate; most Hebrew manuscripts *care; for now there are ten thousand like us*
[c] *11* That is, about 4 ounces or about 115 grams
[d] *12* That is, about 25 pounds or about 12 kilograms
[e] *12* A few Hebrew manuscripts, Septuagint, Vulgate and Syriac; most Hebrew manuscripts may be translated *Absalom, whoever you may be.*
[f] *13* Or *Otherwise, if I had acted treacherously toward him*

18:3–4 Wisdom—One facet of good leadership is the ability to delegate authority to others and leave the results in the hands of God. Waiting in safety was not David's idea, but it seemed best to others, so David agreed. David's strength as a leader lay in having the hearts of his followers, and they in turn put his safety as a high priority. These loyal men did not think that God was done with David as king, and David needed their wisdom.

18:9 ***oak.*** This tree is a terebinth, sometimes called an oak. It was native to the land of Israel and was a strong tree that grew to a height of about 35 feet.

17:29 [o] 1Ch 12:40 [p] 2Sa 16:2; Ro 12:13 **18:2** [q] Jdg 7:16; 1Sa 11:11 [r] 1Sa 26:6 [s] 2Sa 15:19 **18:3** [t] 1Sa 18:7 [u] 2Sa 21:17 **18:6** [v] Jos 17:18 **18:9** [w] 2Sa 14:26 **18:11** [x] 2Sa 3:39 [y] 1Sa 18:4 **18:13** [z] 2Sa 14:19-20 **18:14** [a] 2Sa 2:18; 14:30 **18:15** [b] 2Sa 12:10 **18:16** [c] 2Sa 2:28; 20:22 **18:17** [d] Jos 7:26 [e] Jos 8:29 **18:18** [f] Ge 14:17 [g] Ge 50:5; Nu 32:42; 1Sa 15:12 [h] 2Sa 14:27 **18:19** [i] 2Sa 15:36 [j] ver 31; Jdg 11:36

But Joab replied, "My son, why do you want to go? You don't have any news that will bring you a reward."

23He said, "Come what may, I want to run."

So Joab said, "Run!" Then Ahimaaz ran by way of the plain[a] and outran the Cushite.

24While David was sitting between the inner and outer gates, the watchman[k] went up to the roof of the gateway by the wall. As he looked out, he saw a man running alone.
25The watchman called out to the king and reported it.

The king said, "If he is alone, he must have good news." And the runner came closer and closer.

26Then the watchman saw another runner, and he called down to the gatekeeper, "Look, another man running alone!"

The king said, "He must be bringing good news,[l] too."

27The watchman said, "It seems to me that the first one runs like[m] Ahimaaz son of Zadok."

"He's a good man," the king said. "He comes with good news."

28Then Ahimaaz called out to the king, "All is well!" He bowed down before the king with his face to the ground and said, "Praise be to the LORD your God! He has delivered up those who lifted their hands against my lord the king."

29The king asked, "Is the young man Absalom safe?"

Ahimaaz answered, "I saw great confusion just as Joab was about to send the king's servant and me, your servant, but I don't know what it was."

30The king said, "Stand aside and wait here." So he stepped aside and stood there.
31Then the Cushite arrived and said, "My lord the king, hear the good news! The LORD has vindicated you today by delivering you from the hand of all who rose up against you."

32The king asked the Cushite, "Is the young man Absalom safe?"

The Cushite replied, "May the enemies of my lord the king and all who rise up to harm you be like that young man."[n]

33The king was shaken. He went up to the room over the gateway and wept. As he went, he said: "O my son Absalom! My son, my son Absalom! If only I had died[o] instead of you—O Absalom, my son, my son!"[b][p]

19 [c] Joab was told, "The king is weeping and mourning for Absalom." 2And
for the whole army the victory that day was turned into mourning, because on that day the troops heard it said, "The king is grieving for his son." 3The men stole into the city
that day as men steal in who are ashamed when they flee from battle. 4The king covered his face and cried aloud, "O my son Absalom! O Absalom, my son, my son!"

5Then Joab went into the house to the king and said, "Today you have humiliated all your men, who have just saved your life and the lives of your sons and daughters and the lives of your wives and concubines.
6You love those who hate you and hate those who love you. You have made it clear today that the commanders and their men mean nothing to you. I see that you would be pleased if Absalom were alive today and all of us were dead. 7Now go out and encourage your men. I swear by the LORD that if you don't go out, not a man will be left with you by nightfall. This will be worse for you than all the calamities that have come on you from your youth till now."[q]

8So the king got up and took his seat in the gateway. When the men were told, "The king is sitting in the gateway,[r]" they all came before him.

Meanwhile, the Israelites had fled to their homes.

David Returns to Jerusalem

9Throughout the tribes of Israel, all the people were arguing among themselves, saying, "The king delivered us from the hand of our enemies; he is the one who rescued us from the hand of the Philistines.[s] But now he has fled the country to escape from Absalom;[t] 10and Absalom, whom we
anointed to rule over us, has died in battle.

[a] *23* That is, the plain of the Jordan [b] *33* In Hebrew texts this verse (18:33) is numbered 19:1. [c] In Hebrew texts 19:1-43 is numbered 19:2-44.

18:23 *by way of the plain.* The plain was the floor of the Jordan valley. Ahimaaz took a longer route, but avoided the hilly terrain on the road taken by the Cushite.

18:33 *O my son Absalom.* David's grief can be understood by any parent who has lost a child to vice or crime. Absalom was a rebel, but he had been a little boy born to David in the early years as king in Hebron, and for David he would always be that beloved son. Absalom deserved to die, and David knew it, but he still longed for things to have turned out differently. In a few short years the repercussions of his sin with Bathsheba had destroyed the lives of Amnon, Tamar, and Absalom.

18:33 Despondency—In many ways mental suffering is more intense and devastating than physical suffering. It was hard for David to even imagine taking up life again and going back to Jerusalem as king. It is only the Lord who can give courage in such moments, and He often does it by reminding us of who He is, what He has done in the past, and what He promises to do in the future. Sandwiched in these certainties, we can begin to see that His hand is on us even in our grief.

18:24 [k] 1Sa 14:16; 2Sa 19:8; 2Ki 9:17; Jer 51:12 **18:26** [l] 1Ki 1:42; Isa 52:7; 61:1 **18:27** [m] 2Ki 9:20 **18:32** [n] Jdg 5:31; 1Sa 25:26 **18:33** [o] Ex 32:32 [p] Ge 43:14; 2Sa 19:4; Ro 9:3 **19:7** [q] Pr 14:28 **19:8** [r] 2Sa 15:2 **19:9** [s] 2Sa 8:1-14 [t] 2Sa 15:14

So why do you say nothing about bringing
the king back?"
11King David sent this message to Zadok[u] and Abiathar, the priests: "Ask the
elders of Judah, 'Why should you be the
last to bring the king back to his palace,
since what is being said throughout Israel
has reached the king at his quarters? 12You
are my relatives, my own flesh and blood.
So why should you be the last to bring back
the king?' 13And say to Amasa,[v] 'Are you
not my own flesh and blood?[w] May God
deal with me, be it ever so severely,[x] if you
are not the commander of my army for life
in place of Joab.[y]' "
14He won over the hearts of the men of
Judah so that they were all of one mind.
They sent word to the king, "Return, you
and all your men." 15Then the king returned and went as far as the Jordan.
Now the men of Judah had come to Gilgal[z] to go out and meet the king and bring
him across the Jordan. 16Shimei[a] son of
Gera, the Benjamite from Bahurim, hurried down with the men of Judah to meet
King David. 17With him were a thousand
Benjamites, along with Ziba,[b] the steward of Saul's household,[c] and his fifteen
sons and twenty servants. They rushed
to the Jordan, where the king was. 18They
crossed at the ford to take the king's household over and to do whatever he wished.
When Shimei son of Gera crossed the
Jordan, he fell prostrate before the king
19and said to him, "May my lord not hold
me guilty. Do not remember how your servant did wrong on the day my lord the king
left Jerusalem.[d] May the king put it out of
his mind. 20For I your servant know that I
have sinned, but today I have come here as
the first from the tribes of Joseph to come
down and meet my lord the king."
21Then Abishai[e] son of Zeruiah said,
"Shouldn't Shimei be put to death for this?
He cursed[f] the LORD's anointed."[g]
22David replied, "What does this have to
do with you, you sons of Zeruiah?[h] What
right do you have to interfere? Should anyone be put to death in Israel today?[i] Don't
I know that today I am king over Israel?"
23So the king said to Shimei, "You shall
not die." And the king promised him on
oath.[j]
24Mephibosheth,[k] Saul's grandson, also
went down to meet the king. He had not
taken care of his feet or trimmed his mustache or washed his clothes from the day
the king left until the day he returned safely. 25When he came from Jerusalem to
meet the king, the king asked him, "Why
didn't you go with me,[l] Mephibosheth?"
26He said, "My lord the king, since I your
servant am lame,[m] I said, 'I will have my
donkey saddled and will ride on it, so I can
go with the king.' But Ziba[n] my servant betrayed me. 27And he has slandered your
servant to my lord the king. My lord the
king is like an angel[o] of God; so do whatever you wish. 28All my grandfather's descendants deserved nothing but death[p]
from my lord the king, but you gave your
servant a place among those who eat at
your table.[q] So what right do I have to make
any more appeals to the king?"
29The king said to him, "Why say more?
I order you and Ziba to divide the land."
30Mephibosheth said to the king, "Let
him take everything, now that my lord the
king has returned home safely."
31Barzillai[r] the Gileadite also came down
from Rogelim to cross the Jordan with the
king and to send him on his way from
there. 32Now Barzillai was very old, eighty
years of age. He had provided for the king
during his stay in Mahanaim, for he was
a very wealthy[s] man. 33The king said to
Barzillai, "Cross over with me and stay
with me in Jerusalem, and I will provide
for you."
34But Barzillai answered the king, "How
many more years will I live, that I should go
up to Jerusalem with the king? 35I am now
eighty[t] years old. Can I tell the difference
between what is enjoyable and what is not?
Can your servant taste what he eats and
drinks? Can I still hear the voices of male
and female singers?[u] Why should your servant be an added[v] burden to my lord the

---

19:11 ***elders of Judah.*** David asked his friends the priests, to begin the movement to invite David back to his throne. Apparently he did not want to come into Jerusalem without public support for his rule.

19:13 ***Amasa.*** David's nephew Amasa had commanded the army of Absalom (17:25). When David offered him the position of commander it was probably intended to secure Amasa's allegiance as well as discipline Joab for killing Absalom against David's orders.

19:23 ***the king promised him.*** The king was willing to accept Shimei as a loyal subject if he continued in his loyalty, and he swore that he would not kill Shimei. Apparently David did not trust Shimei, for he later directed Solomon to kill him (1 Kin. 2:8) along with others that he considered dangerous to Solomon's reign. David could not put Shimei to death himself because of his oath, but his son could do it if there was just cause.

19:27 ***do whatever you wish.*** David did not try to decide whether it was Ziba or Mephibosheth who was telling the truth. He commanded that they divide the land. Each was provided for; neither was validated in his claims.

19:11 [u] 2Sa 15:24 **19:13** [v] 2Sa 17:25 [w] Ge 29:14 [x] Ru 1:17; 1Ki 19:2; 8:16 [y] 2Sa 2:13 **19:15** [z] Jos 5:9; 1Sa 11:15 **19:16** [a] 2Sa 16:5-13; 1Ki 2:8 **19:17** [b] 2Sa 9:2; 16:1-2 [c] Ge 43:16 **19:19** [d] 1Sa 22:15; 2Sa 16:6-8 **19:21** [e] 1Sa 26:6 [f] Ex 22:28 [g] 1Sa 12:3; 26:9; 2Sa 16:7-8 **19:22** [h] 2Sa 2:18; 16:10 [i] 1Sa 11:13 **19:23** [j] 1Ki 2:8, 42 **19:24** [k] 2Sa 4:4; 9:6-10 **19:25** [l] 2Sa 16:17 **19:26** [m] Lev 21:18 [n] 2Sa 9:2 **19:27** [o] 1Sa 29:9; 2Sa 14:17, 20 **19:28** [p] 2Sa 16:8; 21:6-9 [q] 2Sa 9:7, 13 **19:31** [r] 2Sa 17:27-29; 1Ki 2:7 **19:32** [s] 1Sa 25:2; 2Sa 17:27 **19:35** [t] Ps 90:10 [u] 2Ch 35:25; Ezr 2:65; Ecc 2:8; 12:1; Isa 5:11-12 [v] 2Sa 15:33

king? 36Your servant will cross over the
Jordan with the king for a short distance,
but why should the king reward me in this
way? 37Let your servant return, that I may
die in my own town near the tomb of my father[w] and mother. But here is your servant
Kimham.[x] Let him cross over with my lord
the king. Do for him whatever you wish."
38The king said, "Kimham shall cross
over with me, and I will do for him whatever you wish. And anything you desire from
me I will do for you."
39So all the people crossed the Jordan,
and then the king crossed over. The king
kissed Barzillai and bid him farewell,[y] and
Barzillai returned to his home.
40When the king crossed over to Gilgal,
Kimham crossed with him. All the troops
of Judah and half the troops of Israel had
taken the king over.
41Soon all the men of Israel were coming
to the king and saying to him, "Why did
our brothers, the men of Judah, steal the
king away and bring him and his household across the Jordan, together with all
his men?"[z]
42All the men of Judah answered the
men of Israel, "We did this because the
king is closely related to us. Why are you
angry about it? Have we eaten any of the
king's provisions? Have we taken anything
for ourselves?"
43Then the men of Israel[a] answered the
men of Judah, "We have ten shares in the
king; so we have a greater claim on David than you have. Why then do you treat
us with contempt? Weren't we the first to
speak of bringing back our king?"
But the men of Judah pressed their
claims even more forcefully than the men
of Israel.

Sheba Rebels Against David

20 Now a troublemaker named Sheba
son of Bikri, a Benjamite, happened
to be there. He sounded the trumpet and
shouted,

"We have no share[b] in David,[c]
no part in Jesse's son![d]
Every man to his tent, Israel!"

2So all the men of Israel deserted David
to follow Sheba son of Bikri. But the men of
Judah stayed by their king all the way from
the Jordan to Jerusalem.
3When David returned to his palace in
Jerusalem, he took the ten concubines[e] he
had left to take care of the palace and put
them in a house under guard. He provided
for them but had no sexual relations with
them. They were kept in confinement till
the day of their death, living as widows.
4Then the king said to Amasa,[f] "Summon the men of Judah to come to me within three days, and be here yourself." 5But
when Amasa went to summon Judah, he
took longer than the time the king had set
for him.
6David said to Abishai,[g] "Now Sheba
son of Bikri will do us more harm than
Absalom did. Take your master's men and
pursue him, or he will find fortified cities
and escape from us."[a] 7So Joab's men and
the Kerethites[h] and Pelethites and all the
mighty warriors went out under the command of Abishai. They marched out from
Jerusalem to pursue Sheba son of Bikri.
8While they were at the great rock
in Gibeon,[i] Amasa came to meet them.
Joab[j] was wearing his military tunic, and
strapped over it at his waist was a belt with
a dagger in its sheath. As he stepped forward, it dropped out of its sheath.
9Joab said to Amasa, "How are you, my
brother?" Then Joab took Amasa by the
beard with his right hand to kiss him. 10Am-
asa was not on his guard against the dagger[k] in Joab's[l] hand, and Joab plunged it into
his belly, and his intestines spilled out on
the ground. Without being stabbed again,
Amasa died. Then Joab and his brother
Abishai pursued Sheba son of Bikri.
11One of Joab's men stood beside Amasa and said, "Whoever favors Joab, and
whoever is for David, let him follow Joab!"
12Amasa lay wallowing in his blood in the
middle of the road, and the man saw that
all the troops came to a halt[m] there. When
he realized that everyone who came up to
Amasa stopped, he dragged him from the
road into a field and threw a garment over
him. 13After Amasa had been removed
from the road, everyone went on with Joab
to pursue Sheba son of Bikri.

---

[a] 6 Or *and do us serious injury*

19:36 Love—Barzillai's acts of hospitality were acts of love: love for the Lord, and love for his king (Mark 9:41). Such true acts of kindness may bring a reward, but the real reward is the pleasure that comes with giving.

20:6 *do us more harm.* Sheba's revolt had more potential for destroying David's reign than Absalom's revolt because it was based on long-standing tribal animosity between Judah and the tribe of Benjamin.

20:9 *my brother.* This was not the first time Joab had killed a man while pretending to have a friendly word with him (3:27). The text does not say whether he suspected Amasa of treachery in his delay, or if Joab was acting out of jealousy, protecting his own long-standing position of leader of David's army.

20:13–22 Strife—Once again David had an opportunity to demonstrate that it was God who had chosen him to be king. If a leader has to contend for his position he is sure to leave rebellion and destruction in his wake.

19:37 [w] Ge 49:29; 1Ki 2:7 [x] ver 40; Jer 41:17
19:39 [y] Ge 31:55; 47:7 **19:41** [z] Jdg 8:1; 12:1
19:43 [a] 2Sa 5:1 **20:1** [b] Ge 31:14 [c] Ge 29:14; 1Ki 12:16
[d] 1Sa 22:7-8; 2Ch 10:16 **20:3** [e] 2Sa 15:16; 16:21-22
20:4 [f] 2Sa 17:25; 19:13 **20:6** [g] 2Sa 21:17
20:7 [h] 1Sa 30:14; 2Sa 8:18; 15:18; 1Ki 1:38 **20:8** [i] Jos 9:3
[j] 2Sa 2:18 **20:10** [k] Jdg 3:21; 2Sa 2:23; 3:27 [l] 1Ki 2:5
20:12 [m] 2Sa 2:23

14 Sheba passed through all the tribes of
Israel to Abel Beth Maakah and through
the entire region of the Bikrites,[a][n] who
gathered together and followed him. 15 All
the troops with Joab came and besieged
Sheba in Abel Beth Maakah.[o] They built
a siege ramp[p] up to the city, and it stood
against the outer fortifications. While they
were battering the wall to bring it down,
16 a wise woman[q] called from the city, "Listen! Listen! Tell Joab to come here so I can
speak to him." 17 He went toward her, and
she asked, "Are you Joab?"
"I am," he answered.
She said, "Listen to what your servant
has to say."
"I'm listening," he said.
18 She continued, "Long ago they used to
say, 'Get your answer at Abel,' and that settled it. 19 We are the peaceful[r] and faithful
in Israel. You are trying to destroy a city
that is a mother in Israel. Why do you want
to swallow up the LORD's inheritance?"[s]
20 "Far be it from me!" Joab replied, "Far
be it from me to swallow up or destroy!
21 That is not the case. A man named Sheba son of Bikri, from the hill country of
Ephraim, has lifted up his hand against
the king, against David. Hand over this
one man, and I'll withdraw from the city."
The woman said to Joab, "His head[t] will
be thrown to you from the wall."
22 Then the woman went to all the people
with her wise advice,[u] and they cut off the
head of Sheba son of Bikri and threw it to
Joab. So he sounded the trumpet, and his
men dispersed from the city, each returning to his home. And Joab went back to the
king in Jerusalem.

David's Officials

23 Joab[v] was over Israel's entire army;
Benaiah son of Jehoiada was over the Kerethites and Pelethites; 24 Adoniram[b][w] was
in charge of forced labor; Jehoshaphat[x] son
of Ahilud was recorder; 25 Sheva was secretary; Zadok[y] and Abiathar were priests;
26 and Ira the Jairite[c] was David's priest.

The Gibeonites Avenged

21 During the reign of David, there was
a famine[z] for three successive years;
so David sought[a] the face of the LORD. The
LORD said, "It is on account of Saul and his
blood-stained house; it is because he put
the Gibeonites to death."
2 The king summoned the Gibeonites[b]
and spoke to them. (Now the Gibeonites
were not a part of Israel but were survivors
of the Amorites; the Israelites had sworn
to spare them, but Saul in his zeal for Israel and Judah had tried to annihilate them.)
3 David asked the Gibeonites, "What shall
I do for you? How shall I make atonement
so that you will bless the LORD's inheritance?"[c]
4 The Gibeonites answered him, "We
have no right to demand silver or gold from
Saul or his family, nor do we have the right
to put anyone in Israel to death."[d]
"What do you want me to do for you?"
David asked.
5 They answered the king, "As for the
man who destroyed us and plotted against
us so that we have been decimated and
have no place anywhere in Israel, 6 let sev-
en of his male descendants be given to us to
be killed and their bodies exposed[e] before
the LORD at Gibeah of Saul—the LORD's
chosen[f] one."
So the king said, "I will give them to
you."
7 The king spared Mephibosheth[g] son of
Jonathan, the son of Saul, because of the
oath[h] before the LORD between David and
Jonathan son of Saul. 8 But the king took
Armoni and Mephibosheth, the two sons
of Aiah's daughter Rizpah,[i] whom she had
borne to Saul, together with the five sons
of Saul's daughter Merab,[d] whom she had
borne to Adriel son of Barzillai the Meho-
lathite.[j] 9 He handed them over to the Gibeonites, who killed them and exposed their
bodies on a hill before the LORD. All sev-
en of them fell together; they were put to
death[k] during the first days of the harvest,
just as the barley harvest was beginning.[l]
10 Rizpah daughter of Aiah took sackcloth and spread it out for herself on a
rock. From the beginning of the harvest

[a] *14* See Septuagint and Vulgate; Hebrew *Berites*.
[b] *24* Some Septuagint manuscripts (see also 1 Kings 4:6 and 5:14); Hebrew *Adoram*
[c] *26* Hebrew; some Septuagint manuscripts and Syriac (see also 23:38) *Ithrite*
[d] *8* Two Hebrew manuscripts, some Septuagint manuscripts and Syriac (see also 1 Samuel 18:19); most Hebrew and Septuagint manuscripts *Michal*

21:1 *because he put the Gibeonites to death.* When the Israelites first came into the Promised Land under the leadership of Joshua, the Gibeonites had deceived them into making a treaty that guaranteed their protection and security (Josh. 9:3–27). Saul had broken that agreement.

21:10 *Rizpah.* Rizpah remained near the bodies, protecting them from scavengers, from the barley harvest to the early rains (late April to October). This heartbreaking devotion from the mother of two of the slain men commended her to David, and finally the bones of Saul and all of his sons were buried in the family grave site.

20:14 [n] Nu 21:16 **20:15** [o] 1Ki 15:20; 2Ki 15:29 [p] 2Ki 19:32; Isa 37:33; Jer 6:6; 32:24 **20:16** [q] 2Sa 14:2 **20:19** [r] Dt 2:26 [s] 1Sa 26:19; 2Sa 21:3 **20:21** [t] 2Sa 4:8 **20:22** [u] Ecc 9:13 **20:23** [v] 2Sa 2:28; 8:16-18; 24:2 **20:24** [w] 1Ki 4:6; 5:14; 12:18; 2Ch 10:18 [x] 2Sa 8:16; 1Ki 4:3 **20:25** [y] 1Sa 2:35; 2Sa 8:17 **21:1** [z] Ge 12:10; Dt 32:24 [a] Ex 32:11 **21:2** [b] Jos 9:15 **21:3** [c] 1Sa 26:19; 2Sa 20:19 **21:4** [d] Nu 35:33-34 **21:6** [e] Nu 25:4 [f] 1Sa 10:24 **21:7** [g] 2Sa 4:4 [h] 1Sa 18:3; 20:8, 15; 2Sa 9:7 **21:8** [i] 2Sa 3:7 [j] 1Sa 18:19 **21:9** [k] 2Sa 16:8 [l] Ru 1:22

till the rain poured down from the heavens on the bodies, she did not let the birds
touch them by day or the wild animals by
night.[m] 11When David was told what Aiah's
daughter Rizpah, Saul's concubine, had
done, 12he went and took the bones of Saul[n]
and his son Jonathan from the citizens of
Jabesh Gilead. (They had stolen their bodies from the public square at Beth Shan,[o]
where the Philistines had hung[p] them after
they struck Saul down on Gilboa.) 13David
brought the bones of Saul and his son Jonathan from there, and the bones of those
who had been killed and exposed were
gathered up.
14They buried the bones of Saul and his
son Jonathan in the tomb of Saul's father
Kish, at Zela[q] in Benjamin, and did everything the king commanded. After that,[r]
God answered prayer[s] in behalf of the land.

Wars Against the Philistines

15Once again there was a battle between
the Philistines[t] and Israel. David went
down with his men to fight against the Philistines, and he became exhausted. 16And
Ishbi-Benob, one of the descendants of
Rapha, whose bronze spearhead weighed
three hundred shekels[a] and who was
armed with a new sword, said he would
kill David. 17But Abishai[u] son of Zeruiah
came to David's rescue; he struck the Philistine down and killed him. Then David's
men swore to him, saying, "Never again
will you go out with us to battle, so that the
lamp[v] of Israel will not be extinguished.[w]"
18In the course of time, there was another battle with the Philistines, at Gob. At
that time Sibbekai[x] the Hushathite killed
Saph, one of the descendants of Rapha.
19In another battle with the Philistines at
Gob, Elhanan son of Jair[b] the Bethlehemite killed the brother of[c] Goliath the Gittite,
who had a spear with a shaft like a weaver's rod.[y]
20In still another battle, which took place
at Gath, there was a huge man with six
fingers on each hand and six toes on each
foot—twenty-four in all. He also was descended from Rapha. 21When he taunted
Israel, Jonathan son of Shimeah,[z] David's
brother, killed him.
22These four were descendants of Rapha
in Gath, and they fell at the hands of David
and his men.

David's Song of Praise

22 David sang[a] to the LORD the words
of this song when the LORD delivered
him from the hand of all his enemies and
from the hand of Saul. 2He said:

"The LORD is my rock,[b] my fortress[c] and
my deliverer;[d]
3 my God is my rock, in whom I take
refuge,[e]
my shield[df] and the horn[eg] of my
salvation.
He is my stronghold,[h] my refuge and
my savior—
from violent people you save me.

4 "I called to the LORD, who is worthy[i] of
praise,
and have been saved from my
enemies.
5 The waves[j] of death swirled about me;
the torrents of destruction
overwhelmed me.
6 The cords of the grave[k] coiled around
me;
the snares of death confronted me.

7 "In my distress[l] I called[m] to the LORD;
I called out to my God.
From his temple he heard my voice;
my cry came to his ears.
8 The earth[n] trembled and quaked,[o]
the foundations[p] of the heavens[f]
shook;
they trembled because he was angry.

---

[a] *16* That is, about 7 1/2 pounds or about 3.5 kilograms [b] *19* See 1 Chron. 20:5; Hebrew *Jaare-Oregim.* [c] *19* See 1 Chron. 20:5; Hebrew does not have *the brother of.* [d] *3* Or *sovereign* [e] *3* *Horn* here symbolizes strength. [f] *8* Hebrew; Vulgate and Syriac (see also Psalm 18:7) *mountains*

21:14 ***God answered prayer.*** It is hard to understand why the death of the descendants of Saul as payment for his treachery was something that would be connected to God hearing prayers for famine. Saul was described as rebellious, and apparently his disobedience was more far reaching than is recorded in Scripture. Possibly the men who were killed had been implicated in killing the Gibeonites. Even if we do not understand, we can always be sure that God is just and God is righteous.

21:16 ***Rapha.*** The Rephaites were giants, a people living in Canaan who were noted for their large size. ***three hundred shekels.*** The spear weighed approximately seven and a half pounds.

22:1 ***words of this song.*** This psalm later became part of the congregational worship of Israel (Ps. 18), but it began as David's personal and earnest expression of praise to the Lord.

22:3 ***the horn of my salvation.*** The horn of an animal is used for protection and defense, so it is a good word picture for a sign of might and power.

22:6 ***death.*** This is the word Sheol, used in Hebrew poetry as a synonym for death. In the Old Testament, Sheol is described as a place of dust, referring to death (Job 17:16), a place of decay (Ps. 16:10), and as a pit (Is. 14:15).

21:10 [m] ver 8; Dt 21:23; 1Sa 17:44 **21:12** [n] 1Sa 31:11-13 [o] Jos 17:11 [p] 1Sa 31:10 **21:14** [q] Jos 18:28 [r] Jos 7:26 [s] 2Sa 24:25 **21:15** [t] 2Sa 5:25 **21:17** [u] 2Sa 20:6 [v] 1Ki 11:36 [w] 2Sa 18:3 **21:18** [x] 1Ch 11:29; 20:4; 27:11 **21:19** [y] 1Sa 17:7 **21:21** [z] 1Sa 16:9 **22:1** [a] Ex 15:1; Jdg 5:1; Ps 18:2-50 **22:2** [b] Dt 32:4; Ps 71:3 [c] Ps 31:3; 91:2 [d] Ps 144:2 **22:3** [e] Dt 32:37; Jer 16:19 [f] Ge 15:1 [g] Lk 1:69 [h] Ps 9:9 **22:4** [i] Ps 48:1; 96:4 **22:5** [j] Ps 69:14-15; 93:4; Jnh 2:3 **22:6** [k] Ps 116:3 **22:7** [l] Ps 120:1 [m] Ps 34:6, 15; 116:4 **22:8** [n] Jdg 5:4; Ps 97:4 [o] Ps 77:18 [p] Job 26:11

[9] Smoke rose from his nostrils;
consuming fire[q] came from his mouth,
burning coals blazed out of it.
[10] He parted the heavens and came down;
dark clouds[r] were under his feet.
[11] He mounted the cherubim and flew;
he soared[a] on the wings of the wind.[s]
[12] He made darkness his canopy around him—
the dark[b] rain clouds of the sky.
[13] Out of the brightness of his presence
bolts of lightning[t] blazed forth.
[14] The LORD thundered[u] from heaven;
the voice of the Most High resounded.
[15] He shot his arrows[v] and scattered the enemy,
with great bolts of lightning he routed them.
[16] The valleys of the sea were exposed
and the foundations of the earth laid bare
at the rebuke[w] of the LORD,
at the blast of breath from his nostrils.

[17] "He reached down from on high[x] and took hold of me;
he drew[y] me out of deep waters.
[18] He rescued me from my powerful enemy,
from my foes, who were too strong for me.
[19] They confronted me in the day of my disaster,
but the LORD was my support.[z]
[20] He brought me out into a spacious[a] place;
he rescued[b] me because he delighted[c] in me.[d]

[21] "The LORD has dealt with me according to my righteousness;[e]
according to the cleanness of my hands[f] he has rewarded me.
[22] For I have kept[g] the ways of the LORD;
I am not guilty of turning from my God.
[23] All his laws are before me;[h]
I have not turned[i] away from his decrees.
[24] I have been blameless[j] before him
and have kept myself from sin.
[25] The LORD has rewarded me according to my righteousness,[k]
according to my cleanness[c] in his sight.

[26] "To the faithful you show yourself faithful,
to the blameless you show yourself blameless,
[27] to the pure[l] you show yourself pure,
but to the devious you show yourself shrewd.[m]
[28] You save the humble,[n]
but your eyes are on the haughty to bring them low.[o]
[29] You, LORD, are my lamp;[p]
the LORD turns my darkness into light.
[30] With your help I can advance against a troop[d];
with my God I can scale a wall.

[31] "As for God, his way is perfect:[q]
The LORD's word is flawless;[r]
he shields all who take refuge in him.
[32] For who is God besides the LORD?
And who is the Rock[s] except our God?
[33] It is God who arms me with strength[e]
and keeps my way secure.
[34] He makes my feet like the feet of a deer;[t]
he causes me to stand on the heights.[u]
[35] He trains my hands[v] for battle;
my arms can bend a bow of bronze.
[36] You make your saving help my shield;[w]
your help has made[f] me great.
[37] You provide a broad path[x] for my feet,
so that my ankles do not give way.

[38] "I pursued my enemies and crushed them;
I did not turn back till they were destroyed.

---

[a] *11* Many Hebrew manuscripts (see also Psalm 18:10); most Hebrew manuscripts *appeared*
[b] *12* Septuagint (see also Psalm 18:11); Hebrew *massed*
[c] *25* Hebrew; Septuagint and Vulgate (see also Psalm 18:24) *to the cleanness of my hands*
[d] *30* Or *can run through a barricade*
[e] *33* Dead Sea Scrolls, some Septuagint manuscripts, Vulgate and Syriac (see also Psalm 18:32); Masoretic Text *who is my strong refuge*
[f] *36* Dead Sea Scrolls; Masoretic Text *shield; / you stoop down to make*

22:22 ***I have kept the ways of the LORD.*** David did not keep the ways of the Lord perfectly. His sins have been written down for the whole world to know throughout the ages. But he never forgot the Lord, always knew that what he did mattered to God, and always turned his steps back to the Lord when he went astray. Like Paul, David ran the race in such a way as to get the prize (1 Cor. 9:24).
22:34 ***the feet of a deer.*** The deer or hind is noted for its swiftness, agility, and surefootedness.
22:35 ***can bend a bow of bronze.*** It would take unusual strength to bend such a bow (see also Job 20:24).

22:9 [q] Ps 97:3; Heb 12:29 **22:10** [r] 1Ki 8:12; Na 1:3 **22:11** [s] Ps 104:3 **22:13** [t] ver 9 **22:14** [u] 1Sa 2:10 **22:15** [v] Dt 32:23 **22:16** [w] Na 1:4 **22:17** [x] Ps 144:7 [y] Ex 2:10 **22:19** [z] Ps 23:4 **22:20** [a] Ps 31:8 [b] Ps 118:5 [c] Ps 22:8 [d] 2Sa 15:26 **22:21** [e] 1Sa 26:23 [f] Ps 24:4 **22:22** [g] Ge 18:19; Ps 128:1; Pr 8:32 **22:23** [h] Dt 6:4-9; Ps 119:30-32 [i] Ps 119:102 **22:24** [j] Ge 6:9; Eph 1:4 **22:25** [k] ver 21 **22:27** [l] Mt 5:8 [m] Lev 26:23-24 **22:28** [n] Ex 3:8; Ps 72:12-13 [o] Isa 2:12, 17; 5:15 **22:29** [p] Ps 27:1 **22:31** [q] Dt 32:4; Mt 5:48 [r] Ps 12:6; 119:140; Pr 30:5-6 **22:32** [s] 1Sa 2:2 **22:34** [t] Hab 3:19 [u] Dt 32:13 **22:35** [v] Ps 144:1 **22:36** [w] Eph 6:16 **22:37** [x] Pr 4:11

39 I crushed[y] them completely, and they
could not rise;
they fell beneath my feet.
40 You armed me with strength for battle;
you humbled my adversaries before me.[z]
41 You made my enemies turn their backs[a]
in flight,
and I destroyed my foes.
42 They cried for help,[b] but there was no
one to save them—[c]
to the LORD, but he did not answer.
43 I beat them as fine as the dust of the
earth;
I pounded and trampled[d] them like
mud[e] in the streets.

44 "You have delivered[f] me from the
attacks of the peoples;
you have preserved[g] me as the head
of nations.
People[h] I did not know now serve me,
45 foreigners cower[i] before me;
as soon as they hear of me, they obey
me.
46 They all lose heart;
they come trembling[a][j] from their
strongholds.

47 "The LORD lives! Praise be to my Rock!
Exalted be my God, the Rock, my
Savior![k]
48 He is the God who avenges me,[l]
who puts the nations under me,
49 who sets me free from my enemies.[m]
You exalted me above my foes;
from a violent man you rescued me.
50 Therefore I will praise you, LORD,
among the nations;
I will sing the praises of your name.[n]

51 "He gives his king great victories;[o]
he shows unfailing kindness to his
anointed,[p]
to David[q] and his descendants
forever."[r]

David's Last Words

23 These are the last words of David:

"The inspired utterance of David son of
Jesse,
the utterance of the man exalted[s] by
the Most High,
the man anointed[t] by the God of Jacob,
the hero of Israel's songs:

2 "The Spirit[u] of the LORD spoke through
me;
his word was on my tongue.
3 The God of Israel spoke,
the Rock[v] of Israel said to me:
'When one rules over people in
righteousness,[w]
when he rules in the fear of God,[x]
4 he is like the light of morning at
sunrise[y]
on a cloudless morning,
like the brightness after rain
that brings grass from the earth.'

5 "If my house were not right with God,
surely he would not have made with
me an everlasting covenant,[z]
arranged and secured in every
part;
surely he would not bring to fruition my
salvation
and grant me my every desire.
6 But evil men are all to be cast aside like
thorns,[a]
which are not gathered with the
hand.
7 Whoever touches thorns
uses a tool of iron or the shaft of a
spear;
they are burned up where they lie."

---

[a] *46* Some Septuagint manuscripts and Vulgate (see also Psalm 18:45); Masoretic Text *they arm themselves*

22:47 *The LORD lives.* This shout of exaltation is the heart cry of every follower of God. The difference between the Living God and the dead idols that entrapped so many in the countries around him stood out very strongly to David.

22:51 *his anointed.* David was anointed by God to be king of Israel. He was set aside for a certain job. Jesus is the ultimate Anointed One, which is the meaning of the Hebrew name Messiah and the Greek name Christ.

23:1 *the hero of Israel's songs.* Of the 150 psalms in the Book of Psalms, 73 are attributed to David by the text. No person in Scriptures is more closely associated with music in the worship of the Lord than King David. He left behind a beautiful record of his heartfelt love of the Lord, his struggles, and his victories.

23:3–4 Fear of God—For centuries certain dynasties of rulers in Europe claimed the divine right to rule. Certainly the Bible teaches that government is ordained of God (Rom. 13). But it also teaches that rulers have a deep stewardship responsibility. They are to rule men in the fear of God. Over and over again it is shown that God sets rulers in place, and also deposes those who consistently rebel against Him.

23:5 *everlasting covenant.* David celebrates his everlasting covenant (7:12–16) here and in Psalm 89.

23:6–7 *evil men.* The worthless, rebellious, or literally "the sons of Belial." This is a term of contempt and scorn, the word that Shimei hurled at David when David was fleeing from the rebellion of his son Absalom (16:7). The word was also used to describe Sheba, the scoundrel from the tribe of Benjamin (20:1). David anticipated God's judgment on the ungodly, who are likened to thorns fit only to be burned.

22:39 [y] Mal 4:3 **22:40** [z] Ps 44:5 **22:41** [a] Ex 23:27 **22:42** [b] Isa 1:15 [c] Ps 50:22 **22:43** [d] Mic 7:10 [e] Isa 10:6; Mic 7:10 **22:44** [f] 2Sa 3:1 [g] Dt 28:13 [h] 2Sa 8:1-14; Isa 55:3-5 **22:45** [i] Ps 66:3; 81:15 **22:46** [j] Mic 7:17 **22:47** [k] Ps 89:26 **22:48** [l] Ps 94:1; 144:2; 1Sa 25:39 **22:49** [m] Ps 140:1,4 **22:50** [n] Ro 15:9* **22:51** [o] Ps 144:9-10 [p] Ps 89:20 [q] 2Sa 7:13 [r] Ps 89:24,29 **23:1** [s] 2Sa 7:8-9; Ps 78:70-71; 89:27 [t] 1Sa 16:12-13; Ps 89:20 **23:2** [u] Mt 22:43; 2Pe 1:21 **23:3** [v] Dt 32:4; 2Sa 22:2,32 [w] Ps 72:2 [x] 2Ch 19:7,9; Isa 11:1-5 **23:4** [y] Jdg 5:31; Ps 89:36 **23:5** [z] Ps 89:29; Isa 55:3 **23:6** [a] Mt 13:40-41

David's Mighty Warriors

8 These are the names of David's mighty
warriors:
Josheb-Basshebeth,[a] a Tahkemonite,[b]
was chief of the Three; he raised his spear
against eight hundred men, whom he
killed[c] in one encounter.
9 Next to him was Eleazar son of Dodai[b]
the Ahohite.[c] As one of the three mighty
warriors, he was with David when they
taunted the Philistines gathered at Pas
Dammim[d] for battle. Then the Israelites
retreated, 10 but Eleazar stood his ground
and struck down the Philistines till his
hand grew tired and froze to the sword.
The LORD brought about a great victory
that day. The troops returned to Eleazar,
but only to strip the dead.
11 Next to him was Shammah son of Agee
the Hararite. When the Philistines banded together at a place where there was a
field full of lentils, Israel's troops fled from
them. 12 But Shammah took his stand in
the middle of the field. He defended it and
struck the Philistines down, and the LORD
brought about a great victory.
13 During harvest time, three of the thirty chief warriors came down to David
at the cave of Adullam,[d] while a band of
Philistines was encamped in the Valley of
Rephaim.[e] 14 At that time David was in the
stronghold,[f] and the Philistine garrison
was at Bethlehem.[g] 15 David longed for water and said, "Oh, that someone would get
me a drink of water from the well near the
gate of Bethlehem!" 16 So the three mighty
warriors broke through the Philistine
lines, drew water from the well near the
gate of Bethlehem and carried it back to
David. But he refused to drink it; instead,
he poured[h] it out before the LORD. 17 "Far
be it from me, LORD, to do this!" he said.
"Is it not the blood[i] of men who went at the
risk of their lives?" And David would not
drink it.
Such were the exploits of the three
mighty warriors.
18 Abishai[j] the brother of Joab son of Zeruiah was chief of the Three.[e] He raised his
spear against three hundred men, whom
he killed, and so he became as famous
as the Three. 19 Was he not held in greater honor than the Three? He became their
commander, even though he was not included among them.
20 Benaiah[k] son of Jehoiada, a valiant
fighter from Kabzeel,[l] performed great exploits. He struck down Moab's two mightiest warriors. He also went down into a pit
on a snowy day and killed a lion. 21 And he
struck down a huge Egyptian. Although
the Egyptian had a spear in his hand, Benaiah went against him with a club. He
snatched the spear from the Egyptian's
hand and killed him with his own spear.
22 Such were the exploits of Benaiah son
of Jehoiada; he too was as famous as the
three mighty warriors. 23 He was held in
greater honor than any of the Thirty, but
he was not included among the Three.
And David put him in charge of his bodyguard.

24 Among the Thirty were:
Asahel[m] the brother of Joab,
Elhanan son of Dodo from Bethle-
hem,
25 Shammah the Harodite,[n]
Elika the Harodite,
26 Helez[o] the Paltite,
Ira son of Ikkesh from Tekoa,
27 Abiezer from Anathoth,[p]
Sibbekai[f] the Hushathite,
28 Zalmon the Ahohite,
Maharai[q] the Netophathite,[r]
29 Heled[g] son of Baanah the Netopha-
thite,
Ithai son of Ribai from Gibeah[s] in
Benjamin,
30 Benaiah the Pirathonite,[t]
Hiddai[h] from the ravines of Gaash,[u]

---

[a] 8 Hebrew; some Septuagint manuscripts suggest *Ish-Bosheth*, that is, *Esh-Baal* (see also 1 Chron. 11:11 *Jashobeam*). [b] 8 Probably a variant of *Hakmonite* (see 1 Chron. 11:11) [c] 8 Some Septuagint manuscripts (see also 1 Chron. 11:11); Hebrew and other Septuagint manuscripts *Three; it was Adino the Eznite who killed eight hundred men* [d] 9 See 1 Chron. 11:13; Hebrew *gathered there.* [e] 18 Most Hebrew manuscripts (see also 1 Chron. 11:20); two Hebrew manuscripts and Syriac *Thirty* [f] 27 Some Septuagint manuscripts (see also 21:18; 1 Chron. 11:29); Hebrew *Mebunnai* [g] 29 Some Hebrew manuscripts and Vulgate (see also 1 Chron. 11:30); most Hebrew manuscripts *Heleb* [h] 30 Hebrew; some Septuagint manuscripts (see also 1 Chron. 11:32) *Hurai*

23:8 *mighty warriors.* The term "mighty men" suggests that these were the elite of David's troops, possibly his personal bodyguards. These men were heroes in the full sense of the word. Their listing must have inspired others to attain such accomplishments.
23:13–14 *Valley of Rephaim.* This valley was a route to Jerusalem. ***Bethlehem.*** David's hometown (1 Sam. 16:1–3) was about six miles south of Jerusalem.
23:15 *get me a drink of water from the well . . . of Bethlehem.* Anyone who has grown up with an especially good well for drinking water can identify with David's craving. The taste of the water from the well at "home" seems more thirst-quenching, more heartening, than any other.

23:16 *poured it out before the LORD.* David was deeply moved by this act of loyalty. He could have let it make him feel important, but instead he dedicated the water to the Lord, knowing that no man's craving should be satisfied at the risk of another man's life.

23:9 [b] 1Ch 27:4 [c] 1Ch 8:4 **23:13** [d] 1Sa 22:1 [e] 2Sa 5:18
23:14 [f] 1Sa 22:4-5 [g] Ru 1:19 **23:16** [h] Ge 35:14
23:17 [i] Lev 17:10-12 **23:18** [j] 2Sa 10:10, 14; 1Ch 11:20
23:20 [k] 2Sa 8:18; 20:23 [l] Jos 15:21 **23:24** [m] 2Sa 2:18
23:25 [n] Jdg 7:1; 1Ch 11:27 **23:26** [o] 1Ch 27:10
23:27 [p] Jos 21:18 **23:28** [q] 1Ch 27:13 [r] 2Ki 25:23; Ne 7:26
23:29 [s] Jos 15:57 **23:30** [t] Jdg 12:13 [u] Jos 24:30

[31] Abi-Albon the Arbathite,
Azmaveth the Barhumite,[v]
[32] Eliahba the Shaalbonite,
the sons of Jashen,
Jonathan [33] son of[a] Shammah the
Hararite,
Ahiam son of Sharar[b] the Hararite,
[34] Eliphelet son of Ahasbai the Maakathite,
Eliam[w] son of Ahithophel[x] the Gilonite,
[35] Hezro the Carmelite,[y]
Paarai the Arbite,
[36] Igal son of Nathan from Zobah,[z]
the son of Hagri,[c]
[37] Zelek the Ammonite,
Naharai the Beerothite, the armor-
bearer of Joab son of Zeruiah,
[38] Ira the Ithrite,[a]
Gareb the Ithrite
[39] and Uriah[b] the Hittite.
There were thirty-seven in all.

David Enrolls the Fighting Men

24 Again[c] the anger of the LORD burned
against Israel, and he incited David
against them, saying, "Go and take a census of[d] Israel and Judah."
[2] So the king said to Joab[e] and the army
commanders[d] with him, "Go throughout
the tribes of Israel from Dan to Beersheba[f]
and enroll the fighting men, so that I may
know how many there are."
[3] But Joab replied to the king, "May the
LORD your God multiply the troops a hundred times over,[g] and may the eyes of my
lord the king see it. But why does my lord
the king want to do such a thing?"
[4] The king's word, however, overruled
Joab and the army commanders; so they
left the presence of the king to enroll the
fighting men of Israel.
[5] After crossing the Jordan, they camped
near Aroer,[h] south of the town in the gorge,
and then went through Gad and on to Jazer.[i]
[6] They went to Gilead and the region of Tah-
tim Hodshi, and on to Dan Jaan and around
toward Sidon.[j] [7] Then they went toward the
fortress of Tyre[k] and all the towns of the Hivites and Canaanites. Finally, they went on
to Beersheba[l] in the Negev[m] of Judah.
[8] After they had gone through the entire
land, they came back to Jerusalem at the
end of nine months and twenty days.
[9] Joab reported the number of the fighting men to the king: In Israel there were
eight hundred thousand able-bodied men
who could handle a sword, and in Judah
five hundred thousand.[n]
[10] David was conscience-stricken[o] after
he had counted the fighting men, and he
said to the LORD, "I have sinned[p] greatly in
what I have done. Now, LORD, I beg you,
take away the guilt of your servant. I have
done a very foolish thing.[q]"
[11] Before David got up the next morning,
the word of the LORD had come to Gad[r] the
prophet, David's seer:[s] [12] "Go and tell David, 'This is what the LORD says: I am giving you three options. Choose one of them
for me to carry out against you.'"
[13] So Gad went to David and said to him,
"Shall there come on you three[e] years of
famine[t] in your land? Or three months of
fleeing from your enemies while they pursue you? Or three days of plague[u] in your
land? Now then, think it over and decide
how I should answer the one who sent me."
[14] David said to Gad, "I am in deep distress. Let us fall into the hands of the LORD,
for his mercy[v] is great; but do not let me fall
into human hands."
[15] So the LORD sent a plague on Israel from that morning until the end of the
time designated, and seventy thousand of
the people from Dan to Beersheba died.[w]
[16] When the angel stretched out his hand to
destroy Jerusalem, the LORD relented[x] concerning the disaster and said to the angel
who was afflicting the people, "Enough!
Withdraw your hand." The angel of the
LORD[y] was then at the threshing floor of
Araunah the Jebusite.

---

[a] *33* Some Septuagint manuscripts (see also 1 Chron. 11:34); Hebrew does not have *son of.* [b] *33* Hebrew; some Septuagint manuscripts (see also 1 Chron. 11:35) *Sakar* [c] *36* Some Septuagint manuscripts (see also 1 Chron. 11:38); Hebrew *Haggadi* [d] *2* Septuagint (see also verse 4 and 1 Chron. 21:2); Hebrew *Joab the army commander* [e] *13* Septuagint (see also 1 Chron. 21:12); Hebrew *seven*

24:3 *why does my lord the king want to do such a thing.* God was angry with Israel, and the numbering and resulting pestilence were a part of His plan to deal with Israel in such a way that they did not become complacent. This incident is not well explained in Scripture. Joab knew that David was acting presumptuously, but at this point David could not see it. Perhaps the census showed a lack of trust in the Lord, and a sense that the might of the nation rested in its armed men.

24:9 *men who could handle a sword.* The numbers given refer only to men of military age. It is impressive that the division of Israel and Judah was so well established. This division would in the end result in a divided kingdom.

24:10 *David was conscience-stricken.* The text does not state precisely what David's sin was. His heart was always sensitive to God's will, and he quickly confessed his sin and sought restoration with the Lord.

23:31 [v] 2Sa 3:16 **23:34** [w] 2Sa 11:3 [x] 2Sa 15:12 **23:35** [y] Jos 12:22 **23:36** [z] 1Sa 14:47 **23:38** [a] 2Sa 20:26; 1Ch 2:53 **23:39** [b] 2Sa 11:3 **24:1** [c] Jos 9:15 [d] 1Ch 27:23 **24:2** [e] 2Sa 20:23 [f] Jdg 20:1; 2Sa 3:10 **24:3** [g] Dt 1:11 **24:5** [h] Dt 2:36; Jos 13:9 [i] Nu 21:32 **24:6** [j] Ge 10:19; Jos 19:28; Jdg 1:31 **24:7** [k] Jos 19:29 [l] Ge 21:22-33 [m] Dt 1:7; Jos 11:3 **24:9** [n] Nu 1:44-46; 1Ch 21:5 **24:10** [o] 1Sa 24:5 [p] 2Sa 12:13 [q] Nu 12:11; 1Sa 13:13 **24:11** [r] 1Sa 22:5 [s] 1Sa 9:9; 1Ch 29:29 **24:13** [t] Dt 28:38-42, 48; Eze 14:21 [u] Lev 26:25 **24:14** [v] Ne 9:28; Ps 51:1; 103:8, 13; 130:4 **24:15** [w] 1Ch 27:24 **24:16** [x] Ge 6:6; 1Sa 15:11 [y] Ex 12:23; Ac 12:23

17When David saw the angel who was
striking down the people, he said to the
LORD, "I have sinned; I, the shepherd,[a] have
done wrong. These are but sheep.[z] What
have they done? Let your hand fall on me
and my family."[a]

David Builds an Altar

18On that day Gad went to David and
said to him, "Go up and build an altar to the
LORD on the threshing floor of Araunah the
Jebusite." 19So David went up, as the LORD
had commanded through Gad. 20When
Araunah looked and saw the king and his
officials coming toward him, he went out
and bowed down before the king with his
face to the ground.
21Araunah said, "Why has my lord the
king come to his servant?"
"To buy your threshing floor," David
answered, "so I can build an altar to the
LORD, that the plague on the people may
be stopped."[b]
22Araunah said to David, "Let my lord
the king take whatever he wishes and offer it up. Here are oxen[c] for the burnt offering, and here are threshing sledges and ox
yokes for the wood. 23Your Majesty, Araunah[b] gives[d] all this to the king." Araunah
also said to him, "May the LORD your God
accept you."
24But the king replied to Araunah, "No,
I insist on paying you for it. I will not sacrifice to the LORD my God burnt offerings
that cost me nothing."[e]
So David bought the threshing floor
and the oxen and paid fifty shekels[c] of silver for them. 25David built an altar[f] to the
LORD there and sacrificed burnt offerings
and fellowship offerings. Then the LORD
answered his prayer[g] in behalf of the land,
and the plague on Israel was stopped.

---

a 17 Dead Sea Scrolls and Septuagint; Masoretic Text does not have *the shepherd.* *b* 23 Some Hebrew manuscripts and Septuagint; most Hebrew manuscripts *King Araunah* *c* 24 That is, about 1 1/4 pounds or about 575 grams

---

24:24 *threshing floor.* The threshing floor was located on Mount Moriah, where Abraham had bound Isaac (Gen. 22:2). Later, Solomon would build the temple at this site (1 Kin. 6:1; 1 Chr. 21:27 — 22:1; 2 Chr. 3:1). ***fifty shekels of silver.*** The fifty shekels of silver paid only for the threshing floor, the oxen, and the implements. The land that surrounded the threshing floor would cost considerably more — six hundred shekels, or 15 pounds of gold (1 Chr. 21:25).

24:25 *burnt offerings and fellowship offerings.* The burnt offering was the principal atoning sacrifice for unintentional sins (Lev. 1:1 – 17; 6:8 – 13). It was completely consumed on the altar, except for the hide, which was given to the officiating priest. The fellowship offering was an optional sacrifice, which did not form any part of the regular offerings required in the tabernacle or temple. It was a voluntary expression of thanksgiving or worship (Lev. 3:1 – 17; 7:11 – 34).

24:17 [z] Ps 74:1 [a] Jnh 1:12 **24:21** [b] Nu 16:44-50
24:22 [c] 1Sa 6:14; 1Ki 19:21 **24:23** [d] Eze 20:40-41
24:24 [e] Mal 1:13-14 **24:25** [f] 1Sa 7:17 [g] 2Sa 21:14

1 KINGS

▶ **AUTHOR:** Both 1 and 2 Kings emphasize God's righteous judgment on idolatry and immorality. The style of these books is similar to that found in Jeremiah. The author of 1 Kings is unknown, but evidence supports the Talmudic tradition that Kings was written by Jeremiah. Clearly, the author was a prophet/historian as evidenced in the prophetic exposé of apostasy.

▶ **TIME:** c. 971–851 B.C. ▶ **KEY VERSES:** 1 Kin. 9:4–5

▶ **THEME:** First Kings continues the saga of the kings of Israel after David. Solomon's reign and the details of the building of the temple take up a major portion of 1 Kings. After Solomon, the kingdom divides, and we have parallel narratives of the northern kingdom, Israel, and the southern kingdom, Judah. The book covers a span of about 120 years. During these years, idolatry becomes the norm, and God is largely forgotten. After Solomon, the main character of the book is Elijah the prophet.

Adonijah Sets Himself Up as King

1 When King David was very old, he
could not keep warm even when they
put covers over him. 2So his attendants
said to him, "Let us look for a young virgin
to serve the king and take care of him. She
can lie beside him so that our lord the king
may keep warm."
3Then they searched throughout Israel
for a beautiful young woman and found
Abishag, a Shunammite,[a] and brought her
to the king. 4The woman was very beautiful; she took care of the king and waited on
him, but the king had no sexual relations
with her.
5Now Adonijah,[b] whose mother was
Haggith, put himself forward and said, "I
will be king." So he got chariots[c] and horses[a] ready, with fifty men to run ahead of
him. 6(His father had never rebuked[d] him
by asking, "Why do you behave as you do?"
He was also very handsome and was born
next after Absalom.)
7Adonijah conferred with Joab[e] son of
Zeruiah and with Abiathar[f] the priest, and
they gave him their support. 8But Zadok[g]
the priest, Benaiah[h] son of Jehoiada, Nathan[i] the prophet, Shimei[j] and Rei and David's special guard[k] did not join Adonijah.
9Adonijah then sacrificed sheep, cattle
and fattened calves at the Stone of Zoheleth near En Rogel.[l] He invited all his
brothers, the king's sons, and all the royal
officials of Judah, 10but he did not invite
Nathan the prophet or Benaiah or the special guard or his brother Solomon.[m]
11Then Nathan asked Bathsheba,[n] Solomon's mother, "Have you not heard that
Adonijah,[o] the son of Haggith, has become
king, and our lord David knows nothing
about it? 12Now then, let me advise[p] you

[a] 5 Or *charioteers*

1:1 *King David was very old.* David was about seventy years old at the time of his death (2 Sam. 5:4; 1 Chr. 29:26–28), and the long years of warfare had doubtlessly taken their physical toll.

1:5 *Adonijah.* The name Adonijah means "the LORD is my Lord." Amnon and Absalom both experienced violent deaths (2 Sam. 13:28–29; 18:14). Kiliab, his second son, apparently died at an early age. Adonijah was David's oldest surviving son.

1:6 *had never rebuked him.* While David had been a most capable leader and a man of deep spiritual sensitivity, he had not exercised proper parental discipline of his children (2 Sam. 13:21–39; 14:18–24).

1:11 *Nathan.* It is a mark of David's integrity that Nathan, who had confronted him with his terrible sin with Bathsheba, was still welcome in the royal household (2 Sam. 12:1–15).

1:11–14 Wisdom—In Old Testament times, messages from God were often given through personal prophecy. Today, believers do not often receive messages through prophecy. God has given the higher privilege of direct access to His wisdom through the ministry of the indwelling Holy Spirit in all who believe. Today believers have access to God's wisdom through His Word, His indwelling Spirit, and counsel from mature Christians.

1:3 [a] Jos 19:18 **1:5** [b] 2Sa 3:4 [c] 2Sa 15:1 **1:6** [d] 2Sa 3:3-4 **1:7** [e] 1Ki 2:22,28; 1Ch 11:6 [f] 1Sa 22:20; 2Sa 20:25 **1:8** [g] 2Sa 20:25 [h] 2Sa 8:18 [i] 2Sa 12:1 [j] 1Ki 4:18 [k] 2Sa 23:8 **1:9** [l] 2Sa 17:17 **1:10** [m] 2Sa 12:24 **1:11** [n] 2Sa 12:24 [o] 2Sa 3:4 **1:12** [p] Pr 15:22

how you can save your own life and the life
of your son Solomon. 13Go in to King David
and say to him, 'My lord the king, did you
not swear[q] to me your servant: "Surely Solomon your son shall be king after me, and
he will sit on my throne"? Why then has
Adonijah become king?' 14While you are
still there talking to the king, I will come
in and add my word to what you have said."
15So Bathsheba went to see the aged
king in his room, where Abishag[r] the Shunammite was attending him. 16Bathsheba
bowed down, prostrating herself before the
king.

"What is it you want?" the king asked.

17She said to him, "My lord, you yourself
swore[s] to me your servant by the LORD your
God: 'Solomon your son shall be king after
me, and he will sit on my throne.' 18But now
Adonijah has become king, and you, my
lord the king, do not know about it. 19He
has sacrificed[t] great numbers of cattle,
fattened calves, and sheep, and has invited all the king's sons, Abiathar the priest
and Joab the commander of the army, but
he has not invited Solomon your servant.
20My lord the king, the eyes of all Israel are
on you, to learn from you who will sit on
the throne of my lord the king after him.
21Otherwise, as soon as my lord the king
is laid to rest[u] with his ancestors, I and my
son Solomon will be treated as criminals."
22While she was still speaking with the
king, Nathan the prophet arrived. 23And
the king was told, "Nathan the prophet
is here." So he went before the king and
bowed with his face to the ground.
24Nathan said, "Have you, my lord the
king, declared that Adonijah shall be
king after you, and that he will sit on your
throne? 25Today he has gone down and sacrificed great numbers of cattle, fattened
calves, and sheep. He has invited all the
king's sons, the commanders of the army
and Abiathar the priest. Right now they are
eating and drinking with him and saying,
'Long live King Adonijah!' 26But me your
servant, and Zadok the priest, and Benaiah son of Jehoiada, and your servant Solomon he did not invite.[v] 27Is this something
my lord the king has done without letting
his servants know who should sit on the
throne of my lord the king after him?"

David Makes Solomon King

28Then King David said, "Call in Bathsheba." So she came into the king's presence and stood before him.
29The king then took an oath: "As surely
as the LORD lives, who has delivered me out
of every trouble,[w] 30I will surely carry out
this very day what I swore[x] to you by the
LORD, the God of Israel: Solomon your son
shall be king after me, and he will sit on my
throne in my place."
31Then Bathsheba bowed down with her
face to the ground, prostrating herself before the king, and said, "May my lord King
David live forever!"
32King David said, "Call in Zadok the
priest, Nathan the prophet and Benaiah
son of Jehoiada." When they came before
the king, 33he said to them: "Take your
lord's servants with you and have Solomon
my son mount my own mule[y] and take him
down to Gihon.[z] 34There have Zadok the
priest and Nathan the prophet anoint[a] him
king over Israel. Blow the trumpet[b] and
shout, 'Long live King Solomon!' 35Then
you are to go up with him, and he is to come
and sit on my throne and reign in my place.
I have appointed him ruler over Israel and
Judah."
36Benaiah son of Jehoiada answered the
king, "Amen! May the LORD, the God of my
lord the king, so declare it. 37As the LORD
was with my lord the king, so may he be
with[c] Solomon to make his throne even
greater[d] than the throne of my lord King
David!"
38So Zadok[e] the priest, Nathan the
prophet, Benaiah son of Jehoiada, the Kerethites[f] and the Pelethites went down and
had Solomon mount King David's mule,
and they escorted him to Gihon.[g] 39Zadok
the priest took the horn of oil[h] from the
sacred tent and anointed Solomon. Then
they sounded the trumpet and all the people shouted,[i] "Long live King Solomon!"
40And all the people went up after him,
playing pipes and rejoicing greatly, so that
the ground shook with the sound.
41Adonijah and all the guests who were
with him heard it as they were finishing
their feast. On hearing the sound of the
trumpet, Joab asked, "What's the meaning
of all the noise in the city?"

1:29 *who has delivered me.* In these words of praise, David celebrated the innumerable times that the Lord had acted on his behalf, to deliver him from his enemies and from his own sins. Some of David's psalms were written in connection with those times of God's deliverance (Ps. 40; 142).

1:38 *the Kerethites and the Pelethites.* These two groups were part of David's bodyguard (2 Sam. 8:18; 15:18; 20:7). Their association with David stretched back to his days among the Philistines, with whom the Kerethites are usually identified (1 Sam. 30:13–14; Ezek. 25:16; Zeph. 2:5).

1:39 *Zadok ... anointed Solomon.* Every priestly anointing would recall the words of Psalm 2, in accordance with the words of the Davidic covenant of 2 Samuel 7. The anointing announced that the anointed one was now the adopted son of the living God.

1:13 [q] ver 30; 1Ch 22:9-13 **1:15** [r] ver 1 **1:17** [s] ver 13, 30 **1:19** [t] ver 9 **1:21** [u] Dt 31:16; 1Ki 2:10 **1:26** [v] ver 8, 10 **1:29** [w] 2Sa 4:9 **1:30** [x] ver 13, 17 **1:33** [y] 2Sa 20:6-7 [z] 2Ch 32:30; 33:14 **1:34** [a] 1Sa 10:1; 16:3, 12; 1Ki 19:16; 2Ki 9:3, 13 [b] ver 25; 2Sa 5:3; 15:10 **1:37** [c] Jos 1:5, 17; 1Sa 20:13 [d] ver 47 **1:38** [e] ver 8 [f] 2Sa 8:18 [g] ver 33 **1:39** [h] Ex 30:23-32; Ps 89:20 [i] ver 34; 1Sa 10:24

[42]Even as he was speaking, Jonathan[j]
son of Abiathar the priest arrived. Adonijah said, "Come in. A worthy man like you
must be bringing good news."[k]
[43]"Not at all!" Jonathan answered. "Our
lord King David has made Solomon king.
[44]The king has sent with him Zadok the
priest, Nathan the prophet, Benaiah son
of Jehoiada, the Kerethites and the Pelethites, and they have put him on the king's
mule, [45]and Zadok the priest and Nathan
the prophet have anointed him king at Gihon. From there they have gone up cheering, and the city resounds[l] with it. That's
the noise you hear. [46]Moreover, Solomon
has taken his seat on the royal throne.
[47]Also, the royal officials have come to
congratulate our lord King David, saying,
'May your God make Solomon's name
more famous than yours and his throne
greater[m] than yours!' And the king bowed
in worship on his bed [48]and said, 'Praise
be to the LORD, the God of Israel, who has
allowed my eyes to see a successor[n] on my
throne today.'"
[49]At this, all Adonijah's guests rose in
alarm and dispersed. [50]But Adonijah, in
fear of Solomon, went and took hold of the
horns[o] of the altar. [51]Then Solomon was
told, "Adonijah is afraid of King Solomon
and is clinging to the horns of the altar. He
says, 'Let King Solomon swear to me today that he will not put his servant to death
with the sword.'"
[52]Solomon replied, "If he shows himself
to be worthy, not a hair[p] of his head will fall
to the ground; but if evil is found in him, he
will die." [53]Then King Solomon sent men,
and they brought him down from the altar. And Adonijah came and bowed down
to King Solomon, and Solomon said, "Go
to your home."

David's Charge to Solomon

2 When the time drew near for David to
die,[q] he gave a charge to Solomon his
son.
[2]"I am about to go the way of all the
earth,"[r] he said. "So be strong,[s] act like a
man, [3]and observe[t] what the LORD your
God requires: Walk in obedience to him,
and keep his decrees and commands, his
laws and regulations, as written in the Law
of Moses. Do this so that you may prosper[u]
in all you do and wherever you go [4]and that
the LORD may keep his promise[v] to me: 'If
your descendants watch how they live, and
if they walk faithfully[w] before me with all
their heart and soul, you will never fail to
have a successor on the throne of Israel.'
[5]"Now you yourself know what Joab[x] son
of Zeruiah did to me—what he did to the
two commanders of Israel's armies, Abner[y]
son of Ner and Amasa[z] son of Jether. He
killed them, shedding their blood in peace-
time as if in battle, and with that blood he
stained the belt around his waist and the
sandals on his feet. [6]Deal with him according to your wisdom,[a] but do not let his gray
head go down to the grave in peace.
[7]"But show kindness to the sons of Barzillai[b] of Gilead and let them be among
those who eat at your table.[c] They stood by
me when I fled from your brother Absalom.
[8]"And remember, you have with you
Shimei[d] son of Gera, the Benjamite from
Bahurim, who called down bitter curses
on me the day I went to Mahanaim. When
he came down to meet me at the Jordan, I
swore[e] to him by the LORD: 'I will not put
you to death by the sword.' [9]But now, do not
consider him innocent. You are a man of
wisdom;[f] you will know what to do to him.
Bring his gray head down to the grave in
blood."

1:50 *took hold of the horns of the altar.* This action was in keeping with the traditional function of the altar as a haven of refuge for those who had committed unintentional crimes (Ex. 21:12–14).

1:53 Forgiveness—Solomon chose to forgive Adonijah for his attempted usurpation of the throne, realizing that Adonijah had legitimate reason to think that he should be the next king. Wiser than his years, young Solomon overlooked the offense of his brother rather than bring any reproach on his reign at this early stage. Sadly, Adonijah proved himself unworthy of his pardon, making another attempt to take the throne after his father David was dead.

2:4 *never fail to have a successor on the throne*. God had made an unconditional covenant with David (2 Sam. 7:12–16; 1 Chr. 17:11–14; Ps. 89), granting him a continual posterity and a royal dynasty. Although the Davidic covenant was an everlasting sacred promise, individual kings through their evil behavior could fail to receive the benefits of the covenant. The line of promise would be preserved, but the time would come when the promised Ruler would not be on an earthly throne (Hos. 3:4). God's prophets predict that the heir to the throne of David will yet reign over a repentant, regathered and restored Israel (Jer. 33:19–26; Ezek. 34:22–31) in fulfillment of the promises of the covenants (Ezek. 37:21–28; Mic. 7:18–20). The New Testament reveals that all this will be realized in Jesus Christ, the Savior King (Acts 3:25–26; 15:16–17; Gal. 3:26–29; Rev. 3:21), who is David's Heir in the ultimate sense (Acts 2:22–36).

2:5–8 *Joab ... Shimei.* David knew that these two men would cause trouble for Solomon if they were not dealt with. Joab had murdered two generals (2 Sam. 3:27; 20:10), killed David's son Absalom (2 Sam. 18:14), and joined Adonijah's conspiracy (1:7,19). Shimei had cursed the king and treated him shamefully as he was fleeing from Absalom (2 Sam. 16:5–13; 19:16–23).

1:42 [j] 2Sa 15:27,36 [k] 2Sa 18:26 **1:45** [l] ver 40
1:47 [m] ver 37; Ge 47:31 **1:48** [n] 2Sa 7:12; 1Ki 3:6
1:50 [o] 1Ki 2:28 **1:52** [p] 1Sa 14:45; 2Sa 14:11
2:1 [q] Ge 47:29; Dt 31:14 **2:2** [r] Jos 23:14 [s] Dt 31:7,23; Jos 1:6 **2:3** [t] Dt 17:14-20; Jos 1:7 [u] 1Ch 22:13
2:4 [v] 2Sa 7:13,25; 1Ki 8:25 [w] 2Ki 20:3; Ps 132:12
2:5 [x] 2Sa 2:18; 18:5,12,14 [y] 2Sa 3:27 [z] 2Sa 20:10
2:6 [a] ver 9 **2:7** [b] 2Sa 17:27; 19:31-39 [c] 2Sa 9:7
2:8 [d] 2Sa 16:5-13 [e] 2Sa 19:18-23 **2:9** [f] ver 6

10 Then David rested with his ancestors and
was buried[g] in the City of David.[h] 11 He had
reigned[i] forty years over Israel—seven years
in Hebron and thirty-three in Jerusalem.
12 So Solomon sat on the throne[j] of his father
David, and his rule was firmly established.[k]

Solomon's Throne Established

13 Now Adonijah, the son of Haggith,
went to Bathsheba, Solomon's mother. Bathsheba asked him, "Do you come
peacefully?"[l]

He answered, "Yes, peacefully." 14 Then
he added, "I have something to say to you."

"You may say it," she replied.

15 "As you know," he said, "the kingdom
was mine. All Israel looked to me as their
king. But things changed, and the kingdom
has gone to my brother; for it has come to
him from the LORD. 16 Now I have one request to make of you. Do not refuse me."

"You may make it," she said.

17 So he continued, "Please ask King Solomon—he will not refuse you—to give me
Abishag[m] the Shunammite as my wife."

18 "Very well," Bathsheba replied, "I will
speak to the king for you."

19 When Bathsheba went to King Solomon to speak to him for Adonijah, the
king stood up to meet her, bowed down to
her and sat down on his throne. He had a
throne brought for the king's mother,[n] and
she sat down at his right hand.[o]

20 "I have one small request to make of
you," she said. "Do not refuse me."

The king replied, "Make it, my mother; I
will not refuse you."

21 So she said, "Let Abishag[p] the Shunammite be given in marriage to your
brother Adonijah."

22 King Solomon answered his mother,
"Why do you request Abishag[q] the Shunammite for Adonijah? You might as well request the kingdom for him—after all, he is
my older brother[r]—yes, for him and for Abiathar the priest and Joab son of Zeruiah!"

23 Then King Solomon swore by the
LORD: "May God deal with me, be it ever so
severely,[s] if Adonijah does not pay with his
life for this request! 24 And now, as surely
as the LORD lives—he who has established
me securely on the throne of my father David and has founded a dynasty for me as he
promised[t]—Adonijah shall be put to death
today!" 25 So King Solomon gave orders to
Benaiah[u] son of Jehoiada, and he struck
down Adonijah and he died.

26 To Abiathar[v] the priest the king said,
"Go back to your fields in Anathoth.[w] You
deserve to die, but I will not put you to
death now, because you carried the ark[x] of
the Sovereign LORD before my father David and shared all my father's hardships."[y]
27 So Solomon removed Abiathar from the
priesthood of the LORD, fulfilling[z] the word
the LORD had spoken at Shiloh about the
house of Eli.

28 When the news reached Joab, who had
conspired with Adonijah though not with
Absalom, he fled to the tent of the LORD and
took hold of the horns[a] of the altar. 29 King
Solomon was told that Joab had fled to the
tent of the LORD and was beside the altar.
Then Solomon ordered Benaiah[b] son of Jehoiada, "Go, strike him down!"

30 So Benaiah entered the tent of the
LORD and said to Joab, "The king says,
'Come out![c]'"

But he answered, "No, I will die here."

Benaiah reported to the king, "This is
how Joab answered me."

31 Then the king commanded Benaiah,
"Do as he says. Strike him down and bury
him, and so clear me and my whole family of the guilt of the innocent blood[d] that
Joab shed. 32 The LORD will repay[e] him for
the blood he shed,[f] because without my father David knowing it he attacked two men
and killed them with the sword. Both of
them—Abner son of Ner, commander of Israel's army, and Amasa[g] son of Jether, commander of Judah's army—were better[h] men
and more upright than he. 33 May the guilt of
their blood rest on the head of Joab and his
descendants forever. But on David and his
descendants, his house and his throne, may
there be the LORD's peace forever."

34 So Benaiah son of Jehoiada went up
and struck down Joab and killed him, and
he was buried at his home out in the country. 35 The king put Benaiah[i] son of Jehoiada over the army in Joab's position and
replaced Abiathar with Zadok[j] the priest.

36 Then the king sent for Shimei[k] and
said to him, "Build yourself a house in Jerusalem and live there, but do not go anywhere else. 37 The day you leave and cross
the Kidron Valley,[l] you can be sure you will
die; your blood will be on your own head."[m]

2:27 ***Abiathar.*** This act fulfilled God's word to Eli, removing the last of his descendants from serving before the Lord (1 Sam. 2:30–33). When Abiathar was removed from office, his influence was greatly restricted. Solomon spared his life in recognition of his past service to God and David (2 Sam. 15:24,29; 1 Chr. 15:11–15).

2:28 ***horns of the altar.*** Because Joab was a murderer (2 Sam. 3:27; 18:14, 20:10), he could not claim the protective sanctity of the horns of the altar, and could not escape execution.

2:35 ***Zadok.*** Zadok was a descendant of Eleazar, the son of Aaron (1 Chr. 6:4–8).

2:10 [g] Ac 2:29; 13:36 [h] 2Sa 5:7 **2:11** [i] 2Sa 5:4,5
2:12 [j] 1Ch 29:23 [k] 2Ch 1:1 **2:13** [l] 1Sa 16:4
2:17 [m] 1Ki 1:3 **2:19** [n] 1Ki 15:13 [o] Ps 45:9 **2:21** [p] 1Ki 1:3
2:22 [q] 2Sa 12:8; 1Ki 1:3 [r] 1Ch 3:2 **2:23** [s] Ru 1:17
2:24 [t] 2Sa 7:11; 1Ch 22:10 **2:25** [u] 2Sa 8:18
2:26 [v] 1Sa 22:20 [w] Jos 21:18 [x] 2Sa 15:24 [y] 1Sa 23:6
2:27 [z] 1Sa 2:27-36 **2:28** [a] 1Ki 1:7,50 **2:29** [b] ver 25
2:30 [c] Ex 21:14 **2:31** [d] Nu 35:33; Dt 19:13; 21:8-9
2:32 [e] Jdg 9:57; Ps 7:16 [f] Jdg 9:24 [g] 2Sa 3:27; 20:10
[h] 2Ch 21:13 **2:35** [i] 1Ki 4:4 [j] ver 27; 1Ch 29:22
2:36 [k] ver 8; 2Sa 16:5 **2:37** [l] 2Sa 15:23 [m] Lev 20:9; Jos 2:19; 2Sa 1:16

38 Shimei answered the king, "What you say is good. Your servant will do as my lord the king has said." And Shimei stayed in Jerusalem for a long time.

39 But three years later, two of Shimei's slaves ran off to Achish[n] son of Maakah, king of Gath, and Shimei was told, "Your slaves are in Gath." **40** At this, he saddled his donkey and went to Achish at Gath in search of his slaves. So Shimei went away and brought the slaves back from Gath.

41 When Solomon was told that Shimei had gone from Jerusalem to Gath and had returned, **42** the king summoned Shimei and said to him, "Did I not make you swear by the LORD and warn you, 'On the day you leave to go anywhere else, you can be sure you will die'? At that time you said to me, 'What you say is good. I will obey.' **43** Why then did you not keep your oath to the LORD and obey the command I gave you?"

44 The king also said to Shimei, "You know in your heart all the wrong[o] you did to my father David. Now the LORD will repay you for your wrongdoing. **45** But King Solomon will be blessed, and David's throne will remain secure[p] before the LORD forever."

46 Then the king gave the order to Benaiah son of Jehoiada, and he went out and struck Shimei down and he died.

The kingdom was now established[q] in Solomon's hands.

Solomon Asks for Wisdom

3 Solomon made an alliance with Pharaoh king of Egypt and married[r] his daughter.[s] He brought her to the City of David[t] until he finished building his palace[u] and the temple of the LORD, and the wall around Jerusalem. **2** The people, however, were still sacrificing at the high places,[v] because a temple had not yet been built for the Name of the LORD. **3** Solomon showed his love[w] for the LORD by walking according to the instructions[x] given him by his father David, except that he offered sacrifices and burned incense on the high places.

4 The king went to Gibeon[y] to offer sacrifices, for that was the most important high place, and Solomon offered a thousand burnt offerings on that altar. **5** At Gibeon the LORD appeared[z] to Solomon during the night in a dream,[a] and God said, "Ask for whatever you want me to give you."

6 Solomon answered, "You have shown great kindness to your servant, my father David, because he was faithful[b] to you and righteous and upright in heart. You have continued this great kindness to him and have given him a son[c] to sit on his throne this very day.

7 "Now, LORD my God, you have made your servant king in place of my father David. But I am only a little child[d] and do not know how to carry out my duties. **8** Your servant is here among the people you have chosen,[e] a great people, too numerous to count or number.[f] **9** So give your servant a discerning[g] heart to govern your people and to distinguish[h] between right and wrong. For who is able[i] to govern this great people of yours?"

10 The Lord was pleased that Solomon had asked for this. **11** So God said to him, "Since you have asked[j] for this and not for long life or wealth for yourself, nor have asked for the death of your enemies but for discernment in administering justice, **12** I will do what you have asked.[k] I will give you a wise[l] and discerning heart, so that there will never have been anyone like you, nor will there ever be. **13** Moreover, I will give you what you have not[m] asked for—both wealth and honor[n]—so that in your lifetime you will have no equal[o] among kings. **14** And if you walk[p] in obedience to me and keep my decrees and commands as David your father did, I will give you a long life."[q] **15** Then Solomon awoke[r]—and he realized it had been a dream.

He returned to Jerusalem, stood before the ark of the Lord's covenant and sacrificed burnt offerings[s] and fellowship offerings.[t] Then he gave a feast[u] for all his court.

3:1 ***made an alliance.*** In the ancient Middle East, political alliances were often ratified by the marriage of the son of one king to the daughter of another. Except in unusual circumstances, the pharaohs of Egypt did not observe this custom. Therefore, the giving of Pharaoh's daughter to Solomon attested to the Israelite king's growing prestige and importance to the Egyptians.

3:7 ***but I am only a little child.*** The term "child" often refers to a servant or to an inexperienced person still in training for a profession. With proper humility, Solomon stressed his relative youth and inexperience.

3:14 Obedience—Because he loved God above all at this time of his life (v. 3), and chose wisdom and discernment for his office, Solomon received even more—riches and honor and distinction. Obedient in many ways, he was accordingly blessed by God. When commands are given by a loving, caring person, obedience must result in blessing. God repeatedly stated this principle (Deut. 5:29—6:24). Saul, David, and Solomon all lost blessing because of disobedience. This was not because of narrowness or rigidity on God's part. He does not give us commands to make our lives harder, or to be harsh and demanding. His commands have blessings built in—He is showing us the best way to live.

3:15 ***ark of the Lord's covenant.*** Although David had brought the ark of the covenant to Jerusalem

2:39 [n] 1Sa 27:2 **2:44** [o] 1Sa 25:39; 2Sa 16:5-13; Eze 17:19 **2:45** [p] 2Sa 7:13; Pr 25:5 **2:46** [q] ver 12; 2Ch 1:1 **3:1** [r] 1Ki 7:8 [s] 1Ki 9:24 [t] 2Sa 5:7 [u] 1Ki 7:1; 9:15, 19 **3:2** [v] Lev 17:3-5; Dt 12:2, 4-5; 1Ki 22:43 **3:3** [w] Dt 6:5; Ps 31:23; 1Co 8:3 [x] 1Ki 2:3; 9:4; 11:4, 6, 38 **3:4** [y] 1Ch 16:39 **3:5** [z] 1Ki 9:2 [a] Nu 12:6; Mt 1:20 **3:6** [b] 1Ki 2:4; 9:4 [c] 1Ki 1:48 **3:7** [d] Nu 27:17; 1Ch 29:1 **3:8** [e] Dt 7:6 [f] Ge 15:5 **3:9** [g] 2Sa 14:17; Jas 1:5 [h] Pr 2:3-9; Heb 5:14 [i] Ps 72:1-2 **3:11** [j] Jas 4:3 **3:12** [k] 1Jn 5:14-15 [l] 1Ki 4:29, 30, 31; 5:12; 10:23; Ecc 1:16 **3:13** [m] Mt 6:33; Eph 3:20 [n] 1Ki 4:21-24; Pr 3:1-2, 16 [o] 1Ki 10:23 **3:14** [p] ver 6; Pr 3:1-2, 16 [q] Ps 61:6; 91:16 **3:15** [r] Ge 41:7 [s] 1Ki 8:65 [t] Mk 6:21 [u] Est 1:3, 9; Da 5:1

A Wise Ruling

16 Now two prostitutes came to the king
and stood before him. 17 One of them said,
"Pardon me, my lord. This woman and I
live in the same house, and I had a baby
while she was there with me. 18 The third
day after my child was born, this woman
also had a baby. We were alone; there was
no one in the house but the two of us.

19 "During the night this woman's son
died because she lay on him. 20 So she got
up in the middle of the night and took my
son from my side while I your servant was
asleep. She put him by her breast and put
her dead son by my breast. 21 The next
morning, I got up to nurse my son—and he
was dead! But when I looked at him closely
in the morning light, I saw that it wasn't the
son I had borne."

22 The other woman said, "No! The living
one is my son; the dead one is yours."

But the first one insisted, "No! The dead one is yours; the living one is mine." And so they argued before the king.

23 The king said, "This one says, 'My son
is alive and your son is dead,' while that one says, 'No! Your son is dead and mine is alive.'"

24 Then the king said, "Bring me a
sword." So they brought a sword for the
king. 25 He then gave an order: "Cut the liv-
ing child in two and give half to one and half to the other."

26 The woman whose son was alive was
deeply moved[v] out of love for her son and said to the king, "Please, my lord, give her the living baby! Don't kill him!"

But the other said, "Neither I nor you shall have him. Cut him in two!"

27 Then the king gave his ruling: "Give
the living baby to the first woman. Do not kill him; she is his mother."

28 When all Israel heard the verdict the
king had given, they held the king in awe, because they saw that he had wisdom[w] from God to administer justice.

Solomon's Officials and Governors

4 So King Solomon ruled over all Israel.
2 And these were his chief officials:

Azariah[x] son of Zadok—the priest;
3 Elihoreph and Ahijah, sons of Shisha—secretaries;
Jehoshaphat[y] son of Ahilud—recorder;
4 Benaiah[z] son of Jehoiada—commander in chief;
Zadok[a] and Abiathar—priests;
5 Azariah son of Nathan—in charge of the district governors;
Zabud son of Nathan—a priest and adviser to the king;
6 Ahishar—palace administrator;
Adoniram son of Abda—in charge of forced labor.

7 Solomon had twelve district governors
over all Israel, who supplied provisions for
the king and the royal household. Each one
had to provide supplies for one month in
the year. 8 These are their names:

Ben-Hur—in the hill country[b] of Ephraim;
9 Ben-Deker—in Makaz, Shaalbim,[c] Beth Shemesh[d] and Elon Bethhanan;
10 Ben-Hesed—in Arubboth (Sokoh[e] and all the land of Hepher[f] were his);
11 Ben-Abinadab—in Naphoth Dor[g] (he was married to Taphath daughter of Solomon);
12 Baana son of Ahilud—in Taanach and Megiddo, and in all of Beth Shan[h] next to Zarethan[i] below Jezreel, from Beth Shan to Abel Meholah[j] across to Jokmeam;[k]
13 Ben-Geber—in Ramoth Gilead (the settlements of Jair[l] son of Manasseh in Gilead were his, as well as the region of Argob in Bashan and its sixty large walled cities[m] with bronze gate bars);
14 Ahinadab son of Iddo—in Mahanaim;[n]
15 Ahimaaz[o]—in Naphtali (he had married Basemath daughter of Solomon);
16 Baana son of Hushai[p]—in Asher and in Aloth;
17 Jehoshaphat son of Paruah—in Issachar;
18 Shimei[q] son of Ela—in Benjamin;

(2 Sam. 6) the tabernacle and its furnishings remained in Gibeon, which served as an important worship center (v. 4; 2 Chr. 1:3–5). After its capture by the Philistines (1 Sam. 5–6), the ark never returned to the tabernacle. The ark was not in the Most Holy Place again until it was placed in Solomon's temple.

3:28 ***wisdom ... justice.*** These important qualities which marked Solomon's reign would characterize the rule of Israel's Messiah in a far greater way (Is. 11:1–5). David's final words to Solomon were, do "according to your wisdom" (2:6). Wisdom does not dwell as a recluse among books in the study. Rather, wisdom stands with confidence at the crossroads of life. Solomon's wisdom was decisive. Through God he was able to observe the actions of others and in this way have a revelation of the truth.

4:7–19 ***twelve district governors.*** These men were responsible for handling lesser administrative tasks and raising revenue for the crown. The districts did not follow tribal boundaries.

4:18 ***Shimei.*** This is not the same Shimei who cursed David (2 Sam. 16:5–13), but probably the man mentioned in 1:8 as a supporter of Solomon.

3:26 [v] Ge 43:30; Isa 49:15; Jer 31:20; Hos 11:8
3:28 [w] ver 9, 11-12; Col 2:3 **4:2** [x] 1Ch 6:10
4:3 [y] 2Sa 8:16 **4:4** [z] 1Ki 2:35 [a] 1Ki 2:27 **4:8** [b] Jos 24:33
4:9 [c] Jdg 1:35 [d] Jos 21:16 **4:10** [e] Jos 15:35 [f] Jos 12:17
4:11 [g] Jos 11:2 **4:12** [h] Jos 17:11; Jdg 5:19 [i] Jos 3:16
[j] 1Ki 19:16 [k] 1Ch 6:68 **4:13** [l] Nu 32:41 [m] Dt 3:4
4:14 [n] Jos 13:26 **4:15** [o] 2Sa 15:27 **4:16** [p] 2Sa 15:32
4:18 [q] 1Ki 1:8

19 Geber son of Uri—in Gilead (the
country of Sihon king of the Amorites and the country of Og[r] king of
Bashan). He was the only governor
over the district.

Solomon's Daily Provisions

20 The people of Judah and Israel were
as numerous as the sand[s] on the seashore;
they ate, they drank and they were happy.
21 And Solomon ruled[t] over all the kingdoms from the Euphrates River[u] to the land
of the Philistines, as far as the border of
Egypt.[v] These countries brought tribute[w]
and were Solomon's subjects all his life.
22 Solomon's daily provisions were thirty
cors[a] of the finest flour and sixty cors[b] of
meal, 23 ten head of stall-fed cattle, twenty
of pasture-fed cattle and a hundred sheep
and goats, as well as deer, gazelles, roe-
bucks and choice fowl. 24 For he ruled over
all the kingdoms west of the Euphrates River, from Tiphsah[x] to Gaza, and had peace[y]
on all sides. 25 During Solomon's lifetime
Judah and Israel, from Dan to Beersheba,[z]
lived in safety,[a] everyone under their own
vine and under their own fig tree.[b]
26 Solomon had four[c] thousand stalls for
chariot horses,[c] and twelve thousand horses.[d]
27 The district governors,[d] each in his
month, supplied provisions for King Solomon and all who came to the king's table.
They saw to it that nothing was lacking.
28 They also brought to the proper place
their quotas of barley and straw for the
chariot horses and the other horses.

Solomon's Wisdom

29 God gave Solomon wisdom[e] and very
great insight, and a breadth of understanding as measureless as the sand on the seashore. 30 Solomon's wisdom was greater
than the wisdom of all the people of the
East,[f] and greater than all the wisdom of
Egypt.[g] 31 He was wiser[h] than anyone else,
including Ethan the Ezrahite—wiser than
Heman, Kalkol and Darda, the sons of
Mahol. And his fame spread to all the surrounding nations. 32 He spoke three thousand proverbs[i] and his songs[j] numbered a
thousand and five. 33 He spoke about plant
life, from the cedar of Lebanon to the hyssop that grows out of walls. He also spoke
about animals and birds, reptiles and fish.
34 From all nations people came to listen to
Solomon's wisdom, sent by all the kings[k] of
the world, who had heard of his wisdom.[e]

Preparations for Building the Temple

5 [f] When Hiram[l] king of Tyre heard that
Solomon had been anointed king to
succeed his father David, he sent his envoys to Solomon, because he had always
been on friendly terms with David. 2 Solomon sent back this message to Hiram:

3 "You know that because of the
wars[m] waged against my father David from all sides, he could not build
a temple for the Name of the LORD his
God until the LORD put his enemies
under his feet. 4 But now the LORD my
God has given me rest[n] on every side,
and there is no adversary or disaster.
5 I intend, therefore, to build a temple[o]
for the Name of the LORD my God, as
the LORD told my father David, when
he said, 'Your son whom I will put on
the throne in your place will build the
temple for my Name.'[p]
6 "So give orders that cedars of Lebanon be cut for me. My men will work
with yours, and I will pay you for your
men whatever wages you set. You
know that we have no one so skilled
in felling timber as the Sidonians."

7 When Hiram heard Solomon's message,
he was greatly pleased and said, "Praise be

---

[a] *22* That is, probably about 5 1/2 tons or about 5 metric tons [b] *22* That is, probably about 11 tons or about 10 metric tons [c] *26* Some Septuagint manuscripts (see also 2 Chron. 9:25); Hebrew *forty* [d] *26* Or *charioteers* [e] *34* In Hebrew texts 4:21-34 is numbered 5:1-14. [f] In Hebrew texts 5:1-18 is numbered 5:15-32.

4:20 *numerous as the sand.* God fulfilled His promise to make Abraham's descendants numerous (Gen. 15:5,18). Solomon's empire extended far beyond the traditional boundaries of Israel. Through this greatly expanded empire, Hebrew people not only traveled to far-flung regions, but they took with them their knowledge of the living God.

4:22 *cors.* A cor was the same size as a homer (Ezek. 45:14); at between six and seven bushels, it was the normal load for a donkey.

4:29 *wisdom.* The three terms used in this verse underscore Solomon's depth of understanding. He was not merely intelligent, able to understand facts and logic; he was also given the ability to apply his intelligence to problems which defy logic, possessing a rare understanding of human beings with all their emotional and spiritual complexities.

4:32–34 *proverbs ... songs.* Solomon was the author of a large part of the Book of Proverbs. He is also traditionally assigned the authorship of the Song of Songs, Psalms 72 and 127, and Ecclesiastes.

5:1 *Hiram.* This Phoenician king ruled over Tyre for 34 years (978–944 B.C.).

5:7 *Praise be to the LORD.* Acknowledging the deities of another people is well known in the Bible (Dan. 3:28) and other ancient Middle Eastern literature. It

4:19 [r] Dt 3:8-10 **4:20** [s] Ge 22:17; 32:12; 1Ki 3:8 **4:21** [t] 2Ch 9:26; Ps 72:11 [u] Jos 1:4; Ps 72:8 [v] Ge 15:18 [w] Ps 68:29 **4:24** [x] Ps 72:11 [y] 1Ch 22:9 **4:25** [z] Jdg 20:1 [a] Jer 23:6 [b] Mic 4:4; Zec 3:10 **4:26** [c] 1Ki 10:26; 2Ch 1:14 **4:27** [d] ver 7 **4:29** [e] 1Ki 3:12 **4:30** [f] Ge 25:6 [g] Ac 7:22 **4:31** [h] 1Ki 3:12; 1Ch 2:6; 6:33; 15:19; Ps 89 Title **4:32** [i] Pr 1:1; Ecc 12:9 [j] SS 1:1 **4:34** [k] 1Ki 10:1; 2Ch 9:23 **5:1** [l] ver 10, 18; 2Sa 5:11; 1Ch 14:1 **5:3** [m] 1Ch 22:8; 28:3 **5:4** [n] 1Ki 4:24; 1Ch 22:9 **5:5** [o] 1Ch 17:12 [p] 2Sa 7:13; 1Ch 22:10

to the LORD today, for he has given David
a wise son to rule over this great nation."
8So Hiram sent word to Solomon:

"I have received the message you
sent me and will do all you want in
providing the cedar and juniper logs.
9My men will haul them down from
Lebanon to the Mediterranean Sea[q],
and I will float them as rafts by sea
to the place you specify. There I will
separate them and you can take them
away. And you are to grant my wish
by providing food[r] for my royal household."

10In this way Hiram kept Solomon supplied with all the cedar and juniper logs he
wanted, 11and Solomon gave Hiram twenty thousand cors[a] of wheat as food for his
household, in addition to twenty thousand
baths[b,c] of pressed olive oil. Solomon continued to do this for Hiram year after year.
12The LORD gave Solomon wisdom,[s] just as
he had promised him. There were peaceful relations between Hiram and Solomon,
and the two of them made a treaty.[t]
13King Solomon conscripted laborers[u]
from all Israel—thirty thousand men.
14He sent them off to Lebanon in shifts of
ten thousand a month, so that they spent
one month in Lebanon and two months
at home. Adoniram[v] was in charge of the
forced labor. 15Solomon had seventy thousand carriers and eighty thousand stonecutters in the hills, 16as well as thirty-three
hundred[d] foremen[w] who supervised the
project and directed the workers. 17At the
king's command they removed from the
quarry[x] large blocks of high-grade stone[y]
to provide a foundation of dressed stone
for the temple. 18The craftsmen of Solomon
and Hiram and workers from Byblos[z] cut
and prepared the timber and stone for the
building of the temple.

Solomon Builds the Temple

6 In the four hundred and eightieth[e] year
after the Israelites came out of Egypt, in
the fourth year of Solomon's reign over Israel, in the month of Ziv, the second month,
he began to build the temple of the LORD.[a]
2The temple[b] that King Solomon built
for the LORD was sixty cubits long, twenty
wide and thirty high.[f] 3The portico at the
front of the main hall of the temple extended the width of the temple, that is twenty
cubits,[g] and projected ten cubits[h] from the
front of the temple. 4He made narrow windows[c] high up in the temple walls. 5Against
the walls of the main hall and inner sanctuary he built a structure around the building, in which there were side rooms.[d] 6The
lowest floor was five cubits[i] wide, the middle floor six cubits[j] and the third floor sev-
en.[k] He made offset ledges around the outside of the temple so that nothing would be
inserted into the temple walls.
7In building the temple, only blocks
dressed[e] at the quarry were used, and no
hammer, chisel or any other iron tool[f] was
heard at the temple site while it was being
built.
8The entrance to the lowest[l] floor was
on the south side of the temple; a stairway
led up to the middle level and from there to
the third. 9So he built the temple and completed it, roofing it with beams and cedar[g]
planks. 10And he built the side rooms all
along the temple. The height of each was
five cubits, and they were attached to the
temple by beams of cedar.
11The word of the LORD came to Solomon: 12"As for this temple you are building,

---

[a] *11* That is, probably about 3,600 tons or about 3,250 metric tons [b] *11* Septuagint (see also 2 Chron. 2:10); Hebrew *twenty cors* [c] *11* That is, about 120,000 gallons or about 440,000 liters
[d] *16* Hebrew; some Septuagint manuscripts (see also 2 Chron. 2:2,18) *thirty-six hundred*
[e] *1* Hebrew; Septuagint *four hundred and fortieth*
[f] *2* That is, about 90 feet long, 30 feet wide and 45 feet high or about 27 meters long, 9 meters wide and 14 meters high [g] *3* That is, about 30 feet or about 9 meters; also in verses 16 and 20 [h] *3* That is, about 15 feet or about 4.5 meters; also in verses 23-26 [i] *6* That is, about 7 1/2 feet or about 2.3 meters; also in verses 10 and 24 [j] *6* That is, about 9 feet or about 2.7 meters [k] *6* That is, about 11 feet or about 3.2 meters [l] *8* Septuagint; Hebrew *middle*

---

does not necessarily imply that Hiram was expressing faith in God.

5:13 *conscripted laborers ... thirty thousand men.* Solomon's long and extensive use of this type of social conscription to accomplish his vast building projects became a source of considerable difficulty for his successor, Rehoboam (12:4).

6:1 *four hundred and eightieth year.* Many scholars take this date as the key date for establishing the time of the Exodus. The division of the kingdom at the death of Solomon can be dated at 930 B.C. (11:41–43). Allowing forty years for Solomon's rule (11:42), the fourth year of his reign would be 966 B.C. If the exodus took place 480 years before 966 B.C., its date was 1446 B.C.

6:2 *temple ... for the LORD.* Solomon followed the floor plan of the tabernacle, but doubled its dimensions. Solomon's temple was constructed on Mount Moriah, the mountain where Abraham was told to offer Isaac as a sacrifice (Gen. 22:2; 2 Chr. 3:1), on the site of the threshing floor of Araunah where God had spoken to David (2 Sam. 24:24). ***cubits.*** The standard cubit was about 18 inches.

6:11 *word of the LORD.* This message to Solomon might have come by means of a prophet. On other occasions, Solomon had more personal encounters with the Lord (3:5; 9:2; 11:11).

5:9 [q] Ezr 3:7 [r] Eze 27:17; Ac 12:20 **5:12** [s] 1Ki 3:12 [t] Am 1:9
5:13 [u] 1Ki 9:15 **5:14** [v] 1Ki 4:6; 2Ch 10:18
5:16 [w] 1Ki 9:23 **5:17** [x] 1Ki 6:7 [y] 1Ch 22:2
5:18 [z] Jos 13:5 **6:1** [a] Ac 7:47 **6:2** [b] Eze 41:1
6:4 [c] Eze 40:16; 41:16 **6:5** [d] ver 16, 19-21; Eze 41:5-6
6:7 [e] Ex 20:25 [f] Dt 27:5 **6:9** [g] ver 14, 38

if you follow my decrees, observe my laws and keep all my commands and obey them, I will fulfill through you the promise[h] I gave to David your father. 13And I will live among the Israelites and will not abandon[i] my people Israel."

14So Solomon built the temple and completed[j] it. 15He lined its interior walls with cedar boards, paneling them from the floor of the temple to the ceiling,[k] and covered the floor of the temple with planks of juniper. 16He partitioned off twenty cubits at the rear of the temple with cedar boards from floor to ceiling to form within the temple an inner sanctuary, the Most Holy Place.[l] 17The main hall in front of this room was forty cubits[a] long. 18The inside of the temple was cedar,[m] carved with gourds and open flowers. Everything was cedar; no stone was to be seen.

19He prepared the inner sanctuary[n] within the temple to set the ark of the covenant[o] of the LORD there. 20The inner sanctuary[p] was twenty cubits long, twenty wide and twenty high. He overlaid the inside with pure gold, and he also overlaid the altar of cedar. 21Solomon covered the inside of the temple with pure gold, and he extended gold chains across the front of the inner sanctuary, which was overlaid with gold. 22So he overlaid the whole interior with gold. He also overlaid with gold the altar that belonged to the inner sanctuary.

23For the inner sanctuary he made a pair of cherubim[q] out of olive wood, each ten cubits high. 24One wing of the first cherub was five cubits long, and the other wing five cubits—ten cubits from wing tip to wing tip. 25The second cherub also measured ten cubits, for the two cherubim were identical in size and shape. 26The height of each cherub was ten cubits. 27He placed the cherubim[r] inside the innermost room of the temple, with their wings spread out. The wing of one cherub touched one wall, while the wing of the other touched the other wall, and their wings touched each other in the middle of the room. 28He overlaid the cherubim with gold.

29On the walls all around the temple, in both the inner and outer rooms, he carved cherubim,[s] palm trees and open flowers. 30He also covered the floors of both the inner and outer rooms of the temple with gold.

31For the entrance to the inner sanctuary he made doors out of olive wood that were one fifth of the width of the sanctuary. 32And on the two olive-wood doors he carved cherubim, palm trees and open flowers, and overlaid the cherubim and palm trees with hammered gold. 33In the same way, for the entrance to the main hall he made doorframes out of olive wood that were one fourth of the width of the hall. 34He also made two doors out of juniper wood, each having two leaves that turned in sockets. 35He carved cherubim, palm trees and open flowers on them and overlaid them with gold hammered evenly over the carvings.

36And he built the inner courtyard of three courses[t] of dressed stone and one course of trimmed cedar beams.

37The foundation of the temple of the LORD was laid in the fourth year, in the month of Ziv. 38In the eleventh year in the month of Bul, the eighth month, the temple was finished in all its details according to its specifications.[u] He had spent seven years building it.

Solomon Builds His Palace

7 It took Solomon thirteen years, however, to complete the construction of his palace.[v] 2He built the Palace[w] of the Forest of Lebanon[x] a hundred cubits long, fifty wide and thirty high,[b] with four rows of cedar columns supporting trimmed cedar beams. 3It was roofed with cedar above the beams that rested on the columns—forty-

[a] 17 That is, about 60 feet or about 18 meters
[b] 2 That is, about 150 feet long, 75 feet wide and 45 feet high or about 45 meters long, 23 meters wide and 14 meters high

6:19 ***ark of the covenant.*** The ark of the covenant (Deut. 10:8) was so named because it housed the two stone tablets of the covenant—the Ten Commandments (Deut. 10:1–5). The ark symbolized the presence of the sovereign God in the midst of His people (8:10–11; Josh. 3:13).
6:20 ***inner sanctuary.*** The Most Holy Place was a cube of thirty feet. ***gold.*** The amount of gold used in this room was about 21 tons or 600 talents (2 Chr. 3:8).
6:23 ***cherubim.*** Cherubim are mighty angelic beings, they were often depicted in the furnishings of the tabernacle and temple. Not a great deal is known about their nature. Cherubim were set to guard the entrance to the garden of Eden (Gen. 3:24). The only extensive description of their appearance is in the Book of Ezekiel (Ezek. 1:5–14; 10:1).
6:31 ***doors out of olive wood.*** A veil or curtain was hung here as well (Ex. 26:31–36; 2 Chr. 3:14).
6:38 **Worship**—in the midst of Solomon's building project he received a prophetic revelation from the Lord (vv. 11–14) in which a promise and a condition were prominent: the Lord would fulfill His promise to David if Solomon obeyed His laws. The temple was the external sign that the Lord would keep His covenant of grace and dwell among the people. Worship can never be divorced from obedience to God's laws in everyday life.
7:1–2 ***Palace of the Forest of Lebanon.*** This building was also apparently used as an armory (10:16–17; Is. 22:8).

6:12 [h] 2Sa 7:12-16; 1Ki 2:4; 9:5 **6:13** [i] Ex 25:8; Lev 26:11; Dt 31:6; Heb 13:5 **6:14** [j] ver 9,38 **6:15** [k] 1Ki 7:7 **6:16** [l] Ex 26:33; Lev 16:2; 1Ki 8:6 **6:18** [m] 1Ki 7:24; Ps 74:6 **6:19** [n] 1Ki 8:6 [o] 1Sa 3:3 **6:20** [p] Eze 41:3-4 **6:23** [q] Ex 37:1-9 **6:27** [r] Ex 25:20; 37:9; 1Ki 8:7; 2Ch 5:8 **6:29** [s] ver 32,35 **6:36** [t] 1Ki 7:12; Ezr 6:4 **6:38** [u] Heb 8:5 **7:1** [v] 1Ki 9:10; 2Ch 8:1 **7:2** [w] 2Sa 7:2 [x] 1Ki 10:17; 2Ch 9:16

five beams, fifteen to a row. 4 Its windows were placed high in sets of three, facing each other. 5 All the doorways had rectangular frames; they were in the front part in sets of three, facing each other.[a]

6 He made a colonnade fifty cubits long and thirty wide.[b] In front of it was a portico, and in front of that were pillars and an overhanging roof.

7 He built the throne hall, the Hall of Justice, where he was to judge,[y] and he covered it with cedar from floor to ceiling.[c][z] 8 And the palace in which he was to live, set farther back, was similar in design. Solomon also made a palace like this hall for Pharaoh's daughter, whom he had married.[a]

9 All these structures, from the outside to the great courtyard and from foundation to eaves, were made of blocks of high-grade stone cut to size and smoothed on their inner and outer faces. 10 The foundations were laid with large stones of good quality, some measuring ten cubits[d] and some eight.[e] 11 Above were high-grade stones, cut to size, and cedar beams. 12 The great courtyard was surrounded by a wall of three courses[b] of dressed stone and one course of trimmed cedar beams, as was the inner courtyard of the temple of the LORD with its portico.

The Temple's Furnishings

13 King Solomon sent to Tyre and brought Huram,[f][c] 14 whose mother was a widow from the tribe of Naphtali and whose father was from Tyre and a skilled craftsman in bronze. Huram was filled with wisdom,[d] with understanding and with knowledge to do all kinds of bronze work. He came to King Solomon and did all[e] the work assigned to him.

15 He cast two bronze pillars,[f] each eighteen cubits high and twelve cubits in circumference.[g] 16 He also made two capitals[g] of cast bronze to set on the tops of the pillars; each capital was five cubits[h] high. 17 A network of interwoven chains adorned the capitals on top of the pillars, seven for each capital. 18 He made pomegranates in two rows[i] encircling each network to decorate the capitals on top of the pillars.[j] He did the same for each capital. 19 The capitals on top of the pillars in the portico were in the shape of lilies, four cubits[k] high. 20 On the capitals of both pillars, above the bowl-shaped part next to the network, were the two hundred pomegranates[h] in rows all around. 21 He erected the pillars at the portico of the temple. The pillar to the south he named Jakin[l] and the one to the north Boaz.[m][i] 22 The capitals on top were in the shape of lilies. And so the work on the pillars was completed.

23 He made the Sea[j] of cast metal, circular in shape, measuring ten cubits from rim to rim and five cubits high. It took a line of thirty cubits[n] to measure around it. 24 Below the rim, gourds encircled it—ten to a cubit. The gourds were cast in two rows in one piece with the Sea.

25 The Sea stood on twelve bulls,[k] three facing north, three facing west, three facing south and three facing east. The Sea rested on top of them, and their hindquarters were toward the center. 26 It was a handbreadth[o] in thickness, and its rim was like the rim of a cup, like a lily blossom. It held two thousand baths.[p]

27 He also made ten movable stands[l] of bronze; each was four cubits long, four wide and three high.[q] 28 This is how the stands were made: They had side panels attached to uprights. 29 On the panels between the uprights were lions, bulls and cherubim—and on the uprights as well.

---

[a] *5* The meaning of the Hebrew for this verse is uncertain. [b] *6* That is, about 75 feet long and 45 feet wide or about 23 meters long and 14 meters wide [c] *7* Vulgate and Syriac; Hebrew *floor* [d] *10* That is, about 15 feet or about 4.5 meters; also in verse 23 [e] *10* That is, about 12 feet or about 3.6 meters [f] *13* Hebrew *Hiram,* a variant of *Huram;* also in verses 40 and 45 [g] *15* That is, about 27 feet high and 18 feet in circumference or about 8.1 meters high and 5.4 meters in circumference [h] *16* That is, about 7 1/2 feet or about 2.3 meters; also in verse 23 [i] *18* Two Hebrew manuscripts and Septuagint; most Hebrew manuscripts *made the pillars, and there were two rows* [j] *18* Many Hebrew manuscripts and Syriac; most Hebrew manuscripts *pomegranates* [k] *19* That is, about 6 feet or about 1.8 meters; also in verse 38 [l] *21* *Jakin* probably means *he establishes.* [m] *21* *Boaz* probably means *in him is strength.* [n] *23* That is, about 45 feet or about 14 meters [o] *26* That is, about 3 inches or about 7.5 centimeters [p] *26* That is, about 12,000 gallons or about 44,000 liters; the Septuagint does not have this sentence. [q] *27* That is, about 6 feet long and wide and about 4 1/2 feet high or about 1.8 meters long and wide and 1.4 meters high

---

7:13–14 *Huram.* Huram (also called Hiram) was of mixed parentage. His father was a Phoenician artisan who had married a widow from the tribe of Naphtali (2 Chr. 2:14). Like his father, Huram had become a master craftsman; his contributions to the work on the temple were extensive.

7:16 *five cubits.* Jeremiah 52:22 agrees with this measurement, but 2 Kings 25:17 records the height as three cubits. This apparent discrepancy may just be a difference in whether the capitals of the pillars were included in the measurement height.

7:21 *Jakin . . . Boaz.* Jakin means "He will establish." Boaz may mean "in Him is strength." Another possible meaning is "He is quick." These two pillars were placed near the porch in front of the temple (2 Chr. 3:17).

7:7 [y] Ps 122:5; Pr 20:8 [z] 1Ki 6:15 **7:8** [a] 1Ki 3:1; 2Ch 8:11 **7:12** [b] 1Ki 6:36 **7:13** [c] 2Ch 2:13 **7:14** [d] Ex 31:2-5; 35:31; 36:1; 2Ch 2:14 [e] 2Ch 4:11,16 **7:15** [f] 2Ki 25:17; 2Ch 3:15; 4:12; Jer 52:17,21 **7:16** [g] 2Ki 25:17 **7:20** [h] 2Ch 3:16; 4:13; Jer 52:23 **7:21** [i] 1Ki 6:3; 2Ch 3:17 **7:23** [j] 2Ki 25:13; 1Ch 18:8; Jer 52:17 **7:25** [k] 2Ch 4:4-5; Jer 52:20 **7:27** [l] ver 38; 2Ch 4:14

Above and below the lions and bulls were
wreaths of hammered work. 30 Each stand[m]
had four bronze wheels with bronze axles,
and each had a basin resting on four supports, cast with wreaths on each side. 31 On
the inside of the stand there was an opening that had a circular frame one cubit[a]
deep. This opening was round, and with its
basework it measured a cubit and a half.[b]
Around its opening there was engraving.
The panels of the stands were square, not
round. 32 The four wheels were under the
panels, and the axles of the wheels were attached to the stand. The diameter of each
wheel was a cubit and a half. 33 The wheels
were made like chariot wheels; the axles,
rims, spokes and hubs were all of cast metal.
34 Each stand had four handles, one on
each corner, projecting from the stand.
35 At the top of the stand there was a circular band half a cubit[c] deep. The supports
and panels were attached to the top of the
stand. 36 He engraved cherubim, lions and
palm trees on the surfaces of the supports
and on the panels, in every available space,
with wreaths all around. 37 This is the way
he made the ten stands. They were all cast
in the same molds and were identical in
size and shape.
38 He then made ten bronze basins,[n] each
holding forty baths[d] and measuring four
cubits across, one basin to go on each of the
ten stands. 39 He placed five of the stands
on the south side of the temple and five on
the north. He placed the Sea on the south
side, at the southeast corner of the temple.
40 He also made the pots[e] and shovels and
sprinkling bowls.

So Huram finished all the work he had
undertaken for King Solomon in the temple
of the LORD:

41 the two pillars;
the two bowl-shaped capitals on top of the pillars;
the two sets of network decorating the two bowl-shaped capitals on top of the pillars;
42 the four hundred pomegranates for the two sets of network (two rows of pomegranates for each network decorating the bowl-shaped capitals[o] on top of the pillars);
43 the ten stands with their ten basins;
44 the Sea and the twelve bulls under it;
45 the pots, shovels and sprinkling bowls.[p]

All these objects that Huram made for
King Solomon for the temple of the LORD
were of burnished bronze. 46 The king had
them cast in clay molds in the plain[q] of the
Jordan between Sukkoth[r] and Zarethan.[s]
47 Solomon left all these things unweighed,[t]
because there were so many; the weight of
the bronze was not determined.
48 Solomon also made all the furnishings
that were in the LORD's temple:

the golden altar;
the golden table[u] on which was the bread of the Presence;[v]
49 the lampstands[w] of pure gold (five on the right and five on the left, in front of the inner sanctuary);
the gold floral work and lamps and tongs;
50 the pure gold basins, wick trimmers, sprinkling bowls, dishes and censers;[x]
and the gold sockets for the doors of the innermost room, the Most Holy Place, and also for the doors of the main hall of the temple.

51 When all the work King Solomon had
done for the temple of the LORD was finished, he brought in the things his father
David had dedicated[y]—the silver and gold
and the furnishings—and he placed them
in the treasuries of the LORD's temple.

The Ark Brought to the Temple

8 Then King Solomon summoned into his
presence at Jerusalem the elders of Israel, all the heads of the tribes and the chiefs[z]
of the Israelite families, to bring up the ark[a]
of the LORD's covenant from Zion, the City of
David.[b] 2 All the Israelites came together to

[a] *31* That is, about 18 inches or about 45 centimeters [b] *31* That is, about 2 1/4 feet or about 68 centimeters; also in verse 32 [c] *35* That is, about 9 inches or about 23 centimeters
[d] *38* That is, about 240 gallons or about 880 liters
[e] *40* Many Hebrew manuscripts, Septuagint, Syriac and Vulgate (see also verse 45 and 2 Chron. 4:11); many other Hebrew manuscripts *basins*

7:40–47 Service—When talents and skills are used in God's service, no work is insignificant. All is deserving of our best because it is done for God (Matt. 10:42). For this task Huram was filled with wisdom, understanding, and skill (v. 14). This description is similar to the description of Bezalel's work on the tabernacle (Ex. 31:2–6). The Holy Spirit is the source of natural gifts as well as the supernatural gifts used in the service of the Lord.

7:48 *furnishings.* The furnishings of the temple were designed to correspond with similar furnishings in the tabernacle (Ex. 25; 30). Although Solomon made ten tables and lampstands instead of one, their functions remained the same, all ten being considered one unit (2 Chr. 29:18).

7:51 *David.* David's personal example of giving (1 Chr. 29:1–9) provided a high model of godly concern in leadership.

8:1 *ark of the LORD's covenant.* The ark had been in Jerusalem for some time (2 Sam. 6), and now it was finally in its proper setting. With the erection of the temple and the placement of the ark, the division of spiritual activities between Gibeon, the location of

7:30 [m] 2Ki 16:17 **7:38** [n] Ex 30:18; 2Ch 4:6 **7:42** [o] ver 20
7:45 [p] Ex 27:3 **7:46** [q] 2Ch 4:17 [r] Ge 33:17; Jos 13:27
[s] Jos 3:16 **7:47** [t] 1Ch 22:3 **7:48** [u] Ex 37:10 [v] Ex 25:30
7:49 [w] Ex 25:31-38 **7:50** [x] 2Ki 25:13 **7:51** [y] 2Sa 8:11
8:1 [z] Nu 7:2 [a] 2Sa 6:17 [b] 2Sa 5:7

King Solomon at the time of the festival[c]
in the month of Ethanim, the seventh
month.[d]
3When all the elders of Israel had arrived, the priests[e] took up the ark, 4and
they brought up the ark of the LORD and
the tent of meeting[f] and all the sacred furnishings in it. The priests and Levites carried them up, 5and King Solomon and the
entire assembly of Israel that had gathered
about him were before the ark, sacrificing[g]
so many sheep and cattle that they could
not be recorded or counted.
6The priests then brought the ark of the
LORD's covenant[h] to its place in the inner
sanctuary of the temple, the Most Holy
Place, and put it beneath the wings of the
cherubim.[i] 7The cherubim spread their
wings over the place of the ark and overshadowed the ark and its carrying poles.
8These poles were so long that their ends
could be seen from the Holy Place in front
of the inner sanctuary, but not from outside the Holy Place; and they are still there
today.[j] 9There was nothing in the ark except the two stone tablets[k] that Moses had
placed in it at Horeb, where the LORD made
a covenant with the Israelites after they
came out of Egypt.
10When the priests withdrew from the
Holy Place, the cloud[l] filled the temple of
the LORD. 11And the priests could not perform their service because of the cloud, for
the glory of the LORD filled his temple.
12Then Solomon said, "The LORD has
said that he would dwell in a dark cloud;[m]
13I have indeed built a magnificent temple
for you, a place for you to dwell[n] forever."
14While the whole assembly of Israel was
standing there, the king turned around and
blessed[o] them. 15Then he said:

"Praise be to the LORD,[p] the God of
Israel, who with his own hand has fulfilled what he promised with his own
mouth to my father David. For he said,
16'Since the day I brought my people
Israel out of Egypt, I have not chosen
a city in any tribe of Israel to have a
temple built so that my Name[q] might
be there, but I have chosen[r] David[s] to
rule my people Israel.'
17"My father David had it in his
heart to build a temple[t] for the Name
of the LORD, the God of Israel. 18But the
LORD said to my father David, 'You did
well to have it in your heart to build a
temple for my Name. 19Nevertheless,
you[u] are not the one to build the temple, but your son, your own flesh and
blood—he is the one who will build
the temple for my Name.'[v]
20"The LORD has kept the promise
he made: I have succeeded David my
father and now I sit on the throne of
Israel, just as the LORD promised, and
I have built[w] the temple for the Name
of the LORD, the God of Israel. 21I have
provided a place there for the ark, in
which is the covenant of the LORD that
he made with our ancestors when he
brought them out of Egypt."

Solomon's Prayer of Dedication

22Then Solomon stood before the altar of
the LORD in front of the whole assembly of
Israel, spread out his hands[x] toward heaven
23and said:

"LORD, the God of Israel, there is no
God like[y] you in heaven above or on
earth below—you who keep your covenant of love[z] with your servants who
continue wholeheartedly in your way.
24You have kept your promise to your
servant David my father; with your
mouth you have promised and with
your hand you have fulfilled it—as it
is today.
25"Now LORD, the God of Israel,
keep for your servant David my father
the promises[a] you made to him when
you said, 'You shall never fail to have
a successor to sit before me on the
throne of Israel, if only your descendants are careful in all they do to walk
before me faithfully as you have done.'
26And now, God of Israel, let your
word that you promised[b] your servant
David my father come true.

---

the tabernacle, and Jerusalem, where the ark had resided in a temporary shelter, was now at an end. The pattern of central worship set up in the wilderness could once again be observed (Deut. 12:1–4).

8:9 *two stone tablets.* The two tablets upon which the Ten Commandments were inscribed were known as the "tablets of the covenant" (Deut. 9:9) and were kept in the ark (Deut. 10:1–5,8) along with the jar of manna (Ex. 16:33–34) and Aaron's rod that budded (Num. 17:10).

8:10–11 *the cloud.* This visible presence of God's dwelling with His people—sometimes called the "shekinah glory"—had also covered the tabernacle when it was inaugurated (Ex. 40:34–35).

8:20 *The LORD has kept.* Israel's God is a keeper of promises. His promise to give Abraham's descendants a land (Gen. 15:13–14,18–21; Josh. 14:12–15) had been provisionally realized (Josh. 21:43–45). Solomon also appropriated God's promise to David (2 Sam. 7:12–18). Subsequent kings in the Davidic line could likewise by faith enjoy the blessings of God promised in the Davidic covenant (Ps. 89:3–4,19–24,27–37).

8:2 [c] 2Ch 7:8 [d] Lev 23:34 **8:3** [e] Nu 7:9; Jos 3:3 **8:4** [f] 1Ki 3:4; 2Ch 1:3 **8:5** [g] 2Sa 6:13 **8:6** [h] 2Sa 6:17 [i] 1Ki 6:19, 27 **8:8** [j] Ex 25:13-15 **8:9** [k] Ex 24:7-8; 25:21; 40:20; Dt 10:2-5; Heb 9:4 **8:10** [l] Ex 40:34-35; 2Ch 7:1-2 **8:12** [m] Ps 18:11; 97:2 **8:13** [n] Ex 15:17; 2Sa 7:13; Ps 132:13 **8:14** [o] 2Sa 6:18 **8:15** [p] 2Sa 7:12-13; 1Ch 29:10, 20; Ne 9:5; Lk 1:68 **8:16** [q] Dt 12:5 [r] 1Sa 16:1 [s] 2Sa 7:4-6, 8 **8:17** [t] 2Sa 7:2; 1Ch 17:1 **8:19** [u] 2Sa 7:5 [v] 2Sa 7:13; 1Ki 5:3, 5 **8:20** [w] 1Ch 28:6 **8:22** [x] Ex 9:29; Ezr 9:5 **8:23** [y] 1Sa 2:2; 2Sa 7:22 [z] Dt 7:9, 12; Ne 1:5; 9:32; Da 9:4 **8:25** [a] 1Ki 2:4 **8:26** [b] 2Sa 7:25

27“But will God really dwell[c] on
earth? The heavens, even the highest heaven, cannot contain[d] you. How
much less this temple I have built!
28Yet give attention to your servant’s
prayer and his plea for mercy, LORD
my God. Hear the cry and the prayer
that your servant is praying in your
presence this day. 29May your eyes be
open[e] toward[f] this temple night and
day, this place of which you said, ‘My
Name[g] shall be there,’ so that you will
hear the prayer your servant prays toward this place. 30Hear the supplication of your servant and of your people Israel when they pray toward this
place. Hear from heaven, your dwelling place, and when you hear, forgive.[h]
31“When anyone wrongs their neighbor and is required to take an oath and
they come and swear the oath[i] before
your altar in this temple, 32then hear
from heaven and act. Judge between
your servants, condemning the guilty
by bringing down on their heads what
they have done, and vindicating the innocent by treating them in accordance
with their innocence.[j]
33“When your people Israel have
been defeated[k] by an enemy because
they have sinned[l] against you, and
when they turn back to you and give
praise to your name, praying and
making supplication to you in this
temple, 34then hear from heaven and
forgive the sin of your people Israel
and bring them back to the land you
gave to their ancestors.
35“When the heavens are shut up
and there is no rain[m] because your
people have sinned against you, and
when they pray toward this place and
give praise to your name and turn
from their sin because you have afflicted them, 36then hear from heaven
and forgive the sin of your servants,
your people Israel. Teach[n] them the
right way[o] to live, and send rain on
the land you gave your people for an
inheritance.
37“When famine[p] or plague comes to
the land, or blight[q] or mildew, locusts
or grasshoppers, or when an enemy be-
sieges them in any of their cities, whatever disaster or disease may come,
38and when a prayer or plea is made by
anyone among your people Israel—being aware of the afflictions of their own
hearts, and spreading out their hands
toward this temple— 39then hear from
heaven, your dwelling place. Forgive
and act; deal with everyone according
to all they do, since you know[r] their
hearts (for you alone know every human heart), 40so that they will fear[s] you
all the time they live in the land you
gave our ancestors.
41“As for the foreigner who does
not belong to your people Israel but
has come from a distant land because
of your name— 42for they will hear
of your great name and your mighty
hand[t] and your outstretched arm—
when they come and pray toward
this temple, 43then hear from heaven,
your dwelling place. Do whatever the
foreigner asks of you, so that all the
peoples of the earth may know[u] your
name and fear[v] you, as do your own
people Israel, and may know that this
house I have built bears your Name.
44“When your people go to war
against their enemies, wherever you
send them, and when they pray to the

8:27 ***God.*** God is infinite; no mere building, no matter how wonderful, can contain Him. God rules from heaven in a realm far superior to anything that man can imagine. Unlike the pagan gods who were thought to actually live in the temples built for them, He is not limited by time or space (Acts 7:48; 17:24). Yet God has committed Himself to fellowship with men, walking among them on the earth and being their God. Incredibly, He has chosen to dwell in the hearts of human beings. The true believer is the temple that God desires (1 Cor. 3:16–19).

8:29–30 The Temple in the Life of Israel—Once Solomon built the temple, it became the primary location for the ceremonial worship of Israel. But it was also to be a house of prayer (Is. 56:7), a special place where God’s people could rightly maintain their individual relationships with God. The temple was a place for repentance and forgiveness (Luke 18:10–14). It was a place for petitions to be brought to God. The temple was the central point of worship and life for Israel. Even today in many European towns, beautiful church buildings stand in the town square as a testament to the centrality that the church once had in the life of the community.

Too often we fall into a practice that makes ceremony itself the central thing or in some cases the only thing. Here, we can see what mattered most was not the ritualistic practices but communication with God. This passage and others like it give clarity to many of the claims of the prophets mentioned later in Scripture. If the people had been praying and listening to God as a part of the act of worship, surely they would have been more obedient to His commands, especially in view of the fact that prophets continually rebuked them.

8:41 ***foreigner.*** Unlike God’s people or resident aliens within the commonwealth of Israel (Deut. 10:18–19), foreigners had no particular claim on the ear of God. But the Israelites expected foreigners to be drawn to God by the way His people worshiped Him.

8:27 [c] Ac 7:48 [d] 2Ch 2:6; Ps 139:7-16; Isa 66:1; Jer 23:24
8:29 [e] 2Ch 7:15; Ne 1:6 [f] Da 6:10 [g] Dt 12:11
8:30 [h] Ps 85:2 **8:31** [i] Ex 22:11 **8:32** [j] Dt 25:1
8:33 [k] Lev 26:17; Dt 28:25 [l] Lev 26:39 **8:35** [m] Lev 26:19; Dt 28:24 **8:36** [n] 1Sa 12:23; Ps 25:4; 94:12 [o] Ps 5:8; 27:11; Jer 6:16 **8:37** [p] Lev 26:26 [q] Dt 28:22 **8:39** [r] 1Sa 16:7; 1Ch 28:9; Ps 11:4; Jer 17:10; Jn 2:24; Ac 1:24
8:40 [s] Ps 130:4 **8:42** [t] Dt 3:24 **8:43** [u] 1Sa 17:46; 2Ki 19:19 [v] Ps 102:15

LORD toward the city you have chosen
and the temple I have built for your
Name, 45then hear from heaven their
prayer and their plea, and uphold their
cause.

46"When they sin against you—for
there is no one who does not sin[w]—
and you become angry with them and
give them over to their enemies, who
take them captive[x] to their own lands,
far away or near; 47and if they have a
change of heart in the land where they
are held captive, and repent and plead[y]
with you in the land of their captors
and say, 'We have sinned, we have
done wrong, we have acted wicked-
ly';[z] 48and if they turn back to you with
all their heart[a] and soul in the land of
their enemies who took them captive,
and pray[b] to you toward the land you
gave their ancestors, toward the city
you have chosen and the temple[c] I
have built for your Name; 49then from
heaven, your dwelling place, hear
their prayer and their plea, and uphold
their cause. 50And forgive your people,
who have sinned against you; forgive
all the offenses they have committed
against you, and cause their captors to
show them mercy;[d] 51for they are your
people and your inheritance,[e] whom
you brought out of Egypt, out of that
iron-smelting furnace.[f]

52"May your eyes be open to your
servant's plea and to the plea of your
people Israel, and may you listen to
them whenever they cry out to you.
53For you singled them out from all
the nations of the world to be your
own inheritance,[g] just as you declared
through your servant Moses when
you, Sovereign LORD, brought our ancestors out of Egypt."

54When Solomon had finished all these
prayers and supplications to the LORD, he
rose from before the altar of the LORD,
where he had been kneeling with his hands
spread out toward heaven. 55He stood and
blessed[h] the whole assembly of Israel in a
loud voice, saying:

56"Praise be to the LORD, who has
given rest[i] to his people Israel just as
he promised. Not one word has failed
of all the good promises[j] he gave
through his servant Moses. 57May the
LORD our God be with us as he was
with our ancestors; may he never leave
us nor forsake[k] us. 58May he turn our
hearts[l] to him, to walk in obedience to
him and keep the commands, decrees
and laws he gave our ancestors. 59And
may these words of mine, which I have
prayed before the LORD, be near to the
LORD our God day and night, that he
may uphold the cause of his servant
and the cause of his people Israel according to each day's need, 60so that
all the peoples[m] of the earth may know
that the LORD is God and that there is
no other.[n] 61And may your hearts be
fully committed[o] to the LORD our God,
to live by his decrees and obey his
commands, as at this time."

The Dedication of the Temple

62Then the king and all Israel with him
offered sacrifices before the LORD. 63Sol-
omon offered a sacrifice of fellowship offerings to the LORD: twenty-two thousand
cattle and a hundred and twenty thousand
sheep and goats. So the king and all the
Israelites dedicated the temple of the LORD.

64On that same day the king consecrated
the middle part of the courtyard in front of
the temple of the LORD, and there he offered
burnt offerings, grain offerings and the fat
of the fellowship offerings, because the
bronze altar[p] that stood before the LORD
was too small to hold the burnt offerings,
the grain offerings and the fat of the fellowship offerings.

65So Solomon observed the festival[q] at
that time, and all Israel with him—a vast
assembly, people from Lebo Hamath[r] to
the Wadi of Egypt.[s] They celebrated it before the LORD our God for seven days and
seven days more, fourteen days in all. 66On
the following day he sent the people away.
They blessed the king and then went home,
joyful and glad in heart for all the good

8:54 *rose from ... kneeling.* Chronicles adds that Solomon's prayer and blessing were accompanied by heavenly fire that consumed the sacrifice on the altar (2 Chr. 7:1–3).

8:58 Regeneration—Solomon prayed for an ability given by God that would allow the people to live according to the covenant which had been given at the time of Moses. Solomon was aware that the nation's history was full of examples of the people turning away from God and from His written revelation. Ultimately, the promise of God to the nation of Israel was that there would be a new covenant given to them which would be internalized and which would be brought about by the Holy Spirit (Jer. 31)—the new covenant which was ratified in Jesus' blood (1 Cor. 11:25). Believers today have a power which enables us to live according to God's word—the Holy Spirit who is the agent of our regeneration.

8:60 *all the peoples of the earth.* This verse does not limit God to the Jews but includes the Gentiles as well.

8:46 [w] Pr 20:9; Ecc 7:20; Ro 3:9; 1Jn 1:8-10 [x] Lev 26:33-39; Dt 28:64 **8:47** [y] Lev 26:40; Ne 1:6 [z] Ps 106:6; Da 9:5 **8:48** [a] Dt 4:29; Jer 29:12-14 [b] Da 6:10 [c] Jnh 2:4 **8:50** [d] 2Ch 30:9; Ps 106:46 **8:51** [e] Dt 4:20; 9:29; Ne 1:10 [f] Jer 11:4 **8:53** [g] Ex 19:5; Dt 9:26-29 **8:55** [h] ver 14; 2Sa 6:18 **8:56** [i] Dt 12:10 [j] Jos 21:45; 23:15 **8:57** [k] Dt 31:6; Jos 1:5; Heb 13:5 **8:58** [l] Ps 119:36 **8:60** [m] Jos 4:24; 1Sa 17:46 [n] Dt 4:35; 1Ki 18:39; Jer 10:10-12 **8:61** [o] 1Ki 11:4; 15:3, 14; 2Ki 20:3 **8:64** [p] 2Ch 4:1 **8:65** [q] ver 2; Lev 23:34 [r] Nu 34:8; Jos 13:5; Jdg 3:3; 2Ki 14:25 [s] Ge 15:18

things the LORD had done for his servant David and his people Israel.

The LORD Appears to Solomon

9 When Solomon had finished[t] building the temple of the LORD and the royal palace, and had achieved all he had desired to do, **2**the LORD appeared[u] to him a second time, as he had appeared to him at Gibeon. **3**The LORD said to him:

> "I have heard[v] the prayer and plea you have made before me; I have consecrated this temple, which you have built, by putting my Name there forever. My eyes[w] and my heart will always be there.
>
> **4**"As for you, if you walk before me faithfully with integrity of heart[x] and uprightness, as David[y] your father did, and do all I command and observe my decrees and laws, **5**I will establish[z] your royal throne over Israel forever, as I promised David your father when I said, 'You shall never fail[a] to have a successor on the throne of Israel.'
>
> **6**"But if you[*a*] or your descendants turn away[b] from me and do not observe the commands and decrees I have given you[*a*] and go off to serve other gods and worship them, **7**then I will cut off Israel from the land[c] I have given them and will reject this temple I have consecrated for my Name.[d] Israel will then become a byword[e] and an object of ridicule[f] among all peoples. **8**This temple will become a heap of rubble. All[*b*] who pass by will be appalled and will scoff and say, 'Why has the LORD done such a thing to this land and to this temple?'[g] **9**People will answer, 'Because they have forsaken the LORD their God, who brought their ancestors out of Egypt, and have embraced other gods, worshiping and serving them—that is why the LORD brought all this disaster on them.'"

Solomon's Other Activities

10At the end of twenty years, during which Solomon built these two buildings—the temple of the LORD and the royal palace— **11**King Solomon gave twenty towns in Galilee to Hiram king of Tyre, because Hiram had supplied him with all the cedar and juniper and gold[h] he wanted. **12**But when Hiram went from Tyre to see the towns that Solomon had given him, he was not pleased with them. **13**"What kind of towns are these you have given me, my brother?" he asked. And he called them the Land of Kabul,[*c*i] a name they have to this day. **14**Now Hiram had sent to the king 120 talents[*d*] of gold.

15Here is the account of the forced labor King Solomon conscripted[j] to build the LORD's temple, his own palace, the terraces,[*e*k] the wall of Jerusalem, and Hazor,[l] Megiddo and Gezer.[m] **16**(Pharaoh king of Egypt had attacked and captured Gezer. He had set it on fire. He killed its Canaanite inhabitants and then gave it as a wedding gift to his daughter, Solomon's wife. **17**And Solomon rebuilt Gezer.) He built up Lower Beth Horon,[n] **18**Baalath,[o] and Tadmor[*f*] in the desert, within his land, **19**as well as all his store cities[p] and the towns for his chariots[q] and for his horses[*g*]—whatever he desired to build in Jerusalem, in Lebanon and throughout all the territory he ruled.

20There were still people left from the Amorites, Hittites, Perizzites, Hivites and Jebusites (these peoples were not Israelites). **21**Solomon conscripted the descendants[r] of all these peoples remaining in the land—whom the Israelites could not exterminate[*h*s]—to serve as slave labor,[t] as it is to this day. **22**But Solomon did not make slaves[u] of any of the Israelites; they were his fighting men, his government officials, his officers, his captains, and the commanders of his chariots and charioteers. **23**They were also the chief officials[v]

---

a 6 The Hebrew is plural. *b* 8 See some Septuagint manuscripts, Old Latin, Syriac, Arabic and Targum; Hebrew *And though this temple is now imposing, all* *c* 13 *Kabul* sounds like the Hebrew for *good-for-nothing.* *d* 14 That is, about 4 1/2 tons or about 4 metric tons *e* 15 Or *the Millo*; also in verse 24 *f* 18 The Hebrew may also be read *Tamar.* *g* 19 Or *charioteers* *h* 21 The Hebrew term refers to the irrevocable giving over of things or persons to the LORD, often by totally destroying them.

9:2 *second time.* God had appeared previously to Solomon in Gibeon (3:4–15). The Lord's warning was a necessary reminder for Solomon, who eventually did compromise the conditions required for enjoying God's blessing (11:1–11).

9:12 *he was not pleased with them.* Hiram's displeasure with Solomon's gift would later result in Solomon's redeeming the towns by repaying the debt in another manner (2 Chr. 8:1–2).

9:14 *120 talents.* A talent was said to be the full load one man could easily carry. It was equal to three thousand shekels, or about 70 pounds.

9:16 *Gezer.* Gezer had been a strong Canaanite city, a part of Ephraim's territorial assignment. Ephraim had never taken Gezer; however, Egypt had conquered the city. Its key location on the edge of the lowlands west of Jerusalem made it a splendid gift for Pharaoh to give on the occasion of his daughter's marriage to Solomon.

9:1 [t] 1Ki 7:1; 2Ch 8:6 **9:2** [u] 1Ki 3:5 **9:3** [v] 2Ki 20:5; Ps 10:17 [w] Dt 11:12; 1Ki 8:29 **9:4** [x] Ge 17:1 [y] 1Ki 15:5 **9:5** [z] 1Ch 22:10 [a] 2Sa 7:15; 1Ki 2:4 **9:6** [b] 2Sa 7:14 **9:7** [c] 2Ki 17:23; 25:21 [d] Jer 7:14 [e] Ps 44:14 [f] Dt 28:37 **9:8** [g] Dt 29:24; Jer 22:8-9 **9:11** [h] 2Ch 8:2 **9:13** [i] Jos 19:27 **9:15** [j] Jos 16:10; 1Ki 5:13 [k] ver 24; 2Sa 5:9 [l] Jos 19:36 [m] Jos 17:11 **9:17** [n] Jos 16:3; 2Ch 8:5 **9:18** [o] Jos 19:44 **9:19** [p] ver 1 [q] 1Ki 4:26 **9:21** [r] Ge 9:25-26 [s] Jos 15:63; 17:12; Jdg 1:21,27,29 [t] Ezr 2:55,58 **9:22** [u] Lev 25:39 **9:23** [v] 1Ki 5:16

in charge of Solomon's projects—550 officials supervising those who did the work.

24 After Pharaoh's daughter[w] had come up from the City of David to the palace Solomon had built for her, he constructed the terraces.[x]

25 Three[y] times a year Solomon sacrificed burnt offerings and fellowship offerings on the altar he had built for the LORD, burning incense before the LORD along with them, and so fulfilled the temple obligations.

26 King Solomon also built ships[z] at Ezion Geber,[a] which is near Elath in Edom, on the shore of the Red Sea.[a] 27 And Hiram sent his men—sailors[b] who knew the sea—to serve in the fleet with Solomon's men. 28 They sailed to Ophir[c] and brought back 420 talents[b] of gold, which they delivered to King Solomon.

The Queen of Sheba Visits Solomon

10 When the queen of Sheba[d] heard about the fame of Solomon and his relationship to the LORD, she came to test Solomon with hard questions.[e] 2 Arriving at Jerusalem with a very great caravan—with camels carrying spices, large quantities of gold, and precious stones—she came to Solomon and talked with him about all that she had on her mind. 3 Solomon answered all her questions; nothing was too hard for the king to explain to her. 4 When the queen of Sheba saw all the wisdom of Solomon and the palace he had built, 5 the food on his table,[f] the seating of his officials, the attending servants in their robes, his cupbearers, and the burnt offerings he made at[c] the temple of the LORD, she was overwhelmed.

6 She said to the king, "The report I heard in my own country about your achievements and your wisdom is true. 7 But I did not believe these things until I came and saw with my own eyes. Indeed, not even half was told me; in wisdom and wealth[g] you have far exceeded the report I heard. 8 How happy your people must be! How happy your officials, who continually stand before you and hear[h] your wisdom! 9 Praise[i] be to the LORD your God, who has delighted in you and placed you on the throne of Israel. Because of the LORD's eternal love for Israel, he has made you king to maintain justice[j] and righteousness."

10 And she gave the king 120 talents[d] of gold,[k] large quantities of spices, and precious stones. Never again were so many spices brought in as those the queen of Sheba gave to King Solomon.

11 (Hiram's ships brought gold from Ophir;[l] and from there they brought great cargoes of almugwood[e] and precious stones. 12 The king used the almugwood to make supports[f] for the temple of the LORD and for the royal palace, and to make harps and lyres for the musicians. So much almugwood has never been imported or seen since that day.)

13 King Solomon gave the queen of Sheba all she desired and asked for, besides what he had given her out of his royal bounty. Then she left and returned with her retinue to her own country.

Solomon's Splendor

14 The weight of the gold[m] that Solomon received yearly was 666 talents,[g] 15 not including the revenues from merchants and traders and from all the Arabian kings and the governors of the territories.

16 King Solomon made two hundred large shields[n] of hammered gold; six hundred shekels[h] of gold went into each shield. 17 He also made three hundred small shields of hammered gold, with three minas[i] of gold in each shield. The king put them in the Palace of the Forest of Lebanon.[o]

18 Then the king made a great throne covered with ivory and overlaid with fine gold.

---

[a] *26* Or *the Sea of Reeds* [b] *28* That is, about 16 tons or about 14 metric tons [c] *5* Or *the ascent by which he went up to* [d] *10* That is, about 4 1/2 tons or about 4 metric tons [e] *11* Probably a variant of *algumwood;* also in verse 12 [f] *12* The meaning of the Hebrew for this word is uncertain. [g] *14* That is, about 25 tons or about 23 metric tons [h] *16* That is, about 15 pounds or about 6.9 kilograms; also in verse 29 [i] *17* That is, about 3 3/4 pounds or about 1.7 kilograms; or perhaps reference is to double minas, that is, about 7 1/2 pounds or about 3.5 kilograms.

9:26 ***Ezion Geber.*** Ezion Geber was at the head of the modern Gulf of Aqaba. Its key location as an outlet to the Red Sea and the regions beyond made it commercially important to Solomon and to Hiram, his Phoenician trading partner (2 Chr. 8:17–18).

9:28 ***Ophir.*** The exact location of Ophir is a mystery. Some have speculated that it may have been in Africa, since it was reached by sea (1 Kin. 22:48). It was certainly a celebrated gold area, the source of much of the wealth David and Solomon used to pay for their vast building projects (1 Chr. 29:4).

10:1 ***Sheba.*** Located in southwestern Arabia (present-day Yemen), Sheba was the homeland of the Sabeans, a people whose far-flung commercial enterprises stretched from Syria to east Africa to distant India. The Sabeans dealt in such precious commodities as gold, gemstones, perfumes, and rare spices.

10:9 ***Praise be to the LORD your God.*** The queen's acknowledgement of Solomon's God and the Lord's covenant faithfulness towards Israel does not necessarily mean that she made a commitment of personal faith in the Lord. She may simply have been expressing respect for Solomon's God (see 5:7).

9:24 [w] 1Ki 3:1; 7:8 [x] 2Sa 5:9; 1Ki 11:27; 2Ch 32:5 **9:25** [y] Ex 23:14; 2Ch 8:12-13, 16 **9:26** [z] 1Ki 22:48 [a] Nu 33:35; Dt 2:8 **9:27** [b] 1Ki 10:11; Eze 27:8 **9:28** [c] 1Ch 29:4 **10:1** [d] Ge 10:7,28; Mt 12:42; Lk 11:31 [e] Jdg 14:12 **10:5** [f] 1Ch 26:16 **10:7** [g] 1Ch 29:25 **10:8** [h] Pr 8:34 **10:9** [i] 1Ki 5:7 [j] 2Sa 8:15; Ps 33:5; 72:2 **10:10** [k] ver 2 **10:11** [l] Ge 10:29; 1Ki 9:27-28 **10:14** [m] 1Ki 9:28 **10:16** [n] 1Ki 14:26-28 **10:17** [o] 1Ki 7:2

19The throne had six steps, and its back
had a rounded top. On both sides of the
seat were armrests, with a lion standing
beside each of them. 20Twelve lions stood
on the six steps, one at either end of each
step. Nothing like it had ever been made for
any other kingdom. 21All King Solomon's
goblets were gold, and all the household
articles in the Palace of the Forest of Lebanon were pure gold. Nothing was made
of silver, because silver was considered of
little value in Solomon's days. 22The king
had a fleet of trading ships[a][p] at sea along
with the ships of Hiram. Once every three
years it returned, carrying gold, silver and
ivory, and apes and baboons.
23King Solomon was greater in riches[q]
and wisdom[r] than all the other kings of the
earth. 24The whole world sought audience
with Solomon to hear the wisdom[s] God had
put in his heart. 25Year after year, everyone
who came brought a gift—articles of silver
and gold, robes, weapons and spices, and
horses and mules.
26Solomon accumulated chariots and
horses;[t] he had fourteen hundred chariots and twelve thousand horses,[b] which he
kept in the chariot cities and also with him
in Jerusalem. 27The king made silver as
common[u] in Jerusalem as stones, and cedar as plentiful as sycamore-fig trees in the
foothills. 28Solomon's horses were imported from Egypt and from Kue[c]—the royal
merchants purchased them from Kue at
the current price. 29They imported a chariot from Egypt for six hundred shekels of
silver, and a horse for a hundred and fifty.[d]
They also exported them to all the kings of
the Hittites[v] and of the Arameans.

Solomon's Wives

11 King Solomon, however, loved many
foreign women[w] besides Pharaoh's
daughter—Moabites, Ammonites, Edomites, Sidonians and Hittites. 2They were
from nations about which the LORD had
told the Israelites, "You must not intermarry[x] with them, because they will surely turn
your hearts after their gods." Nevertheless,
Solomon held fast to them in love. 3He had
seven hundred wives of royal birth and
three hundred concubines, and his wives
led him astray. 4As Solomon grew old, his
wives turned his heart after other gods,
and his heart was not fully devoted[y] to the
LORD his God, as the heart of David his father had been. 5He followed Ashtoreth[z] the
goddess of the Sidonians, and Molek[a] the
detestable god of the Ammonites. 6So Solomon did evil in the eyes of the LORD; he did
not follow the LORD completely, as David
his father had done.
7On a hill east[b] of Jerusalem, Solomon
built a high place for Chemosh[c] the detestable god of Moab, and for Molek[d] the detestable god of the Ammonites. 8He did the
same for all his foreign wives, who burned
incense and offered sacrifices to their gods.

---

[a] 22 Hebrew *of ships of Tarshish* [b] 26 Or *charioteers* [c] 28 Probably *Cilicia*
[d] 29 That is, about 3 3/4 pounds or about 1.7 kilograms

10:26 *fourteen hundred chariots.* Shalmaneser III of Assyria reported that at the battle of Qarqar (853 B.C.) he faced a combined enemy chariot force of 3,900, some two thousand of which were supplied by Israel.

10:27 *silver ... cedar.* Under Solomon, Israel enjoyed its greatest period of prosperity. This time of prosperity and peace also must have allowed for the growth of scholarship and for arts and music.

11:1 *many foreign women.* Taking foreign wives violated the Lord's prohibitions against marrying Canaanite women (v. 2; Ex. 34:12–17; Deut. 7:1–3); taking many wives violated the standard of monogamy established at the beginning (Gen. 2:24–25), and resulted in rampant polygamy, something God had also forbidden to Israel's future kings (Deut. 17:17).

11:1–2 Materialism—Even before Israel crossed over the Jordan and entered the promised land, God had given special instructions for the nation's future kings, warning them against materialism: they were not to collect horses, women, or gold for themselves (Deut. 17:16–17). However, King Solomon did all three, resulting in his downfall. He owned many horses (4:26); he gathered hundreds of wives and concubines (v. 3); and he possessed much gold and silver (10:14–27). The gathering of material wealth, when gained honestly, is not prohibited in the Bible. Improper love of possessions, however, is idolatry. We can own things, but things must not own us.

11:1–4 Unfaithfulness—Solomon was affected by the contemporary practices of the surrounding culture. Entering into a political marriage was a means to consolidate a relationship with a neighboring monarch, and Solomon followed this custom at the expense of obedience to God. Unfaithfulness creeps into our lives when our hearts are more closely attuned to contemporary culture and peer pressure than to the voice of God. The heinousness of Solomon's unfaithfulness stands in contrast with the abundance of God's favor and the plainness of His commands (vv. 9–10).

11:3 *seven hundred ... three hundred.* If the reference to 60 queens and 80 concubines in Song of Songs 6:8 is to Solomon's wives, it represents a much earlier period in Solomon's reign.

11:4 *not fully devoted.* Although it is true that David did not always live up to God's standards, he was loyal to God and trusted Him implicitly, even when he was rebuked for his sins (2 Sam. 12:13; Ps. 32:1–5; 53:1–5).

11:7 *high place.* The use of high places in association with the worship of foreign gods shows the terrible danger that the high places presented to Israel (3:2–4; 14:23; Mic. 1:3). ***Molek.*** The worship of Molek was associated with Baal worship and with human sacrifice (Jer. 7:31–32; 19:5–6; 32:35).

10:22 [p] 1Ki 9:26 **10:23** [q] 1Ki 3:13 [r] 1Ki 4:30
10:24 [s] 1Ki 3:9, 12, 28 **10:26** [t] Dt 17:16; 1Ki 4:26; 9:19; 2Ch 1:14; 9:25 **10:27** [u] Dt 17:17 **10:29** [v] 2Ki 7:6-7
11:1 [w] Dt 17:17; Ne 13:26 **11:2** [x] Ex 34:16; Dt 7:3-4
11:4 [y] 1Ki 8:61; 9:4 **11:5** [z] ver 33; Jdg 2:13; 2Ki 23:13
[a] ver 7 **11:7** [b] 2Ki 23:13 [c] Nu 21:29; Jdg 11:24
[d] Lev 20:2-5; Ac 7:43

9The LORD became angry with Solomon
because his heart had turned away from
the LORD, the God of Israel, who had appeared[e] to him twice. 10Although he had
forbidden Solomon to follow other gods,[f]
Solomon did not keep the LORD's command.[g] 11So the LORD said to Solomon,
"Since this is your attitude and you have
not kept my covenant and my decrees,
which I commanded you, I will most certainly tear[h] the kingdom away from you
and give it to one of your subordinates.
12Nevertheless, for the sake of David your
father, I will not do it during your lifetime.
I will tear it out of the hand of your son.
13Yet I will not tear the whole kingdom
from him, but will give him one tribe[i] for
the sake[j] of David my servant and for the
sake of Jerusalem, which I have chosen."[k]

Solomon's Adversaries

14Then the LORD raised up against Solomon an adversary, Hadad the Edomite,
from the royal line of Edom. 15Earlier when
David was fighting with Edom, Joab the
commander of the army, who had gone up
to bury the dead, had struck down all the
men in Edom.[l] 16Joab and all the Israelites
stayed there for six months, until they had
destroyed all the men in Edom. 17But Hadad, still only a boy, fled to Egypt with some
Edomite officials who had served his father.
18They set out from Midian and went to Paran.[m] Then taking people from Paran with
them, they went to Egypt, to Pharaoh king
of Egypt, who gave Hadad a house and land
and provided him with food.
19Pharaoh was so pleased with Hadad
that he gave him a sister of his own wife,
Queen Tahpenes, in marriage. 20The sister
of Tahpenes bore him a son named Genubath, whom Tahpenes brought up in the
royal palace. There Genubath lived with
Pharaoh's own children.
21While he was in Egypt, Hadad heard
that David rested with his ancestors and
that Joab the commander of the army was
also dead. Then Hadad said to Pharaoh,
"Let me go, that I may return to my own
country."
22"What have you lacked here that you
want to go back to your own country?"
Pharaoh asked.
"Nothing," Hadad replied, "but do let
me go!"
23And God raised up against Solomon
another adversary,[n] Rezon son of Eliada,
who had fled from his master, Hadadezer[o]
king of Zobah. 24When David destroyed
Zobah's army, Rezon gathered a band of
men around him and became their leader; they went to Damascus,[p] where they
settled and took control. 25Rezon was Israel's adversary as long as Solomon lived,
adding to the trouble caused by Hadad. So
Rezon ruled in Aram[q] and was hostile toward Israel.

Jeroboam Rebels Against Solomon

26Also, Jeroboam son of Nebat rebelled[r]
against the king. He was one of Solomon's
officials, an Ephraimite from Zeredah, and
his mother was a widow named Zeruah.
27Here is the account of how he rebelled
against the king: Solomon had built the terraces[a][s] and had filled in the gap in the wall
of the city of David his father. 28Now Jeroboam was a man of standing,[t] and when
Solomon saw how well[u] the young man did
his work, he put him in charge of the whole
labor force of the tribes of Joseph.
29About that time Jeroboam was going
out of Jerusalem, and Ahijah[v] the prophet
of Shiloh met him on the way, wearing a
new cloak. The two of them were alone out
in the country, 30and Ahijah took hold of
the new cloak he was wearing and tore[w] it
into twelve pieces. 31Then he said to Jeroboam, "Take ten pieces for yourself, for this
is what the LORD, the God of Israel, says:
'See, I am going to tear[x] the kingdom out
of Solomon's hand and give you ten tribes.
32But for the sake of my servant David and
the city of Jerusalem, which I have chosen out of all the tribes of Israel, he will
have one tribe. 33I will do this because they
have[b] forsaken me and worshiped[y] Ashtoreth the goddess of the Sidonians, Chemosh the god of the Moabites, and Molek
the god of the Ammonites, and have not
walked in obedience to me, nor done what
is right in my eyes, nor kept my decrees[z]
and laws as David, Solomon's father, did.

---

[a] 27 Or *the Millo* [b] 33 Hebrew; Septuagint, Vulgate and Syriac *because he has*

11:13 *one tribe.* The one tribe left to the house of David was Judah, the principal tribe of the southern kingdom. By this time, Simeon had assimilated with Judah (12:17–21).

11:14 *Hadad the Edomite.* Hadad was one of the survivors who had escaped when David defeated the Edomite army (2 Sam. 8:13–14). Pharaoh's ready reception and favorable treatment of Hadad probably had political ramifications, the pharaoh seeing him as a potential future ally on Israel's border.

11:26 *Jeroboam.* At first a trusted official for Solomon (v. 28), Jeroboam came under his wrath and fled to Egypt. Eventually, Jeroboam was instrumental in bringing about the prophesied schism of the country (12:2–19). He became the first king of the northern kingdom (12:20).

11:31–32 *ten tribes . . . one tribe.* The twelfth tribe might be Simeon, which was absorbed by Judah; it is

11:9 [e] ver 2-3; 1Ki 3:5; 9:2 **11:10** [f] 1Ki 9:6 [g] 1Ki 6:12
11:11 [h] ver 31; 1Ki 12:15-16; 2Ki 17:21 **11:13** [i] 1Ki 12:20
[j] 2Sa 7:15 [k] Dt 12:11 **11:15** [l] Dt 20:13; 2Sa 8:14; 1Ch 18:12
11:18 [m] Nu 10:12 **11:23** [n] ver 14 [o] 2Sa 8:3
11:24 [p] 2Sa 8:5; 10:8,18 **11:25** [q] 2Sa 10:19
11:26 [r] 2Sa 20:21; 1Ki 12:2; 2Ch 13:6 **11:27** [s] 1Ki 9:24
11:28 [t] Ru 2:1 [u] Pr 22:29 **11:29** [v] 1Ki 12:15; 14:2;
2Ch 9:29 **11:30** [w] 1Sa 15:27 **11:31** [x] ver 11
11:33 [y] ver 5-7 [z] 1Ki 3:3

34“‘But I will not take the whole kingdom out of Solomon’s hand; I have made him ruler all the days of his life for the sake of David my servant, whom I chose and who obeyed my commands and decrees. 35I will take the kingdom from his son’s hands and give you ten tribes. 36I will give one tribe[a] to his son so that David my servant may always have a lamp[b] before me in Jerusalem, the city where I chose to put my Name. 37However, as for you, I will take you, and you will rule over all that your heart desires;[c] you will be king over Israel. 38If you do whatever I command you and walk in obedience to me and do what is right in my eyes by obeying my decrees[d] and commands, as David my servant did, I will be with you. I will build you a dynasty[e] as enduring as the one I built for David and will give Israel to you. 39I will humble David’s descendants because of this, but not forever.’ ”

40Solomon tried to kill Jeroboam, but Jeroboam fled to Egypt, to Shishak[f] the king, and stayed there until Solomon’s death.

Solomon’s Death

41As for the other events of Solomon’s reign—all he did and the wisdom he displayed—are they not written in the book of the annals of Solomon? 42Solomon reigned in Jerusalem over all Israel forty years. 43Then he rested with his ancestors and was buried in the city of David his father. And Rehoboam[g] his son succeeded him as king.

Israel Rebels Against Rehoboam

12 Rehoboam went to Shechem, for all Israel had gone there to make him king. 2When Jeroboam son of Nebat heard this (he was still in Egypt, where he had fled[h] from King Solomon), he returned from[a] Egypt. 3So they sent for Jeroboam, and he and the whole assembly of Israel went to Rehoboam and said to him: 4“Your father put a heavy yoke[i] on us, but now lighten the harsh labor and the heavy yoke he put on us, and we will serve you.”

5Rehoboam answered, “Go away for three days and then come back to me.” So the people went away.

6Then King Rehoboam consulted the elders[j] who had served his father Solomon during his lifetime. “How would you advise me to answer these people?” he asked.

7They replied, “If today you will be a servant to these people and serve them and give them a favorable answer,[k] they will always be your servants.”

8But Rehoboam rejected the advice the elders gave him and consulted the young men who had grown up with him and were serving him. 9He asked them, “What is your advice? How should we answer these people who say to me, ‘Lighten the yoke your father put on us’?”

10The young men who had grown up with him replied, “These people have said to you, ‘Your father put a heavy yoke on us, but make our yoke lighter.’ Now tell them, ‘My little finger is thicker than my father’s waist. 11My father laid on you a heavy yoke; I will make it even heavier. My father scourged you with whips; I will scourge you with scorpions.’ ”

12Three days later Jeroboam and all the people returned to Rehoboam, as the king had said, “Come back to me in three days.” 13The king answered the people harshly. Rejecting the advice given him by the elders, 14he followed the advice of the young men and said, “My father made your yoke heavy; I will make it even heavier. My father scourged[l] you with whips; I will scourge you with scorpions.” 15So the king did not listen to the people, for this turn of events was from the LORD,[m] to fulfill the word the LORD had spoken to Jeroboam son of Nebat through Ahijah[n] the Shilonite.

---

[a] 2 Or *he remained in*

---

also possible that Benjamin existed for some time as a “buffer state” between Israel and Judah, linked at times with the southern kingdom (2 Chr. 11:3).

11:36 *a lamp.* This is an image of one of the divinely intended functions of the kings of ancient Israel. In the midst of the darkness of a pagan world, the Davidic kings were to be a lamp to the nations, in anticipation of the coming Messiah who would be the Light of the World (2 Sam. 21:17; 2 Kin. 8:19; 2 Chr. 21:7; John 1:1–9).

11:40 *Shishak.* Shishak (or Sheshonq I, 945–924 B.C.) was the first pharaoh of Egypt’s strong twenty-second dynasty. Ironically, this future destroyer of Israel appears here as a protector of one of its future kings.

11:41 *the book of the annals of Solomon.* This book is mentioned only here; compare the references to the book of the annals of the kings of Israel (14:19) and the book of the annals of the kings of Judah (14:29). It is likely that the author of the books of Kings drew on these sources.

12:1 *Shechem.* Shechem was an important center of Israelite activity. It was the first place mentioned in Canaan with reference to Abraham (Gen. 12:6). It was also one of the Levitical cities of refuge (Num. 35:6). By going for his coronation to a place with ancient ties to the history of his people, and which was situated in the region of the northern tribes, Rehoboam doubtless believed that he was making a strategic move.

12:15 *from the LORD.* Even at this crucial time of national schism, God was sovereignly working through human events to accomplish His will, which had been made known through earlier prophecy (11:29–39). ***to fulfill the word.*** All things derive their origin and

11:36 [a] ver 13; 1Ki 12:17 [b] 1Ki 15:4; 2Ki 8:19
11:37 [c] 2Sa 3:21 **11:38** [d] Dt 17:19 [e] Jos 1:5; 2Sa 7:11,27
11:40 [f] 2Ch 12:2 **11:43** [g] 1Ki 14:21; Mt 1:7
12:2 [h] 1Ki 11:40 **12:4** [i] 1Sa 8:11-18; 1Ki 4:20-28
12:6 [j] 1Ki 4:2 **12:7** [k] Pr 15:1 **12:14** [l] Ex 1:14; 5:5-9, 16-18
12:15 [m] ver 24; Dt 2:30; Jdg 14:4; 2Ch 22:7; 25:20
[n] 1Ki 11:29

16When all Israel saw that the king refused to listen to them, they answered the king:

"What share do we have in David,
  what part in Jesse's son?
To your tents, Israel![o]
  Look after your own house, David!"

So the Israelites went home. 17But as for the Israelites who were living in the towns of Judah,[p] Rehoboam still ruled over them.

18King Rehoboam sent out Adoniram,[a][q] who was in charge of forced labor, but all Israel stoned him to death. King Rehoboam, however, managed to get into his chariot and escape to Jerusalem. 19So Israel has been in rebellion against the house of David[r] to this day.

20When all the Israelites heard that Jeroboam had returned, they sent and called him to the assembly and made him king over all Israel. Only the tribe of Judah remained loyal to the house of David.[s]

21When Rehoboam arrived in Jerusalem, he mustered all Judah and the tribe of Benjamin—a hundred and eighty thousand able young men—to go to war[t] against Israel and to regain the kingdom for Rehoboam son of Solomon.

22But this word of God came to Shemaiah[u] the man of God: 23"Say to Rehoboam son of Solomon king of Judah, to all Judah and Benjamin, and to the rest of the people, 24'This is what the LORD says: Do not go up to fight against your brothers, the Israelites. Go home, every one of you, for this is my doing.'" So they obeyed the word of the LORD and went home again, as the LORD had ordered.

Golden Calves at Bethel and Dan

25Then Jeroboam fortified Shechem[v] in the hill country of Ephraim and lived there. From there he went out and built up Peniel.[b][w]

26Jeroboam thought to himself, "The kingdom will now likely revert to the house of David. 27If these people go up to offer sacrifices at the temple of the LORD in Jerusalem,[x] they will again give their allegiance to their lord, Rehoboam king of Judah. They will kill me and return to King Rehoboam."

28After seeking advice, the king made two golden calves.[y] He said to the people, "It is too much for you to go up to Jerusalem. Here are your gods, Israel, who brought you up out of Egypt."[z] 29One he set up in Bethel,[a] and the other in Dan.[b] 30And this thing became a sin;[c] the people came to worship the one at Bethel and went as far as Dan to worship the other.[c]

31Jeroboam built shrines[d] on high places and appointed priests[e] from all sorts of

---

[a] *18* Some Septuagint manuscripts and Syriac (see also 4:6 and 5:14); Hebrew *Adoram* [b] *25* Hebrew *Penuel*, a variant of *Peniel* [c] *30* Probable reading of the original Hebrew text; Masoretic Text *people went to the one as far as Dan*

---

destiny from God. They are determined, controlled, and directed from beginning to end by His wise and sovereign counsel. His plan encompasses everything that comes to pass, including all ends and all the ways and means to those ends. His plan also incorporates the folly of men in their deliberations, advice, and decisions, without compelling them to it by external constraint. In fact, God's Word reveals the solemn truth that His plan encompasses even the sin, ungodliness, and evil of men in their motivations and aspirations, their thoughts, words, and deeds, without eliminating their full responsibility for it (Acts 2:22–23; 4:27–28).

12:16 *What share do we have in David?* The ancient rivalry felt by the northern tribes now came to a peak in resentment against the tribe of Judah and the house of David

12:17 *towns of Judah.* The southern section of the land also included the tribal allotment of Simeon. But Simeon by this time had been absorbed by Judah, their allotment was "within the territory of Judah" (Josh. 19:1).

12:20 *made him king.* The coronation of Jeroboam had been prophesied by Ahijah the prophet of the Lord (11:29–31). Nonetheless, the actual coronation apparently was done apart from priest or prophet of the Lord; there was no divine anointing, no true religious ceremony. Only the kings of the southern kingdom would have the sanction of the Davidic covenant (2 Sam. 7).

12:22 *Shemaiah.* According to 2 Chronicles 12:15, Iddo the prophet and Shemaiah together wrote a history of Rehoboam's reign.

12:28 *two golden calves.* Not only would they strike a familiar chord from Israel's history, but the two calves would arouse the interest of the remaining Canaanites in the northern kingdom. The result of Jeroboam's action was religious confusion and apostasy; this was the first time that a deliberate attempt had been made to establish a heterodox doctrine, an unauthorized variation of the true religion. It appears that Jeroboam was doing the same thing that Aaron did, presenting the calves as representations of God, and thus luring people away from true worship.

12:29 *Bethel.* Bethel was north of Jerusalem in Benjamite territory, it had enjoyed a prominent place in Israelite history throughout the earlier patriarchal period (Gen. 28:10–21). Dan was in the north; before its capture by the Danites it had a reputation as a center for pagan worship (Judg. 18:30). Jeroboam's choice of these two sites was a brilliant move. He had one site in the northernmost part of his kingdom and another in the southernmost part; both had long ties to Israel's past, and eliminated the need for long, tedious treks to Jerusalem.

12:31 *not Levites.* Jeroboam's new religious institutions included starting a new religious order that

12:16 [o] 2Sa 20:1 **12:17** [p] 1Ki 11:13, 36
12:18 [q] 2Sa 20:24; 1Ki 4:6; 5:14 **12:19** [r] 2Ki 17:21
12:20 [s] 1Ki 11:13, 32 **12:21** [t] 2Ch 11:1
12:22 [u] 2Ch 12:5-7 **12:25** [v] Jdg 9:45 [w] Jdg 8:8, 17
12:27 [x] Dt 12:5-6 **12:28** [y] Ex 32:4; 2Ki 10:29; 17:16 [z] Ex 32:8 **12:29** [a] Ge 28:19 [b] Jdg 18:27-31
12:30 [c] 1Ki 13:34; 2Ki 17:21 **12:31** [d] 1Ki 13:32 [e] Nu 3:10; 1Ki 13:33; 2Ki 17:32; 2Ch 11:14-15; 13:9

people, even though they were not Levites. **32**He instituted a festival on the fifteenth day of the eighth[f] month, like the festival held in Judah, and offered sacrifices on the altar. This he did in Bethel, sacrificing to the calves he had made. And at Bethel he also installed priests at the high places he had made. **33**On the fifteenth day of the eighth month, a month of his own choosing, he offered sacrifices on the altar he had built at Bethel.[g] So he instituted the festival for the Israelites and went up to the altar to make offerings.

The Man of God From Judah

13 By the word of the LORD a man of God[h] came from Judah to Bethel,[i] as Jeroboam was standing by the altar to make an offering. **2**By the word of the LORD he cried out against the altar: "Altar, altar! This is what the LORD says: 'A son named Josiah[j] will be born to the house of David. On you he will sacrifice the priests of the high places who make offerings here, and human bones will be burned on you.'" **3**That same day the man of God gave a sign:[k] "This is the sign the LORD has declared: The altar will be split apart and the ashes on it will be poured out."

4When King Jeroboam heard what the man of God cried out against the altar at Bethel, he stretched out his hand from the altar and said, "Seize him!" But the hand he stretched out toward the man shriveled up, so that he could not pull it back. **5**Also, the altar was split apart and its ashes poured out according to the sign given by the man of God by the word of the LORD.

6Then the king said to the man of God, "Intercede[l] with the LORD your God and pray for me that my hand may be restored." So the man of God interceded with the LORD, and the king's hand was restored and became as it was before.

7The king said to the man of God, "Come home with me for a meal, and I will give you a gift."[m]

8But the man of God answered the king, "Even if you were to give me half your possessions,[n] I would not go with you, nor would I eat bread[o] or drink water here. **9**For I was commanded by the word of the LORD: 'You must not eat bread or drink water or return by the way you came.'" **10**So he took another road and did not return by the way he had come to Bethel.

11Now there was a certain old prophet living in Bethel, whose sons came and told him all that the man of God had done there that day. They also told their father what he had said to the king. **12**Their father asked them, "Which way did he go?" And his sons showed him which road the man of God from Judah had taken. **13**So he said to his sons, "Saddle the donkey for me." And when they had saddled the donkey for him, he mounted it **14**and rode after the man of God. He found him sitting under an oak tree and asked, "Are you the man of God who came from Judah?"

"I am," he replied.

15So the prophet said to him, "Come home with me and eat."

16The man of God said, "I cannot turn back and go with you, nor can I eat bread[p] or drink water with you in this place. **17**I have been told by the word of the LORD: 'You must not eat bread or drink water there or return by the way you came.'"

18The old prophet answered, "I too am a prophet, as you are. And an angel said to me by the word of the LORD: 'Bring him back with you to your house so that he may eat bread and drink water.'" (But he was lying[q] to him.) **19**So the man of God returned with him and ate and drank in his house.

20While they were sitting at the table, the

---

did not include the Levites; setting up shrines at high places (3:2–3); and replacing the Festival of Tabernacles with a fall festival of the eighth month. His various attempts at religious innovation would quickly incur God's wrath and earn him a reputation that would live in infamy (13:33–34; 22:52).

13:4–5 *Seize him!* The life and character of Jeroboam stands in stark contrast to that of King David. When David was told that he would become king, he never forgot that it was God who gave him the position, and God who would maintain it. Jeroboam, however, seemed to think that he would only stay in office by his own efforts. When David was confronted with his sin by Nathan the prophet, he humbly confessed (2 Sam. 12:13). The wicked Jeroboam sought to arrest his accuser.

13:6 *the LORD your God.* This language may be simply deferential to the prophet, but here it may indicate recognition by Jeroboam that he was no longer really serving the living God.

13:7–8 *a gift*. The prophet was not just being ungracious, he was following a direct command from God. In biblical times, sharing a meal was more than just a social custom. It implied an intimate fellowship. Great religious ceremonies from the Passover to the Lord's Table center on people eating together. The prophet did not want his act of mercy to suggest that God accepted Jeroboam's deviant worship, or leave the impression that a touch from God could be bought and paid for. Giving a gift can be an easy way to avoid the really important matter of changing lives and lifestyles. If a person is convinced that by his giving he is rewarding a church or a pastor, then it becomes impossible for that church or pastor to have any kind of prophetic ministry to that individual. Instead, they become his debtor.

13:11 *a certain old prophet.* This prophet was clearly an apostate. He had not spoken against Jeroboam; instead, he boldly lied to the Lord's true prophet.

13:19 *returned with him.* The man of God had

12:32 [f] Lev 23:33-34; Nu 29:12 **12:33** [g] Nu 15:39; 1Ki 13:1; Am 7:13 **13:1** [h] 2Ki 23:17 [i] 1Ki 12:32-33 **13:2** [j] 2Ki 23:15-16, 20 **13:3** [k] Jdg 6:17; Isa 7:14; Jn 2:11; 1Co 1:22 **13:6** [l] Ex 8:8; 9:28; 10:17; Lk 6:27-28; Ac 8:24; Jas 5:16 **13:7** [m] 1Sa 9:7; 2Ki 5:15 **13:8** [n] Nu 22:18; 24:13 [o] ver 16 **13:16** [p] ver 8 **13:18** [q] Dt 13:3

word of the LORD came to the old prophet who had brought him back. 21 He cried out to the man of God who had come from Judah, "This is what the LORD says: 'You have defied[r] the word of the LORD and have not kept the command the LORD your God gave you. 22 You came back and ate bread and drank water in the place where he told you not to eat or drink. Therefore your body will not be buried in the tomb of your ancestors.'"

23 When the man of God had finished eating and drinking, the prophet who had brought him back saddled his donkey for him. 24 As he went on his way, a lion[s] met him on the road and killed him, and his body was left lying on the road, with both the donkey and the lion standing beside it. 25 Some people who passed by saw the body lying there, with the lion standing beside the body, and they went and reported it in the city where the old prophet lived.

26 When the prophet who had brought him back from his journey heard of it, he said, "It is the man of God who defied the word of the LORD. The LORD has given him over to the lion, which has mauled him and killed him, as the word of the LORD had warned him."

27 The prophet said to his sons, "Saddle the donkey for me," and they did so. 28 Then he went out and found the body lying on the road, with the donkey and the lion standing beside it. The lion had neither eaten the body nor mauled the donkey. 29 So the prophet picked up the body of the man of God, laid it on the donkey, and brought it back to his own city to mourn for him and bury him. 30 Then he laid the body in his own tomb, and they mourned over him and said, "Alas, my brother!"[t]

31 After burying him, he said to his sons, "When I die, bury me in the grave where the man of God is buried; lay my bones[u] beside his bones. 32 For the message he declared by the word of the LORD against the altar in Bethel and against all the shrines on the high places[v] in the towns of Samaria[w] will certainly come true."[x]

33 Even after this, Jeroboam did not change his evil ways, but once more appointed priests for the high places from all sorts[y] of people. Anyone who wanted to become a priest he consecrated for the high places. 34 This was the sin[z] of the house of Jeroboam that led to its downfall and to its destruction[a] from the face of the earth.

Ahijah's Prophecy Against Jeroboam

14 At that time Abijah son of Jeroboam became ill, 2 and Jeroboam said to his wife, "Go, disguise yourself, so you won't be recognized as the wife of Jeroboam. Then go to Shiloh. Ahijah[b] the prophet is there—the one who told me I would be king over this people. 3 Take ten loaves of bread[c] with you, some cakes and a jar of honey, and go to him. He will tell you what will happen to the boy." 4 So Jeroboam's wife did what he said and went to Ahijah's house in Shiloh.

Now Ahijah could not see; his sight was gone because of his age. 5 But the LORD had told Ahijah, "Jeroboam's wife is coming to ask you about her son, for he is ill, and you are to give her such and such an answer. When she arrives, she will pretend to be someone else."

6 So when Ahijah heard the sound of her footsteps at the door, he said, "Come in, wife of Jeroboam. Why this pretense? I have been sent to you with bad news. 7 Go, tell Jeroboam that this is what the LORD, the God of Israel, says: 'I raised you up from among the people and appointed you ruler[d] over my people Israel. 8 I tore[e] the kingdom away from the house of David and gave it to you, but you have not been like my servant David, who kept my commands and followed me with all his heart, doing only what was right[f] in my eyes. 9 You have done more evil than all who lived before you. You have made for yourself other gods, idols[g] made of metal; you have aroused my anger and turned your back on me.[h]

---

withstood Jeroboam's persuasions; he probably came expecting just such pressure. Sadly, he made the mistake of letting down his guard when he had passed the test he was expecting. There is never any excuse for violating God's clear instructions, and he paid a terrible price for his disobedience.

13:24 ***a lion.*** The way the lion stood by both the man of God and his donkey shows that the lion did not kill for food but was God's executioner (vv. 25–26,28).

13:32 ***towns of Samaria.*** The city of Samaria did not, in fact, come into being for nearly half a century (16:24), but the author mentions it here from his own later perspective.

13:33 ***evil ways.*** Rather than learning from the report of this incident, Jeroboam was even more set in his evil ways. His apostasy would earn for him his reputation as the one who "had caused Israel to commit [sin]" (16:26).

14:4 ***Shiloh.*** Located about twenty miles north of Jerusalem, Shiloh had been the religious center for the nation during the time of the judges and was the location of the tabernacle (Josh. 18:1; 1 Sam. 1:3). The city was destroyed by the Philistines after the loss of the ark (1 Sam. 4:1–11; Jer. 7:12–15). ***could not see.*** Although he was blind, Ahijah could "see" by means of the revelation of the living God.

13:21 [r] ver 26 **13:24** [s] 1Ki 20:36 **13:30** [t] Jer 22:18 **13:31** [u] 2Ki 23:18 **13:32** [v] ver 2; Lev 26:30 [w] 1Ki 16:24, 28 [x] 2Ki 23:16 **13:33** [y] 1Ki 12:31; 2Ch 11:15; 13:9 **13:34** [z] 1Ki 12:30 [a] 1Ki 14:10 **14:2** [b] 1Sa 28:8; 2Sa 14:2; 1Ki 11:29 **14:3** [c] 1Sa 9:7 **14:7** [d] 2Sa 12:7-8; 1Ki 16:2 **14:8** [e] 1Ki 11:31, 33, 38 [f] 1Ki 15:5 **14:9** [g] Ex 34:17; 1Ki 12:28; 2Ch 11:15 [h] Ne 9:26; Ps 50:17; Eze 23:35

[10]"'Because of this, I am going to bring
disaster on the house of Jeroboam. I will
cut off from Jeroboam every last male in
Israel—slave or free.[a][i] I will burn up the
house of Jeroboam as one burns dung, un-
til it is all gone.[j] [11]Dogs[k] will eat those belonging to Jeroboam who die in the city,
and the birds will feed on those who die in
the country. The LORD has spoken!'
[12]"As for you, go back home. When you
set foot in your city, the boy will die. [13]All
Israel will mourn for him and bury him. He
is the only one belonging to Jeroboam who
will be buried, because he is the only one in
the house of Jeroboam in whom the LORD,
the God of Israel, has found anything good.[l]
[14]"The LORD will raise up for himself
a king over Israel who will cut off the
family of Jeroboam. Even now this is beginning to happen.[b] [15]And the LORD will
strike Israel, so that it will be like a reed
swaying in the water. He will uproot[m]
Israel from this good land that he gave
to their ancestors and scatter them beyond the Euphrates River, because they
aroused[n] the LORD's anger by making
Asherah[o] poles.[c] [16]And he will give Israel
up because of the sins[p] Jeroboam has committed and has caused Israel to commit."
[17]Then Jeroboam's wife got up and
left and went to Tirzah.[q] As soon as she
stepped over the threshold of the house,
the boy died. [18]They buried him, and all Israel mourned for him, as the LORD had said
through his servant the prophet Ahijah.
[19]The other events of Jeroboam's reign,
his wars and how he ruled, are written in
the book of the annals of the kings of Israel. [20]He reigned for twenty-two years and
then rested with his ancestors. And Nadab
his son succeeded him as king.

Rehoboam King of Judah

[21]Rehoboam son of Solomon was king
in Judah. He was forty-one years old when
he became king, and he reigned seventeen years in Jerusalem, the city the LORD
had chosen out of all the tribes of Israel in
which to put his Name. His mother's name
was Naamah; she was an Ammonite.[r]
[22]Judah[s] did evil in the eyes of the LORD.
By the sins they committed they stirred
up his jealous anger[t] more than those
who were before them had done. [23]They
also set up for themselves high places, sacred stones[u] and Asherah poles on every
high hill and under every spreading tree.[v]
[24]There were even male shrine prostitutes[w]
in the land; the people engaged in all the
detestable practices of the nations the LORD
had driven out before the Israelites.
[25]In the fifth year of King Rehoboam,
Shishak king of Egypt attacked[x] Jerusalem. [26]He carried off the treasures of the
temple[y] of the LORD and the treasures of
the royal palace. He took everything, including all the gold shields[z] Solomon had
made. [27]So King Rehoboam made bronze
shields to replace them and assigned these
to the commanders of the guard on duty at
the entrance to the royal palace. [28]When-
ever the king went to the LORD's temple,
the guards bore the shields, and afterward
they returned them to the guardroom.
[29]As for the other events of Rehoboam's
reign, and all he did, are they not written
in the book of the annals of the kings of

---

[a] *10* Or *Israel—every ruler or leader* [b] *14* The meaning of the Hebrew for this sentence is uncertain. [c] *15* That is, wooden symbols of the goddess Asherah; here and elsewhere in 1 Kings

---

14:11 ***Dogs.*** Dogs were scavengers, and in the Middle East they came to symbolize the dregs of society (2 Kin. 8:13).

14:14 ***cut off the family.*** As prophesied here, the end of Jeroboam's reign would soon be accomplished (15:27—16:7).

14:15 ***Asherah poles.*** This refers to the wooden poles or images associated with the worship of the goddess Asherah (Judg. 3:7; 2 Kin. 23:4). Worship of this pagan goddess would become one of the sins that would bring about the downfall of the northern kingdom (2 Kin. 17:9–11).

14:17 ***Tirzah.*** Famed for its beauty (Song 6:4), Tirzah was a royal retreat and the capital of the northern kingdom's first two dynasties (15:33).

14:19 ***the book of the annals of the kings of Israel.*** This book is mentioned 15 times in Kings. Apparently it was an official record of events in the southern kingdom down to the days of Jehoiakim. This work should not be confused with the biblical books of Chronicles, which were written much later, after the exile.

14:20 ***He reigned.*** Each of the subsequent kings of Israel was judged against the example of the wickedness of Jeroboam (15:34). Only with Ahab was a worse pattern set (16:31).

14:23 ***high places.*** The high places were a problem throughout the history of Judah and Israel (Mic. 1:3). At times, the worship offered on them may have been done sincerely, in true worship of God (3:2–4; 2 Kin. 12:3). But these were also the places in which Canaanite worship rites were practiced, and images set up to honor Baal and Asherah. Even when the worship on the high places was not mixed with pagan rituals, it was not in accord with the law of Moses (see 2 Chr. 1:3).

14:24 ***detestable practices.*** This is an exceedingly strong term; it describes perverted activities that impelled God to dispossess the Canaanite peoples from their land (Deut. 18:9–12).

14:26 ***treasures of the temple of the LORD.*** The sacking of the temple is particularly shocking when we think of the long and detailed description of Solomon's building and furnishing of the house of the Lord.

14:10 [i] Dt 32:36; 1Ki 21:21; 2Ki 9:8-9; 14:26 [j] 1Ki 15:29 **14:11** [k] 1Ki 16:4; 21:24 **14:13** [l] 2Ch 12:12; 19:3 **14:15** [m] Dt 29:28; 2Ki 15:29; 17:6; Ps 52:5 [n] Jos 23:15-16 [o] Ex 34:13; Dt 12:3 **14:16** [p] 1Ki 12:30; 13:34; 15:30,34; 16:2 **14:17** [q] ver 12; 1Ki 15:33; 16:6-9 **14:21** [r] ver 31; 1Ki 11:1; 2Ch 12:13 **14:22** [s] 2Ch 12:1 [t] Dt 32:21; Ps 78:58; 1Co 10:22 **14:23** [u] Dt 16:22; 2Ki 17:9-10; Eze 16:24-25 [v] Dt 12:2; Isa 57:5 **14:24** [w] Dt 23:17; 1Ki 15:12; 2Ki 23:7 **14:25** [x] 1Ki 11:40; 2Ch 12:2 **14:26** [y] 1Ki 15:15,18 [z] 1Ki 10:17

Judah? 30There was continual warfare[a]
between Rehoboam and Jeroboam. 31And
Rehoboam rested with his ancestors and
was buried with them in the City of David.
His mother's name was Naamah; she was
an Ammonite.[b] And Abijah[a] his son succeeded him as king.

Abijah King of Judah

15 In the eighteenth year of the reign of
Jeroboam son of Nebat, Abijah[b] became king of Judah, 2and he reigned in
Jerusalem three years. His mother's name
was Maakah[c] daughter of Abishalom.[c]
3He committed all the sins his father had
done before him; his heart was not fully
devoted[d] to the LORD his God, as the heart
of David his forefather had been. 4Never-
theless, for David's sake the LORD his God
gave him a lamp[e] in Jerusalem by raising
up a son to succeed him and by making Jerusalem strong. 5For David had done what
was right in the eyes of the LORD and had
not failed to keep[f] any of the LORD's commands all the days of his life—except in
the case of Uriah[g] the Hittite.
6There was war[h] between Abijah[d] and
Jeroboam throughout Abijah's lifetime.
7As for the other events of Abijah's reign,
and all he did, are they not written in the
book of the annals of the kings of Judah? There was war between Abijah and
Jeroboam. 8And Abijah rested with his
ancestors and was buried in the City of
David. And Asa his son succeeded him as
king.

Asa King of Judah

9In the twentieth year of Jeroboam king
of Israel, Asa became king of Judah, 10and
he reigned in Jerusalem forty-one years.
His grandmother's name was Maakah[i]
daughter of Abishalom.
11Asa did what was right in the eyes of
the LORD, as his father David had done.
12He expelled the male shrine prostitutes[j]
from the land and got rid of all the idols his
ancestors had made. 13He even deposed his
grandmother Maakah from her position as
queen mother, because she had made a repulsive image for the worship of Asherah.
Asa cut it down[k] and burned it in the Kidron Valley. 14Although he did not remove
the high places, Asa's heart was fully committed[l] to the LORD all his life. 15He brought
into the temple of the LORD the silver and
gold and the articles that he and his father
had dedicated.[m]
16There was war[n] between Asa and Baasha king of Israel throughout their reigns.
17Baasha king of Israel went up against
Judah and fortified Ramah[o] to prevent
anyone from leaving or entering the territory of Asa king of Judah.

---

a 31 Some Hebrew manuscripts and Septuagint (see also 2 Chron. 12:16); most Hebrew manuscripts *Abijam* *b 1* Some Hebrew manuscripts and Septuagint (see also 2 Chron. 12:16); most Hebrew manuscripts *Abijam*; also inverses 7 and 8
c 2 A variant of *Absalom*; also in verse 10
d 6 Some Hebrew manuscripts and Syriac *Abijam* (that is, Abijah); most Hebrew manuscripts *Rehoboam*

15:2 ***Maakah.*** Elsewhere she is described as "the daughter of Uriel of Gibeah" (2 Chr. 13:2), and "the daughter of Absalom" (2 Chr. 11:21). It is thought that she was the granddaughter of Absalom; the daughter of Uriel of Gibeah and Absalom's daughter Tamar (2 Sam. 14:27). She was the favorite of Rehoboam's many wives. The fact that she is mentioned in connection with both her son Abijah and her grandson Asa (vv. 10,12) makes it appear that she was an important figure, probably wielding a good deal of influence.

15:4 ***for David's sake.*** That is, because of God's love for David and the promise He had made to him (2 Sam. 7). ***lamp.*** This is one of the lovely images of God's intended blessing on the Davidic house.

15:5 Perseverance—The lamp of God was still shining in Jerusalem during the reign of Abijah, even though he was not wholly devoted to the Lord, nor was his father who reigned before him. In spite of the sins of Abijah and his father, God continued to let His light shine in Jerusalem for the sake of David, whose heart was all for the Lord. In a similar way, our actions will affect the generations which follow us. If we are committed to God's ways, and willing to stand for what is right, our children will benefit; if we selfishly follow our own pleasures, our children often are left picking up the pieces.

15:10 ***His grandmother's name was Maakah.*** Literally "mother's." It is apparent from verse 2 that Maakah was Asa's grandmother. It is important to remember that many times the Hebrews used the terms "father, mother, son, daughter" loosely, to indicate ancestry rather than exact generation (v. 3).

15:13 ***He even deposed.*** Asa's many spiritual activities (2 Chr. 14:2–5; 15:1–18) are telescoped into a few statements here. Although the reforms mentioned took place early in Asa's reign (2 Chr. 14:2–5), the chronicler indicates that the deposing of Maakah took place in the fifteenth year of his rule (895 B.C.). Maakah's removal came as a result of a time of covenant renewal (2 Chr. 15:1–16) and a consequent reaction against her vile idolatry.

15:14 ***high places.*** In some instances, the high places were places where the Lord was worshiped (1 Sam. 9:12); in other cases they were used for pagan purposes (2 Chr. 14:2–3).

15:17 ***Ramah.*** Ramah was about five and a half miles north of Jerusalem on the main north-south commercial route through the land, and it was therefore of great importance to both kingdoms. It gave east-west access to both the foothills of Ephraim and the Mediterranean coast, so it was of strategic military importance as well. Baasha was striking a blow for control of the center of the land.

14:30 [a] 1Ki 12:21; 15:6 **14:31** [b] ver 21; 2Ch 12:16
15:2 [c] 2Ch 11:20; 13:2 **15:3** [d] 1Ki 11:4; Ps 119:80
15:4 [e] 2Sa 21:17; 1Ki 11:36; 2Ch 21:7 **15:5** [f] 1Ki 9:4; 14:8
[g] 2Sa 11:2-27; 12:9 **15:6** [h] 1Ki 14:30 **15:10** [i] ver 2
15:12 [j] 1Ki 14:24; 22:46 **15:13** [k] Ex 32:20 **15:14** [l] ver 3;
1Ki 8:61; 22:43 **15:15** [m] 1Ki 7:51 **15:16** [n] ver 32
15:17 [o] Jos 18:25; 1Ki 12:27

18 Asa then took all the silver and gold
that was left in the treasuries of the LORD's
temple[p] and of his own palace. He entrusted it to his officials and sent[q] them to
Ben-Hadad[r] son of Tabrimmon, the son of
Hezion, the king of Aram, who was ruling
in Damascus. 19 "Let there be a treaty between me and you," he said, "as there was
between my father and your father. See, I
am sending you a gift of silver and gold.
Now break your treaty with Baasha king of
Israel so he will withdraw from me."
20 Ben-Hadad agreed with King Asa and
sent the commanders of his forces against
the towns of Israel. He conquered[s] Ijon,
Dan, Abel Beth Maakah and all Kinnereth in addition to Naphtali. 21 When Baasha heard this, he stopped building Ramah and withdrew to Tirzah. 22 Then King
Asa issued an order to all Judah—no one
was exempt—and they carried away from
Ramah the stones and timber Baasha had
been using there. With them King Asa built
up Geba[t] in Benjamin, and also Mizpah.
23 As for all the other events of Asa's
reign, all his achievements, all he did and
the cities he built, are they not written in
the book of the annals of the kings of Judah? In his old age, however, his feet became diseased. 24 Then Asa rested with his
ancestors and was buried with them in the
city of his father David. And Jehoshaphat[u]
his son succeeded him as king.

Nadab King of Israel

25 Nadab son of Jeroboam became king
of Israel in the second year of Asa king
of Judah, and he reigned over Israel two
years. 26 He did evil in the eyes of the LORD,
following the ways of his father[v] and committing the same sin his father had caused
Israel to commit.
27 Baasha son of Ahijah from the tribe
of Issachar plotted against him, and he
struck him down[w] at Gibbethon,[x] a Philistine town, while Nadab and all Israel were
besieging it. 28 Baasha killed Nadab in the
third year of Asa king of Judah and succeeded him as king.
29 As soon as he began to reign, he killed
Jeroboam's whole family.[y] He did not leave
Jeroboam anyone that breathed, but destroyed them all, according to the word of
the LORD given through his servant Ahijah the Shilonite. 30 This happened because
of the sins[z] Jeroboam had committed and
had caused Israel to commit, and because
he aroused the anger of the LORD, the God
of Israel.
31 As for the other events of Nadab's reign,
and all he did, are they not written in the
book of the annals of the kings of Israel?
32 There was war[a] between Asa and Baasha
king of Israel throughout their reigns.

Baasha King of Israel

33 In the third year of Asa king of Judah,
Baasha son of Ahijah became king of all
Israel in Tirzah, and he reigned twenty-
four years. 34 He did evil[b] in the eyes of the
LORD, following the ways of Jeroboam and
committing the same sin Jeroboam had
caused Israel to commit.
16 Then the word of the LORD came to
Jehu[c] son of Hanani[d] concerning Baasha: 2 "I lifted you up from the dust[e] and
appointed you ruler[f] over my people Israel,
but you followed the ways of Jeroboam and
caused[g] my people Israel to sin and to arouse
my anger by their sins. 3 So I am about to
wipe out Baasha and his house,[h] and I will
make your house like that of Jeroboam son
of Nebat. 4 Dogs[i] will eat those belonging
to Baasha who die in the city, and birds
will feed on those who die in the country."
5 As for the other events of Baasha's reign,
what he did and his achievements, are they
not written in the book of the annals[j] of the
kings of Israel? 6 Baasha rested with his ancestors and was buried in Tirzah.[k] And Elah
his son succeeded him as king.
7 Moreover, the word of the LORD came[l]
through the prophet Jehu[m] son of Hanani
to Baasha and his house, because of all the
evil he had done in the eyes of the LORD,
arousing his anger by the things he did, becoming like the house of Jeroboam—and
also because he destroyed it.

15:18–19 Unfaithfulness—Asa's life was a mixture of good and evil, faithfulness and faithlessness. He took a stand against the rampant idolatry, removing male cult prostitutes and idolatrous worship, and even demoting his own grandmother to reduce her evil influence (v. 13). Yet later in his life, he signally failed to trust God for either safety or health. When Baasha, king of Israel, attacked him, he sought help from the Syrians (vv. 17–18) rather than from God, and resented and rejected the prophetic rebuke he received (2 Chr. 16:7–10). Near the end of his life, Asa suffered a crippling disease in his feet; yet even in this "he did not seek help from the LORD, but only from the physicians" (2 Chr. 16:12).

15:25 *Nadab.* His name means "Generous" or "Noble," but he did not live up to his name.

15:29 *according to the word of the LORD.* The death of Nadab was in line with the prophetic fulfillment of God's judgment on the house of Jeroboam (14:9,16). Nonetheless, the manner of his death was condemned by God through His prophet Jehu (16:7).

16:1–7 *Jehu.* This Jehu is not to be confused with Jehu the king of Israel (2 Kin. 9:2). Jehu the prophet came from the southern kingdom; his long prophetic ministry lasted into the days of Jehoshaphat. Like his father before him, he confronted sin fearlessly, even in the royal house (2 Chr. 16:7–10).

15:18 [p] ver 15; 1Ki 14:26 [q] 2Ki 12:18 [r] 1Ki 11:23-24 **15:20** [s] Jdg 18:29; 2Sa 20:14; 2Ki 15:29 **15:22** [t] Jos 18:24; 21:17 **15:24** [u] Mt 1:8 **15:26** [v] 1Ki 12:30; 14:16 **15:27** [w] 1Ki 14:14 [x] Jos 19:44; 21:23 **15:29** [y] 1Ki 14:10, 14 **15:30** [z] 1Ki 14:9, 16 **15:32** [a] ver 16 **15:34** [b] ver 26; 1Ki 12:28-29; 13:33; 14:16 **16:1** [c] ver 7; 2Ch 19:2; 20:34 [d] 2Ch 16:7 **16:2** [e] 1Sa 2:8 [f] 1Ki 14:7-9 [g] 1Ki 15:34 **16:3** [h] ver 11; 1Ki 14:10; 15:29; 21:22 **16:4** [i] 1Ki 14:11 **16:5** [j] 1Ki 14:19; 15:31 **16:6** [k] 1Ki 14:17; 15:33 **16:7** [l] 1Ki 15:27,29 [m] ver 1

Elah King of Israel

8 In the twenty-sixth year of Asa king of
Judah, Elah son of Baasha became king of
Israel, and he reigned in Tirzah two years.
9 Zimri, one of his officials, who had command of half his chariots, plotted against
him. Elah was in Tirzah at the time, getting drunk[n] in the home of Arza, the palace administrator[o] at Tirzah. 10 Zimri came
in, struck him down and killed him in the
twenty-seventh year of Asa king of Judah.
Then he succeeded him as king.
11 As soon as he began to reign and was
seated on the throne, he killed off Baasha's
whole family.[p] He did not spare a single
male, whether relative or friend. 12 So Zimri destroyed the whole family of Baasha,
in accordance with the word of the LORD
spoken against Baasha through the prophet Jehu— 13 because of all the sins Baasha and his son Elah had committed and
had caused Israel to commit, so that they
aroused the anger of the LORD, the God of
Israel, by their worthless idols.[q]
14 As for the other events of Elah's reign,
and all he did, are they not written in the
book of the annals of the kings of Israel?

Zimri King of Israel

15 In the twenty-seventh year of Asa king
of Judah, Zimri reigned in Tirzah seven
days. The army was encamped near Gibbethon,[r] a Philistine town. 16 When the Israelites in the camp heard that Zimri had
plotted against the king and murdered him,
they proclaimed Omri, the commander of
the army, king over Israel that very day
there in the camp. 17 Then Omri and all the
Israelites with him withdrew from Gibbethon and laid siege to Tirzah. 18 When Zimri
saw that the city was taken, he went into the
citadel of the royal palace and set the palace
on fire around him. So he died, 19 because of
the sins he had committed, doing evil in the
eyes of the LORD and following the ways of
Jeroboam and committing the same sin Jeroboam had caused Israel to commit.
20 As for the other events of Zimri's reign,
and the rebellion he carried out, are they
not written in the book of the annals of the
kings of Israel?

Omri King of Israel

21 Then the people of Israel were split into
two factions; half supported Tibni son of
Ginath for king, and the other half supported Omri. 22 But Omri's followers proved
stronger than those of Tibni son of Ginath.
So Tibni died and Omri became king.
23 In the thirty-first year of Asa king of
Judah, Omri became king of Israel, and he
reigned twelve years, six of them in Tirzah.[s]
24 He bought the hill of Samaria from Shemer for two talents[a] of silver and built a city
on the hill, calling it Samaria,[t] after Shemer,
the name of the former owner of the hill.
25 But Omri did evil[u] in the eyes of the
LORD and sinned more than all those before him. 26 He followed completely the
ways of Jeroboam son of Nebat, committing the same sin Jeroboam had caused[v]
Israel to commit, so that they aroused the
anger of the LORD, the God of Israel, by
their worthless idols.[w]
27 As for the other events of Omri's reign,
what he did and the things he achieved, are
they not written in the book of the annals
of the kings of Israel? 28 Omri rested with
his ancestors and was buried in Samaria.
And Ahab his son succeeded him as king.

Ahab Becomes King of Israel

29 In the thirty-eighth year of Asa king
of Judah, Ahab son of Omri became king
of Israel, and he reigned in Samaria over
Israel twenty-two years. 30 Ahab son of
Omri did more[x] evil in the eyes of the LORD
than any of those before him. 31 He not only
considered it trivial to commit the sins of
Jeroboam son of Nebat, but he also married[y] Jezebel daughter[z] of Ethbaal king of
the Sidonians, and began to serve Baal[a]
and worship him. 32 He set up an altar for
Baal in the temple[b] of Baal that he built in
Samaria. 33 Ahab also made an Asherah
pole[c] and did more[d] to arouse the anger of

a 24 That is, about 150 pounds or about 68 kilograms

16:10 *Zimri.* Zimri's treacherous act was the prophesied judgment on Baasha and Elah for their wickedness.
16:23 *Omri.* Omri's exploits are commemorated in the Moabite Stone and the Assyrian annals. Indeed, he was so important to the Assyrians that they called Israel "the House of Omri" long after his death. Yet the author of Kings describes little of Omri's achievements, because he did evil in the eyes of the Lord.
16:30 *Ahab.* In Ahab we come to the very lowest point in the degeneration of the spiritual life of the kings of Israel. Each of the kings of the northern kingdom had been guilty of walking in the steps of Jeroboam, but Ahab's sins made Jeroboam's look trivial. His greatest crime was his promotion of Baal worship as the state religion.
16:31 *Jezebel.* Ahab's marriage to Jezebel was politically important and demonstrated the rising prominence of Israel's third dynasty. Her father was both king and priest of Baal in Sidon; similarly, Jezebel was princess and priestess of Baal. Her Phoenician name was Abizebel, meaning "My Father [Baal] is Noble." The Hebrew scribes purposely dropped a letter from her name, calling her Jezebel, "Lacking Honor." ***began to serve Baal and worship him.*** Ahab completely abandoned even a skewed worship of God, and became a full-fledged worshiper of Baal.

16:9 [n] 2Ki 9:30-33 [o] 1Ki 18:3 **16:11** [p] ver 3
16:13 [q] Dt 32:21; 1Sa 12:21; Isa 41:29 **16:15** [r] Jos 19:44; 1Ki 15:27 **16:23** [s] 1Ki 15:21 **16:24** [t] 1Ki 13:32; Jn 4:4
16:25 [u] Dt 4:25; Mic 6:16 **16:26** [v] ver 19 [w] Dt 32:21
16:30 [x] ver 25; 1Ki 14:9 **16:31** [y] Dt 7:3; 1Ki 11:2 [z] Jdg 18:7; 2Ki 9:34 [a] 2Ki 10:18; 17:16 **16:32** [b] 2Ki 10:21, 27; 11:18 **16:33** [c] 2Ki 13:6 [d] ver 29,30; 1Ki 14:9; 21:25

the LORD, the God of Israel, than did all the
kings of Israel before him.
34In Ahab's time, Hiel of Bethel rebuilt
Jericho. He laid its foundations at the cost
of his firstborn son Abiram, and he set up
its gates at the cost of his youngest son Segub, in accordance with the word of the
LORD spoken by Joshua son of Nun.[e]

Elijah Announces a Great Drought

17 Now Elijah[f] the Tishbite, from Tish-
be[a] in Gilead,[g] said to Ahab, "As the
LORD, the God of Israel, lives, whom I
serve, there will be neither dew nor rain[h]
in the next few years except at my word."

Elijah Fed by Ravens

2Then the word of the LORD came to Elijah:
3"Leave here, turn eastward and hide in the
Kerith Ravine, east of the Jordan. **4**You will
drink from the brook, and I have directed
the ravens[i] to supply you with food there."
5So he did what the LORD had told him.
He went to the Kerith Ravine, east of the
Jordan, and stayed there. **6**The ravens
brought him bread and meat in the morning[j] and bread and meat in the evening,
and he drank from the brook.

Elijah and the Widow at Zarephath

7Some time later the brook dried up because there had been no rain in the land.
8Then the word of the LORD came to him:
9"Go at once to Zarephath[k] in the region
of Sidon and stay there. I have directed a
widow[l] there to supply you with food." **10**So
he went to Zarephath. When he came to the
town gate, a widow was there gathering
sticks. He called to her and asked, "Would
you bring me a little water in a jar so I may
have a drink?"[m] **11**As she was going to get
it, he called, "And bring me, please, a piece
of bread."
12"As surely as the LORD your God lives,"
she replied, "I don't have any bread—only
a handful of flour in a jar and a little olive
oil[n] in a jug. I am gathering a few sticks to
take home and make a meal for myself and
my son, that we may eat it—and die."
13Elijah said to her, "Don't be afraid. Go
home and do as you have said. But first
make a small loaf of bread for me from
what you have and bring it to me, and then
make something for yourself and your son.
14For this is what the LORD, the God of Israel, says: 'The jar of flour will not be used
up and the jug of oil will not run dry until
the day the LORD sends rain on the land.'"
15She went away and did as Elijah had
told her. So there was food every day for
Elijah and for the woman and her family.
16For the jar of flour was not used up and
the jug of oil did not run dry, in keeping
with the word of the LORD spoken by Elijah.
17Some time later the son of the woman who owned the house became ill. He
grew worse and worse, and finally stopped
breathing. **18**She said to Elijah, "What do you
have against me, man of God? Did you come
to remind me of my sin[o] and kill my son?"
19"Give me your son," Elijah replied. He
took him from her arms, carried him to the
upper room where he was staying, and laid
him on his bed. **20**Then he cried out to the
LORD, "LORD my God, have you brought
tragedy even on this widow I am staying
with, by causing her son to die?" **21**Then
he stretched[p] himself out on the boy three
times and cried out to the LORD, "LORD my
God, let this boy's life return to him!"
22The LORD heard Elijah's cry, and the
boy's life returned to him, and he lived.
23Elijah picked up the child and carried
him down from the room into the house.
He gave him to his mother and said, "Look,
your son is alive!"
24Then the woman said to Elijah, "Now I

[a] *1* Or *Tishbite, of the settlers*

16:34 ***rebuilt Jericho.*** Jericho had been semi-occupied at various times (Judg. 3:13), but not as a permanently occupied fortified city. Either Hiel offered his sons as foundation sacrifices, or they died in some mishap. However it happened, Joshua's curse was carried out.

17:1 ***Elijah.*** No prophet had arisen since Moses who was like Elijah. His name means "The LORD is God," a statement which was the core of his message to the unbelieving nation. ***dew nor rain.*** Elijah's pronouncement was an immediate challenge: Baal was supposed to govern the weather, but Elijah was declaring him powerless before the Living God.

17:6 ***ravens.*** It is interesting to note that ravens were considered unclean birds (Lev. 11:15).

17:9 ***Zarephath.*** Zarephath was in Phoenician territory, seven miles south of Sidon, the stronghold of Baal. The Lord's sustaining Elijah first by a raven and then by a widow provided the prophet with a dramatic test of faith at the outset of his ministry. The widow, too, would be taught the value of trusting in God alone.

17:14 ***will not run dry.*** While an apostate Israelite nation suffered because of the drought, God supplied the daily necessities to a non-Israelite who willingly took Him at His word. Both the prophet and the widow were reminded of the value of personal trust in Him who alone is sufficient to meet every need (Phil. 4:19).

17:17–23 Resurrection—Resurrection from the dead was not a miracle ordinary people expected to see, even from a prophet of God. This widow, however, would have had reason to hope for God's help. She had opened her home to Elijah, and she had seen firsthand His power and the results of complete trust in Him. Yet it was not until she had seen the miracle of her son brought back to life that she expressed faith in God.

16:34 [e] Jos 6:26 **17:1** [f] Mal 4:5; Jas 5:17 [g] Jdg 12:4 [h] Dt 10:8; 1Ki 18:1; 2Ki 3:14; Lk 4:25 **17:4** [i] Ge 8:7 **17:6** [j] Ex 16:8 **17:9** [k] Ob 1:20 [l] Lk 4:26 **17:10** [m] Ge 24:17; Jn 4:7 **17:12** [n] ver 1; 2Ki 4:2 **17:18** [o] 2Ki 3:13; Lk 5:8 **17:21** [p] 2Ki 4:34; Ac 20:10

know[q] that you are a man of God and that
the word of the LORD from your mouth is
the truth."[r]

Elijah and Obadiah

18 After a long time, in the third[s] year,
the word of the LORD came to Elijah:
"Go and present yourself to Ahab, and I
will send rain[t] on the land." 2So Elijah went
to present himself to Ahab.

Now the famine was severe in Samaria,
3and Ahab had summoned Obadiah, his
palace administrator.[u] (Obadiah was a devout believer[v] in the LORD. 4While Jezebel[w]
was killing off the LORD's prophets, Obadiah had taken a hundred prophets and hidden[x] them in two caves, fifty in each, and
had supplied them with food and water.)
5Ahab had said to Obadiah, "Go through
the land to all the springs and valleys. Maybe we can find some grass to keep the horses and mules alive so we will not have to
kill any of our animals." 6So they divided
the land they were to cover, Ahab going in
one direction and Obadiah in another.

7As Obadiah was walking along, Elijah
met him. Obadiah recognized[y] him, bowed
down to the ground, and said, "Is it really
you, my lord Elijah?"

8"Yes," he replied. "Go tell your master,
'Elijah is here.'"

9"What have I done wrong," asked Obadiah, "that you are handing your servant over
to Ahab to be put to death? 10As surely as
the LORD your God lives, there is not a nation or kingdom where my master has not
sent someone to look[z] for you. And whenever a nation or kingdom claimed you were
not there, he made them swear they could
not find you. 11But now you tell me to go to
my master and say, 'Elijah is here.' 12I don't
know where the Spirit[a] of the LORD may carry you when I leave you. If I go and tell Ahab
and he doesn't find you, he will kill me. Yet
I your servant have worshiped the LORD
since my youth. 13Haven't you heard, my
lord, what I did while Jezebel was killing
the prophets of the LORD? I hid a hundred
of the LORD's prophets in two caves, fifty in
each, and supplied them with food and water. 14And now you tell me to go to my master and say, 'Elijah is here.' He will kill me!"

15Elijah said, "As the LORD Almighty
lives, whom I serve, I will surely present[b]
myself to Ahab today."

Elijah on Mount Carmel

16So Obadiah went to meet Ahab and
told him, and Ahab went to meet Elijah.
17When he saw Elijah, he said to him, "Is
that you, you troubler[c] of Israel?"

18"I have not made trouble for Israel," Elijah replied. "But you[d] and your father's family have. You have abandoned[e] the LORD's
commands and have followed the Baals.
19Now summon the people from all over
Israel to meet me on Mount Carmel.[f] And
bring the four hundred and fifty prophets
of Baal and the four hundred prophets of
Asherah, who eat at Jezebel's table."

20So Ahab sent word throughout all Israel and assembled the prophets on Mount
Carmel. 21Elijah went before the people
and said, "How long will you waver[g] between two opinions? If the LORD is God,
follow him; but if Baal is God, follow him."

But the people said nothing.

22Then Elijah said to them, "I am the
only one of the LORD's prophets left,[h] but
Baal has four hundred and fifty prophets.[i]
23Get two bulls for us. Let Baal's prophets
choose one for themselves, and let them cut
it into pieces and put it on the wood but not
set fire to it. I will prepare the other bull
and put it on the wood but not set fire to it.
24Then you call on the name of your god,
and I will call on the name of the LORD. The
god who answers by fire[j]—he is God."

Then all the people said, "What you say
is good."

25Elijah said to the prophets of Baal,
"Choose one of the bulls and prepare it
first, since there are so many of you. Call
on the name of your god, but do not light
the fire." 26So they took the bull given them
and prepared it.

Then they called on the name of Baal
from morning till noon. "Baal, answer us!"
they shouted. But there was no response;[k]
no one answered. And they danced around
the altar they had made.

18:3 *Obadiah.* Although tradition has sometimes identified them, this Obadiah is probably not the author of the prophetic book of that name. It is clear that this Obadiah was a man of great faith, whose heroic actions give us a more balanced picture of the situation people of faith endured in Israel at this time.

18:18 *Baals.* The wording indicates that Ahab had a practice of attending services at various local shrines where this deity was worshiped.

18:19 *Baal ... Asherah.* The worship of Baal and Asherah held a constant fascination for Israel from earliest times (Ex. 34:13; Num. 25; Judg. 2:13) and eventually caused Israel's demise (2 Kin. 17:16–18).

18:21 *two opinions.* We are confronted today with a choice no less momentous than the Israelites' choice between the Lord and Baal. Here is a broad road that leads down to destruction; there, a way narrow and difficult that leads upward to life (Matt. 7:13–14). God doesn't share devotion with anything or anyone. We have to make the choice to be on God's side—we cannot serve two masters. We will either gratify self, conforming to the corrupt pattern of this present age, or glorify Him who alone is worthy of worship.

17:24 [q] Jn 3:2; 16:30 [r] Ps 119:43; Jn 17:17 **18:1** [s] 1Ki 17:1; Lk 4:25; Jas 5:17 [t] Dt 28:12 **18:3** [u] 1Ki 16:9 [v] Ne 7:2 **18:4** [w] 2Ki 9:7 [x] ver 13; Isa 16:3 **18:7** [y] 2Ki 1:8 **18:10** [z] 1Ki 17:3 **18:12** [a] 2Ki 2:16; Eze 3:14; Ac 8:39 **18:15** [b] 1Ki 17:1 **18:17** [c] Jos 7:25; 1Ki 21:20; Ac 16:20 **18:18** [d] 1Ki 16:31,33; 21:25 [e] 2Ch 15:2 **18:19** [f] Jos 19:26 **18:21** [g] Jos 24:15; 2Ki 17:41; Mt 6:24 **18:22** [h] 1Ki 19:10 [i] ver 19 **18:24** [j] ver 38; 1Ch 21:26 **18:26** [k] Ps 115:4-5; Jer 10:5; 1Co 8:4; 12:2

27At noon Elijah began to taunt them.
"Shout louder!" he said. "Surely he is a god!
Perhaps he is deep in thought, or busy, or
traveling. Maybe he is sleeping and must
be awakened."[l] 28So they shouted louder
and slashed[m] themselves with swords and
spears, as was their custom, until their
blood flowed. 29Midday passed, and they
continued their frantic prophesying until the time for the evening sacrifice.[n] But
there was no response, no one answered,
no one paid attention.[o]
30Then Elijah said to all the people,
"Come here to me." They came to him, and
he repaired the altar[p] of the LORD, which
had been torn down. 31Elijah took twelve
stones, one for each of the tribes descended
from Jacob, to whom the word of the LORD
had come, saying, "Your name shall be Israel."[q] 32With the stones he built an altar in
the name[r] of the LORD, and he dug a trench
around it large enough to hold two seahs[a]
of seed. 33He arranged[s] the wood, cut the
bull into pieces and laid it on the wood.
Then he said to them, "Fill four large jars
with water and pour it on the offering and
on the wood."
34"Do it again," he said, and they did it
again.
"Do it a third time," he ordered, and they
did it the third time. 35The water ran down
around the altar and even filled the trench.
36At the time of sacrifice, the prophet
Elijah stepped forward and prayed: "LORD,
the God of Abraham,[t] Isaac and Israel, let it
be known[u] today that you are God in Israel
and that I am your servant and have done
all these things at your command.[v] 37An-
swer me, LORD, answer me, so these people
will know that you, LORD, are God, and that
you are turning their hearts back again."
38Then the fire[w] of the LORD fell and
burned up the sacrifice, the wood, the
stones and the soil, and also licked up the
water in the trench.
39When all the people saw this, they fell
prostrate and cried, "The LORD—he is God!
The LORD—he is God!"[x]
40Then Elijah commanded them, "Seize
the prophets of Baal. Don't let anyone get
away!" They seized them, and Elijah had
them brought down to the Kishon Valley[y]
and slaughtered[z] there.
41And Elijah said to Ahab, "Go, eat and
drink, for there is the sound of a heavy
rain." 42So Ahab went off to eat and drink,
but Elijah climbed to the top of Carmel,
bent down to the ground and put his face
between his knees.[a]
43"Go and look toward the sea," he told
his servant. And he went up and looked.
"There is nothing there," he said.
Seven times Elijah said, "Go back."
44The seventh time the servant reported,
"A cloud[b] as small as a man's hand is rising
from the sea."
So Elijah said, "Go and tell Ahab, 'Hitch
up your chariot and go down before the
rain stops you.'"
45Meanwhile, the sky grew black with
clouds, the wind rose, a heavy rain started
falling and Ahab rode off to Jezreel. 46The
power[c] of the LORD came on Elijah and,
tucking his cloak into his belt,[d] he ran
ahead of Ahab all the way to Jezreel.

Elijah Flees to Horeb

19 Now Ahab told Jezebel everything
Elijah had done and how he had
killed[e] all the prophets with the sword. 2So
Jezebel sent a messenger to Elijah to say,
"May the gods deal with me, be it ever so
severely,[f] if by this time tomorrow I do not
make your life like that of one of them."
3Elijah was afraid[b] and ran[g] for his life.
When he came to Beersheba in Judah, he
left his servant there, 4while he himself
went a day's journey into the wilderness.
He came to a broom bush, sat down under
it and prayed that he might die. "I have had
enough, LORD," he said. "Take my life;[h] I am
no better than my ancestors." 5Then he lay
down under the bush and fell asleep.[i]

---

[a] 32 That is, probably about 24 pounds or about 11 kilograms [b] 3 Or *Elijah saw*

18:27 *busy, or traveling.* "Traveling" is a euphemism with the same meaning as our euphemism "on a comfort break." Elijah was piling on the sarcasm—a god is not supposed to have embarrassing bodily functions.

18:30 *repaired the altar.* This was an earlier altar that had been used by the true people of God. Elijah avoided all contact with the altar that was associated with Baal.

18:36 *LORD, the God of Abraham, Isaac and Israel.* This phrase, so characteristic of worship in the early period (Gen. 50:24; Ex. 3:6), reminded Elijah's hearers that the God who had made the covenant with Abraham was still the God of the northern kingdom, and the nation's only hope of life, protection, and blessing (Deut. 30:20).

18:46 *tucking his cloak into his belt.* This enabled Elijah to run freely the 13 miles to Jezreel.

19:3 *ran for his life.* One may ask why a man who had seen God's mighty power should give way to fear, but we must realize that God did not criticize Elijah for his reaction. Elijah was not a superhero but a man with a nature like ours (James 5:17). He had seen a great victory on Mount Carmel, but he also knew that Jezebel was still in power, the faith of the people was still weak, at best, and his life truly was in danger. To run for his life did not necessarily indicate lack of trust; running is sometimes just the act of prudence.

19:5 *Get up and eat.* God's response to Elijah's fear

18:27 [l] Hab 2:19 **18:28** [m] Lev 19:28; Dt 14:1
18:29 [n] Ex 29:41 [o] ver 26 **18:30** [p] 1Ki 19:10
18:31 [q] Ge 32:28; 35:10; 2Ki 17:34 **18:32** [r] Col 3:17
18:33 [s] Ge 22:9; Lev 1:6-8 **18:36** [t] Ex 3:6; Mt 22:32
[u] 1Ki 8:43; 2Ki 19:19 [v] Nu 16:28 **18:38** [w] Lev 9:24;
Jdg 6:21; 1Ch 21:26; 2Ch 7:1; Job 1:16 **18:39** [x] ver 24
18:40 [y] Jdg 4:7 [z] Dt 13:5; 18:20; 2Ki 10:24-25
18:42 [a] ver 19-20; Jas 5:18 **18:44** [b] Lk 12:54
18:46 [c] 2Ki 3:15 [d] 2Ki 4:29; 9:1 **19:1** [e] 1Ki 18:40
19:2 [f] 1Ki 20:10; 2Ki 6:31; Ru 1:17 **19:3** [g] Ge 31:21
19:4 [h] Nu 11:15; Jer 20:18; Jnh 4:8 **19:5** [i] Ge 28:11

All at once an angel touched him and
said, "Get up and eat." 6He looked around,
and there by his head was some bread
baked over hot coals, and a jar of water.
He ate and drank and then lay down again.
7The angel of the LORD came back a second time and touched him and said, "Get
up and eat, for the journey is too much
for you." 8So he got up and ate and drank.
Strengthened by that food, he traveled forty[j] days and forty nights until he reached
Horeb,[k] the mountain of God. 9There he
went into a cave[l] and spent the night.

The LORD Appears to Elijah

And the word of the LORD came to him:
"What are you doing here, Elijah?"
10He replied, "I have been very zealous[m]
for the LORD God Almighty. The Israelites
have rejected your covenant, torn down
your altars, and put your prophets to death
with the sword. I am the only one left,[n] and
now they are trying to kill me too."
11The LORD said, "Go out and stand on
the mountain[o] in the presence of the LORD,
for the LORD is about to pass by."
Then a great and powerful wind[p] tore
the mountains apart and shattered the
rocks before the LORD, but the LORD was
not in the wind. After the wind there was
an earthquake, but the LORD was not in the
earthquake. 12After the earthquake came
a fire, but the LORD was not in the fire.
And after the fire came a gentle whisper.[q]
13When Elijah heard it, he pulled his cloak
over his face[r] and went out and stood at the
mouth of the cave.
Then a voice said to him, "What are you
doing here, Elijah?"
14He replied, "I have been very zealous
for the LORD God Almighty. The Israelites
have rejected your covenant, torn down
your altars, and put your prophets to death
with the sword. I am the only one left,[s] and
now they are trying to kill me too."
15The LORD said to him, "Go back the
way you came, and go to the Desert of Damascus. When you get there, anoint Hazael[t] king over Aram. 16Also, anoint[u] Jehu
son of Nimshi king over Israel, and anoint
Elisha[v] son of Shaphat from Abel Meholah
to succeed you as prophet. 17Jehu will put
to death any who escape the sword of Hazael,[w] and Elisha will put to death any who
escape the sword of Jehu. 18Yet I reserve[x]
seven thousand in Israel—all whose knees
have not bowed down to Baal and whose
mouths have not kissed[y] him."

The Call of Elisha

19So Elijah went from there and found
Elisha son of Shaphat. He was plowing
with twelve yoke of oxen, and he himself
was driving the twelfth pair. Elijah went
up to him and threw his cloak[z] around him.
20Elisha then left his oxen and ran after
Elijah. "Let me kiss my father and mother
goodbye,"[a] he said, "and then I will come
with you."
"Go back," Elijah replied. "What have I
done to you?"
21So Elisha left him and went back. He
took his yoke of oxen[b] and slaughtered
them. He burned the plowing equipment to
cook the meat and gave it to the people, and
they ate. Then he set out to follow Elijah
and became his servant.[c]

Ben-Hadad Attacks Samaria

20 Now Ben-Hadad[d] king of Aram mustered his entire army. Accompanied
by thirty-two kings with their horses and
chariots, he went up and besieged Samaria and attacked it. 2He sent messengers
into the city to Ahab king of Israel, saying, "This is what Ben-Hadad says: 3'Your

---

and discouragement was to give him the very tangible, physical encouragement of food and rest.

19:7 *the angel of the LORD.* This term sometimes refers to God Himself (Ex. 3:2–6), and other times it seems to refer simply to a heavenly messenger (2 Kin. 1:3; 19:35).

19:8 *Horeb.* The name Horeb refers to Mount Sinai itself, "the mountain of God" (Ex. 3:1).

19:11 *the LORD was not in the earthquake.* Although each of the things mentioned in these verses could signal God's presence (Ex. 40:38; Zech. 14:4–5; Acts 2:2–3), Elijah learned that God is not just the God of the spectacular.

19:12 *gentle whisper.* This is often translated "a still small voice." Elijah had called for fire and national revival. What Elijah did not see was that God was already quietly at work in the lives of many people (v. 18).

19:18 *have not bowed.* In times of widespread drift and deliberate deviation from biblical standards of doctrine and ethics, it is easy to suffer from an "Elijah complex." We think that we alone have been on fire for God when everyone else has rejected His covenant, profaned His altars, and persecuted His prophets. Whenever we are tempted to imagine that we are the only ones left to represent the cause of the gospel, we are also open to the dangers of self-pity and self-righteousness. But we are not alone when we belong to the family of God. In every age, God has preserved faithful people who rejoice in Him and are on fire for the truth.

20:1 *Ben-Hadad.* Ben-Hadad II (860–842 B.C.) was king of Aram, the ancient name for the area which is Syria today.

20:2 *Ahab.* When he is associated with his wicked wife Jezebel, Ahab appears as thoroughly evil. But in this chapter he appears as a capable leader in a time of international turmoil, and as a person who had some sense of the power and presence of God (vv. 13–14).

19:8 [j] Ex 24:18; 34:28; Dt 9:9-11, 18; Mt 4:2 [k] Ex 3:1
19:9 [l] Ex 33:22 **19:10** [m] Nu 25:13 [n] 1Ki 18:4, 22; Ro 11:3*
19:11 [o] Ex 24:12 [p] Eze 1:4; 37:7 **19:12** [q] Job 4:16; Zec 4:6
19:13 [r] ver 9; Ex 3:6 **19:14** [s] ver 10 **19:15** [t] 2Ki 8:7-15
19:16 [u] 2Ki 9:1-3, 6 [v] ver 21; 2Ki 2:9, 15 **19:17** [w] 2Ki 8:12, 29, 9.14, 13.3, 7, 22 **19:18** [x] Ro 11:1* [y] Hos 13:2
19:19 [z] 2Ki 2:8, 14 **19:20** [a] Mt 8:21-22; Lk 9:61
19:21 [b] 2Sa 24:22 [c] ver 16 **20:1** [d] 1Ki 15:18; 22:31; 2Ki 6:24

silver and gold are mine, and the best of your wives and children are mine.' "

4The king of Israel answered, "Just as you say, my lord the king. I and all I have are yours."

5The messengers came again and said, "This is what Ben-Hadad says: 'I sent to demand your silver and gold, your wives and your children. 6But about this time tomorrow I am going to send my officials to search your palace and the houses of your officials. They will seize everything you value and carry it away.' "

7The king of Israel summoned all the elders of the land and said to them, "See how this man is looking for trouble![e] When he sent for my wives and my children, my silver and my gold, I did not refuse him."

8The elders and the people all answered, "Don't listen to him or agree to his demands."

9So he replied to Ben-Hadad's messengers, "Tell my lord the king, 'Your servant will do all you demanded the first time, but this demand I cannot meet.' " They left and took the answer back to Ben-Hadad.

10Then Ben-Hadad sent another message to Ahab: "May the gods deal with me, be it ever so severely, if enough dust[f] remains in Samaria to give each of my men a handful."

11The king of Israel answered, "Tell him: 'One who puts on his armor should not boast[g] like one who takes it off.' "

12Ben-Hadad heard this message while he and the kings were drinking[h] in their tents,[a] and he ordered his men: "Prepare to attack." So they prepared to attack the city.

Ahab Defeats Ben-Hadad

13Meanwhile a prophet came to Ahab king of Israel and announced, "This is what the LORD says: 'Do you see this vast army? I will give it into your hand today, and then you will know[i] that I am the LORD.' "

14"But who will do this?" asked Ahab.

The prophet replied, "This is what the LORD says: 'The junior officers under the provincial commanders will do it.' "

"And who will start[j] the battle?" he asked.

The prophet answered, "You will."

15So Ahab summoned the 232 junior officers under the provincial commanders. Then he assembled the rest of the Israelites, 7,000 in all. 16They set out at noon while Ben-Hadad and the 32 kings allied with him were in their tents getting drunk.[k] 17The junior officers under the provincial commanders went out first.

Now Ben-Hadad had dispatched scouts, who reported, "Men are advancing from Samaria."

18He said, "If they have come out for peace, take them alive; if they have come out for war, take them alive."

19The junior officers under the provincial commanders marched out of the city with the army behind them 20and each one struck down his opponent. At that, the Arameans fled, with the Israelites in pursuit. But Ben-Hadad king of Aram escaped on horseback with some of his horsemen. 21The king of Israel advanced and overpowered the horses and chariots and inflicted heavy losses on the Arameans.

22Afterward, the prophet[l] came to the king of Israel and said, "Strengthen your position and see what must be done, because next spring[m] the king of Aram will attack you again."

23Meanwhile, the officials of the king of Aram advised him, "Their gods are gods[n] of the hills. That is why they were too strong for us. But if we fight them on the plains, surely we will be stronger than they. 24Do this: Remove all the kings from their commands and replace them with other officers. 25You must also raise an army like the one you lost—horse for horse and chariot for chariot—so we can fight Israel on the plains. Then surely we will be stronger than they." He agreed with them and acted accordingly.

26The next spring[o] Ben-Hadad mustered the Arameans and went up to Aphek[p] to fight against Israel. 27When the Israelites were also mustered and given provisions, they marched out to meet them. The Israelites camped opposite them like two small flocks of goats, while the Arameans covered the countryside.[q]

28The man of God came up and told the king of Israel, "This is what the LORD says:

---

[a] *12* Or *in Sukkoth*; also in verse 16

20:13 ***a prophet.*** This prophet was not named, but his true message reminds us that there were still many prophets who were faithful to the Lord (18:13; 20:35).

20:23 ***gods of the hills.*** The Aramean advisers reflected traditional ancient Middle Eastern theological concepts. Their gods were limited to certain geographical locations.

20:26 ***Aphek.*** This is not the Philistine city where the ark was lost (1 Sam. 4:1), but another location just east of the Jordan in northern Gilead. They were launching their second campaign in the Jordan valley, but they would learn that the power of the living God is not limited to the mountains as they had hoped.

20:28 ***not a god of the valleys.*** The God of Israel is Lord of the universe, and there is no limit to His power and authority. Not only are we responsible to Him as individuals, but so are the social, economic, and political institutions of the world. Just as it was

20:7 [e] 2Ki 5:7 **20:10** [f] 2Sa 22:43; 1Ki 19:2 **20:11** [g] Pr 27:1; Jer 9:23 **20:12** [h] ver 16; 1Ki 16:9 **20:13** [i] ver 28; Ex 6:7 **20:14** [j] Jdg 1:1 **20:16** [k] ver 12; 1Ki 16:9 **20:22** [l] ver 13 [m] ver 26; 2Sa 11:1 **20:23** [n] 1Ki 14:23; Ro 1:21-23 **20:26** [o] ver 22 [p] 2Ki 13:17 **20:27** [q] Jdg 6:6; 1Sa 13:6

'Because the Arameans think the LORD is a god of the hills and not a god[r] of the valleys, I will deliver this vast army into your hands, and you will know[s] that I am the LORD.'"

29 For seven days they camped opposite each other, and on the seventh day the battle was joined. The Israelites inflicted a hundred thousand casualties on the Aramean foot soldiers in one day. 30 The rest of them escaped to the city of Aphek,[t] where the wall collapsed on twenty-seven thousand of them. And Ben-Hadad fled to the city and hid[u] in an inner room.

31 His officials said to him, "Look, we have heard that the kings of Israel are merciful. Let us go to the king of Israel with sackcloth[v] around our waists and ropes around our heads. Perhaps he will spare your life."

32 Wearing sackcloth around their waists and ropes around their heads, they went to the king of Israel and said, "Your servant Ben-Hadad says: 'Please let me live.'"

The king answered, "Is he still alive? He is my brother."

33 The men took this as a good sign and were quick to pick up his word. "Yes, your brother Ben-Hadad!" they said.

"Go and get him," the king said. When Ben-Hadad came out, Ahab had him come up into his chariot.

34 "I will return the cities[w] my father took from your father," Ben-Hadad offered. "You may set up your own market areas in Damascus,[x] as my father did in Samaria."

Ahab said, "On the basis of a treaty[y] I will set you free." So he made a treaty with him, and let him go.

A Prophet Condemns Ahab

35 By the word of the LORD one of the company of the prophets said to his companion, "Strike me with your weapon," but he refused.[z]

36 So the prophet said, "Because you have not obeyed the LORD, as soon as you leave me a lion[a] will kill you." And after the man went away, a lion found him and killed him.

37 The prophet found another man and said, "Strike me, please." So the man struck him and wounded him. 38 Then the prophet went and stood by the road waiting for the king. He disguised himself with his headband down over his eyes. 39 As the king passed by, the prophet called out to him, "Your servant went into the thick of the battle, and someone came to me with a captive and said, 'Guard this man. If he is missing, it will be your life for his life,[b] or you must pay a talent[a] of silver.' 40 While your servant was busy here and there, the man disappeared."

"That is your sentence," the king of Israel said. "You have pronounced it yourself."

41 Then the prophet quickly removed the headband from his eyes, and the king of Israel recognized him as one of the prophets. 42 He said to the king, "This is what the LORD says: 'You have set free a man I had determined should die.[b][c] Therefore it is your life for his life,[d] your people for his people.'" 43 Sullen and angry,[e] the king of Israel went to his palace in Samaria.

Naboth's Vineyard

21 Some time later there was an incident involving a vineyard belonging to Naboth[f] the Jezreelite. The vineyard was in Jezreel,[g] close to the palace of Ahab king of Samaria. 2 Ahab said to Naboth, "Let me have your vineyard to use for a vegetable garden, since it is close to my palace. In exchange I will give you a better vineyard or, if you prefer, I will pay you whatever it is worth."

3 But Naboth replied, "The LORD forbid that I should give you the inheritance[h] of my ancestors."

4 So Ahab went home, sullen and angry[i] because Naboth the Jezreelite had said, "I will not give you the inheritance of my ancestors." He lay on his bed sulking and refused to eat.

5 His wife Jezebel came in and asked him, "Why are you so sullen? Why won't you eat?"

6 He answered her, "Because I said to Naboth the Jezreelite, 'Sell me your vineyard; or if you prefer, I will give you another vineyard in its place.' But he said, 'I will not give you my vineyard.'"

7 Jezebel his wife said, "Is this how you

---

[a] *39* That is, about 75 pounds or about 34 kilograms
[b] *42* The Hebrew term refers to the irrevocable giving over of things or persons to the LORD, often by totally destroying them.

---

presumption for the Arameans to think that God was bound by geography, it is also presumption to think that if we follow the laws of morality in our private lives, we can violate them in our social, economic, and political relationships. Separation of church and state should not mean separation of God and state. The nation that violates the moral laws of God will eventually suffer defeat.

20:43 ***Sullen and angry.*** Rather than repenting of his sin, Ahab felt ill used by God and resented his punishment, adamantly refusing to change his ways.

21:1 ***Samaria.*** Samaria was Ahab's capital city; sometimes its name is used to represent all Israel (2 Kin. 1:3; 2 Chr. 24:23; Jon. 3:6).

21:2 ***Let me have your vineyard.*** All the land was the Lord's, who granted it to each Israelite tribe and family, and provisions were made so that the land could not be permanently sold out of the family to whom it had been given (Lev. 25:23–28; Num. 36:2–9). In this sense, the vineyard was not Naboth's to dispose of. It belonged to his descendants as much as it did to him.

20:28 [r] ver 23 [s] ver 13 **20:30** [t] ver 26 [u] 1Ki 22:25; 2Ch 18:24 **20:31** [v] Ge 37:34 **20:34** [w] 1Ki 15:20 [x] Jer 49:23-27 [y] Ex 23:32 **20:35** [z] 1Ki 13:21; 2Ki 2:3-7 **20:36** [a] 1Ki 13:24 **20:39** [b] 2Ki 10.24 **20:42** [c] Jer 48:10 [d] ver 39; Jos 2:14; 1Ki 22:31-37 **20:43** [e] 1Ki 21:4 **21:1** [f] 2Ki 9:21 [g] 1Ki 18:45-46 **21:3** [h] Lev 25:23; Nu 36:7; Eze 46:18 **21:4** [i] 1Ki 20:43

act as king over Israel? Get up and eat!
Cheer up. I'll get you the vineyard[j] of Naboth the Jezreelite."
8So she wrote letters in Ahab's name,
placed his seal[k] on them, and sent them to
the elders and nobles who lived in Naboth's
city with him. 9In those letters she wrote:

> "Proclaim a day of fasting and seat
> Naboth in a prominent place among
> the people. 10But seat two scoundrels[l]
> opposite him and have them bring
> charges that he has cursed[m] both God
> and the king. Then take him out and
> stone him to death."

11So the elders and nobles who lived in
Naboth's city did as Jezebel directed in
the letters she had written to them. 12They
proclaimed a fast[n] and seated Naboth in a
prominent place among the people. 13Then
two scoundrels came and sat opposite
him and brought charges against Naboth
before the people, saying, "Naboth has
cursed both God and the king." So they
took him outside the city and stoned him
to death.[o] 14Then they sent word to Jezebel:
"Naboth has been stoned to death."
15As soon as Jezebel heard that Naboth had been stoned to death, she said to
Ahab, "Get up and take possession of the
vineyard[p] of Naboth the Jezreelite that he
refused to sell you. He is no longer alive,
but dead." 16When Ahab heard that Naboth
was dead, he got up and went down to take
possession of Naboth's vineyard.
17Then the word of the LORD came to Elijah
the Tishbite: 18"Go down to meet Ahab king
of Israel, who rules in Samaria. He is now
in Naboth's vineyard, where he has gone to
take possession of it. 19Say to him, 'This is
what the LORD says: Have you not murdered
a man and seized his property?' Then say
to him, 'This is what the LORD says: In the
place where dogs licked up Naboth's blood,[q]
dogs[r] will lick up your blood—yes, yours!'"
20Ahab said to Elijah, "So you have
found me, my enemy!"[s]
"I have found you," he answered, "because you have sold[t] yourself to do evil in
the eyes of the LORD. 21He says, 'I am going to bring disaster on you. I will wipe out
your descendants and cut off from Ahab
every last male[u] in Israel—slave or free.[a]
22I will make your house[v] like that of Jeroboam son of Nebat and that of Baasha son
of Ahijah, because you have aroused my
anger and have caused Israel to sin.'[w]
23"And also concerning Jezebel the LORD
says: 'Dogs[x] will devour Jezebel by the wall
of[b] Jezreel.'
24"Dogs[y] will eat those belonging to
Ahab who die in the city, and the birds will
feed on those who die in the country."
25(There was never[z] anyone like Ahab,
who sold himself to do evil in the eyes of
the LORD, urged on by Jezebel his wife.
26He behaved in the vilest manner by going after idols, like the Amorites[a] the LORD
drove out before Israel.)
27When Ahab heard these words, he tore
his clothes, put on sackcloth[b] and fasted. He
lay in sackcloth and went around meekly.
28Then the word of the LORD came to Elijah the Tishbite: 29"Have you noticed how
Ahab has humbled himself before me? Because he has humbled himself, I will not
bring this disaster in his day, but I will bring
it on his house in the days of his son."[c]

Micaiah Prophesies Against Ahab

22 For three years there was no war between Aram and Israel. 2But in the
third year Jehoshaphat king of Judah went
down to see the king of Israel. 3The king of
Israel had said to his officials, "Don't you
know that Ramoth Gilead[d] belongs to us
and yet we are doing nothing to retake it
from the king of Aram?"
4So he asked Jehoshaphat, "Will you go
with me to fight[e] against Ramoth Gilead?"
Jehoshaphat replied to the king of Israel,
"I am as you are, my people as your people,
my horses as your horses." 5But Jehosha-

---

[a] 21 Or *Israel—every ruler or leader* [b] 23 Most Hebrew manuscripts; a few Hebrew manuscripts, Vulgate and Syriac (see also 2 Kings 9:26) *the plot of ground at*

21:13 *outside the city.* God's law was followed in the manner and place of his death (Lev. 24:14–16,23), although his execution was an outrage, based on false testimony, lies, greed, and refusal to honor the laws concerning the land.

21:19 *Have you not murdered.* In Genesis 9:6 the principle was established that those who shed human blood must have their blood shed by other humans. Ahab had previously allowed his wicked wife Jezebel to plot the murder of an innocent landowner in order to obtain his vineyard. As a result, God determined that both Ahab and Jezebel would die bloody deaths, and this is exactly what happened (22:34–38; 2 Kin. 9:30–37). How tragic that these two brilliant, capable, and talented members of royalty, whose lives could have brought so much blessing to Israel, would instead bring about their own downfall by choosing the path of wickedness rather than the path of life.

21:27 *When Ahab heard these words.* The vacillating nature of Ahab's conduct is seen clearly in verses 25–29. He did great evil, under the influence of his evil wife. Nevertheless, he could at times display real courage (22:34–35) and even real humility before God (21:29). His life is a sad picture of what happens when we are ruled by our own passions rather than by God.

22:4 *Jehoshaphat.* Jehoshaphat was the fourth king of the southern kingdom. He was related to

21:7 [j] 1Sa 8:14 **21:8** [k] Ge 38:18; Est 3:12; 8:8, 10 **21:10** [l] Ac 6:11 [m] Ex 22:28; Lev 24:15-16 **21:12** [n] Isa 58:4 **21:13** [o] 2Ki 9:26 **21:15** [p] 1Sa 8:14 **21:19** [q] 2Ki 9:26; Ps 9:12; Isa 14:20 [r] 1Ki 22:38 **21:20** [s] 1Ki 18:17 [t] ver 25; 2Ki 17:17; Ro 7:14 **21:21** [u] 1Ki 14:10; 2Ki 9:8 **21:22** [v] 1Ki 15:29; 16:3 [w] 1Ki 12:30 **21:23** [x] 2Ki 9:10, 34-36 **21:24** [y] 1Ki 14:11; 16:4 **21:25** [z] ver 20; 1Ki 16:33 **21:26** [a] Ge 15:16; Lev 18:25-30; 2Ki 21:11 **21:27** [b] Ge 37:34; 2Sa 3:31; 2Ki 6:30 **21:29** [c] 2Ki 9:26 **22:3** [d] Dt 4:43; Jos 21:38 **22:4** [e] 2Ki 3:7

phat also said to the king of Israel, "First
seek the counsel[f] of the LORD."
6 So the king of Israel brought together
the prophets—about four hundred men—
and asked them, "Shall I go to war against
Ramoth Gilead, or shall I refrain?"
"Go,"[g] they answered, "for the Lord will
give it into the king's hand."
7 But Jehoshaphat asked, "Is there no longer a prophet[h] of the LORD here whom we
can inquire of?"
8 The king of Israel answered Jehoshaphat, "There is still one prophet through
whom we can inquire of the LORD, but I
hate[i] him because he never prophesies anything good[j] about me, but always bad. He is
Micaiah son of Imlah."
"The king should not say such a thing,"
Jehoshaphat replied.
9 So the king of Israel called one of his
officials and said, "Bring Micaiah son of
Imlah at once."
10 Dressed in their royal robes, the king
of Israel and Jehoshaphat king of Judah
were sitting on their thrones at the threshing floor[k] by the entrance of the gate of Samaria, with all the prophets prophesying
before them. 11 Now Zedekiah son of Kenaanah had made iron horns[l] and he declared, "This is what the LORD says: 'With
these you will gore the Arameans until
they are destroyed.'"
12 All the other prophets were prophesying the same thing. "Attack Ramoth Gilead
and be victorious," they said, "for the LORD
will give it into the king's hand."
13 The messenger who had gone to summon Micaiah said to him, "Look, the other
prophets without exception are predicting
success for the king. Let your word agree
with theirs, and speak favorably."
14 But Micaiah said, "As surely as the
LORD lives, I can tell him only what the
LORD tells me."[m]
15 When he arrived, the king asked him,
"Micaiah, shall we go to war against Ramoth Gilead, or not?"
"Attack and be victorious," he answered,
"for the LORD will give it into the king's hand."
16 The king said to him, "How many times
must I make you swear to tell me nothing
but the truth in the name of the LORD?"
17 Then Micaiah answered, "I saw all Israel scattered on the hills like sheep without a shepherd,[n] and the LORD said, 'These
people have no master. Let each one go
home in peace.'"
18 The king of Israel said to Jehoshaphat,
"Didn't I tell you that he never prophesies
anything good about me, but only bad?"
19 Micaiah continued, "Therefore hear
the word of the LORD: I saw the LORD sitting on his throne[o] with all the multitudes[p]
of heaven standing around him on his right
and on his left. 20 And the LORD said, 'Who
will entice Ahab into attacking Ramoth
Gilead and going to his death there?'
"One suggested this, and another that.
21 Finally, a spirit came forward, stood before the LORD and said, 'I will entice him.'
22 "'By what means?' the LORD asked.
"'I will go out and be a deceiving[q] spirit
in the mouths of all his prophets,' he said.
"'You will succeed in enticing him,' said
the LORD. 'Go and do it.'
23 "So now the LORD has put a deceiving
spirit in the mouths of all these prophets[r]
of yours. The LORD has decreed disaster
for you."
24 Then Zedekiah[s] son of Kenaanah
went up and slapped[t] Micaiah in the face.
"Which way did the spirit from[a] the LORD
go when he went from me to speak to you?"
he asked.
25 Micaiah replied, "You will find out on
the day you go to hide[u] in an inner room."
26 The king of Israel then ordered, "Take
Micaiah and send him back to Amon the
ruler of the city and to Joash the king's son
27 and say, 'This is what the king says: Put
this fellow in prison[v] and give him nothing
but bread and water until I return safely.'"
28 Micaiah declared, "If you ever return
safely, the LORD has not spoken[w] through
me." Then he added, "Mark my words, all
you people!"

---

a 24 Or *Spirit of*

Ahab through the marriage of his son Jehoram to Ahab's daughter Athaliah (2 Kin. 8:18–27).

22:9 *Micaiah.* The prophet Micaiah is not known except in connection with this incident (2 Chr. 18:8–27).

22:14 *I can tell him only what the LORD tells me.* Unless a prophecy is truly directed by God, it is valueless. Micaiah's response was what one would expect from a godly man, but his first statement to Ahab (v. 15) is a little puzzling. It seems that Micaiah was playing with Ahab a little, pointing out to him the futility of asking for favorable prophecy rather than true prophecy. It seems obvious that Micaiah (or God through Micaiah), was in no way deceiving Ahab, since Ahab was instantly aware that he had not been given a real prophecy.

22:16–17 *truth.* All of us wish to hear good news, not bad. We want to hear the favorable, the acceptable, the words that bring us happiness and do not condemn. It can be tempting to speak only what will be well-received even if it is not true, but neither God nor man is served by untruth. While the truth should always be spoken in love (Eph. 4:15), it must be the sole content of what we say. The prophet had to speak only the truth, or he would no longer have been a prophet—his words were the words of the Lord spoken in His name. Our words should be true because, if we are His people, we speak in His name.

22:5 [f] Ex 33:7; 2Ki 3:11 **22:6** [g] 1Ki 18:19 **22:7** [h] 2Ki 3:11 **22:8** [i] Am 5:10 [j] Isa 5:20 **22:10** [k] ver 6 **22:11** [l] Dt 33:17; Zec 1:18-21 **22:14** [m] Nu 22:18; 24:13; 1Ki 18:10, 15 **22:17** [n] ver 34-36; Nu 27:17; Mt 9:36 **22:19** [o] Isa 6:1; Eze 1:26; Da 7:9 [p] Job 1:6; 2:1; Ps 103:20-21; Mt 18:10; Heb 1:7, 14 **22:22** [q] Jdg 9:23; 1Sa 16:14; 18:10; 19:9; Eze 14:9; 2Th 2:11 **22:23** [r] Eze 14:9 **22:24** [s] ver 11 [t] Ac 23:2 **22:25** [u] 1Ki 20:30 **22:27** [v] 2Ch 16:10 **22:28** [w] Dt 18:22

Ahab Killed at Ramoth Gilead

29So the king of Israel and Jehoshaphat
king of Judah went up to Ramoth Gilead.
30The king of Israel said to Jehoshaphat,
"I will enter the battle in disguise,[x] but you
wear your royal robes." So the king of Israel disguised himself and went into battle.

31Now the king of Aram had ordered
his thirty-two chariot commanders, "Do
not fight with anyone, small or great, except the king[y] of Israel." 32When the chariot commanders saw Jehoshaphat, they
thought, "Surely this is the king of Israel."
So they turned to attack him, but when
Jehoshaphat cried out, 33the chariot commanders saw that he was not the king of
Israel and stopped pursuing him.

34But someone drew his bow[z] at random
and hit the king of Israel between the sections of his armor. The king told his chariot driver, "Wheel around and get me out
of the fighting. I've been wounded." 35All
day long the battle raged, and the king was
propped up in his chariot facing the Arameans. The blood from his wound ran onto
the floor of the chariot, and that evening he
died. 36As the sun was setting, a cry spread
through the army: "Every man to his town.
Every man to his land!"[a]

37So the king died and was brought
to Samaria, and they buried him there.
38They washed the chariot at a pool in Samaria (where the prostitutes bathed),[a] and
the dogs[b] licked up his blood, as the word
of the LORD had declared.

39As for the other events of Ahab's reign,
including all he did, the palace he built and
adorned with ivory,[c] and the cities he fortified, are they not written in the book of the
annals of the kings of Israel? 40Ahab rested
with his ancestors. And Ahaziah his son
succeeded him as king.

Jehoshaphat King of Judah

41Jehoshaphat son of Asa became king
of Judah in the fourth year of Ahab king of
Israel. 42Jehoshaphat was thirty-five years
old when he became king, and he reigned in
Jerusalem twenty-five years. His mother's
name was Azubah daughter of Shilhi. 43In
everything he followed the ways of his father Asa[d] and did not stray from them; he did
what was right in the eyes of the LORD. The
high places,[e] however, were not removed,
and the people continued to offer sacrifices
and burn incense there.[b] 44Jehoshaphat was
also at peace with the king of Israel.

45As for the other events of Jehoshaphat's reign, the things he achieved and
his military exploits, are they not written
in the book of the annals of the kings of
Judah? 46He rid the land of the rest of the
male shrine prostitutes[f] who remained
there even after the reign of his father Asa.
47There was then no king[g] in Edom; a provincial governor ruled.

48Now Jehoshaphat built a fleet of trading ships[c][h] to go to Ophir for gold, but they
never set sail—they were wrecked at Ezion
Geber. 49At that time Ahaziah son of Ahab
said to Jehoshaphat, "Let my men sail with
yours," but Jehoshaphat refused.

50Then Jehoshaphat rested with his ancestors and was buried with them in the
city of David his father. And Jehoram his
son succeeded him as king.

Ahaziah King of Israel

51Ahaziah son of Ahab became king of
Israel in Samaria in the seventeenth year of
Jehoshaphat king of Judah, and he reigned
over Israel two years. 52He did evil[i] in the
eyes of the LORD, because he followed the
ways of his father and mother and of Jeroboam son of Nebat, who caused Israel to
sin. 53He served and worshiped Baal[j] and
aroused the anger of the LORD, the God of
Israel, just as his father[k] had done.

---

[a] 38 Or *Samaria and cleaned the weapons*
[b] 43 In Hebrew texts this sentence (22:43b) is numbered 22:44, and 22:44-53 is numbered 22:45-54.
[c] 48 Hebrew *of ships of Tarshish*

22:38 *the dogs licked up his blood.* Elijah's grisly prophecy concerning the house of Ahab came to pass here (21:19–24).

22:39 *adorned with ivory.* Archaeological excavations at Samaria have illustrated the nature of Ahab's palace, a house with luxurious decorations made of ivory.

22:46 *male shrine prostitutes.* Apparently male prostitution was a part of the debased religious practices of Baal worship (14:24).

22:53 Conclusion—The story does not end here but is continued in 2 Kings. The division of the Book of Kings is not original, but was done for convenience when the Bible was translated into Greek in the second century B.C.

22:30 [x] 2Ch 35:32 **22:31** [y] 2Sa 17:2 **22:34** [z] 2Ch 35:23 **22:36** [a] 2Ki 14:12 **22:38** [b] 1Ki 21:19 **22:39** [c] 2Ch 9:17; Am 3:15 **22:43** [d] 2Ch 17:3 [e] 1Ki 3:2; 15:14; 2Ki 12:3 **22:46** [f] Dt 23:17; 1Ki 14:24; 15:12 **22:47** [g] 2Sa 8:14; 2Ki 3:9; 8:20 **22:48** [h] 1Ki 9:26; 10:22 **22:52** [i] 1Ki 15:26; 21:25 **22:53** [j] Jdg 2:11 [k] 1Ki 16:30-32

2 KINGS

▸ **AUTHOR:** This book, thought to originally be part of 1 Kings, is similar to the Book of Jeremiah. It has been observed that the omission of Jeremiah's ministry in the account of King Josiah and his successors may indicate that Jeremiah himself was the recorder of the events. The last two chapters were evidently added to the book after the Babylonian captivity and written by someone other than Jeremiah.

▸ **TIME:** 853 – 560 B.C. ▸ **KEY VERSES:** 2 Kin. 17:22 – 23

▸ **THEME:** Both Elijah in 1 Kings and Elisha in 2 Kings are prime examples of how prophets functioned in Israel. They fearlessly confronted kings. They were involved in miracles. Both seemed to always be involved in the middle of some political controversy. Most importantly, they called on God and got results. In 2 Kings, Israel's story begins with the reign of Ahab's son, Ahaziah, continues with the capture and deportation of Israel to Assyria in 722 B.C., and ends with Judah's fall in 587 B.C., when Nebuchadnezzar burns the temple and palace in Jerusalem and deports many people back to Babylon.

The LORD's Judgment on Ahaziah

1 After Ahab's death, Moab[a] rebelled
against Israel. 2Now Ahaziah had fall-
en through the lattice of his upper room in
Samaria and injured himself. So he sent
messengers,[b] saying to them, "Go and consult Baal-Zebub,[c] the god of Ekron,[d] to see
if I will recover[e] from this injury."
3But the angel[f] of the LORD said to Elijah[g]
the Tishbite, "Go up and meet the messengers of the king of Samaria and ask them,
'Is it because there is no God in Israel[h] that
you are going off to consult Baal-Zebub,
the god of Ekron?' 4Therefore this is what
the LORD says: 'You will not leave[i] the bed
you are lying on. You will certainly die!'"
So Elijah went.
5When the messengers returned to the
king, he asked them, "Why have you come
back?"
6"A man came to meet us," they replied.
"And he said to us, 'Go back to the king
who sent you and tell him, "This is what
the LORD says: Is it because there is no God
in Israel that you are sending messengers
to consult Baal-Zebub, the god of Ekron?
Therefore you will not leave the bed you
are lying on. You will certainly die!"'"
7The king asked them, "What kind of
man was it who came to meet you and told
you this?"
8They replied, "He had a garment of
hair[a][j] and had a leather belt around his
waist."
The king said, "That was Elijah the Tishbite."
9Then he sent[k] to Elijah a captain[l] with
his company of fifty men. The captain went
up to Elijah, who was sitting on the top of a
hill, and said to him, "Man of God, the king
says, 'Come down!'"
10Elijah answered the captain, "If I am
a man of God, may fire come down from
heaven and consume you and your fifty
men!" Then fire[m] fell from heaven and consumed the captain and his men.

[a] 8 Or *He was a hairy man*

1:2 *Ahaziah.* The account of his brief, wicked reign begins in 1 Kings 22:51. The division of the Book of Kings into two parts was for the convenience of the translators, as is indicated by the fact that Ahaziah's reign carries over from one book to the other without a break.

1:6 Unbelief—Just as in the days of Ahaziah, men and women today often will turn to everything but the one genuine source of truth. But because there is no help or life or power in man's gods, man's ideas and philosophies, belief in them will end only in wasted, ineffective lives, and eventually in eternal death. True joy and meaning in life can only be found through trust in God.

1:8 *A garment of hair.* This may refer to Elijah's garments, but the usual translation of "hairy man" is supported by the ancient versions.

1:10 *fire . . . from heaven.* Heavenly fire could signal divine judgment (Gen. 19:24). Elijah had already called down such fire in his contest with the prophets

1:1 [a] Ge 19:37; 2Sa 8:2; 2Ki 3:5 **1:2** [b] ver 16 [c] Mk 3:22 [d] 1Sa 6:2; Isa 2:6; 14:29; Mt 10:25 [e] Jdg 18:5; 2Ki 8:7-10 **1:3** [f] ver 15; Ge 16:7 [g] 1Ki 17:1 [h] 1Sa 28:8 **1:4** [i] ver 6, 16; Ps 41:8 **1:8** [j] 1Ki 18:7; Zec 13:4; Mt 3:4; Mk 1:6 **1:9** [k] 2Ki 6:14 [l] Ex 18:25; Isa 3:3 **1:10** [m] 1Ki 18:38; Lk 9:54; Rev 11:5; 13:13

11 At this the king sent to Elijah another captain with his fifty men. The captain
said to him, "Man of God, this is what the
king says, 'Come down at once!'"
12 "If I am a man of God," Elijah replied,
"may fire come down from heaven and
consume you and your fifty men!" Then the
fire of God fell from heaven and consumed
him and his fifty men.
13 So the king sent a third captain with
his fifty men. This third captain went up
and fell on his knees before Elijah. "Man
of God," he begged, "please have respect
for my life[n] and the lives of these fifty men,
your servants! 14 See, fire has fallen from
heaven and consumed the first two captains and all their men. But now have respect for my life!"
15 The angel[o] of the LORD said to Elijah,
"Go down with him; do not be afraid[p] of
him." So Elijah got up and went down with
him to the king.
16 He told the king, "This is what the
LORD says: Is it because there is no God in
Israel for you to consult that you have sent
messengers[q] to consult Baal-Zebub, the
god of Ekron? Because you have done this,
you will never leave[r] the bed you are lying
on. You will certainly die!" 17 So he died,[s]
according to the word of the LORD that Elijah had spoken.
Because Ahaziah had no son, Joram[a][t]
succeeded him as king in the second year
of Jehoram son of Jehoshaphat king of Judah. 18 As for all the other events of Ahaziah's reign, and what he did, are they not
written in the book of the annals of the
kings of Israel?

Elijah Taken Up to Heaven

2 When the LORD was about to take[u] Elijah up to heaven in a whirlwind,[v] Elijah
and Elisha[w] were on their way from Gilgal.[x] 2 Elijah said to Elisha, "Stay here;[y] the
LORD has sent me to Bethel."
But Elisha said, "As surely as the LORD
lives and as you live, I will not leave you."[z]
So they went down to Bethel.
3 The company[a] of the prophets at Bethel came out to Elisha and asked, "Do you
know that the LORD is going to take your
master from you today?"
"Yes, I know," Elisha replied, "so be quiet."
4 Then Elijah said to him, "Stay here, Elisha; the LORD has sent me to Jericho.[b]"
And he replied, "As surely as the LORD
lives and as you live, I will not leave you."
So they went to Jericho.
5 The company[c] of the prophets at Jericho
went up to Elisha and asked him, "Do you
know that the LORD is going to take your
master from you today?"
"Yes, I know," he replied, "so be quiet."
6 Then Elijah said to him, "Stay here;[d] the
LORD has sent me to the Jordan."[e]
And he replied, "As surely as the LORD
lives and as you live, I will not leave you."[f]
So the two of them walked on.
7 Fifty men from the company of the
prophets went and stood at a distance,
facing the place where Elijah and Elisha
had stopped at the Jordan. 8 Elijah took his
cloak,[g] rolled it up and struck[h] the water
with it. The water divided[i] to the right and
to the left, and the two of them crossed over
on dry[j] ground.
9 When they had crossed, Elijah said to
Elisha, "Tell me, what can I do for you before I am taken from you?"
"Let me inherit a double[k] portion of your
spirit,"[l] Elisha replied.
10 "You have asked a difficult thing," Elijah said, "yet if you see me when I am tak-
en from you, it will be yours—otherwise,
it will not."
11 As they were walking along and talking together, suddenly a chariot of fire[m]
and horses of fire appeared and separated the two of them, and Elijah went up to
heaven[n] in a whirlwind.[o] 12 Elisha saw this
and cried out, "My father! My father! The
chariots[p] and horsemen of Israel!" And Elisha saw him no more. Then he took hold of
his garment and tore[q] it in two.

---

[a] 17 Hebrew *Jehoram,* a variant of *Joram*

---

of Baal (1 Kin. 18:36–38). If this fire was lightning, the episode would have been a particularly significant slap in the face of their religion, showing that Baal was not the god of the storm he was reputed to be. The God of Israel was—and is—the Lord of creation.

2:3 ***take.*** The same Hebrew word is used for Enoch's entrance to heaven (Gen. 5:24). The work that God was about to do had been divinely revealed to many of God's servants (vv. 3,5). This widespread knowledge of God's purpose would protect against later denials by cynical persons that the event had ever taken place.

2:9 ***double portion.*** In material things, the principal heir received a double portion of his father's goods. Elisha wanted the principle of primary inheritance to apply to spiritual things. Far from being a selfish request, Elisha's petition reflects his humble acknowledgment that if Elijah's ministry were to continue through him, it would take special God-given spiritual power.

2:11 ***heaven.*** The Bible does not give very much information about exactly what happens to the believer after death. This verse says that Elijah "went up to heaven," and it is assumed that he went to the same place to which Enoch had been taken up (Heb. 11:5). Jesus assured the thief on the cross that he would be in "paradise" with Him (Luke 23:43), a place

1:13 [n] 1Sa 26:21; Ps 72:14 **1:15** [o] ver 3 [p] Isa 51:12; 57:11; Jer 1:17; Eze 2:6 **1:16** [q] ver 2 [r] ver 4 **1:17** [s] 2Ki 8:15; Jer 20:6; 28:17 [t] 2Ki 3:1; 8:16 **2:1** [u] Ge 5:24; Heb 11:5 [v] ver 11; 1Ki 19:11; Isa 5:28; 66:15; Jer 4:13; Na 1:3 [w] 1Ki 19:16, 21 [x] Dt 11:30; 2Ki 4:38 **2:2** [y] ver 6 [z] Ru 1:16; 1Sa 1:26; 2Ki 4:30 **2:3** [a] 1Sa 10:5; 2Ki 4:1, 38 **2:4** [b] Jos 3:16; 6:26 **2:5** [c] ver 3 **2:6** [d] ver 2 [e] Jos 3:15 [f] Ru 1:16 **2:8** [g] 1Ki 19:19 [h] ver 14 [i] Ex 14:21 [j] Ex 14:22, 29 **2:9** [k] Dt 21:17 [l] Nu 11:17 **2:11** [m] 2Ki 6:17; Ps 68:17; 104:3, 4; Isa 66:15; Hab 3:8; Zec 6:1 [n] Ge 5:24 [o] ver 1 **2:12** [p] 2Ki 6:17; 13:14 [q] Ge 37:29

13Elisha then picked up Elijah's cloak
that had fallen from him and went back
and stood on the bank of the Jordan. 14He
took the cloak[r] that had fallen from Elijah
and struck[s] the water with it. "Where now
is the LORD, the God of Elijah?" he asked.
When he struck the water, it divided to the
right and to the left, and he crossed over.
15The company[t] of the prophets from Jericho, who were watching, said, "The spirit[u] of Elijah is resting on Elisha." And they
went to meet him and bowed to the ground
before him. 16"Look," they said, "we your
servants have fifty able men. Let them go
and look for your master. Perhaps the Spirit[v]
of the LORD has picked him up[w] and set him
down on some mountain or in some valley."
"No," Elisha replied, "do not send them."
17But they persisted until he was too
embarrassed[x] to refuse. So he said, "Send
them." And they sent fifty men, who
searched for three days but did not find
him. 18When they returned to Elisha, who
was staying in Jericho, he said to them,
"Didn't I tell you not to go?"

Healing of the Water

19The people of the city said to Elisha,
"Look, our lord, this town is well situated,
as you can see, but the water is bad and the
land is unproductive."
20"Bring me a new bowl," he said, "and
put salt in it." So they brought it to him.
21Then he went out to the spring and
threw[y] the salt into it, saying, "This is what
the LORD says: 'I have healed this water.
Never again will it cause death or make
the land unproductive.'" 22And the water
has remained pure[z] to this day, according
to the word Elisha had spoken.

Elisha Is Jeered

23From there Elisha went up to Bethel.
As he was walking along the road, some
boys came out of the town and jeered[a] at
him. "Get out of here, baldy!" they said.
"Get out of here, baldy!" 24He turned
around, looked at them and called down a
curse[b] on them in the name[c] of the LORD.
Then two bears came out of the woods and
mauled forty-two of the boys. 25And he
went on to Mount Carmel[d] and from there
returned to Samaria.

Moab Revolts

3 Joram[a][e] son of Ahab became king of Israel in Samaria in the eighteenth year of
Jehoshaphat king of Judah, and he reigned
twelve years. 2He did evil[f] in the eyes of the
LORD, but not as his father[g] and mother had
done. He got rid of the sacred stone[h] of Baal
that his father had made. 3Nevertheless he
clung to the sins[i] of Jeroboam son of Nebat,
which he had caused Israel to commit; he
did not turn away from them.
4Now Mesha king of Moab[j] raised sheep,
and he had to pay the king of Israel a tribute of a hundred thousand lambs[k] and the
wool of a hundred thousand rams. 5But after Ahab died, the king of Moab rebelled[l]
against the king of Israel. 6So at that time
King Joram set out from Samaria and mobilized all Israel. 7He also sent this message to Jehoshaphat king of Judah: "The
king of Moab has rebelled against me. Will
you go with me to fight[m] against Moab?"
"I will go with you," he replied. "I am

---

[a] *1* Hebrew *Jehoram,* a variant of *Joram;* also in verse 6

---

of which Paul also had a brief glimpse (2 Cor. 12:1–4). While we do not have a clear picture of what it is like, we know that God will provide a place of beauty and rest for all His children.

2:15 *The spirit of Elijah.* The prophets witnessed both the miracle of Elijah (v. 8) and the similar miracle of Elisha. In this way there would be common agreement that Elisha was the successor of Elijah. They bowed, not in worship, but in respect and submission to the will of God.

2:17 *he was too embarrassed.* Although these words may indicate Elisha's sense of shame on behalf of his disciples for their disbelief, the use of the phrase elsewhere indicates that it means Elisha was worn out, no longer willing to resist (8:11). He came to the point where he gave in to their request.

2:23 *Get out of here, baldy!* The words of these youths indicate their disbelief of Elijah's "going up" into heaven and their disrespect for God's prophet. God did not tolerate blasphemy against Himself by the demeaning of Elijah's departure, or the abuse of his prophet, whom He had called for an important task at a critical period in Israel's history.

3:2 *sacred stone of Baal.* Probably this was a stone pillar or statue erected by Ahab and bearing an inscription and image of the god Baal. Although it was put away temporarily, it apparently was not destroyed, because it later became one of the objects of Jehu's purge (10:26–27).

3:4 *Mesha king of Moab.* The existence of this Moabite king is confirmed by an inscription on a pillar known as the Moabite Stone. The inscription indicates that Omri had conquered the plains of Moab north of the Arnon River, and that the area remained under Israelite control throughout Ahab's reign. Thus the events of this chapter probably took place after Jehoram's accession and shortly before Jehoshaphat's death in 847 B.C. ***raised sheep.*** This Hebrew word is used only of Mesha and of Amos, the prophet (Amos 1:1).

3:7 *Will you go with me.* Because Jehoshaphat was related to the throne of the northern kingdom through the marriage of his son Jehoram to Ahab's daughter Athaliah, it could be presumed that he would be available as an ally.

2:14 [r] 1Ki 19:19 [s] ver 8 **2:15** [t] ver 7; 1Sa 10:5 [u] Nu 11:17
2:16 [v] 1Ki 18:12 [w] Ac 8:39 **2:17** [x] 2Ki 8:11
2:21 [y] Ex 15:25; 2Ki 4:41; 6:6 **2:22** [z] Ex 15:25
2:23 [a] Ex 22:28; 2Ch 36:16; Job 19:18; Ps 31:18
2:24 [b] Ge 4:11; Ne 13:25-27 [c] Dt 18:19 **2:25** [d] 1Ki 18:20; 2Ki 4:25 **3:1** [e] 2Ki 1:17 **3:2** [f] 1Ki 15:26 [g] 1Ki 16:30-32 [h] Ex 23:24; 2Ki 10:18, 26-28 **3:3** [i] 1Ki 12:28-32; 14:9, 16
3:4 [j] Ge 19:37; 2Ki 1:1 [k] Ezr 7:17; Isa 16:1 **3:5** [l] 2Ki 1:1
3:7 [m] 1Ki 22:4

as you are, my people as your people, my horses as your horses.”

8“By what route shall we attack?” he asked.

“Through the Desert of Edom,” he answered.

9So the king of Israel set out with the king of Judah and the king of Edom.[n] After a roundabout march of seven days, the army had no more water for themselves or for the animals with them.

10“What!” exclaimed the king of Israel. “Has the LORD called us three kings together only to deliver us into the hands of Moab?”

11But Jehoshaphat asked, “Is there no prophet of the LORD here, through whom we may inquire[o] of the LORD?”

An officer of the king of Israel answered, “Elisha[p] son of Shaphat is here. He used to pour water on the hands of Elijah.[a][q]”

12Jehoshaphat said, “The word[r] of the LORD is with him.” So the king of Israel and Jehoshaphat and the king of Edom went down to him.

13Elisha said to the king of Israel, “Why do you want to involve me? Go to the prophets of your father and the prophets of your mother.”

“No,” the king of Israel answered, “because it was the LORD who called us three kings together to deliver us into the hands of Moab.”

14Elisha said, “As surely as the LORD Almighty lives, whom I serve, if I did not have respect for the presence of Jehoshaphat king of Judah, I would not pay any attention to you. 15But now bring me a harpist.”[s]

While the harpist was playing, the hand[t] of the LORD came on Elisha 16and he said, “This is what the LORD says: I will fill this valley with pools of water. 17For this is what the LORD says: You will see neither wind nor rain, yet this valley will be filled with water,[u] and you, your cattle and your other animals will drink. 18This is an easy[v] thing in the eyes of the LORD; he will also deliver Moab into your hands. 19You will overthrow every fortified city and every major town. You will cut down every good tree, stop up all the springs, and ruin every good field with stones.”

20The next morning, about the time[w] for offering the sacrifice, there it was—water flowing from the direction of Edom! And the land was filled with water.[x]

21Now all the Moabites had heard that the kings had come to fight against them; so every man, young and old, who could bear arms was called up and stationed on the border. 22When they got up early in the morning, the sun was shining on the water. To the Moabites across the way, the water looked red—like blood. 23“That’s blood!” they said. “Those kings must have fought and slaughtered each other. Now to the plunder, Moab!”

24But when the Moabites came to the camp of Israel, the Israelites rose up and fought them until they fled. And the Israelites invaded the land and slaughtered the Moabites. 25They destroyed the towns, and each man threw a stone on every good field until it was covered. They stopped up all the springs and cut down every good tree. Only Kir Hareseth[y] was left with its stones in place, but men armed with slings surrounded it and attacked it.

26When the king of Moab saw that the battle had gone against him, he took with him seven hundred swordsmen to break through to the king of Edom, but they failed. 27Then he took his firstborn[z] son, who was to succeed him as king, and offered him as a sacrifice on the city wall. The fury against Israel was great; they withdrew and returned to their own land.

The Widow’s Olive Oil

4 The wife of a man from the company[a] of the prophets cried out to Elisha, “Your servant my husband is dead, and you know that he revered the LORD. But now his creditor[b] is coming to take my two boys as his slaves.”

2Elisha replied to her, “How can I help you? Tell me, what do you have in your house?”

“Your servant has nothing there at all,” she said, “except a small jar of olive oil.”[c]

3Elisha said, “Go around and ask all your neighbors for empty jars. Don’t ask for just a few. 4Then go inside and shut the door behind you and your sons. Pour oil into all the jars, and as each is filled, put it to one side.”

5She left him and shut the door behind

---

a 11 That is, he was Elijah’s personal servant.

3:14 ***I would not pay any attention to you.*** As a devotee of Baal, Jehoram had no claim on the favor of God. Nevertheless, he would enjoy the benefits of God’s grace toward Jehoshaphat.

3:20 ***filled with water.*** The dry stream beds can easily overflow their banks in downpours of rain. Even distant areas can be flooded by water from faraway mountain streams swelled by heavy rains.

4:1 ***The wife of a man.*** The fate of widows was perilous in the ancient Middle East. A practical test of biblical piety was to observe how those in power treated widows and orphans (Job 24:21; Ps. 146:9).

3:9 [n] 1Ki 22:47 **3:11** [o] Ge 25:22; 1Ki 22:7 [p] Ge 20:7 [q] 1Ki 19:16 **3:12** [r] Nu 11:17 **3:15** [s] 1Sa 16:23 [t] Jer 15:17; Eze 1:3 **3:17** [u] Ps 107:35; Isa 32:2; 35:6; 41:18 **3:18** [v] Ge 18:14; 2Ki 20:10; Isa 49:6; Jer 32:17, 27; Mk 10:27 **3:20** [w] Ex 29:39-40 [x] Ex 17:6 **3:25** [y] ver 19; Isa 15:1; 16:7; Jer 48:31, 36 **3:27** [z] Dt 12:31; 2Ki 16:3; 21:6; 2Ch 28:3; Ps 106:38; Jer 19:4-5; Am 2:1; Mic 6:7 **4:1** [a] 1Sa 10:5; 2Ki 2:3 [b] Ex 22:26; Lev 25:39-43; Ne 5:3-5; Job 22:6; 24:9 **4:2** [c] 1Ki 17:12

her and her sons. They brought the jars to
her and she kept pouring. 6When all the
jars were full, she said to her son, "Bring
me another one."
But he replied, "There is not a jar left."
Then the oil stopped flowing.
7She went and told the man of God,[d] and
he said, "Go, sell the oil and pay your debts.
You and your sons can live on what is left."

The Shunammite's Son Restored to Life

8One day Elisha went to Shunem.[e] And
a well-to-do woman was there, who urged
him to stay for a meal. So whenever he
came by, he stopped there to eat. 9She
said to her husband, "I know that this man
who often comes our way is a holy man
of God. 10Let's make a small room on the
roof and put in it a bed and a table, a chair
and a lamp for him. Then he can stay[f] there
whenever he comes to us."
11One day when Elisha came, he went
up to his room and lay down there. 12He
said to his servant Gehazi, "Call the Shunammite."[g] So he called her, and she stood
before him. 13Elisha said to him, "Tell her,
'You have gone to all this trouble for us.
Now what can be done for you? Can we
speak on your behalf to the king or the
commander of the army?'"
She replied, "I have a home among my
own people."
14"What can be done for her?" Elisha
asked.
Gehazi said, "She has no son, and her
husband is old."
15Then Elisha said, "Call her." So he
called her, and she stood in the doorway.
16"About this time[h] next year," Elisha said,
"you will hold a son in your arms."
"No, my lord!" she objected. "Please,
man of God, don't mislead your servant!"
17But the woman became pregnant, and
the next year about that same time she gave
birth to a son, just as Elisha had told her.
18The child grew, and one day he went
out to his father, who was with the reapers.[i]
19He said to his father, "My head! My head!"
His father told a servant, "Carry him to
his mother." 20After the servant had lifted
him up and carried him to his mother, the
boy sat on her lap until noon, and then he
died. 21She went up and laid him on the
bed[j] of the man of God, then shut the door
and went out.
22She called her husband and said,
"Please send me one of the servants and
a donkey so I can go to the man of God
quickly and return."
23"Why go to him today?" he asked. "It's
not the New Moon[k] or the Sabbath."
"That's all right," she said.
24She saddled the donkey and said to her
servant, "Lead on; don't slow down for me
unless I tell you." 25So she set out and came
to the man of God at Mount Carmel.[l]
When he saw her in the distance, the man
of God said to his servant Gehazi, "Look!
There's the Shunammite! 26Run to meet her
and ask her, 'Are you all right? Is your husband all right? Is your child all right?'"
"Everything is all right," she said.
27When she reached the man of God at
the mountain, she took hold of his feet. Gehazi came over to push her away, but the
man of God said, "Leave her alone! She is
in bitter distress,[m] but the LORD has hidden
it from me and has not told me why."
28"Did I ask you for a son, my lord?"
she said. "Didn't I tell you, 'Don't raise my
hopes'?"
29Elisha said to Gehazi, "Tuck your cloak
into your belt,[n] take my staff[o] in your hand
and run. Don't greet anyone you meet, and
if anyone greets you, do not answer. Lay
my staff on the boy's face."
30But the child's mother said, "As surely
as the LORD lives and as you live, I will not
leave you." So he got up and followed her.
31Gehazi went on ahead and laid the
staff on the boy's face, but there was no
sound or response. So Gehazi went back
to meet Elisha and told him, "The boy has
not awakened."
32When Elisha reached the house, there
was the boy lying dead on his couch.[p]
33He went in, shut the door on the two of
them and prayed[q] to the LORD. 34Then he

4:10 ***small room.*** The flat roofs of houses in this time were used as extra living space, and often a small room would be built on the roof which could be reached from outside. This accommodated a guest while providing privacy. Recognizing Elisha as one of God's chosen servants, the Shunammite woman was especially concerned that the normal measures of hospitality be applied even more fully.

4:12–13 Thankfulness—Both Elijah and the Shunammite woman illustrate the vitally important teaching of Scripture: Be thankful; be ready both to receive and to give; express your thankfulness always with words and deeds. Too many blessings, kind words, and thoughtful actions go thankless until it is too late. The kindness and love expressed to Elijah registered in his heart and mind. His loving question should be our question in response to kindness: "What can I do for you?"

4:23 ***New Moon ... Sabbath.*** There was no work on these days, so they would be more suitable for going to see the prophet (Ex. 20:9–12; Amos 8:5).

4:27 ***the LORD has hidden it.*** The prophets did not know everything, but only what God made known to them (5:26).

4:33 ***prayed to the LORD.*** Elisha's actions demonstrate that his faith was in the person and power of God alone, and not in the staff that symbolized his prophetic office. The restoration of the boy's life is a demonstration that life itself is in the hands of God.

4:7 [d] 1Ki 12:22 **4:8** [e] Jos 19:18 **4:10** [f] Mt 10:41; Ro 12:13 **4:12** [g] 2Ki 8:1 **4:16** [h] Ge 18:10 **4:18** [i] Ru 2:3 **4:21** [j] ver 32 **4:23** [k] Nu 10:10; 1Ch 23:31; Ps 81:3 **4:25** [l] 1Ki 18:20; 2Ki 2:25 **4:27** [m] 1Sa 1:15 **4:29** [n] 1Ki 18:46; 2Ki 2:8, 14; 9:1 [o] Ex 4:2; 7:19; 14:16 **4:32** [p] ver 21 **4:33** [q] 1Ki 17:20; Mt 6:6

got on the bed and lay on the boy, mouth to mouth, eyes to eyes, hands to hands. As he stretched[r] himself out on him, the boy's body grew warm. 35Elisha turned away and walked back and forth in the room and then got on the bed and stretched out on him once more. The boy sneezed seven times[s] and opened his eyes.[t]

36Elisha summoned Gehazi and said, "Call the Shunammite." And he did. When she came, he said, "Take your son."[u] 37She came in, fell at his feet and bowed to the ground. Then she took her son and went out.

Death in the Pot

38Elisha returned to Gilgal[v] and there was a famine[w] in that region. While the company of the prophets was meeting with him, he said to his servant, "Put on the large pot and cook some stew for these prophets."

39One of them went out into the fields to gather herbs and found a wild vine and picked as many of its gourds as his garment could hold. When he returned, he cut them up into the pot of stew, though no one knew what they were. 40The stew was poured out for the men, but as they began to eat it, they cried out, "Man of God, there is death in the pot!" And they could not eat it.

41Elisha said, "Get some flour." He put it into the pot and said, "Serve it to the people to eat." And there was nothing harmful in the pot.[x]

Feeding of a Hundred

42A man came from Baal Shalishah,[y] bringing the man of God twenty loaves[z] of barley bread[a] baked from the first ripe grain, along with some heads of new grain. "Give it to the people to eat," Elisha said.

43"How can I set this before a hundred men?" his servant asked.

But Elisha answered, "Give it to the people to eat.[b] For this is what the LORD says: 'They will eat and have some left over.[c]'" 44Then he set it before them, and they ate and had some left over, according to the word of the LORD.

Naaman Healed of Leprosy

5 Now Naaman was commander of the army of the king of Aram.[d] He was a great man in the sight of his master and highly regarded, because through him the LORD had given victory to Aram. He was a valiant soldier, but he had leprosy.[a][e]

2Now bands of raiders[f] from Aram had gone out and had taken captive a young girl from Israel, and she served Naaman's wife. 3She said to her mistress, "If only my master would see the prophet[g] who is in Samaria! He would cure him of his leprosy."

4Naaman went to his master and told him what the girl from Israel had said. 5"By all means, go," the king of Aram replied. "I will send a letter to the king of Israel." So Naaman left, taking with him ten talents[b] of silver, six thousand shekels[c] of gold and ten sets of clothing.[h] 6The letter that he took to the king of Israel read: "With this letter I am sending my servant Naaman to you so that you may cure him of his leprosy."

7As soon as the king of Israel read the letter,[i] he tore his robes and said, "Am I God?[j] Can I kill and bring back to life?[k] Why does this fellow send someone to me to be cured of his leprosy? See how he is trying to pick a quarrel[l] with me!"

8When Elisha the man of God heard that the king of Israel had torn his robes, he sent him this message: "Why have you torn your robes? Have the man come to me and he will know that there is a prophet[m] in Israel." 9So Naaman went with his horses and chariots and stopped at the door of Elisha's house. 10Elisha sent a messenger to say to him, "Go, wash[n] yourself seven times[o] in the Jordan, and your flesh will be restored and you will be cleansed."

11But Naaman went away angry and said, "I thought that he would surely come out to me and stand and call on the name of

---

[a] *1* The Hebrew for *leprosy* was used for various diseases affecting the skin; also in verses 3, 6, 7, 11 and 27. [b] *5* That is, about 750 pounds or about 340 kilograms [c] *5* That is, about 150 pounds or about 69 kilograms

---

4:36 Resurrection—When the writer of Hebrews tells us about those "Women [who] received back their dead, raised to life again" (Heb. 11:35), he is probably referring to the two women about whom we read in 1 Kings 17:8–24 and 2 Kings 4:8–37. Many similarities can be seen between these two resurrection miracles, but it is clear that neither prophet followed a "resurrection formula." God is not bound to follow certain procedures or respond to incantations. Instead, He heals whom He will, in what way He wills.

4:41 *flour.* The meal or flour had no magical properties, Elisha's faith in the living God effected the miraculous cure.

5:1 *king of Aram.* The king of Aram (or Syria) was Ben-Hadad II (860–842 B.C.). He was a constant threat against the northern kingdom and would lead an invasion against it later (6:24—7:20).

5:3 *the prophet who is in Samaria.* Although Elisha traveled frequently and may sometimes have lived at Mount Carmel (4:25), he apparently maintained a residence in the capital city of Samaria (2:25; 6:9—7:20).

5:7 *tore his robes.* While such letters of introduction were common in the ancient Middle East, Ben-Hadad's frequent forays against Israel made the king suspicious that the Arameans were seeking a pretext for another attack. Tearing one's robes was a sign of grief or agitation.

5:10 *wash ... in the Jordan.* Elisha's instructions

4:34 [r] 1Ki 17:21; Ac 20:10 **4:35** [s] Jos 6:15 [t] 2Ki 8:5 **4:36** [u] Heb 11:35 **4:38** [v] 2Ki 2:1 [w] Lev 26:26; 2Ki 8:1 **4:41** [x] Ex 15:25; 2Ki 2:21 **4:42** [y] 1Sa 9:4 [z] Mt 14:17; 15:36 [a] 1Sa 9:7 **4:43** [b] Lk 9:13 [c] Mt 14:20; Jn 6:12 **5:1** [d] Ge 10:22; 2Sa 10:19 [e] Ex 4:6; Nu 12:10; Lk 4:27 **5:2** [f] 2Ki 6:23; 13:20; 24:2 **5:3** [g] Ge 20:7 **5:5** [h] ver 22; Ge 24:53; Jdg 14:12; 1Sa 9:7 **5:7** [i] 2Ki 19:14 [j] Ge 30:2 [k] Dt 32:39; 1Sa 2:6 [l] 1Ki 20:7 **5:8** [m] 1Ki 22:7 **5:10** [n] Jn 9:7 [o] Ge 33:3; Lev 14:7

the LORD his God, wave his hand[p] over the
spot and cure me of my leprosy. 12Are not
Abana and Pharpar, the rivers of Damascus, better than all the waters[q] of Israel?
Couldn't I wash in them and be cleansed?"
So he turned and went off in a rage.[r]
13Naaman's servants went to him and
said, "My father,[s] if the prophet had told
you to do some great thing, would you not
have done it? How much more, then, when
he tells you, 'Wash and be cleansed'!" 14So
he went down and dipped himself in the
Jordan seven times,[t] as the man of God had
told him, and his flesh was restored[u] and
became clean like that of a young boy.[v]
15Then Naaman and all his attendants
went back to the man of God[w]. He stood before him and said, "Now I know[x] that there
is no God in all the world except in Israel.
So please accept a gift[y] from your servant."
16The prophet answered, "As surely as
the LORD lives, whom I serve, I will not accept a thing." And even though Naaman
urged him, he refused.[z]
17"If you will not," said Naaman, "please
let me, your servant, be given as much
earth[a] as a pair of mules can carry, for your
servant will never again make burnt offerings and sacrifices to any other god but the
LORD. 18But may the LORD forgive your servant for this one thing: When my master
enters the temple of Rimmon to bow down
and he is leaning[b] on my arm and I have to
bow there also—when I bow down in the
temple of Rimmon, may the LORD forgive
your servant for this."
19"Go in peace,"[c] Elisha said.
After Naaman had traveled some distance, 20Gehazi, the servant of Elisha the
man of God, said to himself, "My master
was too easy on Naaman, this Aramean, by
not accepting from him what he brought.
As surely as the LORD[d] lives, I will run after
him and get something from him."
21So Gehazi hurried after Naaman.
When Naaman saw him running toward
him, he got down from the chariot to meet
him. "Is everything all right?" he asked.
22"Everything is all right," Gehazi answered. "My master sent me to say, 'Two
young men from the company of the prophets have just come to me from the hill country of Ephraim. Please give them a talent[a]
of silver and two sets of clothing.'"[e]
23"By all means, take two talents," said
Naaman. He urged Gehazi to accept them,
and then tied up the two talents of silver
in two bags, with two sets of clothing. He
gave them to two of his servants, and they
carried them ahead of Gehazi. 24When
Gehazi came to the hill, he took the things
from the servants and put them away in the
house. He sent the men away and they left.
25When he went in and stood before his
master, Elisha asked him, "Where have
you been, Gehazi?"
"Your servant didn't go anywhere," Gehazi answered.
26But Elisha said to him, "Was not my
spirit with you when the man got down
from his chariot to meet you? Is this the
time[f] to take money or to accept clothes—
or olive groves and vineyards, or flocks and
herds, or male and female slaves?[g] 27Naa-
man's leprosy[h] will cling to you and to your
descendants forever." Then Gehazi[i] went
from Elisha's presence and his skin was
leprous—it had become as white as snow.[j]

An Axhead Floats

6 The company[k] of the prophets said to
Elisha, "Look, the place where we meet
with you is too small for us. 2Let us go to
the Jordan, where each of us can get a
pole; and let us build a place there for us
to meet."
And he said, "Go."
3Then one of them said, "Won't you
please come with your servants?"
"I will," Elisha replied. 4And he went
with them.
They went to the Jordan and began to cut
down trees. 5As one of them was cutting

[a] 22 That is, about 75 pounds or about 34 kilograms

illustrate the fact that simple obedience to God's will, even if it is not what we imagined, is the only road to receiving God's blessings.

5:15 *no God ... except in Israel.* Naaman is an unusual example of a foreigner who came to faith in God.

5:17 *earth.* Naaman's unusual request may refer back to God's instructions to the Israelites in the desert (Ex. 20:24). Altars built for the worship of the Lord were to be made of earth or undressed stones, perhaps to avoid the possibility of the altar itself becoming an object of veneration.

5:23 *talents.* A talent was an enormous amount of silver—equal to 3,000 shekels, or about 75 pounds.

5:26 *my spirit with you.* The use of the term *spirit* suggests not only Elisha's knowledge but also his strong feelings for Gehazi.

5:26–27 Worldliness—Naaman, in gratitude, urged Elisha to receive a gift, but Elisha steadfastly refused. The prophet wanted the new convert to understand clearly that the God of Israel cannot be bribed. His gifts are bestowed because of His gracious heart. Gehazi's sin was serious—it involved covetousness, lying, misrepresentation of the prophet and, more importantly, brought disgrace on the name of the God of Israel. Gehazi was acting in his own self-interest rather than for the cause of God. When we choose according to the values of unregenerate men, we are worldly and damage the interests of God's kingdom.

5:11 [p] Ex 7:19 **5:12** [q] Isa 8:6 [r] Pr 14:17,29; 19:11; 29:11 **5:13** [s] 2Ki 6:21; 13:14 **5:14** [t] Ge 33:3; Lev 14:7; Jos 6:15 [u] Ex 4:7 [v] Job 33:25; Lk 4:27 **5:15** [w] Jos 2:11 [x] Jos 4:24; 1Sa 17:46; Da 2:47 [y] 1Sa 9:7; 25:27 **5:16** [z] ver 20,26; Ge 14:23; Da 5:17 **5:17** [a] Ex 20:24 **5:18** [b] 2Ki 7:2 **5:19** [c] 1Sa 1:17; Ac 15:33 **5:20** [d] Ex 20:7 **5:22** [e] ver 5; Ge 45:22 **5:26** [f] ver 16 [g] Jer 45:5 **5:27** [h] Nu 12:10; 2Ki 15:5 [i] Col 3:5 [j] Ex 4:6 **6:1** [k] 1Sa 10:5; 2Ki 4:38

down a tree, the iron axhead fell into the
water. "Oh no, my lord!" he cried out. "It
was borrowed!"
6The man of God asked, "Where did
it fall?" When he showed him the place,
Elisha cut a stick and threw[l] it there, and
made the iron float. 7"Lift it out," he said.
Then the man reached out his hand and
took it.

Elisha Traps Blinded Arameans

8Now the king of Aram was at war with
Israel. After conferring with his officers,
he said, "I will set up my camp in such and
such a place."
9The man of God sent word to the king[m]
of Israel: "Beware of passing that place,
because the Arameans are going down
there." 10So the king of Israel checked on
the place indicated by the man of God.
Time and again Elisha warned[n] the king,
so that he was on his guard in such places.
11This enraged the king of Aram. He
summoned his officers and demanded of
them, "Tell me! Which of us is on the side
of the king of Israel?"
12"None of us, my lord the king[o]," said
one of his officers, "but Elisha, the prophet
who is in Israel, tells the king of Israel the
very words you speak in your bedroom."
13"Go, find out where he is," the king
ordered, "so I can send men and capture
him." The report came back: "He is in Dothan."[p] 14Then he sent[q] horses and chariots and a strong force there. They went by
night and surrounded the city.
15When the servant of the man of God
got up and went out early the next morning, an army with horses and chariots had
surrounded the city. "Oh no, my lord! What
shall we do?" the servant asked.
16"Don't be afraid,"[r] the prophet answered. "Those who are with us are more[s]
than those who are with them."
17And Elisha prayed, "Open his eyes,
LORD, so that he may see." Then the LORD
opened the servant's eyes, and he looked
and saw the hills full of horses and chariots[t] of fire all around Elisha.
18As the enemy came down toward him,
Elisha prayed to the LORD, "Strike this
army with blindness."[u] So he struck them
with blindness, as Elisha had asked.
19Elisha told them, "This is not the road
and this is not the city. Follow me, and I will
lead you to the man you are looking for."
And he led them to Samaria.
20After they entered the city, Elisha said,
"LORD, open the eyes of these men so they
can see." Then the LORD opened their eyes
and they looked, and there they were, inside Samaria.
21When the king of Israel saw them, he
asked Elisha, "Shall I kill them, my father?[v]
Shall I kill them?"
22"Do not kill them," he answered.
"Would you kill those you have captured[w]
with your own sword or bow? Set food and
water before them so that they may eat and
drink and then go back to their master."
23So he prepared a great feast for them,
and after they had finished eating and
drinking, he sent them away, and they returned to their master. So the bands[x] from
Aram stopped raiding Israel's territory.

Famine in Besieged Samaria

24Some time later, Ben-Hadad[y] king
of Aram mobilized his entire army and
marched up and laid siege[z] to Samaria.
25There was a great famine[a] in the city;
the siege lasted so long that a donkey's
head sold for eighty shekels[a] of silver, and
a quarter of a cab[b] of seed pods[c][b] for five
shekels.[d]

---

[a] *25* That is, about 2 pounds or about 920 grams
[b] *25* That is, probably about 1/4 pound or about 100 grams [c] *25* Or *of doves' dung* [d] *25* That is, about 2 ounces or about 58 grams

---

6:6 *made the iron float.* At a time when most tools were still made of bronze, an iron blade was valuable.
6:13 *Dothan.* Dothan was in the central highlands of Israel. It is mentioned only here and in Genesis 37:17, when Joseph was sold to the Midianites.
6:15 *servant of the man of God.* Since Gehazi had become a leper (5:27), this is probably another servant. However, Gehazi is mentioned again in 8:4 as one who was still faithfully representing the miracles done through Elisha.
6:16–17 Understanding the Big Picture—Spiritually, we don't often make the personal progress we should. We fall back into old patterns of behavior too easily. We feel like God has left us out there alone to fight with our internal weaknesses as well as external forces that often seem to overpower us.
We're like Elisha's servant who couldn't see the full reality. We don't have a big enough vision to see what God is doing around us and in us. We're too wrapped up in our own physical and emotional reality. We're so full of ourselves that there's no room for God and the new vision He can bring to our lives.

Curiously, this story doesn't contain any record of the servant's response to what he saw. Did that new vision dramatically change his life? Did he forever understand the extent of God's protective care? Maybe that happened, or maybe like most of us, he was only able to catch a glimpse. We must live by faith that the full reality is represented by those brief and beautiful glimpses of the bigger picture.
6:19 *I will lead you.* Elisha's words are technically true, although he was undoubtedly misleading and deceiving the Arameans. The fact that he did not use his unfair advantage to kill Israel's enemies is worthy of notice.
6:25 *donkey's head.* Donkeys were unclean for

6:6 [l] Ex 15:25; 2Ki 2:21 **6:9** [m] ver 12 **6:10** [n] Jer 11:18 **6:12** [o] ver 9 **6:13** [p] Ge 37:17 **6:14** [q] 2Ki 1:9 **6:16** [r] Ge 15:1 [s] 2Ch 32:7; Ps 55:18; Ro 8:31; 1Jn 4:4 **6:17** [t] 2Ki 2:11, 12; Ps 68:17; Zec 6:1-7 **6:18** [u] Ge 19:11; Ac 13:11 **6:21** [v] 2Ki 5:13 **6:22** [w] Dt 20:11; 2Ch 28:8-15; Ro 12:20 **6:23** [x] 2Ki 5:2 **6:24** [y] 1Ki 15:18; 20:1; 2Ki 8:7 [z] Dt 28:52 **6:25** [a] Lev 26:26; Ru 1:1 [b] Isa 36:12

26As the king of Israel was passing by on
the wall, a woman cried to him, "Help me,
my lord the king!"
27The king replied, "If the LORD does not
help you, where can I get help for you? From
the threshing floor? From the winepress?"
28Then he asked her, "What's the matter?"
She answered, "This woman said to me,
'Give up your son so we may eat him today,
and tomorrow we'll eat my son.' 29So we
cooked my son and ate[c] him. The next day
I said to her, 'Give up your son so we may
eat him,' but she had hidden him."
30When the king heard the woman's
words, he tore[d] his robes. As he went along
the wall, the people looked, and they saw
that, under his robes, he had sackcloth[e] on
his body. 31He said, "May God deal with
me, be it ever so severely, if the head of Elisha son of Shaphat remains on his shoulders today!"
32Now Elisha was sitting in his house,
and the elders[f] were sitting with him. The
king sent a messenger ahead, but before
he arrived, Elisha said to the elders, "Don't
you see how this murderer[g] is sending
someone to cut off my head?[h] Look, when
the messenger comes, shut the door and
hold it shut against him. Is not the sound
of his master's footsteps behind him?"
33While he was still talking to them, the
messenger came down to him.
The king said, "This disaster is from the
LORD. Why should I wait[i] for the LORD any
longer?"
7 Elisha replied, "Hear the word of the
LORD. This is what the LORD says: About
this time tomorrow, a seah[a] of the finest
flour will sell for a shekel[b] and two seahs[c] of
barley for a shekel[j] at the gate of Samaria."
2The officer on whose arm the king was
leaning[k] said to the man of God, "Look,
even if the LORD should open the floodgates[l] of the heavens, could this happen?"
"You will see it with your own eyes," answered Elisha, "but you will not eat[m] any
of it!"

The Siege Lifted

3Now there were four men with leprosy[dn]
at the entrance of the city gate. They said to
each other, "Why stay here until we die? 4If
we say, 'We'll go into the city'—the famine
is there, and we will die. And if we stay here,
we will die. So let's go over to the camp of
the Arameans and surrender. If they spare
us, we live; if they kill us, then we die."
5At dusk they got up and went to the
camp of the Arameans. When they reached
the edge of the camp, no one was there, 6for
the Lord had caused the Arameans to hear
the sound[o] of chariots and horses and a
great army, so that they said to one another, "Look, the king of Israel has hired[p] the
Hittite[q] and Egyptian kings to attack us!"
7So they got up and fled[r] in the dusk and
abandoned their tents and their horses and
donkeys. They left the camp as it was and
ran for their lives.
8The men who had leprosy[s] reached the
edge of the camp, entered one of the tents
and ate and drank. Then they took silver,
gold and clothes, and went off and hid them.
They returned and entered another tent and
took some things from it and hid them also.
9Then they said to each other, "What
we're doing is not right. This is a day of
good news and we are keeping it to ourselves. If we wait until daylight, punishment will overtake us. Let's go at once and
report this to the royal palace."
10So they went and called out to the city
gatekeepers and told them, "We went into
the Aramean camp and no one was there—
not a sound of anyone—only tethered horses and donkeys, and the tents left just as
they were." 11The gatekeepers shouted the
news, and it was reported within the palace.
12The king got up in the night and said
to his officers, "I will tell you what the Arameans have done to us. They know we
are starving; so they have left the camp to
hide[t] in the countryside, thinking, 'They
will surely come out, and then we will take
them alive and get into the city.'"
13One of his officers answered, "Have

[a] *1* That is, probably about 12 pounds or about 5.5 kilograms of flour; also in verses 16 and 18 [b] *1* That is, about 2/5 ounce or about 12 grams; also in verses 16 and 18 [c] *1* That is, probably about 20 pounds or about 9 kilograms of barley; also in verses 16 and 18 [d] *3* The Hebrew for *leprosy* was used for various diseases affecting the skin; also in verse 8.

---

food (Lev. 11:3). ***seed pods.*** This is literally translated as "doves' dung." It is not known whether this term is meant to refer to the actual manure of doves or pigeons, or whether it is a slang term for some kind of bean or seed (some translations, including this one, say "seed pods" or "locust beans").

6:28 ***eat him.*** Israel had been warned that national disobedience could reduce the people to such a loathsome deed (Lev. 26:29; Deut. 28:53–57).

7:3 ***men with leprosy.*** Because lepers were excluded from the city (Lev. 13:4–6; Num. 5:2–3), and avoided by all, they probably were ignored by the invaders and had been left to their fate. If the ordinary people of the city were suffering from hunger, these men must have been in even worse plight. They concluded that they had nothing to lose by going to the other side.

7:9 ***good news.*** Good news and good fortune had to be shared (Prov. 15:27; 21:17), and the men feared that failure to do so might merit divine punishment.

6:29 [c] Lev 26:29; Dt 28:53-55 **6:30** [d] 2Ki 18:37; Isa 22:15 [e] Ge 37:34; 1Ki 21:27 **6:32** [f] Eze 8:1; 14:1; 20:1 [g] 1Ki 18:4 [h] ver 31 **6:33** [i] Lev 24:11; Job 2:9; 14:14; Isa 40:31 **7:1** [j] ver 16 **7:2** [k] 2Ki 5:18 [l] ver 19; Ge 7:11; Ps 78:23; Mal 3:10 [m] ver 17 **7:3** [n] Lev 13:45-46; Nu 5:1-4 **7:6** [o] Ex 14:24; 2Sa 5:24; Eze 1:24 [p] 2Sa 10:6; Jer 46:21 [q] Nu 13:29 **7:7** [r] Jdg 7:21; Ps 48:4-6; Pr 28:1; Isa 30:17 **7:8** [s] Isa 33:23; 35:6 **7:12** [t] Jos 8:4; 2Ki 6:25-29

some men take five of the horses that are
left in the city. Their plight will be like that
of all the Israelites left here—yes, they will
only be like all these Israelites who are
doomed. So let us send them to find out
what happened."
14So they selected two chariots with their
horses, and the king sent them after the
Aramean army. He commanded the drivers, "Go and find out what has happened."
15They followed them as far as the Jordan,
and they found the whole road strewn with
the clothing and equipment the Arameans
had thrown away in their headlong flight.
So the messengers returned and reported
to the king. 16Then the people went out and
plundered[u] the camp of the Arameans. So
a seah of the finest flour sold for a shekel,
and two seahs of barley sold for a shekel,[v]
as the LORD had said.
17Now the king had put the officer on
whose arm he leaned in charge of the gate,
and the people trampled him in the gateway, and he died,[w] just as the man of God
had foretold when the king came down to
his house. 18It happened as the man of God
had said to the king: "About this time tomorrow, a seah of the finest flour will sell
for a shekel and two seahs of barley for a
shekel at the gate of Samaria."
19The officer had said to the man of God,
"Look, even if the LORD should open the
floodgates[x] of the heavens, could this happen?" The man of God had replied, "You
will see it with your own eyes, but you will
not eat any of it!" 20And that is exactly
what happened to him, for the people trampled him in the gateway, and he died.

The Shunammite's Land Restored

8 Now Elisha had said to the woman[y]
whose son he had restored to life, "Go
away with your family and stay for a while
wherever you can, because the LORD has
decreed a famine[z] in the land that will last
seven years."[a] 2The woman proceeded to
do as the man of God said. She and her
family went away and stayed in the land of
the Philistines seven years.
3At the end of the seven years she came
back from the land of the Philistines and
went to appeal to the king for her house
and land. 4The king was talking to Gehazi, the servant of the man of God, and had
said, "Tell me about all the great things Elisha has done." 5Just as Gehazi was telling
the king how Elisha had restored[b] the dead
to life, the woman whose son Elisha had
brought back to life came to appeal to the
king for her house and land.
Gehazi said, "This is the woman, my lord
the king, and this is her son whom Elisha
restored to life." 6The king asked the woman about it, and she told him.
Then he assigned an official to her case
and said to him, "Give back everything that
belonged to her, including all the income
from her land from the day she left the
country until now."

Hazael Murders Ben-Hadad

7Elisha went to Damascus,[c] and Ben-Hadad[d] king of Aram was ill. When the king
was told, "The man of God has come all the
way up here," 8he said to Hazael,[e] "Take a
gift[f] with you and go to meet the man of
God. Consult[g] the LORD through him; ask
him, 'Will I recover from this illness?'"
9Hazael went to meet Elisha, taking with
him as a gift forty camel-loads of all the
finest wares of Damascus. He went in and
stood before him, and said, "Your son Ben-
Hadad king of Aram has sent me to ask,
'Will I recover from this illness?'"
10Elisha answered, "Go and say to him,
'You will certainly recover.'[h] Nevertheless,[a] the LORD has revealed to me that he
will in fact die." 11He stared at him with a
fixed gaze until Hazael was embarrassed.[i]
Then the man of God began to weep.[j]

[a] *10* The Hebrew may also be read *Go and say, 'You will certainly not recover,' for.*

8:1 Kindness—Performing an act of kindness can be compared to throwing sand in the wind. You can be sure some of it will come back to you. The woman mentioned here could give glowing testimony to this. She had been led to feed and house the prophet Elisha (4:8–10), and this act of kindness produced good fruit. Through Elisha's prayers, her child was born and restored (ch. 4), and now Elisha warned her of the coming famine. God always remembers our acts of kindness (Mal. 3:16). In fact, the only thing God "forgets" about us is our confessed sins (Jer. 31:34).

8:3 *went to appeal to the king.* The Shunammite woman had not renounced or sold her property, but merely had left during the previous famine. Moreover, she had returned within seven years (Deut. 15:1–6; Ruth 4:3–4). Since the property was still legally hers, she pressed her claim to the king himself.

8:4 *Gehazi.* At this point, Gehazi was still faithful to the ministry of Elisha.

8:6 *Give back everything.* We get a complex picture of King Jehoram. At times he was so angry with Elisha that he wished him dead (6:31), yet even then he was in mourning for his people. In this section, his righteous judgment should be contrasted with the wretched behavior of the wicked Ahab (1 Kin. 21:1–16).

8:10 *You will certainly recover.* Elisha was answering Ben-Hadad's exact question: his illness was not deadly, in the natural course of things he would have recovered. However, Elisha also knew that Ben-Hadad's life would be taken by his servant Hazael.

8:11 *embarrassed.* Elisha had reached the end of his ability to resist his emotions and wept over the suffering that Hazael would bring.

7:16 [u] Isa 33:4,23 [v] ver 1 **7:17** [w] ver 2; 2Ki 6:32 **7:19** [x] ver 2 **8:1** [y] 2Ki 4:8-37 [z] Lev 26:26; Dt 28:22; Ru 1:1 [a] Ge 12:10; Ps 105:16; Hag 1:11 **8:5** [b] 2Ki 4:35 **8:7** [c] 2Sa 8:5; 1Ki 11:24 [d] 2Ki 6:24 **8:8** [e] 1Ki 19:15 [f] Ge 32:20; 1Sa 9:7; 2Ki 1:2 [g] Jdg 18:5 **8:10** [h] Isa 38:1 **8:11** [i] Jdg 3:25 [j] Lk 19:41

12“Why is my lord weeping?” asked Hazael.
“Because I know the harm[k] you will do
to the Israelites,” he answered. “You will
set fire to their fortified places, kill their
young men with the sword, dash[l] their little
children[m] to the ground, and rip open[n] their
pregnant women.”
13Hazael said, “How could your servant,
a mere dog,[o] accomplish such a feat?”
“The LORD has shown me that you will
become king[p] of Aram,” answered Elisha.
14Then Hazael left Elisha and returned
to his master. When Ben-Hadad asked,
“What did Elisha say to you?” Hazael replied, “He told me that you would certainly
recover.” 15But the next day he took a thick
cloth, soaked it in water and spread it over
the king’s face, so that he died.[q] Then Hazael succeeded him as king.

Jehoram King of Judah

16In the fifth year of Joram[r] son of Ahab
king of Israel, when Jehoshaphat was king
of Judah, Jehoram[s] son of Jehoshaphat began his reign as king of Judah. 17He was
thirty-two years old when he became king,
and he reigned in Jerusalem eight years.
18He followed the ways of the kings of Israel, as the house of Ahab had done, for he
married a daughter[t] of Ahab. He did evil
in the eyes of the LORD. 19Nevertheless, for
the sake of his servant David, the LORD
was not willing to destroy[u] Judah. He had
promised to maintain a lamp[v] for David
and his descendants forever.
20In the time of Jehoram, Edom rebelled
against Judah and set up its own king.[w]
21So Jehoram[a] went to Zair with all his
chariots. The Edomites surrounded him
and his chariot commanders, but he rose
up and broke through by night; his army,
however, fled back home. 22To this day
Edom has been in rebellion[x] against Judah.
Libnah[y] revolted at the same time.
23As for the other events of Jehoram’s
reign, and all he did, are they not written
in the book of the annals of the kings of
Judah? 24Jehoram rested with his ancestors and was buried with them in the City
of David. And Ahaziah his son succeeded
him as king.

Ahaziah King of Judah

25In the twelfth[z] year of Joram son of
Ahab king of Israel, Ahaziah son of Jehoram king of Judah began to reign. 26Aha-
ziah was twenty-two years old when he
became king, and he reigned in Jerusalem
one year. His mother’s name was Athaliah,[a] a granddaughter of Omri[b] king of Israel. 27He followed the ways of the house of
Ahab[c] and did evil[d] in the eyes of the LORD,
as the house of Ahab had done, for he was
related by marriage to Ahab’s family.
28Ahaziah went with Joram son of Ahab
to war against Hazael king of Aram at Ramoth Gilead.[e] The Arameans wounded Joram; 29so King Joram returned to Jezreel[f]
to recover from the wounds the Arameans
had inflicted on him at Ramoth[b] in his battle with Hazael[g] king of Aram.
Then Ahaziah son of Jehoram king of Judah went down to Jezreel to see Joram son
of Ahab, because he had been wounded.

Jehu Anointed King of Israel

9 The prophet Elisha summoned a man
from the company[h] of the prophets and
said to him, “Tuck your cloak into your
belt,[i] take this flask of olive oil[j] with you
and go to Ramoth Gilead.[k] 2When you get
there, look for Jehu son of Jehoshaphat, the
son of Nimshi. Go to him, get him away
from his companions and take him into
an inner room. 3Then take the flask and
pour the oil[l] on his head and declare, ‘This
is what the LORD says: I anoint you king
over Israel.’ Then open the door and run;
don’t delay!”

[a] 21 Hebrew *Joram,* a variant of *Jehoram;* also in verses 23 and 24 [b] 29 Hebrew *Ramah,* a variant of *Ramoth*

8:13 *dog.* In the ancient Middle East, dogs were despised as scavengers and unclean animals. Shalmaneser III of Assyria noted Hazael’s accession to the throne with the words: “Hazael, son of nobody, seizes the throne.”

8:16 *Joram ... Jehoram.* These are variant spellings of the same name; the two kings were brothers-in-law since Jehoram of Judah had married the sister of Joram of Israel.

8:16–19 Apostasy—The complete picture of Jehoram’s shameful apostasy is presented by the chronicler (2 Chr. 21:2–26). There were two powerful influences in Jehoram’s life, one good and one evil; sadly, the evil influence prevailed. His father, Jehoshaphat, was one of the few godly kings of Judah, but Jehoram’s wife was Athaliah, daughter of Jezebel, who influenced him to worship Baal (v. 18). Jehoram’s life of unfaithfulness earned God’s judgment, and he died a lonely and miserable death. Nevertheless, the Lord remained committed to His covenant promise (v. 19). Human unfaithfulness cannot destroy God’s purpose of salvation.

8:27 *the ways of the house of Ahab.* The lowest point of Israel’s religious apostasy was reached in the reign of Ahab and his wicked wife Jezebel (1 Kin. 16:31).

9:2 *Jehu.* The name Jehu means “The LORD is He.”

8:12 [k] 1Ki 19:17; 2Ki 10:32; 12:17; 13:3,7 [l] Ps 137:9; Isa 13:16; Hos 13:16; Na 3:10; Lk 19:44 [m] Ge 34:29 [n] 2Ki 15:16; Am 1:13 **8:13** [o] 1Sa 17:43; 2Sa 3:8 [p] 1Ki 19:15 **8:15** [q] 2Ki 1:17 **8:16** [r] 2Ki 1:17; 3:1 [s] 2Ch 21:1-4 **8:18** [t] ver 26; 2Ki 11:1 **8:19** [u] Ge 6:13 [v] 2Sa 21:17; 7:13; 1Ki 11:36; Rev 21:23 **8:20** [w] 1Ki 22:47 **8:22** [x] Ge 27:40 [y] Nu 33:20; Jos 21:13; 2Ki 19:8 **8:25** [z] 2Ki 9:29 **8:26** [a] ver 18 [b] 1Ki 16:23 **8:27** [c] 1Ki 16:30 [d] 1Ki 15:26 **8:28** [e] Dt 4:43; 1Ki 22:3,29 **8:29** [f] 2Ki 9:15 [g] 1Ki 19:15,17 **9:1** [h] 1Sa 10:5 [i] 2Ki 4:29 [j] 1Sa 10:1 [k] 2Ki 8:28 **9:3** [l] 1Ki 19:16

4So the young prophet went to Ramoth
Gilead. 5When he arrived, he found the
army officers sitting together. "I have a
message for you, commander," he said.
"For which of us?" asked Jehu.
"For you, commander," he replied.
6Jehu got up and went into the house.
Then the prophet poured the oil[m] on Jehu's
head and declared, "This is what the LORD,
the God of Israel, says: 'I anoint you king
over the LORD's people Israel. 7You are to
destroy the house of Ahab your master,
and I will avenge[n] the blood of my servants[o] the prophets and the blood of all
the LORD's servants shed by Jezebel.[p] 8The
whole house[q] of Ahab will perish. I will
cut off from Ahab every last male[r] in Israel—slave or free.[a] 9I will make the house
of Ahab like the house of Jeroboam[s] son of
Nebat and like the house of Baasha[t] son of
Ahijah. 10As for Jezebel, dogs[u] will devour
her on the plot of ground at Jezreel, and
no one will bury her.'" Then he opened the
door and ran.
11When Jehu went out to his fellow officers, one of them asked him, "Is everything all right? Why did this maniac[v] come
to you?"
"You know the man and the sort of
things he says," Jehu replied.
12"That's not true!" they said. "Tell us."
Jehu said, "Here is what he told me: 'This
is what the LORD says: I anoint you king
over Israel.'"
13They quickly took their cloaks and
spread[w] them under him on the bare steps.
Then they blew the trumpet[x] and shouted,
"Jehu is king!"

Jehu Kills Joram and Ahaziah

14So Jehu son of Jehoshaphat, the son of
Nimshi, conspired against Joram. (Now
Joram and all Israel had been defending
Ramoth Gilead[y] against Hazael king of
Aram, 15but King Joram[b] had returned to
Jezreel to recover[z] from the wounds the Arameans had inflicted on him in the battle
with Hazael king of Aram.) Jehu said, "If
you desire to make me king, don't let anyone slip out of the city to go and tell the
news in Jezreel." 16Then he got into his
chariot and rode to Jezreel, because Joram
was resting there and Ahaziah[a] king of Judah had gone down to see him.
17When the lookout[b] standing on the
tower in Jezreel saw Jehu's troops approaching, he called out, "I see some troops
coming."
"Get a horseman," Joram ordered. "Send
him to meet them and ask, 'Do you come
in peace?[c]'"
18The horseman rode off to meet Jehu
and said, "This is what the king says: 'Do
you come in peace?'"
"What do you have to do with peace?"
Jehu replied. "Fall in behind me."
The lookout reported, "The messenger
has reached them, but he isn't coming
back."
19So the king sent out a second horseman. When he came to them he said, "This
is what the king says: 'Do you come in
peace?'"
Jehu replied, "What do you have to do
with peace? Fall in behind me."
20The lookout reported, "He has reached
them, but he isn't coming back either. The
driving is like[d] that of Jehu son of Nimshi—he drives like a maniac."
21"Hitch up my chariot," Joram ordered.
And when it was hitched up, Joram king
of Israel and Ahaziah king of Judah rode
out, each in his own chariot, to meet Jehu.
They met him at the plot of ground that had
belonged to Naboth[e] the Jezreelite. 22When
Joram saw Jehu he asked, "Have you come
in peace, Jehu?"
"How can there be peace," Jehu replied,
"as long as all the idolatry and witchcraft
of your mother Jezebel[f] abound?"
23Joram turned about and fled, calling
out to Ahaziah, "Treachery,[g] Ahaziah!"
24Then Jehu drew his bow[h] and shot
Joram between the shoulders. The arrow

[a] 8 Or *Israel—every ruler or leader* [b] 15 Hebrew *Jehoram*, a variant of *Joram*; also in verses 17 and 21-24

9:6 *poured the oil.* The last part of the Lord's threefold command to Elijah had been carried out (8:7–13; 1 Kin. 19:15–21). In the Old Testament, anointing was customarily reserved for a king (2 Sam. 2:4) or the high priest (Ex. 40:13).

9:13 *cloaks.* This action was a mark of homage fit for a king (Matt. 21:8). This scene is reminiscent of the anointing of King Solomon (1 Kin. 1:34).

9:21 *belonged to Naboth.* Ahab's dynasty ended on the very stolen property that occasioned the divine sentence of judgment (1 Kin. 21:17–24). Ahab's unlawful seizure of the land of Naboth was regarded as one of his most heinous crimes.

9:22 *idolatry and witchcraft of . . . Jezebel.* Jezebel's spiritual adultery had brought vile demonic practices into the kingdom and sealed its doom (1 Kin. 21:25–26). As God had said, such activities would surely bring about the nation's demise (Deut. 28:25–26). Jehu justified his actions as a judgment on Jezebel's sins.

9:23 *Treachery.* In reality, Joram and Ahaziah were the true traitors, the ones who had led the people in rebellion against God and sealed their own doom by their disobedience.

9:6 [m] 1Ki 19:16; 2Ch 22:7 **9:7** [n] Ge 4:24; Rev 6:10 [o] Dt 32:43 [p] 1Ki 18:4; 21:15 **9:8** [q] 2Ki 10:17 [r] Dt 32:36; 1Sa 25:22; 1Ki 21:21; 2Ki 14:26 **9:9** [s] 1Ki 14:10; 15:29; 16:3, 11 [t] 1Ki 16:3 **9:10** [u] ver 35-36; 1Ki 21:23 **9:11** [v] Jer 29:26; Jn 10:20; Ac 26:24 **9:13** [w] Mt 21:8; Lk 19:36 [x] 2Sa 15:10; 1Ki 1:34, 39 **9:14** [y] Dt 4:43; 2Ki 8:28 **9:15** [z] 2Ki 8:29 **9:16** [a] 2Ch 22:7 **9:17** [b] Isa 21:6 [c] 1Sa 16:4 **9:20** [d] 2Sa 18:27 **9:21** [e] ver 26; 1Ki 21:1-7, 15-19 **9:22** [f] 1Ki 16:30-33; 18:19; 2Ch 21:13; Rev 2:20 **9:23** [g] 2Ki 11:14 **9:24** [h] 1Ki 22:34

pierced his heart and he slumped down in
his chariot. 25 Jehu said to Bidkar, his chariot officer, "Pick him up and throw him on
the field that belonged to Naboth the Jezreelite. Remember how you and I were riding together in chariots behind Ahab his
father when the LORD spoke this prophecy[i]
against him: 26 'Yesterday I saw the blood
of Naboth[j] and the blood of his sons, declares the LORD, and I will surely make you
pay for it on this plot of ground, declares
the LORD.'[a] Now then, pick him up and
throw him on that plot, in accordance with
the word of the LORD."[k]

27 When Ahaziah king of Judah saw
what had happened, he fled up the road to
Beth Haggan.[b] Jehu chased him, shouting,
"Kill him too!" They wounded him in his
chariot on the way up to Gur near Ibleam,[l]
but he escaped to Megiddo[m] and died there.
28 His servants took him by chariot[n] to Jerusalem and buried him with his ancestors
in his tomb in the City of David. 29 (In the
eleventh[o] year of Joram son of Ahab, Ahaziah had become king of Judah.)

Jezebel Killed

30 Then Jehu went to Jezreel. When Jezebel heard about it, she put on eye makeup,[p]
arranged her hair and looked out of a window. 31 As Jehu entered the gate, she asked,
"Have you come in peace, you Zimri,[q] you
murderer of your master?"[c]

32 He looked up at the window and
called out, "Who is on my side? Who?"
Two or three eunuchs looked down at him.
33 "Throw her down!" Jehu said. So they
threw her down, and some of her blood
spattered the wall and the horses as they
trampled her underfoot.[r]

34 Jehu went in and ate and drank. "Take
care of that cursed woman," he said, "and
bury her, for she was a king's daughter."[s]
35 But when they went out to bury her, they
found nothing except her skull, her feet
and her hands. 36 They went back and told
Jehu, who said, "This is the word of the
LORD that he spoke through his servant
Elijah the Tishbite: On the plot of ground at
Jezreel dogs[t] will devour Jezebel's flesh.[d][u]
37 Jezebel's body will be like dung[v] on the
ground in the plot at Jezreel, so that no one
will be able to say, 'This is Jezebel.'"

Ahab's Family Killed

10 Now there were in Samaria[w] seventy
sons[x] of the house of Ahab. So Jehu
wrote letters and sent them to Samaria: to
the officials of Jezreel,[e][y] to the elders and
to the guardians[z] of Ahab's children. He
said, 2 "You have your master's sons with
you and you have chariots and horses, a
fortified city and weapons. Now as soon
as this letter reaches you, 3 choose the best
and most worthy of your master's sons and
set him on his father's throne. Then fight
for your master's house."

4 But they were terrified and said, "If two
kings could not resist him, how can we?"

5 So the palace administrator, the city
governor, the elders and the guardians
sent this message to Jehu: "We are your
servants[a] and we will do anything you say.
We will not appoint anyone as king; you do
whatever you think best."

6 Then Jehu wrote them a second letter,
saying, "If you are on my side and will obey
me, take the heads of your master's sons
and come to me in Jezreel by this time tomorrow."

Now the royal princes, seventy of them,
were with the leading men of the city,
who were rearing them. 7 When the letter
arrived, these men took the princes and
slaughtered all seventy[b] of them. They put
their heads[c] in baskets and sent them to
Jehu in Jezreel. 8 When the messenger arrived, he told Jehu, "They have brought the
heads of the princes."

Then Jehu ordered, "Put them in two
piles at the entrance of the city gate until
morning."

9 The next morning Jehu went out. He
stood before all the people and said, "You
are innocent. It was I who conspired against
my master and killed him, but who killed
all these? 10 Know, then, that not a word
the LORD has spoken against the house of
Ahab will fail. The LORD has done what he
announced[d] through his servant Elijah."[e]
11 So Jehu[f] killed everyone in Jezreel who

[a] *26* See 1 Kings 21:19. [b] *27* Or *fled by way of the garden house* [c] *31* Or *"Was there peace for Zimri, who murdered his master?"* [d] *36* See 1 Kings 21:23. [e] *1* Hebrew; some Septuagint manuscripts and Vulgate *of the city*

10:1 *seventy sons.* Ahab's "seventy sons" probably included the children of his concubines, as well as grandchildren.

10:9 Righteousness—Jehu declared Ahab's "leading men" (v. 6) innocent of the death of Ahab's seventy sons. The Hebrew word translates literally as "just" or "righteous." They were righteous in the same sense that Jehu himself was (v. 30), in that God had ordered the death of Ahab's family and they were actually carrying out God's orders. However, this did not mean that these men could be considered righteous in any other sense. They had already thrown in their lot with Ahab and his wicked ways, they were his "great men," and as such, they had to meet the same fate as the rest of his family (v. 11). They had almost accidentally been obedient to God's will, but their hearts were still for the enemy.

10:10 *the LORD has done what he announced.*

9:25 [i] 1Ki 21:19-22,24-29 **9:26** [j] 1Ki 21:19 [k] 1Ki 21:29 **9:27** [l] Jdg 1:27 [m] 2Ki 23:29 **9:28** [n] 2Ki 14:20; 23:30 **9:29** [o] 2Ki 8:25 **9:30** [p] Jer 4:30; Eze 23:40 **9:31** [q] 1Ki 16:9-10 **9:33** [r] Ps 7:5 **9:34** [s] 1Ki 16:31; 21:25 **9:36** [t] Ps 68:23; Jer 15:3 [u] 1Ki 21:23 **9:37** [v] Ps 83:10; Isa 5:25; Jer 8:2; 9:22; 16:4; 25:33, Zep 1:17 **10:1** [w] 1Ki 13:32 [x] Jdg 8:30 [y] 1Ki 21:1 [z] ver 5 **10:5** [a] Jos 9:8; 1Ki 20:4,32 **10:7** [b] 1Ki 21:21 [c] 2Sa 4:8 **10:10** [d] 2Ki 9:7-10 [e] 1Ki 21:29 **10:11** [f] Hos 1:4

remained of the house of Ahab, as well as
all his chief men, his close friends and his
priests, leaving him no survivor.[g]
12 Jehu then set out and went toward Samaria. At Beth Eked of the Shepherds, 13 he
met some relatives of Ahaziah king of Judah and asked, "Who are you?"
They said, "We are relatives of Ahaziah,[h]
and we have come down to greet the families of the king and of the queen mother.[i]"
14 "Take them alive!" he ordered. So they
took them alive and slaughtered them by
the well of Beth Eked—forty-two of them.
He left no survivor.
15 After he left there, he came upon Jehonadab[j] son of Rekab,[k] who was on his
way to meet him. Jehu greeted him and
said, "Are you in accord with me, as I am
with you?"
"I am," Jehonadab answered.
"If so," said Jehu, "give me your hand."[l]
So he did, and Jehu helped him up into the
chariot. 16 Jehu said, "Come with me and
see my zeal[m] for the LORD." Then he had
him ride along in his chariot.
17 When Jehu came to Samaria, he killed
all who were left there of Ahab's family;[n]
he destroyed them, according to the word
of the LORD spoken to Elijah.

Servants of Baal Killed

18 Then Jehu brought all the people together and said to them, "Ahab served[o]
Baal a little; Jehu will serve him much.
19 Now summon[p] all the prophets of Baal,
all his servants and all his priests. See that
no one is missing, because I am going to
hold a great sacrifice for Baal. Anyone who
fails to come will no longer live." But Jehu
was acting deceptively in order to destroy
the servants of Baal.
20 Jehu said, "Call an assembly[q] in hon-
or of Baal." So they proclaimed it. 21 Then
he sent word throughout Israel, and all
the servants of Baal came; not one stayed
away. They crowded into the temple of Baal
until it was full from one end to the other.
22 And Jehu said to the keeper of the wardrobe, "Bring robes for all the servants of
Baal." So he brought out robes for them.
23 Then Jehu and Jehonadab son of Rekab went into the temple of Baal. Jehu
said to the servants of Baal, "Look around
and see that no one who serves the LORD
is here with you—only servants of Baal."
24 So they went in to make sacrifices and
burnt offerings. Now Jehu had posted
eighty men outside with this warning: "If
one of you lets any of the men I am placing
in your hands escape, it will be your life
for his life."[r]
25 As soon as Jehu had finished making
the burnt offering, he ordered the guards
and officers: "Go in and kill[s] them; let no
one escape."[t] So they cut them down with
the sword. The guards and officers threw
the bodies out and then entered the inner shrine of the temple of Baal. 26 They
brought the sacred stone[u] out of the temple
of Baal and burned it. 27 They demolished
the sacred stone of Baal and tore down the
temple[v] of Baal, and people have used it for
a latrine to this day.
28 So Jehu[w] destroyed Baal worship in Israel. 29 However, he did not turn away from
the sins[x] of Jeroboam son of Nebat, which
he had caused Israel to commit—the worship of the golden calves[y] at Bethel[z] and
Dan.
30 The LORD said to Jehu, "Because you
have done well in accomplishing what is
right in my eyes and have done to the house
of Ahab all I had in mind to do, your descendants will sit on the throne of Israel
to the fourth generation."[a] 31 Yet Jehu was
not careful[b] to keep the law of the LORD,
the God of Israel, with all his heart. He did
not turn away from the sins[c] of Jeroboam,
which he had caused Israel to commit.
32 In those days the LORD began to reduce[d] the size of Israel. Hazael[e] overpowered the Israelites throughout their terri-

---

Evaluating Jehu is difficult. His praise for the ministry of the prophets of God and his stated respect for the word of God commend him to us, but later he did not exhibit faithfulness to the Lord (10:31).

10:15 ***Jehonadab.*** The name Jehonadab means "The LORD is Noble." He was an ascetic, nomadic Rekabite. These people were known for their faithfulness to God and to the austere regulations laid down by Jehonadab (Jer. 35:1–16).

10:21 ***temple of Baal.*** This was the temple constructed by Ahab (1 Kin. 16:32).

10:21–24 Worship—At times Israel imported pagan ideas and practices into their worship and attempted to mix them with the worship of the Lord. The extremity of this apostasy was reached when Ahab erected an altar for Baal, the fertility god of the Canaanites, in a temple built for Baal in Samaria (1 Kin. 16:32). The participants in Baal worship engaged not only in immoral sexual orgies but in the detestable practice of child sacrifice (Num. 25:1–8; Jer. 19:5). God could not tolerate such behavior and Jehu's purge was the punishment that He had promised for disobedience.

10:29 ***the golden calves.*** Jehu's destruction of Baal worship was a political act. His continuing of the state worship policies established by Jeroboam clearly shows his disregard for true spiritual revival in Israel.

10:32 ***the LORD began to reduce the size of Israel.*** The attacks of Hazael were part of God's judgment on Israel.

10:11 [g] ver 14; Job 18:19 **10:13** [h] 2Ki 8:24, 29; 2Ch 22:8 [i] 1Ki 2:19 **10:15** [j] Jer 35:6, 14-19 [k] 1Ch 2:55; Jer 35:2 [l] Ezr 10:19; Eze 17:18 **10:16** [m] Nu 25:13; 1Ki 19:10 **10:17** [n] 2Ki 9:8 **10:18** [o] Jdg 2:11; 1Ki 16:31-32 **10:19** [p] 1Ki 18:19; 22:6 **10:20** [q] Ex 32:5; Joel 1:14 **10:24** [r] 1Ki 20:39 **10:25** [s] Ex 22:20; 2Ki 11:18 [t] 1Ki 18:40 **10:26** [u] 1Ki 14:23 **10:27** [v] 1Ki 16:32 **10:28** [w] 1Ki 19:17 **10:29** [x] 1Ki 12:30 [y] 1Ki 12:28-29 [z] 1Ki 12:32 **10:30** [a] ver 35; 2Ki 15:12 **10:31** [b] Pr 4:23 [c] 1Ki 12:30 **10:32** [d] 2Ki 13:25 [e] 1Ki 19:17; 2Ki 8:12

tory 33east of the Jordan in all the land of
Gilead (the region of Gad, Reuben and Manasseh), from Aroer[f] by the Arnon Gorge
through Gilead to Bashan.
34As for the other events of Jehu's reign,
all he did, and all his achievements, are
they not written in the book of the annals[g]
of the kings of Israel?
35Jehu rested with his ancestors and was
buried in Samaria. And Jehoahaz his son
succeeded him as king. 36The time that
Jehu reigned over Israel in Samaria was
twenty-eight years.

Athaliah and Joash

11 When Athaliah[h] the mother of Ahaziah saw that her son was dead, she
proceeded to destroy the whole royal family. 2But Jehosheba, the daughter of King Jehoram[a] and sister of Ahaziah, took Joash[i]
son of Ahaziah and stole him away from
among the royal princes, who were about
to be murdered. She put him and his nurse
in a bedroom to hide him from Athaliah;
so he was not killed.[j] 3He remained hidden
with his nurse at the temple of the LORD for
six years while Athaliah ruled the land.
4In the seventh year Jehoiada sent for
the commanders of units of a hundred,
the Carites[k] and the guards and had them
brought to him at the temple of the LORD.
He made a covenant with them and put
them under oath at the temple of the LORD.
Then he showed them the king's son. 5He
commanded them, saying, "This is what
you are to do: You who are in the three
companies that are going on duty on the
Sabbath[l]—a third of you guarding the royal palace,[m] 6a third at the Sur Gate, and a
third at the gate behind the guard, who
take turns guarding the temple— 7and
you who are in the other two companies
that normally go off Sabbath duty are all
to guard the temple for the king. 8Station
yourselves around the king, each of you
with weapon in hand. Anyone who approaches your ranks[b] is to be put to death.
Stay close to the king wherever he goes."
9The commanders of units of a hundred
did just as Jehoiada the priest ordered.
Each one took his men—those who were
going on duty on the Sabbath and those
who were going off duty—and came to Jehoiada the priest. 10Then he gave the commanders the spears and shields[n] that had
belonged to King David and that were in
the temple of the LORD. 11The guards, each
with weapon in hand, stationed themselves
around the king—near the altar and the
temple, from the south side to the north
side of the temple.
12Jehoiada brought out the king's son
and put the crown on him; he presented
him with a copy of the covenant[o] and proclaimed him king. They anointed[p] him, and
the people clapped their hands[q] and shouted, "Long live the king!"[r]
13When Athaliah heard the noise made
by the guards and the people, she went to
the people at the temple of the LORD. 14She
looked and there was the king, standing by
the pillar,[s] as the custom was. The officers
and the trumpeters were beside the king,
and all the people of the land were rejoicing and blowing trumpets.[t] Then Athaliah
tore[u] her robes and called out, "Treason!
Treason!"[v]
15Jehoiada the priest ordered the commanders of units of a hundred, who were
in charge of the troops: "Bring her out
between the ranks[c] and put to the sword
anyone who follows her." For the priest had
said, "She must not be put to death in the
temple[w] of the LORD." 16So they seized her
as she reached the place where the horses enter[x] the palace grounds, and there she
was put to death.[y]
17Jehoiada then made a covenant[z] between the LORD and the king and people
that they would be the LORD's people. He
also made a covenant between the king
and the people.[a] 18All the people of the
land went to the temple[b] of Baal and tore it

[a] 2 Hebrew *Joram,* a variant of *Jehoram*
[b] 8 Or *approaches the precincts* [c] 15 Or *out from the precincts*

11:1 *Athaliah.* This name means "The LORD is Exalted." Sadly, she did not live up to her name, and instead exalted herself.
11:2 *Jehosheba.* Josephus says that Jehosheba was Ahaziah's half sister. As the wife of the high priest Jehoiada, her marriage, and her relation to the royal house made it possible for her to rescue and hide her nephew Joash.
11:3 *hidden ... at the temple of the LORD.* Joash was to inherit the promises of the Davidic covenant. His righteous reign may be attributed in part to his early years spent in the house of the Lord and to the godly instruction and protection of his aunt Jehosheba and her husband.
11:9 *did just as ... the priest ordered.* The remarkably willing obedience of the royal guard would seem to indicate that even her own followers were disgusted by Athaliah's wickedness.
11:12 *a copy of the covenant.* Deuteronomy prescribed the duties of the king with regard to the preservation of God's law (Deut. 17:18). By putting a copy of the Law in Joash's hand and the crown on his head, Jehoiada presented him as the rightful heir to the throne.
11:17 *covenant.* Covenant renewal was particularly necessary after the usurpation by the wicked Athaliah.

10:33 [f] Nu 32:34; Dt 2:36; Jdg 11:26; Isa 17:2 **10:34** [g] 1Ki 15:31 **11:1** [h] 2Ki 8:18 **11:2** [i] ver 21; 2Ki 12:1 [j] Jdg 9:5 **11:4** [k] ver 19 **11:5** [l] 1Ch 9:25 [m] 1Ki 14:27 **11:10** [n] 2Sa 8:7; 1Ch 18:7 **11:12** [o] Ex 25:16; 2Ki 23:3 [p] 1Sa 9:16; 1Ki 1:39 [q] Ps 47:1; 98:8; Isa 55:12 [r] 1Sa 10:24 **11:14** [s] 1Ki 7:15; 2Ki 23:3; 2Ch 34:31 [t] 1Ki 1:39 [u] Ge 37:29 [v] 2Ki 9:23 **11:15** [w] 1Ki 2:30 **11:16** [x] Ne 3:28; Jer 31:40 [y] Ge 4:14 **11:17** [z] Ex 24:8; 2Sa 5:3; 2Ch 15:12; 23:3; 29:10; 34:31; Ezr 10:3 [a] 2Ki 23:3; Jer 34:8 **11:18** [b] 1Ki 16:32

down. They smashed[c] the altars and idols
to pieces and killed Mattan the priest[d] of
Baal in front of the altars.
Then Jehoiada the priest posted guards
at the temple of the LORD. 19He took with
him the commanders of hundreds, the Carites,[e] the guards and all the people of the
land, and together they brought the king
down from the temple of the LORD and went
into the palace, entering by way of the gate
of the guards. The king then took his place
on the royal throne. 20All the people of the
land rejoiced,[f] and the city was calm, because Athaliah had been slain with the
sword at the palace.
21Joash[a] was seven years old when he
began to reign.[b]

Joash Repairs the Temple

12[c] In the seventh year of Jehu, Joash[dg]
became king, and he reigned in Jerusalem forty years. His mother's name was
Zibiah; she was from Beersheba. 2Joash
did what was right in the eyes of the LORD
all the years Jehoiada the priest instructed
him. 3The high places,[h] however, were not
removed; the people continued to offer sacrifices and burn incense there.
4Joash said to the priests, "Collect[i] all
the money that is brought as sacred offerings[j] to the temple of the LORD—the
money collected in the census,[k] the money
received from personal vows and the money brought voluntarily[l] to the temple. 5Let
every priest receive the money from one of
the treasurers, then use it to repair whatever damage is found in the temple."
6But by the twenty-third year of King
Joash the priests still had not repaired the
temple. 7Therefore King Joash summoned
Jehoiada the priest and the other priests and
asked them, "Why aren't you repairing the
damage done to the temple? Take no more
money from your treasurers, but hand it
over for repairing the temple." 8The priests
agreed that they would not collect any more
money from the people and that they would
not repair the temple themselves.
9Jehoiada the priest took a chest and
bored a hole in its lid. He placed it beside
the altar, on the right side as one enters the
temple of the LORD. The priests who guarded the entrance[m] put into the chest all the
money[n] that was brought to the temple of
the LORD. 10Whenever they saw that there
was a large amount of money in the chest,
the royal secretary[o] and the high priest
came, counted the money that had been
brought into the temple of the LORD and
put it into bags. 11When the amount had
been determined, they gave the money to
the men appointed to supervise the work
on the temple. With it they paid those who
worked on the temple of the LORD—the
carpenters and builders, 12the masons
and stonecutters.[p] They purchased timber and blocks of dressed stone for the
repair of the temple of the LORD, and met
all the other expenses of restoring the
temple.
13The money brought into the temple
was not spent for making silver basins,
wick trimmers, sprinkling bowls, trumpets or any other articles of gold[q] or silver
for the temple of the LORD; 14it was paid to
the workers, who used it to repair the temple. 15They did not require an accounting
from those to whom they gave the money to
pay the workers, because they acted with
complete honesty.[r] 16The money from the
guilt offerings[s] and sin offerings[et] was not
brought into the temple of the LORD; it belonged[u] to the priests.
17About this time Hazael[v] king of Aram
went up and attacked Gath and captured it.
Then he turned to attack Jerusalem. 18But
Joash king of Judah took all the sacred
objects dedicated by his predecessors—
Jehoshaphat, Jehoram and Ahaziah, the
kings of Judah—and the gifts he himself
had dedicated and all the gold found in the
treasuries of the temple of the LORD and
of the royal palace, and he sent[w] them to
Hazael king of Aram, who then withdrew[x]
from Jerusalem.
19As for the other events of the reign of
Joash, and all he did, are they not written
in the book of the annals of the kings of
Judah? 20His officials[y] conspired against
him and assassinated[z] him at Beth Millo,[a]

---

[a] *21* Hebrew *Jehoash*, a variant of *Joash* [b] *21* In Hebrew texts this verse (11:21) is numbered 12:1.
[c] In Hebrew texts 12:1-21 is numbered 12:2-22.
[d] *1* Hebrew *Jehoash*, a variant of *Joash*; also in verses 2, 4, 6, 7 and 18 [e] *16* Or *purification offerings*

11:20 *rejoiced . . . calm.* The joy of the people and the peacefulness of the land were marks of God's blessing to the restored Davidic dynasty.

12:2 *all the years Jehoiada the priest instructed him.* Sadly, after Jehoiada's death Joash's reign took a different turn; nonetheless, he was one of the few kings of Judah who showed some signs of righteousness.

12:3 *high places.* Although the high places seem to have been used at times for the worship of the true God, they were also strongly associated with Canaanite religious rites (1 Kin. 3:2–4; 14:23). Apostasy would become a besetting sin later in Joash's reign (2 Chr. 24:17–19,24).

12:17 *Hazael king of Aram.* The Aramean invasion recorded here took place late in Joash's reign. The king fell into apostasy and this invasion came as a judgment of his wickedness.

12:20 *conspired against him.* Joash had been

11:18 [c] Dt 12:3 [d] 1Ki 18:40; 2Ki 10:25; 23:20
11:19 [e] ver 4 **11:20** [f] Pr 11:10; 28:12; 29:2
12:1 [g] 2Ki 11:2 **12:3** [h] 1Ki 3:3; 2Ki 14:4; 15:35; 18:4
12:4 [i] 2Ki 22:4 [j] Ex 35:5 [k] Ex 30:12 [l] Ex 35:29; 1Ch 29:3-9
12:9 [m] Jer 35:4 [n] 2Ch 24:8; Mk 12:41; Lk 21:1
12:10 [o] 2Sa 8:17 **12:12** [p] 2Ki 22:5-6 **12:13** [q] 1Ki 7:48-51; 2Ch 24:14 **12:15** [r] 2Ki 22:7; 1Co 4:2
12:16 [s] Lev 5:14-19; Nu 18:9 [t] Lev 4:1-35 [u] Lev 7:7
12:17 [v] 2Ki 8:12 **12:18** [w] 1Ki 15:18; 2Ch 21:16-17
[x] 1Ki 15:21 **12:20** [y] 2Ki 14:5 [z] 2Ch 24:25 [a] Jdg 9:6

on the road down to Silla. 21 The officials who murdered him were Jozabad son of Shimeath and Jehozabad son of Shomer. He died and was buried with his ancestors in the City of David. And Amaziah his son succeeded him as king.

Jehoahaz King of Israel

13 In the twenty-third year of Joash son of Ahaziah king of Judah, Jehoahaz son of Jehu became king of Israel in Samaria, and he reigned seventeen years. 2 He did evil[b] in the eyes of the LORD by following the sins of Jeroboam son of Nebat, which he had caused Israel to commit, and he did not turn away from them. 3 So the LORD's anger[c] burned against Israel, and for a long time he kept them under the power[d] of Hazael king of Aram and Ben-Hadad[e] his son.

4 Then Jehoahaz sought[f] the LORD's favor, and the LORD listened to him, for he saw[g] how severely the king of Aram was oppressing[h] Israel. 5 The LORD provided a deliverer[i] for Israel, and they escaped from the power of Aram. So the Israelites lived in their own homes as they had before. 6 But they did not turn away from the sins[j] of the house of Jeroboam, which he had caused Israel to commit; they continued in them. Also, the Asherah pole[a][k] remained standing in Samaria.

7 Nothing had been left[l] of the army of Jehoahaz except fifty horsemen, ten chariots and ten thousand foot soldiers, for the king of Aram had destroyed the rest and made them like the dust[m] at threshing time.

8 As for the other events of the reign of Jehoahaz, all he did and his achievements, are they not written in the book of the annals of the kings of Israel? 9 Jehoahaz rested with his ancestors and was buried in Samaria. And Jehoash[b] his son succeeded him as king.

Jehoash King of Israel

10 In the thirty-seventh year of Joash king of Judah, Jehoash son of Jehoahaz became king of Israel in Samaria, and he reigned sixteen years. 11 He did evil in the eyes of the LORD and did not turn away from any of the sins of Jeroboam son of Nebat, which he had caused Israel to commit; he continued in them.

12 As for the other events of the reign of Jehoash, all he did and his achievements, including his war against Amaziah[n] king of Judah, are they not written in the book of the annals[o] of the kings of Israel? 13 Jehoash rested with his ancestors, and Jeroboam[p] succeeded him on the throne. Jehoash was buried in Samaria with the kings of Israel.

14 Now Elisha had been suffering from the illness from which he died. Jehoash king of Israel went down to see him and wept over him. "My father! My father!" he cried. "The chariots[q] and horsemen of Israel!"

15 Elisha said, "Get a bow and some arrows,"[r] and he did so. 16 "Take the bow in your hands," he said to the king of Israel. When he had taken it, Elisha put his hands on the king's hands.

17 "Open the east window," he said, and he opened it. "Shoot!"[s] Elisha said, and he shot. "The LORD's arrow of victory, the arrow of victory over Aram!" Elisha declared. "You will completely destroy the Arameans at Aphek."[t]

18 Then he said, "Take the arrows," and the king took them. Elisha told him, "Strike the ground." He struck it three times and stopped. 19 The man of God was angry with

[a] 6 That is, a wooden symbol of the goddess Asherah; here and elsewhere in 2 Kings
[b] 9 Hebrew *Joash*, a variant of *Jehoash*; also in verses 12-14 and 25

severely wounded in Hazael's invasion (2 Chr. 24:24–25), and then fell victim to dissent and unpopularity that culminated in his assassination. Because of Joash's apostasy and murder of Zechariah, Jehoiada's son (2 Chr. 24:17–22), the king was not laid to rest in the royal tombs (2 Chr. 24:25).

13:2 ***evil ... the sins of Jeroboam.*** After the end of the house of Omri in Jehu's purge, the kings of Israel reverted to the level of syncretism that had been established by Jeroboam I, indulging in a skewed religion in which worship of the Lord was mixed with idolatry.

13:4 ***sought the LORD's favor.*** Although Jehoahaz did not follow the Lord exclusively, God graciously heard his genuine plea for help. In His long-suffering mercy, God often deals patiently with people and blesses them in spite of their failures (1 Kin. 21:25–29; 2 Pet. 3:9).

13:6 Unbelief—No one is bound to continue following a path of sin. We always have the option of turning to God. However, the tendency to maintain things as they are and have been, to resist change no matter how urgently needed or how right it may be, or how much good it promises, is powerful. We cling to the known, the familiar, no matter how unsatisfying and ineffective it may be or how unhappy it may make us. Changing direction is not easy or painless, but the good news is that it really can be done. God is loving and forgiving, and when we repent of sin, He gives us the power to overcome it.

13:14 ***My father.*** The grief of Jehoash at the impending death of Elisha shows that, like his father Jehoahaz, this Israelite king possessed some genuine spirituality. The line of Jehu had its good moments and received some reward from the Lord (10:30). However, none of this line or any other of the kings of Israel served God with all their hearts.

13:18 ***He struck it three times and stopped.***

13:2 [b] 1Ki 12:26-33 **13:3** [c] Dt 31:17; Jdg 2:14 [d] 1Ki 8:12; 12:17; 19:17 [e] ver 24 **13:4** [f] Dt 4:29; Ps 78:34 [g] Ex 3:7; Dt 26:7 [h] 2Ki 14:26 **13:5** [i] ver 25; 2Ki 14:25,27 **13:6** [j] 1Ki 12.30 [k] 1Ki 16:33 **13:7** [l] 2Ki 10:32-33 [m] 2Sa 22:43 **13:12** [n] 2Ki 14:15 [o] 1Ki 15:31 **13:13** [p] 2Ki 14:23; Hos 1:1 **13:14** [q] 2Ki 2:12 **13:15** [r] 1Sa 20:20 **13:17** [s] Jos 8:18 [t] 1Ki 20:26

him and said, "You should have struck the ground five or six times; then you would have defeated Aram and completely destroyed it. But now you will defeat it only three times."[u]

20Elisha died and was buried.

Now Moabite raiders[v] used to enter the country every spring. 21Once while some Israelites were burying a man, suddenly they saw a band of raiders; so they threw the man's body into Elisha's tomb. When the body touched Elisha's bones, the man came to life[w] and stood up on his feet.

22Hazael king of Aram oppressed[x] Israel throughout the reign of Jehoahaz. 23But the LORD was gracious to them and had compassion and showed concern for them because of his covenant[y] with Abraham, Isaac and Jacob. To this day he has been unwilling to destroy[z] them or banish them from his presence.[a]

24Hazael king of Aram died, and Ben-Hadad[b] his son succeeded him as king. 25Then Jehoash son of Jehoahaz recaptured from Ben-Hadad son of Hazael the towns he had taken in battle from his father Jehoahaz. Three times[c] Jehoash defeated him, and so he recovered[d] the Israelite towns.

Amaziah King of Judah

14 In the second year of Jehoash[a] son of Jehoahaz king of Israel, Amaziah son of Joash king of Judah began to reign. 2He was twenty-five years old when he became king, and he reigned in Jerusalem twenty-nine years. His mother's name was Jehoaddan; she was from Jerusalem. 3He did what was right in the eyes of the LORD, but not as his father David had done. In everything he followed the example of his father Joash. 4The high places,[e] however, were not removed; the people continued to offer sacrifices and burn incense there.

5After the kingdom was firmly in his grasp, he executed[f] the officials[g] who had murdered his father the king. 6Yet he did not put the children of the assassins to death, in accordance with what is written in the Book of the Law[h] of Moses where the LORD commanded: "Parents are not to be put to death for their children, nor children put to death for their parents; each will die for their own sin."[b][i]

7He was the one who defeated ten thousand Edomites in the Valley of Salt[j] and captured Sela[k] in battle, calling it Joktheel, the name it has to this day.

8Then Amaziah sent messengers to Jehoash son of Jehoahaz, the son of Jehu, king of Israel, with the challenge: "Come, let us face each other in battle."

9But Jehoash king of Israel replied to Amaziah king of Judah: "A thistle[l] in Lebanon sent a message to a cedar in Lebanon, 'Give your daughter to my son in marriage.' Then a wild beast in Lebanon came along and trampled the thistle underfoot. 10You have indeed defeated Edom and now you are arrogant.[m] Glory in your victory, but stay at home! Why ask for trouble and cause your own downfall and that of Judah also?"

11Amaziah, however, would not listen, so Jehoash king of Israel attacked. He and Amaziah king of Judah faced each other at Beth Shemesh[n] in Judah. 12Judah was routed by Israel, and every man fled to his home.[o] 13Jehoash king of Israel captured Amaziah king of Judah, the son of Joash, the son of Ahaziah, at Beth Shemesh. Then Jehoash went to Jerusalem and broke down the wall[p] of Jerusalem from the Ephraim Gate[q] to the Corner Gate[r]—a section about four hundred cubits long.[c] 14He took all the gold and silver and all the articles found in the temple of the LORD and in the treasuries

---

[a] *1* Hebrew *Joash*, a variant of *Jehoash*; also in verses 13, 23 and 27 [b] *6* Deut. 24:16 [c] *13* That is, about 600 feet or about 180 meters

---

Jehoash's half-hearted compliance with Elisha's instructions exposed his weak faith and illustrated God's unfavorable evaluation of his character (v. 11).

13:21 ***came to life.*** There was no magic in Elisha's bones; this was a demonstration of the power of God associated with His servant.

13:23 ***showed concern for them.*** This glimpse of the wonderful mercy of the living God is like a drink of fresh water in the midst of the sad tale of the northern kingdom.

14:1 ***Amaziah.*** The name Amaziah means "The LORD is Mighty." He was one of the few godly kings in the kingdom of Judah.

14:4 ***high places.*** Like his father Joash before him (12:3), Amaziah allowed worship at the high places to continue. This practice blossomed into open idolatry in the reigns of subsequent kings (16:4; 21:3).

14:9–10 Pride—Amaziah's conquest of the formidable city of Sela atop the seemingly unapproachable cliffs of the Wadi Musa was a monumental accomplishment. Rather than recognize God's hand in this feat, Amaziah became proud and fell into spiritual compromise (2 Chr. 25:5–16). A little success can sometimes be a dangerous thing. Failure to acknowledge God's power leads to personal pride, and such pride leads inevitably to downfall. God will not share His glory.

14:11 ***Beth Shemesh.*** The name of the city means "House of the Sun," indicating that there had once been a temple to the sun god there in Canaanite times. Beth Shemesh was in the Valley of Sorek, about 15 miles west of Jerusalem. This was the town where

13:19 [u] ver 25 **13:20** [v] 2Ki 3:7; 24:2 **13:21** [w] Mt 27:52 **13:22** [x] 1Ki 19:17; 2Ki 8:12 **13:23** [y] Ge 13:16-17; Ex 2:24 [z] Dt 29:20 [a] Ex 33:15; 2Ki 14:27; 17:18; 24:3,20 **13:24** [b] ver 3 **13:25** [c] ver 18,19 [d] 2Ki 10:32 **14:4** [e] 2Ki 12:3; 16:4 **14:5** [f] 2Ki 21:24 [g] 2Ki 12:20 **14:6** [h] Dt 28:61 [i] Nu 26:11; Job 21:20; Jer 31:30; 44:3; Eze 18:4,20 **14:7** [j] 2Sa 8:13; 2Ch 25:11 [k] Jdg 1:36 **14:9** [l] Jdg 9:8-15 **14:10** [m] Dt 8:14; 2Ch 26:16; 32:25 **14:11** [n] Jos 15:10 **14:12** [o] 2Sa 18:17 **14:13** [p] 1Ki 3:1; 2Ch 33:14; 36:19; Jer 39:2 [q] Ne 8:16; 12:39 [r] 2Ch 25:23; Jer 31:38; Zec 14:10

of the royal palace. He also took hostages
and returned to Samaria.
15As for the other events of the reign
of Jehoash, what he did and his achievements, including his war[s] against Amaziah
king of Judah, are they not written in the
book of the annals of the kings of Israel?
16Jehoash rested with his ancestors and
was buried in Samaria with the kings of
Israel. And Jeroboam his son succeeded
him as king.
17Amaziah son of Joash king of Judah
lived for fifteen years after the death of Jehoash son of Jehoahaz king of Israel. 18As
for the other events of Amaziah's reign, are
they not written in the book of the annals
of the kings of Judah?
19They conspired[t] against him in Jerusalem, and he fled to Lachish,[u] but they sent
men after him to Lachish and killed him
there. 20He was brought back by horse[v]
and was buried in Jerusalem with his ancestors, in the City of David.
21Then all the people of Judah took Azariah,[aw] who was sixteen years old, and
made him king in place of his father Amaziah. 22He was the one who rebuilt Elath[x]
and restored it to Judah after Amaziah
rested with his ancestors.

Jeroboam II King of Israel

23In the fifteenth year of Amaziah son
of Joash king of Judah, Jeroboam[y] son
of Jehoash king of Israel became king in
Samaria, and he reigned forty-one years.
24He did evil in the eyes of the LORD and did
not turn away from any of the sins of Jeroboam son of Nebat, which he had caused
Israel to commit.[z] 25He was the one who restored the boundaries of Israel from Lebo
Hamath[a] to the Dead Sea,[bb] in accordance
with the word of the LORD, the God of Israel, spoken through his servant Jonah[c] son
of Amittai, the prophet from Gath Hepher.
26The LORD had seen how bitterly everyone in Israel, whether slave or free,[d]
was suffering;[ce] there was no one to help
them.[f] 27And since the LORD had not said
he would blot out[g] the name of Israel from
under heaven, he saved[h] them by the hand
of Jeroboam son of Jehoash.
28As for the other events of Jeroboam's
reign, all he did, and his military achievements, including how he recovered for Israel both Damascus[i] and Hamath,[j] which had
belonged to Judah, are they not written in
the book of the annals[k] of the kings of Israel? 29Jeroboam rested with his ancestors,
the kings of Israel. And Zechariah his son
succeeded him as king.

Azariah King of Judah

15 In the twenty-seventh year of Jeroboam king of Israel, Azariah[dl] son of
Amaziah king of Judah began to reign. 2He
was sixteen years old when he became king,
and he reigned in Jerusalem fifty-two years.
His mother's name was Jekoliah; she was
from Jerusalem. 3He did what was right in
the eyes of the LORD, just as his father Amaziah had done. 4The high places, however,
were not removed; the people continued to
offer sacrifices and burn incense there.
5The LORD afflicted[m] the king with leprosy[e] until the day he died, and he lived in
a separate house.[fn] Jotham[o] the king's son
had charge of the palace[p] and governed the
people of the land.

---

[a] *21* Also called *Uzziah* [b] *25* Hebrew *the Sea of the Arabah* [c] *26* Or *Israel was suffering. They were without a ruler or leader, and* [d] *1* Also called *Uzziah*; also in verses 6, 7, 8, 17, 23 and 27 [e] *5* The Hebrew for *leprosy* was used for various diseases affecting the skin. [f] *5* Or *in a house where he was relieved of responsibilities*

---

the holy ark was taken after its "wanderings" among the Philistines.

14:17 *fifteen years.* The notice of fifteen years of life for Amaziah suggests he was released after the death of Jehoash for an additional period (782–767 B.C.). If so, he reigned alongside his son Azariah (or Uzziah), whose 52-year reign began in 792 B.C. (15:2).

14:23 *forty-one years.* Jeroboam II had a very long reign. His 41 years included 10 years as coregent with his father Jehoash (792–782 B.C.).

14:25 *Jonah.* Once again a prophet of God gave direction to a king. The reference to Jonah here provides the historical setting for the famous prophet (Jon. 1:1).

14:28 *his military achievements.* The Scriptures emphasize Jeroboam's military prowess. Yet Jeroboam's might may have also been economic. The well-known Samaritan Ostraca, which may date from this period, record the delivery to Samaria of fine oil and barley produced on the royal estates.

14:29 *Zechariah.* The brief reign of Zechariah is noted in 15:8–12. He was the fourth in the line of Jehu to reign in Israel, in fulfillment of God's gracious promise to Jehu (10:30).

15:1 *Azariah.* Also called Uzziah (2 Chr. 26:1), this king is credited with 52 years of reign. This figure includes 10 years during which his father Amaziah was held captive (792–782 B.C.). The latter part of Azariah's reign was tainted by his intrusion into the priestly office (2 Chr. 26:16–19), an act that resulted in his being stricken with leprosy (v. 5). This condition put his son Jotham on the throne to rule with him and handle public matters relative to the royal office. The nature of Jotham's duties (v. 5), the assigning of a full 52 years of reign to Azariah, and Isaiah's dating of his call to the year of Azariah's (or Uzziah's) death (Is. 6:1) may indicate that Azariah retained the power of the throne until the end.

15:5 *leprosy.* The events that brought about this affliction are described in 2 Chronicles 26:16–21.

14:15 [s] 2Ki 13:12 **14:19** [t] 2Ki 12:20 [u] Jos 10:3; 2Ki 18:14, 17 **14:20** [v] 2Ki 9:28 **14:21** [w] 2Ki 15:1; 2Ch 26:23 **14:22** [x] 1Ki 9:26; 2Ki 16:6 **14:23** [y] 2Ki 13:13 **14:24** [z] 1Ki 15:30 **14:25** [a] Nu 13:21; 1Ki 8:65 [b] Dt 3:17 [c] Jnh 1:1; Mt 12:39 **14:26** [d] Dt 32:36 [e] 2Ki 13:4 [f] Ps 18:41; 22:11; 72:12; 107:12; Isa 63:5; La 1:7 **14:27** [g] 2Ki 13:23 [h] Jdg 6:14 **14:28** [i] 2Sa 8:5; 1Ki 11:24 [j] 2Ch 8:3 [k] 1Ki 15:31 **15:1** [l] ver 32; 2Ki 14:21 **15:5** [m] Ge 12:17 [n] Lev 13:46 [o] 2Ch 27:1 [p] Ge 41:40

6As for the other events of Azariah's
reign, and all he did, are they not written
in the book of the annals of the kings of
Judah? 7Azariah rested[q] with his ancestors and was buried near them in the City
of David. And Jotham[r] his son succeeded
him as king.

Zechariah King of Israel

8In the thirty-eighth year of Azariah
king of Judah, Zechariah son of Jeroboam became king of Israel in Samaria, and
he reigned six months. 9He did evil[s] in the
eyes of the LORD, as his predecessors had
done. He did not turn away from the sins
of Jeroboam son of Nebat, which he had
caused Israel to commit.

10Shallum son of Jabesh conspired
against Zechariah. He attacked him in
front of the people,[a] assassinated[t] him and
succeeded him as king. 11The other events
of Zechariah's reign are written in the
book of the annals[u] of the kings of Israel.
12So the word of the LORD spoken to Jehu
was fulfilled:[v] "Your descendants will sit
on the throne of Israel to the fourth generation."[b]

Shallum King of Israel

13Shallum son of Jabesh became king
in the thirty-ninth year of Uzziah king of
Judah, and he reigned in Samaria[w] one
month. 14Then Menahem son of Gadi went
from Tirzah[x] up to Samaria. He attacked
Shallum son of Jabesh in Samaria, assassinated[y] him and succeeded him as king.

15The other events of Shallum's reign,
and the conspiracy he led, are written in
the book of the annals[z] of the kings of Israel.

16At that time Menahem, starting out
from Tirzah, attacked Tiphsah[a] and everyone in the city and its vicinity, because they
refused to open[b] their gates. He sacked
Tiphsah and ripped open all the pregnant
women.

Menahem King of Israel

17In the thirty-ninth year of Azariah
king of Judah, Menahem son of Gadi became king of Israel, and he reigned in Samaria ten years. 18He did evil in the eyes
of the LORD. During his entire reign he did
not turn away from the sins of Jeroboam
son of Nebat, which he had caused Israel
to commit.

19Then Pul[c][c] king of Assyria invaded the
land, and Menahem gave him a thousand
talents[d] of silver to gain his support and
strengthen his own hold on the kingdom.
20Menahem exacted this money from Israel. Every wealthy person had to contribute
fifty shekels[e] of silver to be given to the
king of Assyria. So the king of Assyria
withdrew[d] and stayed in the land no longer.

21As for the other events of Menahem's
reign, and all he did, are they not written
in the book of the annals of the kings of
Israel? 22Menahem rested with his ancestors. And Pekahiah his son succeeded him
as king.

Pekahiah King of Israel

23In the fiftieth year of Azariah king of
Judah, Pekahiah son of Menahem became
king of Israel in Samaria, and he reigned
two years. 24Pekahiah did evil in the eyes
of the LORD. He did not turn away from
the sins of Jeroboam son of Nebat, which
he had caused Israel to commit. 25One of
his chief officers, Pekah[e] son of Remaliah,
conspired against him. Taking fifty men
of Gilead with him, he assassinated[f] Pekahiah, along with Argob and Arieh, in the
citadel of the royal palace at Samaria. So
Pekah killed Pekahiah and succeeded him
as king.

---

[a] *10* Hebrew; some Septuagint manuscripts *in Ibleam* [b] *12* 2 Kings 10:30 [c] *19* Also called *Tiglath-Pileser* [d] *19* That is, about 38 tons or about 34 metric tons [e] *20* That is, about 1 1/4 pounds or about 575 grams

---

15:12 *fourth generation.* Jehu had been promised a continuing posterity into the fourth generation as a reward for carrying out his divine commission (10:30), but after the death of Zechariah in 752 B.C., Israel plunged into a period of degeneracy, bloody conspiracies and international intrigue that would bring about its demise in 722 B.C.

15:17 *Menahem.* This wicked king came into power by assassination and established his authority by brutal acts against humanity. Ironically, his name means "Comforter."

15:19 *Pul.* Pul is a second Babylonian name for the Assyrian king Tiglath-Pileser III (745–727 B.C.; 1 Chr. 5:26). Although he came to the throne as a usurper from the ranks of the military, he would prove a competent king. Under Tiglath-Pileser III and his successors, Assyria became the dominant power in the Middle East for well over a century (747–612 B.C.).

15:23 *Pekahiah.* Pekahiah means "The LORD has Opened the Eyes." After an evil reign of two years, a usurper "closed his eyes" for him.

15:25 Murder — Sometimes a corrupt leader needs to be taken out of power, but when this is done by coup and murder, the new leader ends up being just as bad as the old one. He lives in fear that someone will do the same thing to him; in an attempt to keep his position, he will exercise the same control and perpetrate the same kind of abuses as the leader he deposed. A vicious cycle is begun, as we can see from the succession of murders and new kings in Israel. Anytime leadership changes through conniving and coup, even if actual murder is not part of the picture, problems in trust and confidence will result.

15:7 [q] Isa 6:1; 14:28 [r] ver 5 **15:9** [s] 1Ki 15:26 **15:10** [t] 2Ki 12:20 **15:11** [u] 1Ki 15:31 **15:12** [v] 2Ki 10:30 **15:13** [w] ver 1,8 **15:14** [x] 1Ki 14:17 [y] 2Ki 12:20 **15:15** [z] 1Ki 15:31 **15:16** [a] 1Ki 4:24 [b] 2Ki 8:12; Hos 13:16 **15:19** [c] 1Ch 5:6,26 **15:20** [d] 2Ki 12:18 **15:25** [e] 2Ch 28:6; Isa 7:1 [f] 2Ki 12:20

26 The other events of Pekahiah's reign, and all he did, are written in the book of the annals of the kings of Israel.

Pekah King of Israel

27 In the fifty-second year of Azariah king of Judah, Pekah[g] son of Remaliah[h] became king of Israel in Samaria, and he reigned twenty years. 28 He did evil in the eyes of the LORD. He did not turn away from the sins of Jeroboam son of Nebat, which he had caused Israel to commit.

29 In the time of Pekah king of Israel, Tiglath-Pileser[i] king of Assyria came and took Ijon,[j] Abel Beth Maakah, Janoah, Kedesh and Hazor. He took Gilead and Galilee, including all the land of Naphtali,[k] and deported[l] the people to Assyria. 30 Then Hoshea[m] son of Elah conspired against Pekah son of Remaliah. He attacked and assassinated[n] him, and then succeeded him as king in the twentieth year of Jotham son of Uzziah.

31 As for the other events of Pekah's reign, and all he did, are they not written in the book of the annals of the kings of Israel?

Jotham King of Judah

32 In the second year of Pekah son of Remaliah king of Israel, Jotham[o] son of Uzziah king of Judah began to reign. 33 He was twenty-five years old when he became king, and he reigned in Jerusalem sixteen years. His mother's name was Jerusha daughter of Zadok. 34 He did what was right[p] in the eyes of the LORD, just as his father Uzziah had done. 35 The high places,[q] however, were not removed; the people continued to offer sacrifices and burn incense there. Jotham rebuilt the Upper Gate[r] of the temple of the LORD.

36 As for the other events of Jotham's reign, and what he did, are they not written in the book of the annals of the kings of Judah? 37 (In those days the LORD began to send Rezin[s] king of Aram and Pekah son of Remaliah against Judah.) 38 Jotham rested with his ancestors and was buried with them in the City of David, the city of his father. And Ahaz his son succeeded him as king.

Ahaz King of Judah

16 In the seventeenth year of Pekah son of Remaliah, Ahaz[t] son of Jotham king of Judah began to reign. 2 Ahaz was twenty years old when he became king, and he reigned in Jerusalem sixteen years. Unlike David his father, he did not do what was right[u] in the eyes of the LORD his God. 3 He followed the ways of the kings of Israel and even sacrificed his son[v] in the fire, engaging in the detestable[w] practices of the nations the LORD had driven out before the Israelites. 4 He offered sacrifices and burned incense at the high places, on the hilltops and under every spreading tree.[x]

5 Then Rezin[y] king of Aram and Pekah son of Remaliah king of Israel marched up to fight against Jerusalem and besieged Ahaz, but they could not overpower him. 6 At that time, Rezin[z] king of Aram recovered Elath[a] for Aram by driving out the people of Judah. Edomites then moved into Elath and have lived there to this day.

7 Ahaz sent messengers to say to Tiglath-Pileser[b] king of Assyria, "I am your servant and vassal. Come up and save[c] me out of the hand of the king of Aram and of the king of Israel, who are attacking me." 8 And Ahaz took the silver and gold found in the temple of the LORD and in the treasuries of the royal palace and sent it as a gift[d] to the king of Assyria. 9 The king of Assyria complied by attacking Damascus[e] and capturing it. He deported its inhabitants to Kir[f] and put Rezin to death.

15:27 *Pekah.* Because Hoshea's nine-year reign (17:1) began in 732 B.C., Pekah's twenty years must have included a time of kingship in his own district during the unsettled days of Shallum, Menahem, and Pekahiah (752–740 B.C.). Apparently Pekah rode the crest of anti-Assyrian sentiment.

15:30 *Hoshea ... conspired.* The annals of Tiglath-Pileser III record Hoshea's heavy tribute and the Assyrian king's claim that he himself set the new Israelite king in office.

15:32 *Jotham.* Jotham's reign was partly righteous. After the purge of Ahaziah and Athaliah (9:27–29; 11:13–16), the kings of Judah who reigned in relative righteousness were Joash (12:2–3), Amaziah (14:3–4), and Azariah (15:3–4). A positive righteousness would be modeled by Hezekiah (18:3–6) and again by Josiah (22:2).

16:1 *Ahaz ... began to reign.* The seventeenth year of Pekah was 736–735 B.C. Ahaz's 16 year reign apparently ended in 720 B.C. If so, like Jotham before him, Ahaz must have lived on another four years after giving up his rule. Hezekiah's first year of independent rule began in 715 B.C., 14 years before Sennacherib's invasion of Judah and his siege of Jerusalem in 701 B.C.

16:3 *sacrificed his son in the fire.* According to the author of Chronicles, this rite was connected with the Baal worship practiced in the Valley of Ben Hinnom (2 Chr. 28:2–3). Ahaz was an apostate who personally led his people in the religious worship practices of Canaan.

16:7 *sent messengers ... king of Assyria.* Tiglath-Pileser's records list the tribute of both Hoshea and Ahaz.

15:27 [g] 2Ch 28:6; Isa 7:1 [h] Isa 7:4 **15:29** [i] 2Ki 16:7; 17:6; 1Ch 5:26; 2Ch 28:20; Jer 50:17 [j] 1Ki 15:20 [k] 2Ki 16:9; 17:24; 2Ch 16:4; Isa 9:1 [l] 2Ki 24:14-16; 1Ch 5:22; Isa 14:6, 17; 36:17; 45:13 **15:30** [m] 2Ki 17:1 [n] 2Ki 12:20 **15:32** [o] 1Ch 5:17 **15:34** [p] ver 3; 1Ki 14:8; 2Ch 26:4-5 **15:35** [q] 2Ki 12:3 [r] 2Ch 23:20 **15:37** [s] 2Ki 16:5; Isa 7:1 **16:1** [t] Isa 1:1; 14:28 **16:2** [u] 1Ki 14:8 **16:3** [v] Lev 18:21; 2Ki 21:6 [w] Lev 18:3; Dt 9:4; 12:31 **16:4** [x] Dt 12:2; Eze 6:13 **16:5** [y] 2Ki 15:37; Isa 7:1, 4 **16:6** [z] Isa 9:12 [a] 2Ki 14:22; 2Ch 26:2 **16:7** [b] 2Ki 15:29 [c] Isa 2:6; Jer 2:18; Eze 16:28; Hos 10:6 **16:8** [d] 2Ki 12:18 **16:9** [e] 2Ki 15:29 [f] Isa 22:6; Am 1:5; 9:7

10Then King Ahaz went to Damascus
to meet Tiglath-Pileser king of Assyria.
He saw an altar in Damascus and sent
to Uriah[g] the priest a sketch of the altar,
with detailed plans for its construction.
11So Uriah the priest built an altar in accordance with all the plans that King Ahaz
had sent from Damascus and finished it
before King Ahaz returned. **12**When the
king came back from Damascus and saw
the altar, he approached it and presented
offerings[a][h] on it. **13**He offered up his burnt
offering[i] and grain offering, poured out his
drink offering, and splashed the blood of
his fellowship offerings[j] against the altar.
14As for the bronze altar[k] that stood before
the LORD, he brought it from the front of the
temple—from between the new altar and
the temple of the LORD—and put it on the
north side of the new altar.

15King Ahaz then gave these orders to
Uriah the priest: "On the large new altar,
offer the morning[l] burnt offering and the
evening grain offering, the king's burnt offering and his grain offering, and the burnt
offering of all the people of the land, and
their grain offering and their drink offering. Splash against this altar the blood of
all the burnt offerings and sacrifices. But I
will use the bronze altar for seeking guidance."[m] **16**And Uriah the priest did just as
King Ahaz had ordered.

17King Ahaz cut off the side panels
and removed the basins from the movable stands. He removed the Sea from the
bronze bulls that supported it and set it on
a stone base.[n] **18**He took away the Sabbath
canopy[b] that had been built at the temple
and removed the royal entryway outside
the temple of the LORD, in deference to the
king of Assyria.[o]

19As for the other events of the reign of
Ahaz, and what he did, are they not written in the book of the annals of the kings
of Judah? **20**Ahaz rested with his ancestors
and was buried with them in the City of David. And Hezekiah his son succeeded him
as king.

Hoshea Last King of Israel

17 In the twelfth year of Ahaz king of
Judah, Hoshea[p] son of Elah became
king of Israel in Samaria, and he reigned
nine years. **2**He did evil in the eyes of the
LORD, but not like the kings of Israel who
preceded him.

3Shalmaneser[q] king of Assyria came up
to attack Hoshea, who had been Shalmaneser's vassal and had paid him tribute. **4**But
the king of Assyria discovered that Hoshea
was a traitor, for he had sent envoys to So[c]
king of Egypt, and he no longer paid tribute
to the king of Assyria, as he had done year
by year. Therefore Shalmaneser seized
him and put him in prison. **5**The king of
Assyria invaded the entire land, marched
against Samaria and laid siege[r] to it for
three years. **6**In the ninth year of Hoshea,
the king of Assyria captured Samaria[s] and
deported[t] the Israelites to Assyria. He settled them in Halah, in Gozan[u] on the Habor
River and in the towns of the Medes.

Israel Exiled Because of Sin

7All this took place because the Israelites had sinned[v] against the LORD their
God, who had brought them up out of
Egypt[w] from under the power of Pharaoh
king of Egypt. They worshiped other gods
8and followed the practices of the nations[x]
the LORD had driven out before them, as
well as the practices that the kings of Israel had introduced. **9**The Israelites secretly did things against the LORD their God
that were not right. From watchtower to
fortified city[y] they built themselves high
places in all their towns. **10**They set up sacred stones and Asherah poles[z] on every
high hill and under every spreading tree.[a]
11At every high place they burned incense,
as the nations whom the LORD had driven
out before them had done. They did wicked things that aroused the LORD's anger.
12They worshiped idols,[b] though the LORD
had said, "You shall not do this."[d] **13**The

---

[a] 12 Or *and went up* [b] 18 Or *the dais of his throne* (see Septuagint) [c] 4 *So* is probably an abbreviation for *Osorkon.* [d] 12 Exodus 20:4,5

16:10–16 Vanity—The king of Israel was commanded to pattern his reign according to God's Word, but Ahaz apparently thought his own ideas were better. Once the Word of God has been set aside, there is no stopping point for presumptuous spirituality and immoral activities. Such practices may be aesthetically and humanly pleasing, but Jesus designated them as vain worship because they are based upon precepts and traditions of men, rather than on God's holy and sufficient Word (Matt. 15:7–9).

16:18 *the king of Assyria.* Ahaz was more interested in imitating the foreign king than in following God. His use of the altar to make sacrifices to God and his many other religious innovations underscored Ahaz's essential paganism (2 Chr. 28:2–4,22–25). He went so far in his apostasy as to shut the doors of the temple (2 Chr. 28:24).

17:1 *twelfth year.* Hoshea became king in 732 B.C., so the twelve years of Ahaz indicate a period of coregency with his father Jotham.

17:3 *Shalmaneser.* Shalmaneser V succeeded Tiglath-Pileser III as king of Assyria in 727 B.C.

17:7 *Israelites had sinned.* The reason for the fall of Samaria and the end of the northern kingdom was clearly its spiritual failure; they had turned away from the living God.

16:10 [g] Isa 8:2 **16:12** [h] 2Ch 26:16 **16:13** [i] Lev 6:8-13 [j] Lev 7:11-21 **16:14** [k] 2Ch 4:1 **16:15** [l] Ex 29:38-41 [m] 1Sa 9:9 **16:17** [n] 1Ki 7:27 **16:18** [o] Eze 16:28 **17:1** [p] 2Ki 15:30 **17:3** [q] 2Ki 18:9-12; Hos 10:14 **17:5** [r] Hos 13:16 **17:6** [s] Hos 13:16 [t] Dt 28:36,64; 2Ki 18:10-11 [u] 1Ch 5:26 **17:7** [v] Jos 23:16; Jdg 6:10 [w] Ex 14:15-31 **17:8** [x] Lev 18:3; Dt 18:9; 2Ki 16:3 **17:9** [y] 2Ki 18:8 **17:10** [z] Ex 34:13; Mic 5:14 [a] 1Ki 14:23 **17:12** [b] Ex 20:4

LORD warned Israel and Judah through all
his prophets and seers:[c] "Turn from your
evil ways.[d] Observe my commands and decrees, in accordance with the entire Law
that I commanded your ancestors to obey
and that I delivered to you through my servants the prophets."
14 But they would not listen and were as
stiff-necked[e] as their ancestors, who did
not trust in the LORD their God. 15 They
rejected his decrees and the covenant[f] he
had made with their ancestors and the
statutes he had warned them to keep. They
followed worthless idols[g] and themselves
became worthless. They imitated the nations[h] around them although the LORD had
ordered them, "Do not do as they do."
16 They forsook all the commands of the
LORD their God and made for themselves
two idols cast in the shape of calves,[i] and
an Asherah[j] pole. They bowed down to all
the starry hosts,[k] and they worshiped Baal.[l]
17 They sacrificed[m] their sons and daughters in the fire. They practiced divination
and sought omens[n] and sold[o] themselves
to do evil in the eyes of the LORD, arousing
his anger.
18 So the LORD was very angry with Israel and removed them from his presence.
Only the tribe of Judah was left, 19 and even
Judah did not keep the commands of the
LORD their God. They followed the practices Israel had introduced.[p] 20 Therefore the
LORD rejected all the people of Israel; he afflicted them and gave them into the hands
of plunderers,[q] until he thrust them from
his presence.
21 When he tore[r] Israel away from the
house of David, they made Jeroboam son of
Nebat their king.[s] Jeroboam enticed Israel
away from following the LORD and caused
them to commit a great sin. 22 The Israelites persisted in all the sins of Jeroboam
and did not turn away from them 23 until
the LORD removed them from his presence,
as he had warned through all his servants
the prophets. So the people of Israel were
taken from their homeland into exile in Assyria, and they are still there.

Samaria Resettled

24 The king of Assyria[t] brought people
from Babylon, Kuthah, Avva, Hamath and
Sepharvaim[u] and settled them in the towns
of Samaria to replace the Israelites. They
took over Samaria and lived in its towns.
25 When they first lived there, they did not
worship the LORD; so he sent lions[v] among
them and they killed some of the people.
26 It was reported to the king of Assyria:
"The people you deported and resettled in
the towns of Samaria do not know what the
god of that country requires. He has sent
lions among them, which are killing them
off, because the people do not know what
he requires."
27 Then the king of Assyria gave this order:
"Have one of the priests you took captive
from Samaria go back to live there and
teach the people what the god of the land requires." 28 So one of the priests who had been
exiled from Samaria came to live in Bethel
and taught them how to worship the LORD.
29 Nevertheless, each national group
made its own gods in the several towns[w]
where they settled, and set them up in the
shrines[x] the people of Samaria had made
at the high places.[y] 30 The people from

17:14–18 Israel's Disobedience—These verses are a good summary of the spiritual departure from God that led to Israel's eventual downfall. The people of Israel didn't listen and three specific results are recorded:

1. *The Israelites refused to believe.* All the fulfilled promises, all the history of God's saving acts were simply ignored. It didn't matter what God had done. They had ears to hear and eyes to see, yet failed to do so.
2. *They rejected God's laws and covenant.* They willfully turned their backs on the way of living that God had directed them toward.
3. *They worshiped idols.* They actually worshiped anything and everything but what they were instructed to worship. In spite of God's clear mandate to them to have no other gods before Him, the Israelites were easily influenced by any culture they came in contact with.

The common denominator here is the will. This was willful rebellion. We are no different. Every day each of us, by an act of our own will, does something disobedient. We worry unnecessarily, we have fears for aspects of our lives that we know God has promised to protect and care for. Sometimes we simply don't care what God has said. We'd rather do what we want because it feels good or because His way is too difficult. We are truly sinners in need of a forgiving God.

17:21 *Jeroboam enticed Israel away from following the LORD.* Jeroboam had initiated the false worship that set the standard for all of Israel's idolatrous activities. The worship of the calves at Dan and Bethel, and Israel's fascination with Baal worship (1 Kin. 12:28–29; 16:32–33), are repeatedly cited as the chief causes of Israel's spiritual defeat and political collapse.

17:24 *king of Assyria.* This was probably Sargon II (722–705 B.C.), although the practice described here was continued by later kings as well. Such a mixing of populations was designed to break down ethnic distinctions and weaken the loyalties that the people had. It would also help create a sense of empire. Samaria. This was the whole region where the repopulation took place; eventually the inhabitants would be called Samaritans.

17:13 [c] 1Sa 9:9 [d] Jer 18:11; 25:5; 35:15 **17:14** [e] Ex 32:9; Dt 31:27; Ac 7:51 **17:15** [f] Dt 29:25 [g] Dt 32:21; Ro 1:21-23 [h] Dt 12:30-31 **17:16** [i] 1Ki 12:28 [j] 1Ki 14:15,23 [k] 2Ki 21:3 [l] 1Ki 16:31 **17:17** [m] Dt 18:10-12; 2Ki 16:3 [n] Lev 19:26 [o] 1Ki 21:20 **17:19** [p] 1Ki 14:22-23; 2Ki 16:3 **17:20** [q] 2Ki 15:29 **17:21** [r] 1Ki 11:11 [s] 1Ki 12:20 **17:24** [t] Ezr 4:2,10 [u] 2Ki 18:34 **17:25** [v] Ge 37:20 **17:29** [w] Jer 2:28 [x] 1Ki 12:31 [y] Mic 4:5

Babylon made Sukkoth Benoth, those from
Kuthah made Nergal, and those from Hamath made Ashima; 31the Avvites made
Nibhaz and Tartak, and the Sepharvites
burned their children in the fire as sacrifices to Adrammelek[z] and Anammelek, the
gods of Sepharvaim.[a] 32They worshiped
the LORD, but they also appointed all sorts[b]
of their own people to officiate for them as
priests in the shrines at the high places.
33They worshiped the LORD, but they also
served their own gods in accordance with
the customs of the nations from which they
had been brought.

34To this day they persist in their former
practices. They neither worship the LORD
nor adhere to the decrees and regulations,
the laws and commands that the LORD gave
the descendants of Jacob, whom he named
Israel.[c] 35When the LORD made a covenant
with the Israelites, he commanded them:
"Do not worship[d] any other gods or bow
down to them, serve them or sacrifice to
them. 36But the LORD, who brought you up
out of Egypt with mighty power and outstretched arm,[e] is the one you must worship.
To him you shall bow down and to him offer sacrifices. 37You must always be careful[f] to keep the decrees and regulations, the
laws and commands he wrote for you. Do
not worship other gods. 38Do not forget[g] the
covenant I have made with you, and do not
worship other gods. 39Rather, worship the
LORD your God; it is he who will deliver you
from the hand of all your enemies."

40They would not listen, however, but
persisted in their former practices. 41Even
while these people were worshiping the
LORD,[h] they were serving their idols. To
this day their children and grandchildren
continue to do as their ancestors did.

Hezekiah King of Judah

18 In the third year of Hoshea son of
Elah king of Israel, Hezekiah[i] son of
Ahaz king of Judah began to reign. 2He
was twenty-five years old when he became
king, and he reigned in Jerusalem twenty-
nine years.[j] His mother's name was Abijah[a] daughter of Zechariah. 3He did what
was right in the eyes of the LORD, just as his
father David[k] had done. 4He removed[l] the
high places, smashed the sacred stones[m]
and cut down the Asherah poles. He broke
into pieces the bronze snake[n] Moses had
made, for up to that time the Israelites had
been burning incense to it. (It was called
Nehushtan.[b])

5Hezekiah trusted[o] in the LORD, the God
of Israel. There was no one like him among
all the kings of Judah, either before him or
after him. 6He held fast[p] to the LORD and
did not stop following him; he kept the
commands the LORD had given Moses.
7And the LORD was with him; he was successful[q] in whatever he undertook. He rebelled[r] against the king of Assyria and did
not serve him. 8From watchtower to fortified city,[s] he defeated the Philistines, as far
as Gaza and its territory.

9In King Hezekiah's fourth year,[t] which
was the seventh year of Hoshea son of Elah
king of Israel, Shalmaneser king of Assyria marched against Samaria and laid siege
to it. 10At the end of three years the Assyrians took it. So Samaria was captured in
Hezekiah's sixth year, which was the ninth
year of Hoshea king of Israel. 11The king[u]
of Assyria deported Israel to Assyria and

---

[a] 2 Hebrew *Abi*, a variant of *Abijah*
[b] 4 *Nehushtan* sounds like the Hebrew for both *bronze* and *snake*.

17:33 *worshiped the LORD, but they also served their own gods.* This is the classic example of syncretism, the attempt to mix the worship of the true God with other religious traditions and beliefs. The apostate religion of the people of Samaria caused them to be rejected by the faithful Jews who returned from the Exile (Ezra 4:1–5), and by the time of the New Testament, hostility was very strong between the two groups (John 4:9; 8:48).

18:1 *the third year of Hoshea.* The 29 years of Hezekiah's reign thus included a period of coregency with his father Ahaz before he ruled independently (715–699 B.C.). The name Hezekiah means "The LORD Has Strengthened."

18:3 *He did what was right in the eyes of the LORD.* Hezekiah was the first king since David who served the Lord with all his heart.

18:4 *high places.* Consistently, the kings who preceded Hezekiah are criticized by the author for not destroying the high places (15:34–35). While there were traditions of worship of the true God at these locations, far too often they became sites for the licentious worship of Baal and Asherah. Hezekiah's reforms included not only the destruction of the pagan cult objects introduced in the days of his apostate father Ahaz, but the bronze serpent that had been preserved since the days of Moses (2 Chr. 29–31). Symbols all too easily can be made into objects of veneration.

18:5 *no one like him.* Hezekiah's faith was unparalleled by any other king who had preceded him after the time of David; Josiah's adherence to the law would be extolled in a similar manner (23:25).

18:6 Obedience—The obedience of Hezekiah provides a powerful lesson for all of God's people. He "clung" to the Lord, staying true to God and His commandments. He must have faced strong opposition as he eliminated practices which had been going on for generations, and destroyed objects which had long been considered sacred, but he knew that God's approval was more important than human approbation. In the same way, we must be willing to serve God before we please those around us.

17:31 [z] 2Ki 19:37 [a] ver 24 **17:32** [b] 1Ki 12:31 **17:34** [c] Ge 32:28; 35:10; 1Ki 18:31 **17:35** [d] Ex 20:5; Jdg 6:10 **17:36** [e] Ex 3:20; 6:6; Ps 136:12 **17:37** [f] Dt 5:32 **17:38** [g] Dt 4:23; 6:12 **17:41** [h] ver 32-33; 1Ki 18:21; Mt 6:24 **18:1** [i] Isa 1:1; 2Ch 28:27 **18:2** [j] Isa 38:5 **18:3** [k] Isa 38:5 **18:4** [l] 2Ch 31:1 [m] Ex 23:24 [n] Nu 21:9 **18:5** [o] 2Ki 19:10; 23:25 **18:6** [p] Dt 10:20; Jos 23:8 **18:7** [q] Ge 39:3; 1Sa 18:14 [r] 2Ki 16:7 **18:8** [s] 2Ki 17:9; Isa 14:29 **18:9** [t] Isa 1:1 **18:11** [u] Isa 37:12

settled them in Halah, in Gozan on the Habor River and in towns of the Medes. 12This
happened because they had not obeyed the
LORD their God, but had violated his covenant[v]—all that Moses the servant of the
LORD commanded.[w] They neither listened
to the commands[x] nor carried them out.
13In the fourteenth year of King Hezekiah's reign, Sennacherib king of Assyria
attacked all the fortified cities of Judah[y]
and captured them. 14So Hezekiah king
of Judah sent this message to the king of
Assyria at Lachish: "I have done wrong.[z]
Withdraw from me, and I will pay whatever you demand of me." The king of Assyria exacted from Hezekiah king of Judah
three hundred talents[a] of silver and thirty
talents[b] of gold. 15So Hezekiah gave[a] him
all the silver that was found in the temple
of the LORD and in the treasuries of the royal palace.
16At this time Hezekiah king of Judah
stripped off the gold with which he had
covered the doors and doorposts of the
temple of the LORD, and gave it to the king
of Assyria.

Sennacherib Threatens Jerusalem

17The king of Assyria sent his supreme
commander,[b] his chief officer and his field
commander with a large army, from Lachish to King Hezekiah at Jerusalem. They
came up to Jerusalem and stopped at the
aqueduct of the Upper Pool,[c] on the road to
the Washerman's Field. 18They called for
the king; and Eliakim[d] son of Hilkiah the
palace administrator, Shebna[e] the secretary, and Joah son of Asaph the recorder
went out to them.
19The field commander said to them,
"Tell Hezekiah:

"'This is what the great king, the
king of Assyria, says: On what are
you basing this confidence of yours?
20You say you have the counsel and
the might for war—but you speak
only empty words. On whom are you
depending, that you rebel against me?
21Look, I know you are depending on
Egypt,[f] that splintered reed of a staff,[g]
which pierces the hand of anyone who
leans on it! Such is Pharaoh king of
Egypt to all who depend on him. 22But
if you say to me, "We are depending on
the LORD our God"—isn't he the one
whose high places and altars Hezekiah removed, saying to Judah and Jerusalem, "You must worship before this
altar in Jerusalem"?
23"'Come now, make a bargain with
my master, the king of Assyria: I will
give you two thousand horses—if you
can put riders on them! 24How can you
repulse one officer[h] of the least of my
master's officials, even though you
are depending on Egypt for chariots
and horsemen[c]? 25Furthermore, have
I come to attack and destroy this place
without word from the LORD?[i] The
LORD himself told me to march against
this country and destroy it.'"

26Then Eliakim son of Hilkiah, and
Shebna and Joah said to the field commander, "Please speak to your servants
in Aramaic,[j] since we understand it. Don't
speak to us in Hebrew in the hearing of the
people on the wall."
27But the commander replied, "Was it
only to your master and you that my master sent me to say these things, and not to
the people sitting on the wall—who, like
you, will have to eat their own excrement
and drink their own urine?"
28Then the commander stood and called
out in Hebrew, "Hear the word of the great
king, the king of Assyria! 29This is what
the king says: Do not let Hezekiah deceive[k]
you. He cannot deliver you from my hand.

[a] *14* That is, about 11 tons or about 10 metric tons
[b] *14* That is, about 1 ton or about 1 metric ton
[c] *24* Or *charioteers*

18:13 *fourteenth year.* Hezekiah's fourteenth year of sole rule was 701 B.C. The details of the generally rebellious situation that provoked Sennacherib to invade the western portion of his empire are recounted in his annals, where Hezekiah is particularly mentioned for his involvement in the whole affair.

18:17 *supreme commander ... chief officer ... field commander.* These titles suggest persons of high station in Assyria.

18:20 *On whom are you depending?* Perhaps Hezekiah's reputation for trusting in God was already widely known (v. 5). Trusting became the focal point of the Assyrian's psychological warfare (vv. 19–22,24–30).

18:21 *splintered reed.* Actually, Sennacherib's warning against confidence in Egypt was well taken, the point having been made previously by Isaiah (Is. 30:3–5; 31:1–3).

18:25 *The LORD himself told me.* The Assyrians may have been aware of prophecies concerning the judgment of Judah and Jerusalem and Assyria's own role as God's avengers (Is. 10:5–11). The remark was intended to introduce stark terror into the hearts of the people of Jerusalem (2 Chr. 32:18) by pointing out that now even their God was against them.

18:25 Self-Righteousness—The Assyrians were God's instrument for punishing Israel (Is. 10:5–10), but this fact was not due to any righteousness or virtue on Assyria's part. Rather, their attitude was blasphemous and proud (19:22). The lesson for the powerful king of Assyria is the lesson for kings, nations, and all individuals: no one may boast before the Lord (1 Cor. 1:29).

18:12 [v] 2Ki 17:15 [w] Da 9:6,10 [x] 1Ki 9:6 **18:13** [y] 2Ch 32:1; Isa 1:7; Mic 1:9 **18:14** [z] Isa 24:5 **18:15** [a] 1Ki 15:18; 2Ki 16:8 **18:17** [b] Isa 20:1 [c] 2Ki 20:20; 2Ch 32:4,30; Isa 7:3 **18:18** [d] 2Ki 19:2; Isa 22:20 [e] Isa 22:15 **18:21** [f] Isa 20:5; Eze 29:6 [g] Isa 30:5,7 **18:24** [h] Isa 10:8 **18:25** [i] 2Ki 19:6, 22 **18:26** [j] Ezr 4:7 **18:29** [k] 2Ki 19:10

30 Do not let Hezekiah persuade you to trust
in the LORD when he says, 'The LORD will
surely deliver us; this city will not be given
into the hand of the king of Assyria.'
31 "Do not listen to Hezekiah. This is
what the king of Assyria says: Make peace
with me and come out to me. Then each of
you will eat fruit from your own vine and
fig tree[l] and drink water from your own
cistern,[m] 32 until I come and take you to a
land like your own—a land of grain and
new wine, a land of bread and vineyards, a
land of olive trees and honey. Choose life[n]
and not death!
"Do not listen to Hezekiah, for he is
misleading you when he says, 'The LORD
will deliver us.' 33 Has the god[o] of any nation ever delivered his land from the hand
of the king of Assyria? 34 Where are the
gods of Hamath[p] and Arpad?[q] Where are
the gods of Sepharvaim, Hena and Ivvah?
Have they rescued Samaria from my hand?
35 Who of all the gods of these countries has
been able to save his land from me? How
then can the LORD deliver Jerusalem from
my hand?"[r]
36 But the people remained silent and
said nothing in reply, because the king had
commanded, "Do not answer him."
37 Then Eliakim son of Hilkiah the palace administrator, Shebna the secretary,
and Joah son of Asaph the recorder went to
Hezekiah, with their clothes torn,[s] and told
him what the field commander had said.

Jerusalem's Deliverance Foretold

19 When King Hezekiah heard this,
he tore[t] his clothes and put on sackcloth and went into the temple of the LORD.
2 He sent Eliakim the palace administrator, Shebna the secretary and the leading
priests, all wearing sackcloth, to the prophet Isaiah[u] son of Amoz. 3 They told him,
"This is what Hezekiah says: This day is a
day of distress and rebuke and disgrace, as
when children come to the moment of birth
and there is no strength to deliver them. 4 It
may be that the LORD your God will hear all
the words of the field commander, whom
his master, the king of Assyria, has sent
to ridicule[v] the living God, and that he will
rebuke[w] him for the words the LORD your
God has heard. Therefore pray for the remnant that still survives."
5 When King Hezekiah's officials came
to Isaiah, 6 Isaiah said to them, "Tell your
master, 'This is what the LORD says: Do not
be afraid of what you have heard—those
words with which the underlings of the
king of Assyria have blasphemed[x] me.
7 Listen! When he hears a certain report, I
will make him want to return to his own
country, and there I will have him cut down
with the sword.[y]' "
8 When the field commander heard that
the king of Assyria had left Lachish,[z] he
withdrew and found the king fighting
against Libnah.
9 Now Sennacherib received a report that
Tirhakah, the king of Cush,[a] was marching
out to fight against him. So he again sent
messengers to Hezekiah with this word:
10 "Say to Hezekiah king of Judah: Do not
let the god you depend[a] on deceive[b] you
when he says, 'Jerusalem will not be giv-
en into the hands of the king of Assyria.'
11 Surely you have heard what the kings
of Assyria have done to all the countries,
destroying them completely. And will you
be delivered? 12 Did the gods of the nations
that were destroyed by my predecessors
deliver[c] them—the gods of Gozan,[d] Harran,[e] Rezeph and the people of Eden who
were in Tel Assar? 13 Where is the king of
Hamath or the king of Arpad? Where are
the kings of Lair, Sepharvaim, Hena and
Ivvah?"[f]

[a] 9 That is, the upper Nile region

18:33 *the god of any nation.* The field commander's assertion that none of the gods of the nations who had opposed Assyria had withstood the Assyrian king is another aspect of the continued psychological warfare and evidence of the field commander's awareness of Isaiah's prophetic words (Is. 10:7 – 11).

19:2 *Isaiah.* The ministry of the great prophet Isaiah had begun in the year that Uzziah (or Azariah) died (Is. 6:1), nearly four decades earlier (740 B.C.). Once Isaiah had sought out Judah's godless King Ahaz to minister to him (Is. 7:3); now the prophet was being sought by the godly Hezekiah (the details of 18:13—20:19 are also recorded in Is. 36 – 39).

19:4 *hear ... rebuke.* The first verb does not suggest that God is unaware of the words of the field commander. Rather, the words describe God as determining to redress the wrong.

19:6 *Do not be afraid.* Isaiah's prophecy was one of comfort. Not only would Sennacherib fail to conquer Jerusalem, but he would face a violent death upon his return home. Both points of this prophetic message would come true, although Sennacherib was not assassinated until 20 years later (c. 681 B.C.). In his annals Sennacherib boasts of five more campaigns; however, he makes no mention of any other invasions of Judah.

19:9 *Tirhakah, the king of Cush.* Since Tirhakah did not become king until 690 B.C., there is an apparent problem with the chronology of this verse. However, it is possible that the biblical author merely calls Tirhakah by the title he was best known by at the time of writing.

19:12 *Eden.* This is not the Eden of Genesis, but an area known today as Bit-Adini, south of Haran (Ezek. 27:23; Amos 1:5).

18:31 [l] Nu 13:23; 1Ki 4:25 [m] Jer 14:3; La 4:4
18:32 [n] Dt 8:7-9; 30:19 **18:33** [o] 2Ki 19:12; Isa 10:10-11
18:34 [p] 2Ki 17:24; 19:13 [q] Isa 10:9 **18:35** [r] Ps 2:1-2
18:37 [s] 2Ki 6:30 **19:1** [t] Ge 37:34; 1Ki 21:27; 2Ch 32:20-22
19:2 [u] Isa 1:1 **19:4** [v] 2Ki 18:35 [w] 2Sa 16:12
19:6 [x] 2Ki 18:25 **19:7** [y] ver 37 **19:8** [z] 2Ki 18:14
19:10 [a] 2Ki 18:5 [b] 2Ki 18:29 **19:12** [c] 2Ki 18:33 [d] 2Ki 17:6
[e] Ge 11:31 **19:13** [f] 2Ki 18:34

Hezekiah's Prayer

14Hezekiah received the letter from the
messengers and read it. Then he went up
to the temple of the LORD and spread it out
before the LORD. 15And Hezekiah prayed
to the LORD: "LORD, the God of Israel, enthroned between the cherubim,[g] you alone
are God over all the kingdoms of the earth.
You have made heaven and earth. 16Give
ear,[h] LORD, and hear;[i] open your eyes,[j]
LORD, and see; listen to the words Sennacherib has sent to ridicule the living God.

17"It is true, LORD, that the Assyrian
kings have laid waste these nations and
their lands. 18They have thrown their gods
into the fire and destroyed them, for they
were not gods[k] but only wood and stone,
fashioned by human hands.[l] 19Now, LORD
our God, deliver us from his hand, so that
all the kingdoms[m] of the earth may know[n]
that you alone, LORD, are God."

Isaiah Prophesies Sennacherib's Fall

20Then Isaiah son of Amoz sent a message to Hezekiah: "This is what the LORD,
the God of Israel, says: I have heard[o] your
prayer concerning Sennacherib king of
Assyria. 21This is the word that the LORD
has spoken against him:

"'Virgin Daughter[p] Zion
despises you and mocks[q] you.
Daughter Jerusalem
tosses her head[r] as you flee.
22 Who is it you have ridiculed and
blasphemed?
Against whom have you raised your
voice
and lifted your eyes in pride?
Against the Holy One[s] of Israel!
23 By your messengers
you have ridiculed the Lord.
And you have said,[t]
"With my many chariots[u]
I have ascended the heights of the
mountains,
the utmost heights of Lebanon.
I have cut down its tallest cedars,
the choicest of its junipers.
I have reached its remotest parts,
the finest of its forests.
24 I have dug wells in foreign lands
and drunk the water there.
With the soles of my feet
I have dried up all the streams of
Egypt."

25 "'Have you not heard?[v]
Long ago I ordained it.
In days of old I planned[w] it;
now I have brought it to pass,
that you have turned fortified cities
into piles of stone.[x]
26 Their people, drained of power,
are dismayed[y] and put to shame.
They are like plants in the field,
like tender green shoots,[z]
like grass sprouting on the roof,
scorched[a] before it grows up.

27 "'But I know[b] where you are
and when you come and go
and how you rage against me.
28 Because you rage against me
and because your insolence has
reached my ears,
I will put my hook[c] in your nose
and my bit[d] in your mouth,
and I will make you return[e]
by the way you came.'

29"This will be the sign[f] for you, Hezekiah:

"This year you will eat what grows by
itself,[g]
and the second year what springs
from that.
But in the third year sow and reap,
plant vineyards[h] and eat their fruit.
30 Once more a remnant of the kingdom of
Judah
will take root[i] below and bear fruit
above.
31 For out of Jerusalem will come a
remnant,
and out of Mount Zion a band of
survivors.

19:15 ***You have made heaven and earth.*** The conflict mentioned in this chapter involves far more than the kings of Egypt, Assyria, or Judah. The warfare is one in which the gods of the pagan world would dishonor the true and living God of Israel. Hezekiah's prayer was addressed to the God who alone is sovereign over all the kingdoms of the world. His sovereignty is related to the fact of creation; He is the God who made heaven and earth. The heathen gods are born in corrupted human imaginations, and backed by a rebellious angel (Satan), but God is the one who owns and controls the universe.

19:21 ***Daughter Zion.*** As elsewhere in the OT (Zeph. 3:14) note that this phrase is written "daughter Zion," without the "of." Zion (Jerusalem) is like a daughter to God, who He will protect and guard only as a father would.

19:22 ***Holy One of Israel.*** This title is characteristic of Isaiah's own manner of referring to God. He uses the phrase 26 times (Is. 6:3). Sennacherib needed to know that his boastful pride blasphemed the sovereign and holy God of all nations.

19:30 ***remnant . . . will take root.*** The promises in these verses were both for the immediate situation and ultimately for the final regathering of the Jewish people into their land in the time of the coming Messiah.

19:15 [g] Ex 25:22 **19:16** [h] Ps 31:2 [i] 1Ki 8:29 [j] ver 4; 2Ch 6:40 **19:18** [k] Isa 44:9-11; Jer 10:3-10 [l] Ps 115:4; Ac 17:29 **19:19** [m] 1Ki 8:43 [n] Ps 83:18 **19:20** [o] 2Ki 20:5 **19:21** [p] Jer 14:17; La 2:13 [q] Ps 22:7-8 [r] Job 16:4; Ps 109:25 **19:22** [s] Ps 71:22; Isa 5:24 **19:23** [t] Isa 10:18 [u] Ps 20:7 **19:25** [v] Isa 40:21,28 [w] Isa 10:5; 45:7 [x] Mic 1:6 **19:26** [y] Ps 6:10 [z] Isa 4:2 [a] Ps 129:6 **19:27** [b] Ps 139:1-4 **19:28** [c] Eze 19:9; 29:4 [d] Isa 30:28 [e] ver 33 **19:29** [f] 2Ki 20:8-9; Lk 2:12 [g] Lev 25:5 [h] Ps 107:37 **19:30** [i] 2Ch 32:22-23

"The zeal[j] of the LORD Almighty will accomplish this.

32"Therefore this is what the LORD says
concerning the king of Assyria:

"'He will not enter this city
or shoot an arrow here.
He will not come before it with shield
or build a siege ramp against it.
33 By the way that he came he will return;[k]
he will not enter this city,
declares the LORD.
34 I will defend[l] this city and save it,
for my sake and for the sake of
David[m] my servant.'"

35That night the angel of the LORD[n]
went out and put to death a hundred and
eighty-five thousand in the Assyrian camp.
When the people got up the next morning—there were all the dead bodies![o] 36So
Sennacherib king of Assyria broke camp
and withdrew. He returned to Nineveh[p]
and stayed there.
37One day, while he was worshiping
in the temple of his god Nisrok, his sons
Adrammelek and Sharezer killed him with
the sword,[q] and they escaped to the land of
Ararat.[r] And Esarhaddon[s] his son succeeded him as king.

Hezekiah's Illness

20 In those days Hezekiah became ill
and was at the point of death. The
prophet Isaiah son of Amoz went to him
and said, "This is what the LORD says: Put
your house in order, because you are going
to die; you will not recover."
2Hezekiah turned his face to the wall
and prayed to the LORD, 3"Remember,[t]
LORD, how I have walked before you faithfully[u] and with wholehearted devotion and
have done what is good in your eyes." And
Hezekiah wept bitterly.
4Before Isaiah had left the middle court,
the word of the LORD came to him: 5"Go
back and tell Hezekiah, the ruler of my
people, 'This is what the LORD, the God of
your father David, says: I have heard[v] your
prayer and seen your tears;[w] I will heal you.
On the third day from now you will go up
to the temple of the LORD. 6I will add fifteen
years to your life. And I will deliver you
and this city from the hand of the king of
Assyria. I will defend[x] this city for my sake
and for the sake of my servant David.'"
7Then Isaiah said, "Prepare a poultice of
figs." They did so and applied it to the boil,[y]
and he recovered.
8Hezekiah had asked Isaiah, "What will
be the sign that the LORD will heal me and
that I will go up to the temple of the LORD
on the third day from now?"
9Isaiah answered, "This is the LORD's
sign[z] to you that the LORD will do what he
has promised: Shall the shadow go forward
ten steps, or shall it go back ten steps?"
10"It is a simple matter for the shadow
to go forward ten steps," said Hezekiah.
"Rather, have it go back ten steps."
11Then the prophet Isaiah called on the
LORD, and the LORD made the shadow go
back[a] the ten steps it had gone down on the
stairway of Ahaz.

Envoys From Babylon

12At that time Marduk-Baladan son of
Baladan king of Babylon sent Hezekiah
letters and a gift, because he had heard of
Hezekiah's illness. 13Hezekiah received the
envoys and showed them all that was in his
storehouses—the silver, the gold, the spices
and the fine olive oil—his armory and everything found among his treasures. There
was nothing in his palace or in all his kingdom that Hezekiah did not show them.
14Then Isaiah the prophet went to King
Hezekiah and asked, "What did those men
say, and where did they come from?"
"From a distant land," Hezekiah replied.
"They came from Babylon."
15The prophet asked, "What did they see
in your palace?"

19:32 *not enter this city.* While Sennacherib later boasted of taking some 46 Judean cities, with reference to Jerusalem he could only report that he made Hezekiah "prisoner in Jerusalem, his royal residence, like a bird in a cage." God's defense and deliverance of Jerusalem demonstrated His faithfulness to the Davidic covenant.

19:37 *killed him with the sword.* The events depicted here took place 20 years after God's deliverance of Jerusalem. When his father was assassinated, Esarhaddon took the throne and ruled from 681 to 668 B.C.

20:3 *I have walked before you.* Hezekiah's prayer recognized that although all of life is in God's hands, God is also a rewarder of those who faithfully serve Him (Deut. 5:30–33; 30:15–16).

20:7 *poultice of figs.* The practice of applying figs to an ulcerated sore is well attested in the records of the ancient Middle East, being mentioned as early as 2000 B.C.

20:12 *Marduk-Baladan.* This was a Chaldean king who twice ruled in Babylon (721–710, 703 B.C.). A perennial enemy of Assyria, he was twice defeated by them and cast out from Babylon. His search for allies in his resistance to Assyria may have occasioned the embassy to Hezekiah, especially because he had heard of Hezekiah's miraculous deliverance from the Assyrian army (2 Chr. 32:31).

20:13 *showed them all that was in his storehouses.* One of the remarkable features of the Bible is the fact that it does not gloss over the faults of its best heroes and heroines. This account of the foolishness of Hezekiah follows immediately on the narrative of his great trust in the Lord (vv. 1–11).

19:31 [j] Isa 9:7 **19:33** [k] ver 28 **19:34** [l] 2Ki 20:6 [m] 1Ki 11:12-13 **19:35** [n] Ex 12:23 [o] Job 24:24 **19:36** [p] Ge 10:11; Jnh 1:2 **19:37** [q] ver 7 [r] Ge 8:4 [s] Ezr 4:2 **20:3** [t] Ne 13:22 [u] 2Ki 18:3-6 **20:5** [v] 1Sa 9:16; 1Ki 9:3; 2Ki 19:20 [w] Ps 39:12; 56:8 **20:6** [x] 2Ki 19:34 **20:7** [y] Isa 38:21 **20:9** [z] Dt 13:2; Jer 44:29 **20:11** [a] Jos 10:13

"They saw everything in my palace,"
Hezekiah said. "There is nothing among
my treasures that I did not show them."
16Then Isaiah said to Hezekiah, "Hear
the word of the LORD: 17The time will surely come when everything in your palace,
and all that your predecessors have stored
up until this day, will be carried off to Babylon.[b] Nothing will be left, says the LORD.
18And some of your descendants,[c] your
own flesh and blood who will be born to
you, will be taken away, and they will become eunuchs in the palace of the king of
Babylon."
19"The word of the LORD you have spoken is good," Hezekiah replied. For he
thought, "Will there not be peace and security in my lifetime?"
20As for the other events of Hezekiah's
reign, all his achievements and how he
made the pool[d] and the tunnel by which
he brought water into the city, are they not
written in the book of the annals of the
kings of Judah? 21Hezekiah rested with his
ancestors. And Manasseh his son succeeded him as king.

Manasseh King of Judah

21 Manasseh was twelve years old when
he became king, and he reigned in
Jerusalem fifty-five years. His mother's
name was Hephzibah.[e] 2He did evil[f] in
the eyes of the LORD, following the detestable practices[g] of the nations the LORD had
driven out before the Israelites. 3He rebuilt
the high places[h] his father Hezekiah had
destroyed; he also erected altars to Baal[i]
and made an Asherah pole, as Ahab king
of Israel had done. He bowed down to all
the starry hosts[j] and worshiped them. 4He
built altars[k] in the temple of the LORD, of
which the LORD had said, "In Jerusalem
I will put my Name."[l] 5In the two courts[m]
of the temple of the LORD, he built altars
to all the starry hosts. 6He sacrificed his
own son[n] in the fire, practiced divination,
sought omens, and consulted mediums and
spiritists.[o] He did much evil in the eyes of
the LORD, arousing his anger.
7He took the carved Asherah pole[p] he
had made and put it in the temple, of which
the LORD had said to David and to his son
Solomon, "In this temple and in Jerusalem,
which I have chosen out of all the tribes of
Israel, I will put my Name[q] forever. 8I will
not again[r] make the feet of the Israelites
wander from the land I gave their ancestors, if only they will be careful to do everything I commanded them and will keep
the whole Law that my servant Moses[s]
gave them." 9But the people did not listen.
Manasseh led them astray, so that they did
more evil[t] than the nations[u] the LORD had
destroyed before the Israelites.
10The LORD said through his servants the
prophets: 11"Manasseh king of Judah has
committed these detestable sins. He has
done more evil[v] than the Amorites[w] who
preceded him and has led Judah into sin
with his idols. 12Therefore this is what the
LORD, the God of Israel, says: I am going
to bring such disaster[x] on Jerusalem and
Judah that the ears of everyone who hears
of it will tingle.[y] 13I will stretch out over Jerusalem the measuring line used against
Samaria and the plumb line[z] used against
the house of Ahab. I will wipe[a] out Jerusalem as one wipes a dish, wiping it and
turning it upside down. 14I will forsake[b] the
remnant[c] of my inheritance and give them
into the hands of enemies. They will be
looted and plundered by all their enemies;

20:16–18 Vanity—How much better for Israel's welfare if Hezekiah had been interested in introducing the Babylonian envoys to his God rather than to the treasures of the nation. The prophet's rebuke confirms that Hezekiah's action arose from a vain desire to impress the Babylonians with the externals of his kingdom. Human pride, and the vain hope that deliverance will come from man, must be forsaken if God's blessing is to be experienced.

20:19 *The word of the LORD . . . is good.* Hezekiah's response seems a little heartless. He did verbally acknowledge God's right to decide, but it does not appear that he had any real sense of the trouble his folly would bring on the people.

20:20 *the pool and the tunnel.* Hezekiah dug a tunnel between the spring of Gihon and the Pool of Siloam to bring a ready supply of water within the eastern wall of Jerusalem. This tunnel is still in existence, a crooked shaft 1,750 feet long.

21:1 *Manasseh.* This wicked king's fifty-five year reign was the longest of any of the kings of the divided kingdom. Externally, the period was one of political stability. It is known as the Assyrian Peace, an era in which the kings Esarhaddon (681–668 B.C.) and Ashurbanipal (668–626 B.C.) reigned and brought the Assyrian Empire to its zenith. However, the length of Manasseh's reign does not indicate a good rule, but rather God's persevering mercy and faithfulness to the Davidic covenant (2 Chr. 33:10–13).

21:3 *starry hosts.* Worship of heavenly bodies was strictly forbidden (Deut. 4:19; 17:2–7) and was condemned strongly by Israel's prophets (Is. 47:13; Amos 5:26). Yet Manasseh paid no attention to either the law or the prophets (2 Chr. 33:2–10).

21:4 *altars in the temple of the LORD.* All that had been accomplished by the godly kings of Judah was undone by this reprobate. But wicked as Manasseh was, God heard his prayer when he repented (2 Chr. 33:12–16).

20:17 [b] 2Ki 24:13; 25:13; 2Ch 36:10; Jer 27:22; 52:17-23
20:18 [c] 2Ki 24:15; 2Ch 33:11; Da 1:3 **20:20** [d] Ne 3:16
21:1 [e] Isa 62:4 **21:2** [f] Jer 15:4 [g] 2Ki 16:3 **21:3** [h] 2Ki 18:4
[i] Jdg 6:28; 1Ki 16:32 [j] Dt 17:3; 2Ki 17:16 **21:4** [k] Jer 32:34
[l] 2Sa 7:13; 1Ki 8:29 **21:5** [m] 1Ki 7:12; 2Ki 23:12
21:6 [n] Lev 18:21; Dt 18:10; 2Ki 16:3; 17:17 [o] Lev 19:31
21:7 [p] Dt 16:21; 2Ki 23:4 [q] 2Sa 7:13; 1Ki 8:29; 9:3; 2Ki 23:27;
Jer 32:34 **21:8** [r] 2Sa 7:10 [s] 2Ki 18:12 **21:9** [t] Pr 29:12
[u] Dt 9:4 **21:11** [v] 2Ki 24:3-4 [w] Ge 15:16; 1Ki 21:26
21:12 [x] 2Ki 23:26; 24:3; Jer 15:4 [y] 1Sa 3:11; Jer 19:3
21:13 [z] Isa 34:11; La 2:8; Am 7:7-9 [a] 2Ki 23:27
21:14 [b] Ps 78:58-60 [c] 2Ki 19:4; Mic 2:12

15they have done evil[d] in my eyes and have
aroused[e] my anger from the day their ancestors came out of Egypt until this day."
16Moreover, Manasseh also shed so
much innocent blood[f] that he filled Jerusalem from end to end—besides the sin that
he had caused Judah to commit, so that
they did evil in the eyes of the LORD.
17As for the other events of Manasseh's
reign, and all he did, including the sin he
committed, are they not written in the book
of the annals of the kings of Judah? 18Ma-
nasseh rested with his ancestors and was
buried in his palace garden,[g] the garden of
Uzza. And Amon his son succeeded him
as king.

Amon King of Judah

19Amon was twenty-two years old when
he became king, and he reigned in Jerusalem two years. His mother's name was
Meshullemeth daughter of Haruz; she was
from Jotbah. 20He did evil[h] in the eyes of
the LORD, as his father Manasseh had done.
21He followed completely the ways of his
father, worshiping the idols his father had
worshiped, and bowing down to them. 22He
forsook the LORD, the God of his ancestors,
and did not walk[i] in obedience to him.
23Amon's officials conspired against
him and assassinated[j] the king in his palace. 24Then the people of the land killed[k] all
who had plotted against King Amon, and
they made Josiah his son king in his place.
25As for the other events of Amon's
reign, and what he did, are they not written in the book of the annals of the kings of
Judah? 26He was buried in his tomb in the
garden[l] of Uzza. And Josiah his son succeeded him as king.

The Book of the Law Found

22 Josiah was eight years old when he
became king, and he reigned in Jerusalem thirty-one years. His mother's name
was Jedidah daughter of Adaiah; she was
from Bozkath.[m] 2He did what was right[n]
in the eyes of the LORD and followed completely the ways of his father David, not
turning aside to the right[o] or to the left.
3In the eighteenth year of his reign, King
Josiah sent the secretary, Shaphan[p] son of
Azaliah, the son of Meshullam, to the temple of the LORD. He said: 4"Go up to Hilkiah the high priest and have him get ready
the money that has been brought into the
temple of the LORD, which the doorkeepers have collected[q] from the people. 5Have
them entrust it to the men appointed to supervise the work on the temple. And have
these men pay the workers who repair[r]
the temple of the LORD— 6the carpenters,
the builders and the masons. Also have
them purchase timber and dressed stone
to repair the temple.[s] 7But they need not
account for the money entrusted to them,
because they are honest in their dealings."[t]
8Hilkiah the high priest said to Shaphan
the secretary, "I have found the Book of the
Law[u] in the temple of the LORD." He gave it
to Shaphan, who read it. 9Then Shaphan
the secretary went to the king and reported to him: "Your officials have paid out the
money that was in the temple of the LORD
and have entrusted it to the workers and
supervisors at the temple." 10Then Shaphan the secretary informed the king,
"Hilkiah the priest has given me a book."
And Shaphan read from it in the presence
of the king.[v]
11When the king heard the words of the
Book of the Law, he tore his robes. 12He
gave these orders to Hilkiah the priest,
Ahikam[w] son of Shaphan, Akbor son of
Micaiah, Shaphan the secretary and Asaiah the king's attendant: 13"Go and inquire
of the LORD for me and for the people and
for all Judah about what is written in this
book that has been found. Great is the

21:15 *from the day.* The story of the Old Testament is not a record of God's anger, but of His mercy and the delay of His just wrath.

21:23 *conspired against him.* No reason is assigned for the conspiracy that brought about Amon's assassination. While it may have had some connection with the international crisis that precipitated Ashurbanipal's renewed attention to the west, Amon's own wickedness may have provided sufficient cause.

22:1 *Josiah.* The name Josiah means "The LORD Supports." Like the name of Cyrus (Is. 44:28; 45:1) and of the city of Bethlehem (Mic. 5:2), the name Josiah was announced by a prophet long before the time of his birth (1 Kin. 13:1–2).

22:2 *not turning aside.* Not many rulers can rival Josiah's thirty-eight years of perseverance in righteousness. Some begin with high ideals and a commitment to do what is right in the sight of the Lord, but they soon learn that compromise is the art of politics. Compromise can be right and good. We ought to think more highly of others than ourselves and be willing to let go of our own preferences and opinions for the good of others. However, good can never result from compromising God's revealed ethics, morality, and justice. We must learn to live like Josiah, putting obedience to God before comfort and popular acceptance.

22:4 *Hilkiah the high priest.* This man was a major figure in the revival of true religion that young Josiah accomplished. The work of restoring the temple was under his direction.

22:8 *the Book of the Law.* This may mean either parts or all of the Pentateuch. Although it was placed by the side of the ark of the covenant (Deut. 31:26), it may have been lost, set aside, or hidden during the wicked reigns of Manasseh and Amon.

21:15 [d] Ex 32:22 [e] Jer 25:7 **21:16** [f] 2Ki 24:4 **21:18** [g] ver 26 **21:20** [h] ver 2-6 **21:22** [i] 1Ki 11:33 **21:23** [j] 2Ki 12:20; 2Ch 33:24-25 **21:24** [k] 2Ki 14:5 **21:26** [l] ver 18 **22:1** [m] Jos 15:39 **22:2** [n] Dt 17:19 [o] Dt 5:32 **22:3** [p] 2Ch 34:20; Jer 39:14 **22:4** [q] 2Ki 12:4-5 **22:5** [r] 2Ki 12:5, 11-14 **22:6** [s] 2Ki 12:11-12 **22:7** [t] 2Ki 12:15 **22:8** [u] Dt 31:24 **22:10** [v] Jer 36:21 **22:12** [w] 2Ki 25:22; Jer 26:24

LORD's anger[x] that burns against us because those who have gone before us have
not obeyed the words of this book; they
have not acted in accordance with all that
is written there concerning us."
[14]Hilkiah the priest, Ahikam, Akbor,
Shaphan and Asaiah went to speak to the
prophet Huldah, who was the wife of Shallum son of Tikvah, the son of Harhas, keeper of the wardrobe. She lived in Jerusalem,
in the New Quarter.
[15]She said to them, "This is what the
LORD, the God of Israel, says: Tell the man
who sent you to me, [16]'This is what the
LORD says: I am going to bring disaster[y]
on this place and its people, according to
everything written in the book[z] the king
of Judah has read. [17]Because they have
forsaken[a] me and burned incense to other gods and aroused my anger by all the
idols their hands have made,[a] my anger
will burn against this place and will not
be quenched.' [18]Tell the king of Judah,
who sent you to inquire[b] of the LORD, 'This
is what the LORD, the God of Israel, says
concerning the words you heard: [19]Be-
cause your heart was responsive and you
humbled[c] yourself before the LORD when
you heard what I have spoken against this
place and its people—that they would become a curse[bd] and be laid waste[e]—and because you tore your robes and wept in my
presence, I also have heard you, declares
the LORD. [20]Therefore I will gather you to
your ancestors, and you will be buried in
peace.[f] Your eyes will not see all the disaster I am going to bring on this place.'"
So they took her answer back to the king.

Josiah Renews the Covenant

23 Then the king called together all the
elders of Judah and Jerusalem. [2]He
went up to the temple of the LORD with the
people of Judah, the inhabitants of Jerusalem, the priests and the prophets—all
the people from the least to the greatest.
He read[g] in their hearing all the words of
the Book of the Covenant, which had been
found in the temple of the LORD. [3]The king
stood by the pillar and renewed the covenant[h] in the presence of the LORD—to follow[i] the LORD and keep his commands, statutes and decrees with all his heart and all
his soul, thus confirming the words of the
covenant written in this book. Then all the
people pledged themselves to the covenant.
[4]The king ordered Hilkiah the high
priest, the priests next in rank and the
doorkeepers[j] to remove[k] from the temple
of the LORD all the articles made for Baal
and Asherah and all the starry hosts. He
burned them outside Jerusalem in the
fields of the Kidron Valley and took the
ashes to Bethel. [5]He did away with the
idolatrous priests appointed by the kings
of Judah to burn incense on the high places
of the towns of Judah and on those around
Jerusalem—those who burned incense
to Baal, to the sun and moon, to the constellations and to all the starry hosts.[l] [6]He
took the Asherah pole from the temple of
the LORD to the Kidron Valley outside Jerusalem and burned it there. He ground it
to powder and scattered the dust over the
graves of the common people.[m] [7]He also
tore down the quarters of the male shrine
prostitutes[n] that were in the temple of the
LORD, the quarters where women did weaving for Asherah.
[8]Josiah brought all the priests from the
towns of Judah and desecrated the high
places, from Geba[o] to Beersheba, where the
priests had burned incense. He broke down
the gateway at the entrance of the Gate
of Joshua, the city governor, which was
on the left of the city gate. [9]Although the
priests of the high places did not serve[p] at

[a] 17 *Or by everything they have done* [b] 19 That is, their names would be used in cursing (see Jer. 29:22); or, others would see that they are cursed.

22:14 *the prophet Huldah.* Huldah is one of only a few women mentioned in Scripture as a prophetess. She served at the same time as other godly prophets, such as Jeremiah and Zephaniah, and some have suggested that her husband Shallum was a relative of Jeremiah (Jer. 32:7–12).

23:2 *He read ... the words of the Book.* Like Moses (Ex. 24:3–8) and Joshua (Josh. 8:34–35) before him, Josiah followed the ancient standard for godly leadership (Deut. 17:18–20; 31:9–13) and assembled the people to renew the covenant.

23:3 Knowing the Will of God—Christians often act as if learning the will of God is some mysterious process fraught with the danger of making all kinds of mistakes. This passage points to the fact that most of what we need to know about the will of God is contained in the Scriptures. The best place to *learn* the will of God is from reading the Bible. The only way to *do* the will of God is to obey the teaching of the Bible. God may have more specific plans for each of us, but His basic plan for all of us is to do what He says as revealed in His written word.

23:5 *idolatrous priests.* This term is also used by Zephaniah to describe the priests who led the rites associated with Baal and with star worship of various kinds (Zeph. 1:4). These priests had been appointed by Judah's past kings but functioned outside the divinely established priesthood.

23:6 *Asherah pole.* Although they had been destroyed by Hezekiah, these wooden images had been reintroduced by Manasseh (21:7) and also by Amon (21:21).

22:13 [x] Dt 29:24-28; 31:17 **22:16** [y] Dt 31:29; Jos 23:15 [z] Dt 29:27; Da 9:11 **22:17** [a] Dt 29:25-27 **22:18** [b] 2Ch 34:26; Jer 21:2 **22:19** [c] Ex 10:3; 1Ki 21:29; Ps 51:17; Isa 57:15; Mic 6:8 [d] Jer 26:6 [e] Lev 26:31 **22:20** [f] Isa 57:1 **23:2** [g] Dt 31:11; 2Ki 22:8 **23:3** [h] 2Ki 11:14,17 [i] Dt 13:4 **23:4** [j] 2Ki 25:18 [k] 2Ki 21:7 **23:5** [l] 2Ki 21:3; Jer 8:2 **23:6** [m] Jer 26:23 **23:7** [n] 1Ki 14:24; 15:12; Eze 16:16 **23:8** [o] 1Ki 15:22 **23:9** [p] Eze 44:10-14

the altar of the LORD in Jerusalem, they ate
unleavened bread with their fellow priests.
10He desecrated Topheth,[q] which was in
the Valley of Ben Hinnom,[r] so no one could
use it to sacrifice their son[s] or daughter in
the fire to Molek. 11He removed from the
entrance to the temple of the LORD the horses that the kings of Judah had dedicated to
the sun. They were in the court[a] near the
room of an official named Nathan-Melek.
Josiah then burned the chariots dedicated
to the sun.[t]
12He pulled down the altars the kings of
Judah had erected on the roof[u] near the upper room of Ahaz, and the altars Manasseh
had built in the two courts[v] of the temple
of the LORD. He removed them from there,
smashed them to pieces and threw the rubble into the Kidron Valley. 13The king also
desecrated the high places that were east of
Jerusalem on the south of the Hill of Corruption—the ones Solomon[w] king of Israel had
built for Ashtoreth the vile goddess of the Sidonians, for Chemosh the vile god of Moab,
and for Molek the detestable god of the people of Ammon. 14Josiah smashed[x] the sacred stones and cut down the Asherah poles
and covered the sites with human bones.
15Even the altar[y] at Bethel, the high place
made by Jeroboam[z] son of Nebat, who had
caused Israel to sin—even that altar and
high place he demolished. He burned the
high place and ground it to powder, and
burned the Asherah pole also. 16Then Josiah[a] looked around, and when he saw
the tombs that were there on the hillside,
he had the bones removed from them
and burned on the altar to defile it, in accordance with the word of the LORD proclaimed by the man of God who foretold
these things.
17The king asked, "What is that tomb-
stone I see?"
The people of the city said, "It marks the
tomb of the man of God who came from
Judah and pronounced against the altar of
Bethel the very things you have done to it."
18"Leave it alone," he said. "Don't let anyone disturb his bones[b]." So they spared his
bones and those of the prophet who had
come from Samaria.
19Just as he had done at Bethel, Josiah
removed all the shrines at the high places that the kings of Israel had built in the
towns of Samaria and that had aroused the
LORD's anger. 20Josiah slaughtered[c] all the
priests of those high places on the altars
and burned human bones[d] on them. Then
he went back to Jerusalem.
21The king gave this order to all the people: "Celebrate the Passover[e] to the LORD
your God, as it is written in this Book of
the Covenant." 22Neither in the days of the
judges who led Israel nor in the days of the
kings of Israel and the kings of Judah had
any such Passover been observed. 23But
in the eighteenth year of King Josiah, this
Passover was celebrated to the LORD in Jerusalem.
24Furthermore, Josiah got rid of the mediums and spiritists,[f] the household gods,[g]
the idols and all the other detestable things
seen in Judah and Jerusalem. This he did
to fulfill the requirements of the law written in the book that Hilkiah the priest
had discovered in the temple of the LORD.
25Neither before nor after Josiah was there
a king like him who turned[h] to the LORD
as he did—with all his heart and with all
his soul and with all his strength, in accordance with all the Law of Moses.
26Nevertheless, the LORD did not turn
away from the heat of his fierce anger,
which burned against Judah because of
all that Manasseh[i] had done to arouse his

---

[a] *11* The meaning of the Hebrew for this word is uncertain.

23:10 ***Topheth.*** This appears to have been a place in the valley of Hinnom where human sacrifices were made to Molek (Jer. 7:31–32; 32:35). ***in the fire to Molek.*** Some think that Molek was a god of the Ammonites (1 Kin. 11:5), or that Molek was the name of a type of child sacrifice associated with Baal worship (Jer. 19:5–6). Evidence of such child sacrifice has been found in the excavations at the Phoenician city of Carthage.

23:18 ***the prophet ... from Samaria.*** The prophet from Samaria was the old prophet of Bethel (1 Kin. 13:11). Samaria is the name for an entire area, not just the city that was later the capital of the northern kingdom (1 Kin. 13:32; 16:23–24). After the death of the man of God who had denounced Jeroboam's altar at Bethel, the aged prophet of Bethel requested that at his death he should be buried in Bethel beside that prophet of Judah.

23:22 ***any such Passover.*** The restoration of religious places was part of the revival of spiritual worship. Although Hezekiah had held a Passover (2 Chr. 30), he had done so with some modification of the law (2 Chr. 30:13–20). Accordingly, Josiah's meeting of the strict requirements of the law (2 Chr. 35:1–19) was truly unparalleled since the days of the judges.

23:25 ***Neither before nor after ... was there a king like him.*** Like his grandfather Hezekiah, who was famed for being without equal in his trust of the Lord (18:5), Josiah was truly a righteous king. Because of their outstanding examples of godliness, the authors of Kings and Chronicles devote considerable space to their reigns.

23:26–27 **Unfaithfulness**—The revival under Josiah, recorded in chapters 22 and 23, was like a stay of execution. It gave Judah some additional time but it was too little, too late. The die had been cast in Manasseh's reign as God threatened to "wipe

23:10 [q] Isa 30:33; Jer 7:31,32; 19:6 [r] Jos 15:8 [s] Lev 18:21; Dt 18:10 **23:11** [t] Dt 4:19 **23:12** [u] Jer 19:13; Zep 1:5 [v] 2Ki 21:5 **23:13** [w] 1Ki 11:7 **23:14** [x] Ex 23:24; Dt 7:5,25 **23:15** [y] 1Ki 13:1-3 [z] 1Ki 12:33 **23:16** [a] 1Ki 13:2 **23:18** [b] 1Ki 13:31 **23:20** [c] Ex 22:20; 2Ki 10:25; 11:18 [d] 1Ki 13:2 **23:21** [e] Ex 12:11; Nu 9:2; Dt 16:1-8 **23:24** [f] Lev 19:31; Dt 18:11; 2Ki 21:6 [g] Ge 31:19 **23:25** [h] 2Ki 18:5 **23:26** [i] 2Ki 21:12; Jer 15:4

anger. 27So the LORD said, "I will remove[j]
Judah also from my presence[k] as I removed
Israel, and I will reject Jerusalem, the city I
chose, and this temple, about which I said,
'My Name shall be there.'[a]"
28As for the other events of Josiah's
reign, and all he did, are they not written
in the book of the annals of the kings of
Judah?
29While Josiah was king, Pharaoh Necho[l] king of Egypt went up to the Euphrates
River to help the king of Assyria. King Josiah marched out to meet him in battle, but
Necho faced him and killed him at Megiddo.[m] 30Josiah's servants brought his body
in a chariot[n] from Megiddo to Jerusalem
and buried him in his own tomb. And the
people of the land took Jehoahaz son of Josiah and anointed him and made him king
in place of his father.

Jehoahaz King of Judah

31Jehoahaz[o] was twenty-three years old
when he became king, and he reigned in Jerusalem three months. His mother's name
was Hamutal[p] daughter of Jeremiah; she
was from Libnah. 32He did evil in the eyes
of the LORD, just as his predecessors had
done. 33Pharaoh Necho put him in chains
at Riblah[q] in the land of Hamath[r] so that he
might not reign in Jerusalem, and he imposed on Judah a levy of a hundred talents[b]
of silver and a talent[c] of gold. 34Pharaoh
Necho made Eliakim[s] son of Josiah king
in place of his father Josiah and changed
Eliakim's name to Jehoiakim. But he took
Jehoahaz and carried him off to Egypt, and
there he died.[t] 35Jehoiakim paid Pharaoh
Necho the silver and gold he demanded. In
order to do so, he taxed the land and exacted the silver and gold from the people of
the land according to their assessments.[u]

Jehoiakim King of Judah

36Jehoiakim[v] was twenty-five years old
when he became king, and he reigned in
Jerusalem eleven years. His mother's name
was Zebidah daughter of Pedaiah; she was
from Rumah. 37And he did evil in the eyes
of the LORD, just as his predecessors had
done.

24 During Jehoiakim's reign, Nebuchadnezzar[w] king of Babylon invaded the land, and Jehoiakim became his
vassal for three years. But then he turned
against Nebuchadnezzar and rebelled.
2The LORD sent Babylonian,[d] Aramean,[x]
Moabite and Ammonite raiders against
him to destroy[y] Judah, in accordance
with the word of the LORD proclaimed by
his servants the prophets. 3Surely these
things happened to Judah according to
the LORD's command,[z] in order to remove
them from his presence because of the sins
of Manasseh[a] and all he had done, 4includ-
ing the shedding of innocent blood.[b] For
he had filled Jerusalem with innocent
blood, and the LORD was not willing to
forgive.
5As for the other events of Jehoiakim's
reign, and all he did, are they not written
in the book of the annals of the kings of
Judah? 6Jehoiakim rested[c] with his ancestors. And Jehoiachin his son succeeded
him as king.
7The king of Egypt[d] did not march out
from his own country again, because the
king of Babylon[e] had taken all his territory,
from the Wadi of Egypt to the Euphrates
River.

---

a 27 1 Kings 8:29 *b* 33 That is, about 3 3/4 tons or about 3.4 metric tons *c* 33 That is, about 75 pounds or about 34 kilograms *d* 2 Or *Chaldean*

---

out Jerusalem as one wipes a dish" (21:13) because Manasseh did more evil than the other nations whom the Lord had destroyed. In the light of Jeremiah 18:7–8 we must assume that Josiah's people responded only externally to God's principles and not from the heart. Unfaithfulness was deeply rooted, and professions of religion could not change them from the inside.

23:29 ***Pharaoh Necho.*** During the long years of Josiah's reign (640–609 B.C.), Assyrian power had steadily crumbled until, as Nahum had predicted, Nineveh itself had fallen (612 B.C.). The surviving Assyrian forces had regrouped at Harran. Because Egypt was a long-standing ally of Assyria, Necho journeyed northward to help the beleaguered Assyrians. Josiah's deployment of his forces to the valley of Megiddo was an attempt to prevent the Egyptians from aiding the Assyrian forces at Haran. Although Pharaoh Necho was delayed sufficiently so that Haran was lost to the Assyrians, Josiah's action ultimately cost him his life (2 Chr. 35:20–25).

23:31 ***Jehoahaz.*** Jehoahaz, also called Shallum (Jer. 22:11), was Josiah's third son (24:18; 1 Chr. 3:15).

23:34 ***carried him off to Egypt, and there he died.*** The curse for Judah's disobedience was beginning to fall (Deut. 28:64–68).

23:37 ***he did evil.*** Jehoiakim's short reign was noted for its extreme wickedness (2 Chr. 36:5–8). Jeremiah depicts him as a despicable monster who took advantage of his people (Jer. 22:13–14,17), filled the land with every sort of vice and violence (Jer. 18:18–20), and opposed all that was holy (Jer. 25:1–7). Unlike his father Josiah, who led the nation in reformation at the hearing of the Word of God (22:11; 23:1–25), Jehoiakim went so far as to cut up and burn a scroll of Scripture (Jer. 36:21–24) and to kill Uriah, a true prophet of God (Jer. 26:20–23).

24:2 ***Babylonian.*** This name originally applied to certain inhabitants of southern Mesopotamia, but by this time the term had come to be identified with the Babylonians, and Babylonia was called Chaldea. After the fall of the Babylonian Empire, the term *Chaldean* came to mean "soothsayer" (Dan. 2:2).

23:27 [j] 2Ki 21:13 [k] 2Ki 18:11 **23:29** [l] Jer 46:2 [m] Zec 12:11
23:30 [n] 2Ki 9:28 **23:31** [o] 1Ch 3:15; Jer 22:11 [p] 2Ki 24:18
23:33 [q] 2Ki 25:6 [r] 1Ki 8:65 **23:34** [s] 1Ch 3:15; 2Ch 36:5-8
[t] Jer 22:12; Eze 19:3-4 **23:35** [u] ver 33 **23:36** [v] Jer 26:1
24:1 [w] Jer 25:1,9; Da 1:1 **24:2** [x] Jer 35:11 [y] Jer 25:9
24:3 [z] 2Ki 18:25 [a] 2Ki 21:12; 23:26 **24:4** [b] 2Ki 21:16
24:6 [c] Jer 22:19 **24:7** [d] Ge 15:18 [e] Jer 37:5-7; 46:2

Jehoiachin King of Judah

8 Jehoiachin[f] was eighteen years old when he became king, and he reigned in Jerusalem three months. His mother's name was Nehushta daughter of Elnathan; she was from Jerusalem. 9 He did evil in the eyes of the LORD, just as his father had done.

10 At that time the officers of Nebuchadnezzar[g] king of Babylon advanced on Jerusalem and laid siege to it, 11 and Nebuchadnezzar himself came up to the city while his officers were besieging it. 12 Jehoiachin king of Judah, his mother, his attendants, his nobles and his officials all surrendered[h] to him.

In the eighth year of the reign of the king of Babylon, he took Jehoiachin prisoner. 13 As the LORD had declared,[i] Nebuchadnezzar removed the treasures[j] from the temple of the LORD and from the royal palace, and cut up the gold articles[k] that Solomon[l] king of Israel had made for the temple of the LORD. 14 He carried all Jerusalem into exile:[m] all the officers and fighting men, and all the skilled workers and artisans—a total of ten thousand. Only the poorest[n] people of the land were left.

15 Nebuchadnezzar took Jehoiachin captive to Babylon. He also took from Jerusalem to Babylon the king's mother,[o] his wives, his officials and the prominent people[p] of the land. 16 The king of Babylon also deported to Babylon the entire force of seven thousand fighting men, strong and fit for war, and a thousand skilled workers and artisans.[q] 17 He made Mattaniah, Jehoiachin's uncle, king in his place and changed his name to Zedekiah.[r]

Zedekiah King of Judah

18 Zedekiah[s] was twenty-one years old when he became king, and he reigned in Jerusalem eleven years. His mother's name was Hamutal[t] daughter of Jeremiah; she was from Libnah. 19 He did evil in the eyes of the LORD, just as Jehoiakim had done. 20 It was because of the LORD's anger that all this happened to Jerusalem and Judah, and in the end he thrust[u] them from his presence.

The Fall of Jerusalem

Now Zedekiah rebelled against the king of Babylon.

25 So in the ninth year of Zedekiah's reign, on the tenth day of the tenth month, Nebuchadnezzar[v] king of Babylon marched against Jerusalem with his whole army. He encamped outside the city and built siege works[w] all around it. 2 The city was kept under siege until the eleventh year of King Zedekiah.

3 By the ninth day of the fourth[a] month the famine[x] in the city had become so severe that there was no food for the people to eat. 4 Then the city wall was broken through,[y] and the whole army fled at night through the gate between the two walls near the king's garden, though the Babylonians[b] were surrounding[z] the city. They fled toward the Arabah,[c] 5 but the Babylonian[d] army pursued the king and overtook him in the plains of Jericho. All his soldiers were separated from him and scattered,[a] 6 and he was captured.[b]

He was taken to the king of Babylon at Riblah,[c] where sentence was pronounced on him. 7 They killed the sons of Zedekiah before his eyes. Then they put out his eyes, bound him with bronze shackles and took him to Babylon.[d]

8 On the seventh day of the fifth month, in the nineteenth year of Nebuchadnezzar king of Babylon, Nebuzaradan commander of the imperial guard, an official of the king of Babylon, came to Jerusalem. 9 He

---

a 3 Probable reading of the original Hebrew text (see Jer. 52:6); Masoretic Text does not have *fourth*.
b 4 Or *Chaldeans*; also in verses 13, 25 and 26
c 4 Or *the Jordan Valley* *d* 5 Or *Chaldean*; also in verses 10 and 24

24:8 *Jehoiachin.* Because the scriptural description of Jehoiachin seems to represent him as a mature young man (Jer. 22:24–30; Ezek. 19:6), Jehoiachin's age at accession was probably eighteen rather than eight, as given elsewhere in some manuscripts (compare 2 Chr. 36:9).
24:12 *Jehoiachin.* Jehoiakim apparently had died before Nebuchadnezzar arrived at Jerusalem, because it was Jehoiachin who was carried off captive with other leaders of Judah (such as Ezekiel; Ezek. 1:1).
24:14–16 *carried.* The people of Israel lost their freedom and independence because of their own perpetually iniquitous ways. To be exiled is to be torn away from everything familiar, from everything traditional, from all identifiable scenery, and forced to live in a place where one has no identity and no roots. The people's whole sense of national identity was bound to their land, the place God had given them, and to be torn from that land was the ultimate evidence that God had rejected them.
24:15 *took Jehoiachin captive.* Jehoiachin's captivity was prophesied in Jeremiah 22:24–27. Jehoiachin's eventual release is recorded in 25:27–30 and Jeremiah 52:31–34.
24:17 *Mattaniah.* This was Josiah's youngest son (1 Chr. 3:15). He reigned until the fall of Jerusalem in 586 B.C.
25:7 *put out his eyes.* The last thing Zedekiah saw was the reward of his sinful folly—the horrible spectacle of his own loved ones being put to death. He would carry this picture with him until his own death in a Babylonian prison (Jer. 52:11).

24:8 [f] 1Ch 3:16 **24:10** [g] Da 1:1 **24:12** [h] 2Ki 25:27; Jer 22:24-30; 24:1; 25:1; 29:2; 52:28 **24:13** [i] 2Ki 20:17 [j] 2Ki 25:15; Isa 39:6 [k] 2Ki 25:14; Jer 20:5 [l] 1Ki 7:51 **24:14** [m] Jer 24:1; 52:28 [n] 2Ki 25:12; Jer 40:7; 52:16 **24:15** [o] Jer 22:24-28 [p] Est 2:6; Eze 17:12-14 **24:16** [q] Jer 52:28 **24:17** [r] 1Ch 3:15; 2Ch 36:11; Jer 37:1 **24:18** [s] Jer 52:1 [t] 2Ki 23:31 **24:20** [u] Dt 4:26; 29:27 **25:1** [v] Jer 34:1-7 [w] Eze 24:2 **25:3** [x] Jer 14:18; La 4:9 **25:4** [y] Eze 33:21 [z] Jer 4:17 **25:5** [a] Eze 12:14 **25:6** [b] Jer 34:21-22 [c] 2Ki 23:33 **25:7** [d] Jer 21:7; 32:4-5; Eze 12:11

set fire[e] to the temple of the LORD, the royal palace and all the houses of Jerusalem. Every important building he burned down.[f] [10]The whole Babylonian army under the commander of the imperial guard broke down the walls[g] around Jerusalem. [11]Nebuzaradan the commander of the guard carried into exile[h] the people who remained in the city, along with the rest of the populace and those who had deserted to the king of Babylon.[i] [12]But the commander left behind some of the poorest people[j] of the land to work the vineyards and fields.

[13]The Babylonians broke up the bronze pillars, the movable stands and the bronze Sea that were at the temple of the LORD and they carried the bronze to Babylon. [14]They also took away the pots, shovels, wick trimmers, dishes and all the bronze articles[k] used in the temple service. [15]The commander of the imperial guard took away the censers and sprinkling bowls—all that were made of pure gold or silver.

[16]The bronze from the two pillars, the Sea and the movable stands, which Solomon had made for the temple of the LORD, was more than could be weighed. [17]Each pillar[l] was eighteen cubits[a] high. The bronze capital on top of one pillar was three cubits[b] high and was decorated with a network and pomegranates of bronze all around. The other pillar, with its network, was similar.

[18]The commander of the guard took as prisoners Seraiah[m] the chief priest, Zephaniah[n] the priest next in rank and the three doorkeepers. [19]Of those still in the city, he took the officer in charge of the fighting men, and five royal advisers. He also took the secretary who was chief officer in charge of conscripting the people of the land and sixty of the conscripts who were found in the city. [20]Nebuzaradan the commander took them all and brought them to the king of Babylon at Riblah. [21]There at Riblah, in the land of Hamath, the king had them executed.

So Judah went into captivity, away from her land.[o]

[22]Nebuchadnezzar king of Babylon appointed Gedaliah[p] son of Ahikam, the son of Shaphan, to be over the people he had left behind in Judah. [23]When all the army officers and their men heard that the king of Babylon had appointed Gedaliah as governor, they came to Gedaliah at Mizpah—Ishmael son of Nethaniah, Johanan son of Kareah, Seraiah son of Tanhumeth the Netophathite, Jaazaniah the son of the Maakathite, and their men. [24]Gedaliah took an oath to reassure them and their men. "Do not be afraid of the Babylonian officials," he said. "Settle down in the land and serve the king of Babylon, and it will go well with you."

[25]In the seventh month, however, Ishmael son of Nethaniah, the son of Elishama, who was of royal blood, came with ten men and assassinated Gedaliah and also the men of Judah and the Babylonians who were with him at Mizpah. [26]At this, all the people from the least to the greatest, together with the army officers, fled to Egypt[q] for fear of the Babylonians.

Jehoiachin Released

[27]In the thirty-seventh year of the exile of Jehoiachin king of Judah, in the year Awel-Marduk became king of Babylon, he released Jehoiachin[r] king of Judah from prison. He did this on the twenty-seventh day of the twelfth month. [28]He spoke kindly to him and gave him a seat of honor[s] higher than those of the other kings who were with him in Babylon. [29]So Jehoiachin put aside his prison clothes and for the rest of his life ate regularly at the king's table.[t] [30]Day by day the king gave Jehoiachin a regular allowance as long as he lived.[u]

---

[a] *17* That is, about 27 feet or about 8.1 meters
[b] *17* That is, about 4 1/2 feet or about 1.4 meters

25:10 ***broke down the walls.*** These walls would lie in ruins for a century and a half (Neh. 2:11—6:16).
25:17 ***three cubits.*** This may be the height of the capitals not including the ornamental work; 1 Kings 7:16 and Jeremiah 52:22 say five cubits.
25:18 ***Seraiah.*** Although Seraiah was executed (v. 21), his son Jozadak was deported (1 Chr. 6:15). Through Jozadak's line would come Ezra, the priest and great reformer, who one day would return to Jerusalem and take up Seraiah's work (Ezra 7:1).
25:22 ***Gedaliah.*** Gedaliah's father Ahikam had supported Jeremiah in his struggles with the apostate officials of Judah (Jer. 26:24). The prophet Jeremiah was allowed to stay and assist Gedaliah in the process of reconstruction (Jer. 39:11–14; 40:1–6).
25:27 ***Awel-Marduk.*** This king succeeded Nebuchadnezzar and reigned a short time (561–560 B.C.). Tablets from the reign of Nabonidus (555–539 B.C.) record the daily rations of Jehoiachin who is called "Yaukin, king of the land of Yahud (Judah)."
25:28 ***spoke kindly.*** Awel-Marduk's kindness toward Jehoiachin brings the books of Kings to an end on a ray of hope. Exile was neither the end of Israel nor of the Davidic line.

25:9 [e] Isa 60:7 [f] Ps 74:3-8; Jer 2:15; Am 2:5; Mic 3:12
25:10 [g] Ne 1:3 **25:11** [h] 2Ki 24:14 [i] 2Ki 24:1
25:12 [j] 2Ki 24:14 **25:14** [k] Ex 27:3; 1Ki 7:47-50
25:17 [l] 1Ki 7:15-22 **25:18** [m] 1Ch 6:14; Ezr 7:1; Ne 11:11
[n] Jer 21:1; 29:25 **25:21** [o] Ge 12:7; Dt 28:64; Jos 23:13; 2Ki 23:27 **25:22** [p] Jer 39:14; 40:5,7 **25:26** [q] Isa 30:2; Jer 43:7 **25:27** [r] 2Ki 24:12; Jer 52:31-34 **25:28** [s] Ezr 5:5; Ne 2:1; Da 2:48 **25:29** [t] 2Sa 9:7 **25:30** [u] Est 2:9; Jer 28:4

1 CHRONICLES

▶ **AUTHOR:** Tradition in the Jewish Talmud supports Ezra the priest as the author of 1 Chronicles. The content points to priestly authorship because of the emphasis on the temple, the priesthood, and the theocratic line of David in the southern kingdom of Judah. Ezra was an educated scribe (Ezra 7:6), and according to the apocryphal book of 2 Maccabees 2:13–15, Nehemiah collected an extensive library which was available to Ezra for his use in compiling Chronicles.

▶ **TIME:** c. 1004–971 B.C. ▶ **KEY VERSES:** 1 Chr. 7:11–14

▶ **THEME:** First Chronicles is largely a retelling of the texts of 1 and 2 Samuel with administrative details and the roles that the various tribes and alliances played in the events of the nation. We don't see the family conflict with Michal when the ark is brought to Jerusalem or the affair with Bathsheba and its fallout. When it comes to succession, all we are told is that David chose Solomon to succeed him. This is a primary document of the history of Israel.

Historical Records From Adam to Abraham

To Noah's Sons

1 Adam,[a] Seth, Enosh, 2 Kenan,[b] Mahalalel,[c] Jared,[d] 3 Enoch,[e] Methuselah,[f] Lamech,[g] Noah.[h]

4 The sons of Noah:[a][i]
Shem, Ham and Japheth.[j]

The Japhethites

5 The sons[b] of Japheth:
Gomer, Magog, Madai, Javan, Tubal, Meshek and Tiras.
6 The sons of Gomer:
Ashkenaz, Riphath[c] and Togarmah.
7 The sons of Javan:
Elishah, Tarshish, the Kittites and the Rodanites.

The Hamites

8 The sons of Ham:
Cush, Egypt, Put and Canaan.
9 The sons of Cush:
Seba, Havilah, Sabta, Raamah and Sabteka.
The sons of Raamah:
Sheba and Dedan.
10 Cush was the father[d] of
Nimrod, who became a mighty warrior on earth.
11 Egypt was the father of
the Ludites, Anamites, Lehabites,
Naphtuhites, 12 Pathrusites, Kaslu-
hites (from whom the Philistines came) and Caphtorites.
13 Canaan was the father of
Sidon his firstborn,[e] and of the Hittites, 14 Jebusites, Amorites, Girgashites, 15 Hivites, Arkites, Sinites,
16 Arvadites, Zemarites and Hamathites.

The Semites

17 The sons of Shem:
Elam, Ashur, Arphaxad, Lud and Aram.
The sons of Aram:[f]
Uz, Hul, Gether and Meshek.
18 Arphaxad was the father of Shelah,
and Shelah the father of Eber.
19 Two sons were born to Eber:
One was named Peleg,[g] because in

[a] *4* Septuagint; Hebrew does not have this line.
[b] *5 Sons* may mean *descendants* or *successors* or *nations*; also in verses 6-9, 17 and 23.
[c] *6* Many Hebrew manuscripts and Vulgate (see also Septuagint and Gen. 10:3); most Hebrew manuscripts *Diphath*
[d] *10 Father* may mean *ancestor* or *predecessor* or *founder*; also in verses 11, 13, 18 and 20.
[e] *13* Or *of the Sidonians, the foremost*
[f] *17* One Hebrew manuscript and some Septuagint manuscripts (see also Gen. 10:23); most Hebrew manuscripts do not have this line.
[g] *19 Peleg* means *division*.

1:1 ***Adam, Seth, Enosh.*** Including the names of these pre-flood people along with the rest of the genealogical record indicates that the chronicler had no question of their historical identity.

1:18 ***Eber.*** Eber was the ancestor of Abraham, Isaac, and Jacob. The name Hebrew, a derivative of Eber's name, was applied to the Israelites.

1:19 ***the earth was divided.*** This refers to the division of the earth's population by the scattering of

1:1 [a] Ge 5:1-32; Lk 3:36-38 **1:2** [b] Ge 5:9 [c] Ge 5:12 [d] Ge 5:15 **1:3** [e] Ge 5:18; Jude 1:14 [f] Ge 5:21 [g] Ge 5:25 [h] Ge 5:29 **1:4** [i] Ge 6:10; 10:1 [j] Ge 5:32

his time the earth was divided; his brother was named Joktan.
20 Joktan was the father of
Almodad, Sheleph, Hazarmaveth, Jerah, 21 Hadoram, Uzal, Diklah, 22 Obal,[a] Abimael, Sheba, 23 Ophir, Havilah and Jobab. All these were sons of Joktan.

24 Shem,[k] Arphaxad,[b] Shelah,
25 Eber, Peleg, Reu,
26 Serug, Nahor, Terah
27 and Abram (that is, Abraham).

The Family of Abraham

28 The sons of Abraham:
Isaac and Ishmael.

Descendants of Hagar

29 These were their descendants:
Nebaioth the firstborn of Ishmael, Kedar, Adbeel, Mibsam,
30 Mishma, Dumah, Massa, Hadad,
Tema, 31 Jetur, Naphish and Kedemah. These were the sons of Ishmael.

Descendants of Keturah

32 The sons born to Keturah, Abraham's concubine:[l]
Zimran, Jokshan, Medan, Midian, Ishbak and Shuah.
The sons of Jokshan:
Sheba and Dedan.[m]
33 The sons of Midian:
Ephah, Epher, Hanok, Abida and Eldaah.
All these were descendants of Keturah.

Descendants of Sarah

34 Abraham[n] was the father of Isaac.[o]
The sons of Isaac:
Esau and Israel.[p]

Esau's Sons

35 The sons of Esau:[q]
Eliphaz, Reuel,[r] Jeush, Jalam and Korah.
36 The sons of Eliphaz:
Teman, Omar, Zepho,[c] Gatam and Kenaz;
by Timna: Amalek.[d][s]
37 The sons of Reuel:[t]
Nahath, Zerah, Shammah and Mizzah.

The People of Seir in Edom

38 The sons of Seir:
Lotan, Shobal, Zibeon, Anah, Dishon, Ezer and Dishan.
39 The sons of Lotan:
Hori and Homam. Timna was Lotan's sister.
40 The sons of Shobal:
Alvan,[e] Manahath, Ebal, Shepho and Onam.
The sons of Zibeon:
Aiah and Anah.[u]
41 The son of Anah:
Dishon.
The sons of Dishon:
Hemdan,[f] Eshban, Ithran and Keran.
42 The sons of Ezer:
Bilhan, Zaavan and Akan.[g]
The sons of Dishan[h]:
Uz and Aran.

The Rulers of Edom

43 These were the kings who reigned in Edom before any Israelite king reigned:
Bela son of Beor, whose city was named Dinhabah.
44 When Bela died, Jobab son of Zerah from Bozrah succeeded him as king.
45 When Jobab died, Husham from the land of the Temanites[v] succeeded him as king.
46 When Husham died, Hadad son of Bedad, who defeated Midian in the country of Moab, succeeded him as king. His city was named Avith.

[a] *22* Some Hebrew manuscripts and Syriac (see also Gen. 10:28); most Hebrew manuscripts *Ebal* [b] *24* Hebrew; some Septuagint manuscripts *Arphaxad, Cainan* (see also note at Gen. 11:10) [c] *36* Many Hebrew manuscripts, some Septuagint manuscripts and Syriac (see also Gen. 36:11); most Hebrew manuscripts *Zephi* [d] *36* Some Septuagint manuscripts (see also Gen. 36:12); Hebrew *Gatam, Kenaz, Timna and Amalek* [e] *40* Many Hebrew manuscripts and some Septuagint manuscripts (see also Gen. 36:23); most Hebrew manuscripts *Alian* [f] *41* Many Hebrew manuscripts and some Septuagint manuscripts (see also Gen. 36:26); most Hebrew manuscripts *Hamran* [g] *42* Many Hebrew and Septuagint manuscripts (see also Gen. 36:27); most Hebrew manuscripts *Zaavan, Jaakan* [h] *42* See Gen. 36:28; Hebrew *Dishon*, a variant of *Dishan*

the human race following the judgment of God on the tower of Babel.

1:36 ***Timna.*** Timna was Eliphaz's concubine (Gen. 36:12). Her son Amalek was the founder of the Amalekites, a people that became one of Israel's most persistent enemies (Ex. 17:8–16; Deut. 25:17–19; 1 Sam. 15:1–3).

1:38 ***Seir.*** Seir was the patriarchal name of the pre-Edomite population in the region east and south of the Dead Sea (Gen. 36:20–30). ***Lotan.*** Lotan was Timna's brother, and Timna was the concubine of Esau's son. This is how the people of Seir and the descendants of Esau were related, and together these two people groups became the kingdom of Edom.

1:43 ***the kings ... in Edom.*** Although the kings of Edom ruled in succession, they were not part of a dynasty. Apparently Edom did not have a capital, and its kings ruled from their own cities.

1:24 [k] Ge 10:21-25; Lk 3:34-36 **1:32** [l] Ge 22:24 [m] Ge 10:7 **1:34** [n] Lk 3:34 [o] Ge 21:2-3; Mt 1:2; Ac 7:8 [p] Ge 17:5; 25:25-26 **1:35** [q] Ge 36:19 [r] Ge 36:4 **1:36** [s] Ex 17:14 **1:37** [t] Ge 36:17 **1:40** [u] Ge 36:2 **1:45** [v] Ge 36:11

47 When Hadad died, Samlah from Masrekah succeeded him as king.
48 When Samlah died, Shaul from Rehoboth on the river[a] succeeded him as
king.
49 When Shaul died, Baal-Hanan son of
Akbor succeeded him as king.
50 When Baal-Hanan died, Hadad succeeded him as king. His city was
named Pau,[b] and his wife's name
was Mehetabel daughter of Matred,
the daughter of Me-Zahab. 51 Hadad
also died.

The chiefs of Edom were:
Timna, Alvah, Jetheth, 52 Oholibamah, Elah, Pinon, 53 Kenaz, Teman,
Mibzar, 54 Magdiel and Iram. These
were the chiefs of Edom.

Israel's Sons

2 These were the sons of Israel:
Reuben, Simeon, Levi, Judah, Issachar, Zebulun, 2 Dan, Joseph, Benjamin, Naphtali, Gad and Asher.

Judah

To Hezron's Sons

3 The sons of Judah:[w]
Er, Onan and Shelah.[x] These three
were born to him by a Canaanite
woman, the daughter of Shua.[y] Er,
Judah's firstborn, was wicked in the
LORD's sight; so the LORD put him to
death.[z] 4 Judah's daughter-in-law[a]
Tamar[b] bore Perez[c] and Zerah to
Judah. He had five sons in all.
5 The sons of Perez:[d]
Hezron[e] and Hamul.
6 The sons of Zerah:
Zimri, Ethan, Heman, Kalkol and
Darda[c]—five in all.
7 The son of Karmi:
Achar,[d][f] who brought trouble on Is-
rael by violating the ban on taking
devoted things.[e][g]
8 The son of Ethan:
Azariah.
9 The sons born to Hezron[h] were:
Jerahmeel, Ram and Caleb.[f]

From Ram Son of Hezron

10 Ram[i] was the father of
Amminadab[j], and Amminadab the
father of Nahshon,[k] the leader of
the people of Judah. 11 Nahshon was
the father of Salmon,[g] Salmon the
father of Boaz, 12 Boaz[l] the father of
Obed and Obed the father of Jesse.[m]
13 Jesse[n] was the father of
Eliab[o] his firstborn; the second
son was Abinadab, the third Shimea, 14 the fourth Nethanel, the fifth
Raddai, 15 the sixth Ozem and the
seventh David. 16 Their sisters were
Zeruiah[p] and Abigail. Zeruiah's[q]
three sons were Abishai, Joab[r] and
Asahel. 17 Abigail was the mother of
Amasa,[s] whose father was Jether
the Ishmaelite.

Caleb Son of Hezron

18 Caleb son of Hezron had children by
his wife Azubah (and by Jerioth).
These were her sons: Jesher, Shobab and Ardon. 19 When Azubah
died, Caleb[t] married Ephrath, who
bore him Hur. 20 Hur was the father
of Uri, and Uri the father of Bezalel.[u]
21 Later, Hezron, when he was sixty
years old, married the daughter
of Makir the father of Gilead.[v] He
made love to her, and she bore him
Segub. 22 Segub was the father of
Jair, who controlled twenty-three
towns in Gilead. 23 (But Geshur and
Aram captured Havvoth Jair,[h][w] as
well as Kenath[x] with its surrounding

[a] *48* Possibly the Euphrates [b] *50* Many Hebrew manuscripts, some Septuagint manuscripts, Vulgate and Syriac (see also Gen. 36:39); most Hebrew manuscripts *Pai* [c] *6* Many Hebrew manuscripts, some Septuagint manuscripts and Syriac (see also 1 Kings 4:31); most Hebrew manuscripts *Dara* [d] *7 Achar* means *trouble*; *Achar* is called *Achan* in Joshua. [e] *7* The Hebrew term refers to the irrevocable giving over of things or persons to the LORD, often by totally destroying them. [f] *9* Hebrew *Kelubai*, a variant of *Caleb* [g] *11* Septuagint (see also Ruth 4:21); Hebrew *Salma* [h] *23* Or *captured the settlements of Jair*

1:51 *chiefs.* The word "chiefs" usually referred to military leaders (Gen. 36:40–43).

2:1–55 Family—The Hebrew nation, descended through Abraham, kept one of the most carefully preserved family records of all time. To be associated with the family of Israel was to be identified with the God of Israel, and the history of this people is closely associated with the things that God taught each of these ancestors.

2:10 *Nahshon.* This genealogy is selective, focusing on the members important to the lineage of David. Nahshon was head of the tribe of Judah at the time of the wilderness march from Sinai to Kadesh Barnea (Num. 1:7; 2:3; 7:12). He was more than five generations removed from Judah.

2:16 *sisters.* Sisters are not usually mentioned in ancient genealogies. However this genealogy pays particular attention to the family of David, and as his sister's sons were important members of his military units, the sisters are listed.

2:18 *Caleb.* This Caleb is not the famous companion of Joshua (Num. 13:6; Josh. 14:6–7), who lived several centuries later during the conquest of Canaan.

2:3 [w] Ge 29:35; 38:2-10 [x] Ge 38:5 [y] Ge 38:2 [z] Nu 26:19 **2:4** [a] Ge 11:31 [b] Ge 38:11-30 [c] Ge 38:29 **2:5** [d] Ge 46:12 [e] Nu 26:21 **2:7** [f] Jos 7:1 [g] Jos 6:18 **2:9** [h] Nu 26:21 **2:10** [i] Lk 3:32-33 [j] Ex 6:23 [k] Nu 1:7 **2:12** [l] Ru 2:1 [m] Ru 4:17 **2:13** [n] Ru 4:17 [o] 1Sa 16:6 **2:16** [p] 1Sa 26:6 [q] 2Sa 2:18 [r] 2Sa 2:13 **2:17** [s] 2Sa 17:25 **2:19** [t] ver 42, 50 **2:20** [u] Ex 31:2 **2:21** [v] Nu 27:1 **2:23** [w] Nu 32:41; Dt 3:14; Jos 13:30 [x] Nu 32:42

settlements—sixty towns.) All these
were descendants of Makir the father of Gilead.
24 After Hezron died in Caleb Ephrathah, Abijah the wife of Hezron bore
him Ashhur[y] the father[a] of Tekoa.

Jerahmeel Son of Hezron

25 The sons of Jerahmeel the firstborn of
Hezron:
Ram his firstborn, Bunah, Oren,
Ozem and[b] Ahijah. 26 Jerahmeel had
another wife, whose name was Ata-
rah; she was the mother of Onam.
27 The sons of Ram the firstborn of Jerahmeel:
Maaz, Jamin and Eker.
28 The sons of Onam:
Shammai and Jada.
The sons of Shammai:
Nadab and Abishur.
29 Abishur's wife was named Abihail,
who bore him Ahban and Molid.
30 The sons of Nadab:
Seled and Appaim. Seled died without children.
31 The son of Appaim:
Ishi, who was the father of Sheshan.
Sheshan was the father of Ahlai.
32 The sons of Jada, Shammai's brother:
Jether and Jonathan. Jether died
without children.
33 The sons of Jonathan:
Peleth and Zaza.
These were the descendants of Jerahmeel.
34 Sheshan had no sons—only daughters.
He had an Egyptian servant named
Jarha. 35 Sheshan gave his daughter
in marriage to his servant Jarha,
and she bore him Attai.
36 Attai was the father of Nathan,
Nathan the father of Zabad,[z]
37 Zabad the father of Ephlal,
Ephlal the father of Obed,
38 Obed the father of Jehu,
Jehu the father of Azariah,
39 Azariah the father of Helez,
Helez the father of Eleasah,
40 Eleasah the father of Sismai,
Sismai the father of Shallum,
41 Shallum the father of Jekamiah,
and Jekamiah the father of Elishama.

The Clans of Caleb

42 The sons of Caleb[a] the brother of Jerahmeel:
Mesha his firstborn, who was the father of Ziph, and his son Mareshah,[c]
who was the father of Hebron.
43 The sons of Hebron:
Korah, Tappuah, Rekem and Shema.
44 Shema was the father of Raham,
and Raham the father of Jorkeam.
Rekem was the father of Shammai.
45 The son of Shammai was Maon[b],
and Maon was the father of Beth
Zur.[c]
46 Caleb's concubine Ephah was the
mother of Haran, Moza and Gazez.
Haran was the father of Gazez.
47 The sons of Jahdai:
Regem, Jotham, Geshan, Pelet,
Ephah and Shaaph.
48 Caleb's concubine Maakah was the
mother of Sheber and Tirhanah.
49 She also gave birth to Shaaph the
father of Madmannah[d] and to Sheva the father of Makbenah and Gib-
ea. Caleb's daughter was Aksah.[e]
50 These were the descendants of
Caleb.

The sons of Hur[f] the firstborn of Ephrathah:
Shobal the father of Kiriath Jearim,[g]
51 Salma the father of Bethlehem,
and Hareph the father of Beth Ga-
der.
52 The descendants of Shobal the father
of Kiriath Jearim were:
Haroeh, half the Manahathites,
53 and the clans of Kiriath Jearim:
the Ithrites,[h] Puthites, Shumath-
ites and Mishraites. From these descended the Zorathites and Eshtao-
lites.
54 The descendants of Salma:
Bethlehem, the Netophathites,[i] At-
roth Beth Joab, half the Manahathites, the Zorites, 55 and the clans
of scribes[d] who lived at Jabez: the
Tirathites, Shimeathites and Su-
cathites. These are the Kenites[j] who
came from Hammath,[k] the father of
the Rekabites.[e][l]

The Sons of David

3 These were the sons of David[m] born to
him in Hebron:
The firstborn was Amnon the son of
Ahinoam of Jezreel;[n]
the second, Daniel the son of Abigail[o] of Carmel;

---

[a] 24 *Father* may mean *civic leader* or *military leader*; also in verses 42, 45, 49-52 and possibly elsewhere. [b] 25 Or *Oren and Ozem, by*
[c] 42 The meaning of the Hebrew for this phrase is uncertain. [d] 55 Or *of the Sopherites*
[e] 55 Or *father of Beth Rekab*

2:51 *father of Bethlehem.* The chronicler recorded Caleb's genealogy because of the significance of Bethlehem, the birthplace of King David. One of Caleb's descendants, Salma, was the founder of Bethlehem.
3:1–5 *sons of David.* The fact that David had six sons by six wives in Hebron does not condone

2:24 [y] 1Ch 4:5 **2:36** [z] 1Ch 11:41 **2:42** [a] ver 19
2:45 [b] Jos 15:55 [c] Jos 15:58 **2:49** [d] Jos 15:31 [e] Jos 15:16
2:50 [f] 1Ch 4:4 [g] ver 19 **2:53** [h] 2Sa 23:38
2:54 [i] Ezr 2:22; Ne 7:26; 12:28 **2:55** [j] Ge 15:19; Jdg 1:16; Jdg 4:11 [k] Jos 19:35 [l] 2Ki 10:15,23; Jer 35:2-19
3:1 [m] 1Ch 14:3; 28:5 [n] Jos 15:56 [o] 1Sa 25:42

2 the third, Absalom the son of Maakah daughter of Talmai king of Geshur;
the fourth, Adonijah[p] the son of
Haggith;
3 the fifth, Shephatiah the son of Abital;
and the sixth, Ithream, by his wife
Eglah.
4 These six were born to David in Hebron,[q] where he reigned seven years
and six months.[r]
David reigned in Jerusalem thirty-three
years, 5and these were the children born
to him there:
Shammua,[a] Shobab, Nathan and
Solomon. These four were by Bathsheba[bs] daughter of Ammiel. 6There
were also Ibhar, Elishua,[c] Eliphelet,
7Nogah, Nepheg, Japhia, 8Elishama,
Eliada and Eliphelet—nine in all.
9All these were the sons of David,
besides his sons by his concubines.
And Tamar[t] was their sister.[u]

The Kings of Judah

10 Solomon's son was Rehoboam,[v]
Abijah his son,
Asa his son,
Jehoshaphat[w] his son,
11 Jehoram[dx] his son,
Ahaziah[y] his son,
Joash[z] his son,
12 Amaziah[a] his son,
Azariah his son,
Jotham[b] his son,
13 Ahaz[c] his son,
Hezekiah[d] his son,
Manasseh[e] his son,
14 Amon[f] his son,
Josiah[g] his son.
15 The sons of Josiah:
Johanan the firstborn,
Jehoiakim[h] the second son,
Zedekiah[i] the third,
Shallum[j] the fourth.
16 The successors of Jehoiakim:
Jehoiachin[ek] his son,
and Zedekiah.[l]

The Royal Line After the Exile

17 The descendants of Jehoiachin the
captive:
Shealtiel[m] his son, 18Malkiram, Pedaiah, Shenazzar,[n] Jekamiah, Hosh-
ama and Nedabiah.[o]
19 The sons of Pedaiah:
Zerubbabel[p] and Shimei.
The sons of Zerubbabel:
Meshullam and Hananiah.
Shelomith was their sister.
20 There were also five others:
Hashubah, Ohel, Berekiah, Hasadi-
ah and Jushab-Hesed.
21 The descendants of Hananiah:
Pelatiah and Jeshaiah, and the sons
of Rephaiah, of Arnan, of Obadiah
and of Shekaniah.
22 The descendants of Shekaniah:
Shemaiah and his sons:
Hattush,[q] Igal, Bariah, Neariah and
Shaphat—six in all.
23 The sons of Neariah:
Elioenai, Hizkiah and Azrikam—
three in all.
24 The sons of Elioenai:
Hodaviah, Eliashib, Pelaiah, Akkub, Johanan, Delaiah and Ana-
ni—seven in all.

Other Clans of Judah

4 The descendants of Judah:[r]
Perez, Hezron,[s] Karmi, Hur and
Shobal.
2 Reaiah son of Shobal was the father
of Jahath, and Jahath the father of
Ahumai and Lahad. These were the
clans of the Zorathites.

---

[a] 5 Hebrew *Shimea*, a variant of *Shammua*
[b] 5 One Hebrew manuscript and Vulgate (see also Septuagint and 2 Samuel 11:3); most Hebrew manuscripts *Bathshua*
[c] 6 Two Hebrew manuscripts (see also 2 Samuel 5:15 and 1 Chron. 14:5); most Hebrew manuscripts *Elishama*
[d] 11 Hebrew *Joram*, a variant of *Jehoram*
[e] 16 Hebrew *Jeconiah*, a variant of *Jehoiachin*; also in verse 17

---

polygamy. David had apparently followed the custom of marrying the daughters of neighboring kings to create allies, in spite of the warning Moses gave for the kings to avoid accumulating many wives (Deut. 17:17). Jesus refers back to creation when He addresses the concept of single partners for life (Matt. 19:1–12), so it is clear that even though some polygamy was practiced, it has never been God's plan for marriage.

3:19 ***Pedaiah.*** Zerubbabel here is designated as a son of Pedaiah, but elsewhere (Ezra 3:2,8; 5:2; Neh. 12:1; Hag. 1:12,14; 2:2,23) as a son of Pedaiah's brother Shealtiel (v. 17). It is likely that Shealtiel had died while Zerubbabel was young, and that the youth was raised by his uncle Pedaiah. This relationship may explain Luke's statement that Zerubbabel was "the son of Shealtiel" (Luke 3:27), who was a descendant of David through his son Nathan.

4:1 ***descendants of Judah.*** The chronicler here refers to other persons and events relative to Judah's genealogy (2:3–17). In the list in this verse Perez is Judah's son, Hezron is his grandson, Karmi his nephew, Hur the grandson of Hezron, and Shobal the grandson of Hur.

3:2 [p] 1Ki 2:22 **3:4** [q] 2Sa 5:4; 1Ch 29:27 [r] 2Sa 2:11; 5:5 **3:5** [s] 2Sa 11:3; 12:24 **3:9** [t] 2Sa 13:1 [u] 1Ch 14:4 **3:10** [v] 1Ki 11:43; 14:21-31; 2Ch 12:16 [w] 2Ch 17:1-21:3 **3:11** [x] 2Ki 8:16-24; 2Ch 21:1 [y] 2Ch 22:1-10 [z] 2Ki 11:1-12:21 **3:12** [a] 2Ki 14:1-22; 2Ch 25:1-28 [b] Isa 1:1; Hos 1:1; Mic 1:1 **3:13** [c] 2Ki 16:1-20; 2Ch 28:1; Isa 7:1 [d] 2Ki 18:1-20:21; 2Ch 29:1; Jer 26:19 [e] 2Ch 33:1 **3:14** [f] 2Ki 21:19-26; 2Ch 33:21; Zep 1:1 [g] 2Ch 34:1; Jer 1:2; 3:6; 25:3 **3:15** [h] 2Ki 23:34 [i] Jer 37:1 [j] 2Ki 23:31 **3:16** [k] 2Ki 24:6,8; Mt 1:11 [l] 2Ki 24:18 **3:17** [m] Ezr 3:2 **3:18** [n] Ezr 1:8; 5:14 [o] Jer 22:30 **3:19** [p] Ezr 2:2; 3:2; 5:2; Ne 7:7; 12:1; Hag 1:1; 2:2; Zec 4:6 **3:22** [q] Ezr 8:2-3 **4:1** [r] Ge 29:35; 46:12; 1Ch 2:3 [s] Nu 26:21

3 These were the sons[a] of Etam:
Jezreel, Ishma and Idbash. Their sister was named Hazzelelponi. 4 Penuel was the father of Gedor, and Ezer
the father of Hushah.
These were the descendants of Hur,[t]
the firstborn of Ephrathah and father[b] of Bethlehem.[u]
5 Ashhur[v] the father of Tekoa had two
wives, Helah and Naarah.
6 Naarah bore him Ahuzzam, Hepher,
Temeni and Haahashtari. These
were the descendants of Naarah.
7 The sons of Helah:
Zereth, Zohar, Ethnan, 8 and Koz,
who was the father of Anub and
Hazzobebah and of the clans of
Aharhel son of Harum.

9 Jabez was more honorable than his
brothers. His mother had named him Jabez,[c] saying, "I gave birth to him in pain."
10 Jabez cried out to the God of Israel, "Oh,
that you would bless me and enlarge my
territory! Let your hand be with me, and
keep me from harm so that I will be free
from pain." And God granted his request.

11 Kelub, Shuhah's brother, was the father of Mehir, who was the father of
Eshton. 12 Eshton was the father of
Beth Rapha, Paseah and Tehinnah
the father of Ir Nahash.[d] These were
the men of Rekah.
13 The sons of Kenaz:
Othniel[w] and Seraiah.
The sons of Othniel:
Hathath and Meonothai.[e] 14 Meonothai was the father of Ophrah.
Seraiah was the father of Joab,
the father of Ge Harashim.[f] It was
called this because its people were
skilled workers.
15 The sons of Caleb son of Jephunneh:
Iru, Elah and Naam.
The son of Elah:
Kenaz.
16 The sons of Jehallelel:
Ziph, Ziphah, Tiria and Asarel.
17 The sons of Ezrah:
Jether, Mered, Epher and Jalon. One
of Mered's wives gave birth to Miriam,[x] Shammai and Ishbah the father of Eshtemoa. 18 (His wife from
the tribe of Judah gave birth to Jered
the father of Gedor, Heber the father
of Soko, and Jekuthiel the father of
Zanoah.[y]) These were the children
of Pharaoh's daughter Bithiah,
whom Mered had married.
19 The sons of Hodiah's wife, the sister of
Naham:
the father of Keilah[z] the Garmite,
and Eshtemoa the Maakathite.[a]
20 The sons of Shimon:
Amnon, Rinnah, Ben-Hanan and Ti-
lon.
The descendants of Ishi:
Zoheth and Ben-Zoheth.
21 The sons of Shelah[b] son of Judah:
Er the father of Lekah, Laadah the
father of Mareshah and the clans of
the linen workers at Beth Ashbea,
22 Jokim, the men of Kozeba, and Joash and Saraph, who ruled in Moab
and Jashubi Lehem. (These records
are from ancient times.) 23 They
were the potters who lived at Neta-
im and Gederah; they stayed there
and worked for the king.

Simeon

24 The descendants of Simeon:[c]
Nemuel, Jamin, Jarib,[d] Zerah and
Shaul;
25 Shallum was Shaul's son, Mibsam
his son and Mishma his son.
26 The descendants of Mishma:
Hammuel his son, Zakkur his son
and Shimei his son.
27 Shimei had sixteen sons and six
daughters, but his brothers did not have
many children; so their entire clan did not

---

[a] 3 Some Septuagint manuscripts (see also Vulgate); Hebrew *father* [b] 4 *Father* may mean *civic leader* or *military leader*; also in verses 12, 14, 17, 18 and possibly elsewhere. [c] 9 *Jabez* sounds like the Hebrew for *pain*. [d] 12 Or *of the city of Nahash* [e] 13 Some Septuagint manuscripts and Vulgate; Hebrew does not have *and Meonothai*. [f] 14 *Ge Harashim* means *valley of skilled workers*.

4:4 *Ephrathah.* Ephrathah is the wife of the early Caleb (2:19) and the mother of Hur, whose son Salma was the "father of Bethlehem." The names of Bethlehem and Ephrath are closely connected (Gen. 35:19; Ruth 4:11), and the birthplace of the anticipated Messiah is called Bethlehem Ephrathah (Mic. 5:2).

4:9–10 Providence—This passage does not say why or how Jabez was more honorable than his brothers. At the least, he recognized that God is the source of all blessings, and Jabez asked God to bless him. James said that we have not because we ask not (James 4:2–3), and then goes on to address the issue of selfish motives in prayer. Paul encourages believers not to be anxious, but to make our requests to God, with prayer and thanksgiving (Phil. 4:6). It is clear that it is right to ask God for the things that we believe are good, to thank Him for them, and to keep in mind that we can trust Him to meet all of our needs.

4:15 *Caleb.* This is the Caleb who was the friend and colleague of Joshua (Josh. 14:6–7).

4:21 *Er.* The fact that Shelah named his son "Er" indicates that he followed the levirate custom of raising up a child in the name of a deceased brother (Gen. 38:6–11).

4:24 *Simeon.* The tribe of Simeon had no land allotted to them (Jos 19:1–9) because they were a small tribe. They settled in the territory of Judah.

4:4 [t] 1Ch 2:50 [u] Ru 1:19 **4:5** [v] 1Ch 2:24
4:13 [w] Jos 15:17 **4:17** [x] Ex 15:20 **4:18** [y] Jos 15:34
4:19 [z] Jos 15:44 [a] Dt 3:14 **4:21** [b] Ge 38:5
4:24 [c] Ge 29:33 [d] Nu 26:12

become as numerous as the people of Judah. 28They lived in Beersheba,[e] Moladah,[f]
Hazar Shual, 29Bilhah, Ezem,[g] Tolad, 30Be-
thuel, Hormah,[h] Ziklag, 31Beth Markaboth,
Hazar Susim, Beth Biri and Shaaraim.[i]
These were their towns until the reign of
David. 32Their surrounding villages were
Etam, Ain,[j] Rimmon, Token and Ashan[k]—
five towns— 33and all the villages around
these towns as far as Baalath.[a] These were
their settlements. And they kept a genealogical record.

34Meshobab, Jamlech, Joshah son of
Amaziah, 35Joel, Jehu son of Joshibi-
ah, the son of Seraiah, the son of Asi-
el, 36also Elioenai, Jaakobah, Jeshoha-
iah, Asaiah, Adiel, Jesimiel, Benaiah,
37and Ziza son of Shiphi, the son of
Allon, the son of Jedaiah, the son of
Shimri, the son of Shemaiah.

38The men listed above by name were
leaders of their clans. Their families increased greatly, 39and they went to the
outskirts of Gedor[l] to the east of the valley
in search of pasture for their flocks. 40They
found rich, good pasture, and the land was
spacious, peaceful and quiet.[m] Some Hamites had lived there formerly.
41The men whose names were listed
came in the days of Hezekiah king of Judah. They attacked the Hamites in their
dwellings and also the Meunites[n] who were
there and completely destroyed[b] them, as
is evident to this day. Then they settled in
their place, because there was pasture for
their flocks. 42And five hundred of these
Simeonites, led by Pelatiah, Neariah, Rephaiah and Uzziel, the sons of Ishi, invaded
the hill country of Seir.[o] 43They killed the
remaining Amalekites[p] who had escaped,
and they have lived there to this day.

Reuben

5 The sons of Reuben[q] the firstborn of
Israel (he was the firstborn, but when
he defiled his father's marriage bed,[r] his
rights as firstborn were given to the sons
of Joseph[s] son of Israel;[t] so he could not be
listed in the genealogical record in accordance with his birthright,[u] 2and though Judah[v] was the strongest of his brothers and
a ruler[w] came from him, the rights of the
firstborn[x] belonged to Joseph)— 3the sons
of Reuben[y] the firstborn of Israel:
Hanok, Pallu,[z] Hezron and Karmi.
4The descendants of Joel:
Shemaiah his son, Gog his son,
Shimei his son, 5Micah his son,
Reaiah his son, Baal his son,
6and Beerah his son, whom Tiglath-
Pileser[c][a] king of Assyria took into
exile. Beerah was a leader of the
Reubenites.
7Their relatives by clans,[b] listed according to their genealogical records:
Jeiel the chief, Zechariah, 8and Bela
son of Azaz, the son of Shema, the
son of Joel. They settled in the area
from Aroer[c] to Nebo and Baal Meon.
9To the east they occupied the land
up to the edge of the desert that extends to the Euphrates River, because their livestock had increased
in Gilead.[d]
10During Saul's reign they waged
war against the Hagrites[e], who were
defeated at their hands; they occupied
the dwellings of the Hagrites throughout the entire region east of Gilead.

Gad

11The Gadites[f] lived next to them in Bashan, as far as Salekah:[g]
12Joel was the chief, Shapham the second, then Janai and Shaphat, in Bashan.
13Their relatives, by families, were:
Michael, Meshullam, Sheba, Jorai,
Jakan, Zia and Eber—seven in all.
14These were the sons of Abihail son
of Huri, the son of Jaroah, the son of
Gilead, the son of Michael, the son of
Jeshishai, the son of Jahdo, the son
of Buz.
15Ahi son of Abdiel, the son of Guni,
was head of their family.
16The Gadites lived in Gilead, in Bashan
and its outlying villages, and on all
the pasturelands of Sharon as far as
they extended.
17All these were entered in the genealogical records during the reigns of Jotham[h]
king of Judah and Jeroboam[i] king of Israel.

18The Reubenites, the Gadites and the
half-tribe of Manasseh had 44,760 men
ready for military service[j]—able-bodied

[a] *33* Some Septuagint manuscripts (see also Joshua 19:8); Hebrew *Baal* [b] *41* The Hebrew term refers to the irrevocable giving over of things or persons to the LORD, often by totally destroying them.
[c] *6* Hebrew *Tilgath-Pilneser,* a variant of *Tiglath-Pileser;* also in verse 26

5:9 edge of the desert ... the Euphrates River. The Reubenites had pushed east into the wilderness, so they were the first to be deported by the Assyrians (v. 6).

4:28 [e] Ge 21:14 [f] Jos 15:26 **4:29** [g] Jos 15:29 **4:30** [h] Nu 14:45 **4:31** [i] Jos 15:36 **4:32** [j] Nu 34:11 [k] Jos 15:42 **4:39** [l] Jos 15:58 **4:40** [m] Jdg 18:7-10 **4:41** [n] 2Ch 20:1; 26:7 **4:42** [o] Ge 14:6 **4:43** [p] 1Sa 15:8; 30:17; 2Sa 8:12; Est 3:1; 9:16 **5:1** [q] Ge 29:32 [r] Ge 35:22; 49:4 [s] Ge 48:16, 22; 49:26 [t] Ge 48:5 [u] 1Ch 26:10 **5:2** [v] Ge 49:10, 12 [w] 1Sa 9:16; 12:12; 2Sa 6:21; 1Ch 11:2; 2Ch 7:18; Ps 60:7; Mic 5:2; Mt 2:6 [x] Ge 25:31 **5:3** [y] Ge 29:32; 46:9; Ex 6:14; Nu 26:5-11 [z] Nu 26:5 **5:6** [a] ver 26; 2Ki 15:19; 16:10; 2Ch 28:20 **5:7** [b] ver 17 **5:8** [c] Nu 32:34 **5:9** [d] Nu 32:26; Jos 22:9 **5:10** [e] ver 18-21 **5:11** [f] Jos 13:24-28 [g] Dt 3:10; Jos 13:11 **5:17** [h] 2Ki 15:32 [i] 2Ki 14:16, 28 **5:18** [j] Nu 1:3

men who could handle shield and sword,
who could use a bow, and who were trained
for battle. 19They waged war against the
Hagrites, Jetur,[k] Naphish and Nodab.
20They were helped[l] in fighting them, and
God delivered the Hagrites and all their allies into their hands, because they cried[m]
out to him during the battle. He answered
their prayers, because they trusted[n] in him.
21They seized the livestock of the Hagrites—fifty thousand camels, two hundred
fifty thousand sheep and two thousand
donkeys. They also took one hundred thousand people captive, 22and many others fell
slain, because the battle[o] was God's. And
they occupied the land until the exile.[p]

The Half-Tribe of Manasseh

23The people of the half-tribe of Manasseh were numerous; they settled in the land
from Bashan to Baal Hermon, that is, to Senir (Mount Hermon).[q]
24These were the heads of their families:
Epher, Ishi, Eliel, Azriel, Jeremiah, Hodaviah and Jahdiel. They were brave warriors,
famous men, and heads of their families.
25But they were unfaithful[r] to the God of
their ancestors and prostituted[s] themselves
to the gods of the peoples of the land, whom
God had destroyed before them. 26So the
God of Israel stirred up the spirit of Pul[t]
king of Assyria (that is, Tiglath-Pileser[u]
king of Assyria), who took the Reubenites,
the Gadites and the half-tribe of Manasseh
into exile. He took them to Halah,[v] Habor,
Hara and the river of Gozan, where they
are to this day.

Levi

6 [a] The sons of Levi:[w]
Gershon, Kohath and Merari.
2The sons of Kohath:
Amram, Izhar, Hebron and Uzziel.
3The children of Amram:
Aaron, Moses and Miriam.
The sons of Aaron:
Nadab, Abihu,[x] Eleazar and Ithamar.
4Eleazar was the father of Phinehas,
Phinehas the father of Abishua,
5Abishua the father of Bukki,
Bukki the father of Uzzi,
6Uzzi the father of Zerahiah,
Zerahiah the father of Meraioth,
7Meraioth the father of Amariah,
Amariah the father of Ahitub,
8Ahitub the father of Zadok,[y]
Zadok the father of Ahimaaz,
9Ahimaaz the father of Azariah,
Azariah the father of Johanan,
10Johanan the father of Azariah[z] (it
was he who served as priest in the
temple Solomon built in Jerusalem),
11Azariah the father of Amariah,
Amariah the father of Ahitub,
12Ahitub the father of Zadok,
Zadok the father of Shallum,
13Shallum the father of Hilkiah,[a]
Hilkiah the father of Azariah,
14Azariah the father of Seraiah,[b]
and Seraiah the father of Jozadak.[b]

---

[a] In Hebrew texts 6:1-15 is numbered 5:27-41, and 6:16-81 is numbered 6:1-66. [b] *14* Hebrew *Jehozadak,* a variant of *Jozadak;* also in verse 15

5:25 Unbelief—In marriage, adultery is the ultimate breach of trust, breaking a solemn promise of faithfulness and commitment. These tribes of Israel acted just like adulterers when they chose idols instead of the living God. Like a prostitute who has chosen crudity, vulgarity, and cheap finery instead of the steady faithful love and fine clothing from her husband, so Israel had believed a lie and abandoned their covenant with the living God.

5:26 *Tiglath-Pileser.* The famous king Tiglath-Pileser, who reigned around 745–727 B.C., has gone down in Assyrian annals as one of the most powerful rulers of the neo-Assyrian period (v. 6).

6:1–60 Family—Families are usually marked by certain traits or characteristics. Because the Levites were the designated priests, they had a special responsibility to have a reputation for uprightness and faithfulness, but all Israelites were a representation of God to the nations around them. If we are a part of the family of God, we should ask ourselves if we look like God. When people see us, do they see His characteristics?

6:1 *Levi.* All religious personnel involved in tabernacle or temple ministry had to be members of the tribe of Levi. Aaron himself was a Levite, and from the beginning of the priesthood his descendants were designated as the only ones who could serve as high priests (6:16–25; Ex. 28:1).

6:2–4 *Kohath.* This son of Levi was the one to whom the office of priest became exclusively connected. Every priest had to be a Levite, but not every Levite could become a priest. The high priests were descended from Aaron, Kohath's grandson. ***Eleazar.*** Beginning with Eleazar, the genealogy traces the line of high priests through Jozadak, the priest who went into Babylonian exile with his people (v. 15). ***Ithamar.*** Another line of high priests began with Ithamar, including such persons as Eli, Ahimelek, and Abiathar. In the days of David the priestly service was divided between the Eleazar and the Ithamar priests. Solomon rejected the Ithamar priesthood, and accepted only the priests descended from Eleazar (1 Kin. 2:26–27). From Eleazar to Jozadak, there were at least 22 high priests in unbroken succession.

6:8 *Zadok.* This priest, not the same person as the Zadok of verse 12, was the one selected by David to serve along with Ahimelek the son of Abiathar as high priest (2 Sam. 8:17).

6:14 *Jozadak.* The last priest in the list was carried into Babylon (v. 15). He was the father of Joshua, the priest who returned from Babylon with Zerubbabel to rebuild the temple and reestablish the Jewish community (Hag. 1:12,14).

5:19 [k] ver 10; Ge 25:15; 1Ch 1:31 **5:20** [l] Ps 37:40 [m] 1Ki 8:44; 2Ch 13:14; 14:11; Ps 20:7-9; 22:5 [n] Ps 26:1; Da 6:23 **5:22** [o] 2Ch 32:8 [p] 2Ki 15:29; 17:6 **5:23** [q] Dt 3:8, 9; SS 4:8 **5:25** [r] Dt 32:15-18; 2Ki 17:7; 1Ch 9:1; 2Ch 26:16 [s] Ex 34:15 **5:26** [t] 2Ki 15:19 [u] 2Ki 15:29 [v] 2Ki 17:6; 18:11 **6:1** [w] Ge 46:11; Ex 6:16; Nu 26:57; 1Ch 23:6 **6:3** [x] Lev 10:1 **6:8** [y] 2Sa 8:17; 15:27; Ezr 7:2 **6:10** [z] 1Ki 4:2; 6:1; 2Ch 3:1; 26:17-18 **6:13** [a] 2Ki 22:1-20; 2Ch 34:9; 35:8 **6:14** [b] 2Ki 25:18; Ezr 2:2; Ne 11:11

15 Jozadak[c] was deported when the LORD sent Judah and Jerusalem into exile by the hand of Nebuchadnezzar.

16 The sons of Levi:[d]
Gershon,[a] Kohath and Merari.[e]
17 These are the names of the sons of Gershon:
Libni and Shimei.
18 The sons of Kohath:
Amram, Izhar, Hebron and Uzziel.
19 The sons of Merari:[f]
Mahli and Mushi.
These are the clans of the Levites listed according to their fathers:
20 Of Gershon:
Libni his son, Jahath his son,
Zimmah his son, 21 Joah his son,
Iddo his son, Zerah his son
and Jeatherai his son.
22 The descendants of Kohath:
Amminadab his son, Korah[g] his son,
Assir his son, 23 Elkanah his son,
Ebiasaph his son, Assir his son,
24 Tahath his son, Uriel[h] his son,
Uzziah his son and Shaul his son.
25 The descendants of Elkanah:
Amasai, Ahimoth,
26 Elkanah his son,[b] Zophai his son,
Nahath his son, 27 Eliab his son,
Jeroham his son, Elkanah[i] his son
and Samuel[j] his son.[c]
28 The sons of Samuel:
Joel[d][k] the firstborn
and Abijah the second son.
29 The descendants of Merari:
Mahli, Libni his son,
Shimei his son, Uzzah his son,
30 Shimea his son, Haggiah his son
and Asaiah his son.

The Temple Musicians

31 These are the men[l] David put in charge
of the music[m] in the house of the LORD after the ark came to rest there. 32 They ministered with music before the tabernacle,
the tent of meeting, until Solomon built the
temple of the LORD in Jerusalem. They performed their duties according to the regulations laid down for them.
33 Here are the men who served, together
with their sons:
From the Kohathites:
Heman,[n] the musician,
the son of Joel,[o] the son of Samuel,
34 the son of Elkanah,[p] the son of Jeroham,
the son of Eliel, the son of Toah,
35 the son of Zuph, the son of Elkanah,
the son of Mahath, the son of Amasai,
36 the son of Elkanah, the son of Joel,
the son of Azariah, the son of Zephaniah,
37 the son of Tahath, the son of Assir,
the son of Ebiasaph, the son of Korah,[q]
38 the son of Izhar,[r] the son of Kohath,
the son of Levi, the son of Israel;
39 and Heman's associate Asaph,[s] who served at his right hand:
Asaph son of Berekiah, the son of Shimea,[t]
40 the son of Michael, the son of Baaseiah,[e]
the son of Malkijah, 41 the son of Ethni,
the son of Zerah, the son of Adaiah,
42 the son of Ethan, the son of Zimmah,
the son of Shimei, 43 the son of Jahath,
the son of Gershon, the son of Levi;
44 and from their associates, the Merarites, at his left hand:
Ethan son of Kishi, the son of Abdi,
the son of Malluk, 45 the son of Hashabiah,
the son of Amaziah, the son of Hilkiah,
46 the son of Amzi, the son of Bani,
the son of Shemer, 47 the son of Mahli,
the son of Mushi, the son of Merari,
the son of Levi.

48 Their fellow Levites[u] were assigned to all
the other duties of the tabernacle, the house
of God. 49 But Aaron and his descendants
were the ones who presented offerings on
the altar[v] of burnt offering and on the altar

[a] *16* Hebrew *Gershom,* a variant of *Gershon;* also in verses 17, 20, 43, 62 and 71 [b] *26* Some Hebrew manuscripts, Septuagint and Syriac; most Hebrew manuscripts *Ahimoth* [26]*and Elkanah. The sons of Elkanah:* [c] *27* Some Septuagint manuscripts (see also 1 Samuel 1:19,20 and 1 Chron. 6:33,34); Hebrew does not have *and Samuel his son.*
[d] *28* Some Septuagint manuscripts and Syriac (see also 1 Samuel 8:2 and 1 Chron. 6:33); Hebrew does not have *Joel.* [e] *40* Most Hebrew manuscripts; some Hebrew manuscripts, one Septuagint manuscript and Syriac *Maaseiah*

6:17 *Gershon.* The purpose of this genealogy is to list the principal offspring of the sons of Levi who were not priests, but servants in the temple.

6:22 *Amminadab.* Amminadab is another name for Izhar (v. 18) who otherwise appears as the father of Korah (6:37–38; Ex. 6:21; Num. 16:1).

6:28 *Samuel.* Samuel's ancestors were described as Ephraimites (1 Sam. 1:1). Although Samuel was an Ephraimite because he lived in a city in the tribal territory of Ephraim, this genealogy makes it clear that he was a Levite. Levites lived in their own cities among all the tribes, because they did not receive a land inheritance. As a Levite, he could be trained under Eli (1 Sam. 2:11), and later officiate at public services that included sacrifices (1 Sam. 9:13; 10:8).

6:15 [c] 2Ki 25:18; Ne 12:1; Hag 1:1, 14; 2:2, 4; Zec 6:11 **6:16** [d] Ge 29:34; Ex 6:16; Nu 3:17-20 [e] Nu 26:57 **6:19** [f] Ge 46:11; 1Ch 23:21; 24:26 **6:22** [g] Ex 6:24 **6:24** [h] 1Ch 15:5 **6:27** [i] 1Sa 1:1 [j] 1Sa 1:20 **6:28** [k] ver 33; 1Sa 8:2 **6:31** [l] 1Ch 25:1; 2Ch 29:25-26; Ne 12:45 [m] 1Ch 9:33; 15:19; Ezr 3:10; Ps 68:25 **6:33** [n] 1Ki 4:31; 1Ch 15:17; 25:1 [o] ver 28 **6:34** [p] 1Sa 1:1 **6:37** [q] Ex 6:24 **6:38** [r] Ex 6:21 **6:39** [s] 1Ch 25:1, 9; 2Ch 29:13; Ne 11:17 [t] 1Ch 15:17 **6:48** [u] 1Ch 23:32 **6:49** [v] Ex 27:1-8

of incense[w] in connection with all that was
done in the Most Holy Place, making atonement for Israel, in accordance with all that
Moses the servant of God had commanded.

50 These were the descendants of Aaron:
Eleazar his son, Phinehas his son,
Abishua his son, 51 Bukki his son,
Uzzi his son, Zerahiah his son,
52 Meraioth his son, Amariah his son,
Ahitub his son, 53 Zadok[x] his son
and Ahimaaz his son.

54 These were the locations of their settlements[y] allotted as their territory (they were
assigned to the descendants of Aaron who
were from the Kohathite clan, because the
first lot was for them):
55 They were given Hebron in Judah
with its surrounding pasturelands.
56 But the fields and villages around
the city were given to Caleb son of Jephunneh.[z]
57 So the descendants of Aaron were
given Hebron (a city of refuge), and
Libnah,[a][a] Jattir,[b] Eshtemoa, 58 Hilen,
Debir,[c] 59 Ashan,[d] Juttah[b] and Beth
Shemesh, together with their pasturelands. 60 And from the tribe of Benjamin they were given Gibeon,[c] Geba,
Alemeth and Anathoth,[e] together with
their pasturelands.
The total number of towns distributed among the Kohathite clans came
to thirteen.
61 The rest of Kohath's descendants were
allotted ten towns from the clans of half the
tribe of Manasseh.
62 The descendants of Gershon, clan by
clan, were allotted thirteen towns from the
tribes of Issachar, Asher and Naphtali, and
from the part of the tribe of Manasseh that
is in Bashan.
63 The descendants of Merari, clan by
clan, were allotted twelve towns from the
tribes of Reuben, Gad and Zebulun.
64 So the Israelites gave the Levites these
towns[f] and their pasturelands. 65 From the
tribes of Judah, Simeon and Benjamin they
allotted the previously named towns.
66 Some of the Kohathite clans were giv-
en as their territory towns from the tribe
of Ephraim.
67 In the hill country of Ephraim they
were given Shechem (a city of refuge),
and Gezer,[d][g] 68 Jokmeam,[h] Beth Horon,[i] 69 Aijalon[j] and Gath Rimmon,[k] together with their pasturelands.
70 And from half the tribe of Manasseh the Israelites gave Aner and Bile-
am, together with their pasturelands,
to the rest of the Kohathite clans.

71 The Gershonites[l] received the following:
From the clan of the half-tribe of Manasseh
they received Golan in Bashan[m] and
also Ashtaroth, together with their
pasturelands;
72 from the tribe of Issachar
they received Kedesh, Daberath,[n]
73 Ramoth and Anem, together with
their pasturelands;
74 from the tribe of Asher
they received Mashal, Abdon,[o]
75 Hukok[p] and Rehob,[q] together with
their pasturelands;
76 and from the tribe of Naphtali
they received Kedesh in Galilee,
Hammon[r] and Kiriathaim,[s] together with their pasturelands.

77 The Merarites (the rest of the Levites)
received the following:
From the tribe of Zebulun
they received Jokneam, Kartah,[e]
Rimmono and Tabor, together with
their pasturelands;
78 from the tribe of Reuben across the
Jordan east of Jericho
they received Bezer[t] in the wilderness, Jahzah, 79 Kedemoth[u] and
Mephaath, together with their pasturelands;

---

[a] 57 See Joshua 21:13; Hebrew *given the cities of refuge: Hebron, Libnah.* [b] 59 Syriac (see also Septuagint and Joshua 21:16); Hebrew does not have *Juttah.* [c] 60 See Joshua 21:17; Hebrew does not have *Gibeon.* [d] 67 See Joshua 21:21; Hebrew *given the cities of refuge: Shechem, Gezer.* [e] 77 See Septuagint and Joshua 21:34; Hebrew does not have *Jokneam, Kartah.*

6:57 *Hebron.* The law specified that if a person killed another unintentionally he could find sanctuary in one of six specified cities, and there wait in safety for the trial (Num. 35:6–27). No one could take revenge as long as he was in the city of refuge. These six cities were included among the 48 Levitical cities, and Hebron, located in Judah, was one of them.

6:61—7:27 Family—In any family record, some of the names have strong memories associated with them. The reputations may be good or bad, but they are all a part of the family reputation. It is comforting to know that the family that produced Saul, the unfaithful king, is the same line that produced Saul, who became the faithful apostle Paul.

6:67 *Shechem.* Shechem was both a Levitical city and a city of refuge. Shechem was especially significant in Israel. It was the site of Abraham's first altar in Canaan (Gen. 12:6–7), the place where Jacob bought a piece of land (Gen. 33:19), and the location of the first capital of the northern kingdom (1 Kin. 12:25).

6:76 *Kedesh.* Kedesh was another of the six cities of refuge. It was the most northern of the three west of the Jordan.

6:78 *Bezer.* Bezer was also a city of refuge, the farthest south of those east of the Jordan.

6:49 [w] Ex 30:1-7, 10; 2Ch 26:18 **6:53** [x] 2Sa 8:17 **6:54** [y] Nu 31:10 **6:56** [z] Jos 14:13; 15:13 **6:57** [a] Nu 33:20 [b] Jos 15:48 **6:58** [c] Jos 10:3 **6:59** [d] Jos 15:42 **6:60** [e] Jer 1:1 **6:64** [f] Nu 35:1-8; Jos 21:3, 41-42 **6:67** [g] Jos 10:33 **6:68** [h] 1Ki 4:12 [i] Jos 10:10 **6:69** [j] Jos 10:12 [k] Jos 19:45 **6:71** [l] 1Ch 23:7 [m] Jos 20:8 **6:72** [n] Jos 19:12 **6:74** [o] Jos 19:28 **6:75** [p] Jos 19:34 [q] Nu 13:21 **6:76** [r] Jos 19:28 [s] Nu 32:37 **6:78** [t] Jos 20:8 **6:79** [u] Dt 2:26

80 and from the tribe of Gad
they received Ramoth in Gilead,[v]
Mahanaim,[w] 81 Heshbon and Jazer,[x]
together with their pasturelands.[y]

Issachar

7 The sons of Issachar:[z]
Tola, Puah,[a] Jashub and Shimron—
four in all.
2 The sons of Tola:
Uzzi, Rephaiah, Jeriel, Jahmai, Ib-
sam and Samuel—heads of their
families. During the reign of David, the descendants of Tola listed
as fighting men in their genealogy
numbered 22,600.
3 The son of Uzzi:
Izrahiah.
The sons of Izrahiah:
Michael, Obadiah, Joel and Ishiah.
All five of them were chiefs. 4 According to their family genealogy,
they had 36,000 men ready for battle, for they had many wives and
children.
5 The relatives who were fighting men
belonging to all the clans of Issachar, as listed in their genealogy,
were 87,000 in all.

Benjamin

6 Three sons of Benjamin:[b]
Bela, Beker and Jediael.
7 The sons of Bela:
Ezbon, Uzzi, Uzziel, Jerimoth and
Iri, heads of families—five in all.
Their genealogical record listed
22,034 fighting men.
8 The sons of Beker:
Zemirah, Joash, Eliezer, Elioenai,
Omri, Jeremoth, Abijah, Anathoth
and Alemeth. All these were the
sons of Beker. 9 Their genealogical
record listed the heads of families
and 20,200 fighting men.
10 The son of Jediael:
Bilhan.
The sons of Bilhan:
Jeush, Benjamin, Ehud, Kenaanah,
Zethan, Tarshish and Ahishahar.
11 All these sons of Jediael were
heads of families. There were 17,200
fighting men ready to go out to war.
12 The Shuppites and Huppites were the
descendants of Ir, and the Hushites[a]
the descendants of Aher.

Naphtali

13 The sons of Naphtali:[c]
Jahziel, Guni, Jezer and Shillem[b]—
the descendants of Bilhah.

Manasseh

14 The descendants of Manasseh:[d]
Asriel was his descendant through
his Aramean concubine. She gave
birth to Makir the father of Gilead.[e]
15 Makir took a wife from among the
Huppites and Shuppites. His sister's
name was Maakah.
Another descendant was named Zelophehad,[f] who had only daughters.
16 Makir's wife Maakah gave birth
to a son and named him Peresh. His
brother was named Sheresh, and his
sons were Ulam and Rakem.
17 The son of Ulam:
Bedan.
These were the sons of Gilead[g] son of
Makir, the son of Manasseh. 18 His
sister Hammoleketh gave birth to
Ishhod, Abiezer[h] and Mahlah.
19 The sons of Shemida were:
Ahian, Shechem, Likhi and Aniam.

Ephraim

20 The descendants of Ephraim:[i]
Shuthelah, Bered his son,
Tahath his son, Eleadah his son,
Tahath his son, 21 Zabad his son
and Shuthelah his son.
Ezer and Elead were killed by the
native-born men of Gath, when they
went down to seize their livestock.
22 Their father Ephraim mourned for
them many days, and his relatives
came to comfort him. 23 Then he made
love to his wife again, and she became
pregnant and gave birth to a son. He
named him Beriah,[c] because there had

[a] 12 Or *Ir. The sons of Dan: Hushim,* (see Gen. 46:23); Hebrew does not have *The sons of Dan.* [b] 13 Some Hebrew and Septuagint manuscripts (see also Gen. 46:24 and Num. 26:49); most Hebrew manuscripts *Shallum* [c] 23 *Beriah* sounds like the Hebrew for *misfortune.*

6:80 *Ramoth in Gilead.* Another city of refuge, Ramoth, was directly east of the Jordan. In this way the cities of refuge were distributed throughout the land so that any Israelite could be within a few miles of one of them. All six cities were assigned to the Levites, with Hebron designated for the priests (Deut. 17:8–13; 19:17–21).

7:14 *Manasseh ... Makir.* Manasseh was the son of Joseph, and his son was Makir. Makir's daughter became the wife of Judah's grandson Hezron (2:21), which joined the two tribes of Judah and Manasseh.

7:15 *Zelophehad, who had only daughters.* This man had no sons, so Moses made provision for inheritance rights for daughters in such cases (Num. 36:1–9).

7:20–21 *Tahath ... Shuthelah.* The repetition of these two names illustrates the custom of sons being named for their grandfathers or more remote ancestors.

6:80 [v] Jos 20:8 [w] Ge 32:2 **6:81** [x] Nu 21:32 [y] 2Ch 11:14 **7:1** [z] Ge 30:18; Nu 26:23 [a] Ge 46:13 **7:6** [b] Ge 46:21; Nu 26:38; 1Ch 8:1-40 **7:13** [c] Ge 30:8; 46:24 **7:14** [d] Ge 41:51; Jos 17:1; 1Ch 5:23 [e] Nu 26:30 **7:15** [f] Nu 26:33; 36:1-12 **7:17** [g] Nu 26:30; 1Sa 12:11 **7:18** [h] Jos 17:2 **7:20** [i] Ge 41:52; Nu 1:33; 26:35

been misfortune in his family. 24His
daughter was Sheerah, who built Lower and Upper Beth Horon[j] as well as
Uzzen Sheerah.
25 Rephah was his son, Resheph his son,[a]
Telah his son, Tahan his son,
26 Ladan his son, Ammihud his son,
Elishama his son, 27Nun his son
and Joshua his son.
28Their lands and settlements included
Bethel and its surrounding villages, Naa-
ran to the east, Gezer[k] and its villages to
the west, and Shechem and its villages all
the way to Ayyah and its villages. 29Along
the borders of Manasseh were Beth Shan,[l]
Taanach, Megiddo and Dor,[m] together with
their villages. The descendants of Joseph
son of Israel lived in these towns.

Asher

30 The sons of Asher:[n]
Imnah, Ishvah, Ishvi and Beriah.
Their sister was Serah.
31 The sons of Beriah:
Heber and Malkiel, who was the father of Birzaith.
32 Heber was the father of Japhlet, Shomer and Hotham and of their sister
Shua.
33 The sons of Japhlet:
Pasak, Bimhal and Ashvath.
These were Japhlet's sons.
34 The sons of Shomer:
Ahi, Rohgah,[b] Hubbah and Aram.
35 The sons of his brother Helem:
Zophah, Imna, Shelesh and Amal.
36 The sons of Zophah:
Suah, Harnepher, Shual, Beri, Im-
rah, 37Bezer, Hod, Shamma, Shil-
shah, Ithran[c] and Beera.
38 The sons of Jether:
Jephunneh, Pispah and Ara.
39 The sons of Ulla:
Arah, Hanniel and Rizia.
40All these were descendants of Asher—
heads of families, choice men, brave warriors and outstanding leaders. The number
of men ready for battle, as listed in their
genealogy, was 26,000.

The Genealogy of Saul the Benjamite

8 Benjamin[o] was the father of Bela his
firstborn,
Ashbel the second son, Aharah the
third,
2 Nohah the fourth and Rapha the
fifth.
3 The sons of Bela were:
Addar,[p] Gera, Abihud,[d] 4Abishua,
Naaman, Ahoah,[q] 5Gera, Shephu-
phan and Huram.
6 These were the descendants of Ehud,[r]
who were heads of families of those
living in Geba and were deported to
Manahath:
7 Naaman, Ahijah, and Gera, who deported them and who was the father
of Uzza and Ahihud.
8 Sons were born to Shaharaim in Moab
after he had divorced his wives Hushim and Baara. 9By his wife Hodesh he had Jobab, Zibia, Mesha,
Malkam, 10Jeuz, Sakia and Mir-
mah. These were his sons, heads of
families. 11By Hushim he had Abi-
tub and Elpaal.
12 The sons of Elpaal:
Eber, Misham, Shemed (who built
Ono[s] and Lod with its surrounding
villages), 13and Beriah and Shema,
who were heads of families of those
living in Aijalon[t] and who drove out
the inhabitants of Gath.[u]
14 Ahio, Shashak, Jeremoth, 15Zebadiah,
Arad, Eder, 16Michael, Ishpah and
Joha were the sons of Beriah.
17 Zebadiah, Meshullam, Hizki, Heber,
18Ishmerai, Izliah and Jobab were
the sons of Elpaal.
19 Jakim, Zikri, Zabdi, 20Elienai, Zillethai, Eliel, 21Adaiah, Beraiah
and Shimrath were the sons of
Shimei.
22 Ishpan, Eber, Eliel, 23Abdon, Zikri,
Hanan, 24Hananiah, Elam, Antho-
thijah, 25Iphdeiah and Penuel were
the sons of Shashak.
26 Shamsherai, Shehariah, Athaliah,
27Jaareshiah, Elijah and Zikri were
the sons of Jeroham.
28All these were heads of families, chiefs
as listed in their genealogy, and they lived
in Jerusalem.

---

[a] *25* Some Septuagint manuscripts; Hebrew does not have *his son.* [b] *34* Or *of his brother Shomer: Rohgah* [c] *37* Possibly a variant of *Jether*
[d] *3* Or *Gera the father of Ehud*

8:1 *Benjamin.* The reason for this second and much more detailed genealogy of Benjamin is its focus on the genealogy of King Saul (vv. 29–40).

8:9 *Mesha.* There was a well-known Moabite king named Mesha. Both the Scriptures (2 Kin. 3:4) and the Moabite Stone attest to this fact. The reference here to Mesha as a son of Shaharaim and Hodesh, his Moabite wife (v. 8), suggests that the Illustrious Moabite king may have had a Benjamite father, but the evidence is not conclusive.

8:28 *chiefs ... lived in Jerusalem.* This city was not taken by David until approximately 1004 B.C., so the line of Benjamin was traced to at least that time. Even after David took the city, there may have been Benjamites who still lived there, for David gave Benjamites positions of responsibility in his government (11:31; 12:1–7,29).

7:24 [j] Jos 10:10; 16:3,5 **7:28** [k] Jos 10:33; 16:7
7:29 [l] Jos 17:11 [m] Jos 11:2 **7:30** [n] Ge 46:17; Nu 1:40; 26:44
8:1 [o] Ge 46:21; 1Ch 7:6 **8:3** [p] Ge 46:21 **8:4** [q] 2Sa 23:9
8:6 [r] Jdg 3:12-30; 1Ch 2:52 **8:12** [s] Ezr 2:33; Ne 6:2; 7:37; 11:35 **8:13** [t] Jos 10:12 [u] Jos 11:22

29 Jeiel[a] the father[b] of Gibeon lived in
Gibeon.[v]
His wife's name was Maakah,
30 and his firstborn son was Abdon,
followed by Zur, Kish, Baal, Ner,[c]
Nadab, 31 Gedor, Ahio, Zeker 32 and
Mikloth, who was the father of
Shimeah. They too lived near their
relatives in Jerusalem.
33 Ner[w] was the father of Kish,[x] Kish the
father of Saul[y], and Saul the father
of Jonathan, Malki-Shua, Abinadab
and Esh-Baal.[d][z]
34 The son of Jonathan:[a]
Merib-Baal,[e][b] who was the father of
Micah.
35 The sons of Micah:
Pithon, Melek, Tarea and Ahaz.
36 Ahaz was the father of Jehoaddah, Jehoaddah was the father of
Alemeth, Azmaveth and Zimri,
and Zimri was the father of Moza.
37 Moza was the father of Binea; Ra-
phah was his son, Eleasah his son
and Azel his son.
38 Azel had six sons, and these were their
names:
Azrikam, Bokeru, Ishmael, Sheari-
ah, Obadiah and Hanan. All these
were the sons of Azel.
39 The sons of his brother Eshek:
Ulam his firstborn, Jeush the second
son and Eliphelet the third. 40 The
sons of Ulam were brave warriors
who could handle the bow. They had
many sons and grandsons—150 in
all.
All these were the descendants of Benjamin.[c]

9 All Israel was listed in the genealogies recorded in the book of the kings of Israel and Judah. They were taken captive to Babylon because of their unfaithfulness.[d]

The People in Jerusalem

2 Now the first to resettle on their own property in their own towns[e] were some Israelites, priests, Levites and temple servants.[f]

3 Those from Judah, from Benjamin, and from Ephraim and Manasseh who lived in Jerusalem were:
4 Uthai son of Ammihud, the son of
Omri, the son of Imri, the son of
Bani, a descendant of Perez son of
Judah.[g]
5 Of the Shelanites[f]:
Asaiah the firstborn and his sons.
6 Of the Zerahites:
Jeuel.
The people from Judah numbered
690.
7 Of the Benjamites:
Sallu son of Meshullam, the son of
Hodaviah, the son of Hassenuah;
8 Ibneiah son of Jeroham; Elah son of
Uzzi, the son of Mikri; and Meshullam son of Shephatiah, the son of
Reuel, the son of Ibnijah.
9 The people from Benjamin, as listed
in their genealogy, numbered 956.
All these men were heads of their
families.
10 Of the priests:
Jedaiah; Jehoiarib; Jakin;
11 Azariah son of Hilkiah, the son of
Meshullam, the son of Zadok, the
son of Meraioth, the son of Ahitub,
the official in charge of the house of
God;
12 Adaiah son of Jeroham, the son of
Pashhur,[h] the son of Malkijah; and

[a] *29* Some Septuagint manuscripts (see also 9:35); Hebrew does not have *Jeiel.* [b] *29 Father* may mean *civic leader* or *military leader.* [c] *30* Some Septuagint manuscripts (see also 9:36); Hebrew does not have *Ner.* [d] *33* Also known as *Ish-Bosheth* [e] *34* Also known as *Mephibosheth* [f] *5* See Num. 26:20; Hebrew *Shilonites.*

8:30 *Kish.* Kish was the father of Saul (v. 33; 9:39). In this passage the relationship between Jeiel and Kish is unclear because Kish is also named as the son of Ner (v. 33). However, in 9:35–39 the lineage is clearly traced from Jeiel to Ner to Kish and finally to Saul.

8:32 *Jerusalem.* Jerusalem remained under Jebusite control until David conquered it (2 Sam. 5:6–19). Perhaps at this time the Benjamites lived among the Jebusites.

8:33 *Esh-Baal.* Esh-Baal was evidently Saul's youngest son, since he was not named in the genealogies of the beginning of Saul's reign (1 Sam. 14:49). Usually called Ish-bosheth, which means "man of the shameful thing," he reigned for a short time after his father's death (2 Sam. 2:10).

9:1 Unfaithfulness—Blatant disobedience always leads to disaster. God is serious about working righteousness in our lives, and He knows the changes that both trials and blessings can bring to our hearts. He will not leave us in a state of lethargy and peace if we need to be ignited. Sometimes He will test us to see if we are serious about walking with Him. Like the Israelites, we need to ask ourselves if we are obedient or compromising.

9:2 *Israelites.* The deportation of Israel by the Assyrians from 734 to 722 B.C. resulted in Israel's dispersion throughout the eastern Mediterranean world. However, it is apparent from this verse that some of them joined their Judean brethren in the return from Babylon after 539 B.C.

9:3 *Ephraim and Manasseh.* Both of these tribes were from the northern kingdom, or Israel. This is another confirmation that the returning community included Israelites as well as Judeans. It is very possible that some of those in the northern tribes, who had remained faithful to the Lord, may have migrated into Judah before Assyria took Israel captive.

8:29 [v] Jos 9:3 **8:33** [w] 1Sa 28:19 [x] 1Sa 9:1 [y] 1Sa 14:49 [z] 2Sa 2:8 **8:34** [a] 2Sa 9:12 [b] 2Sa 4:4 **8:40** [c] Nu 26:38 **9:1** [d] 1Ch 5:25 **9:2** [e] Jos 9:27; Ezr 2:70 [f] Ezr 2:43,58; 8:20; Ne 7:60 **9:4** [g] Ge 38:29; 46:12 **9:12** [h] Ezr 2:38; 10:22; Ne 10:3; Jer 21:1; 38:1

Maasai son of Adiel, the son of Jahzerah, the son of Meshullam, the son of Meshillemith, the son of Immer.
13 The priests, who were heads of families, numbered 1,760. They were able men, responsible for ministering in the house of God.
14 Of the Levites:
Shemaiah son of Hasshub, the son of Azrikam, the son of Hashabiah, a Merarite;
15 Bakbakkar, Heresh, Galal and Mattaniah[i] son of Mika, the son of Zikri, the son of Asaph;
16 Obadiah son of Shemaiah, the son of Galal, the son of Jeduthun; and Berekiah son of Asa, the son of Elkanah, who lived in the villages of the Netophathites.[j]
17 The gatekeepers:[k]
Shallum, Akkub, Talmon, Ahiman and their fellow Levites, Shallum their chief
18 being stationed at the King's Gate[l] on the east, up to the present time. These were the gatekeepers belonging to the camp of the Levites.
19 Shallum[m] son of Kore, the son of Ebiasaph, the son of Korah, and his fellow gatekeepers from his family (the Korahites) were responsible for guarding the thresholds of the tent just as their ancestors had been responsible for guarding the entrance to the dwelling of the LORD.
20 In earlier times Phinehas[n] son of Eleazar was the official in charge of the gatekeepers, and the LORD was with him.
21 Zechariah[o] son of Meshelemiah was the gatekeeper at the entrance to the tent of meeting.
22 Altogether, those chosen to be gatekeepers[p] at the thresholds numbered 212. They were registered by genealogy in their villages. The gatekeepers had been assigned to their positions of trust by David and Samuel the seer.[q]
23 They and their descendants were in charge of guarding the gates of the house of the LORD—the house called the tent of meeting.
24 The gatekeepers were on the four sides: east, west, north and south.
25 Their fellow Levites in their villages had to come from time to time and share their duties for seven-day[r] periods.
26 But the four principal gatekeepers, who were Levites, were entrusted with the responsibility for the rooms and treasuries[s] in the house of God.
27 They would spend the night stationed around the house of God,[t] because they had to guard it; and they had charge of the key[u] for opening it each morning.

28 Some of them were in charge of the articles used in the temple service; they counted them when they were brought in and when they were taken out.
29 Others were assigned to take care of the furnishings and all the other articles of the sanctuary,[v] as well as the special flour and wine, and the olive oil, incense and spices.
30 But some[w] of the priests took care of mixing the spices.
31 A Levite named Mattithiah, the firstborn son of Shallum the Korahite, was entrusted with the responsibility for baking the offering bread.
32 Some of the Kohathites, their fellow Levites, were in charge of preparing for every Sabbath the bread set out on the table.[x]
33 Those who were musicians,[y] heads of Levite families, stayed in the rooms of the temple and were exempt from other duties because they were responsible for the work day and night.[z]
34 All these were heads of Levite families, chiefs as listed in their genealogy, and they lived in Jerusalem.

The Genealogy of Saul

35 Jeiel[a] the father[a] of Gibeon lived in Gibeon.
His wife's name was Maakah,
36 and his firstborn son was Abdon, followed by Zur, Kish, Baal, Ner, Nadab,
37 Gedor, Ahio, Zechariah and Mikloth.
38 Mikloth was the father of Shimeam. They too lived near their relatives in Jerusalem.
39 Ner[b] was the father of Kish,[c] Kish the father of Saul, and Saul the father of Jonathan,[d] Malki-Shua, Abinadab and Esh-Baal.[b e]
40 The son of Jonathan:
Merib-Baal,[c f] who was the father of Micah.
41 The sons of Micah:
Pithon, Melek, Tahrea and Ahaz.[d]
42 Ahaz was the father of Jadah, Jadah[e] was the father of Alemeth, Azmaveth and Zimri, and Zimri was the father of Moza.
43 Moza was the father of Binea; Rephaiah was his son, Eleasah his son and Azel his son.

[a] 35 *Father* may mean *civic leader* or *military leader.* [b] 39 Also known as *Ish-Bosheth* [c] 40 Also known as *Mephibosheth* [d] 41 Vulgate and Syriac (see also Septuagint and 8:35); Hebrew does not have *and Ahaz.* [e] 42 Some Hebrew manuscripts and Septuagint (see also 8:36); most Hebrew manuscripts *Jarah, Jarah*

9:19 *Korah.* As descendants of Kohath (Ex. 6:18) Korah and his line had close connections with the priesthood. They could not be priests, but they ministered closely with the temple, first as carriers of the holy objects (Num. 4:5 – 15), and later as gatekeepers.

9:15 [i] 2Ch 20:14; Ne 11:22 **9:16** [j] Ne 12:28
9:17 [k] ver 22; 1Ch 26:1; 2Ch 8:14; 31:14; Ezr 2:42; Ne 7:45

9:18 [l] 1Ch 26:14; Eze 43:1; 46:1 **9:19** [m] Jer 35:4
9:20 [n] Nu 25:7-13 **9:21** [o] 1Ch 26:2, 14 **9:22** [p] ver 17; 1Ch 26:1-2; 2Ch 31:15, 18 [q] 1Sa 9:9 **9:25** [r] 2Ki 11:5; 2Ch 23:8 **9:26** [s] 1Ch 26:22 **9:27** [t] Nu 3:38; 1Ch 23:30-32 [u] Isa 22:22 **9:29** [v] Nu 3:28; 1Ch 23:29
9:30 [w] Ex 30:23-25 **9:32** [x] Lev 24:5-8; 1Ch 23:29, 2Ch 13:11 **9:33** [y] 1Ch 6:31; 25:1-31 [z] Ps 134:1
9:35 [a] 1Ch 8:29 **9:39** [b] 1Ch 8:33 [c] 1Sa 9:1 [d] 1Sa 13:22
[e] 2Sa 2:8 **9:40** [f] 2Sa 4:4

44 Azel had six sons, and these were their
names:
Azrikam, Bokeru, Ishmael, Sheari-
ah, Obadiah and Hanan. These were
the sons of Azel.

Saul Takes His Life

10 Now the Philistines fought against
Israel; the Israelites fled before them,
and many fell dead on Mount Gilboa. 2 The
Philistines were in hot pursuit of Saul and
his sons, and they killed his sons Jonathan,
Abinadab and Malki-Shua. 3 The fighting
grew fierce around Saul, and when the archers overtook him, they wounded him.
4 Saul said to his armor-bearer, "Draw
your sword and run me through, or these
uncircumcised fellows will come and
abuse me."
But his armor-bearer was terrified and
would not do it; so Saul took his own sword
and fell on it. 5 When the armor-bearer saw
that Saul was dead, he too fell on his sword
and died. 6 So Saul and his three sons died,
and all his house died together.
7 When all the Israelites in the valley saw
that the army had fled and that Saul and
his sons had died, they abandoned their
towns and fled. And the Philistines came
and occupied them.
8 The next day, when the Philistines came
to strip the dead, they found Saul and his
sons fallen on Mount Gilboa. 9 They stripped
him and took his head and his armor, and
sent messengers throughout the land of the
Philistines to proclaim the news among
their idols and their people. 10 They put his
armor in the temple of their gods and hung
up his head in the temple of Dagon.[g]
11 When all the inhabitants of Jabesh Gilead[h] heard what the Philistines had done
to Saul, 12 all their valiant men went and
took the bodies of Saul and his sons and
brought them to Jabesh. Then they buried
their bones under the great tree in Jabesh,
and they fasted seven days.
13 Saul died[i] because he was unfaithful[j]
to the LORD; he did not keep[k] the word of
the LORD and even consulted a medium[l] for
guidance, 14 and did not inquire of the LORD.
So the LORD put him to death and turned[m]
the kingdom[n] over to David son of Jesse.

David Becomes King Over Israel

11 All Israel[o] came together to David at
Hebron[p] and said, "We are your own
flesh and blood. 2 In the past, even while
Saul was king, you were the one who led
Israel on their military campaigns.[q] And
the LORD your God said to you, 'You will
shepherd[r] my people Israel, and you will
become their ruler.[s]'"
3 When all the elders of Israel had come to
King David at Hebron, he made a covenant
with them at Hebron before the LORD, and
they anointed[t] David king over Israel, as the
LORD had promised through Samuel.

David Conquers Jerusalem

4 David and all the Israelites marched to
Jerusalem (that is, Jebus). The Jebusites[u]
who lived there 5 said to David, "You will
not get in here." Nevertheless, David captured the fortress of Zion—which is the
City of David.
6 David had said, "Whoever leads the
attack on the Jebusites will become commander in chief." Joab[v] son of Zeruiah went
up first, and so he received the command.
7 David then took up residence in the fortress, and so it was called the City of David.
8 He built up the city around it, from the terraces[a][w] to the surrounding wall, while Joab
restored the rest of the city. 9 And David became more and more powerful,[x] because
the LORD Almighty was with him.

[a] 8 Or *the Millo*

10:4 *uncircumcised.* For the Hebrew, circumcision was a sign of God's promise through Abraham to them. The uncircumcised were those outside the promise, often their enemies. ***abuse.*** The abuse of the Philistines might take the form of cutting off Saul's thumbs and big toes, which would leave him crippled and humiliated (Judg. 1:6–7). Whatever they did would have been meant to belittle Saul, his kingdom, and his God. ***was terrified.*** The armor-bearer was not afraid of Saul. He was afraid of God. He was afraid of killing one who had been anointed king over Israel and who belonged to God who had set him apart. ***sword and fell on it.*** Suicide was very rare among Hebrews of Old Testament times.

10:10 *Dagon.* Dagon was worshiped by the Philistines and other peoples in Syria and northwest Mesopotamia as the god of grain. Apparently the Philistines celebrated military victory by bringing a trophy of their success back to their temple where it could be displayed as a tribute to the might of their god.

10:14 *put him to death.* This statement is shocking in its bluntness. In the final analysis, Saul's death was not by his own hand, but by the hand of God. The Lord let Saul pursue a course that led to death.

11:1–2 Unity—The history of events between the death of Saul and the beginning of David's reign over all Israel is omitted by the chronicler, but is narrated in 2 Samuel 2–4. The fighting between the house of David and the house of Saul continued until Saul's son Ish-Bosheth was killed. Israel could not be unified as long as some were trying to be loyal to Saul. God had already rejected Saul and chosen David, but until Saul's house was gone, the people could not focus on God's choice for king. We as believers often find ourselves in a state of disunity because we are mixed up with our own agendas instead of seeing God's plan.

11:8 *He built up the city.* Once David occupied Mount Ophel, the original and very small area of

10:10 [g] Jdg 16:23 **10:11** [h] Jdg 21:8 **10:13** [i] 2Sa 1:1 [j] 1Sa 15:23; 1Ch 5:25 [k] 1Sa 13:13 [l] Lev 19:31; 20:6; Dt 18:9-14; 1Sa 28:7 **10:14** [m] 1Ch 12:23 [n] 1Sa 13:14; 15:28 **11:1** [o] 1Ch 9:1 [p] Ge 13:18; 23:19 **11:2** [q] 1Sa 18:5, 16 [r] Ps 78:71; Mt 2:6 [s] 1Ch 5:2 **11:3** [t] 1Sa 16:1-13 **11:4** [u] Ge 10:16; 15:18-21; Jos 3:10; 15:8; Jdg 1:21; 19:10 **11:6** [v] 2Sa 2:13; 8:16 **11:8** [w] 2Sa 5:9; 2Ch 32:5 **11:9** [x] 2Sa 3:1; Est 9:4

David's Mighty Warriors

10These were the chiefs of David's
mighty warriors—they, together with all
Israel,[y] gave his kingship strong support to
extend it over the whole land, as the LORD
had promised[z]— 11this is the list of David's
mighty warriors:[a]

Jashobeam,[a] a Hakmonite, was chief of
the officers[b]; he raised his spear against
three hundred men, whom he killed in one
encounter.

12Next to him was Eleazar son of Dodai
the Ahohite, one of the three mighty warriors. 13He was with David at Pas Dammim
when the Philistines gathered there for battle. At a place where there was a field full of
barley, the troops fled from the Philistines.
14But they took their stand in the middle of
the field. They defended it and struck the
Philistines down, and the LORD brought
about a great victory.[b]

15Three of the thirty chiefs came down
to David to the rock at the cave of Adullam,
while a band of Philistines was encamped
in the Valley[c] of Rephaim. 16At that time
David was in the stronghold,[d] and the Philistine garrison was at Bethlehem. 17Da-
vid longed for water and said, "Oh, that
someone would get me a drink of water
from the well near the gate of Bethlehem!"
18So the Three broke through the Philistine lines, drew water from the well near
the gate of Bethlehem and carried it back
to David. But he refused to drink it; instead,
he poured[e] it out to the LORD. 19"God forbid that I should do this!" he said. "Should
I drink the blood of these men who went at
the risk of their lives?" Because they risked
their lives to bring it back, David would not
drink it.

Such were the exploits of the three
mighty warriors.

20Abishai[f] the brother of Joab was chief
of the Three. He raised his spear against
three hundred men, whom he killed, and
so he became as famous as the Three. 21He
was doubly honored above the Three and
became their commander, even though he
was not included among them.

22Benaiah son of Jehoiada, a valiant
fighter from Kabzeel,[g] performed great exploits. He struck down Moab's two mightiest warriors. He also went down into a pit
on a snowy day and killed a lion.[h] 23And
he struck down an Egyptian who was five
cubits[c] tall. Although the Egyptian had a
spear like a weaver's rod[i] in his hand, Benaiah went against him with a club. He
snatched the spear from the Egyptian's
hand and killed him with his own spear.
24Such were the exploits of Benaiah son of
Jehoiada; he too was as famous as the three
mighty warriors. 25He was held in greater
honor than any of the Thirty, but he was
not included among the Three. And David
put him in charge of his bodyguard.

26The mighty warriors were:
Asahel[j] the brother of Joab,
Elhanan son of Dodo from Bethlehem,
27Shammoth[k] the Harorite,
Helez the Pelonite,
28Ira son of Ikkesh from Tekoa,
Abiezer[l] from Anathoth,
29Sibbekai[m] the Hushathite,
Ilai the Ahohite,
30Maharai the Netophathite,
Heled son of Baanah the Netophathite,
31Ithai son of Ribai from Gibeah in
Benjamin,
Benaiah[n] the Pirathonite,[o]
32Hurai from the ravines of Gaash,
Abiel the Arbathite,
33Azmaveth the Baharumite,
Eliahba the Shaalbonite,
34the sons of Hashem the Gizonite,
Jonathan son of Shagee the Hararite,
35Ahiam son of Sakar the Hararite,
Eliphal son of Ur,
36Hepher the Mekerathite,
Ahijah the Pelonite,
37Hezro the Carmelite,
Naarai son of Ezbai,
38Joel the brother of Nathan,
Mibhar son of Hagri,
39Zelek the Ammonite,
Naharai the Berothite, the armor-
bearer of Joab son of Zeruiah,
40Ira the Ithrite,
Gareb the Ithrite,

---

[a] 11 Possibly a variant of *Jashob-Baal*
[b] 11 Or *Thirty*; some Septuagint manuscripts *Three* (see also 2 Samuel 23:8)
[c] 23 That is, about 7 feet 6 inches or about 2.3 meters

Jerusalem, he greatly enlarged it by building retaining walls along the Kidron valley to the east and south and the Tyropoeon valley to the west. Between these walls and the top of the hill he built terraces, so that various buildings could be constructed there.

11:18 *poured it out to the LORD.* Even though he had been longing for a drink from his "home well," David never considered sending any of his brave supporters to get it for him. When they risked their lives to bring it to him, David responded by pouring it on the ground, as if it had been a blood offering for God. The Israelites were strictly forbidden to eat blood (Lev. 3:17; Deut. 12:23), and David considered this water to be in the same category. Only God should receive such a sacrifice (Gen. 35:14).

11:23 *five cubits.* The Egyptian was about seven and a half feet tall.

11:10 [y] ver 1 [z] ver 3; 1Ch 12:23 **11:11** [a] 2Sa 17:10
11:14 [b] Ex 14:30; 1Sa 11:13 **11:15** [c] 1Ch 14:9; Isa 17:5
11:16 [d] 2Sa 5:17 **11:18** [e] Dt 12:16 **11:20** [f] 1Sa 26:6
11:22 [g] Jos 15:21 [h] 1Sa 17:36 **11:23** [i] 1Sa 17:7
11:26 [j] 2Sa 2:18 **11:27** [k] 1Ch 27:8 **11:28** [l] 1Ch 27:12
11:29 [m] 2Sa 21:18 **11:31** [n] 1Ch 27:14 [o] Jdg 12:13

41 Uriah[p] the Hittite,
Zabad[q] son of Ahlai,
42 Adina son of Shiza the Reubenite,
who was chief of the Reubenites,
and the thirty with him,
43 Hanan son of Maakah,
Joshaphat the Mithnite,
44 Uzzia the Ashterathite,[r]
Shama and Jeiel the sons of Hotham
the Aroerite,
45 Jediael son of Shimri,
his brother Joha the Tizite,
46 Eliel the Mahavite,
Jeribai and Joshaviah the sons of El-
naam,
Ithmah the Moabite,
47 Eliel, Obed and Jaasiel the Mezobaite.

Warriors Join David

12 These were the men who came to David at Ziklag,[s] while he was banished
from the presence of Saul son of Kish (they
were among the warriors who helped him
in battle; 2 they were armed with bows and
were able to shoot arrows or to sling stones
right-handed or left-handed;[t] they were relatives of Saul[u] from the tribe of Benjamin):

3 Ahiezer their chief and Joash the
sons of Shemaah the Gibeathite; Jeziel
and Pelet the sons of Azmaveth; Berakah, Jehu the Anathothite, 4 and Ishmaiah the Gibeonite, a mighty warrior
among the Thirty, who was a leader of
the Thirty; Jeremiah, Jahaziel, Johanan, Jozabad the Gederathite,[a v] 5 Elu-
zai, Jerimoth, Bealiah, Shemariah and
Shephatiah the Haruphite; 6 Elkanah,
Ishiah, Azarel, Joezer and Jashobeam
the Korahites; 7 and Joelah and Zebadiah the sons of Jeroham from Gedor.[w]

8 Some Gadites[x] defected to David at his
stronghold in the wilderness. They were
brave warriors, ready for battle and able
to handle the shield and spear. Their faces
were the faces of lions,[y] and they were as
swift as gazelles[z] in the mountains.
9 Ezer was the chief,
Obadiah the second in command, Eliab the third,
10 Mishmannah the fourth, Jeremiah the
fifth,
11 Attai the sixth, Eliel the seventh,
12 Johanan the eighth, Elzabad the ninth,
13 Jeremiah the tenth and Makbannai
the eleventh.
14 These Gadites were army commanders; the least was a match for a hundred,[a]
and the greatest for a thousand.[b] 15 It was
they who crossed the Jordan in the first
month when it was overflowing all its
banks,[c] and they put to flight everyone
living in the valleys, to the east and to the
west.
16 Other Benjamites[d] and some men from
Judah also came to David in his stronghold. 17 David went out to meet them and
said to them, "If you have come to me in
peace to help me, I am ready for you to join
me. But if you have come to betray me to
my enemies when my hands are free from
violence, may the God of our ancestors see
it and judge you."
18 Then the Spirit[e] came on Amasai,[f]
chief of the Thirty, and he said:

"We are yours, David!
We are with you, son of Jesse!
Success,[g] success to you,
and success to those who help you,
for your God will help you."

So David received them and made them
leaders of his raiding bands.
19 Some of the tribe of Manasseh defected to David when he went with the Philistines to fight against Saul. (He and his men
did not help the Philistines because, after
consultation, their rulers sent him away.
They said, "It will cost us our heads if he
deserts to his master Saul.")[h] 20 When David went to Ziklag,[i] these were the men of
Manasseh who defected to him: Adnah,
Jozabad, Jediael, Michael, Jozabad, Elihu
and Zillethai, leaders of units of a thousand
in Manasseh. 21 They helped David against
raiding bands, for all of them were brave
warriors, and they were commanders in
his army. 22 Day after day men came to help
David, until he had a great army, like the
army of God.[b]

---

[a] 4 In Hebrew texts the second half of this verse (*Jeremiah . . . Gederathite*) is numbered 12:5, and 12:5-40 is numbered 12:6-41. [b] 22 Or *a great and mighty army*

11:41 *Uriah.* This is the same Uriah who was the husband of Bathsheba. The fact that Uriah was one of the mighty men of valor, who did so much to establish David as king, makes David's betrayal of Uriah doubly tragic (2 Sam. 11).

12:2 *relatives of Saul from the tribe of Benjamin.* There is a curious little play on words here. Benjamin means "son of the right hand." These Benjamites could shoot and sling with either the right hand or the left hand, which made them particularly versatile in battle. They were more than "sons of the right hand" to David. They were "sons of the left hand" as well.

12:15 *in the first month.* The first month was Nisan, corresponding approximately to April, the time of spring rains. Ordinarily a person could not cross the Jordan at flood stage, but the fact that the Gadites were not stopped by the floods is a testimony of their unusual courage.

11:41 [p] 2Sa 11:6 [q] 1Ch 2:36 **11:44** [r] Dt 1:4 **12:1** [s] Jos 15:31; 1Sa 27:2-6 **12:2** [t] Jdg 3:15; 20:16 [u] 2Sa 3:19 **12:4** [v] Jos 15:36 **12:7** [w] Jos 15:58 **12:8** [x] Ge 30:11 [y] 2Sa 17:10 [z] 2Sa 2:18 **12:14** [a] Lev 26:8 [b] Dt 32:30 **12:15** [c] Jos 3:15 **12:16** [d] 2Sa 3:19 **12:18** [e] Jdg 3:10; 6:34; 1Ch 28:12; 2Ch 15:1; 20:14; 24:20 [f] 2Sa 17:25 [g] 1Sa 25:5-6 **12:19** [h] 1Sa 29:2-11 **12:20** [i] 1Sa 27:6

Others Join David at Hebron

23These are the numbers of the men
armed for battle who came to David at Hebron[j] to turn[k] Saul's kingdom over to him,
as the LORD had said:[l]
24from Judah, carrying shield and
spear—6,800 armed for battle;
25from Simeon, warriors ready for battle—7,100;
26from Levi—4,600, 27including Jehoiada, leader of the family of Aaron,
with 3,700 men, 28and Zadok,[m] a
brave young warrior, with 22 officers from his family;
29from Benjamin,[n] Saul's tribe—3,000,
most[o] of whom had remained loyal
to Saul's house until then;
30from Ephraim, brave warriors, famous in their own clans—20,800;
31from half the tribe of Manasseh, designated by name to come and make
David king—18,000;
32from Issachar, men who understood
the times and knew what Israel
should do[p]—200 chiefs, with all
their relatives under their command;
33from Zebulun, experienced soldiers
prepared for battle with every type
of weapon, to help David with undivided loyalty—50,000;
34from Naphtali—1,000 officers, together with 37,000 men carrying shields
and spears;
35from Dan, ready for battle—28,600;
36from Asher, experienced soldiers prepared for battle—40,000;
37and from east of the Jordan, from Reuben, Gad and the half-tribe of Manasseh, armed with every type of
weapon—120,000.
38All these were fighting men who volunteered to serve in the ranks. They came
to Hebron fully determined to make David
king over all Israel.[q] All the rest of the Israelites were also of one mind to make David king. 39The men spent three days there
with David, eating and drinking,[r] for their
families had supplied provisions for them.
40Also, their neighbors from as far away
as Issachar, Zebulun and Naphtali came
bringing food on donkeys, camels, mules
and oxen. There were plentiful supplies[s] of
flour, fig cakes, raisin[t] cakes, wine, olive oil,
cattle and sheep, for there was joy[u] in Israel.

Bringing Back the Ark

13 David conferred with each of his officers, the commanders of thousands
and commanders of hundreds. 2He then
said to the whole assembly of Israel, "If it
seems good to you and if it is the will of
the LORD our God, let us send word far and
wide to the rest of our people throughout
the territories of Israel, and also to the
priests and Levites who are with them in
their towns and pasturelands, to come and
join us. 3Let us bring the ark of our God
back to us,[v] for we did not inquire[w] of[a] it[b]
during the reign of Saul." 4The whole assembly agreed to do this, because it seemed
right to all the people.
5So David assembled all Israel,[x] from the
Shihor River[y] in Egypt to Lebo Hamath,[z]
to bring the ark of God from Kiriath Jearim.[a] 6David and all Israel went to Baalah[b]
of Judah (Kiriath Jearim) to bring up from
there the ark of God the LORD, who is enthroned between the cherubim[c]—the ark
that is called by the Name.
7They moved the ark of God from Abinadab's[d] house on a new cart, with Uzzah and
Ahio guiding it. 8David and all the Israelites were celebrating with all their might

a 3 Or *we neglected*   *b* 3 Or *him*

12:28 *Zadok.* This Zadok was probably the same Zadok who was first appointed by David as priest at Gibeon (16:39). The office of priest was not incompatible with that of warrior, as Phinehas showed (Num. 25:6–9; Josh. 22:13–30).

12:32 Wisdom—The men of Issachar were dealing with the issue of "the LORD's anointed." There was no longer any question that David was the Lord's choice, and that Saul had been replaced, but the timing was crucial. It would do no good to anoint David if it took rebellion and treason to place him on the throne. Men who gain power by trickery usually assume that others will be ready to do likewise, and dishonesty and intrigue are not a good foundation for a God-honoring nation. It is sometimes hard to wait for God's timing, or even hard to tell just what His timing is, but if we ask for wisdom, He will give it to us (James 1:5).

13:3 *the ark of our God.* This was the ark of the covenant that contained a copy of the Ten Commandments (Ex. 25:10–22). Besides holding the stone tablets, the ark represented the presence of the living God among the Israelites.

13:5 Commitment—One of David's first official actions upon becoming king was to bring the ark of God to Jerusalem. The ark had been in Kiriath Jearim since the time it was returned by the Philistines when Samuel was a boy (1 Sam. 6:20—7:1). Moving the ark to Jerusalem was a sign of David's commitment to place the Lord first in his reign.

13:6 *the LORD, who is enthroned between the cherubim.* On each side of the ark of the covenant were two cherubim. They extended their wings over the cover, also called the mercy seat (Ex. 25:17–22), and the glory of God was perceived as sitting on top of the ark, as a King sits on a throne. ***that is called by the Name.*** In Deuteronomy, the presence of God is often spoken of as the presence of His name (Deut. 12:1–14).

12:23 [j] 2Sa 2:3-4 [k] 1Ch 10:14 [l] 1Sa 16:1; 1Ch 11:10
12:28 [m] 2Sa 8:17; 1Ch 6:8; 15:11; 16:39; 27:17
12:29 [n] 2Sa 3:19 [o] 2Sa 2:8-9 **12:32** [p] Est 1:13
12:38 [q] 2Sa 5:1-3; 1Ch 9:1 **12:39** [r] 2Sa 3:20; Isa 25:6-8
12:40 [s] 2Sa 16:1; 17:29 [t] 1Sa 25:18 [u] 1Ch 29:22
13:3 [v] 1Sa 7:1-2 [w] 2Ch 1:5 **13:5** [x] 1Ch 11:1; 15:3
[y] Jos 13:3 [z] Nu 13:21 [a] 1Sa 6:21; 7:2 **13:6** [b] Jos 15:9;
2Sa 6:2 [c] Ex 25:22; 2Ki 19:15 **13:7** [d] Nu 4:15; 1Sa 7:1

before God, with songs and with harps,
lyres, timbrels, cymbals and trumpets.[e]
9When they came to the threshing floor
of Kidon, Uzzah reached out his hand to
steady the ark, because the oxen stumbled.
10The LORD's anger[f] burned against Uzzah,
and he struck him down[g] because he had
put his hand on the ark. So he died there
before God.
11Then David was angry because the
LORD's wrath had broken out against Uzzah, and to this day that place is called Perez Uzzah.[a][h]
12David was afraid of God that day and
asked, "How can I ever bring the ark of
God to me?" 13He did not take the ark to
be with him in the City of David. Instead,
he took it to the house of Obed-Edom[i] the
Gittite. 14The ark of God remained with the
family of Obed-Edom in his house for three
months, and the LORD blessed his household[j] and everything he had.

David's House and Family

14 Now Hiram king of Tyre sent messengers to David, along with cedar logs,[k]
stonemasons and carpenters to build a
palace for him. 2And David knew that the
LORD had established him as king over Israel and that his kingdom had been highly
exalted[l] for the sake of his people Israel.
3In Jerusalem David took more wives
and became the father of more sons[m] and
daughters. 4These are the names of the
children born to him there:[n] Shammua,
Shobab, Nathan, Solomon, 5Ibhar, Elishua,
Elpelet, 6Nogah, Nepheg, Japhia, 7Elisha-
ma, Beeliada[b] and Eliphelet.

David Defeats the Philistines

8When the Philistines heard that David
had been anointed king over all Israel,[o]
they went up in full force to search for him,
but David heard about it and went out to
meet them. 9Now the Philistines had come
and raided the Valley[p] of Rephaim; 10so
David inquired of God: "Shall I go and attack the Philistines? Will you deliver them
into my hands?"
The LORD answered him, "Go, I will deliver them into your hands."
11So David and his men went up to Baal
Perazim,[q] and there he defeated them. He
said, "As waters break out, God has broken
out against my enemies by my hand." So that
place was called Baal Perazim.[c] 12The Philistines had abandoned their gods there, and
David gave orders to burn[r] them in the fire.[s]
13Once more the Philistines raided the
valley;[t] 14so David inquired of God again,
and God answered him, "Do not go directly
after them, but circle around them and attack them in front of the poplar trees. 15As
soon as you hear the sound of marching in
the tops of the poplar trees, move out to battle, because that will mean God has gone
out in front of you to strike the Philistine
army." 16So David did as God commanded
him, and they struck down the Philistine
army, all the way from Gibeon[u] to Gezer.[v]
17So David's fame[w] spread throughout
every land, and the LORD made all the nations fear[x] him.

The Ark Brought to Jerusalem

15 After David had constructed buildings for himself in the City of David,
he prepared[y] a place for the ark of God and
pitched[z] a tent for it. 2Then David said, "No
one but the Levites[a] may carry[b] the ark of
God, because the LORD chose them to carry
the ark of the LORD and to minister[c] before
him forever."

---

[a] *11 Perez Uzzah* means *outbreak against Uzzah.*
[b] *7* A variant of *Eliada*
[c] *11 Baal Perazim* means *the lord who breaks out.*

13:9 *threshing floor of Kidon.* Also called "the threshing floor of Nakon" (2 Sam. 6:6), this hard flat surface was used for separating the grain kernels from the straw and husks.

13:11 *Perez Uzzah.* Perez Uzzah means "outbreak against Uzzah." The ark should have been carried on poles by Levites (Num. 4:14–15). This direction for transporting the holy things was very clear, and should have been remembered.

14:1–2 *Hiram king of Tyre.* A powerful ruler of the Phoenician city-state of Tyre, Hiram is mentioned in the Scriptures and in other sources. He was a contemporary of both David and Solomon. He helped build David's house, and he also supplied material for the temple and other building projects in Solomon's reign (1 Kin. 9:10).

14:3 *took more wives.* See the note for 3:1–5.

14:4 *children.* The first four listed here are all sons of Bathsheba (3:5).

15:1 *place for the ark.* The place for the ark was in the tent in the City of David. The original tabernacle built in Moses' day had been placed at Shiloh (Josh. 18:1). It remained there until the capture of the ark by the Philistines (1 Sam. 4:1–11), when it was evidently moved to Nob, just two miles from Jerusalem (1 Sam. 21:1–6). Then it was moved to a high place at Gibeon (2 Chr. 1:3), about two miles north of Saul's city Gibeah. When David became king, he left the Mosaic tabernacle at Gibeon and appointed the priest Zadok to attend to its ministry (16:39). Even after he had built a new tabernacle on Mount Zion and brought the ark into it, the original tent remained at Gibeon. Solomon brought the ark from Mount Zion and the tabernacle of Moses from Gibeon and placed them in the new temple he had built on Mount Moriah (2 Chr. 5:4–5).

15:2 *No one ... but the Levites.* According to the provisions of the Law, the ark was to be carried only

13:8 [e] 2Sa 6:5; 1Ch 15:16, 19, 24; 2Ch 5:12; Ps 92:3
13:10 [f] 1Ch 15:13, 15 [g] Lev 10:2 **13:11** [h] 1Ch 15:13; Ps 7:11 **13:13** [i] 1Ch 15:18, 24; 16:38; 26:4-5, 15
13:14 [j] 2Sa 6:11; 1Ch 26:4-5 **14:1** [k] 2Ch 2:3; Ezr 3:7
14:2 [l] Nu 24:7; Dt 26:19 **14:3** [m] 1Ch 3:1 **14:4** [n] 1Ch 3:9
14:8 [o] 1Ch 11:1 **14:9** [p] ver 13; Jos 15:8; 1Ch 11:15
14:11 [q] Isa 28:21 **14:12** [r] Ex 32:20 [s] Jos 7:15
14:13 [t] ver 9 **14:16** [u] Jos 9:3 [v] Jos 10:33
14:17 [w] Jos 6:27; 2Ch 26:8 [x] Ex 15:14-16; Dt 2:25
15:1 [y] Ps 132:1-18 [z] 1Ch 16:1; 17:1 **15:2** [a] Nu 4:15; Dt 10:8; 2Ch 5:5 [b] Dt 31:9 [c] 1Ch 23:13

3 David assembled all Israel[d] in Jerusalem to bring up the ark of the LORD to the
place he had prepared for it. 4 He called together the descendants of Aaron and the
Levites:
5 From the descendants of Kohath,
Uriel the leader and 120 relatives;
6 from the descendants of Merari,
Asaiah the leader and 220 relatives;
7 from the descendants of Gershon,[a]
Joel the leader and 130 relatives;
8 from the descendants of Elizaphan,[e]
Shemaiah the leader and 200 relatives;
9 from the descendants of Hebron,[f]
Eliel the leader and 80 relatives;
10 from the descendants of Uzziel,
Amminadab the leader and 112 relatives.
11 Then David summoned Zadok[g] and
Abiathar[h] the priests, and Uriel, Asaiah,
Joel, Shemaiah, Eliel and Amminadab the
Levites. 12 He said to them, "You are the
heads of the Levitical families; you and
your fellow Levites are to consecrate[i] yourselves and bring up the ark of the LORD, the
God of Israel, to the place I have prepared
for it. 13 It was because you, the Levites,[j] did
not bring it up the first time that the LORD
our God broke out in anger against us.[k] We
did not inquire of him about how to do it in
the prescribed way." 14 So the priests and
Levites consecrated themselves in order
to bring up the ark of the LORD, the God
of Israel. 15 And the Levites carried the ark
of God with the poles on their shoulders,
as Moses had commanded[l] in accordance
with the word of the LORD.
16 David told the leaders of the Levites to
appoint their fellow Levites as musicians[m]
to make a joyful sound with musical instruments: lyres, harps and cymbals.[n]
17 So the Levites appointed Heman[o] son
of Joel; from his relatives, Asaph[p] son of
Berekiah; and from their relatives the Merarites,[q] Ethan son of Kushaiah; 18 and with
them their relatives next in rank: Zechariah,[b] Jaaziel, Shemiramoth, Jehiel, Unni,
Eliab, Benaiah, Maaseiah, Mattithiah,
Eliphelehu, Mikneiah, Obed-Edom[r] and
Jeiel,[c] the gatekeepers.
19 The musicians Heman,[s] Asaph and
Ethan were to sound the bronze cymbals;
20 Zechariah, Jaaziel,[d] Shemiramoth, Jehiel, Unni, Eliab, Maaseiah and Benaiah were to play the lyres according to
alamoth,[e] 21 and Mattithiah, Eliphelehu,
Mikneiah, Obed-Edom, Jeiel and Azaziah
were to play the harps, directing according to *sheminith*.[e] 22 Kenaniah the head Levite was in charge of the singing; that was
his responsibility because he was skillful
at it.
23 Berekiah and Elkanah were to be
doorkeepers for the ark. 24 Shebaniah,
Joshaphat, Nethanel, Amasai, Zechariah, Benaiah and Eliezer the priests were
to blow trumpets[t] before the ark of God.
Obed-Edom and Jehiah were also to be
doorkeepers for the ark.
25 So David and the elders of Israel and
the commanders of units of a thousand
went to bring up the ark[u] of the covenant
of the LORD from the house of Obed-Edom,
with rejoicing. 26 Because God had helped
the Levites who were carrying the ark of

[a] 7 Hebrew *Gershom*, a variant of *Gershon*
[b] 18 Three Hebrew manuscripts and most Septuagint manuscripts (see also verse 20 and 16:5); most Hebrew manuscripts *Zechariah son and* or *Zechariah, Ben and*
[c] 18 Hebrew; Septuagint (see also verse 21) *Jeiel and Azaziah*
[d] 20 See verse 18; Hebrew *Aziel*, a variant of *Jaaziel*.
[e] 20,21 Probably a musical term

by the Levites, by means of poles inserted through corner rings (Num. 4:14–15).

15:11 *Zadok.* The other line of the priesthood descended from Aaron's son Eleazar, and included Zadok (6:8). During David's time representatives of both Ithamar and Eleazar served. Zadok served at the tabernacle at Gibeon, and Abiathar served as chief priest at Jerusalem. When Solomon became king, Abiathar was deposed and Zadok ministered as high priest at the temple (1 Kin. 2:26–27,35). The dismissal of Abiathar as priest was in accordance with the Lord's word to Eli because of the unfaithfulness of Eli's sons (1 Sam. 2:27–36). ***Abiathar.*** The transition from the rule of Saul to David involved a transition from the old Mosaic tabernacle to the new place David had established on Mount Zion in preparation for the temple (v. 1). Abiathar's father, the priest Ahimelek, was in charge of the old tabernacle when it left Shiloh and was moved to Nob (1 Sam. 21:1). Ahimelek was Eli's great-grandson (1 Sam. 14:3; 22:9). Eli is considered to have been a descendant of Aaron's son Ithamar.

15:17 *Heman.* The musician Heman was the grandson of the prophet Samuel (6:33). He is probably the same Heman who appears in the superscription of Psalm 88. ***Asaph.*** Asaph was leader of the Gershonite Levites (6:39–43). Asaph and his sons ministered primarily as singers (25:1–2; 2 Chr. 20:14) and composers, as their superscriptions suggest (Ps. 50; 73–83). ***Ethan.*** Ethan was the head of the Merarite division of musicians (6:44). He may be the composer of Psalm 89.

15:20 *play the lyres according to alamoth.* The meaning of "*alamoth*" is uncertain. It may mean a soprano voice.

15:21 *harps ... according to sheminith.* The meaning of "*sheminith*" is uncertain, but it is apparently a musical term, perhaps derived from the Hebrew word for eighth, referring to musical scales.

15:24 *Obed-Edom.* It is likely that Obed-Edom in this verse was the same person who had custody of the ark in the months before it was brought to Jerusalem (13:13–14). He apparently was a Levite and certainly a righteous man.

15:3 [d] 1Ki 8:1; 1Ch 13:5 **15:8** [e] Ex 6:22 **15:9** [f] Ex 6:18 **15:11** [g] 1Ch 12:28 [h] 1Sa 22:20 **15:12** [i] Ex 19:14-15; Lev 11:44; 2Ch 35:6 **15:13** [j] 1Ki 8:4 [k] 2Sa 6:3; 1Ch 13:7-10 **15:15** [l] Ex 25:14; Nu 4:5,15 **15:16** [m] Ps 68:25 [n] 1Ch 13:8; 25:1; Ne 12:27,36 **15:17** [o] 1Ch 6:33 [p] 1Ch 6:39 [q] 1Ch 6:44 **15:18** [r] 1Ch 26:4-5 **15:19** [s] 1Ch 25:6 **15:24** [t] ver 28; 1Ch 16:6; 2Ch 7:6 **15:25** [u] 1Ch 13:13; 2Ch 1:4

the covenant of the LORD, seven bulls and
seven rams[v] were sacrificed. 27 Now David
was clothed in a robe of fine linen, as were
all the Levites who were carrying the ark,
and as were the musicians, and Kenaniah,
who was in charge of the singing of the
choirs. David also wore a linen ephod. 28 So
all Israel brought up the ark of the covenant
of the LORD with shouts, with the sounding
of rams' horns[w] and trumpets, and of cymbals, and the playing of lyres and harps.

29 As the ark of the covenant of the LORD
was entering the City of David, Michal
daughter of Saul watched from a window.
And when she saw King David dancing
and celebrating, she despised him in her
heart.

Ministering Before the Ark

16 They brought the ark of God and
set it inside the tent that David had
pitched[x] for it, and they presented burnt
offerings and fellowship offerings before
God. 2 After David had finished sacrificing
the burnt offerings and fellowship offerings, he blessed[y] the people in the name of
the LORD. 3 Then he gave a loaf of bread, a
cake of dates and a cake of raisins to each
Israelite man and woman.

4 He appointed some of the Levites to
minister[z] before the ark of the LORD, to extol,[a] thank, and praise the LORD, the God
of Israel: 5 Asaph was the chief, and next
to him in rank were Zechariah, then Jaaziel,[b] Shemiramoth, Jehiel, Mattithiah, Eliab, Benaiah, Obed-Edom and Jeiel. They
were to play the lyres and harps, Asaph
was to sound the cymbals, 6 and Benaiah
and Jahaziel the priests were to blow the
trumpets regularly before the ark of the
covenant of God.

7 That day David first appointed Asaph
and his associates to give praise[a] to the
LORD in this manner:

8 Give praise[b] to the LORD, proclaim his
name;
make known among the nations[c]
what he has done.
9 Sing to him, sing praise[d] to him;
tell of all his wonderful acts.
10 Glory in his holy name;
let the hearts of those who seek the
LORD rejoice.
11 Look to the LORD and his strength;
seek[e] his face always.

12 Remember[f] the wonders he has done,
his miracles,[g] and the judgments he
pronounced,
13 you his servants, the descendants of
Israel,
his chosen ones, the children of
Jacob.
14 He is the LORD our God;
his judgments[h] are in all the earth.

15 He remembers[c] his covenant forever,
the promise he made, for a thousand
generations,
16 the covenant[i] he made with Abraham,
the oath he swore to Isaac.
17 He confirmed it to Jacob[j] as a decree,
to Israel as an everlasting covenant:
18 "To you I will give the land of Canaan[k]
as the portion you will inherit."

19 When they were but few in number,[l]
few indeed, and strangers in it,
20 they[d] wandered from nation to nation,
from one kingdom to another.
21 He allowed no one to oppress them;
for their sake he rebuked kings:[m]

---

[a] *4* Or *petition*; or *invoke* [b] *5* See 15:18,20; Hebrew *Jeiel*, possibly another name for *Jaaziel*. [c] *15* Some Septuagint manuscripts (see also Psalm 105:8); Hebrew *Remember* [d] *18-20* One Hebrew manuscript, Septuagint and Vulgate (see also Psalm 105:12); most Hebrew manuscripts *inherit, / [19] though you are but few in number, / few indeed, and strangers in it." / [20] They*

15:29 *Michal daughter of Saul.* Michal was David's first wife, whom he married before Saul started pursuing him (1 Sam. 18:27; 19:11–17). When David was hiding from Saul, Michal was given in marriage to another (1 Sam. 25:44). One of the conditions of David's peace agreement with Abner was that Michal be returned to him (2 Sam. 3:13–16). The Bible does not say why Michal despised David, but it seems probable that the real source of her attitude was bitterness about her life. If she had no understanding of God's hand in her life and the life of the nation, seeing David's joyful abandonment before the Lord would have been galling.

16:3 *he gave.* David's distribution of food was in line with the nature of the peace offerings. Such offerings often accompanied occasions of praise and thanksgiving such as this one. They were unique in that they provided a common meal in which all participated before God—the offerer, his family and friends, and the priests (Lev. 7:11–14,28–34; Deut. 12:17–19).

16:4 *Levites.* The appointment of Levites described here was of a more permanent nature than that of 15:1–24, which concerned the immediate task of moving the ark into Jerusalem. Some of the same persons were involved, as verses 5 and 6 make clear.

16:7 *give praise to the LORD.* David's musical abilities are well-known, both as a harpist (1 Sam. 16:18) and as the writer of many of the psalms. This psalm consists of three different parts. Each portion correlates with part of another psalm. Verses 8–22 correspond with Psalm 105:1–15; verses 23–33 with Psalm 96:1–13; and verses 34–36 with Psalm 106:1, 47–48.

16:12–16 Obedience—"Remember the wonders he has done ..." and for those of us who are believers, "proclaim the Lord's death until he comes" (1 Cor. 11:23–26). Remembering is connected to obedience, only when we remember His commands can we obey Him.

15:26 [v] Nu 23:1-4,29 **15:28** [w] 1Ch 13:8 **16:1** [x] 1Ch 15:1 **16:2** [y] Ex 39:43 **16:4** [z] 1Ch 15:2 **16:7** [a] 2Sa 23:1 **16:8** [b] ver 34; Ps 136:1 [c] 2Ki 19:19 **16:9** [d] Ex 15:1 **16:11** [e] 1Ch 28:9; 2Ch 7:14; Ps 24:6; 119:2,58 **16:12** [f] Ps 77:11 [g] Ps 78:43 **16:14** [h] Isa 26:9 **16:16** [i] Ge 12:7; 15:18; 17:2; 22:16-18; 26:3; 28:13; 35:11 **16:17** [j] Ge 35:9-12 **16:18** [k] Ge 13:14-17 **16:19** [l] Ge 34:30; Dt 7:7 **16:21** [m] Ge 12:17; 20:3; Ex 7:15-18

22 "Do not touch my anointed ones;
do my prophets[n] no harm."

23 Sing to the LORD, all the earth;
proclaim his salvation day after day.
24 Declare his glory among the nations,
his marvelous deeds among all peoples.

25 For great is the LORD and most worthy of praise;[o]
he is to be feared[p] above all gods.[q]
26 For all the gods of the nations are idols,
but the LORD made the heavens.[r]
27 Splendor and majesty are before him;
strength and joy are in his dwelling place.

28 Ascribe to the LORD, all you families of nations,
ascribe to the LORD glory and strength.[s]
29 Ascribe to the LORD the glory due his name;
bring an offering and come before him.
Worship the LORD in the splendor of his[a] holiness.[t]
30 Tremble[u] before him, all the earth!
The world is firmly established; it cannot be moved.

31 Let the heavens rejoice, let the earth be glad;[v]
let them say among the nations, "The LORD reigns![w]"
32 Let the sea resound, and all that is in it;[x]
let the fields be jubilant, and everything in them!
33 Let the trees[y] of the forest sing,
let them sing for joy before the LORD,
for he comes to judge[z] the earth.

34 Give thanks[a] to the LORD, for he is good;[b]
his love endures forever.[c]
35 Cry out, "Save us, God our Savior;[d]
gather us and deliver us from the nations,
that we may give thanks to your holy name,
and glory in your praise."
36 Praise be to the LORD, the God of Israel,[e]
from everlasting to everlasting.

Then all the people said "Amen" and "Praise the LORD."

37David left Asaph and his associates before the ark of the covenant of the LORD to
minister there regularly, according to each
day's requirements.[f] 38He also left Obed-
Edom[g] and his sixty-eight associates to
minister with them. Obed-Edom son of Jeduthun, and also Hosah,[h] were gatekeepers.
39David left Zadok[i] the priest and his
fellow priests before the tabernacle of
the LORD at the high place in Gibeon[j] 40to

[a] 29 Or *LORD with the splendor of*

16:22 *anointed.* In this context "anointed ones" means those set apart for God's service, not necessarily literally anointed with oil.

16:29 The Meaning of Worship—Worship refers to the honor and praise given in thought or deed to a person or thing. The Bible teaches that God alone is worthy of worship (Ps. 29:2). But it also records accounts of those who worshiped inappropriately: people (Acts 14:8–18); false gods (2 Kin. 10:19); images and idols (Is. 2:8); heavenly bodies (2 Kin. 21:3); Satan (Rev. 13:4); and demons (Rev. 9:20).

True worship involves at least three important elements:

1. *Reverence.* This includes the honor and respect directed toward the Lord in thought and feeling. Jesus said that those who worship God must do so "in the spirit and in the truth" (John 4:24). The term *spirit* speaks of the personal nature of worship. It is from my person to God's person and involves the intellect, emotions, and will. The word *truth* speaks of the content of worship. God is pleased when we worship Him, understanding His true character.
2. *Public expression.* This was particularly prevalent in the Old Testament because of the sacrificial system. For example, when a believer received a particular blessing for which he wanted to thank God, it was not sufficient to say it privately; he expressed his thanks publicly with a thank offering (Lev. 7:12).
3. *Service.* The words for worship in both Testaments originally referred to the labor of slaves for the master. Worship especially includes the joyful service which Christians render to Christ their Master. The concept of worship involves much more than church attendance once or twice a week. It involves an entire life of obedience, service and praise to God.

16:33 *trees . . . sing.* This is a figure of speech called personification, in which inanimate things are spoken of as if they had human characteristics. Because the whole creation was negatively affected by the fall of humanity into sin, it could not be restored to perfection and could not truly rejoice until humanity was redeemed. ***he comes.*** When the Lord returns to the earth, all creation will burst out in praise.

16:38 *Obed-Edom.* There are two men by this name in this verse. The first is the Obed-Edom whose house sheltered the ark for three months (13:14) and who was a doorkeeper (15:24). The second was also a gatekeeper, a son of Jeduthun.

16:39 *Zadok.* Until the temple of Solomon was completed, there were two legitimate places for community worship—the Mosaic tabernacle at Gibeon, and David's tabernacle on Mount Zion. Zadok, a descendant of Eleazar, served at Gibeon, while Abiathar, a descendant of Ithamar, served at Jerusalem (see note for 15:11).

16:22 [n] Ge 20:7 **16:25** [o] Ps 48:1 [p] Ps 76:7; 89:7 [q] Dt 32:39 **16:26** [r] Lev 19:4; Ps 102:25 **16:28** [s] Ps 29:1-2 **16:29** [t] Ps 29:1-2 **16:30** [u] Ps 114:7 **16:31** [v] Isa 44:23; 49:13 [w] Ps 93:1 **16:32** [x] Ps 98:7 **16:33** [y] Isa 55:12 [z] Ps 96:10; 98:9 **16:34** [a] ver 8 [b] Na 1:7 [c] 2Ch 5:13; 7:3; Ezr 3:11; Ps 136:1-26; Jer 33:11 **16:35** [d] Mic 7:7 **16:36** [e] Dt 27:15; 1Ki 8:15; Ps 72:18-19 **16:37** [f] 2Ch 8:14 **16:38** [g] 1Ch 13:13 [h] 1Ch 26:10 **16:39** [i] 2Sa 8:17; 1Ch 15:11 [j] 1Ki 3:4; 2Ch 1:3

present burnt offerings to the LORD on the altar of burnt offering regularly, morning and evening, in accordance with everything written in the Law[k] of the LORD, which he had given Israel. 41With them were Heman[l] and Jeduthun and the rest of those chosen and designated by name to give thanks to the LORD, "for his love endures forever." 42Heman and Jeduthun were responsible for the sounding of the trumpets and cymbals and for the playing of the other instruments for sacred song.[m] The sons of Jeduthun were stationed at the gate.

43Then all the people left, each for their own home, and David returned home to bless his family.

God's Promise to David

17 After David was settled in his palace, he said to Nathan the prophet, "Here I am, living in a house of cedar, while the ark of the covenant of the LORD is under a tent.[n]"

2Nathan replied to David, "Whatever you have in mind,[o] do it, for God is with you."

3But that night the word of God came to Nathan, saying:

4"Go and tell my servant David, 'This is what the LORD says: You[p] are not the one to build me a house to dwell in. 5I have not dwelt in a house from the day I brought Israel up out of Egypt to this day. I have moved from one tent site to another, from one dwelling place to another. 6Wherever I have moved with all the Israelites, did I ever say to any of their leaders[a] whom I commanded to shepherd my people, "Why have you not built me a house of cedar?"'

7"Now then, tell my servant David, 'This is what the LORD Almighty says: I took you from the pasture, from tending the flock, and appointed you ruler[q] over my people Israel. 8I have been with you wherever you have gone, and I have cut off all your enemies from before you. Now I will make your name like the names of the greatest men on earth. 9And I will provide a place for my people Israel and will plant them so that they can have a home of their own and no longer be disturbed. Wicked people will not oppress them anymore, as they did at the beginning 10and have done ever since the time I appointed leaders[r] over my people Israel. I will also subdue all your enemies.

"'I declare to you that the LORD will build a house for you: 11When your days are over and you go to be with your ancestors, I will raise up your offspring to succeed you, one of your own sons, and I will establish his kingdom. 12He is the one who will build[s] a house for me, and I will establish his throne forever.[t] 13I will be his father,[u] and he will be my son.[v] I will never take my love away from him, as I took it away from your predecessor. 14I will set him over my house and my kingdom forever; his throne[w] will be established forever.[x]'"

15Nathan reported to David all the words of this entire revelation.

David's Prayer

16Then King David went in and sat before the LORD, and he said:

"Who am I, LORD God, and what is my family, that you have brought me this far? 17And as if this were not enough in your sight, my God, you have spoken about the future of the house of your servant. You, LORD God, have looked on me as though I were the most exalted of men.

18"What more can David say to you for honoring your servant? For you know your servant, 19LORD. For the sake[y] of your servant and according to your will, you have done this great thing and made known all these great promises.[z]

[a] 6 Traditionally *judges*; also in verse 10

16:41 *Jeduthun.* This was probably another name for the musician Ethan, who is usually named together with Asaph and Heman (15:17,19; 6:33,39,44).
16:42 *instruments for sacred song.* It is difficult to overemphasize the importance of music in Old Testament worship. The Book of Psalms in itself, and constant references to choral and orchestral ministry demonstrate the significance of music as the people worshiped their Creator (9:33; 15:16–24; 16:4–6; 25:1–31).
17:1 *Nathan the prophet.* Nathan was a prophet at the time of both David and Solomon. He was closely connected with both kings, and was trusted as a faithful spokesman of God (2 Sam. 7:2–3; 12:1–15; 1 Kin. 1:8–38,45; 2 Chr. 29:25). The "records of Nathan the prophet" provided a source for the composition of the books of Chronicles (29:29; 2 Chr. 9:29). ***a house of cedar.*** Cedar paneling was too expensive to be used in an ordinary home.
17:9 *I will provide a place.* This did not mean that Israel would move to another land, but it was a restating of God's promise that they were meant to inherit the land (Gen. 13:14–17; 15:18–21; 17:8; Ex. 3:16–17; 6:8; Deut. 1:8; Josh. 1:2–5).
17:16–18 Thankfulness—As with David, God's willingness to bless us is not because we are great but because He is good. His purpose is for us to be like Him, and to bless us and establish us forever with Him through Christ (John 14).

16:40 [k] Ex 29:38; Nu 28:1-8 **16:41** [l] 1Ch 6:33; 25:1-6; 2Ch 5:13 **16:42** [m] 2Ch 7:6 **17:1** [n] 1Ch 15:1 **17:2** [o] 2Ch 6:7 **17:4** [p] 1Ch 28:3 **17:7** [q] 2Sa 6:21 **17:10** [r] Jdg 2:16 **17:12** [s] 1Ki 5:5 [t] 2Ch 7:18 **17:13** [u] 2Co 6:18 [v] Lk 1:32; Heb 1:5* **17:14** [w] 1Ki 2:12; 1Ch 28:5 [x] Ps 132:11; Jer 33:17 **17:19** [y] 2Sa 7:16-17; 2Ki 20:6; Isa 9:7; 37:35; 55:3 [z] 2Sa 7:25

20“There is no one like you, LORD,
and there is no God but you,[a] as we
have heard with our own ears. 21And
who is like your people Israel—the
one nation on earth whose God went
out to redeem[b] a people for himself,
and to make a name for yourself, and
to perform great and awesome wonders by driving out nations from before your people, whom you redeemed
from Egypt? 22You made your people
Israel your very own forever,[c] and you,
LORD, have become their God.
23“And now, LORD, let the promise[d]
you have made concerning your servant and his house be established forever. Do as you promised, 24so that it
will be established and that your name
will be great forever. Then people will
say, ‘The LORD Almighty, the God over
Israel, is Israel’s God!’ And the house
of your servant David will be established before you.
25“You, my God, have revealed
to your servant that you will build a
house for him. So your servant has
found courage to pray to you. 26You,
LORD, are God! You have promised
these good things to your servant.
27Now you have been pleased to bless
the house of your servant, that it may
continue forever in your sight;[e] for
you, LORD, have blessed it, and it will
be blessed forever.”

David’s Victories

18 In the course of time, David defeated the Philistines and subdued them,
and he took Gath and its surrounding villages from the control of the Philistines.
2David also defeated the Moabites,[f] and
they became subject to him and brought
him tribute.
3Moreover, David defeated Hadadezer
king of Zobah,[g] in the vicinity of Hamath,
when he went to set up his monument at[a]
the Euphrates River.[h] 4David captured a
thousand of his chariots, seven thousand
charioteers and twenty thousand foot soldiers. He hamstrung[i] all but a hundred of
the chariot horses.
5When the Arameans of Damascus[j]
came to help Hadadezer king of Zobah,
David struck down twenty-two thousand
of them. 6He put garrisons in the Aramean kingdom of Damascus, and the Arameans became subject to him and brought
him tribute. The LORD gave David victory
wherever he went.
7David took the gold shields carried by
the officers of Hadadezer and brought
them to Jerusalem. 8From Tebah[b] and Kun,
towns that belonged to Hadadezer, David
took a great quantity of bronze, which Solomon used to make the bronze Sea,[k] the
pillars and various bronze articles.
9When Tou king of Hamath heard that
David had defeated the entire army of Hadadezer king of Zobah, 10he sent his son
Hadoram to King David to greet him and
congratulate him on his victory in battle
over Hadadezer, who had been at war with
Tou. Hadoram brought all kinds of articles
of gold, of silver and of bronze.
11King David dedicated these articles
to the LORD, as he had done with the silver and gold he had taken from all these
nations: Edom[l] and Moab, the Ammonites
and the Philistines, and Amalek.[m]
12Abishai son of Zeruiah struck down
eighteen thousand Edomites[n] in the Valley
of Salt. 13He put garrisons in Edom, and
all the Edomites became subject to David.
The LORD gave David victory wherever he
went.

David’s Officials

14David reigned[o] over all Israel,[p] doing
what was just and right for all his people.
15Joab[q] son of Zeruiah was over the army;
Jehoshaphat son of Ahilud was recorder;
16Zadok[r] son of Ahitub and Ahimelek[c][s] son
of Abiathar were priests; Shavsha was secretary; 17Benaiah son of Jehoiada was over
the Kerethites and Pelethites;[t] and David’s
sons were chief officials at the king’s side.

[a] 3 Or *to restore his control over* [b] 8 Hebrew *Tibhath*, a variant of *Tebah* [c] 16 Some Hebrew manuscripts, Vulgate and Syriac (see also 2 Samuel 8:17); most Hebrew manuscripts *Abimelek*

17:20 *no God but you.* This is a clear assertion of the uniqueness of Israel’s God. Statements such as “all gods” and “the gods of the nations” in David’s song of thanksgiving (16:25–26) must be understood in the light of this clear confession that there is only one living God.

18:1 *took Gath.* This is the only record of David taking a Philistine city, although he had defeated the Philistines many times in battle. Gath was the Philistine city closest to Israelite territory, so it posed the greatest threat to Israel.

18:2 *Moabites.* David’s great-grandmother Ruth was a Moabitess (Ruth 4:13–17), and David had sent his own family to Moab for protection when he was hiding from Saul (1 Sam. 22:3–4). Yet Moab had been an enemy of Israel (Num. 23), and would be again (Ezek. 25:9).

18:11 *dedicated . . . to the LORD.* The fact that David dedicated all the spoils of war to God suggests that he viewed the battles as campaigns initiated and led by God. When Solomon built the temple, he brought all the dedicated things into the temple treasuries (2 Chr. 5:1).

18:17 *Kerethites . . . Pelethites.* These were companies of soldiers, probably mercenaries from Philistia (1 Sam. 30:14; 2 Sam. 15:18; Ezek. 25:16).

17:20 [a] Ex 8:10; 9:14; 15:11; Isa 44:6; 46:9 **17:21** [b] Ex 6:6 **17:22** [c] Ex 19:5-6 **17:23** [d] 1Ki 8:25 **17:27** [e] Ps 16:11; 21:6 **18:2** [f] Nu 21:29 **18:3** [g] 1Ch 19:6 [h] Ge 2:14 **18:4** [i] Ge 49:6 **18:5** [j] 2Ki 16:9; 1Ch 19:6 **18:8** [k] 1Ki 7:23; 2Ch 4:12, 15-16 **18:11** [l] Nu 24:18 [m] Nu 24:20 **18:12** [n] 1Ki 11:15 **18:14** [o] 1Ch 29:26 [p] 1Ch 11:1 **18:15** [q] 2Sa 5:6-8; 1Ch 11:6 **18:16** [r] 2Sa 8:17; 1Ch 6:8 [s] 1Ch 24:6 **18:17** [t] 1Sa 30:14; 2Sa 8:18; 15:18

David Defeats the Ammonites

19 In the course of time, Nahash king of the Ammonites[u] died, and his son succeeded him as king. 2David thought, "I will show kindness to Hanun son of Nahash, because his father showed kindness to me." So David sent a delegation to express his sympathy to Hanun concerning his father.

When David's envoys came to Hanun in the land of the Ammonites to express sympathy to him, 3the Ammonite commanders said to Hanun, "Do you think David is honoring your father by sending envoys to you to express sympathy? Haven't his envoys come to you only to explore and spy out[v] the country and overthrow it?" 4So Hanun seized David's envoys, shaved them, cut off their garments at the buttocks, and sent them away.

5When someone came and told David about the men, he sent messengers to meet them, for they were greatly humiliated. The king said, "Stay at Jericho till your beards have grown, and then come back."

6When the Ammonites realized that they had become obnoxious[w] to David, Hanun and the Ammonites sent a thousand talents[a] of silver to hire chariots and charioteers from Aram Naharaim,[b] Aram Maakah and Zobah.[x] 7They hired thirty-two thousand chariots and charioteers, as well as the king of Maakah with his troops, who came and camped near Medeba,[y] while the Ammonites were mustered from their towns and moved out for battle.

8On hearing this, David sent Joab out with the entire army of fighting men. 9The Ammonites came out and drew up in battle formation at the entrance to their city, while the kings who had come were by themselves in the open country.

10Joab saw that there were battle lines in front of him and behind him; so he selected some of the best troops in Israel and deployed them against the Arameans. 11He put the rest of the men under the command of Abishai[z] his brother, and they were deployed against the Ammonites. 12Joab said, "If the Arameans are too strong for me, then you are to rescue me; but if the Ammonites are too strong for you, then I will rescue you. 13Be strong, and let us fight bravely for our people and the cities of our God. The LORD will do what is good in his sight."

14Then Joab and the troops with him advanced to fight the Arameans, and they fled before him. 15When the Ammonites realized that the Arameans were fleeing, they too fled before his brother Abishai and went inside the city. So Joab went back to Jerusalem.

16After the Arameans saw that they had been routed by Israel, they sent messengers and had Arameans brought from beyond the Euphrates River, with Shophak the commander of Hadadezer's army leading them.

17When David was told of this, he gathered all Israel[a] and crossed the Jordan; he advanced against them and formed his battle lines opposite them. David formed his lines to meet the Arameans in battle, and they fought against him. 18But they fled before Israel, and David killed seven thousand of their charioteers and forty thousand of their foot soldiers. He also killed Shophak the commander of their army.

19When the vassals of Hadadezer saw that they had been routed by Israel, they made peace with David and became subject to him.

So the Arameans were not willing to help the Ammonites anymore.

The Capture of Rabbah

20 In the spring, at the time when kings go off to war, Joab led out the armed forces. He laid waste the land of the Ammonites and went to Rabbah[b] and besieged it, but David remained in Jerusalem. Joab attacked Rabbah and left it in ruins.[c] 2David took the crown from the head of their king[c]—its weight was found to be a talent[d] of gold, and it was set with precious stones—and it was placed on David's head.

a 6 That is, about 38 tons or about 34 metric tons
b 6 That is, Northwest Mesopotamia
c 2 Or *of Milkom,* that is, Molek
d 2 That is, about 75 pounds or about 34 kilograms

19:1 *Nahash.* Nahash was reigning in Saul's earliest years (1 Sam. 11:1); the present incident must have occurred early in David's reign at Jerusalem.

19:3 Slander—The delegation was treated scandalously, and David's motives were slanderously attacked. Of course there were no grounds for such suspicions. Men who themselves act basely toward their neighbors are most likely to suspect such behavior in others. One of the marks of a godly person is that he does not slander with his tongue (Ps. 15:3).

19:4 *shaved . . . cut off.* Hebrew men were proud of their beards and scrupulously modest in their attire. The Ammonites had humiliated David's men in the most offensive way possible.

19:6 *a thousand talents.* A talent is about 75 pounds.

19:19 *became subject to him.* This did not mean that the vassals became David's slaves but, instead, that they now pledged their allegiance to the nation of Israel.

20:1 *David remained in Jerusalem.* This is the time that David committed adultery with Bathsheba (2 Sam. 11). The chronicler omits this story, not because it is unsavory, but because it has no bearing on his theme. He is showing how the Davidic dynasty was the fulfillment of God's promises.

20:2 *crown.* The crown David took was ceremonial and not for wearing, since it weighed about 75

19:1 [u] Ge 19:38; Jdg 10:17-11:33; 2Ch 20:1-2; Zep 2:8-11
19:3 [v] Nu 21:32 **19:6** [w] Ge 34:30 [x] 1Ch 18:3, 5, 9
19:7 [y] Nu 21:30; Jos 13:9, 16 **19:11** [z] 1Sa 26:6
19:17 [a] 1Ch 9:1 **20:1** [b] Dt 3:11; 2Sa 12:26 [c] Am 1:13-15

He took a great quantity of plunder from
the city 3and brought out the people who
were there, consigning them to labor with
saws and with iron picks and axes.[d] David
did this to all the Ammonite towns. Then
David and his entire army returned to Jerusalem.

War With the Philistines

4In the course of time, war broke out
with the Philistines, at Gezer.[e] At that time
Sibbekai the Hushathite killed Sippai, one
of the descendants of the Rephaites,[f] and
the Philistines were subjugated.
5In another battle with the Philistines,
Elhanan son of Jair killed Lahmi the brother of Goliath the Gittite, who had a spear
with a shaft like a weaver's rod.[g]
6In still another battle, which took place
at Gath, there was a huge man with six
fingers on each hand and six toes on each
foot—twenty-four in all. He also was descended from Rapha. 7When he taunted
Israel, Jonathan son of Shimea, David's
brother, killed him.
8These were descendants of Rapha in
Gath, and they fell at the hands of David
and his men.

David Counts the Fighting Men

21 Satan[h] rose up against Israel and incited David to take a census[i] of Israel.
2So David said to Joab and the commanders of the troops, "Go and count[j] the Israelites from Beersheba to Dan. Then report
back to me so that I may know how many
there are."
3But Joab replied, "May the LORD multiply his troops a hundred times over.[k] My
lord the king, are they not all my lord's subjects? Why does my lord want to do this?
Why should he bring guilt on Israel?"
4The king's word, however, overruled
Joab; so Joab left and went throughout
Israel and then came back to Jerusalem.
5Joab reported the number of the fighting
men to David: In all Israel[l] there were one
million one hundred thousand men who
could handle a sword, including four hundred and seventy thousand in Judah.
6But Joab did not include Levi and Benjamin in the numbering, because the king's
command was repulsive to him. 7This command was also evil in the sight of God; so
he punished Israel.
8Then David said to God, "I have sinned
greatly by doing this. Now, I beg you, take

---

pounds. David put the crown on his head to demonstrate that he had vanquished the Ammonites and now reigned over them as well.

20:7 *Shimea.* This was David's older brother, the third son of Jesse (2:13).

20:8 *of Rapha in Gath.* Goliath was from Gath (1 Sam. 17:4).

21:1 Temptation by Satan—The role of Satan as the Christian's opponent is well summed up by the meaning of the name Satan, which means "adversary." He is also called "the devil," meaning "accuser." He can appear as a dragon (Rev. 12:3–4,9) or as a beautifully deceptive "angel of light" (2 Cor. 11:14). He stands hatefully opposed to all the work of God and promotes defiance among men (Job 2:4–5). When Satan sinned he was expelled from heaven (Luke 10:18), although apparently he still had some access to God (Job 2:4–5). A multitude of angels joined him in his rebellion and subsequently became the demons mentioned often in the biblical record (Matt. 12:24; Rev. 12:7). Although Satan's doom was secured by Jesus' death on the cross (John 16:11), he will continue to hinder God's program until he and his angels are destroyed (Matt. 25:41).

The terrifying work of Satan in the unbeliever is described in Scripture as follows: he blinds their minds (2 Cor. 4:4); he takes the Word of God from their hearts (Luke 8:12); and he controls them (Acts 13:8). In regard to Christians, Satan may accuse them (Rev. 12:10), devour their testimony for Christ (1 Pet. 5:8–9), deceive them (Col. 2:8), hinder their work (1 Thess. 2:18), tempt them to immorality (1 Cor. 7:5), and even be used by God to discipline Christians (1 Cor. 5:5; 2 Cor. 12:7).

The Christian's response to Satan is to recognize his power and deception (2 Cor. 2:11; Eph. 6:11), to adhere steadfastly to the faith (1 Pet. 5:9) to resist him openly (James 4:7), and not to give him opportunities. In practice, the best way to oppose him is to be a growing Christian. Believers can respond to temptation by Satan with confidence. We know that nothing can separate us from the love of God (Rom. 8:38–39). Also in light of Satan's tremendous power to blind men to the gospel, Christians must always be aggressively and compassionately witnessing to the lost in order to snatch them from his control.

21:2 *David said.* Samuel attributed David's impulse to number the people to God Himself (2 Sam. 24:1) while here it is attributed to Satan (v. 1). The apparent contradiction can be resolved by recognizing that though Satan is the author of all evil, he cannot exercise his evil intentions apart from the permission of God. Moreover, God could use Satan to accomplish His own purposes of judgment (1 Kin. 22:19–23; Job 1) or discipline (as here with David). ***Go and count.*** David's plan to take a census was not evil in itself, for the Lord Himself at other times had commanded the Israelites to be counted (Num. 1). The problem seems to have been David's presumptuous attitude. He apparently wanted to have a number to look at, instead of remembering that no matter how many or few were the Israelites, their strength was always in the Lord. ***Beersheba to Dan.*** This was the traditional way of describing all of Israel from south to north. The distance is about 150 miles.

21:3 *bring guilt.* Joab's warning was David's chance to repent of his intention to number the people for his own purposes. God does not entice us to evil (James 1:13–15; 4:7–8), and even though God was using Satan in this situation, David was still the one who decided to sin (v. 17). God knew what was in David's heart, and either through Joab's rebuke or through David carrying out his sinful thoughts, God intended to deal with David's attitude.

20:3 [d] Dt 29:11 **20:4** [e] Jos 10:33 [f] Ge 14:5 **20:5** [g] 1Sa 17:7 **21:1** [h] 2Ch 18:21; Ps 109:6 [i] 2Ch 14:8; 25:5 **21:2** [j] 1Ch 27:23-24 **21:3** [k] Dt 1:11 **21:5** [l] 1Ch 9:1

away the guilt of your servant. I have done
a very foolish thing."
9The LORD said to Gad,[m] David's seer,[n]
10"Go and tell David, 'This is what the LORD
says: I am giving you three options. Choose
one of them for me to carry out against
you.'"
11So Gad went to David and said to him,
"This is what the LORD says: 'Take your
choice: 12three years of famine,[o] three
months of being swept away[a] before your
enemies, with their swords overtaking you,
or three days of the sword[p] of the LORD[q]—
days of plague in the land, with the angel
of the LORD ravaging every part of Israel.'
Now then, decide how I should answer the
one who sent me."
13David said to Gad, "I am in deep distress. Let me fall into the hands of the
LORD, for his mercy[r] is very great; but do
not let me fall into human hands."
14So the LORD sent a plague on Israel,
and seventy thousand men of Israel fell
dead.[s] 15And God sent an angel[t] to destroy
Jerusalem.[u] But as the angel was doing so,
the LORD saw it and relented[v] concerning
the disaster and said to the angel who was
destroying[w] the people, "Enough! Withdraw your hand." The angel of the LORD
was then standing at the threshing floor of
Araunah[b] the Jebusite.
16David looked up and saw the angel of
the LORD standing between heaven and
earth, with a drawn sword in his hand extended over Jerusalem. Then David and the
elders, clothed in sackcloth, fell facedown.[x]
17David said to God, "Was it not I who
ordered the fighting men to be counted?
I, the shepherd,[c] have sinned and done
wrong. These are but sheep.[y] What have
they done? LORD my God, let your hand fall
on me and my family,[z] but do not let this
plague remain on your people."

David Builds an Altar

18Then the angel of the LORD ordered
Gad to tell David to go up and build an altar to the LORD on the threshing floor[a] of
Araunah the Jebusite. 19So David went up
in obedience to the word that Gad had spoken in the name of the LORD.
20While Araunah was threshing wheat,[b]
he turned and saw the angel; his four sons
who were with him hid themselves. 21Then
David approached, and when Araunah
looked and saw him, he left the threshing
floor and bowed down before David with
his face to the ground.
22David said to him, "Let me have the
site of your threshing floor so I can build
an altar to the LORD, that the plague on the
people may be stopped. Sell it to me at the
full price."
23Araunah said to David, "Take it! Let
my lord the king do whatever pleases him.
Look, I will give the oxen for the burnt offerings, the threshing sledges for the wood,
and the wheat for the grain offering. I will
give all this."
24But King David replied to Araunah,
"No, I insist on paying the full price. I will
not take for the LORD what is yours, or sacrifice a burnt offering that costs me nothing."
25So David paid Araunah six hundred
shekels[d] of gold for the site. 26David built
an altar to the LORD there and sacrificed
burnt offerings and fellowship offerings.
He called on the LORD, and the LORD answered him with fire[c] from heaven on the
altar of burnt offering.
27Then the LORD spoke to the angel, and
he put his sword back into its sheath. 28At
that time, when David saw that the LORD
had answered him on the threshing floor
of Araunah the Jebusite, he offered sacrifices there. 29The tabernacle of the LORD,
which Moses had made in the wilderness,
and the altar of burnt offering were at that
time on the high place at Gibeon.[d] 30But
David could not go before it to inquire of
God, because he was afraid of the sword
of the angel of the LORD.
22 Then David said, "The house of the
LORD God[e] is to be here, and also the
altar of burnt offering for Israel."

[a] *12* Hebrew; Septuagint and Vulgate (see also 2 Samuel 24:13) *of fleeing* [b] *15* Hebrew *Ornan*, a variant of *Araunah*; also in verses 18-28
[c] *17* Probable reading of the original Hebrew text (see 2 Samuel 24:17 and note); Masoretic Text does not have *the shepherd*. [d] *25* That is, about 15 pounds or about 6.9 kilograms

21:9 *seer.* Gad was a prophet, one who received revelations from the Lord (1 Sam. 22:5).

21:15 *to destroy Jerusalem.* When God saw David's repentance and heard his intercessory prayer (v. 17), He relented and stopped the destroying angel. God responded to David's heartfelt prayer. One of the most important aspects of intercessory prayer is how it turns the heart of the one praying toward God, and aligns the intercessor with God's attitudes and purposes.

21:24 *costs me nothing.* David showed a clear perception of the essence of sacrifice. Every prayer, every sacrifice must come from the heart and labor of the one who offers these things to God. No one can have a relationship with God for or on the behalf of someone else.

21:29 *tabernacle ... which Moses had made.* The Old Testament account does not fully trace the movement of the tabernacle after Shiloh, but it did end up first at Nob and finally at Gibeon (15:1).

22:1 *The house of the LORD God.* As long as the ark remained at Kiriath Jearim and the tabernacle of Moses was at Nob and Gibeon, it was impossible for

21:9 [m] 1Sa 22:5 [n] 1Sa 9:9 **21:12** [o] Dt 32:24 [p] Eze 30:25 [q] Ge 19:13 **21:13** [r] Ps 6:4; 86:15; 130:4,7 **21:14** [s] 1Ch 27:24 **21:15** [t] Ge 32:1 [u] Ps 125:2 [v] Ge 6:6; Ex 32:14 [w] Ge 19:13 **21:16** [x] Nu 14:5; Jos 7:6 **21:17** [y] 2Sa 7:8; Ps 74:1 [z] Jnh 1:12 **21:18** [a] 2Ch 3:1 **21:20** [b] Jdg 6:11 **21:26** [c] Lev 9:24; Jdg 6:21 **21:29** [d] 1Ki 3:4; 1Ch 16:39 **22:1** [e] Ge 28:17; 1Ch 21:18-29; 2Ch 3:1

Preparations for the Temple

2So David gave orders to assemble the foreigners[f] residing in Israel, and from among them he appointed stonecutters[g] to prepare dressed stone for building the house of God. 3He provided a large amount of iron to make nails for the doors of the gateways and for the fittings, and more bronze than could be weighed.[h] 4He also provided more cedar logs[i] than could be counted, for the Sidonians and Tyrians had brought large numbers of them to David.

5David said, "My son Solomon is young[j] and inexperienced, and the house to be built for the LORD should be of great magnificence and fame and splendor in the sight of all the nations. Therefore I will make preparations for it." So David made extensive preparations before his death.

6Then he called for his son Solomon and charged him to build[k] a house for the LORD, the God of Israel. 7David said to Solomon: "My son, I had it in my heart[l] to build[m] a house for the Name[n] of the LORD my God. 8But this word of the LORD came to me: 'You have shed much blood and have fought many wars.[o] You are not to build a house for my Name,[p] because you have shed much blood on the earth in my sight. 9But you will have a son who will be a man of peace[q] and rest, and I will give him rest from all his enemies on every side. His name will be Solomon,[a][r] and I will grant Israel peace and quiet[s] during his reign. 10He is the one who will build a house for my Name.[t] He will be my son,[u] and I will be his father. And I will establish the throne of his kingdom over Israel forever.'[v]

11"Now, my son, the LORD be with[w] you, and may you have success and build the house of the LORD your God, as he said you would. 12May the LORD give you discretion and understanding[x] when he puts you in command over Israel, so that you may keep the law of the LORD your God. 13Then you will have success if you are careful to observe the decrees and laws[y] that the LORD gave Moses for Israel. Be strong and courageous.[z] Do not be afraid or discouraged.

14"I have taken great pains to provide for the temple of the LORD a hundred thousand talents[b] of gold, a million talents[c] of silver, quantities of bronze and iron too great to be weighed, and wood and stone. And you may add to them.[a] 15You have many workers: stonecutters, masons and carpenters, as well as those skilled in every kind of work 16in gold and silver, bronze and iron—craftsmen[b] beyond number. Now begin the work, and the LORD be with you."

17Then David ordered[c] all the leaders of Israel to help his son Solomon. 18He said to them, "Is not the LORD your God with you? And has he not granted you rest[d] on every side?[e] For he has given the inhabitants of the land into my hands, and the land is subject to the LORD and to his people. 19Now devote your heart and soul to seeking the LORD your God.[f] Begin to build the sanctuary of the LORD God, so that you may bring the ark of the covenant of the LORD and the sacred articles belonging to God into the temple that will be built for the Name of the LORD."

The Levites

23 When David was old and full of years, he made his son Solomon[g] king over Israel.[h]

2He also gathered together all the leaders of Israel, as well as the priests and Levites. 3The Levites thirty years old or more[i] were counted, and the total number of men was thirty-eight thousand.[j] 4David said, "Of these, twenty-four thousand are to be in charge[k] of the work of the temple of the LORD and six thousand are to be officials and judges.[l] 5Four thousand are to be gatekeepers and four thousand are to praise the LORD with the musical instruments[m] I have provided for that purpose."[n]

[a] *9 Solomon* sounds like and may be derived from the Hebrew for *peace.* [b] *14* That is, about 3,750 tons or about 3,400 metric tons [c] *14* That is, about 37,500 tons or about 34,000 metric tons

worship to be carried out in the manner originally intended. When the house of God was built, the ark and the altar would be together once again.

22:5 *young and inexperienced.* Solomon was born about halfway through David's reign. At the time that David began to gather building materials, Solomon was probably not over 18 years old.

22:13 Zeal—David says in Psalm 71, "Since my youth, God, you have taught me, and to this day I declare your marvelous deeds" (v. 17). Wherever he went, David proclaimed the goodness and majesty of God, and now he saw the temple and the centrality of worship as the pinnacle of his service for God. He could encourage Solomon to proceed with confidence because he knew he was doing God's will.

22:18 *subject to the LORD.* The conquest of the land began in Joshua's time and was completed under David. It had been a long process, including times of great disobedience and others of great faith. There is an element of submission in this statement, relating both to the Israelites and the land itself.

23:1 *his son Solomon king.* This phrasing suggests that this is an official appointment, perhaps in the role of coregent with David. It was later ratified by the whole nation (29:22).

22:2 [f] 1Ki 9:21; Isa 56:6 [g] 1Ki 5:17-18 **22:3** [h] ver 14; 1Ki 7:47; 1Ch 29:2-5 **22:4** [i] 1Ki 5:6 **22:5** [j] 1Ki 3:7; 1Ch 29:1 **22:6** [k] Ac 7:47 **22:7** [l] 1Ch 17:2 [m] 2Sa 7:2; 1Ki 8:17 [n] Dt 12:5, 11 **22:8** [o] 1Ki 5:3 [p] 1Ch 28:3 **22:9** [q] 1Ki 5:4 [r] 2Sa 12:24 [s] 1Ki 4:20 **22:10** [t] 1Ch 17:12 [u] 2Sa 7:13 [v] 2Sa 7:14; 2Ch 6:15 **22:11** [w] ver 16 **22:12** [x] 1Ki 3:9-12; 2Ch 1:10 **22:13** [y] 1Ch 28:7 [z] Dt 31:6; Jos 1:6-9; 1Ch 28:20 **22:14** [a] ver 3; 1Ch 29:2-5, 19 **22:16** [b] ver 11; 2Ch 2:7 **22:17** [c] 1Ch 28:1-6 **22:18** [d] ver 9; 1Ch 23:25 [e] 2Sa 7:1 **22:19** [f] ver 7; 1Ki 8:6; 1Ch 20:9; 2Ch 5:7; 7:14 **23:1** [g] 1Ki 1:33-39; 1Ch 28:5 [h] 1Ki 1:30; 1Ch 29:28 **23:3** [i] ver 24; Nu 8:24 [j] Nu 4:3-49 **23:4** [k] Ezr 3:8 [l] 1Ch 26:29; 2Ch 19:8 **23:5** [m] 1Ch 15:16 [n] Ne 12:45

[6]David separated[o] the Levites into divisions corresponding to the sons of Levi: Gershon, Kohath and Merari.

Gershonites

[7]Belonging to the Gershonites:
Ladan and Shimei.
[8]The sons of Ladan:
Jehiel the first, Zetham and Joel—three in all.
[9]The sons of Shimei:
Shelomoth, Haziel and Haran—three in all.
These were the heads of the families of Ladan.
[10]And the sons of Shimei:
Jahath, Ziza,[a] Jeush and Beriah.
These were the sons of Shimei—four in all.
[11]Jahath was the first and Ziza the second, but Jeush and Beriah did not have many sons; so they were counted as one family with one assignment.

Kohathites

[12]The sons of Kohath:[p]
Amram, Izhar, Hebron and Uzziel—four in all.
[13]The sons of Amram:[q]
Aaron and Moses.
Aaron was set apart,[r] he and his descendants forever, to consecrate the most holy things, to offer sacrifices before the LORD, to minister before him and to pronounce blessings[s] in his name forever. [14]The sons of Moses the man[t] of God were counted as part of the tribe of Levi.
[15]The sons of Moses:
Gershom and Eliezer.[u]
[16]The descendants of Gershom:[v]
Shubael was the first.
[17]The descendants of Eliezer:
Rehabiah was the first.
Eliezer had no other sons, but the sons of Rehabiah were very numerous.
[18]The sons of Izhar:
Shelomith was the first.
[19]The sons of Hebron:[w]
Jeriah the first, Amariah the second, Jahaziel the third and Jekameam the fourth.
[20]The sons of Uzziel:
Micah the first and Ishiah the second.

Merarites

[21]The sons of Merari:[x]
Mahli and Mushi.
The sons of Mahli:
Eleazar and Kish.
[22]Eleazar died without having sons: he had only daughters. Their cousins, the sons of Kish, married them.
[23]The sons of Mushi:
Mahli, Eder and Jerimoth—three in all.

[24]These were the descendants of Levi
by their families—the heads of families
as they were registered under their names
and counted individually, that is, the workers twenty years old or more[y] who served
in the temple of the LORD. [25]For David had
said, "Since the LORD, the God of Israel, has
granted rest[z] to his people and has come to
dwell in Jerusalem forever, [26]the Levites no
longer need to carry the tabernacle or any
of the articles used in its service."[a] [27]Ac-
cording to the last instructions of David,
the Levites were counted from those twenty years old or more.
[28]The duty of the Levites was to help Aaron's descendants in the service of the temple of the LORD: to be in charge of the courtyards, the side rooms, the purification[b] of all
sacred things and the performance of other
duties at the house of God. [29]They were in
charge of the bread set out on the table,[c] the
special flour for the grain offerings,[d] the
thin loaves made without yeast, the baking and the mixing, and all measurements
of quantity and size.[e] [30]They were also to
stand every morning to thank and praise
the LORD. They were to do the same in the
evening[f] [31]and whenever burnt offerings
were presented to the LORD on the Sabbaths,
at the New Moon[g] feasts and at the appointed festivals.[h] They were to serve before the
LORD regularly in the proper number and in
the way prescribed for them.
[32]And so the Levites[i] carried out their
responsibilities for the tent of meeting,[j] for

[a] *10* One Hebrew manuscript, Septuagint and Vulgate (see also verse 11); most Hebrew manuscripts *Zina*

23:26 *no longer need to carry.* When the tabernacle was replaced by a permanent building, the role of the Levites changed. This is another aspect of the subdued land. The Israelites were there to stay.

23:30 Praise—This is a beautiful picture of daily praise, thanking the Lord for the day that begins and the day that ends. As believers, we don't need someone else to thank the Lord on our behalf. We need to praise Him. The value of praise is that it lifts our hearts to God's heart. It keeps us thinking about Him and worshiping Him. Life can be almost overwhelming at times, and a habit of praising God lifts our thoughts above our troubles and focuses on who He is and what He has done.

23:32 *Holy Place.* This referred to the outer room of the tabernacle. The Most Holy Place was only approached by the high priest.

23:6 [o] 2Ch 8:14; 29:25 **23:12** [p] Ex 6:18 **23:13** [q] Ex 6:20; 28:1 [r] Ex 30:7-10; Dt 21:5 [s] Nu 6:23 **23:14** [t] Dt 33:1 **23:15** [u] Ex 18:4 **23:16** [v] 1Ch 26:24-28 **23:19** [w] 1Ch 24:23 **23:21** [x] 1Ch 24:26 **23:24** [y] Nu 4:3; 10:17,21 **23:25** [z] 1Ch 22:9 **23:26** [a] Nu 4:5, 15; 7:9; Dt 10:8 **23:28** [b] 2Ch 29:15; Ne 13:9; Mal 3:3 **23:29** [c] Ex 25:30 [d] Lev 2:4-7; 6:20-23 [e] Lev 19:35-36; 1Ch 9:29, 32 **23:30** [f] 1Ch 9:33; Ps 134:1 **23:31** [g] 2Ki 4:23 [h] Lev 23:4; Nu 28:9-29:39; Isa 1:13-14; Col 2:16 **23:32** [i] Nu 1:53; 1Ch 6:48 [j] Nu 3:6-8, 38

the Holy Place and, under their relatives
the descendants of Aaron, for the service
of the temple of the LORD.[k]

The Divisions of Priests

24 These were the divisions[l] of the descendants of Aaron:[m]
The sons of Aaron were Nadab, Abihu,
Eleazar and Ithamar.[n] 2But Nadab and Abihu died before their father did,[o] and they
had no sons; so Eleazar and Ithamar served
as the priests. 3With the help of Zadok[p] a
descendant of Eleazar and Ahimelek a descendant of Ithamar, David separated them
into divisions for their appointed order of
ministering. 4A larger number of leaders
were found among Eleazar's descendants
than among Ithamar's, and they were divided accordingly: sixteen heads of families from Eleazar's descendants and eight
heads of families from Ithamar's descendants. 5They divided them impartially by
casting lots,[q] for there were officials of the
sanctuary and officials of God among the
descendants of both Eleazar and Ithamar.
6The scribe Shemaiah son of Nethanel,
a Levite, recorded their names in the presence of the king and of the officials: Zadok
the priest, Ahimelek[r] son of Abiathar and
the heads of families of the priests and of
the Levites—one family being taken from
Eleazar and then one from Ithamar.

7The first lot fell to Jehoiarib,
the second to Jedaiah,[s]
8the third to Harim,[t]
the fourth to Seorim,
9the fifth to Malkijah,
the sixth to Mijamin,
10the seventh to Hakkoz,
the eighth to Abijah,[u]
11the ninth to Jeshua,
the tenth to Shekaniah,
12the eleventh to Eliashib,
the twelfth to Jakim,
13the thirteenth to Huppah,
the fourteenth to Jeshebeab,
14the fifteenth to Bilgah,
the sixteenth to Immer,[v]
15the seventeenth to Hezir,[w]
the eighteenth to Happizzez,
16the nineteenth to Pethahiah,
the twentieth to Jehezkel,
17the twenty-first to Jakin,
the twenty-second to Gamul,
18the twenty-third to Delaiah
and the twenty-fourth to Maaziah.

19This was their appointed order of ministering when they entered the temple of
the LORD, according to the regulations prescribed for them by their ancestor Aaron,
as the LORD, the God of Israel, had commanded him.

The Rest of the Levites

20As for the rest of the descendants of Levi:[x]
from the sons of Amram: Shubael;
from the sons of Shubael: Jehdeiah.
21As for Rehabiah,[y] from his sons:
Ishiah was the first.
22From the Izharites: Shelomoth;
from the sons of Shelomoth: Jahath.
23The sons of Hebron:[z] Jeriah the first,[a]
Amariah the second, Jahaziel the
third and Jekameam the fourth.
24The son of Uzziel: Micah;
from the sons of Micah: Shamir.
25The brother of Micah: Ishiah;
from the sons of Ishiah: Zechariah.
26The sons of Merari:[a] Mahli and Mushi.
The son of Jaaziah: Beno.
27The sons of Merari:
from Jaaziah: Beno, Shoham, Zakkur and Ibri.
28From Mahli: Eleazar, who had no sons.
29From Kish: the son of Kish:
Jerahmeel.
30And the sons of Mushi: Mahli, Eder
and Jerimoth.

These were the Levites, according to
their families. 31They also cast lots,[b] just
as their relatives the descendants of Aaron
did, in the presence of King David and of
Zadok, Ahimelek, and the heads of families of the priests and of the Levites. The
families of the oldest brother were treated
the same as those of the youngest.

The Musicians

25 David, together with the commanders of the army, set apart some of the
sons of Asaph,[c] Heman[d] and Jeduthun[e] for
the ministry of prophesying,[f] accompanied
by harps, lyres and cymbals.[g] Here is the
list of the men[h] who performed this service:[i]

a 23 Two Hebrew manuscripts and some Septuagint manuscripts (see also 23:19); most Hebrew manuscripts *The sons of Jeriah:*

24:1 ***descendants of Aaron.*** See notes 6:2–4; 15:11.

24:10 ***Abijah.*** This Abijah may be the ancestor of Zechariah, father of John the Baptist, who is named in Luke 1:5.

24:20–21 ***descendants of Levi.*** The nonpriestly Levites also were divided by clan to determine their service rotation.

25:1 ***prophesying, accompanied by harps, lyres and cymbals.*** The role of prophet was not limited to a prediction or proclamation in words. Vocal and instrumental music could be a kind of prophetic message, usually in the form of praise (1 Sam. 10:5–6).

23:32 [k] 2Ch 23:18; 31:2; Eze 44:14 **24:1** [l] 1Ch 23:6; 28:13; 2Ch 5:11; 8:14; 23:8; 31:2; 35:4, 5; Ezr 6:18 [m] Nu 3:2-4 [n] Ex 6:23 **24:2** [o] Lev 10:1-2; Nu 3:4 **24:3** [p] 2Sa 8:17 **24:5** [q] ver 31; 1Ch 25:8 **24:6** [r] 1Ch 18:16 **24:7** [s] Ezr 2:36; Ne 12:6 **24:8** [t] Ezr 2:39; Ne 10:5 **24:10** [u] Ne 12:4, 17; Lk 1:5 **24:14** [v] Jer 20:1 **24:15** [w] Ne 10:20 **24:20** [x] 1Ch 23:6 **24:21** [y] 1Ch 23:17 **24:23** [z] 1Ch 23:19 **24:26** [a] 1Ch 6:19; 23:21 **24:31** [b] ver 5 **25:1** [c] 1Ch 6:39 [d] 1Ch 6:33 [e] 1Ch 16:41, 42; Ne 11:17 [f] 1Sa 10:5; 2Ki 3:15 [g] 1Ch 15:16 [h] 1Ch 6:31 [i] 2Ch 5:12; 8:14; 34:12; 35:15; Ezr 3:10

2From the sons of Asaph:
Zakkur, Joseph, Nethaniah and Asarelah. The sons of Asaph were under the supervision of Asaph, who prophesied under the king's supervision.
3As for Jeduthun, from his sons:[j]
Gedaliah, Zeri, Jeshaiah, Shimei,[a] Hashabiah and Mattithiah, six in all, under the supervision of their father Jeduthun, who prophesied, using the harp[k] in thanking and praising the LORD.
4As for Heman, from his sons:
Bukkiah, Mattaniah, Uzziel, Shubael and Jerimoth; Hananiah, Hanani, Eliathah, Giddalti and Romamti-Ezer; Joshbekashah, Mallothi, Hothir and
Mahazioth. 5(All these were sons of Heman the king's seer. They were given him through the promises of God to exalt him. God gave Heman fourteen sons and three daughters.)

6All these men were under the supervision of their father[l] for the music of the temple of the LORD, with cymbals, lyres and harps, for the ministry at the house of God. Asaph, Jeduthun and Heman[m] were under the supervision of the king.[n] 7Along
with their relatives—all of them trained and skilled in music for the LORD—they numbered 288. 8Young and old alike, teacher as well as student, cast lots[o] for their duties.

9The first lot, which was for Asaph,[p] fell to Joseph,
his sons and relatives[b] 12[c]
the second to Gedaliah,
him and his relatives and sons 12
10the third to Zakkur,
his sons and relatives 12
11the fourth to Izri,[d]
his sons and relatives 12
12the fifth to Nethaniah,
his sons and relatives 12
13the sixth to Bukkiah,
his sons and relatives 12
14the seventh to Jesarelah,[e]
his sons and relatives 12
15the eighth to Jeshaiah,
his sons and relatives 12
16the ninth to Mattaniah,
his sons and relatives 12
17the tenth to Shimei,
his sons and relatives 12
18the eleventh to Azarel,[f]
his sons and relatives 12
19the twelfth to Hashabiah,
his sons and relatives 12
20the thirteenth to Shubael,
his sons and relatives 12
21the fourteenth to Mattithiah,
his sons and relatives 12
22the fifteenth to Jerimoth,
his sons and relatives 12
23the sixteenth to Hananiah,
his sons and relatives 12
24the seventeenth to Joshbekashah,
his sons and relatives 12
25the eighteenth to Hanani,
his sons and relatives 12
26the nineteenth to Mallothi,
his sons and relatives 12
27the twentieth to Eliathah,
his sons and relatives 12
28the twenty-first to Hothir,
his sons and relatives 12
29the twenty-second to Giddalti,
his sons and relatives 12
30the twenty-third to Mahazioth,
his sons and relatives 12
31the twenty-fourth to Romamti-Ezer,
his sons and relatives 12.[q]

The Gatekeepers

26 The divisions of the gatekeepers:[r]
From the Korahites: Meshelemiah son of Kore, one of the sons of Asaph.
2Meshelemiah had sons:
Zechariah[s] the firstborn,
Jediael the second,
Zebadiah the third,
Jathniel the fourth,
3Elam the fifth,
Jehohanan the sixth
and Eliehoenai the seventh.
4Obed-Edom also had sons:
Shemaiah the firstborn,
Jehozabad the second,
Joah the third,
Sakar the fourth,
Nethanel the fifth,
5Ammiel the sixth,
Issachar the seventh

[a] *3* One Hebrew manuscript and some Septuagint manuscripts (see also verse 17); most Hebrew manuscripts do not have *Shimei.* [b] *9* See Septuagint; Hebrew does not have *his sons and relatives.* [c] *9* See the total in verse 7; Hebrew does not have *twelve.* [d] *11* A variant of *Zeri* [e] *14* A variant of *Asarelah* [f] *18* A variant of *Uzziel*

25:2 under the king's supervision. This underscored the leading role that David took in the religious life of the nation.

26:1 – 32 Duty—Our duties include all of the activities required to fulfill an assigned service. We are not praised for doing these jobs, and sometimes only the Lord sees what we have done. The temple servants knew that their jobs were "for" the Lord, but they were not personally very visible among the hundreds who did similar tasks. From the gatekeepers to the guardians of the treasures, faithfulness was the moral obligation, or duty, of each officer. For us as believers, the moral obligation is the same. We are never off duty.

25:3 [j] 1Ch 16:41-42 [k] Ge 4:21; Ps 33:2 **25:6** [l] 1Ch 15:16 [m] 1Ch 15:19 [n] 2Ch 23:18; 29:25 **25:8** [o] 1Ch 26:13 **25:9** [p] 1Ch 6:39 **25:31** [q] 1Ch 9:33 **26:1** [r] 1Ch 9:17 **26:2** [s] 1Ch 9:21

and Peullethai the eighth.
(For God had blessed Obed-Edom.[t])
6 Obed-Edom's son Shemaiah also had
sons, who were leaders in their father's family because they were
very capable men. 7The sons of
Shemaiah: Othni, Rephael, Obed
and Elzabad; his relatives Elihu and
Semakiah were also able men. 8All
these were descendants of Obed-
Edom; they and their sons and their
relatives were capable men with the
strength to do the work—descendants of Obed-Edom, 62 in all.
9 Meshelemiah had sons and relatives,
who were able men—18 in all.
10 Hosah the Merarite had sons: Shimri
the first (although he was not the
firstborn, his father had appointed
him the first),[u] 11Hilkiah the second,
Tabaliah the third and Zechariah
the fourth. The sons and relatives of
Hosah were 13 in all.
12These divisions of the gatekeepers,
through their leaders, had duties for ministering[v] in the temple of the LORD, just
as their relatives had. 13Lots[w] were cast
for each gate, according to their families,
young and old alike.
14The lot for the East Gate[x] fell to Shelemiah.[a] Then lots were cast for his son
Zechariah,[y] a wise counselor, and the lot
for the North Gate fell to him. 15The lot for
the South Gate fell to Obed-Edom,[z] and the
lot for the storehouse fell to his sons. 16The
lots for the West Gate and the Shalleketh
Gate on the upper road fell to Shuppim and
Hosah.
Guard was alongside of guard: 17There
were six Levites a day on the east, four a
day on the north, four a day on the south
and two at a time at the storehouse. 18As
for the court[b] to the west, there were four at
the road and two at the court[b] itself.
19These were the divisions of the gatekeepers who were descendants of Korah
and Merari.[a]

The Treasurers and Other Officials

20Their fellow Levites[b] were[c] in charge
of the treasuries of the house of God and
the treasuries for the dedicated things.[c]
21The descendants of Ladan, who were
Gershonites through Ladan and who were
heads of families belonging to Ladan the
Gershonite,[d] were Jehieli, 22the sons of Jehieli, Zetham and his brother Joel. They
were in charge of the treasuries[e] of the temple of the LORD.
23From the Amramites, the Izharites, the
Hebronites and the Uzzielites:[f]
24 Shubael,[g] a descendant of Gershom
son of Moses, was the official in
charge of the treasuries. 25His relatives through Eliezer: Rehabiah his
son, Jeshaiah his son, Joram his son,
Zikri his son and Shelomith[h] his son.
26Shelomith and his relatives were
in charge of all the treasuries for the
things dedicated[i] by King David, by
the heads of families who were the
commanders of thousands and commanders of hundreds, and by the
other army commanders. 27Some of
the plunder taken in battle they dedicated for the repair of the temple of
the LORD. 28And everything dedicated by Samuel the seer[j] and by Saul
son of Kish, Abner son of Ner and
Joab son of Zeruiah, and all the other dedicated things were in the care
of Shelomith and his relatives.
29 From the Izharites: Kenaniah and his
sons were assigned duties away
from the temple, as officials and
judges[k] over Israel.
30 From the Hebronites: Hashabiah[l] and
his relatives—seventeen hundred
able men—were responsible in Israel
west of the Jordan for all the work of
the LORD and for the king's service.
31As for the Hebronites,[m] Jeriah was
their chief according to the genealogical records of their families. In
the fortieth[n] year of David's reign a
search was made in the records, and
capable men among the Hebronites
were found at Jazer in Gilead. 32Je-
riah had twenty-seven hundred relatives, who were able men and heads
of families, and King David put them
in charge of the Reubenites, the Gadites and the half-tribe of Manasseh
for every matter pertaining to God
and for the affairs of the king.

Army Divisions

27 This is the list of the Israelites—heads
of families, commanders of thousands
and commanders of hundreds, and their

[a] *14* A variant of *Meshelemiah* [b] *18* The meaning of the Hebrew for this word is uncertain. [c] *20* Septuagint; Hebrew *As for the Levites, Ahijah was*

26:14 *lot for the East Gate.* The East Gate was the most important because it led straight into the main entrance of the temple.
27:1 *heads of families, commanders.* Apparently a professional standing army is being described here, one that was divided into twelve corps.

26:5 [t] 2Sa 6:10; 1Ch 13:13; 16:38 **26:10** [u] Dt 21:16; 1Ch 5:1 **26:12** [v] 1Ch 9:22 **26:13** [w] 1Ch 24:5,31; 25:8 **26:14** [x] 1Ch 9:18 [y] 1Ch 9:21 **26:15** [z] 1Ch 13:13; 2Ch 25:24 **26:19** [a] 2Ch 35:15; Ne 7:1; Eze 44:11 **26:20** [b] 2Ch 24:5 [c] 1Ch 28:12 **26:21** [d] 1Ch 23:7; 29:8 **26:22** [e] 1Ch 9:26 **26:23** [f] Nu 3:27 **26:24** [g] 1Ch 23:16 **26:25** [h] 1Ch 23:18 **26:26** [i] 2Sa 8:11 **26:28** [j] 1Sa 9:9 **26:29** [k] Dt 17:8-13; 1Ch 23:4; Ne 11:16 **26:30** [l] 1Ch 27:17 **26:31** [m] 1Ch 23:19 [n] 2Sa 5:4

officers, who served the king in all that concerned the army divisions that were on duty month by month throughout the year. Each division consisted of 24,000 men.

2 In charge of the first division, for the first month, was Jashobeam[o] son of Zabdiel. There were 24,000 men in his division. 3He was a descendant of Perez and chief of all the army officers for the first month.
4 In charge of the division for the second month was Dodai[p] the Ahohite; Mikloth was the leader of his division. There were 24,000 men in his division.
5 The third army commander, for the third month, was Benaiah[q] son of Jehoiada the priest. He was chief and there were 24,000 men in his division. 6This was the Benaiah who was a mighty warrior among the Thirty and was over the Thirty. His son Ammizabad was in charge of his division.
7 The fourth, for the fourth month, was Asahel[r] the brother of Joab; his son Zebadiah was his successor. There were 24,000 men in his division.
8 The fifth, for the fifth month, was the commander Shamhuth[s] the Izrahite. There were 24,000 men in his division.
9 The sixth, for the sixth month, was Ira[t] the son of Ikkesh the Tekoite. There were 24,000 men in his division.
10 The seventh, for the seventh month, was Helez[u] the Pelonite, an Ephraimite. There were 24,000 men in his division.
11 The eighth, for the eighth month, was Sibbekai[v] the Hushathite, a Zerahite. There were 24,000 men in his division.
12 The ninth, for the ninth month, was Abiezer[w] the Anathothite, a Benjamite. There were 24,000 men in his division.
13 The tenth, for the tenth month, was Maharai[x] the Netophathite, a Zerahite. There were 24,000 men in his division.
14 The eleventh, for the eleventh month, was Benaiah[y] the Pirathonite, an Ephraimite. There were 24,000 men in his division.
15 The twelfth, for the twelfth month, was Heldai[z] the Netophathite, from the family of Othniel.[a] There were 24,000 men in his division.

Leaders of the Tribes

16 The leaders of the tribes of Israel:

over the Reubenites: Eliezer son of Zikri;
over the Simeonites: Shephatiah son of Maakah;
17 over Levi: Hashabiah[b] son of Kemuel;
over Aaron: Zadok;[c]
18 over Judah: Elihu, a brother of David;
over Issachar: Omri son of Michael;
19 over Zebulun: Ishmaiah son of Obadiah;
over Naphtali: Jerimoth son of Azriel;
20 over the Ephraimites: Hoshea son of Azaziah;
over half the tribe of Manasseh: Joel son of Pedaiah;
21 over the half-tribe of Manasseh in Gilead: Iddo son of Zechariah;
over Benjamin: Jaasiel son of Abner;
22 over Dan: Azarel son of Jeroham.

These were the leaders of the tribes of Israel.

23David did not take the number of the
men twenty years old or less,[d] because the
LORD had promised to make Israel as numerous as the stars[e] in the sky. 24Joab son
of Zeruiah began to count the men but did
not finish. God's wrath came on Israel on
account of this numbering,[f] and the number was not entered in the book[a] of the annals of King David.

The King's Overseers

25Azmaveth son of Adiel was in charge of the royal storehouses.

Jonathan son of Uzziah was in charge of the storehouses in the outlying districts, in the towns, the villages and the watchtowers.

26Ezri son of Kelub was in charge of the workers who farmed the land.

---

a 24 Septuagint; Hebrew *number*

27:2 *Jashobeam.* A connection can be made here to the list of David's mighty men, which is also headed by Jashobeam (11:11 – 12). He was one of "the Three," which meant that he was regarded as unusually heroic.
27:4 *Dodai.* Dodai's son Eleazar was the second of the mighty men included in the first trio along with Jashobeam (11:12).
27:5 *Benaiah.* As the son of a priest, Benaiah was from the tribe of Levi. In the earlier list of mighty men he was celebrated for killing a lion and a gigantic Egyptian (11:22 – 23). Because of this kind of courage, he was honored among the thirty mighty men, though he was not one of "the Three" (11:24). Later he was named as commander of the entire Israelite army (2 Kin. 4:4).
27:7 *Asahel.* David's nephew Asahel (2:15 – 16) was among the thirty mighty men, but did not achieve a position among "the Three" (11:26).
27:11 – 12 *Sibbekai ... Abiezer.* These two men were also members of the elite thirty mighty men. (11:28 – 29).
27:18 *Elihu.* This brother of David is usually called Eliab (1 Sam. 16:6).

27:2 [o] 2Sa 23:8; 1Ch 11:11 **27:4** [p] 2Sa 23:9 **27:5** [q] 2Sa 23:20 **27:7** [r] 2Sa 2:18; 1Ch 11:26 **27:8** [s] 1Ch 11:27 **27:9** [t] 2Sa 23:26; 1Ch 11:28 **27:10** [u] 2Sa 23:26; 1Ch 11:27 **27:11** [v] 2Sa 21:18 **27:12** [w] 2Sa 23:27; 1Ch 11:28 **27:13** [x] 2Sa 23:28; 1Ch 11:30 **27:14** [y] 1Ch 11:31 **27:15** [z] 2Sa 23:29 [a] Jos 15:17 **27:17** [b] 1Ch 26:30 [c] 2Sa 8:17; 1Ch 12:28 **27:23** [d] 1Ch 21:2-5 [e] Ge 15:5 **27:24** [f] 2Sa 24:15; 1Ch 21:7

27Shimei the Ramathite was in charge of
the vineyards.
Zabdi the Shiphmite was in charge of the
produce of the vineyards for the wine vats.
28Baal-Hanan the Gederite was in
charge of the olive and sycamore-fig[g] trees
in the western foothills.
Joash was in charge of the supplies of
olive oil.
29Shitrai the Sharonite was in charge of
the herds grazing in Sharon.
Shaphat son of Adlai was in charge of
the herds in the valleys.
30Obil the Ishmaelite was in charge of
the camels.
Jehdeiah the Meronothite was in charge
of the donkeys.
31Jaziz the Hagrite[h] was in charge of the
flocks.
All these were the officials in charge of
King David's property.

32Jonathan, David's uncle, was a counselor, a man of insight and a scribe. Jehiel son of Hakmoni took care of the king's sons.
33Ahithophel[i] was the king's counselor.
Hushai[j] the Arkite was the king's confidant.
34Ahithophel was succeeded by Jehoiada son of Benaiah and by Abiathar.[k]
Joab[l] was the commander of the royal army.

David's Plans for the Temple

28 David summoned all the officials[m] of Israel to assemble at Jerusalem: the officers over the tribes, the commanders of the divisions in the service of the king, the commanders of thousands and commanders of hundreds, and the officials in charge of all the property and livestock belonging to the king and his sons, together with the palace officials, the warriors and all the brave fighting men.
2King David rose to his feet and said:
"Listen to me, my fellow Israelites, my people. I had it in my heart[n] to build a house as a place of rest for the ark of the covenant of the LORD, for the footstool[o] of our God,
and I made plans to build it. 3But God said
to me,[p] 'You are not to build a house for my Name,[q] because you are a warrior and have shed blood.'[r]
4"Yet the LORD, the God of Israel, chose me[s] from my whole family[t] to be king over Israel forever. He chose Judah[u] as leader, and from the tribe of Judah he chose my family, and from my father's sons he was
pleased to make me king over all Israel. 5Of
all my sons—and the LORD has given me many[v]—he has chosen my son Solomon[w] to sit on the throne of the kingdom of the
LORD over Israel. 6He said to me: 'Solomon
your son is the one who will build my house and my courts, for I have chosen him to be
my son,[x] and I will be his father. 7I will
establish his kingdom forever if he is unswerving in carrying out my commands and laws,[y] as is being done at this time.'
8"So now I charge you in the sight of all Israel and of the assembly of the LORD, and in the hearing of our God: Be careful to follow all the commands[z] of the LORD your God, that you may possess this good land and pass it on as an inheritance to your descendants forever.[a]

27:29 ***Sharonite.*** A fertile plain between Israelite and Philistine territory, Sharon was ideal for grazing cattle and sheep. It is appropriate that someone from Sharon, who knew the land and all its seasonal changes, should be in charge of the livestock.
27:30 ***Ishmaelite.*** As inhabitants of the desert, the Ishmaelites were at home with the breeding and use of camels.
28:2 ***footstool.*** The word "footstool" is a metaphor describing either the ark of the covenant or the tabernacle as the earthly base of God's activity. The words make a little picture of God on His throne in heaven, resting His feet on the earth.
28:4–6 Government of Israel—The government of Israel was under two important headings; the laws, and the leaders. *The laws*—The "commandments," especially the Ten Commandments, revealed God's holiness and set up a divine standard of righteousness for the people to follow (Ex. 20:1–17). The judgments governed the social life of the people (Ex. 21). The ordinances included the sacrifices that showed that blood must be shed for the forgiveness of sins (Lev. 1–17). *The leaders*—At first Moses was the primary leader; then he was replaced by Joshua. After Joshua's death the nation was governed for many years by judges who were usually raised up by God to oppose a specific enemy. Finally, at the people's request, God granted them a king, thus establishing the monarchy (1 Sam. 8:6–17).
Through most of Israel's history four leadership roles can be seen:

1. *The king* was the Lord's representative who ruled the people, but only as the Lord's servant. He led in war (1 Sam. 8:20) and made judicial decisions (2 Sam. 15:2); but could not make law, since he himself was under the law (Deut. 17:14–20).
2. *The priest* taught the Lord's laws and officiated at the offering of sacrifices (Lev. 1:5).
3. *The prophet* was the man of God who spoke for God and gave divine pronouncements for the present or the future.
4. *The wise man* produced literary works stressing practical wisdom (Prov. 1:1), taught discipline of character to the young (Prov. 22:17), and gave counsel to the king (2 Sam. 16:20).

28:6 ***be my son, and I will be his father.*** This remarkable statement not only shows that the Davidic kings enjoyed unparalleled access to the Lord as His adopted sons (17:3; Ps. 2:7), but it anticipates the absolute sonship of the Son of David, Jesus Christ (Acts 13:33; Heb. 1:5).

27:28 [g] 1Ki 10:27; 2Ch 1:15 **27:31** [h] 1Ch 5:10
27:33 [i] 2Sa 15:12 [j] 2Sa 15:37 **27:34** [k] 1Ki 1:7 [l] 1Ch 11:6
28:1 [m] 1Ch 11:10; 27:1-31 **28:2** [n] 1Ch 17:2 [o] Ps 99:5; 132:7 **28:3** [p] 2Sa 7:5 [q] 1Ch 22:8 [r] 1Ki 5:3; 1Ch 17:4
28:4 [s] 1Ch 17:23, 27; 2Ch 6:6 [t] 1Sa 16:1-13 [u] Ge 49:10; 1Ch 5:2 **28:5** [v] 1Ch 3:1 [w] 1Ch 22:9; 23:1
28:6 [x] 2Sa 7:13; 1Ch 22:9-10 **28:7** [y] 1Ch 22:13
28:8 [z] Dt 6:1 [a] Dt 4:1

9“And you, my son Solomon, acknowledge the God of your father, and serve him with wholehearted devotion[b] and with a willing mind, for the LORD searches every heart[c] and understands every desire and every thought. If you seek him,[d] he will be found by you; but if you forsake[e] him, he will reject[f] you forever. 10Consider now, for the LORD has chosen you to build a house as the sanctuary. Be strong and do the work.”

11Then David gave his son Solomon the plans[g] for the portico of the temple, its buildings, its storerooms, its upper parts, its inner rooms and the place of atonement. 12He gave him the plans of all that the Spirit[h] had put in his mind for the courts of the temple of the LORD and all the surrounding rooms, for the treasuries of the temple of God and for the treasuries for the dedicated things.[i] 13He gave him instructions for the divisions[j] of the priests and Levites, and for all the work of serving in the temple of the LORD, as well as for all the articles to be used in its service. 14He designated the weight of gold for all the gold articles to be used in various kinds of service, and the weight of silver for all the silver articles to be used in various kinds of service: 15the weight of gold for the gold lampstands[k] and their lamps, with the weight for each lampstand and its lamps; and the weight of silver for each silver lampstand and its lamps, according to the use of each lampstand; 16the weight of gold for each table[l] for consecrated bread; the weight of silver for the silver tables; 17the weight of pure gold for the forks, sprinkling bowls[m] and pitchers; the weight of gold for each gold dish; the weight of silver for each silver dish; 18and the weight of the refined gold for the altar of incense.[n] He also gave him the plan for the chariot,[o] that is, the cherubim of gold that spread their wings and overshadow[p] the ark of the covenant of the LORD.

19“All this,” David said, “I have in writing as a result of the LORD’s hand on me, and he enabled me to understand all the details[q] of the plan.[r]”

20David also said to Solomon his son, “Be strong and courageous,[s] and do the work. Do not be afraid or discouraged, for the LORD God, my God, is with you. He will not fail you or forsake[t] you until all the work for the service of the temple of the LORD is finished.[u] 21The divisions of the priests and Levites are ready for all the work on the temple of God, and every willing person skilled[v] in any craft will help you in all the work. The officials and all the people will obey your every command.”

Gifts for Building the Temple

29 Then King David said to the whole assembly: “My son Solomon, the one whom God has chosen, is young and inexperienced.[w] The task is great, because this palatial structure is not for man but for the LORD God. 2With all my resources I have provided for the temple of my God—gold[x] for the gold work, silver for the silver, bronze for the bronze, iron for the iron and wood for the wood, as well as onyx for the settings, turquoise,[a][y] stones of various colors, and all kinds of fine stone and marble—all of these in large quantities.[z] 3Besides, in my devotion to the temple of my God I now give my personal treasures of gold and silver for the temple of my God, over and above everything I have provided[a] for this holy temple: 4three thousand talents[b] of gold (gold of Ophir)[b] and seven thousand talents[c] of refined silver,[c] for the overlaying of the walls of the buildings, 5for the gold work and the silver work, and for all the work to be done by the craftsmen. Now, who is willing to consecrate themselves to the LORD today?”

6Then the leaders of families, the officers of the tribes of Israel, the commanders of thousands and commanders of hundreds, and the officials[d] in charge of the king’s work gave willingly.[e] 7They[f] gave toward

a 2 The meaning of the Hebrew for this word is uncertain. *b* 4 That is, about 110 tons or about 100 metric tons *c* 4 That is, about 260 tons or about 235 metric tons

28:19 *the LORD’s hand on me.* The plans for the temple were from God, just as the plans of the tabernacle of Moses were. This was extremely important, for God had stressed the necessity of making the tabernacle exactly according to His instructions (Ex. 38:22; 39:5–7,42–43). The Israelites would need to know that this permanent building was God’s plan, not just David’s.

28:20 *Be strong and courageous.* David’s charge to Solomon is very similar to the charge given to Joshua when Moses handed over the leadership of Israel to him (Josh. 1:6–9).

29:4 Generosity—It is extremely difficult to assign a modern monetary value to ancient goods and services, but we might compare David’s gift for the temple to approximately one billion, eight hundred thousand dollars in gold, and eighty-four million in silver. This kind of personal wealth is astounding, but for David, its value was significant only as provision for the temple for the Lord. He never lost sight of the fact that both honor and riches come from God. They are His to give, His to use, and His to remove.

29:7 *five thousand talents.* This represents about

28:9 [b] 1Ch 29:19 [c] 1Sa 16:7; Ps 7:9 [d] Ps 40:16; Jer 29:13 [e] Jos 24:20; 2Ch 15:2 [f] Ps 44:23 **28:11** [g] Ex 25:9 **28:12** [h] 1Ch 12:18 [i] 1Ch 26:20 **28:13** [j] 1Ch 24:1 **28:15** [k] Ex 25:31 **28:16** [l] Ex 25:23 **28:17** [m] Ex 27:3 **28:18** [n] Ex 30:1-10 [o] Ex 25:18-22 [p] Ex 25:20 **28:19** [q] 1Ki 6:38 [r] Ex 25:9 **28:20** [s] Dt 31:6; 1Ch 22:13; 2Ch 19:11; Hag 2:4 [t] Dt 4:31; Jos 24:20 [u] 1Ki 6:14; 2Ch 7:11 **28:21** [v] Ex 35:25-36:5 **29:1** [w] 1Ki 3:7; 1Ch 22:5; 2Ch 13:7 **29:2** [x] ver 7, 14, 16; Ezr 1:4; 6:5; Hag 2:8 [y] Isa 54:11 [z] 1Ch 22:2-5 **29:3** [a] 2Ch 24:10; 31:3; 35:8 **29:4** [b] Ge 10:29 [c] 1Ch 22:14 **29:6** [d] 1Ch 27:1; 28:1 [e] ver 9; Ex 25:1-8; 35:20-29; 36:2; 2Ch 24:10; Ezr 7:15 **29:7** [f] Ex 25:2; Ne 7:70-71

the work on the temple of God five thousand talents[a] and ten thousand darics[b] of
gold, ten thousand talents[c] of silver, eighteen thousand talents[d] of bronze and a
hundred thousand talents[e] of iron. 8Any-
one who had precious stones[g] gave them
to the treasury of the temple of the LORD in
the custody of Jehiel the Gershonite.[h] 9The
people rejoiced at the willing response of
their leaders, for they had given freely and
wholeheartedly[i] to the LORD. David the
king also rejoiced greatly.

David's Prayer

10David praised the LORD in the presence
of the whole assembly, saying,

"Praise be to you, LORD,
the God of our father Israel,
from everlasting to everlasting.
11 Yours, LORD, is the greatness and the power[j]
and the glory and the majesty and the splendor,
for everything in heaven and earth is yours.[k]
Yours, LORD, is the kingdom;
you are exalted as head over all.[l]
12 Wealth and honor[m] come from you;
you are the ruler[n] of all things.
In your hands are strength and power
to exalt and give strength to all.
13 Now, our God, we give you thanks,
and praise your glorious name.

14"But who am I, and who are my people, that we should be able to give as generously as this? Everything comes from
you, and we have given you only what
comes from your hand. 15We are foreigners and strangers[o] in your sight, as were
all our ancestors. Our days on earth are
like a shadow,[p] without hope. 16LORD our
God, all this abundance that we have provided for building you a temple for your
Holy Name comes from your hand, and
all of it belongs to you. 17I know, my God,
that you test the heart[q] and are pleased
with integrity. All these things I have giv-
en willingly and with honest intent. And
now I have seen with joy how willingly
your people who are here have given to
you.[r] 18LORD, the God of our fathers Abraham, Isaac and Israel, keep these desires
and thoughts in the hearts of your people
forever, and keep their hearts loyal to you.
19And give my son Solomon the wholehearted devotion[s] to keep your commands,
statutes and decrees[t] and to do everything
to build the palatial structure for which I
have provided."[u]

20Then David said to the whole assembly, "Praise the LORD your God." So they all
praised the LORD, the God of their fathers;
they bowed down, prostrating themselves
before the LORD and the king.

Solomon Acknowledged as King

21The next day they made sacrifices to
the LORD and presented burnt offerings to
him:[v] a thousand bulls, a thousand rams
and a thousand male lambs, together with
their drink offerings, and other sacrifices
in abundance for all Israel. 22They ate and
drank with great joy[w] in the presence of the
LORD that day.

Then they acknowledged Solomon son of
David as king a second time, anointing him
before the LORD to be ruler and Zadok[x] to

[a] 7 That is, about 190 tons or about 170 metric tons
[b] 7 That is, about 185 pounds or about 84 kilograms
[c] 7 That is, about 380 tons or about 340 metric tons
[d] 7 That is, about 675 tons or about 610 metric tons
[e] 7 That is, about 3,800 tons or about 3,400 metric tons

---

190 tons of gold. ***ten thousand darics.*** This is about 185 pounds of gold. ***eighteen thousand talents.*** This was equivalent to about 675 tons. ***a hundred thousand talents.*** This was approximately 3,750 tons.

29:10 ***praised the LORD.*** David modeled before the people the worship of the living God. He started with praise for God's goodness, greatness, and glory, and then acknowledged his place under the care and blessing of God.

29:14–15 All That We Have—Even though David was king and could accumulate whatever he wanted, he was more conscious of the need to give, particularly to God. How can anyone strive to accumulate, if you know in the long run that none of what you've gathered is really yours? Generosity is the natural outcome of a right perspective on possessions.

Verse 15 points to two other elements that indicate a basis for generosity. David understood where his real home was, namely with God. If a king regards himself as an alien in his own land, how much more should we? Somehow he resisted the temptation to regard the land as his to do with as he wished. He understood the brevity of life. Why spend time accumulating when we can't take it with us? Living with this perspective allows us to be transparent before God. We can be in sync with God because we're keeping nothing from Him. What we have has value only as it furthers the kingdom, and God is quite capable of supplying everything we need to be able to live.

It also means we're functioning clearly in the context of the biblical mandate of stewardship. We're here to have dominion (Gen. 1:28) but with the end that God is honored by what we do.

29:18 ***God of our fathers Abraham, Isaac and Israel.*** These familiar words identify the Israelites with the promises of God to their forefathers, and to the God of those promises.

29:22 ***king a second time.*** This refers to the ratification of Solomon's kingship (see note for 23:1).

29:8 [g] Ex 35:27 [h] 1Ch 26:21 **29:9** [i] 1Ki 8:61; 2Co 9:7
29:11 [j] Ps 24:8; 59:17; 62:11 [k] Ps 89:11 [l] Rev 5:12-13
29:12 [m] 2Ch 1:12 [n] 2Ch 20:6; Ro 11:36 **29:15** [o] Ps 39:12;
Heb 11:13 [p] Job 14:2 **29:17** [q] Ps 139:23; Pr 15:11; 17:3;
Jer 11:20; 17:10 [r] 1Ch 28:9; Ps 15:1-5 **29:19** [s] 1Ch 28:9
[t] Ps 72:1 [u] 1Ch 22:14 **29:21** [v] 1Ki 8:62
29:22 [w] 1Ch 23:1 [x] 1Ki 1:33-39

be priest. 23So Solomon sat on the throne[y]
of the LORD as king in place of his father
David. He prospered and all Israel obeyed
him. 24All the officers and warriors, as well
as all of King David's sons, pledged their
submission to King Solomon.
25The LORD highly exalted Solomon in
the sight of all Israel and bestowed on him
royal splendor[z] such as no king over Israel
ever had before.[a]

The Death of David

26David son of Jesse was king[b] over
all Israel. 27He ruled over Israel forty
years—seven in Hebron and thirty-three
in Jerusalem.[c] 28He died[d] at a good old
age, having enjoyed long life, wealth and
honor. His son Solomon succeeded him as
king.[e]
29As for the events of King David's
reign, from beginning to end, they are
written in the records of Samuel the seer,[f]
the records of Nathan[g] the prophet and the
records of Gad[h] the seer, 30together with
the details of his reign and power, and the
circumstances that surrounded him and
Israel and the kingdoms of all the other
lands.

29:23 *throne of the LORD.* The position of king may have passed from David to Solomon, but the throne was the Lord's. Eventually Jesus, the Son of David and the Son of God would sit on that throne and reign forever (Luke 1:32).

29:23 [y] 1Ki 2:12 **29:25** [z] 2Ch 1:1, 12 [a] 1Ki 3:13; Ecc 2:9 **29:26** [b] 1Ch 18:14 **29:27** [c] 2Sa 5:4-5; 1Ki 2:11; 1Ch 3:4 **29:28** [d] Ge 15:15; Ac 13:36 [e] 1Ch 23:1 **29:29** [f] 1Sa 9:9 [g] 2Sa 7:2 [h] 1Sa 22:5

2 CHRONICLES

▶ **AUTHOR:** The sources of 1 and 2 Chronicles include multiple official and prophetic records. In addition to these, the author-compiler had access to genealogical lists and documents, such as the message and letters of Sennacherib (2 Chr. 32:10–17). It seems likely that Ezra was the author as Jewish tradition suggests.

▶ **TIME:** c. 991–538 B.C. ▶ **KEY VERSE:** 2 Chr. 7:14

▶ **THEME:** Second Chronicles begins with Solomon's reign and ends with the fall of Jerusalem. It covers more extensively the details involved in the building and dedication of the temple. The kings of Judah are detailed down through the last king, Zedekiah, who is exiled to Babylon in 587 B.C. It largely ignores what happens in the northern kingdom after the split into two nations.

Solomon Asks for Wisdom

1 Solomon son of David established[a] himself firmly over his kingdom, for the LORD his God was with[b] him and made him exceedingly great.[c]

2Then Solomon spoke to all Israel[d]—to the commanders of thousands and commanders of hundreds, to the judges and to all the leaders in Israel, the heads of families— 3and Solomon and the whole assembly went to the high place at Gibeon, for God's tent of meeting[e] was there, which Moses[f] the LORD's servant had made in the wilderness. 4Now David had brought up the ark[g] of God from Kiriath Jearim to the place he had prepared for it, because he had pitched a tent[h] for it in Jerusalem. 5But the bronze altar[i] that Bezalel[j] son of Uri, the son of Hur, had made was in Gibeon in front of the tabernacle of the LORD; so Solomon and the assembly inquired[k] of him there. 6Solomon went up to the bronze altar before the LORD in the tent of meeting and offered a thousand burnt offerings on it.

7That night God appeared[l] to Solomon and said to him, "Ask for whatever you want me to give you."

8Solomon answered God, "You have shown great kindness to David my father and have made me[m] king in his place. 9Now, LORD God, let your promise[n] to my father David be confirmed, for you have made me king over a people who are as numerous as the dust of the earth.[o] 10Give me wisdom and knowledge, that I may lead[p] this people, for who is able to govern this great people of yours?"

11God said to Solomon, "Since this is your heart's desire and you have not asked for wealth,[q] possessions or honor, nor for the death of your enemies, and since you have not asked for a long life but for wisdom and knowledge to govern my people over whom I have made you king, 12therefore wisdom and knowledge will be given you. And I will also give you wealth, possessions and honor,[r] such as no king who was before you ever had and none after you will have.[s]"

1:3 *high place.* In the Old Testament the high places were usually associated with pagan worship (Num. 22:41). The Israelites were specifically charged to destroy these places of worship so that they would not become a snare and lead them into idol worship (Num. 33:53; Deut. 12:3). Nevertheless, Israelites often chose the high places to worship (1 Sam. 9:12). The high place at Gibeon was the location of the Mosaic tabernacle and the great bronze altar throughout David's reign (see note for 1 Kin. 14:23).

1:10 *lead.* This refers to the totality of Solomon's life. As king he would lead by example as well as by edict.

1:11–12 Wisdom—There's significance here in what Solomon didn't ask for. He didn't ask for honor, money, a long life, or the death of his enemies. He didn't ask for the things that would be on the top of most people's lists. He didn't ask for what would make life comfortable and easy. He asked for what would make life good. He asked for wisdom with an eye toward how he would rule, knowing that the quality of his reign largely depended on the quality of his judgments in dealing with people and issues. His priority was his service to others rather than doing what was supposedly best for his personal well-being.

What would be an equivalent today? A corporate executive wanting to know how to make his company

1:1 [a] 1Ki 2:12,26; 2Ch 12:1 [b] Ge 21:22; 39:2; Nu 14:43 [c] 1Ch 29:25 **1:2** [d] 1Ch 9:1; 28:1 **1:3** [e] Ex 36:8 [f] Ex 40:18 **1:4** [g] 2Sa 6:2; 1Ch 15:25 [h] 2Sa 6:17; 1Ch 15:1 **1:5** [i] Ex 38:2 [j] Ex 31:2 [k] 1Ch 13:3 **1:7** [l] 2Ch 7:12 **1:8** [m] 1Ch 23:1; 28:5 **1:9** [n] 2Sa 7:25; 1Ki 8:25 [o] Ge 12:2 **1:10** [p] Nu 27:17; 2Sa 5:2; Pr 8:15-16 **1:11** [q] Dt 17:17 **1:12** [r] 1Ch 29:12 [s] 1Ch 29:25; 2Ch 9:22; Ne 13:26

13Then Solomon went to Jerusalem from
the high place at Gibeon, from before the
tent of meeting. And he reigned over Israel.
14Solomon accumulated chariots[t] and
horses; he had fourteen hundred chariots
and twelve thousand horses,[a] which he
kept in the chariot cities and also with him
in Jerusalem. 15The king made silver and
gold[u] as common in Jerusalem as stones,
and cedar as plentiful as sycamore-fig
trees in the foothills. 16Solomon's horses were imported from Egypt and from
Kue[b]—the royal merchants purchased
them from Kue at the current price. 17They
imported a chariot[v] from Egypt for six
hundred shekels[c] of silver, and a horse for
a hundred and fifty.[d] They also exported
them to all the kings of the Hittites and of
the Arameans.

Preparations for Building the Temple

2[e] Solomon gave orders to build a temple[w]
for the Name of the LORD and a royal
palace for himself.[x] 2He conscripted 70,000
men as carriers and 80,000 as stonecutters in the hills and 3,600 as foremen over
them.[y]
3Solomon sent this message to Hiram[f][z]
king of Tyre:

> "Send me cedar logs[a] as you did for
> my father David when you sent him
> cedar to build a palace to live in. 4Now
> I am about to build a temple[b] for the
> Name of the LORD my God and to ded-
> icate it to him for burning fragrant in-
> cense[c] before him, for setting out the
> consecrated bread[d] regularly, and for
> making burnt offerings[e] every morn-
> ing and evening and on the Sabbaths,[f]
> at the New Moons and at the appoint-
> ed festivals of the LORD our God. This
> is a lasting ordinance for Israel.
> 5"The temple I am going to build will
> be great,[g] because our God is greater
> than all other gods.[h] 6But who is able
> to build a temple for him, since the
> heavens, even the highest heavens,
> cannot contain him?[i] Who then am I[j]
> to build a temple for him, except as a
> place to burn sacrifices before him?
> 7"Send me, therefore, a man skilled
> to work in gold and silver, bronze and
> iron, and in purple, crimson and blue
> yarn, and experienced in the art of en-
> graving, to work in Judah and Jerusa-
> lem with my skilled workers,[k] whom
> my father David provided.
> 8"Send me also cedar, juniper and
> algum[g] logs from Lebanon, for I know
> that your servants are skilled in cut-
> ting timber there. My servants will
> work with yours 9to provide me with
> plenty of lumber, because the temple
> I build must be large and magnificent.
> 10I will give your servants, the woods-
> men who cut the timber, twenty thou-
> sand cors[h] of ground wheat, twenty
> thousand cors[i] of barley, twenty thou-
> sand baths[j] of wine and twenty thou-
> sand baths of olive oil.[l]"

[a] 14 Or *charioteers* [b] 16 Probably Cilicia [c] 17 That is, about 15 pounds or about 6.9 kilograms [d] 17 That is, about 3 3/4 pounds or about 1.7 kilograms [e] In Hebrew texts 2:1 is numbered 1:18, and 2:2-18 is numbered 2:1-17. [f] 3 Hebrew *Huram*, a variant of *Hiram*; also in verses 11 and 12 [g] 8 Probably a variant of *almug* [h] 10 That is, probably about 3,600 tons or about 3,200 metric tons of wheat [i] 10 That is, probably about 3,000 tons or about 2,700 metric tons of barley [j] 10 That is, about 120,000 gallons or about 440,000 liters

contribute for the good of society as opposed to focusing exclusively on profit? A manager being more interested in seeing his staff happy and functioning well rather than getting ahead himself? A father making personal sacrifices for the health of his own family?

1:14 *chariots.* A chariot force of 1,400 units was a significant achievement for Israel, a nation located primarily in hilly terrain where chariots were of limited value. ***horses.*** Moses warned the future kings not to multiply horses for themselves, nor were they to send people back to Egypt to multiply horses (Deut. 17:16). The number of horses that Solomon had for his 1,400 chariots was probably about 4,000.

1:17 *six hundred shekels of silver.* It is often difficult to assign a price in modern currency to the goods and services of the ancient world. This verse suggests that a chariot cost as much as four horses. ***exported.*** Solomon had a thriving business in horses and chariots. Because Israel was on the route between Asia and Africa, such goods would go through Israel and become subject to Solomon's heavy import and export taxes.

2:3 *Hiram king of Tyre.* Also called Huram, he was the same Phoenician ruler who had provided men and materials for David's palace.

2:5 *our God is greater than all other gods.* Solomon's statement means that God is the only true God, not that He is the greatest among many lesser ones. All pagan "gods" are not gods at all (1 Cor. 8:4–5; 10:20).

2:6 Heaven — God is omnipresent. This means that He is everywhere present at all times. There are no bounds or limitations to His presence. But in a special sense, God does have a center for His existence. This is described by Solomon as the "highest heavens," an expression also used by Moses (Deut. 10:14). His title "LORD Almighty" (1 Sam. 1:3) suggests that the dwelling of God is populated by angels and other heavenly beings. It is here that His throne is situated (Is. 6:1). In this sphere His will is done perfectly (Dan. 4:35).

2:10 *wheat ... barley.* The amount of wheat and barley was about 125,000 bushels, or 3,750 tons of each. ***wine ... oil.*** Twenty thousand baths of wine and oil was approximately 115,000 gallons of each.

1:14 [t] 1Sa 8:11; 1Ki 4:26; 9:19 **1:15** [u] 1Ki 9:28; Isa 60:5 **1:17** [v] SS 1:9 **2:1** [w] Dt 12:5 [x] Ecc 2:4 **2:2** [y] ver 18; 2Ch 10:4 **2:3** [z] 2Sa 5:11 [a] 1Ch 14:1 **2:4** [b] ver 1; Dt 12:5 [c] Ex 30:7 [d] Ex 25:30 [e] Ex 29:42; 2Ch 13:11 [f] Nu 28:9-10 **2:5** [g] 1Ch 22:5; Ps 135:5 [h] 1Ch 16:25 **2:6** [i] 1Ki 8:27; 2Ch 6:18; Jer 23:24 [j] Ex 3:11 **2:7** [k] ver 13-14; Ex 35:31; 1Ch 22:16 **2:10** [l] Ezr 3:7

11 Hiram king of Tyre replied by letter to Solomon:

> "Because the LORD loves[m] his people, he has made you their king."

12 And Hiram added:

> "Praise be to the LORD, the God of Israel, who made heaven and earth![n] He has given King David a wise son, endowed with intelligence and discernment, who will build a temple for the LORD and a palace for himself.
>
> 13 "I am sending you Huram-Abi,[o] a man of great skill, 14 whose mother was from Dan[p] and whose father was from Tyre. He is trained[q] to work in gold and silver, bronze and iron, stone and wood, and with purple and blue[r] and crimson yarn and fine linen. He is experienced in all kinds of engraving and can execute any design given to him. He will work with your skilled workers and with those of my lord, David your father.
>
> 15 "Now let my lord send his servants the wheat and barley and the olive oil[s] and wine he promised, 16 and we will cut all the logs from Lebanon that you need and will float them as rafts by sea down to Joppa.[t] You can then take them up to Jerusalem."

17 Solomon took a census of all the foreigners[u] residing in Israel, after the census[v] his father David had taken; and they were found to be 153,600. 18 He assigned[w] 70,000 of them to be carriers and 80,000 to be stonecutters in the hills, with 3,600 foremen over them to keep the people working.

Solomon Builds the Temple

3 Then Solomon began to build[x] the temple of the LORD[y] in Jerusalem on Mount Moriah, where the LORD had appeared to his father David. It was on the threshing floor of Araunah[a][z] the Jebusite, the place provided by David. 2 He began building on the second day of the second month in the fourth year of his reign.[a]

3 The foundation Solomon laid for building the temple of God was sixty cubits long and twenty cubits wide[b][b] (using the cubit of the old standard). 4 The portico at the front of the temple was twenty cubits[c] long across the width of the building and twenty[d] cubits high.

He overlaid the inside with pure gold. 5 He paneled the main hall with juniper and covered it with fine gold and decorated it with palm tree[c] and chain designs. 6 He adorned the temple with precious stones. And the gold he used was gold of Parvaim. 7 He overlaid the ceiling beams, doorframes, walls and doors of the temple with gold, and he carved cherubim[d] on the walls.

8 He built the Most Holy Place,[e] its length corresponding to the width of the temple—twenty cubits long and twenty cubits wide. He overlaid the inside with six hundred talents[e] of fine gold. 9 The gold nails[f] weighed fifty shekels.[f] He also overlaid the upper parts with gold.

10 For the Most Holy Place he made a pair[g] of sculptured cherubim and overlaid them with gold. 11 The total wingspan of the cherubim was twenty cubits. One wing of the first cherub was five cubits[g]

---

a *1* Hebrew *Ornan,* a variant of *Araunah*
b *3* That is, about 90 feet long and 30 feet wide or about 27 meters long and 9 meters wide
c *4* That is, about 30 feet or about 9 meters; also in verses 8, 11 and 13
d *4* Some Septuagint and Syriac manuscripts; Hebrew *and a hundred and twenty*
e *8* That is, about 23 tons or about 21 metric tons
f *9* That is, about 1 1/4 pounds or about 575 grams
g *11* That is, about 7 1/2 feet or about 2.3 meters; also in verse 15

2:12 Prudence—The wisdom and generosity of King Hiram toward Solomon showed him to be a prudent king. He wanted things to go well for Solomon because he liked and respected his father David, and good neighbors created stability for both nations.
2:14 *whose mother was from Dan.* His mother was an Israelite from the tribe of Dan.
3:1 *Mount Moriah.* This was the mountain where Abraham brought his son Isaac to sacrifice him (Gen. 22) and where the Lord provided a ram instead. It was suitable that this place where Abraham showed such incredible obedience should be the site of the temple that dealt with the issues of sacrifice and sin. ***threshing floor of Araunah.*** It was here that David saw the angel of death and prayed for the people (2 Sam. 24).
3:2 *second day of the second month.* The second month fell in our month of April.
3:3 *cubit of the old standard.* The Israelites had two standard cubits, one about 17 inches and the other about 20 inches. The temple was probably made on the cubit that measured a little over 17 inches, which means that its foundation was approximately 90 feet long and 30 feet wide. The tabernacle that Moses made in the wilderness was about 45 feet long and 15 feet wide (Ex. 26:15–37). More details of the temple are in 1 Kings 5–7.
3:5 *main hall.* This room was the holy place, or sanctuary (1 Kin. 6:17).
3:8 *Most Holy Place.* The "holy of holies," or Most Holy Place, was the inner sanctuary where the ark of the covenant was kept. This room was cubical, 30 feet on a side. ***six hundred talents.*** The room was overlaid with about 23 tons of gold.
3:9 *nails . . . gold.* Gold by itself is too soft to use for nails, so the nails mentioned here must have been plated with gold, as the weight would indicate.

2:11 [m] 1Ki 10:9; 2Ch 9:8 **2:12** [n] Ne 9:6; Ps 8:3; 33:6; 102:25 **2:13** [o] 1Ki 7:13 **2:14** [p] Ex 31:6 [q] Ex 35:31 [r] Ex 35:35 **2:15** [s] ver 10; Ezr 3:7 **2:16** [t] Jos 19:46; Jnh 1:3 **2:17** [u] 1Ch 22:2 [v] 2Sa 24:2 **2:18** [w] ver 2; 1Ch 22:2; 2Ch 8:8 **3:1** [x] Ac 7:47 [y] Ge 28:17 [z] 2Sa 24:18; 1Ch 21:18 **3:2** [a] Ezr 5:11 **3:3** [b] Eze 41:2 **3:5** [c] Eze 40:16 **3:7** [d] Ge 3:24; 1Ki 6:29-35; Eze 41:18 **3:8** [e] Ex 26:33 **3:9** [f] Ex 26:32 **3:10** [g] Ex 25:18

long and touched the temple wall, while its
other wing, also five cubits long, touched
the wing of the other cherub. 12Similarly
one wing of the second cherub was five
cubits long and touched the other temple
wall, and its other wing, also five cubits
long, touched the wing of the first cherub.
13The wings of these cherubim[h] extended
twenty cubits. They stood on their feet, facing the main hall.[a]
14He made the curtain[i] of blue, purple
and crimson yarn and fine linen, with
cherubim[j] worked into it.
15For the front of the temple he made two
pillars,[k] which together were thirty-five cubits[b] long, each with a capital[l] five cubits
high. 16He made interwoven chains[c][m] and
put them on top of the pillars. He also made
a hundred pomegranates[n] and attached
them to the chains. 17He erected the pillars
in the front of the temple, one to the south
and one to the north. The one to the south
he named Jakin[d] and the one to the north
Boaz.[e]

The Temple's Furnishings

4 He made a bronze altar[o] twenty cubits
long, twenty cubits wide and ten cubits
high.[f] 2He made the Sea[p] of cast metal, circular in shape, measuring ten cubits from
rim to rim and five cubits[g] high. It took a
line of thirty cubits[h] to measure around it.
3Below the rim, figures of bulls encircled
it—ten to a cubit.[i] The bulls were cast in
two rows in one piece with the Sea.
4The Sea stood on twelve bulls, three
facing north, three facing west, three facing south and three facing east.[q] The Sea
rested on top of them, and their hindquarters were toward the center. 5It was a handbreadth[j] in thickness, and its rim was like
the rim of a cup, like a lily blossom. It held
three thousand baths.[k]
6He then made ten basins[r] for washing
and placed five on the south side and five
on the north. In them the things to be used
for the burnt offerings[s] were rinsed, but
the Sea was to be used by the priests for
washing.
7He made ten gold lampstands[t] according to the specifications[u] for them and
placed them in the temple, five on the south
side and five on the north.
8He made ten tables[v] and placed them in
the temple, five on the south side and five
on the north. He also made a hundred gold
sprinkling bowls.[w]
9He made the courtyard[x] of the priests,
and the large court and the doors for the
court, and overlaid the doors with bronze.
10He placed the Sea on the south side, at the
southeast corner.
11And Huram also made the pots and
shovels and sprinkling bowls.
So Huram finished[y] the work he had undertaken for King Solomon in the temple
of God:

---

[a] 13 Or *facing inward* [b] 15 That is, about 53 feet or about 16 meters [c] 16 Or possibly *made chains in the inner sanctuary*; the meaning of the Hebrew for this phrase is uncertain. [d] 17 *Jakin* probably means *he establishes.* [e] 17 *Boaz* probably means *in him is strength.* [f] 1 That is, about 30 feet long and wide and 15 feet high or about 9 meters long and wide and 4.5 meters high [g] 2 That is, about 7 1/2 feet or about 2.3 meters [h] 2 That is, about 45 feet or about 14 meters [i] 3 That is, about 18 inches or about 45 centimeters [j] 5 That is, about 3 inches or about 7.5 centimeters [k] 5 That is, about 18,000 gallons or about 66,000 liters

---

3:13 *twenty cubits.* The wings of the cherubim spanned the entire width of the room.

3:14 *the curtain.* This was a heavy curtain between the holy place and the Most Holy Place. It shielded the ark and cherubim from view, and as God was visualized as sitting on the mercy seat under the wings of the cherubim (see note for 1 Chr. 13:6), it also shielded even the priests from the most intimate presence of God. The veil between the holy place and the Most Holy Place was ripped in two when Jesus died on the cross (Matt. 27:51). The tearing of the temple curtain is seen as a symbol that through Jesus, believers have direct access to the Lord God (Heb. 6:19; 9:1 — 10:20).

3:15 *thirty-five cubits ... five cubits.* The pillars were about 53 feet tall with a 7 foot capital on top.

3:17 *Jakin ... Boaz.* The names of the two pillars mean "He Establishes" and "In Him Is Strength."

4:2 *Sea of cast metal.* The Sea was a receptacle for water corresponding to the much smaller bronze basin of the Mosaic tabernacle (Ex. 30:17 – 21). The basin provided water for the priests to wash their hands and feet in preparation for ministering at the altar. The Sea served the same purpose. It was huge — 15 feet in diameter and 45 feet in circumference.

4:5 *three thousand baths.* When filled with about 27,000 gallons of water the sea would have weighed about 108 tons.

4:6 *ten basins.* Each basin held 40 baths, or about 230 gallons (1 Kin. 7:38). They could accommodate large animals, such as oxen. The law of burnt offerings required certain parts of the animal to be washed in water before it was placed on the altar (Lev. 1:9,13).

4:7 *ten gold lampstands.* The wilderness tabernacle had only one lampstand (Ex. 25:31), but the temple had ten.

4:8 *ten tables.* There had been only one table in the tabernacle (Ex. 25:23). The increase reflects the grandeur of the temple, as well as the large number of people to be served.

4:9 *courtyard of the priests.* There were areas in and about the temple that only the priests could enter. One of these was the area immediately surrounding it and enclosed by a separating wall, the "courtyard of the priests." ***large court.*** The large court was an outer area where the people in general could go.

3:13 [h] Ex 25:18 **3:14** [i] Ex 26:31,33; Heb 9:3 [j] Ge 3:24 **3:15** [k] 1Ki 7:15; Rev 3:12 [l] 1Ki 7:22 **3:16** [m] 1Ki 7:17 [n] 1Ki 7:20 **4:1** [o] Ex 20:24; 27:1-2; 40:6; 1Ki 8:64; 2Ki 16:14 **4:2** [p] Rev 4:6; 15:2 **4:4** [q] Nu 2:3-25; Eze 48:30-34; Rev 21:13 **4:6** [r] Ex 30:18 [s] Ne 13:5,9; Eze 40:38 **4:7** [t] Ex 25:31 [u] Ex 25:40 **4:8** [v] Ex 25:23 [w] Nu 4:14 **4:9** [x] 1Ki 6:36; 2Ki 21:5; 2Ch 33:5 **4:11** [y] 1Ki 7:14

12 the two pillars;
the two bowl-shaped capitals on top of the pillars;
the two sets of network decorating the two bowl-shaped capitals on top of the pillars;
13 the four hundred pomegranates for the two sets of network (two rows of pomegranates for each network, decorating the bowl-shaped capitals on top of the pillars);
14 the stands[z] with their basins;
15 the Sea and the twelve bulls under it;
16 the pots, shovels, meat forks and all related articles.

All the objects that Huram-Abi[a] made for
King Solomon for the temple of the LORD
were of polished bronze. 17 The king had
them cast in clay molds in the plain of the
Jordan between Sukkoth[b] and Zarethan.[a]
18 All these things that Solomon made
amounted to so much that the weight of the
bronze[c] could not be calculated.

19 Solomon also made all the furnishings
that were in God's temple:

the golden altar;
the tables[d] on which was the bread of the Presence;
20 the lampstands[e] of pure gold with their lamps, to burn in front of the inner sanctuary as prescribed;
21 the gold floral work and lamps and tongs (they were solid gold);
22 the pure gold wick trimmers, sprinkling bowls, dishes[f] and censers;[g] and the gold doors of the temple: the inner doors to the Most Holy Place and the doors of the main hall.

5 When all the work Solomon had done
for the temple of the LORD was finished,[h] he brought in the things his father
David had dedicated[i]—the silver and gold
and all the furnishings—and he placed
them in the treasuries of God's temple.

The Ark Brought to the Temple

2 Then Solomon summoned to Jerusa-
lem the elders of Israel, all the heads of the
tribes and the chiefs of the Israelite families, to bring up the ark[j] of the LORD's covenant from Zion, the City of David. 3 And
all the Israelites[k] came together to the king
at the time of the festival in the seventh
month.

4 When all the elders of Israel had arrived, the Levites took up the ark, 5 and
they brought up the ark and the tent of
meeting and all the sacred furnishings in
it. The Levitical priests[l] carried them up;
6 and King Solomon and the entire assembly of Israel that had gathered about him
were before the ark, sacrificing so many
sheep and cattle that they could not be recorded or counted.

7 The priests then brought the ark[m] of
the LORD's covenant to its place in the inner sanctuary of the temple, the Most Holy
Place, and put it beneath the wings of the
cherubim. 8 The cherubim[n] spread their
wings over the place of the ark and covered
the ark and its carrying poles. 9 These poles
were so long that their ends, extending from
the ark, could be seen from in front of the inner sanctuary, but not from outside the Holy
Place; and they are still there today. 10 There
was nothing in the ark except[o] the two tablets[p] that Moses had placed in it at Horeb,
where the LORD made a covenant with the
Israelites after they came out of Egypt.

11 The priests then withdrew from the
Holy Place. All the priests who were there
had consecrated themselves, regardless of
their divisions.[q] 12 All the Levites who were

[a] 17 Hebrew *Zeredatha*, a variant of *Zarethan*

4:14 ***stands.*** The stands had four bronze wheels (1 Kin. 7:27–37).
4:17 ***cast in clay molds.*** Many bronze products were made at a place in the Jordan valley about 35 miles north of the Dead Sea. Archaeologists have uncovered evidence of this work in an area where the clay is suitable for bronze casting.
4:19 ***golden altar.*** This altar was used for offering incense (Ex. 30:1–10; 1 Kin. 7:48). It was in the holy place just in front of the veil.
4:22 ***inner doors.*** The tabernacle had a veil between the "Most Holy Place" where the ark was, and the "house," or holy place. Solomon's temple had a set of doors there as well.
5:2 ***ark of the LORD's covenant.*** Though David had built a tabernacle, or tent, on Mount Zion to house the ark (1 Chr. 15:1), it was still separate from the original tabernacle and bronze altar at Gibeon. Completing Solomon's temple made it possible for the ark and the altar to be in the same place for the first time since the Israelites lost the ark to the Philistines during the days when the tabernacle was at Shiloh and Samuel was a little boy (1 Sam. 4–6).
5:3 ***festival.*** Since this was the seventh month, the festival was the Festival of Tabernacles. This was an appropriate occasion for moving the ark to a permanent location because the festival commemorated Israel's wandering in the wilderness when the ark had no permanent place (Lev. 23:39–43).
5:5 ***tent of meeting.*** This tent was the Mosaic tabernacle. Solomon ended worship at the high place at Gibeon by dismantling the tabernacle and bringing it and all its furnishings to Jerusalem.
5:9 ***still there today.*** The ark was supposed to remain safely in the temple forever. At the time of the writing of this book (probably between 460 and 430 B.C.), the temple had been destroyed and the ark was gone. No one knows what happened to ark after Nebuchadnezzar destroyed Jerusalem in 586 B.C.
5:12 ***Asaph, Heman, Jeduthun.*** These men were

4:14 [z] 1Ki 7:27-30 **4:16** [a] 1Ki 7:13 **4:17** [b] Ge 33:17
4:18 [c] 1Ki 7:23 **4:19** [d] Ex 25:23,30 **4:20** [e] Ex 25:31
4:22 [f] Nu 7:14 [g] Lev 10:1 **5:1** [h] 1Ki 6:14 [i] 2Sa 8:11
5:2 [j] Nu 3:31; 2Sa 6:12; 1Ch 15:25 **5:3** [k] 1Ch 9:1; 2Ch 7:8-10 **5:5** [l] Nu 3:31; 1Ch 15:2 **5:7** [m] Rev 11:19
5:8 [n] Ge 3:24 **5:10** [o] Heb 9:4 [p] Ex 16:34; Dt 10:2
5:11 [q] 1Ch 24:1

musicians[r]—Asaph, Heman, Jeduthun and their sons and relatives—stood on the east side of the altar, dressed in fine linen and playing cymbals, harps and lyres. They were accompanied by 120 priests sounding trumpets.[s] 13The trumpeters and musicians joined in unison to give praise and thanks to the LORD. Accompanied by trumpets, cymbals and other instruments, the singers raised their voices in praise to the LORD and sang:

"He is good;
his love endures forever."[t]

Then the temple of the LORD was filled with the cloud, 14and the priests could not perform[u] their service because of the cloud,[v] for the glory[w] of the LORD filled the temple of God.

6 Then Solomon said, "The LORD has said that he would dwell in a dark cloud;[x] 2I have built a magnificent temple for you, a place for you to dwell forever.[y]"

3While the whole assembly of Israel was standing there, the king turned around and blessed them. 4Then he said:

"Praise be to the LORD, the God of Israel, who with his hands has fulfilled what he promised with his mouth to my father David. For he said, 5'Since the day I brought my people out of Egypt, I have not chosen a city in any tribe of Israel to have a temple built so that my Name might be there, nor have I chosen anyone to be ruler over my people Israel. 6But now I have chosen Jerusalem[z] for my Name[a] to be there, and I have chosen David[b] to rule my people Israel.'

7"My father David had it in his heart[c] to build a temple for the Name of the LORD, the God of Israel. 8But the LORD said to my father David, 'You did well to have it in your heart to build a temple for my Name. 9Nevertheless, you are not the one to build the temple, but your son, your own flesh and blood—he is the one who will build the temple for my Name.'

10"The LORD has kept the promise he made. I have succeeded David my father and now I sit on the throne of Israel, just as the LORD promised, and I have built the temple for the Name of the LORD, the God of Israel. 11There I have placed the ark, in which is the covenant[d] of the LORD that he made with the people of Israel."

Solomon's Prayer of Dedication

12Then Solomon stood before the altar of the LORD in front of the whole assembly of Israel and spread out his hands. 13Now he had made a bronze platform,[e] five cubits long, five cubits wide and three cubits high,[a] and had placed it in the center of the outer court. He stood on the platform and then knelt down[f] before the whole assembly of Israel and spread out his hands toward heaven. 14He said:

"LORD, the God of Israel, there is no God like you[g] in heaven or on earth—you who keep your covenant of love[h] with your servants who continue wholeheartedly in your way. 15You have kept your promise to your servant David my father; with your mouth you have promised[i] and with your hand you have fulfilled it—as it is today.

16"Now, LORD, the God of Israel, keep for your servant David my father the promises you made to him when you said, 'You shall never fail[j] to have a successor to sit before me on the throne of Israel, if only your descendants are careful in all they do to walk before me according to my law,[k] as you have done.' 17And now, LORD, the God of Israel, let your word that you promised your servant David come true.

a *13* That is, about 7 1/2 feet long and wide and 4 1/2 feet high or about 2.3 meters long and wide and 1.4 meters high

---

the heads of the divisions of Levitical musicians (1 Chr. 6:33,39; 25:1).

5:13 Praise—Praise and worship are simply recognizing the perfections and worthiness of the Lord. His loving-kindness never runs out or diminishes. Everyday His mercy and grace exist in perfection on our behalf. A time for daily praise is one of the best ways to grow closer to God.

6:2 *to dwell forever.* It did not occur to Solomon that one day the glory of the Lord would depart from this temple and it would be destroyed (Ezek. 10:18).

6:14 *there is no God like you.* Solomon's acclamation is echoed by every child of God who reflects on God's faithfulness and mercy to those who "walk before Him" with "all their hearts." It is not that Solomon considered other gods to be valid, but he was in a position to see the kind of trust that pagans put in their gods, and how whimsical and unfaithful these "gods" were.

6:16 *if only your descendants are careful.* Solomon was recognizing that the covenant was dependent on the people remaining faithful to God, and he wanted his line to walk with God as David had. Even though future generations did not imitate David, God's faithfulness was carried out through Jesus, the Son of David (Matt. 9:27; 15:22; 22:41–45).

5:12 [r] 1Ki 10:12; 1Ch 25:1; Ps 68:25 [s] 1Ch 13:8; 15:24 **5:13** [t] 1Ch 16:34,41; 2Ch 7:3; 20:21; Ezr 3:11; Ps 100:5; 136:1; Jer 33:11 **5:14** [u] Ex 40:35; Rev 15:8 [v] Ex 19:16 [w] Ex 29:43; 2Ch 7:2 **6:1** [x] Ex 19:9; 1Ki 8:12-50 **6:2** [y] Ezr 6:12; 7:15; Ps 135:21 **6:6** [z] Dt 12:5; Isa 14:1 [a] Ex 20:24; 2Ch 12:13 [b] 1Ch 28:4 **6:7** [c] 1Sa 10:7; 1Ch 17:2; 28:2; Ac 7:46 **6:11** [d] Dt 10:2; 2Ch 5:10; Ps 25:10; 50:5 **6:13** [e] Ne 8:4 [f] Ps 95:6 **6:14** [g] Ex 8:10; 15:11 [h] Dt 7:9 **6:15** [i] 1Ch 22:10 **6:16** [j] 2Sa 7:13,15; 1Ki 2:4; 2Ch 7:18; 23:3 [k] Ps 132:12

18“But will God really dwell[l] on earth
with humans? The heavens,[m] even the
highest heavens, cannot contain you.
How much less this temple I have built!
19Yet, LORD my God, give attention to
your servant’s prayer and his plea for
mercy. Hear the cry and the prayer
that your servant is praying in your
presence. 20May your eyes[n] be open
toward this temple day and night, this
place of which you said you would put
your Name[o] there. May you hear[p] the
prayer your servant prays toward this
place. 21Hear the supplications of your
servant and of your people Israel when
they pray toward this place. Hear from
heaven, your dwelling place; and when
you hear, forgive.[q]
22“When anyone wrongs their
neighbor and is required to take an
oath[r] and they come and swear the
oath before your altar in this temple, 23then hear from heaven and act.
Judge between your servants, condemning[s] the guilty and bringing
down on their heads what they have
done, and vindicating the innocent by
treating them in accordance with their
innocence.
24“When your people Israel have
been defeated[t] by an enemy because
they have sinned against you and
when they turn back and give praise
to your name, praying and making
supplication before you in this temple,
25then hear from heaven and forgive
the sin of your people Israel and bring
them back to the land you gave to them
and their ancestors.
26“When the heavens are shut up
and there is no rain[u] because your
people have sinned against you, and
when they pray toward this place and
give praise to your name and turn
from their sin because you have afflicted them, 27then hear from heaven
and forgive[v] the sin of your servants,
your people Israel. Teach them the
right way to live, and send rain on the
land you gave your people for an inheritance.
28“When famine[w] or plague comes
to the land, or blight or mildew, locusts
or grasshoppers, or when enemies besiege them in any of their cities, whatever disaster or disease may come,
29and when a prayer or plea is made
by anyone among your people Israel—
being aware of their afflictions and
pains, and spreading out their hands
toward this temple— 30then hear from
heaven, your dwelling place. Forgive,[x]
and deal with everyone according
to all they do, since you know their
hearts (for you alone know the human
heart),[y] 31so that they will fear you[z]
and walk in obedience to you all the
time they live in the land you gave our
ancestors.
32“As for the foreigner who does not
belong to your people Israel but has
come[a] from a distant land because
of your great name and your mighty
hand[b] and your outstretched arm—
when they come and pray toward this
temple, 33then hear from heaven, your
dwelling place. Do whatever the foreigner[c] asks of you, so that all the peoples of the earth may know your name
and fear you, as do your own people
Israel, and may know that this house I
have built bears your Name.
34“When your people go to war
against their enemies,[d] wherever you
send them, and when they pray[e] to you
toward this city you have chosen and
the temple I have built for your Name,
35then hear from heaven their prayer
and their plea, and uphold their cause.
36“When they sin against you—for
there is no one who does not sin[f]—and
you become angry with them and give
them over to the enemy, who takes
them captive[g] to a land far away or
near; 37and if they have a change of
heart[h] in the land where they are held

6:23 ***hear from heaven.*** Solomon’s request that God hear from heaven underscored God’s transcendence. Although God had chosen to be present on earth at the temple, He is also beyond the limits of the temple building.

6:25 ***bring them back.*** This statement is a hint of the future captivity and deportation of God’s disobedient people (Deut. 28:29–30). When the exile to Babylon became a reality, the temple was destroyed and no one could pray at that place as before. But even in those days, God’s people directed their prayer toward Jerusalem (Dan. 6:10).

6:32–33 ***As for the foreigner.*** God made His covenant exclusively with Israel, the nation descended from Abraham, but He did so for the purpose of attracting the nations to Himself, the Creator of all people. A foreigner who embraced the Lord as God would be numbered among God’s people.

6:36 ***there is no one who does not sin.*** This statement is repeated in the New Testament (Rom. 3:23; 1 John 1:8–10). ***takes them captive.*** Solomon’s speech anticipated the possibility of exile (v. 25), something that had already taken place by the time Chronicles was written.

6:18 [l] Rev 21:3 [m] 2Ch 2:6; Ps 11:4; Isa 40:22; 66:1; Ac 7:49
6:20 [n] Ex 3:16; Ps 34:15 [o] Dt 12:11 [p] 2Ch 7:14; 30:20
6:21 [q] Ps 51:1; Isa 33:24; 40:2; 43:25; 44:22; 55:7; Mic 7:18
6:22 [r] Ex 22:11 **6:23** [s] Isa 3:11; 65:6; Mt 16:27
6:24 [t] Lev 26:17 **6:26** [u] Lev 26:19; Dt 11:17; 28:24; 2Sa 1:21; 1Ki 17:1 **6:27** [v] ver 30, 39; 2Ch 7:14
6:28 [w] 2Ch 20:9 **6:30** [x] ver 27 [y] 1Sa 16:7; 1Ch 28:9; Ps 7:9; 44:21; Pr 16:2; 17:3 **6:31** [z] Ps 103:11, 13; Pr 8:13
6:32 [a] 2Ch 9:6; Jn 12:20; Ac 8:27 [b] Ex 3:19, 20
6:33 [c] 2Ch 7:14 **6:34** [d] Dt 28:7 [e] 1Ch 5:20
6:36 [f] Job 15:14; Ps 143:2; Ecc 7:20; Jer 17:9; Jas 3:1; 1Jn 1:8-10 [g] Lev 26:44 **6:37** [h] 2Ch 7:14; 33:12, 19, 23; Jer 29:13

captive, and repent and plead with you
in the land of their captivity and say,
'We have sinned, we have done wrong
and acted wickedly'; 38and if they
turn back to you with all their heart
and soul in the land of their captivity
where they were taken, and pray toward the land you gave their ancestors, toward the city you have chosen
and toward the temple I have built for
your Name; 39then from heaven, your
dwelling place, hear their prayer and
their pleas, and uphold their cause.
And forgive your people, who have
sinned against you.

40"Now, my God, may your eyes be
open and your ears attentive[i] to the
prayers offered in this place.

41 "Now arise,[j] LORD God, and come
to your resting place,[k]
you and the ark of your might.
May your priests,[l] LORD God, be
clothed with salvation,
may your faithful people rejoice
in your goodness.[m]
42 LORD God, do not reject your
anointed one.
Remember the great love[n]
promised to David your
servant."

The Dedication of the Temple

7 When Solomon finished praying, fire[o]
came down from heaven and consumed
the burnt offering and the sacrifices, and
the glory of the LORD filled[p] the temple.[q]
2The priests could not enter[r] the temple of
the LORD because the glory[s] of the LORD
filled it. 3When all the Israelites saw the
fire coming down and the glory of the
LORD above the temple, they knelt on the
pavement with their faces to the ground,
and they worshiped and gave thanks to the
LORD, saying,

"He is good;
his love endures forever."[t]

4Then the king and all the people offered
sacrifices before the LORD. 5And King Solomon offered a sacrifice of twenty-two
thousand head of cattle and a hundred
and twenty thousand sheep and goats. So
the king and all the people dedicated the
temple of God. 6The priests took their positions, as did the Levites[u] with the LORD's
musical instruments,[v] which King David
had made for praising the LORD and which
were used when he gave thanks, saying,
"His love endures forever." Opposite the
Levites, the priests blew their trumpets,
and all the Israelites were standing.

7Solomon consecrated the middle part of
the courtyard in front of the temple of the
LORD, and there he offered burnt offerings
and the fat of the fellowship offerings, because the bronze altar he had made could
not hold the burnt offerings, the grain offerings and the fat portions.

8So Solomon observed the festival[w] at
that time for seven days, and all Israel with
him—a vast assembly, people from Lebo
Hamath to the Wadi of Egypt.[x] 9On the
eighth day they held an assembly, for they

7:1 Miracles—This event marks the third of four events when supernatural fire fell from heaven. The first occurred during the dedication of the tabernacle in the days of Moses (Lev. 9:24). The second happened when David dedicated a piece of ground to the Lord that later became the site of Solomon's temple (1 Chr. 21:26). The final occurrence transpired on Mount Carmel when Elijah prayed for fire to consume his offering (1 Kin. 18:38). We often think that a miracle will convince an unbeliever of the reality of the living God, and sometimes it does. But sensing the presence of God, or seeing His work, does not equal believing. The Israelites often backslid, even after miraculous events, and even the miracles of Jesus did not convince all that He was the Messiah (Matt. 11:20–24).

7:3 Need for Worship—The first reason for worship is simply that God commands it (1 Chr. 16:29; Matt. 4:10). The first four of the Ten Commandments charge men and women to worship the one true God and Him alone (Ex. 20:3–10). To allow anything or anyone other than God to have a position of lordship over us constitutes gross disobedience to the will of God and incurs His terrible wrath (Ex. 20:5; Deut. 27:15). Eventually all peoples will bow to God anyway, even if they do so unwillingly (Phil. 2:10).

An equally important reason for worship is that God is worthy of our worship. He designed us for worship. He alone possesses the attributes that merit our worship and service. Among these are goodness (Ps. 100:5), mercy (Ex. 4:31), holiness (Ps. 99:5,9), and creative power (Rev. 4:11). When men of biblical times clearly saw the unveiled glory of God, they could not help but fall prostrate in worship. Examples of this response can be seen in the actions of Moses (Ex. 34:5–8), Isaiah (Is. 6), Paul (Acts 9:3–6), and John (Rev. 1:9–17).

A final reason for worship is that men and women need to give it. People cannot find personal fulfillment apart from the glad submission of themselves in worshipful obedience to God. He is the Creator and they are the creatures (Rev. 4:11). We are made to worship God. If we do anything less, we fail to be who God created us to be. One who worships God not only participates in the occupation of heaven (Rev. 7:9–12), but also finds joyful satisfaction in the present time (Rom. 12:2; Col. 3:24).

7:8 *festival.* The festival was the Festival of Tabernacles, which began on the fifteenth day of the seventh month and continued through the twenty-second day (see note for 5:3). ***Lebo Hamath ... Wadi of Egypt.*** These geographical locations specify the extent of Solomon's early kingdom from north to south.

7:9 *dedication of the altar.* This is the same dedication referred to in 5:3.

6:40 [i] 2Ch 7:15; Ne 1:6, 11; Ps 17:1, 6 **6:41** [j] Isa 33:10 [k] 1Ch 28:2 [l] Ps 132:16 [m] Ps 116:12 **6:42** [n] Ps 89:24, 28; Isa 55:3 **7:1** [o] Lev 9:24; 1Ki 18:38 [p] Ex 16:10 [q] Ps 26:8 **7:2** [r] 1Ki 8:11 [s] Ex 29:43; 40:35; 2Ch 5:14 **7:3** [t] 1Ch 16:34; 2Ch 5:13; 20:21 **7:6** [u] 1Ch 15:16 [v] 2Ch 5:12 **7:8** [w] 2Ch 30:26 [x] Ge 15:18

had celebrated the dedication of the altar
for seven days and the festival[y] for seven
days more. 10On the twenty-third day of
the seventh month he sent the people to
their homes, joyful and glad in heart for
the good things the LORD had done for David and Solomon and for his people Israel.

The LORD Appears to Solomon

11When Solomon had finished the temple of the LORD and the royal palace, and
had succeeded in carrying out all he had
in mind to do in the temple of the LORD and
in his own palace, 12the LORD appeared to
him at night and said:

"I have heard your prayer and have
chosen this place for myself[z] as a temple for sacrifices.

13"When I shut up the heavens so
that there is no rain,[a] or command
locusts to devour the land or send a
plague among my people, 14if my people, who are called by my name, will
humble[b] themselves and pray and seek
my face[c] and turn[d] from their wicked
ways, then I will hear from heaven,
and I will forgive[e] their sin and will
heal[f] their land. 15Now my eyes will
be open and my ears attentive to the
prayers offered in this place.[g] 16I have
chosen[h] and consecrated this temple
so that my Name may be there forever. My eyes and my heart will always
be there.

17"As for you, if you walk before me
faithfully[i] as David your father did,
and do all I command, and observe
my decrees and laws, 18I will establish your royal throne, as I covenanted with David your father when I said,
'You shall never fail to have a successor[j] to rule over Israel.'[k]

19"But if you[a] turn away[l] and forsake[m] the decrees and commands I
have given you[a] and go off to serve
other gods and worship them, 20then
I will uproot[n] Israel from my land,[o]
which I have given them, and will
reject this temple I have consecrated
for my Name. I will make it a byword
and an object of ridicule[p] among all
peoples. 21This temple will become a
heap of rubble. All[b] who pass by will
be appalled and say,[q] 'Why has the
LORD done such a thing to this land
and to this temple?' 22People will answer, 'Because they have forsaken the
LORD, the God of their ancestors, who
brought them out of Egypt, and have
embraced other gods, worshiping and
serving them—that is why he brought
all this disaster on them.'"

Solomon's Other Activities

8 At the end of twenty years, during
which Solomon built the temple of the
LORD and his own palace, 2Solomon rebuilt
the villages that Hiram[c] had given him,
and settled Israelites in them. 3Solomon
then went to Hamath Zobah and captured
it. 4He also built up Tadmor in the desert
and all the store cities he had built in Hamath. 5He rebuilt Upper Beth Horon[r] and
Lower Beth Horon as fortified cities, with
walls and with gates and bars, 6as well as
Baalath and all his store cities, and all the
cities for his chariots and for his horses[d]—
whatever he desired to build in Jerusalem,
in Lebanon and throughout all the territory
he ruled.

7There were still people left from the Hittites, Amorites, Perizzites, Hivites and Jebusites[s] (these people were not Israelites).
8Solomon conscripted[t] the descendants of

---

[a] *19* The Hebrew is plural. [b] *21* See some Septuagint manuscripts, Old Latin, Syriac, Arabic and Targum; Hebrew *And though this temple is now so imposing, all* [c] *2* Hebrew *Huram,* a variant of *Hiram;* also in verse 18 [d] *6* Or *charioteers*

7:10 *sent the people to their homes.* The people returned to their huts, or booths, where they stayed as a part of the Festival of Tabernacles. Few if any Israelites used tents for their housing at this time.
7:11 *temple of the LORD ... royal palace.* Since it took Solomon 13 years to build his palace and 20 years in all to build both it and the temple, these events are halfway through Solomon's 40-year reign.
7:14 Prayer—This promise to hear, if the people will pray, is directly linked to the covenant promises that God made with the Israelites (Deut. 28–30). Blessings were linked to obedience, curses linked to rebellion, and the promise that God would hear if they repented was the reminder that God had eternal commitment to them. Even nations outside this covenant have taken great comfort in remembering this promise. God always hears the sincere prayers of His people, and Christians are directed to pray for the leaders of the nations (1 Tim. 2:1–2).
8:4 *Tadmor.* Solomon built and fortified cities such as Tadmor because they were on vital caravan routes. These fortified cities provided protection to his caravans and became the customs points at which Solomon collected taxes. ***store cities.*** Facilities were scattered throughout Solomon's outlying provinces to provide warehouses for his armies and merchantmen, as well as to store produce and other tributes paid by the vassal states (1 Kin. 9:19).
8:5 *Upper Beth Horon and Lower Beth Horon.* These cities were strategically located near the border between Judah and the northern tribal districts, along a major mountain pass to the Mediterranean (Josh. 10:10; 1 Sam. 13:18).

7:9 [y] Lev 23:36 **7:12** [z] Dt 12:5 **7:13** [a] 2Ch 6:26-28; Am 4:7 **7:14** [b] Lev 26:41; 2Ch 6:37; Jas 4:10 [c] 1Ch 16:11 [d] Isa 55:7; Zec 1:4 [e] 2Ch 6:27 [f] 2Ch 30:20; Isa 30:26; 57:18 **7:15** [g] 2Ch 6:40 **7:16** [h] ver 12; 2Ch 6:6 **7:17** [i] 1Ki 9:4 **7:18** [j] 2Ch 6:16 [k] 2Sa 7:13; 2Ch 13:5 **7:19** [l] Dt 28:15 [m] Lev 26:14,33 **7:20** [n] Dt 29:28 [o] 1Ki 14:15 [p] Dt 28:37 **7:21** [q] Dt 29:24 **8:5** [r] 1Ch 7:24; 2Ch 14:7 **8:7** [s] Ge 10:16 **8:8** [t] 1Ki 4:6; 9:21

all these people remaining in the land—whom the Israelites had not destroyed—to serve as slave labor, as it is to this day. 9But Solomon did not make slaves of the Israelites for his work; they were his fighting men, commanders of his captains, and commanders of his chariots and charioteers. 10They were also King Solomon's chief officials—two hundred and fifty officials supervising the men.

11Solomon brought Pharaoh's daughter[u] up from the City of David to the palace he had built for her, for he said, "My wife must not live in the palace of David king of Israel, because the places the ark of the LORD has entered are holy."

12On the altar[v] of the LORD that he had built in front of the portico, Solomon sacrificed burnt offerings to the LORD, 13according to the daily requirement[w] for offerings commanded by Moses for the Sabbaths,[x] the New Moons and the three[y] annual festivals—the Festival of Unleavened Bread, the Festival of Weeks[z] and the Festival of Tabernacles. 14In keeping with the ordinance of his father David, he appointed the divisions[a] of the priests for their duties, and the Levites[b] to lead the praise and to assist the priests according to each day's requirement. He also appointed the gatekeepers[c] by divisions for the various gates, because this was what David the man of God[d] had ordered.[e] 15They did not deviate from the king's commands to the priests or to the Levites in any matter, including that of the treasuries.

16All Solomon's work was carried out, from the day the foundation of the temple of the LORD was laid until its completion. So the temple of the LORD was finished.

17Then Solomon went to Ezion Geber and Elath on the coast of Edom. 18And Hiram sent him ships commanded by his own men, sailors who knew the sea. These, with Solomon's men, sailed to Ophir and brought back four hundred and fifty talents*[a]* of gold,[f] which they delivered to King Solomon.

The Queen of Sheba Visits Solomon

9 When the queen of Sheba[g] heard of Solomon's fame, she came to Jerusalem to test him with hard questions. Arriving with a very great caravan—with camels carrying spices, large quantities of gold, and precious stones—she came to Solomon and talked with him about all she had on her mind. 2Solomon answered all her questions; nothing was too hard for him to explain to her. 3When the queen of Sheba saw the wisdom of Solomon,[h] as well as the palace he had built, 4the food on his table, the seating of his officials, the attending servants in their robes, the cupbearers in their robes and the burnt offerings he made at*[b]* the temple of the LORD, she was overwhelmed.

5She said to the king, "The report I heard in my own country about your achievements and your wisdom is true. 6But I did not believe what they said until I came[i] and saw with my own eyes. Indeed, not even half the greatness of your wisdom was told me; you have far exceeded the report I heard. 7How happy your people must be! How happy your officials, who continually stand before you and hear your wisdom! 8Praise be to the LORD your God, who has delighted in you and placed you on his throne[j] as king to rule for the LORD your God. Because of the love of your God for Israel and his desire to uphold them forever, he has made you king[k] over them, to maintain justice and righteousness."

9Then she gave the king 120 talents*[c]* of gold,[l] large quantities of spices, and precious stones. There had never been such spices as those the queen of Sheba gave to King Solomon.

10(The servants of Hiram and the servants of Solomon brought gold from Ophir;[m] they also brought algumwood*[d]* and precious stones. 11The king used the algumwood to make steps for the temple of the LORD and for the royal palace, and to make harps and lyres for the musicians. Nothing like them had ever been seen in Judah.)

12King Solomon gave the queen of Sheba all she desired and asked for; he gave her more than she had brought to him. Then she left and returned with her retinue to her own country.

a *18* That is, about 17 tons or about 15 metric tons
b *4* Or *and the ascent by which he went up to*
c *9* That is, about 4 1/2 tons or about 4 metric tons
d *10* Probably a variant of *almugwood*

8:18 *Hiram.* The Phoenicians were world famous mariners, so when Solomon undertook a merchant marine enterprise he called once more on his good friend Hiram, king of Tyre. ***Ophir.*** A source of finest gold (1 Chr. 29:4); the location of Ophir is not known, except that it was reached by sea. People have speculated that it may have been in South Arabia, India, or Africa.

9:1 *Sheba.* Sheba was more than a thousand miles south of Israel, at the southern end of the Arabian peninsula.

9:8 *Praise be to the LORD your God.* The language of politeness in the ancient world does not necessarily suggest that the Queen of Sheba was converted. Visiting dignitaries customarily praised the god of the host nation.

8:11 [u] 1Ki 3:1; 7:8 **8:12** [v] 1Ki 8:64; 2Ch 4:1; 15:8 **8:13** [w] Ex 29:38; Nu 28:3 [x] Nu 28:9 [y] Ex 23:14; Dt 16:16 [z] Ex 23:16 **8:14** [a] 1Ch 24:1 [b] 1Ch 25:1 [c] 1Ch 9:17; 26:1 [d] Ne 12:24,36 [e] 1Ch 23:6; Ne 12:45 **8:18** [f] 2Ch 9:9 **9:1** [g] Ge 10:7; Eze 23:42; Mt 12:42; Lk 11:31 **9:3** [h] 1Ki 5:12 **9:6** [i] 2Ch 6:32 **9:8** [j] 1Ki 2:12; 1Ch 17:14; 28:5; 29:23; 2Ch 13:8 [k] 2Ch 2:11 **9:9** [l] 2Ch 8:18 **9:10** [m] 2Ch 8:18

Solomon's Splendor

13The weight of the gold that Solomon
received yearly was 666 talents,[a] 14not including the revenues brought in by merchants and traders. Also all the kings of
Arabia[n] and the governors of the territories
brought gold and silver to Solomon.
15King Solomon made two hundred large
shields of hammered gold; six hundred
shekels[b] of hammered gold went into each
shield. 16He also made three hundred small
shields[o] of hammered gold, with three hundred shekels[c] of gold in each shield. The
king put them in the Palace of the Forest
of Lebanon.[p]
17Then the king made a great throne
covered with ivory[q] and overlaid with
pure gold. 18The throne had six steps, and
a footstool of gold was attached to it. On
both sides of the seat were armrests, with a
lion standing beside each of them. 19Twelve
lions stood on the six steps, one at either
end of each step. Nothing like it had ever
been made for any other kingdom. 20All
King Solomon's goblets were gold, and all
the household articles in the Palace of the
Forest of Lebanon were pure gold. Nothing was made of silver, because silver was
considered of little value in Solomon's day.
21The king had a fleet of trading ships[d]
manned by Hiram's[e] servants. Once every
three years it returned, carrying gold, silver and ivory, and apes and baboons.
22King Solomon was greater in riches
and wisdom than all the other kings of the
earth.[r] 23All the kings[s] of the earth sought
audience with Solomon to hear the wisdom
God had put in his heart. 24Year after year,
everyone who came brought a gift[t]—articles of silver and gold, and robes, weapons
and spices, and horses and mules.
25Solomon had four thousand stalls for
horses and chariots,[u] and twelve thousand
horses,[f] which he kept in the chariot cities and also with him in Jerusalem. 26He
ruled[v] over all the kings from the Euphrates River[w] to the land of the Philistines,
as far as the border of Egypt.[x] 27The king
made silver as common in Jerusalem as
stones, and cedar as plentiful as sycamore-
fig trees in the foothills. 28Solomon's horses were imported from Egypt and from all
other countries.

Solomon's Death

29As for the other events of Solomon's
reign, from beginning to end, are they
not written in the records of Nathan[y] the
prophet, in the prophecy of Ahijah[z] the
Shilonite and in the visions of Iddo the seer
concerning Jeroboam[a] son of Nebat? 30Sol-
omon reigned in Jerusalem over all Israel
forty years. 31Then he rested with his ancestors and was buried in the city of David[b]
his father. And Rehoboam his son succeeded him as king.

Israel Rebels Against Rehoboam

10 Rehoboam went to Shechem, for all
Israel had gone there to make him
king. 2When Jeroboam[c] son of Nebat heard
this (he was in Egypt, where he had fled[d]
from King Solomon), he returned from
Egypt. 3So they sent for Jeroboam, and he
and all Israel[e] went to Rehoboam and said
to him: 4"Your father put a heavy yoke on
us,[f] but now lighten the harsh labor and
the heavy yoke he put on us, and we will
serve you."

---

[a] *13* That is, about 25 tons or about 23 metric tons [b] *15* That is, about 15 pounds or about 6.9 kilograms [c] *16* That is, about 7 1/2 pounds or about 3.5 kilograms [d] *21* Hebrew *of ships that could go to Tarshish* [e] *21* Hebrew *Huram*, a variant of *Hiram* [f] *25* Or *charioteers*

9:13 *The weight of gold ... 666 talents.* Solomon's annual income in gold amounted to 25 tons. This figure probably reflects the annual revenues of the entire nation through taxes.

9:14 *kings ... governors ... brought.* The gold and silver that the kings and governors brought to Solomon was tribute, a form of taxation on vassal states, not a voluntary gift.

9:15 *shields of hammered gold.* The targets or shields of beaten gold were for decorative or ceremonial purpose, not the armory. Gold was too expensive, too heavy, and too soft to use in battle.

9:26 *to the land of the Philistines.* Most of the kings of Israel had continuing trouble with the Philistines, even though they were able to subdue every other surrounding neighbor. David had some success against the Philistines (1 Chr. 18:1), and later Jehoshaphat managed to exact tribute from some of them (17:11).

9:29 *Nathan the prophet.* This is the same Nathan that rebuked David for his adultery and murder (2 Sam. 12:1–15). He was a confidant and counselor to both David and Solomon (1 Kin. 1:8–11). ***Ahijah ... Iddo.*** Ahijah and Iddo were contemporaries who compiled the accounts of both Jeroboam and Rehoboam (12:15).

9:31 *Rehoboam.* Rehoboam was a son of Solomon by his wife Naamah of Ammon (12:13). He was 41 when he began to rule, so he must have been born during the period when Solomon ruled alongside David (1 Chr. 29:22–23).

10:1 *Shechem.* Rehoboam probably chose Shechem as the place to be crowned because a rift had begun to develop between the northern and southern tribes (1 Kin. 11:26–40).

10:4 Wisdom — Bravado is different than wisdom. Saying that one is going to be tough is different than being wise. Short of despotic force, no king can rule a people who do not trust him, and even if there is not outright rebellion, the resistance makes an unhappy

9:14 [n] 2Ch 17:11; Isa 21:13; Jer 25:24; Eze 27:21; 30:5
9:16 [o] 2Ch 12:9 [p] 1Ki 7:2 **9:17** [q] 1Ki 22:39
9:22 [r] 1Ki 3:13; 2Ch 1:12 **9:23** [s] 1Ki 4:34
9:24 [t] 2Ch 32:23; Ps 45:12; 68:29; 72:10; Isa 18:7
9:25 [u] 1Sa 8:11; 1Ki 4:26 **9:26** [v] 1Ki 4:21 [w] Ps 72:8-9
[x] Ge 15:18-21 **9:29** [y] 2Sa 7:2; 1Ch 29:29 [z] 1Ki 11:29
[a] 2Ch 10:2 **9:31** [b] 1Ki 2:10 **10:2** [c] 2Ch 9:29 [d] 1Ki 11:40
10:3 [e] 1Ch 9:1 **10:4** [f] 2Ch 2:2

5Rehoboam answered, "Come back to
me in three days." So the people went away.
6Then King Rehoboam consulted the elders[g] who had served his father Solomon
during his lifetime. "How would you advise
me to answer these people?" he asked.
7They replied, "If you will be kind to
these people and please them and give
them a favorable answer,[h] they will always
be your servants."
8But Rehoboam rejected[i] the advice the
elders[j] gave him and consulted the young
men who had grown up with him and were
serving him. 9He asked them, "What is
your advice? How should we answer these
people who say to me, 'Lighten the yoke
your father put on us'?"
10The young men who had grown up
with him replied, "The people have said
to you, 'Your father put a heavy yoke on
us, but make our yoke lighter.' Now tell
them, 'My little finger is thicker than my
father's waist. 11My father laid on you a
heavy yoke; I will make it even heavier.
My father scourged you with whips; I will
scourge you with scorpions.'"
12Three days later Jeroboam and all the
people returned to Rehoboam, as the king
had said, "Come back to me in three days."
13The king answered them harshly. Rejecting the advice of the elders, 14he followed
the advice of the young men and said, "My
father made your yoke heavy; I will make it
even heavier. My father scourged you with
whips; I will scourge you with scorpions."
15So the king did not listen to the people,
for this turn of events was from God,[k] to
fulfill the word the LORD had spoken to
Jeroboam son of Nebat through Ahijah
the Shilonite.[l]
16When all Israel[m] saw that the king refused to listen to them, they answered the
king:

"What share do we have in David,[n]
  what part in Jesse's son?
To your tents, Israel!
  Look after your own house, David!"

So all the Israelites went home. 17But as for
the Israelites who were living in the towns
of Judah, Rehoboam still ruled over them.
18King Rehoboam sent out Adoniram,[a][o]
who was in charge of forced labor, but the
Israelites stoned him to death. King Rehoboam, however, managed to get into his
chariot and escape to Jerusalem. 19So Israel has been in rebellion against the house
of David to this day.

11 When Rehoboam arrived in Jerusalem,[p] he mustered Judah and Benjamin—a hundred and eighty thousand able
young men—to go to war against Israel
and to regain the kingdom for Rehoboam.
2But this word of the LORD came to Shemaiah[q] the man of God: 3"Say to Rehoboam son of Solomon king of Judah and to
all Israel in Judah and Benjamin, 4'This is
what the LORD says: Do not go up to fight
against your fellow Israelites.[r] Go home,
every one of you, for this is my doing.'"
So they obeyed the words of the LORD and
turned back from marching against Jeroboam.

Rehoboam Fortifies Judah

5Rehoboam lived in Jerusalem and built
up towns for defense in Judah: 6Bethlehem,
Etam, Tekoa, 7Beth Zur, Soko, Adullam,
8Gath, Mareshah, Ziph, 9Adoraim, Lachish, Azekah, 10Zorah, Aijalon and Hebron. These were fortified cities in Judah
and Benjamin. 11He strengthened their defenses and put commanders in them, with
supplies of food, olive oil and wine. 12He
put shields and spears in all the cities, and
made them very strong. So Judah and Benjamin were his.
13The priests and Levites from all their
districts throughout Israel sided with him.
14The Levites[s] even abandoned their pasturelands and property[t] and came to Judah and Jerusalem, because Jeroboam
and his sons had rejected them as priests
of the LORD 15when he appointed[u] his own
priests[v] for the high places and for the goat[w]
and calf[x] idols he had made. 16Those from
every tribe of Israel[y] who set their hearts
on seeking the LORD, the God of Israel,
followed the Levites to Jerusalem to offer

[a] 18 Hebrew *Hadoram,* a variant of *Adoniram*

---

nation. Like many other people, Rehoboam mistook conciliation for weakness, and lost his chance to have influence with most of the nation. It is important to remember that the outcome of this encounter was just what God wanted. Rehoboam was reaping the fruits of his father's (and his own) indifference to God.

10:15 *this turn of events was from God.* Human foolishness and decisions often achieve God's purposes. Solomon's defection from God late in his reign had already disqualified his descendants from ruling over all Israel (1 Kin. 11:9–13). Rehoboam initiated the split with his own foolish actions.

11:13 *all their districts.* Though Israel and Judah had split into two kingdoms, the priests and Levites of Israel sided with Judah. One reason for this was that they knew that Rehoboam was of the lineage of David, and therefore part of God's covenant promise to David. Another reason was that Jeroboam had established his own religious cult, which had no need for the true priests of God (1 Kin. 12:24–33).

11:16 *followed ... to Jerusalem.* Once the legitimate religious leaders had left Israel, the worshipers of God in the northern kingdom could no longer worship in good conscience, so they either made

10:6 [g] Job 8:8-9; 12:12; 15:10; 32:7 **10:7** [h] Pr 15:1
10:8 [i] 2Sa 17:14 [j] Pr 13:20 **10:15** [k] 2Ch 11:4; 25:16-20
[l] 1Ki 11:29 **10:16** [m] 1Ch 9:1 [n] ver 19; 2Sa 20:1
10:18 [o] 1Ki 5:14 **11:1** [p] 1Ki 12:21 **11:2** [q] 2Ch 12:5-7, 15
11:4 [r] 2Ch 28:8-11 **11:14** [s] Nu 35:2-5 [t] 2Ch 13:9
11:15 [u] 1Ki 13:33 [v] 1Ki 12:31 [w] Lev 17:7 [x] 1Ki 12:28; 2Ch 13:8 **11:16** [y] 2Ch 15:9

sacrifices to the LORD, the God of their ancestors. 17They strengthened[z] the kingdom of Judah and supported Rehoboam son of Solomon three years, following the ways of David and Solomon during this time.

Rehoboam's Family

18Rehoboam married Mahalath, who was the daughter of David's son Jerimoth and of Abihail, the daughter of Jesse's son Eliab. 19She bore him sons: Jeush, Shemariah and Zaham. 20Then he married Maakah[a] daughter of Absalom, who bore him Abijah,[b] Attai, Ziza and Shelomith. 21Rehoboam loved Maakah daughter of Absalom more than any of his other wives and concubines. In all, he had eighteen wives[c] and sixty concubines, twenty-eight sons and sixty daughters.

22Rehoboam appointed Abijah[d] son of Maakah as crown prince among his brothers, in order to make him king. 23He acted wisely, dispersing some of his sons throughout the districts of Judah and Benjamin, and to all the fortified cities. He gave them abundant provisions and took many wives for them.

Shishak Attacks Jerusalem

12 After Rehoboam's position as king was established[e] and he had become strong,[f] he and all Israel[a] with him abandoned the law of the LORD. 2Because they had been unfaithful[g] to the LORD, Shishak[h] king of Egypt attacked Jerusalem in the fifth year of King Rehoboam. 3With twelve hundred chariots and sixty thousand horsemen and the innumerable troops of Libyans, Sukkites and Cushites[b][i] that came with him from Egypt, 4he captured the fortified cities[j] of Judah and came as far as Jerusalem.

5Then the prophet Shemaiah[k] came to Rehoboam and to the leaders of Judah who had assembled in Jerusalem for fear of Shishak, and he said to them, "This is what the LORD says, 'You have abandoned me; therefore, I now abandon[l] you to Shishak.'"

6The leaders of Israel and the king humbled themselves and said, "The LORD is just."[m]

7When the LORD saw that they humbled themselves, this word of the LORD came to Shemaiah: "Since they have humbled themselves, I will not destroy them but will soon give them deliverance.[n] My wrath will not be poured out on Jerusalem through Shishak. 8They will, however, become subject[o] to him, so that they may learn the difference between serving me and serving the kings of other lands."

9When Shishak king of Egypt attacked Jerusalem, he carried off the treasures of the temple of the LORD and the treasures of the royal palace. He took everything, including the gold shields[p] Solomon had made. 10So King Rehoboam made bronze shields to replace them and assigned these to the commanders of the guard on duty at the entrance to the royal palace. 11Whenever the king went to the LORD's temple, the guards went with him, bearing the shields, and afterward they returned them to the guardroom.

12Because Rehoboam humbled himself, the LORD's anger turned from him, and he was not totally destroyed. Indeed, there was some good[q] in Judah.

13King Rehoboam established himself firmly in Jerusalem and continued as king. He was forty-one years old when he became king, and he reigned seventeen years in Jerusalem, the city the LORD had chosen out of all the tribes of Israel in which to put his Name.[r] His mother's name was Naamah; she was an Ammonite. 14He did evil because he had not set his heart on seeking the LORD.

15As for the events of Rehoboam's reign,

---

[a] *1* That is, Judah, as frequently in 2 Chronicles
[b] *3* That is, people from the upper Nile region

---

pilgrimages to Jerusalem, or moved there (1 Kin. 12:25–33). At the time of the Babylonian captivity (36:10) the northern kingdom was already captured by Assyria (2 Kin. 17), but there were many representatives from the northern tribes living in Judah.

11:22 *Abijah.* Rehoboam named his son Abijah as the next king to ensure a smooth succession following his death. Abijah probably served under or alongside Rehoboam, just as Solomon had served under David (1 Chr. 23:1).

12:2 *Egypt.* Egypt was beginning to recover from a long period of decline and wanted to reestablish control over Israel. God used their ambitions to discipline Rehoboam for abandoning the Lord.

12:3 *Libyans, Sukkites.* The Lybians were also known as the Lubim. The Sukkites were other desert tribes, probably from western Libya. ***Cushites.*** These famous Ethiopian warriors originated in the lands south of Egypt.

12:6 Righteousness—The king and princes of Judah recognized that the Lord was righteous, even in leaving them in the hands of Shishak. What they did not know, was the difference between being the "vassal" of the righteous Lord, and the vassal of the unrighteous Shishak. Like the Israelites, we count on the righteousness and graciousness of the Lord toward us. It is good to know that He is unfailing in His loving-kindness, but it is not something to presume upon, as if our conforming to His image does not really matter.

12:9 *carried off the treasures.* Judah was now a vassal state of Egypt.

11:17 [z] 2Ch 12:1 **11:20** [a] 1Ki 15:2 [b] 2Ch 13:2 **11:21** [c] Dt 17:17 **11:22** [d] Dt 21:15-17 **12:1** [e] ver 13 [f] 2Ch 11:17 **12:2** [g] 1Ki 14:22-24 [h] 1Ki 11:40 **12:3** [i] 2Ch 16:8; Na 3:9 **12:4** [j] 2Ch 11:10 **12:5** [k] 2Ch 11:2 [l] Dt 28:15; 2Ch 15:2 **12:6** [m] Ex 9:27; Da 9:14 **12:7** [n] 1Ki 21:29; Ps 78:38 **12:8** [o] Dt 28:48 **12:9** [p] 2Ch 9:16 **12:12** [q] 1Ki 14:13; 2Ch 19:3 **12:13** [r] Dt 12:5; 2Ch 6:6

from beginning to end, are they not written in the records of Shemaiah[s] the prophet
and of Iddo the seer that deal with genealogies? There was continual warfare between Rehoboam and Jeroboam. 16Reho-
boam rested with his ancestors and was
buried in the City of David. And Abijah[t]
his son succeeded him as king.

Abijah King of Judah

13 In the eighteenth year of the reign
of Jeroboam, Abijah became king of
Judah, 2and he reigned in Jerusalem three
years. His mother's name was Maakah,[a] a
daughter[b] of Uriel of Gibeah.

There was war between Abijah[u] and Jeroboam.[v] 3Abijah went into battle with an
army of four hundred thousand able fighting men, and Jeroboam drew up a battle
line against him with eight hundred thousand able troops.

4Abijah stood on Mount Zemaraim,[w] in
the hill country of Ephraim, and said, "Jeroboam and all Israel,[x] listen to me! 5Don't
you know that the LORD, the God of Israel,
has given the kingship of Israel to David
and his descendants forever[y] by a covenant
of salt?[z] 6Yet Jeroboam son of Nebat, an
official of Solomon son of David, rebelled[a]
against his master. 7Some worthless
scoundrels[b] gathered around him and opposed Rehoboam son of Solomon when he
was young and indecisive and not strong
enough to resist them.

8"And now you plan to resist the kingdom of the LORD, which is in the hands of
David's descendants. You are indeed a vast
army and have with you the golden calves[c]
that Jeroboam made to be your gods.
9But didn't you drive out the priests of the
LORD,[d] the sons of Aaron, and the Levites,
and make priests of your own as the peoples of other lands do? Whoever comes to
consecrate himself with a young bull[e] and
seven rams may become a priest of what
are not gods.[f]

10"As for us, the LORD is our God, and we
have not forsaken him. The priests who
serve the LORD are sons of Aaron, and the
Levites assist them. 11Every morning and
evening[g] they present burnt offerings and
fragrant incense to the LORD. They set out
the bread on the ceremonially clean table[h]
and light the lamps on the gold lampstand
every evening. We are observing the requirements of the LORD our God. But you
have forsaken him. 12God is with us; he is
our leader. His priests with their trumpets
will sound the battle cry against you.[i] People of Israel, do not fight against the LORD,[j]
the God of your ancestors, for you will not
succeed."

13Now Jeroboam had sent troops around
to the rear, so that while he was in front
of Judah the ambush[k] was behind them.
14Judah turned and saw that they were being attacked at both front and rear. Then
they cried out[l] to the LORD. The priests
blew their trumpets 15and the men of Judah raised the battle cry. At the sound of
their battle cry, God routed Jeroboam and
all Israel[m] before Abijah and Judah. 16The
Israelites fled before Judah, and God delivered[n] them into their hands. 17Abijah and
his troops inflicted heavy losses on them,
so that there were five hundred thousand
casualties among Israel's able men. 18The
Israelites were subdued on that occasion,
and the people of Judah were victorious because they relied[o] on the LORD, the God of
their ancestors.

19Abijah pursued Jeroboam and took
from him the towns of Bethel, Jeshanah
and Ephron, with their surrounding villages. 20Jeroboam did not regain power

[a] 2 Most Septuagint manuscripts and Syriac (see also 11:20 and 1 Kings 15:2); Hebrew *Micaiah*
[b] 2 Or *granddaughter*

13:2 *His mother's name was Maakah.* Maakah is a variation of "Michaiah." She is the daughter of "Uriel of Gibeah" in this passage, as well as the "daughter of Absalom" (11:21). It is thought that she was the granddaughter of Absalom, the daughter of Uriel of Gibeah and Absalom's daughter Tamar (2 Sam. 14:27). The terms "father, mother, son, daughter" were often used in talking of ancestors instead of generations. Jesus is referred to as the "Son of David" (Matt. 9:27; 15:22; 22:42), which is clearly a reference to His ancestry.

13:5 *covenant of salt.* Salt was a preservative and symbolized durability, so a covenant of salt was one that would not be broken. Sometimes covenant makers each took a pinch of salt and mixed it, to show that just as the salt could not be separated, so the promise could not be set aside.

13:6 *Yet Jeroboam.* The throne had been promised to David's line forever, yet the promise was contingent on the faithfulness of his descendants (7:18–19). Because Solomon had turned from God, part of the kingdom was taken from him, and Jeroboam was chosen by God through the prophet Ahijah to rule over the part of the kingdom that was taken from Solomon (10:2). So far this story mirrors the events in the lives of Saul and David. But unlike David, Jeroboam did not wait for the Lord to deliver the promised kingdom to him. Jeroboam took his place by force, and immediately turned from God. His name became a byword, synonymous with "bad king." (See also 1 Kin. 11–14.)

13:7 *when he was young and indecisive.* Abijah's version of the nation's division put his father in a relatively good light. Rehoboam was 41 years old when he became king (12:13).

12:15 [s] 2Ch 9:29; 11:2 **12:16** [t] 2Ch 11:20
13:2 [u] 2Ch 11:20 [v] 1Ki 15:6 **13:4** [w] Jos 18:22 [x] 1Ch 11:1
13:5 [y] 2Sa 7:13 [z] Lev 2:13; Nu 18:19 **13:6** [a] 1Ki 11:26
13:7 [b] Jdg 9:4 **13:8** [c] 1Ki 12:28; 2Ch 11:15
13:9 [d] 2Ch 11:14-15 [e] Ex 29:35-36 [f] Jer 2:11
13:11 [g] Ex 29:39; 2Ch 2:4 [h] Lev 24:5-9 **13:12** [i] Nu 10:8-9 [j] Ac 5:39 **13:13** [k] Jos 8:9 **13:14** [l] 2Ch 14:11
13:15 [m] 2Ch 14:12 **13:16** [n] 2Ch 16:8 **13:18** [o] 1Ch 5:20; 2Ch 14:11; Ps 22:5

during the time of Abijah. And the LORD
struck him down and he died.
21But Abijah grew in strength. He married fourteen wives and had twenty-two
sons and sixteen daughters.
22The other events of Abijah's reign,
what he did and what he said, are written
in the annotations of the prophet Iddo.
14[a] And Abijah rested with his ancestors
and was buried in the City of David.
Asa his son succeeded him as king, and in
his days the country was at peace for ten
years.

Asa King of Judah

2Asa did what was good and right in the
eyes of the LORD his God. 3He removed
the foreign altars and the high places,
smashed the sacred stones and cut down
the Asherah poles.[b][p] 4He commanded
Judah to seek the LORD, the God of their
ancestors, and to obey his laws and commands. 5He removed the high places and
incense altars[q] in every town in Judah, and
the kingdom was at peace under him. 6He
built up the fortified cities of Judah, since
the land was at peace. No one was at war
with him during those years, for the LORD
gave him rest.[r]
7"Let us build up these towns," he said to
Judah, "and put walls around them, with
towers, gates and bars. The land is still
ours, because we have sought the LORD
our God; we sought him and he has giv-
en us rest on every side." So they built and
prospered.
8Asa had an army of three hundred
thousand men from Judah, equipped with
large shields and with spears, and two hundred and eighty thousand from Benjamin,
armed with small shields and with bows.
All these were brave fighting men.
9Zerah the Cushite[s] marched out against
them with an army of thousands upon
thousands and three hundred chariots,
and came as far as Mareshah.[t] 10Asa went
out to meet him, and they took up battle
positions in the Valley of Zephathah near
Mareshah.
11Then Asa called[u] to the LORD his God
and said, "LORD, there is no one like you
to help the powerless against the mighty.
Help us, LORD our God, for we rely[v] on you,
and in your name[w] we have come against
this vast army. LORD, you are our God; do
not let mere mortals prevail[x] against you."
12The LORD struck down[y] the Cushites
before Asa and Judah. The Cushites fled,
13and Asa and his army pursued them
as far as Gerar.[z] Such a great number of
Cushites fell that they could not recover;
they were crushed before the LORD and
his forces. The men of Judah carried off a
large amount of plunder. 14They destroyed
all the villages around Gerar, for the terror[a] of the LORD had fallen on them. They
looted all these villages, since there was
much plunder there. 15They also attacked
the camps of the herders and carried off
droves of sheep and goats and camels.
Then they returned to Jerusalem.

Asa's Reform

15 The Spirit of God came on[b] Azariah
son of Oded. 2He went out to meet Asa
and said to him, "Listen to me, Asa and all
Judah and Benjamin. The LORD is with you[c]
when you are with him.[d] If you seek[e] him,
he will be found by you, but if you forsake
him, he will forsake you.[f] 3For a long time
Israel was without the true God, without a
priest to teach[g] and without the law.[h] 4But
in their distress they turned to the LORD,
the God of Israel, and sought him,[i] and he
was found by them. 5In those days it was not
safe to travel about,[j] for all the inhabitants
of the lands were in great turmoil. 6One nation was being crushed by another and one

[a] In Hebrew texts 14:1 is numbered 13:23, and 14:2-15 is numbered 14:1-14. [b] 3 That is, wooden symbols of the goddess Asherah; here and elsewhere in 2 Chronicles

14:2–4 Faithfulness—King Asa chose to be faithful to God as he began his reign. His people enjoyed ten years of peace because of Asa's obedience. For each one of us there is a peace that comes with faithfulness to God. This does not necessarily mean that outer circumstances are uncomplicated, but in our hearts the peace of God can still reign. Like Asa, our actions affect the lives of those around us. We are created to have an eternal relationship with God, and that begins in the life of faith, believing that He is who He says He is and that we need Him. "Now faith is confidence in what we hope for and assurance about what we do not see" (Heb. 11:1).

14:3 *sacred stones ... Asherah poles.* Sacred stones were stone posts associated with Canaanite fertility rites. Asherah was a Canaanite goddess associated with Baal worship. Asherah poles were trees or groves that were symbolic parts of Asherah worship.

14:9 *Zerah the Cushite.* Since Egypt was strong at this time (12:3) and fully in control of its own territory, it is likely that Zerah and his large army were mercenaries of the Egyptian king Osorkon I (914–874 B.C.), successor of Shishak. ***Mareshah.*** Mareshah was one of Asa's important fortified cities, about 25 miles southwest of Jerusalem (11:8). It was near the Via Maris, the coastal highway connecting Egypt and Canaan, making it strategically important.

14:13 *Gerar.* Gerar was at the frontier between Egypt and Canaan and might have been in Egyptian territory at this time.

14:3 [p] Ex 34:13; Dt 7:5; 1Ki 15:12-14 **14:5** [q] 2Ch 34:4,7 **14:6** [r] 1Ch 22:9; 2Ch 15:15 **14:9** [s] 2Ch 12:3; 16:8 [t] 2Ch 11:8 **14:11** [u] 2Ch 13:14 [v] 2Ch 13:18 [w] 1Sa 17:45 [x] 1Sa 14:6; Ps 9:19 **14:12** [y] 2Ch 13:15 **14:13** [z] Ge 10:19 **14:14** [a] Ge 35:5; 2Ch 17:10 **15:1** [b] Nu 11:25,26; 24:2; 2Ch 20:14; 24:20 **15:2** [c] ver 4,15; 2Ch 20:17 [d] Jas 4:8 [e] Jer 29:13 [f] 1Ch 28:9; 2Ch 24:20 **15:3** [g] Lev 10:11 [h] 2Ch 17:9; La 2:9 **15:4** [i] Dt 4:29 **15:5** [j] Jdg 5:6

city by another,[k] because God was troubling them with every kind of distress. 7But as for you, be strong[l] and do not give up, for your work will be rewarded."[m]

8When Asa heard these words and the prophecy of Azariah son of[a] Oded the prophet, he took courage. He removed the detestable idols from the whole land of Judah and Benjamin and from the towns he had captured[n] in the hills of Ephraim. He repaired the altar[o] of the LORD that was in front of the portico of the LORD's temple.

9Then he assembled all Judah and Benjamin and the people from Ephraim, Manasseh and Simeon who had settled among them, for large numbers[p] had come over to him from Israel when they saw that the LORD his God was with him.

10They assembled at Jerusalem in the third month of the fifteenth year of Asa's reign. 11At that time they sacrificed to the LORD seven hundred head of cattle and seven thousand sheep and goats from the plunder[q] they had brought back. 12They entered into a covenant[r] to seek the LORD,[s] the God of their ancestors, with all their heart and soul. 13All who would not seek the LORD, the God of Israel, were to be put to death,[t] whether small or great, man or woman. 14They took an oath to the LORD with loud acclamation, with shouting and with trumpets and horns. 15All Judah rejoiced about the oath because they had sworn it wholeheartedly. They sought God[u] eagerly, and he was found by them. So the LORD gave them rest[v] on every side.

16King Asa also deposed his grandmother Maakah from her position as queen mother, because she had made a repulsive image for the worship of Asherah.[w] Asa cut it down, broke it up and burned it in the Kidron Valley. 17Although he did not remove the high places from Israel, Asa's heart was fully committed to the LORD all his life. 18He brought into the temple of God the silver and gold and the articles that he and his father had dedicated.

19There was no more war until the thirty-fifth year of Asa's reign.

Asa's Last Years

16 In the thirty-sixth year of Asa's reign Baasha[x] king of Israel went up against Judah and fortified Ramah to prevent anyone from leaving or entering the territory of Asa king of Judah.

2Asa then took the silver and gold out of the treasuries of the LORD's temple and of his own palace and sent it to Ben-Hadad king of Aram, who was ruling in Damascus. 3"Let there be a treaty[y] between me and you," he said, "as there was between my father and your father. See, I am sending you silver and gold. Now break your treaty with Baasha king of Israel so he will withdraw from me."

4Ben-Hadad agreed with King Asa and sent the commanders of his forces against the towns of Israel. They conquered Ijon, Dan, Abel Maim[b] and all the store cities of Naphtali. 5When Baasha heard this, he stopped building Ramah and abandoned his work. 6Then King Asa brought all the men of Judah, and they carried away from Ramah the stones and timber Baasha had been using. With them he built up Geba and Mizpah.

7At that time Hanani[z] the seer came to Asa king of Judah and said to him: "Because you relied on the king of Aram and not on the LORD your God, the army of the king of Aram has escaped from your hand. 8Were not the Cushites[c][a] and Libyans a mighty army with great numbers of chariots and horsemen[d]? Yet when you relied on the LORD, he delivered[b] them into your hand. 9For the eyes[c] of the LORD range throughout the earth to strengthen those whose hearts are fully committed to him. You have done a foolish[d] thing, and from now on you will be at war."

10Asa was angry with the seer because of this; he was so enraged that he put him

---

[a] 8 Vulgate and Syriac (see also Septuagint and verse 1); Hebrew does not have *Azariah son of.*
[b] 4 Also known as *Abel Beth Maakah*
[c] 8 That is, people from the upper Nile region
[d] 8 Or *charioteers*

15:10 *third month.* This quite likely locates this festival at the time of the firstfruits, the Festival of Weeks (Lev. 23:15–21; Num. 28:26–31).

15:16 *Maakah.* It appears that "mother" is used in the sense of ancestress; Maakah was the mother of Asa's father, Abijah (13:2). Still, Asa demoted her from her position as queen mother because she set up pagan idols — a courageous and delicate task for anyone, even a king.

15:17 Perseverance — Asa started his reign with a determination to serve the Lord and to abolish idol worship. Azariah the prophet spurred him on to finish the job, to get rid of idols in his land and the land just captured. Paul talks about fighting the good fight, finishing the course, keeping the faith (2 Tim. 4:7). We all need people like Azariah in our lives, who encourage us to keep on being faithful. In the same manner, we need to encourage others to persevere to the end.

16:6 *Geba and Mizpah.* Geba was just east of Ramah, and Mizpah was between Ramah and Bethel. Fortifying these two cities effectively stopped Israel from rebuilding Ramah because it was now between two of Asa's fortresses.

16:7–9 *Hanani the seer.* Hanani was probably the father of another prophet, Jehu, who once challenged King Jehoshaphat of Judah (19:2; 20:34).

15:6 [k] Mt 24:7 **15:7** [l] Jos 1:7,9 [m] Ps 58:11
15:8 [n] 2Ch 13:19 [o] 2Ch 8:12 **15:9** [p] 2Ch 11:16-17
15:11 [q] 2Ch 14:13 **15:12** [r] 2Ki 11:17; 2Ch 23:16; 34:31
[s] 1Ch 16:11 **15:13** [t] Ex 22:20; Dt 13:9-16
15:15 [u] Dt 4:29 [v] 1Ch 22:9; 2Ch 14:7 **15:16** [w] Ex 34:13; 2Ch 14:2-5 **16:1** [x] Jer 41:9 **16:3** [y] 2Ch 20:35
16:7 [z] 1Ki 16:1 **16:8** [a] 2Ch 12:3; 14:9 [b] 2Ch 13:16
16:9 [c] Pr 15:3; Jer 16:17; Zec 4:10 [d] 1Sa 13:13

in prison. At the same time Asa brutally oppressed some of the people.

11 The events of Asa's reign, from beginning to end, are written in the book of the kings of Judah and Israel. 12 In the thirty-ninth year of his reign Asa was afflicted with a disease in his feet. Though his disease was severe, even in his illness he did not seek help from the LORD,[e] but only from the physicians. 13 Then in the forty-first year of his reign Asa died and rested with his ancestors. 14 They buried him in the tomb that he had cut out for himself in the City of David. They laid him on a bier covered with spices and various blended perfumes,[f] and they made a huge fire[g] in his honor.

Jehoshaphat King of Judah

17 Jehoshaphat his son succeeded him as king and strengthened himself against Israel. 2 He stationed troops in all the fortified cities of Judah and put garrisons in Judah and in the towns of Ephraim that his father Asa had captured.[h]

3 The LORD was with Jehoshaphat because he followed the ways of his father David[i] before him. He did not consult the Baals 4 but sought[j] the God of his father and followed his commands rather than the practices of Israel. 5 The LORD established the kingdom under his control; and all Judah brought gifts[k] to Jehoshaphat, so that he had great wealth and honor.[l] 6 His heart was devoted[m] to the ways of the LORD; furthermore, he removed the high places[n] and the Asherah poles[o] from Judah.[p]

7 In the third year of his reign he sent his officials Ben-Hail, Obadiah, Zechariah, Nethanel and Micaiah to teach[q] in the towns of Judah. 8 With them were certain Levites[r]—Shemaiah, Nethaniah, Zebadiah, Asahel, Shemiramoth, Jehonathan, Adonijah, Tobijah and Tob-Adonijah—and the priests Elishama and Jehoram. 9 They taught throughout Judah, taking with them the Book of the Law[s] of the LORD; they went around to all the towns of Judah and taught the people.

10 The fear[t] of the LORD fell on all the kingdoms of the lands surrounding Judah, so that they did not go to war against Jehoshaphat. 11 Some Philistines brought Jehoshaphat gifts and silver as tribute, and the Arabs[u] brought him flocks:[v] seven thousand seven hundred rams and seven thousand seven hundred goats.

12 Jehoshaphat became more and more powerful; he built forts and store cities in Judah 13 and had large supplies in the towns of Judah. He also kept experienced fighting men in Jerusalem. 14 Their enrollment[w] by families was as follows:

From Judah, commanders of units of 1,000:
Adnah the commander, with 300,000 fighting men;
15 next, Jehohanan the commander, with 280,000;
16 next, Amasiah son of Zikri, who volunteered[x] himself for the service of the LORD, with 200,000.
17 From Benjamin:[y]
Eliada, a valiant soldier, with 200,000 men armed with bows and shields;
18 next, Jehozabad, with 180,000 men armed for battle.

19 These were the men who served the king, besides those he stationed in the fortified cities[z] throughout Judah.[a]

Micaiah Prophesies Against Ahab

18 Now Jehoshaphat had great wealth and honor,[b] and he allied[c] himself with Ahab[d] by marriage. 2 Some years later he went down to see Ahab in Samaria. Ahab slaughtered many sheep and cattle for him and the people with him and urged him to attack Ramoth Gilead. 3 Ahab king of Israel asked Jehoshaphat king of Judah, "Will you go with me against Ramoth Gilead?"

Jehoshaphat replied, "I am as you are, and my people as your people; we will join you in the war." 4 But Jehoshaphat also said to the king of Israel, "First seek the counsel of the LORD."

5 So the king of Israel brought together the prophets—four hundred men—and asked them, "Shall we go to war against Ramoth Gilead, or shall I not?"

17:2 ***towns of Ephraim.*** Ephraim is a synonym for Israel. The cities referred to here are mentioned also in 15:8.

17:13–18 ***experienced fighting men.*** Jehoshaphat's men were grouped into three divisions of Judeans with a total number of 780,000 and two divisions of Benjamites numbering 380,000. The Hebrew word for thousand can mean family, or clan, (Judg. 6:15; 1 Sam. 10:19; Mic. 5:2). In that case, the 780,000 would be 780 companies, and the 380,000 would be 380 companies, and the total warriors would be nearer to 78,000 and 38,000.

18:2 ***Ramoth Gilead.*** This important city was some 35 miles east of Beth Shan and was controlled by the Arameans. It was also one of the Israelite cities of refuge (Josh. 20:8; 1 Chr. 6:80).

18:5 ***prophets.*** These prophets were probably prophets of Baal or Asherah (1 Kin. 18:19), the Canaanite gods worshiped by Ahab's wife Jezebel.

16:12 [e] Jer 17:5-6 **16:14** [f] Ge 50:2; Jn 19:39-40 [g] 2Ch 21:19; Jer 34:5 **17:2** [h] 2Ch 15:8 **17:3** [i] 1Ki 22:43 **17:4** [j] 1Ki 12:28; 2Ch 22:9 **17:5** [k] 1Sa 10:27 [l] 2Ch 18:1 **17:6** [m] 1Ki 8:61; 2Ch 15:17 [n] 1Ki 15:14; 2Ch 19:3; 20:33 [o] Ex 34:13 [p] 2Ch 21:12 **17:7** [q] Lev 10:11; Dt 6:4-9; 2Ch 15:3; 35:3 **17:8** [r] 2Ch 19:8; Ne 8:7-8 **17:9** [s] Dt 6:4-9; 28:61 **17:10** [t] Ge 35:5; Dt 2:25; 2Ch 14:14 **17:11** [u] 2Ch 9:14; 26:8 [v] 2Ch 21:16 **17:14** [w] 2Sa 24:2 **17:16** [x] Jdg 5:9; 1Ch 29:9 **17:17** [y] Nu 1:36 **17:19** [z] 2Ch 11:10 [a] 2Ch 25:5 **18:1** [b] 2Ch 17:5 [c] 2Ch 19:1-3; 22:3 [d] 2Ch 21:6

"Go," they answered, "for God will give
it into the king's hand."
6But Jehoshaphat asked, "Is there no longer a prophet of the LORD here whom we
can inquire of?"
7The king of Israel answered Jehoshaphat, "There is still one prophet through
whom we can inquire of the LORD, but I
hate him because he never prophesies anything good about me, but always bad. He is
Micaiah son of Imlah."
"The king should not say such a thing,"
Jehoshaphat replied.
8So the king of Israel called one of his
officials and said, "Bring Micaiah son of
Imlah at once."
9Dressed in their royal robes, the king of
Israel and Jehoshaphat king of Judah were
sitting on their thrones at the threshing
floor by the entrance of the gate of Samaria, with all the prophets prophesying before them. 10Now Zedekiah son of Kenaanah had made iron horns, and he declared,
"This is what the LORD says: 'With these
you will gore the Arameans until they are
destroyed.'"
11All the other prophets were prophesying the same thing. "Attack Ramoth Gilead[e] and be victorious," they said, "for the
LORD will give it into the king's hand."
12The messenger who had gone to summon Micaiah said to him, "Look, the other
prophets without exception are predicting
success for the king. Let your word agree
with theirs, and speak favorably."
13But Micaiah said, "As surely as the
LORD lives, I can tell him only what my
God says."[f]
14When he arrived, the king asked him,
"Micaiah, shall we go to war against Ramoth Gilead, or shall I not?"
"Attack and be victorious," he answered,
"for they will be given into your hand."
15The king said to him, "How many times
must I make you swear to tell me nothing
but the truth in the name of the LORD?"
16Then Micaiah answered, "I saw all Israel[g] scattered on the hills like sheep without a shepherd,[h] and the LORD said, 'These
people have no master. Let each one go
home in peace.'"
17The king of Israel said to Jehoshaphat,
"Didn't I tell you that he never prophesies
anything good about me, but only bad?"
18Micaiah continued, "Therefore hear
the word of the LORD: I saw the LORD sitting on his throne[i] with all the multitudes
of heaven standing on his right and on his
left. 19And the LORD said, 'Who will entice
Ahab king of Israel into attacking Ramoth
Gilead and going to his death there?'
"One suggested this, and another that.
20Finally, a spirit came forward, stood before the LORD and said, 'I will entice him.'
"'By what means?' the LORD asked.
21"'I will go and be a deceiving spirit[j] in
the mouths of all his prophets,' he said.
"'You will succeed in enticing him,' said
the LORD. 'Go and do it.'
22"So now the LORD has put a deceiving spirit in the mouths of these prophets
of yours.[k] The LORD has decreed disaster
for you."
23Then Zedekiah son of Kenaanah
went up and slapped[l] Micaiah in the face.
"Which way did the spirit from[a] the LORD
go when he went from me to speak to you?"
he asked.
24Micaiah replied, "You will find out on
the day you go to hide in an inner room."
25The king of Israel then ordered, "Take
Micaiah and send him back to Amon the
ruler of the city and to Joash the king's son,
26and say, 'This is what the king says: Put
this fellow in prison[m] and give him nothing
but bread and water until I return safely.'"
27Micaiah declared, "If you ever return
safely, the LORD has not spoken through
me." Then he added, "Mark my words, all
you people!"

Ahab Killed at Ramoth Gilead

28So the king of Israel and Jehoshaphat
king of Judah went up to Ramoth Gilead.
29The king of Israel said to Jehoshaphat,
"I will enter the battle in disguise, but you
wear your royal robes." So the king of Israel disguised[n] himself and went into battle.
30Now the king of Aram had ordered his
chariot commanders, "Do not fight with
anyone, small or great, except the king of
Israel." 31When the chariot commanders
saw Jehoshaphat, they thought, "This is
the king of Israel." So they turned to attack him, but Jehoshaphat cried out,[o] and

[a] 23 Or *Spirit of*

18:11 *prophesying.* The true prophet's words come directly from God, and they show God's thoughts, and sometimes His plans. These false prophets were speaking authoritatively, probably accompanied with such ravings and demonstrations as would show their power and ability to see the future (1 Kin. 18:26–29).

18:15 *nothing but the truth.* Ahab knew from experience that his prophets told him what they thought he wanted to hear, not the truth. Because their prophecies agreed with Micaiah's, he knew that Micaiah must have been mocking when he prophesied success.

18:22 *deceiving spirit.* The spirits who stood before the Lord were both angels and demons, none of whom could act without God's permission. God allowed this spirit to work in the mouths of the false prophets to accomplish His own purposes of judgment (1 Chr. 21:1; Job 1).

18:11 [e] 2Ch 22:5 **18:13** [f] Nu 22:18, 20, 35
18:16 [g] 1Ch 9:1 [h] Nu 27:17; Eze 34:5-8 **18:18** [i] Da 7:9
18:21 [j] 1Ch 21:1; Job 1:6; Zec 3:1; Jn 8:44
18:22 [k] Job 12:16; Isa 19:14; Eze 14:9 **18:23** [l] Jer 20:2; Mk 14:65; Ac 23:2 **18:26** [m] 2Ch 16:10; Heb 11:36
18:29 [n] 1Sa 28:8 **18:31** [o] 2Ch 13:14

the LORD helped him. God drew them away
from him, 32 for when the chariot commanders saw that he was not the king of
Israel, they stopped pursuing him.
33 But someone drew his bow at random and hit the king of Israel between the
breastplate and the scale armor. The king
told the chariot driver, "Wheel around and
get me out of the fighting. I've been wounded." 34 All day long the battle raged, and the
king of Israel propped himself up in his
chariot facing the Arameans until evening.
Then at sunset he died.[p]

19 When Jehoshaphat king of Judah
returned safely to his palace in Jerusalem, 2 Jehu[q] the seer, the son of Hanani,
went out to meet him and said to the king,
"Should you help the wicked[r] and love[a]
those who hate the LORD?[s] Because of this,
the wrath[t] of the LORD is on you. 3 There is,
however, some good[u] in you, for you have
rid the land of the Asherah poles[v] and have
set your heart on seeking God.[w]"

Jehoshaphat Appoints Judges

4 Jehoshaphat lived in Jerusalem, and he
went out again among the people from Beersheba to the hill country of Ephraim and
turned them back to the LORD, the God of
their ancestors. 5 He appointed judges[x] in
the land, in each of the fortified cities of
Judah. 6 He told them, "Consider carefully
what you do,[y] because you are not judging
for mere mortals[z] but for the LORD, who is
with you whenever you give a verdict. 7 Now
let the fear of the LORD be on you. Judge
carefully, for with the LORD our God there is
no injustice[a] or partiality[b] or bribery."
8 In Jerusalem also, Jehoshaphat appointed some of the Levites, priests and
heads of Israelite families to administer[c]
the law of the LORD and to settle disputes.
And they lived in Jerusalem. 9 He gave
them these orders: "You must serve faithfully and wholeheartedly in the fear of the
LORD. 10 In every case that comes before
you from your people who live in the cities—whether bloodshed or other concerns
of the law, commands, decrees or regulations—you are to warn them not to sin
against the LORD;[d] otherwise his wrath will
come on you and your people. Do this, and
you will not sin.
11 "Amariah the chief priest will be over
you in any matter concerning the LORD,
and Zebadiah son of Ishmael, the leader
of the tribe of Judah, will be over you in
any matter concerning the king, and the
Levites will serve as officials before you.
Act with courage,[e] and may the LORD be
with those who do well."

Jehoshaphat Defeats Moab and Ammon

20 After this, the Moabites and Ammonites with some of the Meunites[b][f]
came to wage war against Jehoshaphat.
2 Some people came and told Jehoshaphat, "A vast army is coming against you
from Edom,[c] from the other side of the
Dead Sea. It is already in Hazezon Tamar[g]"
(that is, En Gedi). 3 Alarmed, Jehoshaphat
resolved to inquire of the LORD, and he proclaimed a fast[h] for all Judah. 4 The people of
Judah came together to seek help from the
LORD; indeed, they came from every town
in Judah to seek him.
5 Then Jehoshaphat stood up in the assembly of Judah and Jerusalem at the
temple of the LORD in the front of the new
courtyard 6 and said:

"LORD, the God of our ancestors,[i]
are you not the God who is in heav-
en?[j] You rule over all the kingdoms[k]
of the nations. Power and might are in
your hand, and no one can withstand
you. 7 Our God, did you not drive out
the inhabitants of this land before your
people Israel and give it forever to the
descendants of Abraham your friend?[l]
8 They have lived in it and have built in
it a sanctuary[m] for your Name, saying,
9 'If calamity comes upon us, whether
the sword of judgment, or plague or
famine,[n] we will stand in your presence before this temple that bears
your Name and will cry out to you in
our distress, and you will hear us and
save us.'
10 "But now here are men from Ammon, Moab and Mount Seir, whose

[a] 2 Or *and make alliances with* [b] 1 Some Septuagint manuscripts; Hebrew *Ammonites* [c] 2 One Hebrew manuscript; most Hebrew manuscripts, Septuagint and Vulgate *Aram*

18:33 *at random.* From the human perspective, this was a chance shot. From God's perspective, chance had no part in it. Ahab's disguise could not foil God's plan.

19:3 Repentance—Repentance is never by word only. It is always followed by actions which show that the attitude of repentance is really present. Part of repentance is acknowledging that God is right and that He knows how we should live. It was the change in Jehoshaphat's actions that proved his change of heart.

19:4 *hill country of Ephraim.* The hill country of Ephraim became the northern border of Judah after the division into two kingdoms. This is another way of saying that the whole country was brought back to the Lord.

18:34 [p] 2Ch 22:5 **19:2** [q] 1Ki 16:1 [r] 2Ch 16:2-9 [s] Ps 139:21-22 [t] 2Ch 24:18; 32:25; Ps 7:11 **19:3** [u] 1Ki 14:13; 2Ch 12:12 [v] 2Ch 17:6 [w] 2Ch 18:1; 20:35; 25:7; Ezr 7:10 **19:5** [x] Ge 47:6; Ex 18:26 **19:6** [y] Lev 19:15 [z] Dt 1:17; 16:18-20; 17:8-13 **19:7** [a] Ge 18:25; Dt 32:4 [b] Dt 10:17; Job 34:19; Ro 2:11; Col 3:25 **19:8** [c] 2Ch 17:8-9 **19:10** [d] Dt 17:8-13 **19:11** [e] 1Ch 20:20 **20:1** [f] 1Ch 4:41 **20:2** [g] Ge 14:7 **20:3** [h] 1Sa 7:6; 2Ch 19:3; Ezr 8:21; Jer 36:9; Jnh 3:5,7 **20:6** [i] Mt 6:9 [j] Dt 4:39 [k] 1Ch 29:11-12 **20:7** [l] Isa 41:8; Jas 2:23 **20:8** [m] 2Ch 6:20 **20:9** [n] 2Ch 6:28

territory you would not allow Israel to
invade when they came from Egypt;[o]
so they turned away from them and
did not destroy them. 11See how they
are repaying us by coming to drive us
out of the possession[p] you gave us as
an inheritance. 12Our God, will you
not judge them?[q] For we have no power
to face this vast army that is attacking
us. We do not know what to do, but our
eyes are on you.[r]"

13All the men of Judah, with their wives
and children and little ones, stood there before the LORD.

14Then the Spirit[s] of the LORD came on
Jahaziel son of Zechariah, the son of Benaiah, the son of Jeiel, the son of Mattaniah,
a Levite and descendant of Asaph, as he
stood in the assembly.

15He said: "Listen, King Jehoshaphat
and all who live in Judah and Jerusalem!
This is what the LORD says to you: 'Do not
be afraid or discouraged[t] because of this
vast army. For the battle[u] is not yours, but
God's. 16Tomorrow march down against
them. They will be climbing up by the Pass
of Ziz, and you will find them at the end of
the gorge in the Desert of Jeruel. 17You will
not have to fight this battle. Take up your
positions; stand firm and see[v] the deliverance the LORD will give you, Judah and
Jerusalem. Do not be afraid; do not be discouraged. Go out to face them tomorrow,
and the LORD will be with you.' "

18Jehoshaphat bowed down[w] with his
face to the ground, and all the people of
Judah and Jerusalem fell down in worship
before the LORD. 19Then some Levites from
the Kohathites and Korahites stood up and
praised the LORD, the God of Israel, with a
very loud voice.

20Early in the morning they left for the
Desert of Tekoa. As they set out, Jehoshaphat stood and said, "Listen to me, Judah
and people of Jerusalem! Have faith[x] in
the LORD your God and you will be upheld;
have faith in his prophets and you will be
successful.[y]" 21After consulting the people,
Jehoshaphat appointed men to sing to the
LORD and to praise him for the splendor of
his[a] holiness[z] as they went out at the head
of the army, saying:

> "Give thanks to the LORD,
> for his love endures forever."[a]

22As they began to sing and praise, the
LORD set ambushes[b] against the men of
Ammon and Moab and Mount Seir who
were invading Judah, and they were defeated. 23The Ammonites[c] and Moabites
rose up against the men from Mount Seir[d]
to destroy and annihilate them. After they
finished slaughtering the men from Seir,
they helped to destroy one another.[e]

24When the men of Judah came to the
place that overlooks the desert and looked
toward the vast army, they saw only dead
bodies lying on the ground; no one had escaped. 25So Jehoshaphat and his men went
to carry off their plunder, and they found
among them a great amount of equipment
and clothing[b] and also articles of value—
more than they could take away. There was
so much plunder that it took three days to
collect it. 26On the fourth day they assembled in the Valley of Berakah, where they
praised the LORD. This is why it is called
the Valley of Berakah[c] to this day.

27Then, led by Jehoshaphat, all the men
of Judah and Jerusalem returned joyfully
to Jerusalem, for the LORD had given them
cause to rejoice over their enemies. 28They
entered Jerusalem and went to the temple of
the LORD with harps and lyres and trumpets.

29The fear[f] of God came on all the surrounding kingdoms when they heard how
the LORD had fought[g] against the enemies
of Israel. 30And the kingdom of Jehoshaphat was at peace, for his God had given
him rest[h] on every side.

The End of Jehoshaphat's Reign

31So Jehoshaphat reigned over Judah.
He was thirty-five years old when he became king of Judah, and he reigned in Jerusalem twenty-five years. His mother's

[a] 21 Or *him with the splendor of* [b] 25 Some Hebrew manuscripts and Vulgate; most Hebrew manuscripts *corpses* [c] 26 *Berakah* means *praise.*

20:14 *Jahaziel.* As a member of the Asaph division of the Levites (1 Chr. 6:39; 15:17–19; 16:7) Jahaziel was probably a musician. The spiritual work of the musicians was closely linked with prophecy (1 Chr. 25:1).

20:19 *Kohathites ... Korahites.* The Kohathites were members of the Levitical division of Heman the singer (1 Chr. 6:33). The Korahites were a subdivision of the Kohathites (1 Chr. 6:37,39) who were employed as gatekeepers to the temple.

20:21 Thankfulness—More necessary than guns for soldiers, more important than strategy, is the giving of thanks to God. Judah faced a literal, physical battle involving great odds. They sent their singers out first, singing praises to God and thanking Him for His everlasting loving-kindness. Is this the way we face battles in our lives? Do we first thank God for who He is, what He has done, and for His faithfulness to us?

20:26 *Valley of Berakah.* The Judeans renamed Ziz "the Valley of Berakah," meaning "praise," to remind themselves of God's goodness.

20:10 [o] Nu 20:14-21; Dt 2:4-6,9, 18-19 **20:11** [p] Ps 83:1-12 **20:12** [q] Jdg 11:27 [r] Ps 25:15; 121:1-2 **20:14** [s] 2Ch 15:1 **20:15** [t] 2Ch 32:7 [u] Ex 14:13-14; 1Sa 17:47 **20:17** [v] Ex 14:13; 2Ch 15:2 **20:18** [w] Ex 4:31 **20:20** [x] Isa 7:9 [y] Ge 39:3; Pr 16:3 **20:21** [z] 1Ch 16:29; Ps 29:2 [a] 2Ch 5:13; Ps 136:1 **20:22** [b] Jdg 7:22; 2Ch 13:13 **20:23** [c] Ge 19:38 [d] 2Ch 21:8 [e] Jdg 7:22; 1Sa 14:20; Eze 38:21 **20:29** [f] Ge 35:5; Dt 2:25; 2Ch 14:14; 17:10 [g] Ex 14:14 **20:30** [h] 1Ch 22:9; 2Ch 14:6-7; 15:15

name was Azubah daughter of Shilhi. 32 He followed the ways of his father Asa and did not stray from them; he did what was right in the eyes of the LORD. 33 The high places,[i] however, were not removed, and the people still had not set their hearts on the God of their ancestors.

34 The other events of Jehoshaphat's reign, from beginning to end, are written in the annals of Jehu[j] son of Hanani, which are recorded in the book of the kings of Israel.

35 Later, Jehoshaphat king of Judah made an alliance[k] with Ahaziah king of Israel, whose ways were wicked.[l] 36 He agreed with him to construct a fleet of trading ships.[a] After these were built at Ezion Geber, 37 Eliezer son of Dodavahu of Mareshah prophesied against Jehoshaphat, saying, "Because you have made an alliance with Ahaziah, the LORD will destroy what you have made." The ships[m] were wrecked and were not able to set sail to trade.[b]

21 Then Jehoshaphat rested with his ancestors and was buried with them in the City of David. And Jehoram[n] his son succeeded him as king. 2 Jehoram's brothers, the sons of Jehoshaphat, were Azariah, Jehiel, Zechariah, Azariahu, Michael and Shephatiah. All these were sons of Jehoshaphat king of Israel.[c] 3 Their father had given them many gifts[o] of silver and gold and articles of value, as well as fortified cities[p] in Judah, but he had given the kingdom to Jehoram because he was his firstborn son.

Jehoram King of Judah

4 When Jehoram established[q] himself firmly over his father's kingdom, he put all his brothers[r] to the sword along with some of the officials of Israel. 5 Jehoram was thirty-two years old when he became king, and he reigned in Jerusalem eight years. 6 He followed the ways of the kings of Israel,[s] as the house of Ahab had done, for he married a daughter of Ahab.[t] He did evil in the eyes of the LORD. 7 Nevertheless, because of the covenant the LORD had made with David,[u] the LORD was not willing to destroy the house of David.[v] He had promised to maintain a lamp[w] for him and his descendants forever.

8 In the time of Jehoram, Edom[x] rebelled against Judah and set up its own king. 9 So Jehoram went there with his officers and all his chariots. The Edomites surrounded him and his chariot commanders, but he rose up and broke through by night. 10 To this day Edom has been in rebellion against Judah.

Libnah[y] revolted at the same time, because Jehoram had forsaken the LORD, the God of his ancestors. 11 He had also built high places on the hills of Judah and had caused the people of Jerusalem to prostitute themselves and had led Judah astray.

12 Jehoram received a letter from Elijah[z] the prophet, which said:

> "This is what the LORD, the God of your father[a] David, says: 'You have not followed the ways of your father Jehoshaphat or of Asa[b] king of Judah. 13 But you have followed the ways of the kings of Israel, and you have led Judah and the people of Jerusalem to prostitute themselves, just as the house of Ahab did.[c] You have also murdered your own brothers, members of your own family, men who were better[d] than you. 14 So now the LORD is about to strike your people, your sons, your wives and everything that is yours, with a heavy blow. 15 You yourself will be very ill with a lingering disease[e] of the bowels, until the disease causes your bowels to come out.'"

16 The LORD aroused against Jehoram the hostility of the Philistines and of the Arabs[f] who lived near the Cushites. 17 They attacked Judah, invaded it and carried off all the goods found in the king's palace, together with his sons and wives. Not a son was left to him except Ahaziah,[d] the youngest.[g]

---

[a] 36 Hebrew *of ships that could go to Tarshish*
[b] 37 Hebrew *sail for Tarshish*
[c] 2 That is, Judah, as frequently in 2 Chronicles
[d] 17 Hebrew *Jehoahaz,* a variant of *Ahaziah*

20:34 ***Jehu.*** The son of the prophet Hanani, Jehu was a prophet himself (19:2). He is mentioned in 1 Kings in connection with the kings of Israel, and was therefore a good source of information about both the northern and southern kingdoms.

20:35 ***Ahaziah.*** Ahaziah was the son of Ahab. He succeeded his father and reigned for two years (1 Kin. 22:51). Ahaziah was injured in a fall and turned to the Philistine gods rather than to the Lord for healing (2 Kin. 1:2).

21:11 ***prostitute.*** Israel's relationship with God was like a marriage relationship. Worship of other gods was a violation in the same way that prostitution violates a marriage. It not only says that the true husband is not worthy of respect, it is a rejection of the whole idea of the faithfulness and care of the true husband.

21:12 ***Elijah the prophet.*** Though 1 and 2 Kings pay considerable attention to Elijah (1 Kin. 17:1—2 Kin. 2:18), the books of Chronicles mention him only here. He had been taken up into heaven after King Ahaziah's death (2 Kin. 1:17; 2:1).

20:33 [i] 2Ch 17:6; 19:3 **20:34** [j] 1Ki 16:1
20:35 [k] 2Ch 16:3 [l] 2Ch 19:1-3 **20:37** [m] 1Ki 9:26; 2Ch 9:21
21:1 [n] 1Ch 3:11 **21:3** [o] 2Ch 11:23 [p] 2Ch 11:10
21:4 [q] 1Ki 2:12 [r] Jdg 9:5 **21:6** [s] 1Ki 12:28-30 [t] 2Ch 18:1; 22:3 **21:7** [u] 2Sa 7:13 [v] 2Sa 7:15; 2Ch 23:3 [w] 2Sa 21:17; 1Ki 11:36 **21:8** [x] 2Ch 20:22-23 **21:10** [y] Nu 33:20
21:12 [z] 2Ki 1:16 17 [a] 2Ch 17:3-6 [b] 2Ch 14:2
21:13 [c] ver 6, 11; 1Ki 16:29-33 [d] ver 4; 1Ki 2:32
21:15 [e] ver 18-19; Nu 12:10 **21:16** [f] 2Ch 17:10-11; 22:1; 26:7 **21:17** [g] 2Ki 12:18; 2Ch 22:1; 25:23; Joel 3:5

18After all this, the LORD afflicted Jehoram with an incurable disease of the bowels. 19In the course of time, at the end of the
second year, his bowels came out because
of the disease, and he died in great pain.
His people made no funeral fire in his hon-
or,[h] as they had for his predecessors.
20Jehoram was thirty-two years old
when he became king, and he reigned in
Jerusalem eight years. He passed away, to
no one's regret, and was buried[i] in the City
of David, but not in the tombs of the kings.

Ahaziah King of Judah

22 The people[j] of Jerusalem[k] made Ahaziah, Jehoram's youngest son, king
in his place, since the raiders,[l] who came
with the Arabs into the camp, had killed all
the older sons. So Ahaziah son of Jehoram
king of Judah began to reign.
2Ahaziah was twenty-two[a] years old
when he became king, and he reigned in
Jerusalem one year. His mother's name
was Athaliah, a granddaughter of Omri.
3He too followed[m] the ways of the house
of Ahab,[n] for his mother encouraged him
to act wickedly. 4He did evil in the eyes of
the LORD, as the house of Ahab had done,
for after his father's death they became his
advisers, to his undoing. 5He also followed
their counsel when he went with Joram[b]
son of Ahab king of Israel to wage war
against Hazael king of Aram at Ramoth
Gilead.[o] The Arameans wounded Joram;
6so he returned to Jezreel to recover from
the wounds they had inflicted on him at
Ramoth[c] in his battle with Hazael[p] king
of Aram.
Then Ahaziah[d] son of Jehoram king of
Judah went down to Jezreel to see Joram
son of Ahab because he had been wounded.
7Through Ahaziah's[q] visit to Joram,
God brought about Ahaziah's downfall.
When Ahaziah arrived, he went out with
Joram to meet Jehu son of Nimshi, whom
the LORD had anointed to destroy the house
of Ahab. 8While Jehu was executing judgment on the house of Ahab,[r] he found the
officials of Judah and the sons of Ahaziah's
relatives, who had been attending Ahaziah, and he killed them. 9He then went in
search of Ahaziah, and his men captured
him while he was hiding[s] in Samaria. He
was brought to Jehu and put to death. They
buried him, for they said, "He was a son of
Jehoshaphat, who sought[t] the LORD with
all his heart." So there was no one in the
house of Ahaziah powerful enough to retain the kingdom.

Athaliah and Joash

10When Athaliah the mother of Ahaziah saw that her son was dead, she proceeded to destroy the whole royal family
of the house of Judah. 11But Jehosheba,[e]
the daughter of King Jehoram, took Joash
son of Ahaziah and stole him away from
among the royal princes who were about to
be murdered and put him and his nurse in a
bedroom. Because Jehosheba,[e] the daughter of King Jehoram and wife of the priest
Jehoiada, was Ahaziah's sister, she hid the
child from Athaliah so she could not kill
him. 12He remained hidden with them at
the temple of God for six years while Athaliah ruled the land.
23 In the seventh year Jehoiada showed
his strength. He made a covenant
with the commanders of units of a hundred: Azariah son of Jeroham, Ishmael son
of Jehohanan, Azariah son of Obed, Maaseiah son of Adaiah, and Elishaphat son
of Zikri. 2They went throughout Judah and
gathered the Levites[u] and the heads of Israelite families from all the towns. When
they came to Jerusalem, 3the whole assem-

[a] *2* Some Septuagint manuscripts and Syriac (see also 2 Kings 8:26); Hebrew *forty-two*
[b] *5* Hebrew *Jehoram,* a variant of *Joram;* also in verses 6 and 7 [c] *6* Hebrew *Ramah,* a variant of *Ramoth* [d] *6* Some Hebrew manuscripts, Septuagint, Vulgate and Syriac (see also 2 Kings 8:29); most Hebrew manuscripts *Azariah*
[e] *11* Hebrew *Jehoshabeath,* a variant of *Jehosheba*

21:20 *tombs of the kings.* These tombs were a royal cemetery in Jerusalem where most of the kings of David's dynasty were buried. (Asa was an exception, 16:14.)

22:1 *Ahaziah.* Ahaziah of Judah was the namesake of his uncle from Israel. His father Jehoram had married a sister of Ahab's son Ahaziah (1 Kin. 22:40; 2 Kin. 8:18).

22:5 *Joram son of Ahab.* Joram succeeded his brother Ahaziah because Ahaziah had no son of his own (2 Kin. 1:17). Joram is a short form of Jehoram. He is called this to distinguish him from his brother-in-law Jehoram who was king of Judah. ***Hazael.*** Hazael was the king of Damascus who came to power after assassinating Ben-Hadad (2 Kin. 8:7–15). Elijah had prophesied that this would come about and had even commissioned Elisha to anoint Hazael to his new position (1 Kin. 19:15). Elisha wept after he had anointed Hazael, for he knew that Hazael would cruelly kill many Israelites. ***Ramoth Gilead.*** Ahab and Jehoshaphat had tried to recover this city from Aramean domination 12 years earlier (18:3).

22:10 *the whole royal family.* Most of the royal family that Athaliah murdered were her own grandchildren. She wanted to stamp out the Davidic dynasty and bring Judah back under Israelite control. Satan had been diligent in his attempts to thwart the plans of God, and because the Davidic line was directly linked to the Messiah, this would have been a strategic move. It is not unlike the murder of the baby boys by Herod at the time of Jesus' birth (Matt. 2:10–18).

23:3 Unity—Unity is only unity when we are "the

21:19 [h] 2Ch 16:14 **21:20** [i] 2Ch 24:25; 28:27; 33:20; Jer 22:18, 28 **22:1** [j] 2Ch 33:25; 36:1 [k] 2Ch 23:20-21; 26:1 [l] 2Ch 21:16-17 **22:3** [m] 2Ch 18:1 [n] 2Ch 21:6
22:5 [o] 2Ch 18:11, 34 **22:6** [p] 1Ki 19:15; 2Ki 8:13-15; 9:15
22:7 [q] 2Ki 9:16; 2Ch 10:15 **22:8** [r] 2Ki 10:13
22:9 [s] Jdg 9:5 [t] 2Ch 17:4 **23:2** [u] Nu 35:2-5

bly made a covenant[v] with the king at the temple of God.

Jehoiada said to them, "The king's son shall reign, as the LORD promised concerning the descendants of David.[w] 4Now this is what you are to do: A third of you priests and Levites who are going on duty on the Sabbath are to keep watch at the doors, 5a third of you at the royal palace and a third at the Foundation Gate, and all the others are to be in the courtyards of the temple of the LORD. 6No one is to enter the temple of the LORD except the priests and Levites on duty; they may enter because they are consecrated, but all the others are to observe[x] the LORD's command not to enter.[a] 7The Levites are to station themselves around the king, each with weapon in hand. Anyone who enters the temple is to be put to death. Stay close to the king wherever he goes."

8The Levites and all the men of Judah did just as Jehoiada the priest ordered.[y] Each one took his men—those who were going on duty on the Sabbath and those who were going off duty—for Jehoiada the priest had not released any of the divisions.[z] 9Then he gave the commanders of units of a hundred the spears and the large and small shields that had belonged to King David and that were in the temple of God. 10He stationed all the men, each with his weapon in his hand, around the king—near the altar and the temple, from the south side to the north side of the temple.

11Jehoiada and his sons brought out the king's son and put the crown on him; they presented him with a copy[a] of the covenant and proclaimed him king. They anointed him and shouted, "Long live the king!"

12When Athaliah heard the noise of the people running and cheering the king, she went to them at the temple of the LORD. 13She looked, and there was the king,[b] standing by his pillar[c] at the entrance. The officers and the trumpeters were beside the king, and all the people of the land were rejoicing and blowing trumpets, and musicians with their instruments were leading the praises. Then Athaliah tore her robes and shouted, "Treason! Treason!"

14Jehoiada the priest sent out the commanders of units of a hundred, who were in charge of the troops, and said to them: "Bring her out between the ranks[b] and put to the sword anyone who follows her." For the priest had said, "Do not put her to death at the temple of the LORD." 15So they seized her as she reached the entrance of the Horse Gate[d] on the palace grounds, and there they put her to death.

16Jehoiada then made a covenant[e] that he, the people and the king[c] would be the LORD's people. 17All the people went to the temple of Baal and tore it down. They smashed the altars and idols and killed[f] Mattan the priest of Baal in front of the altars.

18Then Jehoiada placed the oversight of the temple of the LORD in the hands of the Levitical priests,[g] to whom David had made assignments in the temple,[h] to present the burnt offerings of the LORD as written in the Law of Moses, with rejoicing and singing, as David had ordered. 19He also stationed gatekeepers[i] at the gates of the LORD's temple so that no one who was in any way unclean might enter.

20He took with him the commanders of hundreds, the nobles, the rulers of the people and all the people of the land and brought the king down from the temple of the LORD. They went into the palace through the Upper Gate[j] and seated the king on the royal throne. 21All the people of the land rejoiced, and the city was calm, because Athaliah had been slain with the sword.[k]

Joash Repairs the Temple

24 Joash was seven years old when he became king, and he reigned in Jerusalem forty years. His mother's name was Zibiah; she was from Beersheba. 2Joash did what was right in the eyes of the LORD[l] all the years of Jehoiada the priest. 3Jehoiada chose two wives for him, and he had sons and daughters.

4Some time later Joash decided to restore the temple of the LORD. 5He called together the priests and Levites and said to them, "Go to the towns of Judah and collect the money[m] due annually from all Israel,[n] to repair the temple of your God. Do it now." But the Levites[o] did not act at once.

6Therefore the king summoned Jehoiada the chief priest and said to him, "Why haven't you required the Levites to bring in from Judah and Jerusalem the tax imposed by Moses the servant of the LORD and by the assembly of Israel for the tent of the covenant law?"[p]

[a] 6 Or *are to stand guard where the LORD has assigned them* [b] 14 Or *out from the precincts* [c] 16 Or *covenant between the LORD and the people and the king that they* (see 2 Kings 11:17)

same" on issues of the truth. The removal of Athaliah could not have occurred without the cooperation and teamwork of everyone. Knowing that they were doing God's will gave them great courage.

23:11 ***the covenant.*** The covenant was a copy of the Law of Moses, part of which outlined the king's covenant privileges and duties (Deut. 17:18–20; 1 Chr. 29:19). ***anointed him.*** Anointing was a sign and seal of the king's appointment by God (1 Sam. 16:3; 1 Kin. 1:39).

23:3 [v] 2Ki 11:17 [w] 2Sa 7:12; 1Ki 2:4; 2Ch 6:16; 7:18; 21:7 **23:6** [x] 1Ch 23:28-29; Zec 3:7 **23:8** [y] 2Ki 11:9 [z] 1Ch 24:1 **23:11** [a] Ex 25:16; Dt 17:18; 1Sa 10:24 **23:13** [b] 1Ki 1:41 [c] 1Ki 7:15 **23:15** [d] Ne 3:28; Jer 31:40 **23:16** [e] 2Ch 29:10; 34:31; Ne 9:38 **23:17** [f] Dt 13:6-9 **23:18** [g] 1Ch 23:28-32; 2Ch 5:5 [h] 1Ch 23:6; 25:6 **23:19** [i] 1Ch 9:22 **23:20** [j] 2Ki 15:35 **23:21** [k] 2Ch 22:1 **24:2** [l] 2Ch 25:2; 26:5 **24:5** [m] Ex 30:16; Ne 10:32-33; Mt 17:24 [n] 1Ch 11:1 [o] 1Ch 26:20 **24:6** [p] Ex 30:12-16; Nu 1:50

7 Now the sons of that wicked woman Athaliah had broken into the temple of God and had used even its sacred objects for the Baals.

8 At the king's command, a chest was made and placed outside, at the gate of the temple of the LORD. 9 A proclamation was then issued in Judah and Jerusalem that they should bring to the LORD the tax that Moses the servant of God had required of Israel in the wilderness. 10 All the officials and all the people brought their contributions gladly,[q] dropping them into the chest until it was full. 11 Whenever the chest was brought in by the Levites to the king's officials and they saw that there was a large amount of money, the royal secretary and the officer of the chief priest would come and empty the chest and carry it back to its place. They did this regularly and collected a great amount of money. 12 The king and Jehoiada gave it to those who carried out the work required for the temple of the LORD. They hired[r] masons and carpenters to restore the LORD's temple, and also workers in iron and bronze to repair the temple.

13 The men in charge of the work were diligent, and the repairs progressed under them. They rebuilt the temple of God according to its original design and reinforced it. 14 When they had finished, they brought the rest of the money to the king and Jehoiada, and with it were made articles for the LORD's temple: articles for the service and for the burnt offerings, and also dishes and other objects of gold and silver. As long as Jehoiada lived, burnt offerings were presented continually in the temple of the LORD.

15 Now Jehoiada was old and full of years, and he died at the age of a hundred and thirty. 16 He was buried with the kings in the City of David, because of the good he had done in Israel for God and his temple.

The Wickedness of Joash

17 After the death of Jehoiada, the officials of Judah came and paid homage to the king, and he listened to them. 18 They abandoned[s] the temple of the LORD, the God of their ancestors, and worshiped Asherah poles and idols.[t] Because of their guilt, God's anger[u] came on Judah and Jerusalem. 19 Although the LORD sent prophets to the people to bring them back to him, and though they testified against them, they would not listen.[v]

20 Then the Spirit[w] of God came on Zechariah[x] son of Jehoiada the priest. He stood before the people and said, "This is what God says: 'Why do you disobey the LORD's commands? You will not prosper.[y] Because you have forsaken the LORD, he has forsaken[z] you.' "

21 But they plotted against him, and by order of the king they stoned[a] him to death[b] in the courtyard of the LORD's temple.[c] 22 King Joash did not remember the kindness Zechariah's father Jehoiada had shown him but killed his son, who said as he lay dying, "May the LORD see this and call you to account."[d]

23 At the turn of the year,[a] the army of Aram marched against Joash; it invaded Judah and Jerusalem and killed all the leaders of the people.[e] They sent all the plunder to their king in Damascus. 24 Although the Aramean army had come with only a few men,[f] the LORD delivered into their hands a much larger army.[g] Because Judah had forsaken the LORD, the God of their ancestors, judgment was executed on Joash. 25 When the Arameans withdrew, they left Joash severely wounded. His officials conspired against him for murdering the son of Jehoiada the priest, and they killed him in his bed. So he died and was buried[h] in the City of David, but not in the tombs of the kings.

---

[a] *23* Probably in the spring

24:7 *sacred objects.* The sacred objects included gold, silver, and other valuables collected as tribute from defeated enemies and presented to God as spoils of war, acknowledging that the victory was His and for His purposes (2 Sam. 8:10 – 11).

24:14 *As long as Jehoiada lived.* All of Jehoiada's life, Judah enjoyed a revival of the true worship of God.

24:20 – 21 *Zechariah son of Jehoiada.* This priest is not the prophet of the same name who wrote the Book of Zechariah, nor is he the Zechariah mentioned by Jesus (Matt. 23:35). Zechariah, whose father rescued the young Joash, may even have been raised like a brother to King Joash. The "Zechariah son of Berekiah," that Jesus refers to was probably the prophet who wrote the Book of Zechariah (Zech. 1:7), although the reference to his death is found only in the Gospels.

24:22 Martyrs — Zechariah is one of the pre-Christian martyrs who gave his life for his faith in God. Some of these faithful ones are listed in Hebrews 11; some are known only to God. Jesus predicted that those killed for their faith would actually increase in the last days (Matt. 10:21; 24:9) and during the coming great tribulation, the ranks of the martyrs will swell to unprecedented size (Rev. 7:14). The "offense" of martyrs is their relationship with God; their comfort is that God knows, and He keeps them faithful to the end (2 Tim. 4:8).

24:24 *judgment was executed.* God arranged for Israel's defeat and Joash's death in fulfillment of Zechariah's dying cry for justice (v. 22). Judgment for evil does not always come so quickly, but it is just as inevitable, no matter how long it is delayed.

24:10 [q] Ex 25:2; 1Ch 29:3, 6, 9 **24:12** [r] 2Ch 34:11 **24:18** [s] ver 4; Jos 24:20; 2Ch 7:19 [t] Ex 34:13; 1Ki 14:23; 2Ch 33:3; Jer 17:2 [u] Jos 22:20; 2Ch 19:2 **24:19** [v] Nu 11:29; Jer 7:25; Zec 1:4 **24:20** [w] Jdg 3:10; 1Ch 12:18; 2Ch 20:14 [x] Mt 23:35; Lk 11:51 [y] Nu 14:41 [z] Dt 31:17; 2Ch 15:2 **24:21** [a] Jos 7:25; Ac 7:58-59 [b] Ne 9:26; Jer 26:21 [c] Jer 20:2; Mt 23:35 **24:22** [d] Ge 9:5 **24:23** [e] 2Ki 12:17-18 **24:24** [f] 2Ch 14:9; 16:8; 20:2, 12 [g] Lev 26:23-25; Dt 28:25 **24:25** [h] 2Ch 21:20

26Those who conspired against him
were Zabad,[a] son of Shimeath an Ammonite woman, and Jehozabad, son of Shim-
rith[b][i] a Moabite woman.[j] 27The account of
his sons, the many prophecies about him,
and the record of the restoration of the temple of God are written in the annotations
on the book of the kings. And Amaziah his
son succeeded him as king.

Amaziah King of Judah

25 Amaziah was twenty-five years
old when he became king, and he
reigned in Jerusalem twenty-nine years.
His mother's name was Jehoaddan; she
was from Jerusalem. 2He did what was
right in the eyes of the LORD, but not wholeheartedly.[k] 3After the kingdom was firmly in his control, he executed the officials
who had murdered his father the king. 4Yet
he did not put their children to death, but
acted in accordance with what is written
in the Law, in the Book of Moses,[l] where
the LORD commanded: "Parents shall not
be put to death for their children, nor children be put to death for their parents; each
will die for their own sin."[c][m]

5Amaziah called the people of Judah
together and assigned them according to
their families to commanders of thousands
and commanders of hundreds for all Judah
and Benjamin. He then mustered[n] those
twenty years old[o] or more and found that
there were three hundred thousand men
fit for military service,[p] able to handle the
spear and shield. 6He also hired a hundred
thousand fighting men from Israel for a
hundred talents[d] of silver.

7But a man of God came to him and said,
"Your Majesty, these troops from Israel[q]
must not march with you, for the LORD is
not with Israel—not with any of the people of Ephraim. 8Even if you go and fight
courageously in battle, God will overthrow
you before the enemy, for God has the power to help or to overthrow."[r]

9Amaziah asked the man of God, "But
what about the hundred talents I paid for
these Israelite troops?"

The man of God replied, "The LORD can
give you much more than that."[s]

10So Amaziah dismissed the troops who
had come to him from Ephraim and sent
them home. They were furious with Judah
and left for home in a great rage.[t]

11Amaziah then marshaled his strength
and led his army to the Valley of Salt,
where he killed ten thousand men of Seir.
12The army of Judah also captured ten
thousand men alive, took them to the top
of a cliff and threw them down so that all
were dashed to pieces.[u]

13Meanwhile the troops that Amaziah
had sent back and had not allowed to take
part in the war raided towns belonging to
Judah from Samaria to Beth Horon. They
killed three thousand people and carried
off great quantities of plunder.

14When Amaziah returned from slaughtering the Edomites, he brought back the
gods of the people of Seir. He set them up
as his own gods,[v] bowed down to them and
burned sacrifices to them. 15The anger of the
LORD burned against Amaziah, and he sent
a prophet to him, who said, "Why do you
consult this people's gods, which could not
save[w] their own people from your hand?"

16While he was still speaking, the king
said to him, "Have we appointed you an
adviser to the king? Stop! Why be struck
down?"

So the prophet stopped but said, "I know
that God has determined to destroy you,
because you have done this and have not
listened to my counsel."

17After Amaziah king of Judah consulted
his advisers, he sent this challenge to Jehoash[e] son of Jehoahaz, the son of Jehu, king
of Israel: "Come, let us face each other in
battle."

18But Jehoash king of Israel replied to
Amaziah king of Judah: "A thistle[x] in Lebanon sent a message to a cedar in Lebanon, 'Give your daughter to my son in marriage.' Then a wild beast in Lebanon came
along and trampled the thistle underfoot.
19You say to yourself that you have defeated Edom, and now you are arrogant and
proud. But stay at home! Why ask for trouble and cause your own downfall and that
of Judah also?"

---

[a] *26* A variant of *Jozabad* [b] *26* A variant of *Shomer* [c] *4* Deut. 24:16 [d] *6* That is, about 3 3/4 tons or about 3.4 metric tons; also in verse 9
[e] *17* Hebrew *Joash*, a variant of *Jehoash*; also in verses 18, 21, 23 and 25

25:7 *these troops from Israel must not march with you.* As long as Israel was in rebellion against God, He would not bless any alliance with them. ***Ephraim.*** Ephraim was the dominant tribe in Israel, so the whole kingdom was sometimes referred to as Ephraim (Hos. 4:15 – 19).

25:11 *Valley of Salt.* This valley was probably in the desert south of the Dead Sea. ***men of Seir.*** These people were Edomites, descendants of Esau.

25:18 *thistle ... cedar.* The thistle represents Amaziah, and the cedar, Joash. It was arrogant for the weak, insignificant Amaziah to suppose that he could defeat Joash. ***wild beast.*** The wild beast that tramples the bush represents the war that Amaziah was so eager to pursue.

25:19 Vanity—Those who reject God's counsel in favor of their own way are taking counsel against Him; their devisings are in vain and will come to nothing (Ps. 2:12). Refusing God's counsel, though seeking counsel from others, Amaziah decided to challenge the king of Israel to war (v. 17). It is hard to imagine how he thought he could succeed under such

24:26 [i] 2Ki 12:21 [j] Ru 1:4 **25:2** [k] ver 14; 1Ki 8:61; 2Ch 24:2 **25:4** [l] Dt 28:61 [m] Nu 26:11; Dt 24:16 **25:5** [n] 2Sa 24:2 [o] Ex 30:14 [p] Nu 1:3; 1Ch 21:1; 2Ch 17:14-19 **25:7** [q] 2Ch 16:2-9; 19:1-3 **25:8** [r] 2Ch 14:11; 20:6 **25:9** [s] Dt 8:18; Pr 10:22 **25:10** [t] ver 13 **25:12** [u] Ps 141:6; Ob 1:3 **25:14** [v] Ex 20:3; 2Ch 28:23; Isa 44:15 **25:15** [w] Ps 96:5; Isa 36:20 **25:18** [x] Jdg 9:8-15

20 Amaziah, however, would not listen,
for God so worked that he might deliver
them into the hands of Jehoash, because
they sought the gods of Edom.[y] 21 So Jehoash king of Israel attacked. He and Amaziah king of Judah faced each other at Beth
Shemesh in Judah. 22 Judah was routed by
Israel, and every man fled to his home.
23 Jehoash king of Israel captured Amaziah
king of Judah, the son of Joash, the son of
Ahaziah,[a] at Beth Shemesh. Then Jehoash
brought him to Jerusalem and broke down
the wall of Jerusalem from the Ephraim
Gate[z] to the Corner Gate[a]—a section about
four hundred cubits[b] long. 24 He took all the
gold and silver and all the articles found in
the temple of God that had been in the care
of Obed-Edom,[b] together with the palace
treasures and the hostages, and returned
to Samaria.
25 Amaziah son of Joash king of Judah
lived for fifteen years after the death of
Jehoash son of Jehoahaz king of Israel.
26 As for the other events of Amaziah's
reign, from beginning to end, are they not
written in the book of the kings of Judah
and Israel? 27 From the time that Amaziah
turned away from following the LORD, they
conspired against him in Jerusalem and
he fled to Lachish[c], but they sent men after
him to Lachish and killed him there. 28 He
was brought back by horse and was buried with his ancestors in the City of Judah.[c]

Uzziah King of Judah

26 Then all the people of Judah[d] took
Uzziah,[d] who was sixteen years old,
and made him king in place of his father
Amaziah. 2 He was the one who rebuilt
Elath and restored it to Judah after Amaziah rested with his ancestors.
3 Uzziah was sixteen years old when he
became king, and he reigned in Jerusalem
fifty-two years. His mother's name was
Jekoliah; she was from Jerusalem. 4 He
did what was right in the eyes of the LORD,
just as his father Amaziah had done. 5 He
sought God during the days of Zechariah,
who instructed him in the fear[e] of God.[e] As
long as he sought the LORD, God gave him
success.[f]
6 He went to war against the Philistines[g]
and broke down the walls of Gath, Jabneh
and Ashdod.[h] He then rebuilt towns near
Ashdod and elsewhere among the Philistines. 7 God helped him against the Philistines and against the Arabs[i] who lived in
Gur Baal and against the Meunites.[j] 8 The
Ammonites[k] brought tribute to Uzziah, and
his fame spread as far as the border of Egypt,
because he had become very powerful.
9 Uzziah built towers in Jerusalem at
the Corner Gate,[l] at the Valley Gate[m] and
at the angle of the wall, and he fortified
them. 10 He also built towers in the wilderness and dug many cisterns, because he
had much livestock in the foothills and in
the plain. He had people working his fields
and vineyards in the hills and in the fertile
lands, for he loved the soil.
11 Uzziah had a well-trained army, ready
to go out by divisions according to their
numbers as mustered by Jeiel the secretary
and Maaseiah the officer under the direction of Hananiah, one of the royal officials.
12 The total number of family leaders over
the fighting men was 2,600. 13 Under their
command was an army of 307,500 men
trained for war, a powerful force to support the king against his enemies. 14 Uzziah provided shields, spears, helmets, coats
of armor, bows and slingstones for the entire army.[n] 15 In Jerusalem he made devices
invented for use on the towers and on the
corner defenses so that soldiers could shoot
arrows and hurl large stones from the walls.
His fame spread far and wide, for he was
greatly helped until he became powerful.
16 But after Uzziah became powerful,
his pride[o] led to his downfall.[p] He was unfaithful[q] to the LORD his God, and entered
the temple of the LORD to burn incense[r] on
the altar of incense. 17 Azariah[s] the priest
with eighty other courageous priests of the
LORD followed him in. 18 They confronted
King Uzziah and said, "It is not right for
you, Uzziah, to burn incense to the LORD.
That is for the priests,[t] the descendants[u]
of Aaron,[v] who have been consecrated to
burn incense.[w] Leave the sanctuary, for
you have been unfaithful; and you will not
be honored by the LORD God."

[a] *23* Hebrew *Jehoahaz,* a variant of *Ahaziah*
[b] *23* That is, about 600 feet or about 180 meters
[c] *28* Most Hebrew manuscripts; some Hebrew manuscripts, Septuagint, Vulgate and Syriac (see also 2 Kings 14:20) *David*
[d] *1* Also called *Azariah*
[e] *5* Many Hebrew manuscripts, Septuagint and Syriac; other Hebrew manuscripts *vision*

circumstances. One of the delusions that goes with rejection of God is a false confidence in ones' own powers of understanding.

25:27 ***Lachish.*** The fact that Amaziah reached the city of Lachish on the border with Philistia, some 25 miles from Jerusalem, suggests that he may have been seeking sanctuary among the Philistines.

26:2 ***Elath.*** On the eastern arm of the Red Sea, Elath was technically in Edomite territory (8:17), but it was regularly under Israel or Judah throughout Old Testament times (21:8–10).

26:15 ***devices.*** This is one of the earliest references to catapults, which seem to have been defensive weapons, since their users were on the towers and in the corners.

25:20 [y] 1Ki 12:15; 2Ch 10:15; 22:7 **25:23** [z] 2Ki 14:13; Ne 8:16; 12:39 [a] 2Ch 26:9; Jer 31:38 **25:24** [b] 1Ch 26:15 **25:27** [c] Jos 10:3 **26:1** [d] 2Ch 22:1 **26:5** [e] 2Ch 15:2; 24:2; Da 1:17 [f] 2Ch 27:6 **26:6** [g] Isa 2:6; 11:14; 14:29; Jer 25:20 [h] Am 1:8; 3:9 **26:7** [i] 2Ch 21:16 [j] 2Ch 20:1 **26:8** [k] Ge 19:38; 2Ch 17:11 **26:9** [l] 2Ki 14:13; 2Ch 25:23 [m] Ne 2:13; 3:13 **26:14** [n] Jer 46:4 **26:16** [o] 2Ki 14:10 [p] Dt 32:15; 2Ch 25:19 [q] 1Ch 5:25 [r] 2Ki 16:12 **26:17** [s] 1Ki 4:2; 1Ch 6:10 **26:18** [t] Nu 16:39 [u] Nu 18:1-7 [v] Ex 30:7 [w] 1Ch 6:49

19 Uzziah, who had a censer in his hand
ready to burn incense, became angry.
While he was raging at the priests in their
presence before the incense altar in the
LORD's temple, leprosy[a][x] broke out on his
forehead. 20 When Azariah the chief priest
and all the other priests looked at him, they
saw that he had leprosy on his forehead, so
they hurried him out. Indeed, he himself
was eager to leave, because the LORD had
afflicted him.
21 King Uzziah had leprosy until the day
he died. He lived in a separate house[b][y]—
leprous, and banned from the temple of
the LORD. Jotham his son had charge of the
palace and governed the people of the land.
22 The other events of Uzziah's reign,
from beginning to end, are recorded by
the prophet Isaiah[z] son of Amoz. 23 Uzziah[a]
rested with his ancestors and was buried
near them in a cemetery that belonged to
the kings, for people said, "He had leprosy." And Jotham his son succeeded him as
king.[b]

Jotham King of Judah

27 Jotham[c] was twenty-five years
old when he became king, and he
reigned in Jerusalem sixteen years. His
mother's name was Jerusha daughter of
Zadok. 2 He did what was right in the eyes
of the LORD, just as his father Uzziah had
done, but unlike him he did not enter the
temple of the LORD. The people, however,
continued their corrupt practices. 3 Jotham
rebuilt the Upper Gate of the temple of the
LORD and did extensive work on the wall
at the hill of Ophel.[d] 4 He built towns in the
hill country of Judah and forts and towers
in the wooded areas.
5 Jotham waged war against the king
of the Ammonites[e] and conquered them.
That year the Ammonites paid him a hundred talents[c] of silver, ten thousand cors[d]
of wheat and ten thousand cors[e] of barley.
The Ammonites brought him the same
amount also in the second and third years.
6 Jotham grew powerful[f] because he
walked steadfastly before the LORD his
God.
7 The other events in Jotham's reign, including all his wars and the other things
he did, are written in the book of the kings
of Israel and Judah. 8 He was twenty-five
years old when he became king, and he
reigned in Jerusalem sixteen years. 9 Jotham rested with his ancestors and was
buried in the City of David. And Ahaz his
son succeeded him as king.

Ahaz King of Judah

28 Ahaz[g] was twenty years old when
he became king, and he reigned in
Jerusalem sixteen years. Unlike David his
father, he did not do what was right in the
eyes of the LORD. 2 He followed the ways of
the kings of Israel and also made idols[h] for
worshiping the Baals. 3 He burned sacrifices in the Valley of Ben Hinnom[i] and sacrificed his children[j] in the fire, engaging in
the detestable[k] practices of the nations the
LORD had driven out before the Israelites.
4 He offered sacrifices and burned incense
at the high places, on the hilltops and under every spreading tree.
5 Therefore the LORD his God delivered

---

[a] *19* The Hebrew for *leprosy* was used for various diseases affecting the skin; also in verses 20, 21 and 23. [b] *21* Or *in a house where he was relieved of responsibilities* [c] *5* That is, about 3 3/4 tons or about 3.4 metric tons [d] *5* That is, probably about 1,800 tons or about 1,600 metric tons of wheat [e] *5* That is, probably about 1,500 tons or about 1,350 metric tons of barley

---

26:19 *leprosy.* Leprosy was any kind of serious skin condition (Lev. 13:1—14:32). Today the term "leprosy" refers technically only to Hansen's disease. The Law viewed leprosy as a breach of God's own holiness; it was a graphic symbol of defilement.

26:22 *Isaiah.* Isaiah the prophet witnessed the last years of Uzziah, but very little about Uzziah is included in the Book of Isaiah. The books of Kings and Chronicles frequently refer to further details written about the kings, but they were not part of the Scripture, so we know very little about these records.

27:1 *sixteen years.* Jotham's sixteen years began eleven years before Uzziah died. This suggests that Uzziah had leprosy for more than a decade before he died.

27:3 *Upper Gate.* This gate connected the temple and the royal palace. ***wall at the hill of Ophel.*** Ophel was the original Jebusite area of Jerusalem. Its walls dated back hundreds of years and must have required regular maintenance.

27:6 Truth—In the face of deep moral corruption among his people, Jotham set his course to act on God's truth. There is always blessing in obedience, even if the blessing is not the sort that the rest of the world can see.

28:1 did not do what was right in the eyes of the LORD. During Ahaz's reign Isaiah and Micah prophesied in Judah, and Hosea prophesied in Israel.

28:3 *Valley of Ben Hinnom.* This valley was just outside the western wall of Jerusalem. It was a dumping ground for all kinds of refuse, much of which was burned. The valley itself became a symbol of impurity. It was used as a site of pagan worship, including human sacrifice (2 Kin. 23:10; Jer. 7:31–32; 19:2–6; 32:35). ***detestable practices of the nations.*** Worshipers of the Ammonite god Molek practiced human and child sacrifice (Lev. 18:21; 20:2–5; Deut. 12:31).

28:4 *every spreading tree.* Canaanite nature cults focused on evergreens, probably as symbols of perpetual fertility (see note for 14:3).

26:19 [x] Nu 12:10; 2Ki 5:25-27 **26:21** [y] Ex 4:6; Lev 13:46; 14:8; Nu 5:2; 19:12 **26:22** [z] 2Ki 15:1; Isa 1:1; 6:1 **26:23** [a] Isa 1:1; 6:1 [b] 2Ki 14:21; 15:7; Am 1:1 **27:1** [c] 2Ki 15:5,32; 1Ch 3:12 **27:3** [d] 2Ch 33:14; Ne 3:26 **27:5** [e] Ge 19:38 **27:6** [f] 2Ch 26:5 **28:1** [g] 1Ch 3:13; Isa 1:1 **28:2** [h] Ex 34:17; 2Ch 22:3 **28:3** [i] Jos 15:8; 2Ki 23:10 [j] Lev 18:21; 2Ki 3:27; 2Ch 33:6; Eze 20:26 [k] Dt 18:9; 2Ch 33:2

him into the hands of the king of Aram.[l]
The Arameans defeated him and took
many of his people as prisoners and
brought them to Damascus.
He was also given into the hands of the
king of Israel, who inflicted heavy casualties on him. 6 In one day Pekah[m] son of
Remaliah killed a hundred and twenty
thousand soldiers in Judah[n]—because
Judah had forsaken the LORD, the God of
their ancestors. 7 Zikri, an Ephraimite warrior, killed Maaseiah the king's son, Azrikam the officer in charge of the palace, and
Elkanah, second to the king. 8 The men of
Israel took captive from their fellow Israelites who were from Judah[o] two hundred
thousand wives, sons and daughters. They
also took a great deal of plunder, which
they carried back to Samaria.[p]
9 But a prophet of the LORD named Oded
was there, and he went out to meet the
army when it returned to Samaria. He
said to them, "Because the LORD, the God
of your ancestors, was angry[q] with Judah,
he gave them into your hand. But you have
slaughtered them in a rage that reaches to
heaven.[r] 10 And now you intend to make the
men and women of Judah and Jerusalem
your slaves.[s] But aren't you also guilty of
sins against the LORD your God? 11 Now listen to me! Send back your fellow Israelites
you have taken as prisoners, for the LORD's
fierce anger rests on you.[t]"
12 Then some of the leaders in Ephraim—Azariah son of Jehohanan, Berekiah son of Meshillemoth, Jehizkiah son of
Shallum, and Amasa son of Hadlai—confronted those who were arriving from the
war. 13 "You must not bring those prisoners
here," they said, "or we will be guilty before the LORD. Do you intend to add to our
sin and guilt? For our guilt is already great,
and his fierce anger rests on Israel."
14 So the soldiers gave up the prisoners
and plunder in the presence of the officials
and all the assembly. 15 The men designated
by name took the prisoners, and from the
plunder they clothed all who were naked.
They provided them with clothes and sandals, food and drink,[u] and healing balm.
All those who were weak they put on donkeys. So they took them back to their fellow
Israelites at Jericho, the City of Palms,[v] and
returned to Samaria.
16 At that time King Ahaz sent to the
kings[a] of Assyria[w] for help. 17 The Edomites[x] had again come and attacked Judah
and carried away prisoners,[y] 18 while the
Philistines[z] had raided towns in the foothills and in the Negev of Judah. They
captured and occupied Beth Shemesh, Aijalon[a] and Gederoth, as well as Soko, Timnah and Gimzo, with their surrounding
villages. 19 The LORD had humbled Judah
because of Ahaz king of Israel,[b] for he had
promoted wickedness in Judah and had
been most unfaithful[b] to the LORD. 20 Tiglath-Pileser[c][c] king of Assyria came to him,
but he gave him trouble instead of help.[d]
21 Ahaz took some of the things from the
temple of the LORD and from the royal palace and from the officials and presented
them to the king of Assyria, but that did
not help him.
22 In his time of trouble King Ahaz became even more unfaithful[e] to the LORD.
23 He offered sacrifices to the gods[f] of

a *16* Most Hebrew manuscripts; one Hebrew manuscript, Septuagint and Vulgate (see also 2 Kings 16:7) *king* *b* *19* That is, Judah, as frequently in 2 Chronicles *c* *20* Hebrew *Tilgath-Pilneser*, a variant of *Tiglath-Pileser*

28:6 *Pekah.* Pekah, who assassinated Pekahiah son of Menahem so that he could become king of Israel (2 Kin. 15:23–27), reigned for 20 years. He was murdered in a plot headed by Hoshea, the last king of Israel. ***because Judah had forsaken the LORD.*** Pekah was not offended by Judah's godlessness and did not himself initiate this purge. God used Pekah to carry out His judgment.
28:9 *Oded.* The prophet Oded is mentioned only here. ***slaughtered them in a rage.*** God used the Israelite armies to carry out His judgment on Judah (v. 6), but He never intended for the Israelites to enjoy it.
28:13 *our guilt is already great.* Within ten years the Assyrians would capture Samaria and deport all of the Israelites, treating them far more cruelly than they were treating the Judeans. The Israelites brought this judgment on themselves not only by this incident, but by the whole course of the history of their unfaithfulness to God.
28:16 *kings of Assyria.* The kings of Assyria were Tiglath-Pileser III, Shalamaneser V, and Sargon II.
28:18 *Beth Shemesh ... Gimzo.* All these places were near valleys that led up to central Judah from the surrounding plains. Control of them meant control of Judah itself. Because Ahaz understood this, he appealed to Assyria.
28:20 *Tiglath-Pileser.* Tiglath-Pileser brought the Mesopotamian influence over the countries of the eastern Mediterranean to its highest point. He undertook a campaign against Arpad in Syria and terrorized Menahem of Israel so much that Menahem paid him a huge bribe to be left alone (2 Kin. 15:19). Tiglath returned to the west again, and Ahaz scrambled for protection against Syria and Israel (2 Kin. 16:5–7; Is. 7:1–2). The Assyrians overran Damascus and replaced the assassinated Pekah of Israel with Hoshea (2 Kin. 15:30), but they did not assist Ahaz. The king of Judah's troubles with the Edomites, Philistines, Arameans, and even the Israelites (Is. 7:1) were over for the time being, but at great cost.
28:23 Unbelief—Looking to the gods of his enemies, foolishly believing that the gods had aided his

28:5 [l] Isa 7:1 **28:6** [m] 2Ki 15:25,27 [n] ver 8; Isa 9:21; 11:13
28:8 [o] Dt 28:25-41; 2Ch 11:4 [p] 2Ch 29:9
28:9 [q] 2Ch 25:15; Isa 10:6; 47:6; Zec 1:15 [r] Ezr 9:6; Rev 18:5
28:10 [s] Lev 25:39-46 **28:11** [t] 2Ch 11:4; Jas 2:13
28:15 [u] 2Ki 6:22; Pr 25:21-22 [v] Dt 34:3; Jdg 1:16
28:16 [w] 2Ki 16:7 **28:17** [x] Ps 137:7; Isa 34:5 [y] 2Ch 29:9
28:18 [z] Eze 16:27,57 [a] Jos 10:12 **28:19** [b] 2Ch 21:2
28:20 [c] 2Ki 15:29; 1Ch 5:6 [d] 2Ki 16:7 **28:22** [e] Jer 5:3
28:23 [f] 2Ch 25:14

Damascus, who had defeated him; for he
thought, "Since the gods of the kings of
Aram have helped them, I will sacrifice to
them so they will help me."[g] But they were
his downfall and the downfall of all Israel.
24Ahaz gathered together the furnishings from the temple of God[h] and cut them
in pieces. He shut the doors[i] of the LORD's
temple and set up altars[j] at every street
corner in Jerusalem. 25In every town in Judah he built high places to burn sacrifices
to other gods and aroused the anger of the
LORD, the God of his ancestors.
26The other events of his reign and all his
ways, from beginning to end, are written in
the book of the kings of Judah and Israel.
27Ahaz rested[k] with his ancestors and was
buried[l] in the city of Jerusalem, but he was
not placed in the tombs of the kings of Israel. And Hezekiah his son succeeded him
as king.

Hezekiah Purifies the Temple

29 Hezekiah[m] was twenty-five years
old when he became king, and he
reigned in Jerusalem twenty-nine years.
His mother's name was Abijah daughter of
Zechariah. 2He did what was right in the
eyes of the LORD, just as his father David[n]
had done.
3In the first month of the first year of his
reign, he opened the doors of the temple of
the LORD and repaired[o] them. 4He brought
in the priests and the Levites, assembled
them in the square on the east side 5and
said: "Listen to me, Levites! Consecrate[p]
yourselves now and consecrate the temple of the LORD, the God of your ancestors.
Remove all defilement from the sanctuary.
6Our parents[q] were unfaithful;[r] they did
evil in the eyes of the LORD our God and
forsook him. They turned their faces away
from the LORD's dwelling place and turned
their backs on him. 7They also shut the
doors of the portico and put out the lamps.
They did not burn incense or present any
burnt offerings at the sanctuary to the God
of Israel. 8Therefore, the anger of the LORD
has fallen on Judah and Jerusalem; he has
made them an object of dread and horror[s]
and scorn,[t] as you can see with your own
eyes. 9This is why our fathers have fallen
by the sword and why our sons and daughters and our wives are in captivity.[u] 10Now I
intend to make a covenant[v] with the LORD,
the God of Israel, so that his fierce anger
will turn away from us. 11My sons, do not
be negligent now, for the LORD has chosen
you to stand before him and serve him,[w] to
minister[x] before him and to burn incense."
12Then these Levites[y] set to work:
from the Kohathites,
Mahath son of Amasai and Joel son of Azariah;
from the Merarites,
Kish son of Abdi and Azariah son of Jehallelel;
from the Gershonites,
Joah son of Zimmah and Eden[z] son of Joah;
13from the descendants of Elizaphan,
Shimri and Jeiel;
from the descendants of Asaph,[a]
Zechariah and Mattaniah;
14from the descendants of Heman,
Jehiel and Shimei;
from the descendants of Jeduthun,
Shemaiah and Uzziel.
15When they had assembled their fellow
Levites and consecrated themselves, they
went in to purify[b] the temple of the LORD, as
the king had ordered, following the word of
the LORD. 16The priests went into the sanctuary of the LORD to purify it. They brought
out to the courtyard of the LORD's temple
everything unclean that they found in the
temple of the LORD. The Levites took it and
carried it out to the Kidron Valley.[c] 17They
began the consecration on the first day of
the first month, and by the eighth day of
the month they reached the portico of the
LORD. For eight more days they consecrated the temple of the LORD itself, finishing
on the sixteenth day of the first month.
18Then they went in to King Hezekiah
and reported: "We have purified the entire
temple of the LORD, the altar of burnt offering with all its utensils, and the table for
setting out the consecrated bread, with all
its articles. 19We have prepared and consecrated all the articles[d] that King Ahaz removed in his unfaithfulness while he was
king. They are now in front of the LORD's
altar."

---

enemies in their victory, Ahaz went farther from God into unbelief. Ahaz committed two grievous sins. He ascribed to another source what was God's doing, and he placed his faith in what was imagined, to bring success to himself. There is never a time when God is out of control. Even if things do not turn out the way we wish they would, we can be sure that if we keep our minds and attitudes in line with God's ways, we will eventually see these events from His perspective.

29:9 *in captivity.* Under the wicked leadership of Ahaz, many of the people of Judah had been taken captive by Rezin of Damascus and Pekah of Israel (28:5–8).

29:12 *Kohathites ... Merarites ... Gershonites.* Hezekiah summoned the leaders of the three major Levitical clans, two leaders from each clan.

28:23 [g] Jer 44:17-18 **28:24** [h] 2Ki 16:18 [i] 2Ch 29:7 [j] 2Ch 30:14 **28:27** [k] Isa 14:28-32 [l] 2Ch 21:20; 24:25 **29:1** [m] 1Ch 3:13 **29:2** [n] 2Ch 28:1; 34:2 **29:3** [o] 2Ch 28:24 **29:5** [p] 2Ch 35:6 **29:6** [q] Ps 106:6-47; Jer 2:27 [r] 1Ch 5:25; Eze 8:16 **29:8** [s] Dt 28:25; 2Ch 24:18 [t] Jer 18:16; 19:8; 25:9, 18 **29:9** [u] 2Ch 28:5-8, 17 **29:10** [v] 2Ch 15:12; 23:16 **29:11** [w] Nu 3:6; 8:6, 14 [x] 1Ch 15:2 **29:12** [y] Nu 3:17-20 [z] 2Ch 31:15 **29:13** [a] 1Ch 6:39 **29:15** [b] ver 5; 1Ch 23:28; 2Ch 30:12 **29:16** [c] 2Sa 15:23 **29:19** [d] 2Ch 28:24

20 Early the next morning King Hezekiah gathered the city officials together and went up to the temple of the LORD. 21 They brought seven bulls, seven rams, seven male lambs and seven male goats as a sin offering[a][e] for the kingdom, for the sanctuary and for Judah. The king commanded the priests, the descendants of Aaron, to offer these on the altar of the LORD. 22 So they slaughtered the bulls, and the priests took the blood and splashed it against the altar; next they slaughtered the rams and splashed their blood against the altar; then they slaughtered the lambs and splashed their blood[f] against the altar. 23 The goats for the sin offering were brought before the king and the assembly, and they laid their hands[g] on them. 24 The priests then slaughtered the goats and presented their blood on the altar for a sin offering to atone[h] for all Israel, because the king had ordered the burnt offering and the sin offering for all Israel.

25 He stationed the Levites in the temple of the LORD with cymbals, harps and lyres in the way prescribed by David[i] and Gad[j] the king's seer and Nathan the prophet; this was commanded by the LORD through his prophets. 26 So the Levites stood ready with David's instruments,[k] and the priests with their trumpets.[l]

27 Hezekiah gave the order to sacrifice the burnt offering on the altar. As the offering began, singing to the LORD began also, accompanied by trumpets and the instruments[m] of David king of Israel. 28 The whole assembly bowed in worship, while the musicians played and the trumpets sounded. All this continued until the sacrifice of the burnt offering was completed.

29 When the offerings were finished, the king and everyone present with him knelt down and worshiped.[n] 30 King Hezekiah and his officials ordered the Levites to praise the LORD with the words of David and of Asaph the seer. So they sang praises with gladness and bowed down and worshiped.

31 Then Hezekiah said, "You have now dedicated yourselves to the LORD. Come and bring sacrifices[o] and thank offerings to the temple of the LORD." So the assembly brought sacrifices and thank offerings, and all whose hearts were willing[p] brought burnt offerings.

32 The number of burnt offerings the assembly brought was seventy bulls, a hundred rams and two hundred male lambs—all of them for burnt offerings to the LORD. 33 The animals consecrated as sacrifices amounted to six hundred bulls and three thousand sheep and goats. 34 The priests, however, were too few to skin all the burnt offerings;[q] so their relatives the Levites helped them until the task was finished and until other priests had been consecrated,[r] for the Levites had been more conscientious in consecrating themselves than the priests had been. 35 There were burnt offerings in abundance, together with the fat[s] of the fellowship offerings[t] and the drink offerings[u] that accompanied the burnt offerings.

So the service of the temple of the LORD was reestablished. 36 Hezekiah and all the people rejoiced at what God had brought about for his people, because it was done so quickly.

Hezekiah Celebrates the Passover

30 Hezekiah sent word to all Israel and Judah and also wrote letters to Ephraim and Manasseh,[v] inviting them to come to the temple of the LORD in Jerusalem and celebrate the Passover[w] to the LORD, the God of Israel. 2 The king and his officials and the whole assembly in Jerusalem decided to celebrate[x] the Passover in the second month. 3 They had not been able to celebrate it at the regular time because not enough priests had consecrated[y] themselves and the people had not assembled in Jerusalem. 4 The plan seemed right both to

[a] 21 Or *purification offering*; also in verses 23 and 24

29:21 ***bulls . . . rams . . . lambs . . . goats.*** The law required the sacrifice of these animals for atonement of sin in general (Lev. 1:3 – 13). On the other hand, the sacrifice of goats atoned for specific sins (Lev. 4:1 — 5:13). Here the priests offered seven of each kind to signify the wholeness of their repentance.

29:24 ***all Israel.*** The repetition of "all Israel" here suggests that Hezekiah meant to include all twelve tribes, including the northern kingdom (30:1 – 9).

29:30 ***the words of David and of Asaph.*** This refers to the psalms of David and Asaph (1 Chr. 6:39; 15:17; 16:5; 25:1), many of them in the Book of Psalms. The people of Judah used these psalms for community worship and private meditation.

29:31 ***thank offerings.*** Sometimes called "peace" or "fellowship" offerings, thank offerings celebrated the relationship gained by the offerings of atonement (Lev. 3:1 – 17; 7:11 – 36). The thank offerings included people and priests in a great banquet together, all in fellowship with God.

29:34 ***priests . . . were too few.*** Under Ahaz the priests and Levites had been stripped of their duties. Now, 20 years later, there were not enough priests.

30:1 ***sent word to all Israel.*** Though the kingdom of Israel had split more than two centuries before, Hezekiah never lost sight of the fact that God's covenant was made with all twelve tribes and that His promises included them all (Ezek. 37:15 – 28).

29:21 [e] Lev 4:13-14 **29:22** [f] Lev 4:18 **29:23** [g] Lev 4:15 **29:24** [h] Ex 29:36; Lev 4:26 **29:25** [i] 1Ch 25:6; 2Ch 8:14 [j] 1Sa 22:5; 2Sa 24:11 **29:26** [k] 1Ch 15:16 [l] 1Ch 15:24; 23:5; 2Ch 5:12 **29:27** [m] 2Ch 23:18 **29:29** [n] 2Ch 20:18 **29:31** [o] Heb 13:15-16 [p] Ex 25:2; 35:22 **29:34** [q] 2Ch 35:11 [r] 2Ch 30:3, 15 **29:35** [s] Ex 29:13; Lev 3:16 [t] Lev 7:11-21 [u] Nu 15:5-10 **30:1** [v] Ge 41:52 [w] Ex 12:11; Nu 28:16 **30:2** [x] Nu 9:10 **30:3** [y] 2Ch 29:34

the king and to the whole assembly. 5They
decided to send a proclamation throughout
Israel, from Beersheba to Dan,[z] calling the
people to come to Jerusalem and celebrate
the Passover to the LORD, the God of Israel.
It had not been celebrated in large numbers
according to what was written.
6At the king's command, couriers went
throughout Israel and Judah with letters
from the king and from his officials, which
read:

"People of Israel, return to the LORD,
the God of Abraham, Isaac and Israel, that he may return to you who are
left, who have escaped from the hand
of the kings of Assyria. 7Do not be like
your parents[a] and your fellow Israelites, who were unfaithful to the LORD,
the God of their ancestors, so that he
made them an object of horror,[b] as you
see. 8Do not be stiff-necked,[c] as your
ancestors were; submit to the LORD.
Come to his sanctuary, which he has
consecrated forever. Serve the LORD
your God, so that his fierce anger[d] will
turn away from you. 9If you return[e]
to the LORD, then your fellow Israelites and your children will be shown
compassion[f] by their captors and will
return to this land, for the LORD your
God is gracious and compassionate.[g]
He will not turn his face from you if
you return to him."

10The couriers went from town to town
in Ephraim and Manasseh, as far as Zebulun, but people scorned and ridiculed[h]
them. 11Nevertheless, some from Asher,
Manasseh and Zebulun humbled themselves and went to Jerusalem.[i] 12Also in
Judah the hand of God was on the people to
give them unity[j] of mind to carry out what
the king and his officials had ordered, following the word of the LORD.
13A very large crowd of people assembled in Jerusalem to celebrate the Festival
of Unleavened Bread[k] in the second month.
14They removed the altars[l] in Jerusalem
and cleared away the incense altars and
threw them into the Kidron Valley.[m]
15They slaughtered the Passover lamb
on the fourteenth day of the second month.
The priests and the Levites were ashamed
and consecrated[n] themselves and brought
burnt offerings to the temple of the LORD.
16Then they took up their regular positions[o] as prescribed in the Law of Moses the man of God. The priests splashed
against the altar the blood handed to them
by the Levites. 17Since many in the crowd
had not consecrated themselves, the Levites had to kill[p] the Passover lambs for all
those who were not ceremonially clean and
could not consecrate their lambs[a] to the
LORD. 18Although most of the many people
who came from Ephraim, Manasseh, Issachar and Zebulun had not purified themselves,[q] yet they ate the Passover, contrary
to what was written. But Hezekiah prayed
for them, saying, "May the LORD, who is
good, pardon everyone 19who sets their
heart on seeking God—the LORD, the God
of their ancestors—even if they are not
clean according to the rules of the sanctuary." 20And the LORD heard[r] Hezekiah and
healed[s] the people.[t]
21The Israelites who were present in
Jerusalem celebrated the Festival of Unleavened Bread[u] for seven days with great
rejoicing, while the Levites and priests
praised the LORD every day with resounding instruments dedicated to the LORD.[b]
22Hezekiah spoke encouragingly to all
the Levites, who showed good understanding of the service of the LORD. For the seven
days they ate their assigned portion and offered fellowship offerings and praised[c] the
LORD, the God of their ancestors.
23The whole assembly then agreed to
celebrate[v] the festival seven more days;
so for another seven days they celebrated
joyfully. 24Hezekiah king of Judah provided[w] a thousand bulls and seven thousand
sheep and goats for the assembly, and the
officials provided them with a thousand

[a] 17 Or *consecrate themselves* [b] 21 Or *priests sang to the LORD every day, accompanied by the LORD's instruments of praise* [c] 22 Or *and confessed their sins to*

30:8 *Come to his sanctuary.* People who were not priests were not allowed to enter the temple. This phrase is a figure of speech for serving the Lord.
30:9 *If you return to the LORD.* Hezekiah was referring to the covenant (Deut. 28–30) which promised that obedience would lead to blessing in the land, and disobedience would result in exile.
30:10 *as far as Zebulun.* Zebulun was probably the northernmost territory of Israel at this time because Naphtali had been taken by Tiglath-Pileser III (2 Kin. 15:29).
30:17 *Levites had to kill.* Traditionally the slaughter of the Passover lamb was performed by the head of the family (Ex. 12:3–6). But on this occasion many were not ritually purified, and the Levites acted on their behalf.
30:22 *who showed good understanding.* The Levites' ministry included teaching (17:8–10). The people of Israel had had virtually no consistent teaching of God's revelation for 200 years, apart from the witness of the prophets such as Elijah, Elisha, Hosea, and Amos.

30:5 [z] Jdg 20:1 **30:7** [a] Ps 78:8, 57; 106:6; Eze 20:18 [b] 2Ch 29:8 **30:8** [c] Ex 32:9 [d] Nu 25:4; 2Ch 29:10 **30:9** [e] Dt 30:2-5; Isa 1:16; 55:7 [f] 1Ki 8:50; Ps 106:46 [g] Ex 34:6-7; Dt 4:31; Mic 7:18 **30:10** [h] 2Ch 36:16 **30:11** [i] ver 25 **30:12** [j] Jer 32:39; Eze 11:19; Php 2:13 **30:13** [k] Nu 28:16 **30:14** [l] 2Ch 28:24 [m] 2Sa 15:23 **30:15** [n] 2Ch 29:34 **30:16** [o] 2Ch 35:10 **30:17** [p] 2Ch 29:34 **30:18** [q] Ex 12:43-49; Nu 9:6-10 **30:20** [r] 2Ch 6:20 [s] 2Ch 7:14; Mal 4:2 [t] Jas 5:16 **30:21** [u] Ex 12:15, 17; 13:6 **30:23** [v] 1Ki 8:65; 2Ch 7:9 **30:24** [w] 1Ki 8:5; 2Ch 29:34; 35:7; Ezr 6:17; 8:35

bulls and ten thousand sheep and goats. A great number of priests consecrated themselves. 25 The entire assembly of Judah rejoiced, along with the priests and Levites and all who had assembled from Israel[x], including the foreigners who had come from Israel and also those who resided in Judah. 26 There was great joy in Jerusalem, for since the days of Solomon[y] son of David king of Israel there had been nothing like this in Jerusalem. 27 The priests and the Levites stood to bless[z] the people, and God heard them, for their prayer reached heaven, his holy dwelling place.

31 When all this had ended, the Israelites who were there went out to the towns of Judah, smashed the sacred stones and cut down[a] the Asherah poles. They destroyed the high places and the altars throughout Judah and Benjamin and in Ephraim and Manasseh. After they had destroyed all of them, the Israelites returned to their own towns and to their own property.

Contributions for Worship

2 Hezekiah[b] assigned the priests and Levites to divisions[c]—each of them according to their duties as priests or Levites—to offer burnt offerings and fellowship offerings, to minister,[d] to give thanks and to sing praises[e] at the gates of the LORD's dwelling.[f] 3 The king contributed[g] from his own possessions for the morning and evening burnt offerings and for the burnt offerings on the Sabbaths, at the New Moons and at the appointed festivals as written in the Law of the LORD.[h] 4 He ordered the people living in Jerusalem to give the portion[i] due the priests and Levites so they could devote themselves to the Law of the LORD. 5 As soon as the order went out, the Israelites generously gave the firstfruits[j] of their grain, new wine,[k] olive oil and honey and all that the fields produced. They brought a great amount, a tithe of everything. 6 The people of Israel and Judah who lived in the towns of Judah also brought a tithe[l] of their herds and flocks and a tithe of the holy things dedicated to the LORD their God, and they piled them in heaps.[m] 7 They began doing this in the third month and finished in the seventh month.[n] 8 When Hezekiah and his officials came and saw the heaps, they praised the LORD and blessed[o] his people Israel.

9 Hezekiah asked the priests and Levites about the heaps; 10 and Azariah the chief priest, from the family of Zadok,[p] answered, "Since the people began to bring their contributions to the temple of the LORD, we have had enough to eat and plenty to spare, because the LORD has blessed his people, and this great amount is left over."[q]

11 Hezekiah gave orders to prepare storerooms in the temple of the LORD, and this was done. 12 Then they faithfully brought in the contributions, tithes and dedicated gifts. Konaniah,[r] a Levite, was the overseer in charge of these things, and his brother Shimei was next in rank. 13 Jehiel, Azaziah, Nahath, Asahel, Jerimoth, Jozabad,[s] Eliel, Ismakiah, Mahath and Benaiah were assistants of Konaniah and Shimei his brother. All these served by appointment of King Hezekiah and Azariah the official in charge of the temple of God.

14 Kore son of Imnah the Levite, keeper of the East Gate, was in charge of the freewill offerings given to God, distributing the contributions made to the LORD and also the consecrated gifts. 15 Eden,[t] Miniamin, Jeshua, Shemaiah, Amariah and Shekaniah assisted him faithfully in the towns[u] of the priests, distributing to their fellow priests according to their divisions, old and young alike.

30:25 *foreigners.* The strangers were aliens who lived in Israel and Judah and who could come to the festivals because they adhered to God and the Law (Deut. 16:11; 26:11; 29:11; 31:12).

30:26 Heaven—Solomon asked God to hear the prayers of the people as they directed their prayers toward the temple in Jerusalem, and to respond from His dwelling in heaven (2 Chr. 6:21). The people, nearly 200 years after Solomon made this prayer, sought the Lord, and He heard them. There is great joy among the people when they realize that God hears them from heaven, and there is great joy in heaven when one sinner repents (Luke 15:7).

31:2 *Hezekiah assigned.* The long interruption (28:24) of Judah's official worship in the time of Ahaz brought chaos to their religious life. David had originally organized the Levitical system, but because of the years of neglect, Hezekiah had to reorganize it.

31:3 *New Moons.* The new moon celebrations came at the appearance of the new moon, the beginning of another month (Num. 28:11–15). ***appointed festivals.*** The fixed festivals were the Passover and Festival of Unleavened Bread (Lev. 23:4–8); Festival of Weeks or Pentecost (Lev. 23:15–22); and the Festival of Tabernacles (Lev. 23:33–43).

31:5 *firstfruits.* The early harvests of grain, particularly barley, were being reaped at this time. The Passover had been held a month late (30:2) and it was now the third month. The first fruits began appearing at the time of the late Passover, and the harvests were fully gathered in some 50 days later, at the time of Pentecost (Lev. 23:9–22). ***a tithe.*** A tenth of the harvest belonged to the Levites (Num. 18:21–24).

30:25 [x] ver 11 **30:26** [y] 2Ch 7:8 **30:27** [z] Ex 39:43; Nu 6:23; Dt 26:15; 2Ch 23:18; Ps 68:5 **31:1** [a] 2Ki 18:4; 2Ch 32:12; Isa 36:7 **31:2** [b] 2Ch 29:9 [c] 1Ch 24:1 [d] 1Ch 15:2 [e] Ps 7:17; 9:2; 47:6; 71:22 [f] 1Ch 23:28-32 **31:3** [g] 1Ch 29:3; 2Ch 35:7; Eze 45:17 [h] Nu 28:1-29:40 **31:4** [i] Nu 18:8; Dt 18:8; Ne 13:10; Mal 2:7 **31:5** [j] Nu 18:12, 24; Ne 13:12; Eze 44:30 [k] Dt 12:17 **31:6** [l] Lev 27:30; Ne 13:10-12 [m] Dt 14:28; Ru 3:7 **31:7** [n] Ex 23:16 **31:8** [o] Ps 144:13-15 **31:10** [p] 2Sa 8:17 [q] Ex 36:5; Eze 44:30; Mal 3:10-12 **31:12** [r] 2Ch 35:9 **31:13** [s] 2Ch 35:9 **31:15** [t] 2Ch 29:12 [u] Jos 21:9-19

16 In addition, they distributed to the males three years old or more whose names were in the genealogical records[v]—all who would enter the temple of the LORD to perform the daily duties of their various tasks, according to their responsibilities and their divisions. 17 And they distributed to the priests enrolled by their families in the genealogical records and likewise to the Levites twenty years old or more, according to their responsibilities and their divisions. 18 They included all the little ones, the wives, and the sons and daughters of the whole community listed in these genealogical records. For they were faithful in consecrating themselves.

19 As for the priests, the descendants of Aaron, who lived on the farmlands around their towns or in any other towns,[w] men were designated by name to distribute portions to every male among them and to all who were recorded in the genealogies of the Levites.

20 This is what Hezekiah did throughout Judah, doing what was good and right and faithful[x] before the LORD his God. 21 In everything that he undertook in the service of God's temple and in obedience to the law and the commands, he sought his God and worked wholeheartedly. And so he prospered.[y]

Sennacherib Threatens Jerusalem

32 After all that Hezekiah had so faithfully done, Sennacherib[z] king of Assyria came and invaded Judah. He laid siege to the fortified cities, thinking to conquer them for himself. 2 When Hezekiah saw that Sennacherib had come and that he intended to wage war against Jerusalem,[a] 3 he consulted with his officials and military staff about blocking off the water from the springs outside the city, and they helped him. 4 They gathered a large group of people who blocked all the springs[b] and the stream that flowed through the land. "Why should the kings[a] of Assyria come and find plenty of water?" they said. 5 Then he worked hard repairing all the broken sections of the wall[c] and building towers on it. He built another wall outside that one and reinforced the terraces[b][d] of the City of David. He also made large numbers of weapons[e] and shields.

6 He appointed military officers over the people and assembled them before him in the square at the city gate and encouraged them with these words: 7 "Be strong and courageous.[f] Do not be afraid or discouraged[g] because of the king of Assyria and the vast army with him, for there is a greater power with us than with him.[h] 8 With him is only the arm of flesh,[i] but with us[j] is the LORD our God to help us and to fight our battles."[k] And the people gained confidence from what Hezekiah the king of Judah said.

9 Later, when Sennacherib king of Assyria and all his forces were laying siege to Lachish,[l] he sent his officers to Jerusalem with this message for Hezekiah king of Judah and for all the people of Judah who were there:

10 "This is what Sennacherib king of Assyria says: On what are you basing your confidence,[m] that you remain in Jerusalem under siege? 11 When Hezekiah says, 'The LORD our God will save us from the hand of the king of Assyria,' he is misleading[n] you, to let you die of hunger and thirst. 12 Did not Hezekiah himself remove this god's high places and altars, saying to Judah and Jerusalem, 'You must worship before one altar[o] and burn sacrifices on it'?

13 "Do you not know what I and my predecessors have done to all the peoples of the other lands? Were the gods of those nations ever able to deliver their land from my hand?[p] 14 Who of all the gods of these nations that my

---

a 4 Hebrew; Septuagint and Syriac *king*
b 5 Or *the Millo*

31:17 *genealogical records ... according to their responsibilities and their divisions.* All temple servants had to descend from Levi, but the priests had to trace their genealogy specifically to Aaron (1 Chr. 6:49 – 53).

32:1 *Sennacherib.* In Hezekiah's fourteenth year, Sennacherib invaded Judah and eventually laid siege to Jerusalem (2 Kin. 18:13 – 17). One of the most imperialistic of Assyria's kings, Sennacherib undertook many military campaigns to the west. In his own inscriptions he boasts of having taken many of Judah's cities, a claim supported by the parallel account in 2 Kings.

32:3 *blocking off the water.* Hezekiah managed to stop the water by concealing the springs outside the city and then digging a tunnel to bring them to the Pool of Siloam inside the city walls. Hezekiah hid the source of water and made it unavailable to the enemy (2 Kin. 20:20). The Siloam Inscription describes how workmen constructed the 1,800 foot tunnel connecting the springs of Gihon to the Pool of Siloam.

32:5 *reinforced the terraces.* This refers to extensive terracing that surrounded the ancient hills of Ophel and Mount Zion. The work of extending the hills of Jerusalem was first undertaken by David (1 Chr. 11:7 – 8) and continued by Solomon (1 Kin. 9:15).

32:9 *laying siege to Lachish.* Both the Old Testament and Assyrian inscriptions document the siege against Lachish, an important fortified city west of Jerusalem and near the great coastal route (11:9). Its capture by Assyria would cut off access to Jerusalem from the west and would give Assyria control of the coast.

31:16 [v] 1Ch 23:3; Ezr 3:4 **31:19** [w] ver 12-15; Lev 25:34; Nu 35:2-5 **31:20** [x] 2Ki 20:3; 22:2 **31:21** [y] Dt 29:9 **32:1** [z] 2Ki 18:13-19; Isa 36:1; 37:9, 17, 37 **32:2** [a] Isa 22:7; Jer 1:15 **32:4** [b] 2Ki 18:17; 20:20; Isa 22:9, 11; Na 3:14 **32:5** [c] 2Ch 25:23; Isa 22:10 [d] 1Ki 9:24; 1Ch 11:8 [e] Isa 22:8 **32:7** [f] Dt 31:6; 1Ch 22:13 [g] 2Ch 20:15 [h] Nu 14:9; 2Ki 6:16 **32:8** [i] Job 40:9; Isa 52:10; Jer 17:5; 32:21 [j] Dt 3:22; 1Sa 17:45; 2Ch 13:12 [k] 1Ch 5:22; 2Ch 20:17; Ps 20:7; Isa 28:6 **32:9** [l] Jos 10:3, 31 **32:10** [m] Eze 29:16 **32:11** [n] Isa 37:10 **32:12** [o] 2Ch 31:1 **32:13** [p] ver 15

predecessors destroyed has been able
to save his people from me? How then
can your god deliver you from my
hand? 15Now do not let Hezekiah deceive[q] you and mislead you like this.
Do not believe him, for no god of any
nation or kingdom has been able to deliver[r] his people from my hand or the
hand of my predecessors.[s] How much
less will your god deliver you from my
hand!"

16Sennacherib's officers spoke further
against the LORD God and against his
servant Hezekiah. 17The king also wrote
letters[t] ridiculing[u] the LORD, the God of Israel, and saying this against him: "Just as
the gods[v] of the peoples of the other lands
did not rescue their people from my hand,
so the god of Hezekiah will not rescue his
people from my hand." 18Then they called
out in Hebrew to the people of Jerusalem
who were on the wall, to terrify them and
make them afraid in order to capture the
city. 19They spoke about the God of Jerusalem as they did about the gods of the other
peoples of the world—the work of human
hands.[w]

20King Hezekiah and the prophet Isaiah
son of Amoz cried out in prayer to heaven
about this. 21And the LORD sent an angel,[x]
who annihilated all the fighting men and
the commanders and officers in the camp
of the Assyrian king. So he withdrew to his
own land in disgrace. And when he went
into the temple of his god, some of his sons,
his own flesh and blood, cut him down
with the sword.[y]

22So the LORD saved Hezekiah and the
people of Jerusalem from the hand of Sennacherib king of Assyria and from the
hand of all others. He took care of them[a]
on every side. 23Many brought offerings to
Jerusalem for the LORD and valuable gifts[z]
for Hezekiah king of Judah. From then on
he was highly regarded by all the nations.

Hezekiah's Pride, Success and Death

24In those days Hezekiah became ill and
was at the point of death. He prayed to the
LORD, who answered him and gave him a
miraculous sign. 25But Hezekiah's heart
was proud[a] and he did not respond to the
kindness shown him; therefore the LORD's
wrath[b] was on him and on Judah and Jerusalem. 26Then Hezekiah repented[c] of
the pride of his heart, as did the people of
Jerusalem; therefore the LORD's wrath did
not come on them during the days of Hezekiah.[d]

27Hezekiah had very great wealth and
honor,[e] and he made treasuries for his silver and gold and for his precious stones,
spices, shields and all kinds of valuables.
28He also made buildings to store the harvest of grain, new wine and olive oil; and
he made stalls for various kinds of cattle,
and pens for the flocks. 29He built villages
and acquired great numbers of flocks and
herds, for God had given him very great
riches.[f]

30It was Hezekiah who blocked[g] the upper outlet of the Gihon[h] spring and channeled the water down to the west side of the
City of David. He succeeded in everything
he undertook. 31But when envoys were sent
by the rulers of Babylon[i] to ask him about
the miraculous sign[j] that had occurred in
the land, God left him to test[k] him and to
know everything that was in his heart.

32The other events of Hezekiah's reign
and his acts of devotion are written in the
vision of the prophet Isaiah son of Amoz
in the book of the kings of Judah and Israel. 33Hezekiah rested with his ancestors
and was buried on the hill where the tombs
of David's descendants are. All Judah and
the people of Jerusalem honored him when
he died. And Manasseh his son succeeded
him as king.

Manasseh King of Judah

33 Manasseh[l] was twelve years old
when he became king, and he
reigned in Jerusalem fifty-five years. 2He
did evil in the eyes of the LORD,[m] following
the detestable[n] practices of the nations the
LORD had driven out before the Israelites.
3He rebuilt the high places his father Hez-

[a] 22 Hebrew; Septuagint and Vulgate *He gave them rest*

32:18 *in Hebrew.* Aramaic had become the language of international communication and diplomacy and there was no reason to continue the dialogue in Hebrew except to traumatize the people.
32:20 *the prophet Isaiah.* By now the prophet Isaiah had been involved in public ministry to the kings of Judah for nearly 40 years (26:22; Is. 6:1). He had considerable prestige and was especially important as a counselor of young Hezekiah (Is. 37:1–7).
32:25 *heart was proud.* Hezekiah had received Babylonian envoys who had come to congratulate him on his recovery, and probably to enlist his support in their struggle against Assyria (2 Kin. 20:12–19). Their visit ignited his desire to show off the treasures of his kingdom, and this treasure was eventually seized by the same Babylonians (2 Kin. 20:16–18; Is. 39:6–7).
32:31 *test.* This test was not for God's benefit, but for Hezekiah's.

32:15 [q] Isa 37:10 [r] Da 3:15 [s] Ex 5:2 **32:17** [t] Isa 37:14 [u] Ps 74:22; Isa 37:4, 17 [v] 2Ki 19:12 **32:19** [w] 2Ki 19:18; Ps 115:4-8; Isa 2:8; 17:8 **32:21** [x] Ge 19:13 [y] 2Ki 19:7 **32:23** [z] 2Ch 9:24; 17:5; Isa 45:14; Zec 14:16-17 **32:25** [a] 2Ki 14:10; 2Ch 26:16 [b] 2Ch 19:2; 24:18 **32:26** [c] Jer 26:18-19 [d] 2Ch 34:27,28; Isa 39:8 **32:27** [e] 1Ch 29:12 **32:29** [f] 1Ch 29:12 **32:30** [g] 2Ki 18:17 [h] 1Ki 1:33 **32:31** [i] Isa 39:1 [j] ver 24; Isa 38:7 [k] Ge 22:1; Dt 8:16 **33:1** [l] 1Ch 3:13 **33:2** [m] Jer 15:4 [n] Dt 18:9; 2Ch 28:3

ekiah had demolished; he also erected altars to the Baals and made Asherah poles.[o] He bowed down[p] to all the starry hosts and worshiped them. 4He built altars in the temple of the LORD, of which the LORD had said, "My Name[q] will remain in Jerusalem forever." 5In both courts of the temple of the LORD,[r] he built altars to all the starry hosts. 6He sacrificed his children[s] in the fire in the Valley of Ben Hinnom, practiced divination and witchcraft, sought omens, and consulted mediums[t] and spiritists.[u] He did much evil in the eyes of the LORD, arousing his anger.

7He took the image he had made and put it in God's temple,[v] of which God had said to David and to his son Solomon, "In this temple and in Jerusalem, which I have chosen out of all the tribes of Israel, I will put my Name forever. 8I will not again make the feet of the Israelites leave the land[w] I assigned to your ancestors, if only they will be careful to do everything I commanded them concerning all the laws, decrees and regulations given through Moses." 9But Manasseh led Judah and the people of Jerusalem astray, so that they did more evil than the nations the LORD had destroyed before the Israelites.[x]

10The LORD spoke to Manasseh and his people, but they paid no attention. 11So the LORD brought against them the army commanders of the king of Assyria, who took Manasseh prisoner,[y] put a hook in his nose, bound him with bronze shackles[z] and took him to Babylon. 12In his distress he sought the favor of the LORD his God and humbled[a] himself greatly before the God of his ancestors. 13And when he prayed to him, the LORD was moved by his entreaty and listened to his plea; so he brought him back to Jerusalem and to his kingdom. Then Manasseh knew that the LORD is God.

14Afterward he rebuilt the outer wall of the City of David, west of the Gihon[b] spring in the valley, as far as the entrance of the Fish Gate[c] and encircling the hill of Ophel;[d] he also made it much higher. He stationed military commanders in all the fortified cities in Judah.

15He got rid of the foreign gods and removed[e] the image from the temple of the LORD, as well as all the altars he had built on the temple hill and in Jerusalem; and he threw them out of the city. 16Then he restored the altar of the LORD and sacrificed fellowship offerings and thank offerings[f] on it, and told Judah to serve the LORD, the God of Israel. 17The people, however, continued to sacrifice at the high places, but only to the LORD their God.

18The other events of Manasseh's reign, including his prayer to his God and the words the seers spoke to him in the name of the LORD, the God of Israel, are written in the annals of the kings of Israel.[a] 19His prayer and how God was moved by his entreaty, as well as all his sins and unfaithfulness, and the sites where he built high places and set up Asherah poles and idols before he humbled[g] himself—all these are written in the records of the seers.[b][h] 20Manasseh rested with his ancestors and was buried[i] in his palace. And Amon his son succeeded him as king.

Amon King of Judah

21Amon[j] was twenty-two years old when he became king, and he reigned in

[a] *18* That is, Judah, as frequently in 2 Chronicles
[b] *19* One Hebrew manuscript and Septuagint; most Hebrew manuscripts *of Hozai*

33:4 *My name will remain in Jerusalem forever.* The point was that God had the exclusive right to inhabit the temple, as opposed to the deities Manasseh introduced (v. 5).

33:6 *sacrificed his children in the fire.* Like Ahaz, Manasseh practiced human sacrifice, going so far as to offer up his own children (28:3). ***practiced divination.*** Divination is an attempt to determine the plans and purposes of the gods so that one can avoid their hostility or take advantage of their favors (Is. 2:6; Jer. 27:9). ***witchcraft, sought omens.*** Witchcraft and seeking omens attempt to bring about desired results by employing magical or mystical rituals. ***mediums and spiritists.*** Mediums are those who claim to contact and consult with the dead. Spiritists are the "knowing ones" whose specialty is also communication with the dead in the hope of acquiring information inaccessible to the living. All such practices were common among Canaanite and other pagan religions and were to be strictly avoided by God's people (Deut. 13:1–6; 18:9–14).

33:11 *Babylon.* For some time Babylon had been part of the Assyrian Empire, though it had broken free on occasion, especially under the leadership of Marduk-Baladan, Hezekiah's contemporary (2 Kin. 20:12). Ashurbanipal brought Babylon back under Assyrian domination. He was the king who took Manasseh to Babylon as a prisoner.

33:14 *wall of the City of David.* The term "City of David" originally referred to Mount Zion alone (1 Chr. 11:5) but eventually designated the entire city, including Mount Ophel, the original Jebusite settlement. ***Gihon.*** Gihon was the spring that was the main source of water for Jerusalem. It was in the Kidron valley near the northeastern brow of Mount Zion. ***Fish Gate.*** The Fish Gate was in the center of the wall north of the temple. Manasseh's construction was a total distance of about 750 yards.

33:20 *buried in his palace.* Manasseh had truly converted (v. 13), but his prior sin had been so heinous that he was denied burial in the royal cemetery.

33:3 [o] Dt 16:21-22 [p] Dt 17:3; 2Ch 31:1 **33:4** [q] 2Ch 7:16 **33:5** [r] 2Ch 4:9 **33:6** [s] Lev 18:21; Dt 18:10; 2Ch 28:3 [t] Lev 19:31 [u] 1Sa 28:13 **33:7** [v] 2Ch 7:16 **33:8** [w] 2Sa 7:10 **33:9** [x] Jer 15:4 **33:11** [y] Dt 28:36 [z] Ps 149:8 **33:12** [a] 2Ch 6:37; 32:26; 1Pe 5:6 **33:14** [b] 1Ki 1:33 [c] Ne 3:3; 12:39; Zep 1:10 [d] 2Ch 27:3; Ne 3:26 **33:15** [e] ver 3-7; 2Ki 23:12 **33:16** [f] Lev 7:11-18 **33:19** [g] 2Ch 6:37 [h] 2Ki 21:17 **33:20** [i] 2Ki 21:18; 2Ch 21:20 **33:21** [j] 1Ch 3:14

Jerusalem two years. 22He did evil in the
eyes of the LORD, as his father Manasseh
had done. Amon worshiped and offered
sacrifices to all the idols Manasseh had
made. 23But unlike his father Manasseh, he
did not humble[k] himself before the LORD;
Amon increased his guilt.
24Amon's officials conspired against
him and assassinated him in his palace.
25Then the people[l] of the land killed all who
had plotted against King Amon, and they
made Josiah his son king in his place.

Josiah's Reforms

34 Josiah[m] was eight years old when
he became king,[n] and he reigned in
Jerusalem thirty-one years. 2He did what
was right in the eyes of the LORD and followed the ways of his father David,[o] not
turning aside to the right or to the left.
3In the eighth year of his reign, while
he was still young, he began to seek the
God[p] of his father David. In his twelfth
year he began to purge Judah and Jerusalem of high places, Asherah poles and
idols. 4Under his direction the altars of the
Baals were torn down; he cut to pieces the
incense altars that were above them, and
smashed the Asherah poles[q] and the idols.
These he broke to pieces and scattered over
the graves of those who had sacrificed to
them.[r] 5He burned[s] the bones of the priests
on their altars, and so he purged Judah
and Jerusalem. 6In the towns of Manasseh, Ephraim and Simeon, as far as Naphtali, and in the ruins around them, 7he tore
down the altars and the Asherah poles
and crushed the idols to powder[t] and cut
to pieces all the incense altars throughout
Israel. Then he went back to Jerusalem.
8In the eighteenth year of Josiah's reign,
to purify the land and the temple, he sent
Shaphan son of Azaliah and Maaseiah the
ruler of the city, with Joah son of Joahaz,
the recorder, to repair the temple of the
LORD his God.
9They went to Hilkiah[u] the high priest
and gave him the money that had been
brought into the temple of God, which the
Levites who were the gatekeepers had
collected from the people of Manasseh,
Ephraim and the entire remnant of Israel and from all the people of Judah and
Benjamin and the inhabitants of Jerusalem. 10Then they entrusted it to the men
appointed to supervise the work on the
LORD's temple. These men paid the workers who repaired and restored the temple.
11They also gave money[v] to the carpenters
and builders to purchase dressed stone,
and timber for joists and beams for the
buildings that the kings of Judah had allowed to fall into ruin.[w]
12The workers labored faithfully.[x] Over
them to direct them were Jahath and Obadiah, Levites descended from Merari, and
Zechariah and Meshullam, descended from
Kohath. The Levites—all who were skilled
in playing musical instruments—[y] 13had
charge of the laborers[z] and supervised all
the workers from job to job. Some of the
Levites were secretaries, scribes and gatekeepers.

The Book of the Law Found

14While they were bringing out the money that had been taken into the temple of
the LORD, Hilkiah the priest found the Book
of the Law of the LORD that had been given
through Moses. 15Hilkiah said to Shaphan
the secretary, "I have found the Book of the
Law[a] in the temple of the LORD." He gave it
to Shaphan.
16Then Shaphan took the book to the
king and reported to him: "Your officials
are doing everything that has been committed to them. 17They have paid out the
money that was in the temple of the LORD
and have entrusted it to the supervisors
and workers." 18Then Shaphan the secretary informed the king, "Hilkiah the priest
has given me a book." And Shaphan read
from it in the presence of the king.
19When the king heard the words of the
Law,[b] he tore[c] his robes. 20He gave these
orders to Hilkiah, Ahikam son of Shaphan[d], Abdon son of Micah,[a] Shaphan the
secretary and Asaiah the king's attendant:
21"Go and inquire of the LORD for me and
for the remnant in Israel and Judah about
what is written in this book that has been
found. Great is the LORD's anger that is
poured out[e] on us because those who have
gone before us have not kept the word of
the LORD; they have not acted in accordance with all that is written in this book."

[a] 20 Also called *Akbor son of Micaiah*

34:3 *Asherah poles.* See note for 14:3.

34:5 *burned the bones of the priests.* This act of Josiah, which took place at Bethel, fulfilled the words of the prophet of Judah in the days of Jeroboam I, king of Israel (1 Kin. 13:1–2; 2 Kin. 23:15–16). The prophet had mentioned Josiah by name three hundred years before.

34:8 *Shaphan.* Shaphan was a scribe or secretary of the king (v. 15). He was responsible for state records that must have included the original temple plans and specifications. The temple was repaired strictly according to its original pattern. ***Joah . . . the recorder.*** The recorder kept the royal diaries. Official happenings were duly noted and recorded for posterity. The work of men like Joah provided sources for later historians such as the author of Chronicles (1 Chr. 18:15).

33:23 [k] ver 12; Ex 10:3; 2Ch 7:14; Ps 18:27; 147:6; Pr 3:34
33:25 [l] 2Ch 22:1 **34:1** [m] 1Ch 3:14 [n] Zep 1:1
34:2 [o] 2Ch 29:2 **34:3** [p] 1Ki 13:2; 1Ch 16:11; 2Ch 15:2; 33:17,22 **34:4** [q] Ex 34:13 [r] Ex 32:20; Lev 26:30; 2Ki 23:11; Mic 1:5 **34:5** [s] 1Ki 13:2 **34:7** [t] Ex 32:20; 2Ch 31:1
34:9 [u] 1Ch 6:13; 2Ch 35:8 **34:11** [v] 2Ch 24:12 [w] 2Ch 33:4-7 **34:12** [x] 2Ki 12:15 [y] 1Ch 25:1
34:13 [z] 1Ch 23:4 **34:15** [a] 2Ki 22:8; Ezr 7:6; Ne 8:1
34:19 [b] Dt 28:3-68 [c] Jos 7:6; Isa 36:22; 37:1
34:20 [d] 2Ki 22:3 **34:21** [e] 2Ch 29:8; La 2:4; 4:11; Eze 36:18

22 Hilkiah and those the king had sent with him[a] went to speak to the prophet[f] Huldah, who was the wife of Shallum son of Tokhath,[b] the son of Hasrah,[c] keeper of the wardrobe. She lived in Jerusalem, in the New Quarter.

23 She said to them, "This is what the LORD, the God of Israel, says: Tell the man who sent you to me, 24 'This is what the LORD says: I am going to bring disaster[g] on this place and its people[h]—all the curses[i] written in the book that has been read in the presence of the king of Judah. 25 Because they have forsaken me[j] and burned incense to other gods and aroused my anger by all that their hands have made,[d] my anger will be poured out on this place and will not be quenched.' 26 Tell the king of Judah, who sent you to inquire of the LORD, 'This is what the LORD, the God of Israel, says concerning the words you heard: 27 Because your heart was responsive[k] and you humbled[l] yourself before God when you heard what he spoke against this place and its people, and because you humbled yourself before me and tore your robes and wept in my presence, I have heard you, declares the LORD. 28 Now I will gather you to your ancestors,[m] and you will be buried in peace. Your eyes will not see all the disaster I am going to bring on this place and on those who live here.'"[n]

So they took her answer back to the king.

29 Then the king called together all the elders of Judah and Jerusalem. 30 He went up to the temple of the LORD[o] with the people of Judah, the inhabitants of Jerusalem, the priests and the Levites—all the people from the least to the greatest. He read in their hearing all the words of the Book of the Covenant, which had been found in the temple of the LORD. 31 The king stood by his pillar[p] and renewed the covenant[q] in the presence of the LORD—to follow[r] the LORD and keep his commands, statutes and decrees with all his heart and all his soul, and to obey the words of the covenant written in this book.

32 Then he had everyone in Jerusalem and Benjamin pledge themselves to it; the people of Jerusalem did this in accordance with the covenant of God, the God of their ancestors.

33 Josiah removed all the detestable[s] idols from all the territory belonging to the Israelites, and he had all who were present in Israel serve the LORD their God. As long as he lived, they did not fail to follow the LORD, the God of their ancestors.

Josiah Celebrates the Passover

35 Josiah celebrated the Passover[t] to the LORD in Jerusalem, and the Passover lamb was slaughtered on the fourteenth day of the first month. 2 He appointed the priests to their duties and encouraged them in the service of the LORD's temple. 3 He said to the Levites, who instructed[u] all Israel and who had been consecrated to the LORD: "Put the sacred ark in the temple that Solomon son of David king of Israel built. It is not to be carried about on your shoulders. Now serve the LORD your God and his people Israel. 4 Prepare yourselves by families in your divisions,[v] according to the instructions written by David king of Israel and by his son Solomon.

5 "Stand in the holy place with a group of Levites for each subdivision of the families of your fellow Israelites, the lay people. 6 Slaughter the Passover lambs, consecrate yourselves[w] and prepare the lambs for your fellow Israelites, doing what the LORD commanded through Moses."

---

[a] 22 One Hebrew manuscript, Vulgate and Syriac; most Hebrew manuscripts do not have *had sent with him.* [b] 22 Also called *Tikvah* [c] 22 Also called *Harhas* [d] 25 Or *by everything they have done*

34:22 *the prophet Huldah.* Huldah is one of four female prophets named in the Old Testament. The other three are Miriam (Ex. 15:20), Deborah (Judg. 4:4), and Noadiah (Neh. 6:14).

34:24 *all the curses written in the book.* Both Deuteronomy and Leviticus had long lists of blessings for obedience and curses for rebellion, which were part of the conditions attached to the covenant with Israel (Deut. 28–30).

34:25 Apostasy—In all of life, no greater sin, no more serious or sadder error could be made than to forsake God and believe other gods. Such an act cuts one off from all of the loving care, the wisdom and discipline of the Creator God. Apostasy grieves God, and it grieves those who love God.

34:31 *the covenant ... to follow the LORD.* Very few of the kings of Judah promised to follow the Lord as Josiah did. After David, only Joash, Hezekiah, and Josiah made such public commitments (23:3; 29:10; 1 Chr. 17:7–14).

35:3 *Put the sacred ark in the temple ... It is not to be carried about on your shoulders.* The ark had apparently been removed from the temple. Who removed it and when or why is not known, but plenty of wicked kings could have done it. Manasseh's vehement opposition to God must have kept the ark in constant jeopardy, so perhaps it had been removed for protection. The only proper way to carry the ark was on the shoulders of the priests (Num. 4:5; 6:1).

35:6 *Slaughter the Passover lambs.* The Levites were standing in for the people in the sacrifice of the Passover lambs. This became the tradition from that time on, with the result that the priests gained influence and power.

34:22 [f] Ex 15:20; Ne 6:14 **34:24** [g] Pr 16:4; Isa 3:9; Jer 40:2; 42:10; 44:2, 11 [h] 2Ch 36:14-20 [i] Dt 28:15-68 **34:25** [j] 2Ch 33:3-6; Jer 22:9 **34:27** [k] 2Ch 12:7; 32:26 [l] Ex 10:3; 2Ch 6:37 **34:28** [m] 2Ch 35:20-25 [n] 2Ch 32:26 **34:30** [o] 2Ki 23:2; Ne 8:1-3 **34:31** [p] 1Ki 7:15; 2Ki 11:14 [q] 2Ki 11:17; 2Ch 23:16; 29:10 [r] Dt 13:4 **34:33** [s] ver 3-7; Dt 18:9 **35:1** [t] Ex 12:1-30; Nu 9:3; 28:16 **35:3** [u] Dt 33:10; 1Ch 23:26; 2Ch 5:7; 17:7 **35:4** [v] ver 10; 1Ch 9:10-13; 24:1; 2Ch 8:14; Ezr 6:18 **35:6** [w] Lev 11:44; 2Ch 29:5, 15

7 Josiah provided for all the lay people who were there a total of thirty thousand lambs and goats for the Passover offerings,[x] and also three thousand cattle—all from the king's own possessions.[y]

8 His officials also contributed[z] voluntarily to the people and the priests and Levites. Hilkiah,[a] Zechariah and Jehiel, the officials in charge of God's temple, gave the priests twenty-six hundred Passover offerings and three hundred cattle. 9 Also Konaniah[b] along with Shemaiah and Nethanel, his brothers, and Hashabiah, Jeiel and Jozabad,[c] the leaders of the Levites, provided five thousand Passover offerings and five hundred head of cattle for the Levites.

10 The service was arranged and the priests stood in their places with the Levites in their divisions[d] as the king had ordered.[e] 11 The Passover lambs were slaughtered,[f] and the priests splashed against the altar the blood handed to them, while the Levites skinned the animals. 12 They set aside the burnt offerings to give them to the subdivisions of the families of the people to offer to the LORD, as it is written in the Book of Moses. They did the same with the cattle. 13 They roasted the Passover animals over the fire as prescribed,[g] and boiled the holy offerings in pots, caldrons and pans and served them quickly to all the people. 14 After this, they made preparations for themselves and for the priests, because the priests, the descendants of Aaron, were sacrificing the burnt offerings and the fat portions[h] until nightfall. So the Levites made preparations for themselves and for the Aaronic priests.

15 The musicians,[i] the descendants of Asaph, were in the places prescribed by David, Asaph, Heman and Jeduthun the king's seer. The gatekeepers at each gate did not need to leave their posts, because their fellow Levites made the preparations for them.

16 So at that time the entire service of the LORD was carried out for the celebration of the Passover and the offering of burnt offerings on the altar of the LORD, as King Josiah had ordered. 17 The Israelites who were present celebrated the Passover at that time and observed the Festival of Unleavened Bread for seven days. 18 The Passover had not been observed like this in Israel since the days of the prophet Samuel; and none of the kings of Israel had ever celebrated such a Passover as did Josiah, with the priests, the Levites and all Judah and Israel who were there with the people of Jerusalem. 19 This Passover was celebrated in the eighteenth year of Josiah's reign.

The Death of Josiah

20 After all this, when Josiah had set the temple in order, Necho king of Egypt went up to fight at Carchemish[j] on the Euphrates,[k] and Josiah marched out to meet him in battle. 21 But Necho sent messengers to him, saying, "What quarrel is there, king of Judah, between you and me? It is not you I am attacking at this time, but the house with which I am at war. God has told[l] me to hurry; so stop opposing God, who is with me, or he will destroy you."

22 Josiah, however, would not turn away from him, but disguised[m] himself to engage him in battle. He would not listen to what Necho had said at God's command but went to fight him on the plain of Megiddo.

23 Archers[n] shot King Josiah, and he told his officers, "Take me away; I am badly wounded." 24 So they took him out of his chariot, put him in his other chariot and brought him to Jerusalem, where he died. He was buried in the tombs of his ancestors, and all Judah and Jerusalem mourned for him.

25 Jeremiah composed laments for Josiah, and to this day all the male and female singers commemorate Josiah in the laments.[o] These became a tradition in Israel and are written in the Laments.

35:13 *holy offerings.* The other holy offerings, distinguished from the Passover offering, were the cattle slaughtered for thank, or peace offerings (v. 7).

35:18 *since the days of the prophet Samuel.* It had been almost four hundred years since the days of Samuel.

35:20 *to fight at Carchemish.* Carchemish was one of the last strongholds of Assyria to resist the onslaught of the rising neo-Babylonian kingdom. The Babylonians and Medes were on their way to subdue Haran and Carchemish. Necho, more afraid of the Babylonians than the Assyrians, was hoping to get to Carchemish in time to assist his Assyrian allies in their time of need. Josiah was an ally of Babylon, so he went to Megiddo to intercept the Egyptians.

35:21 *God has told me.* God sometimes spoke to pagan rulers about a course of action He wanted them to take (36:22; Gen. 20:6; 41:25; Dan. 2:28). Necho did not know the source of his divine leading, but God did direct him, displaying His sovereignty over even the wicked and unbelieving powers of this world (Is. 44:28–45).

35:22 *Megiddo.* The major route from Egypt to the upper Euphrates was the Via Maris, or Way of the Sea. This route went up the coast of Israel before turning inland through the mountain pass at Megiddo. It crossed the plain of Jezreel, crossed the Jordan near the Sea of Galilee, and went on through Damascus where it joined the north-south route to upper Syria. If Josiah could control the pass at Megiddo, he could control the movement of traffic on that vital route.

35:7 [x] 2Ch 30:24 [y] 2Ch 31:3 **35:8** [z] 1Ch 29:3; 2Ch 29:31-36 [a] 1Ch 6:13 **35:9** [b] 2Ch 31:12 [c] 2Ch 31:13 **35:10** [d] ver 4; Ezr 6:18 [e] 2Ch 30:16 **35:11** [f] 2Ch 29:22, 34; 30:17 **35:13** [g] Ex 12:2-11; Lev 6:25; 1Sa 2:13-15 **35:14** [h] Ex 29:13 **35:15** [i] 1Ch 25:1; 26:12-19; 2Ch 29:30; Ne 12:46; Ps 68:25 **35:20** [j] Isa 10:9; Jer 46:2 [k] Ge 2:14 **35:21** [l] 1Ki 13:18; 2Ki 18:25 **35:22** [m] Jdg 5:19; 1Sa 28:8; 2Ch 18:29 **35:23** [n] 1Ki 22:34 **35:25** [o] Jer 22:10, 15-16

26The other events of Josiah's reign and
his acts of devotion in accordance with
what is written in the Law of the LORD—
27all the events, from beginning to end, are
written in the book of the kings of Israel
36 and Judah. 1And the people of the
land took Jehoahaz son of Josiah
and made him king in Jerusalem in place
of his father.

Jehoahaz King of Judah

2Jehoahaz[a] was twenty-three years old
when he became king, and he reigned
in Jerusalem three months. 3The king
of Egypt dethroned him in Jerusalem and imposed on Judah a levy of a
hundred talents[b] of silver and a talent[c] of
gold. 4The king of Egypt made Eliakim, a
brother of Jehoahaz, king over Judah and
Jerusalem and changed Eliakim's name
to Jehoiakim. But Necho[p] took Eliakim's
brother Jehoahaz and carried him off to
Egypt.

Jehoiakim King of Judah

5Jehoiakim[q] was twenty-five years old
when he became king, and he reigned in
Jerusalem eleven years. He did evil in the
eyes of the LORD his God. 6Nebuchadnez-
zar[r] king of Babylon attacked him and
bound him with bronze shackles to take
him to Babylon.[s] 7Nebuchadnezzar also
took to Babylon articles from the temple
of the LORD and put them in his temple[d]
there.[t]
8The other events of Jehoiakim's reign,
the detestable things he did and all that
was found against him, are written in
the book of the kings of Israel and Judah.
And Jehoiachin his son succeeded him as
king.

Jehoiachin King of Judah

9Jehoiachin[u] was eighteen[e] years old
when he became king, and he reigned in
Jerusalem three months and ten days. He
did evil in the eyes of the LORD. 10In the
spring, King Nebuchadnezzar sent for
him and brought him to Babylon,[v] together with articles of value from the temple of
the LORD, and he made Jehoiachin's uncle,[f]
Zedekiah, king over Judah and Jerusalem.

Zedekiah King of Judah

11Zedekiah[w] was twenty-one years old
when he became king, and he reigned in
Jerusalem eleven years. 12He did evil in the
eyes of the LORD[x] his God and did not humble[y] himself before Jeremiah the prophet,
who spoke the word of the LORD. 13He also
rebelled against King Nebuchadnezzar,
who had made him take an oath[z] in God's
name. He became stiff-necked[a] and hardened his heart and would not turn to the
LORD, the God of Israel. 14Furthermore, all
the leaders of the priests and the people became more and more unfaithful,[b] following
all the detestable practices of the nations
and defiling the temple of the LORD, which
he had consecrated in Jerusalem.

The Fall of Jerusalem

15The LORD, the God of their ancestors,
sent word to them through his messengers[c]
again and again,[d] because he had pity on

[a] 2 Hebrew *Joahaz*, a variant of *Jehoahaz*; also in verse 4 [b] 3 That is, about 3 3/4 tons or about 3.4 metric tons [c] 3 That is, about 75 pounds or about 34 kilograms [d] 7 Or *palace* [e] 9 One Hebrew manuscript, some Septuagint manuscripts and Syriac (see also 2 Kings 24:8); most Hebrew manuscripts *eight* [f] 10 Hebrew *brother*, that is, relative (see 2 Kings 24:17)

36:3 *king of Egypt.* After Assyria's defeat at Harran and Carchemish, the Egyptian army withdrew south of the Euphrates, dominating Syria and Judah. Judah became an Egyptian vassal state, which explains why Necho could depose Jehoahaz and require tribute.

36:6 *Nebuchadnezzar.* Nebuchadnezzar was leading a campaign against Carchemish when he succeeded his father. He drove Egypt out of Syria and Judah and took some Jewish captives, including Daniel, back to Babylon (Dan. 1:1). At the same time, Jehoiakim changed his loyalty from Necho to Nebuchadnezzar and remained a trusted vassal for three years. (2 Kin. 24:1). But then Jehoiakim rebelled against Babylon, and in about 602 B.C. Nebuchadnezzar returned to Jerusalem to punish him. ***to take him to Babylon.*** Jehoiakim was not actually taken to Babylon since he reigned until 598 B.C. and died of natural causes in Jerusalem (Jer. 22:18).

36:7 *took ... articles from the temple of the LORD.* The Babylonian king looted the temple of much of its treasure, fulfilling the prophecy made to Hezekiah a century earlier (32:31). ***his temple.*** His temple was the temple of the Babylonians' patron god Marduk.

36:10 *Zedekiah.* Zedekiah was the youngest of the four sons of Josiah, and the third to rule over Judah (v. 1). He became king by Nebuchadnezzar's appointment, showing Judah's status as a Babylonian vassal (v. 3).

36:12 *Jeremiah.* Jeremiah was the famous prophet who composed the Book of Jeremiah, which included his words to Zedekiah (Jer. 21:3–7; 32:5).

36:14 *all the detestable practices of the nations.* This statement refers primarily to idolatry and all the immorality and perversity that went with it. God's covenant with Israel required them to be different from the nations in this key respect (Ex. 23:24; Lev. 26:1; Deut. 4:15–20,25–28; 18:9–14; 27:14–15).

36:4 [p] Jer 22:10-12 **36:5** [q] Jer 22:18; 26:1; 35:1
36:6 [r] Jer 25:9; 27:6; Eze 29:18 [s] 2Ch 33:11; Eze 19:9; Da 1:1
36:7 [t] 2Ki 24:13; Ezr 1:7; Da 1:2 **36:9** [u] Jer 22:24-28; 52:31
36:10 [v] ver 18; 2Ki 20:17; Ezr 1:7; Jer 22:25; 24:1; 29:1; 37:1; Eze 17:12 **36:11** [w] 2Ki 24:17; Jer 27:1; 28:1
36:12 [x] Jer 37:1-39:18 [y] Dt 8:3; 2Ch 7:14; 33:23; Jer 21:3-7
36:13 [z] Eze 17:13 [a] 2Ki 17:14; 2Ch 30:8 **36:14** [b] 1Ch 5:25
36:15 [c] Isa 5:4; 44:26; Jer 7:25; Hag 1:13; Zec 1:4; Mal 2:7; 3:1 [d] Jer 7:13,25; 25:3-4; 35:14,15; 44:4-6

his people and on his dwelling place. 16But
they mocked God's messengers, despised
his words and scoffed[e] at his prophets until
the wrath[f] of the LORD was aroused against
his people and there was no remedy.[g] 17He
brought up against them the king of the
Babylonians,[a] who killed their young men
with the sword in the sanctuary, and did
not spare young men[h] or young women,
the elderly or the infirm. God gave them
all into the hands of Nebuchadnezzar.[i] 18He
carried to Babylon all the articles[j] from
the temple of God, both large and small,
and the treasures of the LORD's temple and
the treasures of the king and his officials.
19They set fire[k] to God's temple[l] and broke
down the wall[m] of Jerusalem; they burned
all the palaces and destroyed[n] everything
of value there.[o]

20He carried into exile[p] to Babylon the
remnant, who escaped from the sword, and
they became servants[q] to him and his successors until the kingdom of Persia came
to power. 21The land enjoyed its sabbath
rests;[r] all the time of its desolation it rested,[s] until the seventy years[t] were completed in fulfillment of the word of the LORD
spoken by Jeremiah.

22In the first year of Cyrus[u] king of Persia, in order to fulfill the word of the LORD
spoken by Jeremiah, the LORD moved the
heart of Cyrus king of Persia to make a
proclamation throughout his realm and
also to put it in writing:

23"This is what Cyrus king of Persia
says:

> "'The LORD, the God of heaven, has given me all the kingdoms of the earth and he has appointed[v] me to build a temple for him at Jerusalem in Judah. Any of his people among you may go up, and may the LORD their God be with them.'"

[a] 17 Or *Chaldeans*

36:16 Unbelief—There is a line of divine patience that a nation can cross, bringing doom upon that country. In 586 B.C. Judah stepped over that mark. Prior to this God had graciously given His people many opportunities to repent of their unbelief. When we earnestly pray for our country as commanded by God (1 Tim. 2:1–2) we are asking to be kept from overstepping the limit of God's patience. About three thousand years ago, Solomon succinctly said, "Righteousness exalts a nation, but sin condemns any people" (Prov. 14:34).

36:17 king of the Babylonians. The Babylonian king, Nebuchadnezzar, reigned from 605 to 562 B.C. He became an instrument of God's judgment all through Judah's last years and well into the Exile (Dan. 2:37–38; 5:18–19).

36:20 until the kingdom of Persia. Cyrus conquered Babylon in 539 B.C. and allowed the Jews to return to Jerusalem the following year.

36:21 sabbath. According to the Law of Moses, the land was to lie fallow every seventh year (Lev. 25:4). Judah's exile in Babylon allowed the land to enjoy the sabbaths it had missed because of disobedience (Lev. 26:33–35). ***Jeremiah.*** In two places (Jer. 25:12; 29:10) Jeremiah predicted the Exile and its length (Dan. 9:2).

36:22 the first year of Cyrus. The first year refers to the first year of Cyrus' rule over Babylon, not his first year over Media and Persia. He began to rule Media and Persia in 550 B.C. Twelve years later he brought Babylon under his control and issued his famous decree, known from the Old Testament (Ezra 1:2–4) and from his own records, the Cylinder of Cyrus. Jeremiah's seventy years were from about 609 to 539 B.C. ***the LORD moved the heart.*** Cyrus was both a mighty monarch and the instrument by whom God delivered His people from exile, returned them to their land, and rebuilt the temple (Is. 44:28–45). Like many rulers who encountered the Living God, Cyrus recognized and even extolled His power as the God of Israel, but this was not the same as abandoning all other gods and following the Lord alone.

36:23 Providence—God is the Lord of the universe. He not only rules over those who are called by His name, but He also moves upon the hearts and minds of others whom He chooses to use in the fulfillment of His purpose. It was part of God's plan for the Jews to be taken captive by Babylon, and for Babylon to be taken by Persia. Cyrus had been chosen and ordained for his role in returning the Jews to their own land, and was even called by name by Isaiah the prophet (Is. 44:28; 45:1). It is not always possible to understand the things that the Lord is doing, but we can still rejoice in His providence, confident that the Judge of all the earth will do right (Gen. 18:25).

36:16 [e] 2Ki 2:23; Pr 1:25; Jer 5:13 [f] Ezr 5:12; Pr 1:30-31 [g] 2Ch 30:10; Pr 29:1; Zec 1:2 **36:17** [h] Jer 6:11 [i] Ezr 5:12; Jer 32:28 **36:18** [j] ver 7, 10 **36:19** [k] Jer 11:16; 17:27; 21:10, 14; 22:7; 32:29; 39:8; La 4:11; Eze 20:47; Am 2:5; Zec 11:1 [l] 1Ki 9:8-9 [m] 2Ki 14:13 [n] La 2:6 [o] Ps 79:1-3 **36:20** [p] Lev 26:44; 2Ki 24:14; Ezr 2:1; Ne 7:6 [q] Jer 27:7 **36:21** [r] Lev 25:4; 26:34 [s] 1Ch 22:9 [t] Jer 1:1; 25:11; 27:22; 29:10; 40:1; Da 9:2; Zec 1:12; 7:5 **36:22** [u] Isa 44:28; 45:1, 13; Jer 25:12; 29:10; Da 1:21; 6:28; 10:1 **36:23** [v] Jdg 4:10

EZRA

▶ **AUTHOR:** Although Ezra is not specifically named as the author, Jewish tradition attributes the book to him. This seems appropriate as portions of the book are written in the first person, from Ezra's point of view (7:28—9:15). Similar to Chronicles, this book has a strong priestly emphasis. Ezra was a direct descendant of Aaron through Eleazar, Phinehas, and Zadok, and so came from a long and illustrious priestly line. It is believed that Ezra had access to the extensive library of written documents gathered by Nehemiah and that this was one of the sources used in writing this book as well as Chronicles.

▶ **TIME:** c. 538–457 B.C. ▶ **KEY VERSE:** Ezra 1:3

▶ **THEME:** Many scholars think Ezra and Nehemiah belong together as one book. Together they tell parts of the same story. The Exile is over and the temple is to be rebuilt along with the wall of Jerusalem despite considerable opposition. While Nehemiah's perspective is that of a civil servant and building contractor, Ezra is a teacher of the law and a priest, and as such, provides leadership by bringing God's Word to the people and by restoring proper worship. When the people respond to the Word and reestablish their relationship with God through worship, the building process is renewed and completed.

Cyrus Helps the Exiles to Return

1 In the first year of Cyrus king of Persia,
in order to fulfill the word of the LORD
spoken by Jeremiah,[a] the LORD moved the
heart[b] of Cyrus king of Persia to make a
proclamation throughout his realm and
also to put it in writing:

2"This is what Cyrus king of Persia
says:
"'The LORD, the God of heaven, has
given me all the kingdoms of the earth
and he has appointed[c] me to build[d] a
temple for him at Jerusalem in Judah.
3Any of his people among you may go
up to Jerusalem in Judah and build the
temple of the LORD, the God of Israel,
the God who is in Jerusalem, and may
their God be with them. 4And in any
locality where survivors[e] may now be
living, the people are to provide them
with silver and gold, with goods and
livestock, and with freewill offerings[f]
for the temple of God in Jerusalem.'"[g]

5Then the family heads of Judah and Benjamin,[h] and the priests and Levites—everyone whose heart God had moved[i]—prepared to go up and build the house[j] of the
LORD in Jerusalem. 6All their neighbors assisted them with articles of silver and gold,
with goods and livestock, and with valuable
gifts, in addition to all the freewill offerings.
7Moreover, King Cyrus brought out
the articles belonging to the temple of the
LORD, which Nebuchadnezzar had carried

1:1 ***first year of Cyrus.*** This refers to the first year of Cyrus' reign over Babylon. Cyrus the Great, the founder of the Persian Empire and the Achaemenid dynasty, conquered Babylon in 539 B.C. The events in the Book of Ezra were taking place at the same time as the latter part of the Book of Daniel, after the overthrow of Belshazzar by the Medes and Persians, and the absorption of Babylon into the Persian Empire (Dan. 5:28,30–31; 6:28). ***Jeremiah.*** Jeremiah had prophesied that the Babylonian captivity would last 70 years (Jer. 25:11; 29:10) after which the Lord would judge Babylon (Jer. 25:12–14). ***to make a proclamation.*** One hundred and forty years before Cyrus the Great was even born, Isaiah the prophet called him by name, foretelling the decree he would issue allowing the Israelites to return to their homeland (Is. 44:28; 45:14).

1:4 ***the people are to provide them.*** The assistance that the Israelites were to receive from their non-Jewish neighbors in rebuilding the temple was similar to the help an earlier generation received from the Egyptians before the Exodus (Ex. 12:33–36). In a sense, the return to Jerusalem to rebuild the temple was a second exodus (Is. 43:14–21; 48:20–21).

1:7 ***which Nebuchadnezzar had carried away.***

1:1 [a] Jer 25:11-12; 29:10-14 [b] 2Ch 36:22,23
1:2 [c] Isa 44:28; 45:13 [d] Ezr 5:13 **1:4** [e] Isa 10:20-22
[f] Nu 15:3; Ps 50:14; 54:6; 116:17 [g] Ezr 4:3; 5:13; 6:3, 14
1:5 [h] Ezr 4:1; Ne 11:4 [i] ver 1; Ex 35:20-22; 2Ch 36:22; Hag 1:14; Php 2:13 [j] Ps 127:1

away from Jerusalem and had placed in the
temple of his god.[a][k] 8Cyrus king of Persia
had them brought by Mithredath the trea-
surer, who counted them out to Sheshbazzar[l] the prince of Judah.
9This was the inventory:

gold dishes	30
silver dishes	1,000
silver pans[b]	29
10 gold bowls	30
matching silver bowls	410
other articles	1,000

11In all, there were 5,400 articles of gold
and of silver. Sheshbazzar brought all
these along with the exiles when they came
up from Babylon to Jerusalem.

The List of the Exiles Who Returned

2 Now these are the people of the province who came up from the captivity of
the exiles,[m] whom Nebuchadnezzar king
of Babylon[n] had taken captive to Babylon
(they returned to Jerusalem and Judah,
each to their own town,[o] 2in company with
Zerubbabel,[p] Joshua,[q] Nehemiah, Seraiah,[r]
Reelaiah, Mordecai, Bilshan, Mispar, Bigvai, Rehum and Baanah):

The list of the men of the people of Israel:

3 the descendants of Parosh[s]	2,172
4 of Shephatiah	372
5 of Arah	775
6 of Pahath-Moab (through the line of Jeshua and Joab)	2,812
7 of Elam	1,254
8 of Zattu	945
9 of Zakkai	760
10 of Bani	642
11 of Bebai	623
12 of Azgad	1,222
13 of Adonikam[t]	666
14 of Bigvai	2,056
15 of Adin	454
16 of Ater (through Hezekiah)	98
17 of Bezai	323
18 of Jorah	112
19 of Hashum	223
20 of Gibbar	95
21 the men of Bethlehem[u]	123
22 of Netophah	56
23 of Anathoth	128
24 of Azmaveth	42
25 of Kiriath Jearim,[c] Kephirah and Beeroth	743
26 of Ramah[v] and Geba	621
27 of Mikmash	122
28 of Bethel and Ai[w]	223
29 of Nebo	52
30 of Magbish	156
31 of the other Elam	1,254
32 of Harim	320
33 of Lod, Hadid and Ono	725
34 of Jericho[x]	345
35 of Senaah	3,630

36The priests:

the descendants of Jedaiah[y] (through the family of Jeshua)	973
37 of Immer[z]	1,052
38 of Pashhur[a]	1,247
39 of Harim[b]	1,017

40The Levites:[c]

the descendants of Jeshua[d] and Kadmiel (of the line of Hodaviah)	74

41The musicians:[e]

the descendants of Asaph	128

42The gatekeepers[f] of the temple:

the descendants of Shallum, Ater, Talmon, Akkub, Hatita and Shobai	139

43The temple servants:[g]

the descendants of
Ziha, Hasupha, Tabbaoth,

---

[a] 7 Or *gods* [b] 9 The meaning of the Hebrew for this word is uncertain. [c] 25 See Septuagint (see also Neh. 7:29); Hebrew *Kiriath Arim.*

See 2 Kings 24:1–7,11–13; 25:8–17; 2 Chronicles 36:5–19; Daniel 1:2.

1:8 *Sheshbazzar.* Ezra 5:2 and 5:16 appear to identify Sheshbazzar and Zerubbabel as one and the same person. The name Sheshbazzar occurs in only two passages (vv. 8–11; 5:14–16) and both times are related to official Persian actions. It is possible, and considered likely, that Sheshbazzar was the Persian name for Zerubbabel.

2:2 *Nehemiah ... Mordecai.* The Nehemiah mentioned here is not the same man who rebuilt the walls of Jerusalem 90 years later. The Mordecai in this verse is also considered to be a different man than the one who figured so prominently in the Book of Esther.

2:40–42 *The Levites ... The musicians ... The gatekeepers of the temple.* The Levites assisted the priests in the temple and in teaching the people the Law. The singers were also Levites and had the responsibility of praising God with music (1 Chr. 15:16). Although only 128 singers returned to Jerusalem, at one time there had been as many as four thousand who praised the Lord with musical instruments in Solomon's temple (1 Chr. 23:5). The gatekeepers were another set of Levites who prevented unauthorized people from entering the restricted area of the temple.

2:43 *The temple servants.* The temple servants, also called the "Nethinim," means "given ones" or

1:7 [k] 2Ki 24:13; 2Ch 36:7, 10; Ezr 5:14; 6:5 **1:8** [l] Ezr 5:14
2:1 [m] 2Ch 36:20; Ne 7:6 [n] 2Ki 24:16; 25:12 [o] Ne 7:73
2:2 [p] 1Ch 3:19 [q] Ezr 3:2 [r] Ne 10:2 **2:3** [s] Ezr 8:3
2:13 [t] Ezr 8:13 **2:21** [u] Mic 5:2 **2:26** [v] Jos 18:25
2:28 [w] Ge 12:8 **2:34** [x] 1Ki 16:34; 2Ch 28:15
2:36 [y] 1Ch 24:7 **2:37** [z] 1Ch 24:14 **2:38** [a] 1Ch 9:12
2:39 [b] 1Ch 24:8 **2:40** [c] Ge 29:34; Nu 3:9; Dt 18:6-7; 1Ch 16:4; Ezr 7:7; 8:15; Ne 12:24 [d] Ezr 3:9
2:41 [e] 1Ch 15:16 **2:42** [f] 1Sa 3:15; 1Ch 9:17
2:43 [g] 1Ch 9:2; Ne 11:21

[44]Keros, Siaha, Padon,
[45]Lebanah, Hagabah, Akkub,
[46]Hagab, Shalmai, Hanan,
[47]Giddel, Gahar, Reaiah,
[48]Rezin, Nekoda, Gazzam,
[49]Uzza, Paseah, Besai,
[50]Asnah, Meunim, Nephusim,
[51]Bakbuk, Hakupha, Harhur,
[52]Bazluth, Mehida, Harsha,
[53]Barkos, Sisera, Temah,
[54]Neziah and Hatipha

[55]The descendants of the servants of Solomon:

the descendants of
Sotai, Hassophereth, Peruda,
[56]Jaala, Darkon, Giddel,
[57]Shephatiah, Hattil,
Pokereth-Hazzebaim and Ami

[58]The temple servants[h] and the descendants of the servants of Solomon 392

[59]The following came up from the
towns of Tel Melah, Tel Harsha, Kerub, Addon and Immer, but they could not show that their families were descended[i] from Israel:

[60]The descendants of
Delaiah, Tobiah and Nekoda 652

[61]And from among the priests:

The descendants of
Hobaiah, Hakkoz and Barzillai (a man who had married a daughter of Barzillai the Gileadite[j] and was called by that name).

[62]These searched for their family
records, but they could not find them and so were excluded from the priesthood[k] as unclean.
[63]The governor ordered them not to eat any of the most sacred food[l] until there was a priest ministering with the Urim and Thummim.[m]

[64]The whole company numbered
42,360,
[65]besides their 7,337 male and female slaves; and they also had 200 male and female singers.[n]
[66]They had 736 horses,[o] 245 mules,
[67]435 camels and 6,720 donkeys.

[68]When they arrived at the house of the
LORD in Jerusalem, some of the heads of the families[p] gave freewill offerings toward the rebuilding of the house of God on its site.
[69]According to their ability they gave to the treasury for this work 61,000 darics[a] of gold, 5,000 minas[b] of silver and 100 priestly garments.
[70]The priests, the Levites, the musicians, the gatekeepers and the temple servants settled in their own towns, along with some of the other people, and the rest of the Israelites settled in their towns.[q]

Rebuilding the Altar

3 When the seventh month came and the Israelites had settled in their towns,[r] the people assembled[s] together as one in Jerusalem.
[2]Then Joshua[t] son of Jozadak[u] and his fellow priests and Zerubbabel son of Shealtiel[v] and his associates began to build the altar of the God of Israel to sacrifice burnt offerings on it, in accordance with what is written in the Law of Moses[w] the man of God.
[3]Despite their fear[x] of the peoples around them, they built the altar on its foundation and sacrificed burnt offerings on it to the LORD, both the morning and evening sacrifices.[y]
[4]Then in accordance with what is written, they celebrated the Festival of Tabernacles[z] with the required number of burnt offerings prescribed for

[a] *69* That is, about 1,100 pounds or about 500 kilograms [b] *69* That is, about 3 tons or about 2.8 metric tons

"dedicated ones." In 1 Chronicles 9:2, the temple servants are distinguished from the priests and the Levites. Jewish tradition identifies the temple servants with the Gibeonites who had been assigned by Joshua to assist the Levites in more menial tasks (Josh. 9:27).

2:63 *Urim and Thummim.* The Urim and Thummim were somehow used to determine God's will (Ex. 28:30). It is not known exactly what they were, but it has been speculated that they were special sacred stones, used for casting lots.

2:64 *42,360.* The individual numbers listed in chapter 2 add up to only 29,818. The difference is accounted for because the larger total includes women, who are not named in the lists.

2:65 *male and female singers.* These men and women are thought to be other than the choir of the temple (v. 41). They were probably professional singers employed for banquets and feasts (2 Chr. 35:25; Eccl. 2:7–8). It could be that some of the Jews achieved prosperity and a degree of luxury in Babylon. They had not, after all, been enslaved in exile, but only restricted from returning to their land.

3:1 *seventh month.* The seventh month was a sacred month to the Jewish people. The first day of the month was the Festival of Trumpets (Num. 29:1–6), the tenth day was the Day of Atonement (Num. 29:7–11), and the fifteenth day was the Festival of Tabernacles (Num. 29:12–38).

3:2–3 *Joshua.* This is believed to be the same person as the priest Joshua mentioned by the prophets Haggai and Zechariah (Hag. 1:1; Zech. 3:1).

3:4 *Festival of Tabernacles.* The Festival of Booths, or Tabernacles, was a festival instituted as a remembrance of the earlier generations' wanderings in the wilderness (Num. 29:13–38).

2:58 [h] 1Ki 9:21; 1Ch 9:2 **2:59** [i] Nu 1:18 **2:61** [j] 2Sa 17:27 **2:62** [k] Nu 3:10; 16:39-40 **2:63** [l] Lev 2:3, 10 [m] Ex 28:30; Nu 27:21 **2:65** [n] 2Sa 19:35 **2:66** [o] Isa 66:20 **2:68** [p] Ex 25:2 **2:70** [q] ver 1; 1Ch 9:2; Ne 11:3-4 **3:1** [r] Ne 7:73; 8:1 [s] Lev 23:24 **3:2** [t] Ezr 2:2; Ne 12:1, 8; Hag 2:2 [u] Hag 1:1; Zec 6:11 [v] 1Ch 3:17 [w] Ex 20:24; Dt 12:5-6 **3:3** [x] Ezr 4:4; Da 9:25 [y] Ex 29:39; Nu 28:1-8 **3:4** [z] Ex 23:16; Nu 29:12-38; Ne 8:14-18; Zec 14:16-19

each day. 5After that, they presented the
regular burnt offerings, the New Moon[a]
sacrifices and the sacrifices for all the appointed sacred festivals of the LORD,[b] as
well as those brought as freewill offerings
to the LORD. 6On the first day of the seventh
month they began to offer burnt offerings
to the LORD, though the foundation of the
LORD's temple had not yet been laid.

Rebuilding the Temple

7Then they gave money to the masons
and carpenters, and gave food and drink
and olive oil to the people of Sidon and
Tyre, so that they would bring cedar logs[c]
by sea from Lebanon[d] to Joppa, as authorized by Cyrus[e] king of Persia.
8In the second month of the second year
after their arrival at the house of God in
Jerusalem, Zerubbabel[f] son of Shealtiel,
Joshua son of Jozadak and the rest of the
people (the priests and the Levites and all
who had returned from the captivity to Jerusalem) began the work. They appointed
Levites twenty[g] years old and older to supervise the building of the house of the
LORD. 9Joshua[h] and his sons and brothers
and Kadmiel and his sons (descendants of
Hodaviah[a]) and the sons of Henadad and
their sons and brothers—all Levites—
joined together in supervising those working on the house of God.
10When the builders laid[i] the foundation of the temple of the LORD, the priests
in their vestments and with trumpets,[j] and
the Levites (the sons of Asaph) with cymbals, took their places to praise[k] the LORD,
as prescribed by David[l] king of Israel.[m]
11With praise and thanksgiving they sang
to the LORD:

"He is good;
his love toward Israel endures
forever."[n]

And all the people gave a great shout[o] of
praise to the LORD, because the foundation
of the house of the LORD was laid. 12But
many of the older priests and Levites and
family heads, who had seen the former
temple,[p] wept aloud when they saw the
foundation of this temple being laid, while
many others shouted for joy. 13No one
could distinguish the sound of the shouts
of joy[q] from the sound of weeping, because
the people made so much noise. And the
sound was heard far away.

Opposition to the Rebuilding

4 When the enemies of Judah and Benjamin heard that the exiles were building
a temple for the LORD, the God of Israel,
2they came to Zerubbabel and to the heads
of the families and said, "Let us help you
build because, like you, we seek your God
and have been sacrificing to him since the
time of Esarhaddon[r] king of Assyria, who
brought us here."[s]
3But Zerubbabel, Joshua and the rest
of the heads of the families of Israel answered, "You have no part with us in building a temple to our God. We alone will
build it for the LORD, the God of Israel, as
King Cyrus, the king of Persia, commanded us."[t]
4Then the peoples around them set out to
discourage the people of Judah and make
them afraid to go on building.[b][u] 5They
bribed officials to work against them and
frustrate their plans during the entire reign
of Cyrus king of Persia and down to the
reign of Darius king of Persia.

Later Opposition Under Xerxes and Artaxerxes

6At the beginning of the reign of Xerxes,[c][v] they lodged an accusation against
the people of Judah and Jerusalem.[w]

---

[a] 9 Hebrew *Yehudah,* a variant of *Hodaviah*
[b] 4 Or *and troubled them as they built*
[c] 6 Hebrew *Ahasuerus*

3:11 Patience—In spite of Israel's history of sin, leading to the broken empire, captivity, exile, the destruction of the temple and walls of Jerusalem, God still had not forgotten His people. Joy filled the hearts of the Israelites, for God's love had endured. Patiently, faithfully, He was keeping every promise. He is equally faithful and patient to each of us, even though we so often miss the mark. He does not give us up, but showers us with benefits and never ceases to show us His unchanging persistent love.

4:1 *the enemies of Judah.* The enemies of Judah were the Samaritans. Esarhaddon (v. 2), who ruled Assyria from 681–669 B.C., had transported the conquered people of the northern kingdom to other lands. He then brought people from elsewhere into Palestine. These foreigners intermarried with the Hebrews who were left in the land. Their offspring became the Samaritans mentioned in the New Testament.

4:4–5 Persecution—Israel encountered hostility when they returned to their land. At first glance it might seem that Israel was at fault for turning down help. These people said they had been offering sacrifices to Yahweh. This did not mean, however, that they had ceased to serve their idols (2 Kin. 17:29–35). Whatever their hidden reasons for offering help, it would not have been in favor of the Israelites. Their underlying hostility became obvious as they succeeded in hindering the work on the temple.

4:6 *Xerxes.* When Darius I died (486 B.C.) his son Xerxes reigned (485–465 B.C.). This is the same king who appears in the Book of Esther.

3:5 [a] Nu 28:3, 11, 14; Col 2:16 [b] Lev 23:1-44; Nu 29:39
3:7 [c] 1Ch 14:1 [d] Isa 35:2 [e] Ezr 1:2-4; 6:3 **3:8** [f] Zec 4:9
[g] 1Ch 23:24 **3:9** [h] Ezr 2:40 **3:10** [i] Ezr 5:16 [j] Nu 10:2;
1Ch 16:6 [k] 1Ch 25:1 [l] 1Ch 6:31 [m] Zec 6:12
3:11 [n] 1Ch 16:34, 41; 2Ch 7:3; Ps 107:1; 118:1 [o] Ne 12:24
3:12 [p] Hag 2:3, 9 **3:13** [q] Job 8:21; Ps 27:6; Isa 16:9
4:2 [r] 2Ki 17:24; 19:37 [s] 2Ki 17:41 **4:3** [t] Ezr 1:1-4; Ne 2:20
4:4 [u] Ezr 3:3 **4:6** [v] Est 1:1; Da 9:1 [w] Est 3:13; 9:5

7 And in the days of Artaxerxes[x] king of Persia, Bishlam, Mithredath, Tabeel and the rest of his associates wrote a letter to Artaxerxes. The letter was written in Aramaic script and in the Aramaic[y] language.[a,b]

8 Rehum the commanding officer and Shimshai the secretary wrote a letter against Jerusalem to Artaxerxes the king as follows:

9 Rehum the commanding officer and Shimshai the secretary, together with the rest of their associates[z]—the judges, officials and administrators over the people from Persia, Uruk and Babylon, the Elamites of Susa, 10 and the other people whom the great and honorable Ashurbanipal deported and settled in the city of Samaria and elsewhere in Trans-Euphrates.[a]

11 (This is a copy of the letter they sent him.)

To King Artaxerxes,

From your servants in Trans-Euphrates:

12 The king should know that the people who came up to us from you have gone to Jerusalem and are rebuilding that rebellious and wicked city. They are restoring the walls and repairing the foundations.[b]

13 Furthermore, the king should know that if this city is built and its walls are restored, no more taxes, tribute or duty[c] will be paid, and eventually the royal revenues will suffer.[c] 14 Now since we are under obligation to the palace and it is not proper for us to see the king dishonored, we are sending this message to inform the king, 15 so that a search may be made in the archives[d] of your predecessors. In these records you will find that this city is a rebellious city, troublesome to kings and provinces, a place with a long history of sedition. That is why this city was destroyed.[e] 16 We inform the king that if this city is built and its walls are restored, you will be left with nothing in Trans-Euphrates.

17 The king sent this reply:

To Rehum the commanding officer, Shimshai the secretary and the rest of their associates living in Samaria and elsewhere in Trans-Euphrates:[f]

Greetings.

18 The letter you sent us has been read and translated in my presence. 19 I issued an order and a search was made, and it was found that this city has a long history of revolt[g] against kings and has been a place of rebellion and sedition. 20 Jerusalem has had powerful kings ruling over the whole of Trans-Euphrates,[h] and taxes, tribute and duty were paid to them. 21 Now issue an order to these men to stop work, so that this city will not be rebuilt until I so order. 22 Be careful not to neglect this matter. Why let this threat grow, to the detriment of the royal interests?[i]

23 As soon as the copy of the letter of King Artaxerxes was read to Rehum and Shimshai the secretary and their associates,[j] they went immediately to the Jews in Jerusalem and compelled them by force to stop.

24 Thus the work on the house of God in Jerusalem came to a standstill until the second year of the reign of Darius[k] king of Persia.

Tattenai's Letter to Darius

5 Now Haggai[l] the prophet and Zechariah[m] the prophet, a descendant of Iddo, prophesied[n] to the Jews in Judah and Jerusalem in the name of the God of Israel, who was over them. 2 Then Zerubbabel[o] son of Shealtiel and Joshua[p] son of Jozadak set to work[q] to rebuild the house of God in Jerusalem. And the prophets of God were with them, supporting them.

3 At that time Tattenai,[r] governor of Trans-Euphrates, and Shethar-Bozenai[s] and their associates went to them and asked, "Who authorized you to rebuild this temple and to finish it?"[t] 4 They[d] also asked, "What are the names of those who are constructing this building?" 5 But the eye of their God[u] was watching over the elders of the Jews, and they were not stopped until a report could go to Darius and his written reply be received.

[a] 7 Or *written in Aramaic and translated*
[b] 7 The text of 4:8–6:18 is in Aramaic. [c] *13* The meaning of the Aramaic for this clause is uncertain. [d] *4* See Septuagint; Aramaic *We.*

4:21 ***this city will not be rebuilt.*** The Persian king Artaxerxes ordered the Jewish people to cease their work on the temple. Years later at the request of Nehemiah the decision was reviewed (Neh. 2:1 – 8).

4:24 ***Darius king of Persia.*** This is not the same Darius as the Darius of Daniel 5 and 6.

4:7 [x] Ezr 7:1; Ne 2:1 [y] 2Ki 18:26; Isa 36:11; Da 2:4 **4:9** [z] Ezr 5:6; 6:6, 13 **4:10** [a] ver 17; Ne 4:2

4:12 [b] Ezr 5:3, 9 **4:13** [c] Ezr 7:24; Ne 5:4 **4:15** [d] Ezr 5:17; 6:1 [e] Est 3:8 **4:17** [f] ver 10 **4:19** [g] 2Ki 18:7 **4:20** [h] Ge 15:18-21; Ex 23:31; Jos 1:4; 1Ki 4:21; 1Ch 18:3; Ps 72:8-11 **4:22** [i] Da 6:2 **4:23** [j] ver 9 **4:24** [k] Ne 2:1-8; Da 9:25; Hag 1:1, 15; Zec 1:1 **5:1** [l] Ezr 6:14; Hag 1:1, 3, 12; 2:1, 10, 20 [m] Zec 1:1; 7:1 [n] Hag 1:14-2:9; Zec 4:9-10; 8:9 **5:2** [o] 1Ch 3:19; Hag 1:14; 2:21; Zec 4:6-10 [p] Ezr 2:2; 3:2 [q] ver 8; Hag 2:2-5 **5:3** [r] Ezr 6:6 [s] Ezr 6:6 [t] ver 9; Ezr 1:3; 4:12 **5:5** [u] 2Ki 25:28; Ezr 7:6, 9, 28; 8:18, 22, 31; Ne 2:8, 18; Ps 33:18; Isa 66:14

[6]This is a copy of the letter that Tattenai, governor of Trans-Euphrates, and Shethar-Bozenai and their associates, the officials of Trans-Euphrates, sent to King Darius. [7]The report they sent him read as follows:

To King Darius:

Cordial greetings.

[8]The king should know that we went to the district of Judah, to the temple of the great God. The people are building it with large stones and placing the timbers in the walls. The work[v] is being carried on with diligence and is making rapid progress under their direction.

[9]We questioned the elders and asked them, "Who authorized you to rebuild this temple and to finish it?"[w] [10]We also asked them their names, so that we could write down the names of their leaders for your information.

[11]This is the answer they gave us:

"We are the servants of the God of heaven and earth, and we are rebuilding the temple[x] that was built many years ago, one that a great king of Israel built and finished. [12]But because our ancestors angered[y] the God of heaven, he gave them into the hands of Nebuchadnezzar the Chaldean, king of Babylon, who destroyed this temple and deported the people to Babylon.[z]

[13]"However, in the first year of Cyrus king of Babylon, King Cyrus issued a decree[a] to rebuild this house of God. [14]He even removed from the temple[a] of Babylon the gold and silver articles of the house of God, which Nebuchadnezzar had taken from the temple in Jerusalem and brought to the temple[a] in Babylon.[b] Then King Cyrus gave them to a man named Sheshbazzar,[c] whom he had appointed governor, [15]and he told him, 'Take these articles and go and deposit them in the temple in Jerusalem. And rebuild the house of God on its site.'

[16]"So this Sheshbazzar came and laid the foundations of the house of God[d] in Jerusalem. From that day to the present it has been under construction but is not yet finished."

[17]Now if it pleases the king, let a search be made in the royal archives[e] of Babylon to see if King Cyrus did in fact issue a decree to rebuild this house of God in Jerusalem. Then let the king send us his decision in this matter.

The Decree of Darius

6 King Darius then issued an order, and they searched in the archives[f] stored in the treasury at Babylon. [2]A scroll was found in the citadel of Ecbatana in the province of Media, and this was written on it:

Memorandum:

[3]In the first year of King Cyrus, the king issued a decree concerning the temple of God in Jerusalem:

Let the temple be rebuilt as a place to present sacrifices, and let its foundations be laid.[g] It is to be sixty cubits[b] high and sixty cubits wide, [4]with three courses[h] of large stones and one of timbers. The costs are to be paid by the royal treasury.[i] [5]Also, the gold[j] and silver articles of the house of God, which Nebuchadnezzar took from the temple in Jerusalem and brought to Babylon, are to be returned to their places in the temple in Jerusalem; they are to be deposited in the house of God.[k]

[6]Now then, Tattenai,[l] governor of Trans-Euphrates, and Shethar-Bozenai[m] and you other officials of that province, stay away from there. [7]Do not interfere with the work on this temple of God. Let the governor of the Jews and the Jewish elders rebuild this house of God on its site.

[8]Moreover, I hereby decree what you are to do for these elders of the Jews in the construction of this house of God:

Their expenses are to be fully paid out of the royal treasury,[n] from the revenues[o] of Trans-Euphrates, so that the work will not stop. [9]Whatever is needed—young bulls, rams, male lambs for burnt offerings[p] to the God

[a] *14 Or palace* [b] *3* That is, about 90 feet or about 27 meters

5:12 *our ancestors angered the God of heaven.* Although the Jewish people acknowledged that Nebuchadnezzar destroyed the first temple, they traced the cause not to his power, but to their sin and God's judgment.

6:2 *Ecbatana.* This city, also called "Achmetha," was the summer residence of the Persian kings.

6:3 *It is to be sixty cubits high and sixty cubits wide.* Though the complete dimensions are not given, it is likely that the second temple was built on the foundation stones that were still in place from the time of Solomon (1 Kin. 6:2).

6:8–10 *Moreover.* Not only could Tattenai not stop reconstruction of the temple, he also had to fund its completion.

5:8 [v] ver 2 **5:9** [w] Ezr 4:12 **5:11** [x] 1Ki 6:1; 2Ch 3:1-2 **5:12** [y] 2Ch 36:16 [z] Dt 21:10; 28:36; 2Ki 24:1; 25:8, 9, 11; Jer 1:3 **5:13** [a] Ezr 1:1 **5:14** [b] Ezr 1:7; 6:5; Da 5:2 [c] 1Ch 3:18 **5:16** [d] Ezr 3:10; 6:15 **5:17** [e] Ezr 4:15; 6:1, 2 **6:1** [f] Ezr 4:15; 5:17 **6:3** [g] Ezr 3:10; Hag 2:3 **6:4** [h] 1Ki 6:36 [i] ver 8; Ezr 7:20 **6:5** [j] 1Ch 29:2 [k] Ezr 1:7; 5:14 **6:6** [l] Ezr 5:3 [m] Ezr 5:3 **6:8** [n] ver 4 [o] 1Sa 9:20 **6:9** [p] Lev 1:3, 10

of heaven, and wheat, salt, wine and olive oil, as requested by the priests in Jerusalem—must be given them daily without fail, 10so that they may offer sacrifices pleasing to the God of heaven and pray for the well-being of the king and his sons.[q]

11Furthermore, I decree that if anyone defies this edict, a beam is to be pulled from their house and they are to be impaled[r] on it. And for this crime their house is to be made a pile of rubble.[s] 12May God, who has caused his Name to dwell there,[t] overthrow any king or people who lifts a hand to change this decree or to destroy this temple in Jerusalem.

I Darius[u] have decreed it. Let it be carried out with diligence.

Completion and Dedication of the Temple

13Then, because of the decree King Darius had sent, Tattenai, governor of Trans-Euphrates, and Shethar-Bozenai and their associates[v] carried it out with diligence. 14So the elders of the Jews continued to build and prosper under the preaching[w] of Haggai the prophet and Zechariah, a descendant of Iddo. They finished building the temple according to the command of the God of Israel and the decrees of Cyrus,[x] Darius[y] and Artaxerxes,[z] kings of Persia. 15The temple was completed on the third day of the month Adar, in the sixth year of the reign of King Darius.[a]

16Then the people of Israel—the priests, the Levites and the rest of the exiles—celebrated the dedication[b] of the house of God with joy. 17For the dedication of this house of God they offered[c] a hundred bulls, two hundred rams, four hundred male lambs and, as a sin offering[α] for all Israel, twelve male goats, one for each of the tribes of Israel. 18And they installed the priests in their divisions[d] and the Levites in their groups[e] for the service of God at Jerusalem, according to what is written in the Book of Moses.[f]

The Passover

19On the fourteenth day of the first month, the exiles celebrated the Passover.[g] 20The priests and Levites had purified themselves and were all ceremonially clean. The Levites slaughtered[h] the Passover lamb for all the exiles, for their relatives the priests and for themselves. 21So the Israelites who had returned from the exile ate it, together with all who had separated themselves[i] from the unclean practices[j] of their Gentile neighbors in order to seek the LORD,[k] the God of Israel. 22For seven days they celebrated with joy the Festival of Unleavened Bread,[l] because the LORD had filled them with joy by changing the attitude[m] of the king of Assyria so that he assisted them in the work on the house of God, the God of Israel.

Ezra Comes to Jerusalem

7 After these things, during the reign of Artaxerxes[n] king of Persia, Ezra son of Seraiah, the son of Azariah, the son of Hilkiah,[o] 2the son of Shallum, the son of Zadok,[p] the son of Ahitub,[q] 3the son of Amariah, the son of Azariah, the son of Meraioth, 4the son of Zerahiah, the son of Uzzi, the son of Bukki, 5the son of Abishua, the son of Phinehas, the son of Eleazar, the son of Aaron the chief priest— 6this Ezra[r] came up from Babylon. He was a teacher well versed in the Law of Moses, which the LORD, the God of Israel, had given. The king had granted him everything he asked, for the hand of the LORD his God was on him.[s] 7Some of the Israelites, including priests, Levites, musicians, gatekeepers and temple servants, also came up to Jerusalem in the seventh year of King Artaxerxes.[t]

α 17 Or *purification offering*

6:16 *celebrated the dedication ... with joy.* Some have suggested that Psalms 145–148 were used to celebrate the completion of the rebuilding of the temple.

6:19 *celebrated the Passover.* This celebration must have been exceptionally memorable; it was the first time since the captivity that the people were able to celebrate according to the law, with sacrifices offered in the temple (v. 20).

6:21 *Gentile neighbors.* The term probably refers to the people who had been transplanted into Palestine by the Assyrians.

6:22 Providence—The situation the Jews faced seemed hopeless. But God in His providence caused Cyrus to look favorably upon the Jews and allow them to return to their homeland. What seemed impossible became possible through God. Sometimes it is easy for us to forget that even in the worst of times and circumstances God is still on His throne.

7:1–5 *After these things.* The events of chapter 6 took place during the reign of King Darius. The temple was completed and dedicated in 515 B.C. Chapter 7 jumps forward many years to the reign of Artaxerxes (464–424 B.C.). Thus, between chapters 6 and 7 there is a gap of approximately 60 years. During this period the events of the Book of Esther took place.

7:6 *a teacher well versed in the Law of Moses.* A scribe was one who copied and studied the law. After

6:10 q Ezr 7:23; 1Ti 2:1-2 **6:11** r Dt 21:22-23; Est 2:23; 5:14; 9:14 s Ezr 7:26; Da 2:5; 3:29 **6:12** t Ex 20:24; Dt 12:5; 1Ki 9:3; 2Ch 6:2 u ver 14 **6:13** v Ezr 4:9 **6:14** w Ezr 5:1 x Ezr 1:1-4 y ver 12 z Ezr 7:1; Ne 2:1 **6:15** a Zec 1:1; 4:9 **6:16** b 1Ki 8:63; 2Ch 7:5 **6:17** c 2Sa 6:13; 2Ch 29:21; 30:24; Ezr 8:35 **6:18** d 1Ch 23:6; 2Ch 35:4; Lk 1:5 e 1Ch 24:1 f Nu 3:6-9; 8:9-11; 18:1-32 **6:19** g Ex 12:11; Nu 28:16 **6:20** h 2Ch 30:15, 17; 35:11 **6:21** i Ezr 9:1; Ne 9:2 j Dt 18:9; Ezr 9:11; Eze 36:25 k 1Ch 22:19; Ps 14:2 **6:22** l Ex 12:17 m Ezr 1:1 **7:1** n Ezr 4:7; 6:14; Ne 2:1 o 2Ki 22:4 **7:2** p 1Ki 1:8; 1Ch 6:8 q Ne 11:11 **7:6** r Ne 12:36 s Ezr 5:5; Isa 41:20 **7:7** t Ezr 8:1

8 Ezra arrived in Jerusalem in the fifth
month of the seventh year of the king. 9 He
had begun his journey from Babylon on
the first day of the first month, and he arrived in Jerusalem on the first day of the
fifth month, for the gracious hand of his
God was on him.[u] 10 For Ezra had devoted
himself to the study and observance of the
Law of the LORD, and to teaching[v] its decrees and laws in Israel.

King Artaxerxes' Letter to Ezra

11 This is a copy of the letter King Artaxerxes had given to Ezra the priest, a teacher of the Law, a man learned in matters
concerning the commands and decrees of
the LORD for Israel:

12 Artaxerxes, king of kings,[w]

To Ezra the priest, teacher of the Law
of the God of heaven:

Greetings.

13 Now I decree that any of the Israelites in my kingdom, including priests
and Levites, who volunteer to go to Jerusalem with you, may go. 14 You are
sent by the king and his seven advisers[x] to inquire about Judah and Jerusalem with regard to the Law of your
God, which is in your hand. 15 Moreover, you are to take with you the silver
and gold that the king and his advisers
have freely given[y] to the God of Israel,
whose dwelling[z] is in Jerusalem, 16 together with all the silver and gold[a] you
may obtain from the province of Babylon, as well as the freewill offerings
of the people and priests for the temple
of their God in Jerusalem.[b] 17 With this
money be sure to buy bulls, rams and
male lambs,[c] together with their grain
offerings and drink offerings,[d] and sacrifice[e] them on the altar of the temple of
your God in Jerusalem.
18 You and your fellow Israelites
may then do whatever seems best
with the rest of the silver and gold, in
accordance with the will of your God.
19 Deliver[f] to the God of Jerusalem all
the articles entrusted to you for worship in the temple of your God. 20 And
anything else needed for the temple of
your God that you are responsible to
supply, you may provide from the royal treasury.[g]
21 Now I, King Artaxerxes, decree
that all the treasurers of Trans-Euphrates are to provide with diligence whatever Ezra the priest, the teacher of the
Law of the God of heaven, may ask of
you— 22 up to a hundred talents[a] of silver, a hundred cors[b] of wheat, a hundred baths[c] of wine, a hundred baths[c]
of olive oil, and salt without limit.
23 Whatever the God of heaven has prescribed, let it be done with diligence for
the temple of the God of heaven. Why
should his wrath fall on the realm of
the king and of his sons?[h] 24 You are
also to know that you have no authority to impose taxes, tribute or duty[i] on
any of the priests, Levites, musicians,
gatekeepers, temple servants or other
workers at this house of God.[j]
25 And you, Ezra, in accordance
with the wisdom of your God, which
you possess, appoint[k] magistrates
and judges to administer justice to
all the people of Trans-Euphrates—
all who know the laws of your God.
And you are to teach[l] any who do not
know them. 26 Whoever does not obey
the law of your God and the law of
the king must surely be punished by
death, banishment, confiscation of
property, or imprisonment.[d][m]

27 Praise be to the LORD, the God of our ancestors, who has put it into the king's heart[n]
to bring honor[o] to the house of the LORD in
Jerusalem in this way 28 and who has ex-

[a] *22* That is, about 3 3/4 tons or about 3.4 metric tons [b] *22* That is, probably about 18 tons or about 16 metric tons [c] *22* That is, about 600 gallons or about 2,200 liters [d] *26* The text of 7:12-26 is in Aramaic.

---

the Exile, the office of scribe came into prominence, in some ways replacing the prophet in importance, and eventually eclipsing the role of the priest. In the Gospels, numerous references are made to the scribes as ones who were considered spiritual leaders of the people.

7:9 ***first month ... fifth month.*** The first month corresponds to March-April, the fifth month to July-August. ***the gracious hand of his God.*** Ezra was grateful for God's protection even more since the route he traveled was dangerous because of rebellion in Egypt and the fact that spring was the time armies began their campaigns.

7:9–10 Obedience. Ezra followed God's command and made his paramount exercise the study, practice, and teaching of God's law. The "gracious hand of his God" was upon Ezra, for he had "had devoted himself to the study and observance of the Law of the LORD." That same command is for us also. We don't always know when we as Christians are being watched by others, but if we are diligent to obey, our lives will point to Christ.

7:22 ***a hundred talents of silver.*** One hundred talents of silver weighed nearly four tons. One hundred kors of wheat amounted to about 625 bushels; one hundred baths of wine or oil equaled about six hundred gallons each.

7:9 [u] ver 6 **7:10** [v] ver 25; Dt 33:10; Ne 8:1-8 **7:12** [w] Eze 26:7; Da 2:37 **7:14** [x] Est 1:14 **7:15** [y] 1Ch 29:6 [z] 1Ch 29:6, 9; 2Ch 6:2 **7:16** [a] Ezr 8:25 [b] Zec 6:10 **7:17** [c] 2Ki 3:4 [d] Nu 15:5-12 [e] Dt 12:5-11 **7:19** [f] Ezr 5:14; Jer 27:22 **7:20** [g] Ezr 6:4 **7:23** [h] Ezr 6:10 **7:24** [i] Ezr 4:13 [j] Ezr 8:36 **7:25** [k] Ex 18:21, 26; Dt 16:18 [l] ver 10; Lev 10:11 **7:26** [m] Ezr 6:11 **7:27** [n] Ezr 1:1; 6:22 [o] 1Ch 29:12

tended his good favor[p] to me before the king and his advisers and all the king's powerful officials. Because the hand of the LORD my God was on me,[q] I took courage and gathered leaders from Israel to go up with me.

List of the Family Heads Returning With Ezra

8 These are the family heads and those registered with them who came up with me from Babylon during the reign of King Artaxerxes:[r]

2 of the descendants of Phinehas, Gershom;
of the descendants of Ithamar, Daniel;
of the descendants of David, Hattush
3 of the descendants of Shekaniah;[s]

of the descendants of Parosh,[t] Zechariah, and with him were registered 150 men;
4 of the descendants of Pahath-Moab,[u] Eliehoenai son of Zerahiah, and with him 200 men;
5 of the descendants of Zattu,[a] Shekaniah son of Jahaziel, and with him 300 men;
6 of the descendants of Adin,[v] Ebed son of Jonathan, and with him 50 men;
7 of the descendants of Elam, Jeshaiah son of Athaliah, and with him 70 men;
8 of the descendants of Shephatiah, Zebadiah son of Michael, and with him 80 men;
9 of the descendants of Joab, Obadiah son of Jehiel, and with him 218 men;
10 of the descendants of Bani,[b] Shelomith son of Josiphiah, and with him 160 men;
11 of the descendants of Bebai, Zechariah son of Bebai, and with him 28 men;
12 of the descendants of Azgad, Johanan son of Hakkatan, and with him 110 men;
13 of the descendants of Adonikam,[w] the last ones, whose names were Eliphelet, Jeuel and Shemaiah, and with them 60 men;
14 of the descendants of Bigvai, Uthai and Zakkur, and with them 70 men.

The Return to Jerusalem

15 I assembled them at the canal that
flows toward Ahava,[x] and we camped there
three days. When I checked among the
people and the priests, I found no Levites[y]
there. 16 So I summoned Eliezer, Ariel, Shemaiah, Elnathan, Jarib, Elnathan, Nathan,
Zechariah and Meshullam, who were leaders, and Joiarib and Elnathan, who were
men of learning, 17 and I ordered them to go
to Iddo, the leader in Kasiphia. I told them
what to say to Iddo and his fellow Levites,
the temple servants[z] in Kasiphia, so that
they might bring attendants to us for the
house of our God. 18 Because the gracious
hand of our God was on us,[a] they brought
us Sherebiah, a capable man, from the descendants of Mahli son of Levi, the son of
Israel, and Sherebiah's sons and brothers,
18 in all; 19 and Hashabiah, together with
Jeshaiah from the descendants of Merari, and his brothers and nephews, 20 in
all. 20 They also brought 220 of the temple
servants[b]—a body that David and the officials had established to assist the Levites.
All were registered by name.
21 There, by the Ahava Canal,[c] I proclaimed a fast, so that we might humble
ourselves before our God and ask him for a
safe journey[d] for us and our children, with
all our possessions. 22 I was ashamed to ask
the king for soldiers[e] and horsemen to protect us from enemies on the road, because
we had told the king, "The gracious hand of
our God is on everyone[f] who looks to him,
but his great anger is against all who forsake him.[g]" 23 So we fasted[h] and petitioned
our God about this, and he answered our
prayer.
24 Then I set apart twelve of the leading
priests, namely, Sherebiah,[i] Hashabiah and
ten of their brothers, 25 and I weighed out[j] to
them the offering of silver and gold and the
articles that the king, his advisers, his officials and all Israel present there had donat-
ed for the house of our God. 26 I weighed out
to them 650 talents[c] of silver, silver articles
weighing 100 talents,[d] 100 talents[d] of gold,
27 20 bowls of gold valued at 1,000 darics,[e]
and two fine articles of polished bronze, as
precious as gold.
28 I said to them, "You as well as these
articles are consecrated to the LORD.[k] The
silver and gold are a freewill offering to the

[a] 5 Some Septuagint manuscripts (also 1 Esdras 8:32); Hebrew does not have *Zattu.* [b] *10* Some Septuagint manuscripts (also 1 Esdras 8:36); Hebrew does not have *Bani.* [c] *26* That is, about 24 tons or about 22 metric tons [d] *26* That is, about 3 3/4 tons or about 3.4 metric tons [e] *27* That is, about 19 pounds or about 8.4 kilograms

8:17 *Kasiphia.* The significance of Kasiphia is uncertain, but it is thought that there may have been a Jewish sanctuary or temple there.

8:22 *looks to him.* Ezra knew that God would protect him; he wasn't afraid to "stick his neck out" even though it might have been more comfortable to have the security of soldiers as escorts. In our own lives, it is the same. Our responsibility is obedience, no matter what. Our safety is God's responsibility.

7:28 [p] 2Ki 25:28 [q] Ezr 5:5; 9:9 **8:1** [r] Ezr 7:7
8:3 [s] 1Ch 3:22 [t] Ezr 2:3 **8:4** [u] Ezr 2:6
8:6 [v] Ezr 2:15; Ne 7:20; 10:16 **8:13** [w] Ezr 2:13
8:15 [x] ver 21,31 [y] Ezr 2:40; 7:7 **8:17** [z] Ezr 2:43
8:18 [a] Ezr 5:5 **8:20** [b] 1Ch 9:2; Ezr 2:43 **8:21** [c] ver 15; 2Ch 20:3 [d] Ps 5:8; 107:7 **8:22** [e] Ne 2:9; Ezr 7:6,9,28
[f] Ezr 5:5 [g] Dt 31:17; 2Ch 15:2 **8:23** [h] 2Ch 20:3; 33:13
8:24 [i] ver 18 **8:25** [j] ver 33; Ezr 7:15,16
8:28 [k] Lev 21:6; 22:2-3

LORD, the God of your ancestors. 29Guard
them carefully until you weigh them out in
the chambers of the house of the LORD in
Jerusalem before the leading priests and
the Levites and the family heads of Israel."
30Then the priests and Levites received the
silver and gold and sacred articles that had
been weighed out to be taken to the house
of our God in Jerusalem.
31On the twelfth day of the first month
we set out from the Ahava Canal[l] to go to
Jerusalem. The hand of our God was on
us, and he protected us from enemies and
bandits along the way. 32So we arrived in
Jerusalem, where we rested three days.[m]
33On the fourth day, in the house of our
God, we weighed out the silver and gold
and the sacred articles into the hands of
Meremoth[n] son of Uriah, the priest. Eleazar son of Phinehas was with him, and so
were the Levites Jozabad son of Jeshua and
Noadiah son of Binnui.[o] 34Everything was
accounted for by number and weight, and
the entire weight was recorded at that time.
35Then the exiles who had returned
from captivity sacrificed burnt offerings
to the God of Israel: twelve bulls for all Israel, ninety-six rams, seventy-seven male
lambs and, as a sin offering,[a] twelve male
goats.[p] All this was a burnt offering to the
LORD. 36They also delivered the king's orders[q] to the royal satraps and to the governors of Trans-Euphrates, who then gave
assistance to the people and to the house
of God.[r]

Ezra's Prayer About Intermarriage

9 After these things had been done, the
leaders came to me and said, "The people of Israel, including the priests and the
Levites, have not kept themselves separate[s] from the neighboring peoples with
their detestable practices, like those of
the Canaanites, Hittites, Perizzites, Jebusites, Ammonites,[t] Moabites, Egyptians
and Amorites.[u] 2They have taken some of
their daughters[v] as wives for themselves
and their sons, and have mingled the holy
race[w] with the peoples around them. And
the leaders and officials have led the way
in this unfaithfulness."[x]
3When I heard this, I tore my tunic and
cloak, pulled hair from my head and beard
and sat down appalled. 4Then everyone
who trembled[y] at the words of the God of
Israel gathered around me because of this
unfaithfulness of the exiles. And I sat there
appalled until the evening sacrifice.
5Then, at the evening sacrifice,[z] I rose
from my self-abasement, with my tunic
and cloak torn, and fell on my knees with
my hands spread out to the LORD my God
6and prayed:

"I am too ashamed and disgraced,
my God, to lift up my face to you, because our sins are higher than our
heads and our guilt has reached to the
heavens.[a] 7From the days of our ancestors[b] until now, our guilt has been
great. Because of our sins, we and our
kings and our priests have been subjected to the sword[c] and captivity,[d] to
pillage and humiliation[e] at the hand of
foreign kings, as it is today.
8"But now, for a brief moment, the
LORD our God has been gracious[f] in
leaving us a remnant[g] and giving us
a firm place[b][h] in his sanctuary, and so
our God gives light to our eyes[i] and a
little relief in our bondage. 9Though
we are slaves,[j] our God has not forsak-
en us in our bondage. He has shown
us kindness[k] in the sight of the kings
of Persia: He has granted us new life
to rebuild the house of our God and
repair its ruins,[l] and he has given us
a wall of protection in Judah and Jerusalem.
10"But now, our God, what can we
say after this? For we have forsaken
the commands[m] 11you gave through
your servants the prophets when you
said: 'The land you are entering to possess is a land polluted[n] by the corruption of its peoples. By their detestable
practices[o] they have filled it with their
impurity from one end to the other.
12Therefore, do not give your daughters in marriage to their sons or take
their daughters for your sons. Do not
seek a treaty of friendship with them[p]
at any time, that you may be strong
and eat the good things of the land and
leave it to your children as an everlasting inheritance.'
13"What has happened to us is a result of our evil deeds and our great
guilt, and yet, our God, you have punished us less than our sins deserved[q]
and have given us a remnant like this.

[a] *35* Or *purification offering* [b] *8* Or *a foothold*

9:2 *taken some of their daughters as wives for themselves.* Intermarrying with people who did not worship the One True God was expressly forbidden (Ex. 34:16; Deut. 7:3). While there are instances of marriages to non-Israelites being blessed (Rahab, Ruth), these were cases where the woman had clearly taken a stand as a believer in Yahweh, renouncing her old religion.

9:13–14 *punished us less than our sins deserved.* Israel was guilty and deserved whatever

8:31 [l] ver 15 **8:32** [m] Ge 40:13; Ne 2:11 **8:33** [n] Ne 3:4, 21 [o] Ne 3:24 **8:35** [p] 2Ch 29:21; Ezr 6:17 **8:36** [q] Ezr 7:21-24 [r] Est 9:3 **9:1** [s] Ezr 6:21; Ne 9:2 [t] Ge 19:38 [u] Ex 13:5 **9:2** [v] Ex 34:16 [w] Ex 22:31 [x] Ezr 10:2 **9:4** [y] Ezr 10:3 **9:5** [z] Ex 29:41 **9:6** [a] 2Ch 28:9; Job 42:6; Ps 38:4; Rev 18:5 **9:7** [b] 2Ch 29:6 [c] Eze 21:1-32 [d] Dt 28:64 [e] Dt 28:37 **9:8** [f] Ps 25:16; Isa 33:2 [g] Ge 45:7 [h] Ecc 12:11; Isa 22:23 [i] Ps 13:3 **9:9** [j] Ex 1:14; Ne 9:36 [k] Ezr 7:28 [l] Ps 69:35; Isa 43:1; Jer 32:44 **9:10** [m] Dt 11:8; Isa 1:19-20 **9:11** [n] Lev 18:25-28 [o] Dt 9:4 **9:12** [p] Ex 34:15; Dt 7:3; 23:6 **9:13** [q] Job 11:6; Ps 103:10

14Shall we then break your commands
again and intermarry[r] with the peoples who commit such detestable practices? Would you not be angry enough
with us to destroy us,[s] leaving us no
remnant[t] or survivor? 15LORD, the God
of Israel, you are righteous![u] We are
left this day as a remnant. Here we
are before you in our guilt, though because of it not one of us can stand[v] in
your presence.[w]"

The People's Confession of Sin

10 While Ezra was praying and confessing,[x] weeping and throwing himself down before the house of God, a large
crowd of Israelites—men, women and
children—gathered around him. They too
wept bitterly. 2Then Shekaniah son of Jehiel, one of the descendants of Elam, said to
Ezra, "We have been unfaithful[y] to our God
by marrying foreign women from the peoples around us. But in spite of this, there
is still hope for Israel.[z] 3Now let us make a
covenant[a] before our God to send away[b] all
these women and their children, in accordance with the counsel of my lord and of
those who fear the commands of our God.
Let it be done according to the Law. 4Rise
up; this matter is in your hands. We will
support you, so take courage and do it."
5So Ezra rose up and put the leading
priests and Levites and all Israel under
oath[c] to do what had been suggested. And
they took the oath. 6Then Ezra withdrew
from before the house of God and went to
the room of Jehohanan son of Eliashib.
While he was there, he ate no food and
drank no water,[d] because he continued to
mourn over the unfaithfulness of the exiles.
7A proclamation was then issued
throughout Judah and Jerusalem for all
the exiles to assemble in Jerusalem. 8Any-
one who failed to appear within three days
would forfeit all his property, in accordance with the decision of the officials and
elders, and would himself be expelled from
the assembly of the exiles.
9Within the three days, all the men of
Judah and Benjamin[e] had gathered in Jerusalem. And on the twentieth day of the
ninth month, all the people were sitting in
the square before the house of God, greatly distressed by the occasion and because
of the rain. 10Then Ezra the priest stood
up and said to them, "You have been unfaithful; you have married foreign women,
adding to Israel's guilt. 11Now honor[a] the
LORD, the God of your ancestors, and do his
will. Separate yourselves from the peoples
around you and from your foreign wives."[f]
12The whole assembly responded with a
loud voice:[g] "You are right! We must do as
you say. 13But there are many people here
and it is the rainy season; so we cannot
stand outside. Besides, this matter cannot
be taken care of in a day or two, because we
have sinned greatly in this thing. 14Let our
officials act for the whole assembly. Then
let everyone in our towns who has married a foreign woman come at a set time,
along with the elders and judges[h] of each
town, until the fierce anger[i] of our God in
this matter is turned away from us." 15Only
Jonathan son of Asahel and Jahzeiah son
of Tikvah, supported by Meshullam and
Shabbethai[j] the Levite, opposed this.
16So the exiles did as was proposed. Ezra
the priest selected men who were family
heads, one from each family division, and

[a] 11 Or *Now make confession to*

punishment God gave them. God would have been just in consuming them, even to the point of leaving no remnant or survivor. But in His great mercy, God provided a way out for Israel. In an even greater way, He provided a way out for all mankind. Sin is always sin, no matter how small it may seem to us. God would be justified in destroying us all for only one sin. God is just. This means that He cannot tolerate sin even a little bit. But He is also more loving, kind, and compassionate than we can comprehend. In His mercy, He provided the way out. He sent His son to pay the price of our sin for us. In this way His justice was satisfied, and at the same time His love provided a way to save us.

9:15 *We are left this day as a remnant.* It is true that Israel was rebellious and evil at times in her history. Kings and Chronicles record how wicked they had become. But the people who returned to rebuild the temple were a chastened and different generation from the one taken into captivity. The men and women who went back were determined to obey God's laws and would not tolerate idolatry. While the returning Jews succeeded in ridding themselves of heathen idol worship, they created another problem. They set in motion a legalistic system that culminated with a people who valued their interpretation of the law over the Scriptures. The condition progressed until Jesus spoke out against their extremism and their lack of mercy and compassion (Matt. 23:1–36).

10:3 Fear of God—When one thinks of fear, usually what comes to mind is dread and alarm—an unpleasant emotion caused by the anticipation of danger or a threat. But the fear of God is another thing. We tremble and obey Him, not out of dread but out of deep reverence for an almighty God. The covenant the men of Israel made with God was the most binding form of covenant a person could make. They were pledging "in the fear of God" to do as they promised.

10:9 *the ninth month.* The ninth month, Kislev, corresponds to November-December.

9:14 [r] Ne 13:27 [s] Dt 9:8 [t] Dt 9:14 **9:15** [u] Ge 18:25; Ps 51:4; Jer 12:1; Da 9:7 [v] Ne 9:33; Ps 130:3; Mal 3:2 [w] 1Ki 8:47 **10:1** [x] 2Ch 20:9; Da 9:20 **10:2** [y] Ezr 9:2; Ne 13:27 [z] Dt 30:8-10 **10:3** [a] 2Ch 34:31 [b] Ex 34:16; Dt 7:2-3; Ezr 9:4 **10:5** [c] Ne 5:12; 13:25 **10:6** [d] Ex 34:28; Dt 9:18 **10:9** [e] Ezr 1:5 **10:11** [f] ver 3; Dt 24:1; Ne 9:2; Mal 2:10-16 **10:12** [g] Jos 6:5 **10:14** [h] Dt 16:18 [i] Nu 25:4; 2Ch 29:10; 30:8 **10:15** [j] Ne 11:16

all of them designated by name. On the first
day of the tenth month they sat down to investigate the cases, 17 and by the first day of
the first month they finished dealing with all
the men who had married foreign women.

Those Guilty of Intermarriage

18 Among the descendants of the priests,
the following had married foreign
women:[k]

From the descendants of Joshua[l] son
of Jozadak, and his brothers: Maaseiah, Eliezer, Jarib and Gedaliah.
19 (They all gave their hands[m] in
pledge to put away their wives, and
for their guilt they each presented a
ram from the flock as a guilt offering.)[n]

20 From the descendants of Immer:[o]
Hanani and Zebadiah.
21 From the descendants of Harim:[p]
Maaseiah, Elijah, Shemaiah, Jehiel
and Uzziah.
22 From the descendants of Pashhur:[q]
Elioenai, Maaseiah, Ishmael, Nethanel, Jozabad and Elasah.

23 Among the Levites:[r]

Jozabad, Shimei, Kelaiah (that is,
Kelita), Pethahiah, Judah and Eliezer.
24 From the musicians:
Eliashib.[s]
From the gatekeepers:
Shallum, Telem and Uri.

25 And among the other Israelites:

From the descendants of Parosh:[t]
Ramiah, Izziah, Malkijah, Mijamin,
Eleazar, Malkijah and Benaiah.
26 From the descendants of Elam:[u]
Mattaniah, Zechariah, Jehiel, Abdi,
Jeremoth and Elijah.
27 From the descendants of Zattu:
Elioenai, Eliashib, Mattaniah, Jeremoth, Zabad and Aziza.
28 From the descendants of Bebai:
Jehohanan, Hananiah, Zabbai and
Athlai.
29 From the descendants of Bani:
Meshullam, Malluk, Adaiah, Jashub, Sheal and Jeremoth.
30 From the descendants of Pahath-
Moab:
Adna, Kelal, Benaiah, Maaseiah,
Mattaniah, Bezalel, Binnui and Manasseh.
31 From the descendants of Harim:
Eliezer, Ishijah, Malkijah, Shemaiah, Shimeon, 32 Benjamin, Malluk
and Shemariah.
33 From the descendants of Hashum:
Mattenai, Mattattah, Zabad, Eliphelet, Jeremai, Manasseh and Shimei.
34 From the descendants of Bani:
Maadai, Amram, Uel, 35 Benaiah,
Bedeiah, Keluhi, 36 Vaniah, Meremoth, Eliashib, 37 Mattaniah, Mattenai and Jaasu.
38 From the descendants of Binnui:[a]
Shimei, 39 Shelemiah, Nathan, Adaiah, 40 Maknadebai, Shashai, Sha-
rai, 41 Azarel, Shelemiah, Shemariah, 42 Shallum, Amariah and
Joseph.
43 From the descendants of Nebo:
Jeiel, Mattithiah, Zabad, Zebina,
Jaddai, Joel and Benaiah.

44 All these had married foreign women,
and some of them had children by these
wives.[b]

---

[a] *37,38* See Septuagint (also 1 Esdras 9:34); Hebrew *Jaasu* [38]*and Bani and Binnui,* [b] *44* Or *and they sent them away with their children*

10:18 [k] Jdg 3:6 [l] Ezr 2:2 **10:19** [m] 2Ki 10:15 [n] Lev 5:15; 6:6 **10:20** [o] 1Ch 24:14 **10:21** [p] 1Ch 24:8

10:22 [q] 1Ch 9:12 **10:23** [r] Ne 8:7; 9:4 **10:24** [s] Ne 3:1; 12:10; 13:7,28 **10:25** [t] Ezr 2:3 **10:26** [u] ver 2

NEHEMIAH

▶ **AUTHOR:** It is apparent that much of this book came from Nehemiah's personal memoirs. The account is extremely vivid and frank. Obviously, 1:1—7:5; 12:27–43; and 13:4–31 are the "words of Nehemiah." Some scholars state that Nehemiah composed the above portions and compiled the rest. Others feel that Ezra wrote 7:6—12:26 and 12:44—13:3, then put together the rest using Nehemiah's diary. Nehemiah 7:5–73 and Ezra 2:1–70 are almost identical, but both lists may have been pulled from an existing record of the same period.

▶ **TIME:** 444–425 B.C. ▶ **KEY VERSE:** Neh. 6:15

▶ **THEME:** Nehemiah's role in rebuilding the temple and the walls of Jerusalem is more political than physical, as he deals with the new political situation arising in Persia and in Jerusalem. He also serves as the general contractor who pulls together the raw materials and the workers while orchestrating the rebuilding process. Within all his work, there is an underlying understanding that he has been called by God to do this work and is fulfilling God's purposes. When the people don't follow through with adhering to the law, Nehemiah is just as forceful as Ezra in calling the people back to repentance and obedience.

Nehemiah's Prayer

1 The words of Nehemiah son of Hakaliah:

In the month of Kislev[a] in the twentieth year, while I was in the citadel of Susa,
2Hanani,[b] one of my brothers, came from Judah with some other men, and I questioned them about the Jewish remnant[c] that had survived the exile, and also about Jerusalem.
3They said to me, "Those who survived the exile and are back in the province are in great trouble and disgrace. The wall of Jerusalem is broken down, and its gates have been burned with fire.[d]"
4When I heard these things, I sat down and wept.[e] For some days I mourned and fasted[f] and prayed before the God of heaven.
5Then I said:

"LORD, the God of heaven, the great and awesome God,[g] who keeps his covenant of love[h] with those who love him and keep his commandments,
6let your ear be attentive and your eyes open to hear[i] the prayer[j] your servant is praying before you day and night for your servants, the people of Israel. I confess the sins we Israelites, including myself and my father's family, have committed against you.
7We have acted very wickedly[k] toward you. We have not obeyed the commands, decrees and laws you gave your servant Moses.
8"Remember[l] the instruction you gave your servant Moses, saying, 'If

1:1 ***Nehemiah.*** Nehemiah, whose name means "The LORD Comforts," was a highly placed statesman associated with Ezra in the work of reestablishing the people of Judah in the Promised Land. ***the twentieth year.*** This is a reference to the twentieth year of rule of Artaxerxes I Longimanus (456–424 B.C.). It was he who had commissioned Ezra to return to Jerusalem (Ezra 7:1). ***the citadel of Susa.*** The capital, or fortified royal palace, was built on an acropolis about 150 miles north of the Persian Gulf, in present day Iran. This is the city where Daniel received his vision about the rams and goats (Dan. 8:2) and the home of Mordecai and Esther (Esth. 1:2).
1:2 ***came from Judah . . . Jerusalem.*** The journey from Susa to Jerusalem, which covered nearly one thousand miles, probably took about four months.

1:5 Obedience—The covenant of God with the Israelites had been made with the understanding that obedience would bring God's great blessings, and the result of rebellion would be curses, one of which was captivity (Deut. 28–30). God had been patient for a long time, but eventually the nation was overpowered, and many of the people taken into captivity. Nehemiah acknowledged not only the necessity of obedience, but the confidence that he had that God would answer his prayer because God said He would hear and bless the obedient.

1:1 [a] Ne 10:1; Zec 7:1 **1:2** [b] Ne 7:2 [c] Jer 52:28
1:3 [d] 2Ki 25:10; Ne 2:3, 13, 17 **1:4** [e] Ps 137:1 [f] Ezr 9:4
1:5 [g] Dt 7:21; Ne 4:14 [h] Ex 20:6; Da 9:4 **1:6** [i] 1Ki 8:29
[j] Da 9:17 **1:7** [k] Dt 28:14-15; Ps 106:6 **1:8** [l] 2Ki 20:3

you are unfaithful, I will scatter[m] you among the nations, [9]but if you return to me and obey my commands, then even if your exiled people are at the farthest horizon, I will gather[n] them from there and bring them to the place I have chosen as a dwelling for my Name.'[o]

[10]"They are your servants and your people, whom you redeemed by your great strength and your mighty hand.[p]
[11]Lord, let your ear be attentive[q] to the prayer of this your servant and to the prayer of your servants who delight in revering your name. Give your servant success today by granting him favor in the presence of this man."

I was cupbearer[r] to the king.

Artaxerxes Sends Nehemiah to Jerusalem

2 In the month of Nisan in the twentieth year of King Artaxerxes,[s] when wine was brought for him, I took the wine and gave it to the king. I had not been sad in his presence before, [2]so the king asked me, "Why does your face look so sad when you are not ill? This can be nothing but sadness of heart."

I was very much afraid, [3]but I said to the king, "May the king live forever![t] Why should my face not look sad when the city[u] where my ancestors are buried lies in ruins, and its gates have been destroyed by fire?[v]"

[4]The king said to me, "What is it you want?"

Then I prayed to the God of heaven, [5]and I answered the king, "If it pleases the king and if your servant has found favor in his sight, let him send me to the city in Judah where my ancestors are buried so that I can rebuild it."

[6]Then the king[w], with the queen sitting beside him, asked me, "How long will your journey take, and when will you get back?" It pleased the king to send me; so I set a time.

[7]I also said to him, "If it pleases the king, may I have letters to the governors of Trans-Euphrates,[x] so that they will provide me safe-conduct until I arrive in Judah? [8]And may I have a letter to Asaph, keeper of the royal park, so he will give me timber to make beams for the gates of the citadel[y] by the temple and for the city wall and for the residence I will occupy?" And because the gracious hand of my God was on me,[z] the king granted my requests. [9]So I went to the governors of Trans-Euphrates and gave them the king's letters. The king had also sent army officers and cavalry[a] with me.

[10]When Sanballat[b] the Horonite and Tobiah[c] the Ammonite official heard about this, they were very much disturbed that someone had come to promote the welfare of the Israelites.[d]

Nehemiah Inspects Jerusalem's Walls

[11]I went to Jerusalem, and after staying there three days[e] [12]I set out during the night with a few others. I had not told anyone what my God had put in my heart to do for Jerusalem. There were no mounts with me except the one I was riding on.

[13]By night I went out through the Valley Gate[f] toward the Jackal[a] Well and the Dung Gate,[g] examining the walls[h] of Jerusalem, which had been broken down, and its gates, which had been destroyed by fire. [14]Then I moved on toward the Fountain Gate[i] and the King's Pool,[j] but there was not enough room for my mount to get through; [15]so I went up the valley by night, examining the wall. Finally, I turned back and reentered through the Valley Gate. [16]The officials did not know where I had gone or what I was doing, because as yet I had said nothing to the Jews or the priests or nobles or officials or any others who would be doing the work.

[17]Then I said to them, "You see the trouble we are in: Jerusalem lies in ruins, and its gates have been burned with fire.[k] Come, let us rebuild the wall[l] of Jerusalem, and we

[a] 13 Or *Serpent* or *Fig*

1:11 *cupbearer to the king.* As the king's cupbearer, Nehemiah held an honored position. His constant proximity to the king of Persia made him privy to the state secrets and personal affairs of the king.
2:2 *face look so sad.* Persian monarchs believed that just being in their presence would make any person happy. Yet, Nehemiah was about to request the emperor's permission to go to Jerusalem, suggesting that he would rather be somewhere other than in the emperor's presence. In addition to this, it was Artaxerxes himself who had ordered the work on the wall to be stopped (Ezra 4:21–23). Nehemiah had reason to be afraid.
2:4 *I prayed.* Even though Nehemiah had come into the presence of the king, he never left the presence of God.
2:8 *the royal park . . . timber.* Jerusalem had plenty of limestone for building projects, but timber was scarce.
2:10 *the Ammonite.* At the time of Nehemiah, the Ammonites (Gen. 19:38) had pushed west into the land vacated by Judah. The prospect of a strong Jewish community in newly fortified Jerusalem would have seemed threatening.

1:8 [m] Lev 26:33 **1:9** [n] Dt 30:4 [o] 1Ki 8:48; Jer 29:14 **1:10** [p] Ex 32:11; Dt 9:29 **1:11** [q] ver 6 [r] Ge 40:1 **2:1** [s] Ezr 7:1 **2:3** [t] 1Ki 1:31; Da 2:4; 5:10; 6:6,21 [u] Ps 137:6 [v] Ne 1:3 **2:6** [w] Ne 5:14; 13:6 **2:7** [x] Ezr 8:36 **2:8** [y] Ne 7:2 [z] ver 18; Ezr 5:5; 7:6 **2:9** [a] Ezr 8:22 **2:10** [b] ver 19; Ne 4:1,7 [c] Ne 4:3; 13:4-7 [d] Est 10:3 **2:11** [e] Ge 40:13 **2:13** [f] 2Ch 26:9 [g] Ne 3:13 [h] Ne 1:3 **2:14** [i] Ne 3:15 [j] 2Ki 18:17 **2:17** [k] Ne 1:3 [l] Ps 102:16; Isa 30:13; 58:12

will no longer be in disgrace.[m]" 18 I also told
them about the gracious hand of my God
on me[n] and what the king had said to me.

They replied, "Let us start rebuilding."
So they began this good work.

19 But when Sanballat the Horonite, Tobiah the Ammonite official and Geshem[o]
the Arab heard about it, they mocked and
ridiculed us.[p] "What is this you are doing?"
they asked. "Are you rebelling against the
king?"

20 I answered them by saying, "The God
of heaven will give us success. We his servants will start rebuilding, but as for you,
you have no share[q] in Jerusalem or any
claim or historic right to it."

Builders of the Wall

3 Eliashib[r] the high priest and his fellow
priests went to work and rebuilt[s] the
Sheep Gate.[t] They dedicated it and set its
doors in place, building as far as the Tower
of the Hundred, which they dedicated, and
as far as the Tower of Hananel.[u] 2 The men
of Jericho[v] built the adjoining section, and
Zakkur son of Imri built next to them.

3 The Fish Gate[w] was rebuilt by the sons
of Hassenaah. They laid its beams and
put its doors and bolts and bars in place.
4 Meremoth son of Uriah, the son of Hakkoz, repaired the next section. Next to
him Meshullam son of Berekiah, the son
of Meshezabel, made repairs, and next to
him Zadok son of Baana also made repairs.
5 The next section was repaired by the men
of Tekoa,[x] but their nobles would not put
their shoulders to the work under their supervisors.[a]

6 The Jeshanah[b] Gate[y] was repaired by
Joiada son of Paseah and Meshullam son
of Besodeiah. They laid its beams and put
its doors with their bolts and bars in place.
7 Next to them, repairs were made by men
from Gibeon[z] and Mizpah—Melatiah of
Gibeon and Jadon of Meronoth—places under the authority of the governor of
Trans-Euphrates. 8 Uzziel son of Harhaiah,
one of the goldsmiths, repaired the next
section; and Hananiah, one of the perfume-
makers, made repairs next to that. They restored Jerusalem as far as the Broad Wall.[a]
9 Rephaiah son of Hur, ruler of a half-district of Jerusalem, repaired the next section. 10 Adjoining this, Jedaiah son of Ha-
rumaph made repairs opposite his house,
and Hattush son of Hashabneiah made repairs next to him. 11 Malkijah son of Harim
and Hasshub son of Pahath-Moab repaired
another section and the Tower of the Ovens.[b] 12 Shallum son of Hallohesh, ruler of
a half-district of Jerusalem, repaired the
next section with the help of his daughters.

13 The Valley Gate[c] was repaired by Hanun and the residents of Zanoah.[d] They
rebuilt it and put its doors with their bolts
and bars in place. They also repaired a
thousand cubits[c] of the wall as far as the
Dung Gate.[e]

14 The Dung Gate was repaired by Malkijah son of Rekab, ruler of the district of
Beth Hakkerem.[f] He rebuilt it and put its
doors with their bolts and bars in place.

15 The Fountain Gate was repaired by
Shallun son of Kol-Hozeh, ruler of the district of Mizpah. He rebuilt it, roofing it over
and putting its doors and bolts and bars
in place. He also repaired the wall of the
Pool of Siloam,[d][g] by the King's Garden, as
far as the steps going down from the City
of David. 16 Beyond him, Nehemiah son
of Azbuk, ruler of a half-district of Beth
Zur,[h] made repairs up to a point opposite
the tombs[e][i] of David, as far as the artificial
pool and the House of the Heroes.

17 Next to him, the repairs were made
by the Levites under Rehum son of Bani.
Beside him, Hashabiah, ruler of half the
district of Keilah,[j] carried out repairs for
his district. 18 Next to him, the repairs were
made by their fellow Levites under Binnui[f]
son of Henadad, ruler of the other half-district of Keilah. 19 Next to him, Ezer son of
Jeshua, ruler of Mizpah, repaired another
section, from a point facing the ascent to
the armory as far as the angle of the wall.
20 Next to him, Baruch son of Zabbai zealously repaired another section, from the
angle to the entrance of the house of Eliashib the high priest. 21 Next to him, Meremoth[k] son of Uriah, the son of Hakkoz, repaired another section, from the entrance
of Eliashib's house to the end of it.

22 The repairs next to him were made by

---

[a] 5 Or *their Lord* or *the governor* [b] 6 Or *Old*
[c] 13 That is, about 1,500 feet or about 450 meters
[d] 15 Hebrew *Shelah,* a variant of *Shiloah,* that is, Siloam [e] 16 Hebrew; Septuagint, some Vulgate manuscripts and Syriac *tomb* [f] 18 Two Hebrew manuscripts and Syriac (see also Septuagint and verse 24); most Hebrew manuscripts *Bavvai*

2:18 ***the gracious hand of my God on me.*** Nehemiah emphasized that it was not just his own idea to rebuild the wall of Jerusalem. The idea had come to him from the Lord (vv. 8,12).

3:8 ***the Broad Wall.*** The Broad Wall was probably built in the seventh century B.C. by Hezekiah to accommodate the influx of refugees from the fall of Samaria in 722 B.C. (2 Chr. 32:5).

3:15 ***Pool of Siloam.*** This pool is also known as the Pool of Shela.

2:17 [m] Eze 5:14 **2:18** [n] 2Sa 2:7 **2:19** [o] Ne 6:1,2,6 [p] Ps 44:13-16 **2:20** [q] Ezr 4:3 **3:1** [r] Ezr 10:24 [s] Isa 58:12 [t] ver 32; Ne 12:39 [u] Ne 12:39; Jer 31:38; Zec 14:10 **3:2** [v] Ne 7:36 **3:3** [w] 2Ch 33:14; Ne 12:39 **3:5** [x] 2Sa 14:2 **3:6** [y] Ne 12:39 **3:7** [z] Jos 9:3; Ne 2:7 **3:8** [a] Ne 12:38 **3:11** [b] Ne 12:38 **3:13** [c] 2Ch 26:9 [d] Jos 15:34 [e] Ne 2:13 **3:14** [f] Jer 6:1 **3:15** [g] Isa 8:6; Jn 9:7 **3:16** [h] Jos 15:58 [i] Ac 2:29 **3:17** [j] Jos 15:44 **3:21** [k] Ezr 8:33

the priests from the surrounding region. 23 Beyond them, Benjamin and Hasshub made repairs in front of their house; and next to them, Azariah son of Maaseiah, the son of Ananiah, made repairs beside his house. 24 Next to him, Binnui[l] son of Henadad repaired another section, from Azariah's house to the angle and the corner, 25 and Palal son of Uzai worked opposite the angle and the tower projecting from the upper palace near the court of the guard.[m] Next to him, Pedaiah son of Parosh[n] 26 and the temple servants[o] living on the hill of Ophel[p] made repairs up to a point opposite the Water Gate[q] toward the east and the projecting tower. 27 Next to them, the men of Tekoa[r] repaired another section, from the great projecting tower[s] to the wall of Ophel.

28 Above the Horse Gate,[t] the priests made repairs, each in front of his own house. 29 Next to them, Zadok son of Immer made repairs opposite his house. Next to him, Shemaiah son of Shekaniah, the guard at the East Gate, made repairs. 30 Next to him, Hananiah son of Shelemiah, and Hanun, the sixth son of Zalaph, repaired another section. Next to them, Meshullam son of Berekiah made repairs opposite his living quarters. 31 Next to him, Malkijah, one of the goldsmiths, made repairs as far as the house of the temple servants and the merchants, opposite the Inspection Gate, and as far as the room above the corner; 32 and between the room above the corner and the Sheep Gate[u] the goldsmiths and merchants made repairs.

Opposition to the Rebuilding

4 [a] When Sanballat[v] heard that we were rebuilding the wall, he became angry and was greatly incensed. He ridiculed the Jews, 2 and in the presence of his associates[w] and the army of Samaria, he said, "What are those feeble Jews doing? Will they restore their wall? Will they offer sacrifices? Will they finish in a day? Can they bring the stones back to life from those heaps of rubble[x]—burned as they are?"

3 Tobiah[y] the Ammonite, who was at his side, said, "What they are building—even a fox climbing up on it would break down their wall of stones!"[z]

4 Hear us, our God, for we are despised.[a]
Turn their insults back on their own heads.
Give them over as plunder in a land of captivity. 5 Do not cover up their guilt[b] or blot out their sins from your sight,[c] for they have thrown insults in the face of[b] the builders.

6 So we rebuilt the wall till all of it reached half its height, for the people worked with all their heart.

7 But when Sanballat, Tobiah,[d] the Arabs, the Ammonites and the people of Ashdod heard that the repairs to Jerusalem's walls had gone ahead and that the gaps were being closed, they were very angry. 8 They all plotted together[e] to come and fight against Jerusalem and stir up trouble against it. 9 But we prayed to our God and posted a guard day and night to meet this threat.

10 Meanwhile, the people in Judah said, "The strength of the laborers[f] is giving out, and there is so much rubble that we cannot rebuild the wall."

11 Also our enemies said, "Before they know it or see us, we will be right there among them and will kill them and put an end to the work."

12 Then the Jews who lived near them came and told us ten times over, "Wherever you turn, they will attack us."

13 Therefore I stationed some of the people behind the lowest points of the wall at the exposed places, posting them by families, with their swords, spears and bows. 14 After I looked things over, I stood up and said to the nobles, the officials and the rest of the people, "Don't be afraid[g] of them. Remember[h] the Lord, who is great and awesome,[i] and fight[j] for your families, your sons and your daughters, your wives and your homes."

15 When our enemies heard that we were aware of their plot and that God had frustrated it,[k] we all returned to the wall, each to our own work.

16 From that day on, half of my men did the work, while the other half were equipped with spears, shields, bows and armor. The officers posted themselves behind all the people of Judah 17 who were building the wall. Those who carried materials did their work with one hand and held a weapon[l] in the other, 18 and each of the builders wore his sword at his side as he worked. But the man who sounded the trumpet[m] stayed with me.

---

[a] In Hebrew texts 4:1-6 is numbered 3:33-38, and 4:7-23 is numbered 4:1-17. [b] 5 Or *have aroused your anger before*

4:2 ***bring the stones back to life.*** When limestone is subjected to intense heat, it becomes unsuitable for building. The stones from the burned wall would not be useable.

4:9 Prayer—It is difficult to work in a hostile environment. Ambition, courage, and preparation are important in a situation like this, and so is prayer. If we are not careful to ask God to protect us, our fear can cripple us as much as the animosity of our enemies. No matter how prepared we may be for a crisis, the power of God is the ultimate factor in determining whether we win or lose.

3:24 [l] Ezr 8:33 **3:25** [m] Jer 32:2; 37:21; 39:14 [n] Ezr 2:3 **3:26** [o] Ne 7:46; 11:21 [p] 2Ch 33:14 [q] Ne 8:1, 3, 16; 12:37 **3:27** [r] ver 5 [s] Ps 48:12 **3:28** [t] 2Ki 11:16; 2Ch 23:15; Jer 31:40 **3:32** [u] ver 1; Jn 5:2 **4:1** [v] Ne 2:10 **4:2** [w] Ezr 4:9-10 [x] Ps 79:1; Jer 26:18 **4:3** [y] Ne 2:10 [z] Job 13:12; 15:3 **4:4** [a] Ps 44:13; 79:12; 123:3-4; Jer 33:24 **4:5** [b] Isa 2:9; La 1:22 [c] 2Ki 14:27; Ps 51:1; 69:27-28; 109:14; Jer 18:23 **4:7** [d] Ne 2:10 **4:8** [e] Ps 2:2; 83:1-18 **4:10** [f] 1Ch 23:4 **4:14** [g] Ge 28:15; Nu 14:9; Dt 1:29 [h] Ne 1:8 [i] Ne 1:5 [j] 2Sa 10:12 **4:15** [k] 2Sa 17:14; Job 5:12 **4:17** [l] Ps 149:6 **4:18** [m] Nu 10:2

19Then I said to the nobles, the officials and the rest of the people, "The work is extensive and spread out, and we are widely separated from each other along the wall. 20Wherever you hear the sound of the trumpet,[n] join us there. Our God will fight[o] for us!"

21So we continued the work with half the men holding spears, from the first light of dawn till the stars came out. 22At that time I also said to the people, "Have every man and his helper stay inside Jerusalem at night, so they can serve us as guards by night and as workers by day." 23Neither I nor my brothers nor my men nor the guards with me took off our clothes; each had his weapon, even when he went for water.[a]

Nehemiah Helps the Poor

5 Now the men and their wives raised a great outcry against their fellow Jews. 2Some were saying, "We and our sons and daughters are numerous; in order for us to eat and stay alive, we must get grain."

3Others were saying, "We are mortgaging our fields,[p] our vineyards and our homes to get grain during the famine."[q]

4Still others were saying, "We have had to borrow money to pay the king's tax[r] on our fields and vineyards. 5Although we are of the same flesh and blood[s] as our fellow Jews and though our children are as good as theirs, yet we have to subject our sons and daughters to slavery.[t] Some of our daughters have already been enslaved, but we are powerless, because our fields and our vineyards belong to others."[u]

6When I heard their outcry and these charges, I was very angry. 7I pondered them in my mind and then accused the nobles and officials. I told them, "You are charging your own people interest!"[v] So I called together a large meeting to deal with them 8and said: "As far as possible, we have bought[w] back our fellow Jews who were sold to the Gentiles. Now you are selling your own people, only for them to be sold back to us!" They kept quiet, because they could find nothing to say.[x]

9So I continued, "What you are doing is not right. Shouldn't you walk in the fear of our God to avoid the reproach[y] of our Gentile enemies? 10I and my brothers and my men are also lending the people money and grain. But let us stop charging interest![z] 11Give back to them immediately their fields, vineyards, olive groves and houses, and also the interest[a] you are charging them—one percent of the money, grain, new wine and olive oil."

12"We will give it back," they said. "And we will not demand anything more from them. We will do as you say."

Then I summoned the priests and made the nobles and officials take an oath[b] to do what they had promised. 13I also shook[c] out the folds of my robe and said, "In this way may God shake out of their house and possessions anyone who does not keep this promise. So may such a person be shaken out and emptied!"

At this the whole assembly said, "Amen,"[d] and praised the LORD. And the people did as they had promised.

14Moreover, from the twentieth year of King Artaxerxes,[e] when I was appointed to be their governor[f] in the land of Judah, until his thirty-second year—twelve years—neither I nor my brothers ate the food allotted to the governor. 15But the earlier governors—those preceding me—placed a heavy burden on the people and took forty shekels[b] of silver from them in addition to food and wine. Their assistants also lorded it over the people. But out of reverence for God[g] I did not act like that. 16Instead,[h] I devoted myself to the work on this wall. All my men were assembled there for the work; we[c] did not acquire any land.

17Furthermore, a hundred and fifty Jews and officials ate at my table, as well as those who came to us from the surrounding nations. 18Each day one ox, six choice

---

a *23* The meaning of the Hebrew for this clause is uncertain. *b* *15* That is, about 1 pound or about 460 grams *c* *16* Most Hebrew manuscripts; some Hebrew manuscripts, Septuagint, Vulgate and Syriac *I*

5:7 *charging ... interest.* It was not wrong to lend money to a fellow Jew, or even to lend money at interest to a non-Jewish person, but it was forbidden to charge interest to a fellow Jew (Ex. 22:25; Deut. 23:19–20). The people had already fallen back into disobedience.

5:9 Fear of God—Fear of God is the knowledge that God has the right to judge our actions for good or evil. It is the basis for keeping the commandments which concern other men. We do not murder because it is taking the life of one who bears the image and likeness of God. We deal honestly with one another, we do not covet our neighbor's possessions, or abridge any of his rights, because those things are given to him by God, and our neighbor belongs to God who created him. If we do not walk in the fear of the Lord, we demonstrate our pride and presumption to those who are watching us.

5:11 *one percent.* This is probably a reference to the interest the nobles and rulers had been charging.

5:15 *earlier governors.* Several former governors had paid their own expenses with the people's taxes. During his twelve year administration (444–432 B.C.),

4:20 [n] Eze 33:3 [o] Ex 14:14; Dt 1:30; 20:4; Jos 10:14
5:3 [p] Ps 109:11 [q] Ge 47:23 **5:4** [r] Ezr 4:13 **5:5** [s] Ge 29:14 [t] Lev 25:39-43, 47; 2Ki 4:1; Isa 50:1 [u] Dt 15:7-11; 2Ki 4:1
5:7 [v] Ex 22:25-27; Lev 25:35-37; Dt 23:19-20; 24:10-13
5:8 [w] Lev 25:47 [x] Jer 34:8 **5:9** [y] Isa 52:5
5:10 [z] Ex 22:25 **5:11** [a] Isa 58:6 **5:12** [b] Ezr 10:5
5:13 [c] Mt 10:14; Ac 18:6 [d] Dt 27:15-26 **5:14** [e] Ne 2:6; 13:6 [f] Ge 42:6; Ezr 6:7; Jer 40:7; Hag 1:1 **5:15** [g] Ge 20:11
5:16 [h] 2Th 3:7-10

sheep and some poultry[i] were prepared
for me, and every ten days an abundant
supply of wine of all kinds. In spite of all
this, I never demanded the food allotted to
the governor, because the demands were
heavy on these people.
19Remember[j] me with favor, my God, for
all I have done for these people.

Further Opposition to the Rebuilding

6 When word came to Sanballat, Tobiah,[k]
Geshem[l] the Arab and the rest of our
enemies that I had rebuilt the wall and not
a gap was left in it—though up to that time
I had not set the doors in the gates— 2San-
ballat and Geshem sent me this message:
"Come, let us meet together in one of the
villages[a] on the plain of Ono.[m]"
But they were scheming to harm me; 3so
I sent messengers to them with this reply:
"I am carrying on a great project and cannot go down. Why should the work stop
while I leave it and go down to you?" 4Four
times they sent me the same message, and
each time I gave them the same answer.
5Then, the fifth time, Sanballat[n] sent his
aide to me with the same message, and in
his hand was an unsealed letter 6in which
was written:

"It is reported among the nations—
and Geshem[b][o] says it is true—that you
and the Jews are plotting to revolt, and
therefore you are building the wall.
Moreover, according to these reports
you are about to become their king
7and have even appointed prophets to
make this proclamation about you in
Jerusalem: 'There is a king in Judah!'
Now this report will get back to the
king; so come, let us meet together."

8I sent him this reply: "Nothing like what
you are saying is happening; you are just
making it up out of your head."
9They were all trying to frighten us,
thinking, "Their hands will get too weak
for the work, and it will not be completed."
But I prayed, "Now strengthen my
hands."
10One day I went to the house of Shemaiah son of Delaiah, the son of Mehetabel,
who was shut in at his home. He said, "Let
us meet in the house of God, inside the
temple[p], and let us close the temple doors,
because men are coming to kill you—by
night they are coming to kill you."
11But I said, "Should a man like me run
away? Or should someone like me go into
the temple to save his life? I will not go!"
12I realized that God had not sent him,
but that he had prophesied against me[q]
because Tobiah and Sanballat[r] had hired
him. 13He had been hired to intimidate me
so that I would commit a sin by doing this,
and then they would give me a bad name
to discredit me.[s]

14Remember[t] Tobiah and Sanballat,[u] my
God, because of what they have done; remember also the prophet[v] Noadiah and
how she and the rest of the prophets[w] have
been trying to intimidate me. 15So the wall
was completed on the twenty-fifth of Elul,
in fifty-two days.

Opposition to the Completed Wall

16When all our enemies heard about this,
all the surrounding nations were afraid
and lost their self-confidence, because they
realized that this work had been done with
the help of our God.
17Also, in those days the nobles of Judah
were sending many letters to Tobiah, and
replies from Tobiah kept coming to them.
18For many in Judah were under oath to
him, since he was son-in-law to Shekaniah
son of Arah, and his son Jehohanan had
married the daughter of Meshullam son of
Berekiah. 19Moreover, they kept reporting
to me his good deeds and then telling him
what I said. And Tobiah sent letters to intimidate me.
7 After the wall had been rebuilt and I had
set the doors in place, the gatekeepers,[x]
the musicians[y] and the Levites[z] were appointed. 2I put in charge of Jerusalem my
brother Hanani,[a] along with Hananiah[b] the
commander of the citadel,[c] because he was
a man of integrity and feared[d] God more

[a] 2 Or *in Kephirim* [b] 6 Hebrew *Gashmu*, a variant of *Geshem*

Nehemiah did not collect taxes from the people, although as the governor he had the right to.

6:2 *the plain of Ono.* The plain of Ono was about twenty miles northwest of Jerusalem.

6:10 *Shemaiah.* Shemaiah was a false prophet, not the Levite of the same name who helped build the wall (3:29) or the priest who sealed the covenant with Nehemiah (10:8). Whether he was pretending to represent God, or was speaking with "authority" because he claimed that he had inside information, Shemaiah's strategy was to get Nehemiah sidetracked.

6:16 Providence—The fact that the Jews were able to finish the wall so quickly and with such singleness of purpose said even to their enemies that it was God who had helped them. God always provides everything we need to do His work. It is when we get off on our own agendas that we are short of energy and resources. Like Nehemiah, we need to pray for God's direct guidance, and then pray to keep our focus on His plan.

7:1 *gatekeepers ... musicians ... Levites.* The Levites were assistants to the priests (Num. 18:1–4) who guarded and cleaned the sanctuary. The gate-

5:18 [i] 1Ki 4:23 **5:19** [j] Ge 8:1; 2Ki 20:3; Ne 1:8; 13:14, 22, 31 **6:1** [k] Ne 2:10 [l] Ne 2:19 **6:2** [m] 1Ch 8:12 **6:5** [n] Ne 2:10 **6:6** [o] Ne 2:19 **6:10** [p] Nu 18:7 **6:12** [q] Eze 13:22-23 [r] Ne 2:10 **6:13** [s] Jer 20:10 **6:14** [t] Ne 1:8 [u] Ne 2:10 [v] Ex 15:20; Eze 13:17-23; Ac 21:9; Rev 2:20 [w] Ne 13:29; Jer 23:9-40; Zec 13:2-3 **7:1** [x] 1Ch 9:27; 26:12-19; Ne 6:1, 15 [y] Ps 68:25 [z] Ne 8:9 **7:2** [a] Ne 1:2 [b] Ne 10:23 [c] Ne 2:8 [d] 1Ki 18:3

than most people do. 3I said to them, "The
gates of Jerusalem are not to be opened until the sun is hot. While the gatekeepers are
still on duty, have them shut the doors and
bar them. Also appoint residents of Jerusalem as guards, some at their posts and
some near their own houses."

The List of the Exiles Who Returned

4Now the city was large and spacious,
but there were few people in it,[e] and the
houses had not yet been rebuilt. 5So my
God put it into my heart to assemble the
nobles, the officials and the common people for registration by families. I found the
genealogical record of those who had been
the first to return. This is what I found written there:

6These are the people of the province who came up from the captivity
of the exiles[f] whom Nebuchadnezzar
king of Babylon had taken captive
(they returned to Jerusalem and Judah, each to his own town, 7in company with Zerubbabel,[g] Joshua, Nehemiah, Azariah, Raamiah, Nahamani,
Mordecai, Bilshan, Mispereth, Bigvai,
Nehum and Baanah):

The list of the men of Israel:

8the descendants of Parosh 2,172
9of Shephatiah 372
10of Arah 652
11of Pahath-Moab (through
the line of Jeshua and Joab) 2,818
12of Elam 1,254
13of Zattu 845
14of Zakkai 760
15of Binnui 648
16of Bebai 628
17of Azgad 2,322
18of Adonikam 667
19of Bigvai 2,067
20of Adin[h] 655
21of Ater (through Hezekiah) 98
22of Hashum 328
23of Bezai 324
24of Hariph 112
25of Gibeon 95
26the men of Bethlehem and
Netophah[i] 188
27of Anathoth[j] 128
28of Beth Azmaveth 42
29of Kiriath Jearim, Kephirah[k]
and Beeroth[l] 743
30of Ramah and Geba 621
31of Mikmash 122
32of Bethel and Ai[m] 123
33of the other Nebo 52
34of the other Elam 1,254
35of Harim 320
36of Jericho[n] 345
37of Lod, Hadid and Ono[o] 721
38of Senaah 3,930

39The priests:

the descendants of Jedaiah
(through the family of
Jeshua) 973
40of Immer 1,052
41of Pashhur 1,247
42of Harim 1,017

43The Levites:

the descendants of Jeshua
(through Kadmiel through
the line of Hodaviah) 74

44The musicians:[p]

the descendants of Asaph 148

45The gatekeepers:[q]

the descendants of
Shallum, Ater, Talmon,
Akkub, Hatita and Shobai 138

46The temple servants:[r]

the descendants of
Ziha, Hasupha, Tabbaoth,
47Keros, Sia, Padon,
48Lebana, Hagaba, Shalmai,
49Hanan, Giddel, Gahar,
50Reaiah, Rezin, Nekoda,
51Gazzam, Uzza, Paseah,
52Besai, Meunim, Nephusim,
53Bakbuk, Hakupha, Harhur,
54Bazluth, Mehida, Harsha,
55Barkos, Sisera, Temah,
56Neziah and Hatipha

57The descendants of the servants of
Solomon:

the descendants of
Sotai, Sophereth, Perida,
58Jaala, Darkon, Giddel,
59Shephatiah, Hattil,
Pokereth-Hazzebaim and Amon

---

keepers and musicians were also Levites (1 Chr. 9:17–19; 26:12–19).

7:3 ***gates.*** The gates of a city normally opened at sunrise. If an enemy mounted a surprise attack at sunrise, he would find a city just beginning to wake up. By keeping the gates closed a little longer, the city was safer.

7:4 ***there were few people.*** For the size of the city, Jerusalem was underpopulated. Even though it had been 90 years since people had returned under Zerubbabel to live there, Jerusalem still had a lot of undeveloped space within the walls renewed by Nehemiah.

7:5 ***my God put it into my heart.*** Nehemiah attributed to the Lord the idea of a census that would show the distribution of the population. If he knew the population pattern in the capital and the countryside, he could then determine which districts could best afford to lose a portion of their inhabitants to Jerusalem.

7:4 [e] Ne 11:1 **7:6** [f] 2Ch 36:20; Ezr 2:1-70; Ne 1:2 **7:7** [g] 1Ch 3:19; Ezr 2:2 **7:20** [h] Ezr 8:6 **7:26** [i] 2Sa 23:28; 1Ch 2:54 **7:27** [j] Jos 21:18 **7:29** [k] Jos 18:26 [l] Jos 18:25 **7:32** [m] Ge 12:8 **7:36** [n] Ne 3:2 **7:37** [o] 1Ch 8:12 **7:44** [p] Ne 11:23 **7:45** [q] 1Ch 9:17 **7:46** [r] Ne 3:26

60 The temple servants and the descendants of the servants of Solomon[s] 392

61 The following came up from the towns of Tel Melah, Tel Harsha, Kerub, Addon and Immer, but they could not show that their families were descended from Israel:

62 the descendants of Delaiah, Tobiah and Nekoda 642

63 And from among the priests:

the descendants of Hobaiah, Hakkoz and Barzillai (a man who had married a daughter of Barzillai the Gileadite and was called by that name).

64 These searched for their family records, but they could not find
them and so were excluded from the
priesthood as unclean. 65 The governor, therefore, ordered them not to eat any of the most sacred food until there should be a priest ministering with the Urim and Thummim.[t]

66 The whole company numbered
42,360, 67 besides their 7,337 male and female slaves; and they also had 245
male and female singers. 68 There were
736 horses, 245 mules,[a] 69 435 camels and 6,720 donkeys.

70 Some of the heads of the families contributed to the work. The governor gave to the treasury 1,000 darics[b] of gold, 50 bowls and 530 garments for
priests. 71 Some of the heads of the
families[u] gave to the treasury for the work 20,000 darics[c] of gold and 2,200
minas[d] of silver. 72 The total given by
the rest of the people was 20,000 darics of gold, 2,000 minas[e] of silver and 67 garments for priests.[v]

73 The priests, the Levites, the gatekeepers, the musicians and the temple servants,[w] along with certain of the people and the rest of the Israelites, settled in their own towns.[x]

Ezra Reads the Law

8 When the seventh month came and the Israelites had settled in their towns,[y]
1 all the people came together as one in
the square before the Water Gate.[z] They told Ezra the teacher of the Law to bring out the Book of the Law of Moses,[a] which the LORD had commanded for Israel.

2 So on the first day of the seventh month[b] Ezra the priest brought the Law[c] before the assembly, which was made up of men and women and all who were able
to understand. 3 He read it aloud from daybreak till noon as he faced the square before the Water Gate[d] in the presence of the

---

a *68* Some Hebrew manuscripts (see also Ezra 2:66); most Hebrew manuscripts do not have this verse. *b* *70* That is, about 19 pounds or about 8.4 kilograms *c* *71* That is, about 375 pounds or about 170 kilograms; also in verse 72 *d* *71* That is, about 1 1/3 tons or about 1.2 metric tons *e* *72* That is, about 1 1/4 tons or about 1.1 metric tons

---

7:70 *darics.* One thousand gold darics would weigh about nineteen pounds.
8:2 *first day of the seventh month.* The wall had been completed on the twenty-fifth day of the sixth month (6:15) so this event took place just a few days after the completion of the wall. ***men and women and all who were able to understand.*** This is a more specific list of those gathered than is usual. "All who could hear" includes older children, as well as adults.
8:3 Reading God's Word—There are many parts of the world today that still have limited access to the Bible and below-average literacy rates. Even if they could obtain a Bible they might not be able to read it. Other areas of the world have a well-educated population and freedom to pursue any religion they choose. Throughout much of history, the only access to Scripture was through someone who read it in a public or church setting. Today most of the western world has access to audio recordings of the Bible or to numerous printed versions. Here are some suggestions to aid you in receiving the greatest benefit from reading or listening to the Bible:

- *Read the Bible prayerfully.* Ask the Spirit of God to meet your heart's need as you read (Ps. 119:18).
- *Read the Bible thoughtfully.* Think about the meaning and implications of what you are reading.
- *Read the Bible carefully.* Take careful note not only of the words that are used but also of how they relate to one another.
- *Read the Bible repeatedly.* It may be of great help to read the same portion over and over again each day for a month's time. This is a good way for the words to take root in your heart. If you are reading a short book, read it every day. Divide longer books up into manageable portions of two or three chapters and read that portion through every day.
- *Read the Bible extensively.* Sometimes it is of great help to read large portions of the Word of God through at one sitting. If you do this, do it at a time when you are alert and not likely to be disturbed during your reading.
- *Read the Bible regularly.* It is good to have a particular time every day when you habitually give yourself to the reading of the Word of God.
- *Read the Bible faithfully.* Inevitably there will be days when you will fail to read the Bible. Do not let your momentary lapse discourage you. Faithfully resume your practice of reading God's Word.
- *Read the Bible obediently.* Because the Bible is God's Word written to you, it is essential to obey it (Ex. 12:24).

7:60 [s] 1Ch 9:2 **7:65** [t] Ex 28:30; Ne 8:9 **7:71** [u] 1Ch 29:7 **7:72** [v] Ex 25:2 **7:73** [w] Ne 1:10; Ps 34:22; 103:21; 113:1; 135:1 [x] Ezr 3:1; Ne 11:1 [y] Ezr 3:1 **8:1** [z] Ne 3:26 [a] Dt 28:61; 2Ch 34:15; Ezr 7:6 **8:2** [b] Lev 23:23-25; Nu 29:1-6 [c] Dt 31:11 **8:3** [d] Ne 3:26

men, women and others who could understand. And all the people listened attentively to the Book of the Law.
[4]Ezra the teacher of the Law stood on a
high wooden platform[e] built for the occasion. Beside him on his right stood Mattithiah, Shema, Anaiah, Uriah, Hilkiah and
Maaseiah; and on his left were Pedaiah,
Mishael, Malkijah, Hashum, Hashbadda-
nah, Zechariah and Meshullam.
[5]Ezra opened the book. All the people
could see him because he was standing[f]
above them; and as he opened it, the people all stood up. [6]Ezra praised the LORD, the
great God; and all the people lifted their
hands[g] and responded, "Amen! Amen!"
Then they bowed down and worshiped the
LORD with their faces to the ground.
[7]The Levites[h]—Jeshua, Bani, Sherebiah,
Jamin, Akkub, Shabbethai, Hodiah, Maaseiah, Kelita, Azariah, Jozabad, Hanan
and Pelaiah—instructed[i] the people in the
Law while the people were standing there.
[8]They read from the Book of the Law of
God, making it clear[a] and giving the meaning so that the people understood what was
being read.
[9]Then Nehemiah the governor, Ezra the
priest and teacher of the Law, and the Levites[j] who were instructing the people said
to them all, "This day is holy to the LORD
your God. Do not mourn or weep."[k] For all
the people had been weeping as they listened to the words of the Law.
[10]Nehemiah said, "Go and enjoy choice
food and sweet drinks, and send some to
those who have nothing[l] prepared. This
day is holy to our Lord. Do not grieve, for
the joy[m] of the LORD is your strength."
[11]The Levites calmed all the people, saying, "Be still, for this is a holy day. Do not
grieve."
[12]Then all the people went away to eat
and drink, to send portions of food and to
celebrate with great joy,[n] because they now
understood the words that had been made
known to them.
[13]On the second day of the month, the
heads of all the families, along with the
priests and the Levites, gathered around
Ezra the teacher to give attention to the
words of the Law. [14]They found written in
the Law, which the LORD had commanded
through Moses, that the Israelites were to
live in temporary shelters during the festival of the seventh month [15]and that they
should proclaim this word and spread it
throughout their towns and in Jerusalem:
"Go out into the hill country and bring back
branches from olive and wild olive trees,
and from myrtles, palms and shade trees, to
make temporary shelters"—as it is written.[b]
[16]So the people went out and brought
back branches and built themselves temporary shelters on their own roofs, in their
courtyards, in the courts of the house of
God and in the square by the Water Gate
and the one by the Gate of Ephraim.[o] [17]The
whole company that had returned from
exile built temporary shelters and lived in
them. From the days of Joshua son of Nun
until that day, the Israelites had not celebrated[p] it like this. And their joy was very great.
[18]Day after day, from the first day to the
last, Ezra read[q] from the Book of the Law of
God. They celebrated the festival for seven
days, and on the eighth day, in accordance
with the regulation,[r] there was an assembly.

[a] 8 Or *God, translating it* [b] 15 See Lev. 23:37-40.

- *Read the Bible thankfully.* Thank God for the gift He has given us in Scripture. Thank Him that you have the freedom or the opportunity to read the Bible at all.

8:5 *the people all stood up.* Standing signified their reverence for the Word. This gesture later became characteristic of the Jewish people in synagogue services.

8:6 *lifted their hands.* The people answered "Amen" and lifted their hands, indicating their participation with Ezra in prayer.

8:9 God's Word Convicts—One of the great proofs that the Bible is really God's inspired Word is its unique ability to convict men and women of their sins. There are many biblical stories that point to this phenomenon where people realize the extent of their sin and the need to repent of it.

Under Josiah's rule a copy of God's Word is found in the temple. When it is read both the king and the people are convicted of their sins in not keeping God's law. Afterwards a great revival occurs (2 Chr. 34:14–28).

When Nehemiah returns to Israel to help the returning Jews rebuild the gates of Jerusalem, he assembles the people and has the Scriptures read to them for three hours a day. This soon causes them to confess their sin (Neh. 9:3).

In the New Testament we see many instances where the Holy Spirit uses God's Word to convict people of their sin. At Pentecost Peter uses the Scriptures to rebuke Israel for crucifying its Messiah. The result of his sermon is three thousand souls being convicted and accepting Christ (Acts 2:37,41).

8:9–10 Repentance—Once the people understood the Word of God, they wept. They had heard the high standard of the law, recognized their low standing before the Lord, and were convicted. Weeping and sorrow for sin are part of repentance. But the other part of repentance is change. With change comes joy. The joy of the Lord is the joy that springs up in our hearts because of our relationship to the Lord. It is a God-given gladness found when we are in communion with God. When our goal is to know more about the Lord, the byproduct is His joy.

8:17 *From the days of Joshua.* The reference here is to the construction of booths. The people of Israel

8:4 [e] 2Ch 6:13 **8:5** [f] Jdg 3:20 **8:6** [g] Ex 4:31; Ezr 9:5; 1Ti 2:8 **8:7** [h] Ezr 10:23 [i] Lev 10:11; 2Ch 17:7 **8:9** [j] Ne 7:1,65,70 [k] Dt 12:7,12; 16:14-15 **8:10** [l] 1Sa 25:8; Lk 14:12-14 [m] Lev 23:40; Dt 12:18; 16:11, 14-15 **8:12** [n] Est 9:22 **8:16** [o] 2Ki 14:13; Ne 12:39 **8:17** [p] 2Ch 7:8; 8:13; 30:21 **8:18** [q] Dt 31:11 [r] Lev 23:36, 40; Nu 29:35

The Israelites Confess Their Sins

9 On the twenty-fourth day of the same
month, the Israelites gathered together,
fasting and wearing sackcloth and putting
dust on their heads.[s] **2**Those of Israelite descent had separated themselves from all
foreigners.[t] They stood in their places and
confessed their sins and the sins of their
ancestors.[u] **3**They stood where they were
and read from the Book of the Law of the
LORD their God for a quarter of the day, and
spent another quarter in confession and in
worshiping the LORD their God. **4**Standing
on the stairs of the Levites[v] were Jeshua,
Bani, Kadmiel, Shebaniah, Bunni, Sherebiah, Bani and Kenani. They cried out with
loud voices to the LORD their God. **5**And the
Levites—Jeshua, Kadmiel, Bani, Hashabneiah, Sherebiah, Hodiah, Shebaniah and
Pethahiah—said: "Stand up and praise the
LORD your God,[w] who is from everlasting to
everlasting.[a]"

"Blessed be your glorious name, and
may it be exalted above all blessing
and praise. **6**You alone are the LORD.[x]
You made the heavens,[y] even the highest heavens, and all their starry host,
the earth[z] and all that is on it, the seas[a]
and all that is in them.[b] You give life
to everything, and the multitudes of
heaven worship you.

7"You are the LORD God, who chose
Abram and brought him out of Ur of
the Chaldeans[c] and named him Abraham.[d] **8**You found his heart faithful to
you, and you made a covenant with
him to give to his descendants the land
of the Canaanites, Hittites, Amorites,
Perizzites, Jebusites and Girgashites.[e]
You have kept your promise[f] because
you are righteous.[g]

9"You saw the suffering of our ancestors in Egypt;[h] you heard their cry
at the Red Sea.[b][i] **10**You sent signs[j] and
wonders against Pharaoh, against all
his officials and all the people of his
land, for you knew how arrogantly the
Egyptians treated them. You made a
name[k] for yourself, which remains to
this day. **11**You divided the sea before
them,[l] so that they passed through it
on dry ground, but you hurled their
pursuers into the depths, like a stone
into mighty waters.[m] **12**By day you led[n]
them with a pillar of cloud,[o] and by
night with a pillar of fire to give them
light on the way they were to take.

13"You came down on Mount Sinai;[p]
you spoke[q] to them from heaven. You
gave them regulations and laws that
are just[r] and right, and decrees and
commands that are good.[s] **14**You made
known to them your holy Sabbath[t] and
gave them commands, decrees and
laws through your servant Moses.
15In their hunger you gave them bread
from heaven[u] and in their thirst you
brought them water from the rock;[v]
you told them to go in and take possession of the land you had sworn with
uplifted hand to give them.[w]

16"But they, our ancestors, became arrogant and stiff-necked, and
they did not obey your commands.[x]
17They refused to listen and failed
to remember[y] the miracles you per-

[a] 5 Or *God for ever and ever* [b] 9 Or *the Sea of Reeds*

had celebrated the Feast of Tabernacles since the days of Joshua (1 Kin. 8:65; 2 Chr. 7:9; Ezra 3:4).

9:1 *the twenty-fourth day of the same month.* The people's public worship had begun on the first day of the seventh month (8:2). More than three weeks later, the people were still engaged in public worship. ***fasting, and wearing sackcloth ... dust.*** These are all traditional signs of mourning.

9:2 *separated ... from all foreigners.* The separation was a sacred separation from foreign persons who worshiped other gods and whose practices might have brought harm to the integrity of the worship of the Lord.

9:3 *confession.* When this word is used with God as its object, as in this verse, it refers to the praise of God. They were acknowledging His attributes and worthiness of praise.

9:6 *You alone are the LORD.* One of the fundamental teachings of Scripture is that God is not one among many. He alone is the living God (Deut. 6:4).

9:7 *You are the LORD God.* The word order of the Hebrew text is striking: "You are He, Yahweh (the) God." The use of the definite article marks Him as "the true God."

9:9 *suffering of our ancestors in Egypt.* The Book of Exodus tells about the plight of the Israelites in Egypt and their complaint to the Lord for deliverance. It then speaks of God's mercy in His response to the people's need. This verse suggests that before the people expressed their hurt, the Lord was already aware of their troubles.

9:11 Persecution—No one asks for or welcomes persecution. But history has borne out the fact that when believers are persecuted they draw close to the Lord. They are keenly aware that they are dependent on Him for strength, endurance, and even sustenance. Some of the sweetest times with the Lord are the times when unbelievers pity us for our tribulation. Times of rest bring independence of spirit. This is when it helps to go back and remember the things that the Lord has done in the past and rejoice, and to remember that He is sufficient for future persecution as well.

9:1 [s] Jos 7:6; 1Sa 4:12 **9:2** [t] Ne 13:3,30 [u] Ezr 10:11; Ps 106:6 **9:4** [v] Ezr 10:23 **9:5** [w] Ps 78:4 **9:6** [x] Dt 6:4 [y] 2Ki 19:15 [z] Ge 1:1; Isa 37:16 [a] Ps 95:5 [b] Dt 10:14 **9:7** [c] Ge 11:31 [d] Ge 17:5 **9:8** [e] Ge 15:18-21 [f] Jos 21:45 [g] Ge 15:6; Ezr 9:15 **9:9** [h] Ex 3:7 [i] Ex 14:10-30 **9:10** [j] Ex 10:1 [k] Jer 32:20; Da 9:15 **9:11** [l] Ex 14:21; Ps 78:13 [m] Ex 15:4-5,10; Heb 11:29 **9:12** [n] Ex 15:13 [o] Ex 13:21 **9:13** [p] Ex 19:11 [q] Ex 19:19 [r] Ps 119:137 [s] Ex 20:1 **9:14** [t] Ge 2:3; Ex 20:8-11 **9:15** [u] Ex 16:4; Jn 6:31 [v] Ex 17:6; Nu 20:7-13 [w] Dt 1:8,21 **9:16** [x] Dt 1:26-33; 31:29 **9:17** [y] Ps 78:42

formed among them. They became
stiff-necked and in their rebellion appointed a leader in order to return to
their slavery.[z] But you are a forgiving
God, gracious and compassionate,
slow to anger[a] and abounding in love.[b]
Therefore you did not desert them,[c]
18even when they cast for themselves
an image of a calf[d] and said, 'This is
your god, who brought you up out of
Egypt,' or when they committed awful
blasphemies.

19"Because of your great compassion you did not abandon them in the
wilderness. By day the pillar of cloud
did not fail to guide them on their path,
nor the pillar of fire by night to shine
on the way they were to take. 20You
gave your good Spirit[e] to instruct
them. You did not withhold your manna[f] from their mouths, and you gave
them water[g] for their thirst. 21For forty
years you sustained them in the wilderness; they lacked nothing,[h] their
clothes did not wear out nor did their
feet become swollen.[i]

22"You gave them kingdoms and nations, allotting to them even the remotest frontiers. They took over the country of Sihon[a][j] king of Heshbon and the
country of Og king of Bashan.[k] 23You
made their children as numerous as
the stars in the sky, and you brought
them into the land that you told their
parents to enter and possess. 24Their
children went in and took possession
of the land.[l] You subdued before them
the Canaanites, who lived in the land;
you gave the Canaanites into their
hands, along with their kings and the
peoples of the land, to deal with them
as they pleased. 25They captured fortified cities and fertile land; they took
possession of houses filled with all
kinds of good things, wells already
dug, vineyards, olive groves and fruit
trees in abundance. They ate to the full
and were well-nourished;[m] they reveled in your great goodness.[n]

26"But they were disobedient and rebelled against you; they turned their
backs on your law.[o] They killed your
prophets,[p] who had warned them in
order to turn them back to you; they
committed awful blasphemies.[q] 27So
you delivered them into the hands of
their enemies,[r] who oppressed them.
But when they were oppressed they
cried out to you. From heaven you
heard them, and in your great compassion[s] you gave them deliverers,
who rescued them from the hand of
their enemies.

28"But as soon as they were at rest,
they again did what was evil in your
sight. Then you abandoned them to
the hand of their enemies so that they
ruled over them. And when they cried
out to you again, you heard from heav-
en, and in your compassion you delivered them[t] time after time.

29"You warned them in order to
turn them back to your law, but they
became arrogant[u] and disobeyed your
commands. They sinned against your
ordinances, of which you said, 'The
person who obeys them will live by
them.'[v] Stubbornly they turned their
backs on you, became stiff-necked and
refused to listen.[w] 30For many years
you were patient with them. By your
Spirit you warned them through your
prophets.[x] Yet they paid no attention,
so you gave them into the hands of
the neighboring peoples. 31But in your
great mercy you did not put an end[y] to
them or abandon them, for you are a
gracious and merciful God.

32"Now therefore, our God, the
great God, mighty[z] and awesome, who
keeps his covenant of love,[a] do not let
all this hardship seem trifling in your
eyes—the hardship that has come on
us, on our kings and leaders, on our
priests and prophets, on our ancestors
and all your people, from the days of
the kings of Assyria until today. 33In
all that has happened to us, you have
remained righteous;[b] you have acted
faithfully, while we acted wickedly.[c]

a 22 One Hebrew manuscript and Septuagint; most Hebrew manuscripts *Sihon, that is, the country of the*

9:26 *killed your prophets.* Jesus also directed this charge against the rebellious people of His time (Matt. 23:31).

9:30–31 Patience—Nehemiah writes, "You had patience with them." This is the same eternal God who still patiently bears with His people. Even as born-again believers we struggle with sin, and we are thankful that He is patient with us as we grow in the grace and knowledge of our Lord and Savior, Jesus Christ (2 Pet. 3:18). This patience does not mean that He is tolerant of sin, but that He knows that it takes perseverance to walk as a Christian. He gives us time to grow. Indeed, God is patient to the whole world, not wishing for any to perish, but for all to come to repentance (2 Pet. 3:9).

9:32 *covenant.* God's covenant and loyalty are unbreakable (2 Tim. 2:11–13). ***today.*** "Today" refers to the time of the great revival under Ezra (8:1–2).

9:17 [z] Nu 14:1-4 [a] Ex 34:6 [b] Nu 14:17-19 [c] Ps 78:11 **9:18** [d] Ex 32:4 **9:20** [e] Nu 11:17; Isa 63:11, 14 [f] Ex 16:15 [g] Ex 17:6 **9:21** [h] Dt 2:7 [i] Dt 8:4 **9:22** [j] Nu 21:21 [k] Nu 21:33 **9:24** [l] Jos 11:23 **9:25** [m] Dt 6:10-12 [n] Nu 13:27; Dt 32:12-15 **9:26** [o] 1Ki 14:9 [p] Mt 21:35-36 [q] Jdg 2:12-13 **9:27** [r] Jdg 2:14 [s] Ps 106:45 **9:28** [t] Ps 106:43 **9:29** [u] Ps 5:5; Isa 2:11; Jer 43:2 [v] Dt 30:16 [w] Zec 7:11-12 **9:30** [x] 2Ki 17:13-18; 2Ch 36:16 **9:31** [y] Isa 48:9; Jer 4:27 **9:32** [z] Ps 24:8 [a] Dt 7:9 **9:33** [b] Ge 18:25 [c] Jer 44:3; Da 9:7-8, 14

[34]Our kings,[d] our leaders, our priests
and our ancestors[e] did not follow your
law; they did not pay attention to your
commands or the statutes you warned
them to keep. [35]Even while they were
in their kingdom, enjoying your great
goodness[f] to them in the spacious and
fertile land you gave them, they did
not serve you[g] or turn from their evil
ways.

[36]"But see, we are slaves[h] today,
slaves in the land you gave our ancestors so they could eat its fruit and the
other good things it produces. [37]Be-
cause of our sins, its abundant harvest
goes to the kings you have placed over
us. They rule over our bodies and our
cattle as they please. We are in great
distress.[i]

The Agreement of the People

[38]"In view of all this, we are making a
binding agreement,[j] putting it in writing,[k]
and our leaders, our Levites and our priests
are affixing their seals to it."[a]

10 [b] Those who sealed it were:

Nehemiah the governor, the son of Hakaliah.

Zedekiah, [2]Seraiah,[l] Azariah, Jeremiah,
[3]Pashhur,[m] Amariah, Malkijah,
[4]Hattush, Shebaniah, Malluk,
[5]Harim,[n] Meremoth, Obadiah,
[6]Daniel, Ginnethon, Baruch,
[7]Meshullam, Abijah, Mijamin,
[8]Maaziah, Bilgai and Shemaiah.
These were the priests.

[9]The Levites:[o]

Jeshua son of Azaniah, Binnui of the sons of Henadad, Kadmiel,
[10]and their associates: Shebaniah,
Hodiah, Kelita, Pelaiah, Hanan,
[11]Mika, Rehob, Hashabiah,
[12]Zakkur, Sherebiah, Shebaniah,
[13]Hodiah, Bani and Beninu.

[14]The leaders of the people:

Parosh, Pahath-Moab, Elam, Zattu, Bani,
[15]Bunni, Azgad, Bebai,
[16]Adonijah, Bigvai, Adin,[p]
[17]Ater, Hezekiah, Azzur,
[18]Hodiah, Hashum, Bezai,
[19]Hariph, Anathoth, Nebai,
[20]Magpiash, Meshullam, Hezir,[q]
[21]Meshezabel, Zadok, Jaddua,
[22]Pelatiah, Hanan, Anaiah,
[23]Hoshea, Hananiah,[r] Hasshub,
[24]Hallohesh, Pilha, Shobek,
[25]Rehum, Hashabnah, Maaseiah,
[26]Ahiah, Hanan, Anan,
[27]Malluk, Harim and Baanah.

[28]"The rest of the people—priests,
Levites, gatekeepers, musicians, temple servants[s] and all who separated
themselves from the neighboring peoples[t] for the sake of the Law of God,
together with their wives and all their
sons and daughters who are able to
understand— [29]all these now join
their fellow Israelites the nobles, and
bind themselves with a curse and an
oath[u] to follow the Law of God given
through Moses the servant of God and
to obey carefully all the commands,
regulations and decrees of the LORD
our Lord.

[30]"We promise not to give our
daughters in marriage to the peoples
around us or take their daughters for
our sons.[v]

[31]"When the neighboring peoples
bring merchandise or grain to sell on
the Sabbath,[w] we will not buy from
them on the Sabbath or on any holy
day. Every seventh year we will forgo
working the land[x] and will cancel all
debts.[y]

[32]"We assume the responsibility for
carrying out the commands to give
a third of a shekel[c] each year for the
service of the house of our God: [33]for
the bread set out on the table;[z] for the
regular grain offerings and burnt offerings; for the offerings on the Sabbaths, at the New Moon[a] feasts and

[a] *38* In Hebrew texts this verse (9:38) is numbered 10:1. [b] In Hebrew texts 10:1-39 is numbered 10:2-40. [c] *32* That is, about 1/8 ounce or about 4 grams

9:38 ***In view of all this.*** The psalm ends in action, not just sentiment. The intent was to bring the participants in this time of worship and remembrance to a commitment to change behavior and to pledge to mirror God's faithfulness.

10:1 ***Those who sealed it.*** The way a person in official capacity "signed" a document in the ancient world was similar to the use of a wax seal. A personally distinctive seal was pressed into soft clay. The pattern of the seal identified the official who had issued the document.

10:30 ***promise not to give our daughters.*** Marriage with non-Jewish people was strictly forbidden in Scriptures (Ex. 34:12–16; Deut. 7:3; Josh. 23:12–13; Judg. 3:6). Ezra had dealt very decisively with those who had married foreign wives, and this was still in their memory (Ezra 9–10).

9:34 [d] 2Ki 23:11 [e] Jer 44:17 **9:35** [f] Isa 63:7 [g] Dt 28:45-48 **9:36** [h] Dt 28:48; Ezr 9:9 **9:37** [i] Dt 28:33; La 5:5 **9:38** [j] 2Ch 23:16 [k] Isa 44:5 **10:2** [l] Ezr 2:2 **10:3** [m] 1Ch 9:12 **10:5** [n] 1Ch 24:8 **10:9** [o] Ne 12:1 **10:16** [p] Ezr 8:6 **10:20** [q] 1Ch 24:15 **10:23** [r] Ne 7:2 **10:28** [s] Ps 135:1 [t] 2Ch 6:26; Ne 9:2 **10:29** [u] Nu 5:21; Ps 119:106 **10:30** [v] Ex 34:16; Dt 7:3; Ne 13:23 **10:31** [w] Ne 13:16, 18; Jer 17:27; Eze 23:38; Am 8:5 [x] Ex 23:11; Lev 25:1-7 [y] Dt 15:1 **10:33** [z] Lev 24:6 [a] Nu 10:10; Ps 81:3; Isa 1:14

at the appointed festivals; for the holy
offerings; for sin offerings[a] to make
atonement for Israel; and for all the
duties of the house of our God.[b]
34“We—the priests, the Levites
and the people—have cast lots[c] to
determine when each of our families
is to bring to the house of our God at
set times each year a contribution of
wood[d] to burn on the altar of the LORD
our God, as it is written in the Law.
35“We also assume responsibility
for bringing to the house of the LORD
each year the firstfruits[e] of our crops
and of every fruit tree.[f]
36“As it is also written in the Law,
we will bring the firstborn[g] of our sons
and of our cattle, of our herds and of
our flocks to the house of our God, to
the priests ministering there.[h]
37“Moreover, we will bring to the
storerooms of the house of our God,
to the priests, the first of our ground
meal, of our grain offerings, of the
fruit of all our trees and of our new
wine and olive oil.[i] And we will bring
a tithe[j] of our crops to the Levites,[k] for
it is the Levites who collect the tithes
in all the towns where we work.[l] 38A
priest descended from Aaron is to accompany the Levites when they receive the tithes, and the Levites are to
bring a tenth of the tithes[m] up to the
house of our God, to the storerooms of
the treasury. 39The people of Israel, including the Levites, are to bring their
contributions of grain, new wine and
olive oil to the storerooms, where the
articles for the sanctuary and for the
ministering priests, the gatekeepers
and the musicians are also kept.
“We will not neglect the house of
our God.”[n]

The New Residents of Jerusalem

11 Now the leaders of the people settled
in Jerusalem. The rest of the people
cast lots to bring one out of every ten of
them to live in Jerusalem,[o] the holy city,[p]
while the remaining nine were to stay in
their own towns.[q] 2The people commended all who volunteered to live in Jerusalem.
3These are the provincial leaders who
settled in Jerusalem (now some Israelites, priests, Levites, temple servants and
descendants of Solomon’s servants lived
in the towns of Judah, each on their own
property in the various towns,[r] 4while other people from both Judah and Benjamin[s]
lived in Jerusalem):[t]

From the descendants of Judah:

Athaiah son of Uzziah, the son of
Zechariah, the son of Amariah, the
son of Shephatiah, the son of Mahalalel, a descendant of Perez; 5and Maaseiah son of Baruch, the son of Kol-
Hozeh, the son of Hazaiah, the son of
Adaiah, the son of Joiarib, the son of
Zechariah, a descendant of Shelah.
6The descendants of Perez who lived
in Jerusalem totaled 468 men of standing.

7From the descendants of Benjamin:

Sallu son of Meshullam, the son of
Joed, the son of Pedaiah, the son of
Kolaiah, the son of Maaseiah, the son
of Ithiel, the son of Jeshaiah, 8and his
followers, Gabbai and Sallai—928
men. 9Joel son of Zikri was their chief
officer, and Judah son of Hassenuah
was over the New Quarter of the city.

10From the priests:

Jedaiah; the son of Joiarib; Jakin;
11Seraiah[u] son of Hilkiah, the son of
Meshullam, the son of Zadok, the son
of Meraioth, the son of Ahitub,[v] the
official in charge of the house of God,
12and their associates, who carried on
work for the temple—822 men; Adaiah
son of Jeroham, the son of Pelaliah,
the son of Amzi, the son of Zechariah, the son of Pashhur, the son of Malkijah, 13and his associates, who were
heads of families—242 men; Amash-
sai son of Azarel, the son of Ahzai, the
son of Meshillemoth, the son of Immer,
14and his[b] associates, who were men of
standing—128. Their chief officer was
Zabdiel son of Haggedolim.

15From the Levites:

Shemaiah son of Hasshub, the son
of Azrikam, the son of Hashabiah,
the son of Bunni; 16Shabbethai[w] and
Jozabad,[x] two of the heads of the Levites, who had charge of the outside
work of the house of God; 17Mattani-
ah[y] son of Mika, the son of Zabdi, the
son of Asaph,[z] the director who led in
thanksgiving and prayer; Bakbukiah,

[a] 33 Or *purification offerings* [b] 14 Most Septuagint manuscripts; Hebrew *their*

11:1 ***cast lots.*** Casting lots was considered a good way to determine God’s will when there was no other clear direction. Solomon wrote, “The lot is cast into the lap, but its every decision is from the LORD” (Prov. 16:33). ***one out of every ten.*** This was the proportion determined in order to bring the population of Jerusalem to the level deemed necessary for its strength and viability.

10:33 [b] 2Ch 24:5 **10:34** [c] Lev 16:8 [d] Ne 13:31
10:35 [e] Ex 22:29; 23:19; Nu 18:12 [f] Dt 26:1-11
10:36 [g] Ex 13:2; Nu 18:14-16 [h] Ne 13:31
10:37 [i] Lev 23:17; Nu 18:12 [j] Lev 27:30; Nu 18:21
[k] Dt 14:22-29 [l] Eze 44:30 **10:38** [m] Nu 18:26
10:39 [n] Dt 12:6; Ne 13:11, 12 **11:1** [o] Ne 7:4 [p] ver 18;
Isa 48:2; 52:1; 64:10; Zec 14:20-21 [q] Ne 7:73
11:3 [r] 1Ch 9:2-3; Ezr 2:1 **11:4** [s] Ezr 1:5 [t] Ezr 2:70
11:11 [u] 2Ki 25:18; Ezr 2:2 [v] Ezr 7:2 **11:16** [w] Ezr 10:15
[x] Ezr 8:33 **11:17** [y] 1Ch 9:15; Ne 12:8 [z] 2Ch 5:12

second among his associates; and
Abda son of Shammua, the son of Galal, the son of Jeduthun.[a] 18 The Levites
in the holy city[b] totaled 284.

19 The gatekeepers:

Akkub, Talmon and their associates,
who kept watch at the gates—172 men.

20 The rest of the Israelites, with the
priests and Levites, were in all the towns
of Judah, each on their ancestral property.
21 The temple servants[c] lived on the hill of
Ophel, and Ziha and Gishpa were in charge
of them.

22 The chief officer of the Levites in Jerusalem was Uzzi son of Bani, the son of
Hashabiah, the son of Mattaniah,[d] the son
of Mika. Uzzi was one of Asaph's descendants, who were the musicians responsible
for the service of the house of God. 23 The
musicians[e] were under the king's orders,
which regulated their daily activity.

24 Pethahiah son of Meshezabel, one of
the descendants of Zerah[f] son of Judah,
was the king's agent in all affairs relating
to the people.

25 As for the villages with their fields,
some of the people of Judah lived in Kiriath Arba[g] and its surrounding settlements,
in Dibon[h] and its settlements, in Jekabzeel
and its villages, 26 in Jeshua, in Moladah, in
Beth Pelet,[i] 27 in Hazar Shual, in Beersheba[j]
and its settlements, 28 in Ziklag,[k] in Meko-
nah and its settlements, 29 in En Rimmon,
in Zorah,[l] in Jarmuth,[m] 30 Zanoah, Adullam[n] and their villages, in Lachish[o] and its
fields, and in Azekah[p] and its settlements.
So they were living all the way from Beersheba[q] to the Valley of Hinnom.

31 The descendants of the Benjamites
from Geba[r] lived in Mikmash,[s] Aija, Bethel and its settlements, 32 in Anathoth,[t] Nob[u]
and Ananiah, 33 in Hazor,[v] Ramah and Gittaim,[w] 34 in Hadid, Zeboim[x] and Neballat,
35 in Lod and Ono,[y] and in Ge Harashim.

36 Some of the divisions of the Levites of
Judah settled in Benjamin.

Priests and Levites

12 These were the priests[z] and Levites
who returned with Zerubbabel[a] son
of Shealtiel and with Joshua:[b]

Seraiah,[c] Jeremiah, Ezra,
2 Amariah, Malluk, Hattush,
3 Shekaniah, Rehum, Meremoth,
4 Iddo,[d] Ginnethon,[a] Abijah,[e]
5 Mijamin,[b] Moadiah, Bilgah,
6 Shemaiah, Joiarib, Jedaiah,[f]
7 Sallu, Amok, Hilkiah and Jedaiah.

These were the leaders of the priests and
their associates in the days of Joshua.

8 The Levites were Jeshua, Binnui, Kadmiel, Sherebiah, Judah, and also Mattaniah,[g] who, together with his associates, was
in charge of the songs of thanksgiving.
9 Bakbukiah and Unni, their associates,
stood opposite them in the services.

10 Joshua was the father of Joiakim, Joiakim the father of Eliashib,[h] Eliashib the
father of Joiada, 11 Joiada the father of Jonathan, and Jonathan the father of Jaddua.

12 In the days of Joiakim, these were the
heads of the priestly families:

of Seraiah's family, Meraiah;
of Jeremiah's, Hananiah;
13 of Ezra's, Meshullam;
of Amariah's, Jehohanan;
14 of Malluk's, Jonathan;
of Shekaniah's,[c] Joseph;
15 of Harim's, Adna;
of Meremoth's,[d] Helkai;
16 of Iddo's,[i] Zechariah;
of Ginnethon's, Meshullam;
17 of Abijah's, Zikri;
of Miniamin's and of Moadiah's, Piltai;
18 of Bilgah's, Shammua;
of Shemaiah's, Jehonathan;
19 of Joiarib's, Mattenai;
of Jedaiah's, Uzzi;
20 of Sallu's, Kallai;
of Amok's, Eber;
21 of Hilkiah's, Hashabiah;
of Jedaiah's, Nethanel.

22 The family heads of the Levites in the
days of Eliashib, Joiada, Johanan and Jaddua, as well as those of the priests, were
recorded in the reign of Darius the Persian.
23 The family heads among the descendants
of Levi up to the time of Johanan son of
Eliashib were recorded in the book of the
annals. 24 And the leaders of the Levites[j]

---

a *4* Many Hebrew manuscripts and Vulgate (see also verse 16); most Hebrew manuscripts *Ginnethoi* *b* *5* A variant of *Miniamin* *c* *14* Very many Hebrew manuscripts, some Septuagint manuscripts and Syriac (see also verse 3); most Hebrew manuscripts *Shebaniah's* *d* *15* Some Septuagint manuscripts (see also verse 3); Hebrew *Meraioth's*

11:25 ***Kiriath Arba.*** Kiriath Arba is another name for Hebron.

12:1 ***Zerubbabel.*** The return of Zerubbabel is recorded in Ezra 1–6. ***Joshua.*** Joshua is Joshua the priest. ***Ezra.*** This is not the priest who wrote the book of the same name.

12:22 ***Darius.*** Darius refers to Darius II (Nothus), who ruled Persia from 423 to 405 B.C.

12:23 ***the book of the annals.*** The book of the annals was an official record of the heads of the fathers' houses.

11:17 [a] 1Ch 25:1 **11:18** [b] Rev 21:2 **11:21** [c] Ezr 2:43; Ne 3:26 **11:22** [d] 1Ch 9:15 **11:23** [e] Ne 7:44 **11:24** [f] Ge 38:30 **11:25** [g] Ge 35:27; Jos 14:15 [h] Nu 21:30 **11:26** [i] Jos 15:27 **11:27** [j] Ge 21:14 **11:28** [k] 1Sa 27:6 **11:29** [l] Jos 15:33 [m] Jos 10:3 **11:30** [n] Jos 15:35 [o] Jos 10:3 [p] Jos 10:10 [q] Jos 15:28 **11:31** [r] Jos 21:17; Isa 10:29 [s] 1Sa 13:2 **11:32** [t] Jos 21:18; Isa 10:30 [u] 1Sa 21:1 **11:33** [v] Jos 11:1 [w] 2Sa 4:3 **11:34** [x] 1Sa 13:18 **11:35** [y] 1Ch 8:12 **12:1** [z] Ne 10:1-8 [a] 1Ch 3:19 [b] Ezr 2:2 [c] Ezr 2:2 **12:4** [d] Zec 1:1 [e] Lk 1:5 **12:6** [f] 1Ch 24:7 **12:8** [g] Ne 11:17 **12:10** [h] Ezr 10:24 **12:16** [i] ver 4 **12:24** [j] Ezr 2:40

were Hashabiah, Sherebiah, Jeshua son of
Kadmiel, and their associates, who stood
opposite them to give praise and thanksgiving, one section responding to the other,
as prescribed by David the man of God.
25Mattaniah, Bakbukiah, Obadiah, Meshullam, Talmon and Akkub were gatekeepers who guarded the storerooms at the
gates. **26**They served in the days of Joiakim
son of Joshua, the son of Jozadak, and in
the days of Nehemiah the governor and of
Ezra the priest, the teacher of the Law.

Dedication of the Wall of Jerusalem

27At the dedication[k] of the wall of Jerusalem, the Levites were sought out from
where they lived and were brought to Jerusalem to celebrate joyfully the dedication
with songs of thanksgiving and with the
music of cymbals,[l] harps and lyres.[m] **28**The
musicians also were brought together
from the region around Jerusalem—from
the villages of the Netophathites,[n] **29**from
Beth Gilgal, and from the area of Geba
and Azmaveth, for the musicians had built
villages for themselves around Jerusalem.
30When the priests and Levites had purified themselves ceremonially, they purified
the people,[o] the gates and the wall.
31I had the leaders of Judah go up on
top of[a] the wall. I also assigned two large
choirs to give thanks. One was to proceed
on top of[b] the wall to the right, toward the
Dung Gate.[p] **32**Hoshaiah and half the leaders of Judah followed them, **33**along with
Azariah, Ezra, Meshullam, **34**Judah, Benjamin,[q] Shemaiah, Jeremiah, **35**as well
as some priests with trumpets,[r] and also
Zechariah son of Jonathan, the son of Shemaiah, the son of Mattaniah, the son of Micaiah, the son of Zakkur, the son of Asaph,
36and his associates—Shemaiah, Azarel,
Milalai, Gilalai, Maai, Nethanel, Judah
and Hanani—with musical instruments[s]
prescribed by David the man of God.[t] Ezra[u]
the teacher of the Law led the procession.
37At the Fountain Gate[v] they continued directly up the steps of the City of David on
the ascent to the wall and passed above the
site of David's palace to the Water Gate[w]
on the east.
38The second choir proceeded in the opposite direction. I followed them on top
of[c] the wall, together with half the people—past the Tower of the Ovens[x] to the
Broad Wall,[y] **39**over the Gate of Ephraim,[z]
the Jeshanah[d] Gate,[a] the Fish Gate,[b] the
Tower of Hananel[c] and the Tower of the
Hundred,[d] as far as the Sheep Gate.[e] At the
Gate of the Guard they stopped.
40The two choirs that gave thanks then
took their places in the house of God; so
did I, together with half the officials, **41**as
well as the priests—Eliakim, Maaseiah,
Miniamin, Micaiah, Elioenai, Zechariah
and Hananiah with their trumpets— **42**and
also Maaseiah, Shemaiah, Eleazar, Uzzi,
Jehohanan, Malkijah, Elam and Ezer. The
choirs sang under the direction of Jezra-
hiah. **43**And on that day they offered great
sacrifices, rejoicing because God had given
them great joy. The women and children
also rejoiced. The sound of rejoicing in Jerusalem could be heard far away.
44At that time men were appointed to be
in charge of the storerooms[f] for the contributions, firstfruits and tithes.[g] From the
fields around the towns they were to bring
into the storerooms the portions required
by the Law for the priests and the Levites,
for Judah was pleased with the ministering priests and Levites.[h] **45**They performed
the service of their God and the service of
purification, as did also the musicians and
gatekeepers, according to the commands
of David[i] and his son Solomon.[j] **46**For long
ago, in the days of David and Asaph,[k] there
had been directors for the musicians and
for the songs of praise[l] and thanksgiving
to God. **47**So in the days of Zerubbabel and
of Nehemiah, all Israel contributed the daily portions for the musicians and the gatekeepers. They also set aside the portion for
the other Levites, and the Levites set aside
the portion for the descendants of Aaron.[m]

---

[a] 31 Or *go alongside* [b] 31 Or *proceed alongside*
[c] 38 Or *them alongside* [d] 39 Or *Old*

12:27 *dedication of the wall.* After the completion of Jerusalem's wall (ch. 6), the people repented and renewed their commitment to the Lord (chs. 8–10). The repopulation of Jerusalem was ordered, so the dedication was delayed.

12:31–46 Praise—Nehemiah choreographed a dramatic demonstration of praise, thanksgiving, and celebration on top of the wall. It was a wholehearted celebration to the Lord, and a visible victory dance before Israel's enemies. This time of praise had been preceded by repentance and reorganization of their duties to the temple and the city of Jerusalem. Praise that rises deep in the heart is always praise that comes from knowing that we are in good standing with God. We have repented of our sins and set our hearts and minds on obedience. God is good, His ways are infinitely right, and He is worthy of all of our enthusiastic worship.

12:43 *sacrifices.* The sacrifices offered at the dedication of the wall probably were not burnt offerings, but peace offerings in which the people shared a common meal. The dedication was an occasion for great rejoicing, and men, women, and children took part.

12:27 [k] Dt 20:5 [l] 2Sa 6:5 [m] 1Ch 15:16,28; 25:6; Ps 92:3
12:28 [n] 1Ch 2:54; 9:16 **12:30** [o] Ex 19:10; Job 1:5
12:31 [p] Ne 2:13 **12:34** [q] Ezr 1:5 **12:35** [r] Ezr 3:10
12:36 [s] 1Ch 15:16 [t] 2Ch 8:14 [u] Ezr 7:6 **12:37** [v] Ne 2:14; 3:15 [w] Ne 3:26 **12:38** [x] Ne 3:11 [y] Ne 3:8
12:39 [z] 2Ki 14:13; Ne 8:16 [a] Ne 3:6 [b] 2Ch 33:14; Ne 3:3 [c] Ne 3:1 [d] Ne 3:1 [e] Ne 3:1 **12:44** [f] Ne 13:4,13 [g] Lev 27:30 [h] Dt 18:8 **12:45** [i] 1Ch 25:1; 2Ch 8:14 [j] 1Ch 6:31; 23:5
12:46 [k] 2Ch 35:15 [l] 2Ch 29:27; Ps 137:4
12:47 [m] Nu 18:21; Dt 18:8

Nehemiah's Final Reforms

13 On that day the Book of Moses was read aloud in the hearing of the people and there it was found written that no Ammonite or Moabite should ever be admitted into the assembly of God,[n] 2because they had not met the Israelites with food and water but had hired Balaam[o] to call a curse down on them.[p] (Our God, however, turned the curse into a blessing.)[q] 3When the people heard this law, they excluded from Israel all who were of foreign descent.[r]

4Before this, Eliashib the priest had been put in charge of the storerooms[s] of the house of our God. He was closely associated with Tobiah,[t] 5and he had provided him with a large room formerly used to store the grain offerings and incense and temple articles, and also the tithes[u] of grain, new wine and olive oil prescribed for the Levites, musicians and gatekeepers, as well as the contributions for the priests.

6But while all this was going on, I was not in Jerusalem, for in the thirty-second year of Artaxerxes[v] king of Babylon I had returned to the king. Some time later I asked his permission 7and came back to Jerusalem. Here I learned about the evil thing Eliashib[w] had done in providing Tobiah a room in the courts of the house of God. 8I was greatly displeased and threw all Tobiah's household goods out of the room.[x] 9I gave orders to purify the rooms,[y] and then I put back into them the equipment of the house of God, with the grain offerings and the incense.

10I also learned that the portions assigned to the Levites had not been given to them,[z] and that all the Levites and musicians responsible for the service had gone back to their own fields. 11So I rebuked the officials and asked them, "Why is the house of God neglected?"[a] Then I called them together and stationed them at their posts.

12All Judah brought the tithes[b] of grain, new wine and olive oil into the storerooms.[c] 13I put Shelemiah the priest, Zadok the scribe, and a Levite named Pedaiah in charge of the storerooms and made Hanan son of Zakkur, the son of Mattaniah, their assistant, because they were considered trustworthy. They were made responsible for distributing the supplies to their fellow Levites.[d]

14Remember[e] me for this, my God, and do not blot out what I have so faithfully done for the house of my God and its services.

15In those days I saw people in Judah treading winepresses on the Sabbath and bringing in grain and loading it on donkeys, together with wine, grapes, figs and all other kinds of loads. And they were bringing all this into Jerusalem on the Sabbath.[f] Therefore I warned them against selling food on that day. 16People from Tyre who lived in Jerusalem were bringing in fish and all kinds of merchandise and selling them in Jerusalem on the Sabbath[g] to the people of Judah. 17I rebuked the nobles of Judah and said to them, "What is this wicked thing you are doing—desecrating the Sabbath day? 18Didn't your ancestors do the same things, so that our God brought all this calamity on us and on this city? Now you are stirring up more wrath against Israel by desecrating the Sabbath."[h]

19When evening shadows fell on the gates of Jerusalem before the Sabbath,[i] I ordered the doors to be shut and not opened until the Sabbath was over. I stationed some of my own men at the gates so that no load could be brought in on the Sabbath day. 20Once or twice the merchants and sellers of all kinds of goods spent the night outside Jerusalem. 21But I warned them and said, "Why do you spend the night by the wall? If you do this again, I will arrest you." From that time on they no longer came on the Sabbath. 22Then I commanded the Levites to purify themselves and go and guard the gates in order to keep the Sabbath day holy.

Remember[j] me for this also, my God, and show mercy to me according to your great love.

23Moreover, in those days I saw men of Judah who had married[k] women from Ashdod, Ammon and Moab.[l] 24Half of their children spoke the language of Ashdod or the language of one of the other peoples, and did not know how to speak the language of Judah. 25I rebuked them and called curses down on them. I beat some of

---

13:4–9 ***Tobiah.*** Tobiah was an Ammonite (2:10).

13:23–24 ***men of Judah who had married women from Ashdod, Ammon and Moab.*** The problem of Jews marrying foreigners had been dealt with thirty years before by Ezra (Ezra 9–10).

13:25 ***rebuked them ... beat some of the men ... pulled out their hair.*** It is unnerving to read this list of verbs and imagine the scene. These were not the dispassionate remarks of someone giving a seminar. Nehemiah forced them to comply to the will of God in this matter. After all, this was the principal issue that had led to Israel's captivity in the beginning.

13:1 [n] ver 23; Dt 23:3 **13:2** [o] Nu 22:3-11 [p] Nu 23:7; Dt 23:3 [q] Nu 23:11; Dt 23:4-5 **13:3** [r] ver 23; Ne 9:2 **13:4** [s] Ne 12:44 [t] Ne 2:10 **13:5** [u] Lev 27:30; Nu 18:21 **13:6** [v] Ne 2:6; 5:14 **13:7** [w] Ezr 10:24 **13:8** [x] Mt 21:12-13; Jn 2:13-16 **13:9** [y] 1Ch 23:28; 2Ch 29:5 **13:10** [z] Dt 12:19 **13:11** [a] Ne 10:37-39; Hag 1:1-9 **13:12** [b] 2Ch 31:6 [c] 1Ki 7:51; Ne 10:37-39; Mal 3:10 **13:13** [d] Ne 12:44; Ac 6:1-5 **13:14** [e] Ge 8:1 **13:15** [f] Ex 20:8-11; 34:21; Dt 5:12-15; Ne 10:31 **13:16** [g] Ne 10:31 **13:18** [h] Ne 10:31; Jer 17:21-23 **13:19** [i] Lev 23:32 **13:22** [j] Ge 8:1; Ne 12:30 **13:23** [k] Ezr 9:1-2; Mal 2:11 [l] ver 1; Ne 10:30

the men and pulled out their hair. I made them take an oath[m] in God's name and said: "You are not to give your daughters in marriage to their sons, nor are you to take their daughters in marriage for your sons or for yourselves. 26Was it not because of marriages like these that Solomon king of Israel sinned? Among the many nations there was no king like him.[n] He was loved by his God,[o] and God made him king over all Israel, but even he was led into sin by foreign women.[p] 27Must we hear now that you too are doing all this terrible wickedness and are being unfaithful to our God by marrying[q] foreign women?"

28One of the sons of Joiada son of Eliashib[r] the high priest was son-in-law to Sanballat[s] the Horonite. And I drove him away from me.

29Remember[t] them, my God, because they defiled the priestly office and the covenant of the priesthood and of the Levites.

30So I purified the priests and the Levites of everything foreign,[u] and assigned them duties, each to his own task. 31I also made provision for contributions of wood[v] at designated times, and for the firstfruits.

Remember[w] me with favor, my God.

13:28 ***son-in-law to Sanballat.*** The marriage was particularly offensive because it formed a treasonable alliance with Israel's enemies and compromised the purity of the high priesthood.

13:25 [m] Ezr 10:5 **13:26** [n] 1Ki 3:13; 2Ch 1:12 [o] 2Sa 12:25 [p] 1Ki 11:3 **13:27** [q] Ezr 9:14; 10:2 **13:28** [r] Ezr 10:24 [s] Ne 2:10 **13:29** [t] Ne 6:14 **13:30** [u] Ne 10:30 **13:31** [v] Ne 10:34 [w] ver 14, 22; Ge 8:1

ESTHER

▶ **AUTHOR:** Even though the author's identity is not given in the text, it is obvious from the intimate knowledge of Persian customs and etiquette, the citadel in Susa, and the details of the reign of King Xerxes, that the author lived in Persia during this period. The love expressed here for the Jewish people and the author's knowledge of Jewish customs further suggest Jewish authorship. It is also thought that this Persian Jew was either an eyewitness to the events or knew an eyewitness. It may be that this author had access to the detailed records kept by Mordecai.

▶ **TIME:** c. 483 – 473 B.C. ▶ **KEY VERSE:** Esth. 4:14

▶ **THEME:** Esther is unique among the Scriptures for two reasons: God is not mentioned by name once, and the heroine is a woman who is part of the harem of a foreign king. The events of the book take place about 30 years before Nehemiah, after the temple in Jerusalem was rebuilt but before the walls were refinished. Esther probably helped to pave the way for Nehemiah's work. The book fits well within the tapestry of the Old Testament. Just as in so many other Old Testament narratives, God provides the means to preserve His people in the face of a severe crisis. It is still read aloud as part of the Purim celebration by Jewish people.

Queen Vashti Deposed

1 This is what happened during the time
of Xerxes,[a][a] the Xerxes who ruled over
127 provinces[b] stretching from India to
Cush[b];[c] 2At that time King Xerxes reigned
from his royal throne in the citadel of
Susa,[d] 3and in the third year of his reign
he gave a banquet[e] for all his nobles and
officials. The military leaders of Persia and
Media, the princes, and the nobles of the
provinces were present.
4For a full 180 days he displayed the vast
wealth of his kingdom and the splendor
and glory of his majesty. 5When these days
were over, the king gave a banquet, lasting
seven days,[f] in the enclosed garden[g] of the
king's palace, for all the people from the
least to the greatest who were in the citadel of Susa. 6The garden had hangings of
white and blue linen, fastened with cords
of white linen and purple material to silver
rings on marble pillars. There were couches[h] of gold and silver on a mosaic pavement
of porphyry, marble, mother-of-pearl and
other costly stones. 7Wine was served in
goblets of gold, each one different from the
other, and the royal wine was abundant, in
keeping with the king's liberality.[i] 8By the
king's command each guest was allowed
to drink with no restrictions, for the king
instructed all the wine stewards to serve
each man what he wished.
9Queen Vashti also gave a banquet[j] for the
women in the royal palace of King Xerxes.
10On the seventh day, when King Xerxes
was in high spirits[k] from wine,[l] he commanded the seven eunuchs who served
him—Mehuman, Biztha, Harbona,[m] Bigtha, Abagtha, Zethar and Karkas— 11to
bring[n] before him Queen Vashti, wearing
her royal crown, in order to display her
beauty[o] to the people and nobles, for she
was lovely to look at. 12But when the atten-

[a] *1* Hebrew *Ahasuerus*; here and throughout Esther [b] *1* That is, the upper Nile region

1:1 *Xerxes.* The kingdom of Xerxes extended from India (the region drained by the Indus River) to Ethiopia (northern Sudan). The Persian Kingdom under Xerxes was divided into smaller areas called provinces and larger divisions called satrapies.

1:6 *white and blue . . . purple.* These were the royal colors of the Persians.

1:8 *no restrictions.* The usual Persian custom was that guests at a banquet were required to drink each time the king raised his cup.

1:10 *eunuchs.* These were eunuchs who were castrated for the purpose of acting as harem attendants. They would have had the physical strength and stamina of any man, but not be a sexual threat to the king's women.

1:1 [a] Ezr 4:6; Da 9:1 [b] Est 9:30; Da 3:2; 6:1 [c] Est 8:9 **1:2** [d] Ezr 4:9; Ne 1:1; Est 2:8 **1:3** [e] 1Ki 3:15; Est 2:18 **1:5** [f] Jdg 14:17 [g] 2Ki 21:18; Est 7:7-8 **1:6** [h] Est 7:8; Eze 23:41; Am 3:12; 6:4 **1:7** [i] Est 2:18; Da 5:2 **1:9** [j] 1Ki 3:15 **1:10** [k] Jdg 16:25; Ru 3:7 [l] Ge 14:18; Est 3:15; 5:6; 7:2; Pr 31:4-7; Da 5:1-4 [m] Est 7:9 **1:11** [n] SS 2:4 [o] Ps 45:11; Eze 16:14

dants delivered the king's command, Queen Vashti refused to come. Then the king became furious and burned with anger.[p]

13 Since it was customary for the king to consult experts in matters of law and justice, he spoke with the wise men who understood the times[q] 14 and were closest to the king—Karshena, Shethar, Admatha, Tarshish, Meres, Marsena and Memukan, the seven nobles[r] of Persia and Media who had special access to the king and were highest in the kingdom.

15 "According to law, what must be done to Queen Vashti?" he asked. "She has not obeyed the command of King Xerxes that the eunuchs have taken to her."

16 Then Memukan replied in the presence of the king and the nobles, "Queen Vashti has done wrong, not only against the king but also against all the nobles and the peoples of all the provinces of King Xerxes. 17 For the queen's conduct will become known to all the women, and so they will despise their husbands and say, 'King Xerxes commanded Queen Vashti to be brought before him, but she would not come.' 18 This very day the Persian and Median women of the nobility who have heard about the queen's conduct will respond to all the king's nobles in the same way. There will be no end of disrespect and discord.[s]

19 "Therefore, if it pleases the king,[t] let him issue a royal decree and let it be written in the laws of Persia and Media, which cannot be repealed,[u] that Vashti is never again to enter the presence of King Xerxes. Also let the king give her royal position to someone else who is better than she. 20 Then when the king's edict is proclaimed throughout all his vast realm, all the women will respect their husbands, from the least to the greatest."

21 The king and his nobles were pleased with this advice, so the king did as Memukan proposed. 22 He sent dispatches to all parts of the kingdom, to each province in its own script and to each people in their own language,[v] proclaiming that every man should be ruler over his own household, using his native tongue.

Esther Made Queen

2 Later when King Xerxes' fury had subsided,[w] he remembered Vashti and what she had done and what he had decreed about her. 2 Then the king's personal attendants proposed, "Let a search be made for beautiful young virgins for the king. 3 Let the king appoint commissioners in every province of his realm to bring all these beautiful young women into the harem at the citadel of Susa. Let them be placed under the care of Hegai, the king's eunuch, who is in charge of the women; and let beauty treatments be given to them. 4 Then let the young woman who pleases the king be queen instead of Vashti." This advice appealed to the king, and he followed it.

5 Now there was in the citadel of Susa a Jew of the tribe of Benjamin, named Mordecai son of Jair, the son of Shimei, the son of Kish,[x] 6 who had been carried into exile from Jerusalem by Nebuchadnezzar king of Babylon, among those taken captive with Jehoiachin[a][y] king of Judah.[z] 7 Mordecai had a cousin named Hadassah, whom he had brought up because she had neither father nor mother. This young woman, who was also known as Esther,[a] had a lovely figure[b] and was beautiful. Mordecai had taken her as his own daughter when her father and mother died.

8 When the king's order and edict had been proclaimed, many young women were brought to the citadel of Susa[c] and put under the care of Hegai. Esther also was taken to the king's palace and entrusted to Hegai, who had charge of the harem. 9 She pleased him and won his favor.[d] Immediately he provided her with her beauty treatments and special food.[e] He assigned to her seven female attendants selected

[a] 6 Hebrew *Jeconiah,* a variant of *Jehoiachin*

1:16–18 *Memukan.* Acting as spokesman for the others, Memukan responded shrewdly by enlarging the offense beyond a personal affront to the king. The Hebrew word used for despise occurs only here in the Old Testament.

2:5 *Kish.* Some think this may have been the Kish who was the father of King Saul (1 Sam. 9:1–2). It was not uncommon to refer to someone as "the son of" a more distant ancestor (Matt. 15:22).

2:6 *had been carried into exile.* This verse is a little confusing, as the Hebrew text does not indicate the subject of the verb "had been carried into exile." It seems highly unlikely that it could be Mordecai, because if he had been among those carried to Babylon, he would probably not have been alive in the time of Xerxes. If the name Kish does not refer to a more distant ancestor, he may have been the one taken into captivity. Whatever the case, it is obvious that Mordecai and his family were among those descended from the captives taken to Babylon in the days of Nebuchadnezzar.

2:7 *Hadassah.* Hadassah is a Hebrew name that means "Myrtle." Esther is a Persian name meaning "Star." Jewish people in that time customarily had two names when they lived in places other than Israel. One would be their secular name, which was understood by their adopted culture, and the other would be their sacred name, given in Hebrew.

2:8 *Esther also was taken.* We cannot determine whether Esther went willingly or reluctantly to the palace complex. But perhaps God was already preparing her for the work he had for her to do.

1:12 [p] Ge 39:19; Est 2:21; 7:7; Pr 19:12 **1:13** [q] 1Ch 12:32; Jer 10:7; Da 2:12 **1:14** [r] 2Ki 25:19; Ezr 7:14
1:18 [s] Pr 19:13; 27:15 **1:19** [t] Ecc 8:4 [u] Est 8:8; Da 6:8, 12
1:22 [v] Ne 13:24; Est 8:9; Eph 5:22-24; 1Ti 2:12
2:1 [w] Est 1:19-20; 7:10 **2:5** [x] 1Sa 9:1; Est 3:2
2:6 [y] 2Ki 24:6, 15, 2Ch 36:10, 20 [z] Da 1:1-5; 5:13
2:7 [a] Ge 41:45 [b] Ge 39:6 **2:8** [c] ver 3, 15; Ne 1:1; Est 1:2; Da 8:2 **2:9** [d] Ge 39:21 [e] ver 3, 12; Ge 37:3; 1Sa 9:22-24; 2Ki 25:30; Eze 16:9-13; Da 1:5

from the king's palace and moved her and her attendants into the best place in the harem.

10 Esther had not revealed her nationality and family background, because Mordecai had forbidden her to do so.[f] 11 Every day he walked back and forth near the courtyard of the harem to find out how Esther was and what was happening to her.

12 Before a young woman's turn came to go in to King Xerxes, she had to complete twelve months of beauty treatments prescribed for the women, six months with oil of myrrh and six with perfumes[g] and cosmetics. 13 And this is how she would go to the king: Anything she wanted was given her to take with her from the harem to the king's palace. 14 In the evening she would go there and in the morning return to another part of the harem to the care of Shaashgaz, the king's eunuch who was in charge of the concubines.[h] She would not return to the king unless he was pleased with her and summoned her by name.[i]

15 When the turn came for Esther (the young woman Mordecai had adopted, the daughter of his uncle Abihail[j]) to go to the king,[k] she asked for nothing other than what Hegai, the king's eunuch who was in charge of the harem, suggested. And Esther won the favor[l] of everyone who saw her. 16 She was taken to King Xerxes in the royal residence in the tenth month, the month of Tebeth, in the seventh year of his reign.

17 Now the king was attracted to Esther more than to any of the other women, and she won his favor and approval more than any of the other virgins. So he set a royal crown on her head and made her queen[m] instead of Vashti. 18 And the king gave a great banquet,[n] Esther's banquet, for all his nobles and officials.[o] He proclaimed a holiday throughout the provinces and distributed gifts with royal liberality.[p]

Mordecai Uncovers a Conspiracy

19 When the virgins were assembled a second time, Mordecai was sitting at the king's gate.[q] 20 But Esther had kept secret her family background and nationality just as Mordecai had told her to do, for she continued to follow Mordecai's instructions as she had done when he was bringing her up.[r]

21 During the time Mordecai was sitting at the king's gate, Bigthana[a] and Teresh, two of the king's officers[s] who guarded the doorway, became angry[t] and conspired to assassinate King Xerxes. 22 But Mordecai found out about the plot and told Queen Esther, who in turn reported it to the king, giving credit to Mordecai. 23 And when the report was investigated and found to be true, the two officials were impaled[u] on poles. All this was recorded in the book of the annals[v] in the presence of the king.

Haman's Plot to Destroy the Jews

3 After these events, King Xerxes honored Haman son of Hammedatha, the Agagite,[w] elevating him and giving him a seat of honor higher than that of all the other nobles. 2 All the royal officials at the king's gate knelt down and paid honor to Haman, for the king had commanded this concerning him. But Mordecai would not kneel down or pay him honor.

3 Then the royal officials at the king's gate asked Mordecai, "Why do you disobey the king's command?"[x] 4 Day after day they spoke to him but he refused to comply.[y] Therefore they told Haman about it to see whether Mordecai's behavior would be tolerated, for he had told them he was a Jew.

5 When Haman saw that Mordecai would not kneel down or pay him honor, he was enraged.[z] 6 Yet having learned who Mordecai's people were, he scorned the idea

[a] 21 Hebrew *Bigthan,* a variant of *Bigthana*

2:14 ***concubines.*** These women lived unfortunate, though highly pampered lives. If the king never called them again, they were destined to remain secluded in the harem for the rest of their lives.

2:21 ***sitting at the king's gate.*** In ancient cities, the gates were the "courthouse" of the town, where official business was carried out (Deut. 22:13 – 15). The "king's gate" may have served a similar purpose.

3:1 ***the Agagite.*** Some believe Agagite is a reference to the historical district of Agag within the Persian Empire. Others believe this term more likely links Haman's descent to the Amalekites. These descendants of Esau (Gen. 36:12) were ancient enemies of the Hebrews (Ex. 17:8). Agag, a king of the Amalekites, was captured by King Saul (1 Sam. 15:8). If Haman was descended from the Amalekites, and Mordecai from the family of Saul (v. 5), then the irritation Haman had for Mordecai could have been a symptom of a long-standing family hostility.

3:2 ***knelt down and paid honor.*** It is not known whether the bowing was required as an act of worship to the king's man, or merely as an overt sign of deep respect. If such obeisance indicated worship, Mordecai's reason for refusal is obvious. If it was merely a sign of respect, he may not have been able to bring himself to show such honor to one who was an ancestral enemy.

3:5 – 6 ***enraged.*** If Haman was of Amalekite ancestry, it could be that this was the cause of his deep hatred. Also, it is possible that Haman simply could not stand to see anyone who did not properly respect his position.

2:10 [f] ver 20 **2:12** [g] Pr 27:9; SS 1:3; Isa 3:24
2:14 [h] 1Ki 11:3; SS 6:8; Da 5:2 [i] Est 4:11 **2:15** [j] Est 9:29
[k] Ps 45:14 [l] Ge 18:3; 30:27; Est 5:8 **2:17** [m] Est 1:11;
Eze 16:9-13 **2:18** [n] 1Ki 3:15; Est 1:3 [o] Ge 40:20 [p] Est 1:7
2:19 [q] ver 21; Est 3:2; 4:2; 5:13 **2:20** [r] ver 10
2:21 [s] Ge 40:2; Est 6:2 [t] Est 1:12; 3:5; 5:9; 7:7
2:23 [u] Ge 40:19; Ps 7:14-16; Pr 26:27 [v] Est 6:1; 10:2
3:1 [w] ver 10; Ex 17:8-16; Nu 24:7; Dt 25:17-19; 1Sa 14:48;
Est 5:11 **3:3** [x] Est 5:9; Da 3:12 **3:4** [y] Ge 39:10
3:5 [z] Est 2:21; 5:9

of killing only Mordecai. Instead Haman looked for a way[a] to destroy[b] all Mordecai's people, the Jews,[c] throughout the whole kingdom of Xerxes.

7 In the twelfth year of King Xerxes, in the first month, the month of Nisan, the *pur*[d] (that is, the lot[e]) was cast in the presence of Haman to select a day and month. And the lot fell on[*a*] the twelfth month, the month of Adar.[f]

8 Then Haman said to King Xerxes, "There is a certain people dispersed among the peoples in all the provinces of your kingdom who keep themselves separate. Their customs[g] are different from those of all other people, and they do not obey[h] the king's laws; it is not in the king's best interest to tolerate them.[i] 9 If it pleases the king, let a decree be issued to destroy them, and I will give ten thousand talents[*b*] of silver to the king's administrators for the royal treasury."[j]

10 So the king took his signet ring[k] from his finger and gave it to Haman son of Hammedatha, the Agagite, the enemy of the Jews. 11 "Keep the money," the king said to Haman, "and do with the people as you please."

12 Then on the thirteenth day of the first month the royal secretaries were summoned. They wrote out in the script of each province and in the language[l] of each people all Haman's orders to the king's satraps, the governors of the various provinces and the nobles of the various peoples. These were written in the name of King Xerxes himself and sealed[m] with his own ring. 13 Dispatches were sent by couriers to all the king's provinces with the order to destroy, kill and annihilate all the Jews[n]—young and old, women and children—on a single day, the thirteenth day of the twelfth month, the month of Adar,[o] and to plunder[p] their goods. 14 A copy of the text of the edict was to be issued as law in every province and made known to the people of every nationality so they would be ready for that day.[q]

15 The couriers went out, spurred on by the king's command, and the edict was issued in the citadel of Susa.[r] The king and Haman sat down to drink,[s] but the city of Susa was bewildered.[t]

Mordecai Persuades Esther to Help

4 When Mordecai learned of all that had been done, he tore his clothes,[u] put on sackcloth and ashes,[v] and went out into the city, wailing[w] loudly and bitterly. 2 But he went only as far as the king's gate,[x] because no one clothed in sackcloth was allowed to enter it. 3 In every province to which the edict and order of the king came, there was great mourning among the Jews, with fasting, weeping and wailing. Many lay in sackcloth and ashes.

4 When Esther's eunuchs and female attendants came and told her about Mordecai, she was in great distress. She sent clothes for him to put on instead of his sackcloth, but he would not accept them. 5 Then Esther summoned Hathak, one of the king's eunuchs assigned to attend her, and ordered him to find out what was troubling Mordecai and why.

6 So Hathak went out to Mordecai in the open square of the city in front of the king's gate. 7 Mordecai told him everything that had happened to him, including the exact amount of money Haman had promised to pay into the royal treasury for the destruction of the Jews.[y] 8 He also gave him a copy

a 7 Septuagint; Hebrew does not have *And the lot fell on.* *b* 9 That is, about 375 tons or about 340 metric tons

3:7 pur *(that is, the lot).* The casting of lots was common in ancient times. Haman's casting a lot at the beginning of the year to determine the best time to destroy the Jewish people fits in with the culture of the day, as the Babylonians believed that the gods gathered at the beginning of each year to establish the destiny of human beings. The word *pur* is the basis for the name of the new feast in chapter 9.

3:8 Slander—Haman was sly. He devised an accusation to convince the king that the Jews were a dangerous and treasonous people. His accusation contained a clever mixture of truth and falsehood. The laws of the Jewish people were admittedly different, but this was not unusual, nor was it a threat to Persia, which contained many minorities. Not only was accusing the whole Jewish nation of civil disobedience a lie, it was also intended to lead to something much worse: murder.

3:10 *ring.* The king's signet ring symbolized his authority. He would have used this signet as a stamp to authorize official documents.

3:15 *Haman sat down to drink.* Haman was so unconcerned about the death sentence he was placing on the Jewish people that he sat down comfortably to relax while the city was in confusion.

4:1–2 *sackcloth and ashes.* Sackcloth and ashes were used as a visible sign of mourning, indicating a sense of desolation.

4:3 *fasting.* It is interesting to note that throughout the entire Book of Esther, God is not mentioned by name even once. One assumes that Esther's fasting was accompanied by prayer, but it is never mentioned. Fasting was a religious custom, and we know the Jews relied on God for their safety. Many think the author of Esther was writing the story to a secular audience, and this is the reason for God's actual name being left out.

3:6 [a] Pr 16:25 [b] Ps 74:8; 83:4 [c] Est 9:24 **3:7** [d] Est 9:24, 26 [e] Lev 16:8; 1Sa 10:21 [f] ver 13; Ezr 6:15; Est 9:19 **3:8** [g] Ac 16:20-21 [h] Jer 29:7; Da 6:13 [i] Ezr 4:15 **3:9** [j] Est 7:4 **3:10** [k] Ge 41:42; Est 7:6; 8:2 **3:12** [l] Ne 13:24 [m] Ge 38:18; 1Ki 21:8; Est 8:8-10 **3:13** [n] 1Sa 15:3; Ezr 4:6; Est 8:10-14 [o] ver 7 [p] Est 8:11; 9:10 **3:14** [q] Est 8:8; 9:1 **3:15** [r] Est 8:14 [s] Est 1:10 [t] Est 8:15 **4:1** [u] Nu 14:6 [v] 2Sa 13:19; Eze 27:30-31; Jnh 3:5-6 [w] Ex 11:6; Ps 30:11 **4:2** [x] Est 2:19 **4:7** [y] Est 3:9; 7:4

of the text of the edict for their annihilation, which had been published in Susa, to show to Esther and explain it to her, and he told him to instruct her to go into the king's presence to beg for mercy and plead with him for her people.

9Hathak went back and reported to Esther what Mordecai had said. 10Then she instructed him to say to Mordecai, 11"All the king's officials and the people of the royal provinces know that for any man or woman who approaches the king in the inner court without being summoned[z] the king has but one law:[a] that they be put to death unless the king extends the gold scepter[b] to them and spares their lives. But thirty days have passed since I was called to go to the king."

12When Esther's words were reported to Mordecai, 13he sent back this answer: "Do not think that because you are in the king's house you alone of all the Jews will escape. 14For if you remain silent[c] at this time, relief[d] and deliverance[e] for the Jews will arise from another place, but you and your father's family will perish. And who knows but that you have come to your royal position for such a time as this?"[f]

15Then Esther sent this reply to Mordecai: 16"Go, gather together all the Jews who are in Susa, and fast[g] for me. Do not eat or drink for three days, night or day. I and my attendants will fast as you do. When this is done, I will go to the king, even though it is against the law. And if I perish, I perish."[h]

17So Mordecai went away and carried out all of Esther's instructions.

Esther's Request to the King

5 On the third day Esther put on her royal robes[i] and stood in the inner court of the palace, in front of the king's[j] hall. The king was sitting on his royal throne in the hall, facing the entrance. 2When he saw Queen Esther standing in the court, he was pleased with her and held out to her the gold scepter that was in his hand. So Esther approached and touched the tip of the scepter.[k]

3Then the king asked, "What is it, Queen Esther? What is your request? Even up to half the kingdom,[l] it will be given you."

4"If it pleases the king," replied Esther, "let the king, together with Haman, come today to a banquet I have prepared for him."

5"Bring Haman at once," the king said, "so that we may do what Esther asks."

So the king and Haman went to the banquet Esther had prepared. 6As they were drinking wine,[m] the king again asked Esther, "Now what is your petition? It will be given you. And what is your request? Even up to half the kingdom,[n] it will be granted."[o]

7Esther replied, "My petition and my request is this: 8If the king regards me with favor[p] and if it pleases the king to grant my petition and fulfill my request, let the king and Haman come tomorrow to the banquet[q] I will prepare for them. Then I will answer the king's question."

Haman's Rage Against Mordecai

9Haman went out that day happy and in high spirits. But when he saw Mordecai at the king's gate and observed that he neither rose nor showed fear in his presence, he was filled with rage[r] against Mordecai.[s] 10Nevertheless, Haman restrained himself and went home.

Calling together his friends and Zeresh,[t] his wife, 11Haman boasted[u] to them about his vast wealth, his many sons,[v] and all the ways the king had honored him and how he had elevated him above the other nobles and officials. 12"And that's not all," Haman added. "I'm the only person[w] Queen Esther invited to accompany the king to the banquet she gave. And she has invited me along with the king tomorrow. 13But all this gives me no satisfaction as long as I see that Jew Mordecai sitting at the king's gate.[x]"

4:11 *without being summoned.* Esther understood that Mordecai was asking her to risk her life. She would be taking her life into her hands to go uncalled to the king in any circumstances; the fact that she had not been called for a month probably meant that she was even more unsure of her reception.

4:14 *for such a time as this.* Even though this verse does not directly mention God, Mordecai obviously believed that Esther was made queen through God's design, and she would be acting as God's agent to deliver His people.

4:16 Self-Denial—Even though Esther must have been afraid, knowing that she was breaking the law, she decided to trust God. Her statement "if I perish, I perish," was not despair, but willingness to act however God willed, recognizing that the consequences were in His hands. Self-denial is not easy, but God never fails His children.

5:2 *he was pleased with her.* When Esther illegally entered the king's court, he was pleased by her appearance and decided to overlook her offense. In this scene we again see the hand of God.

5:8 *tomorrow ... Then I will answer the king's question.* Why did Esther delay in telling the king her real request? Perhaps she was afraid, and used the intervening time to strengthen her courage. But it seems that here also is God's hand, for the delay provided time for the king's sleepless night and the events that followed.

4:11 [z] Est 2:14 [a] Da 2:9 [b] Est 5:1,2; 8:4 **4:14** [c] Ecc 3:7; Isa 62:1; Am 5:13 [d] Est 9:16,22 [e] Ge 45:7; Dt 28:29 [f] Ge 50:20 **4:16** [g] 2Ch 20:3; Est 9:31 [h] Ge 43:14 **5:1** [i] Est 4:16; Eze 16:13 [j] Est 6:4; Pr 21:1 **5:2** [k] Est 4:11; 8:4; Pr 21:1 **5:3** [l] Est 7:2; Da 5:16; Mk 6:23 **5:6** [m] Est 1:10 [n] Mk 6:23 [o] Est 7:2; 9:12 **5:8** [p] Est 2:15; 7:3; 8:5 [q] 1Ki 3:15; Est 6:14 **5:9** [r] Est 2:21; Pr 14:17 [s] Est 3:3,5 **5:10** [t] Est 6:13 **5:11** [u] Pr 13:16 [v] Est 9:7-10, 13 **5:12** [w] Job 22:29; Pr 16:18; 29:23 **5:13** [x] Est 2:19

14His wife Zeresh and all his friends said to him, "Have a pole set up, reaching to a height of fifty cubits,[a][y] and ask the king in the morning to have Mordecai impaled[z] on it. Then go with the king to the banquet and enjoy yourself." This suggestion delighted Haman, and he had the pole set up.

Mordecai Honored

6 That night the king could not sleep;[a] so he ordered the book of the chronicles,[b] the record of his reign, to be brought in and read to him. 2It was found recorded there that Mordecai had exposed Bigthana and Teresh, two of the king's officers who guarded the doorway, who had conspired to assassinate King Xerxes.

3"What honor and recognition has Mordecai received for this?" the king asked.

"Nothing has been done for him,"[c] his attendants answered.

4The king said, "Who is in the court?" Now Haman had just entered the outer court of the palace to speak to the king about impaling Mordecai on the pole he had set up for him.

5His attendants answered, "Haman is standing in the court."

"Bring him in," the king ordered.

6When Haman entered, the king asked him, "What should be done for the man the king delights to honor?"

Now Haman thought to himself, "Who is there that the king would rather honor than me?" 7So he answered the king, "For the man the king delights to honor, 8have them bring a royal robe[d] the king has worn and a horse[e] the king has ridden, one with a royal crest placed on its head. 9Then let the robe and horse be entrusted to one of the king's most noble princes. Let them robe the man the king delights to honor, and lead him on the horse through the city streets, proclaiming before him, 'This is what is done for the man the king delights to honor![f]' "

10"Go at once," the king commanded Haman. "Get the robe and the horse and do just as you have suggested for Mordecai the Jew, who sits at the king's gate. Do not neglect anything you have recommended."

11So Haman got[g] the robe and the horse. He robed Mordecai, and led him on horseback through the city streets, proclaiming before him, "This is what is done for the man the king delights to honor!"

12Afterward Mordecai returned to the king's gate. But Haman rushed home, with his head covered[h] in grief, 13and told Zeresh[i] his wife and all his friends everything that had happened to him.

His advisers and his wife Zeresh said to him, "Since Mordecai, before whom your downfall[j] has started, is of Jewish origin, you cannot stand against him—you will surely come to ruin!" 14While they were still talking with him, the king's eunuchs arrived and hurried Haman away to the banquet[k] Esther had prepared.

Haman Impaled

7 So the king and Haman went to Queen Esther's banquet,[l] 2and as they were drinking wine[m] on the second day, the king again asked, "Queen Esther, what is your petition? It will be given you. What is your request? Even up to half the kingdom,[n] it will be granted.[o]"

3Then Queen Esther answered, "If I have found favor[p] with you, Your Majesty, and if it pleases you, grant me my life—this is my petition. And spare my people—this is my request. 4For I and my people have been sold to be destroyed, killed and annihilated.[q] If we had merely been sold as male and female slaves, I would have kept quiet, because no such distress would justify disturbing the king.[b]"

5King Xerxes asked Queen Esther, "Who is he? Where is he—the man who has dared to do such a thing?"

6Esther said, "An adversary and enemy! This vile Haman!"

Then Haman was terrified before the king and queen. 7The king got up in a rage,[r] left his wine and went out into the palace garden.[s] But Haman, realizing that the king had already decided his fate,[t] stayed behind to beg Queen Esther for his life.

---

[a] *14* That is, about 75 feet or about 23 meters
[b] *4* Or *quiet, but the compensation our adversary offers cannot be compared with the loss the king would suffer*

5:14 *pole.* The pole's height, 50 cubits, was about 75 feet.

6:1 *the king could not sleep.* Within this chapter we observe a series of events that point unmistakably to God's sovereign hand. Only because of the "chance happening" of his sleepless night did the king learn of Mordecai's past loyalty.

6:4 *had just entered the outer court.* Here again is the Lord's hand at work on behalf of his people. No sooner had Mordecai's reward been discussed than Haman appeared in the court.

6:10 *Jew.* The term "Jew," derived from Judah, came into use during the Exile because the people were primarily from the southern kingdom of Judah.

7:3 *my people—this is my request.* Esther disclosed her real identity to the king in her plea for the lives of her people.

7:6 *This vile Haman.* In Haman's evil plan to kill his enemy he had unwittingly threatened the queen's life.

5:14 [y] Est 7:9 [z] Ezr 6:11; Est 6:4 **6:1** [a] Da 2:1; 6:18 [b] Est 2:23; 10:2 **6:3** [c] Ecc 9:13-16 **6:8** [d] Ge 41:42; Isa 52:1 [e] 1Ki 1:33 **6:9** [f] Ge 41:43 **6:11** [g] Ge 41:42 **6:12** [h] 2Sa 15:30; Jer 14:3, 4; Mic 3:7 **6:13** [i] Est 5:10 [j] Ps 57:6; Pr 26:27; 28:18 **6:14** [k] 1Ki 3:15; Est 5:8 **7:1** [l] Ge 40:20-22; Mt 22:1-14 **7:2** [m] Est 1:10 [n] Est 5:3 [o] Est 9:12 **7:3** [p] Est 2:15 **7:4** [q] Est 3:9 **7:7** [r] Ge 34:7; Est 1:12; Pr 19:12; 20:1-2 [s] 2Ki 21:18 [t] Est 6:13

8Just as the king returned from the palace garden to the banquet hall, Haman was falling on the couch[u] where Esther was reclining.[v]

The king exclaimed, "Will he even molest the queen while she is with me in the house?"[w]

As soon as the word left the king's mouth, they covered Haman's face.[x] 9Then Harbona,[y] one of the eunuchs attending the king, said, "A pole reaching to a height of fifty cubits[a][z] stands by Haman's house. He had it set up for Mordecai, who spoke up to help the king."

The king said, "Impale him on it!"[a] 10So they impaled Haman[b] on the pole[c] he had set up for Mordecai.[d] Then the king's fury subsided.[e]

The King's Edict in Behalf of the Jews

8 That same day King Xerxes gave Queen Esther the estate of Haman,[f] the enemy of the Jews. And Mordecai came into the presence of the king, for Esther had told how he was related to her. 2The king took off his signet ring,[g] which he had reclaimed from Haman, and presented it to Mordecai. And Esther appointed him over Haman's estate.[h]

3Esther again pleaded with the king, falling at his feet and weeping. She begged him to put an end to the evil plan of Haman the Agagite, which he had devised against the Jews. 4Then the king extended the gold scepter[i] to Esther and she arose and stood before him.

5"If it pleases the king," she said, "and if he regards me with favor and thinks it the right thing to do, and if he is pleased with me, let an order be written overruling the dispatches that Haman son of Hammedatha, the Agagite, devised and wrote to destroy the Jews in all the king's provinces. 6For how can I bear to see disaster fall on my people? How can I bear to see the destruction of my family?"[j]

7King Xerxes replied to Queen Esther and to Mordecai the Jew, "Because Haman attacked the Jews, I have given his estate to Esther, and they have impaled him on the pole he set up. 8Now write another decree[k] in the king's name in behalf of the Jews as seems best to you, and seal it with the king's signet ring[l]—for no document written in the king's name and sealed with his ring can be revoked."[m]

9At once the royal secretaries were summoned—on the twenty-third day of the third month, the month of Sivan. They wrote out all Mordecai's orders to the Jews, and to the satraps, governors and nobles of the 127 provinces stretching from India to Cush.[b][n] These orders were written in the script of each province and the language of each people and also to the Jews in their own script and language.[o] 10Mordecai wrote in the name of King Xerxes, sealed the dispatches with the king's signet ring, and sent them by mounted couriers, who rode fast horses especially bred for the king.

11The king's edict granted the Jews in every city the right to assemble and protect themselves; to destroy, kill and annihilate the armed men of any nationality or province who might attack them and their women and children,[c] and to plunder[p] the property of their enemies. 12The day appointed for the Jews to do this in all the provinces of King Xerxes was the thirteenth day of the twelfth month, the month of Adar.[q] 13A copy of the text of the edict was to be issued as law in every province and made known to the people of every nationality so that the Jews would be ready on that day[r] to avenge themselves on their enemies.

14The couriers, riding the royal horses, went out, spurred on by the king's command, and the edict was issued in the citadel of Susa.

The Triumph of the Jews

15When Mordecai[s] left the king's presence, he was wearing royal garments of blue and white, a large crown of gold and a purple robe of fine linen.[t] And the city of Susa held a joyous celebration.[u] 16For the Jews it was a time of happiness and joy,[v] gladness and honor.[w] 17In every province and in every city to which the edict of the king came, there was joy[x] and gladness among the Jews, with feasting and cele-

a 9 That is, about 75 feet or about 23 meters
b 9 That is, the upper Nile region *c* 11 Or *province, together with their women and children, who might attack them;*

7:8 ***covered Haman's face.*** The covering of his face signified that he was condemned to death.
8:2 ***he had reclaimed from Haman.*** Mordecai was given Haman's position as prime minister.
8:8 ***no document written in the king's name ... can be revoked.*** In the Persian Empire, a royal decree could not be altered, but a second one could be written that effectively invalidated the first.
8:17 ***became Jews.*** This is the only place in the Old Testament that refers to conversion to Judaism. Before, a person was a Jew if he or she was born so, and now it appears as a religion to which one could convert.

7:8 [u] Est 1:6 [v] Ge 39:14 [w] Ge 34:7 [x] Est 6:12
7:9 [y] Est 1:10 [z] Est 5:14 [a] Ps 7:14-16; 9:16; Pr 11:5-6; 26:27; Mt 7:2 **7:10** [b] Pr 10:28 [c] Est 9:25 [d] Da 6:24 [e] Est 2:1
8:1 [f] Est 2:7; 7:6; Pr 22:22-23 **8:2** [g] Ge 41:42; Est 3:10 [h] Pr 13:22; Da 2:48 **8:4** [i] Est 4:11; 5:2 **8:6** [j] Est 7:4; 9:1
8:8 [k] Est 3:12-14 [l] Ge 41:42 [m] Est 1:19; Da 6:15
8:9 [n] Est 1:1 [o] Est 1:22 **8:11** [p] Est 9:10, 15, 16
8:12 [q] Est 3:13; 9:1 **8:13** [r] Est 3:14 **8:15** [s] Est 9:4 [t] Ge 41:42 [u] Est 3:15 **8:16** [v] Ps 97:10-12 [w] Ps 112:4
8:17 [x] Est 9:19, 27; Ps 35:27; Pr 11:10

brating. And many people of other nationalities became Jews because fear[y] of the
Jews had seized them.[z]

9 On the thirteenth day of the twelfth
month, the month of Adar,[a] the edict
commanded by the king was to be carried out. On this day the enemies of the
Jews had hoped to overpower them, but
now the tables were turned and the Jews
got the upper hand[b] over those who hated
them.[c] 2The Jews assembled in their cities[d]
in all the provinces of King Xerxes to attack those determined to destroy them. No
one could stand against them,[e] because the
people of all the other nationalities were
afraid of them. 3And all the nobles of the
provinces, the satraps, the governors and
the king's administrators helped the Jews,[f]
because fear of Mordecai had seized them.
4Mordecai was prominent[g] in the palace;
his reputation spread throughout the provinces, and he became more and more powerful.[h]

5The Jews struck down all their enemies with the sword, killing and destroying them,[i] and they did what they pleased
to those who hated them. 6In the citadel of
Susa, the Jews killed and destroyed five
hundred men. 7They also killed Parshan-
datha, Dalphon, Aspatha, 8Poratha, Ada-
lia, Aridatha, 9Parmashta, Arisai, Aridai
and Vaizatha, 10the ten sons[j] of Haman
son of Hammedatha, the enemy of the
Jews. But they did not lay their hands on
the plunder.[k]

11The number of those killed in the citadel of Susa was reported to the king that
same day. 12The king said to Queen Esther,
"The Jews have killed and destroyed five
hundred men and the ten sons of Haman in
the citadel of Susa. What have they done in
the rest of the king's provinces? Now what
is your petition? It will be given you. What
is your request? It will also be granted."[l]

13"If it pleases the king," Esther answered, "give the Jews in Susa permission
to carry out this day's edict tomorrow also,
and let Haman's ten sons[m] be impaled[n] on
poles."

14So the king commanded that this be
done. An edict was issued in Susa, and
they impaled[o] the ten sons of Haman.
15The Jews in Susa came together on the
fourteenth day of the month of Adar, and
they put to death in Susa three hundred
men, but they did not lay their hands on
the plunder.[p]

16Meanwhile, the remainder of the Jews
who were in the king's provinces also assembled to protect themselves and get relief[q] from their enemies.[r] They killed seventy-five thousand of them[s] but did not
lay their hands on the plunder. 17This happened on the thirteenth day of the month
of Adar, and on the fourteenth they rested
and made it a day of feasting[t] and joy.

18The Jews in Susa, however, had assembled on the thirteenth and fourteenth, and
then on the fifteenth they rested and made
it a day of feasting and joy.

19That is why rural Jews—those living
in villages—observe the fourteenth of the
month of Adar[u] as a day of joy and feasting, a day for giving presents to each other.[v]

Purim Established

20Mordecai recorded these events, and
he sent letters to all the Jews throughout
the provinces of King Xerxes, near and far,
21to have them celebrate annually the fourteenth and fifteenth days of the month of
Adar 22as the time when the Jews got relief[w] from their enemies, and as the month
when their sorrow was turned into joy and
their mourning into a day of celebration.[x]
He wrote them to observe the days as days
of feasting and joy and giving presents of
food[y] to one another and gifts to the poor.

23So the Jews agreed to continue the celebration they had begun, doing what Mordecai had written to them. 24For Haman
son of Hammedatha, the Agagite,[z] the enemy of all the Jews, had plotted against the
Jews to destroy them and had cast the *pur*[a]
(that is, the lot[b]) for their ruin and destruction. 25But when the plot came to the king's
attention,[a] he issued written orders that the
evil scheme Haman had devised against
the Jews should come back onto his own
head,[c] and that he and his sons should be
impaled[d] on poles.[e] 26(Therefore these days
were called Purim, from the word *pur*.[f])
Because of everything written in this letter and because of what they had seen and
what had happened to them, 27the Jews
took it on themselves to establish the custom that they and their descendants and all

[a] 25 Or *when Esther came before the king*

9:7–10 *ten sons of Haman.* The patterns of reprisal and revenge were so deeply ingrained in the culture of the ancient Middle East that the survival of even one of these sons might mean trouble for the next generation of Jews.

9:26–28 *Purim.* Purim (from the word *pur,* referring to the lots Haman cast to determine the best day for destroying the Jews; 3:7) reminds the Jews of God's deliverance from their day of destruction.

8:17 [y] Ex 15:14, 16; Dt 11:25 [z] Est 9:3 **9:1** [a] Est 8:12 [b] Jer 29:4-7 [c] Est 3:12-14; Pr 22:22-23 **9:2** [d] ver 15-18 [e] Est 8:11, 17; Ps 71:13, 24 **9:3** [f] Ezr 8:36 **9:4** [g] Ex 11:3 [h] 2Sa 3:1; 1Ch 11:9 **9:5** [i] Ezr 4:6 **9:10** [j] Est 5:11 [k] Ge 14:23; 1Sa 14:32; Est 3:13; 8:11 **9:12** [l] Est 5:6; 7:2 **9:13** [m] Est 5:11 [n] Dt 21:22-23 **9:14** [o] Ezr 6:11 **9:15** [p] Ge 14:23; Est 8:11 **9:16** [q] Est 4:14 [r] Dt 25:19 [s] 1Ch 4:43 **9:17** [t] 1Ki 3:15 **9:19** [u] Est 3:7 [v] ver 22; Dt 16:11, 14; Ne 8:10, 12; Est 2:9; Rev 11:10 **9:22** [w] Est 4:14 [x] Ne 8:12; Ps 30:11-12 [y] 2Ki 25:30 **9:24** [z] Ex 17:8-16 [a] Est 3:7 [b] Lev 16:8 **9:25** [c] Ps 7:16 [d] Dt 21:22-23 [e] Est 7:10 **9:26** [f] ver 20; Est 3:7

who join them should without fail observe
these two days every year, in the way prescribed and at the time appointed. 28 These
days should be remembered and observed
in every generation by every family, and
in every province and in every city. And
these days of Purim should never fail to
be celebrated by the Jews—nor should the
memory of these days die out among their
descendants.
29 So Queen Esther, daughter of Abihail,[g]
along with Mordecai the Jew, wrote with
full authority to confirm this second letter
concerning Purim. 30 And Mordecai sent
letters to all the Jews in the 127 provinces[h]
of Xerxes' kingdom—words of goodwill
and assurance— 31 to establish these days
of Purim at their designated times, as Mordecai the Jew and Queen Esther had decreed for them, and as they had established
for themselves and their descendants in regard to their times of fasting[i] and lamentation.[j] 32 Esther's decree confirmed these
regulations about Purim, and it was written down in the records.

The Greatness of Mordecai

10 King Xerxes imposed tribute
throughout the empire, to its distant
shores.[k] 2 And all his acts of power and
might, together with a full account of the
greatness of Mordecai,[l] whom the king had
promoted,[m] are they not written in the book
of the annals[n] of the kings of Media and
Persia? 3 Mordecai the Jew was second[o] in
rank[p] to King Xerxes,[q] preeminent among
the Jews, and held in high esteem by his
many fellow Jews, because he worked for
the good of his people and spoke up for the
welfare of all the Jews.[r]

9:29 [g] Est 2:15 **9:30** [h] Est 1:1 **9:31** [i] Est 4:16 [j] Est 4:1-3 **10:1** [k] Ps 72:10; 97:1; Isa 24:15 **10:2** [l] Est 8:15; 9:4 [m] Ge 41:44 [n] Est 2:23 **10:3** [o] Da 5:7 [p] Ge 41:43 [q] Ge 41:40 [r] Ne 2:10; Jer 29:4-7; Da 6:3

JOB

▶ **AUTHOR:** The author of Job is unknown and there are no textual hints as to his identity. The non-Hebraic cultural background may point to a Gentile authorship, but an interesting school of thought maintains that Moses may have written this book. The land of Uz (1:1) is directly adjacent to Midian, where Moses lived for 40 years. Perhaps the oldest book of the Bible, set in the time of the patriarchs (Abraham, Isaac, Jacob, and Joseph), it is conceivable that Moses obtained a record of the dialogue left by Job or Elihu.

▶ **TIME:** Unknown ▶ **KEY VERSE:** Job 13:15

▶ **THEME:** There are many things that set Job apart from the rest of Scripture. Its dramatic format is unique. It is a story that is not part of the flow of the history of Israel. And the thematic focus is narrower than other books of its size. A classic work of literature, its primary subject matter is the most basic question man has of God: Why do we suffer? The Book of Job is the biblical text that addresses this issue head-on, and the dramatic nature of the story intensifies the conflict of ideas and understanding between God and man.

Prologue

1 In the land of Uz[a] there lived a man
whose name was Job.[b] This man was
blameless[c] and upright; he feared God[d]
and shunned evil. 2He had seven sons and
three daughters,[e] 3and he owned seven
thousand sheep, three thousand camels,
five hundred yoke of oxen and five hundred donkeys, and had a large number of
servants. He was the greatest man[f] among
all the people of the East.
4His sons used to hold feasts in their
homes on their birthdays, and they would
invite their three sisters to eat and drink
with them. 5When a period of feasting had
run its course, Job would make arrangements for them to be purified. Early in the
morning he would sacrifice a burnt offering[g] for each of them, thinking, "Perhaps
my children have sinned[h] and cursed God[i]
in their hearts." This was Job's regular custom.
6One day the angels[a][j] came to present
themselves before the LORD, and Satan[b]

[a] 6 Hebrew *the sons of God* [b] 6 Hebrew *satan* means *adversary.*

1:1 *Uz.* The precise location of Uz is unknown, but it may have been near Edom. Some of the other towns and peoples mentioned in this book are known to have been located near Edom, so it is logical to assume that Uz was in the same area.
1:2 Why Do We Suffer?—Scripture points us to multiple reasons for suffering. Here, as in Job's case, suffering somehow is involved in God's purposes, and we are to learn from it. The New Testament echoes this teaching in James 1 where it says to "Consider it pure joy, my brothers and sisters, whenever you face trials of many kinds, because you know that the testing of your faith produces perseverance" (James 1:2–3). Suffering also happens as a result of our own sin. David suffered many family trials because of his sin with Bathsheba. Other times we suffer directly because of our faith, as martyrs have done for centuries. Sometimes living out our faith comes in direct conflict with the ruling powers, and we suffer because of it. Still other times we suffer because we live in a fallen world where things go wrong or natural disasters occur.

Both Peter and Paul advise us to commit our pain and suffering to God, realizing He is faithful to work out all things for our good and God's glory (Rom. 8:28; 1 Pet. 4:9). This lesson is often learned over a whole lifetime as we see in numerous Psalms and in the lives of many biblical characters.
1:6 *the angels.* In the Hebrew, this is literally translated "sons of God." Celestial beings or angels are called "sons of God" because they had no parents. They were created by God to serve Him (2:1; 4:18; Ps. 103:20). This can also mean a group of saints (Gen. 6:2). Adam was also called "the son of God" (Luke 3:38) because God was his Creator rather than having a human father and mother. Here Satan is said to be among them. ***Satan.*** At some point after creation, Satan, who was the highest created angel

1:1 [a] Jer 25:20 [b] Eze 14:14, 20; Jas 5:11 [c] Ge 6:9; 17:1 [d] Ge 22:12; Ex 18:21 **1:2** [e] Job 42:13 **1:3** [f] Job 29:25 **1:5** [g] Ge 8:20; Job 42:8 [h] Job 8:4 [i] 1Ki 21:10, 13 **1:6** [j] Job 38:7

also came with them.[k] 7The LORD said to
Satan, "Where have you come from?"
Satan answered the LORD, "From roaming throughout the earth, going back and
forth on it."[l]

8Then the LORD said to Satan, "Have you
considered my servant Job?[m] There is no
one on earth like him; he is blameless and
upright, a man who fears God and shuns
evil."[n]

9"Does Job fear God for nothing?"[o] Satan replied. 10"Have you not put a hedge
around him and his household and everything he has?[p] You have blessed the work
of his hands, so that his flocks and herds
are spread throughout the land.[q] 11But
now stretch out your hand and strike everything he has,[r] and he will surely curse
you to your face."[s]

12The LORD said to Satan, "Very well,
then, everything he has is in your power,
but on the man himself do not lay a finger."
Then Satan went out from the presence
of the LORD.

13One day when Job's sons and daughters were feasting and drinking wine at the
oldest brother's house, 14a messenger came
to Job and said, "The oxen were plowing
and the donkeys were grazing nearby,
15and the Sabeans[t] attacked and made off
with them. They put the servants to the
sword, and I am the only one who has escaped to tell you!"

16While he was still speaking, another
messenger came and said, "The fire of God
fell from the heavens[u] and burned up the
sheep and the servants,[v] and I am the only
one who has escaped to tell you!"

17While he was still speaking, another messenger came and said, "The Chaldeans[w] formed three raiding parties and
swept down on your camels and made off
with them. They put the servants to the
sword, and I am the only one who has escaped to tell you!"

18While he was still speaking, yet another messenger came and said, "Your sons
and daughters were feasting and drinking
wine at the oldest brother's house, 19when
suddenly a mighty wind[x] swept in from the
desert and struck the four corners of the
house. It collapsed on them and they are
dead, and I am the only one who has escaped to tell you!"

20At this, Job got up and tore his robe[y]
and shaved his head. Then he fell to the
ground in worship[z] 21and said:

"Naked I came from my mother's womb,
and naked I will depart.[a][a]
The LORD gave and the LORD has taken
away;[b]
may the name of the LORD be
praised."[c]

22In all this, Job did not sin by charging
God with wrongdoing.[d]

2 On another day the angels[b] came to
present themselves before the LORD,
and Satan also came with them[e] to present
himself before him. 2And the LORD said to
Satan, "Where have you come from?"
Satan answered the LORD, "From roaming throughout the earth, going back and
forth on it."

3Then the LORD said to Satan, "Have you
considered my servant Job? There is no
one on earth like him; he is blameless and

---

a 21 Or *will return there* b 1 Hebrew *the sons of God*

(Ezek. 28:12–15), aspired to be as God Himself (Is. 14:13–14). As a result, he was barred from his heavenly position (Ezek. 28:16) and took a large number of angels with him in his rebellion, over whom he rules (Matt. 12:24). Jesus said that He saw Satan fall from heaven (Luke 10:18), but this chapter in Job, and the incident of the lying spirit with the false prophets of Ahab (2 Chr. 18:8–22), indicate that Satan still had access to heaven and heavenly counsels. God can and does limit Satan (1:12). The cross defeated Satan (John 12:31), but the final judgment will not occur until the end of the millennium (Rev. 20:10). In the meantime, Satan tries to thwart and defeat the work of God. God sometimes uses Satan to teach a lesson (1 Chr. 21; 2 Cor. 12:7–10), but it is still God who is in control.

1:7 ***The LORD.*** The Hebrew word Yahweh, usually translated "the LORD," is the personal name of the true God of the Old Testament (Ex. 3:14–15). It is the particular name of God in covenantal relations with His people Israel (Ex. 6:1–6; 19:3–8).

1:8 ***blameless and upright.*** The Lord was not saying that Job was sinless, but He was saying that Job had his priorities right. Job feared the Lord and it showed in his life.

1:10 ***hedge.*** No harm could come to Job unless the Lord permitted it (v. 12). Believers today should take great comfort from the biblical teaching that the Lord protects His people—whether by a cloud (Ex. 14:19–20), or by a wall of fiery chariots (2 Kin. 6:17), or through guardian angels (Heb. 1:14).

1:11 ***curse.*** The sin of cursing God is a pivotal issue for the Book of Job. Job feared that his children might think or speak irreverently of God (v. 5). But Satan asserted that Job would "surely curse" God if his prosperity and blessings were removed. Even Job's wife urged him to "Curse God and die" (2:9).

1:15 ***Sabeans.*** The Sabeans were nomadic raiders from Sheba, probably located in southwestern Arabia, in present-day Yemen.

1:17 ***Chaldeans.*** The Chaldeans were part of various west Semitic marauding tribes active in the middle Euphrates from the twelfth to the ninth centuries B.C. They migrated eastward into Assyria and then Babylonia, and were the forerunners of the Chaldean or neo-Babylonian dynasty established by Nebuchadnezzar's father.

1:6 [k] Job 2:1 **1:7** [l] 1Pe 5:8 **1:8** [m] Jos 1:7; Job 42:7-8 [n] ver 1 **1:9** [o] 1Ti 6:5 **1:10** [p] Ps 34:7 [q] ver 3; Job 29:6; 31:25; Ps 128:1-2 **1:11** [r] Job 19:21 [s] Job 2:5 **1:15** [t] Ge 10:7; Job 6:19 **1:16** [u] Ge 19:24 [v] Lev 10:2; Nu 11:1-3 **1:17** [w] Ge 11:28,31 **1:19** [x] Jer 4:11; 13:24 **1:20** [y] Ge 37:29 [z] 1Pe 5:6 **1:21** [a] Ecc 5:15; 1Ti 6:7 [b] 1Sa 2:7 [c] Job 2:10; Eph 5:20; 1Th 5:18 **1:22** [d] Job 2:10 **2:1** [e] Job 1:6

upright, a man who fears God and shuns
evil.[f] And he still maintains his integrity,[g]
though you incited me against him to ruin
him without any reason."[h]
4"Skin for skin!" Satan replied. "A man
will give all he has for his own life. 5But
now stretch out your hand and strike his
flesh and bones,[i] and he will surely curse
you to your face."[j]
6The LORD said to Satan, "Very well,
then, he is in your hands; but you must
spare his life."[k]
7So Satan went out from the presence
of the LORD and afflicted Job with painful
sores from the soles of his feet to the crown
of his head.[l] 8Then Job took a piece of broken pottery and scraped himself with it as
he sat among the ashes.[m]
9His wife said to him, "Are you still
maintaining your integrity? Curse God
and die!"
10He replied, "You are talking like a foolish[a] woman. Shall we accept good from
God, and not trouble?"[n]
In all this, Job did not sin in what he said.[o]

11When Job's three friends, Eliphaz the
Temanite,[p] Bildad the Shuhite[q] and Zophar the Naamathite, heard about all the
troubles that had come upon him, they set
out from their homes and met together by
agreement to go and sympathize with him
and comfort him.[r] 12When they saw him
from a distance, they could hardly recognize him; they began to weep aloud, and
they tore their robes and sprinkled dust on
their heads.[s] 13Then they sat on the ground
with him for seven days and seven nights.[t]
No one said a word to him, because they
saw how great his suffering was.

Job Speaks

3 After this, Job opened his mouth and
cursed the day of his birth. 2He said:

3 "May the day of my birth perish,
and the night that said, 'A boy is
conceived!'[u]
4 That day—may it turn to darkness;
may God above not care about it;
may no light shine on it.
5 May gloom and utter darkness[v] claim it
once more;
may a cloud settle over it;
may blackness overwhelm it.
6 That night—may thick darkness[w]
seize it;
may it not be included among the
days of the year
nor be entered in any of the months.
7 May that night be barren;
may no shout of joy be heard in it.
8 May those who curse days[b] curse that
day,
those who are ready to rouse
Leviathan.[x]
9 May its morning stars become dark;
may it wait for daylight in vain
and not see the first rays of
dawn,[y]
10 for it did not shut the doors of the
womb on me
to hide trouble from my eyes.

11 "Why did I not perish at birth,
and die as I came from the womb?[z]
12 Why were there knees to receive me[a]
and breasts that I might be nursed?
13 For now I would be lying down[b] in
peace;
I would be asleep and at rest[c]
14 with kings and rulers of the earth,[d]
who built for themselves places now
lying in ruins,[e]
15 with princes[f] who had gold,
who filled their houses with silver.[g]
16 Or why was I not hidden away in the
ground like a stillborn child,[h]
like an infant who never saw the light
of day?
17 There the wicked cease from turmoil,
and there the weary are at rest.[i]

---

[a] 10 The Hebrew word rendered *foolish* denotes moral deficiency. [b] 8 Or *curse the sea*

2:10 *good ... trouble.* This comment of Job's is one of the central themes of the whole book. A person of faith will trust in God through prosperity or adversity, even if they are unable to understand why bad things happen (Hab. 3:17–19).

2:11 *Temanite ... Shuhite ... Naamathite.* A Temanite was probably an Edomite from Teman in northern Edom, and a Naamathite probably came from Naameh, a mountainous area in northwestern Arabia. From this context, it can be assumed that a Shuhite was also a person from a certain town, unknown in modern times.

3:1 *cursed the day.* The Hebrew word for "cursed," meaning "to hold in contempt," is elsewhere employed of cursing God (Ex. 22:28; Lev. 24:15) or cursing one's parents (Ex. 21:17). Job expressed a strong malediction against the day of his birth and the night of his conception, but he did not commit blasphemy. He did not curse the Chaldeans, or Sabeans, much less God. Neither did he express thoughts of suicide.

3:8 *curse.* Job employed two separate Hebrew words translated "curse," different from the term in verse 1. He wished that the popular magicians who cast spells on the day for their clients could have cast a spell on his day so that he never could have been born. He was not endorsing pagan magic, but was speaking vividly and forcefully to express his agony and despair.

2:3 [f] Job 1:1,8 [g] Job 27:6 [h] Job 9:17 **2:5** [i] Job 19:20 [j] Job 1:11 **2:6** [k] Job 1:12 **2:7** [l] Dt 28:35; Job 7:5 **2:8** [m] Job 42:6; Jer 6:26; Eze 27:30; Mt 11:21 **2:10** [n] Job 1:21 [o] Job 1:22; Ps 39:1; Jas 1:12; 5:11 **2:11** [p] Ge 36:11; Jer 49:7 [q] Ge 25:2 [r] Job 42:11; Ro 12:15 **2:12** [s] Jos 7:6; Ne 9:1; La 2:10; Eze 27:30 **2:13** [t] Ge 50:10; Eze 3:15 **3:3** [u] Job 10:18-19; Jer 20:14-18 **3:5** [v] Job 10:21,22; Ps 23:4; Jer 2:6; 13:16 **3:6** [w] Job 23:17 **3:8** [x] Job 41:1,8,10,25 **3:9** [y] Job 41:18 **3:11** [z] Job 10:18 **3:12** [a] Ge 30:3; Isa 66:12 **3:13** [b] Job 17:13 [c] Job 7:8-10, 21; 10:22; 14:10-12; 19:27; 21:13,23 **3:14** [d] Job 12:17 [e] Job 15:28 **3:15** [f] Job 12:21 [g] Job 27:17 **3:16** [h] Ps 58:8; Ecc 6:3 **3:17** [i] Job 17:16

18 Captives also enjoy their ease;
they no longer hear the slave driver's shout.[j]
19 The small and the great are there,
and the slaves are freed from their owners.

20 "Why is light given to those in misery,
and life to the bitter of soul,[k]
21 to those who long for death that does not come,[l]
who search for it more than for hidden treasure,[m]
22 who are filled with gladness
and rejoice when they reach the grave?
23 Why is life given to a man
whose way is hidden,
whom God has hedged in?[n]
24 For sighing has become my daily food;[o]
my groans pour out like water.[p]
25 What I feared has come upon me;
what I dreaded[q] has happened to me.
26 I have no peace, no quietness;
I have no rest,[r] but only turmoil."

Eliphaz

4 Then Eliphaz the Temanite replied:

2 "If someone ventures a word with you,
will you be impatient?
But who can keep from speaking?[s]
3 Think how you have instructed many,
how you have strengthened feeble hands.[t]
4 Your words have supported those who stumbled;
you have strengthened faltering knees.[u]
5 But now trouble comes to you, and you are discouraged;
it strikes[v] you, and you are dismayed.[w]
6 Should not your piety be your confidence[x]
and your blameless[y] ways your hope?

7 "Consider now: Who, being innocent, has ever perished?[z]
Where were the upright ever destroyed?[a]
8 As I have observed, those who plow evil[b]
and those who sow trouble reap it.[c]
9 At the breath of God[d] they perish;
at the blast of his anger they are no more.[e]
10 The lions may roar and growl,
yet the teeth of the great lions are broken.[f]
11 The lion perishes for lack of prey,[g]
and the cubs of the lioness are scattered.

12 "A word was secretly brought to me,
my ears caught a whisper[h] of it.[i]
13 Amid disquieting dreams in the night,
when deep sleep falls on people,[j]
14 fear and trembling seized me
and made all my bones shake.[k]
15 A spirit glided past my face,
and the hair on my body stood on end.
16 It stopped,
but I could not tell what it was.
A form stood before my eyes,
and I heard a hushed voice:
17 'Can a mortal be more righteous than God?[l]
Can even a strong man be more pure than his Maker?[m]
18 If God places no trust in his servants,
if he charges his angels with error,[n]
19 how much more those who live in houses of clay,[o]
whose foundations[p] are in the dust,[q]

3:20–22 *long for death.* Even though Job longed for death, he was not considering suicide. The context of the other passages indicates that Job merely wished that the Lord would let him die (7:15–21; 10:18–22).
3:23 *whom God has hedged in?* The irony is that Job perceived God's hedge as keeping him from a desirable death instead of seeing it as God's protection of his life.
4:7 *Who, being innocent, has ever perished?* Eliphaz concluded that since Job was suffering, he must have sin in his life. Eliphaz supported the retribution doctrine: God supports the righteous but abandons the wicked.
4:8 *sow trouble reap it.* It can be true that planting wicked actions will yield a crop of trauma, but the converse is not necessarily true. Hard times can come to anyone, and the crop that is harvested in hard times depends on whether or not we continue to follow God in times of trouble.
4:13 *disquieting dreams in the night.* Eliphaz appealed to a vision to authenticate his theology, but all dreams do not come from God. The "reader" of this book has different information, for God pulled aside the curtain of heaven to reveal the true background for Job's troubles.

4:19 Death—We live in houses of clay, and our foundations are in the dust. We may presume upon tomorrow, having illusions of permanence, but suddenly the cords of our tent are pulled up and our existence collapses. We perish, more readily than a moth encircling a flame. Surely the transience of life, the reality of death, and the certainty of judgment should move us to pray that the Eternal God will teach us to number our days so we can use them wisely (Ps. 90:12). This awareness gives us a sense of urgency in turning from sin and serving our Savior.

3:18 [j] Job 39:7 **3:20** [k] 1Sa 1:10; Jer 20:18; Eze 27:30-31 **3:21** [l] Rev 9:6 [m] Pr 2:4 **3:23** [n] Job 19:6, 8, 12; Ps 88:8; La 3:7 **3:24** [o] Job 6:7; 33:20 [p] Ps 42:3, 4 **3:25** [q] Job 30:15 **3:26** [r] Job 7:4, 14 **4:2** [s] Job 32:20 **4:3** [t] Isa 35:3; Heb 12:12 **4:4** [u] Isa 35:3; Heb 12:12 **4:5** [v] Job 19:21 [w] Job 6:14 **4:6** [x] Pr 3:26 [y] Job 1:1 **4:7** [z] Job 36:7 [a] Job 8:20; Ps 37:25 **4:8** [b] Job 15:35 [c] Pr 22:8; Hos 10:13; Gal 6:7-8 **4:9** [d] Job 15:30; Isa 30:33; 2Th 2:8 [e] Job 40:13 **4:10** [f] Job 5:15; Ps 58:6 **4:11** [g] Job 27:14; Ps 34:10 **4:12** [h] Job 26:14 [i] Job 33:14 **4:13** [j] Job 33:15 **4:14** [k] Jer 23:9; Hab 3:16 **4:17** [l] Job 9:2 [m] Job 35:10 **4:18** [n] Job 15:15 **4:19** [o] Job 10:9 [p] Job 22:16 [q] Ge 2:7

who are crushed more readily than a
moth!
20 Between dawn and dusk they are
broken to pieces;
unnoticed, they perish forever.[r]
21 Are not the cords of their tent pulled up,[s]
so that they die without wisdom?'[t]

5 "Call if you will, but who will answer
you?
To which of the holy ones[u] will you
turn?
2 Resentment kills a fool,
and envy slays the simple.[v]
3 I myself have seen a fool taking root,[w]
but suddenly his house was cursed.[x]
4 His children are far from safety,[y]
crushed in court[z] without a defender.
5 The hungry consume his harvest,[a]
taking it even from among thorns,
and the thirsty pant after his wealth.
6 For hardship does not spring from the
soil,
nor does trouble sprout from the
ground.
7 Yet man is born to trouble[b]
as surely as sparks fly upward.

8 "But if I were you, I would appeal to
God;
I would lay my cause before him.[c]
9 He performs wonders that cannot be
fathomed,[d]
miracles that cannot be counted.
10 He provides rain for the earth;
he sends water on the countryside.[e]
11 The lowly he sets on high,[f]
and those who mourn are lifted to
safety.
12 He thwarts the plans[g] of the crafty,
so that their hands achieve no
success.
13 He catches the wise in their craftiness,[h]
and the schemes of the wily are swept
away.
14 Darkness[i] comes upon them in the
daytime;
at noon they grope as in the night.[j]
15 He saves the needy[k] from the sword in
their mouth;
he saves them from the clutches of
the powerful.[l]
16 So the poor have hope,
and injustice shuts its mouth.[m]

17 "Blessed is the one whom God
corrects;[n]
so do not despise the discipline[o] of
the Almighty.[a][p]
18 For he wounds, but he also binds up;[q]
he injures, but his hands also heal.[r]
19 From six calamities he will rescue you;
in seven no harm will touch you.[s]
20 In famine[t] he will deliver you from
death,
and in battle from the stroke of the
sword.[u]
21 You will be protected from the lash of
the tongue,[v]
and need not fear[w] when destruction
comes.
22 You will laugh at destruction and
famine,
and need not fear the wild animals.[x]
23 For you will have a covenant with the
stones[y] of the field,
and the wild animals will be at peace
with you.[z]
24 You will know that your tent is secure;
you will take stock of your property
and find nothing missing.[a]
25 You will know that your children will
be many,[b]
and your descendants like the grass
of the earth.[c]
26 You will come to the grave in full
vigor,[d]
like sheaves gathered in season.

27 "We have examined this, and it is true.
So hear it and apply it to yourself."

Job

6 Then Job replied:

2 "If only my anguish could be weighed
and all my misery be placed on the
scales![e]

[a] 17 Hebrew *Shaddai*; here and throughout Job

5:17 *corrects.* Eliphaz insinuated that since Job's suffering was a result of God's discipline for his sin, Job should not reject what God was trying to teach him. While it is true that God sometimes disciplines people for their own good (Prov. 3:11–12; Heb. 12:7), Eliphaz was suggesting that trouble in one's life necessarily means that one is being disciplined. Once again, the reader of this book has insight that the participants in the story do not have. Job's troubles do indeed teach him more about God, but the troubles originated because God was showing Satan that His followers are not following Him for what they get, but because of who He is.

5:23 covenant with the stones of the field. Stones in the field are a significant hindrance to farming, just as wild animals or lack of rain are a hindrance. Eliphaz was saying that one who accepts the discipline of the Almighty will not find himself fighting the elements of nature. It is true that God is a deliverer, a healer, and one who disciplines his followers. We can safely trust Him to care for us. But having disaster, wounds, or failure is not necessarily a sign of God's discipline.

4:20 [r] Job 14:2, 20; 20:7; Ps 90:5-6 **4:21** [s] Job 8:22 [t] Job 18:21; 36:12 **5:1** [u] Job 15:15 **5:2** [v] Pr 12:16 **5:3** [w] Ps 37:35; Jer 12:2 [x] Job 24:18 **5:4** [y] Job 4:11 [z] Am 5:12 **5:5** [a] Job 18:8-10 **5:7** [b] Job 14:1 **5:8** [c] Ps 35:23; 50:15 **5:9** [d] Job 42:3; Ps 40:5 **5:10** [e] Job 36:28 **5:11** [f] Ps 113:7-8 **5:12** [g] Ne 4:15; Ps 33:10 **5:13** [h] 1Co 3:19* **5:14** [i] Job 12:25 [j] Dt 28:29 **5:15** [k] Ps 35:10 [l] Job 4:10 **5:16** [m] Ps 107:42 **5:17** [n] Jas 1:12 [o] Ps 94:12; Pr 3:11 [p] Heb 12:5-11 **5:18** [q] Isa 30:26 [r] 1Sa 2:6 **5:19** [s] Ps 34:19; 91:10 **5:20** [t] Ps 33:19 [u] Ps 144:10 **5:21** [v] Ps 31:20 [w] Ps 91:5 **5:22** [x] Ps 91:13; Eze 34:25 **5:23** [y] Ps 91:12 [z] Isa 11:6-9 **5:24** [a] Job 8:6 **5:25** [b] Ps 112:2 [c] Ps 72:16; Isa 44:3-4 **5:26** [d] Ge 15:15 **6:2** [e] Job 31:6

3 It would surely outweigh the sand[f] of the seas—
no wonder my words have been impetuous.[g]
4 The arrows[h] of the Almighty are in me,[i]
my spirit drinks[j] in their poison;
God's terrors[k] are marshaled against me.[l]
5 Does a wild donkey bray when it has grass,
or an ox bellow when it has fodder?
6 Is tasteless food eaten without salt,
or is there flavor in the sap of the mallow[a]?
7 I refuse to touch it;
such food makes me ill.[m]

8 "Oh, that I might have my request,
that God would grant what I hope for,[n]
9 that God would be willing to crush me,
to let loose his hand and cut off my life![o]
10 Then I would still have this consolation—
my joy in unrelenting pain—
that I had not denied the words[p] of the Holy One.[q]

11 "What strength do I have, that I should still hope?
What prospects, that I should be patient?[r]
12 Do I have the strength of stone?
Is my flesh bronze?
13 Do I have any power to help myself,[s]
now that success has been driven from me?

14 "Anyone who withholds kindness from a friend
forsakes the fear of the Almighty.
15 But my brothers are as undependable as intermittent streams,[t]
as the streams that overflow
16 when darkened by thawing ice
and swollen with melting snow,
17 but that stop flowing in the dry season,
and in the heat[u] vanish from their channels.
18 Caravans turn aside from their routes;
they go off into the wasteland and perish.
19 The caravans of Tema[v] look for water,
the traveling merchants of Sheba look in hope.
20 They are distressed, because they had been confident;
they arrive there, only to be disappointed.[w]
21 Now you too have proved to be of no help;
you see something dreadful and are afraid.[x]
22 Have I ever said, 'Give something on my behalf,
pay a ransom for me from your wealth,
23 deliver me from the hand of the enemy,
rescue me from the clutches of the ruthless'?

24 "Teach me, and I will be quiet;[y]
show me where I have been wrong.
25 How painful are honest words![z]
But what do your arguments prove?
26 Do you mean to correct what I say,
and treat my desperate words as wind?[a]
27 You would even cast lots[b] for the fatherless
and barter away your friend.

28 "But now be so kind as to look at me.
Would I lie to your face?[c]
29 Relent, do not be unjust;
reconsider, for my integrity is at stake.[b][d]
30 Is there any wickedness on my lips?[e]
Can my mouth not discern[f] malice?

7 "Do not mortals have hard service[g] on earth?[h]
Are not their days like those of hired laborers?[i]

[a] *6* The meaning of the Hebrew for this phrase is uncertain. [b] *29* Or *my righteousness still stands*

6:9 Prayer—Job thought it would be better to die than to endure all the pain and suffering that resulted from the tragedies he had experienced. He could not know that the fact that he was alive was actually because God had protected him. This prayer should be a great comfort to believers. We cannot always see God's hedge of protection in a traumatic situation. We can cry out for relief, when God wants us to endure. He knows far more about our situation than we do, and we can trust Him, even as we anguish over unanswered prayer.

6:10 *still have this consolation.* Job's single comfort was that he had not denied God, even though he believed that God was the one who had wounded him.

6:15 *intermittent streams.* A brook is a stream that only carries water during the rainy season. Other times of the year it is a dry path. Job was likening his friends to a dry stream.

6:24 *show me.* If Job's friends could show him error in his ways, Job was willing to listen. The problem was that Job's friends were reasoning backwards. They were assuming that they knew his error, based on the extent of Job's suffering. But they had their formula wrong. Sinners may suffer, but suffering does not equal sin or the Lord's discipline.

6:3 [f] Pr 27:3 [g] Job 23:2 **6:4** [h] Ps 38:2 [i] Job 16:12, 13 [j] Job 21:20 [k] Job 30:15 [l] Ps 88:15-18 **6:7** [m] Job 3:24 **6:8** [n] Job 14:13 **6:9** [o] Nu 11:15; 1Ki 19:4 **6:10** [p] Job 22:22; 23:12 [q] Lev 19:2; Isa 57:15 **6:11** [r] Job 21:4 **6:13** [s] Job 26:2 **6:15** [t] Ps 38:11; Jer 15:18 **6:17** [u] Job 24:19 **6:19** [v] Ge 25:15; Isa 21:14 **6:20** [w] Jer 14:3 **6:21** [x] Ps 38:11 **6:24** [y] Ps 39:1 **6:25** [z] Ecc 12:11 **6:26** [a] Job 8:2; 15:3 **6:27** [b] Joel 3:3; Na 3:10; 2Pe 2:3 **6:28** [c] Job 27:4; 33:1, 3; 36:3, 4 **6:29** [d] Job 23:7, 10; 34:5, 36; 42:6 **6:30** [e] Job 27:4 [f] Job 12:11 **7:1** [g] Job 14:14; Isa 40:2 [h] Job 5:7 [i] Job 14:6

2 Like a slave longing for the evening shadows,
or a hired laborer waiting to be paid,[j]
3 so I have been allotted months of futility,
and nights of misery have been assigned to me.[k]
4 When I lie down I think, 'How long before I get up?'[l]
The night drags on, and I toss and turn until dawn.
5 My body is clothed with worms[m] and scabs,
my skin is broken and festering.

6 "My days are swifter than a weaver's shuttle,[n]
and they come to an end without hope.[o]
7 Remember, O God, that my life is but a breath;[p]
my eyes will never see happiness again.[q]
8 The eye that now sees me will see me no longer;
you will look for me, but I will be no more.[r]
9 As a cloud vanishes and is gone,
so one who goes down to the grave[s] does not return.[t]
10 He will never come to his house again;
his place[u] will know him no more.[v]

11 "Therefore I will not keep silent;[w]
I will speak out in the anguish of my spirit,
I will complain in the bitterness of my soul.[x]
12 Am I the sea, or the monster of the deep,[y]
that you put me under guard?
13 When I think my bed will comfort me
and my couch will ease my complaint,[z]
14 even then you frighten me with dreams
and terrify[a] me with visions,
15 so that I prefer strangling and death,[b]
rather than this body of mine.
16 I despise my life;[c] I would not live forever.
Let me alone; my days have no meaning.
17 "What is mankind that you make so much of them,
that you give them so much attention,[d]
18 that you examine them every morning
and test them every moment?[e]
19 Will you never look away from me,
or let me alone even for an instant?[f]
20 If I have sinned, what have I done to you,[g]
you who see everything we do?
Why have you made me your target?[h]
Have I become a burden to you?[a]
21 Why do you not pardon my offenses
and forgive my sins?[i]
For I will soon lie down in the dust;[j]
you will search for me, but I will be no more."

Bildad

8 Then Bildad the Shuhite replied:

2 "How long will you say such things?
Your words are a blustering wind.[k]
3 Does God pervert justice?[l]
Does the Almighty pervert what is right?[m]
4 When your children sinned against him,
he gave them over to the penalty of their sin.[n]
5 But if you will seek God earnestly
and plead[o] with the Almighty,
6 if you are pure and upright,
even now he will rouse himself on your behalf[p]
and restore you to your prosperous state.[q]
7 Your beginnings will seem humble,
so prosperous[r] will your future be.

8 "Ask the former generation[s]
and find out what their ancestors learned,
9 for we were born only yesterday and know nothing,[t]
and our days on earth are but a shadow.[u]

[a] *20* A few manuscripts of the Masoretic Text, an ancient Hebrew scribal tradition and Septuagint; most manuscripts of the Masoretic Text *I have become a burden to myself.*

7:6 *hope.* Job's choice of the word "hope" in the context of the weaver's shuttle may convey a double meaning. The Hebrew word for "hope" sounds like the Hebrew word that means "thread" or "cord."
7:20 *what have I done to you.* Job, too, was assuming that his troubles came from God. Job did not believe that he had sinned in a way that would cause God to bring trouble on him. This may sound presumptuous, as if Job thought he was without any sin at all. But we remember that God Himself referred to Job as upright and blameless. God was not finding fault with the way that Job was living out his life of faith in God.
8:3 *Does God pervert justice?* Bildad was saying that Job and his children received what they deserved.
8:6 *if you are pure and upright.* This was actually the way God described Job (1:8; 2:3). Bildad's concept that one must "get right with God" was not erroneous. But his error was his assumption that loss of possessions was equal with loss of God's favor.

7:2 [j] Lev 19:13 **7:3** [k] Job 16:7; Ps 6:6 **7:4** [l] Dt 28:67 **7:5** [m] Job 17:14; Isa 14:11 **7:6** [n] Job 9:25 [o] Job 13:15; 17:11, 15 **7:7** [p] Ps 78:39; Jas 4:14 [q] Job 9:25 **7:8** [r] Job 20:7, 9, 21 **7:9** [s] Job 11:8 [t] 2Sa 12:23; Job 30:15 **7:10** [u] Job 27:21, 23 [v] Job 8:18 **7:11** [w] Ps 40:9 [x] 1Sa 1:10 **7:12** [y] Eze 32:2-3 **7:13** [z] Job 9:27 **7:14** [a] Job 9:34 **7:15** [b] 1Ki 19:4 **7:16** [c] Job 9:21; 10:1 **7:17** [d] Ps 8:4; 144:3; Heb 2:6 **7:18** [e] Job 14:3 **7:19** [f] Job 9:18 **7:20** [g] Job 35:6 [h] Job 16:12 **7:21** [i] Job 10:14 [j] Job 10:9; Ps 104:29 **8:2** [k] Job 6:26 **8:3** [l] Dt 32:4; 2Ch 19:7; Ro 3:5 [m] Ge 18:25 **8:4** [n] Job 1:19 **8:5** [o] Job 11:13 **8:6** [p] Ps 7:6 [q] Job 5:24 **8:7** [r] Job 42:12 **8:8** [s] Dt 4:32; 32:7; Job 15:18 **8:9** [t] Ge 47:9 [u] 1Ch 29:15; Job 7:6

10 Will they not instruct you and tell you?
Will they not bring forth words from their understanding?
11 Can papyrus grow tall where there is no marsh?
Can reeds thrive without water?
12 While still growing and uncut,
they wither more quickly than grass.[v]
13 Such is the destiny of all who forget God;[w]
so perishes the hope of the godless.[x]
14 What they trust in is fragile[a];
what they rely on is a spider's web.[y]
15 They lean on the web,[z] but it gives way;
they cling to it, but it does not hold.[a]
16 They are like a well-watered plant in the sunshine,
spreading its shoots[b] over the garden;[c]
17 it entwines its roots around a pile of rocks
and looks for a place among the stones.
18 But when it is torn from its spot,
that place disowns it and says, 'I never saw you.'[d]
19 Surely its life withers[e] away,
and[b] from the soil other plants grow.[f]
20 "Surely God does not reject one who is blameless[g]
or strengthen the hands of evildoers.[h]
21 He will yet fill your mouth with laughter[i]
and your lips with shouts of joy.[j]
22 Your enemies will be clothed in shame,[k]
and the tents of the wicked will be no more."[l]

Job

9 Then Job replied:

2 "Indeed, I know that this is true.
But how can mere mortals prove their innocence before God?[m]
3 Though they wished to dispute with him,
they could not answer him one time out of a thousand.[n]
4 His wisdom[o] is profound, his power is vast.[p]
Who has resisted him and come out unscathed?[q]
5 He moves mountains without their knowing it
and overturns them in his anger.[r]
6 He shakes the earth[s] from its place
and makes its pillars tremble.[t]
7 He speaks to the sun and it does not shine;
he seals off the light of the stars.[u]
8 He alone stretches out the heavens[v]
and treads on the waves of the sea.[w]
9 He is the Maker of the Bear[c] and Orion,
the Pleiades and the constellations of the south.[x]
10 He performs wonders[y] that cannot be fathomed,
miracles that cannot be counted.[z]
11 When he passes me, I cannot see him;
when he goes by, I cannot perceive him.[a]
12 If he snatches away, who can stop him?[b]
Who can say to him, 'What are you doing?'[c]
13 God does not restrain his anger;
even the cohorts of Rahab[d] cowered at his feet.
14 "How then can I dispute with him?
How can I find words to argue with him?
15 Though I were innocent, I could not answer him;[e]
I could only plead[f] with my Judge for mercy.
16 Even if I summoned him and he responded,
I do not believe he would give me a hearing.
17 He would crush me[g] with a storm[h]
and multiply[i] my wounds for no reason.[j]
18 He would not let me catch my breath
but would overwhelm me with misery.[k]

---

a 14 The meaning of the Hebrew for this word is uncertain. *b 19* Or *Surely all the joy it has / is that* *c 9* Or *of Leo*

8:13 Such is the destiny of all who forget God. Bildad falsely deduced that one can always determine the cause by looking at the effect. We can know that the people around us suffer, but it is not given to us to know the spiritual causes, if any, behind this suffering.

9:3 Though they wished to dispute with him. The word "dispute" indicates a legal argument, not a quarrel. Job was seeking justice. He did not think he had sinned (as his friends indicated) so that God would punish him.

9:17 crush me with a storm. Job saw God as Lord of the heavens (vv. 7–8) and assumed that it was God who sent the windstorm that destroyed his children. Job did not know that it was Satan who sought to destroy him, and that God drew a line of protection around him.

8:12 [v] Ps 129:6; Jer 17:6 **8:13** [w] Ps 9:17 [x] Job 11:20; 13:16; 15:34; Pr 10:28 **8:14** [y] Isa 59:5 **8:15** [z] Job 27:18 [a] Ps 49:11 **8:16** [b] Ps 80:11 [c] Ps 37:35; Jer 11:16 **8:18** [d] Job 7:8; Ps 37:36 **8:19** [e] Job 20:5 [f] Ecc 1:4 **8:20** [g] Job 1:1 [h] Job 21:30 **8:21** [i] Job 5:22 [j] Ps 126:2; 132:16 **8:22** [k] Ps 35:26; 109:29; 132:18 [l] Job 18:6, 14, 21 **9:2** [m] Job 4:17; Ps 143:2; Ro 3:20 **9:3** [n] Job 10:2; 40:2 **9:4** [o] Job 11:6 [p] Job 36:5 [q] 2Ch 13:12 **9:5** [r] Mic 1:4 **9:6** [s] Isa 2:21; Hag 2:6; Heb 12:26 [t] Job 26:11 **9:7** [u] Isa 13:10; Eze 32:8 **9:8** [v] Ge 1:6; Ps 104:2-3 [w] Job 38:16; Ps 77:19 **9:9** [x] Ge 1:16; Job 38:31; Am 5:8 **9:10** [y] Ps 71:15 [z] Job 5:9 **9:11** [a] Job 23:8-9; 35:14 **9:12** [b] Job 11:10 [c] Isa 45:9; Ro 9:20 **9:13** [d] Job 26:12; Ps 89:10; Isa 30:7; 51:9 **9:15** [e] Job 10:15 [f] Job 8:5 **9:17** [g] Job 16:12 [h] Job 30:22 [i] Job 16:14 [j] Job 2:3 **9:18** [k] Job 7:19; 27:2

19 If it is a matter of strength, he is
mighty!
And if it is a matter of justice, who
can challenge him[a]?
20 Even if I were innocent, my mouth
would condemn me;
if I were blameless, it would
pronounce me guilty.

21 "Although I am blameless,[l]
I have no concern for myself;
I despise my own life.[m]
22 It is all the same; that is why I say,
'He destroys both the blameless and
the wicked.'[n]
23 When a scourge[o] brings sudden death,
he mocks the despair of the
innocent.[p]
24 When a land falls into the hands of the
wicked,[q]
he blindfolds its judges.[r]
If it is not he, then who is it?

25 "My days are swifter than a runner;[s]
they fly away without a glimpse of
joy.
26 They skim past like boats of papyrus,[t]
like eagles swooping down on their
prey.[u]
27 If I say, 'I will forget my complaint,[v]
I will change my expression, and
smile,'
28 I still dread[w] all my sufferings,
for I know you will not hold me
innocent.[x]
29 Since I am already found guilty,
why should I struggle in vain?[y]
30 Even if I washed myself with soap
and my hands[z] with cleansing
powder,[a]
31 you would plunge me into a slime pit
so that even my clothes would
detest me.

32 "He is not a mere mortal like me that I
might answer him,[b]
that we might confront each other in
court.[c]
33 If only there were someone to mediate
between us,[d]
someone to bring us together,
34 someone to remove God's rod from me,[e]
so that his terror would frighten me
no more.
35 Then I would speak up without fear of
him,
but as it now stands with me, I
cannot.[f]

10 "I loathe my very life;[g]
therefore I will give free rein to my
complaint
and speak out in the bitterness of my
soul.[h]
2 I say to God: Do not declare me guilty,
but tell me what charges[i] you have
against me.
3 Does it please you to oppress me,[j]
to spurn the work of your hands,[k]
while you smile on the plans of the
wicked?[l]
4 Do you have eyes of flesh?
Do you see as a mortal sees?[m]
5 Are your days like those of a mortal
or your years like those of a strong
man,[n]
6 that you must search out my faults
and probe after my sin[o]—
7 though you know that I am not guilty
and that no one can rescue me from
your hand?

8 "Your hands shaped[p] me and made me.
Will you now turn and destroy me?
9 Remember that you molded me like
clay.[q]
Will you now turn me to dust again?[r]
10 Did you not pour me out like milk
and curdle me like cheese,
11 clothe me with skin and flesh
and knit me together[s] with bones and
sinews?
12 You gave me life[t] and showed me
kindness,
and in your providence watched over
my spirit.

13 "But this is what you concealed in your
heart,
and I know that this was in your
mind:[u]

---

a 19 See Septuagint; Hebrew *me.*

10:1–3 Affliction—In the face of his adversities, Job despaired of life, but he continued to plead with God in prayer for an answer. Job's friends saw all suffering in a mathematical equation with sin. If these friends were right, that would reduce our relationship with God to a formula that says, "If you are good, God will rescue you, and if you are bad, God will abandon you to suffering." The converse of that statement says, "If you are suffering, you are bad, and because I am not suffering, I am good." It is often in the converse that a formula is shown to be faulty. Who can really claim to be good? We are all sinners in need of a savior.

10:7 *I am not guilty ... no one can rescue me from your hand.* Job thought that God was unjust in oppressing him, yet he realized that there is no one higher than God to deliver him from God. Job's thinking was twisted in much the same way that his friends' was. He was equating innocence with peace, and he could not imagine any reason why God would not rescue him.

9:21 [l] Job 1:1 [m] Job 7:16 **9:22** [n] Job 10:8; Ecc 9:2, 3; Eze 21:3 **9:23** [o] Heb 11:36 [p] Job 24:1, 12 **9:24** [q] Job 10:3; 16:11 [r] Job 12:6 **9:25** [s] Job 7:6 **9:26** [t] Isa 18:2 [u] Hab 1:8 **9:27** [v] Job 7:11 **9:28** [w] Job 3:25; Ps 119:120 [x] Job 7:21 **9:29** [y] Ps 37:33 **9:30** [z] Job 31:7 [a] Jer 2:22 **9:32** [b] Ro 9:20 [c] Ps 143:2; Ecc 6:10 **9:33** [d] 1Sa 2:25 **9:34** [e] Job 13:21; Ps 39:10 **9:35** [f] Job 13:21 **10:1** [g] 1Ki 19:4 [h] Job 7:11 **10:2** [i] Job 9:29 **10:3** [j] Job 9:22 [k] Job 14:15; Ps 138:8; Isa 64:8 [l] Job 21:16; 22:18 **10:4** [m] 1Sa 16:7 **10:5** [n] Ps 90:2, 4; 2Pe 3:8 **10:6** [o] Job 14:16 **10:8** [p] Ps 119:73 **10:9** [q] Isa 64:8 [r] Ge 2:7 **10:11** [s] Ps 139:13, 15 **10:12** [t] Job 33:4 **10:13** [u] Job 23:13

14 If I sinned, you would be watching me
and would not let my offense go
unpunished.[v]
15 If I am guilty—woe to me![w]
Even if I am innocent, I cannot lift my
head,[x]
for I am full of shame
and drowned in[a] my affliction.
16 If I hold my head high, you stalk me
like a lion[y]
and again display your awesome
power against me.[z]
17 You bring new witnesses against me[a]
and increase your anger toward me;[b]
your forces come against me wave
upon wave.

18 "Why then did you bring me out of the
womb?[c]
I wish I had died before any eye
saw me.
19 If only I had never come into being,
or had been carried straight from the
womb to the grave!
20 Are not my few days[d] almost over?[e]
Turn away from me[f] so I can have a
moment's joy
21 before I go to the place of no return,[g]
to the land of gloom and utter
darkness,[h]
22 to the land of deepest night,
of utter darkness and disorder,
where even the light is like darkness."

Zophar

11 Then Zophar the Naamathite replied:

2 "Are all these words to go unanswered?[i]
Is this talker to be vindicated?
3 Will your idle talk reduce others to
silence?
Will no one rebuke you when you
mock?[j]
4 You say to God, 'My beliefs are
flawless[k]
and I am pure[l] in your sight.'
5 Oh, how I wish that God would speak,
that he would open his lips against
you
6 and disclose to you the secrets of
wisdom,[m]
for true wisdom has two sides.
Know this: God has even forgotten
some of your sin.[n]

7 "Can you fathom[o] the mysteries of God?
Can you probe the limits of the
Almighty?
8 They are higher than the heavens[p]
above—what can you do?
They are deeper than the depths
below—what can you know?
9 Their measure is longer than the earth
and wider than the sea.

10 "If he comes along and confines you in
prison
and convenes a court, who can
oppose him?[q]
11 Surely he recognizes deceivers;
and when he sees evil, does he not
take note?[r]
12 But the witless can no more become
wise
than a wild donkey's colt can be born
human.[b]

13 "Yet if you devote your heart[s] to him
and stretch out your hands to him,[t]
14 if you put away the sin that is in your
hand
and allow no evil[u] to dwell in your
tent,[v]
15 then, free of fault, you will lift up your
face;[w]
you will stand firm and without fear.
16 You will surely forget your trouble,[x]
recalling it only as waters gone by.[y]
17 Life will be brighter than noonday,[z]
and darkness will become like
morning.
18 You will be secure, because there is
hope;
you will look about you and take your
rest[a] in safety.[b]

[a] 15 Or *and aware of* [b] 12 Or *wild donkey can be born tame*

10:18 *bring me out of the womb.* Job wondered how the God who so carefully fashioned him in the womb (vv. 9–11) could turn against him. This was the desperate cry of a sufferer blind to the fact that God was working good out of all the tragic events of his life.

11:4 *My beliefs are flawless.* Zophar exaggerated what Job had said about his innocence (9:14–21) to make Job look foolish.

11:7 *Can you probe the limits of the Almighty?* Zophar was correct in saying that understanding the depths of God is beyond man. But the fact that we cannot know everything about God does not mean that we cannot know anything about Him, nor that it is wrong to try to know and understand Him better.

11:13 *stretch out your hands to him.* Stretching out the hands was a posture of prayer as well as of praise (Ps. 134:2). Assuming that Job was suffering because of his iniquity, this was not bad advice.

11:15 *stand firm and without fear.* There is peace and comfort for those who have repented of their sin and turned to God. This is true and important to remember. But Zophar's presupposition that iniquity causes suffering kept him from understanding what Job's struggle was.

10:14 [v] Job 7:21 **10:15** [w] Job 9:13; Isa 3:11 [x] Job 9:15 **10:16** [y] Isa 38:13; La 3:10 [z] Job 5:9 **10:17** [a] Job 16:8 [b] Ru 1:21 **10:18** [c] Job 3:11 **10:20** [d] Job 14:1 [e] Job 7:19 [f] Job 7:16 **10:21** [g] 2Sa 12:23; Job 3:13; 16:22 [h] Ps 23:4; 88:12 **11:2** [i] Job 8:2 **11:3** [j] Job 17:2; 21:3 **11:4** [k] Job 6:10 [l] Job 10:7 **11:6** [m] Job 9:4 [n] Ezr 9:13; Job 15:5 **11:7** [o] Ecc 3:11; Ro 11:33 **11:8** [p] Job 22:12 **11:10** [q] Job 9:12; Rev 3:7 **11:11** [r] Job 34:21-25; Ps 10:14 **11:13** [s] 1Sa 7:3; Ps 78:8 [t] Ps 88:9 **11:14** [u] Ps 101:4 [v] Job 22:23 **11:15** [w] Job 22:26; 1Jn 3:21 **11:16** [x] Isa 65:16 [y] Job 22:11 **11:17** [z] Job 22:28; Ps 37:6; Isa 58:8, 10 **11:18** [a] Ps 3:5 [b] Lev 26:6; Pr 3:24

19 You will lie down, with no one to make
you afraid,[c]
and many will court your favor.[d]
20 But the eyes of the wicked will fail,[e]
and escape will elude them;[f]
their hope will become a dying
gasp."[g]

Job 12

12 Then Job replied:

2 "Doubtless you are the only people who
matter,
and wisdom will die with you![h]
3 But I have a mind as well as you;
I am not inferior to you.
Who does not know all these things?[i]
4 "I have become a laughingstock[j] to my
friends,
though I called on God and he
answered[k]—
a mere laughingstock, though
righteous and blameless![l]
5 Those who are at ease have contempt
for misfortune
as the fate of those whose feet are
slipping.
6 The tents of marauders are
undisturbed,[m]
and those who provoke God are
secure[n]—
those God has in his hand.[a]
7 "But ask the animals, and they will
teach you,
or the birds in the sky, and they will
tell you;
8 or speak to the earth, and it will teach
you,
or let the fish in the sea inform you.
9 Which of all these does not know
that the hand of the LORD has done
this?[o]
10 In his hand is the life of every creature
and the breath of all mankind.[p]
11 Does not the ear test words
as the tongue tastes food?[q]
12 Is not wisdom found among the aged?[r]
Does not long life bring
understanding?[s]
13 "To God belong wisdom[t] and power;[u]
counsel and understanding are his.[v]
14 What he tears down[w] cannot be rebuilt;[x]
those he imprisons cannot be
released.
15 If he holds back the waters,[y] there is
drought;[z]
if he lets them loose, they devastate
the land.[a]
16 To him belong strength and insight;
both deceived and deceiver are his.[b]
17 He leads rulers away stripped[c]
and makes fools of judges.[d]
18 He takes off the shackles[e] put on by
kings
and ties a loincloth[b] around their
waist.
19 He leads priests away stripped
and overthrows officials long
established.[f]
20 He silences the lips of trusted advisers
and takes away the discernment of
elders.[g]
21 He pours contempt on nobles
and disarms the mighty.
22 He reveals the deep things of darkness[h]
and brings utter darkness[i] into the
light.[j]
23 He makes nations great, and destroys
them;[k]
he enlarges nations,[l] and disperses
them.
24 He deprives the leaders of the earth of
their reason;
he makes them wander in a trackless
waste.[m]
25 They grope in darkness with no light;[n]
he makes them stagger like
drunkards.[o]

13 "My eyes have seen all this,
my ears have heard and understood
it.
2 What you know, I also know;
I am not inferior to you.[p]
3 But I desire to speak to the Almighty
and to argue my case with God.[q]
4 You, however, smear me with lies;[r]
you are worthless physicians, all of
you!
5 If only you would be altogether silent!
For you, that would be wisdom.[s]
6 Hear now my argument;
listen to the pleas of my lips.

[a] 6 Or *those whose god is in their own hand*
[b] 18 Or *shackles of kings / and ties a belt*

12:13 *counsel and understanding are his.* Job was sure that he did not understand what was happening to him, but he knew that God did know the answer.
13:4 *smear me with lies.* Job's friends were accusing him of hidden sin, offering a false formula for peace with God, and assuming that they had a greater understanding both of Job and of God's ways than they really did. False doctrine, even if held with sincerity, is still a lie.

11:19 [c] Lev 26:6 [d] Isa 45:14 **11:20** [e] Dt 28:65; Job 17:5 [f] Job 27:22; 34:22 [g] Job 8:13 **12:2** [h] Job 17:10

12:3 [i] Job 13:2 **12:4** [j] Job 21:3 [k] Ps 91:15 [l] Job 6:29 **12:6** [m] Job 22:18 [n] Job 9:24; 21:9 **12:9** [o] Isa 41:20 **12:10** [p] Job 27:3; 33:4; Ac 17:28 **12:11** [q] Job 34:3 **12:12** [r] Job 15:10 [s] Job 32:7,9 **12:13** [t] Job 11:6 [u] Job 9:4 [v] Job 32:8; 38:36 **12:14** [w] Job 19:10 [x] Job 37:7; Isa 25:2 **12:15** [y] 1Ki 8:35 [z] 1Ki 17:1 [a] Ge 7:11 **12:16** [b] Job 13:7,9 **12:17** [c] Job 19:9 [d] Job 3:14 **12:18** [e] Ps 116:16 **12:19** [f] Job 24:12,22; 34:20,28; 35:9 **12:20** [g] Job 32:9 **12:22** [h] 1Co 4:5 [i] Job 3:5 [j] Da 2:22 **12:23** [k] Jer 25:9 [l] Ps 107:38; Isa 9:3; 26:15 **12:24** [m] Ps 107:40 **12:25** [n] Job 5:14 [o] Ps 107:27; Isa 24:20 **13:2** [p] Job 12:3 **13:3** [q] Job 23:3-4 **13:4** [r] Ps 119:69; Jer 23:32 **13:5** [s] Pr 17:28

7 Will you speak wickedly on God's behalf?
Will you speak deceitfully for him?[t]
8 Will you show him partiality?[u]
Will you argue the case for God?
9 Would it turn out well if he examined you?
Could you deceive him as you might deceive a mortal?[v]
10 He would surely call you to account
if you secretly showed partiality.
11 Would not his splendor[w] terrify you?
Would not the dread of him fall on you?
12 Your maxims are proverbs of ashes;
your defenses are defenses of clay.

13 "Keep silent and let me speak;
then let come to me what may.
14 Why do I put myself in jeopardy
and take my life in my hands?
15 Though he slay me, yet will I hope[x] in him;[y]
I will surely[a] defend my ways to his face.[z]
16 Indeed, this will turn out for my deliverance,[a]
for no godless person would dare come before him!
17 Listen carefully to what I say;[b]
let my words ring in your ears.
18 Now that I have prepared my case,[c]
I know I will be vindicated.
19 Can anyone bring charges against me?[d]
If so, I will be silent and die.[e]

20 "Only grant me these two things, God,
and then I will not hide from you:
21 Withdraw your hand[f] far from me,
and stop frightening me with your terrors.
22 Then summon me and I will answer,[g]
or let me speak, and you reply to me.[h]
23 How many wrongs and sins have I committed?[i]
Show me my offense and my sin.
24 Why do you hide your face[j]
and consider me your enemy?[k]
25 Will you torment a windblown leaf?[l]
Will you chase after dry chaff?[m]
26 For you write down bitter things against me
and make me reap the sins of my youth.[n]
27 You fasten my feet in shackles;[o]
you keep close watch on all my paths
by putting marks on the soles of my feet.

28 "So man wastes away like something rotten,
like a garment eaten by moths.[p]

14 "Mortals, born of woman,
are of few days and full of trouble.[q]
2 They spring up like flowers[r] and wither away;[s]
like fleeting shadows,[t] they do not endure.
3 Do you fix your eye on them?[u]
Will you bring them[b] before you for judgment?[v]
4 Who can bring what is pure[w] from the impure?[x]
No one![y]
5 A person's days are determined;
you have decreed the number of his months[z]
and have set limits he cannot exceed.
6 So look away from him and let him alone,[a]
till he has put in his time like a hired laborer.[b]

7 "At least there is hope for a tree:
If it is cut down, it will sprout again,
and its new shoots will not fail.
8 Its roots may grow old in the ground
and its stump die in the soil,
9 yet at the scent of water it will bud
and put forth shoots like a plant.
10 But a man dies and is laid low;
he breathes his last and is no more.[c]
11 As the water of a lake dries up
or a riverbed becomes parched and dry,[d]
12 so he lies down and does not rise;
till the heavens are no more,[e] people will not awake
or be roused from their sleep.[f]

13 "If only you would hide me in the grave
and conceal me till your anger has passed![g]

---

[a] 15 Or *He will surely slay me; I have no hope — / yet I will* [b] 3 Septuagint, Vulgate and Syriac; Hebrew *me*

13:12 *maxims ... defenses.* The quickest way to make ourselves look silly is to try to explain something that we don't understand. Prayer is far more helpful than worthless counsel.
13:21 *Withdraw your hand ... frightening me.* Job was not cocky as he turned to plead his case before God. His requests were safe and wise for any believer who struggles with what life has handed him. Job asked God not to give up on him, and he asked God to keep him from being overpowered by the terror and majesty of God. Job knew very well that he was far below God, and that all that God is and does could be totally overwhelming to him.
14:13 *hide me ... till your anger is passed.* Job's wish for the grave to be a temporary hiding place from God's wrath differed dramatically from his earlier remarks concerning the grave (7:9–10;

13:7 [t] Job 36:4 **13:8** [u] Lev 19:15 **13:9** [v] Job 12:16; Gal 6:7 **13:11** [w] Job 31:23 **13:15** [x] Job 7:6 [y] Ps 23:4; Pr 14:32 [z] Job 27:5 **13:16** [a] Isa 12:1 **13:17** [b] Job 21:2 **13:18** [c] Job 23:4 **13:19** [d] Job 40:4; Isa 50:8 [e] Job 10:8 **13:21** [f] Ps 39:10 **13:22** [g] Job 14:15 [h] Job 9:16 **13:23** [i] 1Sa 26:18 **13:24** [j] Dt 32:20; Ps 13:1; Isa 8:17 [k] Job 19:11; La 2:5 **13:25** [l] Lev 26:36 [m] Job 21:18; Isa 42:3 **13:26** [n] Ps 25:7 **13:27** [o] Job 33:11 **13:28** [p] Isa 50:9; Jas 5:2 **14:1** [q] Job 5:7; Ecc 2:23 **14:2** [r] Jas 1:10 [s] Ps 90:5-6 [t] Job 8:9 **14:3** [u] Ps 8:4; 144:3 [v] Ps 143:2 **14:4** [w] Ps 51:10 [x] Eph 2:1-3 [y] Jn 3:6; Ro 5:12 **14:5** [z] Job 21:21 **14:6** [a] Job 7:19 [b] Job 7:1, 2; Ps 39:13 **14:10** [c] Job 13:19 **14:11** [d] Isa 19:5 **14:12** [e] Rev 20:11; 21:1 [f] Ac 3:21 **14:13** [g] Isa 26:20

If only you would set me a time
and then remember me!
14 If someone dies, will they live again?
All the days of my hard service
I will wait for my renewal[a] to come.
15 You will call and I will answer you;[h]
you will long for the creature your
hands have made.
16 Surely then you will count my steps[i]
but not keep track of my sin.[j]
17 My offenses will be sealed up in a bag;[k]
you will cover over my sin.[l]

18 "But as a mountain erodes and crumbles
and as a rock is moved from its place,
19 as water wears away stones
and torrents wash away the soil,
so you destroy a person's hope.[m]
20 You overpower them once for all, and
they are gone;
you change their countenance and
send them away.
21 If their children are honored, they do
not know it;
if their offspring are brought low,
they do not see it.[n]
22 They feel but the pain of their own
bodies
and mourn only for themselves."

Eliphaz

15 Then Eliphaz the Temanite replied:

2 "Would a wise person answer with
empty notions
or fill their belly with the hot east
wind?[o]
3 Would they argue with useless words,
with speeches that have no value?
4 But you even undermine piety
and hinder devotion to God.
5 Your sin prompts your mouth;
you adopt the tongue of the crafty.[p]
6 Your own mouth condemns you, not
mine;
your own lips testify against you.[q]

7 "Are you the first man ever born?[r]
Were you brought forth before the
hills?[s]
8 Do you listen in on God's council?[t]
Do you have a monopoly on wisdom?
9 What do you know that we do not know?
What insights do you have that we do
not have?[u]
10 The gray-haired and the aged[v] are on
our side,
men even older than your father.
11 Are God's consolations[w] not enough for
you,
words[x] spoken gently to you?[y]
12 Why has your heart[z] carried you away,
and why do your eyes flash,
13 so that you vent your rage against God
and pour out such words from your
mouth?

14 "What are mortals, that they could be
pure,
or those born of woman,[a] that they
could be righteous?[b]
15 If God places no trust in his holy ones,
if even the heavens are not pure in his
eyes,[c]
16 how much less mortals, who are vile
and corrupt,[d]
who drink up evil like water![e]

17 "Listen to me and I will explain to you;
let me tell you what I have seen,
18 what the wise have declared,
hiding nothing received from their
ancestors[f]
19 (to whom alone the land was given
when no foreigners moved among
them):
20 All his days the wicked man suffers
torment,
the ruthless man through all the
years stored up for him.[g]
21 Terrifying sounds fill his ears;[h]
when all seems well, marauders
attack him.[i]
22 He despairs of escaping the realm of
darkness;
he is marked for the sword.[j]
23 He wanders about[k] for food like a
vulture;
he knows the day of darkness is at
hand.[l]
24 Distress and anguish fill him with
terror;

a 14 Or *release*

10:18–22). He attributed the cause of his suffering to God's wrath because he assumed the retribution dogma that the righteous are always blessed and the wicked will eventually experience God's judgment. It did not occur to Job that he was being tested.

14:14 ***live again.*** Job had some understanding of man's potential for immortality. The answer to his question comes in the New Testament with an emphatic "Yes!" by Jesus (John 11:23–26; 1 Cor. 15:3–57).

15:21 ***Terrifying sounds.*** Eliphaz began his subtle argument to prove that Job was a wicked man. He alluded to Job's dread, the same word translated *feared* in 3:25, as an implicit indicator that Job was wicked.

15:24 ***Distress . . . terror.*** In contrast to 14:20 where Job complained to God that He overpowered people, Eliphaz said that the wicked man's (by implication, Job's) own fears overpower him. Eliphaz's statement may have been true, but that did not mean it applied to Job. Job did not understand God's ways correctly, but

14:15 [h] Job 13:22 **14:16** [i] Ps 139:1-3; Pr 5:21; Jer 32:19 [j] Job 10:6 **14:17** [k] Dt 32:34 [l] Hos 13:12 **14:19** [m] Job 7:6 **14:21** [n] Ecc 9:5; Isa 63:16 **15:2** [o] Job 6:26 **15:5** [p] Job 5:13 **15:6** [q] Lk 19:22 **15:7** [r] Job 38:21 [s] Ps 90:2; Pr 8:25 **15:8** [t] Ro 11:34; 1Co 2:11 **15:9** [u] Job 13:2 **15:10** [v] Job 32:6-7 **15:11** [w] 2Co 1:3-4 [x] Zec 1:13 [y] Job 36:16 **15:12** [z] Job 11:13 **15:14** [a] Job 14:4; 25:4 [b] Pr 20:9; Ecc 7:20 **15:15** [c] Job 4:18; 25:5 **15:16** [d] Ps 14:1 [e] Job 34:7; Pr 19:28 **15:18** [f] Job 8:8 **15:20** [g] Job 24:1; 27:13-23 **15:21** [h] Job 18:11; 20:25 [i] Job 27:20; 1Th 5:3 **15:22** [j] Job 19:29; 27:14 **15:23** [k] Ps 59:15; 109:10 [l] Job 18:12

troubles overwhelm him, like a king
poised to attack,
25 because he shakes his fist at God
and vaunts himself against the
Almighty,[m]
26 defiantly charging against him
with a thick, strong shield.

27 "Though his face is covered with fat
and his waist bulges with flesh,[n]
28 he will inhabit ruined towns
and houses where no one lives,[o]
houses crumbling to rubble.[p]
29 He will no longer be rich and his wealth
will not endure,[q]
nor will his possessions spread over
the land.
30 He will not escape the darkness;[r]
a flame[s] will wither his shoots,
and the breath of God's mouth[t] will
carry him away.
31 Let him not deceive himself by trusting
what is worthless,[u]
for he will get nothing in return.
32 Before his time[v] he will wither,[w]
and his branches will not flourish.[x]
33 He will be like a vine stripped of its
unripe grapes,[y]
like an olive tree shedding its
blossoms.
34 For the company of the godless will be
barren,
and fire will consume the tents of
those who love bribes.[z]
35 They conceive trouble and give birth to
evil;[a]
their womb fashions deceit."

Job 16

16 Then Job replied:

2 "I have heard many things like these;
you are miserable comforters, all of
you![b]
3 Will your long-winded speeches never
end?
What ails you that you keep on
arguing?[c]
4 I also could speak like you,
if you were in my place;
I could make fine speeches against you
and shake my head[d] at you.
5 But my mouth would encourage you;
comfort from my lips would bring
you relief.

6 "Yet if I speak, my pain is not relieved;
and if I refrain, it does not go away.
7 Surely, God, you have worn me out;[e]
you have devastated my entire
household.
8 You have shriveled me up—and it has
become a witness;
my gauntness[f] rises up and testifies
against me.[g]
9 God assails me and tears[h] me in his
anger
and gnashes his teeth at me;[i]
my opponent fastens on me his
piercing eyes.[j]
10 People open their mouths[k] to jeer at me;
they strike my cheek[l] in scorn
and unite together against me.[m]
11 God has turned me over to the ungodly
and thrown me into the clutches of
the wicked.[n]
12 All was well with me, but he
shattered me;
he seized me by the neck and
crushed me.[o]
He has made me his target;[p]
13 his archers surround me.
Without pity, he pierces[q] my kidneys
and spills my gall on the ground.
14 Again and again[r] he bursts upon me;
he rushes at me like a warrior.[s]

15 "I have sewed sackcloth[t] over my skin
and buried my brow in the dust.
16 My face is red with weeping,
dark shadows ring my eyes;
17 yet my hands have been free of violence[u]
and my prayer is pure.

18 "Earth, do not cover my blood;[v]
may my cry never be laid to rest![w]

---

neither did Eliphaz. Job was overpowered by Satan's attacks, and he could not see what God was doing. Eliphaz assumed that because Job was overpowered, it was because he had behaved arrogantly towards God.

15:31 *trusting what is worthless.* Eliphaz was entirely right in his comments about the fruitlessness of a wicked life, and that the Lord will bring the wicked into judgment. But Eliphaz did not have the concept that in this life the wicked can appear to prosper, and the righteous can appear to struggle. Judgment may not fall in this life.

15:34 *fire will consume.* In mentioning the fire that consumes the tents of the wicked, Eliphaz implied that the fire of God that destroyed Job's sheep and servants (1:16) was a direct result of Job's corruption.

16:7 – 17 Afflictions—One of the clear lessons of the Book of Job is that it is possible to give false and insensitive counsel to one who is experiencing affliction and testing. When we suffer, some of the lessons learned are for us, some of the lessons are for others who are watching, and some are for the Kingdom of God. We may not know in this life what all of the implications are. Our afflictions are designed by God to drive us out of ourselves to the Eternal God who is our refuge and who supports us with His everlasting arms (Deut. 33:27). As friends of the afflicted, we must be sympathetic, loving, and kind, remembering that

15:25 [m] Job 36:9 **15:27** [n] Ps 17:10 **15:28** [o] Isa 5:9 [p] Job 3:14 **15:29** [q] Job 27:16-17 **15:30** [r] Job 5:14 [s] Job 22:20 [t] Job 4:9 **15:31** [u] Isa 59:4 **15:32** [v] Ecc 7:17 [w] Job 22:16; Ps 55:23 [x] Job 18:16 **15:33** [y] Hab 3:17 **15:34** [z] Job 8:22 **15:35** [a] Ps 7:14; Isa 59:4; Hos 10:13 **16:2** [b] Job 13:4 **16:3** [c] Job 6:26 **16:4** [d] Ps 22:7; 109:25; La 2:15; Zep 2:15; Mt 27:39 **16:7** [e] Job 7:3 **16:8** [f] Job 19:20 [g] Job 10:17 **16:9** [h] Hos 6:1 [i] Ps 35:16; La 2:16; Ac 7:54 [j] Job 13:24 **16:10** [k] Ps 22:13 [l] Isa 50:6; La 3:30; Mic 5:1; Ac 23:2 [m] Ps 35:15 **16:11** [n] Job 1:15, 17 **16:12** [o] Job 9:17 [p] La 3:12 **16:13** [q] Job 20:24 **16:14** [r] Job 9:17 [s] Joel 2:7 **16:15** [t] Ge 37:34 **16:17** [u] Isa 59:6; Jnh 3:8 **16:18** [v] Isa 26:21 [w] Ps 66:18-19

19 Even now my witness[x] is in heaven;
my advocate is on high.
20 My intercessor is my friend[a]
as my eyes pour out[y] tears to God;
21 on behalf of a man he pleads[z] with God
as one pleads for a friend.

22 "Only a few years will pass
before I take the path of no return.[a]

17 [1]My spirit is broken,
my days are cut short,
the grave awaits me.[b]
2 Surely mockers[c] surround me;
my eyes must dwell on their hostility.

3 "Give me, O God, the pledge you demand.[d]
Who else will put up security[e] for me?[f]
4 You have closed their minds to understanding;
therefore you will not let them triumph.
5 If anyone denounces their friends for reward,
the eyes of their children will fail.[g]

6 "God has made me a byword[h] to everyone,
a man in whose face people spit.
7 My eyes have grown dim with grief;[i]
my whole frame is but a shadow.
8 The upright are appalled at this;
the innocent are aroused[j] against the ungodly.
9 Nevertheless, the righteous[k] will hold to their ways,
and those with clean hands[l] will grow stronger.

10 "But come on, all of you, try again!
I will not find a wise man among you.[m]
11 My days have passed, my plans are shattered.
Yet the desires of my heart[n]
12 turn night into day;
in the face of the darkness light is near.
13 If the only home I hope for is the grave,[o]
if I spread out my bed in the realm of darkness,
14 if I say to corruption,[p] 'You are my father,'
and to the worm,[q] 'My mother' or 'My sister,'
15 where then is my hope—[r]
who can see any hope for me?
16 Will it go down to the gates of death?[s]
Will we descend together into the dust?"

Bildad

18 Then Bildad the Shuhite replied:

2 "When will you end these speeches?
Be sensible, and then we can talk.
3 Why are we regarded as cattle
and considered stupid in your sight?[t]
4 You who tear yourself[u] to pieces in your anger,
is the earth to be abandoned for your sake?
Or must the rocks be moved from their place?

5 "The lamp of a wicked man is snuffed out;[v]
the flame of his fire stops burning.
6 The light in his tent becomes dark;
the lamp beside him goes out.
7 The vigor of his step is weakened;[w]
his own schemes[x] throw him down.[y]
8 His feet thrust him into a net;[z]
he wanders into its mesh.
9 A trap seizes him by the heel;
a snare holds him fast.
10 A noose is hidden for him on the ground;
a trap lies in his path.

[a] 20 Or *My friends treat me with scorn*

often only God has the answers. If we have suffered similarly, we have comfort to offer (2 Cor. 1:6–7), and if we have not suffered similarly, we can support our friends in prayer and practical service.

16:21 *as one pleads.* Job was expressing the need for an intercessor. This need anticipated Jesus Christ, who is our Intercessor (Heb. 7:25) and Advocate (1 John 2:1).

17:3 *pledge.* In another legal metaphor, Job appealed to God by laying down a pledge, that is, by providing bail. The use of the same metaphor in Psalm 119:121–122 to indicate the psalmist's request for relief from his "oppressors" may suggest that Job was pleading for God to demonstrate confidence in his innocence.

17:9 *the righteous will hold to their ways.* Job seems to be entertaining a little sarcasm here. He had referred to himself as a byword, one at whom men spit. Then he said that the righteous will grow stronger, which was not a reference to himself, even though he still did not think he deserved the trouble that had fallen upon him. He was probably referring to his friends, who considered themselves righteous, with clean hands, and who repeatedly strengthened their position and arguments.

18:4 *who tear yourself . . . in your anger.* This may be Bildad's response to Job's allegation that God had torn Job in His anger (16:13).

18:8–10 *net . . . trap.* Six different Hebrew synonyms for various types of nets and snares emphasize the many imminent dangers that God has designed for the wicked to ensure that they will be caught in their wickedness.

16:19 [x] Ge 31:50; Ro 1:9; 1Th 2:5 **16:20** [y] La 2:19
16:21 [z] Ps 9:4 **16:22** [a] Ecc 12:5 **17:1** [b] Ps 88:3-4
17:2 [c] 1Sa 1:6-7 **17:3** [d] Ps 119:122 [e] Pr 6:1 [f] Isa 38:14
17:5 [g] Job 11:20 **17:6** [h] Job 30:9 **17:7** [i] Job 16:8
17:8 [j] Job 22:19 **17:9** [k] Pr 4:18 [l] Job 22:30
17:10 [m] Job 12:2 **17:11** [n] Job 7:6 **17:13** [o] Job 3:13
17:14 [p] Job 13:28; 30:28,30; Ps 16:10 [q] Job 21:26
17:15 [r] Job 7:6 **17:16** [s] Job 3:17-19; Jnh 2:6
18:3 [t] Ps 73:22 **18:4** [u] Job 13:14 **18:5** [v] Job 21:17; Pr 13:9; 20:20; 24:20 **18:7** [w] Pr 4:12 [x] Job 5:13 [y] Job 15:6
18:8 [z] Job 22:10; Ps 9:15; 35:7

[11] Terrors startle him on every side[a]
and dog[b] his every step.
[12] Calamity is hungry[c] for him;
disaster is ready for him when he falls.
[13] It eats away parts of his skin;
death's firstborn devours his limbs.[d]
[14] He is torn from the security of his tent[e]
and marched off to the king of terrors.
[15] Fire resides[a] in his tent;
burning sulfur[f] is scattered over his dwelling.
[16] His roots dry up below[g]
and his branches wither above.[h]
[17] The memory of him perishes from the earth;
he has no name in the land.[i]
[18] He is driven from light into the realm of darkness[j]
and is banished from the world.
[19] He has no offspring[k] or descendants[l]
among his people,
no survivor where once he lived.[m]
[20] People of the west are appalled at his fate;[n]
those of the east are seized with horror.
[21] Surely such is the dwelling[o] of an evil man;
such is the place of one who does not know God."[p]

Job 19

19 Then Job replied:

[2] "How long will you torment me
and crush me with words?
[3] Ten times now you have reproached me;
shamelessly you attack me.
[4] If it is true that I have gone astray,
my error[q] remains my concern alone.
[5] If indeed you would exalt yourselves above me[r]
and use my humiliation against me,
[6] then know that God has wronged me[s]
and drawn his net[t] around me.

[7] "Though I cry, 'Violence!' I get no response;[u]
though I call for help, there is no justice.[v]
[8] He has blocked my way so I cannot pass;[w]
he has shrouded my paths in darkness.[x]
[9] He has stripped[y] me of my honor
and removed the crown from my head.[z]
[10] He tears me down[a] on every side till I am gone;
he uproots my hope[b] like a tree.[c]
[11] His anger[d] burns against me;
he counts me among his enemies.[e]
[12] His troops advance in force;[f]
they build a siege ramp[g] against me
and encamp around my tent.

[13] "He has alienated my family[h] from me;
my acquaintances are completely estranged from me.[i]
[14] My relatives have gone away;
my closest friends have forgotten me.
[15] My guests and my female servants
count me a foreigner;
they look on me as on a stranger.
[16] I summon my servant, but he does not answer,
though I beg him with my own mouth.
[17] My breath is offensive to my wife;
I am loathsome to my own family.
[18] Even the little boys[j] scorn me;
when I appear, they ridicule me.
[19] All my intimate friends[k] detest me;[l]
those I love have turned against me.
[20] I am nothing but skin and bones;[m]
I have escaped only by the skin of my teeth.[b]

[a] 15 Or *Nothing he had remains* [b] 20 Or *only by my gums*

18:21 *evil man.* Bildad believed that the evidence he had exhibited in verses 5–20 implicated Job himself as the wicked one. Bildad was right that, in the end, the wicked will perish dramatically. But in this life they are not necessarily judged. If it were that simple, that the wicked never prospered and the righteous always thrived, people might try to be followers of God just for the blessings. The whole thrust of the Book of Job is that God Himself is reason enough to follow God, whether or not there is prosperity (1:9–11).

19:7 Despondency—The despondency of Job was a swollen river into which many streams had poured. He had experienced the loss of family, property, and health. Wife and friends had misunderstood him. The suffering saint felt tormented, crushed with the irrelevant words of critics who should have comforted instead of corrected him. Crying out for help, Job received none and came to the conclusion that there is no justice anywhere. The interesting thing about Job is that while he may have despaired of hearing from God, he never doubted that God was there and knew what was going on.

19:8 *He has blocked my way.* Job felt fenced in by God, when it was really Satan who had been mistreating him (1:10; 3:23). The only fence from God was a hedge of protection.

18:11 [a] Job 15:21; Jer 6:25; 20:3 [b] Job 20:8
18:12 [c] Isa 8:21 **18:13** [d] Zec 14:12 **18:14** [e] Job 8:22
18:15 [f] Ps 11:6 **18:16** [g] Isa 5:24; Hos 9:1-16; Am 2:9
[h] Job 15:30; Mal 4:1 **18:17** [i] Ps 34:16; Pr 2:22; 10:7
18:18 [j] Job 5:14 **18:19** [k] Jer 22:30 [l] Isa 14:22
[m] Job 27:14-15 **18:20** [n] Ps 37:13; Jer 50:27,31
18:21 [o] Job 21:28 [p] Jer 9:3; 1Th 4:5 **19:4** [q] Job 6:24
19:5 [r] Ps 35:26; 38:16; 55:12 **19:6** [s] Job 27:2 [t] Job 18:8
19:7 [u] Job 30:20 [v] Job 9:24; Hab 1:2-4 **19:8** [w] Job 3:23; La 3:7 [x] Job 30:26 **19:9** [y] Job 12:17 [z] Ps 89:39,44; La 5:16 **19:10** [a] Job 12:14 [b] Job 7:6 [c] Job 24:20
19:11 [d] Job 16:9 [e] Job 13:24 **19:12** [f] Job 16:13
[g] Job 30:12 **19:13** [h] Ps 69:8 [i] Job 16:7; Ps 88:8
19:18 [j] 2Ki 2:23 **19:19** [k] Ps 55:12-13 [l] Ps 38:11
19:20 [m] Job 33:21; Ps 102:5

21 "Have pity on me, my friends, have pity,
for the hand of God has struck me.
22 Why do you pursue[n] me as God does?
Will you never get enough of my flesh?[o]

23 "Oh, that my words were recorded,
that they were written on a scroll,[p]
24 that they were inscribed with an iron tool on[a] lead,
or engraved in rock forever!
25 I know that my redeemer[bq] lives,[r]
and that in the end he will stand on the earth.[c]
26 And after my skin has been destroyed,
yet[d] in[e] my flesh I will see God;[s]
27 I myself will see him
with my own eyes—I, and not another.
How my heart yearns[t] within me!

28 "If you say, 'How we will hound him,
since the root of the trouble lies in him,[f]'
29 you should fear the sword yourselves;
for wrath will bring punishment by the sword,[u]
and then you will know that there is judgment.[g]"[v]

Zophar

20 Then Zophar the Naamathite replied:
2 "My troubled thoughts prompt me to answer
because I am greatly disturbed.
3 I hear a rebuke[w] that dishonors me,
and my understanding inspires me to reply.

4 "Surely you know how it has been from of old,
ever since mankind[h] was placed on the earth,
5 that the mirth of the wicked is brief,
the joy of the godless lasts but a moment.[x]
6 Though the pride of the godless person reaches to the heavens
and his head touches the clouds,[y]
7 he will perish forever,[z] like his own dung;
those who have seen him will say,
'Where is he?'[a]
8 Like a dream[b] he flies away,[c] no more to be found,
banished[d] like a vision of the night.[e]
9 The eye that saw him will not see him again;
his place will look on him no more.[f]
10 His children[g] must make amends to the poor;
his own hands must give back his wealth.[h]
11 The youthful vigor[i] that fills his bones
will lie with him in the dust.[j]

12 "Though evil is sweet in his mouth
and he hides it under his tongue,
13 though he cannot bear to let it go
and lets it linger in his mouth,[k]
14 yet his food will turn sour in his stomach;
it will become the venom of serpents within him.
15 He will spit out the riches he swallowed;
God will make his stomach vomit them up.
16 He will suck the poison[l] of serpents;
the fangs of an adder will kill him.[m]
17 He will not enjoy the streams,
the rivers flowing with honey[n] and cream.[o]
18 What he toiled for he must give back uneaten;
he will not enjoy the profit from his trading.
19 For he has oppressed the poor and left them destitute;[p]
he has seized houses he did not build.

20 "Surely he will have no respite from his craving;[q]
he cannot save himself by his treasure.

[a] 24 Or *and* [b] 25 Or *vindicator* [c] 25 Or *on my grave* [d] 26 Or *And after I awake, / though this body has been destroyed, / then* [e] 26 Or *destroyed, / apart from* [f] 28 Many Hebrew manuscripts, Septuagint and Vulgate; most Hebrew manuscripts *me* [g] 29 Or *sword, / that you may come to know the Almighty* [h] 4 Or *Adam*

19:25 *I know that my redeemer lives.* Job's longing for a mediator (9:33) and his desire for someone to plead on his behalf with God (16:19–21) may suggest that he was thinking of someone other than God. Here was a strong, resolute hope for a mediator between God and humanity. Ultimately Job's longing for a vindicator or mediator was fulfilled in Jesus Christ (1 Tim. 2:5).
19:26 *in my flesh I will see God.* Job was stating his strong belief in the eternality of the soul, and even of the resurrected body, although it was not until Christ's resurrection that followers of the Living God understood all the implications of this belief (1 Cor. 15:12–19).
19:29 *fear the sword.* Job anticipated the reaction of his friends to his stated confidence that some day he would see God face-to-face.
20:20 *no respite.* In stating that the wicked person knows no quietness, Zophar implied that Job had received what he deserved.

19:22 [n] Job 13:25; 16:11 [o] Ps 69:26 **19:23** [p] Isa 30:8 **19:25** [q] Ps 78:35; Pr 23:11; Isa 43:14; Jer 50:34 [r] Job 16:19 **19:26** [s] Ps 17:15; Mt 5:8; 1Co 13:12; 1Jn 3:2 **19:27** [t] Ps 73:26 **19:29** [u] Job 15:22 [v] Job 22:4; Ps 1:5; 9:7 **20:3** [w] Job 19:3 **20:5** [x] Job 8:12; Ps 37:35-36; 73:19 **20:6** [y] Isa 14:13-14; Ob 1:3-4 **20:7** [z] Job 4:20 [a] Job 7:10; 8:18 **20:8** [b] Ps 73:20 [c] Job 27:21-23 [d] Job 18:18 [e] Ps 90:5 **20:9** [f] Job 7:8 **20:10** [g] Job 5:4 [h] Job 27:16-17 **20:11** [i] Job 13:26 [j] Job 21:26 **20:13** [k] Nu 11:18-20 **20:16** [l] Dt 32:32 [m] Dt 32:24 **20:17** [n] Dt 32:13 [o] Job 29:6 **20:19** [p] Job 24:4, 14; 35:9 **20:20** [q] Ecc 5:12-14

21 Nothing is left for him to devour;
his prosperity will not endure.[r]
22 In the midst of his plenty, distress will overtake him;
the full force of misery will come upon him.
23 When he has filled his belly,
God will vent his burning anger against him
and rain down his blows on him.[s]
24 Though he flees[t] from an iron weapon,
a bronze-tipped arrow pierces him.
25 He pulls it out of his back,
the gleaming point out of his liver.
Terrors[u] will come over him;[v]
26 total darkness[w] lies in wait for his treasures.
A fire unfanned will consume him[x]
and devour what is left in his tent.
27 The heavens will expose his guilt;
the earth will rise up against him.[y]
28 A flood will carry off his house,[z]
rushing waters[a] on the day of God's wrath.[a]
29 Such is the fate God allots the wicked,
the heritage appointed for them by God."[b]

Job 21

Then Job replied:

2 "Listen carefully to my words;
let this be the consolation you give me.
3 Bear with me while I speak,
and after I have spoken, mock on.[c]

4 "Is my complaint directed to a human being?
Why should I not be impatient?[d]
5 Look at me and be appalled;
clap your hand over your mouth.[e]
6 When I think about this, I am terrified;
trembling seizes my body.
7 Why do the wicked live on,
growing old and increasing in power?[f]
8 They see their children established around them,
their offspring before their eyes.[g]
9 Their homes are safe and free from fear;[h]
the rod of God is not on them.
10 Their bulls never fail to breed;
their cows calve and do not miscarry.[i]
11 They send forth their children as a flock;
their little ones dance about.
12 They sing to the music of timbrel and lyre;
they make merry to the sound of the pipe.[j]
13 They spend their years in prosperity[k]
and go down to the grave in peace.[b]
14 Yet they say to God, 'Leave us alone![l]
We have no desire to know your ways.[m]
15 Who is the Almighty, that we should serve him?
What would we gain by praying to him?'[n]
16 But their prosperity is not in their own hands,
so I stand aloof from the plans of the wicked.

17 "Yet how often is the lamp of the wicked snuffed out?[o]
How often does calamity come upon them,
the fate God allots in his anger?
18 How often are they like straw before the wind,
like chaff[p] swept away by a gale?
19 It is said, 'God stores up the punishment of the wicked for their children.'[q]

[a] 28 Or The possessions in his house will be carried off, / washed away *[b] 13 Or in an instant*

20:27 *heavens will expose his guilt.* Zophar apparently reversed Job's appeal to the earth and heavens (16:18–19) for vindication. He argued that the heavens and earth would bear witness not to Job's innocence, but to his iniquity.

20:29 *the heritage appointed for them by God.* In contrast to his previous words (11:13–20) Zophar seemed to be suggesting that it was too late for Job to repent. It is true, as Zophar says (v. 5) that the wicked and godless will be judged. But that does not mean either that Job was one of the wicked, or that the judgment of the wicked would be in this life (Luke 16:19–25).

21:7 *Why do the wicked live on ... ?* With a rhetorical question, Job began exposing the loopholes in the retribution dogma—the belief that suffering always indicates God's punishment of a person. Other biblical writers also agonized over the prosperity of the wicked (Ps. 37; 73; Jer. 12:1–4), but Scriptures affirm that God is controlling everything to accomplish His good purpose (Rom. 8:28).

21:9 *safe and free from fear.* Job reacted to Eliphaz's argument (15:21–24) that although the wicked live peacefully for a while, they live in terror of inevitable destruction.

21:17 *lamp of the wicked snuffed out.* The rhetorical questions introduced by "how often" expected the answer, "not very often." Job challenged Bildad's belief that the wicked person's light does go out (18:5–6).

21:19 *wicked for their children.* Job denied the dogma that even if a wicked person prospers temporarily, his children will be punished. Job's position is sustained by other passages in the Bible (Deut. 24:16; John 9:1–3).

20:21 [r] Job 15:29 **20:23** [s] Ps 78:30-31 **20:24** [t] Isa 24:18; Am 5:19 **20:25** [u] Job 18:11 [v] Job 16:13 **20:26** [w] Job 18:18 [x] Ps 21:9 **20:27** [y] Dt 31:28 **20:28** [z] Dt 28:31 [a] Job 21:17,20,30 **20:29** [b] Job 27:13 **21:3** [c] Job 16:10 **21:4** [d] Job 6:11 **21:5** [e] Jdg 18:19; Job 29:9; 40:4 **21:7** [f] Job 12:6; Ps 73:3; Jer 12:1; Hab 1:13 **21:8** [g] Ps 17:14 **21:9** [h] Ps 73:5 **21:10** [i] Ex 23:26 **21:12** [j] Ps 81:2 **21:13** [k] Job 36:11 **21:14** [l] Job 22:17 [m] Pr 1:29 **21:15** [n] Ex 5:2; Job 34:9; Mal 3:14 **21:17** [o] Job 18:5 **21:18** [p] Job 13:25; Ps 1:4 **21:19** [q] Ex 20:5; Jer 31:29; Eze 18:2

Let him repay the wicked, so that
they themselves will
experience it!
20 Let their own eyes see their destruction;
let them drink[r] the cup of the wrath
of the Almighty.[s]
21 For what do they care about the
families they leave behind
when their allotted months[t] come to
an end?

22 "Can anyone teach knowledge to God,[u]
since he judges even the highest?[v]
23 One person dies in full vigor,
completely secure and at ease,
24 well nourished in body,[a]
bones rich with marrow.[w]
25 Another dies in bitterness of soul,
never having enjoyed anything good.
26 Side by side they lie in the dust,
and worms cover them both.[x]

27 "I know full well what you are thinking,
the schemes by which you would
wrong me.
28 You say, 'Where now is the house of the
great,[y]
the tents where the wicked lived?'[z]
29 Have you never questioned those who
travel?
Have you paid no regard to their
accounts—
30 that the wicked are spared from the day
of calamity,[a]
that they are delivered from[b] the day
of wrath?[b]
31 Who denounces their conduct to their
face?
Who repays them for what they have
done?
32 They are carried to the grave,
and watch is kept over their tombs.
33 The soil in the valley is sweet to them;[c]
everyone follows after them,
and a countless throng goes[c] before
them.[d]

34 "So how can you console me[e] with your
nonsense?
Nothing is left of your answers but
falsehood!"

Eliphaz

22 Then Eliphaz the Temanite replied:

2 "Can a man be of benefit to God?[f]
Can even a wise person benefit him?
3 What pleasure would it give the
Almighty if you were righteous?
What would he gain if your ways
were blameless?

4 "Is it for your piety that he rebukes you
and brings charges against you?[g]
5 Is not your wickedness great?
Are not your sins[h] endless?
6 You demanded security[i] from your
relatives for no reason;
you stripped people of their clothing,
leaving them naked.
7 You gave no water to the weary
and you withheld food from the
hungry,[j]
8 though you were a powerful man,
owning land—
an honored man,[k] living on it.
9 And you sent widows away empty-
handed[l]
and broke the strength of the
fatherless.
10 That is why snares are all around you,
why sudden peril terrifies you,
11 why it is so dark[m] you cannot see,
and why a flood of water covers
you.[n]

12 "Is not God in the heights of heaven?[o]
And see how lofty are the highest
stars!
13 Yet you say, 'What does God know?[p]
Does he judge through such
darkness?[q]
14 Thick clouds[r] veil him, so he does not
see us
as he goes about in the vaulted
heavens.'
15 Will you keep to the old path
that the wicked have trod?

[a] *24* The meaning of the Hebrew for this word is uncertain. [b] *30* Or *wicked are reserved for the day of calamity, / that they are brought forth to* [c] *33* Or *them, / as a countless throng went*

22:2 ***Can a man be of benefit to God?*** The implication of Eliphaz's rhetorical question—that man cannot put God under any obligation that God must repay—was a valid theological principle that the Lord Himself corroborates in 41:11. However, his application of that principle to Job's circumstances (vv. 3–5) was invalid, for it was based on the faulty assumption that the righteous are always blessed and the wicked always experience God's judgment on earth.
22:3–4 ***righteous ... piety.*** The same Hebrew root words ("integrity" and "fear of God") had earlier been used by Eliphaz in his courteous remarks about Job (4:6). In these verses Eliphaz is being sarcastic.
22:6–9 ***naked ... weary ... widows.*** These trumped up charges were categorically denied by Job (29:11–17; 31:13–22), and God's own witness to Satan revealed to the reader that the charges were false (1:8).

21:20 [r] Ps 75:8; Isa 51:17 [s] Jer 25:15; Rev 14:10 **21:21** [t] Job 14:5 **21:22** [u] Job 35:11; 36:22; Isa 40:13-14; Ro 11:34 [v] Ps 82:1 **21:24** [w] Pr 3:8 **21:26** [x] Job 24:20; Ecc 9:2-3; Isa 14:11 **21:28** [y] Job 1:3; 12:21; 31:37 [z] Job 8:22 **21:30** [a] Pr 16:4 [b] Job 20:22, 28; 2Pe 2:9 **21:33** [c] Job 3:22; 17:16; 24:24 [d] Job 3:19 **21:34** [e] Job 16:2 **22:2** [f] Lk 17:10 **22:4** [g] Job 14:3; 19:29; Ps 143:2 **22:5** [h] Job 11:6; 15:5 **22:6** [i] Ex 22:26; Dt 24:6, 17; Eze 18:12, 16 **22:7** [j] Job 31:17, 21, 31 **22:8** [k] Isa 3:3; 9:15 **22:9** [l] Job 24:3, 21 **22:11** [m] Job 5:14 [n] Ps 69:1-2; 124:4-5; La 3:54 **22:12** [o] Job 11:8 **22:13** [p] Ps 10:11; Isa 29:15 [q] Eze 8:12 **22:14** [r] Job 26:9

16 They were carried off before their time,[s]
their foundations washed away by a flood.[t]
17 They said to God, 'Leave us alone!
What can the Almighty do to us?'[u]
18 Yet it was he who filled their houses with good things,[v]
so I stand aloof from the plans of the wicked.[w]
19 The righteous see their ruin and rejoice;[x]
the innocent mock[y] them, saying,
20 'Surely our foes are destroyed,
and fire[z] devours their wealth.'

21 "Submit to God and be at peace with him;
in this way prosperity will come to you.[a]
22 Accept instruction from his mouth
and lay up his words in your heart.
23 If you return[b] to the Almighty, you will be restored:[c]
If you remove wickedness far from your tent[d]
24 and assign your nuggets to the dust,
your gold of Ophir to the rocks in the ravines,[e]
25 then the Almighty will be your gold,
the choicest silver for you.[f]
26 Surely then you will find delight in the Almighty[g]
and will lift up your face to God.
27 You will pray to him,[h] and he will hear you,
and you will fulfill your vows.
28 What you decide on will be done,
and light will shine on your ways.
29 When people are brought low and you say, 'Lift them up!'
then he will save the downcast.[i]
30 He will deliver even one who is not innocent,
who will be delivered through the cleanness of your hands."[j]

Job 23

Then Job replied:

2 "Even today my complaint[k] is bitter;[l]
his hand[a] is heavy in spite of[b] my groaning.
3 If only I knew where to find him;
if only I could go to his dwelling!
4 I would state my case[m] before him
and fill my mouth with arguments.
5 I would find out what he would answer me,
and consider what he would say to me.
6 Would he vigorously oppose me?[n]
No, he would not press charges against me.
7 There the upright can establish their innocence before him,[o]
and there I would be delivered forever from my judge.

8 "But if I go to the east, he is not there;
if I go to the west, I do not find him.
9 When he is at work in the north, I do not see him;
when he turns to the south, I catch no glimpse of him.[p]
10 But he knows the way that I take;
when he has tested me,[q] I will come forth as gold.[r]
11 My feet have closely followed his steps;[s]
I have kept to his way without turning aside.[t]
12 I have not departed from the commands of his lips;[u]
I have treasured the words of his mouth more than my daily bread.[v]

13 "But he stands alone, and who can oppose him?
He does whatever he pleases.[w]
14 He carries out his decree against me,
and many such plans he still has in store.[x]
15 That is why I am terrified before him;
when I think of all this, I fear him.
16 God has made my heart faint;[y]
the Almighty[z] has terrified me.
17 Yet I am not silenced by the darkness,[a]
by the thick darkness that covers my face.

24

"Why does the Almighty not set times for judgment?[b]
Why must those who know him look in vain for such days?[c]
2 There are those who move boundary stones;[d]
they pasture flocks they have stolen.

[a] 2 Septuagint and Syriac; Hebrew / *the hand on me* [b] 2 Or *heavy on me in*

22:18 *I stand aloof from the plans of the wicked.* Eliphaz was repeating Job (21:16).
22:30 *cleanness of your hands.* This was actually fulfilled through Job's prayer for the three friends (42:8–10).
23:13 *stands alone.* When Job contemplated the unique power and sovereign freedom of God, he was terrified (13:21).
24:2 *boundary stones.* Removing landmarks was tantamount to stealing land. The landmarks set boundaries, and moving them would have been like moving surveyor's stakes (Deut. 27:17).

22:16 [s] Job 15:32 [t] Job 14:19; Mt 7:26-27 **22:17** [u] Job 21:15 **22:18** [v] Job 12:6 [w] Job 21:16 **22:19** [x] Ps 58:10; 107:42 [y] Ps 52:6 **22:20** [z] Job 15:30 **22:21** [a] Ps 34:8-10 **22:23** [b] Job 8:5; Isa 31:6; Zec 1:3 [c] Isa 19:22; Ac 20:32 [d] Job 11:14 **22:24** [e] Job 31:25 **22:25** [f] Isa 33:6 **22:26** [g] Job 27:10; Isa 58:14 **22:27** [h] Job 33:26; 34:28; Isa 58:9 **22:29** [i] Mt 23:12; 1Pe 5:5 **22:30** [j] Job 42:7-8 **23:2** [k] Job 7:11 [l] Job 6:3 **23:4** [m] Job 13:18 **23:6** [n] Job 9:4 **23:7** [o] Job 13:3 **23:9** [p] Job 9:11 **23:10** [q] Ps 66:10; 139:1-3 [r] 1Pe 1:7 **23:11** [s] Ps 17:5 [t] Ps 44:18 **23:12** [u] Job 6:10 [v] Jn 4:32,34 **23:13** [w] Ps 115:3 **23:14** [x] 1Th 3:3 **23:16** [y] Dt 20:3; Ps 22:14; Jer 51:46 [z] Job 27:2 **23:17** [a] Job 19:8 **24:1** [b] Jer 46:10 [c] Ac 1:7 **24:2** [d] Dt 19:14; 27:17; Pr 23:10

3 They drive away the orphan's donkey
and take the widow's ox in pledge.[e]
4 They thrust the needy from the path
and force all the poor[f] of the land into hiding.[g]
5 Like wild donkeys in the desert,
the poor go about their labor[h] of foraging food;
the wasteland provides food for their children.
6 They gather fodder in the fields
and glean in the vineyards of the wicked.
7 Lacking clothes, they spend the night naked;
they have nothing to cover themselves in the cold.[i]
8 They are drenched by mountain rains
and hug[j] the rocks for lack of shelter.
9 The fatherless[k] child is snatched from the breast;
the infant of the poor is seized for a debt.
10 Lacking clothes, they go about naked;
they carry the sheaves, but still go hungry.
11 They crush olives among the terraces[a];
they tread the winepresses, yet suffer thirst.
12 The groans of the dying rise from the city,
and the souls of the wounded cry out for help.[l]
But God charges no one with wrongdoing.[m]

13 "There are those who rebel against the light,[n]
who do not know its ways
or stay in its paths.[o]
14 When daylight is gone, the murderer rises up,
kills the poor and needy,
and in the night steals forth like a thief.[p]
15 The eye of the adulterer watches for dusk;[q]
he thinks, 'No eye will see me,'[r]
and he keeps his face concealed.
16 In the dark, thieves break into houses,[s]
but by day they shut themselves in;
they want nothing to do with the light.[t]
17 For all of them, midnight is their morning;
they make friends with the terrors of darkness.
18 "Yet they are foam[u] on the surface of the water;[v]
their portion of the land is cursed,
so that no one goes to the vineyards.
19 As heat and drought snatch away the melted snow,[w]
so the grave[x] snatches away those who have sinned.
20 The womb forgets them,
the worm feasts on them;
the wicked are no longer remembered[y]
but are broken like a tree.[z]
21 They prey on the barren and childless woman,
and to the widow they show no kindness.[a]
22 But God drags away the mighty by his power;
though they become established, they have no assurance of life.[b]
23 He may let them rest in a feeling of security,[c]
but his eyes are on their ways.[d]
24 For a little while they are exalted, and then they are gone;[e]
they are brought low and gathered up like all others;
they are cut off like heads of grain.[f]

25 "If this is not so, who can prove me false
and reduce my words to nothing?"[g]

Bildad

25 Then Bildad the Shuhite replied:

2 "Dominion and awe belong to God;[h]
he establishes order in the heights of heaven.
3 Can his forces be numbered?
On whom does his light not rise?[i]
4 How then can a mortal be righteous before God?
How can one born of woman be pure?[j]
5 If even the moon[k] is not bright
and the stars are not pure in his eyes,[l]
6 how much less a mortal, who is but a maggot—
a human being,[m] who is only a worm!"[n]

a 11 The meaning of the Hebrew for this word is uncertain.

24:16 *break into houses.* The walls of houses were built of mud bricks, through which thieves could dig.
24:24 *brought low.* Job was not so much arguing that the wicked would not prosper (vv. 18–25), as he was saying that everyone is brought low.
25:6 *worm.* What a contrast to the words of God (Gen. 1:26–31) when He made humans in His own image and declared them "very good." Bildad was conscious of the great gap between God and man, but unlike Job, he did not feel that he could make the connection of communication that Job was striving for.

24:3 [e] Dt 24:6, 10, 12, 17; Job 22:6 **24:4** [f] Job 29:12; 30:25; Ps 41:1 [g] Pr 28:28 **24:5** [h] Ps 104:23 **24:7** [i] Ex 22:27; Job 22:6 **24:8** [j] La 4:5 **24:9** [k] Dt 24:17 **24:12** [l] Eze 26:15 [m] Job 9:23 **24:13** [n] Jn 3:19-20 [o] Isa 5:20 **24:14** [p] Ps 10:9 **24:15** [q] Pr 7:8-9 [r] Ps 10:11 **24:16** [s] Ex 22:2; Mt 6:19 [t] Jn 3:20 **24:18** [u] Job 9:26 [v] Job 22:16 **24:19** [w] Job 6:17 [x] Job 21:13 **24:20** [y] Job 18:17; Pr 10:7 [z] Ps 31:12; Da 4:14 **24:21** [a] Job 22:9 **24:22** [b] Dt 28:66 **24:23** [c] Job 12:6 [d] Job 11:11 **24:24** [e] Job 14:21; Ps 37:10 [f] Isa 17:5 **24:25** [g] Job 6:28; 27:4 **25:2** [h] Job 9:4; Rev 1:6 **25:3** [i] Jas 1:17 **25:4** [j] Job 4:17; 14:4 **25:5** [k] Job 31:26 [l] Job 15:15 **25:6** [m] Job 7:17 [n] Ps 22:6

Job 26

26 Then Job replied:

2 "How you have helped the powerless![o]
How you have saved the arm that is feeble![p]
3 What advice you have offered to one without wisdom!
And what great insight you have displayed!
4 Who has helped you utter these words?
And whose spirit spoke from your mouth?

5 "The dead are in deep anguish,[q]
those beneath the waters and all that live in them.
6 The realm of the dead[r] is naked before God;
Destruction[a] lies uncovered.[s]
7 He spreads out the northern skies[t] over empty space;
he suspends the earth over nothing.
8 He wraps up the waters[u] in his clouds,[v]
yet the clouds do not burst under their weight.
9 He covers the face of the full moon,
spreading his clouds[w] over it.
10 He marks out the horizon on the face of the waters[x]
for a boundary between light and darkness.[y]
11 The pillars of the heavens quake,
aghast at his rebuke.
12 By his power he churned up the sea;[z]
by his wisdom[a] he cut Rahab to pieces.
13 By his breath the skies became fair;
his hand pierced the gliding serpent.[b]
14 And these are but the outer fringe of his works;
how faint the whisper we hear of him!
Who then can understand the thunder of his power?"[c]

Job's Final Word to His Friends

27 And Job continued his discourse:[d]

2 "As surely as God lives, who has denied me justice,[e]
the Almighty, who has made my life bitter,[f]
3 as long as I have life within me,
the breath of God[g] in my nostrils,
4 my lips will not say anything wicked,
and my tongue will not utter lies.[h]
5 I will never admit you are in the right;
till I die, I will not deny my integrity.[i]
6 I will maintain my innocence and never let go of it;
my conscience will not reproach me as long as I live.[j]

7 "May my enemy be like the wicked,
my adversary like the unjust!
8 For what hope have the godless[k] when they are cut off,
when God takes away their life?[l]
9 Does God listen to their cry
when distress comes upon them?[m]
10 Will they find delight in the Almighty?[n]
Will they call on God at all times?

11 "I will teach you about the power of God;
the ways of the Almighty I will not conceal.
12 You have all seen this yourselves.
Why then this meaningless talk?

13 "Here is the fate God allots to the wicked,
the heritage a ruthless man receives from the Almighty:[o]

---

[a] 6 Hebrew *Abaddon*

26:4 *whose spirit spoke from your mouth?* The contrast between Bildad's comments about God (ch. 25) and Job's worshipful declaration of God's majesty (vv. 7 – 14) indicate the difference in the level of their understanding of who God is.
26:6 *The realm of the dead . . . Destruction.* "The realm of the dead" and "destruction" were fearful, hidden concepts to Job and his contemporaries, but they held no secrets for the all-knowing God.
26:7 *suspends the earth over nothing.* Job's comments on the suspension of the earth, the manner of clouds (v. 8) and the horizon (v. 10) speak much for his powers of observation as well as the inspiration of Scripture.
27:2 *who has made my life bitter.* Though Job repeatedly complained of a bitter spirit (7:11; 10:1), the Lord did not cause him to respond that way. Job's responses only exposed the attitude that lay deep within his being. The message of the Lord for Job was that no matter what the circumstances, one should resolutely trust in God (40:8; 42:1 – 6).
27:5 *admit you are in the right.* Job maintained that his friends were erroneous in their reasoning, and to agree with them would be to compromise his integrity.
27:12 *meaningless talk?* Job maintained that the actions of his friends were foolish, considering the knowledge of God that they should have had.
27:13 *heritage of a ruthless man.* Job likened the foolishness of his friends to wickedness, and indeed it is wicked to knowingly misrepresent God. The rest of the chapter is a satirical paraphrase of the friends' teaching about the fate of the wicked (24:18 – 25), which Job has thrown back in his friends' faces.

26:2 [o] Job 6:12 [p] Ps 71:9 **26:5** [q] Ps 88:10 **26:6** [r] Ps 139:8 [s] Job 41:11; Pr 15:11; Heb 4:13 **26:7** [t] Job 9:8 **26:8** [u] Pr 30:4 [v] Job 37:11 **26:9** [w] Job 22:14; Ps 97:2 **26:10** [x] Pr 8:27, 29 [y] Job 38:8-11 **26:12** [z] Ex 14:21; Isa 51:15; Jer 31:35 [a] Job 12:13 **26:13** [b] Isa 27:1 **26:14** [c] Job 36:29 **27:1** [d] Job 29:1 **27:2** [e] Job 34:5 [f] Job 9:18 **27:3** [g] Job 32:8; 33:4 **27:4** [h] Job 6:28 **27:5** [i] Job 2:9; 13:15 **27:6** [j] Job 2:3 **27:8** [k] Job 8:13 [l] Job 11:20; Lk 12:20 **27:9** [m] Job 35:12; Pr 1:28; Isa 1:15; Jer 14:12; Mic 3:4 **27:10** [n] Job 22:26 **27:13** [o] Job 15:20; 20:29

14 However many his children, their fate is
the sword;[p]
his offspring will never have enough
to eat.[q]
15 The plague will bury those who survive
him,
and their widows will not weep for
them.[r]
16 Though he heaps up silver like dust
and clothes like piles of clay,[s]
17 what he lays up the righteous will wear,[t]
and the innocent will divide his silver.
18 The house he builds is like a moth's
cocoon,[u]
like a hut[v] made by a watchman.
19 He lies down wealthy, but will do so no
more;[w]
when he opens his eyes, all is gone.
20 Terrors overtake him like a flood;[x]
a tempest snatches him away in the
night.[y]
21 The east wind carries him off, and he is
gone;
it sweeps him out of his place.[z]
22 It hurls itself against him without
mercy[a]
as he flees headlong from its power.[b]
23 It claps its hands in derision
and hisses him out of his place."[c]

Interlude: Where Wisdom Is Found

28 There is a mine for silver
and a place where gold is refined.
2 Iron is taken from the earth,
and copper is smelted from ore.[d]
3 Mortals put an end to the darkness;[e]
they search out the farthest recesses
for ore in the blackest darkness.
4 Far from human dwellings they cut a
shaft,
in places untouched by human feet;
far from other people they dangle
and sway.
5 The earth, from which food comes,[f]
is transformed below as by fire;
6 lapis lazuli comes from its rocks,
and its dust contains nuggets of gold.
7 No bird of prey knows that hidden path,
no falcon's eye has seen it.
8 Proud beasts do not set foot on it,
and no lion prowls there.
9 People assault the flinty rock with their
hands
and lay bare the roots of the
mountains.
10 They tunnel through the rock;
their eyes see all its treasures.
11 They search[a] the sources of the rivers
and bring hidden things to light.

12 But where can wisdom be found?[g]
Where does understanding dwell?
13 No mortal comprehends its worth;[h]
it cannot be found in the land of the
living.
14 The deep says, "It is not in me";
the sea says, "It is not with me."
15 It cannot be bought with the finest gold,
nor can its price be weighed out in
silver.[i]
16 It cannot be bought with the gold of
Ophir,
with precious onyx or lapis lazuli.
17 Neither gold nor crystal can compare
with it,
nor can it be had for jewels of gold.[j]
18 Coral and jasper are not worthy of
mention;
the price of wisdom is beyond rubies.[k]
19 The topaz of Cush cannot compare
with it;
it cannot be bought with pure gold.[l]

20 Where then does wisdom come from?
Where does understanding dwell?[m]
21 It is hidden from the eyes of every
living thing,
concealed even from the birds in the
sky.
22 Destruction[b][n] and Death say,
"Only a rumor of it has reached our
ears."
23 God understands the way to it
and he alone knows where it dwells,[o]
24 for he views the ends of the earth[p]
and sees everything under the
heavens.[q]
25 When he established the force of the
wind
and measured out the waters,[r]
26 when he made a decree for the rain
and a path for the thunderstorm,[s]
27 then he looked at wisdom and
appraised it;
he confirmed it and tested it.
28 And he said to the human race,
"The fear of the Lord—that is wisdom,
and to shun evil is understanding."[t]

---

[a] 11 Septuagint, Aquila and Vulgate; Hebrew *They dam up* [b] 22 Hebrew *Abaddon*

28:13–19 *not.* Every verse in this whole stanza has the Hebrew word for "not" at least once, stressing the absence of wisdom or even the desire for wisdom. The rhetorical questions concerning the whereabouts of wisdom and understanding (v. 12) receive an emphatic answer: not anywhere in the land of the living or dead.

28:28 *fear of the Lord.* To fear God is to acknowledge that God has the right to judge our actions for good or evil. Job had talked a lot about injustice and his innocence, but he was solidly aware that only God has wisdom, and in the end, his fear of the Lord was greater than his protestations of blamelessness.

27:14 [p] Dt 28:41; Job 15:22; Hos 9:13 [q] Job 20:10 **27:15** [r] Ps 78:64 **27:16** [s] Zec 9:3 **27:17** [t] Pr 28:8; Ecc 2:26 **27:18** [u] Job 8:14 [v] Isa 1:8 **27:19** [w] Job 7:8 **27:20** [x] Job 15:21 [y] Job 20:8 **27:21** [z] Job 7:10; 21:18 **27:22** [a] Jer 13:14; Eze 5:11; 24:14 [b] Job 11:20 **27:23** [c] Job 18:18 **28:2** [d] Dt 8:9 **28:3** [e] Ecc 1:13 **28:5** [f] Ps 104:14 **28:12** [g] Ecc 7:24 **28:13** [h] Pr 3:15; Mt 13:44-46 **28:15** [i] Pr 3:13-14; 8:10-11; 16:16 **28:17** [j] Pr 16:16 **28:18** [k] Pr 3:15 **28:19** [l] Pr 8:19 **28:20** [m] ver 23,28 **28:22** [n] Job 26:6 **28:23** [o] Pr 8:22-31 **28:24** [p] Ps 33:13-14 [q] Pr 15:3 **28:25** [r] Job 12:15; Ps 135:7 **28:26** [s] Job 37:3, 8, 11; 38:25, 27 **28:28** [t] Dt 4:6; Ps 111:10; Pr 1:7; 9:10

Job's Final Defense

29 Job continued his discourse:[u]

[2] "How I long for the months gone by,
for the days when God watched over me,[v]
[3] when his lamp shone on my head
and by his light I walked through darkness![w]
[4] Oh, for the days when I was in my prime,
when God's intimate friendship blessed my house,[x]
[5] when the Almighty was still with me
and my children were around me,
[6] when my path was drenched with cream[y]
and the rock[z] poured out for me streams of olive oil.[a]

[7] "When I went to the gate[b] of the city
and took my seat in the public square,
[8] the young men saw me and stepped aside
and the old men rose to their feet;
[9] the chief men refrained from speaking
and covered their mouths with their hands;[c]
[10] the voices of the nobles were hushed,
and their tongues stuck to the roof of their mouths.[d]
[11] Whoever heard me spoke well of me,
and those who saw me commended me,
[12] because I rescued the poor[e] who cried for help,
and the fatherless[f] who had none to assist them.[g]
[13] The one who was dying blessed me;[h]
I made the widow's[i] heart sing.
[14] I put on righteousness[j] as my clothing;
justice was my robe and my turban.
[15] I was eyes[k] to the blind
and feet to the lame.
[16] I was a father to the needy;[l]
I took up the case of the stranger.
[17] I broke the fangs of the wicked
and snatched the victims from their teeth.[m]

[18] "I thought, 'I will die in my own house,
my days as numerous as the grains of sand.[n]
[19] My roots will reach to the water,[o]
and the dew will lie all night on my branches.
[20] My glory will not fade;
the bow[p] will be ever new in my hand.'[q]

[21] "People listened to me expectantly,
waiting in silence for my counsel.
[22] After I had spoken, they spoke no more;
my words fell gently on their ears.[r]
[23] They waited for me as for showers
and drank in my words as the spring rain.
[24] When I smiled at them, they scarcely believed it;
the light of my face was precious to them.[a]
[25] I chose the way for them and sat as their chief;
I dwelt as a king[s] among his troops;
I was like one who comforts mourners.[t]

30 "But now they mock me,[u]
men younger than I,
whose fathers I would have disdained
to put with my sheep dogs.
[2] Of what use was the strength of their hands to me,
since their vigor had gone from them?
[3] Haggard from want and hunger,
they roamed[b] the parched land
in desolate wastelands at night.
[4] In the brush they gathered salt herbs,
and their food[c] was the root of the broom bush.
[5] They were banished from human society,
shouted at as if they were thieves.
[6] They were forced to live in the dry stream beds,
among the rocks and in holes in the ground.
[7] They brayed among the bushes
and huddled in the undergrowth.
[8] A base and nameless brood,
they were driven out of the land.

[9] "And now those young men mock me[v] in song;[w]
I have become a byword[x] among them.
[10] They detest me and keep their distance;
they do not hesitate to spit in my face.[y]

---

a 24 The meaning of the Hebrew for this clause is uncertain. *b* 3 Or *gnawed* *c* 4 Or *fuel*

29:12 ***rescued the poor.*** Considering Job's account of his life when he was prosperous, Eliphaz's accusations of Job sending the widows away empty and crushing the orphans (22:9) was a calculated insult.

29:14 ***put on righteousness . . . turban.*** This vivid portrait of Job was a stark contrast to his present condition, with his flesh being "clothed" in worms and dust.

29:1 [u] Job 13:12; 27:1 **29:2** [v] Jer 31:28 **29:3** [w] Job 11:17 **29:4** [x] Ps 25:14; Pr 3:32 **29:6** [y] Job 20:17 [z] Ps 81:16 [a] Dt 32:13 **29:7** [b] Job 31:21 **29:9** [c] Job 21:5 **29:10** [d] Ps 137:6 **29:12** [e] Job 24:4 [f] Job 31:17,21 [g] Ps 72:12; Pr 21:13 **29:13** [h] Job 31:20 [i] Job 22:9 **29:14** [j] Job 27:6; Ps 132:9; Isa 59:17; 61:10; Eph 6:14 **29:15** [k] Nu 10:31 **29:16** [l] Job 24:4; Pr 29:7 **29:17** [m] Ps 3:7 **29:18** [n] Ps 30:6 **29:19** [o] Job 18:16; Jer 17:8 **29:20** [p] Ps 18:34 [q] Ge 49:24 **29:22** [r] Dt 32:2 **29:25** [s] Job 1:3; 31:37 [t] Job 4:4 **30:1** [u] Job 12:4 **30:9** [v] Ps 69:11 [w] Job 12:4; La 3:14,63 [x] Job 17:6 **30:10** [y] Nu 12:14; Dt 25:9; Isa 50:6; Mt 26:67

11 Now that God has unstrung my bow
and afflicted me,[z]
they throw off restraint[a] in my
presence.
12 On my right the tribe[a] attacks;
they lay snares for my feet,[b]
they build their siege ramps
against me.[c]
13 They break up my road;[d]
they succeed in destroying me.
'No one can help him,' they say.
14 They advance as through a gaping
breach;
amid the ruins they come rolling in.
15 Terrors overwhelm me;[e]
my dignity is driven away as by the
wind,
my safety vanishes like a cloud.[f]

16 "And now my life ebbs away;[g]
days of suffering grip me.
17 Night pierces my bones;
my gnawing pains never rest.
18 In his great power God becomes like
clothing to me[b];
he binds me like the neck of my
garment.
19 He throws me into the mud,[h]
and I am reduced to dust and ashes.

20 "I cry out to you, God, but you do not
answer;[i]
I stand up, but you merely look at me.
21 You turn on me ruthlessly;[j]
with the might of your hand[k] you
attack me.[l]
22 You snatch me up and drive me before
the wind;[m]
you toss me about in the storm.[n]
23 I know you will bring me down to
death,[o]
to the place appointed for all the
living.[p]

24 "Surely no one lays a hand on a broken
man
when he cries for help in his distress.[q]
25 Have I not wept for those in trouble?
Has not my soul grieved for the
poor?[r]
26 Yet when I hoped for good, evil came;
when I looked for light, then came
darkness.[s]
27 The churning inside me never stops;[t]
days of suffering confront me.
28 I go about blackened,[u] but not by the
sun;
I stand up in the assembly and cry for
help.[v]
29 I have become a brother of jackals,[w]
a companion of owls.[x]
30 My skin grows black and peels;[y]
my body burns with fever.[z]
31 My lyre is tuned to mourning,[a]
and my pipe to the sound of wailing.

31 "I made a covenant with my eyes
not to look lustfully at a young
woman.[b]
2 For what is our lot from God above,
our heritage from the Almighty on
high?[c]
3 Is it not ruin[d] for the wicked,
disaster for those who do wrong?[e]
4 Does he not see my ways[f]
and count my every step?[g]

5 "If I have walked with falsehood
or my foot has hurried after deceit[h]—
6 let God weigh me in honest scales[i]
and he will know that I am
blameless—
7 if my steps have turned from the
path,[j]
if my heart has been led by my
eyes,
or if my hands[k] have been defiled,
8 then may others eat what I have
sown,[l]
and may my crops be uprooted.[m]

9 "If my heart has been enticed[n] by a
woman,
or if I have lurked at my neighbor's
door,
10 then may my wife grind another man's
grain,
and may other men sleep with her.[o]

---

a *12* The meaning of the Hebrew for this word is uncertain. *b* *18* Hebrew; Septuagint *power he grasps my clothing*

30:11 ***unstrung my bow.*** A bow that is not strung up is not ready for use. This was a terrible contrast to his former life, described in 29:20, where Job referred to himself as having his bowstring renewed. A bow that is being used has its string replaced regularly so that the bow can operate at its maximum strength.

30:21 ***might of your hand.*** Job blamed God's strong hand, which Satan could not move, for calamities that were actually caused by the hand of Satan (1:11 – 12,18 – 19).

31:5 ***If.*** The word "if" was a part of a formula used by accused persons to swear their innocence. The full oath formula was, in effect, "If I am guilty of this crime, may God impose that curse." Because of hesitation about speaking a curse, the person swearing the oath would normally use an abbreviated version. By contrast, Job used the full formula four times, which demonstrated his confidence that he would be acquitted.

30:11 [z] Ru 1:21 [a] Ps 32:9 **30:12** [b] Ps 140:4-5 [c] Job 19:12 **30:13** [d] Isa 3:12 **30:15** [e] Job 31:23; Ps 55:4-5 [f] Job 3:25; Hos 13:3 **30:16** [g] Job 3:24; Ps 22:14; 42:4 **30:19** [h] Ps 69:2, 14 **30:20** [i] Job 19:7 **30:21** [j] Job 19:6, 22 [k] Job 16:9, 14 [l] Job 10:3 **30:22** [m] Job 27:21 [n] Job 9:17 **30:23** [o] Job 9:22; 10:8 [p] Job 3:19 **30:24** [q] Job 19:7 **30:25** [r] Job 24:4; Ps 35:13-14; Ro 12:15 **30:26** [s] Job 3:25-26; 19:8; Jer 8:15 **30:27** [t] La 2:11 **30:28** [u] Ps 38:6; 42:9; 43:2 [v] Job 19:7 **30:29** [w] Ps 44:19 [x] Ps 102:6; Mic 1:8 **30:30** [y] La 4:8 [z] Ps 102:3 **30:31** [a] Isa 24:8 **31:1** [b] Mt 5:28 **31:2** [c] Job 20:29 **31:3** [d] Job 21:30 [e] Job 34:22 **31:4** [f] 2Ch 16:9 [g] Pr 5:21 **31:5** [h] Mic 2:11 **31:6** [i] Job 6:2; 27:5-6 **31:7** [j] Job 23:11 [k] Job 9:30 **31:8** [l] Lev 26:16; Job 20:18 [m] Mic 6:15 **31:9** [n] Job 24:15 **31:10** [o] Dt 28:30; Jer 8:10

11 For that would have been wicked,
a sin to be judged.[p]
12 It is a fire[q] that burns to Destruction[a];[r]
it would have uprooted my harvest.[s]

13 "If I have denied justice to any of my servants,
whether male or female,
when they had a grievance against me,[t]
14 what will I do when God confronts me?
What will I answer when called to account?
15 Did not he who made me in the womb make them?
Did not the same one form us both within our mothers?[u]

16 "If I have denied the desires of the poor[v]
or let the eyes of the widow[w] grow weary,
17 if I have kept my bread to myself,
not sharing it with the fatherless[x]—
18 but from my youth I reared them as a father would,
and from my birth I guided the widow—
19 if I have seen anyone perishing for lack of clothing,[y]
or the needy[z] without garments,
20 and their hearts did not bless me
for warming them with the fleece from my sheep,
21 if I have raised my hand against the fatherless,[a]
knowing that I had influence in court,
22 then let my arm fall from the shoulder,
let it be broken off at the joint.[b]
23 For I dreaded destruction from God,
and for fear of his splendor[c] I could not do such things.

24 "If I have put my trust in gold[d]
or said to pure gold, 'You are my security,'[e]
25 if I have rejoiced over my great wealth,[f]
the fortune my hands had gained,
26 if I have regarded the sun[g] in its radiance
or the moon moving in splendor,
27 so that my heart was secretly enticed
and my hand offered them a kiss of homage,
28 then these also would be sins to be judged,[h]
for I would have been unfaithful to God on high.

29 "If I have rejoiced at my enemy's misfortune[i]
or gloated over the trouble that came to him[j]—
30 I have not allowed my mouth to sin
by invoking a curse against their life—
31 if those of my household have never said,
'Who has not been filled with Job's meat?'[k]—
32 but no stranger had to spend the night in the street,
for my door was always open to the traveler[l]—
33 if I have concealed[m] my sin as people do,[b]
by hiding[n] my guilt in my heart
34 because I so feared the crowd[o]
and so dreaded the contempt of the clans
that I kept silent and would not go outside—

35 ("Oh, that I had someone to hear me![p]
I sign now my defense—let the Almighty answer me;
let my accuser[q] put his indictment in writing.
36 Surely I would wear it on my shoulder,
I would put it on like a crown.
37 I would give him an account of my every step;
I would present it to him as to a ruler.[r])—

38 "if my land cries out against me[s]
and all its furrows are wet with tears,
39 if I have devoured its yield without payment[t]
or broken the spirit of its tenants,[u]
40 then let briers[v] come up instead of wheat
and stinkweed instead of barley."

The words of Job are ended.

Elihu

32 So these three men stopped answering Job, because he was righteous in

[a] 12 Hebrew *Abaddon* [b] 33 Or *as Adam did*

31:27 *my hand offered them a kiss of homage.* This phrase refers to the apparent ancient custom of kissing the hand as a prelude to the superstitious and idolatrous act of throwing a kiss to the heavenly bodies.

32:1 *righteous in his own eyes.* Job's friends accused him of self-righteousness because of his denial of the sins they ascribed to him. Job considered himself blameless (and so did God), but he was not without sin. Job needed to see how he compared to God's utter holiness, in spite of the fact that he had none of the unconfessed sins that his friends accused him of.

31:11 [p] Ge 38:24; Lev 20:10; Dt 22:22-24 **31:12** [q] Job 15:30 [r] Job 26:6 [s] Job 20:28 **31:13** [t] Dt 24:14-15 **31:15** [u] Job 10:3 **31:16** [v] Job 5:16; 20:19 [w] Job 22:9 **31:17** [x] Job 22:7; 29:12 **31:19** [y] Job 22:6 [z] Job 24:4 **31:21** [a] Job 22:9 **31:22** [b] Job 38:15 **31:23** [c] Job 13:11 **31:24** [d] Job 22:25 [e] Mt 6:24; Mk 10:24 **31:25** [f] Ps 62:10 **31:26** [g] Eze 8:16 **31:28** [h] Dt 17:2-7 **31:29** [i] Ob 1:12 [j] Pr 17:5; 24:17-18 **31:31** [k] Job 22:7 **31:32** [l] Ge 19:2-3; Ro 12:13 **31:33** [m] Pr 28:13 [n] Ge 3:8 **31:34** [o] Ex 23:2 **31:35** [p] Job 19:7; 30:28 [q] Job 27:7; 35:14 **31:37** [r] Job 1:3; 29:25 **31:38** [s] Ge 4:10 **31:39** [t] 1Ki 21:19 [u] Lev 19:13; Jas 5:4 **31:40** [v] Ge 3:18

his own eyes.[w] 2But Elihu son of Barakel
the Buzite,[x] of the family of Ram, became
very angry with Job for justifying himself rather than God.[y] 3He was also angry
with the three friends, because they had
found no way to refute Job, and yet had
condemned him.[a] 4Now Elihu had waited
before speaking to Job because they were
older than he. 5But when he saw that the
three men had nothing more to say, his anger was aroused.

6So Elihu son of Barakel the Buzite said:

"I am young in years,
and you are old;[z]
that is why I was fearful,
not daring to tell you what I know.
7I thought, 'Age should speak;
advanced years should teach wisdom.'
8But it is the spirit[b] in a person,
the breath of the Almighty,[a] that
gives them understanding.[b]
9It is not only the old[c] who are wise,[c]
not only the aged who understand
what is right.

10"Therefore I say: Listen to me;
I too will tell you what I know.
11I waited while you spoke,
I listened to your reasoning;
while you were searching for words,
12 I gave you my full attention.
But not one of you has proved Job
wrong;
none of you has answered his
arguments.
13Do not say, 'We have found wisdom;[d]
let God, not a man, refute him.'
14But Job has not marshaled his words
against me,
and I will not answer him with your
arguments.

15"They are dismayed and have no more
to say;
words have failed them.
16Must I wait, now that they are silent,
now that they stand there with no
reply?
17I too will have my say;
I too will tell what I know.
18For I am full of words,
and the spirit within me compels me;
19inside I am like bottled-up wine,
like new wineskins ready to burst.
20I must speak and find relief;
I must open my lips and reply.
21I will show no partiality,[e]
nor will I flatter anyone;
22for if I were skilled in flattery,
my Maker would soon take me away.

33 "But now, Job, listen to my words;
pay attention to everything I say.[f]
2I am about to open my mouth;
my words are on the tip of my
tongue.
3My words come from an upright heart;
my lips sincerely speak what I know.[g]
4The Spirit of God has made me;[h]
the breath of the Almighty[i] gives me
life.
5Answer me[j] then, if you can;
stand up[k] and argue your case
before me.
6I am the same as you in God's sight;
I too am a piece of clay.[l]
7No fear of me should alarm you,
nor should my hand be heavy on
you.[m]

8"But you have said in my hearing—
I heard the very words—
9'I am pure,[n] I have done no wrong;[o]
I am clean and free from sin.
10Yet God has found fault with me;
he considers me his enemy.[p]
11He fastens my feet in shackles;[q]
he keeps close watch on all my
paths.'[r]

12"But I tell you, in this you are not right,
for God is greater than any mortal.[s]
13Why do you complain to him[t]
that he responds to no one's words[d]?
14For God does speak[u]—now one way,
now another—
though no one perceives it.
15In a dream,[v] in a vision of the night,
when deep sleep falls on people
as they slumber in their beds,
16he may speak[w] in their ears
and terrify them with warnings,
17to turn them from wrongdoing
and keep them from pride,

---

[a] *3* Masoretic Text; an ancient Hebrew scribal tradition *Job, and so had condemned God*
[b] *8* Or *Spirit*; also in verse 18
[c] *9* Or *many*; or *great*
[d] *13* Or *that he does not answer for any of his actions*

32:2 *became very angry.* Elihu's first mistake was in dealing with a delicate situation while he was angry. He did use the same arguments as the three friends, but he did not understand the whole situation any better than they did. Only the reader is aware of the counsel that took place in heaven (ch. 1).

33:12 *in this you are not right.* Elihu was correct in saying that God was not answerable to Job. God does not ever have to explain Himself to us, even though He often graciously does so. Job had great respect for God, and understood the fear of the Lord (28:28). He was persistent in asking God for an answer, and in the end, God did reply.

32:1 [w] Job 10:7; 33:9 **32:2** [x] Ge 22:21 [y] Job 27:5; 30:21 **32:6** [z] Job 15:10 **32:8** [a] Job 27:3; 33:4 [b] Pr 2:6 **32:9** [c] 1Co 1:26 **32:13** [d] Jer 9:23 **32:21** [e] Lev 19:15; Job 13:10; Mt 22:16 **33:1** [f] Job 13:6 **33:3** [g] Job 6:28; 27:4; 36:4 **33:4** [h] Ge 2:7; Job 10:3 [i] Job 27:3 **33:5** [j] ver 32 [k] Job 13:18 **33:6** [l] Job 4:19 **33:7** [m] Job 9:34; 13:21; 2Co 2:4 **33:9** [n] Job 10:7 [o] Job 13:23; 16:17 **33:10** [p] Job 13:24 **33:11** [q] Job 13:27 [r] Job 14:16 **33:12** [s] Ecc 7:20 **33:13** [t] Job 40:2; Isa 45:9 **33:14** [u] Ps 62:11 **33:15** [v] Job 4:13 **33:16** [w] Job 36:10, 15

18 to preserve them from the pit,[x]
their lives from perishing by the sword.[a][y]

19 "Or someone may be chastened on a bed of pain
with constant distress in their bones,[z]
20 so that their body finds food[a] repulsive
and their soul loathes the choicest meal.[b]
21 Their flesh wastes away to nothing,
and their bones, once hidden, now stick out.[c]
22 They draw near to the pit,
and their life to the messengers of death.[b][d]
23 Yet if there is an angel at their side,
a messenger, one out of a thousand,
sent to tell them how to be upright,[e]
24 and he is gracious to that person and says to God,
'Spare them from going down to the pit;[f]
I have found a ransom for them—
25 let their flesh be renewed like a child's;
let them be restored as in the days of their youth'[g]—
26 then that person can pray to God and find favor with him,[h]
they will see God's face and shout for joy;[i]
he will restore them to full well-being.[j]
27 And they will go to others and say,
'I have sinned,[k] I have perverted what is right,[l]
but I did not get what I deserved.[m]
28 God has delivered me from going down to the pit,
and I shall live to enjoy the light of life.'[n]

29 "God does all these things to a person[o]—
twice, even three times—
30 to turn them back from the pit,
that the light of life[p] may shine on them.

31 "Pay attention, Job, and listen to me;
be silent, and I will speak.
32 If you have anything to say, answer me;
speak up, for I want to vindicate you.
33 But if not, then listen to me;
be silent, and I will teach you wisdom.[q]"

34 Then Elihu said:

2 "Hear my words, you wise men;
listen to me, you men of learning.
3 For the ear tests words
as the tongue tastes food.[r]
4 Let us discern for ourselves what is right;
let us learn together what is good.[s]

5 "Job says, 'I am innocent,[t]
but God denies me justice.[u]
6 Although I am right,
I am considered a liar;
although I am guiltless,
his arrow inflicts an incurable wound.'[v]
7 Is there anyone like Job,
who drinks scorn like water?[w]
8 He keeps company with evildoers;
he associates with the wicked.[x]
9 For he says, 'There is no profit
in trying to please God.'[y]

10 "So listen to me, you men of understanding.
Far be it from God to do evil,[z]
from the Almighty to do wrong.[a]
11 He repays everyone for what they have done;[b]
he brings on them what their conduct deserves.[c]
12 It is unthinkable that God would do wrong,
that the Almighty would pervert justice.[d]
13 Who appointed him over the earth?
Who put him in charge of the whole world?[e]
14 If it were his intention
and he withdrew his spirit[c] and breath,[f]
15 all humanity would perish together
and mankind would return to the dust.[g]

[a] 18 Or *from crossing the river* [b] 22 Or *to the place of the dead* [c] 14 Or *Spirit*

33:30 *to turn them back from the pit.* Again, one of Job's advisors had some correct understanding of God, but he mistakenly applied it to Job. It is true that the chastening of pain or trouble sometimes causes men to turn to God and repent of wickedness. But Job's problem was not perverting what was right (v. 27). For him, the answer for the purpose of his pain could not be "to turn [him] back from the pit." Without claiming that Job was sin free, God had called him blameless and upright (1:8).

34:8 *associates with the wicked.* There was no justice in this charge against Job.

34:12 *do wrong ... pervert justice.* Elihu was unhappy with Job's persistent charges that God was unjust (9:22–24; 24:1–25), and this was a proper concern. The judge of all the earth will always do right (Rev. 15:3).

33:18 [x] ver 22,24,28,30 [y] Job 15:22 **33:19** [z] Job 30:17 **33:20** [a] Ps 107:18 [b] Job 3:24; 6:6 **33:21** [c] Job 16:8; 19:20 **33:22** [d] Ps 88:3 **33:23** [e] Mic 6:8 **33:24** [f] Isa 38:17 **33:25** [g] 2Ki 5:14 **33:26** [h] Job 34:28 [i] Job 22:26 [j] Ps 50:15; 51:12 **33:27** [k] 2Sa 12:13 [l] Lk 15:21 [m] Ro 6:21 **33:28** [n] Job 22:28 **33:29** [o] 1Co 12:6; Eph 1:11; Php 2:13 **33:30** [p] Ps 56:13 **33:33** [q] Ps 34:11 **34:3** [r] Job 12:11 **34:4** [s] 1Th 5:21 **34:5** [t] Job 33:9 [u] Job 27:2 **34:6** [v] Job 6:4 **34:7** [w] Job 15:16 **34:8** [x] Job 22:15; Ps 50:18 **34:9** [y] Job 21:15; 35:3 **34:10** [z] Ge 18:25 [a] Dt 32:4; Job 8:3; Ro 9:14 **34:11** [b] Ps 62:12; Mt 16:27; Ro 2:6; 2Co 5:10 [c] Jer 32:19; Eze 33:20 **34:12** [d] Job 8:3 **34:13** [e] Job 38:4,6 **34:14** [f] Ps 104:29 **34:15** [g] Ge 3:19; Job 9:22

16 "If you have understanding, hear this;
listen to what I say.
17 Can someone who hates justice
govern?[h]
Will you condemn the just and
mighty One?[i]
18 Is he not the One who says to kings,
'You are worthless,'
and to nobles, 'You are wicked,'[j]
19 who shows no partiality[k] to princes
and does not favor the rich over the
poor,[l]
for they are all the work of his
hands?[m]
20 They die in an instant, in the middle of
the night;[n]
the people are shaken and they pass
away;
the mighty are removed without
human hand.[o]

21 "His eyes are on the ways of mortals;
he sees their every step.[p]
22 There is no deep shadow,[q] no utter
darkness,[r]
where evildoers can hide.
23 God has no need to examine people
further,
that they should come before him for
judgment.[s]
24 Without inquiry he shatters the mighty[t]
and sets up others in their place.[u]
25 Because he takes note of their deeds,
he overthrows them in the night and
they are crushed.
26 He punishes them for their wickedness
where everyone can see them,
27 because they turned from following
him[v]
and had no regard for any of his
ways.[w]
28 They caused the cry of the poor to come
before him,
so that he heard the cry of the needy.[x]
29 But if he remains silent, who can
condemn him?
If he hides his face, who can see him?
Yet he is over individual and nation
alike,
30 to keep the godless from ruling,
from laying snares for the people.[y]

31 "Suppose someone says to God,
'I am guilty but will offend no more.
32 Teach me what I cannot see;[z]
if I have done wrong, I will not do so
again.'[a]
33 Should God then reward you on your
terms,
when you refuse to repent?[b]
You must decide, not I;
so tell me what you know.

34 "Men of understanding declare,
wise men who hear me say to me,
35 'Job speaks without knowledge;[c]
his words lack insight.'
36 Oh, that Job might be tested to the
utmost
for answering like a wicked man![d]
37 To his sin he adds rebellion;
scornfully he claps his hands[e]
among us
and multiplies his words against
God."[f]

35

Then Elihu said:

2 "Do you think this is just?
You say, 'I am in the right, not God.'
3 Yet you ask him, 'What profit is it
to me,[a]
and what do I gain by not sinning?'[g]

4 "I would like to reply to you
and to your friends with you.
5 Look up at the heavens[h] and see;
gaze at the clouds so high above you.[i]
6 If you sin, how does that affect him?
If your sins are many, what does that
do to him?[j]
7 If you are righteous, what do you give
to him,[k]
or what does he receive[l] from your
hand?[m]
8 Your wickedness only affects humans
like yourself,
and your righteousness only other
people.

9 "People cry out[n] under a load of
oppression;

[a] 3 Or *you*

34:16 *hear this.* As indicated by the singular Hebrew verb translated "hear," Elihu was addressing Job directly in verses 16–33.
34:24 *shatters the mighty.* Job was a mighty man who was broken. Elihu's implication is that Job was a worker of iniquity (v. 22).
34:37 To his sin he adds rebellion. Job was stubborn, but he was not rebellious. He was willing to accept punishment if he deserved it (31:5–6).
35:6 *If you sin.* This is the same argument used by Eliphaz (22:2). The point that Elihu was making here and through verse 8, is that God's stature is not affected either by the sinfulness or righteousness of man. He cannot be diminished by sin nor made greater by righteousness. This is a true and important point. But it leaves out the understanding that God created man to be in His image, and He does care about the actions of man. God wants men to live blamelessly (ch. 1), and it is good to want to please God.

34:17 [h] 2Sa 23:3-4 [i] Job 40:8 **34:18** [j] Ex 22:28
34:19 [k] Dt 10:17; Ac 10:34 [l] Lev 19:15 [m] Job 10:3
34:20 [n] Ex 12:29 [o] Job 12:19 **34:21** [p] Job 31:4; Pr 15:3
34:22 [q] Am 9:2-3 [r] Ps 139:12 **34:23** [s] Job 11:11
34:24 [t] Job 12:19 [u] Da 2:21 **34:27** [v] Ps 28:5; Isa 5:12
[w] 1Sa 15:11 **34:28** [x] Ex 22:23; Job 35:9; Jas 5:4
34:30 [y] Pr 29:2-12 **34:32** [z] Job 35:11; Ps 25:4 [a] Job 33:27
34:33 [b] Job 41:11 **34:35** [c] Job 35:16; 38:2
34:36 [d] Job 22:15 **34:37** [e] Job 27:23 [f] Job 23:2
35:3 [g] Job 9:29-31; 34:9 **35:5** [h] Ge 15:5 [i] Job 22:12
35:6 [j] Pr 8:36 **35:7** [k] Ro 11:35 [l] Pr 9:12 [m] Job 22:2-3;
Lk 17:10 **35:9** [n] Ex 2:23

they plead for relief from the arm of
the powerful.[o]
10 But no one says, 'Where is God my
Maker,[p]
who gives songs in the night,[q]
11 who teaches[r] us more than he teaches[a]
the beasts of the earth
and makes us wiser than[b] the birds in
the sky?'
12 He does not answer[s] when people cry
out
because of the arrogance of the
wicked.
13 Indeed, God does not listen to their
empty plea;
the Almighty pays no attention to it.[t]
14 How much less, then, will he listen
when you say that you do not see
him,[u]
that your case[v] is before him
and you must wait for him,
15 and further, that his anger never
punishes
and he does not take the least notice
of wickedness.[c]
16 So Job opens his mouth with empty
talk;
without knowledge he multiplies
words."[w]

36

Elihu continued:

2 "Bear with me a little longer and I will
show you
that there is more to be said in God's
behalf.
3 I get my knowledge from afar;
I will ascribe justice to my Maker.[x]
4 Be assured that my words are not
false;[y]
one who has perfect knowledge[z] is
with you.

5 "God is mighty, but despises no one;[a]
he is mighty, and firm in his
purpose.[b]
6 He does not keep the wicked alive[c]
but gives the afflicted their rights.[d]
7 He does not take his eyes off the
righteous;[e]
he enthrones them with kings[f]
and exalts them forever.
8 But if people are bound in chains,[g]
held fast by cords of affliction,
9 he tells them what they have done—
that they have sinned arrogantly.[h]
10 He makes them listen[i] to correction
and commands them to repent of
their evil.[j]
11 If they obey and serve him,[k]
they will spend the rest of their days
in prosperity
and their years in contentment.
12 But if they do not listen,
they will perish by the sword[d][l]
and die without knowledge.[m]

13 "The godless in heart[n] harbor
resentment;
even when he fetters them, they do
not cry for help.
14 They die in their youth,
among male prostitutes of the
shrines.[o]
15 But those who suffer he delivers in their
suffering;
he speaks to them in their affliction.

16 "He is wooing[p] you from the jaws of
distress
to a spacious place free from
restriction,
to the comfort of your table[q] laden
with choice food.
17 But now you are laden with the
judgment due the wicked;
judgment and justice have taken hold
of you.[r]
18 Be careful that no one entices you by
riches;
do not let a large bribe turn you
aside.[s]
19 Would your wealth or even all your
mighty efforts
sustain you so you would not be in
distress?

---

[a] *10,11* Or *night,* / [11]*who teaches us by*
[b] *11* Or *us wise by* [c] *15* Symmachus, Theodotion and Vulgate; the meaning of the Hebrew for this word is uncertain. [d] *12* Or *will cross the river*

35:12 Pride—Elihu accused Job of pride because Job had declared his own righteousness (32:1). But Elihu's presumption and self-righteousness became even more excessive than Job's as he developed his pompous speech against Job (36:4). Later Elihu would understand that God had accepted Job, while his "friends" were condemned. Even knowledge about God and commitment to God can become a source of pride that blinds us to other things that God is doing, both in ourselves and in others.

35:13 ***empty plea.*** Elihu was assuming that Job had no answer from God because God knew that Job's cry was empty.

36:2 ***said in God's behalf.*** Elihu believed that he was speaking for God and that he was setting Job straight. It is interesting to note that God asked Job to pray for the other three friends (42:7–10), but no word, either of censure or praise, was said about Elihu.

36:6–14 ***does not keep the wicked alive.*** Elihu repeats the concept that the wicked are judged by being cut off and the repentant are rewarded.

35:9 [o] Job 12:19 **35:10** [p] Job 27:10; Isa 51:13 [q] Ps 42:8; 149:5; Ac 16:25 **35:11** [r] Ps 94:12 **35:12** [s] Pr 1:28
35:13 [t] Job 27:9; Pr 15:29; Isa 1:15; Jer 11:11
35:14 [u] Job 9:11 [v] Ps 37:6 **35:16** [w] Job 34:35, 37
36:3 [x] Job 8:3; 37:23 **36:4** [y] Job 33:3 [z] Job 37:5, 16, 23
36:5 [a] Ps 22:24 [b] Job 12:13 **36:6** [c] Job 8:22 [d] Job 5:15
36:7 [e] Ps 33:18 [f] Ps 113:8 **36:8** [g] Ps 107:10, 14
36:9 [h] Job 15:25 **36:10** [i] Job 33:16 [j] 2Ki 17:13
36:11 [k] Isa 1:19 **36:12** [l] Job 15:22 [m] Job 4:21
36:13 [n] Ro 2:5 **36:14** [o] Dt 23:17 **36:16** [p] Hos 2:14
[q] Ps 23:5 **36:17** [r] Job 22:11 **36:18** [s] Job 34:33

20 Do not long for the night,[t]
to drag people away from their
homes.[a]
21 Beware of turning to evil,[u]
which you seem to prefer to
affliction.[v]

22 "God is exalted in his power.
Who is a teacher like him?[w]
23 Who has prescribed his ways for him,[x]
or said to him, 'You have done
wrong'?[y]
24 Remember to extol his work,[z]
which people have praised in song.[a]
25 All humanity has seen it;
mortals gaze on it from afar.
26 How great is God—beyond our
understanding![b]
The number of his years is past
finding out.[c]

27 "He draws up the drops of water,
which distill as rain to the streams[b];[d]
28 the clouds pour down their moisture
and abundant showers fall on
mankind.[e]
29 Who can understand how he spreads
out the clouds,
how he thunders from his pavilion?[f]
30 See how he scatters his lightning about
him,
bathing the depths of the sea.
31 This is the way he governs[c] the nations[g]
and provides food in abundance.[h]
32 He fills his hands with lightning
and commands it to strike its mark.[i]
33 His thunder announces the coming
storm;
even the cattle make known its
approach.[d]

37 "At this my heart pounds
and leaps from its place.
2 Listen! Listen to the roar of his voice,
to the rumbling that comes from his
mouth.[j]
3 He unleashes his lightning beneath the
whole heaven
and sends it to the ends of the earth.
4 After that comes the sound of his roar;
he thunders with his majestic voice.
When his voice resounds,
he holds nothing back.
5 God's voice thunders in marvelous
ways;
he does great things beyond our
understanding.[k]
6 He says to the snow,[l] 'Fall on the earth,'
and to the rain shower, 'Be a mighty
downpour.'[m]
7 So that everyone he has made may
know his work,
he stops all people from their labor.[e][n]
8 The animals take cover;
they remain in their dens.[o]
9 The tempest comes out from its
chamber,
the cold from the driving winds.
10 The breath of God produces ice,
and the broad waters become frozen.[p]
11 He loads the clouds with moisture;
he scatters his lightning through
them.[q]
12 At his direction they swirl around
over the face of the whole earth
to do whatever he commands them.[r]
13 He brings the clouds to punish people,[s]
or to water his earth and show his
love.[t]

14 "Listen to this, Job;
stop and consider God's wonders.
15 Do you know how God controls the
clouds
and makes his lightning flash?

---

[a] *20* The meaning of the Hebrew for verses 18-20 is uncertain. [b] *27* Or *distill from the mist as rain* [c] *31* Or *nourishes* [d] *33* Or *announces his coming— / the One zealous against evil* [e] *7* Or *work, / he fills all people with fear by his power*

36:23 *You have done wrong.* This is probably the most accurate warning that Elihu gives to Job. Even though Job was sure that God would vindicate his actions (and the reader knows that God saw Job as blameless and upright), he could not defend his position without telling God that He had done wrong. God cannot sin, nor will He tempt people to sin.
36:24 *extol his work.* This is the best advice that Elihu gave Job, and indeed, it was something that Job had already done (26:5–14; 28:1–28). Exalting God for who He is and what He has done is one of the best ways to gain perspective when we are in trouble or despair.
36:26 *How great is God.* As Elihu begins to praise God, his anger with Job disappears, and he speaks accurately and joyfully of the things that he knows about God. From here to the end of chapter 37 Elihu is praising God. The speeches of Elihu are the most difficult of the friends' admonitions to analyze, and scholars are not in total agreement about which charges by Elihu are discerning and which charges are misapplied "conventional wisdom." Like all mixtures of truth and misunderstanding, Elihu's discourse needs careful sorting.
37:7 *stops all people from their labor.* God uses the winter storm to stop man so that he cannot work, but instead may recognize the work of God.
37:12 *direction.* This is a nautical term which literally means "steerings" or "rope-pullings" (Prov. 15) and portrays God as the wise Captain who skillfully charts the course for the clouds, which respond obediently to His hand at the helm.

36:20 [t] Job 34:20,25 **36:21** [u] Ps 66:18 [v] Heb 11:25
36:22 [w] Isa 40:13; 1Co 2:16 **36:23** [x] Job 34:13 [y] Job 8:3
36:24 [z] Ps 92:5; 138:5 [a] Ps 59:16; Rev 15:3
36:26 [b] 1Co 13:12 [c] Job 10:5; Ps 90:2; 102:24; Heb 1:12
36:27 [d] Job 38:28; Ps 147:8 **36:28** [e] Job 5:10
36:29 [f] Job 26:14; 37:16 **36:31** [g] Job 37:13 [h] Ps 136:25; Ac 14:17 **36:32** [i] Job 37:12,15 **37:2** [j] Ps 29:3-9
37:5 [k] Job 5:9 **37:6** [l] Job 38:22 [m] Job 36:27
37:7 [n] Job 12:14 **37:8** [o] Job 38:40; Ps 104:22
37:10 [p] Job 38:29-30; Ps 147:17 **37:11** [q] Job 36:27,29
37:12 [r] Ps 148:8 **37:13** [s] 1Sa 12:17 [t] Ex 9:18; 1Ki 18:45; Job 38:27

16 Do you know how the clouds hang
poised,
those wonders of him who has
perfect knowledge?[u]
17 You who swelter in your clothes
when the land lies hushed under the
south wind,
18 can you join him in spreading out the
skies,[v]
hard as a mirror of cast bronze?

19 "Tell us what we should say to him;
we cannot draw up our case because
of our darkness.
20 Should he be told that I want to speak?
Would anyone ask to be
swallowed up?
21 Now no one can look at the sun,
bright as it is in the skies
after the wind has swept them clean.
22 Out of the north he comes in golden
splendor;
God comes in awesome majesty.
23 The Almighty is beyond our reach and
exalted in power;[w]
in his justice[x] and great
righteousness, he does not
oppress.[y]
24 Therefore, people revere him,[z]
for does he not have regard for all the
wise[a] in heart?[a]"

The LORD Speaks

38 Then the LORD spoke to Job out of the
storm.[b] He said:

2 "Who is this that obscures my plans
with words without knowledge?[c]
3 Brace yourself like a man;
I will question you,
and you shall answer me.[d]

4 "Where were you when I laid the earth's
foundation?[e]
Tell me, if you understand.
5 Who marked off its dimensions?[f] Surely
you know!
Who stretched a measuring line
across it?
6 On what were its footings set,
or who laid its cornerstone[g]—
7 while the morning stars sang together
and all the angels[b] shouted for joy?

8 "Who shut up the sea behind doors[h]
when it burst forth from the womb,[i]
9 when I made the clouds its garment
and wrapped it in thick darkness,
10 when I fixed limits for it[j]
and set its doors and bars in place,[k]
11 when I said, 'This far you may come
and no farther;
here is where your proud waves halt'?[l]

12 "Have you ever given orders to the
morning,
or shown the dawn its place,
13 that it might take the earth by the edges
and shake the wicked[m] out of it?
14 The earth takes shape like clay under a
seal;
its features stand out like those of a
garment.
15 The wicked are denied their light,[n]
and their upraised arm is broken.[o]

16 "Have you journeyed to the springs of
the sea
or walked in the recesses of the
deep?[p]
17 Have the gates of death[q] been shown to
you?
Have you seen the gates of the
deepest darkness?
18 Have you comprehended the vast
expanses of the earth?[r]
Tell me, if you know all this.

19 "What is the way to the abode of light?
And where does darkness reside?
20 Can you take them to their places?
Do you know the paths[s] to their
dwellings?
21 Surely you know, for you were already
born![t]
You have lived so many years!

22 "Have you entered the storehouses of
the snow[u]
or seen the storehouses of the hail,

[a] 24 *Or for he does not have regard for any who think they are wise.* [b] 7 Hebrew *the sons of God*

37:18 *hard as a mirror of cast bronze.* Ancient mirrors were firm and unbreakable because they were made of polished bronze.

37:24 *regard ... wise in heart?* Even though Elihu had claimed earlier to be one who "has perfect knowledge" (36:4), he knew that God does not give preferential treatment, even to the wise.

38:2 *words without knowledge?* The theme of the first speech of the Lord is given here. Job did not know what he was talking about. God quite quickly points out that there is a wide gap in understanding between God and man. God was not saying that Job had sinned in the way that his friends had accused him, but He was saying that Job had been presumptuous with his superficial knowledge of divine things. Job, along with his friends, had to learn that suffering may serve a purpose known only to God. In that case, a follower of God will submit even to loss and trauma, without complaint, for the glory of God.

38:10 *I fixed limits.* If God controls the sea and places boundaries on it, He can place boundaries on anything else that will affect mankind.

37:16 [u] Job 36:4 **37:18** [v] Job 9:8; Ps 104:2; Isa 44:24 **37:23** [w] Job 9:4; 36:4; 1Ti 6:16 [x] Job 8:3 [y] Isa 63:9; Eze 18:23, 32 **37:24** [z] Mt 10:28 [a] Mt 11:25 **38:1** [b] Job 40:6 **38:2** [c] Job 35:16; 42:3; 1Ti 1:7 **38:3** [d] Job 40:7 **38:4** [e] Ps 104:5; Pr 8:29 **38:5** [f] Pr 8:29; Isa 40:12 **38:6** [g] Job 26:7 **38:8** [h] Jer 5:22 [i] Ge 1:9-10 **38:10** [j] Ps 33:7; 104:9 [k] Job 26:10 **38:11** [l] Ps 89:9 **38:13** [m] Ps 104:35 **38:15** [n] Job 18:5 [o] Ps 10:15 **38:16** [p] Ps 77:19 **38:17** [q] Ps 9:13 **38:18** [r] Job 28:24 **38:20** [s] Job 26:10 **38:21** [t] Job 15:7 **38:22** [u] Job 37:6

23 which I reserve for times of trouble,[v]
for days of war and battle?[w]
24 What is the way to the place where the
lightning is dispersed,
or the place where the east winds are
scattered over the earth?
25 Who cuts a channel for the torrents of
rain,
and a path for the thunderstorm,[x]
26 to water[y] a land where no one lives,
an uninhabited desert,
27 to satisfy a desolate wasteland
and make it sprout with grass?[z]
28 Does the rain have a father?[a]
Who fathers the drops of dew?
29 From whose womb comes the ice?
Who gives birth to the frost from the
heavens[b]
30 when the waters become hard as stone,
when the surface of the deep is
frozen?[c]

31 "Can you bind the chains[a] of the
Pleiades?
Can you loosen Orion's belt?[d]
32 Can you bring forth the constellations
in their seasons[b]
or lead out the Bear[c] with its cubs?
33 Do you know the laws[e] of the heavens?
Can you set up God's[d] dominion over
the earth?

34 "Can you raise your voice to the clouds
and cover yourself with a flood of
water?[f]
35 Do you send the lightning bolts on their
way?[g]
Do they report to you, 'Here we are'?
36 Who gives the ibis wisdom[e][h]
or gives the rooster understanding?[f][i]
37 Who has the wisdom to count the
clouds?
Who can tip over the water jars of the
heavens
38 when the dust becomes hard
and the clods of earth stick together?

39 "Do you hunt the prey for the lioness
and satisfy the hunger of the lions[j]
40 when they crouch in their dens[k]
or lie in wait in a thicket?
41 Who provides food for the raven[l]
when its young cry out to God
and wander about for lack of food?[m]

39 "Do you know when the mountain
goats[n] give birth?
Do you watch when the doe bears her
fawn?
2 Do you count the months till they bear?
Do you know the time they give
birth?
3 They crouch down and bring forth their
young;
their labor pains are ended.
4 Their young thrive and grow strong in
the wilds;
they leave and do not return.

5 "Who let the wild donkey[o] go free?
Who untied its ropes?
6 I gave it the wasteland[p] as its home,
the salt flats as its habitat.[q]
7 It laughs at the commotion in the town;
it does not hear a driver's shout.[r]
8 It ranges the hills for its pasture
and searches for any green thing.

9 "Will the wild ox[s] consent to serve
you?
Will it stay by your manger at night?
10 Can you hold it to the furrow with a
harness?
Will it till the valleys behind you?
11 Will you rely on it for its great
strength?
Will you leave your heavy work to it?
12 Can you trust it to haul in your grain
and bring it to your threshing floor?

13 "The wings of the ostrich flap joyfully,
though they cannot compare
with the wings and feathers of the
stork.
14 She lays her eggs on the ground
and lets them warm in the sand,
15 unmindful that a foot may crush them,
that some wild animal may trample
them.
16 She treats her young harshly,[t] as if they
were not hers;
she cares not that her labor was in
vain,

[a] *31* Septuagint; Hebrew *beauty* [b] *32* Or *the morning star in its season* [c] *32* Or *out Leo* [d] *33* Or *their* [e] *36* That is, wisdom about the flooding of the Nile [f] *36* That is, understanding of when to crow; the meaning of the Hebrew for this verse is uncertain.

38:26 *where no one lives.* Though God utilizes meteorological elements to intervene in human affairs, He also uses them in areas that lie outside the human realm, for the sake of the land itself.
38:32 *the Bear.* This is a reference to the constellation known as Ursa Major, also called the Big Dipper.
39:1 *Do you know.* God continues His probing of Job. He has shown His control of the earth and seas, the elements and the heavens, and now He shows the splendor and mysteries of the wild forces of nature, which are also all in God's control.
39:5 *let the wild donkey go free?* God shows his compassion even for beasts of burden. This contrasts sharply with Job's complaints about God not noticing the oppression by the wicked (24:1 – 12).

38:23 [v] Isa 30:30; Eze 13:11 [w] Ex 9:18; Jos 10:11; Rev 16:21 **38:25** [x] Job 28:26 **38:26** [y] Job 36:27 **38:27** [z] Ps 104:14; 107:35 **38:28** [a] Ps 147:8; Jer 14:22 **38:29** [b] Ps 147:16-17 **38:30** [c] Job 37:10 **38:31** [d] Job 9:9; Am 5:8 **38:33** [e] Ps 148:6; Jer 31:36 **38:34** [f] Job 22:11; 36:27-28 **38:35** [g] Job 36:32; 37:3 **38:36** [h] Job 9:4 [i] Job 32:8; Ps 51:6; Ecc 2:26 **38:39** [j] Ps 104:21 **38:40** [k] Job 37:8 **38:41** [l] Lk 12:24 [m] Ps 147:9; Mt 6:26 **39:1** [n] Dt 14:5 **39:5** [o] Job 6:5; 11:12; 24:5 **39:6** [p] Job 24:5; Ps 107:34; Jer 2:24 [q] Hos 8:9 **39:7** [r] Job 3:18 **39:9** [s] Nu 23:22; Dt 33:17 **39:16** [t] La 4:3

17 for God did not endow her with wisdom
or give her a share of good sense.[u]
18 Yet when she spreads her feathers to run,
she laughs at horse and rider.

19 "Do you give the horse its strength
or clothe its neck with a flowing mane?
20 Do you make it leap like a locust,[v]
striking terror with its proud snorting?[w]
21 It paws fiercely, rejoicing in its strength,
and charges into the fray.[x]
22 It laughs at fear, afraid of nothing;
it does not shy away from the sword.
23 The quiver rattles against its side,
along with the flashing spear and lance.
24 In frenzied excitement it eats up the ground;
it cannot stand still when the trumpet sounds.[y]
25 At the blast of the trumpet[z] it snorts, 'Aha!'
It catches the scent of battle from afar,
the shout of commanders and the battle cry.[a]

26 "Does the hawk take flight by your wisdom
and spread its wings toward the south?
27 Does the eagle soar at your command
and build its nest on high?[b]
28 It dwells on a cliff and stays there at night;
a rocky crag is its stronghold.
29 From there it looks for food;[c]
its eyes detect it from afar.
30 Its young ones feast on blood,
and where the slain are, there it is."[d]

40

The LORD said to Job:[e]

2 "Will the one who contends with the Almighty correct him?
Let him who accuses God answer him!"

3 Then Job answered the LORD:

4 "I am unworthy[f]—how can I reply to you?
I put my hand over my mouth.[g]
5 I spoke once, but I have no answer[h]—
twice, but I will say no more."[i]

6 Then the LORD spoke to Job out of the storm:[j]

7 "Brace yourself like a man;
I will question you,
and you shall answer me.[k]

8 "Would you discredit my justice?[l]
Would you condemn me to justify yourself?
9 Do you have an arm like God's,[m]
and can your voice thunder like his?[n]
10 Then adorn yourself with glory and splendor,
and clothe yourself in honor and majesty.[o]
11 Unleash the fury of your wrath,[p]
look at all who are proud and bring them low,[q]
12 look at all who are proud and humble them,[r]
crush[s] the wicked where they stand.
13 Bury them all in the dust together;
shroud their faces in the grave.
14 Then I myself will admit to you
that your own right hand can save you.[t]

15 "Look at Behemoth,
which I made along with you
and which feeds on grass like an ox.
16 What strength it has in its loins,
what power in the muscles of its belly!
17 Its tail sways like a cedar;
the sinews of its thighs are close-knit.
18 Its bones are tubes of bronze,
its limbs like rods of iron.
19 It ranks first among the works of God,[u]
yet its Maker can approach it with his sword.
20 The hills bring it their produce,[v]
and all the wild animals play[w] nearby.
21 Under the lotus plants it lies,
hidden among the reeds in the marsh.
22 The lotuses conceal it in their shadow;
the poplars by the stream[x] surround it.
23 A raging river does not alarm it;
it is secure, though the Jordan should surge against its mouth.

39:30 ***where the slain are, there it is.*** The animals that feed on the blood of the slain prevent the spread of disease. This too, is part of God's intricate plan.
40:8 ***condemn me to justify yourself?*** Because Job had been arguing against the inflexible retribution dogma, which views suffering as God's punishment for sin, Job had to condemn God in order to maintain his own innocence.
40:15 ***Behemoth.*** Suggestions for the identity of this beast include the elephant, the hippopotamus, or a dinosaur. The name means "great beast," and the description most nearly fits a dinosaur, as neither the elephant nor the hippo has a tail like a cedar.

39:17 [u] Job 35:11 **39:20** [v] Joel 2:4-5 [w] Jer 8:16
39:21 [x] Jer 8:6 **39:24** [y] Jer 4:5, 19; Eze 7:14; Am 3:6
39:25 [z] Jos 6:5 [a] Am 1:14; 2:2 **39:27** [b] Jer 49:16; Ob 1:4
39:29 [c] Job 9:26 **39:30** [d] Mt 24:28; Lk 17:37
40:1 [e] Job 10:2; 13:3; 23:4; 31:35; 33:13
40:4 [f] Job 42:6 [g] Job 29:9 **40:5** [h] Job 9:3 [i] Job 9:15
40:6 [j] Job 38:1 **40:7** [k] Job 38:3; 42:4
40:8 [l] Job 27:2; Ro 3:3 **40:9** [m] 2Ch 32:8 [n] Job 37:5; Ps 29:3-4 **40:10** [o] Ps 93:1; 104:1
40:11 [p] Isa 42:25; Na 1:6 [q] Isa 2:11, 12, 17; Da 4:37
40:12 [r] 1Sa 2:7 [s] Isa 13:11; 63:2-3, 6
40:14 [t] Ps 20:6; 60:5; 108:6 **40:19** [u] Job 41:33
40:20 [v] Ps 104:14 [w] Ps 104:26
40:22 [x] Isa 44:4

[24] Can anyone capture it by the eyes,
or trap it and pierce its nose?[y]

41 [a] "Can you pull in Leviathan[z] with a fishhook
or tie down its tongue with a rope?
[2] Can you put a cord through its nose
or pierce its jaw with a hook?[a]
[3] Will it keep begging you for mercy?
Will it speak to you with gentle words?
[4] Will it make an agreement with you
for you to take it as your slave for life?[b]
[5] Can you make a pet of it like a bird
or put it on a leash for the young women in your house?
[6] Will traders barter for it?
Will they divide it up among the merchants?
[7] Can you fill its hide with harpoons
or its head with fishing spears?
[8] If you lay a hand on it,
you will remember the struggle and never do it again!
[9] Any hope of subduing it is false;
the mere sight of it is overpowering.
[10] No one is fierce enough to rouse it.[c]
Who then is able to stand against me?[d]
[11] Who has a claim against me that I must pay?[e]
Everything under heaven belongs to me.[f]

[12] "I will not fail to speak of Leviathan's limbs,
its strength and its graceful form.
[13] Who can strip off its outer coat?
Who can penetrate its double coat of armor[b]?
[14] Who dares open the doors of its mouth,
ringed about with fearsome teeth?
[15] Its back has[c] rows of shields
tightly sealed together;
[16] each is so close to the next
that no air can pass between.
[17] They are joined fast to one another;
they cling together and cannot be parted.
[18] Its snorting throws out flashes of light;
its eyes are like the rays of dawn.[g]
[19] Flames stream from its mouth;
sparks of fire shoot out.
[20] Smoke pours from its nostrils
as from a boiling pot over burning reeds.
[21] Its breath[h] sets coals ablaze,
and flames dart from its mouth.[i]
[22] Strength resides in its neck;
dismay goes before it.
[23] The folds of its flesh are tightly joined;
they are firm and immovable.
[24] Its chest is hard as rock,
hard as a lower millstone.
[25] When it rises up, the mighty are terrified;
they retreat before its thrashing.
[26] The sword that reaches it has no effect,
nor does the spear or the dart or the javelin.
[27] Iron it treats like straw
and bronze like rotten wood.
[28] Arrows do not make it flee;
slingstones are like chaff to it.
[29] A club seems to it but a piece of straw;
it laughs at the rattling of the lance.
[30] Its undersides are jagged potsherds,
leaving a trail in the mud like a threshing sledge.[j]
[31] It makes the depths churn like a boiling caldron
and stirs up the sea like a pot of ointment.
[32] It leaves a glistening wake behind it;
one would think the deep had white hair.
[33] Nothing on earth is its equal[k]—
a creature without fear.
[34] It looks down on all that are haughty;
it is king over all that are proud.[l]"

Job

42 Then Job replied to the LORD:

[2] "I know that you can do all things;[m]
no purpose of yours can be thwarted.[n]
[3] You asked, 'Who is this that obscures my plans without knowledge?'[o]
Surely I spoke of things I did not understand,
things too wonderful for me to know.[p]

[4] "You said, 'Listen now, and I will speak;
I will question you,
and you shall answer me.'[q]
[5] My ears had heard of you[r]
but now my eyes have seen you.[s]

[a] In Hebrew texts 41:1-8 is numbered 40:25-32, and 41:9-34 is numbered 41:1-26. [b] *13* Septuagint; Hebrew *double bridle* [c] *15* Or *Its pride is its*

41:1 *Leviathan.* The identity of Leviathan, which is a transliteration for the Hebrew word "sea monster," or "sea serpent," is disputed. His description (vv. 12–18) sounds like the traditional dragon. He is a sea animal, an uncontrollable giant.

42:4 *you shall answer me.* Job was completely done with his complaints of injustice. He knew that his presuppositions were wrong, and that he needed God's wisdom.

42:5 Conviction—Job was not convicted of a particular sin, but of too small a view of God. In the Bible, the revelation of the character and person of God is the criterion for proper self-evaluation (Is. 6:5). Job

40:24 [y] Job 41:2,7,26 **41:1** [z] Job 3:8; Ps 104:26; Isa 27:1 **41:2** [a] Isa 37:29 **41:4** [b] Ex 21:6 **41:10** [c] Job 3:8 [d] Jer 50:44 **41:11** [e] Ro 11:35 [f] Ex 19:5; Dt 10:14; Ps 24:1; 50:12; 1Co 10:26 **41:18** [g] Job 3:9 **41:21** [h] Isa 40:7 [i] Ps 18:8 **41:30** [j] Isa 41:15 **41:33** [k] Job 40:19 **41:34** [l] Job 28:8 **42:2** [m] Ge 18:14; Mt 19:26 [n] 2Ch 20:6 **42:3** [o] Job 38:2 [p] Ps 40:5; 131:1; 139:6 **42:4** [q] Job 38:3; 40:7 **42:5** [r] Job 26:14; Ro 10:17 [s] Jdg 13:22; Isa 6:5; Eph 1:17-18

6Therefore I despise myself[t]
and repent in dust and ashes."[u]

Epilogue

7After the LORD had said these things to
Job, he said to Eliphaz the Temanite, "I am
angry with you and your two friends,[v] because you have not spoken the truth about
me, as my servant Job has. 8So now take
seven bulls and seven rams[w] and go to my
servant Job and sacrifice a burnt offering[x]
for yourselves. My servant Job will pray for
you, and I will accept his prayer[y] and not
deal with you according to your folly.[z] You
have not spoken the truth about me, as my
servant Job has." 9So Eliphaz the Temanite, Bildad the Shuhite and Zophar the Naamathite did what the LORD told them; and
the LORD accepted Job's prayer.
10After Job had prayed for his friends,
the LORD restored his fortunes[a] and gave
him twice as much as he had before.[b] 11All
his brothers and sisters and everyone who
had known him before[c] came and ate with
him in his house. They comforted and consoled him over all the trouble the LORD had
brought on him, and each one gave him a
piece of silver[a] and a gold ring.
12The LORD blessed the latter part of
Job's life more than the former part. He
had fourteen thousand sheep, six thousand camels, a thousand yoke of oxen and
a thousand donkeys. 13And he also had
seven sons and three daughters. 14The
first daughter he named Jemimah, the second Keziah and the third Keren-Happuch.
15Nowhere in all the land were there found
women as beautiful as Job's daughters, and
their father granted them an inheritance
along with their brothers.
16After this, Job lived a hundred and forty years; he saw his children and their children to the fourth generation. 17And so Job
died, an old man and full of years.[d]

---

[a] *11* Hebrew *him a kesitah*; a kesitah was a unit of money of unknown weight and value.

---

regretted that his trust in God had been so imperfect, for he now understood God in a new way.

42:6 *repent in dust and ashes.* Dust and ashes were a sign of mourning. Job could not retract more fully.

42:7 *spoken the truth about me, as my servant Job has.* Even though God had just shown Job his presumption, God still validated Job's doggedly held position that God had not brought suffering on him because of sin in his life.

42:10 *After Job had prayed ... the LORD restored his fortunes.* Not only did God deal with Job's presumption and the wrong ideas of his friends, but He provided the perfect way to restore their relationship with each other, as well as with God.

42:6 [t] Job 40:4 [u] Ezr 9:6 **42:7** [v] Job 32:3 **42:8** [w] Nu 23:1,29 [x] Job 1:5 [y] Ge 20:17; Jas 5:15-16; 1Jn 5:16 [z] Job 22:30 **42:10** [a] Dt 30:3; Ps 14:7 [b] Job 1:3; Ps 85:1-3; 126:5-6 **42:11** [c] Job 19:13 **42:17** [d] Ge 15:15; 25:8

PSALMS

▶ **AUTHOR:** Seventy-five of the psalms in the book are designated as Davidic: 3–9; 11–32; 34–41; 51–65; 68–70; 86; 101; 103; 108–110; 122; 124; 131; 133; and 138–145. The New Testament tells us that the "anonymous" Psalms 2 and 95 were also written by David. In addition to these, 12 are by Asaph, a priest who headed the service of music; ten are by the sons of Korah, a guild of singers and composers; two are by Solomon, Israel's most powerful king; one is by Moses; one by Heman, a wise man; and one is by Ethan, another wise man. The remaining fifty psalms are anonymous, but tradition attributes them to Ezra.

▶ **TIME:** c. 1410–430 B.C. ▶ **KEY VERSE:** Ps. 19:14

▶ **THEME:** A collection of songs that literally covers hundreds of years of Jewish history from the patriarchs down through the postexilic period, the Book of Psalms is practical and personal as well as scenic and magnificently beautiful. The Psalms teach us how to pray, how to grieve, how to rejoice, and how to worship. Any Christian who makes building a relationship with God a priority in his or her life will find great spiritual nourishment in the Psalms. It is the prayer book for all who believe in the God of the universe. Jesus used it as such, and so should we.

BOOK I

Psalms 1–41

Psalm 1

1 Blessed is the one
who does not walk[a] in step with the wicked
or stand in the way that sinners take
or sit[b] in the company of mockers,
2 but whose delight[c] is in the law of the LORD,[d]
and who meditates[e] on his law day and night.
3 That person is like a tree[f] planted by streams of water,[g]
which yields its fruit[h] in season
and whose leaf does not wither—
whatever they do prospers.[i]

4 Not so the wicked!
They are like chaff[j]
that the wind blows away.
5 Therefore the wicked will not stand[k] in the judgment,[l]
nor sinners in the assembly of the righteous.

1:1 Success—Psalm 1 sets the tone for the whole Book of Psalms. It contrasts the ways of life of the blessed man and the wicked man. Being blessed or successful is not a once for all time, dramatic event, but rather a lifetime of choosing to follow God and His commandments. Success happens when we move from grudging acceptance to enthusiastic delight in absorbing and then following God's laws and mandates. Nothing provides more resources. No motivational speakers will set us on a better course. No degrees will give us more of a life-changing education.

At first glance this kind of lifestyle may not look like the most exciting way to live. We can go through life, plodding along this way, without anybody even noticing. It's a lifestyle that doesn't fill up trophy cases or result in monuments being created. It can, however, end with "Well done, good and faithful servant" from our Lord. The excitement is in the results of being in a position to help family and friends grow. Success comes from being in a relationship with God that means fruitfulness by His definition.

1:1 *Blessed is the one.* Hebrew wisdom literature and poetry is filled with descriptions of two favorite characters: "the righteous man" and "wisdom" (often personified as "she"). In this context, "the righteous man" is a literary tool used to represent those who love and desire to please God, rather than an actual individual.

1:2 *meditates.* Biblical meditation is focusing the mind on Scripture or the attributes and actions of God.

1:3 *prospers.* This is not a guarantee of the future financial worth of the righteous; rather, the righteous person is always useful and productive to the Lord.

1:1 [a] Pr 4:14 [b] Ps 26:4; Jer 15:17 **1:2** [c] Ps 119:16, 35 [d] Ps 119:1 [e] Jos 1:8 **1:3** [f] Ps 128:3 [g] Jer 17:8 [h] Eze 47:12 [i] Ge 39:3 **1:4** [j] Job 21:18; Isa 17:13 **1:5** [k] Ps 5:5 [l] Ps 9:7-8, 16

6 For the LORD watches over[m] the way of
the righteous,
but the way of the wicked leads to
destruction.[n]

Psalm 2

1 Why do the nations conspire[a]
and the peoples plot[o] in vain?
2 The kings[p] of the earth rise up
and the rulers band together
against the LORD and against his
anointed,[q] saying,
3 "Let us break their chains
and throw off their shackles."[r]

4 The One enthroned in heaven laughs;[s]
the Lord scoffs at them.
5 He rebukes them in his anger
and terrifies them in his wrath,[t]
saying,
6 "I have installed my king
on Zion, my holy mountain."

7 I will proclaim the LORD's decree:

He said to me, "You are my son;
today I have become your father.[u]
8 Ask me,
and I will make the nations your
inheritance,
the ends of the earth[v] your possession.
9 You will break them with a rod of iron[b];[w]
you will dash them to pieces[x] like
pottery.[y]"

10 Therefore, you kings, be wise;
be warned, you rulers of the earth.
11 Serve the LORD with fear
and celebrate his rule[z] with
trembling.[a]
12 Kiss his son,[b] or he will be angry
and your way will lead to your
destruction,
for his wrath[c] can flare up in a moment.
Blessed are all who take refuge[d] in
him.

Psalm 3[c]

A psalm of David. When he fled from his son Absalom.[e]

1 LORD, how many are my foes!
How many rise up against me!
2 Many are saying of me,
"God will not deliver him.[f]"[d]

3 But you, LORD, are a shield[g] around me,
my glory, the One who lifts my head
high.[h]
4 I call out to the LORD,
and he answers me from his holy
mountain.[i]

5 I lie down and sleep;[j]
I wake again, because the LORD
sustains me.
6 I will not fear[k] though tens of thousands
assail me on every side.

7 Arise,[l] LORD!
Deliver me,[m] my God!
Strike[n] all my enemies on the jaw;
break the teeth[o] of the wicked.

8 From the LORD comes deliverance.[p]
May your blessing be on your people.

Psalm 4[e]

For the director of music. With stringed instruments. A psalm of David.

1 Answer me when I call to you,
my righteous God.
Give me relief from my distress;
have mercy[q] on me and hear my
prayer.[r]

---

[a] *1* Hebrew; Septuagint *rage* [b] *9* Or *will rule them with an iron scepter* (see Septuagint and Syriac) [c] In Hebrew texts 3:1-8 is numbered 3:2-9. [d] *2* The Hebrew has *Selah* (a word of uncertain meaning) here and at the end of verses 4 and 8. [e] In Hebrew texts 4:1-8 is numbered 4:2-9.

1:6 *watches over the way.* The verb "watches" in this context refers not just to God's awareness, but to an intimate, personal knowledge (101:4). God is intimately involved with the way of the righteous, but has no connection with the way of the ungodly, except in judgment (146:9).

2:1 *Why do the nations conspire.* David, the human author of this psalm (Acts 4:24–26), was probably referring to the nations that confronted him and his legitimate heirs to the throne of Israel. But the Davidic kings were mere shadows of the coming great King, the Savior Jesus. Consequently, in a larger sense, this verse refers to any attack on Jesus and His divine kingdom. This assault occurred in its most dramatic form at the cross, but resistance to God's kingdom has continued.

2:12 *Kiss his son.* All peoples are presented with a clear choice. They can either love and respect the Lord's anointed, and so experience His great blessing, or they can refuse to submit, and incur God's wrath.

3:title *When he fled from his son Absalom.* The history behind this psalm is recorded in 1 Samuel 15.

3:7 *Strike ... on the jaw.* In the poetic imagery that David uses, his enemies are like powerful beasts whose strength is in their jaws and whose terror is in their teeth. God's strike at the source of their strength means that they are no longer a threat.

4:1 *my righteous God.* This phrase can also be translated "O my righteous God." It has two meanings: only God is righteous, and all of a person's righteousness is found in Him alone.

1:6 [m] Ps 37:18; 2Ti 2:19 [n] Ps 9:6 **2:1** [o] Ps 21:11 **2:2** [p] Ps 48:4 [q] Ps 74:18,23; Jn 1:41; Ac 4:25-26* **2:3** [r] Jer 5:5 **2:4** [s] Ps 37:13; 59:8; Pr 1:26 **2:5** [t] Ps 21:9; 78:49-50 **2:7** [u] Ac 13:33*; Heb 1:5* **2:8** [v] Ps 22:27 **2:9** [w] Rev 12:5 [x] Ps 89:23 [y] Rev 2:27* **2:11** [z] Heb 12:28 [a] Ps 119:119-120 **2:12** [b] Jn 5:23 [c] Rev 6:16 [d] Ps 34:8; Ro 9:33 **3:Title** [e] 2Sa 15:14 **3:2** [f] Ps 71:11 **3:3** [g] Ge 15:1; Ps 28:7 [h] Ps 27:6 **3:4** [i] Ps 2:6 **3:5** [j] Lev 26:6; Pr 3:24 **3:6** [k] Ps 27:3 **3:7** [l] Ps 7:6 [m] Ps 6:4 [n] Job 16:10 [o] Ps 58:6 **3:8** [p] Isa 43:3,11 **4:1** [q] Ps 25:16 [r] Ps 17:6

2 How long will you people turn my glory
into shame?
How long will you love delusions and
seek false gods[a]?[b][s]
3 Know that the LORD has set apart his
faithful servant[t] for himself;
the LORD hears[u] when I call to him.

4 Tremble and[c] do not sin;[v]
when you are on your beds,[w]
search your hearts and be silent.
5 Offer the sacrifices of the righteous
and trust in the LORD.[x]

6 Many, LORD, are asking, "Who will
bring us prosperity?"
Let the light of your face shine on us.[y]
7 Fill my heart[z] with joy[a]
when their grain and new wine
abound.

8 In peace I will lie down and sleep,[b]
for you alone, LORD,
make me dwell in safety.[c]

Psalm 5[d]

*For the director of music. For pipes.
A psalm of David.*

1 Listen to my words, LORD,
consider my lament.
2 Hear my cry for help,[d]
my King and my God,[e]
for to you I pray.

3 In the morning,[f] LORD, you hear my
voice;
in the morning I lay my requests
before you
and wait expectantly.
4 For you are not a God who is pleased
with wickedness;
with you, evil people[g] are not
welcome.
5 The arrogant[h] cannot stand[i]
in your presence.
You hate[j] all who do wrong;
6 you destroy those who tell lies.[k]
The bloodthirsty and deceitful
you, LORD, detest.
7 But I, by your great love,
can come into your house;
in reverence I bow down[l]
toward your holy temple.

8 Lead me, LORD, in your righteousness[m]
because of my enemies—
make your way straight[n] before me.
9 Not a word from their mouth can be
trusted;
their heart is filled with malice.
Their throat is an open grave;[o]
with their tongues they tell lies.[p]
10 Declare them guilty, O God!
Let their intrigues be their downfall.
Banish them for their many sins,[q]
for they have rebelled[r] against you.
11 But let all who take refuge in you be glad;
let them ever sing for joy.[s]
Spread your protection over them,
that those who love your name[t] may
rejoice in you.[u]

12 Surely, LORD, you bless the righteous;
you surround them[v] with your favor
as with a shield.

Psalm 6[e]

*For the director of music. With stringed
instruments. According to* sheminith.[f]
A psalm of David.

1 LORD, do not rebuke me in your anger[w]
or discipline me in your wrath.
2 Have mercy on me, LORD, for I am faint;
heal me,[x] LORD, for my bones are in
agony.[y]
3 My soul is in deep anguish.[z]
How long,[a] LORD, how long?

4 Turn, LORD, and deliver me;
save me because of your unfailing
love.[b]

---

[a] 2 Or *seek lies* [b] 2 The Hebrew has *Selah* (a word of uncertain meaning) here and at the end of verse 4. [c] 4 Or *In your anger* (see Septuagint) [d] In Hebrew texts 5:1-12 is numbered 5:2-13. [e] In Hebrew texts 6:1-10 is numbered 6:2-11. [f] Title: Probably a musical term

---

4:4 *Tremble and do not sin.* These words are cited by Paul in the New Testament (Eph. 4:26). This is a good description of what righteous indignation should look like.

4:7 *their grain and new wine.* The joy God gives transcends the joy of the harvest. Agricultural produce, the result of abundant rain on fertile soil, was a blessing of God on His people. But there is something greater than full barns and overflowing cisterns—the joy of God's presence.

5:7 *your holy temple.* David was a leader in reforming the worship of God in Jerusalem, and he established a structure for the worship that would take place in the temple to be built by Solomon. David uses the word "temple" in anticipation of the future glorious building; all later generations of Hebrew worshipers would understand their own worship better because of the use of this word in these psalms.

5:9 *Their throat is an open grave.* Paul echoed the words of these verses in describing the depravity of all people (Rom. 3:13).

6:4 *because of your unfailing love.* Perhaps the most significant single term in the Hebrew text regarding the character of God is the word rendered "unfailing love" here. The Hebrew word describes what some prefer to call the "loyal love" or "lovingkindness" of God.

4:2 [s] Ps 31:6 **4:3** [t] Ps 31:23 [u] Ps 6:8 **4:4** [v] Eph 4:26* [w] Ps 77:6 **4:5** [x] Dt 33:19; Ps 37:3 **4:6** [y] Nu 6:25 **4:7** [z] Ac 14:17 [a] Isa 9:3 **4:8** [b] Ps 3:5 [c] Lev 25:18 **5:2** [d] Ps 3:4 [e] Ps 84:3 **5:3** [f] Ps 88:13 **5:4** [g] Ps 11:5; 92:15 **5:5** [h] Ps 73:3 [i] Ps 1:5 [j] Ps 11:5 **5:6** [k] Ps 55:23; Rev 21:8 **5:7** [l] Ps 138:2 **5:8** [m] Ps 31:1 [n] Ps 27:11 **5:9** [o] Lk 11:44 [p] Ro 3:13* **5:10** [q] Ps 9:16 [r] Ps 107:11 **5:11** [s] Ps 2:12 [t] Ps 69:36 [u] Isa 65:13 **5:12** [v] Ps 32:7 **6:1** [w] Ps 38:1 **6:2** [x] Hos 6:1 [y] Ps 22:14; 31:10 **6:3** [z] Jn 12:27 [a] Ps 90:13 **6:4** [b] Ps 17:13

5 Among the dead no one proclaims your
name.
Who praises you from the grave?[c]
6 I am worn out[d] from my groaning.
All night long I flood my bed with weeping
and drench my couch with tears.[e]
7 My eyes grow weak[f] with sorrow;
they fail because of all my foes.

8 Away from me,[g] all you who do evil,[h]
for the LORD has heard my weeping.
9 The LORD has heard my cry for mercy;[i]
the LORD accepts my prayer.
10 All my enemies will be overwhelmed
with shame and anguish;
they will turn back and suddenly be
put to shame.[j]

Psalm 7[a]

A shiggaion[b] of David, which he sang to the LORD concerning Cush, a Benjamite.

1 LORD my God, I take refuge in you;
save and deliver me from all who
pursue me,[k]
2 or they will tear me apart like a lion[l]
and rip me to pieces with no one to
rescue[m] me.

3 LORD my God, if I have done this
and there is guilt on my hands[n]—
4 if I have repaid my ally with evil
or without cause have robbed my
foe—
5 then let my enemy pursue and
overtake me;
let him trample my life to the ground
and make me sleep in the dust.[c]

6 Arise,[o] LORD, in your anger;
rise up against the rage of my
enemies.[p]
Awake,[q] my God; decree justice.
7 Let the assembled peoples gather
around you,
while you sit enthroned over them on
high.
8 Let the LORD judge the peoples.
Vindicate me, LORD, according to my
righteousness,[r]
according to my integrity, O Most
High.
9 Bring to an end the violence of the
wicked
and make the righteous secure—[s]
you, the righteous God[t]
who probes minds and hearts.[u]
10 My shield[d] is God Most High,
who saves the upright in heart.[v]
11 God is a righteous judge,[w]
a God who displays his wrath every
day.
12 If he does not relent,
he[e] will sharpen his sword;[x]
he will bend and string his bow.
13 He has prepared his deadly weapons;
he makes ready his flaming arrows.
14 Whoever is pregnant with evil
conceives trouble and gives birth[y] to
disillusionment.
15 Whoever digs a hole and scoops it out
falls into the pit they have made.[z]
16 The trouble they cause recoils on them;
their violence comes down on their
own heads.

17 I will give thanks to the LORD because
of his righteousness;[a]
I will sing the praises[b] of the name of
the LORD Most High.

Psalm 8[f]

For the director of music. According to gittith.[g] *A psalm of David.*

1 LORD, our Lord,
how majestic is your name in all the
earth!

You have set your glory
in the heavens.[c]
2 Through the praise of children and
infants
you have established a stronghold[d]
against your enemies,
to silence the foe[e] and the avenger.

---

[a] In Hebrew texts 7:1-17 is numbered 7:2-18.
[b] Title: Probably a literary or musical term
[c] *5* The Hebrew has *Selah* (a word of uncertain meaning) here. [d] *10* Or *sovereign* [e] *12* Or *If anyone does not repent, / God* [f] In Hebrew texts 8:1-9 is numbered 8:2-10. [g] Title: Probably a musical term

---

6:6–7 *groaning.* The sighing and tears of this psalm are to be understood as responses to the psalmist's physical afflictions experienced at the hands of his enemies, and also to reflect the seriousness with which he felt the weight and burden of his own sinfulness. All affliction is not directly related to sin; however, it is an occasion when a spiritual accounting with God should be taken and in which the believer should be inclined to strengthen himself in God.
7:1 *I take refuge in you.* The dominant message in the Book of Psalms is twofold: (1) God is good, and (2) life is difficult. The life of faith is lived between these two realities.
7:12 *If he does not relent.* God abhors sin, but He is also merciful, giving people the opportunity to repent before they are punished for their wickedness.

7:14 *conceives trouble.* These words are echoed in the apostle James' description of the progress of sin (James 1:14–15).

6:5 [c] Ps 30:9; 88:10-12; Ecc 9:10; Isa 38:18 **6:6** [d] Ps 69:3 [e] Ps 42:3 **6:7** [f] Ps 31:9 **6:8** [g] Ps 119:115 [h] Mt 7:23; Lk 13:27 **6:9** [i] Ps 116:1 **6:10** [j] Ps 71:24; 73:19 **7:1** [k] Ps 31:15 **7:2** [l] Isa 38:13 [m] Ps 50:22 **7:3** [n] 1Sa 24:11; Isa 59:3 **7:6** [o] Ps 94:2 [p] Ps 138:7 [q] Ps 44:23 **7:8** [r] Ps 18:20; 96:13 **7:9** [s] Ps 37:23 [t] Jer 11:20 [u] 1Ch 28:9; Ps 26:2; Rev 2:23 **7:10** [v] Ps 125:4 **7:11** [w] Ps 50:6 **7:12** [x] Dt 32:41 **7:14** [y] Job 15:35; Isa 59:4; Jas 1:15 **7:15** [z] Job 4:8 **7:17** [a] Ps 71:15-16 [b] Ps 9:2 **8:1** [c] Ps 57:5; 113:4; 148:13 **8:2** [d] Mt 21:16* [e] Ps 44:16; 1Co 1:27

3 When I consider your heavens,[f]
the work of your fingers,
the moon and the stars,[g]
which you have set in place,
4 what is mankind that you are mindful
of them,
human beings that you care for
them?[a][h]

5 You have made them[b] a little lower than
the angels[c]
and crowned them[b] with glory and
honor.[i]
6 You made them rulers[j] over the works
of your hands;
you put everything under their[d]
feet:[k]
7 all flocks and herds,
and the animals of the wild,
8 the birds in the sky,
and the fish in the sea,
all that swim the paths of the seas.

9 LORD, our Lord,
how majestic is your name in all the
earth![l]

Psalm 9[e,f]

For the director of music. To the tune of "The Death of the Son." A psalm of David.

1 I will give thanks to you, LORD, with all
my heart;[m]
I will tell of all your wonderful
deeds.[n]
2 I will be glad and rejoice[o] in you;
I will sing the praises of your name,[p]
O Most High.

3 My enemies turn back;
they stumble and perish before you.
4 For you have upheld my right and my
cause,[q]
sitting enthroned as the righteous
judge.[r]
5 You have rebuked the nations and
destroyed the wicked;
you have blotted out their name[s] for
ever and ever.
6 Endless ruin has overtaken my
enemies,
you have uprooted their cities;
even the memory of them[t] has
perished.

7 The LORD reigns forever;
he has established his throne[u] for
judgment.
8 He rules the world in righteousness[v]
and judges the peoples with equity.
9 The LORD is a refuge for the oppressed,
a stronghold in times of trouble.[w]
10 Those who know your name[x] trust in
you,
for you, LORD, have never forsaken[y]
those who seek you.

11 Sing the praises of the LORD, enthroned
in Zion;[z]
proclaim among the nations[a] what he
has done.[b]
12 For he who avenges blood[c] remembers;
he does not ignore the cries of the
afflicted.

13 LORD, see how my enemies[d]
persecute me!
Have mercy and lift me up from the
gates of death,
14 that I may declare your praises[e]
in the gates of Daughter Zion,
and there rejoice in your salvation.[f]

---

[a] 4 Or *what is a human being that you are mindful of him, / a son of man that you care for him?* [b] 5 Or *him* [c] 5 Or *than God* [d] 6 Or *made him ruler . . . ; / . . . his* [e] Psalms 9 and 10 may originally have been a single acrostic poem in which alternating lines began with the successive letters of the Hebrew alphabet. In the Septuagint they constitute one psalm. [f] In Hebrew texts 9:1-20 is numbered 9:2-21.

8:5 *a little lower than the angels.* Mankind stands at the summit of God's creation. The Septuagint, an ancient Greek translation of the Old Testament, translates the Hebrew word meaning "God" (*elohim*) as "angels." The author of Hebrews bases his argument in 2:5 – 9 on this translation, and both readings are true. God made man (human beings) in His own image, just a little lower than angels. God created human beings as majestic creatures who were to rule over His creation. In our fallen state, we are profoundly disfigured, a perversion of the majesty God intended. However, Jesus restores those who put their trust in Him. In Christ, we recover majesty; in Him, we become the people that God wants us to be. Whenever we feel worthless, the words of this psalm should encourage us. We and all other human beings are valuable because God Himself created us in His own glorious image.

8:9 *LORD, our Lord.* The first word is the divine name Yahweh. The second Hebrew word translated "our Lord" speaks of the One in control: "our Sovereign."

9:1 *with all my heart.* Real praise is not half-hearted; it involves one's whole being (146:2). The words of these two verses are characteristic of the praise of God in the Psalms. He is to be praised for His works and His name. His name represents who He is; His works represent what He does.

9:10 *Those who know your name.* Those in Old Testament times who "knew the name of the Lord" were those who looked forward with saving faith to God's promised redemption, just as we look back with saving faith to the redemption accomplished.

9:14 *Daughter Zion.* This endearing term for Jerusalem indicated the close relationship and nurturing care God had for His people.

8:3 [f] Ps 89:11 [g] Ps 136:9 **8:4** [h] Job 7:17; Ps 144:3; Heb 2:6 **8:5** [i] Ps 21:5; 103:4 **8:6** [j] Ge 1:28 [k] 1Co 15:25,27*; Eph 1:22; Heb 2:6-8* **8:9** [l] ver 1 **9:1** [m] Ps 86:12 [n] Ps 26:7 **9:2** [o] Ps 5:11 [p] Ps 92:1; 83:18 **9:4** [q] Ps 140:12 [r] 1Pe 2:23 **9:5** [s] Pr 10:7 **9:6** [t] Ps 34:16 **9:7** [u] Ps 89:14 **9:8** [v] Ps 96:13 **9:9** [w] Ps 32:7 **9:10** [x] Ps 91:14 [y] Ps 37:28 **9:11** [z] Ps 76:2 [a] Ps 107:22 [b] Ps 105:1 **9:12** [c] Ge 9:5 **9:13** [d] Ps 38:19 **9:14** [e] Ps 106:2 [f] Ps 13:5; 51:12

15 The nations have fallen into the pit they have dug;[g]
their feet are caught in the net they have hidden.[h]
16 The LORD is known by his acts of justice;
the wicked are ensnared by the work of their hands.[a]
17 The wicked go down to the realm of the dead,[i]
all the nations that forget God.[j]
18 But God will never forget the needy;
the hope[k] of the afflicted[l] will never perish.
19 Arise, LORD, do not let mortals triumph;
let the nations be judged in your presence.
20 Strike them with terror, LORD;
let the nations know they are only mortal.[m]

Psalm 10[b]

1 Why, LORD, do you stand far off?[n]
Why do you hide yourself[o] in times of trouble?

2 In his arrogance the wicked man hunts down the weak,
who are caught in the schemes he devises.
3 He boasts[p] about the cravings of his heart;
he blesses the greedy and reviles the LORD.
4 In his pride the wicked man does not seek him;
in all his thoughts there is no room for God.[q]
5 His ways are always prosperous;
your laws are rejected by[c] him;
he sneers at all his enemies.
6 He says to himself, "Nothing will ever shake me."
He swears, "No one will ever do me harm."[r]

7 His mouth is full[s] of lies and threats;[t]
trouble and evil are under his tongue.[u]
8 He lies in wait near the villages;
from ambush he murders the innocent.[v]
His eyes watch in secret for his victims;
9 like a lion in cover he lies in wait.
He lies in wait to catch the helpless;[w]
he catches the helpless and drags them off in his net.
10 His victims are crushed, they collapse;
they fall under his strength.
11 He says to himself, "God will never notice;[x]
he covers his face and never sees."

12 Arise, LORD! Lift up your hand,[y] O God.
Do not forget the helpless.[z]
13 Why does the wicked man revile God?
Why does he say to himself,
"He won't call me to account"?
14 But you, God, see the trouble[a] of the afflicted;
you consider their grief and take it in hand.
The victims commit themselves to you;[b]
you are the helper[c] of the fatherless.
15 Break the arm of the wicked man;[d]
call the evildoer to account for his wickedness
that would not otherwise be found out.

16 The LORD is King for ever and ever;[e]
the nations[f] will perish from his land.
17 You, LORD, hear the desire of the afflicted;[g]
you encourage them, and you listen to their cry,
18 defending the fatherless[h] and the oppressed,[i]
so that mere earthly mortals will never again strike terror.

---

[a] *16* The Hebrew has *Higgaion* and *Selah* (words of uncertain meaning) here; *Selah* occurs also at the end of verse 20. [b] Psalms 9 and 10 may originally have been a single acrostic poem in which alternating lines began with the successive letters of the Hebrew alphabet. In the Septuagint they constitute one psalm. [c] *5* See Septuagint; Hebrew / *they are haughty, and your laws are far from*

10:1 *Why.* Psalm 10 is found as the second half of Psalm 9 in the Septuagint, the ancient Greek translation of the Hebrew Scripture.

10:3 *the greedy.* The verb "to boast," as translated here, is most commonly rendered "praise." The wicked offer praise, but not to the Lord. Rather, their hearts offer praise and worship to their own greedy desires. Their desires know no divinely set limits, since the wicked do not seek Him, but live with the conscious thought that there is no God (v. 4).

10:11 *God will never notice.* The wicked behave the way they do because they doubt that the Lord knows, cares, or will act. They want to believe that there will be no final judgment, so they feel free to do as they please. But the truth is that God will establish justice.

9:15 [g] Ps 7:15-16 [h] Ps 35:8; 57:6 **9:17** [i] Ps 49:14 [j] Job 8:13; Ps 50:22 **9:18** [k] Ps 71:5; Pr 23:18 [l] Ps 12:5 **9:20** [m] Ps 62:9; Isa 31:3 **10:1** [n] Ps 22:1, 11 [o] Ps 13:1 **10:3** [p] Ps 94:4 **10:4** [q] Ps 14:1; 36:1 **10:6** [r] Rev 18:7 **10:7** [s] Ro 3:14* [t] Ps 73:8 [u] Ps 140:3 **10:8** [v] Ps 94:6 **10:9** [w] Ps 17:12; 59:3; 140:5 **10:11** [x] Job 22:13 **10:12** [y] Ps 17:7; Mic 5:9 [z] Ps 9:12 **10:14** [a] Ps 22:11 [b] Ps 37:5 [c] Ps 68:5 **10:15** [d] Ps 37:17 **10:16** [e] Ps 29:10 [f] Dt 8:20 **10:17** [g] 1Ch 29:18; Ps 34:15 **10:18** [h] Ps 82:3 [i] Ps 9:9

Psalm 11

For the director of music. Of David.

1 In the LORD I take refuge.[j]
How then can you say to me:
"Flee like a bird to your mountain.
2 For look, the wicked bend their bows;
they set their arrows[k] against the strings
to shoot from the shadows
at the upright in heart.[l]
3 When the foundations[m] are being destroyed,
what can the righteous do?"

4 The LORD is in his holy temple;[n]
the LORD is on his heavenly throne.[o]
He observes everyone on earth;[p]
his eyes examine[q] them.
5 The LORD examines the righteous,[r]
but the wicked, those who love violence,
he hates with a passion.[s]
6 On the wicked he will rain
fiery coals and burning sulfur;[t]
a scorching wind[u] will be their lot.

7 For the LORD is righteous,[v]
he loves justice;[w]
the upright will see his face.[x]

Psalm 12[a]

For the director of music. According to sheminith.[b] *A psalm of David.*

1 Help, LORD, for no one is faithful anymore;[y]
those who are loyal have vanished from the human race.
2 Everyone lies to their neighbor;
they flatter with their lips
but harbor deception in their hearts.[z]

3 May the LORD silence all flattering lips
and every boastful tongue—[a]
4 those who say,
"By our tongues we will prevail;
our own lips will defend us—who is lord over us?"

5 "Because the poor are plundered and the needy groan,
I will now arise," says the LORD.
"I will protect them[b] from those who malign them."
6 And the words of the LORD are flawless,[c]
like silver purified in a crucible,
like gold[c] refined seven times.

7 You, LORD, will keep the needy safe
and will protect us forever from the wicked,[d]
8 who freely strut[e] about
when what is vile is honored by the human race.

Psalm 13[d]

For the director of music. A psalm of David.

1 How long, LORD? Will you forget me forever?
How long will you hide your face[f] from me?
2 How long must I wrestle with my thoughts[g]
and day after day have sorrow in my heart?
How long will my enemy triumph over me?[h]

3 Look on me and answer,[i] LORD my God.
Give light to my eyes,[j] or I will sleep in death,[k]
4 and my enemy will say, "I have overcome him,[l]"
and my foes will rejoice when I fall.

5 But I trust in your unfailing love;[m]
my heart rejoices in your salvation.[n]
6 I will sing[o] the LORD's praise,
for he has been good to me.

---

[a] In Hebrew texts 12:1-8 is numbered 12:2-9.
[b] Title: Probably a musical term
[c] 6 Probable reading of the original Hebrew text; Masoretic Text *earth*
[d] In Hebrew texts 13:1-6 is numbered 13:2-6.

11:1 *In the LORD I take refuge.* In contrast to the surrounding psalms of lament (9; 10; 12), this psalm expresses great trust in the Almighty Lord.
11:3 *When the foundations are being destroyed.* The wicked may taunt, but in fact the foundations are not destroyed and will never be.
11:5 *The LORD examines.* Undergoing trials and suffering is not necessarily a mark of sin or of God's disfavor. Such tests will show the true allegiance of our hearts.
12:2 *lies.* The very foundation of a nation is undermined when falsehood prevails. Every aspect of life—home, business, social life—is based on truth. Falsehood breeds suspicion and distrust, which will destroy the very fabric of society and civilization.
12:6 *words ... are flawless.* In contrast to the idle words of the wicked, the words of God are altogether trustworthy. The eternal and steadfast nature of the Lord Himself stands behind His words. He will establish justice just as He has promised to David (v. 5).
13:1 *How long, LORD?* The Lord allows David to pour out his anxiety before Him. But by the end of David's prayer, the Lord has granted him a correct perspective on his situation. David's only option is to trust in the sovereign mercy of his loving God.
13:5 *your unfailing love.* This word refers to God's loyal love or loving-kindness, His faithfulness to His commitment to take care of His people.

11:1 [j] Ps 56:11 **11:2** [k] Ps 7:13 [l] Ps 64:3-4 **11:3** [m] Ps 82:5 **11:4** [n] Ps 18:6 [o] Ps 103:19 [p] Ps 33:13 [q] Ps 34:15-16 **11:5** [r] Ge 22:1; Jas 1:12 [s] Ps 5:5 **11:6** [t] Eze 38:22 [u] Jer 4:11-12 **11:7** [v] Ps 7:9, 11; 45:7 [w] Ps 33:5 [x] Ps 17:15 **12:1** [y] Isa 57:1 **12:2** [z] Ps 10:7; 41:6; 55:21; Ro 16:18 **12:3** [a] Da 7:8; Rev 13:5 **12:5** [b] Ps 10:18; 34:6 **12:6** [c] 2Sa 22:31; Ps 18:30; Pr 30:5 **12:7** [d] Ps 37:28 **12:8** [e] Ps 55:10-11 **13:1** [f] Job 13:24; Ps 44:24 **13:2** [g] Ps 42:4 [h] Ps 42:9 **13:3** [i] Ps 5:1 [j] Ezr 9:8 [k] Jer 51:39 **13:4** [l] Ps 25:2 **13:5** [m] Ps 52:8 [n] Ps 9:14 **13:6** [o] Ps 116:7

Psalm 14

For the director of music. Of David.

1 The fool[a] says in his heart,
"There is no God."[p]
They are corrupt, their deeds are vile;
there is no one who does good.

2 The LORD looks down from heaven[q]
on all mankind
to see if there are any who understand,[r]
any who seek God.
3 All have turned away, all have become
corrupt;[s]
there is no one who does good,[t]
not even one.[u]

4 Do all these evildoers know nothing?[v]

They devour my people[w] as though
eating bread;
they never call on the LORD.[x]
5 But there they are, overwhelmed with
dread,
for God is present in the company of
the righteous.
6 You evildoers frustrate the plans of the
poor,
but the LORD is their refuge.[y]

7 Oh, that salvation for Israel would come
out of Zion!
When the LORD restores[z] his
people,
let Jacob rejoice and Israel be glad!

Psalm 15

A psalm of David.

1 LORD, who may dwell in your sacred
tent?[a]
Who may live on your holy
mountain?[b]

2 The one whose walk is blameless,
who does what is righteous,
who speaks the truth[c] from their
heart;
3 whose tongue utters no slander,[d]
who does no wrong to a neighbor,
and casts no slur on others;
4 who despises a vile person
but honors[e] those who fear the LORD;
who keeps an oath[f] even when it hurts,
and does not change their mind;
5 who lends money to the poor without
interest;[g]
who does not accept a bribe[h] against
the innocent.

Whoever does these things
will never be shaken.[i]

Psalm 16

A miktam[b] of David.

1 Keep me safe,[j] my God,
for in you I take refuge.[k]

2 I say to the LORD, "You are my Lord;
apart from you I have no good thing."[l]
3 I say of the holy people who are in the
land,[m]
"They are the noble ones in whom is
all my delight."
4 Those who run after other gods[n] will
suffer[o] more and more.
I will not pour out libations of blood
to such gods
or take up their names[p] on my lips.
5 LORD, you alone are my portion[q] and
my cup;[r]
you make my lot secure.
6 The boundary lines have fallen for me
in pleasant places;
surely I have a delightful
inheritance.[s]
7 I will praise the LORD, who
counsels me;[t]
even at night[u] my heart instructs me.

---

a 1 The Hebrew words rendered *fool* in Psalms denote one who is morally deficient. *b* Title: Probably a literary or musical term

---

14:1 *fool.* This word does not refer to mental inability, but to moral and spiritual insensitivity. A fool is one who lives a life of "practical atheism," the view that if even there is a God, it really does not matter to one's life.

14:4 *know nothing.* The wicked lack knowledge of God's truth. Although people may be brilliant in their chosen fields, they can still be morally insensitive and spiritually closed to the issues that have eternal consequences.

15:1 *who may dwell in your sacred tent?* No one except Jesus the Messiah is righteous enough to approach God. But there have always been those who stand before God as forgiven sinners, whose righteousness comes as a gift from God. We may come boldly into God's presence because our sins have been covered by Christ's blood.

15:2 *The one whose walk is blameless, who does what is righteous.* The Lord commands us to be holy (1 Pet. 1:15–16), and He also gives us the power to become holy (2 Thess. 2:16–17).

16:5 *my portion.* This phrase refers to the Promised Land. God had given this inheritance to His people (Deut. 6:1–3). However, there was a greater inheritance for the Levites, who did not receive a share in the land (Num. 26:62); their share of the inheritance was in the Lord. David had an ancestral inheritance in the land. As king, he also had extensive royal holdings. But he realized that no inheritance was greater than his relationship with Almighty God.

14:1 [p] Ps 10:4 **14:2** [q] Ps 33:13 [r] Ps 92:6 **14:3** [s] Ps 58:3 [t] Ps 143:2 [u] Ro 3:10-12* **14:4** [v] Ps 82:5 [w] Ps 27:2 [x] Ps 79:6; Isa 64:7 **14:6** [y] Ps 9:9; 40:17 **14:7** [z] Ps 53:6 **15:1** [a] Ps 27:5-6 [b] Ps 24:3-5 **15:2** [c] Ps 24:4; Zec 8:3, 16; Eph 4:25 **15:3** [d] Ex 23:1 **15:4** [e] Ac 28:10 [f] Jdg 11:35 **15:5** [g] Ex 22:25 [h] Ex 23:8; Dt 16:19 [i] 2Pe 1:10 **16:1** [j] Ps 17:8 [k] Ps 7:1 **16:2** [l] Ps 73:25 **16:3** [m] Ps 101:6 **16:4** [n] Ps 106:37-38 [o] Ps 32:10 [p] Ex 23:13 **16:5** [q] Ps 73:26 [r] Ps 23:5 **16:6** [s] Ps 78:55; Jer 3:19 **16:7** [t] Ps 73:24 [u] Ps 77:6

8 I keep my eyes always on the LORD.
With him at my right hand,[v] I will not be shaken.
9 Therefore my heart is glad[w] and my tongue rejoices;
my body also will rest secure,[x]
10 because you will not abandon me to the realm of the dead,
nor will you let your faithful[a] one see decay.[y]
11 You make known to me the path of life;[z]
you will fill me with joy in your presence,[a]
with eternal pleasures[b] at your right hand.

Psalm 17

A prayer of David.

1 Hear me, LORD, my plea is just;
listen to my cry.[c]
Hear my prayer—
it does not rise from deceitful lips.[d]
2 Let my vindication come from you;
may your eyes see what is right.
3 Though you probe my heart,
though you examine me at night and test me,[e]
you will find that I have planned no evil;[f]
my mouth has not transgressed.[g]
4 Though people tried to bribe me,
I have kept myself from the ways of the violent
through what your lips have commanded.
5 My steps have held to your paths;[h]
my feet have not stumbled.[i]
6 I call on you, my God, for you will answer me;[j]
turn your ear to me[k] and hear my prayer.[l]
7 Show me the wonders of your great love,[m]
you who save by your right hand[n]
those who take refuge in you from their foes.
8 Keep me as the apple of your eye;[o]
hide me in the shadow of your wings
9 from the wicked who are out to destroy me,
from my mortal enemies who surround me.[p]
10 They close up their callous hearts,[q]
and their mouths speak with arrogance.[r]
11 They have tracked me down, they now surround me,[s]
with eyes alert, to throw me to the ground.
12 They are like a lion[t] hungry for prey,
like a fierce lion crouching in cover.
13 Rise up, LORD, confront them, bring them down;[u]
with your sword rescue me from the wicked.
14 By your hand save me from such people, LORD,
from those of this world[v] whose reward is in this life.
May what you have stored up for the wicked fill their bellies;
may their children gorge themselves on it,
and may there be leftovers[w] for their little ones.
15 As for me, I will be vindicated and will see your face;
when I awake, I will be satisfied with seeing your likeness.[x]

a 10 Or *holy*

16:10 *realm of the dead.* Not much is known of the ancient Hebrew's concept of life after death. The "realm of the dead" seems to be a dreaded place, shrouded in mystery.

17:3 *probe my heart.* David knew that God had done what he was requesting even before he asked. That is, God knew David's needs and what was in his heart. David's prayer helped him to focus on the source of his strength and to reaffirm his determination to live a pure life.

17:4 God's Word Corrects—There are many symbols for God's Word that can be found in the Bible itself. It can be thought of as a mirror (James 1:23–25), a seed (1 Pet. 1:23), a lamp (Ps. 119:105), a sword (Eph. 6:17), and even food (Heb. 5:12–14). But the Bible also serves as a measuring rod that can be used as a standard against which to measure our beliefs.

God Himself sometimes uses His Word to correct us as he did with David. "Do good to your servant according to your word, LORD ... Before I was afflicted I went astray, but now I obey your word" (Ps. 119:65,67).

There are times when God's Word can correct believers when they are in honest and unintentional error. Aquila and Priscilla, a godly Christian couple, used the Scriptures to help a young preacher named Apollos (Acts 18:24–28). Paul does the same thing for some former disciples of John the Baptist that he met in the city of Ephesus (Acts 19:1–7)

17:14 *whose reward is in this life.* The wicked live their lives with only the pursuit of the pleasures of this world in mind. The righteous should not try to obtain what this life can offer, but instead pursue God and His ways.

17:15 *will see your face.* In the Old Testament there is no well-developed theology of heaven, yet there are times when the faith of the writer rises to utter statements of hope of resurrection and of life eternal with God. It would appear that such a view

16:8 [v] Ps 73:23 **16:9** [w] Ps 4:7; 30:11 [x] Ps 4:8 **16:10** [y] Ac 13:35* **16:11** [z] Mt 7:14 [a] Ac 2:25-28* [b] Ps 36:7-8 **17:1** [c] Ps 61:1 [d] Isa 29:13 **17:3** [e] Ps 26:2; 66:10 [f] Job 23:10; Jer 50:20 [g] Ps 39:1 **17:5** [h] Ps 44:18; 119:133 [i] Ps 18:36 **17:6** [j] Ps 86:7 [k] Ps 116:2 [l] Ps 88:2 **17:7** [m] Ps 31:21 [n] Ps 20:6 **17:8** [o] Dt 32:10 **17:9** [p] Ps 31:20; 109:3 **17:10** [q] Ps 73:7 [r] 1Sa 2:3 **17:11** [s] Ps 37:14; 88:17 **17:12** [t] Ps 7:2; 10:9 **17:13** [u] Ps 7:12; 22:20; 73:18 **17:14** [v] Lk 16:8 [w] Ps 73:3-7 **17:15** [x] Nu 12:8; Ps 4:6-7; 16:11; 1Jn 3:2

Psalm 18[a]

For the director of music. Of David the servant of the LORD. He sang to the LORD the words of this song when the LORD delivered him from the hand of all his enemies and from the hand of Saul. He said:

1 I love you, LORD, my strength.

2 The LORD is my rock,[y] my fortress and my deliverer;
my God is my rock, in whom I take refuge,
my shield[b][z] and the horn[c] of my salvation,[a] my stronghold.

3 I called to the LORD, who is worthy of praise,[b]
and I have been saved from my enemies.
4 The cords of death[c] entangled me;
the torrents[d] of destruction overwhelmed me.
5 The cords of the grave coiled around me;
the snares of death[e] confronted me.

6 In my distress I called to the LORD;
I cried to my God for help.
From his temple he heard my voice;[f]
my cry came before him, into his ears.
7 The earth trembled and quaked,[g]
and the foundations of the mountains shook;
they trembled because he was angry.[h]
8 Smoke rose from his nostrils;
consuming fire[i] came from his mouth,
burning coals blazed out of it.
9 He parted the heavens and came down;[j]
dark clouds were under his feet.
10 He mounted the cherubim[k] and flew;
he soared on the wings of the wind.[l]
11 He made darkness his covering,[m] his canopy around him—
the dark rain clouds of the sky.
12 Out of the brightness of his presence[n] clouds advanced,
with hailstones and bolts of lightning.[o]
13 The LORD thundered[p] from heaven;
the voice of the Most High resounded.[d]
14 He shot his arrows and scattered the enemy,
with great bolts of lightning he routed them.[q]
15 The valleys of the sea were exposed
and the foundations of the earth laid bare
at your rebuke,[r] LORD,
at the blast of breath from your nostrils.

16 He reached down from on high and took hold of me;
he drew me out of deep waters.[s]
17 He rescued me from my powerful enemy,
from my foes, who were too strong for me.[t]
18 They confronted me in the day of my disaster,
but the LORD was my support.[u]
19 He brought me out into a spacious place;[v]
he rescued me because he delighted in me.[w]

20 The LORD has dealt with me according to my righteousness;
according to the cleanness of my hands[x] he has rewarded me.
21 For I have kept the ways of the LORD;[y]
I am not guilty of turning[z] from my God.

[a] In Hebrew texts 18:1-50 is numbered 18:2-51.
[b] 2 Or *sovereign* [c] 2 *Horn* here symbolizes strength. [d] 13 Some Hebrew manuscripts and Septuagint (see also 2 Samuel 22:14); most Hebrew manuscripts *resounded, / amid hailstones and bolts of lightning*

was always a part of godly faith, even though dim in comparison with the later revelation through Christ. Both Psalms 16 and 17 are testimonies to a growing faith that entrance into God's presence would be the fruit of a relationship with God in this life. The afflictions on earth cause faith to look forward to a time after this life when one will behold God's face in righteousness, and faith in God will be vindicated by seeing God.

18:1 *I love you, LORD.* Twice in the Psalms the poet declares a love for God (116:1). Here an unusual word for love is used, referring to compassion as deep as a mother's love. The text for this psalm is also found in 2 Samuel 22.

18:2 *The LORD is my rock.* This is a particularly apt image for David, who many times had to hide in the mountains for security (1 Sam. 26:1,20).

18:5–6 *distress.* As the title of Psalm 18 indicates, this poem of praise was composed in the midst of very trying times (2 Sam. 22:1). Once again, David had become the object of Saul's uncontrollable rage; in his bouts of paranoia, Saul mistakenly suspected that David was laying the foundation of a revolt against his own royal position. How foolish David would have been had he said, "In my distress I took the matter into my own hands." Rather he said, "In my distress I called to the LORD." We have no other option when caught in our distressing situations. Otherwise we compound the suffering.

18:11–12 *darkness . . . brightness.* The references to darkness speak of the hiddenness of God. He cannot be completely understood by those whom He has created. The references to brightness speak of God's holiness.

18:2 [y] Ps 19:14 [z] Ps 59:11 [a] Ps 75:10 **18:3** [b] Ps 48:1
18:4 [c] Ps 116:3 [d] Ps 124:4 **18:5** [e] Ps 116:3
18:6 [f] Ps 34:15 **18:7** [g] Jdg 5:4 [h] Ps 68:7-8
18:8 [i] Ps 50:3 **18:9** [j] Ps 144:5 **18:10** [k] Ps 80:1
[l] Ps 104:3 **18:11** [m] Dt 4:11; Ps 97:2 **18:12** [n] Ps 104:2
[o] Ps 97:3 **18:13** [p] Ps 29:3; 104:7 **18:14** [q] Ps 144:6
18:15 [r] Ps 76:6; 106:9 **18:16** [s] Ps 144:7 **18:17** [t] Ps 35:10
18:18 [u] Ps 59:16 **18:19** [v] Ps 31:8 [w] Ps 118:5
18:20 [x] Ps 24:4 **18:21** [y] 2Ch 34:33 [z] Ps 119:102

22 All his laws are before me;[a]
I have not turned away from his
decrees.
23 I have been blameless before him
and have kept myself from sin.
24 The LORD has rewarded me according
to my righteousness,[b]
according to the cleanness of my
hands in his sight.

25 To the faithful[c] you show yourself
faithful,
to the blameless you show yourself
blameless,
26 to the pure you show yourself pure,
but to the devious you show yourself
shrewd.[d]
27 You save the humble
but bring low those whose eyes are
haughty.[e]
28 You, LORD, keep my lamp burning;
my God turns my darkness into
light.[f]
29 With your help[g] I can advance against a
troop*[a]*;
with my God I can scale a wall.

30 As for God, his way is perfect:[h]
The LORD's word is flawless;[i]
he shields all who take refuge[j] in
him.
31 For who is God besides the LORD?[k]
And who is the Rock[l] except our
God?
32 It is God who arms me with strength[m]
and keeps my way secure.
33 He makes my feet like the feet of a
deer;[n]
he causes me to stand on the heights.[o]
34 He trains my hands for battle;[p]
my arms can bend a bow of bronze.
35 You make your saving help my shield,
and your right hand sustains[q] me;
your help has made me great.
36 You provide a broad path for my feet,
so that my ankles do not give way.

37 I pursued my enemies[r] and overtook
them;
I did not turn back till they were
destroyed.
38 I crushed them so that they could not
rise;[s]
they fell beneath my feet.[t]
39 You armed me with strength for
battle;
you humbled my adversaries
before me.
40 You made my enemies turn their backs[u]
in flight,
and I destroyed[v] my foes.
41 They cried for help, but there was no
one to save them[w]—
to the LORD, but he did not answer.[x]
42 I beat them as fine as windblown dust;
I trampled them*[b]* like mud in the
streets.
43 You have delivered me from the attacks
of the people;
you have made me the head of
nations.[y]
People I did not know[z] now serve me,
44 foreigners[a] cower before me;
as soon as they hear of me, they
obey me.
45 They all lose heart;
they come trembling from their
strongholds.[b]

46 The LORD lives! Praise be to my Rock!
Exalted be God my Savior![c]
47 He is the God who avenges me,
who subdues nations[d] under me,
48 who saves[e] me from my enemies.
You exalted me above my foes;
from a violent man you rescued me.
49 Therefore I will praise you, LORD,
among the nations;
I will sing[f] the praises of your
name.[g]

50 He gives his king great victories;
he shows unfailing love to his
anointed,
to David[h] and to his descendants
forever.[i]

a *29* Or *can run through a barricade* *b* *42* Many Hebrew manuscripts, Septuagint, Syriac and Targum (see also 2 Samuel 22:43); Masoretic Text *I poured them out*

18:35 ***your saving help my shield.*** The use of battle armor as an image of God's provision for the righteous is found in both the Old and New Testaments (Eph. 6:10–20).

18:41 ***They cried . . . to the LORD.*** Apparently, in the extremes of battle, the enemies of David found no help from their gods, so they screamed aloud to David's God for deliverance. But God would not answer them. There is only one prayer from the wicked to which He gladly listens—the prayer of repentance.

18:43 ***head of nations.*** David gained his empire by the work of the Lord on his behalf. But David's empire was only a picture of the kingdom of God that will one day be governed by David's greater Son, the Lord Jesus.

18:49 ***among the nations.*** By proclaiming the victories of God to the Gentiles, David was calling for the nations to respond in faith. How fitting that Paul would cite this verse (or its parallel in 2 Sam. 22:50) in Romans 15:9 as an indicator of God's ongoing intention to bring His salvation to all people.

18:22 [a] Ps 119:30 **18:24** [b] 1Sa 26:23 **18:25** [c] 1Ki 8:32; Ps 62:12; Mt 5:7 **18:26** [d] Pr 3:34 **18:27** [e] Pr 6:17 **18:28** [f] Job 18:6; 29:3 **18:29** [g] Heb 11:34 **18:30** [h] Dt 32:4; Rev 15:3 [i] Ps 12:6 [j] Ps 17:7 **18:31** [k] Dt 32:39; 86:8; Isa 45:5,6,14,18,21 [l] Dt 32:31; 1Sa 2:2 **18:32** [m] Isa 45:5 **18:33** [n] Hab 3:19 [o] Dt 32:13 **18:34** [p] Ps 144:1 **18:35** [q] Ps 119:116 **18:37** [r] Ps 37:20; 44:5 **18:38** [s] Ps 36:12 [t] Ps 47:3 **18:40** [u] Ps 21:12 [v] Ps 94:23 **18:41** [w] Ps 50:22 [x] Job 27:9; Pr 1:28 **18:43** [y] 2Sa 8:1-14 [z] Isa 52:15; 55:5 **18:44** [a] Ps 66:3 **18:45** [b] Mic 7:17 **18:46** [c] Ps 51:14 **18:47** [d] Ps 47:3 **18:48** [e] Ps 59:1 **18:49** [f] Ps 108:1 [g] Ro 15:9* **18:50** [h] Ps 144:10 [i] Ps 89:4

Psalm 19[a]

For the director of music. A psalm of David.

1 The heavens[j] declare[k] the glory of God;
the skies proclaim the work of his hands.
2 Day after day they pour forth speech;
night after night they reveal knowledge.[l]
3 They have no speech, they use no words;
no sound is heard from them.
4 Yet their voice[b] goes out into all the earth,
their words to the ends of the world.[m]
In the heavens God has pitched a tent[n]
for the sun.
5 It is like a bridegroom coming out of his chamber,
like a champion rejoicing to run his course.
6 It rises at one end of the heavens
and makes its circuit to the other;[o]
nothing is deprived of its warmth.

7 The law of the LORD is perfect,
refreshing the soul.[p]
The statutes of the LORD are trustworthy,[q]
making wise the simple.[r]
8 The precepts of the LORD are right,[s]
giving joy to the heart.
The commands of the LORD are radiant,
giving light to the eyes.
9 The fear of the LORD is pure,
enduring forever.
The decrees of the LORD are firm,
and all of them are righteous.[t]

10 They are more precious than gold,[u]
than much pure gold;
they are sweeter than honey,
than honey from the honeycomb.
11 By them your servant is warned;
in keeping them there is great reward.
12 But who can discern their own errors?
Forgive my hidden faults.[v]
13 Keep your servant also from willful sins;
may they not rule over me.
Then I will be blameless,
innocent of great transgression.

14 May these words of my mouth and this meditation of my heart
be pleasing[w] in your sight,
LORD, my Rock[x] and my Redeemer.[y]

Psalm 20[c]

For the director of music. A psalm of David.

1 May the LORD answer you when you are in distress;
may the name of the God of Jacob[z] protect you.[a]
2 May he send you help from the sanctuary[b]
and grant you support from Zion.
3 May he remember[c] all your sacrifices
and accept your burnt offerings.[d][d]
4 May he give you the desire of your heart[e]
and make all your plans succeed.
5 May we shout for joy over your victory
and lift up our banners[f] in the name of our God.

May the LORD grant all your requests.[g]

6 Now this I know:
The LORD gives victory to his anointed.[h]
He answers him from his heavenly sanctuary
with the victorious power of his right hand.

---

a In Hebrew texts 19:1-14 is numbered 19:2-15. *b* 4 Septuagint, Jerome and Syriac; Hebrew *measuring line* *c* In Hebrew texts 20:1-9 is numbered 20:2-10. *d* 3 The Hebrew has *Selah* (a word of uncertain meaning) here.

19:1 *The heavens declare.* All of creation reveals God's glory and majesty (Rom. 1:18–20).
19:4 *a tent for the sun.* In the ancient Middle East, the sun was often thought of as a god. In this poem, the sun is but the stunning workmanship of the Creator, glorifying the God who made it.
19:7–8 *The law of the LORD.* The world reveals God's glory, and the Word reveals His saving grace. God's law (or teaching) is described as "perfect," which is best understood here as "complete." This law needs no alteration in part or in whole. It has power to bring deep and radical change in the inner life or soul. It is God's great instrument in conversion (James 1:18; 1 Pet. 1:23). The Word of God is spoken of as God's "testimony" because it is His own instruction concerning His person and purpose. In Scripture, God testifies concerning Himself, His Son, and sinners. God's Word is sure (2 Pet. 1:19), and may be trusted because He is faithful (1 Tim. 1:15). To those wise in their own eyes, the truth of God is hidden (Matt. 11:25), but to the simple the Scriptures give wisdom that leads to salvation (2 Tim. 3:15).
19:14 *my Redeemer.* God is the One who purchases our freedom from any bondage or slavery. The principal meaning of the word is "defender of family rights."
20:5 *victory.* In the immediate context, victory is used to describe daily deliverance from the rigors of the battle and the victory over the enemy. But the Lord's deliverance of us from our spiritual troubles should prompt the same type of praise.
20:6 *his right hand.* This is a slogan that describes God's powerful deliverance of the Israelites from Egypt (17:7; 44:3; 118:16; Ex. 15:6).

19:1 [j] Isa 40:22 [k] Ps 50:6; Ro 1:19 **19:2** [l] Ps 74:16
19:4 [m] Ro 10:18* [n] Ps 104:2 **19:6** [o] Ps 113:3; Ecc 1:5
19:7 [p] Ps 23:3 [q] Ps 93:5; 111:7 [r] Ps 119:98-100
19:8 [s] Ps 12:6; 119:128 **19:9** [t] Ps 119:138, 142
19:10 [u] Pr 8:10 **19:12** [v] Ps 51:2; 90:8; 139:6
19:14 [w] Ps 104:34 [x] Ps 18:2 [y] Isa 47:4 **20:1** [z] Ps 46:7, 11
[a] Ps 91:14 **20:2** [b] Ps 3:4 **20:3** [c] Ac 10:4 [d] Ps 51:19
20:4 [e] Ps 21:2; 145:16, 19 **20:5** [f] Ps 9:14; 60:4 [g] 1Sa 1:17
20:6 [h] Ps 28:8; 41:11; Isa 58:9

[7]Some trust in chariots and some in
horses,[i]
but we trust in the name of the LORD
our God.[j]
[8]They are brought to their knees and fall,
but we rise up[k] and stand firm.[l]
[9]LORD, give victory to the king!
Answer us[m] when we call!

Psalm 21[a]

For the director of music. A psalm of David.

[1]The king rejoices in your strength, LORD.
How great is his joy in the victories
you give![n]
[2]You have granted him his heart's
desire[o]
and have not withheld the request of
his lips.[b]
[3]You came to greet him with rich
blessings
and placed a crown of pure gold[p] on
his head.
[4]He asked you for life, and you gave it to
him—
length of days, for ever and ever.[q]
[5]Through the victories[r] you gave, his
glory is great;
you have bestowed on him splendor
and majesty.
[6]Surely you have granted him unending
blessings
and made him glad with the joy[s] of
your presence.[t]
[7]For the king trusts in the LORD;
through the unfailing love of the
Most High
he will not be shaken.
[8]Your hand will lay hold[u] on all your
enemies;
your right hand will seize your foes.
[9]When you appear for battle,
you will burn them up as in a blazing
furnace.
The LORD will swallow them up in his
wrath,
and his fire will consume them.[v]
[10]You will destroy their descendants from
the earth,
their posterity from mankind.[w]
[11]Though they plot evil[x] against you
and devise wicked schemes,[y] they
cannot succeed.
[12]You will make them turn their backs[z]
when you aim at them with drawn
bow.
[13]Be exalted in your strength, LORD;
we will sing and praise your might.

Psalm 22[c]

For the director of music. To the tune of "The Doe of the Morning." A psalm of David.

[1]My God, my God, why have you
forsaken me?[a]
Why are you so far[b] from saving me,
so far from my cries of anguish?
[2]My God, I cry out by day, but you do not
answer,
by night,[c] but I find no rest.[d]
[3]Yet you are enthroned as the Holy One;[d]
you are the one Israel praises.[e][e]
[4]In you our ancestors put their trust;
they trusted and you delivered them.
[5]To you they cried out and were saved;
in you they trusted and were not put
to shame.[f]
[6]But I am a worm[g] and not a man,
scorned by everyone,[h] despised[i] by
the people.
[7]All who see me mock me;
they hurl insults,[j] shaking their
heads.[k]
[8]"He trusts in the LORD," they say,
"let the LORD rescue him.[l]
Let him deliver him,
since he delights[m] in him."
[9]Yet you brought me out of the womb;[n]
you made me trust in you, even at my
mother's breast.
[10]From birth[o] I was cast on you;
from my mother's womb you have
been my God.

---

a In Hebrew texts 21:1-13 is numbered 21:2-14. *b* 2 The Hebrew has *Selah* (a word of uncertain meaning) here. *c* In Hebrew texts 22:1-31 is numbered 22:2-32. *d* 2 Or *night, and am not silent* *e* 3 Or *Yet you are holy, / enthroned on the praises of Israel*

21:2 ***his heart's desire.*** The Lord gives people their aspirations when they are derived from a fundamental desire for God's honor and glory (20:4; 37:4; 145:19).
21:9 ***in his wrath.*** This may refer to any period of God's judgment, but compare to "the day of the LORD" (Joel 2:1; Zeph. 1:14).
22:1 ***My God, my God, why have you forsaken me?*** David used these words to express a painful sense of separation from God at a time of great trouble (38:21). These were the very words used by Christ while in agony on the cross (Matt. 27:46; Mark 15:34).
22:6 ***despised by the people.*** When David was at his lowest, his enemies ridiculed his faith in the Lord. These words also describe the experience of the Savior who endured the verbal abuse of His tormentors (Matt. 27:27–31,39–44).

20:7 [i] Ps 33:17; Isa 31:1 [j] 2Ch 32:8 **20:8** [k] Mic 7:8 [l] Ps 37:23 **20:9** [m] Ps 3:7; 17:6 **21:1** [n] Ps 59:16-17 **21:2** [o] Ps 37:4 **21:3** [p] 2Sa 12:30 **21:4** [q] Ps 61:5-6; 91:16; 133:3 **21:5** [r] Ps 18:50 **21:6** [s] Ps 43:4 [t] 1Ch 17:27 **21:8** [u] Isa 10:10 **21:9** [v] Ps 50:3; La 2:2; Mal 4:1 **21:10** [w] Dt 28:18; Ps 37:28 **21:11** [x] Ps 2:1 [y] Ps 10:2 **21:12** [z] Ps 7:12-13; 18:40 **22:1** [a] Mt 27:46*; Mk 15:34* [b] Ps 10:1 **22:2** [c] Ps 42:3 **22:3** [d] Ps 99:9 [e] Dt 10:21 **22:5** [f] Isa 49:23 **22:6** [g] Job 25:6; Isa 41:14 [h] Ps 31:11 [i] Isa 49:7; 53:3 **22:7** [j] Mt 27:39,44 [k] Mk 15:29 **22:8** [l] Ps 91:14 [m] Mt 27:43 **22:9** [n] Ps 71:6 **22:10** [o] Isa 46:3

11 Do not be far from me,
for trouble is near
and there is no one to help.[p]
12 Many bulls[q] surround me;
strong bulls of Bashan[r] encircle me.
13 Roaring lions[s] that tear their prey
open their mouths wide[t] against me.
14 I am poured out like water,
and all my bones are out of joint.[u]
My heart has turned to wax;
it has melted[v] within me.
15 My mouth[a] is dried up like a potsherd,
and my tongue sticks to the roof of
my mouth;[w]
you lay me in the dust[x] of death.
16 Dogs[y] surround me,
a pack of villains encircles me;
they pierce[bz] my hands and my feet.
17 All my bones are on display;
people stare[a] and gloat over me.[b]
18 They divide my clothes among them
and cast lots[c] for my garment.
19 But you, LORD, do not be far from me.
You are my strength; come quickly[d]
to help me.
20 Deliver me from the sword,
my precious life[e] from the power of
the dogs.
21 Rescue me from the mouth of the lions;
save me from the horns of the wild
oxen.
22 I will declare your name to my people;
in the assembly I will praise you.[f]
23 You who fear the LORD, praise him![g]
All you descendants of Jacob, honor
him!
Revere him,[h] all you descendants of
Israel!
24 For he has not despised or scorned
the suffering of the afflicted one;
he has not hidden his face[i] from him
but has listened to his cry for help.[j]
25 From you comes the theme of my praise
in the great assembly;[k]
before those who fear you[c] I will
fulfill my vows.[l]
26 The poor will eat[m] and be satisfied;
those who seek the LORD will praise
him—[n]
may your hearts live forever!
27 All the ends of the earth[o]
will remember and turn to the LORD,
and all the families of the nations
will bow down before him,[p]
28 for dominion belongs to the LORD[q]
and he rules over the nations.
29 All the rich[r] of the earth will feast and
worship;
all who go down to the dust[s] will
kneel before him—
those who cannot keep themselves
alive.
30 Posterity[t] will serve him;
future generations will be told about
the Lord.
31 They will proclaim his righteousness,
declaring to a people yet unborn:[u]
He has done it!

Psalm 23

A psalm of David.

1 The LORD is my shepherd,[v] I lack
nothing.[w]
2 He makes me lie down in green
pastures,
he leads me beside quiet waters,[x]
3 he refreshes my soul.[y]
He guides me along the right paths[z]
for his name's sake.
4 Even though I walk
through the darkest valley,[da]
I will fear no evil,[b]
for you are with me;[c]
your rod and your staff,
they comfort me.

---

[a] *15* Probable reading of the original Hebrew text; Masoretic Text *strength* [b] *16* Dead Sea Scrolls and some manuscripts of the Masoretic Text, Septuagint and Syriac; most manuscripts of the Masoretic Text *me, / like a lion* [c] *25* Hebrew *him* [d] *4* Or *the valley of the shadow of death*

22:15 *my tongue sticks to the roof of my mouth.* Jesus' words "I am thirsty" (John 19:28) also expressed the pain of terrible thirst.
22:16 *they pierce my hands and my feet.* This verse explicitly predicts the crucifixion of the Lord Jesus Christ. The words were a figure of speech for David, but they were literally true for Jesus.
22:18 *cast lots for my garment.* This text was directly fulfilled by the soldiers who gambled at the foot of the cross for the possession of Jesus' robe (Matt. 27:35).
22:27 *all the families of the nations.* This is speaking of the eventual spread of the gospel of redemption to the whole world, fulfilling God's promise to bless all nations through Abraham's descendants (Gen. 12:3).
23:1 *The LORD is my shepherd.* Even though the word "king" does not appear in it, this psalm is a description of what it means to be a good ruler. Moreover, the psalm prophetically speaks of Jesus. He is the Good Shepherd whose flock trusts in Him (John 10:1 – 18) and the King whose perfect rule will be established (Luke 23:2 – 3).
23:4 *through the darkest valley.* The awareness of our own mortality often comes with sickness,

22:11 [p] Ps 72:12 **22:12** [q] Ps 68:30 [r] Dt 32:14 **22:13** [s] Ps 17:12 [t] Ps 35:21 **22:14** [u] Ps 31:10 [v] Job 30:16; Da 5:6 **22:15** [w] Ps 38:10; Jn 19:28 [x] Ps 104:29 **22:16** [y] Ps 59:6 [z] Isa 53:5; Zec 12:10; Jn 19:34 **22:17** [a] Lk 23:35 [b] Lk 23:27 **22:18** [c] Mt 27:35*; Lk 23:34; Jn 19:24* **22:19** [d] Ps 70:5 **22:20** [e] Ps 35:17 **22:22** [f] Heb 2:12* **22:23** [g] Ps 86:12; 135:19 [h] Ps 33:8 **22:24** [i] Ps 69:17 [j] Heb 5:7 **22:25** [k] Ps 35:18 [l] Ecc 5:4 **22:26** [m] Ps 107:9 [n] Ps 40:16 **22:27** [o] Ps 2:8 [p] Ps 86:9 **22:28** [q] Ps 47:7-8 **22:29** [r] Ps 45:12 [s] Isa 26:19 **22:30** [t] Ps 102:28 **22:31** [u] Ps 78:6 **23:1** [v] Isa 40:11; Jn 10:11; 1Pe 2:25 [w] Php 4:19 **23:2** [x] Eze 34:14; Rev 7:17 **23:3** [y] Ps 19:7 [z] Ps 5:8; 85:13 **23:4** [a] Job 10:21-22 [b] Ps 3:6; 27:1 [c] Isa 43:2

5 You prepare a table before me
in the presence of my enemies.
You anoint my head with oil;[d]
my cup[e] overflows.
6 Surely your goodness and love will follow me
all the days of my life,
and I will dwell in the house of the LORD
forever.

Psalm 24

Of David. A psalm.

1 The earth is the LORD's,[f] and everything in it,
the world, and all who live in it;[g]
2 for he founded it on the seas
and established it on the waters.

3 Who may ascend the mountain[h] of the LORD?
Who may stand in his holy place?[i]
4 The one who has clean hands[j] and a pure heart,[k]
who does not trust in an idol
or swear by a false god.[a]

5 They will receive blessing from the LORD
and vindication from God their Savior.
6 Such is the generation of those who seek him,
who seek your face,[l] God of Jacob.[b,c]

7 Lift up your heads, you gates;[m]
be lifted up, you ancient doors,
that the King of glory[n] may come in.
8 Who is this King of glory?
The LORD strong and mighty,
the LORD mighty in battle.[o]
9 Lift up your heads, you gates;
lift them up, you ancient doors,
that the King of glory may come in.
10 Who is he, this King of glory?
The LORD Almighty—
he is the King of glory.

Psalm 25[d]

Of David.

1 In you, LORD my God,
I put my trust.[p]

2 I trust in you;[q]
do not let me be put to shame,
nor let my enemies triumph over me.
3 No one who hopes in you
will ever be put to shame,[r]
but shame will come on those
who are treacherous without cause.

4 Show me your ways, LORD,
teach me your paths.[s]
5 Guide me in your truth and teach me,
for you are God my Savior,
and my hope is in you all day long.
6 Remember, LORD, your great mercy and love,[t]
for they are from of old.
7 Do not remember the sins of my youth[u]
and my rebellious ways;
according to your love[v] remember me,
for you, LORD, are good.

8 Good and upright[w] is the LORD;
therefore he instructs[x] sinners in his ways.
9 He guides[y] the humble in what is right
and teaches them[z] his way.
10 All the ways of the LORD are loving and faithful[a]
toward those who keep the demands of his covenant.[b]
11 For the sake of your name,[c] LORD,
forgive my iniquity, though it is great.

---

[a] 4 Or *swear falsely* [b] 6 Two Hebrew manuscripts and Syriac (see also Septuagint); most Hebrew manuscripts *face, Jacob* [c] 6 The Hebrew has *Selah* (a word of uncertain meaning) here and at the end of verse 10. [d] This psalm is an acrostic poem, the verses of which begin with the successive letters of the Hebrew alphabet.

---

trials, and hardship. But the Lord our protector can lead us through these dark and difficult valleys to eternal life with Him. There is no need to fear death's power (1 Cor. 15:25–27). Our Lord has already traveled this road and come through the valley of darkness. Because He lives, we too shall live. Death is not our final destiny.

23:6 *the house of the LORD forever.* God's promise for the Israelites was not just for the enjoyment of this life in the land of promise; it was also for the full enjoyment of the life to come in His presence (16:9–11; 17:15; 49:15).

24:1 Affirming God's Ownership of the World—Whose world is this anyway? David, of course, who lived in the hills with the animals, had a firm answer. It is God's world. This statement should shape our thinking about a great deal of life. We should have a heightened sense of stewardship to care for God's creation. We should look to God more to understand what is important and what is not important. Seeing God's creation every day should help make praise and thanksgiving a way of life. It should also help us desire to understand God's redemptive acts in history and in our lives.

24:4 *clean hands and a pure heart.* God looks at a person's actions and also at the attitudes of the heart.

24:9 *that the King of glory may come in.* When Jesus came, the meaning of this ancient poem became clear (Matt. 21:1–10; Rev. 19:11–16).

25:3 *who hopes in you.* Waiting on the Lord is the equivalent of hoping in Him (25:5; 40:1).

25:7 *sins of my youth.* Both the sins of immaturity and the transgressions of adulthood need forgiveness (1 John 1:9).

23:5 [d] Ps 92:10 [e] Ps 16:5 **24:1** [f] Ex 9:29; Job 41:11; Ps 89:11 [g] 1Co 10:26* **24:3** [h] Ps 2:6 [i] Ps 15:1; 65:4 **24:4** [j] Job 17:9 [k] Mt 5:8 **24:6** [l] Ps 27:8 **24:7** [m] Isa 26:2 [n] Ps 97:6; 1Co 2:8 **24:8** [o] Ps 76:3-6 **25:1** [p] Ps 86:4 **25:2** [q] Ps 41:11 **25:3** [r] Isa 49:23 **25:4** [s] Ex 33:13 **25:6** [t] Ps 103:17; Isa 63:7, 15 **25:7** [u] Job 13:26; Jer 3:25 [v] Ps 51:1 **25:8** [w] Ps 92:15 [x] Ps 32:8 **25:9** [y] Ps 23:3 [z] Ps 27:11 **25:10** [a] Ps 40:11 [b] Ps 103:18 **25:11** [c] Ps 31:3; 79:9

12 Who, then, are those who fear the LORD?
He will instruct them in the ways[d]
they should choose.[a]
13 They will spend their days in
prosperity,[e]
and their descendants will inherit the
land.[f]
14 The LORD confides[g] in those who fear him;
he makes his covenant known[h] to
them.
15 My eyes are ever on the LORD,[i]
for only he will release my feet from
the snare.

16 Turn to me[j] and be gracious to me,
for I am lonely and afflicted.
17 Relieve the troubles of my heart
and free me from my anguish.[k]
18 Look on my affliction and my distress[l]
and take away all my sins.
19 See how numerous are my enemies[m]
and how fiercely they hate me!

20 Guard my life[n] and rescue me;
do not let me be put to shame,
for I take refuge in you.
21 May integrity[o] and uprightness
protect me,
because my hope, LORD,[b] is in you.

22 Deliver Israel,[p] O God,
from all their troubles!

Psalm 26

Of David.

1 Vindicate me, LORD,
for I have led a blameless life;[q]
I have trusted[r] in the LORD
and have not faltered.[s]
2 Test me,[t] LORD, and try me,
examine my heart and my mind;[u]
3 for I have always been mindful of your
unfailing love
and have lived[v] in reliance on your
faithfulness.

4 I do not sit[w] with the deceitful,
nor do I associate with hypocrites.
5 I abhor[x] the assembly of evildoers
and refuse to sit with the wicked.
6 I wash my hands in innocence,[y]
and go about your altar, LORD,
7 proclaiming aloud your praise
and telling of all your wonderful
deeds.[z]

8 LORD, I love[a] the house where you live,
the place where your glory dwells.
9 Do not take away my soul along with
sinners,
my life with those who are
bloodthirsty,[b]
10 in whose hands are wicked schemes,
whose right hands are full of bribes.[c]
11 I lead a blameless life;
deliver me[d] and be merciful to me.

12 My feet stand on level ground;[e]
in the great congregation[f] I will
praise the LORD.

Psalm 27

Of David.

1 The LORD is my light[g] and my
salvation[h]—
whom shall I fear?
The LORD is the stronghold of my life—
of whom shall I be afraid?[i]

2 When the wicked advance against me
to devour[c] me,
it is my enemies and my foes
who will stumble and fall.[j]
3 Though an army besiege me,
my heart will not fear;[k]
though war break out against me,
even then I will be confident.[l]

4 One thing[m] I ask from the LORD,
this only do I seek:
that I may dwell in the house of the LORD
all the days of my life,[n]
to gaze on the beauty of the LORD
and to seek him in his temple.

[a] 12 Or *ways he chooses* [b] 21 Septuagint; Hebrew does not have LORD. [c] 2 Or *slander*

25:14 *in those who fear him.* Those who fear the Lord pay attention to His instructions and thus learn the secrets of God's wisdom (111:10; Prov. 1:7; 3:32).
25:19 *they hate me.* This psalm is a prayer for forgiveness, instruction, and protection from the forces of darkness which are oppressing the writer. His most prominent trial is hostility from enemies. The animosity which the psalmist encountered was not primarily personal, but was the result of his identification with God's cause. Therefore, he could ask the Lord to look upon Him and vindicate him in the face of his afflictions. The writer's suffering had its roots in the origins of redemptive history (Gen. 3:15)—there would be enmity between the seed of the woman and the seed of the serpent, between the godly and the ungodly. Jesus also reminded his disciples that hatred directed against his servants on His account was to be expected (John 15:18–20).

26:3 *your unfailing love.* The loyal love (13:5) of God is the recurring focus of the Book of Psalms.
26:9 *Do not take away my soul.* On the basis of his protests of integrity (vv. 1–2), David prays for divine discrimination (4:3). God distinguishes those who have responded to His grace from those who have not.

25:12 [d] Ps 37:23 **25:13** [e] Pr 19:23 [f] Ps 37:11
25:14 [g] Pr 3:32 [h] Jn 7:17 **25:15** [i] Ps 141:8
25:16 [j] Ps 69:16 **25:17** [k] Ps 107:6 **25:18** [l] 2Sa 16:12
25:19 [m] Ps 3:1 **25:20** [n] Ps 86:2 **25:21** [o] Ps 41:12
25:22 [p] Ps 130:8 **26:1** [q] Ps 7:8; Pr 20:7 [r] Ps 28:7
[s] 2Ki 20:3; Heb 10:23 **26:2** [t] Ps 17:3 [u] Ps 7:9
26:3 [v] 2Ki 20:3 **26:4** [w] Ps 1:1 **26:5** [x] Ps 31:6; 139:21
26:6 [y] Ps 73:13 **26:7** [z] Ps 9:1 **26:8** [a] Ps 27:4
26:9 [b] Ps 28:3 **26:10** [c] 1Sa 8:3 **26:11** [d] Ps 69:18
26:12 [e] Ps 27:11; 40:2 [f] Ps 22:22 **27:1** [g] Isa 60:19
[h] Ex 15:2 [i] Ps 118:6 **27:2** [j] Ps 9:3; 14:4 **27:3** [k] Ps 3:6
[l] Job 4:6 **27:4** [m] Ps 90:17 [n] Ps 23:6; 26:8

5 For in the day of trouble
he will keep me safe in his dwelling;
he will hide me[o] in the shelter of his sacred tent
and set me high upon a rock.[p]
6 Then my head will be exalted[q]
above the enemies who surround me;
at his sacred tent I will sacrifice[r] with shouts of joy;
I will sing and make music to the LORD.

7 Hear my voice when I call, LORD;
be merciful to me and answer me.[s]
8 My heart says of you, "Seek his face!"
Your face, LORD, I will seek.
9 Do not hide your face[t] from me,
do not turn your servant away in anger;
you have been my helper.
Do not reject me or forsake me,
God my Savior.
10 Though my father and mother forsake me,
the LORD will receive me.
11 Teach me your way, LORD;
lead me in a straight path[u]
because of my oppressors.
12 Do not turn me over to the desire of my foes,
for false witnesses[v] rise up against me,
spouting malicious accusations.

13 I remain confident of this:
I will see the goodness of the LORD[w]
in the land of the living.[x]
14 Wait[y] for the LORD;
be strong and take heart
and wait for the LORD.

Psalm 28

Of David.

1 To you, LORD, I call;
you are my Rock,
do not turn a deaf ear to me.
For if you remain silent,[z]
I will be like those who go down to the pit.[a]
2 Hear my cry for mercy[b]
as I call to you for help,
as I lift up my hands
toward your Most Holy Place.[c]

3 Do not drag me away with the wicked,
with those who do evil,
who speak cordially with their neighbors
but harbor malice in their hearts.[d]
4 Repay them for their deeds
and for their evil work;
repay them for what their hands have done[e]
and bring back on them what they deserve.[f]

5 Because they have no regard for the deeds of the LORD
and what his hands have done,[g]
he will tear them down
and never build them up again.

6 Praise be to the LORD,
for he has heard my cry for mercy.
7 The LORD is my strength[h] and my shield;
my heart trusts[i] in him, and he helps me.
My heart leaps for joy,
and with my song I praise him.[j]

8 The LORD is the strength of his people,
a fortress of salvation for his anointed one.[k]
9 Save your people and bless your inheritance;[l]
be their shepherd[m] and carry them[n] forever.

Psalm 29

A psalm of David.

1 Ascribe to the LORD,[o] you heavenly beings,
ascribe to the LORD glory[p] and strength.
2 Ascribe to the LORD the glory due his name;
worship the LORD in the splendor of his[a] holiness.[q]

---

a 2 Or *LORD with the splendor of*

27:6 *sacrifice with shouts joy.* These are praise offerings that the believers bring to God to celebrate the blessings He gives them (Heb. 13:15).

27:14 *Wait for the LORD.* To wait for the Lord is to demonstrate confident expectation. The Hebrew word for "wait" may also be translated "hope." To hope in God is to wait for His timing and His action (40:1; Is. 40:31).

28:1 *the pit.* This is one of the terms for death in the Psalms (55:23; 143:7).

28:5 *they have no regard.* The language here is similar to that of Paul in Romans 1:18–32. One day even the wicked will have to acknowledge God as their Creator and give Him the glory He deserves.

28:8 *his anointed.* This term acknowledges God's covenant with David, His promise that He would be David's God and David would be His representative. This passage became a heritage of the monarchy, a treasure for each godly king in the Davidic line to go back to for strength and encouragement.

29:1 *you heavenly beings.* This means "sons of gods." This Hebrew phrase refers to spiritual beings who are in the presence of God (see Job 1:6).

29:2 Worship by Israel—The central aspect of

27:5 [o] Ps 17:8; 31:20 [p] Ps 40:2 **27:6** [q] Ps 3:3 [r] Ps 107:22 **27:7** [s] Ps 13:3 **27:9** [t] Ps 69:17 **27:11** [u] Ps 5:8; 25:4; 86:11 **27:12** [v] Mt 26:60; Ac 9:1 **27:13** [w] Ps 31:19 [x] Jer 11:19; Eze 26:20 **27:14** [y] Ps 40:1 **28:1** [z] Ps 83:1 [a] Ps 88:4 **28:2** [b] Ps 138:2; 140:6 [c] Ps 5:7 **28:3** [d] Ps 12:2; Ps 26:9; Jer 9:8 **28:4** [e] 2Ti 4:14; Rev 22:12 [f] Rev 18:6 **28:5** [g] Isa 5:12 **28:7** [h] Ps 18:1 [i] Ps 13:5 [j] Ps 40:3; 69:30 **28:8** [k] Ps 20:6 **28:9** [l] Dt 9:29; Ezr 1:4 [m] Isa 40:11 [n] Dt 1:31; 32:11 **29:1** [o] 1Ch 16:28 [p] Ps 96:7-9 **29:2** [q] 2Ch 20:21

[3]The voice[r] of the LORD is over the waters;
the God of glory thunders,[s]
the LORD thunders over the mighty
waters.
[4]The voice of the LORD is powerful;[t]
the voice of the LORD is majestic.
[5]The voice of the LORD breaks the cedars;
the LORD breaks in pieces the cedars
of Lebanon.[u]
[6]He makes Lebanon leap[v] like a calf,
Sirion[a][w] like a young wild ox.
[7]The voice of the LORD strikes
with flashes of lightning.
[8]The voice of the LORD shakes the desert;
the LORD shakes the Desert of
Kadesh.[x]
[9]The voice of the LORD twists the oaks[b]
and strips the forests bare.
And in his temple all cry, "Glory!"[y]

[10]The LORD sits enthroned over the flood;[z]
the LORD is enthroned as King
forever.[a]
[11]The LORD gives strength to his people;[b]
the LORD blesses his people with
peace.[c]

Psalm 30[c]

A psalm. A song. For the dedication of the temple.[d] Of David.

[1]I will exalt you, LORD,
for you lifted me out of the depths
and did not let my enemies gloat
over me.[d]
[2]LORD my God, I called to you for help,[e]
and you healed me.[f]
[3]You, LORD, brought me up from the
realm of the dead;
you spared me from going down to
the pit.[g]

[4]Sing the praises of the LORD, you his
faithful people;[h]
praise his holy name.[i]
[5]For his anger[j] lasts only a moment,
but his favor lasts a lifetime;
weeping may stay for the night,
but rejoicing comes in the morning.[k]

[6]When I felt secure, I said,
"I will never be shaken."
[7]LORD, when you favored me,
you made my royal mountain[e] stand
firm;
but when you hid your face,[l]
I was dismayed.

[8]To you, LORD, I called;
to the Lord I cried for mercy:
[9]"What is gained if I am silenced,
if I go down to the pit?
Will the dust praise you?
Will it proclaim your faithfulness?[m]
[10]Hear, LORD, and be merciful to me;
LORD, be my help."

[11]You turned my wailing into dancing;
you removed my sackcloth and
clothed me with joy,[n]
[12]that my heart may sing your praises
and not be silent.
LORD my God, I will praise[o] you
forever.[p]

Psalm 31[f]

For the director of music. A psalm of David.

[1]In you, LORD, I have taken refuge;
let me never be put to shame;
deliver me in your righteousness.
[2]Turn your ear to me,
come quickly to my rescue;
be my rock of refuge,[q]
a strong fortress to save me.

---

[a] 6 That is, Mount Hermon [b] 9 Or *LORD makes the deer give birth* [c] In Hebrew texts 30:1-12 is numbered 30:2-13. [d] Title: Or *palace* [e] 7 That is, Mount Zion [f] In Hebrew texts 31:1-24 is numbered 31:2-25.

Israel's worship was the object of their worship, the Lord. While other nations paid homage to many gods, including inanimate objects such as trees and stones, Israel worshiped the one true God. This worship could be private, as a family or corporate as a congregation. Israel's worship occurred in many different contexts and many different elements. It included offering sacrifices (1 Sam. 1:3), adopting a reverent posture (2 Chr. 7:6), verbal praise—either spoken (1 Chr. 16:7) or sung (Ps. 57:7), instrumental praise (Ps. 150:3–5), prayer (2 Chr. 6:14–42), and the great feasts (Lev. 23; 25).

The first place of worship for the people of Israel was the tabernacle constructed by Moses (Ex. 25; 27; 30–31; 35; 40). Solomon's temple in Jerusalem became the permanent place for the central worship of the whole nation when it was completed. The New Testament teaching is that there is no limitation on location for worship. Access to God is direct and immediate (1 Cor. 6:19).

29:6 ***Sirion.*** This was an ancient name for Mount Hermon (Deut. 3:9).

29:10 ***over the flood.*** God is the true victor over all. He even controlled the waters at the height of their destructive power during the flood.

30:3 ***from the realm of the dead.*** David is not reporting a resurrection, but a deliverance from a nearly fatal illness. As in 28:1, the psalmist describes death as a great pit into which a person drops into the enveloping darkness of the unknown.

30:10 ***my help.*** "Help" can also be translated "power" or "strength" (33:20). Jesus promised His disciples that the Holy Spirit would be their Helper (John 14:16).

31:1 ***I have taken refuge.*** This is a psalm of lament, yet David expresses deep trust in God in spite of his afflictions.

29:3 [r] Job 37:5 [s] Ps 18:13 **29:4** [t] Ps 68:33 **29:5** [u] Jdg 9:15 **29:6** [v] Ps 114:4 [w] Dt 3:9 **29:8** [x] Nu 13:26 **29:9** [y] Ps 26:8 **29:10** [z] Ge 6:17 [a] Ps 10:16 **29:11** [b] Ps 28:8 [c] Ps 37:11 **30:1** [d] Ps 25:2; 28:9 **30:2** [e] Ps 88:13 [f] Ps 6:2 **30:3** [g] Ps 28:1; 86:13 **30:4** [h] Ps 149:1 [i] Ps 97:12 **30:5** [j] Ps 103:9 [k] 2Co 4:17 **30:7** [l] Dt 31:17; Ps 104:29 **30:9** [m] Ps 6:5 **30:11** [n] Ps 4:7; Jer 31:4, 13 **30:12** [o] Ps 16:9 [p] Ps 44:8 **31:2** [q] Ps 18:2

3 Since you are my rock and my fortress,[r]
for the sake of your name[s] lead and guide me.
4 Keep me free from the trap that is set for me,
for you are my refuge.[t]
5 Into your hands I commit my spirit;[u]
deliver me, LORD, my faithful God.

6 I hate those who cling to worthless idols;
as for me, I trust in the LORD.[v]
7 I will be glad and rejoice in your love,
for you saw my affliction[w]
and knew the anguish[x] of my soul.
8 You have not given me into the hands[y] of the enemy
but have set my feet in a spacious place.

9 Be merciful to me, LORD, for I am in distress;
my eyes grow weak with sorrow,[z]
my soul and body with grief.
10 My life is consumed by anguish
and my years by groaning;[a]
my strength fails because of my affliction,[a]
and my bones grow weak.[b]
11 Because of all my enemies,
I am the utter contempt of my neighbors[c]
and an object of dread to my closest friends—
those who see me on the street flee from me.
12 I am forgotten as though I were dead;[d]
I have become like broken pottery.
13 For I hear many whispering,
"Terror on every side!"[e]
They conspire against me
and plot to take my life.[f]

14 But I trust[g] in you, LORD;
I say, "You are my God."
15 My times[h] are in your hands;
deliver me from the hands of my enemies,
from those who pursue me.
16 Let your face shine[i] on your servant;
save me in your unfailing love.
17 Let me not be put to shame,[j] LORD,
for I have cried out to you;
but let the wicked be put to shame
and be silent[k] in the realm of the dead.
18 Let their lying lips[l] be silenced,
for with pride and contempt
they speak arrogantly[m] against the righteous.

19 How abundant are the good things[n]
that you have stored up for those who fear you,
that you bestow in the sight of all,[o]
on those who take refuge in you.
20 In the shelter of your presence you hide[p] them
from all human intrigues;[q]
you keep them safe in your dwelling
from accusing tongues.

21 Praise be to the LORD,
for he showed me the wonders of his love[r]
when I was in a city under siege.[s]
22 In my alarm[t] I said,
"I am cut off from your sight!"
Yet you heard my cry[u] for mercy
when I called to you for help.
23 Love the LORD, all his faithful people![v]
The LORD preserves those who are true to him,[w]
but the proud he pays back[x] in full.
24 Be strong and take heart,[y]
all you who hope in the LORD.

Psalm 32

Of David. A maskil.[b]

1 Blessed is the one
whose transgressions are forgiven,
whose sins are covered.[z]
2 Blessed is the one
whose sin the LORD does not count against them[a]
and in whose spirit is no deceit.[b]

3 When I kept silent,
my bones wasted away[c]
through my groaning all day long.

---

[a] *10* Or *guilt* [b] Title: Probably a literary or musical term

---

31:5 *Into your hand I commit my spirit.* With these words, David expressed his complete dependence on God. These very words were spoken by Jesus on the cross shortly before His death (Luke 23:46), and by Stephen when he was stoned (Acts 7:59).

31:15 *My times are in your hands.* Even when we cannot understand the "why," we can trust that God is in control of when each life begins and ends, and also of our times of suffering.

31:22 *In my alarm I said.* The psalmist's emotional response was to accuse God of abandoning him instead of asking for help, yet God still answered his true need.

32:1 *Blessed.* "Blessed" means "happy." It is appropriate that this word is used both of the righteous (1:1) and of the forgiven.

32:3 *kept silent.* When we refuse to admit our sin, we will suffer. David realized that it was not just his feelings that were assaulting him, but the heavy hand of God (38:1,6–8). No matter who else is hurt, the principal offense of any sin is always against the Lord.

31:3 [r] Ps 18:2 [s] Ps 23:3 **31:4** [t] Ps 25:15 **31:5** [u] Lk 23:46; Ac 7:59 **31:6** [v] Jnh 2:8 **31:7** [w] Ps 90:14 [x] Ps 10:14; Jn 10:27 **31:8** [y] Dt 32:30 **31:9** [z] Ps 6:7 **31:10** [a] Ps 13:2 [b] Ps 38:3; 39:11 **31:11** [c] Job 19:13; Ps 38:11; 64:8; Isa 53:4 **31:12** [d] Ps 88:4 **31:13** [e] Jer 20:3, 10; La 2:22 [f] Mt 27:1 **31:14** [g] Ps 140:6 **31:15** [h] Job 24:1; Ps 143:9 **31:16** [i] Nu 6:25; Ps 4:6 **31:17** [j] Ps 25:2-3 [k] Ps 115:17 **31:18** [l] Ps 120:2 [m] Ps 94:4 **31:19** [n] Ro 11:22 [o] Isa 64:4 **31:20** [p] Ps 27:5 [q] Job 5:21 **31:21** [r] Ps 17:7 [s] 1Sa 23:7 **31:22** [t] Ps 116:11 [u] La 3:54 **31:23** [v] Ps 34:9 [w] Ps 145:20 [x] Ps 94:2 **31:24** [y] Ps 27:14 **32:1** [z] Ps 85:2 **32:2** [a] Ro 4:7-8*; 2Co 5:19 [b] Jn 1:47 **32:3** [c] Ps 31:10

4 For day and night
your hand was heavy[d] on me;
my strength was sapped
as in the heat of summer.[a]
5 Then I acknowledged my sin to you
and did not cover up my iniquity.
I said, "I will confess[e]
my transgressions[f] to the LORD."
And you forgave
the guilt of my sin.[g]
6 Therefore let all the faithful pray to you
while you may be found;[h]
surely the rising of the mighty waters
will not reach them.[i]
7 You are my hiding place;
you will protect me from trouble[j]
and surround me with songs of
deliverance.[k]
8 I will instruct[l] you and teach you in the
way you should go;
I will counsel you with my loving eye
on[m] you.
9 Do not be like the horse or the mule,
which have no understanding
but must be controlled by bit and bridle[n]
or they will not come to you.
10 Many are the woes of the wicked,[o]
but the LORD's unfailing love
surrounds the one who trusts[p] in him.
11 Rejoice in the LORD[q] and be glad, you
righteous;
sing, all you who are upright in heart!

Psalm 33

1 Sing joyfully to the LORD, you
righteous;
it is fitting[r] for the upright[s] to praise
him.
2 Praise the LORD with the harp;
make music to him on the
ten-stringed lyre.[t]
3 Sing to him a new song;[u]
play skillfully, and shout for joy.
4 For the word of the LORD is right[v] and
true;
he is faithful in all he does.
5 The LORD loves righteousness and
justice;[w]
the earth is full of his unfailing love.[x]
6 By the word[y] of the LORD the heavens
were made,
their starry host by the breath of his
mouth.
7 He gathers the waters of the sea into
jars[b];
he puts the deep into storehouses.
8 Let all the earth fear the LORD;
let all the people of the world revere
him.[z]
9 For he spoke, and it came to be;
he commanded,[a] and it stood firm.
10 The LORD foils the plans of the nations;[b]
he thwarts the purposes of the
peoples.
11 But the plans of the LORD stand firm
forever,
the purposes[c] of his heart through all
generations.
12 Blessed is the nation whose God is the
LORD,[d]
the people he chose[e] for his
inheritance.
13 From heaven the LORD looks down
and sees all mankind;[f]
14 from his dwelling place[g] he watches
all who live on earth—
15 he who forms[h] the hearts of all,
who considers everything they do.[i]

---

[a] 4 The Hebrew has *Selah* (a word of uncertain meaning) here and at the end of verses 5 and 7.
[b] 7 Or *sea as into a heap*

32:5 What Should Be Done About Sin—There are only two things that the believer should do about his sin: confess it and forsake it. He should never condone or attempt to excuse his sin. Here David confesses his sin and experiences forgiveness. Similarly 1 John 1:9 makes the same point. When the believer confesses his sin, he has the assurance that God "is faithful" (He can be counted on to keep His word) and "just" (He is just in dealing with our sins because He paid the price for them) "forgive us our sins and purify us from all unrighteousness." God is able to cleanse us completely from anything that is inconsistent with His own moral character. Having received forgiveness and cleansing, the believer is to forsake his sin and yield himself completely to God. In so doing, the believer is restored to full fellowship with God.

32:9 *bit and bridle or they will not come to you.* God does not want to drive His people with rules and regulations, the "bit and bridle" of righteousness. Rather, He wants His people to follow Him willingly, that they desire above all to please Him, not just to appease Him.

33:5 *the earth is full.* In spite of the fallen nature of our world, much of the creation remains as it was in the beginning: "very good" (Gen. 1:31). We do have to deal with evil, but every time we see the goodness of God's creation we should rejoice.

33:9 *he spoke, and it came to be.* The creation account in Genesis 1 describes God's spoken word as the controlling element in creation; John 1 shows that Word to be Jesus Christ, God's Son.

33:15 *he who forms the hearts ... who considers.* When we are troubled and weary and suffering, we can never say that God does not notice or understand. He made us carefully, and He continues to watch over all that we do.

32:4 [d] Job 33:7 **32:5** [e] Pr 28:13 [f] Ps 103:12 [g] Lev 26:40 **32:6** [h] Ps 69:13; Isa 55:6 [i] Isa 43:2 **32:7** [j] Ps 9:9 [k] Ex 15:1 **32:8** [l] Ps 25:8 [m] Ps 33:18 **32:9** [n] Pr 26:3 **32:10** [o] Ro 2:9 [p] Pr 16:20 **32:11** [q] Ps 64:10 **33:1** [r] Ps 147:1 [s] Ps 32:11 **33:2** [t] Ps 92:3 **33:3** [u] Ps 96:1 **33:4** [v] Ps 19:8 **33:5** [w] Ps 11:7 [x] Ps 119:64 **33:6** [y] Heb 11:3 **33:8** [z] Ps 67:7; 96:9 **33:9** [a] Ge 1:3; Ps 148:5 **33:10** [b] Isa 8:10 **33:11** [c] Job 23:13 **33:12** [d] Ps 144:15 [e] Ex 19:5; Dt 7:6 **33:13** [f] Job 28:24; Ps 11:4 **33:14** [g] 1Ki 8:39 **33:15** [h] Job 10:8 [i] Jer 32:19

16 No king is saved by the size of his
army;[j]
no warrior escapes by his great
strength.
17 A horse[k] is a vain hope for deliverance;
despite all its great strength it cannot
save.
18 But the eyes[l] of the LORD are on those
who fear him,
on those whose hope is in his
unfailing love,[m]
19 to deliver them from death
and keep them alive in famine.[n]

20 We wait[o] in hope for the LORD;
he is our help and our shield.
21 In him our hearts rejoice,[p]
for we trust in his holy name.
22 May your unfailing love be with us,
LORD,
even as we put our hope in you.

Psalm 34[a,b]

Of David. When he pretended to be insane before Abimelek, who drove him away, and he left.

1 I will extol the LORD at all times;[q]
his praise will always be on my lips.
2 I will glory[r] in the LORD;
let the afflicted hear and rejoice.[s]
3 Glorify the LORD with me;
let us exalt[t] his name together.

4 I sought the LORD,[u] and he
answered me;
he delivered me from all my fears.
5 Those who look to him are radiant;[v]
their faces are never covered with
shame.[w]
6 This poor man called, and the LORD
heard him;
he saved him out of all his troubles.
7 The angel of the LORD[x] encamps around
those who fear him,
and he delivers them.

8 Taste and see that the LORD is good;[y]
blessed is the one who takes refuge[z]
in him.
9 Fear the LORD, you his holy people,
for those who fear him lack
nothing.[a]
10 The lions may grow weak and hungry,
but those who seek the LORD lack no
good thing.[b]
11 Come, my children, listen to me;
I will teach you[c] the fear of the LORD.
12 Whoever of you loves life[d]
and desires to see many good days,
13 keep your tongue from evil
and your lips from telling lies.[e]
14 Turn from evil and do good;[f]
seek peace[g] and pursue it.

15 The eyes of the LORD[h] are on the
righteous,[i]
and his ears are attentive to their
cry;
16 but the face of the LORD is against[j]
those who do evil,[k]
to blot out their name[l] from the
earth.

17 The righteous cry out, and the LORD
hears[m] them;
he delivers them from all their
troubles.
18 The LORD is close[n] to the
brokenhearted[o]
and saves those who are crushed in
spirit.

19 The righteous person may have many
troubles,[p]
but the LORD delivers him from them
all;[q]
20 he protects all his bones,
not one of them will be broken.[r]

21 Evil will slay the wicked;[s]
the foes of the righteous will be
condemned.
22 The LORD will rescue[t] his servants;
no one who takes refuge in him will
be condemned.

---

[a] This psalm is an acrostic poem, the verses of which begin with the successive letters of the Hebrew alphabet. [b] In Hebrew texts 34:1-22 is numbered 34:2-23.

33:18 *hope.* Those who hoped for the Lord's unfailing love were looking forward in faith to the promised redemption, the ultimate fulfillment of the covenants, just as believers today who have the same hope, based on faith in Christ's finished work of redemption.

34:1 *at all times.* The determination of David to praise God is similar to the words of Paul in 1 Thessalonians 5:18. The story behind this psalm may be found in 1 Samuel 21:10–15.

34:7 *The angel of the LORD.* This term is often used interchangeably with the name of God (Ex. 3). When we realize that God Himself is watching over us, there is no need to fear.

34:9 *Fear the LORD.* This is a call to awe, wonder, worship, and reverence (Prov. 1:7). To fear God is to respond to Him in obedience.

34:20 *protects all his bones.* John 19:33–36 shows that the words of this verse were fulfilled in detail in the death of Jesus. Despite the terrible suffering that the Savior endured, none of His bones were broken.

33:16 [j] Ps 44:6 **33:17** [k] Ps 20:7; Pr 21:31
33:18 [l] Job 36:7; Ps 34:15 [m] Ps 147:11 **33:19** [n] Job 5:20
33:20 [o] Ps 130:6 **33:21** [p] Zec 10:7; Jn 16:22
34:1 [q] Ps 71:6; Eph 5:20 **34:2** [r] Jer 9:24; 1Co 1:31
[s] Ps 119:74 **34:3** [t] Lk 1:46 **34:4** [u] Mt 7:7
34:5 [v] Ps 36:9 [w] Ps 25:3 **34:7** [x] 2Ki 6:17; Da 6:22
34:8 [y] 1Pe 2:3 [z] Ps 2:12 **34:9** [a] Ps 23:1 **34:10** [b] Ps 84:11
34:11 [c] Ps 32:8 **34:12** [d] 1Pe 3:10 **34:13** [e] 1Pe 2:22
34:14 [f] Ps 37:27 [g] Heb 12:14 **34:15** [h] Ps 33:18 [i] Job 36:7
34:16 [j] Lev 17:10; Jer 44:11 [k] 1Pe 3:10-12* [l] Pr 10:7
34:17 [m] Ps 145:19 **34:18** [n] Ps 145:18 [o] Isa 57:15
34:19 [p] ver 17 [q] ver 4,6; Pr 24:16 **34:20** [r] Jn 19:36*
34:21 [s] Ps 94:23 **34:22** [t] 1Ki 1:29; Ps 71:23

Psalm 35

Of David.

1 Contend, LORD, with those who contend
with me;
fight[u] against those who fight
against me.
2 Take up shield and armor;
arise[v] and come to my aid.
3 Brandish spear and javelin[a]
against those who pursue me.
Say to me,
"I am your salvation."

4 May those who seek my life
be disgraced[w] and put to shame;
may those who plot my ruin
be turned back in dismay.
5 May they be like chaff[x] before the wind,
with the angel of the LORD driving
them away;
6 may their path be dark and slippery,
with the angel of the LORD pursuing
them.

7 Since they hid their net for me without
cause
and without cause dug a pit for me,
8 may ruin overtake them by surprise—[y]
may the net they hid entangle them,
may they fall into the pit,[z] to their ruin.
9 Then my soul will rejoice[a] in the LORD
and delight in his salvation.[b]
10 My whole being will exclaim,
"Who is like you,[c] LORD?
You rescue the poor from those too
strong[d] for them,
the poor and needy[e] from those who
rob them."

11 Ruthless witnesses[f] come forward;
they question me on things I know
nothing about.
12 They repay me evil for good[g]
and leave me like one bereaved.
13 Yet when they were ill, I put on
sackcloth
and humbled myself with fasting.[h]
When my prayers returned to me
unanswered,
14 I went about mourning
as though for my friend or brother.
I bowed my head in grief
as though weeping for my mother.
15 But when I stumbled, they gathered in
glee;
assailants gathered against me
without my knowledge.
They slandered[i] me without ceasing.
16 Like the ungodly they maliciously
mocked;[b]
they gnashed their teeth[j] at me.

17 How long,[k] Lord, will you look on?
Rescue me from their ravages,
my precious life[l] from these lions.
18 I will give you thanks in the great
assembly;[m]
among the throngs I will praise you.[n]
19 Do not let those gloat over me
who are my enemies without cause;
do not let those who hate me without
reason[o]
maliciously wink the eye.[p]
20 They do not speak peaceably,
but devise false accusations
against those who live quietly in the
land.
21 They sneer[q] at me and say, "Aha! Aha![r]
With our own eyes we have seen it."

22 LORD, you have seen[s] this; do not be
silent.
Do not be far[t] from me, Lord.
23 Awake,[u] and rise to my defense!
Contend for me, my God and Lord.
24 Vindicate me in your righteousness,
LORD my God;
do not let them gloat over me.
25 Do not let them think, "Aha, just what
we wanted!"
or say, "We have swallowed him up."[v]

26 May all who gloat over my distress
be put to shame[w] and confusion;
may all who exalt themselves over me[x]
be clothed with shame and disgrace.

[a] 3 Or *and block the way* [b] 16 Septuagint; Hebrew may mean *Like an ungodly circle of mockers,*

35:2 *come to my aid.* David did not hesitate to call upon God for vindication, comfort, and justice. He placed complete dependence on the Lord.

35:8 *ruin overtake them.* David's response is certainly not an example of turning the other cheek or loving his enemies (Matt. 5:39,44), but it shows David's keen awareness of the battle between good and evil, the reality of wickedness, and his understanding that wickedness is an abomination to the Lord.

35:18 *assembly.* Three times a year, at three of the great annual feasts, all males were required to appear before the Lord in Jerusalem. Each brought his offering to the Lord on these occasions. When they came accompanied by their families, as was often the case, Jerusalem was flooded by a vast horde of people intent upon worshiping God. David viewed speaking before this "great assembly" or the congregation of Israel as the ultimate opportunity for testimony. A constant testimony is given to the world by believers as they give voice to praise Him for His watchful care over them.

35:19 *enemies without cause.* This passage was fulfilled in the suffering of Jesus, the Savior (John 15:23–25).

35:26 *put to shame.* The phrase "shame" does not

35:1 [u] Ps 43:1 **35:2** [v] Ps 62:2 **35:4** [w] Ps 70:2
35:5 [x] Job 21:18; Ps 1:4; Isa 29:5 **35:8** [y] 1Th 5:3 [z] Ps 9:15
35:9 [a] Lk 1:47 [b] Isa 61:10 **35:10** [c] Ex 15:11 [d] Ps 18:17
[e] Ps 37:14 **35:11** [f] Ps 27:12 **35:12** [g] Jn 10:32
35:13 [h] Job 30:25; Ps 69:10 **35:15** [i] Job 30:1,8
35:16 [j] Job 16:9; La 2:16 **35:17** [k] Hab 1:13 [l] Ps 22:20
35:18 [m] Ps 22:25 [n] Ps 22:22 **35:19** [o] Ps 38:19; 69:4;
Jn 15:25* [p] Ps 13:4; Pr 6:13 **35:21** [q] Ps 22:13 [r] Ps 40:15
35:22 [s] Ex 3:7 [t] Ps 10:1; 28:1 **35:23** [u] Ps 44:23
35:25 [v] La 2:16 **35:26** [w] Ps 40:14; 109:29 [x] Ps 38:16

27 May those who delight in my
vindication[y]
shout for joy[z] and gladness;
may they always say, "The LORD be
exalted,
who delights[a] in the well-being of his
servant."

28 My tongue will proclaim your
righteousness,[b]
your praises all day long.

Psalm 36[a]

For the director of music. Of David the servant of the LORD.

1 I have a message from God in my heart
concerning the sinfulness of the
wicked:[b]
There is no fear of God
before their eyes.[c]

2 In their own eyes they flatter
themselves
too much to detect or hate their sin.
3 The words of their mouths[d] are wicked
and deceitful;
they fail to act wisely[e] or do good.[f]
4 Even on their beds they plot evil;[g]
they commit themselves to a sinful
course[h]
and do not reject what is wrong.[i]

5 Your love, LORD, reaches to the heavens,
your faithfulness to the skies.
6 Your righteousness is like the highest
mountains,
your justice like the great deep.[j]
You, LORD, preserve both people and
animals.
7 How priceless is your unfailing love,
O God!
People take refuge in the shadow of
your wings.[k]
8 They feast on the abundance of your
house;[l]
you give them drink from your river[m]
of delights.
9 For with you is the fountain of life;[n]
in your light[o] we see light.

10 Continue your love to those who know
you,
your righteousness to the upright in
heart.
11 May the foot of the proud not come
against me,
nor the hand of the wicked drive me
away.
12 See how the evildoers lie fallen—
thrown down, not able to rise![p]

Psalm 37[c]

Of David.

1 Do not fret because of those who are
evil
or be envious[q] of those who do
wrong;[r]
2 for like the grass they will soon wither,
like green plants they will soon die
away.[s]

3 Trust in the LORD and do good;
dwell in the land[t] and enjoy safe
pasture.[u]
4 Take delight[v] in the LORD,
and he will give you the desires of
your heart.

5 Commit your way to the LORD;
trust in him[w] and he will do this:
6 He will make your righteous reward[x]
shine like the dawn,[y]
your vindication like the noonday sun.

7 Be still[z] before the LORD
and wait patiently[a] for him;
do not fret when people succeed in their
ways,
when they carry out their wicked
schemes.

8 Refrain from anger[b] and turn from
wrath;
do not fret—it leads only to evil.

---

[a] In Hebrew texts 36:1-12 is numbered 36:2-13.
[b] 1 Or *A message from God: The transgression of the wicked / resides in their hearts.*
[c] This psalm is an acrostic poem, the stanzas of which begin with the successive letters of the Hebrew alphabet.

---

refer just to simple embarrassment, but to the revelation of the complete emptiness of wickedness before the judgment seat of God.

36:1 *no fear of God.* Underlying wickedness is a complete disregard for the reality of God in a person's life and in the world.

36:9 *fountain of life.* God's salvation and continuing mercy to His people are often described in terms of life-giving water (Is. 12:3; Jer. 2:13; John 4:1 – 14).

37:1 *Do not fret.* When the wicked seem to prosper, the psalmist calls for patience, a renewed sense of dependence on the Lord, and a new sense of pleasure in knowing Him.

37:4 *the desires of your heart.* Many times, we read this verse as a promise that God will give us anything that we want because He wants us to be happy. In reality, this verse goes much deeper. When we truly delight in God, He plants in our hearts godly desires that He delights to fulfill.

37:7 *Be still before the LORD ... do not fret.* This is not a call to stop caring and go to sleep, but to depend actively on the living Lord, leaving our lives and times in His hands.

35:27 [y] Ps 9:4 [z] Ps 32:11 [a] Ps 40:16; 147:11 **35:28** [b] Ps 51:14 **36:1** [c] Ro 3:18* **36:3** [d] Ps 10:7 [e] Ps 94:8 [f] Jer 4:22 **36:4** [g] Pr 4:16; Mic 2:1 [h] Isa 65:2 [i] Ps 52:3; Ro 12:9 **36:6** [j] Job 11:8; Ps 77:19; Ro 11:33 **36:7** [k] Ru 2:12; Ps 17:8 **36:8** [l] Ps 65:4 [m] Job 20:17; Rev 22:1 **36:9** [n] Jer 2:13 [o] 1Pe 2:9 **36:12** [p] Ps 140:10 **37:1** [q] Pr 23:17-18 [r] Ps 73:3 **37:2** [s] Ps 90:6 **37:3** [t] Dt 30:20 [u] Isa 40:11; Jn 10:9 **37:4** [v] Isa 58:14 **37:5** [w] Ps 4:5; Ps 55:22; Pr 16:3; 1Pe 5:7 **37:6** [x] Mic 7:9 [y] Job 11:17 **37:7** [z] Ps 62:5; La 3:26 [a] Ps 40:1 **37:8** [b] Eph 4:31; Col 3:8

9 For those who are evil will be
destroyed,
but those who hope in the LORD will
inherit the land.[c]
10 A little while, and the wicked will be no
more;[d]
though you look for them, they will
not be found.
11 But the meek will inherit the land[e]
and enjoy peace and prosperity.

12 The wicked plot against the righteous
and gnash their teeth[f] at them;
13 but the Lord laughs at the wicked,
for he knows their day is coming.[g]

14 The wicked draw the sword
and bend the bow[h]
to bring down the poor and needy,[i]
to slay those whose ways are
upright.
15 But their swords will pierce their own
hearts,[j]
and their bows will be broken.

16 Better the little that the righteous have
than the wealth[k] of many wicked;
17 for the power of the wicked will be
broken,[l]
but the LORD upholds the righteous.

18 The blameless spend their days under
the LORD's care,[m]
and their inheritance will endure
forever.
19 In times of disaster they will not wither;
in days of famine they will enjoy
plenty.

20 But the wicked will perish:
Though the LORD's enemies are like
the flowers of the field,
they will be consumed, they will go
up in smoke.[n]

21 The wicked borrow and do not repay,
but the righteous give generously;[o]
22 those the LORD blesses will inherit the
land,
but those he curses[p] will be
destroyed.

23 The LORD makes firm the steps[q]
of the one who delights[r] in him;
24 though he may stumble, he will not
fall,[s]
for the LORD upholds[t] him with his
hand.

25 I was young and now I am old,
yet I have never seen the righteous
forsaken[u]
or their children begging bread.
26 They are always generous and lend
freely;
their children will be a blessing.[a][v]

27 Turn from evil and do good;[w]
then you will dwell in the land
forever.
28 For the LORD loves the just
and will not forsake his faithful
ones.

Wrongdoers will be completely
destroyed[b];
the offspring of the wicked will
perish.[x]
29 The righteous will inherit the land[y]
and dwell in it forever.

30 The mouths of the righteous utter
wisdom,
and their tongues speak what is just.
31 The law of their God is in their hearts;[z]
their feet do not slip.[a]

32 The wicked lie in wait[b] for the
righteous,
intent on putting them to death;
33 but the LORD will not leave them in the
power of the wicked
or let them be condemned when
brought to trial.[c]

34 Hope in the LORD[d]
and keep his way.
He will exalt you to inherit the land;
when the wicked are destroyed, you
will see[e] it.

35 I have seen a wicked and ruthless man
flourishing[f] like a luxuriant native
tree,

---

[a] 26 Or *freely; / the names of their children will be used in blessings* (see Gen. 48:20); or *freely; / others will see that their children are blessed* [b] 28 See Septuagint; Hebrew *They will be protected forever*

37:13 *he knows their day is coming.* The wicked sometimes appear to prosper, but from God's perspective, the flourishing of the wicked is short (Eccl. 3:16 – 17).

37:21 *the righteous give generously.* There are many contrasts between the wicked and the righteous in the wisdom psalms; this one is based on contrasting attitudes toward possessions (15:5; 112:5). Jesus said that such generous givers would be rewarded with "good measure, pressed down, shaken together, and running over" (Luke 6:38).

37:25 *begging bread.* Some interpret these words as referring to spiritual famine — the righteous will never be deprived of the Lord's presence (John 6:35). However, many have taken these words literally and experienced God's miraculous provision for their material needs.

37:27 *Turn from evil.* In this life people must choose either to cling to God and righteousness or to pursue evil.

37:9 [c] Isa 57:13; 60:21 **37:10** [d] Job 7:10; 24:24 **37:11** [e] Mt 5:5 **37:12** [f] Ps 35:16 **37:13** [g] 1Sa 26:10; Ps 2:4 **37:14** [h] Ps 11:2 [i] Ps 35:10 **37:15** [j] Ps 9:16 **37:16** [k] Pr 15:16 **37:17** [l] Job 38:15; Ps 10:15 **37:18** [m] Ps 1:6 **37:20** [n] Ps 102:3 **37:21** [o] Ps 112:5 **37:22** [p] Job 5:3; Pr 3:33 **37:23** [q] 1Sa 2:9 [r] Ps 147:11 **37:24** [s] Pr 24:16 [t] Ps 145:14; 147:6 **37:25** [u] Heb 13:5 **37:26** [v] Ps 147:13 **37:27** [w] Ps 34:14 **37:28** [x] Ps 21:10; Isa 14:20 **37:29** [y] ver 9; Pr 2:21 **37:31** [z] Dt 6:6; Ps 40:8; Isa 51:7 [a] ver 23 **37:32** [b] Ps 10:8 **37:33** [c] Ps 109:31; 2Pe 2:9 **37:34** [d] Ps 27:14 [e] Ps 52:6 **37:35** [f] Job 5:3

36 but he soon passed away and was no more;
though I looked for him, he could not be found.[g]
37 Consider the blameless, observe the upright;
a future awaits those who seek peace.[a][h]
38 But all sinners will be destroyed;
there will be no future[b] for the wicked.[i]
39 The salvation[j] of the righteous comes from the LORD;
he is their stronghold in time of trouble.[k]
40 The LORD helps[l] them and delivers[m] them;
he delivers them from the wicked and saves them,
because they take refuge in him.

Psalm 38[c]

A psalm of David. A petition.

1 LORD, do not rebuke me in your anger
or discipline me in your wrath.[n]
2 Your arrows[o] have pierced me,
and your hand has come down on me.
3 Because of your wrath there is no health in my body;
there is no soundness in my bones[p]
because of my sin.
4 My guilt has overwhelmed me
like a burden too heavy to bear.[q]
5 My wounds fester and are loathsome
because of my sinful folly.[r]
6 I am bowed down and brought very low;
all day long I go about mourning.[s]
7 My back is filled with searing pain;[t]
there is no health in my body.
8 I am feeble and utterly crushed;
I groan[u] in anguish of heart.
9 All my longings lie open before you, Lord;
my sighing[v] is not hidden from you.
10 My heart pounds, my strength fails[w] me;
even the light has gone from my eyes.[x]
11 My friends and companions avoid me
because of my wounds;[y]
my neighbors stay far away.
12 Those who want to kill me set their traps,[z]
those who would harm me talk of my ruin;[a]
all day long they scheme and lie.[b]
13 I am like the deaf, who cannot hear,
like the mute, who cannot speak;
14 I have become like one who does not hear,
whose mouth can offer no reply.
15 LORD, I wait[c] for you;
you will answer,[d] Lord my God.
16 For I said, "Do not let them gloat[e]
or exalt themselves over me when my feet slip."[f]
17 For I am about to fall,
and my pain is ever with me.
18 I confess my iniquity;[g]
I am troubled by my sin.
19 Many have become my enemies[h] without cause[d];
those who hate me without reason[i] are numerous.
20 Those who repay my good with evil[j]
lodge accusations against me,
though I seek only to do what is good.
21 LORD, do not forsake me;
do not be far[k] from me, my God.
22 Come quickly to help me,[l]
my Lord and my Savior.[m]

Psalm 39[e]

For the director of music. For Jeduthun. A psalm of David.

1 I said, "I will watch my ways[n]
and keep my tongue from sin;[o]
I will put a muzzle on my mouth
while in the presence of the wicked."
2 So I remained utterly silent,[p]
not even saying anything good.
But my anguish increased;
3 my heart grew hot within me.

[a] 37 Or *upright; / those who seek peace will have posterity* [b] 38 Or *posterity* [c] In Hebrew texts 38:1-22 is numbered 38:2-23. [d] *19* One Dead Sea Scrolls manuscript; Masoretic Text *my vigorous enemies* [e] In Hebrew texts 39:1-13 is numbered 39:2-14.

37:39 *salvation.* The principal issue here is not regeneration, but sanctification—the daily deliverance of God's people from temptation and evil.

38:1 *do not rebuke me.* David is not saying, "Don't tell me I'm wrong," but "Have mercy on my sinfulness." David's penitent psalms can serve as a model for our own prayers of confession.

38:14 *one who does not hear.* David was determined not to present an opportunity for his enemies to condemn the name of the Lord. His silence foreshadowed the silence of Jesus before His accusers (Mark 14:61).

38:18 *I confess.* David's silence was only before his enemies; to the Lord he willingly confessed his sins.

39:1 *I will watch my ways.* David determined to be silent in suffering so that he would not speak out foolishly.

37:36 [g] Job 20:5 **37:37** [h] Isa 57:1-2 **37:38** [i] Ps 1:4 **37:39** [j] Ps 3:8 [k] Ps 9:9 **37:40** [l] 1Ch 5:20 [m] Isa 31:5 **38:1** [n] Ps 6:1 **38:2** [o] Job 6:4; Ps 32:4 **38:3** [p] Ps 6:2; Isa 1:6 **38:4** [q] Ezr 9:6 **38:5** [r] Ps 69:5 **38:6** [s] Job 30:28; Ps 35:14; 42:9 **38:7** [t] Ps 102:3 **38:8** [u] Ps 22:1 **38:9** [v] Job 3:24; Ps 6:6; 10:17 **38:10** [w] Ps 31:10 [x] Ps 6:7 **38:11** [y] Ps 31:11 **38:12** [z] Ps 140:5 [a] Ps 35:4; 54:3 [b] Ps 35:20 **38:15** [c] Ps 39:7 [d] Ps 17:6 **38:16** [e] Ps 35:26 [f] Ps 13:4 **38:18** [g] Ps 32:5 **38:19** [h] Ps 18:17 [i] Ps 35:19 **38:20** [j] Ps 35:12; 1Jn 3:12 **38:21** [k] Ps 35:22 **38:22** [l] Ps 40:13 [m] Ps 27:1 **39:1** [n] 1Ki 2:4 [o] Job 2:10; Jas 3:2 **39:2** [p] Ps 38:13

While I meditated, the fire burned;
then I spoke with my tongue:

4 "Show me, LORD, my life's end
and the number of my days;[q]
let me know how fleeting my life is.[r]
5 You have made my days[s] a mere
handbreadth;
the span of my years is as nothing
before you.
Everyone is but a breath,[t]
even those who seem secure.[a]

6 "Surely everyone goes around like a
mere phantom;[u]
in vain they rush about,[v] heaping up
wealth
without knowing whose it will
finally be.[w]

7 "But now, Lord, what do I look for?
My hope is in you.[x]
8 Save me[y] from all my transgressions;[z]
do not make me the scorn of fools.
9 I was silent; I would not open my
mouth,[a]
for you are the one who has done this.
10 Remove your scourge from me;
I am overcome by the blow of your
hand.[b]
11 When you rebuke[c] and discipline
anyone for their sin,
you consume their wealth like a
moth[d]—
surely everyone is but a breath.

12 "Hear my prayer, LORD,
listen to my cry for help;
do not be deaf to my weeping.
I dwell with you as a foreigner,[e]
a stranger,[f] as all my ancestors were.
13 Look away from me, that I may enjoy
life again
before I depart and am no more."[g]

Psalm 40[b]

For the director of music. Of David. A psalm.

1 I waited patiently[h] for the LORD;
he turned to me and heard my cry.[i]
2 He lifted me out of the slimy pit,
out of the mud and mire;[j]
he set my feet on a rock[k]
and gave me a firm place to stand.
3 He put a new song[l] in my mouth,
a hymn of praise to our God.
Many will see and fear the LORD
and put their trust in him.

4 Blessed is the one[m]
who trusts in the LORD,[n]
who does not look to the proud,
to those who turn aside to false gods.[c]
5 Many, LORD my God,
are the wonders[o] you have done,
the things you planned for us.
None can compare[p] with you;
were I to speak and tell of your deeds,
they would be too many to declare.

6 Sacrifice and offering you did not
desire—[q]
but my ears you have opened[d]—
burnt offerings[r] and sin offerings[e]
you did not require.
7 Then I said, "Here I am, I have come—
it is written about me in the scroll.[f]
8 I desire to do your will,[s] my God;
your law is within my heart."[t]

---

[a] 5 The Hebrew has *Selah* (a word of uncertain meaning) here and at the end of verse 11. [b] In Hebrew texts 40:1-17 is numbered 40:2-18. [c] 4 Or *to lies* [d] 6 Hebrew; some Septuagint manuscripts *but a body you have prepared for me* [e] 6 Or *purification offerings* [f] 7 Or *come / with the scroll written for me*

39:9 *you are the one who has done this.* David knows that his only chance of deliverance is in God. But he also believes that his trouble has come from God. He is in a quandary. Should he ask for God's help, or should he ask for God to leave him alone?

39:13 *Look away from me.* If God is not going to deliver him, the despondent psalmist asks God to leave him alone. It is rare outside the Book of Job to find language such as this (Job 7:19). The pain of the psalmist was so far from being resolved that he remained in despair until the last verse. Yet the fact that God saves those who call upon Him is described again and again in the Book of Psalms (22:31; 118:21).

40:1 *I waited patiently.* The verb "to wait" expresses a confident trust or faith in the Lord (130:5). David knows that salvation comes only from the Almighty (3:8).

40:6 *my ears you have opened.* God allows us to hear His words, and He also gives us understanding and wisdom to internalize and apply them.

40:7 *Here I am, I have come.* According to Hebrews 10:4–7, Jesus spoke these words to the Father.

40:8 To Know God's Will—Knowing the will of God is not simply a vehicle for finding the right vocation for a life's work. While vocation is important, it is only a small part of God's will. The will of God must be thought of in more comprehensive terms. The will of God is for everyone to live in such a way as to bring honor and glory to God. For different people God may have very different things in mind. We must continually stay in God's Word so that He can make clear to us what His will is for us. We must also be still, listen, and know that He is God.

The first step towards understanding God's will is believing in Christ (John 3:14–16). If we do not accept this gift from God, we will not be saved from judgment (Matt. 7:21). Second, Scripture teaches us that it is God's will for every believer to be sanctified (2 Thess. 2:13–17). Third, the Bible declares God's will as it must be applied to our lives (Deut. 29:29). This fact involves commands to be obeyed, principles to be followed, prohibitions of things to be avoided and living examples to be imitated or shunned. God takes great joy in those who cheerfully do His will.

39:4 [q] Ps 90:12 [r] Ps 103:14 **39:5** [s] Ps 89:45 [t] Ps 62:9 **39:6** [u] 1Pe 1:24 [v] Ps 127:2 [w] Lk 12:20 **39:7** [x] Ps 38:15 **39:8** [y] Ps 51:9 [z] Ps 44:13 **39:9** [a] Job 2:10 **39:10** [b] Job 9:34; Ps 32:4 **39:11** [c] 2Pe 2:16 [d] Job 13:28 **39:12** [e] 1Pe 2:11 [f] Heb 11:13 **39:13** [g] Job 10:21; 14:10 **40:1** [h] Ps 27:14 [i] Ps 34:15 **40:2** [j] Ps 69:14 [k] Ps 27:5 **40:3** [l] Ps 33:3 **40:4** [m] Ps 34:8 [n] Ps 84:12 **40:5** [o] Ps 136:4 [p] Ps 139:18; Isa 55:8 **40:6** [q] 1Sa 15:22; Am 5:22 [r] Isa 1:11 **40:8** [s] Jn 4:34 [t] Ps 37:31

[9]I proclaim your saving acts in the great
assembly;[u]
I do not seal my lips, LORD,
as you know.[v]
[10]I do not hide your righteousness in my
heart;
I speak of your faithfulness[w] and
your saving help.
I do not conceal your love and your
faithfulness
from the great assembly.[x]

[11]Do not withhold your mercy from me,
LORD;
may your love[y] and faithfulness[z]
always protect me.
[12]For troubles[a] without number
surround me;
my sins have overtaken me, and I
cannot see.[b]
They are more than the hairs of my
head,[c]
and my heart fails[d] within me.
[13]Be pleased to save me, LORD;
come quickly, LORD, to help me.[e]

[14]May all who want to take my life
be put to shame and confusion;
may all who desire my ruin[f]
be turned back in disgrace.
[15]May those who say to me, "Aha! Aha!"
be appalled at their own shame.
[16]But may all who seek you
rejoice and be glad in you;
may those who long for your saving
help always say,
"The LORD is great!"[g]

[17]But as for me, I am poor and needy;
may the Lord think of me.
You are my help and my deliverer;
you are my God, do not delay.[h]

Psalm 41[a]

For the director of music. A psalm of David.

[1]Blessed are those who have regard for
the weak;[i]
the LORD delivers them in times of
trouble.
[2]The LORD protects and preserves
them—
they are counted among the blessed
in the land—[j]
he does not give them over to the
desire of their foes.[k]
[3]The LORD sustains them on their
sickbed
and restores them from their bed of
illness.

[4]I said, "Have mercy[l] on me, LORD;
heal me, for I have sinned[m] against
you."
[5]My enemies say of me in malice,
"When will he die and his name
perish?[n]"
[6]When one of them comes to see me,
he speaks falsely,[o] while his heart
gathers slander;[p]
then he goes out and spreads it
around.

[7]All my enemies whisper together[q]
against me;
they imagine the worst for me,
saying,
[8]"A vile disease has afflicted him;
he will never get up from the place
where he lies."
[9]Even my close friend,[r]
someone I trusted,
one who shared my bread,
has turned[b] against me.[s]

[10]But may you have mercy on me, LORD;
raise me up,[t] that I may repay them.
[11]I know that you are pleased with me,[u]
for my enemy does not triumph
over me.[v]
[12]Because of my integrity you uphold me[w]
and set me in your presence forever.[x]

[13]Praise be to the LORD, the God of
Israel,[y]
from everlasting to everlasting.
Amen and Amen.[z]

[a] In Hebrew texts 41:1-13 is numbered 41:2-14.
[b] 9 Hebrew *has lifted up his heel*

Although the Bible is a comprehensive revelation of God's will, there are always decisions we make that Scripture does not directly address. In order to know God's will in these situations we need to be in fellowship with the Lord (1 John 1:6–7), seek principles from the Word (1 Cor. 10:6) , obtain advice from godly counselors (Prov. 11:14), use common sense, and remember that God works through our own minds and He desires for us to do His will (Phil. 2:13).

40:9 *assembly.* In Psalm 35 David prayed for deliverance from his enemies and promised to give God praise before "the great assembly," the congregation of Israel, for that deliverance. Psalm 40 is a joyful account of his deliverance from trouble, and his witness of God's righteousness before the people. The believer is obligated to speak of God's righteous acts toward him, so that others may hear of the goodness and glory of God.

40:11 *your mercy.* This term refers to God's affection for us. David is asking God to surround him with warmth and comfort that is practically maternal.

41:4 *for I have sinned.* In the context of this psalm, this is a general acknowledgement of sin and the need for God's forgiveness and restoration (1 John 1:9).

41:9 *my close friend.* Jesus quoted this verse, noting its fulfillment in Judas (John 13:18).

41:13 *Praise be.* This psalm begins with a blessing

40:9 [u] Ps 22:25 [v] Jos 22:22; Ps 119:13 **40:10** [w] Ps 89:1 [x] Ac 20:20 **40:11** [y] Pr 20:28 [z] Ps 43:3 **40:12** [a] Ps 116:3 [b] Ps 38:4 [c] Ps 69:4 [d] Ps 73:26 **40:13** [e] Ps 70:1 **40:14** [f] Ps 35:4 **40:16** [g] Ps 35:27 **40:17** [h] Ps 70:5 **41:1** [i] Ps 82:3-4; Pr 14:21 **41:2** [j] Ps 37:22 [k] Ps 27:12 **41:4** [l] Ps 6:2 [m] Ps 51:4 **41:5** [n] Ps 38:12 **41:6** [o] Ps 12:2 [p] Pr 26:24 **41:7** [q] Ps 56:5; 71:10-11 **41:9** [r] 2Sa 15:12; Ps 55:12 [s] Job 19:19; Ps 55:20; Mt 26:23; Jn 13:18* **41:10** [t] Ps 3:3 **41:11** [u] Ps 147:11 [v] Ps 25:2 **41:12** [w] Ps 37:17 [x] Job 36:7 **41:13** [y] Ps 72:18 [z] Ps 89:52; 106:48

BOOK II

Psalms 42–72

Psalm 42[a,b]

For the director of music. A maskil[c] of the Sons of Korah.

1 As the deer pants for streams of water,
so my soul pants[a] for you, my God.
2 My soul thirsts[b] for God, for the living God.[c]
When can I go[d] and meet with God?
3 My tears[e] have been my food
day and night,
while people say to me all day long,
"Where is your God?"[f]
4 These things I remember
as I pour out my soul:
how I used to go to the house of God[g]
under the protection of the Mighty One[d]
with shouts of joy and praise[h]
among the festive throng.

5 Why, my soul, are you downcast?[i]
Why so disturbed within me?
Put your hope in God,[j]
for I will yet praise him,
my Savior[k] and my God.

6 My soul is downcast within me;
therefore I will remember you
from the land of the Jordan,
the heights of Hermon—from Mount Mizar.
7 Deep calls to deep
in the roar of your waterfalls;
all your waves and breakers
have swept over me.[l]
8 By day the LORD directs his love,[m]
at night[n] his song[o] is with me—
a prayer to the God of my life.

9 I say to God my Rock,
"Why have you forgotten me?
Why must I go about mourning,[p]
oppressed by the enemy?"
10 My bones suffer mortal agony
as my foes taunt me,
saying to me all day long,
"Where is your God?"

11 Why, my soul, are you downcast?
Why so disturbed within me?
Put your hope in God,
for I will yet praise him,
my Savior and my God.[q]

Psalm 43[a]

1 Vindicate me, my God,
and plead my cause[r]
against an unfaithful nation.
Rescue me from those who are
deceitful and wicked.[s]
2 You are God my stronghold.
Why have you rejected[t] me?
Why must I go about mourning,
oppressed by the enemy?[u]
3 Send me your light[v] and your faithful care,
let them lead me;
let them bring me to your holy mountain,[w]
to the place where you dwell.[x]
4 Then I will go to the altar[y] of God,
to God, my joy and my delight.
I will praise you with the lyre,[z]
O God, my God.

5 Why, my soul, are you downcast?
Why so disturbed within me?
Put your hope in God,
for I will yet praise him,
my Savior and my God.[a]

Psalm 44[e]

For the director of music. Of the Sons of Korah. A maskil.[c]

1 We have heard it with our ears,
O God;
our ancestors have told us[b]
what you did in their days,
in days long ago.

---

[a] In many Hebrew manuscripts Psalms 42 and 43 constitute one psalm. [b] In Hebrew texts 42:1-11 is numbered 42:2-12. [c] Title: Probably a literary or musical term [d] 4 See Septuagint and Syriac; the meaning of the Hebrew for this line is uncertain. [e] In Hebrew texts 44:1-26 is numbered 44:2-27.

---

of God on the righteous; it ends with the righteous blessing their Lord. Here the word "praise" identifies the Lord as the source of our blessing.

42:4 *I used to go to the house of God.* This psalm was written in exile. The psalmist is remembering with longing and tears the times when he was able to worship God in Jerusalem.

42:5 *I will yet praise him.* As is common in the Psalms, the poet is not describing an act of private devotion, but of public praise of the goodness of God. This is praise in words and songs that would be repeated in the midst of the congregation (22:22; Eph. 5:19; Heb. 13:15).

42:6 *the land of the Jordan . . . of Hermon.* These are references to the Promised Land, from which the people were exiled.

43:1 *Vindicate me.* It is believed that Psalm 43 is a continuation of Psalm 42.

43:5 *downcast.* Psalms 42 and 43 reflect a uniform feeling of being cut off from God, rejected and forsaken by Him. There is a common refrain in both psalms in which the author reasons with himself in order to surmount his feelings of depression and

42:1 [a] Ps 119:131 **42:2** [b] Ps 63:1 [c] Jer 10:10 [d] Ps 43:4 **42:3** [e] Ps 80:5 [f] Ps 79:10 **42:4** [g] Isa 30:29 [h] Ps 100:4 **42:5** [i] Ps 38:6; 77:3 [j] La 3:24 [k] Ps 44:3 **42:7** [l] Ps 88:7; Jnh 2:3 **42:8** [m] Ps 57:3 [n] Job 35:10 [o] Ps 63:6; 149:5 **42:9** [p] Ps 38:6 **42:11** [q] Ps 43:5 **43:1** [r] 1Sa 24:15; Ps 26:1; 35:1 [s] Ps 5:6 **43:2** [t] Ps 44:9 [u] Ps 42:9 **43:3** [v] Ps 36:9 [w] Ps 42:4 [x] Ps 84:1 **43:4** [y] Ps 26:6 [z] Ps 33:2 **43:5** [a] Ps 42:6 **44:1** [b] Ex 12:26; Ps 78:3

2 With your hand you drove out[c] the nations
and planted[d] our ancestors;
you crushed the peoples
and made our ancestors flourish.[e]
3 It was not by their sword[f] that they won the land,
nor did their arm bring them victory;
it was your right hand, your arm,[g]
and the light of your face, for you loved[h] them.

4 You are my King[i] and my God,
who decrees[a] victories for Jacob.
5 Through you we push back our enemies;
through your name we trample[j] our foes.
6 I put no trust in my bow,[k]
my sword does not bring me victory;
7 but you give us victory[l] over our enemies,
you put our adversaries to shame.[m]
8 In God we make our boast[n] all day long,
and we will praise your name forever.[b][o]

9 But now you have rejected[p] and humbled us;
you no longer go out with our armies.[q]
10 You made us retreat[r] before the enemy,
and our adversaries have plundered us.
11 You gave us up to be devoured like sheep[s]
and have scattered us among the nations.[t]
12 You sold your people for a pittance,[u]
gaining nothing from their sale.

13 You have made us a reproach to our neighbors,[v]
the scorn[w] and derision of those around us.
14 You have made us a byword among the nations;
the peoples shake their heads[x] at us.
15 I live in disgrace all day long,
and my face is covered with shame
16 at the taunts of those who reproach and revile[y] me,
because of the enemy, who is bent on revenge.

17 All this came upon us,
though we had not forgotten[z] you;
we had not been false to your covenant.
18 Our hearts had not turned[a] back;
our feet had not strayed from your path.
19 But you crushed[b] us and made us a haunt for jackals;
you covered us over with deep darkness.[c]

20 If we had forgotten[d] the name of our God
or spread out our hands to a foreign god,[e]
21 would not God have discovered it,
since he knows the secrets of the heart?[f]
22 Yet for your sake we face death all day long;
we are considered as sheep to be slaughtered.[g]

23 Awake,[h] Lord! Why do you sleep?[i]
Rouse yourself! Do not reject us forever.[j]
24 Why do you hide your face[k]
and forget our misery and oppression?[l]

25 We are brought down to the dust;[m]
our bodies cling to the ground.
26 Rise up[n] and help us;
rescue[o] us because of your unfailing love.

[a] 4 Septuagint, Aquila and Syriac; Hebrew *King, O God; / command* [b] 8 The Hebrew has *Selah* (a word of uncertain meaning) here.

---

loneliness. Prayer is still possible when God seems to be absent, and we can hope in God in the face of present affliction because faith enables the believer to give thanks before the answer is experienced.

44:4 *You are my King.* In this community lament, it is striking that here the speaker is singular. It may be that these words are spoken by Israel's king to the King of glory. As the king of the nation, it was appropriate for him to lead the people in asking for God's renewed favor.

44:9 *you have rejected and humbled us.* The army of Israel was not just a group of soldiers. They were the warriors of the Almighty; their victories were the victories of God, and their defeats were losses that He allowed them to endure. If He ceased accompanying them to battle, they were doomed to failure.

44:17 *we had not forgotten you.* The faithful remnant had to bear the punishment of exile as well as the wicked. Human beings are so interwoven that it is impossible to sin alone. Inevitably others will have to share the burden of our just punishment.

44:22 *as sheep.* These words predict another beloved Son of the Most High who would also feel cast off by the Lord (Is. 53:7; Rom. 8:36).

44:2 [c] Ps 78:55 [d] Ex 15:17 [e] Ps 80:9 **44:3** [f] Dt 8:17; Jos 24:12 [g] Ps 77:15 [h] Dt 4:37; 7:7-8 **44:4** [i] Ps 74:12 **44:5** [j] Ps 108:13 **44:6** [k] Ps 33:16 **44:7** [l] Ps 136:24 [m] Ps 53:5 **44:8** [n] Ps 34:2 [o] Ps 30:12 **44:9** [p] Ps 74:1 [q] Ps 60:1, 10 **44:10** [r] Lev 26:17; Jos 7:8; Ps 89:41 **44:11** [s] Ro 8:36 [t] Dt 4:27; 28:64; Ps 106:27 **44:12** [u] Isa 52:3; Jer 15:13 **44:13** [v] Ps 79:4; 80:6 [w] Dt 28:37 **44:14** [x] Ps 109:25; Jer 24:9 **44:16** [y] Ps 74:10 **44:17** [z] Ps 78:7, 57; Da 9:13 **44:18** [a] Job 23:11 **44:19** [b] Ps 51:8 [c] Job 3:5 **44:20** [d] Ps 78:11 [e] Dt 6:14; Ps 81:9 **44:21** [f] Ps 139:1-2; Jer 17:10 **44:22** [g] Isa 53:7; Ro 8:36* **44:23** [h] Ps 7:6 [i] Ps 78:65 [j] Ps 77:7 **44:24** [k] Job 13:24 [l] Ps 42:9 **44:25** [m] Ps 119:25 **44:26** [n] Ps 35:2 [o] Ps 25:22

Psalm 45[a]

For the director of music. To the tune of "Lilies." Of the Sons of Korah. A maskil.[b] *A wedding song.*

1 My heart is stirred by a noble theme
as I recite my verses for the king;
my tongue is the pen of a skillful
writer.

2 You are the most excellent of men
and your lips have been anointed
with grace,[p]
since God has blessed you forever.

3 Gird your sword[q] on your side, you
mighty one;[r]
clothe yourself with splendor and
majesty.
4 In your majesty ride forth
victoriously[s]
in the cause of truth, humility and
justice;
let your right hand achieve awesome
deeds.
5 Let your sharp arrows pierce the hearts
of the king's enemies;
let the nations fall beneath your feet.
6 Your throne, O God,[c] will last for ever
and ever;[t]
a scepter of justice will be the scepter
of your kingdom.
7 You love righteousness[u] and hate
wickedness;
therefore God, your God, has set you
above your companions
by anointing[v] you with the oil of joy.[w]
8 All your robes are fragrant[x] with myrrh
and aloes and cassia;
from palaces adorned with ivory
the music of the strings makes you
glad.
9 Daughters of kings[y] are among your
honored women;
at your right hand[z] is the royal bride
in gold of Ophir.
10 Listen, daughter, and pay careful
attention:
Forget your people[a] and your father's
house.
11 Let the king be enthralled by your
beauty;
honor[b] him, for he is your lord.[c]
12 The city of Tyre will come with a
gift,[d][d]
people of wealth will seek your favor.
13 All glorious[e] is the princess within her
chamber;
her gown is interwoven with gold.
14 In embroidered garments she is led to
the king;[f]
her virgin companions follow her—
those brought to be with her.
15 Led in with joy and gladness,
they enter the palace of the king.

16 Your sons will take the place of your
fathers;
you will make them princes
throughout the land.

17 I will perpetuate your memory through
all generations;[g]
therefore the nations will praise you[h]
for ever and ever.

Psalm 46[e]

For the director of music. Of the Sons of Korah. According to alamoth.[f] *A song.*

1 God is our refuge[i] and strength,
an ever-present[j] help in trouble.
2 Therefore we will not fear,[k] though the
earth give way[l]
and the mountains fall[m] into the
heart of the sea,

---

[a] In Hebrew texts 45:1-17 is numbered 45:2-18.
[b] Title: Probably a literary or musical term
[c] 6 Here the king is addressed as God's representative.
[d] 12 Or *A Tyrian robe is among the gifts*
[e] In Hebrew texts 46:1-11 is numbered 46:2-12.
[f] Title: Probably a musical term

45:3 *you mighty one.* In the ancient Middle East the king was supposed to be a great warrior. The model in Israel was David, the celebrated champion who defeated the giant Goliath (1 Sam. 17). The term "most mighty" is also a messianic title.
45:6 – 7 *O God . . . God, your God.* The words "Your throne" indicate the messianic direction of the psalm. Here the King is addressed as God, yet it is "God, your God" who anointed Him. The writer to the Hebrews used these verses to assert Jesus' deity (Heb. 1:8 – 9).
45:7 *righteousness.* A person is known by his loves and his hates. If a person "loves" something, he will "hate" its opposite. One who loves justice will hate oppression. One who loves truth will hate falsehood. One who loves kindness will hate cruelty. The psalm deliberately uses very strong verbs: *love* righteousness, *hate* wickedness. We might prefer to be a bit more moderate and tone down the language, but the Scripture calls us to disengage ourselves radically from wickedness, for it is both a virus and a vice.
anointing you. Anointing set aside a particular person for special service to God. In Old Testament times, those who were anointed for special service foreshadowed the Anointed One, the Messiah.
45:9 *Ophir.* Possibly located in southern Arabia or in Africa (2 Chr. 8:17 – 18), this place was known in the Old Testament world as a source of fine gold.
45:14 *embroidered garments.* In the ancient world, the beauty of the bride's gowns might be an expression of her family's wealth, their pride in her, and their love for her.
46:2 *though the earth give way.* God is a refuge for His people against everything actual or imagined.

45:2 [p] Lk 4:22 **45:3** [q] Heb 4:12; Rev 1:16 [r] Isa 9:6 **45:4** [s] Rev 6:2 **45:6** [t] Ps 93:2; 98:9 **45:7** [u] Ps 33:5 [v] Isa 61:1 [w] Ps 21:6; Heb 1:8-9* **45:8** [x] SS 1:3 **45:9** [y] SS 6:8 [z] 1Ki 2:19 **45:10** [a] Dt 21:13 **45:11** [b] Ps 95:6 [c] Isa 54:5 **45:12** [d] Ps 22:29; Isa 49:23 **45:13** [e] Isa 61:10 **45:14** [f] SS 1:4 **45:17** [g] Mal 1:11 [h] Ps 138:4 **46:1** [i] Ps 9:9; 14:6 [j] Dt 4:7 **46:2** [k] Ps 23:4 [l] Ps 82:5 [m] Ps 18:7

3 though its waters roar[n] and foam
and the mountains quake with their surging.[a]

4 There is a river whose streams make glad the city of God,[o]
the holy place where the Most High dwells.
5 God is within her,[p] she will not fall;
God will help[q] her at break of day.
6 Nations[r] are in uproar, kingdoms[s] fall;
he lifts his voice, the earth melts.[t]

7 The LORD Almighty is with us;[u]
the God of Jacob is our fortress.[v]

8 Come and see what the LORD has done,[w]
the desolations[x] he has brought on the earth.
9 He makes wars[y] cease
to the ends of the earth.
He breaks the bow[z] and shatters the spear;
he burns the shields[b] with fire.[a]
10 He says, "Be still, and know that I am God;[b]
I will be exalted[c] among the nations,
I will be exalted in the earth."

11 The LORD Almighty is with us;
the God of Jacob is our fortress.

Psalm 47[c]

For the director of music. Of the Sons of Korah. A psalm.

1 Clap your hands,[d] all you nations;
shout to God with cries of joy.[e]

2 For the LORD Most High is awesome,[f]
the great King[g] over all the earth.
3 He subdued[h] nations under us,
peoples under our feet.
4 He chose our inheritance[i] for us,
the pride of Jacob, whom he loved.[d]

5 God has ascended amid shouts of joy,
the LORD amid the sounding of trumpets.[j]
6 Sing praises[k] to God, sing praises;
sing praises to our King, sing praises.
7 For God is the King of all the earth;[l]
sing to him a psalm[m] of praise.

8 God reigns[n] over the nations;
God is seated on his holy throne.
9 The nobles of the nations assemble
as the people of the God of Abraham,
for the kings[e] of the earth belong to God;[o]
he is greatly exalted.[p]

Psalm 48[f]

A song. A psalm of the Sons of Korah.

1 Great is the LORD,[q] and most worthy of praise,
in the city of our God,[r] his holy mountain.[s]

2 Beautiful[t] in its loftiness,
the joy of the whole earth,
like the heights of Zaphon[g] is Mount Zion,
the city of the Great King.[u]
3 God is in her citadels;
he has shown himself to be her fortress.[v]

4 When the kings joined forces,
when they advanced together,[w]
5 they saw her and were astounded;
they fled in terror.[x]

---

[a] *3* The Hebrew has *Selah* (a word of uncertain meaning) here and at the end of verses 7 and 11. [b] *9* Or *chariots* [c] In Hebrew texts 47:1-9 is numbered 47:2-10. [d] *4* The Hebrew has *Selah* (a word of uncertain meaning) here. [e] *9* Or *shields* [f] In Hebrew texts 48:1-14 is numbered 48:2-15. [g] *2* *Zaphon* was the most sacred mountain of the Canaanites.

46:5 *God is within her.* We do not have an absentee deliverer, a defense that is only sometimes present. The Lord lives with His people and His protection can be counted on.
46:10 *Be still, and know that I am God.* This call for stillness before the Lord is not preparation for worship, but for impending judgment (Hab. 2:20; Zeph. 1:7; Zech. 2:13).
47:4 *whom he loved.* To love means "to make one's choice in." God had chosen the Israelites to be His holy people and, in that way, He loved them. In His dialogue with Nicodemus, Jesus explained that God's love extended to all the nations as well as to Israel (John 3:16).
47:9 *the people of the God of Abraham.* This is the prophetic picture of the ultimate fulfillment of the Abrahamic covenant (Gen. 12:1–3). One day all the peoples of the earth who have come to faith in God through Jesus will discover that they are one people. They are all the true seed of Abraham because they, like Abraham, believed in God (Gen. 15:6; Gal. 3:5–8).
48:1 *Great is the LORD.* Psalm 48 unites with Psalms 46 and 47 to form three great psalms of praise to God for His kingship and His love for the holy city of Jerusalem. This emphasis on Jerusalem has led many scholars to speak of these psalms as "Songs of Zion." ***the city of our God.*** The city of Jerusalem had a particularly dear place in the heart of God's people (1 Kin. 14:21). The city was holy because of the presence of God in the temple.
48:2 *the joy of the whole earth.* As is strongly established in the Book of Psalms, the purpose of God's work in Israel was to draw all nations to Himself. ***city***

46:3 [n] Ps 93:3 **46:4** [o] Ps 48:1,8; Isa 60:14 **46:5** [p] Isa 12:6; Eze 43:7 [q] Ps 37:40 **46:6** [r] Ps 2:1 [s] Ps 68:32 [t] Mic 1:4 **46:7** [u] 2Ch 13:12 [v] Ps 9:9 **46:8** [w] Ps 66:5 [x] Isa 61:4 **46:9** [y] Isa 2:4 [z] Ps 76:3 [a] Eze 39:9 **46:10** [b] Ps 100:3 [c] Isa 2:11 **47:1** [d] Ps 98:8; Isa 55:12 [e] Ps 106:47 **47:2** [f] Dt 7:21 [g] Mal 1:14 **47:3** [h] Ps 18:39,47 **47:4** [i] 1Pe 1:4 **47:5** [j] Ps 68:33; 98:6 **47:6** [k] Ps 68:4; 89:18 **47:7** [l] Zec 14:9 [m] Col 3:16 **47:8** [n] 1Ch 16:31 **47:9** [o] Ps 72:11; 89:18 [p] Ps 97:9 **48:1** [q] Ps 96:4 [r] Ps 46:4 [s] Isa 2:2-3; Mic 4:1; Zec 8:3 **48:2** [t] Ps 50:2; La 2:15 [u] Mt 5:35 **48:3** [v] Ps 46:7 **48:4** [w] 2Sa 10:1-19 **48:5** [x] Ex 15:16

[6]Trembling seized them there,
pain like that of a woman in labor.
[7]You destroyed them like ships of Tarshish
shattered by an east wind.[y]

[8]As we have heard,
so we have seen
in the city of the LORD Almighty,
in the city of our God:
God makes her secure forever.[az]

[9]Within your temple, O God,
we meditate on your unfailing love.[a]
[10]Like your name,[b] O God,
your praise reaches to the ends of the earth;[c]
your right hand is filled with righteousness.
[11]Mount Zion rejoices,
the villages of Judah are glad
because of your judgments.[d]

[12]Walk about Zion, go around her,
count her towers,
[13]consider well her ramparts,
view her citadels,[e]
that you may tell of them
to the next generation.[f]

[14]For this God is our God for ever and ever;
he will be our guide[g] even to the end.

Psalm 49[b]

For the director of music. Of the Sons of Korah. A psalm.

[1]Hear this, all you peoples;[h]
listen, all who live in this world,[i]
[2]both low and high,
rich and poor alike:
[3]My mouth will speak words of wisdom;[j]
the meditation of my heart will give you understanding.[k]
[4]I will turn my ear to a proverb;[l]
with the harp I will expound my riddle:[m]

[5]Why should I fear[n] when evil days come,
when wicked deceivers surround me—
[6]those who trust in their wealth[o]
and boast of their great riches?
[7]No one can redeem the life of another
or give to God a ransom for them—
[8]the ransom for a life is costly,
no payment is ever enough—[p]
[9]so that they should live on[q] forever
and not see decay.
[10]For all can see that the wise die,[r]
that the foolish and the senseless also perish,
leaving their wealth to others.[s]
[11]Their tombs will remain their houses[c] forever,
their dwellings for endless generations,
though they had[d] named[t] lands after themselves.

[12]People, despite their wealth, do not endure;
they are like the beasts that perish.

[13]This is the fate of those who trust in themselves,[u]
and of their followers, who approve their sayings.[e]
[14]They are like sheep and are destined to die;[v]
death will be their shepherd
(but the upright will prevail[w] over them in the morning).
Their forms will decay in the grave,
far from their princely mansions.
[15]But God will redeem me from the realm of the dead;[x]
he will surely take me to himself.[y]
[16]Do not be overawed when others grow rich,
when the splendor of their houses increases;

---

[a] *8* The Hebrew has *Selah* (a word of uncertain meaning) here. [b] In Hebrew texts 49:1-20 is numbered 49:2-21. [c] *11* Septuagint and Syriac; Hebrew *In their thoughts their houses will remain* [d] *11* Or *generations, / for they have* [e] *13* The Hebrew has *Selah* (a word of uncertain meaning) here and at the end of verse 15.

---

of the Great King. Jesus quoted these words in Matthew 5:35, speaking of Jerusalem.
48:12 *Walk about Zion.* Praising the city of Zion was another way of praising God, whose dwelling was there.
49:4 *riddle.* Also translated "dark saying," this word refers to a perplexing moral problem. How do the righteous come to terms with oppressive rich people who seem to have no thought for God?
49:6 *those who trust in their wealth.* The accumulation of material wealth is of no value in the life to come (Mark 10:23). Money can never buy redemption. Only God has the power to deliver us from death and hell.
49:14 *death will be their shepherd.* Death is the great leveler. People who have beauty, riches (vv. 16–17), and power in this world will lose them all at death. They will be stripped of everything except their character or soul. This is why the Scriptures exhort us to pursue character development—God's law, holiness, wisdom, and knowledge—more than anything else.

48:7 [y] Jer 18:17; Eze 27:26 **48:8** [z] Ps 87:5 **48:9** [a] Ps 26:3 **48:10** [b] Dt 28:58; Jos 7:9 [c] Isa 41:10 **48:11** [d] Ps 97:8 **48:13** [e] ver 3; Ps 122:7 [f] Ps 78:6 **48:14** [g] Ps 23:4 **49:1** [h] Ps 78:1 [i] Ps 33:8 **49:3** [j] Ps 37:30 [k] Ps 119:130 **49:4** [l] Ps 78:2 [m] Nu 12:8 **49:5** [n] Ps 23:4 **49:6** [o] Job 31:24 **49:8** [p] Mt 16:26 **49:9** [q] Ps 22:29; 89:48 **49:10** [r] Ecc 2:16 [s] Ecc 2:18,21 **49:11** [t] Ge 4:17; Dt 3:14 **49:13** [u] Lk 12:20 **49:14** [v] Job 24:19; Ps 9:17 [w] Da 7:18; Mal 4:3; 1Co 6:2; Rev 2:26 **49:15** [x] Ps 56:13; Hos 13:14 [y] Ps 73:24

17 for they will take nothing with them
when they die,
their splendor will not descend with
them.[z]
18 Though while they live they count
themselves blessed—[a]
and people praise you when you
prosper—
19 they will join those who have gone
before them,[b]
who will never again see the light[c] of
life.

20 People who have wealth but lack
understanding
are like the beasts that perish.[d]

Psalm 50

A psalm of Asaph.

1 The Mighty One, God, the LORD,[e]
speaks and summons the earth
from the rising of the sun to where it
sets.[f]
2 From Zion, perfect in beauty,[g]
God shines forth.[h]
3 Our God comes[i]
and will not be silent;
a fire devours before him,[j]
and around him a tempest rages.
4 He summons the heavens above,
and the earth,[k] that he may judge his
people:
5 "Gather to me this consecrated people,[l]
who made a covenant[m] with me by
sacrifice."
6 And the heavens proclaim[n] his
righteousness,
for he is a God of justice.[a,b o]

7 "Listen, my people, and I will speak;
I will testify[p] against you, Israel:
I am God, your God.[q]
8 I bring no charges against you
concerning your sacrifices
or concerning your burnt offerings,[r]
which are ever before me.
9 I have no need of a bull[s] from your stall
or of goats from your pens,
10 for every animal of the forest is mine,
and the cattle on a thousand hills.[t]
11 I know every bird in the mountains,
and the insects in the fields are mine.
12 If I were hungry I would not tell you,
for the world[u] is mine, and all that is
in it.
13 Do I eat the flesh of bulls
or drink the blood of goats?

14 "Sacrifice thank offerings[v] to God,
fulfill your vows[w] to the Most High,
15 and call[x] on me in the day of trouble;
I will deliver you, and you will
honor[y] me."

16 But to the wicked person, God says:

"What right have you to recite my laws
or take my covenant on your lips?[z]
17 You hate my instruction
and cast my words behind[a] you.
18 When you see a thief, you join[b] with
him;
you throw in your lot with adulterers.
19 You use your mouth for evil
and harness your tongue to deceit.[c]
20 You sit and testify against your brother[d]
and slander your own mother's son.
21 When you did these things and I kept
silent,[e]
you thought I was exactly[c] like you.
But I now arraign you
and set my accusations[f] before you.

22 "Consider this, you who forget God,[g]
or I will tear you to pieces, with no
one to rescue you:[h]
23 Those who sacrifice thank offerings
honor me,
and to the blameless[d] I will show my
salvation.[i]"

[a] *6* With a different word division of the Hebrew; Masoretic Text *for God himself is judge* [b] *6* The Hebrew has *Selah* (a word of uncertain meaning) here. [c] *21* Or *thought the 'I AM' was* [d] *23* Probable reading of the original Hebrew text; the meaning of the Masoretic Text for this phrase is uncertain.

50:1 *The Mighty One, God, the LORD.* These three titles give a stunning introduction to the poem, a grand display of God Himself in the midst of His people.

50:8 *charges against you concerning your sacrifices.* The sacrifices were commanded by God in Leviticus, but the people had difficulty keeping a godly perspective on the nature of sacrifices. God did not need their offerings—He is already the owner of all the earth. The sacrifices were for their sakes, so that they would understand that sin equals death, and atonement comes by blood.

50:12 *If I were hungry, I would not tell you.* God doesn't hunger for food—and even if He did, He would not need His people to bring it to Him. He hungers for the righteousness of His people.

50:18 *you throw in your lot with adulterers.* In this psalm the Lord brings a legal case against His people for violations of the covenant (v. 4). Verses 7–15 address the formalists, whose major emphasis is on the outward and external observances of the ceremonial law. Verses 16–23 are spoken to wicked members of the community who do not put God's commandments into practice in everyday life. The believer's attitude toward evil is to be one of total rejection: "Do not love the world or anything in the world" (1 John 2:15). There is no neutrality in regard to the moral law, and no approval can be given to those who disobey God's law (Rom. 1:32).

49:17 [z] Ps 17:14; 1Ti 6:7 **49:18** [a] Dt 29:19; Lk 12:19 **49:19** [b] Ge 15:15 [c] Job 33:30 **49:20** [d] Ecc 3:19 **50:1** [e] Jos 22:22 [f] Ps 113:3 **50:2** [g] Ps 48:2 [h] Dt 33:2; Ps 80:1 **50:3** [i] Ps 96:13 [j] Ps 97:3; Da 7:10 **50:4** [k] Dt 4:26; Isa 1:2 **50:5** [l] Ps 30:4 [m] Ex 24:7 **50:6** [n] Ps 89:5 [o] Ps 75:7 **50:7** [p] Ps 81:8 [q] Ex 20:2 **50:8** [r] Ps 40:6; Hos 6:6 **50:9** [s] Ps 69:31 **50:10** [t] Ps 104:24 **50:12** [u] Ex 19:5 **50:14** [v] Heb 13:15 [w] Dt 23:21 **50:15** [x] Ps 81:7 [y] Ps 22:23 **50:16** [z] Isa 29:13 **50:17** [a] Ne 9:26; Ro 2:21-22 **50:18** [b] Ro 1:32; 1Ti 5:22 **50:19** [c] Ps 10:7; 52:2 **50:20** [d] Mt 10:21 **50:21** [e] Ecc 8:11; Isa 42:14 [f] Ps 90:8 **50:22** [g] Job 8:13; Ps 9:17 [h] Ps 7:2 **50:23** [i] Ps 91:16

Psalm 51[a]

For the director of music. A psalm of David. When the prophet Nathan came to him after David had committed adultery with Bathsheba.

1 Have mercy on me, O God,
according to your unfailing love;
according to your great compassion
blot out[j] my transgressions.[k]
2 Wash away[l] all my iniquity
and cleanse[m] me from my sin.

3 For I know my transgressions,
and my sin is always before me.[n]
4 Against you, you only, have I sinned
and done what is evil in your sight;[o]
so you are right in your verdict
and justified when you judge.[p]
5 Surely I was sinful[q] at birth,
sinful from the time my mother conceived me.
6 Yet you desired faithfulness even in the womb;
you taught me wisdom[r] in that secret place.[s]

7 Cleanse me with hyssop,[t] and I will be clean;
wash me, and I will be whiter than snow.[u]
8 Let me hear joy and gladness;[v]
let the bones you have crushed rejoice.
9 Hide your face from my sins[w]
and blot out all my iniquity.

10 Create in me a pure heart,[x] O God,
and renew a steadfast spirit within me.[y]
11 Do not cast me from your presence
or take your Holy Spirit[z] from me.
12 Restore to me the joy of your salvation[a]
and grant me a willing spirit, to sustain me.

13 Then I will teach transgressors your ways,[b]
so that sinners will turn back to you.[c]
14 Deliver me from the guilt of bloodshed,[d] O God,
you who are God my Savior,[e]
and my tongue will sing of your righteousness.[f]
15 Open my lips, Lord,[g]
and my mouth will declare your praise.
16 You do not delight in sacrifice,[h] or I would bring it;
you do not take pleasure in burnt offerings.
17 My sacrifice, O God, is[b] a broken spirit;
a broken and contrite heart[i]
you, God, will not despise.

18 May it please you to prosper Zion,[j]
to build up the walls of Jerusalem.
19 Then you will delight in the sacrifices of the righteous,[k]
in burnt offerings[l] offered whole;
then bulls[m] will be offered on your altar.

---

[a] In Hebrew texts 51:1-19 is numbered 51:3-21.
[b] 17 Or *The sacrifices of God are*

51:1 *Have mercy on me.* This psalm is associated with one of the hardest experiences of David's life, the aftermath of his affair with Bathsheba. For the account of David's sin and the prophet Nathan's rebuke, see 2 Samuel 11:1 – 12:15. according to ***your great compassion.*** David's call for compassion is the only appropriate request for a confessing sinner. No sinner should ask for justice, for that would mean judgment and ruin.

51:4 *Against you.* David had sinned against Bathsheba, Uriah, and the nation he was called to rule. But none of these indictments were as serious as David's offense against God.

51:5 *sinful.* The psalmist should not be misunderstood as teaching that the pollution of human nature results from anything inherently corrupt in sexual relations between husband and wife. We are male and female by the sovereign will and creative power of God (Gen. 1:27). What David confesses, however, is the reality of human depravity (Rom. 5:12). We are inclined to gratify the cravings of our sinful nature, following its desires and thoughts, contradicting God's commands. This is why we must experience radical regeneration by the supernatural power of the Holy Spirit. Apart from that rebirth, we can neither see nor enter the kingdom of God (John 3:3 – 5).

51:7 *hyssop.* Here David refers to the ritual acts of cleansing described in the law of Moses (Lev. 14:4; Num. 19:6).

51:10 – 13 Confession — Confession leads to forgiveness, but what does that look like? Psalm 51 gives us a picture. The results of forgiveness are a clean heart, a renewed spirit, a restored relationship with God, and a joyful experience of God's salvation. God cleans us up. He makes us presentable. He reorients us towards Himself, helping us to focus on what it is right. By forgiving us, God crosses over the canyon of sin that separates us from Him. When you put all this together there is great cause for joy on our part. Forgiveness is more than a theological abstract. It makes the salvation experience deeply personal and emotional in every sense. It takes that which is wrong in our life and makes it right.

51:16 *You do not delight in sacrifice.* God's pleasure is not in the sacrificed animal, but in the willing obedience of His people (Gen. 4:1 – 7; John 4:21 – 24; Rom. 12:1 – 2). The motions of sacrifice not accompanied by a contrite heart are not acceptable to God (Is. 1:12 – 20).

51:1 [j] Ac 3:19 [k] Isa 43:25; Col 2:14 **51:2** [l] 1Jn 1:9 [m] Heb 9:14 **51:3** [n] Isa 59:12 **51:4** [o] Ge 20:6; Lk 15:21 [p] Ro 3:4* **51:5** [q] Job 14:4 **51:6** [r] Pr 2:6 [s] Ps 15:2 **51:7** [t] Lev 14:4; Heb 9:19 [u] Isa 1:18 **51:8** [v] Isa 35:10 **51:9** [w] Jer 16:17 **51:10** [x] Ps 78:37; Ac 15:9 [y] Eze 18:31 **51:11** [z] Eph 4:30 **51:12** [a] Ps 13:5 **51:13** [b] Ac 9:21-22 [c] Ps 22:27 **51:14** [d] 2Sa 12:9 [e] Ps 25:5 [f] Ps 35:28 **51:15** [g] Ps 9:14 **51:16** [h] 1Sa 15:22; Ps 40:6 **51:17** [i] Ps 34:18 **51:18** [j] Ps 102:16; Isa 51:3 **51:19** [k] Ps 4:5 [l] Ps 66:13 [m] Ps 66:15

Psalm 52[a]

For the director of music. A maskil[b] of David. When Doeg the Edomite[n] had gone to Saul and told him: "David has gone to the house of Ahimelek."

1 Why do you boast of evil, you mighty hero?
Why do you boast[o] all day long,
you who are a disgrace in the eyes of God?
2 You who practice deceit,[p]
your tongue plots destruction;
it is like a sharpened razor.[q]
3 You love evil rather than good,
falsehood[r] rather than speaking the truth.[c]
4 You love every harmful word,
you deceitful tongue![s]

5 Surely God will bring you down to everlasting ruin:
He will snatch you up and pluck[t] you from your tent;
he will uproot[u] you from the land of the living.[v]
6 The righteous will see and fear;
they will laugh[w] at you, saying,
7 "Here now is the man
who did not make God his stronghold
but trusted in his great wealth[x]
and grew strong by destroying others!"

8 But I am like an olive tree[y]
flourishing in the house of God;
I trust[z] in God's unfailing love
for ever and ever.
9 For what you have done I will always praise you[a]
in the presence of your faithful people.
And I will hope in your name,
for your name is good.[b]

Psalm 53[d]

For the director of music. According to mahalath.[e] A maskil[b] of David.

1 The fool[c] says in his heart,
"There is no God."[d]
They are corrupt, and their ways are vile;
there is no one who does good.

2 God looks down from heaven[e]
on all mankind
to see if there are any who understand,
any who seek God.[f]
3 Everyone has turned away, all have become corrupt;
there is no one who does good,
not even one.[g]

4 Do all these evildoers know nothing?

They devour my people as though eating bread;
they never call on God.
5 But there they are, overwhelmed with dread,
where there was nothing to dread.[h]
God scattered the bones[i] of those who attacked you;
you put them to shame, for God despised them.

6 Oh, that salvation for Israel would come out of Zion!
When God restores his people,
let Jacob rejoice and Israel be glad!

Psalm 54[f]

For the director of music. With stringed instruments. A maskil[b] of David. When the Ziphites had gone to Saul and said, "Is not David hiding among us?"

1 Save me, O God, by your name;[j]
vindicate me by your might.[k]
2 Hear my prayer, O God;[l]
listen to the words of my mouth.

3 Arrogant foes are attacking me;[m]
ruthless people are trying to kill me[n]—
people without regard for God.[g][o]

---

[a] In Hebrew texts 52:1-9 is numbered 52:3-11.
[b] Title: Probably a literary or musical term
[c] 3 The Hebrew has *Selah* (a word of uncertain meaning) here and at the end of verse 5. [d] In Hebrew texts 53:1-6 is numbered 53:2-7. [e] Title: Probably a musical term [f] In Hebrew texts 54:1-7 is numbered 54:3-9. [g] 3 The Hebrew has *Selah* (a word of uncertain meaning) here.

52:2 *your tongue.* This phrase refers to more than just words. These people used language as a weapon, for they believed that the gods could empower their words to a devastating effect.
52:6 *see and fear.* This fear is a deepened respect for God and a sense of awe before His throne.
52:8 *an olive tree.* An olive tree was a symbol of beauty. In Romans 11:16–24, the olive tree is used as a symbol of the Gentiles who are grafted into the root—the people of God or the church.
53:1 *The fool.* In the Bible, the term "fool" does not indicate mental incompetence, but moral and spiritual insensitivity.
53:5 *scattered the bones.* This is a prophetic pronouncement of the final judgment on the wicked.
54:3 *people without regard for God.* In one of the dark moments of David's life, when the insanely jealous King Saul was bent on destroying him, David was able to lift his heart in supplication, trust, and praise to God. He had been hiding with his men in the hill country south of Jeshimon, but his location

52:Title [n] 1Sa 22:9 **52:1** [o] Ps 94:4 **52:2** [p] Ps 50:19 [q] Ps 57:4 **52:3** [r] Jer 9:5 **52:4** [s] Ps 120:2, 3 **52:5** [t] Isa 22:19 [u] Pr 2:22 [v] Ps 27:13 **52:6** [w] Job 22:19; Ps 37:34; 40:3 **52:7** [x] Ps 49:6 **52:8** [y] Jer 11:16 [z] Ps 13:5 **52:9** [a] Ps 30:12 [b] Ps 54:6 **53:1** [c] Ps 14:1-7; Ro 3:10 [d] Ps 10:4 **53:2** [e] Ps 33:13 [f] 2Ch 15:2 **53:3** [g] Ro 3:10-12* **53:5** [h] Lev 26:17 [i] Eze 6:5 **54:1** [j] Ps 20:1 [k] 2Ch 20:6 **54:2** [l] Ps 5:1; 55:1 **54:3** [m] Ps 86:14 [n] Ps 40:14 [o] Ps 36:1

4 Surely God is my help;[p]
the Lord is the one who sustains me.[q]
5 Let evil recoil[r] on those who slander me;
in your faithfulness[s] destroy them.
6 I will sacrifice a freewill offering[t] to you;
I will praise your name, LORD, for it is good.[u]
7 You have delivered me[v] from all my troubles,
and my eyes have looked in triumph on my foes.[w]

Psalm 55[a]

For the director of music. With stringed instruments. A maskil[b] of David.

1 Listen to my prayer, O God,
do not ignore my plea;[x]
2 hear me and answer me.[y]
My thoughts trouble me and I am distraught[z]
3 because of what my enemy is saying,
because of the threats of the wicked;
for they bring down suffering on me[a]
and assail me in their anger.[b]

4 My heart is in anguish within me;
the terrors[c] of death have fallen on me.
5 Fear and trembling[d] have beset me;
horror has overwhelmed me.
6 I said, "Oh, that I had the wings of a dove!
I would fly away and be at rest.
7 I would flee far away
and stay in the desert;[c]
8 I would hurry to my place of shelter,
far from the tempest and storm.[e]"

9 Lord, confuse the wicked, confound their words,
for I see violence and strife[f] in the city.
10 Day and night they prowl about on its walls;
malice and abuse are within it.
11 Destructive forces[g] are at work in the city;
threats and lies[h] never leave its streets.

12 If an enemy were insulting me,
I could endure it;
if a foe were rising against me,
I could hide.
13 But it is you, a man like myself,
my companion, my close friend,[i]
14 with whom I once enjoyed sweet fellowship
at the house of God,[j]
as we walked about
among the worshipers.

15 Let death take my enemies by surprise;[k]
let them go down alive to the realm of the dead,[l]
for evil finds lodging among them.
16 As for me, I call to God,
and the LORD saves me.
17 Evening,[m] morning[n] and noon
I cry out in distress,
and he hears my voice.
18 He rescues me unharmed
from the battle waged against me,
even though many oppose me.
19 God, who is enthroned from of old,[o]
who does not change—
he will hear[p] them and humble them,
because they have no fear of God.

20 My companion attacks his friends;[q]
he violates his covenant.[r]
21 His talk is smooth as butter,
yet war is in his heart;
his words are more soothing than oil,[s]
yet they are drawn swords.[t]

[a] In Hebrew texts 55:1-23 is numbered 55:2-24.
[b] Title: Probably a literary or musical term
[c] 7 The Hebrew has *Selah* (a word of uncertain meaning) here and in the middle of verse 19.

---

was betrayed to Saul by the people of Ziph (1 Sam. 23:19; 26:1). These were the "strangers" who doubtless stood to profit from David's death. They had no regard for covenant law, which bade the Israelites to love their neighbors as themselves (Lev. 19:18). Nor did they love the Lord their God wholeheartedly (Deut. 6:5), but instead turned their hands against His anointed. Betrayal is a supreme act of treachery, whether in terms of a human being such as David, or of Jesus (Luke 22:48), the anointed Son of God. As such, it merits the most severe punishment from God (Mark 14:21).

54:5 *in your faithfulness destroy.* David did not take vengeance into his own hands. Only the Lord can take revenge.

55:4 *terrors of death.* David's intense pain can be felt in his strong language. The phrase "terrors of death" is unusual. The Hebrew word for "terror" or "dread" is first used in Scripture to describe the horror that Abraham felt in the unnatural darkness that seized him as God was about to come near (Gen. 15:12). The word also described the horrors that would fall on the people of Canaan when the Lord gave the land to the Israelites (Ex. 15:16). To strengthen this feeling, David speaks of fear and trembling and an overwhelming horror (Ezek. 7:18).

55:15 *let them go down alive to the realm of the dead.* David could express his emotions to God in prayer, but judgment or revenge was in God's hands (Rom. 12:19).

54:4 [p] Ps 118:7 [q] Ps 41:12 **54:5** [r] Ps 94:23 [s] Ps 89:49; 143:12 **54:6** [t] Ps 50:14 [u] Ps 52:9 **54:7** [v] Ps 34:6 [w] Ps 59:10 **55:1** [x] Ps 27:9; 61:1 **55:2** [y] Ps 66:19 [z] Ps 77:3; Isa 38:14 **55:3** [a] 2Sa 16:6-8; Ps 17:9 [b] Ps 71:11 **55:4** [c] Ps 116:3 **55:5** [d] Job 21:6; Ps 119:120 **55:8** [e] Isa 4:6 **55:9** [f] Jer 6:7 **55:11** [g] Ps 5:9 [h] Ps 10:7 **55:13** [i] 2Sa 15:12; Ps 41:9 **55:14** [j] Ps 42:4 **55:15** [k] Ps 64:7 [l] Nu 16:30, 33 **55:17** [m] Ps 141:2; Ac 3:1 [n] Ps 5:3 **55:19** [o] Dt 33:27 [p] Ps 78:59 **55:20** [q] Ps 7:4 [r] Ps 89:34 **55:21** [s] Pr 5:3 [t] Ps 28:3; 57:4; 59:7

22 Cast your cares on the LORD
and he will sustain you;[u]
he will never let
the righteous be shaken.[v]
23 But you, God, will bring down the
wicked
into the pit[w] of decay;
the bloodthirsty and deceitful[x]
will not live out half their days.[y]

But as for me, I trust in you.[z]

Psalm 56[a]

For the director of music. To the tune of "A Dove on Distant Oaks." Of David. A miktam.[b] *When the Philistines had seized him in Gath.*

1 Be merciful to me, my God,
for my enemies are in hot pursuit;[a]
all day long they press their attack.
2 My adversaries pursue me all day long;[b]
in their pride many are
attacking me.[c]

3 When I am afraid,[d] I put my trust in
you.
4 In God, whose word I praise—
in God I trust and am not afraid.
What can mere mortals do to me?[e]

5 All day long they twist my words;[f]
all their schemes are for my ruin.
6 They conspire,[g] they lurk,
they watch my steps,
hoping to take my life.[h]
7 Because of their wickedness do not[c] let
them escape;
in your anger, God, bring the nations
down.[i]

8 Record my misery;
list my tears on your scroll[d]—
are they not in your record?[j]
9 Then my enemies will turn back[k]
when I call for help.[l]
By this I will know that God is
for me.[m]

10 In God, whose word I praise,
in the LORD, whose word I praise—
11 in God I trust and am not afraid.
What can man do to me?

12 I am under vows[n] to you, my God;
I will present my thank offerings to
you.
13 For you have delivered me from
death[o]
and my feet from stumbling,
that I may walk before God
in the light of life.[p]

Psalm 57[e]

For the director of music. To the tune of "Do Not Destroy." Of David. A miktam.[b] *When he had fled from Saul into the cave.*

1 Have mercy on me, my God, have
mercy on me,
for in you I take refuge.[q]
I will take refuge in the shadow of your
wings[r]
until the disaster has passed.[s]

2 I cry out to God Most High,
to God, who vindicates me.[t]
3 He sends from heaven and saves me,[u]
rebuking those who hotly
pursue me—[f][v]
God sends forth his love and his
faithfulness.[w]

4 I am in the midst of lions;[x]
I am forced to dwell among ravenous
beasts—
men whose teeth are spears and
arrows,
whose tongues are sharp swords.[y]

5 Be exalted, O God, above the
heavens;
let your glory be over all the earth.[z]

---

[a] In Hebrew texts 56:1-13 is numbered 56:2-14.
[b] Title: Probably a literary or musical term
[c] 7 Probable reading of the original Hebrew text; Masoretic Text does not have *do not.*
[d] 8 Or *misery; / put my tears in your wineskin*
[e] In Hebrew texts 57:1-11 is numbered 57:2-12.
[f] 3 The Hebrew has *Selah* (a word of uncertain meaning) here and at the end of verse 6.

55:22 *Cast your cares on the LORD.* The Lord is the one constant in life, and the one true Friend.
56:1 *Be merciful to me.* David cried out to God because of his overwhelming sense of loss during his time as a fugitive in a foreign land (1 Sam. 21:10 – 15).
56:8 *list my tears on your scroll.* Nothing that happens to us escapes God's notice and care; not a tear falls to the ground that He does not remember. When we suffer, it is a great comfort to know that God is *for* us — everything that we live through will be put to use for our good.
57:title *Saul into the cave.* The narrative of David's life indicates that he twice hid in caves — once in Adullam (1 Sam. 22:1 – 5) which was the setting of Psalm 142, and once in En Gedi (1 Sam. 24:1 – 7), the setting of this poem. In En Gedi, David spared Saul's life even though he had a perfect chance to put Saul out of the way and claim the kingship for himself.
57:1 – 3 *I cry out to God.* Although he had lived a righteous life, David still realized that he did not deserve the protection of God and that if his life was saved it would be by the grace of God. He trusted God to care for him just as a mother hen protects her young by covering them with her wings.
57:5 *Be exalted.* One of the ways in which God exalts Himself is by graciously delivering the needy.

55:22 [u] Ps 37:5; Mt 6:25-34; 1Pe 5:7 [v] Ps 37:24
55:23 [w] Ps 73:18 [x] Ps 5:6 [y] Job 15:32; Pr 10:27 [z] Ps 25:2
56:1 [a] Ps 57:1-3 **56:2** [b] Ps 57:3 [c] Ps 35:1
56:3 [d] Ps 55:4-5 **56:4** [e] Ps 118:6; Heb 13:6
56:5 [f] Ps 41:7 **56:6** [g] Ps 59:3 [h] Ps 71:10 **56:7** [i] Ps 36:12; 55:23 **56:8** [j] Mal 3:16 **56:9** [k] Ps 9:3 [l] Ps 102:2
[m] Ro 8:31 **56:12** [n] Ps 50:14 **56:13** [o] Ps 116:8
[p] Job 33:30 **57:1** [q] Ps 2:12 [r] Ps 17:8 [s] Isa 26:20
57:2 [t] Ps 138:8 **57:3** [u] Ps 18:9, 16 [v] Ps 56:1 [w] Ps 40:11
57:4 [x] Ps 35:17 [y] Ps 55:21; Pr 30:14 **57:5** [z] Ps 108:5

[6]They spread a net for my feet—
I was bowed down[a] in distress.
They dug a pit[b] in my path—
but they have fallen into it themselves.[c]

[7]My heart, O God, is steadfast,
my heart is steadfast;[d]
I will sing and make music.
[8]Awake, my soul!
Awake, harp and lyre![e]
I will awaken the dawn.

[9]I will praise you, Lord, among the nations;
I will sing of you among the peoples.
[10]For great is your love, reaching to the heavens;
your faithfulness reaches to the skies.[f]

[11]Be exalted, O God, above the heavens;
let your glory be over all the earth.[g]

Psalm 58[a]

For the director of music. To the tune of "Do Not Destroy." Of David. A miktam.[b]

[1]Do you rulers indeed speak justly?[h]
Do you judge people with equity?
[2]No, in your heart you devise injustice,
and your hands mete out violence on the earth.[i]

[3]Even from birth the wicked go astray;
from the womb they are wayward, spreading lies.
[4]Their venom is like the venom of a snake,[j]
like that of a cobra that has stopped its ears,
[5]that will not heed the tune of the charmer,
however skillful the enchanter may be.

[6]Break the teeth in their mouths, O God;[k]
LORD, tear out the fangs of those lions![l]
[7]Let them vanish like water that flows away;[m]
when they draw the bow, let their arrows fall short.[n]
[8]May they be like a slug that melts away as it moves along,
like a stillborn child[o] that never sees the sun.

[9]Before your pots can feel the heat of the thorns[p]—
whether they be green or dry—the wicked will be swept away.[cq]
[10]The righteous will be glad when they are avenged,[r]
when they dip their feet in the blood of the wicked.[s]
[11]Then people will say,
"Surely the righteous still are rewarded;
surely there is a God who judges the earth."[t]

Psalm 59[d]

For the director of music. To the tune of "Do Not Destroy." Of David. A miktam.[b] *When Saul had sent men to watch David's house in order to kill him.*

[1]Deliver me from my enemies, O God;[u]
be my fortress against those who are attacking me.
[2]Deliver me from evildoers
and save me from those who are after my blood.[v]

[3]See how they lie in wait for me!
Fierce men conspire[w] against me
for no offense or sin of mine, LORD.
[4]I have done no wrong, yet they are ready to attack me.[x]
Arise to help me; look on my plight!

---

[a] In Hebrew texts 58:1-11 is numbered 58:2-12.
[b] Title: Probably a literary or musical term
[c] 9 The meaning of the Hebrew for this verse is uncertain.
[d] In Hebrew texts 59:1-17 is numbered 59:2-18.

57:7 ***My heart, O God, is steadfast.*** Just as Paul was able to say that he had kept the faith (2 Tim. 4:7), David rejoiced that his trust in God had remained strong.

58:1 ***rulers.*** This may also be translated "mighty ones" or "judges." Although they were merely humans, the wicked judges were behaving as though they claimed divine authority.

58:6 ***Break the teeth in their mouths.*** The wicked are pictured as having powerful teeth, as though they were carnivores, eating the righteous alive. Here David asks God to shatter their teeth, symbolizing the destruction of the power of the wicked over the poor and defenseless.

58:10 ***dip their feet in the blood of the wicked.*** We know that it is wrong to rejoice in the downfall of another human being; the picture of the righteous wading in the blood of their fallen enemies is hard for modern Western Christians to understand. Jesus clearly taught that our attitude towards our enemies should be one of compassion and forgiveness (Matt. 5:43–48; Luke 23:34), but this does not mean that we should take a soft attitude towards sin. Wickedness grieves and angers God, and when wickedness has finally been dealt with, we will rejoice.

59:1 ***Deliver me from my enemies.*** The story behind this psalm of lament is found in 1 Samuel 19:9–17.

59:3 ***for no offense or sin of mine.*** There were times in David's life when he knew that he was suffering because of sin in his life (Ps. 32:1–7), but at other times he was hounded by wicked persons even though he was innocent.

57:6 [a] Ps 145:14 [b] Ps 35:7 [c] Ps 7:15; Pr 28:10
57:7 [d] Ps 108:1 **57:8** [e] Ps 16:9; 30:12; 150:3
57:10 [f] Ps 36:5; 103:11 **57:11** [g] ver 5 **58:1** [h] Ps 82:2
58:2 [i] Ps 94:20; Mal 3:15 **58:4** [j] Ps 140:3; Ecc 10:11
58:6 [k] Ps 3:7 [l] Job 4:10 **58:7** [m] Jos 7:5; Ps 112:10
[n] Ps 64:3 **58:8** [o] Job 3:16 **58:9** [p] Ps 118:12 [q] Pr 10:25
58:10 [r] Ps 64:10; 91:8 [s] Ps 68:23 **58:11** [t] Ps 9:8; 18:20
59:1 [u] Ps 143:9 **59:2** [v] Ps 139:19 **59:3** [w] Ps 56:6
59:4 [x] Ps 35:19, 23

5 You, LORD God Almighty,
you who are the God of Israel,
rouse yourself to punish all the nations;
show no mercy to wicked traitors.[a][y]
6 They return at evening,
snarling like dogs,[z]
and prowl about the city.
7 See what they spew from their mouths—
the words from their lips are sharp as
swords,[a]
and they think, "Who can hear us?"[b]
8 But you laugh at them, LORD;[c]
you scoff at all those nations.[d]

9 You are my strength, I watch for you;
you, God, are my fortress,[e]
10 my God on whom I can rely.

God will go before me
and will let me gloat over those who
slander me.
11 But do not kill them, Lord our shield,[b][f]
or my people will forget.[g]
In your might uproot them
and bring them down.[h]
12 For the sins of their mouths,[i]
for the words of their lips,[j]
let them be caught in their pride.[k]
For the curses and lies they utter,
13 consume them in your wrath,
consume them till they are no more.[l]
Then it will be known to the ends of the
earth
that God rules over Jacob.[m]

14 They return at evening,
snarling like dogs,
and prowl about the city.
15 They wander about for food[n]
and howl if not satisfied.
16 But I will sing of your strength,[o]
in the morning[p] I will sing of your
love;[q]
for you are my fortress,
my refuge in times of trouble.[r]

17 You are my strength, I sing praise to you;
you, God, are my fortress,
my God on whom I can rely.

Psalm 60[c]

For the director of music. To the tune of "The Lily of the Covenant." A miktam[d] of David. For teaching. When he fought Aram Naharaim[e] and Aram Zobah,[f] and when Joab returned and struck down twelve thousand Edomites in the Valley of Salt.

1 You have rejected us,[s] God, and burst
upon us;
you have been angry[t]—now
restore us![u]
2 You have shaken the land[v] and torn it
open;
mend its fractures,[w] for it is quaking.
3 You have shown your people desperate
times;[x]
you have given us wine that makes us
stagger.[y]
4 But for those who fear you, you have
raised a banner
to be unfurled against the bow.[g]

5 Save us and help us with your right
hand,[z]
that those you love[a] may be delivered.
6 God has spoken from his sanctuary:
"In triumph I will parcel out
Shechem[b]
and measure off the Valley of
Sukkoth.
7 Gilead[c] is mine, and Manasseh is mine;
Ephraim is my helmet,
Judah[d] is my scepter.[e]
8 Moab is my washbasin,
on Edom I toss my sandal;
over Philistia I shout in triumph.[f]"

9 Who will bring me to the fortified city?
Who will lead me to Edom?

[a] *5* The Hebrew has *Selah* (a word of uncertain meaning) here and at the end of verse 13.
[b] *11* Or *sovereign* [c] In Hebrew texts 60:1-12 is numbered 60:3-14. [d] Title: Probably a literary or musical term [e] Title: That is, Arameans of Northwest Mesopotamia [f] Title: That is, Arameans of central Syria [g] *4* The Hebrew has *Selah* (a word of uncertain meaning) here.

59:6 *snarling like dogs.* Dogs were unclean animals, semi-wild scavengers rather than the beloved pets of our own day. To call someone a dog or compare him to a dog was a profound insult.
59:11 *do not kill them ... uproot them.* The imprecation or curse in this verse is unusual. Instead of asking for the destruction of the wicked, the psalmist asks for them to be uprooted, to be made fugitives. This would be a constant reminder of the consequences of evil.
59:16–17 *I will sing.* David knew that King Saul had sent a murder squad to track him down and kill him. Yet he arose in the morning with joy in his heart and a song on his lips. This was in contrast to his enemies, who would return to the city each evening after a long, fruitless search for David. They were nervous, irritable, and arrogant.
60:1 *You have rejected us ... burst upon us.* This is a poetic description of an otherwise unknown defeat of the armies of Israel in a battle that was part of the campaign against Aram of Zobah and his Mesopotamian allies (2 Sam. 8). The defeat was so startling that it caused the people of Israel to feel as though God had made the earth tremble.
60:5 *those you love.* This term is particularly endearing (Is. 5:1; Jer. 11:15). God did not merely act for His people out of duty, He loved them.
60:8 *Moab ... Edom ... Philistia.* These traditional enemies of Israel were also enemies of God. The Lord would not allow them to disturb His people.

59:5 [y] Jer 18:23 **59:6** [z] ver 14 **59:7** [a] Ps 57:4 [b] Ps 10:11 **59:8** [c] Ps 37:13; Pr 1:26 [d] Ps 2:4 **59:9** [e] Ps 9:9; 62:2 **59:11** [f] Ps 84:9 [g] Dt 4:9 [h] Ps 106:27 **59:12** [i] Ps 10:7 [j] Pr 12:13 [k] Zep 3:11 **59:13** [l] Ps 104:35 [m] Ps 83:18 **59:15** [n] Job 15:23 **59:16** [o] Ps 21:13 [p] Ps 88:13 [q] Ps 101:1 [r] Ps 46:1 **60:1** [s] 2Sa 5:20; Ps 44:9 [t] Ps 79:5 [u] Ps 80:3 **60:2** [v] Ps 18:7 [w] 2Ch 7:14 **60:3** [x] Ps 71:20 [y] Isa 51:17; Jer 25:16 **60:5** [z] Ps 17:7; 108:6 [a] Ps 127:2 **60:6** [b] Ge 12:6 **60:7** [c] Jos 13:31 [d] Dt 33:17 [e] Ge 49:10 **60:8** [f] 2Sa 8:1

10 Is it not you, God, you who have now
rejected us
and no longer go out with our
armies?[g]
11 Give us aid against the enemy,
for human help is worthless.[h]
12 With God we will gain the victory,
and he will trample down our
enemies.[i]

Psalm 61[a]

For the director of music. With stringed instruments. Of David.

1 Hear my cry, O God;[j]
listen to my prayer.[k]

2 From the ends of the earth I call to
you,
I call as my heart grows faint;[l]
lead me to the rock[m] that is higher
than I.
3 For you have been my refuge,[n]
a strong tower against the foe.[o]

4 I long to dwell[p] in your tent
forever
and take refuge in the shelter of your
wings.[b][q]
5 For you, God, have heard my vows;[r]
you have given me the heritage of
those who fear your name.[s]

6 Increase the days of the king's life,
his years for many generations.[t]
7 May he be enthroned in God's presence
forever;[u]
appoint your love and faithfulness to
protect him.[v]

8 Then I will ever sing in praise of your
name[w]
and fulfill my vows day after day.

Psalm 62[c]

For the director of music. For Jeduthun. A psalm of David.

1 Truly my soul finds rest[x] in God;
my salvation comes from him.
2 Truly he is my rock[y] and my salvation;
he is my fortress, I will never be
shaken.

3 How long will you assault me?
Would all of you throw me down—
this leaning wall,[z] this tottering
fence?
4 Surely they intend to topple me
from my lofty place;
they take delight in lies.
With their mouths they bless,
but in their hearts they curse.[d][a]

5 Yes, my soul, find rest in God;
my hope comes from him.
6 Truly he is my rock and my salvation;
he is my fortress, I will not be
shaken.
7 My salvation and my honor depend on
God[e];
he is my mighty rock, my refuge.[b]
8 Trust in him at all times, you
people;
pour out your hearts to him,[c]
for God is our refuge.

9 Surely the lowborn are but a breath,[d]
the highborn are but a lie.
If weighed on a balance,[e] they are
nothing;
together they are only a breath.
10 Do not trust in extortion
or put vain hope in stolen goods;[f]
though your riches increase,
do not set your heart on them.[g]

11 One thing God has spoken,
two things I have heard:
"Power belongs to you, God,
12 and with you, Lord, is unfailing
love";
and, "You reward everyone
according to what they have done."[h]

---

[a] In Hebrew texts 61:1-8 is numbered 61:2-9. [b] 4 The Hebrew has *Selah* (a word of uncertain meaning) here. [c] In Hebrew texts 62:1-12 is numbered 62:2-13. [d] 4 The Hebrew has *Selah* (a word of uncertain meaning) here and at the end of verse 8. [e] 7 Or / *God Most High is my salvation and my honor*

60:12 *we will gain the victory.* As the title records, this was what happened. David's general Joab led the battle, and under God's hand Israel's enemies were soundly defeated. When the help of man proves useless, often God dramatically provides strength and power so that our boast is solely in Him.

61:2 *the rock that is higher than I.* The imagery of God as a Rock for the believer was introduced by Moses (Deut. 32:4) and is developed elsewhere in the Psalms (62:2; 71:3; 144:1).

61:6 *for many generations.* This phrase refers to David's long rule, but more literally prophesies the eternal rule of Jesus, the King of kings.

62:title *Jeduthun.* Jeduthun was appointed by David as one of those in charge of the music associated with worship (1 Chr. 16:41–42).

62:8 *Trust ... you people.* David addresses the righteous with his lesson of reliance on God. What is true for David is extended to all in the believing community.

62:11 *One thing ... Two things.* It is a convention of wisdom literature to use a number and then raise it by one (Prov. 30:15–31), emphasizing the certainty of the point made.

60:10 [g] Jos 7:12; Ps 44:9; 108:11 **60:11** [h] Ps 146:3 **60:12** [i] Nu 24:18; Ps 44:5 **61:1** [j] Ps 64:1 [k] Ps 86:6 **61:2** [l] Ps 77:3 [m] Ps 18:2 **61:3** [n] Ps 62:7 [o] Pr 18:10 **61:4** [p] Ps 23:6 [q] Ps 91:4 **61:5** [r] Ps 56:12 [s] Ps 86:11 **61:6** [t] Ps 21:4 **61:7** [u] Ps 41:12 [v] Ps 40:11 **61:8** [w] Ps 65:1; 71:22 **62:1** [x] Ps 33:20 **62:2** [y] Ps 89:26 **62:3** [z] Isa 30:13 **62:4** [a] Ps 28:3 **62:7** [b] Ps 46:1; 85:9; Jer 3:23 **62:8** [c] 1Sa 1:15; Ps 42:4; La 2:19 **62:9** [d] Ps 39:5, 11 [e] Isa 40:15 **62:10** [f] Isa 61:8 [g] Job 31:25; 1Ti 6:6-10 **62:12** [h] Job 34:11; Mt 16:27

Psalm 63[a]

A psalm of David. When he was in the Desert of Judah.

1 You, God, are my God,
earnestly I seek you;
I thirst for you,[i]
my whole being longs for you,
in a dry and parched land
where there is no water.

2 I have seen you in the sanctuary[j]
and beheld your power and your glory.
3 Because your love is better than life,[k]
my lips will glorify you.
4 I will praise you as long as I live,[l]
and in your name I will lift up my hands.[m]
5 I will be fully satisfied as with the richest of foods;[n]
with singing lips my mouth will praise you.

6 On my bed I remember you;
I think of you through the watches of the night.[o]
7 Because you are my help,[p]
I sing in the shadow of your wings.
8 I cling to you;
your right hand upholds me.[q]

9 Those who want to kill me will be destroyed;[r]
they will go down to the depths of the earth.[s]
10 They will be given over to the sword
and become food for jackals.
11 But the king will rejoice in God;
all who swear by God will glory in him,[t]
while the mouths of liars will be silenced.

Psalm 64[b]

For the director of music. A psalm of David.

1 Hear me, my God, as I voice my complaint;[u]
protect my life from the threat of the enemy.[v]
2 Hide me from the conspiracy of the wicked,[w]
from the plots of evildoers.
3 They sharpen their tongues like swords
and aim cruel words like deadly arrows.[x]
4 They shoot from ambush at the innocent;[y]
they shoot suddenly, without fear.[z]

5 They encourage each other in evil plans,
they talk about hiding their snares;
they say, "Who will see it[c]?"[a]
6 They plot injustice and say,
"We have devised a perfect plan!"
Surely the human mind and heart are cunning.

7 But God will shoot them with his arrows;
they will suddenly be struck down.
8 He will turn their own tongues against them[b]
and bring them to ruin;
all who see them will shake their heads[c] in scorn.
9 All people will fear;
they will proclaim the works of God
and ponder what he has done.[d]

10 The righteous will rejoice in the LORD
and take refuge in him;[e]
all the upright in heart will glory in him![f]

Psalm 65[d]

For the director of music. A psalm of David. A song.

1 Praise awaits[e] you, our God, in Zion;
to you our vows will be fulfilled.[g]
2 You who answer prayer,
to you all people will come.[h]
3 When we were overwhelmed by sins,[i]
you forgave[f] our transgressions.[j]

---

[a] In Hebrew texts 63:1-11 is numbered 63:2-12.
[b] In Hebrew texts 64:1-10 is numbered 64:2-11.
[c] 5 Or *us* [d] In Hebrew texts 65:1-13 is numbered 65:2-14. [e] 1 Or *befits*; the meaning of the Hebrew for this word is uncertain. [f] 3 Or *made atonement for*

63:title *in the Desert of Judah.* This possibly refers to an incident during the period when Saul was chasing David (1 Sam. 22–24).

63:2 *in the sanctuary.* The sanctuary had been at Nob (1 Sam. 21:1), and it was there that David had sought the presence of the Lord. Later it was moved to Jerusalem (76:1–2).

63:4 *lift up my hands.* To lift the hands to the Lord expresses dependence on Him, coupled with an acknowledgement of His power, wonder, and majesty.

63:8 *your right hand.* The same power of God that delivered Israel from Egypt (Ex. 15:6) would support David—and all other believers in their daily lives.

64:10 *take refuge in him.* By placing our problems into God's hands, we can rest in His sovereign will for our lives. Concerns about the future can be cast aside, for the Lord controls our future and has good plans for us (Rom. 8:28).

65:3 *forgave our transgressions.* David speaks of a coming day when sin will be dealt with fully, when redemption will be completely paid. This took place in the death and resurrection of Jesus Christ (Eph. 1:7).

63:1 [i] Ps 42:2; 84:2 **63:2** [j] Ps 27:4 **63:3** [k] Ps 69:16 **63:4** [l] Ps 104:33 [m] Ps 28:2 **63:5** [n] Ps 36:8 **63:6** [o] Ps 42:8 **63:7** [p] Ps 27:9 **63:8** [q] Ps 18:35 **63:9** [r] Ps 40:14 [s] Ps 55:15 **63:11** [t] Dt 6:13; Ps 21:1; Isa 45:23 **64:1** [u] Ps 55:2 [v] Ps 140:1 **64:2** [w] Ps 56:6; 59:2 **64:3** [x] Ps 58:7 **64:4** [y] Ps 11:2 [z] Ps 55:19 **64:5** [a] Ps 10:11 **64:8** [b] Ps 9:3; Pr 18:7 [c] Ps 22:7 **64:9** [d] Jer 51:10 **64:10** [e] Ps 25:20 [f] Ps 32:11 **65:1** [g] Ps 116:18 **65:2** [h] Isa 66:23 **65:3** [i] Ps 38:4 [j] Heb 9:14

4 Blessed are those you choose[k]
and bring near to live in your courts!
We are filled with the good things of your house,[l]
of your holy temple.

5 You answer us with awesome and righteous deeds,
God our Savior,[m]
the hope of all the ends of the earth
and of the farthest seas,[n]
6 who formed the mountains by your power,
having armed yourself with strength,[o]
7 who stilled the roaring of the seas,[p]
the roaring of their waves,
and the turmoil of the nations.[q]
8 The whole earth is filled with awe at your wonders;
where morning dawns, where evening fades,
you call forth songs of joy.

9 You care for the land and water it;[r]
you enrich it abundantly.
The streams of God are filled with water
to provide the people with grain,[s]
for so you have ordained it.[a]
10 You drench its furrows and level its ridges;
you soften it with showers and bless its crops.
11 You crown the year with your bounty,
and your carts overflow with abundance.
12 The grasslands of the wilderness overflow;[t]
the hills are clothed with gladness.
13 The meadows are covered with flocks[u]
and the valleys are mantled with grain;[v]
they shout for joy and sing.[w]

Psalm 66

For the director of music. A song. A psalm.

1 Shout for joy to God, all the earth![x]
2 Sing the glory of his name;[y]
make his praise glorious.
3 Say to God, "How awesome are your deeds![z]
So great is your power
that your enemies cringe[a] before you.
4 All the earth bows down[b] to you;
they sing praise[c] to you,
they sing the praises of your name."[b]

5 Come and see what God has done,
his awesome deeds[d] for mankind!
6 He turned the sea into dry land,[e]
they passed through the waters on foot—
come, let us rejoice in him.
7 He rules forever[f] by his power,
his eyes watch[g] the nations—
let not the rebellious[h] rise up against him.

8 Praise[i] our God, all peoples,
let the sound of his praise be heard;
9 he has preserved our lives
and kept our feet from slipping.[j]
10 For you, God, tested us;
you refined us like silver.[k]
11 You brought us into prison
and laid burdens[l] on our backs.
12 You let people ride over our heads;[m]
we went through fire and water,
but you brought us to a place of abundance.[n]

13 I will come to your temple with burnt offerings
and fulfill my vows[o] to you—
14 vows my lips promised and my mouth spoke
when I was in trouble.
15 I will sacrifice fat animals to you
and an offering of rams;
I will offer bulls and goats.[p]

16 Come and hear,[q] all you who fear God;
let me tell[r] you what he has done for me.
17 I cried out to him with my mouth;
his praise was on my tongue.
18 If I had cherished sin in my heart,
the Lord would not have listened;[s]

---

[a] 9 Or *for that is how you prepare the land*
[b] 4 The Hebrew has *Selah* (a word of uncertain meaning) here and at the end of verses 7 and 15.

65:9 *You care for the land and water it.* Rainfall is seen here as a gracious visitation of God. This is in keeping with the provisions of God's covenant with Israel (Deut. 28:12). These words have some fulfillment every time the rains bring productivity to the earth.
66:1 *all the earth.* As in Psalm 100:1, the call is not only for the people of Israel, but for the peoples of all the earth to join in the praises of the living God, the Most High (87:7; 96:1–6; 117:1).
66:2 *the glory of his name.* The Lord's name describes His character, so honoring God's name is honoring God Himself (Ex. 3:14–15).
66:8 *Praise our God.* To praise God is to identify Him as the source of our blessing.
66:16 *all you who fear God.* Those who fear God are those who respond in awe and wonder to Him.
66:18 *cherished sin.* Ongoing sin tolerated in a believer's life is one of the main things that blocks effective prayer and hinders growth.

65:4 [k] Ps 4:3; 33:12 [l] Ps 36:8 **65:5** [m] Ps 85:4 [n] Ps 107:23 **65:6** [o] Ps 93:1 **65:7** [p] Mt 8:26 [q] Isa 17:12-13 **65:9** [r] Ps 68:9-10 [s] Ps 46:4; 104:14 **65:12** [t] Job 28:26 **65:13** [u] Ps 144:13 [v] Ps 72:16 [w] Ps 98:8; Isa 55:12 **66:1** [x] Ps 100:1 **66:2** [y] Ps 79:9 **66:3** [z] Ps 65:5 [a] Ps 18:44 **66:4** [b] Ps 22:27 [c] Ps 67:3 **66:5** [d] Ps 106:22 **66:6** [e] Ex 14:22 **66:7** [f] Ps 145:13 [g] Ps 11:4 [h] Ps 140:8 **66:8** [i] Ps 98:4 **66:9** [j] Ps 121:3 **66:10** [k] Ps 17:3; Isa 48:10; Zec 13:9; 1Pe 1:6-7 **66:11** [l] La 1:13 **66:12** [m] Isa 51:23 [n] Isa 43:2 **66:13** [o] Ecc 5:4 **66:15** [p] Nu 6:14; Ps 51:19 **66:16** [q] Ps 34:11 [r] Ps 71:15, 24 **66:18** [s] Job 36:21; Isa 1:15; Jas 4:3

[19] but God has surely listened
and has heard[t] my prayer.
[20] Praise be to God,
who has not rejected[u] my prayer
or withheld his love from me!

Psalm 67[a]

For the director of music. With stringed instruments. A psalm. A song.

[1] May God be gracious to us and bless us
and make his face shine on us—[bv]
[2] so that your ways may be known on earth,
your salvation[w] among all nations.[x]

[3] May the peoples praise you, God;
may all the peoples praise you.
[4] May the nations be glad and sing for joy,
for you rule the peoples with equity[y]
and guide the nations of the earth.
[5] May the peoples praise you, God;
may all the peoples praise you.

[6] The land yields its harvest;[z]
God, our God, blesses us.
[7] May God bless us still,
so that all the ends of the earth will fear him.[a]

Psalm 68[c]

For the director of music. Of David. A psalm. A song.

[1] May God arise, may his enemies be scattered;
may his foes flee[b] before him.
[2] May you blow them away like smoke—[c]
as wax melts[d] before the fire,
may the wicked perish before God.
[3] But may the righteous be glad
and rejoice[e] before God;
may they be happy and joyful.

[4] Sing to God, sing in praise of his name,[f]
extol him who rides on the clouds[dg];
rejoice before him—his name is the LORD.[h]
[5] A father to the fatherless,[i] a defender of widows,[j]
is God in his holy dwelling.[k]
[6] God sets the lonely in families,[el]
he leads out the prisoners[m] with singing;
but the rebellious live in a sun-scorched land.[n]

[7] When you, God, went out[o] before your people,
when you marched through the wilderness,[f]
[8] the earth shook, the heavens poured down rain,[p]
before God, the One of Sinai,[q]
before God, the God of Israel.
[9] You gave abundant showers,[r] O God;
you refreshed your weary inheritance.
[10] Your people settled in it,
and from your bounty, God, you provided[s] for the poor.

[11] The Lord announces the word,
and the women who proclaim it are a mighty throng:
[12] "Kings and armies flee[t] in haste;
the women at home divide the plunder.
[13] Even while you sleep among the sheep pens,[gu]
the wings of my dove are sheathed with silver,
its feathers with shining gold."

---

[a] In Hebrew texts 67:1-7 is numbered 67:2-8. [b] *1* The Hebrew has *Selah* (a word of uncertain meaning) here and at the end of verse 4. [c] In Hebrew texts 68:1-35 is numbered 68:2-36. [d] *4* Or *name, / prepare the way for him who rides through the deserts* [e] *6* Or *the desolate in a homeland* [f] *7* The Hebrew has *Selah* (a word of uncertain meaning) here and at the end of verses 19 and 32. [g] *13* Or *the campfires;* or *the saddlebags*

67:1 *his face shine.* In the language of Aaron's benediction (Num. 6:24–26), the psalmist calls for God to smile on His people.
67:2 *known on earth.* From the beginning God had intended to bring His blessing to all nations, in fulfillment of the provisions of the Abrahamic covenant (Gen. 12:3). This passage anticipates the thrust of world mission that is found in the New Testament (Matt. 28:18–20; Acts 1:8).
67:6 *yields its harvest.* The coming of God's kingdom on earth will be marked by a magnificent increase in production. The curse on the land (Gen. 3:17–19; Rom. 8:22) will be lifted at that time.
68:1 *May God arise.* This psalm is based in part on the Song of Deborah in Judges 5. The presence of the wicked on the earth is an assault on God's holiness and a constant threat to the righteous. Only God's mercy compels Him to delay His judgment (75:2).
68:5–6 *father.* The view of God as Father is not as fully developed in the Old Testament as it is in the New Testament. This passage affords some insight into the character of God as Father. He is not seen in these verses as the Almighty God destroying His foes. He is pictured rather as the Father helping His children in need. He delights in kindly works which bring a happy existence to His children.
68:11 *the women who proclaim it.* This may refer to the women who gave praise to God under the direction of Miriam (Ex. 15:20–21).

66:19 [t] Ps 116:1-2 **66:20** [u] Ps 22:24; 68:35
67:1 [v] Nu 6:24-26; Ps 4:6 **67:2** [w] Isa 52:10 [x] Titus 2:11
67:4 [y] Ps 96:10-13 **67:6** [z] Lev 26:4; Ps 85:12; Eze 34:27
67:7 [a] Ps 33:8 **68:1** [b] Nu 10:35; Isa 33:3
68:2 [c] Hos 13:3 [d] Isa 9:18; Mic 1:4 **68:3** [e] Ps 32:11
68:4 [f] Ps 66:2 [g] Dt 33:26 [h] Ex 6:3; Ps 83:18
68:5 [i] Ps 10:14 [j] Dt 10:18 [k] Dt 26:15 **68:6** [l] Ps 113:9
[m] Ac 12:6 [n] Ps 107:34 **68:7** [o] Ex 13:21; Jdg 4:14
68:8 [p] Jdg 5:4 [q] Ex 19:16, 18 **68:9** [r] Dt 11:11
68:10 [s] Ps 74:19 **68:12** [t] Jos 10:16 **68:13** [u] Ge 49:14

14 When the Almighty[a] scattered[v] the
kings in the land,
it was like snow fallen on Mount
Zalmon.

15 Mount Bashan, majestic mountain,
Mount Bashan, rugged mountain,
16 why gaze in envy, you rugged
mountain,
at the mountain where God chooses[w]
to reign,
where the LORD himself will dwell
forever?
17 The chariots of God are tens of
thousands
and thousands of thousands;[x]
the Lord has come from Sinai into his
sanctuary.[b]
18 When you ascended on high,
you took many captives;[y]
you received gifts from people,[z]
even from[c] the rebellious—
that you,[d] LORD God, might dwell
there.

19 Praise be to the Lord, to God our Savior,[a]
who daily bears our burdens.[b]
20 Our God is a God who saves;
from the Sovereign LORD comes
escape from death.[c]
21 Surely God will crush the heads[d] of his
enemies,
the hairy crowns of those who go on
in their sins.
22 The Lord says, "I will bring them from
Bashan;
I will bring them from the depths of
the sea,[e]
23 that your feet may wade in the blood of
your foes,[f]
while the tongues of your dogs[g] have
their share."

24 Your procession, God, has come into
view,
the procession of my God and King
into the sanctuary.[h]
25 In front are the singers, after them the
musicians;
with them are the young women
playing the timbrels.[i]
26 Praise God in the great congregation;
praise the LORD in the assembly of
Israel.[j]
27 There is the little tribe[k] of Benjamin,
leading them,
there the great throng of Judah's
princes,
and there the princes of Zebulun and
of Naphtali.

28 Summon your power, God[e];
show us your strength, our God, as
you have done before.
29 Because of your temple at Jerusalem
kings will bring you gifts.[l]
30 Rebuke the beast among the reeds,
the herd of bulls[m] among the calves
of the nations.
Humbled, may the beast bring bars of
silver.
Scatter the nations[n] who delight in
war.
31 Envoys will come from Egypt;[o]
Cush[f] will submit herself to God.

32 Sing to God, you kingdoms of the
earth,
sing praise to the Lord,
33 to him who rides[p] across the highest
heavens, the ancient heavens,
who thunders with mighty voice.[q]
34 Proclaim the power[r] of God,
whose majesty is over Israel,
whose power is in the heavens.
35 You, God, are awesome in your
sanctuary;
the God of Israel gives power and
strength to his people.[s]

Praise be to God![t]

Psalm 69[g]

For the director of music. To the tune of "Lilies." Of David.

1 Save me, O God,
for the waters have come up to my
neck.[u]

[a] 14 Hebrew *Shaddai* [b] 17 Probable reading of the original Hebrew text; Masoretic Text *Lord is among them at Sinai in holiness* [c] 18 Or *gifts for people, / even* [d] 18 Or *they* [e] 28 Many Hebrew manuscripts, Septuagint and Syriac; most Hebrew manuscripts *Your God has summoned power for you* [f] 31 That is, the upper Nile region [g] In Hebrew texts 69:1-36 is numbered 69:2-37.

68:14 *the Almighty.* This translates the name "Shaddai," a title that refers to the majesty and strength of the Lord (91:1).

68:18 *you took many captives.* Paul quotes this verse in Ephesians 4:8, applying it to Jesus Christ. ***received gifts.*** When God delivered His people from Egypt, He brought them out with great treasures from the Egyptians (Ex. 12:35–36). These gifts were used by the people of Israel to build the tabernacle (Ex. 35:20–29), where the Lord promised to dwell.

68:29 *kings will bring you gifts.* Royal guests came to Solomon with gifts (1 Kin. 10:1–10); but the ultimate prophetic fulfillment of this verse was in the kings who came to Jerusalem to bring gifts to the infant Jesus (Matt. 2:1–12). One day all kings will show their obedience and humility before Jesus, the great King (2:10–12; 76:11).

69:1 *the waters have come up to my neck.* This highly messianic psalm presents a remarkable

68:14 [v] Jos 10:10 **68:16** [w] Dt 12:5 **68:17** [x] Dt 33:2; Da 7:10 **68:18** [y] Jdg 5:12 [z] Eph 4:8* **68:19** [a] Ps 65:5 [b] Ps 55:22 **68:20** [c] Ps 56:13 **68:21** [d] Ps 110:5; Hab 3:13 **68:22** [e] Nu 21:33 **68:23** [f] Ps 58:10 [g] 1Ki 21:19 **68:24** [h] Ps 63:2 **68:25** [i] Jdg 11:34; 1Ch 13:8 **68:26** [j] Ps 26:12; Isa 48:1 **68:27** [k] 1Sa 9:21 **68:29** [l] Ps 72:10 **68:30** [m] Ps 22:12 [n] Ps 89:10 **68:31** [o] Isa 19:19; 45:14 **68:33** [p] Ps 18:10 [q] Ps 29:4 **68:34** [r] Ps 29:1 **68:35** [s] Ps 29:11 [t] Ps 66:20 **69:1** [u] Jnh 2:5

2 I sink in the miry depths,[v]
where there is no foothold.
I have come into the deep waters;
the floods engulf me.
3 I am worn out calling for help;[w]
my throat is parched.
My eyes fail,[x]
looking for my God.
4 Those who hate me without reason[y]
outnumber the hairs of my head;
many are my enemies without
cause,[z]
those who seek to destroy me.
I am forced to restore
what I did not steal.

5 You, God, know my folly;[a]
my guilt is not hidden from you.[b]

6 Lord, the LORD Almighty,
may those who hope in you
not be disgraced because of me;
God of Israel,
may those who seek you
not be put to shame because of me.
7 For I endure scorn for your sake,[c]
and shame covers my face.[d]
8 I am a foreigner to my own family,
a stranger to my own mother's
children;[e]
9 for zeal for your house consumes me,[f]
and the insults of those who insult
you fall on me.[g]
10 When I weep and fast,[h]
I must endure scorn;
11 when I put on sackcloth,[i]
people make sport of me.
12 Those who sit at the gate mock me,
and I am the song of the drunkards.[j]

13 But I pray to you, LORD,
in the time of your favor;[k]
in your great love,[l] O God,
answer me with your sure salvation.
14 Rescue me from the mire,
do not let me sink;
deliver me from those who hate me,
from the deep waters.[m]
15 Do not let the floodwaters[n] engulf me
or the depths swallow me up[o]
or the pit close its mouth over me.

16 Answer me, LORD, out of the goodness
of your love;[p]
in your great mercy turn to me.
17 Do not hide your face[q] from your
servant;
answer me quickly, for I am in
trouble.[r]
18 Come near and rescue me;
deliver[s] me because of my foes.

19 You know how I am scorned,[t] disgraced
and shamed;
all my enemies are before you.
20 Scorn has broken my heart
and has left me helpless;
I looked for sympathy, but there was
none,
for comforters,[u] but I found none.[v]
21 They put gall in my food
and gave me vinegar for my
thirst.[w]

22 May the table set before them become a
snare;
may it become retribution and[a] a
trap.
23 May their eyes be darkened so they
cannot see,
and their backs be bent forever.[x]
24 Pour out your wrath[y] on them;
let your fierce anger overtake them.
25 May their place be deserted;[z]
let there be no one to dwell in their
tents.[a]

---

[a] 22 Or *snare / and their fellowship become*

---

description of the suffering of Jesus Christ. Psalm 22 describes Jesus' physical sufferings, while Psalm 69 focuses more on His emotional and spiritual suffering. Yet, like Psalm 22, this psalm was written by David approximately a thousand years before the events it describes. Both psalms begin with the sufferings of David but have their full meaning in the sufferings of Jesus. For these reasons, the apostles in the New Testament acknowledge that David was a prophet of God (Acts 2:30).

69:4 ***without cause.*** The Savior suffered affliction even though He was holy, harmless, and undefiled, and so no amount of holiness in His followers can prevent the enmity of a wicked world (John 15:19). In the Sermon on the Mount, Jesus promised blessing and a great reward to His followers who suffered for the sake of righteousness, a cause which is identified with Christ's own person (Matt. 5:10–11). Peter must have taken seriously Jesus' words on this subject, for he reminds believers that if they are reviled for the name of Christ, it is a blessing which indicates that the Spirit of God is resting upon them (1 Pet. 4:14).

69:9 ***zeal for your house consumes me.*** Like Phinehas in Numbers 25, David describes himself as a zealot for the house of the Lord. Jesus' cleansing of the temple was a fulfillment of these words (John 2:17).

69:21 ***gall.*** "Gall" is commonly employed in Scripture as a synonym for poison, or bitterness. When Jesus hung on the cross, He actually was offered some sour wine mixed with gall (probably the bitter herb myrrh), a drink given occasionally to relieve the crucified person's thirst and pain (Matt. 27:34).

69:25 ***May their place be deserted.*** These words were fulfilled in Judas Iscariot. See Acts 1:20, in which the words of this verse are joined to the words of 109:8.

69:2 [v] Ps 40:2 **69:3** [w] Ps 6:6 [x] Ps 119:82; Isa 38:14 **69:4** [y] Jn 15:25* [z] Ps 35:19; 38:19 **69:5** [a] Ps 38:5 [b] Ps 44:21 **69:7** [c] Jer 15:15 [d] Ps 44:15 **69:8** [e] Ps 31:11; Isa 53:3 **69:9** [f] Jn 2:17* [g] Ps 89:50-51; Ro 15:3* **69:10** [h] Ps 35:13 **69:11** [i] Ps 35:13 **69:12** [j] Job 30:9 **69:13** [k] Isa 49:8; 2Co 6:2 [l] Ps 51:1 **69:14** [m] ver 2; Ps 144:7 **69:15** [n] Ps 124:4-5 [o] Nu 16:33 **69:16** [p] Ps 63:3 **69:17** [q] Ps 27:9 [r] Ps 66:14 **69:18** [s] Ps 49:15 **69:19** [t] Ps 22:6 **69:20** [u] Job 16:2 [v] Isa 63:5 **69:21** [w] Mt 27:34; Mk 15:23; Jn 19:28-30 **69:23** [x] Isa 6:9-10; Ro 11:9-10* **69:24** [y] Ps 79:6 **69:25** [z] Mt 23:38 [a] Ac 1:20*

26 For they persecute those you wound
and talk about the pain of those you hurt.[b]
27 Charge them with crime upon crime;[c]
do not let them share in your salvation.[d]
28 May they be blotted out of the book of life[e]
and not be listed with the righteous.[f]

29 But as for me, afflicted and in pain—
may your salvation, God, protect me.[g]

30 I will praise God's name in song[h]
and glorify him[i] with thanksgiving.
31 This will please the LORD more than an ox,
more than a bull with its horns and hooves.[j]
32 The poor will see and be glad[k]—
you who seek God, may your hearts live![l]
33 The LORD hears the needy[m]
and does not despise his captive people.

34 Let heaven and earth praise him,
the seas and all that move in them,[n]
35 for God will save Zion[o]
and rebuild the cities of Judah.[p]
Then people will settle there and possess it;
36 the children of his servants will inherit it,
and those who love his name will dwell there.[q]

Psalm 70[a]

For the director of music. Of David. A petition.

1 Hasten, O God, to save me;
come quickly, LORD, to help me.[r]

2 May those who want to take my life[s]
be put to shame and confusion;
may all who desire my ruin
be turned back in disgrace.[t]
3 May those who say to me, "Aha! Aha!"
turn back because of their shame.
4 But may all who seek you
rejoice and be glad in you;
may those who long for your saving help always say,
"The LORD is great!"

5 But as for me, I am poor and needy;[u]
come quickly to me,[v] O God.
You are my help and my deliverer;
LORD, do not delay.

Psalm 71

1 In you, LORD, I have taken refuge;
let me never be put to shame.[w]
2 In your righteousness, rescue me and deliver me;
turn your ear[x] to me and save me.
3 Be my rock of refuge,
to which I can always go;
give the command to save me,
for you are my rock and my fortress.[y]
4 Deliver me, my God, from the hand of the wicked,[z]
from the grasp of those who are evil and cruel.

5 For you have been my hope, Sovereign LORD,
my confidence[a] since my youth.
6 From birth[b] I have relied on you;
you brought me forth from my mother's womb.[c]
I will ever praise[d] you.
7 I have become a sign[e] to many;
you are my strong refuge.[f]
8 My mouth[g] is filled with your praise,
declaring your splendor[h] all day long.

9 Do not cast[i] me away when I am old;[j]
do not forsake me when my strength is gone.
10 For my enemies speak against me;
those who wait to kill[k] me conspire[l] together.
11 They say, "God has forsaken him;
pursue him and seize him,
for no one will rescue[m] him."
12 Do not be far[n] from me, my God;
come quickly, God, to help[o] me.
13 May my accusers perish in shame;
may those who want to harm me
be covered with scorn and disgrace.[p]

[a] In Hebrew texts 70:1-5 is numbered 70:2-6.

70:2 *be put to shame and confusion.* David prays that those who rejoice in his misery will be proven wrong in their assumption that the Lord is unable to help His people. In this way, the Lord's deliverance of David will result in God's name being glorified—both by the joy of God's people and the shame of His enemies.
71:2 *your righteousness.* The psalmist is concerned with his own plight and also with the character of God. The psalmist's point is that God could display His righteousness by answering the needs of the psalmist, whose life had been lived in constant trust in God.
71:7 *a sign.* The poet declares that the work of God in his life has made him a special sign to the people, similar to the great miracles of God through Moses and Aaron in Egypt (Ex. 7:3; 11:9).

69:26 [b] Isa 53:4; Zec 1:15 **69:27** [c] Ne 4:5 [d] Ps 109:14; Isa 26:10 **69:28** [e] Ex 32:32-33; Lk 10:20; Php 4:3 [f] Eze 13:9 **69:29** [g] Ps 59:1; 70:5 **69:30** [h] Ps 28:7 [i] Ps 34:3 **69:31** [j] Ps 50:9-13 **69:32** [k] Ps 34:2 [l] Ps 22:26 **69:33** [m] Ps 12:5; 68:6 **69:34** [n] Ps 96:11; 148:1; Isa 44:23; 49:13; 55:12 **69:35** [o] Ob 1:17 [p] Ps 51:18; Isa 44:26 **69:36** [q] Ps 37:29; 102:28 **70:1** [r] Ps 40:13 **70:2** [s] Ps 35:4 [t] Ps 35:26 **70:5** [u] Ps 40:17 [v] Ps 141:1 **71:1** [w] Ps 25:2-3; 31:1 **71:2** [x] Ps 17:6 **71:3** [y] Ps 18:2; 31:2-3; 44:4 **71:4** [z] Ps 140:4 **71:5** [a] Job 4:6; Jer 17:7 **71:6** [b] Ps 22:10 [c] Ps 22:9; Isa 46:3 [d] Ps 9:1; 34:1; 52:9; 119:164; 145:2 **71:7** [e] Isa 8:18; 1Co 4:9 [f] 2Sa 22:3; Ps 61:3 **71:8** [g] Ps 51:15; 63:5 [h] Ps 35:28; 96:6; 104:1 **71:9** [i] Ps 51:11 [j] ver 18; Ps 92:14; Isa 46:4 **71:10** [k] Ps 10:8; 59:3; Pr 1:18 [l] Ps 31:13; 56:6; Mt 12:14 **71:11** [m] Ps 7:2 **71:12** [n] Ps 35:22; 38:21 [o] Ps 38:22; 70:1 **71:13** [p] ver 24

14 As for me, I will always have
hope;[q]
I will praise you more and
more.
15 My mouth will tell[r] of your righteous
deeds,
of your saving acts all day long—
though I know not how to relate them
all.
16 I will come and proclaim your mighty
acts,[s] Sovereign LORD;
I will proclaim your righteous deeds,
yours alone.
17 Since my youth, God, you have
taught[t] me,
and to this day I declare your
marvelous deeds.[u]
18 Even when I am old and gray,[v]
do not forsake me, my God,
till I declare your power to the next
generation,
your mighty acts to all who are to
come.[w]

19 Your righteousness, God, reaches to the
heavens,[x]
you who have done great things.[y]
Who is like you, God?[z]
20 Though you have made me see
troubles,[a]
many and bitter,
you will restore[b] my life again;
from the depths of the earth
you will again bring me up.
21 You will increase my honor[c]
and comfort[d] me once more.

22 I will praise you with the harp[e]
for your faithfulness, my God;
I will sing praise to you with the
lyre,[f]
Holy One of Israel.[g]
23 My lips will shout for joy
when I sing praise to you—
I whom you have delivered.[h]
24 My tongue will tell of your righteous
acts
all day long,[i]
for those who wanted to harm me[j]
have been put to shame and
confusion.

Psalm 72

Of Solomon.

1 Endow the king with your justice,
O God,
the royal son with your
righteousness.
2 May he judge your people in
righteousness,[k]
your afflicted ones with justice.

3 May the mountains bring prosperity to
the people,
the hills the fruit of righteousness.
4 May he defend the afflicted among the
people
and save the children of the needy;[l]
may he crush the oppressor.
5 May he endure[a] as long as the sun,
as long as the moon, through all
generations.
6 May he be like rain[m] falling on a mown
field,
like showers watering the earth.
7 In his days may the righteous flourish[n]
and prosperity abound till the moon
is no more.

8 May he rule from sea to sea
and from the River[b][o] to the ends of
the earth.[p]
9 May the desert tribes bow before him
and his enemies lick the dust.
10 May the kings of Tarshish and of
distant shores
bring tribute to him.
May the kings of Sheba[q] and Seba
present him gifts.[r]
11 May all kings bow down to him
and all nations serve him.

12 For he will deliver the needy who cry out,
the afflicted who have no one to help.
13 He will take pity on the weak and the
needy
and save the needy from death.
14 He will rescue[s] them from oppression
and violence,
for precious[t] is their blood in his sight.

---

[a] 5 Septuagint; Hebrew *You will be feared*
[b] 8 That is, the Euphrates

71:22 *the harp ... the lyre.* The psalmist praised God with music, both vocal and instrumental. His worship came from his inner being which was filled with praises to the living God. No matter what form our worship takes, it is worthless unless it comes from the heart.

72:1 *Endow the king with your justice.* Solomon's prayer for his own godly reign is an intensely messianic poem, speaking in ideal terms of the coming of the great King. The psalm calls for a good king to govern Israel under God's blessing. Ultimately this king is the Savior Jesus.

72:8 *May he rule from sea to sea.* The promises of God to Abraham included a promise that his descendants would have dominion over the land of Canaan (Gen. 15:18–21). These verses expand the geographical dimensions to include the entire earth. ***the River.*** This refers to the Euphrates.

72:14 *He will rescue them from oppression.* This verse points to Jesus' death on the cross, when He paid the price to redeem us from the oppression of sin.

71:14 [q] Ps 130:7 **71:15** [r] Ps 35:28; 40:5 **71:16** [s] Ps 106:2 **71:17** [t] Dt 4:5 [u] Ps 26:7 **71:18** [v] ver 9 [w] Ps 22:30, 31; 78:4 **71:19** [x] Ps 36:5; 57:10 [y] Ps 126:2; Lk 1:49 [z] Ps 35:10 **71:20** [a] Ps 60:3 [b] Hos 6:2 **71:21** [c] Ps 18:35 [d] Ps 23:4; 86:17; Isa 12:1; 49:13 **71:22** [e] Ps 33:2 [f] Ps 92:3; 144:9 [g] 2Ki 19:22 **71:23** [h] Ps 103:4 **71:24** [i] Ps 35:28 [j] ver 13 **72:2** [k] Isa 9:7; 11:4-5; 32:1 **72:4** [l] Isa 11:4 **72:6** [m] Dt 32:2; Hos 6:3 **72:7** [n] Ps 92:12; Isa 2:4 **72:8** [o] Ex 23:31 [p] Zec 9:10 **72:10** [q] Ge 10:7 [r] 2Ch 9:24 **72:14** [s] Ps 69:18 [t] 1Sa 26:21; Ps 116:15

15 Long may he live!
May gold from Sheba[u] be given him.
May people ever pray for him
and bless him all day long.
16 May grain abound throughout the land;
on the tops of the hills may it sway.
May the crops flourish like Lebanon[v]
and thrive[a] like the grass of the field.
17 May his name endure forever;[w]
may it continue as long as the sun.[x]

Then all nations will be blessed
through him,[b]
and they will call him blessed.[y]

18 Praise be to the LORD God, the God of
Israel,[z]
who alone does marvelous deeds.[a]
19 Praise be to his glorious name forever;
may the whole earth be filled with his
glory.[b]
Amen and Amen.[c]

20 This concludes the prayers of David son
of Jesse.

BOOK III

Psalms 73–89

Psalm 73

A psalm of Asaph.

1 Surely God is good to Israel,
to those who are pure in heart.[d]

2 But as for me, my feet had almost slipped;
I had nearly lost my foothold.
3 For I envied[e] the arrogant
when I saw the prosperity of the
wicked.[f]

4 They have no struggles;
their bodies are healthy and strong.[c]
5 They are free[g] from common human
burdens;
they are not plagued by human ills.
6 Therefore pride is their necklace;[h]
they clothe themselves with violence.[i]
7 From their callous hearts[j] comes
iniquity[d];
their evil imaginations have no limits.
8 They scoff, and speak with malice;
with arrogance[k] they threaten
oppression.
9 Their mouths lay claim to heaven,
and their tongues take possession of
the earth.
10 Therefore their people turn to them
and drink up waters in abundance.[e]
11 They say, "How would God know?
Does the Most High know anything?"

12 This is what the wicked are like—
always free of care, they go on
amassing wealth.[l]

13 Surely in vain[m] I have kept my heart pure
and have washed my hands in
innocence.[n]
14 All day long I have been afflicted,
and every morning brings new
punishments.

15 If I had spoken out like that,
I would have betrayed your children.

[a] *16* Probable reading of the original Hebrew text; Masoretic Text *Lebanon, / from the city*
[b] *17* Or *will use his name in blessings* (see Gen. 48:20)
[c] *4* With a different word division of the Hebrew; Masoretic Text *struggles at their death; / their bodies are healthy*
[d] *7* Syriac (see also Septuagint); Hebrew *Their eyes bulge with fat*
[e] *10* The meaning of the Hebrew for this verse is uncertain.

72:17 *May his name endure forever.* The name of the great King will be regarded as the greatest in the universe. Paul speaks this way of Jesus' name in Philippians 2:9–11.
72:20 *This concludes the prayers of David.* The superscription of this psalm attributes it to Solomon. It is possible that Solomon wrote this poem as the close of a collection of his father's psalms. Other psalms were later added to this original collection.
73:1 Walking in the Spirit—An important prerequisite to walking in the Spirit is the confession of sin. Sin must be confessed in order to restore fellowship and to continue receiving God's forgiveness (1 John 1:5–10). Confession means that we agree with God about our sin. That involves much more than simply acknowledging the sin. Confession requires an attitude of sorrow for the sin and a willingness to turn from it. It does not mean that we will never commit the same sin again, but it does mean that the attitude of repentance towards the sin is present.

Confession should be made at the moment the Christian becomes aware of sin. The Scriptures actually mention two specific times for confession: before the close of the day (Eph. 4:26) and before the Lord's Supper (1 Cor. 11:27–32). Failure to do the latter is a special cause for discipline from the Lord.

Confession of sin should involve only those who have knowledge of the sin. This means that private sins should be confessed privately; sins between individuals confessed between those involved (Matt. 5:23–24); and public sins confessed publicly (Matt. 18:17). Public confession is normally made for the edification of the church (1 Cor. 14:26).
73:3 *For I envied.* This psalmist is open with the readers concerning his own weakness and doubts; he also shows that he came to the right conclusion in the end: to trust God.
73:12 *always free of care.* It often does appear that ungodly people get away with everything, ending up on the top of the heap and leaving the godly wondering whether their own acts of righteous living are without meaning or purpose.
73:15 *would have betrayed.* Even as he struggled with the apparent lack of reward for righteousness,

72:15 [u] Isa 60:6 **72:16** [v] Ps 104:16 **72:17** [w] Ex 3:15 [x] Ps 89:36 [y] Ge 12:3; Lk 1:48 **72:18** [z] 1Ch 29:10; Ps 41:13; 106:48 [a] Job 5:9 **72:19** [b] Nu 14:21; Ne 9:5 [c] Ps 41:13 **73:1** [d] Mt 5:8 **73:3** [e] Ps 37:1; Pr 23:17 [f] Job 21:7; Jer 12:1 **73:5** [g] Job 21:9 **73:6** [h] Ge 41:42 [i] Ps 109:18 **73:7** [j] Ps 17:10 **73:8** [k] Ps 17:10; Jude 16 **73:12** [l] Ps 49:6 **73:13** [m] Job 21:15; 34:9 [n] Ps 26:6

16 When I tried to understand[o] all this,
it troubled me deeply
17 till I entered the sanctuary[p] of God;
then I understood their final destiny.[q]

18 Surely you place them on slippery
ground;[r]
you cast them down to ruin.
19 How suddenly[s] are they destroyed,
completely swept away by terrors!
20 They are like a dream[t] when one
awakes;[u]
when you arise, Lord,
you will despise them as fantasies.

21 When my heart was grieved
and my spirit embittered,
22 I was senseless[v] and ignorant;
I was a brute beast[w] before you.

23 Yet I am always with you;
you hold me by my right hand.
24 You guide[x] me with your counsel,[y]
and afterward you will take me into
glory.
25 Whom have I in heaven but you?
And earth has nothing I desire
besides you.[z]
26 My flesh and my heart[a] may fail,[b]
but God is the strength of my heart
and my portion forever.

27 Those who are far from you will
perish;[c]
you destroy all who are unfaithful to
you.
28 But as for me, it is good to be near God.[d]
I have made the Sovereign LORD my
refuge;
I will tell of all your deeds.[e]

Psalm 74

A maskil[a] of Asaph.

1 O God, why have you rejected us
forever?[f]
Why does your anger smolder against
the sheep of your pasture?[g]
2 Remember the nation you purchased[h]
long ago,[i]
the people of your inheritance, whom
you redeemed[j]—
Mount Zion, where you dwelt.[k]
3 Turn your steps toward these
everlasting ruins,
all this destruction the enemy has
brought on the sanctuary.

4 Your foes roared[l] in the place where
you met with us;
they set up their standards[m] as signs.
5 They behaved like men wielding axes
to cut through a thicket of trees.[n]
6 They smashed all the carved[o] paneling
with their axes and hatchets.
7 They burned your sanctuary to the
ground;
they defiled the dwelling place of
your Name.
8 They said in their hearts, "We will
crush[p] them completely!"
They burned every place where God
was worshiped in the land.

9 We are given no signs from God;
no prophets[q] are left,
and none of us knows how long this
will be.
10 How long will the enemy mock you,
God?
Will the foe revile[r] your name forever?
11 Why do you hold back your hand, your
right hand?[s]
Take it from the folds of your
garment and destroy them!

12 But God is my King[t] from long ago;
he brings salvation on the earth.

13 It was you who split open the sea[u] by
your power;

---

[a] Title: Probably a literary or musical term

Asaph knew in his heart that such thoughts were wrong. Even when we can't understand the surface facts, God's witness in our spirits lets us know when we are moving down the wrong track.

73:22 ***a brute beast before you.*** An animal has no sense of eternity or divine perspective. When the psalmist wondered about the value of righteousness, his thinking was based only on the present, like an animal, rather than understanding the bigger picture as a being with an eternal soul.

73:28 ***it is good to be near God.*** There are those who may enjoy great wealth and notoriety today, but nothing they have or do will last forever. Compared to a relationship with the living God, nothing else matters.

74:1 ***anger.*** The Babylonian destruction of the temple in 586 B.C. occasioned a crisis of faith among the ancient covenant people. Since the temple served as the external sign of God's covenant with Israel, its destruction may have caused the impression that God's promise to David had been canceled (2 Sam. 7:12–14). The psalmist is deeply conscious that God is angry with the nation, and the reason for His anger is unmistakably clear. The people had forsaken the covenant, and worshiped and served other gods (Deut. 29:25–26). God's anger reminds us of His eternal hatred of all unrighteousness. It is the holiness of God stirred into an appropriate response to sin.

74:12 ***my King from long ago.*** The Lord is King by virtue of His creation of the earth (Ps. 93). He is King because of His special relationship with Israel (44:4; 99:1–3). And He is the coming King who will reign over all (96:13; 97:1–6; 98:6–9).

73:16 [o] Ecc 8:17 **73:17** [p] Ps 77:13 [q] Ps 37:38
73:18 [r] Ps 35:6 **73:19** [s] Isa 47:11 **73:20** [t] Job 20:8
[u] Ps 78:65 **73:22** [v] Ps 49:10; 92:6 [w] Ecc 3:18
73:24 [x] Ps 48:14 [y] Ps 32:8 **73:25** [z] Php 3:8
73:26 [a] Ps 84:2 [b] Ps 40:12 **73:27** [c] Ps 119:155
73:28 [d] Heb 10:22; Jas 4:8 [e] Ps 40:5 **74:1** [f] Dt 29:20;
Ps 44:23 [g] Ps 79:13; 95:7; 100:3 **74:2** [h] Ex 15:16 [i] Dt 32:7
[j] Ex 15:13 [k] Ps 68:16 **74:4** [l] La 2:7 [m] Nu 2:2
74:5 [n] Jer 46:22 **74:6** [o] 1Ki 6:18 **74:8** [p] Ps 83:4
74:9 [q] 1Sa 3:1 **74:10** [r] Ps 44:16 **74:11** [s] La 2:3
74:12 [t] Ps 44:4 **74:13** [u] Ex 14:21

you broke the heads of the monster[v]
in the waters.
14 It was you who crushed the heads of
Leviathan
and gave it as food to the creatures of
the desert.
15 It was you who opened up springs[w] and
streams;
you dried up[x] the ever-flowing rivers.
16 The day is yours, and yours also the
night;
you established the sun and moon.[y]
17 It was you who set all the boundaries[z]
of the earth;
you made both summer and winter.[a]

18 Remember how the enemy has mocked
you, LORD,
how foolish people[b] have reviled your
name.
19 Do not hand over the life of your dove
to wild beasts;
do not forget the lives of your
afflicted[c] people forever.
20 Have regard for your covenant,[d]
because haunts of violence fill the
dark places of the land.
21 Do not let the oppressed[e] retreat in
disgrace;
may the poor and needy[f] praise your
name.
22 Rise up, O God, and defend your cause;
remember how fools[g] mock you all
day long.
23 Do not ignore the clamor of your
adversaries,[h]
the uproar of your enemies, which
rises continually.

Psalm 75[a]

For the director of music. To the tune of "Do Not Destroy." A psalm of Asaph. A song.

1 We praise you, God,
we praise you, for your Name is near;[i]
people tell of your wonderful deeds.[j]

2 You say, "I choose the appointed time;
it is I who judge with equity.
3 When the earth and all its people
quake,[k]
it is I who hold its pillars[l] firm.[b]

4 To the arrogant I say, 'Boast no more,'
and to the wicked, 'Do not lift up your
horns.[c][m]
5 Do not lift your horns against heaven;
do not speak so defiantly.' "

6 No one from the east or the west
or from the desert can exalt
themselves.
7 It is God who judges:[n]
He brings one down, he exalts
another.[o]
8 In the hand of the LORD is a cup
full of foaming wine mixed[p] with
spices;
he pours it out, and all the wicked of the
earth
drink it down to its very dregs.[q]

9 As for me, I will declare[r] this forever;
I will sing praise to the God of Jacob,
10 who says, "I will cut off the horns of all
the wicked,
but the horns of the righteous will be
lifted up."[s]

Psalm 76[d]

For the director of music. With stringed instruments. A psalm of Asaph. A song.

1 God is renowned in Judah;
in Israel his name is great.
2 His tent is in Salem,[t]
his dwelling place in Zion.
3 There he broke the flashing arrows,
the shields and the swords, the
weapons of war.[e][u]

4 You are radiant with light,
more majestic than mountains rich
with game.
5 The valiant lie plundered,
they sleep their last sleep;[v]
not one of the warriors
can lift his hands.

---

[a] In Hebrew texts 75:1-10 is numbered 75:2-11. [b] *3* The Hebrew has *Selah* (a word of uncertain meaning) here. [c] *4 Horns* here symbolize strength; also in verses 5 and 10. [d] In Hebrew texts 76:1-12 is numbered 76:2-13. [e] *3* The Hebrew has *Selah* (a word of uncertain meaning) here and at the end of verse 9.

74:14 *Leviathan.* This creature was used to poetically describe various evil forces over which God has ultimate control and victory. Eventually the Leviathan (Job 41:1 – 10) became a symbol for Satan (Is. 27:1) who is "the dragon, that ancient serpent" (Rev. 20:2).

74:15 *dried up the ever-flowing rivers.* God enabled His people to cross over the Red Sea (Ex. 14) and the River Jordan (Josh. 3).

75:2 *I choose the appointed time.* God will not be rushed, even by His devoted followers. When we grow impatient to see justice done, we must remember that God has a better sense of time than we do.

75:8 *a cup.* This is not a cup of blessing, but of the Lord's wrath. The biblical image of wine and judgment goes back to Jacob's blessing on Judah (Gen. 49:11) and is referred to in Christ's judgment as depicted in Revelation 19:13 – 15.

76:2 *Salem.* Salem is the shortened form of the name Jerusalem.

74:13 [v] Isa 51:9; Eze 29:3 **74:15** [w] Ex 17:6; Nu 20:11 [x] Jos 2:10; 3:13 **74:16** [y] Ge 1:16; Ps 136:7-9 **74:17** [z] Dt 32:8; Ac 17:26 [a] Ge 8:22 **74:18** [b] Dt 32:6; Ps 39:8 **74:19** [c] Ps 9:18 **74:20** [d] Ge 17:7; Ps 106:45 **74:21** [e] Ps 103:6 [f] Ps 35:10 **74:22** [g] Ps 53:1 **74:23** [h] Ps 65:7 **75:1** [i] Ps 145:18 [j] Ps 44:1; 71:16 **75:3** [k] Isa 24:19 [l] 1Sa 2:8 **75:4** [m] Zec 1:21 **75:7** [n] Ps 50:6 [o] 1Sa 2:7; Ps 147:6; Da 2:21 **75:8** [p] Pr 23:30 [q] Job 21:20; Jer 25:15 **75:9** [r] Ps 40:10 **75:10** [s] Ps 89:17; 92:10; 148:14 **76:2** [t] Ge 14:18 **76:3** [u] Ps 46:9 **76:5** [v] Ps 13:3

6 At your rebuke, God of Jacob,
both horse and chariot[w] lie still.

7 It is you alone who are to be feared.[x]
Who can stand[y] before you when you are angry?[z]
8 From heaven you pronounced judgment,
and the land feared[a] and was quiet—
9 when you, God, rose up to judge,[b]
to save all the afflicted of the land.
10 Surely your wrath against mankind brings you praise,[c]
and the survivors of your wrath are restrained.[a]

11 Make vows to the LORD your God and fulfill them;[d]
let all the neighboring lands
bring gifts[e] to the One to be feared.
12 He breaks the spirit of rulers;
he is feared by the kings of the earth.

Psalm 77[b]

For the director of music. For Jeduthun. Of Asaph. A psalm.

1 I cried out to God[f] for help;
I cried out to God to hear me.
2 When I was in distress,[g] I sought the Lord;
at night I stretched out untiring hands,[h]
and I would not be comforted.[i]

3 I remembered you, God, and I groaned;
I meditated, and my spirit grew faint.[c][j]
4 You kept my eyes from closing;
I was too troubled to speak.
5 I thought about the former days,[k]
the years of long ago;
6 I remembered my songs in the night.
My heart meditated and my spirit asked:

7 "Will the Lord reject forever?
Will he never show his favor[l] again?
8 Has his unfailing love vanished forever?
Has his promise[m] failed for all time?
9 Has God forgotten to be merciful?[n]
Has he in anger withheld his compassion?[o]"

10 Then I thought, "To this I will appeal:
the years when the Most High stretched out his right hand.[p]
11 I will remember the deeds of the LORD;
yes, I will remember your miracles[q] of long ago.
12 I will consider all your works
and meditate on all your mighty deeds."

13 Your ways, God, are holy.
What god is as great as our God?[r]
14 You are the God who performs miracles;
you display your power among the peoples.
15 With your mighty arm you redeemed your people,[s]
the descendants of Jacob and Joseph.

16 The waters[t] saw you, God,
the waters saw you and writhed;[u]
the very depths were convulsed.
17 The clouds poured down water,[v]
the heavens resounded with thunder;
your arrows flashed back and forth.
18 Your thunder was heard in the whirlwind,
your lightning lit up the world;
the earth trembled and quaked.[w]

---

[a] *10* Or *Surely the wrath of mankind brings you praise, / and with the remainder of wrath you arm yourself* [b] In Hebrew texts 77:1-20 is numbered 77:2-21. [c] *3* The Hebrew has *Selah* (a word of uncertain meaning) here and at the end of verses 9 and 15.

76:6 ***horse and chariot.*** This verse is referring to the defeat of the army of Pharaoh (Ex. 14:13 – 29; 15).
76:7 ***to be feared.*** For the righteous, the fear of God is a response of awe, wonder, adoration, and worship. For the wicked, the fear of God is terror, for there is no escape from Him (14:5).
76:11 ***bring gifts.*** As one might bring gifts to a king, so the righteous should bring their gifts to God — the ultimate gift being the dedication of their lives to the service of God (Rom. 12:1).
77:3 ***remembered ... faint.*** What he knew of God contrasted with what he was experiencing. The more the psalmist thought about these things, the more troubled he became.
77:7 – 8 ***Will the Lord reject forever?*** Even though we have put our faith in Christ and committed ourselves to obeying His will, this doesn't automatically guarantee total and perpetual immunity from trouble. There will be seasons when God seems remote and we begin to wonder about God's unfailing love. It is in these times that we must hold most firmly to what we know about God, rather than what we feel. God has neither forgotten to show mercy nor stifled His compassion.
77:11 ***I will remember.*** Asaph did not *feel* any more at peace, but he made a conscious decision to turn from his pain and focus his thoughts on the person, works, and wonders of God. When we are in distress, we often feel that it is our right to vent our frustrations and complaints as long as we still feel them, but God doesn't call us to be driven by feelings. Instead, we have to consciously decide to praise God, trusting that the feelings will follow.

76:6 [w] Ex 15:1 **76:7** [x] 1Ch 16:25 [y] Ezr 9:15; Rev 6:17 [z] Ps 2:5; Na 1:6 **76:8** [a] 1Ch 16:30; 2Ch 20:29-30 **76:9** [b] Ps 9:8 **76:10** [c] Ex 9:16; Ro 9:17 **76:11** [d] Ps 50:14; Ecc 5:4-5 [e] 2Ch 32:23; Ps 68:29 **77:1** [f] Ps 3:4 **77:2** [g] Ps 50:15; Isa 26:9, 16 [h] Job 11:13 [i] Ge 37:35 **77:3** [j] Ps 143:4 **77:5** [k] Dt 32:7; Ps 44:1; 143:5; Isa 51:9 **77:7** [l] Ps 85:1 **77:8** [m] 2Pe 3:9 **77:9** [n] Ps 25:6; 40:11; 51:1 [o] Isa 49:15 **77:10** [p] Ps 31:22 **77:11** [q] Ps 143:5 **77:13** [r] Ex 15:11; Ps 71:19; 86:8 **77:15** [s] Ex 6:6; Dt 9:29 **77:16** [t] Ex 14:21, 28; Hab 3:8 [u] Ps 114:4; Hab 3:10 **77:17** [v] Jdg 5:4 **77:18** [w] Jdg 5:4

19 Your path led through the sea,[x]
your way through the mighty waters,
though your footprints were not seen.
20 You led your people[y] like a flock[z]
by the hand of Moses and Aaron.

Psalm 78

A maskil[a] of Asaph.

1 My people, hear my teaching;[a]
listen to the words of my mouth.
2 I will open my mouth with a parable;[b]
I will utter hidden things, things from
of old—
3 things we have heard and known,
things our ancestors have told us.[c]
4 We will not hide them from their
descendants;[d]
we will tell the next generation
the praiseworthy deeds[e] of the LORD,
his power, and the wonders he has
done.
5 He decreed statutes[f] for Jacob[g]
and established the law in Israel,
which he commanded our ancestors
to teach their children,
6 so the next generation would know
them,
even the children yet to be born,[h]
and they in turn would tell their
children.
7 Then they would put their trust in God
and would not forget[i] his deeds
but would keep his commands.[j]
8 They would not be like their ancestors[k]—
a stubborn[l] and rebellious[m]
generation,
whose hearts were not loyal to God,
whose spirits were not faithful to him.
9 The men of Ephraim, though armed
with bows,[n]
turned back on the day of battle;[o]
10 they did not keep God's covenant[p]
and refused to live by his law.
11 They forgot what he had done,[q]
the wonders he had shown them.
12 He did miracles[r] in the sight of their
ancestors
in the land of Egypt,[s] in the region of
Zoan.[t]
13 He divided the sea[u] and led them
through;
he made the water stand up like a
wall.[v]
14 He guided them with the cloud by day
and with light from the fire all night.[w]
15 He split the rocks[x] in the wilderness
and gave them water as abundant as
the seas;

[a] Title: Probably a literary or musical term

77:20 *You led your people like a flock.* Lost in contemplation of the greatness of God, the poet seems thoroughly distracted from his pain. He does not mention it again, not daring to compare it to the greatness of the Almighty.

78:1 *my teaching.* The psalmist uses the vocabulary of the wisdom school to establish himself. "My teaching" is the familiar word *Torah.* The wisdom writers used this word to indicate insight; their instruction is always in accord with the law of Moses (Prov. 1:8; 3:1; 4:2).

78:2 *hidden things.* These are riddles, or instructions with a deeper meaning beyond the surface.

78:4 Israel's History—The biblical history of Israel covers 1,800 years and represents a marvelous panorama of God's gracious working through promise, miracle, blessing, and judgment. Israel begins as only a promise to Abraham (Gen. 12:2). For over four hundred years the people of Israel maintain their belief in that promise while in bondage in Egypt. Finally, in God's perfect timing, He brings the nation out of Egypt with the greatest series of miracles recorded in the Old Testament (Ex. 7–15). This event is called the Exodus, meaning a *going out.* It is the formative event in the history of the nation. It was a great act of redemption and in the Old Testament is the foremost example of God's care for His people (Ps. 77:14–20; 78:12–55; Hos. 11:1).

Once God had redeemed Israel He established His covenant with them at Mount Sinai (Ex. 19:5–8). From that point on He has been their God and they His people. The covenant foretells gracious blessings for obedience and severe judgments for disobedience. The rest of Israel's history demonstrates the certainty of that prophecy. Throughout periods of conquest, judges, monarchy, exile, restoration and Gentile domination, Israel was blessed when she obeyed and judged when she disobeyed. The nation is finally destroyed in A.D. 70, although this event is not described in the New Testament. Many prophecies appear to promise a future redemption (Rom. 11:26).

There are at least three good reasons to study the history of Israel:

1. It sets forth examples to be followed or avoided (1 Cor. 10:6).
2. It shows God's control of historical events (Ps. 78).
3. It serves as a model for all ages of God's kindness and mercy towards His people (Ps. 78).

78:5–7 *statutes.* The history of Israel is told in a series of cycles with steps in each cycle ranging from a firm, dependent hope in God to deep apostasy. One generation would seek the works of God, hope in Him, and follow Him. The next generation would forget the mighty works of God and depart from reliance and confidence in Him. To avert this endless round of making the same mistakes, God commanded His people to make His laws a regular part of their everyday lives (Deut. 6:4–9), so that they could not forget.

78:9 *Ephraim ... turned back.* The poet may be referring to Ephraim's conflict with Jephthah (Judg. 12:1–7).

77:19 [x] Hab 3:15 **77:20** [y] Ex 13:21 [z] Ps 78:52; Isa 63:11
78:1 [a] Isa 51:4; 55:3 **78:2** [b] Ps 49:4; Mt 13:35*
78:3 [c] Ps 44:1 **78:4** [d] Dt 11:19 [e] Ps 26:7; 71:17
78:5 [f] Ps 19:7; 81:5 [g] Ps 147:19 **78:6** [h] Ps 22:31; 102:18
78:7 [i] Dt 6:12 [j] Dt 5:29 **78:8** [k] 2Ch 30:7 [l] Ex 32:9
[m] ver 37; Isa 30:9 **78:9** [n] ver 57; 1Ch 12:2 [o] Jdg 20:39
78:10 [p] 2Ki 17:15 **78:11** [q] Ps 106:13 **78:12** [r] Ps 106:22
[s] Ex 7-12 [t] Nu 13:22 **78:13** [u] Ex 14:21; Ps 136:13 [v] Ex 15:8
78:14 [w] Ex 13:21; Ps 105:39 **78:15** [x] Nu 20:11; 1Co 10:4

16 he brought streams out of a rocky crag
and made water flow down like rivers.
17 But they continued to sin[y] against him,
rebelling in the wilderness against
the Most High.
18 They willfully put God to the test[z]
by demanding the food they craved.[a]
19 They spoke against God;[b]
they said, "Can God really
spread a table in the wilderness?
20 True, he struck the rock,
and water gushed out,[c]
streams flowed abundantly,
but can he also give us bread?
Can he supply meat[d] for his people?"
21 When the LORD heard them, he was
furious;
his fire broke out[e] against Jacob,
and his wrath rose against Israel,
22 for they did not believe in God
or trust[f] in his deliverance.
23 Yet he gave a command to the skies
above
and opened the doors of the heavens;[g]
24 he rained down manna[h] for the people
to eat,
he gave them the grain of heaven.
25 Human beings ate the bread of angels;
he sent them all the food they could
eat.
26 He let loose the east wind[i] from the
heavens
and by his power made the south
wind blow.
27 He rained meat down on them like dust,
birds like sand on the seashore.
28 He made them come down inside their
camp,
all around their tents.
29 They ate till they were gorged—[j]
he had given them what they craved.
30 But before they turned from what they
craved,
even while the food was still in their
mouths,[k]
31 God's anger rose against them;
he put to death the sturdiest[l] among
them,
cutting down the young men of Israel.
32 In spite of all this, they kept on sinning;
in spite of his wonders,[m] they did not
believe.[n]
33 So he ended their days in futility[o]
and their years in terror.
34 Whenever God slew them, they would
seek[p] him;
they eagerly turned to him again.
35 They remembered that God was their
Rock,[q]
that God Most High was their
Redeemer.[r]
36 But then they would flatter him with
their mouths,[s]
lying to him with their tongues;
37 their hearts were not loyal[t] to him,
they were not faithful to his covenant.
38 Yet he was merciful;[u]
he forgave[v] their iniquities[w]
and did not destroy them.
Time after time he restrained his anger
and did not stir up his full wrath.
39 He remembered that they were but
flesh,[x]
a passing breeze[y] that does not return.
40 How often they rebelled[z] against him in
the wilderness[a]
and grieved him[b] in the wasteland!
41 Again and again they put God to the
test;[c]
they vexed the Holy One of Israel.[d]
42 They did not remember his power—
the day he redeemed them from the
oppressor,
43 the day he displayed his signs in Egypt,
his wonders in the region of Zoan.
44 He turned their river into blood;[e]
they could not drink from their
streams.
45 He sent swarms of flies[f] that devoured
them,
and frogs[g] that devastated them.
46 He gave their crops to the grasshopper,
their produce to the locust.[h]
47 He destroyed their vines with hail[i]
and their sycamore-figs with sleet.
48 He gave over their cattle to the hail,
their livestock[j] to bolts of lightning.
49 He unleashed against them his hot
anger,[k]
his wrath, indignation and hostility—
a band of destroying angels.
50 He prepared a path for his anger;
he did not spare them from death
but gave them over to the plague.

78:29 *he had given them what they craved.* When we turn our hearts toward the Lord, our desires will change to match His will. Then He delights to give us our desires because they are right things which will lead to wholeness and goodness (37:4). Without God, we don't have the wisdom to know what we should long for.

78:38 *merciful.* The awesome transcendence of the Lord is complemented in this section (v. 35) by an emphasis on His compassionate mercy.

78:17 [y] Dt 9:22; Isa 63:10; Heb 3:16 **78:18** [z] 1Co 10:9 [a] Ex 16:2; Nu 11:4 **78:19** [b] Nu 21:5

78:20 [c] Nu 20:11 [d] Nu 11:18 **78:21** [e] Nu 11:1
78:22 [f] Dt 1:32; Heb 3:19 **78:23** [g] Ge 7:11; Mal 3:10
78:24 [h] Ex 16:4; Jn 6:31* **78:26** [i] Nu 11:31
78:29 [j] Nu 11:20 **78:30** [k] Nu 11:33 **78:31** [l] Isa 10:16
78:32 [m] ver 11 [n] ver 22 **78:33** [o] Nu 14:29, 35
78:34 [p] Hos 5:15 **78:35** [q] Dt 32:4 [r] Dt 9:26
78:36 [s] Eze 33:31 **78:37** [t] ver 8; Ac 8:21
78:38 [u] Ex 34:6 [v] Isa 48:10 [w] Nu 14:18, 20
78:39 [x] Ge 6:3; Ps 103:14 [y] Job 7:7; Jas 4:14
78:40 [z] Heb 3:16 [a] Ps 95:8; 106:14 [b] Eph 4:30
78:41 [c] Nu 14:22 [d] 2Ki 19:22; Ps 89:18
78:44 [e] Ex 7:20-21; Ps 105:29 **78:45** [f] Ex 8:24; Ps 105:31 [g] Ex 8:2, 6 **78:46** [h] Ex 10:13
78:47 [i] Ex 9:23; Ps 105:32 **78:48** [j] Ex 9:25
78:49 [k] Ex 15:7

51 He struck down all the firstborn of
Egypt,[l]
the firstfruits of manhood in the tents
of Ham.[m]
52 But he brought his people out like a
flock;[n]
he led them like sheep through the
wilderness.
53 He guided them safely, so they were
unafraid;
but the sea engulfed[o] their enemies.[p]
54 And so he brought them to the border of
his holy land,
to the hill country his right hand[q] had
taken.
55 He drove out nations[r] before them
and allotted their lands to them as an
inheritance;[s]
he settled the tribes of Israel in their
homes.

56 But they put God to the test
and rebelled against the Most High;
they did not keep his statutes.
57 Like their ancestors[t] they were disloyal
and faithless,
as unreliable as a faulty bow.[u]
58 They angered him[v] with their high
places;[w]
they aroused his jealousy with their
idols.[x]
59 When God heard them, he was furious;
he rejected Israel[y] completely.
60 He abandoned the tabernacle of Shiloh,[z]
the tent he had set up among humans.
61 He sent the ark of his might[a] into
captivity,[b]
his splendor into the hands of the
enemy.
62 He gave his people over to the sword;
he was furious with his inheritance.
63 Fire consumed[c] their young men,
and their young women had no
wedding songs;[d]
64 their priests were put to the sword,[e]
and their widows could not weep.

65 Then the Lord awoke as from sleep,[f]
as a warrior wakes from the stupor of
wine.
66 He beat back his enemies;
he put them to everlasting shame.[g]
67 Then he rejected the tents of Joseph,
he did not choose the tribe of
Ephraim;
68 but he chose the tribe of Judah,
Mount Zion,[h] which he loved.
69 He built his sanctuary like the heights,
like the earth that he established
forever.
70 He chose David[i] his servant
and took him from the sheep pens;
71 from tending the sheep he brought him
to be the shepherd[j] of his people
Jacob,
of Israel his inheritance.
72 And David shepherded them with
integrity of heart;[k]
with skillful hands he led them.

Psalm 79

A psalm of Asaph.

1 O God, the nations have invaded your
inheritance;[l]
they have defiled your holy temple,
they have reduced Jerusalem to
rubble.[m]
2 They have left the dead bodies of your
servants
as food for the birds of the sky,
the flesh of your own people for the
animals of the wild.[n]
3 They have poured out blood like water
all around Jerusalem,
and there is no one to bury the dead.[o]
4 We are objects of contempt to our
neighbors,
of scorn and derision to those
around us.[p]

5 How long,[q] LORD? Will you be angry[r]
forever?
How long will your jealousy burn like
fire?[s]
6 Pour out your wrath[t] on the nations
that do not acknowledge[u] you,
on the kingdoms
that do not call on your name;[v]

78:58 ***high places.*** These places of worship were associated with the Canaanite worship of Baal and other fertility gods.
78:60 ***the tabernacle of Shiloh.*** This reference to Shiloh, the place where the tabernacle was set up in the time of Eli, places the time of disobedience described here in the latter period of the judges (1 Sam. 1:3).
78:61 ***the ark of his might into captivity.*** This term is an unusual way of speaking of the ark of the covenant which was lost to the Philistines during the battle of Aphek (1 Sam. 4:1–11). At this time the suffering of the people was acute, including even the deaths of priests (1 Sam. 4:17–18).
78:68 ***Mount Zion, which he loved.*** The description of the sanctuary in verses 68–69 suggests that this psalm was written after Solomon's temple was built.
78:71 ***to be the shepherd of his people Jacob.*** The shepherding attributed to David is an ideal; it will be fully realized in the Savior King, Jesus, the true Good Shepherd (Matt. 2:6; John 10:1–18).
79:1 ***your holy temple.*** The destruction described in this verse may be what the Babylonians did in 586 B.C.
79:6 ***Pour out your wrath.*** An imprecation or curse on one's enemies is often found in the psalms of lament (137:7–9). Vengeance is left to the Lord, but such a call for vengeance is based in part on the

78:51 [l] Ex 12:29; Ps 135:8 [m] Ps 105:23; 106:22 **78:52** [n] Ps 77:20 **78:53** [o] Ex 14:28 [p] Ps 106:10 **78:54** [q] Ex 15:17; Ps 44:3 **78:55** [r] Ps 44:2 [s] Jos 13:7 **78:57** [t] Eze 20:27 [u] Hos 7:16 **78:58** [v] Jdg 2:12 [w] Lev 26:30 [x] Ex 20:4; Dt 32:21 **78:59** [y] Dt 32:19 **78:60** [z] Jos 18:1 **78:61** [a] Ps 132:8 [b] 1Sa 4:17 **78:63** [c] Nu 11:1 [d] Jer 7:34; 16:9 **78:64** [e] 1Sa 4:17; 22:18 **78:65** [f] Ps 44:23 **78:66** [g] 1Sa 5:6 **78:68** [h] Ps 87:2 **78:70** [i] 1Sa 16:1 **78:71** [j] 2Sa 5:2; Ps 28:9 **78:72** [k] 1Ki 9:4 **79:1** [l] Ps 74:2 [m] 2Ki 25:9 **79:2** [n] Dt 28:26; Jer 7:33 **79:3** [o] Jer 16:4 **79:4** [p] Ps 44:13; 80:6 **79:5** [q] Ps 74:10 [r] Ps 74:1; 85:5 [s] Dt 29:20; Ps 89:46; Zep 3:8 **79:6** [t] Ps 69:24; Rev 16:1 [u] Jer 10:25; 2Th 1:8 [v] Ps 14:4

7 for they have devoured Jacob
and devastated his homeland.

8 Do not hold against us the sins of past generations;[w]
may your mercy come quickly to meet us,
for we are in desperate need.[x]
9 Help us,[y] God our Savior,
for the glory of your name;
deliver us and forgive our sins
for your name's sake.[z]
10 Why should the nations say,
"Where is their God?"[a]

Before our eyes, make known among the nations
that you avenge[b] the outpoured blood of your servants.
11 May the groans of the prisoners come before you;
with your strong arm preserve those condemned to die.
12 Pay back into the laps[c] of our neighbors seven times[d]
the contempt they have hurled at you, Lord.
13 Then we your people, the sheep of your pasture,[e]
will praise you forever;[f]
from generation to generation
we will proclaim your praise.

Psalm 80[a]

For the director of music. To the tune of "The Lilies of the Covenant." Of Asaph. A psalm.

1 Hear us, Shepherd of Israel,
you who lead Joseph like a flock.[g]
You who sit enthroned between the cherubim,[h]
shine forth 2 before Ephraim,
Benjamin and Manasseh.[i]
Awaken[j] your might;
come and save us.

3 Restore[k] us,[l] O God;
make your face shine on us,
that we may be saved.

4 How long, LORD God Almighty,
will your anger smolder
against the prayers of your people?
5 You have fed them with the bread of tears;
you have made them drink tears by the bowlful.[m]
6 You have made us an object of derision[b]
to our neighbors,
and our enemies mock us.[n]

7 Restore us, God Almighty;
make your face shine on us,
that we may be saved.

8 You transplanted a vine[o] from Egypt;
you drove out[p] the nations and planted it.
9 You cleared the ground for it,
and it took root and filled the land.
10 The mountains were covered with its shade,
the mighty cedars with its branches.
11 Its branches reached as far as the Sea,[c]
its shoots as far as the River.[dq]

12 Why have you broken down its walls[r]
so that all who pass by pick its grapes?
13 Boars from the forest ravage[s] it,
and insects from the fields feed on it.
14 Return to us, God Almighty!
Look down from heaven and see![t]
Watch over this vine,
15 the root your right hand has planted,
the son[e] you have raised up for yourself.

16 Your vine is cut down, it is burned with fire;
at your rebuke[u] your people perish.
17 Let your hand rest on the man at your right hand,
the son of man you have raised up for yourself.
18 Then we will not turn away from you;
revive us, and we will call on your name.

19 Restore us, LORD God Almighty;
make your face shine on us,
that we may be saved.

---

a In Hebrew texts 80:1-19 is numbered 80:2-20.
b *6* Probable reading of the original Hebrew text; Masoretic Text *contention* *c* *11* Probably the Mediterranean *d* *11* That is, the Euphrates
e *15* Or *branch*

---

covenant provisions that God had established with Abraham. God had promised to curse those who cursed Abraham's descendants (Gen. 12:2 – 3).

79:12 *Pay back into the laps of our neighbors seven times the contempt.* While the Israelites' cries for vengeance seem to be missing the concept of "love your neighbor," it is clear that they understand both the seriousness of the offense against God and also the fact that it is God, not they, who must avenge.

80:1 *Shepherd of Israel.* The concept of God as the Good Shepherd who cares for His people is clearly shown by Jesus in John 10:1 – 18. ***enthroned between the cherubim.*** In the Most Holy Place, the ark of the covenant was topped by the mercy seat on which were two cherubim, heavenly symbols of the throne of God (Ex. 25:22).

80:8 *You transplanted a vine from Egypt.* The picture of Israel as God's vine recurs other places in Scripture (see, for example, Is. 5:1 – 25). In the New Testament, Jesus used the same metaphor to describe the relationship of God with all who trust in Him (John 15:1 – 8).

79:8 [w] Isa 64:9 [x] Ps 116:6; 142:6 **79:9** [y] 2Ch 14:11 [z] Ps 25:11; 31:3; Jer 14:7 **79:10** [a] Ps 42:10 [b] Ps 94:1 **79:12** [c] Isa 65:6; Jer 32:18 [d] Ge 4:15 **79:13** [e] Ps 74:1; 95:7 [f] Ps 44:8 **80:1** [g] Ps 77:20 [h] Ex 25:22 **80:2** [i] Nu 2:18-24 [j] Ps 35:23 **80:3** [k] Ps 85:4; La 5:21 [l] Nu 6:25 **80:5** [m] Ps 42:3; Isa 30:20 **80:6** [n] Ps 79:4 **80:8** [o] Isa 5:1-2; Jer 2:21 [p] Jos 13:6; Ac 7:45 **80:11** [q] Ps 72:8 **80:12** [r] Ps 89:40; Isa 5:5 **80:13** [s] Jer 5:6 **80:14** [t] Isa 63:15 **80:16** [u] Ps 39:11; 76:6

Psalm 81[a]

For the director of music. According to gittith.[b] *Of Asaph.*

1 Sing for joy to God our strength;
shout aloud to the God of Jacob![v]
2 Begin the music, strike the timbrel,[w]
play the melodious harp[x] and lyre.

3 Sound the ram's horn at the New Moon,
and when the moon is full, on the day
of our festival;
4 this is a decree for Israel,
an ordinance of the God of Jacob.
5 When God went out against Egypt,[y]
he established it as a statute for
Joseph.

I heard an unknown voice say:[z]

6 "I removed the burden from their
shoulders;[a]
their hands were set free from the
basket.
7 In your distress you called[b] and I
rescued you,
I answered[c] you out of a
thundercloud;
I tested you at the waters of
Meribah.[cd]
8 Hear me, my people,[e] and I will warn
you—
if you would only listen to me, Israel!
9 You shall have no foreign god[f] among
you;
you shall not worship any god other
than me.
10 I am the LORD your God,
who brought you up out of Egypt.[g]
Open wide your mouth and I will fill[h] it.

11 "But my people would not listen to me;
Israel would not submit to me.[i]
12 So I gave them over[j] to their stubborn
hearts
to follow their own devices.

13 "If my people would only listen to me,[k]
if Israel would only follow my ways,
14 how quickly I would subdue[l] their
enemies
and turn my hand against[m] their foes!
15 Those who hate the LORD would cringe
before him,
and their punishment would last
forever.
16 But you would be fed with the finest of
wheat;[n]
with honey from the rock I would
satisfy you."

Psalm 82

A psalm of Asaph.

1 God presides in the great assembly;
he renders judgment[o] among the
"gods":

2 "How long will you[d] defend the unjust
and show partiality[p] to the
wicked?[cq]
3 Defend the weak and the fatherless;[r]
uphold the cause of the poor[s] and the
oppressed.
4 Rescue the weak and the needy;
deliver them from the hand of the
wicked.

5 "The 'gods' know nothing, they
understand nothing.[t]
They walk about in darkness;[u]
all the foundations[v] of the earth are
shaken.

6 "I said, 'You are "gods";[w]
you are all sons of the Most High.'
7 But you will die[x] like mere mortals;
you will fall like every other ruler."

8 Rise up,[y] O God, judge the earth,
for all the nations are your
inheritance.[z]

---

[a] In Hebrew texts 81:1-16 is numbered 81:2-17.
[b] Title: Probably a musical term [c] 7,2 The Hebrew has *Selah* (a word of uncertain meaning) here. [d] 2 The Hebrew is plural.

81:3 *the New Moon.* The New Moon festival is mentioned in association with the Festival of Trumpets (Num. 29:6). Regulations for this festival can be found in the instructions to the Levites during the time of David (1 Chr. 23:31) and Solomon (2 Chr. 2:4). This psalm seems to be a basic instruction on the festival. The language and regulations are as solemn as any in the Torah.

81:7 *I answered you.* The Lord's appearance to Moses on Mount Sinai was God's great revelation of Himself (Ex. 19:20).

81:9 *no foreign god.* Asaph, the chief musician during David's reign, reviews the goodness of God and His marvelous deliverance of Israel from the land of bondage (Ex. 7–12). The plagues sent upon Egypt were meant to accomplish a purpose: first, to show to God's people the power of the true God; and second, to demonstrate to the Egyptians the total inability of their false gods. In spite of these dramatic object lessons against idolatry, Israel began worshiping pagan images almost as soon as they left Egypt.

82:6 *You are gods.* Jesus quoted this verse in His exchange with the religious authorities who wanted to stone Him for declaring Himself to be the Son of God (John 10:31–35). The word translated "gods" here is the same word translated such in verse 1. This word (*elohim*) is used to refer to the one God, to false gods, to angels, or to "mighty ones" (that is, the judges).

81:1 [v] Ps 66:1 **81:2** [w] Ex 15:20 [x] Ps 92:3 **81:5** [y] Ex 11:4 [z] Ps 114:1 **81:6** [a] Isa 9:4 **81:7** [b] Ex 2:23; Ps 50:15 [c] Ex 19:19 [d] Ex 17:7 **81:8** [e] Ps 50:7 **81:9** [f] Ex 20:3; Dt 32:12; Isa 43:12 **81:10** [g] Ex 20:2 [h] Ps 107:9 **81:11** [i] Ex 32:1-6 **81:12** [j] Ac 7:42; Ro 1:24 **81:13** [k] Dt 5:29; Isa 48:18 **81:14** [l] Ps 47:3 [m] Am 1:8 **81:16** [n] Dt 32:14 **82:1** [o] Ps 58:11; Isa 3:13 **82:2** [p] Dt 1:17 [q] Ps 58:1-2; Pr 18:5 **82:3** [r] Dt 24:17 [s] Jer 22:16 **82:5** [t] Ps 14:4; Mic 3:1 [u] Isa 59:9 [v] Ps 11:3 **82:6** [w] Jn 10:34* **82:7** [x] Ps 49:12; Eze 31:14 **82:8** [y] Ps 12:5 [z] Ps 2:8; Rev 11:15

Psalm 83[a]

A song. A psalm of Asaph.

1 O God, do not remain silent;[a]
do not turn a deaf ear,
do not stand aloof, O God.
2 See how your enemies growl,[b]
how your foes rear their heads.[c]
3 With cunning they conspire[d] against
your people;
they plot against those you cherish.
4 "Come," they say, "let us destroy[e] them
as a nation,
so that Israel's name is remembered[f]
no more."

5 With one mind they plot together;[g]
they form an alliance against you—
6 the tents of Edom[h] and the Ishmaelites,
of Moab[i] and the Hagrites,[j]
7 Byblos,[k] Ammon and Amalek,
Philistia, with the people of Tyre.[l]
8 Even Assyria has joined them
to reinforce Lot's descendants.[b][m]

9 Do to them as you did to Midian,[n]
as you did to Sisera and Jabin at the
river Kishon,[o]
10 who perished at Endor
and became like dung[p] on the ground.
11 Make their nobles like Oreb and Zeeb,[q]
all their princes like Zebah and
Zalmunna,[r]
12 who said, "Let us take possession[s]
of the pasturelands of God."

13 Make them like tumbleweed, my God,
like chaff[t] before the wind.
14 As fire consumes the forest
or a flame sets the mountains ablaze,[u]
15 so pursue them with your tempest
and terrify them with your storm.[v]
16 Cover their faces with shame,[w] LORD,
so that they will seek your name.

17 May they ever be ashamed and
dismayed;
may they perish in disgrace.[x]
18 Let them know that you, whose name is
the LORD—
that you alone are the Most High over
all the earth.[y]

Psalm 84[c]

For the director of music. According to gittith.[d]
Of the Sons of Korah. A psalm.

1 How lovely is your dwelling place,[z]
LORD Almighty!
2 My soul yearns,[a] even faints,
for the courts of the LORD;
my heart and my flesh cry out
for the living God.
3 Even the sparrow has found a home,
and the swallow a nest for herself,
where she may have her young—
a place near your altar,[b]
LORD Almighty, my King and my
God.[c]
4 Blessed are those who dwell in your
house;
they are ever praising you.[e]

5 Blessed are those whose strength[d] is in
you,
whose hearts are set on pilgrimage.[e]
6 As they pass through the Valley of
Baka,
they make it a place of springs;
the autumn[f] rains also cover it with
pools.[f]
7 They go from strength to strength,[g]
till each appears[h] before God in Zion.

8 Hear my prayer, LORD God Almighty;
listen to me, God of Jacob.
9 Look on our shield,[g][i] O God;
look with favor on your anointed one.[j]

---

[a] In Hebrew texts 83:1-18 is numbered 83:2-19. [b] 8 The Hebrew has *Selah* (a word of uncertain meaning) here. [c] In Hebrew texts 84:1-12 is numbered 84:2-13. [d] Title: Probably a musical term [e] 4 The Hebrew has *Selah* (a word of uncertain meaning) here and at the end of verse 8. [f] 6 Or *blessings* [g] 9 Or *sovereign*

83:6 *tents of Edom.* The place names in this passage refer to nations on the borders of Israel and Judah. The Hagrites may have come from Arabia (1 Chr. 5:10,19–20).

83:9 *Sisera.* God's victory over Sisera was accomplished through Deborah and Barak (Judg. 4–5). The same God who had battled Israel's enemies in the past would fight all those who might oppose His people in the future.

83:16 *that they will seek your name.* Asaph's first call for God to shame Israel's enemies is redemptive—that the nations might hear, feel shame, repent, and seek the Lord. Yet, if they continued in their wicked path, they would be further confounded and would one day face God in judgment.

84:1 *How lovely is your dwelling place.* This psalm celebrates God's presence in Jerusalem, the city where His temple was built. Today it is not necessary to go to Jerusalem to draw near to God, for God is near to those who trust in His Son (Matt. 28:18–20).

84:6 *the Valley of Baka.* The Valley of Baka, or "Valley of Weeping," refers to the various difficulties that one might face on a pilgrimage. With God, even times of hardship and sorrow can become times of great joy and blessing.

84:9 *your anointed.* The two phrases "our shield" and "your anointed" both point to the same person, the king of Israel (89:3–4). These anointed kings foreshadowed the coming Messiah—the Anointed One.

83:1 [a] Ps 28:1; 35:22 **83:2** [b] Ps 2:1; Isa 17:12 [c] Jdg 8:28; Ps 81:15 **83:3** [d] Ps 31:13 **83:4** [e] Est 3:6 [f] Jer 11:19 **83:5** [g] Ps 2:2 **83:6** [h] Ps 137:7 [i] 2Ch 20:1 [j] Ge 25:16 **83:7** [k] Jos 13:5 [l] Eze 27:3 **83:8** [m] Dt 2:9 **83:9** [n] Jdg 7:1-23 [o] Jdg 4:23-24 **83:10** [p] Zep 1:17 **83:11** [q] Jdg 7:25 [r] Jdg 8:12, 21 **83:12** [s] 2Ch 20:11 **83:13** [t] Ps 35:5; Isa 17:13 **83:14** [u] Dt 32:22; Isa 9:18 **83:15** [v] Job 9:17 **83:16** [w] Ps 109:29; 132:18 **83:17** [x] Ps 35:4 **83:18** [y] Ps 59:13 **84:1** [z] Ps 27:4; 43:3; 132:5 **84:2** [a] Ps 42:1-2 **84:3** [b] Ps 43:4 [c] Ps 5:2 **84:5** [d] Ps 81:1 [e] Jer 31:6 **84:6** [f] Joel 2:23 **84:7** [g] Pr 4:18 [h] Dt 16:16 **84:9** [i] Ps 59:11 [j] 1Sa 16:6; Ps 2:2; 132:17

[10] Better is one day in your courts
than a thousand elsewhere;
I would rather be a doorkeeper[k] in the
house of my God
than dwell in the tents of the
wicked.
[11] For the LORD God is a sun[l] and shield;[m]
the LORD bestows favor and honor;
no good thing does he withhold[n]
from those whose walk is blameless.

[12] LORD Almighty,
blessed[o] is the one who trusts in you.

Psalm 85[a]

For the director of music. Of the Sons of Korah. A psalm.

[1] You, LORD, showed favor to your land;
you restored the fortunes[p] of Jacob.
[2] You forgave[q] the iniquity[r] of your
people
and covered all their sins.[b]
[3] You set aside all your wrath[s]
and turned from your fierce anger.[t]

[4] Restore[u] us again, God our Savior,
and put away your displeasure
toward us.
[5] Will you be angry with us forever?[v]
Will you prolong your anger through
all generations?
[6] Will you not revive[w] us again,
that your people may rejoice in you?
[7] Show us your unfailing love, LORD,
and grant us your salvation.

[8] I will listen to what God the LORD says;
he promises peace[x] to his people, his
faithful servants—
but let them not turn to folly.
[9] Surely his salvation[y] is near those who
fear him,
that his glory[z] may dwell in our land.

[10] Love and faithfulness[a] meet together;
righteousness[b] and peace kiss each
other.
[11] Faithfulness springs forth from the
earth,
and righteousness[c] looks down from
heaven.
[12] The LORD will indeed give what is good,[d]
and our land will yield[e] its harvest.
[13] Righteousness goes before him
and prepares the way for his steps.

Psalm 86

A prayer of David.

[1] Hear me, LORD, and answer[f] me,
for I am poor and needy.
[2] Guard my life, for I am faithful to you;
save your servant who trusts in you.[g]
You are my God; [3] have mercy[h] on me,
Lord,
for I call[i] to you all day long.
[4] Bring joy to your servant, Lord,
for I put my trust[j] in you.

[5] You, Lord, are forgiving and good,
abounding in love[k] to all who call to
you.
[6] Hear my prayer, LORD;
listen to my cry for mercy.
[7] When I am in distress,[l] I call to you,
because you answer me.

[8] Among the gods there is none like
you,[m] Lord;
no deeds can compare with yours.
[9] All the nations you have made
will come and worship[n] before you,
Lord;
they will bring glory[o] to your name.

---

[a] In Hebrew texts 85:1-13 is numbered 85:2-14.
[b] 2 The Hebrew has *Selah* (a word of uncertain meaning) here.

84:11 ***no good thing does he withhold.*** When we go through times of darkness and difficulty, it sometimes seems that God is not giving us what we need. However, God is far wiser than we can ever be, and He never withholds what is good from us. When it seems that He does, we must assume that what we want would not actually be a good thing for us to have.
85:1 ***you restored the fortunes.*** The setting for this psalm appears to be the restoration of the people of God following a great catastrophe—perhaps the Babylonian captivity.
85:2–3 ***You forgave.*** In all its forms, from hideous to petty, sin alienates people from God and is deserving of His punishment. The wonderful message of the Bible is that God will forgive even the most despicable sinner if that sinner repents and turns from wickedness. God's forgiveness is not just an arbitrary overlooking of our sin, but a judicial act whereby He applies the penalty paid by His son to our account. Our sins are thus covered by Jesus' blood, and God considers us righteous.
85:10 ***Love and faithfulness meet together.*** Kindness without truth is hypocrisy, while truth without love and mercy is cruel. Only when the two meet can we experience wholeness and healing.

86:1 ***Hear me.*** A more literal translation from the Hebrew is "bow down your ear." This dramatic phrase of David captures the grandeur of God on high and his own humble position on the earth below.
86:8 ***Among the gods.*** The ancient nations took their sense of identity in part from their ties to their supposed gods. When the nations found out that their "gods" did not exist, they would have to acknowledge that the Lord alone is God. Here David envisions other nations worshiping the true God and thus anticipates the missionary thrust of the New Testament (Ps. 117:1; Matt. 28:18–20).

84:10 [k] 1Ch 23:5 **84:11** [l] Isa 60:19; Rev 21:23 [m] Ge 15:1 [n] Ps 34:10 **84:12** [o] Ps 2:12 **85:1** [p] Ps 14:7; Jer 30:18; Eze 39:25 **85:2** [q] Nu 14:19 [r] Ps 78:38 **85:3** [s] Ps 106:23 [t] Ex 32:12; Dt 13:17; Ps 78:38; Jnh 3:9 **85:4** [u] Ps 80:3,7 **85:5** [v] Ps 79:5 **85:6** [w] Ps 80:18; Hab 3:2 **85:8** [x] Zec 9:10 **85:9** [y] Isa 46:13 [z] Zec 2:5 **85:10** [a] Ps 89:14; Pr 3:3 [b] Ps 72:2-3; Isa 32:17 **85:11** [c] Isa 45:8 **85:12** [d] Ps 84:11; Jas 1:17 [e] Lev 26:4; Ps 67:6; Zec 8:12 **86:1** [f] Ps 17:6 **86:2** [g] Ps 25:2; 31:14 **86:3** [h] Ps 4:1; 57:1 [i] Ps 88:9 **86:4** [j] Ps 25:1; 143:8 **86:5** [k] Ex 34:6; Ne 9:17; Ps 103:8; 145:8; Joel 2:13; Jnh 4:2 **86:7** [l] Ps 50:15 **86:8** [m] Ex 15:11; Dt 3:24; Ps 89:6 **86:9** [n] Ps 66:4; Rev 15:4 [o] Isa 43:7

10 For you are great and do marvelous deeds;[p]
you alone[q] are God.

11 Teach me your way,[r] LORD,
that I may rely on your faithfulness;
give me an undivided[s] heart,
that I may fear your name.
12 I will praise you, Lord my God, with all my heart;
I will glorify your name forever.
13 For great is your love toward me;
you have delivered me from the depths,
from the realm of the dead.

14 Arrogant foes are attacking me, O God;
ruthless people are trying to kill me—
they have no regard for you.[t]
15 But you, Lord, are a compassionate and gracious[u] God,
slow to anger, abounding in love and faithfulness.[v]
16 Turn to me and have mercy on me;
show your strength in behalf of your servant;
save me, because I serve you
just as my mother did.[w]
17 Give me a sign of your goodness,
that my enemies may see it and be put to shame,
for you, LORD, have helped me and comforted me.

Psalm 87

Of the Sons of Korah. A psalm. A song.

1 He has founded his city on the holy mountain.
2 The LORD loves the gates of Zion[x]
more than all the other dwellings of Jacob.
3 Glorious things are said of you,
city of God:[a][y]
4 "I will record Rahab[b][z] and Babylon
among those who acknowledge me—
Philistia too, and Tyre[a], along with Cush[c]—
and will say, 'This one was born in Zion.'"[d][b]
5 Indeed, of Zion it will be said,
"This one and that one were born in her,
and the Most High himself will establish her."
6 The LORD will write in the register[c] of the peoples:
"This one was born in Zion."

7 As they make music[d] they will sing,
"All my fountains[e] are in you."

Psalm 88[e]

A song. A psalm of the Sons of Korah. For the director of music. According to mahalath leannoth.[f] *A* maskil[g] *of Heman the Ezrahite.*

1 LORD, you are the God who saves me;[f]
day and night I cry out[g] to you.
2 May my prayer come before you;
turn your ear to my cry.

3 I am overwhelmed with troubles
and my life draws near to death.[h]

[a] 3 The Hebrew has *Selah* (a word of uncertain meaning) here and at the end of verse 6.
[b] 4 A poetic name for Egypt [c] 4 That is, the upper Nile region [d] 4 Or *"I will record concerning those who acknowledge me: / 'This one was born in Zion.' / Hear this, Rahab and Babylon, / and you too, Philistia, Tyre and Cush."* [e] In Hebrew texts 88:1-18 is numbered 88:2-19. [f] Title: Possibly a tune, "The Suffering of Affliction"
[g] Title: Probably a literary or musical term

86:13 *you have delivered me.* The cold hand of death knocks at everyone's door, whether we dwell in a luxury condominium with security guards or a tenement surrounded by urban blight. The good news, however, is that the Lord has not left us at the mercy of death, but has provided for the deliverance of our souls from the depths of the grave. We can face the future confidently, knowing that, when our bodies die, our spirits will be with Christ, and that one day we shall also experience the resurrection of the body by His mighty power (Phil. 3:20 – 21).
87:1 *He has founded.* God Himself established Zion (or Jerusalem) as the center of true worship. He ordained Solomon to build a temple there so that He could live among the Israelites (1 Kin. 6:13). Zion is holy because of God's declaration (1 Kin. 11:13), His promise, the worship given Him there (1 Kin. 8:14 – 66), the future work of the Savior there (Matt. 21:4 – 11), and the future rule of the King there (Rev. 21).
87:4 *Rahab.* Rahab is a symbolic name for Egypt (Is. 30:7) that has negative connotations, alluding to the arrogance of the Egyptians. ***Babylon.*** Babylon was the proverbial seat of apostasy and idolatry (Gen. 10:10).
87:5 *born in her.* Despite their foreign heritage, the people who worshiped God were considered to have been born in Zion. It appears that this is referring to a spiritual birth, foreshadowing Jesus' teaching about being born again (John 3:1 – 8).
88: title *Heman.* Heman is identified in 1 Kings 4:31 as a gifted wise man, and in 1 Chronicles 15:16 – 19 as one of the musically gifted Levites who ministered in worship during the time of David.
88:1 *God who saves me.* Even in the midst of despair, Heman confesses his faith in God's saving goodness.
88:3 *death.* This is also translated "Sheol," which is the Hebrew word for "hell." It is often linked with the term "pit" as a symbol of the end of earthly existence. The Old Testament has very little to say about what happens to a soul after death, but it is clear that to go to Sheol is the end of all we know.

86:10 [p] Ps 72:18 [q] Dt 6:4; Mk 12:29; 1Co 8:4 **86:11** [r] Ps 25:5 [s] Jer 32:39 **86:14** [t] Ps 54:3 **86:15** [u] Ps 103:8 [v] Ex 34:6; Ne 9:17; Joel 2:13 **86:16** [w] Ps 116:16 **87:2** [x] Ps 78:68 **87:3** [y] Ps 46:4; Isa 60:1 **87:4** [z] Job 9:13 [a] Ps 45:12 [b] Isa 19:25 **87:6** [c] Ps 69:28; Isa 4:3; Eze 13:9 **87:7** [d] Ps 149:3 [e] Ps 36:9 **88:1** [f] Ps 51:14 [g] Ps 22:2; 27:9; Lk 18:7 **88:3** [h] Ps 107:18, 26

[4]I am counted among those who go
down to the pit;[i]
I am like one without strength.
[5]I am set apart with the dead,
like the slain who lie in the grave,
whom you remember no more,
who are cut off[j] from your care.

[6]You have put me in the lowest pit,
in the darkest depths.[k]
[7]Your wrath lies heavily on me;
you have overwhelmed me with all
your waves.[a][l]
[8]You have taken from me my closest
friends[m]
and have made me repulsive to them.
I am confined[n] and cannot escape;
[9] my eyes[o] are dim with grief.

I call[p] to you, LORD, every day;
I spread out my hands[q] to you.
[10]Do you show your wonders to the dead?
Do their spirits rise up and praise
you?[r]
[11]Is your love declared in the grave,
your faithfulness[s] in Destruction[b]?
[12]Are your wonders known in the place
of darkness,
or your righteous deeds in the land of
oblivion?

[13]But I cry to you for help,[t] LORD;
in the morning[u] my prayer comes
before you.[v]
[14]Why, LORD, do you reject[w] me
and hide your face[x] from me?
[15]From my youth I have suffered and
been close to death;
I have borne your terrors[y] and am in
despair.
[16]Your wrath has swept over me;
your terrors have destroyed me.
[17]All day long they surround me like a
flood;[z]
they have completely engulfed me.
[18]You have taken from me friend[a] and
neighbor—
darkness is my closest friend.

Psalm 89[c]

A maskil[d] of Ethan the Ezrahite.

[1]I will sing[b] of the LORD's great love
forever;
with my mouth I will make your
faithfulness known[c]
through all generations.
[2]I will declare that your love stands firm
forever,
that you have established your
faithfulness in heaven itself.[d]
[3]You said, "I have made a covenant with
my chosen one,
I have sworn to David my servant,
[4]'I will establish your line forever
and make your throne firm through
all generations.'"[e][e]

[5]The heavens[f] praise your wonders,
LORD,
your faithfulness too, in the assembly
of the holy ones.
[6]For who in the skies above can compare
with the LORD?
Who is like the LORD among the
heavenly beings?[g]
[7]In the council of the holy ones God is
greatly feared;
he is more awesome than all who
surround him.[h]
[8]Who is like you,[i] LORD God Almighty?
You, LORD, are mighty, and your
faithfulness surrounds you.
[9]You rule over the surging sea;
when its waves mount up, you still
them.[j]
[10]You crushed Rahab[k] like one of the
slain;
with your strong arm you scattered[l]
your enemies.
[11]The heavens are yours, and yours also
the earth;[m]
you founded the world and all that is
in it.[n]
[12]You created the north and the south;
Tabor[o] and Hermon[p] sing for joy[q] at
your name.
[13]Your arm is endowed with power;
your hand is strong, your right hand
exalted.

---

[a] 7 The Hebrew has *Selah* (a word of uncertain meaning) here and at the end of verse 10.
[b] 11 Hebrew *Abaddon* [c] In Hebrew texts 89:1-52 is numbered 89:2-53. [d] Title: Probably a literary or musical term [e] 4 The Hebrew has *Selah* (a word of uncertain meaning) here and at the end of verses 37, 45 and 48.

88:11 *Destruction.* This word is also translated "Abaddon."
89:1 *the LORD's great love.* The lovingkindness of the Lord in this psalm centers on the covenant that He made with David, promising him an eternal dynasty (2 Sam. 7).
89:6 *heavenly beings.* This phrase may mean "sons of gods" or "sons of the mighty." The reference could be to other supposed gods or to angels, members of the heavenly court (Job 1:6).
89:10 *Rahab.* Rahab is a title for Egypt (87:4).
89:13 *Your arm is endowed with power.* God is the great Deliverer; He brandished His arm and hand in delivering His people from Egypt (Ex. 6:6; 15:6).

88:4 [i] Ps 28:1 **88:5** [j] Ps 31:22; Isa 53:8 **88:6** [k] Ps 69:15; La 3:55 **88:7** [l] Ps 42:7 **88:8** [m] Job 19:13; Ps 31:11 [n] Jer 32:2 **88:9** [o] Ps 38:10 [p] Ps 86:3 [q] Job 11:13; Ps 143:6 **88:10** [r] Ps 6:5 **88:11** [s] Ps 30:9 **88:13** [t] Ps 30:2 [u] Ps 5:3 [v] Ps 119:147 **88:14** [w] Ps 43:2 [x] Job 13:24; Ps 13:1 **88:15** [y] Job 6:4 **88:17** [z] Ps 22:16; 124:4 **88:18** [a] ver 8; Job 19:13; Ps 38:11 **89:1** [b] Ps 59:16; Ps 101:1 [c] Ps 36:5; 40:10 **89:2** [d] Ps 36:5 **89:4** [e] 2Sa 7:12-16; 1Ki 8:16; Ps 132:11-12; Isa 9:7; Lk 1:33 **89:5** [f] Ps 19:1 **89:6** [g] Ps 113:5 **89:7** [h] Ps 47:2 **89:8** [i] Ps 71:19 **89:9** [j] Ps 65:7 **89:10** [k] Ps 87:4 [l] Ps 68:1 **89:11** [m] 1Ch 29:11; Ps 24:1 [n] Ge 1:1 **89:12** [o] Jos 19:22 [p] Dt 3:8; Jos 12:1 [q] Ps 98:8

14 Righteousness and justice are the
foundation of your throne;[r]
love and faithfulness go before you.
15 Blessed are those who have learned to
acclaim you,
who walk in the light[s] of your
presence, LORD.
16 They rejoice in your name[t] all day long;
they celebrate your righteousness.
17 For you are their glory and strength,
and by your favor you exalt our
horn.[a][u]
18 Indeed, our shield[b] belongs to the LORD,
our king[v] to the Holy One of Israel.

19 Once you spoke in a vision,
to your faithful people you said:
"I have bestowed strength on a warrior;
I have raised up a young man from
among the people.
20 I have found David[w] my servant;[x]
with my sacred oil I have anointed[y]
him.
21 My hand will sustain him;
surely my arm will strengthen him.[z]
22 The enemy will not get the better of
him;
the wicked will not oppress[a] him.
23 I will crush his foes before him[b]
and strike down his adversaries.[c]
24 My faithful love will be with him,[d]
and through my name his horn[c] will
be exalted.
25 I will set his hand over the sea,
his right hand over the rivers.[e]
26 He will call out to me, 'You are my
Father,[f]
my God, the Rock my Savior.'[g]
27 And I will appoint him to be my
firstborn,[h]
the most exalted[i] of the kings[j] of the
earth.
28 I will maintain my love to him forever,
and my covenant with him will never
fail.[k]
29 I will establish his line forever,
his throne as long as the heavens
endure.[l]

30 "If his sons forsake my law
and do not follow my statutes,
31 if they violate my decrees
and fail to keep my commands,
32 I will punish their sin with the rod,
their iniquity with flogging;[m]
33 but I will not take my love from him,[n]
nor will I ever betray my
faithfulness.
34 I will not violate my covenant
or alter what my lips have uttered.[o]
35 Once for all, I have sworn by my
holiness—
and I will not lie to David—
36 that his line will continue forever
and his throne endure before me like
the sun;
37 it will be established forever like the
moon,
the faithful witness in the sky."

38 But you have rejected,[p] you have
spurned,
you have been very angry with your
anointed one.
39 You have renounced the covenant with
your servant
and have defiled his crown in the
dust.[q]
40 You have broken through all his walls[r]
and reduced his strongholds[s] to ruins.
41 All who pass by have plundered him;
he has become the scorn of his
neighbors.[t]
42 You have exalted the right hand of his
foes;
you have made all his enemies
rejoice.[u]
43 Indeed, you have turned back the edge
of his sword
and have not supported him in
battle.[v]
44 You have put an end to his splendor
and cast his throne to the ground.
45 You have cut short the days of his
youth;
you have covered him with a mantle
of shame.[w]

46 How long, LORD? Will you hide yourself
forever?
How long will your wrath burn like
fire?[x]
47 Remember how fleeting is my life.[y]
For what futility you have created all
humanity!
48 Who can live and not see death,
or who can escape the power of the
grave?[z]

[a] *17 Horn* here symbolizes strong one.
[b] *18* Or *sovereign* [c] *24 Horn* here symbolizes strength.

89:18 ***the Holy One of Israel.*** This is the title that Isaiah used to describe God, following his experience of God's holiness in his memorable vision of God's throne (Is. 6:1–5).
89:29 ***line ... throne.*** These words echo the covenant God made with David (2 Sam. 7:8–17).
89:34 ***I will not violate my covenant.*** God is determined to complete, fulfill, and accomplish His grand plan for David's dynasty (2 Sam. 7:1–24).

89:14 [r] Ps 97:2 **89:15** [s] Ps 44:3 **89:16** [t] Ps 105:3
89:17 [u] Ps 75:10; 92:10; 148:14

89:18 [v] Ps 47:9 **89:20** [w] Ac 13:22 [x] Ps 78:70 [y] 1Sa 16:1, 12 **89:21** [z] Ps 18:35 **89:22** [a] 2Sa 7:10
89:23 [b] Ps 18:40 [c] 2Sa 7:9 **89:24** [d] 2Sa 7:15
89:25 [e] Ps 72:8 **89:26** [f] 2Sa 7:14 [g] 2Sa 22:47
89:27 [h] Col 1:18 [i] Nu 24:7 [j] Rev 1:5; 19:16
89:28 [k] ver 33-34; Isa 55:3 **89:29** [l] ver 4, 36; Dt 11:21; Jer 33:17 **89:32** [m] 2Sa 7:14 **89:33** [n] 2Sa 7:15
89:34 [o] Nu 23:19 **89:38** [p] Dt 32:19; 1Ch 28:9; Ps 44:9
89:39 [q] La 5:16 **89:40** [r] Ps 80:12 [s] La 2:2
89:41 [t] Ps 44:13 **89:42** [u] Ps 13:2; 80:6
89:43 [v] Ps 44:10 **89:45** [w] Ps 44:15; 109:29
89:46 [x] Ps 79:5 **89:47** [y] Job 7:7; Ps 39:5 **89:48** [z] Ps 22:29; 49:9

49 Lord, where is your former great love,
which in your faithfulness you swore to David?
50 Remember, Lord, how your servant has[a] been mocked,[a]
how I bear in my heart the taunts of all the nations,
51 the taunts with which your enemies, LORD, have mocked,
with which they have mocked every step of your anointed one.[b]

52 Praise be to the LORD forever!
Amen and Amen.[c]

BOOK IV

Psalms 90 – 106

Psalm 90

A prayer of Moses the man of God.

1 Lord, you have been our dwelling place[d]
throughout all generations.
2 Before the mountains were born[e]
or you brought forth the whole world,
from everlasting to everlasting you are God.[f]

3 You turn people back to dust,
saying, "Return to dust, you mortals."[g]
4 A thousand years in your sight
are like a day that has just gone by,
or like a watch in the night.[h]
5 Yet you sweep people away[i] in the sleep of death—
they are like the new grass of the morning:
6 In the morning it springs up new,
but by evening it is dry and withered.[j]

7 We are consumed by your anger
and terrified by your indignation.
8 You have set our iniquities before you,
our secret sins[k] in the light of your presence.
9 All our days pass away under your wrath;
we finish our years with a moan.[l]
10 Our days may come to seventy years,
or eighty, if our strength endures;
yet the best of them are but trouble and sorrow,
for they quickly pass, and we fly away.[m]
11 If only we knew the power of your anger!
Your wrath is as great as the fear that is your due.[n]
12 Teach us to number our days,[o]
that we may gain a heart of wisdom.[p]

13 Relent, LORD! How long[q] will it be?
Have compassion on your servants.[r]
14 Satisfy[s] us in the morning with your unfailing love,
that we may sing for joy[t] and be glad all our days.[u]
15 Make us glad for as many days as you have afflicted us,
for as many years as we have seen trouble.
16 May your deeds be shown to your servants,
your splendor to their children.[v]

17 May the favor[b] of the Lord our God rest on us;
establish the work of our hands for us—
yes, establish the work of our hands.[w]

a 50 Or *your servants have* *b* 17 Or *beauty*

89:49 – 51 *which in your faithfulness you swore to David.* The writer complains that God has not been keeping His promises to David (2 Sam. 7:1 – 24). As a result, His people are experiencing harsh treatment from their enemies. There is no resolution to this psalm; it ends with the people, the king, and the psalmist in distress. Yet the inclusion of this psalm among the praises of Israel suggests that God did answer this prayer of His people, just as He did in the case of Psalm 60.

90:1 *Lord.* This is not God's personal name (Ex. 3:14 – 15), but a Hebrew word celebrating His majestic authority.

90:4 *a thousand years . . . a day.* A thousand years may seem long at the time, but in comparison with God's eternal existence, they are nothing.

90:7 *your anger.* The unbelieving Israelites in the wilderness experienced God's anger (Num. 13 – 14). An entire generation spent their lives wandering because of their unbelief and rebellion.

90:10 *seventy years, or eighty.* The point here is not to set a maximum, but to present a context for the brevity of human life. No matter how long people live, death is inevitable.

90:12 Counting Our Days — This prayer of Moses, probably written near the end of his life, gives us some excellent insight into living. We need to seek wisdom, be sober-minded and diligent, and seek to use our time wisely, living in light of the Lord's commands.

- Life is often painful, sometimes very painful but survivable.
- We perpetually fall short of God's plan for us.
- We are loved by an all-powerful yet merciful God who knows all about us.
- The only true satisfaction is in knowing and obeying God.
- Serve God to your fullest because your time here on earth is short.

90:17 *establish the work of our hands.* We need to have a sense of lasting meaning in our lives, something that will continue to the next generation.

89:50 [a] Ps 69:19 **89:51** [b] Ps 74:10 **89:52** [c] Ps 41:13; 72:19 **90:1** [d] Dt 33:27; Eze 11:16 **90:2** [e] Job 15:7; Pr 8:25 [f] Ps 102:24-27 **90:3** [g] Ge 3:19; Job 34:15 **90:4** [h] 2Pe 3:8 **90:5** [i] Ps 73:20; Isa 40:6 **90:6** [j] Mt 6:30; Jas 1:10 **90:8** [k] Ps 19:12 **90:9** [l] Ps 78:33 **90:10** [m] Job 20:8 **90:11** [n] Ps 76:7 **90:12** [o] Ps 39:4 [p] Dt 32:29 **90:13** [q] Ps 6:3 [r] Dt 32:36; Ps 135:14 **90:14** [s] Ps 103:5 [t] Ps 85:6 [u] Ps 31:7 **90:16** [v] Ps 44:1; Hab 3:2 **90:17** [w] Isa 26:12

Psalm 91

1 Whoever dwells in the shelter[x] of the
Most High
will rest in the shadow[y] of the
Almighty.[a]
2 I will say of the LORD, "He is my refuge[z]
and my fortress,
my God, in whom I trust."

3 Surely he will save you
from the fowler's snare[a]
and from the deadly pestilence.[b]
4 He will cover you with his feathers,
and under his wings you will find
refuge;[c]
his faithfulness will be your shield[d]
and rampart.
5 You will not fear[e] the terror of night,
nor the arrow that flies by day,
6 nor the pestilence that stalks in the
darkness,
nor the plague that destroys at midday.
7 A thousand may fall at your side,
ten thousand at your right hand,
but it will not come near you.
8 You will only observe with your eyes
and see the punishment of the wicked.[f]

9 If you say, "The LORD is my refuge,"
and you make the Most High your
dwelling,
10 no harm[g] will overtake you,
no disaster will come near your tent.
11 For he will command his angels[h]
concerning you
to guard you in all your ways;[i]
12 they will lift you up in their hands,
so that you will not strike your foot
against a stone.[j]
13 You will tread on the lion and the cobra;
you will trample the great lion and
the serpent.[k]

14 "Because he[b] loves me," says the LORD,
"I will rescue him;
I will protect him, for he
acknowledges my name.
15 He will call on me, and I will answer
him;
I will be with him in trouble,
I will deliver him and honor him.[l]
16 With long life[m] I will satisfy him
and show him my salvation.[n]"

Psalm 92[c]

A psalm. A song. For the Sabbath day.

1 It is good to praise the LORD
and make music to your name,[o]
O Most High,[p]
2 proclaiming your love in the
morning[q]
and your faithfulness at night,
3 to the music of the ten-stringed lyre
and the melody of the harp.[r]

4 For you make me glad by your deeds,
LORD;
I sing for joy at what your hands have
done.[s]
5 How great are your works,[t] LORD,
how profound your thoughts![u]
6 Senseless people[v] do not know,
fools do not understand,
7 that though the wicked spring up like
grass
and all evildoers flourish,
they will be destroyed forever.

8 But you, LORD, are forever exalted.

9 For surely your enemies, LORD,
surely your enemies will perish;
all evildoers will be scattered.[w]
10 You have exalted my horn[d][x] like that of
a wild ox;
fine oils[y] have been poured on me.
11 My eyes have seen the defeat of my
adversaries;
my ears have heard the rout of my
wicked foes.[z]

---

[a] *1* Hebrew *Shaddai* [b] *14* That is, probably the king [c] In Hebrew texts 92:1-15 is numbered 92:2-16. [d] *10 Horn* here symbolizes strength.

91:1 *in the shelter.* The person who trusts in God is the one who lives close to Him. ***Most High.*** This title emphasizes God's majesty and is parallel to the term "Almighty." Together, the terms "Most High" and "Almighty" speak of God as a mountain-like majesty.
91:4 *feathers ... wings.* Just as chicks take refuge under the wings of the mother hen, so we can take refuge in God's enveloping care.
91:7 *A thousand may fall at your side.* The Israelites in Egypt were spared the danger that touched their neighbors (Ex. 9:26; 10:23; 11:7); similarly, believers in the Lord are protected from Satan's attacks.
91:11 *command his angels concerning you.* These words were used by Satan to tempt the Savior (Matt. 4:5–6).
91:13 *lion and the cobra.* The animal and snake imagery in this verse pictures all kinds of evil that might threaten believers.
91:14 *Because he loves me.* The word used here is not the usual Hebrew word for love. It has the idea of "holding close to," or even "hugging tightly in love" (see Deut. 7:8; 10:15).
92:6 *Senseless people . . . fools.* A foolish or senseless person is not someone with limited intelligence, but rather a person who is spiritually obtuse — someone who ignores God and refuses to accept responsibility.
92:10 *You have exalted my horn.* This is a figure of speech for the psalmist's eventual triumph, the celebration of the psalmist's strength.

91:1 [x] Ps 31:20 [y] Ps 17:8 **91:2** [z] Ps 142:5 **91:3** [a] Ps 124:7; Pr 6:5 [b] 1Ki 8:37 **91:4** [c] Ps 17:8 [d] Ps 35:2 **91:5** [e] Job 5:21 **91:8** [f] Ps 37:34; 58:10; Mal 1:5 **91:10** [g] Pr 12:21 **91:11** [h] Heb 1:14 [i] Ps 34:7 **91:12** [j] Mt 4:6*; Lk 4:10-11* **91:13** [k] Da 6:22; Lk 10:19 **91:15** [l] 1Sa 2:30; Ps 50:15; Jn 12:26 **91:16** [m] Dt 6:2; Ps 21:4 [n] Ps 50:23 **92:1** [o] Ps 147:1 [p] Ps 135:3 **92:2** [q] Ps 89:1 **92:3** [r] 1Sa 10:5; Ne 12:27; Ps 33:2 **92:4** [s] Ps 8:6; 143:5 **92:5** [t] Rev 15:3 [u] Ps 40:5; 139:17; Isa 28:29; Ro 11:33 **92:6** [v] Ps 73:22 **92:9** [w] Ps 68:1; 89:10 **92:10** [x] Ps 89:17 [y] Ps 23:5 **92:11** [z] Ps 54:7; 91:8

[12]The righteous will flourish like a palm tree,
they will grow like a cedar of Lebanon;[a]
[13]planted in the house of the LORD,
they will flourish in the courts of our God.[b]
[14]They will still bear fruit[c] in old age,
they will stay fresh and green,
[15]proclaiming, "The LORD is upright;
he is my Rock, and there is no wickedness in him.[d]"

Psalm 93

[1]The LORD reigns,[e] he is robed in majesty;[f]
the LORD is robed in majesty and armed with strength;[g]
indeed, the world is established, firm and secure.[h]
[2]Your throne was established long ago;
you are from all eternity.[i]
[3]The seas[j] have lifted up, LORD,
the seas have lifted up their voice;
the seas have lifted up their pounding waves.
[4]Mightier than the thunder[k] of the great waters,
mightier than the breakers of the sea—
the LORD on high is mighty.

[5]Your statutes, LORD, stand firm;
holiness[l] adorns your house
for endless days.

Psalm 94

[1]The LORD is a God who avenges.[m]
O God who avenges, shine forth.[n]
[2]Rise up, Judge[o] of the earth;
pay back[p] to the proud what they deserve.
[3]How long, LORD, will the wicked,
how long will the wicked be jubilant?
[4]They pour out arrogant[q] words;
all the evildoers are full of boasting.[r]
[5]They crush your people,[s] LORD;
they oppress your inheritance.
[6]They slay the widow and the foreigner;
they murder the fatherless.
[7]They say, "The LORD does not see;[t]
the God of Jacob takes no notice."

[8]Take notice, you senseless ones[u] among the people;
you fools, when will you become wise?
[9]Does he who fashioned the ear not hear?
Does he who formed the eye not see?[v]
[10]Does he who disciplines nations not punish?
Does he who teaches[w] mankind lack knowledge?
[11]The LORD knows all human plans;
he knows that they are futile.[x]

[12]Blessed is the one you discipline,[y] LORD,
the one you teach[z] from your law;
[13]you grant them relief from days of trouble,
till a pit[a] is dug for the wicked.
[14]For the LORD will not reject his people;[b]
he will never forsake his inheritance.
[15]Judgment will again be founded on righteousness,[c]
and all the upright in heart will follow it.

[16]Who will rise up[d] for me against the wicked?
Who will take a stand for me against evildoers?[e]
[17]Unless the LORD had given me help,[f]
I would soon have dwelt in the silence of death.
[18]When I said, "My foot is slipping,[g]"
your unfailing love, LORD,
supported me.

92:12 *flourish like a palm tree.* This promise does not refer to success as the world counts it—the righteous are not often wealthy or powerful—but rather to spiritual success. Those who are committed to following God's ways will be so alive spiritually that even in old age they will appear young and vibrant.
93:1 *is robed in majesty.* This language describes the victor of one-on-one combat. God is dressed in the garments of victory.
93:4 *the LORD on high is mighty.* The Creator King is infinite in power; no force in the universe competes with Him.
94:2 *Judge of the earth.* Even when the poets call out for divine vengeance, they recognize that God decides when to exercise His wrath and judgment. God's law clearly states that vengeance belongs to Him (Deut. 32:35).
94:6 *slay the widow and the foreigner.* The Israelites had been commanded to comfort widows and orphans and to welcome strangers, as long as those strangers obeyed the law of God (Ex. 22:21–22).
94:12 *Blessed is the one you discipline.* The word "blessed" means "happy." Instruction, even if accompanied by chastening, is always for our ultimate good, and thus shows the depth of God's love for us (Heb. 12:7–11).
94:13 *a pit is dug for the wicked.* "Pit" is one of the words used as a synonym for Sheol (16:10). Digging the "pit" is a way of describing the preparations for the final judgment of the wicked (Rev. 20:11–15).
94:14 *the LORD will not reject his people.* God will not forget His people any more than He will forget or deny Himself (2 Tim. 2:13).
94:18 *your unfailing love.* God's "unfailing love" or "mercy" refers to His loyal, covenant love.

92:12 [a] Ps 1:3; 52:8; Jer 17:8; Hos 14:6 **92:13** [b] Ps 100:4 **92:14** [c] Jn 15:2 **92:15** [d] Job 34:10 **93:1** [e] Ps 97:1 [f] Ps 104:1 [g] Ps 65:6 [h] Ps 96:10 **93:2** [i] Ps 45:6 **93:3** [j] Ps 96:11 **93:4** [k] Ps 65:7 **93:5** [l] Ps 29:2 **94:1** [m] Na 1:2; Ro 12:19 [n] Ps 80:1 **94:2** [o] Ge 18:25 [p] Ps 31:23 **94:4** [q] Ps 31:18 [r] Ps 52:1 **94:5** [s] Isa 3:15 **94:7** [t] Job 22:14; Ps 10:11 **94:8** [u] Ps 92:6 **94:9** [v] Ex 4:11; Pr 20:12 **94:10** [w] Job 35:11; Isa 28:26 **94:11** [x] 1Co 3:20* **94:12** [y] Job 5:17; Heb 12:5 [z] Dt 8:3 **94:13** [a] Ps 55:23 **94:14** [b] 1Sa 12:22; Ps 37:28; Ro 11:2 **94:15** [c] Ps 97:2 **94:16** [d] Nu 10:35; Ps 17:13 [e] Ps 59:2 **94:17** [f] Ps 124:2 **94:18** [g] Ps 38:16

19 When anxiety was great within me,
your consolation brought me joy.
20 Can a corrupt throne be allied with you—
a throne that brings on misery by its decrees?[h]
21 The wicked band together[i] against the righteous
and condemn the innocent[j] to death.
22 But the LORD has become my fortress,
and my God the rock in whom I take refuge.[k]
23 He will repay[l] them for their sins
and destroy them for their wickedness;
the LORD our God will destroy them.

Psalm 95

1 Come, let us sing for joy to the LORD;
let us shout aloud[m] to the Rock[n] of our salvation.
2 Let us come before him[o] with thanksgiving
and extol him with music[p] and song.

3 For the LORD is the great God,[q]
the great King above all gods.[r]
4 In his hand are the depths of the earth,
and the mountain peaks belong to him.
5 The sea is his, for he made it,
and his hands formed the dry land.[s]

6 Come, let us bow down[t] in worship,
let us kneel[u] before the LORD our Maker;[v]
7 for he is our God
and we are the people of his pasture,[w]
the flock under his care.

Today, if only you would hear his voice,
8 "Do not harden your hearts as you did at Meribah,[a][x]
as you did that day at Massah[b] in the wilderness,
9 where your ancestors tested[y] me;
they tried me, though they had seen what I did.
10 For forty years[z] I was angry with that generation;
I said, 'They are a people whose hearts go astray,
and they have not known my ways.'
11 So I declared on oath[a] in my anger,
'They shall never enter my rest.'"[b]

Psalm 96

1 Sing to the LORD[c] a new song;
sing to the LORD, all the earth.
2 Sing to the LORD, praise his name;
proclaim his salvation[d] day after day.
3 Declare his glory among the nations,
his marvelous deeds among all peoples.

4 For great is the LORD and most worthy of praise;[e]
he is to be feared[f] above all gods.[g]
5 For all the gods of the nations are idols,
but the LORD made the heavens.[h]
6 Splendor and majesty are before him;
strength and glory[i] are in his sanctuary.

7 Ascribe to the LORD,[j] all you families of nations,[k]
ascribe to the LORD glory and strength.
8 Ascribe to the LORD the glory due his name;
bring an offering[l] and come into his courts.
9 Worship the LORD in the splendor of his[c] holiness;[m]
tremble[n] before him, all the earth.[o]
10 Say among the nations, "The LORD reigns.[p]"

---

[a] 8 *Meribah* means *quarreling.* [b] 8 *Massah* means *testing.* [c] 9 Or *LORD with the splendor of*

95:1–7 *let us shout aloud.* Along with others (Ps. 96–100), this song was probably sung at the dedication of the temple after it was restored by Ezra and Nehemiah. It was a time of great celebration. The hearts of the people were filled with joy as they sang and shouted to God, whom they declared to be the great King above all gods.
95:6 *bow down . . . worship . . . kneel.* These words amplify each other and call for a reflective, humble approach to God. Worship is joyful and can be done with abandon (v. 1–5); but at other times worship may be quiet reverence of the Almighty (Ps. 134).
95:7–11 *for he is our God.* This whole section is quoted in Hebrews 3:7–11, with a notable introduction: "So, as the Holy Spirit says. . . ." This phrase reminds us that the words of the Psalms, which are the response of the worshiping Israelite community, are also the oracles of God.
95:8 *Meribah.* Also translated "rebellion," this word would remind the Israelites of a time when they had doubted the Lord's provision (Ex. 17:7; Num. 20:13).
96:3 *all peoples.* This is a bold declaration that one day the message of God's mercy will be known the world over, the fulfillment of God's covenant promise to Abraham that through his descendants all nations of the earth would be blessed (Gen. 12:1–3).
96:7 *families of nations.* The allusion to the Abrahamic covenant continues (vv. 2–3; Gen. 12:1–3).
96:10 *The LORD reigns.* This key phrase was the countercultural cry of ancient Israelites in a world that believed that gods could rise and fall. In contrast, the living God remains Ruler for all eternity.

94:20 [h] Ps 58:2 **94:21** [i] Ps 56:6 [j] Ps 106:38; Pr 17:15,26 **94:22** [k] Ps 18:2; 59:9 **94:23** [l] Ps 7:16 **95:1** [m] Ps 81:1 [n] 2Sa 22:47 **95:2** [o] Mic 6:6 [p] Ps 81:2; Eph 5:19 **95:3** [q] Ps 48:1; 145:3 [r] Ps 96:4; 97:9 **95:5** [s] Ge 1:9; Ps 146:6 **95:6** [t] Php 2:10 [u] 2Ch 6:13 [v] Ps 100:3; 149:2; Isa 17:7; Da 6:10-11; Hos 8:14 **95:7** [w] Ps 74:1; 79:13 **95:8** [x] Ex 17:7 **95:9** [y] Nu 14:22; Ps 78:18; 1Co 10:9 **95:10** [z] Ac 7:36; Heb 3:17 **95:11** [a] Nu 14:23 [b] Dt 1:35; Heb 4:3* **96:1** [c] 1Ch 16:23 **96:2** [d] Ps 71:15 **96:4** [e] Ps 18:3; 145:3 [f] Ps 89:7 [g] Ps 95:3 **96:5** [h] Ps 115:15 **96:6** [i] Ps 29:1 **96:7** [j] Ps 29:1 [k] Ps 22:27 **96:8** [l] Ps 45:12; 72:10 **96:9** [m] Ps 29:2 [n] Ps 114:7 [o] Ps 33:8 **96:10** [p] Ps 97:1

The world is firmly established, it
cannot be moved;[q]
he will judge the peoples with equity.[r]
11 Let the heavens rejoice, let the earth be
glad;[s]
let the sea resound, and all that is
in it.
12 Let the fields be jubilant, and
everything in them;
let all the trees of the forest[t] sing for
joy.[u]
13 Let all creation rejoice before the LORD,
for he comes,
he comes to judge[v] the earth.
He will judge the world in
righteousness
and the peoples in his faithfulness.

Psalm 97

1 The LORD reigns,[w] let the earth be
glad;[x]
let the distant shores rejoice.
2 Clouds and thick darkness[y] surround
him;
righteousness and justice are the
foundation of his throne.[z]
3 Fire[a] goes before[b] him
and consumes[c] his foes on every side.
4 His lightning lights up the world;
the earth sees and trembles.[d]
5 The mountains melt[e] like wax before
the LORD,
before the Lord of all the earth.[f]
6 The heavens proclaim his
righteousness,[g]
and all peoples see his glory.[h]

7 All who worship images[i] are put to
shame,[j]
those who boast in idols—
worship him,[k] all you gods!

8 Zion hears and rejoices
and the villages of Judah are glad
because of your judgments,[l] LORD.
9 For you, LORD, are the Most High over
all the earth;[m]
you are exalted[n] far above all gods.
10 Let those who love the LORD hate evil,[o]
for he guards the lives of his faithful
ones[p]
and delivers[q] them from the hand of
the wicked.[r]
11 Light shines[a][s] on the righteous
and joy on the upright in heart.
12 Rejoice in the LORD, you who are
righteous,
and praise his holy name.[t]

Psalm 98

A psalm.

1 Sing to the LORD a new song,[u]
for he has done marvelous things;[v]
his right hand[w] and his holy arm[x]
have worked salvation for him.
2 The LORD has made his salvation
known[y]
and revealed his righteousness to the
nations.
3 He has remembered[z] his love
and his faithfulness to Israel;
all the ends of the earth have seen
the salvation of our God.

4 Shout for joy[a] to the LORD, all the earth,
burst into jubilant song with music;
5 make music to the LORD with the harp,[b]
with the harp and the sound of
singing,[c]
6 with trumpets[d] and the blast of the
ram's horn—
shout for joy before the LORD, the
King.[e]

7 Let the sea resound, and everything in it,
the world, and all who live in it.[f]

---

a 11 One Hebrew manuscript and ancient versions (see also 112:4); most Hebrew manuscripts *Light is sown*

96:11–13 *Let the heavens rejoice ... for he comes.* All creation groans under the curse, but when Christ returns, "the creation itself will be liberated from its bondage to decay and brought into the freedom and glory of the children of God" (Rom. 8:21).

97:2 *Clouds and thick darkness.* These words may be rephrased as "impenetrable clouds," an indicator of the final judgment and God's awesome power (Joel 2:2; Zeph. 1:15).

97:7 *worship him, all you gods.* One day, people will be forced to acknowledge that God is the only one worthy of worship, as they see that the very things they devoted themselves to in rejection of God must bow down to the Creator as Lord.

97:10 *hate.* The righteousness of God evokes a response either of delight or of shame because of sin (Is. 6:5). The subjects of the kingdom, the lovers of God, follow Him by loving what He loves and hating what He hates. "To fear the LORD is to hate evil" (Prov. 8:13). Sin is portrayed in Scripture as an active and powerful force in unrelenting pursuit of its victims (Gen. 4:7; 1 Pet. 5:8), and the believer is called to total war against it.

98:1 *his right hand.* The "right hand" of the Lord is a way of referring to His great salvation of Israel from Egypt (Ex. 15:6; Deut. 4:34). The phrase is like a slogan for the Lord's redemption.

98:2 *revealed his righteousness to the nations.* God's salvation was designed to be a witness to the nations (Deut. 4:6).

96:10 [q] Ps 93:1 [r] Ps 67:4 **96:11** [s] Ps 97:1; 98:7; Isa 49:13 **96:12** [t] Isa 44:23 [u] Ps 65:13 **96:13** [v] Rev 19:11 **97:1** [w] Ps 96:10 [x] Ps 96:11 **97:2** [y] Ex 19:9; Ps 18:11 [z] Ps 89:14 **97:3** [a] Da 7:10 [b] Hab 3:5 [c] Ps 18:8 **97:4** [d] Ps 104:32 **97:5** [e] Ps 46:2,6; Mic 1:4 [f] Jos 3:11 **97:6** [g] Ps 50:6 [h] Ps 19:1 **97:7** [i] Lev 26:1 [j] Jer 10:14 [k] Heb 1:6 **97:8** [l] Ps 48:11 **97:9** [m] Ps 83:18; 95:3 [n] Ex 18:11 **97:10** [o] Ps 34:14; Am 5:15; Ro 12:9 [p] Pr 2:8 [q] Da 3:28 [r] Ps 37:40; Jer 15:21 **97:11** [s] Job 22:28 **97:12** [t] Ps 30:4 **98:1** [u] Ps 96:1 [v] Ps 96:3 [w] Ex 15:6 [x] Isa 52:10 **98:2** [y] Isa 52:10 **98:3** [z] Lk 1:54 **98:4** [a] Isa 44:23 **98:5** [b] Ps 92:3 [c] Isa 51:3 **98:6** [d] Nu 10:10 [e] Ps 47:7 **98:7** [f] Ps 24:1

8 Let the rivers clap their hands,
let the mountains[g] sing together for joy;
9 let them sing before the LORD,
for he comes to judge the earth.
He will judge the world in righteousness
and the peoples with equity.[h]

Psalm 99

1 The LORD reigns,[i]
let the nations tremble;
he sits enthroned between the cherubim,[j]
let the earth shake.
2 Great is the LORD[k] in Zion;
he is exalted[l] over all the nations.
3 Let them praise your great and awesome name[m]—
he is holy.

4 The King is mighty, he loves justice[n]—
you have established equity;[o]
in Jacob you have done
what is just and right.
5 Exalt[p] the LORD our God
and worship at his footstool;
he is holy.

6 Moses[q] and Aaron were among his priests,
Samuel[r] was among those who called on his name;
they called on the LORD
and he answered[s] them.
7 He spoke to them from the pillar of cloud;[t]
they kept his statutes and the decrees he gave them.

8 LORD our God,
you answered them;
you were to Israel a forgiving God,[u]
though you punished their misdeeds.[a]
9 Exalt the LORD our God
and worship at his holy mountain,
for the LORD our God is holy.

Psalm 100

A psalm. For giving grateful praise.

1 Shout for joy[v] to the LORD, all the earth.
2 Worship the LORD with gladness;
come before him[w] with joyful songs.
3 Know that the LORD is God.[x]
It is he who made us,[y] and we are his[b];
we are his people, the sheep of his pasture.[z]

4 Enter his gates with thanksgiving
and his courts with praise;
give thanks to him and praise his name.[a]
5 For the LORD is good[b] and his love endures forever;[c]
his faithfulness[d] continues through all generations.

Psalm 101

Of David. A psalm.

1 I will sing of your love[e] and justice;
to you, LORD, I will sing praise.
2 I will be careful to lead a blameless life—
when will you come to me?

I will conduct the affairs of my house
with a blameless heart.
3 I will not look with approval
on anything that is vile.[f]

I hate what faithless people do;[g]
I will have no part in it.

---

[a] 8 *Or God, / an avenger of the wrongs done to them* [b] 3 *Or and not we ourselves*

98:9 *for he comes.* Creation rejoices at the coming of the Lord because when He establishes His kingdom, the curse will be lifted, and all creation will be freed from its slavery to corruption (Rom. 8:21–22).
99:1 *cherubim.* Cherubim are the angels most closely related to the glory of God. Two gold cherubim graced the mercy seat of the ark of the covenant (Ex. 25:18–22).
99:3 *name—he is holy.* To be holy is to be "distinct from," "separated," "set apart." This is the principal Hebrew word used to describe the transcendence of God (113:4–6).
99:5 *his footstool.* The footstool of the Lord is sometimes said to be the earth (Is. 66:1); but more specifically, Zion is the Lord's footstool (132:7; Is. 60:13). When the Israelites came to the temple in Jerusalem to worship, they pictured themselves as being at the feet of the Creator.
100:1 *Shout for joy to the LORD.* This command is addressed not just to Israel but to all the earth. The Israelites were to be a people who would attract the nations to worship God.
100:3 *the LORD is God.* These words reflect the great confession of faith in Deuteronomy 6:4–9.
100:5 *the LORD is good.* The shout of the goodness of God in this verse is buttressed by an appeal to His love and faithfulness. The Hebrew root for the word for "truth" comes from the word meaning "to be established" or "to be confirmed." From this word also comes the word "amen," meaning "surely" or "truly." God's goodness is based on His loyal love and His truth.
101:1 *love and justice.* God's loyal love is coupled with justice. He does not allow sin to go unnoticed or unpunished, either in His children or in those who oppress them.

98:8 [g] Isa 55:12 **98:9** [h] Ps 96:10 **99:1** [i] Ps 97:1 [j] Ex 25:22 **99:2** [k] Ps 48:1 [l] Ps 97:9; 113:4 **99:3** [m] Ps 76:1 **99:4** [n] Ps 11:7 [o] Ps 98:9 **99:5** [p] Ps 132:7 **99:6** [q] Ex 24:6 [r] Jer 15:1 [s] 1Sa 7:9 **99:7** [t] Ex 33:9 **99:8** [u] Nu 14:20 **100:1** [v] Ps 98:4 **100:2** [w] Ps 95:2 **100:3** [x] Ps 46:10 [y] Job 10:3 [z] Ps 74:1; Eze 34:31 **100:4** [a] Ps 116:17 **100:5** [b] 1Ch 16:34; Ps 25:8 [c] Ezr 3:11; Ps 106:1 [d] Ps 119:90 **101:1** [e] Ps 51:14; 89:1; 145:7 **101:3** [f] Dt 15:9 [g] Ps 40:4

[4]The perverse of heart[h] shall be far
from me;
I will have nothing to do with what is
evil.

[5]Whoever slanders their neighbor[i] in
secret,
I will put to silence;
whoever has haughty eyes[j] and a proud
heart,
I will not tolerate.

[6]My eyes will be on the faithful in the
land,
that they may dwell with me;
the one whose walk is blameless[k]
will minister to me.

[7]No one who practices deceit
will dwell in my house;
no one who speaks falsely
will stand in my presence.

[8]Every morning[l] I will put to silence
all the wicked[m] in the land;
I will cut off every evildoer[n]
from the city of the LORD.[o]

Psalm 102[a]

A prayer of an afflicted person who has grown weak and pours out a lament before the LORD.

[1]Hear my prayer, LORD;
let my cry for help[p] come to you.
[2]Do not hide your face[q] from me
when I am in distress.
Turn your ear to me;
when I call, answer me quickly.

[3]For my days vanish like smoke;[r]
my bones burn like glowing embers.
[4]My heart is blighted and withered like
grass;[s]
I forget to eat my food.
[5]In my distress I groan aloud
and am reduced to skin and bones.
[6]I am like a desert owl,[t]
like an owl among the ruins.
[7]I lie awake;[u] I have become
like a bird alone[v] on a roof.
[8]All day long my enemies taunt me;
those who rail against me use my
name as a curse.
[9]For I eat ashes as my food
and mingle my drink with tears[w]
[10]because of your great wrath,[x]
for you have taken me up and thrown
me aside.
[11]My days are like the evening shadow;[y]
I wither away like grass.

[12]But you, LORD, sit enthroned forever;[z]
your renown endures[a] through all
generations.
[13]You will arise and have compassion[b] on
Zion,
for it is time to show favor to her;
the appointed time has come.
[14]For her stones are dear to your servants;
her very dust moves them to pity.
[15]The nations will fear[c] the name of the
LORD,
all the kings[d] of the earth will revere
your glory.
[16]For the LORD will rebuild Zion
and appear in his glory.[e]
[17]He will respond to the prayer[f] of the
destitute;
he will not despise their plea.

[18]Let this be written[g] for a future
generation,
that a people not yet created[h] may
praise the LORD:
[19]"The LORD looked down[i] from his
sanctuary on high,
from heaven he viewed the earth,
[20]to hear the groans of the prisoners[j]
and release those condemned to
death."
[21]So the name of the LORD will be
declared[k] in Zion
and his praise in Jerusalem
[22]when the peoples and the kingdoms
assemble to worship the LORD.

[23]In the course of my life[b] he broke my
strength;
he cut short my days.
[24]So I said:
"Do not take me away, my God, in the
midst of my days;
your years go on[l] through all
generations.
[25]In the beginning[m] you laid the
foundations of the earth,
and the heavens are the work of your
hands.

---

[a] In Hebrew texts 102:1-28 is numbered 102:2-29.
[b] *23* Or *By his power*

101:4 *nothing to do with what is evil.* The verb "to do" here has the idea of experience or intimate relationship with something or someone.
101:6 *My eyes will be on the faithful.* David made a covenant with his eyes (Job 31:1) to observe the righteous and sustain them in their walk.
102:12 *enthroned forever.* Our days may be just a passing shadow, but God is King forever. He is gracious, loves His people, and promises to favor them.
102:15 *The nations will fear.* A time will come when the Lord will rule over all the earth.
102:25 *In the beginning.* God is eternal and His works are from ancient times. The writer of the Book of Hebrews applies these words of creation and eternality to the Son (v. 25 – 27; Heb. 1:10 – 12).

101:4 [h] Pr 11:20 **101:5** [i] Ps 50:20 [j] Ps 10:5; Pr 6:17 **101:6** [k] Ps 119:1 **101:8** [l] Jer 21:12 [m] Ps 75:10 [n] Ps 118:10-12 [o] Ps 46:4 **102:1** [p] Ex 2:23 **102:2** [q] Ps 69:17 **102:3** [r] Jas 4:14 **102:4** [s] Ps 37:2 **102:6** [t] Job 30:29; Isa 34:11 **102:7** [u] Ps 77:4 [v] Ps 38:11 **102:9** [w] Ps 42:3 **102:10** [x] Ps 38:3 **102:11** [y] Job 14:2 **102:12** [z] Ps 9:7 [a] Ps 135:13 **102:13** [b] Isa 60:10 **102:15** [c] 1Ki 8:43 [d] Ps 138:4 **102:16** [e] Isa 60:1-2 **102:17** [f] Ne 1:6 **102:18** [g] Ro 15:4 [h] Ps 22:31 **102:19** [i] Dt 26:15 **102:20** [j] Ps 79:11 **102:21** [k] Ps 22:22 **102:24** [l] Ps 90:2; Isa 38:10 **102:25** [m] Ge 1:1; Heb 1:10-12*

26 They will perish,[n] but you remain;
they will all wear out like a garment.
Like clothing you will change them
and they will be discarded.
27 But you remain the same,[o]
and your years will never end.
28 The children of your servants[p] will live
in your presence;
their descendants[q] will be established
before you."

Psalm 103

Of David.

1 Praise the LORD, my soul;[r]
all my inmost being, praise his holy
name.
2 Praise the LORD, my soul,
and forget not all his benefits—
3 who forgives all your sins[s]
and heals[t] all your diseases,
4 who redeems your life from the pit
and crowns you with love and
compassion,
5 who satisfies your desires with good
things
so that your youth is renewed like the
eagle's.[u]

6 The LORD works righteousness
and justice for all the oppressed.

7 He made known[v] his ways[w] to Moses,
his deeds[x] to the people of Israel:
8 The LORD is compassionate and
gracious,[y]
slow to anger, abounding in love.
9 He will not always accuse,
nor will he harbor his anger forever;[z]
10 he does not treat us as our sins deserve[a]
or repay us according to our
iniquities.
11 For as high as the heavens are above
the earth,
so great is his love[b] for those who
fear him;
12 as far as the east is from the west,
so far has he removed our
transgressions[c] from us.
13 As a father has compassion[d] on his
children,
so the LORD has compassion on those
who fear him;
14 for he knows how we are formed,[e]
he remembers that we are dust.
15 The life of mortals is like grass,[f]
they flourish like a flower[g] of the
field;
16 the wind blows[h] over it and it is gone,
and its place[i] remembers it no more.
17 But from everlasting to everlasting
the LORD's love is with those who fear
him,
and his righteousness with their
children's children—
18 with those who keep his covenant
and remember to obey his precepts.[j]

19 The LORD has established his throne in
heaven,
and his kingdom rules[k] over all.

20 Praise the LORD, you his angels,[l]
you mighty ones[m] who do his
bidding,
who obey his word.
21 Praise the LORD, all his heavenly hosts,[n]
you his servants who do his will.
22 Praise the LORD, all his works[o]
everywhere in his dominion.

Praise the LORD, my soul.

Psalm 104

1 Praise the LORD, my soul.[p]

LORD my God, you are very great;
you are clothed with splendor and
majesty.

2 The LORD wraps[q] himself in light as
with a garment;
he stretches out the heavens[r] like a
tent
3 and lays the beams[s] of his upper
chambers on their waters.
He makes the clouds[t] his chariot
and rides on the wings of the
wind.[u]

103:1 *Praise the LORD.* To praise the Lord is to remember that He is the source of all our blessings. The psalmist praises the Lord with his entire being (146:2).
103:3 *heals all your diseases.* This cannot be seen as a promise that the godly will never suffer from disease. Many believers have suffered and died of illnesses, despite repeated prayers for healing. Even though He does not always choose to heal, God is the source of all healing. This verse could also be seen as a parallel construction, coupling pardon from iniquity with healing from the disease of sin.
103:8 *compassionate and gracious.* This is a basic description of God in the Old Testament (86:15; Ex. 34:6–7). If God dealt with us according to our sins, no one could stand before Him (130:3).
103:11 *as high as the heavens are above the earth.* There is no way to compare the divine with the mortal; the mercy of God is greater than the heavens.
103:17 *the LORD's love.* God's loyal love is forever.
103:20–22 *Praise the LORD.* The poet began the psalm with a call to his own inner being to respond with praise to God (v. 1); he concludes the psalm with a call to heaven and earth to join him.
104:2 *wraps himself in light.* God is Spirit (John 4:24), and descriptions of Him vary throughout the

102:26 [n] Isa 34:4; Mt 24:35; 2Pe 3:7-10; Rev 20:11
102:27 [o] Mal 3:6; Heb 13:8; Jas 1:17 **102:28** [p] Ps 69:36
[q] Ps 89:4 **103:1** [r] Ps 104:1 **103:3** [s] Ps 130:8 [t] Ex 15:26
103:5 [u] Isa 40:31 **103:7** [v] Ps 99:7; 147:19 [w] Ex 33:13
[x] Ps 106:22 **103:8** [y] Ex 34:6; Ps 86:15; Jas 5:11
103:9 [z] Ps 30:5; Isa 57:16; Jer 3:5, 12; Mic 7:18
103:10 [a] Ezr 9:13 **103:11** [b] Ps 57:10 **103:12** [c] 2Sa 12:13
103:13 [d] Mal 3:17 **103:14** [e] Isa 29:16 **103:15** [f] Ps 90:5
[g] Job 14:2; Jas 1:10; 1Pe 1:24 **103:16** [h] Isa 40:7 [i] Job 7:10
103:18 [j] Dt 7:9 **103:19** [k] Ps 47:2 **103:20** [l] Ps 148:2;
Heb 1:14 [m] Ps 29:1 **103:21** [n] 1Ki 22:19
103:22 [o] Ps 145:10 **104:1** [p] Ps 103:22 **104:2** [q] Da 7:9
[r] Isa 40:22 **104:3** [s] Am 9:6 [t] Isa 19:1 [u] Ps 18:10

4 He makes winds his messengers,[a][v]
flames of fire[w] his servants.

5 He set the earth[x] on its foundations;
it can never be moved.
6 You covered it[y] with the watery depths[z]
as with a garment;
the waters stood above the
mountains.
7 But at your rebuke[a] the waters fled,
at the sound of your thunder they
took to flight;
8 they flowed over the mountains,
they went down into the valleys,
to the place you assigned[b] for them.
9 You set a boundary they cannot cross;
never again will they cover the
earth.

10 He makes springs[c] pour water into the
ravines;
it flows between the mountains.
11 They give water to all the beasts of the
field;
the wild donkeys quench their thirst.
12 The birds of the sky[d] nest by the waters;
they sing among the branches.
13 He waters the mountains[e] from his
upper chambers;
the land is satisfied by the fruit of his
work.
14 He makes grass grow[f] for the cattle,
and plants for people to cultivate—
bringing forth food[g] from the earth:
15 wine[h] that gladdens human hearts,
oil[i] to make their faces shine,
and bread that sustains their hearts.
16 The trees of the LORD are well watered,
the cedars of Lebanon that he
planted.
17 There the birds[j] make their nests;
the stork has its home in the
junipers.
18 The high mountains belong to the wild
goats;
the crags are a refuge for the hyrax.[k]

19 He made the moon to mark the
seasons,[l]
and the sun[m] knows when to go down.
20 You bring darkness,[n] it becomes night,[o]
and all the beasts of the forest[p] prowl.
21 The lions roar for their prey
and seek their food from God.[q]
22 The sun rises, and they steal away;
they return and lie down in their dens.[r]
23 Then people go out to their work,[s]
to their labor until evening.

24 How many are your works,[t] LORD!
In wisdom you made[u] them all;
the earth is full of your creatures.
25 There is the sea,[v] vast and spacious,
teeming with creatures beyond
number—
living things both large and small.
26 There the ships[w] go to and fro,
and Leviathan,[x] which you formed to
frolic there.

27 All creatures look to you
to give them their food[y] at the proper
time.
28 When you give it to them,
they gather it up;
when you open your hand,
they are satisfied[z] with good things.
29 When you hide your face,[a]
they are terrified;
when you take away their breath,
they die and return to the dust.[b]
30 When you send your Spirit,
they are created,
and you renew the face of the ground.

31 May the glory of the LORD endure
forever;
may the LORD rejoice in his works[c]—
32 he who looks at the earth, and it
trembles,[d]
who touches the mountains,[e] and
they smoke.[f]

[a] 4 Or *angels*

Bible. One strong description of Him is "light" (1 John 1:5). Here, light is described as the garment that enfolds His wonder. The first act of God in Genesis was the command for light (Gen. 1:3).

104:5 *set the earth on its foundations.* The poet retells the story of creation from Genesis 1.

104:6 *covered it with the watery depths.* The term "depths" is the same word used in Genesis 1:2.

104:9 *set a boundary.* God promised that never again would the entire earth be covered as in the flood (Gen. 8:21–22).

104:15 *wine ... oil ... bread.* It is clear that the earth was created for human beings and filled with good things for our sake.

104:19 *He made the moon to mark the seasons.* In the ancient world, the heavenly bodies (sun, moon, and stars) were often worshiped as gods. God makes it clear that, far from being objects of worship, these things were created and set in place specifically for humans. The moon is not our god but our servant, set in place to keep track of times and seasons.

104:27 *All creatures look to you.* All creation depends on the Creator for birth, life, and sustenance. Even death is controlled by the Sovereign One.

104:31 *may the LORD rejoice in his works.* The Lord considered His creation "good" from the beginning (Gen. 1:31), and His pleasure in it remains (Prov. 8:30–31).

104:4 [v] Ps 148:8; Heb 1:7* [w] 2Ki 2:11 **104:5** [x] Job 26:7; Ps 24:1-2 **104:6** [y] Ge 7:19 [z] Ge 1:2 **104:7** [a] Ps 18:15 **104:8** [b] Ps 33:7 **104:10** [c] Ps 107:33; Isa 41:18 **104:12** [d] Mt 8:20 **104:13** [e] Ps 147:8; Jer 10:13 **104:14** [f] Job 38:27; Ps 147:8 [g] Ge 1:30; Job 28:5 **104:15** [h] Jdg 9:13 [i] Ps 23:5; 92:10; Lk 7:46 **104:17** [j] ver 12 **104:18** [k] Pr 30:26 **104:19** [l] Ge 1:14 [m] Ps 19:6 **104:20** [n] Isa 45:7 [o] Ps 74:16 [p] Ps 50:10 **104:21** [q] Job 38:39; Ps 145:15; Joel 1:20 **104:22** [r] Job 37:8 **104:23** [s] Ge 3:19 **104:24** [t] Ps 40:5 [u] Pr 3:19 **104:25** [v] Ps 69:34 **104:26** [w] Ps 107:23; Eze 27:9 [x] Job 41:1 **104:27** [y] Job 36:31; Ps 136:25; 145:15; 147:9 **104:28** [z] Ps 145:16 **104:29** [a] Dt 31:17 [b] Job 34:14; Ecc 12:7 **104:31** [c] Ge 1:31 **104:32** [d] Ps 97:4 [e] Ex 19:18 [f] Ps 144:5

33 I will sing[g] to the LORD all my life;
I will sing praise to my God as long
as I live.
34 May my meditation be pleasing to him,
as I rejoice[h] in the LORD.
35 But may sinners vanish[i] from the earth
and the wicked be no more.

Praise the LORD, my soul.

Praise the LORD.[a][j]

Psalm 105

1 Give praise to the LORD,[k] proclaim his
name;[l]
make known among the nations what
he has done.
2 Sing to him,[m] sing praise to him;
tell of all his wonderful acts.
3 Glory in his holy name;
let the hearts of those who seek the
LORD rejoice.
4 Look to the LORD and his strength;
seek his face[n] always.

5 Remember the wonders[o] he has done,
his miracles, and the judgments he
pronounced,[p]
6 you his servants, the descendants of
Abraham,[q]
his chosen[r] ones, the children of
Jacob.
7 He is the LORD our God;
his judgments are in all the earth.

8 He remembers his covenant[s] forever,
the promise he made, for a thousand
generations,
9 the covenant he made with Abraham,[t]
the oath he swore to Isaac.
10 He confirmed it[u] to Jacob as a decree,
to Israel as an everlasting covenant:
11 "To you I will give the land of Canaan[v]
as the portion you will inherit."

12 When they were but few in number,[w]
few indeed, and strangers in it,[x]
13 they wandered from nation to nation,
from one kingdom to another.
14 He allowed no one to oppress[y] them;
for their sake he rebuked kings:[z]
15 "Do not touch[a] my anointed ones;
do my prophets no harm."

16 He called down famine[b] on the land
and destroyed all their supplies of
food;
17 and he sent a man before them—
Joseph, sold as a slave.[c]
18 They bruised his feet with shackles,[d]
his neck was put in irons,
19 till what he foretold[e] came to pass,
till the word of the LORD proved him
true.
20 The king sent and released him,
the ruler of peoples set him free.[f]
21 He made him master of his household,
ruler over all he possessed,
22 to instruct his princes[g] as he pleased
and teach his elders wisdom.

23 Then Israel entered Egypt;[h]
Jacob resided as a foreigner in the
land of Ham.
24 The LORD made his people very fruitful;
he made them too numerous[i] for their
foes,
25 whose hearts he turned[j] to hate his
people,
to conspire[k] against his servants.
26 He sent Moses[l] his servant,
and Aaron, whom he had chosen.[m]
27 They performed[n] his signs among
them,
his wonders in the land of Ham.
28 He sent darkness[o] and made the land
dark—
for had they not rebelled against his
words?
29 He turned their waters into blood,[p]
causing their fish to die.[q]
30 Their land teemed with frogs,[r]
which went up into the bedrooms of
their rulers.

---

[a] *35* Hebrew *Hallelu Yah*; in the Septuagint this line stands at the beginning of Psalm 105.

105:5 *Remember the wonders he has done.* The psalmist calls to memory what God did for His people in fulfillment of the covenant with Abraham (Gen. 12:1–3; 22:16–18).

105:8 *He remembers.* The words of the original promise to Abraham set out the Lord's obligation in strong terms (Gen. 12:1–3).

105:13–15 *wandered ... for their sake he rebuked kings.* The descendants of Abraham have more than once been strangers in a foreign land, but each time the Lord has preserved their identity as a people and has rescued them from destruction. He saved them from the hand of Pharaoh (Exodus), and from the Persians (Esther). Today, the Jews are again scattered, but even though many have forgotten their God, they still do not forget that they are Jews. God's miraculous preservation of the identity of His people indicates that He is not yet finished with them.

105:17 *Joseph.* The story of Joseph's life is told in Genesis 37–50.

105:26–36 *He sent Moses.* The full story of the Israelites' slavery in Egypt and the plagues God sent upon the Egyptians is told in Exodus 1–11.

104:33 [g] Ps 63:4 **104:34** [h] Ps 9:2 **104:35** [i] Ps 37:38 [j] Ps 105:45; 106:48 **105:1** [k] 1Ch 16:34 [l] Ps 99:6 **105:2** [m] Ps 96:1 **105:4** [n] Ps 27:8 **105:5** [o] Ps 40:5 [p] Ps 77:11 **105:6** [q] ver 42 [r] Ps 106:5 **105:8** [s] Ps 106:45; Lk 1:72 **105:9** [t] Ge 12:7; 17:2; 22:16-18; Gal 3:15-18 **105:10** [u] Ge 28:13-15 **105:11** [v] Ge 13:15; 15:18 **105:12** [w] Ge 34:30; Dt 7:7 [x] Ge 23:4; Heb 11:9 **105:14** [y] Ge 35:5 [z] Ge 12:17-20 **105:15** [a] Ge 26:11 **105:16** [b] Ge 41:54; Lev 26:26; Isa 3:1; Eze 4:16 **105:17** [c] Ge 37:28; 45:5; Ac 7:9 **105:18** [d] Ge 40:15 **105:19** [e] Ge 40:20-22 **105:20** [f] Ge 41:14 **105:22** [g] Ge 41:43-44 **105:23** [h] Ge 46:6; Ac 13:17 **105:24** [i] Ex 1:7,9 **105:25** [j] Ex 4:21 [k] Ex 1:6-10; Ac 7:19 **105:26** [l] Ex 3:10 [m] Nu 16:5; 17:5-8 **105:27** [n] Ex 7:8-12:51 **105:28** [o] Ex 10:22 **105:29** [p] Ps 78:44 [q] Ex 7:21 **105:30** [r] Ex 8:2,6

31 He spoke, and there came swarms of flies,[s]
and gnats[t] throughout their country.
32 He turned their rain into hail,[u]
with lightning throughout their land;
33 he struck down their vines[v] and fig trees
and shattered the trees of their country.
34 He spoke, and the locusts came,[w]
grasshoppers without number;
35 they ate up every green thing in their land,
ate up the produce of their soil.
36 Then he struck down all the firstborn[x] in their land,
the firstfruits of all their manhood.
37 He brought out Israel, laden with silver and gold,[y]
and from among their tribes no one faltered.
38 Egypt was glad when they left,
because dread of Israel[z] had fallen on them.
39 He spread out a cloud[a] as a covering,
and a fire to give light at night.[b]
40 They asked,[c] and he brought them quail;[d]
he fed them well with the bread of heaven.[e]
41 He opened the rock,[f] and water gushed out;
it flowed like a river in the desert.

42 For he remembered his holy promise[g]
given to his servant Abraham.
43 He brought out his people with rejoicing,[h]
his chosen ones with shouts of joy;
44 he gave them the lands of the nations,[i]
and they fell heir to what others had toiled for—
45 that they might keep his precepts
and observe his laws.[j]

Praise the LORD.[a]

Psalm 106

1 Praise the LORD.[b]

Give thanks to the LORD, for he is good;[k]
his love endures forever.

2 Who can proclaim the mighty acts[l] of the LORD
or fully declare his praise?
3 Blessed are those who act justly,
who always do what is right.[m]

4 Remember me,[n] LORD, when you show favor to your people,
come to my aid when you save them,
5 that I may enjoy the prosperity[o] of your chosen ones,
that I may share in the joy[p] of your nation
and join your inheritance in giving praise.

6 We have sinned,[q] even as our ancestors did;
we have done wrong and acted wickedly.
7 When our ancestors were in Egypt,
they gave no thought to your miracles;
they did not remember[r] your many kindnesses,
and they rebelled by the sea,[s] the Red Sea.[c]
8 Yet he saved them for his name's sake,[t]
to make his mighty power known.
9 He rebuked[u] the Red Sea, and it dried up;[v]
he led them through[w] the depths as through a desert.
10 He saved them[x] from the hand of the foe;
from the hand of the enemy he redeemed them.[y]
11 The waters covered[z] their adversaries;
not one of them survived.
12 Then they believed his promises
and sang his praise.[a]

13 But they soon forgot[b] what he had done
and did not wait for his plan to unfold.
14 In the desert they gave in to their craving;
in the wilderness they put God to the test.[c]

a 45 Hebrew *Hallelu Yah* *b* 1 Hebrew *Hallelu Yah*; also in verse 48 *c* 7 Or *the Sea of Reeds*; also in verses 9 and 22

105:44 ***gave them the lands of the nations.*** It is believed that this psalm may have been composed after the return from exile in Babylon. A celebration of God's gift of land would have been a tremendous source of encouragement to the people who had just returned to Israel.
106:6 ***sinned, even as our ancestors.*** It is easy to point out the places where people have gone wrong in the past and to marvel at their stupidity and rebellion, but we have to point the finger at ourselves as well.
106:12 ***Then they believed.*** The people had faithlessly rebelled, but God graciously rescued them anyway, proving that His word is true and worth believing.
106:13 ***they soon forgot.*** Faith which is only active in the face of abundant proof is weak and short-lived.

105:31 [s] Ex 8:21-24 [t] Ex 8:16-18 **105:32** [u] Ex 9:22-25 **105:33** [v] Ps 78:47 **105:34** [w] Ex 10:4, 12-15 **105:36** [x] Ex 12:29 **105:37** [y] Ex 12:35 **105:38** [z] Ex 12:33; 15:16 **105:39** [a] Ex 13:21 [b] Ne 9:12; Ps 78:14 **105:40** [c] Ps 78:18, 24 [d] Ex 16:13 [e] Jn 6:31 **105:41** [f] Ex 17:6; Nu 20:11; Ps 78:15-16; 1Co 10:4 **105:42** [g] Ge 15:13-16 **105:43** [h] Ex 15:1-18; Ps 106:12 **105:44** [i] Jos 13:6-7 **105:45** [j] Dt 4:40; 6:21-24 **106:1** [k] Ps 100:5; 105:1 **106:2** [l] Ps 145:4, 12 **106:3** [m] Ps 15:2 **106:4** [n] Ps 119:132 **106:5** [o] Ps 1:3 [p] Ps 118:15 **106:6** [q] Da 9:5 **106:7** [r] Ps 78:11, 42 [s] Ex 14:11-12 **106:8** [t] Ex 9:16 **106:9** [u] Ps 18:15 [v] Ex 14:21; Na 1:4 [w] Isa 63:11-14 **106:10** [x] Ex 14:30 [y] Ps 107:2 **106:11** [z] Ex 14:28; 15:5 **106:12** [a] Ex 15:1-21 **106:13** [b] Ex 15:24 **106:14** [c] 1Co 10:9

15 So he gave them[d] what they asked for,
but sent a wasting disease[e] among them.
16 In the camp they grew envious[f] of Moses
and of Aaron, who was consecrated to the LORD.
17 The earth opened[g] up and swallowed Dathan;
it buried the company of Abiram.
18 Fire blazed[h] among their followers;
a flame consumed the wicked.
19 At Horeb they made a calf[i]
and worshiped an idol cast from metal.
20 They exchanged their glorious God[j]
for an image of a bull, which eats grass.
21 They forgot the God[k] who saved them,
who had done great things[l] in Egypt,
22 miracles in the land of Ham[m]
and awesome deeds by the Red Sea.
23 So he said he would destroy[n] them—
had not Moses, his chosen one,
stood in the breach[o] before him
to keep his wrath from destroying them.

24 Then they despised the pleasant land;[p]
they did not believe[q] his promise.
25 They grumbled[r] in their tents
and did not obey the LORD.
26 So he swore[s] to them with uplifted hand
that he would make them fall in the wilderness,[t]
27 make their descendants fall among the nations
and scatter[u] them throughout the lands.

28 They yoked themselves to the Baal of Peor[v]
and ate sacrifices offered to lifeless gods;
29 they aroused the LORD's anger by their wicked deeds,
and a plague broke out among them.
30 But Phinehas stood up and intervened,
and the plague was checked.[w]
31 This was credited to him[x] as righteousness
for endless generations to come.
32 By the waters of Meribah[y] they angered the LORD,
and trouble came to Moses because of them;
33 for they rebelled against the Spirit of God,
and rash words came from Moses' lips.[az]

34 They did not destroy[a] the peoples
as the LORD had commanded[b] them,
35 but they mingled[c] with the nations
and adopted their customs.
36 They worshiped their idols,[d]
which became a snare to them.
37 They sacrificed their sons[e]
and their daughters to false gods.
38 They shed innocent blood,
the blood of their sons[f] and daughters,
whom they sacrificed to the idols of Canaan,
and the land was desecrated by their blood.
39 They defiled themselves[g] by what they did;
by their deeds they prostituted[h] themselves.

40 Therefore the LORD was angry[i] with his people
and abhorred his inheritance.[j]
41 He gave them into the hands[k] of the nations,
and their foes ruled over them.

---

[a] 33 Or *against his spirit, / and rash words came from his lips*

106:15 *he gave them what they asked for.* When the people rebelliously kept asking for their own desires, God finally let them have their own way — and also let them take the consequences. We don't have to fear that we might accidentally pray for something wrong and then receive a bad gift from the Lord. Even when we pray wrongly, if our hearts are turned towards God, He will redirect our desires and teach us the better way (37:4). However, it is sin if we keep praying for something when we already know that He said no, and we may have to bear consequences that we never dreamed of.

106:20 *exchanged their glorious God.* These words are echoed by Paul in Romans 1:22 – 23.

106:24 – 25 *they did not believe.* The Old Testament books of Exodus and Joshua illustrate God's plan of salvation. The first relates how Israel was brought out of the land of bondage, and the second describes how they were brought into the land of blessing. The wilderness route they traveled was of His choosing, but not the aimless wandering which followed. That sad 40-year episode was a direct result of their sin of unbelief.

106:28 *Baal of Peor.* After Balaam was prevented from cursing the Israelites, he suggested that the Moabites could destroy the Israelites in another way, by leading them into sin against their God (Num. 25).

106:34 *destroy the peoples.* If Israel had obeyed and the Canaanites had been driven out, the people might never have succumbed to the idolatry that marked their existence for hundreds of years.

106:15 [d] Nu 11:31 [e] Isa 10:16 **106:16** [f] Nu 16:1-3
106:17 [g] Dt 11:6 **106:18** [h] Nu 16:35 **106:19** [i] Ex 32:4
106:20 [j] Jer 2:11; Ro 1:23 **106:21** [k] Ps 78:11 [l] Dt 10:21
106:22 [m] Ps 105:27 **106:23** [n] Ex 32:10 [o] Ex 32:11-14
106:24 [p] Dt 8:7; Eze 20:6 [q] Heb 3:18-19
106:25 [r] Nu 14:2 **106:26** [s] Eze 20:15; Heb 3:11
[t] Nu 14:28-35 **106:27** [u] Lev 26:33; Ps 44:11
106:28 [v] Nu 25:2-3; Hos 9:10 **106:30** [w] Nu 25:8
106:31 [x] Nu 25:11-13 **106:32** [y] Nu 20:2-13; Ps 81:7
106:33 [z] Nu 20:8-12 **106:34** [a] Jdg 1:21 [b] Dt 7:16
106:35 [c] Jdg 3:5-6 **106:36** [d] Jdg 2:12
106:37 [e] 2Ki 16:3; 17:17 **106:38** [f] Nu 35:33
106:39 [g] Eze 20:18 [h] Lev 17:7; Nu 15:39
106:40 [i] Jdg 2:14; Ps 78:59 [j] Dt 9:29 **106:41** [k] Jdg 2:14; Ne 9:27

42 Their enemies oppressed them
and subjected them to their power.
43 Many times he delivered them,
but they were bent on rebellion[l]
and they wasted away in their sin.
44 Yet he took note of their distress
when he heard their cry;[m]
45 for their sake he remembered his covenant[n]
and out of his great love[o] he relented.
46 He caused all who held them captive
to show them mercy.[p]

47 Save us, LORD our God,
and gather us[q] from the nations,
that we may give thanks to your holy name
and glory in your praise.

48 Praise be to the LORD, the God of Israel,
from everlasting to everlasting.

Let all the people say, "Amen!"[r]

Praise the LORD.

BOOK V

Psalms 107 – 150

Psalm 107

1 Give thanks to the LORD,[s] for he is good;
his love endures forever.

2 Let the redeemed[t] of the LORD tell their story—
those he redeemed from the hand of the foe,
3 those he gathered[u] from the lands,
from east and west, from north and south.[a]

4 Some wandered in desert[v] wastelands,
finding no way to a city where they could settle.
5 They were hungry and thirsty,
and their lives ebbed away.
6 Then they cried out[w] to the LORD in their trouble,
and he delivered them from their distress.
7 He led them by a straight way[x]
to a city where they could settle.
8 Let them give thanks to the LORD for his unfailing love
and his wonderful deeds for mankind,
9 for he satisfies[y] the thirsty
and fills the hungry with good things.[z]

10 Some sat in darkness,[a] in utter darkness,
prisoners suffering in iron chains,[b]
11 because they rebelled[c] against God's commands
and despised the plans[d] of the Most High.
12 So he subjected them to bitter labor;
they stumbled, and there was no one to help.[e]
13 Then they cried to the LORD in their trouble,
and he saved them from their distress.
14 He brought them out of darkness, the utter darkness,
and broke away their chains.[f]
15 Let them give thanks to the LORD for his unfailing love
and his wonderful deeds for mankind,
16 for he breaks down gates of bronze
and cuts through bars of iron.

17 Some became fools through their rebellious ways
and suffered affliction[g] because of their iniquities.
18 They loathed all food[h]
and drew near the gates of death.[i]
19 Then they cried to the LORD in their trouble,
and he saved them from their distress.
20 He sent out his word[j] and healed them;[k]
he rescued[l] them from the grave.[m]
21 Let them give thanks to the LORD for his unfailing love
and his wonderful deeds for mankind.
22 Let them sacrifice thank offerings[n]
and tell of his works[o] with songs of joy.

---

[a] 3 Hebrew *north and the sea*

106:45 ***he remembered his covenant.*** God's wrath must always be seen in the context of His loyal love and His long forbearance. Even when the people brought down His wrath by their sins, He remained faithful to the covenant.
107:1 ***his love endures forever.*** God's "loyal love" or "mercies" will never end. He is always willing to restore those who call on Him.
107:9 ***he satisfies the thirsty.*** Only God can fulfill the spiritual longings of the human soul.
107:17 ***fools.*** This harsh word emphasizes moral failure (Prov. 1:7; 15:5). These people deserved the trouble they suffered, yet they too may call upon the Lord, and He will deliver and restore them.

106:43 [l] Jdg 2:16-19 **106:44** [m] Jdg 3:9; 10:10
106:45 [n] Lev 26:42; Ps 105:8 [o] Jdg 2:18
106:46 [p] Ezr 9:9; Jer 42:12 **106:47** [q] Ps 147:2
106:48 [r] Ps 41:13 **107:1** [s] Ps 106:1 **107:2** [t] Ps 106:10
107:3 [u] Ps 106:47; Isa 43:5-6 **107:4** [v] Nu 14:33; 32:13
107:6 [w] Ps 50:15 **107:7** [x] Ezr 8:21 **107:9** [y] Ps 22:26; Lk 1:53 [z] Ps 34:10 **107:10** [a] Lk 1:79 [b] Job 36:8
107:11 [c] Ps 106:7; La 3:42 [d] 2Ch 36:16 **107:12** [e] Ps 22:11
107:14 [f] Ps 116:16; Lk 13:16; Ac 12:7 **107:17** [g] Isa 65:6-7; La 3:39 **107:18** [h] Job 33:20 [i] Job 33:22; Ps 9:13; 88:3
107:20 [j] Mt 8:8 [k] Ps 103:3 [l] Job 33:28 [m] Ps 30:3; 49:15
107:22 [n] Lev 7:12; Ps 50:14; 116:17 [o] Ps 9:11; 73:28; 118:17

23 Some went out on the sea in ships;
they were merchants on the mighty waters.
24 They saw the works of the LORD,
his wonderful deeds in the deep.
25 For he spoke[p] and stirred up a tempest[q]
that lifted high the waves.[r]
26 They mounted up to the heavens and went down to the depths;
in their peril their courage melted[s] away.
27 They reeled and staggered like drunkards;
they were at their wits' end.
28 Then they cried out to the LORD in their trouble,
and he brought them out of their distress.
29 He stilled the storm[t] to a whisper;
the waves[u] of the sea[a] were hushed.
30 They were glad when it grew calm,
and he guided them to their desired haven.
31 Let them give thanks to the LORD for his unfailing love
and his wonderful deeds for mankind.
32 Let them exalt him in the assembly[v] of the people
and praise him in the council of the elders.

33 He turned rivers into a desert,[w]
flowing springs into thirsty ground,
34 and fruitful land into a salt waste,[x]
because of the wickedness of those who lived there.
35 He turned the desert into pools of water[y]
and the parched ground into flowing springs;
36 there he brought the hungry to live,
and they founded a city where they could settle.
37 They sowed fields and planted vineyards[z]
that yielded a fruitful harvest;
38 he blessed them, and their numbers greatly increased,[a]
and he did not let their herds diminish.

39 Then their numbers decreased,[b] and they were humbled
by oppression, calamity and sorrow;
40 he who pours contempt on nobles[c]
made them wander in a trackless waste.[d]
41 But he lifted the needy[e] out of their affliction
and increased their families like flocks.
42 The upright see and rejoice,[f]
but all the wicked shut their mouths.[g]

43 Let the one who is wise[h] heed these things
and ponder the loving deeds[i] of the LORD.

Psalm 108[b]

A song. A psalm of David.

1 My heart, O God, is steadfast;
I will sing and make music with all my soul.
2 Awake, harp and lyre!
I will awaken the dawn.
3 I will praise you, LORD, among the nations;
I will sing of you among the peoples.
4 For great is your love, higher than the heavens;
your faithfulness reaches to the skies.
5 Be exalted, O God, above the heavens;
let your glory be over all the earth.[j]

6 Save us and help us with your right hand,
that those you love may be delivered.
7 God has spoken from his sanctuary:
"In triumph I will parcel out Shechem
and measure off the Valley of Sukkoth.
8 Gilead is mine, Manasseh is mine;
Ephraim is my helmet,
Judah[k] is my scepter.
9 Moab is my washbasin,
on Edom I toss my sandal;
over Philistia I shout in triumph."

10 Who will bring me to the fortified city?
Who will lead me to Edom?
11 Is it not you, God, you who have rejected us
and no longer go out with our armies?[l]

---

a 29 Dead Sea Scrolls; Masoretic Text / *their waves*
b In Hebrew texts 108:1-13 is numbered 108:2-14.

107:33 *He turned rivers into a desert.* During the reign of King Ahab of the northern kingdom of Israel, God sentenced the land to three years of drought because of their Baal worship (1 Kin. 17:1–7).

107:43 *who is wise.* There is no wisdom apart from centering in on and responding to the love of God. The psalmist exhorts the readers to review God's history of delivering those in trouble and to praise His great love.

108:title *A song.* This psalm is actually a medley of two other psalms of David. Verses 1–5 are from 57:7–11, and verses 6–13 are from 60:5–12. David is the author of both of these psalms, and 108 is attributed to him as well, even though the arrangement may have been someone else's.

107:25 [p] Ps 105:31 [q] Jnh 1:4 [r] Ps 93:3 **107:26** [s] Ps 22:14 **107:29** [t] Mt 8:26 [u] Ps 89:9 **107:32** [v] Ps 22:22, 25; 35:18 **107:33** [w] 1Ki 17:1; Ps 74:15 **107:34** [x] Ge 13:10; 14:3; 19:25 **107:35** [y] Ps 114:8; Isa 41:18 **107:37** [z] Isa 65:21 **107:38** [a] Ge 12:2; 17:16, 20; Ex 1:7 **107:39** [b] 2Ki 10:32; Eze 5:12 **107:40** [c] Job 12:21 [d] Job 12:24 **107:41** [e] 1Sa 2:8; Ps 113:7-9 **107:42** [f] Job 22:19 [g] Job 5:16; Ps 63:11; Ro 3:19 **107:43** [h] Jer 9:12; Hos 14:9 [i] Ps 64:9 **108:5** [j] Ps 57:5 **108:8** [k] Ge 49:10 **108:11** [l] Ps 44:9

12 Give us aid against the enemy,
for human help is worthless.
13 With God we will gain the victory,
and he will trample down our enemies.

Psalm 109

For the director of music. Of David. A psalm.

1 My God, whom I praise,
do not remain silent,[m]
2 for people who are wicked and deceitful
have opened their mouths against me;
they have spoken against me with lying tongues.[n]
3 With words of hatred[o] they surround me;
they attack me without cause.[p]
4 In return for my friendship they accuse me,
but I am a man of prayer.[q]
5 They repay me evil for good,[r]
and hatred for my friendship.

6 Appoint someone evil to oppose my enemy;
let an accuser[s] stand at his right hand.
7 When he is tried, let him be found guilty,
and may his prayers condemn[t] him.
8 May his days be few;
may another take his place[u] of leadership.
9 May his children be fatherless
and his wife a widow.[v]
10 May his children be wandering beggars;
may they be driven[a] from their ruined homes.
11 May a creditor seize all he has;
may strangers plunder the fruits of his labor.[w]
12 May no one extend kindness to him
or take pity[x] on his fatherless children.
13 May his descendants be cut off,[y]
their names blotted out[z] from the next generation.
14 May the iniquity of his fathers[a] be remembered before the LORD;
may the sin of his mother never be blotted out.
15 May their sins always remain before the LORD,
that he may blot out their name[b] from the earth.

16 For he never thought of doing a kindness,
but hounded to death the poor
and the needy[c] and the brokenhearted.[d]
17 He loved to pronounce a curse—
may it come back on him.[e]
He found no pleasure in blessing—
may it be far from him.
18 He wore cursing[f] as his garment;
it entered into his body like water,[g]
into his bones like oil.
19 May it be like a cloak wrapped about him,
like a belt tied forever around him.
20 May this be the LORD's payment[h] to my accusers,
to those who speak evil[i] of me.

21 But you, Sovereign LORD,
help me for your name's sake;[j]
out of the goodness of your love,[k] deliver me.
22 For I am poor and needy,
and my heart is wounded within me.
23 I fade away like an evening shadow;[l]
I am shaken off like a locust.
24 My knees give[m] way from fasting;
my body is thin and gaunt.
25 I am an object of scorn[n] to my accusers;
when they see me, they shake their heads.[o]

26 Help me,[p] LORD my God;
save me according to your unfailing love.
27 Let them know[q] that it is your hand,
that you, LORD, have done it.

---

[a] 10 Septuagint; Hebrew *sought*

109:8 ***may another take his place of leadership.*** These words (along with 69:25) are quoted in Acts 1:20 as having been fulfilled in the replacement of Judas Iscariot.

109:9 ***fatherless . . . a widow.*** The curses that the psalmist wants to call down on his enemies seem very harsh and unforgiving. It is hard to understand how we should take this kind of language, in the face of Christ's teaching about loving our enemies and doing good to those who hurt us. However, two important points are clear: the psalmist left vengeance in the hands of the Lord, and he also clearly understood the reality of wickedness. We must remember that forgiveness is not saying, "It wasn't really bad." True forgiveness does not pretend that sin did not happen; it recognizes evil, and then releases the desire for vengeance into God's hands. God has promised that He will judge the wicked in the end.

109:27 ***Let them know.*** Even in the psalmist's intense emotional state, he wants to see the name of God defended, proclaimed, and honored.

109:1 [m] Ps 83:1 **109:2** [n] Ps 52:4; 120:2 **109:3** [o] Ps 69:4 [p] Ps 35:7; Jn 15:25 **109:4** [q] Ps 69:13 **109:5** [r] Ps 35:12; 38:20 **109:6** [s] Zec 3:1 **109:7** [t] Pr 28:9 **109:8** [u] Ac 1:20* **109:9** [v] Ex 22:24 **109:11** [w] Job 5:5 **109:12** [x] Isa 9:17 **109:13** [y] Job 18:19; Ps 37:28 [z] Pr 10:7 **109:14** [a] Ex 20:5; Ne 4:5; Jer 18:23 **109:15** [b] Job 18:17; Ps 34:16 **109:16** [c] Ps 37:14,32 [d] Ps 34:18 **109:17** [e] Pr 14:14; Eze 35:6 **109:18** [f] Ps 73:6 [g] Nu 5:22 **109:20** [h] Ps 94:23; 2Ti 4:14 [i] Ps 71:10 **109:21** [j] Ps 79:9 [k] Ps 69:16 **109:23** [l] Ps 102:11 **109:24** [m] Heb 12:12 **109:25** [n] Ps 22:6 [o] Mt 27:39; Mk 15:29 **109:26** [p] Ps 119:86 **109:27** [q] Job 37:7

28 While they curse,[r] may you bless;
may those who attack me be put to shame,
but may your servant rejoice.[s]
29 May my accusers be clothed with disgrace
and wrapped in shame[t] as in a cloak.
30 With my mouth I will greatly extol the LORD;
in the great throng[u] of worshipers I will praise him.
31 For he stands at the right hand[v] of the needy,
to save their lives from those who would condemn them.

Psalm 110

Of David. A psalm.

1 The LORD says[w] to my lord:[a]

"Sit at my right hand
until I make your enemies
a footstool for your feet."[x]

2 The LORD will extend your mighty scepter[y] from Zion, saying,
"Rule in the midst of your enemies!"
3 Your troops will be willing
on your day of battle.
Arrayed in holy splendor,[z]
your young men will come to you
like dew from the morning's womb.[b]

4 The LORD has sworn
and will not change his mind:[a]
"You are a priest forever,[b]
in the order of Melchizedek."[c]

5 The Lord is at your right hand[c];[d]
he will crush kings[e] on the day of his wrath.[f]
6 He will judge the nations,[g] heaping up the dead[h]
and crushing the rulers[i] of the whole earth.
7 He will drink from a brook along the way,[d]
and so he will lift his head high.[j]

Psalm 111[e]

1 Praise the LORD.[f]

I will extol the LORD with all my heart
in the council of the upright and in the assembly.

2 Great are the works[k] of the LORD;
they are pondered by all who delight in them.
3 Glorious and majestic are his deeds,
and his righteousness endures forever.
4 He has caused his wonders to be remembered;
the LORD is gracious and compassionate.[l]
5 He provides food[m] for those who fear him;
he remembers his covenant forever.

6 He has shown his people the power of his works,
giving them the lands of other nations.
7 The works of his hands are faithful and just;
all his precepts are trustworthy.[n]
8 They are established for ever[o] and ever,
enacted in faithfulness and uprightness.

---

[a] *1* Or *Lord*   [b] *3* The meaning of the Hebrew for this sentence is uncertain.   [c] *5* Or *My lord is at your right hand, LORD*   [d] *7* The meaning of the Hebrew for this clause is uncertain.   [e] This psalm is an acrostic poem, the lines of which begin with the successive letters of the Hebrew alphabet.   [f] *1* Hebrew *Hallelu Yah*

110:1 *The LORD.* "LORD" is the translation of the Hebrew name Yahweh (I AM) and refers to God the Father. According to Jesus' interpretation of the passage (Matt. 22:41–45; Mark 12:35–37; Luke 20:41–44), the second *Lord* is a reference to the Son of God in heaven in the presence of the Father. David himself confesses the Son to be his Lord—that is, his master or sovereign. ***at my right hand.*** This position of high honor beside the Father was given to the Savior upon His resurrection and ascension (Acts 2:33–36; 1 Cor. 15:20–28; Col. 3:1; Heb. 1:13). The Savior placing His feet on His foes depicts the utter defeat of the enemies of Christ (1 Cor. 15:25–26; Eph. 1:22–23).

110:3 *Arrayed in holy splendor.* This description of the people who join the King in His great battle fits with Revelation 19:14.

110:4 *a priest.* God is seen appointing the coming Messiah to be a priest (Heb. 7). This was a source of confusion for Jews, as demonstrated by the questions that the New Testament Jews had about the Messiah. Some Dead Sea Scrolls give evidence that more than one Messiah was anticipated. According to Scripture, the Messiah would be a descendant of David (Is. 9:7), but this prophecy presents Him as a priest. This might seem to be a contradiction because true priests had to be descendants of Aaron, but the Messiah is presented as a priest by divine declaration rather than human descent. ***Melchizedek.*** Melchizedek is first mentioned in Genesis 14:18–20. He was a true priest of the Most High God, unrelated to Abraham and living hundreds of years before Aaron. He became a prototype of the Messiah, whose priesthood was not based on connection with the line of Aaron but was by divine decree (Heb. 5:5–11; 6:20; 7:1–28).

111:1 *Praise the LORD.* This translates the Hebrew word *hallelujah.*

109:28 [r] 2Sa 16:12 [s] Isa 65:14 **109:29** [t] Ps 35:26; 132:18 **109:30** [u] Ps 35:18; 111:1 **109:31** [v] Ps 16:8; 73:23; 121:5 **110:1** [w] Mt 22:44*; Mk 12:36*; Lk 20:42*; Ac 2:34* [x] 1Co 15:25 **110:2** [y] Ps 45:6 **110:3** [z] Jdg 5:2; Ps 96:9 **110:4** [a] Nu 23:19 [b] Heb 5:6*; 7:21* [c] Heb 7:15-17* **110:5** [d] Ps 16:8 [e] Ps 2:12 [f] Ps 2:5, Ro 2:5 **110:6** [g] Isa 2:4 [h] Isa 66:24 [i] Ps 68:21 **110:7** [j] Ps 27:6 **111:2** [k] Ps 92:5; 143:5 **111:4** [l] Ps 103:8 **111:5** [m] Mt 6:26, 31-33 **111:7** [n] Ps 19:7; Rev 15:3 **111:8** [o] Isa 40:8; Mt 5:18

[9]He provided redemption[p] for his people;
he ordained his covenant forever—
holy and awesome[q] is his name.

[10]The fear of the LORD is the beginning of wisdom;[r]
all who follow his precepts have good understanding.[s]
To him belongs eternal praise.[t]

Psalm 112[a]

[1]Praise the LORD.[b]

Blessed are those who fear the LORD,[u]
who find great delight[v] in his commands.

[2]Their children will be mighty in the land;
the generation of the upright will be blessed.
[3]Wealth and riches are in their houses,
and their righteousness endures forever.
[4]Even in darkness light dawns[w] for the upright,
for those who are gracious and compassionate and righteous.[x]
[5]Good will come to those who are generous and lend freely,[y]
who conduct their affairs with justice.

[6]Surely the righteous will never be shaken;
they will be remembered[z] forever.
[7]They will have no fear of bad news;
their hearts are steadfast,[a] trusting in the LORD.
[8]Their hearts are secure, they will have no fear;
in the end they will look in triumph on their foes.[b]
[9]They have freely scattered their gifts to the poor,[c]
their righteousness endures forever;
their horn[c] will be lifted[d] high in honor.

[10]The wicked will see[e] and be vexed,
they will gnash their teeth[f] and waste away;[g]
the longings of the wicked will come to nothing.[h]

Psalm 113

[1]Praise the LORD.[d]

Praise the LORD, you his servants;[i]
praise the name of the LORD.
[2]Let the name of the LORD be praised,
both now and forevermore.[j]
[3]From the rising of the sun[k] to the place where it sets,
the name of the LORD is to be praised.

[4]The LORD is exalted[l] over all the nations,
his glory above the heavens.[m]
[5]Who is like the LORD our God,[n]
the One who sits enthroned[o] on high,
[6]who stoops down to look[p]
on the heavens and the earth?

[a] This psalm is an acrostic poem, the lines of which begin with the successive letters of the Hebrew alphabet. [b] *1* Hebrew *Hallelu Yah* [c] *9 Horn* here symbolizes dignity. [d] *1* Hebrew *Hallelu Yah*; also in verse 9

111:9 *redemption.* The psalmists constantly look back to the Exodus, but they also speak of that which was still to come—the redemption of mankind through the Messiah.
111:10 *fear of the LORD.* The fear of the Lord describes an obedient response of wonder and awe before the Most High God.
112:1 *Praise the LORD.* Like Psalm 111, this psalm begins with the Hebrew word "hallelujah." It then picks up where Psalm 111 left off. ***Blessed.*** This word, meaning "manifestly happy," is the same word which begins the Book of Psalms.
112:2 *Their children will be mighty.* Compare the blessings of this psalm with the curses placed on the wicked in 109:6–13.
112:9 *gifts to the poor.* The gracious and compassionate nature of God is also seen in His people, especially in their acts of benevolence toward the poor. The poor are the materially destitute and helpless segments of society—widows, orphans, and aliens—whose rights are more easily violated. Scripture tells us that giving to the poor is lending to the Lord and will be repaid by the Lord (Prov. 19:17). To give freely to the poor literally means "to scatter" God's gifts, which suggests that the poor will be provided for and that abundance will come to the giver as well (2 Cor. 9:8–9). ***their horn.*** The horn is a symbol of power. When used for a righteous person, it speaks of prominence and a lasting sense of worth in his or her life.
113:1 *Praise the LORD.* This psalm of descriptive praise begins and ends with the Hebrew word "hallelujah." This psalm, along with Psalm 114, is traditionally read before the Passover meal.
113:2 *the name of the LORD.* In biblical times there was a close association between a person's name and identity. Praising the name of God centers one's thoughts on His character.
113:4 *exalted over all the nations.* Unlike the manmade gods of the ancient Middle East, the Lord is not limited to a certain tribe or territory. Not only is He supreme over all nations, but His glory cannot be contained in the universe.
113:6 *who stoops down to look.* God is not some far distant deity who set the world in motion and then went about His business. Instead, He is deeply involved in the lives of the people He created and

111:9 [p] Lk 1:68 [q] Ps 99:3; Lk 1:49 **111:10** [r] Pr 9:10 [s] Ecc 12:13 [t] Ps 145:2 **112:1** [u] Ps 128:1 [v] Ps 119:14, 16, 47, 92 **112:4** [w] Job 11:17 [x] Ps 97:11 **112:5** [y] Ps 37:21, 26 **112:6** [z] Pr 10:7 **112:7** [a] Ps 57:7; Pr 1:33 **112:8** [b] Ps 59:10 **112:9** [c] 2Co 9:9* [d] Ps 75:10 **112:10** [e] Ps 86:17 [f] Ps 37:12 [g] Ps 58:7-8 [h] Pr 11:7 **113:1** [i] Ps 135:1 **113:2** [j] Da 2:20 **113:3** [k] Isa 59:19; Mal 1:11 **113:4** [l] Ps 99:2 [m] Ps 8:1; 97:9 **113:5** [n] Ps 89:6 [o] Ps 103:19 **113:6** [p] Ps 11:4; 138:6; Isa 57:15

7 He raises the poor[q] from the dust
and lifts the needy[r] from the ash heap;
8 he seats them[s] with princes,
with the princes of his people.
9 He settles the childless[t] woman in her home
as a happy mother of children.

Praise the LORD.

Psalm 114

1 When Israel came out of Egypt,[u]
Jacob from a people of foreign tongue,
2 Judah became God's sanctuary,
Israel his dominion.

3 The sea looked and fled,[v]
the Jordan turned back;[w]
4 the mountains leaped like rams,
the hills like lambs.

5 Why was it, sea, that you fled?
Why, Jordan, did you turn back?
6 Why, mountains, did you leap like rams,
you hills, like lambs?

7 Tremble, earth,[x] at the presence of the Lord,
at the presence of the God of Jacob,
8 who turned the rock into a pool,
the hard rock into springs of water.[y]

Psalm 115

1 Not to us, LORD, not to us
but to your name be the glory,[z]
because of your love and faithfulness.

2 Why do the nations say,
"Where is their God?"[a]
3 Our God is in heaven;[b]
he does whatever pleases him.[c]
4 But their idols are silver and gold,
made by human hands.[d]
5 They have mouths, but cannot speak,[e]
eyes, but cannot see.
6 They have ears, but cannot hear,
noses, but cannot smell.
7 They have hands, but cannot feel,
feet, but cannot walk,
nor can they utter a sound with their throats.
8 Those who make them will be like them,
and so will all who trust in them.

9 All you Israelites, trust in the LORD—
he is their help and shield.
10 House of Aaron,[f] trust in the LORD—
he is their help and shield.
11 You who fear him, trust in the LORD—
he is their help and shield.

12 The LORD remembers us and will bless us:
He will bless his people Israel,
he will bless the house of Aaron,
13 he will bless those who fear[g] the LORD—
small and great alike.

14 May the LORD cause you to flourish,[h]
both you and your children.
15 May you be blessed by the LORD,
the Maker of heaven[i] and earth.

16 The highest heavens belong to the LORD,[j]
but the earth he has given[k] to mankind.
17 It is not the dead[l] who praise the LORD,
those who go down to the place of silence;
18 it is we who extol the LORD,
both now and forevermore.[m]

Praise the LORD.[a]

Psalm 116

1 I love the LORD,[n] for he heard my voice;
he heard my cry[o] for mercy.
2 Because he turned his ear[p] to me,
I will call on him as long as I live.

---

[a] 18 Hebrew *Hallelu Yah*

---

loves us so much that He came down from His high position to save us (Phil. 2:5–9).

113:9 *childless woman.* In that time and culture, a barren woman was without significance and without joy. The joy of a barren woman who has been given children is a picture of the joy we receive when God stoops down to touch us.

114:1 *out of Egypt.* This psalm recalling the salvation of Israel from Egypt is traditionally read along with Psalm 113 before the Passover meal.

114:2 *Judah became God's sanctuary.* This verse anticipates the New Testament sense of God living among His people (Ezek. 37:26–27; 2 Cor. 6:16–18).

115:1 *to your name be the glory.* This community psalm of praise focuses on the glory of the Lord in the salvation of His people. It is one of the Passover Psalms (115–118; 136), traditionally read or sung after the Passover meal.

115:4–8 *idols.* Like the prophets (Is. 40:18–20; Jer. 10:1–10), the psalms are derisive toward the idols of the nations.

115:18 *Praise the LORD.* Many of the Passover Psalms (115–117) conclude with the Hebrew word "hallelujah."

116:1 *I love the LORD.* This messianic psalm is one of the Passover psalms (113–118). It was probably recited by Jesus on the night of His arrest, the night He celebrated the Passover with His disciples (Luke 22:15).

113:7 [q] 1Sa 2:8 [r] Ps 107:41 **113:8** [s] Job 36:7 **113:9** [t] 1Sa 2:5; Ps 68:6; Isa 54:1 **114:1** [u] Ex 13:3 **114:3** [v] Ex 14:21; Ps 77:16 [w] Jos 3:16 **114:7** [x] Ps 96:9 **114:8** [y] Ex 17:6; Nu 20:11; Ps 107:35 **115:1** [z] Ps 96:8; Isa 48:11; Eze 36:32 **115:2** [a] Ps 42:3; 79:10 **115:3** [b] Ps 103:19 [c] Ps 135:6; Da 4:35 **115:4** [d] Dt 4:28; Jer 10:3-5 **115:5** [e] Jer 10:5 **115:10** [f] Ps 118:3 **115:13** [g] Ps 128:1,4 **115:14** [h] Dt 1:11 **115:15** [i] Ge 1:1; 14:19; Ps 96:5 **115:16** [j] Ps 89:11 [k] Ps 8:6-8 **115:17** [l] Ps 6:5; 88:10-12; Isa 38:18 **115:18** [m] Ps 113:2; Da 2:20 **116:1** [n] Ps 18:1 [o] Ps 66:19 **116:2** [p] Ps 40:1

[3]The cords of death[q] entangled me,
the anguish of the grave came over me;
I was overcome by distress and sorrow.
[4]Then I called on the name[r] of the LORD:
"LORD, save me![s]"

[5]The LORD is gracious and righteous;[t]
our God is full of compassion.
[6]The LORD protects the unwary;
when I was brought low,[u] he saved me.

[7]Return to your rest,[v] my soul,
for the LORD has been good[w] to you.

[8]For you, LORD, have delivered me[x] from death,
my eyes from tears,
my feet from stumbling,
[9]that I may walk before the LORD
in the land of the living.[y]

[10]I trusted[z] in the LORD when I said,
"I am greatly afflicted";
[11]in my alarm I said,
"Everyone is a liar."[a]

[12]What shall I return to the LORD
for all his goodness to me?

[13]I will lift up the cup of salvation
and call on the name[b] of the LORD.
[14]I will fulfill my vows[c] to the LORD
in the presence of all his people.

[15]Precious in the sight[d] of the LORD
is the death of his faithful servants.
[16]Truly I am your servant, LORD;[e]
I serve you just as my mother did;[f]
you have freed me from my chains.

[17]I will sacrifice a thank offering[g] to you
and call on the name of the LORD.
[18]I will fulfill my vows to the LORD
in the presence of all his people,
[19]in the courts[h] of the house of the LORD—
in your midst, Jerusalem.

Praise the LORD.[a]

Psalm 117

[1]Praise the LORD, all you nations;[i]
extol him, all you peoples.
[2]For great is his love toward us,
and the faithfulness of the LORD[j] endures forever.

Praise the LORD.[a]

Psalm 118

[1]Give thanks to the LORD,[k] for he is good;
his love endures forever.[l]

[2]Let Israel say:[m]
"His love endures forever."
[3]Let the house of Aaron say:
"His love endures forever."
[4]Let those who fear the LORD say:
"His love endures forever."

[5]When hard pressed,[n] I cried to the LORD;
he brought me into a spacious place.[o]
[6]The LORD is with me;[p] I will not be afraid.
What can mere mortals do to me?[q]
[7]The LORD is with me; he is my helper.[r]
I look in triumph on my enemies.[s]

[8]It is better to take refuge in the LORD[t]
than to trust in humans.[u]
[9]It is better to take refuge in the LORD
than to trust in princes.[v]
[10]All the nations surrounded me,
but in the name of the LORD I cut them down.[w]
[11]They surrounded me[x] on every side,[y]
but in the name of the LORD I cut them down.
[12]They swarmed around me like bees,[z]
but they were consumed as quickly as burning thorns;[a]
in the name of the LORD I cut them down.
[13]I was pushed back and about to fall,
but the LORD helped me.[b]

[a] 19,2 Hebrew *Hallelu Yah*

116:3 *cords of death.* These words point prophetically to the Savior's anguish on the cross (Matt. 27:27–35).
116:10 *I trusted in the LORD when I said.* This belief is the hope of eternal life articulated in verse 9. Paul quotes this verse (translated "I believed, and therefore have I spoken") as proof of the scriptural hope of the resurrection (2 Cor. 4:13).
116:13 *the cup of salvation.* This psalm is traditionally read after the Passover meal, following the third cup of wine, called the cup of salvation. How appropriate that this Passover psalm would call to mind God's cup of salvation the very night that the Savior was betrayed (Matt. 26:27; Luke 22:14–22).
118:1 *Give thanks.* This is the climax of the group of psalms called the Passover psalms. These psalms were probably sung by Jesus on the night before His death.
118:2 *His love endures forever.* This refrain praises God's loyal, merciful, covenant love throughout the psalm.
118:9 *than to trust in princes.* Although relying on other people is part of living, our ultimate trust can only be placed in the Lord God. Even powerful rulers are limited by their own mortality (146:3).
118:13 *the LORD helped me.* Compare this to Paul's words in 2 Timothy 4:17–18. Deliverance always comes from God.

116:3 [q] Ps 18:4-5 **116:4** [r] Ps 118:5 [s] Ps 22:20 **116:5** [t] Ezr 9:15; Ne 9:8; Ps 103:8; 145:17 **116:6** [u] Ps 19:7; 79:8 **116:7** [v] Jer 6:16; Mt 11:29 [w] Ps 13:6 **116:8** [x] Ps 56:13 **116:9** [y] Ps 27:13 **116:10** [z] 2Co 4:13* **116:11** [a] Ro 3:4 **116:13** [b] Ps 16:5; 80:18

[14] The LORD is my strength[c] and my
defense[a];
he has become my salvation.[d]

[15] Shouts of joy[e] and victory
resound in the tents of the righteous:
"The LORD's right hand[f] has done
mighty things!
[16] The LORD's right hand is lifted
high;
the LORD's right hand has done
mighty things!"
[17] I will not die[g] but live,
and will proclaim[h] what the LORD has
done.
[18] The LORD has chastened me severely,
but he has not given me over to
death.[i]
[19] Open for me the gates[j] of the
righteous;
I will enter and give thanks to the
LORD.
[20] This is the gate of the LORD
through which the righteous may
enter.[k]
[21] I will give you thanks, for you
answered me;[l]
you have become my salvation.

[22] The stone the builders rejected
has become the cornerstone;[m]
[23] the LORD has done this,
and it is marvelous in our eyes.
[24] The LORD has done it this very day;
let us rejoice today and be glad.

[25] LORD, save us!
LORD, grant us success!

[26] Blessed is he who comes[n] in the name
of the LORD.
From the house of the LORD we bless
you.[b]
[27] The LORD is God,
and he has made his light shine[o]
on us.
With boughs in hand, join in the festal
procession
up[c] to the horns of the altar.

[28] You are my God, and I will praise you;
you are my God,[p] and I will exalt[q]
you.

[29] Give thanks to the LORD, for he is good;
his love endures forever.

Psalm 119[d]

א Aleph

[1] Blessed are those whose ways are
blameless,
who walk[r] according to the law of the
LORD.

---

[a] 14 Or *song* [b] 26 The Hebrew is plural.
[c] 27 Or *Bind the festal sacrifice with ropes / and take it* [d] This psalm is an acrostic poem, the stanzas of which begin with successive letters of the Hebrew alphabet; moreover, the verses of each stanza begin with the same letter of the Hebrew alphabet.

118:14 ***my strength and my defense.*** These words are a quotation from "the Song of Moses" (Ex. 15:2); they are also quoted in Isaiah 12:2. The God who delivered the Israelites by dividing the waters of the Red Sea was ready to deliver the psalmist from trouble.
118:19 ***Open for me the gates of the righteous.*** The poet draws on the wording and imagery of Psalm 24. There is only One who can enter the gates of the Lord of His own accord—Jesus, the perfect King of glory.
118:20 ***gate of the LORD.*** The literal reference may be to the gate of Jerusalem, the city of God—or even to a gate of the temple. Jesus declared that He was the gate or door leading to salvation (John 10:9).
118:22 ***the cornerstone.*** The potent imagery of this verse depicts Jesus' rejection by many (Is. 53:3; Mark 8:31; Luke 9:22; 17:25). Jesus elaborated on this prophetic verse with the parable of the vineyard owner. In this parable, the rejection included the murder of the owner's son—a reference to God's only Son (Mark 12:1–12). But, even though the Savior was rejected, He was elevated to the right hand of God (Acts 7:56). The cross, the symbol of Jesus' rejection, has become the symbol of our salvation (1 Cor. 1:18; Heb. 12:2).
118:25 ***save us.*** These words are familiar to us in the transliteration of the Hebrew word "hosanna." The words are so significant that, if the people had not shouted them aloud (Matt. 21:16) when Jesus entered Jerusalem, the stones would have had to shout them (Luke 19:40).
118:26 ***Blessed is he who comes.*** These are the very words that the people used to bless Jesus as He rode into Jerusalem the week before the Passover (Matt. 21:9; Mark 11:9; Luke 19:38).
119:1 ***Blessed are those whose ways are blameless.*** This very lengthy poem is an acrostic. For each of the 22 consonants in the Hebrew alphabet, there are eight verses beginning with that letter. Within the psalm, eight words for God's law occur again and again: law, testimonies, promise, precepts, statutes, commandments, judgments, word. These words elaborate the application of the law of God to daily life and to Israel's destiny. ***the law of the LORD.*** The Hebrew word *torah*, translated "law," basically means "instruction" or "direction." Broadly, it refers to all God's instructions from Moses to the prophets. More strictly, it refers to the first five books of the Old Testament. The law was never designed as a means

116:14 [c] Ps 22:25; Jnh 2:9 **116:15** [d] Ps 72:14
116:16 [e] Ps 119:125; 143:12 [f] Ps 86:16 **116:17** [g] Lev 7:12; Ps 50:14 **116:19** [h] Ps 96:8; 135:2 **117:1** [i] Ro 15:11*
117:2 [j] Ps 100:5 **118:1** [k] 1Ch 16:8 [l] Ps 106:1; 136:1
118:2 [m] Ps 115:9 **118:5** [n] Ps 120:1 [o] Ps 18:19
118:6 [p] Heb 13:6* [q] Ps 27:1; 56:4 **118:7** [r] Ps 54:4
[s] Ps 59:10 **118:8** [t] Ps 40:4 [u] Jer 17:5 **118:9** [v] Ps 146:3
118:10 [w] Ps 18:40 **118:11** [x] Ps 88:17 [y] Ps 3:6
118:12 [z] Dt 1:44 [a] Ps 58:9 **118:13** [b] Ps 86:17; 140:4
118:14 [c] Ex 15:2 [d] Isa 12:2 **118:15** [e] Ps 68:3 [f] Ps 89:13
118:17 [g] Ps 6:5; Hab 1:12 [h] Ex 15:6; Ps 73:28
118:18 [i] 2Co 6:9 **118:19** [j] Isa 26:2 **118:20** [k] Ps 24:7; Isa 35:8; Rev 22:14 **118:21** [l] Ps 116:1
118:22 [m] Mt 21:42; Mk 12:10; Lk 20:17*; Ac 4:11*; 1Pe 2:7*
118:26 [n] Mt 21:9*; Mk 11:9*; Lk 13:35*; 19:38*; Jn 12:13*
118:27 [o] 1Pe 2:9 **118:28** [p] Isa 25:1 [q] Ex 15:2
119:1 [r] Ps 128:1

2 Blessed are those who keep his statutes
and seek him with all their heart—[s]
3 they do no wrong[t]
but follow his ways.
4 You have laid down precepts
that are to be fully obeyed.
5 Oh, that my ways were steadfast
in obeying your decrees!
6 Then I would not be put to shame
when I consider all your commands.
7 I will praise you with an upright heart
as I learn your righteous laws.
8 I will obey your decrees;
do not utterly forsake me.

ב Beth

9 How can a young person stay on the
path of purity?
By living according to your word.[u]
10 I seek you with all my heart;[v]
do not let me stray from your
commands.[w]
11 I have hidden your word in my heart[x]
that I might not sin against you.
12 Praise be to you, LORD;
teach me your decrees.[y]
13 With my lips I recount
all the laws that come from your
mouth.[z]
14 I rejoice in following your statutes
as one rejoices in great riches.
15 I meditate on your precepts[a]
and consider your ways.
16 I delight[b] in your decrees;
I will not neglect your word.

ג Gimel

17 Be good to your servant[c] while I live,
that I may obey your word.
18 Open my eyes that I may see
wonderful things in your law.
19 I am a stranger on earth;[d]
do not hide your commands from me.
20 My soul is consumed[e] with longing
for your laws[f] at all times.
21 You rebuke the arrogant, who are
accursed,
those who stray[g] from your
commands.
22 Remove from me their scorn[h] and
contempt,
for I keep your statutes.
23 Though rulers sit together and
slander me,
your servant will meditate on your
decrees.
24 Your statutes are my delight;
they are my counselors.

ד Daleth

25 I am laid low in the dust;[i]
preserve my life[j] according to your
word.
26 I gave an account of my ways and you
answered me;
teach me your decrees.[k]

---

of salvation; no one could be saved by keeping it. Instead, the law was the means for the Israelites to learn how to live as God's holy people. The psalmists consistently describe the law of God as a great blessing, for it was God's gracious revelation to His people for their own good (Deut. 6:1–3). In the law, God mercifully pointed out the right path to follow. Only mistaken legalistic interpretations of the law prompted the negative statements in the New Testament.

119:9–11 ***your word.*** The Lord designs that His Word should bring purity (v. 9), security (v. 23), freedom (v. 45), hope (v. 49), life (v. 50), light (v. 105), and peace (v. 165).

119:9 God's Word Cleanses—One of the pieces of furniture in the Old Testament tabernacle was called the bronze laver (Ex. 38:8). It was a huge upright bronze bowl filled with water, resting upon a pedestal. The priests would often stop at this laver to perform their ritualistic cleansings. The Word of God is like this laver. Only the Word can remove the filth and dirt from our hearts (1 Pet. 1:22) just as the bronze laver removed the physical impurities from the priests.

How can the Bible cleanse us? It can cleanse us from wrong thoughts (Ps. 19:12; 51:10; Phil. 4:8–9). It can help eliminate fear (Judg. 1:9). It can cleanse us from wrong actions (1 John 1:9). Jesus directly promises all this: "You are already clean because of the word I have spoken to you" (John 15:3).

119:11 Memorizing Scripture—The Bible recognizes the importance of Scripture memorization. By memorizing the Word, we have access to it no matter where we are or what our circumstances. The following benefits can be cited:

- It keeps us from sinning (Ps. 119:11).
- It provides comfort in times of trouble (Ps. 119:52,92).
- It provides daily sustenance for the spiritual life (Deut. 8:3).
- It provides continual and ready guidance in all the situations of life (Prov. 6:20–23).
- It provides the basis for formal and informal instruction of your children (Deut. 6:6–7).

119:16 ***decrees.*** The Hebrew word translated "decrees" refers to something marked out as a boundary, something inscribed or engraved. Hence the word speaks of the permanence of the law, which God Himself had engraved in stone (Ex. 24:12). The same word is often translated "statutes" (2:7).

119:22 ***statutes.*** The Hebrew word translated "statutes" is derived from the verb meaning "to witness" or "to testify." It refers to the Ten Commandments. The commandments were a testimony because they were a witness to the Israelites of their faithfulness or unfaithfulness to the covenant (Deut. 31:26).

119:2 [s] Dt 6:5 **119:3** [t] 1Jn 3:9; 5:18 **119:9** [u] 2Ch 6:16 **119:10** [v] 2Ch 15:15 [w] ver 21, 118 **119:11** [x] Ps 37:31; Lk 2:19, 51 **119:12** [y] ver 26 **119:13** [z] Ps 40:9 **119:15** [a] Ps 1:2 **119:16** [b] Ps 1:2 **119:17** [c] Ps 13:6; 116:7 **119:19** [d] 1Ch 29:15; Ps 39:12; 2Co 5:6; Heb 11:13 **119:20** [e] Ps 42:2; 84:2 [f] Ps 63:1 **119:21** [g] ver 10 **119:22** [h] Ps 39:8 **119:25** [i] Ps 44:25 [j] Ps 143:11 **119:26** [k] Ps 25:4; 27:11; 86:11

27 Cause me to understand the way of your precepts,
that I may meditate on your wonderful deeds.[l]
28 My soul is weary with sorrow;[m]
strengthen me[n] according to your word.
29 Keep me from deceitful ways;
be gracious to me and teach me your law.
30 I have chosen the way of faithfulness;
I have set my heart on your laws.
31 I hold fast[o] to your statutes, LORD;
do not let me be put to shame.
32 I run in the path of your commands,
for you have broadened my understanding.

ה He

33 Teach me,[p] LORD, the way of your decrees,
that I may follow it to the end.[a]
34 Give me understanding, so that I may keep your law
and obey it with all my heart.
35 Direct me in the path of your commands,
for there I find delight.
36 Turn my heart[q] toward your statutes
and not toward selfish gain.[r]
37 Turn my eyes away from worthless things;
preserve my life[s] according to your word.[b]
38 Fulfill your promise[t] to your servant,
so that you may be feared.
39 Take away the disgrace I dread,
for your laws are good.
40 How I long[u] for your precepts!
In your righteousness preserve my life.

ו Waw

41 May your unfailing love come to me, LORD,
your salvation, according to your promise;
42 then I can answer[v] anyone who taunts me,
for I trust in your word.
43 Never take your word of truth from my mouth,
for I have put my hope in your laws.
44 I will always obey your law,
for ever and ever.
45 I will walk about in freedom,
for I have sought out your precepts.
46 I will speak of your statutes before kings[w]
and will not be put to shame,
47 for I delight in your commands
because I love them.
48 I reach out for your commands, which I love,
that I may meditate on your decrees.

ז Zayin

49 Remember your word to your servant,
for you have given me hope.
50 My comfort in my suffering is this:
Your promise preserves my life.[x]
51 The arrogant mock me[y] unmercifully,
but I do not turn[z] from your law.
52 I remember,[a] LORD, your ancient laws,
and I find comfort in them.
53 Indignation grips me[b] because of the wicked,
who have forsaken your law.[c]
54 Your decrees are the theme of my song
wherever I lodge.
55 In the night, LORD, I remember[d] your name,
that I may keep your law.
56 This has been my practice:
I obey your precepts.

ח Heth

57 You are my portion,[e] LORD;
I have promised to obey your words.
58 I have sought your face with all my heart;
be gracious to me[f] according to your promise.[g]
59 I have considered my ways[h]
and have turned my steps to your statutes.
60 I will hasten and not delay
to obey your commands.
61 Though the wicked bind me with ropes,
I will not forget[i] your law.
62 At midnight[j] I rise to give you thanks
for your righteous laws.
63 I am a friend to all who fear you,[k]
to all who follow your precepts.
64 The earth is filled with your love,[l] LORD;
teach me your decrees.

---

[a] *33* Or *follow it for its reward* [b] *37* Two manuscripts of the Masoretic Text and Dead Sea Scrolls; most manuscripts of the Masoretic Text *life in your way*

119:45 *in freedom.* Many think of laws, instructions, and commandments as limiting and restricting, but the law of God paradoxically frees us. It frees us from sin (v. 133) and gives us the peace that comes from following the Lord's instructions (v. 165).

119:56 *precepts.* This Hebrew word means "an appointed thing," "something for which one is given charge." The word has the same idea as "commandment" for both words assume that the One who commands has the authority to "take charge" or "appoint" (v. 4).

119:27 [l] Ps 145:5 **119:28** [m] Ps 107:26 [n] Ps 20:2; 1Pe 5:10 **119:31** [o] Dt 11:22 **119:33** [p] ver 12 **119:36** [q] 1Ki 8:58 [r] Eze 33:31; Mk 7:21-22; Lk 12:15; Heb 13:5 **119:37** [s] Ps 71:20; Isa 33:15 **119:38** [t] 2Sa 7:25 **119:40** [u] ver 20 **119:42** [v] Pr 27:11 **119:46** [w] Mt 10:18; Ac 26:1-2 **119:50** [x] Ro 15:4 **119:51** [y] Jer 20:7 [z] ver 157; Job 23:11; Ps 44:18 **119:52** [a] Ps 103:18 **119:53** [b] Ezr 9:3 [c] Ps 89:30 **119:55** [d] Ps 63:6 **119:57** [e] Ps 16:5; La 3:24 **119:58** [f] 1Ki 13:6 [g] ver 41 **119:59** [h] Lk 15:17-18 **119:61** [i] Ps 140:5 **119:62** [j] Ac 16:25 **119:63** [k] Ps 101:6-7 **119:64** [l] Ps 33:5

ט Teth

65 Do good to your servant
according to your word, LORD.
66 Teach me knowledge and good judgment,
for I trust your commands.
67 Before I was afflicted I went astray,[m]
but now I obey your word.
68 You are good,[n] and what you do is good;
teach me your decrees.[o]
69 Though the arrogant have smeared me with lies,[p]
I keep your precepts with all my heart.
70 Their hearts are callous[q] and unfeeling,
but I delight in your law.
71 It was good for me to be afflicted
so that I might learn your decrees.
72 The law from your mouth is more precious to me
than thousands of pieces of silver and gold.[r]

י Yodh

73 Your hands made me[s] and formed me;
give me understanding to learn your commands.
74 May those who fear you rejoice[t] when they see me,
for I have put my hope in your word.
75 I know, LORD, that your laws are righteous,
and that in faithfulness[u] you have afflicted me.
76 May your unfailing love be my comfort,
according to your promise to your servant.
77 Let your compassion[v] come to me that I may live,
for your law is my delight.
78 May the arrogant[w] be put to shame for wronging me without cause;[x]
but I will meditate on your precepts.
79 May those who fear you turn to me,
those who understand your statutes.
80 May I wholeheartedly follow your decrees,
that I may not be put to shame.

כ Kaph

81 My soul faints[y] with longing for your salvation,
but I have put my hope in your word.
82 My eyes fail,[z] looking for your promise;
I say, "When will you comfort me?"
83 Though I am like a wineskin in the smoke,
I do not forget your decrees.
84 How long[a] must your servant wait?
When will you punish my persecutors?
85 The arrogant dig pits[b] to trap me,
contrary to your law.
86 All your commands are trustworthy;[c]
help me,[d] for I am being persecuted without cause.[e]
87 They almost wiped me from the earth,
but I have not forsaken[f] your precepts.
88 In your unfailing love preserve my life,
that I may obey the statutes of your mouth.

ל Lamedh

89 Your word, LORD, is eternal;[g]
it stands firm in the heavens.
90 Your faithfulness[h] continues through all generations;
you established the earth, and it endures.[i]
91 Your laws endure[j] to this day,
for all things serve you.
92 If your law had not been my delight,
I would have perished in my affliction.
93 I will never forget your precepts,
for by them you have preserved my life.
94 Save me, for I am yours;
I have sought out your precepts.
95 The wicked are waiting to destroy me,
but I will ponder your statutes.
96 To all perfection I see a limit,
but your commands are boundless.

מ Mem

97 Oh, how I love your law!
I meditate[k] on it all day long.
98 Your commands are always with me
and make me wiser[l] than my enemies.
99 I have more insight than all my teachers,
for I meditate on your statutes.
100 I have more understanding than the elders,
for I obey your precepts.[m]

119:70 ***delight.*** This is not the delight of a passive observer, but the delight of a disciple who has staked his life and security on a cause or principle.
119:82 ***your promise.*** The Hebrew term for "promise" is derived from the verb "to say." The term is a general word for God's law, encompassing everything that the Lord has promised and spoken.
119:97 ***how I love your law!*** Fundamentally, the psalmist's attraction to the law is the result of his love for God Himself, his Teacher (vv. 102,132).

119:67 [m] Jer 31:18-19; Heb 12:11 **119:68** [n] Ps 106:1; 107:1; Mt 19:17 [o] ver 12 **119:69** [p] Job 13:4; Ps 109:2 **119:70** [q] Ps 17:10; Isa 6:10; Ac 28:27 **119:72** [r] Ps 19:10; Pr 8:10-11,19 **119:73** [s] Job 10:8; Ps 100:3; 138:8; 139:13-16 **119:74** [t] Ps 34:2 **119:75** [u] Heb 12:5-11 **119:77** [v] ver 41 **119:78** [w] Jer 50:32 [x] ver 86, 161 **119:81** [y] Ps 84:2 **119:82** [z] Ps 69:3; La 2:11 **119:84** [a] Ps 39:4; Rev 6:10 **119:85** [b] Ps 35:7; Jer 18:20, 22 **119:86** [c] Ps 35:19 [d] Ps 109:26 [e] ver 78 **119:87** [f] Isa 58:2 **119:89** [g] Mt 24:34-35; 1Pe 1:25 **119:90** [h] Ps 36:5 [i] Ps 148:6; Ecc 1:4 **119:91** [j] Jer 33:25 **119:97** [k] Ps 1:2 **119:98** [l] Dt 4:6 **119:100** [m] Job 32:7-9

101 I have kept my feet[n] from every evil path
so that I might obey your word.
102 I have not departed from your laws,
for you yourself have taught me.
103 How sweet are your words to my taste,
sweeter than honey[o] to my mouth![p]
104 I gain understanding from your precepts;
therefore I hate every wrong path.[q]

נ Nun

105 Your word is a lamp for my feet,
a light[r] on my path.
106 I have taken an oath[s] and confirmed it,
that I will follow your righteous laws.
107 I have suffered much;
preserve my life, LORD, according to your word.
108 Accept, LORD, the willing praise of my mouth,[t]
and teach me your laws.
109 Though I constantly take my life in my hands,[u]
I will not forget your law.
110 The wicked have set a snare[v] for me,
but I have not strayed[w] from your precepts.
111 Your statutes are my heritage forever;
they are the joy of my heart.
112 My heart is set on keeping your decrees
to the very end.[a][x]

ס Samekh

113 I hate double-minded people,[y]
but I love your law.
114 You are my refuge and my shield;[z]
I have put my hope[a] in your word.
115 Away from me,[b] you evildoers,
that I may keep the commands of my God!
116 Sustain me,[c] my God, according to your promise, and I will live;
do not let my hopes be dashed.[d]
117 Uphold me, and I will be delivered;
I will always have regard for your decrees.
118 You reject all who stray from your decrees,
for their delusions come to nothing.
119 All the wicked of the earth you discard like dross;[e]
therefore I love your statutes.
120 My flesh trembles[f] in fear of you;
I stand in awe of your laws.

ע Ayin

121 I have done what is righteous and just;
do not leave me to my oppressors.
122 Ensure your servant's well-being;[g]
do not let the arrogant oppress me.
123 My eyes fail, looking for your salvation,
looking for your righteous promise.[h]
124 Deal with your servant according to your love
and teach me your decrees.[i]
125 I am your servant;[j] give me discernment
that I may understand your statutes.
126 It is time for you to act, LORD;
your law is being broken.
127 Because I love your commands
more than gold,[k] more than pure gold,
128 and because I consider all your precepts right,
I hate every wrong path.[l]

פ Pe

129 Your statutes are wonderful;
therefore I obey them.
130 The unfolding of your words gives light;[m]
it gives understanding to the simple.[n]
131 I open my mouth and pant,[o]
longing for your commands.[p]
132 Turn to me and have mercy[q] on me,
as you always do to those who love your name.
133 Direct my footsteps according to your word;[r]
let no sin rule[s] over me.
134 Redeem me from human oppression,[t]
that I may obey your precepts.
135 Make your face shine[u] on your servant
and teach me your decrees.
136 Streams of tears[v] flow from my eyes,
for your law is not obeyed.[w]

---

[a] 112 Or *decrees / for their enduring reward*

119:105 ***a light on my path.*** God's word is a guide for everyday living.
119:127 ***commands.*** This word alludes to God's authority to govern His people. The commandments of God help believers to find their way in a world that is filled with confusion, sin, and error.
119:136 ***Streams of tears.*** One of the earmarks of a true believer is the remorse and sorrow that is felt when the person sins and fails to keep God's law.

119:101 [n] Pr 1:15 **119:103** [o] Ps 19:10; Pr 8:11 [p] Pr 24:13-14 **119:104** [q] ver 128 **119:105** [r] Pr 6:23 **119:106** [s] Ne 10:29 **119:108** [t] Hos 14:2; Heb 13:15 **119:109** [u] Jdg 12:3; Job 13:14 **119:110** [v] Ps 140:5; 141:9 [w] ver 10 **119:112** [x] ver 33 **119:113** [y] Jas 1:8 **119:114** [z] Ps 32:7; 91:1 [a] ver 74 **119:115** [b] Ps 6:8; 139:19; Mt 7:23 **119:116** [c] Ps 54:4 [d] Ps 25:2; Ro 5:5; 9:33 **119:119** [e] Eze 22:18, 19 **119:120** [f] Hab 3:16 **119:122** [g] Job 17:3 **119:123** [h] ver 82 **119:124** [i] ver 12 **119:125** [j] Ps 116:16 **119:127** [k] Ps 19:10 **119:128** [l] ver 104, 163 **119:130** [m] Pr 6:23 [n] Ps 19:7 **119:131** [o] Ps 42:1 [p] ver 20 **119:132** [q] Ps 25:16; 106:4 **119:133** [r] Ps 17:5 [s] Ps 19:13; Ro 6:12 **119:134** [t] Ps 142:6; Lk 1:74 **119:135** [u] Nu 6:25; Ps 4:6 **119:136** [v] Jer 9:1, 18 [w] Eze 9:4

צ Tsadhe

137 You are righteous,[x] LORD,
and your laws are right.[y]
138 The statutes you have laid down are righteous;[z]
they are fully trustworthy.
139 My zeal wears me out,[a]
for my enemies ignore your words.
140 Your promises have been thoroughly tested,[b]
and your servant loves them.
141 Though I am lowly and despised,[c]
I do not forget your precepts.
142 Your righteousness is everlasting
and your law is true.[d]
143 Trouble and distress have come upon me,
but your commands give me delight.
144 Your statutes are always righteous;
give me understanding[e] that I may live.

ק Qoph

145 I call with all my heart; answer me, LORD,
and I will obey your decrees.
146 I call out to you; save me
and I will keep your statutes.
147 I rise before dawn[f] and cry for help;
I have put my hope in your word.
148 My eyes stay open through the watches of the night,[g]
that I may meditate on your promises.
149 Hear my voice in accordance with your love;
preserve my life, LORD, according to your laws.
150 Those who devise wicked schemes are near,
but they are far from your law.
151 Yet you are near,[h] LORD,
and all your commands are true.[i]
152 Long ago I learned from your statutes
that you established them to last forever.[j]

ר Resh

153 Look on my suffering[k] and deliver me,
for I have not forgotten[l] your law.
154 Defend my cause[m] and redeem me;[n]
preserve my life according to your promise.
155 Salvation is far from the wicked,
for they do not seek out[o] your decrees.
156 Your compassion, LORD, is great;
preserve my life[p] according to your laws.
157 Many are the foes who persecute me,[q]
but I have not turned from your statutes.
158 I look on the faithless with loathing,[r]
for they do not obey your word.
159 See how I love your precepts;
preserve my life, LORD, in accordance with your love.
160 All your words are true;
all your righteous laws are eternal.

ש Sin and Shin

161 Rulers persecute me[s] without cause,
but my heart trembles at your word.
162 I rejoice in your promise
like one who finds great spoil.[t]
163 I hate and detest falsehood
but I love your law.
164 Seven times a day I praise you
for your righteous laws.
165 Great peace[u] have those who love your law,
and nothing can make them stumble.
166 I wait for your salvation,[v] LORD,
and I follow your commands.
167 I obey your statutes,
for I love them greatly.
168 I obey your precepts and your statutes,
for all my ways are known[w] to you.

ת Taw

169 May my cry come[x] before you, LORD;
give me understanding according to your word.
170 May my supplication come[y] before you;
deliver me[z] according to your promise.
171 May my lips overflow with praise,[a]
for you teach me[b] your decrees.
172 May my tongue sing of your word,
for all your commands are righteous.
173 May your hand be ready to help[c] me,
for I have chosen[d] your precepts.
174 I long for your salvation,[e] LORD,
and your law gives me delight.
175 Let me live[f] that I may praise you,
and may your laws sustain me.

119:149 ***preserve.*** With this word, the psalmist begs God to keep him, to preserve the life that is in his soul. The psalmist does not want his obedience to waver; he asks for a sustained vitality in the time of his trial. The basis for his plea is God's covenantal love and His just nature.

119:159 ***love.*** The "love" of God is a recurring theme in the Book of Psalms, describing His loyal, covenant love and merciful care of His people.

119:162 ***rejoice.*** Jesus also described the "kingdom of God" as a great treasure, one so valuable that it would be worth selling everything one had in order to possess it (Matt. 13:44–46).

119:137 [x] Ezr 9:15; Jer 12:1 [y] Ne 9:13 **119:138** [z] Ps 19:7 **119:139** [a] Ps 69:9; Jn 2:17 **119:140** [b] Ps 12:6 **119:141** [c] Ps 22:6 **119:142** [d] Ps 19:7 **119:144** [e] Ps 19:9 **119:147** [f] Ps 5:3; 57:8; 108:2 **119:148** [g] Ps 63:6 **119:151** [h] Ps 34:18; 145:18 [i] ver 142 **119:152** [j] Lk 21:33 **119:153** [k] La 5:1 [l] Pr 3:1 **119:154** [m] Mic 7:9 [n] 1Sa 24:15 **119:155** [o] Job 5:4 **119:156** [p] 2Sa 24:14 **119:157** [q] Ps 7:1 **119:158** [r] Ps 139:21 **119:161** [s] 1Sa 24:11 **119:162** [t] 1Sa 30:16 **119:165** [u] Pr 3:2; Isa 26:3, 12; 32:17 **119:166** [v] Ge 49:18 **119:168** [w] Pr 5:21 **119:169** [x] Ps 18:6 **119:170** [y] Ps 28:2 [z] Ps 31:2 **119:171** [a] Ps 51:15 [b] Ps 94:12 **119:173** [c] Ps 37:24 [d] Jos 24:22 **119:174** [e] ver 166 **119:175** [f] Isa 55:3

176 I have strayed like a lost sheep.[g]
Seek your servant,
for I have not forgotten your
commands.

Psalm 120

A song of ascents.

1 I call on the LORD in my distress,[h]
and he answers me.
2 Save me, LORD,
from lying lips[i]
and from deceitful tongues.[j]

3 What will he do to you,
and what more besides,
you deceitful tongue?
4 He will punish you with a warrior's
sharp arrows,[k]
with burning coals of the broom bush.

5 Woe to me that I dwell in Meshek,
that I live among the tents of Kedar![l]
6 Too long have I lived
among those who hate peace.
7 I am for peace;
but when I speak, they are for war.

Psalm 121

A song of ascents.

1 I lift up my eyes to the mountains—
where does my help come from?
2 My help comes from the LORD,
the Maker of heaven and earth.[m]

3 He will not let your foot slip—
he who watches over you will not
slumber;
4 indeed, he who watches over Israel
will neither slumber nor sleep.

5 The LORD watches over[n] you—
the LORD is your shade at your right
hand;
6 the sun[o] will not harm you by day,
nor the moon by night.

7 The LORD will keep you from all
harm[p]—
he will watch over your life;
8 the LORD will watch over your coming
and going
both now and forevermore.[q]

Psalm 122

A song of ascents. Of David.

1 I rejoiced with those who said to me,
"Let us go to the house of the LORD."
2 Our feet are standing
in your gates, Jerusalem.

3 Jerusalem is built like a city
that is closely compacted together.
4 That is where the tribes go up—
the tribes of the LORD—
to praise the name of the LORD
according to the statute given to
Israel.
5 There stand the thrones for judgment,
the thrones of the house of David.

6 Pray for the peace of Jerusalem:
"May those who love[r] you be secure.
7 May there be peace within your
walls
and security within your citadels."
8 For the sake of my family and friends,
I will say, "Peace be within you."
9 For the sake of the house of the LORD
our God,
I will seek your prosperity.[s]

119:176 ***like a lost sheep.*** Jesus, the Messiah, described Himself as the Good Shepherd who would lay down His own life in order to protect and rescue His sheep (John 10:11). He affirmed that God does indeed seek lost sinners in order to bring them to Himself (Luke 15:3–7).

120:1 ***I call ... in my distress.*** This psalm is the first of a group of psalms called the Songs of Ascents (120–134). This group of hymns was probably used by pilgrims making their way to Jerusalem to worship the Lord during the three annual feasts—Passover, Pentecost, and Tabernacles (Lev. 23). Since Jerusalem is on a high hill, a traveler always goes "up" to Jerusalem; hence the term "songs of ascents."

120:5 ***Meshek ... Kedar.*** These seem to be examples of the pagan peoples among whom the psalmist had to live.

121:1 ***my eyes to the mountains.*** This Song of Ascents (see Ps. 120) dramatically pictures a traveler approaching the city of Jerusalem.

121:2 ***from the LORD.*** As comforting as the sight of the holy city would be to a pilgrim, the psalmist emphasizes the real reason for rejoicing: God's tender care for His people. ***the Maker.*** We might have expected the psalmist to emphasize God as a loving heavenly Father or a tender and compassionate Savior, but instead he ascribes our everlasting safety to the God of creation. God owns the world because He made it; nothing that happens is beyond Him.

121:6 ***nor the moon by night.*** There is never a time when the Lord is "off duty" and does not see what is happening to His people.

122:1 ***I rejoiced.*** This third Song of Ascents (see Ps. 120) describes the joy of the pilgrim on arriving at Jerusalem to worship God.

122:4 ***the tribes go up.*** This refers to the three annual festivals of ancient Israel (Lev. 23), as well as to any time that an individual or family needed to worship the Lord in the holy city.

122:5 ***thrones for judgment.*** Jerusalem was not only the central place for worship, it was also the site where civil judgments and decisions were made. Religious and civil issues were closely intertwined in the law of God.

122:6 ***the peace of Jerusalem.*** True peace will only come when the Prince of Peace returns to establish His rule (Ps. 98:5–6; Rev. 21:9–27)

119:176 [g] Isa 53:6 **120:1** [h] Ps 102:2; Jnh 2:2
120:2 [i] Pr 12:22 [j] Ps 52:4 **120:4** [k] Ps 45:5
120:5 [l] Ge 25:13; Jer 49:28 **121:2** [m] Ps 115:15; 124:8
121:5 [n] Isa 25:4 **121:6** [o] Ps 91:5; Isa 49:10; Rev 7:16
121:7 [p] Ps 41:2; 91:10-12 **121:8** [q] Dt 28:6
122:6 [r] Ps 51:18 **122:9** [s] Ne 2:10

Psalm 123

A song of ascents.

1 I lift up my eyes to you,
to you who sit enthroned[t] in heaven.
2 As the eyes of slaves look to the hand of their master,
as the eyes of a female slave look to the hand of her mistress,
so our eyes look to the LORD[u] our God,
till he shows us his mercy.
3 Have mercy on us, LORD, have mercy on us,
for we have endured no end of contempt.
4 We have endured no end
of ridicule from the arrogant,
of contempt from the proud.

Psalm 124

A song of ascents. Of David.

1 If the LORD had not been on our side—
let Israel say[v]—
2 if the LORD had not been on our side
when people attacked us,
3 they would have swallowed us alive
when their anger flared against us;
4 the flood would have engulfed us,
the torrent would have swept over us,
5 the raging waters
would have swept us away.

6 Praise be to the LORD,
who has not let us be torn by their teeth.
7 We have escaped like a bird
from the fowler's snare;[w]
the snare has been broken,
and we have escaped.
8 Our help is in the name of the LORD,
the Maker of heaven[x] and earth.

Psalm 125

A song of ascents.

1 Those who trust in the LORD are like Mount Zion,
which cannot be shaken[y] but endures forever.
2 As the mountains surround Jerusalem,
so the LORD surrounds[z] his people
both now and forevermore.

3 The scepter of the wicked will not remain[a]
over the land allotted to the righteous,
for then the righteous might use
their hands to do evil.[b]

4 LORD, do good[c] to those who are good,
to those who are upright in heart.[d]
5 But those who turn[e] to crooked ways[f]
the LORD will banish with the evildoers.

Peace be on Israel.[g]

Psalm 126

A song of ascents.

1 When the LORD restored[h] the fortunes of[a] Zion,
we were like those who dreamed.[b]
2 Our mouths were filled with laughter,
our tongues with songs of joy.[i]
Then it was said among the nations,
"The LORD has done great things[j] for them."
3 The LORD has done great things for us,
and we are filled with joy.[k]

4 Restore our fortunes,[c] LORD,
like streams in the Negev.[l]
5 Those who sow with tears
will reap with songs of joy.[m]
6 Those who go out weeping,
carrying seed to sow,
will return with songs of joy,
carrying sheaves with them.

Psalm 127

A song of ascents. Of Solomon.

1 Unless the LORD builds[n] the house,
the builders labor in vain.
Unless the LORD watches[o] over the city,
the guards stand watch in vain.

---

[a] 1 Or *LORD brought back the captives to*
[b] 1 Or *those restored to health*
[c] 4 Or *Bring back our captives*

123:2 *As the eyes of slaves.* Good servants keep watch over their masters, anticipating their wants and keeping themselves in constant readiness to obey orders. In the same way, we should keep ourselves focused on pleasing God. The more we look at Him, the more we become like Him (2 Cor. 3:18).
124:1 *the LORD had not been on our side.* It is because God is "on our side" that He sent His Son to save the world (John 3:16).
124:6 *Praise be to the LORD.* To bless God is to identify Him as the source of our blessings (103:2).
125:2 *the mountains surround Jerusalem.* Jerusalem is built on one of seven mountain peaks in the region. The mountains provided some protection for the city, since any invading army would have to march through difficult terrain to reach the city.
126:1 *restored the fortunes.* This seventh Song of Ascents (see Ps. 120) comes from the time of the restoration of Jerusalem, following the Babylonian captivity.
126:4 *Restore.* The people who returned were a small percentage of those who had been exiled; the people still prayed that God would complete the restoration of His people to their land.
127:1 *Unless the LORD.* This psalm, the eighth Song

123:1 [t] Ps 11:4; 121:1; 141:8 **123:2** [u] Ps 25:15 **124:1** [v] Ps 129:1 **124:7** [w] Ps 91:3; Pr 6:5 **124:8** [x] Ge 1:1; Ps 121:2; 134:3 **125:1** [y] Ps 46:5 **125:2** [z] Ps 121:8; Zec 2:4-5 **125:3** [a] Ps 89:22; Pr 22:8; Isa 14:5 [b] 1Sa 24:10; Ps 55:20 **125:4** [c] Ps 119:68 [d] Ps 7:10; 36:10; 94:15 **125:5** [e] Job 23:11 [f] Pr 2:15; Isa 59:8 [g] Ps 128:6 **126:1** [h] Ps 85:1; Hos 6:11 **126:2** [i] Job 8:21; Ps 51:14 [j] Ps 71:19 **126:3** [k] Isa 25:9 **126:4** [l] Isa 35:6; 43:19 **126:5** [m] Isa 35:10 **127:1** [n] Ps 78:69 [o] Ps 121:4

2 In vain you rise early
and stay up late,
toiling for food[p] to eat—
for he grants sleep[q] to[a] those he loves.

3 Children are a heritage from the LORD,
offspring a reward[r] from him.
4 Like arrows in the hands of a warrior
are children born in one's youth.
5 Blessed is the man
whose quiver is full of them.
They will not be put to shame
when they contend with their opponents[s] in court.

Psalm 128

A song of ascents.

1 Blessed are all who fear the LORD,[t]
who walk in obedience to him.[u]
2 You will eat the fruit of your labor;[v]
blessings and prosperity[w] will be yours.
3 Your wife will be like a fruitful vine[x]
within your house;
your children will be like olive shoots[y]
around your table.
4 Yes, this will be the blessing
for the man who fears the LORD.

5 May the LORD bless you from Zion;[z]
may you see the prosperity of Jerusalem
all the days of your life.
6 May you live to see your children's children—[a]
peace be on Israel.[b]

Psalm 129

A song of ascents.

1 "They have greatly oppressed me from my youth,"[c]
let Israel say;[d]
2 "they have greatly oppressed me from my youth,
but they have not gained the victory[e] over me.
3 Plowmen have plowed my back
and made their furrows long.
4 But the LORD is righteous;[f]
he has cut me free from the cords of the wicked."

5 May all who hate Zion[g]
be turned back in shame.[h]
6 May they be like grass on the roof,
which withers[i] before it can grow;
7 a reaper cannot fill his hands with it,
nor one who gathers fill his arms.
8 May those who pass by not say to them,
"The blessing of the LORD be on you;
we bless you[j] in the name of the LORD."

Psalm 130

A song of ascents.

1 Out of the depths[k] I cry to you, LORD;
2 Lord, hear my voice.[l]
Let your ears be attentive[m]
to my cry for mercy.

3 If you, LORD, kept a record of sins,
Lord, who could stand?[n]
4 But with you there is forgiveness,[o]
so that we can, with reverence, serve you.[p]

[a] 2 Or *eat— / for while they sleep he provides for*

of Ascents (see Ps. 120), is one of only two psalms attributed to Solomon (see Ps. 72).

127:2 ***toiling for food.*** This phrase captures the essence of those removed from a sense of the Lord in their lives. The food that should give them strength for life and a zest for living only maintains their miserable state.

127:5 ***in court.*** This is referring to the gate of a city where the elders met and where citizens would convene (Ruth 4:1–12).

128:1 ***Blessed.*** This word describes the happiness of those who trust in the Lord and do His will (127:5). ***fear.*** The fear of God is an attitude of respect, a response of reverence and wonder. It is the only appropriate response to our Creator and Redeemer.

128:2 ***the fruit of your labor.*** There is a reward in work and a satisfaction in labor that is a blessing of God (Eccl. 3:9–13).

129:1–4 ***greatly.*** The psalm begins with a litany of suffering, as the people of God acknowledge that throughout their history in the land they have been under constant assault by various peoples.

129:6 ***grass on the roof.*** Sod was sometimes used on the roofs of the houses. After a spring rain, there might be grass growing on the housetop, but this was not grass that flourished; it lacked roots and soon withered under the summer heat.

130:1 ***Out of the depths.*** The placement of this penitential psalm is fitting. We must not be so interested in the destruction of the wicked (Ps. 129) that we fail to understand our own heart before the Lord.

130:3 ***sins.*** Does the Lord keep a record of our sins? The answer is both yes and no. At the end of all things, Christ will sit on the judgment seat, the books will be opened, and everyone will be judged according to the actual record (Rev. 20:11–15). However, if we cry to Him for mercy now in this life, we shall find forgiveness. Then the record of our sins will be cast away into the depth of God's forgetfulness. They are covered by the blood of Jesus.

130:4 ***forgiveness, so that we can, with reverence, serve you.*** God's provision for forgiveness is not to be taken lightly (Rom. 6:1–2). The truly

127:2 [p] Ge 3:17 [q] Job 11:18 **127:3** [r] Ge 33:5 **127:5** [s] Pr 27:11 **128:1** [t] Ps 112:1 [u] Ps 119:1-3 **128:2** [v] Isa 3:10 [w] Ecc 8:12 **128:3** [x] Eze 19:10 [y] Ps 52:8; 144:12 **128:5** [z] Ps 20:2; 134:3 **128:6** [a] Ge 50:23; Job 42:16 [b] Ps 125:5 **129:1** [c] Ps 88:15; Hos 2:15 [d] Ps 124:1 **129:2** [e] Mt 16:18 **129:4** [f] Ps 119:137 **129:5** [g] Mic 4:11 [h] Ps 71:13 **129:6** [i] Ps 37:2 **129:8** [j] Ru 2:4; Ps 118:26 **130:1** [k] Ps 42:7; 69:2; La 3:55 **130:2** [l] Ps 28:2 [m] 2Ch 6:40; Ps 64:1 **130:3** [n] Ps 76:7; 143:2 **130:4** [o] Ex 34:7; Isa 55:7; Jer 33:8 [p] 1Ki 8:40

5 I wait for the LORD,[q] my whole being
waits,
and in his word[r] I put my hope.
6 I wait for the Lord
more than watchmen[s] wait for the
morning,
more than watchmen wait for the
morning.[t]

7 Israel, put your hope[u] in the LORD,
for with the LORD is unfailing
love
and with him is full redemption.
8 He himself will redeem[v] Israel
from all their sins.

Psalm 131

A song of ascents. Of David.

1 My heart is not proud,[w] LORD,
my eyes are not haughty;
I do not concern myself with great
matters
or things too wonderful for me.
2 But I have calmed and quieted
myself,
I am like a weaned child with its
mother;
like a weaned child I am content.[x]

3 Israel, put your hope[y] in the LORD
both now and forevermore.

Psalm 132

A song of ascents.

1 LORD, remember David
and all his self-denial.

2 He swore an oath to the LORD,
he made a vow to the Mighty One of
Jacob:[z]
3 "I will not enter my house
or go to my bed,
4 I will allow no sleep to my eyes
or slumber to my eyelids,
5 till I find a place[a] for the LORD,
a dwelling for the Mighty One of
Jacob."

6 We heard it in Ephrathah,[b]
we came upon it in the fields of
Jaar:[a][c]
7 "Let us go to his dwelling place,[d]
let us worship at his footstool,[e]
saying,
8 'Arise, LORD,[f] and come to your resting
place,
you and the ark of your might.
9 May your priests be clothed with your
righteousness;[g]
may your faithful people sing for joy.'"

10 For the sake of your servant David,
do not reject your anointed one.

11 The LORD swore an oath to David,[h]
a sure oath he will not revoke:
"One of your own descendants[i]
I will place on your throne.
12 If your sons keep my covenant
and the statutes I teach them,
then their sons will sit
on your throne[j] for ever and ever."

13 For the LORD has chosen Zion,[k]
he has desired it for his dwelling,
saying,
14 "This is my resting place for ever and
ever;[l]
here I will sit enthroned, for I have
desired it.
15 I will bless her with abundant
provisions;
her poor I will satisfy with food.[m]

[a] 6 Or *heard of it in Ephrathah, / we found it in the fields of Jearim.* (See 1 Chron. 13:5,6) (And no quotation marks around verses 7-9)

---

forgiven sinner realizes the magnitude of God's grace, remains grateful for Jesus' sacrifice for sins, and lives in the reverence or fear of God (Ps. 128).

130:8 *He himself will redeem.* God had redeemed the people from slavery in Egypt; the psalmist also looked forward to the time when He would redeem the people from slavery to their own sinful natures, through the death and resurrection of Jesus Christ (Gal. 3:13).

131:1 *My heart is not proud.* David presents himself with genuine humility, a delicate balance between self-abasement and arrogant pride. From the life of David, we know that he was not always able to keep this balance. But it was his desire, and at times—by God's grace—a reality in his life.

131:2 *like a weaned child.* A weaned child is comforted just by the presence of his mother, without crying for the more tangible comfort of milk as a younger baby does.

132:1 *remember.* This psalm was one of the 15 Songs of Ascents sung by pilgrims as they approached the holy city to worship. Each year, as they marched and sang, they anticipated that perhaps this was the year that this prophecy would be fulfilled. ***David ... his self-denial.*** If this psalm was written during the period after the exile, these words have a significant meaning. During the years between the return of the people to Jerusalem and the birth of Jesus, there would have been a growing desire on the part of godly people for the Lord to restore David's kingdom in fulfillment of His promise.

132:6 *Ephrathah.* This name refers to the region of Bethlehem (Ruth 1:2).

132:12 *sit on your throne for ever and ever.* The ultimate fulfillment of God's covenant with David (2 Sam. 7:8–16) is in Jesus Christ, the Son of David (Luke 1:32–33; Acts 2:30).

130:5 [q] Ps 27:14; 33:20; Isa 8:17 [r] Ps 119:81 **130:6** [s] Ps 63:6 [t] Ps 119:147 **130:7** [u] Ps 131:3 **130:8** [v] Lk 1:68 **131:1** [w] Ps 101:5; Ro 12:16 **131:2** [x] Mt 18:3; 1Co 14:20 **131:3** [y] Ps 130:7 **132:2** [z] Ge 49:24 **132:5** [a] Ac 7:46 **132:6** [b] 1Sa 17:12 [c] 1Sa 7:2 **132:7** [d] Ps 5:7 [e] Ps 99:5 **132:8** [f] Nu 10:35; Ps 78:61 **132:9** [g] Job 29:14; Isa 61:3, 10 **132:11** [h] Ps 89:3-4, 35 [i] 2Sa 7:12 **132:12** [j] Lk 1:32; Ac 2:30 **132:13** [k] Ps 48:1-2 **132:14** [l] Ps 68:16 **132:15** [m] Ps 107:9; 147:14

[16]I will clothe her priests[n] with salvation,
and her faithful people will ever sing for joy.
[17]"Here I will make a horn[a] grow[o] for David
and set up a lamp[p] for my anointed one.
[18]I will clothe his enemies with shame,[q]
but his head will be adorned with a radiant crown."

Psalm 133

A song of ascents. Of David.

[1]How good and pleasant it is
when God's people live together[r] in unity!

[2]It is like precious oil poured on the head,[s]
running down on the beard,
running down on Aaron's beard,
down on the collar of his robe.
[3]It is as if the dew of Hermon[t]
were falling on Mount Zion.
For there the LORD bestows his blessing,[u]
even life forevermore.[v]

Psalm 134

A song of ascents.

[1]Praise the LORD, all you servants[w] of the LORD
who minister by night[x] in the house of the LORD.
[2]Lift up your hands[y] in the sanctuary
and praise the LORD.

[3]May the LORD bless you from Zion,[z]
he who is the Maker of heaven[a] and earth.

Psalm 135

[1]Praise the LORD.[b]
Praise the name of the LORD;
praise him, you servants[b] of the LORD,
[2]you who minister in the house[c] of the LORD,
in the courts[d] of the house of our God.
[3]Praise the LORD, for the LORD is good;[e]
sing praise to his name, for that is pleasant.[f]
[4]For the LORD has chosen Jacob[g] to be his own,
Israel to be his treasured possession.[h]
[5]I know that the LORD is great,[i]
that our Lord is greater than all gods.[j]
[6]The LORD does whatever pleases him,[k]
in the heavens and on the earth,
in the seas and all their depths.
[7]He makes clouds rise from the ends of the earth;
he sends lightning with the rain[l]
and brings out the wind[m] from his storehouses.[n]

[8]He struck down the firstborn[o] of Egypt,
the firstborn of people and animals.
[9]He sent his signs[p] and wonders into your midst, Egypt,
against Pharaoh and all his servants.[q]
[10]He struck down many[r] nations
and killed mighty kings—
[11]Sihon[s] king of the Amorites,
Og king of Bashan,
and all the kings of Canaan[t]—
[12]and he gave their land as an inheritance,[u]
an inheritance to his people Israel.

[13]Your name, LORD, endures forever,[v]
your renown,[w] LORD, through all generations.
[14]For the LORD will vindicate his people
and have compassion on his servants.[x]

[15]The idols of the nations are silver and gold,
made by human hands.

---

[a] 17 *Horn* here symbolizes strong one, that is, king.
[b] 1 Hebrew *Hallelu Yah*; also in verses 3 and 21

132:16 *joy.* God's presence is a source of joy to the upright. God had chosen Zion as His resting place, and His godly ones sang for joy. When God rules on the throne of the human spirit, joy reigns within.
132:17 *horn . . . lamp.* The words "horn" and "lamp" speak of the Messiah's authority and righteousness (Is. 11:1–5).
133:3 *the dew of Hermon.* This high mountain to the north of Israel received such large amounts of water that it seemed to be a source of moisture for the lands below.
134:1 *all you servants of the LORD.* This psalm concludes the Songs of Ascents. The people who had come to worship at the temple were getting ready to go home, but the priests would remain at the holy temple, continuing to lift up worship to the Lord.
135:8 *the firstborn of Egypt.* The defeat of Egypt was solely the work of the Lord. Israel was merely His instrument; the battle belonged to Him (Ex. 12:12; 15:3).
135:15 *idols of the nations.* The people who returned from Babylon had had their fill of the worship of idols; at long last, the people of Israel were ready to worship the only true God.

132:16 [n] 2Ch 6:41 **132:17** [o] Eze 29:21; Lk 1:69 [p] 1Ki 11:36; 2Ch 21:7 **132:18** [q] Ps 35:26; 109:29 **133:1** [r] Ge 13:8; Heb 13:1 **133:2** [s] Ex 30:25 **133:3** [t] Dt 4:48 [u] Lev 25:21; Dt 28:8 [v] Ps 42:8 **134:1** [w] Ps 135:1-2 [x] 1Ch 9:33 **134:2** [y] Ps 28:2; 1Ti 2:8 **134:3** [z] Ps 128:5 [a] Ps 124:8 **135:1** [b] Ps 113:1; 134:1 **135:2** [c] Lk 2:37 [d] Ps 116:19 **135:3** [e] Ps 119:68 [f] Ps 147:1 **135:4** [g] Dt 10:15; 1Pe 2:9 [h] Ex 19:5; Dt 7:6 **135:5** [i] Ps 48:1 [j] Ps 97:9 **135:6** [k] Ps 115:3 **135:7** [l] Jer 10:13; Zec 10:1 [m] Job 28:25 [n] Job 38:22 **135:8** [o] Ex 12:12; Ps 78:51 **135:9** [p] Dt 6:22 [q] Ps 136:10-15 **135:10** [r] Nu 21:21-25; Ps 136:17-21 **135:11** [s] Nu 21:21 [t] Jos 12:7-24 **135:12** [u] Ps 78:55 **135:13** [v] Ex 3:15 [w] Ps 102:12 **135:14** [x] Dt 32:36

16 They have mouths, but cannot speak,
eyes, but cannot see.
17 They have ears, but cannot hear,
nor is there breath in their mouths.
18 Those who make them will be like them,
and so will all who trust in them.

19 All you Israelites, praise the LORD;
house of Aaron, praise the LORD;
20 house of Levi, praise the LORD;
you who fear him, praise the LORD.
21 Praise be to the LORD from Zion,[y]
to him who dwells in Jerusalem.

Praise the LORD.

Psalm 136

1 Give thanks to the LORD, for he is good.[z]
His love endures forever.[a]
2 Give thanks to the God of gods.[b]
His love endures forever.
3 Give thanks to the Lord of lords:
His love endures forever.

4 to him who alone does great wonders,[c]
His love endures forever.
5 who by his understanding[d] made the heavens,[e]
His love endures forever.
6 who spread out the earth[f] upon the waters,[g]
His love endures forever.
7 who made the great lights[h]—
His love endures forever.
8 the sun to govern[i] the day,
His love endures forever.
9 the moon and stars to govern the night;
His love endures forever.

10 to him who struck down the firstborn[j] of Egypt
His love endures forever.
11 and brought Israel out[k] from among them
His love endures forever.
12 with a mighty hand and outstretched arm;[l]
His love endures forever.

13 to him who divided the Red Sea[a][m] asunder
His love endures forever.
14 and brought Israel through[n] the midst of it,
His love endures forever.
15 but swept Pharaoh and his army into the Red Sea;[o]
His love endures forever.

16 to him who led his people through the wilderness;[p]
His love endures forever.

17 to him who struck down great kings,[q]
His love endures forever.
18 and killed mighty kings[r]—
His love endures forever.
19 Sihon king of the Amorites[s]
His love endures forever.
20 and Og king of Bashan—
His love endures forever.
21 and gave their land[t] as an inheritance,
His love endures forever.
22 an inheritance to his servant Israel.
His love endures forever.

23 He remembered us[u] in our low estate
His love endures forever.
24 and freed us from our enemies.[v]
His love endures forever.
25 He gives food[w] to every creature.
His love endures forever.

26 Give thanks to the God of heaven.
His love endures forever.

Psalm 137

1 By the rivers of Babylon[x] we sat and wept[y]
when we remembered Zion.
2 There on the poplars
we hung our harps,
3 for there our captors asked us for songs,
our tormentors demanded[z] songs of joy;
they said, "Sing us one of the songs of Zion!"

4 How can we sing the songs of the LORD
while in a foreign land?
5 If I forget you, Jerusalem,
may my right hand forget its skill.

[a] 13 Or *the Sea of Reeds*; also in verse 15

135:19 *praise the LORD.* To praise the Lord is to identify Him as the source of all blessings and to be grateful for all that He has given.

136:1 *love.* This word, also translated "mercy" or "loyal love," is the most significant term used in the Psalms to describe the character of God. His love is forever; it is part of His eternal character.

136:4–9 *great wonders.* God's creation of the universe is the grand display of His wisdom. The heavens give a clear presentation of the glory of God (19:1–6). Romans 1:20 teaches that God's "invisible attributes" are clearly seen through the things He has made.

136:23 *remembered us.* It is possible that these words suggest the return of the people of Judah and Jerusalem to their land following the Babylonian captivity.

137:1 *Babylon.* Babylon was one of the great empires in world history. When this psalm was written, the Jews were living there in exile.

137:5 *If I forget you.* The love of the people for

135:21 [y] Ps 134:3 **136:1** [z] Ps 106:1 [a] 1Ch 16:34; 2Ch 20:21 **136:2** [b] Dt 10:17 **136:4** [c] Ps 72:18 **136:5** [d] Pr 3:19; Jer 51:15 [e] Ge 1:1 **136:6** [f] Ge 1:9; Jer 10:12 [g] Ps 24:2 **136:7** [h] Ge 1:14, 16 **136:8** [i] Ge 1:16 **136:10** [j] Ex 12:29; Ps 135:8 **136:11** [k] Ex 6:6; 12:51 **136:12** [l] Dt 4:34; Ps 44:3 **136:13** [m] Ex 14:21; Ps 78:13 **136:14** [n] Ex 14:22 **136:15** [o] Ex 14:27; Ps 135:9 **136:16** [p] Ex 13:18 **136:17** [q] Ps 135:9-12 **136:18** [r] Dt 29:7 **136:19** [s] Nu 21:21-25 **136:21** [t] Jos 12:1 **136:23** [u] Ps 113:7 **136:24** [v] Ps 107:2 **136:25** [w] Ps 104:27; 145:15 **137:1** [x] Eze 1:1, 3 [y] Ne 1:4 **137:3** [z] Ps 80:6

[6]May my tongue cling to the roof[a] of my
mouth
if I do not remember you,
if I do not consider Jerusalem
my highest joy.
[7]Remember, LORD, what the Edomites[b]
did
on the day Jerusalem fell.[c]
"Tear it down," they cried,
"tear it down to its foundations!"
[8]Daughter Babylon, doomed to
destruction,[d]
happy is the one who repays you
according to what you have done
to us.
[9]Happy is the one who seizes your
infants
and dashes them[e] against the rocks.

Psalm 138

Of David.

[1]I will praise you, LORD, with all my
heart;
before the "gods"[f] I will sing your
praise.
[2]I will bow down toward your holy
temple[g]
and will praise your name
for your unfailing love and your
faithfulness,
for you have so exalted your solemn
decree
that it surpasses your fame.[h]
[3]When I called, you answered me;
you greatly emboldened me.

[4]May all the kings of the earth[i] praise
you, LORD,
when they hear what you have
decreed.
[5]May they sing of the ways of the LORD,
for the glory of the LORD is great.

[6]Though the LORD is exalted, he looks
kindly on the lowly;[j]
though lofty, he sees them[k] from afar.
[7]Though I walk[l] in the midst of trouble,
you preserve my life.
You stretch out your hand against the
anger of my foes;[m]
with your right hand[n] you save me.[o]
[8]The LORD will vindicate[p] me;
your love, LORD, endures forever—
do not abandon the works of your
hands.[q]

Psalm 139

For the director of music. Of David. A psalm.

[1]You have searched me,[r] LORD,
and you know[s] me.
[2]You know when I sit and when I rise;[t]
you perceive my thoughts[u] from afar.
[3]You discern my going out and my lying
down;
you are familiar with all my ways.[v]
[4]Before a word is on my tongue
you, LORD, know it completely.[w]
[5]You hem me in[x] behind and before,
and you lay your hand upon me.
[6]Such knowledge is too wonderful
for me,
too lofty[y] for me to attain.

[7]Where can I go from your Spirit?
Where can I flee[z] from your
presence?
[8]If I go up to the heavens,[a] you are there;
if I make my bed[b] in the depths, you
are there.
[9]If I rise on the wings of the dawn,
if I settle on the far side of the sea,

Jerusalem was not just for the place, but for its function in their lives. The place was holy because it was the dwelling place of God and the place of worship and sacrifice for sins.

137:9 *Happy is the one.* The idea of rejoicing and happiness at the violence depicted here is hard to swallow. Like some of the other difficult stories recorded in Scripture (see the Book of Judges), this imprecatory psalm is included with no comments about how God viewed the psalmist's emotion. Elsewhere in Scripture, we receive strict commands condemning taking vengeance into our own hands (Rom. 12:19–21), rejoicing when others suffer (Obad. 12), and refusing to forgive (Matt. 5:43–45; 6:14–15). However, none of these passages are saying that we should pretend that evil doesn't exist. This psalmist's violent reaction to evil should remind us of how seriously God takes sin. He will not allow wickedness to go unpunished.

138:1 *before the "gods."* David is so confident in his faith in the Lord that he is determined to take the name of God into foreign territory.

138:2 *your holy temple.* The use of the word "temple" does not rule out David as the author of this or similar poems (15:1). The Hebrew term is a general one that would fit whatever building was in use in David's day.

138:6 *the lowly.* When man is boastful and conceited before God, he separates himself from God. Yet God bends with a special concern toward those who are humble before Him.

138:8 *love ... endures forever.* God's loyal covenant love will never be rescinded or forgotten.

139:5 *You hem me in behind and before.* The purpose of God's intimate knowledge of His servants is protective and helpful, not judgmental and condemning.

139:7–12 *you are there.* The believer can rejoice and rest in the knowledge that God is present in every place and every situation in life.

137:6 [a] Eze 3:26 **137:7** [b] Jer 49:7; La 4:21-22; Eze 25:12 [c] Ob 1:11 **137:8** [d] Isa 13:1, 19; Jer 25:12, 26; Jer 50:15; Rev 18:6 **137:9** [e] 2Ki 8:12; Isa 13:16 **138:1** [f] Ps 95:3; 96:4 **138:2** [g] 1Ki 8:29; Ps 5:7; 28:2 [h] Isa 42:21 **138:4** [i] Ps 102:15 **138:6** [j] Ps 113:6; Isa 57:15 [k] Pr 3:34; Jas 4:6 **138:7** [l] Ps 23:4 [m] Jer 51:25 [n] Ps 20:6 [o] Ps 71:20 **138:8** [p] Ps 57:2; Php 1:6 [q] Job 10:3, 8; 14:15 **139:1** [r] Ps 17:3 [s] Jer 12:3 **139:2** [t] 2Ki 19:27 [u] Mt 9:4; Jn 2:24 **139:3** [v] Job 31:4 **139:4** [w] Heb 4:13 **139:5** [x] Ps 34:7 **139:6** [y] Job 42:3; Ro 11:33 **139:7** [z] Jer 23:24; Jnh 1:3 **139:8** [a] Am 9:2-3 [b] Pr 15:11

[10]even there your hand will guide me,[c]
your right hand will hold me fast.
[11]If I say, "Surely the darkness will
hide me
and the light become night
around me,"
[12]even the darkness will not be dark[d] to
you;
the night will shine like the day,
for darkness is as light to you.

[13]For you created my inmost being;[e]
you knit me together[f] in my mother's
womb.
[14]I praise you because I am fearfully and
wonderfully made;
your works are wonderful,[g]
I know that full well.
[15]My frame was not hidden from you
when I was made in the secret place,
when I was woven together[h] in the
depths of the earth.[i]
[16]Your eyes saw my unformed body;
all the days ordained for me were
written in your book
before one of them came to be.
[17]How precious to me are your thoughts,[a]
God![j]
How vast is the sum of them!
[18]Were I to count them,
they would outnumber the grains of
sand—
when I awake, I am still with you.

[19]If only you, God, would slay the
wicked![k]
Away from me,[l] you who are
bloodthirsty!
[20]They speak of you with evil intent;
your adversaries misuse your name.[m]
[21]Do I not hate those[n] who hate you,
LORD,
and abhor those who are in rebellion
against you?
[22]I have nothing but hatred for them;
I count them my enemies.
[23]Search me,[o] God, and know my heart;[p]
test me and know my anxious
thoughts.
[24]See if there is any offensive way in me,
and lead me[q] in the way everlasting.

Psalm 140[b]

For the director of music. A psalm of David.

[1]Rescue me,[r] LORD, from evildoers;
protect me from the violent,[s]
[2]who devise evil plans[t] in their hearts
and stir up war every day.
[3]They make their tongues as sharp as[u] a
serpent's;
the poison of vipers[v] is on their lips.[c]

[4]Keep me safe,[w] LORD, from the hands of
the wicked;[x]
protect me from the violent,
who devise ways to trip my feet.
[5]The arrogant have hidden a snare
for me;
they have spread out the cords of
their net
and have set traps[y] for me along my
path.

[6]I say to the LORD, "You are my God."[z]
Hear, LORD, my cry for mercy.[a]
[7]Sovereign LORD,[b] my strong deliverer,
you shield my head in the day of
battle.
[8]Do not grant the wicked[c] their desires,
LORD;
do not let their plans succeed.

---

[a] 17 Or *How amazing are your thoughts concerning me* [b] In Hebrew texts 140:1-13 is numbered 140:2-14. [c] 3 The Hebrew has *Selah* (a word of uncertain meaning) here and at the end of verses 5 and 8.

139:12 *darkness is as light to you.* God can see what is happening to us even under cover of darkness. Nothing can conceal His people from Him.
139:14 God's Omniscience—He is the God who knows. He knows everything that has happened and will happen. He understands all of nature perfectly. In fact He knows everything there is to know. God knows so much that it would be impossible to overstate what He knows. The proper theological term for this attribute of God is: *omniscience.*

God knows all of our thoughts, motives, and deeds. God knows us better than we know ourselves. We are all uneasy with the fact that God knows us so well. Like Adam and Eve, we fear the exposure of our sin.

There is, however, great reason to rejoice in the fact that God knows us so well. He loves us in spite of what He knows about us; in the midst of our sin He still loves us. He knows the worst things there are to know about us and still wants to save us. He also knows the best things about us. When everyone else misunderstands us, He understands us fully. Finally, God knows what we will be. He has a marvelous end in mind that should give us great comfort no matter what our present state.
139:16 *in your book.* The idea is that all human beings, and the structure and meaning of each person's life, are all established from the beginning by God.
139:23 *Search me, God.* It is only when we are aware of our sins that we can repent of them and be healed.
140:6 *You are my God.* David confessed his complete trust in the Lord even though he was surrounded by people plotting his destruction. On the basis of his trust, he pled with the Lord to deliver him.

139:10 [c] Ps 23:3 **139:12** [d] Job 34:22; Da 2:22
139:13 [e] Ps 119:73 [f] Job 10:11 **139:14** [g] Ps 40:5
139:15 [h] Job 10:11 [i] Ps 63:9 **139:17** [j] Ps 40:5
139:19 [k] Isa 11:4 [l] Ps 119:115 **139:20** [m] Jude 15
139:21 [n] 2Ch 19:2; Ps 31:6; 119:113; 119:158
139:23 [o] Job 31:6; Ps 26:2 [p] Jer 11:20 **139:24** [q] Ps 5:8; 143:10; Pr 15:9 **140:1** [r] Ps 17:13 [s] Ps 18:48
140:2 [t] Ps 36:4; 56:6 **140:3** [u] Ps 57:4 [v] Ps 58:4; Jas 3:8
140:4 [w] Ps 141:9 [x] Ps 71:4 **140:5** [y] Ps 31:4; 35:7
140:6 [z] Ps 16:2 [a] Ps 116:1; 143:1 **140:7** [b] Ps 28:8
140:8 [c] Ps 10:2-3

9 Those who surround me proudly rear
their heads;
may the mischief of their lips engulf
them.[d]
10 May burning coals fall on them;
may they be thrown into the fire,[e]
into miry pits, never to rise.
11 May slanderers not be established in
the land;
may disaster hunt down the violent.[f]

12 I know that the LORD secures justice for
the poor
and upholds the cause[g] of the needy.[h]
13 Surely the righteous will praise your
name,[i]
and the upright will live[j] in your
presence.

Psalm 141

A psalm of David.

1 I call to you, LORD, come quickly[k] to me;
hear me[l] when I call to you.
2 May my prayer be set before you like
incense;[m]
may the lifting up of my hands[n] be
like the evening sacrifice.[o]

3 Set a guard over my mouth, LORD;
keep watch over the door of my lips.
4 Do not let my heart be drawn to what is
evil
so that I take part in wicked deeds
along with those who are evildoers;
do not let me eat their delicacies.[p]

5 Let a righteous man strike me—that is
a kindness;
let him rebuke me[q]—that is oil on my
head.[r]
My head will not refuse it,
for my prayer will still be against the
deeds of evildoers.

6 Their rulers will be thrown down from
the cliffs,
and the wicked will learn that my
words were well spoken.
7 They will say, "As one plows and breaks
up the earth,
so our bones have been scattered at
the mouth[s] of the grave."

8 But my eyes are fixed[t] on you,
Sovereign LORD;
in you I take refuge[u]—do not give me
over to death.
9 Keep me safe[v] from the traps set by
evildoers,
from the snares[w] they have laid for me.
10 Let the wicked fall[x] into their own nets,
while I pass by in safety.

Psalm 142[a]

A maskil[b] of David. When he was in the cave. A prayer.

1 I cry aloud to the LORD;
I lift up my voice to the LORD for
mercy.[y]
2 I pour out before him my complaint;[z]
before him I tell my trouble.

3 When my spirit grows faint[a] within me,
it is you who watch over my way.
In the path where I walk
people have hidden a snare for me.
4 Look and see, there is no one at my
right hand;
no one is concerned for me.
I have no refuge;
no one cares[b] for my life.

5 I cry to you, LORD;
I say, "You are my refuge,[c]
my portion[d] in the land of the living."[e]

6 Listen to my cry,[f]
for I am in desperate need;[g]
rescue me from those who pursue me,
for they are too strong for me.

[a] In Hebrew texts 142:1-7 is numbered 142:2-8.
[b] Title: Probably a literary or musical term

140:10 *May burning coals fall.* David recalls the judgment of Sodom and Gomorrah (Gen. 19:12–29) and asks God to once again judge the enemies of the righteous.
140:12 *justice for the poor.* The cause of the poor and afflicted is of special interest to the Lord. He promises to uphold and comfort them (41:1; 72:4; 109:31; Luke 4:18; 6:20).
141:2 *like incense.* The prayers of God's people are also compared to incense in Revelation 8:3–4.
141:3 *Set a guard over my mouth.* David recognized how terribly easy it is to sin in what we say (Prov. 30:32–33; James 3:1–12).
141:5 *Let a righteous man strike me—that is a kindness.* The rebuke of a righteous person, even if it is painful at the time, is designed to bring about good. Sometimes being "nice" isn't really the kindest thing we can do for someone.
141:8 *my eyes are fixed on you.* If we focus on the strength of wickedness, we will be overcome with fear. If we focus on ourselves, we will become absorbed in our difficulties or exalt ourselves in our victories. Only when we focus on God can we achieve balance and health.
142:title *When he was in the cave.* This may refer to one of two occasions when David hid from King Saul in a cave: at En Gedi (Ps. 57; 1 Sam. 24), and at Adullam (1 Sam. 22:1).
142:5 *You are my refuge.* Sometimes God allows us to go through times when we have no one at our right hand, "no one cares," just so that we will be very aware of our need for God.

140:9 [d] Ps 7:16 **140:10** [e] Ps 11:6; 21:9
140:11 [f] Ps 34:21 **140:12** [g] Ps 9:4 [h] Ps 35:10
140:13 [i] Ps 97:12 [j] Ps 11:7 **141:1** [k] Ps 22:19; 70:5
[l] Ps 143:1 **141:2** [m] Rev 5:8; 8:3 [n] 1Ti 2:8 [o] Ex 29:39,41
141:4 [p] Pr 23:6 **141:5** [q] Pr 9:8 [r] Ps 23:5 **141:7** [s] Ps 53:5
141:8 [t] Ps 25:15 [u] Ps 2:12 **141:9** [v] Ps 140:4 [w] Ps 38:12
141:10 [x] Ps 35:8 **142:1** [y] Ps 30:8 **142:2** [z] Isa 26:16
142:3 [a] Ps 140:5; 143:4,7 **142:4** [b] Ps 31:11; Jer 30:17
142:5 [c] Ps 46:1 [d] Ps 16:5 [e] Ps 27:13 **142:6** [f] Ps 17:1
[g] Ps 79:8; 116:6

7 Set me free from my prison,[h]
that I may praise your name.
Then the righteous will gather about me
because of your goodness to me.[i]

Psalm 143

A psalm of David.

1 LORD, hear my prayer,
listen to my cry for mercy;[j]
in your faithfulness[k] and righteousness[l]
come to my relief.
2 Do not bring your servant into
judgment,
for no one living is righteous[m] before
you.
3 The enemy pursues me,
he crushes me to the ground;
he makes me dwell in the darkness
like those long dead.
4 So my spirit grows faint within me;
my heart within me is dismayed.[n]
5 I remember[o] the days of long ago;
I meditate on all your works
and consider what your hands have
done.
6 I spread out my hands[p] to you;
I thirst for you like a parched land.[a]

7 Answer me quickly,[q] LORD;
my spirit fails.
Do not hide your face[r] from me
or I will be like those who go down to
the pit.
8 Let the morning bring me word of your
unfailing love,[s]
for I have put my trust in you.
Show me the way[t] I should go,
for to you I entrust my life.[u]
9 Rescue me from my enemies,[v] LORD,
for I hide myself in you.
10 Teach me to do your will,
for you are my God;
may your good Spirit
lead[w] me on level ground.

11 For your name's sake, LORD, preserve
my life;[x]
in your righteousness,[y] bring me out
of trouble.
12 In your unfailing love, silence my
enemies;
destroy all my foes,[z]
for I am your servant.[a]

Psalm 144

Of David.

1 Praise be to the LORD my Rock,[b]
who trains my hands for war,
my fingers for battle.
2 He is my loving God and my fortress,[c]
my stronghold and my deliverer,
my shield,[d] in whom I take refuge,
who subdues peoples[b] under me.

3 LORD, what are human beings[e] that you
care for them,
mere mortals that you think of them?
4 They are like a breath;
their days are like a fleeting shadow.[f]

5 Part your heavens,[g] LORD, and come
down;
touch the mountains, so that they
smoke.[h]
6 Send forth lightning and scatter the
enemy;
shoot your arrows[i] and rout them.
7 Reach down your hand from on high;
deliver me and rescue me
from the mighty waters,[j]
from the hands of foreigners[k]
8 whose mouths are full of lies,[l]
whose right hands are deceitful.

9 I will sing a new song to you, my God;
on the ten-stringed lyre[m] I will make
music to you,
10 to the One who gives victory to kings,
who delivers his servant David.[n]

From the deadly sword 11 deliver me;
rescue me from the hands of
foreigners
whose mouths are full of lies,
whose right hands are deceitful.[o]

---

[a] *6* The Hebrew has *Selah* (a word of uncertain meaning) here. [b] *2* Many manuscripts of the Masoretic Text, Dead Sea Scrolls, Aquila, Jerome and Syriac; most manuscripts of the Masoretic Text *subdues my people*

143:2 *no one living is righteous.* This is not so much a confession as an observation that everyone is sinful.

143:3 *in the darkness.* To live in darkness is similar to being in the pit (v. 7); this is the reason for the parallel to those who are already dead (Job 10:21–22).

143:11 *For your name's sake.* The requests of the psalmists are often tied to various character traits of God. When we pray "in Jesus name," we pray both in the authority of His name and in the character it represents.

144:4 *like a fleeting shadow.* Human life apart from God is presented in the darkest terms by the Word of God. Briefly stated, it is short and full of trouble (Job 14:1), uncertain (Luke 12:16–20), and empty (Eccl. 1:2). In contrast, Paul the apostle describes the life of the redeemed as being like a victorious soldier, a winning athlete, a successful farmer, a diligent student, and a useable vessel (2 Tim. 2). The redeemed life is marked by peace and purpose now, and eternity with Christ later.

144:11 *rescue me from the hands of foreigners.*

142:7 [h] Ps 146:7 [i] Ps 13:6 **143:1** [j] Ps 140:6 [k] Ps 89:1-2 [l] Ps 71:2 **143:2** [m] Ps 14:3; Ecc 7:20; Ro 3:20 **143:4** [n] Ps 142:3 **143:5** [o] Ps 77:6 **143:6** [p] Ps 63:1; 88:9 **143:7** [q] Ps 69:17 [r] Ps 27:9; 28:1 **143:8** [s] Ps 46:5; 90:14 [t] Ps 27:11 [u] Ps 25:1-2 **143:9** [v] Ps 31:15 **143:10** [w] Ne 9:20; Ps 23:3; 25:4-5 **143:11** [x] Ps 119:25 [y] Ps 31:1 **143:12** [z] Ps 52:5; 54:5 [a] Ps 116:16 **144:1** [b] Ps 18:2,34 **144:2** [c] Ps 59:9; 91:2 [d] Ps 84:9 **144:3** [e] Ps 8:4; Heb 2:6 **144:4** [f] Ps 39:11; 102:11 **144:5** [g] Ps 18:9; Isa 64:1 [h] Ps 104:32 **144:6** [i] Ps 7:12-13; 18:14 **144:7** [j] Ps 69:2 [k] Ps 18:44 **144:8** [l] Ps 12:2 **144:9** [m] Ps 33:2-3 **144:10** [n] Ps 18:50 **144:11** [o] Ps 12:2; Isa 44:20

12 Then our sons in their youth
will be like well-nurtured
plants,[p]
and our daughters will be like pillars
carved to adorn a palace.
13 Our barns will be filled
with every kind of provision.
Our sheep will increase by
thousands,
by tens of thousands in our fields;
14 our oxen will draw heavy loads.[a]
There will be no breaching of walls,
no going into captivity,
no cry of distress in our streets.
15 Blessed is the people[q] of whom this is
true;
blessed is the people whose God is
the LORD.

Psalm 145[b]

A psalm of praise. Of David.

1 I will exalt you,[r] my God the King;[s]
I will praise your name for ever and
ever.
2 Every day I will praise[t] you
and extol your name for ever and ever.

3 Great is the LORD and most worthy of
praise;
his greatness no one can fathom.[u]
4 One generation[v] commends your works
to another;
they tell of your mighty acts.
5 They speak of the glorious splendor of
your majesty—
and I will meditate on your wonderful
works.[cw]
6 They tell of the power of your awesome
works—[x]
and I will proclaim[y] your great deeds.
7 They celebrate your abundant
goodness[z]
and joyfully sing of your
righteousness.[a]

8 The LORD is gracious and
compassionate,[b]
slow to anger and rich in love.[c]

9 The LORD is good[d] to all;
he has compassion on all he has
made.
10 All your works praise you,[e] LORD;
your faithful people extol you.[f]
11 They tell of the glory of your kingdom
and speak of your might,
12 so that all people may know of your
mighty acts[g]
and the glorious splendor of your
kingdom.
13 Your kingdom is an everlasting
kingdom,[h]
and your dominion endures through
all generations.

The LORD is trustworthy in all he
promises
and faithful in all he does.[d]
14 The LORD upholds[i] all who fall
and lifts up all[j] who are bowed down.
15 The eyes of all look to you,
and you give them their food[k] at the
proper time.
16 You open your hand
and satisfy the desires[l] of every living
thing.

17 The LORD is righteous in all his ways
and faithful in all he does.
18 The LORD is near[m] to all who call on
him,[n]
to all who call on him in truth.
19 He fulfills the desires[o] of those who fear
him;
he hears their cry[p] and saves them.
20 The LORD watches over all who love
him,[q]
but all the wicked he will destroy.[r]

21 My mouth will speak[s] in praise of the
LORD.
Let every creature[t] praise his holy
name
for ever and ever.

---

[a] 14 Or *our chieftains will be firmly established*
[b] This psalm is an acrostic poem, the verses of which (including verse 13b) begin with the successive letters of the Hebrew alphabet.
[c] 5 Dead Sea Scrolls and Syriac (see also Septuagint); Masoretic Text *On the glorious splendor of your majesty / and on your wonderful works I will meditate*
[d] 13 One manuscript of the Masoretic Text, Dead Sea Scrolls and Syriac (see also Septuagint); most manuscripts of the Masoretic Text do not have the last two lines of verse 13.

The principal lie of the enemy was that the Lord could not save His people (Is. 36:18–20).

144:15 *Blessed.* This word could also be translated "Happy." The happiness that David describes refers both to external well-being and to internal peace.

145:8 *gracious and compassionate.* In contrast to the popular image of God as stern and critical, God is full of compassion for erring humans—so much so that He sent His own Son to redeem them (John 3:16).

145:13 *an everlasting kingdom.* The rule of God is eternal, and the message of His wonders needs to be delivered to all people in the present time.

145:17 *righteous . . . faithful.* The pairing of these two terms is a powerful description of the character of God. Righteousness alone would lead to our destruction because of our sin, but God is also kind and gracious and has arranged a way for us to be saved.

144:12 [p] Ps 128:3 **144:15** [q] Ps 33:12 **145:1** [r] Ps 30:1; 34:1 [s] Ps 5:2 **145:2** [t] Ps 71:6 **145:3** [u] Job 5:9; Ps 147:5; Ro 11:33 **145:4** [v] Isa 38:19 **145:5** [w] Ps 119:27 **145:6** [x] Ps 66:3 [y] Dt 32:3 **145:7** [z] Isa 63:7 [a] Ps 51:14 **145:8** [b] Ps 86:15 [c] Ex 34:6; Nu 14:18 **145:9** [d] Ps 100:5 **145:10** [e] Ps 19:1 [f] Ps 68:26 **145:12** [g] Ps 105:1 **145:13** [h] 1Ti 1:17; 2Pe 1:11 **145:14** [i] Ps 37:24 [j] Ps 146:8 **145:15** [k] Ps 104:27; 136:25 **145:16** [l] Ps 104:28 **145:18** [m] Dt 4:7 [n] Jn 4:24 **145:19** [o] Ps 37:4 [p] Pr 15:29 **145:20** [q] Ps 31:23; 97:10 [r] Ps 9:5 **145:21** [s] Ps 71:8 [t] Ps 65:2

Psalm 146

1 Praise the LORD.[a]

Praise the LORD,[u] my soul.

2 I will praise the LORD all my life;[v]
I will sing praise to my God as long as I live.
3 Do not put your trust in princes,[w]
in human beings,[x] who cannot save.
4 When their spirit departs, they return to the ground;[y]
on that very day their plans come to nothing.[z]
5 Blessed are those[a] whose help[b] is the God of Jacob,
whose hope is in the LORD their God.

6 He is the Maker of heaven[c] and earth,
the sea, and everything in them—
he remains faithful[d] forever.
7 He upholds the cause of the oppressed[e]
and gives food to the hungry.[f]
The LORD sets prisoners free,[g]
8 the LORD gives sight to the blind,[h]
the LORD lifts up those who are bowed down,
the LORD loves the righteous.
9 The LORD watches over the foreigner
and sustains the fatherless and the widow,[i]
but he frustrates the ways of the wicked.

10 The LORD reigns[j] forever,
your God, O Zion, for all generations.

Praise the LORD.

Psalm 147

1 Praise the LORD.[b]

How good it is to sing praises to our God,
how pleasant[k] and fitting to praise him![l]

2 The LORD builds up Jerusalem;[m]
he gathers the exiles[n] of Israel.
3 He heals the brokenhearted
and binds up their wounds.
4 He determines the number of the stars[o]
and calls them each by name.
5 Great is our Lord[p] and mighty in power;
his understanding has no limit.[q]
6 The LORD sustains the humble[r]
but casts the wicked to the ground.

7 Sing to the LORD[s] with grateful praise;
make music to our God on the harp.

8 He covers the sky with clouds;
he supplies the earth with rain[t]
and makes grass grow[u] on the hills.
9 He provides food[v] for the cattle
and for the young ravens[w] when they call.

10 His pleasure is not in the strength[x] of the horse,[y]
nor his delight in the legs of the warrior;
11 the LORD delights in those who fear him,
who put their hope in his unfailing love.

12 Extol the LORD, Jerusalem;
praise your God, Zion.

13 He strengthens the bars of your gates
and blesses your people within you.
14 He grants peace[z] to your borders
and satisfies you[a] with the finest of wheat.

15 He sends his command[b] to the earth;
his word runs swiftly.
16 He spreads the snow[c] like wool
and scatters the frost[d] like ashes.
17 He hurls down his hail like pebbles.
Who can withstand his icy blast?
18 He sends his word[e] and melts them;
he stirs up his breezes, and the waters flow.

---

[a] *1* Hebrew *Hallelu Yah*; also in verse 10
[b] *1* Hebrew *Hallelu Yah*; also in verse 20

146:3 *in princes.* Even the best of people are not adequate help in times of terrible stress.
146:5 *hope.* Most men are aware that there is more in life than they are getting out of it. They try many things to satisfy their desire for a fuller life. But like Solomon, who gives his testimony in the Book of Ecclesiastes, they find that "things" do not satisfy. Blessedness, or fullness of life, comes to those who have a relationship with God and hope of eternal life with Him.
146:10 *reigns forever.* God's reign is both present and eternal.
147:2 *builds up Jerusalem.* The few people who had returned from captivity faced an immense task. They needed to remember that the work was God's and He would see that it was accomplished.
147:3 *heals the brokenhearted.* God's principle work is always within the human heart (51:10–12).
147:6 *sustains the humble.* God's greatness may be approached only by the humble (James 4:6).
147:9 *food for the cattle.* Jesus describes God's care as extending even to sparrows (Matt. 10:29).
147:10 *His pleasure is not.* The joy that God finds in His "very good" creation (Gen. 1) does not compare with the delight that He takes in humans whose hearts are turned to Him.

146:1 [u] Ps 103:1 **146:2** [v] Ps 104:33 **146:3** [w] Ps 118:9 [x] Isa 2:22 **146:4** [y] Ps 104:29; Ecc 12:7 [z] Ps 33:10; 1Co 2:6 **146:5** [a] Ps 144:15; Jer 17:7 [b] Ps 71:5 **146:6** [c] Ps 115:15; Ac 14:15; Rev 14:7 [d] Ps 117:2 **146:7** [e] Ps 103:6 [f] Ps 107:9 [g] Ps 68:6 **146:8** [h] Mt 9:30 **146:9** [i] Ex 22:22; Dt 10:18; Ps 68:5 **146:10** [j] Ex 15:18; Ps 10:16 **147:1** [k] Ps 135:3 [l] Ps 33:1 **147:2** [m] Ps 102:16 [n] Dt 30:3 **147:4** [o] Isa 40:26 **147:5** [p] Ps 48:1 [q] Isa 40:28 **147:6** [r] Ps 146:8-9 **147:7** [s] Ps 33:3 **147:8** [t] Job 38:26 [u] Ps 104:14 **147:9** [v] Ps 104:27-28; Mt 6:26 [w] Job 38:41 **147:10** [x] 1Sa 16:7 [y] Ps 33:16-17 **147:14** [z] Isa 60:17-18 [a] Ps 132:15 **147:15** [b] Job 37:12 **147:16** [c] Job 37:6 [d] Job 38:29 **147:18** [e] Ps 33:9

19 He has revealed his word to Jacob,
his laws and decrees[f] to Israel.
20 He has done this for no other
nation;[g]
they do not know his laws.[a]

Praise the LORD.

Psalm 148

1 Praise the LORD.[b]

Praise the LORD from the heavens;
praise him in the heights above.
2 Praise him, all his angels;[h]
praise him, all his heavenly hosts.
3 Praise him, sun and moon;
praise him, all you shining stars.
4 Praise him, you highest heavens
and you waters above the skies.[i]

5 Let them praise the name of the LORD,
for at his command[j] they were
created,
6 and he established them for ever and
ever—
he issued a decree[k] that will never
pass away.

7 Praise the LORD from the earth,
you great sea creatures[l] and all ocean
depths,
8 lightning and hail, snow and
clouds,
stormy winds that do his
bidding,[m]
9 you mountains and all hills,[n]
fruit trees and all cedars,
10 wild animals and all cattle,
small creatures and flying birds,
11 kings of the earth and all nations,
you princes and all rulers on earth,
12 young men and women,
old men and children.

13 Let them praise the name of the
LORD,[o]
for his name alone is exalted;
his splendor is above the earth and
the heavens.[p]
14 And he has raised up for his people a
horn,[c][q]
the praise of all his faithful servants,
of Israel, the people close to his
heart.

Praise the LORD.

Psalm 149

1 Praise the LORD.[d][r]

Sing to the LORD a new song,
his praise in the assembly[s] of his
faithful people.

2 Let Israel rejoice in their Maker;[t]
let the people of Zion be glad in their
King.[u]
3 Let them praise his name with
dancing
and make music to him with timbrel
and harp.[v]
4 For the LORD takes delight[w] in his
people;
he crowns the humble with victory.[x]
5 Let his faithful people rejoice[y] in this
honor
and sing for joy on their beds.[z]

6 May the praise of God be in their
mouths[a]
and a double-edged[b] sword in their
hands,
7 to inflict vengeance on the nations
and punishment on the peoples,
8 to bind their kings with fetters,
their nobles with shackles of iron,
9 to carry out the sentence written
against them—[c]
this is the glory of all his faithful
people.[d]

Praise the LORD.

[a] *20* Masoretic Text; Dead Sea Scrolls and Septuagint *nation; / he has not made his laws known to them* [b] *1* Hebrew *Hallelu Yah*; also in verse 14 [c] *14 Horn* here symbolizes strength.
[d] *1* Hebrew *Hallelu Yah*; also in verse 9

147:19 *his word.* God's word goes throughout His creation, causing snow, frost, hail, wind, and every other aspect of weather to obey His command. He has also given His Word to His people. Will we obey as the wind does, or will we be the only element of creation that is unresponsive to Him?
148:5 *at his command they were created.* The reality of God as Creator of the universe is the basis of His claim on our lives.
148:14 *the people close to his heart.* When we consider the meaning of God's holiness (99:1; Is. 6:3) and the reality of His power, the marvel that He approaches us to mercifully provide for us becomes overwhelming.
149:1 *in the assembly.* One of the primary emphases in the Book of Psalms is that the praise of God is to take place in the center of the worshiping community. Praise unites the people of God (33:1 – 3).
149:5 *faithful people.* This term (also translated "godly ones") refers to those who demonstrate in their lives the characteristics of the God whom they serve.
149:6 *double-edged sword.* The focus of the psalm switches from the congregation at worship to the army in training. Israel's army was to be the vanguard for the battle of the Lord. Their training was to have a strong component of praise and worship to God.

147:19 [f] Dt 33:4; Mal 4:4 **147:20** [g] Dt 4:7-8, 32-34 **148:2** [h] Ps 103:20 **148:4** [i] Ge 1:7; 1Ki 8:27 **148:5** [j] Ge 1:1,6; Ps 33:6,9 **148:6** [k] Job 38:33; Ps 89:37; Jer 33:25 **148:7** [l] Ps 74:13-14 **148:8** [m] Ps 147:15-18 **148:9** [n] Isa 44:23; 49:13; 55:12 **148:13** [o] Isa 12:4 [p] Ps 8:1; 113:4 **148:14** [q] Ps 75:10 **149:1** [r] Ps 33:2 [s] Ps 35:18 **149:2** [t] Ps 95:6 [u] Ps 47:6; Zec 9:9 **149:3** [v] Ps 81:2; 150:4 **149:4** [w] Ps 35:27 [x] Ps 132:16 **149:5** [y] Ps 132:16 [z] Job 35:10 **149:6** [a] Ps 66:17 [b] Heb 4:12; Rev 1:16 **149:9** [c] Dt 7:1; Eze 28:26 [d] Ps 148:14

Psalm 150

1 Praise the LORD.[a]

Praise God in his sanctuary;[e]
praise him in his mighty heavens.[f]
2 Praise him for his acts of power;[g]
praise him for his surpassing greatness.[h]
3 Praise him with the sounding of the trumpet,
praise him with the harp and lyre,[i]
4 praise him with timbrel and dancing,[j]
praise him with the strings[k] and pipe,
5 praise him with the clash of cymbals,[l]
praise him with resounding cymbals.

6 Let everything[m] that has breath praise the LORD.

Praise the LORD.

[a] *1* Hebrew *Hallelu Yah*; also in verse 6

150:1 *Praise the LORD.* This psalm is a development of the Hebrew word "hallelujah," meaning "praise the Lord." **Praise** — To praise God is to acknowledge who He is in all His glory. While thanksgiving is given to acknowledge what God has done, praise is given to declare who God is. Here are some facts about praise:

- God alone is worthy of our praise (Ps. 18:3; 113:3).
- It is His will for us to praise Him (Ps. 50:23)
- Praise should be continuous (Ps. 34:1; 71:6) and also public (Ps. 22:25).
- We are to praise God for His holiness (2 Chr. 20:21), grace (Eph. 1:6), goodness (Ps. 135:3), and kindness (Ps. 138:2).
- All nature praises God (Ps. 148).
- The sun, moon, and stars praise Him (Ps. 19:1).
- The angels praise Him (Ps. 148:2).

150:6 *everything that has breath.* The very breath that God gives us should be used to praise Him. As long as we live we should praise our Creator (146:1 – 2). By His breath God created all things (33:6), and by our breath we should adore Him. The Book of Psalms begins with God's blessing on the righteous (1:1) and concludes with all of creation blessing its loving Creator.

150:1 [e] Ps 102:19 [f] Ps 19:1 **150:2** [g] Dt 3:24 [h] Ps 145:5-6 **150:3** [i] Ps 149:3 **150:4** [j] Ex 15:20 [k] Isa 38:20 **150:5** [l] 1Ch 13:8; 15:16 **150:6** [m] Ps 145:21

PROVERBS

▶ **AUTHOR:** Solomon's name appears at the beginning of the three sections that he wrote: 1–9; 10:1—22:16; and 25–29. Only about 800 of the more than 3000 proverbs attributed to Solomon are recorded here. It is likely that Solomon collected and edited proverbs other than his own. The collection of Solomonic proverbs in chapters 25–29 was assembled by the scribes of King Hezekiah. Some of the sayings in Proverbs are quite similar to those found in *The Wisdom of Amenemope*, a document of teachings on civil service by an Egyptian who probably lived between 1000 B.C. and 600 B.C.

▶ **TIME:** c. 950–700 B.C. ▶ **KEY VERSES:** Prov. 3:5–6

▶ **THEME:** The Proverbs are part of what is commonly called the wisdom literature of the Bible. Each society needs a way to pass on what it understands to be the best way to live to succeeding generations. Biblical wisdom literature provided that means for the Jewish community. The Proverbs contain nuggets of truth that endure not only in the Jewish culture, but also make sense today. It contains basic wisdom on how to deal with the most common every day issues that we face. Transcending personality and culture, the simple truth is that if people followed the advice of Proverbs, many of their problems would be reduced dramatically.

Purpose and Theme

1 The proverbs of Solomon[a] son of David,
king of Israel:[b]

2 for gaining wisdom and instruction;
for understanding words of insight;
3 for receiving instruction in prudent behavior,
doing what is right and just and fair;
4 for giving prudence to those who are simple,[ac]
knowledge and discretion[d] to the young—
5 let the wise listen and add to their learning,[e]
and let the discerning get guidance—
6 for understanding proverbs and parables,[f]
the sayings and riddles[g] of the wise.[b]
7 The fear of the LORD[h] is the beginning of knowledge,
but fools[c] despise wisdom and instruction.

Prologue: Exhortations to Embrace Wisdom

Warning Against the Invitation of Sinful Men

8 Listen, my son,[i] to your father's instruction
and do not forsake your mother's teaching.[j]

[a] 4 The Hebrew word rendered *simple* in Proverbs denotes a person who is gullible, without moral direction and inclined to evil.
[b] 6 Or *understanding a proverb, namely, a parable, / and the sayings of the wise, their riddles*
[c] 7 The Hebrew words rendered *fool* in Proverbs, and often elsewhere in the Old Testament, denote a person who is morally deficient.

1:2–3 ***for gaining ... for understanding ... for receiving.*** These verbs refer to the ways we acquire wisdom. Wisdom refers to skill. Instruction could also be translated discipline; it refers to the process of receiving knowledge and applying it to daily life.
1:3 ***right and just and fair.*** Biblical wisdom also has a moral context. It involves all of life and may often involve a change of behavior and a commitment to justice.
1:4 ***knowledge and discretion to the young.*** The young have little experience and are more likely to make mistakes. A wise person has learned by experience how to distinguish what is true, praiseworthy, and good from what is false, shameful, and bad (Rom. 12:1–2).
1:7 ***The fear of the LORD.*** This concept is the most basic ingredient in wisdom. Fools have rejected the fear of the Lord. The term "despise" is strongly negative. Not fearing God is the same as rejecting wisdom outright (Dan. 11:32; John 17:3).
1:8 ***Listen, my son.*** The opening words of wisdom's

1:1 [a] 1Ki 4:29-34 [b] Pr 10:1; 25:1; Ecc 1:1 **1:4** [c] Pr 8:5 [d] Pr 2:10-11; 8:12 **1:5** [e] Pr 9:9 **1:6** [f] Ps 49:4; 78:2 [g] Nu 12:8 **1:7** [h] Job 28:28; Ps 111:10; Pr 9:10; 15:33; Ecc 12:13 **1:8** [i] Pr 4:1 [j] Pr 6:20

9 They are a garland to grace your head
and a chain to adorn your neck.[k]
10 My son, if sinful men entice[l] you,
do not give in[m] to them.[n]
11 If they say, "Come along with us;
let's lie in wait[o] for innocent blood,
let's ambush some harmless soul;
12 let's swallow them alive, like the grave,
and whole, like those who go down to the pit;[p]
13 we will get all sorts of valuable things
and fill our houses with plunder;
14 cast lots with us;
we will all share the loot"—
15 my son, do not go along with them,
do not set foot[q] on their paths;[r]
16 for their feet rush into evil,
they are swift to shed blood.[s]
17 How useless to spread a net
where every bird can see it!
18 These men lie in wait for their own blood;
they ambush only themselves!
19 Such are the paths of all who go after ill-gotten gain;
it takes away the life of those who get it.[t]

Wisdom's Rebuke

20 Out in the open wisdom calls aloud,[u]
she raises her voice in the public square;
21 on top of the wall[a] she cries out,
at the city gate she makes her speech:

22 "How long will you who are simple[v]
love your simple ways?
How long will mockers delight in mockery
and fools hate knowledge?
23 Repent at my rebuke!
Then I will pour out my thoughts to you,
I will make known to you my teachings.
24 But since you refuse to listen when I call[w]
and no one pays attention when I stretch out my hand,
25 since you disregard all my advice
and do not accept my rebuke,
26 I in turn will laugh[x] when disaster strikes you;
I will mock when calamity overtakes you[y]—
27 when calamity overtakes you like a storm,
when disaster sweeps over you like a whirlwind,
when distress and trouble overwhelm you.

28 "Then they will call to me but I will not answer;[z]
they will look for me but will not find me,[a]
29 since they hated knowledge
and did not choose to fear the LORD.[b]
30 Since they would not accept my advice
and spurned my rebuke,[c]
31 they will eat the fruit of their ways
and be filled with the fruit of their schemes.[d]
32 For the waywardness of the simple will kill them,
and the complacency of fools will destroy them;[e]

[a] *21* Septuagint; Hebrew / *at noisy street corners*

instruction come as an appeal from parent to son (a generic term for child)—a theme that continues throughout the book. Both the Old and New Testament have one central teaching for children to understand—obey your parents. The Fifth Commandment makes honoring parents the foundational teaching in human relationships. It is also the only Commandment that comes with a promise, "that you may live long" (Deut. 5:16). Paul's teaching in Ephesians 6:1 echoes what we see here in Proverbs. Obeying parents is the right thing to do.

From obedience springs the ability to deal with all the other important issues of life. The child who has not learned to obey his parents, who are God's representatives in the family, will probably not learn to obey God.

Christ's obedience is the perfect illustration. He was obedient to God the Father even though that obedience resulted in His death (Phil. 2:6–8). Being obedient for Christ meant no qualifications or limitations on that obedience.

1:15–18 *my son, do not go along with them.* The parents speak words of caution. One step on the precipitous path is a step toward destruction. Spreading a net in the sight of the bird one wishes to trap would be a fruitless task. Yet the fool is less sensible than the bird; he will watch the trap being set and get caught in it anyway.

1:19 *takes away the life.* The study of wisdom is a matter of life and death.

1:20–21 *Out in the open wisdom calls aloud.* The word *wisdom* is plural and intensive. This fact calls attention to the word and heightens its meaning.

1:22–27 *How long will you who are simple love your simple ways?* Wisdom addresses the *naive* ones. These are young people who have not yet made up their minds about life or the direction they will take. Wisdom ridicules those who reject her when they come to face the inevitable judgment of their foolishness (Ps. 2:4). Yet wisdom also laughs with joy at God's work and has delight in the people of God (8:30–31).

1:28–33 *I will not answer.* When fools despise wisdom, they must face the results of their choice. Their hatred for wisdom arises out of refusal to fear

1:9 [k] Pr 4:1-9 **1:10** [l] Ge 39:7 [m] Dt 13:8 [n] Pr 16:29; Eph 5:11 **1:11** [o] Ps 10:8 **1:12** [p] Ps 28:1 **1:15** [q] Ps 119:101 [r] Ps 1:1; Pr 4:14 **1:16** [s] Pr 6:18; Isa 59:7 **1:19** [t] Pr 15:27 **1:20** [u] Pr 8:1; 9:1-3, 13-15 **1:22** [v] Pr 8:5; 9:4, 16 **1:24** [w] Isa 65:12; 66:4; Jer 7:13; Zec 7:11 **1:26** [x] Ps 2:4 [y] Pr 6:15; 10:24 **1:28** [z] 1Sa 8:18; Isa 1:15; Jer 11:11; Mic 3:4 [a] Job 27:9; Pr 8:17; Eze 8:18; Zec 7:13 **1:29** [b] Job 21:14 **1:30** [c] ver 25; Ps 81:11 **1:31** [d] Job 4:8; Pr 14:14; Isa 3:11; Jer 6:19 **1:32** [e] Jer 2:19

33 but whoever listens to me will live in
safety[f]
and be at ease, without fear of harm."[g]

Moral Benefits of Wisdom

2 My son, if you accept my words
and store up my commands within
you,
2 turning your ear to wisdom
and applying your heart to
understanding[h]—
3 indeed, if you call out for insight
and cry aloud for understanding,
4 and if you look for it as for silver
and search for it as for hidden
treasure,[i]
5 then you will understand the fear of the
LORD
and find the knowledge of God.[j]
6 For the LORD gives wisdom;[k]
from his mouth come knowledge and
understanding.
7 He holds success in store for the
upright,
he is a shield[l] to those whose walk is
blameless,[m]
8 for he guards the course of the just
and protects the way of his faithful
ones.[n]

9 Then you will understand what is right
and just
and fair—every good path.
10 For wisdom will enter your heart,[o]
and knowledge will be pleasant to
your soul.
11 Discretion will protect you,
and understanding will guard you.[p]

12 Wisdom will save you from the ways of
wicked men,
from men whose words are perverse,
13 who have left the straight paths
to walk in dark ways,[q]
14 who delight in doing wrong
and rejoice in the perverseness of
evil,[r]
15 whose paths are crooked[s]
and who are devious in their ways.[t]

16 Wisdom will save you also from the
adulterous woman,[u]
from the wayward woman with her
seductive words,
17 who has left the partner of her youth
and ignored the covenant she made
before God.[a][v]
18 Surely her house leads down to death
and her paths to the spirits of the
dead.[w]
19 None who go to her return
or attain the paths of life.[x]

20 Thus you will walk in the ways of the
good
and keep to the paths of the
righteous.
21 For the upright will live in the land,[y]
and the blameless will remain in it;
22 but the wicked will be cut off from the
land,[z]
and the unfaithful will be torn from it.[a]

Wisdom Bestows Well-Being

3 My son, do not forget my teaching,[b]
but keep my commands in your
heart,
2 for they will prolong your life many
years[c]
and bring you peace and prosperity.

3 Let love and faithfulness never leave
you;
bind them around your neck,
write them on the tablet of your
heart.[d]
4 Then you will win favor and a good
name
in the sight of God and man.[e]

5 Trust in the LORD[f] with all your heart
and lean not on your own
understanding;

---

[a] 17 Or *covenant of her God*

God (v. 29). Fools bring about their own destruction. In contrast, those who listen to her will find security.

2:1–5 *My son.* These verses begin the second of the "my son" passages and tie the concepts of wisdom and the knowledge of God more closely together. Wisdom is near but not always easy to embrace.

2:5–8 *the fear of the LORD ... the knowledge of God.* When a person seeks wisdom, he or she finds it. Those who know God fear or revere Him. ***success.*** This is another word for wisdom that can also mean "victory."

2:10–11 *wisdom will enter your heart.* This phrase stresses the internalization of wisdom. The proverbs do not merely provide knowledge; they provide insight into practical living.

2:12–15 *the ways of wicked men.* Evil is directly contrasted with wisdom. It is characterized by perverse things such as lies, deceptions, and deviousness.

2:16–19 *the adulterous woman.* The adulteress is described as a flatterer, and flattery is the method used by the adulteress, not only in trapping her victims, but in excusing her sin (30:20). She is unfaithful to her husband and prefers to forget the covenant of her God (2:17).

3:3–4 *love and faithfulness.* These words describe God's character (Ps. 100:5). The apostle John used the Greek equivalent of these words, "grace and truth," to describe Jesus' character in John 1:14.

3:5–6 *Trust in the LORD.* The verb "trust" is complemented by the verb "lean." Trusting in God is a conscious dependence on God, much like leaning on a

1:33 [f] Ps 25:12; Pr 3:23 [g] Ps 112:8 **2:2** [h] Pr 22:17 **2:4** [i] Job 3:21; Pr 3:14; Mt 13:44 **2:5** [j] Pr 1:7 **2:6** [k] 1Ki 3:9, 12; Jas 1:5 **2:7** [l] Pr 30:5-6 [m] Ps 84:11 **2:8** [n] 1Sa 2:9; Ps 66:9 **2:10** [o] Pr 14:33 **2:11** [p] Pr 4:6; 6:22 **2:13** [q] Pr 4:19; Jn 3:19 **2:14** [r] Pr 10:23; Jer 11:15 **2:15** [s] Ps 125:5 [t] Pr 21:8 **2:16** [u] Pr 5:1-6; 6:20-29; 7:5-27 **2:17** [v] Mal 2:14 **2:18** [w] Pr 7:27 **2:19** [x] Ecc 7:26 **2:21** [y] Ps 37:29 **2:22** [z] Job 18:17; Ps 37:38 [a] Dt 28:63; Pr 10:30 **3:1** [b] Pr 4:5 **3:2** [c] Pr 4:10 **3:3** [d] Ex 13:9; Pr 6:21; 7:3; 2Co 3:3 **3:4** [e] 1Sa 2:26; Lk 2:52 **3:5** [f] Ps 37:3, 5

6 in all your ways submit to him,
and he will make your paths[g] straight.[a][h]
7 Do not be wise in your own eyes;[i]
fear the LORD and shun evil.[j]
8 This will bring health to your body[k]
and nourishment to your bones.[l]
9 Honor the LORD with your wealth,
with the firstfruits[m] of all your crops;
10 then your barns will be filled[n] to overflowing,
and your vats will brim over with new wine.[o]

11 My son, do not despise the LORD's discipline,[p]
and do not resent his rebuke,
12 because the LORD disciplines those he loves,[q]
as a father the son he delights in.[b][r]

13 Blessed are those who find wisdom,
those who gain understanding,
14 for she is more profitable than silver
and yields better returns than gold.[s]
15 She is more precious than rubies;[t]
nothing you desire can compare with her.[u]
16 Long life is in her right hand;
in her left hand are riches and honor.[v]
17 Her ways are pleasant ways,
and all her paths are peace.[w]
18 She is a tree of life[x] to those who take hold of her;
those who hold her fast will be blessed.

19 By wisdom the LORD laid the earth's foundations,[y]
by understanding he set the heavens[z] in place;
20 by his knowledge the watery depths were divided,
and the clouds let drop the dew.

21 My son, do not let wisdom and understanding out of your sight,[a]
preserve sound judgment and discretion;
22 they will be life for you,
an ornament to grace your neck.[b]
23 Then you will go on your way in safety,
and your foot will not stumble.[c]
24 When you lie down,[d] you will not be afraid;
when you lie down, your sleep[e] will be sweet.
25 Have no fear of sudden disaster
or of the ruin that overtakes the wicked,
26 for the LORD will be at your side
and will keep your foot[f] from being snared.

27 Do not withhold good from those to whom it is due,
when it is in your power to act.
28 Do not say to your neighbor,
"Come back tomorrow and I'll give it to you"—
when you already have it with you.[g]
29 Do not plot harm against your neighbor,
who lives trustfully near you.
30 Do not accuse anyone for no reason—
when they have done you no harm.

31 Do not envy[h] the violent
or choose any of their ways.

32 For the LORD detests the perverse[i]
but takes the upright into his confidence.[j]
33 The LORD's curse[k] is on the house of the wicked,[l]
but he blesses the home of the righteous.[m]
34 He mocks proud mockers
but shows favor to the humble[n] and oppressed.
35 The wise inherit honor,
but fools get only shame.

---

[a] 6 Or *will direct your paths* [b] 12 Hebrew; Septuagint *loves, / and he chastens everyone he accepts as his child*

---

tree for support. The command to acknowledge Him means to observe Him and get to know Him in the process of living. These are the vital elements of faith that should fill every area of life.

3:9 *the firstfruits of all your crops.* God expects that out of the blessings we receive we should readily give. One aspect of worship is giving. These verses should not be taken as a formula for getting rich. They point to what is the proper response to God's gifts to us, not a return we get for investing.

3:11–12 *the LORD's discipline.* Discipline is the other side of God's grace. We should cherish God's correction in our lives, because God disciplines those he loves (Heb. 2:7–10)

3:13–18 *Blessed.* The Beatitudes of Jesus in the Sermon on the Mount (Matt. 5:3–12) work much the way these verses do. God is pleased with people who discover that wisdom is a priceless treasure.

3:19 *by wisdom . . . laid the earth's foundations.* One of the central themes in Proverbs is the association of wisdom with creation (8:1–36).

3:21 *do not let . . . out of your sight.* This verse encourages the son to keep faith with wisdom. The intent is much like that of the Shema (Deut. 6:4–9).

3:6 [g] 1Ch 28:9 [h] Pr 16:3; Isa 45:13 **3:7** [i] Ro 12:16 [j] Job 1:1; Pr 16:6 **3:8** [k] Pr 4:22 [l] Job 21:24 **3:9** [m] Ex 22:29; 23:19; Dt 26:1-15 **3:10** [n] Dt 28:8 [o] Joel 2:24 **3:11** [p] Job 5:17 **3:12** [q] Pr 13:24; Rev 3:19 [r] Dt 8:5; Heb 12:5-6* **3:14** [s] Job 28:15; Pr 8:19; 16:16 **3:15** [t] Job 28:18 [u] Pr 8:11 **3:16** [v] Pr 8:18 **3:17** [w] Pr 16:7; Mt 11:28-30 **3:18** [x] Ge 2:9; Pr 11:30; Rev 2:7 **3:19** [y] Ps 104:24 [z] Pr 8:27-29 **3:21** [a] Pr 4:20-22 **3:22** [b] Pr 1:8-9 **3:23** [c] Ps 37:24; Pr 4:12 **3:24** [d] Lev 26:6; Ps 3:5 [e] Job 11:18 **3:26** [f] 1Sa 2:9 **3:28** [g] Lev 19:13; Dt 24:15 **3:31** [h] Ps 37:1; Pr 24:1-2 **3:32** [i] Pr 11:20 [j] Job 29:4; Ps 25:14 **3:33** [k] Dt 11:28; Mal 2:2 [l] Zec 5:4 [m] Ps 1:3 **3:34** [n] Jas 4:6*; 1Pe 5:5*

Get Wisdom at Any Cost

4 Listen, my sons,[o] to a father's
instruction;
pay attention and gain
understanding.
2 I give you sound learning,
so do not forsake my teaching.
3 For I too was a son to my father,
still tender, and cherished by my
mother.
4 Then he taught me, and he said to me,
"Take hold of my words with all your
heart;
keep my commands, and you will
live.[p]
5 Get wisdom,[q] get understanding;
do not forget my words or turn away
from them.
6 Do not forsake wisdom, and she will
protect you;[r]
love her, and she will watch over you.
7 The beginning of wisdom is this: Get[a]
wisdom.
Though it cost all[s] you have,[b] get
understanding.[t]
8 Cherish her, and she will exalt you;
embrace her, and she will honor
you.[u]
9 She will give you a garland to grace
your head
and present you with a glorious
crown.[v]"
10 Listen, my son, accept what I say,
and the years of your life will be
many.[w]
11 I instruct[x] you in the way of wisdom
and lead you along straight paths.
12 When you walk, your steps will not be
hampered;
when you run, you will not stumble.[y]
13 Hold on to instruction, do not let it go;
guard it well, for it is your life.[z]
14 Do not set foot on the path of the
wicked
or walk in the way of evildoers.[a]
15 Avoid it, do not travel on it;
turn from it and go on your way.
16 For they cannot rest until they do evil;[b]
they are robbed of sleep till they
make someone stumble.
17 They eat the bread of wickedness
and drink the wine of violence.
18 The path of the righteous[c] is like the
morning sun,
shining ever brighter till the full light
of day.[d]
19 But the way of the wicked is like deep
darkness;[e]
they do not know what makes them
stumble.
20 My son, pay attention to what I say;
turn your ear to my words.[f]
21 Do not let them out of your sight,[g]
keep them within your heart;
22 for they are life to those who find them
and health to one's whole body.[h]
23 Above all else, guard your heart,
for everything you do flows from it.[i]
24 Keep your mouth free of perversity;
keep corrupt talk far from your lips.
25 Let your eyes look straight ahead;
fix your gaze directly before you.
26 Give careful thought to the[c] paths for
your feet[j]
and be steadfast in all your ways.
27 Do not turn to the right or the left;[k]
keep your foot from evil.

Warning Against Adultery

5 My son, pay attention to my wisdom,
turn your ear to my words[l] of
insight,
2 that you may maintain discretion
and your lips may preserve
knowledge.
3 For the lips of the adulterous woman
drip honey,
and her speech is smoother than oil;[m]
4 but in the end she is bitter as gall,[n]
sharp as a double-edged sword.

[a] 7 Or *Wisdom is supreme; therefore get*
[b] 7 Or *wisdom. / Whatever else you get*
[c] 26 Or *Make level*

4:1–4 *I too was a son to my father.* In Israel training in wisdom happened in the home. As his father had taught him, so the son now teaches his own sons, one generation instructing another. The call for parents to teach the things of God to their children is based on Deuteronomy 6:7.
4:5–7 *Get wisdom.* Verses 5–9 present an impassioned plea from the father to his sons to acquire wisdom whatever the cost. The presentation follows a pattern: statement, restatement, embellishment. By making generous use of creative restatement, the ideas come through strongly.
4:9 *garland to grace ... a glorious crown.* These phrases emphasize the supreme value of wisdom. The person who holds wisdom in highest esteem and embraces it will be exalted and honored.
4:20–27 *Above all else, guard your heart.* This section demands constancy of heart and purpose, honesty in speech, steadiness of gaze, and a right goal in walk and life. Setting off on the path of wisdom is no casual thing.
5:1–6 *the lips of the adulterous woman drip honey.* Chapter 5 returns to the theme of the immoral woman (2:16–19). This passage speaks strongly for marital fidelity against all pressure to the contrary.

4:1 [o] Pr 1:8 **4:4** [p] Pr 7:2 **4:5** [q] Pr 16:16 **4:6** [r] 2Th 2:10 **4:7** [s] Mt 13:44-46 [t] Pr 23:23 **4:8** [u] 1Sa 2:30; Pr 3:18 **4:9** [v] Pr 1:8-9 **4:10** [w] Pr 3:2 **4:11** [x] 1Sa 12:23 **4:12** [y] Job 18:7; Pr 3:23 **4:13** [z] Pr 3:22 **4:14** [a] Ps 1:1; Pr 1:15 **4:16** [b] Ps 36:4; Mic 2:1 **4:18** [c] Isa 26:7 [d] 2Sa 23:4; Da 12:3; Mt 5:14; Php 2:15 **4:19** [e] Job 18:5; Pr 2:13; Isa 59:9-10; Jn 12:35 **4:20** [f] Pr 5:1 **4:21** [g] Pr 3:21; 7:1-2 **4:22** [h] Pr 3:8; 12:18 **4:23** [i] Mt 12:34; Lk 6:45 **4:26** [j] Heb 12:13* **4:27** [k] Dt 5:32; 28:14 **5:1** [l] Pr 4:20; 22:17 **5:3** [m] Ps 55:21; Pr 2:16; 7:5 **5:4** [n] Ecc 7:26

[5]Her feet go down to death;
her steps lead straight to the grave.[o]
[6]She gives no thought to the way of life;
her paths wander aimlessly, but she does not know it.[p]

[7]Now then, my sons, listen[q] to me;
do not turn aside from what I say.
[8]Keep to a path far from her,[r]
do not go near the door of her house,
[9]lest you lose your honor to others
and your dignity[a] to one who is cruel,
[10]lest strangers feast on your wealth
and your toil enrich the house of another.
[11]At the end of your life you will groan,
when your flesh and body are spent.
[12]You will say, "How I hated discipline!
How my heart spurned correction![s]
[13]I would not obey my teachers
or turn my ear to my instructors.
[14]And I was soon in serious trouble
in the assembly of God's people."

[15]Drink water from your own cistern,
running water from your own well.
[16]Should your springs overflow in the streets,
your streams of water in the public squares?
[17]Let them be yours alone,
never to be shared with strangers.
[18]May your fountain[t] be blessed,
and may you rejoice in the wife of your youth.[u]
[19]A loving doe, a graceful deer[v]—
may her breasts satisfy you always,
may you ever be intoxicated with her love.
[20]Why, my son, be intoxicated with another man's wife?
Why embrace the bosom of a wayward woman?

[21]For your ways are in full view[w] of the LORD,
and he examines all your paths.[x]
[22]The evil deeds of the wicked ensnare them;[y]
the cords of their sins hold them fast.[z]
[23]For lack of discipline they will die,[a]
led astray by their own great folly.

Warnings Against Folly

6 My son, if you have put up security for your neighbor,[b]
if you have shaken hands in pledge[c] for a stranger,
[2]you have been trapped by what you said,
ensnared by the words of your mouth.
[3]So do this, my son, to free yourself,
since you have fallen into your neighbor's hands:
Go—to the point of exhaustion—[b]
and give your neighbor no rest!
[4]Allow no sleep to your eyes,
no slumber to your eyelids.[d]
[5]Free yourself, like a gazelle from the hand of the hunter,
like a bird from the snare of the fowler.[e]

[6]Go to the ant, you sluggard;[f]
consider its ways and be wise!
[7]It has no commander,
no overseer or ruler,
[8]yet it stores its provisions in summer
and gathers its food at harvest.[g]

[9]How long will you lie there, you sluggard?[h]
When will you get up from your sleep?
[10]A little sleep, a little slumber,
a little folding of the hands to rest[i]—
[11]and poverty[j] will come on you like a thief
and scarcity like an armed man.

[12]A troublemaker and a villain,
who goes about with a corrupt mouth,
[13]who winks maliciously with his eye,[k]
signals with his feet
and motions with his fingers,

[a] 9 Or *years* [b] 3 Or *Go and humble yourself,*

5:5 *Her feet go down to death.* This verse warns us of the deadly effects of immorality. Fornication, adultery, and prostitution lead to personality decay, venereal disease, abortion, separation, and divorce.
5:8–10 *Keep to a path far from her.* Some temptations should be avoided at all cost. A wise son knows this and will not go near an immoral woman. The apostle Paul's instruction to Timothy to flee youthful lusts (2 Tim. 2:22) teaches the same theme.
5:15 *Drink water from your own cistern.* This image is a clear call to marital fidelity.
5:18 *and may you rejoice in the wife of your youth.* We are encouraged to find mutual joy and pleasure in the marriage bed. It is in fact blessed by God.
6:1 *if you have put up security for your neighbor.* This phrase refers to responsibility for someone else's debt as in cosigning a loan. This does not mean we should never be generous, only that we should not promise what we cannot deliver.
6:6 *Go to the ant, you sluggard.* This passage is a warning about laziness. The sluggard is a lazy person who is captive to leisure. He can learn all he needs to know by studying the work habits of the ant.
6:12 *A troublemaker and a villain.* Unlike the sluggard, whose only desire is to take a nap, the troublemaker cannot wait to cause more problems. He delights in creating dissension.

5:5 [o] Pr 7:26-27 **5:6** [p] Pr 30:20 **5:7** [q] Pr 7:24 **5:8** [r] Pr 7:1-27 **5:12** [s] Pr 1:29; 12:1 **5:18** [t] SS 4:12-15 [u] Ecc 9:9; Mal 2:14 **5:19** [v] SS 2:9; 4:5 **5:21** [w] Ps 119:168; Hos 7:2 [x] Job 14:16; Job 31:4; 34:21; Pr 15:3; Jer 16:17; 32:19; Heb 4:13 **5:22** [y] Ps 9:16 [z] Nu 32:23; Ps 7:15-16; Pr 1:31-32 **5:23** [a] Job 4:21; 36:12 **6:1** [b] Pr 17:18 [c] Pr 11:15; 22:26-27 **6:4** [d] Ps 132:4 **6:5** [e] Ps 91:3 **6:6** [f] Pr 20:4 **6:8** [g] Pr 10:4 **6:9** [h] Pr 24:30-34 **6:10** [i] Pr 24:33 **6:11** [j] Pr 24:30-34 **6:13** [k] Ps 35:19

14 who plots evil[l] with deceit in his heart—
he always stirs up conflict.[m]
15 Therefore disaster will overtake him in an instant;
he will suddenly be destroyed—without remedy.[n]

16 There are six things the LORD hates,
seven that are detestable to him:
17 haughty eyes,
a lying tongue,[o]
hands that shed innocent blood,[p]
18 a heart that devises wicked schemes,
feet that are quick to rush into evil,[q]
19 a false witness[r] who pours out lies
and a person who stirs up conflict in the community.[s]

Warning Against Adultery

20 My son, keep your father's command
and do not forsake your mother's teaching.[t]
21 Bind them always on your heart;
fasten them around your neck.[u]
22 When you walk, they will guide you;
when you sleep, they will watch over you;
when you awake, they will speak to you.
23 For this command is a lamp,
this teaching is a light,[v]
and correction and instruction
are the way to life,
24 keeping you from your neighbor's wife,
from the smooth talk of a wayward woman.[w]

25 Do not lust in your heart after her beauty
or let her captivate you with her eyes.
26 For a prostitute can be had for a loaf of bread,
but another man's wife preys on your very life.[x]
27 Can a man scoop fire into his lap
without his clothes being burned?
28 Can a man walk on hot coals
without his feet being scorched?
29 So is he who sleeps[y] with another man's wife;[z]
no one who touches her will go unpunished.

30 People do not despise a thief if he steals
to satisfy his hunger when he is starving.
31 Yet if he is caught, he must pay sevenfold,[a]
though it costs him all the wealth of his house.
32 But a man who commits adultery[b] has no sense;[c]
whoever does so destroys himself.
33 Blows and disgrace are his lot,
and his shame will never[d] be wiped away.

34 For jealousy[e] arouses a husband's fury,[f]
and he will show no mercy when he takes revenge.
35 He will not accept any compensation;
he will refuse a bribe, however great it is.[g]

Warning Against the Adulterous Woman

7 My son,[h] keep my words
and store up my commands within you.
2 Keep my commands and you will live;[i]
guard my teachings as the apple of your eye.
3 Bind them on your fingers;
write them on the tablet of your heart.[j]

6:16 *seven that are detestable to him.* The use of numerical progression—six, even seven—in these proverbs is a rhetorical device that embellishes the poetry and serves as a memory aid. It gives the impression that there is more to be said about the topic. The word "detestable" is the Bible's strongest expression of hatred for wickedness.

6:23 Illumination of God's Word—Illumination is the last of three important steps that God takes to communicate with us. The first step is revelation which occurred when God spoke to the authors of the Bible. The second step was inspiration, which is the process God used to guide them in correctly writing down His message. The third step provides understanding as men and women hear and see God's message. It is a divine process whereby God causes the written revelation to be understood by the human heart.

Christians need this illumination because we are blinded by our fallen fleshly natures (1 Cor. 2:14) and by Satan himself (2 Cor. 4:3–4). The Holy Spirit is the one who illumines us (John 14:26). We see this illumination process at work in Acts 2 when over 3,000 people respond to Peter's message and become followers of Christ. Christians also need this illumination on a day to day basis to help them fully grasp the marvelous message in God's Word. Paul tells us that the Holy Spirit will show these tremendous truths to us as we read the Scriptures (1 Cor. 2:10; 2 Cor. 4:6).

6:30 *if he steals to satisfy his hunger ... starving.* This passage is not condoning theft. It merely contrasts theft with adultery, which never makes sense. For ancient Israelites, marital fidelity was a mark of one's fidelity to God.

7:1–5 *as the apple of your eye.* People should guard wise words as instinctively as they protect the pupil of the eye.

6:14 [l] Mic 2:1 [m] ver 16-19 **6:15** [n] 2Ch 36:16
6:17 [o] Ps 120:2; Pr 12:22 [p] Dt 19:10; Isa 1:15; 59:7
6:18 [q] Ge 6:5 **6:19** [r] Ps 27:12 [s] ver 12-15 **6:20** [t] Pr 1:8
6:21 [u] Pr 3:3; 7:1-3 **6:23** [v] Ps 19:8; 119:105
6:24 [w] Pr 2:16; 7:5 **6:26** [x] Pr 7:22-23; 29:3
6:29 [y] Ex 20:14 [z] Pr 2:16-19; 5:8 **6:31** [a] Ex 22:1-14
6:32 [b] Ex 20:14 [c] Pr 7:7; 9:4, 16 **6:33** [d] Pr 5:9-14
6:34 [e] Nu 5:14 [f] Ge 34:7 **6:35** [g] Job 31:9-11; SS 8:7
7:1 [h] Pr 1:8; 2:1 **7:2** [i] Pr 4:4 **7:3** [j] Dt 6:8; Pr 3:3

4 Say to wisdom, "You are my sister,"
and to insight, "You are my relative."
5 They will keep you from the adulterous woman,
from the wayward woman with her seductive words.[k]

6 At the window of my house
I looked down through the lattice.
7 I saw among the simple,
I noticed among the young men,
a youth who had no sense.[l]
8 He was going down the street near her corner,
walking along in the direction of her house
9 at twilight,[m] as the day was fading,
as the dark of night set in.

10 Then out came a woman to meet him,
dressed like a prostitute and with crafty intent.
11 (She is unruly[n] and defiant,
her feet never stay at home;
12 now in the street, now in the squares,
at every corner she lurks.)[o]
13 She took hold of him[p] and kissed him
and with a brazen face she said:[q]

14 "Today I fulfilled my vows,
and I have food from my fellowship offering[r] at home.
15 So I came out to meet you;
I looked for you and have found you!
16 I have covered my bed
with colored linens from Egypt.
17 I have perfumed my bed[s]
with myrrh,[t] aloes and cinnamon.
18 Come, let's drink deeply of love till morning;
let's enjoy ourselves with love![u]
19 My husband is not at home;
he has gone on a long journey.
20 He took his purse filled with money
and will not be home till full moon."

21 With persuasive words she led him astray;
she seduced him with her smooth talk.[v]
22 All at once he followed her
like an ox going to the slaughter,
like a deer[a] stepping into a noose[b][w]
23 till an arrow pierces[x] his liver,
like a bird darting into a snare,
little knowing it will cost him his life.[y]

24 Now then, my sons, listen[z] to me;
pay attention to what I say.
25 Do not let your heart turn to her ways
or stray into her paths.[a]
26 Many are the victims she has brought down;
her slain are a mighty throng.
27 Her house is a highway to the grave,
leading down to the chambers of death.[b]

Wisdom's Call

8 Does not wisdom call out?[c]
Does not understanding raise her voice?
2 At the highest point along the way,
where the paths meet, she takes her stand;
3 beside the gate leading into the city,
at the entrance, she cries aloud:[d]
4 "To you, O people, I call out;
I raise my voice to all mankind.
5 You who are simple,[e] gain prudence;[f]
you who are foolish, set your hearts on it.[c]
6 Listen, for I have trustworthy things to say;
I open my lips to speak what is right.
7 My mouth speaks what is true,[g]
for my lips detest wickedness.
8 All the words of my mouth are just;
none of them is crooked or perverse.
9 To the discerning all of them are right;
they are upright to those who have found knowledge.
10 Choose my instruction instead of silver,
knowledge rather than choice gold,[h]
11 for wisdom is more precious[i] than rubies,
and nothing you desire can compare with her.[j]

12 "I, wisdom, dwell together with prudence;
I possess knowledge and discretion.[k]

---

[a] 22 Syriac (see also Septuagint); Hebrew *fool*
[b] 22 The meaning of the Hebrew for this line is uncertain. [c] 5 Septuagint; Hebrew *foolish, instruct your minds*

7:15 *I came out to meet you.* All the adulteress does is perverse. Here she presents an offering as a feast for the young man she plans to entrap. She overcomes her target's fear by assuring him that her husband will not come home and discover them together.
7:22 *like a deer stepping into a noose.* This passage uses several unflattering metaphors to describe how a young fool falls into immorality.
8:1 *Does not wisdom call out?* Wisdom, in contrast to foolishness, wants to reach everyone and therefore broadcasts her message publicly, unlike the immoral woman, who uses privacy and deception to achieve her goals. Wisdom is open to all. Her location is at the place of decision, the place of authority, the place of beginnings. She speaks loudly, but only those who adjust their lives to God's truth actually enjoy the spoils of wisdom.

7:5 [k] ver 21; Job 31:9; Pr 2:16; 6:24 **7:7** [l] Pr 1:22; 6:32 **7:9** [m] Job 24:15 **7:11** [n] Pr 9:13; 1Ti 5:13 **7:12** [o] Pr 8:1-36; 23:26-28 **7:13** [p] Ge 39:12 [q] Pr 1:20 **7:14** [r] Lev 7:11-18 **7:17** [s] Est 1:6; Isa 57:7; Eze 23:41; Am 6:4 [t] Ge 37:25 **7:18** [u] Ge 39:7 **7:21** [v] Pr 5:3 **7:22** [w] Job 18:10 **7:23** [x] Job 15:22; 16:13 [y] Pr 6:26; Ecc 7:26; 9:12 **7:24** [z] Pr 1:8-9; 5:7; 8:32 **7:25** [a] Pr 5:7-8 **7:27** [b] Pr 2:18; 5:5; 9:18; Rev 22:15 **8:1** [c] Pr 1:20; 9:3 **8:3** [d] Job 29:7 **8:5** [e] Pr 1:22 [f] Pr 1:4 **8:7** [g] Ps 37:30; Jn 8:14 **8:10** [h] Pr 3:14-15 **8:11** [i] Job 28:17-19 [j] Pr 3:13-15 **8:12** [k] Pr 1:4

13 To fear the LORD is to hate evil;[l]
I hate[m] pride and arrogance,
evil behavior and perverse speech.
14 Counsel and sound judgment are mine;
I have insight, I have power.[n]
15 By me kings reign
and rulers[o] issue decrees that are just;
16 by me princes govern,
and nobles—all who rule on earth.[a]
17 I love those who love me,[p]
and those who seek me find me.[q]
18 With me are riches and honor,[r]
enduring wealth and prosperity.[s]
19 My fruit is better than fine gold;
what I yield surpasses choice silver.[t]
20 I walk in the way of righteousness,
along the paths of justice,
21 bestowing a rich inheritance on those who love me
and making their treasuries full.[u]

22 "The LORD brought me forth as the first of his works,[b,c]
before his deeds of old;
23 I was formed long ages ago,
at the very beginning, when the world came to be.
24 When there were no watery depths, I was given birth,
when there were no springs overflowing with water;[v]
25 before the mountains were settled in place,
before the hills, I was given birth,[w]
26 before he made the world or its fields
or any of the dust of the earth.[x]
27 I was there when he set the heavens in place,[y]
when he marked out the horizon on the face of the deep,
28 when he established the clouds above
and fixed securely the fountains of the deep,
29 when he gave the sea its boundary[z]
so the waters would not overstep his command,[a]
and when he marked out the foundations of the earth.[b]
30 Then I was constantly[d] at his side.[c]
I was filled with delight day after day,
rejoicing always in his presence,
31 rejoicing in his whole world
and delighting in mankind.[d]

32 "Now then, my children, listen to me;
blessed are[e] those who keep my ways.[f]
33 Listen to my instruction and be wise;
do not disregard it.
34 Blessed are those who listen[g] to me,
watching daily at my doors,
waiting at my doorway.
35 For those who find me[h] find life
and receive favor from the LORD.[i]
36 But those who fail to find me harm themselves;[j]
all who hate me love death."

Invitations of Wisdom and Folly

9 Wisdom has built[k] her house;
she has set up[e] its seven pillars.
2 She has prepared her meat and mixed her wine;
she has also set her table.[l]
3 She has sent out her servants, and she calls[m]
from the highest point of the city,[n]
4 "Let all who are simple come to my house!"
To those who have no sense[o] she says,
5 "Come, eat my food
and drink the wine I have mixed.[p]

[a] *16* Some Hebrew manuscripts and Septuagint; other Hebrew manuscripts *all righteous rulers*
[b] *22* Or *way*; or *dominion*
[c] *22* Or *The LORD possessed me at the beginning of his work*; or *The LORD brought me forth at the beginning of his work*
[d] *30* Or *was the artisan*; or *was a little child*
[e] *1* Septuagint, Syriac and Targum; Hebrew *has hewn out*

8:13 *To fear the LORD is to hate evil.* The offer of wisdom is held out only to those who fear God. Coming to wisdom requires coming to God, and coming to God means turning away from all that God hates—evil, pride, and arrogance.

8:15 *By me kings reign and rulers.* Power and authority require the use of wisdom.

8:30–31 *constantly at his side.* With wisdom's skill, God created the universe. A proper study of the universe is a progressive study of God's wisdom. Her greatest joy comes in the finest of the work of God—the sons of men—that is, humankind.

9:1 *seven pillars.* The number seven represents completeness, as it often does in Semitic poetry. That is, it is not that there were precisely seven pillars so much as that the house of wisdom was solidly built and substantial in character.

9:2 *mixed her wine.* Wine was a staple in ancient Israel; but when a feast was special, a homemaker would add aromatic spices to the wine, enlivening the bouquet and improving the taste (Song 8:2). This idea sets up a contrast with the foolish woman. While wisdom is busy, attending to every detail like a gracious hostess, the foolish woman sits at the entrance of her house with very little to do (9:14).

9:4 *all who are simple.* Wisdom makes a point of inviting the naive, meaning those who have not yet made up their minds about their course in life. The person who comes to wisdom has nothing to lose but naiveté. Hebrews 5:14 speaks of a mature person as one who is able to eat and enjoy solid food, in contrast to the naive, who is able only to drink milk.

8:13 [l] Pr 16:6 [m] Jer 44:4 **8:14** [n] Pr 21:22; Ecc 7:19 **8:15** [o] Da 2:21; Ro 13:1 **8:17** [p] 1Sa 2:30; Ps 91:14; Jn 14:21-24 [q] Pr 1:28; Jas 1:5 **8:18** [r] Pr 3:16 [s] Dt 8:18; Mt 6:33 **8:19** [t] Pr 3:13-14; 10:20 **8:21** [u] Pr 24:4 **8:24** [v] Ge 7:11 **8:25** [w] Job 15:7 **8:26** [x] Ps 90:2 **8:27** [y] Pr 3:19 **8:29** [z] Ge 1:9; Job 38:10; Ps 16:6 [a] Ps 104:9 [b] Job 38:5 **8:30** [c] Jn 1:1-3 **8:31** [d] Ps 16:3; 104:1-30 **8:32** [e] Lk 11:28 [f] Ps 119:1-2 **8:34** [g] Pr 3:13, 18 **8:35** [h] Pr 3:13-18 [i] Pr 12:2 **8:36** [j] Pr 15:32 **9:1** [k] Eph 2:20-22; 1Pe 2:5 **9:2** [l] Lk 14:16-23 **9:3** [m] Pr 8:1-3 [n] ver 14 **9:4** [o] Pr 6:32 **9:5** [p] Isa 55:1

[6]Leave your simple ways and you will live;[q]
walk in the way of insight."

[7]Whoever corrects a mocker invites insults;
whoever rebukes the wicked incurs abuse.[r]
[8]Do not rebuke mockers[s] or they will hate you;
rebuke the wise and they will love you.[t]
[9]Instruct the wise and they will be wiser still;
teach the righteous and they will add to their learning.[u]

[10]The fear of the LORD[v] is the beginning of wisdom,
and knowledge of the Holy One is understanding.
[11]For through wisdom[a] your days will be many,
and years will be added to your life.[w]
[12]If you are wise, your wisdom will reward you;
if you are a mocker, you alone will suffer.

[13]Folly is an unruly woman;[x]
she is simple and knows nothing.[y]
[14]She sits at the door of her house,
on a seat at the highest point of the city,[z]
[15]calling out to those who pass by,
who go straight on their way,
[16]"Let all who are simple come to my house!"
To those who have no sense she says,
[17]"Stolen water is sweet;
food eaten in secret is delicious![a]"
[18]But little do they know that the dead are there,
that her guests are deep in the realm of the dead.[b]

Proverbs of Solomon

10 The proverbs of Solomon:[c]

A wise son brings joy to his father,[d]
but a foolish son brings grief to his mother.

[2]Ill-gotten treasures have no lasting value,[e]
but righteousness delivers from death.[f]

[3]The LORD does not let the righteous go hungry,[g]
but he thwarts the craving of the wicked.

[4]Lazy hands make for poverty,[h]
but diligent hands bring wealth.[i]

[5]He who gathers crops in summer is a prudent son,
but he who sleeps during harvest is a disgraceful son.

[6]Blessings crown the head of the righteous,
but violence overwhelms the mouth of the wicked.[b][j]

[7]The name of the righteous[k] is used in blessings,[c]
but the name of the wicked[l] will rot.[m]

[8]The wise in heart accept commands,
but a chattering fool comes to ruin.[n]

[9]Whoever walks in integrity[o] walks securely,[p]
but whoever takes crooked paths will be found out.[q]

[10]Whoever winks maliciously[r] causes grief,
and a chattering fool comes to ruin.

---

[a] 11 Septuagint, Syriac and Targum; Hebrew *me*
[b] 6 Or *righteous, / but the mouth of the wicked conceals violence*
[c] 7 See Gen. 48:20.

9:7 *Whoever corrects a mocker.* This personality is thoroughly set against wisdom (1:22) and scoffs at the things of God (Ps. 1:1). By contrast a wise man accepts correction and responds with gratitude to the one who points out his error.
9:13–18 *Folly is an unruly woman.* This section is a parody of 9:1–6. Like personified wisdom, the woman of folly calls out an invitation. But she is brash, loud, undisciplined, and knows nothing (7:10–12). She cries out in the same words that wisdom has used, but she has no marvelous banquet for her guests, only shabby food, stolen and meager.
9:18 *the dead are there.* Fools cast away all restraint and express their freedom in direct defiance of heaven's moral law for the ordering of our conduct on earth. But they do not know that the end of such perverse behavior is death. The way of wisdom is to turn from such a disastrous course while there is time.
10:1 *The proverbs of Solomon.* This section focuses on the wise son in contrast with the foolish son. Son is used generically for son and daughter.
10:4 *Lazy hands.* Proverbs often links laziness with poverty, and hard work with riches.
10:7 *but the name of the wicked.* In biblical times a person's name was most significant. When a person's name was remembered by future generations for good, that person's life was believed to have been of great value. But when the memory of a name rotted away, it was as though that person had never lived.
10:9 *walks in integrity.* Many of the proverbs contrast two paths of life. This phrase means conforming to God's law as a course of life. Choosing crooked paths is willfully to disdain the guidance God so graciously provided.

9:6 [q] Pr 8:35 **9:7** [r] Pr 23:9 **9:8** [s] Pr 15:12 [t] Ps 141:5 **9:9** [u] Pr 1:5,7 **9:10** [v] Job 28:28; Pr 1:7 **9:11** [w] Pr 3:16; 10:27 **9:13** [x] Pr 7:11 [y] Pr 5:6 **9:14** [z] ver 3 **9:17** [a] Pr 20:17 **9:18** [b] Pr 2:18; 7:26-27 **10:1** [c] Pr 1:1 [d] Pr 15:20; 29:3 **10:2** [e] Pr 21:6 [f] Pr 11:4,19 **10:3** [g] Mt 6:25-34 **10:4** [h] Pr 19:15 [i] Pr 12:24; 13:4; 21:5 **10:6** [j] ver 8, 11, 14 **10:7** [k] Ps 112:6 [l] Ps 109:13 [m] Ps 9:6 **10:8** [n] Mt 7:24-27 **10:9** [o] Isa 33:15 [p] Ps 23:4 [q] Pr 28:18 **10:10** [r] Ps 35:19

11 The mouth of the righteous is a
fountain of life,[s]
but the mouth of the wicked conceals
violence.[t]

12 Hatred stirs up conflict,
but love covers over all wrongs.[u]

13 Wisdom is found on the lips of the
discerning,[v]
but a rod is for the back of one who
has no sense.[w]

14 The wise store up knowledge,
but the mouth of a fool invites ruin.[x]

15 The wealth of the rich is their fortified
city,[y]
but poverty is the ruin of the poor.[z]

16 The wages of the righteous is life,
but the earnings of the wicked are sin
and death.[a]

17 Whoever heeds discipline shows the
way to life,[b]
but whoever ignores correction leads
others astray.

18 Whoever conceals hatred with lying
lips
and spreads slander is a fool.

19 Sin is not ended by multiplying words,
but the prudent hold their tongues.[c]

20 The tongue of the righteous is choice
silver,
but the heart of the wicked is of little
value.

21 The lips of the righteous nourish many,
but fools die for lack of sense.[d]

22 The blessing of the LORD brings
wealth,[e]
without painful toil for it.

23 A fool finds pleasure in wicked
schemes,[f]
but a person of understanding
delights in wisdom.

24 What the wicked dread[g] will overtake
them;
what the righteous desire will be
granted.[h]

25 When the storm has swept by, the
wicked are gone,
but the righteous stand firm[i] forever.[j]

26 As vinegar to the teeth and smoke to
the eyes,
so are sluggards to those who send
them.[k]

27 The fear of the LORD adds length to life,[l]
but the years of the wicked are cut
short.[m]

28 The prospect of the righteous is joy,
but the hopes of the wicked come to
nothing.[n]

29 The way of the LORD is a refuge for the
blameless,
but it is the ruin of those who do evil.[o]

30 The righteous will never be uprooted,
but the wicked will not remain in the
land.[p]

31 From the mouth of the righteous comes
the fruit of wisdom,[q]
but a perverse tongue will be
silenced.

10:12 ***Hatred ... love.*** This verse describes interpersonal relationships, not salvation. When people respond in love to each other, they cover over the sins or offenses that would otherwise come between them.

10:13 ***but a rod is for the back of one.*** Rod refers to punishment, in this case deserved. The phrase "lack of understanding" comes from the Hebrew idiom "lack heart." The one who "lacks heart" is contrasted with the one who is "wise in heart" (10:8).

10:14–15 ***store up knowledge.*** This set of verses contrasts the wise person's pursuit of knowledge with the empty talk of a fool. Wealth is like a fortress. In biblical times only walled cities had any defense against enemy armies.

10:16–17 ***The wages of the righteous is life.*** These verses present the doctrine of the two ways. The righteous are on the way of life but the wicked wander from it.

10:23 ***A fool finds pleasure.*** Pleasure here usually means "joyous laughter." Here the proverb uses the word in a completely negative sense. For the fool, wickedness is only a game. He makes up the rules as he goes along; for losing is only in getting caught. But a person who has understanding takes a longer-term perspective.

10:25 ***the righteous stand firm forever.*** The short-lived nature of the wicked is contrasted with the stability of the righteous. The foundation of righteousness is faith in God, much like the waters that nourish the tree of Psalm 1:3.

10:28 ***hopes ... come to.*** The righteous have something to look forward to; the wicked do not.

10:29 ***The way of the LORD is a refuge for the blameless.*** Different people see the way of the Lord differently. Those who are innocent see it as a shelter from the storm. Those who practice iniquity see it only as a source of condemnation and wrath. The viewer's perspective makes all the difference.

10:31–32 ***the mouth of the righteous comes the fruit of wisdom.*** These verses form another pair of sentences about true and false speech. This repetition with variation indicates the significance of truth and falsehood.

10:11 [s] Ps 37:30; Pr 13:12, 14, 19 [t] ver 6 **10:12** [u] Pr 17:9; 1Co 13:4-7; 1Pe 4:8 **10:13** [v] ver 31 [w] Pr 26:3 **10:14** [x] Pr 18:6, 7 **10:15** [y] Pr 18:11 [z] Pr 19:7 **10:16** [a] Pr 11:18-19 **10:17** [b] Pr 6:23 **10:19** [c] Pr 17:28; Ecc 5:3; Jas 1:19; 3:2-12 **10:21** [d] Pr 5:22-23; Hos 4:1, 6, 14 **10:22** [e] Ge 24:35; Ps 37:22 **10:23** [f] Pr 2:14; 15:21 **10:24** [g] Isa 66:4 [h] Ps 145:17-19; Mt 5:6; 1Jn 5:14-15 **10:25** [i] Ps 15:5 [j] Pr 12:3, 7; Mt 7:24-27 **10:26** [k] Pr 26:6 **10:27** [l] Pr 9:10-11 [m] Job 15:32 **10:28** [n] Job 8:13; Pr 11:7 **10:29** [o] Pr 21:15 **10:30** [p] Ps 37:9, 28-29; Pr 2:20-22 **10:31** [q] Ps 37:30

32 The lips of the righteous know what finds favor,[r]
but the mouth of the wicked only what is perverse.

11

The LORD detests dishonest scales,[s]
but accurate weights find favor with him.[t]

2 When pride comes, then comes disgrace,[u]
but with humility comes wisdom.[v]

3 The integrity of the upright guides them,
but the unfaithful are destroyed by their duplicity.[w]

4 Wealth is worthless in the day of wrath,[x]
but righteousness delivers from death.[y]

5 The righteousness of the blameless makes their paths straight,
but the wicked are brought down by their own wickedness.[z]

6 The righteousness of the upright delivers them,
but the unfaithful are trapped by evil desires.

7 Hopes placed in mortals die with them;
all the promise of[a] their power comes to nothing.[a]

8 The righteous person is rescued from trouble,
and it falls on the wicked instead.[b]

9 With their mouths the godless destroy their neighbors,
but through knowledge the righteous escape.

10 When the righteous prosper, the city rejoices;[c]
when the wicked perish, there are shouts of joy.

11 Through the blessing of the upright a city is exalted,
but by the mouth of the wicked it is destroyed.[d]

12 Whoever derides their neighbor has no sense,[e]
but the one who has understanding holds their tongue.

13 A gossip betrays a confidence,[f]
but a trustworthy person keeps a secret.

14 For lack of guidance a nation falls,[g]
but victory is won through many advisers.[h]

15 Whoever puts up security[i] for a stranger will surely suffer,
but whoever refuses to shake hands in pledge is safe.

16 A kindhearted woman gains honor,[j]
but ruthless men gain only wealth.

17 Those who are kind benefit themselves,
but the cruel bring ruin on themselves.

18 A wicked person earns deceptive wages,
but the one who sows righteousness reaps a sure reward.[k]

19 Truly the righteous attain life,
but whoever pursues evil finds death.

20 The LORD detests those whose hearts are perverse,
but he delights in those whose ways are blameless.[l]

21 Be sure of this: The wicked will not go unpunished,
but those who are righteous will go free.[m]

---

a 7 Two Hebrew manuscripts; most Hebrew manuscripts, Vulgate, Syriac and Targum *When the wicked die, their hope perishes; / all they expected from*

11:1 *The LORD detests dishonest scales.* Dealing fairly with one another is an outgrowth of the command to love one's neighbor as oneself (Lev. 19:18), which in turn is an outgrowth of the central command given to Israel, to love God above all else (Deut. 6:4–9). That is why dishonest scales are an abomination to God.
11:2 *When pride comes.* Many proverbs contrast the arrogant with the humble, as this one does. The Hebrew word for pride comes from a root that means "to boil up"; it refers to a raging arrogance or insolence.
11:10 *When the righteous prosper.* Truly righteous people bring justice to all the inhabitants of a city, and the city experiences true peace. Many of the psalm writers cried for vindication of the righteous and for a cessation of evil (Ps. 69:22–28).
11:13 *A gossip betrays a confidence.* A faithful friend conceals delicate matters that an unfaithful person reveals.
11:14 *through many advisers.* In modern times, as in the past, leaders of nations need adequate counsel. We all need to seek advice from wise and trustworthy people.
11:17 *Those who are kind benefit themselves.* Throughout the Bible, God promises that good actions will return to you in benefits. Behavior that hurts others will hurt you as well.
11:19 *attain life.* Proverbs such as this remind us that the pursuit of righteousness is a matter of life and death.

10:32 [r] Ecc 10:12 **11:1** [s] Lev 19:36; Dt 25:13-16; Pr 20:10, 23 [t] Pr 16:11 **11:2** [u] Pr 16:18 [v] Pr 18:12; 29:23 **11:3** [w] Pr 13:6 **11:4** [x] Eze 7:19; Zep 1:18 [y] Ge 7:1; Pr 10:2 **11:5** [z] Pr 5:21-23 **11:7** [a] Pr 10:28 **11:8** [b] Pr 21:18 **11:10** [c] Pr 28:12 **11:11** [d] Pr 29:8 **11:12** [e] Pr 14:21 **11:13** [f] Lev 19:16; Pr 20:19; 1Ti 5:13 **11:14** [g] Pr 20:18 [h] Pr 15:22; 24:6 **11:15** [i] Pr 6:1 **11:16** [j] Pr 31:31 **11:18** [k] Hos 10:12-13 **11:20** [l] 1Ch 29:17; Ps 119:1; Pr 12:2, 22 **11:21** [m] Pr 16:5

22 Like a gold ring in a pig's snout
is a beautiful woman who shows no discretion.

23 The desire of the righteous ends only in good,
but the hope of the wicked only in wrath.

24 One person gives freely, yet gains even more;
another withholds unduly, but comes to poverty.

25 A generous person will prosper;
whoever refreshes others will be refreshed.[n]

26 People curse the one who hoards grain,
but they pray God's blessing on the one who is willing to sell.

27 Whoever seeks good finds favor,
but evil comes to one who searches for it.[o]

28 Those who trust in their riches will fall,[p]
but the righteous will thrive like a green leaf.[q]

29 Whoever brings ruin on their family will inherit only wind,
and the fool will be servant to the wise.[r]

30 The fruit of the righteous is a tree of life,[s]
and the one who is wise saves lives.

31 If the righteous receive their due[t] on earth,
how much more the ungodly and the sinner!

12 Whoever loves discipline loves knowledge,
but whoever hates correction is stupid.[u]

2 Good people obtain favor from the LORD,
but he condemns those who devise wicked schemes.

3 No one can be established through wickedness,
but the righteous cannot be uprooted.[v]

4 A wife of noble character is her husband's crown,
but a disgraceful wife is like decay in his bones.[w]

5 The plans of the righteous are just,
but the advice of the wicked is deceitful.

6 The words of the wicked lie in wait for blood,
but the speech of the upright rescues them.[x]

7 The wicked are overthrown and are no more,[y]
but the house of the righteous stands firm.[z]

8 A person is praised according to their prudence,
and one with a warped mind is despised.

9 Better to be a nobody and yet have a servant
than pretend to be somebody and have no food.

10 The righteous care for the needs of their animals,
but the kindest acts of the wicked are cruel.

11 Those who work their land will have abundant food,
but those who chase fantasies have no sense.[a]

12 The wicked desire the stronghold of evildoers,
but the root of the righteous endures.

13 Evildoers are trapped by their sinful talk,[b]
and so the innocent escape trouble.[c]

11:22 ***gold ring.*** A golden ring would be ludicrous on a pig's snout. To the ancient Israelites, pigs were unclean and repellent. The immoral person is compared to such an animal, no matter what the outward appearance might be.
11:24–26 ***another withholds unduly.*** These proverbs should shape our attitudes toward wealth: We should share it. Stinginess may lead to poverty. Generosity has the opposite effect. Selfishness is foolish because it only creates enemies and dishonors God.
11:31 ***much more.*** This proverb argues from a premise to a conclusion. Since the righteous will finally find their reward, it follows that the wicked, who are defiant toward God and in conflict with His works, will certainly receive judgment.
12:1 ***But whoever hates correction is stupid.*** Literally "stupid as a cow."
12:4 ***A wife of noble character.*** A husband should rejoice in such a woman because her noble character brings him honor.
12:5–6 ***The plans of the righteous.*** A person's thoughts are the foundation of his or her words and deeds. The words of wicked persons can be like a deadly ambush.
12:9 ***pretend to be somebody.*** This verse contrasts a person who is a "nobody" but has a servant with a person who makes a great display but does not even have food on the table. Pretension destroys those who indulge in it.

11:25 [n] Mt 5:7; 2Co 9:6-9 **11:27** [o] Est 7:10; Ps 7:15-16 **11:28** [p] Job 31:24-28; Ps 49:6; 52:7; Mk 10:25; 1Ti 6:17 [q] Ps 1:3; 92:12-14; Jer 17:8 **11:29** [r] Pr 14:19 **11:30** [s] Jas 5:20 **11:31** [t] Pr 13:21; Jer 25:29; 1Pe 4:18 **12:1** [u] Pr 9:7-9; 15:5, 10, 12, 32 **12:3** [v] Pr 10:25 **12:4** [w] Pr 14:30 **12:6** [x] Pr 14:3 **12:7** [y] Ps 37:36 [z] Pr 10:25 **12:11** [a] Pr 28:19 **12:13** [b] Pr 18:7 [c] Pr 21:23; 2Pe 2:9

14 From the fruit of their lips people are filled with good things,[d]
and the work of their hands brings them reward.[e]

15 The way of fools seems right to them,[f]
but the wise listen to advice.

16 Fools show their annoyance at once,
but the prudent overlook an insult.[g]

17 An honest witness tells the truth,
but a false witness tells lies.[h]

18 The words of the reckless pierce like swords,[i]
but the tongue of the wise brings healing.[j]

19 Truthful lips endure forever,
but a lying tongue lasts only a moment.

20 Deceit is in the hearts of those who plot evil,
but those who promote peace have joy.

21 No harm overtakes the righteous,[k]
but the wicked have their fill of trouble.

22 The LORD detests lying lips,[l]
but he delights in people who are trustworthy.[m]

23 The prudent keep their knowledge to themselves,[n]
but a fool's heart blurts out folly.

24 Diligent hands will rule,
but laziness ends in forced labor.[o]

25 Anxiety weighs down the heart,[p]
but a kind word cheers it up.

26 The righteous choose their friends carefully,
but the way of the wicked leads them astray.

27 The lazy do not roast[a] any game,
but the diligent feed on the riches of the hunt.

28 In the way of righteousness there is life;[q]
along that path is immortality.

13 A wise son heeds his father's instruction,
but a mocker does not respond to rebukes.[r]

2 From the fruit of their lips people enjoy good things,[s]
but the unfaithful have an appetite for violence.

3 Those who guard their lips[t] preserve their lives,[u]
but those who speak rashly will come to ruin.[v]

4 A sluggard's appetite is never filled,
but the desires of the diligent are fully satisfied.

5 The righteous hate what is false,
but the wicked make themselves a stench
and bring shame on themselves.

6 Righteousness guards the person of integrity,
but wickedness overthrows the sinner.[w]

7 One person pretends to be rich, yet has nothing;
another pretends to be poor, yet has great wealth.[x]

8 A person's riches may ransom their life,
but the poor cannot respond to threatening rebukes.

9 The light of the righteous shines brightly,
but the lamp of the wicked is snuffed out.[y]

---

[a] 27 The meaning of the Hebrew for this word is uncertain.

12:16 ***annoyance at once.*** Careless words can make a fool out of us, so we are wise to think before we speak. Whereas the wise man restrains his anger and turns it away, the fool constantly loses his temper (29:11).
12:18–19 ***the tongue of the wise brings healing.*** Many proverbs praise people who speak carefully and truthfully. Speech reflects a person's character. The words of a righteous person soothe the listener.
12:22 ***detests lying lips.*** God detests perversity of the lips and the heart (11:20). The term conveys extreme hatred.
12:25 ***Anxiety weighs down the heart.*** Anxiety loses some of its force in the face of a positive, encouraging word. Barnabas is an example of an encourager in the early church (Acts 4:36).
12:26 ***The righteous choose their friends carefully.*** Our friends help to determine who we will become, and an excellent example inspires us to copy.
12:27 ***The lazy.*** Lazy people do work, they just don't always finish what they start. The cure for their laziness is diligence—to follow through to the end.
13:5 ***The righteous hate what is false.*** The person who hates lying does not merely feel bad about it; he avoids it like the plague.
13:7 ***rich, yet has nothing.*** The paradox of greed causing poverty, and of generosity causing wealth, is a recurring theme in Scripture (Matt. 6:19–21). The point is not how much money you have, but what you do with it.
13:9 ***The light of the righteous shines brightly.*** For an ancient Israelite, an oil lamp would be the only source of light at night. Without it, a person had no way of seeing the path in front of him.

12:14 [d] Pr 13:2; 15:23; 18:20 [e] Isa 3:10-11
12:15 [f] Pr 14:12; 16:2,25; Lk 18:11 **12:16** [g] Pr 29:11
12:17 [h] Pr 14:5,25 **12:18** [i] Ps 57:4 [j] Pr 15:4
12:21 [k] Ps 91:10 **12:22** [l] Pr 6:17; Rev 22:15 [m] Pr 11:20
12:23 [n] Pr 10:14; 13:16 **12:24** [o] Pr 10:4
12:25 [p] Pr 15:13; Isa 50:4 **12:28** [q] Dt 30:15
13:1 [r] Pr 10:1 **13:2** [s] Pr 12:14 **13:3** [t] Jas 3:2 [u] Pr 21:23
[v] Pr 18:7,20-21 **13:6** [w] Pr 11:3,5 **13:7** [x] 2Co 6:10
13:9 [y] Job 18:5; Pr 4:18-19; 24:20

10 Where there is strife, there is pride,
but wisdom is found in those who take advice.

11 Dishonest money dwindles away,[z]
but whoever gathers money little by little makes it grow.

12 Hope deferred makes the heart sick,
but a longing fulfilled is a tree of life.

13 Whoever scorns instruction will pay for it,[a]
but whoever respects a command is rewarded.

14 The teaching of the wise is a fountain of life,[b]
turning a person from the snares of death.[c]

15 Good judgment wins favor,
but the way of the unfaithful leads to their destruction.[a]

16 All who are prudent act with[b] knowledge,
but fools expose their folly.[d]

17 A wicked messenger falls into trouble,
but a trustworthy envoy brings healing.[e]

18 Whoever disregards discipline comes to poverty and shame,
but whoever heeds correction is honored.[f]

19 A longing fulfilled is sweet to the soul,
but fools detest turning from evil.

20 Walk with the wise and become wise,
for a companion of fools suffers harm.[g]

21 Trouble pursues the sinner,
but the righteous[h] are rewarded with good things.

22 A good person leaves an inheritance for their children's children,
but a sinner's wealth is stored up for the righteous.[i]

23 An unplowed field produces food for the poor,
but injustice sweeps it away.

24 Whoever spares the rod hates their children,
but the one who loves their children is careful to discipline them.[j]

25 The righteous eat to their hearts' content,
but the stomach of the wicked goes hungry.[k]

14 The wise woman builds her house,[l]
but with her own hands the foolish one tears hers down.

2 Whoever fears the LORD walks uprightly,
but those who despise him are devious in their ways.

3 A fool's mouth lashes out with pride,
but the lips of the wise protect them.[m]

4 Where there are no oxen, the manger is empty,
but from the strength of an ox come abundant harvests.

5 An honest witness does not deceive,
but a false witness pours out lies.[n]

6 The mocker seeks wisdom and finds none,
but knowledge comes easily to the discerning.

---

[a] *15* Septuagint and Syriac; the meaning of the Hebrew for this phrase is uncertain. [b] *16* Or *prudent protect themselves through*

13:10 *there is pride.* It is self-centeredness and having to push one's own ideas that bring quarrels. The wise know when to speak and when to keep still.
13:11 *Dishonest money dwindles away.* This proverb describes the natural long-term consequences of cheating. People who compromise their honesty to get rich merely postpone the inevitable need to earn their keep. The day comes when their cheating catches up with them, but by then their honest colleagues have become far better at obtaining wealth.
13:14 *fountain of life.* In an arid land such as ancient Judah, a fountain provided water for oneself and for one's flocks. It was a necessity—a source of life. A fountain is also a picture for salvation (Is. 12:1–3).
13:15 *Good judgment wins favor.* Favor with God and other people—a good reputation is highly desirable because it ensures that you won't be alone in life. A good reputation was the first qualification listed by the apostles for deacons in the early church (Acts 6:3).
13:20 *Walk with the wise and become wise.* Our selection of friends (12:26) is extremely important. Pressure from peers is much stronger than many people realize.
13:24 *hates ... loves.* This is the first of several proverbs on parental discipline. A parent's loving discipline is modeled after God's loving correction (3:11–12).
14:1 *wise woman builds her house.* She develops a peaceful setting for family nurture.
14:2 *fears the LORD.* This phrase contrasts starkly with "despises him." Love for uprightness will naturally coincide with love and respect for the most upright One of all, God Himself. Love for perversity will likewise result in hatred for Him. Fear of the Lord as the beginning of wisdom is the central theme of Proverbs (1:7).
14:4 *the manger is empty.* A farmer has to put up with some messes in the barn if he wants the help of an ox. This is not an excuse to be slovenly, but an encouragement to work hard.

13:11 [z] Pr 10:2 **13:13** [a] Nu 15:31; 2Ch 36:16
13:14 [b] Pr 10:11 [c] Pr 14:27 **13:16** [d] Pr 12:23
13:17 [e] Pr 25:13 **13:18** [f] Pr 15:5,31-32 **13:20** [g] Pr 15:31
13:21 [h] Ps 32:10 **13:22** [i] Job 27:17; Ecc 2:26
13:24 [j] Pr 19:18; 22:15; 23:13-14; 29:15,17; Heb 12:7
13:25 [k] Ps 34:10; Pr 10:3 **14:1** [l] Pr 24:3 **14:3** [m] Pr 12:6
14:5 [n] Pr 6:19; 12:17

7 Stay away from a fool,
for you will not find knowledge on their lips.

8 The wisdom of the prudent is to give thought to their ways,
but the folly of fools is deception.[o]

9 Fools mock at making amends for sin,
but goodwill is found among the upright.

10 Each heart knows its own bitterness,
and no one else can share its joy.

11 The house of the wicked will be destroyed,
but the tent of the upright will flourish.[p]

12 There is a way that appears to be right,[q]
but in the end it leads to death.[r]

13 Even in laughter[s] the heart may ache,
and rejoicing may end in grief.

14 The faithless will be fully repaid for their ways,[t]
and the good rewarded for theirs.[u]

15 The simple believe anything,
but the prudent give thought to their steps.

16 The wise fear the LORD and shun evil,[v]
but a fool is hotheaded and yet feels secure.

17 A quick-tempered person does foolish things,[w]
and the one who devises evil schemes is hated.

18 The simple inherit folly,
but the prudent are crowned with knowledge.

19 Evildoers will bow down in the presence of the good,
and the wicked at the gates of the righteous.[x]

20 The poor are shunned even by their neighbors,
but the rich have many friends.[y]

21 It is a sin to despise one's neighbor,[z]
but blessed is the one who is kind to the needy.[a]

22 Do not those who plot evil go astray?
But those who plan what is good find[a] love and faithfulness.

23 All hard work brings a profit,
but mere talk leads only to poverty.

24 The wealth of the wise is their crown,
but the folly of fools yields folly.

25 A truthful witness saves lives,
but a false witness is deceitful.[b]

26 Whoever fears the LORD has a secure fortress,[c]
and for their children it will be a refuge.

27 The fear of the LORD is a fountain of life,
turning a person from the snares of death.[d]

28 A large population is a king's glory,
but without subjects a prince is ruined.

29 Whoever is patient has great understanding,
but one who is quick-tempered displays folly.[e]

30 A heart at peace gives life to the body,
but envy rots the bones.[f]

31 Whoever oppresses the poor shows contempt for their Maker,[g]
but whoever is kind to the needy honors God.

32 When calamity comes, the wicked are brought down,[h]
but even in death the righteous seek refuge in God.[i]

33 Wisdom reposes in the heart of the discerning[j]
and even among fools she lets herself be known.[b]

34 Righteousness exalts a nation,[k]
but sin condemns any people.

[a] 22 Or *show* [b] 33 Hebrew; Septuagint and Syriac *discerning / but in the heart of fools she is not known*

14:12 *There is a way that appears to be right.* Only when it is too late does the deluded person discover that he is on the crowded highway to death. The implication is not that he was tricked, but that he relied too heavily on his own "wisdom" rather than turning in humility to God.

14:19 *at the gates of the righteous.* In an ancient walled city, the gate area would normally be the weakest section of the wall. The city engineers of ancient Canaan developed complex structures to fortify this point. Controlling the gate of a city meant controlling the city.

14:31 *oppresses ... honors.* The theme of "as you treat people, so you treat God" is central to Scripture (Ex. 22:22–24; Matt. 25:31–46).

14:32 *the wicked are brought down.* Some of the proverbs describe deliverance from death itself (11:4). The teaching of life after death is not a major teaching in the Old Testament, but neither is it altogether neglected.

14:34 *Righteousness exalts a nation.* Although each individual is responsible for his or her actions, the effects extend to the whole community.

14:8 [o] ver 24 **14:11** [p] Pr 3:33; 12:7 **14:12** [q] Pr 12:15 [r] Pr 16:25 **14:13** [s] Ecc 2:2 **14:14** [t] Pr 1:31 [u] Pr 12:14 **14:16** [v] Pr 22:3 **14:17** [w] ver 29 **14:19** [x] Pr 11:29 **14:20** [y] Pr 19:4,7 **14:21** [z] Pr 11:12 [a] Ps 41:1; Pr 19:17 **14:25** [b] ver 5 **14:26** [c] Pr 18:10; 19:23; Isa 33:6 **14:27** [d] Pr 13:14 **14:29** [e] Ecc 7:8-9; Jas 1:19 **14:30** [f] Pr 12:4 **14:31** [g] Pr 17:5 **14:32** [h] Pr 6:15 [i] Job 13:15; 2Ti 4:18 **14:33** [j] Pr 2:6-10 **14:34** [k] Pr 11:11

35 A king delights in a wise servant,
but a shameful servant arouses his fury.[l]

15 A gentle answer turns away wrath,[m]
but a harsh word stirs up anger.

2 The tongue of the wise adorns knowledge,
but the mouth of the fool gushes folly.[n]

3 The eyes[o] of the LORD are everywhere,[p]
keeping watch on the wicked and the good.[q]

4 The soothing tongue is a tree of life,
but a perverse tongue crushes the spirit.

5 A fool spurns a parent's discipline,
but whoever heeds correction shows prudence.[r]

6 The house of the righteous contains great treasure,[s]
but the income of the wicked brings ruin.

7 The lips of the wise spread knowledge,
but the hearts of fools are not upright.

8 The LORD detests the sacrifice of the wicked,[t]
but the prayer of the upright pleases him.[u]

9 The LORD detests the way of the wicked,
but he loves those who pursue righteousness.[v]

10 Stern discipline awaits anyone who leaves the path;
the one who hates correction will die.[w]

11 Death and Destruction[a] lie open before the LORD[x]—
how much more do human hearts![y]

12 Mockers resent correction,[z]
so they avoid the wise.

13 A happy heart makes the face cheerful,
but heartache crushes the spirit.[a]

14 The discerning heart seeks knowledge,[b]
but the mouth of a fool feeds on folly.

15 All the days of the oppressed are wretched,
but the cheerful heart has a continual feast.[c]

16 Better a little with the fear of the LORD
than great wealth with turmoil.[d]

17 Better a small serving of vegetables with love
than a fattened calf with hatred.[e]

18 A hot-tempered person stirs up conflict,[f]
but the one who is patient calms a quarrel.[g]

19 The way of the sluggard is blocked with thorns,[h]
but the path of the upright is a highway.

20 A wise son brings joy to his father,[i]
but a foolish man despises his mother.

---

[a] 11 Hebrew *Abaddon*

15:1 ***A gentle answer turns away wrath.*** Often it is not so much what we say but the way we say it that prompts such varied responses as acceptance and anger. For Abigail's gentle words to David when he was angry, see 1 Samuel 25:12–34. Words can have either life-giving or death-producing results.
15:3 ***The eyes of the LORD.*** That they are in every place watching everything chills those who do evil and comforts those who submit to Him (Eccl. 12:14).
15:6 ***The house of the righteous.*** One house is a blessing and the other is ruinous; the reason for this lies in how the house was acquired and how it is being used. The house of the righteous contains great wealth because it is founded on wisdom and a proper response to God. On the other hand, the wicked never gain enough to suit them, and lose what they have because of their deceptive ways.
15:10 ***Stern discipline.*** There is a consequence for those who forsake God's way. This discipline comes as a means of correction. Only the person who hates this correction will die.
15:11 ***how much more do human hearts.*** This is a "how much more" proverb, which impresses on the reader the clarity with which the Lord sees people's hearts. The Hebrew word *sheol,* or "death," connotes the fear of the unknown. The word actually means "the mysterious realm of death." Yet death is no mystery to the Lord. And if the mysterious realm of the dead is known to Him, then surely a person's heart is transparent to Him. This technique of arguing from the greater to the lesser appears in both Testaments.
15:12 ***Mockers resent correction.*** The mocker (14:6) is used as a foil or comparison in Proverbs to expose more sharply the character of the wise. Whereas the lazy person is a comic figure in Proverbs, the mocker is a villain. His basic problem is displayed in his response to correction. He does not learn from it nor does he seek it. The mocker is adamant in his folly.
15:14 ***The discerning heart.*** The person with an understanding heart, another description of the wise, is never satisfied with what he or she knows. The pursuit of wisdom and knowledge are lifelong occupations—never fully realized in this lifetime. But fools, not knowing the extent of their ignorance, continue to pursue folly.
15:18 ***A hot-tempered person stirs up conflict.*** A hot-tempered person can stir up strife where there is none; but a person who has a slow fuse—who is slow to anger—soothes contention (15:1).

14:35 [l] Mt 24:45-51; 25:14-30 **15:1** [m] Pr 25:15 **15:2** [n] Pr 12:23 **15:3** [o] 2Ch 16:9 [p] Job 31:4; Heb 4:13 [q] Job 34:21; Jer 16:17 **15:5** [r] Pr 13:1 **15:6** [s] Pr 8:21 **15:8** [t] Pr 21:27; Isa 1:11; Jer 6:20 [u] ver 29 **15:9** [v] Pr 21:21; 1Ti 6:11 **15:10** [w] Pr 1:31-32; 5:12 **15:11** [x] Job 26:6; Ps 139:8 [y] 2Ch 6:30; Ps 44:21 **15:12** [z] Am 5:10 **15:13** [a] Pr 12:25; 17:22; 18:14 **15:14** [b] Pr 18:15 **15:15** [c] ver 13 **15:16** [d] Ps 37:16-17; Pr 16:8; 1Ti 6:6 **15:17** [e] Pr 17:1 **15:18** [f] Pr 26:21 [g] Ge 13:8 **15:19** [h] Pr 22:5 **15:20** [i] Pr 10:1

[21] Folly brings joy to one who has no sense,[j]
but whoever has understanding keeps a straight course.

[22] Plans fail for lack of counsel,
but with many advisers they succeed.[k]

[23] A person finds joy in giving an apt reply[l]—
and how good is a timely word![m]

[24] The path of life leads upward for the prudent
to keep them from going down to the realm of the dead.

[25] The LORD tears down the house of the proud,[n]
but he sets the widow's boundary stones in place.[o]

[26] The LORD detests the thoughts of the wicked,[p]
but gracious words are pure in his sight.

[27] The greedy bring ruin to their households,
but the one who hates bribes will live.[q]

[28] The heart of the righteous weighs its answers,[r]
but the mouth of the wicked gushes evil.

[29] The LORD is far from the wicked,
but he hears the prayer of the righteous.[s]

[30] Light in a messenger's eyes brings joy to the heart,
and good news gives health to the bones.

[31] Whoever heeds life-giving correction
will be at home among the wise.[t]

[32] Those who disregard discipline despise themselves,[u]
but the one who heeds correction gains understanding.

[33] Wisdom's instruction is to fear the LORD,[v]
and humility comes before honor.[w]

16

To humans belong the plans of the heart,
but from the LORD comes the proper answer of the tongue.[x]

[2] All a person's ways seem pure to them,
but motives are weighed by the LORD.[y]

[3] Commit to the LORD whatever you do,
and he will establish your plans.[z]

[4] The LORD works out everything to its proper end[a]—
even the wicked for a day of disaster.[b]

[5] The LORD detests all the proud of heart.[c]
Be sure of this: They will not go unpunished.[d]

[6] Through love and faithfulness sin is atoned for;
through the fear of the LORD evil is avoided.[e]

[7] When the LORD takes pleasure in anyone's way,
he causes their enemies to make peace with them.

[8] Better a little with righteousness
than much gain[f] with injustice.

15:25 *The LORD tears down the house of the proud.* God will bring about justice in the end. To the haughty, God will give a dose of humility. But for the widow, a completely defenseless person in ancient times, God will provide protection.

15:32 *despise themselves.* The natural instinct for self-preservation is dangerous when it is time to listen to a necessary rebuke.

15:33 *Wisdom's instruction is to fear the LORD.* Knowledge alone does not make a person wiser; the fear of the Lord must accompany it. The same is true of honor.

16:1–2 *the plans of the heart.* These verses contrast human limitations with the sovereignty of God. Man can plan, dream, and hope, but the final outcome is from the Lord. Rather than "resign ourselves to fate," we should trust in God.

16:3 *Commit to the LORD whatever you do.* The verb "commit to" is from a word meaning "to roll." The idea is to "roll your cares onto the Lord." Trusting the Lord with our decisions frees us from preoccupation with our problems (3:5–6).

Dedication is the foundation of commitment. Without it the believer is unable to offer God anything else. Paul explains this dedication process in Romans 12:1–2. He emphasizes three things. First, it is our body which is to be dedicated as a living sacrifice to God. Second, we are to avoid being conformed to this world, but should strive to be transformed by the Word. Finally, by doing this we can discover God's perfect will for our lives.

After the dedication of our bodies, what are we to commit? We are to commit our salvation to God (2 Tim. 1:12). We are to commit our works (Prov. 16:3). Then our goals in life are to be given to Him (Job 5:8; Ps. 37:5). It is difficult but vital to commit our suffering experiences to God (1 Pet. 4:19). Our Lord Jesus did this very thing when He was on earth (1 Pet. 2:23). Finally, in the hour of death, we can with confidence commit our very souls to God (Ps. 31:5). Paul the apostle assures us that any and all such commitments to the Lord will be accepted and honored (1 Cor. 15:58).

16:6 *Through love and faithfulness.* These words can also be translated "by genuine piety." "Atonement" probably alludes to a sacrificial offering, but not apart from a contrite heart.

15:21 [j] Pr 10:23 **15:22** [k] Pr 11:14 **15:23** [l] Pr 12:14 [m] Pr 25:11 **15:25** [n] Pr 12:7 [o] Dt 19:14; Ps 68:5-6; Pr 23:10-11 **15:26** [p] Pr 6:16 **15:27** [q] Ex 23:8; Isa 33:15 **15:28** [r] 1Pe 3:15 **15:29** [s] Ps 145:18-19 **15:31** [t] ver 5 **15:32** [u] Pr 1:7 **15:33** [v] Pr 1:7 [w] Pr 18:12 **16:1** [x] Pr 19:21 **16:2** [y] Pr 21:2 **16:3** [z] Ps 37:5-6; Pr 3:5-6 **16:4** [a] Isa 43:7 [b] Ro 9:22 **16:5** [c] Pr 6:16 [d] Pr 11:20-21 **16:6** [e] Pr 14:16 **16:8** [f] Ps 37:16

9 In their hearts humans plan their
course,
but the LORD establishes their steps.[g]

10 The lips of a king speak as an oracle,
and his mouth does not betray justice.

11 Honest scales and balances belong to
the LORD;
all the weights in the bag are of his
making.[h]

12 Kings detest wrongdoing,
for a throne is established through
righteousness.[i]

13 Kings take pleasure in honest lips;
they value the one who speaks what
is right.[j]

14 A king's wrath is a messenger of death,[k]
but the wise will appease it.

15 When a king's face brightens, it means
life;[l]
his favor is like a rain cloud in spring.

16 How much better to get wisdom than
gold,
to get insight rather than silver![m]

17 The highway of the upright avoids evil;
those who guard their ways preserve
their lives.

18 Pride goes before destruction,
a haughty spirit before a fall.[n]

19 Better to be lowly in spirit along with
the oppressed
than to share plunder with the proud.

20 Whoever gives heed to instruction
prospers,[a]
and blessed is the one who trusts in
the LORD.[o]

21 The wise in heart are called discerning,
and gracious words promote
instruction.[b][p]

22 Prudence is a fountain of life to the
prudent,[q]
but folly brings punishment to fools.

23 The hearts of the wise make their
mouths prudent,
and their lips promote instruction.[c]

24 Gracious words are a honeycomb,
sweet to the soul and healing to the
bones.[r]

25 There is a way that appears to be right,[s]
but in the end it leads to death.[t]

26 The appetite of laborers works for them;
their hunger drives them on.

27 A scoundrel plots evil,
and on their lips it is like a scorching
fire.[u]

28 A perverse person stirs up conflict,[v]
and a gossip separates close friends.[w]

29 A violent person entices their neighbor
and leads them down a path that is
not good.[x]

30 Whoever winks with their eye is
plotting perversity;
whoever purses their lips is bent on
evil.

31 Gray hair is a crown of splendor;[y]
it is attained in the way of
righteousness.

32 Better a patient person than a warrior,
one with self-control than one who
takes a city.

33 The lot is cast into the lap,
but its every decision is from the
LORD.[z]

---

[a] 20 Or *whoever speaks prudently finds what is good* [b] 21 Or *words make a person persuasive*
[c] 23 Or *prudent / and make their lips persuasive*

16:10 *oracle.* This refers to judicial decisions made by the king. Because the nation rested in the king's hands, his first responsibility was to obey God (King Josiah's reform of Israel, 2 Kin. 22). Even the king had to submit to the dictates of justice.

16:15 *life ... his favor.* Successfully courting a powerful person's favor is like seeing rain clouds in a dry land. The phrase about the light of the face in this proverb helps us understand Aaron's benediction in Numbers 6:24–26.

16:17 *The highway of the upright.* This phrase is a metaphor for the way a person lives habitually. An *upright* person's highway or habit is to *depart from evil.* He does not compromise; he consistently strives to do good.

16:24 *Gracious words are a honeycomb.* The Hebrew word for honeycomb is also used in Psalm 19:10–11 with regard to the Word of God. The Israelites saw honey as a healthy food as well as a sweetener. Any comparison to it would connote positive, healthful effects.

16:27–29 *scoundrel ... perverse ... violent person.* These verses all begin in a similar way describing three different types of wicked people. The word "scoundrel" means a man of Belial; this person is a muckraker who uses bad information for evil purposes; he destroys people on purpose. The "perverse" person starts fights between friends. The "violent person" uses his power of persuasion to recruit others to join in his attacks.

16:32 *Better a patient person than a warrior.* Even though one of the most favored persons in the ancient Middle East was the military hero, this proverb suggests that one who is "slow to anger" or who "rules his spirit" is a greater hero than a returning warrior.

16:33 *The lot is cast into the lap.* The use of lots in ancient Israel could easily be confused with luck. But when a *lot* was cast as a means of determining

16:9 [g] Jer 10:23 **16:11** [h] Pr 11:1 **16:12** [i] Pr 25:5 **16:13** [j] Pr 14:35 **16:14** [k] Pr 19:12 **16:15** [l] Job 29:24 **16:16** [m] Pr 8:10, 19 **16:18** [n] Pr 11:2; 18:12 **16:20** [o] Ps 2:12; 34:8; Pr 19:8; Jer 17:7 **16:21** [p] ver 23 **16:22** [q] Pr 13:14 **16:24** [r] Pr 24:13-14 **16:25** [s] Pr 12:15 [t] Pr 14:12 **16:27** [u] Jas 3:6 **16:28** [v] Pr 15:18 [w] Pr 17:9 **16:29** [x] Pr 1:10; 12:26 **16:31** [y] Pr 20:29 **16:33** [z] Pr 18:18; 29:26

17 Better a dry crust with peace and quiet
than a house full of feasting, with strife.[a]

2 A prudent servant will rule over a disgraceful son
and will share the inheritance as one of the family.

3 The crucible for silver and the furnace for gold,[b]
but the LORD tests the heart.[c]

4 A wicked person listens to deceitful lips;
a liar pays attention to a destructive tongue.

5 Whoever mocks the poor shows contempt for their Maker;[d]
whoever gloats over disaster[e] will not go unpunished.[f]

6 Children's children[g] are a crown to the aged,
and parents are the pride of their children.

7 Eloquent lips are unsuited to a godless fool—
how much worse lying lips to a ruler!

8 A bribe is seen as a charm by the one who gives it;
they think success will come at every turn.

9 Whoever would foster love covers over an offense,[h]
but whoever repeats the matter separates close friends.[i]

10 A rebuke impresses a discerning person
more than a hundred lashes a fool.

11 Evildoers foster rebellion against God;
the messenger of death will be sent against them.

12 Better to meet a bear robbed of her cubs
than a fool bent on folly.

13 Evil will never leave the house
of one who pays back evil[j] for good.

14 Starting a quarrel is like breaching a dam;
so drop the matter before a dispute breaks out.[k]

15 Acquitting the guilty and condemning the innocent[l]—
the LORD detests them both.[m]

16 Why should fools have money in hand to buy wisdom,
when they are not able to understand it?[n]

17 A friend loves at all times,
and a brother is born for a time of adversity.

18 One who has no sense shakes hands in pledge
and puts up security for a neighbor.[o]

19 Whoever loves a quarrel loves sin;
whoever builds a high gate invites destruction.

20 One whose heart is corrupt does not prosper;
one whose tongue is perverse falls into trouble.

21 To have a fool for a child brings grief;
there is no joy for the parent of a godless fool.[p]

22 A cheerful heart is good medicine,
but a crushed spirit dries up the bones.[q]

23 The wicked accept bribes[r] in secret
to pervert the course of justice.

24 A discerning person keeps wisdom in view,
but a fool's eyes[s] wander to the ends of the earth.

25 A foolish son brings grief to his father
and bitterness to the mother who bore him.[t]

God's will, the people knew it did not fall indiscriminately. God exercises sovereignty over human affairs (v. 4).

17:1 ***Better a dry crust.*** This expression means "very little" especially in comparison to feasting. But the feasting in this verse is tainted by contention. Feasting could also be part of a sacrifice to God, but even such a feast could be ruined by angry disputes between believers.

17:2 ***A prudent servant.*** Reversals of fortune could happen if the wise servant was sufficiently skillful and the son and his brothers were undeserving. Much of Genesis describes the unexpected rise of a younger son over his older brother (Gen. 25:23–34).

17:4 ***A wicked person listens to deceitful lips.*** This proverb presents the "wicked person" and the "liar" as a parody of the wise. As the righteous person listens with care to the instruction of a teacher, so the wicked person listens with care to the ruinous speech of the unrighteous.

17:7 ***Eloquent lips.*** It is a contradiction in terms for a fool to speak well or for a prince to be a liar.

17:12 ***a bear robbed of her cubs.*** Nothing matches the rage of a mother bear who has been separated from her cubs; yet there is nothing in life more dangerous than the fool in the midst of his folly.

17:15 ***the LORD detests them both.*** Since God is a God of justice, He detests those who pervert justice—both those who declare the innocent guilty and those who declare the guilty innocent.

17:1 [a] Pr 15:16, 17 **17:3** [b] Pr 27:21 [c] 1Ch 29:17; Ps 26:2; Jer 17:10 **17:5** [d] Pr 14:31 [e] Job 31:29 [f] Ob 1:12 **17:6** [g] Pr 13:22 **17:9** [h] Pr 10:12 [i] Pr 16:28 **17:13** [j] Ps 109:4-5; Jer 18:20 **17:14** [k] Pr 20:3 **17:15** [l] Pr 18:5 [m] Ex 23:6-7; Isa 5:23 **17:16** [n] Pr 23:23 **17:18** [o] Pr 6:1-5; 11:15; 22:26-27 **17:21** [p] Pr 10:1 **17:22** [q] Ps 22:15; Pr 15:13 **17:23** [r] Ex 23:8 **17:24** [s] Ecc 2:14 **17:25** [t] Pr 10:1

26 If imposing a fine on the innocent is not good,[u]
surely to flog honest officials is not right.

27 The one who has knowledge uses words with restraint,
and whoever has understanding is even-tempered.[v]

28 Even fools are thought wise if they keep silent,
and discerning if they hold their tongues.[w]

18 An unfriendly person pursues selfish ends
and against all sound judgment starts quarrels.

2 Fools find no pleasure in understanding
but delight in airing their own opinions.[x]

3 When wickedness comes, so does contempt,
and with shame comes reproach.

4 The words of the mouth are deep waters,
but the fountain of wisdom is a rushing stream.

5 It is not good to be partial to the wicked[y]
and so deprive the innocent of justice.[z]

6 The lips of fools bring them strife,
and their mouths invite a beating.

7 The mouths of fools are their undoing,
and their lips are a snare[a] to their very lives.[b]

8 The words of a gossip are like choice morsels;
they go down to the inmost parts.[c]

9 One who is slack in his work
is brother to one who destroys.[d]

10 The name of the LORD is a fortified tower;[e]
the righteous run to it and are safe.

11 The wealth of the rich is their fortified city;[f]
they imagine it a wall too high to scale.

12 Before a downfall the heart is haughty,
but humility comes before honor.[g]

13 To answer before listening—
that is folly and shame.[h]

14 The human spirit can endure in sickness,
but a crushed spirit who can bear?[i]

15 The heart of the discerning acquires knowledge,[j]
for the ears of the wise seek it out.

16 A gift[k] opens the way
and ushers the giver into the presence of the great.

17 In a lawsuit the first to speak seems right,
until someone comes forward and cross-examines.

18 Casting the lot settles disputes[l]
and keeps strong opponents apart.

19 A brother wronged is more unyielding than a fortified city;
disputes are like the barred gates of a citadel.

20 From the fruit of their mouth a person's stomach is filled;
with the harvest of their lips they are satisfied.[m]

21 The tongue has the power of life and death,
and those who love it will eat its fruit.[n]

22 He who finds a wife finds what is good[o]
and receives favor from the LORD.[p]

23 The poor plead for mercy,
but the rich answer harshly.

18:1 ***pursues selfish ends.*** When a person is seeking his own desires, he separates himself from wisdom. His selfishness puts him "against" sound understanding.
18:2 ***Fools find no pleasure in understanding.*** A compulsive talker never listens, only pausing to plan what he will say next. Every speech confirms what a fool he is.
18:8 ***The words of a gossip.*** These words are like delicious sweets. Although they are fun to eat, they ruin the person's health. Gossip is fun to listen to, but it damages the listener's innermost parts.
18:10–11 ***The name of the LORD is a fortified tower.*** The phrase, *name of the Lord*, is a way of speaking of God's person. The righteous turn to God for security. Rich people, by contrast, tend to trust in their wealth.
18:12 ***the heart is haughty.*** The Hebrew word for haughty, ordinarily negative, can also be used positively to mean courage and daring (2 Chr. 17:6). The path to honor, which the proud so covet, is humility.
18:14 ***The human spirit can endure in sickness.*** This proverb affirms the value of coping skills. Sickness can be overcome, but there is no medicine for a *broken spirit*.
18:20 ***stomach ... lips.*** Inner satisfaction comes from true and good speech.
18:22 ***favor from the LORD.*** Problems in marriage arise from breakdowns in communication or mutual respect, not from some flaw in marriage itself (12:4).

17:26 [u] Pr 18:5 **17:27** [v] Pr 14:29; Jas 1:19
17:28 [w] Job 13:5 **18:2** [x] Pr 12:23 **18:5** [y] Lev 19:15; Pr 24:23-25; 28:21 [z] Ps 82:2; Pr 17:15 **18:7** [a] Ps 140:9 [b] Ps 64:8; Pr 10:14; 12:13; 13:3; Ecc 10:12 **18:8** [c] Pr 26:22
18:9 [d] Pr 28:24 **18:10** [e] 2Sa 22:3; Ps 61:3
18:11 [f] Pr 10:15 **18:12** [g] Pr 11:2; 15:33; 16:18
18:13 [h] Pr 20:25; Jn 7:51 **18:14** [i] Pr 15:13; 17:22
18:15 [j] Pr 15:14 **18:16** [k] Ge 32:20 **18:18** [l] Pr 16:33
18:20 [m] Pr 12:14 **18:21** [n] Pr 13:2-3; Mt 12:37
18:22 [o] Pr 12:4 [p] Pr 19:14; 31:10

[24] One who has unreliable friends soon
comes to ruin,
but there is a friend who sticks closer
than a brother.[q]

19

Better the poor whose walk is
blameless
than a fool whose lips are perverse.[r]

[2] Desire without knowledge is not good—
how much more will hasty feet miss
the way![s]

[3] A person's own folly leads to their ruin,
yet their heart rages against the LORD.

[4] Wealth attracts many friends,
but even the closest friend of the poor
person deserts them.[t]

[5] A false witness[u] will not go unpunished,
and whoever pours out lies will not
go free.[v]

[6] Many curry favor with a ruler,[w]
and everyone is the friend of one who
gives gifts.[x]

[7] The poor are shunned by all their
relatives—
how much more do their friends
avoid them!
Though the poor pursue them with
pleading,
they are nowhere to be found.[a][y]

[8] The one who gets wisdom loves life;
the one who cherishes understanding
will soon prosper.[z]

[9] A false witness will not go unpunished,
and whoever pours out lies will
perish.[a]

[10] It is not fitting for a fool[b] to live in
luxury—
how much worse for a slave to rule
over princes![c]

[11] A person's wisdom yields patience;[d]
it is to one's glory to overlook an
offense.

[12] A king's rage is like the roar of a lion,
but his favor is like dew[e] on the
grass.[f]

[13] A foolish child is a father's ruin,[g]
and a quarrelsome wife is like
the constant dripping of a leaky roof.[h]

[14] Houses and wealth are inherited from
parents,[i]
but a prudent wife is from the LORD.[j]

[15] Laziness brings on deep sleep,
and the shiftless go hungry.[k]

[16] Whoever keeps commandments keeps
their life,
but whoever shows contempt for their
ways will die.[l]

[17] Whoever is kind to the poor lends to the
LORD,
and he will reward them for what
they have done.[m]

[18] Discipline your children, for in that
there is hope;
do not be a willing party to their
death.[n]

[19] A hot-tempered person must pay the
penalty;
rescue them, and you will have to do
it again.

[20] Listen to advice and accept discipline,[o]
and at the end you will be counted
among the wise.[p]

[21] Many are the plans in a person's heart,
but it is the LORD's purpose that
prevails.[q]

[22] What a person desires is unfailing love[b];
better to be poor than a liar.

[23] The fear of the LORD leads to life;
then one rests content, untouched by
trouble.[r]

---

[a] 7 The meaning of the Hebrew for this sentence is uncertain. [b] 22 Or *Greed is a person's shame*

19:4 *Wealth attracts many friends.* This proverb speaks of the effects of wealth and poverty on friendship. It does not describe how friends ought to behave, but how many friends actually do. Like a faithful spouse, a faithful friend is priceless (14:20).
19:8 *The one who gets wisdom loves life.* Ultimately to "love life" means to find the Lord in His Word (16:20).
19:10 *is not fitting.* This phrase might also be rendered "is not a pretty sight" (17:7). For the wrong people to rule is an outrage.
19:12 *roar of a lion ... dew on the grass.* These metaphors are especially fitting when a monarch has all power. His rage may be violent and unpredictable, his pleasure gracious and restorative. A good king will display rage and spread favor for the right reasons.
19:13 *A foolish child ... a quarrelsome wife.* The family exists as the basic unit of a godly society. Two threats against the family are pictured in this proverb. One is the wayward son. The second is an emotionally unstable wife.
19:21 *Many are the plans in a person's heart.* A wise person commits his or her plans to the Lord (16:3). A person whose plans oppose the Lord (as in Ps. 2:1–3) may actually become God's enemy. But the person whose ways are from God will certainly succeed (16:1,9).
19:22 *unfailing love.* Unfailing love may also mean "beauty." Faithfulness is beautiful, whereas deception is a disfigurement of character (3:14; 31:18).

18:24 [q] Pr 17:17; Jn 15:13-15 **19:1** [r] Pr 28:6 **19:2** [s] Pr 29:20 **19:4** [t] Pr 14:20 **19:5** [u] Ex 23:1 [v] Dt 19:19; Pr 21:28 **19:6** [w] Pr 29:26 [x] Pr 17:8; 18:16 **19:7** [y] ver 4; Ps 38:11 **19:8** [z] Pr 16:20 **19:9** [a] ver 5 **19:10** [b] Pr 26:1 [c] Pr 30:21-23; Ecc 10:5-7 **19:11** [d] Pr 16:32 **19:12** [e] Ps 133:3 [f] Pr 16:14-15 **19:13** [g] Pr 10:1 [h] Pr 21:9 **19:14** [i] 2Co 12:14 [j] Pr 18:22 **19:15** [k] Pr 6:9; 10:4 **19:16** [l] Pr 16:17; Lk 10:28 **19:17** [m] Mt 10:42; 2Co 9:6-8 **19:18** [n] Pr 13:24; 23:13-14 **19:20** [o] Pr 4:1 [p] Pr 12:15 **19:21** [q] Ps 33:11; Pr 16:9; Isa 14:24,27 **19:23** [r] Ps 25:13; Pr 12:21; 1Ti 4:8

24 A sluggard buries his hand in the dish;
he will not even bring it back to his mouth![s]

25 Flog a mocker, and the simple will learn prudence;
rebuke the discerning, and they will gain knowledge.[t]

26 Whoever robs their father and drives out their mother[u]
is a child who brings shame and disgrace.

27 Stop listening to instruction, my son,
and you will stray from the words of knowledge.

28 A corrupt witness mocks at justice,
and the mouth of the wicked gulps down evil.[v]

29 Penalties are prepared for mockers,
and beatings for the backs of fools.[w]

20 Wine is a mocker and beer a brawler;
whoever is led astray by them is not wise.[x]

2 A king's wrath strikes terror like the roar of a lion;[y]
those who anger him forfeit their lives.[z]

3 It is to one's honor to avoid strife,
but every fool is quick to quarrel.[a]

4 Sluggards do not plow in season;
so at harvest time they look but find nothing.

5 The purposes of a person's heart are deep waters,
but one who has insight draws them out.

6 Many claim to have unfailing love,
but a faithful person who can find?[b]

7 The righteous lead blameless lives;
blessed are their children after them.[c]

8 When a king sits on his throne to judge,
he winnows out all evil with his eyes.[d]

9 Who can say, "I have kept my heart pure;
I am clean and without sin"?[e]

10 Differing weights and differing measures—
the LORD detests them both.[f]

11 Even small children are known by their actions,
so is their conduct really pure[g] and upright?

12 Ears that hear and eyes that see—
the LORD has made them both.[h]

13 Do not love sleep or you will grow poor;[i]
stay awake and you will have food to spare.

14 "It's no good, it's no good!" says the buyer—
then goes off and boasts about the purchase.

15 Gold there is, and rubies in abundance,
but lips that speak knowledge are a rare jewel.

16 Take the garment of one who puts up security for a stranger;
hold it in pledge[j] if it is done for an outsider.[k]

17 Food gained by fraud tastes sweet,[l]
but one ends up with a mouth full of gravel.

18 Plans are established by seeking advice;
so if you wage war, obtain guidance.[m]

19 A gossip betrays a confidence;[n]
so avoid anyone who talks too much.

19:26–27 ***son.*** The desire for a good son—or daughter—is the subject of a significant portion of Proverbs (ch. 1–9). A child who is abusive to his parents shames them and violates God's command (20:20; Ex. 20:12; Deut. 5:16). As an abusive son is shameful, so an obedient son is faithful.
20:1 ***Wine is a mocker.*** This chapter begins with a warning against the abuse of wine, or excessive drinking (see this theme more extensively in 23:29–35). A wise person takes the danger seriously.
20:5 ***draws them out.*** Motivation for behavior is complex. A gifted counselor is able to draw out from a person genuine feelings and motivations, just as someone draws water from a deep well.
20:9 ***Who can say.*** This proverb is a rhetorical question. Everyone sins, a theme that Paul addresses at length in Romans 3:10–23. Anyone who claims never to sin is a liar (1 John 1:8–9). But those who confess their sin obtain forgiveness (Rom. 4:7).
20:11 ***by their actions.*** A pattern established early in life may continue to mark a person for his or her lifetime. Even at a very early age, a person's moral character may be revealed.
20:13 ***sleep.*** While sleep is a gift from God, it can also be a matter of excess and laziness. Hard work is necessary to make a living; laziness leads only to poverty (6:6–9).
20:16 ***Take the garment.*** Clothing could be taken as collateral for a debt (Deut. 24:10–13). If someone assumes responsibility for the debt of an unknown stranger, he or she should be held accountable even to the point of taking his or her clothing as a pledge.
20:17 ***but one ends up with.*** The Scriptures do not say that there is no pleasure in sinning, only that the reward does not last (9:17–18).

19:24 [s] Pr 26:15 **19:25** [t] Pr 9:9; 21:11 **19:26** [u] Pr 28:24 **19:28** [v] Job 15:16 **19:29** [w] Pr 26:3 **20:1** [x] Pr 31:4 **20:2** [y] Pr 19:12 [z] Pr 8:36 **20:3** [a] Pr 17:14 **20:6** [b] Ps 12:1 **20:7** [c] Ps 37:25-26; 112:2 **20:8** [d] ver 26; Pr 25:4-5 **20:9** [e] 1Ki 8:46; Ecc 7:20; 1Jn 1:8 **20:10** [f] ver 23; Pr 11:1 **20:11** [g] Mt 7:16 **20:12** [h] Ps 94:9 **20:13** [i] Pr 6:11; 19:15 **20:16** [j] Ex 22:26 [k] Pr 27:13 **20:17** [l] Pr 9:17 **20:18** [m] Pr 11:14; 24:6 **20:19** [n] Pr 11:13

20 If someone curses their father or mother,[o]
their lamp will be snuffed out in pitch darkness.[p]

21 An inheritance claimed too soon
will not be blessed at the end.

22 Do not say, "I'll pay you back for this wrong!"[q]
Wait for the LORD, and he will avenge you.[r]

23 The LORD detests differing weights,
and dishonest scales do not please him.[s]

24 A person's steps are directed by the LORD.
How then can anyone understand their own way?[t]

25 It is a trap to dedicate something rashly
and only later to consider one's vows.[u]

26 A wise king winnows out the wicked;
he drives the threshing wheel over them.[v]

27 The human spirit is[a] the lamp of the LORD
that sheds light on one's inmost being.

28 Love and faithfulness keep a king safe;
through love his throne is made secure.[w]

29 The glory of young men is their strength,
gray hair the splendor of the old.[x]

30 Blows and wounds scrub[y] away evil,
and beatings purge the inmost being.

21 In the LORD's hand the king's heart is a stream of water
that he channels toward all who please him.

2 A person may think their own ways are right,
but the LORD weighs the heart.[z]

3 To do what is right and just
is more acceptable to the LORD than sacrifice.[a]

4 Haughty eyes[b] and a proud heart—
the unplowed field of the wicked—produce sin.

5 The plans of the diligent lead to profit[c]
as surely as haste leads to poverty.

6 A fortune made by a lying tongue
is a fleeting vapor and a deadly snare.[bd]

7 The violence of the wicked will drag them away,
for they refuse to do what is right.

8 The way of the guilty is devious,[e]
but the conduct of the innocent is upright.

9 Better to live on a corner of the roof
than share a house with a quarrelsome wife.[f]

10 The wicked crave evil;
their neighbors get no mercy from them.

11 When a mocker is punished, the simple gain wisdom;
by paying attention to the wise they get knowledge.[g]

12 The Righteous One[c] takes note of the house of the wicked
and brings the wicked to ruin.[h]

---

[a] 27 Or *A person's words are* [b] 6 Some Hebrew manuscripts, Septuagint and Vulgate; most Hebrew manuscripts *vapor for those who seek death* [c] 12 Or *The righteous person*

20:20 ***If someone curses.*** This proverb is about breaking the Fifth Commandment, "Honor your father and your mother" (Ex. 20:12). The term for "curses" is based on a word that means "to treat lightly, to regard as insignificant." The statement "their lamp will be snuffed out in pitch darkness," is a symbol of eternal damnation.
20:25 ***to dedicate something rashly.*** Several proverbs warn against making rash promises about holy things, then withdrawing the promises later (Eccl. 5:1–7). It is better never to vow than to vow and then change one's mind.
20:26 ***A wise king winnows out the wicked.*** This royal proverb presents discipline as a merciful act. To punish wickedness is entirely appropriate. When the wicked are separated and punished with the severity that their crimes demand, all of society benefits. Ideally, the king in Israel mirrored God's character.
20:30 ***Blows and wounds scrub away evil.*** Suffering cleanses. No one wants to be hurt, but God can bring good out of any evil and make us better through hardship.
21:1 ***the king's heart is a stream of water.*** A person can look at a river and think that it is following a random pattern, but the water is following the direction of God's hand. So is the king.
21:3 ***To do what is right and just.*** This proverb affirms, as do Psalm 40:6–8; Micah 6:8, and numerous other passages in the Bible, that righteous living is more important than sacrifice (1 Sam. 15:22).
21:6 ***A fortune made by a lying tongue.*** If you have to lie to gain your "treasure," you are ultimately choosing death to your dreams. There is no stability in anything gained by a lie.
21:9 ***a corner of the roof.*** Ancient Israelite roofs were flat and could be used as a deck or terrace. On occasion people would build a temporary shelter on a part of the roof. Here, the harried husband finds he prefers to live on the housetop rather than below with the nagging words of his wife.
21:10 ***The wicked crave evil.*** Wicked persons typically refuse to think of anyone but themselves.

20:20 [o] Pr 30:11 [p] Ex 21:17; Job 18:5 **20:22** [q] Pr 24:29 [r] Ro 12:19 **20:23** [s] ver 10 **20:24** [t] Jer 10:23 **20:25** [u] Ecc 5:2,4-5 **20:26** [v] ver 8 **20:28** [w] Pr 29:14 **20:29** [x] Pr 16:31 **20:30** [y] Pr 22:15 **21:2** [z] Pr 16:2; 24:12; Lk 16:15 **21:3** [a] 1Sa 15:22; Pr 15:8; Isa 1:11; Hos 6:6; Mic 6:6-8 **21:4** [b] Pr 6:17 **21:5** [c] Pr 10:4; 28:22 **21:6** [d] 2Pe 2:3 **21:8** [e] Pr 2:15 **21:9** [f] Pr 25:24 **21:11** [g] Pr 19:25 **21:12** [h] Pr 14:11

13 Whoever shuts their ears to the cry of
the poor
will also cry out and not be answered.[i]
14 A gift given in secret soothes anger,
and a bribe concealed in the cloak
pacifies great wrath.[j]
15 When justice is done, it brings joy to the
righteous
but terror to evildoers.[k]
16 Whoever strays from the path of
prudence
comes to rest in the company of the
dead.[l]
17 Whoever loves pleasure will become
poor;
whoever loves wine and olive oil will
never be rich.[m]
18 The wicked become a ransom[n] for the
righteous,
and the unfaithful for the upright.
19 Better to live in a desert
than with a quarrelsome and nagging
wife.[o]
20 The wise store up choice food and olive
oil,
but fools gulp theirs down.
21 Whoever pursues righteousness and love
finds life, prosperity[a] and honor.[p]
22 One who is wise can go up against the
city of the mighty[q]
and pull down the stronghold in
which they trust.
23 Those who guard their mouths[r] and
their tongues
keep themselves from calamity.[s]
24 The proud and arrogant person[t]—
"Mocker" is his name—
behaves with insolent fury.
25 The craving of a sluggard will be the
death of him,[u]
because his hands refuse to work.
26 All day long he craves for more,
but the righteous give without
sparing.[v]
27 The sacrifice of the wicked is
detestable[w]—
how much more so when brought
with evil intent![x]
28 A false witness will perish,[y]
but a careful listener will testify
successfully.
29 The wicked put up a bold front,
but the upright give thought to their
ways.
30 There is no wisdom,[z] no insight, no
plan
that can succeed against the LORD.[a]
31 The horse is made ready for the day of
battle,
but victory rests with the LORD.[b]

22 A good name is more desirable than
great riches;
to be esteemed is better than silver or
gold.[c]
2 Rich and poor have this in common:
The LORD is the Maker of them all.[d]
3 The prudent see danger and take
refuge,[e]
but the simple keep going and pay the
penalty.[f]
4 Humility is the fear of the LORD;
its wages are riches and honor and
life.
5 In the paths of the wicked are snares
and pitfalls,[g]
but those who would preserve their
life stay far from them.
6 Start children off on the way they
should go,[h]
and even when they are old they will
not turn from it.

[a] 21 Or *righteousness*

21:15 ***When justice is done, it brings joy.*** Doing justice is not a heavy obligation that weighs a person down. For the righteous, promoting justice is a joy.
21:16 ***the company of the dead.*** The term *dead* is a frightful one, meaning "shades" (9:18). Death in these verses may speak of physical death rather than spiritual death (as is the case in James 1).
21:21 ***life, prosperity and honor.*** It is possible that these three ideas go together to mean "a more abundant life." The pursuit of righteousness is its own reward. But added rewards are found in fullness of life, achieving righteousness, and receiving honor. All these things are gifts from the Lord (15:9).
21:28 ***A false witness will perish.*** A large number of proverbs focus on bearing false witness (19:28). The problem with a false witness is that his lies pervert justice for others.
22:2 ***The LORD is the Maker of them all.*** This sentence repeats the theme of riches (v. 1). God makes both the rich and the poor. This means that those who favor the rich over the poor (James 2) have not only missed the point of creation, they have insulted the Creator (14:31).
22:4 ***Humility is the fear of the LORD.*** The writer of this proverb makes humility synonymous with the fear of the Lord. True humility begins with a proper attitude toward God. In such a spirit of submission to God, true fear of God is exhibited.
22:6 ***Start children off.*** This verse, like the other

21:13 [i] Mt 18:30-34; Jas 2:13 **21:14** [j] Pr 18:16; 19:6 **21:15** [k] Pr 10:29 **21:16** [l] Ps 49:14 **21:17** [m] Pr 23:20-21, 29-35 **21:18** [n] Pr 11:8; Isa 43:3 **21:19** [o] ver 9 **21:21** [p] Mt 5:6 **21:22** [q] Ecc 9:15-16 **21:23** [r] Jas 3:2 [s] Pr 12:13; 13:3 **21:24** [t] Ps 1:1; Pr 1:22; Isa 16:6; Jer 48:29 **21:25** [u] Pr 13:4 **21:26** [v] Ps 37:26; Mt 5:42; Eph 4:28 **21:27** [w] Isa 66:3; Jer 6:20; Am 5:22 [x] Pr 15:8 **21:28** [y] Pr 19:5 **21:30** [z] Jer 9:23 [a] Isa 8:10; Ac 5:39 **21:31** [b] Ps 3:8; 33:12-19; Isa 31:1 **22:1** [c] Ecc 7:1 **22:2** [d] Job 31:15 **22:3** [e] Pr 14:16 [f] Pr 27:12 **22:5** [g] Pr 15:19 **22:6** [h] Eph 6:4

7 The rich rule over the poor,
and the borrower is slave to the lender.

8 Whoever sows injustice reaps calamity,[i]
and the rod they wield in fury will be broken.[j]

9 The generous will themselves be blessed,[k]
for they share their food with the poor.[l]

10 Drive out the mocker, and out goes strife;
quarrels and insults are ended.[m]

11 One who loves a pure heart and who speaks with grace
will have the king for a friend.[n]

12 The eyes of the LORD keep watch over knowledge,
but he frustrates the words of the unfaithful.

13 The sluggard says, "There's a lion outside![o]
I'll be killed in the public square!"

14 The mouth of an adulterous woman is a deep pit;[p]
a man who is under the LORD's wrath falls into it.[q]

15 Folly is bound up in the heart of a child,
but the rod of discipline will drive it far away.[r]

16 One who oppresses the poor to increase his wealth
and one who gives gifts to the rich—
both come to poverty.

Thirty Sayings of the Wise

Saying 1

17 Pay attention and turn your ear to the sayings of the wise;[s]
apply your heart to what I teach,
18 for it is pleasing when you keep them in your heart
and have all of them ready on your lips.
19 So that your trust may be in the LORD,
I teach you today, even you.
20 Have I not written thirty sayings for you,
sayings of counsel and knowledge,
21 teaching you to be honest and to speak the truth,[t]
so that you bring back truthful reports
to those you serve?

Saying 2

22 Do not exploit the poor[u] because they are poor
and do not crush the needy in court,[v]
23 for the LORD will take up their case[w]
and will exact life for life.[x]

Saying 3

24 Do not make friends with a hot-tempered person,
do not associate with one easily angered,
25 or you may learn their ways
and get yourself ensnared.[y]

Saying 4

26 Do not be one who shakes hands in pledge[z]
or puts up security for debts;
27 if you lack the means to pay,
your very bed will be snatched from under you.[a]

---

proverbs, contains a wise statement that is usually true. Who your child turns out to be is a reflection of your parenting. As God has taught elsewhere in His word, parents are to teach their children the way of the Lord. Not only are they to teach it purposefully, but they are to do it constantly—when they talk and sit and walk and lay down and get up (Deut. 6:7–8). If children see their parents speaking kindly, being forgiving and gracious, gentle and understanding, children will want these character attributes, too. But even more important, if the parents teach that they depend upon God to build kindly habits in themselves, children will know that it is to the Lord that one turns for help in every part of life. Training children undoubtedly involves everything from wiping feet and closing doors to saying "please" and "thank you," and "I am sorry." But the most important training that a child receives is the continual teaching and daily example of their parents' dependence on the Lord.

22:10 ***the mocker.*** This kind of person should be expelled from the community because his influence is harmful to everyone. The wise know that the scorner is not a laughing matter, because he is laughing at holy things, at God Himself.

22:12 ***The eyes of the LORD.*** God is the final arbiter of knowledge and justice. The eyes of human beings are simply not trustworthy.

22:13 ***There's a lion outside!*** This proverb about lazy people pokes fun at how the lazy invent all sorts of excuses for avoiding work and risk.

22:17–24:22 Proverbs Concerning Various Situations—Verse 17 marks a new section of Proverbs. Three elements distinguish this section: (1) the change from one-verse units to multiple-verse units; (2) section headings that are embedded in the text; and (3) the affinity of this section for ancient Egyptian wisdom texts.

22:17–21 ***turn your ear.*** These introductory words call the reader to pay attention and to prepare to learn about and worship God. The advice emphasizes strongly that a person's trust must be in the Lord.

22:8 [i] Job 4:8 [j] Ps 125:3 **22:9** [k] 2Co 9:6 [l] Pr 19:17
22:10 [m] Pr 18:6; 26:20 **22:11** [n] Pr 16:13; Mt 5:8
22:13 [o] Pr 26:13 **22:14** [p] Pr 2:16; 5:3-5; 7:5; 23:27
[q] Ecc 7:26 **22:15** [r] Pr 13:24; 23:14 **22:17** [s] Pr 5:1
22:21 [t] Lk 1:3-4; 1Pe 3:15 **22:22** [u] Zec 7:10 [v] Ex 23:6; Mal 3:5 **22:23** [w] Ps 12:5 [x] 1Sa 25:39; Pr 23:10-11
22:25 [y] 1Co 15:33 **22:26** [z] Pr 11:15 **22:27** [a] Pr 17:18

Saying 5

28 Do not move an ancient boundary stone[b]
set up by your ancestors.

Saying 6

29 Do you see someone skilled in their work?
They will serve[c] before kings;
they will not serve before officials of low rank.

Saying 7

23 When you sit to dine with a ruler,
note well what[a] is before you,
2 and put a knife to your throat
if you are given to gluttony.
3 Do not crave his delicacies,[d]
for that food is deceptive.

Saying 8

4 Do not wear yourself out to get rich;
do not trust your own cleverness.
5 Cast but a glance at riches, and they are gone,
for they will surely sprout wings
and fly off to the sky like an eagle.[e]

Saying 9

6 Do not eat the food of a begrudging host,
do not crave his delicacies;[f]
7 for he is the kind of person
who is always thinking about the cost.[b]
"Eat and drink," he says to you,
but his heart is not with you.
8 You will vomit up the little you have eaten
and will have wasted your compliments.

Saying 10

9 Do not speak to fools,
for they will scorn your prudent words.[g]

Saying 11

10 Do not move an ancient boundary stone[h]
or encroach on the fields of the fatherless,
11 for their Defender[i] is strong;
he will take up their case against you.[j]

Saying 12

12 Apply your heart to instruction
and your ears to words of knowledge.

Saying 13

13 Do not withhold discipline from a child;
if you punish them with the rod, they will not die.
14 Punish them with the rod
and save them from death.

Saying 14

15 My son, if your heart is wise,
then my heart will be glad indeed;
16 my inmost being will rejoice
when your lips speak what is right.[k]

Saying 15

17 Do not let your heart envy[l] sinners,
but always be zealous for the fear of the LORD.
18 There is surely a future hope for you,
and your hope will not be cut off.[m]

Saying 16

19 Listen, my son, and be wise,
and set your heart on the right path:
20 Do not join those who drink too much wine[n]
or gorge themselves on meat,
21 for drunkards and gluttons become poor,[o]
and drowsiness clothes them in rags.

Saying 17

22 Listen to your father, who gave you life,
and do not despise your mother when she is old.[p]
23 Buy the truth and do not sell it—
wisdom, instruction and insight as well.[q]

---

[a] *1* Or *who* [b] *7* Or *for as he thinks within himself, / so he is;* or *for as he puts on a feast, / so he is*

22:28 *Do not move an ancient boundary.* The ancient Israelites regarded respect for the posted landmark as more than a question of private property. They saw it as a basic part of civil life. People must feel a certain sense of public trust and fairness for society to function.

23:4–5 *Do not wear yourself out to get rich.* These verses call for moderation in work. Although the proverbs discourage laziness (22:13), they also discourage any overworking whose purpose is greater wealth.

23:13–14 *if you punish them with the rod.* This language was designed to motivate overly permissive parents, who were afraid of damaging children with any kind of discipline, or of making rules and enforcing them. There is no call here for abuse. Loving discipline does not destroy rebellious children; it does them a big favor.

23:15 *if your heart is wise.* Wisdom is an outgrowth of a proper response to discipline. That wisdom in turn is immediately discernible to the father and brings joy that must be expressed.

23:21 *for drunkards and gluttons.* These kinds of people have no self-control, and this fact plagues them. Hebrew culture gave a prominent place to eating and drinking, but it had little tolerance for drunkenness and gluttony.

22:28 [b] Dt 19:14; Pr 23:10 **22:29** [c] Ge 41:46
23:3 [d] ver 6-8 **23:5** [e] Pr 27:24 **23:6** [f] Ps 141:4
23:9 [g] Pr 1:7; 9:7; Mt 7:6 **23:10** [h] Dt 19:14; Pr 22:28
23:11 [i] Job 19:25 [j] Pr 22:22-23 **23:16** [k] ver 24; Pr 27:11
23:17 [l] Ps 37:1; Pr 28:14 **23:18** [m] Ps 9:18; Pr 24:14, 19-20
23:20 [n] Isa 5:11, 22; Ro 13:13; Eph 5:18 **23:21** [o] Pr 21:17
23:22 [p] Lev 19:32; Pr 1:8; 30:17; Eph 6:1-2 **23:23** [q] Pr 4:7

24 The father of a righteous child has
great joy;
a man who fathers a wise son rejoices
in him.[r]
25 May your father and mother rejoice;
may she who gave you birth be
joyful!

Saying 18

26 My son,[s] give me your heart
and let your eyes delight in my
ways,[t]
27 for an adulterous woman is a deep pit,[u]
and a wayward wife is a narrow well.
28 Like a bandit she lies in wait[v]
and multiplies the unfaithful among
men.

Saying 19

29 Who has woe? Who has sorrow?
Who has strife? Who has complaints?
Who has needless bruises? Who has
bloodshot eyes?
30 Those who linger over wine,[w]
who go to sample bowls of mixed
wine.
31 Do not gaze at wine when it is red,
when it sparkles in the cup,
when it goes down smoothly!
32 In the end it bites like a snake
and poisons like a viper.
33 Your eyes will see strange sights,
and your mind will imagine
confusing things.
34 You will be like one sleeping on the
high seas,
lying on top of the rigging.
35 "They hit me," you will say, "but I'm not
hurt!
They beat me, but I don't feel it!
When will I wake up
so I can find another drink?"

Saying 20

24 Do not envy[x] the wicked,
do not desire their company;
2 for their hearts plot violence,
and their lips talk about making
trouble.[y]

Saying 21

3 By wisdom a house is built,[z]
and through understanding it is
established;
4 through knowledge its rooms are filled
with rare and beautiful treasures.[a]

Saying 22

5 The wise prevail through great power,
and those who have knowledge
muster their strength.
6 Surely you need guidance to wage war,
and victory is won through many
advisers.[b]

Saying 23

7 Wisdom is too high for fools;
in the assembly at the gate they must
not open their mouths.

Saying 24

8 Whoever plots evil
will be known as a schemer.
9 The schemes of folly are sin,
and people detest a mocker.

Saying 25

10 If you falter in a time of trouble,
how small is your strength![c]
11 Rescue those being led away to death;
hold back those staggering toward
slaughter.[d]
12 If you say, "But we knew nothing about
this,"
does not he who weighs[e] the heart
perceive it?
Does not he who guards your life
know it?
Will he not repay everyone according
to what they have done?[f]

Saying 26

13 Eat honey, my son, for it is good;
honey from the comb is sweet to your
taste.
14 Know also that wisdom is like honey
for you:
If you find it, there is a future hope
for you,
and your hope will not be cut off.[g]

23:29–35 *Who has woe?* Along with Isaiah's celebrated description of debauchery (Is. 19:11–15), this section is one of the sharpest attacks on drunkenness in the Bible (vv. 19–21). The satire is razor sharp and the imagery vivid.

24:6 The Will of God—Common sense tells us that God often works through circumstances and through wise counsel to reveal His will for us. A number of biblical examples illustrate this principle:

- God directed Abraham to substitute a ram, whose horns had become entangled in a thicket, for the life of Isaac (Gen. 22:13)
- God arranged for Pharaoh's daughter to be bathing in the river Nile at the exact time the baby Moses floated by in an ark of bulrushes (Ex. 2:1–10).
- Paul's young nephew happened to overhear a plot to kill his uncle. He then reported it to the authorities who saved Paul's life (Acts 23:11–35).

In light of the above, the Christian should ask himself, "Is the Lord showing me something through these circumstances?" We can also take great comfort in Paul's reminder to the Romans that God causes all things to "works for the good of those who love him, who have been called according to his purpose" (Rom. 8:28).

23:24 [r] ver 15-16; Pr 10:1; 15:20 **23:26** [s] Pr 3:1; 5:1-6 [t] Ps 18:21; Pr 4:4 **23:27** [u] Pr 22:14 **23:28** [v] Pr 7:11-12; Ecc 7:26 **23:30** [w] Ps 75:8; Isa 5:11; Eph 5:18 **24:1** [x] Ps 37:1; 73:3; Pr 3:31-32; 23:17-18 **24:2** [y] Ps 10:7 **24:3** [z] Pr 14:1 **24:4** [a] Pr 8:21 **24:6** [b] Pr 11:14; 20:18; Lk 14:31 **24:10** [c] Job 4:5; Jer 51:46; Heb 12:3 **24:11** [d] Ps 82:4; Isa 58:6-7 **24:12** [e] Pr 21:2 [f] Job 34:11; Ps 62:12; Ro 2:6* **24:14** [g] Ps 119:103; Pr 16:24; 23:18

Saying 27

15 Do not lurk like a thief near the house
of the righteous,
do not plunder their dwelling place;
16 for though the righteous fall seven
times, they rise again,
but the wicked stumble when
calamity strikes.[h]

Saying 28

17 Do not gloat[i] when your enemy falls;
when they stumble, do not let your
heart rejoice,[j]
18 or the LORD will see and disapprove
and turn his wrath away from them.

Saying 29

19 Do not fret[k] because of evildoers
or be envious of the wicked,
20 for the evildoer has no future hope,
and the lamp of the wicked will be
snuffed out.[l]

Saying 30

21 Fear the LORD and the king,[m] my son,
and do not join with rebellious officials,
22 for those two will send sudden
destruction on them,
and who knows what calamities they
can bring?

Further Sayings of the Wise

23 These also are sayings of the wise:[n]

To show partiality[o] in judging is not
good:[p]
24 Whoever says to the guilty, "You are
innocent,"[q]
will be cursed by peoples and
denounced by nations.
25 But it will go well with those who
convict the guilty,
and rich blessing will come on them.

26 An honest answer
is like a kiss on the lips.

27 Put your outdoor work in order
and get your fields ready;
after that, build your house.

28 Do not testify against your neighbor
without cause[r]—
would you use your lips to mislead?
29 Do not say, "I'll do to them as they have
done to me;
I'll pay them back for what they did."[s]

30 I went past the field of a sluggard,[t]
past the vineyard of someone who
has no sense;
31 thorns had come up everywhere,
the ground was covered with weeds,
and the stone wall was in ruins.
32 I applied my heart to what I observed
and learned a lesson from what I saw:
33 A little sleep, a little slumber,
a little folding of the hands to rest[u]—
34 and poverty will come on you like a
thief
and scarcity like an armed man.[v]

More Proverbs of Solomon

25 These are more proverbs[w] of Solomon, compiled by the men of Hezekiah king of Judah:[x]

2 It is the glory of God to conceal a
matter;
to search out a matter is the glory of
kings.[y]
3 As the heavens are high and the earth
is deep,
so the hearts of kings are
unsearchable.

4 Remove the dross from the silver,
and a silversmith can produce a
vessel;
5 remove wicked officials from the king's
presence,[z]
and his throne will be established[a]
through righteousness.[b]

6 Do not exalt yourself in the king's
presence,
and do not claim a place among his
great men;
7 it is better for him to say to you, "Come
up here,"[c]
than for him to humiliate you before
his nobles.

24:21–22 *Fear the LORD and the king.* This proverb relates most fully to the Davidic kings, who were God's regents on earth; one way the ancient Israelites could show respect for God was to respect the king.
25:1 *These are more proverbs of Solomon.* After the first collection of proverbs from Solomon (10:1–22:16) and proverbs from foreign sources (22:17–24:22; 24:23–34) comes a collection of proverbs attributed to Solomon, but which were not compiled until the time of Hezekiah. The following observations can be made: (1) The wisdom tradition concerning Solomon was prodigious; (2) Israel's interest in wisdom was particularly centered in times of relative peace; (3) Hezekiah's involvement in this activity was a mark of the strength of his rule and the sense he had of restoring Solomon's glory.
25:6 *Do not exalt yourself.* Knowing your place is a recurring theme in the Bible. It is humiliating to be told to remove yourself from a seat of honor. Jesus spoke of the same need for deference (Luke 14:11).
25:7 *What you have seen with your eyes.* This phrase reflects the custom in the ancient world of never looking directly in the eyes of a superior until told to do so (Is. 6:5).

24:16 [h] Job 5:19; Ps 34:19; Mic 7:8 **24:17** [i] Ob 1:12 [j] Job 31:29 **24:19** [k] Ps 37:1 **24:20** [l] Job 18:5; Pr 13:9; 23:17-18 **24:21** [m] Ro 13:1-5; 1Pe 2:17 **24:23** [n] Pr 1:6 [o] Lev 19:15 [p] Pr 28:21 **24:24** [q] Pr 17:15 **24:28** [r] Ps 7:4; Pr 25:18; Eph 4:25 **24:29** [s] Pr 20:22; Mt 5:38-41; Ro 12:17 **24:30** [t] Pr 6:6-11; 26:13-16 **24:33** [u] Pr 6:10 **24:34** [v] Pr 10:4; Ecc 10:18 **25:1** [w] 1Ki 4:32 [x] Pr 1:1 **25:2** [y] Pr 16:10-15 **25:5** [z] Pr 20:8 [a] 2Sa 7:13 [b] Pr 16:12; 29:14 **25:7** [c] Lk 14:7-10

What you have seen with your eyes
8 do not bring[a] hastily to court,
for what will you do in the end
if your neighbor puts you to shame?[d]

9 If you take your neighbor to court,
do not betray another's confidence,
10 or the one who hears it may shame you
and the charge against you will
stand.

11 Like apples[b] of gold in settings of silver[e]
is a ruling rightly given.
12 Like an earring of gold or an ornament
of fine gold
is the rebuke of a wise judge to a
listening ear.[f]

13 Like a snow-cooled drink at harvest
time
is a trustworthy messenger to the one
who sends him;
he refreshes the spirit of his master.[g]
14 Like clouds and wind without rain
is one who boasts of gifts never
given.

15 Through patience a ruler can be
persuaded,[h]
and a gentle tongue can break a
bone.[i]

16 If you find honey, eat just enough—
too much of it, and you will vomit.[j]
17 Seldom set foot in your neighbor's
house—
too much of you, and they will hate
you.

18 Like a club or a sword or a sharp arrow
is one who gives false testimony
against a neighbor.[k]
19 Like a broken tooth or a lame foot
is reliance on the unfaithful in a time
of trouble.
20 Like one who takes away a garment on
a cold day,
or like vinegar poured on a wound,
is one who sings songs to a heavy
heart.

21 If your enemy is hungry, give him food
to eat;
if he is thirsty, give him water to
drink.
22 In doing this, you will heap burning
coals[l] on his head,
and the LORD will reward you.[m]

23 Like a north wind that brings
unexpected rain
is a sly tongue—which provokes a
horrified look.

24 Better to live on a corner of the roof
than share a house with a
quarrelsome wife.[n]

25 Like cold water to a weary soul
is good news from a distant land.[o]
26 Like a muddied spring or a polluted
well
are the righteous who give way to the
wicked.

27 It is not good to eat too much honey,[p]
nor is it honorable to search out
matters that are too deep.[q]

28 Like a city whose walls are broken
through
is a person who lacks self-control.

26 Like snow in summer or rain[r] in
harvest,
honor is not fitting for a fool.[s]
2 Like a fluttering sparrow or a darting
swallow,
an undeserved curse does not come
to rest.[t]
3 A whip for the horse, a bridle for the
donkey,[u]
and a rod for the backs of fools![v]
4 Do not answer a fool according to his
folly,
or you yourself will be just like him.[w]
5 Answer a fool according to his folly,
or he will be wise in his own eyes.[x]
6 Sending a message by the hands of a
fool[y]
is like cutting off one's feet or
drinking poison.
7 Like the useless legs of one who is lame
is a proverb in the mouth of a fool.[z]
8 Like tying a stone in a sling
is the giving of honor to a fool.[a]
9 Like a thornbush in a drunkard's hand
is a proverb in the mouth of a fool.[b]

[a] 7,8 Or *nobles / on whom you had set your eyes. / 8Do not go* [b] *11* Or possibly *apricots*

25:15 *Through patience a ruler can be persuaded.* In this passage the general rule that a gentle answer turns away wrath is applied to a particular and most difficult situation.

25:21–22 *burning coals.* The words of Jesus in Matthew 5:43–48 have direct ties to these verses. They speak of God's judgment (Ps. 120:4; 140:10); the idea is that an act of kindness to your enemy may cause him or her to feel ashamed. This is just one way to overcome evil with good (Rom. 12:20).

26:4–5 *according to his folly.* Some people have called the two proverbs here contradictory, but that is not necessarily true. The phrase appears twice as a play on words with two shades of meaning. On the one hand, it means "avoid the temptation to stoop to his level"; that is do not use his methods, "lest you also be like him." On the other hand, it means "avoid the temptation to ignore him altogether"; that is, respond in some way, or else he will become wise in his own eyes and his folly will get worse.

25:8 [d] Mt 5:25-26 **25:11** [e] ver 12; Pr 15:23 **25:12** [f] ver 11; Ps 141:5; Pr 13:18; 15:31 **25:13** [g] Pr 10:26; 13:17 **25:15** [h] Ecc 10:4 [i] Pr 15:1 **25:16** [j] ver 27 **25:18** [k] Ps 57:4; Pr 12:18 **25:22** [l] Ps 18:8 [m] 2Sa 16:12; 2Ch 28:15; Mt 5:44; Ro 12:20* **25:24** [n] Pr 21:9 **25:25** [o] Pr 15:30 **25:27** [p] ver 16 [q] Pr 27:2; Mt 23:12 **26:1** [r] 1Sa 12:17 [s] ver 8; Pr 19:10 **26:2** [t] Nu 23:8; Dt 23:5 **26:3** [u] Ps 32:9 [v] Pr 10:13 **26:4** [w] ver 5; Isa 36:21 **26:5** [x] ver 4; Pr 3:7 **26:6** [y] Pr 10:26 **26:7** [z] ver 9 **26:8** [a] ver 1 **26:9** [b] ver 7

10 Like an archer who wounds at random
is one who hires a fool or any
passer-by.
11 As a dog returns to its vomit,[c]
so fools repeat their folly.[d]
12 Do you see a person wise in their own
eyes?[e]
There is more hope for a fool than for
them.[f]

13 A sluggard says,[g] "There's a lion in the
road,
a fierce lion roaming the streets!"[h]
14 As a door turns on its hinges,
so a sluggard turns on his bed.[i]
15 A sluggard buries his hand in the dish;
he is too lazy to bring it back to his
mouth.[j]
16 A sluggard is wiser in his own eyes
than seven people who answer
discreetly.

17 Like one who grabs a stray dog by the
ears
is someone who rushes into a quarrel
not their own.

18 Like a maniac shooting
flaming arrows of death
19 is one who deceives their neighbor
and says, "I was only joking!"

20 Without wood a fire goes out;
without a gossip a quarrel dies down.[k]
21 As charcoal to embers and as wood to
fire,
so is a quarrelsome person for
kindling strife.[l]
22 The words of a gossip are like choice
morsels;
they go down to the inmost parts.[m]

23 Like a coating of silver dross on
earthenware
are fervent[a] lips with an evil heart.
24 Enemies disguise themselves with their
lips,[n]
but in their hearts they harbor deceit.[o]
25 Though their speech is charming,[p] do
not believe them,
for seven abominations fill their
hearts.[q]
26 Their malice may be concealed by
deception,
but their wickedness will be exposed
in the assembly.
27 Whoever digs a pit[r] will fall into it;[s]
if someone rolls a stone, it will roll
back on them.[t]
28 A lying tongue hates those it hurts,
and a flattering mouth[u] works ruin.

27 Do not boast[v] about tomorrow,
for you do not know what a day may
bring.[w]
2 Let someone else praise you, and not
your own mouth;
an outsider, and not your own lips.[x]

3 Stone is heavy and sand[y] a burden,
but a fool's provocation is heavier
than both.

4 Anger is cruel and fury overwhelming,
but who can stand before jealousy?[z]

5 Better is open rebuke
than hidden love.

6 Wounds from a friend can be
trusted,
but an enemy multiplies kisses.[a]

7 One who is full loathes honey from the
comb,
but to the hungry even what is bitter
tastes sweet.

8 Like a bird that flees its nest[b]
is anyone who flees from home.

9 Perfume[c] and incense bring joy to the
heart,
and the pleasantness of a friend
springs from their heartfelt advice.

10 Do not forsake your friend or a friend
of your family,
and do not go to your relative's house
when disaster[d] strikes you—
better a neighbor nearby than a
relative far away.

11 Be wise, my son, and bring joy to my
heart;[e]
then I can answer anyone who treats
me with contempt.[f]

12 The prudent see danger and take
refuge,
but the simple keep going and pay the
penalty.[g]

---

a 23 Hebrew; Septuagint *smooth*

26:23 Like a coating of silver dross on earthenware. The meaning of this proverb is similar to Jesus' remarks to His enemies that they were like whitewashed tombs (Matt. 23:27). No amount of painting on the outside changes the value of the rotten interior. ***26:24–26 exposed in the assembly.*** A person who hates says one thing but stores up anger within. He may find that his hatred hurts him, when in his life there is so much falsehood that no one believes him no matter how gracious and truthful he might be at times. ***27:7 to the hungry.*** Those who are full do not appreciate what they have, while to those who are hungry anything tastes good.

26:11 [c] 2Pe 2:22* [d] Ex 8:15; Ps 85:8 **26:12** [e] Pr 3:7 [f] Pr 29:20 **26:13** [g] Pr 6:6-11; 24:30-34 [h] Pr 22:13 **26:14** [i] Pr 6:9 **26:15** [j] Pr 19:24 **26:20** [k] Pr 22:10 **26:21** [l] Pr 14:17; 15:18 **26:22** [m] Pr 18:8 **26:24** [n] Ps 31:18 [o] Ps 41:6; Pr 10:18; 12:20 **26:25** [p] Ps 28:3 [q] Jer 9:4-8 **26:27** [r] Ps 7:15 [s] Est 6:13 [t] Est 2:23; 7:9; Ps 35:8; 141:10; Pr 28:10; 29:6; Isa 50:11 **26:28** [u] Ps 12:3; Pr 29:5 **27:1** [v] 1Ki 20:11 [w] Mt 6:34; Lk 12:19-20; Jas 4:13-16 **27:2** [x] Pr 25:27 **27:3** [y] Job 6:3 **27:4** [z] Nu 5:14 **27:6** [a] Ps 141:5; Pr 28:23 **27:8** [b] Isa 16:2 **27:9** [c] Est 2:12; Ps 45:8 **27:10** [d] Pr 17:17; 18:24 **27:11** [e] Pr 10:1; 23:15-16 [f] Ge 24:60 **27:12** [g] Pr 22:3

13 Take the garment of one who puts up security for a stranger;
hold it in pledge if it is done for an outsider.[h]
14 If anyone loudly blesses their neighbor early in the morning,
it will be taken as a curse.
15 A quarrelsome wife is like the dripping[i] of a leaky roof in a rainstorm;
16 restraining her is like restraining the wind
or grasping oil with the hand.
17 As iron sharpens iron,
so one person sharpens another.
18 The one who guards a fig tree will eat its fruit,[j]
and whoever protects their master will be honored.[k]
19 As water reflects the face,
so one's life reflects the heart.[a]
20 Death and Destruction[b] are never satisfied,[l]
and neither are human eyes.[m]
21 The crucible for silver and the furnace for gold,[n]
but people are tested by their praise.
22 Though you grind a fool in a mortar,
grinding them like grain with a pestle,
you will not remove their folly from them.
23 Be sure you know the condition of your flocks,[o]
give careful attention to your herds;
24 for riches do not endure forever,[p]
and a crown is not secure for all generations.
25 When the hay is removed and new growth appears
and the grass from the hills is gathered in,
26 the lambs will provide you with clothing,
and the goats with the price of a field.
27 You will have plenty of goats' milk to feed your family
and to nourish your female servants.

28

The wicked flee[q] though no one pursues,[r]
but the righteous are as bold as a lion.[s]
2 When a country is rebellious, it has many rulers,
but a ruler with discernment and knowledge maintains order.
3 A ruler[c] who oppresses the poor
is like a driving rain that leaves no crops.
4 Those who forsake instruction praise the wicked,
but those who heed it resist them.
5 Evildoers do not understand what is right,
but those who seek the LORD understand it fully.
6 Better the poor whose walk is blameless
than the rich whose ways are perverse.[t]
7 A discerning son heeds instruction,
but a companion of gluttons disgraces his father.[u]
8 Whoever increases wealth by taking interest[v] or profit from the poor
amasses it for another,[w] who will be kind to the poor.[x]
9 If anyone turns a deaf ear to my instruction,
even their prayers are detestable.[y]
10 Whoever leads the upright along an evil path
will fall into their own trap,[z]
but the blameless will receive a good inheritance.
11 The rich are wise in their own eyes;
one who is poor and discerning sees how deluded they are.
12 When the righteous triumph, there is great elation;[a]
but when the wicked rise to power, people go into hiding.[b]

[a] 19 Or *so others reflect your heart back to you*
[b] 20 Hebrew *Abaddon*
[c] 3 Or *A poor person*

27:17 *iron sharpens iron.* This may also be translated as applying to the will; "let iron sharpen iron, and so let a person sharpen his friend." The idea is that people grow from interaction with one another.
28:4–5 *Those who forsake instruction.* When a person abandons God's law, he or she loses all sense of right and praises the wicked (Rom. 1:28–32). Since true justice is from God, the ungodly have trouble understanding it. This is why the fear of the Lord is the beginning of wisdom (1:7).
28:7 *a companion of gluttons.* One way of breaking God's law is to be a companion of gluttons (23:20–21). This is why Jesus' enemies charged Him with associating with gluttons and winebibbers. Such accusations were attacks on His faithfulness to God (Matt. 11:19).
28:8 *interest or profit.* Profit gained by charging interest or high "profit margins" is unjust. God will help the poor eventually at their exploiter's expense.

27:13 [h] Pr 20:16 **27:15** [i] Est 1:18; Pr 19:13 **27:18** [j] 1Co 9:7 [k] Lk 19:12-27 **27:20** [l] Pr 30:15-16; Hab 2:5 [m] Ecc 1:8; 6:7 **27:21** [n] Pr 17:3 **27:23** [o] Pr 12:10 **27:24** [p] Pr 23:5 **28:1** [q] 2Ki 7:7 [r] Lev 26:17; Ps 53:5 [s] Ps 138:3 **28:6** [t] Pr 19:1 **28:7** [u] Pr 23:19-21 **28:8** [v] Ex 18:21 [w] Job 27:17; Pr 13:22 [x] Ps 112:9; Pr 14:31; Lk 14:12-14 **28:9** [y] Ps 66:18; 109:7; Pr 15:8; Isa 1:13 **28:10** [z] Pr 26:27 **28:12** [a] 2Ki 11:20 [b] Pr 11:10; 29:2

13 Whoever conceals their sins[c] does not prosper,
but the one who confesses and renounces them finds mercy.[d]

14 Blessed is the one who always trembles before God,
but whoever hardens their heart falls into trouble.

15 Like a roaring lion or a charging bear
is a wicked ruler over a helpless people.

16 A tyrannical ruler practices extortion,
but one who hates ill-gotten gain will enjoy a long reign.

17 Anyone tormented by the guilt of murder
will seek refuge[e] in the grave;
let no one hold them back.

18 The one whose walk is blameless is kept safe,
but the one whose ways are perverse will fall[f] into the pit.[a]

19 Those who work their land will have abundant food,
but those who chase fantasies will have their fill of poverty.[g]

20 A faithful person will be richly blessed,
but one eager to get rich will not go unpunished.[h]

21 To show partiality is not good[i]—
yet a person will do wrong for a piece of bread.[j]

22 The stingy are eager to get rich
and are unaware that poverty awaits them.[k]

23 Whoever rebukes a person will in the end gain favor
rather than one who has a flattering tongue.[l]

24 Whoever robs their father or mother[m]
and says, "It's not wrong,"
is partner to one who destroys.[n]

25 The greedy stir up conflict,
but those who trust in the LORD[o] will prosper.

26 Those who trust in themselves are fools,[p]
but those who walk in wisdom are kept safe.

27 Those who give to the poor will lack nothing,[q]
but those who close their eyes to them receive many curses.

28 When the wicked rise to power, people go into hiding;[r]
but when the wicked perish, the righteous thrive.

29 Whoever remains stiff-necked after many rebukes
will suddenly be destroyed—without remedy.[s]

2 When the righteous thrive, the people rejoice;[t]
when the wicked rule, the people groan.[u]

3 A man who loves wisdom brings joy to his father,[v]
but a companion of prostitutes squanders his wealth.[w]

4 By justice a king gives a country stability,[x]
but those who are greedy for[b] bribes tear it down.

5 Those who flatter their neighbors
are spreading nets for their feet.

6 Evildoers are snared by their own sin,[y]
but the righteous shout for joy and are glad.

7 The righteous care about justice for the poor,[z]
but the wicked have no such concern.

8 Mockers stir up a city,
but the wise turn away anger.[a]

9 If a wise person goes to court with a fool,
the fool rages and scoffs, and there is no peace.

10 The bloodthirsty hate a person of integrity
and seek to kill the upright.[b]

11 Fools give full vent to their rage,
but the wise bring calm in the end.[c]

12 If a ruler listens to lies,
all his officials become wicked.

[a] *18* Syriac (see Septuagint); Hebrew *into one*
[b] *4* Or *who give*

28:14 *Blessed is the one.* This is a repeat of Psalm 1:1 about a person who is in awe of God. The person who never thinks of God faces calamity.
28:23 *Whoever rebukes a person.* Constructive criticism has more value than flattery, which aims only to win people's affection.
28:25–26 *Those who trust in themselves.* One of the main causes of strife is pride; trust in God leads to blessing.
29:5 *spreading nets.* Flattery is a lie. If you flatter your neighbor you are making a trap of some kind for him. God never lies. He always tells the truth, and so should we.

28:13 [c] Job 31:33 [d] Ps 32:1-5; 1Jn 1:9 **28:17** [e] Ge 9:6 **28:18** [f] Pr 10:9 **28:19** [g] Pr 12:11 **28:20** [h] ver 22; Pr 10:6; 1Ti 6:9 **28:21** [i] Pr 18:5 [j] Eze 13:19 **28:22** [k] ver 20; Pr 23:6 **28:23** [l] Pr 27:5-6 **28:24** [m] Pr 19:26 [n] Pr 18:9 **28:25** [o] Pr 29:25 **28:26** [p] Ps 4:5; Pr 3:5 **28:27** [q] Dt 15:7; 24:19; Pr 19:17; 22:9 **28:28** [r] ver 12 **29:1** [s] 2Ch 36:16; Pr 6:15 **29:2** [t] Est 8:15 [u] Pr 28:12 **29:3** [v] Pr 10:1 [w] Pr 5:8-10; Lk 15:11-32 **29:4** [x] Pr 8:15-16 **29:6** [y] Ecc 9:12 **29:7** [z] Job 29:16; Ps 41:1; Pr 31:8-9 **29:8** [a] Pr 11:11; 16:14 **29:10** [b] 1Jn 3:12 **29:11** [c] Pr 12:16; 19:11

13 The poor and the oppressor have this in common:
The LORD gives sight to the eyes of both.[d]

14 If a king judges the poor with fairness,
his throne will be established forever.[e]

15 A rod and a reprimand impart wisdom,
but a child left undisciplined disgraces its mother.[f]

16 When the wicked thrive, so does sin,
but the righteous will see their downfall.[g]

17 Discipline your children, and they will give you peace;
they will bring you the delights you desire.[h]

18 Where there is no revelation, people cast off restraint;
but blessed is the one who heeds wisdom's instruction.[i]

19 Servants cannot be corrected by mere words;
though they understand, they will not respond.

20 Do you see someone who speaks in haste?
There is more hope for a fool than for them.[j]

21 A servant pampered from youth
will turn out to be insolent.

22 An angry person stirs up conflict,
and a hot-tempered person commits many sins.[k]

23 Pride brings a person low,
but the lowly in spirit gain honor.[l]

24 The accomplices of thieves are their own enemies;
they are put under oath and dare not testify.[m]

25 Fear of man will prove to be a snare,
but whoever trusts in the LORD[n] is kept safe.

26 Many seek an audience with a ruler,[o]
but it is from the LORD that one gets justice.

27 The righteous detest the dishonest;
the wicked detest the upright.[p]

Sayings of Agur

30 The sayings of Agur son of Jakeh—an inspired utterance.

This man's utterance to Ithiel:

"I am weary, God,
but I can prevail.[a]
2 Surely I am only a brute, not a man;
I do not have human understanding.
3 I have not learned wisdom,
nor have I attained to the knowledge of the Holy One.[q]
4 Who has gone up[r] to heaven and come down?
Whose hands[s] have gathered up the wind?
Who has wrapped up the waters[t] in a cloak?[u]
Who has established all the ends of the earth?
What is his name,[v] and what is the name of his son?
Surely you know!

5 "Every word of God is flawless;[w]
he is a shield[x] to those who take refuge in him.
6 Do not add[y] to his words,
or he will rebuke you and prove you a liar.

---

[a] *1* With a different word division of the Hebrew; Masoretic Text *utterance to Ithiel, / to Ithiel and Ukal:*

29:13 *The poor and the oppressor.* God is responsible for giving life to both. Jesus attested that God causes rain to fall on the just and the unjust (Matt. 5:45).
29:18 *Where there is no revelation.* Without God's revelation of the law, the people flounder. True happiness is discovered within the constraints of revelation, in the counsel of the Savior.
29:23 *Pride brings a person low.* Pride, inordinate self-esteem, causes others to lose respect for the conceited egotist. In contrast to this, humility draws honor from others. However, pride takes many forms and is not always the adornment of just the conceited egotist.
29:26 *it is from the LORD that one gets justice.* God controls human affairs. Therefore it makes more sense to seek the Lord first before stooping to seek the favor of human rulers.
30:1 *The sayings of Agur.* This verse starts an entirely new section of Proverbs. Like Lemuel (31:1–9), Agur was a non-Hebrew contributor to the Book of Proverbs. He came to faith in the God of Israel in a foreign land.
30:4 *What is his name . . . ?* This verse gives the riddle that perplexed Agur. The questions all culminate in the last two lines. The Old Testament would answer that "His name" is the Lord God, but did not have a name for His Son. This riddle was to remain unsolved until Jesus answered it for Nicodemus (John 3:13). These verses form one of the most straightforward messianic texts in the Bible.

29:13 [d] Pr 22:2; Mt 5:45 **29:14** [e] Ps 72:1-5; Pr 16:12 **29:15** [f] Pr 10:1; 13:24; 17:21,25 **29:16** [g] Ps 37:35-36; 58:10; 91:8; 92:11 **29:17** [h] ver 15; Pr 10:1 **29:18** [i] Ps 1:1-2; 119:1-2; Jn 13:17 **29:20** [j] Pr 26:12; Jas 1:19 **29:22** [k] Pr 14:17; 15:18; 26:21 **29:23** [l] Pr 11:2; 15:33; 16:18; Isa 66:2; Mt 23:12 **29:24** [m] Lev 5:1 **29:25** [n] Pr 28:25 **29:26** [o] Pr 19:6 **29:27** [p] ver 10 **30:3** [q] Pr 9:10 **30:4** [r] Ps 24:1-2; Jn 3:13; Eph 4:7-10 [s] Ps 104:3; Isa 40:12 [t] Job 26:8; 38:8-9 [u] Ge 1:2 [v] Rev 19:12 **30:5** [w] Ps 12:6; 18:30 [x] Ge 15:1; Ps 84:11 **30:6** [y] Dt 4:2; 12:32; Rev 22:18

7 "Two things I ask of you, LORD;
do not refuse me before I die:
8 Keep falsehood and lies far from me;
give me neither poverty nor riches,
but give me only my daily bread.[z]
9 Otherwise, I may have too much and
disown[a] you
and say, 'Who is the LORD?'[b]
Or I may become poor and steal,
and so dishonor the name of my God.[c]

10 "Do not slander a servant to their master,
or they will curse you, and you will
pay for it.

11 "There are those who curse their
fathers
and do not bless their mothers;[d]
12 those who are pure in their own eyes[e]
and yet are not cleansed of their filth;[f]
13 those whose eyes are ever so haughty,[g]
whose glances are so disdainful;
14 those whose teeth[h] are swords
and whose jaws are set with knives[i]
to devour[j] the poor[k] from the earth
and the needy from among mankind.[l]

15 "The leech has two daughters.
'Give! Give!' they cry.

"There are three things that are never
satisfied,[m]
four that never say, 'Enough!':
16 the grave,[n] the barren womb,
land, which is never satisfied with
water,
and fire, which never says, 'Enough!'

17 "The eye that mocks[o] a father,
that scorns an aged mother,
will be pecked out by the ravens of the
valley,
will be eaten by the vultures.[p]

18 "There are three things that are too
amazing for me,
four that I do not understand:
19 the way of an eagle in the sky,
the way of a snake on a rock,
the way of a ship on the high seas,
and the way of a man with a young
woman.

20 "This is the way of an adulterous
woman:
She eats and wipes her mouth
and says, 'I've done nothing wrong.'[q]

21 "Under three things the earth trembles,
under four it cannot bear up:
22 a servant who becomes king,[r]
a godless fool who gets plenty to eat,
23 a contemptible woman who gets
married,
and a servant who displaces her
mistress.

24 "Four things on earth are small,
yet they are extremely wise:
25 Ants are creatures of little strength,
yet they store up their food in the
summer;[s]
26 hyraxes[t] are creatures of little power,
yet they make their home in the crags;
27 locusts[u] have no king,
yet they advance together in ranks;
28 a lizard can be caught with the hand,
yet it is found in kings' palaces.

29 "There are three things that are stately
in their stride,
four that move with stately bearing:
30 a lion, mighty among beasts,
who retreats before nothing;
31 a strutting rooster, a he-goat,
and a king secure against revolt.[a]

32 "If you play the fool and exalt yourself,
or if you plan evil,
clap your hand over your mouth![v]
33 For as churning cream produces butter,
and as twisting the nose produces
blood,
so stirring up anger produces strife."

Sayings of King Lemuel

31 The sayings[w] of King Lemuel—an inspired utterance his mother taught him.

2 Listen, my son! Listen, son of my womb!
Listen, my son, the answer to my
prayers![x]
3 Do not spend your strength[b] on women,
your vigor on those who ruin kings.[y]

---

[a] *31* The meaning of the Hebrew for this phrase is uncertain. [b] *3* Or *wealth*

30:19 ***young woman.*** This term could also read maid or virgin in this context.

30:20 ***This is the way.*** This verse contrasts with the way of verse 19; this way is awful whereas the former is wonderful. The *adulterous woman* regards her illicit sexual relations without remorse.

30:24–28 ***Four things on earth are small.*** This numerical proverb speaks of four creatures that are small in size but amazing in behavior. Each of these small creatures has a behavioral trait from which wise people can learn.

30:32–33 ***clap your hand over your mouth.*** This phrase means "stop it." The idea is if you are in the middle of making trouble and suddenly realize your foolishness, stop right then before things get worse.

31:1 ***The sayings of King Lemuel.*** This verse begins a new section of material from a non-Israelite source.

30:8 [z] Mt 6:11 **30:9** [a] Jos 24:27; Isa 1:4; 59:13 [b] Dt 6:12; 8:10-14; Hos 13:6 [c] Dt 8:12 **30:11** [d] Pr 20:20 **30:12** [e] Pr 16:2; Lk 18:11 [f] Jer 2:23, 35 **30:13** [g] 2Sa 22:28; Job 41:34; Ps 131:1; Pr 6:17 **30:14** [h] Job 4:11; 29:17; Ps 3:7 [i] Ps 57:4 [j] Job 24:9; Ps 14:4 [k] Am 8:4; Mic 2:2 [l] Job 19:22 **30:15** [m] Pr 27:20 **30:16** [n] Pr 27:20; Isa 5:14; 14:9, 11; Hab 2:5 **30:17** [o] Dt 21:18-21; Pr 23:22 [p] Job 15:23 **30:20** [q] Pr 5:6 **30:22** [r] Pr 19:10; 29:2 **30:25** [s] Pr 6:6-8 **30:26** [t] Ps 104:18 **30:27** [u] Ex 10:4 **30:32** [v] Job 21:5; 29:9 **31:1** [w] Pr 22:17 **31:2** [x] Jdg 11:30; Isa 49:15 **31:3** [y] Dt 17:17; 1Ki 11:3; Ne 13:26; Pr 5:1-14

4 It is not for kings, Lemuel—
it is not for kings to drink wine,[z]
not for rulers to crave beer,
5 lest they drink[a] and forget what has been decreed,[b]
and deprive all the oppressed of their rights.
6 Let beer be for those who are perishing,
wine[c] for those who are in anguish!
7 Let them drink[d] and forget their poverty
and remember their misery no more.

8 Speak[e] up for those who cannot speak for themselves,
for the rights of all who are destitute.
9 Speak up and judge fairly;
defend the rights of the poor and needy.[f]

Epilogue: The Wife of Noble Character

10 [a]A wife of noble character[g] who can find?[h]
She is worth far more than rubies.
11 Her husband[i] has full confidence in her
and lacks nothing of value.[j]
12 She brings him good, not harm,
all the days of her life.
13 She selects wool and flax
and works with eager hands.[k]
14 She is like the merchant ships,
bringing her food from afar.
15 She gets up while it is still night;
she provides food for her family
and portions for her female servants.
16 She considers a field and buys it;
out of her earnings she plants a vineyard.
17 She sets about her work vigorously;
her arms are strong for her tasks.
18 She sees that her trading is profitable,
and her lamp does not go out at night.
19 In her hand she holds the distaff
and grasps the spindle with her fingers.
20 She opens her arms to the poor
and extends her hands to the needy.[l]
21 When it snows, she has no fear for her household;
for all of them are clothed in scarlet.
22 She makes coverings for her bed;
she is clothed in fine linen and purple.
23 Her husband is respected at the city gate,
where he takes his seat among the elders[m] of the land.
24 She makes linen garments and sells them,
and supplies the merchants with sashes.
25 She is clothed with strength and dignity;
she can laugh at the days to come.
26 She speaks with wisdom,
and faithful instruction is on her tongue.[n]
27 She watches over the affairs of her household
and does not eat the bread of idleness.
28 Her children arise and call her blessed;
her husband also, and he praises her:
29 "Many women do noble things,
but you surpass them all."
30 Charm is deceptive, and beauty is fleeting;
but a woman who fears the LORD is to be praised.
31 Honor her for all that her hands have done,
and let her works bring her praise[o] at the city gate.

---

[a] *10* Verses 10-31 are an acrostic poem, the verses of which begin with the successive letters of the Hebrew alphabet.

31:4–5 ***lest they drink and forget what has been decreed.*** In this passage the consumption of strong drink is linked to injustice.
31:10 ***A wife of noble character.*** Proverbs 31:10–31 is an acrostic poem; each verse begins with a successive letter to the Hebrew alphabet. As the Book of Proverbs begins with a Purpose and Theme (1:1–7), which gives the goals of wisdom in general terms, so now it concludes with this Epilogue, which presents them in a case study.
31:20–22 ***to the poor.*** The excellent woman works not to get rich, but to give to the poor. She can be concerned for others because she has provided for her own family.
31:26 ***faithful instruction is on her tongue.*** This attribute of kindness in a woman is valued far above physical charm in God's sight. Peter describes real beauty as a product of the heart and not the combination of certain physical features (1 Pet. 3:1–5).
31:30–31 ***Charm.*** Charm, which could be translated "graciousness", like beauty, can deceive us about the true nature of someone's character. But if a woman fears the Lord, that is trustworthy and more worthy of praise than physical comeliness.

31:4 [z] Pr 20:1; Ecc 10:16-17; Isa 5:22 **31:5** [a] 1Ki 16:9 [b] Pr 16:12; Hos 4:11 **31:6** [c] Ge 14:18 **31:7** [d] Est 1:10 **31:8** [e] 1Sa 19:4; Job 29:12-17 **31:9** [f] Lev 19:15; Dt 1:16; Pr 24:23; 29:7; Isa 1:17; Jer 22:16 **31:10** [g] Ru 3:11; Pr 12:4; 18:22 [h] Pr 8:35; 19:14 **31:11** [i] Ge 2:18 [j] Pr 12:4 **31:13** [k] 1Ti 2:9-10 **31:20** [l] Dt 15:11; Eph 4:28; Heb 13:16 **31:23** [m] Ex 3:16; Ru 4:1, 11; Pr 12:4 **31:26** [n] Pr 10:31 **31:31** [o] Pr 11:16

ECCLESIASTES

▶ **AUTHOR:** The author calls himself "the son of David, king in Jerusalem" in 1:1. Solomonic authorship is the traditional Christian position, although some scholars, along with the Talmud, believe the work was later edited during the time of Hezekiah or possibly Ezra. The proverbs in this book are similar to those in the Book of Proverbs (Eccl. 7; 10). According to 12:9, the Teacher collected and arranged many proverbs, perhaps referring to the two Solomonic collections in Proverbs.

▶ **TIME:** c. 935 B.C. ▶ **KEY VERSE:** Eccl. 2:24

▶ **THEME:** Ecclesiastes is a Greek word that is usually translated "the preacher" or "the teacher." The book was likely written late in Solomon's life, when he could see that the glorious era of his kingdom was beginning to decline. He had it all, power, prestige, pleasure, but none of that provides ultimate satisfaction. That fulfillment comes only through a relationship with God and obedience to His word. It is important to note that the arguments of the book are more thematic than linear. The same topics are addressed in different ways at different points within the work.

Everything Is Meaningless

1 The words of the Teacher,[a][a] son of David, king in Jerusalem:[b]

2 "Meaningless! Meaningless!"
says the Teacher.
"Utterly meaningless!
Everything is meaningless."[c]
3 What do people gain from all their labors
at which they toil under the sun?[d]
4 Generations come and generations go,
but the earth remains forever.[e]
5 The sun rises and the sun sets,
and hurries back to where it rises.[f]
6 The wind blows to the south
and turns to the north;
round and round it goes,
ever returning on its course.
7 All streams flow into the sea,
yet the sea is never full.
To the place the streams come from,
there they return again.[g]
8 All things are wearisome,
more than one can say.
The eye never has enough of seeing,[h]
nor the ear its fill of hearing.
9 What has been will be again,
what has been done will be done again;[i]
there is nothing new under the sun.
10 Is there anything of which one can say,
"Look! This is something new"?
It was here already, long ago;
it was here before our time.

[a] *1* Or *the leader of the assembly*; also in verses 2 and 12

1:1 *the Teacher.* This word denotes a function or a profession. It literally means "one who assembles or gathers people together." Thus the word refers to Solomon as a person who convened an assembly of the wise in order to explore in a formal manner the meaning of life.
1:2 *Meaningless!* This phrase translates the Hebrew superlative, familiar from such phrases as "Song of Songs" and "holy of holies." Here it might express "the ultimate absurdity" or "utter emptiness." The word in the Hebrew means "breath" or "vapor" and thus speaks of life as "quickly passing." Life is like a vapor; indeed, it is like the thinnest of vapors. So wherever we read this word in Ecclesiastes, we should think not simply of what is "meaningless," but more importantly, that which in our lives is "quickly passing" (v. 14; 6:12). This is one of the key terms in the Book of Ecclesiastes, for it is found 38 times here, but only 34 times throughout the rest of the Old Testament. The teaching of the Preacher is to realize that life is a fleeting thing that needs to be savored and enjoyed as a gift from God.
1:4 *Generations.* This term suggests both the human actors and the natural phenomena as well. With the verb "go" we have the first of a series of antitheses in Ecclesiastes. ***the earth remains forever.*** Only God is eternal and everlasting in the fullest sense. But compared to the lives of humankind, the earth abides with little change.

1:1 [a] ver 12; Ecc 7:27; 12:10 [b] Pr 1:1 **1:2** [c] Ps 39:5-6; 62:9; 144:4; Ecc 12:8; Ro 8:20-21 **1:3** [d] Ecc 2:11,22; 3:9; 5:15-16 **1:4** [e] Ps 104:5; 119:90 **1:5** [f] Ps 19:5-6 **1:7** [g] Job 36:28 **1:8** [h] Pr 27:20 **1:9** [i] Ecc 2:12; 3:15

11 No one remembers the former
generations,
and even those yet to come
will not be remembered
by those who follow them.[j]

Wisdom Is Meaningless

12 I, the Teacher,[k] was king over Israel in
Jerusalem. 13 I applied my mind to study
and to explore by wisdom all that is done
under the heavens. What a heavy burden
God has laid on mankind![l] 14 I have seen all
the things that are done under the sun; all
of them are meaningless, a chasing after
the wind.[m]

15 What is crooked cannot be
straightened;[n]
what is lacking cannot be counted.

16 I said to myself, "Look, I have increased in wisdom more than anyone who
has ruled over Jerusalem before me;[o] I
have experienced much of wisdom and
knowledge." 17 Then I applied myself to
the understanding of wisdom,[p] and also of
madness and folly,[q] but I learned that this,
too, is a chasing after the wind.

18 For with much wisdom comes much
sorrow;
the more knowledge, the more grief.[r]

Pleasures Are Meaningless

2 I said to myself, "Come now, I will test
you with pleasure[s] to find out what is
good." But that also proved to be meaningless. 2 "Laughter,"[t] I said, "is madness. And
what does pleasure accomplish?" 3 I tried
cheering myself with wine,[u] and embracing folly[v]—my mind still guiding me with
wisdom. I wanted to see what was good for
people to do under the heavens during the
few days of their lives.
4 I undertook great projects: I built houses for myself[w] and planted vineyards.[x] 5 I
made gardens and parks and planted all
kinds of fruit trees in them. 6 I made reservoirs to water groves of flourishing trees.
7 I bought male and female slaves and had
other slaves who were born in my house.
I also owned more herds and flocks than
anyone in Jerusalem before me. 8 I amassed
silver and gold[y] for myself, and the treasure of kings and provinces. I acquired
male and female singers,[z] and a harem[a]
as well—the delights of a man's heart. 9 I
became greater by far than anyone in Jerusalem before me.[a] In all this my wisdom
stayed with me.

10 I denied myself nothing my eyes
desired;
I refused my heart no pleasure.
My heart took delight in all my labor,
and this was the reward for all my toil.
11 Yet when I surveyed all that my hands
had done
and what I had toiled to achieve,
everything was meaningless, a chasing
after the wind;[b]
nothing was gained under the sun.[c]

Wisdom and Folly Are Meaningless

12 Then I turned my thoughts to consider
wisdom,
and also madness and folly.[d]
What more can the king's successor do
than what has already been done?[e]
13 I saw that wisdom[f] is better than folly,[g]
just as light is better than darkness.
14 The wise have eyes in their heads,
while the fool walks in the darkness;
but I came to realize
that the same fate overtakes them
both.[h]

15 Then I said to myself,

"The fate of the fool will overtake me
also.
What then do I gain by being wise?"[i]
I said to myself,
"This too is meaningless."

---

[a] 8 The meaning of the Hebrew for this phrase is uncertain.

1:13 *under the heavens.* This is a synonymous expression for "under the sun" (vv. 3,9); it refers to life as it is lived by people on earth.
1:14 *chasing after the wind.* This phrase does not occur in the Hebrew Bible outside of Ecclesiastes. Seven of its nine occurrences (v. 14; 2:11,17,26; 4:4,6; 6:9) follow "vanity" statements. The phrase explains the nature of life according to the Preacher. Life is real, but quickly passing; any attempt to slow it is futile.
2:1 *Come now, I will test you.* The Preacher uses a literary device of conversing with himself as a way of describing his thought processes. ***pleasure.*** A new test is proposed, following the test of wisdom. It is the test of "joy."
2:2 *madness.* Solomon labels the lighter side of pleasure and joy as sheer madness, but even the weightier aspects of laughter cause Solomon to ask if anything substantial is really achieved. As Solomon writes in Proverbs 14:13, "Even in laughter the heart may ache, and rejoicing may end in grief."
2:10 *my eyes desired.* Solomon had limitless ability to fulfill any and all of his desires.
2:11 *everything was meaningless.* At the end of his grand quest for possessions and experiences, Solomon concluded that it was "meaningless" or a "vapor," a chasing after the wind. That is, even with all he had done and experienced, there was still a sense that nothing lasting or enduring had been achieved.

1:11 [j] Ecc 2:16 **1:12** [k] ver 1 **1:13** [l] Ge 3:17; Ecc 3:10 **1:14** [m] Ecc 2:11, 17 **1:15** [n] Ecc 7:13 **1:16** [o] 1Ki 3:12; 4:30; Ecc 2:9 **1:17** [p] Ecc 7:23 [q] Ecc 2:3, 12; 7:25 **1:18** [r] Ecc 2:23; 12:12 **2:1** [s] Ecc 7:4; 8:15; Lk 12:19 **2:2** [t] Pr 14:13; Ecc 7:6 **2:3** [u] ver 24-25; Ecc 3:12-13 [v] Ecc 1:17 **2:4** [w] 1Ki 7:1-12 [x] SS 8:11 **2:8** [y] 1Ki 9:28; 10:10, 14, 21 [z] 2Sa 19:35 **2:9** [a] 1Ch 29:25; Ecc 1:16 **2:11** [b] Ecc 1:14 [c] Ecc 1:3 **2:12** [d] Ecc 1:17 [e] Ecc 1:9; 7:25 **2:13** [f] Ecc 7:19; 9:18 [g] Ecc 7:11-12 **2:14** [h] Ps 49:10; Pr 17:24; Ecc 3:19; 6:6; 7:2; 9:3, 11-12 **2:15** [i] Ecc 6:8

16 For the wise, like the fool, will not be
long remembered;
the days have already come when
both have been forgotten.[j]
Like the fool, the wise too must die!

Toil Is Meaningless

17 So I hated life, because the work that
is done under the sun was grievous to me.
All of it is meaningless, a chasing after
the wind.[k] 18 I hated all the things I had
toiled for under the sun, because I must
leave them to the one who comes after
me.[l] 19 And who knows whether that person will be wise or foolish? Yet they will
have control over all the fruit of my toil
into which I have poured my effort and
skill under the sun. This too is meaningless. 20 So my heart began to despair over
all my toilsome labor under the sun. 21 For
a person may labor with wisdom, knowledge and skill, and then they must leave
all they own to another who has not toiled
for it. This too is meaningless and a great
misfortune. 22 What do people get for all the
toil and anxious striving with which they
labor under the sun?[m] 23 All their days their
work is grief and pain;[n] even at night their
minds do not rest. This too is meaningless.
24 A person can do nothing better than
to eat and drink[o] and find satisfaction
in their own toil.[p] This too, I see, is from
the hand of God,[q] 25 for without him, who
can eat or find enjoyment? 26 To the person who pleases him, God gives wisdom,
knowledge and happiness, but to the sinner
he gives the task of gathering and storing
up wealth[r] to hand it over to the one who
pleases God.[s] This too is meaningless, a
chasing after the wind.

A Time for Everything

3 There is a time[t] for everything,
and a season for every activity under
the heavens:

2 a time to be born and a time to die,
a time to plant and a time to uproot,
3 a time to kill and a time to heal,
a time to tear down and a time to
build,
4 a time to weep and a time to laugh,
a time to mourn and a time to dance,
5 a time to scatter stones and a time to
gather them,
a time to embrace and a time to
refrain from embracing,
6 a time to search and a time to give up,
a time to keep and a time to throw
away,
7 a time to tear and a time to mend,
a time to be silent[u] and a time to
speak,
8 a time to love and a time to hate,
a time for war and a time for peace.

9 What do workers gain from their toil?[v]
10 I have seen the burden God has laid on
the human race.[w] 11 He has made everything beautiful in its time.[x] He has also
set eternity in the human heart; yet[a] no
one can fathom[y] what God has done from

[a] *11* *Or also placed ignorance in the human heart, so that*

2:17 *So I hated life.* Such hatred of life is astonishing since the one who finds wisdom also finds life, according to Proverbs 3:16. But the Preacher's dissatisfaction was related to the quickly passing nature of everything (1:2), including the good things.

2:21 *This too is meaningless and a great misfortune.* The term *misfortune* here may mean "calamity" or "ruin." There is a sense of sadness that runs through this section. Nothing that we gain in this life can be carried on into the life to come.

2:24 *eat and drink.* The Preacher concludes that all good is located only in God. This phrase marks one of the central affirmations of the book (3:12,22; 8:15; 9:7); in the midst of a world of trouble, a believer is able to seize the moment in joy from God. Only God supplies the key to the meaning of life. Without Him, genuine meaning, satisfaction, and enjoyment in life are ultimately elusive.

2:26 *God gives wisdom, knowledge and happiness.* One of the words used most frequently in Ecclesiastes to describe God's relationship to individuals is a verb "to give." It appears 11 times with God as the subject. Joy is God's gift to the man who is good in His sight. God has designed us so that true joy is possible only through Him.

3:1–15 *There is a time for everything.* Some regard the Book of Ecclesiastes as describing life apart from God. But clearly this text describes life that is lived in relationship with God. Through these words, the Preacher is not saying that everything has an opportune time according to which one should choose one action or the other. Rather, he teaches that all events are in the hand of God, who makes everything happen in the time He judges appropriate.

3:5 *a time to scatter stones.* In times of peace, stones were cleared from the fields allowing for cultivation. In wartime, the rocks were thrown on the fields to make them unusable (2 Kin. 3:19,25).

3:7 *a time to tear and a time to mend.* When bad news came, it was customary to rip one's garments to show grief (2 Sam. 13:31). When the problem passed, it was just as well to sew the garment back together.

3:9 *What do workers gain.* This is the same question posed in 1:3. The answer here is that all of life unfolds at the appointment of God. All the toiling of man cannot change the time, circumstances, and control of events that God has reserved for Himself.

3:11 *set eternity in the human heart.* This phrase refers to a deep-seated, compulsive drive to transcend our mortality by knowing the meaning and destiny of the world. Because we are made in the image of God, we have an inborn inquisitiveness about eternal realities. We can find peace only when

2:16 [j] Ecc 1:11; 9:5 **2:17** [k] Ecc 4:2 **2:18** [l] Ps 39:6; 49:10 **2:22** [m] Ecc 1:3; 3:9 **2:23** [n] Job 5:7; 14:1; Ecc 1:18 **2:24** [o] Ecc 8:15; 1Co 15:32 [p] Ecc 3:22 [q] Ecc 3:12-13; 5:17-19; 9:7-10 **2:26** [r] Job 27:17 [s] Pr 13:22 **3:1** [t] ver 11, 17; Ecc 8:6 **3:7** [u] Am 5:13 **3:9** [v] Ecc 1:3 **3:10** [w] Ecc 1:13 **3:11** [x] ver 1 [y] Job 11:7; Ecc 8:17

beginning to end.[z] 12I know that there is
nothing better for people than to be happy
and to do good while they live. 13That each
of them may eat and drink,[a] and find satisfaction[b] in all their toil—this is the gift of
God.[c] 14I know that everything God does
will endure forever; nothing can be added
to it and nothing taken from it. God does it
so that people will fear him.[d]

15 Whatever is has already been,[e]
  and what will be has been before;[f]
  and God will call the past to
    account.[a]

16And I saw something else under the
sun:

In the place of judgment—wickedness
    was there,
  in the place of justice—wickedness
    was there.

17I said to myself,

"God will bring into judgment[g]
  both the righteous and the wicked,
for there will be a time for every
    activity,
  a time to judge every deed."[h]

18I also said to myself, "As for humans,
God tests them so that they may see that
they are like the animals.[i] 19Surely the fate
of human beings[j] is like that of the animals;
the same fate awaits them both: As one
dies, so dies the other. All have the same
breath[b]; humans have no advantage over
animals. Everything is meaningless. 20All
go to the same place; all come from dust,
and to dust all return.[k] 21Who knows if the
human spirit rises upward[l] and if the spirit
of the animal goes down into the earth?"
22So I saw that there is nothing better
for a person than to enjoy their work,[m] because that is their lot.[n] For who can bring
them to see what will happen after them?

Oppression, Toil, Friendlessness

4 Again I looked and saw all the oppression[o] that was taking place under the
sun:

I saw the tears of the oppressed—
  and they have no comforter;
power was on the side of their
    oppressors—
  and they have no comforter.[p]
2 And I declared that the dead,[q]
  who had already died,
are happier than the living,
  who are still alive.[r]
3 But better than both
  is the one who has never been born,[s]
who has not seen the evil
  that is done under the sun.[t]

4And I saw that all toil and all achievement spring from one person's envy of another. This too is meaningless, a chasing
after the wind.[u]

5 Fools fold their hands[v]
  and ruin themselves.
6 Better one handful with tranquillity
  than two handfuls with toil[w]
  and chasing after the wind.

7Again I saw something meaningless
under the sun:

8 There was a man all alone;
  he had neither son nor brother.
There was no end to his toil,
  yet his eyes were not content[x] with
    his wealth.
"For whom am I toiling," he asked,
  "and why am I depriving myself of
    enjoyment?"
This too is meaningless—
  a miserable business!

9 Two are better than one,
  because they have a good return for
    their labor:

[a] 15 Or *God calls back the past* [b] 19 Or *spirit*

we come to know our eternal Creator. Even then, we know God only in part (1 Cor. 13:12).

3:12–13 *nothing better ... be happy.* As in 2:24, the advice of the Preacher is to seize the day in the joy of God. Biblical faith is a call for joy, even when we live in a wicked world and under terrible stress; this is because we find true joy in the living God.

3:16–17 *wickedness was there.* It was outrageous that in the very establishments where people should expect justice, they could find only wickedness. The Preacher warns the wicked judges that God, the final Judge, will come to rectify all wrongdoing and bring true justice.

3:20 *All go to the same place.* Both humans and beasts die and go to the grave. But this is not the end for human beings—they will face eternal life or death.

4:1 *they have no comforter.* So much pain can come to the downtrodden that they may even despair of life (1 Kin. 19:4). Only when the oppressed go into the house of God will they gain perspective (5:1–6; Ps. 73:17).

4:3 *who has never been born.* So powerfully wrong and so lonely is the suffering of the oppressed, that Solomon, with a good deal of poetic license similar to Job 3:3–10, argues that nonexistence could be preferred over existence.

4:8 *yet his eyes were not content.* Man is in love with what is vanishing. The antidote for covetousness is to replace sinful desire for increase in wealth, with a strong passion for doing the will of God (1 John 2:17).

4:9–12 *Two are better than one.* Throughout this section there is an emphasis on the obvious

3:11 [z] Job 28:23; Ro 11:33 **3:13** [a] Ecc 2:3 [b] Ps 34:12 [c] Dt 12:7, 18; Ecc 2:24; 5:19 **3:14** [d] Job 23:15; Ecc 5:7; 7:18; 8:12-13; Jas 1:17 **3:15** [e] Ecc 6:10 [f] Ecc 1:9 **3:17** [g] Job 19:29; Ecc 11:9; Mt 16:27; Ro 2:6-8; 2Th 1:6-7 [h] ver 1 **3:18** [i] Ps 73:22 **3:19** [j] Ecc 2:14 **3:20** [k] Ge 2:7; 3:19; Job 34:15 **3:21** [l] Ecc 12:7 **3:22** [m] Ecc 2:24; 5:18 [n] Job 31:2 **4:1** [o] Ps 12:5; Ecc 3:16 [p] La 1:16 **4:2** [q] Jer 20:17-18; 22:10 [r] Job 3:17; 10:18 **4:3** [s] Job 3:16; Ecc 6:3 [t] Job 3:22 **4:4** [u] Ecc 1:14 **4:5** [v] Pr 6:10 **4:6** [w] Pr 15:16-17; 16:8 **4:8** [x] Pr 27:20

10 If either of them falls down,
one can help the other up.
But pity anyone who falls
and has no one to help them up.
11 Also, if two lie down together, they will keep warm.
But how can one keep warm alone?
12 Though one may be overpowered,
two can defend themselves.
A cord of three strands is not quickly broken.

Advancement Is Meaningless

13Better a poor but wise youth than an
old but foolish king who no longer knows
how to heed a warning. 14The youth may
have come from prison to the kingship, or
he may have been born in poverty within
his kingdom. 15I saw that all who lived and
walked under the sun followed the youth,
the king's successor. 16There was no end
to all the people who were before them.
But those who came later were not pleased
with the successor. This too is meaningless, a chasing after the wind.

Fulfill Your Vow to God

5[a] Guard your steps when you go to the
house of God. Go near to listen rather
than to offer the sacrifice of fools, who do
not know that they do wrong.

2 Do not be quick with your mouth,
do not be hasty in your heart
to utter anything before God.[y]
God is in heaven
and you are on earth,
so let your words be few.[z]
3 A dream[a] comes when there are many cares,
and many words mark the speech of a fool.[b]

4When you make a vow to God, do not
delay to fulfill it.[c] He has no pleasure in
fools; fulfill your vow.[d] 5It is better not
to make a vow than to make one and not
fulfill it.[e] 6Do not let your mouth lead you
into sin. And do not protest to the temple
messenger, "My vow was a mistake." Why
should God be angry at what you say and
destroy the work of your hands? 7Much
dreaming and many words are meaningless. Therefore fear God.[f]

Riches Are Meaningless

8If you see the poor oppressed[g] in a district, and justice and rights denied, do not
be surprised at such things; for one official
is eyed by a higher one, and over them both
are others higher still. 9The increase from
the land is taken by all; the king himself
profits from the fields.

10 Whoever loves money never has enough;
whoever loves wealth is never
satisfied with their income.
This too is meaningless.
11 As goods increase,
so do those who consume them.
And what benefit are they to the owners
except to feast their eyes on them?
12 The sleep of a laborer is sweet,
whether they eat little or much,
but as for the rich, their abundance
permits them no sleep.[h]

13I have seen a grievous evil under the sun:[i]

wealth hoarded to the harm of its owners,
14 or wealth lost through some misfortune,
so that when they have children
there is nothing left for them to inherit.
15 Everyone comes naked from their mother's womb,
and as everyone comes, so they depart.[j]
They take nothing from their toil[k]
that they can carry in their hands.[l]

16This too is a grievous evil:

As everyone comes, so they depart,
and what do they gain,
since they toil for the wind?[m]
17 All their days they eat in darkness,
with great frustration, affliction and anger.

---

[a] In Hebrew texts 5:1 is numbered 4:17, and 5:2-20 is numbered 5:1-19.

---

benefits of companions. The intimacy and sharing of life brings relief for the problem of isolation and loneliness. A companion can offer assistance, comfort, and defense — a threefold cord.

5:1 ***Guard your steps.*** This means behave yourself. The idea of righteous behavior is rephrased at the end of the section in the words: "fear God" (5:7).

5:4–5 ***When you make a vow to God.*** One should not attempt to bribe God with a hasty vow. The first part of this verse is almost identical to Deuteronomy 23:21. See the later example of the lie of Ananias and Sapphira (Acts 5:1–11).

5:7 ***fear God.*** This is a central theme of the Book of Ecclesiastes. It does not mean to be afraid of God (Ex. 20:2). It means to have reverence, awe, and wonder in response to His glory.

5:10 ***is never satisfied.*** Desire always outruns possessions, no matter how vast acquisitions may grow.

5:15 ***as everyone comes, so they depart.*** The maxim that "you can't take it with you" is affirmed here (2:21).

5:2 [y] Jdg 11:35 [z] Job 6:24; Pr 10:19; 20:25 **5:3** [a] Job 20:8 [b] Ecc 10:14 **5:4** [c] Dt 23:21; Jdg 11:35; Ps 119:60 [d] Nu 30:2; Ps 66:13-14; 76:11 **5:5** [e] Nu 30:2-4; Pr 20:25; Jnh 2:9; Ac 5:4 **5:7** [f] Ecc 3:14; 12:13 **5:8** [g] Ps 12:5; Ecc 4:1 **5:12** [h] Job 20:20 **5:13** [i] Ecc 6:1-2 **5:15** [j] Job 1:21 [k] Ps 49:17; 1Ti 6:7 [l] Ecc 1:3 **5:16** [m] Pr 11:29; Ecc 1:3

18This is what I have observed to be
good: that it is appropriate for a person
to eat, to drink[n] and to find satisfaction in
their toilsome labor[o] under the sun during
the few days of life God has given them—
for this is their lot. 19Moreover, when God
gives someone wealth and possessions,[p]
and the ability to enjoy them,[q] to accept
their lot[r] and be happy in their toil—this is
a gift of God.[s] 20They seldom reflect on the
days of their life, because God keeps them
occupied with gladness of heart.[t]

6 I have seen another evil under the sun,
and it weighs heavily on mankind:
2God gives some people wealth, possessions and honor, so that they lack nothing
their hearts desire, but God does not grant
them the ability to enjoy them,[u] and strangers enjoy them instead. This is meaningless, a grievous evil.[v]

3A man may have a hundred children
and live many years; yet no matter how
long he lives, if he cannot enjoy his prosperity and does not receive proper burial, I
say that a stillborn[w] child is better off than
he.[x] 4It comes without meaning, it departs
in darkness, and in darkness its name is
shrouded. 5Though it never saw the sun or
knew anything, it has more rest than does
that man— 6even if he lives a thousand
years twice over but fails to enjoy his prosperity. Do not all go to the same place?

7 Everyone's toil is for their mouth,
yet their appetite is never satisfied.[y]
8 What advantage have the wise over
fools?[z]
What do the poor gain
by knowing how to conduct
themselves before others?
9 Better what the eye sees
than the roving of the appetite.
This too is meaningless,
a chasing after the wind.[a]

10 Whatever exists has already been
named,
and what humanity is has been
known;
no one can contend
with someone who is stronger.
11 The more the words,
the less the meaning,
and how does that profit anyone?

12For who knows what is good for a person in life, during the few and meaningless
days[b] they pass through like a shadow?[c]
Who can tell them what will happen under
the sun after they are gone?

Wisdom

7 A good name is better than fine
perfume,[d]
and the day of death better than the
day of birth.
2 It is better to go to a house of mourning
than to go to a house of feasting,
for death[e] is the destiny[f] of everyone;
the living should take this to heart.
3 Frustration is better than laughter,[g]
because a sad face is good for the
heart.
4 The heart of the wise is in the house of
mourning,
but the heart of fools is in the house
of pleasure.[h]
5 It is better to heed the rebuke[i] of a wise
person
than to listen to the song of fools.
6 Like the crackling of thorns[j] under the
pot,
so is the laughter[k] of fools.
This too is meaningless.

7 Extortion turns a wise person into a
fool,
and a bribe[l] corrupts the heart.

8 The end of a matter is better than its
beginning,
and patience[m] is better than pride.
9 Do not be quickly provoked[n] in your
spirit,
for anger resides in the lap of fools.

5:19 *this is a gift of God.* God has separated the gift of enjoying something from the gift of the object itself so that we might be driven back to the Giver.
6:2 *God does not grant them the ability.* Prosperity without the divine gift of enjoyment amounts to nothing (5:19).
6:6 *Do not all go to the same place?* That *same place* is the grave (3:20). If a long life terminates in death with no prospect of anything else, will that life have been worthwhile? Long life without knowing God and without the power to enjoy it is indeed frustrating and useless.
6:12 *like a shadow.* This phrase is a confirmation of the meaning of the Hebrew word translated vanity. Life passes away quickly, like a vapor. ***what will happen ... after they are gone?*** The implied answer is that only God knows what will happen to us after death. Rather than imply that nothing exists beyond the grave, this book teaches that each person's life will be reviewed by God after death.
7:2–4 *house of mourning.* We may learn more about the meaning of life in the *house of mourning* than in the *house of feasting.*
7:9 *anger resides in the lap of fools.* Anger is a destructive flood, working all kinds of havoc in our lives. It often leads to protracted and bitter strife (Prov. 30:33). It disrupts and disunites families (1 Sam. 20:30) and may lead to murder (Gen. 4:4–5; 49:6).

5:18 [n] Ecc 2:3 [o] Ecc 2:10, 24 **5:19** [p] 1Ch 29:12; 2Ch 1:12 [q] Ecc 6:2 [r] Job 31:2 [s] Ecc 2:24; 3:13 **5:20** [t] Dt 12:7, 18 **6:2** [u] Ps 17:14; Ecc 5:19 [v] Ecc 5:13 **6:3** [w] Job 3:16; Ecc 4:3 [x] Job 3:3 **6:7** [y] Pr 16:26; 27:20 **6:8** [z] Ecc 2:15 **6:9** [a] Ecc 1:14 **6:12** [b] Job 10:20 [c] Job 14:2; Ps 39:6; Jas 4:14 **7:1** [d] Pr 22:1; SS 1:3 **7:2** [e] Pr 11:19 [f] Ps 90:12 **7:3** [g] Pr 14:13 **7:4** [h] Ecc 2:1; Jer 16:8 **7:5** [i] Ps 141:5; Pr 13:18; 15:31-32 **7:6** [j] Ps 58:9; 118:12 [k] Ecc 2:2 **7:7** [l] Ex 18:21; 23:8; Dt 16:19 **7:8** [m] Pr 14:29; Gal 5:22; Eph 4:2 **7:9** [n] Mt 5:22; Pr 14:17; Jas 1:19

10 Do not say, "Why were the old days
better than these?"
For it is not wise to ask such
questions.

11 Wisdom, like an inheritance, is a good
thing[o]
and benefits those who see the sun.[p]
12 Wisdom is a shelter
as money is a shelter,
but the advantage of knowledge is this:
Wisdom preserves those who have it.

13 Consider what God has done:[q]

Who can straighten
what he has made crooked?[r]
14 When times are good, be happy;
but when times are bad, consider this:
God has made the one
as well as the other.
Therefore, no one can discover
anything about their future.

15 In this meaningless life[s] of mine I have
seen both of these:

the righteous perishing in their
righteousness,
and the wicked living long in their
wickedness.[t]
16 Do not be overrighteous,
neither be overwise—
why destroy yourself?
17 Do not be overwicked,
and do not be a fool—
why die before your time?[u]
18 It is good to grasp the one
and not let go of the other.
Whoever fears God[v] will avoid all
extremes.[a]

19 Wisdom[w] makes one wise person more
powerful[x]
than ten rulers in a city.

20 Indeed, there is no one on earth who is
righteous,[y]
no one who does what is right and
never sins.[z]

21 Do not pay attention to every word
people say,
or you[a] may hear your servant
cursing you—
22 for you know in your heart
that many times you yourself have
cursed others.

23 All this I tested by wisdom and I said,

"I am determined to be wise"[b]—
but this was beyond me.
24 Whatever exists is far off and most
profound—
who can discover it?[c]
25 So I turned my mind to understand,
to investigate and to search out
wisdom and the scheme of things[d]
and to understand the stupidity of
wickedness
and the madness of folly.[e]

26 I find more bitter than death
the woman who is a snare,[f]
whose heart is a trap
and whose hands are chains.
The man who pleases God will escape
her,
but the sinner she will ensnare.[g]

27 "Look," says the Teacher,[b][h] "this is
what I have discovered:

"Adding one thing to another to
discover the scheme of things—
28 while I was still searching
but not finding—
I found one upright man among a
thousand,
but not one upright woman[i] among
them all.
29 This only have I found:
God created mankind upright,
but they have gone in search of many
schemes."

---

a 18 Or *will follow them both* *b* 27 Or *the leader of the assembly*

7:13 can straighten what he has made crooked? The bend that needs straightening is the presence of afflictions and adversities in life. Both prosperity and adversity come from the hand of God. For prosperity give thanks, but in adversity reflect on the goodness and the comprehensiveness of the plan of God.
7:15 *the righteous perishing.* There are inequities in life that will always be a mystery (3:16 – 4:3; 8:14).
7:16 – 18 *Do not be overrighteous.* Few verses in Ecclesiastes are more susceptible to incorrect interpretation than these. This one is not the so-called golden mean that advises: "Don't be too holy and don't be too wicked; sin to a moderate degree." The Preacher was warning instead about pseudo-religiosity and showy forms of worship as well as self-righteousness and judgmental legalism.
7:20 Individual Sin — The depravity of humanity is verifiable. In Romans 3:23, Paul echoes this when he says, "for all have sinned and fall short of the glory of God." All we have to do is watch the news or check the headlines and we are forced to deal with this reality. Each individual man, woman, and child needs the righteousness of God. Without God's righteousness no one can ever enter or stand in God's presence. We all need new life in Christ because we are all sinners.
7:24 *who can discover it?* The theme of wisdom's inaccessibility also appears in Job 28. The answer to this search for wisdom is that God can find wisdom (Job 28:23 – 28).
7:29 *God created mankind upright.* God created humans to do right. They have preferred to search out their own path.

7:11 [o] Pr 8:10-11; Ecc 2:13 [p] Ecc 11:7 **7:13** [q] Ecc 2:24 [r] Ecc 1:15 **7:15** [s] Job 7:7 [t] Ecc 8:12-14; Jer 12:1 **7:17** [u] Job 15:32; Ps 55:23 **7:18** [v] Ecc 3:14 **7:19** [w] Ecc 2:13 [x] Ecc 9:13-18 **7:20** [y] Ps 14:3 [z] 1Ki 8:46; 2Ch 6:36; Pr 20:9; Ro 3:23 **7:21** [a] Pr 30:10 **7:23** [b] Ecc 1:17; Ro 1:22 **7:24** [c] Job 28:12 **7:25** [d] Job 28:3 [e] Ecc 1:17 **7:26** [f] Ex 10:7; Jdg 14:15 [g] Pr 2:16-19; 5:3-5; 7:23; 22:14 **7:27** [h] Ecc 1:1 **7:28** [i] 1Ki 11:3

8 Who is like the wise?
Who knows the explanation of things?
A person's wisdom brightens their face
and changes its hard appearance.

Obey the King

2 Obey the king's command, I say, because you took an oath before God. 3 Do not be in a hurry to leave the king's presence.[j] Do not stand up for a bad cause, for he will do whatever he pleases. 4 Since a king's word is supreme, who can say to him, "What are you doing?[k]"

5 Whoever obeys his command will come
to no harm,
and the wise heart will know the
proper time and procedure.
6 For there is a proper time and
procedure for every matter,[l]
though a person may be weighed
down by misery.

7 Since no one knows the future,
who can tell someone else what is to
come?
8 As no one has power over the wind to
contain it,
so[a] no one has power over the time of
their death.
As no one is discharged in time of war,
so wickedness will not release those
who practice it.

9 All this I saw, as I applied my mind to everything done under the sun. There is a time when a man lords it over others to his own[b] hurt. 10 Then too, I saw the wicked buried[m]—those who used to come and go from the holy place and receive praise[c] in the city where they did this. This too is meaningless.

11 When the sentence for a crime is not quickly carried out, people's hearts are filled with schemes to do wrong. 12 Although a wicked person who commits a hundred crimes may live a long time, I know that it will go better[n] with those who fear God,[o] who are reverent before him.[p] 13 Yet because the wicked do not fear God,[q] it will not go well with them, and their days[r] will not lengthen like a shadow.

14 There is something else meaningless that occurs on earth: the righteous who get what the wicked deserve, and the wicked who get what the righteous deserve.[s] This too, I say, is meaningless.[t] 15 So I commend the enjoyment of life[u], because there is nothing better for a person under the sun than to eat and drink[v] and be glad.[w] Then joy will accompany them in their toil all the days of the life God has given them under the sun.

16 When I applied my mind to know wisdom[x] and to observe the labor that is done on earth[y]—people getting no sleep day or night— 17 then I saw all that God has done.[z] No one can comprehend what goes on under the sun. Despite all their efforts to search it out, no one can discover its meaning. Even if the wise claim they know, they cannot really comprehend it.[a]

A Common Destiny for All

9 So I reflected on all this and concluded that the righteous and the wise and what they do are in God's hands, but no one knows whether love or hate awaits them.[b] 2 All share a common destiny—the righteous and the wicked, the good and the bad,[d] the clean and the unclean, those who offer sacrifices and those who do not.

As it is with the good,
so with the sinful;
as it is with those who take oaths,
so with those who are afraid to take
them.[c]

3 This is the evil in everything that happens under the sun: The same destiny overtakes all.[d] The hearts of people, moreover, are full of evil and there is madness in their hearts while they live,[e] and afterward they join the dead.[f] 4 Anyone who is among the living has hope[e]—even a live dog is better off than a dead lion!

---

[a] 8 Or *over the human spirit to retain it, / and so* [b] 9 Or *to their* [c] 10 Some Hebrew manuscripts and Septuagint (Aquila); most Hebrew manuscripts *and are forgotten* [d] 2 Septuagint (Aquila), Vulgate and Syriac; Hebrew does not have *and the bad.* [e] 4 Or *What then is to be chosen? With all who live, there is hope*

8:1 *brightens their face and changes its hard appearance.* This idiom is an image of a person who is stable. Out of the depths of experience and understanding, that person is able to enjoy life and build up others.

8:8 *power over the wind to contain it.* The word for *wind* is also translated *spirit.* In this context it could mean "life force" (3:19). God is in charge.

8:15 *eat and drink and be glad.* In contrast to the search for the meaning of all things is the contentment that a wise, loving God gives to those who will receive His gifts. Here is one of the central themes of Ecclesiastes. The Preacher marks the end of the third major section of his book with this refrain. The wicked person (the fool) decides that the best thing to do is "to eat and drink and be merry" with no thought given to the living God. But the righteous person (the wise) can enjoy life while thinking of God and His good gifts.

9:1 *whether love or hate.* Sometimes in Hebrew two opposites together are a way of saying "everything." Love and hate are best viewed as words for God's favor and disfavor.

8:3 [j] Ecc 10:4 **8:4** [k] Job 9:12; Est 1:19; Da 4:35 **8:6** [l] Ecc 3:1 **8:10** [m] Ecc 1:11 **8:12** [n] Dt 12:28; Ps 37:11, 18-19; Pr 1:32-33; Isa 3:10-11 [o] Ex 1:20 [p] Ecc 3:14 **8:13** [q] Ecc 3:14; Isa 3:11 [r] Dt 4:40; Job 5:26; Ps 34:12; Isa 65:20 **8:14** [s] Job 21:7; Ps 73:14; Mal 3:15 [t] Ecc 7:15 **8:15** [u] Ps 42:8 [v] Ex 32:6; Ecc 2:3 [w] Ecc 2:24; 3:12-13; 5:18; 9:7 **8:16** [x] Ecc 1:17 [y] Ecc 1:13 **8:17** [z] Job 28:3 [a] Job 5:9; 28:23; Ecc 3:11; Ro 11:33 **9:1** [b] Dt 33:3; Job 12:10; Ecc 10:14 **9:2** [c] Job 9:22; Ecc 2:14; 6:6; 7:2 **9:3** [d] Job 9:22; Ecc 2:14 [e] Jer 11:8; 13:10; 16:12; 17:9 [f] Job 21:26

5 For the living know that they will die,
but the dead know nothing;[g]
they have no further reward,
and even their name[h] is forgotten.[i]
6 Their love, their hate
and their jealousy have long since vanished;
never again will they have a part
in anything that happens under the sun.[j]

7 Go, eat your food with gladness, and
drink your wine[k] with a joyful heart,[l] for
God has already approved what you do.
8 Always be clothed in white,[m] and always
anoint your head with oil. 9 Enjoy life with
your wife,[n] whom you love, all the days of
this meaningless life that God has given
you under the sun—all your meaningless
days. For this is your lot[o] in life and in your
toilsome labor under the sun. 10 Whatever[p]
your hand finds to do, do it with all your
might,[q] for in the realm of the dead,[r] where
you are going, there is neither working nor
planning nor knowledge nor wisdom.[s]

11 I have seen something else under the
sun:

The race is not to the swift
or the battle to the strong,[t]
nor does food come to the wise[u]
or wealth to the brilliant
or favor to the learned;
but time and chance[v] happen to them all.[w]

12 Moreover, no one knows when their
hour will come:

As fish are caught in a cruel net,
or birds are taken in a snare,
so people are trapped by evil times[x]
that fall unexpectedly upon them.[y]

Wisdom Better Than Folly

13 I also saw under the sun this example of wisdom[z] that greatly impressed me:
14 There was once a small city with only a
few people in it. And a powerful king came
against it, surrounded it and built huge
siege works against it. 15 Now there lived in
that city a man poor but wise, and he saved
the city by his wisdom. But nobody remembered that poor man.[a] 16 So I said, "Wisdom
is better than strength." But the poor man's
wisdom is despised, and his words are no
longer heeded.[b]

17 The quiet words of the wise are more to be heeded
than the shouts of a ruler of fools.
18 Wisdom[c] is better than weapons of war,
but one sinner destroys much good.

10 As dead flies give perfume a bad smell,
so a little folly[d] outweighs wisdom and honor.
2 The heart of the wise inclines to the right,
but the heart of the fool to the left.
3 Even as fools walk along the road,
they lack sense
and show everyone[e] how stupid they are.
4 If a ruler's anger rises against you,
do not leave your post;[f]
calmness can lay great offenses to rest.[g]

5 There is an evil I have seen under the sun,
the sort of error that arises from a ruler:
6 Fools are put in many high positions,[h]
while the rich occupy the low ones.
7 I have seen slaves on horseback,
while princes go on foot like slaves.[i]

8 Whoever digs a pit may fall into it;[j]
whoever breaks through a wall may be bitten by a snake.[k]
9 Whoever quarries stones may be injured by them;
whoever splits logs may be endangered by them.[l]

9:5 *the dead know nothing.* This is not a flat denial of any hope beyond the grave. The point of view is limited to what can be known strictly from the human point of view, "under the sun."
9:8 *Always be clothed in white.* It was difficult in ancient times to keep white clothing clean (see analogy in Is. 1:18). White clothing and ointments — oil — were symbols of joy and purity.
9:11 *not to the swift ... to the strong ... wise ... brilliant ... learned.* We would like to think that the best always win, that the deserving are always rewarded. But our experience shows that these expectations are not always realized. These five assets were enjoyed by individuals. But while some planned and counted on their assets, God in the end determined their lot.
9:14–18 *There was once a small city.* Here is a parable about how an unstoppable military operation against a small city was prevented by the wisdom of one poor but wise man. The conclusion is that wisdom is preferable to strength, and should be heeded.
10:1 *dead flies give perfume a bad smell.* Just as one fly can ruin a whole batch of ointment, so an ounce of folly will spoil a pound of wisdom.
10:2 *The heart of the wise inclines to the right.* In ancient thought, the right hand was the place of honor and favor, while the left hand was the reverse.

9:5 [g] Job 14:21 [h] Ps 9:6 [i] Ecc 1:11; 2:16; Isa 26:14
9:6 [j] Job 21:21 **9:7** [k] Nu 6:20 [l] Ecc 2:24; 8:15
9:8 [m] Ps 23:5; Rev 3:4 **9:9** [n] Pr 5:18 [o] Job 31:2
9:10 [p] 1Sa 10:7 [q] Ecc 11:6; Ro 12:11; Col 3:23 [r] Nu 16:33 [s] Ecc 2:24 **9:11** [t] Am 2:14-15 [u] Job 32:13; Isa 47:10; Jer 9:23 [v] Ecc 2:14 [w] Dt 8:18 **9:12** [x] Pr 29:6 [y] Ps 73:22; Ecc 2:14; 8:7 **9:13** [z] 2Sa 20:22 **9:15** [a] Ge 40:14; Ecc 1:11; 2:16; 4:13 **9:16** [b] Pr 21:22; Ecc 7:19 **9:18** [c] ver 16
10:1 [d] Pr 13:16; 18:2 **10:3** [e] Pr 13:16; 18:2 **10:4** [f] Ecc 8:3 [g] Pr 16:14; 25:15 **10:6** [h] Pr 29:2 **10:7** [i] Pr 19:10
10:8 [j] Ps 7:15; 57:6; Pr 26:27 [k] Est 2:23; Ps 9:16; Am 5:19
10:9 [l] Pr 26:27

10 If the ax is dull
and its edge unsharpened,
more strength is needed,
but skill will bring success.

11 If a snake bites before it is charmed,
the charmer receives no fee.[m]

12 Words from the mouth of the wise are gracious,[n]
but fools are consumed by their own lips.[o]
13 At the beginning their words are folly;
at the end they are wicked madness—
14 and fools multiply words.[p]

No one knows what is coming—
who can tell someone else what will happen after them?[q]

15 The toil of fools wearies them;
they do not know the way to town.

16 Woe to the land whose king was a servant[a][r]
and whose princes feast in the morning.
17 Blessed is the land whose king is of noble birth
and whose princes eat at a proper time—
for strength and not for drunkenness.[s]

18 Through laziness, the rafters sag;
because of idle hands, the house leaks.[t]

19 A feast is made for laughter,
wine[u] makes life merry,
and money is the answer for everything.

20 Do not revile the king[v] even in your thoughts,
or curse the rich in your bedroom,
because a bird in the sky may carry your words,
and a bird on the wing may report what you say.

Invest in Many Ventures

11 Ship[w] your grain across the sea;
after many days you may receive a return.[x]
2 Invest in seven ventures, yes, in eight;
you do not know what disaster may come upon the land.

3 If clouds are full of water,
they pour rain on the earth.
Whether a tree falls to the south or to the north,
in the place where it falls, there it will lie.
4 Whoever watches the wind will not plant;
whoever looks at the clouds will not reap.

5 As you do not know the path of the wind,[y]
or how the body is formed[b] in a mother's womb,[z]
so you cannot understand the work of God,
the Maker of all things.

6 Sow your seed in the morning,
and at evening let your hands not be idle,[a]
for you do not know which will succeed,
whether this or that,
or whether both will do equally well.

Remember Your Creator While Young

7 Light is sweet,
and it pleases the eyes to see the sun.[b]
8 However many years anyone may live,
let them enjoy them all.
But let them remember[c] the days of darkness,
for there will be many.
Everything to come is meaningless.

9 You who are young, be happy while you are young,
and let your heart give you joy in the days of your youth.
Follow the ways of your heart
and whatever your eyes see,
but know that for all these things
God will bring you into judgment.[d]

[a] 16 Or *king is a child* [b] 5 Or *know how life* (or *the spirit*) */ enters the body being formed*

10:10 ***If the ax is dull.*** The wise person will sharpen the ax. A person of limited training will have to work harder, as though with a dull ax, than someone wiser whose tools are maintained.
10:17 ***Blessed is the land.*** Useful nobility expresses itself in a sense of responsibility and deference to social order. This verse is an argument for propriety.
11:1 ***Ship your grain across the sea.*** Verses 1–6 emphasize the element of risk and uncertainty in commercial and agricultural enterprises. Thus if the preceding proverbs in chapter 10 deal with royalty and leaders, these in verses 1–6 deal with common people. Men and women must venture forth judiciously if they are ever to realize a gain, even though there is always a certain amount of risk.
11:2 ***in seven ventures, yes, in eight.*** This urges us to be generous to as many as possible—and then some.
11:4 ***will not plant ... will not reap.*** The person who is so cautious that he must wait for the ideal time before he makes a move is doomed to fail.
11:9 ***Follow the ways of your heart.*** This verse is not an invitation to live sinfully in sensual pleasure (as

10:11 [m] Ps 58:5; Isa 3:3 **10:12** [n] Pr 10:32 [o] Pr 10:14; 14:3; 15:2; 18:7 **10:14** [p] Pr 15:2; Ecc 5:3; 6:12; 8:7 [q] Ecc 9:1 **10:16** [r] Isa 3:4-5, 12 **10:17** [s] Dt 14:26; 1Sa 25:36; Pr 31:4 **10:18** [t] Pr 20:4; 24:30-34 **10:19** [u] Ge 14:18; Jdg 9:13 **10:20** [v] Ex 22:28 **11:1** [w] ver 6; Isa 32:20; Hos 10:12 [x] Dt 24:19; Pr 19:17; Mt 10:42 **11:5** [y] Jn 3:8-10 [z] Ps 139:14-16 **11:6** [a] Ecc 9:10 **11:7** [b] Ecc 7:11 **11:8** [c] Ecc 12:1 **11:9** [d] Job 19:29; Ecc 2:24; 3:17; 12:14; Ro 14:10

10 So then, banish anxiety[e] from your heart
and cast off the troubles of your body,
for youth and vigor are meaningless.[f]

12 Remember[g] your Creator
in the days of your youth,
before the days of trouble[h] come
and the years approach when you will say,
"I find no pleasure in them"—
2 before the sun and the light
and the moon and the stars grow dark,
and the clouds return after the rain;
3 when the keepers of the house tremble,
and the strong men stoop,
when the grinders cease because they are few,
and those looking through the windows grow dim;
4 when the doors to the street are closed
and the sound of grinding fades;
when people rise up at the sound of birds,
but all their songs grow faint;[i]
5 when people are afraid of heights
and of dangers in the streets;
when the almond tree blossoms
and the grasshopper drags itself along
and desire no longer is stirred.
Then people go to their eternal home[j]
and mourners[k] go about the streets.

6 Remember him—before the silver cord is severed,
and the golden bowl is broken;
before the pitcher is shattered at the spring,
and the wheel broken at the well,
7 and the dust returns[l] to the ground it came from,
and the spirit returns to God[m] who gave it.[n]

8 "Meaningless! Meaningless!" says the Teacher.[a]
"Everything is meaningless![o]"

The Conclusion of the Matter

9 Not only was the Teacher wise, but he
also imparted knowledge to the people. He
pondered and searched out and set in order
many proverbs.[p] 10 The Teacher searched
to find just the right words, and what he
wrote was upright and true.[q]
11 The words of the wise are like goads,
their collected sayings like firmly embedded nails[r]—given by one shepherd.[b] 12 Be
warned, my son, of anything in addition
to them.

Of making many books there is no end, and much study wearies the body.[s]

13 Now all has been heard;
here is the conclusion of the matter:
Fear God and keep his commandments,[t]
for this is the duty of all mankind.[u]
14 For God will bring every deed into judgment,[v]
including every hidden thing,[w]
whether it is good or evil.

[a] 8 Or *the leader of the assembly*; also in verses 9 and 10 [b] 11 Or *Shepherd*

Num. 15:39 describes). Instead, it urges young people to enjoy themselves completely while not forgetting that God will review the quality of their life (3:17; 12:14).

12:1–8 *Remember your Creator.* Most interpreters have argued that this poem is an allegory of old age.

12:2 *before . . . grow dark.* The person is losing his sight.

12:4 *sound of grinding fades.* A depiction of toothless old age when eating only soft foods makes little or no noise.

12:6 *the wheel broken at the well.* The system of veins and arteries radiating out from the heart might have appeared to the ancients like the spokes on a wheel.

12:11 *The words of the wise are like goads.* Just as an ox goad prods an animal in the right direction, so will the words of this book, when they are properly understood. ***firmly embedded nails.*** The nails or "pegs" referred to here are the same as in 2 Chronicles 3:9 and Jeremiah 10:4. These are hooks in tents where families hung the clothes and pots needed for everyday life. Here they refer to mental hooks giving stability and perspective to life.

12:13 *keep his commandments.* The commandments of the law are in view here. Jesus summed them up as to "love the Lord your God" and "your neighbor as yourself" (Matt. 22:34–40). We are whole or complete only when we fear God and obey His commandments. What profit is there in living? If we follow what this book has said, we will have a relationship with God and find life in Him.

11:10 [e] Ps 94:19 [f] Ecc 2:24 **12:1** [g] Ecc 11:8 [h] 2Sa 19:35 **12:4** [i] Jer 25:10 **12:5** [j] Job 17:13; 10:21 [k] Jer 9:17; Am 5:16 **12:7** [l] Ge 3:19; Job 34:15; Ps 146:4 [m] Ecc 3:21 [n] Job 20:8; Zec 12:1 **12:8** [o] Ecc 1:2 **12:9** [p] 1Ki 4:32 **12:10** [q] Pr 22:20-21 **12:11** [r] Ezr 9:8 **12:12** [s] Ecc 1:18 **12:13** [t] Dt 4:2; 10:12 [u] Mic 6:8 **12:14** [v] Ecc 3:17 [w] Mt 10:26; 1Co 4:5

SONG OF SONGS

▶ **AUTHOR:** According to 1 Kings 4:32, Solomon wrote 1,005 songs, but this eulogy of love stood out among them as the "song of songs." Tradition strongly favors Solomon as the author of this book. Solomon is specifically mentioned seven times, and he is identified as the groom. There is also evidence in the book of incredible royal luxury and expensive imported goods, things that characterized Solomon's reign.

▶ **TIME:** c. 965 B.C. ▶ **KEY VERSE:** Song 7:10

▶ **THEME:** Song of Songs, or Song of Solomon as it is sometimes known, is a one of kind love poem that concentrates on elements of the physical attraction between the sexes. It is possible that the Shulammite maiden was Abishag, who attended to David in his last days. Like Jesus' presence at a wedding, Song of Songs is an indication of God's blessing on the physical union of man and woman. God created us for each other, and we should delight in physical intimacy within the context of marriage that God has sanctioned for us.

---

1 Solomon's Song of Songs.[a]

She[a]

[2] Let him kiss me with the kisses of his mouth—
for your love[b] is more delightful than wine.
[3] Pleasing is the fragrance of your perfumes;[c]
your name[d] is like perfume poured out.
No wonder the young women[e] love you!
[4] Take me away with you—let us hurry!
Let the king bring me into his chambers.[f]

Friends

We rejoice and delight in you[b];
we will praise your love more than wine.

She

How right they are to adore you!

[5] Dark am I, yet lovely,[g]
daughters of Jerusalem,[h]
dark like the tents of Kedar,
like the tent curtains of Solomon.[c]
[6] Do not stare at me because I am dark,
because I am darkened by the sun.
My mother's sons were angry with me
and made me take care of the vineyards;[i]
my own vineyard I had to neglect.
[7] Tell me, you whom I love,
where you graze your flock
and where you rest your sheep[j] at midday.
Why should I be like a veiled woman
beside the flocks of your friends?

[a] The main male and female speakers (identified primarily on the basis of the gender of the relevant Hebrew forms) are indicated by the captions *He* and *She* respectively. The words of others are marked *Friends*. In some instances the divisions and their captions are debatable.
[b] 4 The Hebrew is masculine singular.
[c] 5 Or *Salma*

1:1 ***Song of Songs.*** Like the superlative expressions "holy of holies" or "King of kings," *Song of Songs* means "the loveliest of songs." There are two principal speakers in this book, the woman (She, the Shulammite) and the man (He, Solomon).
1:2 ***for your love is more delightful than wine.*** The Hebrew noun used here means sexual love, as it clearly does in Ezekiel 16:8. This is the Hebrew word that most approximates the Greek word *eros*. In the Song of Songs, this plural word (a mark of intensity) speaks of divinely blessed lovemaking.
1:3 ***Pleasing is the fragrance of your perfumes.*** It was customary in biblical times to rub the body with fragrant oils after a bath in preparation for a festive occasion (Ruth 3:3).
1:5 ***Dark am I, yet lovely.*** The Shulammite compares her dark coloring acquired from long hours working in the vineyards (v. 6) with the lighter complexion of the city maidens. The point here is her class and station in life. Unlike the young women of the court in Jerusalem who had been raised in comfort and conditions of ease, this woman had worked as a field hand in the sun. She knows her beauty is not diminished by her more rugged manner of living.
1:7 ***you whom I love.*** Here the woman mentally

1:1 [a] 1Ki 4:32 **1:2** [b] SS 4:10 **1:3** [c] SS 4:10 [d] Ecc 7:1 [e] Ps 45:14 **1:4** [f] Ps 45:15 **1:5** [g] SS 2:14; 4:3 [h] SS 2:7; 5:8; 5:16 **1:6** [i] Ps 69:8; SS 8:12 **1:7** [j] SS 3:1-4; Isa 13:20

Friends

[8]If you do not know, most beautiful of
women,[k]
follow the tracks of the sheep
and graze your young goats
by the tents of the shepherds.

He

[9]I liken you, my darling, to a mare
among Pharaoh's chariot horses.[l]
[10]Your cheeks[m] are beautiful with
earrings,
your neck with strings of jewels.[n]
[11]We will make you earrings of gold,
studded with silver.

She

[12]While the king was at his table,
my perfume spread its fragrance.[o]
[13]My beloved is to me a sachet of myrrh
resting between my breasts.
[14]My beloved is to me a cluster of henna[p]
blossoms
from the vineyards of En Gedi.[q]

He

[15]How beautiful[r] you are, my darling!
Oh, how beautiful!
Your eyes are doves.[s]

She

[16]How handsome you are, my beloved!
Oh, how charming!
And our bed is verdant.

He

[17]The beams of our house are cedars;[t]
our rafters are firs.

She[a]

2 I am a rose[b][u] of Sharon,[v]
a lily[w] of the valleys.

He

[2]Like a lily among thorns
is my darling among the young
women.

She

[3]Like an apple[c] tree among the trees of
the forest
is my beloved[x] among the young men.
I delight[y] to sit in his shade,
and his fruit is sweet to my taste.[z]
[4]Let him lead me to the banquet hall,[a]
and let his banner[b] over me be love.
[5]Strengthen me with raisins,
refresh me with apples,[c]
for I am faint with love.[d]
[6]His left arm is under my head,
and his right arm embraces me.[e]
[7]Daughters of Jerusalem, I charge you[f]
by the gazelles and by the does of the
field:
Do not arouse or awaken love
until it so desires.[g]

[8]Listen! My beloved!
Look! Here he comes,
leaping across the mountains,
bounding over the hills.[h]
[9]My beloved is like a gazelle[i] or a young
stag.[j]
Look! There he stands behind our
wall,
gazing through the windows,
peering through the lattice.
[10]My beloved spoke and said to me,
"Arise, my darling,
my beautiful one, come with me.
[11]See! The winter is past;
the rains are over and gone.
[12]Flowers appear on the earth;
the season of singing has come,
the cooing of doves
is heard in our land.
[13]The fig tree forms its early fruit;[k]
the blossoming[l] vines spread their
fragrance.
Arise, come, my darling;
my beautiful one, come with me."

[a] Or *He* [b] *1* Probably a member of the crocus family [c] *3* Or possibly *apricot*; here and elsewhere in Song of Songs

---

addresses Solomon, her husband. She pictures him as the shepherd of Israel.

1:8 *follow the tracks of the sheep.* It would be better if she returned to the borders of Lebanon and the life of the farm rather than live alone and anxious in Solomon's palace. The point of this verse is that one should always count the cost of marriage to a particular person before the marriage.

1:13 *My beloved is to me a sachet of myrrh.* This verse refers to an oriental custom for a woman to wear a small bag of myrrh, a perfumed ointment, around her neck at night. All the next day a lovely fragrance would linger about her.

1:17 *The beams of our house are cedars.* As the Shulammite lies on their wedding bed (v. 16), she observes the marvelous cedar beams above her head. The opulence of Solomon's personal and public buildings in Jerusalem is well documented (1 Kin. 7:1–12).

2:3 *Like an apple tree.* Raisin cakes (v. 5) and apples are symbols for sexual passion in ancient love songs.

2:4 *to the banquet hall.* The literal meaning of the phrase is "the house of wine," used because of the role that wine plays not only in feasting, but especially in weddings in biblical cultures (1:2). In the Bible, wine is a symbol of joy (Ps. 104:15).

2:8 *bounding over the hills.* This is the young bride's imaginative way of recalling the joy she experienced at her husband's arrival.

2:11–13 *The winter is past.* By this Solomon means that the time of joy has come; it is the summer of their love. Solomon may have come at a time of great beauty in the fields and forests where the

1:8 [k]SS 5:9; 6:1 **1:9** [l]2Ch 1:17 **1:10** [m]SS 5:13 [n]Isa 61:10 **1:12** [o]SS 4:11-14 **1:14** [p]SS 4:13 [q]1Sa 23:29 **1:15** [r]SS 4:7 [s]SS 2:14; 4:1; 5:2, 12; 6:9 **1:17** [t]1Ki 6:9 **2:1** [u]Isa 35:1 [v]S 1Ch 27:29 [w]SS 5:13; Hos 14:5 **2:3** [x]SS 1:14 [y]SS 1:4 [z]SS 4:16 **2:4** [a]Est 1:11 [b]Nu 1:52 **2:5** [c]SS 7:8 [d]SS 5:8 **2:6** [e]SS 8:3 **2:7** [f]SS 5:8 [g]SS 3:5; 8:4 **2:8** [h]ver 17; SS 8:14 **2:9** [i]2Sa 2:18 [j]ver 17; SS 8:14 **2:13** [k]Isa 28:4; Jer 24:2; Hos 9:10; Mic 7:1; Na 3:12 [l]SS 7:12

He

14 My dove[m] in the clefts of the rock,
in the hiding places on the mountainside,
show me your face,
let me hear your voice;
for your voice is sweet,
and your face is lovely.[n]
15 Catch for us the foxes,[o]
the little foxes
that ruin the vineyards,[p]
our vineyards that are in bloom.[q]

She

16 My beloved is mine and I am his;[r]
he browses among the lilies.[s]
17 Until the day breaks
and the shadows flee,[t]
turn, my beloved,[u]
and be like a gazelle
or like a young stag[v]
on the rugged hills.[a][w]

3 All night long on my bed
I looked[x] for the one my heart loves;
I looked for him but did not find him.
2 I will get up now and go about the city,
through its streets and squares;
I will search for the one my heart loves.
So I looked for him but did not find him.
3 The watchmen found me
as they made their rounds in the city.[y]
"Have you seen the one my heart loves?"
4 Scarcely had I passed them
when I found the one my heart loves.
I held him and would not let him go
till I had brought him to my mother's house,[z]
to the room of the one who conceived me.[a]
5 Daughters of Jerusalem, I charge you[b]
by the gazelles and by the does of the field:
Do not arouse or awaken love
until it so desires.[c]
6 Who is this coming up from the wilderness[d]
like a column of smoke,
perfumed with myrrh[e] and incense
made from all the spices[f] of the merchant?
7 Look! It is Solomon's carriage,
escorted by sixty warriors,[g]
the noblest of Israel,
8 all of them wearing the sword,
all experienced in battle,
each with his sword at his side,
prepared for the terrors of the night.[h]
9 King Solomon made for himself the carriage;
he made it of wood from Lebanon.
10 Its posts he made of silver,
its base of gold.
Its seat was upholstered with purple,
its interior inlaid with love.
Daughters of Jerusalem, 11 come out,
and look, you daughters of Zion.[i]
Look[b] on King Solomon wearing a crown,
the crown with which his mother crowned him
on the day of his wedding,
the day his heart rejoiced.[j]

He

4 How beautiful you are, my darling!
Oh, how beautiful!
Your eyes behind your veil are doves.[k]
Your hair is like a flock of goats
descending from the hills of Gilead.[l]
2 Your teeth are like a flock of sheep just shorn,
coming up from the washing.
Each has its twin;
not one of them is alone.[m]
3 Your lips are like a scarlet ribbon;

[a] 17 Or *the hills of Bether* [b] 10,11 Or *interior lovingly inlaid / by the daughters of Jerusalem. / 11Come out, you daughters of Zion, / and look*

---

young woman lived; he uses the beauty of creation to describe the ripeness of time for their love.

2:15 *Catch for us the foxes.* The Shulammite's brothers called on Solomon to catch them the foxes. Many times they had seen little foxes creep into the vineyards they tended and destroy the roots by gnawing on them.

3:1 *on my bed.* This is a dream that took place before they were married. The young woman was becoming concerned about what she would be getting into in the royal marriage.

3:3 *Have you seen.* Her frantic search for her beloved is initially unsuccessful.

3:4 *the one my heart loves.* At last she finds him and in her dream takes him to her mother's house. The worry of his absence is intolerable to her; she wants him to move back with her to her familiar home and lifestyle.

3:7 *Solomon's carriage.* This was a sedan chair with poles projecting from the front and back so that a person could be carried by several bearers. (vv. 9–10). The Shulammite was being carried to the wedding and to her groom on Solomon's own couch.

4:1 *How beautiful you are.* Solomon lavishly praises his bride's great beauty. He uses verbal symbols of loveliness to paint a picture of the breathtaking charm of the Shulammite. Dove's eyes are a picture of purity, innocence, and beauty. The king compared the movement of her flowing hair to the graceful movement of a flock of goats in their descent down from Mount Gilead.

4:2–5 *teeth ... lips ... neck ... breasts.* The king

2:14 [m] Ge 8:8; SS 1:15 [n] SS 1:5; 8:13 **2:15** [o] Jdg 15:4 [p] SS 1:6 [q] SS 7:12 **2:16** [r] SS 7:10 [s] SS 4:5; 6:3 **2:17** [t] SS 4:6 [u] SS 1:14 [v] ver 9 [w] ver 8 **3:1** [x] SS 5:6; Isa 26:9 **3:3** [y] SS 5:7 **3:4** [z] SS 8:2 [a] SS 6:9 **3:5** [b] SS 2:7 [c] SS 8:4 **3:6** [d] SS 8:5 [e] SS 1:13; 4:6, 14 [f] Ex 30:34 **3:7** [g] 1Sa 8:11 **3:8** [h] Job 15:22; Ps 91:5 **3:11** [i] Isa 4:4 [j] Isa 62:5 **4:1** [k] SS 1:15; 5:12 [l] SS 6:5; Mic 7:14 **4:2** [m] SS 6:6

your mouth[n] is lovely.
Your temples behind your veil
are like the halves of a pomegranate.[o]
4 Your neck is like the tower[p] of David,
built with courses of stone[a];
on it hang a thousand shields,[q]
all of them shields of warriors.
5 Your breasts[r] are like two fawns,
like twin fawns of a gazelle[s]
that browse among the lilies.[t]
6 Until the day breaks
and the shadows flee,[u]
I will go to the mountain of myrrh[v]
and to the hill of incense.
7 You are altogether beautiful,[w] my darling;
there is no flaw in you.

8 Come with me from Lebanon, my bride,[x]
come with me from Lebanon.
Descend from the crest of Amana,
from the top of Senir,[y] the summit of Hermon,[z]
from the lions' dens
and the mountain haunts of leopards.
9 You have stolen my heart, my sister, my bride;
you have stolen my heart
with one glance of your eyes,
with one jewel of your necklace.[a]
10 How delightful[b] is your love[c], my sister, my bride!
How much more pleasing is your love than wine,
and the fragrance of your perfume
more than any spice!
11 Your lips drop sweetness as the honeycomb, my bride;
milk and honey are under your tongue.[d]
The fragrance of your garments
is like the fragrance of Lebanon.[e]
12 You are a garden locked up, my sister, my bride;
you are a spring enclosed, a sealed fountain.[f]
13 Your plants are an orchard of pomegranates[g]
with choice fruits,
with henna[h] and nard,
14 nard and saffron,
calamus and cinnamon,[i]
with every kind of incense tree,
with myrrh[j] and aloes
and all the finest spices.[k]
15 You are[b] a garden fountain,
a well of flowing water
streaming down from Lebanon.

She

16 Awake, north wind,
and come, south wind!
Blow on my garden,
that its fragrance may spread everywhere.
Let my beloved come into his garden
and taste its choice fruits.[l]

He

5 I have come into my garden, my sister, my bride;[m]
I have gathered my myrrh with my spice.
I have eaten my honeycomb and my honey;
I have drunk my wine and my milk.[n]

Friends

Eat, friends, and drink;
drink your fill of love.

She

2 I slept but my heart was awake.
Listen! My beloved is knocking:
"Open to me, my sister, my darling,
my dove, my flawless[o] one.[p]
My head is drenched with dew,
my hair with the dampness of the night."
3 I have taken off my robe—
must I put it on again?
I have washed my feet—
must I soil them again?

---

[a] *4* The meaning of the Hebrew for this phrase is uncertain. [b] *15* Or *I am* (spoken by *She*)

---

rhapsodizes of the perfection of her physical features. Her beauty is exquisite.

4:9 *my sister, my bride.* This strange pairing of words was based on the idea that in marriage a couple became "related." The woman was dignified as a member of the king's family.

4:11 *lips . . . milk and honey.* The sweetness of his bride's kisses are like food to him (5:1; compare 1:2).

4:12 *a garden locked up . . . a spring enclosed.* Solomon evokes thoughts of refreshment and delight. His use of the words "enclosed" and "sealed" indicate, in a poetic manner, his wife's virginity on their wedding night. This was the treasure she brought to him, and which she charged the other young women in the court to maintain for their wedding nights as well (2:7).

4:16 *Let my beloved come into his garden.* The bride is now ready to accept her lover for the first time to her "garden". She calls on the wind to blow through. That is, she is ready to make love to her husband for the first time.

5:1 *I have drunk my wine and my milk.* At the conclusion of their lovemaking, the groom speaks of his complete satisfaction in his beautiful bride.

5:2 – 7 *I slept.* These words begin a section (vv. 2 – 8) that most likely is another dream sequence (3:1 – 5). The bride dreams that her lover is coming to her, but she has already washed, removed her robe, and gotten into bed (v. 3). She finally goes to the door to let

4:3 [n] SS 5:16 [o] SS 6:7 **4:4** [p] SS 7:4 [q] Eze 27:10 **4:5** [r] SS 7:3 [s] Pr 5:19 [t] SS 2:16; 6:2-3 **4:6** [u] SS 2:17 [v] ver 14 **4:7** [w] SS 1:15 **4:8** [x] SS 5:1 [y] Dt 3:9 [z] 1Ch 5:23 **4:9** [a] Ge 41:42 **4:10** [b] SS 7:6 [c] SS 1.2 **4:11** [d] Ps 19:10; SS 5:1 [e] Hos 14:6 **4:12** [f] Pr 5:15-18 **4:13** [g] SS 6:11; 7:12 [h] SS 1:14 **4:14** [i] Ex 30:23 [j] SS 3:6 [k] SS 1:12 **4:16** [l] SS 2:3; 5:1 **5:1** [m] SS 4:8 [n] SS 4:11; Isa 55:1 **5:2** [o] SS 4:7 [p] SS 6:9

[4]My beloved thrust his hand through the
latch-opening;
my heart began to pound for him.
[5]I arose to open for my beloved,
and my hands dripped with myrrh,[q]
my fingers with flowing myrrh,
on the handles of the bolt.
[6]I opened for my beloved,[r]
but my beloved had left; he was
gone.[s]
My heart sank at his departure.[a]
I looked[t] for him but did not find him.
I called him but he did not answer.
[7]The watchmen found me
as they made their rounds in the city.[u]
They beat me, they bruised me;
they took away my cloak,
those watchmen of the walls!
[8]Daughters of Jerusalem, I charge you[v]—
if you find my beloved,
what will you tell him?
Tell him I am faint with love.[w]

Friends

[9]How is your beloved better than others,
most beautiful of women?[x]
How is your beloved better than others,
that you so charge us?

She

[10]My beloved is radiant and ruddy,
outstanding among ten thousand.[y]
[11]His head is purest gold;
his hair is wavy
and black as a raven.
[12]His eyes are like doves[z]
by the water streams,
washed in milk,[a]
mounted like jewels.
[13]His cheeks[b] are like beds of spice[c]
yielding perfume.
His lips are like lilies[d]
dripping with myrrh.
[14]His arms are rods of gold
set with topaz.
His body is like polished ivory
decorated with lapis lazuli.[e]
[15]His legs are pillars of marble
set on bases of pure gold.
His appearance is like Lebanon,[f]
choice as its cedars.
[16]His mouth[g] is sweetness itself;
he is altogether lovely.
This is my beloved,[h] this is my friend,
daughters of Jerusalem.[i]

Friends

6 Where has your beloved[j] gone,
most beautiful of women?[k]
Which way did your beloved turn,
that we may look for him with you?

She

[2]My beloved has gone[l] down to his
garden,[m]
to the beds of spices,[n]
to browse in the gardens
and to gather lilies.
[3]I am my beloved's and my beloved is
mine;[o]
he browses among the lilies.[p]

He

[4]You are as beautiful as Tirzah,[q] my
darling,
as lovely as Jerusalem,[r]
as majestic as troops with banners.[s]
[5]Turn your eyes from me;
they overwhelm me.
Your hair is like a flock of goats
descending from Gilead.[t]
[6]Your teeth are like a flock of sheep
coming up from the washing.
Each has its twin,
not one of them is missing.[u]
[7]Your temples behind your veil[v]
are like the halves of a
pomegranate.[w]
[8]Sixty queens[x] there may be,
and eighty concubines,[y]
and virgins beyond number;
[9]but my dove,[z] my perfect one,[a] is
unique,
the only daughter of her mother,
the favorite of the one who bore her.[b]
The young women saw her and called
her blessed;
the queens and concubines praised
her.

---

[a] 6 Or *heart had gone out to him when he spoke*

---

him in, but he is gone. Her sorrow at this drives her into the city to search for him.

5:8–9 *Daughters of Jerusalem.* She asks for help in her search, but the daughters question what is so special about the one for whom she seeks.

6:1 *that we may look for him with you?* The chorus members now join in the search. In the dream sequence, we suspect that the chorus is well aware of his location. It is only the bride who needs to discover his whereabouts.

6:3 *I am my beloved's and my beloved is mine.* These words are an inversion of the words of 2:16; compare also 7:10. ***he browses among the lilies.*** With these words the bride comes to terms with the reality that, as much as she and the king are in love, he still has other responsibilities and so does she. His work as king makes him the shepherd of his people, yet his love for her does not necessarily diminish because of his devotion to his work.

6:8–9 *Sixty ... eighty.* This use of numbers is a rhetorical device to emphasize that the bride alone is Solomon's love.

5:5 [q] ver 13 **5:6** [r] SS 6:1 [s] SS 6:2 [t] SS 3:1 **5:7** [u] SS 3:3 **5:8** [v] SS 2:7; 3:5 [w] SS 2:5 **5:9** [x] SS 1:8; 6:1 **5:10** [y] Ps 45:2 **5:12** [z] SS 1:15; 4:1 [a] Ge 49:12 **5:13** [b] SS 1:10 [c] SS 6:2 [d] SS 2:1 **5:14** [e] Job 28:6 **5:15** [f] 1Ki 4:33; SS 7:4 **5:16** [g] SS 4:3 [h] SS 7:9 [i] SS 1:5 **6:1** [j] SS 5:6 [k] SS 1:8 **6:2** [l] SS 5:6 [m] SS 4:12 [n] SS 5:13 **6:3** [o] SS 7:10 [p] SS 2:16 **6:4** [q] Jos 12:24 [r] Ps 48:2; 50:2 [s] ver 10 **6:5** [t] SS 4:1 **6:6** [u] SS 4:2 **6:7** [v] Ge 24:65 [w] SS 4:3 **6:8** [x] Ps 45:9 [y] Ge 22:24 **6:9** [z] SS 1:15 [a] SS 5:2 [b] SS 3:4

Friends

10 Who is this that appears like the dawn,
fair as the moon, bright as the sun,
majestic as the stars in procession?

He

11 I went down to the grove of nut trees
to look at the new growth in the valley,
to see if the vines had budded
or the pomegranates were in bloom.[c]
12 Before I realized it,
my desire set me among the royal chariots of my people.[a]

Friends

13 Come back, come back, O Shulammite;
come back, come back, that we may gaze on you!

He

Why would you gaze on the Shulammite
as on the dance[d] of Mahanaim?[b]

7 [c] How beautiful your sandaled feet,
O prince's[e] daughter!
Your graceful legs are like jewels,
the work of an artist's hands.
2 Your navel is a rounded goblet
that never lacks blended wine.
Your waist is a mound of wheat
encircled by lilies.
3 Your breasts[f] are like two fawns,
like twin fawns of a gazelle.
4 Your neck is like an ivory tower.[g]
Your eyes are the pools of Heshbon[h]
by the gate of Bath Rabbim.
Your nose is like the tower of Lebanon[i]
looking toward Damascus.
5 Your head crowns you like Mount Carmel.[j]
Your hair is like royal tapestry;
the king is held captive by its tresses.
6 How beautiful[k] you are and how pleasing,
my love, with your delights![l]
7 Your stature is like that of the palm,
and your breasts[m] like clusters of fruit.
8 I said, "I will climb the palm tree;
I will take hold of its fruit."
May your breasts be like clusters of grapes on the vine,
the fragrance of your breath like apples,[n]
9 and your mouth like the best wine.

She

May the wine go straight to my beloved,[o]
flowing gently over lips and teeth.[d]
10 I belong to my beloved,
and his desire[p] is for me.[q]
11 Come, my beloved, let us go to the countryside,
let us spend the night in the villages.[e]
12 Let us go early to the vineyards[r]
to see if the vines have budded,[s]
if their blossoms[t] have opened,
and if the pomegranates[u] are in bloom[v]—
there I will give you my love.
13 The mandrakes[w] send out their fragrance,
and at our door is every delicacy,
both new and old,
that I have stored up for you, my beloved.[x]

8 If only you were to me like a brother,
who was nursed at my mother's breasts!
Then, if I found you outside,
I would kiss you,
and no one would despise me.
2 I would lead you
and bring you to my mother's house[y]—
she who has taught me.
I would give you spiced wine to drink,
the nectar of my pomegranates.
3 His left arm is under my head
and his right arm embraces me.[z]
4 Daughters of Jerusalem, I charge you:
Do not arouse or awaken love
until it so desires.[a]

Friends

5 Who is this coming up from the wilderness[b]
leaning on her beloved?

---

[a] 12 Or *among the chariots of Amminadab*; or *among the chariots of the people of the prince* [b] 13 In Hebrew texts this verse (6:13) is numbered 7:1. [c] In Hebrew texts 7:1-13 is numbered 7:2-14. [d] 9 Septuagint, Aquila, Vulgate and Syriac; Hebrew *lips of sleepers* [e] 11 Or *the henna bushes*

6:13 *Come back, come back, O Shulammite.* The chorus calls the bride back from her daydreams and reminds her that she is Solomon's queen.
7:1 *Your graceful legs.* The Hebrew wording suggests not only her form but also the fluid motion of her dance (6:13).
7:7–8 *like that of the palm.* This is a sexual image that has its basis in the pollination of palm trees. To fertilize a female palm tree, the gardener climbs the male tree and takes some of its flowers. Then he climbs the female tree and ties the pollen-bearing flowers among its branches.
7:13 *The mandrakes.* The yellow fruit of the mandrake was small, sweet-tasting and fragrant. It was considered a love potion (Gen. 30:16).
8:3 *left . . . right.* The repetition of 2:6–7 punctuates both the joy of sexual intimacy with marriage and the warnings against sexual activity before marriage.

6:11 [c] SS 7:12 **6:13** [d] Ex 15:20 **7:1** [e] Ps 45:13
7:3 [f] SS 4:5 **7:4** [g] Ps 144:12; SS 4:4 [h] Nu 21:26 [i] SS 5:15
7:5 [j] Isa 35:2 **7:6** [k] SS 1:15 [l] SS 4:10 **7:7** [m] SS 4:5
7:8 [n] SS 2:5 **7:9** [o] SS 5:16 **7:10** [p] Ps 45:11 [q] SS 2:16; 6:3
7:12 [r] SS 1:6 [s] SS 2:15 [t] SS 2:13 [u] SS 4:13 [v] SS 6:11
7:13 [w] Ge 30:14 [x] SS 4:16 **8:2** [y] SS 3:4 **8:3** [z] SS 2:6
8:4 [a] SS 2:7; 3:5 **8:5** [b] SS 3:6

She

Under the apple tree I roused you;
there your mother conceived[c] you,
there she who was in labor gave you birth.
6 Place me like a seal over your heart,
like a seal on your arm;
for love[d] is as strong as death,
its jealousy[ae] unyielding as the grave.
It burns like blazing fire,
like a mighty flame.[b]
7 Many waters cannot quench love;
rivers cannot sweep it away.
If one were to give
all the wealth of one's house for love,
it[c] would be utterly scorned.[f]

Friends

8 We have a little sister,
and her breasts are not yet grown.
What shall we do for our sister
on the day she is spoken for?
9 If she is a wall,
we will build towers of silver on her.
If she is a door,
we will enclose her with panels of cedar.

She

10 I am a wall,
and my breasts are like towers.
Thus I have become in his eyes
like one bringing contentment.
11 Solomon had a vineyard[g] in Baal Hamon;
he let out his vineyard to tenants.
Each was to bring for its fruit
a thousand shekels[dh] of silver.
12 But my own vineyard[i] is mine to give;
the thousand shekels are for you, Solomon,
and two hundred[e] are for those who tend its fruit.

He

13 You who dwell in the gardens
with friends in attendance,
let me hear your voice!

She

14 Come away, my beloved,
and be like a gazelle[j]
or like a young stag[k]
on the spice-laden mountains.[l]

---

[a] 6 Or *ardor* [b] 6 Or *fire, / like the very flame of the LORD* [c] 7 Or *he* [d] 11 That is, about 25 pounds or about 12 kilograms; also in verse 12 [e] 12 That is, about 5 pounds or about 2.3 kilograms

---

8:6 *like a seal.* This is a symbol of possession or ownership. The Shulammite wants the king to feel a total ownership of her in his heart. She is committed only to him; and she wants him to be completely committed to her. As long as she resides in his heart, she feels secure.
8:7 *quench ... scorned.* The point of this verse is that true love cannot be destroyed or purchased.
8:10 *I am a wall ... towers.* The woman explains that she has been virtuous in youth and that she will remain faithful in her adulthood.
8:14 *spice-laden mountains.* That is she wants him to return to her loving embrace (1:13).

8:5 [c] SS 3:4 **8:6** [d] SS 1:2 [e] Nu 5:14 **8:7** [f] Pr 6:35 **8:11** [g] Ecc 2:4 [h] Isa 7:23 **8:12** [i] SS 1:6 **8:14** [j] Pr 5:19 [k] SS 2:9 [l] SS 2:8, 17

ISAIAH

▶ **AUTHOR:** Although there is much argument regarding the unity of the work, Isaiah is the commonly accepted author of this book. He was from a distinguished Jewish family and his education is evident in his impressive vocabulary and style. The New Testament writers John, Paul, Matthew, and Luke, as well as Jesus himself, all quote from the Book of Isaiah and credit him with its authorship. This great poet was uncompromising, sincere, and compassionate. Isaiah maintained close contact with the royal court, but his exhortations against alliances with foreign powers were not always well received.

▶ **TIME:** c. 740–680 B.C. ▶ **KEY VERSES:** Is. 9:6–7

▶ **THEME:** Because of the length of the book and Isaiah's interactions with the politics of the time, we probably get a better picture of Isaiah's ministry than we do of any of the other prophets. It also contains more of the well-known, classic prophecy texts than any other book. One commentator calls Isaiah the "Romans" of the Old Testament, as in Isaiah we get a broad perspective on how and why God is working in history. Both God's holiness and grace come clearly into perspective through a careful study of this book.

1 The vision[a] concerning Judah and Jerusalem[b] that Isaiah son of Amoz saw[c]
during the reigns of Uzziah,[d] Jotham,
Ahaz[e] and Hezekiah, kings of Judah.

A Rebellious Nation

2 Hear me, you heavens! Listen, earth!
For the LORD has spoken:[f]
"I reared children and brought them up,
but they have rebelled[g] against me.
3 The ox knows its master,
the donkey its owner's manger,
but Israel does not know,[h]
my people do not understand."

4 Woe to the sinful nation,
a people whose guilt is great,
a brood of evildoers,[i]
children given to corruption!
They have forsaken the LORD;
they have spurned the Holy One[j] of Israel
and turned their backs on him.

5 Why should you be beaten anymore?
Why do you persist in rebellion?[k]
Your whole head is injured,
your whole heart afflicted.[l]
6 From the sole of your foot to the top of your head
there is no soundness[m]—
only wounds and welts
and open sores,
not cleansed or bandaged[n]
or soothed with olive oil.[o]

7 Your country is desolate,[p]
your cities burned with fire;
your fields are being stripped by foreigners
right before you,
laid waste as when overthrown by strangers.
8 Daughter Zion is left
like a shelter in a vineyard,
like a hut[q] in a cucumber field,
like a city under siege.

1:1 ***Isaiah son of Amoz.*** God sent His message through Isaiah to Judah, the people of the southern kingdom—specifically to their magistrates, priests, and prophets in Jerusalem. The nation had been divided into two parts: Judah (the southern kingdom) and Israel (the northern kingdom). While Isaiah's message was primarily for the southern kingdom, it was also for the northern kingdom. The entire nation was heading down a path of sin and idolatry that would end in destruction. Isaiah lived to see the nation of Assyria take the northern kingdom into captivity in 722 B.C. The record of Isaiah's visions contains the revelations that God gave during the reigns of Uzziah (792–740 B.C.), Jotham (752–736 B.C.), Ahaz (736–720 B.C.), and Hezekiah (729–699 B.C.). God never changes, and this revelation is still relevant for His people today.

1:1 [a] Nu 12:6 [b] Isa 40:9 [c] Isa 2:1 [d] 2Ch 26:22 [e] 2Ki 16:1
1:2 [f] Mic 1:2 [g] Isa 30:1,9; 65:2 **1:3** [h] Jer 8:7; 9:3,6
1:4 [i] Isa 14:20 [j] Isa 5:19,24 **1:5** [k] Isa 31:6 [l] Isa 33:6,24
1:6 [m] Ps 38:3 [n] Isa 30:26; Jer 8:22 [o] Lk 10:34
1:7 [p] Lev 26:34 **1:8** [q] Job 27:18

[9]Unless the LORD Almighty
had left us some survivors,[r]
we would have become like Sodom,
we would have been like Gomorrah.[s]
[10]Hear the word of the LORD,[t]
you rulers of Sodom;[u]
listen to the instruction[v] of our God,
you people of Gomorrah!
[11]"The multitude of your sacrifices—
what are they to me?" says the
LORD.
"I have more than enough of burnt
offerings,
of rams and the fat of fattened
animals;[w]
I have no pleasure
in the blood of bulls[x] and lambs and
goats.[y]
[12]When you come to appear before me,
who has asked this of you,[z]
this trampling of my courts?
[13]Stop bringing meaningless
offerings![a]
Your incense[b] is detestable to me.
New Moons, Sabbaths and
convocations[c]—
I cannot bear your worthless
assemblies.
[14]Your New Moon feasts and your
appointed festivals[d]
I hate with all my being.
They have become a burden to me;
I am weary[e] of bearing them.
[15]When you spread out your hands in
prayer,
I hide[f] my eyes from you;
even when you offer many prayers,
I am not listening.

Your hands are full of blood![g]

[16]Wash and make yourselves clean.
Take your evil deeds out of my sight;[h]
stop doing wrong.[i]
[17]Learn to do right; seek justice.[j]
Defend the oppressed.[a]
Take up the cause of the fatherless;[k]
plead the case of the widow.

[18]"Come now, let us settle the matter,"[l]
says the LORD.
"Though your sins are like scarlet,
they shall be as white as snow;[m]
though they are red as crimson,
they shall be like wool.
[19]If you are willing and obedient,
you will eat the good things of the
land;[n]
[20]but if you resist and rebel,
you will be devoured by the sword."[o]
For the mouth of the LORD
has spoken.[p]

[21]See how the faithful city
has become a prostitute![q]
She once was full of justice;
righteousness used to dwell in her—
but now murderers!
[22]Your silver has become dross,
your choice wine is diluted with
water.
[23]Your rulers are rebels,
partners with thieves;
they all love bribes[r]
and chase after gifts.
They do not defend the cause of the
fatherless;
the widow's case does not come
before them.[s]

[a] *17 Or justice. / Correct the oppressor*

1:9 *LORD Almighty.* Isaiah describes God as ruler over all powers in heaven and earth through His command of His angelic armies. ***survivors.*** Though God punished His sinful people, he always preserved survivors, or a remnant (Gen. 22:16–17; Ex. 34:6–7; Mic. 7:19–20; Rom. 9:29; 11:15). ***Sodom ... Gomorrah.*** These two cities were regarded as the epitome of sinfulness. It was a scathing condemnation to say that Jerusalem had become like those cities.

1:18–20 The Message of the Prophets—These verses contain the essence of the prophet's message to Israel, which is also meant for us today. We need to recognize the reality of our condition. We are a stiff-necked and rebellious people, who would rather do what we want, when we want. Even today, we want the benefits of God's grace without accepting any accountability to God.

Just as in the days of Isaiah, God's people attempt to replace obedience with ceremony. We ignore God's commands to care for the destitute, and we lose sight of God's requirements for justice and righteousness. Each of us stands before God dirty and bloody, saying we are still His people, when we are clearly not ready to fellowship with a holy God. We need to be cleaned up first.

Our God is a redeeming God who knows how to deal with sin. Although there is no rebellion that goes beyond His reach, the remedy has to be His. The first step in obedience is repentance—turning away from the direction we are going in order to see God.

1:18 *settle the matter.* This term means "to come to a legal decision." It is not an invitation to negotiate or compromise. The people were to come to an agreement with God concerning the enormous gravity of their sin. God was not declaring His people innocent of wickedness, but He was prepared to pardon their sins if they would repent and turn to Him.

1:20 *has spoken.* The verb "has spoken" indicates finality (contrast the verb "says" in v. 18). God had graciously extended His offer of mercy over a significant period of time, but this was the only offer He made. They could not "cut another deal" with Him (40:5; 55:11).

1:9 [r] Isa 10:20-22; 37:4, 31-32 [s] Ge 19:24; Ro 9:29* **1:10** [t] Isa 28:14 [u] Isa 3:9; Eze 16:49; Ro 9:29; Rev 11:8 [v] Isa 8:20 **1:11** [w] Ps 50:8 [x] Jer 6:20 [y] 1Sa 15:22; Mal 1:10 **1:12** [z] Ex 23:17 **1:13** [a] Isa 66:3 [b] Jer 7:9 [c] 1Ch 23:31 **1:14** [d] Lev 23:1-44; Nu 28:11-29:39; Isa 29:1 [e] Isa 7:13; 43:22, 24 **1:15** [f] Isa 8:17; 59:2; Mic 3:4 [g] Isa 59:3 **1:16** [h] Isa 52:11 [i] Isa 55:7; Jer 25:5 **1:17** [j] Zep 2:3 [k] Ps 82:3 **1:18** [l] Isa 41:1; 43:9, 26 [m] Ps 51:7; Rev 7:14 **1:19** [n] Dt 30:15-16; Isa 55:2 **1:20** [o] Isa 3:25; 65:12 [p] Isa 34:16; 40:5; 58:14; Mic 4:4 **1:21** [q] Isa 57:3-9; Jer 2:20 **1:23** [r] Ex 23:8 [s] Isa 10:2; Jer 5:28; Eze 22:6-7; Zec 7:10

24 Therefore the Lord, the LORD Almighty,
the Mighty One of Israel, declares:
"Ah! I will vent my wrath on my foes
and avenge[t] myself on my enemies.
25 I will turn my hand against you;[a]
I will thoroughly purge away your dross
and remove all your impurities.[u]
26 I will restore your leaders as in days of old,[v]
your rulers as at the beginning.
Afterward you will be called
the City of Righteousness,[w]
the Faithful City.[x]"

27 Zion will be delivered with justice,
her penitent ones with righteousness.[y]
28 But rebels and sinners will both be broken,
and those who forsake the LORD will perish.[z]

29 "You will be ashamed because of the sacred oaks[a]
in which you have delighted;
you will be disgraced because of the gardens[b]
that you have chosen.
30 You will be like an oak with fading leaves,
like a garden without water.
31 The mighty man will become tinder
and his work a spark;
both will burn together,
with no one to quench the fire.[c]"

The Mountain of the LORD

2 This is what Isaiah son of Amoz saw concerning Judah and Jerusalem:[d]

2 In the last days
the mountain[e] of the LORD's temple will be established
as the highest of the mountains;
it will be exalted above the hills,
and all nations will stream to it.

3 Many peoples will come and say,

"Come, let us go up to the mountain of the LORD,
to the temple of the God of Jacob.
He will teach us his ways,
so that we may walk in his paths."
The law[f] will go out from Zion,
the word of the LORD from Jerusalem.[g]
4 He will judge between the nations
and will settle disputes for many peoples.
They will beat their swords into plowshares
and their spears into pruning hooks.[h]
Nation will not take up sword against nation,[i]
nor will they train for war anymore.

5 Come, descendants of Jacob,[j]
let us walk in the light[k] of the LORD.

The Day of the LORD

6 You, LORD, have abandoned[l] your people,
the descendants of Jacob.
They are full of superstitions from the East;
they practice divination like the Philistines[m]
and embrace[n] pagan customs.[o]

[a] 25 That is, against Jerusalem

1:27 *delivered.* The Hebrew word for "delivered" means "ransomed" or "freed" from another's ownership through the payment of a price. ***penitent.*** Zion's penitents, those who turned their backs on idolatry and injustice, found freedom from sin and judgment.
1:29 *sacred oaks ... gardens.* These sacred oaks and the gardens with sacred groves for fertility rites were part of idol worship, which the people had chosen instead of worshiping only the Living God.
2:2 *In the last days.* The last days refer to the conditions in Christ's (the Messiah's) future kingdom. At the time of the writing of the Book of Isaiah, no one had a clear idea of what the coming of the Messiah would mean. They believed that, under His rule, earthly kingdoms and authorities would vanish, and everything would at last be the way God originally planned before the fall (Gen. 3:1–22). But they did not yet have an understanding of Christ dying on the cross for the sins of the whole world, or of the church age. Isaiah was looking forward to what Christians are still looking forward to—what we call the second coming, or return of Christ (Acts 1:11; Rev. 21–22).
2:4 *nor will they train for war anymore.* The Old Testament term for "peace" meant soundness or completeness. Just as man can never be truly at peace apart from his Creator, so a nation of sinful humanity cannot truly achieve peace apart from God. Men or nations will be rebellious, self-centered, and at odds with each other unless their harmony with God is restored. This can only happen when, person by person, peace is provided by the Prince of Peace, Jesus Christ. To look forward to the day when there will be this peace for the whole world is to understand the magnitude of God's promise in this passage.
2:6 *You, LORD, have abandoned.* This was a present condition—but not a permanent condition—for the Israelites. God's covenant with Israel had always been based on their obedience, and the Israelites (or house of Jacob) were finally going to experience the results of their disobedience (Deut. 27–30). ***full of superstitions from the East ... divination.*** Copying other religions and participating in the occult practices of peoples of Canaan were strictly forbidden (Deut. 18:9–14). Whoever did these things was detestable to the Lord.

1:24 [t] Isa 35:4; 59:17; 61:2; 63:4 **1:25** [u] Eze 22:22; Mal 3:3 **1:26** [v] Jer 33:7, 11 [w] Isa 33:5; 62:1; Zec 8:3 [x] Isa 60:14; 62:2 **1:27** [y] Isa 35:10; 62:12; 63:4 **1:28** [z] Ps 9:5; Isa 24:20; 66:24; 2Th 1:8-9 **1:29** [a] Isa 57:5 [b] Isa 65:3; 66:17 **1:31** [c] Isa 5:24; 9:18-19; 26:11; 33:14; 66:15-16, 24 **2:1** [d] Isa 1:1 **2:2** [e] Isa 27:13; 56:7; 66:20; Mic 4:7 **2:3** [f] Isa 51:4, 7 [g] Lk 24:47 **2:4** [h] Joel 3:10 [i] Ps 46:9; Isa 9:5; 11:6-9; 32:18; Hos 2:18; Zec 9:10 **2:5** [j] Isa 58:1 [k] Isa 60:1, 19-20; 1Jn 1:5, 7 **2:6** [l] Dt 31:17 [m] 2Ki 1:2 [n] Pr 6:1 [o] 2Ki 16:7

7 Their land is full of silver and gold;
there is no end to their treasures.
Their land is full of horses;[p]
there is no end to their chariots.[q]
8 Their land is full of idols;[r]
they bow down to the work of their hands,
to what their fingers[s] have made.
9 So people will be brought low[t]
and everyone humbled[u]—
do not forgive them.[a][v]

10 Go into the rocks, hide in the ground
from the fearful presence of the LORD
and the splendor of his majesty![w]
11 The eyes of the arrogant will be humbled
and human pride[x] brought low;
the LORD alone will be exalted in that day.

12 The LORD Almighty has a day in store
for all the proud and lofty,
for all that is exalted[y]
(and they will be humbled),[z]
13 for all the cedars of Lebanon, tall and lofty,
and all the oaks of Bashan,[a]
14 for all the towering mountains
and all the high hills,[b]
15 for every lofty tower
and every fortified wall,[c]
16 for every trading ship[b][d]
and every stately vessel.
17 The arrogance of man will be brought low
and human pride humbled;
the LORD alone will be exalted in that day,[e]
18 and the idols will totally disappear.[f]

19 People will flee to caves in the rocks
and to holes in the ground
from the fearful presence of the LORD
and the splendor of his majesty,
when he rises to shake the earth.[g]
20 In that day people will throw away
to the moles and bats[h]
their idols of silver and idols of gold,
which they made to worship.
21 They will flee to caverns in the rocks
and to the overhanging crags
from the fearful presence of the LORD
and the splendor of his majesty,
when he rises to shake the earth.[i]
22 Stop trusting in mere humans,[j]
who have but a breath in their nostrils.
Why hold them in esteem?[k]

Judgment on Jerusalem and Judah

3 See now, the Lord,
the LORD Almighty,
is about to take from Jerusalem and Judah
both supply and support:
all supplies of food[l] and all supplies of water,[m]
2 the hero and the warrior,[n]
the judge and the prophet,
the diviner and the elder,[o]
3 the captain of fifty and the man of rank,
the counselor, skilled craftsman and clever enchanter.

4 "I will make mere youths their officials;
children will rule over them."[p]

5 People will oppress each other—
man against man, neighbor against neighbor.[q]
The young will rise up against the old,
the nobody against the honored.

6 A man will seize one of his brothers
in his father's house, and say,
"You have a cloak, you be our leader;
take charge of this heap of ruins!"
7 But in that day he will cry out,
"I have no remedy.[r]
I have no food or clothing in my house;
do not make me the leader of the people."

8 Jerusalem staggers,
Judah is falling;[s]
their words[t] and deeds are against the LORD,
defying[u] his glorious presence.

---

[a] 9 Or *not raise them up* [b] 16 Hebrew *every ship of Tarshish*

2:7 *full of silver and gold . . . full of horses.* The king was not to multiply horses, wives, or gold and silver for himself, for this would cause his heart to turn away from the Lord (Deut. 17:14–17).

2:8 *full of idols.* Idolatry was forbidden in the Ten Commandments (Ex. 20:4; Deut. 13), and it was a flagrant rebellion against the Lord who had rescued them from the land of Egypt and redeemed them from slavery. It was a seduction to unfaithfulness and was to be punished with death.

2:19 *caves in the rocks . . . fearful presence of the LORD.* Men will want to hide from the Lord whom they have not been willing to obey (Rev. 6:15–17).

3:4 *mere youths . . . children.* The rulers would be incompetent and inexperienced.

3:8 *against the LORD.* Prior to entering Canaan, Moses had the blessings and the curses of the law of God recited to the people, warning of the serious consequences of unbelief. Unfaithfulness would result in captivity, worldwide dispersion, and aimless

2:7 [p] Dt 17:16 [q] Isa 31:1; Mic 5:10 **2:8** [r] Isa 10:9-11 [s] Isa 17:8 **2:9** [t] Ps 62:9 [u] Isa 5:15 [v] Ne 4:5 **2:10** [w] 2Th 1:9; Rev 6:15-16 **2:11** [x] Isa 5:15; 37:23 **2:12** [y] Isa 24:4, 21; Mal 4:1 [z] Job 40:11 **2:13** [a] Zec 11:2 **2:14** [b] Isa 30:25; 40:4 **2:15** [c] Isa 25:2, 12 **2:16** [d] 1Ki 10:22 **2:17** [e] ver 11 **2:18** [f] Isa 21:9 **2:19** [g] Heb 12:26 **2:20** [h] Lev 11:19 **2:21** [i] ver 19 **2:22** [j] Ps 146:3; Jer 17:5 [k] Ps 8:4; 144:3; Isa 40:15; Jas 4:14 **3:1** [l] Lev 26:26 [m] Isa 5:13; Eze 4:16 **3:2** [n] Eze 17:13 [o] 2Ki 24:14; Isa 9:14-15 **3:4** [p] Ecc 10:16 *fn* **3:5** [q] Isa 9:19; Jer 9:8; Mic 7:2, 6 **3:7** [r] Eze 34:4; Hos 5:13 **3:8** [s] Isa 1:7 [t] Isa 9:15, 17 [u] Ps 73:9, 11

[9]The look on their faces testifies against
them;
they parade their sin like Sodom;[v]
they do not hide it.
Woe to them!
They have brought disaster[w] upon
themselves.

[10]Tell the righteous it will be well[x] with
them,
for they will enjoy the fruit of their
deeds.[y]
[11]Woe to the wicked!
Disaster[z] is upon them!
They will be paid back
for what their hands have done.

[12]Youths[a] oppress my people,
women rule over them.
My people, your guides lead you
astray;[b]
they turn you from the path.

[13]The LORD takes his place in court;
he rises to judge[c] the people.
[14]The LORD enters into judgment[d]
against the elders and leaders of his
people:
"It is you who have ruined my vineyard;
the plunder[e] from the poor is in your
houses.
[15]What do you mean by crushing my
people[f]
and grinding the faces of the poor?"
declares the Lord,
the LORD Almighty.

[16]The LORD says,
"The women of Zion[g] are haughty,
walking along with outstretched necks,
flirting with their eyes,
strutting along with swaying hips,
with ornaments jingling on their
ankles.
[17]Therefore the Lord will bring sores on
the heads of the women of Zion;
the LORD will make their scalps bald."

[18]In that day the Lord will snatch away
their finery: the bangles and headbands
and crescent necklaces,[h] [19]the earrings
and bracelets and veils, [20]the headdress-
es[i] and anklets and sashes, the perfume
bottles and charms, [21]the signet rings and
nose rings, [22]the fine robes and the capes
and cloaks, the purses [23]and mirrors, and
the linen garments and tiaras and shawls.

[24]Instead of fragrance[j] there will be a
stench;
instead of a sash,[k] a rope;
instead of well-dressed hair, baldness;[l]
instead of fine clothing, sackcloth;[m]
instead of beauty,[n] branding.
[25]Your men will fall by the sword,[o]
your warriors in battle.
[26]The gates of Zion will lament and
mourn;[p]
destitute, she will sit on the ground.[q]

4 [1]In that day seven women
will take hold of one man[r]
and say, "We will eat our own food[s]
and provide our own clothes;
only let us be called by your name.
Take away our disgrace!"[t]

The Branch of the LORD

[2]In that day the Branch of the LORD[u] will
be beautiful and glorious, and the fruit[v]
of the land will be the pride and glory of
the survivors in Israel. [3]Those who are
left in Zion, who remain[w] in Jerusalem,
will be called holy,[x] all who are recorded[y]
among the living in Jerusalem. [4]The Lord
will wash away the filth[z] of the women of
Zion; he will cleanse the bloodstains[a] from
Jerusalem by a spirit[a] of judgment[b] and a
spirit[a] of fire.[c] [5]Then the LORD will create
over all of Mount Zion and over those who
assemble there a cloud of smoke by day
and a glow of flaming fire by night;[d] over
everything the glory[b][e] will be a canopy. [6]It
will be a shelter[f] and shade from the heat
of the day, and a refuge[g] and hiding place
from the storm and rain.

[a] 4 Or *the Spirit* [b] 5 Or *over all the glory there*

wandering among the Gentile nations (Deut. 28). Joshua gave the same warning after bringing them into the land (Josh. 24). Both warnings went unheeded. From a historical perspective, it is easy to be appalled at the people's heedlessness. They ignored specific and direct commands, apparently knowing well that they were courting disaster. But, if we as believers examine ourselves carefully, we might be appalled at our own unfaithfulness in certain areas. God's directives are always there for a reason, and unfaithfulness, even in little things, causes a rift in our relationship with God.

3:16 ***women of Zion.*** The plural "women" suggests the women of the city as well as a personification of Jerusalem. The list of finery (v. 18–23), whether applied figuratively to the city of Jerusalem or to specific women, indicated a preoccupation with frivolity and wealth.

4:1 ***Take away our disgrace.*** It was considered a sign of inadequacy to have no children.

4:2 ***In that day.*** Isaiah is speaking of the future revelation of the glory of the Lord on earth (2:2–4). ***the Branch of the LORD.*** Jesus Christ is the fruitful Branch (Jer. 23:5; Zech. 3:8). The reign of Jesus, the King of Creation, will be marked by plenty. The earth will be released from its curse, producing all that God intended it to produce in the beginning.

3:9 [v] Ge 13:13 [w] Pr 8:36; Ro 6:23 **3:10** [x] Dt 28:1-14 [y] Ps 128:2 **3:11** [z] Dt 28:15-68 **3:12** [a] ver 4 [b] Isa 9:16 **3:13** [c] Mic 6:2 **3:14** [d] Job 22:4 [e] Job 24:9; Jas 2:6 **3:15** [f] Ps 94:5 **3:16** [g] SS 3:11 **3:18** [h] Jdg 8:21 **3:20** [i] Ex 39:28 **3:24** [j] Est 2:12 [k] Pr 31:24 [l] Isa 22:12 [m] La 2:10; Eze 27:30-31 [n] 1Pe 3:3 **3:25** [o] Isa 1:20 **3:26** [p] Jer 14:2 [q] La 2:10 **4:1** [r] Isa 13:12 [s] 2Th 3:12 [t] Ge 30:23 **4:2** [u] Isa 11:1-5; 53:2; Jer 23:5-6; Zec 3:8; 6:12 [v] Ps 72:16 **4:3** [w] Ro 11:5 [x] Isa 52:1; 60:21 [y] Lk 10:20 **4:4** [z] Isa 3:24 [a] Isa 1:15 [b] Isa 28:6 [c] Isa 1:31; Mt 3:11 **4:5** [d] Ex 13:21 [e] Isa 60:1 **4:6** [f] Ps 27:5 [g] Isa 25:4

The Song of the Vineyard

5 I will sing for the one I love
a song about his vineyard:[h]
My loved one had a vineyard
on a fertile hillside.
2 He dug it up and cleared it of
stones
and planted it with the choicest
vines.[i]
He built a watchtower in it
and cut out a winepress as well.
Then he looked for a crop of good
grapes,
but it yielded only bad fruit.[j]

3 "Now you dwellers in Jerusalem and
people of Judah,
judge between me and my
vineyard.[k]
4 What more could have been done for
my vineyard
than I have done for it?[l]
When I looked for good grapes,
why did it yield only bad?
5 Now I will tell you
what I am going to do to my
vineyard:
I will take away its hedge,
and it will be destroyed;
I will break down its wall,[m]
and it will be trampled.[n]
6 I will make it a wasteland,
neither pruned nor cultivated,
and briers and thorns[o] will grow
there.
I will command the clouds
not to rain on it."

7 The vineyard[p] of the LORD Almighty
is the nation of Israel,
and the people of Judah
are the vines he delighted in.
And he looked for justice,[q] but saw
bloodshed;
for righteousness, but heard cries of
distress.

Woes and Judgments

8 Woe[r] to you who add house to house
and join field to field[s]
till no space is left
and you live alone in the land.

9 The LORD Almighty has declared in my
hearing:[t]

"Surely the great houses will become
desolate,[u]
the fine mansions left without
occupants.
10 A ten-acre vineyard will produce only a
bath[a] of wine;
a homer[b] of seed will yield only an
ephah[c] of grain."[v]

11 Woe to those who rise early in the
morning
to run after their drinks,
who stay up late at night
till they are inflamed with wine.[w]
12 They have harps and lyres at their
banquets,
pipes and timbrels and wine,
but they have no regard[x] for the deeds
of the LORD,
no respect for the work of his hands.[y]
13 Therefore my people will go into exile[z]
for lack of understanding;[a]
those of high rank will die of hunger
and the common people will be
parched with thirst.
14 Therefore Death[b] expands its jaws,
opening wide its mouth;[c]
into it will descend their nobles and
masses
with all their brawlers and revelers.
15 So people will be brought low[d]
and everyone humbled,[e]
the eyes of the arrogant[f] humbled.
16 But the LORD Almighty will be exalted
by his justice,[g]
and the holy God will be proved holy[h]
by his righteous acts.
17 Then sheep will graze as in their own
pasture;[i]
lambs will feed[d] among the ruins of
the rich.

18 Woe to those who draw sin along with
cords of deceit,
and wickedness[j] as with cart ropes,

---

[a] *10* That is, about 6 gallons or about 22 liters
[b] *10* That is, probably about 360 pounds or about 160 kilograms [c] *10* That is, probably about 36 pounds or about 16 kilograms [d] *17* Septuagint; Hebrew / *strangers will eat*

5:4 ***What more could have been done for my vineyard.*** This is a rhetorical question. There was nothing more that God could or should have done to bring forth good fruit from His vineyard. The failure was on the part of the people, not God (John 15:1).
5:6 ***briers and thorns.*** Briers and thorns symbolize the anarchy that will take over the land after the exile (3:4–5). ***not to rain.*** As God promised in His covenant on Mount Sinai, sufficient rainfall would come to the people who were faithful to His commands, but the rain would be withheld if the people were rebellious (Deut. 28:12,23–24).
5:14 ***Death.*** This word is used for the grave or the place where the body goes after death. Its meaning is not precise, but this word is sometimes translated "hell" where the context considers the "grave" in a negative sense.
5:18 ***deceit.*** A falsehood is a lie. Those who "draw

5:1 [h] Ps 80:8-9 **5:2** [i] Jer 2:21 [j] Mt 21:19; Mk 11:13; Lk 13:6 **5:3** [k] Mt 21:40 **5:4** [l] 2Ch 36:15; Jer 2:5-7; Mic 6:3-4; Mt 23:37 **5:5** [m] Ps 80:12 [n] Isa 28:3, 18; La 1:15; Lk 21:24 **5:6** [o] Isa 7:23, 24; Heb 6:8 **5:7** [p] Ps 80:8 [q] Isa 59:15 **5:8** [r] Jer 22:13 [s] Mic 2:2; Hab 2:9-12 **5:9** [t] Isa 22:14 [u] Isa 6:11-12; Mt 23:38 **5:10** [v] Lev 26:26 **5:11** [w] Pr 23:29-30 **5:12** [x] Job 34:27 [y] Ps 28:5; Am 6:5-6 **5:13** [z] Hos 4:6 [a] Isa 1:3; Hos 4:6 **5:14** [b] Pr 30:16 [c] Nu 16:30 **5:15** [d] Isa 10:33 [e] Isa 2:9 [f] Isa 2:11 **5:16** [g] Isa 28:17; 30:18; 33:5; 61:8 [h] Isa 29:23 **5:17** [i] Isa 7:25; Zep 2:6, 14 **5:18** [j] Isa 59:4-8; Jer 23:14

19 to those who say, "Let God hurry;
let him hasten his work
so we may see it.
The plan of the Holy One of Israel—
let it approach, let it come into
view,
so we may know it."[k]

20 Woe to those who call evil good
and good evil,
who put darkness for light
and light for darkness,[l]
who put bitter for sweet
and sweet for bitter.[m]

21 Woe to those who are wise in their own
eyes[n]
and clever in their own sight.

22 Woe to those who are heroes at
drinking wine[o]
and champions at mixing
drinks,
23 who acquit the guilty for a bribe,[p]
but deny justice[q] to the innocent.[r]
24 Therefore, as tongues of fire lick up
straw
and as dry grass sinks down in the
flames,
so their roots will decay[s]
and their flowers blow away like
dust;
for they have rejected the law of the
LORD Almighty
and spurned the word[t] of the Holy
One of Israel.
25 Therefore the LORD's anger[u] burns
against his people;
his hand is raised and he strikes
them down.
The mountains shake,
and the dead bodies are like refuse[v]
in the streets.
Yet for all this, his anger is not turned
away,[w]
his hand is still upraised.[x]

26 He lifts up a banner for the distant
nations,
he whistles[y] for those at the ends of
the earth.[z]
Here they come,
swiftly and speedily!
27 Not one of them grows tired or
stumbles,
not one slumbers or sleeps;
not a belt is loosened at the waist,[a]
not a sandal strap is broken.[b]
28 Their arrows are sharp,[c]
all their bows[d] are strung;
their horses' hooves seem like flint,
their chariot wheels like a whirlwind.
29 Their roar is like that of the lion,[e]
they roar like young lions;
they growl as they seize[f] their prey
and carry it off with no one to
rescue.[g]
30 In that day they will roar over it
like the roaring of the sea.[h]
And if one looks at the land,
there is only darkness and distress;[i]
even the sun will be darkened[j] by
clouds.

Isaiah's Commission

6 In the year that King Uzziah[k] died,[l] I
saw the Lord,[m] high and exalted, seated
on a throne;[n] and the train of his robe filled
the temple. 2 Above him were seraphim,[o]
each with six wings: With two wings they
covered their faces, with two they covered
their feet,[p] and with two they were flying.
3 And they were calling to one another:

"Holy, holy, holy is the LORD Almighty;
the whole earth is full of his glory."[q]

---

sin along with cords of deceit" are those who are dragging sin behind them with ropes of lies. Essentially, these lies are the various ways people have of justifying sin. They are not ashamed of their sin, but are quite openly attached to it, carrying it wherever they go. Of course, the big lie is the lie that sin does not matter, that judgment will not come. The truth is that the fruits of sin always catch up with us, and, unless we make peace with God through Christ, the judgment for sin will follow.

6:1 ***King Uzziah died.*** King Uzziah died in 740 B.C., signaling the end of an age. He is described as a good king (2 Chr. 26:1–15), but in his pride he was unfaithful to God (2 Chr. 26:16–23), and he died a leper. He was succeeded by his son Jotham, who did right, and then by wicked Ahaz (7:1). The relative prosperity of the first half of the eighth century was replaced by the Syro-Ephraimite wars and the Assyrian campaigns into Israel.

6:3 ***Holy, holy, holy.*** To say the word "holy" twice in Hebrew is to describe someone as "most holy." To say the word three times intensifies the idea to the highest level. ***the whole earth is full of his glory.*** We know that the glory of God transcends the universe, yet this phrase emphasizes God's closeness to His creation—His involvement with the earth and its people.

We know that our greatest failing is not realizing who God is nor what His character is like. This is particularly true in the case of God's holiness. To be holy means "to be set apart." God is set apart from the power, practice, and presence of sin, and is set apart to absolute righteousness and goodness. There is no sin in God and God can have nothing to do with sin. If we are to approach God, we must do so on God's terms. We must be made holy by God's action in Christ.

Most of our lives are so caught up in the mundane

5:19 [k] Jer 17:15; Eze 12:22; 2Pe 3:4 **5:20** [l] Mt 6:22-23; Lk 11:34-35 [m] Am 5:7 **5:21** [n] Pr 3:7; Ro 12:16; 1Co 3:18-20 **5:22** [o] Pr 23:20 **5:23** [p] Ex 23:8 [q] Isa 10:2 [r] Ps 94:21; Jas 5:6 **5:24** [s] Job 18:16 [t] Isa 8:6; 30:9, 12 **5:25** [u] 2Ki 22:13 [v] 2Ki 9:37 [w] Jer 4:8; Da 9:16 [x] Isa 9:12, 17, 21; 10:4 **5:26** [y] Isa 7:18; Zec 10:8 [z] Dt 28:49; Isa 13:5; 18:3 **5:27** [a] Job 12:18 [b] Joel 2:7-8 **5:28** [c] Ps 45:5 [d] Ps 7:12 **5:29** [e] Jer 51:38; Zep 3:3; Zec 11:3 [f] Isa 10:6; 49:24-25 [g] Isa 42:22; Mic 5:8 **5:30** [h] Lk 21:25 [i] Isa 8:22; Jer 4:23-28 [j] Joel 2:10 **6:1** [k] 2Ch 26:22, 23 [l] 2Ki 15:7 [m] Jn 12:41 [n] Rev 4:2 **6:2** [o] Rev 4:8 [p] Eze 1:11 **6:3** [q] Ps 72:19; Rev 4:8

4At the sound of their voices the doorposts
and thresholds shook and the temple was
filled with smoke.
5"Woe to me!" I cried. "I am ruined! For I
am a man of unclean lips, and I live among
a people of unclean lips,[r] and my eyes have
seen the King,[s] the LORD Almighty."
6Then one of the seraphim flew to me
with a live coal in his hand, which he had
taken with tongs from the altar. 7With it he
touched my mouth and said, "See, this has
touched your lips;[t] your guilt is taken away
and your sin atoned for.[u]"
8Then I heard the voice[v] of the Lord saying, "Whom shall I send? And who will go
for us?"

And I said, "Here am I. Send me!"
9He said, "Go[w] and tell this people:

"'Be ever hearing, but never
understanding;
be ever seeing, but never
perceiving.'[x]
10Make the heart of this people calloused;[y]
make their ears dull
and close their eyes.[a]
Otherwise they might see with their
eyes,
hear with their ears,[z]
understand with their hearts,
and turn and be healed."[a]

11Then I said, "For how long, Lord?"[b]
And he answered:

"Until the cities lie ruined[c]
and without inhabitant,
until the houses are left deserted
and the fields ruined and ravaged,
12until the LORD has sent everyone far away[d]
and the land is utterly forsaken.[e]
13And though a tenth remains[f] in the land,
it will again be laid waste.
But as the terebinth and oak
leave stumps when they are cut down,
so the holy seed will be the stump in
the land."[g]

The Sign of Immanuel

7 When Ahaz son of Jotham, the son of
Uzziah, was king of Judah, King Rezin[h]
of Aram[i] and Pekah[j] son of Remaliah king
of Israel marched up to fight against Jerusalem, but they could not overpower it.
2Now the house of David[k] was told,
"Aram has allied itself with[b] Ephraim[l]";
so the hearts of Ahaz and his people were
shaken, as the trees of the forest are shak-
en by the wind.
3Then the LORD said to Isaiah, "Go out,
you and your son Shear-Jashub,[c] to meet
Ahaz at the end of the aqueduct of the Upper Pool, on the road to the Launderer's
Field.[m] 4Say to him, 'Be careful, keep calm[n]
and don't be afraid.[o] Do not lose heart[p] because of these two smoldering stubs[q] of
firewood—because of the fierce anger[r] of
Rezin and Aram and of the son of Remaliah. 5Aram, Ephraim and Remaliah's son

---

[a] 9,10 Hebrew; Septuagint '*You will be ever hearing, but never understanding; / you will be ever seeing, but never perceiving.' / 10This people's heart has become calloused; / they hardly hear with their ears, / and they have closed their eyes*
[b] 2 Or *has set up camp in*
[c] 3 *Shear-Jashub* means *a remnant will return.*

---

that we don't understand and experience God's holiness as we should. There is little appreciation or understanding of the sacred "otherness" of God. We have too often reduced Him to only friend and advisor. We do so at our own peril; for it is that sacred "otherness" that brings us to our knees. That is where the relationship needs to begin. Isaiah received God's call in that position. He recognized God's holiness and his own uncleanness and the need for God to purify him before he would be fit to serve as a prophet.

The experience of coming to understand God's holiness is simultaneously humbling, challenging, and exhilarating. We touch the fullness of our potential as we are touched and purified by God in Christ's sacrifice for us.

6:6 *live coal . . . from the altar.* Brought face to face with the holiness of the Lord, Isaiah was stunned by his own uncleanness. Without taking any action on his own, Isaiah was offered forgiveness and cleansing. This was a unique event, especially for Isaiah, but not the last time that the Lord reached out to man to offer forgiveness and cleansing. Salvation through Christ is a gift, not received through works (Eph. 2:8–9).

6:10 *heart . . . dull.* Isaiah's call was to a very discouraging ministry. People with "calloused" hearts were insensitive. They were "padded" with self-satisfaction so they could not feel the prick of the Lord's words. The more Isaiah proclaimed the Word of God, the less response he received from the people. In truth, the call of God was for faithfulness to God, to His word, and to the call itself.

6:13 *tenth.* A "tenth" is one of Isaiah's expressions for the "survivors."

7:1 *When.* The next five chapters contain a series of prophecies related specifically to the Syro-Ephraimite wars—the invasion of Judah by Rezin and Pekah (2 Kin. 16). These prophecies aimed to call Judah back to faith in God.

7:2 *house of David.* The king was descended from David and was referred to as "from the house of David." ***Ephraim.*** The word Ephraim represents the northern kingdom of Israel.

7:3 *Shear-Jashub.* The name of Isaiah's son meant "a remnant will return." This name referred to a coming exile and the salvation of the remaining faithful, although all of those events occurred long after Isaiah's lifetime.

7:4 *son of Remaliah.* The son of Remaliah is Pekah, king of Israel.

6:5 [r] Jer 9:3-8 [s] Jer 51:57 **6:7** [t] Jer 1:9 [u] 1Jn 1:7
6:8 [v] Ac 9:4 **6:9** [w] Eze 3:11 [x] Mt 13:15*; Lk 8:10*
6:10 [y] Dt 32:15; Ps 119:70 [z] Jer 5:21 [a] Mt 13:13-15; Mk 4:12*; Ac 28:26-27* **6:11** [b] Ps 79:5 [c] Lev 26:31
6:12 [d] Dt 28:64 [e] Jer 4:29 **6:13** [f] Isa 1:9 [g] Job 14:7
7:1 [h] 2Ki 15:37 [i] 2Ch 28:5 [j] 2Ki 15:25 **7:2** [k] ver 13; Isa 22:22 [l] Isa 9:9 **7:3** [m] 2Ki 18:17; Isa 36:2
7:4 [n] Isa 30:15 [o] Isa 35:4 [p] Dt 20:3 [q] Zec 3:2 [r] Isa 10:24

have plotted your ruin, saying, 6“Let us invade Judah; let us tear it apart and divide
it among ourselves, and make the son of
Tabeel king over it.” 7Yet this is what the
Sovereign LORD says:

“ ‘It will not take place,
it will not happen,[s]
8 for the head of Aram is Damascus,[t]
and the head of Damascus is only
Rezin.
Within sixty-five years
Ephraim will be too shattered[u] to be a
people.
9 The head of Ephraim is Samaria,
and the head of Samaria is only
Remaliah’s son.
If you do not stand firm in your faith,[v]
you will not stand at all.’ ”[w]

10Again the LORD spoke to Ahaz, 11“Ask
the LORD your God for a sign, whether
in the deepest depths or in the highest
heights.”
12But Ahaz said, “I will not ask; I will not
put the LORD to the test.”
13Then Isaiah said, “Hear now, you
house of David! Is it not enough to try the
patience of humans? Will you try the patience of my God[x] also? 14Therefore the
Lord himself will give you[a] a sign: The virgin[b] will conceive and give birth to a son,[y]
and[c] will call him Immanuel.[d z] 15He will be
eating curds and honey[a] when he knows
enough to reject the wrong and choose the
right, 16for before the boy knows[b] enough
to reject the wrong and choose the right,
the land of the two kings you dread will be
laid waste.[c] 17The LORD will bring on you
and on your people and on the house of
your father a time unlike any since Ephraim broke away[d] from Judah—he will bring
the king of Assyria.[e]”

Assyria, the LORD’s Instrument

18In that day the LORD will whistle[f] for
flies from the Nile delta in Egypt and for
bees from the land of Assyria.[g] 19They will
all come and settle in the steep ravines
and in the crevices[h] in the rocks, on all the
thornbushes and at all the water holes. 20In
that day the Lord will use[i] a razor hired
from beyond the Euphrates River—the
king of Assyria[j]—to shave your head and
private parts, and to cut off your beard
also. 21In that day, a person will keep alive
a young cow and two goats. 22And because of the abundance of the milk they
give, there will be curds to eat. All who remain in the land will eat curds and honey.
23In that day, in every place where there
were a thousand vines worth a thousand
silver shekels,[e] there will be only briers
and thorns.[k] 24Hunters will go there with
bow and arrow, for the land will be covered with briers and thorns. 25As for all
the hills once cultivated by the hoe, you
will no longer go there for fear of the briers and thorns; they will become places
where cattle are turned loose and where
sheep run.[l]

Isaiah and His Children as Signs

8 The LORD said to me, “Take a large
scroll[m] and write on it with an ordinary pen: Maher-Shalal-Hash-Baz.”[f n] 2So
I called in Uriah[o] the priest and Zechariah son of Jeberekiah as reliable witnesses

[a] 14 The Hebrew is plural. [b] 14 Or *young woman* [c] 14 Masoretic Text; Dead Sea Scrolls *son, and he* or *son, and they* [d] 14 *Immanuel* means *God with us.* [e] 23 That is, about 25 pounds or about 12 kilograms [f] 1 *Maher-Shalal-Hash-Baz* means *quick to the plunder, swift to the spoil*; also in verse 3.

7:6 *son of Tabeel.* Tabeel means “good for nothing.” Syria and Israel wanted to place an incompetent puppet king over Judah.
7:12 *not ask . . . not put the LORD to the test.* In the mouth of the wicked Ahaz, these words rang hollow. Ahaz was continually testing the Lord’s patience by his disobedience.
7:14 *Immanuel.* The Christian church traditionally has seen this verse as a prophecy of the Christ child, in whose incarnation God became present in physical form with mankind. The name “Immanuel” means “God with us.” Christ, as a descendant of the house of David, fulfills the requirements of the sign and reinforces Isaiah’s message that the nation’s destiny does not rest with a foreign people, but with the God of Sinai.
7:15 *curds and honey.* Curds and honey contrast with “bread and wine” from cultivated lands and symbolically represent the Judean’s simple diet after the Assyrian invasion. Thus, the Child, similar to Isaiah’s son Shear-Jashub (v. 3), would be identified with the remnant.
7:16 *for before.* Similar prophecies were spoken of the child’s birth and Isaiah’s other son, Maher-Shalal-Hash-Baz (8:3). Israel and Syria would be destroyed before the child and Isaiah’s son would reach maturity (see 8:4, where Syria is referred to as Damascus and Israel as Samaria). It is not uncommon for biblical prophecies to have one level of fulfillment in the immediate future and a final fulfillment many years later in the person and work of the Savior, Jesus. Thus, the birth of Isaiah’s son could have been a sign to King Ahaz. However, this would have been an early fulfillment, not the ultimate fulfillment. It was the coming of Jesus, God’s only Son, which was the complete fulfillment.
7:20 *shave . . . beard.* This was a symbol of humiliation.
8:2 *Zechariah son of Jeberekiah.* This was not the Zechariah who wrote the Book of Zechariah.

7:7 [s] Isa 8:10; Ac 4:25 **7:8** [t] Ge 14:15 [u] Isa 17:1-3
7:9 [v] 2Ch 20:20 [w] Isa 8:6-8; 30:12-14 **7:13** [x] Isa 25:1
7:14 [y] Lk 1:31 [z] Isa 8:8, 10; Mt 1:23* **7:15** [a] ver 22
7:16 [b] Isa 8:4 [c] Isa 17:3; Hos 5:9, 13; Am 1:3-5
7:17 [d] 1Ki 12:16 [e] 2Ch 28:20 **7:18** [f] Isa 5:26 [g] Isa 13:5
7:19 [h] Isa 2:19 **7:20** [i] Isa 10:15 [j] Isa 8:7; 10:5
7:23 [k] Isa 5:6 **7:25** [l] Isa 5:17 **8:1** [m] Isa 30:8; Hab 2:2
[n] ver 3; Hab 2:2 **8:2** [o] 2Ki 16:10

for me. [3]Then I made love to the prophetess, and she conceived and gave birth to a
son. And the LORD said to me, "Name him
Maher-Shalal-Hash-Baz. [4]For before the
boy knows[p] how to say 'My father' or 'My
mother,' the wealth of Damascus and the
plunder of Samaria will be carried off by
the king of Assyria.[q]"

[5]The LORD spoke to me again:

[6]"Because this people has rejected[r]
the gently flowing waters of Shiloah[s]
and rejoices over Rezin
and the son of Remaliah,[t]
[7]therefore the Lord is about to bring
against them
the mighty floodwaters[u] of the
Euphrates—
the king of Assyria[v] with all his
pomp.
It will overflow all its channels,
run over all its banks
[8]and sweep on into Judah, swirling
over it,
passing through it and reaching up to
the neck.
Its outspread wings will cover the
breadth of your land,
Immanuel[a]!"[w]

[9]Raise the war cry,[b][x] you nations, and be
shattered!
Listen, all you distant lands.
Prepare[y] for battle, and be shattered!
Prepare for battle, and be shattered!
[10]Devise your strategy, but it will be
thwarted;[z]
propose your plan, but it will not
stand,[a]
for God is with us.[c][b]

[11]This is what the LORD says to me with
his strong hand upon me,[c] warning me not
to follow[d] the way of this people:

[12]"Do not call conspiracy[e]
everything this people calls a
conspiracy;
do not fear what they fear,
and do not dread it.[f]
[13]The LORD Almighty is the one you are
to regard as holy,[g]
he is the one you are to fear,
he is the one you are to dread.[h]
[14]He will be a holy place;[i]
for both Israel and Judah he will be
a stone that causes people to stumble
and a rock that makes them fall.[j]
And for the people of Jerusalem he
will be
a trap and a snare.[k]
[15]Many of them will stumble;[l]
they will fall and be broken,
they will be snared and captured."

[16]Bind up this testimony of warning
and seal[m] up God's instruction
among my disciples.
[17]I will wait[n] for the LORD,
who is hiding[o] his face from the
descendants of Jacob.
I will put my trust in him.

[18]Here am I, and the children the LORD
has given me.[p] We are signs[q] and symbols
in Israel from the LORD Almighty, who
dwells on Mount Zion.[r]

The Darkness Turns to Light

[19]When someone tells you to consult[s]
mediums and spiritists, who whisper and
mutter,[t] should not a people inquire of their
God? Why consult the dead on behalf of
the living? [20]Consult God's instruction[u]
and the testimony of warning. If anyone
does not speak according to this word, they
have no light[v] of dawn. [21]Distressed and

[a] *8 Immanuel* means *God with us.* [b] *9* Or *Do your worst* [c] *10* Hebrew *Immanuel*

8:3 *the prophetess.* Isaiah's wife was a prophetess in her own right. It is possible that this was a new wife, following the death of the mother of Shear-Jashub (7:3). ***Maher-Shalal-Hash-Baz.*** The child's name means "Speed the Spoil, Hasten the Plunder."

8:4 *plunder of Samaria ... king of Assyria.* This was a specific prediction of the fall of Samaria to the Assyrians in 722 B.C. This prophecy must have been written shortly before that time, as the fulfillment would come before the new child would be able to speak.

8:8 *Immanuel.* Isaiah bestowed on Judah the name of the promised Child, Immanuel, which means "God with us" (7:14), because it would be preserved only because God was with that nation.

8:14 *a stone that causes people to stumble and a rock that makes them fall.* God is a stone of stumbling for unbelievers (Ps. 118:22; Luke 20:17–18; Rom. 9:33; 1 Pet. 2:6–8).

8:16 *testimony ... instruction.* The testimony refers to a legal transaction. The instruction refers to God's instruction revealed through Isaiah. Isaiah's disciples put his prophecies in the form of a legal transaction, probably to prove their authenticity when they were fulfilled (see vv. 1–2; compare Jer. 28:9; 32:12–14).

8:18 *children.* Isaiah's name means "Jehovah has saved," and his two sons' names speak of the impending judgment of God (7:3; 8:3). They were symbols of God's intentions for the nation.

8:19 *consult mediums and spiritists.* This indicates that the people were involved in necromancy, the practice of conjuring up the spirits of the dead in order to influence events. This practice, as well as the use of any mediums or spiritists, was strictly forbidden (Deut. 18:9–14).

8:4 [p] Isa 7:16 [q] Isa 7:8 **8:6** [r] Isa 5:24 [s] Jn 9:7 [t] Isa 7:1 **8:7** [u] Isa 17:12-13 [v] Isa 7:20 **8:8** [w] Isa 7:14 **8:9** [x] Isa 17:12-13 [y] Joel 3:9 **8:10** [z] Job 5:12 [a] Isa 7:7 [b] Isa 7:14; Ro 8:31 **8:11** [c] Eze 3:14 [d] Eze 2:8 **8:12** [e] Isa 7:2; 30:1 [f] 1Pe 3:14* **8:13** [g] Nu 20:12 [h] Isa 29:23 **8:14** [i] Isa 4:6; Eze 11:16 [j] Lk 2:34; Ro 9:33*; 1Pe 2:8* [k] Isa 24:17-18 **8:15** [l] Isa 28:13; 59:10; Lk 20:18; Ro 9:32 **8:16** [m] Isa 29:11-12 **8:17** [n] Hab 2:3 [o] Dt 31:17; Isa 54:8 **8:18** [p] Heb 2:13* [q] Lk 2:34 [r] Ps 9:11 **8:19** [s] 1Sa 28:8 [t] Isa 29:4 **8:20** [u] Isa 1:10; Lk 16:29 [v] Mic 3:6

hungry, they will roam through the land;
when they are famished, they will become
enraged and, looking upward, will curse[w]
their king and their God. 22 Then they will
look toward the earth and see only distress
and darkness and fearful gloom, and they
will be thrust into utter darkness.[x]

9 [a] Nevertheless, there will be no more
gloom for those who were in distress.
In the past he humbled the land of Zebulun
and the land of Naphtali,[y] but in the future
he will honor Galilee of the nations, by the
Way of the Sea, beyond the Jordan—

2 The people walking in darkness
have seen a great light;[z]
on those living in the land of deep
darkness[a]
a light has dawned.[b]
3 You have enlarged the nation
and increased their joy;
they rejoice before you
as people rejoice at the harvest,
as warriors rejoice
when dividing the plunder.
4 For as in the day of Midian's defeat,[c]
you have shattered
the yoke[d] that burdens them,
the bar across their shoulders,[e]
the rod of their oppressor.[f]
5 Every warrior's boot used in battle
and every garment rolled in blood
will be destined for burning,[g]
will be fuel for the fire.
6 For to us a child is born,[h]
to us a son is given,[i]
and the government[j] will be on his
shoulders.
And he will be called
Wonderful Counselor,[k] Mighty God,[l]
Everlasting Father, Prince of Peace.[m]
7 Of the greatness of his government and
peace
there will be no end.[n]
He will reign on David's throne
and over his kingdom,
establishing and upholding it
with justice[o] and righteousness
from that time on and forever.
The zeal[p] of the LORD Almighty
will accomplish this.

[a] In Hebrew texts 9:1 is numbered 8:23, and 9:2-21 is numbered 9:1-20.

9:1 *in distress.* The ancient tribal allotments of Zebulun and Naphtali (Josh. 19:10–16,32–39), which included Galilee, were the first to feel the brunt of the Assyrian invasions (2 Kin. 15:29). Galilee of the nations, by ***the Way of the Sea, beyond the Jordan.*** These three phrases indicate administrative districts of the Assyrian conqueror Tiglath-Pileser III as a result of the three campaigns he waged in the west around 733 B.C. The city of Capernaum is "by the Way of the Sea," (Galilee) in the region of Zebulun and Naphtali. This is where Jesus began his ministry, in fulfillment of the prophecy of Isaiah 9:1–2 (Matt. 4:15–16).

9:2 *have seen a great light.* The light stands for God's blessings, presence, and revelation, fulfilled in Jesus who came in the flesh (Matt. 4:15–16). The coming of Jesus revealed the mercy and grace of God in the same way that the rising sun reveals the nature of the land it shines upon. All history is labeled from that definitive moment: before the Light, or after the Light (John 1:9).

9:6–7 *a child.* In this triumphant song Isaiah rejoices as though the promised Child of the house of David has already been born. The Child's birthright involves authority and rule, while His character is depicted with descriptive names. As "Wonderful" and "Counselor," He represents the sum of wisdom and knowledge, and His divinity is established clearly by the title "mighty God." The Fatherhood of the Messiah is eternal, which again demonstrates His identity with God (John 10:30). Finally, as the "Prince of Peace" He brings peace into the world by His atoning death on the cross, paying the price of human sin and reconciling us to God. The line of David will be the human line for the source of these blessings, (2 Sam. 7:8–16; Luke 1:32–33) and the divine nature of the Messiah will guarantee their permanence.

9:7 The Son of God—In Luke 24:25–27 Jesus goes to great lengths to help two of his disciples understand what the Jewish Scriptures (the Old Testament) said about Him. Throughout the Old Testament there are numerous passages that point towards Jesus Christ in several ways. This prophecy in Isaiah is one of the most important of these passages. Here He is spoken of as a son before He became a man (see also Gal. 4:4). Micah prophesies His birth, but also states that His "origins are from of old, from ancient times" (Mic. 5:2). John says that He existed "in the beginning" before anything was created (John 1:1–3).

Even before He was born of Mary, He appeared to men in the Old Testament as the "Angel of the LORD." It is clear that this is no ordinary angel because He is identified as God (Ex. 3:2). He pardons sin (Ex. 23:20–21), and He is worshiped (Josh. 5:13–15). While these passages do not say that this member of the Godhead was the preincarnate Christ, we may conclude that they are the same person since their work is the same.

While Christ occasionally appeared to men in the Old Testament, He took on a physical, human body when He was conceived in Mary's womb. This incomparable event of God's becoming man in Jesus Christ is called the incarnation. This miracle was prophesied hundreds of years previously (7:14) and was fulfilled historically when Christ was born (Luke 2:7). Thus Christ, the sinless God-man, was qualified to become our Redeemer (2 Cor. 5:21).

As a man, Christ experienced normal physical, mental, social, and spiritual growth as others did (Luke 2:52). He had pain, hunger, thirst, fatigue, temptation, pleasure, rest, and even lack of knowledge (Mark 13:32). Because of His complete humanity He can be sympathetic and compassionate toward us (Heb. 4:15).

8:21 [w] Rev 16:11 **8:22** [x] ver 20; Isa 5:30
9:1 [y] 2Ki 15:29 **9:2** [z] Eph 5:8 [a] Lk 1:79 [b] Mt 4:15-16*
9:4 [c] Jdg 7:25 [d] Isa 14:25 [e] Isa 10:27 [f] Isa 14:4; 49:26; 51:13; 54:14 **9:5** [g] Isa 2:4 **9:6** [h] Isa 53:2; Lk 2:11 [i] Jn 3:16 [j] Mt 28:18 [k] Isa 28:29 [l] Isa 10:21; 11:2 [m] Isa 26:3, 12; 66:12 **9:7** [n] Da 2:44; Lk 1:33 [o] Isa 11:4; 16:5; 32:1, 16 [p] Isa 37:32; 59:17

The LORD's Anger Against Israel

8 The Lord has sent a message against Jacob;
it will fall on Israel.
9 All the people will know it—
Ephraim and the inhabitants of Samaria[q]—
who say with pride
and arrogance[r] of heart,
10 "The bricks have fallen down,
but we will rebuild with dressed stone;
the fig trees have been felled,
but we will replace them with cedars."
11 But the LORD has strengthened Rezin's[s] foes against them
and has spurred their enemies on.
12 Arameans[t] from the east and Philistines[u] from the west
have devoured[v] Israel with open mouth.

Yet for all this, his anger is not turned away,
his hand is still upraised.[w]

13 But the people have not returned to him who struck[x] them,
nor have they sought[y] the LORD Almighty.
14 So the LORD will cut off from Israel both head and tail,
both palm branch and reed[z] in a single day;[a]
15 the elders[b] and dignitaries are the head,
the prophets who teach lies are the tail.
16 Those who guide[c] this people mislead them,
and those who are guided are led astray.[d]
17 Therefore the Lord will take no pleasure in the young men,[e]
nor will he pity[f] the fatherless and widows,
for everyone is ungodly[g] and wicked,[h]
every mouth speaks folly.[i]

Yet for all this, his anger is not turned away,
his hand is still upraised.[j]

18 Surely wickedness burns like a fire;[k]
it consumes briers and thorns,
it sets the forest thickets ablaze,[l]
so that it rolls upward in a column of smoke.
19 By the wrath[m] of the LORD Almighty
the land will be scorched
and the people will be fuel for the fire;[n]
they will not spare one another.[o]
20 On the right they will devour,
but still be hungry;[p]
on the left they will eat,[q]
but not be satisfied.
Each will feed on the flesh of their own offspring[a]:
21 Manasseh will feed on Ephraim, and Ephraim on Manasseh;
together they will turn against Judah.[r]

Yet for all this, his anger is not turned away,
his hand is still upraised.[s]

10 Woe to those who make unjust laws,
to those who issue oppressive decrees,[t]
2 to deprive[u] the poor of their rights
and withhold justice from the oppressed of my people,[v]
making widows their prey
and robbing the fatherless.
3 What will you do on the day of reckoning,[w]
when disaster[x] comes from afar?
To whom will you run for help?[y]
Where will you leave your riches?
4 Nothing will remain but to cringe among the captives[z]
or fall among the slain.[a]

Yet for all this, his anger is not turned away,[b]
his hand is still upraised.

[a] 20 Or *arm*

While Christ was fully man He was also fully God, as these facts indicate: He is called God (John 1:1; Heb. 1:8); He did works that only God could do, such as forgive sins (Mark 2:7) and create (Col. 1:16); He had attributes that only God could have, such as truth (John 14:6) and omniscience (John 2:24–25); and He claimed equality with God (John 10:30).

The question may be raised as to whether Christ lost anything of deity when He became a man (Phil. 2:6–8). While there is an inscrutable mystery involved in this unparalleled act of condescension, one can be certain that He lost none of God's attributes, because He was still God (John 20:28). He is fully God and fully man united in one person forever. Even now, at the right hand of God, He is the God-man (1 Tim. 2:5). The great condescension of the Son of God in becoming a man serves eternally as a perfect model of humility and self-giving love (Phil. 2:8).

9:8 *message against Jacob.* The message was a judgment against the northern kingdom. The Lord would destroy it and its capital, Samaria.

10:1 *Woe.* Woe is a chilling word when spoken by God (5:8–23; 10:5). The leaders who make laws that affect a community for good or evil bear a fearful responsibility before God, whether they acknowledge it or not.

10:3 *from afar.* The Assyrians were the devastation that came from afar.

9:9 [q] Isa 7:9 [r] Isa 46:12 **9:11** [s] Isa 7:8 **9:12** [t] 2Ki 16:6 [u] 2Ch 28:18 [v] Ps 79:7 [w] Isa 5:25 **9:13** [x] Jer 5:3 [y] Isa 31:1; Hos 7:7,10 **9:14** [z] Isa 19:15 [a] Rev 18:8 **9:15** [b] Isa 3:2-3 **9:16** [c] Mt 15:14; 23:16,24 [d] Isa 3:12 **9:17** [e] Jer 18:21 [f] Isa 27:11 [g] Isa 10:6 [h] Isa 1:4 [i] Mt 12:34 [j] Isa 5:25 **9:18** [k] Mal 4:1 [l] Ps 83:14 **9:19** [m] Isa 13:9,13 [n] Isa 1:31 [o] Mic 7:2,6 **9:20** [p] Lev 26:26 [q] Isa 49:26 **9:21** [r] 2Ch 28:6 [s] Isa 5:25 **10:1** [t] Ps 58:2 **10:2** [u] Isa 3:14 [v] Isa 5:23 **10:3** [w] Job 31:14; Hos 9:7 [x] Lk 19:44 [y] Isa 20:6 **10:4** [z] Isa 24:22 [a] Isa 22:2; 34:3; 66:16 [b] Isa 5:25

God's Judgment on Assyria

5 "Woe to the Assyrian,[c] the rod of my anger,
in whose hand is the club[d] of my wrath![e]
6 I send him against a godless[f] nation,
I dispatch him against a people who anger me,[g]
to seize loot and snatch plunder,[h]
and to trample them down like mud in the streets.
7 But this is not what he intends,[i]
this is not what he has in mind;
his purpose is to destroy,
to put an end to many nations.
8 'Are not my commanders[j] all kings?' he says.
9 'Has not Kalno[k] fared like Carchemish?[l]
Is not Hamath like Arpad,
and Samaria[m] like Damascus?[n]
10 As my hand seized the kingdoms of the idols,[o]
kingdoms whose images excelled those of Jerusalem and Samaria—
11 shall I not deal with Jerusalem and her images
as I dealt with Samaria and her idols?' "

12 When the Lord has finished all his
work[p] against Mount Zion[q] and Jerusalem,
he will say, "I will punish the king of Assyria[r] for the willful pride of his heart and
the haughty look in his eyes. 13 For he says:

" 'By the strength of my hand I have done this,[s]
and by my wisdom, because I have understanding.
I removed the boundaries of nations,
I plundered their treasures;[t]
like a mighty one I subdued[a] their kings.
14 As one reaches into a nest,[u]
so my hand reached for the wealth[v] of the nations;
as people gather abandoned eggs,
so I gathered all the countries;
not one flapped a wing,
or opened its mouth to chirp.' "

15 Does the ax raise itself above the person who swings it,
or the saw boast against the one who uses it?[w]
As if a rod were to wield the person who lifts it up,
or a club[x] brandish the one who is not wood!
16 Therefore, the Lord, the LORD Almighty,
will send a wasting disease[y] upon his sturdy warriors;
under his pomp[z] a fire will be kindled
like a blazing flame.
17 The Light of Israel will become a fire,[a]
their Holy One[b] a flame;
in a single day it will burn and consume
his thorns[c] and his briers.[d]
18 The splendor of his forests[e] and fertile fields
it will completely destroy,
as when a sick person wastes away.
19 And the remaining trees of his forests will be so few[f]
that a child could write them down.

The Remnant of Israel

20 In that day[g] the remnant of Israel,
the survivors of Jacob,
will no longer rely[h] on him
who struck them down[i]
but will truly rely[j] on the LORD,
the Holy One of Israel.
21 A remnant[k] will return,[b] a remnant of Jacob
will return to the Mighty God.[l]
22 Though your people be like the sand by the sea, Israel,
only a remnant will return.[m]
Destruction has been decreed,[n]
overwhelming and righteous.

[a] 13 Or *treasures; / I subdued the mighty,*
[b] 21 Hebrew *shear-jashub* (see 7:3 and note); also in verse 22

10:5 *Assyrian.* Though God uses sinners as instruments of His will (7:17; 13:5), they will still be held accountable for their own wickedness. In this, God shows that He is just in all His ways (Hab. 1 – 3).
10:6 *a godless nation.* The ungodly nation is Judah (v. 11 – 12).
10:9 *Kalno . . . Damascus.* This is a list of cities that had already fallen to Assyria.
10:10 *idols ... images.* The Assyrians had conquered the nations who had false gods. Surely, they believed, they would also have an easy time against "Jerusalem and her idols." Only the Living God was to be worshiped by the Israelites, but they had repeatedly broken that command (Ex. 20:4 – 6; Judg. 2:19).
10:15 *Does . . . the saw boast.* The saw that boasted was the Assyrian army. They were an instrument in the hands of God.
10:16 *sturdy warriors.* The sturdy warriors who come under judgment are the Assyrians.
10:20 *remnant.* The Hebrew word used here for "remnant" is different than the word used in 1:9. The difference may be considered slight; it is the difference between those who were left, or remained (10:20,22), and those who survived (1:9).
10:22 *a remnant.* Most of the people of the northern kingdom were carried off into captivity. But some

10:5 [c] Isa 14:25; Zep 2:13 [d] Jer 51:20 [e] Isa 13:3,5,13; 30:30; 66:14 **10:6** [f] Isa 9:17 [g] Isa 9:19 [h] Isa 5:29 **10:7** [i] Ge 50:20; Ac 4:23-28 **10:8** [j] 2Ki 18:24 **10:9** [k] Ge 10:10 [l] 2Ch 35:20 [m] 2Ki 17:6 [n] 2Ki 16:9 **10:10** [o] 2Ki 19:18 **10:12** [p] Isa 28:21-22; 65:7 [q] 2Ki 19:31 [r] Jer 50:18 **10:13** [s] Isa 37:24; Da 4:30 [t] Eze 28:4 **10:14** [u] Jer 49:16; Ob 1:4 [v] Job 31:25 **10:15** [w] Isa 45:9; Ro 9:20-21 [x] ver 5 **10:16** [y] ver 18; Isa 17:4 [z] Isa 8:7 **10:17** [a] Isa 31:9 [b] Isa 37:23 [c] Nu 11:1-3 [d] Isa 9:18 **10:18** [e] 2Ki 19:23 **10:19** [f] Isa 21:17 **10:20** [g] Isa 11:10,11 [h] 2Ki 16:7 [i] 2Ch 28:20 [j] Isa 17:7 **10:21** [k] Isa 6:13 [l] Isa 9:6 **10:22** [m] Ro 9:27-28 [n] Isa 28:22; Da 9:27

23 The Lord, the LORD Almighty, will
carry out
the destruction decreed upon the
whole land.[o]

24 Therefore this is what the Lord, the
LORD Almighty, says:

"My people who live in Zion,[p]
do not be afraid of the Assyrians,
who beat[q] you with a rod
and lift up a club against you, as
Egypt did.
25 Very soon[r] my anger against you will end
and my wrath[s] will be directed to
their destruction."
26 The LORD Almighty will lash[t] them
with a whip,
as when he struck down Midian[u] at
the rock of Oreb;
and he will raise his staff over the waters,[v]
as he did in Egypt.
27 In that day their burden will be lifted
from your shoulders,
their yoke[w] from your neck;[x]
the yoke will be broken
because you have grown so fat.[a]

28 They enter Aiath;
they pass through Migron;[y]
they store supplies at Mikmash.[z]
29 They go over the pass, and say,
"We will camp overnight at Geba."
Ramah[a] trembles;
Gibeah of Saul flees.
30 Cry out, Daughter Gallim![b]
Listen, Laishah!
Poor Anathoth![c]
31 Madmenah is in flight;
the people of Gebim take cover.
32 This day they will halt at Nob;[d]
they will shake their fist
at the mount of Daughter Zion,[e]
at the hill of Jerusalem.

33 See, the Lord, the LORD Almighty,
will lop off the boughs with great
power.
The lofty trees will be felled,
the tall[f] ones will be brought low.
34 He will cut down the forest thickets
with an ax;
Lebanon will fall before the Mighty
One.

The Branch From Jesse

11 A shoot will come up from the stump
of Jesse;[g]
from his roots a Branch[h] will bear
fruit.
2 The Spirit[i] of the LORD will rest on him—
the Spirit of wisdom[j] and of
understanding,
the Spirit of counsel and of might,[k]
the Spirit of the knowledge and fear
of the LORD—
3 and he will delight in the fear of the
LORD.

He will not judge by what he sees with
his eyes,[l]
or decide by what he hears with his
ears;[m]
4 but with righteousness[n] he will judge
the needy,
with justice[o] he will give decisions for
the poor[p] of the earth.
He will strike[q] the earth with the rod of
his mouth;
with the breath[r] of his lips he will slay
the wicked.

---

[a] 27 Hebrew; Septuagint *broken / from your shoulders*

Israelites made their way to Judah and became part of the southern kingdom. These people and their descendants would act as a remnant by preserving the names of the northern tribes among the people of God.

10:28–32 *Aiath . . . Jerusalem.* These verses depict Isaiah's vision of the king of Assyria's relentless march south over difficult terrain from Aiath (or Ai), which was ten miles north of Jerusalem on a point overlooking the city. The cities as listed in these verses are closer and closer to the capital at Jerusalem.

10:32 *they.* "They" refers to Assyria, the enemy.

10:33–34 *bough . . . thickets.* The bough and the thickets are the Assyrian leaders and the Assyrian army. The point is that God will bring judgment on the instruments He used to judge Israel.

11:1 *a shoot will come up from the stump of Jesse.* Jesse was King David's father (1 Sam. 16:10–13). As David inaugurated a kingdom of righteousness and peace, the new David—the "rod" or "root" (53:2) from David's line—will establish an incomparably greater kingdom. The words "rod" and "root" are messianic terms. They are figurative words for the great descendant of the household of David, the Seed of the woman promised in Genesis 3:15, Jesus Christ Himself (Matt. 1:17).

11:2 *Spirit.* As in the case of David (1 Sam. 16:13), the Messiah would be empowered by the Holy Spirit (4:4; 42:1; 48:16; 59:21; 61:1; Luke 3:22), who was the Agent for establishing God's kingdom (Gen. 1:1–2; Judg. 3:10; 6:34; 1 Sam. 10:6). ***wisdom and of understanding.*** The Messiah will be the ideal king. He will embody the administrative skill to govern with righteousness and justice far more than even Solomon (1 Kin. 3:9), who asked for those gifts when he became king. ***counsel.*** The Holy Spirit's "counsel" is not advice, but authoritative plans and decisions. ***fear of the LORD.*** The Messiah would demonstrate in all His life the correct response to God; He would honor and obey Him (Ex. 20:20).

11:4 *judge.* In this context, judge does not mean to bring people to account, but to act on their behalf. As

---

10:23 [o] Isa 28:22; Ro 9:27-28* **10:24** [p] Ps 87:5-6 [q] Ex 5:14 **10:25** [r] Isa 17:14 [s] ver 5; Da 11:36 **10:26** [t] Isa 37:36-38 [u] Isa 9:4 [v] Ex 14:16 **10:27** [w] Isa 9:4 [x] Isa 14:25 **10:28** [y] 1Sa 14:2 [z] 1Sa 13:2 **10:29** [a] Jos 18:25 **10:30** [b] 1Sa 25:44 [c] Ne 11:32 **10:32** [d] 1Sa 21:1 [e] Jer 6:23 **10:33** [f] Am 2:9 **11:1** [g] ver 10; Isa 9:7; Rev 5:5 [h] Isa 4:2 **11:2** [i] Isa 42:1; 48:16; 61:1; Mt 3:16; Jn 1:32-33 [j] Eph 1:17 [k] 2Ti 1:7 **11:3** [l] Jn 7:24 [m] Jn 2:25 **11:4** [n] Ps 72:2 [o] Isa 9:7 [p] Isa 3:14 [q] Mal 4:6 [r] Job 4:9; 2Th 2:8

5 Righteousness will be his belt
and faithfulness[s] the sash around his waist.[t]

6 The wolf will live with the lamb,[u]
the leopard will lie down with the goat,
the calf and the lion and the yearling[a] together;
and a little child will lead them.
7 The cow will feed with the bear,
their young will lie down together,
and the lion will eat straw like the ox.
8 The infant will play near the cobra's den,
and the young child will put its hand into the viper's nest.
9 They will neither harm nor destroy[v]
on all my holy mountain,
for the earth[w] will be filled with the knowledge[x] of the LORD
as the waters cover the sea.

10 In that day the Root of Jesse will stand
as a banner[y] for the peoples; the nations[z]
will rally to him,[a] and his resting place[b]
will be glorious. 11 In that day[c] the Lord will
reach out his hand a second time to reclaim
the surviving remnant of his people from
Assyria,[d] from Lower Egypt, from Upper
Egypt, from Cush,[b] from Elam,[e] from Babylonia,[c] from Hamath and from the islands[f]
of the Mediterranean.

12 He will raise a banner for the nations
and gather the exiles of Israel;
he will assemble the scattered people[g] of Judah
from the four quarters of the earth.
13 Ephraim's jealousy will vanish,
and Judah's enemies[d] will be destroyed;
Ephraim will not be jealous of Judah,
nor Judah hostile toward Ephraim.[h]
14 They will swoop down on the slopes of Philistia to the west;
together they will plunder the people to the east.
They will subdue Edom[i] and Moab,[j]
and the Ammonites will be subject to them.
15 The LORD will dry up
the gulf of the Egyptian sea;
with a scorching wind he will sweep his hand[k]
over the Euphrates River.[l]
He will break it up into seven streams
so that anyone can cross over in sandals.
16 There will be a highway[m] for the remnant of his people
that is left from Assyria,
as there was for Israel
when they came up from Egypt.[n]

Songs of Praise

12 In that day you will say:

"I will praise[o] you, LORD.
Although you were angry with me,
your anger has turned away
and you have comforted me.
2 Surely God is my salvation;
I will trust[p] and not be afraid.
The LORD, the LORD himself, is my strength and my defense[e];
he has become my salvation.[q]"
3 With joy you will draw water[r]
from the wells of salvation.

4 In that day you will say:

"Give praise to the LORD, proclaim his name;[s]
make known among the nations what he has done,
and proclaim that his name is exalted.
5 Sing[t] to the LORD, for he has done glorious things;[u]
let this be known to all the world.

[a] 6 Hebrew; Septuagint *lion will feed* [b] 11 That is, the upper Nile region [c] 11 Hebrew *Shinar* [d] 13 Or *hostility* [e] 2 Or *song*

the Judge of His people, God sentences the wicked and offers protection and defense for the innocent and oppressed. ***rod of his mouth ... breath of his lips.*** This concept is repeated in Revelation 19:15, when the Lord Jesus returns with power and great glory.

11:6–9 *wolf will live with the lamb ... neither harm nor destroy.* This picture of cruel beasts regenerated with a new nature that makes them protect their natural prey portrays a reign of peace and security. This can only be realized in the return of the Messiah to establish the kingdom of God (65:17–25; Rev. 21:1–8).

11:10 *the nations.* The revelation of the Messiah is for people of all nations.

11:11 *a second time.* The "second time" may refer to the remnant coming back to the land in 538 B.C., in contrast to the first exodus from Egypt. Beyond that, it could also refer to the remnant's coming to Christ in the present age (Rom. 11:5) or to its future return to Christ (Rom. 11:11–27; Rev. 7:4–8).

12:1 *In that day.* The day refers to the day that the Lord rescues His people, whether it was the return of the remnant or the future return of Christ as portrayed in the Book of Revelation.

12:2 *my strength and my defense.* This psalm of redemption is based on the first psalm of redemption in Exodus (Ex. 15:2; Ps. 118:14).

12:3 *wells of salvation.* In an arid land, the provision of wells and springs was regarded as a divine gift. Hebrew poets often associate water with salvation (Ex. 17:1–7).

11:5 [s] Isa 25:1 [t] Eph 6:14 **11:6** [u] Isa 65:25 **11:9** [v] Job 5:23 [w] Ps 98:2-3; Isa 52:10 [x] Isa 45:6, 14; Hab 2:14 **11:10** [y] Jn 12:32 [z] Isa 49:23; Lk 2:32 [a] Ro 15:12* [b] Isa 14:3; 28:12; 32:17-18 **11:11** [c] Isa 10:20 [d] Isa 19:24; Hos 11:11; Mic 7:12; Zec 10:10 [e] Ge 10:22 [f] Isa 42:4, 10, 12; 66:19 **11:12** [g] Zep 3:10 **11:13** [h] Jer 3:18; Eze 37:16-17, 22; Hos 1:11 **11:14** [i] Da 11:41; Joel 3:19 [j] Isa 16:14; 25:10 **11:15** [k] Isa 19:16 [l] Isa 7:20 **11:16** [m] Isa 19:23; 62:10 [n] Ex 14:26-31 **12:1** [o] Isa 25:1 **12:2** [p] Isa 26:3 [q] Ex 15:2; Ps 118:14 **12:3** [r] Jn 4:10, 14 **12:4** [s] Ps 105:1; Isa 24:15 **12:5** [t] Ex 15:1 [u] Ps 98:1

6 Shout aloud and sing for joy, people of Zion,
for great is the Holy One of Israel[v]
among you.[w]"

A Prophecy Against Babylon

13 A prophecy against Babylon that Isaiah son of Amoz saw:

2 Raise a banner[x] on a bare hilltop,
shout to them;
beckon to them
to enter the gates of the nobles.
3 I have commanded those I prepared for battle;
I have summoned my warriors[y] to carry out my wrath—
those who rejoice[z] in my triumph.

4 Listen, a noise on the mountains,
like that of a great multitude![a]
Listen, an uproar among the kingdoms,
like nations massing together!
The LORD Almighty is mustering
an army for war.
5 They come from faraway lands,
from the ends of the heavens[b]—
the LORD and the weapons of his wrath—
to destroy[c] the whole country.

6 Wail,[d] for the day[e] of the LORD is near;
it will come like destruction from the Almighty.[a]
7 Because of this, all hands will go limp,
every heart will melt with fear.[f]
8 Terror[g] will seize them,
pain and anguish will grip them;
they will writhe like a woman in labor.
They will look aghast at each other,
their faces aflame.[h]

9 See, the day of the LORD is coming
—a cruel day, with wrath and fierce anger—
to make the land desolate
and destroy the sinners within it.
10 The stars of heaven and their constellations
will not show their light.
The rising sun[i] will be darkened[j]
and the moon will not give its light.[k]
11 I will punish[l] the world for its evil,
the wicked for their sins.
I will put an end to the arrogance of the haughty
and will humble the pride of the ruthless.
12 I will make people[m] scarcer than pure gold,
more rare than the gold of Ophir.
13 Therefore I will make the heavens tremble;[n]
and the earth will shake from its place
at the wrath of the LORD Almighty,
in the day of his burning anger.

14 Like a hunted gazelle,
like sheep without a shepherd,[o]
they will all return to their own people,
they will flee to their native land.[p]
15 Whoever is captured will be thrust through;
all who are caught will fall[q] by the sword.[r]
16 Their infants[s] will be dashed to pieces before their eyes;
their houses will be looted and their wives violated.

17 See, I will stir up[t] against them the Medes,
who do not care for silver
and have no delight in gold.[u]
18 Their bows will strike down the young men;
they will have no mercy on infants,
nor will they look with compassion on children.
19 Babylon, the jewel of kingdoms,
the pride and glory[v] of the Babylonians,[b]
will be overthrown[w] by God
like Sodom and Gomorrah.[x]

[a] 6 Hebrew *Shaddai* [b] 19 Or *Chaldeans*

13:1 ***prophecy against ... that Isaiah ... saw.*** The Book of Isaiah takes a major turn at chapter 13, which continues through chapter 27. The focus in this extended section is first on the Lord's judgments against the nations, through chapter 23, followed by an end-time prophecy in chapters 24–27. ***Babylon.*** Babylon was the crown jewel of the Assyrian Empire. This burden may refer to its destruction around 689 B.C. when Sennacherib quelled a rebellion there. Yet the Lord's overthrow of Babylon, the "jewel of kingdoms" (v. 19), symbolizes His triumph over the world (v. 11). Babylon is the epitome of religion and culture in the ancient Middle East. Thus the burden is indirectly against all nations, especially Assyria (14:24–27). Peter uses the term Babylon symbolically in the New Testament (1 Pet. 5:13), as does John (Rev. 14:8; 18:2,10–21).

13:6 ***the day of the LORD.*** This designated "day" refers to a time of unusual activity of God in the lives of people, for judgment or for mercy. ***is near.*** The basic idea of this term is not that of approaching a fixed date, but that the day of the Lord is about to burst into one's world. The day of the Lord is imminent—able to happen at any time—not because people have almost reached it as a destination, but because it may burst in upon people without further warning.

12:6 [v] Isa 49:26 [w] Zep 3:14-17 **13:2** [x] Jer 50:2; 51:27 **13:3** [y] Joel 3:11 [z] Ps 149:2 **13:4** [a] Joel 3:14 **13:5** [b] Isa 5:26 [c] Isa 24:1 **13:6** [d] Eze 30:2 [e] Isa 2:12; Joel 1:15 **13:7** [f] Eze 21:7 **13:8** [g] Isa 21:4 [h] Na 2:10 **13:10** [i] Isa 24:23 [j] Isa 5:30; Rev 8:12 [k] Eze 32:7; Mt 24:29*; Mk 13:24* **13:11** [l] Isa 3:11; 11:4; 26:21 **13:12** [m] Isa 4:1 **13:13** [n] Isa 34:4; 51:6; Hag 2:6 **13:14** [o] 1Ki 22:17 [p] Jer 50:16 **13:15** [q] Jer 51:4 [r] Isa 14:19; Jer 50:25 **13:16** [s] Ps 137:9 **13:17** [t] Jer 51:1 [u] Pr 6:34-35 **13:19** [v] Da 4:30 [w] Rev 14:8 [x] Ge 19:24

20 She will never be inhabited[y]
or lived in through all generations;
there no nomads[z] will pitch their tents,
there no shepherds will rest their flocks.
21 But desert creatures[a] will lie there,
jackals will fill her houses;
there the owls will dwell,
and there the wild goats will leap about.
22 Hyenas will inhabit her strongholds,[b]
jackals[c] her luxurious palaces.
Her time is at hand,[d]
and her days will not be prolonged.

14 The LORD will have compassion[e] on Jacob;
once again he will choose[f] Israel
and will settle them in their own land.
Foreigners[g] will join them
and unite with the descendants of Jacob.
2 Nations will take them
and bring[h] them to their own place.
And Israel will take possession of the nations[i]
and make them male and female servants in the LORD's land.
They will make captives of their captors
and rule over their oppressors.[j]

3 On the day the LORD gives you relief[k]
from your suffering and turmoil and from
the harsh labor forced on you, 4 you will
take up this taunt[l] against the king of Babylon:

How the oppressor[m] has come to an end!
How his fury[a] has ended!
5 The LORD has broken the rod of the wicked,[n]
the scepter of the rulers,
6 which in anger struck down peoples[o]
with unceasing blows,
and in fury subdued nations
with relentless aggression.[p]
7 All the lands are at rest and at peace;
they break into singing.[q]
8 Even the junipers[r] and the cedars of Lebanon
gloat over you and say,
"Now that you have been laid low,
no one comes to cut us down."
9 The realm of the dead[s] below is all astir
to meet you at your coming;
it rouses the spirits of the departed to greet you—
all those who were leaders in the world;
it makes them rise from their thrones—
all those who were kings over the nations.
10 They will all respond,
they will say to you,
"You also have become weak, as we are;
you have become like us."[t]
11 All your pomp has been brought down to the grave,
along with the noise of your harps;
maggots are spread out beneath you
and worms[u] cover you.
12 How you have fallen[v] from heaven,
morning star,[w] son of the dawn!
You have been cast down to the earth,
you who once laid low the nations!
13 You said in your heart,
"I will ascend[x] to the heavens;
I will raise my throne[y]
above the stars of God;
I will sit enthroned on the mount of assembly,
on the utmost heights of Mount Zaphon.[b]

[a] *4* Dead Sea Scrolls, Septuagint and Syriac; the meaning of the word in the Masoretic Text is uncertain. [b] *13* Or *of the north*; Zaphon was the most sacred mountain of the Canaanites.

13:21–22 *owls ... jackals.* With the exception of the goat, all of the animals mentioned in these verses are unclean. This image created a clear message to the people of Israel of a place that was desolate and unfit to inhabit.

14:4 *Babylon.* Babylon is often used in Scripture for Satan's kingdom. This passage can be read with a double point of view. One, as if it were talking about an unnamed political king; and two, as a reference to and description of Satan's career. Both views are sobering and worth taking note of.

14:8 *the junipers ... gloat.* The trees will no longer be cut down to construct machines of war.

14:9 *The realm of the dead below is all astir.* The commotion in the "grave" when the king of Babylon (or Satan; see Rev. 20:1–3) arrives contrasts sharply with the rest on earth when he is gone (v. 7).

14:12 *fallen from heaven.* This is a figure of speech meaning cast down from an exalted political position. Jesus said, "And you, Capernaum, will you be lifted to the heavens? No, you will go down to Hades" (Luke 10:15); and, apparently with the same meaning, "I saw Satan fall like lightning from heaven" (Luke 10:18). The "son of the dawn," called Lucifer or Day Star in Hebrew, is the planet Venus. The poetic language of this verse describes the aspiration of this brightest star to climb to the zenith of the heavens and its extinction before the rising sun. This is an apt summary of the failed goal of Satan (or the king of Babylon, v. 4), who wanted to grasp universal and eternal domination (Ezek. 28:14–16; Rev. 12:12–13; 20:2).

13:20 [y] Isa 14:23; 34:10-15 [z] 2Ch 17:11 **13:21** [a] Rev 18:2 **13:22** [b] Isa 25:2 [c] Isa 34:13 [d] Jer 51:33 **14:1** [e] Ps 102:13; Isa 49:10, 13; 54:7-8, 10 [f] Isa 41:8; 44:1; 49:7; Zec 1:17; 2:12 [g] Eph 2:12-19 **14:2** [h] Isa 60:9 [i] Isa 49:7, 23 [j] Isa 60:14; 61:5 **14:3** [k] Isa 11:10 **14:4** [l] Hab 2:6 [m] Isa 9:4 **14:5** [n] Ps 125:3 **14:6** [o] Isa 10:14 [p] Isa 47:6 **14:7** [q] Ps 98:1; 126:1-3 **14:8** [r] Eze 31:16 **14:9** [s] Eze 32:21 **14:10** [t] Eze 32:21 **14:11** [u] Isa 51:8 **14:12** [v] Isa 34:4; Lk 10:18 [w] 2Pe 1:19; Rev 2:28; 8:10; 9:1 **14:13** [x] Da 5:23; 8:10; Mt 11:23 [y] Eze 28:2; 2Th 2:4

14 I will ascend above the tops of the clouds;
I will make myself like the Most High."[z]
15 But you are brought down to the realm of the dead,
to the depths[a] of the pit.
16 Those who see you stare at you,
they ponder your fate:[b]
"Is this the man who shook the earth
and made kingdoms tremble,
17 the man who made the world a wilderness,[c]
who overthrew its cities
and would not let his captives go home?"
18 All the kings of the nations lie in state,
each in his own tomb.
19 But you are cast out[d] of your tomb
like a rejected branch;
you are covered with the slain,
with those pierced by the sword,
those who descend to the stones of the pit.[e]
Like a corpse trampled underfoot,
20 you will not join them in burial,
for you have destroyed your land
and killed your people.

Let the offspring[f] of the wicked[g]
never be mentioned[h] again.
21 Prepare a place to slaughter his children
for the sins of their ancestors;[i]
they are not to rise to inherit the land
and cover the earth with their cities.
22 "I will rise up against them,"
declares the LORD Almighty.
"I will wipe out Babylon's name and survivors,
her offspring and descendants,[j]"
declares the LORD.
23 "I will turn her into a place for owls[k]
and into swampland;
I will sweep her with the broom of destruction,"
declares the LORD Almighty.
24 The LORD Almighty has sworn,[l]
"Surely, as I have planned, so it will be,
and as I have purposed, so it will happen.[m]
25 I will crush the Assyrian[n] in my land;
on my mountains I will trample him down.
His yoke[o] will be taken from my people,
and his burden removed from their shoulders.[p]"
26 This is the plan[q] determined for the whole world;
this is the hand[r] stretched out over all nations.
27 For the LORD Almighty has purposed,
and who can thwart him?
His hand is stretched out, and who can turn it back?[s]

A Prophecy Against the Philistines

28 This prophecy[t] came in the year King
Ahaz[u] died:
29 Do not rejoice, all you Philistines,[v]
that the rod that struck you is broken;
from the root of that snake will spring up a viper,[w]
its fruit will be a darting, venomous serpent.
30 The poorest of the poor will find pasture,
and the needy[x] will lie down in safety.[y]
But your root I will destroy by famine;[z]
it will slay[a] your survivors.
31 Wail, you gate![b] Howl, you city!
Melt away, all you Philistines!
A cloud of smoke comes from the north,[c]
and there is not a straggler in its ranks.
32 What answer shall be given
to the envoys[d] of that nation?
"The LORD has established Zion,[e]
and in her his afflicted people will find refuge.[f]"

14:14 ***I will make myself like the Most High.*** This is the most outrageous of the arrogant desires of Satan (or of this unnamed king). He wanted to surpass the Most High, a term for the Lord that is often used in connection with the nations of the world (Ps. 87:5; 91:1; 92:1). This statement strongly speaks of Satan (v. 12), who purposes to work against God in every possible way. Satan's sin is centered in pride, the desire to be in submission to no one, not even God (1 Tim. 3:6). Ezekiel saw Satan's work in the king of Tyre (Ezek. 28), and Isaiah sees the parallel between the character and goals of Satan and this unnamed Babylonian king.
14:28 ***Ahaz.*** King Ahaz died in 720 B.C.
14:29 ***rod.*** The rod is probably a metaphor for the Assyrian king (10:5).

14:31 ***gate.*** The gate of a walled city was its weakest point. When the gate fell, the city could be taken. ***from the north.*** The Assyrian army would come from the north.

14:14 [z] Isa 47:8; 2Th 2:4 **14:15** [a] Mt 11:23; Lk 10:15 **14:16** [b] Jer 50:23 **14:17** [c] Joel 2:3 **14:19** [d] Isa 22:16-18 [e] Jer 41:7-9 **14:20** [f] Job 18:19 [g] Isa 1:4 [h] Ps 21:10 **14:21** [i] Ex 20:5; Lev 26:39 **14:22** [j] 1Ki 14:10; Job 18:19 **14:23** [k] Isa 34:11-15; Zep 2:14 **14:24** [l] Isa 45:23 [m] Ac 4:28 **14:25** [n] Isa 10:5, 12 [o] Isa 9:4 [p] Isa 10:27 **14:26** [q] Isa 23:9 [r] Ex 15:12 **14:27** [s] 2Ch 20:6; Isa 43:13; Da 4:35 **14:28** [t] Isa 13:1 [u] 2Ki 16:20 **14:29** [v] 2Ch 26:6 [w] Isa 11:8 **14:30** [x] Isa 3:15 [y] Isa 7:21-22 [z] Isa 8:21; 9:20; 51:19 [a] Jer 25:16 **14:31** [b] Isa 3:26 [c] Jer 1:14 **14:32** [d] Isa 37:9 [e] Ps 87:2, 5; Isa 44:28; 54:11 [f] Isa 4:6; Jas 2:5

A Prophecy Against Moab

15 A prophecy against Moab:[g]

Ar in Moab is ruined,[h]
destroyed in a night!
Kir in Moab is ruined,
destroyed in a night!
2 Dibon goes up to its temple,
to its high places[i] to weep;
Moab wails over Nebo and Medeba.
Every head is shaved[j]
and every beard cut off.
3 In the streets they wear sackcloth;
on the roofs and in the public
squares[k]
they all wail,
prostrate with weeping.[l]
4 Heshbon and Elealeh[m] cry out,
their voices are heard all the way to
Jahaz.
Therefore the armed men of Moab cry
out,
and their hearts are faint.

5 My heart cries out over Moab;[n]
her fugitives flee as far as Zoar,
as far as Eglath Shelishiyah.
They go up the hill to Luhith,
weeping as they go;
on the road to Horonaim[o]
they lament their destruction.[p]
6 The waters of Nimrim are dried up[q]
and the grass is withered;[r]
the vegetation is gone
and nothing green is left.
7 So the wealth they have acquired[s] and
stored up
they carry away over the Ravine of
the Poplars.
8 Their outcry echoes along the border of
Moab;
their wailing reaches as far as
Eglaim,
their lamentation as far as Beer Elim.
9 The waters of Dimon[a] are full of
blood,
but I will bring still more upon
Dimon[a]—
a lion[t] upon the fugitives of Moab
and upon those who remain in the
land.

16 Send lambs[u] as tribute
to the ruler of the land,
from Sela,[v] across the desert,
to the mount of Daughter Zion.[w]
2 Like fluttering birds
pushed from the nest,[x]
so are the women of Moab
at the fords of the Arnon.[y]

3 "Make up your mind," Moab says.
"Render a decision.
Make your shadow like night—
at high noon.
Hide the fugitives,[z]
do not betray the refugees.
4 Let the Moabite fugitives stay with you;
be their shelter from the destroyer."

The oppressor[a] will come to an end,
and destruction will cease;
the aggressor will vanish from the
land.
5 In love a throne[b] will be established;
in faithfulness a man will sit on it—
one from the house[b] of David[c]—
one who in judging seeks justice[d]
and speeds the cause of
righteousness.
6 We have heard of Moab's[e] pride[f]—
how great is her arrogance!—
of her conceit, her pride and her
insolence;
but her boasts are empty.

[a] 9 *Dimon*, a wordplay on *Dibon* (see verse 2), sounds like the Hebrew for *blood*. [b] 5 Hebrew *tent*

15:1 ***Moab.*** For the origin of the people of Moab, see the story of Lot and his daughters in Genesis 19:30–38 (also Num. 22–25; Deut. 1:5).
15:2 ***high places.*** High places were sites of pagan worship (16:12).
15:5 ***heart cries out.*** Isaiah does not rejoice in the downfall of Moab. He knew that the judgment from God was righteous, and he remembered that Moab had been a treacherous enemy to his nation, yet his heart cried out in pity. It is the mark of God's people that they do not rejoice in the downfall of the wicked, even though they may be glad to be free from oppression.
15:9 ***Dimon.*** The term Dimon sounds like "blood" in Hebrew. ***lion.*** Fleeing from one tragedy after another in their flight southward, the refugees turned to Judah in the west for asylum (16:1–5). A remnant would survive in Moab, as would be the case with Israel (1:9; 6:13; 10:20; 11:16)—but not with Assyria (14:22) and Philistia (14:30).
16:5 ***a throne will be established.*** Moab's salvation ultimately lies in the coming one, Jesus the Messiah, whose throne will be established (9:1–7; 11:1–5; Amos 9:11–12; Acts 15:16–17).
16:6 ***pride.*** In the end, it was the pride and the haughtiness and the wrath of Moab that brought the nation into judgment. The pride of Moab is not the honest pride in a difficult task well done, but the pride of a haughty, disdainful people who considered themselves above remonstrance. The third element of Moab's downfall, wrath, is closely linked with pride. A people who consider themselves the center of interest and importance lose their natural inhibition. They feel free to indulge in wrath because they are convinced that whatever they do is right.

15:1 [g] Isa 11:14 [h] Jer 48:24,41 **15:2** [i] Jer 48:35 [j] Lev 21:5 **15:3** [k] Jer 48:38 [l] Isa 22:4 **15:4** [m] Nu 32:3 **15:5** [n] Jer 48:31 [o] Jer 48:3,34 [p] Jer 4:20; 48:5 **15:6** [q] Isa 19:5-7; Jer 48:34 [r] Joel 1:12 **15:7** [s] Isa 30:6; Jer 48:36 **15:9** [t] 2Ki 17:25 **16:1** [u] 2Ki 3:4 [v] 2Ki 14:7 [w] Isa 10:32 **16:2** [x] Pr 27:8 [y] Nu 21:13-14; Jer 48:20 **16:3** [z] 1Ki 18:4 **16:4** [a] Isa 9:4 **16:5** [b] Da 7:14; Mic 4:7 [c] Lk 1:32 [d] Isa 9:7 **16:6** [e] Am 2:1; Zep 2:8 [f] Ob 1:3; Zep 2:10

7 Therefore the Moabites wail,[g]
they wail together for Moab.
Lament and grieve
for the raisin cakes[h] of Kir Hareseth.[i]
8 The fields of Heshbon wither,
the vines of Sibmah also.
The rulers of the nations
have trampled down the choicest
vines,
which once reached Jazer
and spread toward the desert.
Their shoots spread out
and went as far as the sea.[a]
9 So I weep,[j] as Jazer weeps,
for the vines of Sibmah.
Heshbon and Elealeh,
I drench you with tears!
The shouts of joy over your ripened
fruit
and over your harvests[k] have been
stilled.
10 Joy and gladness are taken away from
the orchards;[l]
no one sings or shouts in the
vineyards;
no one treads[m] out wine at the presses,[n]
for I have put an end to the shouting.
11 My heart laments for Moab[o] like a harp,
my inmost being[p] for Kir Hareseth.
12 When Moab appears at her high place,
she only wears herself out;
when she goes to her shrine[q] to pray,
it is to no avail.[r]

13 This is the word the LORD has already
spoken concerning Moab. 14 But now the
LORD says: "Within three years, as a servant bound by contract would count them,
Moab's splendor and all her many people
will be despised,[s] and her survivors will be
very few and feeble."[t]

A Prophecy Against Damascus

17 A prophecy against Damascus:[u]

"See, Damascus will no longer be a city
but will become a heap of ruins.[v]
2 The cities of Aroer will be deserted
and left to flocks,[w] which will lie
down,
with no one to make them afraid.[x]
3 The fortified city will disappear from
Ephraim,
and royal power from Damascus;
the remnant of Aram will be
like the glory[y] of the Israelites,"[z]
declares the LORD Almighty.

4 "In that day the glory of Jacob will fade;
the fat of his body will waste[a] away.
5 It will be as when reapers harvest the
standing grain,
gathering[b] the grain in their arms—
as when someone gleans heads of
grain
in the Valley of Rephaim.
6 Yet some gleanings will remain,[c]
as when an olive tree is beaten,[d]
leaving two or three olives on the
topmost branches,
four or five on the fruitful boughs,"
declares the LORD, the God
of Israel.

7 In that day people will look[e] to their
Maker
and turn their eyes to the Holy One[f]
of Israel.
8 They will not look to the altars,
the work of their hands,[g]
and they will have no regard for the
Asherah poles[b]
and the incense altars their fingers
have made.

9 In that day their strong cities, which
they left because of the Israelites, will be
like places abandoned to thickets and undergrowth. And all will be desolation.

10 You have forgotten[h] God your Savior;[i]
you have not remembered the Rock,
your fortress.

[a] 8 Probably the Dead Sea [b] 8 That is, wooden symbols of the goddess Asherah

16:8 *vines.* The vines refers to Moab.
16:9 *Heshbon and Elealeh.* These cities were among the principal settlements in ancient Moab (15:4).
16:12 *high place . . . shrine.* As long as people worship false gods, they will be doomed to pain, judgment, and recurring trouble (15:2–4). Even when the people weary of the false gods and try to pray to the one true God, they will not be able to communicate with Him because they have not repented and renounced the false gods.
16:14 *Within three years.* A former prophecy against Moab (15:2) would be realized within three years, perhaps referring to the quelling of a rebellion against Sargon in 715 B.C. However, a remnant would remain (15:9). Moab had far more hope for salvation than did either Babylon or Philistia.
17:3 *fortified city.* This city may be Samaria, the capital city. ***Ephraim.*** Ephraim designates northern Israel.
17:5 *Rephaim.* The word "Rephaim" is the Hebrew word for "shades" or "ghosts." The "Valley of Rephaim" is the valley of death.
17:6 *remain.* A remnant would be left (10:20) even though it would be pitifully small.
17:10 *forgotten.* Forgetting God is letting the truth of God fade by ignoring Him. In the end, such neglect is unbelief, refusing to believe in God and refusing to

16:7 [g] Jer 48:20 [h] 1Ch 16:3 [i] 2Ki 3:25 **16:9** [j] Isa 15:3 [k] Jer 40:12 **16:10** [l] Isa 24:7-8 [m] Jdg 9:27 [n] Job 24:11 **16:11** [o] Isa 15:5 [p] Isa 63:15; Hos 11:8; Php 2:1 **16:12** [q] Isa 15:2 [r] 1Ki 18:29 **16:14** [s] Isa 25:10; Jer 48:42 [t] Isa 21:17 **17:1** [u] Ge 14:15; Jer 49:23; Ac 9:2 [v] Isa 25:2; Am 1:3; Zec 9:1 **17:2** [w] Isa 7:21; Eze 25:5 [x] Jer 7:33; Mic 4:4 **17:3** [y] ver 4; Hos 9:11 [z] Isa 7:8, 16; 8:4 **17:4** [a] Isa 10:16 **17:5** [b] ver 11; Jer 51:33; Joel 3:13; Mt 13:30 **17:6** [c] Dt 4:27; Isa 24:13 [d] Isa 27:12 **17:7** [e] Isa 10:20 [f] Mic 7:7 **17:8** [g] Isa 2:18, 20; 30:22 **17:10** [h] Isa 51:13 [i] Ps 68:19; Isa 12:2

Therefore, though you set out the finest
plants
and plant imported vines,
11 though on the day you set them out, you
make them grow,
and on the morning[j] when you plant
them, you bring them to bud,
yet the harvest will be as nothing[k]
in the day of disease and incurable
pain.[l]
12 Woe to the many nations that rage—
they rage like the raging sea![m]
Woe to the peoples who roar—
they roar like the roaring of great
waters!
13 Although the peoples roar like the roar
of surging waters,
when he rebukes[n] them they flee[o] far
away,
driven before the wind like chaff[p] on
the hills,
like tumbleweed before a gale.[q]
14 In the evening, sudden terror!
Before the morning, they are gone![r]
This is the portion of those who loot us,
the lot of those who plunder us.

A Prophecy Against Cush

18 Woe to the land of whirring wings[a]
along the rivers of Cush,[b][s]
2 which sends envoys by sea
in papyrus[t] boats over the water.

Go, swift messengers,
to a people tall and smooth-skinned,
to a people feared far and wide,
an aggressive[u] nation of strange
speech,
whose land is divided by rivers.[v]

3 All you people of the world,
you who live on the earth,
when a banner[w] is raised on the
mountains,
you will see it,
and when a trumpet sounds,
you will hear it.

4 This is what the LORD says to me:
"I will remain quiet and will look on
from my dwelling place,[x]
like shimmering heat in the sunshine,
like a cloud of dew[y] in the heat of
harvest."
5 For, before the harvest, when the
blossom is gone
and the flower becomes a ripening
grape,
he will cut off the shoots with pruning
knives,
and cut down and take away the
spreading branches.[z]
6 They will all be left to the mountain
birds of prey
and to the wild animals;[a]
the birds will feed on them all summer,
the wild animals all winter.

7 At that time gifts will be brought to the
LORD Almighty

from a people tall and smooth-skinned,
from a people feared far and wide,
an aggressive nation of strange speech,
whose land is divided by rivers—

the gifts will be brought to Mount Zion, the
place of the Name of the LORD Almighty.[b]

A Prophecy Against Egypt

19 A prophecy[c] against Egypt:[d]

See, the LORD rides on a swift cloud[e]
and is coming to Egypt.
The idols of Egypt tremble before him,
and the hearts of the Egyptians melt[f]
with fear.

2 "I will stir up Egyptian against
Egyptian—
brother will fight against brother,[g]
neighbor against neighbor,
city against city,
kingdom against kingdom.[h]

[a] *1* Or *of locusts* [b] *1* That is, the upper Nile region

believe His Word. The safe caring place, the Refuge from storms, is forgotten. God becomes like a friend whom you never visit any more or think much about and finally do not remember at all. This slippery slope takes us far from the Rock of our refuge, the God of our Salvation.

17:11 ***bring them to bud.*** This phrase may allude to the ancient practice of force-blooming potted plants and allowing them to die. Pagans believed that this reenactment of the life cycle would secure fertile fields. But even after performing this rite, the harvest would be in ruin. Just as the choice vines of the Lord's vineyard disappointed Him (5:1–7), so His errant people would find their harvest hopes shattered.

17:12 ***many nations.*** The many people are the nations that plunder Israel (v. 14).

17:14 ***Before the morning.*** Sennacherib's army would be destroyed between evening time and morning (37:36–38). ***us.*** Isaiah identified himself with his plundered people.

18:1 ***Cush.*** Also called Ethiopia in the Bible, Cush was at the southern end of Isaiah's world. A Cushite dynasty took over Egypt in 715 B.C. and probably sent ambassadors to Jerusalem.

18:5 ***before the harvest ... cut down.*** This is another example of a bad harvest (17:10–11).

18:7 ***place of the Name.*** Note how closely the Lord identifies with Mount Zion. This was the one place for the true worship of God.

19:2 ***Egyptian against Egyptian.*** The political anarchy of the Egyptians has religious roots: their many gods failed them.

17:11 [j] Ps 90:6 [k] Hos 8:7 [l] Job 4:8 **17:12** [m] Ps 18:4; Jer 6:23; Lk 21:25 **17:13** [n] Ps 9:5 [o] Isa 13:14 [p] Isa 41:2, 15-16 [q] Job 21:18 **17:14** [r] 2Ki 19:35 **18:1** [s] Isa 20:3-5; Eze 30:4-5, 9; Zep 2:12; 3:10 **18:2** [t] Ex 2:3 [u] Ge 10:8-9; 2Ch 12:3 [v] ver 7 **18:3** [w] Isa 5:26 **18:4** [x] Isa 26:21; Hos 5:15 [y] Isa 26:19; Hos 14:5 **18:5** [z] Isa 17:10-11; Eze 17:6 **18:6** [a] Isa 56:9; Jer 7:33; Eze 32:4; 39:17 **18:7** [b] Ps 68:31 **19:1** [c] Isa 13:1; Jer 43:12 [d] Ex 12:12; Joel 3:19 [e] Ps 18:10; 104:3; Rev 1:7 [f] Jos 2:11 **19:2** [g] Jdg 7:22; Mt 10:21, 36 [h] 2Ch 20:23

3 The Egyptians will lose heart,
and I will bring their plans to nothing;
they will consult the idols and the spirits of the dead,
the mediums and the spiritists.[i]
4 I will hand the Egyptians over
to the power of a cruel master,
and a fierce king[j] will rule over them,"
declares the Lord, the LORD Almighty.

5 The waters of the river will dry up,[k]
and the riverbed will be parched and dry.
6 The canals will stink;[l]
the streams of Egypt will dwindle and dry up.[m]
The reeds and rushes will wither,[n]
7 also the plants along the Nile,
at the mouth of the river.
Every sown field[o] along the Nile
will become parched, will blow away and be no more.
8 The fishermen[p] will groan and lament,
all who cast hooks[q] into the Nile;
those who throw nets on the water
will pine away.
9 Those who work with combed flax will despair,
the weavers of fine linen[r] will lose hope.
10 The workers in cloth will be dejected,
and all the wage earners will be sick at heart.

11 The officials of Zoan[s] are nothing but fools;
the wise counselors of Pharaoh give senseless advice.
How can you say to Pharaoh,
"I am one of the wise men,[t]
a disciple of the ancient kings"?

12 Where are your wise men[u] now?
Let them show you and make known
what the LORD Almighty
has planned[v] against Egypt.
13 The officials of Zoan have become fools,
the leaders of Memphis[w] are deceived;
the cornerstones of her peoples
have led Egypt astray.
14 The LORD has poured into them
a spirit of dizziness;[x]
they make Egypt stagger in all that she does,
as a drunkard staggers around in his vomit.
15 There is nothing Egypt can do—
head or tail, palm branch or reed.[y]

16 In that day the Egyptians will become
weaklings.[z] They will shudder with fear[a] at
the uplifted hand[b] that the LORD Almighty
raises against them. 17 And the land of Judah will bring terror to the Egyptians; everyone to whom Judah is mentioned will
be terrified, because of what the LORD Almighty is planning[c] against them.
18 In that day five cities in Egypt will
speak the language of Canaan and swear
allegiance[d] to the LORD Almighty. One of
them will be called the City of the Sun.[a]
19 In that day there will be an altar[e] to the
LORD in the heart of Egypt, and a monument[f] to the LORD at its border. 20 It will be
a sign and witness to the LORD Almighty
in the land of Egypt. When they cry out to
the LORD because of their oppressors, he
will send them a savior and defender, and
he will rescue[g] them. 21 So the LORD will
make himself known to the Egyptians,
and in that day they will acknowledge[h] the
LORD. They will worship[i] with sacrifices
and grain offerings; they will make vows
to the LORD and keep them. 22 The LORD will
strike[j] Egypt with a plague; he will strike
them and heal them. They will turn[k] to the
LORD, and he will respond to their pleas
and heal[l] them.
23 In that day there will be a highway[m]
from Egypt to Assyria. The Assyrians will
go to Egypt and the Egyptians to Assyria.
The Egyptians and Assyrians will worship[n] together. 24 In that day Israel will be
the third, along with Egypt and Assyria,
a blessing[b] on the earth. 25 The LORD Almighty will bless them, saying, "Blessed be
Egypt my people,[o] Assyria my handiwork,[p]
and Israel my inheritance.[q]"

---

[a] *18* Some manuscripts of the Masoretic Text, Dead Sea Scrolls, Symmachus and Vulgate; most manuscripts of the Masoretic Text *City of Destruction* [b] *24* Or *Assyria, whose names will be used in blessings* (see Gen. 48:20); or *Assyria, who will be seen by others as blessed*

19:3 *Egyptians.* The principal key for understanding the world of ancient Egypt is the concept of order, or *ma'at*. When the spirit of the Egyptians was demoralized, they lost their sense of order and purpose. This would completely confuse and disarm any aggression and would cause economic and political upheaval.

19:13 *Memphis.* This was Noph, Egypt's ancient capital.

19:19–21 Worship—The prophets spoke of the future when the Gentile nations would come to know God and worship Him. Egypt is one of these nations for which there is a future mercy. The Egyptians will swear allegiance to the true God, institute extensive public worship of God, and become equal partners in the community of believers. This is a remarkable promise from our God, and one that is worth remembering in troubling political times.

19:25 *my people ... my handiwork.* Historically, Egypt and Assyria were enemies. When they change and turn to the Lord (symbolic of all converted

19:3 [i] Isa 8:19; 47:13; Da 2:2, 10 **19:4** [j] Isa 20:4; Jer 46:26; Eze 29:19 **19:5** [k] Jer 51:36 **19:6** [l] Ex 7:18 [m] Isa 37:25; Eze 30:12 [n] Isa 15:6 **19:7** [o] Isa 23:3 **19:8** [p] Eze 47:10 [q] Hab 1:15 **19:9** [r] Pr 7:16; Eze 27:7 **19:11** [s] Nu 13:22 [t] 1Ki 4:30; Ac 7:22 **19:12** [u] 1Co 1:20 [v] Isa 14:24; Ro 9:17 **19:13** [w] Jer 2:16; Eze 30:13, 16 **19:14** [x] Mt 17:17 **19:15** [y] Isa 9:14 **19:16** [z] Jer 51:30; Na 3:13 [a] Heb 10:31 [b] Isa 11:15 **19:17** [c] Isa 14:24 **19:18** [d] Zep 3:9 **19:19** [e] Jos 22:10 [f] Ge 28:18 **19:20** [g] Isa 49:24-26 **19:21** [h] Isa 11:9 [i] Isa 56:7; Mal 1:11 **19:22** [j] Heb 12:11 [k] Isa 45:14; Hos 14:1 [l] Dt 32:39 **19:23** [m] Isa 11:16 [n] Isa 27:13 **19:25** [o] Ps 100:3 [p] Isa 29:23; 45:11; 60:21; 64:8; Eph 2:10 [q] Hos 2:23

A Prophecy Against Egypt and Cush

20 In the year that the supreme commander,[r] sent by Sargon king of Assyria, came to Ashdod and attacked and
captured it— 2 at that time the LORD spoke
through Isaiah son of Amoz.[s] He said to
him, "Take off the sackcloth[t] from your
body and the sandals[u] from your feet."
And he did so, going around stripped[v] and
barefoot.[w]
3 Then the LORD said, "Just as my servant
Isaiah has gone stripped and barefoot for
three years, as a sign[x] and portent against
Egypt and Cush,[a][y] 4 so the king[z] of Assyria will lead away stripped and barefoot
the Egyptian captives and Cushite exiles,
young and old, with buttocks bared—to
Egypt's shame.[a] 5 Those who trusted in
Cush and boasted in Egypt[b] will be dismayed and put to shame. 6 In that day the
people who live on this coast will say, 'See
what has happened to those we relied on,
those we fled to for help[c] and deliverance
from the king of Assyria! How then can we
escape?[d]' "

A Prophecy Against Babylon

21 A prophecy against the Desert[e] by the Sea:

Like whirlwinds sweeping through the southland,[f]
an invader comes from the desert,
from a land of terror.

2 A dire[g] vision has been shown to me:
The traitor betrays,[h] the looter takes loot.
Elam,[i] attack! Media, lay siege!
I will bring to an end all the groaning she caused.

3 At this my body is racked with pain,
pangs seize me, like those of a woman in labor;[j]
I am staggered by what I hear,
I am bewildered by what I see.

4 My heart falters,
fear makes me tremble;
the twilight I longed for
has become a horror to me.

5 They set the tables,
they spread the rugs,
they eat, they drink![k]
Get up, you officers,
oil the shields!

6 This is what the Lord says to me:

"Go, post a lookout
and have him report what he sees.

7 When he sees chariots[l]
with teams of horses,
riders on donkeys
or riders on camels,
let him be alert,
fully alert."

8 And the lookout[b][m] shouted,

"Day after day, my lord, I stand on the watchtower;
every night I stay at my post.

9 Look, here comes a man in a chariot
with a team of horses.
And he gives back the answer:
'Babylon[n] has fallen,[o] has fallen!
All the images of its gods[p]
lie shattered on the ground!' "

10 My people who are crushed on the threshing floor,[q]
I tell you what I have heard
from the LORD Almighty,
from the God of Israel.

A Prophecy Against Edom

11 A prophecy against Dumah[c]:[r]

Someone calls to me from Seir,[s]
"Watchman, what is left of the night?
Watchman, what is left of the night?"

a 3 That is, the upper Nile region; also in verse 5
b 8 Dead Sea Scrolls and Syriac; Masoretic Text *A lion*
c 11 *Dumah*, a wordplay on *Edom*, means *silence* or *stillness*.

Gentiles), they will be healed (v. 22) and blessed by God.

20:2 *sackcloth.* Isaiah replaced the garb of spiritual mourning with the signs of being exiled into captivity.

20:3 *three years.* Three years means "involving three years," a minimum of 14 months, but possibly more.

20:6 *who live on this coast.* This probably refers to the nations, including Judah, bordering on the eastern shore of the Mediterranean Sea, who looked to Egypt to save them from Assyria.

21:2 *Elam ... Media.* Elam, a major part of Persia, and Media were allied in 700 B.C. Perhaps as a part of the Assyrian army (5:26), they helped to bring about the fall of Babylon in 689 B.C., since they certainly did so in 539 B.C. (11:11; 13:17).

21:4 *heart falters.* Isaiah saw that even a longed-for event can have terrible consequences in its wake. The judgment of God on Babylon would not be easy to look at.

21:7 *donkeys ... camels.* The Persians, who overthrew Babylon in 539 B.C., used donkeys and camels in their army.

21:11 *Watchman.* The watchman was the night patrol who kept watch on the city. The metaphor refers to the prophet Isaiah, who, as a guard on the walls,

20:1 [r] 2Ki 18:17 **20:2** [s] Isa 13:1 [t] Zec 13:4; Mt 3:4 [u] Eze 24:17,23 [v] 1Sa 19:24 [w] Mic 1:8 **20:3** [x] Isa 8:18 [y] Isa 37:9; 43:3 **20:4** [z] Isa 19:4 [a] Isa 47:3; Jer 13:22,26 **20:5** [b] 2Ki 18:21; Isa 30:5 **20:6** [c] Isa 10:3 [d] Jer 30:15-17; Mt 23:33; 1Th 5:3; Heb 2:3 **21:1** [e] Isa 13:21; Jer 51:43 [f] Zec 9:14 **21:2** [g] Ps 60:3 [h] Isa 33:1 [i] Isa 22:6; Jer 49:34 **21:3** [j] Ps 48:6; Isa 26:17 **21:5** [k] Jer 51:39,57; Da 5:2 **21:7** [l] ver 9 **21:8** [m] Hab 2:1 **21:9** [n] Rev 14:8 [o] Jer 51:8; Rev 18:2 [p] Isa 46:1; Jer 50:2; 51:44 **21:10** [q] Jer 51:33 **21:11** [r] Ge 25:14 [s] Ge 32:3

[12]The watchman replies,
"Morning is coming, but also the night.
If you would ask, then ask;
and come back yet again."

A Prophecy Against Arabia

[13]A prophecy[t] against Arabia:

You caravans of Dedanites,
who camp in the thickets of Arabia,
[14] bring water for the thirsty;
you who live in Tema,[u]
bring food for the fugitives.
[15]They flee[v] from the sword,
from the drawn sword,
from the bent bow
and from the heat of battle.

[16]This is what the Lord says to me:
"Within one year, as a servant bound by
contract[w] would count it, all the splendor[x]
of Kedar[y] will come to an end. [17]The survivors of the archers, the warriors of Kedar,
will be few.[z]" The LORD, the God of Israel,
has spoken.

A Prophecy About Jerusalem

22 A prophecy[a] against the Valley[b] of Vision:

What troubles you now,
that you have all gone up on the roofs,
[2]you town so full of commotion,
you city of tumult and revelry?[c]
Your slain were not killed by the sword,
nor did they die in battle.
[3]All your leaders have fled together;
they have been captured without using the bow.
All you who were caught were taken prisoner together,
having fled while the enemy was still far away.
[4]Therefore I said, "Turn away from me;
let me weep[d] bitterly.
Do not try to console me
over the destruction of my people."[e]

[5]The Lord, the LORD Almighty, has a day
of tumult and trampling and terror[f]
in the Valley of Vision,
a day of battering down walls
and of crying out to the mountains.
[6]Elam[g] takes up the quiver,[h]
with her charioteers and horses;
Kir[i] uncovers the shield.
[7]Your choicest valleys are full of chariots,
and horsemen are posted at the city gates.[j]
[8]The Lord stripped away the defenses of Judah,
and you looked in that day
to the weapons[k] in the Palace of the Forest.[l]
[9]You saw that the walls of the City of David
were broken through in many places;
you stored up water
in the Lower Pool.[m]
[10]You counted the buildings in Jerusalem
and tore down houses to strengthen the wall.
[11]You built a reservoir between the two walls[n]
for the water of the Old Pool,[o]
but you did not look to the One who made it,
or have regard for the One who planned it long ago.

[12]The Lord, the LORD Almighty,
called you on that day
to weep[p] and to wail,
to tear out your hair[q] and put on sackcloth.[r]
[13]But see, there is joy and revelry,
slaughtering of cattle and killing of sheep,
eating of meat and drinking of wine![s]
"Let us eat and drink," you say,
"for tomorrow we die!"[t]

[14]The LORD Almighty has revealed this
in my hearing:[u] "Till your dying day this
sin will not be atoned[v] for," says the Lord,
the LORD Almighty.

[15]This is what the Lord, the LORD Almighty, says:

"Go, say to this steward,
to Shebna[w] the palace administrator:
[16]What are you doing here and who gave you permission
to cut out a grave[x] for yourself here,
hewing your grave on the height
and chiseling your resting place in the rock?

[17]"Beware, the LORD is about to take firm hold of you
and hurl you away, you mighty man.

---

could see the dawn — the light of salvation — in the east before the others.

21:13 ***caravans of Dedanites.*** The Dedanites may refer to the refugees (v. 15) from Dedan, which was about 90 miles southeast of Tema (v. 14).

22:11 ***reservoir between the two walls.*** The defense of the city depended upon the availability of water within its walls. Hezekiah addressed this need by digging a tunnel beneath the city, connecting the lower pool in Jerusalem's southwestern valley with the old pool, the source of water in the eastern valley.

21:13 [t] Isa 13:1 **21:14** [u] Ge 25:15 **21:15** [v] Isa 13:14 **21:16** [w] Isa 16:14 [x] Isa 17:3 [y] Ps 120:5; Isa 60:7 **21:17** [z] Isa 10:19 **22:1** [a] Isa 13:1 [b] Ps 125:2; Jer 21:13; Joel 3:2, 12, 14 **22:2** [c] Isa 32:13 **22:4** [d] Isa 15:3; Lk 19:41 [e] Jer 9:1 **22:5** [f] La 1:5 **22:6** [g] Isa 21:2 [h] Jer 49:35 [i] 2Ki 16:9 **22:7** [j] 2Ch 32:1-2 **22:8** [k] 2Ch 32:5 [l] 1Ki 7:2 **22:9** [m] 2Ch 32:4 **22:11** [n] 2Ki 25:4; Jer 39:4 [o] 2Ch 32:4 **22:12** [p] Joel 2:17 [q] Mic 1:16 [r] Joel 1:13 **22:13** [s] Isa 5:22; 28:7-8; 56:12; Lk 17:26-29 [t] 1Co 15:32* **22:14** [u] Isa 5:9 [v] Isa 13:11; 26:21; 30:13-14; Eze 24:13 **22:15** [w] 2Ki 18:18; Isa 36:3 **22:16** [x] Mt 27:60

[18]He will roll you up tightly like a ball
and throw[y] you into a large country.
There you will die
and there the chariots you were so proud of
will become a disgrace to your master's house.
[19]I will depose you from your office,
and you will be ousted from your position.

[20]"In that day I will summon my servant,
Eliakim[z] son of Hilkiah. [21]I will clothe
him with your robe and fasten your sash
around him and hand your authority over
to him. He will be a father to those who live
in Jerusalem and to the people of Judah. [22]I
will place on his shoulder the key[a] to the
house of David;[b] what he opens no one can
shut, and what he shuts no one can open.[c]
[23]I will drive him like a peg[d] into a firm
place;[e] he will become a seat[α] of honor[f] for
the house of his father. [24]All the glory of his
family will hang on him: its offspring and
offshoots—all its lesser vessels, from the
bowls to all the jars.

[25]"In that day," declares the LORD Almighty, "the peg[g] driven into the firm place
will give way; it will be sheared off and will
fall, and the load hanging on it will be cut
down." The LORD has spoken.[h]

A Prophecy Against Tyre

23 A prophecy against Tyre:[i]

Wail, you ships[j] of Tarshish![k]
For Tyre is destroyed
and left without house or harbor.
From the land of Cyprus
word has come to them.

[2]Be silent, you people of the island
and you merchants of Sidon,
whom the seafarers have enriched.
[3]On the great waters
came the grain of the Shihor;
the harvest of the Nile[b][l] was the revenue of Tyre,[m]
and she became the marketplace of the nations.

[4]Be ashamed, Sidon,[n] and you fortress of the sea,
for the sea has spoken:
"I have neither been in labor nor given birth;
I have neither reared sons nor
brought up daughters."
[5]When word comes to Egypt,
they will be in anguish at the report from Tyre.

[6]Cross over to Tarshish;
wail, you people of the island.
[7]Is this your city of revelry,[o]
the old, old city,
whose feet have taken her
to settle in far-off lands?
[8]Who planned this against Tyre,
the bestower of crowns,
whose merchants are princes,
whose traders are renowned in the earth?
[9]The LORD Almighty planned it,
to bring down[p] her pride in all her splendor
and to humble[q] all who are renowned[r] on the earth.

[10]Till[c] your land as they do along the Nile,
Daughter Tarshish,
for you no longer have a harbor.
[11]The LORD has stretched out his hand[s] over the sea
and made its kingdoms tremble.
He has given an order concerning Phoenicia
that her fortresses be destroyed.[t]
[12]He said, "No more of your reveling,[u]
Virgin Daughter[v] Sidon, now crushed!

"Up, cross over to Cyprus;
even there you will find no rest."
[13]Look at the land of the Babylonians,[d]
this people that is now of no account!
The Assyrians[w] have made it
a place for desert creatures;
they raised up their siege towers,
they stripped its fortresses bare
and turned it into a ruin.[x]

[14]Wail, you ships of Tarshish;[y]
your fortress is destroyed!

[15]At that time Tyre[z] will be forgotten for
seventy years, the span of a king's life. But
at the end of these seventy years, it will happen to Tyre as in the song of the prostitute:

[α] *23 Or throne* [b] *2,3* Masoretic Text; Dead Sea Scrolls *Sidon, / who cross over the sea; / your envoys [3]are on the great waters. / The grain of the Shihor, / the harvest of the Nile,* [c] *10* Dead Sea Scrolls and some Septuagint manuscripts; Masoretic Text *Go through* [d] *13* Or *Chaldeans*

22:25 *peg ... be cut down.* Even the firmly reliable Eliakim could not sustain the burden of government. Only Immanuel could do that (9:6–7).
23:1 *Tyre.* Tyre was besieged several times over a period of about 400 years before it was finally laid waste by Alexander the Great in 332 B.C.
23:6 *Tarshish.* Tarshish is Tartessus in Spain and represents the most distant place to the ancient Israelites.
23:15 *seventy years.* Seventy years symbolizes a full measure of time, a lifetime.

22:18 [y] Isa 17:13 **22:20** [z] 2Ki 18:18; Isa 36:3
22:22 [a] Rev 3:7 [b] Isa 7:2 [c] Job 12:14
22:23 [d] Zec 10:4 [e] Ezr 9:8 [f] 1Sa 2:7-8; Job 36:7
22:25 [g] ver 23 [h] Isa 46:11; Mic 4:4 **23:1** [i] Jos 19:29; 1Ki 5:1; Jer 47:4; Eze 26,27,28; Joel 3:4-8; Am 1:9-10; Zec 9:2-4 [j] 1Ki 10:22 [k] Ge 10:4; Isa 2:16 *fn*
23:3 [l] Isa 19:7 [m] Eze 27:3 **23:4** [n] Ge 10:15, 19
23:7 [o] Isa 22:2; 32:13 **23:9** [p] Job 40:11 [q] Isa 13:11 [r] Isa 5:13; 9:15 **23:11** [s] Ex 14:21 [t] Isa 25:2; Zec 9:3-4
23:12 [u] Rev 18:22 [v] Isa 47:1 **23:13** [w] Isa 10:5 [x] Isa 10:7
23:14 [y] Isa 2:16 *fn* **23:15** [z] Jer 25:22

16 "Take up a harp, walk through the city,
you forgotten prostitute;
play the harp well, sing many a song,
so that you will be remembered."

17 At the end of seventy years, the LORD
will deal with Tyre. She will return to her
lucrative prostitution[a] and will ply her
trade with all the kingdoms on the face of
the earth. 18 Yet her profit and her earnings
will be set apart for the LORD;[b] they will not
be stored up or hoarded. Her profits will
go to those who live before the LORD,[c] for
abundant food and fine clothes.

The LORD's Devastation of the Earth

24 See, the LORD is going to lay waste
the earth[d]
and devastate it;
he will ruin its face
and scatter its inhabitants—
2 it will be the same
for priest as for people,[e]
for the master as for his servant,
for the mistress as for her servant,
for seller as for buyer,[f]
for borrower as for lender,
for debtor as for creditor.[g]
3 The earth will be completely laid waste
and totally plundered.[h]
The LORD has spoken this word.

4 The earth dries up and withers,
the world languishes and withers,
the heavens[i] languish with the
earth.
5 The earth is defiled[j] by its people;
they have disobeyed[k] the laws,
violated the statutes
and broken the everlasting
covenant.
6 Therefore a curse consumes the earth;
its people must bear their guilt.
Therefore earth's inhabitants are
burned up,[l]
and very few are left.
7 The new wine dries up and the vine
withers;[m]
all the merrymakers groan.[n]
8 The joyful timbrels[o] are stilled,
the noise[p] of the revelers has stopped,
the joyful harp[q] is silent.[r]
9 No longer do they drink wine[s] with a
song;
the beer is bitter[t] to its drinkers.
10 The ruined city lies desolate;
the entrance to every house is barred.
11 In the streets they cry out for wine;
all joy turns to gloom,[u]
all joyful sounds are banished from
the earth.
12 The city is left in ruins,
its gate is battered to pieces.
13 So will it be on the earth
and among the nations,
as when an olive tree is beaten,[v]
or as when gleanings are left after
the grape harvest.

14 They raise their voices, they shout for
joy;[w]
from the west they acclaim the
LORD's majesty.
15 Therefore in the east give glory[x] to the
LORD;
exalt[y] the name of the LORD, the God
of Israel,
in the islands of the sea.
16 From the ends of the earth we hear
singing:
"Glory[z] to the Righteous One."

But I said, "I waste away, I waste away!
Woe to me!
The treacherous betray!
With treachery the treacherous
betray![a]"

23:18 ***her profit ... set apart for the LORD.*** This was not a violation of God's command (Deut. 23:18) which forbade bringing a harlot's pay (v. 17) to the temple. Tyre's destruction was part of the Lord's war against the unrighteous. The spoils would belong to Him as the Victor (Deut. 2:35; Josh. 6:17,19).

24:1–27:12 ***See, the LORD.*** The section describing the Lord's "prophecies" against particular nations (ch. 13–23) is now placed in a larger framework that shows God's triumph over the entire earth for His elect. Chapter 24 focuses on God's overthrow of the corrupted earth; chapter 25 focuses on the responsive praise to His actions. Chapters 26 and 27 focus on God's efforts for His people.

24:4 ***The earth dries up and withers.*** For a similar idea, see Romans 8:22.

24:5 ***laws ... statutes ... covenant.*** The usual language concerning a breach of the covenant is applied more generally to the wicked nations. Perhaps these words speak of that innate sense of right and wrong—the conscience—that God has given to all mankind, but which everyone violates (Acts 24:16; Rom. 1:18–32).

24:14–16 ***raise their voices.*** Isaiah cannot join in the chorus of praise, because he, like Daniel (Dan. 7:28; 8:27), was too overwhelmed by the tragedy that was to come. It is impossible to tell whether the people who praised the Lord were faithful followers who had been oppressed by the treacherous leaders, or whether those who praised were the unfaithful leaders who were beginning to remember the Lord. There comes a time when the Lord does not wait any more, but He carries out the promised punishment for sinful behavior. Those who have trusted in Him will always find their souls secure, but that does not mean that they will not see dreadful sights or perhaps even be martyred for their faith.

23:17 [a] Eze 16:26; Na 3:4; Rev 17:1 **23:18** [b] Ex 28:36; Ps 72:10 [c] Isa 60:5-9; Mic 4:13 **24:1** [d] ver 20; Isa 2:19-21; 33:9 **24:2** [e] Hos 4:9 [f] Eze 7:12 [g] Lev 25:35-37; Dt 23:19-20 **24:3** [h] Isa 6:11-12 **24:4** [i] Isa 2:12 **24:5** [j] Ge 3:17; Nu 35:33 [k] Isa 10:6; 59:12 **24:6** [l] Isa 1:31 **24:7** [m] Joel 1:10-12 [n] Isa 16:8-10 **24:8** [o] Isa 5:12 [p] Jer 7:34; 16:9; 25:10; Hos 2:11 [q] Rev 18:22 [r] Eze 26:13 **24:9** [s] Isa 5:11,22 [t] Isa 5:20 **24:11** [u] Isa 16:10; 32:13; Jer 14:3 **24:13** [v] Isa 17:6 **24:14** [w] Isa 12:6 **24:15** [x] Isa 66:19 [y] Isa 25:3; Mal 1:11 **24:16** [z] Isa 28:5 [a] Isa 21:2; Jer 5:11

17 Terror and pit and snare[b] await you,
people of the earth.
18 Whoever flees at the sound of terror
will fall into a pit;
whoever climbs out of the pit
will be caught in a snare.
The floodgates of the heavens[c] are
opened,
the foundations of the earth shake.[d]
19 The earth is broken up,
the earth is split asunder,[e]
the earth is violently shaken.
20 The earth reels like a drunkard,[f]
it sways like a hut in the wind;
so heavy upon it is the guilt of its
rebellion[g]
that it falls—never to rise again.

21 In that day the LORD will punish[h]
the powers in the heavens above
and the kings on the earth below.
22 They will be herded together
like prisoners[i] bound in a dungeon;[j]
they will be shut up in prison
and be punished[a] after many days.[k]
23 The moon will be dismayed,
the sun[l] ashamed;
for the LORD Almighty will reign[m]
on Mount Zion[n] and in Jerusalem,
and before its elders—with great
glory.[o]

Praise to the LORD

25 LORD, you are my God;
I will exalt you and praise your
name,
for in perfect faithfulness
you have done wonderful things,[p]
things planned[q] long ago.
2 You have made the city a heap of
rubble,[r]
the fortified[s] town a ruin,
the foreigners' stronghold[t] a city no
more;
it will never be rebuilt.
3 Therefore strong peoples will honor
you;
cities of ruthless[u] nations will revere
you.
4 You have been a refuge[v] for the poor,
a refuge for the needy in their
distress,
a shelter from the storm
and a shade from the heat.
For the breath of the ruthless[w]
is like a storm driving against a
wall
5 and like the heat of the desert.
You silence[x] the uproar of
foreigners;
as heat is reduced by the shadow of a
cloud,
so the song of the ruthless is stilled.

6 On this mountain[y] the LORD Almighty
will prepare
a feast[z] of rich food for all peoples,
a banquet of aged wine—
the best of meats and the finest of
wines.[a]
7 On this mountain he will destroy
the shroud[b] that enfolds all
peoples,
the sheet that covers all nations;
8 he will swallow up death[c] forever.
The Sovereign LORD will wipe away the
tears[d]
from all faces;
he will remove his people's disgrace[e]
from all the earth.
The LORD has spoken.

9 In that day they will say,

"Surely this is our God;[f]
we trusted in him, and he saved[g] us.
This is the LORD, we trusted in him;
let us rejoice[h] and be glad in his
salvation."

10 The hand of the LORD will rest on this
mountain;
but Moab[i] will be trampled in their
land
as straw is trampled down in the
manure.
11 They will stretch out their hands in it,
as swimmers stretch out their hands
to swim.
God will bring down[j] their pride[k]
despite the cleverness[b] of their
hands.
12 He will bring down your high fortified
walls
and lay them low;[l]
he will bring them down to the ground,
to the very dust.

---

a 22 Or *released* *b* 11 The meaning of the Hebrew for this word is uncertain.

24:21 ***that day.*** "That day" is the day that the Lord will finally judge the whole world (Rev. 20:11 – 15).
25:5 ***ruthless.*** The use of the term "ruthless" three times in verses 3 – 5 emphasizes divine judgment on the nations represented.
25:8 ***wipe away the tears.*** When the first earth passes away and the tabernacle of God is among men, finally the whole creation will be as it should be, and God will tenderly wipe away the tears of his people (Rev. 7:17; 21:4).

24:17 [b] Jer 48:43 **24:18** [c] Ge 7:11 [d] Ps 18:7 **24:19** [e] Dt 11:6 **24:20** [f] Isa 19:14 [g] Isa 1:2,28; 43:27 **24:21** [h] Isa 10:12 **24:22** [i] Isa 10:4 [j] Isa 42:7,22 [k] Eze 38:8 **24:23** [l] Isa 13:10 [m] Rev 22:5 [n] Heb 12:22 [o] Isa 60:19 **25:1** [p] Ps 98:1 [q] Nu 23:19 **25:2** [r] Isa 17:1 [s] Isa 17:3 [t] Isa 13:22 **25:3** [u] Isa 13:11 **25:4** [v] Isa 4:6; 17:10; 27:5; 33:16 [w] Isa 29:5; 49:25 **25:5** [x] Jer 51:55 **25:6** [y] Isa 2:2 [z] Isa 1:19; Mt 8:11; 22:4 [a] Pr 9:2 **25:7** [b] 2Co 3:15-16; Eph 4:18 **25:8** [c] Hos 13:14; 1Co 15:54-55* [d] Isa 30:19; 35:10; 51:11; 65:19; Rev 7:17; 21:4 [e] Mt 5:11; 1Pe 4:14 **25:9** [f] Isa 40:9 [g] Ps 20:5; Isa 33:22; 35:4; 49:25-26; 60:16 [h] Isa 35:2,10 **25:10** [i] Am 2:1-3 **25:11** [j] Isa 5:25; 14:26; 16:14 [k] Job 40:12 **25:12** [l] Isa 15:1

A Song of Praise

26 In that day this song will be sung in the land of Judah:

We have a strong city;[m]
God makes salvation
its walls[n] and ramparts.
2 Open the gates
that the righteous[o] nation may enter,
the nation that keeps faith.
3 You will keep in perfect peace
those whose minds are steadfast,
because they trust in you.
4 Trust[p] in the LORD forever,
for the LORD, the LORD himself, is the Rock eternal.
5 He humbles those who dwell on high,
he lays the lofty city low;
he levels it to the ground[q]
and casts it down to the dust.
6 Feet trample it down—
the feet of the oppressed,
the footsteps of the poor.[r]

7 The path of the righteous is level;
you, the Upright One, make the way of the righteous smooth.[s]
8 Yes, LORD, walking in the way of your laws,[a][t]
we wait for you;
your name[u] and renown
are the desire of our hearts.
9 My soul yearns for you in the night;
in the morning my spirit longs[v] for you.
When your judgments come upon the earth,
the people of the world learn righteousness.[w]
10 But when grace is shown to the wicked,
they do not learn righteousness;
even in a land of uprightness they go on doing evil[x]
and do not regard[y] the majesty of the LORD.
11 LORD, your hand is lifted high,
but they do not see[z] it.
Let them see your zeal for your people
and be put to shame;
let the fire[a] reserved for your enemies
consume them.

12 LORD, you establish peace for us;
all that we have accomplished you have done for us.
13 LORD our God, other lords[b] besides you
have ruled over us,
but your name alone do we honor.[c]
14 They are now dead,[d] they live no more;
their spirits do not rise.
You punished them and brought them to ruin;[e]
you wiped out all memory of them.
15 You have enlarged the nation, LORD;
you have enlarged the nation.
You have gained glory for yourself;
you have extended all the borders[f] of the land.

16 LORD, they came to you in their distress;[g]
when you disciplined them,
they could barely whisper a prayer.[b]
17 As a pregnant woman about to give birth[h]
writhes and cries out in her pain,
so were we in your presence, LORD.
18 We were with child, we writhed in labor,
but we gave birth[i] to wind.
We have not brought salvation[j] to the earth,
and the people of the world have not come to life.

19 But your dead[k] will live, LORD;
their bodies will rise—
let those who dwell in the dust
wake up and shout for joy—
your dew is like the dew of the morning;
the earth will give birth to her dead.[l]

20 Go, my people, enter your rooms
and shut the doors[m] behind you;
hide[n] yourselves for a little while
until his wrath has passed by.[o]
21 See, the LORD is coming[p] out of his dwelling[q]
to punish[r] the people of the earth for their sins.
The earth will disclose the blood[s] shed on it;
the earth will conceal its slain no longer.

---

[a] 8 Or *judgments* [b] 16 The meaning of the Hebrew for this clause is uncertain.

26:3 *peace.* The result of a settled faith in God is "perfect peace." Faith in God is the only thing that brings inner peace to man. One must come to the point of recognizing his own utter sinfulness and his deep need of a redeemer before he can find peace. Only when one is at peace with God can he have peace with others. Only a mind settled in God can tolerate the changing circumstances of life.

26:8 *wait.* Waiting for—or on—the Lord is a waiting with expectation. Perhaps one could describe it as the difference between waiting for the arrival of an airplane with a loved one arriving, and the waiting one does at a traffic light. (For a similar idea, see 40:31.)

26:18 *gave birth to wind.* Even the faithful followers of the Lord cannot bring new life to the earth. Only God can regenerate the world and its inhabitants. The new life can come only through Jesus Christ, whose coming was still in the future at the time of Isaiah's writing.

26:21 *The earth will disclose the blood shed on it.* In that day of judgment, there will be no unsolved murders, no injustice that is unrevealed.

26:1 [m] Isa 14:32 [n] Isa 60:18 **26:2** [o] Isa 54:14; 58:8; 62:2 **26:4** [p] Isa 12:2; 50:10 **26:5** [q] Isa 25:12 **26:6** [r] Isa 3:15 **26:7** [s] Isa 42:16 **26:8** [t] Isa 56:1 [u] Isa 12:4 **26:9** [v] Ps 63:1; 78:34; Isa 55:6 [w] Mt 6:33 **26:10** [x] Isa 32:6 [y] Isa 22:12-13; Hos 11:7; Jn 5:37-38; Ro 2:4 **26:11** [z] Isa 44:9, 18 [a] Heb 10:27 **26:13** [b] Isa 2:8; 10:5, 11 [c] Isa 63:7 **26:14** [d] Dt 4:28 [e] Isa 10:3 **26:15** [f] Isa 33:17 **26:16** [g] Hos 5:15 **26:17** [h] Jn 16:21 **26:18** [i] Isa 33:11; 59:4 [j] Ps 17:14 **26:19** [k] Isa 25:8; Eph 5:14 [l] Eze 37:1-14; Da 12:2 **26:20** [m] Ex 12:23 [n] Ps 91:1, 4 [o] Ps 30:5; Isa 54:7-8 **26:21** [p] Jude 1:14 [q] Mic 1:3 [r] Isa 13:9, 11; 30:12-14 [s] Job 16:18; Lk 11:50-51

Deliverance of Israel

27 In that day,

the LORD will punish with his sword[t]—
his fierce, great and powerful sword—
Leviathan[u] the gliding serpent,
Leviathan the coiling serpent;
he will slay the monster[v] of the sea.

2 In that day—

"Sing about a fruitful vineyard:[w]
3 I, the LORD, watch over it;
I water[x] it continually.
I guard it day and night
so that no one may harm it.
4 I am not angry.
If only there were briers and thorns confronting me!
I would march against them in battle;
I would set them all on fire.[y]
5 Or else let them come to me for refuge;[z]
let them make peace[a] with me,
yes, let them make peace with me."

6 In days to come Jacob will take root,
Israel will bud and blossom[b]
and fill all the world with fruit.[c]

7 Has the LORD struck her
as he struck[d] down those who struck her?
Has she been killed
as those were killed who killed her?
8 By warfare[a] and exile[e] you contend with her—
with his fierce blast he drives her out,
as on a day the east wind blows.
9 By this, then, will Jacob's guilt be atoned for,
and this will be the full fruit of the removal of his sin:[f]
When he makes all the altar stones
to be like limestone crushed to pieces,
no Asherah poles[b][g] or incense altars
will be left standing.
10 The fortified city stands desolate,[h]
an abandoned settlement, forsaken like the wilderness;
there the calves graze,
there they lie down;[i]
they strip its branches bare.
11 When its twigs are dry, they are broken off
and women come and make fires with them.
For this is a people without understanding;[j]
so their Maker has no compassion on them,
and their Creator[k] shows them no favor.[l]

12 In that day the LORD will thresh from
the flowing Euphrates to the Wadi of
Egypt,[m] and you, Israel, will be gathered[n]
up one by one. 13 And in that day a great
trumpet[o] will sound. Those who were perishing in Assyria and those who were exiled in Egypt[p] will come and worship the
LORD on the holy mountain in Jerusalem.

Woe to the Leaders of Ephraim and Judah

28 Woe to that wreath, the pride of Ephraim's[q] drunkards,
to the fading flower, his glorious beauty,
set on the head of a fertile valley[r]—
to that city, the pride of those laid low by wine![s]

[a] *8* See Septuagint; the meaning of the Hebrew for this word is uncertain. [b] *9* That is, wooden symbols of the goddess Asherah

27:1 ***punish.*** The punishment in this verse links it with 26:21; this verse is the climax of the preceding section. ***Leviathan.*** This creature was used to poetically describe various evil forces over which God has ultimate control and victory (Job 3:8; Ps. 74:14). Eventually Leviathan (Job 41:1) became a symbol for Satan, who is "the dragon, that ancient serpent" (Rev. 20:2).

27:2 ***vineyard.*** The vineyard is Israel (5:7; 27:6). The language of the vineyard is used frequently in Scripture. The good vines are planted or cared for by God and His servants. They are supposed to bear good fruit and be worthy of the care of the Master. Sometimes the fruit is bad, sometimes the servants are unfaithful, but the vines always belong to God (Matt. 21:33–46; Mark 12:1–12; Luke 20:9–19).

27:3 ***watch over it . . . water it.*** The "watcher" of the vineyard contrasts with the one who will lay waste, and watering it "continually" contrasts with the lack of "rain" in 5:6.

27:12 ***thresh . . . be gathered.*** Threshing and gathering describe how the grain is separated from the chaff. The grain is saved or "gathered," and the chaff is thrown away. Threshing can be accomplished by beating the grain heads with flails or driving a cart over the grain to separate the grain from the stalks and husks. The grain is then gathered in baskets and tossed in the air, where the wind blows away the chaff and bits of straw, and the ripe grain falls back down into the basket.

28:1 ***wreath.*** The "wreath" on Ephraim's drunkards is part of a word picture (v. 3) contrasting the debasing actions of a drunkard with the crown of flowers, which was customary to wear at feasts. The incongruity of this image parallels God's view of the debauchery of the Israelites in the beautiful land He had given them.

27:1 [t] Isa 34:6; 66:16 [u] Job 3:8 [v] Ps 74:13 **27:2** [w] Jer 2:21 **27:3** [x] Isa 58:11 **27:4** [y] Isa 10:17; Mt 3:12; Heb 6:8 **27:5** [z] Isa 25:4 [a] Job 22:21; Ro 5:1; 2Co 5:20 **27:6** [b] Hos 14:5-6 [c] Isa 37:31 **27:7** [d] Isa 37:36-38 **27:8** [e] Isa 50:1; 54:7 **27:9** [f] Ro 11:27* [g] Ex 34:13 **27:10** [h] Isa 32:14; Jer 26:6 [i] Isa 17:2 **27:11** [j] Dt 32:28; Isa 1:3; Jer 8:7 [k] Dt 32:18; Isa 43:1, 7, 15; 44:1-2, 21, 24 [l] Isa 9:17 **27:12** [m] Ge 15:18 [n] Dt 30:4; Isa 11:12; 17:6 **27:13** [o] Lev 25:9; Mt 24:31 [p] Isa 19:21, 25 **28:1** [q] ver 3; Isa 9:9 [r] ver 4 [s] Hos 7:5

2 See, the Lord has one who is powerful[t]
and strong.
Like a hailstorm[u] and a destructive
wind,[v]
like a driving rain and a flooding[w]
downpour,
he will throw it forcefully to the
ground.
3 That wreath, the pride of Ephraim's[x]
drunkards,
will be trampled underfoot.
4 That fading flower, his glorious beauty,
set on the head of a fertile valley,[y]
will be like figs[z] ripe before harvest—
as soon as people see them and take
them in hand,
they swallow them.

5 In that day the LORD Almighty
will be a glorious crown,[a]
a beautiful wreath
for the remnant of his people.
6 He will be a spirit of justice[b]
to the one who sits in judgment,[c]
a source of strength
to those who turn back the battle[d] at
the gate.
7 And these also stagger from wine[e]
and reel[f] from beer:
Priests[g] and prophets[h] stagger from
beer
and are befuddled with wine;
they reel from beer,
they stagger when seeing visions,[i]
they stumble when rendering
decisions.
8 All the tables are covered with vomit[j]
and there is not a spot without filth.

9 "Who is it he is trying to teach?[k]
To whom is he explaining his
message?
To children weaned[l] from their milk,[m]
to those just taken from the breast?
10 For it is:
Do this, do that,
a rule for this, a rule for that[a];
a little here, a little there."

11 Very well then, with foreign lips and
strange tongues[n]
God will speak to this people,[o]
12 to whom he said,
"This is the resting place, let the
weary rest";[p]
and, "This is the place of repose"—
but they would not listen.
13 So then, the word of the LORD to them
will become:
Do this, do that,
a rule for this, a rule for that;
a little here, a little there—
so that as they go they will fall
backward;
they will be injured[q] and snared and
captured.[r]

14 Therefore hear the word of the LORD,[s]
you scoffers
who rule this people in Jerusalem.
15 You boast, "We have entered into a
covenant with death,
with the realm of the dead we have
made an agreement.
When an overwhelming scourge
sweeps by,[t]
it cannot touch us,
for we have made a lie[u] our refuge
and falsehood[b] our hiding place.[v]"

16 So this is what the Sovereign LORD
says:

"See, I lay a stone in Zion, a tested
stone,[w]
a precious cornerstone for a sure
foundation;
the one who relies on it
will never be stricken with panic.[x]
17 I will make justice[y] the measuring line
and righteousness the plumb line;[z]
hail will sweep away your refuge, the lie,
and water will overflow your hiding
place.
18 Your covenant with death will be
annulled;
your agreement with the realm of the
dead will not stand.[a]
When the overwhelming scourge
sweeps by,[b]
you will be beaten down[c] by it.

---

[a] *10* Hebrew / *sav lasav sav lasav / kav lakav kav lakav* (probably meaningless sounds mimicking the prophet's words); also in verse 13 [b] *15* Or *false gods*

28:5 *glorious crown.* The crown of the Lord of Hosts, which is Himself, sits in true beauty on the remnant of His people. Unlike the fading beauty of the crown of flowers, the glorious crown will be a lasting beauty.

28:9 *those just taken.* A child was weaned between the ages of three and five, the time for elementary moral education, which is described in verse 10.

28:13 *fall backward . . . injured.* In keeping with their drunken habits, the people would not be able to hear the teaching of the Lord.

28:14 *scoffers.* The scoffers, or scornful, are worse than "fools." Beyond choosing what is bad, they despise what is good (Ps. 1:1).

28:16 *precious cornerstone.* The apostles identified the cornerstone as Jesus Christ (1 Pet. 2:4–6).

28:2 [t] Isa 40:10 [u] Isa 30:30; Eze 13:11 [v] Isa 29:6 [w] Isa 8:7
28:3 [x] ver 1 **28:4** [y] ver 1 [z] Hos 9:10; Na 3:12
28:5 [a] Isa 62:3 **28:6** [b] Isa 11:2-4; 32:1, 16 [c] Jn 5:30
[d] 2Ch 32:8 **28:7** [e] Isa 22:13 [f] Isa 56:10-12 [g] Isa 24:2
[h] Isa 9:15 [i] Isa 29:11; Hos 4:11 **28:8** [j] Jer 48:26
28:9 [k] ver 26; Isa 30:20; 48:17; 50:4; 54:13 [l] Ps 131:2
[m] Heb 5:12-13 **28:11** [n] Isa 33:19 [o] 1Co 14:21*
28:12 [p] Isa 11:10; Mt 11:28-29 **28:13** [q] Mt 21:44 [r] Isa 8:15
28:14 [s] Isa 1:10 **28:15** [t] ver 2, 18; Isa 8:7-8; 30:28;
Da 11:22 [u] Isa 9:15 [v] Isa 29:15 **28:16** [w] Ps 118:22;
Isa 8:14-15; Mt 21:42; Ac 4:11; Eph 2:20 [x] Ro 9:33*; 10:11*;
1Pe 2:6* **28:17** [y] Isa 5:16 [z] 2Ki 21:13 **28:18** [a] Isa 7:7
[b] ver 15 [c] Da 8:13

19 As often as it comes it will carry you
away;[d]
morning after morning, by day and
by night,
it will sweep through."
The understanding of this message
will bring sheer terror.[e]
20 The bed is too short to stretch out on,
the blanket too narrow to wrap
around you.[f]
21 The LORD will rise up as he did at
Mount Perazim,[g]
he will rouse himself as in the Valley
of Gibeon[h]—
to do his work,[i] his strange work,
and perform his task, his alien task.
22 Now stop your mocking,
or your chains will become heavier;
the Lord, the LORD Almighty, has
told me
of the destruction decreed[j] against
the whole land.[k]

23 Listen and hear my voice;
pay attention and hear what I say.
24 When a farmer plows for planting, does
he plow continually?
Does he keep on breaking up and
working the soil?
25 When he has leveled the surface,
does he not sow caraway and scatter
cumin?[l]
Does he not plant wheat in its place,[a]
barley in its plot,[a]
and spelt[m] in its field?
26 His God instructs him
and teaches him the right way.
27 Caraway is not threshed with a sledge,
nor is the wheel of a cart rolled over
cumin;
caraway is beaten out with a rod,
and cumin with a stick.
28 Grain must be ground to make bread;
so one does not go on threshing it
forever.
The wheels of a threshing cart may be
rolled over it,
but one does not use horses to grind
grain.
29 All this also comes from the LORD
Almighty,
whose plan is wonderful,[n]
whose wisdom is magnificent.[o]

Woe to David's City

29 Woe[p] to you, Ariel, Ariel,[q]
the city where David settled!
Add year to year
and let your cycle of festivals[r] go on.
2 Yet I will besiege Ariel;
she will mourn and lament,[s]
she will be to me like an altar
hearth.[b]
3 I will encamp against you on all sides;
I will encircle[t] you with towers
and set up my siege works against
you.
4 Brought low, you will speak from the
ground;
your speech will mumble[u] out of the
dust.
Your voice will come ghostlike from the
earth;
out of the dust your speech will
whisper.

5 But your many enemies will become
like fine dust,
the ruthless hordes like blown chaff.[v]
Suddenly,[w] in an instant,
6 the LORD Almighty will come
with thunder and earthquake[x] and
great noise,
with windstorm and tempest and
flames of a devouring fire.
7 Then the hordes of all the nations[y] that
fight against Ariel,
that attack her and her fortress and
besiege her,
will be as it is with a dream,[z]
with a vision in the night—

[a] 25 The meaning of the Hebrew for this word is uncertain. [b] 2 The Hebrew for *altar hearth* sounds like the Hebrew for *Ariel*.

28:20 *bed ... blanket.* The word picture of the short bed and inadequate covering is an illustration of the inadequacy of any security that is not based on a relationship with the Living God as He has outlined it in Scripture.

28:27 *Caraway ... threshed with a sledge.* Caraway cannot be threshed with a sledge. The cart and sledge are too large for such a fine seed (27:12).

28:29 *plan is wonderful.* The wisdom that the farmer uses to tend his crops comes from God, the source of all good counsel.

29:1 *Ariel.* Ariel probably means "altar" (Ezek. 43:15–16). The destruction and bloodshed in Jerusalem would make the city appear like an altar. The repetition of the term *Ariel* indicates the Lord's sorrow over the state to which His city had fallen. ***where David settled.*** David made Jerusalem his capital and planned the temple that Solomon later built in that city. These words show God's continuing love for His servant David.

29:7 *as it is with a dream.* No city has suffered desolation and later been rebuilt like Jerusalem. One final time the fires of God's wrath will be allowed to burn on the City of Peace. God's eternal purpose will bring the city to its knees. Judgment is God's unwilling work. He never allows the fires of discipline to punish His own for no reason. When His disciplines have accomplished His task, peace is sure to follow.

28:19 [d] 2Ki 24:2 [e] Job 18:11 **28:20** [f] Isa 59:6 **28:21** [g] 1Ch 14:11 [h] Jos 10:10, 12; 1Ch 14:16 [i] Isa 10:12; Lk 19:41-44 **28:22** [j] Isa 10:22 [k] Isa 10:23 **28:25** [l] Mt 23:23 [m] Ex 9:32 **28:29** [n] Isa 9:6 [o] Ro 11:33 **29:1** [p] Isa 22:12-13 [q] 2Sa 5:9 [r] Isa 1:14 **29:2** [s] Isa 3:26; La 2:5 **29:3** [t] Lk 19:43 44 **29:4** [u] Isa 8:19 **29:5** [v] Isa 17:13 [w] Isa 17:14; 1Th 5:3 **29:6** [x] Mt 24:7; Mk 13:8; Lk 21:11; Rev 11:19 **29:7** [y] Mic 4:11-12; Zec 12:9 [z] Job 20:8

8 as when a hungry person dreams of
eating,
but awakens[a] hungry still;
as when a thirsty person dreams of
drinking,
but awakens faint and thirsty still.
So will it be with the hordes of all the
nations
that fight against Mount Zion.

9 Be stunned and amazed,
blind yourselves and be sightless;
be drunk,[b] but not from wine,[c]
stagger, but not from beer.
10 The LORD has brought over you a deep
sleep:
He has sealed your eyes[d] (the
prophets);[e]
he has covered your heads (the
seers).[f]

11 For you this whole vision is nothing but
words sealed[g] in a scroll. And if you give
the scroll to someone who can read, and
say, "Read this, please," they will answer,
"I can't; it is sealed." 12 Or if you give the
scroll to someone who cannot read, and
say, "Read this, please," they will answer,
"I don't know how to read."

13 The Lord says:

"These people come near to me with
their mouth
and honor me with their lips,
but their hearts are far from me.[h]
Their worship of me
is based on merely human rules they
have been taught.[a][i]
14 Therefore once more I will astound
these people
with wonder upon wonder;[j]
the wisdom of the wise[k] will
perish,
the intelligence of the intelligent will
vanish.[l]"
15 Woe to those who go to great
depths
to hide their plans from the LORD,
who do their work in darkness and
think,
"Who sees us?[m] Who will know?"[n]
16 You turn things upside down,
as if the potter were thought to be
like the clay!
Shall what is formed say to the one who
formed it,
"You did not make me"?
Can the pot say to the potter,[o]
"You know nothing"?

17 In a very short time, will not Lebanon
be turned into a fertile field[p]
and the fertile field seem like a
forest?[q]
18 In that day the deaf[r] will hear the words
of the scroll,
and out of gloom and darkness
the eyes of the blind will see.[s]
19 Once more the humble[t] will rejoice in
the LORD;
the needy[u] will rejoice in the Holy
One of Israel.
20 The ruthless will vanish,
the mockers[v] will disappear,
and all who have an eye for evil[w] will
be cut down—
21 those who with a word make someone
out to be guilty,
who ensnare the defender in court[x]
and with false testimony deprive the
innocent of justice.[y]

22 Therefore this is what the LORD, who
redeemed Abraham,[z] says to the descendants of Jacob:

"No longer will Jacob be ashamed;[a]
no longer will their faces grow pale.
23 When they see among them their
children,[b]
the work of my hands,[c]
they will keep my name holy;
they will acknowledge the holiness of
the Holy One of Jacob,
and will stand in awe of the God of
Israel.
24 Those who are wayward[d] in spirit will
gain understanding;[e]
those who complain will accept
instruction."[f]

---

a 13 Hebrew; Septuagint *They worship me in vain; / their teachings are merely human rules*

29:17 *Lebanon ... fertile field.* This is a statement of sharp changes. Lebanon was a land of forests. As valuable as a fertile field was, a forest was even more valuable in Israel and Judah, which did not have large stands of trees suitable for lumber. It would indicate some major economic and physical changes for Lebanon to become a field and for a fertile field to be as valuable as a forest.

29:19 *needy ... rejoice.* God always notices the poor and commands His people to do likewise. The poor and the humble are particularly vulnerable to exploitation, and God in His justice does not forget this when He is dealing with disobedient leaders.

29:21 *with a word ... ensnare ... false testimony.* The central issue in this passage is justice. The evil ones miscarry justice with "a word" or false testimony, "snare" through legal technicalities, and win cases with empty words or lies and clever arguments that obscure true justice.

29:8 [a] Ps 73:20 **29:9** [b] Isa 51:17 [c] Isa 51:21-22 **29:10** [d] Ps 69:23; Isa 6:9-10; Ro 11:8* [e] Mic 3:6 [f] 1Sa 9:9 **29:11** [g] Isa 8:16; Mt 13:11; Rev 5:1-2 **29:13** [h] Eze 33:31 [i] Mt 15:8-9*; Mk 7:6-7*; Col 2:22 **29:14** [j] Hab 1:5 [k] Jer 8:9; 49:7 [l] Isa 6:9-10; 1Co 1:19* **29:15** [m] Ps 10:11-13; 94:7; Isa 57:12 [n] Job 22:13 **29:16** [o] Isa 45:9; 64:8; Ro 9:20-21* **29:17** [p] Ps 84:6 [q] Isa 32:15 **29:18** [r] Mk 7:37 [s] Isa 32:3; 35:5; Mt 11:5 **29:19** [t] Isa 61:1; Mt 5:5; 11:29 [u] Isa 14:30; Mt 11:5; Jas 1:9; 2:5 **29:20** [v] Isa 28:22 [w] Isa 59:4; Mic 2:1 **29:21** [x] Am 5:10, 15 [y] Isa 5:23; 32:7 **29:22** [z] Isa 41:8; 63:16 [a] Isa 49:23 **29:23** [b] Isa 49:20-26 [c] Isa 19:25 **29:24** [d] Isa 28:7; Heb 5:2 [e] Isa 41:20; 60:16 [f] Isa 30:21

Woe to the Obstinate Nation

30 “Woe[g] to the obstinate children,”[h]
declares the LORD,
“to those who carry out plans that are not mine,
forming an alliance,[i] but not by my Spirit,
heaping sin upon sin;
2 who go down to Egypt[j]
without consulting[k] me;
who look for help to Pharaoh’s protection,[l]
to Egypt’s shade for refuge.
3 But Pharaoh’s protection will be to your shame,
Egypt’s shade will bring you disgrace.[m]
4 Though they have officials in Zoan[n]
and their envoys have arrived in Hanes,
5 everyone will be put to shame
because of a people[o] useless to them,
who bring neither help nor advantage,
but only shame and disgrace.”

6 A prophecy concerning the animals of
the Negev:

Through a land of hardship and distress,[p]
of lions and lionesses,
of adders and darting snakes,[q]
the envoys carry their riches on donkeys’ backs,
their treasures[r] on the humps of camels,
to that unprofitable nation,
7 to Egypt, whose help is utterly useless.
Therefore I call her
Rahab the Do-Nothing.

8 Go now, write it on a tablet for them,
inscribe it on a scroll,[s]
that for the days to come
it may be an everlasting witness.
9 For these are rebellious people,
deceitful[t] children,
children unwilling to listen to the LORD’s instruction.[u]
10 They say to the seers,
“See no more visions[v]!”
and to the prophets,
“Give us no more visions of what is right!
Tell us pleasant things,[w]
prophesy illusions.[x]
11 Leave this way,
get off this path,
and stop confronting[y] us
with the Holy One of Israel!”

12 Therefore this is what the Holy One of
Israel says:

“Because you have rejected this message,[z]
relied on oppression[a]
and depended on deceit,
13 this sin will become for you
like a high wall,[b] cracked and bulging,
that collapses[c] suddenly,[d] in an instant.
14 It will break in pieces like pottery,[e]
shattered so mercilessly
that among its pieces not a fragment will be found
for taking coals from a hearth
or scooping water out of a cistern.”

15 This is what the Sovereign LORD, the
Holy One of Israel, says:

“In repentance and rest is your salvation,
in quietness and trust[f] is your strength,
but you would have none of it.
16 You said, ‘No, we will flee on horses.’[g]
Therefore you will flee!
You said, ‘We will ride off on swift horses.’
Therefore your pursuers will be swift!
17 A thousand will flee
at the threat of one;
at the threat of five[h]
you will all flee[i] away,
till you are left
like a flagstaff on a mountaintop,
like a banner on a hill.”

18 Yet the LORD longs[j] to be gracious to you;
therefore he will rise up to show you compassion.
For the LORD is a God of justice.[k]
Blessed are all who wait for him![l]

30:1 ***Woe.*** This is the fourth woe. The rebellious children are Hezekiah’s advisers. To the sin of injustice they add the sin of devising plans independently of God.
30:4 ***Zoan . . . Hanes.*** Zoan, which was in the Nile delta, was the capital of Egypt at this time (19:11 – 13). Hanes was 50 miles south of Cairo.
30:15 ***trust.*** A quiet, patient trust in God provides more strength for a follower of God than any alliance with any other person or system. When danger threatens, it is difficult not to look for ways to use one’s own strength. It is also difficult to maintain inward composure and not trust in external sources of help. Even if we cannot imagine how we can be helped, if we are trusting God, we can have confidence and therefore have peace that He will not forsake us in our hour of need. God may use our strength or the help of others, but, when we turn to God first, we can learn which resources, if any, are the ones He wants us to use. When God is first, then our decisions are wise.

30:1 [g] Isa 29:15 [h] Isa 1:2 [i] Isa 8:12 **30:2** [j] Isa 31:1 [k] Nu 27:21 [l] Isa 36:9 **30:3** [m] Isa 20:4-5; 36:6 **30:4** [n] Isa 19:11 **30:5** [o] ver 7 **30:6** [p] Ex 5:10, 21; Isa 8:22; Jer 11:4 [q] Dt 8:15 [r] Isa 15:7 **30:8** [s] Isa 8:1; Hab 2:2 **30:9** [t] Isa 28:15; 59:3-4 [u] Isa 1:10 **30:10** [v] Jer 11:21; Am 7:13 [w] 1Ki 22:8 [x] Eze 13:7; Ro 16:18 **30:11** [y] Job 21:14 **30:12** [z] Isa 5:24 [a] Isa 5:7 **30:13** [b] Ps 62:3 [c] 1Ki 20:30 [d] Isa 29:5 **30:14** [e] Ps 2:9; Jer 19:10-11 **30:15** [f] Isa 32:17 **30:16** [g] Isa 31:1, 3 **30:17** [h] Lev 26:8; Jos 23:10 [i] Lev 26:36; Dt 28:25 **30:18** [j] Isa 42:14; 2Pe 3:9, 15 [k] Isa 5:16 [l] Isa 25:9

19People of Zion, who live in Jerusalem,
you will weep no more.[m] How gracious he
will be when you cry for help! As soon as
he hears, he will answer[n] you. 20Although
the Lord gives you the bread[o] of adversity
and the water of affliction, your teachers
will be hidden[p] no more; with your own
eyes you will see them. 21Whether you turn
to the right or to the left, your ears will hear
a voice[q] behind you, saying, "This is the
way; walk in it." 22Then you will desecrate
your idols[r] overlaid with silver and your
images covered with gold; you will throw
them away like a menstrual cloth and say
to them, "Away with you!"

23He will also send you rain[s] for the
seed you sow in the ground, and the food
that comes from the land will be rich and
plentiful. In that day your cattle will graze
in broad meadows.[t] 24The oxen and donkeys that work the soil will eat fodder and
mash, spread out with fork[u] and shovel.
25In the day of great slaughter, when the
towers[v] fall, streams of water will flow[w] on
every high mountain and every lofty hill.
26The moon will shine like the sun,[x] and
the sunlight will be seven times brighter,
like the light of seven full days, when the
LORD binds up the bruises of his people and
heals[y] the wounds he inflicted.

27 See, the Name[z] of the LORD comes from afar,
with burning anger[a] and dense clouds of smoke;
his lips are full of wrath,[b]
and his tongue is a consuming fire.
28 His breath[c] is like a rushing torrent,
rising up to the neck.[d]
He shakes the nations in the sieve[e] of destruction;
he places in the jaws of the peoples
a bit[f] that leads them astray.
29 And you will sing
as on the night you celebrate a holy festival;
your hearts will rejoice
as when people playing pipes go up
to the mountain[g] of the LORD,
to the Rock of Israel.
30 The LORD will cause people to hear his majestic voice
and will make them see his arm coming down
with raging anger and consuming fire,
with cloudburst, thunderstorm and hail.
31 The voice of the LORD will shatter Assyria;[h]
with his rod he will strike[i] them down.
32 Every stroke the LORD lays on them
with his punishing club
will be to the music of timbrels and harps,
as he fights them in battle with the blows of his arm.[j]
33 Topheth[k] has long been prepared;
it has been made ready for the king.
Its fire pit has been made deep and wide,
with an abundance of fire and wood;
the breath of the LORD,
like a stream of burning sulfur,[l]
sets it ablaze.

Woe to Those Who Rely on Egypt

31 Woe to those who go down to Egypt[m] for help,
who rely on horses,
who trust in the multitude of their chariots[n]
and in the great strength of their horsemen,
but do not look to the Holy One of Israel,
or seek help from the LORD.[o]
2 Yet he too is wise[p] and can bring disaster;[q]
he does not take back his words.[r]
He will rise up against that wicked nation,[s]
against those who help evildoers.

30:23–24 ***send you rain.*** The promises that were part of the original Mosaic covenant were in force again. Blessing would extend from field to flock (Deut. 28:11–12).

30:30 ***his arm coming down.*** The strong arm of God had delivered the Israelites from Egypt. Now His arm would descend in judgment (Ex. 6:6).

30:33 ***Topheth.*** Topheth was a place where Judah made human sacrifices to the heathen god Molek. The prophet uses it as a picture of God's vengeance on the wicked. He is not picturing temporal punishment, but everlasting destruction. This punishment will be in a place that is "deep" or inescapable. Then Isaiah draws the picture of the punishment by fire in hell. Some claim that the fire is symbolic, but it should be remembered that the reality is always greater than the symbol. The bliss of the righteous cannot be fully comprehended, and neither can the terror that awaits the wicked.

31:1 ***Woe.*** The fifth woe reaffirms the fourth woe (30:1–33). It, too, was addressed to those who replace faith in the Lord with reliance on Egypt.

31:2 ***wicked nation . . . help evildoers.*** "Evildoers" refer to Judah, and the "wicked nation," Judah's help, refers to Egypt.

30:19 [m] Isa 60:20; 61:3 [n] Ps 50:15; Isa 58:9; 65:24; Mt 7:7-11 **30:20** [o] 1Ki 22:27 [p] Ps 74:9; Am 8:11 **30:21** [q] Isa 29:24 **30:22** [r] Ex 32:4 **30:23** [s] Isa 65:21-22 [t] Ps 65:13 **30:24** [u] Mt 3:12; Lk 3:17 **30:25** [v] Isa 2:15 [w] Isa 41:18 **30:26** [x] Isa 24:23; 60:19-20; Rev 21:23; 22:5 [y] Dt 32:39; Isa 1:5 **30:27** [z] Isa 59:19 [a] Isa 66:14 [b] Isa 10:5 **30:28** [c] Isa 11:4 [d] Isa 8:8 [e] Am 9:9 [f] 2Ki 19:28; Isa 37:29 **30:29** [g] Ps 42:4 **30:31** [h] Isa 10:5, 12 [i] Isa 11:4 **30:32** [j] Isa 11:15; Eze 32:10 **30:33** [k] 2Ki 23:10 [l] Ge 19:24 **31:1** [m] Dt 17:16; Isa 30:2, 5 [n] Isa 2:7 [o] Ps 20:7; Da 9:13 **31:2** [p] Ro 16:27 [q] Isa 45:7 [r] Nu 23:19 [s] Isa 32:6

3 But the Egyptians[t] are mere mortals
and not God;[u]
their horses are flesh and not spirit.
When the LORD stretches out his hand,[v]
those who help will stumble,
those who are helped[w] will fall;
all will perish together.

4 This is what the LORD says to me:

"As a lion[x] growls,
a great lion over its prey—
and though a whole band of shepherds
is called together against it,
it is not frightened by their shouts
or disturbed by their clamor—
so the LORD Almighty will come down[y]
to do battle on Mount Zion and on its
heights.
5 Like birds hovering overhead,
the LORD Almighty will shield[z]
Jerusalem;
he will shield it and deliver[a] it,
he will 'pass over' it and will
rescue it."

6 Return, you Israelites, to the One you
have so greatly revolted against. 7 For in
that day every one of you will reject the
idols of silver and gold[b] your sinful hands
have made.

8 "Assyria[c] will fall by no human sword;
a sword, not of mortals, will devour[d]
them.
They will flee before the sword
and their young men will be put to
forced labor.[e]
9 Their stronghold[f] will fall because of
terror;
at the sight of the battle standard
their commanders will panic,"
declares the LORD,
whose fire[g] is in Zion,
whose furnace is in Jerusalem.

The Kingdom of Righteousness

32 See, a king[h] will reign in
righteousness
and rulers will rule with justice.[i]
2 Each one will be like a shelter[j] from the
wind
and a refuge from the storm,
like streams of water in the desert
and the shadow of a great rock in a
thirsty land.
3 Then the eyes of those who see will no
longer be closed,[k]
and the ears of those who hear will
listen.
4 The fearful heart will know and
understand,[l]
and the stammering tongue will be
fluent and clear.
5 No longer will the fool[m] be called noble
nor the scoundrel be highly
respected.
6 For fools speak folly,[n]
their hearts are bent on evil:
They practice ungodliness[o]
and spread error[p] concerning the
LORD;
the hungry they leave empty[q]
and from the thirsty they withhold
water.
7 Scoundrels use wicked methods,[r]
they make up evil schemes[s]
to destroy the poor with lies,
even when the plea of the needy[t] is
just.
8 But the noble make noble plans,
and by noble deeds[u] they stand.

The Women of Jerusalem

9 You women who are so complacent,
rise up and listen[v] to me;
you daughters who feel secure,[w]
hear what I have to say!
10 In little more than a year
you who feel secure will tremble;
the grape harvest will fail,[x]
and the harvest of fruit will not come.
11 Tremble, you complacent women;
shudder, you daughters who feel
secure!
Strip off your fine clothes[y]
and wrap yourselves in rags.
12 Beat your breasts[z] for the pleasant
fields,
for the fruitful vines
13 and for the land of my people,
a land overgrown with thorns and
briers[a]—
yes, mourn for all houses of merriment
and for this city of revelry.[b]

31:7 ***that day.*** "That day" refers to the day when God will judge the rebellious (24:21; 26:1). God had judged nations from time to time over the ages (Canaan, Egypt, Babylon, Israel, etc.), but the final day of judgment when everything will be made new is still in the future (Rev. 20:11–15).
32:1 ***See.*** The fifth woe concludes with a prophecy about leadership and its effects. ***a king will reign in righteousness.*** The prophecy concerning this king is fulfilled in the Lord Jesus Christ (7:14; 9:1–7; 11:1–5; 28:16; John 10:11). ***rulers.*** The rulers are Jesus' shepherds (1 Pet. 5:2–4).
32:9–11 ***complacent.*** The word "complacent" has connotations of "trust," as one who has taken refuge, or who is secure and without care. These women were complacent, but it was a false security. ***rags.*** Mourning women removed their clothing and wore rags around their waists (Gen. 37:34).

31:3 [t] Isa 36:9 [u] Eze 28:9; 2Th 2:4 [v] Isa 9:17, 21 [w] Isa 30:5-7
31:4 [x] Nu 24:9; Hos 11:10; Am 3:8 [y] Isa 42:13
31:5 [z] Ps 91:4 [a] Isa 37:35; 38:6 **31:7** [b] Isa 2:20; 30:22
31:8 [c] Isa 10:12 [d] Isa 14:25; 37:7 [e] Ge 49:15
31:9 [f] Dt 32:31, 37 [g] Isa 10:17 **32:1** [h] Eze 37:24
[i] Ps 72:1-4; Isa 9:7 **32:2** [j] Isa 4:6 **32:3** [k] Isa 29:18
32:4 [l] Isa 29:24 **32:5** [m] 1Sa 25:25 **32:6** [n] Pr 19:3
[o] Isa 9:17 [p] Isa 9:16 [q] Isa 3:15 **32:7** [r] Jer 5:26-28 [s] Mic 7:3
[t] Isa 61:1 **32:8** [u] Pr 11:25 **32:9** [v] Isa 28:23 [w] Isa 47:8;
Am 6:1; Zep 2:15 **32:10** [x] Isa 5:5-6; 24:7
32:11 [y] Isa 47:2 **32:12** [z] Na 2:7 **32:13** [a] Isa 5:6
[b] Isa 22:2

[14]The fortress[c] will be abandoned,
the noisy city deserted;[d]
citadel and watchtower[e] will become a wasteland forever,
the delight of donkeys,[f] a pasture for flocks,
[15]till the Spirit[g] is poured on us from on high,
and the desert becomes a fertile field,[h]
and the fertile field seems like a forest.[i]
[16]The LORD's justice will dwell in the desert,
his righteousness live in the fertile field.
[17]The fruit of that righteousness will be peace;[j]
its effect will be quietness and confidence[k] forever.
[18]My people will live in peaceful dwelling places,
in secure homes,
in undisturbed places of rest.[l]
[19]Though hail[m] flattens the forest[n]
and the city is leveled[o] completely,
[20]how blessed you will be,
sowing[p] your seed by every stream,
and letting your cattle and donkeys range free.[q]

Distress and Help

33 Woe to you, destroyer,
you who have not been destroyed!
Woe to you, betrayer,
you who have not been betrayed!
When you stop destroying,
you will be destroyed;[r]
when you stop betraying,
you will be betrayed.[s]

[2]LORD, be gracious to us;
we long for you.
Be our strength[t] every morning,
our salvation[u] in time of distress.
[3]At the uproar of your army, the peoples flee;
when you rise up,[v] the nations scatter.
[4]Your plunder, O nations, is harvested as by young locusts;
like a swarm of locusts people pounce on it.

[5]The LORD is exalted,[w] for he dwells on high;
he will fill Zion with his justice[x] and righteousness.[y]
[6]He will be the sure foundation for your times,
a rich store of salvation[z] and wisdom and knowledge;
the fear[a] of the LORD is the key to this treasure.[a]

[7]Look, their brave men cry aloud in the streets;
the envoys[b] of peace weep bitterly.
[8]The highways are deserted,
no travelers are on the roads.[c]
The treaty is broken,
its witnesses[b] are despised,
no one is respected.
[9]The land dries up[d] and wastes away,
Lebanon[e] is ashamed and withers;[f]
Sharon is like the Arabah,
and Bashan and Carmel drop their leaves.

[10]"Now will I arise,[g]" says the LORD.
"Now will I be exalted;
now will I be lifted up.
[11]You conceive[h] chaff,
you give birth[i] to straw;
your breath is a fire[j] that consumes you.
[12]The peoples will be burned to ashes;
like cut thornbushes they will be set ablaze.[k]"

[13]You who are far away,[l] hear[m] what I have done;
you who are near, acknowledge my power!
[14]The sinners in Zion are terrified;
trembling[n] grips the godless:
"Who of us can dwell with the consuming fire?[o]
Who of us can dwell with everlasting burning?"
[15]Those who walk righteously[p]
and speak what is right,[q]
who reject gain from extortion
and keep their hands from accepting bribes,
who stop their ears against plots of murder
and shut their eyes[r] against contemplating evil—

[a] 6 Or *is a treasure from him* [b] 8 Dead Sea Scrolls; Masoretic Text / *the cities*

33:1 *Woe.* The sixth woe differs from the others in that it is addressed to Assyria, not to Judah. By focusing exclusively on Assyria's defeat and Judah's salvation, the prophecy magnifies Judah's exalted King.
33:3 *you rise up.* This passage refers to an exaltation of the heavenly King (vv. 5,10) as He rises to demonstrate His glory and vindicate His justice.
33:4 *plunder.* The plunder of God's war with His enemies belongs to the Lord, the true Victor (23:18; 34:2).
33:9 *Sharon ... Bashan.* Sharon was on the western coastal plain, and Bashan was on the east side of the Jordan.
33:15 *walk righteously.* For a similar description of the person who can approach the Holy One, see

32:14 [c] Isa 13:22 [d] Isa 6:11; 27:10 [e] Isa 34:13 [f] Ps 104:11 **32:15** [g] Isa 11:2; Joel 2:28 [h] Ps 107:35; Isa 35:1-2 [i] Isa 29:17 **32:17** [j] Ps 119:165; Ro 14:17; Jas 3:18 [k] Isa 30:15 **32:18** [l] Hos 2:18-23 **32:19** [m] Isa 28:17; 30:30 [n] Isa 10:19; Zec 11:2 [o] Isa 24:10; 27:10 **32:20** [p] Ecc 11:1 [q] Isa 30:24 **33:1** [r] Hab 2:8; Mt 7:2 [s] Isa 21:2 **33:2** [t] Isa 40:10; 51:9; 59:16 [u] Isa 25:9 **33:3** [v] Isa 59:16-18 **33:5** [w] Ps 97:9 [x] Isa 28:6 [y] Isa 1:26 **33:6** [z] Isa 51:6 [a] Isa 11:2-3; Mt 6:33 **33:7** [b] 2Ki 18:37 **33:8** [c] Jdg 5:6; Isa 35:8 **33:9** [d] Isa 3:26 [e] Isa 2:13; 35:2 [f] Isa 24:4 **33:10** [g] Ps 12:5; Isa 2:21 **33:11** [h] Ps 7:14; Isa 59:4; Jas 1:15 [i] Isa 26:18 [j] Isa 1:31 **33:12** [k] Isa 10:17 **33:13** [l] Ps 48:10; 49:1 [m] Isa 49:1 **33:14** [n] Isa 32:11 [o] Isa 30:30; Heb 12:29 **33:15** [p] Isa 58:8 [q] Ps 15:2; 24:4 [r] Ps 119:37

16 they are the ones who will dwell on the heights,
whose refuge[s] will be the mountain fortress.[t]
Their bread will be supplied,
and water will not fail[u] them.

17 Your eyes will see the king[v] in his beauty
and view a land that stretches afar.[w]
18 In your thoughts you will ponder the former terror:[x]
"Where is that chief officer?
Where is the one who took the revenue?
Where is the officer in charge of the towers?"
19 You will see those arrogant people no more,
people whose speech is obscure,
whose language is strange and incomprehensible.[y]

20 Look on Zion, the city of our festivals;
your eyes will see Jerusalem,
a peaceful abode,[z] a tent that will not be moved;[a]
its stakes will never be pulled up,
nor any of its ropes broken.
21 There the LORD will be our Mighty One.
It will be like a place of broad rivers and streams.[b]
No galley with oars will ride them,
no mighty ship will sail them.
22 For the LORD is our judge,[c]
the LORD is our lawgiver,[d]
the LORD is our king;[e]
it is he who will save[f] us.

23 Your rigging hangs loose:
The mast is not held secure,
the sail is not spread.
Then an abundance of spoils will be divided
and even the lame[g] will carry off plunder.[h]
24 No one living in Zion will say, "I am ill";[i]
and the sins of those who dwell there will be forgiven.[j]

Judgment Against the Nations

34 Come near, you nations, and listen;
pay attention, you peoples![k]
Let the earth[l] hear, and all that is in it,
the world, and all that comes out of it![m]
2 The LORD is angry with all nations;
his wrath is on all their armies.
He will totally destroy[a][n] them,
he will give them over to slaughter.[o]
3 Their slain will be thrown out,
their dead bodies will stink;[p]
the mountains will be soaked with their blood.[q]
4 All the stars in the sky will be dissolved[r]
and the heavens rolled up[s] like a scroll;
all the starry host will fall[t]
like withered leaves from the vine,
like shriveled figs from the fig tree.

5 My sword[u] has drunk its fill in the heavens;
see, it descends in judgment on Edom,[v]
the people I have totally destroyed.[w]
6 The sword of the LORD is bathed in blood,
it is covered with fat—
the blood of lambs and goats,
fat from the kidneys of rams.
For the LORD has a sacrifice in Bozrah
and a great slaughter in the land of Edom.
7 And the wild oxen will fall with them,
the bull calves and the great bulls.[x]
Their land will be drenched with blood,
and the dust will be soaked with fat.

8 For the LORD has a day of vengeance,[y]
a year of retribution, to uphold Zion's cause.

[a] *2* The Hebrew term refers to the irrevocable giving over of things or persons to the LORD, often by totally destroying them; also in verse 5.

Psalm 1:1–2; 15:2; Galatians 5:22–25; and Ephesians 5:1–2.

33:17 *land that stretches afar.* The prophet's land was continually threatened by the Assyrian army. But, in prophetic vision, Isaiah saw a little picture of the beauty of heaven. In the mind of the believer, the trials of the present fade into insignificance if he only contemplates that glorious time when he will dwell in the presence of his King.

33:18 *chief officer.* The chief officer who counted was the one who took tribute (2 Kin. 18:14).

33:19 *people whose speech is obscure.* For a similar idea concerning Israel's enemies, see Deuteronomy 28:49.

33:22 *the LORD is our lawgiver.* The lawgiver is associated with other acts of mercy (Deut. 6:1–3; John 1:14–18); the giving of the law was God's way to point out the correct path for the Israelites to follow. His commitment to set our feet on the right path is one of His acts of mercy.

34:4 *heavens rolled up like a scroll.* The old cosmos will give way to the new (51:6; Matt. 24:29; Rev. 6:13–14; 21:1). ***starry host.*** The starry host here refers to pagan deities (24:21; 2 Kin. 17:16).

34:8 *vengeance.* The Lord has promised that He will one day right the wrongs suffered by His followers, but that vengeance is His and His alone (Deut. 32:35; Rom. 12:19).

33:16 [s] Isa 25:4 [t] Isa 26:1 [u] Isa 49:10 **33:17** [v] Isa 6:5 [w] Isa 26:15 **33:18** [x] Isa 17:14 **33:19** [y] Isa 28:11; Jer 5:15 **33:20** [z] Isa 32:18 [a] Ps 46:5; 125:1-2 **33:21** [b] Isa 41:18; 48:18; 66:12 **33:22** [c] Isa 11:4 [d] Isa 2:3; Jas 4:12 [e] Ps 89:18 [f] Isa 25:9 **33:23** [g] 2Ki 7:8 [h] 2Ki 7:16 **33:24** [i] Isa 30:26 [j] Jer 50:20; 1Jn 1:7-9 **34:1** [k] Isa 41:1; 43:9 [l] Ps 49:1 [m] Dt 32:1 **34:2** [n] Isa 13:5 [o] Isa 30:25 **34:3** [p] Joel 2:20; Am 4:10 [q] ver 7; Eze 14:19; 35:6; 38:22 **34:4** [r] Isa 13:13; 2Pe 3:10 [s] Eze 32:7-8 [t] Joel 2:31; Mt 24:29*; Rev 6:13 **34:5** [u] Dt 32:41-42; Jer 46:10; Eze 21:5 [v] Am 1:11-12 [w] Isa 24:6; Mal 1:4 **34:7** [x] Ps 68:30 **34:8** [y] Isa 63:4

9 Edom's streams will be turned into pitch,
her dust into burning sulfur;
her land will become blazing pitch!
10 It will not be quenched night or day;
its smoke will rise forever.[z]
From generation to generation it will lie desolate;[a]
no one will ever pass through it again.
11 The desert owl[a][b] and screech owl[a] will possess it;
the great owl[a] and the raven will nest there.
God will stretch out over Edom
the measuring line of chaos
and the plumb line[c] of desolation.
12 Her nobles will have nothing there to be called a kingdom,
all her princes[d] will vanish[e] away.
13 Thorns will overrun her citadels,
nettles and brambles her strongholds.[f]
She will become a haunt for jackals,[g]
a home for owls.
14 Desert creatures will meet with hyenas,[h]
and wild goats will bleat to each other;
there the night creatures will also lie down
and find for themselves places of rest.
15 The owl will nest there and lay eggs,
she will hatch them, and care for her young
under the shadow of her wings;
there also the falcons[i] will gather,
each with its mate.

16 Look in the scroll[j] of the LORD and read:

None of these will be missing,
not one will lack her mate.
For it is his mouth[k] that has given the order,
and his Spirit will gather them together.
17 He allots their portions;[l]
his hand distributes them by measure.
They will possess it forever
and dwell there from generation to generation.[m]

Joy of the Redeemed

35 The desert[n] and the parched land will be glad;
the wilderness will rejoice and blossom.[o]
Like the crocus, 2 it will burst into bloom;
it will rejoice greatly and shout for joy.[p]
The glory of Lebanon[q] will be given to it,
the splendor of Carmel[r] and Sharon;
they will see the glory of the LORD,
the splendor of our God.[s]

3 Strengthen the feeble hands,
steady the knees[t] that give way;
4 say to those with fearful hearts,
"Be strong, do not fear;
your God will come,
he will come with vengeance;[u]
with divine retribution
he will come to save you."

5 Then will the eyes of the blind be opened[v]
and the ears of the deaf[w] unstopped.
6 Then will the lame[x] leap like a deer,
and the mute tongue[y] shout for joy.
Water will gush forth in the wilderness
and streams[z] in the desert.
7 The burning sand will become a pool,
the thirsty ground bubbling springs.[a]
In the haunts where jackals[b] once lay,
grass and reeds and papyrus will grow.

8 And a highway[c] will be there;
it will be called the Way of Holiness;[d]
it will be for those who walk on that Way.
The unclean[e] will not journey on it;
wicked fools will not go about on it.

a 11 The precise identification of these birds is uncertain.

34:9 *pitch . . . burning sulfur.* Pitch and burning sulfur may allude to Sodom and Gomorrah (30:33; Gen. 19:24; Ezek. 38:22).

35:1–2 *glad.* Isaiah 35 stands in contrast to Isaiah 34. This chapter opens with the lilt of joy. The Arabah, or desert plain, shall blossom and break into bloom. Centuries before, Moses had warned of a day when the rain of this land would become "powder and dust" (Deut. 28:24). That day came because Israel was disobedient to God. But, at the second coming of Christ (Rev. 20:1–6), Israel will be restored spiritually, and with spiritual restoration comes physical blessing. When judgment is removed, great blessing follows. Restoration follows repentance, and restoration is accompanied by joy.

35:3 *Strengthen the feeble hands.* This phrase is cited in Hebrews 12:12 (Josh. 1:6–7,9,18). We can reassure ourselves with the knowledge that our Savior is coming. In that day, justice will be restored.

35:5–6 *eyes . . . ears . . . lame . . . tongue.* This prophecy of healings was fulfilled by Jesus (Matt. 12:22; Luke 4:18; 7:22), and it was this passage in Isaiah that Jesus referred to when He answered John the Baptist's disciples who asked if He was the Expected One. The reply was somewhat cryptic, but it was something that John would understand in prison, without requiring Jesus to reveal Himself before it was time (Matt. 11:27; Luke 7:22).

34:10 [z] Rev 14:10-11; 19:3 [a] Isa 13:20; 24:1; Eze 29:12; Mal 1:3 **34:11** [b] Zep 2:14; Rev 18:2 [c] 2Ki 21:13; La 2:8 **34:12** [d] Jer 27:20; 39:6 [e] Isa 41:11-12 **34:13** [f] Isa 13:22; 32:13 [g] Ps 44:19; Jer 9:11; 10:22 **34:14** [h] Isa 13:22 **34:15** [i] Dt 14:13 **34:16** [j] Isa 30:8 [k] Isa 1:20; 58:14 **34:17** [l] Isa 17:14; Jer 13:25 [m] ver 10 **35:1** [n] Isa 27:10; 41:18-19 [o] Isa 51:3 **35:2** [p] Isa 25:9; 55:12 [q] Isa 32:15 [r] SS 7:5 [s] Isa 25:9 **35:3** [t] Job 4:4; Heb 12:12 **35:4** [u] Isa 1:24; 34:8 **35:5** [v] Mt 11:5; Jn 9:6-7 [w] Isa 29:18; 50:4 **35:6** [x] Mt 15:30; Jn 5:8-9; Ac 3:8 [y] Isa 32:4; Mt 9:32-33; 12:22; Lk 11:14 [z] Isa 41:18; Jn 7:38 **35:7** [a] Isa 49:10 [b] Isa 13:22 **35:8** [c] Isa 11:16; 33:8; Mt 7:13-14 [d] Isa 4:3; 1Pe 1:15 [e] Isa 52:1

9 No lion[f] will be there,
nor any ravenous beast;[g]
they will not be found there.
But only the redeemed[h] will walk there,
10 and those the LORD has rescued will
return.
They will enter Zion with singing;
everlasting joy[i] will crown their heads.
Gladness and joy will overtake them,
and sorrow and sighing will flee
away.[j]

Sennacherib Threatens Jerusalem

36 In the fourteenth year of King Hezekiah's reign, Sennacherib[k] king of
Assyria attacked all the fortified cities of
Judah and captured them. 2 Then the king
of Assyria sent his field commander with
a large army from Lachish to King Hezekiah at Jerusalem. When the commander
stopped at the aqueduct of the Upper Pool,
on the road to the Launderer's Field,[l] 3 Eliakim[m] son of Hilkiah the palace administrator, Shebna[n] the secretary, and Joah son of
Asaph the recorder went out to him.
4 The field commander said to them, "Tell
Hezekiah:

"'This is what the great king, the
king of Assyria, says: On what are
you basing this confidence of yours?
5 You say you have counsel and might
for war—but you speak only empty
words. On whom are you depending,
that you rebel[o] against me? 6 Look, I
know you are depending on Egypt,[p]
that splintered reed[q] of a staff, which
pierces the hand of anyone who leans
on it! Such is Pharaoh king of Egypt to
all who depend on him. 7 But if you say
to me, "We are depending on the LORD
our God"—isn't he the one whose high
places and altars Hezekiah removed,[r]
saying to Judah and Jerusalem, "You
must worship before this altar"?[s]
8 "'Come now, make a bargain with
my master, the king of Assyria: I will
give you two thousand horses—if you
can put riders on them! 9 How then can
you repulse one officer of the least of
my master's officials, even though you
are depending on Egypt[t] for chariots
and horsemen[a]?[u] 10 Furthermore, have
I come to attack and destroy this land
without the LORD? The LORD himself
told[v] me to march against this country
and destroy it.'"

11 Then Eliakim, Shebna and Joah said to
the field commander, "Please speak to your
servants in Aramaic,[w] since we understand
it. Don't speak to us in Hebrew in the hearing of the people on the wall."
12 But the commander replied, "Was it
only to your master and you that my master sent me to say these things, and not to
the people sitting on the wall—who, like
you, will have to eat their own excrement
and drink their own urine?"
13 Then the commander stood and called
out in Hebrew,[x] "Hear the words of the
great king, the king of Assyria! 14 This is
what the king says: Do not let Hezekiah deceive you. He cannot deliver you! 15 Do not
let Hezekiah persuade you to trust in the
LORD when he says, 'The LORD will surely
deliver us; this city will not be given into
the hand of the king of Assyria.'[y]
16 "Do not listen to Hezekiah. This is
what the king of Assyria says: Make peace
with me and come out to me. Then each of
you will eat fruit from your own vine and
fig tree[z] and drink water from your own
cistern,[a] 17 until I come and take you to a
land like your own—a land of grain and
new wine, a land of bread and vineyards.
18 "Do not let Hezekiah mislead you when
he says, 'The LORD will deliver us.' Have
the gods of any nations ever delivered their
lands from the hand of the king of Assyria?
19 Where are the gods of Hamath and Arpad? Where are the gods of Sepharvaim?
Have they rescued Samaria from my hand?
20 Who of all the gods[b] of these countries
have been able to save their lands from me?
How then can the LORD deliver Jerusalem
from my hand?"

---

[a] 9 Or *charioteers*

35:10 *rescued.* Someone who is rescued is someone who has had a price paid to set him free from captivity. This promise looked forward to the return of the political captives and, in a much fuller sense, to the salvation through Jesus Christ, who gave "his life as a ransom for many" (Matt. 20:28; Mark 10:45; see 1 Tim. 2:6).
36:1 *fourteenth year.* The 14th year of King Hezekiah's sole reign was 701 B.C. ***all.*** In his annals, Sennacherib mentions 46 cities that he attacked.
36:7 *removed.* Hezekiah had destroyed the idolatrous high places and altars that his father Ahaz had built (2 Kin. 18:1–5; 2 Chr. 31:1–3).
36:8 *riders.* Micah referred to Jerusalem's soldiers as merely "troops" (Mic. 5:1) compared to the enormous international army of Assyria.
36:10 *The LORD himself told me.* Ancient Middle Eastern conquerors liked to claim that the gods of their defeated enemies had joined their side (2 Chr. 35:21). These words about the Lord were no more than a boast.
36:11 *Aramaic.* The Syrian language was Aramaic, which was the language of international diplomacy.
36:19 *Have they rescued Samaria ... ?* Like the Assyrian king (10:11), the field commander assumed that different gods were worshiped in Samaria than in Jerusalem.

35:9 [f] Isa 30:6 [g] Isa 34:14 [h] Isa 51:11; 62:12; 63:4
35:10 [i] Isa 25:9 [j] Isa 30:19; 51:11; Rev 7:17; 21:4
36:1 [k] 2Ch 32:1 **36:2** [l] Isa 7:3 **36:3** [m] Isa 22:20-21
[n] 2Ki 18:18 **36:5** [o] 2Ki 18:7 **36:6** [p] Isa 30:2,5
[q] Eze 29:6-7 **36:7** [r] 2Ki 18:4 [s] Dt 12:2-5 **36:9** [t] Isa 31:3
[u] Isa 30:2-5 **36:10** [v] 1Ki 13:18 **36:11** [w] Ezr 4:7
36:13 [x] 2Ch 32:18 **36:15** [y] Isa 37:10 **36:16** [z] 1Ki 4:25;
Zec 3:10 [a] Pr 5:15 **36:20** [b] 1Ki 20:23

21But the people remained silent and
said nothing in reply, because the king had
commanded, "Do not answer him."[c]
22Then Eliakim son of Hilkiah the palace administrator, Shebna the secretary
and Joah son of Asaph the recorder went to
Hezekiah, with their clothes torn, and told
him what the field commander had said.

Jerusalem's Deliverance Foretold

37 When King Hezekiah heard this,
he tore his clothes and put on sackcloth and went into the temple of the LORD.
2He sent Eliakim the palace administrator, Shebna the secretary, and the leading
priests, all wearing sackcloth, to the prophet Isaiah son of Amoz.[d] 3They told him,
"This is what Hezekiah says: This day is
a day of distress and rebuke and disgrace,
as when children come to the moment of
birth[e] and there is no strength to deliver
them. 4It may be that the LORD your God
will hear the words of the field commander, whom his master, the king of Assyria,
has sent to ridicule the living God, and that
he will rebuke him for the words the LORD
your God has heard.[f] Therefore pray for the
remnant[g] that still survives."
5When King Hezekiah's officials came
to Isaiah, 6Isaiah said to them, "Tell your
master, 'This is what the LORD says: Do
not be afraid[h] of what you have heard—
those words with which the underlings of
the king of Assyria have blasphemed me.
7Listen! When he hears a certain report,[i] I
will make him want to return to his own
country, and there I will have him cut down
with the sword.'"
8When the field commander heard that
the king of Assyria had left Lachish, he
withdrew and found the king fighting
against Libnah.[j]
9Now Sennacherib received a report[k]
that Tirhakah, the king of Cush,[a] was
marching out to fight against him. When
he heard it, he sent messengers to Hezekiah with this word: 10"Say to Hezekiah king
of Judah: Do not let the god you depend on
deceive you when he says, 'Jerusalem will
not be given into the hands of the king of
Assyria.'[l] 11Surely you have heard what
the kings of Assyria have done to all the
countries, destroying them completely.
And will you be delivered?[m] 12Did the gods
of the nations that were destroyed by my
predecessors[n] deliver them—the gods of
Gozan, Harran,[o] Rezeph and the people of
Eden who were in Tel Assar? 13Where is
the king of Hamath or the king of Arpad?
Where are the kings of Lair, Sepharvaim,
Hena and Ivvah?"

Hezekiah's Prayer

14Hezekiah received the letter from the
messengers and read it. Then he went up
to the temple of the LORD and spread it out
before the LORD. 15And Hezekiah prayed
to the LORD: 16"LORD Almighty, the God of
Israel, enthroned between the cherubim,
you alone are God[p] over all the kingdoms
of the earth. You have made heaven and
earth. 17Give ear, LORD, and hear;[q] open
your eyes, LORD, and see;[r] listen to all the
words Sennacherib has sent to ridicule the
living God.
18"It is true, LORD, that the Assyrian
kings have laid waste all these peoples and
their lands.[s] 19They have thrown their gods
into the fire and destroyed them,[t] for they
were not gods[u] but only wood and stone,
fashioned by human hands. 20Now, LORD
our God, deliver us from his hand, so that
all the kingdoms of the earth may know
that you, LORD, are the only God.[b][v]"

Sennacherib's Fall

21Then Isaiah son of Amoz[w] sent a message to Hezekiah: "This is what the LORD,
the God of Israel, says: Because you have
prayed to me concerning Sennacherib king
of Assyria, 22this is the word the LORD has
spoken against him:

"Virgin Daughter Zion
despises and mocks you.
Daughter Jerusalem
tosses her head[x] as you flee.

---

[a] *9* That is, the upper Nile region [b] *20* Dead Sea Scrolls (see also 2 Kings 19:19); Masoretic Text *you alone are the LORD*

36:22 *Shebna.* Isaiah had earlier condemned Shebna for presumption (22:15–23). Apparently that was a warning which was heeded, for his attitude was of mourning, repentance, and humility at this time.

37:6 *Do not be afraid.* The Lord commonly reassured His servants with these words (7:4; 35:4; Gen. 15:1; Josh. 1:9). We have no reason to fear if our trust is in the all-powerful God (Heb. 13:6).

37:10 *Say.* Blasphemous and malicious designs against God and His people should motivate us to rely completely on the Lord and earnestly seek His strength. The response of God's people to blasphemers must never be incited by personal feelings, but by the desire that "all the kingdoms of the earth may know that you, LORD, are the only God" (37:20).

37:21 *This is what the LORD, the God of Israel, says.* Hezekiah's plea for help against the Assyrian menace brought a word from the Lord. Hezekiah was assured that the Lord was in absolute charge, even to the extent that the Assyrian king's activities were brought about through God's own plan (37:26). Sennacherib's forces fell before the mighty power of the

36:21 [c] Pr 9:7-8; 26:4 **37:2** [d] Isa 1:1 **37:3** [e] Isa 26:18; 66:9; Hos 13:13 **37:4** [f] Isa 36:13, 18-20 [g] Isa 1:9 **37:6** [h] Isa 7:4 **37:7** [i] ver 9 **37:8** [j] Nu 33:20 **37:9** [k] ver 7 **37:10** [l] Isa 36:15 **37:11** [m] Isa 36:18-20 **37:12** [n] 2Ki 18:11 [o] Ge 11:31; 12:1-4; Ac 7:2 **37:16** [p] Dt 10:17; Ps 86:10; 136:2-3 **37:17** [q] 2Ch 6:40 [r] Da 9:18 **37:18** [s] 2Ki 15:29; Na 2:11-12 **37:19** [t] Isa 26:14 [u] Isa 41:24, 29 **37:20** [v] Ps 46:10 **37:21** [w] ver 2 **37:22** [x] Job 16:4

23 Who is it you have ridiculed and
blasphemed?[y]
Against whom have you raised your
voice
and lifted your eyes in pride?[z]
Against the Holy One of Israel!
24 By your messengers
you have ridiculed the Lord.
And you have said,
'With my many chariots
I have ascended the heights of the
mountains,
the utmost heights of Lebanon.[a]
I have cut down its tallest cedars,
the choicest of its junipers.
I have reached its remotest heights,
the finest of its forests.
25 I have dug wells in foreign lands[a]
and drunk the water there.
With the soles of my feet
I have dried up all the streams of
Egypt.[b]'

26 "Have you not heard?
Long ago I ordained[c] it.
In days of old I planned[d] it;
now I have brought it to pass,
that you have turned fortified cities
into piles of stone.[e]
27 Their people, drained of power,
are dismayed and put to shame.
They are like plants in the field,
like tender green shoots,
like grass sprouting on the roof,[f]
scorched[b] before it grows up.

28 "But I know where you are
and when you come and go[g]
and how you rage[h] against me.
29 Because you rage against me
and because your insolence[i] has
reached my ears,
I will put my hook in your nose[j]
and my bit in your mouth,
and I will make you return
by the way you came.[k]

30 "This will be the sign for you, Hezekiah:

"This year you will eat what grows by
itself,
and the second year what springs
from that.
But in the third year sow and reap,
plant vineyards and eat their fruit.
31 Once more a remnant of the kingdom of
Judah
will take root below and bear fruit[l]
above.
32 For out of Jerusalem will come a
remnant,
and out of Mount Zion a band of
survivors.
The zeal[m] of the LORD Almighty
will accomplish this.

33 "Therefore this is what the LORD says
concerning the king of Assyria:

"He will not enter this city
or shoot an arrow here.
He will not come before it with shield
or build a siege ramp against it.
34 By the way that he came he will return;[n]
he will not enter this city,"
declares the LORD.
35 "I will defend[o] this city and save it,
for my sake[p] and for the sake of
David[q] my servant!"

36 Then the angel of the LORD went out
and put to death a hundred and eighty-five
thousand in the Assyrian[r] camp. When the
people got up the next morning—there
were all the dead bodies! 37 So Sennacherib
king of Assyria broke camp and withdrew.
He returned to Nineveh[s] and stayed there.
38 One day, while he was worshiping
in the temple of his god Nisrok, his sons
Adrammelek and Sharezer killed him with
the sword, and they escaped to the land of
Ararat.[t] And Esarhaddon his son succeeded him as king.

Hezekiah's Illness

38 In those days Hezekiah became ill
and was at the point of death. The
prophet Isaiah son of Amoz[u] went to him
and said, "This is what the LORD says: Put
your house in order,[v] because you are going to die; you will not recover."
2 Hezekiah turned his face to the wall
and prayed to the LORD, 3 "Remember,
LORD, how I have walked[w] before you faithfully and with wholehearted devotion[x] and
have done what is good in your eyes.[y]" And
Hezekiah wept[z] bitterly.

---

[a] 25 Dead Sea Scrolls (see also 2 Kings 19:24); Masoretic Text does not have *in foreign lands.*
[b] 27 Some manuscripts of the Masoretic Text, Dead Sea Scrolls and some Septuagint manuscripts (see also 2 Kings 19:26); most manuscripts of the Masoretic Text *roof / and terraced fields*

---

angel of the Lord (37:36), as a witness to the truth of the Word of God that the king's heart is turned by the hand of the Lord (Prov. 21:1).

37:29 ***my hook in your nose.*** The Assyrians dragged prisoners away with a hook in the nose. The Lord's judgment was coming, and soon the Assyrians would experience being pulled away where they did not want to go.

37:36 ***angel of the LORD … put to death.*** This verse is the fulfillment of God's promise to take vengeance on those who trouble His people (34:8).

37:38 ***Esarhaddon.*** Esarhaddon began his reign in 681 B.C.

37:23 [y] ver 4 [z] Isa 2:11 **37:24** [a] Isa 14:8 **37:25** [b] Dt 11:10 **37:26** [c] Ac 2:23; 4:27-28; 1Pe 2:8 [d] Isa 10:6; 25:1 [e] Isa 25:2 **37:27** [f] Ps 129:6 **37:28** [g] Ps 139:1-3 [h] Ps 2:1 **37:29** [i] Isa 10:12 [j] Isa 30:28; Eze 38:4 [k] ver 34 **37:31** [l] Isa 27:6 **37:32** [m] Isa 9:7 **37:34** [n] ver 29 **37:35** [o] Isa 31.5, 38.6 [p] Isa 43:25; 48:9, 11 [q] 2Ki 20:6 **37:36** [r] Isa 10:12 **37:37** [s] Ge 10:11 **37:38** [t] Ge 8:4; Jer 51:27 **38:1** [u] Isa 37:2 [v] 2Sa 17:23 **38:3** [w] Ne 13:14; Ps 26:3 [x] 1Ch 29:19 [y] Dt 6:18 [z] Ps 6:8

4Then the word of the LORD came to Isaiah: 5"Go and tell Hezekiah, 'This is what
the LORD, the God of your father David,
says: I have heard your prayer and seen
your tears; I will add fifteen years[a] to your
life. 6And I will deliver you and this city
from the hand of the king of Assyria. I will
defend[b] this city.
7" 'This is the LORD's sign[c] to you that the
LORD will do what he has promised: 8I will
make the shadow cast by the sun go back
the ten steps it has gone down on the stairway of Ahaz.' " So the sunlight went back
the ten steps it had gone down.[d]

9A writing of Hezekiah king of Judah after his illness and recovery:

10I said, "In the prime of my life[e]
must I go through the gates of death[f]
and be robbed of the rest of my
years?[g]"
11I said, "I will not again see the LORD
himself
in the land of the living;[h]
no longer will I look on my fellow man,
or be with those who now dwell in
this world.
12Like a shepherd's tent[i] my house
has been pulled down[j] and taken
from me.
Like a weaver I have rolled[k] up my life,
and he has cut me off from the loom;[l]
day and night[m] you made an end
of me.
13I waited patiently till dawn,
but like a lion he broke[n] all my bones;[o]
day and night you made an end
of me.
14I cried like a swift or thrush,
I moaned like a mourning dove.[p]
My eyes grew weak as I looked to the
heavens.
I am being threatened; Lord, come to
my aid!"[q]
15But what can I say?
He has spoken to me, and he himself
has done this.[r]
I will walk humbly[s] all my years
because of this anguish of my soul.[t]
16Lord, by such things people live;
and my spirit finds life in them too.
You restored me to health
and let me live.[u]
17Surely it was for my benefit
that I suffered such anguish.
In your love you kept me
from the pit[v] of destruction;
you have put all my sins[w]
behind your back.[x]
18For the grave[y] cannot praise you,
death cannot sing your praise;[z]
those who go down to the pit[a]
cannot hope for your faithfulness.
19The living, the living—they praise[b] you,
as I am doing today;
parents tell their children[c]
about your faithfulness.
20The LORD will save me,
and we will sing[d] with stringed
instruments[e]
all the days of our lives[f]
in the temple[g] of the LORD.

21Isaiah had said, "Prepare a poultice of figs and apply it to the boil, and he will recover."
22Hezekiah had asked, "What will be the
sign that I will go up to the temple of the
LORD?"

Envoys From Babylon

39 At that time Marduk-Baladan son of Baladan king of Babylon[h] sent Hezekiah letters and a gift, because he had
heard of his illness and recovery. 2Hezeki-
ah received the envoys[i] gladly and showed them what was in his storehouses—the silver, the gold,[j] the spices, the fine olive oil—his entire armory and everything found among his treasures. There was nothing in his palace or in all his kingdom that Hezekiah did not show them.
3Then Isaiah the prophet went to King Hezekiah and asked, "What did those men say, and where did they come from?"
"From a distant land,[k]" Hezekiah replied. "They came to me from Babylon."

38:5 ***add fifteen years to your life.*** Hezekiah had no male heir at the time of his illness. Manasseh, the successor to his throne, was 12 when Hezekiah died (2 Kin. 20:21–21:1).
38:9 ***writing of Hezekiah.*** Scriptures attest to King Hezekiah's interest in devotional literature. Apparently, he instructed his scribes to compile some of the proverbs of Solomon (Prov. 25:1). He ordered the Levites to worship God with the psalms of David and Asaph (2 Chr. 29:30), and the song of praise (v. 10–20) has some similarities with those psalms.
38:22 ***sign.*** Depending on one's attitude, the request for a sign may express either unbelief (Matt. 12:39; John 6:30) or faith (v. 7). The healing of a boil would be the sign that the Lord would save Hezekiah (vv. 20–21).
39:1 ***recovery.*** The miracle of the sundial (38:8) would have held special interest for the astronomy-minded Babylonians (2 Chr. 32:31).
39:2 ***showed them what was in his storehouses.*** Hezekiah was flattered to receive the attention of the Babylonian delegation and wanted to show how important he was.

38:5 [a] 2Ki 18:2 **38:6** [b] Isa 31:5; 37:35 **38:7** [c] Isa 7:11, 14 **38:8** [d] Jos 10:13 **38:10** [e] Ps 102:24 [f] Ps 107:18; 2Co 1:9 [g] Job 17:11 **38:11** [h] Ps 27:13; 116:9 **38:12** [i] 2Co 5:1, 4; 2Pe 1:13-14 [j] Job 4:21 [k] Heb 1:12 [l] Job 7:6 [m] Ps 73:14 **38:13** [n] Ps 51:8 [o] Job 10:16; Da 6:24 **38:14** [p] Isa 59:11 [q] Job 17:3 **38:15** [r] Ps 39:9 [s] 1Ki 21:27 [t] Job 7:11 **38:16** [u] Ps 119:25 **38:17** [v] Ps 30:3 [w] Jer 31:34 [x] Isa 43:25; Mic 7:19 **38:18** [y] Ecc 9:10 [z] Ps 6:5; 88:10-11; 115:17 [a] Ps 30:9 **38:19** [b] Dt 6:7; Ps 118:17; 119:175 [c] Dt 11:19 **38:20** [d] Ps 68:25 [e] Ps 33:2 [f] Ps 116:2 [g] Ps 116:17-19 **39:1** [h] 2Ch 32:31 **39:2** [i] 2Ch 32:31 [j] 2Ki 18:15 **39:3** [k] Dt 28:49

4 The prophet asked, "What did they see
in your palace?"
"They saw everything in my palace,"
Hezekiah said. "There is nothing among
my treasures that I did not show them."
5 Then Isaiah said to Hezekiah, "Hear
the word of the LORD Almighty: 6 The time
will surely come when everything in your
palace, and all that your predecessors have
stored up until this day, will be carried off
to Babylon.[l] Nothing will be left, says the
LORD. 7 And some of your descendants,
your own flesh and blood who will be born
to you, will be taken away, and they will
become eunuchs in the palace of the king
of Babylon.[m]"
8 "The word of the LORD you have spoken
is good," Hezekiah replied. For he thought,
"There will be peace and security in my
lifetime.[n]"

Comfort for God's People

40 Comfort, comfort[o] my people,
says your God.
2 Speak tenderly[p] to Jerusalem,
and proclaim to her
that her hard service has been
completed,[q]
that her sin has been paid for,
that she has received from the LORD's
hand
double[r] for all her sins.

3 A voice of one calling:
"In the wilderness prepare
the way[s] for the LORD[a];
make straight in the desert
a highway for our God.[b][t]
4 Every valley shall be raised up,
every mountain and hill made low;
the rough ground shall become
level,[u]
the rugged places a plain.
5 And the glory of the LORD will be
revealed,
and all people will see it together.[v]
For the mouth of the LORD
has spoken."[w]

6 A voice says, "Cry out."
And I said, "What shall I cry?"
"All people are like grass,[x]
and all their faithfulness is like the
flowers of the field.
7 The grass withers and the flowers fall,
because the breath[y] of the LORD blows
on them.
Surely the people are grass.
8 The grass withers and the flowers fall,
but the word[z] of our God endures
forever.[a]"

9 You who bring good news[b] to Zion,
go up on a high mountain.
You who bring good news to
Jerusalem,[c]
lift up your voice with a shout,
lift it up, do not be afraid;
say to the towns of Judah,
"Here is your God!"[c]

---

[a] 3 Or *A voice of one calling in the wilderness: / "Prepare the way for the LORD* [b] 3 Hebrew; Septuagint *make straight the paths of our God* [c] 9 Or *Zion, bringer of good news, / go up on a high mountain. / Jerusalem, bringer of good news*

40:1–55:13 *Comfort.* This section is addressed to the Babylonian exiles in a prophetic manner. This book of comfort, written about 150 years before the time of Cyrus, promised the exiles from Judah that they would return to Jerusalem (40:1–2). The restoration after the exile pointed to the coming of the Lord's kingdom. In Isaiah's prophecy, this first taste of salvation merges with predictions of the full salvation that Jesus Christ would bring.

40:2–5 Preparing the Way—Biblical scholars think this passage was originally intended to encourage the Israelite exiles, who were looking forward to their return to Israel. The obstacles to getting back home included both a release from slavery and a journey of hundreds of miles on foot through hostile territory. There was also much to be apprehensive about when they arrived home. How were they ever going to be able to rebuild their communities when they were virtually penniless and without resources? Scholars also see this passage as one of the key messianic prophecies. The image of verses 3–4 is that of the ancient Near Eastern practice of "rolling out the red carpet" for a visiting monarch. Mark makes use of these verses to describe the ministry of John the Baptist, as the prophet urges people to prepare for the coming of the Messiah.

Both applications point to the same concepts. God is saying, "Trust Me, I will make it right. I will make a way through the obstacles. No matter how large the obstacles, I will overcome them." We should see these as some of the strongest words of comfort in the Bible.

40:2 *Jerusalem.* In this case, Jerusalem represents the exiles.

40:3 *voice of one calling.* John referred to this passage to explain who he was (John 1:23) as the forerunner of Christ.

40:5 *glory ... will be revealed.* The glory of the Lord is revealed in the restoration of the captives, but in a fuller sense it is revealed in the coming of the Lord Jesus Christ (Luke 2:29–32; John 1:14).

40:9 *good news.* Good news from God to man can always be properly described as "gospel." Here, the glad tidings are that the God who once delivered His captive people from bondage in Egypt is again at hand to rescue and protect His beleaguered Israelites. The assurance that God is with us (7:14; John 1:14) to save is at the heart of the Christian gospel (1 Cor. 15:3–4), and it is always "good news," even when it is something we have heard before.

39:6 [l] 2Ki 24:13; Jer 20:5 **39:7** [m] 2Ki 24:15; Da 1:1-7 **39:8** [n] 2Ch 32:26 **40:1** [o] Isa 12:1; 49:13; 51:3, 12; 52:9; 61:2; 66:13; Jer 31:13; Zep 3:14-17; 2Co 1:3 **40:2** [p] Isa 35:4 [q] Isa 41:11-13; 49:25 [r] Isa 61:7; Jer 16:18; Zec 9:12; Rev 18:6 **40:3** [s] Mal 3:1 [t] Mt 3:3*; Mk 1:3*; Jn 1:23* **40:4** [u] Isa 45:2, 13 **40:5** [v] Isa 52:10; Lk 3:4-6* [w] Isa 1:20; 58:14 **40:6** [x] Job 14:2 **40:7** [y] Job 41:21 **40:8** [z] Isa 55:11; 59:21 [a] Mt 5:18; 1Pe 1:24-25* **40:9** [b] Isa 52:7-10; 61:1; Ro 10:15 [c] Isa 25:9

10 See, the Sovereign LORD comes[d] with power,
and he rules[e] with a mighty arm.[f]
See, his reward[g] is with him,
and his recompense accompanies him.
11 He tends his flock like a shepherd:[h]
He gathers the lambs in his arms
and carries them close to his heart;
he gently leads those that have young.

12 Who has measured the waters[i] in the hollow of his hand,[j]
or with the breadth of his hand marked off the heavens?[k]
Who has held the dust of the earth in a basket,
or weighed the mountains on the scales
and the hills in a balance?
13 Who can fathom the Spirit[a] of the LORD,
or instruct the LORD as his counselor?[l]
14 Whom did the LORD consult to enlighten him,
and who taught him the right way?
Who was it that taught him knowledge,[m]
or showed him the path of understanding?

15 Surely the nations are like a drop in a bucket;
they are regarded as dust on the scales;
he weighs the islands as though they were fine dust.
16 Lebanon is not sufficient for altar fires,
nor its animals[n] enough for burnt offerings.
17 Before him all the nations[o] are as nothing;[p]
they are regarded by him as worthless
and less than nothing.[q]

18 With whom, then, will you compare God?[r]
To what image[s] will you liken him?
19 As for an idol,[t] a metalworker casts it,
and a goldsmith[u] overlays it with gold[v]
and fashions silver chains for it.
20 A person too poor to present such an offering
selects wood that will not rot;
they look for a skilled worker
to set up an idol that will not topple.[w]

21 Do you not know?
Have you not heard?
Has it not been told[x] you from the beginning?
Have you not understood[y] since the earth was founded?[z]
22 He sits enthroned above the circle of the earth,
and its people are like grasshoppers.[a]
He stretches out the heavens like a canopy,[b]
and spreads them out like a tent[c] to live in.
23 He brings princes[d] to naught
and reduces the rulers of this world to nothing.[e]
24 No sooner are they planted,
no sooner are they sown,
no sooner do they take root in the ground,
than he blows[f] on them and they wither,
and a whirlwind sweeps them away like chaff.

25 "To whom will you compare me?[g]
Or who is my equal?" says the Holy One.
26 Lift up your eyes and look to the heavens:[h]
Who created[i] all these?

[a] 13 Or *mind*

40:12–31 God's Sovereignty over the Nations—God controls the destinies of rulers and politicians and public figures, no matter how much power they think they have. When times are rough, we wonder if God is really in charge. We wonder why He lets us get moved around by so many economic and political forces beyond our control. We sometimes wonder if He really even cares about what is going on in the world or our lives. If He really is in charge, does He know what He is doing?

The testimony of Isaiah is a resounding Yes! Nations may rise and fall. Rulers may come and go. God remains both Starter and Finisher. The circumstances that surround us are temporary conditions in the scheme of eternity. As God sustains the stars in heaven and the whole universe, He sustains our lives. We may not be able to say that easily every day, but if we keep coming back to Him, He will not disappoint us.

40:12 *with the breadth of his hand marked.* This verse dramatically imposes images of the grandeur of God.

40:15 *nations are like a drop in a bucket.* Wicked nations have no power to thwart the purposes of God (Ps. 2:1–6).

40:19–20 *idol.* Many idols were made with wood, then overlaid with gold. The poor had to choose the best wood available and hope it was good enough. But of what value is the prayer of a poor man to a plain idol? What is the value of the rich to one covered with gold? To both questions, the answer is "none."

40:26 *who created all these.* The Babylonian gods

40:10 [d] Rev 22:7 [e] Isa 9:6-7 [f] Isa 59:16 [g] Isa 62:11; Rev 22:12 **40:11** [h] Eze 34:23; Mic 5:4; Jn 10:11 **40:12** [i] Job 38:10 [j] Pr 30:4 [k] Heb 1:10-12 **40:13** [l] Ro 11:34*; 1Co 2:16* **40:14** [m] Job 21:22; Col 2:3 **40:16** [n] Ps 50:9-11; Mic 6:7; Heb 10:5-9 **40:17** [o] Isa 30:28 [p] Isa 29:7 [q] Da 4:35 **40:18** [r] Ex 8:10; 1Sa 2:2; Isa 46:5 [s] Ac 17:29 **40:19** [t] Ps 115:4 [u] Isa 41:7; Jer 10:3 [v] Isa 2:20 **40:20** [w] 1Sa 5:3 **40:21** [x] Ps 19:1; 50:6; Ac 14:17 [y] Ro 1:19 [z] Isa 48:13; 51:13 **40:22** [a] Nu 13:33; Ps 104:2; Isa 42:5 [b] Job 22:14 [c] Job 36:29 **40:23** [d] Isa 34:12 [e] Job 12:21; Ps 107:40 **40:24** [f] Isa 41:16 **40:25** [g] ver 18 **40:26** [h] Isa 51:6 [i] Ps 89:11-13; Isa 42:5

He who brings out the starry host[j] one by one
and calls forth each of them by name.
Because of his great power and mighty strength,
not one of them is missing.[k]

27 Why do you complain, Jacob?
Why do you say, Israel,
"My way is hidden from the LORD;
my cause is disregarded by my God"?[l]
28 Do you not know?
Have you not heard?[m]
The LORD is the everlasting[n] God,
the Creator of the ends of the earth.
He will not grow tired or weary,
and his understanding no one can fathom.[o]
29 He gives strength to the weary[p]
and increases the power of the weak.
30 Even youths grow tired and weary,
and young men[q] stumble and fall;
31 but those who hope[r] in the LORD
will renew their strength.[s]
They will soar on wings like eagles;[t]
they will run and not grow weary,
they will walk and not be faint.[u]

The Helper of Israel

41 "Be silent[v] before me, you islands![w]
Let the nations renew their strength!
Let them come forward[x] and speak;
let us meet together[y] at the place of judgment.

2 "Who has stirred[z] up one from the east,[a]
calling him in righteousness to his service[a]?
He hands nations over to him
and subdues kings before him.
He turns them to dust[b] with his sword,
to windblown chaff[c] with his bow.
3 He pursues them and moves on unscathed,
by a path his feet have not traveled before.
4 Who has done this and carried it through,
calling forth the generations from the beginning?[d]
I, the LORD—with the first of them
and with the last[e]—I am he."

5 The islands[f] have seen it and fear;
the ends of the earth tremble.
They approach and come forward;
6 they help each other
and say to their companions, "Be strong!"
7 The metalworker encourages the goldsmith,[g]
and the one who smooths with the hammer
spurs on the one who strikes the anvil.
One says of the welding, "It is good."
The other nails down the idol so it will not topple.

8 "But you, Israel, my servant,
Jacob, whom I have chosen,
you descendants of Abraham[h] my friend,[i]
9 I took you from the ends of the earth,[j]
from its farthest corners I called you.
I said, 'You are my servant';
I have chosen[k] you and have not rejected you.
10 So do not fear, for I am with you;[l]
do not be dismayed, for I am your God.
I will strengthen you and help[m] you;
I will uphold you with my righteous right hand.

11 "All who rage[n] against you
will surely be ashamed and disgraced;[o]
those who oppose[p] you
will be as nothing and perish.[q]
12 Though you search for your enemies,
you will not find them.[r]
Those who wage war against you
will be as nothing[s] at all.
13 For I am the LORD your God
who takes hold of your right hand[t]
and says to you, Do not fear;
I will help[u] you.

[a] 2 Or *east, / whom victory meets at every step*

---

were identified with the heavenly bodies. These words would have been comforting and encouraging to the Israelites who had learned to say no to Babylon and yes to the Lord.

40:27 ***my cause is disregarded.*** The captives in their weariness may have complained that they were forgotten by God.

40:31 ***hope.*** To "hope" for the Lord entails confident expectation and active waiting, never passive resignation.

41:2 ***one from the east.*** This refers to Cyrus, king of Persia (559–530 B.C.; see 46:11).

41:4 ***first ... last.*** The Lord also refers to Himself as the first and last in Revelation 22:13, when He is speaking to the apostle John of the things that will happen at the end of the age. This description speaks of His sovereignty over all time.

40:26 [j] Ps 147:4 [k] Isa 34:16 **40:27** [l] Job 27:2; Lk 18:7-8 **40:28** [m] ver 21 [n] Ps 90:2 [o] Ps 147:5; Ro 11:33 **40:29** [p] Isa 50:4; Jer 31:25 **40:30** [q] Isa 9:17; Jer 6:11; 9:21 **40:31** [r] Lk 18:1 [s] 2Co 4:16 [t] Ex 19:4; Ps 103:5 [u] 2Co 4:1; Heb 12:1-3 **41:1** [v] Hab 2:20; Zec 2:13 [w] Isa 11:11 [x] Isa 48:16 [y] Isa 1:18; 34:1; 50:8 **41:2** [z] Ezr 1:2 [a] ver 25; Isa 45:1, 13 [b] 2Sa 22:43 [c] Isa 40:24 **41:4** [d] ver 26; Isa 46:10 [e] Isa 44:6; 48:12; Rev 1:8, 17; 22:13 **41:5** [f] Eze 26:17-18 **41:7** [g] Isa 40:19 **41:8** [h] Isa 29:22; 51:2; 63:16 [i] 2Ch 20:7; Jas 2:23 **41:9** [j] Isa 11:12 [k] Dt 7:6 **41:10** [l] Jos 1:9; Isa 43:2, 5; Ro 8:31 [m] ver 13-14; Isa 44:2; 49:8 **41:11** [n] Isa 17:12 [o] Isa 45:24 [p] Ex 23:22 [q] Isa 29:8 **41:12** [r] Ps 37:35-36 [s] Isa 17:14 **41:13** [t] Isa 42:6; 45:1 [u] ver 10

14 Do not be afraid, you worm Jacob,
little Israel, do not fear,
for I myself will help you," declares the LORD,
your Redeemer, the Holy One of Israel.
15 "See, I will make you into a threshing sledge,[v]
new and sharp, with many teeth.
You will thresh the mountains and crush them,
and reduce the hills to chaff.
16 You will winnow[w] them, the wind will pick them up,
and a gale will blow them away.
But you will rejoice in the LORD
and glory[x] in the Holy One of Israel.

17 "The poor and needy search for water,[y]
but there is none;
their tongues are parched with thirst.
But I the LORD will answer[z] them;
I, the God of Israel, will not forsake them.
18 I will make rivers flow[a] on barren heights,
and springs within the valleys.
I will turn the desert[b] into pools of water,
and the parched ground into springs.[c]
19 I will put in the desert
the cedar and the acacia, the myrtle and the olive.
I will set junipers in the wasteland,
the fir and the cypress together,[d]
20 so that people may see and know,
may consider and understand,
that the hand of the LORD has done this,
that the Holy One of Israel has created[e] it.

21 "Present your case," says the LORD.
"Set forth your arguments," says Jacob's King.[f]
22 "Tell us, you idols,
what is going to happen.[g]
Tell us what the former things were,
so that we may consider them
and know their final outcome.
Or declare to us the things to come,[h]
23 tell us what the future holds,
so we may know[i] that you are gods.
Do something, whether good or bad,[j]
so that we will be dismayed and filled with fear.
24 But you are less than nothing[k]
and your works are utterly worthless;
whoever chooses you is detestable.[l]

25 "I have stirred up one from the north,[m]
and he comes—
one from the rising sun who calls on my name.
He treads[n] on rulers as if they were mortar,
as if he were a potter treading the clay.
26 Who told of this from the beginning, so we could know,
or beforehand, so we could say, 'He was right'?
No one told of this,
no one foretold it,
no one heard any words[o] from you.
27 I was the first to tell[p] Zion, 'Look, here they are!'
I gave to Jerusalem a messenger of good news.[q]
28 I look but there is no one[r]—
no one among the gods to give counsel,[s]
no one to give answer when I ask them.
29 See, they are all false!
Their deeds amount to nothing;[t]
their images are but wind[u] and confusion.

The Servant of the LORD

42 "Here is my servant, whom I uphold,
my chosen one[v] in whom I delight;
I will put my Spirit[w] on him,
and he will bring justice to the nations.
2 He will not shout or cry out,
or raise his voice in the streets.

41:14 ***Redeemer.*** For Israel, the redeemer was the family protector of distressed relatives, who could avenge murder (Num. 35:19) and redeem indentured slaves (Lev. 25:47–49). When the Lord is called the Redeemer, the title highlights His zeal to defend, protect, and purchase back His people (49:26).
41:16 ***winnow them.*** As threshed grain is tossed in the air or "winnowed" to separate the chaff, so the victorious people of God would be able to "blow away" their enemies.
41:21 ***Present your case.*** The Lord is addressing the idols in this passage. He is pointing out that only the Lord can tell the past or the future; He challenges the idols to prove themselves, but they cannot.
41:24 ***detestable.*** Something that is detestable is something that causes revulsion. If the Lord regards idol worshipers as detestable, we should too.
41:25 ***from the north.*** The conquest of Media by Cyrus (550 B.C.) made him master of the territories north of Babylon. Cyrus did not personally know God (45:4), but he nevertheless called on God's name when he released the exiles (2 Chr. 36:23; Ezra 1:1–4).
42:1 ***my servant.*** The Lord formally presents His servant. This title is identified with Jesus Christ in the New Testament. This is the beginning of the first song of the Suffering Servant (vv. 1–13).

41:15 [v] Mic 4:13 **41:16** [w] Jer 51:2 [x] Isa 45:25 **41:17** [y] Isa 43:20 [z] Isa 30:19 **41:18** [a] Isa 30:25 [b] Isa 43:19 [c] Isa 35:7 **41:19** [d] Isa 60:13 **41:20** [e] Job 12:9 **41:21** [f] Isa 43:15 **41:22** [g] Isa 43:9; 45:21 [h] Isa 46:10 **41:23** [i] Isa 42:9; 44:7-8; 45:3 [j] Jer 10:5 **41:24** [k] Isa 37:19; 44:9; 1Co 8:4 [l] Ps 115:8 **41:25** [m] ver 2 [n] 2Sa 22:43 **41:26** [o] Hab 2:18-19 **41:27** [p] Isa 48:3, 16 [q] Isa 40:9 **41:28** [r] Isa 50:2; 59:16; 63:5 [s] Isa 40:13-14 **41:29** [t] ver 24 [u] Jer 5:13 **42:1** [v] Isa 43:10; Lk 9:35; 1Pe 2:4, 6 [w] Isa 11:2; Mt 3:16-17; Jn 3:34

3 A bruised reed he will not break,
and a smoldering wick he will not snuff out.
In faithfulness he will bring forth justice;[x]
4 he will not falter or be discouraged
till he establishes justice on earth.
In his teaching the islands will put their hope."[y]

5 This is what God the LORD says—
the Creator of the heavens, who stretches them out,
who spreads out the earth with all that springs from it,[z]
who gives breath[a] to its people,
and life to those who walk on it:
6 "I, the LORD, have called[b] you in righteousness;[c]
I will take hold of your hand.
I will keep[d] you and will make you
to be a covenant[e] for the people
and a light for the Gentiles,[f]
7 to open eyes that are blind,[g]
to free[h] captives from prison[i]
and to release from the dungeon
those who sit in darkness.

8 "I am the LORD; that is my name![j]
I will not yield my glory to another[k]
or my praise to idols.
9 See, the former things have taken place,
and new things I declare;
before they spring into being
I announce them to you."

Song of Praise to the LORD

10 Sing to the LORD a new song,[l]
his praise from the ends of the earth,[m]
you who go down to the sea, and all that is in it,[n]
you islands, and all who live in them.
11 Let the wilderness[o] and its towns raise their voices;
let the settlements where Kedar[p] lives rejoice.
Let the people of Sela sing for joy;
let them shout from the mountaintops.[q]
12 Let them give glory[r] to the LORD
and proclaim his praise in the islands.
13 The LORD will march out like a champion,[s]
like a warrior he will stir up his zeal;[t]
with a shout[u] he will raise the battle cry
and will triumph over his enemies.[v]

14 "For a long time I have kept silent,
I have been quiet and held myself back.
But now, like a woman in childbirth,
I cry out, I gasp and pant.
15 I will lay waste[w] the mountains and hills
and dry up all their vegetation;
I will turn rivers into islands
and dry up[x] the pools.
16 I will lead[y] the blind[z] by ways they have not known,
along unfamiliar paths I will guide them;
I will turn the darkness into light before them
and make the rough places smooth.[a]
These are the things I will do;
I will not forsake[b] them.
17 But those who trust in idols,
who say to images, 'You are our gods,'
will be turned back in utter shame.[c]

Israel Blind and Deaf

18 "Hear, you deaf;[d]
look, you blind, and see!
19 Who is blind[e] but my servant,[f]
and deaf like the messenger[g] I send?
Who is blind like the one in covenant[h] with me,
blind like the servant of the LORD?
20 You have seen many things, but you pay no attention;
your ears are open, but you do not listen."[i]

42:3 ***bruised reed ... smoldering wick.*** The Servant will restore that which is broken; He will not break or snuff out the needy.
42:6 ***covenant.*** The Servant will institute a new covenant binding Israel to the Lord (49:8). The prophets refer to this new covenant as a "covenant of peace" (54:10; Ezek. 34:25); an "everlasting covenant" (which is also associated with the Davidic covenant, 55:3); a "new covenant" (Jer. 31:31–34); and most often simply as covenant. ***people.*** The "people" refers to the Gentiles.
42:17 ***idols.*** Why is idolatry so terrible in God's sight? Several reasons may be given. It displays a total ignorance of the true nature and being of the Creator. He is invisible, eternal, all-knowing, and all-present Spirit, without limitations. Idolatry usually reduces the concept of God to an ugly metal or wooden object, which is almost always perceived as evil and bloodthirsty, selfish and capricious. Finally, idolatry provides absolutely no indication of those characteristics closest to God's heart—His love, mercy, grace, and holiness.
42:18–25 ***Hear, you deaf.*** This prophecy, justifying the exile as punishment, consists of two parts. First, the Lord addresses the fact that the people did not listen to Him.

42:3 [x] Ps 72:2 **42:4** [y] Ge 49:10; Mt 12:18-21* **42:5** [z] Ps 24:2 [a] Ac 17:25 **42:6** [b] Isa 43:1 [c] Jer 23:6 [d] Isa 26:3 [e] Isa 49:8 [f] Lk 2:32; Ac 13:47 **42:7** [g] Isa 35:5 [h] Isa 49:9; 61:1 [i] Lk 4:19; 2Ti 2:26; Heb 2:14-15 **42:8** [j] Ex 3:15 [k] Isa 48:11 **42:10** [l] Ps 33:3; 40:3; 98:1 [m] Isa 49:6 [n] 1Ch 16:32; Ps 96:11 **42:11** [o] Isa 32:16 [p] Isa 60:7 [q] Isa 52:7; Na 1:15 **42:12** [r] Isa 24:15 **42:13** [s] Isa 9:6 [t] Isa 26:11 [u] Hos 11:10 [v] Isa 66:14 **42:15** [w] Eze 38:20 [x] Isa 50:2; Na 1:4-6 **42:16** [y] Lk 1:78-79 [z] Isa 32:3 [a] Lk 3:5 [b] Heb 13:5 **42:17** [c] Ps 97:7; Isa 1:29; 44:11; 45:16 **42:18** [d] Isa 35:5 **42:19** [e] Isa 43:8; Eze 12:2 [f] Isa 41:8-9 [g] Isa 44:26 [h] Isa 26:3 **42:20** [i] Jer 6:10

21 It pleased the LORD
for the sake of his righteousness
to make his law[j] great and glorious.
22 But this is a people plundered and looted,
all of them trapped in pits[k]
or hidden away in prisons.[l]
They have become plunder,
with no one to rescue them;
they have been made loot,
with no one to say, "Send them back."
23 Which of you will listen to this
or pay close attention[m] in time to come?
24 Who handed Jacob over to become loot,
and Israel to the plunderers?
Was it not the LORD,
against whom we have sinned?
For they would not follow[n] his ways;
they did not obey his law.
25 So he poured out on them his burning
anger,
the violence of war.
It enveloped them in flames,[o] yet they
did not understand;
it consumed them, but they did not
take it to heart.[p]

Israel's Only Savior

43 But now, this is what the LORD
says—
he who created you, Jacob,
he who formed[q] you, Israel:[r]
"Do not fear, for I have redeemed[s] you;
I have summoned you by name;[t] you
are mine.
2 When you pass through the waters,[u]
I will be with you;[v]
and when you pass through the rivers,
they will not sweep over you.
When you walk through the fire,[w]
you will not be burned;
the flames will not set you ablaze.[x]
3 For I am the LORD your God,[y]
the Holy One of Israel, your Savior;
I give Egypt for your ransom,
Cush[a][z] and Seba in your stead.[a]
4 Since you are precious and honored in
my sight,
and because I love[b] you,
I will give people in exchange for you,
nations in exchange for your life.
5 Do not be afraid,[c] for I am with you;[d]
I will bring your children[e] from the
east
and gather you from the west.
6 I will say to the north, 'Give them up!'
and to the south,[f] 'Do not hold them
back.'
Bring my sons from afar
and my daughters[g] from the ends of
the earth—
7 everyone who is called by my name,[h]
whom I created for my glory,
whom I formed and made.[i]"

8 Lead out those who have eyes but are
blind,[j]
who have ears but are deaf.[k]
9 All the nations gather together[l]
and the peoples assemble.
Which of their gods foretold[m] this
and proclaimed to us the former
things?
Let them bring in their witnesses to
prove they were right,
so that others may hear and say, "It is
true."
10 "You are my witnesses," declares the
LORD,
"and my servant[n] whom I have
chosen,
so that you may know and believe me
and understand that I am he.
Before me no god[o] was formed,
nor will there be one after me.
11 I, even I, am the LORD,
and apart from me there is no savior.[p]
12 I have revealed and saved and
proclaimed—
I, and not some foreign god[q] among
you.
You are my witnesses,[r]" declares the
LORD, "that I am God.
13 Yes, and from ancient days[s] I am he.
No one can deliver out of my hand.
When I act, who can reverse it?"[t]

God's Mercy and Israel's Unfaithfulness

14 This is what the LORD says—
your Redeemer, the Holy One of
Israel:
"For your sake I will send to Babylon
and bring down as fugitives[u] all the
Babylonians,[b][v]
in the ships in which they took pride.

---

[a] *3* That is, the upper Nile region [b] *14* Or *Chaldeans*

42:24 ***sinned.*** The second part of the prophecy addresses the sin of the exiles, which was the reason for the punishment.
43:1 ***this is what the LORD says.*** This statement emphasizes the authority of the words that will follow.
43:14 ***This is what the LORD says.*** The same phrase (v. 1) is used to emphasize the ultimate source of this prophecy, God Himself. ***Redeemer.*** The Lord is described as Redeemer because He zealously defends, protects, and purchases back His people (41:14).

42:21 [j] ver 4 **42:22** [k] Isa 24:18 [l] Isa 24:22 **42:23** [m] Isa 48:18 **42:24** [n] Isa 30:15 **42:25** [o] 2Ki 25:9 [p] Isa 29:13; 47:7; 57:1, 11; Hos 7:9 **43:1** [q] ver 7 [r] Ge 32:28; Isa 44:21 [s] Isa 44:2, 6 [t] Isa 42:6; 45:3-4 **43:2** [u] Isa 8:7 [v] Dt 31:6, 8 [w] Isa 29:6; 30:27 [x] Ps 66:12; Da 3:25-27 **43:3** [y] Ex 20:2 [z] Isa 20:3 [a] Pr 21:18 **43:4** [b] Isa 63:9 **43:5** [c] Isa 44:2 [d] Jer 30:10-11 [e] Isa 41:8 **43:6** [f] Ps 107:3 [g] 2Co 6:18 **43:7** [h] Isa 56:5; 63:19; Jas 2:7 [i] ver 1, 21; Ps 100:3; Eph 2:10 **43:8** [j] Isa 6:9-10 [k] Isa 42:20; Eze 12:2 **43:9** [l] Isa 41:1 [m] Isa 41:26 **43:10** [n] Isa 41:8-9 [o] Isa 44:6, 8 **43:11** [p] Isa 45:21 **43:12** [q] Dt 32:12; Ps 81:9 [r] Isa 44:8 **43:13** [s] Ps 90:2 [t] Job 9:12; Isa 14:27 **43:14** [u] Isa 13:14-15 [v] Isa 23:13

15 I am the LORD, your Holy One,
Israel's Creator, your King."
16 This is what the LORD says—
he who made a way through the sea,
a path through the mighty waters,[w]
17 who drew out[x] the chariots and horses,
the army and reinforcements together,[y]
and they lay there, never to rise again,
extinguished, snuffed out like a wick:
18 "Forget the former things;
do not dwell on the past.
19 See, I am doing a new thing![z]
Now it springs up; do you not perceive it?
I am making a way in the wilderness[a]
and streams in the wasteland.
20 The wild animals honor me,
the jackals[b] and the owls,
because I provide water[c] in the wilderness
and streams in the wasteland,
to give drink to my people, my chosen,
21 the people I formed for myself
that they may proclaim my praise.[d]

22 "Yet you have not called on me, Jacob,
you have not wearied yourselves for[a] me, Israel.[e]
23 You have not brought me sheep for burnt offerings,
nor honored[f] me with your sacrifices.[g]
I have not burdened you with grain offerings
nor wearied you with demands[h] for incense.[i]
24 You have not bought any fragrant calamus[j] for me,
or lavished on me the fat of your sacrifices.
But you have burdened me with your sins
and wearied[k] me with your offenses.[l]

25 "I, even I, am he who blots out
your transgressions,[m] for my own sake,[n]
and remembers your sins no more.[o]
26 Review the past for me,
let us argue the matter together;[p]
state the case[q] for your innocence.
27 Your first father sinned;
those I sent to teach[r] you rebelled against me.
28 So I disgraced the dignitaries of your temple;
I consigned Jacob to destruction[b]
and Israel to scorn.[s]

Israel the Chosen

44 "But now listen, Jacob, my servant,[t]
Israel, whom I have chosen.
2 This is what the LORD says—
he who made you, who formed you in the womb,
and who will help[u] you:
Do not be afraid, Jacob, my servant,
Jeshurun,[c][v] whom I have chosen.
3 For I will pour water[w] on the thirsty land,
and streams on the dry ground;
I will pour out my Spirit[x] on your offspring,
and my blessing on your descendants.[y]
4 They will spring up like grass in a meadow,
like poplar trees[z] by flowing streams.[a]
5 Some will say, 'I belong to the LORD';
others will call themselves by the name of Jacob;
still others will write on their hand,[b] 'The LORD's,'[c]
and will take the name Israel.

The LORD, Not Idols

6 "This is what the LORD says—
Israel's King[d] and Redeemer,[e] the LORD Almighty:
I am the first and I am the last;[f]
apart from me there is no God.
7 Who then is like me? Let him proclaim it.
Let him declare and lay out before me
what has happened since I established my ancient people,
and what is yet to come—
yes, let them foretell[g] what will come.

[a] 22 Or *Jacob; / surely you have grown weary of*
[b] 28 The Hebrew term refers to the irrevocable giving over of things or persons to the LORD, often by totally destroying them.
[c] 2 *Jeshurun* means *the upright one*, that is, Israel.

43:22 *Yet you.* After the splendid and glorious declarations of His faithfulness, the Lord addresses the unfaithfulness of His people.
43:25 *for my own sake.* The Lord chooses to save and forgive. This arises out of His own character (37:35; 42:21; 48:9,11).
44:2 *Jeshurun.* Jeshurun, meaning "upright one," is a poetic word for the nation of Israel (Deut. 32:15).
44:6 *Israel's King.* For background, read Psalm 99, which begins by declaring, "The LORD reigns."

43:16 [w] Ps 77:19; Isa 11:15; 51:10 **43:17** [x] Ps 118:12; Isa 1:31 [y] Ex 14:9 **43:19** [z] 2Co 5:17; Rev 21:5 [a] Ex 17:6; Nu 20:11 **43:20** [b] Isa 13:22 [c] Isa 48:21 **43:21** [d] Ps 102:18; 1Pe 2:9 **43:22** [e] Isa 30:11 **43:23** [f] Zec 7:5-6; Mal 1:6-8 [g] Am 5:25 [h] Jer 7:22 [i] Ex 30:35; Lev 2:1 **43:24** [j] Ex 30:23 [k] Isa 1:14; 7:13 [l] Mal 2:17 **43:25** [m] Ac 3:19 [n] Isa 37:35; Eze 36:22 [o] Isa 38:17; Jer 31:34 **43:26** [p] Isa 1:18 [q] Isa 41:1; 50:8 **43:27** [r] Isa 9:15; 28:7; Jer 5:31 **43:28** [s] Jer 24:9; Eze 5:15 **44:1** [t] ver 21; Jer 30:10; 46:27-28 **44:2** [u] Isa 41:10 [v] Dt 32:15 **44:3** [w] Joel 3:18 [x] Joel 2:28; Ac 2:17 [y] Isa 61:9; 65:23 **44:4** [z] Lev 23:40 [a] Job 40:22 **44:5** [b] Ex 13:9 [c] Zec 8:20-22 **44:6** [d] Isa 41:21 [e] Isa 43:1 [f] Isa 41:4; Rev 1:8,17; 22:13 **44:7** [g] Isa 41:22,26

8 Do not tremble, do not be afraid.
Did I not proclaim this and foretell it long ago?
You are my witnesses. Is there any God[h] besides me?
No, there is no other Rock;[i] I know not one."

9 All who make idols are nothing,
and the things they treasure are worthless.[j]
Those who would speak up for them are blind;
they are ignorant, to their own shame.
10 Who shapes a god and casts an idol,
which can profit nothing?[k]
11 People who do that will be put to shame;[l]
such craftsmen are only human beings.
Let them all come together and take their stand;
they will be brought down to terror and shame.[m]

12 The blacksmith[n] takes a tool
and works with it in the coals;
he shapes an idol with hammers,
he forges it with the might of his arm.[o]
He gets hungry and loses his strength;
he drinks no water and grows faint.
13 The carpenter[p] measures with a line
and makes an outline with a marker;
he roughs it out with chisels
and marks it with compasses.
He shapes it in human form,[q]
human form in all its glory,
that it may dwell in a shrine.[r]
14 He cut down cedars,
or perhaps took a cypress or oak.
He let it grow among the trees of the forest,
or planted a pine, and the rain made it grow.
15 It is used as fuel[s] for burning;
some of it he takes and warms himself,
he kindles a fire and bakes bread.
But he also fashions a god and worships it;
he makes an idol and bows[t] down to it.
16 Half of the wood he burns in the fire;
over it he prepares his meal,
he roasts his meat and eats his fill.
He also warms himself and says,
"Ah! I am warm; I see the fire."
17 From the rest he makes a god, his idol;
he bows down to it and worships.
He prays[u] to it and says,
"Save[v] me! You are my god!"
18 They know nothing, they understand[w] nothing;
their eyes[x] are plastered over so they cannot see,
and their minds closed so they cannot understand.
19 No one stops to think,
no one has the knowledge or understanding[y] to say,
"Half of it I used for fuel;
I even baked bread over its coals,
I roasted meat and I ate.
Shall I make a detestable[z] thing from what is left?
Shall I bow down to a block of wood?"
20 Such a person feeds on ashes;[a] a deluded[b] heart misleads him;
he cannot save himself, or say,
"Is not this thing in my right hand a lie?[c]"

21 "Remember[d] these things, Jacob,
for you, Israel, are my servant.
I have made you, you are my servant;[e]
Israel, I will not forget you.[f]
22 I have swept away[g] your offenses like a cloud,
your sins like the morning mist.
Return[h] to me,
for I have redeemed[i] you."

23 Sing for joy,[j] you heavens, for the LORD has done this;
shout aloud, you earth[k] beneath.
Burst into song, you mountains,[l]
you forests and all your trees,
for the LORD has redeemed Jacob,
he displays his glory[m] in Israel.

Jerusalem to Be Inhabited

24 "This is what the LORD says—
your Redeemer,[n] who formed you in the womb:

I am the LORD,
the Maker of all things,
who stretches out the heavens,[o]
who spreads out the earth by myself,

44:8 *You are my witnesses.* The people of Israel had already witnessed great miracles on their behalf (43:10).

44:9–20 *All who make idols.* This passage skillfully displays the utter absurdity of trusting in idols. Idolatry is a source of shame (v. 11), and it is caused by a deceived heart (v. 20). This is a passage to remember and to come back to, for idolatry was a continual snare to the Israelites. We need to remember in our modern age that we are not immune to this sin; it is the Second Commandment, the reminder that nothing must come between us and our relationship to God.

44:22 *swept away.* The idea of total forgiveness of sins is also found in 40:2 and 43:25.

44:23 *displays his glory.* When He saves, the Lord demonstrates to the world His mercy and His power and His glory.

44:24 *This is what the LORD says.* Because the Lord says it, it will come to pass.

44:8 [h] Isa 43:10 [i] Dt 4:35; 1Sa 2:2 **44:9** [j] Isa 41:24
44:10 [k] Isa 41:29; Jer 10:5; Ac 19:26 **44:11** [l] Isa 1:29
[m] Isa 42:17 **44:12** [n] Isa 40:19; 41:6-7 [o] Jer 10:3-5;
Ac 17:29 **44:13** [p] Isa 41:7 [q] Ps 115:4-7 [r] Jdg 17:4-5
44:15 [s] ver 19 [t] 2Ch 25:14 **44:17** [u] 1Ki 18:26 [v] Isa 45:20
44:18 [w] Isa 1:3 [x] Isa 6:9-10 **44:19** [y] Isa 5:13; 27:11; 45:20
[z] Dt 27:15 **44:20** [a] Ps 102:9 [b] Job 15:31; Ro 1:21-23, 28;
2Th 2:11; 2Ti 3:13 [c] Isa 59:3, 4, 13; Ro 1:25
44:21 [d] Isa 46:8; Zec 10:9 [e] ver 1-2 [f] Isa 49:15
44:22 [g] Isa 43:25; Ac 3:19 [h] Isa 55:7 [i] 1Co 6:20
44:23 [j] Isa 42:10 [k] Ps 148:7 [l] Ps 98:8 [m] Isa 61:3
44:24 [n] Isa 43:14 [o] Isa 42:5

25 who foils[p] the signs of false prophets
and makes fools of diviners,[q]
who overthrows the learning of the
wise[r]
and turns it into nonsense,[s]
26 who carries out the words[t] of his
servants
and fulfills[u] the predictions of his
messengers,

who says of Jerusalem, 'It shall be
inhabited,'
of the towns of Judah, 'They shall be
rebuilt,'
and of their ruins, 'I will restore
them,'[v]
27 who says to the watery deep, 'Be dry,
and I will dry up your streams,'
28 who says of Cyrus,[w] 'He is my shepherd
and will accomplish all that I please;
he will say of Jerusalem,[x] "Let it be
rebuilt,"
and of the temple,[y] "Let its
foundations be laid." '

45 "This is what the LORD says to his
anointed,
to Cyrus, whose right hand I take
hold[z] of
to subdue nations[a] before him
and to strip kings of their armor,
to open doors before him
so that gates will not be shut:
2 I will go before you
and will level[b] the mountains[α];
I will break down gates of bronze
and cut through bars of iron.[c]
3 I will give you hidden treasures,[d]
riches stored in secret places,[e]
so that you may know[f] that I am the
LORD,
the God of Israel, who summons you
by name.[g]
4 For the sake of Jacob my servant,[h]
of Israel my chosen,
I summon you by name
and bestow on you a title of honor,
though you do not acknowledge[i] me.
5 I am the LORD, and there is no other;[j]
apart from me there is no God.[k]
I will strengthen you,[l]
though you have not
acknowledged me,
6 so that from the rising of the sun
to the place of its setting[m]
people may know there is none
besides me.[n]
I am the LORD, and there is no other.
7 I form the light and create darkness,
I bring prosperity and create
disaster;[o]
I, the LORD, do all these things.

8 "You heavens above, rain[p] down my
righteousness;[q]
let the clouds shower it down.
Let the earth open wide,
let salvation[r] spring up,
let righteousness flourish with it;
I, the LORD, have created it.

9 "Woe to those who quarrel[s] with their
Maker,
those who are nothing but potsherds
among the potsherds on the ground.
Does the clay say to the potter,[t]
'What are you making?'
Does your work say,
'The potter has no hands'?

[α] 2 Dead Sea Scrolls and Septuagint; the meaning of the word in the Masoretic Text is uncertain.

44:25 *diviners.* This term refers to people who attempt to foretell the future through occult practices. They are often mentioned along with other practitioners of the occult—all of whom were forbidden in Israel (Deut. 18:10–22). Diviners brought trouble on themselves, and on their nations as well (Deut. 18:10; 2 Kin. 17:17–18; Mic. 3:6–7).
44:28 *Cyrus.* Here, Isaiah mentions by name the king of Persia who would allow the Israelites to return to Jerusalem in 538 B.C. (Ezra 1:1–4). He was a chosen servant of God, even though he was not an Israelite. Isaiah's prophecy was made more than 150 years before it was fulfilled.
45:3 *hidden treasures.* These treasures are an allusion to the fabled wealth of Sardis captured by Cyrus in 546 B.C. ***who summons you by name.*** The Lord specifically named Cyrus and appointed his work before he became king, and even before he was born. Isaiah was ministering from approximately 740 to 701 B.C., which was at least 150 years before Cyrus became prominent. The Lord picked out Cyrus, but He picked out each of us, too, to do good works which He had planned beforehand for us to do (Eph. 2:10).
45:8 *have created it.* In the Middle East, pagan people commonly believed that the fertility of the earth and maintenance of the social order depended on the king's right relationship with a deity. Isaiah was proclaiming the Lord's clear statement that it is the Lord alone who made the earth and blesses it with rain and with righteousness.
45:9 *potsherds.* The ultimate act of insanity committed by the human soul is unfaithfulness. As the prophet Isaiah shows, how inconceivable and ridiculous it would be for a simple piece of pottery to lash out at the craftsman. And yet, that was what Israel had consistently done from the exodus of Egypt to the destruction of the second temple by Titus in A.D. 70. Jonah was a classic example of unfaithfulness. In the Book of Jonah, all nature spontaneously obeyed its Creator. The ocean churned, the fish appeared, the gourd grew, the worm ate, and the east wind blew at the command of God. The only object in that narrative that dared disobey was Jonah the prophet. What

44:25 [p] Ps 33:10 [q] Isa 47:13 [r] 1Co 1:27 [s] 2Sa 15:31; 1Co 1:19-20 **44:26** [t] Zec 1:6 [u] Isa 55:11; Mt 5:18 [v] Isa 49:8-21 **44:28** [w] 2Ch 36:22 [x] Isa 14:32 [y] Ezr 1:2-4 **45:1** [z] Ps 73:23; Isa 41:13; 42:6 [a] Jer 50:35 **45:2** [b] Isa 40:4 [c] Ps 107:16; Jer 51:30 **45:3** [d] Jer 50:37 [e] Jer 41:8 [f] Isa 41:23 [g] Ex 33:12; Isa 43:1 **45:4** [h] Isa 41:8-9 [i] Ac 17:23 **45:5** [j] Isa 44:8 [k] Ps 18:31 [l] Ps 18:39 **45:6** [m] Isa 43:5; Mal 1:11 [n] ver 5, 18 **45:7** [o] Isa 31:2; Am 3:6 **45:8** [p] Ps 72:6; Joel 3:18 [q] Ps 85:11; Isa 60:21; 61:10, 11; Hos 10:12 [r] Isa 12:3 **45:9** [s] Job 15:25 [t] Isa 29:16; Ro 9:20-21*

10 Woe to the one who says to a father,
'What have you begotten?'
or to a mother,
'What have you brought to birth?'

11 "This is what the LORD says—
the Holy One of Israel, and its Maker:
Concerning things to come,
do you question me about my children,
or give me orders about the work of my hands?[u]
12 It is I who made the earth
and created mankind on it.
My own hands stretched out the heavens;[v]
I marshaled their starry hosts.[w]
13 I will raise up Cyrus[a][x] in my righteousness:
I will make all his ways straight.
He will rebuild my city
and set my exiles free,
but not for a price or reward,[y]
says the LORD Almighty."

14 This is what the LORD says:

"The products of Egypt and the merchandise of Cush,[b]
and those tall Sabeans—
they will come over to you
and will be yours;
they will trudge behind you,
coming over to you in chains.[z]
They will bow down before you
and plead[a] with you, saying,
'Surely God is with you,[b] and there is no other;
there is no other god.'"

15 Truly you are a God who has been hiding[c] himself,
the God and Savior of Israel.
16 All the makers of idols will be put to shame and disgraced;[d]
they will go off into disgrace together.
17 But Israel will be saved[e] by the LORD
with an everlasting salvation;[f]
you will never be put to shame or disgraced,
to ages everlasting.

18 For this is what the LORD says—
he who created the heavens,
he is God;
he who fashioned and made the earth,
he founded it;
he did not create it to be empty,[g]
but formed it to be inhabited[h]—
he says:
"I am the LORD,
and there is no other.[i]
19 I have not spoken in secret,[j]
from somewhere in a land of darkness;
I have not said to Jacob's descendants,[k]
'Seek me in vain.'
I, the LORD, speak the truth;
I declare what is right.[l]

20 "Gather together[m] and come;
assemble, you fugitives from the nations.
Ignorant[n] are those who carry[o] about idols of wood,
who pray to gods that cannot save.[p]
21 Declare what is to be, present it—
let them take counsel together.
Who foretold[q] this long ago,
who declared it from the distant past?
Was it not I, the LORD?
And there is no God apart from me,[r]
a righteous God and a Savior;
there is none but me.

22 "Turn[s] to me and be saved,[t]
all you ends of the earth;[u]
for I am God, and there is no other.
23 By myself I have sworn,[v]
my mouth has uttered in all integrity[w]
a word that will not be revoked:[x]
Before me every knee will bow;
by me every tongue will swear.[y]
24 They will say of me, 'In the LORD alone
are deliverance[z] and strength.'"
All who have raged against him
will come to him and be put to shame.[a]
25 But all the descendants of Israel
will find deliverance in the LORD
and will make their boast in him.[b]

---

[a] *13* Hebrew *him* [b] *14* That is, the upper Nile region

---

law of logic would allow a finite and sinful creature to brazenly speak out against the infinite and sovereign Creator of all things? (Compare Romans 9:20.)

45:14 they will come over to you and will be yours. The "you" and "yours" are both feminine singular, referring to the Daughter of Zion.

45:19 in secret ... darkness. The diviners pronounced their mysterious and ambiguous oracles in secret and dark places. The Lord's prophets proclaimed the truth openly to all who would listen.

45:23 By myself I have sworn. The Lord's promise to Abraham was sworn by Himself (Gen. 22:16; Heb. 6:13), and whatever God promises will come to pass, for He cannot lie. The certainty of the Word of the Lord is emphasized strongly in the Book of Isaiah (40:8). ***Before me every knee will bow.*** This promise will be fulfilled in Jesus Christ (Rom. 14:11; 1 Cor. 15:24–25; Phil. 2:10–11).

45:24–25 deliverance. God breaks the stranglehold of nations to secure the release of His people from captivity. In the same way, God also breaks the

45:11 [u] Isa 19:25 **45:12** [v] Ge 2:1; Isa 42:5 [w] Ne 9:6 **45:13** [x] 2Ch 36:22; Isa 41:2 [y] Isa 52:3 **45:14** [z] Isa 14:1-2 [a] Jer 16:19; Zec 8:20-23 [b] 1Co 14:25 **45:15** [c] Ps 44:24 **45:16** [d] Isa 44:9, 11 **45:17** [e] Ro 11:26 [f] Isa 26:4 **45:18** [g] Ge 1:2 [h] Ge 1:26; Isa 42:5 [i] ver 5 **45:19** [j] Isa 48:16 [k] Isa 41:8 [l] Dt 30:11 **45:20** [m] Isa 43:9 [n] Isa 44:19 [o] Isa 46:1; Jer 10:5 [p] Isa 44:17; 46:6-7 **45:21** [q] Isa 41:22 [r] ver 5 **45:22** [s] Zec 12:10 [t] Nu 21:8-9; 2Ch 20:12 [u] Isa 49:6, 12 **45:23** [v] Ge 22:16 [w] Heb 6:13 [x] Isa 55:11 [y] Ps 63:11; Isa 19:18; Ro 14:11*; Php 2:10-11 **45:24** [z] Jer 33:16 [a] Isa 41:11 **45:25** [b] Isa 41:16

Gods of Babylon

46 Bel[c] bows down, Nebo stoops low;
their idols are borne by beasts of burden.[a]
The images that are carried[d] about are burdensome,
a burden for the weary.
2 They stoop and bow down together;
unable to rescue the burden,
they themselves go off into captivity.[e]

3 "Listen[f] to me, you descendants of Jacob,
all the remnant of the people of Israel,
you whom I have upheld since your birth,
and have carried since you were born.
4 Even to your old age and gray hairs[g]
I am he,[h] I am he who will sustain you.
I have made you and I will carry you;
I will sustain you and I will rescue you.

5 "With whom will you compare me or count me equal?
To whom will you liken me that we may be compared?[i]
6 Some pour out gold from their bags
and weigh out silver on the scales;
they hire a goldsmith[j] to make it into a god,
and they bow down and worship it.[k]
7 They lift it to their shoulders and carry[l] it;
they set it up in its place, and there it stands.
From that spot it cannot move.
Even though someone cries out to it, it cannot answer;
it cannot save[m] them from their troubles.

8 "Remember[n] this, keep it in mind,
take it to heart, you rebels.
9 Remember the former things, those of long ago;[o]
I am God, and there is no other;
I am God, and there is none like me.[p]
10 I make known the end from the beginning,
from ancient times,[q] what is still to come.
I say, 'My purpose will stand,[r]
and I will do all that I please.'
11 From the east I summon a bird of prey;
from a far-off land, a man to fulfill my purpose.
What I have said, that I will bring about;
what I have planned, that I will do.
12 Listen[s] to me, you stubborn-hearted,
you who are now far from my righteousness.[t]
13 I am bringing my righteousness near,
it is not far away;
and my salvation will not be delayed.
I will grant salvation to Zion,
my splendor[u] to Israel.

The Fall of Babylon

47 "Go down, sit in the dust,
Virgin Daughter[v] Babylon;
sit on the ground without a throne,
queen city of the Babylonians.[b][w]
No more will you be called
tender or delicate.[x]
2 Take millstones[y] and grind[z] flour;
take off your veil.[a]
Lift up your skirts,[b] bare your legs,
and wade through the streams.
3 Your nakedness[c] will be exposed
and your shame[d] uncovered.
I will take vengeance;[e]
I will spare no one."

4 Our Redeemer—the LORD Almighty is his name[f]—
is the Holy One of Israel.

5 "Sit in silence, go into darkness,[g]
queen city of the Babylonians;
no more will you be called
queen of kingdoms.[h]

---

[a] 1 Or *are but beasts and cattle* [b] 1 Or *Chaldeans*; also in verse 5

---

stranglehold of sin to release his people from spiritual bondage. He does so by pouring forth righteousness through the atoning sacrifice of Jesus Christ on the cross. This is the centerpiece of God's salvation, which is worldwide in its scope. It is the only ground for acceptance by God, the only foundation for fellowship with God, and the only platform of service to God. Those who embrace it find that they are released from sin's guilt and that they are also given strength to have victory over sin. No wonder this all evokes jubilant praise!
46:1 ***Bel ... Nebo.*** Bel, meaning "Lord," was a title of Marduk, Babylon's chief deity. Nebo, Marduk's son, was the god of fate, writing, and wisdom.
46:11 ***From the east I summon a bird of prey.*** The bird of prey refers to Cyrus (41:2) and to the speed and power of his conquests.
47:2 ***grind flour.*** Grinding flour was usually a job for female slaves (Ex. 11:5). ***bare your legs.*** This phrase suggests doing menial labor with overtones of the shame of indecent exposure. A woman who was doing heavy labor may have needed more freedom of movement than was possible without shortening her skirts.
47:3 ***nakedness.*** Nakedness indicates disgrace, impropriety, lack of dignity, and vulnerability (Gen. 9:22–23).

46:1 [c] Isa 21:9; Jer 50:2; 51:44 [d] Isa 45:20 **46:2** [e] Jdg 18:17-18; 2Sa 5:21 **46:3** [f] ver 12 **46:4** [g] Ps 71:18 [h] Isa 43:13 **46:5** [i] Isa 40:18, 25 **46:6** [j] Isa 40:19 [k] Isa 44:17 **46:7** [l] ver 1 [m] Isa 44:17; Isa 45:20 **46:8** [n] Isa 44:21 **46:9** [o] Dt 32:7 [p] Isa 45:5, 21 **46:10** [q] Isa 45:21 [r] Pr 19:21; Ac 5:39 **46:12** [s] ver 3 [t] Ps 119:150; Isa 48:1; Jer 2:5 **46:13** [u] Isa 44:23 **47:1** [v] Isa 23:12 [w] Ps 137:8; Jer 50:42; 51:33; Zec 2:7 [x] Dt 28:56 **47:2** [y] Ex 11:5; Mt 24:41 [z] Jdg 16:21 [a] Ge 24:65 [b] Isa 32:11 **47:3** [c] Eze 16:37; Na 3:5 [d] Isa 20:4 [e] Isa 34:8 **47:4** [f] Jer 50:34 **47:5** [g] Isa 13:10 [h] Isa 13:19

6 I was angry[i] with my people
and desecrated my inheritance;
I gave them into your hand,[j]
and you showed them no mercy.
Even on the aged
you laid a very heavy yoke.
7 You said, 'I am forever—
the eternal queen!'[k]
But you did not consider these things
or reflect[l] on what might happen.[m]

8 "Now then, listen, you lover of pleasure,
lounging in your security[n]
and saying to yourself,
'I am, and there is none besides me.[o]
I will never be a widow[p]
or suffer the loss of children.'
9 Both of these will overtake you
in a moment,[q] on a single day:
loss of children[r] and widowhood.
They will come upon you in full
measure,
in spite of your many sorceries[s]
and all your potent spells.[t]
10 You have trusted[u] in your wickedness
and have said, 'No one sees me.'[v]
Your wisdom[w] and knowledge mislead[x]
you
when you say to yourself,
'I am, and there is none besides me.'
11 Disaster will come upon you,
and you will not know how to conjure
it away.
A calamity will fall upon you
that you cannot ward off with a
ransom;
a catastrophe you cannot foresee
will suddenly[y] come upon you.

12 "Keep on, then, with your magic spells
and with your many sorceries,[z]
which you have labored at since
childhood.
Perhaps you will succeed,
perhaps you will cause terror.
13 All the counsel you have received has
only worn you out![a]
Let your astrologers[b] come forward,
those stargazers who make predictions
month by month,
let them save[c] you from what is
coming upon you.
14 Surely they are like stubble;[d]
the fire will burn them up.
They cannot even save themselves
from the power of the flame.[e]
These are not coals for warmth;
this is not a fire to sit by.
15 That is all they are to you—
these you have dealt with
and labored[f] with since childhood.
All of them go on in their error;
there is not one that can save you.

Stubborn Israel

48 "Listen to this, you descendants of
Jacob,
you who are called by the name of
Israel
and come from the line of Judah,
you who take oaths in the name of the
LORD
and invoke[g] the God of Israel—
but not in truth[h] or righteousness—
2 you who call yourselves citizens of the
holy city[i]
and claim to rely[j] on the God of
Israel—
the LORD Almighty is his name:
3 I foretold the former things[k] long ago,
my mouth announced[l] them and I
made them known;
then suddenly I acted, and they came
to pass.
4 For I knew how stubborn[m] you were;
your neck muscles[n] were iron,
your forehead[o] was bronze.
5 Therefore I told you these things long
ago;
before they happened I announced
them to you
so that you could not say,
'My images brought them about;[p]
my wooden image and metal god
ordained them.'
6 You have heard these things; look at
them all.
Will you not admit them?

"From now on I will tell you of new
things,
of hidden things unknown to you.

47:6 ***you showed them no mercy.*** Babylon's cruel abuse of Israel when the Lord had given them into Babylon's hand would be avenged, as in the case of the Assyrians (10:1–19; 49:25). When God chooses to punish, He is never pleased with a bystander who cheers over the downfall of another.

47:10 ***trusted in your wickedness.*** The selfish pride of the wicked is based in part on believing that there is not an all-knowing, all-seeing God in the universe.

47:12 ***Keep on, then.*** The admonition to "keep on" is facetious. The sorcerers and astrologers have nothing real to offer a person or nation that is having trouble.

48:5 ***I announced them to you.*** God told His people of events that would come to pass in the future so that they would know that it was He, and He alone, who controlled history.

48:6 ***new things ... hidden things.*** God did not tell His people all that the future would unfold. He knew that, if they had possessed such knowledge, they would have misused that knowledge to the detriment of God's plan and themselves.

47:6 [i] 2Ch 28:9 [j] Isa 10:13 **47:7** [k] ver 5; Rev 18:7 [l] Isa 42:23,25 [m] Dt 32:29 **47:8** [n] Isa 32:9 [o] Isa 45:6; Zep 2:15 [p] Rev 18:7 **47:9** [q] Ps 73:19; 1Th 5:3; Rev 18:8-10 [r] Isa 13:18 [s] Na 3:4 [t] Rev 18:23 **47:10** [u] Ps 52:7; 62:10 [v] Isa 29:15 [w] Isa 5:21 [x] Isa 44:20 **47:11** [y] 1Th 5:3 **47:12** [z] ver 9 **47:13** [a] Isa 57:10; Jer 51:58 [b] Isa 44:25 [c] ver 15 **47:14** [d] Isa 5:24; Na 1:10 [e] Isa 10:17; Jer 51:30, 32,58 **47:15** [f] Rev 18:11 **48:1** [g] Isa 58:2 [h] Jer 4:2 **48:2** [i] Isa 52:1 [j] Isa 10:20; Mic 3:11; Ro 2:17 **48:3** [k] Isa 41:22 [l] Isa 45:21 **48:4** [m] Dt 31:27 [n] Ex 32:9; Ac 7:51 [o] Eze 3:9 **48:5** [p] Jer 44:15-18

7 They are created now, and not long ago;
you have not heard of them before today.
So you cannot say,
'Yes, I knew of them.'
8 You have neither heard nor understood;
from of old your ears have not been open.
Well do I know how treacherous you are;
you were called a rebel[q] from birth.
9 For my own name's sake I delay my wrath;[r]
for the sake of my praise I hold it back from you,
so as not to destroy you completely.[s]
10 See, I have refined you, though not as silver;
I have tested you in the furnace[t] of affliction.
11 For my own sake,[u] for my own sake, I do this.
How can I let myself be defamed?[v]
I will not yield my glory to another.[w]

Israel Freed

12 "Listen[x] to me, Jacob,
Israel, whom I have called:
I am he;
I am the first and I am the last.[y]
13 My own hand laid the foundations of the earth,[z]
and my right hand spread out the heavens;[a]
when I summon them,
they all stand up together.[b]
14 "Come together,[c] all of you, and listen:
Which of the idols has foretold these things?
The LORD's chosen ally
will carry out his purpose[d] against Babylon;
his arm will be against the Babylonians.[a]
15 I, even I, have spoken;
yes, I have called[e] him.
I will bring him,
and he will succeed in his mission.

16 "Come near[f] me and listen to this:

"From the first announcement I have not spoken in secret;[g]
at the time it happens, I am there."

And now the Sovereign LORD has sent[h] me,
endowed with his Spirit.
17 This is what the LORD says—
your Redeemer,[i] the Holy One[j] of Israel:
"I am the LORD your God,
who teaches you what is best for you,
who directs[k] you in the way[l] you should go.
18 If only you had paid attention[m] to my commands,
your peace[n] would have been like a river,
your well-being[o] like the waves of the sea.
19 Your descendants would have been like the sand,
your children like its numberless grains;[p]
their name would never be blotted out[q]
nor destroyed from before me."

20 Leave Babylon,
flee[r] from the Babylonians!
Announce this with shouts of joy[s]
and proclaim it.
Send it out to the ends of the earth;
say, "The LORD has redeemed[t] his servant Jacob."
21 They did not thirst[u] when he led them through the deserts;
he made water flow[v] for them from the rock;
he split the rock
and water gushed out.[w]

22 "There is no peace," says the LORD, "for the wicked."[x]

[a] 14 Or *Chaldeans*; also in verse 20

48:11 ***For my own sake.*** God's acts of mercy are His own initiative, springing from the depths of His mercy (37:35; 42:21; 43:25).
48:12 ***Listen to me.*** This section (vv. 12–22) is directed to all Israel and encourages the unrighteous to participate in the Lord's redemption of the nation from Babylon.
48:16 ***his Spirit.*** One of the works of the Holy Spirit is to empower believers and their message. Isaiah recognized this task of the Spirit of God. The prophet had delivered unbelievable prophecies in a time when Assyria reigned supreme, speaking of a day when Babylon would replace the Assyrians. He even named the Persian King Cyrus, who would rescue Judah from Babylon. Knowing that these things were hard to believe, he urged the people to listen. He appealed to them on the basis that the Lord had sent him "and his Spirit." Isaiah's message was not simply the message of a man, but the Word of the Holy Spirit, the teacher and director of God's messengers.
48:20 ***Announce.*** By putting the command "announce" in the present tense, the future salvation is brought vividly into the present.

48:8 [q] Dt 9:7,24; Ps 58:3 **48:9** [r] Ps 78:38; Isa 30:18 [s] Ne 9:31 **48:10** [t] 1Ki 8:51 **48:11** [u] 1Sa 12:22; Isa 37:35 [v] Dt 32:27; Jer 14:7,21; Eze 20:9,14,22,44 [w] Isa 42:8 **48:12** [x] Isa 46:3 [y] Isa 41:4; Rev 1:17; 22:13 **48:13** [z] Heb 1:10-12 [a] Ex 20:11 [b] Isa 40:26 **48:14** [c] Isa 43:9 [d] Isa 46:10-11 **48:15** [e] Isa 45:1 **48:16** [f] Isa 41:1 [g] Isa 45:19 [h] Zec 2:9,11 **48:17** [i] Isa 49:7 [j] Isa 43:14 [k] Isa 49:10 [l] Ps 32:8 **48:18** [m] Dt 32:29 [n] Ps 119:165; Isa 66:12 [o] Isa 45:8 **48:19** [p] Ge 22:17 [q] Isa 56:5; 66:22 **48:20** [r] Jer 50:8; 51:6,45; Zec 2:6-7; Rev 18:4 [s] Isa 49:13 [t] Isa 52:9; 63:9 **48:21** [u] Isa 41:17 [v] Isa 30:25 [w] Ex 17:6; Nu 20:11; Ps 105:41; Isa 35:6 **48:22** [x] Isa 57:21

The Servant of the Lord

49 Listen to me, you islands;
hear this, you distant nations:
Before I was born[y] the Lord
called[z] me;
from my mother's womb he has
spoken my name.
2 He made my mouth like a sharpened
sword,[a]
in the shadow of his hand he
hid me;
he made me into a polished arrow
and concealed me in his quiver.
3 He said to me, "You are my servant,[b]
Israel, in whom I will display my
splendor.[c]"
4 But I said, "I have labored in vain;[d]
I have spent my strength for nothing
at all.
Yet what is due me is in the Lord's
hand,
and my reward[e] is with my God."

5 And now the Lord says—
he who formed me in the womb to be
his servant
to bring Jacob back to him
and gather Israel[f] to himself,
for I am[a] honored[g] in the eyes of the
Lord
and my God has been my strength—
6 he says:
"It is too small a thing for you to be my
servant
to restore the tribes of Jacob
and bring back those of Israel I have
kept.
I will also make you a light for the
Gentiles,[h]
that my salvation may reach to the
ends of the earth."[i]

7 This is what the Lord says—
the Redeemer and Holy One of
Israel[j]—
to him who was despised[k] and abhorred
by the nation,
to the servant of rulers:
"Kings[l] will see you and stand up,
princes will see and bow down,
because of the Lord, who is faithful,
the Holy One of Israel, who has
chosen you."

Restoration of Israel

8 This is what the Lord says:

"In the time of my favor[m] I will answer
you,
and in the day of salvation I will help
you;[n]
I will keep[o] you and will make you
to be a covenant for the people,[p]
to restore the land[q]
and to reassign its desolate
inheritances,
9 to say to the captives,[r] 'Come out,'
and to those in darkness, 'Be free!'

"They will feed beside the roads
and find pasture on every barren
hill.[s]
10 They will neither hunger nor thirst,[t]
nor will the desert heat or the sun
beat down on them.[u]
He who has compassion[v] on them will
guide them
and lead them beside springs[w] of
water.
11 I will turn all my mountains into
roads,
and my highways[x] will be raised up.[y]
12 See, they will come from afar[z]—
some from the north, some from the
west,
some from the region of Aswan.[b]"

13 Shout for joy, you heavens;
rejoice, you earth;
burst into song, you mountains![a]
For the Lord comforts[b] his people
and will have compassion on his
afflicted ones.

14 But Zion said, "The Lord has
forsaken me,
the Lord has forgotten me."

[a] 5 Or *him, / but Israel would not be gathered; / yet I will be* [b] 12 Dead Sea Scrolls; Masoretic Text *Sinim*

49:1–13 *Listen.* This second song of the Suffering Servant (42:1–13) consists of two parts: the Servant's soliloquy (vv. 1–6) and the Lord's oracles to Him (vv. 7–9). The song is followed by Isaiah's elaboration (vv. 9–12), and it concludes with a hymn of praise.
49:2 *mouth like a sharpened sword.* The truth is "sharpened." It cuts through lies and deception like a sharp sword (Eph. 6:17; Heb. 4:12; Rev. 1:16; 19:15).
49:5 *bring Jacob back.* The political mission of Cyrus to bring Jacob back from Babylon (44:28; 45:13) foreshadows the spiritually redemptive mission of the Servant to free His people from their captivity to sin (42:7).
49:6 *for the Gentiles.* The "Gentiles" refers to those who are not Israel.
49:9 *Come out.* This is an allusion to Isaiah's command for the exiles to leave Babylon (48:20).
49:14 *has forsaken me.* The complaint that the Lord had forsaken Zion resembles that in 40:27–31. The Lord disciplined the Israelites briefly because of their sin (54:7; Lam. 5:20–22), but the things that Isaiah was saying about captivity were still in the future. A message such as this would be good to remember in the days of captivity when it seemed that they were waiting a long time for the Lord to rescue them.

49:1 [y] Isa 44:24; 46:3; Mt 1:20 [z] Isa 7:14; 9:6; 44:2; Jer 1:5; Gal 1:15 **49:2** [a] Isa 11:4; Rev 1:16 **49:3** [b] Zec 3:8 [c] Isa 44:23 **49:4** [d] Isa 65:23 [e] Isa 35:4 **49:5** [f] Isa 11:12 [g] Isa 43:4 **49:6** [h] Lk 2:32 [i] Ac 13:47* **49:7** [j] Isa 48:17 [k] Ps 22:6; 69:7-9 [l] Isa 52:15 **49:8** [m] Ps 69:13 [n] 2Co 6:2* [o] Isa 26:3 [p] Isa 42:6 [q] Isa 44:26 **49:9** [r] Isa 42:7; 61:1; Lk 4:19 [s] Isa 41:18 **49:10** [t] Isa 33:16 [u] Ps 121:6; Rev 7:16 [v] Isa 14:1 [w] Isa 35:7 **49:11** [x] Isa 11:16 [y] Isa 40:4 **49:12** [z] Isa 43:5-6 **49:13** [a] Isa 44:23 [b] Isa 40:1

15 "Can a mother forget the baby at her breast
and have no compassion on the child she has borne?
Though she may forget,
I will not forget you![c]
16 See, I have engraved[d] you on the palms of my hands;
your walls[e] are ever before me.
17 Your children hasten back,
and those who laid you waste[f] depart from you.
18 Lift up your eyes and look around;
all your children gather[g] and come to you.
As surely as I live,[h]" declares the LORD,
"you will wear[i] them all as ornaments;
you will put them on, like a bride.

19 "Though you were ruined and made desolate[j]
and your land laid waste,[k]
now you will be too small for your people,[l]
and those who devoured you will be far away.
20 The children born during your bereavement
will yet say in your hearing,
'This place is too small for us;
give us more space to live in.'[m]
21 Then you will say in your heart,
'Who bore me these?
I was bereaved and barren;
I was exiled and rejected.[n]
Who brought these up?
I was left[o] all alone,
but these—where have they come from?'"

22 This is what the Sovereign LORD says:

"See, I will beckon to the nations,
I will lift up my banner[p] to the peoples;
they will bring your sons in their arms
and carry your daughters on their hips.[q]
23 Kings[r] will be your foster fathers,
and their queens your nursing mothers.[s]
They will bow down before you with their faces to the ground;
they will lick the dust[t] at your feet.
Then you will know that I am the LORD;[u]
those who hope in me will not be disappointed."

24 Can plunder be taken from warriors,[v]
or captives be rescued from the fierce[a]?

25 But this is what the LORD says:

"Yes, captives[w] will be taken from warriors,[x]
and plunder retrieved from the fierce;
I will contend with those who contend with you,
and your children I will save.[y]
26 I will make your oppressors[z] eat[a] their own flesh;
they will be drunk on their own blood,[b] as with wine.
Then all mankind will know[c]
that I, the LORD, am your Savior,
your Redeemer, the Mighty One of Jacob."

Israel's Sin and the Servant's Obedience

50 This is what the LORD says:

"Where is your mother's certificate of divorce[d]
with which I sent her away?
Or to which of my creditors
did I sell[e] you?
Because of your sins you were sold;[f]
because of your transgressions your mother was sent away.

[a] 24 Dead Sea Scrolls, Vulgate and Syriac (see also Septuagint and verse 25); Masoretic Text *righteous*

49:15 ***Can a mother forget.*** In the strongest of human ties, the tenderness of the mother for her precious and dependent child, the Lord draws a parallel picture of Himself. Even if the mother could forget, the Lord will never forget. Human parents often fail, but the Lord is the parent who never forgets how much His child needs Him.

49:20 ***too small.*** The complaint that the place is too small is in fact a cause for rejoicing (54:1–3; Zech. 2:4–5), because it means that the Lord would cause His people to grow. This prophecy points to the return of the exiles to Jerusalem, for under Ezra and Nehemiah the exiles built a relatively small city (Ezra 2; Neh. 7). Some view the ultimate fulfillment of this prophecy to be the gathering of the Lord's people at the coming of Jesus' kingdom.

49:22 ***lift up my banner to the peoples.*** The return of the Israelites from all the nations, not only from Babylon, shows that the future salvation of all Israel is in view (Rom. 11:26).

50:1 ***divorce.*** The Lord had put away Israel as a husband might put away a wife, but it was for only a short period of exile (54:5–7; 62:4) and not permanently. Permanent exile would have required a certificate of divorce (Deut. 24:1–4). If the Lord had issued one, He could not have taken Israel back (Jer. 3:1,8). No prophet suggested that God had completely broken His covenant; rather, they predicted God's faithfulness to a remnant who would return (Mic. 4:9–10).

49:15 [c] Isa 44:21 **49:16** [d] SS 8:6 [e] Ps 48:12-13; Isa 62:6 **49:17** [f] Isa 10:6 **49:18** [g] Isa 43:5; 54:7; Isa 60:4 [h] Isa 45:23 [i] Isa 52:1 **49:19** [j] Isa 54:1,3 [k] Isa 5:6 [l] Zec 10:10 **49:20** [m] Isa 54:1-3 **49:21** [n] Isa 5:13 [o] Isa 1:8 **49:22** [p] Isa 11:10 [q] Isa 60:4 **49:23** [r] Isa 60:3, 10-11 [s] Isa 60:16 [t] Ps 72:9 [u] Mic 7:17 **49:24** [v] Mt 12:29; Lk 11:21 **49:25** [w] Isa 14:2 [x] Jer 50:33-34 [y] Isa 25:9; 35:4 **49:26** [z] Isa 9:4 [a] Isa 9:20 [b] Rev 16:6 [c] Eze 39:7 **50:1** [d] Dt 24:1; Jer 3:8; Hos 2:2 [e] Ne 5:5; Mt 18:25 [f] Dt 32:30; Isa 52:3

2 When I came, why was there no one?
When I called, why was there no one to answer?[g]
Was my arm too short[h] to deliver you?
Do I lack the strength[i] to rescue you?
By a mere rebuke I dry up the sea,[j]
I turn rivers into a desert;
their fish rot for lack of water
and die of thirst.
3 I clothe the heavens with darkness
and make sackcloth[k] its covering."

4 The Sovereign LORD has given me a well-instructed tongue,[l]
to know the word that sustains the weary.[m]
He wakens me morning by morning,[n]
wakens my ear to listen like one being instructed.
5 The Sovereign LORD has opened my ears;[o]
I have not been rebellious,[p]
I have not turned away.
6 I offered my back to those who beat[q] me,
my cheeks to those who pulled out my beard;
I did not hide my face
from mocking and spitting.[r]
7 Because the Sovereign LORD helps[s] me,
I will not be disgraced.
Therefore have I set my face like flint,[t]
and I know I will not be put to shame.
8 He who vindicates me is near.
Who then will bring charges against me?[u]
Let us face each other![v]
Who is my accuser?
Let him confront me!
9 It is the Sovereign LORD who helps[w] me.
Who will condemn me?
They will all wear out like a garment;
the moths[x] will eat them up.

10 Who among you fears the LORD
and obeys the word of his servant?[y]
Let the one who walks in the dark,
who has no light,
trust[z] in the name of the LORD
and rely on their God.
11 But now, all you who light fires
and provide yourselves with flaming torches,[a]
go, walk in the light of your fires[b]
and of the torches you have set ablaze.
This is what you shall receive from my hand:
You will lie down in torment.[c]

Everlasting Salvation for Zion

51 "Listen[d] to me, you who pursue righteousness[e]
and who seek the LORD:
Look to the rock from which you were cut
and to the quarry from which you were hewn;
2 look to Abraham,[f] your father,
and to Sarah, who gave you birth.
When I called him he was only one man,
and I blessed him and made him many.[g]
3 The LORD will surely comfort[h] Zion
and will look with compassion on all her ruins;[i]
he will make her deserts like Eden,[j]
her wastelands like the garden of the LORD.
Joy and gladness[k] will be found in her,
thanksgiving and the sound of singing.

---

creditors. If the Lord had sold Israel to creditors (Ex. 21:7; 2 Kin. 4:1; Neh. 5:5), He would not have any authority over its destiny. But the Israelites sold themselves because of their own iniquities (42:23–25). Therefore God as their Redeemer could buy them back (41:14; 52:3). ***your mother.*** The mother is Jerusalem—more specifically, the inhabitants of the preceding generation that had gone into exile.

50:2 ***I came.*** God came to Israel at the time of the exile through the prophets whom He sent. Later God came to this earth through His Servant and Son, Jesus (41:9).

50:4 ***well instructed tongue.*** The third Servant song consists of a reflection by the Servant (vv. 4–9) and the prophet's address to the believing and unbelieving Israel (vv. 10–11).

50:6 ***mocking and spitting.*** This prophecy was fulfilled in the suffering of Jesus Christ (Matt. 27:30).

50:7 ***face like flint.*** Setting one's face like a flint indicates determination in the face of opposition (Ezek. 3:8–9; Luke 9:51).

50:8 ***vindicates.*** God's Servant fully anticipates vindication before the bar of God's justice. He was told to obey God perfectly, and He did. He was sent to suffer sacrificially, and He did. No prosecutor has a case against Him. In a stupendous development, God discloses that the sinners who identify themselves with the Servant may expect the same, although they are not righteous. Sin does carry the death penalty, but identification with the Servant brings exchange and substitution, in which the Servant takes the sinners' place. This makes the justification of sinners both possible and just. Their sins are transferred to Him, and He dies in their place. His shed blood removes their guilt, and they will be declared not guilty. His perfection makes them righteous, and they will be declared righteous. Every accuser will be silenced. Every attempt to have them convicted will be thrown out of court. God is just when He justifies those who belong to the Servant Savior (Rom. 8:31–34).

50:11 ***light fires.*** Those who light fires instead of the Light from God are those who are self-reliant. When the Light comes into the world, some will choose darkness (John 3:17–18).

50:2 [g] Isa 41:28 [h] Nu 11:23; Isa 59:1 [i] Ge 18:14 [j] Ex 14:22; Jos 3:16 **50:3** [k] Rev 6:12 **50:4** [l] Ex 4:12 [m] Mt 11:28 [n] Ps 5:3; 119:147; 143:8 **50:5** [o] Isa 35:5 [p] Mt 26:39; Jn 8:29; 14:31; 15:10; Ac 26:19; Heb 5:8 **50:6** [q] Isa 53:5; Mt 27:30; Mk 14:65; 15:19; Lk 22:63 [r] La 3:30; Mt 26:67 **50:7** [s] Isa 42:1 [t] Eze 3:8-9 **50:8** [u] Isa 43:26; Ro 8:32-34 [v] Isa 41:1 **50:9** [w] Isa 41:10 [x] Job 13:28; Isa 51:8 **50:10** [y] Isa 49:3 [z] Isa 26:4 **50:11** [a] Pr 26:18 [b] Jas 3:6 [c] Isa 65:13-15 **51:1** [d] Isa 46:3 [e] ver 7; Ps 94:15; Ro 9:30-31 **51:2** [f] Isa 29:22; Ro 4:16; Heb 11:11 [g] Ge 12:2 **51:3** [h] Isa 40:1 [i] Isa 52:9 [j] Ge 2:8 [k] Isa 25:9; 66:10

4 "Listen to me, my people;[l]
hear me, my nation:
Instruction will go out from me;
my justice[m] will become a light to the
nations.[n]
5 My righteousness draws near speedily,
my salvation is on the way,[o]
and my arm[p] will bring justice to the
nations.
The islands will look to me
and wait in hope for my arm.
6 Lift up your eyes to the heavens,
look at the earth beneath;
the heavens will vanish like smoke,[q]
the earth will wear out like a garment[r]
and its inhabitants die like flies.
But my salvation will last forever,
my righteousness will never fail.

7 "Hear me, you who know what is right,[s]
you people who have taken my
instruction to heart:[t]
Do not fear the reproach of mere
mortals
or be terrified by their insults.[u]
8 For the moth will eat them up like a
garment;[v]
the worm will devour them like wool.
But my righteousness will last
forever,[w]
my salvation through all
generations."
9 Awake, awake, arm of the LORD,
clothe yourself with strength![x]
Awake, as in days gone by,
as in generations of old.[y]
Was it not you who cut Rahab to
pieces,
who pierced that monster[z] through?
10 Was it not you who dried up the sea,[a]
the waters of the great deep,
who made a road in the depths of the
sea
so that the redeemed might cross
over?
11 Those the LORD has rescued[b] will
return.
They will enter Zion with singing;
everlasting joy will crown their heads.
Gladness and joy[c] will overtake them,
and sorrow and sighing will flee
away.[d]

12 "I, even I, am he who comforts[e] you.
Who are you that you fear mere
mortals,[f]
human beings who are but grass,[g]
13 that you forget[h] the LORD your Maker,[i]
who stretches out the heavens[j]
and who lays the foundations of the
earth,
that you live in constant terror[k] every
day
because of the wrath of the oppressor,
who is bent on destruction?
For where is the wrath of the oppressor?
14 The cowering prisoners will soon be
set free;
they will not die in their dungeon,
nor will they lack bread.[l]
15 For I am the LORD your God,
who stirs up the sea[m] so that its
waves roar—
the LORD Almighty is his name.
16 I have put my words in your mouth[n]
and covered you with the shadow of
my hand[o]—
I who set the heavens in place,
who laid the foundations of the
earth,
and who say to Zion, 'You are my
people.'"

The Cup of the LORD's Wrath

17 Awake, awake![p]
Rise up, Jerusalem,
you who have drunk from the hand of
the LORD
the cup of his wrath,[q]
you who have drained to its dregs
the goblet that makes people stagger.[r]
18 Among all the children[s] she bore
there was none to guide her;[t]
among all the children she reared
there was none to take her by the
hand.
19 These double calamities[u] have come
upon you—
who can comfort you?—
ruin and destruction, famine[v] and
sword—
who can[a] console you?
20 Your children have fainted;
they lie at every street corner,[w]
like antelope caught in a net.
They are filled with the wrath of the
LORD,
with the rebuke of your God.

21 Therefore hear this, you afflicted one,
made drunk,[x] but not with wine.

[a] *19* Dead Sea Scrolls, Septuagint, Vulgate and Syriac; Masoretic Text / *how can I*

51:14 ***prisoners ... in their dungeon.*** The prisoners refer to those who were captive in Babylon. The meaning also extends to all who experience the darkness of sin and alienation from God (48:20; 49:9).
51:19 ***These double calamities.*** The double calamities are the desolation of the land and the destruction of the people.
51:21 ***drunk, but not with wine.*** The cause of drunkenness was not wine, but the "goblet of wrath" (v. 22), the terror of God's judgment.

51:4 [l] Ps 50:7 [m] Isa 2:4 [n] Isa 42:4,6 **51:5** [o] Isa 46:13 [p] Isa 40:10; 63:1,5 **51:6** [q] Mt 24:35; 2Pe 3:10 [r] Ps 102:25-26 **51:7** [s] ver 1 [t] Ps 37:31 [u] Mt 5:11; Ac 5:41 **51:8** [v] Isa 50:9 [w] ver 6 **51:9** [x] Isa 52:1 [y] Dt 4:34 [z] Ps 74:13 **51:10** [a] Ex 14:22 **51:11** [b] Isa 35:9 [c] Jer 33:11 [d] Rev 7:17 **51:12** [e] 2Co 1:4 [f] Ps 118:6; Isa 2:22 [g] Isa 40:6-7; 1Pe 1:24 **51:13** [h] Isa 17:10 [i] Isa 45:11 [j] Ps 104:2; Isa 48:13 [k] Isa 7:4 **51:14** [l] Isa 49:10 **51:15** [m] Jer 31:35 **51:16** [n] Dt 18:18; Isa 59:21 [o] Ex 33:22 **51:17** [p] Isa 52:1 [q] Job 21:20; Rev 14:10; 16:19 [r] Ps 60:3 **51:18** [s] Ps 88:18 [t] Isa 49:21 **51:19** [u] Isa 47:9 [v] Isa 14:30 **51:20** [w] Isa 5:25; Jer 14:16 **51:21** [x] ver 17; Isa 29:9

22 This is what your Sovereign LORD says,
your God, who defends[y] his people:
"See, I have taken out of your hand
the cup[z] that made you stagger;
from that cup, the goblet of my wrath,
you will never drink again.
23 I will put it into the hands of your
tormentors,[a]
who said to you,
'Fall prostrate[b] that we may walk[c] on
you.'
And you made your back like the
ground,
like a street to be walked on."

52 Awake, awake,[d] Zion,
clothe yourself with strength![e]
Put on your garments of splendor,[f]
Jerusalem, the holy city.[g]
The uncircumcised and defiled
will not enter you again.[h]
2 Shake off your dust;[i]
rise up, sit enthroned, Jerusalem.
Free yourself from the chains on your
neck,
Daughter Zion, now a captive.

3 For this is what the LORD says:

"You were sold for nothing,[j]
and without money[k] you will be
redeemed."

4 For this is what the Sovereign LORD
says:

"At first my people went down to Egypt[l]
to live;
lately, Assyria has oppressed them.

5 "And now what do I have here?" declares the LORD.

"For my people have been taken away
for nothing,
and those who rule them mock,[a]"
declares the LORD.
"And all day long
my name is constantly blasphemed.[m]
6 Therefore my people will know[n] my
name;
therefore in that day they will know
that it is I who foretold it.
Yes, it is I."

7 How beautiful on the mountains
are the feet of those who bring good
news,[o]
who proclaim peace,[p]
who bring good tidings,
who proclaim salvation,
who say to Zion,
"Your God reigns!"[q]
8 Listen! Your watchmen[r] lift up their
voices;
together they shout for joy.
When the LORD returns to Zion,
they will see it with their own
eyes.
9 Burst into songs of joy[s] together,
you ruins[t] of Jerusalem,
for the LORD has comforted his
people,
he has redeemed Jerusalem.[u]
10 The LORD will lay bare his holy
arm
in the sight of all the nations,[v]
and all the ends of the earth will see
the salvation[w] of our God.

11 Depart,[x] depart, go out from there!
Touch no unclean thing![y]
Come out from it and be pure,[z]
you who carry the articles of the
LORD's house.
12 But you will not leave in haste[a]
or go in flight;
for the LORD will go before you,[b]
the God of Israel will be your rear
guard.[c]

The Suffering and Glory of the Servant

13 See, my servant[d] will act wisely[b];
he will be raised and lifted up and
highly exalted.[e]
14 Just as there were many who were
appalled at him[c]—
his appearance was so disfigured
beyond that of any human
being
and his form marred beyond human
likeness—

[a] 5 Dead Sea Scrolls and Vulgate; Masoretic Text *wail* [b] *13* Or *will prosper* [c] *14* Hebrew *you*

52:6 *will know my name.* The people are the redeemed exiles, as well as the people who believe in and follow the Servant (Messiah). Isaiah was speaking of a time beyond his own time, to people who were not yet born (1 Pet. 1:10–12). Jesus speaks strongly of this concept when He says, "I know my sheep and my sheep know me" (John 10:11–18).

52:12 *go before you . . . rear guard.* This is an allusion to the pillar of cloud and fire that protected Israel in its flight from Egypt (Ex. 13:21–22; 14:19–20).

52:13—53:12 *See.* The fourth of the Servant songs, which form the central unit of chapters 40–66, begins with the praise of the Father for the work of the Servant.

52:14 *appearance was so disfigured.* This speaks of the physical punishment that the Servant, Jesus Christ, endured when he was bearing the sins of the world on the cross. He was cruelly beaten, even before He was crucified (Matt. 27:27–31; Mark 15:16–20; John 19:1–3).

51:22 [y] Isa 49:25 [z] ver 17 **51:23** [a] Isa 49:26; Jer 25:15-17, 26,28; 49:12 [b] Zec 12:2 [c] Jos 10:24 **52:1** [d] Isa 51:17 [e] Isa 51:9 [f] Ex 28:2,40; Ps 110:3; Zec 3:4 [g] Ne 11:1; Mt 4:5; Rev 21:2 [h] Na 1:15; Rev 21:27 **52:2** [i] Isa 29:4 **52:3** [j] Ps 44:12 [k] Isa 45:13 **52:4** [l] Ge 46:6 **52:5** [m] Eze 36:20; Ro 2:24* **52:6** [n] Isa 49:23 **52:7** [o] Isa 40:9; Ro 10:15* [p] Na 1:15; Eph 6:15 [q] Ps 93:1 **52:8** [r] Isa 62:6 **52:9** [s] Ps 98:4 [t] Isa 51:3 [u] Isa 48:20 **52:10** [v] Isa 66:18 [w] Ps 98:2-3; Lk 3:6 **52:11** [x] Isa 48:20 [y] Isa 1:16; 2Co 6:17* [z] 2Ti 2:19 **52:12** [a] Ex 12:11 [b] Mic 2:13 [c] Ex 14:19 **52:13** [d] Isa 42:1 [e] Isa 57:15; Php 2:9

[15]so he will sprinkle many nations,[a]
and kings will shut their mouths
because of him.
For what they were not told, they will
see,
and what they have not heard, they
will understand.[f]

53 Who has believed our message[g]
and to whom has the arm of the
LORD been revealed?[h]
[2]He grew up before him like a tender
shoot,
and like a root out of dry ground.
He had no beauty or majesty to attract
us to him,
nothing in his appearance[i] that we
should desire him.
[3]He was despised and rejected by
mankind,
a man of suffering, and familiar with
pain.[j]
Like one from whom people hide their
faces
he was despised,[k] and we held him in
low esteem.

[4]Surely he took up our pain
and bore our suffering,[l]
yet we considered him punished by
God,[m]
stricken by him, and afflicted.
[5]But he was pierced for our
transgressions,[n]
he was crushed for our iniquities;
the punishment that brought us peace
was on him,
and by his wounds we are healed.[o]
[6]We all, like sheep, have gone astray,
each of us has turned to our own way;
and the LORD has laid on him
the iniquity of us all.

[7]He was oppressed and afflicted,
yet he did not open his mouth;[p]
he was led like a lamb to the slaughter,
and as a sheep before its shearers is
silent,
so he did not open his mouth.
[8]By oppression[b] and judgment he was
taken away.
Yet who of his generation protested?
For he was cut off from the land of the
living;[q]
for the transgression[r] of my people he
was punished.[c]
[9]He was assigned a grave with the
wicked,
and with the rich[s] in his death,
though he had done no violence,[t]
nor was any deceit in his mouth.[u]

[10]Yet it was the LORD's will[v] to crush[w] him
and cause him to suffer,[x]
and though the LORD makes[d] his life
an offering for sin,
he will see his offspring[y] and prolong
his days,
and the will of the LORD will prosper
in his hand.

[a] 15 Or *so will many nations be amazed at him* (see also Septuagint) [b] 8 Or *From arrest* [c] 8 Or *generation considered / that he was cut off from the land of the living, / that he was punished for the transgression of my people?* [d] 10 Hebrew *though you make*

52:15 ***shut their mouths.*** The kings are silent in stunned respect.

53:1–12 The Suffering Servant—Along with Psalm 22, this Scripture is understood to be one of the key prophetic Old Testament passages pointing to the saving work of Christ. This passage presents the whole idea of the "Suffering Servant," which is one of the central concepts of Isaiah, and for many, Judaism. Christ's fulfillment of this passage in His passion is remarkable. The New Testament writers point often to Isaiah 53 and how Christ fulfilled this prophecy (Matt. 8:17; Luke 23:8–9; John 12:38; Rom. 10:16; 1 Pet. 2:25). It is also the Scripture that Philip explained to the Ethiopian eunuch in Acts 8:32–33.

In the Old Testament sacrificial system people offered animals to atone for sin (Lev. 16). The Bible presents Christ as the ultimate sacrifice that died once and for all for the sins of the world (Heb. 8–10). Our sins are forgiven and we become righteous through Christ's great work on the cross (2 Cor. 5:21).

53:2 ***no beauty or majesty.*** There was nothing in the Promised Servant's appearance to mark His special calling.

53:3 ***despised and rejected.*** The Servant was not received joyfully by the people who needed Him so much (Mark 9:12). ***man of suffering.*** This phrase does not indicate that the Servant would be dour, but that He knew better than anyone the havoc that sin brings into human life, and, as the kindest of friends, He was sorry for the pain of His people.

53:4 ***bore our suffering.*** The Savior Jesus came to suffer and die for the sins of others (Matt. 8:17; Heb. 9:28; 1 Pet. 2:24). Griefs, sorrows, and affliction refer to the consequences of sin.

53:7 ***yet he did not open his mouth.*** Jesus did not open His mouth to defend Himself or to answer the false charges made against Him (Matt. 26:63; Mark 14:61; Luke 23:9; John 19:9).

53:10 ***it was the LORD's will to crush him.*** The Old Testament pointed to the doctrine of the atonement long before Jesus died for our sins (1 Cor. 15:3). In fact, the atonement was part of God's eternal plan (Eph. 1:4–7). The Father was pleased that His Son should die because it would cover up the sins of many and reconcile them to Himself. ***offering for sin.*** The offering for sin, or "guilt offering," was the sacrifice of a ram to secure the Lord's atonement for sin (Lev. 5:6–7,15; 7:1; 14:12; 19:21). Here, the prophet Isaiah describes the Servant Jesus as a guilt offering. ***his offspring.*** If the Spirit of God dwells in us (Rom. 8:9–11), and if we are led by the Spirit, then we are sons of God—His offspring (Rom. 8:14).

52:15 [f] Ro 15:21*; Eph 3:4-5 **53:1** [g] Ro 10:16* [h] Jn 12:38* **53:2** [i] Isa 52:14 **53:3** [j] ver 4, 10; Lk 18:31-33 [k] Ps 22:6; Jn 1:10-11 **53:4** [l] Mt 8:17* [m] Jn 19:7 **53:5** [n] Ro 4:25; 1Co 15:3; Heb 9:28 [o] 1Pe 2:24-25 **53:7** [p] Mk 14:61 **53:8** [q] Da 9:26; Ac 8:32-33* [r] ver 12 **53:9** [s] Mt 27:57-60 [t] Isa 42:1-3 [u] 1Pe 2:22* **53:10** [v] Isa 46:10 [w] ver 5 [x] ver 3 [y] Ps 22:30

[11] After he has suffered,[z]
he will see the light of life[a] and be satisfied[b];
by his knowledge[c] my righteous servant will justify[a] many,
and he will bear their iniquities.
[12] Therefore I will give him a portion among the great,[d][b]
and he will divide the spoils with the strong,[e]
because he poured out his life unto death,[c]
and was numbered with the transgressors.[d]
For he bore the sin of many,
and made intercession for the transgressors.

The Future Glory of Zion

54 "Sing, barren woman,
you who never bore a child;
burst into song, shout for joy,
you who were never in labor;
because more are the children[e] of the desolate woman
than of her who has a husband,[f]"
says the LORD.
[2] "Enlarge the place of your tent,[g]
stretch your tent curtains wide,
do not hold back;
lengthen your cords,
strengthen your stakes.[h]
[3] For you will spread out to the right and to the left;
your descendants will dispossess nations
and settle in their desolate[i] cities.

[4] "Do not be afraid; you will not be put to shame.
Do not fear disgrace; you will not be humiliated.
You will forget the shame of your youth
and remember no more the reproach[j] of your widowhood.
[5] For your Maker is your husband[k]—
the LORD Almighty is his name—
the Holy One of Israel is your Redeemer;[l]
he is called the God of all the earth.[m]
[6] The LORD will call you back[n]
as if you were a wife deserted[o] and distressed in spirit—
a wife who married young,
only to be rejected," says your God.
[7] "For a brief moment[p] I abandoned you,
but with deep compassion I will bring you back.[q]
[8] In a surge of anger[r]
I hid my face from you for a moment,
but with everlasting kindness[s]
I will have compassion on you,"
says the LORD your Redeemer.

[9] "To me this is like the days of Noah,
when I swore that the waters of Noah would never again cover the earth.[t]
So now I have sworn not to be angry[u] with you,
never to rebuke you again.
[10] Though the mountains be shaken[v]
and the hills be removed,
yet my unfailing love for you will not be shaken[w]
nor my covenant[x] of peace be removed,"
says the LORD, who has compassion[y] on you.

[11] "Afflicted[z] city, lashed by storms[a] and not comforted,[b]
I will rebuild you with stones of turquoise,[f][c]
your foundations[d] with lapis lazuli.
[12] I will make your battlements of rubies,
your gates of sparkling jewels,
and all your walls of precious stones.
[13] All your children will be taught by the LORD,[e]
and great will be their peace.[f]
[14] In righteousness you will be established:
Tyranny[g] will be far from you;
you will have nothing to fear.
Terror will be far removed;
it will not come near you.
[15] If anyone does attack you, it will not be my doing;
whoever attacks you will surrender[h] to you.

---

[a] 11 Dead Sea Scrolls (see also Septuagint); Masoretic Text does not have *the light of life.*
[b] 11 Or (with Masoretic Text) *11He will see the fruit of his suffering / and will be satisfied*
[c] 11 Or *by knowledge of him*
[d] 12 Or *many*
[e] 12 Or *numerous*
[f] 11 The meaning of the Hebrew for this word is uncertain.

54:1 *never bore.* The Israelites received a liberation (through the promised Cyrus for the Babylonian exiles, or through the Messiah, in the fullest sense) that they did not work for—it was God's idea.
54:4 *widowhood.* The widowhood was the time without the working presence of God in the lives of the people of God, the time of exile. In the fullest sense, every sinner is a "widow" without God, who has the role of protector and provider.
54:11 *foundations with lapis lazuli.* For a more detailed description of the New Jerusalem, see Revelation 21:18–21. It will be a city of stunning beauty and grand proportions.

53:11 [z] Jn 10:14-18 [a] Ro 5:18-19 **53:12** [b] Php 2:9 [c] Mt 26:28,38,39,42 [d] Mk 15:27*; Lk 22:37*; 23:32 **54:1** [e] Isa 49:20 [f] 1Sa 2:5; Gal 4:27* **54:2** [g] Isa 49:19-20 [h] Ex 35:18; 39:40 **54:3** [i] Isa 49:19 **54:4** [j] Isa 51:7 **54:5** [k] Jer 3:14 [l] Isa 48:17 [m] Isa 6:3 **54:6** [n] Isa 49:14-21 [o] Isa 50:1-2; 62:4,12 **54:7** [p] Isa 26:20 [q] Isa 49:18 **54:8** [r] Isa 60:10 [s] ver 10 **54:9** [t] Ge 8:21 [u] Isa 12:1 **54:10** [v] Ps 46:2 [w] Isa 51:6 [x] Ps 89:34 [y] ver 8 **54:11** [z] Isa 14:32 [a] Isa 28:2; 29:6 [b] Isa 51:19 [c] 1Ch 29:2; Rev 21:18 [d] Isa 28:16; Rev 21:19-20 **54:13** [e] Jn 6:45* [f] Isa 48:18 **54:14** [g] Isa 9:4 **54:15** [h] Isa 41:11-16

16 "See, it is I who created the blacksmith
who fans the coals into flame
and forges a weapon fit for its work.
And it is I who have created the
destroyer to wreak havoc;
17 no weapon forged against you will
prevail,[i]
and you will refute[j] every tongue that
accuses you.
This is the heritage of the servants of
the LORD,
and this is their vindication from me,"
declares the LORD.

Invitation to the Thirsty

55 "Come, all you who are thirsty,[k]
come to the waters;
and you who have no money,
come, buy[l] and eat!
Come, buy wine and milk[m]
without money and without cost.[n]
2 Why spend money on what is not bread,
and your labor on what does not
satisfy?[o]
Listen, listen to me, and eat what is
good,[p]
and you will delight in the richest of
fare.
3 Give ear and come to me;
listen, that you may live.[q]
I will make an everlasting covenant[r]
with you,
my faithful love[s] promised to David.[t]
4 See, I have made him a witness to the
peoples,
a ruler and commander[u] of the
peoples.
5 Surely you will summon nations[v] you
know not,
and nations you do not know will
come running to you,
because of the LORD your God,
the Holy One of Israel,
for he has endowed you with
splendor."[w]

6 Seek the LORD while he may be
found;[x]
call[y] on him while he is near.
7 Let the wicked forsake their ways
and the unrighteous their
thoughts.[z]
Let them turn[a] to the LORD, and he will
have mercy[b] on them,
and to our God, for he will freely
pardon.[c]
8 "For my thoughts are not your thoughts,
neither are your ways my ways,"[d]
declares the LORD.
9 "As the heavens are higher than the
earth,[e]
so are my ways higher than your
ways
and my thoughts than your thoughts.
10 As the rain[f] and the snow
come down from heaven,
and do not return to it
without watering the earth
and making it bud and flourish,
so that it yields seed for the sower
and bread for the eater,[g]
11 so is my word that goes out from my
mouth:
It will not return to me empty,[h]
but will accomplish what I desire
and achieve the purpose[i] for which I
sent it.
12 You will go out in joy
and be led forth in peace;[j]
the mountains and hills
will burst into song before you,
and all the trees[k] of the field
will clap their hands.[l]
13 Instead of the thornbush will grow the
juniper,
and instead of briers[m] the myrtle[n]
will grow.
This will be for the LORD's renown,[o]
for an everlasting sign,
that will endure forever."

54:17 *the servants of the LORD.* Throughout the rest of Isaiah, the word "servants" refers to all saints, Jews and Gentiles (56:6–8; 63:17; 65:8–9,13–15; 66:14), the offspring of the Servant (Jesus).
55:4 *witness.* God's fulfillment of the promises to the house of David, climaxing in the resurrection of Christ, serves as a witness to the nations (43:10,12; 44:8). It shows that He has fulfilled His prophecies and promises, and that He is who He says He is: the King of the universe.
55:6 *while he may be found.* Solomon warned his readers to remember their Creator in the days of their youth, when the evil days have not yet come (Eccl. 12:1). The writer to the Hebrews admonishes his readers, "Today, if you hear his voice, do not harden your hearts" (Ps. 95:7–8; Heb. 4:7). Responding to the call of God is not something to be put off. Hardened hearts become a habit, or evil days may impair our ability to think clearly. If the Lord is calling, respond to Him. We do not know how long we have to live. No one knows whether "this night" his soul may be required (Luke 12:20).
55:9 *higher.* The gulf existing between human and divine nature is expressed here in graphic terms. God functions at the level of pure holiness, and He is motivated by complete love and service to others. The corruption of human nature by sin introduces carnal elements that are totally unknown to the nature of God, and by contrast are base both in character and execution. It is only when we are born again that we can understand the things of the Spirit, the ways of God (John 3:9–21).

54:17 [i] Isa 29:8 [j] Isa 45:24-25 **55:1** [k] Jn 4:14; 7:37 [l] La 5:4; Mt 13:44; Rev 3:18 [m] SS 5:1 [n] Hos 14:4; Mt 10:8; Rev 21:6 **55:2** [o] Ps 22:26; Ecc 6:2; Hos 8:7 [p] Isa 1:19 **55:3** [q] Lev 18:5; Ro 10:5 [r] Isa 61:8 [s] Isa 54:8 [t] Ac 13:34* **55:4** [u] Jer 30:9; Eze 34:23-24 **55:5** [v] Isa 49:6 [w] Isa 60:9 **55:6** [x] Ps 32:6; Isa 49:8; 2Co 6:1-2 [y] Isa 65:24 **55:7** [z] Isa 32:7; 59:7 [a] Isa 44:22 [b] Isa 54:10 [c] Isa 1:18; 40:2 **55:8** [d] Isa 53:6 **55:9** [e] Ps 103:11 **55:10** [f] Isa 30:23 [g] 2Co 9:10 **55:11** [h] Isa 45:23 [i] Isa 44:26 **55:12** [j] Isa 54:10, 13 [k] 1Ch 16:33 [l] Ps 98:8 **55:13** [m] Isa 5:6 [n] Isa 41:19 [o] Isa 63:12

Salvation for Others

56 This is what the LORD says:

"Maintain justice[p]
and do what is right,
for my salvation[q] is close at hand
and my righteousness will soon be revealed.
2 Blessed[r] is the one who does this—
the person who holds it fast,
who keeps the Sabbath[s] without desecrating it,
and keeps their hands from doing any evil."

3 Let no foreigner who is bound to the LORD say,
"The LORD will surely exclude me from his people."
And let no eunuch[t] complain,
"I am only a dry tree."

4 For this is what the LORD says:

"To the eunuchs who keep my Sabbaths,
who choose what pleases me
and hold fast to my covenant—
5 to them I will give within my temple and its walls[u]
a memorial and a name
better than sons and daughters;
I will give them an everlasting name
that will endure forever.[v]
6 And foreigners who bind themselves to the LORD
to minister[w] to him,
to love the name of the LORD,
and to be his servants,
all who keep the Sabbath[x] without desecrating it
and who hold fast to my covenant—
7 these I will bring to my holy mountain[y]
and give them joy in my house of prayer.
Their burnt offerings and sacrifices[z]
will be accepted on my altar;
for my house will be called
a house of prayer for all nations.[a]"[b]
8 The Sovereign LORD declares—
he who gathers the exiles of Israel:
"I will gather[c] still others to them
besides those already gathered."

God's Accusation Against the Wicked

9 Come, all you beasts of the field,[d]
come and devour, all you beasts of the forest!
10 Israel's watchmen[e] are blind,
they all lack knowledge;
they are all mute dogs,
they cannot bark;
they lie around and dream,
they love to sleep.[f]
11 They are dogs with mighty appetites;
they never have enough.
They are shepherds[g] who lack understanding;[h]
they all turn to their own way,
they seek their own gain.[i]
12 "Come," each one cries, "let me get wine!
Let us drink our fill of beer!
And tomorrow will be like today,
or even far better."[j]

57 The righteous perish,[k]
and no one takes it to heart;[l]
the devout are taken away,
and no one understands
that the righteous are taken away
to be spared from evil.[m]
2 Those who walk uprightly[n]
enter into peace;
they find rest as they lie in death.

3 "But you—come here, you children of a sorceress,
you offspring of adulterers[o] and prostitutes![p]
4 Who are you mocking?
At whom do you sneer
and stick out your tongue?
Are you not a brood of rebels,
the offspring of liars?
5 You burn with lust among the oaks
and under every spreading tree;[q]
you sacrifice your children[r] in the ravines
and under the overhanging crags.
6 The idols[s] among the smooth stones of the ravines are your portion;
indeed, they are your lot.

56:3 *foreigner.* In speaking of the foreigner who joined himself to the Lord, Isaiah was not speaking of the foreign wives that the returning exiles would have married (Ezra 9:1–4). Those foreign wives were considered a corrupting influence because they had not become followers of the Living God. The foreigners that Isaiah was prophesying about would be converted to worship the true Lord (44:5).

56:5 *everlasting.* This word links this passage with 55:13.

56:9 *beasts.* The unclean, ravenous beasts summoned to attack the ungodly community are hostile nations (Jer. 12:8–9; Ezek. 34:5,8).

56:11 *dogs.* The dog was not highly regarded in biblical culture, and to the Jews they were unclean.

57:5 *sacrifice your children.* Killing the children was associated with the worship of Molek and with demon worship (30:33; 2 Kin. 23:10; Ps. 106:37–38; Jer. 7:31).

56:1 [p] Isa 1:17 [q] Ps 85:9 **56:2** [r] Ps 119:2 [s] Ex 20:8, 10; Isa 58:13 **56:3** [t] Jer 38:7 *fn*; Ac 8:27 **56:5** [u] Isa 26:1; 60:18 [v] Isa 48:19; 55:13 **56:6** [w] Isa 60:7, 10; 61:5 [x] ver 2, 4 **56:7** [y] Isa 2:2 [z] Ro 12:1; Heb 13:15 [a] Mt 21:13*; Lk 19:46* [b] Mk 11:17* **56:8** [c] Isa 11:12; 60:3-11; Jn 10:16 **56:9** [d] Isa 18:6; Jer 12:9 **56:10** [e] Eze 3:17 [f] Na 3:18 **56:11** [g] Eze 34:2 [h] Isa 1:3 [i] Isa 57:17; Eze 13:19; Mic 3:11 **56:12** [j] Ps 10:6; Lk 12:18-19 **57:1** [k] Ps 12:1 [l] Isa 42:25 [m] 2Ki 22:20 **57:2** [n] Isa 26:7 **57:3** [o] Mt 16:4 [p] Isa 1:21 **57:5** [q] 2Ki 16:4 [r] Lev 18:21; Ps 106:37-38; Eze 16:20 **57:6** [s] Jer 3:9

Yes, to them you have poured out drink offerings[t]
and offered grain offerings.
In view of all this, should I relent?[u]
7 You have made your bed on a high and lofty hill;[v]
there you went up to offer your sacrifices.
8 Behind your doors and your doorposts
you have put your pagan symbols.
Forsaking me, you uncovered your bed,
you climbed into it and opened it wide;
you made a pact with those whose beds you love,[w]
and you looked with lust on their naked bodies.[x]
9 You went to Molek[a] with olive oil
and increased your perfumes.
You sent your ambassadors[b][y] far away;
you descended to the very realm of the dead!
10 You wearied yourself by such going about,
but you would not say, 'It is hopeless.'[z]
You found renewal of your strength,
and so you did not faint.

11 "Whom have you so dreaded and feared[a]
that you have not been true to me,
and have neither remembered[b] me
nor taken this to heart?
Is it not because I have long been silent[c]
that you do not fear me?
12 I will expose your righteousness and your works,[d]
and they will not benefit you.
13 When you cry out[e] for help,
let your collection of idols save you!
The wind will carry all of them off,
a mere breath will blow them away.
But whoever takes refuge in me
will inherit the land[f]
and possess my holy mountain."[g]

Comfort for the Contrite

14 And it will be said:

"Build up, build up, prepare the road!
Remove the obstacles out of the way of my people."[h]
15 For this is what the high and exalted[i] One says—
he who lives forever,[j] whose name is holy:
"I live in a high and holy place,
but also with the one who is contrite[k] and lowly in spirit,[l]
to revive the spirit of the lowly
and to revive the heart of the contrite.[m]
16 I will not accuse them forever,
nor will I always be angry,[n]
for then they would faint away because of me—
the very people I have created.
17 I was enraged by their sinful greed;[o]
I punished them, and hid my face in anger,
yet they kept on in their willful ways.[p]
18 I have seen their ways, but I will heal[q] them;
I will guide them and restore comfort[r]
to Israel's mourners,
19 creating praise on their lips.[s]
Peace, peace,[t] to those far and near,"[u]
says the LORD. "And I will heal them."
20 But the wicked[v] are like the tossing sea,
which cannot rest,
whose waves cast up mire and mud.
21 "There is no peace,"[w] says my God, "for the wicked."[x]

True Fasting

58 "Shout it aloud,[y] do not hold back.
Raise your voice like a trumpet.
Declare to my people their rebellion[z]
and to the descendants of Jacob their sins.
2 For day after day they seek[a] me out;
they seem eager to know my ways,
as if they were a nation that does what is right
and has not forsaken the commands of its God.
They ask me for just decisions
and seem eager for God to come near[b] them.

[a] 9 Or *to the king* [b] 9 Or *idols*

57:12 *your righteousness.* This phrase is stated in sarcasm or irony. The people had found a counterfeit life in idolatry and immorality that would only lead to death.
57:14 *Build up.* This verse is based on 40:1–4. The phrase "build up" resembles "every valley shall be raised up."
57:16 *will not accuse them forever.* God was addressing the human failure to keep His good laws, but humans will always fail. God knew this, so He created a way of salvation, a way to heal the problem of sin (v. 18). He knew that they needed to be radically rescued, for the law was powerless to save them (Rom. 2–8).
58:2 *eager to know my ways ... eager for God to come near.* Unfortunately, one can really enjoy all the religious ritual without really wanting to know God. God can always tell the difference between the heart that is turned toward Him and the heart that is devoted to religious form.

57:6 [t] Jer 7:18 [u] Jer 5:9, 29; 9:9 **57:7** [v] Jer 3:6; Eze 16:16 **57:8** [w] Eze 16:26; 23:7 [x] Eze 23:18 **57:9** [y] Eze 23:16, 40 **57:10** [z] Jer 2:25; 18:12 **57:11** [a] Pr 29:25 [b] Jer 2:32; 3:21 [c] Ps 50:21 **57:12** [d] Isa 29:15; Mic 3:2-4, 8 **57:13** [e] Jer 22:20; 30:15 [f] Ps 37:9 [g] Isa 65:9-11 **57:14** [h] Isa 62:10; Jer 18:15 **57:15** [i] Isa 52:13 [j] Dt 33:27 [k] Ps 147:3 [l] Ps 34:18; 51:17; Isa 66:2 [m] Isa 61:1 **57:16** [n] Ps 85:5; 103:9; Mic 7:18 **57:17** [o] Isa 56:11 [p] Isa 1:4 **57:18** [q] Isa 30:26 [r] Isa 61:1-3 **57:19** [s] Isa 6:7; Heb 13:15 [t] Eph 2:17 [u] Ac 2:39 **57:20** [v] Job 18:5-21 **57:21** [w] Isa 59:8 [x] Isa 48:22 **58:1** [y] Isa 40:6 [z] Isa 48:8 **58:2** [a] Isa 48:1; Titus 1:16; Jas 4:8 [b] Isa 29:13

3 'Why have we fasted,'[c] they say,
'and you have not seen it?
Why have we humbled ourselves,
and you have not noticed?'[d]

"Yet on the day of your fasting, you do
as you please[e]
and exploit all your workers.
4 Your fasting ends in quarreling and
strife,[f]
and in striking each other with
wicked fists.
You cannot fast as you do today
and expect your voice to be heard[g] on
high.
5 Is this the kind of fast[h] I have chosen,
only a day for people to humble[i]
themselves?
Is it only for bowing one's head like a
reed
and for lying in sackcloth and ashes?[j]
Is that what you call a fast,
a day acceptable to the LORD?

6 "Is not this the kind of fasting I have
chosen:
to loose the chains of injustice[k]
and untie the cords of the yoke,
to set the oppressed[l] free
and break every yoke?
7 Is it not to share your food with the
hungry[m]
and to provide the poor wanderer
with shelter[n]—
when you see the naked, to clothe[o] them,
and not to turn away from your own
flesh and blood?[p]
8 Then your light will break forth like the
dawn,[q]
and your healing[r] will quickly appear;
then your righteousness[a] will go before
you,
and the glory of the LORD will be your
rear guard.[s]
9 Then you will call,[t] and the LORD will
answer;
you will cry for help, and he will say:
Here am I.

"If you do away with the yoke of
oppression,
with the pointing finger[u] and
malicious talk,[v]
10 and if you spend yourselves in behalf of
the hungry
and satisfy the needs of the
oppressed,[w]
then your light[x] will rise in the darkness,
and your night will become like the
noonday.[y]
11 The LORD will guide you always;
he will satisfy your needs[z] in a
sun-scorched land
and will strengthen your frame.
You will be like a well-watered garden,[a]
like a spring[b] whose waters never fail.
12 Your people will rebuild the ancient
ruins[c]
and will raise up the age-old
foundations;[d]
you will be called Repairer of Broken
Walls,
Restorer of Streets with Dwellings.

13 "If you keep your feet from breaking
the Sabbath[e]
and from doing as you please on my
holy day,
if you call the Sabbath a delight[f]
and the LORD's holy day honorable,
and if you honor it by not going your
own way
and not doing as you please or
speaking idle words,
14 then you will find your joy[g] in the LORD,
and I will cause you to ride in
triumph on the heights[h] of the
land
and to feast on the inheritance of
your father Jacob."
For the mouth of the LORD
has spoken.[i]

Sin, Confession and Redemption

59 Surely the arm of the LORD is not
too short[j] to save,
nor his ear too dull to hear.[k]
2 But your iniquities have separated
you from your God;
your sins have hidden his face from you,
so that he will not hear.[l]

[a] 8 Or *your righteous One*

58:6 *to loose ... and untie ... free.* Love is right at the top of the list in relating to God and to other people (1 John 4:7–21). Once again, the Lord is defining true religion. It is always horizontal (directed toward other people) as well as vertical (directed toward God). If we love God, we will be just and merciful to other people (Mic. 6:8; James 1:26–27).

59:2 The Effects of Sin—Sin, regardless of how serious, always has an effect—separation. Sin separates one from God. This separation from God is death. Adam was told that if he ate of the tree of the knowledge of good and evil he would die (Gen. 3:3). Adam ate of the tree anyway and immediately died spiritually—his soul was separated from God—and he then began to die physically. The entrance of sin into the world brought with it death (Rom. 5:12; 6:23). That man is a sinner is proven by the fact that he dies—where there is death, there is sin. Sin's penalty, death, can be remedied by life—union with God. This is achieved by belief in Jesus, who died to pay the penalty of man's sin (Rom. 5:21). For one who

58:3 [c] Lev 16:29 [d] Mal 3:14 [e] Isa 22:13; Zec 7:5-6 **58:4** [f] 1Ki 21:9-13; Isa 59:6 [g] Isa 59:2 **58:5** [h] Zec 7:5 [i] 1Ki 21:27 [j] Job 2:8 **58:6** [k] Ne 5:10-11 [l] Jer 34:9 **58:7** [m] Eze 18:16; Lk 3:11 [n] Isa 16:4; Heb 13:2 [o] Job 31:19-20; Mt 25:36 [p] Ge 29:14; Lk 10:31-32 **58:8** [q] Job 11:17 [r] Isa 30:26 [s] Ex 14:19 **58:9** [t] Ps 50:15 [u] Pr 6:13 [v] Ps 12:2; Isa 59:13 **58:10** [w] Dt 15:7-8 [x] Isa 42:16 [y] Job 11:17 **58:11** [z] Ps 107:9 [a] SS 4:15 [b] Jn 4:14 **58:12** [c] Isa 49:8 [d] Isa 44:28 **58:13** [e] Isa 56:2 [f] Ps 84:2, 10 **58:14** [g] Job 22:26 [h] Dt 32:13 [i] Isa 1:20 **59:1** [j] Nu 11:23; Isa 50:2 [k] Isa 58:9; 65:24 **59:2** [l] Isa 1:15; 58:4

3 For your hands are stained with blood,[m]
your fingers with guilt.
Your lips have spoken falsely,
and your tongue mutters wicked things.
4 No one calls for justice;
no one pleads a case with integrity.
They rely on empty arguments, they utter lies;
they conceive trouble and give birth to evil.[n]
5 They hatch the eggs of vipers
and spin a spider's web.[o]
Whoever eats their eggs will die,
and when one is broken, an adder is hatched.
6 Their cobwebs are useless for clothing;
they cannot cover themselves with what they make.[p]
Their deeds are evil deeds,
and acts of violence[q] are in their hands.
7 Their feet rush into sin;
they are swift to shed innocent blood.[r]
They pursue evil schemes;[s]
acts of violence mark their ways.[t]
8 The way of peace they do not know;
there is no justice in their paths.
They have turned them into crooked roads;
no one who walks along them will know peace.[u]

9 So justice is far from us,
and righteousness does not reach us.
We look for light, but all is darkness;[v]
for brightness, but we walk in deep shadows.
10 Like the blind[w] we grope along the wall,
feeling our way like people without eyes.
At midday we stumble[x] as if it were twilight;
among the strong, we are like the dead.[y]
11 We all growl like bears;
we moan mournfully like doves.[z]
We look for justice, but find none;
for deliverance, but it is far away.
12 For our offenses[a] are many in your sight,
and our sins testify[b] against us.
Our offenses are ever with us,
and we acknowledge our iniquities:
13 rebellion and treachery against the LORD,
turning our backs[c] on our God,
inciting revolt and oppression,[d]
uttering lies[e] our hearts have conceived.
14 So justice is driven back,
and righteousness[f] stands at a distance;
truth[g] has stumbled in the streets,
honesty cannot enter.
15 Truth is nowhere to be found,
and whoever shuns evil becomes a prey.

The LORD looked and was displeased
that there was no justice.
16 He saw that there was no one,[h]
he was appalled that there was no one to intervene;
so his own arm achieved salvation[i] for him,
and his own righteousness sustained him.
17 He put on righteousness as his breastplate,[j]
and the helmet[k] of salvation on his head;
he put on the garments[l] of vengeance
and wrapped himself in zeal[m] as in a cloak.
18 According to what they have done,
so will he repay
wrath to his enemies
and retribution to his foes;
he will repay the islands their due.
19 From the west,[n] people will fear the name of the LORD,
and from the rising of the sun,[o] they will revere his glory.
For he will come like a pent-up flood
that the breath of the LORD drives along.[a]

[a] 19 Or *When enemies come in like a flood, / the Spirit of the LORD will put them to flight*

---

believes in Jesus, the penalty of sin is broken. He will die physically but physical death for him is only the doorway into the presence of God.

Sin has an effect upon the believer, for it mars his fellowship with God. Sin in the believer's life is a terrible thing and is not to be tolerated. While it is probable that the believer will sin, it is never necessary for him to do so (1 John 2:1).

59:5 *eggs of vipers.* The viper is a poisonous snake (Acts 28:3–6).

59:7–8 *feet rush into sin.* This passage is cited in Romans 3:15–17 to document the universal aspect of sin.

59:9 So. "So" links Israel's repentance with the prophet's reprimand. With the pronoun "us," Isaiah identified himself with his people's sins (Ezek. 9:6–7; Dan. 9:5).

59:16 *no one.* God's salvation does not depend on humans (Ezek. 22:30).

59:17 *righteousness as his breastplate.* This idea of the righteous warrior is repeated in Ephesians 6:13–17. Right standing with God is our protection, as surely as the warrior depends on the heavy body shield over his heart to protect him from the arrows of the enemy.

59:3 [m] Isa 1:15 **59:4** [n] Job 15:35; Ps 7:14 **59:5** [o] Job 8:14 **59:6** [p] Isa 28:20 [q] Isa 58:4 **59:7** [r] Pr 6:17 [s] Mk 7:21-22 [t] Ro 3:15-17* **59:8** [u] Isa 57:21; Lk 1:79 **59:9** [v] Isa 5:30; 8:20 **59:10** [w] Dt 28:29 [x] Isa 8:15 [y] La 3:6 **59:11** [z] Isa 38:14; Eze 7:16 **59:12** [a] Ezr 9:6 [b] Isa 3:9 **59:13** [c] Pr 30:9; Mt 10:33; Titus 1:16 [d] Isa 5:7 [e] Mk 7:21-22 **59:14** [f] Isa 1:21 [g] Isa 48:1 **59:16** [h] Isa 41:28 [i] Ps 98:1; Isa 63:5 **59:17** [j] Eph 6:14 [k] Eph 6:17; 1Th 5:8 [l] Isa 63:3 [m] Isa 9:7 **59:19** [n] Isa 49:12 [o] Ps 113:3

20 "The Redeemer will come to Zion,
to those in Jacob who repent of their sins,"[p]
declares the LORD.

21 "As for me, this is my covenant with them," says the LORD. "My Spirit,[q] who is on you, will not depart from you, and my words that I have put in your mouth will always be on your lips, on the lips of your children and on the lips of their descendants—from this time on and forever," says the LORD.

The Glory of Zion

60 "Arise,[r] shine, for your light[s] has come,
and the glory of the LORD rises upon you.
2 See, darkness covers the earth
and thick darkness[t] is over the peoples,
but the LORD rises upon you
and his glory appears over you.
3 Nations[u] will come to your light,
and kings[v] to the brightness of your dawn.

4 "Lift up your eyes and look about you:
All assemble[w] and come to you;
your sons come from afar,
and your daughters[x] are carried on the hip.[y]
5 Then you will look and be radiant,
your heart will throb and swell with joy;
the wealth on the seas will be brought to you,
to you the riches of the nations will come.
6 Herds of camels will cover your land,
young camels of Midian[z] and Ephah.[a]
And all from Sheba[b] will come,
bearing gold and incense[c]
and proclaiming the praise[d] of the LORD.
7 All Kedar's[e] flocks will be gathered to you,
the rams of Nebaioth will serve you;
they will be accepted as offerings on my altar,
and I will adorn my glorious temple.[f]
8 "Who are these[g] that fly along like clouds,
like doves to their nests?
9 Surely the islands[h] look to me;
in the lead are the ships of Tarshish,[a][i]
bringing[j] your children from afar,
with their silver and gold,
to the honor of the LORD your God,
the Holy One of Israel,
for he has endowed you with splendor.[k]

10 "Foreigners[l] will rebuild your walls,
and their kings[m] will serve you.
Though in anger I struck you,
in favor I will show you compassion.[n]

[a] 9 Or *the trading ships*

59:20 *The Redeemer will come.* The Redeemer comes in the person of Jesus Christ.
59:21 *My Spirit.* God promised that His Spirit and His Word would never be lost to His people. The covenant that He made with them affirms that the Word is firm and unshakable. It may not be performed immediately, but the hearers can be assured of its truth. He also promised that He would always be present with His people through the Spirit. This is a promise that continues to be comforting to the people of God, and it must have brought particular comfort to the people who lived in the "silent" years between the preaching of Malachi and the coming of John the Baptist.
59:21 Inspiration of God's Word—The word *inspiration* occurs only once in the New Testament in 2 Timothy 3:16. Paul says there "All Scripture is God-breathed." God takes the initiative in communicating with us. Divine inspiration logically follows divine revelation. In revelation God speaks to man's ear, while by inspiration He guides the pen to ensure that the imparted message is correctly written down. God's intent is to give His people a right understanding of His revelation and a permanent record of His dealings with mankind. The authority of the Bible is from God Himself.

Bible authors understood that their writings were being guided by the Spirit of God, even as they wrote them. Peter said this was true of Old Testament authors (2 Pet. 1:20–21). He then stated his own letters were inspired by God (2 Pet. 3:1–2). Finally, he pointed out this was also true concerning Paul's writings (2 Pet. 3:15).

This means that the Bible is more than just the wise insights of men who desired to follow God. God worked in the thinking of the biblical writers so the message they wrote was also God's message. While the writings certainly display the individual characteristics of all of the different authors, there is also an overall divine influence that unifies the Bible as no other book.
60:1 *Arise, shine.* This command is directed to Zion (v. 14), which is both the recipient of God's light and the reflector of it. It is difficult to imagine the world without the knowledge of Christ, yet each believer who remembers his life before he was born again can testify to the power of the light of the gospel. It is a great joy to come from the darkness of sin and doubt to the light of forgiveness and knowledge of Jesus Christ. What a joyful command, to "shine" for the Savior.
60:9 *ships of Tarshish.* The reference to the ships of Tarshish alludes to the wealth of King Solomon (2:16; 1 Kin. 10:22).

59:20 [p] Ac 2:38-39; Ro 11:26-27* **59:21** [q] Isa 11:2; 44:3 **60:1** [r] Isa 52:2 [s] Eph 5:14 **60:2** [t] Jer 13:16; Col 1:13 **60:3** [u] Isa 45:14; Rev 21:24 [v] Isa 49:23 **60:4** [w] Isa 11:12 [x] Isa 43:6 [y] Isa 49:20-22 **60:6** [z] Ge 25:2 [a] Ge 25:4 [b] Ps 72:10 [c] Isa 43:23; Mt 2:11 [d] Isa 42:10 **60:7** [e] Ge 25:13 [f] ver 13; Hag 2:3,7,9 **60:8** [g] Isa 49:21 **60:9** [h] Isa 11:11 [i] Isa 2:16 *fn* [j] Isa 14:2; 43:6 [k] Isa 55:5 **60:10** [l] Isa 14:1-2 [m] Isa 49:23; Rev 21:24 [n] Isa 54:8

11 Your gates[o] will always stand open,
they will never be shut, day or night,
so that people may bring you the wealth
of the nations[p]—
their kings[q] led in triumphal
procession.
12 For the nation or kingdom that will not
serve[r] you will perish;
it will be utterly ruined.

13 "The glory of Lebanon[s] will come to you,
the juniper, the fir and the cypress
together,[t]
to adorn my sanctuary;
and I will glorify the place for my feet.[u]
14 The children of your oppressors[v] will
come bowing before you;
all who despise you will bow down[w]
at your feet
and will call you the City of the LORD,
Zion[x] of the Holy One of Israel.

15 "Although you have been forsaken[y] and
hated,
with no one traveling[z] through,
I will make you the everlasting pride[a]
and the joy[b] of all generations.
16 You will drink the milk of nations
and be nursed[c] at royal breasts.
Then you will know that I, the LORD, am
your Savior,
your Redeemer,[d] the Mighty One of
Jacob.
17 Instead of bronze I will bring you gold,
and silver in place of iron.
Instead of wood I will bring you bronze,
and iron in place of stones.
I will make peace your governor
and well-being your ruler.
18 No longer will violence be heard in your
land,
nor ruin or destruction within your
borders,
but you will call your walls Salvation[e]
and your gates Praise.
19 The sun will no more be your light by
day,
nor will the brightness of the moon
shine on you,
for the LORD will be your everlasting
light,[f]
and your God will be your glory.[g]
20 Your sun[h] will never set again,
and your moon will wane no more;
the LORD will be your everlasting light,
and your days of sorrow[i] will end.
21 Then all your people will be righteous[j]
and they will possess[k] the land
forever.
They are the shoot I have planted,[l]
the work of my hands,[m]
for the display of my splendor.[n]
22 The least of you will become a
thousand,
the smallest a mighty nation.
I am the LORD;
in its time I will do this swiftly."

The Year of the LORD's Favor

61 The Spirit[o] of the Sovereign LORD is
on me,
because the LORD has anointed[p] me
to proclaim good news to the poor.[q]
He has sent me to bind up[r] the
brokenhearted,
to proclaim freedom for the captives[s]
and release from darkness for the
prisoners,[a]
2 to proclaim the year of the LORD's favor[t]
and the day of vengeance[u] of our
God,
to comfort[v] all who mourn,
3 and provide for those who grieve in
Zion—
to bestow on them a crown of beauty
instead of ashes,
the oil of joy
instead of mourning,
and a garment of praise
instead of a spirit of despair.
They will be called oaks of
righteousness,
a planting of the LORD
for the display of his splendor.[w]

4 They will rebuild the ancient ruins[x]
and restore the places long
devastated;
they will renew the ruined cities
that have been devastated for
generations.

a 1 Hebrew; Septuagint *the blind*

60:12 *not serve you will perish.* The nation and kingdom that does not serve Zion, where Christ now reigns (Acts 2:29–36), shall perish (John 3:18; Heb. 2:3; 9:27; 10:27).

60:18–20 *No longer.* These verses form the basis for the description of the New Jerusalem in the new heaven and earth (Rev. 21:1,23; 22:5).

60:18 *Salvation ... Praise.* Judging from the figurative language in verses 15–22, especially verse 17, God's salvation and Israel's praise will be the city's defense (Zech. 2:4–5).

61:1 *me.* The "me" featured so prominently here is the same as the Servant in 42:1; 49:1; 50:4; 52:13. The Servant is the Messiah, the Lord Jesus Christ. This verse is the passage from Isaiah that Jesus read in the synagogue at the beginning of His ministry (Luke 4:16–21). When He finished reading it, He said, "Today this scripture is fulfilled in your hearing."

61:2 *day of vengeance.* The day of God's vengeance is yet to come. This is the "day" that the Book of Revelation is talking about (Rev. 11:14–19).

60:11 [o] ver 18; Isa 62:10; Rev 21:25 [p] ver 5; Rev 21:26 [q] Ps 149:8 **60:12** [r] Isa 14:2 **60:13** [s] Isa 35:2 [t] Isa 41:19 [u] 1Ch 28:2; Ps 132:7 **60:14** [v] Isa 14:2 [w] Isa 49:23; Rev 3:9 [x] Heb 12:22 **60:15** [y] Isa 1:7-9; 6:12 [z] Isa 33:8 [a] Isa 4:2 [b] Isa 65:18 **60:16** [c] Isa 49:23; 66:11, 12 [d] Isa 59:20 **60:18** [e] Isa 26:1 **60:19** [f] Rev 22:5 [g] Zec 2:5; Rev 21:23 **60:20** [h] Isa 30:26 [i] Isa 35:10 **60:21** [j] Rev 21:27 [k] Ps 37:11, 22; Isa 57:13; 61:7 [l] Mt 15:13 [m] Isa 19:25; 29:23; Eph 2:10 [n] Isa 52:1 **61:1** [o] Isa 11:2 [p] Ps 45:7 [q] Mt 11:5; Lk 7:22 [r] Isa 57:15 [s] Isa 42:7; 49:9 **61:2** [t] Isa 49:8; Lk 4:18-19* [u] Isa 34:8 [v] Isa 57:18; Mt 5:4 **61:3** [w] Isa 60:20-21 **61:4** [x] Isa 49:8; Eze 36:33; Am 9:14

[5]Strangers[y] will shepherd your flocks;
foreigners will work your fields and vineyards.
[6]And you will be called priests[z] of the LORD,
you will be named ministers of our God.
You will feed on the wealth[a] of nations,
and in their riches you will boast.
[7]Instead of your shame
you will receive a double[b] portion,
and instead of disgrace
you will rejoice in your inheritance.
And so you will inherit a double portion in your land,
and everlasting joy will be yours.

[8]"For I, the LORD, love justice;[c]
I hate robbery and wrongdoing.
In my faithfulness I will reward my people
and make an everlasting covenant[d] with them.
[9]Their descendants will be known among the nations
and their offspring among the peoples.
All who see them will acknowledge
that they are a people the LORD has blessed."

[10]I delight greatly in the LORD;
my soul rejoices[e] in my God.
For he has clothed me with garments of salvation
and arrayed me in a robe of his righteousness,[f]
as a bridegroom adorns his head like a priest,
and as a bride[g] adorns herself with her jewels.
[11]For as the soil makes the sprout come up
and a garden causes seeds to grow,
so the Sovereign LORD will make righteousness[h]
and praise spring up before all nations.

Zion's New Name

62 For Zion's sake I will not keep silent,
for Jerusalem's sake I will not remain quiet,
till her vindication[i] shines out like the dawn,
her salvation like a blazing torch.
[2]The nations[j] will see your vindication,
and all kings your glory;
you will be called by a new name[k]
that the mouth of the LORD will bestow.
[3]You will be a crown[l] of splendor in the LORD's hand,
a royal diadem in the hand of your God.
[4]No longer will they call you Deserted,[m]
or name your land Desolate.
But you will be called Hephzibah,[a]
and your land Beulah[b];
for the LORD will take delight[n] in you,
and your land will be married.[o]
[5]As a young man marries a young woman,
so will your Builder marry you;
as a bridegroom rejoices over his bride,
so will your God rejoice[p] over you.

[6]I have posted watchmen[q] on your walls, Jerusalem;
they will never be silent day or night.
You who call on the LORD,
give yourselves no rest,
[7]and give him no rest[r] till he establishes Jerusalem
and makes her the praise of the earth.

[8]The LORD has sworn by his right hand
and by his mighty arm:
"Never again will I give your grain[s]
as food for your enemies,
and never again will foreigners drink the new wine
for which you have toiled;

---

[a] 4 *Hephzibah* means *my delight is in her.*
[b] 4 *Beulah* means *married.*

61:10 Christ's Righteousness—One of the most awesome requirements made upon men and women by God is that they be righteous, that is, conform to His ethical and moral standards (Ps. 15:2; Mic. 6:8). Since God is holy He cannot allow sinners into His presence (Is. 6:3–5). We sinners cannot save ourselves or make ourselves righteous. Only God's intervention can save us and make us righteous. God sent Christ, who never sinned, to die for our sins and thus satisfy His own wrath towards us and our sin. God, at the cross, treated Christ as though He had committed our sins even though He was righteous. On the other hand, when we believe in Christ, He treats us as though we were as righteous as Himself (2 Cor. 5:21). It is as if God deposits in our spiritual account the very worth of Christ, much as though He were a banker adding an inexhaustible deposit to our bank account.

62:2 *a new name.* A new name, like new clothing, signified a new status (Gen. 17:5,15; 32:28; Rev. 2:17).

62:4 *Hephzibah ... Beulah.* The name "Hephzibah" means "my delight is in her"—in this case, it is the Lord's delight—and "Beulah" means "married." Both of these names are symbolic, pointing to a time when Israel's relationship with the Lord is restored.

62:6 *You who call on the LORD.* The "watchmen," or prophets, were intercessors. They prayed that the Lord's promises would be fulfilled.

62:8 *The LORD has sworn.* When God made the promise to Abraham (Heb. 6:13), He swore by Himself; so here He again swears in His own name. There is no greater name than the name of the Lord, and He cannot lie—this is the surest promise man can receive.

61:5 [y] Isa 14:1-2 **61:6** [z] Ex 19:6; 1Pe 2:5 [a] Isa 60:11 **61:7** [b] Isa 40:2; Zec 9:12 **61:8** [c] Ps 11:7; Isa 5:16 [d] Isa 55:3 **61:10** [e] Isa 25:9; Hab 3:18 [f] Ps 132:9; Isa 52:1 [g] Isa 49:18; Rev 21:2 **61:11** [h] Ps 85:11 **62:1** [i] Isa 1:26 **62:2** [j] Isa 52:10; 60:3 [k] ver 4, 12 **62:3** [l] Isa 28:5; Zec 9:16; 1Th 2:19 **62:4** [m] Isa 54:6 [n] Jer 32:41; Zep 3:17 [o] Jer 3:14; Hos 2:19 **62:5** [p] Isa 65:19 **62:6** [q] Isa 52:8; Eze 3:17 **62:7** [r] Mt 15:21-28; Lk 18:1-8 **62:8** [s] Dt 28:30-33; Isa 1:7; Jer 5:17

9 but those who harvest it will eat it
and praise the LORD,
and those who gather the grapes will
drink it
in the courts of my sanctuary."
10 Pass through, pass through the gates![t]
Prepare the way for the people.
Build up, build up the highway![u]
Remove the stones.
Raise a banner[v] for the nations.
11 The LORD has made proclamation
to the ends of the earth:
"Say to Daughter Zion,[w]
'See, your Savior comes![x]
See, his reward is with him,
and his recompense accompanies
him.'"[y]
12 They will be called[z] the Holy People,[a]
the Redeemed[b] of the LORD;
and you will be called Sought After,
the City No Longer Deserted.[c]

God's Day of Vengeance and Redemption

63 Who is this coming from Edom,
from Bozrah,[d] with his garments
stained crimson?
Who is this, robed in splendor,
striding forward in the greatness of
his strength?

"It is I, proclaiming victory,
mighty to save."[e]

2 Why are your garments red,
like those of one treading the
winepress?
3 "I have trodden the winepress[f] alone;
from the nations no one was
with me.
I trampled them in my anger
and trod them down in my wrath;[g]
their blood spattered my garments,[h]
and I stained all my clothing.
4 It was for me the day of vengeance;
the year for me to redeem had come.
5 I looked, but there was no one[i] to help,
I was appalled that no one gave
support;
so my own arm[j] achieved salvation
for me,
and my own wrath sustained me.[k]
6 I trampled the nations in my anger;
in my wrath I made them drunk[l]
and poured their blood[m] on the
ground."

Praise and Prayer

7 I will tell of the kindnesses[n] of the LORD,
the deeds for which he is to be praised,
according to all the LORD has done
for us—
yes, the many good things
he has done for Israel,
according to his compassion[o] and
many kindnesses.
8 He said, "Surely they are my people,[p]
children who will be true to me";
and so he became their Savior.
9 In all their distress he too was
distressed,
and the angel of his presence[q] saved
them.[a]
In his love and mercy he redeemed[r]
them;
he lifted them up and carried[s] them
all the days of old.
10 Yet they rebelled[t]
and grieved his Holy Spirit.[u]
So he turned and became their enemy[v]
and he himself fought against them.
11 Then his people recalled[b] the days of old,
the days of Moses and his people—
where is he who brought them through
the sea,[w]
with the shepherd of his flock?
Where is he who set
his Holy Spirit[x] among them,
12 who sent his glorious arm of power
to be at Moses' right hand,
who divided the waters[y] before them,
to gain for himself everlasting
renown,
13 who led[z] them through the depths?
Like a horse in open country,
they did not stumble;[a]
14 like cattle that go down to the plain,
they were given rest by the Spirit of
the LORD.
This is how you guided your people
to make for yourself a glorious name.

---

[a] 9 Or *Savior* [9] *in their distress. / It was no envoy or angel / but his own presence that saved them*
[b] 11 Or *But may he recall*

63:1 *Edom.* Edom epitomized Israel's enemies (Ps. 137:7; Lam. 4:21–22; Ezek. 25:12; 35:1–5; Obad. 13–14). It was famous for its winemaking (v. 3). ***Bozrah.*** Bozrah was the chief town of Edom.
63:3 *I.* The pronoun "I" refers to Christ in Revelation 19:5.
63:11 *set his Holy Spirit among them.* This refers to the presence of the Holy Spirit on Moses and his helpers in the desert (Num. 11:17,25).
63:12 *glorious arm.* This verse refers to God dividing the Red Sea (Ex. 15:6; 14:16,21; Ps. 78:13). Isaiah is reminding his hearers of the mighty acts that God did in the past, as well as the things that He has promised to do in the future. Such perspective is often helpful when one is bearing difficult times in the present.

62:10 [t] Isa 60:11 [u] Isa 11:16; 57:14 [v] Isa 11:10
62:11 [w] Zec 9:9; Mt 21:5 [x] Rev 22:12 [y] Isa 40:10
62:12 [z] ver 4 [a] 1Pe 2:9 [b] Isa 35:9 [c] Isa 42:16
63:1 [d] Am 1:12 [e] Zep 3:17 **63:3** [f] Rev 14:20; 19:15
[g] Isa 22:5 [h] Rev 19:13 **63:5** [i] Isa 41:28 [j] Ps 44:3; 98:1
[k] Isa 59:16 **63:6** [l] Isa 29:9 [m] Isa 34:3 **63:7** [n] Isa 54:8
[o] Ps 51:1; Eph 2:4 **63:8** [p] Isa 51:4 **63:9** [q] Ex 33:14
[r] Dt 7:7-8 [s] Dt 1:31 **63:10** [t] Ps 78:40 [u] Ps 51:11; Ac 7:51;
Eph 4:30 [v] Ps 106:40 **63:11** [w] Ex 14:22,30 [x] Nu 11:17
63:12 [y] Ex 14:21-22; Isa 11:15 **63:13** [z] Dt 32:12 [a] Jer 31:9

15 Look down from heaven[b] and see,
from your lofty throne,[c] holy and glorious.
Where are your zeal[d] and your might?
Your tenderness and compassion[e] are withheld from us.
16 But you are our Father,
though Abraham does not know us
or Israel acknowledge[f] us;
you, LORD, are our Father,
our Redeemer[g] from of old is your name.
17 Why, LORD, do you make us wander from your ways
and harden our hearts so we do not revere[h] you?
Return[i] for the sake of your servants,
the tribes that are your inheritance.
18 For a little while your people possessed your holy place,
but now our enemies have trampled down your sanctuary.[j]
19 We are yours from of old;
but you have not ruled over them,
they have not been called[a] by your name.

64 [b] Oh, that you would rend the heavens[k] and come down,[l]
that the mountains[m] would tremble before you!
2 As when fire sets twigs ablaze
and causes water to boil,
come down to make your name known to your enemies
and cause the nations to quake[n] before you!
3 For when you did awesome[o] things that we did not expect,
you came down, and the mountains trembled before you.
4 Since ancient times no one has heard,
no ear has perceived,
no eye has seen any God besides you,
who acts on behalf of those who wait for him.[p]
5 You come to the help of those who gladly do right,[q]
who remember your ways.
But when we continued to sin against them,
you were angry.
How then can we be saved?
6 All of us have become like one who is unclean,
and all our righteous[r] acts are like filthy rags;
we all shrivel up like a leaf,[s]
and like the wind our sins sweep us away.
7 No one[t] calls on your name
or strives to lay hold of you;
for you have hidden[u] your face from us
and have given us over[v] to[c] our sins.
8 Yet you, LORD, are our Father.[w]
We are the clay, you are the potter;[x]
we are all the work of your hand.
9 Do not be angry[y] beyond measure, LORD;
do not remember our sins[z] forever.
Oh, look on us, we pray,
for we are all your people.
10 Your sacred cities have become a wasteland;
even Zion is a wasteland, Jerusalem a desolation.
11 Our holy and glorious temple,[a] where our ancestors praised you,
has been burned with fire,
and all that we treasured[b] lies in ruins.
12 After all this, LORD, will you hold yourself back?[c]
Will you keep silent[d] and punish us beyond measure?

Judgment and Salvation

65 "I revealed myself to those who did not ask for me;
I was found by those who did not seek me.[e]
To a nation[f] that did not call on my name,
I said, 'Here am I, here am I.'
2 All day long I have held out my hands
to an obstinate people,[g]
who walk in ways not good,
pursuing their own imaginations[h]—
3 a people who continually provoke me
to my very face,[i]
offering sacrifices in gardens[j]
and burning incense on altars of brick;

---

[a] 19 Or *We are like those you have never ruled, / like those never called* [b] In Hebrew texts 64:1 is numbered 63:19b, and 64:2-12 is numbered 64:1-11. [c] 7 Septuagint, Syriac and Targum; Hebrew *have made us melt because of*

64:4 *no eye has seen.* Paul cites this verse with some changes in 1 Corinthians 2:9.
64:10 *wasteland ... desolation.* The prophetic picture of devastation of the land is probably referring to the time of the Babylonian invasion.
65:1 *those who did not ask for me.* Paul saw his ministry to the Gentiles as a fulfillment of this promise (Rom. 10:20–21).

63:15 [b] Dt 26:15; Ps 80:14 [c] Ps 123:1 [d] Isa 9:7; 26:11 [e] Jer 31:20; Hos 11:8

63:16 [f] Job 14:21 [g] Isa 41:14; 44:6 **63:17** [h] Isa 29:13 [i] Nu 10:36 **63:18** [j] Ps 74:3-8 **64:1** [k] Ps 18:9; 144:5 [l] Mic 1:3 [m] Ex 19:18 **64:2** [n] Ps 99:1; Jer 5:22; 33:9 **64:3** [o] Ps 65:5 **64:4** [p] Isa 30:18; 1Co 2:9* **64:5** [q] Isa 26:8 **64:6** [r] Isa 46:12; 48:1 [s] Ps 90:5-6 **64:7** [t] Isa 59:4 [u] Dt 31:18; Isa 1:15; 54:8 [v] Isa 9:18 **64:8** [w] Isa 63:16 [x] Isa 29:16 **64:9** [y] Isa 57:17; 60:10 [z] Isa 43:25 **64:11** [a] Ps 74:3-7 [b] La 1:7,10 **64:12** [c] Ps 74:10-11; Isa 42:14 [d] Ps 83:1 **65:1** [e] Hos 1:10; Ro 9:24-26; 10:20* [f] Eph 2:12 **65:2** [g] Isa 1:2,23; Ro 10:21* [h] Ps 81:11-12; Isa 66:18 **65:3** [i] Job 1:11 [j] Isa 1:29

4 who sit among the graves
and spend their nights keeping secret vigil;
who eat the flesh of pigs,[k]
and whose pots hold broth of impure meat;
5 who say, 'Keep away; don't come near me,
for I am too sacred[l] for you!'
Such people are smoke in my nostrils,
a fire that keeps burning all day.

6 "See, it stands written before me:
I will not keep silent[m] but will pay back[n] in full;
I will pay it back into their laps[o]—
7 both your sins[p] and the sins of your ancestors,"[q]
says the LORD.
"Because they burned sacrifices on the mountains
and defied me on the hills,[r]
I will measure into their laps
the full payment for their former deeds."

8 This is what the LORD says:

"As when juice is still found in a cluster of grapes
and people say, 'Don't destroy it,
there is still a blessing in it,'
so will I do in behalf of my servants;
I will not destroy them all.
9 I will bring forth descendants[s] from Jacob,
and from Judah those who will possess[t] my mountains;
my chosen people will inherit them,
and there will my servants live.[u]
10 Sharon[v] will become a pasture for flocks,
and the Valley of Achor[w] a resting place for herds,
for my people who seek[x] me.

11 "But as for you who forsake[y] the LORD
and forget my holy mountain,
who spread a table for Fortune
and fill bowls of mixed wine for Destiny,
12 I will destine you for the sword,[z]
and all of you will fall in the slaughter;
for I called but you did not answer,[a]
I spoke but you did not listen.[b]
You did evil in my sight
and chose what displeases me."

13 Therefore this is what the Sovereign LORD says:

"My servants will eat,[c]
but you will go hungry;
my servants will drink,
but you will go thirsty;[d]
my servants will rejoice,
but you will be put to shame.[e]
14 My servants will sing
out of the joy of their hearts,
but you will cry out[f]
from anguish of heart
and wail in brokenness of spirit.
15 You will leave your name
for my chosen ones to use in their curses;[g]
the Sovereign LORD will put you to death,
but to his servants he will give another name.
16 Whoever invokes a blessing in the land
will do so by the one true God;[h]
whoever takes an oath in the land
will swear[i] by the one true God.
For the past troubles will be forgotten
and hidden from my eyes.

New Heavens and a New Earth

17 "See, I will create
new heavens and a new earth.[j]
The former things will not be remembered,[k]
nor will they come to mind.
18 But be glad and rejoice[l] forever
in what I will create,
for I will create Jerusalem to be a delight
and its people a joy.
19 I will rejoice[m] over Jerusalem
and take delight in my people;
the sound of weeping and of crying[n]
will be heard in it no more.

20 "Never again will there be in it
an infant who lives but a few days,
or an old man who does not live out his years;[o]
the one who dies at a hundred
will be thought a mere child;
the one who fails to reach[a] a hundred
will be considered accursed.

[a] 20 Or *the sinner who reaches*

65:10 *Sharon ... Valley of Achor.* Sharon, on the coastal plain in the west, and the Valley of Achor, near Jericho in the east, represent the whole land.
65:17 *new heavens and a new earth.* As God fashioned the existing heavens and earth, so He will fashion a new cosmos that will be ready for His presence and for the enjoyment of His people (Rev. 21:4).
65:20 *the one who fails to reach a hundred will be considered accursed.* In the coming kingdom the life spans will be much greater. People will not be affected by disease and aging in the same way as in our present age. This time probably refers to the millennial kingdom (Rev. 20:1–6).

65:4 [k] Lev 11:7 **65:5** [l] Mt 9:11; Lk 7:39; 18:9-12 **65:6** [m] Ps 50:3 [n] Jer 16:18 [o] Ps 79:12 **65:7** [p] Isa 22:14 [q] Ex 20:5 [r] Isa 57:7 **65:9** [s] Isa 45:19 [t] Am 9:11-15 [u] Isa 32:18 **65:10** [v] Isa 35:2 [w] Jos 7:26 [x] Isa 51:1 **65:11** [y] Dt 29:24-25; Isa 1:28 **65:12** [z] Isa 27:1 [a] Pr 1:24-25; Isa 41:28; 66:4 [b] 2Ch 36:15-16; Jer 7:13 **65:13** [c] Isa 1:19 [d] Isa 41:17 [e] Isa 44:9 **65:14** [f] Mt 8:12; Lk 13:28 **65:15** [g] Zec 8:13 **65:16** [h] Ps 31:5 [i] Isa 19:18 **65:17** [j] Isa 66:22; 2Pe 3:13 [k] Isa 43:18; Jer 3:16 **65:18** [l] Ps 98:1-9; Isa 25:9 **65:19** [m] Isa 35:10; 62:5 [n] Isa 25:8; Rev 7:17 **65:20** [o] Ecc 8:13

21 They will build houses[p] and dwell in
them;
they will plant vineyards and eat
their fruit.[q]
22 No longer will they build houses and
others live in them,
or plant and others eat.
For as the days of a tree,[r]
so will be the days[s] of my people;
my chosen ones will long enjoy
the work of their hands.
23 They will not labor in vain,
nor will they bear children doomed to
misfortune;
for they will be a people blessed[t] by the
LORD,
they and their descendants[u] with
them.
24 Before they call[v] I will answer;
while they are still speaking[w] I will
hear.
25 The wolf and the lamb[x] will feed
together,
and the lion will eat straw like the ox,
and dust will be the serpent's[y] food.
They will neither harm nor destroy
on all my holy mountain,"
says the LORD.

Judgment and Hope

66 This is what the LORD says:

"Heaven is my throne,[z]
and the earth is my footstool.[a]
Where is the house[b] you will build
for me?
Where will my resting place be?
2 Has not my hand made all these
things,[c]
and so they came into being?"
declares the LORD.

"These are the ones I look on with
favor:
those who are humble and contrite in
spirit,[d]
and who tremble at my word.[e]
3 But whoever sacrifices a bull[f]
is like one who kills a person,
and whoever offers a lamb
is like one who breaks a dog's
neck;
whoever makes a grain offering
is like one who presents pig's blood,
and whoever burns memorial incense[g]
is like one who worships an idol.
They have chosen their own ways,[h]
and they delight in their
abominations;
4 so I also will choose harsh treatment
for them
and will bring on them what they
dread.[i]
For when I called, no one answered,[j]
when I spoke, no one listened.
They did evil[k] in my sight
and chose what displeases me."[l]

5 Hear the word of the LORD,
you who tremble at his word:
"Your own people who hate[m] you,
and exclude you because of my name,
have said,
'Let the LORD be glorified,
that we may see your joy!'
Yet they will be put to shame.[n]
6 Hear that uproar from the city,
hear that noise from the temple!
It is the sound of the LORD
repaying[o] his enemies all they
deserve.

7 "Before she goes into labor,[p]
she gives birth;
before the pains come upon her,
she delivers a son.[q]
8 Who has ever heard of such things?
Who has ever seen[r] things like this?
Can a country be born in a day
or a nation be brought forth in a
moment?
Yet no sooner is Zion in labor
than she gives birth to her children.
9 Do I bring to the moment of birth[s]
and not give delivery?" says the
LORD.
"Do I close up the womb
when I bring to delivery?" says your
God.
10 "Rejoice[t] with Jerusalem and be glad
for her,
all you who love[u] her;
rejoice greatly with her,
all you who mourn over her.

65:25 *wolf . . . lamb.* This picture is also presented in 11:6 – 9. It is a picture of regenerated nature that will occur in the new heavens and new earth.

66:1 *Where is the house.* No place on earth can accommodate the transcendent God. Even the temple built by Solomon, which was filled with the glory of the Lord (1 Kin. 8:11), did not really contain the Lord. He called it a "a temple for my Name" (1 Kin. 8:18).

66:3 *like one who kills a person.* This may refer to child sacrifice (57:5). ***like one who breaks a dog's neck ... like one who presents pig's blood.*** The dog and the pig were both unclean animals; this may refer to a pagan practice.

66:6 *uproar from the city ... noise from the temple ... enemies.* Isaiah heard the sound of noise from the city and the temple, the Lord giving His enemies what they deserved. This prophecy may find its fulfillment at the Lord's second coming (66:17; 2 Thess. 1:7 – 10).

65:21 [p] Isa 32:18 [q] Isa 37:30; Am 9:14 **65:22** [r] Ps 92:12-14 [s] Ps 21:4; 91:16 **65:23** [t] Dt 28:3-12; Isa 61:9 [u] Ac 2:39 **65:24** [v] Isa 55:6 [w] Da 9:20-23; 10:12 **65:25** [x] Isa 11:6 [y] Ge 3:14; Mic 7:17 **66:1** [z] Mt 23:22 [a] 1Ki 8:27; Mt 5:34-35 [b] 2Sa 7:7; Jn 4:20-21; Ac 7:49*; 17:24 **66:2** [c] Isa 40:26; Ac 7:50* [d] Isa 57:15; Mt 5:3-4; Lk 18:13-14 [e] Ezr 9:4 **66:3** [f] Isa 1:11 [g] Lev 2:2 [h] Isa 57:17 **66:4** [i] Pr 10:24 [j] Pr 1:24; Jer 7:13 [k] 2Ki 21:2, 4, 6 [l] Isa 65:12 **66:5** [m] Ps 38:20; Isa 60:15 [n] Lk 13:17 **66:6** [o] Isa 65:6; Joel 3:7 **66:7** [p] Isa 54:1 [q] Rev 12:5 **66:8** [r] Isa 64:4 **66:9** [s] Isa 37:3 **66:10** [t] Dt 32:43; Ro 15:10 [u] Ps 26:8

11 For you will nurse[v] and be satisfied
at her comforting breasts;
you will drink deeply
and delight in her overflowing
abundance."

12 For this is what the LORD says:

"I will extend peace to her like a river,[w]
and the wealth[x] of nations like a
flooding stream;
you will nurse and be carried[y] on her
arm
and dandled on her knees.
13 As a mother comforts her child,
so will I comfort[z] you;
and you will be comforted over
Jerusalem."
14 When you see this, your heart will
rejoice
and you will flourish like grass;
the hand of the LORD will be made
known to his servants,
but his fury[a] will be shown to his
foes.
15 See, the LORD is coming with fire,
and his chariots[b] are like a
whirlwind;
he will bring down his anger with fury,
and his rebuke[c] with flames of fire.
16 For with fire[d] and with his sword[e]
the LORD will execute judgment on all
people,
and many will be those slain by the
LORD.

17 "Those who consecrate and purify
themselves to go into the gardens,[f] following one who is among those who
eat the flesh of pigs,[g] rats and other unclean things—they will meet their end[h]
together with the one they follow," declares the LORD.

18 "And I, because of what they have
planned and done, am about to come[a] and
gather the people of all nations and languages, and they will come and see my
glory.

19 "I will set a sign[i] among them, and I
will send some of those who survive to the
nations—to Tarshish,[j] to the Libyans[b] and
Lydians[k] (famous as archers), to Tubal[l]
and Greece, and to the distant islands[m]
that have not heard of my fame or seen my
glory.[n] They will proclaim my glory among
the nations. 20 And they will bring all your
people, from all the nations, to my holy
mountain in Jerusalem as an offering to
the LORD—on horses, in chariots and wagons, and on mules and camels," says the
LORD. "They will bring them, as the Israelites bring their grain offerings, to the temple of the LORD in ceremonially clean vessels.[o] 21 And I will select some of them also
to be priests[p] and Levites," says the LORD.

22 "As the new heavens and the new
earth[q] that I make will endure before me,"
declares the LORD, "so will your name and
descendants endure.[r] 23 From one New
Moon to another and from one Sabbath[s] to
another, all mankind will come and bow
down[t] before me," says the LORD. 24 "And
they will go out and look on the dead bodies of those who rebelled against me; the
worms[u] that eat them will not die, the fire
that burns them will not be quenched,[v] and
they will be loathsome to all mankind."

[a] *18* The meaning of the Hebrew for this clause is uncertain. [b] *19* Some Septuagint manuscripts *Put* (Libyans); Hebrew *Pul*

66:16 *fire ... sword.* The Divine Warrior comes with fire and sword (Luke 21:24; Rev. 19:11–15). The word picture promises judgment and punishment.

66:23 *all mankind will come and bow down before me.* In the end, every person will bow to the Lord, whether they were followers of God or not. This idea is repeated in more detail in Romans 14:11, 1 Corinthians 15:24–25, Philippians 2:10, and Revelation 15:4.

66:24 *the fire that burns them will not be quenched.* This verse is cited by Jesus in Mark 9:44,46,48. The imagery is drawn from the valley of Hinnom that was Jerusalem's garbage dump, where unclean corpses decomposed and were burned. The final eternal punishment is the lake of fire (Rev. 20:1–15). Although the Book of Isaiah depicts God's coming salvation, it closes with a strong statement of the judgment of the wicked.

66:11 [v] Isa 60:16 **66:12** [w] Isa 48:18 [x] Ps 72:3; Isa 60:5; 61:6 [y] Isa 60:4 **66:13** [z] Isa 40:1; 2Co 1:4 **66:14** [a] Isa 10:5 **66:15** [b] Ps 68:17 [c] Ps 9:5 **66:16** [d] Isa 30:30 [e] Isa 27:1 **66:17** [f] Isa 1:29 [g] Lev 11:7 [h] Ps 37:20; Isa 1:28 **66:19** [i] Isa 11:10; 49:22 [j] Isa 2:16 [k] Eze 27:10 [l] Ge 10:2 [m] Isa 11:11 [n] 1Ch 16:24; Isa 24:15 **66:20** [o] Isa 52:11 **66:21** [p] Ex 19:6; Isa 61:6; 1Pe 2:5,9 **66:22** [q] Isa 65:17; Heb 12:26-27; 2Pe 3:13; Rev 21:1 [r] Jn 10:27-29; 1Pe 1:4-5 **66:23** [s] Eze 46:1-3 [t] Isa 19:21 **66:24** [u] Isa 14:11 [v] Isa 1:31; Mk 9:48*

JEREMIAH

▶ **AUTHOR:** Jeremiah was the son of Hilkiah the priest and lived just over two miles north of Jerusalem. The book clearly states that Jeremiah is its author, and that he dictated all his prophecies to his secretary Baruch. A first copy of the work was destroyed by the king, after which Jeremiah produced a more complete edition (36–38). The only segment of this book not credited to Jeremiah is chapter 52. This supplement is almost identical to 2 Kings 24:18—25:30, and may have been added by Baruch. Daniel alludes to Jeremiah's prophecy of the seventy-year captivity (25:11–14; 29:10; Dan. 9:2), and Jeremiah's authorship is also confirmed by Ecclesiasticus, Josephus, and the Talmud.

▶ **TIME:** c. 627–580 B.C. ▶ **KEY VERSES:** Jer. 7:23–24

▶ **THEME:** In the Book of Jeremiah we get an intimate picture of this prophet's life and thoughts. He was constantly rejected for speaking God's message, often lamenting to God. For this fact he is often called the weeping prophet. His ministry begins in 627 B.C., during the reign of King Josiah, who brought about reform after finding the Book of Deuteronomy in the temple. By that time Judah was a weak kingdom that was subject to the major political forces of the day, which were Egypt and Babylon. While Josiah's reform was certainly a step in the right direction, many of the people didn't follow through on the implications of what the law taught. Jeremiah demonstrated God's perspective on the political upheaval going on throughout Judah in his day.

1 The words of Jeremiah son of Hilkiah,
one of the priests at Anathoth[a] in the
territory of Benjamin. 2The word of the
LORD came to him in the thirteenth year of
the reign of Josiah son of Amon king of Judah, 3and through the reign of Jehoiakim[b]
son of Josiah king of Judah, down to the
fifth month of the eleventh year of Zedekiah[c] son of Josiah king of Judah, when the
people of Jerusalem went into exile.[d]

The Call of Jeremiah

4The word of the LORD came to me, saying,

5 "Before I formed you in the womb I
knew[a][e] you,
before you were born[f] I set you apart;
I appointed you as a prophet to the
nations.[g]"

6"Alas, Sovereign LORD," I said, "I do not
know how to speak;[h] I am too young."[i]
7But the LORD said to me, "Do not say, 'I
am too young.' You must go to everyone I
send you to and say whatever I command
you. 8Do not be afraid[j] of them, for I am
with you[k] and will rescue you," declares
the LORD.
9Then the LORD reached out his hand
and touched[l] my mouth and said to me,
"I have put my words in your mouth.[m]

[a] 5 Or *chose*

1:1 ***Jeremiah.*** The name probably means either "the Lord exalts" or "the Lord establishes."
1:4 ***The word of the LORD came to me, saying.*** This was a standard way of introducing a divine oracle at the beginning of a prophetic book. Jeremiah did not speak out of his own imagination. He spoke as God revealed His word and will.
1:5 ***Before I formed you in the womb I knew you.*** Jeremiah was keenly aware that the call of God in his life had been determined by God from before his conception. As God's word became a reality in his life, the prophet understood that God knew him and had called him to proclaim a critical message at a crucial point in the history of the nation. The word "knew" refers to an intimate knowledge that comes from relationship and personal commitment.
1:8 ***I am with you and will rescue you.*** Twice in his call (v. 19), God reassured Jeremiah of His presence and protection. In moments of personal crisis, Jeremiah prays these words back to God (20:11).
1:9 ***I have put my words in your mouth.*** This verse gives us an understanding of the dual nature

1:1 [a] Jos 21:18; 1Ch 6:60; Jer 32:7-9 **1:3** [b] 2Ki 23:34 [c] 2Ki 24:17; Jer 39:2 [d] Jer 52:15 **1:5** [e] Ps 139:16 [f] Isa 49:1 [g] ver 10; Jer 25:15-26 **1:6** [h] Ex 4:10; 6:12 [i] 1Ki 3:7 **1:8** [j] Eze 2:6 [k] Jos 1:5; Jer 15:20 **1:9** [l] Isa 6:7 [m] Ex 4:12

10See, today I appoint you over nations
and kingdoms to uproot and tear down,
to destroy and overthrow, to build and to
plant."[n]
11The word of the LORD came to me:
"What do you see, Jeremiah?"[o]
"I see the branch of an almond tree," I
replied.
12The LORD said to me, "You have seen
correctly, for I am watching[a] to see that my
word is fulfilled."
13The word of the LORD came to me
again: "What do you see?"[p]
"I see a pot that is boiling," I answered.
"It is tilting toward us from the north."
14The LORD said to me, "From the north
disaster will be poured out on all who live
in the land. 15I am about to summon all the
peoples of the northern kingdoms," declares the LORD.

"Their kings will come and set up their
thrones
in the entrance of the gates of
Jerusalem;
they will come against all her
surrounding walls
and against all the towns of Judah.[q]
16I will pronounce my judgments on my
people
because of their wickedness[r] in
forsaking me,[s]
in burning incense to other gods[t]
and in worshiping what their hands
have made.

17"Get yourself ready! Stand up and say
to them whatever I command you. Do not
be terrified[u] by them, or I will terrify you
before them. 18Today I have made you[v] a
fortified city, an iron pillar and a bronze
wall to stand against the whole land—
against the kings of Judah, its officials, its
priests and the people of the land. 19They
will fight against you but will not overcome you, for I am with you[w] and will rescue[x] you," declares the LORD.

Israel Forsakes God

2 The word of the LORD came to me: 2"Go
and proclaim in the hearing of Jerusalem:

"This is what the LORD says:

"'I remember the devotion of your
youth,[y]
how as a bride you loved me
and followed me through the
wilderness,[z]
through a land not sown.
3Israel was holy[a] to the LORD,[b]
the firstfruits[c] of his harvest;
all who devoured[d] her were held guilty,[e]
and disaster overtook them,'"
declares the LORD.

4Hear the word of the LORD, you
descendants of Jacob,
all you clans of Israel.

5This is what the LORD says:

"What fault did your ancestors find
in me,
that they strayed so far from me?
They followed worthless idols
and became worthless[f] themselves.
6They did not ask, 'Where is the LORD,
who brought us up out of Egypt[g]
and led us through the barren
wilderness,
through a land of deserts[h] and
ravines,[i]
a land of drought and utter darkness,
a land where no one travels and no
one lives?'
7I brought you into a fertile land
to eat its fruit and rich produce.[j]
But you came and defiled my land
and made my inheritance detestable.[k]
8The priests did not ask,
'Where is the LORD?'

---

[a] *12* The Hebrew for *watching* sounds like the Hebrew for *almond tree.*

---

of Scripture. The message is the Lord's; its expression is accomplished through His servants the prophets (Heb. 1:1).

1:10 ***I appoint you over nations.*** The nations were instruments in God's purpose of revealing Himself. The Lord would use Babylon to punish Judah, and then He would use the Persians to punish Babylon.

1:11 ***I see the branch of an almond tree.*** God confirmed His call to Jeremiah with two visions. The first vision involved an almond tree, which blossoms when other trees are still dormant. The almond tree served as a harbinger of spring, as though it "watched over" the beginning of the season. In a similar fashion, God was "watching over" His word, ready to bring judgment on Israel.

1:13 ***I see a pot that is boiling ... It is tilting toward us from the north.*** This is the second vision God used to confirm Jeremiah's call. Judgment was coming from the north.

1:17 ***Get yourself ready!*** This means tuck your robe into your belt so you can run.

1:18 ***a fortified city.*** This military language indicates that God would fight for Jeremiah. His defense system could not be battered down or tunneled under by men and armies.

2:1–3 ***as a bride you loved me.*** Chapter 2 is presented in the form of a covenant lawsuit, an indictment brought by God against His people. Jeremiah challenged the people of Judah to remember God.

2:8 ***priests ... leaders ... prophets.*** Those who should have known God most intimately did not

---

1:10 [n] Jer 18:7-10; 24:6; 31:4, 28 **1:11** [o] Jer 24:3; Am 7:8 **1:13** [p] Zec 4:2 **1:15** [q] Jer 4:16; 9:11 **1:16** [r] Dt 28:20 [s] Jer 17:13 [t] Jer 7:9; 19:4 **1:17** [u] Eze 2:6 **1:18** [v] Isa 50:7 **1:19** [w] Jer 20:11 [x] ver 8 **2:2** [y] Eze 16:8-14, 60; Hos 2:15 [z] Dt 2:7 **2:3** [a] Dt 7:6 [b] Ex 19:6 [c] Jas 1:18; Rev 14:4 [d] Isa 41:11; Jer 30:16 [e] Jer 50:7 **2:5** [f] 2Ki 17:15 **2:6** [g] Hos 13:4 [h] Dt 8:15 [i] Dt 32:10 **2:7** [j] Nu 13:27; Dt 8:7-9; 11:10-12 [k] Ps 106:34-39; Jer 16:18

Those who deal with the law did not
know me;[l]
the leaders rebelled against me.
The prophets prophesied by Baal,[m]
following worthless idols.[n]
9 "Therefore I bring charges[o] against you
again,"
declares the LORD.
"And I will bring charges against
your children's children.
10 Cross over to the coasts of Cyprus and
look,
send to Kedar[a] and observe
closely;
see if there has ever been anything
like this:
11 Has a nation ever changed its gods?
(Yet they are not gods[p] at all.)
But my people have exchanged their
glorious[q] God
for worthless idols.
12 Be appalled at this, you heavens,
and shudder with great horror,"
declares the LORD.
13 "My people have committed two sins:
They have forsaken me,
the spring of living water,[r]
and have dug their own cisterns,
broken cisterns that cannot hold
water.
14 Is Israel a servant, a slave[s] by
birth?
Why then has he become plunder?
15 Lions[t] have roared;
they have growled at him.
They have laid waste[u] his land;
his towns are burned and
deserted.
16 Also, the men of Memphis[v] and
Tahpanhes[w]
have cracked your skull.
17 Have you not brought this on
yourselves[x]
by forsaking the LORD your God
when he led you in the way?
18 Now why go to Egypt[y]
to drink water from the Nile[b]?[z]
And why go to Assyria
to drink water from the Euphrates?
19 Your wickedness will punish you;
your backsliding[a] will rebuke[b] you.
Consider then and realize
how evil and bitter[c] it is for you
when you forsake the LORD your God
and have no awe[d] of me,"
declares the Lord,
the LORD Almighty.
20 "Long ago you broke off your yoke[e]
and tore off your bonds;
you said, 'I will not serve you!'
Indeed, on every high hill[f]
and under every spreading tree[g]
you lay down as a prostitute.
21 I had planted[h] you like a choice vine[i]
of sound and reliable stock.
How then did you turn against me
into a corrupt,[j] wild vine?
22 Although you wash yourself with
soap
and use an abundance of cleansing
powder,
the stain of your guilt is still
before me,"
declares the Sovereign LORD.
23 "How can you say, 'I am not
defiled;[k]
I have not run after the Baals'?[l]
See how you behaved in the valley;[m]
consider what you have done.
You are a swift she-camel
running[n] here and there,
24 a wild donkey[o] accustomed to the
desert,
sniffing the wind in her craving—
in her heat who can restrain her?
Any males that pursue her need not tire
themselves;
at mating time they will find her.
25 Do not run until your feet are bare
and your throat is dry.
But you said, 'It's no use!
I love foreign gods,[p]
and I must go after them.'
26 "As a thief is disgraced[q] when he is
caught,
so the people of Israel are
disgraced—
they, their kings and their officials,
their priests and their prophets.

[a] *10* In the Syro-Arabian desert [b] *18* Hebrew *Shihor*; that is, a branch of the Nile

---

know Him at all. The rulers transgressed against God and His covenant. The prophets prophesied in the name of Baal rather than God.

2:13 ***broken cisterns.*** The people could have chosen a "spring of living water." Instead they chose broken cisterns that would have been useless for sustaining life.

2:15 ***Lions have roared.*** Assyria laid waste to Israel and Judah during several invasions between 734 and 701 B.C.

2:16 ***the men of Memphis and Tahpanhes.*** Egypt forced Judah into a vassal relationship.

2:19 ***backsliding.*** Israel had turned in every direction for help except to the true source of safety and security.

2:23–25 ***a swift she-camel.*** The image is that of a camel who is in heat, vividly portraying Israel's lust for foreign gods.

2:8 [l] Jer 4:22 [m] Jer 23:13 [n] Jer 16:19 **2:9** [o] Eze 20:35-36; Mic 6:2 **2:11** [p] Isa 37:19; Jer 16:20 [q] Ps 106:20; Ro 1:23 **2:13** [r] Ps 36:9; Jn 4:14 **2:14** [s] Ex 4:22 **2:15** [t] Jer 4:7; 50:17 [u] Isa 1:7 **2:16** [v] Isa 19:13 [w] Jer 43:7-9 **2:17** [x] Jer 4:18 **2:18** [y] Isa 30:2 [z] Jos 13:3 **2:19** [a] Jer 3:11, 22 [b] Isa 3:9; Hos 5:5 [c] Job 20:14; Am 8:10 [d] Ps 36:1 **2:20** [e] Lev 26:13 [f] Isa 57:7; Jer 17:2 [g] Dt 12:2 **2:21** [h] Ex 15:17 [i] Ps 80:8 [j] Isa 5:4 **2:23** [k] Pr 30:12 [l] Jer 9:14 [m] Jer 7:31 [n] ver 33; Jer 31:22 **2:24** [o] Jer 14:6 **2:25** [p] Dt 32:16; Jer 3:13; 14:10 **2:26** [q] Jer 48:27

27 They say to wood, 'You are my father,'
and to stone,[r] 'You gave me birth.'
They have turned their backs to me
and not their faces;[s]
yet when they are in trouble,[t] they say,
'Come and save us!'
28 Where then are the gods[u] you made for
yourselves?
Let them come if they can save you
when you are in trouble![v]
For you, Judah, have as many gods
as you have towns.[w]

29 "Why do you bring charges against me?
You have all[x] rebelled against me,"
declares the LORD.
30 "In vain I punished your people;
they did not respond to correction.
Your sword has devoured your
prophets[y]
like a ravenous lion.

31 "You of this generation, consider the
word of the LORD:

"Have I been a desert to Israel
or a land of great darkness?[z]
Why do my people say, 'We are free to
roam;
we will come to you no more'?
32 Does a young woman forget her
jewelry,
a bride her wedding ornaments?
Yet my people have forgotten me,
days without number.
33 How skilled you are at pursuing love!
Even the worst of women can learn
from your ways.
34 On your clothes is found
the lifeblood[a] of the innocent poor,
though you did not catch them
breaking in.[b]
Yet in spite of all this
35 you say, 'I am innocent;
he is not angry with me.'
But I will pass judgment[c] on you
because you say, 'I have not sinned.'[d]
36 Why do you go about so much,
changing[e] your ways?
You will be disappointed by Egypt[f]
as you were by Assyria.
37 You will also leave that place
with your hands on your head,[g]
for the LORD has rejected those you
trust;
you will not be helped[h] by them.

3 "If a man divorces[i] his wife
and she leaves him and marries
another man,
should he return to her again?
Would not the land be completely
defiled?
But you have lived as a prostitute with
many lovers[j]—
would you now return to me?"
declares the LORD.
2 "Look up to the barren heights and see.
Is there any place where you have not
been ravished?
By the roadside[k] you sat waiting for
lovers,
sat like a nomad in the desert.
You have defiled the land[l]
with your prostitution and
wickedness.
3 Therefore the showers have been
withheld,[m]
and no spring rains[n] have fallen.
Yet you have the brazen look of a
prostitute;
you refuse to blush with shame.[o]
4 Have you not just called to me:
'My Father,[p] my friend from my
youth,[q]
5 will you always be angry?[r]
Will your wrath continue forever?'
This is how you talk,
but you do all the evil you can."

Unfaithful Israel

6 During the reign of King Josiah, the
LORD said to me, "Have you seen what
faithless Israel has done? She has gone up
on every high hill and under every spreading tree[s] and has committed adultery[t]

2:32 ***Yet my people have forgotten me.*** In the ancient world, those women who were not slaves normally possessed a variety of rings, bracelets, and ornaments made from gold, silver, or bronze. Many of these were exquisite in appearance and were frequently inlaid with semiprecious stones. Ornaments of this kind were commonly part of the wedding finery of a bride. The nation Israel, however, which was God's bride, had behaved in a completely unnatural fashion by presuming to forget the God to whom the people were so intimately bound by the Sinai covenant. In forgetting their God for so long a time they had actually rejected Him and His claims upon them, a prospect which Jeremiah found almost impossible to believe.
3:1 ***If a man divorces his wife.*** Deuteronomy 24:1–4 forbids a man to remarry his divorced wife if she has remarried and been divorced in the meantime. The implication is that the woman has been defiled by the second marriage. After forsaking God, Israel had taken many other lovers, that is, the nation worshiped many other gods. Yet the Lord in His mercy still extended His loving hand to His unfaithful bride.
3:3 ***showers . . . spring rains.*** There were two types of rain that fell in Israel in the spring from March to early April. These were vital for the fields and crops.
3:6 ***During the reign of King Josiah.*** The reign of

2:27 [r] Jer 3:9 [s] Jer 18:17; 32:33 [t] Jdg 10:10; Isa 26:16
2:28 [u] Isa 45:20 [v] Dt 32:37 [w] 2Ki 17:29; Jer 11:13
2:29 [x] Jer 5:1; 6:13; Da 9:11 **2:30** [y] Ne 9:26; Ac 7:52; 1Th 2:15 **2:31** [z] Isa 45:19 **2:34** [a] 2Ki 21:16 [b] Ex 22:2
2:35 [c] Jer 25:31 [d] 1Jn 1:8, 10 **2:36** [e] Jer 31:22 [f] Isa 30:2, 3, 7 **2:37** [g] 2Sa 13:19 [h] Jer 37:7 **3:1** [i] Dt 24:1-4 [j] Jer 2:20, 25; Eze 16:26, 29 **3:2** [k] Ge 38:14; Eze 16:25 [l] Jer 2:7 **3:3** [m] Lev 26:19 [n] Jer 14:4 [o] Jer 6:15; 8:12; Zep 3:5 **3:4** [p] ver 19 [q] Jer 2:2 **3:5** [r] Ps 103:9; Isa 57:16
3:6 [s] Jer 17:2 [t] Jer 2:20

there. 7 I thought that after she had done
all this she would return to me but she did
not, and her unfaithful sister[u] Judah saw
it. 8 I gave faithless Israel her certificate of
divorce and sent her away because of all
her adulteries. Yet I saw that her unfaithful
sister Judah had no fear;[v] she also went out
and committed adultery. 9 Because Israel's
immorality mattered so little to her, she
defiled the land[w] and committed adultery
with stone[x] and wood.[y] 10 In spite of all this,
her unfaithful sister Judah did not return
to me with all her heart, but only in pretense,[z]" declares the LORD.

11 The LORD said to me, "Faithless Israel is more righteous[a] than unfaithful[b] Judah. 12 Go, proclaim this message toward
the north:[c]

"'Return,[d] faithless Israel,' declares the LORD,
'I will frown on you no longer,
for I am faithful,' declares the LORD,
'I will not be angry[e] forever.
13 Only acknowledge[f] your guilt—
you have rebelled against the LORD your God,
you have scattered your favors to foreign gods[g]
under every spreading tree,[h]
and have not obeyed[i] me,'"
declares the LORD.

14 "Return,[j] faithless people," declares the
LORD, "for I am your husband. I will choose
you—one from a town and two from a
clan—and bring you to Zion. 15 Then I will
give you shepherds[k] after my own heart,
who will lead you with knowledge and understanding. 16 In those days, when your
numbers have increased greatly in the
land," declares the LORD, "people will no
longer say, 'The ark of the covenant of the
LORD.' It will never enter their minds or be
remembered;[l] it will not be missed, nor will
another one be made. 17 At that time they
will call Jerusalem The Throne[m] of the
LORD, and all nations will gather in Jerusalem to honor[n] the name of the LORD. No
longer will they follow the stubbornness of
their evil hearts.[o] 18 In those days the people of Judah will join the people of Israel,[p]
and together[q] they will come from a northern[r] land to the land[s] I gave your ancestors
as an inheritance.

19 "I myself said,

"'How gladly would I treat you like my children
and give you a pleasant land,
the most beautiful inheritance of any nation.'
I thought you would call me 'Father'[t]
and not turn away from following me.
20 But like a woman unfaithful to her husband,
so you, Israel, have been unfaithful to me,"
declares the LORD.

21 A cry is heard on the barren heights,[u]
the weeping and pleading of the people of Israel,
because they have perverted their ways
and have forgotten the LORD their God.

22 "Return,[v] faithless people;
I will cure[w] you of backsliding."

"Yes, we will come to you,
for you are the LORD our God.
23 Surely the idolatrous commotion on the hills
and mountains is a deception;
surely in the LORD our God
is the salvation[x] of Israel.
24 From our youth shameful[y] gods have consumed
the fruits of our ancestors' labor—
their flocks and herds,
their sons and daughters.
25 Let us lie down in our shame,[z]
and let our disgrace cover us.
We have sinned against the LORD our God,
both we and our ancestors;
from our youth[a] till this day
we have not obeyed the LORD our God."

Josiah (640–609 B.C.) followed the idolatrous reigns of Manasseh (697–642 B.C.) and Amon (642–640 B.C.).

3:8 ***faithless Israel . . . all her adulteries.*** Because of Israel's adultery, the Lord presented her with a certificate of divorce based on Deuteronomy 24:1–4. As a consequence, in 722 B.C. Israel was taken captive by Assyria, and Samaria was destroyed. Judah looked on but did not learn from Israel's example.

3:15 ***Then I will give you shepherds.*** Throughout the Bible God provides shepherds for His people to watch over them, guide them, care for them, and lead them. From Moses in the Old Testament to Jesus in the New, God provides faithful, devoted leaders after His own heart.

3:16 ***when your numbers have increased greatly.*** God ordained that His shepherds would lead Israel through a time of blessing, increase in numbers, and material prosperity.

3:19 ***give you a pleasant land.*** The possession of the land was always dependent on the covenant faithfulness of Israel to their God. The Lord's desire has always been to bless His people.

3:23 ***the hills and mountains.*** The mountains were centers of idol worship and thus were strongholds of falsehood. True salvation or deliverance could be found only in the true God of Israel.

3:7 [u] Eze 16:46 **3:8** [v] Eze 16:47; 23:11 **3:9** [w] ver 2 [x] Isa 57:6 [y] Jer 2:27 **3:10** [z] Jer 12:2 **3:11** [a] Eze 16:52; 23:11 [b] ver 7 **3:12** [c] 2Ki 17:3-6 [d] ver 14; Jer 31:21, 22; Eze 33:11 [e] Ps 86:15 **3:13** [f] Dt 30:1-3; Jer 14:20; 1Jn 1:9 [g] Jer 2:25 [h] Dt 12:2 [i] ver 25 **3:14** [j] Hos 2:19 **3:15** [k] Ac 20:28 **3:16** [l] Isa 65:17 **3:17** [m] Jer 17:12; Eze 43:7 [n] Isa 60:9 [o] Jer 11:8 **3:18** [p] Hos 1:11 [q] Isa 11:13; Jer 50:4 [r] Jer 16:15; 31:8 [s] Am 9:15 **3:19** [t] ver 4; Isa 63:16 **3:21** [u] ver 2 **3:22** [v] Hos 14:4 [w] Jer 33:6; Hos 6:1 **3:23** [x] Ps 3:8; Jer 17:14 **3:24** [y] Hos 9:10 **3:25** [z] Ezr 9:6 [a] Jer 22:21

4 "If you, Israel, will return,[b]
then return to me,"
declares the LORD.
"If you put your detestable idols[c] out of
my sight
and no longer go astray,
2 and if in a truthful, just and righteous
way
you swear,[d] 'As surely as the LORD
lives,'[e]
then the nations will invoke blessings[f]
by him
and in him they will boast."

3 This is what the LORD says to the people
of Judah and to Jerusalem:

"Break up your unplowed ground[g]
and do not sow among thorns.[h]
4 Circumcise yourselves to the LORD,
circumcise your hearts,[i]
you people of Judah and inhabitants
of Jerusalem,
or my wrath[j] will flare up and burn like
fire
because of the evil you have done—
burn with no one to quench[k] it.

Disaster From the North

5 "Announce in Judah and proclaim in
Jerusalem and say:
'Sound the trumpet throughout the
land!'
Cry aloud and say:
'Gather together!
Let us flee to the fortified cities!'[l]
6 Raise the signal to go to Zion!
Flee for safety without delay!
For I am bringing disaster from the
north,[m]
even terrible destruction."

7 A lion[n] has come out of his lair;
a destroyer of nations has set out.
He has left his place
to lay waste[o] your land.
Your towns will lie in ruins[p]
without inhabitant.
8 So put on sackcloth,[q]
lament and wail,
for the fierce anger[r] of the LORD
has not turned away from us.

9 "In that day," declares the LORD,
"the king and the officials will lose
heart,
the priests will be horrified,
and the prophets will be appalled."[s]

10 Then I said, "Alas, Sovereign LORD!
How completely you have deceived[t] this
people and Jerusalem by saying, 'You will
have peace,'[u] when the sword is at our
throats!"
11 At that time this people and Jerusalem
will be told, "A scorching wind[v] from the
barren heights in the desert blows toward
my people, but not to winnow or cleanse;
12 a wind too strong for that comes from me.
Now I pronounce my judgments[w] against
them."

13 Look! He advances like the clouds,[x]
his chariots[y] come like a whirlwind,[z]
his horses are swifter than eagles.[a]
Woe to us! We are ruined!
14 Jerusalem, wash[b] the evil from your
heart and be saved.
How long will you harbor wicked
thoughts?
15 A voice is announcing from Dan,[c]
proclaiming disaster from the hills of
Ephraim.
16 "Tell this to the nations,
proclaim concerning Jerusalem:
'A besieging army is coming from a
distant land,
raising a war cry[d] against the cities
of Judah.

4:2 *the LORD lives.* This phrase was regularly used in oaths. When spoken by those faithful to the covenant, it should have been a sign of truth, judgment, and righteousness. Failure to be willing to owe God their faithfulness and worship brought terrible consequences to Israel, the northern kingdom, and then to Judah, and resulted in failure of the nations to be converted as well. Because Israel would not give glory to God, the rest of the world could not.

4:4 *Circumcise yourselves to the LORD.* Circumcision was a sign of the covenant relationship between Israel and God (Gen. 17:10–14). The intent of God was always that the outward symbol should be a sign of a reality of total devotion to Him (Deut. 10:12–21).

4:5 *Sound the trumpet throughout the land.* Jeremiah announced the judgment of Judah and Jerusalem with the alarming sound of a trumpet, literally a shofar made of a ram's horn. This was the instrument used to sound the alarm when an enemy attacked a city.

4:7 *of his lair.* Destruction would come as a terrible surprise, like a lion hiding and then pouncing on its prey. The desolation of the land and the deportation of the people would be the result.

4:8 *put on sackcloth.* This material was a rough-textured fabric that was worn as a sign of mourning or distress (6:21).

4:13 *He advances like the clouds.* Judah had become the foe of God, and He would use the nation's international foes to discipline the nation. The imagery of clouds and chariots like a whirlwind portrays the thoroughness and swiftness of God's judgment.

4:15 *Dan ... hills of Ephraim.* Dan was the most northern tribe of Israel. Ephraim was the southernmost region of the northern kingdom of Israel. The message is that just as Israel had been subjugated, Judah was also in danger.

4:1 [b] Jer 3:1,22; Joel 2:12 [c] Jer 35:15 **4:2** [d] Dt 10:20; Isa 65:16 [e] Jer 12:16 [f] Ge 22:18; Gal 3:8 **4:3** [g] Hos 10:12 [h] Mk 4:18 **4:4** [i] Dt 10:16; Jer 9:26; Ro 2:28-29 [j] Zep 2:2 [k] Am 5:6 **4:5** [l] Jos 10:20; Jer 8:14 **4:6** [m] Jer 1:13-15; 50:3 **4:7** [n] 2Ki 24:1; Jer 2:15 [o] Isa 1:7 [p] Jer 25:9 **4:8** [q] Isa 22:12; Jer 6:26 [r] Jer 30:24 **4:9** [s] Isa 29:9 **4:10** [t] 2Th 2:11 [u] Jer 14:13 **4:11** [v] Eze 17:10, Hos 13:15 **4:12** [w] Jer 1:16 **4:13** [x] Isa 19:1 [y] Isa 66:15 [z] Isa 5:28 [a] Dt 28:49; Hab 1:8 **4:14** [b] Jas 4:8 **4:15** [c] Jer 8:16 **4:16** [d] Eze 21:22

17 They surround[e] her like men guarding
a field,
because she has rebelled[f] against me,'"
declares the LORD.
18 "Your own conduct and actions[g]
have brought this on you.[h]
This is your punishment.
How bitter[i] it is!
How it pierces to the heart!"

19 Oh, my anguish, my anguish![j]
I writhe in pain.
Oh, the agony of my heart!
My heart pounds within me,
I cannot keep silent.[k]
For I have heard the sound of the
trumpet;
I have heard the battle cry.[l]
20 Disaster follows disaster;[m]
the whole land lies in ruins.
In an instant my tents[n] are destroyed,
my shelter in a moment.
21 How long must I see the battle
standard
and hear the sound of the trumpet?

22 "My people are fools;[o]
they do not know me.[p]
They are senseless children;
they have no understanding.
They are skilled in doing evil;[q]
they know not how to do good."[r]

23 I looked at the earth,
and it was formless and empty;[s]
and at the heavens,
and their light was gone.
24 I looked at the mountains,
and they were quaking;[t]
all the hills were swaying.
25 I looked, and there were no people;
every bird in the sky had flown
away.[u]
26 I looked, and the fruitful land was a
desert;
all its towns lay in ruins
before the LORD, before his fierce
anger.

27 This is what the LORD says:

"The whole land will be ruined,
though I will not destroy[v] it
completely.
28 Therefore the earth will mourn[w]
and the heavens above grow dark,[x]
because I have spoken and will not
relent,[y]
I have decided and will not turn
back.[z]"

29 At the sound of horsemen and archers[a]
every town takes to flight.[b]
Some go into the thickets;
some climb up among the rocks.
All the towns are deserted;[c]
no one lives in them.

30 What are you doing,[d] you devastated
one?
Why dress yourself in scarlet
and put on jewels[e] of gold?
Why highlight your eyes with makeup?[f]
You adorn yourself in vain.
Your lovers[g] despise you;
they want to kill you.

31 I hear a cry as of a woman in labor,[h]
a groan as of one bearing her first
child—
the cry of Daughter Zion gasping for
breath,[i]
stretching out her hands[j] and saying,
"Alas! I am fainting;
my life is given over to murderers."

Not One Is Upright

5 "Go up and down[k] the streets of
Jerusalem,
look around and consider,
search through her squares.
If you can find but one person[l]
who deals honestly and seeks the
truth,
I will forgive[m] this city.
2 Although they say, 'As surely as the
LORD lives,'[n]
still they are swearing falsely."

4:19 ***my anguish, my anguish.*** Anguish here means *bowels* or *belly,* a reference to the internal organs. In ancient Middle Eastern thought, the internal organs were the seat of emotions and feelings.
4:23 ***it was formless and empty.*** This Hebrew phrase is the same one used in Genesis 1:2 to describe the chaos before the ordering of the cosmos. ***their light was gone.*** The prophets spoke of darkness as part of God's judgment on the world. Here the lack of light describes the disastrous effects of sin on creation, particularly on the land of Judah.
4:24 ***they were quaking.*** The symbols of stability and of strength would be shaken as by an earthquake. Birds would disappear as Hosea had proclaimed (Hos. 4:3). In Genesis 1, the creation of the birds of the heavens depicts the fulfillment of the creative process. In Jeremiah and Hosea, the removal of the birds symbolizes the reversal of creation.
4:28 ***the heavens above grow dark.*** The dark skies are associated with God's judgment.

5:1 ***one person who deals honestly.*** Similar to Abraham's plea that Sodom be saved on account of the few faithful people among its inhabitants (Gen. 18:16–33), so Jeremiah summoned the people to search the city of Jerusalem for one just and righteous person.

4:17 [e] 2Ki 25:1, 4 [f] Jer 5:23 **4:18** [g] Ps 107:17; Isa 50:1 [h] Jer 2:17 [i] Jer 2:19 **4:19** [j] Isa 16:11; 22:4; Jer 9:10 [k] Jer 20:9 [l] Nu 10:9 **4:20** [m] Ps 42:7; Eze 7:26 [n] Jer 10:20 **4:22** [o] Jer 10:8 [p] Jer 2:8 [q] Jer 13:23; 1Co 14:20 [r] Ro 16:19 **4:23** [s] Ge 1:2 **4:24** [t] Isa 5:25; Eze 38:20 **4:25** [u] Jer 9:10; 12:4; Zep 1:3 **4:27** [v] Jer 5:10, 18; 12:12; 30:11; 46:28 **4:28** [w] Jer 12:4, 11; 14:2; Hos 4:3 [x] Isa 5:30; 50:3 [y] Nu 23:19 [z] Jer 23:20; 30:24 **4:29** [a] Jer 6:23 [b] 2Ki 25:4 [c] ver 7 **4:30** [d] Isa 10:3-4 [e] Eze 23:40 [f] 2Ki 9:30 [g] La 1:2; Eze 23:9, 22 **4:31** [h] Jer 13:21 [i] Isa 42:14 [j] Isa 1:15; La 1:17 **5:1** [k] 2Ch 16:9; Eze 22:30 [l] Ge 18:32 [m] Ge 18:24 **5:2** [n] Jer 4:2

3 LORD, do not your eyes[o] look for truth?
You struck[p] them, but they felt no pain;
you crushed them, but they refused correction.[q]
They made their faces harder than stone[r]
and refused to repent.
4 I thought, "These are only the poor;
they are foolish,
for they do not know[s] the way of the LORD,
the requirements of their God.
5 So I will go to the leaders[t]
and speak to them;
surely they know the way of the LORD,
the requirements of their God."
But with one accord they too had broken off the yoke
and torn off the bonds.[u]
6 Therefore a lion from the forest will attack them,
a wolf from the desert will ravage them,
a leopard[v] will lie in wait near their towns
to tear to pieces any who venture out,
for their rebellion is great
and their backslidings many.[w]
7 "Why should I forgive you?
Your children have forsaken me
and sworn[x] by gods that are not gods.[y]
I supplied all their needs,
yet they committed adultery[z]
and thronged to the houses of prostitutes.
8 They are well-fed, lusty stallions,
each neighing for another man's wife.[a]
9 Should I not punish them for this?"[b]
declares the LORD.
"Should I not avenge myself
on such a nation as this?

10 "Go through her vineyards and ravage them,
but do not destroy them completely.[c]
Strip off her branches,
for these people do not belong to the LORD.
11 The people of Israel and the people of Judah
have been utterly unfaithful[d] to me,"
declares the LORD.
12 They have lied about the LORD;
they said, "He will do nothing!
No harm will come to us;[e]
we will never see sword or famine.[f]
13 The prophets[g] are but wind
and the word is not in them;
so let what they say be done to them."

14 Therefore this is what the LORD God
Almighty says:

"Because the people have spoken these words,
I will make my words in your mouth[h] a fire[i]
and these people the wood it consumes.
15 People of Israel," declares the LORD,
"I am bringing a distant nation[j] against you—
an ancient and enduring nation,
a people whose language[k] you do not know,
whose speech you do not understand.
16 Their quivers are like an open grave;
all of them are mighty warriors.
17 They will devour[l] your harvests and food,
devour[m] your sons and daughters;
they will devour[n] your flocks and herds,
devour your vines and fig trees.
With the sword they will destroy
the fortified cities in which you trust.[o]

18 "Yet even in those days," declares the
LORD, "I will not destroy[p] you completely.
19 And when the people ask,[q] 'Why has the
LORD our God done all this to us?' you will
tell them, 'As you have forsaken me and
served foreign gods[r] in your own land, so
now you will serve foreigners[s] in a land not
your own.'

5:3 *they refused correction.* The Hebrew term translated *correction* means "chastisement" or "discipline." Sometimes it means "instruction." In the Prophets, it generally refers to God's attempt to teach His children faithfulness by means of discipline or punishment (7:28). But despite the words of Jeremiah and other prophets, Israel refused "correction" and continued down the path of self-destruction.

5:5 *broken off the yoke.* Jeremiah paints a picture of Judah as oxen that are wandering aimlessly through the field, guided by their own desires. They are exposed to the elements and the wild animals of the forest and desert.

5:7 *they committed adultery.* The prophets generally refer to cultic prostitution as adultery. Such immoral behavior violated covenant law (Ex. 20:14) and set in motion the curses of the covenant.

5:9 *Should I not punish them for this?* The Hebrew word translated *punish* (9:9), literally meaning "to visit," can be used of the visitation of God in mercy (Ps. 65:9) or in wrath. Here it clearly refers to wrath.

5:13 *The prophets are but wind.* False prophets like Hananiah (28:11) had foretold a time of peace and deliverance from the domination and destructiveness of their enemies. But their word was like an empty breeze. The very sword they denied would seal their fate.

5:17 *They will devour.* The word devour is used four times in this verse to paint an image of the enemy as consuming field, flock, and fortifications.

5:3 [o] 2Ch 16:9 [p] Isa 9:13 [q] Jer 2:30; Zep 3:2 [r] Jer 7:26; 19:15; Eze 3:8-9 **5:4** [s] Jer 8:7 **5:5** [t] Mic 3:1,9 [u] Ps 2:3; Jer 2:20 **5:6** [v] Hos 13:7 [w] Jer 30:14 **5:7** [x] Jos 23:7; Zep 1:5 [y] Dt 32:21; Jer 2:11; Gal 4:8 [z] Nu 25:1 **5:8** [a] Jer 29:23; Eze 22:11 **5:9** [b] ver 29; Jer 9:9 **5:10** [c] Jer 4:27 **5:11** [d] Jer 3:20 **5:12** [e] Jer 23:17 [f] 2Ch 36:16; Jer 14:13 **5:13** [g] Jer 14:15 **5:14** [h] Jer 1:9; Hos 6:5 [i] Jer 23:29 **5:15** [j] Dt 28:49; Isa 5:26; Jer 4:16 [k] Isa 28:11 **5:17** [l] Lev 26:16; Jer 8:16 [m] Dt 28:32; Jer 50:7, 17 [n] Dt 28:31 [o] Dt 28:33 **5:18** [p] Jer 4:27 **5:19** [q] Dt 29:24-26; 1Ki 9:9 [r] Jer 16:13 [s] Dt 28:48

20 "Announce this to the descendants of
Jacob
and proclaim it in Judah:
21 Hear this, you foolish and senseless
people,
who have eyes[t] but do not see,
who have ears but do not hear:[u]
22 Should you not fear[v] me?" declares the
LORD.
"Should you not tremble in my
presence?
I made the sand a boundary for the sea,
an everlasting barrier it cannot
cross.
The waves may roll, but they cannot
prevail;
they may roar, but they cannot
cross it.
23 But these people have stubborn and
rebellious[w] hearts;
they have turned aside and gone
away.
24 They do not say to themselves,
'Let us fear the LORD our God,
who gives autumn and spring rains[x] in
season,
who assures us of the regular weeks
of harvest.'[y]
25 Your wrongdoings have kept these
away;
your sins have deprived you of good.

26 "Among my people are the wicked
who lie in wait[z] like men who snare
birds
and like those who set traps to catch
people.
27 Like cages full of birds,
their houses are full of deceit;[a]
they have become rich[b] and powerful
28 and have grown fat[c] and sleek.
Their evil deeds have no limit;
they do not seek justice.
They do not promote the case of the
fatherless;[d]
they do not defend the just cause of
the poor.[e]
29 Should I not punish them for this?"
declares the LORD.
"Should I not avenge myself
on such a nation as this?

30 "A horrible[f] and shocking thing
has happened in the land:
31 The prophets prophesy lies,[g]
the priests rule by their own authority,
and my people love it this way.
But what will you do in the end?

Jerusalem Under Siege

6 "Flee for safety, people of Benjamin!
Flee from Jerusalem!
Sound the trumpet in Tekoa![h]
Raise the signal over Beth
Hakkerem![i]
For disaster looms out of the north,[j]
even terrible destruction.
2 I will destroy Daughter Zion,
so beautiful and delicate.
3 Shepherds[k] with their flocks will come
against her;
they will pitch their tents around[l] her,
each tending his own portion."

4 "Prepare for battle against her!
Arise, let us attack at noon![m]
But, alas, the daylight is fading,
and the shadows of evening grow
long.
5 So arise, let us attack at night
and destroy her fortresses!"

6 This is what the LORD Almighty says:

"Cut down the trees[n]
and build siege ramps[o] against
Jerusalem.
This city must be punished;
it is filled with oppression.
7 As a well pours out its water,
so she pours out her wickedness.
Violence[p] and destruction[q] resound in
her;
her sickness and wounds are ever
before me.

5:20 ***descendants of Jacob.*** Even after the northern kingdom had been destroyed, the prophets still spoke of Israel. There was not a complete destruction of the northern tribes, as is commonly thought.
5:26–28 ***the wicked.*** Those responsible for the welfare of the whole populace had abused their positions by exploiting the lesser elements of Israelite society. The picture presented is one of birds, or the poor, being ensnared by great men who were building wealth at the expense of orphans and the needy (Deut. 10:18).
5:31 ***prophets ... priests.*** The deterioration of the leadership of the land reached the very people who were supposed to be the mainstays of righteousness among the people. Both offices had succumbed to the temptation of abusing their power, rejecting their responsible roles as messengers and servants of God.
6:4–5 ***Prepare for battle against her.*** Prepare can also be translated "make holy." It refers to ritual sanctification performed in preparation for battle. The words are overheard in the camps of the enemies who are about to come against Jerusalem. Sorcerers and diviners were called upon to perform sacrifices to determine the will of the gods and assure a successful outcome in battle.
6:6 ***Cut down the trees and build siege ramps.*** A siege ramp was a ramp of wood, stone, and sand that sloped toward the wall of a city. Armored siege machines could go up the ramp and attack the city walls.
6:7 ***Violence and destruction.*** Jerusalem had once been a city that had peace, justice, and righteousness.

5:21 [t] Isa 6:10; Eze 12:2 [u] Mt 13:15; Mk 8:18
5:22 [v] Dt 28:58 **5:23** [w] Dt 21:18 **5:24** [x] Ps 147:8; Joel 2:23 [y] Ge 8:22; Ac 14:17 **5:26** [z] Ps 10:8; Pr 1:11
5:27 [a] Jer 9:6 [b] Jer 12:1 **5:28** [c] Dt 32:15 [d] Zec 7:10 [e] Isa 1:23; Jer 7:6 **5:30** [f] Jer 23:14; Hos 6:10
5:31 [g] Eze 13:6; Mic 2:11 **6:1** [h] 2Ch 11:6 [i] Ne 3:14 [j] Jer 4:6
6:3 [k] Jer 12:10 [l] 2Ki 25:4; Lk 19:43 **6:4** [m] Jer 15:8
6:6 [n] Dt 20:19-20 [o] Jer 32:24 **6:7** [p] Ps 55:9; Eze 7:11,23 [q] Jer 20:8

8 Take warning, Jerusalem,
or I will turn away[r] from you
and make your land desolate
so no one can live in it."

9 This is what the LORD Almighty says:

"Let them glean the remnant of Israel
as thoroughly as a vine;
pass your hand over the branches again,
like one gathering grapes."

10 To whom can I speak and give warning?
Who will listen to me?
Their ears are closed[a][s]
so they cannot hear.
The word[t] of the LORD is offensive to them;
they find no pleasure in it.
11 But I am full of the wrath[u] of the LORD,
and I cannot hold it in.[v]

"Pour it out on the children in the street
and on the young men[w] gathered together;
both husband and wife will be caught in it,
and the old, those weighed down with years.
12 Their houses will be turned over to others,[x]
together with their fields and their wives,[y]
when I stretch out my hand[z]
against those who live in the land,"
declares the LORD.
13 "From the least to the greatest,
all are greedy for gain;[a]
prophets and priests alike,
all practice deceit.[b]
14 They dress the wound of my people
as though it were not serious.
'Peace, peace,' they say,
when there is no peace.[c]
15 Are they ashamed of their detestable conduct?
No, they have no shame at all;
they do not even know how to blush.[d]
So they will fall among the fallen;
they will be brought down when I punish them,"
says the LORD.

16 This is what the LORD says:

"Stand at the crossroads and look;
ask for the ancient paths,[e]
ask where the good way[f] is, and walk in it,
and you will find rest[g] for your souls.
But you said, 'We will not walk in it.'
17 I appointed watchmen[h] over you and said,
'Listen to the sound of the trumpet!'
But you said, 'We will not listen.'[i]
18 Therefore hear, you nations;
you who are witnesses,
observe what will happen to them.
19 Hear, you earth:[j]
I am bringing disaster on this people,
the fruit of their schemes,[k]
because they have not listened to my words
and have rejected my law.[l]
20 What do I care about incense from Sheba
or sweet calamus[m] from a distant land?
Your burnt offerings are not acceptable;[n]
your sacrifices[o] do not please me."[p]

21 Therefore this is what the LORD says:

"I will put obstacles before this people.
Parents and children alike will stumble[q] over them;
neighbors and friends will perish."

22 This is what the LORD says:

"Look, an army is coming
from the land of the north;[r]
a great nation is being stirred up
from the ends of the earth.
23 They are armed with bow and spear;
they are cruel and show no mercy.[s]
They sound like the roaring sea
as they ride on their horses;[t]
they come like men in battle formation
to attack you, Daughter Zion."

---

[a] 10 Hebrew *uncircumcised*

Under the siege of the Babylonians in 588–586 B.C. conditions were unspeakable (see the Book of Lamentations).

6:11 ***I am full of the wrath of the LORD.*** Jeremiah's own emotions reveal his identification with God's feelings about Judah. The prophet was both angry and weary with the entire nation, both young and old.

6:13 ***all are greedy for gain.*** The accusation of covetousness suggests monetary gain by means of deception and fraud. Even those called to guide the nation in its covenant relationship had defrauded God and man.

6:15 ***they do not even know how to blush.*** The people had lost all sense of what was right before God.

6:16–17 ***ancient paths.*** This phrase probably refers to the Sinai covenant and the Book of Deuteronomy, as Jeremiah called the people back to former days of steadfast devotion.

6:20 ***Your burnt offerings are not acceptable.*** There is a common misconception that in the Old Testament, prior to the cross, God was primarily interested in outward and formal religious rites, such as circumcision, Sabbath-day observance, and animal sacrifices. Nothing could be more removed from the truth. In both Testaments, God is basically concerned with the attitudes of the heart (Deut. 10:6).

6:8 [r] Eze 23:18; Hos 9:12 **6:10** [s] Ac 7:51 [t] Jer 20:8
6:11 [u] Jer 7:20 [v] Job 32:20; Jer 20:9 [w] Jer 9:21
6:12 [x] Dt 28:30 [y] Jer 8:10; 38:22 [z] Isa 5:25
6:13 [a] Isa 56:11 [b] Jer 8:10 **6:14** [c] Jer 4:10; 8:11; Eze 13:10
6:15 [d] Jer 3:3; 8:10-12 **6:16** [e] Jer 18:15 [f] Ps 119:3
[g] Mt 11:29 **6:17** [h] Eze 3:17 [i] Jer 11:7-8; 25:4
6:19 [j] Isa 1:2; Jer 22:29 [k] Pr 1:31 [l] Jer 8:9 **6:20** [m] Ex 30:23
[n] Am 5:22 [o] Ps 50:8-10; Jer 7:21; Mic 6:7-8 [p] Isa 1:11
6:21 [q] Isa 8:14 **6:22** [r] Jer 1:15; 10:22 **6:23** [s] Isa 13:18
[t] Jer 4:29

24 We have heard reports about them,
and our hands hang limp.
Anguish[u] has gripped us,
pain like that of a woman in labor.[v]
25 Do not go out to the fields
or walk on the roads,
for the enemy has a sword,
and there is terror on every side.[w]
26 Put on sackcloth,[x] my people,
and roll in ashes;[y]
mourn with bitter wailing
as for an only son,[z]
for suddenly the destroyer
will come upon us.

27 "I have made you a tester[a] of metals
and my people the ore,
that you may observe
and test their ways.
28 They are all hardened rebels,[b]
going about to slander.[c]
They are bronze and iron;[d]
they all act corruptly.
29 The bellows blow fiercely
to burn away the lead with fire,
but the refining goes on in vain;
the wicked are not purged out.
30 They are called rejected silver,
because the LORD has rejected
them."[e]

False Religion Worthless

7 This is the word that came to Jeremiah
from the LORD: 2 "Stand[f] at the gate of
the LORD's house and there proclaim this
message:
"'Hear the word of the LORD, all you people of Judah who come through these gates
to worship the LORD. 3 This is what the LORD
Almighty, the God of Israel, says: Reform
your ways[g] and your actions, and I will let
you live in this place. 4 Do not trust in deceptive[h] words and say, "This is the temple of the LORD, the temple of the LORD, the
temple of the LORD!" 5 If you really change
your ways and your actions and deal with
each other justly,[i] 6 if you do not oppress the
foreigner, the fatherless or the widow and
do not shed innocent blood[j] in this place,
and if you do not follow other gods[k] to your
own harm, 7 then I will let you live in this
place, in the land[l] I gave your ancestors for
ever and ever. 8 But look, you are trusting in
deceptive words that are worthless.
9 "'Will you steal and murder, commit
adultery and perjury,[a] burn incense to
Baal[m] and follow other gods[n] you have not
known, 10 and then come and stand before
me in this house,[o] which bears my Name,
and say, "We are safe"—safe to do all these
detestable things? 11 Has this house,[p] which
bears my Name, become a den of robbers[q]
to you? But I have been watching![r] declares
the LORD.
12 "'Go now to the place in Shiloh[s] where
I first made a dwelling for my Name, and
see what I did[t] to it because of the wickedness of my people Israel. 13 While you were
doing all these things, declares the LORD,
I spoke to you again and again,[u] but you
did not listen;[v] I called you, but you did not
answer.[w] 14 Therefore, what I did to Shiloh
I will now do to the house that bears my
Name,[x] the temple you trust in, the place
I gave to you and your ancestors. 15 I will
thrust you from my presence, just as I did
all your fellow Israelites, the people of
Ephraim.'[y]

---

[a] 9 Or *and swear by false gods*

6:26 ***roll in ashes.*** This action symbolically expressed sorrow and despair.
6:27 ***I have made you a tester.*** Jeremiah would act as the nation's assayer, the one who tests or evaluates quality or purity.
6:29–30 ***the refining goes on in vain.*** Jeremiah assesses Judah as a refiner purifies silver, using lead to remove impurities (9:7). The lead is consumed, so the dross in the silver ore cannot be purged. This results in the refiner discarding the ore because it is so impure that the smelting process is not worth the energy it takes. Similarly God rejects those whose wickedness cannot be refined.
7:2 ***Stand at the gate.*** The parallel in 26:2 suggests the proclamation was made in the outer court of the temple, where Jeremiah would have been guaranteed a large audience.
7:4 ***Do not trust in deceptive words.*** Trust conveys the sense of security and confidence that the people had in their holy place. They believed that since God had chosen Jerusalem as His dwelling, had promised that a Davidic king would remain on the throne forever, and had delivered the city from attack in the days of Hezekiah and Isaiah, He would never allow the city or the temple to be destroyed. ***the temple of the LORD.*** The Israelites believed that the building guaranteed their security whether or not they obeyed the provisions of the covenant. This false hope was a lie (3:23; 7:9).
7:10 ***stand before me.*** This means "to place (oneself) in submissive service to someone." Entering the temple of God in such a manner, while worshiping other gods, was incomprehensible. Furthermore, for the people to think that they were secure enough to perform perverted abominations was the ultimate hypocrisy.
7:11 ***den of robbers.*** Like thieves hiding in a cave for safety, Judah attempted to hide behind the sanctuary of the temple for protection from the divine hand of judgment. But the Lord had seen the hypocrisy of Israel's ways. Jesus quoted this verse when He cleansed the second temple (Matt. 21:13).

6:24 [u] Jer 4:19 [v] Jer 4:31; 50:41-43 **6:25** [w] Jer 49:29
6:26 [x] Jer 4:8 [y] Jer 25:34; Mic 1:10 [z] Zec 12:10
6:27 [a] Jer 9:7 **6:28** [b] Jer 5:23 [c] Jer 9:4 [d] Eze 22:18
6:30 [e] Ps 119:119; Jer 7:29; Hos 9:17 **7:2** [f] Jer 17:19
7:3 [g] Jer 18:11; 26:13 **7:4** [h] Mic 3:11 **7:5** [i] Jer 22:3
7:6 [j] Jer 2:34; 19:4 [k] Dt 8:19 **7:7** [l] Dt 4:40
7:9 [m] Jer 11:13, 17 [n] Ex 20:3 **7:10** [o] Jer 32:34;
Eze 23:38-39 **7:11** [p] Isa 56:7 [q] Mt 21:13*; Mk 11:17*;
Lk 19:46* [r] Jer 29:23 **7:12** [s] Jos 18:1 [t] 1Sa 4:10-11, 22;
Ps 78:60-64 **7:13** [u] 2Ch 36:15 [v] Isa 65:12 [w] Jer 35:17
7:14 [x] 1Ki 9:7 **7:15** [y] Ps 78:67

16“So do not pray for this people nor offer any plea[z] or petition for them; do not
plead with me, for I will not listen to you.
17Do you not see what they are doing in the
towns of Judah and in the streets of Jerusalem? 18The children gather wood, the fathers light the fire, and the women knead
the dough and make cakes to offer to the
Queen of Heaven.[a] They pour out drink
offerings[b] to other gods to arouse[c] my
anger. 19But am I the one they are provoking? declares the LORD. Are they not
rather harming themselves, to their own
shame?[d]
20“ ‘Therefore this is what the Sovereign
LORD says: My anger[e] and my wrath will
be poured out on this place—on man and
beast, on the trees of the field and on the
crops of your land—and it will burn and
not be quenched.
21“ ‘This is what the LORD Almighty, the
God of Israel, says: Go ahead, add your
burnt offerings to your other sacrifices[f]
and eat[g] the meat yourselves! 22For when
I brought your ancestors out of Egypt and
spoke to them, I did not just give them
commands about burnt offerings and sacrifices,[h] 23but I gave them this command:
Obey[i] me, and I will be your God and you
will be my people.[j] Walk in obedience to
all I command you, that it may go well[k]
with you. 24But they did not listen or pay
attention;[l] instead, they followed the stubborn inclinations of their evil hearts. They
went backward and not forward. 25From
the time your ancestors left Egypt until
now, day after day, again and again I sent
you my servants the prophets.[m] 26But they
did not listen to me or pay attention. They
were stiff-necked and did more evil than
their ancestors.’[n]
27“When you tell[o] them all this, they will
not listen[p] to you; when you call to them,
they will not answer. 28Therefore say
to them, ‘This is the nation that has not
obeyed the LORD its God or responded to
correction. Truth has perished; it has vanished from their lips.
29“ ‘Cut off[q] your hair and throw it away;
take up a lament on the barren heights, for
the LORD has rejected and abandoned[r] this
generation that is under his wrath.

The Valley of Slaughter

30“ ‘The people of Judah have done
evil in my eyes, declares the LORD. They
have set up their detestable idols[s] in the
house that bears my Name and have
defiled[t] it. 31They have built the high
places of Topheth[u] in the Valley of Ben
Hinnom to burn their sons and daughters[v] in the fire—something I did not
command, nor did it enter my mind.[w] 32So
beware, the days are coming, declares
the LORD, when people will no longer call
it Topheth or the Valley of Ben Hinnom,
but the Valley of Slaughter,[x] for they will
bury[y] the dead in Topheth until there is no
more room. 33Then the carcasses of this
people will become food[z] for the birds and
the wild animals, and there will be no
one to frighten them away. 34I will bring
an end to the sounds[a] of joy and gladness
and to the voices of bride and bridegroom[b]
in the towns of Judah and the streets of
Jerusalem, for the land will become desolate.[c]

7:16 *do not pray for this people.* God's instruction to Jeremiah indicates the extreme depravity of Jerusalem's inhabitants (11:14; 14:11). No manner of intercession was to be made on behalf of Judah. God would not hear Jeremiah's appeals.

7:18 *the Queen of Heaven.* This is a reference to the goddess Ishtar, who was worshiped in open-air cultic centers throughout the eastern Mediterranean region and Mesopotamia. Worship of Ishtar involved the preparation of special cakes that bore the goddess's image, as well as drink offerings (44:19). The family cooperation in the idolatrous worship of Ishtar stood in direct opposition to the covenant demands that a father instruct his children in the ways of the Lord (Deut. 6:4–9).

7:21 *add your burnt offerings to your other sacrifices.* Because the people had missed the true meaning of the Lord's worship, they could multiply their offerings as much as they liked and it would do them no good. The Lord cared for none of their sacrifices. To Him they were simply meat.

7:23 *that it may go well with you.* God required that His people obey His voice. Obedience would bring blessing. When the prophets lashed out against sacrifice, it was not against the sacrificial system as God had established it, but against the corruption of that system as the people practiced it. The same thing is found in the New Testament passages that seemingly speak against the law. Both the New Testament writers and the Hebrew prophets denounce the abuses of divine systems in human hands.

7:26 *did not listen ... They were stiff-necked.* These phrases suggest a cold rebuff to the will and work of God. Jeremiah, like Isaiah before him (Is. 6:9,10), was told that the people would not respond to his message.

7:29 *Cut off your hair.* This practice was a way of expressing mourning and grief. The act may also have symbolized that Judah had rejected the covenant relationship just as if they had broken a Nazirite vow, a sign of personal devotion that required the hair not to be cut (Num. 6:1–21).

7:33 *carcasses of this people.* Unburied corpses left to the elements and animals were regarded as a horrible desecration in the ancient Middle East.

7:16 [z] Ex 32:10; Dt 9:14; Jer 15:1 **7:18** [a] Jer 44:17-19 [b] Jer 19:13 [c] 1Ki 14:9 **7:19** [d] Jer 9:19 **7:20** [e] Jer 42:18; La 2:3-5 **7:21** [f] Isa 1:11; Am 5:21-22 [g] Hos 8:13 **7:22** [h] 1Sa 15:22; Ps 51:16; Hos 6:6 **7:23** [i] Ex 19:5 [j] Lev 26:12 [k] Ex 15:26 **7:24** [l] Ps 81:11-12; Jer 11:8 **7:25** [m] Jer 25:4 **7:26** [n] Jer 16:12 **7:27** [o] Eze 2:7 [p] Eze 3:7 **7:29** [q] Job 1:20; Isa 15:2; Mic 1:16 [r] Jer 6:30 **7:30** [s] Eze 7:20-22 [t] Jer 32:34 **7:31** [u] 2Ki 23:10 [v] Ps 106:38 [w] Jer 19:5 **7:32** [x] Jer 19:6 [y] Jer 19:11 **7:33** [z] Dt 28:26 **7:34** [a] Isa 24:8; Eze 26:13 [b] Rev 18:23 [c] Lev 26:34

8 "'At that time, declares the LORD, the bones of the kings and officials of Judah, the bones of the priests and prophets, and the bones of the people of Jerusalem will be removed from their graves.
2They will be exposed to the sun and the moon and all the stars of the heavens, which they have loved and served[d] and which they have followed and consulted and worshiped. They will not be gathered up or buried, but will be like dung lying on the ground.
3Wherever I banish them, all the survivors of this evil nation will prefer death to life,[e] declares the LORD Almighty.'

Sin and Punishment

4"Say to them, 'This is what the LORD says:

"'When people fall down, do they not get up?[f]
When someone turns away, do they not return?
5Why then have these people turned away?
Why does Jerusalem always turn away?
They cling to deceit;[g]
they refuse to return.[h]
6I have listened attentively,
but they do not say what is right.
None of them repent[i] of their wickedness,
saying, "What have I done?"
Each pursues their own course[j]
like a horse charging into battle.
7Even the stork in the sky
knows her appointed seasons,
and the dove, the swift and the thrush
observe the time of their migration.
But my people do not know[k]
the requirements of the LORD.

8"'How can you say, "We are wise,
for we have the law[l] of the LORD,"
when actually the lying pen of the scribes
has handled it falsely?
9The wise[m] will be put to shame;
they will be dismayed and trapped.
Since they have rejected the word[n] of the LORD,
what kind of wisdom do they have?
10Therefore I will give their wives to other men
and their fields to new owners.[o]
From the least to the greatest,
all are greedy for gain;[p]
prophets and priests alike,
all practice deceit.
11They dress the wound of my people
as though it were not serious.
"Peace, peace," they say,
when there is no peace.[q]
12Are they ashamed of their detestable conduct?
No, they have no shame[r] at all;
they do not even know how to blush.
So they will fall among the fallen;
they will be brought down when they are punished,[s]
says the LORD.[t]

13"'I will take away their harvest,
declares the LORD.
There will be no grapes on the vine.[u]
There will be no figs[v] on the tree,
and their leaves will wither.[w]
What I have given them
will be taken[x] from them.[a]'"

14Why are we sitting here?
Gather together!
Let us flee to the fortified cities[y]
and perish there!
For the LORD our God has doomed us to perish
and given us poisoned water[z] to drink,
because we have sinned[a] against him.
15We hoped for peace[b]
but no good has come,
for a time of healing
but there is only terror.[c]
16The snorting of the enemy's horses
is heard from Dan;[d]
at the neighing of their stallions
the whole land trembles.
They have come to devour
the land and everything in it,
the city and all who live there.

17"See, I will send venomous snakes[e]
among you,
vipers that cannot be charmed,[f]
and they will bite you,"
declares the LORD.

[a] *13* The meaning of the Hebrew for this sentence is uncertain.

8:1–3 *the sun and the moon and all the stars of the heavens.* The gods and goddesses to whom Jerusalem looked for deliverance would stand over the people's desecrated corpses, which are pictured here as dung. Those who survived the siege and attack as exiles and slaves would prefer death over life.

8:7 *appointed seasons.* Whereas the birds follow their instincts to migrate, the people of Israel refused to follow God's promptings to obey His covenant. Note that God still refers to the people of Judah as "my people" even though they continued to rebel against Him.

8:17 *I will send venomous snakes among you.* Judgment by means of poisonous snakes is described in Numbers 21:6.

8:2 [d] 2Ki 23:5; Ac 7:42 **8:3** [e] Job 3:22; Rev 9:6 **8:4** [f] Pr 24:16 **8:5** [g] Jer 5:27 [h] Jer 7:24; 9:6 **8:6** [i] Rev 9:20 [j] Ps 14:1-3 **8:7** [k] Isa 1:3; Jer 5:4-5 **8:8** [l] Ro 2:17 **8:9** [m] Jer 6:15 [n] Jer 6:19 **8:10** [o] Jer 6:12 [p] Isa 56:11 **8:11** [q] Jer 6:14 **8:12** [r] Jer 3:3 [s] Ps 52:5-7; Isa 3:9 [t] Jer 6:15 **8:13** [u] Joel 1:7 [v] Lk 13:6 [w] Mt 21:19 [x] Jer 5:17 **8:14** [y] Jer 4:5; 35:11 [z] Dt 29:18; Jer 9:15; 23:15 [a] Jer 14:7,20 **8:15** [b] ver 11 [c] Jer 14:19 **8:16** [d] Jer 4:15 **8:17** [e] Nu 21:6; Dt 32:24 [f] Ps 58:5

18 You who are my Comforter[a] in sorrow,
my heart is faint[g] within me.
19 Listen to the cry of my people
from a land far away:[h]
"Is the LORD not in Zion?
Is her King no longer there?"

"Why have they aroused my anger with their images,
with their worthless foreign idols?"[i]

20 "The harvest is past,
the summer has ended,
and we are not saved."

21 Since my people are crushed, I am crushed;
I mourn,[j] and horror grips me.
22 Is there no balm in Gilead?[k]
Is there no physician there?
Why then is there no healing[l]
for the wound of my people?

9 [b] 1 Oh, that my head were a spring of water
and my eyes a fountain of tears!
I would weep[m] day and night
for the slain of my people.[n]
2 Oh, that I had in the desert
a lodging place for travelers,
so that I might leave my people
and go away from them;
for they are all adulterers,[o]
a crowd of unfaithful people.

3 "They make ready their tongue
like a bow, to shoot lies;[p]
it is not by truth
that they triumph[c] in the land.
They go from one sin to another;
they do not acknowledge me,"
declares the LORD.
4 "Beware of your friends;
do not trust anyone in your clan.[q]
For every one of them is a deceiver,[d][r]
and every friend a slanderer.
5 Friend deceives friend,
and no one speaks the truth.
They have taught their tongues to lie;
they weary themselves with sinning.
6 You[e] live in the midst of deception;[s]
in their deceit they refuse to acknowledge me,"
declares the LORD.

7 Therefore this is what the LORD Almighty says:

"See, I will refine[t] and test[u] them,
for what else can I do
because of the sin of my people?
8 Their tongue[v] is a deadly arrow;
it speaks deceitfully.
With their mouths they all speak cordially to their neighbors,
but in their hearts they set traps[w] for them.
9 Should I not punish them for this?"
declares the LORD.
"Should I not avenge[x] myself
on such a nation as this?"

10 I will weep and wail for the mountains
and take up a lament concerning the wilderness grasslands.
They are desolate and untraveled,
and the lowing of cattle is not heard.
The birds[y] have all fled
and the animals are gone.

11 "I will make Jerusalem a heap of ruins,
a haunt of jackals;[z]
and I will lay waste the towns of Judah
so no one can live there."[a]

12 Who is wise[b] enough to understand
this? Who has been instructed by the LORD
and can explain it? Why has the land been
ruined and laid waste like a desert that no
one can cross?
13 The LORD said, "It is because they have
forsaken my law, which I set before them;

[a] *18* The meaning of the Hebrew for this word is uncertain. [b] In Hebrew texts 9:1 is numbered 8:23, and 9:2-26 is numbered 9:1-25. [c] *3* Or *lies; / they are not valiant for truth* [d] *4* Or *a deceiving Jacob* [e] *6* That is, Jeremiah (the Hebrew is singular)

8:20 *harvest is past.* This proverb reflects the sense of helplessness in the early fall. The harvest was meager and the oppression persisted. Even Jeremiah was deeply hurt — this translates a Hebrew word derived from the verb meaning "to break," "to shatter"; in other words, the prophet's spirit was broken over the fate of his people.
8:22 *Is there no balm in Gilead?* The region of Gilead was known for its balsam ointment (Gen. 37:25). There is no healing, physical or spiritual, for a people intent on rebelling against God.
9:1 *my eyes a fountain of tears.* Jeremiah, who is known as the "weeping prophet," identified personally with the suffering of his people. Here he expresses his desire for a reserve of tears that would flow without stopping.
9:3 *They make ready their tongue like a bow.* Once falseness takes hold in a community or nation, it seems to pervade every area of life. Such a condition is what Jeremiah describes here. There was falsity in every relation. There was a lack of fidelity and trust.
9:4 *Beware of your friends.* The personal affairs of the people were characterized by deceit, slander, and mistrust. Ethical standards had collapsed.
9:8 *Their tongue is a deadly arrow.* Jeremiah returns to the imagery of bow and arrow to depict Judah's deceit (v. 3). The picture is of a person speaking peaceably to his neighbor while lying in wait to ambush him.
9:13 *have not obeyed.* The word "obey," which comes from the Hebrew word meaning "to hear," implies an active response to the hearing of God's word. Instead of walking according to God's law, the people

8:18 [g] La 5:17 **8:19** [h] Jer 9:16 [i] Dt 32:21 **8:21** [j] Jer 14:17 **8:22** [k] Ge 37:25 [l] Jer 30:12 **9:1** [m] Jer 13:17; La 2:11, 18 [n] Isa 22:4 **9:2** [o] Jer 5:7-8; 23:10; Hos 4:2 **9:3** [p] Ps 64:3 **9:4** [q] Mic 7:5-6 [r] Ge 27:35 **9:6** [s] Jer 5:27 **9:7** [t] Isa 1:25 [u] Jer 6:27 **9:8** [v] ver 3 [w] Jer 5:26 **9:9** [x] Jer 5:9, 29 **9:10** [y] Jer 4:25; 12:4; Hos 4:3 **9:11** [z] Isa 34:13 [a] Isa 25:2; Jer 26:9 **9:12** [b] Ps 107:43; Hos 14:9

they have not obeyed me or followed my
law.[c] 14Instead, they have followed[d] the
stubbornness of their hearts;[e] they have
followed the Baals, as their ancestors
taught them." 15Therefore this is what the
LORD Almighty, the God of Israel, says:
"See, I will make this people eat bitter food[f]
and drink poisoned water.[g] 16I will scatter
them among nations[h] that neither they nor
their ancestors have known,[i] and I will pursue them with the sword[j] until I have made
an end of them."[k]

17This is what the LORD Almighty says:

"Consider now! Call for the wailing
women[l] to come;
send for the most skillful of them.
18Let them come quickly
and wail over us
till our eyes overflow with tears
and water streams from our eyelids.[m]
19The sound of wailing is heard from Zion:
'How ruined[n] we are!
How great is our shame!
We must leave our land
because our houses are in ruins.'"

20Now, you women, hear the word of the
LORD;
open your ears to the words of his
mouth.
Teach your daughters how to wail;
teach one another a lament.[o]
21Death has climbed in through our
windows
and has entered our fortresses;
it has removed the children from the
streets
and the young men[p] from the public
squares.

22Say, "This is what the LORD declares:

"'Dead bodies will lie
like dung[q] on the open field,
like cut grain behind the reaper,
with no one to gather them.'"

23This is what the LORD says:

"Let not the wise boast of their wisdom[r]
or the strong boast of their strength[s]
or the rich boast of their riches,[t]
24but let the one who boasts boast[u] about
this:
that they have the understanding to
know me,
that I am the LORD,[v] who exercises
kindness,[w]
justice and righteousness[x] on earth,
for in these I delight,"
declares the LORD.

25"The days are coming," declares the
LORD, "when I will punish all who are circumcised only in the flesh[y]— 26Egypt, Judah, Edom, Ammon, Moab and all who live
in the wilderness in distant places.[a][z] For
all these nations are really uncircumcised,
and even the whole house of Israel is uncircumcised in heart.[a]"

God and Idols

10 Hear what the LORD says to you, people of Israel. 2This is what the LORD
says:

"Do not learn the ways of the nations[b]
or be terrified by signs in the
heavens,
though the nations are terrified by
them.
3For the practices of the peoples are
worthless;
they cut a tree out of the forest,
and a craftsman[c] shapes it with his
chisel.
4They adorn it with silver and gold;
they fasten it with hammer and nails
so it will not totter.[d]
5Like a scarecrow in a cucumber field,
their idols cannot speak;[e]
they must be carried
because they cannot walk.[f]
Do not fear them;
they can do no harm
nor can they do any good."[g]
6No one is like you, LORD;
you are great,[h]
and your name is mighty in power.

a 26 Or wilderness and who clip the hair by their foreheads

---

walked according to the dictates or stubbornness of their own hearts.
9:18 *Let them come quickly.* There is urgency in summoning the skilled mourners to lead the people in tearful lament over the imminent destruction of Judah.
9:21 *Death has climbed.* The Canaanite god of death, Mot, was believed to enter a household through an open window to bring adversity, destruction and death.
9:24 *kindness, justice and righteousness on earth.* True knowledge of God resulting from an intimate relationship with Him will be demonstrated in a person's character. God demands these attributes of his followers.
10:2 *the ways of the nations.* The Gentiles worshiped natural phenomena by means of handmade icons and symbolic imagery. ***signs in the heavens.*** These were astral deities (8:1–3) worshiped in the days of Manasseh and reinstituted following the death of Josiah and the collapse of his reforms.
10:6–7 *No one is like you, LORD.* This phrase expresses one of the great teachings of the prophets—

9:13 [c] 2Ch 7:19; Ps 89:30-32 **9:14** [d] Jer 2:8,23 [e] Jer 7:24 **9:15** [f] La 3:15 [g] Jer 8:14 **9:16** [h] Lev 26:33 [i] Dt 28:64 [j] Eze 5:2 [k] Jer 44:27; Eze 5:12 **9:17** [l] 2Ch 35:25; Ecc 12:5; Am 5:16 **9:18** [m] Jer 14:17 **9:19** [n] Jer 4:13 **9:20** [o] Isa 32:9-13 **9:21** [p] 2Ch 36:17 **9:22** [q] Jer 8:2 **9:23** [r] Ecc 9:11 [s] 1Ki 20:11 [t] Eze 28:4-5 **9:24** [u] 1Co 1:31*; Gal 6:14 [v] 2Co 10:17* [w] Ps 51:1; Mic 7:18 [x] Ps 36:6 **9:25** [y] Ro 2:8-9 **9:26** [z] Jer 25:23 [a] Lev 26:41; Ac 7:51; Ro 2:28 **10:2** [b] Lev 20:23 **10:3** [c] Isa 40:19 **10:4** [d] Isa 41:7 **10:5** [e] 1Co 12:2 [f] Ps 115:5,7 [g] Isa 41:24; 46:7 **10:6** [h] Ps 48:1

7 Who should not fear you,
King of the nations?[i]
This is your due.
Among all the wise leaders of the nations
and in all their kingdoms,
there is no one like you.
8 They are all senseless and foolish;[j]
they are taught by worthless wooden idols.
9 Hammered silver is brought from Tarshish
and gold from Uphaz.
What the craftsman and goldsmith have made[k]
is then dressed in blue and purple—
all made by skilled workers.
10 But the LORD is the true God;
he is the living God, the eternal King.
When he is angry, the earth trembles;
the nations cannot endure his wrath.[l]

11 "Tell them this: 'These gods, who did
not make the heavens and the earth, will
perish[m] from the earth and from under the
heavens.'"[a]

12 But God made the earth by his power;
he founded the world by his wisdom
and stretched out the heavens[n] by his understanding.
13 When he thunders,[o] the waters in the heavens roar;
he makes clouds rise from the ends of the earth.
He sends lightning with the rain[p]
and brings out the wind from his storehouses.

14 Everyone is senseless and without knowledge;
every goldsmith is shamed by his idols.
The images he makes are a fraud;
they have no breath in them.
15 They are worthless,[q] the objects of mockery;
when their judgment comes, they will perish.
16 He who is the Portion[r] of Jacob is not like these,
for he is the Maker of all things,[s]
including Israel, the people of his inheritance[t]—
the LORD Almighty is his name.[u]

Coming Destruction

17 Gather up your belongings[v] to leave the land,
you who live under siege.
18 For this is what the LORD says:
"At this time I will hurl[w] out
those who live in this land;
I will bring distress on them
so that they may be captured."
19 Woe to me because of my injury!
My wound[x] is incurable!
Yet I said to myself,
"This is my sickness, and I must endure[y] it."
20 My tent[z] is destroyed;
all its ropes are snapped.
My children are gone from me and are no more;[a]
no one is left now to pitch my tent
or to set up my shelter.
21 The shepherds are senseless
and do not inquire of the LORD;
so they do not prosper
and all their flock is scattered.[b]
22 Listen! The report is coming—
a great commotion from the land of the north!
It will make the towns of Judah desolate,
a haunt of jackals.[c]

[a] *11* The text of this verse is in Aramaic.

---

the incomparability of God. God is not simply better than other gods; He alone is the living God.

10:9 *made by skilled workers.* No matter how skilled the idol makers were, the fabricated icons were lifeless, deteriorating, false gods who were no more powerful or wise than their makers.

10:10 *the LORD is the true God.* Jeremiah speaks of Israel's God not only as living, but also as being the true God and the nation's everlasting King. He thus governs His covenant people by principles of truth, and with a power that far surpasses the might of earthly kings. Whereas pagan gods cannot alter the course of nature in the slightest degree, even though their worshipers believed very much to the contrary, the God of Sinai is the Creator of nature. He can punish the wicked by storm, flood, earthquake, or pestilence, and strike terror into the hearts of all those who oppose Him.

10:12 *he founded the world.* Jeremiah emphasizes the creative power of God, drawing on the imagery of Job 38 and Psalm 8. Jeremiah was reminding the people of Judah that their God not only created the universe but also governs its ongoing life.

10:17 *Gather up your belongings to leave the land.* The Assyrian stone reliefs of Shalmaneser III depict captives transporting household goods on their heads as they go into exile in the eastern reaches of the empire. Soon this would be the fate of the people of Judah.

10:19 *Woe to me.* Jeremiah personally identified with Judah and the destruction of Jerusalem. The injuries inflicted upon Judah were severe.

10:7 [i] Ps 22:28; Rev 15:4 **10:8** [j] Isa 40:19; Jer 4:22 **10:9** [k] Ps 115:4; Isa 40:19 **10:10** [l] Ps 76:7 **10:11** [m] Ps 96:5; Isa 2:18 **10:12** [n] Ge 1:1,8; Job 9:8; Isa 40:22 **10:13** [o] Job 36:29 [p] Ps 135:7 **10:15** [q] Isa 41:24; Jer 14:22 **10:16** [r] Dt 32:9; Ps 119:57 [s] ver 12 [t] Ps 74:2 [u] Jer 31:35; 32:18 **10:17** [v] Eze 12:3-12 **10:18** [w] 1Sa 25:29 **10:19** [x] Jer 14:17 [y] Mic 7:9 **10:20** [z] Jer 4:20 [a] Jer 31:15; La 1:5 **10:21** [b] Jer 23:2 **10:22** [c] Jer 9:11

Jeremiah's Prayer

23 LORD, I know that people's lives are not
their own;
it is not for them to direct their steps.[d]
24 Discipline me, LORD, but only in due
measure—
not in your anger,[e]
or you will reduce me to nothing.[f]
25 Pour out your wrath on the nations[g]
that do not acknowledge you,
on the peoples who do not call on
your name.[h]
For they have devoured[i] Jacob;
they have devoured him completely
and destroyed his homeland.[j]

The Covenant Is Broken

11 This is the word that came to Jeremiah from the LORD: 2"Listen to the
terms of this covenant and tell them to the
people of Judah and to those who live in
Jerusalem. 3Tell them that this is what the
LORD, the God of Israel, says: 'Cursed[k] is
the one who does not obey the terms of
this covenant— 4the terms I commanded
your ancestors when I brought them out of
Egypt, out of the iron-smelting furnace.[l]' I
said, 'Obey[m] me and do everything I command you, and you will be my people,[n] and
I will be your God. 5Then I will fulfill the
oath I swore[o] to your ancestors, to give
them a land flowing with milk and honey'—the land you possess today."
I answered, "Amen, LORD."
6The LORD said to me, "Proclaim all these
words in the towns of Judah and in the
streets of Jerusalem: 'Listen to the terms
of this covenant and follow[p] them. 7From
the time I brought your ancestors up from
Egypt until today, I warned them again
and again,[q] saying, "Obey me." 8But they
did not listen or pay attention;[r] instead,
they followed the stubbornness of their evil
hearts. So I brought on them all the curses[s]
of the covenant I had commanded them to
follow but that they did not keep.'"
9Then the LORD said to me, "There is a
conspiracy[t] among the people of Judah and
those who live in Jerusalem. 10They have returned to the sins of their ancestors,[u] who
refused to listen to my words. They have
followed other gods[v] to serve them. Both Israel and Judah have broken the covenant I
made with their ancestors. 11Therefore this
is what the LORD says: 'I will bring on them
a disaster[w] they cannot escape. Although
they cry[x] out to me, I will not listen[y] to
them. 12The towns of Judah and the people
of Jerusalem will go and cry out to the gods
to whom they burn incense,[z] but they will
not help them at all when disaster[a] strikes.
13You, Judah, have as many gods as you
have towns; and the altars you have set up
to burn incense[b] to that shameful[c] god Baal
are as many as the streets of Jerusalem.'
14"Do not pray[d] for this people or offer
any plea or petition for them, because I will
not listen[e] when they call to me in the time
of their distress.

15 "What is my beloved doing in my
temple
as she, with many others, works out
her evil schemes?
Can consecrated meat avert your
punishment?
When you engage in your wickedness,
then you rejoice.[a]"

16 The LORD called you a thriving olive
tree
with fruit beautiful in form.
But with the roar of a mighty storm
he will set it on fire,[f]
and its branches will be broken.[g]

17The LORD Almighty, who planted[h] you,
has decreed disaster for you, because the
people of both Israel and Judah have done
evil and aroused my anger by burning incense to Baal.[i]

[a] 15 Or *Could consecrated meat avert your punishment? / Then you would rejoice*

11:2 ***Listen to the terms of this covenant.*** Jeremiah's message from the Lord here is strongly associated with the Book of Deuteronomy. The word translated "terms" is the Hebrew name of the Book of Deuteronomy; it is also used to refer to the terms of the covenant. A covenant is a legal treaty or relationship between individuals, between nations, or—in the case of Israel—between a nation and its God. The covenant specified rights, obligations and responsibilities of the parties entering into the agreement.

11:4 ***iron-smelting furnace.*** This terminology comes directly from Deuteronomy 4:20, which is set in a context of a warning against worshiping idols.

11:5 ***I will fulfill the oath.*** The blessing of land, as promised to Abraham, was dependent upon the covenant loyalty of the people.

11:11 ***bring on them a disaster.*** Because the heart of the nation was evil, God would bring disaster upon the people. God's justice is inescapable when sin is intrinsic to one's character. Even if the people were to cry out in distress, God would not listen.

11:17 ***planted.*** This term recalls the theme of Jeremiah 2:21, the idea that God had established Israel as His choicest vine. However, here the context is the impending doom that would result from the evil done by the Lord's people.

10:23 [d] Pr 20:24 **10:24** [e] Ps 6:1; 38:1 [f] Jer 30:11 **10:25** [g] Zep 3:8 [h] Job 18:21; Ps 14:4 [i] Ps 79:7; Jer 8:16 [j] Ps 79:6-7 **11:3** [k] Dt 27:26; Gal 3:10 **11:4** [l] Dt 4:20; 1Ki 8:51 [m] Ex 24:8 [n] Jer 7:23; 31:33 **11:5** [o] Ex 13:5; Dt 7:12; Ps 105:8-11 **11:6** [p] Dt 15:5; Ro 2:13; Jas 1:22 **11:7** [q] 2Ch 36:15 **11:8** [r] Jer 7:26 [s] Lev 26:14-43 **11:9** [t] Eze 22:25 **11:10** [u] Dt 9:7 [v] Jdg 2:12-13 **11:11** [w] 2Ki 22:16 [x] Jer 14:12; Eze 8:18 [y] ver 14; Pr 1:28; Isa 1:15; Zec 7:13 **11:12** [z] Jer 44:17 [a] Dt 32:37 **11:13** [b] Jer 7:9 [c] Jer 3:24 **11:14** [d] Ex 32:10 [e] ver 11 **11:16** [f] Jer 21:14 [g] Isa 27:11; Ro 11:17-24 **11:17** [h] Isa 5:2; Jer 12:2 [i] Jer 7:9

Plot Against Jeremiah

18Because the LORD revealed their plot to
me, I knew it, for at that time he showed me
what they were doing. 19I had been like a
gentle lamb led to the slaughter; I did not
realize that they had plotted[j] against me,
saying,

"Let us destroy the tree and its fruit;
let us cut him off from the land of the living,[k]
that his name be remembered[l] no more."

20But you, LORD Almighty, who judge righteously
and test the heart and mind,[m]
let me see your vengeance on them,
for to you I have committed my cause.

21Therefore this is what the LORD says
about the people of Anathoth who are
threatening to kill you,[n] saying, "Do not
prophesy in the name of the LORD or you
will die[o] by our hands"— 22therefore this
is what the LORD Almighty says: "I will
punish them. Their young men[p] will die
by the sword, their sons and daughters by
famine. 23Not even a remnant[q] will be left
to them, because I will bring disaster on
the people of Anathoth in the year of their
punishment.[r]"

Jeremiah's Complaint

12 You are always righteous,[s] LORD,
when I bring a case before you.
Yet I would speak with you about your justice:
Why does the way of the wicked prosper?[t]
Why do all the faithless live at ease?

2You have planted[u] them, and they have taken root;
they grow and bear fruit.
You are always on their lips
but far from their hearts.[v]

3Yet you know me, LORD;
you see me and test[w] my thoughts about you.
Drag them off like sheep to be butchered!
Set them apart for the day of slaughter![x]

4How long will the land lie parched[y]
and the grass in every field be withered?[z]
Because those who live in it are wicked,
the animals and birds have perished.[a]
Moreover, the people are saying,
"He will not see what happens to us."

God's Answer

5"If you have raced with men on foot
and they have worn you out,
how can you compete with horses?
If you stumble[a] in safe country,
how will you manage in the thickets[b] by[b] the Jordan?

6Your relatives, members of your own family—
even they have betrayed you;
they have raised a loud cry against you.[c]
Do not trust them,
though they speak well of you.[d]

7"I will forsake my house,
abandon[e] my inheritance;
I will give the one I love
into the hands of her enemies.

8My inheritance has become to me
like a lion in the forest.
She roars at me;
therefore I hate her.[f]

9Has not my inheritance become to me
like a speckled bird of prey
that other birds of prey surround and attack?
Go and gather all the wild beasts;
bring them to devour.[g]

[a] 5 Or *you feel secure only* [b] 5 Or *the flooding of*

11:20 ***let me see your vengeance on them.*** Jeremiah appealed for vindication to God as the one true righteous judge. "Heart" refers to the seat of intellect and will. "Vengeance" describes God's fury and anger against sin that demands punishment.

11:21–23 ***the people of Anathoth.*** These people insisted that Jeremiah not prophesy in the name of the Lord. If Jeremiah had yielded to their demand, he would have repudiated his calling, his person, and his God. The threat of death to Jeremiah was answered by punishment of the young men as well as their children. The prediction of death by famine was fulfilled when the city was besieged by the Babylonians in the days of Zedekiah.

12:4 ***How long will the land lie parched.*** Jeremiah's question related to God's delay of judgment on the people of the land. "land lie parched ... grass in every field be withered ... animals and birds have perished" are phrases that are recurring themes in Jeremiah and other prophetic texts (4:28; 40:7; Zeph. 1:3). In spite of past chastisement, the people believed that God would not bring their country to an end.

12:5–6 ***If you have raced with men on foot.*** God's response to Jeremiah's question (v. 4) comes in the form of two metaphorical questions. The first metaphor of foot racing was designed to teach Jeremiah that the obstacles he faced in his hometown were meager compared to those he would encounter before the kings of Judah and Babylon (the horses). ***safe country.*** This second metaphor was designed to remind the prophet of the impending turmoil he would have to endure in proclaiming the message of judgment to an unrepentant leadership. The relatively peaceful setting of Anathoth, with its minor opposition from treacherous family members, served to prepare Jeremiah to struggle against greater antagonists.

11:19 [j] Jer 18:18; 20:10 [k] Job 28:13; Isa 53:8 [l] Ps 83:4 **11:20** [m] Ps 7:9 **11:21** [n] Jer 12:6 [o] Jer 26:8, 11; 38:4 **11:22** [p] Jer 18:21 **11:23** [q] Jer 6:9 [r] Jer 23:12 **12:1** [s] Ezr 9:15 [t] Jer 5:27-28 **12:2** [u] Jer 11:17 [v] Isa 29:13; Jer 3:10; Mt 15:8; Titus 1:16 **12:3** [w] Ps 7:9; 11:5; 139:1-4; Jer 11:20 [x] Jer 17:18 **12:4** [y] Jer 4:28 [z] Joel 1:10-12 [a] Jer 4:25; 9:10 **12:5** [b] Jer 49:19; 50:44 **12:6** [c] Pr 26:24-25; Jer 9:4 [d] Ps 12:2 **12:7** [e] Jer 7:29 **12:8** [f] Hos 9:15; Am 6:8 **12:9** [g] Isa 56:9; Jer 15:3; Eze 23:25

10 Many shepherds[h] will ruin my vineyard
and trample down my field;
they will turn my pleasant field
into a desolate wasteland.[i]
11 It will be made a wasteland,
parched and desolate before me;[j]
the whole land will be laid waste
because there is no one who cares.
12 Over all the barren heights in the desert
destroyers will swarm,
for the sword of the LORD[k] will devour
from one end of the land to the other;[l]
no one will be safe.
13 They will sow wheat but reap thorns;
they will wear themselves out but
gain nothing.[m]
They will bear the shame of their
harvest
because of the LORD's fierce anger."[n]

14 This is what the LORD says: "As for all
my wicked neighbors who seize the inheritance I gave my people Israel, I will uproot[o]
them from their lands and I will uproot the
people of Judah from among them. 15 But
after I uproot them, I will again have compassion and will bring[p] each of them back
to their own inheritance and their own
country. 16 And if they learn well the ways
of my people and swear by my name, saying, 'As surely as the LORD lives'[q]—even
as they once taught my people to swear
by Baal[r]—then they will be established
among my people.[s] 17 But if any nation does
not listen, I will completely uproot and destroy[t] it," declares the LORD.

A Linen Belt

13 This is what the LORD said to me: "Go
and buy a linen belt and put it around
your waist, but do not let it touch water."
2 So I bought a belt, as the LORD directed,
and put it around my waist.
3 Then the word of the LORD came to me
a second time: 4 "Take the belt you bought
and are wearing around your waist, and go
now to Perath[a] and hide it there in a crev-
ice in the rocks." 5 So I went and hid it at
Perath, as the LORD told me.[u]
6 Many days later the LORD said to me,
"Go now to Perath and get the belt I told
you to hide there." 7 So I went to Perath and
dug up the belt and took it from the place
where I had hidden it, but now it was ruined and completely useless.
8 Then the word of the LORD came to me:
9 "This is what the LORD says: 'In the same
way I will ruin the pride of Judah and the
great pride[v] of Jerusalem. 10 These wicked
people, who refuse to listen to my words,
who follow the stubbornness of their
hearts[w] and go after other gods[x] to serve
and worship them, will be like this belt—
completely useless! 11 For as a belt is bound
around the waist, so I bound all the people
of Israel and all the people of Judah to me,'
declares the LORD, 'to be my people for my
renown[y] and praise and honor.[z] But they
have not listened.'[a]

Wineskins

12 "Say to them: 'This is what the LORD,
the God of Israel, says: Every wineskin
should be filled with wine.' And if they say
to you, 'Don't we know that every wineskin should be filled with wine?' 13 then tell
them, 'This is what the LORD says: I am going to fill with drunkenness[b] all who live
in this land, including the kings who sit on
David's throne, the priests, the prophets
and all those living in Jerusalem. 14 I will
smash them one against the other, parents
and children alike, declares the LORD. I will
allow no pity or mercy or compassion[c] to
keep me from destroying[d] them.'"

[a] 4 Or possibly *to the Euphrates*; similarly in verses 5-7

12:10–11 ***Many shepherds.*** This phrase refers to the foreign kings who had come as agents of God to judge Judah. The repetition of the word "desolate" describes the complete devastation of Judah (Is. 6:11). Because of sin, the land that once saw God's bounteous blessing would experience His devastating judgment.
12:15 ***after I uproot them.*** This verse offers a glimmer of hope in the middle of a prophecy of judgment. In the midst of His judgment, God would remember His covenant with Abraham. Eventually He would return and have compassion on His people.
12:16 ***swear by my name.*** Only the everlasting love of God provides an answer to what God will do in a life that turns from an oath to a false god to an oath to serve the Lord. What unfathomable blessing can be ours from a God like this when we pledge our allegiance to Him. He asks our allegiance, and He asks us to truly learn the ways that He has established for His people.
13:1–5 ***linen belt.*** This was an article of clothing that was like a short skirt or kilt worn by men. Jeremiah was not supposed to wash it.
13:6–7 ***ruined and completely useless.*** Because Jeremiah's girdle was dirty and then was exposed to the elements, it was ruined and useless.
13:8–11 ***refuse to listen to my words ... follow the stubbornness of their hearts ... go after other gods.*** As Jeremiah's waistband was ruined, so Judah's pride would be reduced to ruin. Pride describes the self-exalting conduct that characterized Israel in its love for idols. This pride is explained in a triplet of verbal phrases.
13:14 ***I will smash them one against the other.*** The wine jars of God's wrath would be smashed and broken together, a picture of a devastated nation.

12:10 [h] Jer 23:1 [i] Isa 5:1-7 **12:11** [j] ver 4; Isa 42:25; Jer 23:10 **12:12** [k] Jer 47:6 [l] Jer 3:2 **12:13** [m] Lev 26:20; Dt 28:38; Mic 6:15; Hag 1:6 [n] Jer 4:26 **12:14** [o] Zec 2:7-9 **12:15** [p] Am 9:14-15 **12:16** [q] Jer 4:2 [r] Jos 23:7 [s] Isa 49:6; Jer 3:17 **12:17** [t] Isa 60:12 **13:5** [u] Ex 40:16 **13:9** [v] Lev 26:19 **13:10** [w] Jer 11:8; 16:12 [x] Jer 9:14 **13:11** [y] Jer 32:20; 33:9 [z] Ex 19:5-6 [a] Jer 7:26 **13:13** [b] Ps 60:3; 75:8; Isa 51:17; 63:6; Jer 51:57 **13:14** [c] Jer 16:5 [d] Dt 29:20; Eze 5:10

Threat of Captivity

15 Hear and pay attention,
do not be arrogant,
for the LORD has spoken.
16 Give glory[e] to the LORD your God
before he brings the darkness,
before your feet stumble[f]
on the darkening hills.
You hope for light,
but he will turn it to utter darkness
and change it to deep gloom.[g]
17 If you do not listen,[h]
I will weep in secret
because of your pride;
my eyes will weep bitterly,
overflowing with tears,[i]
because the LORD's flock[j] will be
taken captive.[k]

18 Say to the king and to the queen
mother,
"Come down from your thrones,
for your glorious crowns
will fall from your heads."
19 The cities in the Negev will be shut up,
and there will be no one to open
them.
All Judah[l] will be carried into exile,
carried completely away.

20 Look up and see
those who are coming from the
north.[m]
Where is the flock[n] that was entrusted
to you,
the sheep of which you boasted?
21 What will you say when the LORD sets
over you
those you cultivated as your special
allies?[o]
Will not pain grip you
like that of a woman in labor?[p]
22 And if you ask yourself,
"Why has this happened to me?"—
it is because of your many sins[q]
that your skirts have been torn off
and your body mistreated.[r]
23 Can an Ethiopian[a] change his skin
or a leopard its spots?
Neither can you do good
who are accustomed to doing evil.

24 "I will scatter you like chaff[s]
driven by the desert wind.[t]
25 This is your lot,
the portion[u] I have decreed for you,"
declares the LORD,
"because you have forgotten me
and trusted in false gods.
26 I will pull up your skirts over your face
that your shame may be seen[v]—
27 your adulteries and lustful neighings,
your shameless prostitution![w]
I have seen your detestable acts
on the hills and in the fields.[x]
Woe to you, Jerusalem!
How long will you be unclean?"[y]

Drought, Famine, Sword

14 This is the word of the LORD that came
to Jeremiah concerning the drought:
2 "Judah mourns,[z]
her cities languish;
they wail for the land,
and a cry goes up from Jerusalem.
3 The nobles send their servants for water;
they go to the cisterns
but find no water.[a]
They return with their jars unfilled;
dismayed and despairing,
they cover their heads.[b]
4 The ground is cracked
because there is no rain in the land;[c]
the farmers are dismayed
and cover their heads.
5 Even the doe in the field
deserts her newborn fawn
because there is no grass.[d]
6 Wild donkeys stand on the barren
heights[e]
and pant like jackals;
their eyes fail
for lack of food."

7 Although our sins testify[f] against us,
do something, LORD, for the sake of
your name.
For we have often rebelled;[g]
we have sinned[h] against you.

---

a 23 Hebrew *Cushite* (probably a person from the upper Nile region)

13:16 *Give glory to the LORD your God.* This means exalt and worship Him. The verse warns of the consequences of failing to glorify God. Four Hebrew synonyms for darkness are found in this verse, deepening the impression of divine displeasure meted out against God's people.
13:20 *those who are coming from the north.* This phrase refers to Babylon.
13:23 *Can an Ethiopian change his skin.* The negative rhetorical question confirmed Judah's inability to change its own ways. The nation had reinforced its habit of doing evil (4:22) for so long that it did not know how to do good.
13:26–27 *your skirts over your face.* This phrase meant public exposure (v. 22). Since Judah had lustfully sought adulterous relationships with foreign gods and goddesses, God would expose and bring to shame its actions.
14:2 *mourns.* This is a general word for grief over the dead. It describes the dark gloom of weeping and wailing.

13:16 [e] Jos 7:19 [f] Jer 23:12 [g] Isa 59:9 **13:17** [h] Mal 2:2 [i] Jer 9:1 [j] Ps 80:1; Jer 23:1 [k] Jer 14:18 **13:19** [l] Jer 20:4; 52:30 **13:20** [m] Jer 6:22; Hab 1:6 [n] Jer 23:2 **13:21** [o] Jer 38:22 [p] Jer 4:31 **13:22** [q] Jer 9:2-6; 16:10-12 [r] Eze 16:37; Na 3:5-6 **13:24** [s] Ps 1:4 [t] Lev 26:33 **13:25** [u] Job 20:29; Mt 24:51 **13:26** [v] La 1:8; Eze 16:37; Hos 2:10 **13:27** [w] Jer 2:20 [x] Eze 6:13 [y] Hos 8:5 **14:2** [z] Isa 3:26; Jer 8:21 **14:3** [a] 2Ki 18:31; Job 6:19-20 [b] 2Sa 15:30 **14:4** [c] Jer 3:3 **14:5** [d] Isa 15:6 **14:6** [e] Job 39:5-6; Jer 2:24 **14:7** [f] Hos 5:5 [g] Jer 5:6 [h] Jer 8:14

8 You who are the hope[i] of Israel,
its Savior in times of distress,
why are you like a stranger in the land,
like a traveler who stays only a night?
9 Why are you like a man taken by
surprise,
like a warrior powerless to save?[j]
You are among[k] us, LORD,
and we bear your name;[l]
do not forsake us!

10 This is what the LORD says about this
people:

"They greatly love to wander;
they do not restrain their feet.[m]
So the LORD does not accept[n] them;
he will now remember[o] their
wickedness
and punish them for their sins."[p]

11 Then the LORD said to me, "Do not
pray[q] for the well-being of this people. 12 Although they fast, I will not listen to their
cry;[r] though they offer burnt offerings[s] and
grain offerings, I will not accept[t] them. Instead, I will destroy them with the sword,
famine and plague."
13 But I said, "Alas, Sovereign LORD! The
prophets keep telling them, 'You will not
see the sword or suffer famine.[u] Indeed, I
will give you lasting peace in this place.'"
14 Then the LORD said to me, "The prophets are prophesying lies[v] in my name. I
have not sent[w] them or appointed them or
spoken to them. They are prophesying to
you false visions,[x] divinations,[y] idolatries[a]
and the delusions of their own minds.
15 Therefore this is what the LORD says
about the prophets who are prophesying
in my name: I did not send them, yet they
are saying, 'No sword or famine will touch
this land.' Those same prophets will perish[z] by sword and famine.[a] 16 And the people they are prophesying to will be thrown
out into the streets of Jerusalem because of
the famine and sword. There will be no one
to bury[b] them, their wives, their sons and
their daughters.[c] I will pour out on them the
calamity they deserve.[d]

17 "Speak this word to them:

"'Let my eyes overflow with tears[e]
night and day without ceasing;
for the Virgin Daughter, my people,
has suffered a grievous wound,
a crushing blow.[f]
18 If I go into the country,
I see those slain by the sword;
if I go into the city,
I see the ravages of famine.[g]
Both prophet and priest
have gone to a land they know not.'"

19 Have you rejected Judah completely?[h]
Do you despise Zion?
Why have you afflicted us
so that we cannot be healed?[i]
We hoped for peace
but no good has come,
for a time of healing
but there is only terror.[j]
20 We acknowledge our wickedness, LORD,
and the guilt of our ancestors;
we have indeed sinned[k] against you.
21 For the sake of your name[l] do not
despise us;
do not dishonor your glorious throne.[m]
Remember your covenant with us
and do not break it.
22 Do any of the worthless idols of the
nations bring rain?[n]
Do the skies themselves send down
showers?
No, it is you, LORD our God.
Therefore our hope is in you,
for you are the one who does all this.

15 Then the LORD said to me: "Even if
Moses[o] and Samuel[p] were to stand
before me, my heart would not go out to
this people.[q] Send them away from my
presence![r] Let them go! 2 And if they ask

[a] 14 Or *visions, worthless divinations*

14:8 ***hope ... Savior.*** Jeremiah pleaded with God on the basis of God's name and character. Instead of having an intimate relationship with Judah, God had become like a stranger or a traveler in the land, because the people worshiped other gods.

14:10 ***They greatly love to wander.*** "Love" describes voluntary desire. "Wander" describes a repetitive back and forth movement—in this case, of seeking every possible occasion for sin. Because no one displayed any restraint from sin, God could not violate His holy character and accept the people of Judah.

14:13 ***I will give you lasting peace.*** Jeremiah complained to the Lord about false prophets who were proclaiming a message of peace instead of war and pestilence. These pretentious prophets presumed upon God's mercy and promise of deliverance as demonstrated in the days of Hezekiah and Isaiah, when Jerusalem was miraculously rescued from the siege of Sennacherib's army.

14:21–22 ***For the sake of your name.*** The people's plea for God's mercy was based on His character. Entreaties based on divine character and attributes are common in the Psalms. At stake was God's reputation and the blessing that would come to the people, but here the obligations of the people to the Lord are disregarded.

15:2 ***death ... sword ... starvation ... captivity.*** These all would be the outcome of God's judgment. He would use foreign armies as instruments of judgment (14:11–12).

14:8 [i] Jer 17:13 **14:9** [j] Isa 50:2 [k] Jer 8:19 [l] Isa 63:19; Jer 15:16 **14:10** [m] Ps 119:101; Jer 2:25 [n] Jer 6:20; Am 5:22 [o] Hos 9:9 [p] Jer 44:21-23; Hos 8:13 **14:11** [q] Ex 32:10 **14:12** [r] Isa 1:15; Jer 11:11 [s] Jer 7:21 [t] Jer 6:20 **14:13** [u] Jer 5:12 **14:14** [v] Jer 27:14 [w] Jer 23:21,32 [x] Jer 23:16 [y] Eze 12:24 **14:15** [z] Eze 14:9 [a] Jer 5:12-13 **14:16** [b] Ps 79:3 [c] Jer 7:33 [d] Pr 1:31 **14:17** [e] Jer 9:1 [f] Jer 8:21 **14:18** [g] Eze 7:15 **14:19** [h] Jer 7:29 [i] Jer 30:12-13 [j] Jer 8:15 **14:20** [k] Da 9:7-8 **14:21** [l] ver 7 [m] Jer 3:17 **14:22** [n] Ps 135:7 **15:1** [o] Ex 32:11; Nu 14:13-20 [p] 1Sa 7:9 [q] Jer 7:16; Eze 14:14, 20 [r] 2Ki 17:20

you, 'Where shall we go?' tell them, 'This is what the LORD says:

"'Those destined for death, to death;
those for the sword, to the sword;[s]
those for starvation, to starvation;[t]
those for captivity, to captivity.'[u]

3"I will send four kinds of destroyers[v]
against them," declares the LORD, "the
sword to kill and the dogs to drag away and
the birds[w] and the wild animals to devour
and destroy.[x] 4I will make them abhorrent[y]
to all the kingdoms of the earth[z] because
of what Manasseh[a] son of Hezekiah king
of Judah did in Jerusalem.

5"Who will have pity[b] on you,
Jerusalem?
Who will mourn for you?
Who will stop to ask how you are?
6You have rejected[c] me," declares the
LORD.
"You keep on backsliding.
So I will reach out[d] and destroy you;
I am tired of holding back.
7I will winnow them with a winnowing
fork
at the city gates of the land.
I will bring bereavement and
destruction on my people,[e]
for they have not changed their
ways.
8I will make their widows more
numerous
than the sand of the sea.
At midday I will bring a destroyer[f]
against the mothers of their young
men;
suddenly I will bring down on them
anguish and terror.
9The mother of seven will grow faint[g]
and breathe her last.
Her sun will set while it is still day;
she will be disgraced and humiliated.
I will put the survivors to the sword[h]
before their enemies,"
declares the LORD.

10Alas, my mother, that you gave me
birth,[i]
a man with whom the whole land
strives and contends![j]
I have neither lent[k] nor borrowed,
yet everyone curses me.

11The LORD said,

"Surely I will deliver you[l] for a good
purpose;
surely I will make your enemies
plead[m] with you
in times of disaster and times of
distress.

12"Can a man break iron—
iron from the north[n]—or bronze?

13"Your wealth and your treasures
I will give as plunder, without charge,[o]
because of all your sins
throughout your country.[p]
14I will enslave you to your enemies
in[a] a land you do not know,[q]
for my anger will kindle a fire[r]
that will burn against you."

15LORD, you understand;
remember me and care for me.
Avenge me on my persecutors.[s]
You are long-suffering—do not take me
away;
think of how I suffer reproach for
your sake.[t]
16When your words came, I ate[u] them;
they were my joy and my heart's
delight,[v]
for I bear your name,[w]
LORD God Almighty.
17I never sat[x] in the company of revelers,
never made merry with them;
I sat alone because your hand was on me
and you had filled me with
indignation.

---

a 14 Some Hebrew manuscripts, Septuagint and Syriac (see also 17:4); most Hebrew manuscripts *I will cause your enemies to bring you / into*

15:3–4 *I will send four kinds of destroyers.* The judgment of Judah is described. The imagery of dogs, birds, and beasts devouring human flesh vividly illustrates not only death, but desecration. The basis for this desecration is the defilement of Jerusalem that took place during the reign of Manasseh, when idolatry reigned in the temple courts and children were sacrificed to Molek (7:31).
15:7–8 *winnow them with a winnowing fork.* Like wheat chaff that is scattered by the winnowing fork and the wind, the people of Judah would be dispersed. The population would be decimated. The further ravaging of the land is revealed in the numerous widows who would be left in the wake of the death of the men of Judah.
15:9 *The mother of seven.* The blessing of seven sons was the ultimate hope for ancient mothers and fathers. But the utmost horror was to lose all seven in death, resulting in the loss of one's heirs.
15:10 *yet everyone curses me.* To curse someone in ancient Israel was to invoke condemnation on that person with a prescribed formula.
15:16 *your words came, I ate them.* Eating the words of the Lord means to internalize them and allow their meaning to become a reality in one's life.
15:17 *I never sat in the company of revelers.* Jeremiah's isolation was the result of his obedience to the word and calling of God.

15:2 [s] Jer 43:11 [t] Jer 14:12 [u] Rev 13:10 **15:3** [v] Lev 26:16 [w] Dt 28:26 [x] Lev 26:22; Eze 14:21 **15:4** [y] Jer 24:9; 29:18 [z] Dt 28:25 [a] 2Ki 21:2; 23:26-27 **15:5** [b] Isa 51:19; Jer 13:14; 21:7; Na 3:7 **15:6** [c] Jer 6:19; 7:24 [d] Zep 1:4 **15:7** [e] Jer 18:21 **15:8** [f] Jer 6:4 **15:9** [g] 1Sa 2:5 [h] Jer 21:7 **15:10** [i] Job 3:1 [j] Jer 1:19 [k] Lev 25:36 **15:11** [l] Jer 40:4 [m] Jer 21:1-2; 37:3; 42:1-3 **15:12** [n] Jer 28:14 **15:13** [o] Ps 44:12 [p] Jer 17:3 **15:14** [q] Dt 28:36; Jer 16:13 [r] Dt 32:22; Ps 21:9 **15:15** [s] Jer 12:3 [t] Ps 69:7-9 **15:16** [u] Eze 3:3; Rev 10:10 [v] Ps 119:72, 103 [w] Jer 14:9 **15:17** [x] Ps 1:1; 26:4-5; Jer 16:8

[18]Why is my pain unending
and my wound grievous and
incurable?[y]
You are to me like a deceptive brook,
like a spring that fails.[z]

[19]Therefore this is what the LORD says:

"If you repent, I will restore you
that you may serve[a] me;
if you utter worthy, not worthless,
words,
you will be my spokesman.
Let this people turn to you,
but you must not turn to them.
[20]I will make you a wall to this people,
a fortified wall of bronze;
they will fight against you
but will not overcome you,
for I am with you
to rescue and save you,"[b]
declares the LORD.
[21]"I will save you from the hands of the
wicked
and deliver[c] you from the grasp of the
cruel."[d]

Day of Disaster

16 Then the word of the LORD came to
me: [2]"You must not marry[e] and have
sons or daughters in this place." [3]For this
is what the LORD says about the sons and
daughters born in this land and about the
women who are their mothers and the men
who are their fathers:[f] [4]"They will die of
deadly diseases. They will not be mourned
or buried[g] but will be like dung lying on
the ground.[h] They will perish by sword and
famine, and their dead bodies will become
food for the birds and the wild animals."[i]
[5]For this is what the LORD says: "Do not
enter a house where there is a funeral meal;
do not go to mourn or show sympathy, because I have withdrawn my blessing, my
love and my pity from this people," declares the LORD. [6]"Both high and low will
die in this land.[j] They will not be buried
or mourned, and no one will cut[k] themselves or shave[l] their head for the dead. [7]No
one will offer food to comfort those who
mourn[m] for the dead—not even for a father
or a mother—nor will anyone give them a
drink to console them.
[8]"And do not enter a house where there
is feasting and sit down to eat and drink.[n]
[9]For this is what the LORD Almighty, the
God of Israel, says: Before your eyes and in
your days I will bring an end to the sounds[o]
of joy and gladness and to the voices of
bride and bridegroom in this place.[p]
[10]"When you tell these people all this
and they ask you, 'Why has the LORD decreed such a great disaster against us?
What wrong have we done? What sin have
we committed against the LORD our God?'[q]
[11]then say to them, 'It is because your ancestors forsook me,' declares the LORD,
'and followed other gods and served and
worshiped them. They forsook me and did
not keep my law.[r] [12]But you have behaved
more wickedly than your ancestors.[s] See
how all of you are following the stubbornness of your evil hearts[t] instead of obeying
me. [13]So I will throw you out of this land
into a land neither you nor your ancestors
have known,[u] and there you will serve other gods[v] day and night, for I will show you
no favor.'[w]
[14]"However, the days are coming," declares the LORD, "when it will no longer
be said, 'As surely as the LORD lives, who
brought the Israelites up out of Egypt,'[x]
[15]but it will be said, 'As surely as the LORD
lives, who brought the Israelites up out
of the land of the north and out of all the
countries where he had banished them.'[y]
For I will restore[z] them to the land I gave
their ancestors.
[16]"But now I will send for many fishermen," declares the LORD, "and they will
catch them.[a] After that I will send for many
hunters, and they will hunt[b] them down on
every mountain and hill and from the crevices of the rocks.[c] [17]My eyes are on all their
ways; they are not hidden[d] from me, nor is
their sin concealed from my eyes.[e] [18]I will
repay them double[f] for their wickedness
and their sin, because they have defiled my
land[g] with the lifeless forms of their vile

15:18 *like a spring that fails.* This simile is a vivid picture of the arid regions in the Middle East, where water is at a premium.

16:1–2 *You must not marry.* In the case of Jeremiah, the prohibition against marriage was both a sign to the nation and a blight against his name among the people. Celibacy was abnormal; large families were indicative of God's blessing upon a household. Jeremiah faced life with God as his sole comfort and support.

16:10 *Why has the LORD decreed.* The trio of questions posed by the people indicates their lack of understanding of God's word. The people of Judah had missed the purpose for which they were chosen, to manifest to the world the nature and character of God by living as the people of God.

16:16 *many fishermen ... many hunters.* These words refer to the Babylonian armies that would scour the land for Judah's rebels. Hunting and fishing imagery as a metaphor for deportation is also found in Ezekiel 12:3 and Amos 4:2.

15:18 [y] Jer 30:15; Mic 1:9 [z] Job 6:15 **15:19** [a] Zec 3:7 **15:20** [b] Jer 20:11; Eze 3:8 **15:21** [c] Jer 50:34 [d] Ge 48:16 **16:2** [e] 1Co 7:26-27 **16:3** [f] Jer 6:21 **16:4** [g] Jer 25:33 [h] Ps 83:10; Jer 9:22 [i] Ps 79:1-3; Jer 15:3; 34:20 **16:6** [j] Eze 9:5-6 [k] Lev 19:28 [l] Jer 41:5; 47:5 **16:7** [m] Eze 24:17; Hos 9:4 **16:8** [n] Ecc 7:2-4; Jer 15:17 **16:9** [o] Isa 24:8; Eze 26:13; Hos 2:11 [p] Rev 18:23 **16:10** [q] Dt 29:24; Jer 5:19 **16:11** [r] Dt 29:25-26; 1Ki 9:9; Ps 106:35-43; Jer 22:9 **16:12** [s] Jer 7:26 [t] Ecc 9:3; Jer 13:10 **16:13** [u] Dt 28:36; Jer 5:19 [v] Dt 4:28 [w] Jer 15:5 **16:14** [x] Dt 15:15; Jer 23:7-8 **16:15** [y] Isa 11:11; Jer 23:8 [z] Jer 24:6 **16:16** [a] Am 4:2; Hab 1:14-15 [b] Am 9:3; Mic 7:2 [c] 1Sa 26:20 **16:17** [d] 1Co 4:5; Heb 4:13 [e] Pr 15:3 **16:18** [f] Isa 40:2; Rev 18:6 [g] Nu 35:34; Jer 2:7

images and have filled my inheritance with
their detestable idols."

19 LORD, my strength and my fortress,
my refuge in time of distress,
to you the nations will come[h]
from the ends of the earth and say,
"Our ancestors possessed nothing but
false gods,[i]
worthless idols that did them no good.
20 Do people make their own gods?
Yes, but they are not gods!"[j]

21 "Therefore I will teach them—
this time I will teach them
my power and might.
Then they will know
that my name is the LORD.

17 "Judah's sin is engraved with an iron
tool,[k]
inscribed with a flint point,
on the tablets of their hearts[l]
and on the horns of their altars.
2 Even their children remember
their altars and Asherah poles[a][m]
beside the spreading trees
and on the high hills.[n]
3 My mountain in the land
and your[b] wealth and all your
treasures
I will give away as plunder,[o]
together with your high places,[p]
because of sin throughout your
country.[q]
4 Through your own fault you will lose
the inheritance[r] I gave you.
I will enslave you to your enemies[s]
in a land[t] you do not know,
for you have kindled my anger,
and it will burn[u] forever."
5 This is what the LORD says:

"Cursed is the one who trusts in man,[v]
who draws strength from mere flesh
and whose heart turns away from the
LORD.
6 That person will be like a bush in the
wastelands;
they will not see prosperity when it
comes.
They will dwell in the parched places of
the desert,
in a salt[w] land where no one lives.
7 "But blessed is the one who trusts[x] in
the LORD,
whose confidence is in him.
8 They will be like a tree planted by the
water
that sends out its roots by the stream.
It does not fear when heat comes;
its leaves are always green.
It has no worries in a year of drought[y]
and never fails to bear fruit."[z]

9 The heart[a] is deceitful above all things
and beyond cure.
Who can understand it?

10 "I the LORD search the heart[b]
and examine the mind,[c]
to reward[d] each person according to
their conduct,
according to what their deeds
deserve."[e]

11 Like a partridge that hatches eggs it did
not lay
are those who gain riches by unjust
means.
When their lives are half gone, their
riches will desert them,
and in the end they will prove to be
fools.[f]

12 A glorious throne,[g] exalted from the
beginning,
is the place of our sanctuary.
13 LORD, you are the hope[h] of Israel;
all who forsake[i] you will be put to
shame.

a 2 That is, wooden symbols of the goddess Asherah *b* 2,3 Or *hills* / [3]*and the mountains of the land. / Your*

16:19–20 *strength ... fortress ... refuge.* Jeremiah knew that his only place of safety was in God. The scope of Jeremiah's hope is universal. The Gentiles, among whom the people of Judah would be exiled, would come to the God of Israel in fulfillment of the promise of Genesis 12:1–3.
17:3 *your high places, because of sin.* Jerusalem and the other cities of Judah were demolished and plundered by the Babylonians. The remaining treasures of the temple of God were carried by Nebuchadnezzar's army to Babylon. Even the idolatrous cultic centers were destroyed (15:13–14).
17:4 *will lose the inheritance.* This phrase, when used in the context of land, usually refers to letting the land lie fallow during the sabbatical year (Ex. 23:10–11). Judah's captivity would provide rest for the land from the idolatrous activities of its people.
17:5 *Cursed is the one.* One cannot trust in both God and humankind.
17:7 *blessed is the one who trusts in the LORD.* The basic element in a life of faith is stability. Man depending upon his own strength is unstable. But faith in God brings stability.
17:11 *Like a partridge that hatches eggs it did not lay.* The teaching of Jeremiah 17:1–10 is supported by a proverb based on the common belief that the partridge hatched eggs other than its own. When the young birds recognized that the partridge was not their mother, they would leave her. Similarly, a man who unjustly gains wealth will be abandoned by the wealth and then be known as a fool.
17:12–13 *A glorious throne.* This phrase refers to the temple in Jerusalem and the ark of the covenant,

16:19 [h] Isa 2:2; Jer 3:17 [i] Ps 4:2 **16:20** [j] Ps 115:4-7; Isa 37:19; Jer 2:11 **17:1** [k] Job 19:24 [l] Pr 3:3; 2Co 3:3 **17:2** [m] 2Ch 24:18 [n] Jer 2:20 **17:3** [o] 2Ki 24:13 [p] Jer 26:18; Mic 3:12 [q] Jer 15:13 **17:4** [r] La 5:2 [s] Dt 28:48; Jer 12:7 [t] Jer 16:13 [u] Jer 7:20; 15:14 **17:5** [v] Isa 2:22; 30:1-3 **17:6** [w] Dt 29:23; Job 39:6 **17:7** [x] Ps 34:8; 40:4; Pr 16:20 **17:8** [y] Jer 14:1-6 [z] Ps 1:3; 92:12-14 **17:9** [a] Ecc 9:3; Mt 13:15; Mk 7:21-22 **17:10** [b] 1Sa 16:7; Rev 2:23 [c] Ps 17:3; 139:23; Jer 11:20; 20:12; Ro 8:27 [d] Ps 62:12; Jer 32:19 [e] Ro 2:6 **17:11** [f] Lk 12:20 **17:12** [g] Jer 3:17 **17:13** [h] Jer 14:8 [i] Isa 1:28; Jer 2:17

Those who turn away from you will be written in the dust
because they have forsaken the LORD,
the spring of living water.

14 Heal me, LORD, and I will be healed;
save me and I will be saved,
for you are the one I praise.[j]
15 They keep saying to me,
"Where is the word of the LORD?
Let it now be fulfilled!"[k]
16 I have not run away from being your shepherd;
you know I have not desired the day of despair.
What passes my lips is open before you.
17 Do not be a terror[l] to me;
you are my refuge[m] in the day of disaster.
18 Let my persecutors be put to shame,
but keep me from shame;
let them be terrified,
but keep me from terror.
Bring on them the day of disaster;
destroy them with double destruction.[n]

Keeping the Sabbath Day Holy

19 This is what the LORD said to me:
"Go and stand at the Gate of the People,[a]
through which the kings of Judah go in and
out; stand also at all the other gates of Jerusalem.[o] 20 Say to them, 'Hear the word of
the LORD, you kings of Judah and all people
of Judah and everyone living in Jerusalem[p]
who come through these gates.[q] 21 This is
what the LORD says: Be careful not to carry a load on the Sabbath[r] day or bring it
through the gates of Jerusalem. 22 Do not
bring a load out of your houses or do any
work on the Sabbath, but keep the Sabbath
day holy, as I commanded your ancestors.[s]
23 Yet they did not listen or pay attention;[t]
they were stiff-necked[u] and would not listen or respond to discipline.[v] 24 But if you
are careful to obey me, declares the LORD,
and bring no load through the gates of this
city on the Sabbath, but keep the Sabbath
day holy by not doing any work on it, 25 then
kings who sit on David's throne[w] will come
through the gates of this city with their officials. They and their officials will come
riding in chariots and on horses, accompanied by the men of Judah and those living
in Jerusalem, and this city will be inhabited forever. 26 People will come from the
towns of Judah and the villages around
Jerusalem, from the territory of Benjamin
and the western foothills, from the hill
country and the Negev,[x] bringing burnt offerings and sacrifices, grain offerings and
incense, and bringing thank offerings to
the house of the LORD. 27 But if you do not
obey[y] me to keep the Sabbath day holy by
not carrying any load as you come through
the gates of Jerusalem on the Sabbath day,
then I will kindle an unquenchable fire[z] in
the gates of Jerusalem that will consume
her fortresses.'"[a]

At the Potter's House

18 This is the word that came to Jeremiah from the LORD: 2 "Go down to the
potter's house, and there I will give you
my message." 3 So I went down to the potter's house, and I saw him working at the
wheel. 4 But the pot he was shaping from
the clay was marred in his hands; so the
potter formed it into another pot, shaping
it as seemed best to him.
5 Then the word of the LORD came to me.
6 He said, "Can I not do with you, Israel, as
this potter does?" declares the LORD. "Like
clay[b] in the hand of the potter, so are you in
my hand, Israel. 7 If at any time I announce
that a nation or kingdom is to be uprooted,[c]
torn down and destroyed, 8 and if that nation I warned repents of its evil, then I will
relent[d] and not inflict on it the disaster[e] I
had planned. 9 And if at another time I announce that a nation or kingdom is to be
built[f] up and planted, 10 and if it does evil[g]
in my sight and does not obey me, then I
will reconsider[h] the good I had intended to
do for it.

---

[a] 19 Or *Army*

---

the symbol of God's presence and sovereignty over the nations.

17:17 ***Do not be a terror to me.*** This refers to physical, emotional, or mental horror.

17:18 ***Let my persecutors be put to shame.*** Jeremiah called for his persecutors to be ashamed and dismayed, to be dishonored and demoralized. The prophet also called upon the Lord to confirm the message of judgment in the day of doom and double destruction.

17:21–22 ***Be careful.*** This same phrasing is used in Deuteronomy 4:15 in a warning against idolatry. The sanctity of the Sabbath was a most serious matter. The Sabbath stood as a sign of creation and the covenant relationship between God and Israel.

18:4–6 ***was marred in his hands.*** The potter's vessel was marred and thus unsuitable for its intended purpose. The potter's remolding of the clay into an acceptable and unblemished work symbolized God's action in reforming Israel. The people had become marred and defiled and had to be reformed into a vessel fit to be identified with the Lord.

17:14 [j] Ps 109:1 **17:15** [k] Isa 5:19; 2Pe 3:4 **17:17** [l] Ps 88:15-16 [m] Jer 16:19; Na 1:7 **17:18** [n] Ps 35:1-8 **17:19** [o] Jer 7:2; 26:2 **17:20** [p] Jer 19:3 [q] Jer 22:2 **17:21** [r] Nu 15:32-36; Ne 13:15-21; Jn 5:10 **17:22** [s] Ex 20:8; 31:13; Isa 56:2-6; Eze 20:12 **17:23** [t] Jer 7:26 [u] Jer 19:15 [v] Jer 7:28 **17:25** [w] 2Sa 7:13; Isa 9:7; Jer 22:2, 4; Lk 1:32 **17:26** [x] Jer 32:44; 33:13; Zec 7:7 **17:27** [y] Jer 22:5 [z] Jer 7:20 [a] 2Ki 25:9; Am 2:5 **18:6** [b] Isa 45:9; Ro 9:20-21 **18:7** [c] Jer 1:10 **18:8** [d] Jer 26:13; Jnh 3:8-10 [e] Eze 18:21; Hos 11:8-9 **18:9** [f] Jer 1:10; 31:28 **18:10** [g] Eze 33:18 [h] 1Sa 2:29-30

11“Now therefore say to the people of Judah and those living in Jerusalem, ‘This
is what the LORD says: Look! I am preparing a disaster[i] for you and devising a plan
against you. So turn[j] from your evil ways,[k]
each one of you, and reform your ways and
your actions.’ 12But they will reply, ‘It’s no
use.[l] We will continue with our own plans;
we will all follow the stubbornness of our
evil hearts.’”

13Therefore this is what the LORD says:

“Inquire among the nations:
 Who has ever heard anything like
  this?[m]
A most horrible[n] thing has been done
 by Virgin Israel.
14Does the snow of Lebanon
 ever vanish from its rocky slopes?
Do its cool waters from distant sources
 ever stop flowing?[a]
15Yet my people have forgotten me;
 they burn incense to worthless idols,[o]
which made them stumble in their
  ways,
 in the ancient paths.[p]
They made them walk in byways,
 on roads not built up.[q]
16Their land will be an object of horror[r]
 and of lasting scorn;[s]
all who pass by will be appalled
 and will shake their heads.[t]
17Like a wind[u] from the east,
 I will scatter them before their
  enemies;
I will show them my back and not my
  face[v]
 in the day of their disaster.”

18They said, “Come, let’s make plans[w]
against Jeremiah; for the teaching of the
law by the priest[x] will not cease, nor will
counsel from the wise, nor the word from
the prophets.[y] So come, let’s attack him
with our tongues[z] and pay no attention to
anything he says.”

19Listen to me, LORD;
 hear what my accusers are saying!
20Should good be repaid with evil?
 Yet they have dug a pit[a] for me.
Remember that I stood before you
 and spoke in their behalf[b]
 to turn your wrath away from them.
21So give their children over to famine;[c]
 hand them over to the power of the
  sword.
Let their wives be made childless and
  widows;[d]
 let their men be put to death,
 their young men slain by the sword in
  battle.
22Let a cry[e] be heard from their houses
 when you suddenly bring invaders
  against them,
for they have dug a pit to capture me
 and have hidden snares[f] for my feet.
23But you, LORD, know
 all their plots to kill[g] me.
Do not forgive[h] their crimes
 or blot out their sins from your sight.
Let them be overthrown before you;
 deal with them in the time of your
  anger.

19 This is what the LORD says: “Go and
buy a clay jar from a potter.[i] Take
along some of the elders[j] of the people and
of the priests 2and go out to the Valley of
Ben Hinnom,[k] near the entrance of the
Potsherd Gate. There proclaim the words
I tell you, 3and say, ‘Hear the word of the
LORD, you kings[l] of Judah and people of Jerusalem. This is what the LORD Almighty,
the God of Israel, says: Listen! I am going
to bring a disaster[m] on this place that will
make the ears of everyone who hears of it
tingle.[n] 4For they have forsaken[o] me and
made this a place of foreign gods; they

[a] *14* The meaning of the Hebrew for this sentence is uncertain.

18:13–14 *Who has ever heard anything like this?* Negative rhetorical questions show the absurdity of Israel’s rebellion. ***snow of Lebanon.*** This describes the Mount Hermon watershed that erupts in numerous springs, providing most of the water for the Jordan River. God’s blessing was often demonstrated in the provision of water from rocks in arid regions (Ex. 17:6).
18:15 *burn incense to worthless idols.* Foreign deities such as Baal and Asherah were represented by empty and ineffective cultic figurines.
18:17 *Like a wind from the east.* This line refers to the scorching late-spring sirocco wind from the northern Arabian desert.
18:19–20 *they have dug a pit for me.* Jeremiah reminded the Lord how he had interceded for the people and had asked God to turn away His wrath and judgment. But instead of showing their appreciation for Jeremiah’s intervention, the people prepared his grave.
19:3 *Hear the word of the LORD.* This key word of the Deuteronomic code (Deut. 6:4) calls for a decision regarding the content of the message. ***ears of everyone who hears it tingle.*** This expression is used to refer to a harsh, ringing judgment announcement (1 Sam. 3:11).
19:4–5 *the blood of the innocent.* This phrase refers to the murderous act of child sacrifice (7:31). Human sacrifice was known among the Phoenicians, Moabites, and Canaanites. This abominable practice, performed in the name of religious worship, was explicitly forbidden in the covenant (Deut. 12:31).

18:11 [i] Jer 4:6 [j] 2Ki 17:13; Isa 1:16-19 [k] Jer 7:3 **18:12** [l] Isa 57:10; Jer 2:25 **18:13** [m] Isa 66:8; Jer 2:10 [n] Jer 5:30 **18:15** [o] Jer 10:15 [p] Jer 6:16 [q] Isa 57:14; 62:10 **18:16** [r] Jer 25:9 [s] Jer 19:8 [t] Ps 22:7 **18:17** [u] Jer 13:24 [v] Jer 2:27 **18:18** [w] Jer 11:19 [x] Mal 2:7 [y] Jer 5:13 [z] Ps 52:2 **18:20** [a] Ps 35:7; 57:6 [b] Ps 106:23 **18:21** [c] Jer 11:22 [d] Ps 109:9 **18:22** [e] Jer 6:26 [f] Ps 140:5 **18:23** [g] Jer 11:21 [h] Ps 109:14 **19:1** [i] Jer 18:2 [j] Nu 11:17 **19:2** [k] Jos 15:8 **19:3** [l] Jer 17:20 [m] Jer 6:19 [n] 1Sa 3:11 **19:4** [o] Dt 28:20; Isa 65:11

have burned incense[p] in it to gods that neither they nor their ancestors nor the kings
of Judah ever knew, and they have filled
this place with the blood of the innocent.[q]
5They have built the high places of Baal to
burn their children[r] in the fire as offerings
to Baal—something I did not command
or mention, nor did it enter my mind.[s] 6So
beware, the days are coming, declares the
LORD, when people will no longer call this
place Topheth or the Valley of Ben Hinnom,[t] but the Valley of Slaughter.[u]
7"'In this place I will ruin[a] the plans of
Judah and Jerusalem. I will make them
fall by the sword before their enemies,[v] at
the hands of those who want to kill them,
and I will give their carcasses[w] as food[x]
to the birds and the wild animals. 8I will
devastate this city and make it an object
of horror and scorn;[y] all who pass by will
be appalled and will scoff because of all its
wounds. 9I will make them eat[z] the flesh of
their sons and daughters, and they will eat
one another's flesh because their enemies[a]
will press the siege so hard against them to
destroy them.'
10"Then break the jar[b] while those who go
with you are watching, 11and say to them,
'This is what the LORD Almighty says: I will
smash[c] this nation and this city just as this
potter's jar is smashed and cannot be repaired. They will bury[d] the dead in Topheth
until there is no more room. 12This is what
I will do to this place and to those who live
here, declares the LORD. I will make this city
like Topheth. 13The houses[e] in Jerusalem
and those of the kings of Judah will be defiled like this place, Topheth—all the houses where they burned incense on the roofs
to all the starry hosts[f] and poured out drink
offerings[g] to other gods.'"
14Jeremiah then returned from Topheth,
where the LORD had sent him to prophesy, and
stood in the court[h] of the LORD's temple and
said to all the people, 15"This is what the LORD
Almighty, the God of Israel, says: 'Listen! I
am going to bring on this city and all the villages around it every disaster I pronounced
against them, because they were stiff-necked[i]
and would not listen to my words.'"

Jeremiah and Pashhur

20 When the priest Pashhur son of Immer,[j] the official[k] in charge of the
temple of the LORD, heard Jeremiah prophesying these things, 2he had Jeremiah the
prophet beaten[l] and put in the stocks[m] at the
Upper Gate of Benjamin[n] at the LORD's temple. 3The next day, when Pashhur released
him from the stocks, Jeremiah said to him,
"The LORD's name for you is not Pashhur,
but Terror on Every Side.[o] 4For this is what
the LORD says: 'I will make you a terror to
yourself and to all your friends; with your
own eyes[p] you will see them fall by the
sword of their enemies. I will give[q] all Judah into the hands of the king of Babylon,
who will carry[r] them away to Babylon or
put them to the sword. 5I will deliver all the
wealth[s] of this city into the hands of their
enemies—all its products, all its valuables
and all the treasures of the kings of Judah.
They will take it away[t] as plunder and carry it off to Babylon. 6And you, Pashhur, and
all who live in your house will go into exile
to Babylon. There you will die and be buried, you and all your friends to whom you
have prophesied[u] lies.'"

Jeremiah's Complaint

7You deceived[b] me, LORD, and I was
deceived[b];
you overpowered me and prevailed.
I am ridiculed all day long;
everyone mocks me.

---

[a] 7 The Hebrew for *ruin* sounds like the Hebrew for *jar* (see verses 1 and 10). [b] 7 Or *persuaded*

19:9 *I will make them eat the flesh of their sons.* The gruesome practice of cannibalism appears, recalling the words of Deuteronomy 28:53. After years of siege resulting in severe famine, the people would resort to eating human flesh in order to survive. This prophecy was literally fulfilled in 586 B.C. when Nebuchadnezzar invaded Judah, and again in A.D. 70 when Titus destroyed Jerusalem.

20:1 *Pashhur ... the official in charge of the temple.* A person in this position had to be a priest. He had oversight of the temple, the temple guards, entry into the courts, and so on. Jeremiah's proclamations against the city and the temple were of grave concern to Pashhur because of the threat to the continuation of the cult in which he was involved.

20:2 *Upper Gate of Benjamin.* This portal provided access into the temple courtyards from the north, the direction of Benjamin's territory.

20:3–4 *Terror on Every Side.* As Pashhur had been a terror to Jeremiah, so he would become a terror to himself, his family, and his associates.

20:6 *Pashhur, and all who live in your house.* Pashhur's whole family and his close associates, who had opposed Jeremiah, would be deported to Babylon because Pashhur had prophesied lies. Pashhur apparently had announced that Jerusalem would not suffer destruction.

20:7 *You deceived me, LORD, and I was deceived.* A play on words is intended by using two forms of the same word, which means "to deceive." Jeremiah claimed that the Lord had seduced him and that he had succumbed to the temptation.

19:4 [p] Lev 18:21 [q] 2Ki 21:16; Jer 2:34 **19:5** [r] Lev 18:21; Ps 106:37-38 [s] Jer 7:31; 32:35 **19:6** [t] Jos 15:8 [u] Jer 7:32 **19:7** [v] Lev 26:17; Dt 28:25 [w] Jer 16:4; 34:20 [x] Ps 79:2 **19:8** [y] Jer 18:16 **19:9** [z] Lev 26:29; Dt 28:49-57; La 4:10 [a] Isa 9:20 **19:10** [b] ver 1 **19:11** [c] Ps 2:9; Isa 30:14 [d] Jer 7:32 **19:13** [e] Jer 32:29; 52:13 [f] Dt 4:19; Ac 7:42 [g] Jer 7:18; Eze 20:28 **19:14** [h] 2Ch 20:5; Jer 26:2 **19:15** [i] Ne 9:16; Jer 7:26; 17:23 **20:1** [j] 1Ch 24:14 [k] 2Ki 25:18 **20:2** [l] Jer 1:19 [m] Job 13:27 [n] Jer 37:13; 38:7; Zec 14:10 **20:3** [o] ver 10 **20:4** [p] Jer 29:21 [q] Jer 21:10 [r] Jer 52:27 **20:5** [s] Jer 17:3 [t] 2Ki 20:17 **20:6** [u] Jer 14:15; La 2:14

8 Whenever I speak, I cry out
proclaiming violence and
destruction.[v]
So the word of the LORD has
brought me
insult and reproach[w] all day long.
9 But if I say, "I will not mention his word
or speak anymore in his name,"
his word is in my heart like a fire,[x]
a fire shut up in my bones.
I am weary of holding it in;[y]
indeed, I cannot.
10 I hear many whispering,
"Terror[z] on every side!
Denounce[a] him! Let's denounce him!"
All my friends[b]
are waiting for me to slip,[c] saying,
"Perhaps he will be deceived;
then we will prevail[d] over him
and take our revenge on him."

11 But the LORD[e] is with me like a mighty
warrior;
so my persecutors[f] will stumble and
not prevail.[g]
They will fail and be thoroughly
disgraced;[h]
their dishonor will never be forgotten.
12 LORD Almighty, you who examine the
righteous
and probe the heart and mind,[i]
let me see your vengeance[j] on them,
for to you I have committed[k] my
cause.

13 Sing to the LORD!
Give praise to the LORD!
He rescues[l] the life of the needy
from the hands of the wicked.

14 Cursed be the day I was born![m]
May the day my mother bore me not
be blessed!
15 Cursed be the man who brought my
father the news,
who made him very glad, saying,
"A child is born to you—a son!"
16 May that man be like the towns[n]
the LORD overthrew without pity.
May he hear wailing in the morning,
a battle cry at noon.
17 For he did not kill me in the womb,[o]
with my mother as my grave,
her womb enlarged forever.
18 Why did I ever come out of the womb
to see trouble and sorrow
and to end my days in shame?[p]

God Rejects Zedekiah's Request

21 The word came to Jeremiah from
the LORD when King Zedekiah[q] sent
to him Pashhur[r] son of Malkijah and the
priest Zephaniah[s] son of Maaseiah. They
said: 2 "Inquire[t] now of the LORD for us because Nebuchadnezzar[a][u] king of Babylon
is attacking us. Perhaps the LORD will perform wonders[v] for us as in times past so
that he will withdraw from us."
3 But Jeremiah answered them, "Tell
Zedekiah, 4 'This is what the LORD, the
God of Israel, says: I am about to turn[w]
against you the weapons of war that are
in your hands, which you are using to fight
the king of Babylon and the Babylonians[b]
who are outside the wall besieging[x] you.
And I will gather them inside this city. 5 I
myself will fight against you with an outstretched hand[y] and a mighty arm in furious anger and in great wrath. 6 I will strike
down those who live in this city—both
man and beast—and they will die of a
terrible plague.[z] 7 After that, declares the
LORD, I will give Zedekiah[a] king of Judah,
his officials and the people in this city who
survive the plague, sword and famine, into
the hands of Nebuchadnezzar king of Babylon[b] and to their enemies who want to kill
them. He will put them to the sword; he
will show them no mercy or pity or compassion.'[c]
8 "Furthermore, tell the people, 'This
is what the LORD says: See, I am setting

[a] 2 Hebrew *Nebuchadrezzar,* of which *Nebuchadnezzar* is a variant; here and often in Jeremiah and Ezekiel [b] 4 Or *Chaldeans;* also in verse 9

20:8 *insult and reproach.* Jeremiah had faithfully proclaimed the Lord's word of judgment and destruction, but the prophecy had not been fulfilled, thus opening the prophet up to criticism.
20:11 *the LORD is with me.* In order for a prophet to endure the pain and suffering that goes with the job, he needs to be aware of God's presence, power and approval.
20:12 *you who examine the righteous.* God tests (6:27; 17:10) and judges the righteous, those who walk uprightly in His ways and truth.
20:14–15 *Cursed be the day.* In ancient Israel, to curse God or one's parents was an offense punishable by death. Jeremiah avoided committing a capital offense by cursing his conception and birth, and hence his call from God.
21:2 *Inquire now of the LORD.* This phrase means to seek His will.
21:5 *with an outstretched hand.* Because the people of Judah had become God's enemies, God would fight against them. The divine instruments by which Israel had gained freedom from Egypt (Ex. 15:6; Deut. 6:21) and deliverance from their enemies would be used against them.
21:8–9 *the way of life and the way of death.* Death would come to those who attempted to

20:8 [v] Jer 6:7 [w] 2Ch 36:16; Jer 6:10 **20:9** [x] Ps 39:3 [y] Job 32:18-20; Ac 4:20 **20:10** [z] Ps 31:13; Jer 6:25 [a] Isa 29:21 [b] Ps 41:9 [c] Lk 11:53-54 [d] 1Ki 19:2 **20:11** [e] Jer 1:8; Ro 8:31 [f] Jer 17:18 [g] Jer 15:20 [h] Jer 23:40 **20:12** [i] Jer 17:10 [j] Ps 54:7; 59:10 [k] Ps 62:8; Jer 11:20 **20:13** [l] Ps 35:10 **20:14** [m] Job 3:3; Jer 15:10 **20:16** [n] Ge 19:25 **20:17** [o] Job 10:18-19 **20:18** [p] Ps 90:9 **21:1** [q] 2Ki 24:18; Jer 52:1 [r] Jer 38:1 [s] 2Ki 25:18; Jer 29:25; 37:3 **21:2** [t] Jer 37:3,7 [u] 2Ki 25:1 [v] Ps 44:1-4; Jer 32:17 **21:4** [w] Jer 32:5 [x] Jer 37:8-10 **21:5** [y] Jer 6:12 **21:6** [z] Jer 14:12 **21:7** [a] 2Ki 25:7; Jer 52:9 [b] Jer 37:17; 39:5 [c] 2Ch 36:17; Eze 7:9; Hab 1:6

before you the way of life and the way of
death. 9Whoever stays in this city will die
by the sword, famine or plague.[d] But whoever goes out and surrenders to the Babylonians who are besieging you will live; they
will escape with their lives.[e] 10I have determined to do this city harm[f] and not good,
declares the LORD. It will be given into the
hands[g] of the king of Babylon, and he will
destroy it with fire.'[h]

11"Moreover, say to the royal house[i] of Judah, 'Hear the word of the LORD. 12This is
what the LORD says to you, house of David:

"'Administer justice[j] every morning;
  rescue from the hand of the oppressor
  the one who has been robbed,
or my wrath will break out and burn like
    fire
  because of the evil you have done—
  burn with no one to quench[k] it.
13 I am against[l] you, Jerusalem,
  you who live above this valley[m]
  on the rocky plateau, declares the
    LORD—
you who say, "Who can come
    against us?
  Who can enter our refuge?"[n]
14 I will punish you as your deeds[o] deserve,
  declares the LORD.
I will kindle a fire[p] in your forests[q]
  that will consume everything around
    you.'"

Judgment Against Wicked Kings

22 This is what the LORD says: "Go
down to the palace of the king of
Judah and proclaim this message there:
2'Hear the word of the LORD to you, king
of Judah, you who sit on David's throne[r]—
you, your officials and your people who
come through these gates.[s] 3This is what
the LORD says: Do what is just[t] and right.
Rescue from the hand of the oppressor[u] the
one who has been robbed. Do no wrong or
violence to the foreigner, the fatherless or
the widow,[v] and do not shed innocent blood
in this place. 4For if you are careful to carry out these commands, then kings[w] who
sit on David's throne will come through
the gates of this palace, riding in chariots
and on horses, accompanied by their officials and their people. 5But if you do not
obey[x] these commands, declares the LORD,
I swear[y] by myself that this palace will become a ruin.'"

6For this is what the LORD says about the
palace of the king of Judah:

"Though you are like Gilead to me,
  like the summit of Lebanon,
I will surely make you like a
    wasteland,[z]
  like towns not inhabited.
7 I will send destroyers[a] against you,
  each man with his weapons,
and they will cut[b] up your fine cedar
    beams
  and throw them into the fire.

8"People from many nations will pass
by this city and will ask one another, 'Why
has the LORD done such a thing to this great
city?'[c] 9And the answer will be: 'Because
they have forsaken the covenant of the
LORD their God and have worshiped and
served other gods.[d]'"

10 Do not weep for the dead[e] king or
    mourn[f] his loss;
  rather, weep bitterly for him who is
    exiled,
because he will never return
  nor see his native land again.

---

survive the siege of Jerusalem; life was possible through surrender to the Chaldeans (Babylonians).

21:10 *I have determined.* This phrase describes the fixed intention of God, which in this context was against Jerusalem. The result would be adversity rather than good.

21:13 *come against us.* Attacking armies generally approached Jerusalem from the north along an elevated ridge.

22:1 *Go ... king of Judah ... proclaim this message.* This is the first of three messages directed at specific kings of Judah. Shallum, the fourth son of Josiah, was placed on the throne by the people of Judah, but he was dethroned after three months by Pharaoh Necho. Shallum was imprisoned and taken captive to Egypt (2 Chr. 36:1–4). Eliakim (Jehoiakim), Shallum's brother, was placed on the throne as an Egyptian vassal. Necho maintained control of Palestine until Nebuchadnezzar defeated Egypt at the Battle of Carchemish in 605 B.C. Shallum died without returning from Egypt, in fulfillment of Jeremiah's prophecy.

22:2 *who sit on David's throne.* Jeremiah's prophecy was addressed to three groups: the kings who are of David's lineage, the kings' servants, and "your people who come through these gates." The last phrase may refer to the citizens in general or to personnel who regularly entered the palace gates.

22:3 *Do what is just and right.* For all practical purposes these two terms are synonymous. One could not have one without the other.

22:6–7 *Gilead ... Lebanon.* The territories were sources for timber for the royal palaces. These luxurious residences would be reduced to deserted wilderness and set ablaze if the kings disobeyed the covenant.

22:9 *worshiped ... other gods.* The pagan nations would recognize that the destruction of Jerusalem was the result of Judah's violation of its covenant with God. The people of Judah had exchanged their God for alien deities, whom they worshiped and served.

21:9 [d] Jer 14:12 [e] Jer 38:2, 17; 39:18; 45:5 **21:10** [f] Jer 44:11, 27; Am 9:4 [g] Jer 32:28; 38:2-3 [h] Jer 52:13 **21:11** [i] Jer 13:18 **21:12** [j] Jer 22:3 [k] Isa 1:31 **21:13** [l] Eze 13:8 [m] Ps 125:2 [n] Jer 49:4; Ob 1:3-4 **21:14** [o] Isa 3:10-11 [p] 2Ch 36:19; Jer 52:13 [q] Eze 20:47 **22:2** [r] Jer 17:25; Lk 1:32 [s] Jer 17:20 **22:3** [t] Mic 6:8; Zec 7:9 [u] Ps 72:4; Jer 21:12 [v] Ex 22:22 **22:4** [w] Jer 17:25 **22:5** [x] Jer 17:27 [y] Heb 6:13 **22:6** [z] Mic 3:12 **22:7** [a] Jer 4:7 [b] Isa 10:34 **22:8** [c] Dt 29:25-26; 1Ki 9:8-9; Jer 16:10-11 **22:9** [d] 2Ki 22:17; 2Ch 34:25 **22:10** [e] Ecc 4:2 [f] ver 18

11For this is what the LORD says about Shallum[a][g] son of Josiah, who succeeded his father as king of Judah but has gone from
this place: "He will never return. 12He will
die[h] in the place where they have led him
captive; he will not see this land again."

13"Woe to him who builds[i] his palace by
unrighteousness,
his upper rooms by injustice,
making his own people work for
nothing,
not paying[j] them for their labor.
14He says, 'I will build myself a great
palace[k]
with spacious upper rooms.'
So he makes large windows in it,
panels it with cedar[l]
and decorates it in red.

15"Does it make you a king
to have more and more cedar?
Did not your father have food and
drink?
He did what was right and just,[m]
so all went well[n] with him.
16He defended the cause of the poor and
needy,[o]
and so all went well.
Is that not what it means to know me?"
declares the LORD.
17"But your eyes and your heart
are set only on dishonest gain,
on shedding innocent blood[p]
and on oppression and extortion."

18Therefore this is what the LORD says
about Jehoiakim son of Josiah king of Judah:

"They will not mourn for him:
'Alas, my brother! Alas, my sister!'
They will not mourn for him:
'Alas, my master! Alas, his
splendor!'
19He will have the burial of a donkey—
dragged away and thrown[q]
outside the gates of Jerusalem."

20"Go up to Lebanon and cry out,
let your voice be heard in Bashan,
cry out from Abarim,[r]
for all your allies are crushed.
21I warned you when you felt secure,
but you said, 'I will not listen!'
This has been your way from your
youth;[s]
you have not obeyed[t] me.
22The wind will drive all your shepherds
away,
and your allies will go into exile.
Then you will be ashamed and
disgraced
because of all your wickedness.
23You who live in 'Lebanon,[b]'
who are nestled in cedar
buildings,
how you will groan when pangs come
upon you,
pain[u] like that of a woman in
labor!

24"As surely as I live," declares the LORD,
"even if you, Jehoiachin[c][v] son of Jehoiakim king of Judah, were a signet ring on
my right hand, I would still pull you off.
25I will deliver[w] you into the hands of those
who want to kill you, those you fear—Nebuchadnezzar king of Babylon and the Babylonians.[d] 26I will hurl[x] you and the mother
who gave you birth into another country,
where neither of you was born, and there
you both will die. 27You will never come
back to the land you long to return to."

28Is this man Jehoiachin a despised,
broken pot,[y]
an object no one wants?
Why will he and his children be hurled[z]
out,
cast into a land[a] they do not know?
29O land,[b] land, land,
hear the word of the LORD!
30This is what the LORD says:
"Record this man as if childless,[c]
a man who will not prosper[d] in his
lifetime,
for none of his offspring will prosper,
none will sit on the throne[e] of David
or rule anymore in Judah."

---

[a] *11* Also called *Jehoahaz* [b] *23* That is, the palace in Jerusalem (see 1 Kings 7:2)
[c] *24* Hebrew *Koniah,* a variant of *Jehoiachin;* also in verse 28 [d] *25* Or *Chaldeans*

22:13 *not paying them for their labor.* The king was supposed to be the guardian of his people, but Jehoiakim enslaved his fellow Israelites to build his self-aggrandizing palaces.

22:18–19 *He will have the burial of a donkey.* A king of such despicable character as Jehoiakim deserved no lament. Instead of proper funeral rites due a king, Jehoiakim would receive an ignoble burial, like an animal, alone and unlamented.

22:22–23 *The wind will drive all your shepherds away.* The winds of adversity and invasion would carry off Judah's leaders and allies alike. The nation would be ashamed that it had entered into such futile associations.

22:24–27 *Jehoiachin.* Jehoiachin succeeded his father in 598 B.C. under the threat of siege from Babylon as a result of Jehoiakim's rebellion. Jehoiachin reigned for three months until he and his family were exiled to Babylon by Nebuchadnezzar (2 Kin. 24:6–16). Eventually Jehoiachin was released from prison after the death of Nebuchadnezzar.

22:11 [g] 2Ki 23:31 **22:12** [h] 2Ki 23:34 **22:13** [i] Mic 3:10; Hab 2:9 [j] Lev 19:13; Jas 5:4 **22:14** [k] Isa 5:8-9 [l] 2Sa 7:2 **22:15** [m] 2Ki 23:25 [n] Ps 128:2; Isa 3:10 **22:16** [o] Ps 72:1-4, 12-13 **22:17** [p] 2Ki 24:4 **22:19** [q] Jer 36:30 **22:20** [r] Nu 27:12 **22:21** [s] Jer 3:25; 32:30 [t] Jer 7:23-28 **22:23** [u] Jer 4:31 **22:24** [v] 2Ki 24:6, 8; Jer 37:1 **22:25** [w] 2Ki 24:16; Jer 34:20 **22:26** [x] 2Ki 24:8; 2Ch 36:10 **22:28** [y] Ps 31:12; Jer 48:38; Hos 8:8 [z] Jer 15:1 [a] Jer 17:4 **22:29** [b] Jer 6:19; Mic 1:2 **22:30** [c] 1Ch 3:18; Mt 1:12 [d] Jer 10:21 [e] Ps 94:20

The Righteous Branch

23 "Woe to the shepherds[f] who are destroying and scattering[g] the sheep of
my pasture!"[h] declares the LORD. 2There-
fore this is what the LORD, the God of Israel,
says to the shepherds who tend my people:
"Because you have scattered my flock and
driven them away and have not bestowed
care on them, I will bestow punishment on
you for the evil[i] you have done," declares
the LORD. 3"I myself will gather the remnant[j] of my flock out of all the countries
where I have driven them and will bring
them back to their pasture, where they will
be fruitful and increase in number. 4I will
place shepherds[k] over them who will tend
them, and they will no longer be afraid[l] or
terrified, nor will any be missing,[m]" declares the LORD.

5"The days are coming," declares the
LORD,
"when I will raise up for David[a] a
righteous Branch,[n]
a King who will reign[o] wisely
and do what is just and right[p] in the
land.
6In his days Judah will be saved
and Israel will live in safety.
This is the name[q] by which he will be
called:
The LORD Our Righteous
Savior.[r]

7"So then, the days are coming," declares
the LORD, "when people will no longer say,
'As surely as the LORD lives, who brought
the Israelites up out of Egypt,'[s] 8but they
will say, 'As surely as the LORD lives, who
brought the descendants of Israel up out
of the land of the north and out of all the
countries where he had banished them.'
Then they will live in their own land."[t]

Lying Prophets

9Concerning the prophets:

My heart is broken within me;
all my bones tremble.
I am like a drunken man,
like a strong man overcome by wine,
because of the LORD
and his holy words.[u]
10The land is full of adulterers;[v]
because of the curse[b] the land lies
parched
and the pastures[w] in the wilderness
are withered.[x]
The prophets follow an evil course
and use their power unjustly.

11"Both prophet and priest are godless;[y]
even in my temple[z] I find their
wickedness,"
declares the LORD.
12"Therefore their path will become
slippery;[a]
they will be banished to darkness
and there they will fall.
I will bring disaster on them
in the year they are punished,[b]"
declares the LORD.

13"Among the prophets of Samaria
I saw this repulsive thing:
They prophesied by Baal[c]
and led my people Israel astray.
14And among the prophets of Jerusalem
I have seen something horrible:[d]
They commit adultery and live a lie.[e]
They strengthen the hands of
evildoers,[f]
so that not one of them turns from
their wickedness.
They are all like Sodom[g] to me;
the people of Jerusalem are like
Gomorrah."[h]

15Therefore this is what the LORD Almighty says concerning the prophets:

"I will make them eat bitter food
and drink poisoned water,[i]
because from the prophets of Jerusalem
ungodliness has spread throughout
the land."

[a] 5 Or *up from David's line* [b] 10 Or *because of these things*

23:3 *I myself will gather the remnant.* The kings of Israel had caused the dispersion of the nation; but the Lord would mercifully bring about the restoration of the remnant. This concept was a popular one with many of the prophets. (Is. 1:9; 10:20–23). The blessing of restoration and prosperity as a consequence of repentance is outlined in Deuteronomy 30:1–10.

23:5 *a righteous Branch.* Beginning with Isaiah 4:2 this term is used of the promised Messiah (33:15; Zech. 3:8). This great king will reign with justice and righteousness. This ideal was founded on God's promise to David (2 Sam. 7:16).

23:7–8 *the days are coming.* The future restoration of Israel would exceed anything in the past; it would surpass even the first exodus, the deliverance from Egypt.

23:9–10 *My heart is broken within me.* Jeremiah's dismay over the false prophets weakened him mentally and physically, so much so that he felt drunken from the inner turmoil.

23:15 *I will make them eat bitter food.* This word refers to bitterness and death by poison. According to Deuteronomy 18:20, the consequence of false prophecy was death.

23:1 [f] Jer 10:21; Eze 34:1-10; Zec 11:15-17 [g] Isa 56:11 [h] Eze 34:31 **23:2** [i] Jer 21:12 **23:3** [j] Isa 11:10-12; Jer 32:37; Eze 34:11-16 **23:4** [k] Jer 3:15; 31:10; Eze 34:23 [l] Jer 30:10; 46:27-28 [m] Jn 6:39 **23:5** [n] Isa 4:2 [o] Isa 9:7 [p] Isa 11:1; Zec 6:12 **23:6** [q] Jer 33:16; Mt 1:21-23 [r] Ro 3:21-22; 1Co 1:30 **23:7** [s] Jer 16:14 **23:8** [t] Isa 43:5-6; Am 9:14-15 **23:9** [u] Jer 20:8-9 **23:10** [v] Jer 9:2 [w] Ps 107:34; Jer 9:10 [x] Hos 4:2-3 **23:11** [y] Jer 6:13; 8:10; Zep 3:4 [z] Jer 7:10 **23:12** [a] Ps 35:6; Jer 13:16 [b] Jer 11:23 **23:13** [c] Jer 2:8 **23:14** [d] Jer 5:30 [e] Jer 29:23 [f] Eze 13:22 [g] Ge 18:20 [h] Isa 1:9-10; Jer 20:16 **23:15** [i] Jer 8:14; 9:15

16This is what the LORD Almighty says:

“Do not listen[j] to what the prophets are
prophesying to you;
they fill you with false hopes.
They speak visions[k] from their own
minds,
not from the mouth[l] of the LORD.
17 They keep saying to those who despise
me,
‘The LORD says: You will have
peace.’[m]
And to all who follow the stubbornness[n]
of their hearts
they say, ‘No harm[o] will come to you.’
18 But which of them has stood in the
council of the LORD
to see or to hear his word?
Who has listened and heard his
word?
19 See, the storm[p] of the LORD
will burst out in wrath,
a whirlwind swirling down
on the heads of the wicked.
20 The anger[q] of the LORD will not turn
back[r]
until he fully accomplishes
the purposes of his heart.
In days to come
you will understand it clearly.
21 I did not send[s] these prophets,
yet they have run with their message;
I did not speak to them,
yet they have prophesied.
22 But if they had stood in my council,
they would have proclaimed my
words to my people
and would have turned[t] them from their
evil ways
and from their evil deeds.

23 “Am I only a God nearby,[u]”
declares the LORD,
“and not a God far away?
24 Who can hide[v] in secret places
so that I cannot see them?”
declares the LORD.
“Do not I fill heaven and earth?”[w]
declares the LORD.

25“I have heard what the prophets say
who prophesy lies[x] in my name. They say,
‘I had a dream![y] I had a dream!’ 26How long
will this continue in the hearts of these lying prophets, who prophesy the delusions[z]
of their own minds? 27They think the
dreams they tell one another will make my
people forget[a] my name, just as their ancestors forgot[b] my name through Baal worship. 28Let the prophet who has a dream
recount the dream, but let the one who has
my word speak it faithfully. For what has
straw to do with grain?” declares the LORD.
29“Is not my word like fire,”[c] declares the
LORD, “and like a hammer that breaks a
rock in pieces?
30“Therefore,” declares the LORD, “I am
against[d] the prophets[e] who steal from one
another words supposedly from me. 31Yes,”
declares the LORD, “I am against the prophets who wag their own tongues and yet
declare, ‘The LORD declares.’[f] 32Indeed,
I am against those who prophesy false
dreams,[g]” declares the LORD. “They tell
them and lead my people astray with their
reckless lies, yet I did not send or appoint
them. They do not benefit[h] these people in
the least,” declares the LORD.

False Prophecy

33“When these people, or a prophet or a
priest, ask you, ‘What is the message[i] from
the LORD?’ say to them, ‘What message? I
will forsake[j] you, declares the LORD.’ 34If a
prophet or a priest or anyone else claims,
‘This is a message[k] from the LORD,’ I will
punish[l] them and their household. 35This
is what each of you keeps saying to your
friends and other Israelites: ‘What is the
LORD’s answer?’[m] or ‘What has the LORD
spoken?’ 36But you must not mention ‘a
message from the LORD’ again, because
each one’s word becomes their own message. So you distort[n] the words of the living
God, the LORD Almighty, our God. 37This is
what you keep saying to a prophet: ‘What is
the LORD’s answer to you?’ or ‘What has the
LORD spoken?’ 38Although you claim, ‘This
is a message from the LORD,’ this is what

23:16 *visions from their own minds.* Visions were commonly understood to be a means of receiving a message from God (or the gods). The term *vision* used here and in Jeremiah 14:14 is also found in Daniel 1:17 and 8:1; plus it is used in other prophetic books to describe a divine revelation (Is. 1:1; Mic. 3:6).

23:19 *the storm of the LORD.* This is a symbol of God’s judgment (Is. 29:6).

23:21–22 *I did not send these prophets.* A true prophet must be sent by God with a word from God. A true prophet of God calls people to repentance of sin or evil and to renewed faith.

23:26 *the delusions of their own minds.* The character of the false prophets was based on lies and deceit. Their deception was apparent because their goal was to draw the people into idolatry with their fanciful dreams, leading people to forget God and follow Baal (2:8).

23:28–29 *what has straw to do with grain.* This poetic interlude compares dream and word. A dream is like dead straw. It is lifeless and fleeting. But God’s word contains life like a head of grain. It has the force of fire and a hammer.

23:38–40 *a message from the LORD.* False prophets could not speak an oracle. The disgrace that

23:16 [j] Jer 27:9-10, 14; Mt 7:15 [k] Jer 14:14 [l] Jer 9:20
23:17 [m] Jer 8:11 [n] Jer 13:10 [o] Jer 5:12; Am 9:10; Mic 3:11
23:19 [p] Jer 25:32; 30:23 **23:20** [q] 2Ki 23:26 [r] Jer 30:24
23:21 [s] Jer 14:14; 27:15 **23:22** [t] Jer 25:5; Zec 1:4
23:23 [u] Ps 139:1-10 **23:24** [v] Job 22:12-14 [w] 1Ki 8:27
23:25 [x] Jer 14:14 [y] ver 28, 32; Jer 29:8 **23:26** [z] 1Ti 4:1-2
23:27 [a] Dt 13:1-3; Jer 29:8 [b] Jdg 3:7; 8:33-34
23:29 [c] Jer 5:14 **23:30** [d] Ps 34:16 [e] Dt 18:20; Jer 14:15
23:31 [f] ver 17 **23:32** [g] ver 25 [h] Jer 7:8; La 2:14
23:33 [i] Mal 1:1 [j] ver 39 **23:34** [k] La 2:14 [l] Zec 13:3
23:35 [m] Jer 33:3; 42:4 **23:36** [n] Gal 1:7-8; 2Pe 3:16

the LORD says: You used the words, 'This
is a message from the LORD,' even though I
told you that you must not claim, 'This is a
message from the LORD.' 39Therefore, I will
surely forget you and cast[o] you out of my
presence along with the city I gave to you
and your ancestors. 40I will bring on you
everlasting disgrace[p]—everlasting shame
that will not be forgotten."

Two Baskets of Figs

24 After Jehoiachin[a][q] son of Jehoiakim
king of Judah and the officials, the
skilled workers and the artisans of Judah
were carried into exile from Jerusalem to
Babylon by Nebuchadnezzar king of Babylon, the LORD showed me two baskets of
figs[r] placed in front of the temple of the
LORD. 2One basket had very good figs, like
those that ripen early; the other basket
had very bad[s] figs, so bad they could not
be eaten.

3Then the LORD asked me, "What do you
see,[t] Jeremiah?"

"Figs," I answered. "The good ones are
very good, but the bad ones are so bad they
cannot be eaten."

4Then the word of the LORD came to me:
5"This is what the LORD, the God of Israel,
says: 'Like these good figs, I regard as good
the exiles from Judah, whom I sent away
from this place to the land of the Babylonians.[b] 6My eyes will watch over them for
their good, and I will bring them back[u] to
this land. I will build[v] them up and not tear
them down; I will plant them and not uproot them. 7I will give them a heart to know
me, that I am the LORD. They will be my
people,[w] and I will be their God, for they
will return[x] to me with all their heart.[y]

8" 'But like the bad[z] figs, which are so bad
they cannot be eaten,' says the LORD, 'so
will I deal with Zedekiah king of Judah,
his officials[a] and the survivors[b] from Jerusalem, whether they remain in this land
or live in Egypt.[c] 9I will make them abhorrent[d] and an offense to all the kingdoms
of the earth, a reproach and a byword,[e] a
curse[c][f] and an object of ridicule, wherever I banish[g] them. 10I will send the sword,[h]
famine and plague[i] against them until they
are destroyed from the land I gave to them
and their ancestors.' "

Seventy Years of Captivity

25 The word came to Jeremiah concerning all the people of Judah in
the fourth year of Jehoiakim[j] son of Josiah
king of Judah, which was the first year of
Nebuchadnezzar[k] king of Babylon. 2So Jeremiah the prophet said to all the people of
Judah[l] and to all those living in Jerusalem:
3For twenty-three years—from the thirteenth year of Josiah[m] son of Amon king
of Judah until this very day—the word of
the LORD has come to me and I have spoken
to you again and again,[n] but you have not
listened.[o]

4And though the LORD has sent all his
servants the prophets[p] to you again and
again, you have not listened or paid any attention. 5They said, "Turn now, each of you,
from your evil ways and your evil practices, and you can stay in the land the LORD
gave to you and your ancestors for ever and
ever. 6Do not follow other gods[q] to serve
and worship them; do not arouse my anger
with what your hands have made. Then I
will not harm you."

7"But you did not listen to me," declares
the LORD, "and you have aroused my anger
with what your hands have made,[r] and you
have brought harm[s] to yourselves."

8Therefore the LORD Almighty says
this: "Because you have not listened
to my words, 9I will summon[t] all the
peoples of the north[u] and my servant[v]
Nebuchadnezzar king of Babylon," declares the LORD, "and I will bring them
against this land and its inhabitants and
against all the surrounding nations. I
will completely destroy[d] them and make
them an object of horror and scorn,[w] and
an everlasting ruin. 10I will banish from
them the sounds[x] of joy and gladness,
the voices of bride and bridegroom,[y] the
sound of millstones[z] and the light of the
lamp.[a] 11This whole country will become
a desolate wasteland,[b] and these nations
will serve the king of Babylon seventy
years.[c]

---

[a] 1 Hebrew *Jeconiah,* a variant of *Jehoiachin*
[b] 5 Or *Chaldeans*
[c] 9 That is, their names will be used in cursing (see 29:22); or, others will see that they are cursed.
[d] 9 The Hebrew term refers to the irrevocable giving over of things or persons to the LORD, often by totally destroying them.

---

resulted from the false prophets would last for an extended period of time: Its memory would endure forever (20:11).

24:4–7 *Like these good figs.* These are identified with the deported exiles, including Jehoiachin's royal household, whom God set apart. God would bring back the captives, establish them in the land, and multiply their crops.

25:3 *I have spoken to you again and again.* This phrase describes Jeremiah's diligence and persistence.

25:9 *my servant Nebuchadnezzar.* This expression does not imply that the Babylonian monarch worshiped Israel's God, but simply that he was used

23:39 [o] Jer 7:15 **23:40** [p] Jer 20:11; Eze 5:14-15
24:1 [q] 2Ki 24:16; 2Ch 36:9; Jer 29:2 [r] Am 8:1-2
24:2 [s] Isa 5:4 **24:3** [t] Jer 1:11; Am 8:2 **24:6** [u] Jer 29:10; Eze 11:17 [v] Jer 33:7; 42:10 **24:7** [w] Isa 51:16; Jer 31:33; Heb 8:10 [x] Jer 32:40 [y] Eze 11:19 **24:8** [z] Jer 29:17 [a] Jer 39:6 [b] Jer 39:9 [c] Jer 44:1,26 **24:9** [d] Jer 15:4; 34:17 [e] Dt 28:25; 1Ki 9:7 [f] Jer 29:18 [g] Dt 28:37
24:10 [h] Isa 51:19 [i] Jer 27:8 **25:1** [j] 2Ki 24:2; Jer 36:1 [k] 2Ki 24:1 **25:2** [l] Jer 18:11 **25:3** [m] Jer 1:2 [n] Jer 11:7; 26:5 [o] Jer 7:26 **25:4** [p] Jer 7:25 **25:6** [q] Dt 8:19
25:7 [r] Dt 32:21 [s] 2Ki 21:15 **25:9** [t] Isa 13:3-5 [u] Jer 1:15 [v] Jer 27:6 [w] Jer 18:16 **25:10** [x] Isa 24:8; Eze 26:13 [y] Jer 7:34 [z] Ecc 12:3-4 [a] Rev 18:22-23 **25:11** [b] Jer 4:26-27; 12:11-12 [c] 2Ch 36:21

12"But when the seventy years[d] are fulfilled, I will punish the king of Babylon and
his nation, the land of the Babylonians,[a] for
their guilt," declares the LORD, "and will
make it desolate[e] forever. 13I will bring
on that land all the things I have spoken
against it, all that are written in this book
and prophesied by Jeremiah against all
the nations. 14They themselves will be enslaved[f] by many nations[g] and great kings;
I will repay[h] them according to their deeds
and the work of their hands."

The Cup of God's Wrath

15This is what the LORD, the God of Israel, said to me: "Take from my hand this cup[i]
filled with the wine of my wrath and make
all the nations to whom I send you drink it.
16When they drink it, they will stagger[j] and
go mad[k] because of the sword I will send
among them."

17So I took the cup from the LORD's
hand and made all the nations to whom
he sent[l] me drink it: 18Jerusalem and the
towns of Judah, its kings and officials, to
make them a ruin and an object of horror
and scorn, a curse[bm]—as they are today;[n]
19Pharaoh king of Egypt, his attendants,
his officials and all his people, 20and all
the foreign people there; all the kings of
Uz;[o] all the kings of the Philistines (those
of Ashkelon,[p] Gaza, Ekron, and the people
left at Ashdod); 21Edom, Moab and Ammon;[q] 22all the kings of Tyre and Sidon;[r]
the kings of the coastlands[s] across the sea;
23Dedan, Tema, Buz and all who are in distant places[c];[t] 24all the kings of Arabia[u] and
all the kings of the foreign people who live
in the wilderness; 25all the kings of Zimri,
Elam[v] and Media; 26and all the kings of the
north,[w] near and far, one after the other—
all the kingdoms on the face of the earth.
And after all of them, the king of Sheshak[dx]
will drink it too.

27"Then tell them, 'This is what the LORD
Almighty, the God of Israel, says: Drink,
get drunk[y] and vomit, and fall to rise no
more because of the sword[z] I will send
among you.' 28But if they refuse to take the
cup from your hand and drink, tell them,
'This is what the LORD Almighty says: You
must drink it! 29See, I am beginning to
bring disaster[a] on the city that bears my
Name,[b] and will you indeed go unpunished?[c] You will not go unpunished, for I
am calling down a sword on all[d] who live
on the earth, declares the LORD Almighty.'

30"Now prophesy all these words against
them and say to them:

"'The LORD will roar[e] from on high;
  he will thunder[f] from his holy
    dwelling
  and roar mightily against his land.
He will shout like those who tread the
    grapes,
  shout against all who live on the
    earth.
31The tumult will resound to the ends of
    the earth,
  for the LORD will bring charges[g]
    against the nations;
he will bring judgment on all mankind
  and put the wicked to the sword,'"
declares the LORD.

32This is what the LORD Almighty says:

"Look! Disaster is spreading
  from nation to nation;[h]
a mighty storm[i] is rising
  from the ends of the earth."

33At that time those slain[j] by the LORD will
be everywhere—from one end of the earth
to the other. They will not be mourned or
gathered[k] up or buried,[l] but will be like
dung lying on the ground.

---

[a] 12 Or *Chaldeans* [b] 18 That is, their names to be used in cursing (see 29:22); or, to be seen by others as cursed [c] 23 Or *who clip the hair by their foreheads* [d] 26 *Sheshak* is a cryptogram for Babylon.

---

by God to fulfill His purposes (as in the case of Cyrus, who is called the Lord's "anointed" in Is. 45:1).

25:16 *drink . . . stagger and go mad.* This triad sequence depicts the judgment process by which the sword of the Lord subdues those opposed to Him. The state of drunkenness was condemned in the Old Testament: to drink the cup and stagger was to display one's guilt (Num. 5:19–28).

25:18 *to make them a ruin and an object of horror and scorn, a curse.* The list of nations that would be made to drink from the cup of the Lord's judgment begins with Judah and Jerusalem, which would be made a source of derision (19:8).

25:27–28 *Drink, get drunk and vomit.* These terms for progressive inebriation emphasize the extent of judgment that would flow from God's cup of wrath. Those who refused the cup would be forced to drink.

25:30 *The LORD will roar from on high.* Generally this phrase refers to God's abode on Mount Zion (Joel 3:16; Amos 1:2).

25:31 *The tumult will resound.* This tumult refers to a thunderous judgment resulting from God's "covenant lawsuit" against the nations. Though they had not received the law like Judah and Israel, the Gentiles would be judged because they were "wicked." The word "wicked" refers to the guilt associated with the breach of ethical standards, including violating the poor and needy and abusing the oppressed.

25:12 [d] Jer 29:10 [e] Isa 13:19-22; 14:22-23
25:14 [f] Jer 27:7 [g] Jer 50:9; 51:27-28 [h] Jer 51:6
25:15 [i] Isa 51:17; Ps 75:8; Rev 14:10 **25:16** [j] Na 3:11
[k] Jer 51:7 **25:17** [l] Jer 1:10 **25:18** [m] Jer 24:9 [n] Jer 44:22
25:20 [o] Job 1:1 [p] Jer 47:5 **25:21** [q] Jer 49:1
25:22 [r] Jer 47:4 [s] Jer 31:10 **25:23** [t] Jer 9:26; 49:32
25:24 [u] 2Ch 9:14 **25:25** [v] Ge 10:22 **25:26** [w] Jer 50:3, 9
[x] Jer 51:41 **25:27** [y] ver 16, 28; Hab 2:16 [z] Eze 21:4
25:29 [a] Jer 13:12-14 [b] 1Pe 4:17 [c] Pr 11:31 [d] ver 30-31
25:30 [e] Isa 16:10; 42:13 [f] Joel 3:16; Am 1:2
25:31 [g] Hos 4:1; Joel 3:2; Mic 6:2 **25:32** [h] Isa 34:2
[i] Jer 23:19 **25:33** [j] Isa 66:16; Eze 39:17-20 [k] Jer 16:4
[l] Ps 79:3

34 Weep and wail, you shepherds;
roll[m] in the dust, you leaders of the
flock.
For your time to be slaughtered[n] has
come;
you will fall like the best of the
rams.[a]
35 The shepherds will have nowhere to
flee,
the leaders of the flock no place to
escape.[o]
36 Hear the cry of the shepherds,
the wailing of the leaders of the flock,
for the LORD is destroying their
pasture.
37 The peaceful meadows will be laid
waste
because of the fierce anger of the
LORD.
38 Like a lion[p] he will leave his lair,
and their land will become desolate
because of the sword[b] of the oppressor
and because of the LORD's fierce
anger.

Jeremiah Threatened With Death

26 Early in the reign of Jehoiakim[q] son
of Josiah king of Judah, this word
came from the LORD: 2 "This is what the
LORD says: Stand in the courtyard[r] of the
LORD's house and speak to all the people
of the towns of Judah who come to worship in the house of the LORD. Tell[s] them
everything I command you; do not omit[t] a
word. 3 Perhaps they will listen and each
will turn[u] from their evil ways. Then I will
relent[v] and not inflict on them the disaster I was planning because of the evil they
have done. 4 Say to them, 'This is what the
LORD says: If you do not listen[w] to me and
follow my law,[x] which I have set before you,
5 and if you do not listen to the words of my
servants the prophets, whom I have sent to
you again and again (though you have not
listened[y]), 6 then I will make this house like
Shiloh[z] and this city a curse[c][a] among all
the nations of the earth.'"
7 The priests, the prophets and all the
people heard Jeremiah speak these words
in the house of the LORD. 8 But as soon as
Jeremiah finished telling all the people everything the LORD had commanded him
to say, the priests, the prophets and all the
people seized him and said, "You must die!
9 Why do you prophesy in the LORD's name
that this house will be like Shiloh and this
city will be desolate and deserted?"[b] And
all the people crowded around Jeremiah in
the house of the LORD.
10 When the officials of Judah heard
about these things, they went up from the
royal palace to the house of the LORD and
took their places at the entrance of the New
Gate of the LORD's house. 11 Then the priests
and the prophets said to the officials and
all the people, "This man should be sentenced to death[c] because he has prophesied against this city. You have heard it
with your own ears!"
12 Then Jeremiah said to all the officials[d]
and all the people: "The LORD sent me to
prophesy[e] against this house and this city
all the things you have heard.[f] 13 Now reform[g] your ways and your actions and
obey the LORD your God. Then the LORD
will relent and not bring the disaster he
has pronounced against you. 14 As for me,
I am in your hands;[h] do with me whatever
you think is good and right. 15 Be assured,
however, that if you put me to death, you
will bring the guilt of innocent blood on
yourselves and on this city and on those
who live in it, for in truth the LORD has sent
me to you to speak all these words in your
hearing."
16 Then the officials[i] and all the people
said to the priests and the prophets, "This
man should not be sentenced to death![j] He
has spoken to us in the name of the LORD
our God."

---

[a] *34* Septuagint; Hebrew *fall and be shattered like fine pottery* [b] *38* Some Hebrew manuscripts and Septuagint (see also 46:16 and 50:16); most Hebrew manuscripts *anger* [c] *6* That is, its name will be used in cursing (see 29:22); or, others will see that it is cursed.

25:37 *because of the fierce anger of the LORD.* Human anger is an emotion. God's anger is an aspect of the righteous administration of His laws—natural, moral, and spiritual.

26:2 *do not omit a word.* Jeremiah was told to speak unsparingly with unwavering boldness.

26:3 *Perhaps they will listen.* The introduction to the judgment oracle is expressed in conditional terms. If the people repented of evil, the Lord would relent from the calamity He was threatening to bring on them.

26:6 *then I will make this house like Shiloh.* This city was not far from Jerusalem. The people could see the effects of its destruction by the Philistines in 1050 B.C., a destruction that overtook it even though it was the first resting place of the ark of the covenant. Jeremiah uses Shiloh as an illustration of the coming judgment of Jerusalem even though the temple of God had been built there.

26:13 *obey the LORD your God.* Jeremiah gives the Lord's assurance that if we, like Judah, turn to obey Him, our future will be changed from punishment to blessing.

26:15 *if you put me to death.* Jeremiah defended himself and pointed to the potential sin of shedding innocent blood. He had already accused the leaders of Jerusalem of child sacrifices in the Hinnom valley (2:34; 19:4).

25:34 [m] Jer 6:26 [n] Isa 34:6; Jer 50:27 **25:35** [o] Job 11:20 **25:38** [p] Jer 4:7 **26:1** [q] 2Ki 23:36 **26:2** [r] Jer 19:14 [s] Jer 1:17; Mt 28:20; Ac 20:27 [t] Dt 4:2 **26:3** [u] Jer 36:7 [v] Jer 18:8 **26:4** [w] Lev 26:14 [x] 1Ki 9:6 **26:5** [y] Jer 25:4 **26:6** [z] Jos 18:1 [a] 2Ki 22:19 **26:9** [b] Jer 9:11 **26:11** [c] Dt 18:20; Jer 18:23; 38:4; Mt 26:66; Ac 6:11 **26:12** [d] Jer 1:18 [e] Am 7:15; Ac 4:18-20; 5:29 [f] ver 2, 15 **26:13** [g] Jer 7:5; Joel 2:12-14 **26:14** [h] Jer 38:5 **26:16** [i] Ac 23:9 [j] Ac 5:34-39; 23:29

17Some of the elders of the land stepped forward and said to the entire assembly of people, 18"Micah[k] of Moresheth prophesied in the days of Hezekiah king of Judah. He told all the people of Judah, 'This is what the LORD Almighty says:

"'Zion[l] will be plowed like a field,
Jerusalem will become a heap of rubble,[m]
the temple hill[n] a mound overgrown with thickets.'[a][o]

19"Did Hezekiah king of Judah or anyone else in Judah put him to death? Did not Hezekiah[p] fear the LORD and seek his favor? And did not the LORD relent,[q] so that he did not bring the disaster[r] he pronounced against them? We are about to bring a terrible disaster[s] on ourselves!"

20(Now Uriah son of Shemaiah from Kiriath Jearim[t] was another man who prophesied in the name of the LORD; he prophesied the same things against this city and this land as Jeremiah did. 21When King Jehoiakim[u] and all his officers and officials heard his words, the king was determined to put him to death. But Uriah heard of it and fled[v] in fear to Egypt. 22King Jehoiakim, however, sent Elnathan[w] son of Akbor to Egypt, along with some other men. 23They brought Uriah out of Egypt and took him to King Jehoiakim, who had him struck down with a sword and his body thrown into the burial place of the common people.)

24Furthermore, Ahikam[x] son of Shaphan supported Jeremiah, and so he was not handed over to the people to be put to death.

Judah to Serve Nebuchadnezzar

27 Early in the reign of Zedekiah[b][y] son of Josiah king of Judah, this word came to Jeremiah from the LORD: 2This is what the LORD said to me: "Make a yoke[z] out of straps and crossbars and put it on your neck. 3Then send word to the kings of Edom, Moab, Ammon,[a] Tyre and Sidon through the envoys who have come to Jerusalem to Zedekiah king of Judah. 4Give them a message for their masters and say, 'This is what the LORD Almighty, the God of Israel, says: "Tell this to your masters: 5With my great power and outstretched arm[b] I made the earth and its people and the animals that are on it, and I give[c] it to anyone I please. 6Now I will give all your countries into the hands of my servant[d] Nebuchadnezzar[e] king of Babylon; I will make even the wild animals subject to him.[f] 7All nations will serve[g] him and his son and his grandson until the time[h] for his land comes; then many nations and great kings will subjugate[i] him.

8"'"If, however, any nation or kingdom will not serve Nebuchadnezzar king of Babylon or bow its neck under his yoke, I will punish that nation with the sword, famine and plague, declares the LORD, until I destroy it by his hand. 9So do not listen to your prophets, your diviners, your interpreters of dreams, your mediums[j] or your sorcerers who tell you, 'You will not serve the king of Babylon.' 10They prophesy lies[k] to you that will only serve to remove you far from your lands; I will banish you and you will perish. 11But if any nation will bow its neck under the yoke[l] of the king of Babylon and serve him, I will let that nation remain in its own land to till it and to live there, declares the LORD."'"

12I gave the same message to Zedekiah king of Judah. I said, "Bow your neck under the yoke of the king of Babylon; serve him and his people, and you will live. 13Why

---

a *18* Micah 3:12 *b* *1* A few Hebrew manuscripts and Syriac (see also 27:3,12 and 28:1); most Hebrew manuscripts *Jehoiakim* (Most Septuagint manuscripts do not have this verse.)

26:18 ***Micah of Moresheth.*** In the reign of Hezekiah, Micah had announced the impending destruction of Jerusalem by the Assyrians (Mic. 3:12). Yet because of the repentance of Hezekiah and the inhabitants, the city was spared from the onslaught of the Assyrian army under Sennacherib (701 B.C.).

26:24 ***Ahikam son of Shaphan.*** This man, along with his father, served as a scribe under Josiah when the Book of the Law was found in the temple (2 Kin. 22:8–14). Ahikam's brother Gemariah also opposed Jehoiakim's burning of Jeremiah's scroll (36:25). This faithful family was supportive of Jeremiah and was instrumental in saving his life.

27:2–3 ***a yoke out of straps.*** These are wooden bars or beams that attach to a pair of oxen with leather bands. The symbolic act of wearing the yoke would communicate bondage, restraint, and enslavement.

27:7 ***All nations will serve him and his son and his grandson.*** Following the death of Nebuchadnezzar in 562 B.C., his heirs and successors retained control of Babylon for only 24 years. Babylon fell without a battle to Cyrus and the Persian armies in 539 B.C., and later to Alexander the Great of Greece.

27:9–10 ***do not listen.*** The way kings summoned various prophet-diviners to give them direction is well known from the Book of Daniel (Dan. 2:2; 5:7). Besides prophets, there were diviners, like Balaam (Num. 22–24), who were prohibited from practicing their craft in Israel (Deut. 18:9–14). The collective effort of these diviners to determine the fate of their nations failed. Like the false prophets of Judah, they heralded a message of rebellion and resistance against Babylon. Only Jeremiah stood for the truth. The Lord would punish Judah through Nebuchadnezzar.

26:18 [k] Mic 1:1 [l] Isa 2:3 [m] Ne 4:2; Jer 9:11 [n] Mic 4:1; Zec 8:3 [o] Jer 17:3 **26:19** [p] 2Ch 32:24-26; Isa 37:14-20 [q] Ex 32:14; 2Sa 24:16 [r] Jer 44:7 [s] Hab 2:10 **26:20** [t] Jos 9:17 **26:21** [u] 1Ki 19:2 [v] Mt 10:23 **26:22** [w] Jer 36:12, 25 **26:24** [x] 2Ki 22:12 **27:1** [y] 2Ch 36:11 **27:2** [z] Jer 28:10, 13 **27:3** [a] Jer 25:21 **27:5** [b] Dt 9:29 [c] Ps 115:16 **27:6** [d] Jer 25:9 [e] Jer 21:7; Eze 29:18-20 [f] Jer 28:14; Da 2:37-38 **27:7** [g] 2Ch 36:20 [h] Jer 25:12 [i] Jer 25:14; Da 5:28 **27:9** [j] Dt 18:11 **27:10** [k] Jer 23:25 **27:11** [l] Jer 21:9

will you and your people die[m] by the sword,
famine and plague with which the LORD has
threatened any nation that will not serve
the king of Babylon? 14 Do not listen to the
words of the prophets who say to you, 'You
will not serve the king of Babylon,' for they
are prophesying lies[n] to you. 15 'I have not
sent[o] them,' declares the LORD. 'They are
prophesying lies in my name.[p] Therefore, I
will banish you and you will perish,[q] both
you and the prophets who prophesy to you.'"
16 Then I said to the priests and all these
people, "This is what the LORD says: Do not
listen to the prophets who say, 'Very soon
now the articles[r] from the LORD's house will
be brought back from Babylon.' They are
prophesying lies to you. 17 Do not listen to
them. Serve the king of Babylon, and you
will live. Why should this city become a
ruin? 18 If they are prophets and have the
word of the LORD, let them plead[s] with the
LORD Almighty that the articles remaining in the house of the LORD and in the palace of the king of Judah and in Jerusalem
not be taken to Babylon. 19 For this is what
the LORD Almighty says about the pillars,
the bronze Sea,[t] the movable stands and
the other articles[u] that are left in this city,
20 which Nebuchadnezzar king of Babylon
did not take away when he carried[v] Jehoiachin[a][w] son of Jehoiakim king of Judah into
exile from Jerusalem to Babylon, along with
all the nobles of Judah and Jerusalem—
21 yes, this is what the LORD Almighty, the
God of Israel, says about the things that are
left in the house of the LORD and in the palace of the king of Judah and in Jerusalem:
22 'They will be taken[x] to Babylon and there
they will remain until the day[y] I come for
them,' declares the LORD. 'Then I will bring[z]
them back and restore them to this place.'"

The False Prophet Hananiah

28 In the fifth month of that same year,
the fourth year, early in the reign of
Zedekiah[a] king of Judah, the prophet Hananiah son of Azzur, who was from Gibeon,[b] said to me in the house of the LORD in
the presence of the priests and all the people: 2 "This is what the LORD Almighty, the
God of Israel, says: 'I will break the yoke[c]
of the king of Babylon. 3 Within two years
I will bring back to this place all the articles[d] of the LORD's house that Nebuchadnezzar king of Babylon removed from here
and took to Babylon. 4 I will also bring back
to this place Jehoiachin[a][e] son of Jehoiakim
king of Judah and all the other exiles from
Judah who went to Babylon,' declares the
LORD, 'for I will break the yoke of the king
of Babylon.'"
5 Then the prophet Jeremiah replied to
the prophet Hananiah before the priests
and all the people who were standing in
the house of the LORD. 6 He said, "Amen!
May the LORD do so! May the LORD fulfill
the words you have prophesied by bringing the articles of the LORD's house and all
the exiles back to this place from Babylon.
7 Nevertheless, listen to what I have to say
in your hearing and in the hearing of all
the people: 8 From early times the prophets
who preceded you and me have prophesied
war, disaster and plague[f] against many
countries and great kingdoms. 9 But the
prophet who prophesies peace will be recognized as one truly sent by the LORD only
if his prediction comes true.[g]"
10 Then the prophet Hananiah took the
yoke[h] off the neck of the prophet Jeremiah
and broke it, 11 and he said[i] before all the
people, "This is what the LORD says: 'In the
same way I will break the yoke of Nebuchadnezzar king of Babylon off the neck of
all the nations within two years.'" At this,
the prophet Jeremiah went on his way.
12 After the prophet Hananiah had broken
the yoke off the neck of the prophet Jeremiah, the word of the LORD came to Jeremiah: 13 "Go and tell Hananiah, 'This is what
the LORD says: You have broken a wooden
yoke, but in its place you will get a yoke of
iron. 14 This is what the LORD Almighty, the
God of Israel, says: I will put an iron yoke[j]
on the necks of all these nations to make
them serve[k] Nebuchadnezzar king of Babylon, and they will serve him. I will even
give him control over the wild animals.[l]'"

---

[a] 20,4 Hebrew *Jeconiah*, a variant of *Jehoiachin*

27:21–22 *about the things.* Jeremiah's message from the Lord is presented in detail. The remaining vessels in the temple, as well as in the king's palace, would be carried to Babylon until the Lord restored His people. In the midst of a prophetic message against the false prophets, Jeremiah spoke a message of hope and restoration. Destruction was imminent, but God does not forget His people. He would restore the righteous remnant.

28:1–4 *Hananiah son of Azzur.* This prophet believed that God's message for Judah was one of imminent deliverance—within two years—from servitude to the king of Babylon. Hananiah also prophesied the return of the holy vessels taken by Nebuchadnezzar from the temple. Furthermore, Hananiah espoused the popular belief that the kingship of Zedekiah was illegitimate and that God would restore Jehoiachin to the throne in Jerusalem.

28:7–9 *war, disaster and plague.* Hananiah's message of peace and prosperity ran contrary to the long tradition of the genuine Hebrew prophets. Amos, Hosea, Micah, Joel, and Nahum spoke words of judgment and destruction against the great kingdoms like Assyria and Egypt.

27:13 [m] Eze 18:31 **27:14** [n] Jer 14:14 **27:15** [o] Jer 23:21 [p] Jer 29:9 [q] Jer 6:15 **27:16** [r] 2Ki 24:13; 2Ch 36:7, 10; Jer 28:3; Da 1:2 **27:18** [s] 1Sa 7:8 **27:19** [t] 2Ki 25:13 [u] Jer 52:17-23 **27:20** [v] 2Ch 36:10; Jer 24:1 [w] Jer 22:24 **27:22** [x] 2Ki 25:13 [y] 2Ch 36:21 [z] Ezr 1:7; 7:19 **28:1** [a] Jer 27:1,3 [b] Jos 9:3 **28:2** [c] Jer 27:12 **28:3** [d] 2Ki 24:13 **28:4** [e] Jer 22:24-27 **28:8** [f] Lev 26:14-17; Isa 5:5-7 **28:9** [g] Dt 18:22 **28:10** [h] Jer 27:2 **28:11** [i] Jer 14:14; 27:10 **28:14** [j] Dt 28:48 [k] Jer 25:11 [l] Jer 27:6

15Then the prophet Jeremiah said to
Hananiah the prophet, "Listen, Hananiah! The LORD has not sent[m] you, yet you
have persuaded this nation to trust in lies.[n]
16Therefore this is what the LORD says: 'I
am about to remove you from the face of
the earth.[o] This very year you are going to
die, because you have preached rebellion[p]
against the LORD.'"
17In the seventh month of that same year,
Hananiah the prophet died.

A Letter to the Exiles

29 This is the text of the letter that the
prophet Jeremiah sent from Jerusa-
lem to the surviving elders among the exiles and to the priests, the prophets and all
the other people Nebuchadnezzar had carried into exile from Jerusalem to Babylon.[q]
2(This was after King Jehoiachin[a][r] and the
queen mother, the court officials and the
leaders of Judah and Jerusalem, the skilled
workers and the artisans had gone into exile from Jerusalem.) 3He entrusted the letter to Elasah son of Shaphan and to Gemariah son of Hilkiah, whom Zedekiah king
of Judah sent to King Nebuchadnezzar in
Babylon. It said:

4This is what the LORD Almighty,
the God of Israel, says to all those I
carried[s] into exile from Jerusalem to
Babylon: 5"Build[t] houses and settle
down; plant gardens and eat what they
produce. 6Marry and have sons and
daughters; find wives for your sons
and give your daughters in marriage,
so that they too may have sons and
daughters. Increase in number there;
do not decrease. 7Also, seek the peace
and prosperity of the city to which I
have carried you into exile. Pray[u] to
the LORD for it, because if it prospers,
you too will prosper." 8Yes, this is what
the LORD Almighty, the God of Israel,
says: "Do not let the prophets and diviners among you deceive[v] you. Do not
listen to the dreams you encourage
them to have.[w] 9They are prophesying
lies[x] to you in my name. I have not sent
them," declares the LORD.

10This is what the LORD says: "When
seventy years[y] are completed for Babylon, I will come to you and fulfill my
good promise to bring you back[z] to this
place. 11For I know the plans[a] I have
for you," declares the LORD, "plans
to prosper you and not to harm you,
plans to give you hope and a future.
12Then you will call on me and come
and pray to me, and I will listen[b] to
you. 13You will seek[c] me and find me
when you seek me with all your heart.[d]
14I will be found by you," declares the
LORD, "and will bring you back[e] from
captivity.[b] I will gather you from all
the nations and places where I have
banished you," declares the LORD,
"and will bring you back to the place
from which I carried you into exile."[f]

[a] 2 Hebrew *Jeconiah*, a variant of *Jehoiachin*
[b] 14 Or *will restore your fortunes*

28:15–16 *you have persuaded this nation to trust in lies.* Hananiah had not been sent by God, but he had led the people astray with a lie. As a result, Hananiah would die that very year.

29:2 *after.* This parenthetical passage provides background from 2 Kings 24:12–16 concerning the deportation of Jehoiachin to Babylon in 597 B.C. This method of eliminating leaders and leaving the peasant population to pay taxes to the kingdom was learned from the Assyrians and was designed to reduce the likelihood of rebellion.

29:4 *to all those I carried into exile.* Jeremiah reminded the exiled community that ultimately it was God, not Nebuchadnezzar, who had caused them to be taken to Babylon.

29:10 *When seventy years are completed.* The concept of 70 years of Babylonian captivity is reiterated from Jeremiah 25:12. The number 70 symbolizes completion and fulfillment of God's sovereign plans for creation and human history. The completion of the years of the kingdom of Babylon would also be the completion of Judah's exile.

29:11 A Hope and a Future—This text comes from a letter from Jeremiah to the exiles from Judah who were living in Babylon (vv. 4–9). The exiles must have had a lot of questions about their situation before they heard from Jeremiah. Had God abandoned them forever? How could they serve God properly while under the domination of the nation of Babylon? When would the exile end? Would they ever see Jerusalem again? What was the plan?

The answer that Jeremiah wrote to them probably wasn't satisfactory for all. They still would have had questions. Many would have wanted more specific answers. They would have wanted to know how long they would be in Babylon. They would have asked if they could do anything to hasten their return. These are not unlike the questions we ask of God on a daily basis.

Perhaps the best way to describe the content of Jeremiah's letter is to say that he is pointing to the fact that all the specifics are wrapped up in their relationship with God. The promises are ultimate promises. If we seek Him, we will find Him. God Himself is our hope. Shouldn't knowing this give us all the direction we need? Isn't this what our faith is all about? On the basis of knowing what God has done and what He has promised to do, we will move ahead in trust. We may not see the path clearly, but we know He does lead and He is leading us.

29:14 *I will be found by you.* Those who seek God with a whole heart will find Him and experience His renewal. ***will bring you back.*** God was the captor, and He would restore His people from captivity.

28:15 [m] Jer 29:31 [n] Jer 20:6; 29:21; La 2:14; Eze 13:6
28:16 [o] Ge 7:4 [p] Dt 13:5; Jer 29:32 **29:1** [q] 2Ch 36:10
29:2 [r] 2Ki 24:12; Jer 22:24-28 **29:4** [s] Jer 24:5
29:5 [t] ver 28 **29:7** [u] Ezr 6:10; 1Ti 2:1-2 **29:8** [v] Jer 37:9
[w] Jer 23:27 **29:9** [x] Jer 14:14; 27:15 **29:10** [y] 2Ch 36:21;
Jer 25:12; Da 9:2 [z] Jer 21:22 **29:11** [a] Ps 40:5
29:12 [b] Ps 145:19 **29:13** [c] Mt 7:7 [d] Dt 4:29; Jer 24:7
29:14 [e] Dt 30:3; Jer 30:3 [f] Jer 23:3-4

15 You may say, "The LORD has raised up prophets for us in Babylon," 16 but this is what the LORD says about the king who sits on David's throne and all the people who remain in this city, your fellow citizens who did not go with you into exile— 17 yes, this is what the LORD Almighty says: "I will send the sword, famine and plague[g] against them and I will make them like figs[h] that are so bad they cannot be eaten. 18 I will pursue them with the sword, famine and plague and will make them abhorrent[i] to all the kingdoms of the earth, a curse[a] and an object of horror,[j] of scorn and reproach, among all the nations where I drive them. 19 For they have not listened to my words,"[k] declares the LORD, "words that I sent to them again and again by my servants the prophets.[l] And you exiles have not listened either," declares the LORD.

20 Therefore, hear the word of the LORD, all you exiles whom I have sent[m] away from Jerusalem to Babylon. 21 This is what the LORD Almighty, the God of Israel, says about Ahab son of Kolaiah and Zedekiah son of Maaseiah, who are prophesying lies[n] to you in my name: "I will deliver them into the hands of Nebuchadnezzar king of Babylon, and he will put them to death before your very eyes. 22 Because of them, all the exiles from Judah who are in Babylon will use this curse: 'May the LORD treat you like Zedekiah and Ahab, whom the king of Babylon burned[o] in the fire.' 23 For they have done outrageous things in Israel; they have committed adultery[p] with their neighbors' wives, and in my name they have uttered lies—which I did not authorize. I know[q] it and am a witness to it," declares the LORD.

Message to Shemaiah

24 Tell Shemaiah the Nehelamite, 25 "This is what the LORD Almighty, the God of Israel, says: You sent letters in your own name to all the people in Jerusalem, to the priest Zephaniah[r] son of Maaseiah, and to all the other priests. You said to Zephaniah, 26 'The LORD has appointed you priest in place of Jehoiada to be in charge of the house of the LORD; you should put any maniac[s] who acts like a prophet into the stocks[t] and neck-irons. 27 So why have you not reprimanded Jeremiah from Anathoth, who poses as a prophet among you? 28 He has sent this message[u] to us in Babylon: It will be a long time.[v] Therefore build[w] houses and settle down; plant gardens and eat what they produce.'"

29 Zephaniah the priest, however, read the letter to Jeremiah the prophet. 30 Then the word of the LORD came to Jeremiah: 31 "Send this message to all the exiles: 'This is what the LORD says about Shemaiah[x] the Nehelamite: Because Shemaiah has prophesied to you, even though I did not send[y] him, and has persuaded you to trust in lies, 32 this is what the LORD says: I will surely punish Shemaiah the Nehelamite and his descendants.[z] He will have no one left among this people, nor will he see the good[a] things I will do for my people, declares the LORD, because he has preached rebellion[b] against me.'"

Restoration of Israel

30 This is the word that came to Jeremiah from the LORD: 2 "This is what the LORD, the God of Israel, says: 'Write[c] in a book all the words I have spoken to you. 3 The days are coming,' declares the LORD, 'when I will bring[d] my people Israel and Judah back from captivity[b] and restore[e] them to the land I gave their ancestors to possess,' says the LORD."

4 These are the words the LORD spoke concerning Israel and Judah: 5 "This is what the LORD says:

"'Cries of fear[f] are heard—
    terror, not peace.
6 Ask and see:
    Can a man bear children?
Then why do I see every strong man
    with his hands on his stomach like a woman in labor,[g]
    every face turned deathly pale?

---

[a] 18 That is, their names will be used in cursing (see verse 22); or, others will see that they are cursed. [b] 3 Or *will restore the fortunes of my people Israel and Judah*

29:21 ***Ahab son of Kolaiah and Zedekiah son of Maaseiah.*** These two were the prophets spoken of in Jeremiah 29:15. They were accused by Jeremiah of a deplorable crime; prophesying the imminent collapse of Babylon and the restoration of the captives to Jerusalem. Such false prophecy urging rebellion against God was a capital offense (Deut. 14:5–10). The prophetic punishment of Ahab and Zedekiah was death by command of Nebuchadnezzar.

30:2 ***Write ... all the words.*** The oracles of Jeremiah were recorded by the scribe Baruch (ch. 36). "Book" refers to any type of writing medium, from a clay tablet to a parchment scroll. Jeremiah's oracles were recorded on a scroll (36:2).

30:6 ***hands on his stomach.*** This phrase symbolizes the agony of God's people who had become like defenseless pregnant women in the midst of delivery before their enemies (4:31; 6:24).

29:17 [g] Jer 27:8 [h] Jer 24:8-10 **29:18** [i] Jer 15:4 [j] Dt 28:25; Jer 42:18 **29:19** [k] Jer 6:19 [l] Jer 25:4 **29:20** [m] Jer 24:5 **29:21** [n] ver 9; Jer 14:14 **29:22** [o] Da 3:6 **29:23** [p] Jer 23:14 [q] Heb 4:13 **29:25** [r] 2Ki 25:18; Jer 21:1 **29:26** [s] 2Ki 9:11; Hos 9:7; Jn 10:20 [t] Jer 20:2 **29:28** [u] ver 1 [v] ver 10 [w] ver 5 **29:31** [x] ver 24 [y] Jer 14:14; 28:15 **29:32** [z] 1Sa 2:30-33 [a] ver 10 [b] Jer 28:16 **30:2** [c] Isa 30:8 **30:3** [d] Jer 29:14 [e] Jer 16:15 **30:5** [f] Jer 6:25 **30:6** [g] Jer 4:31

7 How awful that day[h] will be!
No other will be like it.
It will be a time of trouble[i] for Jacob,
but he will be saved[j] out of it.

8 "'In that day,' declares the LORD Almighty,
'I will break the yoke[k] off their necks
and will tear off their bonds;
no longer will foreigners enslave them.[l]
9 Instead, they will serve the LORD their God
and David[m] their king,[n]
whom I will raise up for them.

10 "'So do not be afraid,[o] Jacob my servant;[p]
do not be dismayed, Israel,'
declares the LORD.
'I will surely save[q] you out of a distant place,
your descendants from the land of their exile.
Jacob will again have peace and security,[r]
and no one will make him afraid.
11 I am with you and will save you,'
declares the LORD.
'Though I completely destroy all the nations
among which I scatter you,
I will not completely destroy[s] you.
I will discipline[t] you but only in due measure;
I will not let you go entirely unpunished.'[u]

12 "This is what the LORD says:

"'Your wound is incurable,
your injury beyond healing.[v]
13 There is no one to plead your cause,
no remedy for your sore,
no healing[w] for you.
14 All your allies[x] have forgotten you;
they care nothing for you.
I have struck you as an enemy[y] would
and punished you as would the cruel,[z]
because your guilt is so great
and your sins[a] so many.
15 Why do you cry out over your wound,
your pain that has no cure?
Because of your great guilt and many sins
I have done these things to you.

16 "'But all who devour[b] you will be devoured;
all your enemies will go into exile.[c]
Those who plunder[d] you will be plundered;
all who make spoil of you I will despoil.
17 But I will restore you to health
and heal your wounds,'
declares the LORD,
'because you are called an outcast,[e]
Zion for whom no one cares.'

18 "This is what the LORD says:

"'I will restore the fortunes[f] of Jacob's tents
and have compassion[g] on his dwellings;
the city will be rebuilt[h] on her ruins,
and the palace will stand in its proper place.
19 From them will come songs[i] of thanksgiving[j]
and the sound of rejoicing.[k]
I will add to their numbers,[l]
and they will not be decreased;
I will bring them honor,[m]
and they will not be disdained.
20 Their children[n] will be as in days of old,
and their community will be established[o] before me;
I will punish all who oppress them.
21 Their leader[p] will be one of their own;
their ruler will arise from among them.
I will bring him near[q] and he will come close to me—
for who is he who will devote himself
to be close to me?'
declares the LORD.

30:8 ***In that day.*** The day of the Lord was an ordained time of horror and distress for Israel and Judah, out of which the Lord would save them. Jeremiah expressed the hope of release from the bondage of the yoke of Babylon according to the Lord's timing (25:12) and not that of men (28:11).
30:12 ***Your wound is incurable.*** God's hand of judgment had brought serious harm to the nation, a mortal wound unless God intervened.
30:13 ***remedy.*** This refers to the growth of new skin over an open wound.
30:14 ***All your allies have forgotten you.*** Israel's allies were the surrounding nations like Assyria, Egypt, Phoenicia, Ammon, and Edom, with whom it had made political and religious alliances. These nations had quickly forgotten Judah; they shrank back or were defeated by Nebuchadnezzar.
30:17 ***I will restore you to health.*** Restoration and healing of Israel came in two forms: retribution against its enemies and healing of its wounds.
30:18 ***Jacob's tents ... dwellings ... city ... palace.*** These phrases emphasize God's work in rebuilding the homes and cities of His returning exiles, from the peasant population to the administration.
30:21 ***Their leader will be one of their own.*** Israel's leaders would no longer be appointed by foreign kings, and foreign rulers would not preside over Israel's lands.

30:7 [h] Isa 2:12; Joel 2:11 [i] Zep 1:15 [j] ver 10 **30:8** [k] Isa 9:4 [l] Eze 34:27 **30:9** [m] Isa 55:3-4; Lk 1:69; Ac 2:30; 13:23 [n] Eze 34:23-24; 37:24; Hos 3:5 **30:10** [o] Isa 43:5; Jer 46:27-28 [p] Isa 44:2 [q] Jer 29:14 [r] Isa 35:9 **30:11** [s] Jer 4:27; 46:28 [t] Jer 10:24 [u] Am 9:8 **30:12** [v] Jer 15:18 **30:13** [w] Jer 8:22; 14:19; 46:11 **30:14** [x] Jer 22:20; La 1:2 [y] Job 13:24 [z] Job 30:21 [a] Jer 5:6 **30:16** [b] Isa 33:1; Jer 2:3; 10:25 [c] Isa 14:2; Joel 3:4-8 [d] Jer 50:10 **30:17** [e] Jer 33:24 **30:18** [f] ver 3; Jer 31:23 [g] Ps 102:13 [h] Jer 31:4, 24, 38 **30:19** [i] Isa 35:10; 51:11 [j] Isa 51:3 [k] Ps 126:1-2; Jer 31:4 [l] Jer 33:22 [m] Isa 60:9 **30:20** [n] Isa 54:13; Jer 31:17 [o] Isa 54:14 **30:21** [p] ver 9 [q] Nu 16:5

22 "'So you will be my people,
and I will be your God.'"

23 See, the storm[r] of the LORD
will burst out in wrath,
a driving wind swirling down
on the heads of the wicked.
24 The fierce anger[s] of the LORD will not
turn back[t]
until he fully accomplishes
the purposes of his heart.
In days to come
you will understand[u] this.

31 "At that time," declares the LORD, "I
will be the God[v] of all the families of
Israel, and they will be my people."
2 This is what the LORD says:

"The people who survive the sword
will find favor[w] in the wilderness;
I will come to give rest[x] to Israel."

3 The LORD appeared to us in the past,[a]
saying:

"I have loved[y] you with an everlasting
love;
I have drawn[z] you with unfailing
kindness.
4 I will build you up again,
and you, Virgin Israel, will be rebuilt.
Again you will take up your timbrels
and go out to dance with the joyful.[a]
5 Again you will plant vineyards
on the hills of Samaria;[b]
the farmers will plant them
and enjoy their fruit.[c]
6 There will be a day when watchmen cry
out
on the hills of Ephraim,
'Come, let us go up to Zion,
to the LORD our God.'"[d]

7 This is what the LORD says:

"Sing with joy for Jacob;
shout for the foremost[e] of the nations.
Make your praises heard, and say,
'LORD, save[f] your people,
the remnant[g] of Israel.'
8 See, I will bring them from the land of
the north[h]
and gather[i] them from the ends of the
earth.
Among them will be the blind[j] and the
lame,[k]
expectant mothers and women in
labor;
a great throng will return.
9 They will come with weeping;[l]
they will pray as I bring them back.
I will lead[m] them beside streams of
water
on a level[n] path where they will not
stumble,
because I am Israel's father,[o]
and Ephraim is my firstborn son.

10 "Hear the word of the LORD, you
nations;
proclaim it in distant coastlands:[p]
'He who scattered Israel will gather[q]
them
and will watch over his flock like a
shepherd.'[r]
11 For the LORD will deliver Jacob
and redeem[s] them from the hand of
those stronger[t] than they.
12 They will come and shout for joy on the
heights[u] of Zion;
they will rejoice in the bounty[v] of the
LORD—
the grain, the new wine and the olive
oil,[w]
the young of the flocks and herds.
They will be like a well-watered
garden,[x]
and they will sorrow[y] no more.
13 Then young women will dance and be
glad,
young men and old as well.
I will turn their mourning[z] into
gladness;
I will give them comfort and joy[a]
instead of sorrow.

[a] 3 Or *LORD has appeared to us from afar*

31:3 *everlasting love ... unfailing kindness.* These strong words are in parallel and point toward a love characterized by loyalty, a king of covenant love. Out of His faithfulness to the covenants God established with Abraham and Moses, and out of His great love, God established the nation Israel for His glory and for hers. The Lord would also deliver His people from captivity and reestablish them by His love.

31:4 *Virgin Israel.* Earlier in Jeremiah, this expression was used sadly in depicting the departure of Israel from faith in God (14:17). Here the image is reversed. Israel is rebuilt in the manner of her former betrothal (2:2), having become again a virgin bride to God. ***go out to dance with the joyful.*** A joyful celebration of marriage and festival throughout villages is in view here (v. 13).

31:6 *watchmen.* This time the watchman's purpose is not to warn the people about oncoming armies but to call them to come with joy to the holy city.

31:9 *I am Israel's father.* This text is one of the few cases in the Old Testament where the fatherhood of God is portrayed directly (Deut. 32:6; Is. 63:16). Israel was familiar with the idea of God as Father, but it was not until the teaching of Jesus that the phrase took on the importance that we understand it to have in our lives today.

31:12 *the bounty of the LORD.* The blessings of the goodness of the Lord are bountiful crops, flocks, and vineyards (Ps. 65).

30:23 [r] Jer 23:19 **30:24** [s] Jer 4:8 [t] Jer 4:28 [u] Jer 23:19-20
31:1 [v] Jer 30:22 **31:2** [w] Nu 14:20 [x] Ex 33:14
31:3 [y] Dt 4:37 [z] Hos 11:4 **31:4** [a] Jer 30:19
31:5 [b] Jer 50:19 [c] Isa 65:21; Am 9:14 **31:6** [d] Isa 2:3; Jer 50:4-5; Mic 4:2 **31:7** [e] Dt 28:13; Isa 61:9 [f] Ps 14:7; 28:9 [g] Isa 37:31 **31:8** [h] Jer 3:18; 23:8 [i] Dt 30:4; Eze 34:12-14 [j] Isa 42:16 [k] Eze 34:16; Mic 4:6 **31:9** [l] Ps 126:5 [m] Isa 63:13 [n] Isa 49:11 [o] Ex 4:22; Jer 3:4 **31:10** [p] Isa 66:19; Jer 25:22 [q] Jer 50:19 [r] Isa 40:11; Eze 34:12 **31:11** [s] Isa 44:23; 48:20 [t] Ps 142:6 **31:12** [u] Eze 17:23; Mic 4:1 [v] Joel 3:18 [w] Hos 2:21-22 [x] Isa 58:11 [y] Isa 65:19; Jn 16:22; Rev 7:17
31:13 [z] Isa 61:3 [a] Ps 30:11; Isa 51:11

14 I will satisfy[b] the priests with abundance,
and my people will be filled with my bounty,"
declares the LORD.

15 This is what the LORD says:

"A voice is heard in Ramah,[c]
mourning and great weeping,
Rachel weeping for her children
and refusing to be comforted,[d]
because they are no more."[e]

16 This is what the LORD says:

"Restrain your voice from weeping
and your eyes from tears,[f]
for your work will be rewarded,[g]"
declares the LORD.
"They will return[h] from the land of the enemy.
17 So there is hope for your descendants,"
declares the LORD.
"Your children will return to their own land.

18 "I have surely heard Ephraim's moaning:
'You disciplined[i] me like an unruly calf,[j]
and I have been disciplined.
Restore[k] me, and I will return,
because you are the LORD my God.
19 After I strayed,[l]
I repented;
after I came to understand,
I beat[m] my breast.
I was ashamed and humiliated
because I bore the disgrace of my youth.'
20 Is not Ephraim my dear son,
the child in whom I delight?
Though I often speak against him,
I still remember[n] him.
Therefore my heart yearns for him;
I have great compassion[o] for him,"
declares the LORD.

21 "Set up road signs;
put up guideposts.
Take note of the highway,[p]
the road that you take.
Return,[q] Virgin[r] Israel,
return to your towns.
22 How long will you wander,[s]
unfaithful[t] Daughter Israel?
The LORD will create a new thing on earth—
the woman will return to[a] the man."

23 This is what the LORD Almighty, the
God of Israel, says: "When I bring them
back from captivity,[b][u] the people in the land
of Judah and in its towns will once again
use these words: 'The LORD bless you, you
prosperous city,[v] you sacred mountain.'[w]
24 People will live[x] together in Judah and all
its towns—farmers and those who move
about with their flocks. 25 I will refresh the
weary and satisfy the faint."[y]
26 At this I awoke[z] and looked around. My
sleep had been pleasant to me.
27 "The days are coming," declares the
LORD, "when I will plant[a] the kingdoms
of Israel and Judah with the offspring of
people and of animals. 28 Just as I watched
over them to uproot and tear down, and to
overthrow, destroy and bring disaster,[b] so I
will watch over them to build and to plant,"[c]
declares the LORD. 29 "In those days people
will no longer say,

'The parents[d] have eaten sour grapes,
and the children's teeth are set on edge.'[e]

30 Instead, everyone will die for their own
sin;[f] whoever eats sour grapes—their own
teeth will be set on edge.

31 "The days are coming," declares the LORD,
"when I will make a new covenant[g]
with the people of Israel
and with the people of Judah.

[a] 22 Or *will protect* [b] 23 Or *I restore their fortunes*

31:14 *I will satisfy the priests with abundance.* The theme of joy is summarized in God's intention to fill the priests and the people with abundance. Jeremiah gave the people hope and comfort in facing the poverty and oppression of exile and captivity.
31:19 *I beat my breast.* This indicates an outward demonstration of remorse over sin and change of life (Ezek. 21:12).
31:21 *signs . . . guideposts.* These would point out the way to the people's homeland. More importantly, Israel was instructed to set its heart toward the way that is the path of faith in its God.
31:27 *I will plant the kingdoms of Israel.* God would plant and multiply the seed of man and animal in the land of Judah.
31:28 *to build and to plant.* These are the same terms used in Jeremiah's call (1:10).
31:31–34 The New Covenant—The New Covenant is called "new" in contrast to the covenant with Moses which is called "old" (Jer. 31:32; Heb. 8:6–13) because the new accomplishes what the old could only point to, that is, the salvation of believers through the death and resurrection of Jesus Christ. Four provisions are made in this covenant: (1) *Regeneration*—God will put His law in their inward parts and write it in their hearts (31:33), (2) *A national restoration*—Yahweh will be their God and the nation will be His people (31:33), (3) *Personal ministry of*

31:14 [b] ver 25 **31:15** [c] Jos 18:25 [d] Ge 37:35 [e] Jer 10:20; Mt 2:17-18* **31:16** [f] Isa 25:8; 30:19 [g] Ru 2:12 [h] Jer 30:3; Eze 11:17 **31:18** [i] Job 5:17 [j] Hos 4:16 [k] Ps 80:3 **31:19** [l] Eze 36:31 [m] Eze 21:12; Lk 18:13 **31:20** [n] Hos 4:4; 11:8 [o] Isa 55:7; 63:15; Mic 7:18 **31:21** [p] Jer 50:5 [q] Isa 52:11 [r] ver 4 **31:22** [s] Jer 2:23 [t] Jer 3:6 **31:23** [u] Jer 30:18 [v] Isa 1:26 [w] Ps 48:1; Zec 8:3 **31:24** [x] Zec 8:4-8 **31:25** [y] Jn 4:14 **31:26** [z] Zec 4:1 **31:27** [a] Eze 36:9-11; Hos 2:23 **31:28** [b] Jer 18:8; 44:27 [c] Jer 1:10 **31:29** [d] La 5:7 [e] Eze 18:2 **31:30** [f] Isa 3:11; Gal 6:7 **31:31** [g] Jer 32:40; Eze 37:26; Lk 22:20; Heb 8:8-12*; 10:16-17

32 It will not be like the covenant[h]
I made with their ancestors[i]
when I took them by the hand
to lead them out of Egypt,
because they broke my covenant,
though I was a husband to[a] them,[b]"
declares the LORD.
33 "This is the covenant I will make with
the people of Israel
after that time," declares the LORD.
"I will put my law in their minds
and write it on their hearts.[j]
I will be their God,
and they will be my people.[k]
34 No longer will they teach[l] their
neighbor,
or say to one another, 'Know the
LORD,'
because they will all know[m] me,
from the least of them to the
greatest,"
declares the LORD.
"For I will forgive[n] their wickedness
and will remember their sins[o] no
more."

35 This is what the LORD says,

he who appoints[p] the sun
to shine by day,
who decrees the moon and stars
to shine by night,[q]
who stirs up the sea
so that its waves roar—
the LORD Almighty is his name:[r]
36 "Only if these decrees[s] vanish from my
sight,"
declares the LORD,
"will Israel[t] ever cease
being a nation before me."

37 This is what the LORD says:

"Only if the heavens above can be
measured[u]
and the foundations of the earth
below be searched out
will I reject[v] all the descendants of
Israel
because of all they have done,"
declares the LORD.

38 "The days are coming," declares the
LORD, "when this city will be rebuilt[w] for
me from the Tower of Hananel[x] to the
Corner Gate.[y] 39 The measuring line will
stretch from there straight to the hill of
Gareb and then turn to Goah. 40 The whole
valley[z] where dead bodies[a] and ashes are
thrown, and all the terraces out to the Kidron Valley[b] on the east as far as the corner of the Horse Gate,[c] will be holy[d] to the
LORD. The city will never again be uprooted or demolished."

Jeremiah Buys a Field

32 This is the word that came to Jeremiah from the LORD in the tenth[e]
year of Zedekiah king of Judah, which
was the eighteenth[f] year of Nebuchadnezzar. 2 The army of the king of Babylon was
then besieging Jerusalem, and Jeremiah
the prophet was confined in the courtyard
of the guard[g] in the royal palace of Judah.
3 Now Zedekiah king of Judah had imprisoned him there, saying, "Why do you
prophesy[h] as you do? You say, 'This is what
the LORD says: I am about to give this city
into the hands of the king of Babylon, and
he will capture[i] it. 4 Zedekiah king of Judah will not escape[j] the Babylonians[c] but
will certainly be given into the hands of
the king of Babylon, and will speak with
him face to face and see him with his own

[a] 32 Hebrew; Septuagint and Syriac / *and I turned away from* [b] 32 Or *was their master*
[c] 4 Or *Chaldeans*; also in verses 5, 24, 25, 28, 29 and 43

the Holy Spirit—they will all be taught individually by God (31:34) and (4) *Full justification*—their sins will be forgiven and completely removed (31:34). The New Covenant is made sure by the blood that Jesus shed on Calvary's cross. The blood that guarantees to Israel its New Covenant also provides for the forgiveness of sins for the believers who comprise the church. Jesus' payment for sin is more than adequate to pay for the sins of all who will believe in Him.

31:32 ***the covenant I made with their ancestors.*** The old covenant demanded adherence to stipulations (Ex. 19:1–23:33) which the people were unable to keep. Above all other commandments, the people were commanded to love and serve God and abandon all others (Deut. 6:4–5). This they did not do. From the wilderness period (Ex. 32:1–10; Num. 25:1–9) until the days of Manasseh, the history of Israel was permeated with idolatrous activity. ***husband.*** As Hosea was to Gomer, the Lord had been a faithful and devoted husband to Israel (Hos. 1:2).

31:33 ***the covenant I will make.*** The new covenant, as the old, would be initiated by God Himself. ***after that time.*** This expression looks forward to the time of fulfillment of the new covenant, which found fruition in the life, death, and resurrection of Jesus Christ.

31:34 ***No longer will they teach their neighbor.*** Knowledge of God is a major theme of Jeremiah (2:8; 4:22; 5:4; 8:7).

31:36–37 ***if these decrees vanish.*** The foundation of the new covenant is as sure as the God who maintains creation. At the peak of Judah's apostasy, shortly before the destruction of the nation by Babylon in divine judgment, the Lord emphatically reaffirmed His covenant relationship with the Jewish people.

31:32 [h] Ex 24:8 [i] Dt 5:3 **31:33** [j] 2Co 3:3 [k] Jer 24:7; Heb 10:16 **31:34** [l] 1Jn 2:27 [m] Jn 6:45 [n] Isa 54:13; Jer 33:8; 50:20 [o] Mic 7:19; Ro 11:27; Heb 10:17* **31:35** [p] Ps 136:7-9 [q] Ge 1:16 [r] Jer 10:16 **31:36** [s] Isa 54:9-10; Jer 33:20-26 [t] Ps 89:36-37 **31:37** [u] Jer 33:22 [v] Jer 33:24-26; Ro 11:1-5 **31:38** [w] Jer 30:18 [x] Ne 3:1 [y] 2Ki 14:13; Zec 14:10 **31:40** [z] Jer 7:31-32 [a] Jer 8:2 [b] 2Sa 15:23; Jn 18:1 [c] 2Ki 11:16 [d] Joel 3:17; Zec 14:21 **32:1** [e] 2Ki 25:1 [f] Jer 25:1; 39:1 **32:2** [g] Ne 3:25; Jer 37:21 **32:3** [h] Jer 26:8-9 [i] ver 28; Jer 34:2-3 **32:4** [j] Jer 38:18, 23; 39:5-7; 52:9

eyes. 5He will take[k] Zedekiah to Babylon,
where he will remain until I deal with him,
declares the LORD. If you fight against the
Babylonians, you will not succeed.'"[l]
6Jeremiah said, "The word of the LORD
came to me: 7Hanamel son of Shallum your
uncle is going to come to you and say, 'Buy
my field at Anathoth, because as nearest
relative it is your right and duty[m] to buy it.'
8"Then, just as the LORD had said, my
cousin Hanamel came to me in the courtyard of the guard and said, 'Buy my field
at Anathoth in the territory of Benjamin.
Since it is your right to redeem it and possess it, buy it for yourself.'
"I knew that this was the word of the
LORD; 9so I bought the field at Anathoth
from my cousin Hanamel and weighed
out for him seventeen shekels[a] of silver.[n]
10I signed and sealed the deed, had it witnessed,[o] and weighed out the silver on the
scales. 11I took the deed of purchase—the
sealed copy containing the terms and conditions, as well as the unsealed copy—
12and I gave this deed to Baruch[p] son of
Neriah,[q] the son of Mahseiah, in the presence of my cousin Hanamel and of the
witnesses who had signed the deed and of
all the Jews sitting in the courtyard of the
guard.
13"In their presence I gave Baruch these
instructions: 14'This is what the LORD Almighty, the God of Israel, says: Take these
documents, both the sealed and unsealed
copies of the deed of purchase, and put
them in a clay jar so they will last a long
time. 15For this is what the LORD Almighty,
the God of Israel, says: Houses, fields and
vineyards will again be bought in this
land.'[r]
16"After I had given the deed of purchase
to Baruch son of Neriah, I prayed to the
LORD:

> 17"Ah, Sovereign LORD,[s] you have made
> the heavens and the earth by your
> great power and outstretched arm.[t]
> Nothing is too hard[u] for you. 18You
> show love[v] to thousands but bring the
> punishment for the parents' sins into
> the laps of their children[w] after them.
> Great and mighty God, whose name is
> the LORD Almighty,[x] 19great are your
> purposes and mighty are your deeds.[y]
> Your eyes are open to the ways of all
> mankind;[z] you reward each person
> according to their conduct and as
> their deeds deserve.[a] 20You performed
> signs and wonders in Egypt[b] and have
> continued them to this day, in Isra-
> el and among all mankind, and have
> gained the renown that is still yours.
> 21You brought your people Israel out
> of Egypt with signs and wonders, by
> a mighty hand[c] and an outstretched
> arm and with great terror.[d] 22You gave
> them this land you had sworn to give
> their ancestors, a land flowing with
> milk and honey.[e] 23They came in and
> took possession[f] of it, but they did not
> obey you or follow your law;[g] they did
> not do what you commanded them to
> do. So you brought all this disaster[h] on
> them.
> 24"See how the siege ramps are
> built up to take the city. Because of
> the sword, famine and plague,[i] the
> city will be given into the hands of
> the Babylonians who are attacking it.
> What you said[j] has happened, as you
> now see. 25And though the city will be
> given into the hands of the Babyloni-
> ans, you, Sovereign LORD, say to me,
> 'Buy the field with silver and have the
> transaction witnessed.'"

26Then the word of the LORD came to
Jeremiah: 27"I am the LORD, the God of all
mankind.[k] Is anything too hard for me?
28Therefore this is what the LORD says: I
am about to give this city into the hands
of the Babylonians and to Nebuchadnezzar[l] king of Babylon, who will capture it.[m]
29The Babylonians who are attacking this
city will come in and set it on fire; they
will burn it down,[n] along with the houses[o] where the people aroused my anger by
burning incense on the roofs to Baal and
by pouring out drink offerings[p] to other
gods.

---

[a] 9 That is, about 7 ounces or about 200 grams

32:6–8 *at Anathoth.* The Lord instructed Jeremiah to purchase a field in his hometown three miles north of Jerusalem.
32:13–15 *clay jar.* Examples of storage jars that served as safety-deposit vessels have been excavated in Judah. The Dead Sea Scrolls were also stored in ceramic vessels, aiding their preservation for almost two thousand years. The illustrated message of the purchase was assurance and confirmation that restoration of the land was certain.
32:20–21 *signs and wonders in Egypt.* The great historical demonstration of God's loyal love was the exodus of Israel from Egypt. The miracles that accompanied the exodus made God known among the nations such as Moab (Num. 22–24).
32:27 *the God of all mankind.* God was Lord over Israel and Judah, and Lord over the nations (27:11), including mighty Babylon (25:15–26).

32:5 [k] Jer 39:7; Eze 12:13 [l] Jer 21:4 **32:7** [m] Lev 25:24-25; Ru 4:3-4; Mt 27:10* **32:9** [n] Ge 23:16 **32:10** [o] Ru 4:9 **32:12** [p] ver 16; Jer 36:4; 43:3,6; 45:1 [q] Jer 51:59 **32:15** [r] ver 43-44; Jer 30:18; Am 9:14-15 **32:17** [s] Jer 1:6 [t] 2Ki 19:15; Ps 102:25 [u] Mt 19:26 **32:18** [v] Dt 5:10 [w] Ex 20:5 [x] Jer 10:16 **32:19** [y] Isa 28:29 [z] Pr 5:21; Jer 16:17 [a] Jer 17:10; Mt 16:27 **32:20** [b] Ex 9:16 **32:21** [c] Ex 6:6; 1Ch 17:21; Da 9:15 [d] Dt 26:8 **32:22** [e] Ex 3:8; Jer 11:5 **32:23** [f] Ps 44:2; 78:54-55 [g] Ne 9:26; Jer 11:8 [h] Da 9:14 **32:24** [i] Jer 14:12 [j] Dt 4:25-26; Jos 23:15-16 **32:27** [k] Nu 16:22 **32:28** [l] 2Ch 36:17 [m] ver 3 **32:29** [n] 2Ch 36:19; Jer 21:10; 37:8, 10; 52:13 [o] Jer 19:13 [p] Jer 44:18

30“The people of Israel and Judah have
done nothing but evil in my sight from
their youth;[q] indeed, the people of Israel
have done nothing but arouse my anger[r]
with what their hands have made,[s] declares
the LORD. 31From the day it was built until now, this city has so aroused my anger
and wrath that I must remove[t] it from my
sight. 32The people of Israel and Judah
have provoked me by all the evil[u] they
have done—they, their kings and officials,
their priests and prophets, the people of Judah and those living in Jerusalem. 33They
turned their backs[v] to me and not their faces; though I taught[w] them again and again,
they would not listen or respond to discipline. 34They set up their vile images in the
house that bears my Name and defiled[x] it.
35They built high places for Baal in the Valley of Ben Hinnom to sacrifice their sons
and daughters to Molek,[y] though I never
commanded—nor did it enter my mind[z]—
that they should do such a detestable thing
and so make Judah sin.

36“You are saying about this city, ‘By the
sword, famine and plague[a] it will be giv-
en into the hands of the king of Babylon’;
but this is what the LORD, the God of Israel,
says: 37I will surely gather[b] them from all
the lands where I banish them in my furious anger and great wrath; I will bring
them back to this place and let them live
in safety.[c] 38They will be my people,[d] and
I will be their God. 39I will give them singleness[e] of heart and action, so that they
will always fear me and that all will then
go well for them and for their children after them. 40I will make an everlasting covenant[f] with them: I will never stop doing
good to them, and I will inspire them to fear
me, so that they will never turn away from
me.[g] 41I will rejoice in doing them good[h]
and will assuredly plant[i] them in this land
with all my heart and soul.

42“This is what the LORD says: As I have
brought all this great calamity on this people, so I will give them all the prosperity
I have promised[j] them. 43Once more fields
will be bought[k] in this land of which you
say, ‘It is a desolate waste, without people
or animals, for it has been given into the
hands of the Babylonians.’ 44Fields will be
bought for silver, and deeds[l] will be signed,
sealed and witnessed in the territory of
Benjamin, in the villages around Jerusalem, in the towns of Judah and in the towns
of the hill country, of the western foothills
and of the Negev,[m] because I will restore[n]
their fortunes,[a] declares the LORD.”

Promise of Restoration

33 While Jeremiah was still confined
in the courtyard[o] of the guard, the
word of the LORD came to him a second
time: 2“This is what the LORD says, he who
made the earth,[p] the LORD who formed it
and established it—the LORD is his name:[q]
3‘Call[r] to me and I will answer you and tell
you great and unsearchable things you do
not know.’ 4For this is what the LORD, the
God of Israel, says about the houses in this
city and the royal palaces of Judah that
have been torn down to be used against the
siege[s] ramps[t] and the sword 5in the fight
with the Babylonians[b]: ‘They will be filled
with the dead bodies of the people I will
slay in my anger and wrath.[u] I will hide
my face[v] from this city because of all its
wickedness.

6“ ‘Nevertheless, I will bring health and
healing to it; I will heal my people and will
let them enjoy abundant peace and security. 7I will bring Judah[w] and Israel back
from captivity[c][x] and will rebuild them as
they were before.[y] 8I will cleanse[z] them
from all the sin they have committed
against me and will forgive[a] all their sins
of rebellion against me. 9Then this city will
bring me renown, joy, praise[b] and honor[c]
before all nations on earth that hear of all

[a] 44 Or *will bring them back from captivity*
[b] 5 Or *Chaldeans* [c] 7 Or *will restore the fortunes of Judah and Israel*

32:39 ***singleness of heart and action.*** Because the Lord had written on the heart of the people a new covenant (31:33), no longer would they worship other deities and turn to foreign nations for help. The word “way” is often used in Jeremiah to denote the character of a person’s life, whether evil (4:18) or good (7:23).
32:40 ***everlasting covenant.*** This expression is also found in Isaiah 55:3; Ezekiel 16:60; 37:26. In Ezekiel it is equated with a covenant of peace that God will establish with His people. This covenant will be everlasting, unlike the Sinai covenant which had been broken and ignored for so long.
33:1 ***While Jeremiah was still confined.*** A chronological tie is made to 32:2 (588 B.C.). Jeremiah had been placed under palace court guard because of what his enemies regarded as “seditious speeches,” announcing the fall of Jerusalem and giving advice to Zedekiah to surrender to Nebuchadnezzar.
33:8 ***cleanse ... forgive.*** Forgiveness is described with these two terms. The word “cleanse” describes ritual purification of what is physically or spiritually unclean or defiled, like Israel and Judah (2:23; 7:30). “Forgive” in the Old Testament is used only with God as the subject as He forgives man. This fact helps us understand the reaction of the scribes when they heard Jesus forgiving sins (Mark 2:7).

32:30 [q] Jer 22:21 [r] Jer 8:19 [s] Jer 25:7 **32:31** [t] 2Ki 23:27; 24:3 **32:32** [u] Isa 1:4-6; Da 9:8 **32:33** [v] Jer 2:27; Eze 8:16 [w] Jer 7:13 **32:34** [x] Jer 7:30 **32:35** [y] Lev 18:21 [z] Jer 7:31; 19:5 **32:36** [a] ver 24 **32:37** [b] Jer 23:3,6 [c] Dt 30:3; Eze 34:28 **32:38** [d] Jer 24:7; 2Co 6:16* **32:39** [e] Eze 11:19 **32:40** [f] Isa 55:3 [g] Jer 24:7 **32:41** [h] Dt 30:9 [i] Jer 24:6; 31:28; Am 9:15 **32:42** [j] Jer 31:28 **32:43** [k] ver 15 **32:44** [l] ver 10 [m] Jer 17:26 [n] Jer 33:7, 11, 26 **33:1** [o] Jer 32:2-3; 37:21; 38:28 **33:2** [p] Jer 10:16 [q] Ex 3:15; 15:3 **33:3** [r] Isa 55:6; Jer 29:12 **33:4** [s] Eze 4:2 [t] Jer 32:24; Hab 1:10 **33:5** [u] Jer 21:4-7 [v] Isa 8:17 **33:7** [w] Jer 32:44 [x] Jer 30:3; Am 9:14 [y] Isa 1:26 **33:8** [z] Heb 9:13-14 [a] Jer 31:34; Mic 7:18; Zec 13:1 **33:9** [b] Jer 13:11 [c] Isa 62:7; Jer 3:17

the good things I do for it; and they will
be in awe and will tremble at the abundant
prosperity and peace I provide for it.’
10“This is what the LORD says: ‘You say
about this place, “It is a desolate waste,
without people or animals.”[d] Yet in the
towns of Judah and the streets of Jerusalem that are deserted, inhabited by neither
people nor animals, there will be heard
once more 11the sounds of joy and gladness,[e] the voices of bride and bridegroom,
and the voices of those who bring thank
offerings[f] to the house of the LORD, saying,

“Give thanks to the LORD Almighty,
for the LORD is good;[g]
his love endures forever.”[h]

For I will restore the fortunes of the land as
they were before,’ says the LORD.
12“This is what the LORD Almighty
says: ‘In this place, desolate[i] and without
people or animals—in all its towns there
will again be pastures for shepherds to
rest their flocks.[j] 13In the towns of the hill
country, of the western foothills and of the
Negev,[k] in the territory of Benjamin, in
the villages around Jerusalem and in the
towns of Judah, flocks will again pass under the hand[l] of the one who counts them,’
says the LORD.
14“ ‘The days are coming,’ declares the
LORD, ‘when I will fulfill the good promise[m]
I made to the people of Israel and Judah.

15“ ‘In those days and at that time
I will make a righteous[n] Branch[o]
sprout from David’s line;
he will do what is just and right in the
land.
16In those days Judah will be saved[p]
and Jerusalem will live in
safety.
This is the name by which it[a] will be
called:
The LORD Our Righteous Savior.’[q]

17For this is what the LORD says: ‘David will
never fail[r] to have a man to sit on the throne
of Israel, 18nor will the Levitical[s] priests
ever fail to have a man to stand before me
continually to offer burnt offerings, to burn
grain offerings and to present sacrifices.[t]’ ”
19The word of the LORD came to Jeremiah: 20“This is what the LORD says: ‘If you
can break my covenant with the day[u] and
my covenant with the night, so that day
and night no longer come at their appointed time, 21then my covenant[v] with David
my servant—and my covenant with the
Levites who are priests ministering before me—can be broken and David will
no longer have a descendant to reign on
his throne.[w] 22I will make the descendants
of David my servant and the Levites who
minister before me as countless[x] as the
stars in the sky and as measureless as the
sand on the seashore.’ ”
23The word of the LORD came to Jeremiah: 24“Have you not noticed that these
people are saying, ‘The LORD has rejected the two kingdoms[b][y] he chose’? So they
despise[z] my people and no longer regard
them as a nation.[a] 25This is what the LORD
says: ‘If I have not made my covenant with
day and night[b] and established the laws of
heaven and earth,[c] 26then I will reject[d] the
descendants of Jacob[e] and David my servant and will not choose one of his sons
to rule over the descendants of Abraham,
Isaac and Jacob. For I will restore their fortunes[c][f] and have compassion on them.’ ”

Warning to Zedekiah

34 While Nebuchadnezzar king of Babylon and all his army and all the kingdoms and peoples[g] in the empire he ruled
were fighting against Jerusalem[h] and all
its surrounding towns, this word came to
Jeremiah from the LORD: 2“This is what the
LORD, the God of Israel, says: Go to Zedekiah[i] king of Judah and tell him, ‘This is what
the LORD says: I am about to give this city
into the hands of the king of Babylon, and
he will burn it down.[j] 3You will not escape
from his grasp but will surely be captured
and given into his hands.[k] You will see the
king of Babylon with your own eyes, and
he will speak with you face to face. And
you will go to Babylon.
4“ ‘Yet hear the LORD’s promise to you,
Zedekiah king of Judah. This is what the
LORD says concerning you: You will not die

[a] 16 Or *he* [b] 24 Or *families* [c] 26 Or *will bring them back from captivity*

33:13 *flocks will again pass under.* The term "flocks" is used to depict the Israelites as they returned from captivity into the fold of the holy city of Jerusalem.
33:16 *will live in safety.* Following the devastation of the Babylonian onslaught, Jerusalem would exist under divine protection.
33:17 *David will never fail.* The Davidic covenant of divine succession is reiterated (2 Sam. 7:12–16). The Levitical priesthood would likewise be heirs to a divine succession in overseeing the sacrificial system in the Jerusalem temple. Jesus, as Priest and King, fulfills both offices in the New Covenant.
34:3 *You will not escape from his grasp.* Though Zedekiah attempted to flee to Jericho, Nebuchadnezzar's forces captured and brought him to Riblah for a face to face meeting with Nebuchadnezzar (32:3,4).

33:10 [d] Jer 32:43 **33:11** [e] Isa 51:3 [f] Lev 7:12 [g] 1Ch 16:8; Ps 136:1 [h] 1Ch 16:34; 2Ch 5:13; Ps 100:4-5 **33:12** [i] Jer 32:43 [j] Isa 65:10; Eze 34:11-15 **33:13** [k] Jer 17:26 [l] Lev 27:32 **33:14** [m] Jer 29:10 **33:15** [n] Ps 72:2 [o] Isa 4:2; 11:1; Jer 23:5 **33:16** [p] Isa 45:17 [q] 1Co 1:30 **33:17** [r] 2Sa 7:13; 1Ki 2:4; Ps 89:29-37; Lk 1:33 **33:18** [s] Dt 18:1 [t] Heb 13:15 **33:20** [u] Ps 89:36 **33:21** [v] Ps 89:34 [w] 2Ch 7:18 **33:22** [x] Ge 15:5 **33:24** [y] Eze 37:22 [z] Ne 4:4 [a] Jer 30:17 **33:25** [b] Jer 31:35-36 [c] Ps 74:16-17 **33:26** [d] Jer 31:37 [e] Isa 14:1 [f] ver 7 **34:1** [g] Jer 27:7 [h] 2Ki 25:1; Jer 39:1 **34:2** [i] 2Ch 36:11 [j] ver 22; Jer 32:29; 37:8 **34:3** [k] 2Ki 25:7; Jer 21:7; 32:4

by the sword; 5you will die peacefully. As
people made a funeral fire[l] in honor of your
predecessors, the kings who ruled before
you, so they will make a fire in your honor
and lament, "Alas,[m] master!" I myself make
this promise, declares the LORD.' "
6Then Jeremiah the prophet told all this
to Zedekiah king of Judah, in Jerusalem,
7while the army of the king of Babylon
was fighting against Jerusalem and the
other cities of Judah that were still holding
out—Lachish[n] and Azekah.[o] These were
the only fortified cities left in Judah.

Freedom for Slaves

8The word came to Jeremiah from the
LORD after King Zedekiah had made a
covenant with all the people[p] in Jerusalem
to proclaim freedom[q] for the slaves. 9Ev-
eryone was to free their Hebrew slaves,
both male and female; no one was to hold
a fellow Hebrew in bondage.[r] 10So all the
officials and people who entered into this
covenant agreed that they would free their
male and female slaves and no longer hold
them in bondage. They agreed, and set
them free. 11But afterward they changed
their minds and took back the slaves they
had freed and enslaved them again.
12Then the word of the LORD came to
Jeremiah: 13"This is what the LORD, the
God of Israel, says: I made a covenant with
your ancestors[s] when I brought them out
of Egypt, out of the land of slavery. I said,
14'Every seventh year each of you must
free any fellow Hebrews who have sold
themselves to you. After they have served
you six years, you must let them go free.'[a][t]
Your ancestors, however, did not listen to
me or pay attention[u] to me. 15Recently you
repented and did what is right in my sight:
Each of you proclaimed freedom to your
own people.[v] You even made a covenant before me in the house that bears my Name.[w]
16But now you have turned around[x] and
profaned[y] my name; each of you has taken
back the male and female slaves you had
set free to go where they wished. You have
forced them to become your slaves again.
17"Therefore this is what the LORD says:
You have not obeyed me; you have not proclaimed freedom to your own people. So I
now proclaim 'freedom' for you,[z] declares
the LORD—'freedom' to fall by the sword,
plague and famine. I will make you abhorrent to all the kingdoms of the earth.[a]
18Those who have violated my covenant and
have not fulfilled the terms of the covenant
they made before me, I will treat like the calf
they cut in two and then walked between its
pieces.[b] 19The leaders of Judah and Jerusalem, the court officials,[c] the priests and all
the people of the land who walked between
the pieces of the calf, 20I will deliver[d] into
the hands of their enemies who want to kill
them.[e] Their dead bodies will become food
for the birds and the wild animals.[f]
21"I will deliver Zedekiah[g] king of Judah
and his officials[h] into the hands of their enemies who want to kill them, to the army of
the king of Babylon, which has withdrawn[i]
from you. 22I am going to give the order,
declares the LORD, and I will bring them
back to this city. They will fight against it,
take[j] it and burn[k] it down. And I will lay
waste the towns of Judah so no one can
live there."

The Rekabites

35 This is the word that came to Jeremiah from the LORD during the reign of
Jehoiakim[l] son of Josiah king of Judah: 2"Go
to the Rekabite[m] family and invite them to
come to one of the side rooms[n] of the house
of the LORD and give them wine to drink."

---

a *14* Deut. 15:12

34:5 *you will die peacefully.* Jeremiah proclaimed the destruction of Jerusalem and the death of its inhabitants by sword, pestilence, and famine. The particular implications for Zedekiah are outlined here. He would not be executed by the sword. According to 2 Kings 25:6–7, his sons were killed before his eyes and then his eyes were put out before being taken to Babylon.

34:8 *Zedekiah had made a covenant with all the people.* A legal agreement was made between Zedekiah and the people of Jerusalem during the Babylonian siege to release from bondage all Hebrew slaves.

34:12–14 *This is what the LORD . . . says.* Jeremiah, a faithful steward of the word of God, began his attack against Judah's leaders by recounting the teaching of the law on the matter of emancipating slaves (Ex. 21:2–6; Deut. 15:12–15). He reminded the people that their forefathers were slaves in Egypt, and that God had freed them from slavery and oppression.

34:16 *turned around and profaned my name.* When the princes of Judah emancipated their Hebrew slaves, it demonstrated their covenant faithfulness and devotion to God (v. 10). But when the righteous decision was reversed (v. 11), the name of God was profaned. The name of God sums up and represents His attributes, character, and work. That name had been defiled by the breach of covenant in the same way that the people had defiled the land with their idolatry (16:18).

34:18–19 *the calf they cut in two.* The covenant ceremony is outlined. The main ritual of the two-party covenant began with cutting the sacrificial animal in half, after which the two participants would walk together between the parts (Gen. 15). The divided animal portrayed the potential fate of one who broke the covenant stipulations.

35:2 *the Rekabite family.* This clan was a tightly knit group of descendants of the Kenites (Judg. 1:16;

34:5 [l] 2Ch 16:14; 21:19 [m] Jer 22:18 **34:7** [n] Jos 10:3 [o] Jos 10:10; 2Ch 11:9 **34:8** [p] 2Ki 11:17 [q] Ex 21:2; Lev 25:10, 39-41; Ne 5:5-8 **34:9** [r] Lev 25:39-46 **34:13** [s] Ex 24:8 **34:14** [t] Ex 21:2 [u] Dt 15:12; 2Ki 17:14 **34:15** [v] ver 8 [w] Jer 7:10-11; 32:34 **34:16** [x] Eze 3:20; 18:24 [y] Ex 20:7; Lev 19:12 **34:17** [z] Mt 7:2; Gal 6:7 [a] Dt 28:25, 64; Jer 29:18 **34:18** [b] Ge 15:10 **34:19** [c] Zep 3:3-4 **34:20** [d] Jer 21:7 [e] Jer 11:21 [f] Dt 28:26; Jer 7:33; 19:7 **34:21** [g] Jer 32:4 [h] Jer 39:6; 52:24-27 [i] Jer 37:5 **34:22** [j] Jer 39:1-2 [k] Jer 39:8 **35:1** [l] 2Ch 36:5 **35:2** [m] 2Ki 10:15; 1Ch 2:55 [n] 1Ki 6:5

3So I went to get Jaazaniah son of Jeremiah, the son of Habazziniah, and his brothers and all his sons—the whole family of the Rekabites. 4I brought them into the house of the LORD, into the room of the sons of Hanan son of Igdaliah the man of God.[o] It was next to the room of the officials, which was over that of Maaseiah son of Shallum[p] the doorkeeper.[q] 5Then I set bowls full of wine and some cups before the Rekabites and said to them, "Drink some wine."

6But they replied, "We do not drink wine, because our forefather Jehonadab[a][r] son of Rekab gave us this command: 'Neither you nor your descendants must ever drink wine.[s] 7Also you must never build houses, sow seed or plant vineyards; you must never have any of these things, but must always live in tents.[t] Then you will live a long time in the land[u] where you are nomads.' 8We have obeyed everything our forefather[v] Jehonadab son of Rekab commanded us. Neither we nor our wives nor our sons and daughters have ever drunk wine 9or built houses to live in or had vineyards, fields or crops.[w] 10We have lived in tents and have fully obeyed everything our forefather Jehonadab commanded us. 11But when Nebuchadnezzar king of Babylon invaded[x] this land, we said, 'Come, we must go to Jerusalem[y] to escape the Babylonian[b] and Aramean armies.' So we have remained in Jerusalem."

12Then the word of the LORD came to Jeremiah, saying: 13"This is what the LORD Almighty, the God of Israel, says: Go and tell the people of Judah and those living in Jerusalem, 'Will you not learn a lesson[z] and obey my words?' declares the LORD. 14'Jehonadab son of Rekab ordered his descendants not to drink wine and this command has been kept. To this day they do not drink wine, because they obey their forefather's command. But I have spoken to you again and again,[a] yet you have not obeyed[b] me. 15Again and again I sent all my servants the prophets[c] to you. They said, "Each of you must turn[d] from your wicked ways and reform[e] your actions; do not follow other gods to serve them. Then you will live in the land[f] I have given to you and your ancestors." But you have not paid attention or listened[g] to me. 16The descendants of Jehonadab son of Rekab have carried out the command their forefather[h] gave them, but these people have not obeyed me.'

17"Therefore this is what the LORD God Almighty, the God of Israel, says: 'Listen! I am going to bring on Judah and on everyone living in Jerusalem every disaster[i] I pronounced against them. I spoke to them, but they did not listen;[j] I called to them, but they did not answer.'"[k]

18Then Jeremiah said to the family of the Rekabites, "This is what the LORD Almighty, the God of Israel, says: 'You have obeyed the command of your forefather Jehonadab and have followed all his instructions and have done everything he ordered.' 19Therefore this is what the LORD Almighty, the God of Israel, says: 'Jehonadab son of Rekab will never fail[l] to have a descendant to serve[m] me.'"

Jehoiakim Burns Jeremiah's Scroll

36 In the fourth year of Jehoiakim[n] son of Josiah king of Judah, this word came to Jeremiah from the LORD: 2"Take a scroll[o] and write on it all the words I have spoken to you concerning Israel, Judah and all the other nations from the time I began speaking to you in the reign of Josiah[p] till now. 3Perhaps[q] when the people of Judah hear[r] about every disaster I plan to inflict on them, they will each turn[s] from their wicked ways; then I will forgive[t] their wickedness and their sin."

4So Jeremiah called Baruch[u] son of Neriah, and while Jeremiah dictated[v] all the words the LORD had spoken to him, Baruch wrote them on the scroll.[w] 5Then Jeremiah told Baruch, "I am restricted; I am not allowed to go to the LORD's temple. 6So you go to the house of the LORD on a day of fasting[x] and read to the people from the scroll the words of the LORD that you wrote as

[a] *6* Hebrew *Jonadab*, a variant of *Jehonadab*; here and often in this chapter [b] *11* Or *Chaldean*

1 Chr. 2:55). They lived as nomads, rejecting all forms of urban and agrarian life. They refused to drink wine or strong drink and would not cultivate vineyards. They also would not plant any other crops. They were invited by Jeremiah into one of the chambers surrounding the courtyard of the temple of God for a symbolic demonstration.

35:13–16 ***obey their forefather's command.*** The Rekabites held to the teaching of their forefather, while the Israelites continually rebelled against the teaching of God.

36:2 ***Take a scroll and write on it.*** The usual material for a scroll was parchment (a kind of leather), though Egyptian papyrus was also available. The contents of the scroll were the oracles dating from the days of Josiah, at the advent of Jeremiah's ministry (626 B.C.).

36:6 ***read ... from the scroll.*** This scroll was to be read on a day of fasting, a time set aside by official declaration of the king or priests (v. 9) in a period of national crisis.

35:4 [o] Dt 33:1 [p] 1Ch 9:19 [q] 2Ki 12:9 **35:6** [r] 2Ki 10:15 [s] Lev 10:9; Nu 6:2-4; Lk 1:15 **35:7** [t] Heb 11:9 [u] Ex 20:12; Eph 6:2-3 **35:8** [v] Pr 1:8; Col 3:20 **35:9** [w] 1Ti 6:6 **35:11** [x] 2Ki 24:1 [y] Jer 8:14 **35:13** [z] Jer 6:10; 32:33 **35:14** [a] Jer 7:13; 25:3 [b] Isa 30:9 **35:15** [c] Jer 7:25 [d] Jer 26:3 [e] Isa 1:16-17; Jer 4:1; 18:11; Eze 18:30 [f] Jer 25:5 [g] Jer 7:26 **35:16** [h] Mal 1:6 **35:17** [i] Jos 23:15; Jer 21:4-7 [j] Pr 1:24; Ro 10:21 [k] Isa 65:12; 66:4; Jer 7:13 **35:19** [l] Jer 33:17 [m] Jer 15:19 **36:1** [n] 2Ch 36:5 **36:2** [o] Ex 17:14; Jer 30:2; Hab 2:2 [p] Jer 1:2; 25:3 **36:3** [q] ver 7; Eze 12:3 [r] Mk 4:12 [s] Jer 26:3; Jnh 3:8; Ac 3:19 [t] Jer 18:8 **36:4** [u] Jer 32:12 [v] ver 18 [w] Eze 2:9 **36:6** [x] ver 9

I dictated. Read them to all the people of
Judah who come in from their towns. 7 Perhaps they will bring their petition before
the LORD and will each turn[y] from their
wicked ways, for the anger[z] and wrath pronounced against this people by the LORD
are great."
8 Baruch son of Neriah did everything
Jeremiah the prophet told him to do; at
the LORD's temple he read the words of the
LORD from the scroll. 9 In the ninth month[a]
of the fifth year of Jehoiakim son of Josiah
king of Judah, a time of fasting[b] before the
LORD was proclaimed for all the people in
Jerusalem and those who had come from
the towns of Judah. 10 From the room of
Gemariah son of Shaphan the secretary,[c]
which was in the upper courtyard at the entrance of the New Gate[d] of the temple, Baruch read to all the people at the LORD's temple the words of Jeremiah from the scroll.
11 When Micaiah son of Gemariah, the
son of Shaphan, heard all the words of the
LORD from the scroll, 12 he went down to the
secretary's room in the royal palace, where
all the officials were sitting: Elishama the
secretary, Delaiah son of Shemaiah, Elnathan[e] son of Akbor, Gemariah son of
Shaphan, Zedekiah son of Hananiah, and
all the other officials. 13 After Micaiah told
them everything he had heard Baruch read
to the people from the scroll, 14 all the officials sent Jehudi[f] son of Nethaniah, the son
of Shelemiah, the son of Cushi, to say to
Baruch, "Bring the scroll from which you
have read to the people and come." So Baruch son of Neriah went to them with the
scroll in his hand. 15 They said to him, "Sit
down, please, and read it to us."
So Baruch read it to them. 16 When they
heard all these words, they looked at each
other in fear and said to Baruch, "We must report all these words to the king." 17 Then they
asked Baruch, "Tell us, how did you come
to write all this? Did Jeremiah dictate it?"
18 "Yes," Baruch replied, "he dictated[g] all
these words to me, and I wrote them in ink
on the scroll."
19 Then the officials said to Baruch, "You
and Jeremiah, go and hide.[h] Don't let anyone know where you are."
20 After they put the scroll in the room of
Elishama the secretary, they went to the
king in the courtyard and reported everything to him. 21 The king sent Jehudi[i] to get
the scroll, and Jehudi brought it from the
room of Elishama the secretary and read
it to the king[j] and all the officials standing
beside him. 22 It was the ninth month and
the king was sitting in the winter apart-
ment,[k] with a fire burning in the firepot in
front of him. 23 Whenever Jehudi had read
three or four columns of the scroll, the king
cut them off with a scribe's knife and threw
them into the firepot, until the entire scroll
was burned in the fire.[l] 24 The king and all
his attendants who heard all these words
showed no fear,[m] nor did they tear their
clothes.[n] 25 Even though Elnathan, Delaiah
and Gemariah urged the king not to burn
the scroll, he would not listen to them. 26 Instead, the king commanded Jerahmeel, a
son of the king, Seraiah son of Azriel and
Shelemiah son of Abdeel to arrest[o] Baruch
the scribe and Jeremiah the prophet. But
the LORD had hidden[p] them.
27 After the king burned the scroll containing the words that Baruch had written
at Jeremiah's dictation,[q] the word of the
LORD came to Jeremiah: 28 "Take another scroll and write on it all the words that
were on the first scroll, which Jehoiakim
king of Judah burned up. 29 Also tell Jehoiakim king of Judah, 'This is what the
LORD says: You burned that scroll and said,
"Why did you write on it that the king of
Babylon would certainly come and destroy
this land and wipe from it[r] both man and
beast?" 30 Therefore this is what the LORD
says about Jehoiakim king of Judah: He
will have no one to sit on the throne of David; his body will be thrown out[s] and exposed to the heat by day and the frost by
night. 31 I will punish him and his children
and his attendants for their wickedness; I
will bring on them and those living in Jerusalem and the people of Judah every disaster[t] I pronounced against them, because
they have not listened.'"
32 So Jeremiah took another scroll and
gave it to the scribe Baruch son of Neriah,
and as Jeremiah dictated,[u] Baruch wrote[v]

36:8 *Baruch . . . did everything Jeremiah . . . told him to do.* As a faithful disciple, Baruch read from the book of God's words in the temple of the Lord. This act closely parallels the reading of the Book of the Law in the temple after it was discovered there under Josiah (2 Chron. 34:29–31).

36:20–24 *the king cut them off with a scribe's knife.* Jehoiakim showed no signs of fear or lamentation, unlike Josiah when the Book of the Law was read in his hearing (2 Kin. 22:11–13). Instead he cuts the scroll up and throws it into a fire.

36:29–31 *tell Jehoiakim king of Judah.* Indictment and judgment against Jehoiakim is pronounced. The indictment was declared because he destroyed the scroll of the Word of the Lord. First, the Davidic lineage would not continue through him. His son would rule for only three months before Nebuchadnezzar deported Jehoiachin to Babylon, where he died. Second, the king's body would be treated disgracefully after his death. As the king had cast the scroll into the fire, so his body would be cast from the royal palace. Third, the royal household would experience the destructive judgment that had been proclaimed in the words of the original scroll.

36:7 [y] Jer 26:3 [z] Dt 31:17 **36:9** [a] ver 22 [b] 2Ch 20:3
36:10 [c] Jer 52:25 [d] Jer 26:10 **36:12** [e] Jer 26:22
36:14 [f] ver 21 **36:18** [g] ver 4 **36:19** [h] 1Ki 17:3
36:21 [i] ver 14 [j] 2Ki 22:10 **36:22** [k] Am 3:15
36:23 [l] 1Ki 22:8 **36:24** [m] Ps 36:1 [n] Ge 37:29; 2Ki 22:11; Isa 37:1 **36:26** [o] Mt 23:34 [p] Jer 15:21 **36:27** [q] ver 4
36:29 [r] Isa 30:10 **36:30** [s] Jer 22:19 **36:31** [t] Pr 29:1
36:32 [u] ver 4 [v] Ex 34:1

on it all the words of the scroll that Jehoiakim king of Judah had burned[w] in the fire.
And many similar words were added to
them.

Jeremiah in Prison

37 Zedekiah[x] son of Josiah was made
king[y] of Judah by Nebuchadnezzar
king of Babylon; he reigned in place of Jehoiachin[a][z] son of Jehoiakim. 2 Neither he
nor his attendants nor the people of the
land paid any attention[a] to the words the
LORD had spoken through Jeremiah the
prophet.

3 King Zedekiah, however, sent Jehukal
son of Shelemiah with the priest Zephaniah[b] son of Maaseiah to Jeremiah the prophet with this message: "Please pray[c] to the
LORD our God for us."

4 Now Jeremiah was free to come and
go among the people, for he had not yet
been put in prison.[d] 5 Pharaoh's army had
marched out of Egypt,[e] and when the Babylonians[b] who were besieging Jerusalem
heard the report about them, they withdrew[f] from Jerusalem.[g]

6 Then the word of the LORD came to
Jeremiah the prophet: 7 "This is what the
LORD, the God of Israel, says: Tell the king
of Judah, who sent you to inquire[h] of me,
'Pharaoh's army, which has marched out to
support you, will go back to its own land, to
Egypt.[i] 8 Then the Babylonians will return
and attack this city; they will capture it and
burn[j] it down.'

9 "This is what the LORD says: Do not
deceive[k] yourselves, thinking, 'The Babylonians will surely leave us.' They will
not! 10 Even if you were to defeat the entire
Babylonian[c] army that is attacking you
and only wounded men were left in their
tents, they would come out and burn this
city down."

11 After the Babylonian army had withdrawn[l] from Jerusalem because of Pharaoh's army, 12 Jeremiah started to leave the
city to go to the territory of Benjamin to get
his share of the property[m] among the people there. 13 But when he reached the Benjamin Gate, the captain of the guard, whose
name was Irijah son of Shelemiah, the son
of Hananiah, arrested him and said, "You
are deserting to the Babylonians!"

14 "That's not true!" Jeremiah said. "I am
not deserting to the Babylonians." But Irijah would not listen to him; instead, he arrested[n] Jeremiah and brought him to the
officials. 15 They were angry with Jeremiah
and had him beaten[o] and imprisoned in the
house[p] of Jonathan the secretary, which
they had made into a prison.

16 Jeremiah was put into a vaulted cell
in a dungeon, where he remained a long
time. 17 Then King Zedekiah sent for him
and had him brought to the palace, where
he asked[q] him privately,[r] "Is there any word
from the LORD?"

"Yes," Jeremiah replied, "you will be delivered[s] into the hands of the king of Babylon."

18 Then Jeremiah said to King Zedekiah,
"What crime[t] have I committed against
you or your attendants or this people, that
you have put me in prison? 19 Where are
your prophets who prophesied to you, 'The
king of Babylon will not attack you or this
land'? 20 But now, my lord the king, please
listen. Let me bring my petition before you:
Do not send me back to the house of Jonathan the secretary, or I will die there."

21 King Zedekiah then gave orders for
Jeremiah to be placed in the courtyard of
the guard and given a loaf of bread from the
street of the bakers each day until all the
bread[u] in the city was gone.[v] So Jeremiah
remained in the courtyard of the guard.[w]

---

[a] *1* Hebrew *Koniah*, a variant of *Jehoiachin*
[b] *5* Or *Chaldeans*; also in verses 8, 9, 13 and 14
[c] *10* Or *Chaldean*; also in verse 11

37:2 *Neither he nor his attendants nor the people of the land paid any attention.* It is eminently possible and easy to reject God's message. As Zedekiah and all the people did, so can we deliberately refuse to heed the Lord, even when events have shown the truth of His message.

37:5 *Pharaoh's army had marched out of Egypt.* In late spring or early summer 588 B.C., Pharaoh Hophra led the Egyptian army into southern Palestine. The Babylonian forces withdrew their siege of Jerusalem to confront the Egyptians. Zedekiah hoped the Babylonians would be defeated, but his hopes proved to be in vain.

37:9 *Do not deceive yourselves.* To think that the brief respite caused by the Egyptian appearance in the southern coastal plain was proof of imminent deliverance, as the false prophets declared, was an exercise in self-deception and futile imagination.

37:14–16 *I am not deserting to the Babylonians.* Jeremiah denied the accusation of defection, but to no avail. Irijah arrested the prophet and arraigned him before the court of princes. Prison space was lacking in Jerusalem due to the crowded conditions of the siege, so a prison had to be devised.

37:17–19 *Then King Zedekiah sent for him and had him brought to the palace.* Fearing possible exposure and opposition from his courtiers, Zedekiah secretly summoned Jeremiah and asked of him a word from the Lord. He seems to have earnestly desired a word from God but could not come to grips with the reality and respond appropriately. Jeremiah appealed to Zedekiah's sense of justice and decency and asked to be released from prison. Zedekiah consented.

36:32 [w] ver 23 **37:1** [x] 2Ki 24:17 [y] Eze 17:13 [z] 2Ki 24:8, 12; 2Ch 36:10; Jer 22:24 **37:2** [a] 2Ki 24:19; 2Ch 36:12, 14 **37:3** [b] Jer 29:25; 52:24 [c] 1Ki 13:6; Jer 21:1-2; 42:2 **37:4** [d] ver 15; Jer 32:2 **37:5** [e] Eze 17:15 [f] Jer 34:21 [g] 2Ki 24:7 **37:7** [h] 2Ki 22:18 [i] Jer 2:36; La 4:17 **37:8** [j] Jer 34:22; 39:8 **37:9** [k] Jer 29:8 **37:11** [l] ver 5 **37:12** [m] Jer 32:9 **37:14** [n] Jer 40:4 **37:15** [o] Jer 20:2 [p] Jer 38:26 **37:17** [q] Jer 15:11 [r] Jer 38:16 [s] Jer 21:7 **37:18** [t] 1Sa 26:18; Jn 10:32; Ac 25:8 **37:21** [u] Isa 33:16; Jer 38:9 [v] 2Ki 25:3; Jer 52:6 [w] Jer 32:2; 38:6, 13, 28

Jeremiah Thrown Into a Cistern

38 Shephatiah son of Mattan, Gedaliah son of Pashhur, Jehukal[a][x] son of
Shelemiah, and Pashhur son of Malkijah
heard what Jeremiah was telling all the
people when he said, **2**"This is what the
LORD says: 'Whoever stays in this city will
die by the sword, famine or plague,[y] but
whoever goes over to the Babylonians[b] will
live. They will escape with their lives; they
will live.'[z] **3**And this is what the LORD says:
'This city will certainly be given into the
hands of the army of the king of Babylon,
who will capture it.'"[a]
4Then the officials[b] said to the king,
"This man should be put to death.[c] He is
discouraging the soldiers who are left in
this city, as well as all the people, by the
things he is saying to them. This man is
not seeking the good of these people but
their ruin."
5"He is in your hands," King Zedekiah
answered. "The king can do nothing to oppose you."
6So they took Jeremiah and put him into
the cistern of Malkijah, the king's son,
which was in the courtyard of the guard.[d]
They lowered Jeremiah by ropes into the
cistern; it had no water in it, only mud, and
Jeremiah sank down into the mud.
7But Ebed-Melek,[e] a Cushite,[c] an official[d][f] in the royal palace, heard that they
had put Jeremiah into the cistern. While
the king was sitting in the Benjamin Gate,[g]
8Ebed-Melek went out of the palace and
said to him, **9**"My lord the king, these men
have acted wickedly in all they have done
to Jeremiah the prophet. They have thrown
him into a cistern, where he will starve to
death when there is no longer any bread[h]
in the city."
10Then the king commanded Ebed-Melek the Cushite, "Take thirty men from here
with you and lift Jeremiah the prophet out
of the cistern before he dies."
11So Ebed-Melek took the men with him
and went to a room under the treasury
in the palace. He took some old rags and
worn-out clothes from there and let them
down with ropes to Jeremiah in the cistern.
12Ebed-Melek the Cushite said to Jeremiah,
"Put these old rags and worn-out clothes
under your arms to pad the ropes." Jeremiah did so, **13**and they pulled him up with
the ropes and lifted him out of the cistern.
And Jeremiah remained in the courtyard
of the guard.[i]

Zedekiah Questions Jeremiah Again

14Then King Zedekiah sent for Jeremiah the prophet and had him brought to the
third entrance to the temple of the LORD. "I
am going to ask you something," the king
said to Jeremiah. "Do not hide[j] anything
from me."
15Jeremiah said to Zedekiah, "If I give
you an answer, will you not kill me? Even
if I did give you counsel, you would not listen to me."
16But King Zedekiah swore this oath secretly[k] to Jeremiah: "As surely as the LORD
lives, who has given us breath,[l] I will neither kill you nor hand you over to those
who want to kill you."[m]
17Then Jeremiah said to Zedekiah, "This
is what the LORD God Almighty, the God
of Israel, says: 'If you surrender to the officers of the king of Babylon, your life will
be spared and this city will not be burned
down; you and your family will live.[n] **18**But
if you will not surrender to the officers of
the king of Babylon, this city will be giv-
en into the hands[o] of the Babylonians and
they will burn[p] it down; you yourself will
not escape[q] from them.'"
19King Zedekiah said to Jeremiah, "I am
afraid[r] of the Jews who have gone over[s] to
the Babylonians, for the Babylonians may
hand me over to them and they will mistreat me."
20"They will not hand you over," Jeremiah replied. "Obey[t] the LORD by doing what
I tell you. Then it will go well with you, and
your life[u] will be spared. **21**But if you refuse
to surrender, this is what the LORD has re-

---

a 1 Hebrew *Jukal,* a variant of *Jehukal*
b 2 Or *Chaldeans;* also in verses 18, 19 and 23
c 7 Probably from the upper Nile region *d* 7 Or *a eunuch*

38:2–3 *Whoever stays in this city.* Verse 2 is almost an exact duplicate of 21:9. Jeremiah said the choice was between life under the Babylonians and death among the ruins of Jerusalem. Such a statement was treasonous, as was the statement that Jerusalem must fall.

38:7 *Ebed-Melek.* This man took special care to obtain rags for Jeremiah to cushion his armpits, preventing the ropes from cutting his skin. A foreigner, a once despised Cushite (from Egypt), he cared more for the prophet of God than did the king and the princes of Jeremiah's own people.

38:17 *Then Jeremiah said to Zedekiah.* Jeremiah repeated to the king the message recorded in Jeremiah 38:2–3. Surrender would spare the life of the king, and the city's failure to surrender would bring death and destruction.

38:20–23 *Then it will go well with you.* Jeremiah tried to settle Zedekiah's fears and to resolve his moral and ethical dilemma by reassuring him that surrender would result in his personal safety. But if the king refused to surrender to Nebuchadnezzar, the word of judgment would fall. Women and children would be handed over to Nebuchadnezzar and Jerusalem would be destroyed.

38:1 [x] Jer 37:3 **38:2** [y] Jer 34:17 [z] Jer 21:9; 39:18; 45:5 **38:3** [a] Jer 21:4, 10; 32:3 **38:4** [b] Jer 36:12 [c] Jer 26:11 **38:6** [d] Jer 37:21 **38:7** [e] Jer 39:16 [f] Ac 8:27 [g] Job 29:7 **38:9** [h] Jer 37:21 **38:13** [i] Jer 37:21 **38:14** [j] 1Sa 3:17 **38:16** [k] Jer 37:17 [l] Isa 42:5; 57:16 [m] ver 4 **38:17** [n] 2Ki 24:12; Jer 21:9 **38:18** [o] ver 3; Jer 34:3 [p] Jer 37:8 [q] Jer 24:8; 32:4 **38:19** [r] Isa 51:12; Jn 12:42 [s] Jer 39:9 **38:20** [t] Jer 11:4 [u] Isa 55:3

vealed to me: 22All the women[v] left in the
palace of the king of Judah will be brought
out to the officials of the king of Babylon.
Those women will say to you:

"'They misled you and overcame you—
those trusted friends of yours.
Your feet are sunk in the mud;
your friends have deserted you.'

23"All your wives and children[w] will be
brought out to the Babylonians. You yourself will not escape from their hands but
will be captured[x] by the king of Babylon;
and this city will[a] be burned down."
24Then Zedekiah said to Jeremiah, "Do
not let anyone know about this conversation, or you may die. 25If the officials hear
that I talked with you, and they come to you
and say, 'Tell us what you said to the king
and what the king said to you; do not hide it
from us or we will kill you,' 26then tell them,
'I was pleading with the king not to send me
back to Jonathan's house[y] to die there.'"
27All the officials did come to Jeremiah
and question him, and he told them everything the king had ordered him to say. So
they said no more to him, for no one had
heard his conversation with the king.
28And Jeremiah remained in the courtyard of the guard[z] until the day Jerusalem
was captured.

The Fall of Jerusalem

39 This is how Jerusalem was taken: 1In
the ninth year of Zedekiah king of
Judah, in the tenth month, Nebuchadnezzar king of Babylon marched against Jerusalem with his whole army and laid siege[a]
to it. 2And on the ninth day of the fourth
month of Zedekiah's eleventh year, the city
wall was broken through. 3Then all the officials[b] of the king of Babylon came and
took seats in the Middle Gate: Nergal-Sharezer of Samgar, Nebo-Sarsekim a chief
officer, Nergal-Sharezer a high official and
all the other officials of the king of Babylon. 4When Zedekiah king of Judah and
all the soldiers saw them, they fled; they
left the city at night by way of the king's
garden, through the gate between the two
walls, and headed toward the Arabah.[b]
5But the Babylonian[c] army pursued
them and overtook Zedekiah[c] in the plains
of Jericho. They captured him and took
him to Nebuchadnezzar king of Babylon
at Riblah[d] in the land of Hamath, where
he pronounced sentence on him. 6There at
Riblah the king of Babylon slaughtered the
sons of Zedekiah before his eyes and also
killed all the nobles of Judah. 7Then he put
out Zedekiah's eyes[e] and bound him with
bronze shackles to take him to Babylon.[f]
8The Babylonians[d] set fire[g] to the royal palace and the houses of the people
and broke down the walls[h] of Jerusalem.
9Nebuzaradan commander of the imperial
guard carried into exile to Babylon the people who remained in the city, along with
those who had gone over to him, and the
rest of the people.[i] 10But Nebuzaradan the
commander of the guard left behind in the
land of Judah some of the poor people, who
owned nothing; and at that time he gave
them vineyards and fields.
11Now Nebuchadnezzar king of Babylon
had given these orders about Jeremiah
through Nebuzaradan commander of the
imperial guard: 12"Take him and look after
him; don't harm[j] him but do for him whatever he asks." 13So Nebuzaradan the commander of the guard, Nebushazban a chief
officer, Nergal-Sharezer a high official and
all the other officers of the king of Babylon
14sent and had Jeremiah taken out of the
courtyard of the guard.[k] They turned him
over to Gedaliah son of Ahikam,[l] the son
of Shaphan, to take him back to his home.
So he remained among his own people.[m]
15While Jeremiah had been confined in
the courtyard of the guard, the word of the
LORD came to him: 16"Go and tell Ebed-Melek[n] the Cushite, 'This is what the LORD Almighty, the God of Israel, says: I am about
to fulfill my words against this city—
words concerning disaster,[o] not prosperity. At that time they will be fulfilled before
your eyes. 17But I will rescue[p] you on that
day, declares the LORD; you will not be giv-
en into the hands of those you fear. 18I will
save you; you will not fall by the sword[q]
but will escape with your life,[r] because you
trust[s] in me, declares the LORD.'"

[a] 23 Or *and you will cause this city to* [b] 4 Or *the Jordan Valley* [c] 5 Or *Chaldean* [d] 8 Or *Chaldeans*

39:1 ***king of Babylon marched against Jerusalem with his whole army and laid siege to it.*** The Babylonian siege began in December 589 B.C. and ended about 30 months later when the walls of Jerusalem were breached.
39:3–7 ***all the officials of the king of Babylon.*** When Zedekiah saw the Babylonian officers enter the gate on the north side of Jerusalem, he and his men left at night through another gate on the south side of the city. They were captured near Jericho and taken to Riblah to meet Nebuchadnezzar.
39:8–10 ***The Babylonians set fire.*** In addition to the royal palace and homes of the inhabitants, Jeremiah 52:13 includes the "temple of the LORD" among the buildings burned in Jerusalem. ***poor people.*** Typically the Babylonians deported the upper classes, such as court officials, merchants, artisans, and craftsmen, and left behind peasants to work the fields.
39:18 ***will escape with your life, because you trust in me.*** Ebed-Melek experienced the power and grace of God in the deliverance of his life simply because he exercised faith.

38:22 [v] Jer 6:12 **38:23** [w] 2Ki 25:6 [x] Jer 41:10 **38:26** [y] Jer 37:15 **38:28** [z] Jer 37:21; 39:14 **39:1** [a] 2Ki 25:1; Jer 52:4; Eze 24:2 **39:3** [b] Jer 21:4 **39:5** [c] Jer 32:4 [d] 2Ki 23:33 **39:7** [e] Eze 12:13 [f] Jer 32:5 **39:8** [g] Jer 38:18 [h] Ne 1:3 **39:9** [i] Jer 40:1 **39:12** [j] Pr 16:7; 1Pe 3:13 **39:14** [k] Jer 38:28 [l] 2Ki 22:12 [m] Jer 40:5 **39:16** [n] Jer 38:7 [o] Jer 21:10; Da 9:12 **39:17** [p] Ps 41:1-2 **39:18** [q] Jer 45:5 [r] Jer 21:9; 38:2 [s] Jer 17:7

Jeremiah Freed

40 The word came to Jeremiah from the LORD after Nebuzaradan commander of the imperial guard had released him at Ramah. He had found Jeremiah bound in chains among all the captives from Jerusalem and Judah who were being carried into exile to Babylon. 2When the commander of the guard found Jeremiah, he said to him, "The LORD your God decreed this disaster for this place.[t] 3And now the LORD has brought it about; he has done just as he said he would. All this happened because you people sinned[u] against the LORD and did not obey[v] him. 4But today I am freeing you from the chains on your wrists. Come with me to Babylon, if you like, and I will look after you; but if you do not want to, then don't come. Look, the whole country lies before you; go wherever you please."[w] 5However, before Jeremiah turned to go,[a] Nebuzaradan added, "Go back to Gedaliah[x] son of Ahikam, the son of Shaphan, whom the king of Babylon has appointed over the towns of Judah, and live with him among the people, or go anywhere else you please."[y]

Then the commander gave him provisions and a present and let him go. 6So Jeremiah went to Gedaliah son of Ahikam at Mizpah[z] and stayed with him among the people who were left behind in the land.

Gedaliah Assassinated

7When all the army officers and their men who were still in the open country heard that the king of Babylon had appointed Gedaliah son of Ahikam as governor over the land and had put him in charge of the men, women and children who were the poorest[a] in the land and who had not been carried into exile to Babylon, 8they came to Gedaliah at Mizpah[b]—Ishmael[c] son of Nethaniah, Johanan and Jonathan the sons of Kareah, Seraiah son of Tanhumeth, the sons of Ephai the Netophathite,[d] and Jaazaniah[b] the son of the Maakathite,[e] and their men. 9Gedaliah son of Ahikam, the son of Shaphan, took an oath to reassure them and their men. "Do not be afraid to serve[f] the Babylonians,[c]" he said. "Settle down in the land and serve the king of Babylon, and it will go well with you.[g] 10I myself will stay at Mizpah[h] to represent you before the Babylonians who come to us, but you are to harvest the wine, summer fruit and olive oil, and put them in your storage jars, and live in the towns you have taken over."[i]

11When all the Jews in Moab,[j] Ammon, Edom and all the other countries heard that the king of Babylon had left a remnant in Judah and had appointed Gedaliah son of Ahikam, the son of Shaphan, as governor over them, 12they all came back to the land of Judah, to Gedaliah at Mizpah, from all the countries where they had been scattered.[k] And they harvested an abundance of wine and summer fruit.

13Johanan son of Kareah and all the army officers still in the open country came to Gedaliah at Mizpah[l] 14and said to him, "Don't you know that Baalis king of the Ammonites[m] has sent Ishmael son of Nethaniah to take your life?" But Gedaliah son of Ahikam did not believe them.

15Then Johanan son of Kareah said privately to Gedaliah in Mizpah, "Let me go and kill Ishmael son of Nethaniah, and no one will know it. Why should he take your life and cause all the Jews who are gathered around you to be scattered and the remnant of Judah to perish?"

16But Gedaliah son of Ahikam said to Johanan son of Kareah, "Don't do such a thing! What you are saying about Ishmael is not true."

41 In the seventh month Ishmael[n] son of Nethaniah, the son of Elishama, who was of royal blood and had been one of the king's officers, came with ten men to Gedaliah son of Ahikam at Mizpah. While they were eating together there, 2Ishmael[o] son of Nethaniah and the ten men who were with him got up and struck down Gedaliah son of Ahikam, the son of Shaphan, with the sword, killing the one whom the king of Babylon had appointed[p] as governor over the land.[q] 3Ishmael also killed all

---

[a] 5 Or *Jeremiah answered* [b] 8 Hebrew *Jezaniah,* a variant of *Jaazaniah* [c] 9 Or *Chaldeans*; also in verse 10

40:2–3 *the LORD has brought it about; he has done just as he said.* Prophets whose words were deemed verified were generally treated well by peoples of the ancient Middle East.

40:4–5 *today I am freeing you from the chains.* Jeremiah was released from bondage and given three options: (1) to go with Nebuzaradan to Babylon and enjoy special treatment and protection there; (2) to remain in the care of Gedaliah, the district governor at Mizpah; (3) to live in the land as he chose.

40:7–10 *army officers.* This phrase refers to the surviving Jewish commanders of the armies in the towns throughout Judah who had fled into the rugged hill country. Among the list of escaped leaders was Ishmael, a member of the royal family and a court officer (41:1).

40:11–12 *the Jews.* Those who had escaped the Babylonian onslaught into neighboring states returned home and began working the fields, vineyards, and orchards.

40:13–16 *Johanan.* This man led a group of leaders to Gedaliah to warn him of a plot by Ishmael. He even asked for permission to kill the plotter, Ishmael. Unfortunately, Gedaliah was far too trusting of Ishmael and didn't take the warning seriously enough.

40:2 [t] Jer 50:7 **40:3** [u] Da 9:11 [v] Dt 29:24-28; Ro 2:5-9
40:4 [w] Ge 13:9; Jer 39:11-12 **40:5** [x] 2Ki 25:22 [y] Jer 39:14
40:6 [z] Jdg 20:1; 1Sa 7:5-17 **40:7** [a] Jer 39:10
40:8 [b] ver 13 [c] ver 14; Jer 41:1,2 [d] 2Sa 23:28 [e] Dt 3:14
40:9 [f] Jer 27:11 [g] Jer 38:20 **40:10** [h] ver 6 [i] Dt 1:39
40:11 [j] Nu 25:1 **40:12** [k] Jer 43:5 **40:13** [l] ver 8
40:14 [m] 2Sa 10:1-19; Jer 25:21; 41:10 **41:1** [n] Jer 40:8
41:2 [o] Ps 41:9; 109:5 [p] Jer 40:5 [q] 2Sa 3:27; 20:9-10

the men of Judah who were with Gedaliah at Mizpah, as well as the Babylonian[a] soldiers who were there.

4The day after Gedaliah's assassination, before anyone knew about it, 5eighty men who had shaved off their beards,[r] torn their clothes and cut themselves came from Shechem,[s] Shiloh[t] and Samaria,[u] bringing grain offerings and incense with them to the house of the LORD.[v] 6Ishmael son of Nethaniah went out from Mizpah to meet them, weeping[w] as he went. When he met them, he said, "Come to Gedaliah son of Ahikam." 7When they went into the city, Ishmael son of Nethaniah and the men who were with him slaughtered them and threw them into a cistern. 8But ten of them said to Ishmael, "Don't kill us! We have wheat and barley, olive oil and honey, hidden in a field."[x] So he let them alone and did not kill them with the others. 9Now the cistern where he threw all the bodies of the men he had killed along with Gedaliah was the one King Asa[y] had made as part of his defense[z] against Baasha[a] king of Israel. Ishmael son of Nethaniah filled it with the dead.

10Ishmael made captives of all the rest of the people[b] who were in Mizpah—the king's daughters along with all the others who were left there, over whom Nebuzaradan commander of the imperial guard had appointed Gedaliah son of Ahikam. Ishmael son of Nethaniah took them captive and set out to cross over to the Ammonites.[c]

11When Johanan[d] son of Kareah and all the army officers who were with him heard about all the crimes Ishmael son of Nethaniah had committed, 12they took all their men and went to fight Ishmael son of Nethaniah. They caught up with him near the great pool[e] in Gibeon. 13When all the people[f] Ishmael had with him saw Johanan son of Kareah and the army officers who were with him, they were glad. 14All the people Ishmael had taken captive at Mizpah turned and went over to Johanan son of Kareah. 15But Ishmael son of Nethaniah and eight of his men escaped[g] from Johanan and fled to the Ammonites.

Flight to Egypt

16Then Johanan son of Kareah and all the army officers who were with him led away all the people of Mizpah who had survived,[h] whom Johanan had recovered from Ishmael son of Nethaniah after Ishmael had assassinated Gedaliah son of Ahikam—the soldiers, women, children and court officials he had recovered from Gibeon. 17And they went on, stopping at Geruth Kimham[i] near Bethlehem on their way to Egypt[j] 18to escape the Babylonians.[b] They were afraid[k] of them because Ishmael son of Nethaniah had killed Gedaliah[l] son of Ahikam, whom the king of Babylon had appointed as governor over the land.

42 Then all the army officers, including Johanan[m] son of Kareah and Jezaniah[c] son of Hoshaiah, and all the people from the least to the greatest[n] approached 2Jeremiah the prophet and said to him, "Please hear our petition and pray[o] to the LORD your God for this entire remnant.[p] For as you now see, though we were once many, now only a few[q] are left. 3Pray that the LORD your God will tell us where we should go and what we should do."[r]

4"I have heard you," replied Jeremiah the prophet. "I will certainly pray[s] to the LORD your God as you have requested; I will tell you everything the LORD says and will keep nothing back from you."[t]

5Then they said to Jeremiah, "May the LORD be a true and faithful witness[u] against us if we do not act in accordance with everything the LORD your God sends you to tell us. 6Whether it is favorable or unfavorable, we will obey the LORD our God, to whom we are sending you, so that it will go well[v] with us, for we will obey[w] the LORD our God."

7Ten days later the word of the LORD came to Jeremiah. 8So he called together Johanan son of Kareah and all the army officers[x] who were with him and all the people from the least to the greatest. 9He said to them, "This is what the LORD, the God of Israel, to whom you sent me to present your petition, says:[y] 10'If you stay in this land, I will build[z] you up and not tear you down; I will plant[a] you and not uproot you,[b] for I have relented concerning the disaster I have inflicted on you.[c] 11Do not be afraid of the king of Babylon,[d] whom you

---

[a] 3 Or *Chaldean* [b] 18 Or *Chaldeans*
[c] 1 Hebrew; Septuagint (see also 43:2) *Azariah*

41:11–12 *they took all their men.* After Ishmael assassinated Gedaliah, Johanan gathered forces to fight Ishmael's army at Gibeon. Then he started for Egypt and safety.

42:1–3 *said to him.* The people asked Jeremiah to intercede with the Lord on their behalf.

42:4–6 *I will certainly pray.* Jeremiah cautiously agreed to pray to God. He asked the people to agree to abide by the answer he received. The people responded with an oath of obedience, calling upon the Lord as witness.

41:5 [r] Lev 19:27 [s] Ge 33:18; Jdg 9:1-57; 1Ki 12:1 [t] Jos 18:1 [u] 1Ki 16:24 [v] 2Ki 25:9 **41:6** [w] 2Sa 3:16 **41:8** [x] Isa 45:3 **41:9** [y] 1Ki 15:22; 2Ch 16:6 [z] Jdg 6:2 [a] 2Ch 16:1 **41:10** [b] Jer 40:7, 12 [c] Jer 40:14 **41:11** [d] Jer 40:8 **41:12** [e] 2Sa 2:13 **41:13** [f] ver 10 **41:15** [g] Job 21:30; Pr 28:17 **41:16** [h] Jer 43:4 **41:17** [i] 2Sa 19:37 [j] Jer 42:14 **41:18** [k] Isa 51:12; Jer 42:16; Lk 12:4-5 [l] Jer 40:5 **42:1** [m] Jer 40:13; 41:11 [n] Jer 6:13; 44:12 **42:2** [o] Jer 36:7; Ac 8:24; Jas 5:16 [p] Isa 1:9 [q] Lev 26:22; La 1:1 **42:3** [r] Ps 86:11; Pr 3:6 **42:4** [s] Ex 8:29; 1Sa 12:23 [t] 1Ki 22:14; 1Sa 3:17 **42:5** [u] Ge 31:50 **42:6** [v] Dt 5:29; 6:3; Jer 7:23 [w] Ex 24:7; Jos 24:24 **42:8** [x] ver 1 **42:9** [y] 2Ki 22:15 **42:10** [z] Jer 24:6 [a] Jer 31:28 [b] Eze 36:36 [c] Jer 18:8 **42:11** [d] Jer 27:11

now fear.[e] Do not be afraid of him, declares
the LORD, for I am with you and will save[f]
you and deliver you from his hands.[g] 12I
will show you compassion so that he will
have compassion on you and restore you
to your land.'[h]
13"However, if you say, 'We will not stay
in this land,' and so disobey[i] the LORD your
God, 14and if you say, 'No, we will go and
live in Egypt,[j] where we will not see war or
hear the trumpet or be hungry for bread,'
15then hear the word of the LORD, you remnant of Judah. This is what the LORD Almighty, the God of Israel, says: 'If you are
determined to go to Egypt and you do go to
settle there, 16then the sword[k] you fear will
overtake you there, and the famine you
dread will follow you into Egypt, and there
you will die. 17Indeed, all who are determined to go to Egypt to settle there will die
by the sword, famine and plague;[l] not one
of them will survive or escape the disaster I
will bring on them.' 18This is what the LORD
Almighty, the God of Israel, says: 'As my
anger and wrath[m] have been poured out on
those who lived in Jerusalem,[n] so will my
wrath be poured out on you when you go to
Egypt. You will be a curse[a] and an object of
horror,[o] a curse[a] and an object of reproach;
you will never see this place again.'[p]
19"Remnant of Judah, the LORD has told
you, 'Do not go to Egypt.'[q] Be sure of this:
I warn you today 20that you made a fatal
mistake when you sent me to the LORD your
God and said, 'Pray to the LORD our God for
us; tell us everything he says and we will
do it.'[r] 21I have told you today, but you still
have not obeyed the LORD your God in all
he sent me to tell you.[s] 22So now, be sure of
this: You will die by the sword, famine and
plague[t] in the place where you want to go
to settle."[u]

43 When Jeremiah had finished telling
the people all the words of the LORD
their God—everything the LORD had sent
him to tell them[v]— 2Azariah son of Hoshaiah and Johanan[w] son of Kareah and all the
arrogant men said to Jeremiah, "You are
lying! The LORD our God has not sent you
to say, 'You must not go to Egypt to settle
there.' 3But Baruch son of Neriah is inciting you against us to hand us over to the
Babylonians,[b] so they may kill us or carry
us into exile to Babylon."[x]
4So Johanan son of Kareah and all the
army officers and all the people disobeyed
the LORD's command[y] to stay in the land
of Judah.[z] 5Instead, Johanan son of Kareah and all the army officers led away all
the remnant of Judah who had come back
to live in the land of Judah from all the
nations where they had been scattered.[a]
6They also led away all those whom Nebuzaradan commander of the imperial guard
had left with Gedaliah son of Ahikam, the
son of Shaphan—the men, the women, the
children and the king's daughters. And
they took Jeremiah the prophet and Baruch son of Neriah along with them. 7So
they entered Egypt in disobedience to the
LORD and went as far as Tahpanhes.[b]
8In Tahpanhes[c] the word of the LORD
came to Jeremiah: 9"While the Jews are
watching, take some large stones with you
and bury them in clay in the brick pavement at the entrance to Pharaoh's palace
in Tahpanhes. 10Then say to them, 'This
is what the LORD Almighty, the God of Israel, says: I will send for my servant[d] Nebuchadnezzar king of Babylon, and I will
set his throne over these stones I have
buried here; he will spread his royal canopy above them. 11He will come and attack
Egypt,[e] bringing death to those destined
for death, captivity to those destined for
captivity, and the sword to those destined
for the sword.[f] 12He will set fire to the temples of the gods[g] of Egypt; he will burn
their temples and take their gods captive.
As a shepherd picks[h] his garment clean of
lice, so he will pick Egypt clean and depart. 13There in the temple of the sun[c] in
Egypt he will demolish the sacred pillars
and will burn down the temples of the gods
of Egypt.'"

Disaster Because of Idolatry

44 This word came to Jeremiah concerning all the Jews living in Lower Egypt—in Migdol,[i] Tahpanhes[j] and
Memphis[k]—and in Upper Egypt:[l] 2"This
is what the LORD Almighty, the God of
Israel, says: You saw the great disaster I
brought on Jerusalem and on all the towns

[a] *18* That is, your name will be used in cursing (see 29:22); or, others will see that you are cursed.
[b] *3* Or *Chaldeans* [c] *13* Or *in Heliopolis*

42:15 *determined.* This expression indicates the fixed intentions of the people. The announcement of judgment against the disobedient evacuees echoes Jeremiah's earlier pronouncements against Judah. The very thing they were trying to escape from would meet them in Egypt.

43:4–7 *all the people disobeyed.* Johanan led the migration to Egypt, against the direction of the Lord through Jeremiah.

43:10 *these stones.* These symbolized the strong foundation of Nebuchadnezzar's empire, the point from which he would spread his canopy.

42:11 [e] Nu 14:9 [f] Isa 43:5 [g] Jer 1:8; Ro 8:31 **42:12** [h] Ps 106:44-46 **42:13** [i] Jer 44:16 **42:14** [j] Nu 11:4-5 **42:16** [k] Eze 11:8 **42:17** [l] ver 22; Jer 44:13 **42:18** [m] Dt 29:18-20; Jer 7:20 [n] 2Ch 36:19; Jer 39:1-9 [o] Jer 29:18 [p] Jer 22:10 **42:19** [q] Dt 17:16; Isa 30:7 **42:20** [r] ver 2 **42:21** [s] Eze 2:7; Zec 7:11-12 **42:22** [t] ver 17; Eze 6:11 [u] Hos 9:6 **43:1** [v] Jer 26:8; 42:9-22 **43:2** [w] Jer 42:1 **43:3** [x] Jer 38:4 **43:4** [y] Jer 42:5-6 [z] Jer 42:10 **43:5** [a] Jer 40:12 **43:7** [b] Jer 2:16; 44:1 **43:8** [c] Jer 2:16 **43:10** [d] Isa 44:28; Jer 25:9; 27:6 **43:11** [e] Jer 46:13-26; Eze 29:19-20 [f] Jer 15:2; 44:13; Zec 11:9 **43:12** [g] Jer 46:25; Eze 30:13 [h] Ps 104:2; 109:18-19 **44:1** [i] Ex 14:2 [j] Jer 43:7,8 [k] Isa 19:13 [l] Isa 11:11; Jer 46:14

of Judah. Today they lie deserted and in ruins[m] 3because of the evil they have done. They aroused my anger by burning incense to and worshiping other gods[n] that neither they nor you nor your ancestors[o] ever knew. 4Again and again[p] I sent my servants the prophets,[q] who said, 'Do not do this detestable thing that I hate!' 5But they did not listen or pay attention; they did not turn from their wickedness or stop burning incense to other gods.[r] 6Therefore, my fierce anger was poured out; it raged against the towns of Judah and the streets of Jerusalem and made them the desolate ruins they are today.

7"Now this is what the LORD God Almighty, the God of Israel, says: Why bring such great disaster[s] on yourselves by cutting off from Judah the men and women,[t] the children and infants, and so leave yourselves without a remnant? 8Why arouse my anger with what your hands have made,[u] burning incense to other gods in Egypt, where you have come to live?[v] You will destroy yourselves and make yourselves a curse[a] and an object of reproach[w] among all the nations on earth. 9Have you forgotten the wickedness committed by your ancestors and by the kings and queens of Judah and the wickedness committed by you and your wives in the land of Judah and the streets of Jerusalem?[x] 10To this day they have not humbled themselves or shown reverence, nor have they followed my law[y] and the decrees I set before you and your ancestors.[z]

11"Therefore this is what the LORD Almighty, the God of Israel, says: I am determined to bring disaster[a] on you and to destroy all Judah. 12I will take away the remnant[b] of Judah who were determined to go to Egypt to settle there. They will all perish in Egypt; they will fall by the sword or die from famine. From the least to the greatest, they will die by sword or famine.[c] They will become a curse and an object of horror, a curse and an object of reproach.[d] 13I will punish those who live in Egypt with the sword, famine and plague,[e] as I punished Jerusalem. 14None of the remnant of Judah who have gone to live in Egypt will escape or survive to return to the land of Judah, to which they long to return and live; none will return except a few fugitives."[f]

15Then all the men who knew that their wives were burning incense to other gods, along with all the women who were present—a large assembly—and all the people living in Lower and Upper Egypt, said to Jeremiah, 16"We will not listen[g] to the message you have spoken to us in the name of the LORD! 17We will certainly do everything we said we would:[h] We will burn incense to the Queen of Heaven[i] and will pour out drink offerings to her just as we and our ancestors, our kings and our officials did in the towns of Judah and in the streets of Jerusalem. At that time we had plenty of food and were well off and suffered no harm.[j] 18But ever since we stopped burning incense to the Queen of Heaven and pouring out drink offerings to her, we have had nothing and have been perishing by sword and famine.[k]"

19The women added, "When we burned incense to the Queen of Heaven[l] and poured out drink offerings to her, did not our husbands know that we were making cakes impressed with her image and pouring out drink offerings to her?"

20Then Jeremiah said to all the people, both men and women, who were answering him, 21"Did not the LORD remember[m] and call to mind the incense[n] burned in the towns of Judah and the streets of Jerusalem[o] by you and your ancestors,[p] your kings and your officials and the people of the land? 22When the LORD could no longer endure your wicked actions and the detestable things you did, your land became a curse[q] and a desolate waste without inhabitants, as it is today.[r] 23Because you have burned incense and have sinned against the LORD and have not obeyed him or followed his law or his decrees or his stipulations, this disaster[s] has come upon you, as you now see."[t]

24Then Jeremiah said to all the people, including the women,[u] "Hear the word of the LORD, all you people of Judah in Egypt.[v]

---

[a] 8 That is, your name will be used in cursing (see 29:22); or, others will see that you are cursed; also in verse 12; similarly in verse 22.

44:8 ***arouse.*** This term indicates willful, stubborn rebellion against God, which provoked His anger.

44:10 ***they have not humbled themselves.*** The present generation of Jews had learned nothing from the past failures of the nation. The people were not broken in heart, only more stubborn.

44:13 ***I will punish those who live in Egypt.*** The Jews in Egypt would suffer the same judgment as those in Jerusalem. Only a small remnant would survive to tell their story.

44:18 ***Queen of Heaven.*** The people reasoned that when they stopped worshiping the Queen of Heaven in the days of Josiah's reform, their king was killed and their land was overrun and destroyed.

44:24 ***including the women.*** The focus here is on the stubbornness of the women who persisted in

44:2 [m] Isa 6:11; Jer 9:11; 34:22 **44:3** [n] ver 8; Dt 13:6-11; 29:26 [o] Dt 32:17; Jer 19:4 **44:4** [p] Jer 7:13 [q] Jer 7:25; 25:4; 26:5 **44:5** [r] Jer 11:8-10 **44:7** [s] Jer 26:19 [t] Jer 51:22 **44:8** [u] Jer 25:6-7 [v] 1Co 10:22 [w] Jer 42:18 **44:9** [x] ver 17, 21 **44:10** [y] Jos 1:7 [z] 1Ki 9:6-9 **44:11** [a] Jer 21:10; Am 9:4 **44:12** [b] ver 7 [c] Isa 1:28 [d] Jer 29:18; 42:15-18 **44:13** [e] Jer 42:17 **44:14** [f] ver 28; Jer 22:24-27; Ro 9:27 **44:16** [g] Jer 11:8-10 **44:17** [h] Dt 23:23 [i] ver 25; Jer 7:18 [j] Hos 2:5-13 **44:18** [k] Mal 3:13-15 **44:19** [l] Jer 7:18 **44:21** [m] Isa 64:9; Jer 14:10 [n] Jer 11:13 [o] ver 9 [p] Ps 79:8 **44:22** [q] Jer 25:18 [r] Ge 19:13; Ps 107:33-34 **44:23** [s] Jer 40:2 [t] 1Ki 9:9; Jer 7:13-15; Da 9:11-12 **44:24** [u] ver 15 [v] Jer 43:7

25This is what the LORD Almighty, the God
of Israel, says: You and your wives have
done what you said you would do when you
promised, 'We will certainly carry out the
vows we made to burn incense and pour out
drink offerings to the Queen of Heaven.'[w]
"Go ahead then, do what you promised!
Keep your vows![x] 26But hear the word of
the LORD, all you Jews living in Egypt: 'I
swear[y] by my great name,' says the LORD,
'that no one from Judah living anywhere
in Egypt will ever again invoke my name
or swear, "As surely as the Sovereign LORD
lives."[z] 27For I am watching over them for
harm,[a] not for good; the Jews in Egypt
will perish by sword and famine until
they are all destroyed. 28Those who escape the sword and return to the land of
Judah from Egypt will be very few.[b] Then
the whole remnant of Judah who came to
live in Egypt will know whose word will
stand—mine or theirs.[c]
29" 'This will be the sign to you that I
will punish you in this place,' declares
the LORD, 'so that you will know that my
threats of harm against you will surely
stand.'[d] 30This is what the LORD says: 'I am
going to deliver Pharaoh[e] Hophra king of
Egypt into the hands of his enemies who
want to kill him, just as I gave Zedekiah[f]
king of Judah into the hands of Nebuchadnezzar king of Babylon, the enemy who
wanted to kill him.' "[g]

A Message to Baruch

45 When Baruch[h] son of Neriah wrote
on a scroll the words Jeremiah the
prophet dictated in the fourth year of Jehoiakim[i] son of Josiah king of Judah, Jeremiah said this to Baruch: 2"This is what
the LORD, the God of Israel, says to you,
Baruch: 3You said, 'Woe to me! The LORD
has added sorrow to my pain; I am worn
out with groaning[j] and find no rest.' 4But
the LORD has told me to say to you, 'This is
what the LORD says: I will overthrow what I
have built and uproot what I have planted,[k]
throughout the earth.[l] 5Should you then
seek great things for yourself? Do not seek
them.[m] For I will bring disaster on all people, declares the LORD, but wherever you go
I will let you escape with your life.' "[n]

A Message About Egypt

46 This is the word of the LORD that
came to Jeremiah the prophet concerning the nations:[o]

2Concerning Egypt:

This is the message against the army of
Pharaoh Necho[p] king of Egypt, which was
defeated at Carchemish[q] on the Euphrates
River by Nebuchadnezzar king of Babylon
in the fourth year of Jehoiakim[r] son of Josiah king of Judah:

3"Prepare your shields,[s] both large and small,
and march out for battle!
4Harness the horses,
mount the steeds!
Take your positions
with helmets on!
Polish[t] your spears,
put on your armor![u]
5What do I see?
They are terrified,
they are retreating,
their warriors are defeated.
They flee[v] in haste
without looking back,
and there is terror[w] on every side,"
declares the LORD.
6"The swift cannot flee[x]
nor the strong escape.
In the north by the River Euphrates
they stumble and fall.[y]

7"Who is this that rises like the Nile,
like rivers of surging waters?[z]
8Egypt rises like the Nile,
like rivers of surging waters.
She says, 'I will rise and cover the earth;
I will destroy cities and their people.'

---

their idolatry. Nothing could make them abandon their vows to worship the Queen of Heaven.

44:26–27 *by my great name.* The name of God reveals His quality and character in dealing with humankind.

44:28 *the whole remnant of Judah.* A small remnant would survive and see the fulfillment of God's word as revealed through Jeremiah. Their own hopes of prosperity in Egypt would vanish, and the sign of God's work against them would be the fall of Pharaoh Hophra of Egypt. In 570 B.C., Hophra was overthrown in a military coup by his own general, Amasis. Three years later he was executed in fulfillment of Jeremiah's prophecy.

45:2–3 *to you, Baruch.* Jeremiah addressed Baruch in light of the scribe's sorrow. Baruch lamented his plight in the same manner that Jeremiah had done (15:10). He also suffered mental anguish and personal rejection from his people due to his association with Jeremiah (36:15–19).

46:1 *concerning the nations.* This verse introduces a collection of oracles. The text moves generally from the west—Egypt—to the east—Elam and Babylon. Scattered throughout the oracles are brief messages of the restoration of Israel and Judah. The main message of these oracles is the sovereignty of God over all the nations of the earth.

44:25 [w] ver 17 [x] Eze 20:39 **44:26** [y] Ge 22:16; Isa 48:1; Heb 6:13-17 [z] Dt 32:40; Ps 50:16 **44:27** [a] Jer 31:28 **44:28** [b] ver 13-14; Isa 10:19 [c] ver 17, 25-26 **44:29** [d] Pr 19:21 **44:30** [e] Jer 46:26; Eze 30:21 [f] 2Ki 25:1-7 [g] Jer 39:5 **45:1** [h] Jer 32:12; 36:4, 18, 32 [i] 2Ch 36:5 **45:3** [j] Ps 69:3 **45:4** [k] Jer 11:17 [l] Isa 5:5-7; Jer 18:7-10 **45:5** [m] Mt 6:25-27, 33 [n] Jer 21:9; 38:2; 39:18 **46:1** [o] Jer 1:10; 25:15-38 **46:2** [p] 2Ki 23:29 [q] 2Ch 35:20 [r] Jer 45:1 **46:3** [s] Isa 21:5; Jer 51:11-12 **46:4** [t] Eze 21:9-11 [u] 1Sa 17:5, 38; 2Ch 26:14; Ne 4:16 **46:5** [v] ver 21 [w] Jer 49:29 **46:6** [x] Isa 30:16 [y] ver 12, 16; Da 11:19 **46:7** [z] Jer 47:2

9 Charge, you horses!
Drive furiously, you charioteers![a]
March on, you warriors—men of Cush[a]
and Put who carry shields,
men of Lydia[b] who draw the bow.
10 But that day[c] belongs to the Lord, the LORD Almighty—
a day of vengeance, for vengeance on his foes.
The sword will devour[d] till it is satisfied,
till it has quenched its thirst with blood.
For the Lord, the LORD Almighty, will offer sacrifice[e]
in the land of the north by the River Euphrates.

11 "Go up to Gilead and get balm,[f]
Virgin[g] Daughter Egypt.
But you try many medicines in vain;
there is no healing[h] for you.
12 The nations will hear of your shame;
your cries will fill the earth.
One warrior will stumble over another;
both will fall[i] down together."

13 This is the message the LORD spoke to
Jeremiah the prophet about the coming of
Nebuchadnezzar king of Babylon to attack
Egypt:[j]

14 "Announce this in Egypt, and proclaim it in Migdol;
proclaim it also in Memphis and Tahpanhes:[k]
'Take your positions and get ready,
for the sword devours those around you.'
15 Why will your warriors be laid low?
They cannot stand, for the LORD will push them down.[l]
16 They will stumble[m] repeatedly;
they will fall[n] over each other.
They will say, 'Get up, let us go back
to our own people and our native lands,
away from the sword of the oppressor.'
17 There they will exclaim,
'Pharaoh king of Egypt is only a loud noise;
he has missed his opportunity.[o]'
18 "As surely as I live," declares the King,[p]
whose name is the LORD Almighty,
"one will come who is like Tabor[q]
among the mountains,
like Carmel[r] by the sea.
19 Pack your belongings for exile,[s]
you who live in Egypt,
for Memphis will be laid waste
and lie in ruins without inhabitant.

20 "Egypt is a beautiful heifer,
but a gadfly is coming
against her from the north.[t]
21 The mercenaries[u] in her ranks
are like fattened calves.
They too will turn and flee[v] together,
they will not stand their ground,
for the day[w] of disaster is coming upon them,
the time for them to be punished.
22 Egypt will hiss like a fleeing serpent
as the enemy advances in force;
they will come against her with axes,
like men who cut down trees.
23 They will chop down her forest,"
declares the LORD,
"dense though it be.
They are more numerous than locusts,[x]
they cannot be counted.
24 Daughter Egypt will be put to shame,
given into the hands of the people of the north.[y]"

25 The LORD Almighty, the God of Israel, says: "I am about to bring punishment
on Amon god of Thebes,[z] on Pharaoh, on
Egypt and her gods[a] and her kings, and on
those who rely[b] on Pharaoh. 26 I will give
them into the hands[c] of those who want
to kill them—Nebuchadnezzar king[d] of
Babylon and his officers. Later, however,
Egypt will be inhabited[e] as in times past,"
declares the LORD.

27 "Do not be afraid,[f] Jacob my servant;
do not be dismayed, Israel.
I will surely save you out of a distant place,
your descendants from the land of their exile.[g]
Jacob will again have peace and security,
and no one will make him afraid.

a 9 That is, the upper Nile region

46:10–12 ***that day belongs to the Lord.*** This time the day is a day of vengeance in which Egypt is punished for the death of Josiah. The imagery of a devouring sword is also found in Jeremiah 2:30. Egypt's demise is pictured as a sacrificial feast. As there was no healing balm for sinful Judah, so now Egypt was mortally wounded, stumbling to its death.

46:15–17 ***Why will your warriors be laid low?*** God subduing powerful nations and their gods (v. 25) in judgment is a prominent theme in these oracles.

46:18 ***King ... LORD Almighty.*** The term "Almighty" can literally be translated "of armies." God is the true and sovereign King over all the armies of heaven and earth.

46:25–26 ***her gods and her kings.*** The gods and goddesses of Egypt were punished in the defeat of the people who worshiped them.

46:9 [a] Jer 47:3 [b] Isa 66:19 **46:10** [c] Joel 1:15 [d] Dt 32:42 [e] Zep 1:7 **46:11** [f] Jer 8:22 [g] Isa 47:1 [h] Jer 30:13; Mic 1:9 **46:12** [i] Isa 19:4; Na 3:8-10 **46:13** [j] Isa 19:1 **46:14** [k] Jer 43:8 **46:15** [l] Isa 66:15-16 **46:16** [m] Lev 26:37 [n] ver 6 **46:17** [o] Isa 19:11-16 **46:18** [p] Jer 48:15 [q] Jos 19:22 [r] 1Ki 18:42 **46:19** [s] Isa 20:4 **46:20** [t] ver 24; Jer 47:2 **46:21** [u] 2Ki 7:6 [v] ver 5 [w] Ps 37:13 **46:23** [x] Jdg 7:12 **46:24** [y] Jer 1:15 **46:25** [z] Eze 30:14; Na 3:8 [a] Jer 43:12 [b] Isa 20:6 **46:26** [c] Jer 44:30 [d] Eze 32:11 [e] Eze 29:11-16 **46:27** [f] Isa 41:13; 43:5 [g] Isa 11:11; Jer 50:19

28 Do not be afraid, Jacob my servant,
for I am with you,"[h] declares the LORD.
"Though I completely destroy[i] all the nations
among which I scatter you,
I will not completely destroy you.
I will discipline you but only in due measure;
I will not let you go entirely unpunished."

A Message About the Philistines

47 This is the word of the LORD that
came to Jeremiah the prophet concerning the Philistines before Pharaoh attacked Gaza:[j]

2 This is what the LORD says:
"See how the waters are rising in the north;[k]
they will become an overflowing torrent.
They will overflow the land and everything in it,
the towns and those who live in them.
The people will cry out;
all who dwell in the land will wail
3 at the sound of the hooves of galloping steeds,
at the noise of enemy chariots
and the rumble of their wheels.
Parents will not turn to help their children;
their hands will hang limp.
4 For the day has come
to destroy all the Philistines
and to remove all survivors
who could help Tyre[l] and Sidon.[m]
The LORD is about to destroy the Philistines,[n]
the remnant from the coasts of Caphtor.[a][o]
5 Gaza will shave[p] her head in mourning;
Ashkelon[q] will be silenced.
You remnant on the plain,
how long will you cut yourselves?

6 "'Alas, sword[r] of the LORD,
how long till you rest?
Return to your sheath;
cease and be still.'
7 But how can it rest
when the LORD has commanded it,
when he has ordered it
to attack Ashkelon and the coast?"

A Message About Moab

48 Concerning Moab:
This is what the LORD Almighty, the God
of Israel, says:

"Woe to Nebo,[s] for it will be ruined.
Kiriathaim[t] will be disgraced and captured;
the stronghold[b] will be disgraced and shattered.
2 Moab will be praised[u] no more;
in Heshbon[c][v] people will plot her downfall:
'Come, let us put an end to that nation.'
You, the people of Madmen,[d] will also be silenced;
the sword will pursue you.
3 Cries of anguish arise from Horonaim,[w]
cries of great havoc and destruction.
4 Moab will be broken;
her little ones will cry out.[e]
5 They go up the hill to Luhith,[x]
weeping bitterly as they go;
on the road down to Horonaim
anguished cries over the destruction are heard.
6 Flee! Run for your lives;
become like a bush[f] in the desert.[y]
7 Since you trust in your deeds and riches,
you too will be taken captive,
and Chemosh[z] will go into exile,[a]
together with his priests and officials.
8 The destroyer will come against every town,
and not a town will escape.
The valley will be ruined
and the plateau destroyed,
because the LORD has spoken.
9 Put salt on Moab,
for she will be laid waste[g];
her towns will become desolate,
with no one to live in them.

10 "A curse on anyone who is lax in doing the LORD's work!
A curse on anyone who keeps their sword[b] from bloodshed![c]

11 "Moab has been at rest[d] from youth,
like wine left on its dregs,[e]
not poured from one jar to another—
she has not gone into exile.

---

[a] 4 That is, Crete [b] 1 Or *captured; / Misgab* [c] 2 The Hebrew for *Heshbon* sounds like the Hebrew for *plot.* [d] 2 The name of the Moabite town Madmen sounds like the Hebrew for *be silenced.* [e] 4 Hebrew; Septuagint / *proclaim it to Zoar* [f] 6 Or *like Aroer* [g] 9 Or *Give wings to Moab, / for she will fly away*

47:6–7 *sword of the LORD.* This image is used often to portray divine judgment (12:2; 46:10,14,16).
48:6–8 *a bush.* This bush is a type of juniper that ekes out its stunted growth in the wilderness, hiding in crevasses of rock. ***exile.*** Taking a deity captive was a well-known Middle Eastern custom. The national statue of the patron deity was seized, and it was believed that the captured god could no longer protect its people.

46:28 [h] Isa 8:9-10 [i] Jer 4:27 **47:1** [j] Ge 10:19; Am 1:6; Zec 9:5-7 **47:2** [k] Isa 8:7; 14:31 **47:4** [l] Am 1:9-10; Zec 9:2-4 [m] Jer 25:22 [n] Ge 10:14; Joel 3:4 [o] Dt 2:23 **47:5** [p] Jer 41:5; Mic 1:16 [q] Jer 25:20 **47:6** [r] Jer 12:12 **48:1** [s] Nu 32:38 [t] Nu 32:37 **48:2** [u] Isa 16:14 [v] Nu 21:25 **48:3** [w] Isa 15:5 **48:5** [x] Isa 15:5 **48:6** [y] Jer 17:6 **48:7** [z] Nu 21:29 [a] Isa 46:1-2; Jer 49:3 **48:10** [b] Jer 47:6 [c] 1Ki 20:42; 2Ki 13:15-19 **48:11** [d] Zec 1:15 [e] Zep 1:12

So she tastes as she did,
and her aroma is unchanged.
12 But days are coming,"
declares the LORD,
"when I will send men who pour from pitchers,
and they will pour her out;
they will empty her pitchers
and smash her jars.
13 Then Moab will be ashamed[f] of Chemosh,
as Israel was ashamed
when they trusted in Bethel.

14 "How can you say, 'We are warriors,[g]
men valiant in battle'?
15 Moab will be destroyed and her towns invaded;
her finest young men will go down in the slaughter,[h]"
declares the King,[i] whose name is the LORD Almighty.[j]
16 "The fall of Moab is at hand;[k]
her calamity will come quickly.
17 Mourn for her, all who live around her,
all who know her fame;
say, 'How broken is the mighty scepter,
how broken the glorious staff!'

18 "Come down from your glory
and sit on the parched ground,[l]
you inhabitants of Daughter Dibon,[m]
for the one who destroys Moab
will come up against you
and ruin your fortified cities.[n]
19 Stand by the road and watch,
you who live in Aroer.[o]
Ask the man fleeing and the woman escaping,
ask them, 'What has happened?'
20 Moab is disgraced, for she is shattered.
Wail[p] and cry out!
Announce by the Arnon[q]
that Moab is destroyed.
21 Judgment has come to the plateau—
to Holon, Jahzah[r] and Mephaath,[s]
22 to Dibon,[t] Nebo and Beth Diblathaim,
23 to Kiriathaim, Beth Gamul and Beth Meon,[u]
24 to Kerioth[v] and Bozrah—
to all the towns of Moab, far and near.
25 Moab's horn[a][w] is cut off;
her arm[x] is broken,"
declares the LORD.

26 "Make her drunk,[y]
for she has defied the LORD.
Let Moab wallow in her vomit;
let her be an object of ridicule.
27 Was not Israel the object of your ridicule?[z]
Was she caught among thieves,
that you shake your head[a] in scorn[b]
whenever you speak of her?
28 Abandon your towns and dwell among the rocks,
you who live in Moab.
Be like a dove[c] that makes its nest
at the mouth of a cave.[d]

29 "We have heard of Moab's pride[e]—
how great is her arrogance!—
of her insolence, her pride, her conceit
and the haughtiness of her heart.
30 I know her insolence but it is futile,"
declares the LORD,
"and her boasts accomplish nothing.
31 Therefore I wail[f] over Moab,
for all Moab I cry out,
I moan for the people of Kir Hareseth.[g]
32 I weep for you, as Jazer weeps,
you vines of Sibmah.[h]
Your branches spread as far as the sea[b];
they reached as far as[c] Jazer.
The destroyer has fallen
on your ripened fruit and grapes.
33 Joy and gladness are gone
from the orchards and fields of Moab.
I have stopped the flow of wine[i] from the presses;
no one treads them with shouts of joy.[j]
Although there are shouts,
they are not shouts of joy.

34 "The sound of their cry rises
from Heshbon to Elealeh[k] and Jahaz,[l]
from Zoar[m] as far as Horonaim[n] and Eglath Shelishiyah,
for even the waters of Nimrim are dried up.[o]
35 In Moab I will put an end
to those who make offerings on the high places[p]
and burn incense[q] to their gods,"
declares the LORD.

[a] 25 *Horn* here symbolizes strength.
[b] 32 Probably the Dead Sea [c] 32 Two Hebrew manuscripts and Septuagint; most Hebrew manuscripts *as far as the Sea of*

48:17 *Mourn for her, all who live around her.* A note of sarcasm is communicated. The nations around Moab, like Judah, who was attacked by Moab's mercenaries, were called upon to lament Moab's destruction.
48:18 *Come down from your glory.* The haughty Moab was shamed by the destruction of its fortresses.
48:26–29 *Make her drunk.* Judgment is portrayed in the form of drunkenness to the point of vomiting, the result of Moab's mockery of Israel (25:15–29).
48:33 *Joy and gladness are gone.* The joy once heard echoing from the vineyards and winepresses had vanished before the horrifying sound of horses' hoofbeats and clashing weapons.

48:13 [f] Hos 10:6 **48:14** [g] Ps 33:16 **48:15** [h] Jer 50:27 [i] Jer 46:18 [j] Jer 51:57 **48:16** [k] Isa 13:22 **48:18** [l] Isa 47:1 [m] Nu 21:30; Jos 13:9 [n] ver 8 **48:19** [o] Dt 2:36 **48:20** [p] Isa 16:7 [q] Nu 21:13 **48:21** [r] Nu 21:23; Isa 15:4 [s] Jos 13:18 **48:22** [t] Jos 13:9,17 **48:23** [u] Jos 13:17 **48:24** [v] Am 2:2 **48:25** [w] Ps 75:10 [x] Ps 10:15; Eze 30:21 **48:26** [y] Jer 25:16,27 **48:27** [z] Jer 2:26 [a] Job 16:4; Jer 18:16 [b] Mic 7:8-10 **48:28** [c] Ps 55:6-7 [d] Jdg 6:2 **48:29** [e] Job 40:12; Isa 16:6 **48:31** [f] Isa 15:5-8 [g] 2Ki 3:25 **48:32** [h] Isa 16:8-9 **48:33** [i] Isa 16:10 [j] Joel 1:12 **48:34** [k] Nu 32:3 [l] Isa 15:4 [m] Ge 13:10 [n] Isa 15:5 [o] Isa 15:6 **48:35** [p] Isa 15:2; 16:12 [q] Jer 11:13

36 "So my heart laments[r] for Moab like the
music of a pipe;
it laments like a pipe for the people of
Kir Hareseth.
The wealth they acquired[s] is gone.
37 Every head is shaved[t]
and every beard cut off;
every hand is slashed
and every waist is covered with
sackcloth.[u]
38 On all the roofs in Moab
and in the public squares
there is nothing but mourning,
for I have broken Moab
like a jar[v] that no one wants,"
declares the LORD.
39 "How shattered she is! How they wail!
How Moab turns her back in shame!
Moab has become an object of ridicule,
an object of horror to all those
around her."

40 This is what the LORD says:

"Look! An eagle is swooping[w] down,
spreading its wings[x] over Moab.
41 Kerioth[a] will be captured
and the strongholds taken.
In that day the hearts of Moab's warriors
will be like the heart of a woman in
labor.[y]
42 Moab will be destroyed[z] as a nation[a]
because she defied[b] the LORD.
43 Terror and pit and snare[c] await you,
you people of Moab,"
declares the LORD.
44 "Whoever flees[d] from the terror
will fall into a pit,
whoever climbs out of the pit
will be caught in a snare;
for I will bring on Moab
the year[e] of her punishment,"
declares the LORD.

45 "In the shadow of Heshbon
the fugitives stand helpless,
for a fire has gone out from Heshbon,
a blaze from the midst of Sihon;[f]
it burns the foreheads of Moab,
the skulls[g] of the noisy boasters.
46 Woe to you, Moab![h]
The people of Chemosh are destroyed;
your sons are taken into exile
and your daughters into captivity.

47 "Yet I will restore[i] the fortunes of Moab
in days to come,"
declares the LORD.

Here ends the judgment on Moab.

A Message About Ammon

49 Concerning the Ammonites:[j]

This is what the LORD says:
"Has Israel no sons?
Has Israel no heir?
Why then has Molek[b] taken possession
of Gad?
Why do his people live in its towns?
2 But the days are coming,"
declares the LORD,
"when I will sound the battle cry[k]
against Rabbah[l] of the Ammonites;
it will become a mound of ruins,
and its surrounding villages will be
set on fire.
Then Israel will drive out
those who drove her out,[m]"
says the LORD.
3 "Wail, Heshbon, for Ai[n] is destroyed!
Cry out, you inhabitants of Rabbah!
Put on sackcloth and mourn;
rush here and there inside the walls,
for Molek will go into exile,[o]
together with his priests and officials.
4 Why do you boast of your valleys,
boast of your valleys so fruitful?
Unfaithful Daughter Ammon,
you trust in your riches[p] and say,
'Who will attack me?'[q]
5 I will bring terror on you
from all those around you,"
declares the Lord,
the LORD Almighty.
"Every one of you will be driven away,
and no one will gather the fugitives.

6 "Yet afterward, I will restore[r] the
fortunes of the Ammonites,"
declares the LORD.

A Message About Edom

7 Concerning Edom:[s]

This is what the LORD Almighty says:

"Is there no longer wisdom in Teman?[t]
Has counsel perished from the
prudent?
Has their wisdom decayed?
8 Turn and flee, hide in deep caves,
you who live in Dedan,[u]
for I will bring disaster on Esau
at the time when I punish him.

[a] *41* Or *The cities* [b] *1* Or *their king*; also in verse 3

48:40–44 ***An eagle is swooping down.*** The imagery is that of Babylon spreading its ravaging armies over Moab like an eagle spreading its wings. ***she defied.*** Moab's chief sin was pride, considering itself greater than the God of Israel. Its pride would be turned to fear and terror, and then the nation would be taken captive.
49:1–2 ***Rabbah.*** This was the patron deity of the Ammonites and is pictured here as taking possession of the land formerly belonging to the Gadites, a process that began in the days of the judges.

48:36 [r] Isa 16:11 [s] Isa 15:7 **48:37** [t] Isa 15:2; Jer 41:5 [u] Ge 37:34 **48:38** [v] Jer 22:28 **48:40** [w] Dt 28:49; Hab 1:8 [x] Isa 8:8 **48:41** [y] Isa 21:3 **48:42** [z] Ps 83:4; Isa 16:14 [a] ver 2 [b] ver 26 **48:43** [c] Isa 24:17 **48:44** [d] 1Ki 19:17; Isa 24:18 [e] Jer 11:23 **48:45** [f] Nu 21:21, 26-28 [g] Nu 24:17 **48:46** [h] Nu 21:29 **48:47** [i] Jer 12:15; 49:6, 39 **49:1** [j] Am 1:13; Zep 2:8-9 **49:2** [k] Jer 4:19 [l] Dt 3:11 [m] Isa 14:2; Eze 21:28-32; 25:2-11 **49:3** [n] Jos 8:28 [o] Jer 48:7 **49:4** [p] Jer 9:23; 1Ti 6:17 [q] Jer 21:13 **49:6** [r] ver 39; Jer 48:47 **49:7** [s] Ge 25:30; Eze 25:12 [t] Ge 36:11, 15, 34 **49:8** [u] Jer 25:23

9 If grape pickers came to you,
would they not leave a few grapes?
If thieves came during the night,
would they not steal only as much as they wanted?
10 But I will strip Esau bare;
I will uncover his hiding places,
so that he cannot conceal himself.
His armed men are destroyed,
also his allies and neighbors,
so there is no one[v] to say,
11 'Leave your fatherless children;[w] I will keep them alive.
Your widows too can depend on me.' "

12 This is what the LORD says: "If those
who do not deserve to drink the cup[x] must
drink it, why should you go unpunished?[y]
You will not go unpunished, but must drink
it. 13 I swear[z] by myself," declares the LORD,
"that Bozrah[a] will become a ruin and a
curse,[a] an object of horror and reproach;
and all its towns will be in ruins forever."

14 I have heard a message from the LORD;
an envoy was sent to the nations to say,
"Assemble yourselves to attack it!
Rise up for battle!"

15 "Now I will make you small among the nations,
despised by mankind.
16 The terror you inspire
and the pride of your heart have deceived you,
you who live in the clefts of the rocks,
who occupy the heights of the hill.
Though you build your nest[b] as high as the eagle's,
from there I will bring you down,"
declares the LORD.
17 "Edom will become an object of horror;[c]
all who pass by will be appalled and will scoff
because of all its wounds.[d]
18 As Sodom and Gomorrah[e] were overthrown,
along with their neighboring towns,"
says the LORD,
"so no one will live there;
no people will dwell[f] in it.

19 "Like a lion coming up from Jordan's thickets[g]
to a rich pastureland,
I will chase Edom from its land in an instant.
Who is the chosen one I will appoint for this?
Who is like me and who can challenge me?[h]
And what shepherd can stand against me?"

20 Therefore, hear what the LORD has planned against Edom,
what he has purposed[i] against those who live in Teman:
The young of the flock[j] will be dragged away;
their pasture will be appalled at their fate.
21 At the sound of their fall the earth will tremble;[k]
their cry[l] will resound to the Red Sea.[b]
22 Look! An eagle will soar and swoop[m] down,
spreading its wings over Bozrah.
In that day the hearts of Edom's warriors
will be like the heart of a woman in labor.[n]

A Message About Damascus

23 Concerning Damascus:[o]

"Hamath[p] and Arpad[q] are dismayed,
for they have heard bad news.
They are disheartened,
troubled like[c] the restless sea.[r]
24 Damascus has become feeble,
she has turned to flee
and panic has gripped her;
anguish and pain have seized her,
pain like that of a woman in labor.
25 Why has the city of renown not been abandoned,
the town in which I delight?
26 Surely, her young men will fall in the streets;
all her soldiers will be silenced[s] in that day,"
declares the LORD Almighty.
27 "I will set fire[t] to the walls of Damascus;
it will consume the fortresses of Ben-Hadad.[u]"

---

[a] *13* That is, its name will be used in cursing (see 29:22); or, others will see that it is cursed.
[b] *21* Or *the Sea of Reeds*
[c] *23* Hebrew *on* or *by*

49:9–11 ***grape pickers.*** This imagery is derived from 6:9, but there was no real remnant left in Edom. The nation had been totally ravaged and stripped bare, with only women and children left alive to work the land.

49:17–19 ***appalled.*** Like Israel, Judah, Egypt, Moab, and Ammon, Edom would be destroyed and would become an object of derision. Like the lion that emerges from the thickets along the lower Jordan and seizes its prey, God would attack the Edomites through His appointed instrument.

49:10 [v] Mal 1:2-5 **49:11** [w] Hos 14:3
49:12 [x] Jer 25:15 [y] Jer 25:28-29 **49:13** [z] Ge 22:16
[a] Ge 36:33; Isa 34:6 **49:16** [b] Job 39:27; Am 9:2
49:17 [c] ver 13 [d] Jer 50:13; Eze 35:7 **49:18** [e] Ge 19:24; Dt 29:23 [f] ver 33 **49:19** [g] Jer 12:5 [h] Jer 50:44
49:20 [i] Isa 14:27 [j] Jer 50:45 **49:21** [k] Eze 26:15
[l] Jer 50:46; Eze 26:18 **49:22** [m] Hos 8:1 [n] Isa 13:8; Jer 48:40-41 **49:23** [o] Ge 14:15; 2Ch 16:2; Ac 9:2
[p] Isa 10:9; Am 6:2; Zec 9:2 [q] 2Ki 18:34 [r] Ge 49:4; Isa 57:20
49:26 [s] Jer 50:30 **49:27** [t] Jer 43:12; Am 1:4
[u] 1Ki 15:18

A Message About Kedar and Hazor

28Concerning Kedar[v] and the kingdoms of Hazor, which Nebuchadnezzar king of Babylon attacked:

This is what the LORD says:

"Arise, and attack Kedar
and destroy the people of the East.[w]
29 Their tents and their flocks will be taken;
their shelters will be carried off
with all their goods and camels.
People will shout to them,
'Terror[x] on every side!'

30 "Flee quickly away!
Stay in deep caves, you who live in Hazor,"
declares the LORD.
"Nebuchadnezzar king of Babylon has plotted against you;
he has devised a plan against you.

31 "Arise and attack a nation at ease,
which lives in confidence,"
declares the LORD,
"a nation that has neither gates nor bars;[y]
its people live far from danger.
32 Their camels will become plunder,
and their large herds will be spoils of war.
I will scatter to the winds those who are in distant places[a][z]
and will bring disaster on them from every side,"
declares the LORD.
33 "Hazor will become a haunt of jackals,
a desolate[a] place forever.
No one will live there;
no people will dwell[b] in it."

A Message About Elam

34This is the word of the LORD that came
to Jeremiah the prophet concerning Elam,[c]
early in the reign of Zedekiah[d] king of Judah:

35This is what the LORD Almighty says:

"See, I will break the bow[e] of Elam,
the mainstay of their might.
36 I will bring against Elam the four winds[f]
from the four quarters of heaven;
I will scatter them to the four winds,
and there will not be a nation
where Elam's exiles do not go.
37 I will shatter Elam before their foes,
before those who want to kill them;
I will bring disaster on them,
even my fierce anger,"[g]
declares the LORD.
"I will pursue them with the sword[h]
until I have made an end of them.
38 I will set my throne in Elam
and destroy her king and officials,"
declares the LORD.

39 "Yet I will restore[i] the fortunes of Elam
in days to come,"
declares the LORD.

A Message About Babylon

50 This is the word the LORD spoke
through Jeremiah the prophet concerning Babylon[j] and the land of the Babylonians[b]:

2 "Announce and proclaim[k] among the nations,
lift up a banner and proclaim it;
keep nothing back, but say,
'Babylon will be captured;[l]
Bel[m] will be put to shame,
Marduk[n] filled with terror.
Her images will be put to shame
and her idols filled with terror.'
3 A nation from the north will attack her
and lay waste her land.
No one will live[o] in it;
both people and animals[p] will flee away.

4 "In those days, at that time,"
declares the LORD,
"the people of Israel and the people of Judah together[q]
will go in tears[r] to seek[s] the LORD their God.
5 They will ask the way to Zion
and turn their faces toward it.
They will come[t] and bind themselves to the LORD
in an everlasting covenant[u]
that will not be forgotten.

---

[a] 32 Or *who clip the hair by their foreheads*
[b] 1 Or *Chaldeans*; also in verses 8, 25, 35 and 45

49:30–33 *Hazor will become a haunt of jackals.* Nebuchadnezzar's destructive army would attack the tent villages of Kedar and Hazor. The oases would be left to the jackals for habitation (9:11; 10:22). The Bedouin peoples would be scattered afar, as if by the hot desert winds.
49:34–36 *break the bow.* The Elamites were famous for their skilled archers (Is. 22:6), who became an important part of the Persian army under Cyrus. ***four winds.*** This expression indicates the military might that the Lord musters against His enemies (Ezek. 37:9).
50:2–3 *Bel will be put to shame.* Bel was a title like Baal, meaning "Lord," another name for Babylon's patron deity, Marduk. The oracle begins with a defamation of the gods of Babylon. The term translated "images" means animal droppings. The Hebrew prophets are openly contemptuous of idols and speak of them with ridicule.

49:28 [v] Ge 25:13 [w] Jdg 6:3 **49:29** [x] Jer 6:25; 46:5 **49:31** [y] Eze 38:11 **49:32** [z] Jer 9:26 **49:33** [a] Jer 10:22 [b] ver 18; Jer 51:37 **49:34** [c] Ge 10:22 [d] 2Ki 24:18 **49:35** [e] Isa 22:6 **49:36** [f] ver 32 **49:37** [g] Jer 30:24 [h] Jer 9:16 **49:39** [i] Jer 48:47 **50:1** [j] Ge 10:10; Isa 13:1 **50:2** [k] Jer 4:16 [l] Jer 51:31 [m] Isa 46:1 [n] Jer 51:47 **50:3** [o] ver 13; Isa 14:22-23 [p] Zep 1:3 **50:4** [q] Jer 3:18; Hos 1:11 [r] Ezr 3:12; Jer 31:9 [s] Hos 3:5 **50:5** [t] Jer 33:7 [u] Isa 55:3; Jer 32:40; Heb 8:6-10

6 "My people have been lost sheep;[v]
their shepherds have led them astray
and caused them to roam on the mountains.
They wandered over mountain and hill[w]
and forgot their own resting place.[x]
7 Whoever found them devoured them;
their enemies said, 'We are not guilty,[y]
for they sinned against the LORD, their verdant pasture,
the LORD, the hope[z] of their ancestors.'

8 "Flee[a] out of Babylon;
leave the land of the Babylonians,
and be like the goats that lead the flock.
9 For I will stir up and bring against Babylon
an alliance of great nations from the land of the north.
They will take up their positions against her,
and from the north she will be captured.
Their arrows will be like skilled warriors
who do not return empty-handed.
10 So Babylonia[a] will be plundered;
all who plunder her will have their fill,"
declares the LORD.

11 "Because you rejoice and are glad,
you who pillage my inheritance,[b]
because you frolic like a heifer threshing grain
and neigh like stallions,
12 your mother will be greatly ashamed;
she who gave you birth will be disgraced.
She will be the least of the nations—
a wilderness, a dry land, a desert.
13 Because of the LORD's anger she will not be inhabited
but will be completely desolate.
All who pass Babylon will be appalled;
they will scoff[c] because of all her wounds.[d]

14 "Take up your positions around Babylon,
all you who draw the bow.[e]
Shoot at her! Spare no arrows,
for she has sinned against the LORD.
15 Shout[f] against her on every side!
She surrenders, her towers fall,
her walls[g] are torn down.
Since this is the vengeance[h] of the LORD,
take vengeance on her;
do to her[i] as she has done to others.
16 Cut off from Babylon the sower,
and the reaper with his sickle at harvest.
Because of the sword[j] of the oppressor
let everyone return to their own people,[k]
let everyone flee to their own land.[l]

17 "Israel is a scattered flock
that lions[m] have chased away.
The first to devour them
was the king[n] of Assyria;
the last to crush their bones
was Nebuchadnezzar[o] king[p] of Babylon."

18 Therefore this is what the LORD Almighty, the God of Israel, says:

"I will punish the king of Babylon and his land
as I punished the king[q] of Assyria.[r]
19 But I will bring[s] Israel back to their own pasture,
and they will graze on Carmel and Bashan;
their appetite will be satisfied
on the hills[t] of Ephraim and Gilead.
20 In those days, at that time,"
declares the LORD,
"search will be made for Israel's guilt,
but there will be none,
and for the sins[u] of Judah,
but none will be found,
for I will forgive[v] the remnant[w] I spare.

21 "Attack the land of Merathaim
and those who live in Pekod.[x]
Pursue, kill and completely destroy[b] them,"
declares the LORD.
"Do everything I have commanded you.
22 The noise[y] of battle is in the land,
the noise of great destruction!

[a] 10 Or *Chaldea* [b] 21 The Hebrew term refers to the irrevocable giving over of things or persons to the LORD, often by totally destroying them; also in verse 26.

50:11–13 *you who pillage my inheritance.* Babylon's plunder would be its punishment for gloating over Judah's demise and the abuse of God's heritage. Babylon would "be a wilderness." Defamation, drought, dehabitation, desolation, and derision were Babylon's destiny (18:16; 19:8; 49:17).

50:21–28 *completely destroy them.* The tables would be turned on Babylon. The Lord God had launched His vengeful weapons upon the city through His anointed servant Cyrus (2 Chr. 36:22,23; Is 45:1).

50:6 [v] Isa 53:6; Mt 9:36; 10:6 [w] Jer 3:6; Eze 34:6 [x] ver 19 **50:7** [y] Jer 2:3 [z] Jer 14:8 **50:8** [a] Isa 48:20; Jer 51:6; Rev 18:4 **50:11** [b] Isa 47:6 **50:13** [c] Jer 18:16 [d] Jer 49:17 **50:14** [e] ver 29,42 **50:15** [f] Jer 51:14 [g] Jer 51:44,58 [h] Jer 51:6 [i] Ps 137:8; Rev 18:6 **50:16** [j] Jer 25:38 [k] Isa 13:14 [l] Jer 51:9 **50:17** [m] Jer 2:15 [n] 2Ki 17:6 [o] 2Ki 24:10,14 [p] 2Ki 25:7 **50:18** [q] Isa 10:12 [r] Eze 31:3 **50:19** [s] Jer 31:10; Eze 34:13 [t] Jer 31:5; 33:12 **50:20** [u] Mic 7:18,19 [v] Jer 31:34 [w] Isa 1:9 **50:21** [x] Eze 23:23 **50:22** [y] Jer 4:19-21; 51:54

23 How broken and shattered
is the hammer of the whole earth!
How desolate[z] is Babylon
among the nations!
24 I set a trap[a] for you, Babylon,
and you were caught before you knew it;
you were found and captured[b]
because you opposed[c] the LORD.
25 The LORD has opened his arsenal
and brought out the weapons[d] of his wrath,
for the Sovereign LORD Almighty has work to do
in the land of the Babylonians.[e]
26 Come against her from afar.
Break open her granaries;
pile her up like heaps of grain.
Completely destroy[f] her
and leave her no remnant.
27 Kill all her young bulls;
let them go down to the slaughter!
Woe to them! For their day has come,
the time for them to be punished.
28 Listen to the fugitives and refugees from Babylon
declaring in Zion[g]
how the LORD our God has taken vengeance,[h]
vengeance for his temple.

29 "Summon archers against Babylon,
all those who draw the bow.[i]
Encamp all around her;
let no one escape.
Repay[j] her for her deeds;[k]
do to her as she has done.
For she has defied[l] the LORD,
the Holy One of Israel.
30 Therefore, her young men[m] will fall in the streets;
all her soldiers will be silenced in that day,"
declares the LORD.
31 "See, I am against[n] you, you arrogant one,"
declares the Lord, the LORD Almighty,
"for your day has come,
the time for you to be punished.
32 The arrogant one will stumble and fall
and no one will help her up;
I will kindle a fire[o] in her towns
that will consume all who are around her."

33 This is what the LORD Almighty says:

"The people of Israel are oppressed,[p]
and the people of Judah as well.
All their captors hold them fast,
refusing to let them go.[q]
34 Yet their Redeemer is strong;
the LORD Almighty[r] is his name.
He will vigorously defend their cause[s]
so that he may bring rest[t] to their land,
but unrest to those who live in Babylon.

35 "A sword[u] against the Babylonians!"
declares the LORD—
"against those who live in Babylon
and against her officials and wise[v] men!
36 A sword against her false prophets!
They will become fools.
A sword against her warriors![w]
They will be filled with terror.
37 A sword against her horses and chariots[x]
and all the foreigners in her ranks!
They will become weaklings.[y]
A sword against her treasures!
They will be plundered.
38 A drought on[a] her waters!
They will dry[z] up.
For it is a land of idols,[a]
idols that will go mad with terror.

39 "So desert creatures and hyenas will live there,
and there the owl will dwell.
It will never again be inhabited
or lived in from generation to generation.[b]
40 As I overthrew Sodom and Gomorrah[c]
along with their neighboring towns,"
declares the LORD,
"so no one will live there;
no people will dwell in it.

41 "Look! An army is coming from the north;[d]
a great nation and many kings
are being stirred up from the ends of the earth.[e]
42 They are armed with bows[f] and spears;
they are cruel and without mercy.[g]
They sound like the roaring sea[h]
as they ride on their horses;
they come like men in battle formation
to attack you, Daughter Babylon.[i]
43 The king of Babylon has heard reports about them,
and his hands hang limp.

[a] 38 Or *A sword against*

50:34 ***their Redeemer is strong.*** One who secured the freedom of a kinsman, protecting family rights, was called a kinsmen redeemer. Here God, the Redeemer of Israel (Is. 47:4), offers to obtain the legal freedom of His people from captivity.

50:23 [z] Isa 14:16 **50:24** [a] Da 5:30-31 [b] Jer 51:31 [c] Job 9:4 **50:25** [d] Isa 13:5 [e] Jer 51:25,55

50:26 [f] Isa 14:22-23 **50:28** [g] Isa 48:20; Jer 51:10 [h] ver 15 **50:29** [i] ver 14 [j] Rev 18:6 [k] Jer 51:56 [l] Isa 47:10 **50:30** [m] Isa 13:18; Jer 49:26 **50:31** [n] Jer 21:13 **50:32** [o] Jer 21:14; 49:27 **50:33** [p] Isa 58:6 [q] Isa 14:17 **50:34** [r] Jer 51:19 [s] Jer 15:21; 51:36 [t] Isa 14:7 **50:35** [u] Jer 47:6 [v] Da 5:7 **50:36** [w] Jer 49:22 **50:37** [x] Jer 51:21 [y] Jer 51:30; Na 3:13 **50:38** [z] Jer 51:36 [a] ver 2 **50:39** [b] Isa 13:19-22; 34:13-15; Jer 51:37; Rev 18:2 **50:40** [c] Ge 19:24 **50:41** [d] Jer 6:22 [e] Isa 13:4; Jer 51:22-28 **50:42** [f] ver 14 [g] Isa 13:18 [h] Isa 5:30 [i] Jer 6:23

Anguish has gripped him,
pain like that of a woman in labor.
44 Like a lion coming up from Jordan's thickets
to a rich pastureland,
I will chase Babylon from its land in an instant.
Who is the chosen[j] one I will appoint for this?
Who is like me and who can challenge me?[k]
And what shepherd can stand against me?"
45 Therefore, hear what the LORD has planned against Babylon,
what he has purposed[l] against the land of the Babylonians:
The young of the flock will be dragged away;
their pasture will be appalled at their fate.
46 At the sound of Babylon's capture the earth will tremble;
its cry[m] will resound among the nations.

51 This is what the LORD says:
"See, I will stir up the spirit of a destroyer
against Babylon and the people of Leb Kamai.[a]
2 I will send foreigners to Babylon
to winnow[n] her and to devastate her land;
they will oppose her on every side
in the day of her disaster.
3 Let not the archer string his bow,[o]
nor let him put on his armor.[p]
Do not spare her young men;
completely destroy[b] her army.
4 They will fall[q] down slain in Babylon,[c]
fatally wounded in her streets.[r]
5 For Israel and Judah have not been forsaken[s]
by their God, the LORD Almighty,
though their land[d] is full of guilt[t]
before the Holy One of Israel.

6 "Flee[u] from Babylon!
Run for your lives!
Do not be destroyed because of her sins.[v]
It is time for the LORD's vengeance;[w]
he will repay[x] her what she deserves.
7 Babylon was a gold cup[y] in the LORD's hand;
she made the whole earth drunk.
The nations drank her wine;
therefore they have now gone mad.
8 Babylon will suddenly fall[z] and be broken.
Wail over her!
Get balm[a] for her pain;
perhaps she can be healed.

9 " 'We would have healed Babylon,
but she cannot be healed;
let us leave[b] her and each go to our own land,
for her judgment[c] reaches to the skies,
it rises as high as the heavens.'

10 " 'The LORD has vindicated[d] us;
come, let us tell in Zion
what the LORD our God has done.'[e]

11 "Sharpen the arrows,[f]
take up the shields![g]
The LORD has stirred up the kings of the Medes,[h]
because his purpose[i] is to destroy Babylon.
The LORD will take vengeance,
vengeance for his temple.[j]
12 Lift up a banner against the walls of Babylon!
Reinforce the guard,
station the watchmen,
prepare an ambush!
The LORD will carry out his purpose,
his decree against the people of Babylon.
13 You who live by many waters[k]
and are rich in treasures,[l]
your end has come,
the time for you to be destroyed.
14 The LORD Almighty has sworn by himself:[m]
I will surely fill you with troops, as with a swarm of locusts,[n]
and they will shout[o] in triumph over you.

---

a 1 *Leb Kamai* is a cryptogram for Chaldea, that is, Babylonia. *b* 3 The Hebrew term refers to the irrevocable giving over of things or persons to the LORD, often by totally destroying them.
c 4 Or *Chaldea* *d* 5 Or *Almighty, / and the land of the Babylonians*

51:6–10 *Babylon was a gold cup.* The imagery of Babylon's cup of fury from 25:15–19 is reversed. Here Babylon's cup is broken by the Lord. ***Get balm.*** As in the case of Judah (8:22), decadent Babylon was beyond healing and had to be abandoned. The destruction of Babylon was the vindication of the justice of God. Jeremiah's prediction (25:12–14) would be realized: Israel would be made righteous through God's work.

50:44 [j] Nu 16:5 [k] Job 41:10; Isa 46:9; Jer 49:19 **50:45** [l] Ps 33:11; Isa 14:24; Jer 51:11 **50:46** [m] Rev 18:9-10 **51:2** [n] Isa 41:16; Jer 15:7; Mt 3:12 **51:3** [o] Jer 50:29 [p] Jer 46:4 **51:4** [q] Isa 13:15 [r] Jer 49:26; 50:30 **51:5** [s] Isa 54:6-8 [t] Hos 4:1 **51:6** [u] Jer 50:8 [v] Nu 16:26; Rev 18:4 [w] Jer 50:15 [x] Jer 25:14 **51:7** [y] Jer 25:15-16; Rev 14:8-10; 17:4 **51:8** [z] Isa 21:9; Rev 14:8 [a] Jer 46:11 **51:9** [b] Isa 13:14; Jer 50:16 [c] Rev 18:4-5 **51:10** [d] Mic 7:9 [e] Jer 50:28 **51:11** [f] Jer 50:9 [g] Jer 46:4 [h] ver 28 [i] Jer 50:45 [j] Jer 50:28 **51:13** [k] Rev 17:1, 15 [l] Isa 45:3; Hab 2:9 **51:14** [m] Am 6:8 [n] ver 27; Na 3:15 [o] Jer 50:15

15 "He made the earth by his power;
he founded the world by his wisdom
and stretched[p] out the heavens by his understanding.
16 When he thunders,[q] the waters in the heavens roar;
he makes clouds rise from the ends of the earth.
He sends lightning with the rain
and brings out the wind from his storehouses.[r]

17 "Everyone is senseless and without knowledge;
every goldsmith is shamed by his idols.
The images he makes are a fraud;[s]
they have no breath in them.
18 They are worthless,[t] the objects of mockery;
when their judgment comes, they will perish.
19 He who is the Portion of Jacob is not like these,
for he is the Maker of all things,
including the people of his inheritance—
the LORD Almighty is his name.

20 "You are my war club,[u]
my weapon for battle—
with you I shatter[v] nations,
with you I destroy kingdoms,
21 with you I shatter horse and rider,[w]
with you I shatter chariot and driver,
22 with you I shatter man and woman,
with you I shatter old man and youth,
with you I shatter young man and young woman,[x]
23 with you I shatter shepherd and flock,
with you I shatter farmer and oxen,
with you I shatter governors and officials.[y]

24 "Before your eyes I will repay[z] Babylon
and all who live in Babylonia[a] for all the
wrong they have done in Zion," declares
the LORD.

25 "I am against you, you destroying mountain,
you who destroy the whole earth,"
declares the LORD.
"I will stretch out my hand against you,
roll you off the cliffs,
and make you a burned-out mountain.[a]
26 No rock will be taken from you for a cornerstone,
nor any stone for a foundation,
for you will be desolate[b] forever,"
declares the LORD.

27 "Lift up a banner[c] in the land!
Blow the trumpet among the nations!
Prepare the nations for battle against her;
summon against her these kingdoms:[d]
Ararat,[e] Minni and Ashkenaz.[f]
Appoint a commander against her;
send up horses like a swarm of locusts.
28 Prepare the nations for battle against her—
the kings of the Medes,[g]
their governors and all their officials,
and all the countries they rule.
29 The land trembles and writhes,
for the LORD's purposes against Babylon stand—
to lay waste the land of Babylon
so that no one will live there.[h]
30 Babylon's warriors[i] have stopped fighting;
they remain in their strongholds.
Their strength is exhausted;
they have become weaklings.[j]
Her dwellings are set on fire;
the bars[k] of her gates are broken.
31 One courier[l] follows another
and messenger follows messenger
to announce to the king of Babylon
that his entire city is captured,
32 the river crossings seized,
the marshes set on fire,
and the soldiers terrified.[m]"

33 This is what the LORD Almighty, the
God of Israel, says:

"Daughter Babylon is like a threshing floor[n]
at the time it is trampled;
the time to harvest[o] her will soon come."

34 "Nebuchadnezzar[p] king of Babylon has devoured us,
he has thrown us into confusion,
he has made us an empty jar.

---

[a] 24 Or *Chaldea*; also in verse 35

51:20–26 *You are my war club.* Babylon had been God's implement for judgment against the nations, and Judah in particular.
51:29–32 *Babylon's warriors have stopped fighting.* The Nabonidus Chronicle, an ancient text describing the fall of Babylon, reports that "Cyrus entered Babylon without a battle." By the time Cyrus reached Babylon, he had conquered all of Babylonia except for the capital city, cutting off roads and supply routes.

51:15 [p] Ge 1:1; Job 9:8; Ps 104:2 **51:16** [q] Ps 18:11-13 [r] Ps 135:7; Jnh 1:4 **51:17** [s] Isa 44:20; Hab 2:18-19 **51:18** [t] Jer 18:15 **51:20** [u] Isa 10:5 [v] Mic 4:13 **51:21** [w] Ex 15:1 **51:22** [x] 2Ch 36:17; Isa 13:17-18 **51:23** [y] ver 57 **51:24** [z] Jer 50:15 **51:25** [a] Zec 4:7 **51:26** [b] ver 29; Isa 13:19-22; Jer 50:12 **51:27** [c] Isa 13:2; Jer 50:2 [d] Jer 25:14 [e] Ge 8:4 [f] Ge 10:3 **51:28** [g] ver 11 **51:29** [h] ver 43; Isa 13:20 **51:30** [i] Jer 50:36 [j] Isa 19:16 [k] Isa 45:2; La 2:9; Na 3:13 **51:31** [l] 2Sa 18:19-31 **51:32** [m] Jer 50:36 **51:33** [n] Isa 21:10 [o] Isa 17:5; Hos 6:11 **51:34** [p] Jer 50:17

Like a serpent he has swallowed us
and filled his stomach with our
delicacies,
and then has spewed us out.
35 May the violence done to our flesh[a] be
on Babylon,"
say the inhabitants of Zion.
"May our blood be on those who live in
Babylonia,"
says Jerusalem.[q]

36 Therefore this is what the LORD says:

"See, I will defend your cause[r]
and avenge[s] you;
I will dry up[t] her sea
and make her springs dry.
37 Babylon will be a heap of ruins,
a haunt[u] of jackals,
an object of horror and scorn,
a place where no one lives.[v]
38 Her people all roar like young
lions,
they growl like lion cubs.
39 But while they are aroused,
I will set out a feast for them
and make them drunk,
so that they shout with laughter—
then sleep forever and not awake,"
declares the LORD.[w]
40 "I will bring them down
like lambs to the slaughter,
like rams and goats.

41 "How Sheshak[b][x] will be captured,[y]
the boast of the whole earth
seized!
How desolate Babylon will be
among the nations!
42 The sea will rise over Babylon;
its roaring waves[z] will cover her.
43 Her towns will be desolate,
a dry and desert land,
a land where no one lives,
through which no one travels.[a]
44 I will punish Bel[b] in Babylon
and make him spew out[c] what he has
swallowed.
The nations will no longer stream to
him.
And the wall[d] of Babylon will
fall.

45 "Come out[e] of her, my people!
Run[f] for your lives!
Run from the fierce anger of the
LORD.
46 Do not lose heart or be afraid[g]
when rumors[h] are heard in the land;
one rumor comes this year, another the
next,
rumors of violence in the land
and of ruler against ruler.
47 For the time will surely come
when I will punish the idols[i] of
Babylon;
her whole land will be disgraced[j]
and her slain will all lie fallen within
her.
48 Then heaven and earth and all that is in
them
will shout[k] for joy over Babylon,
for out of the north[l]
destroyers will attack her,"
declares the LORD.

49 "Babylon must fall because of Israel's
slain,
just as the slain in all the earth
have fallen because of Babylon.[m]
50 You who have escaped the sword,
leave[n] and do not linger!
Remember[o] the LORD in a distant land,
and call to mind Jerusalem."

51 "We are disgraced,[p]
for we have been insulted
and shame covers our faces,
because foreigners have entered
the holy places of the LORD's house."[q]

52 "But days are coming," declares the
LORD,
"when I will punish her idols,[r]
and throughout her land
the wounded will groan.
53 Even if Babylon ascends to the heavens[s]
and fortifies her lofty stronghold,
I will send destroyers[t] against her,"
declares the LORD.

54 "The sound of a cry comes from
Babylon,
the sound of great destruction[u]
from the land of the Babylonians.[c]
55 The LORD will destroy Babylon;
he will silence her noisy din.
Waves[v] of enemies will rage like great
waters;
the roar of their voices will resound.

---

[a] 35 Or *done to us and to our children*
[b] 41 *Sheshak* is a cryptogram for Babylon.
[c] 54 Or *Chaldeans*

51:47–48 ***the time will surely come.*** This expression usually introduces a message of divine intervention into history. ***punish the idols of Babylon.*** The city was known for its thousands of images of its numerous gods and goddesses. As the king claimed to conquer nations in the name of his patron deity, so the gods of the defeated would be punished along with their worshipers. The devastation of decadent Babylon would be no cause for mourning among the nations. Instead, the nations would sing joyfully of Babylon's fall.

51:35 [q] ver 24; Ps 137:8 **51:36** [r] Ps 140:12; Jer 50:34; La 3:58 [s] ver 6; Ro 12:19 [t] Jer 50:38 **51:37** [u] Isa 13:22; Rev 18:2 [v] Jer 50:13,39 **51:39** [w] ver 57 **51:41** [x] Jer 25:26 [y] Isa 13:19 **51:42** [z] Isa 8:7 **51:43** [a] ver 29,62; Isa 13:20; Jer 2:6 **51:44** [b] Isa 46:1 [c] ver 34 [d] ver 58; Jer 50:15 **51:45** [e] Rev 18:4 [f] ver 6; Isa 48:20; Jer 50:8 **51:46** [g] Jer 46:27 [h] 2Ki 19:7 **51:47** [i] ver 52; Isa 46:1-2; Jer 50:2 [j] Jer 50:12 **51:48** [k] Isa 44:23; Rev 18:20 [l] ver 11 **51:49** [m] Ps 137:8; Jer 50:29 **51:50** [n] ver 45 [o] Ps 137:6 **51:51** [p] Ps 44:13-16; 79:4 [q] La 1:10 **51:52** [r] ver 47 **51:53** [s] Ge 11:4; Isa 14:13-14 [t] Jer 49:16 **51:54** [u] Jer 50:22 **1:55** [v] Ps 18:4

56 A destroyer[w] will come against
Babylon;
her warriors will be captured,
and their bows will be broken.[x]
For the LORD is a God of retribution;
he will repay[y] in full.
57 I will make her officials and wise men
drunk,
her governors, officers and warriors
as well;
they will sleep[z] forever and not awake,"
declares the King,[a] whose name is the
LORD Almighty.

58 This is what the LORD Almighty says:

"Babylon's thick wall[b] will be
leveled
and her high gates set on fire;
the peoples[c] exhaust themselves for
nothing,
the nations' labor is only fuel for the
flames."[d]

59 This is the message Jeremiah the
prophet gave to the staff officer Seraiah
son of Neriah,[e] the son of Mahseiah, when
he went to Babylon with Zedekiah[f] king
of Judah in the fourth[g] year of his reign.
60 Jeremiah had written on a scroll[h] about
all the disasters that would come upon
Babylon—all that had been recorded concerning Babylon. 61 He said to Seraiah,
"When you get to Babylon, see that you
read all these words aloud. 62 Then say,
'LORD, you have said you will destroy this
place, so that neither people nor animals
will live in it; it will be desolate[i] forever.'
63 When you finish reading this scroll, tie a
stone to it and throw it into the Euphrates.
64 Then say, 'So will Babylon sink to rise no
more because of the disaster I will bring on
her. And her people[j] will fall.' "

The words of Jeremiah end[k] here.

The Fall of Jerusalem

52 Zedekiah[l] was twenty-one years
old when he became king, and he
reigned in Jerusalem eleven years. His
mother's name was Hamutal daughter of
Jeremiah; she was from Libnah.[m] 2 He did
evil in the eyes of the LORD, just as Jehoiakim[n] had done. 3 It was because of the
LORD's anger that all this happened to Jerusalem and Judah,[o] and in the end he thrust
them from his presence.

Now Zedekiah rebelled[p] against the
king of Babylon.
4 So in the ninth year of Zedekiah's reign,
on the tenth[q] day of the tenth month, Nebuchadnezzar king of Babylon marched
against Jerusalem[r] with his whole army.
They encamped outside the city and built
siege works all around it.[s] 5 The city was
kept under siege until the eleventh year of
King Zedekiah.
6 By the ninth day of the fourth month the
famine in the city had become so severe
that there was no food for the people to eat.[t]
7 Then the city wall was broken through,
and the whole army fled. They left the city
at night through the gate between the two
walls near the king's garden, though the
Babylonians[a] were surrounding the city.
They fled toward the Arabah,[b] 8 but the
Babylonian[c] army pursued King Zedekiah
and overtook him in the plains of Jericho.
All his soldiers were separated from him
and scattered, 9 and he was captured.[u]
He was taken to the king of Babylon
at Riblah[v] in the land of Hamath,[w] where
he pronounced sentence on him. 10 There
at Riblah the king of Babylon killed the
sons[x] of Zedekiah before his eyes; he also
killed all the officials of Judah. 11 Then he
put out Zedekiah's eyes, bound him with
bronze shackles and took him to Babylon,
where he put him in prison till the day of
his death.[y]
12 On the tenth day of the fifth[z] month,
in the nineteenth year of Nebuchadnezzar
king of Babylon, Nebuzaradan[a] commander of the imperial guard, who served the
king of Babylon, came to Jerusalem. 13 He
set fire[b] to the temple[c] of the LORD, the
royal palace and all the houses of Jerusalem. Every important building he burned
down. 14 The whole Babylonian army, under the commander of the imperial guard,
broke down all the walls[d] around Jerusalem. 15 Nebuzaradan the commander of the
guard carried into exile some of the poorest people and those who remained in the
city, along with the rest of the craftsmen[d]
and those who had deserted to the king of
Babylon. 16 But Nebuzaradan left behind[e]
the rest of the poorest people of the land to
work the vineyards and fields.

[a] 7 Or *Chaldeans*; also in verse 17 [b] 7 Or *the Jordan Valley* [c] 8 Or *Chaldean*; also in verse 14
[d] 15 Or *the populace*

52:13–16 *set fire to the temple of the LORD.* The entire city of Jerusalem was burned, from the temple to the royal palace to the houses. The city walls were demolished. Leading citizens and some of the poor were deported under Nebuzaradan's command, leaving only a remnant of peasant farmers to work the fields, vineyards, and orchards.

51:56 [w] ver 48 [x] Ps 46:9 [y] ver 6; Ps 94:1-2; Hab 2:8
51:57 [z] Ps 76:5; Jer 25:27 [a] Jer 46:18; 48:15
51:58 [b] ver 44 [c] ver 64 [d] Hab 2:13 **51:59** [e] Jer 36:4
[f] Jer 52:1 [g] Jer 28:1 **51:60** [h] Jer 30:2; 36:2
51:62 [i] Isa 13:20; Jer 50:13, 39 **51:64** [j] ver 58 [k] Job 31:40
52:1 [l] 2Ki 24:17 [m] Jos 10:29; 2Ki 8:22 **52:2** [n] Jer 36:30
52:3 [o] Isa 3:1 [p] Eze 17:12-16 **52:4** [q] Zec 8:19 [r] 2Ki 25:1-7;
Jer 39:1 [s] Eze 24:1-2 **52:6** [t] Isa 3:1 **52:9** [u] Jer 32:4
[v] Nu 34:11 [w] Nu 13:21 **52:10** [x] Jer 22:30
52:11 [y] Eze 12:13 **52:12** [z] Zec 7:5; 8:19 [a] Jer 39:9
52:13 [b] 2Ch 36:19; Ps 74:8; La 2:6 [c] Ps 79:1; Mic 3:12
52:14 [d] Ne 1:3 **52:16** [e] Jer 40:6

17The Babylonians broke up the bronze
pillars,[f] the movable stands[g] and the
bronze Sea[h] that were at the temple of the
LORD and they carried all the bronze to
Babylon.[i] 18They also took away the pots,
shovels, wick trimmers, sprinkling bowls,
dishes and all the bronze articles used in
the temple service.[j] 19The commander of
the imperial guard took away the basins,
censers,[k] sprinkling bowls, pots, lampstands, dishes and bowls used for drink
offerings—all that were made of pure gold
or silver.
20The bronze from the two pillars, the
Sea and the twelve bronze bulls under it,
and the movable stands, which King Solomon had made for the temple of the LORD,
was more than could be weighed.[l] 21Each
pillar was eighteen cubits high and twelve
cubits in circumference[a]; each was four
fingers thick, and hollow.[m] 22The bronze
capital[n] on top of one pillar was five cubits[b]
high and was decorated with a network
and pomegranates of bronze all around.
The other pillar, with its pomegranates,
was similar. 23There were ninety-six pomegranates on the sides; the total number of
pomegranates[o] above the surrounding network was a hundred.
24The commander of the guard took as
prisoners Seraiah[p] the chief priest, Zephaniah[q] the priest next in rank and the three
doorkeepers. 25Of those still in the city, he
took the officer in charge of the fighting
men, and seven royal advisers. He also
took the secretary who was chief officer
in charge of conscripting the people of the
land, sixty of whom were found in the city.
26Nebuzaradan[r] the commander took them
all and brought them to the king of Babylon
at Riblah. 27There at Riblah, in the land of
Hamath, the king had them executed.
So Judah went into captivity, away[s] from
her land. 28This is the number of the people
Nebuchadnezzar carried into exile:[t]

in the seventh year, 3,023 Jews;
29 in Nebuchadnezzar's eighteenth year,
832 people from Jerusalem;
30 in his twenty-third year,
745 Jews taken into exile by Nebuzaradan the commander of the
imperial guard.
There were 4,600 people in all.

Jehoiachin Released

31In the thirty-seventh year of the exile
of Jehoiachin king of Judah, in the year
Awel-Marduk became king of Babylon, on
the twenty-fifth day of the twelfth month,
he released Jehoiachin king of Judah and
freed him from prison. 32He spoke kindly
to him and gave him a seat of honor higher than those of the other kings who were
with him in Babylon. 33So Jehoiachin put
aside his prison clothes and for the rest of
his life ate regularly at the king's table.[u]
34Day by day the king of Babylon gave Jehoiachin a regular allowance[v] as long as he
lived, till the day of his death.

---

[a] *21* That is, about 27 feet high and 18 feet in circumference or about 8.1 meters high and 5.4 meters in circumference [b] *22* That is, about 7 1/2 feet or about 2.3 meters

---

52:31–34 *Awel-Marduk.* Nebuchadnezzar's son became king next but only reigned for two years. Jehoiachin was released from prison during his reign and pardoned. He was provided with food and given a seat of honor in Babylon. This restoration was symbolic of the future restoration of Israel and Judah to their homeland.

52:17 [f] 1Ki 7:15 [g] 1Ki 7:27-37 [h] 1Ki 7:23 [i] Jer 27:19-22 **52:18** [j] Ex 27:3; 1Ki 7:45 **52:19** [k] 1Ki 7:50 **52:20** [l] 1Ki 7:47 **52:21** [m] 1Ki 7:15 **52:22** [n] 1Ki 7:16 **52:23** [o] 1Ki 7:20 **52:24** [p] 2Ki 25:18 [q] Jer 21:1; 37:3 **52:26** [r] ver 12 **52:27** [s] Jer 20:4 **52:28** [t] 2Ki 24:14-16; 2Ch 36:20 **52:33** [u] 2Sa 9:7 **52:34** [v] 2Sa 9:10

LAMENTATIONS

▶ **AUTHOR:** The universal consensus of early Jewish and Christian tradition attributes this book to Jeremiah. Even though the author is unnamed in the book, the superscription to Lamentations in the Septuagint states: "And it came to pass, after Israel had been carried away captive and Jerusalem had become desolate, that Jeremiah sat weeping, and lamented with this lamentation over Jerusalem saying. . . ." The Talmud, as well as many other ancient sources, also supports this position.

▶ **TIME:** c. 586 B.C. ▶ **KEY VERSES:** Lam. 3:22–23

▶ **THEME:** A lament is a vehicle for working through sorrow. While grief is expressed in words, its resolution is in God and the hope He gives for the future. In a way, the lamentation process is one of coming to grips with all that God wants us to see about our present circumstances. For the people of Judah to lose a country meant not only the loss of the homeland, but the loss of God's presence and power to sustain the people in that land. It is hard for people who have never experienced such loss to understand the depth of grief expressed in this book.

1 [a] How deserted lies the city,
once so full of people!
How like a widow[a] is she,
who once was great[b] among the nations!
She who was queen among the provinces
has now become a slave.[c]

2 Bitterly she weeps[d] at night,
tears are on her cheeks.
Among all her lovers[e]
there is no one to comfort her.
All her friends have betrayed[f] her;
they have become her enemies.[g]

3 After affliction and harsh labor,
Judah has gone into exile.[h]
She dwells among the nations;
she finds no resting place.[i]
All who pursue her have overtaken her
in the midst of her distress.

4 The roads to Zion mourn,
for no one comes to her appointed festivals.
All her gateways are desolate,[j]
her priests groan,
her young women grieve,
and she is in bitter anguish.[k]

5 Her foes have become her masters;
her enemies are at ease.
The LORD has brought her grief[l]
because of her many sins.
Her children have gone into exile,[m]
captive before the foe.

6 All the splendor has departed
from Daughter Zion.[n]
Her princes are like deer
that find no pasture;
in weakness they have fled
before the pursuer.

7 In the days of her affliction and wandering
Jerusalem remembers all the treasures
that were hers in days of old.

[a] This chapter is an acrostic poem, the verses of which begin with the successive letters of the Hebrew alphabet.

1:1 ***How.*** This exclamatory word is used frequently in laments and funeral songs. It expresses astonishment, sorrow, and dismay (2:1; 4:1).

1:2 ***Among all her lovers.*** Verse 19 describes Judah's sin of turning away from God and toward the gods of Canaan (Jer. 3:1–6). Also, the sins of Judah often involved the sexual forms of pagan worship that characterized the Canaanite people.

1:4 ***The roads to Zion mourn.*** When the temple was built, Zion was used to describe the hill on which the temple was located. Later, the name came to stand for the whole city. The roads "mourned" because there would no longer be throngs of pilgrims traveling to Jerusalem to worship at the temple.

1:5 ***Her children have gone into exile.*** God had warned Israel in Leviticus 26:41 that captivity in a foreign land would be the result of continued sinning.

1:7 ***In the days of her affliction and wandering.***

1:1 [a] Isa 47:8 [b] 1Ki 4:21 [c] Isa 3:26; Jer 40:9 **1:2** [d] Ps 6:6 [e] Jer 3:1 [f] Jer 4:30; Mic 7:5 [g] ver 16 **1:3** [h] Jer 13:19 [i] Dt 28:65 **1:4** [j] Jer 9:11 [k] Joel 1:8-13 **1:5** [l] Jer 30:15 [m] Jer 39:9; 52:28-30 **1:6** [n] Jer 13:18

When her people fell into enemy
hands,
there was no one to help her.[o]
Her enemies looked at her
and laughed at her destruction.

8 Jerusalem has sinned[p] greatly
and so has become unclean.
All who honored her despise her,
for they have all seen her naked;[q]
she herself groans[r]
and turns away.

9 Her filthiness clung to her skirts;
she did not consider her future.[s]
Her fall[t] was astounding;
there was none to comfort[u] her.
"Look, LORD, on my affliction,[v]
for the enemy has triumphed."

10 The enemy laid hands
on all her treasures;[w]
she saw pagan nations
enter her sanctuary[x]—
those you had forbidden[y]
to enter your assembly.

11 All her people groan[z]
as they search for bread;[a]
they barter their treasures for food
to keep themselves alive.
"Look, LORD, and consider,
for I am despised."

12 "Is it nothing to you, all you who
pass by?[b]
Look around and see.
Is any suffering like my suffering[c]
that was inflicted on me,
that the LORD brought on me
in the day of his fierce anger?[d]

13 "From on high he sent fire,
sent it down into my bones.[e]
He spread a net for my feet
and turned me back.
He made me desolate,[f]
faint[g] all the day long.

14 "My sins have been bound into a yoke[a];[h]
by his hands they were woven
together.
They have been hung on my neck,
and the Lord has sapped my strength.
He has given me into the hands[i]
of those I cannot withstand.

15 "The Lord has rejected
all the warriors in my midst;[j]
he has summoned an army[k] against me
to[b] crush my young men.[l]
In his winepress the Lord has trampled
Virgin Daughter Judah.

16 "This is why I weep
and my eyes overflow with tears.[m]
No one is near to comfort[n] me,
no one to restore my spirit.
My children are destitute
because the enemy has prevailed."[o]

17 Zion stretches out her hands,[p]
but there is no one to comfort her.
The LORD has decreed for Jacob
that his neighbors become his foes;
Jerusalem has become
an unclean thing among them.

18 "The LORD is righteous,
yet I rebelled[q] against his command.
Listen, all you peoples;
look on my suffering.[r]
My young men and young women
have gone into exile.[s]

19 "I called to my allies
but they betrayed me.
My priests and my elders
perished[t] in the city
while they searched for food
to keep themselves alive.

20 "See, LORD, how distressed[u] I am!
I am in torment[v] within,
and in my heart I am disturbed,
for I have been most rebellious.
Outside, the sword bereaves;
inside, there is only death.[w]

a 14 Most Hebrew manuscripts; many Hebrew manuscripts and Septuagint *He kept watch over my sins* *b* 15 Or *has set a time for me* / *when he will*

The emphasis is on Jerusalem's utter helplessness as her enemies ridiculed her miseries (v. 21).

1:10 *nations enter her sanctuary.* Since God's people had not preserved the sanctuary of their hearts from pollution, they had no reason to be amazed when their enemies desecrated the earthly sanctuary. As a rule, Gentiles were forbidden to enter the congregation of the Lord.

1:13 *he sent fire ... into my bones.* Jerusalem's suffering is portrayed, using several metaphors: (1) fire from heaven, (2) a hunter's net spread to trap animals, (3) an animal yoke fastened about the head of a person, and (4) the crushing of grapes in a winepress. The purpose of Jerusalem's suffering was to bring about a turning or repentance.

1:15 *Virgin Daughter Judah.* Jerusalem (Judah) was supposed to be the chaste bride of God. Instead, she had become a polluted harlot because her people worshiped other gods than the God with whom they covenanted.

1:16 *comfort.* The real comforter of Judah is God. But because of Judah's sin, God would not come to their assistance.

1:7 [o] Jer 37:7; La 4:17 **1:8** [p] ver 20; Isa 59:2-13 [q] Jer 13:22,26 [r] ver 21,22 **1:9** [s] Dt 32:28-29; Isa 47:7; Eze 24:13 [t] Jer 13:18 [u] Ecc 4:1; Jer 16:7 [v] Ps 25:18 **1:10** [w] Isa 64:11 [x] Ps 74:7-8; Jer 51:51 [y] Dt 23:3 **1:11** [z] Ps 38:8 [a] Jer 52:6 **1:12** [b] Jer 18:16 [c] ver 18 [d] Isa 13:13; Jer 30:24 **1:13** [e] Job 30:30 [f] Jer 44:6 [g] Hab 3:16 **1:14** [h] Dt 28:48; Isa 47:6 [i] Jer 32:5 **1:15** [j] Jer 37:10 [k] Isa 41:2 [l] Isa 28:18; Jer 18:21 **1:16** [m] La 2:11,18; 3:48-49 [n] Ps 69:20; Ecc 4:1 [o] ver 2; Jer 13:17; 14:17 **1:17** [p] Jer 4:31 **1:18** [q] 1Sa 12:14 [r] ver 12 [s] Dt 28:32,41 **1:19** [t] Jer 14:15; La 2:20 **1:20** [u] Jer 4:19 [v] La 2:11 [w] Dt 32:25; Eze 7:15

21 "People have heard my groaning,[x]
but there is no one to comfort me.[y]
All my enemies have heard of my distress;
they rejoice[z] at what you have done.
May you bring the day[a] you have announced
so they may become like me.

22 "Let all their wickedness come before you;
deal with them
as you have dealt with me
because of all my sins.[b]
My groans are many
and my heart is faint."

2 [a] How the Lord has covered Daughter Zion
with the cloud of his anger[b]![c]
He has hurled down the splendor of Israel
from heaven to earth;
he has not remembered his footstool[d]
in the day of his anger.

2 Without pity[e] the Lord has swallowed[f] up
all the dwellings of Jacob;
in his wrath he has torn down
the strongholds[g] of Daughter Judah.
He has brought her kingdom and its princes
down to the ground[h] in dishonor.

3 In fierce anger he has cut off
every horn[c,d][i] of Israel.
He has withdrawn his right hand[j]
at the approach of the enemy.
He has burned in Jacob like a flaming fire
that consumes everything around it.[k]

4 Like an enemy he has strung his bow;[l]
his right hand is ready.
Like a foe he has slain
all who were pleasing to the eye;[m]
he has poured out his wrath like fire[n]
on the tent of Daughter Zion.

5 The Lord is like an enemy;[o]
he has swallowed up Israel.
He has swallowed up all her palaces
and destroyed her strongholds.[p]
He has multiplied mourning and lamentation
for Daughter Judah.[q]

6 He has laid waste his dwelling like a garden;
he has destroyed his place of meeting.[r]
The LORD has made Zion forget
her appointed festivals and her Sabbaths;[s]
in his fierce anger he has spurned
both king and priest.[t]

7 The Lord has rejected his altar
and abandoned his sanctuary.
He has given the walls of her palaces[u]
into the hands of the enemy;
they have raised a shout in the house of the LORD
as on the day of an appointed festival.

8 The LORD determined to tear down
the wall around Daughter Zion.
He stretched out a measuring line[v]
and did not withhold his hand from destroying.
He made ramparts and walls lament;
together they wasted away.[w]

9 Her gates[x] have sunk into the ground;
their bars he has broken and destroyed.
Her king and her princes are exiled[y]
among the nations,
the law[z] is no more,
and her prophets no longer find
visions[a] from the LORD.

10 The elders of Daughter Zion
sit on the ground in silence;
they have sprinkled dust on their heads[b]
and put on sackcloth.[c]
The young women of Jerusalem
have bowed their heads to the ground.[d]

[a] This chapter is an acrostic poem, the verses of which begin with the successive letters of the Hebrew alphabet. [b] *1* Or *How the Lord in his anger / has treated Daughter Zion with contempt* [c] *3* Or *off / all the strength*; or *every king* [d] *3 Horn* here symbolizes strength.

1:21 *All my enemies.* Those who previously had been friends of Judah (v. 2) became Judah's enemies. ***bring the day.*** Several times the "day" of God's wrath is mentioned in the Book of Lamentations (2:1,21 – 22). The term is used to refer not only to the time of Jerusalem's fall in the past, but also to a future day when God would rectify all of the wrongs that the nations had committed against Israel and God.
2:1 *his anger.* This word is a firm expression of God's displeasure with wickedness and sin. Yet God's anger never shuts us off from His compassion (Ps. 77:9).
2:3 *withdrawn his right hand.* Usually the right hand of God is understood as the instrument of help for God's people stretched out against their enemies (Ex. 15:6; Ps. 20:6). Here God's hand is withdrawn from the enemies, leaving the people of God at their mercy.
2:9 *the law is no more.* These words do not suggest the end of the law, but rather the ceasing of the work of the law in the lives of the people for their blessing (Deut. 6:1 – 3).
2:10 *they have sprinkled dust on their heads.* This custom was a common sign of mourning in Israel

1:21 [x] ver 8 [y] ver 4 [z] La 2:15 [a] Isa 47:11; Jer 30:16 **1:22** [b] Ne 4:5 **2:1** [c] La 3:44 [d] Ps 99:5; 132:7 **2:2** [e] La 3:43 [f] Ps 21:9 [g] Ps 89:39-40; Mic 5:11 [h] Isa 25:12 **2:3** [i] Ps 75:5, 10 [j] Ps 74:11 [k] Isa 42:25; Jer 21:4-5, 14 **2:4** [l] Job 16:13; La 3:12-13 [m] Eze 24:16, 25 [n] Isa 42:25; Jer 7:20 **2:5** [o] Jer 30:14 [p] ver 2 [q] Jer 9:17-20 **2:6** [r] Jer 52:13 [s] La 1:4; Zep 3:18 [t] La 4:16 **2:7** [u] Ps 74:7-8; Isa 64:11; Jer 33:4-5 **2:8** [v] 2Ki 21:13; Isa 34:11 [w] Isa 3:26 **2:9** [x] Ne 1:3 [y] Dt 28:36; 2Ki 24:15 [z] 2Ch 15:3 [a] Jer 14:14 **2:10** [b] Job 2:12 [c] Isa 15:3 [d] Job 2:13; Isa 3:26

11 My eyes fail from weeping,[e]
I am in torment within[f];
my heart is poured out[g] on the ground
because my people are destroyed,
because children and infants faint[h]
in the streets of the city.

12 They say to their mothers,
"Where is bread and wine?"
as they faint like the wounded
in the streets of the city,
as their lives ebb away
in their mothers' arms.[i]

13 What can I say for you?
With what can I compare you,
Daughter Jerusalem?
To what can I liken you,
that I may comfort you,
Virgin Daughter Zion?[j]
Your wound is as deep as the sea.[k]
Who can heal you?

14 The visions of your prophets
were false and worthless;
they did not expose your sin
to ward off your captivity.[l]
The prophecies they gave you
were false and misleading.[m]

15 All who pass your way
clap their hands at you;[n]
they scoff[o] and shake their heads
at Daughter Jerusalem:
"Is this the city that was called
the perfection of beauty,[p]
the joy of the whole earth?"[q]

16 All your enemies open their mouths
wide against you;[r]
they scoff and gnash their teeth[s]
and say, "We have swallowed her up.[t]
This is the day we have waited for;
we have lived to see it."

17 The LORD has done what he planned;
he has fulfilled his word,
which he decreed long ago.[u]
He has overthrown you without pity,[v]
he has let the enemy gloat over you,
he has exalted the horn[a] of your
foes.[w]

18 The hearts of the people
cry out to the Lord.[x]
You walls of Daughter Zion,
let your tears[y] flow like a river
day and night;[z]
give yourself no relief,
your eyes no rest.[a]

19 Arise, cry out in the night,
as the watches of the night begin;
pour out your heart[b] like water
in the presence of the Lord.[c]
Lift up your hands to him
for the lives of your children,
who faint[d] from hunger
at every street corner.

20 "Look, LORD, and consider:
Whom have you ever treated like
this?
Should women eat their offspring,[e]
the children they have cared for?[f]
Should priest and prophet be killed[g]
in the sanctuary of the Lord?

21 "Young and old lie together
in the dust of the streets;
my young men and young women
have fallen by the sword.[h]
You have slain them in the day of your
anger;
you have slaughtered them without
pity.[i]

22 "As you summon to a feast day,
so you summoned against me terrors[j]
on every side.
In the day of the LORD's anger
no one escaped or survived;
those I cared for and reared[k]
my enemy has destroyed."

3[b] I am the man who has seen affliction
by the rod of the LORD's wrath.[l]
2 He has driven me away and made me
walk
in darkness[m] rather than light;
3 indeed, he has turned his hand
against me[n]
again and again, all day long.

[a] *17 Horn* here symbolizes strength. [b] This chapter is an acrostic poem; the verses of each stanza begin with the successive letters of the Hebrew alphabet, and the verses within each stanza begin with the same letter.

---

and in other countries of the ancient world. ***young women of Jerusalem.*** Their sadness was increased by the knowledge that this was not a time for marriage and family. Even though their lives had been spared, they had lost their futures.

2:15 *shake their heads.* This was a common expression of derision (Ps. 22:7; 109:25; Jer. 19:8). Losing face in the ancient Middle East was a terrible evil.

2:18 *You walls.* The wall of the people's hearts was more impenetrable than the wall of the city of Jerusalem (vv. 7–8).

2:19 *Arise.* The call is for people to awaken and scream for mercy from the Lord. ***Lift up your hands.*** This refers to a posture of prayer (1:17; Ps. 134:2).

2:20 *Should women eat their offspring.* So desperate were the scenes of starvation in Jerusalem that women actually fought over whose deceased child would be eaten next.

2:11 [e] La 1:16; 3:48-51 [f] La 1:20 [g] ver 19; Ps 22:14 [h] La 4:4
2:12 [i] La 4:4 **2:13** [j] Isa 37:22 [k] Jer 14:17; La 1:12
2:14 [l] Isa 58:1 [m] Jer 2:8; 23:25-32, 33-40; 29:9; Eze 13:3; 22:28 **2:15** [n] Eze 25:6 [o] Jer 19:8 [p] Ps 50:2 [q] Ps 48:2
2:16 [r] Ps 56:2; La 3:46 [s] Job 16:9 [t] Ps 35:25
2:17 [u] Dt 28:15-45 [v] ver 2; Eze 5:11 [w] Ps 89:42
2:18 [x] Ps 119:145 [y] La 1:16 [z] Jer 9:1 [a] La 3:49
2:19 [b] 1Sa 1:15; Ps 62:8 [c] Isa 26:9 [d] Isa 51:20
2:20 [e] Dt 28:53; Jer 19:9 [f] La 4:10 [g] Ps 78:64; Jer 14:15
2:21 [h] 2Ch 36:17; Ps 78:62-63; Jer 6:11 [i] Jer 13:14; La 3:43; Zec 11:6 **2:22** [j] Ps 31:13; Jer 6:25 [k] Hos 9:13
3:1 [l] Job 19:21; Ps 88:7 **3:2** [m] Jer 4:23 **3:3** [n] Isa 5:25

4 He has made my skin and my flesh
grow old
and has broken my bones.[o]
5 He has besieged me and surrounded me
with bitterness[p] and hardship.[q]
6 He has made me dwell in darkness
like those long dead.[r]

7 He has walled me in so I cannot escape;[s]
he has weighed me down with chains.[t]
8 Even when I call out or cry for help,
he shuts out my prayer.[u]
9 He has barred my way with blocks of
stone;
he has made my paths crooked.[v]

10 Like a bear lying in wait,
like a lion in hiding,
11 he dragged me from the path and
mangled[w] me
and left me without help.
12 He drew his bow[x]
and made me the target[y] for his
arrows.[z]

13 He pierced my heart
with arrows from his quiver.[a]
14 I became the laughingstock[b] of all my
people;
they mock me in song[c] all day long.
15 He has filled me with bitter herbs
and given me gall to drink.[d]

16 He has broken my teeth with gravel;[e]
he has trampled me in the dust.
17 I have been deprived of peace;
I have forgotten what prosperity is.
18 So I say, "My splendor is gone
and all that I had hoped from the
LORD."[f]

19 I remember my affliction and my
wandering,
the bitterness and the gall.
20 I well remember them,
and my soul is downcast[g] within me.[h]
21 Yet this I call to mind
and therefore I have hope:

22 Because of the LORD's great love we are
not consumed,
for his compassions never fail.[i]
23 They are new every morning;
great is your faithfulness.[j]
24 I say to myself, "The LORD is my
portion;[k]
therefore I will wait for him."

25 The LORD is good to those whose hope
is in him,
to the one who seeks him;[l]
26 it is good to wait quietly
for the salvation of the LORD.[m]
27 It is good for a man to bear the yoke
while he is young.

28 Let him sit alone in silence,[n]
for the LORD has laid it on him.
29 Let him bury his face in the dust—
there may yet be hope.[o]
30 Let him offer his cheek to one who
would strike him,[p]
and let him be filled with disgrace.

31 For no one is cast off
by the Lord forever.[q]
32 Though he brings grief, he will show
compassion,
so great is his unfailing love.[r]
33 For he does not willingly bring
affliction
or grief to anyone.[s]

34 To crush underfoot
all prisoners in the land,
35 to deny people their rights
before the Most High,
36 to deprive them of justice—
would not the Lord see such things?[t]

37 Who can speak and have it happen
if the Lord has not decreed it?[u]
38 Is it not from the mouth of the Most
High
that both calamities and good things
come?[v]

3:4 ***He has made my skin and my flesh grow old.*** This imagery suggests the ebbing and wasting away of Jeremiah's life and that of the nation.

3:9 ***He has barred my way with blocks of stone.*** A common practice of the Assyrians was to wall up prisoners in extremely confined places and leave them to die.

3:15 ***filled me with bitter herbs.*** Called "wormwood" in other translations, this was a bitter herb used to flavor some drinks.

3:16 ***He has broken my teeth with gravel.*** The people had sensed that they were so associated with dust and sackcloth—symbols of mourning—that it was as though they fed on dirt. The dust became gravel which broke the people's teeth.

3:22 ***his compassions never fail.*** This verse seems to contradict all that had been written up to this point (2:1–5). Yet the very fact that there was a prophet left to write these words and a remnant left to read them showed that not every person in Jerusalem had been consumed.

3:23 ***great is your faithfulness.*** Here is the heart of the Book of Lamentations. The comforting, compassionate character of God dominates the wreckage of every other institution and office. God remains "full of grace and truth" in every situation (John 1:14; see Ex. 34:6).

3:29 ***bury his face in the dust.*** This expression is a figure of speech for conquest. The phrase pictures a captive lying face down with the conqueror's foot on his back.

3:4 [o] Ps 51:8; Isa 38:13; Jer 50:17 **3:5** [p] ver 19 [q] Jer 23:15
3:6 [r] Ps 88:5-6 **3:7** [s] Job 3:23 [t] Jer 40:4
3:8 [u] Job 30:20; Ps 22:2 **3:9** [v] Isa 63:17; Hos 2:6
3:11 [w] Hos 6:1 **3:12** [x] La 2:4 [y] Job 7:20 [z] Ps 7:12-13; 38:2
3:13 [a] Job 6:4 **3:14** [b] Jer 20:7 [c] Job 30:9
3:15 [d] Jer 9:15 **3:16** [e] Pr 20:17 **3:18** [f] Job 17:15
3:20 [g] Ps 42:5 [h] Ps 42:11 **3:22** [i] Ps 78:38; Mal 3:6
3:23 [j] Zep 3:5 **3:24** [k] Ps 16:5 **3:25** [l] Isa 25:9; 30:18
3:26 [m] Ps 37:7; 40:1 **3:28** [n] Jer 15:17 **3:29** [o] Jer 31:17
3:30 [p] Job 16:10; Isa 50:6 **3:31** [q] Ps 94:14; Isa 54:7
3:32 [r] Ps 78:38; Hos 11:8 **3:33** [s] Eze 33:11
3:36 [t] Jer 22:3; Hab 1:13 **3:37** [u] Ps 33:9-11
3:38 [v] Job 2:10; Isa 45:7; Jer 32:42

39 Why should the living complain
when punished for their sins?[w]
40 Let us examine our ways and test them,[x]
and let us return to the LORD.[y]
41 Let us lift up our hearts and our hands
to God in heaven,[z] and say:
42 "We have sinned and rebelled[a]
and you have not forgiven.[b]
43 "You have covered yourself with anger
and pursued us;
you have slain without pity.[c]
44 You have covered yourself with a cloud[d]
so that no prayer[e] can get through.
45 You have made us scum[f] and refuse
among the nations.
46 "All our enemies have opened their
mouths
wide against us.[g]
47 We have suffered terror and pitfalls,[h]
ruin and destruction.[i]"
48 Streams of tears flow from my eyes[j]
because my people are destroyed.[k]
49 My eyes will flow unceasingly,
without relief,[l]
50 until the LORD looks down
from heaven and sees.[m]
51 What I see brings grief to my soul
because of all the women of my city.
52 Those who were my enemies without
cause
hunted me like a bird.[n]
53 They tried to end my life in a pit[o]
and threw stones at me;
54 the waters closed over my head,[p]
and I thought I was about to perish.
55 I called on your name, LORD,
from the depths of the pit.[q]
56 You heard my plea:[r] "Do not close your
ears
to my cry for relief."
57 You came near when I called you,
and you said, "Do not fear."[s]
58 You, Lord, took up my case;[t]
you redeemed my life.[u]
59 LORD, you have seen the wrong done
to me.[v]
Uphold my cause!
60 You have seen the depth of their
vengeance,
all their plots against me.[w]
61 LORD, you have heard their insults,
all their plots against me—
62 what my enemies whisper and mutter
against me all day long.[x]
63 Look at them! Sitting or standing,
they mock me in their songs.
64 Pay them back what they deserve, LORD,
for what their hands have done.[y]
65 Put a veil over their hearts,[z]
and may your curse be on them!
66 Pursue them in anger and destroy them
from under the heavens of the LORD.

4 [a] How the gold has lost its luster,
the fine gold become dull!
The sacred gems are scattered
at every street corner.[a]
2 How the precious children of Zion,
once worth their weight in gold,
are now considered as pots of clay,
the work of a potter's hands!
3 Even jackals offer their breasts
to nurse their young,
but my people have become heartless
like ostriches in the desert.[b]
4 Because of thirst the infant's tongue
sticks to the roof of its mouth;[c]
the children beg for bread,
but no one gives it to them.[d]
5 Those who once ate delicacies
are destitute in the streets.
Those brought up in royal purple[e]
now lie on ash heaps.[f]
6 The punishment of my people
is greater than that of Sodom,[g]
which was overthrown in a moment
without a hand turned to help her.
7 Their princes were brighter than snow
and whiter than milk,
their bodies more ruddy than rubies,
their appearance like lapis lazuli.

[a] This chapter is an acrostic poem, the verses of which begin with the successive letters of the Hebrew alphabet.

3:44 *with a cloud.* So long as sin festered, God's wrath was a cloud or veil through which no prayer could penetrate—including the prayers of the people and the prayers of Jeremiah.
3:52–54 *end my life in a pit.* Jeremiah speaks not only of his own experience of being cast into a pit (Jer. 38:4–6), but also of his pain and grief over the wretched condition of his fellow countrymen. The pit is a metaphor for the grave or extreme danger (Ps. 28:1; 40:2).
3:64–66 *Pay them.* The request for divine vindication is an expression of a longing for God's righteousness and the success of His kingdom and His truth.
4:1 2 *sacred gems are scattered.* The Babylonian army looted the temple and overturned all its huge stones.
4:4 *the infant's tongue.* The theme of thirsting and starving children is revisited (2:11–13).

3:39 [w] Jer 30:15; Mic 7:9 **3:40** [x] 2Co 13:5 [y] Ps 119:59; 139:23-24 **3:41** [z] Ps 25:1; 28:2 **3:42** [a] Da 9:5 [b] Jer 5:7-9 **3:43** [c] La 2:2, 17, 21 **3:44** [d] Ps 97:2 [e] ver 8 **3:45** [f] 1Co 4:13 **3:46** [g] La 2:16 **3:47** [h] Jer 48:43 [i] Isa 24:17-18; 51:19 **3:48** [j] La 1:16 [k] La 2:11 **3:49** [l] Jer 14:17 **3:50** [m] Isa 63:15 **3:52** [n] Ps 35:7 **3:53** [o] Jer 37:16 **3:54** [p] Ps 69:2; Jnh 2:3-5 **3:55** [q] Ps 130:1; Jnh 2:2 **3:56** [r] Ps 55:1 **3:57** [s] Isa 41:10 **3:58** [t] Jer 51:36 [u] Ps 34:22; Jer 50:34 **3:59** [v] Jer 18:19-20 **3:60** [w] Jer 11:20; 18:18 **3:62** [x] Eze 36:3 **3:64** [y] Ps 28:4 **3:65** [z] Isa 6:10 **4:1** [a] Eze 7:19 **4:3** [b] Job 39:16 **4:4** [c] Ps 22:15 [d] La 2:11, 12 **4:5** [e] Jer 6:2 [f] Am 6:3-7 **4:6** [g] Ge 19:25

[8]But now they are blacker[h] than soot;
they are not recognized in the streets.
Their skin has shriveled on their bones;[i]
it has become as dry as a stick.

[9]Those killed by the sword are better off
than those who die of famine;
racked with hunger, they waste away
for lack of food from the field.[j]

[10]With their own hands compassionate
women
have cooked their own children,[k]
who became their food
when my people were destroyed.

[11]The LORD has given full vent to his
wrath;
he has poured out his fierce anger.
He kindled a fire[l] in Zion
that consumed her foundations.[m]

[12]The kings of the earth did not believe,
nor did any of the peoples of the world,
that enemies and foes could enter
the gates of Jerusalem.[n]

[13]But it happened because of the sins of
her prophets
and the iniquities of her priests,[o]
who shed within her
the blood of the righteous.

[14]Now they grope through the streets
as if they were blind.[p]
They are so defiled with blood[q]
that no one dares to touch their
garments.

[15]"Go away! You are unclean!" people cry
to them.
"Away! Away! Don't touch us!"
When they flee and wander about,
people among the nations say,
"They can stay here no longer."[r]

[16]The LORD himself has scattered them;
he no longer watches over them.[s]
The priests are shown no honor,
the elders[t] no favor.

[17]Moreover, our eyes failed,
looking in vain[u] for help;[v]
from our towers we watched
for a nation[w] that could not save us.

[18]People stalked us at every step,
so we could not walk in our streets.
Our end was near, our days were
numbered,
for our end had come.[x]

[19]Our pursuers were swifter
than eagles[y] in the sky;
they chased us[z] over the mountains
and lay in wait for us in the desert.

[20]The LORD's anointed,[a] our very life
breath,
was caught in their traps.[b]
We thought that under his shadow
we would live among the nations.

[21]Rejoice and be glad, Daughter Edom,
you who live in the land of Uz.
But to you also the cup[c] will be passed;
you will be drunk and stripped
naked.[d]

[22]Your punishment will end, Daughter
Zion;[e]
he will not prolong your exile.
But he will punish your sin, Daughter
Edom,
and expose your wickedness.[f]

5 Remember, LORD, what has happened
to us;
look, and see our disgrace.[g]
[2]Our inheritance[h] has been turned over
to strangers,
our homes[i] to foreigners.
[3]We have become fatherless,
our mothers are widows.[j]
[4]We must buy the water we drink;
our wood can be had only at a price.[k]
[5]Those who pursue us are at our heels;
we are weary[l] and find no rest.
[6]We submitted to Egypt and Assyria[m]
to get enough bread.
[7]Our ancestors sinned and are no more,
and we bear their punishment.[n]
[8]Slaves[o] rule over us,
and there is no one to free us from
their hands.[p]
[9]We get our bread at the risk of our lives
because of the sword in the desert.
[10]Our skin is hot as an oven,
feverish from hunger.[q]

4:10 *cooked their own children.* This verse describes the horrible effects of the long siege that were alluded to in 2:20. This unimaginable horror could only have occurred in the most inhumane conditions of human suffering.

5:2–3 *Our inheritance.* The Promised Land had been a gift from the Lord to Abraham. This inheritance was a kind of "down payment" on the future reign of God that would include the restoration of His people to that land. God demonstrated that He owned all nations and that Israel was to be His instrument for blessing all the nations on the earth. Yet in their present condition, the people of Israel seemed to be the most helpless of all peoples.

5:10 *Our skin is hot as an oven.* Disease would have been rampant during the siege.

4:8 [h] Job 30:28 [i] Ps 102:3-5 **4:9** [j] Jer 15:2; 16:4
4:10 [k] Lev 26:29; Dt 28:53-57; Jer 19:9; La 2:20; Eze 5:10
4:11 [l] Jer 17:27 [m] Dt 32:22; Jer 7:20; Eze 22:31
4:12 [n] 1Ki 9:9; Jer 21:13 **4:13** [o] Jer 5:31; 6:13; Eze 22:28; Mic 3:11 **4:14** [p] Isa 59:10 [q] Jer 2:34; 19:4
4:15 [r] Lev 13:46 **4:16** [s] Isa 9:14-16 [t] La 5:12
4:17 [u] Isa 20:5; Eze 29:16 [v] La 1:7 [w] Jer 37:7
4:18 [x] Eze 7:2-12; Am 8:2 **4:19** [y] Dt 28:49 [z] Isa 5:26-28
4:20 [a] 2Sa 19:21 [b] Jer 39:5; Eze 12:12-13; 19:4,8
4:21 [c] Jer 25:15 [d] Isa 34:6-10; Am 1:11-12; Ob 1:16
4:22 [e] Isa 40:2; Jer 33:8 [f] Ps 137:7; Mal 1:4 **5:1** [g] Ps 44:13-16; 89:50 **5:2** [h] Ps 79:1 [i] Zep 1:13 **5:3** [j] Jer 15:8; 18:21
5:4 [k] Isa 3:1 **5:5** [l] Ne 9:37 **5:6** [m] Hos 9:3
5:7 [n] Jer 14:20; 16:12 **5:8** [o] Ne 5:15 [p] Zec 11:6
5:10 [q] La 4:8-9

11 Women have been violated[r] in Zion,
and virgins in the towns of Judah.
12 Princes have been hung up by their hands;
elders are shown no respect.[s]
13 Young men toil at the millstones;
boys stagger under loads of wood.
14 The elders are gone from the city gate;
the young men have stopped their music.[t]
15 Joy is gone from our hearts;
our dancing has turned to mourning.[u]
16 The crown[v] has fallen from our head.
Woe to us, for we have sinned![w]
17 Because of this our hearts[x] are faint,
because of these things our eyes[y] grow dim
18 for Mount Zion, which lies desolate,[z]
with jackals prowling over it.

19 You, LORD, reign forever;
your throne endures[a] from generation to generation.
20 Why do you always forget us?[b]
Why do you forsake us so long?
21 Restore[c] us to yourself, LORD, that we may return;
renew our days as of old
22 unless you have utterly rejected us
and are angry with us beyond measure.[d]

5:16 ***The crown has fallen from our head.*** This phrase expresses the loss of Judah's position of honor.
5:17 ***our hearts are faint . . . our eyes grow dim.*** The normal zest for life was gone. Death would be better than a horrible existence during the siege of Jerusalem.
5:18 ***jackals prowling over it.*** The idea of wild animals roaming the holy city where the people of God once came in glad worship was the final indignity.
5:19 ***You, LORD, reign forever.*** God's eternal rule and reign are a hope and support during the bleakest moments of suffering and despair (Ps. 80:1; 103:19).

5:11 [r] Zec 14:2 **5:12** [s] La 4:16 **5:14** [t] Isa 24:8; Jer 7:34 **5:15** [u] Jer 25:10 **5:16** [v] Ps 89:39 [w] Isa 3:11 **5:17** [x] Isa 1:5 [y] Ps 6:7 **5:18** [z] Mic 3:12 **5:19** [a] Ps 45:6; 102:12,24-27 **5:20** [b] Ps 13:1; 44:24 **5:21** [c] Ps 80:3 **5:22** [d] Isa 64:9

EZEKIEL

▸ **AUTHOR:** There is strong evidence in favor of Ezekiel's authorship of this book. The first person singular is used throughout the book, indicating that it is the work of one person. This person is actually identified in 1:3 and 24:24 as Ezekiel. The unity and integrity of Ezekiel's prophetic record are supported and the style, language, and thematic development are consistent throughout the book. Like Jeremiah, Ezekiel was a priest who was called to be a prophet of the Lord. Ezekiel was privileged to receive a number of visions of the power and plan of God, and he was careful and artistic in his written presentation.

▸ **TIME:** c. 592 – 570 B.C. ▸ **KEY VERSES:** Ezek. 36:33 – 35

▸ **THEME:** Ezekiel was an exilic prophet, meaning he prophesied to the exiles in Babylon. He was one of the 10,000 taken there by Nebuchadnezzar in 597 B.C. (2 Kin. 24:14). The book contains a series of prophetic messages, which represents a lifetime of ministry to the exiles in Babylon. Ezekiel sees himself as a watchman or lookout, compelled to warn people of coming danger and of the need for personal responsibility to an awesome, all-seeing, all-knowing God. The last half of the book is more concerned with encouraging the people to hope for God's promise of restoration back to the land of Israel. The restoration of the temple is a key element of chapters 40 – 48.

Ezekiel's Inaugural Vision

1 In my thirtieth year, in the fourth month
on the fifth day, while I was among the
exiles[a] by the Kebar River, the heavens
were opened[b] and I saw visions[c] of God.
2On the fifth of the month—it was the
fifth year of the exile of King Jehoiachin[d]—
3the word of the LORD came to Ezekiel the
priest, the son of Buzi, by the Kebar River
in the land of the Babylonians.[a] There the
hand of the LORD was on him.[e]
4I looked, and I saw a windstorm coming out of the north[f]—an immense cloud
with flashing lightning and surrounded by
brilliant light. The center of the fire looked
like glowing metal,[g] 5and in the fire was
what looked like four living creatures.[h]
In appearance their form was human,[i]
6but each of them had four faces[j] and four
wings. 7Their legs were straight; their feet
were like those of a calf and gleamed like
burnished bronze.[k] 8Under their wings on
their four sides they had human hands.[l] All
four of them had faces and wings, 9and the
wings of one touched the wings of another.
Each one went straight ahead; they did not
turn as they moved.[m]

[a] 3 Or *Chaldeans*

1:1 ***In my thirtieth year.*** This most likely refers to Ezekiel's age. He was preparing to become a priest when the Babylonians attacked Judah in 597 B.C. ***I saw visions of God.*** As with all the true prophets of ancient Israel, the visitation of God was at His initiative, calling certain people to special responsibilities. The word "vision" is derived from the common Hebrew verb meaning "to see," rather than from the specific verb used for prophetic vision as in Isaiah 1.
1:3 ***the word of the LORD.*** Ezekiel uses this introductory phrase 50 times in this book. It always introduces a divine message and sometimes a new section. ***Ezekiel.*** The name comes from the verb meaning "to seize, to hold fast," coupled with the term meaning "God." Thus Ezekiel's name indicates that he was a man whom God had seized.
1:4 ***windstorm ... immense cloud ... flashing lightning.*** Compare the descriptions of divine appearance in Exodus 19:16 – 20; Psalm 18:7 – 15; and Micah 1:2 – 4.
1:5 ***four living creatures.*** These creatures are related to the cherubim — celestial beings associated with God's holiness and glory, and sometimes poetically with storm winds upon which God travels (Ps. 18:10). There are two basic approaches to understanding them: as a highly symbolic representation of deity, or as highly symbolic representations of angelic beings who serve in God's presence. Probably they are angels, since God Himself is not revealed until the end of the section (v. 26).

1:1 [a] Eze 11:24-25 [b] Mt 3:16; Ac 7:56 [c] Ex 24:10
1:2 [d] 2Ki 24:15 **1:3** [e] 2Ki 3:15; Eze 3:14,22 **1:4** [f] Jer 1:14
[g] Eze 8:2 **1:5** [h] Rev 4:6 [i] ver 26 **1:6** [j] Eze 10:14
1:7 [k] Da 10:6; Rev 1:15 **1:8** [l] Eze 10:8 **1:9** [m] Eze 10:22

10 Their faces looked like this: Each of the four had the face of a human being, and on the right side each had the face of a lion, and on the left the face of an ox; each also had the face of an eagle.[n] 11 Such were their faces. They each had two wings[o] spreading out upward, each wing touching that of the creature on either side; and each had two other wings covering its body. 12 Each one went straight ahead. Wherever the spirit would go, they would go, without turning as they went. 13 The appearance of the living creatures was like burning coals of fire or like torches. Fire moved back and forth among the creatures; it was bright, and lightning[p] flashed out of it. 14 The creatures sped back and forth like flashes of lightning.[q]

15 As I looked at the living creatures, I saw a wheel on the ground beside each creature with its four faces. 16 This was the appearance and structure of the wheels: They sparkled like topaz,[r] and all four looked alike. Each appeared to be made like a wheel intersecting a wheel. 17 As they moved, they would go in any one of the four directions the creatures faced; the wheels did not change direction[s] as the creatures went. 18 Their rims were high and awesome, and all four rims were full of eyes[t] all around.

19 When the living creatures moved, the wheels beside them moved; and when the living creatures rose from the ground, the wheels also rose. 20 Wherever the spirit would go, they would go,[u] and the wheels would rise along with them, because the spirit of the living creatures was in the wheels. 21 When the creatures moved, they also moved; when the creatures stood still, they also stood still; and when the creatures rose from the ground, the wheels rose along with them, because the spirit of the living creatures was in the wheels.[v]

22 Spread out above the heads of the living creatures was what looked something like a vault,[w] sparkling like crystal, and awesome. 23 Under the vault their wings were stretched out one toward the other, and each had two wings covering its body. 24 When the creatures moved, I heard the sound of their wings, like the roar of rushing waters, like the voice[x] of the Almighty,[a] like the tumult of an army.[y] When they stood still, they lowered their wings.

25 Then there came a voice from above the vault over their heads as they stood with lowered wings. 26 Above the vault over their heads was what looked like a throne of lapis lazuli,[z] and high above on the throne was a figure like that of a man.[a] 27 I saw that from what appeared to be his waist up he looked like glowing metal, as if full of fire, and that from there down he looked like fire; and brilliant light surrounded him.[b] 28 Like the appearance of a rainbow[c] in the clouds on a rainy day, so was the radiance around him.[d]

This was the appearance of the likeness of the glory[e] of the LORD. When I saw it, I fell facedown,[f] and I heard the voice of one speaking.

Ezekiel's Call to Be a Prophet

2 He said to me, "Son of man,[b] stand[g] up on your feet and I will speak to you." 2 As he spoke, the Spirit came into me and raised me[h] to my feet, and I heard him speaking to me.

3 He said: "Son of man, I am sending you

a 24 Hebrew *Shaddai* *b* 1 The Hebrew phrase *ben adam* means *human being*. The phrase *son of man* is retained as a form of address here and throughout Ezekiel because of its possible association with "Son of Man" in the New Testament.

1:10 *human being ... lion ... ox ... eagle.* Composite fantastic figures in these classic combinations have been found in Mesopotamian and Egyptian iconography. The idealized strengths of each figure were thus presumed to reside in these living beings.
1:18 *rims ... full of eyes.* The wheels had an exquisite beauty and an animate intelligence.
1:19–21 *spirit ... in the wheels.* The prophet stresses the association of the wheels with the living beings, as well as the beings' ability to travel where they wished. It appears that the wheels represented the flexibility and mobility of the living beings. This is a pictorial representation of God's omnipresence.
1:24 *Almighty.* This is the divine name *Shaddai*, most likely based on a word meaning "mountain," to suggest God's omnipotence and majesty (10:5).
1:26 *throne.* While Isaiah describes the elevation of the Lord's throne (Is. 6:1), Ezekiel focuses on its beauty.
1:27–28 *glory of the LORD.* The "glory" indicates the wonder, majesty, and worthiness of the living God. Amid the wheels, the beings, the colors, and the dazzling light was a figure who appeared like a man (v. 26). Compare the vision of Daniel who saw One "like a son of man" (Dan. 7:13). ***I fell facedown.*** The prophet's response was to fall down in worship and submission. All believers should recognize God's great glory and fall down in humble submission before Him (Phil. 2:10–11).
2:1 *Son of man.* Ezekiel uses this phrase more than 90 times to refer to himself. It emphasizes his humanity in his God-given role as a spokesman for God. The meaning of the phrase is "human one." In the Old Testament, only Daniel 7:13 and 8:17 also employ this phrase. In the New Testament, "Son of man" is used frequently by Jesus for Himself. With this phrase Jesus was calling Himself "the Human One"—the long-awaited Messiah who came as God in the flesh (Luke 21:27; John 1:14; 2 John 7).
2:2 *the Spirit came into me.* This reference to the indwelling of the Holy Spirit in God's prophet is of great importance. The visions and messages of Ezekiel were revelations from the living God.

1:10 [n] Eze 10:14; Rev 4:7 **1:11** [o] Isa 6:2 **1:13** [p] Rev 4:5 **1:14** [q] Ps 29:7 **1:16** [r] Eze 10:9-11; Da 10:6 **1:17** [s] ver 9 **1:18** [t] Eze 10:12; Rev 4:6 **1:20** [u] ver 12 **1:21** [v] Eze 10:17 **1:22** [w] Eze 10:1 **1:24** [x] Eze 10:5; 43:2; Da 10:6; Rev 1:15; 19:6 [y] 2Ki 7:6 **1:26** [z] Ex 24:10; Eze 10:1 [a] Rev 1:13 **1:27** [b] Eze 8:2 **1:28** [c] Ge 9:13; Rev 10:1 [d] Rev 4:2 [e] Eze 8:4 [f] Eze 3:23; Da 8:17; Rev 1:17 **2:1** [g] Da 10:11 **2:2** [h] Eze 3:24; Da 8:18

to the Israelites, to a rebellious nation that
has rebelled against me; they and their ancestors have been in revolt against me to
this very day.[i] 4The people to whom I am
sending you are obstinate and stubborn.[j]
Say to them, 'This is what the Sovereign
LORD says.' 5And whether they listen or fail
to listen[k]—for they are a rebellious people[l]—they will know that a prophet has
been among them.[m] 6And you, son of man,
do not be afraid[n] of them or their words.
Do not be afraid, though briers and thorns[o]
are all around you and you live among
scorpions. Do not be afraid of what they
say or be terrified by them, though they are
a rebellious people.[p] 7You must speak my
words to them, whether they listen or fail
to listen, for they are rebellious.[q] 8But you,
son of man, listen to what I say to you. Do
not rebel like that rebellious people;[r] open
your mouth and eat[s] what I give you."
9Then I looked, and I saw a hand[t]
stretched out to me. In it was a scroll,
10which he unrolled before me. On both
sides of it were written words of lament
and mourning and woe.[u]

3 And he said to me, "Son of man, eat
what is before you, eat this scroll; then
go and speak to the people of Israel." 2So
I opened my mouth, and he gave me the
scroll to eat.
3Then he said to me, "Son of man, eat
this scroll I am giving you and fill your
stomach with it." So I ate[v] it, and it tasted
as sweet as honey[w] in my mouth.
4He then said to me: "Son of man, go now
to the people of Israel and speak my words
to them. 5You are not being sent to a people
of obscure speech and strange language,[x]
but to the people of Israel— 6not to many
peoples of obscure speech and strange
language, whose words you cannot understand. Surely if I had sent you to them,
they would have listened to you.[y] 7But the
people of Israel are not willing to listen to
you because they are not willing to listen
to me, for all the Israelites are hardened
and obstinate.[z] 8But I will make you as unyielding and hardened as they are.[a] 9I will
make your forehead like the hardest stone,
harder than flint. Do not be afraid of them
or terrified by them, though they are a rebellious people.[b]"
10And he said to me, "Son of man, listen
carefully and take to heart all the words I
speak to you. 11Go now to your people in
exile and speak to them. Say to them, 'This
is what the Sovereign LORD says,' whether
they listen or fail to listen.[c]"
12Then the Spirit lifted me up,[d] and I
heard behind me a loud rumbling sound as
the glory of the LORD rose from the place
where it was standing.[a] 13It was the sound
of the wings of the living creatures brush-
ing against each other and the sound of
the wheels beside them, a loud rumbling
sound.[e] 14The Spirit then lifted me up and
took me away, and I went in bitterness and
in the anger of my spirit, with the strong
hand of the LORD on me. 15I came to the
exiles who lived at Tel Aviv near the Kebar
River.[f] And there, where they were living,
I sat among them for seven days[g]—deeply
distressed.

Ezekiel's Task as Watchman

16At the end of seven days the word of
the LORD came to me:[h] 17"Son of man, I
have made you a watchman[i] for the people
of Israel; so hear the word I speak and give

a 12 Probable reading of the original Hebrew text; Masoretic Text *sound—may the glory of the LORD be praised from his place*

2:5 *they are a rebellious people.* God told Ezekiel to take His Word to the sons of Israel. These people were to hear what the Lord Himself was to say to them. Listening or not listening, belief or unbelief, would not change what was spoken. Our belief or unbelief has no effect on what God tells us or what the Bible says. His word remains true. By its very nature, it is worthy of belief.

2:6 *briers ... thorns ... scorpions.* These images vividly portray the nature of the rebellious opponents of Ezekiel's warnings. God told Ezekiel not to allow fear to hinder his message, whether or not the message was wanted (v. 7).

2:10 *lament and mourning and woe.* The unusual feature of writing on both sides of a scroll indicates the magnitude of the nation's transgressions and its need for words of grief (Zech. 5:3; Rev. 5:1). Although Ezekiel would later bring words of comfort and consolation (ch. 33–48), his first prophecies from God contained only sorrow and sadness.

3:1–3 *eat this scroll.* The symbolic act of eating the scroll demonstrated that Ezekiel internalized the message in preparation for speaking to the people.

3:8–9 *I will make you as unyielding and hardened as they are.* There may have been an intentional pun on Ezekiel's name, which means "strongly seized by God" (see 1:3) or "God strengthens." Double meanings in biblical names are common.

3:14 *I went into bitterness and in the anger of my spirit.* Ezekiel's human perspective caused him to focus on the distasteful calling of delivering a message that would not be well received. The prophet was angry and appalled. But God was present to help him deal with these feelings and then move him on to live and work among the captives.

3:17 *a watchman.* He stood on the city wall guarding against any external or internal threat. He would sound an alarm upon sighting impending danger (2 Sam. 18:24). God made Ezekiel a spiritual watchman over His people.

2:3 [i] Jer 3:25; Eze 20:8-24 **2:4** [j] Eze 3:7 **2:5** [k] Eze 3:11 [l] Eze 3:27 [m] Eze 33:33 **2:6** [n] Jer 1:8, 17 [o] Isa 9:18; Mic 7:4 [p] Eze 3:9 **2:7** [q] Jer 1:7; Eze 3:10-11 **2:8** [r] Isa 50:5 [s] Jer 15:16; Rev 10:9 **2:9** [t] Eze 8:3 **2:10** [u] Rev 8:13 **3:3** [v] Jer 15:16 [w] Ps 19:10; Ps 119:103; Rev 10:9-10 **3:5** [x] Isa 28:11; Jnh 1:2 **3:6** [y] Mt 11:21-23 **3:7** [z] Eze 2:4; Jn 15:20-23 **3:8** [a] Jer 1:18 **3:9** [b] Isa 50:7; Eze 2:6; Mic 3:8 **3:11** [c] Eze 2:4-5, 7 **3:12** [d] Eze 8:3; Ac 8:39 **3:13** [e] Eze 1:24; 10:5, 16-17 **3:15** [f] Ps 137:1 [g] Job 2:13 **3:16** [h] Jer 42:7 **3:17** [i] Isa 52:8; Jer 6:17; Eze 33:7-9

them warning from me. 18When I say to a wicked person, 'You will surely die,' and you do not warn them or speak out to dissuade them from their evil ways in order to save their life, that wicked person will die for[a] their sin, and I will hold you accountable for their blood.[j] 19But if you do warn the wicked person and they do not turn from their wickedness or from their evil ways, they will die for their sin; but you will have saved yourself.[k]

20"Again, when a righteous person turns from their righteousness and does evil, and I put a stumbling block before them, they will die. Since you did not warn them, they will die for their sin. The righteous things that person did will not be remembered, and I will hold you accountable for their blood.[l] 21But if you do warn the righteous person not to sin and they do not sin, they will surely live because they took warning, and you will have saved yourself.[m]"

22The hand of the LORD[n] was on me there, and he said to me, "Get up and go[o] out to the plain,[p] and there I will speak to you." 23So I got up and went out to the plain. And the glory of the LORD was standing there, like the glory I had seen by the Kebar River,[q] and I fell facedown.[r]

24Then the Spirit came into me and raised me[s] to my feet. He spoke to me and said: "Go, shut yourself inside your house. 25And you, son of man, they will tie with ropes; you will be bound so that you cannot go out among the people.[t] 26I will make your tongue stick to the roof of your mouth so that you will be silent and unable to rebuke them, for they are a rebellious people.[u] 27But when I speak to you, I will open your mouth and you shall say to them, 'This is what the Sovereign LORD says.'[v] Whoever will listen let them listen, and whoever will refuse let them refuse; for they are a rebellious people.[w]

Siege of Jerusalem Symbolized

4 "Now, son of man, take a block of clay, put it in front of you and draw the city of Jerusalem on it. 2Then lay siege to it: Erect siege works against it, build a ramp[x] up to it, set up camps against it and put battering rams around it.[y] 3Then take an iron pan, place it as an iron wall between you and the city and turn your face toward it. It will be under siege, and you shall besiege it. This will be a sign[z] to the people of Israel.[a]

4"Then lie on your left side and put the sin of the people of Israel upon yourself.[b] You are to bear their sin for the number of days you lie on your side. 5I have assigned you the same number of days as the years of their sin. So for 390 days you will bear the sin of the people of Israel.

6"After you have finished this, lie down again, this time on your right side, and bear the sin of the people of Judah. I have assigned you 40 days, a day for each year.[b] 7Turn your face toward the siege of Jerusalem and with bared arm prophesy against her. 8I will tie you up with ropes so that you cannot turn from one side to the other until you have finished the days of your siege.[c]

9"Take wheat and barley, beans and lentils, millet and spelt;[d] put them in a storage

---

a *18* Or *in;* also in verses 19 and 20 *b* *4* Or *upon your side*

3:20 ***when a righteous person turns from their righteousness and does evil.*** The prophet's responsibility was to warn, if he saw apostasy taking place. If he did not, he became culpable too. Even for the most devoted and the most saintly, righteousness can become something to spurn and iniquity can become something to embrace. God says that repudiation of righteousness leads to death.

3:26 ***silent and unable to rebuke them.*** This phrase qualified what was meant by Ezekiel's being mute. The idea may be better stated as "not be a legal mediator." During his "mute" period, Ezekiel would not be allowed to speak as a mediator on behalf of the people before God, their Judge.

3:27 ***Whoever will listen let them listen.*** Jesus used this warning often in His teaching (Mark 4:23). The phrasing emphasizes individual responsibility and readiness to accept the divine message.

4:1 ***take a block of clay.*** The tablet would have been soft enough to inscribe with a stylus.

4:2 ***lay siege.*** The city of Jerusalem would come under siege, meaning that the Babylonians would surround the city and cut off its outside supplies. The purpose was to starve its inhabitants into submission. By his symbolic drawing, Ezekiel may have been commanded to do what other "prophets" of the nations might do. That is, the hired "prophets" of pagan nations might use such a drawing as a device for invoking the gods to bring about the event graphically described. In Ezekiel's case, the drawing was the opposite of what the people wanted. As they sat in captivity, the worst news would have been that the holy city had been destroyed.

4:3 ***an iron pan.*** This was a plate that Ezekiel possessed as a priest; it was for baking grain for the cereal offerings (Lev. 2:5; 6:21). Here its purpose was to represent a wall between Ezekiel and the city.

4:7 ***Turn your face toward the siege.*** As horrible as it was, the siege ultimately showed God's faithfulness to His covenant established in the days of Moses — that idolatry and disobedience would bring curses, which would include being conquered, captured and removed from the land (Deut. 28:15 – 68).

4:8 ***tie you up.*** Ezekiel was bound while lying on either side for the entire 430 days, but the activities described in Ezekiel 4:9 – 17 show that his lying down and being tied up occurred only during parts of each day.

3:18 [j] ver 20; Eze 33:6 **3:19** [k] 2Ki 17:13; Eze 14:14, 20; Ac 18:6; 20:26; 1Ti 4:14-16 **3:20** [l] Ps 125:5; Eze 18:24; 33:12, 18 **3:21** [m] Ac 20:31 **3:22** [n] Eze 1:3 [o] Ac 9:6 [p] Eze 8:4 **3:23** [q] Eze 1:1 [r] Eze 1:28 **3:24** [s] Eze 2:2 **3:25** [t] Eze 4:8 **3:26** [u] Eze 2:5; 24:27; 33:22 **3:27** [v] ver 11 [w] Eze 12:3; 24:27; 33:22 **4:2** [x] Jer 6:6 [y] Eze 21:22 **4:3** [z] Isa 8:18; 20:3; Eze 12:3-6; 24:24, 27 [a] Jer 39:1 **4:6** [b] Nu 14:34; Da 9:24-26; 12:11-12 **4:8** [c] Eze 3:25 **4:9** [d] Isa 28:25

jar and use them to make bread for yourself. You are to eat it during the 390 days you lie on your side. 10Weigh out twenty shekels[a] of food to eat each day and eat it at set times. 11Also measure out a sixth of a hin[b] of water and drink it at set times. 12Eat the food as you would a loaf of barley bread; bake it in the sight of the people, using human excrement[e] for fuel." 13The LORD said, "In this way the people of Israel will eat defiled food among the nations where I will drive them."[f]

14Then I said, "Not so, Sovereign LORD![g] I have never defiled myself. From my youth until now I have never eaten anything found dead[h] or torn by wild animals. No impure meat has ever entered my mouth.[i]"

15"Very well," he said, "I will let you bake your bread over cow dung instead of human excrement."

16He then said to me: "Son of man, I am about to cut off[j] the food supply in Jerusalem. The people will eat rationed food in anxiety and drink rationed water in despair,[k] 17for food and water will be scarce. They will be appalled at the sight of each other and will waste away because of[c] their sin.[l]

God's Razor of Judgment

5 "Now, son of man, take a sharp sword and use it as a barber's razor[m] to shave[n] your head and your beard.[o] Then take a set of scales and divide up the hair. 2When the days of your siege come to an end, burn a third of the hair inside the city. Take a third and strike it with the sword all around the city. And scatter a third to the wind. For I will pursue them with drawn sword.[p] 3But take a few hairs and tuck them away in the folds of your garment.[q] 4Again, take a few of these and throw them into the fire and burn them up. A fire will spread from there to all Israel.

5"This is what the Sovereign LORD says: This is Jerusalem, which I have set in the center of the nations, with countries all around her. 6Yet in her wickedness she has rebelled against my laws and decrees more than the nations and countries around her. She has rejected my laws and has not followed my decrees.[r]

7"Therefore this is what the Sovereign LORD says: You have been more unruly than the nations around you and have not followed my decrees or kept my laws. You have not even[d] conformed to the standards of the nations around you.[s]

8"Therefore this is what the Sovereign LORD says: I myself am against you, Jerusalem, and I will inflict punishment on you in the sight of the nations.[t] 9Because of all your detestable idols, I will do to you what I have never done before and will never do again.[u] 10Therefore in your midst parents will eat their children, and children will eat their parents.[v] I will inflict punishment on you and will scatter all your survivors to the winds.[w] 11Therefore as surely as I live, declares the Sovereign LORD, because you have defiled my sanctuary with all your vile images[x] and detestable practices,[y] I myself will shave you; I will not look on you with pity or spare you.[z] 12A third of your people will die of the plague or perish by famine inside you; a third will fall by the sword outside your walls; and a third I will scatter to the winds and pursue with drawn sword.[a]

13"Then my anger will cease and my wrath[b] against them will subside, and I will be avenged.[c] And when I have spent my wrath on them, they will know that I the LORD have spoken in my zeal.

14"I will make you a ruin and a reproach among the nations around you, in the sight of all who pass by.[d] 15You will be a reproach and a taunt, a warning and an object of horror to the nations around you when I inflict punishment on you in anger

[a] *10* That is, about 8 ounces or about 230 grams
[b] *11* That is, about 2/3 quart or about 0.6 liter
[c] *17* Or *away in*
[d] *7* Most Hebrew manuscripts; some Hebrew manuscripts and Syriac *You have*

4:17 *waste away because of their sin.* The people had broken their covenant with God, and He had no choice but to bring upon them the promised consequences of their disobedience (Lev. 26:14–29).

5:1 *a barber's razor to shave your head and your beard.* Shaving the head was an act showing shame or disgrace in Hebrew culture (7:18). It also represented a type of pagan mourning forbidden by the law (27:31). Shaving the head was a mark of defilement, making a priest like Ezekiel ritually unclean, and so unable to perform his duties in the temple (Lev. 21:5). This message was telling the people that they were about to be humiliated and defiled.

5:2 *a third.* Each citizen of Jerusalem would suffer one of the three fates depicted by each of the three mounds of hair: (1) some would be burned along with the city or would die from plague, famine, or other siege conditions (5:12; 2 Kin. 25:9); (2) some would be murdered by the sword during the attack (5:12; 2 Kin. 25:18–21); and (3) some would be scattered in the wind—referring to the exile (5:12; 2 Kin. 25:11–17).

5:9–17 *what I have never done.* The elements in God's judgment on the people for their sins can be enumerated in this way: (1) a judgment that will be worse in extent than ever before; (2) a terrible famine

4:12 [e] Isa 36:12 **4:13** [f] Hos 9:3 **4:14** [g] Jer 1:6; Eze 9:8; 20:49 [h] Lev 11:39 [i] Ex 22:31; Dt 14:3; Ac 10:14
4:16 [j] Ps 105:16; Eze 5:16 [k] ver 10-11; Lev 26:26; Isa 3:1; Eze 12:19 **4:17** [l] Lev 26:39; Eze 24:23; 33:10
5:1 [m] Isa 7:20 [n] Eze 44:20 [o] Lev 21:5 **5:2** [p] ver 12; Lev 26:33 **5:3** [q] Jer 39:10 **5:6** [r] Jer 11:10; Eze 16:47-51; Zec 7:11 **5:7** [s] 2Ch 33:9; Jer 2:10-11; Eze 16:47
5:8 [t] Eze 15:7 **5:9** [u] Da 9:12; Mt 24:21 **5:10** [v] Lev 26:29; La 2:20 [w] Lev 26:33; Ps 44:11; Eze 12:14; Zec 2:6
5:11 [x] Eze 7:20 [y] 2Ch 36:14; Eze 8:6 [z] Eze 7:4,9
5:12 [a] ver 2, 17; Jer 15:2; 21:9; Eze 6:11-12; 12:14
5:13 [b] Eze 21:17; 36:6 [c] Isa 1:24 **5:14** [d] Lev 26:32; Ne 2:17; Ps 74:3-10; 79:1-4

and in wrath and with stinging rebuke.[e] I
the LORD have spoken.[f] 16When I shoot at
you with my deadly and destructive arrows
of famine, I will shoot to destroy you. I will
bring more and more famine upon you and
cut off your supply of food.[g] 17I will send
famine and wild beasts against you, and
they will leave you childless. Plague and
bloodshed[h] will sweep through you, and
I will bring the sword against you. I the
LORD have spoken.[i]"

Doom for the Mountains of Israel

6 The word of the LORD came to me: 2"Son
of man, set your face against the mountains[j] of Israel; prophesy against them 3and
say: 'You mountains of Israel, hear the
word of the Sovereign LORD. This is what
the Sovereign LORD says to the mountains
and hills, to the ravines and valleys:[k] I am
about to bring a sword against you, and I
will destroy your high places.[l] 4Your altars
will be demolished and your incense altars[m] will be smashed; and I will slay your
people in front of your idols. 5I will lay the
dead bodies of the Israelites in front of their
idols, and I will scatter your bones[n] around
your altars. 6Wherever you live, the towns
will be laid waste and the high places demolished, so that your altars will be laid
waste and devastated, your idols[o] smashed
and ruined, your incense altars[p] broken
down, and what you have made wiped out.[q]
7Your people will fall slain among you, and
you will know that I am the LORD.

8" 'But I will spare some, for some of you
will escape[r] the sword when you are scattered among the lands and nations.[s] 9Then
in the nations where they have been carried captive, those who escape will remember me—how I have been grieved[t] by their
adulterous hearts, which have turned away
from me, and by their eyes, which have
lusted after their idols.[u] They will loathe
themselves for the evil they have done and
for all their detestable practices.[v] 10And
they will know that I am the LORD; I did
not threaten in vain to bring this calamity
on them.

11" 'This is what the Sovereign LORD says:
Strike your hands together and stamp your
feet and cry out "Alas!" because of all the
wicked and detestable practices of the people of Israel, for they will fall by the sword,
famine and plague.[w] 12One who is far away
will die of the plague, and one who is near
will fall by the sword, and anyone who survives and is spared will die of famine. So
will I pour out my wrath on them.[x] 13And
they will know that I am the LORD, when
their people lie slain among their idols
around their altars, on every high hill
and on all the mountaintops, under every
spreading tree and every leafy oak[y]—places where they offered fragrant incense to
all their idols.[z] 14And I will stretch out my
hand[a] against them and make the land
a desolate waste from the desert to Dib-
lah[a]—wherever they live. Then they will
know that I am the LORD.[b]' "

The End Has Come

7 The word of the LORD came to me: 2"Son
of man, this is what the Sovereign LORD
says to the land of Israel:

" 'The end![c] The end has come
upon the four corners[d] of the
land!

[a] *14* Most Hebrew manuscripts; a few Hebrew manuscripts *Riblah*

---

that will lead to cannibalism; (3) pestilence, meaning plagues and diseases associated with famine; (4) violent death by sword or wild beasts; and (5) the scattering and killing of a remnant. These punishments would come as the result of the people's idolatry.

6:2–3 ***mountains and hills.*** Also translated "high places," these were originally elevated locations for worship of the god Baal and other deities of the Canaanite pantheon. The term "high place" could be used of any location, whether hilltop or valley. Before entering the Promised Land, the Hebrews had been commanded to abolish all the high places where idols were worshiped (Num. 33:52).

6:4–6 ***slay your people ... lay the dead bodies ... scatter your bones.*** These phrases refer to God's judgment. Dead people lying unburied and bones scattered around signify the ultimate defilement of the land. God would bring this upon them because they had defiled and desecrated themselves by worshiping in the pagan high places.

6:13 ***And they will know that I am the LORD.*** As in verses 7 and 10, the Lord states the purpose of the coming destruction of His city and many of its people. The use of God's personal name further emphasizes the intent to bring His people back to a personal, intimate relationship with Himself.

6:13 God's Desire for Exclusiveness—God's point throughout the Book of Ezekiel is the same; His relationship with us is exclusive. He doesn't share that primary God-man relationship with anybody else or anything. As a model for exclusiveness, Ezekiel uses the marriage relationship. Exclusiveness is the boundary that provides the shape to that relationship. It is the same with our relationship with God. When we violate God's desire for exclusiveness, we ruin our relationship with Him. God designed us for Himself alone. If we have anything less than an exclusive relationship with Him, we become less than what we were created to be.

7:2–3 ***The end!*** Three uses of this key word stressed that the fulfillment of the prophecy was at hand.

5:15 [e] 1Ki 9:7; Jer 22:8-9; 24:9 [f] Eze 25:17 **5:16** [g] Dt 32:24
5:17 [h] Eze 38:22 [i] Eze 14:21 **6:2** [j] Eze 36:1
6:3 [k] Eze 36:4 [l] Lev 26:30 **6:4** [m] 2Ch 14:5
6:5 [n] Jer 8:1-2 **6:6** [o] Mic 1:7; Zec 13:2 [p] Lev 26:30
[q] Isa 6:11; Eze 5:14 **6:8** [r] Jer 44:28 [s] Isa 6:13; Jer 44:14;
Eze 12:16; 14:22 **6:9** [t] Ps 78:40; Isa 7:13 [u] Eze 20:7, 24
[v] Eze 20:43; 36:31 **6:11** [w] Eze 5:12; 21:14, 17; 25:6
6:12 [x] Eze 5:12 **6:13** [y] Isa 57:5 [z] 1Ki 14:23; Jer 2:20;
Eze 20:28; Hos 4:13 **6:14** [a] Isa 5:25 [b] Eze 14:13
7:2 [c] Am 8:2, 10 [d] Rev 7:1; 20:8

3 The end is now upon you,
and I will unleash my anger against you.
I will judge you according to your conduct
and repay you for all your detestable practices.
4 I will not look on you with pity;[e]
I will not spare you.
I will surely repay you for your conduct
and for the detestable practices among you.

" 'Then you will know that I am the LORD.'

5 "This is what the Sovereign LORD says:

" 'Disaster![f] Unheard-of[a] disaster!
See, it comes!
6 The end has come!
The end has come!
It has roused itself against you.
See, it comes!
7 Doom has come upon you,
upon you who dwell in the land.
The time has come! The day is near![g]
There is panic, not joy, on the mountains.
8 I am about to pour out my wrath[h] on you
and spend my anger against you.
I will judge you according to your conduct
and repay you for all your detestable practices.[i]
9 I will not look on you with pity;
I will not spare you.
I will repay you for your conduct
and for the detestable practices among you.

" 'Then you will know that it is I the LORD who strikes you.

10 " 'See, the day!
See, it comes!
Doom has burst forth,
the rod[j] has budded,
arrogance has blossomed!
11 Violence has arisen,[b]
a rod to punish the wicked.
None of the people will be left,
none of that crowd—
none of their wealth,
nothing of value.[k]
12 The time has come!
The day has arrived!
Let not the buyer rejoice
nor the seller grieve,
for my wrath is on the whole crowd.[l]
13 The seller will not recover
the property that was sold—
as long as both buyer and seller live.
For the vision concerning the whole crowd
will not be reversed.
Because of their sins, not one of them
will preserve their life.[m]

14 " 'They have blown the trumpet,
they have made all things ready,
but no one will go into battle,
for my wrath is on the whole crowd.
15 Outside is the sword;
inside are plague and famine.
Those in the country
will die by the sword;
those in the city
will be devoured by famine and plague.[n]
16 The fugitives who escape
will flee to the mountains.
Like doves[o] of the valleys,
they will all moan,
each for their own sins.[p]
17 Every hand will go limp;[q]
every leg will be wet with urine.
18 They will put on sackcloth
and be clothed with terror.[r]
Every face will be covered with shame,
and every head will be shaved.[s]

19 " 'They will throw their silver into the streets,
and their gold will be treated as a thing unclean.
Their silver and gold
will not be able to deliver them
in the day of the LORD's wrath.[t]
It will not satisfy their hunger
or fill their stomachs,
for it has caused them to stumble[u] into sin.[v]

---

[a] 5 Most Hebrew manuscripts; some Hebrew manuscripts and Syriac *Disaster after*
[b] 11 Or *The violent one has become*

7:10 *the rod has budded.* The flowering of the rod indicates that the time to bring judgment was ripe. These words describe one whose time had come, a person marked by arrogance. In this case, it pictures the chosen instrument of God (Num. 17:5) with whom He would discipline Jerusalem and Judah—namely Nebuchadnezzar, king of Babylon and the characteristic representative of the arrogant and evil Babylonians.
7:12 *Let not the buyer rejoice.* The fact of coming judgment was so certain, and its effects would be so lasting and devastating, that transactions of buying and selling would be concluded improperly or not at all.
7:16–19 *The fugitives who escape.* Those left alive would hide in the hills and be characterized by four things: (1) mourning; displaying their humiliation over sin by wearing sackcloth and shaving their heads (Is. 15:2); (2) weakness; (3) horror; and (4) disgust and disillusionment over wealth.

7:4 [e] Eze 5:11 **7:5** [f] 2Ki 21:12 **7:7** [g] Eze 12:23; Zep 1:14
7:8 [h] Isa 42:25; Eze 9:8; 14:19; Na 1:6 [i] Eze 20:8, 21; 36:19
7:10 [j] Ps 89:32; Isa 10:5 **7:11** [k] Jer 16:6; Zep 1:18
7:12 [l] ver 7; Isa 5:13-14; Eze 30:3 **7:13** [m] Lev 25:24-28
7:15 [n] Dt 32:25; Jer 14:18; La 1:20; Eze 5:12
7:16 [o] Isa 59:11 [p] Ezr 9:15; Eze 6:8 **7:17** [q] Isa 13:7; Eze 21:7; 22:14 **7:18** [r] Ps 55:5 [s] Isa 15:2-3; Eze 27:31; Am 8:10 **7:19** [t] Eze 13:5; Zep 1:7, 18 [u] Eze 14:3 [v] Pr 11:4

20 They took pride in their beautiful
jewelry
and used it to make their detestable
idols.
They made it into vile images;[w]
therefore I will make it a thing
unclean for them.
21 I will give their wealth as plunder to
foreigners
and as loot to the wicked of the earth,
who will defile it.[x]
22 I will turn my face[y] away from the
people,
and robbers will desecrate the place I
treasure.
They will enter it
and will defile it.

23 "'Prepare chains!
For the land is full of bloodshed,[z]
and the city is full of violence.
24 I will bring the most wicked of nations
to take possession of their houses.
I will put an end to the pride of the
mighty,
and their sanctuaries[a] will be
desecrated.[b]
25 When terror comes,
they will seek peace in vain.[c]
26 Calamity upon calamity[d] will come,
and rumor upon rumor.
They will go searching for a vision from
the prophet,
priestly instruction in the law will
cease,
the counsel of the elders will come to
an end.[e]
27 The king will mourn,
the prince will be clothed with
despair,[f]
and the hands of the people of the
land will tremble.
I will deal with them according to their
conduct,[g]
and by their own standards I will
judge them.

"'Then they will know that I am the LORD.[h]'"

Idolatry in the Temple

8 In the sixth year, in the sixth month on
the fifth day, while I was sitting in my
house and the elders[i] of Judah were sitting
before[j] me, the hand of the Sovereign LORD
came on me there.[k] 2 I looked, and I saw a
figure like that of a man.[a] From what appeared to be his waist down he was like
fire, and from there up his appearance was
as bright as glowing metal.[l] 3 He stretched
out what looked like a hand and took me
by the hair of my head. The Spirit lifted me
up[m] between earth and heaven and in visions of God he took me to Jerusalem, to
the entrance of the north gate of the inner
court, where the idol that provokes to jealousy[n] stood. 4 And there before me was the
glory[o] of the God of Israel, as in the vision
I had seen in the plain.[p]
5 Then he said to me, "Son of man, look
toward the north." So I looked, and in the
entrance north of the gate of the altar I saw
this idol[q] of jealousy.
6 And he said to me, "Son of man, do
you see what they are doing—the utterly
detestable[r] things the Israelites are doing
here, things that will drive me far from my
sanctuary? But you will see things that are
even more detestable."
7 Then he brought me to the entrance to
the court. I looked, and I saw a hole in the
wall. 8 He said to me, "Son of man, now dig
into the wall." So I dug into the wall and
saw a doorway there.
9 And he said to me, "Go in and see the
wicked and detestable things they are doing here." 10 So I went in and looked, and I
saw portrayed all over the walls all kinds
of crawling things and unclean animals
and all the idols of Israel.[s] 11 In front of them
stood seventy elders of Israel, and Jaazaniah son of Shaphan was standing among
them. Each had a censer[t] in his hand, and a
fragrant cloud of incense[u] was rising.
12 He said to me, "Son of man, have you
seen what the elders of Israel are doing in
the darkness, each at the shrine of his own
idol? They say, 'The LORD does not see[v] us;
the LORD has forsaken the land.'" 13 Again,
he said, "You will see them doing things
that are even more detestable."
14 Then he brought me to the entrance of
the north gate of the house of the LORD, and

[a] 2 Or *saw a fiery figure*

7:20 *pride in their beautiful jewelry.* The people had sinned horribly when they crafted idols out of the temple treasures and then worshiped what their hands had made (Rom. 1:25).
8:5–6 *drive me far from my sanctuary.* The people thought that just because the temple stood among them, whatever wrong they might do could not bring ultimate disaster. They thought the temple guaranteed their security. They did not realize that their evil had actually caused God to leave His temple, which would then no longer be their protection.
8:11 *seventy elders.* These men were the nation's leaders (Num. 11:16–25).
8:13–14 *Tammuz.* This was a fertility god. The women were crying out to the idol because they had no children or because the crops were failing. In the sixth month, August-September, Tammuz was

7:20 [w] Jer 7:30 **7:21** [x] 2Ki 24:13 **7:22** [y] Eze 39:23-24 **7:23** [z] 2Ki 21:16 **7:24** [a] Eze 24:21 [b] 2Ch 7:20; Eze 28:7 **7:25** [c] Eze 13:10, 16 **7:26** [d] Jer 4:20 [e] Isa 47:11; Eze 20:1-3; Mic 3:6 **7:27** [f] Ps 109:19; Eze 26:16 [g] Eze 18:20 [h] ver 4 **8:1** [i] Eze 14:1 [j] Eze 33:31 [k] Eze 1:1-3 **8:2** [l] Eze 1:4, 26-27 **8:3** [m] Eze 3:12; 11:1 [n] Ex 20:5; Dt 32:16 **8:4** [o] Eze 1:28 [p] Eze 3:22 **8:5** [q] Ps 78:58; Jer 32:34 **8:6** [r] Eze 5:11 **8:10** [s] Ex 20:4 **8:11** [t] Nu 16:17 [u] Nu 16:35 **8:12** [v] Ps 10:11; Isa 29:15; Eze 9:9

I saw women sitting there, mourning the
god Tammuz. 15 He said to me, "Do you see
this, son of man? You will see things that
are even more detestable than this."
16 He then brought me into the inner court
of the house of the LORD, and there at the
entrance to the temple, between the portico
and the altar,[w] were about twenty-five men.
With their backs toward the temple of the
LORD and their faces toward the east, they
were bowing down to the sun in the east.[x]
17 He said to me, "Have you seen this, son
of man? Is it a trivial matter for the people
of Judah to do the detestable things they
are doing here? Must they also fill the land
with violence[y] and continually arouse my
anger?[z] Look at them putting the branch
to their nose! 18 Therefore I will deal with
them in anger; I will not look on them with
pity[a] or spare them. Although they shout in
my ears, I will not listen[b] to them."

Judgment on the Idolaters

9 Then I heard him call out in a loud voice,
"Bring near those who are appointed to
execute judgment on the city, each with a
weapon in his hand." 2 And I saw six men
coming from the direction of the upper
gate, which faces north, each with a deadly weapon in his hand. With them was a
man clothed in linen[c] who had a writing kit
at his side. They came in and stood beside
the bronze altar.
3 Now the glory[d] of the God of Israel went
up from above the cherubim,[e] where it had
been, and moved to the threshold of the
temple. Then the LORD called to the man
clothed in linen who had the writing kit at
his side 4 and said to him, "Go throughout
the city of Jerusalem and put a mark[f] on
the foreheads of those who grieve and lament[g] over all the detestable things that are
done in it.[h]"
5 As I listened, he said to the others, "Follow him through the city and kill, without
showing pity[i] or compassion. 6 Slaughter
the old men, the young men and women,
the mothers and children, but do not touch
anyone who has the mark. Begin at my
sanctuary." So they began with the old
men[j] who were in front of the temple.[k]
7 Then he said to them, "Defile the temple
and fill the courts with the slain. Go!" So
they went out and began killing throughout the city. 8 While they were killing and I
was left alone, I fell facedown,[l] crying out,
"Alas, Sovereign LORD! Are you going to
destroy the entire remnant of Israel in this
outpouring of your wrath on Jerusalem?[m]"
9 He answered me, "The sin of the people
of Israel and Judah is exceedingly great;
the land is full of bloodshed and the city is
full of injustice.[n] They say, 'The LORD has
forsaken the land; the LORD does not see.'[o]
10 So I will not look on them with pity[p] or
spare them, but I will bring down on their
own heads what they have done.[q]"
11 Then the man in linen with the writing
kit at his side brought back word, saying,
"I have done as you commanded."

God's Glory Departs From the Temple

10 I looked, and I saw the likeness of a
throne[r] of lapis lazuli[s] above the vault[t]
that was over the heads of the cherubim.
2 The LORD said to the man clothed in lin-
en,[u] "Go in among the wheels[v] beneath the
cherubim. Fill[w] your hands with burning
coals from among the cherubim and scatter them over the city." And as I watched,
he went in.
3 Now the cherubim were standing on the
south side of the temple when the man went
in, and a cloud filled the inner court. 4 Then
the glory of the LORD[x] rose from above the
cherubim and moved to the threshold of the
temple. The cloud filled the temple, and the
court was full of the radiance of the glory of the LORD. 5 The sound of the wings of
the cherubim could be heard as far away
as the outer court, like the voice[y] of God
Almighty[a] when he speaks.
6 When the LORD commanded the man in
linen, "Take fire from among the wheels,

[a] 5 Hebrew *El-Shaddai*

thought to "die" with the scorched land. Worshipers would wail over his death and cry for his resurgence.

8:17–18 *putting the branch to their nose.* This action is not mentioned elsewhere. In the context it appears to be (1) a ritualistic gesture used in idol worship, or (2) an action indicative of the extensive violence which was occurring in Judah as a result of idolatry.

9:5–6 *Follow him through the city.* The universality of this judgment is shocking to us; but this is in line with divine judgments from the time of the flood in Genesis to the final judgment described in Revelation.

9:6–7 *my sanctuary.* The corrupt spiritual leaders had been practicing idolatry and immorality in the temple itself (8:3–16). Judgment would begin with them because they had led the nation astray.

9:9 *sin ... bloodshed ... injustice.* These three reasons are given as the offenses that deserve this terrible outpouring of God's wrath. The people and especially rich rulers willfully chose to believe that God did not see or care what injustices went on.

10:3–5 *a cloud filled the inner court.* The cloud represented God's glory (as in 1:4), which was seen moving from the inner court to the threshold of the temple. From there it filled the temple.

8:16 [w] Joel 2:17 [x] Dt 4:19; 17:3; Job 31:28; Jer 2:27; Eze 11:1, 12 **8:17** [y] Eze 9:9 [z] Eze 16:26 **8:18** [a] Eze 9:10; 24:14 [b] Isa 1:15; Jer 11:11; Mic 3:4; Zec 7:13 **9:2** [c] Lev 16:4; Eze 10:2; Rev 15:6 **9:3** [d] Eze 10:4 [e] Eze 11:22 **9:4** [f] Ex 12:7; 2Co 1:22; Rev 7:3; 9:4 [g] Ps 119:136; Jer 13:17; Eze 21:6 [h] Ps 119:53 **9:5** [i] Eze 5:11 **9:6** [j] Eze 8:11-13, 16 [k] 2Ch 36:17; Jer 25:29; 1Pe 4:17 **9:8** [l] Jos 7:6 [m] Eze 11:13; Am 7:1-6 **9:9** [n] Eze 22:29 [o] Job 22:13; Eze 8:12 **9:10** [p] Eze 7:4; 8:18 [q] Isa 65:6; Eze 11:21 **10:1** [r] Rev 4:2 [s] Ex 24:10 [t] Eze 1:22 **10:2** [u] Eze 9:2 [v] Eze 1:15 [w] Rev 8:5 **10:4** [x] Eze 1:28; 9:3 **10:5** [y] Job 40:9; Eze 1:24

from among the cherubim," the man went in and stood beside a wheel. 7Then one of the cherubim reached out his hand to the fire that was among them. He took up some of it and put it into the hands of the man in linen, who took it and went out. 8(Under the wings of the cherubim could be seen what looked like human hands.)[z]

9I looked, and I saw beside the cherubim four wheels, one beside each of the cherubim; the wheels sparkled like topaz.[a] 10As for their appearance, the four of them looked alike; each was like a wheel intersecting a wheel. 11As they moved, they would go in any one of the four directions the cherubim faced; the wheels did not turn about[a] as the cherubim went. The cherubim went in whatever direction the head faced, without turning as they went. 12Their entire bodies, including their backs, their hands and their wings, were completely full of eyes,[b] as were their four wheels.[c] 13I heard the wheels being called "the whirling wheels." 14Each of the cherubim[d] had four faces:[e] One face was that of a cherub, the second the face of a human being, the third the face of a lion, and the fourth the face of an eagle.[f]

15Then the cherubim rose upward. These were the living creatures[g] I had seen by the Kebar River. 16When the cherubim moved, the wheels beside them moved; and when the cherubim spread their wings to rise from the ground, the wheels did not leave their side. 17When the cherubim stood still, they also stood still; and when the cherubim rose, they rose with them, because the spirit of the living creatures was in them.[h]

18Then the glory of the LORD departed from over the threshold of the temple and stopped above the cherubim.[i] 19While I watched, the cherubim spread their wings and rose from the ground, and as they went, the wheels went with them.[j] They stopped at the entrance of the east gate of the LORD's house, and the glory of the God of Israel was above them.

20These were the living creatures I had seen beneath the God of Israel by the Kebar River,[k] and I realized that they were cherubim. 21Each had four faces[l] and four wings,[m] and under their wings was what looked like human hands. 22Their faces had the same appearance as those I had seen by the Kebar River. Each one went straight ahead.

God's Sure Judgment on Jerusalem

11 Then the Spirit lifted me up and brought me to the gate of the house of the LORD that faces east. There at the entrance of the gate were twenty-five men, and I saw among them Jaazaniah son of Azzur and Pelatiah son of Benaiah, leaders of the people.[n] 2The LORD said to me, "Son of man, these are the men who are plotting evil and giving wicked advice in this city. 3They say, 'Haven't our houses been recently rebuilt? This city is a pot,[o] and we are the meat in it.'[p] 4Therefore prophesy[q] against them; prophesy, son of man."

5Then the Spirit of the LORD came on me, and he told me to say: "This is what the LORD says: That is what you are saying, you leaders in Israel, but I know what is going through your mind.[r] 6You have killed many people in this city and filled its streets with the dead.[s]

7"Therefore this is what the Sovereign LORD says: The bodies you have thrown there are the meat and this city is the pot, but I will drive you out of it.[t] 8You fear the sword, and the sword is what I will bring against you, declares the Sovereign LORD.[u] 9I will drive you out of the city and deliver you into the hands[v] of foreigners and inflict punishment on you.[w] 10You will fall by the sword, and I will execute judgment on you at the borders of Israel.[x] Then you will know that I am the LORD. 11This city will not be a pot[y] for you, nor will you be the meat in it; I will execute judgment on you at the borders of Israel. 12And you will know that I am the LORD, for you have not followed my decrees[z] or kept my laws but have conformed to the standards of the nations around you.[a]"

13Now as I was prophesying, Pelatiah[b] son of Benaiah died. Then I fell facedown and cried out in a loud voice, "Alas, Sovereign LORD! Will you completely destroy the remnant of Israel?[c]"

---

[a] *11* Or *aside*

10:9–17 ***One face was that of a cherub.*** Whereas one of the four faces in 1:10 is a bull, here it is a cherub. These are ancient sculptures with animal bodies and wings but human faces. The difference of the faces between 1:10 and 10:14 should not be called an error; it is possible that the images that Ezekiel saw were changing from time to time.

10:20–22 ***and I realized that they were cherubim.*** They sometimes serve as guardians (Gen. 3:24). They are associated with God's throne and presence (the mercy seat on the ark, Ex. 25:18–22; 1 Chr. 13:6). They are also associated with God's chariot-like throne (v. 1; 1:20–26; Ps. 18:10).

11:3 ***houses ... rebuilt.*** These officials were proclaiming that the inhabitants of Jerusalem were as secure behind the city's walls as meat was safe in its cooking pot. There was no impending doom, they said; therefore, new construction projects were encouraged.

11:13 ***Alas, Sovereign LORD!*** Ezekiel's reaction showed that Pelatiah, one of the corrupt city leaders

10:8 [z] Eze 1:8 **10:9** [a] Eze 1:15-16; Rev 21:20 **10:12** [b] Rev 4:6-8 [c] Eze 1:15-21 **10:14** [d] 1Ki 7:36 [e] Eze 1:6 [f] Eze 1:10; Rev 4:7 **10:15** [g] Eze 1:3, 5 **10:17** [h] Eze 1:20-21 **10:18** [i] Ps 18:10 **10:19** [j] Eze 11:1, 22 **10:20** [k] Eze 1:1 **10:21** [l] Eze 41:18 [m] Eze 1:6 **11:1** [n] Eze 8:16; 10:19; 43:4-5 **11:3** [o] Jer 1:13; Eze 24:3 [p] ver 7, 11 **11:4** [q] Eze 3:4, 17 **11:5** [r] Jer 17:10 **11:6** [s] Eze 7:23; 22:6 **11:7** [t] Eze 24:3-13, Mic 3:2-3 **11:8** [u] Pr 10:24 **11:9** [v] Ps 106:41 [w] Dt 28:36; Eze 5:8 **11:10** [x] 2Ki 14:25 **11:11** [y] ver 3 **11:12** [z] Lev 18:4; Eze 18:9 [a] Eze 8:10 **11:13** [b] ver 1 [c] Eze 9:8

The Promise of Israel's Return

14The word of the LORD came to me:
15"Son of man, the people of Jerusalem
have said of your fellow exiles and all the
other Israelites, 'They are far away from
the LORD; this land was given to us as our
possession.'[d]
16"Therefore say: 'This is what the Sovereign LORD says: Although I sent them
far away among the nations and scattered
them among the countries, yet for a little
while I have been a sanctuary[e] for them in
the countries where they have gone.'
17"Therefore say: 'This is what the Sovereign LORD says: I will gather you from the
nations and bring you back from the countries where you have been scattered, and I
will give you back the land of Israel again.'[f]
18"They will return to it and remove all its
vile images[g] and detestable idols.[h] 19I will
give them an undivided heart[i] and put a
new spirit in them; I will remove from them
their heart of stone[j] and give them a heart
of flesh.[k] 20Then they will follow my decrees
and be careful to keep my laws.[l] They will
be my people, and I will be their God.[m] 21But
as for those whose hearts are devoted to
their vile images and detestable idols, I will
bring down on their own heads what they
have done, declares the Sovereign LORD.[n]"
22Then the cherubim, with the wheels beside them, spread their wings, and the glory
of the God of Israel was above them.[o] 23The
glory[p] of the LORD went up from within the
city and stopped above the mountain[q] east
of it. 24The Spirit[r] lifted me up and brought
me to the exiles in Babylonia[a] in the vision[s]
given by the Spirit of God.
Then the vision I had seen went up from
me, 25and I told the exiles everything the
LORD had shown me.[t]

The Exile Symbolized

12 The word of the LORD came to me:
2"Son of man, you are living among a
rebellious people. They have eyes to see but
do not see and ears to hear but do not hear,
for they are a rebellious people.[u]
3"Therefore, son of man, pack your belongings for exile and in the daytime, as
they watch, set out and go from where you
are to another place. Perhaps[v] they will
understand,[w] though they are a rebellious
people.[x] 4During the daytime, while they
watch, bring out your belongings packed
for exile. Then in the evening, while they
are watching, go out like those who go into
exile.[y] 5While they watch, dig through the
wall and take your belongings out through
it. 6Put them on your shoulder as they are
watching and carry them out at dusk. Cover your face so that you cannot see the
land, for I have made you a sign[z] to the Israelites."
7So I did as I was commanded.[a] During
the day I brought out my things packed for
exile. Then in the evening I dug through
the wall with my hands. I took my belongings out at dusk, carrying them on my
shoulders while they watched.
8In the morning the word of the LORD
came to me: 9"Son of man, did not the Israelites, that rebellious people, ask you,
'What are you doing?'[b]
10"Say to them, 'This is what the Sovereign LORD says: This prophecy concerns
the prince in Jerusalem and all the Israelites who are there.' 11Say to them, 'I am a
sign to you.'
"As I have done, so it will be done to
them. They will go into exile as captives.[c]

---

[a] 24 Or *Chaldea*

(v. 1), was struck dead by God as undeniable proof that the prophet's message would come true. Ezekiel himself was awestruck and asked if this meant that God would not after all preserve a remnant.

11:15 *your fellow exiles.* The people in Jerusalem (representative of Judah) regarded the exiles as sinners because they had been deported to Babylon.

11:16 *I have been a sanctuary.* God explained to Ezekiel that the Hebrews taken captive and spread among foreign lands were actually the remnant whom God was protecting. God Himself would continue as their sanctuary—a word in Hebrew that literally means a "holy place."

11:18–20 *They will . . . remove all its vile images and detestable idols.* When the remnant returned to the land, they would abolish idolatry. At that time God would establish a new covenant with them (Jer. 31:31–34). Then God would pour out His Spirit (36:26–27; Joel 2:28–29) so that His people would become united in purpose and empowered to maintain their righteousness. They would finally and truly become His people (Ex. 6:6–8).

11:23 *The glory of the LORD went up.* The Hebrew term for "glory" literally means of "weight" or "significance" and refers to the wonder and majesty of the living God.

11:24–25 *The Spirit lifted me up.* Ezekiel's visions are not merely dreams; they were inspired by God Himself and thus were prophetic. ***Babylonia.*** This is an also translated Chaldea.

12:3–7 *pack your belongings for exile.* Ezekiel's next visual demonstration warned the captives already in Babylon that they should not expect a quick return to Jerusalem. He had already shown that the city would soon fall (ch. 4–5) and those not killed would be led into exile. These exiles should have understood Ezekiel's meaning.

12:11–14 *They will go into exile as captives.* Speaking in 592 B.C., Ezekiel predicted the

11:15 [d] Eze 33:24 **11:16** [e] Ps 90:1; 91:9; Isa 8:14 **11:17** [f] Jer 3:18; 24:5-6; Eze 28:25; 34:13 **11:18** [g] Eze 5:11 [h] Eze 37:23 **11:19** [i] Jer 32:39 [j] Zec 7:12 [k] Eze 18:31; 36:26; 2Co 3:3 **11:20** [l] Ps 105:45 [m] Eze 14:11; 36:26-28 **11:21** [n] Eze 9:10; 16:43 **11:22** [o] Eze 10:19 **11:23** [p] Eze 8:4; 10:4 [q] Zec 14:4 **11:24** [r] Eze 8:3 [s] 2Co 12:2-4 **11:25** [t] Eze 3:4,11 **12:2** [u] Isa 6:10; Eze 2:6-8; Mt 13:15 **12:3** [v] Jer 36:3 [w] Jer 26:3 [x] 2Ti 2:25-26 **12:4** [y] ver 12; Jer 39:4 **12:6** [z] ver 12; Isa 8:18; 20:3; Eze 4:3; 24:24 **12:7** [a] Eze 24:18; 37:10 **12:9** [b] Eze 17:12; 20:49; 24:19 **12:11** [c] 2Ki 25:7; Jer 15:2; 52:15

12"The prince among them will put his things on his shoulder at dusk[d] and leave, and a hole will be dug in the wall for him to go through. He will cover his face so that he cannot see the land.[e] 13I will spread my net[f] for him, and he will be caught in my snare;[g] I will bring him to Babylonia, the land of the Chaldeans, but he will not see[h] it, and there he will die.[i] 14I will scatter to the winds all those around him—his staff and all his troops—and I will pursue them with drawn sword.[j]

15"They will know that I am the LORD, when I disperse them among the nations and scatter them through the countries. 16But I will spare a few of them from the sword, famine and plague, so that in the nations where they go they may acknowledge all their detestable practices. Then they will know that I am the LORD.[k]"

17The word of the LORD came to me: 18"Son of man, tremble as you eat your food,[l] and shudder in fear as you drink your water. 19Say to the people of the land: 'This is what the Sovereign LORD says about those living in Jerusalem and in the land of Israel: They will eat their food in anxiety and drink their water in despair, for their land will be stripped of everything[m] in it because of the violence of all who live there.[n] 20The inhabited towns will be laid waste and the land will be desolate. Then you will know that I am the LORD.[o]'"

There Will Be No Delay

21The word of the LORD came to me: 22"Son of man, what is this proverb you have in the land of Israel: 'The days go by and every vision comes to nothing'?[p] 23Say to them, 'This is what the Sovereign LORD says: I am going to put an end to this proverb, and they will no longer quote it in Israel.' Say to them, 'The days are near when every vision will be fulfilled.[q] 24For there will be no more false visions or flattering divinations[r] among the people of Israel. 25But I the LORD will speak what I will, and it shall be fulfilled without delay. For in your days, you rebellious people, I will fulfill whatever I say, declares the Sovereign LORD.[s]'"

26The word of the LORD came to me: 27"Son of man, the Israelites are saying, 'The vision he sees is for many years from now, and he prophesies about the distant future.'[t]

28"Therefore say to them, 'This is what the Sovereign LORD says: None of my words will be delayed any longer; whatever I say will be fulfilled, declares the Sovereign LORD.'"

False Prophets Condemned

13 The word of the LORD came to me: 2"Son of man, prophesy against the prophets of Israel who are now prophesying. Say to those who prophesy out of their own imagination: 'Hear the word of the LORD![u] 3This is what the Sovereign LORD says: Woe to the foolish[a] prophets[v] who follow their own spirit and have seen nothing![w] 4Your prophets, Israel, are like jackals among ruins. 5You have not gone up to the breaches in the wall to repair[x] it for the people of Israel so that it will stand firm in the battle on the day of the LORD.[y] 6Their visions are false and their divinations a lie. Even though the LORD has not sent them, they say, "The LORD declares," and expect him to fulfill their words.[z] 7Have you not seen false visions and uttered lying divinations when you say, "The LORD declares," though I have not spoken?

[a] 3 Or *wicked*

---

deportation of Jerusalem's population to Babylon six years later and prophesied exactly what would happen to their leader Zedekiah. The king would attempt to escape by night, secretly and in disguise; but he would be caught and blinded by the Babylonians, then carried off to Babylon where he would later die.

12:15–16 *They will know that I am the LORD.* The defeat of God's people would not indicate the Lord's lack of strength, but the serious consequences of sin against Him. Yet He would demonstrate that His purpose had always been to restore His people to Himself (Heb. 12:1–11). Through the difficult experience, His people would learn that their God was both holy and loving. Sin offended Him, but He still would reach out to restore the sinner.

12:22 *The days go by and every vision comes to nothing.* This proverb among the exiles indicates how hardened they were to Ezekiel's prophecies. Although already captive, the people were cynical and apathetic, mistakenly thinking that a delay in judgment meant no judgment, at least in their lifetime (vv. 25,27–28; 2 Pet. 3:3–4).

12:23–25 *The days are near when every vision will be fulfilled.* This proverb would replace the old one (v. 22), and false prophets opposing Ezekiel would cease to speak. The exiles would live to see the judgment on Jerusalem fulfilled.

13:2–4 *jackals among ruins.* The word translated "ruins" conveys the idea of open, desolate places. In the immediate context (v. 5), the jackals are pictured roaming amid the rubble of ruined city walls. The prophets were fools because they confused their own thoughts with God's. They were like jackals among the ruins because they scavenged for themselves while causing, ignoring, and profiting from the human wreckage surrounding them.

13:5 *the day of the LORD.* This phrase refers to times when God triumphs (7:19; 30:3). It is particularly used by the prophets to describe those periods in which

12:12 [d] Jer 39:4 [e] Jer 52:7 **12:13** [f] Eze 17:20; 19:8; Hos 7:12 [g] Isa 24:17-18 [h] Jer 39:7 [i] Jer 52:11; Eze 17:16 **12:14** [j] 2Ki 25:5; Eze 5:10, 12 **12:16** [k] Jer 22:8-9; Eze 6:8-10; 14:22 **12:18** [l] La 5:9; Eze 4:16 **12:19** [m] Eze 6:6-14; Mic 7:13; Zec 7:14 [n] Eze 4:16; 23:33 **12:20** [o] Isa 7:23-24; Jer 4:7 **12:22** [p] Eze 11:3; Am 6:3; 2Pe 3:4 **12:23** [q] Ps 37:13; Joel 2:1; Zep 1:14 **12:24** [r] Jer 14:14; Eze 13:23; Zec 13:2-4 **12:25** [s] Isa 14:24; Hab 1:5 **12:27** [t] Da 10:14 **13:2** [u] ver 17; Jer 23:16; 37:19 **13:3** [v] La 2:14 [w] Jer 23:25-32 **13:5** [x] Isa 58:12; Eze 22:30 [y] Eze 7:19 **13:6** [z] Jer 28:15; Eze 22:28

8“ ‘Therefore this is what the Sovereign LORD says: Because of your false words and lying visions, I am against you, declares the Sovereign LORD. 9My hand will be against the prophets who see false visions and utter lying divinations. They will not belong to the council of my people or be listed in the records[a] of Israel, nor will they enter the land of Israel. Then you will know that I am the Sovereign LORD.[b]

10“ ‘Because they lead my people astray,[c] saying, “Peace,” when there is no peace, and because, when a flimsy wall is built, they cover it with whitewash,[d] 11therefore tell those who cover it with whitewash that it is going to fall. Rain will come in torrents, and I will send hailstones hurtling down, and violent winds will burst forth.[e] 12When the wall collapses, will people not ask you, “Where is the whitewash you covered it with?”

13“ ‘Therefore this is what the Sovereign LORD says: In my wrath I will unleash a violent wind, and in my anger hailstones[f] and torrents of rain will fall with destructive fury.[g] 14I will tear down the wall you have covered with whitewash and will level it to the ground so that its foundation[h] will be laid bare. When it[a] falls,[i] you will be destroyed in it; and you will know that I am the LORD. 15So I will pour out my wrath against the wall and against those who covered it with whitewash. I will say to you, “The wall is gone and so are those who whitewashed it, 16those prophets of Israel who prophesied to Jerusalem and saw visions of peace for her when there was no peace, declares the Sovereign LORD.[j]” ’

17“Now, son of man, set your face against the daughters[k] of your people who prophesy out of their own imagination. Prophesy against them[l] 18and say, ‘This is what the Sovereign LORD says: Woe to the women who sew magic charms on all their wrists and make veils of various lengths for their heads in order to ensnare people. Will you ensnare the lives of my people but preserve your own? 19You have profaned[m] me among my people for a few handfuls of barley and scraps of bread. By lying to my people, who listen to lies, you have killed those who should not have died and have spared those who should not live.[n]

20“ ‘Therefore this is what the Sovereign LORD says: I am against your magic charms with which you ensnare people like birds and I will tear them from your arms; I will set free the people that you ensnare like birds. 21I will tear off your veils and save my people from your hands, and they will no longer fall prey to your power. Then you will know that I am the LORD.[o] 22Because you disheartened the righteous with your lies, when I had brought them no grief, and because you encouraged the wicked not to turn from their evil ways and so save their lives,[p] 23therefore you will no longer see false visions or practice divination.[q] I will save my people from your hands. And then you will know that I am the LORD.[r]’ ”

Idolaters Condemned

14 Some of the elders of Israel came to me and sat down in front of me.[s] 2Then the word of the LORD came to me: 3“Son of man, these men have set up idols in their hearts and put wicked stumbling blocks[t] before their faces. Should I let them inquire of me at all?[u] 4Therefore speak to them and tell them, ‘This is what the Sovereign LORD says: When any of the Israelites set up idols in their hearts and put a wicked stumbling block before their faces and then go to a prophet, I the LORD will answer them myself in keeping with their great idolatry. 5I will do this to recapture the hearts of the people of Israel, who have all deserted[v] me for their idols.’[w]

6“Therefore say to the people of Israel, ‘This is what the Sovereign LORD says: Repent! Turn from your idols and renounce all your detestable practices![x]

---

a 14 Or *the city*

God delivers people or judges them (Joel 2:1; Zeph. 1:7). In that day, God will actively bring about His purposes for the world; He will rescue the righteous and judge evildoers.

13:10 – 16 ***you will be destroyed in it.*** The false prophets would experience God's wrath — just as the walls of Jerusalem which were being constructed at that time would be destroyed. Jerusalem would be conquered and captured for the sins of its inhabitants. The preaching of a false peace had prompted people to build for a "certain" future, but only the opposite was certain. The false prophets had deceived the people with false hopes of comfort and prosperity (v. 10). Their deception placed them not only at odds with God's truth, but also with God Himself. Their destruction was certain.

13:17 – 19 ***set your face against the daughters of your people.*** The Hebrew women who were false prophetesses were confusing their own ideas with God's and casting magic death spells through sorcery or witchcraft (Lev. 19:26).

14:1 – 3 ***Some of the elders of Israel.*** God revealed to Ezekiel that this group consisted of double-minded men (1 Kin. 18:21; Matt. 6:24; James 1:5 – 8). Outwardly, they came to seek a word from God through His true prophet Ezekiel, but in their hearts they harbored loyalties to other gods.

14:5 ***recapture the hearts of the people of Israel.*** These words announce God's restorative purpose (Prov. 3:12; Rev. 3:19) in allowing sin to run its course.

13:9 [a] Jer 17:13 [b] Eze 20:38 **13:10** [c] Jer 50:6 [d] Eze 7:25; 22:28 **13:11** [e] Eze 38:22 **13:13** [f] Rev 11:19; 16:21 [g] Ex 9:25; Isa 30:30 **13:14** [h] Mic 1:6 [i] Jer 6:15 **13:16** [j] Isa 57:21; Jer 6:14 **13:17** [k] Rev 2:20 [l] ver 2 **13:19** [m] Eze 20:39; 22:26 [n] Pr 28:21 **13:21** [o] Ps 91:3 **13:22** [p] Jer 23:14; Eze 33:14-16 **13:23** [q] ver 6; Eze 12:24 [r] Mic 3:6 **14:1** [s] Eze 8:1; 20:1 **14:3** [t] ver 7; Eze 7:19 [u] Isa 1:15; Eze 20:31 **14:5** [v] Zec 11:8 [w] Jer 2:11 **14:6** [x] Isa 2:20; 30:22

7"'When any of the Israelites or any foreigner[y] residing in Israel separate themselves from me and set up idols in their hearts and put a wicked stumbling block before their faces and then go to a prophet to inquire of me, I the LORD will answer them myself. 8I will set my face against[z] them and make them an example and a byword.[a] I will remove them from my people. Then you will know that I am the LORD.

9"'And if the prophet[b] is enticed[c] to utter a prophecy, I the LORD have enticed that prophet, and I will stretch out my hand against him and destroy him from among my people Israel.[d] 10They will bear their guilt—the prophet will be as guilty as the one who consults him. 11Then the people of Israel will no longer stray[e] from me, nor will they defile themselves anymore with all their sins. They will be my people, and I will be their God, declares the Sovereign LORD.[f]'"

Jerusalem's Judgment Inescapable

12The word of the LORD came to me: 13"Son of man, if a country sins against me by being unfaithful and I stretch out my hand against it to cut off its food supply[g] and send famine upon it and kill its people and their animals,[h] 14even if these three men—Noah,[i] Daniel[a][j] and Job[k]—were in it, they could save only themselves by their righteousness,[l] declares the Sovereign LORD.

15"Or if I send wild beasts[m] through that country and they leave it childless and it becomes desolate so that no one can pass through it because of the beasts,[n] 16as surely as I live, declares the Sovereign LORD, even if these three men were in it, they could not save their own sons or daughters. They alone would be saved, but the land would be desolate.[o]

17"Or if I bring a sword[p] against that country and say, 'Let the sword pass throughout the land,' and I kill its people and their animals,[q] 18as surely as I live, declares the Sovereign LORD, even if these three men were in it, they could not save their own sons or daughters. They alone would be saved.

19"Or if I send a plague into that land and pour out my wrath[r] on it through bloodshed, killing its people and their animals,[s] 20as surely as I live, declares the Sovereign LORD, even if Noah, Daniel and Job were in it, they could save neither son nor daughter. They would save only themselves by their righteousness.[t]

21"For this is what the Sovereign LORD says: How much worse will it be when I send against Jerusalem my four dreadful judgments—sword and famine and wild beasts and plague—to kill its men and their animals![u] 22Yet there will be some survivors—sons and daughters who will be brought out of it.[v] They will come to you, and when you see their conduct[w] and their actions, you will be consoled regarding the disaster I have brought on Jerusalem—every disaster I have brought on it. 23You will be consoled when you see their conduct and their actions, for you will know that I have done nothing in it without cause, declares the Sovereign LORD.[x]"

Jerusalem as a Useless Vine

15 The word of the LORD came to me: 2"Son of man, how is the wood of a vine[y] different from that of a branch from any of the trees in the forest? 3Is wood ever taken from it to make anything useful? Do they make pegs from it to hang things on? 4And after it is thrown on the fire as fuel and the fire burns both ends and chars the middle, is it then useful for anything?[z] 5If it was not useful for anything when it was whole, how much less can it be made into something useful when the fire has burned it and it is charred?

6"Therefore this is what the Sovereign LORD says: As I have given the wood of the vine among the trees of the forest as fuel for the fire, so will I treat the people living in Jerusalem. 7I will set my face against[a] them. Although they have come out of the fire, the fire will yet consume them. And when I set my face against them, you will know that I am the LORD.[b] 8I will make the land desolate[c] because they have been unfaithful,[d] declares the Sovereign LORD."

[a] 14 Or *Danel,* a man of renown in ancient literature; also in verse 20

14:8 *I will remove them from my people.* The unrepentant idolater would be separated not only from God, but also from God's people (13:9). This experience would be a strong visual warning and an international example—proverb—of God's absolute honoring of His promise to punish disobedience with cursing (Lev. 20:1–7).

14:9–11 *They will bear their guilt.* The relationship between God's sovereignty and human responsibility is implicit in these verses. God allows false preaching for His own inscrutable purposes, but the preacher is held accountable for the content of the message. These were Israelite false prophets who deliberately ignored the truth and mixed it with falsehood.

15:6 *the vine among the trees of the forest.* Unlike an olive tree whose wood is also useful, the vine has only one use, to bear grapes.

15:6–8 *the fire will yet consume them.* God had designed the people of Israel for a particular purpose, to bring glory to His name by living faithfully to His covenant and by bringing the nations to the

14:7 [y] Ex 12:48; 20:10 **14:8** [z] Eze 15:7 [a] Eze 5:15 **14:9** [b] Jer 14:15 [c] Jer 4:10 [d] 1Ki 22:23 **14:11** [e] Eze 48:11 [f] Eze 11:19-20; 37:23 **14:13** [g] Lev 26:26 [h] Eze 5:16; 6:14; 15:8 **14:14** [i] Ge 6:8 [j] ver 20; Eze 28:3; Da 1:6; 6:13 [k] Job 1:1 [l] Job 42:9; Jer 15:1; Eze 18:20 **14:15** [m] Eze 5:17 [n] Lev 26:22 **14:16** [o] Eze 18:20 **14:17** [p] Lev 26:25; Eze 5:12; 21:3-4 [q] Eze 25:13; Zep 1:3 **14:19** [r] Eze 7:8 [s] Eze 38:22 **14:20** [t] ver 14 **14:21** [u] Jer 15:3; Eze 5:17; 33:27; Am 4:6-10; Rev 6:8 **14:22** [v] Eze 12:16 [w] Eze 20:43 **14:23** [x] Jer 22:8-9 **15:2** [y] Isa 5:1-7; Jer 2:21; Hos 10:1 **15:4** [z] Eze 19:14; Jn 15:6 **15:7** [a] Ps 34:16; Eze 14:8 [b] Isa 24:18; Am 9:1-4 **15:8** [c] Eze 14:13 [d] Eze 17:20

Jerusalem as an Adulterous Wife

16 The word of the LORD came to me:
2"Son of man, confront Jerusalem
with her detestable practices[e] 3and say,
'This is what the Sovereign LORD says to
Jerusalem: Your ancestry[f] and birth were
in the land of the Canaanites; your father
was an Amorite and your mother a Hittite.[g]
4On the day you were born[h] your cord was
not cut, nor were you washed with water
to make you clean, nor were you rubbed
with salt or wrapped in cloths. 5No one
looked on you with pity or had compassion enough to do any of these things for
you. Rather, you were thrown out into the
open field, for on the day you were born
you were despised.
6" 'Then I passed by and saw you kicking
about in your blood, and as you lay there in
your blood I said to you, "Live!"[a][i] 7I made
you grow[j] like a plant of the field. You grew
and developed and entered puberty. Your
breasts had formed and your hair had
grown, yet you were stark naked.[k]
8" 'Later I passed by, and when I looked
at you and saw that you were old enough
for love, I spread the corner of my garment[l]
over you and covered your naked body. I
gave you my solemn oath and entered into
a covenant with you, declares the Sovereign LORD, and you became mine.[m]
9" 'I bathed you with water and washed[n]
the blood from you and put ointments
on you. 10I clothed you with an embroidered[o] dress and put sandals of fine leather on you. I dressed you in fine linen[p] and
covered you with costly garments.[q] 11I
adorned you with jewelry:[r] I put bracelets[s]
on your arms and a necklace[t] around your
neck, 12and I put a ring on your nose,[u] earrings on your ears and a beautiful crown[v]
on your head. 13So you were adorned with
gold and silver; your clothes were of fine
linen and costly fabric and embroidered
cloth. Your food was honey, olive oil[w] and
the finest flour. You became very beautiful
and rose to be a queen.[x] 14And your fame[y]
spread among the nations on account of
your beauty,[z] because the splendor I had
given you made your beauty perfect, declares the Sovereign LORD.
15" 'But you trusted in your beauty and
used your fame to become a prostitute.
You lavished your favors on anyone who
passed by[a] and your beauty became his.[b]
16You took some of your garments to make
gaudy high places, where you carried on
your prostitution.[c] You went to him, and
he possessed your beauty.[b] 17You also
took the fine jewelry I gave you, the jewelry made of my gold and silver, and you
made for yourself male idols and engaged
in prostitution with them.[d] 18And you took
your embroidered clothes to put on them,
and you offered my oil and incense before
them. 19Also the food I provided for you—
the flour, olive oil and honey I gave you to
eat—you offered as fragrant incense before them. That is what happened, declares
the Sovereign LORD.[e]
20" 'And you took your sons and daughters[f] whom you bore to me[g] and sacrificed
them as food to the idols. Was your prostitution not enough?[h] 21You slaughtered my
children and sacrificed them to the idols.[i]

a 6 A few Hebrew manuscripts, Septuagint and Syriac; most Hebrew manuscripts repeat *and as you lay there in your blood I said to you, "Live!"*
b 16 The meaning of the Hebrew for this sentence is uncertain.

---

knowledge of the Lord. Instead, Israel had become like the pagan nations around them.

16:2 *confront Jerusalem with her detestable practices.* What follows is an animated development of the dreary story, designed to teach errant Jerusalem the real nature of her character in the eyes of God. The word "abominations" describes that which makes one physically ill.

16:3 *your father was an Amorite and your mother a Hittite.* These shocking words refer to the cultural and moral origins of Jerusalem. Ancient Canaan was inhabited by Semitic and non-Semitic peoples. The Amorites and Hittites are associated in Scripture with the southern hill country, where Jerusalem is (Num. 13:29). The point is that non-Israelites founded this city. Jebusites controlled it when the Israelites entered the land under Joshua (Josh. 15:8). Israel did not obtain full control of the city until David conquered it (2 Sam. 5:6–7). In other words, Israel was not as pure as it thought it was.

16:4 *nor were you rubbed with salt.* God reminds Jerusalem that He had rescued them from being like an abandoned newborn child—unwashed, unsanitary, and exposed to the elements to die. God alone has given her glory.

16:6 *Live!* Ezekiel warned the Jews remaining in Jerusalem to repent, reminding them that not merely their existence, but their living relation to God, was dependent upon His free grace. God alone is the Author of eternal life, just as He is Creator of all life (John 5:24).

16:7–9 *Your breasts had formed.* The city is compared to a young woman, mature and lovely. Yet it was naked and bare until God covered it with a relationship of covenantal love. This began when David moved the ark of the covenant there and God established the covenant with David (2 Sam. 6:1–7:17).

16:15 *you trusted in your beauty.* These words indict God's people for forgetting that their fame and fortune were God's gifts and not their own doing (v. 14). They relied on themselves and their gifts instead of on God. They came to believe that their material wealth and health as a nation absolutely

16:2 [e] Eze 20:4; 22:2 **16:3** [f] Eze 21:30 [g] ver 45
16:4 [h] Hos 2:3 **16:6** [i] Ex 19:4 **16:7** [j] Dt 1:10 [k] Ex 1:7
16:8 [l] Ru 3:9 [m] Jer 2:2; Hos 2:7, 19-20 **16:9** [n] Ru 3:3
16:10 [o] Ex 26:36 [p] Eze 27:16 [q] ver 18 **16:11** [r] Eze 23:40
[s] Isa 3:19; Eze 23:42 [t] Ge 41:42 **16:12** [u] Isa 3:21
[v] Isa 28:5; Jer 13:18 **16:13** [w] 1Sa 10:1 [x] Dt 32:13-14;
1Ki 4:21 **16:14** [y] 1Ki 10:24 [z] La 2:15 **16:15** [a] ver 25
[b] Isa 57:8; Jer 2:20; Eze 23:3; 27:3 **16:16** [c] 2Ki 23:7
16:17 [d] Eze 7:20 **16:19** [e] Hos 2:8 **16:20** [f] Jer 7:31
[g] Ex 13:2 [h] Ps 106:37-38; Isa 57:5; Eze 23:37
16:21 [i] 2Ki 17:17; Jer 19:5

22In all your detestable practices and your
prostitution you did not remember the days
of your youth,[j] when you were naked and
bare, kicking about in your blood.[k]
23“ ‘Woe! Woe to you, declares the Sovereign LORD. In addition to all your other
wickedness, 24you built a mound for yourself and made a lofty shrine[l] in every public square.[m] 25At every street corner you
built your lofty shrines and degraded your
beauty, spreading your legs with increasing promiscuity to anyone who passed
by.[n] 26You engaged in prostitution with the
Egyptians, your neighbors with large genitals, and aroused my anger[o] with your increasing promiscuity.[p] 27So I stretched out
my hand[q] against you and reduced your
territory; I gave you over to the greed of
your enemies, the daughters of the Philistines,[r] who were shocked by your lewd conduct. 28You engaged in prostitution with
the Assyrians[s] too, because you were in-
satiable; and even after that, you still were
not satisfied. 29Then you increased your
promiscuity to include Babylonia,[a][t] a land
of merchants, but even with this you were
not satisfied.
30“ ‘I am filled with fury against you,[b]
declares the Sovereign LORD, when you do
all these things, acting like a brazen prostitute![u] 31When you built your mounds at
every street corner and made your lofty
shrines[v] in every public square, you were
unlike a prostitute, because you scorned
payment.
32“ ‘You adulterous wife! You prefer
strangers to your own husband! 33All prostitutes receive gifts, but you give gifts[w] to
all your lovers, bribing them to come to you
from everywhere for your illicit favors.[x]
34So in your prostitution you are the opposite of others; no one runs after you for
your favors. You are the very opposite, for
you give payment and none is given to you.
35“ ‘Therefore, you prostitute, hear the
word of the LORD! 36This is what the Sovereign LORD says: Because you poured out
your lust and exposed your naked body
in your promiscuity with your lovers, and
because of all your detestable idols, and
because you gave them your children's
blood,[y] 37therefore I am going to gather all
your lovers, with whom you found pleasure, those you loved as well as those you
hated. I will gather them against you from
all around and will strip you in front of
them, and they will see you stark naked.[z]
38I will sentence you to the punishment
of women who commit adultery and who
shed blood;[a] I will bring on you the blood
vengeance of my wrath and jealous anger.[b]
39Then I will deliver you into the hands of
your lovers, and they will tear down your
mounds and destroy your lofty shrines.
They will strip you of your clothes and take
your fine jewelry and leave you stark naked.[c] 40They will bring a mob against you,
who will stone[d] you and hack you to pieces
with their swords. 41They will burn down[e]
your houses and inflict punishment on you
in the sight of many women.[f] I will put a
stop[g] to your prostitution, and you will no
longer pay your lovers. 42Then my wrath
against you will subside and my jealous
anger will turn away from you; I will be
calm and no longer angry.[h]
43“ ‘Because you did not remember[i] the
days of your youth but enraged me with all
these things, I will surely bring down[j] on
your head what you have done, declares
the Sovereign LORD. Did you not add lewdness to all your other detestable practices?[k]
44“ ‘Everyone who quotes proverbs will
quote this proverb about you: “Like mother, like daughter.” 45You are a true daughter of your mother, who despised her husband and her children; and you are a true
sister of your sisters, who despised their
husbands and their children. Your mother
was a Hittite and your father an Amorite.[l]
46Your older sister was Samaria, who lived
to the north of you with her daughters;
and your younger sister, who lived to the
south of you with her daughters, was Sodom.[m] 47You not only followed their ways
and copied their detestable practices, but
in all your ways you soon became more

[a] 29 Or *Chaldea* [b] 30 Or *How feverish is your heart,*

---

demonstrated God's approval of their spiritual life, even though they were becoming spiritually corrupt.

16:27–29 *engaged in prostitution.* Jerusalem's kings had sought political alliances with Assyria (2 Kin. 15:17–20) and Babylon (2 Kin. 20:12–19) instead of relying on their God for security. Probably a part of the treaty-making ceremonies was to worship the other nation's god. For Israel to do this would be a violation of the First Commandment.

16:36 *poured out your lust.* Jerusalem was filthy spiritually because the city had soiled itself by worshiping foreign idols and practicing infanticide (vv. 20–21; Deut. 12:29–32).

16:41 *I will put a stop to your prostitution.* During the captivity, Israel would abandon idolatry and polytheism, as Ezekiel predicted. God's anger over the people's sin would be satisfied.

16:44–47 *Samaria ... Sodom.* Along with Jerusalem, these three are presented as sisters in the religiously and morally corrupt cultures in Canaan. Ezekiel even makes the point that Jerusalem had become more corrupt than the other two.

16:22 [j] Jer 2:2; Hos 11:1 [k] ver 6 **16:24** [l] ver 31; Isa 57:7 [m] Ps 78:58; Jer 2:20; 3:2; Eze 20:28 **16:25** [n] ver 15; Pr 9:14 **16:26** [o] Eze 8:17 [p] Eze 20:8; 23:19-21 **16:27** [q] Eze 20:33 [r] 2Ch 28:18 **16:28** [s] 2Ki 16:7 **16:29** [t] Eze 23:14-17 **16:30** [u] Jer 3:3 **16:31** [v] ver 24 **16:33** [w] Isa 30:6; 57:9 [x] Hos 8:9-10 **16:36** [y] Jer 19:5; Eze 23:10 **16:37** [z] Jer 13:22 **16:38** [a] Eze 23:45 [b] Lev 20:10; Eze 23:25 **16:39** [c] Eze 23:26; Hos 2:3 **16:40** [d] Jn 8:5,7 **16:41** [e] Dt 13:16 [f] Eze 23:10 [g] Eze 23:27,48 **16:42** [h] Isa 54:9; Eze 5:13; 39:29 **16:43** [i] Ps 78:42 [j] Eze 22:31 [k] ver 22; Eze 11:21 **16:45** [l] Eze 23:2 **16:46** [m] Ge 13:10-13; Eze 23:4

depraved than they.[n] 48 As surely as I live,
declares the Sovereign LORD, your sister
Sodom and her daughters never did what
you and your daughters have done.[o]
49 " 'Now this was the sin of your sister
Sodom:[p] She and her daughters were arrogant,[q] overfed and unconcerned; they did
not help the poor and needy.[r] 50 They were
haughty and did detestable things before
me. Therefore I did away with them as you
have seen.[s] 51 Samaria did not commit half
the sins you did. You have done more detestable things than they, and have made
your sisters seem righteous by all these
things you have done.[t] 52 Bear your disgrace, for you have furnished some justification for your sisters. Because your
sins were more vile than theirs, they appear more righteous than you. So then, be
ashamed and bear your disgrace, for you
have made your sisters appear righteous.
53 " 'However, I will restore[u] the fortunes
of Sodom and her daughters and of Samaria and her daughters, and your fortunes
along with them, 54 so that you may bear
your disgrace[v] and be ashamed of all you
have done in giving them comfort. 55 And
your sisters, Sodom with her daughters
and Samaria with her daughters, will return to what they were before; and you
and your daughters will return to what
you were before.[w] 56 You would not even
mention your sister Sodom in the day of
your pride, 57 before your wickedness was
uncovered. Even so, you are now scorned
by the daughters of Edom[a][x] and all her
neighbors and the daughters of the Philistines—all those around you who despise
you. 58 You will bear the consequences of
your lewdness and your detestable practices, declares the LORD.[y]
59 " 'This is what the Sovereign LORD
says: I will deal with you as you deserve,
because you have despised my oath by
breaking the covenant.[z] 60 Yet I will remember the covenant I made with you in the
days of your youth, and I will establish an
everlasting covenant[a] with you. 61 Then you
will remember your ways and be ashamed[b]
when you receive your sisters, both those
who are older than you and those who are
younger. I will give them to you as daughters, but not on the basis of my covenant
with you. 62 So I will establish my covenant
with you, and you will know that I am the
LORD.[c] 63 Then, when I make atonement[d] for
you for all you have done, you will remember and be ashamed and never again open
your mouth[e] because of your humiliation,
declares the Sovereign LORD.[f] ' "

Two Eagles and a Vine

17 The word of the LORD came to me:
2 "Son of man, set forth an allegory
and tell it to the Israelites as a parable.[g]
3 Say to them, 'This is what the Sovereign
LORD says: A great eagle[h] with powerful
wings, long feathers and full plumage of
varied colors came to Lebanon.[i] Taking
hold of the top of a cedar, 4 he broke off its
topmost shoot and carried it away to a land
of merchants, where he planted it in a city
of traders.
5 " 'He took one of the seedlings of the
land and put it in fertile soil. He planted
it like a willow by abundant water,[j] 6 and
it sprouted and became a low, spreading
vine. Its branches turned toward him, but
its roots remained under it. So it became
a vine and produced branches and put out
leafy boughs.
7 " 'But there was another great eagle
with powerful wings and full plumage. The
vine now sent out its roots toward him from
the plot where it was planted and stretched
out its branches to him for water.[k] 8 It had
been planted in good soil by abundant water so that it would produce branches, bear
fruit and become a splendid vine.'

---

[a] 57 Many Hebrew manuscripts and Syriac; most Hebrew manuscripts, Septuagint and Vulgate *Aram*

16:53–59 *despised my oath by breaking the covenant.* The punishment of the exile and captivity was appropriate. The clear promise of the covenant was that blessings and curses were dependent upon Israel's obedience or disobedience (Ex. 24; Lev. 26; Deut. 28–29).

16:60–63 *Yet I will remember.* Despite Jerusalem's disobedience to the Mosaic covenant and the resulting punishment, the covenant with Abraham—*My covenant*—would still be honored. Fulfillment of the covenant with Abraham did not depend on the people's faithfulness; God had made the promise and he would keep it (Gen. 15; 17:7–8; Lev. 26:40–45; Ps. 145:13). The everlasting covenant had been made with Abraham before the Hebrew nation even existed. This covenant would be remembered and reestablished with the exiled Judeans. At that time, God's people would be ashamed by the contrast between their faithlessness and God's faithfulness and the fact that they were being exalted over those who were less sinful—Sodom and Samaria. The people of these other sinful nations would also inherit land, but only by God's grace, because no such covenant was made with them.

17:2–10 *set forth an allegory and tell it ... as a parable.* Both of these words can be used to refer to an allegory. The "parable" primarily refers to a comparison between two things. A "riddle" was sometimes used as a political contest of mental competition between kings, in which the loser would submit to the winner and be killed. The details of the allegory: *great eagle* is the king of Babylon (v. 12);

16:47 [n] 2Ki 21:9; Eze 5:7 **16:48** [o] Mt 10:15; 11:23-24 **16:49** [p] Ge 13:13 [q] Ps 138:6 [r] Eze 18:7, 12, 16; Lk 12:16-20 **16:50** [s] Ge 18:20-21; 19:5 **16:51** [t] Jer 3:8-11 **16:53** [u] Isa 19:24-25 **16:54** [v] Jer 2:26; Eze 14:22 **16:55** [w] Mal 3:4 **16:57** [x] 2Ki 16:6 **16:58** [y] Eze 23:49 **16:59** [z] Eze 17:19 **16:60** [a] Jer 32:40; Eze 37:26 **16:61** [b] Eze 20:43 **16:62** [c] Jer 24:7; Eze 20:37, 43-44; Hos 2:19-20 **16:63** [d] Ps 65:3; 79:9 [e] Ro 3:19 [f] Ps 39:9; Da 9:7-8 **17:2** [g] Eze 20:49 **17:3** [h] Hos 8:1 [i] Jer 22:23 **17:5** [j] Dt 8:7-9; Isa 44:4 **17:7** [k] Eze 31:4

9"Say to them, 'This is what the Sovereign LORD says: Will it thrive? Will it not be uprooted and stripped of its fruit so that it withers? All its new growth will wither. It will not take a strong arm or many people to pull it up by the roots. 10It has been planted,[l] but will it thrive? Will it not wither completely when the east wind strikes it—wither away in the plot where it grew?' "

11Then the word of the LORD came to me: 12"Say to this rebellious people, 'Do you not know what these things mean?[m]' Say to them: 'The king of Babylon went to Jerusalem and carried off her king and her nobles,[n] bringing them back with him to Babylon.[o] 13Then he took a member of the royal family and made a treaty with him, putting him under oath.[p] He also carried away the leading men of the land, 14so that the kingdom would be brought low,[q] unable to rise again, surviving only by keeping his treaty. 15But the king rebelled[r] against him by sending his envoys to Egypt to get horses and a large army.[s] Will he succeed? Will he who does such things escape? Will he break the treaty and yet escape?[t]

16" 'As surely as I live, declares the Sovereign LORD, he shall die[u] in Babylon, in the land of the king who put him on the throne, whose oath he despised and whose treaty he broke.[v] 17Pharaoh[w] with his mighty army and great horde will be of no help to him in war, when ramps[x] are built and siege works erected to destroy many lives.[y] 18He despised the oath by breaking the covenant. Because he had given his hand in pledge[z] and yet did all these things, he shall not escape.

19" 'Therefore this is what the Sovereign LORD says: As surely as I live, I will repay him for despising my oath and breaking my covenant.[a] 20I will spread my net[b] for him, and he will be caught in my snare. I will bring him to Babylon and execute judgment[c] on him there because he was unfaithful to me. 21All his choice troops will fall by the sword,[d] and the survivors[e] will be scattered to the winds.[f] Then you will know that I the LORD have spoken.

22" 'This is what the Sovereign LORD says: I myself will take a shoot from the very top of a cedar and plant it; I will break off a tender sprig from its topmost shoots and plant it on a high and lofty mountain.[g] 23On the mountain heights of Israel I will plant it; it will produce branches and bear fruit and become a splendid cedar. Birds of every kind will nest in it; they will find shelter in the shade of its branches.[h] 24All the trees of the forest[i] will know that I the LORD bring down the tall tree and make the low tree grow tall. I dry up the green tree and make the dry tree flourish.

" 'I the LORD have spoken, and I will do it.[j]' "

The One Who Sins Will Die

18 The word of the LORD came to me: 2"What do you people mean by quoting this proverb about the land of Israel:

" 'The parents eat sour grapes,
and the children's teeth are set on edge'?[k]

3"As surely as I live, declares the Sovereign LORD, you will no longer quote this proverb in Israel. 4For everyone belongs to me, the parent as well as the child—both alike belong to me. The one who sins is the one who will die.[l]

Lebanon symbolizes Canaan, of which Jerusalem (v. 12) is the major city; *the top of a cedar* is the king of Jerusalem and Judah (v. 12); topmost shootrefers to the nobility of Judah; the *city of traders* is Babylon; *seedlings* is a member of the royal family (v. 13); the *fertile field* is the land where this royal offspring would rule (vv. 13–14); *another great eagle* is the king of Egypt (v. 15); and the *vine* is the remnant and ruler left in Judah. This remnant failed to prosper because they made a treaty with the Egyptian Pharaoh. As a result, even the remnant was slain and scattered by Babylon's army (vv. 15–21).

17:11–21 ***Say to this rebellious people.*** Since Ezekiel had preached earlier about Jerusalem's past abominations (ch. 16), the people were likely charging God with unfairness in punishing the present population. Ezekiel points out that present and past sins make God's actions just and fair. In this section, the Lord explains His grounds for using Babylon to judge Judah.

17:22 ***I myself will take.*** In contrast to human kings, God declared that He personally would pick out, plant, and make prominent "a tender sprig". Cedar branches are symbolic of rulers on the Davidic throne (vv. 3–4,12–13) and elsewhere of a line of David's descendants prophesied to produce the Messiah (2 Sam. 7:16; Is. 11:1–5; Jer. 22:24–30; Zech. 6:9–13; Matt. 1:1–17).

17:23–24 ***make the dry tree flourish.*** What was accomplished in the restoration under Zerubbabel was a fulfillment of this promise. But as is often the case, in biblical prophecy, the greater fulfillment is still to come in the reign of the Savior King.

18:2–3 ***set on edge.*** The Hebrew word that is rendered here is literally "made dull" but can refer to a sour sensation. The main idea of the proverb is that children are affected by their parents' behavioral choices just as eating sour grapes produces a bitter taste. However, the people were interpreting and applying this proverb incorrectly; therefore, God said they should not use it any longer.

18:4 ***The one who sins is the one who will die.*** In this verse, the physical, earthly consequences

17:10 [l] Hos 13:15 **17:12** [m] Eze 12:9 [n] 2Ki 24:15 [o] Eze 24:19 **17:13** [p] 2Ch 36:13 **17:14** [q] Eze 29:14 **17:15** [r] Jer 52:3 [s] Dt 17:16 [t] Jer 34:3; 38:18 **17:16** [u] Jer 52:11; Eze 12:13 [v] 2Ki 24:17 **17:17** [w] Jer 37:7 [x] Eze 4:2 [y] Isa 36:6; Jer 37:5; Eze 29:6-7 **17:18** [z] 1Ch 29:24 **17:19** [a] Eze 16:59 **17:20** [b] Eze 12:13; 32:3 [c] Jer 2:35; Eze 20:36 **17:21** [d] Eze 12:14 [e] 2Ki 25:11 [f] 2Ki 25:5 **17:22** [g] Jer 23:5; Eze 20:40; 36:1,36; 37:22 **17:23** [h] Ps 92:12; Isa 2:2; Eze 31:6; Da 4:12; Hos 14:5-7; Mt 13:32 **17:24** [i] Ps 96:12 [j] Eze 19:12; 21:26; 22:14; Am 9:11 **18:2** [k] Isa 3:15; Jer 31:29; La 5:7 **18:4** [l] ver 20; Isa 42:5; Ro 6:23

5 "Suppose there is a righteous man
who does what is just and right.
6 He does not eat at the mountain[m]
shrines
or look to the idols[n] of Israel.
He does not defile his neighbor's wife
or have sexual relations with a
woman during her period.
7 He does not oppress[o] anyone,
but returns what he took in pledge[p]
for a loan.
He does not commit robbery
but gives his food to the hungry
and provides clothing for the naked.[q]
8 He does not lend to them at interest
or take a profit from them.[r]
He withholds his hand from doing
wrong
and judges fairly[s] between two
parties.
9 He follows my decrees
and faithfully keeps my laws.
That man is righteous;[t]
he will surely live,[u]
declares the Sovereign LORD.

10 "Suppose he has a violent son, who
sheds blood[v] or does any of these other
things[a] 11 (though the father has done none
of them):

"He eats at the mountain shrines.
He defiles his neighbor's wife.
12 He oppresses the poor[w] and needy.
He commits robbery.
He does not return what he took in
pledge.
He looks to the idols.
He does detestable things.[x]
13 He lends at interest and takes a profit.[y]

Will such a man live? He will not! Because he has done all these detestable things, he is to be put to death; his blood will be on his own head.[z]

14 "But suppose this son has a son who
sees all the sins his father commits, and though he sees them, he does not do such things:[a]

15 "He does not eat at the mountain
shrines
or look to the idols of Israel.
He does not defile his neighbor's wife.
16 He does not oppress anyone
or require a pledge for a loan.
He does not commit robbery
but gives his food to the hungry
and provides clothing for the
naked.[b]
17 He withholds his hand from
mistreating the poor
and takes no interest or profit from
them.
He keeps my laws and follows my
decrees.

He will not die for his father's sin; he will
surely live. 18 But his father will die for
his own sin, because he practiced extortion, robbed his brother and did what was wrong among his people.

19 "Yet you ask, 'Why does the son not
share the guilt of his father?' Since the son has done what is just and right and has been careful to keep all my decrees, he
will surely live.[c] 20 The one who sins is the
one who will die. The child will not share the guilt of the parent, nor will the parent share the guilt of the child. The righteousness of the righteous will be credited to them, and the wickedness of the wicked will be charged against them.[d]

21 "But if a wicked person turns away
from all the sins they have committed and keeps all my decrees and does what is just and right, that person will surely live;
they will not die.[e] 22 None of the offenses
they have committed will be remembered against them. Because of the righteous
things they have done, they will live.[f] 23 Do
I take any pleasure in the death of the wicked? declares the Sovereign LORD. Rather, am I not pleased[g] when they turn from their ways and live?[h]

24 "But if a righteous person turns from
their righteousness and commits sin and does the same detestable things the wicked person does, will they live? None of the righteous things that person has done will be remembered. Because of the unfaithfulness they are guilty of and because of the sins they have committed, they will die.[i]

25 "Yet you say, 'The way of the Lord is

[a] 10 Or *things to a brother*

of sinful behavior are being addressed (3:16 – 21; 33:12 – 20; Deut. 30:15 – 20).

18:6 *have sexual relations with a woman during her period.* In ancient Israel, intimacy during the woman's menstrual period was prohibited. The Old Testament does not explain the reason for this, but it may be tied to the special role of blood for the atoning of sin (Lev. 15:19 – 33).

18:19 – 32 *Why does the son not share the guilt of his father?* In this passage, Ezekiel further clarifies his teaching on individual responsibility for sin by answering certain questions that reflect what his audience might be thinking in response to his previous message. God's response to their questions through Ezekiel is, in part, also composed of questions.

18:6 [m] Eze 22:9 [n] Dt 4:19; Eze 6:13; 20:24
18:7 [o] Ex 22:21 [p] Ex 22:26; Dt 24:12 [q] Dt 15:11; Mt 25:36
18:8 [r] Ex 22:25; Lev 25:35-37; Dt 23:19-20 [s] Zec 8:16
18:9 [t] Hab 2:4 [u] Lev 18:5; Eze 20:11; Am 5:4
18:10 [v] Ex 21:12 **18:12** [w] Am 4:1 [x] 2Ki 21:11; Isa 59:6-7; Jer 22:17; Eze 8:6, 17 **18:13** [y] Ex 22:25 [z] Eze 33:4-5
18:14 [a] 2Ch 34:21; Pr 23:24 **18:16** [b] Ps 41:1; Isa 58:10
18:19 [c] Ex 20:5; Dt 5:9; Jer 15:4; Zec 1:3-6
18:20 [d] Dt 24:16; 1Ki 8:32; 2Ki 14:6; Isa 3:11; Mt 16:27; Ro 2:9 **18:21** [e] Eze 33:12, 19 **18:22** [f] Ps 18:20-24; Isa 43:25; Mic 7:19 **18:23** [g] Ps 147:11 [h] Eze 33:11; 1Ti 2:4
18:24 [i] 1Sa 15:11; 2Ch 24:17-20; Eze 3:20; 20:27; 2Pe 2:20-22

not just.' Hear, you Israelites: Is my way unjust?[j] Is it not your ways that are unjust? 26If
a righteous person turns from their righteousness and commits sin, they will die for
it; because of the sin they have committed
they will die. 27But if a wicked person turns
away from the wickedness they have committed and does what is just and right, they
will save their life.[k] 28Because they consider all the offenses they have committed and
turn away from them, that person will surely live; they will not die. 29Yet the Israelites
say, 'The way of the Lord is not just.' Are my
ways unjust, people of Israel? Is it not your
ways that are unjust?

30"Therefore, you Israelites, I will judge
each of you according to your own ways,
declares the Sovereign LORD. Repent![l] Turn
away from all your offenses; then sin will
not be your downfall.[m] 31Rid yourselves of
all the offenses you have committed, and
get a new heart[n] and a new spirit. Why will
you die, people of Israel?[o] 32For I take no
pleasure in the death of anyone, declares
the Sovereign LORD. Repent and live![p]

A Lament Over Israel's Princes

19 "Take up a lament[q] concerning the
princes[r] of Israel 2and say:

"'What a lioness was your mother
among the lions!
She lay down among them
and reared her cubs.
3 She brought up one of her cubs,
and he became a strong lion.
He learned to tear the prey
and he became a man-eater.
4 The nations heard about him,
and he was trapped in their pit.
They led him with hooks
to the land of Egypt.[s]

5 "'When she saw her hope unfulfilled,
her expectation gone,
she took another of her cubs
and made him a strong lion.[t]
6 He prowled among the lions,
for he was now a strong lion.
He learned to tear the prey
and he became a man-eater.[u]
7 He broke down[a] their strongholds
and devastated[v] their towns.
The land and all who were in it
were terrified by his roaring.
8 Then the nations[w] came against him,
those from regions round about.
They spread their net for him,
and he was trapped in their pit.[x]
9 With hooks they pulled him into a cage
and brought him to the king of
Babylon.[y]
They put him in prison,
so his roar was heard no longer
on the mountains of Israel.[z]

10 "'Your mother was like a vine in your
vineyard[b]
planted by the water;
it was fruitful and full of branches
because of abundant water.[a]
11 Its branches were strong,
fit for a ruler's scepter.
It towered high
above the thick foliage,
conspicuous for its height
and for its many branches.[b]
12 But it was uprooted[c] in fury
and thrown to the ground.
The east wind made it shrivel,
it was stripped of its fruit;
its strong branches withered
and fire consumed them.[d]
13 Now it is planted in the desert,[e]
in a dry and thirsty land.[f]
14 Fire spread from one of its main[c]
branches
and consumed[g] its fruit.
No strong branch is left on it
fit for a ruler's scepter.'[h]

"This is a lament and is to be used as a lament."

Rebellious Israel Purged

20 In the seventh year, in the fifth month
on the tenth day, some of the elders of
Israel came to inquire of the LORD, and they
sat down in front of me.[i]

2Then the word of the LORD came to me:
3"Son of man, speak to the elders of Israel
and say to them, 'This is what the Sovereign LORD says: Have you come to inquire[j]
of me? As surely as I live, I will not let
you inquire of me, declares the Sovereign
LORD.[k]'

[a] 7 Targum (see Septuagint); Hebrew *He knew*
[b] 10 Two Hebrew manuscripts; most Hebrew manuscripts *your blood*
[c] 14 Or *from under its*

19:2–10 *lioness ... vine in your vineyard.* Most likely both of these terms represented the nation of Israel since each was a "mother" of kings—the "cubs" and the "branches." The vine and lion images are common symbols for Hebrew royalty and nationality (15:1–6; 17:1–10; Gen. 49:9).

19:13 *in a dry and thirsty land.* To anyone who loved the covenantal promises focused on God's worship in Jerusalem, any alternative to Jerusalem was akin to living in the desert.

20:2–4 *I will not let you inquire of me.* God explains to Ezekiel that the elders of Israel had forfeited any right to inquire of Him due to the abominations of

18:25 [j] Ge 18:25; Jer 12:1; Eze 33:17; Zep 3:5; Mal 2:17; 3:13-15 **18:27** [k] Isa 1:18
18:30 [l] Mt 3:2 [m] Eze 7:3; 33:20; Hos 12:6
18:31 [n] Ps 51:10 [o] Isa 1:16-17; Eze 11:19; 36:26
18:32 [p] Eze 33:11 **19:1** [q] Eze 26:17; 27:2,32 [r] 2Ki 24:6
19:4 [s] 2Ki 23:33-34; 2Ch 36:4
19:5 [t] 2Ki 23:34 **19:6** [u] 2Ki 24:9; 2Ch 36:9
19:7 [v] Eze 30:12 **19:8** [w] 2Ki 24:2 [x] 2Ki 24:11
19:9 [y] 2Ch 36:6 [z] 2Ki 24:15
19:10 [a] Ps 80:8-11 **19:11** [b] Eze 31:3; Da 4:11
19:12 [c] Eze 17:10 [d] Isa 27:11; Eze 20:17; Hos 13:15
19:13 [e] Eze 20:35 [f] Hos 2:3
19:14 [g] Eze 20:47 [h] Eze 15:4 **20:1** [i] Eze 8:1
20:3 [j] Eze 14:3 [k] Mic 3:7

[4]"Will you judge them? Will you judge
them, son of man? Then confront them
with the detestable practices of their ancestors[l] [5]and say to them: 'This is what the
Sovereign LORD says: On the day I chose[m]
Israel, I swore with uplifted hand to the descendants of Jacob and revealed myself to
them in Egypt. With uplifted hand I said to
them, "I am the LORD your God."[n] [6]On that
day I swore to them that I would bring them
out of Egypt into a land I had searched out
for them, a land flowing with milk and
honey,[o] the most beautiful of all lands.[p]
[7]And I said to them, "Each of you, get rid
of the vile images[q] you have set your eyes
on, and do not defile yourselves with the
idols of Egypt. I am the LORD your God."[r]

[8]" 'But they rebelled against me and
would not listen to me; they did not get
rid of the vile images they had set their
eyes on, nor did they forsake the idols of
Egypt.[s] So I said I would pour out my wrath
on them and spend my anger against them
in Egypt.[t] [9]But for the sake of my name, I
brought them out of Egypt.[u] I did it to keep
my name from being profaned in the eyes
of the nations among whom they lived and
in whose sight I had revealed myself to the
Israelites. [10]Therefore I led them out of
Egypt and brought them into the wilderness.[v] [11]I gave them my decrees and made
known to them my laws, by which the person who obeys them will live.[w] [12]Also I
gave them my Sabbaths as a sign[x] between
us, so they would know that I the LORD
made them holy.

[13]" 'Yet the people of Israel rebelled[y]
against me in the wilderness. They did not
follow my decrees but rejected my laws—
by which the person who obeys them will
live—and they utterly desecrated my Sabbaths. So I said I would pour out my wrath[z]
on them and destroy them in the wilderness.[a] [14]But for the sake of my name I did
what would keep it from being profaned
in the eyes of the nations in whose sight I
had brought them out.[b] [15]Also with uplifted
hand I swore to them in the wilderness that
I would not bring them into the land I had
given them—a land flowing with milk and
honey, the most beautiful of all lands[c]—
[16]because they rejected my laws and did
not follow my decrees and desecrated my
Sabbaths. For their hearts[d] were devoted
to their idols.[e] [17]Yet I looked on them with
pity and did not destroy them or put an end
to them in the wilderness. [18]I said to their
children in the wilderness, "Do not follow
the statutes of your parents[f] or keep their
laws or defile yourselves with their idols.
[19]I am the LORD your God;[g] follow my decrees and be careful to keep my laws.[h]
[20]Keep my Sabbaths holy, that they may
be a sign between us. Then you will know
that I am the LORD your God."[i]

[21]" 'But the children rebelled against me:
They did not follow my decrees, they were
not careful to keep my laws, of which I said,
"The person who obeys them will live by
them," and they desecrated my Sabbaths.
So I said I would pour out my wrath on
them and spend my anger against them
in the wilderness. [22]But I withheld[j] my
hand, and for the sake of my name I did
what would keep it from being profaned
in the eyes of the nations in whose sight I
had brought them out. [23]Also with uplifted
hand I swore to them in the wilderness that
I would disperse them among the nations
and scatter[k] them through the countries,
[24]because they had not obeyed my laws
but had rejected my decrees and desecrated my Sabbaths,[l] and their eyes lusted after[m] their parents' idols.[n] [25]So I gave[o] them
other statutes that were not good and laws
through which they could not live;[p] [26]I defiled them through their gifts—the sacrifice of every firstborn—that I might fill
them with horror so they would know that
I am the LORD.[q]'

---

their fathers. All the people are responsible for their own sins, and this does not mean that these Hebrews were paying for sins their ancestors had committed. Instead, the present generation of Hebrews in exile had clearly shown their failure to learn practical lessons from history, and thus had condemned themselves to repeat many mistakes. These leaders came to God with questions, but the questions were foolish and demonstrated the people's sinfulness. God gives a remedial review of their past.

20:11 ***the person who obeys them will live.*** Following their exodus from slavery in Egypt, God began to sanctify the Israelites by revealing to them a code of law and entering a covenant relationship with them on a Creator-creature basis. This does not teach that eternal salvation can be earned by good works, but that the quality of the believer's physical and spiritual life on earth are related to his or her obedience to the living God.

20:12 ***gave them my Sabbaths.*** This is an important verse for understanding the Sabbath (Ex. 20:8–11; Deut. 5:12–15). Sabbath means "rest." That is, the Sabbath was a day to cease all ordinary work or labor, as clearly emphasized in Exodus 20:8–11. The Sabbath was to serve as a sign of God's covenantal relationship with His people, Israel.

20:20 ***Keep my Sabbaths holy.*** This word means "to treat as holy," "to observe as distinct," and "to consecrate." God commands that His Sabbaths be continually maintained by His people as sacred—distinct and separate from ordinary days.

20:4 [l] Eze 16:2; 22:2; Mt 23:32 **20:5** [m] Dt 7:6 [n] Ex 6:7
20:6 [o] Ex 3:8; Jer 32:22 [p] Dt 8:7; Ps 48:2; Da 8:9
20:7 [q] Ex 20:4 [r] Ex 20:2; Lev 18:3; Dt 29:18 **20:8** [s] Eze 7:8
[t] Isa 63:10 **20:9** [u] Eze 36:22; 39:7 **20:10** [v] Ex 13:18
20:11 [w] Lev 18:5; Dt 4:7-8; Ro 10:5 **20:12** [x] Ex 31:13
20:13 [y] Ps 78:40 [z] Dt 9:8 [a] Nu 14:29; Ps 95:8-10; Isa 56:6
20:14 [b] Eze 36:23 **20:15** [c] Ps 95:11; 106:26
20:16 [d] Nu 15:39 [e] Am 5:26 **20:18** [f] Zec 1:4
20:19 [g] Ex 20:2 [h] Dt 5:32-33; 6:1-2; 8:1; 11:1; 12:1
20:20 [i] Jer 17:22 **20:22** [j] Ps 78:38 **20:23** [k] Lev 26:33;
Dt 28:64 **20:24** [l] ver 13 [m] Eze 6:9 [n] ver 16
20:25 [o] Ps 81:12 [p] 2Th 2:11 **20:26** [q] 2Ki 17:17

27“Therefore, son of man, speak to the
people of Israel and say to them, ‘This is
what the Sovereign LORD says: In this also
your ancestors blasphemed[r] me by being
unfaithful to me:[s] 28When I brought them
into the land[t] I had sworn to give them and
they saw any high hill or any leafy tree,
there they offered their sacrifices, made offerings that aroused my anger, presented
their fragrant incense and poured out their
drink offerings.[u] 29Then I said to them:
What is this high place you go to?’ ” (It is
called Bamah[a] to this day.)

Rebellious Israel Renewed

30“Therefore say to the Israelites: ‘This is
what the Sovereign LORD says: Will you defile yourselves[v] the way your ancestors did
and lust after their vile images?[w] 31When
you offer your gifts—the sacrifice of your
children[x] in the fire—you continue to defile
yourselves with all your idols to this day.
Am I to let you inquire of me, you Israelites? As surely as I live, declares the Sovereign LORD, I will not let you inquire of me.[y]
32“ ‘You say, “We want to be like the nations, like the peoples of the world, who
serve wood and stone.” But what you have
in mind will never happen. 33As surely as
I live, declares the Sovereign LORD, I will
reign over you with a mighty hand and
an outstretched arm and with outpoured
wrath.[z] 34I will bring you from the nations[a]
and gather you from the countries where
you have been scattered—with a mighty
hand and an outstretched arm and with
outpoured wrath.[b] 35I will bring you into
the wilderness of the nations and there,
face to face, I will execute judgment[c] upon
you. 36As I judged your ancestors in the
wilderness of the land of Egypt, so I will
judge you, declares the Sovereign LORD.[d]
37I will take note of you as you pass under my rod,[e] and I will bring you into the
bond of the covenant.[f] 38I will purge[g] you
of those who revolt and rebel against me.
Although I will bring them out of the land
where they are living, yet they will not enter the land of Israel. Then you will know
that I am the LORD.[h]
39“ ‘As for you, people of Israel, this is
what the Sovereign LORD says: Go and
serve your idols,[i] every one of you! But afterward you will surely listen to me and no
longer profane my holy name with your
gifts and idols.[j] 40For on my holy mountain,
the high mountain of Israel, declares the
Sovereign LORD, there in the land all the
people of Israel will serve me, and there I
will accept them. There I will require your
offerings[k] and your choice gifts,[b] along
with all your holy sacrifices.[l] 41I will accept
you as fragrant incense when I bring you
out from the nations and gather you from
the countries where you have been scattered, and I will be proved holy[m] through
you in the sight of the nations.[n] 42Then
you will know that I am the LORD,[o] when I
bring you into the land of Israel,[p] the land
I had sworn with uplifted hand to give to
your ancestors. 43There you will remember
your conduct and all the actions by which
you have defiled yourselves, and you will
loathe yourselves for all the evil you have
done.[q] 44You will know that I am the LORD,
when I deal with you for my name’s sake[r]
and not according to your evil ways and
your corrupt practices, you people of Israel, declares the Sovereign LORD.[s]’ ”

Prophecy Against the South

45The word of the LORD came to me:
46“Son of man, set your face toward the
south; preach against the south and prophesy against[t] the forest of the southland.[u]

---

[a] 29 *Bamah* means *high place.* [b] 40 Or *and the gifts of your firstfruits*

20:32 *We want to be like the nations.* Chosen to be a nation separate from sin and secular ways—a special instrument to reveal God’s glory—Israel’s consistent tendency was to identify with the neighboring ungodly nations and to take on their idolatrous ways (Ex. 19:5).

20:33–36 *I will bring you from the nations.* The judgment of captivity in Babylon had begun in the deportations of 605 and 597 B.C. and would be continued with Jerusalem’s fall in 586 B.C. However, God also promised to restore Judah and to judge her enemies with fury (Deut. 4:34). This refers to the Persian conquest of Babylon in 539 B.C. and to the three returns of the Jews to their land and the rebuilding of their homeland (538–330 B.C.), yet Israel would again be taken captive and made to wander throughout the nations during the Roman occupation.

20:37 *I will take note of you as you pass under my rod.* This is the way a shepherd counts and controls his sheep (Lev. 27:32; Jer. 33:13).

20:39 *Go and serve your idols, every one of you!* This is an ironic command; the rest of the verse indicates that God was giving the stubborn people over to what they had decided. God grants each one a destiny consistent with his or her decisions.

20:44 *You will know that I am the LORD.* The promise of this verse is that the Lord will gather the nation of Israel from places where they have been dispersed and that they will repent because of the evil things they have done.

20:46–47 *toward the south.* This refers to the land of Judah—the southern kingdom—which had more trees then than now.

20:27 [r] Ro 2:24 [s] Eze 18:24 **20:28** [t] Ps 78:55,58 [u] Eze 6:13 **20:30** [v] ver 43 [w] Jer 16:12 **20:31** [x] Eze 16:20 [y] Ps 106:37-39; Jer 7:31 **20:33** [z] Jer 21:5 **20:34** [a] 2Co 6:17* [b] Isa 27:12-13; Jer 44:6; La 2:4 **20:35** [c] Jer 2:35 **20:36** [d] Nu 11:1-35; 1Co 10:5-10 **20:37** [e] Lev 27:32; Jer 33:13 [f] Eze 16:62 **20:38** [g] Eze 34:17-22; Am 9:9-10 [h] Ps 95:11; Jer 44:14; Eze 13:9; Mal 3:3; Heb 4:3 **20:39** [i] Jer 44:25 [j] Isa 1:13; Eze 43:7; Am 4:4 **20:40** [k] Isa 60:7 [l] Isa 56:7; Mal 3:4 **20:41** [m] Eze 28:25; 36:23 [n] Eze 11:17 **20:42** [o] Eze 38:23 [p] Eze 34:13; 36:24 **20:43** [q] Eze 6:9; 16:61; Hos 5:15 **20:44** [r] Eze 36:22 [s] Eze 24:24 **20:46** [t] Eze 21:2; Am 7:16 [u] Isa 30:6; Jer 13:19

[47]Say to the southern forest: 'Hear the word
of the LORD. This is what the Sovereign
LORD says: I am about to set fire to you,
and it will consume all your trees, both
green and dry. The blazing flame will not
be quenched, and every face from south to
north will be scorched by it.[v] [48]Everyone
will see that I the LORD have kindled it; it
will not be quenched.[w]' "

[49]Then I said, "Sovereign LORD, they
are saying of me, 'Isn't he just telling parables?[x]' "[a]

Babylon as God's Sword of Judgment

21 [b] The word of the LORD came to me:
[2]"Son of man, set your face against
Jerusalem and preach against the sanctuary. Prophesy against[y] the land of Israel [3]and say to her: 'This is what the LORD
says: I am against you.[z] I will draw my
sword from its sheath and cut off from
you both the righteous and the wicked.[a]
[4]Because I am going to cut off the righteous and the wicked, my sword will be
unsheathed against everyone from south
to north.[b] [5]Then all people will know that
I the LORD have drawn my sword from its
sheath; it will not return[c] again.'[d]

[6]"Therefore groan, son of man! Groan
before them with broken heart and bitter
grief.[e] [7]And when they ask you, 'Why are
you groaning?' you shall say, 'Because of the
news that is coming. Every heart will melt
with fear and every hand go limp;[f] every
spirit will become faint and every leg will
be wet with urine.' It is coming! It will surely take place, declares the Sovereign LORD."

[8]The word of the LORD came to me: [9]"Son
of man, prophesy and say, 'This is what the
Lord says:

" 'A sword, a sword,
sharpened and polished—
[10]sharpened for the slaughter,[g]
polished to flash like lightning!

" 'Shall we rejoice in the scepter of my
royal son? The sword despises every such
stick.

[11]" 'The sword is appointed to be
polished,[h]
to be grasped with the hand;
it is sharpened and polished,
made ready for the hand of the slayer.
[12]Cry out and wail, son of man,
for it is against my people;
it is against all the princes of Israel.
They are thrown to the sword
along with my people.
Therefore beat your breast.[i]

[13]" 'Testing will surely come. And what if
even the scepter, which the sword despises,
does not continue? declares the Sovereign
LORD.'

[14]"So then, son of man, prophesy
and strike your hands[j] together.
Let the sword strike twice,
even three times.
It is a sword for slaughter—
a sword for great slaughter,
closing in on them from every side.[k]
[15]So that hearts may melt with fear[l]
and the fallen be many,
I have stationed the sword for
slaughter[c]
at all their gates.
Look! It is forged to strike like
lightning,
it is grasped for slaughter.[m]
[16]Slash to the right, you sword,
then to the left,
wherever your blade is turned.
[17]I too will strike my hands[n] together,
and my wrath[o] will subside.
I the LORD have spoken."

[18]The word of the LORD came to me:
[19]"Son of man, mark out two roads for the
sword of the king of Babylon to take, both
starting from the same country. Make a
signpost where the road branches off to
the city. [20]Mark out one road for the sword
to come against Rabbah of the Ammonites[p]
and another against Judah and fortified
Jerusalem. [21]For the king of Babylon will
stop at the fork in the road, at the junction
of the two roads, to seek an omen: He will
cast lots[q] with arrows, he will consult his
idols, he will examine the liver.[r] [22]Into his
right hand will come the lot for Jerusalem,

---

a *49* In Hebrew texts 20:45-49 is numbered 21:1-5.
b In Hebrew texts 21:1-32 is numbered 21:6-37.
c *15* Septuagint; the meaning of the Hebrew for this word is uncertain.

21:6 ***broken heart.*** This phrase translates words that literally mean "breaking loins," suggesting great emotional upheaval.
21:12 ***Cry out and wail ... beat your breast.*** Ezekiel was told to add verbal groans and a physical gesture to his musical message. In that culture, these actions displayed great grief and sorrow (Jer. 31:19).
21:14–17 ***strike twice ... three times.*** This was a numeric device (Prov. 6:16) used here to emphasize the extent and effectiveness of the sword's employment against Judah.
21:19–20 ***Make a signpost.*** Ezekiel was to place a signpost at a fork in the road leading to the capital cities of Ammon and Judah.
21:21 ***cast lots with arrows.*** There was a method of casting lots using arrows inscribed with names. They were shaken about in the quiver and then dropped to the ground like throwing dice. ***examine***

20:47 [v] Isa 9:18-19; 13:8; Jer 21:14 **20:48** [w] Jer 7:20
20:49 [x] Mt 13:13; Jn 16:25 **21:2** [y] Eze 20:46
21:3 [z] Jer 21:13 [a] ver 9-11; Job 9:22 **21:4** [b] Eze 20:47
21:5 [c] ver 30 [d] Na 1:9 **21:6** [e] Isa 22:4 **21:7** [f] Eze 22:14; 7:17 **21:10** [g] Ps 110:5-6; Isa 34:5-6 **21:11** [h] Jer 46:4
21:12 [i] Jer 31:19 **21:14** [j] Nu 24:10 [k] Eze 6:11; 30:24
21:15 [l] 2Sa 17:10 [m] Ps 22:14 **21:17** [n] ver 14; Eze 22:13
[o] Eze 5:13 **21:20** [p] Dt 3:11; Jer 49:2; Am 1:14
21:21 [q] Pr 16:33 [r] Nu 22:7; 23:23

where he is to set up battering rams, to
give the command to slaughter, to sound
the battle cry, to set battering rams against
the gates, to build a ramp and to erect siege
works.[s] 23It will seem like a false omen to
those who have sworn allegiance to him,
but he will remind[t] them of their guilt and
take them captive.

24"Therefore this is what the Sovereign LORD says: 'Because you people have
brought to mind your guilt by your open rebellion, revealing your sins in all that you
do—because you have done this, you will
be taken captive.

25" 'You profane and wicked prince of Israel, whose day has come, whose time of
punishment has reached its climax,[u] 26this
is what the Sovereign LORD says: Take off
the turban, remove the crown.[v] It will not
be as it was: The lowly will be exalted and
the exalted will be brought low.[w] 27A ruin!
A ruin! I will make it a ruin! The crown will
not be restored until he to whom it rightfully belongs shall come; to him I will give it.'[x]

28"And you, son of man, prophesy and
say, 'This is what the Sovereign LORD says
about the Ammonites[y] and their insults:

" 'A sword,[z] a sword,
drawn for the slaughter,
polished to consume
and to flash like lightning!
29 Despite false visions concerning you
and lying divinations about you,
it will be laid on the necks
of the wicked who are to be slain,
whose day has come,
whose time of punishment has
reached its climax.[a]

30 " 'Let the sword return to its sheath.[b]
In the place where you were created,
in the land of your ancestry,[c]
I will judge you.
31 I will pour out my wrath on you
and breathe out my fiery anger[d]
against you;
I will deliver you into the hands of
brutal men,
men skilled in destruction.[e]
32 You will be fuel for the fire,[f]
your blood will be shed in your land,
you will be remembered[g] no more;
for I the LORD have spoken.' "

Judgment on Jerusalem's Sins

22 The word of the LORD came to me:

2"Son of man, will you judge her? Will
you judge this city of bloodshed?[h] Then confront her with all her detestable practices[i]
3and say: 'This is what the Sovereign LORD
says: You city that brings on herself doom
by shedding blood[j] in her midst and defiles
herself by making idols, 4you have become
guilty because of the blood you have shed[k]
and have become defiled by the idols you
have made. You have brought your days to
a close, and the end of your years has come.[l]
Therefore I will make you an object of scorn
to the nations and a laughingstock to all the
countries.[m] 5Those who are near and those
who are far away will mock you, you infamous city, full of turmoil.

6" 'See how each of the princes of Israel who are in you uses his power to shed
blood.[n] 7In you they have treated father and
mother with contempt;[o] in you they have
oppressed the foreigner and mistreated the
fatherless and the widow.[p] 8You have despised my holy things and desecrated my
Sabbaths.[q] 9In you are slanderers[r] who are
bent on shedding blood; in you are those
who eat at the mountain shrines[s] and commit lewd acts.[t] 10In you are those who dishonor their father's bed; in you are those
who violate women during their period,
when they are ceremonially unclean.[u] 11In
you one man commits a detestable offense
with his neighbor's wife, another shamefully defiles his daughter-in-law,[v] and another
violates his sister,[w] his own father's daughter. 12In you are people who accept bribes[x]
to shed blood; you take interest and make a
profit from the poor. You extort unjust gain
from your neighbors.[y] And you have forgotten me, declares the Sovereign LORD.

---

the liver. Sheep livers from sacrificed animals were studied. The shades and shapes of various sections of the organ were the basis for a positive or negative prediction.

21:26–27 *turban ... crown.* These stand for the priesthood and kingship. Both would be removed from Judah.

21:28 *about the Ammonites.* The Ammonites joined other nations east of the Jordan in raiding Judean territory, in return for protection from Nebuchadnezzar. Later, during the reign of Zedekiah, Ammon, Moab, Edom, and others conspired against Babylon, but with false hopes of help from Egypt (Jer. 27:3–11).

22:1–5 *You have brought your days to a close.* The city was ripe for judgment. When such hypocrisy is exposed and punishment is executed before the world, God's people become lasting objects of ridicule.

22:6–12 *the princes of Israel.* Jerusalem's princes had shed the blood of innocent people (7:27; 11:1; 12:10; 19:1; 21:13). These evil leaders had been (1) taking advantage of parents and the weak; (2) rejecting God and His covenant, leading to ungodliness and inhumanity; (3) murdering the innocent by slandering them; (4) preferring idolatrous religion and its

21:22 [s] Eze 4:2; 26:9 **21:23** [t] Nu 5:15 **21:25** [u] Eze 35:5 **21:26** [v] Jer 13:18 [w] Ps 75:7; Eze 17:24 **21:27** [x] Ps 2:6; Jer 23:5-6; Eze 37:24; Hag 2:21-22 **21:28** [y] Zep 2:8 [z] Jer 12:12 **21:29** [a] ver 25; Eze 22:28; 35:5 **21:30** [b] Jer 47:6 [c] Eze 16:3 **21:31** [d] Eze 22:20-21 [e] Jer 51:20-23 **21:32** [f] Mal 4:1 [g] Eze 25:10 **22:2** [h] Eze 24:6, 9; Na 3:1 [i] Eze 16:2 **22:3** [j] ver 6, 13, 27; Eze 23:37, 45 **22:4** [k] 2Ki 21:16 [l] Eze 21:25 [m] Eze 5:14 **22:6** [n] Isa 1:23 **22:7** [o] Dt 5:16; 27:16 [p] Ex 22:21-22 **22:8** [q] Eze 23:38-39 **22:9** [r] Lev 19:16 [s] Eze 18:11 [t] Hos 4:10, 14 **22:10** [u] Lev 18:8, 19 **22:11** [v] Lev 18:15 [w] Lev 18:9; 2Sa 13:14 **22:12** [x] Dt 27:25; Mic 7:3 [y] Lev 19:13

[13]"'I will surely strike my hands[z] together at the unjust gain[a] you have made and at the blood[b] you have shed in your midst. [14]Will your courage endure or your hands be strong in the day I deal with you? I the LORD have spoken,[c] and I will do it.[d] [15]I will disperse you among the nations and scatter[e] you through the countries; and I will put an end to your uncleanness.[f] [16]When you have been defiled[a] in the eyes of the nations, you will know that I am the LORD.'"

[17]Then the word of the LORD came to me: [18]"Son of man, the people of Israel have become dross[g] to me; all of them are the copper, tin, iron and lead left inside a furnace. They are but the dross of silver.[h] [19]Therefore this is what the Sovereign LORD says: 'Because you have all become dross, I will gather you into Jerusalem. [20]As silver, copper, iron, lead and tin are gathered into a furnace to be melted with a fiery blast, so will I gather you in my anger and my wrath and put you inside the city and melt you.[i] [21]I will gather you and I will blow on you with my fiery wrath, and you will be melted inside her. [22]As silver is melted[j] in a furnace, so you will be melted inside her, and you will know that I the LORD have poured out my wrath on you.'"[k]

[23]Again the word of the LORD came to me: [24]"Son of man, say to the land, 'You are a land that has not been cleansed or rained on in the day of wrath.'[l] [25]There is a conspiracy[m] of her princes[b] within her like a roaring lion tearing its prey; they devour people,[n] take treasures and precious things and make many widows[o] within her. [26]Her priests do violence to my law[p] and profane my holy things; they do not distinguish between the holy and the common;[q] they teach that there is no difference between the unclean and the clean;[r] and they shut their eyes to the keeping of my Sabbaths, so that I am profaned among them.[s] [27]Her officials within her are like wolves tearing their prey; they shed blood and kill people to make unjust gain.[t] [28]Her prophets whitewash[u] these deeds for them by false visions and lying divinations. They say, 'This is what the Sovereign LORD says'—when the LORD has not spoken.[v] [29]The people of the land practice extortion and commit robbery; they oppress the poor and needy and mistreat the foreigner,[w] denying them justice.[x]

[30]"I looked for someone among them who would build up the wall[y] and stand before me in the gap on behalf of the land so I would not have to destroy it, but I found no one.[z] [31]So I will pour out my wrath on them and consume them with my fiery anger, bringing down[a] on their own heads all they have done, declares the Sovereign LORD.[b]"

Two Adulterous Sisters

23 The word of the LORD came to me: [2]"Son of man, there were two women, daughters of the same mother.[c] [3]They became prostitutes in Egypt,[d] engaging in prostitution[e] from their youth. In that land their breasts were fondled and their virgin bosoms caressed. [4]The older was named Oholah, and her sister was Oholibah. They were mine and gave birth to sons and daughters. Oholah is Samaria, and Oholibah is Jerusalem.

[5]"Oholah engaged in prostitution while she was still mine; and she lusted after her lovers, the Assyrians[f]—warriors[g] [6]clothed in blue, governors and commanders, all of them handsome young men, and mounted horsemen. [7]She gave herself as a prostitute to all the elite of the Assyrians and defiled herself with all the idols of everyone she lusted after.[h] [8]She did not give up the prostitution she began in Egypt,[i] when during her youth men slept with her, caressed her virgin bosom and poured out their lust on her.[j]

[9]"Therefore I delivered her into the hands[k] of her lovers, the Assyrians, for whom she lusted.[l] [10]They stripped[m] her naked, took away her sons and daughters and killed her with the sword. She became a byword among women,[n] and punishment was inflicted on her.[o]

---

[a] 16 Or *When I have allotted you your inheritance*
[b] 25 Septuagint; Hebrew *prophets*

---

immoral rituals; (5) engaging in sexual immorality with neighbors, family, and relatives; and (6) loving money and using it to get ahead of fellow citizens.

22:26 *Her priests.* Those who were supposed to be leaders were not examples of separation from worldly ways (Ex. 19:6). Some at least were motivated by monetary gain (Mic. 3:11).

22:30 *looked for someone among them.* God could not find a spiritual leader to guide the people in godliness.

23:4 *Oholah.* In Hebrew, Oholah means "her own tabernacle" and ***Oholibah*** means "My tabernacle is in her." These seem to refer to God's sanctuaries in each land or, in a distinct usage, to the tent shrines for Canaanite idols as opposed to God's true temple.

23:9–10 *They stripped her naked.* This means to be stripped bare and so put to great shame. Ezekiel is reminding his audience of how God already had judged Samaria through Assyrian conquest and captivity in 722 B.C. (2 Kin. 17:5–41).

22:13 [z] Eze 21:17 [a] Isa 33:15 [b] ver 3 **22:14** [c] Eze 24:14 [d] Eze 17:24; 21:7 **22:15** [e] Dt 4:27; Zec 7:14 [f] Eze 23:27 **22:18** [g] Ps 119:119; Isa 1:22 [h] Jer 6:28-30 **22:20** [i] Mal 3:2 **22:22** [j] Isa 1:25 [k] Eze 20:8, 33 **22:24** [l] Eze 24:13 **22:25** [m] Jer 11:9 [n] Hos 6:9 [o] Jer 15:8 **22:26** [p] Mal 2:7-8 [q] Eze 44:23 [r] Lev 10:10 [s] 1Sa 2:12-17; Jer 2:8, 26; Hag 2:11-14 **22:27** [t] Isa 1:23 **22:28** [u] Eze 13:10 [v] Eze 13:2, 6-7 **22:29** [w] Ex 22:21; 23:9 [x] Isa 5:7 **22:30** [y] Eze 13:5 [z] Ps 106:23; Jer 5:1 **22:31** [a] Eze 16:43 [b] Eze 7:8-9; 9:10; Ro 2:8 **23:2** [c] Jer 3:7; Eze 16:45 **23:3** [d] Jos 24:14 [e] Lev 17:7 **23:5** [f] 2Ki 16:7; Hos 5:13 [g] Hos 8:9 **23:7** [h] Hos 5:3; 6:10 **23:8** [i] Ex 32:4 [j] Eze 16:15 **23:9** [k] 2Ki 18:11 [l] Hos 11:5 **23:10** [m] Hos 2:10 [n] Eze 16:41 [o] Eze 16:36

11"Her sister Oholibah saw this, yet in
her lust and prostitution she was more depraved than her sister.[p] 12She too lusted
after the Assyrians—governors and commanders, warriors in full dress, mounted
horsemen, all handsome young men.[q] 13I
saw that she too defiled herself; both of
them went the same way.

14"But she carried her prostitution
still further. She saw men portrayed on
a wall,[r] figures of Chaldeans[a] portrayed
in red,[s] 15with belts around their waists
and flowing turbans on their heads; all of
them looked like Babylonian chariot officers, natives of Chaldea.[b] 16As soon as she
saw them, she lusted after them and sent
messengers to them in Chaldea. 17Then
the Babylonians came to her, to the bed
of love, and in their lust they defiled her.
After she had been defiled by them, she
turned away from them in disgust. 18When
she carried on her prostitution openly and
exposed her naked body, I turned away[t]
from her in disgust, just as I had turned
away from her sister.[u] 19Yet she became
more and more promiscuous as she recalled the days of her youth, when she was
a prostitute in Egypt. 20There she lusted
after her lovers, whose genitals were like
those of donkeys and whose emission was
like that of horses. 21So you longed for the
lewdness of your youth, when in Egypt
your bosom was caressed and your young
breasts fondled.[c][v]

22"Therefore, Oholibah, this is what the
Sovereign LORD says: I will stir up your
lovers against you, those you turned away
from in disgust, and I will bring them
against you from every side[w]— 23the Babylonians[x] and all the Chaldeans, the men
of Pekod[y] and Shoa and Koa, and all the
Assyrians with them, handsome young
men, all of them governors and commanders, chariot officers and men of high rank,
all mounted on horses.[z] 24They will come
against you with weapons,[d] chariots and
wagons[a] and with a throng of people; they
will take up positions against you on every side with large and small shields and
with helmets. I will turn you over to them
for punishment,[b] and they will punish you
according to their standards. 25I will direct
my jealous anger against you, and they
will deal with you in fury. They will cut off
your noses and your ears, and those of you
who are left will fall by the sword. They
will take away your sons and daughters,[c]
and those of you who are left will be consumed by fire.[d] 26They will also strip[e] you
of your clothes and take your fine jewelry.[f]
27So I will put a stop[g] to the lewdness and
prostitution you began in Egypt. You will
not look on these things with longing or
remember Egypt anymore.

28"For this is what the Sovereign LORD
says: I am about to deliver you into the
hands[h] of those you hate, to those you
turned away from in disgust. 29They will
deal with you in hatred and take away
everything you have worked for. They
will leave you stark naked, and the shame
of your prostitution will be exposed.
Your lewdness and promiscuity[i] 30have
brought this on you, because you lusted
after the nations and defiled yourself with
their idols.[j] 31You have gone the way of
your sister; so I will put her cup[k] into your
hand.[l]

32"This is what the Sovereign LORD says:

"You will drink your sister's cup,
  a cup large and deep;
it will bring scorn and derision,
  for it holds so much.[m]
33You will be filled with drunkenness and
    sorrow,
  the cup of ruin and desolation,
  the cup of your sister Samaria.[n]
34You will drink it[o] and drain it dry
  and chew on its pieces—
  and you will tear your breasts.

I have spoken, declares the Sovereign
LORD.

35"Therefore this is what the Sovereign
LORD says: Since you have forgotten[p] me
and turned your back on me,[q] you must
bear the consequences of your lewdness
and prostitution."

---

[a] 14 Or *Babylonians* [b] 15 Or *Babylonia*; also in verse 16 [c] 21 Syriac (see also verse 3); Hebrew *caressed because of your young breasts*
[d] 24 The meaning of the Hebrew for this word is uncertain.

23:14 *She saw men portrayed on a wall.* These lines tell how Judean envoys to Babylon became enamored of Babylonian rulers and their power through pictures (Jer. 22:14) on their palace and temple walls.
23:17–18 *After she had been defiled by them.* This is an allusion to Judah's turning in disappointment and disgust from relying on Babylon to relying on Egypt (2 Kin. 23:28–24:1). God's alienation from Jerusalem is an allusion to the city's coming defeat by Nebuchadnezzar.
23:32–34 *You will drink your sister's cup.* The cup is often symbolic of God's judgment (Ps. 75:7–8; Jer. 25:15–29). The phrase portrays how completely Judah would drink the cup of wrath, breaking what was already broken. ***tear your breasts.*** This image gives a picture of the resultant agony and anguish.

23:11 [p] Jer 3:8-11; Eze 16:51 **23:12** [q] 2Ki 16:7-15; 2Ch 28:16 **23:14** [r] Eze 8:10 [s] Jer 22:14
23:18 [t] Ps 78:59; 106:40; Jer 6:8 [u] Jer 12:8; Am 5:21
23:21 [v] Eze 16:26 **23:22** [w] Eze 16:37
23:23 [x] 2Ki 20:14-18 [y] Jer 50:21 [z] 2Ki 24:2
23:24 [a] Jer 47:3; Eze 26:7, 10; Na 2:4 [b] Jer 39:5-6
23:25 [c] ver 47 [d] Eze 20:47-48 **23:26** [e] Jer 13:22 [f] Isa 3:18-23; Eze 16:39 **23:27** [g] Eze 16:41
23:28 [h] Jer 34:20 **23:29** [i] Dt 28:48 **23:30** [j] Eze 6:9
23:31 [k] Jer 25:15 [l] 2Ki 21:13 **23:32** [m] Ps 60:3; Isa 51:17; Jer 25:15 **23:33** [n] Jer 25:15-16 **23:34** [o] Ps 75:8; Isa 51:17 **23:35** [p] Isa 17:10; Jer 3:21 [q] 1Ki 14:9

36The LORD said to me: “Son of man, will
you judge Oholah and Oholibah? Then confront[r] them with their detestable practices,[s]
37for they have committed adultery and
blood is on their hands. They committed
adultery with their idols; they even sacrificed their children, whom they bore to me,
as food for them.[t] 38They have also done
this to me: At that same time they defiled
my sanctuary and desecrated my Sabbaths. 39On the very day they sacrificed
their children to their idols, they entered
my sanctuary and desecrated[u] it. That is
what they did in my house.[v]

40“They even sent messengers for men
who came from far away,[w] and when they
arrived you bathed yourself for them, applied eye makeup[x] and put on your jewelry.[y] 41You sat on an elegant couch,[z] with a
table[a] spread before it on which you had
placed the incense and olive oil that belonged to me.

42“The noise of a carefree crowd was
around her; drunkards were brought from
the desert along with men from the rabble, and they put bracelets[b] on the wrists
of the woman and her sister and beautiful
crowns on their heads.[c] 43Then I said about
the one worn out by adultery, ‘Now let them
use her as a prostitute,[d] for that is all she
is.’ 44And they slept with her. As men sleep
with a prostitute, so they slept with those
lewd women, Oholah and Oholibah. 45But
righteous judges will sentence them to the
punishment of women who commit adultery and shed blood, because they are adulterous and blood is on their hands.[e]

46“This is what the Sovereign LORD says:
Bring a mob[f] against them and give them
over to terror and plunder. 47The mob will
stone them and cut them down with their
swords; they will kill their sons and daughters and burn[g] down their houses.[h]

48“So I will put an end to lewdness in
the land, that all women may take warning and not imitate you.[i] 49You will suffer
the penalty for your lewdness and bear
the consequences of your sins of idolatry.
Then you will know that I am the Sovereign LORD.[j]”

Jerusalem as a Cooking Pot

24 In the ninth year, in the tenth month
on the tenth day, the word of the
LORD came to me:[k] 2“Son of man, record
this date, this very date, because the king
of Babylon has laid siege to Jerusalem this
very day.[l] 3Tell this rebellious people[m] a
parable[n] and say to them: ‘This is what the
Sovereign LORD says:

“ ‘Put on the cooking pot;[o] put it on
and pour water into it.
4 Put into it the pieces of meat,
all the choice pieces—the leg and the
shoulder.
Fill it with the best of these bones;
5 take the pick of the flock.[p]
Pile wood beneath it for the bones;
bring it to a boil
and cook the bones in it.[q]

6“ ‘For this is what the Sovereign LORD says:

“ ‘Woe to the city of bloodshed,[r]
to the pot now encrusted,
whose deposit will not go away!
Take the meat out piece by piece
in whatever order[s] it comes.

7“ ‘For the blood she shed is in her midst:
She poured it on the bare rock;
she did not pour it on the ground,
where the dust would cover it.[t]
8 To stir up wrath and take revenge
I put her blood on the bare rock,
so that it would not be covered.

9“ ‘Therefore this is what the Sovereign
LORD says:

“ ‘Woe to the city of bloodshed!
I, too, will pile the wood high.
10 So heap on the wood
and kindle the fire.
Cook the meat well,
mixing in the spices;
and let the bones be charred.
11 Then set the empty pot on the coals
till it becomes hot and its copper
glows,
so that its impurities may be melted
and its deposit burned away.[u]
12 It has frustrated all efforts;
its heavy deposit has not been
removed,
not even by fire.

13“ ‘Now your impurity is lewdness. Because I tried to cleanse you but you would
not be cleansed from your impurity, you
will not be clean again until my wrath
against you has subsided.[v]

24:1–2 *record this date.* This would be a bitter reminder of God’s trustworthiness to do what He promised through the prophets.
24:5 *flock.* The flock was symbolic of God’s chosen people (ch. 34). ***bones.*** Bones were sometimes used as fuel for fire.
24:6 *deposit will not go away.* God does not play favorites; His judgment would fall equally on all inhabitants of the city, for they all had sinned.

23:36 [r] Eze 16:2 [s] Isa 58:1; Eze 22:2; Mic 3:8
23:37 [t] Eze 16:36 **23:39** [u] 2Ki 21:4 [v] Jer 7:10

23:40 [w] Isa 57:9 [x] 2Ki 9:30 [y] Jer 4:30; Eze 16:13-19
23:41 [z] Est 1:6; Pr 7:17; Am 6:4 [a] Isa 65:11; Eze 44:16
23:42 [b] Ge 24:30 [c] Eze 16:11-12 **23:43** [d] ver 3
23:45 [e] Lev 20:10; Eze 16:38; Hos 6:5
23:46 [f] Eze 16:40 **23:47** [g] 2Ch 36:19 [h] 2Ch 36:17; Eze 16:40-41 **23:48** [i] 2Pe 2:6
23:49 [j] Eze 7:4; 9:10; 20:38 **24:1** [k] Eze 8:1
24:2 [l] 2Ki 25:1; Jer 39:1; 52:4
24:3 [m] Isa 1:2; Eze 2:3,6 [n] Eze 17:2; 20:49 [o] Jer 1:13; Eze 11:3 **24:5** [p] Jer 52:10 [q] Jer 52:24-27
24:6 [r] Eze 22:2 [s] Ob 1:11; Na 3:10
24:7 [t] Lev 17:13 **24:11** [u] Jer 21:10; Eze 22:15
24:13 [v] Jer 6:28-30; Eze 16:42; 22:24

14“‘I the LORD have spoken. The time has come for me to act. I will not hold back; I will not have pity, nor will I relent. You will be judged according to your conduct and your actions,[w] declares the Sovereign LORD.[x]’”

Ezekiel’s Wife Dies

15The word of the LORD came to me: 16“Son of man, with one blow I am about to take away from you the delight of your eyes. Yet do not lament or weep or shed any tears.[y] 17Groan quietly; do not mourn for the dead. Keep your turban fastened and your sandals on your feet; do not cover your mustache and beard or eat the customary food of mourners.[z]”

18So I spoke to the people in the morning, and in the evening my wife died. The next morning I did as I had been commanded.

19Then the people asked me, “Won’t you tell us what these things have to do with us?[a] Why are you acting like this?”

20So I said to them, “The word of the LORD came to me: 21Say to the people of Israel, ‘This is what the Sovereign LORD says: I am about to desecrate my sanctuary—the stronghold in which you take pride, the delight of your eyes,[b] the object of your affection. The sons and daughters[c] you left behind will fall by the sword.[d] 22And you will do as I have done. You will not cover your mustache and beard or eat the customary food of mourners.[e] 23You will keep your turbans on your heads and your sandals on your feet. You will not mourn[f] or weep but will waste away because of[a] your sins and groan among yourselves.[g] 24Ezekiel will be a sign[h] to you; you will do just as he has done. When this happens, you will know that I am the Sovereign LORD.’

25“And you, son of man, on the day I take away their stronghold, their joy and glory, the delight of their eyes, their heart’s desire, and their sons and daughters[i] as well— 26on that day a fugitive will come to tell you[j] the news. 27At that time your mouth will be opened; you will speak with him and will no longer be silent. So you will be a sign to them, and they will know that I am the LORD.[k]”

A Prophecy Against Ammon

25 The word of the LORD came to me: 2“Son of man, set your face against the Ammonites[l] and prophesy against them.[m] 3Say to them, ‘Hear the word of the Sovereign LORD. This is what the Sovereign LORD says: Because you said “Aha![n]” over my sanctuary when it was desecrated and over the land of Israel when it was laid waste and over the people of Judah when they went into exile,[o] 4therefore I am going to give you to the people of the East[p] as a possession. They will set up their camps and pitch their tents among you; they will eat your fruit and drink your milk.[q] 5I will turn Rabbah[r] into a pasture for camels and Ammon into a resting place for sheep.[s] Then you will know that I am the LORD. 6For this is what the Sovereign LORD says: Because you have clapped your hands and stamped your feet, rejoicing with all the malice of your heart against the land of Israel,[t] 7therefore I will stretch out my hand[u] against you and give you as plunder to the nations. I will wipe you out from among the nations and exterminate you from the countries. I will destroy[v] you, and you will know that I am the LORD.[w]’”

A Prophecy Against Moab

8“This is what the Sovereign LORD says: ‘Because Moab[x] and Seir said, “Look,

---

a 23 Or *away in*

24:16 *do not lament or weep.* This command of God may be one of the hardest ever given to one of His servants. The picture of Ezekiel’s wife dying and Ezekiel not being allowed to grieve illustrated God’s pain over the death of His wife—Jerusalem—and His inability to mourn because the nation deserved the punishment. Ezekiel was called by God to “be a sign to the exiles” by demonstrating what they should do in response to the “death” of their desire and delight—their nation and its capital city. What Ezekiel was commanded to accept and do illustrated the degree of personal sacrifice and separation from ordinary life that the prophetic ministry often required. A long period of mourning was normal in the ancient Middle East.

24:21 *the object of your affection.* The Judeans had the wrong kind of pride about the temple. Instead of the temple being a place of worship and the house of God, the Judeans took pride in the building as a sign of their importance.

24:22–24 *sign.* When Jerusalem fell, God would prove Himself as trustworthy and righteous, and Ezekiel as His true prophet (v. 27). ***you will know that I am the Sovereign LORD.*** The trials that the Israelites were going through would prompt them to depend on the Lord and know that He is holy.

25:2 *set your face against the Ammonites.* This country corresponds roughly to the present-day country of Jordan with its capital Amman.

25:4 *people of the East.* This is another title for the Babylonians (21:31). Ancient historical records mention Ammon’s subjugation by Nebuchadnezzar five years after the fall of Jerusalem. Arab invaders came to dominate the territory, and Persian control began about 530 B.C.

25:8–12 *Moab and Seir.* Moab was south of Ammon

24:14 [w] Eze 36:19 [x] Eze 18:30 **24:16** [y] Jer 13:17; 16:5; 22:10 **24:17** [z] Jer 16:7 **24:19** [a] Eze 12:9; 37:18 **24:21** [b] Ps 27:4 [c] Eze 23:25 [d] Jer 7:14, 15; Eze 23:47 **24:22** [e] Jer 16:7 **24:23** [f] Job 27:15 [g] Ps 78:64 **24:24** [h] Isa 20:3; Eze 4:3; 12:11 **24:25** [i] Jer 11:22 **24:26** [j] 1Sa 4:12; Job 1:15-19 **24:27** [k] Eze 3:26; 33:22 **25:2** [l] Eze 21:28; Zep 2:8-9 [m] Jer 49:1-6 **25:3** [n] Eze 26:2; 36:2 [o] Pr 17:5 **25:4** [p] Jdg 6:3 [q] Dt 28:33, 51; Jdg 6:33 **25:5** [r] Dt 3:11; Eze 21:20 [s] Isa 17:2 **25:6** [t] Ob 1:12; Zep 2:8 **25:7** [u] Zep 1:4 [v] Eze 21:31 [w] Am 1:14-15 **25:8** [x] Jer 48:1; Am 2:1

Judah has become like all the other nations,” **9**therefore I will expose the flank of Moab, beginning at its frontier towns—Beth Jeshimoth[y], Baal Meon[z] and Kiriathaim[a]—the glory of that land. **10**I will give Moab along with the Ammonites to the people of the East as a possession, so that the Ammonites will not be remembered[b] among the nations; **11**and I will inflict punishment on Moab. Then they will know that I am the LORD.’”

A Prophecy Against Edom

12“This is what the Sovereign LORD says: ‘Because Edom[c] took revenge on Judah and became very guilty by doing so, **13**therefore this is what the Sovereign LORD says: I will stretch out my hand against Edom and kill both man and beast.[d] I will lay it waste, and from Teman to Dedan[e] they will fall by the sword. **14**I will take vengeance on Edom by the hand of my people Israel, and they will deal with Edom in accordance with my anger[f] and my wrath; they will know my vengeance, declares the Sovereign LORD.’”

A Prophecy Against Philistia

15“This is what the Sovereign LORD says: ‘Because the Philistines[g] acted in vengeance and took revenge with malice in their hearts, and with ancient hostility sought to destroy Judah, **16**therefore this is what the Sovereign LORD says: I am about to stretch out my hand against the Philistines,[h] and I will wipe out the Kerethites[i] and destroy those remaining along the coast. **17**I will carry out great vengeance on them and punish them in my wrath. Then they will know that I am the LORD, when I take vengeance on them.’”

A Prophecy Against Tyre

26 In the eleventh month of the twelfth[*a*] year, on the first day of the month, the word of the LORD came to me: **2**“Son of man, because Tyre[j] has said of Jerusalem, ‘Aha![k] The gate to the nations is broken, and its doors have swung open to me; now that she lies in ruins I will prosper,’ **3**therefore this is what the Sovereign LORD says: I am against you, Tyre, and I will bring many nations against you, like the sea[l] casting up its waves. **4**They will destroy[m] the walls of Tyre[n] and pull down her towers; I will scrape away her rubble and make her a bare rock. **5**Out in the sea[o] she will become a place to spread fishnets, for I have spoken, declares the Sovereign LORD. She will become plunder[p] for the nations, **6**and her settlements on the mainland will be ravaged by the sword. Then they will know that I am the LORD.

7“For this is what the Sovereign LORD says: From the north I am going to bring against Tyre Nebuchadnezzar[*b*q] king of Babylon, king of kings,[r] with horses and chariots,[s] with horsemen and a great army. **8**He will ravage your settlements on the mainland with the sword; he will set up siege works[t] against you, build a ramp[u] up to your walls and raise his shields against you. **9**He will direct the blows of his battering rams against your walls and demolish your towers with his weapons. **10**His horses will be so many that they will cover you with dust. Your walls will tremble at the noise of the warhorses, wagons and chariots[v] when he enters your gates as men enter a city whose walls have been broken through. **11**The hooves[w] of his horses will trample all your streets; he will kill your people with the sword, and your strong pillars[x] will fall to the ground.[y] **12**They will plunder your wealth and loot your merchandise; they will break down your walls and demolish your fine houses and throw your stones, timber and rubble into the sea.[z] **13**I will put an end[a] to your noisy songs, and the music of your harps[b] will be heard no more.[c] **14**I will make you a bare rock, and you will become a place to spread fishnets. You will never be rebuilt,[d] for I the LORD have spoken, declares the Sovereign LORD.

---

a *1* Probable reading of the original Hebrew text; Masoretic Text does not have *month of the twelfth.*
b 7 Hebrew *Nebuchadrezzar,* of which *Nebuchadnezzar* is a variant; here and often in Ezekiel and Jeremiah

---

and east of the Dead Sea. Seir (Edom) was located south of Moab. They were the descendants of Esau.

25:15 *Philistines.* The Philistines were along the Mediterranean coast in southwest Palestine.

25:16 *Kerethites.* This term was used here as a substitute term for some or all of the Philistines who had migrated from Crete. Their remote ancestors were Aegeans.

26:2 *Tyre.* Tyre was a major seaport and the leading city in Phoenicia (present-day Lebanon). ***has said.*** The past tense could refer to an event that had not yet taken place, using a Hebrew idiom which describes a future event so certain that it can be expressed as having already been accomplished (Is. 9:6; 52:13–53:12).

26:7–14 *I will make you a bare rock.* This prophecy of Tyre' fate had two steps. First the Babylonian army under Nebuchadnezzar laid siege to it, and Persia defeated it in about 525 B.C. Then in 322 B.C. Alexander the Great defeated it again when his army built a causeway a half a mile long between the shore and the city on its island. He tore down defensive walls to build the causeway.

25:9 [y] Nu 33:49 [z] Nu 32:3; Jos 13:17 [a] Nu 32:37; Jos 13:19 **25:10** [b] Eze 21:32 **25:12** [c] 2Ch 28:17 **25:13** [d] Eze 29:8 [e] Jer 25:23 **25:14** [f] Eze 35:11 **25:15** [g] 2Ch 28:18 **25:16** [h] Jer 47:1-7 [i] 1Sa 30:14; Zep 2:4-5 **26:2** [j] 2Sa 5:11; Isa 23 [k] Eze 25:3 **26:3** [l] Isa 5:30; Jer 50:42; 51:42 **26:4** [m] Isa 23:1, 11 [n] Am 1:10 **26:5** [o] Eze 27:32 [p] Eze 29:19 **26:7** [q] Jer 27:6 [r] Ezr 7:12; Da 2:37 [s] Eze 23:24; Na 2:3-4 **26:8** [t] Jer 6:6 [u] Eze 21:22 **26:10** [v] Jer 4:13 **26:11** [w] Isa 5:28 [x] Jer 43:13 [y] Isa 26:5 **26:12** [z] Isa 23:8; Eze 27:3-27; 28:8 **26:13** [a] Jer 7:34 [b] Isa 14:11 [c] Jer 25:10; Rev 18:22 **26:14** [d] Job 12:14; Mal 1:4

15 “This is what the Sovereign LORD says
to Tyre: Will not the coastlands[e] tremble[f]
at the sound of your fall, when the wounded groan and the slaughter takes place in
you? 16 Then all the princes of the coast will
step down from their thrones and lay aside
their robes and take off their embroidered
garments. Clothed[g] with terror, they will sit
on the ground, trembling[h] every moment,
appalled[i] at you. 17 Then they will take up
a lament[j] concerning you and say to you:

“ ‘How you are destroyed, city of
renown,
peopled by men of the sea!
You were a power on the seas,
you and your citizens;
you put your terror
on all who lived there.[k]
18 Now the coastlands tremble
on the day of your fall;
the islands in the sea
are terrified at your collapse.’[l]

19 “This is what the Sovereign LORD says:
When I make you a desolate city, like cities
no longer inhabited, and when I bring the
ocean depths over you and its vast waters
cover you,[m] 20 then I will bring you down
with those who go down to the pit,[n] to the
people of long ago. I will make you dwell
in the earth below, as in ancient ruins, with
those who go down to the pit, and you will
not return or take your place*[a]* in the land of
the living.[o] 21 I will bring you to a horrible
end and you will be no more. You will be
sought, but you will never again be found,
declares the Sovereign LORD.”[p]

A Lament Over Tyre

27 The word of the LORD came to me:
2 “Son of man, take up a lament concerning Tyre. 3 Say to Tyre, situated at the
gateway to the sea,[q] merchant of peoples
on many coasts, ‘This is what the Sovereign LORD says:

“ ‘You say, Tyre,
“I am perfect in beauty.[r]”
4 Your domain was on the high seas;
your builders brought your beauty to
perfection.
5 They made all your timbers
of juniper from Senir*[b]*;[s]
they took a cedar from Lebanon
to make a mast for you.
6 Of oaks[t] from Bashan
they made your oars;
of cypress wood*[c]* from the coasts of
Cyprus[u]
they made your deck, adorned with
ivory.
7 Fine embroidered linen from Egypt was
your sail
and served as your banner;
your awnings were of blue and purple[v]
from the coasts of Elishah.
8 Men of Sidon and Arvad[w] were your
oarsmen;
your skilled men, Tyre, were aboard
as your sailors.[x]
9 Veteran craftsmen of Byblos[y] were on
board
as shipwrights to caulk your seams.
All the ships of the sea and their sailors
came alongside to trade for your
wares.

10 “ ‘Men of Persia,[z] Lydia and Put[a]
served as soldiers in your army.
They hung their shields and helmets on
your walls,
bringing you splendor.
11 Men of Arvad and Helek
guarded your walls on every side;
men of Gammad
were in your towers.
They hung their shields around your
walls;
they brought your beauty to
perfection.

12 “ ‘Tarshish[b] did business with you because of your great wealth of goods;[c] they
exchanged silver, iron, tin and lead for your
merchandise.
13 “ ‘Greece, Tubal and Meshek[d] did business with you; they traded human beings[e]
and articles of bronze for your wares.
14 “ ‘Men of Beth Togarmah[f] exchanged
chariot horses, cavalry horses and mules
for your merchandise.

a 20 Septuagint; Hebrew *return, and I will give glory* *b* 5 That is, Mount Hermon *c* 6 Targum; the Masoretic Text has a different division of the consonants.

27:1–25 ***take up a lament concerning Tyre.*** Prosperity often leads to pride, which results in the abandonment of God (Deut. 18:11–14). Jerusalem and Tyre both claimed to be unique, the former because of her exclusive claim to true religion and the latter because of the exclusive emphasis on material gain. Yet the wealth of Tyre vanished quickly.
27:6 ***Bashan.*** This was the broad and fertile plateau east of the Sea of Galilee and the upper Jordan.
27:8 ***Sidon.*** Sidon was a Phoenician seaport about 30 miles north of Tyre. The two cities were rivals but Tyre tended to dominate.
27:10–11 ***Lydia and Put.*** Or Lud, in western Asia Minor, and Libya, in northern Africa.
27:13 ***Greece, Tubal and Meshek.*** Tubal and Meshek are thought to have been in eastern Asia Minor or modern Turkey.
27:14 ***Togarmah.*** This phrase may refer to the people of Armenia in eastern Asia Minor (38:6).

26:15 [e] Eze 27:35 [f] Jer 49:21 **26:16** [g] Job 8:22 [h] Hos 11:10 [i] Eze 32:10 **26:17** [j] Eze 19:1; 27:32 [k] Isa 14:12 **26:18** [l] Isa 23:5; 41:5; Eze 27:35 **26:19** [m] Isa 8:7-8 **26:20** [n] Eze 32:18; Am 9:2; Jnh 2:2,6 [o] Eze 32:24,30 **26:21** [p] Eze 27:36; 28:19; Rev 18:21 **27:3** [q] ver 33 [r] Eze 28:2 **27:5** [s] Dt 3:9 **27:6** [t] Nu 21:33; Jer 22:20; Zec 11:2 [u] Ge 10:4; Isa 23:12 **27:7** [v] Ex 25:4; Jer 10:9 **27:8** [w] Ge 10:18 [x] 1Ki 9:27 **27:9** [y] Jos 13:5; 1Ki 5:18 **27:10** [z] Eze 38:5 [a] Eze 30:5 **27:12** [b] Ge 10:4 [c] ver 18,33 **27:13** [d] Ge 10:2; Isa 66:19; Eze 38:2 [e] Rev 18:13 **27:14** [f] Ge 10:3; Eze 38:6

15“ ‘The men of Rhodes[a][g] traded with
you, and many coastlands[h] were your customers; they paid you with ivory[i] tusks and
ebony.
16“ ‘Aram[b][j] did business with you because of your many products; they exchanged turquoise,[k] purple fabric, embroidered work, fine linen, coral and rubies for
your merchandise.
17“ ‘Judah and Israel traded with you;
they exchanged wheat from Minnith[l] and
confections,[c] honey, olive oil and balm for
your wares.
18“ ‘Damascus[m] did business with you
because of your many products and great
wealth of goods. They offered wine from
Helbon, wool from Zahar 19and casks of
wine from Izal in exchange for your wares:
wrought iron, cassia and calamus.
20“ ‘Dedan traded in saddle blankets with
you.
21“ ‘Arabia and all the princes of Kedar[n]
were your customers; they did business
with you in lambs, rams and goats.
22“ ‘The merchants of Sheba[o] and Raamah traded with you; for your merchandise
they exchanged the finest of all kinds of
spices[p] and precious stones, and gold.
23“ ‘Harran,[q] Kanneh and Eden[r] and merchants of Sheba, Ashur and Kilmad traded
with you. 24In your marketplace they traded with you beautiful garments, blue fabric,
embroidered work and multicolored rugs
with cords twisted and tightly knotted.

25“ ‘The ships of Tarshish[s] serve
as carriers for your wares.
You are filled with heavy cargo
as you sail the sea.
26Your oarsmen take you
out to the high seas.
But the east wind[t] will break you to
pieces
far out at sea.
27Your wealth,[u] merchandise and wares,
your mariners, sailors and
shipwrights,
your merchants and all your soldiers,
and everyone else on board
will sink into the heart of the sea
on the day of your shipwreck.
28The shorelands will quake[v]
when your sailors cry out.
29All who handle the oars
will abandon their ships;
the mariners and all the sailors
will stand on the shore.
30They will raise their voice
and cry bitterly over you;
they will sprinkle dust[w] on their heads
and roll[x] in ashes.[y]
31They will shave their heads because of
you
and will put on sackcloth.
They will weep[z] over you with anguish
of soul
and with bitter mourning.[a]
32As they wail and mourn over you,
they will take up a lament[b]
concerning you:
“Who was ever silenced like Tyre,
surrounded by the sea?”
33When your merchandise went out on
the seas,
you satisfied many nations;
with your great wealth[c] and your wares
you enriched the kings of the earth.
34Now you are shattered by the sea
in the depths of the waters;
your wares and all your company
have gone down with you.[d]
35All who live in the coastlands[e]
are appalled at you;
their kings shudder with horror
and their faces are distorted with
fear.
36The merchants among the nations scoff
at you;[f]
you have come to a horrible end
and will be no more.[g]’ ”

A Prophecy Against the King of Tyre

28 The word of the LORD came to me:
2“Son of man, say to the ruler of Tyre,
‘This is what the Sovereign LORD says:

a 15 Septuagint; Hebrew *Dedan* *b* 16 Most Hebrew manuscripts; some Hebrew manuscripts and Syriac *Edom* *c* 17 The meaning of the Hebrew for this word is uncertain.

27:15 *Rhodes.* This may have been Dedan which was a major trading center in the southern Aegean Sea.
27:17 *balm.* Balm was an aromatic resin or other gummy substance that may have had medicinal value (Jer. 8:22).
27:19 *cassia.* Cassia was either a type of cinnamon tree or a plant from which perfume and incense were made. ***calamus.*** This refers to an oil-producing reed found in swamps.
27:21 *Kedar.* Kedar was a nomadic tribe in Arabia.
27:22 *Sheba and Raamah.* These places were located near Arabia (Gen. 10:6–7).
27:23 *Kanneh and Eden ... Kilmad.* These three places were probably in Mesopotamia, most likely south of Haran.
28:2 *In the pride of your heart.* Ezekiel rebuked the king of Tyre for imagining that by his wisdom he had acquired his riches of silver and gold. He had filled the city with violence because of the abundance and

27:15 [g] Ge 10:7 [h] Jer 25:22 [i] 1Ki 10:22; Rev 18:12 **27:16** [j] Jdg 10:6; Isa 7:1-8 [k] Eze 28:13 **27:17** [l] Jdg 11:33 **27:18** [m] Ge 14:15; Eze 47:16-18 **27:21** [n] Ge 25:13; Isa 60:7 **27:22** [o] Ge 10:7,28; 1Ki 10:1-2; Isa 60:6 [p] Ge 43:11 **27:23** [q] 2Ki 19:12 [r] Isa 37:12 **27:25** [s] Isa 2:16 *fn* **27:26** [t] Ps 48:7; Jer 18:17 **27:27** [u] Pr 11:4 **27:28** [v] Eze 26:15 **27:30** [w] 2Sa 1:2 [x] Jer 6:26 [y] Rev 18:18-19 **27:31** [z] Isa 16:9 [a] Isa 22:12; Eze 7:18 **27:32** [b] Eze 26:17 **27:33** [c] ver 12; Eze 28:4-5 **27:34** [d] Zec 9:4 **27:35** [e] Eze 26:15 **27:36** [f] Jer 18:16; 19:8; 49:17; 50:13; Zep 2:15 [g] Ps 37:10,36; Eze 26:21

"'In the pride of your heart
you say, "I am a god;
I sit on the throne[h] of a god
in the heart of the seas."
But you are a mere mortal and not a god,
though you think you are as wise as a god.[i]
3 Are you wiser than Daniel[a]?[j]
Is no secret hidden from you?
4 By your wisdom and understanding
you have gained wealth for yourself
and amassed gold and silver
in your treasuries.[k]
5 By your great skill in trading
you have increased your wealth,
and because of your wealth
your heart has grown proud.[l]

6 "'Therefore this is what the Sovereign LORD says:

"'Because you think you are wise,
as wise as a god,
7 I am going to bring foreigners against you,
the most ruthless of nations;[m]
they will draw their swords against
your beauty and wisdom
and pierce your shining splendor.
8 They will bring you down to the pit,[n]
and you will die a violent death
in the heart of the seas.[o]
9 Will you then say, "I am a god,"
in the presence of those who kill you?
You will be but a mortal, not a god,
in the hands of those who slay you.
10 You will die the death of the uncircumcised[p]
at the hands of foreigners.

I have spoken, declares the Sovereign LORD.'"

11 The word of the LORD came to me:
12 "Son of man, take up a lament[q] concerning the king of Tyre and say to him: 'This
is what the Sovereign LORD says:

"'You were the seal of perfection,
full of wisdom and perfect in beauty.[r]
13 You were in Eden,[s]
the garden of God;[t]
every precious stone adorned you:
carnelian, chrysolite and emerald,
topaz, onyx and jasper,
lapis lazuli, turquoise[u] and beryl.[b]
Your settings and mountings[c] were made of gold;
on the day you were created they were prepared.
14 You were anointed[v] as a guardian cherub,[w]
for so I ordained you.
You were on the holy mount of God;
you walked among the fiery stones.
15 You were blameless in your ways
from the day you were created
till wickedness was found in you.
16 Through your widespread trade
you were filled with violence,[x]
and you sinned.
So I drove you in disgrace from the mount of God,
and I expelled you, guardian cherub,[y]
from among the fiery stones.
17 Your heart became proud[z]
on account of your beauty,
and you corrupted your wisdom
because of your splendor.
So I threw you to the earth;
I made a spectacle of you before kings.
18 By your many sins and dishonest trade
you have desecrated your sanctuaries.
So I made a fire come out from you,
and it consumed you,
and I reduced you to ashes[a] on the ground
in the sight of all who were watching.
19 All the nations who knew you
are appalled at you;
you have come to a horrible end
and will be no more.[b]'"

[a] *3* Or *Danel,* a man of renown in ancient literature
[b] *13* The precise identification of some of these precious stones is uncertain.
[c] *13* The meaning of the Hebrew for this phrase is uncertain.

---

unrighteousness of his trade. God would therefore bring a ruthless nation against him.

28:10 *the death of the uncircumcised.* This term denotes a disgraceful death (31:18).

28:12 *king of Tyre.* The lamentation is for the king of Tyre because he is exhibiting the character and attitudes of Satan. ***seal of perfection.*** This is more literally "the one sealing a plan." In effect, the king affixed the official seal of his signet ring to the plans that made Tyre one of the leading centers of commerce in that day.

28:14 *cherub.* Satan was a created being (v. 13). He does not have the characteristics of God. He belonged to the order of angels called cherubim. ***the holy mount of God.*** The focus here seems to be on the king of Tyre' attempt to enter into the council of the gods. So instead of the verse referring to the king's presence In Jerusalem, it could refer more logically to a Phoenician ritual, the celebration of their patron god Melqart's fiery resurrection. This king wanted to imitate Melqart.

28:15 *blameless.* Satan was not created evil. ***wickedness.*** The Bible does not say where this iniquity came from, but his sin was pride (1 Tim. 3:6).

28:16–19 *widespread trade.* The expression is most easily and appropriately applied to the human king who was the driving force behind the development of Tyre's commercial empire.

28:17 *on account of your beauty.* This was part of the sin of pride, which made Satan want to be like the Most High (Is. 14:13–14). ***threw you to the earth.*** Jesus said that He saw Satan fall (Luke 10:18).

28:2 [h] Isa 14:13 [i] Ps 9:20; 82:6-7; Isa 31:3; 2Th 2:4 **28:3** [j] Da 1:20; 5:11-12 **28:4** [k] Zec 9:3 **28:5** [l] Job 31:25; Ps 52:7; 62:10; Hos 12:8; 13:6 **28:7** [m] Eze 30:11; 31:12; 32:12; Hab 1:6 **28:8** [n] Eze 32:30 [o] Eze 27:27 **28:10** [p] Eze 31:18; 32:19, 24 **28:12** [q] Eze 19:1 [r] Eze 27:2-4 **28:13** [s] Ge 2:8 [t] Eze 31:8-9 [u] Eze 27:16 **28:14** [v] Ex 30:26; 40:9 [w] Ex 25:17-20 **28:16** [x] Hab 2:17 [y] Ge 3:24 **28:17** [z] Eze 31:10 **28:18** [a] Mal 4:3 **28:19** [b] Jer 51:64; Eze 26:21; 27:36

A Prophecy Against Sidon

20The word of the LORD came to me:
21"Son of man, set your face against[c] Sidon;[d] prophesy against her 22and say: 'This
is what the Sovereign LORD says:

"'I am against you, Sidon,
and among you I will display my
glory.[e]
You will know that I am the LORD,
when I inflict punishment[f] on you
and within you am proved to be holy.
23I will send a plague upon you
and make blood flow in your streets.
The slain will fall within you,
with the sword against you on every
side.
Then you will know that I am the LORD.[g]

24"'No longer will the people of Israel
have malicious neighbors who are painful
briers and sharp thorns.[h] Then they will
know that I am the Sovereign LORD.
25"'This is what the Sovereign LORD
says: When I gather[i] the people of Israel
from the nations where they have been
scattered,[j] I will be proved holy[k] through
them in the sight of the nations. Then they
will live in their own land, which I gave to
my servant Jacob.[l] 26They will live there
in safety[m] and will build houses and plant
vineyards; they will live in safety when I
inflict punishment on all their neighbors
who maligned them. Then they will know
that I am the LORD their God.[n]'"

A Prophecy Against Egypt

Judgment on Pharaoh

29 In the tenth year, in the tenth month
on the twelfth day, the word of the
LORD came to me:[o] 2"Son of man, set your
face against Pharaoh king of Egypt[p] and
prophesy against him and against all
Egypt.[q] 3Speak to him and say: 'This is
what the Sovereign LORD says:

"'I am against you, Pharaoh[r] king of
Egypt,
you great monster[s] lying among your
streams.
You say, "The Nile belongs to me;
I made it for myself."
4But I will put hooks[t] in your jaws
and make the fish of your streams
stick to your scales.
I will pull you out from among your
streams,
with all the fish sticking to your
scales.[u]
5I will leave you in the desert,
you and all the fish of your streams.
You will fall on the open field
and not be gathered or picked up.
I will give you as food
to the beasts of the earth and the
birds of the sky.[v]

6Then all who live in Egypt will know that
I am the LORD.

"'You have been a staff of reed[w] for
the people of Israel. 7When they grasped
you with their hands, you splintered[x] and
you tore open their shoulders; when they
leaned on you, you broke and their backs
were wrenched.[a][y]
8"'Therefore this is what the Sovereign
LORD says: I will bring a sword against you
and kill both man and beast.[z] 9Egypt will
become a desolate wasteland. Then they
will know that I am the LORD.
"'Because you said, "The Nile is mine; I
made it,[a]" 10therefore I am against you and
against your streams, and I will make the
land of Egypt a ruin and a desolate waste
from Migdol to Aswan,[b] as far as the border of Cush.[b] 11The foot of neither man nor
beast will pass through it; no one will live
there for forty years.[c] 12I will make the land
of Egypt desolate among devastated lands,
and her cities will lie desolate forty years
among ruined cities. And I will disperse
the Egyptians among the nations and scatter them through the countries.[d]

---

[a] 7 Syriac (see also Septuagint and Vulgate); Hebrew *and you caused their backs to stand*
[b] 10 That is, the upper Nile region

28:24 *painful briers and sharp thorns.* These words refer to the nations around Israel who had been enemies and evil influences. When the judgments were executed fully, these nations would no longer be able to harass and oppress Israel.
29:3 *great monster.* The Pharaoh is pictured here as a crocodile. Pharaoh's arrogant pride is described by his words about the Nile River, "I made it for myself."
29:4–5 *I will put hooks in your jaws.* Whereas verse 3 explains why Pharaoh would be punished, these verses explain how the punishment would be accomplished. The imagery pictures a crocodile being caught, carried out of the water onto land, and left as carrion.
29:8 *sword.* Here is another reference to the Babylonian army under Nebuchadnezzar, the predicted human instrument of God's coming wrath (21:1–7, 9–11,19–20).
29:10 *Migdol to Aswan, as far as the border of Cush.* This phrase refers to places most likely near the northern and southern boundaries of ancient Egypt, indicating the totality of the land (Judg. 20:1). The desolation would extend to the land south of Egypt — ancient Nubia, which is modern Sudan.

28:21 [c] Eze 6:2 [d] Ge 10:15; Jer 25:22 **28:22** [e] Eze 39:13 [f] Eze 30:19 **28:23** [g] Eze 38:22 **28:24** [h] Nu 33:55; Jos 23:13; Eze 2:6 **28:25** [i] Ps 106:47; Jer 32:37 [j] Isa 11:12 [k] Eze 20:41 [l] Jer 23:8; Eze 11:17; 34:27; 37:25 **28:26** [m] Jer 23:6 [n] Isa 65:21; Jer 32:15; Eze 38:8; Am 9:14-15 **29:1** [o] ver 17; Eze 26:1 **29:2** [p] Jer 25:19 [q] Isa 19:1-17; Jer 46:2; Eze 30:1-26; 31:1-18; 32:1-32 **29:3** [r] Jer 44:30 [s] Ps 74:13; Isa 27:1; Eze 32:2 **29:4** [t] 2Ki 19:28 [u] Eze 38:4 **29:5** [v] Jer 7:33; 34:20; Eze 32:4-6; 39:4 **29:6** [w] 2Ki 18:21; Isa 36:6 **29:7** [x] Isa 36:6 [y] Eze 17:15-17 **29:8** [z] Eze 14:17; 32:11-13 **29:9** [a] Eze 30:7-8, 13-19 **29:10** [b] Eze 30:6 **29:11** [c] Eze 32:13 **29:12** [d] Jer 46:19; Eze 30:7,23,26

13“‘Yet this is what the Sovereign LORD
says: At the end of forty years I will gather
the Egyptians from the nations where they
were scattered. 14I will bring them back
from captivity and return them to Upper
Egypt,[e] the land of their ancestry. There
they will be a lowly[f] kingdom. 15It will be
the lowliest of kingdoms and will never
again exalt itself above the other nations.[g] I
will make it so weak that it will never again
rule over the nations. 16Egypt will no longer be a source of confidence[h] for the people of Israel but will be a reminder of their
sin in turning to her for help. Then they will
know that I am the Sovereign LORD.[i]’”

Nebuchadnezzar’s Reward

17In the twenty-seventh year, in the first
month on the first day, the word of the
LORD came to me:[j] 18“Son of man, Nebuchadnezzar[k] king of Babylon drove his
army in a hard campaign against Tyre; every head was rubbed bare[l] and every shoulder made raw. Yet he and his army got no
reward from the campaign he led against
Tyre. 19Therefore this is what the Sovereign LORD says: I am going to give Egypt
to Nebuchadnezzar king of Babylon, and
he will carry off its wealth. He will loot and
plunder the land as pay for his army.[m] 20I
have given him Egypt as a reward for his
efforts because he and his army did it for
me, declares the Sovereign LORD.[n]

21“On that day I will make a horn[a][o] grow
for the Israelites, and I will open your
mouth[p] among them. Then they will know
that I am the LORD.[q]”

A Lament Over Egypt

30 The word of the LORD came to me:
2“Son of man, prophesy and say:
‘This is what the Sovereign LORD says:

“‘Wail[r] and say,
“Alas for that day!”
3For the day is near,[s]
the day of the LORD[t] is near—
a day of clouds,
a time of doom for the nations.
4A sword will come against Egypt,
and anguish will come upon Cush.[b]
When the slain fall in Egypt,
her wealth will be carried away
and her foundations torn down.[u]

5Cush and Libya,[v] Lydia and all Arabia,
Kub and the people[w] of the covenant land
will fall by the sword along with Egypt.

6“‘This is what the LORD says:

“‘The allies of Egypt will fall
and her proud strength will fail.
From Migdol to Aswan[x]
they will fall by the sword within her,
declares the Sovereign LORD.
7“‘They will be desolate
among desolate lands,
and their cities will lie
among ruined cities.[y]
8Then they will know that I am the LORD,
when I set fire to Egypt
and all her helpers are crushed.

9“‘On that day messengers will go out
from me in ships to frighten Cush[z] out of
her complacency. Anguish[a] will take hold
of them on the day of Egypt’s doom, for it
is sure to come.[b]

10“‘This is what the Sovereign LORD
says:

“‘I will put an end to the hordes of Egypt
by the hand of Nebuchadnezzar king
of Babylon.[c]
11He and his army—the most ruthless of
nations[d]—
will be brought in to destroy the land.
They will draw their swords against
Egypt
and fill the land with the slain.
12I will dry up[e] the waters of the Nile[f]
and sell the land to an evil nation;
by the hand of foreigners
I will lay waste the land and
everything in it.

I the LORD have spoken.

13“‘This is what the Sovereign LORD
says:

“‘I will destroy the idols[g]
and put an end to the images in
Memphis.[h]
No longer will there be a prince in
Egypt,[i]
and I will spread fear throughout the
land.

---

a *21 Horn* here symbolizes strength. *b* *4* That is, the upper Nile region; also in verses 5 and 9

29:14–15 *Upper Egypt.* This was southern Egypt. It would thereafter never again dominate other nations.
29:18 *every head was rubbed bare.* The siege of Tyre was protracted, lasting about 13 years.
29:21 *On that day.* This refers to the day when Egypt would fall to Babylon, and a prophecy about the Messiah should not be read into this text.
30:5 *Cush.* This refers to the area south of Egypt toward modern Ethiopia.
30:9 *day of Egypt’s doom.* This was the day that Egypt and her allies would be conquered. It was part of a larger period of God’s judgment on the nations outside Israel by means of Babylon; in fact, Ezekiel describes the Babylonians as “messengers” sent from God Himself.
30:13–19 *Memphis.* Memphis, or ancient Noph, was a significant city in Egypt. It was capital of the Old Kingdom in the third century B.C.

29:14 [e] Eze 30:14 [f] Eze 17:14 **29:15** [g] Zec 10:11
29:16 [h] Isa 36:4,6 [i] Isa 30:2; Hos 8:13 **29:17** [j] Eze 24:1
29:18 [k] Jer 27:6; Eze 26:7-8 [l] Jer 48:37
29:19 [m] Jer 43:10-13; Eze 30:4, 10, 24-25
29:20 [n] Isa 10:6-7; 45:1; Jer 25:9 **29:21** [o] Ps 132:17
[p] Eze 33:22 [q] Eze 24:27 **30:2** [r] Isa 13:6 **30:3** [s] Eze 7:7; Joel 2:1, 11; Ob 1:15 [t] ver 18; Eze 7:12, 19
30:4 [u] Eze 29:19 **30:5** [v] Eze 27:10 [w] Jer 25:20
30:6 [x] Eze 29:10 **30:7** [y] Eze 29:12 **30:9** [z] Isa 18:1-2
[a] Isa 23:5 [b] Eze 32:9-10 **30:10** [c] Eze 29:19
30:11 [d] Eze 28:7 **30:12** [e] Isa 19:6 [f] Eze 29:9
30:13 [g] Jer 43:12 [h] Isa 19:13 [i] Zec 10:11

14 I will lay[j] waste Upper Egypt,
set fire to Zoan[k]
and inflict punishment on Thebes.[l]
15 I will pour out my wrath on Pelusium,
the stronghold of Egypt,
and wipe out the hordes of Thebes.
16 I will set fire to Egypt;
Pelusium will writhe in agony.
Thebes will be taken by storm;
Memphis will be in constant distress.
17 The young men of Heliopolis[m] and Bubastis
will fall by the sword,
and the cities themselves will go into captivity.
18 Dark will be the day at Tahpanhes
when I break the yoke of Egypt;[n]
there her proud strength will come to an end.
She will be covered with clouds,
and her villages will go into captivity.[o]
19 So I will inflict punishment on Egypt,
and they will know that I am the LORD.'"

Pharaoh's Arms Are Broken

20 In the eleventh year, in the first month
on the seventh day, the word of the LORD
came to me:[p] 21 "Son of man, I have broken
the arm[q] of Pharaoh king of Egypt. It has
not been bound up to be healed[r] or put in a
splint so that it may become strong enough
to hold a sword. 22 Therefore this is what the
Sovereign LORD says: I am against Pharaoh
king of Egypt.[s] I will break both his arms,
the good arm as well as the broken one,
and make the sword fall from his hand.[t]
23 I will disperse the Egyptians among the
nations and scatter them through the countries.[u] 24 I will strengthen[v] the arms of the
king of Babylon and put my sword[w] in his
hand, but I will break the arms of Pharaoh,
and he will groan before him like a mortally wounded man. 25 I will strengthen the
arms of the king of Babylon, but the arms
of Pharaoh will fall limp. Then they will
know that I am the LORD, when I put my
sword into the hand of the king of Babylon
and he brandishes it against Egypt. 26 I will
disperse the Egyptians among the nations
and scatter them through the countries.
Then they will know that I am the LORD.[x]"

Pharaoh as a Felled Cedar of Lebanon

31 In the eleventh year,[y] in the third
month on the first day, the word of
the LORD came to me:[z] 2 "Son of man, say to
Pharaoh king of Egypt and to his hordes:

"'Who can be compared with you in majesty?
3 Consider Assyria, once a cedar in Lebanon,
with beautiful branches
overshadowing the forest;
it towered on high,
its top above the thick foliage.[a]
4 The waters nourished it,
deep springs made it grow tall;
their streams flowed
all around its base
and sent their channels
to all the trees of the field.
5 So it towered higher
than all the trees of the field;
its boughs increased
and its branches grew long,
spreading because of abundant waters.[b]
6 All the birds of the sky
nested in its boughs,
all the animals of the wild
gave birth under its branches;
all the great nations
lived in its shade.[c]
7 It was majestic in beauty,
with its spreading boughs,
for its roots went down
to abundant waters.
8 The cedars[d] in the garden of God
could not rival it,
nor could the junipers
equal its boughs,
nor could the plane trees
compare with its branches—
no tree in the garden of God
could match its beauty.[e]
9 I made it beautiful
with abundant branches,
the envy of all the trees of Eden[f]
in the garden of God.[g]

10 "'Therefore this is what the Sovereign
LORD says: Because the great cedar towered over the thick foliage, and because it
was proud[h] of its height, 11 I gave it into the
hands of the ruler of the nations, for him

30:21 ***I have broken the arm of Pharaoh.*** The prophecy refers to Pharaoh Hophra's unsuccessful attempt to relieve the siege of Jerusalem just a few months earlier (29:2,6–7). God used Nebuchadnezzar to defeat the Egyptian army.
31:4 ***The waters nourished it.*** These waters were the Tigris and Euphrates rivers. They were important for agricultural fertility and fostered the development of great cities along trade routes.
31:10–14 ***hands of the ruler of the nations.*** The meaning is that Assyria had been cut down by Babylon. The picturesque conclusion to this second message of chapter 31 indicates that all the other nations that observe Assyria's ruin would share its destiny of death.

30:14 [j] Eze 29:14 [k] Ps 78:12,43 [l] Jer 46:25 **30:17** [m] Ge 41:45 **30:18** [n] Lev 26:13 [o] ver 3 **30:20** [p] Eze 26:1; 29:17; 31:1 **30:21** [q] Jer 48:25 [r] Jer 30:13; 46:11 **30:22** [s] Jer 46:25 [t] Ps 37:17 **30:23** [u] Eze 29:12 **30:24** [v] Zec 10:6, 12 [w] Eze 21:14; Zep 2:12 **30:26** [x] Eze 29:12 **31:1** [y] Jer 52:5 [z] Eze 30:20 **31:3** [a] Isa 10:34 **31:5** [b] Eze 17:5 **31:6** [c] Eze 17:23; Mt 13:32 **31:8** [d] Ps 80:10 [e] Ge 2:8-9 **31:9** [f] Ge 2:8 [g] Ge 13:10; Eze 28:13 **31:10** [h] Isa 14:13-14; Eze 28:17

to deal with according to its wickedness.
I cast it aside,[i] 12and the most ruthless of
foreign nations[j] cut it down and left it. Its
boughs fell on the mountains and in all the
valleys;[k] its branches lay broken in all the
ravines of the land. All the nations of the
earth came out from under its shade and
left it.[l] 13All the birds settled on the fallen
tree, and all the wild animals lived among
its branches.[m] 14Therefore no other trees
by the waters are ever to tower proudly on
high, lifting their tops above the thick foliage. No other trees so well-watered are
ever to reach such a height; they are all
destined for death,[n] for the earth below,
among mortals who go down to the realm
of the dead.[o]

15"'This is what the Sovereign LORD
says: On the day it was brought down to
the realm of the dead I covered the deep
springs with mourning for it; I held back
its streams, and its abundant waters were
restrained. Because of it I clothed Lebanon
with gloom, and all the trees of the field
withered away. 16I made the nations tremble[p] at the sound of its fall when I brought
it down to the realm of the dead to be with
those who go down to the pit. Then all
the trees[q] of Eden, the choicest and best
of Lebanon, the well-watered trees, were
consoled[r] in the earth below.[s] 17They too,
like the great cedar, had gone down to the
realm of the dead, to those killed by the
sword,[t] along with the armed men who
lived in its shade among the nations.

18"'Which of the trees of Eden can be
compared with you in splendor and majesty? Yet you, too, will be brought down with
the trees of Eden to the earth below; you
will lie among the uncircumcised,[u] with
those killed by the sword.

"'This is Pharaoh and all his hordes, declares the Sovereign LORD.'"

A Lament Over Pharaoh

32 In the twelfth year, in the twelfth
month on the first day, the word of
the LORD came to me:[v] 2"Son of man, take
up a lament[w] concerning Pharaoh king of
Egypt and say to him:

"'You are like a lion[x] among the
nations;
you are like a monster in the seas
thrashing about in your streams,
churning the water with your feet
and muddying the streams.[y]

3"'This is what the Sovereign LORD says:

"'With a great throng of people
I will cast my net over you,
and they will haul you up in my net.[z]
4I will throw you on the land
and hurl you on the open field.
I will let all the birds of the sky settle on
you
and all the animals of the wild gorge
themselves on you.[a]
5I will spread your flesh on the mountains
and fill the valleys[b] with your remains.
6I will drench the land with your flowing
blood[c]
all the way to the mountains,
and the ravines will be filled with
your flesh.
7When I snuff you out, I will cover the
heavens
and darken their stars;
I will cover the sun with a cloud,
and the moon will not give its light.[d]
8All the shining lights in the heavens
I will darken over you;
I will bring darkness over your land,
declares the Sovereign LORD.
9I will trouble the hearts of many peoples
when I bring about your destruction
among the nations,
among[a] lands you have not known.
10I will cause many peoples to be
appalled at you,
and their kings will shudder with
horror because of you
when I brandish my sword before
them.
On the day[e] of your downfall
each of them will tremble
every moment for his life.[f]

11"'For this is what the Sovereign LORD
says:

"'The sword of the king of Babylon[g]
will come against you.
12I will cause your hordes to fall
by the swords of mighty men—
the most ruthless of all nations.[h]
They will shatter the pride of Egypt,
and all her hordes will be
overthrown.[i]
13I will destroy all her cattle
from beside abundant waters
no longer to be stirred by the foot of man
or muddied by the hooves of cattle.[j]

---

a 9 Hebrew; Septuagint *bring you into captivity among the nations, / to*

31:18 ***Pharaoh and all his hordes.*** If Assyria, the greatest nation, had fallen to the Babylonians, surely a nation less great (Egypt) would also fall.
32:2 ***lion ... monster.*** These words depict Egypt as proud and powerful.

31:11 [i] Da 5:20 **31:12** [j] Eze 28:7 [k] Eze 32:5; 35:8 [l] Eze 32:11-12; Da 4:14 **31:13** [m] Isa 18:6; Eze 29:5; 32:4

31:14 [n] Ps 82:7 [o] Ps 63:9; Eze 26:20; 32:24 **31:16** [p] Eze 26:15 [q] Isa 14:8 [r] Eze 14:22; 32:31 [s] Isa 14:15; Eze 32:18 **31:17** [t] Ps 9:17 **31:18** [u] Jer 9:26; Eze 32:19, 21 **32:1** [v] Eze 31:1; 33:21 **32:2** [w] Eze 19:1; 27:2 [x] Eze 19:3,6; Na 2:11-13 [y] Eze 29:3; 34:18 **32:3** [z] Eze 12:13 **32:4** [a] Isa 18:6; Eze 31:12-13 **32:5** [b] Eze 31:12 **32:6** [c] Isa 34:3 **32:7** [d] Isa 13:10; 34:4; Eze 30:3; Joel 2:2,31; 3:15; Mt 24:29; Rev 8:12 **32:10** [e] Jer 46:10 [f] Eze 26:16; 27:35 **32:11** [g] Jer 46:26 **32:12** [h] Eze 28:7 [i] Eze 31:11-12 **32:13** [j] Eze 29:8,11

14Then I will let her waters settle
and make her streams flow like oil,
declares the Sovereign LORD.
15When I make Egypt desolate
and strip the land of everything in it,
when I strike down all who live there,
then they will know that I am the
LORD.[k]'

16"This is the lament[l] they will chant for her. The daughters of the nations will chant it; for Egypt and all her hordes they will chant it, declares the Sovereign LORD."

Egypt's Descent Into the Realm of the Dead

17In the twelfth year, on the fifteenth day
of the month, the word of the LORD came to
me:[m] 18"Son of man, wail for the hordes of
Egypt and consign[n] to the earth below both
her and the daughters of mighty nations,
along with those who go down to the pit.[o]
19Say to them, 'Are you more favored than
others? Go down and be laid among the uncircumcised.'[p] 20They will fall among those
killed by the sword. The sword is drawn;
let her be dragged[q] off with all her hordes.
21From within the realm of the dead[r] the
mighty leaders will say of Egypt and her allies, 'They have come down and they lie with the uncircumcised, with those killed by the sword.'
22"Assyria is there with her whole army;
she is surrounded by the graves of all her
slain, all who have fallen by the sword.
23Their graves are in the depths of the pit[s]
and her army lies around her grave. All who had spread terror in the land of the living are slain, fallen by the sword.
24"Elam[t] is there, with all her hordes
around her grave. All of them are slain, fallen by the sword.[u] All who had spread terror in the land of the living[v] went down uncircumcised to the earth below. They bear their shame with those who go down
to the pit.[w] 25A bed is made for her among
the slain, with all her hordes around her grave. All of them are uncircumcised, killed by the sword. Because their terror had spread in the land of the living, they bear their shame with those who go down to the pit; they are laid among the slain.
26"Meshek and Tubal[x] are there, with
all their hordes around their graves. All of them are uncircumcised, killed by the sword because they spread their terror in
the land of the living. 27But they do not lie
with the fallen warriors of old,[a] who went down to the realm of the dead with their weapons of war—their swords placed under their heads and their shields[b] resting on their bones—though these warriors also had terrorized the land of the living.
28"You too, Pharaoh, will be broken and
will lie among the uncircumcised, with those killed by the sword.
29"Edom[y] is there, her kings and all her
princes; despite their power, they are laid with those killed by the sword. They lie with the uncircumcised, with those who go down to the pit.[z]
30"All the princes of the north[a] and all
the Sidonians[b] are there; they went down with the slain in disgrace despite the terror caused by their power. They lie uncircumcised with those killed by the sword and bear their shame with those who go down to the pit.
31"Pharaoh—he and all his army—will
see them and he will be consoled[c] for all his hordes that were killed by the sword,
declares the Sovereign LORD. 32Although
I had him spread terror in the land of the living, Pharaoh and all his hordes will be laid among the uncircumcised, with those killed by the sword, declares the Sovereign LORD."

Renewal of Ezekiel's Call as Watchman

33 The word of the LORD came to me:
2"Son of man, speak to your people
and say to them: 'When I bring the sword[d] against a land, and the people of the land choose one of their men and make him
their watchman,[e] 3and he sees the sword
coming against the land and blows the
trumpet[f] to warn the people, 4then if anyone hears the trumpet but does not heed

[a] 27 Septuagint; Hebrew *warriors who were uncircumcised* [b] 27 Probable reading of the original Hebrew text; Masoretic Text *punishment*

32:14 *streams flow like oil.* This phrase is not used anywhere else. It pictures the time following massive killing when the Nile and its tributaries would experience a "deadly" calm.

32:24 *Elam is there.* Elam was east and southeast of Assyria in what is now Iran. The people of Elam were descended from one of the sons of Shem (Gen. 10:22; 1 Chr. 1:17).

32:30 *princes of the north.* This is a reference to lands that are north of Israel like Tyre and Sidon.

32:31 *Pharaoh ... will see.* Now the message (vv. 17–32) comes full circle. The point is that Egypt and Pharaoh will die like the other nations at the hand of the living God who judges every nation with justice.

33:2 *your people.* This phrase refers to fellow Israelites in exile with Ezekiel, now including the people of Judah deported to Babylon after Nebuchadnezzar.

32:15 [k] Ex 7:5; 14:4, 18; Ps 107:33-34; Eze 6:7 **32:16** [l] 2Sa 1:17; 2Ch 35:25; Eze 26:17 **32:17** [m] ver 1 **32:18** [n] Jer 1:10 [o] Eze 31:14, 16; Mic 1:8 **32:19** [p] ver 29-30; Eze 28:10; 31:18 **32:20** [q] Ps 28:3 **32:21** [r] Isa 14:9 **32:23** [s] Isa 14:15 **32:24** [t] Ge 10:22 [u] Jer 49:37 [v] Job 28:13 [w] Eze 26:20 **32:26** [x] Ge 10:2; Eze 27:13 **32:29** [y] Isa 34:5-15; Jer 49:7; Eze 35:15; Ob 1:1 [z] Eze 25:12-14 **32:30** [a] Jer 25:26; Eze 38:6; 39:2 [b] Jer 25:22; Eze 28:21 **32:31** [c] Eze 14:22; 31:16 **33:2** [d] Jer 12:12 [e] Eze 3:11 **33:3** [f] Hos 8:1

the warning[g] and the sword comes and takes their life, their blood will be on their own head.[h] **5**Since they heard the sound of the trumpet but did not heed the warning, their blood will be on their own head. If they had heeded the warning, they would have saved themselves. **6**But if the watchman sees the sword coming and does not blow the trumpet to warn the people and the sword comes and takes someone's life, that person's life will be taken because of their sin, but I will hold the watchman accountable for their blood.'[i]

7"Son of man, I have made you a watchman for the people of Israel; so hear the word I speak and give them warning from me.[j] **8**When I say to the wicked, 'You wicked person, you will surely die,[k]' and you do not speak out to dissuade them from their ways, that wicked person will die for[a] their sin, and I will hold you accountable for their blood.[l] **9**But if you do warn the wicked person to turn from their ways and they do not do so, they will die for their sin, though you yourself will be saved.[m]

10"Son of man, say to the Israelites, 'This is what you are saying: "Our offenses and sins weigh us down, and we are wasting away[n] because of[b] them. How then can we live?[o]"' **11**Say to them, 'As surely as I live, declares the Sovereign LORD, I take no pleasure in the death of the wicked, but rather that they turn from their ways and live.[p] Turn! Turn from your evil ways! Why will you die, people of Israel?'[q]

12"Therefore, son of man, say to your people, 'If someone who is righteous disobeys, that person's former righteousness will count for nothing. And if someone who is wicked repents, that person's former wickedness will not bring condemnation. The righteous person who sins will not be allowed to live even though they were formerly righteous.'[r] **13**If I tell a righteous person that they will surely live, but then they trust in their righteousness and do evil, none of the righteous things that person has done will be remembered; they will die for the evil they have done.[s] **14**And if I say to a wicked person, 'You will surely die,' but they then turn away from their sin and do what is just[t] and right— **15**if they give back what they took in pledge for a loan, return what they have stolen,[u] follow the decrees that give life, and do no evil—that person will surely live; they will not die.[v] **16**None of the sins that person has committed will be remembered against them. They have done what is just and right; they will surely live.[w]

17"Yet your people say, 'The way of the Lord is not just.' But it is their way that is not just. **18**If a righteous person turns from their righteousness and does evil, they will die for it.[x] **19**And if a wicked person turns away from their wickedness and does what is just and right, they will live by doing so. **20**Yet you Israelites say, 'The way of the Lord is not just.' But I will judge each of you according to your own ways."

Jerusalem's Fall Explained

21In the twelfth year of our exile, in the tenth month on the fifth day, a man who had escaped[y] from Jerusalem came to me and said, "The city has fallen![z]" **22**Now the evening before the man arrived, the hand of the LORD was on me,[a] and he opened my mouth[b] before the man came to me in the morning. So my mouth was opened and I was no longer silent.[c]

23Then the word of the LORD came to me: **24**"Son of man, the people living in those ruins[d] in the land of Israel are saying, 'Abraham was only one man, yet he possessed the land. But we are many; surely the land has been given to us as our possession.'[e] **25**Therefore say to them, 'This is what the Sovereign LORD says: Since you eat meat with the blood[f] still in it and look to your idols and shed blood, should you then possess the land?[g] **26**You rely on your sword, you do detestable things, and each of you defiles his neighbor's wife.[h] Should you then possess the land?'

27"Say this to them: 'This is what the Sovereign LORD says: As surely as I live, those who are left in the ruins will fall by the sword, those out in the country I will give to the wild animals to be devoured, and those in strongholds and caves will

---

[a] *8* Or *in*; also in verse 9 [b] *10* Or *away in*

33:12–20 *I will judge each of you according to your own ways.* God presents His rationale in these verses for deciding who would be rewarded with life and who would suffer death; He would save those who repent and turn to Him, but would condemn those who trust in themselves and do evil. After presenting His rationale, God declares that His judgment is just and fair—certainly more just than the practices of the Israelites.

33:25–26 *Should you then possess the land?* Ezekiel confronted his people with specific examples of their past and present refusal to obey God's revealed will for their lives (18:6,10; 22:11; Ex. 20:4–5,13; Lev. 7:26–27; 17:10–14; Deut. 12:16,23). Was it not then reasonable that God would punish the present generation by removing them from the land, at least temporarily? The writer of Hebrews, after using the example of Israel's failure to enter the land, admonished the church in a similar way (Heb. 4:1).

33:4 [g] 2Ch 25:16 [h] Jer 6:17; Eze 18:13; Zec 1:4; Ac 18:6 **33:6** [i] Eze 3:18 **33:7** [j] Jer 26:2; Eze 3:17 **33:8** [k] ver 14 [l] Eze 18:4 **33:9** [m] Eze 3:17-19 **33:10** [n] Eze 24:23 [o] Lev 26:39; Eze 4:17 **33:11** [p] Eze 18:32; 2Pe 3:9 [q] Eze 18:23 **33:12** [r] 2Ch 7:14; Eze 3:20 **33:13** [s] Eze 18:24; Heb 10:38; 2Pe 2:20-21 **33:14** [t] Eze 18:27 **33:15** [u] Ex 22:1-4; Lev 6:2-5 [v] Eze 20:11; Lk 19:8 **33:16** [w] Isa 43:25; Eze 18:22 **33:18** [x] Eze 3:20; Eze 18:26 **33:21** [y] Eze 24:26 [z] 2Ki 25:4, 10; Jer 39:1-2; Eze 32:1 **33:22** [a] Eze 1:3 [b] Lk 1:64 [c] Eze 3:26-27; 24:27 **33:24** [d] Eze 36:4 [e] Isa 51:2; Jer 40:7; Eze 11:15; Ac 7:5 **33:25** [f] Ge 9:4; Dt 12:16 [g] Jer 7:9-10; Eze 22:6, 27 **33:26** [h] Eze 22:11

die of a plague.[i] 28I will make the land a desolate waste, and her proud strength will come to an end, and the mountains of Israel will become desolate so that no one will cross them. 29Then they will know that I am the LORD, when I have made the land a desolate waste because of all the detestable things they have done.'

30"As for you, son of man, your people are talking together about you by the walls and at the doors of the houses, saying to each other, 'Come and hear the message that has come from the LORD.' 31My people come to you, as they usually do, and sit before[j] you to hear your words, but they do not put them into practice. Their mouths speak of love, but their hearts are greedy for unjust gain.[k] 32Indeed, to them you are nothing more than one who sings love songs with a beautiful voice and plays an instrument well, for they hear your words but do not put them into practice.[l]

33"When all this comes true—and it surely will—then they will know that a prophet has been among them.[m]"

The LORD Will Be Israel's Shepherd

34 The word of the LORD came to me: 2"Son of man, prophesy against the shepherds of Israel; prophesy and say to them: 'This is what the Sovereign LORD says: Woe to you shepherds of Israel who only take care of yourselves! Should not shepherds take care of the flock?[n] 3You eat the curds, clothe yourselves with the wool and slaughter the choice animals, but you do not take care of the flock.[o] 4You have not strengthened the weak or healed the sick or bound up the injured. You have not brought back the strays or searched for the lost. You have ruled them harshly and brutally.[p] 5So they were scattered because there was no shepherd,[q] and when they were scattered they became food for all the wild animals.[r] 6My sheep wandered over all the mountains and on every high hill. They were scattered over the whole earth, and no one searched or looked for them.[s]

7" 'Therefore, you shepherds, hear the word of the LORD: 8As surely as I live, declares the Sovereign LORD, because my flock lacks a shepherd and so has been plundered and has become food for all the wild animals, and because my shepherds did not search for my flock but cared for themselves rather than for my flock, 9therefore, you shepherds, hear the word of the LORD: 10This is what the Sovereign LORD says: I am against[t] the shepherds and will hold them accountable for my flock. I will remove them from tending the flock so that the shepherds can no longer feed themselves. I will rescue[u] my flock from their mouths, and it will no longer be food for them.[v]

11" 'For this is what the Sovereign LORD says: I myself will search for my sheep and look after them. 12As a shepherd[w] looks after his scattered flock when he is with them, so will I look after my sheep. I will rescue them from all the places where they were scattered on a day of clouds and darkness.[x] 13I will bring them out from the nations and gather them from the countries, and I will bring them into their own land. I will pasture them on the mountains of Israel, in the ravines and in all the settlements in the land.[y] 14I will tend them in a good pasture, and the mountain heights of Israel[z] will be their grazing land. There they will lie down in good grazing land, and there they will feed in a rich pasture[a] on the mountains of Israel.[b] 15I myself will tend my sheep and have them lie down, declares the Sovereign LORD.[c] 16I will search for the lost and bring back the strays. I will bind up the injured and strengthen the weak,[d] but the sleek and the strong I will destroy. I will shepherd the flock with justice.[e]

17" 'As for you, my flock, this is what the Sovereign LORD says: I will judge between one sheep and another, and between rams and goats.[f] 18Is it not enough for you to feed on the good pasture? Must you also trample the rest of your pasture with your feet? Is it not enough for you to drink clear water? Must you also muddy the rest with your feet? 19Must my flock feed on what you have trampled and drink what you have muddied with your feet?

33:30–33 ***hear your words, but they do not put them into practice.*** This section contrasts the actions and attitudes of the exiles with the life of God's prophet Ezekiel. The exiles had claimed to go to the prophet to receive God's revelation, but their behavior was inconsistent with their stated beliefs. Their true desire was for entertainment, not for divine enlightenment. If the fall of Jerusalem failed to awaken them spiritually, nothing would. Yet it certainly would open their eyes to the divine truth of Ezekiel's preaching. In these verses then, God also comforted and consoled Ezekiel.

34:7–10 ***did not search for my flock.*** The crimes of Israel's leaders come under review before their punishment is pronounced.

34:11–16 ***a day of clouds and darkness.*** This was the day Jerusalem fell (30:1–5). It may also speak of the future day of deliverance when God will seek out His sheep. Israel, though guilty and misguided, would eventually be rescued by the divine Good Shepherd and restored to the Promised Land (ch. 33–39).

33:27 [i] 1Sa 13:6; Isa 2:19; Jer 42:22; Eze 39:4 **33:31** [j] Eze 8:1 [k] Ps 78:36-37; Isa 29:13; Eze 22:27; Mt 13:22; 1Jn 3:18 **33:32** [l] Mk 6:20 **33:33** [m] 1Sa 3:20; Jer 28:9; Eze 2:5 **34:2** [n] Ps 78:70-72; Isa 40:11; Jer 3:15; 23:1; Mic 3:11; Jn 10:11; 21:15-17 **34:3** [o] Isa 56:11; Eze 22:27; Zec 11:16 **34:4** [p] Zec 11:15-17 **34:5** [q] Nu 27:17 [r] ver 28; Isa 56:9 **34:6** [s] Ps 142:4; 1Pe 2:25 **34:10** [t] Jer 21:13 [u] Ps 72:14 [v] 1Sa 2:29-30; Zec 10:3 **34:12** [w] Isa 40:11; Jer 31:10; Lk 19:10 [x] Eze 30:3 **34:13** [y] Jer 23:3 **34:14** [z] Eze 20:40 [a] Ps 23:2 [b] Eze 36:29-30 **34:15** [c] Ps 23:1-2 **34:16** [d] Mic 4:6 [e] Isa 10:16; Lk 5:32 **34:17** [f] Mt 25:32-33

20“ ‘Therefore this is what the Sovereign LORD says to them: See, I myself will
judge between the fat sheep and the lean
sheep. 21Because you shove with flank and
shoulder, butting all the weak sheep with
your horns[g] until you have driven them
away, 22I will save my flock, and they
will no longer be plundered. I will judge
between one sheep and another.[h] 23I will
place over them one shepherd, my servant
David, and he will tend[i] them; he will tend
them and be their shepherd. 24I the LORD
will be their God,[j] and my servant David
will be prince among them. I the LORD
have spoken.[k]

25“ ‘I will make a covenant of peace with
them and rid the land of savage beasts[l]
so that they may live in the wilderness
and sleep in the forests in safety.[m] 26I
will make them and the places surrounding my hill a blessing.[a][n] I will send down
showers in season;[o] there will be showers
of blessing.[p] 27The trees will yield their
fruit and the ground will yield its crops;
the people will be secure in their land.
They will know that I am the LORD, when
I break the bars of their yoke[q] and rescue
them from the hands of those who enslaved them.[r] 28They will no longer be
plundered by the nations, nor will wild animals devour them. They will live in safety, and no one will make them afraid.[s]
29I will provide for them a land renowned[t]
for its crops, and they will no longer be
victims of famine[u] in the land or bear the
scorn[v] of the nations.[w] 30Then they will
know that I, the LORD their God, am with
them and that they, the Israelites, are my
people, declares the Sovereign LORD.[x]
31You are my sheep, the sheep of my pasture,[y] and I am your God, declares the Sovereign LORD.’ ”

A Prophecy Against Edom

35 The word of the LORD came to me:
2“Son of man, set your face against
Mount Seir; prophesy against it 3and say:
‘This is what the Sovereign LORD says:
I am against you, Mount Seir, and I will
stretch out my hand[z] against you and
make you a desolate waste.[a] 4I will turn
your towns into ruins and you will be desolate. Then you will know that I am the
LORD.[b]

5“ ‘Because you harbored an ancient
hostility and delivered the Israelites
over to the sword at the time of their
calamity, the time their punishment
reached its climax,[c] 6therefore as surely as I live, declares the Sovereign LORD,
I will give you over to bloodshed and
it will pursue you.[d] Since you did not
hate bloodshed, bloodshed will pursue
you. 7I will make Mount Seir a desolate
waste and cut off from it all who come
and go. 8I will fill your mountains with
the slain; those killed by the sword will
fall on your hills and in your valleys and
in all your ravines.[e] 9I will make you
desolate forever; your towns will not be
inhabited. Then you will know that I am
the LORD.[f]

10“ ‘Because you have said, “These two
nations and countries will be ours and
we will take possession[g] of them,” even
though I the LORD was there, 11therefore
as surely as I live, declares the Sovereign LORD, I will treat you in accordance
with the anger[h] and jealousy you showed
in your hatred of them and I will make
myself known among them when I judge
you.[i] 12Then you will know that I the LORD
have heard all the contemptible things
you have said against the mountains of
Israel. You said, “They have been laid
waste and have been given over to us to
devour.[j]” 13You boasted against me and
spoke against me without restraint, and
I heard it.[k] 14This is what the Sovereign
LORD says: While the whole earth rejoices,
I will make you desolate.[l] 15Because you
rejoiced[m] when the inheritance of Israel
became desolate, that is how I will treat
you. You will be desolate, Mount Seir,[n] you
and all of Edom.[o] Then they will know that
I am the LORD.’ ”

[a] *26* Or *I will cause them and the places surrounding my hill to be named in blessings* (see Gen. 48:20); or *I will cause them and the places surrounding my hill to be seen as blessed*

34:23–24 *I will place ... he will tend.* The change from the pronoun *I* to *he* in this verse indicates that God would continue operating as the Chief Shepherd through this chosen future ruler from the Davidic line. He is the Messiah—God's only Son and His servant.

34:25–31 *covenant of peace.* These exiles were encouraged through these promises (37:26–28; 38:11–13; 39:25–29; Is. 54:10): (1) security from foreign aggressor nations; (2) showers of blessing, meaning productivity and prosperity; and (3) the certainty that the Lord is Israel's God and desires reunion with His people and a lasting relationship built on a new covenant (Jer. 31:31–34; Heb. 8:6).

35:6–9 *desolate waste.* Having stated why Edom deserved judgment, Ezekiel explained how the nation would be punished. The punishment would include widespread death and unrelieved destruction (Is. 34:6–8; 63:1–6; Jer. 49:7–13).

34:21 [g] Dt 33:17 **34:22** [h] Ps 72:12-14; Jer 23:2-3 **34:23** [i] Isa 40:11 **34:24** [j] Eze 36:28 [k] Jer 30:9 **34:25** [l] Lev 26:6 [m] Isa 11:6-9; Hos 2:18 **34:26** [n] Ge 12:2 [o] Ps 68:9 [p] Dt 11:13-15; Isa 44:3 **34:27** [q] Lev 26:13 [r] Jer 30:8 **34:28** [s] Jer 30:10; Eze 39:26 **34:29** [t] Isa 4:2 [u] Eze 36:29 [v] Eze 36:6 [w] Eze 36:15 **34:30** [x] Eze 14:11; 37:27 **34:31** [y] Ps 100:3; Jer 23:1 **35:3** [z] Jer 6:12 [a] Eze 25:12-14 **35:4** [b] ver 9 **35:5** [c] Ps 137:7; Eze 21:29 **35:6** [d] Isa 63:2-6 **35:8** [e] Eze 31:12 **35:9** [f] Jer 49:13 **35:10** [g] Ps 83:12; Eze 36:2,5 **35:11** [h] Eze 25:14 [i] Ps 9:16; Mt 7:2 **35:12** [j] Jer 50:7 **35:13** [k] Da 11:36 **35:14** [l] Jer 51:48 **35:15** [m] Ob 1:12 [n] ver 3 [o] Isa 34:5-6, 11; Jer 50:11-13; La 4:21

Hope for the Mountains of Israel

36 "Son of man, prophesy to the mountains of Israel and say, 'Mountains of Israel, hear the word of the LORD. 2This is what the Sovereign LORD says: The enemy said of you, "Aha![p] The ancient heights[q] have become our possession.[r]"' 3Therefore prophesy and say, 'This is what the Sovereign LORD says: Because they ravaged and crushed you from every side so that you became the possession of the rest of the nations and the object of people's malicious talk and slander,[s] 4therefore, mountains of Israel, hear the word of the Sovereign LORD: This is what the Sovereign LORD says to the mountains and hills, to the ravines and valleys,[t] to the desolate ruins and the deserted towns that have been plundered and ridiculed by the rest of the nations around you[u]— 5this is what the Sovereign LORD says: In my burning zeal I have spoken against the rest of the nations, and against all Edom, for with glee and with malice in their hearts they made my land their own possession so that they might plunder its pastureland.'[v] 6Therefore prophesy concerning the land of Israel and say to the mountains and hills, to the ravines and valleys: 'This is what the Sovereign LORD says: I speak in my jealous wrath because you have suffered the scorn of the nations.[w] 7Therefore this is what the Sovereign LORD says: I swear with uplifted hand that the nations around you will also suffer scorn.

8" 'But you, mountains of Israel, will produce branches and fruit[x] for my people Israel, for they will soon come home. 9I am concerned for you and will look on you with favor; you will be plowed and sown, 10and I will cause many people to live on you—yes, all of Israel. The towns will be inhabited and the ruins rebuilt.[y] 11I will increase the number of people and animals living on you, and they will be fruitful and become numerous. I will settle people on you as in the past[z] and will make you prosper more than before.[a] Then you will know that I am the LORD. 12I will cause people, my people Israel, to live on you. They will possess you, and you will be their inheritance;[b] you will never again deprive them of their children.

13" 'This is what the Sovereign LORD says: Because some say to you, "You devour people[c] and deprive your nation of its children," 14therefore you will no longer devour people or make your nation childless, declares the Sovereign LORD. 15No longer will I make you hear the taunts of the nations, and no longer will you suffer the scorn of the peoples or cause your nation to fall, declares the Sovereign LORD.[d]' "

Israel's Restoration Assured

16Again the word of the LORD came to me: 17"Son of man, when the people of Israel were living in their own land, they defiled it by their conduct and their actions. Their conduct was like a woman's monthly uncleanness in my sight.[e] 18So I poured out[f] my wrath on them because they had shed blood in the land and because they had defiled it with their idols. 19I dispersed them among the nations, and they were scattered[g] through the countries; I judged them according to their conduct and their actions.[h] 20And wherever they went among the nations they profaned[i] my holy name, for it was said of them, 'These are the LORD's people, and yet they had to leave his land.'[j] 21I had concern for my holy name, which the people of Israel profaned among the nations where they had gone.[k]

22"Therefore say to the Israelites, 'This is what the Sovereign LORD says: It is not for your sake, people of Israel, that I am going to do these things, but for the sake of my holy name, which you have profaned[l] among the nations where you have gone.[m] 23I will show the holiness of my great name, which has been profaned among the nations, the name you have profaned among them. Then the nations will know that I am the LORD, declares the Sovereign LORD, when I am proved holy[n] through you before their eyes.[o]

36:1–7 *The ancient heights.* This was a term for Israel because the hill country was central to the country's geography. God is glorified and the exiles comforted by the following: (1) exposing the crimes of the enemies of His nation; (2) exonerating His land from false charges; and (3) executing judgment and justice against the foreign nations.

36:12 *my people Israel.* Despite all their sinfulness, which the book has taken enormous pains to detail and describe, the nation was still referred to as the people of God. They would finally and forever take possession of their land, symbolized by the mountains and the central hills of Palestine, which are personified as "you" in this verse.

36:19 *according to their conduct and their actions.* Israel had been hypocritical and unholy; they had not separated themselves or made themselves distinct from the pagan world around them (v. 18). God had given His people the Promised Land as a place where they could show the world the difference it makes to follow the true God (Deut. 7:1–11). They failed to follow God, so He forced them out of the land. Through either their obedience or their disobedience, God would demonstrate to the watching world His personality, power, and plans.

36:2 [p] Eze 25:3 [q] Dt 32:13 [r] Eze 35:10 **36:3** [s] Ps 44:13-14 **36:4** [t] Eze 6:3 [u] Dt 11:11; Ps 79:4; Eze 34:28 **36:5** [v] Jer 50:11; Eze 25:12-14; 35:10, 15 **36:6** [w] Ps 123:3-4; Eze 34:29 **36:8** [x] Isa 27:6 **36:10** [y] ver 33; Isa 49:17-23 **36:11** [z] Mic 7:14 [a] Jer 31:28; Eze 16:55 **36:12** [b] Eze 47:14, 22 **36:13** [c] Nu 13:32 **36:15** [d] Ps 89:50-51; Eze 34:29 **36:17** [e] Jer 2:7 **36:18** [f] 2Ch 34:21 **36:19** [g] Dt 28:64 [h] Eze 39:24 **36:20** [i] Ro 2:24 [j] Isa 52:5; Jer 33:24; Eze 12:16 **36:21** [k] Ps 74:18; Isa 48:9 **36:22** [l] Ro 2:24* [m] Ps 106:8 **36:23** [n] Eze 20:41 [o] Ps 126:2; Isa 5:16

[24]"'For I will take you out of the nations; I will gather you from all the countries and bring you back into your own land.[p] [25]I will sprinkle[q] clean water on you, and you will be clean; I will cleanse[r] you from all your impurities and from all your idols.[s] [26]I will give you a new heart[t] and put a new spirit in you; I will remove from you your heart of stone and give you a heart of flesh.[u] [27]And I will put my Spirit[v] in you and move you to follow my decrees and be careful to keep my laws. [28]Then you will live in the land I gave your ancestors; you will be my people,[w] and I will be your God.[x] [29]I will save you from all your uncleanness. I will call for the grain and make it plentiful and will not bring famine[y] upon you. [30]I will increase the fruit of the trees and the crops of the field, so that you will no longer suffer disgrace among the nations because of famine.[z] [31]Then you will remember your evil ways and wicked deeds, and you will loathe yourselves for your sins and detestable practices.[a] [32]I want you to know that I am not doing this for your sake, declares the Sovereign LORD. Be ashamed and disgraced for your conduct, people of Israel![b]

[33]"'This is what the Sovereign LORD says: On the day I cleanse you from all your sins, I will resettle your towns, and the ruins will be rebuilt. [34]The desolate land will be cultivated instead of lying desolate in the sight of all who pass through it. [35]They will say, "This land that was laid waste has become like the garden of Eden;[c] the cities that were lying in ruins, desolate and destroyed, are now fortified and inhabited.[d]" [36]Then the nations around you that remain will know that I the LORD have rebuilt what was destroyed and have replanted what was desolate. I the LORD have spoken, and I will do it.'[e]

[37]"This is what the Sovereign LORD says: Once again I will yield to Israel's plea and do this for them: I will make their people as numerous as sheep, [38]as numerous as the flocks for offerings[f] at Jerusalem during her appointed festivals. So will the ruined cities be filled with flocks of people. Then they will know that I am the LORD."

The Valley of Dry Bones

37 The hand of the LORD was on me,[g] and he brought me out by the Spirit[h] of the LORD and set me in the middle of a valley;[i] it was full of bones.[j] [2]He led me back and forth among them, and I saw a great many bones on the floor of the valley, bones that were very dry. [3]He asked me, "Son of man, can these bones live?"

I said, "Sovereign LORD, you alone know.[k]"

[4]Then he said to me, "Prophesy to these bones and say to them, 'Dry bones, hear the word of the LORD![l] [5]This is what the Sovereign LORD says to these bones: I will make breath[a] enter you, and you will come to life.[m] [6]I will attach tendons to you and make flesh come upon you and cover you with skin; I will put breath in you, and you will come to life. Then you will know that I am the LORD.[n]'"

[7]So I prophesied as I was commanded. And as I was prophesying, there was a noise, a rattling sound, and the bones came together, bone to bone. [8]I looked, and tendons and flesh appeared on them and skin covered them, but there was no breath in them.

[9]Then he said to me, "Prophesy to the breath;[o] prophesy, son of man, and say to it, 'This is what the Sovereign LORD says: Come, breath, from the four winds and breathe into these slain, that they may

[a] 5 The Hebrew for this word can also mean *wind* or *spirit* (see verses 6-14).

36:25 *sprinkle clean water on you.* This symbolized cleansing from sin.

36:27 *I will put my Spirit in you.* The regenerating and empowering work of the Holy Spirit on individuals would not only restore the people physically to the land, but would restore them spiritually, by giving them a new heart and new spirit to help them follow Him and do His will (11:19–20; 18:31; 37:14; Jer. 31:31–34; Joel 2:28–29; Rom. 7:7–8:11).

36:28–30 *you will be my people.* The purpose of the Mosaic covenant would finally be realized (Deut. 26:16–19; 29:13; 30:8). The Israelites would become a people dedicated to God's ways.

36:31–32 *not doing this for your sake.* The restoration from the exile would recover God's glorious reputation among the nations and erase the guilt of the Israelites' sin. This is all a product of God's favor on the Israelites — even though they had done nothing to merit such mercy.

37:4 *Prophesy to these bones.* Ezekiel's prophecies had often been directed to people as deaf as these old, dry bones.

37:5 *breath.* This word is translated as wind or spirit in other places. The breath sent by God into the lifeless bodies symbolizes the Holy Spirit who brings renewal, regeneration, and rebirth (John 3:5–8; 6:44; 7:37–39; Rom. 8:9–11).

37:6 *you will come to life.* This passage is not about resurrection from physical death, but rebirth from spiritual death brought about by divine power. Psalm 87 is another text that speaks of spiritual rebirth. The point of Jesus' words to Nicodemus in John 3 was that he should have known and understood the concept of a second birth.

36:24 [p] Eze 34:13; 37:21 **36:25** [q] Heb 9:13; 10:22 [r] Ps 51:2,7 [s] Zec 13:2 **36:26** [t] Jer 24:7 [u] Ps 51:10; Eze 11:19 **36:27** [v] Eze 37:14 **36:28** [w] Jer 30:22 [x] Eze 14:11; 37:14,27 **36:29** [y] Eze 34:29 **36:30** [z] Lev 26:4-5; Eze 34:27; Hos 2:21-22 **36:31** [a] Eze 6:9; 20:43 **36:32** [b] Dt 9:5 **36:35** [c] Joel 2:3 [d] Isa 51:3 **36:36** [e] Eze 17:22; 22:14; 37:14; 39:27-28 **36:38** [f] 1Ki 8:63; 2Ch 35:7-9 **37:1** [g] Eze 1:3; 8:3 [h] Eze 11:24; Lk 4:1; Ac 8:39 [i] Jer 7:32 [j] Jer 8:2; Eze 40:1 **37:3** [k] Dt 32:39; 1Sa 2:6; Isa 26:19 **37:4** [l] Jer 22:29 **37:5** [m] Ge 2:7; Ps 104:29-30 **37:6** [n] Eze 38:23; Joel 2:27; 3:17 **37:9** [o] Ps 104:30

live.'" 10So I prophesied as he commanded me, and breath entered them; they came to life and stood up on their feet—a vast army.[p]

11Then he said to me: "Son of man, these bones are the people of Israel. They say, 'Our bones are dried up and our hope is gone; we are cut off.'[q] 12Therefore prophesy and say to them: 'This is what the Sovereign LORD says: My people, I am going to open your graves and bring you up from them; I will bring you back to the land of Israel.[r] 13Then you, my people, will know that I am the LORD, when I open your graves and bring you up from them. 14I will put my Spirit[s] in you and you will live, and I will settle you in your own land. Then you will know that I the LORD have spoken, and I have done it, declares the LORD.[t]'"

One Nation Under One King

15The word of the LORD came to me: 16"Son of man, take a stick of wood and write on it, 'Belonging to Judah and the Israelites[u] associated with him.[v]' Then take another stick of wood, and write on it, 'Belonging to Joseph (that is, to Ephraim) and all the Israelites associated with him.' 17Join them together into one stick so that they will become one in your hand.[w]

18"When your people ask you, 'Won't you tell us what you mean by this?'[x] 19say to them, 'This is what the Sovereign LORD says: I am going to take the stick of Joseph—which is in Ephraim's hand—and of the Israelite tribes associated with him, and join it to Judah's stick. I will make them into a single stick of wood, and they will become one in my hand.'[y] 20Hold before their eyes the sticks you have written on 21and say to them, 'This is what the Sovereign LORD says: I will take the Israelites out of the nations where they have gone. I will gather them from all around and bring them back into their own land.[z] 22I will make them one nation in the land, on the mountains of Israel. There will be one king over all of them and they will never again be two nations or be divided into two kingdoms.[a] 23They will no longer defile[b] themselves with their idols and vile images or with any of their offenses, for I will save them from all their sinful backsliding,[a] and I will cleanse them. They will be my people, and I will be their God.[c]

24"'My servant David[d] will be king over them, and they will all have one shepherd.[e] They will follow my laws and be careful to keep my decrees.[f] 25They will live in the land I gave to my servant Jacob, the land where your ancestors lived.[g] They and their children and their children's children will live there forever,[h] and David my servant will be their prince forever.[i] 26I will make a covenant of peace[j] with them; it will be an everlasting covenant. I will establish them and increase their numbers,[k] and I will put my sanctuary among them forever.[l] 27My dwelling place[m] will be with them; I will be their God, and they will be my people.[n] 28Then the nations will know that I the LORD make Israel holy,[o] when my sanctuary is among them forever.'"

The LORD's Great Victory Over the Nations

38 The word of the LORD came to me: 2"Son of man, set your face against Gog, of the land of Magog,[p] the chief prince of[b] Meshek and Tubal;[q] prophesy against him 3and say: 'This is what the Sovereign LORD says: I am against you, Gog, chief prince of[c] Meshek and Tubal.[r] 4I will turn

a 23 Many Hebrew manuscripts (see also Septuagint); most Hebrew manuscripts *all their dwelling places where they sinned* *b* 2 Or *the prince of Rosh,* *c* 3 Or *Gog, prince of Rosh,*

37:10 ***a vast army.*** The dead bones in the valley (vv. 1–2) must have looked like the aftermath of a horrible military defeat in which there were no survivors even to bury the dead.

37:11–14 ***these bones.*** The bones symbolize the whole house of Israel. This identification picks up on imagery already used: (1) those identified as dry or spiritually dead; (2) those identified as despondent and dejected, with no apparent hope of being "resurrected" as the people of the living God; and (3) those described as disassembled and dispersed before being rejoined and rebuilt. The major thrust of this passage is the coming spiritual rebirth of God's chosen people through the agency of His Spirit.

37:24–25 ***My servant David.*** This title refers to the Messiah and King who would come from David's line to save Israel (2 Sam. 7:8–16).

37:26–28 ***my sanctuary among them.*** The sanctuary or holy place of the living God is His dwelling place among His people (Zeph. 3:15–18). ***my sanctuary.*** This is a synonym for tabernacle. Both can be used of God's dwelling in the midst of His people in the wilderness. Here they point to the future dwelling of the living God in the midst of His people forevermore.

38:2 ***Son of man.*** This is a title for Ezekiel emphasizing his humanity, even though his message was from God. The proper names in this prophecy do not have to be specifically identified for an understanding of the main message.

38:3 ***Gog.*** This leader or king only appears in Scripture here and in Revelation 20:8. Several ideas about his identity have been suggested but none are completely convincing.

37:10 [p] Rev 11:11 **37:11** [q] La 3:54 **37:12** [r] Dt 32:39; 1Sa 2:6; Isa 26:19; Hos 13:14; Am 9:14-15 **37:14** [s] Joel 2:28-29 [t] Eze 36:27-28, 36 **37:16** [u] 1Ki 12:20; 2Ch 10:17-19 [v] Nu 17:2-3; 2Ch 15:9 **37:17** [w] ver 24; Isa 11:13; Jer 50:4; Hos 1:11 **37:18** [x] Eze 24:19 **37:19** [y] Zec 10:6 **37:21** [z] Isa 43:5-6; Eze 36:24; 39:27 **37:22** [a] Isa 11:13; Jer 3:18; Hos 1:11 **37:23** [b] Eze 36:25; 43:7 [c] Eze 11:18; 36:28 **37:24** [d] Hos 3:5 [e] Isa 40:11; Eze 34:23 [f] Ps 78:70-71 **37:25** [g] Eze 28:25 [h] Am 9:15 [i] Isa 11:1 **37:26** [j] Isa 55:3 [k] Jer 30:19 [l] Eze 16:62 **37:27** [m] Lev 26:11; Jn 1:14 [n] 2Co 6:16* **37:28** [o] Ex 31:13; Eze 20:12 **38:2** [p] Ge 10:2 [q] Rev 20:8 **38:3** [r] Eze 39:1

you around, put hooks[s] in your jaws and
bring you out with your whole army—your
horses, your horsemen fully armed, and a
great horde with large and small shields,
all of them brandishing their swords.[t] 5Per-
sia, Cush[au] and Put[v] will be with them, all
with shields and helmets, 6also Gomer[w]
with all its troops, and Beth Togarmah[x]
from the far north with all its troops—the
many nations with you.
7" 'Get ready; be prepared,[y] you and all
the hordes gathered about you, and take
command of them. 8After many days[z] you
will be called to arms. In future years you
will invade a land that has recovered from
war, whose people were gathered from
many nations[a] to the mountains of Israel,
which had long been desolate. They had
been brought out from the nations, and
now all of them live in safety.[b] 9You and
all your troops and the many nations with
you will go up, advancing like a storm;[c] you
will be like a cloud[d] covering the land.
10" 'This is what the Sovereign LORD says:
On that day thoughts will come into your
mind and you will devise an evil scheme.[e]
11You will say, "I will invade a land of unwalled villages; I will attack a peaceful and
unsuspecting people—all of them living
without walls and without gates and bars.[f]
12I will plunder and loot and turn my hand
against the resettled ruins and the people
gathered from the nations, rich in livestock
and goods, living at the center of the land.[b]"
13Sheba[g] and Dedan and the merchants of
Tarshish and all her villages[c] will say to
you, "Have you come to plunder? Have you
gathered your hordes to loot, to carry off
silver and gold, to take away livestock and
goods and to seize much plunder?[h]" '
14"Therefore, son of man, prophesy and
say to Gog: 'This is what the Sovereign
LORD says: In that day, when my people Israel are living in safety,[i] will you not take
notice of it? 15You will come from your
place in the far north, you and many nations with you, all of them riding on horses, a great horde, a mighty army.[j] 16You
will advance against my people Israel like
a cloud[k] that covers the land. In days to
come, Gog, I will bring you against my
land, so that the nations may know me
when I am proved holy through you before their eyes.[l]
17" 'This is what the Sovereign LORD
says: You are the one I spoke of in former
days by my servants the prophets of Israel.
At that time they prophesied for years that
I would bring you against them. 18This is
what will happen in that day: When Gog
attacks the land of Israel, my hot anger will
be aroused, declares the Sovereign LORD.
19In my zeal and fiery wrath I declare that
at that time there shall be a great earthquake in the land of Israel.[m] 20The fish in
the sea, the birds in the sky, the beasts of
the field, every creature that moves along
the ground, and all the people on the face
of the earth will tremble at my presence.
The mountains will be overturned, the
cliffs will crumble and every wall will fall
to the ground.[n] 21I will summon a sword[o]
against Gog on all my mountains, declares
the Sovereign LORD. Every man's sword
will be against his brother.[p] 22I will execute
judgment[q] on him with plague and bloodshed; I will pour down torrents of rain,
hailstones[r] and burning sulfur on him and
on his troops and on the many nations with
him. 23And so I will show my greatness
and my holiness, and I will make myself
known in the sight of many nations. Then
they will know that I am the LORD.[s]'

39 "Son of man, prophesy against Gog
and say: 'This is what the Sovereign LORD says: I am against you, Gog,
chief prince of[d] Meshek and Tubal.[t] 2I will
turn you around and drag you along. I will
bring you from the far north and send you
against the mountains of Israel. 3Then I
will strike your bow[u] from your left hand
and make your arrows[v] drop from your
right hand. 4On the mountains of Israel
you will fall, you and all your troops and
the nations with you. I will give you as food
to all kinds of carrion birds and to the wild
animals.[w] 5You will fall in the open field,
for I have spoken, declares the Sovereign

[a] 5 That is, the upper Nile region [b] 12 The Hebrew for this phrase means *the navel of the earth.* [c] 13 Or *her strong lions* [d] 1 Or *Gog, prince of Rosh,*

38:8 ***After many days . . . In future years.*** The first phrase usually denotes an indefinite time period, sometimes extending into the distant future or the end times (Dan. 8:26). The second phrase frequently points to messianic times or to the times when Israel is regathered. From Ezekiel's viewpoint, he was predicting a time in the very distant future—the end times. Unless the passage refers to spiritual warfare, the invasion of Israel and the subsequent time of confident and carefree peace are still future events. ***live in safety.*** This phrase indicates that the Israel of this passage is secure; the nation is not safe from attack, but it is safe from defeat.

38:18–23 ***my hot anger will be aroused.*** These verses speak of God defending His nation against Gog and his army with supernatural and earthshaking methods. Unusually strong language concerning the wrath of God is found in these verses.

38:4 [s] 2Ki 19:28 [t] Eze 29:4; Da 11:40 **38:5** [u] Ge 10:6 [v] Eze 27:10 **38:6** [w] Ge 10:2 [x] Eze 27:14 **38:7** [y] Isa 8:9 **38:8** [z] Isa 24:22 [a] Isa 11:11 [b] Jer 23:6 **38:9** [c] Isa 28:2 [d] Jer 4:13; Joel 2:2 **38:10** [e] Ps 36:4; Mic 2:1 **38:11** [f] Jer 49:31; Zec 2:4 **38:13** [g] Eze 27:22 [h] Isa 10:6; Jer 15:13 **38:14** [i] ver 8; Zec 2:5 **38:15** [j] Eze 39:2 **38:16** [k] ver 9 [l] Isa 29:23; Eze 39:21 **38:19** [m] Ps 18:7; Eze 5:13; Hag 2:6,21 **38:20** [n] Hos 4:3; Na 1:5 **38:21** [o] Eze 14:17 [p] 1Sa 14:20; 2Ch 20:23; Hag 2:22 **38:22** [q] Isa 66:16; Jer 25:31 [r] Ps 18:12; Rev 16:21 **38:23** [s] Eze 36:23 **39:1** [t] Eze 38:2,3 **39:3** [u] Hos 1:5 [v] Ps 76:3 **39:4** [w] ver 17-20; Eze 29:5; 33:27

LORD. 6I will send fire[x] on Magog and on those who live in safety in the coastlands,[y] and they will know that I am the LORD.

7"'I will make known my holy name among my people Israel. I will no longer let my holy name be profaned,[z] and the nations will know that I the LORD am the Holy One in Israel.[a] 8It is coming! It will surely take place, declares the Sovereign LORD. This is the day I have spoken of.

9"'Then those who live in the towns of Israel will go out and use the weapons for fuel and burn them up—the small and large shields, the bows and arrows, the war clubs and spears. For seven years they will use them for fuel.[b] 10They will not need to gather wood from the fields or cut it from the forests, because they will use the weapons for fuel. And they will plunder those who plundered them and loot those who looted them, declares the Sovereign LORD.[c]

11"'On that day I will give Gog a burial place in Israel, in the valley of those who travel east of the Sea. It will block the way of travelers, because Gog and all his hordes will be buried there. So it will be called the Valley of Hamon Gog.[a][d]

12"'For seven months the Israelites will be burying them in order to cleanse the land.[e] 13All the people of the land will bury them, and the day I display my glory[f] will be a memorable day for them, declares the Sovereign LORD. 14People will be continually employed in cleansing the land. They will spread out across the land and, along with others, they will bury any bodies that are lying on the ground.

"'After the seven months they will carry out a more detailed search. 15As they go through the land, anyone who sees a human bone will leave a marker beside it until the gravediggers bury it in the Valley of Hamon Gog, 16near a town called Hamonah.[b] And so they will cleanse the land.'

17"Son of man, this is what the Sovereign LORD says: Call out to every kind of bird[g] and all the wild animals: 'Assemble and come together from all around to the sacrifice I am preparing for you, the great sacrifice on the mountains of Israel. There you will eat flesh and drink blood. 18You will eat the flesh of mighty men and drink the blood of the princes of the earth as if they were rams and lambs, goats and bulls—all of them fattened animals from Bashan.[h] 19At the sacrifice I am preparing for you, you will eat fat till you are glutted and drink blood till you are drunk. 20At my table you will eat your fill of horses and riders, mighty men and soldiers of every kind,' declares the Sovereign LORD.[i]

21"I will display my glory among the nations, and all the nations will see the punishment I inflict and the hand I lay on them.[j] 22From that day forward the people of Israel will know that I am the LORD their God. 23And the nations will know that the people of Israel went into exile for their sin, because they were unfaithful to me. So I hid my face from them and handed them over to their enemies, and they all fell by the sword.[k] 24I dealt with them according to their uncleanness and their offenses, and I hid my face from them.[l]

25"Therefore this is what the Sovereign LORD says: I will now restore the fortunes of Jacob[c][m] and will have compassion[n] on all the people of Israel, and I will be zealous for my holy name.[o] 26They will forget their shame and all the unfaithfulness they showed toward me when they lived in safety[p] in their land with no one to make them afraid.[q] 27When I have brought them back from the nations and have gathered them from the countries of their enemies, I will be proved holy through them in the sight of many nations.[r] 28Then they will know that I am the LORD their God, for though I sent them into exile among the nations, I will gather them to their own land, not leaving any behind. 29I will no longer hide my face from them, for I will pour out my Spirit[s] on the people of Israel, declares the Sovereign LORD."

---

a *11 Hamon Gog* means *hordes of Gog.*
b *16 Hamonah* means *horde.* c *25* Or *now bring Jacob back from captivity*

39:6 *I will send fire.* Often fire from the Lord has the form of lightning bolts (1 Kin. 18:38).

39:12 *cleanse the land.* The law of Moses prescribed the sacrifice of a heifer to cleanse the land if a murdered person was found in a region (Deut. 21:1–9).

39:17–20 *Call out to every kind of bird.* A poem or song is addressed to the scavenging birds and beasts who come to the multitude of dead bodies (vv. 14–16). Whether figurative or not, the passage powerfully pictures God's sovereign control over the complete conquest of Israel's future and most ferocious enemies (Rev. 19:11–21). The meal would be a divinely prepared sacrifice served at God's table.

39:21–22 *my glory among the nations.* The universal knowledge of the living God of Israel will be based finally on the outcome of the battle described in chapters 38 and 39. Ezekiel followed the great theme of biblical theology begun in Genesis 12:3 that the ultimate purpose of God in His choice of Abraham and Sarah was to make His blessings known to all the families of the earth. God will demonstrate His glory both among the nations and among His chosen people Israel.

39:6 x Eze 30:8; Am 1:4 y Jer 25:22 **39:7** z Ex 20:7 a Isa 12:6; Eze 36:16,23 **39:9** b Ps 46:9 **39:10** c Isa 14:2; 33:1; Hab 2:8 **39:11** d Eze 38:2 **39:12** e Dt 21:23 **39:13** f Eze 28:22 **39:17** g Rev 19:17 **39:18** h Ps 22:12; Jer 51:40 **39:20** i Rev 19:17-18 **39:21** j Ex 9:16; Isa 37:20; Eze 38:16 **39:23** k Isa 1:15; 59:2; Jer 22:8-9; 44:23 **39:24** l Jer 2:17, 19; 4:18; Eze 36:19 **39:25** m Jer 33:7; Eze 34:13 n Jer 30:18 o Isa 27:12-13 **39:26** p 1Ki 4:25 q Isa 17:2; Eze 34:28; Mic 4:4 **39:27** r Eze 36:23-24; 37:21; 38:16 **39:29** s Joel 2:28; Ac 2:17

The Temple Area Restored

40 In the twenty-fifth year of our exile, at the beginning of the year, on the tenth of the month, in the fourteenth year after the fall of the city[t]—on that very day the hand of the LORD was on me[u] and he took me there. 2In visions[v] of God he took me to the land of Israel and set me on a very high mountain,[w] on whose south side were some buildings that looked like a city. 3He took me there, and I saw a man whose appearance was like bronze;[x] he was standing in the gateway with a linen cord and a measuring rod[y] in his hand. 4The man said to me, "Son of man, look carefully and listen closely and pay attention to everything I am going to show you, for that is why you have been brought here. Tell[z] the people of Israel everything you see.[a]"

The East Gate to the Outer Court

5I saw a wall completely surrounding the temple area. The length of the measuring rod in the man's hand was six long cubits,[a] each of which was a cubit and a handbreadth. He measured[b] the wall; it was one measuring rod thick and one rod high.

6Then he went to the east gate.[c] He climbed its steps and measured the threshold of the gate; it was one rod deep. 7The alcoves[d] for the guards were one rod long and one rod wide, and the projecting walls between the alcoves were five cubits[b] thick. And the threshold of the gate next to the portico facing the temple was one rod deep.

8Then he measured the portico of the gateway; 9it[c] was eight cubits[d] deep and its jambs were two cubits[e] thick. The portico of the gateway faced the temple.

10Inside the east gate were three alcoves on each side; the three had the same measurements, and the faces of the projecting walls on each side had the same measurements. 11Then he measured the width of the entrance of the gateway; it was ten cubits and its length was thirteen cubits.[f] 12In front of each alcove was a wall one cubit high, and the alcoves were six cubits square. 13Then he measured the gateway from the top of the rear wall of one alcove to the top of the opposite one; the distance was twenty-five cubits[g] from one parapet opening to the opposite one. 14He measured along the faces of the projecting walls all around the inside of the gateway—sixty cubits.[h] The measurement was up to the portico[i] facing the courtyard.[j][e] 15The distance from the entrance of the gateway to the far end of its portico was fifty cubits.[k] 16The alcoves and the projecting walls inside the gateway were surmounted by narrow parapet openings all around, as was the portico; the openings all around faced inward. The faces of the projecting walls were decorated with palm trees.[f]

The Outer Court

17Then he brought me into the outer court.[g] There I saw some rooms and a pavement that had been constructed all around the court; there were thirty rooms[h] along the pavement.[i] 18It abutted the sides of the gateways and was as wide as they were long; this was the lower pavement. 19Then he measured the distance from the inside of the lower gateway to the outside of the inner court;[j] it was a hundred cubits[l][k] on the east side as well as on the north.

---

[a] *5* That is, about 11 feet or about 3.2 meters; also in verse 12. The long cubit of about 21 inches or about 53 centimeters is the basic unit of measurement of length throughout chapters 40–48. [b] *7* That is, about 8 3/4 feet or about 2.7 meters; also in verse 48
[c] *8,9* Many Hebrew manuscripts, Septuagint, Vulgate and Syriac; most Hebrew manuscripts *gateway facing the temple; it was one rod deep. 9Then he measured the portico of the gateway; it*
[d] *9* That is, about 14 feet or about 4.2 meters
[e] *9* That is, about 3 1/2 feet or about 1 meter
[f] *11* That is, about 18 feet wide and 23 feet long or about 5.3 meters wide and 6.9 meters long
[g] *13* That is, about 44 feet or about 13 meters; also in verses 21, 25, 29, 30, 33 and 36 [h] *14* That is, about 105 feet or about 32 meters
[i] *14* Septuagint; Hebrew *projecting wall*
[j] *14* The meaning of the Hebrew for this verse is uncertain. [k] *15* That is, about 88 feet or about 27 meters; also in verses 21, 25, 29, 33 and 36
[l] *19* That is, about 175 feet or about 53 meters; also in verses 23, 27 and 47

40:1 *In the twenty-fifth year of our exile.* The actual date would have been about 573 B.C. This final vision of the temple in the book is one of God returning to dwell in the midst of His people who are now restored in their homeland. These are difficult chapters to interpret because of how easy it is to get bogged down in the architectural details. The writing is apocalyptic in style and expresses in symbolic manner how God would restore Israel in the future.

40:3–5 *a linen chord and a measuring rod in his hand.* This man with a measuring rod is a kind of angelic architect who serves as both a guide and an interpreter for Ezekiel. ***Tell the people of Israel everything you see.*** The details of the temple would have been of great importance and enormous interest to the exiles because the temple was the focal point of all of their worship.

40:7 *cubits ... rod.* A cubit was about 21 inches long. A measuring rod was six cubits or ten and one-half feet in length.

40:16 *palm trees.* These were common decorations that were also found in Solomon's temple (1 Kin. 6:29–35).

40:1 [t] 2Ki 25:7; Jer 39:1-10; 52:4-11; Eze 33:21 [u] Eze 1:3 **40:2** [v] Da 7:1,7 [w] Eze 17:22; Rev 21:10 **40:3** [x] Eze 1:7; Da 10:6; Rev 1:15 [y] Eze 47:3; Zec 2:1-2; Rev 11:1; 21:15 **40:4** [z] Jer 26:2 [a] Eze 44:5 **40:5** [b] Eze 42:20 **40:6** [c] Eze 8:16 **40:7** [d] ver 36 **40:14** [e] Ex 27:9 **40:16** [f] ver 21-22; 2Ch 3:5; Eze 41:26 **40:17** [g] Rev 11:2 [h] Eze 41:6 [i] Eze 42:1 **40:19** [j] Eze 46:1 [k] ver 23, 27

The North Gate

20Then he measured the length and
width of the north gate, leading into the
outer court. 21Its alcoves[l]—three on each
side—its projecting walls and its portico
had the same measurements as those of the
first gateway. It was fifty cubits long and
twenty-five cubits wide. 22Its openings, its
portico[m] and its palm tree decorations had
the same measurements as those of the
gate facing east. Seven steps led up to it,
with its portico opposite them. 23There was
a gate to the inner court facing the north
gate, just as there was on the east. He measured from one gate to the opposite one; it
was a hundred cubits.[n]

The South Gate

24Then he led me to the south side and I
saw the south gate. He measured its jambs
and its portico, and they had the same
measurements as the others. 25The gateway and its portico had narrow openings
all around, like the openings of the others.
It was fifty cubits long and twenty-five cubits wide.[o] 26Seven steps led up to it, with
its portico opposite them; it had palm tree
decorations on the faces of the projecting
walls on each side.[p] 27The inner court[q] also
had a gate facing south, and he measured
from this gate to the outer gate on the south
side; it was a hundred cubits.

The Gates to the Inner Court

28Then he brought me into the inner
court through the south gate, and he measured the south gate; it had the same measurements[r] as the others. 29Its alcoves, its
projecting walls and its portico had the
same measurements as the others. The
gateway and its portico had openings all
around. It was fifty cubits long and twenty-five cubits wide. 30(The porticoes[s] of
the gateways around the inner court were
twenty-five cubits wide and five cubits
deep.) 31Its portico[t] faced the outer court;
palm trees decorated its jambs, and eight
steps led up to it.

32Then he brought me to the inner court
on the east side, and he measured the gateway; it had the same measurements as the
others. 33Its alcoves, its projecting walls
and its portico had the same measurements
as the others. The gateway and its portico
had openings all around. It was fifty cubits
long and twenty-five cubits wide. 34Its portico[u] faced the outer court; palm trees decorated the jambs on either side, and eight
steps led up to it.

35Then he brought me to the north gate[v]
and measured it. It had the same measurements as the others, 36as did its alcoves,[w]
its projecting walls and its portico, and it
had openings all around. It was fifty cubits
long and twenty-five cubits wide. 37Its portico[a] faced the outer court; palm trees decorated the jambs on either side, and eight
steps led up to it.

The Rooms for Preparing Sacrifices

38A room with a doorway was by the
portico in each of the inner gateways,
where the burnt offerings[x] were washed.
39In the portico of the gateway were two
tables on each side, on which the burnt offerings,[y] sin offerings[b][z] and guilt offerings[a]
were slaughtered. 40By the outside wall of
the portico of the gateway, near the steps at
the entrance of the north gateway were two
tables, and on the other side of the steps
were two tables. 41So there were four tables on one side of the gateway and four
on the other—eight tables in all—on which
the sacrifices were slaughtered. 42There
were also four tables of dressed stone[b] for
the burnt offerings, each a cubit and a half
long, a cubit and a half wide and a cubit
high.[c] On them were placed the utensils for
slaughtering the burnt offerings and the
other sacrifices.[c] 43And double-pronged
hooks, each a handbreadth[d] long, were attached to the wall all around. The tables
were for the flesh of the offerings.

The Rooms for the Priests

44Outside the inner gate, within the inner
court, were two rooms, one[e] at the side of
the north gate and facing south, and another at the side of the south[f] gate and facing
north. 45He said to me, "The room facing
south is for the priests who guard the temple,[d] 46and the room facing north[e] is for the
priests who guard the altar.[f] These are the
sons of Zadok,[g] who are the only Levites
who may draw near to the LORD to minister
before him.[h]"

---

[a] *37* Septuagint (see also verses 31 and 34); Hebrew *jambs* [b] *39* Or *purification offerings* [c] *42* That is, about 2 2/3 feet long and wide and 21 inches high or about 80 centimeters long and wide and 53 centimeters high [d] *43* That is, about 3 1/2 inches or about 9 centimeters [e] *44* Septuagint; Hebrew *were rooms for singers, which were* [f] *44* Septuagint; Hebrew *east*

40:22 *Seven steps led up to it.* This would indicate that the temple area is a huge raised area, built up above the level of the surrounding land.

40:38–43 *two tables on each side, on which the burnt offerings . . . were slaughtered.* Ezekiel observes a room where the animals are slaughtered and washed for sacrificial offerings. These sacrifices point to the ultimate sacrifice; the sacrifice of God's only Son on the cross once for all (Heb. 7:20–28; 9:25–30).

40:44–47 *room . . . for the priests.* The guide explains that the chamber on the north side is for the priests who run the day-to-day operations of the temple. The chamber on the south side is for the priests who perform the sacrifices.

40:21 [l] ver 7 **40:22** [m] ver 49 **40:23** [n] ver 19 **40:25** [o] ver 33 **40:26** [p] ver 22 **40:27** [q] ver 32 **40:28** [r] ver 35 **40:30** [s] ver 21 **40:31** [t] ver 22 **40:34** [u] ver 22 **40:35** [v] Eze 44:4; 47:2 **40:36** [w] ver 7 **40:38** [x] 2Ch 4:6; Eze 42:13 **40:39** [y] Eze 46:2 [z] Lev 4:3,28 [a] Lev 7:1 **40:42** [b] Ex 20:25 [c] ver 39 **40:45** [d] 1Ch 9:23 **40:46** [e] Eze 42:13 [f] Nu 18:5 [g] 1Ki 2:35 [h] Nu 16:5; Eze 43:19; 44:15; 45:4; 48:11

47 Then he measured the court: It was
square—a hundred cubits long and a hundred cubits wide. And the altar was in front
of the temple.

The New Temple

48 He brought me to the portico of the
temple[i] and measured the jambs of the portico; they were five cubits wide on either
side. The width of the entrance was fourteen cubits[a] and its projecting walls were[b]
three cubits[c] wide on either side. 49 The portico[j] was twenty cubits[d] wide, and twelve[e]
cubits[f] from front to back. It was reached
by a flight of stairs,[g] and there were pillars[k]
on each side of the jambs.

41 Then the man brought me to the main
hall[l] and measured the jambs; the
width of the jambs was six cubits[h] on each
side.[i] 2 The entrance was ten cubits[j] wide,
and the projecting walls on each side of it
were five cubits[k] wide. He also measured
the main hall; it was forty cubits long and
twenty cubits wide.[l][m]
3 Then he went into the inner sanctuary
and measured the jambs of the entrance;
each was two cubits[m] wide. The entrance
was six cubits wide, and the projecting
walls on each side of it were seven cubits[n]
wide. 4 And he measured the length of the
inner sanctuary; it was twenty cubits, and
its width was twenty cubits across the end
of the main hall.[n] He said to me, "This is the
Most Holy Place.[o]"
5 Then he measured the wall of the temple; it was six cubits thick, and each side
room around the temple was four cubits[o]
wide. 6 The side rooms were on three levels, one above another, thirty[p] on each level. There were ledges all around the wall of
the temple to serve as supports for the side
rooms, so that the supports were not inserted into the wall of the temple.[q] 7 The side
rooms all around the temple were wider at
each successive level. The structure surrounding the temple was built in ascending
stages, so that the rooms widened as one
went upward. A stairway[r] went up from
the lowest floor to the top floor through
the middle floor.
8 I saw that the temple had a raised base
all around it, forming the foundation of
the side rooms. It was the length of the
rod, six long cubits. 9 The outer wall of the
side rooms was five cubits thick. The open
area between the side rooms of the temple
10 and the priests' rooms was twenty cubits
wide all around the temple. 11 There were
entrances to the side rooms from the open
area, one on the north and another on the
south; and the base adjoining the open
area was five cubits wide all around.
12 The building facing the temple courtyard on the west side was seventy cubits[p]
wide. The wall of the building was five cubits thick all around, and its length was
ninety cubits.[q]
13 Then he measured the temple; it was a
hundred cubits[r] long, and the temple courtyard and the building with its walls were
also a hundred cubits long. 14 The width of
the temple courtyard on the east, including the front of the temple, was a hundred
cubits.[s]
15 Then he measured the length of the
building facing the courtyard at the rear of
the temple, including its galleries[t] on each
side; it was a hundred cubits.
The main hall, the inner sanctuary and
the portico facing the court, 16 as well as the
thresholds and the narrow windows[u] and
galleries around the three of them—everything beyond and including the threshold was covered with wood. The floor, the
wall up to the windows, and the windows
were covered.[v] 17 In the space above the
outside of the entrance to the inner sanctuary and on the walls at regular intervals
all around the inner and outer sanctuary
18 were carved[w] cherubim[x] and palm trees.[y]
Palm trees alternated with cherubim.
Each cherub had two faces:[z] 19 the face of a

[a] *48* That is, about 25 feet or about 7.4 meters
[b] *48* Septuagint; Hebrew *entrance was*
[c] *48* That is, about 5 1/4 feet or about 1.6 meters
[d] *49* That is, about 35 feet or about 11 meters
[e] *49* Septuagint; Hebrew *eleven*
[f] *49* That is, about 21 feet or about 6.4 meters
[g] *49* Hebrew; Septuagint *Ten steps led up to it*
[h] *1* That is, about 11 feet or about 3.2 meters; also in verses 3, 5 and 8
[i] *1* One Hebrew manuscript and Septuagint; most Hebrew manuscripts *side, the width of the tent*
[j] *2* That is, about 18 feet or about 5.3 meters
[k] *2* That is, about 8 3/4 feet or about 2.7 meters; also in verses 9, 11 and 12
[l] *2* That is, about 70 feet long and 35 feet wide or about 21 meters long and 11 meters wide
[m] *3* That is, about 3 1/2 feet or about 1.1 meters; also in verse 22
[n] *3* That is, about 12 feet or about 3.7 meters
[o] *5* That is, about 7 feet or about 2.1 meters
[p] *12* That is, about 123 feet or about 37 meters
[q] *12* That is, about 158 feet or about 48 meters
[r] *13* That is, about 175 feet or about 53 meters; also in verses 14 and 15

41:1–4 *Then the man brought me to the main hall.* The basic temple has three areas: the outer area, the holy place or "nave," and the inner area or the "Most Holy Place." The innermost room is the focal point of the whole structure. Only the High Priest could enter it and then only once a year on the Day of Atonement.

41:13–15 *Then he measured the temple.* Ezekiel would likely have found pleasure in the symmetrical precision of the temple. It would have meant that it all fit together perfectly. There was nothing that was out of place. This may represent the order and harmony in God's future kingdom.

40:48 [i] 1Ki 6:2 **40:49** [j] ver 22; 1Ki 6:3 [k] 1Ki 7:15
41:1 [l] ver 23 **41:2** [m] 2Ch 3:3 **41:4** [n] 1Ki 6:20
[o] Ex 26:33; Heb 9:3-8 **41:6** [p] Eze 40:17 [q] 1Ki 6:5
41:7 [r] 1Ki 6:8 **41:14** [s] Eze 40:47 **41:15** [t] Eze 42:3
41:16 [u] 1Ki 6:4 [v] ver 25-26; 1Ki 6:15; Eze 42:3
41:18 [w] 1Ki 6:18 [x] Ex 37:7; 2Ch 3:7 [y] 1Ki 6:29; 7:36
[z] Eze 10:21

human being toward the palm tree on one side and the face of a lion toward the palm tree on the other. They were carved all around the whole temple.[a] 20From the floor to the area above the entrance, cherubim and palm trees were carved on the wall of the main hall.

21The main hall[b] had a rectangular doorframe, and the one at the front of the Most Holy Place was similar. 22There was a wooden altar[c] three cubits[a] high and two cubits square[b]; its corners, its base[c] and its sides were of wood. The man said to me, "This is the table[d] that is before the LORD." 23Both the main hall[e] and the Most Holy Place had double doors.[f] 24Each door had two leaves—two hinged leaves[g] for each door. 25And on the doors of the main hall were carved cherubim and palm trees like those carved on the walls, and there was a wooden overhang on the front of the portico. 26On the sidewalls of the portico were narrow windows with palm trees carved on each side. The side rooms of the temple also had overhangs.[h]

The Rooms for the Priests

42 Then the man led me northward into the outer court and brought me to the rooms[i] opposite the temple courtyard[j] and opposite the outer wall on the north side.[k] 2The building whose door faced north was a hundred cubits long and fifty cubits wide.[d] 3Both in the section twenty cubits[e] from the inner court and in the section opposite the pavement of the outer court, gallery[l] faced gallery at the three levels.[m] 4In front of the rooms was an inner passageway ten cubits wide and a hundred cubits[f] long.[g] Their doors were on the north.[n] 5Now the upper rooms were narrower, for the galleries took more space from them than from the rooms on the lower and middle floors of the building. 6The rooms on the top floor had no pillars, as the courts had; so they were smaller in floor space than those on the lower and middle floors. 7There was an outer wall parallel to the rooms and the outer court; it extended in front of the rooms for fifty cubits. 8While the row of rooms on the side next to the outer court was fifty cubits long, the row on the side nearest the sanctuary was a hundred cubits long. 9The lower rooms had an entrance[o] on the east side as one enters them from the outer court.

10On the south side[h] along the length of the wall of the outer court, adjoining the temple courtyard and opposite the outer wall, were rooms[p] 11with a passageway in front of them. These were like the rooms on the north; they had the same length and width, with similar exits and dimensions. Similar to the doorways on the north 12were the doorways of the rooms on the south. There was a doorway at the beginning of the passageway that was parallel to the corresponding wall extending eastward, by which one enters the rooms.

13Then he said to me, "The north[q] and south rooms facing the temple courtyard are the priests' rooms, where the priests who approach the LORD will eat the most holy offerings. There they will put the most holy offerings—the grain offerings, the sin offerings[i][r] and the guilt offerings[s]—for the place is holy.[t] 14Once the priests enter the holy precincts, they are not to go into the outer court until they leave behind the garments[u] in which they minister, for these are holy. They are to put on other clothes before they go near the places that are for the people.[v]"

15When he had finished measuring what was inside the temple area, he led me out by the east gate[w] and measured the area all around: 16He measured the east side with the measuring rod; it was five hundred cubits.[j,k] 17He measured the north side; it

[a] 22 That is, about 5 1/4 feet or about 1.5 meters [b] 22 Septuagint; Hebrew *long* [c] 22 Septuagint; Hebrew *length* [d] 2 That is, about 175 feet long and 88 feet wide or about 53 meters long and 27 meters wide [e] 3 That is, about 35 feet or about 11 meters [f] 4 Septuagint and Syriac; Hebrew *and one cubit* [g] 4 That is, about 18 feet wide and 175 feet long or about 5.3 meters wide and 53 meters long [h] 10 Septuagint; Hebrew *Eastward* [i] 13 Or *purification offerings* [j] 16 See Septuagint of verse 17; Hebrew *rods*; also in verses 18 and 19. [k] 16 Five hundred cubits equal about 875 feet or about 265 meters; also in verses 17, 18 and 19.

41:22 *This is the table that is before the LORD.* This is a reference to the table that held the showbread or bread of the Presence (Ex. 25:23–30), a reminder that man lives his whole life constantly in the divine presence. When God is not present to bless His people, their worship is unacceptable, because such worship will inevitably be merely formal and devoid of blessing. When God is present with His people in worship, they are then enabled to worship.

42:1–14 *Then the man led me . . . into the outer court.* At this point the text has given us many details of the physical descriptions of the temple. No references have been made to God's spiritual presence. Ezekiel has set the scene for the return of the Lord to His temple and city.

42:13–14 *where the priests who approach the LORD will eat.* This chapter focuses on the buildings designed for the use of the priests. They were used for storage, changing, and eating.

42:15–20 *he led me out.* After seeing the inside of the temple area, the guide takes Ezekiel to see the surrounding grounds.

41:19 [a] Eze 10:14 **41:21** [b] ver 1 **41:22** [c] Ex 30:1 [d] Ex 25:23; Eze 23:41; 44:16; Mal 1:7, 12 **41:23** [e] ver 1 [f] 1Ki 6:32 **41:24** [g] 1Ki 6:34 **41:26** [h] ver 15-16; Eze 40:16 **42:1** [i] ver 13 [j] Eze 41:12-14 [k] Eze 40:17 **42:3** [l] Eze 41:15 [m] Eze 41:16 **42:4** [n] Eze 46:19 **42:9** [o] Eze 44:5; 46:19 **42:10** [p] ver 1 **42:13** [q] Eze 40:46 [r] Lev 10:17; 6:25 [s] Lev 14:13 [t] Ex 29:31; Lev 6:29; 7:6; 10:12-13; Nu 18:9-10 **42:14** [u] Eze 44:19 [v] Ex 29:9; Lev 8:7-9 **42:15** [w] Eze 43:1

was five hundred cubits[a] by the measuring rod. 18He measured the south side; it was five hundred cubits by the measuring rod. 19Then he turned to the west side and measured; it was five hundred cubits by the measuring rod. 20So he measured[x] the area on all four sides. It had a wall around it,[y] five hundred cubits long and five hundred cubits wide,[z] to separate the holy from the common.[a]

God's Glory Returns to the Temple

43 Then the man brought me to the gate facing east,[b] 2and I saw the glory of the God of Israel coming from the east. His voice was like the roar of rushing waters,[c] and the land was radiant with his glory.[d] 3The vision I saw was like the vision I had seen when he[b] came to destroy the city and like the visions I had seen by the Kebar River, and I fell facedown. 4The glory[e] of the LORD entered the temple through the gate facing east.[f] 5Then the Spirit[g] lifted me up[h] and brought me into the inner court, and the glory of the LORD filled the temple.

6While the man was standing beside me, I heard someone speaking to me from inside the temple. 7He said: "Son of man, this is the place of my throne and the place for the soles of my feet. This is where I will live among the Israelites forever. The people of Israel will never again defile my holy name—neither they nor their kings—by their prostitution and the funeral offerings[c] for their kings at their death.[d][i] 8When they placed their threshold next to my threshold and their doorposts beside my doorposts, with only a wall between me and them, they defiled my holy name by their detestable practices. So I destroyed them in my anger. 9Now let them put away from me their prostitution and the funeral offerings for their kings, and I will live among them forever.[j]

10"Son of man, describe the temple to the people of Israel, that they may be ashamed[k] of their sins. Let them consider its perfection, 11and if they are ashamed of all they have done, make known to them the design of the temple—its arrangement, its exits and entrances—its whole design and all its regulations[e] and laws. Write these down before them so that they may be faithful to its design and follow all its regulations.[l]

12"This is the law of the temple: All the surrounding area[m] on top of the mountain will be most holy. Such is the law of the temple.

The Great Altar Restored

13"These are the measurements of the altar[n] in long cubits,[f] that cubit being a cubit and a handbreadth: Its gutter is a cubit deep and a cubit wide, with a rim of one span[g] around the edge. And this is the height of the altar: 14From the gutter on the ground up to the lower ledge that goes around the altar it is two cubits high, and the ledge is a cubit wide.[h] From this lower ledge to the upper ledge that goes around the altar it is four cubits high, and that ledge is also a cubit wide.[i] 15Above that, the altar hearth is four cubits high, and four horns[o] project upward from the hearth. 16The altar hearth is square, twelve cubits[j] long and twelve cubits wide. 17The upper ledge also is square, fourteen cubits[k] long and fourteen cubits wide. All around the altar is a gutter of one cubit with a rim of half a cubit.[l] The steps[p] of the altar face east."

18Then he said to me, "Son of man, this is what the Sovereign LORD says: These will be the regulations for sacrificing burnt offerings[q] and splashing blood[r] against the altar when it is built: 19You are to give a young bull[s] as a sin offering[m] to the Levitical priests of the family of Zadok,[t] who come near[u] to minister before me, declares the Sovereign LORD. 20You are to take some of its blood and put it on the four horns of

---

a 17 Septuagint; Hebrew *rods* *b* 3 Some Hebrew manuscripts and Vulgate; most Hebrew manuscripts *I* *c* 7 Or *the memorial monuments*; also in verse 9 *d* 7 Or *their high places*
e 11 Some Hebrew manuscripts and Septuagint; most Hebrew manuscripts *regulations and its whole design* *f* 13 That is, about 21 inches or about 53 centimeters; also in verses 14 and 17. The long cubit is the basic unit for linear measurement throughout Ezekiel 40–48. *g* 13 That is, about 11 inches or about 27 centimeters *h* 14 That is, about 3 1/2 feet high and 1 3/4 feet wide or about 105 centimeters high and 53 centimeters wide
i 14 That is, about 7 feet high and 1 3/4 feet wide or about 2.1 meters high and 53 centimeters wide
j 16 That is, about 21 feet or about 6.4 meters
k 17 That is, about 25 feet or about 7.4 meters
l 17 That is, about 11 inches or about 27 centimeters
m 19 Or *purification offering*; also in verses 21, 22 and 25

43:2 *the glory of the God of Israel coming.* Nineteen years before, Ezekiel had a vision of the Lord leaving His temple (10:18–22; 11:22–24). Now he gets a chance to see His return. Ezekiel's response is one of being overwhelmed with awe.

43:3 *the Kebar River.* This was where the Jewish exiles were located in Babylonia.

43:7–12 *I will live among the Israelites forever.* When God left Jerusalem, it rapidly moved towards destruction. Here, when God returned, everything was rebuilt as a permanent dwelling. The Lord stipulated that Israel was not to defile God's holiness as it had done in the past.

43:20–23 *purifying ... burnt offering.* These suggest purification and cleansing from sin. Because

42:20 [x] Eze 40:5 [y] Zec 2:5 [z] Eze 45:2; Rev 21:16 [a] Eze 22:26 **43:1** [b] Eze 10:19; 42:15; 44:1; 46:1 **43:2** [c] Rev 1:15 [d] Isa 6:3; Eze 11:23; Rev 18:1 **43:4** [e] Eze 1:28 [f] Eze 10:19 **43:5** [g] Eze 11:24 [h] Eze 3:12; 8:3 **43:7** [i] Lev 26:30 **43:9** [j] Eze 37:26-28 **43:10** [k] Eze 16:61 **43:11** [l] Eze 44:5 **43:12** [m] Eze 40:2 **43:13** [n] 2Ch 4:1 **43:15** [o] Ex 27:2 **43:17** [p] Ex 20:26 **43:18** [q] Ex 40:29 [r] Lev 1:5, 11; Heb 9:21-22 **43:19** [s] Lev 4:3; Eze 45:18-19 [t] Eze 44:15 [u] Nu 16:40; Eze 40:46

the altar and on the four corners of the upper ledge[v] and all around the rim, and so
purify the altar[w] and make atonement for
it. **21**You are to take the bull for the sin offering and burn it in the designated part
of the temple area outside the sanctuary.[x]
22"On the second day you are to offer a
male goat without defect for a sin offering,
and the altar is to be purified as it was purified with the bull. **23**When you have finished purifying it, you are to offer a young
bull and a ram from the flock, both without
defect.[y] **24**You are to offer them before the
LORD, and the priests are to sprinkle salt[z]
on them and sacrifice them as a burnt offering to the LORD.
25"For seven days[a] you are to provide a
male goat daily for a sin offering; you are
also to provide a young bull and a ram
from the flock, both without defect.[b] **26**For
seven days they are to make atonement for
the altar and cleanse it; thus they will dedicate it. **27**At the end of these days, from the
eighth day[c] on, the priests are to present
your burnt offerings and fellowship offerings[d] on the altar. Then I will accept you,
declares the Sovereign LORD."

The Priesthood Restored

44 Then the man brought me back to
the outer gate of the sanctuary, the
one facing east,[e] and it was shut. **2**The LORD
said to me, "This gate is to remain shut.
It must not be opened; no one may enter
through it.[f] It is to remain shut because
the LORD, the God of Israel, has entered
through it. **3**The prince himself is the only
one who may sit inside the gateway to eat
in the presence[g] of the LORD. He is to enter
by way of the portico of the gateway and go
out the same way.[h]"
4Then the man brought me by way of
the north gate to the front of the temple. I
looked and saw the glory of the LORD filling the temple[i] of the LORD, and I fell facedown.[j]
5The LORD said to me, "Son of man, look
carefully, listen closely and give attention
to everything I tell you concerning all the
regulations and instructions regarding the
temple of the LORD. Give attention to the entrance to the temple and all the exits of the
sanctuary.[k] **6**Say to rebellious Israel,[l] 'This
is what the Sovereign LORD says: Enough
of your detestable practices, people of Israel! **7**In addition to all your other detestable practices, you brought foreigners uncircumcised in heart[m] and flesh into my
sanctuary, desecrating my temple while
you offered me food, fat and blood, and you
broke my covenant.[n] **8**Instead of carrying
out your duty in regard to my holy things,
you put others in charge of my sanctuary.[o]
9This is what the Sovereign LORD says: No
foreigner uncircumcised in heart and flesh
is to enter my sanctuary, not even the foreigners who live among the Israelites.[p]
10" 'The Levites who went far from me
when Israel went astray[q] and who wandered from me after their idols must bear
the consequences of their sin.[r] **11**They may
serve in my sanctuary, having charge of
the gates of the temple and serving in it;
they may slaughter the burnt offerings[s]
and sacrifices for the people and stand before the people and serve them.[t] **12**But because they served them in the presence of
their idols and made the people of Israel
fall into sin, therefore I have sworn with
uplifted hand[u] that they must bear the consequences of their sin, declares the Sovereign LORD.[v] **13**They are not to come near
to serve me as priests or come near any of
my holy things or my most holy offerings;
they must bear the shame[w] of their detestable practices.[x] **14**And I will appoint them
to guard the temple for all the work that is
to be done in it.[y]
15" 'But the Levitical priests, who are descendants of Zadok and who guarded my
sanctuary when the Israelites went astray
from me, are to come near to minister before me; they are to stand before me to offer sacrifices of fat and blood, declares the
Sovereign LORD.[z] **16**They alone are to enter
my sanctuary; they alone are to come near
my table[a] to minister before me and serve
me as guards.[b]

---

of the sinlessness—without blemish—of the sacrifice, the people for whom the sacrifice is made are declared acceptable before God (v. 27; Ex. 29:14; Lev. 3; 4:12).

44:1–3 ***This gate is to remain shut.*** Today this is known as the "Golden Gate" and dates from several centuries after Christ. It is walled shut today in accordance with an Islamic tradition.

44:4–9 ***I looked ... I fell facedown.*** Ezekiel experiences another awe-inspiring vision of God's glory leading him to bow in worship (1:28–2:1). God demands that His renewed people follow His regulations exactly. He emphasizes the necessity of holiness and righteousness, especially in light of Israel's past.

44:11–14 ***They may serve in my sanctuary.*** God explains to Ezekiel why the Levites would be limited to certain types of temple ministry. The Levites (with the exception of the sons of Zadok; v. 15) could not be priests but could be ministers (servants or attendants). They could not serve in the inner court or temple, where the holy things are located; but they could oversee the general operation of the temple complex.

43:20 [v] ver 17 [w] Lev 16:19 **43:21** [x] Ex 29:14; Heb 13:11 **43:23** [y] Ex 29:1 **43:24** [z] Lev 2:13; Mk 9:49-50 **43:25** [a] Lev 8:33 [b] Ex 29:37 **43:27** [c] Lev 9:1 [d] Lev 17:5 **44:1** [e] Eze 43:1 **44:2** [f] Eze 43:4-5 **44:3** [g] Ex 24:9-11 [h] Eze 46:2,8 **44:4** [i] Isa 6:4; Rev 15:8 [j] Eze 1:28; 3:23 **44:5** [k] Eze 40:4; 43:10-11 **44:6** [l] Eze 3:9 **44:7** [m] Lev 26:41 [n] Ge 17:14; Ex 12:48; Lev 22:25 **44:8** [o] Lev 22:2; Nu 18:7 **44:9** [p] Joel 3:17; Zec 14:21 **44:10** [q] 2Ki 23:8 [r] Nu 18:23 **44:11** [s] 2Ch 29:34 [t] Nu 3:5-37; 16:9; 1Ch 26:12-19 **44:12** [u] Ps 106:26 [v] 2Ki 16:10-16 **44:13** [w] Eze 16:61 [x] Nu 18:3 **44:14** [y] Nu 18:4; 1Ch 23:28-32 **44:15** [z] Jer 33:18; Eze 40:46; Zec 3:7 **44:16** [a] Eze 41:22 [b] Nu 18:5

17" 'When they enter the gates of the inner court, they are to wear linen clothes;[c] they must not wear any woolen garment while ministering at the gates of the inner court or inside the temple. 18They are to wear linen turbans[d] on their heads and linen undergarments[e] around their waists. They must not wear anything that makes them perspire.[f] 19When they go out into the outer court where the people are, they are to take off the clothes they have been ministering in and are to leave them in the sacred rooms, and put on other clothes, so that the people are not consecrated[g] through contact with their garments.[h]

20" 'They must not shave their heads or let their hair grow long, but they are to keep the hair of their heads trimmed.[i] 21No priest is to drink wine when he enters the inner court.[j] 22They must not marry widows or divorced women; they may marry only virgins of Israelite descent or widows of priests.[k] 23They are to teach my people the difference between the holy and the common[l] and show them how to distinguish between the unclean and the clean.[m]

24" 'In any dispute, the priests are to serve as judges[n] and decide it according to my ordinances. They are to keep my laws and my decrees for all my appointed festivals, and they are to keep my Sabbaths holy.[o]

25" 'A priest must not defile himself by going near a dead person; however, if the dead person was his father or mother, son or daughter, brother or unmarried sister, then he may defile himself.[p] 26After he is cleansed, he must wait seven days.[q] 27On the day he goes into the inner court of the sanctuary to minister in the sanctuary, he is to offer a sin offering[a] for himself, declares the Sovereign LORD.

28" 'I am to be the only inheritance[r] the priests have. You are to give them no possession in Israel; I will be their possession. 29They will eat the grain offerings, the sin offerings and the guilt offerings; and everything in Israel devoted[b] to the LORD[s] will belong to them.[t] 30The best of all the firstfruits[u] and of all your special gifts will belong to the priests. You are to give them the first portion of your ground meal[v] so that a blessing[w] may rest on your household.[x] 31The priests must not eat anything, whether bird or animal, found dead or torn by wild animals.[y]

Israel Fully Restored

45 " 'When you allot the land as an inheritance,[z] you are to present to the LORD a portion of the land as a sacred district, 25,000 cubits[c] long and 20,000[d] cubits[e] wide; the entire area will be holy.[a] 2Of this, a section 500 cubits[f] square[b] is to be for the sanctuary, with 50 cubits[g] around it for open land. 3In the sacred district, measure off a section 25,000 cubits long and 10,000 cubits[h] wide. In it will be the sanctuary, the Most Holy Place. 4It will be the sacred portion of the land for the priests,[c] who minister in the sanctuary and who draw near to minister before the LORD. It will be a place for their houses as well as a holy place for the sanctuary.[d] 5An area 25,000 cubits long and 10,000 cubits wide will belong to the Levites, who serve in the temple, as their possession for towns to live in.[i][e]

6" 'You are to give the city as its property an area 5,000 cubits[j] wide and 25,000 cubits long, adjoining the sacred portion; it will belong to all Israel.[f]

7" 'The prince will have the land bordering each side of the area formed by the

[a] 27 Or *purification offering*; also in verse 29
[b] 29 The Hebrew term refers to the irrevocable giving over of things or persons to the LORD.
[c] 1 That is, about 8 miles or about 13 kilometers; also in verses 3, 5 and 6 [d] 1 Septuagint (see also verses 3 and 5 and 48:9); Hebrew *10,000* [e] 1 That is, about 6 1/2 miles or about 11 kilometers
[f] 2 That is, about 875 feet or about 265 meters
[g] 2 That is, about 88 feet or about 27 meters
[h] 3 That is, about 3 1/3 miles or about 5.3 kilometers; also in verse 5 [i] 5 Septuagint; Hebrew *temple; they will have as their possession 20 rooms* [j] 6 That is, about 1 2/3 miles or about 2.7 kilometers

44:23 *They are to teach my people the difference between the holy and the common.* These verses speak of holiness in conduct. These regulations continued practices already prescribed in the law of Moses (Lev. 10:6,9; 21:1 – 7,10,14). Their aim was to help the priests avoid conformity to the immoral and idolatrous religious rituals and conduct among the pagan nations. The priests, then and in the future, have the responsibility of modeling and maintaining the highest standards of morality, self-control, self-denial, discipline, and obedience to God's will.

44:28 *I will be their possession.* God was to be the priests' inheritance in all respects; they were not to inherit land or cities.

45:1 – 5 *a sacred district.* A distinct or holy section was to be allocated for God. This area would be divided into two equal sections. One would be the portion for the Zadokites. In the center of this part of the holy district is the holy square-mile environs for the temple. The other half of the holy district would be the portion given to the Levites. All this is holy; God owns it.

45:6 *the city.* Most likely the city is Jerusalem.

45:7 – 8 *The prince . . . my princes.* Their identity is

44:17 [c] Ex 39:27-28; Rev 19:8 **44:18** [d] Ex 28:39; Isa 3:20 [e] Ex 28:42 [f] Lev 16:4 **44:19** [g] Lev 6:27; Eze 46:20 [h] Lev 6:10-11; Eze 42:14 **44:20** [i] Lev 21:5; Nu 6:5 **44:21** [j] Lev 10:9 **44:22** [k] Lev 21:7 **44:23** [l] Eze 22:26 [m] Mal 2:7 **44:24** [n] Dt 17:8-9; 1Ch 23:4 [o] 2Ch 19:8 **44:25** [p] Lev 21:1-4 **44:26** [q] Nu 19:14 **44:28** [r] Nu 18:20; Dt 10:9; 18:1-2; Jos 13:33 **44:29** [s] Lev 27:21 [t] Nu 18:9, 14 **44:30** [u] Nu 18:12-13 [v] Nu 15:18-21 [w] Mal 3:10 [x] Ne 10:35 37 **44:31** [y] Ex 22:31; Lev 22:8 **45:1** [z] Eze 47:21-22 [a] Eze 48:8-9, 29 **45:2** [b] Eze 42:20 **45:4** [c] Eze 40:46 [d] Eze 48:10-11 **45:5** [e] Eze 48:13 **45:6** [f] Eze 48:15-18

sacred district and the property of the city. It will extend westward from the west side and eastward from the east side, running lengthwise from the western to the eastern border parallel to one of the tribal portions.[g] [8]This land will be his possession in Israel. And my princes will no longer oppress my people but will allow the people of Israel to possess the land according to their tribes.[h]

[9]" 'This is what the Sovereign LORD says: You have gone far enough, princes of Israel! Give up your violence and oppression and do what is just and right.[i] Stop dispossessing my people, declares the Sovereign LORD. [10]You are to use accurate scales,[j] an accurate ephah[a][k] and an accurate bath.[b] [11]The ephah[l] and the bath are to be the same size, the bath containing a tenth of a homer and the ephah a tenth of a homer; the homer is to be the standard measure for both. [12]The shekel[c] is to consist of twenty gerahs.[m] Twenty shekels plus twenty-five shekels plus fifteen shekels equal one mina.[d]

[13]" 'This is the special gift you are to offer: a sixth of an ephah[e] from each homer of wheat and a sixth of an ephah[f] from each homer of barley. [14]The prescribed portion of olive oil, measured by the bath, is a tenth of a bath[g] from each cor (which consists of ten baths or one homer, for ten baths are equivalent to a homer). [15]Also one sheep is to be taken from every flock of two hundred from the well-watered pastures of Israel. These will be used for the grain offerings, burnt offerings[n] and fellowship offerings to make atonement[o] for the people, declares the Sovereign LORD. [16]All the people of the land will be required to give this special offering to the prince in Israel. [17]It will be the duty of the prince to provide the burnt offerings, grain offerings and drink offerings at the festivals, the New Moons and the Sabbaths[p]—at all the appointed festivals of Israel. He will provide the sin offerings,[h] grain offerings, burnt offerings and fellowship offerings to make atonement for the Israelites.[q]

[18]" 'This is what the Sovereign LORD says: In the first month[r] on the first day you are to take a young bull without defect[s] and purify the sanctuary.[t] [19]The priest is to take some of the blood of the sin offering and put it on the doorposts of the temple, on the four corners of the upper ledge[u] of the altar[v] and on the gateposts of the inner court. [20]You are to do the same on the seventh day of the month for anyone who sins unintentionally[w] or through ignorance; so you are to make atonement for the temple.

[21]" 'In the first month on the fourteenth day you are to observe the Passover,[x] a festival lasting seven days, during which you shall eat bread made without yeast. [22]On that day the prince is to provide a bull as a sin offering for himself and for all the people of the land.[y] [23]Every day during the seven days of the festival he is to provide seven bulls and seven rams[z] without defect as a burnt offering to the LORD, and a male goat for a sin offering.[a] [24]He is to provide as a grain offering[b] an ephah for each bull and an ephah for each ram, along with a hin[i] of olive oil for each ephah.[c]

[25]" 'During the seven days of the festival,[d] which begins in the seventh month on the fifteenth day, he is to make the same provision for sin offerings, burnt offerings, grain offerings and oil.[e]

---

[a] *10* An ephah was a dry measure having the capacity of about 3/5 bushel or about 22 liters.
[b] *10* A bath was a liquid measure equaling about 6 gallons or about 22 liters.
[c] *12* A shekel weighed about 2/5 ounce or about 12 grams.
[d] *12* That is, 60 shekels; the common mina was 50 shekels. Sixty shekels were about 1 1/2 pounds or about 690 grams.
[e] *13* That is, probably about 6 pounds or about 2.7 kilograms
[f] *13* That is, probably about 5 pounds or about 2.3 kilograms
[g] *14* That is, about 2 1/2 quarts or about 2.2 liters
[h] *17* Or *purification offerings*; also in verses 19, 22, 23 and 25
[i] *24* That is, about 1 gallon or about 3.8 liters

---

unknown (44:3), but the allotted area is on both sides of the holy district. The prince and God's princes of the Messianic Period—in contrast to previous leaders of Israel (11:1–13; 14:1–11,20–22; 34:1–10) will not be greedy for riches and real estate but will give the land that remains to the people.

45:10–11 ***You are to use accurate scales.*** The merchants were exhorted to use accurate measures. They must not cheat anymore when weighing produce (Lev. 19:35; Amos 8:5; Mic. 6:10–12). God called for an end to dishonesty and deceit; a time is coming when all such scheming will end (37:15–28).

45:18 ***In the first month on the first day.*** This is an annual day of purifying the temple sanctuary. In the light of Jesus' death on the cross, the actions of the prince symbolize and emphasize that God has made atonement for all through the sacrifice of the Messiah. The prince represents the people in these actions of worship.

45:21 ***you are to observe the Passover, a festival lasting seven days.*** In this passage the Festivals of Passover and Tabernacles are observed (Ex. 12:1–14; Lev. 23:5–8,33–43; Num. 28:16–25). The dates are in relation to the Levitical calendar, the Jewish religious year. The procedures as well are very similar to those of the Mosaic system. These festivals commemorate God's faithfulness to His promises.

45:7 [g] Eze 48:21 **45:8** [h] Nu 26:53; Eze 46:18 **45:9** [i] Jer 22:3; Zec 7:9-10; 8:16 **45:10** [j] Dt 25:15; Pr 11:1; Am 8:4-6; Mic 6:10-11 [k] Lev 19:36 **45:11** [l] Isa 5:10 **45:12** [m] Ex 30:13; Lev 27:25; Nu 3:47 **45:15** [n] Lev 1:4 [o] Lev 6:30 **45:17** [p] Lev 23:38; Isa 66:23 [q] 1Ki 8:62; 2Ch 31:3; Eze 46:4-12 **45:18** [r] Ex 12:2 [s] Lev 22:20; Heb 9:14 [t] Lev 16:16,33 **45:19** [u] Eze 43:17 [v] Lev 16:18-19; Eze 43:20 **45:20** [w] Lev 4:27 **45:21** [x] Ex 12:11; Lev 23:5-6 **45:22** [y] Lev 4:14 **45:23** [z] Job 42:8 [a] Nu 28:16-25 **45:24** [b] Nu 28:12-13 [c] Eze 46:5-7 **45:25** [d] Dt 16:13 [e] Lev 23:34-43; Nu 29:12-38

46 "'This is what the Sovereign LORD says: The gate of the inner court[f] facing east[g] is to be shut on the six working days, but on the Sabbath day and on the day of the New Moon[h] it is to be opened. **2**The prince is to enter from the outside through the portico[i] of the gateway and stand by the gatepost. The priests are to sacrifice his burnt offering and his fellowship offerings. He is to bow down in worship at the threshold of the gateway and then go out, but the gate will not be shut until evening.[j] **3**On the Sabbaths and New Moons the people of the land are to worship in the presence of the LORD at the entrance of that gateway.[k] **4**The burnt offering the prince brings to the LORD on the Sabbath day is to be six male lambs and a ram, all without defect. **5**The grain offering given with the ram is to be an ephah,[a] and the grain offering with the lambs is to be as much as he pleases, along with a hin[b] of olive oil for each ephah.[l] **6**On the day of the New Moon[m] he is to offer a young bull, six lambs and a ram, all without defect. **7**He is to provide as a grain offering one ephah with the bull, one ephah with the ram, and with the lambs as much as he wants to give, along with a hin of oil for each ephah.[n] **8**When the prince enters, he is to go in through the portico[o] of the gateway, and he is to come out the same way.[p]

9"'When the people of the land come before the LORD at the appointed festivals,[q] whoever enters by the north gate to worship is to go out the south gate; and whoever enters by the south gate is to go out the north gate. No one is to return through the gate by which they entered, but each is to go out the opposite gate. **10**The prince is to be among them, going in when they go in and going out when they go out.[r] **11**At the feasts and the appointed festivals, the grain offering is to be an ephah with a bull, an ephah with a ram, and with the lambs as much as he pleases, along with a hin of oil for each ephah.[s]

12"'When the prince provides[t] a freewill offering[u] to the LORD—whether a burnt offering or fellowship offerings—the gate facing east is to be opened for him. He shall offer his burnt offering or his fellowship offerings as he does on the Sabbath day. Then he shall go out, and after he has gone out, the gate will be shut.[v]

13"'Every day you are to provide a year-old lamb without defect for a burnt offering to the LORD; morning by morning you shall provide it.[w] **14**You are also to provide with it morning by morning a grain offering, consisting of a sixth of an ephah[c] with a third of a hin[d] of oil to moisten the flour. The presenting of this grain offering to the LORD is a lasting ordinance.[x] **15**So the lamb and the grain offering and the oil shall be provided morning by morning for a regular[y] burnt offering.[z]

16"'This is what the Sovereign LORD says: If the prince makes a gift from his inheritance to one of his sons, it will also belong to his descendants; it is to be their property by inheritance.[a] **17**If, however, he makes a gift from his inheritance to one of his servants, the servant may keep it until the year of freedom;[b] then it will revert to the prince. His inheritance belongs to his sons only; it is theirs. **18**The prince must not take any of the inheritance[c] of the people, driving them off their property. He is to give his sons their inheritance out of his own property, so that not one of my people will be separated from their property.'"

19Then the man brought me through the entrance[d] at the side of the gate to the sacred rooms facing north, which belonged to the priests, and showed me a place at the western end. **20**He said to me, "This is the place where the priests are to cook the guilt offering and the sin offering[e] and bake the grain offering, to avoid bringing them into the outer court and consecrating[e] the people."[f]

21He then brought me to the outer court and led me around to its four corners, and I saw in each corner another court. **22**In the four corners of the outer court were enclosed[f] courts, forty cubits long and thirty cubits wide;[g] each of the courts in the

[a] *5* That is, probably about 35 pounds or about 16 kilograms; also in verses 7 and 11 [b] *5* That is, about 1 gallon or about 3.8 liters; also in verses 7 and 11 [c] *14* That is, probably about 6 pounds or about 2.7 kilograms [d] *14* That is, about 1 1/2 quarts or about 1.3 liters [e] *20* Or *purification offering* [f] *22* The meaning of the Hebrew for this word is uncertain. [g] *22* That is, about 70 feet long and 53 feet wide or about 21 meters long and 16 meters wide

46:1 – 8 ***The prince is to enter.*** What the rituals signified under the law was fulfilled by the Messiah. At the time of this prince, certain promises were being fulfilled and the covenants consummated in the Messianic Age (40:6 – 16,28 – 37; 43:18 – 27; Ex. 20:8 – 11).

46:9 ***No one is to return through the gate by which they entered.*** The prescribed protocol was probably to ensure an orderly procession and service. Such regulations would be needed on the special festival days due to the participation of large numbers of people.

46:14 ***a lasting ordinance.*** This is a change from the provisions in the law (Num. 28:5). God's people cannot be reminded too often of God's provisions for them; nor can they thank Him too much or too frequently.

46:1 [f] Eze 40:19 [g] 1Ch 9:18 [h] ver 6; Isa 66:23 **46:2** [i] ver 8 [j] ver 12; Eze 44:3 **46:3** [k] Lk 1:10 **46:5** [l] ver 11; Eze 45:24 **46:6** [m] ver 1; Nu 10:10 **46:7** [n] Eze 45:24 **46:8** [o] ver 2 [p] Eze 44:3 **46:9** [q] Ex 23:14; 34:20 **46:10** [r] 2Sa 6:14-15; Ps 42:4 **46:11** [s] ver 5 **46:12** [t] Eze 45:17 [u] Lev 7:16 [v] ver 2 **46:13** [w] Ex 29:38; Nu 28:3 **46:14** [x] Da 8:11 **46:15** [y] Ex 29:42 [z] Ex 29:38; Nu 28:5-6 **46:16** [a] 2Ch 21:3 **46:17** [b] Lev 25:10 **46:18** [c] Lev 25:23; Eze 45:8; Mic 2:1-2 **46:19** [d] Eze 42:9 **46:20** [e] Lev 6:27 [f] Zec 14:20

four corners was the same size. 23 Around the inside of each of the four courts was a ledge of stone, with places for fire built all around under the ledge. 24 He said to me, "These are the kitchens where those who minister at the temple are to cook the sacrifices of the people."

The River From the Temple

47 The man brought me back to the entrance to the temple, and I saw water[g] coming out from under the threshold of the temple toward the east (for the temple faced east). The water was coming down from under the south side of the temple, south of the altar.[h] 2 He then brought me out through the north gate and led me around the outside to the outer gate facing east, and the water was trickling from the south side.

3 As the man went eastward with a measuring line[i] in his hand, he measured off a thousand cubits[a] and then led me through water that was ankle-deep. 4 He measured off another thousand cubits and led me through water that was knee-deep. He measured off another thousand and led me through water that was up to the waist. 5 He measured off another thousand, but now it was a river that I could not cross, because the water had risen and was deep enough to swim in—a river that no one could cross.[j] 6 He asked me, "Son of man, do you see this?"

Then he led me back to the bank of the river. 7 When I arrived there, I saw a great number of trees on each side of the river.[k] 8 He said to me, "This water flows toward the eastern region and goes down into the Arabah,[b][l] where it enters the Dead Sea. When it empties into the sea, the salty water there becomes fresh.[m] 9 Swarms of living creatures will live wherever the river flows. There will be large numbers of fish, because this water flows there and makes the salt water fresh; so where the river flows everything will live.[n] 10 Fishermen[o] will stand along the shore; from En Gedi[p] to En Eglaim there will be places for spreading nets.[q] The fish will be of many kinds[r]—like the fish of the Mediterranean Sea.[s] 11 But the swamps and marshes will not become fresh; they will be left for salt.[t] 12 Fruit trees of all kinds will grow on both banks of the river.[u] Their leaves will not wither, nor will their fruit[v] fail. Every month they will bear fruit, because the water from the sanctuary flows to them. Their fruit will serve for food and their leaves for healing.[w]"

The Boundaries of the Land

13 This is what the Sovereign LORD says: "These are the boundaries[x] of the land that you will divide among the twelve tribes of Israel as their inheritance, with two portions for Joseph.[y] 14 You are to divide it equally among them. Because I swore with uplifted hand to give it to your ancestors, this land will become your inheritance.[z]

15 "This is to be the boundary of the land:

"On the north side it will run from the Mediterranean Sea by the Hethlon road[a] past Lebo Hamath to Zedad, 16 Berothah[c][b] and Sibraim (which lies on the border between Damascus and Hamath),[c] as far as Hazer Hattikon, which is on the border of Hauran. 17 The boundary will extend from the sea to Hazar Enan,[d] along the northern border of Damascus, with the border of Hamath to the north. This will be the northern boundary.[d]

18 "On the east side the boundary will run between Hauran and Damascus, along the Jordan between Gilead and the land of Israel, to the Dead Sea and as far as Tamar.[e] This will be the eastern boundary.

19 "On the south side it will run from Tamar as far as the waters of Meribah Kadesh,[e] then along the Wadi of Egypt[f] to the Mediterranean Sea.[g] This will be the southern boundary.

20 "On the west side, the Mediterranean Sea will be the boundary to a point opposite Lebo Hamath.[h] This will be the western boundary.[i]

[a] 3 That is, about 1,700 feet or about 530 meters
[b] 8 Or *the Jordan Valley*
[c] 15,16 See Septuagint and 48:1; Hebrew *road to go into Zedad, 16Hamath, Berothah.*
[d] 17 Hebrew *Enon,* a variant of *Enan*
[e] 18 See Syriac; Hebrew *Israel. You will measure to the Dead Sea.*

46:24 *These are the kitchens.* These were kitchen areas for the people to boil their sacrifices. The temple was a place for sacrificing, cooking, and eating. To combine the two elements is healthy for spiritual fellowship.

47:7–12 *the water from the sanctuary flows to them.* The living water that God will provide has immeasurable power to renew, restore, and resurrect life. The water is a river of healing and the source of abundant life for everything and everyone.

47:14 *You are to divide it equally.* Equality of inheritance is stressed. The unilateral and unconditional nature of the Abrahamic covenant is suggested; this inheritance is a free gift of God's grace which God's people did and could do nothing to deserve.

47:1 [g] Isa 55:1 [h] Ps 46:4; Joel 3:18; Rev 22:1 **47:3** [i] Eze 40:3 **47:5** [j] Isa 11:9; Hab 2:14 **47:7** [k] ver 12; Rev 22:2 **47:8** [l] Dt 3:17; Jos 3:16 [m] Isa 41:18 **47:9** [n] Isa 12:3; 55:1; Jn 4:14; 7:37-38 **47:10** [o] Mt 4:19 [p] Jos 15:62 [q] Eze 26:5 [r] Ps 104:25; Mt 13:47 [s] Nu 34:6 **47:11** [t] Dt 29:23 **47:12** [u] ver 7; Rev 22:2 [v] Ps 1:3 [w] Ge 2:9; Jer 17:8 **47:13** [x] Nu 34:2-12 [y] Ge 48:5 **47:14** [z] Ge 12:7; Dt 1:8; Eze 20:5-6 **47:15** [a] Eze 48:1 **47:16** [b] 2Sa 8:8 [c] Nu 13:21; Eze 48:1 **47:17** [d] Eze 48:1 **47:19** [e] Dt 32:51 [f] Isa 27:12 [g] Eze 48:28 **47:20** [h] Eze 48:1 [i] Nu 34:6

21"You are to distribute this land among
yourselves according to the tribes of Israel.
22You are to allot it as an inheritance for
yourselves and for the foreigners[j] residing
among you and who have children. You are
to consider them as native-born Israelites;
along with you they are to be allotted an
inheritance among the tribes of Israel.[k] 23In
whatever tribe a foreigner resides, there
you are to give them their inheritance," declares the Sovereign LORD.

The Division of the Land

48 "These are the tribes, listed by name:
At the northern frontier, Dan[l] will
have one portion; it will follow the Hethlon
road[m] to Lebo Hamath;[n] Hazar Enan and
the northern border of Damascus next to
Hamath will be part of its border from the
east side to the west side.
2"Asher[o] will have one portion; it will
border the territory of Dan from east to
west.
3"Naphtali[p] will have one portion; it will
border the territory of Asher from east to
west.
4"Manasseh[q] will have one portion; it
will border the territory of Naphtali from
east to west.
5"Ephraim[r] will have one portion; it will
border the territory of Manasseh[s] from east
to west.[t]
6"Reuben[u] will have one portion; it will
border the territory of Ephraim from east
to west.
7"Judah[v] will have one portion; it will
border the territory of Reuben from east
to west.
8"Bordering the territory of Judah from
east to west will be the portion you are to
present as a special gift. It will be 25,000
cubits[a] wide, and its length from east to
west will equal one of the tribal portions;
the sanctuary will be in the center of it.[w]
9"The special portion you are to offer
to the LORD will be 25,000 cubits long and
10,000 cubits[b] wide.[x] 10This will be the sacred portion for the priests. It will be 25,000
cubits long on the north side, 10,000 cubits
wide on the west side, 10,000 cubits wide
on the east side and 25,000 cubits long on
the south side. In the center of it will be the
sanctuary of the LORD.[y] 11This will be for
the consecrated priests, the Zadokites,[z]
who were faithful in serving me[a] and did
not go astray as the Levites did when the
Israelites went astray.[b] 12It will be a special gift to them from the sacred portion of
the land, a most holy portion, bordering the
territory of the Levites.
13"Alongside the territory of the priests,
the Levites will have an allotment 25,000
cubits long and 10,000 cubits wide. Its total
length will be 25,000 cubits and its width
10,000 cubits.[c] 14They must not sell or exchange any of it. This is the best of the
land and must not pass into other hands,
because it is holy to the LORD.[d]
15"The remaining area, 5,000 cubits[c]
wide and 25,000 cubits long, will be for the
common use of the city, for houses and for
pastureland. The city will be in the center
of it 16and will have these measurements:
the north side 4,500 cubits,[d] the south side
4,500 cubits, the east side 4,500 cubits, and
the west side 4,500 cubits.[e] 17The pastureland for the city will be 250 cubits[e] on the
north, 250 cubits on the south, 250 cubits
on the east, and 250 cubits on the west.
18What remains of the area, bordering on
the sacred portion and running the length
of it, will be 10,000 cubits on the east side
and 10,000 cubits on the west side. Its produce will supply food for the workers of
the city.[f] 19The workers from the city who
farm it will come from all the tribes of Israel. 20The entire portion will be a square,
25,000 cubits on each side. As a special gift
you will set aside the sacred portion, along
with the property of the city.
21"What remains on both sides of the
area formed by the sacred portion and
the property of the city will belong to the
prince. It will extend eastward from the
25,000 cubits of the sacred portion to
the eastern border, and westward from the
25,000 cubits to the western border. Both
these areas running the length of the tribal portions will belong to the prince, and
the sacred portion with the temple sanctuary will be in the center of them.[g] 22So the
property of the Levites and the property of
the city will lie in the center of the area that
belongs to the prince. The area belonging
to the prince will lie between the border of
Judah and the border of Benjamin.

---

[a] *8* That is, about 8 miles or about 13 kilometers; also in verses 9, 10, 13, 15, 20 and 21 [b] *9* That is, about 3 1/3 miles or about 5.3 kilometers; also in verses 10, 13 and 18 [c] *15* That is, about 1 2/3 miles or about 2.7 kilometers [d] *16* That is, about 1 1/2 miles or about 2.4 kilometers; also in verses 30, 32, 33 and 34 [e] *17* That is, about 440 feet or about 135 meters

---

47:21–23 *and for the foreigners.* Non-Israelites who married and settled within the Jewish communities were to be accepted as native Israelites, qualified to share in the territorial inheritance of whatever tribe they joined (Lev. 19:34).

48:1 *These are the tribes.* The land would be divided into thirteen parts. The division makes it clear that all who believe have a place.

47:22 [j] Isa 14:1 [k] Nu 26:55-56; Isa 56:6-7; Ro 10:12; Eph 2:12-16; 3:6; Col 3:11 **48:1** [l] Ge 30:6 [m] Eze 47:15-17 [n] Eze 47:20 **48:2** [o] Jos 19:24-31 **48:3** [p] Jos 19:32-39 **48:4** [q] Jos 17:1-11 **48:5** [r] Jos 16:5-9 [s] Jos 17:7-10 [t] Jos 17:17 **48:6** [u] Jos 13:15-21 **48:7** [v] Jos 15:1-63 **48:8** [w] ver 21 **48:9** [x] Eze 45:1 **48:10** [y] ver 21; Eze 45:3-4 **48:11** [z] 2Sa 8:17 [a] Lev 8:35 [b] Eze 14:11; 44:15 **48:13** [c] Eze 45:5 **48:14** [d] Lev 25:34; 27:10, 28 **48:16** [e] Rev 21:16 **48:18** [f] Eze 45:6 **48:21** [g] ver 8, 10; Eze 45:7

23"As for the rest of the tribes: Benjamin[h]
will have one portion; it will extend from
the east side to the west side.
24"Simeon[i] will have one portion; it will
border the territory of Benjamin from east
to west.
25"Issachar[j] will have one portion; it will
border the territory of Simeon from east
to west.
26"Zebulun[k] will have one portion; it will
border the territory of Issachar from east
to west.
27"Gad[l] will have one portion; it will border the territory of Zebulun from east to
west.
28"The southern boundary of Gad
will run south from Tamar[m] to the waters of Meribah Kadesh, then along
the Wadi of Egypt to the Mediterranean
Sea.[n]
29"This is the land you are to allot as an
inheritance to the tribes of Israel, and these
will be their portions," declares the Sovereign LORD.

The Gates of the New City

30"These will be the exits of the city: Beginning on the north side, which is 4,500 cubits long,
31the gates of the city will be named
after the tribes of Israel. The three gates on
the north side will be the gate of Reuben,
the gate of Judah and the gate of Levi.
32"On the east side, which is 4,500 cubits
long, will be three gates: the gate of Joseph,
the gate of Benjamin and the gate of Dan.
33"On the south side, which measures
4,500 cubits, will be three gates: the gate of
Simeon, the gate of Issachar and the gate
of Zebulun.
34"On the west side, which is 4,500 cubits
long, will be three gates: the gate of Gad,
the gate of Asher and the gate of Naphtali.
35"The distance all around will be 18,000
cubits.[a]

"And the name of the city from that time on will be:

THE LORD IS THERE.[o]"

[a] *35* That is, about 6 miles or about 9.5 kilometers

48:31 *named after the tribes of Israel.* The gates are named after the original twelve tribes (Rev. 21:12–13). The gate for Joseph represents the two tribes of Manasseh and Ephraim.

48:35 *THE LORD IS THERE.* This return of the Lord and the regathering of His people is predicted by Ezekiel in 11:17; 20:33–44; 37:15–28 and 39:21–29. The Lord was forced to depart from the city and the temple because of the wickedness of the Israelites (8:6; 10:18). But here, Ezekiel foresees the return of God in all His glory to His people, His temple, and His land. This was a powerful message in its context. Ezekiel and his immediate audience were far away from their homeland. This vision of the coming restoration would have inspired much hope in the faithful.

48:23 [h] Jos 18:11-28 **48:24** [i] Ge 29:33; Jos 19:1-9 **48:25** [j] Jos 19:17-23 **48:26** [k] Jos 19:10-16 **48:27** [l] Jos 13:24-28 **48:28** [m] Ge 14:7 [n] Eze 47:19 **48:35** [o] Isa 12:6; 24:23; Jer 3:17; 14:9; 33:16; Joel 3:21; Zec 2:10; Rev 21:3

DANIEL

▶ **AUTHOR:** Daniel's life and ministry bridge the entire seventy-year period of Babylonian captivity. This claims Daniel as author, and it uses the first person from 7:2 onward. The Jewish Talmud supports this claim, and Christ attributed a quote from 9:27 to the "prophet Daniel" (Matt. 24:15). Daniel's wisdom and divinely given interpretive abilities brought him into a position of prominence, especially in the courts of Nebuchadnezzar and Darius.

▶ **TIME:** c. 605–536 B.C. ▶ **KEY VERSES:** Dan. 2:20–22

▶ **THEME:** Daniel is one of very few heroes in the Bible whose record is flawless. He is an example of how to live and work as a believer in a hostile environment; a man of action while at the same time fully aware of his dependence on God. The important prophecies in Daniel have inspired many interpretations over the years. Many have attempted to identify the various elements of the prophecies and apply them to contemporary figures.

Daniel's Training in Babylon

1 In the third year of the reign of Jehoiakim king of Judah, Nebuchadnezzar[a]
king of Babylon came to Jerusalem and besieged it.[b] 2And the Lord delivered Jehoiakim king of Judah into his hand, along
with some of the articles from the temple
of God. These he carried off to the temple
of his god in Babylonia[a] and put in the treasure house of his god.[c]
3Then the king ordered Ashpenaz, chief
of his court officials, to bring into the
king's service some of the Israelites from
the royal family and the nobility[d]— 4young
men without any physical defect, handsome, showing aptitude for every kind of
learning, well informed, quick to understand, and qualified to serve in the king's
palace. He was to teach them the language
and literature of the Babylonians.[b] 5The
king assigned them a daily amount of food
and wine[e] from the king's table. They were
to be trained for three years, and after that
they were to enter the king's service.[f]
6Among those who were chosen were
some from Judah: Daniel,[g] Hananiah, Mishael and Azariah. 7The chief official gave
them new names: to Daniel, the name Belteshazzar;[h] to Hananiah, Shadrach; to Mishael, Meshach; and to Azariah, Abednego.[i]

[a] 2 Hebrew *Shinar* [b] 4 Or *Chaldeans*

1:1 ***Jehoiakim king of Judah.*** Jehoiakim was an evil king who sided first with the Egyptians and then with the Babylonians, until he finally decided to rebel. His independence was short-lived, however, and he remained under Babylonian domination until his death (2 Kin. 23:34—24:6).

1:2 ***the temple of his god.*** These articles taken from the temple appear later, on the night of Belshazzar's feast (ch. 5). Eventually they were returned to Zerubbabel, who brought them back to Israel (Ezra 1:7).

1:3 ***chief of his court officials.*** In ancient Middle Eastern monarchies, royal harems were typically superintended by men who had been emasculated and were considered reliable to serve in that capacity. A eunuch was often regarded as a privileged official. Some have speculated that Daniel and his friends were eunuchs, but there is no specific statement in the book to this effect.

1:4 ***language and literature.*** The language of most of Mesopotamia was Akkadian, which was written in cuneiform script. Over the centuries the Babylonians and Assyrians produced a massive body of literature of all types. Though Aramaic had begun to replace Akkadian by the time of Nebuchadnezzar, scholars continued to study and write literature in their classical tongue. ***Babylonians.*** This name was commonly applied to Babylonians in general, and also to the guild of astrologers, diviners, and other practitioners of wisdom to which Daniel was being introduced (v. 17; 2:2; 3:8).

1:7 ***names.*** Daniel means "God is my Judge"; Belteshazzar means "Lady protect the king," referring to the goddess Sarpanitu, wife of the god Marduk. Hananiah means "The Lord is gracious"; Shadrach means "I am fearful of the God." Mishael means "Who is what God is?" Meshach means "I am of little account." Azariah means "The Lord has helped me"; Abednego means "Servant of [the god] Nebo."

1:1 [a] 2Ki 24:1 [b] 2Ch 36:6 **1:2** [c] 2Ch 36:7; Jer 27:19-20; Zec 5:5-11 **1:3** [d] 2Ki 20:18; 24:15; Isa 39:7 **1:5** [e] ver 8, 10 [f] ver 19 **1:6** [g] Eze 14:14 **1:7** [h] Da 4:8; 5:12 [i] Da 2:49; 3:12

8But Daniel resolved not to defile[j] himself with the royal food and wine, and he
asked the chief official for permission not
to defile himself this way. 9Now God had
caused the official to show favor[k] and compassion[l] to Daniel, 10but the official told
Daniel, "I am afraid of my lord the king,
who has assigned your[a] food and drink.
Why should he see you looking worse than
the other young men your age? The king
would then have my head because of you."
11Daniel then said to the guard whom
the chief official had appointed over Daniel, Hananiah, Mishael and Azariah,
12"Please test your servants for ten days:
Give us nothing but vegetables to eat and
water to drink. 13Then compare our appearance with that of the young men who
eat the royal food, and treat your servants
in accordance with what you see." 14So he
agreed to this and tested them for ten days.
15At the end of the ten days they looked
healthier and better nourished than any
of the young men who ate the royal food.[m]
16So the guard took away their choice food
and the wine they were to drink and gave
them vegetables instead.[n]
17To these four young men God gave
knowledge and understanding[o] of all kinds
of literature and learning.[p] And Daniel
could understand visions and dreams of
all kinds.[q]
18At the end of the time[r] set by the king
to bring them into his service, the chief official presented them to Nebuchadnezzar.
19The king talked with them, and he found
none equal to Daniel, Hananiah, Mishael
and Azariah; so they entered the king's
service.[s] 20In every matter of wisdom and
understanding about which the king questioned them, he found them ten times better
than all the magicians and enchanters in
his whole kingdom.[t]
21And Daniel remained there until the
first year of King Cyrus.[u]

Nebuchadnezzar's Dream

2 In the second year of his reign, Nebuchadnezzar had dreams;[v] his mind was
troubled[w] and he could not sleep.[x] 2So the
king summoned the magicians,[y] enchanters, sorcerers[z] and astrologers[b][a] to tell him
what he had dreamed.[b] When they came in
and stood before the king, 3he said to them,
"I have had a dream that troubles[c] me and I
want to know what it means.[c]"
4Then the astrologers answered the
king,[d][d] "May the king live forever![e] Tell
your servants the dream, and we will interpret it."
5The king replied to the astrologers,
"This is what I have firmly decided: If you
do not tell me what my dream was and interpret it, I will have you cut into pieces[f]
and your houses turned into piles of rubble.[g] 6But if you tell me the dream and explain it, you will receive from me gifts and
rewards and great honor.[h] So tell me the
dream and interpret it for me."
7Once more they replied, "Let the king
tell his servants the dream, and we will interpret it."
8Then the king answered, "I am certain
that you are trying to gain time, because
you realize that this is what I have firmly
decided: 9If you do not tell me the dream,
there is only one penalty[i] for you. You have
conspired to tell me misleading and wicked things, hoping the situation will change.
So then, tell me the dream, and I will know
that you can interpret it for me."[j]
10The astrologers answered the king,
"There is no one on earth who can do what
the king asks! No king, however great
and mighty, has ever asked such a thing
of any magician or enchanter or astrolo-
ger.[k] 11What the king asks is too difficult.
No one can reveal it to the king except the
gods,[l] and they do not live among humans."
12This made the king so angry and furious[m] that he ordered the execution[n] of all
the wise men of Babylon. 13So the decree
was issued to put the wise men to death,
and men were sent to look for Daniel and
his friends to put them to death.[o]
14When Arioch, the commander of the
king's guard, had gone out to put to death
the wise men of Babylon, Daniel spoke to
him with wisdom and tact. 15He asked the

[a] *10* The Hebrew for *your* and *you* in this verse is plural. [b] *2* Or *Chaldeans*; also in verses 4, 5 and 10 [c] *3* Or *was* [d] *4* At this point the Hebrew text has *in Aramaic*, indicating that the text from here through the end of chapter 7 is in Aramaic.

1:8 *defile himself.* The issue here was not the richness of the food or the alcohol. The king's table no doubt included unclean meats and food which had not been prepared according to the law. In addition, both meat and wines may well have already been offered to idols.

2:2 *magicians.* The word translated "magicians" refers to those who use a pen—most likely, those learned in the sacred writings of the Babylonians.

2:8 *gain time.* Nebuchadnezzar obviously did not have any faith in the integrity of his wise men or in the reality of their wisdom. He wanted to know for sure that the interpretation of his dream was a supernatural revelation, not just a clever story to please a king.

2:11 *except the gods.* The wise men were forced to acknowledge their own limitations. As far as they knew, they were doomed because the gods who had the answers did not speak with men.

1:8 [j] Eze 4:13-14 **1:9** [k] Ge 39:21; Pr 16:7 [l] 1Ki 8:50; Ps 106:46 **1:15** [m] Ex 23:25 **1:16** [n] ver 12-13 **1:17** [o] 1Ki 3:12 [p] Da 2:23; Jas 1:5 [q] Da 2:19, 30; 7:1; 8:1 **1:18** [r] ver 5 **1:19** [s] Ge 41:46 **1:20** [t] 1Ki 4:30; Da 2:13, 28 **1:21** [u] Da 6:28; 10:1 **2:1** [v] Job 33:15, 18; Da 4:5 [w] Ge 41:8 [x] Est 6:1; Da 6:18 **2:2** [y] Ge 41:8 [z] Ex 7:11 [a] ver 10; Da 5:7 [b] Da 4:6 **2:3** [c] Da 4:5 **2:4** [d] Ezr 4:7 [e] Da 3:9; 5:10 **2:5** [f] ver 12 [g] Ezr 6:11; Da 3:29 **2:6** [h] ver 48; Da 5:7, 16 **2:9** [i] Est 4:11 [j] Isa 41:22-24 **2:10** [k] ver 27 **2:11** [l] Da 5:11 **2:12** [m] Da 3:13, 19 [n] ver 5 **2:13** [o] Da 1:20

king's officer, "Why did the king issue such
a harsh decree?" Arioch then explained the
matter to Daniel. 16 At this, Daniel went in
to the king and asked for time, so that he
might interpret the dream for him.
17 Then Daniel returned to his house and
explained the matter to his friends Hananiah, Mishael and Azariah.[p] 18 He urged them
to plead for mercy[q] from the God of heaven
concerning this mystery,[r] so that he and his
friends might not be executed with the rest
of the wise men of Babylon. 19 During the
night the mystery[s] was revealed to Daniel
in a vision.[t] Then Daniel praised the God of
heaven 20 and said:

"Praise be to the name of God for ever
and ever;[u]
wisdom and power[v] are his.
21 He changes times and seasons;[w]
he deposes[x] kings and raises up
others.
He gives wisdom[y] to the wise
and knowledge to the discerning.
22 He reveals deep and hidden things;[z]
he knows what lies in darkness,[a]
and light[b] dwells with him.
23 I thank and praise you, God of my
ancestors:[c]
You have given me wisdom[d] and
power,
you have made known to me what we
asked of you,
you have made known to us the
dream of the king."

Daniel Interprets the Dream

24 Then Daniel went to Arioch,[e] whom
the king had appointed to execute the wise
men of Babylon, and said to him, "Do not
execute the wise men of Babylon. Take me
to the king, and I will interpret his dream
for him."
25 Arioch took Daniel to the king at once
and said, "I have found a man among the
exiles from Judah[f] who can tell the king
what his dream means."
26 The king asked Daniel (also called Belteshazzar),[g] "Are you able to tell me what I
saw in my dream and interpret it?"
27 Daniel replied, "No wise man, enchanter, magician or diviner can explain to the
king the mystery he has asked about,[h]
28 but there is a God in heaven who reveals
mysteries.[i] He has shown King Nebuchadnezzar what will happen in days to come.[j]
Your dream and the visions that passed
through your mind[k] as you were lying in
bed are these:
29 "As Your Majesty was lying there,
your mind turned to things to come, and
the revealer of mysteries showed you what
is going to happen. 30 As for me, this mystery has been revealed[l] to me, not because
I have greater wisdom than anyone else
alive, but so that Your Majesty may know
the interpretation and that you may understand what went through your mind.
31 "Your Majesty looked, and there before
you stood a large statue—an enormous,
dazzling statue,[m] awesome in appearance.
32 The head of the statue was made of pure
gold, its chest and arms of silver, its belly
and thighs of bronze, 33 its legs of iron, its
feet partly of iron and partly of baked clay.
34 While you were watching, a rock was
cut out, but not by human hands.[n] It struck
the statue on its feet of iron and clay and
smashed them.[o] 35 Then the iron, the clay,
the bronze, the silver and the gold were
all broken to pieces and became like chaff
on a threshing floor in the summer. The
wind swept them away[p] without leaving a
trace. But the rock that struck the statue
became a huge mountain[q] and filled the
whole earth.
36 "This was the dream, and now we will
interpret it to the king. 37 Your Majesty, you
are the king of kings.[r] The God of heaven
has given you dominion[s] and power and
might and glory; 38 in your hands he has
placed all mankind and the beasts of the
field and the birds in the sky. Wherever
they live, he has made you ruler over them
all.[t] You are that head of gold.
39 "After you, another kingdom will arise,

2:18 ***plead for mercy from the God of heaven.*** Daniel and his friends knew the same thing that the other wise men did: only God could possibly reveal the king's dream. But, unlike the other wise men, they knew that their God would answer when they called on Him.

2:28 ***in days to come.*** This is an expression used frequently for the end times when God will intervene in human history to establish His eternal kingdom (Is. 2:2; Hos. 3:5; Mic. 4:1–3).

2:31 ***a large statue.*** The statue that Nebuchadnezzar saw represented four kingdoms that would rule over all the earth.

2:37 ***The God of heaven has given you dominion.*** The rulers of the nations of the world may not recognize God's authority, but that does not alter the fact that they have their positions only through His permission.

2:38 ***head of gold.*** The first worldwide empire, the head of gold, was Babylon.

2:39 ***another kingdom will arise, inferior to yours.*** The second empire, the chest and arms of silver, was Medo-Persia. Just as silver is inferior to gold, Medo-Persia was inferior to Babylon, not in size but in its effectiveness in governing its people. ***third kingdom, one of bronze.*** The third kingdom would be the Greek Empire.

2:17 [p] Da 1:6 **2:18** [q] Isa 37:4 [r] Jer 33:3 **2:19** [s] ver 28 [t] Job 33:15; Da 1:17 **2:20** [u] Ps 113:2; 145:1-2 [v] Jer 32:19 **2:21** [w] Da 7:25 [x] Job 12:19; Ps 75:6-7 [y] Jas 1:5 **2:22** [z] Job 12:22; Ps 25:14; Da 5:11 [a] Ps 139:11-12; Jer 23:24; Heb 4:13 [b] Isa 45:7; Jas 1:17 **2:23** [c] Ex 3:15 [d] Da 1:17 **2:24** [e] ver 14 **2:25** [f] Da 1:6; 5:13; 6:13 **2:26** [g] Da 1:7 **2:27** [h] ver 10 **2:28** [i] Ge 40:8; Am 4:13 [j] Ge 49:1; Da 10:14 [k] Da 4:5 **2:30** [l] Isa 45:3; Da 1:17; Am 4:13 **2:31** [m] Hab 1:7 **2:34** [n] Zec 4:6 [o] ver 44-45; Ps 2:9; Isa 60:12; Da 8:25 **2:35** [p] Ps 1:4; 37:10; Isa 17:13 [q] Isa 2:3; Mic 4:1 **2:37** [r] Eze 26:7 [s] Jer 27:7 **2:38** [t] Jer 27:6; Da 4:21-22

inferior to yours. Next, a third kingdom, one of bronze, will rule over the whole earth. 40Finally, there will be a fourth kingdom, strong as iron—for iron breaks and smashes everything—and as iron breaks things to pieces, so it will crush and break all the others.[u] 41Just as you saw that the feet and toes were partly of baked clay and partly of iron, so this will be a divided kingdom; yet it will have some of the strength of iron in it, even as you saw iron mixed with clay. 42As the toes were partly iron and partly clay, so this kingdom will be partly strong and partly brittle. 43And just as you saw the iron mixed with baked clay, so the people will be a mixture and will not remain united, any more than iron mixes with clay.

44"In the time of those kings, the God of heaven will set up a kingdom that will never be destroyed, nor will it be left to another people. It will crush[v] all those kingdoms[w] and bring them to an end, but it will itself endure forever.[x] 45This is the meaning of the vision of the rock[y] cut out of a mountain, but not by human hands[z]—a rock that broke the iron, the bronze, the clay, the silver and the gold to pieces.

"The great God has shown the king what will take place in the future. The dream is true and its interpretation is trustworthy."

46Then King Nebuchadnezzar fell prostrate[a] before Daniel and paid him honor and ordered that an offering[b] and incense be presented to him. 47The king said to Daniel, "Surely your God is the God of gods[c] and the Lord of kings[d] and a revealer of mysteries,[e] for you were able to reveal this mystery."

48Then the king placed Daniel in a high position and lavished many gifts on him. He made him ruler over the entire province of Babylon and placed him in charge of all its wise men.[f] 49Moreover, at Daniel's request the king appointed Shadrach, Meshach and Abednego administrators over the province of Babylon,[g] while Daniel himself remained at the royal court.

The Image of Gold and the Blazing Furnace

3 King Nebuchadnezzar made an image[h] of gold, sixty cubits high and six cubits wide,[a] and set it up on the plain of Dura in the province of Babylon. 2He then summoned the satraps, prefects, governors, advisers, treasurers, judges, magistrates and all the other provincial officials[i] to come to the dedication of the image he had set up. 3So the satraps, prefects, governors, advisers, treasurers, judges, magistrates and all the other provincial officials assembled for the dedication of the image that King Nebuchadnezzar had set up, and they stood before it.

4Then the herald loudly proclaimed, "Nations and peoples of every language,[j] this is what you are commanded to do: 5As soon as you hear the sound of the horn, flute, zither, lyre, harp, pipe and all kinds of music, you must fall down and worship the image of gold that King Nebuchadnezzar has set up.[k] 6Whoever does not fall down and worship will immediately be thrown into a blazing furnace."[l]

7Therefore, as soon as they heard the sound of the horn, flute, zither, lyre, harp and all kinds of music, all the nations and peoples of every language fell down and worshiped the image of gold that King Nebuchadnezzar had set up.[m]

8At this time some astrologers[b][n] came forward and denounced the Jews. 9They

---

[a] *1* That is, about 90 feet high and 9 feet wide or about 27 meters high and 2.7 meters wide
[b] *8* Or *Chaldeans*

2:40 *fourth kingdom, strong as iron.* The fourth kingdom, the legs of iron, is the only one not specifically identified within the Book of Daniel. Rome is the most likely choice, for it succeeded Greece, and was certainly a very strong empire.

2:41–45 *will be a divided kingdom.* Some believe that this is a reference to the Roman Empire's decline, when the kingdom was divided and the fabric of the empire was weakening in the early centuries after Christ. In this case the "kingdom which will never be destroyed" (obviously the kingdom of God) is a spiritual kingdom introduced by Christ at His first coming, and the mountain that grew from the rock would be a reference to the spread of Christianity, which eventually was named the state religion of the Roman Empire.

Others believe that verses 41–45 point to future events that have not yet been fulfilled. When this vision is compared with the four beasts of chapter 7, it seems clear that the fourth kingdom is yet to come. It is theorized that the kingdom of iron does actually refer to the Roman Empire, which will be revived in some form in the last days, perhaps as a ten-nation confederacy (the ten toes, or the ten horns of the beast of chapter 7). In this case, the "kingdom that will never be destroyed" is a literal kingdom to be established by Jesus Christ at the second coming, at which time He will destroy the kingdoms of the world (Rev. 19:15).

3:1 *cubits.* Nebuchadnezzar's image was 90 to 100 feet tall. The odd proportions of this figure (a normal human height-to-width ratio is about 4:1 rather than 10:1) may indicate that the height includes a base or pedestal.

3:2 *satraps.* Satraps were the chief officials of the provinces of the empire.

2:40 [u] Da 7:7,23 **2:44** [v] Ps 2:9; 1Co 15:24 [w] Isa 60:12 [x] Ps 145:13; Isa 9:7; Da 4:34; 6:26; 7:14,27; Mic 4:7,13; Lk 1:33 **2:45** [y] Isa 28:16 [z] Da 8:25 **2:46** [a] Da 8:17; Ac 10:25 [b] Ac 14:13 **2:47** [c] Da 11:36 [d] Da 4:25 [e] ver 22, 28 **2:48** [f] ver 6; Da 4:9; 5:11 **2:49** [g] Da 1:7
3:1 [h] Isa 46:6; Jer 16:20; Hab 2:19 **3:2** [i] ver 27; Da 6:7
3:4 [j] Da 4:1; 6:25 **3:5** [k] ver 10,15 **3:6** [l] ver 11,15,21; Jer 29:22; Da 6:7; Mt 13:42,50; Rev 13:15 **3:7** [m] ver 5
3:8 [n] Da 2:10

said to King Nebuchadnezzar, "May the
king live forever![o] 10Your Majesty has issued a decree[p] that everyone who hears
the sound of the horn, flute, zither, lyre,
harp, pipe and all kinds of music must
fall down and worship the image of gold,[q]
11and that whoever does not fall down and
worship will be thrown into a blazing furnace. 12But there are some Jews whom you
have set over the affairs of the province of
Babylon—Shadrach, Meshach and Abednego[r]—who pay no attention[s] to you, Your
Majesty. They neither serve your gods
nor worship the image of gold you have
set up."[t]

13Furious[u] with rage, Nebuchadnezzar summoned Shadrach, Meshach and
Abednego. So these men were brought
before the king, 14and Nebuchadnezzar said to them, "Is it true, Shadrach,
Meshach and Abednego, that you do
not serve my gods[v] or worship the image[w] of gold I have set up? 15Now when
you hear the sound of the horn, flute, zither, lyre, harp, pipe and all kinds of music,
if you are ready to fall down and worship
the image I made, very good. But if you do
not worship it, you will be thrown immediately into a blazing furnace. Then what
god[x] will be able to rescue[y] you from my
hand?"

16Shadrach, Meshach and Abednego[z] replied to him, "King Nebuchadnezzar, we
do not need to defend ourselves before you
in this matter. 17If we are thrown into the
blazing furnace, the God we serve is able
to deliver[a] us from it, and he will deliver[b]
us[α] from Your Majesty's hand. 18But even
if he does not, we want you to know, Your
Majesty, that we will not serve your gods
or worship the image of gold you have
set up.[c]"

19Then Nebuchadnezzar was furious
with Shadrach, Meshach and Abednego,
and his attitude toward them changed. He
ordered the furnace heated seven[d] times
hotter than usual 20and commanded some
of the strongest soldiers in his army to tie
up Shadrach, Meshach and Abednego and
throw them into the blazing furnace. 21So
these men, wearing their robes, trousers,
turbans and other clothes, were bound and
thrown into the blazing furnace. 22The
king's command was so urgent and the
furnace so hot that the flames of the fire
killed the soldiers who took up Shadrach,
Meshach and Abednego,[e] 23and these
three men, firmly tied, fell into the blazing furnace.

24Then King Nebuchadnezzar leaped to
his feet in amazement and asked his advisers, "Weren't there three men that we tied
up and threw into the fire?"

They replied, "Certainly, Your Majesty."

25He said, "Look! I see four men walking around in the fire, unbound and unharmed, and the fourth looks like a son of
the gods."

26Nebuchadnezzar then approached the
opening of the blazing furnace and shouted, "Shadrach, Meshach and Abednego,
servants of the Most High God,[f] come out!
Come here!"

So Shadrach, Meshach and Abednego
came out of the fire, 27and the satraps,
prefects, governors and royal advisers[g]
crowded around them.[h] They saw that the
fire[i] had not harmed their bodies, nor was
a hair of their heads singed; their robes
were not scorched, and there was no smell
of fire on them.

28Then Nebuchadnezzar said, "Praise
be to the God of Shadrach, Meshach and
Abednego, who has sent his angel[j] and
rescued his servants! They trusted[k] in
him and defied the king's command and
were willing to give up their lives rather
than serve or worship any god except their
own God.[l] 29Therefore I decree[m] that the
people of any nation or language who say
anything against the God of Shadrach,
Meshach and Abednego be cut into pieces and their houses be turned into piles of
rubble,[n] for no other god can save[o] in this
way."

30Then the king promoted Shadrach,
Meshach and Abednego in the province of
Babylon.[p]

[α] 17 Or *If the God we serve is able to deliver us, then he will deliver us from the blazing furnace and*

3:18 *But even if he does not.* The faithful men knew that God could deliver them (v. 17), yet they were also aware that God could have chosen not to do so. Faith in God may not translate into victory in every circumstance (Heb. 11:32–39). To these men the outcome was irrelevant, for what was at stake was not God's ability or their own lives, but their faith and obedience to serve Him regardless of the cost.

3:25 *I see four men walking.* The fourth man walking with the three friends in the furnace may have been an angel. Many believe that this was an appearance of the pre-incarnate Christ.

3:28 *Praise be to the God of Shadrach, Meshach and Abednego.* Pagan cultures did not deny the existence of other gods, even those of other peoples. Nebuchadnezzar was impressed with the God of Israel, but that did not mean that he recognized that God is the only true god.

3:9 [o] Ne 2:3; Da 5:10; 6:6 **3:10** [p] Da 6:12 [q] ver 4-6
3:12 [r] Da 2:49 [s] Da 6:13 [t] Est 3:3 **3:13** [u] Da 2:12
3:14 [v] Isa 46:1; Jer 50:2 [w] ver 1 **3:15** [x] Isa 36:18-20
[y] Ex 5:2; 2Ch 32:15 **3:16** [z] Da 1:7 **3:17** [a] Ps 27:1-2
[b] Job 5:19; Jer 1:8 **3:18** [c] ver 28; Jos 24:15
3:19 [d] Lev 26:18-28 **3:22** [e] Da 1:7 **3:26** [f] Da 4:2, 34
3:27 [g] ver 2 [h] Isa 43:2; Heb 11:32-34 [i] Da 6:23
3:28 [j] Ps 34:7; Da 6:22; Ac 5:19 [k] Job 13:15; Ps 26:1; 84:12;
Jer 17:7 [l] ver 18 **3:29** [m] Da 6:26 [n] Ezr 6:11 [o] Da 6:27
3:30 [p] Da 2:49

Nebuchadnezzar's Dream of a Tree

4 [a] King Nebuchadnezzar,

To the nations and peoples of every
language,[q] who live in all the earth:

May you prosper greatly![r]

2It is my pleasure to tell you about
the miraculous signs[s] and wonders
that the Most High God[t] has performed for me.

3How great are his signs,
how mighty his wonders![u]
His kingdom is an eternal kingdom;
his dominion endures[v] from
generation to generation.

4I, Nebuchadnezzar, was at home in
my palace, contented[w] and prosperous.
5I had a dream[x] that made me afraid.
As I was lying in bed, the images and
visions that passed through my mind[y]
terrified me. 6So I commanded that all
the wise men of Babylon be brought
before me to interpret[z] the dream for
me. 7When the magicians,[a] enchanters, astrologers[b] and diviners[b] came,
I told them the dream, but they could
not interpret it for me.[c] 8Finally, Daniel
came into my presence and I told him
the dream. (He is called Belteshazzar,[d]
after the name of my god, and the spirit of the holy gods[e] is in him.)
9I said, "Belteshazzar, chief[f] of the
magicians, I know that the spirit of
the holy gods[g] is in you, and no mystery is too difficult for you. Here is my
dream; interpret it for me. 10These are
the visions I saw while lying in bed:[h]
I looked, and there before me stood a
tree in the middle of the land. Its height
was enormous.[i] 11The tree grew large
and strong and its top touched the sky;
it was visible to the ends of the earth.
12Its leaves were beautiful, its fruit
abundant, and on it was food for all.
Under it the wild animals found shelter, and the birds lived in its branches;[j]
from it every creature was fed.
13"In the visions I saw while lying
in bed,[k] I looked, and there before me
was a holy one,[l] a messenger,[c] coming down from heaven. 14He called in
a loud voice: 'Cut down the tree and
trim off its branches; strip off its leaves
and scatter its fruit. Let the animals
flee from under it and the birds from
its branches.[m] 15But let the stump and
its roots, bound with iron and bronze,
remain in the ground, in the grass of
the field.
"'Let him be drenched with the dew
of heaven, and let him live with the animals among the plants of the earth.
16Let his mind be changed from that
of a man and let him be given the mind
of an animal, till seven times[d] pass by
for him.[n]
17"'The decision is announced by
messengers, the holy ones declare the
verdict, so that the living may know
that the Most High[o] is sovereign[p] over
all kingdoms on earth and gives them
to anyone he wishes and sets over
them the lowliest[q] of people.'
18"This is the dream that I, King
Nebuchadnezzar, had. Now, Belteshazzar, tell me what it means, for
none of the wise men in my kingdom
can interpret it for me.[r] But you can,[s]
because the spirit of the holy gods is
in you."[t]

Daniel Interprets the Dream

19Then Daniel (also called Belteshazzar) was greatly perplexed for a time,
and his thoughts terrified[u] him. So the
king said, "Belteshazzar, do not let the
dream or its meaning alarm you."
Belteshazzar answered, "My lord,
if only the dream applied to your enemies and its meaning to your adversaries! 20The tree you saw, which grew
large and strong, with its top touching
the sky, visible to the whole earth,
21with beautiful leaves and abundant

[a] In Aramaic texts 4:1-3 is numbered 3:31-33, and 4:4-37 is numbered 4:1-34. [b] 7 Or *Chaldeans* [c] 13 Or *watchman*; also in verses 17 and 23 [d] 16 Or *years*; also in verses 23, 25 and 32

4:1 ***King Nebuchadnezzar.*** These verses are a royal proclamation by Nebuchadnezzar concerning the God of Israel, in which the king celebrated what God had done for him and extolled His power and dominion.

4:8 ***my god.*** This refers to Marduk. Nebuchadnezzar was still a pagan, but he also recognized that Daniel had the spirit of his God, and that Daniel's God was different from other gods.

4:9 ***chief of the magicians.*** Daniel's position as head magician did not mean that he practiced sorcery or witchcraft, a thing clearly forbidden by the law (Deut. 18:10–11). In the pluralistic Babylonian society, Daniel's relationship with the God of Israel would automatically have been categorized as another form of magic, or astrology, or divination, the "wisdom" of the day. He received the honor and position of one who has favor with the gods.

4:16 ***seven times.*** These times could refer to years, months, weeks, days, or hours. Most take them as years, as elsewhere in the book (7:25).

4:20 ***tree.*** In the Old Testament, a tree is a common symbol for a ruler (Judg. 9:7–15; Ezek. 31:2–14; Zech. 11:1–2).

4:1 [q] Da 3:4 [r] Da 6:25 **4:2** [s] Ps 74:9 [t] Da 3:26 **4:3** [u] Ps 105:27; Da 6:27 [v] Da 2:44 **4:4** [w] Ps 30:6 **4:5** [x] Da 2:1 [y] Da 2:28 **4:6** [z] Da 2:2 **4:7** [a] Ge 41:8 [b] Isa 44:25; Da 2:2 [c] Da 2:10 **4:8** [d] Da 1:7 [e] Da 5:11, 14 **4:9** [f] Da 2:48 [g] Da 5:11-12 **4:10** [h] ver 5 [i] Eze 31:3-4 **4:12** [j] Eze 17:23; Mt 13:32 **4:13** [k] Da 7:1 [l] ver 23; Dt 33:2; Da 8:13 **4:14** [m] Eze 31:12; Mt 3:10 **4:16** [n] ver 23, 32 **4:17** [o] ver 2, 25; Ps 83:18 [p] Jer 27:5-7; Da 2:21; 5:18-21 [q] Da 11:21 **4:18** [r] Ge 41:8; Da 5:8, 15 [s] Ge 41:15 [t] ver 7-9 **4:19** [u] Da 7:15, 28; 8:27; 10:16-17

fruit, providing food for all, giving
shelter to the wild animals, and having nesting places in its branches for
the birds— 22Your Majesty, you are
that tree![v] You have become great and
strong; your greatness has grown until
it reaches the sky, and your dominion
extends to distant parts of the earth.[w]
23"Your Majesty saw a holy one,[x] a
messenger, coming down from heav-
en and saying, 'Cut down the tree and
destroy it, but leave the stump, bound
with iron and bronze, in the grass of
the field, while its roots remain in the
ground. Let him be drenched with the
dew of heaven; let him live with the
wild animals, until seven times pass
by for him.'[y]
24"This is the interpretation, Your
Majesty, and this is the decree[z] the
Most High has issued against my lord
the king: 25You will be driven away
from people and will live with the wild
animals; you will eat grass like the ox
and be drenched with the dew of heav-
en. Seven times will pass by for you
until you acknowledge that the Most
High[a] is sovereign over all kingdoms
on earth and gives them to anyone he
wishes.[b] 26The command to leave the
stump of the tree with its roots[c] means
that your kingdom will be restored
to you when you acknowledge that
Heaven rules.[d] 27Therefore, Your Majesty, be pleased to accept my advice:
Renounce your sins by doing what is
right, and your wickedness by being
kind to the oppressed.[e] It may be that
then your prosperity will continue.[f]"

The Dream Is Fulfilled

28All this happened[g] to King Nebuchadnezzar. 29Twelve months later, as
the king was walking on the roof of
the royal palace of Babylon, 30he said,
"Is not this the great Babylon I have
built as the royal residence, by my
mighty power and for the glory of my
majesty?"[h]
31Even as the words were on
his lips, a voice came from heav-
en, "This is what is decreed for you,
King Nebuchadnezzar: Your royal authority has been taken from
you. 32You will be driven away from
people and will live with the wild animals; you will eat grass like the ox.
Seven times will pass by for you until
you acknowledge that the Most High is
sovereign over all kingdoms on earth
and gives them to anyone he wishes."
33Immediately what had been said
about Nebuchadnezzar was fulfilled.
He was driven away from people and
ate grass like the ox. His body was
drenched with the dew of heaven until
his hair grew like the feathers of an
eagle and his nails like the claws of a
bird.[i]

34At the end of that time, I, Nebuchadnezzar, raised my eyes toward
heaven, and my sanity was restored.
Then I praised the Most High; I honored and glorified him who lives forever.[j]

His dominion is an eternal dominion;
his kingdom endures from generation
to generation.[k]
35 All the peoples of the earth
are regarded as nothing.[l]
He does as he pleases[m]
with the powers of heaven
and the peoples of the earth.
No one can hold back his hand
or say to him: "What have you done?"[n]

36At the same time that my sanity
was restored, my honor and splendor
were returned to me for the glory of
my kingdom.[o] My advisers and nobles
sought me out, and I was restored to
my throne and became even greater
than before. 37Now I, Nebuchadnezzar, praise and exalt and glorify the
King of heaven, because everything
he does is right and all his ways are
just.[p] And those who walk in pride he
is able to humble.[q]

The Writing on the Wall

5 King Belshazzar gave a great banquet[r]
for a thousand of his nobles and drank

4:23 *a messenger.* The term "messenger" means "waking one," one who is constantly alert. The parallel "holy one" suggests that the messenger is either the Lord Himself or one of His angels (3:28; 6:22; 8:16; 10:13).

4:32 *until you acknowledge that the Most High is sovereign.* Nebuchadnezzar would become insane, yet in his animal-like state he would learn more of God than he ever had before. The chastisement of God is always for a holy and helpful purpose, if we will accept it.

5:1 *King Belshazzar.* Belshazzar is called the king and the son of Nebuchadnezzar. Other ancient records, however, seem to dispute both facts. These records indicate that Belshazzar was the son of Nabonidus, the last king of Babylon. It is possible that Belshazzar was the grandson of Nebuchadnezzar. In ancient writings, the term *father* is often used to indicate ancestry rather than immediate family (2 Kin.

4:22 [v] 2Sa 12:7 [w] Jer 27:7; Da 2:37-38; 5:18-19
4:23 [x] ver 13 [y] Da 5:21 **4:24** [z] Job 40:12; Ps 107:40
4:25 [a] ver 17; Ps 83:18 [b] Jer 27:5; Da 5:21 **4:26** [c] ver 15
[d] Da 2:37 **4:27** [e] Isa 55:6-7 [f] 1Ki 21:29; Ps 41:3; Eze 18:22
4:28 [g] Nu 23:19 **4:30** [h] Isa 37:24-25; Da 5:20; Hab 2:4
4:33 [i] Da 5:20-21 **4:34** [j] Da 12:7; Rev 4:10 [k] Ps 145:13;
Da 2:44; 5:21; 6:26; Lk 1:33 **4:35** [l] Isa 40:17 [m] Ps 115:3;
135:6 [n] Isa 45:9; Ro 9:20 **4:36** [o] Pr 22:4 **4:37** [p] Dt 32:4;
Ps 33:4-5 [q] Ex 18:11; Job 40:11-12; Da 5:20,23
5:1 [r] Est 1:3

wine with them. 2While Belshazzar was drinking his wine, he gave orders to bring in the gold and silver goblets[s] that Nebuchadnezzar his father[a] had taken from the temple in Jerusalem, so that the king and his nobles, his wives and his concubines might drink from them.[t] 3So they brought in the gold goblets that had been taken from the temple of God in Jerusalem, and the king and his nobles, his wives and his concubines drank from them. 4As they drank the wine, they praised the gods of gold and silver, of bronze, iron, wood and stone.[u]

5Suddenly the fingers of a human hand appeared and wrote on the plaster of the wall, near the lampstand in the royal palace. The king watched the hand as it wrote. 6His face turned pale and he was so frightened[v] that his legs became weak[w] and his knees were knocking.

7The king summoned the enchanters, astrologers[b] and diviners.[x] Then he said to these wise[y] men of Babylon, "Whoever reads this writing and tells me what it means will be clothed in purple and have a gold chain placed around his neck,[z] and he will be made the third highest ruler in the kingdom."[a]

8Then all the king's wise men came in, but they could not read the writing or tell the king what it meant.[b] 9So King Belshazzar became even more terrified[c] and his face grew more pale. His nobles were baffled.

10The queen,[c] hearing the voices of the king and his nobles, came into the banquet hall. "May the king live forever!"[d] she said. "Don't be alarmed! Don't look so pale! 11There is a man in your kingdom who has the spirit of the holy gods[e] in him. In the time of your father he was found to have insight and intelligence and wisdom[f] like that of the gods. Your father, King Nebuchadnezzar, appointed him chief of the magicians, enchanters, astrologers and diviners.[g] 12He did this because Daniel, whom the king called Belteshazzar,[h] was found to have a keen mind and knowledge and understanding, and also the ability to interpret dreams, explain riddles and solve difficult problems.[i] Call for Daniel, and he will tell you what the writing means."

13So Daniel was brought before the king, and the king said to him, "Are you Daniel, one of the exiles my father the king brought from Judah?[j] 14I have heard that the spirit of the gods is in you and that you have insight, intelligence and outstanding wisdom. 15The wise men and enchanters were brought before me to read this writing and tell me what it means, but they could not explain it. 16Now I have heard that you are able to give interpretations and to solve difficult problems. If you can read this writing and tell me what it means, you will be clothed in purple and have a gold chain placed around your neck, and you will be made the third highest ruler in the kingdom."

17Then Daniel answered the king, "You may keep your gifts for yourself and give your rewards to someone else.[k] Nevertheless, I will read the writing for the king and tell him what it means.

18"Your Majesty, the Most High God gave your father Nebuchadnezzar sovereignty and greatness and glory and splendor.[l] 19Because of the high position he gave him, all the nations and peoples of every language dreaded and feared him. Those the king wanted to put to death, he put to death;[m] those he wanted to spare, he spared; those he wanted to promote, he promoted; and those he wanted to humble, he humbled. 20But when his heart became arrogant and hardened with pride,[n] he was deposed from his royal throne and stripped[o] of his glory.[p] 21He was driven away from people and given the mind of an animal; he lived with the wild donkeys and ate grass like the ox; and his body was drenched with the dew of heaven, until he acknowledged that the Most High God is sovereign[q] over all kingdoms on earth and sets over them anyone he wishes.[r]

22"But you, Belshazzar, his son,[d] have not humbled[s] yourself, though you knew all this. 23Instead, you have set yourself up against[t] the Lord of heaven. You had the goblets from his temple brought to you, and you and your nobles, your wives and

---

a 2 Or *ancestor*; or *predecessor*; also in verses 11, 13 and 18 *b* 7 Or *Chaldeans*; also in verse 11 *c* 10 Or *queen mother* *d* 22 Or *descendant*; or *successor*

14:3). Belshazzar may have served as vice-regent while his father was still living (Nabonidus seems to have spent a number of the years of his reign in Arabia). Thus, he would have been acting as king, even if he was not officially king. Note that Darius the Mede was also called king, even though he served Cyrus (v. 31; 6:6).

5:7 *third highest ruler.* Assuming that Belshazzar was acting as regent for his father Nabonidus, the "third ruler" would have been next in line for the throne.

5:11 *the spirit of the holy gods.* This is the same expression used by Nebuchadnezzar (4:8–9,18).

5:13 *Daniel, one of the exiles.* Daniel was an old man by this time, possibly 80 years old or older.

5:2 [s] 2Ki 24:13; Jer 52:19 [t] Est 1:7; Da 1:2 **5:4** [u] Ps 135:15-18; Hab 2:19; Rev 9:20 **5:6** [v] Da 4:5 [w] Eze 7:17 **5:7** [x] Isa 44:25 [y] Da 4:6-7 [z] Ge 41:42 [a] Da 2:5-6, 48; 6:2-3 **5:8** [b] Da 2:10, 27 **5:9** [c] Isa 21:4 **5:10** [d] Da 3:9 **5:11** [e] Da 4:8-9, 19 [f] ver 14; Da 1:17 [g] Da 2:47-48 **5:12** [h] Da 1:7 [i] ver 14-16; Da 6:3 **5:13** [j] Da 6:13 **5:17** [k] 2Ki 5:16 **5:18** [l] Jer 27:7; Da 2:37-38 **5:19** [m] Da 2:12-13; 3:6 **5:20** [n] Da 4:30 [o] Jer 13:18 [p] Job 40:12; Isa 14:13-15 **5:21** [q] Eze 17:24 [r] Da 4:16-17, 35 **5:22** [s] Ex 10:3; 2Ch 33:23 **5:23** [t] Jer 50:29

your concubines drank wine from them.
You praised the gods of silver and gold, of
bronze, iron, wood and stone, which cannot see or hear or understand.[u] But you did
not honor the God who holds in his hand
your life[v] and all your ways.[w] **24**Therefore
he sent the hand that wrote the inscription.
25"This is the inscription that was written:

MENE, MENE, TEKEL, PARSIN

26"Here is what these words mean:

Mene[a]: God has numbered the
days[x] of your reign and
brought it to an end.[y]
27 *Tekel*[b]: You have been weighed on
the scales and found want-
ing.[z]
28 *Peres*[c]: Your kingdom is divided
and given to the Medes[a] and
Persians."[b]

29Then at Belshazzar's command, Daniel was clothed in purple, a gold chain was
placed around his neck, and he was proclaimed the third highest ruler in the kingdom.
30That very night Belshazzar,[c] king of
the Babylonians,[d] was slain,[d] **31**and Darius[e] the Mede took over the kingdom, at the
age of sixty-two.[e]

Daniel in the Den of Lions

6[f] It pleased Darius[f] to appoint 120 satraps[g] to rule throughout the kingdom,
2with three administrators over them, one
of whom was Daniel.[h] The satraps were
made accountable[i] to them so that the king
might not suffer loss. **3**Now Daniel so distinguished himself among the administrators and the satraps by his exceptional
qualities that the king planned to set him
over the whole kingdom.[j] **4**At this, the administrators and the satraps tried to find
grounds for charges against Daniel in his
conduct of government affairs, but they
were unable to do so. They could find no
corruption in him, because he was trustworthy and neither corrupt nor negligent.
5Finally these men said, "We will never
find any basis for charges against this man
Daniel unless it has something to do with
the law of his God."[k]
6So these administrators and satraps
went as a group to the king and said: "May
King Darius live forever![l] **7**The royal administrators, prefects, satraps, advisers
and governors[m] have all agreed that the
king should issue an edict and enforce
the decree that anyone who prays to any
god or human being during the next thirty days, except to you, Your Majesty, shall
be thrown into the lions' den.[n] **8**Now, Your
Majesty, issue the decree and put it in
writing so that it cannot be altered—in
accordance with the law of the Medes and
Persians, which cannot be repealed."[o] **9**So
King Darius put the decree in writing.
10Now when Daniel learned that the decree had been published, he went home to his
upstairs room where the windows opened
toward[p] Jerusalem. Three times a day he
got down on his knees[q] and prayed, giving
thanks to his God, just as he had done before.[r] **11**Then these men went as a group and
found Daniel praying and asking God for
help. **12**So they went to the king and spoke
to him about his royal decree: "Did you
not publish a decree that during the next
thirty days anyone who prays to any god
or human being except to you, Your Majesty, would be thrown into the lions' den?"
The king answered, "The decree
stands—in accordance with the law of the
Medes and Persians, which cannot be repealed."[s]

---

[a] *26 Mene* can mean *numbered* or *mina* (a unit of money). [b] *27 Tekel* can mean *weighed* or *shekel.* [c] *28 Peres* (the singular of *Parsin*) can mean *divided* or *Persia* or *a half mina* or *a half shekel.* [d] *30* Or *Chaldeans* [e] *31* In Aramaic texts this verse (5:31) is numbered 6:1. [f] In Aramaic texts 6:1-28 is numbered 6:2-29.

5:25–28 *MENE, MENE, TEKEL, PARSIN.* Mene means "numbered." The repetition is for emphasis. God had numbered the days of Belshazzar's kingdom, and the time was up. TEKEL means "weighed." God had weighed Belshazzar's character, and he did not measure up. PARSIN (the plural of PERES) means "divided." That very night Babylon would be divided and defeated by the Medes and the Persians.

5:30 *That very night.* That very evening (October 12, 539 B.C.), Babylon fell to the Persian army commanded by Gubaru.

5:31 *Darius the Mede.* Darius the Mede is mentioned by name only in the Book of Daniel. He cannot be the famous Darius I Hystaspes because Darius I was not a Mede, and he lived too late (522–486 B.C.) to be a contemporary of Daniel. It is believed that "Darius the Mede" was Gubaru, a governor appointed by Cyrus. Ancient literary sources indicate that this official took over immediately in Babylon until Cyrus appointed his own son Cambyses as co-ruler around 538 B.C. Why Gubaru might have been called Darius is uncertain, though ancient rulers often took other names for themselves.

6:3 *exceptional qualities.* This probably refers to Daniel's surpassing ability to do his job well and perhaps also indicates a commendable attitude.

6:5 *the law of his God.* Daniel had such integrity that, even after a life spent in government circles, his enemies could find nothing against him. His devotion to God was so well known that these men were confident that Daniel would obey His law even if it would cost him his life.

5:23 [u] Ps 115:4-8; Hab 2:19 [v] Job 12:10 [w] Job 31:4; Jer 10:23 **5:26** [x] Jer 27:7 [y] Isa 13:6 **5:27** [z] Ps 62:9 **5:28** [a] Isa 13:17 [b] Da 6:28 **5:30** [c] ver 1 [d] Isa 21:9; Jer 51:31 **5:31** [e] Da 6:1; 9:1 **6:1** [f] Da 5:31 [g] Est 1:1 **6:2** [h] Da 2:48-49 [i] Ezr 4:22 **6:3** [j] Ge 41:41; Est 10:3; Da 5:12-14 **6:5** [k] Ac 24:13-16 **6:6** [l] Ne 2:3; Da 2:4 **6:7** [m] Da 3:2 [n] Ps 59:3; 64:2-6; Da 3:6 **6:8** [o] Est 1:19 **6:10** [p] 1Ki 8:48-49 [q] Ps 95:6 [r] Ac 5:29 **6:12** [s] Est 1:19; Da 3:8-12

13 Then they said to the king, "Daniel,
who is one of the exiles from Judah,[t] pays
no attention[u] to you, Your Majesty, or to the
decree you put in writing. He still prays
three times a day." 14 When the king heard
this, he was greatly distressed;[v] he was determined to rescue Daniel and made every
effort until sundown to save him.
15 Then the men went as a group to King
Darius and said to him, "Remember, Your
Majesty, that according to the law of the
Medes and Persians no decree or edict that
the king issues can be changed."[w]
16 So the king gave the order, and they
brought Daniel and threw him into the lions' den.[x] The king said to Daniel, "May
your God, whom you serve continually,
rescue[y] you!"
17 A stone was brought and placed over
the mouth of the den, and the king sealed[z]
it with his own signet ring and with the
rings of his nobles, so that Daniel's situation might not be changed. 18 Then the king
returned to his palace and spent the night
without eating[a] and without any entertainment being brought to him. And he could
not sleep.[b]
19 At the first light of dawn, the king got
up and hurried to the lions' den. 20 When
he came near the den, he called to Daniel
in an anguished voice, "Daniel, servant of
the living God, has your God, whom you
serve continually, been able to rescue you
from the lions?"[c]
21 Daniel answered, "May the king live
forever![d] 22 My God sent his angel,[e] and he
shut the mouths of the lions.[f] They have not
hurt me, because I was found innocent in
his sight.[g] Nor have I ever done any wrong
before you, Your Majesty."
23 The king was overjoyed and gave orders to lift Daniel out of the den. And when
Daniel was lifted from the den, no wound[h]
was found on him, because he had trusted[i]
in his God.
24 At the king's command, the men who
had falsely accused Daniel were brought in
and thrown into the lions' den,[j] along with
their wives and children.[k] And before they
reached the floor of the den, the lions overpowered them and crushed all their bones.[l]
25 Then King Darius wrote to all the nations and peoples of every language in all
the earth:

"May you prosper greatly![m]

26 "I issue a decree that in every part
of my kingdom people must fear and
reverence the God of Daniel.[n]

"For he is the living God
 and he endures forever;
his kingdom will not be destroyed,
 his dominion will never end.[o]
27 He rescues and he saves;
 he performs signs and wonders[p]
 in the heavens and on the earth.
He has rescued Daniel
 from the power of the lions."[q]

28 So Daniel prospered during the reign
of Darius and the reign of Cyrus[a][r] the Persian.

Daniel's Dream of Four Beasts

7 In the first year of Belshazzar[s] king of
Babylon, Daniel had a dream, and visions passed through his mind[t] as he was
lying in bed. He wrote[u] down the substance
of his dream.
2 Daniel said: "In my vision at night I
looked, and there before me were the four
winds of heaven[v] churning up the great
sea. 3 Four great beasts,[w] each different
from the others, came up out of the sea.
4 "The first was like a lion,[x] and it had
the wings of an eagle.[y] I watched until its
wings were torn off and it was lifted from
the ground so that it stood on two feet like
a human being, and the mind of a human
was given to it.

---

[a] 28 Or *Darius, that is, the reign of Cyrus*

6:13 *who is one of the exiles from Judah.* Daniel's accusers did not describe him as governor (v. 2), but as a captive from another land, in order to implicate him as a treasonous and dangerous person.
6:14 *was greatly distressed.* It is clear that Darius had not factored Daniel into the situation in the beginning. He never had the intention of harming him.
6:23 *he had trusted in his God.* Daniel's faithfulness got him into trouble; faith got him out of it (Heb. 11:33).
6:24 *their wives and children.* The entire families of the wicked conspirators were destroyed because the Persians, like the Hebrews and other peoples, considered guilt a collective responsibility (Num. 16:1–35; Josh. 7).
6:28 *and the reign of Cyrus.* Gubaru, or Darius, served Cyrus for about one year, after which Cyrus appointed his son Cambyses as regent over Babylon.
7:1 *the first year of Belshazzar.* Chapter 5 records Belshazzar's death, indicating that the Book of Daniel is not arranged chronologically.
7:3 *Four great beasts.* These four beasts represent kings or kingdoms, like the four metals of the statue in chapter 2.
7:4 *like a lion, and it had the wings of an eagle.* There has been almost universal agreement from the early centuries until today that this beast represents Babylon. It is also agreed that the visions of chapters 2 and 7 speak of the same four kingdoms.

6:13 [t] Da 2:25; 5:13 [u] Est 3:8; Da 3:12 **6:14** [v] Mk 6:26
6:15 [w] Est 8:8 **6:16** [x] ver 7 [y] Job 5:19; Ps 37:39-40
6:17 [z] Mt 27:66 **6:18** [a] 2Sa 12:17 [b] Est 6:1; Da 2:1
6:20 [c] Da 3:17 **6:21** [d] Da 2:4 **6:22** [e] Da 3:28
[f] Ps 91:11-13; Heb 11:33 [g] Ac 12:11; 2Ti 4:17
6:23 [h] Da 3:27 [i] 1Ch 5:20 **6:24** [j] Dt 19:18-19; Est 7:9-10;
Ps 54:5 [k] Dt 24:16; 2Ki 14:6 [l] Isa 38:13 **6:25** [m] Da 4:1
6:26 [n] Ps 99:1-3; Da 3:29 [o] Da 2:44; 4:34 **6:27** [p] Da 4:3
[q] ver 22 **6:28** [r] 2Ch 36:22; Da 1:21 **7:1** [s] Da 5:1
[t] Da 1:17 [u] Jer 36:4 **7:2** [v] Rev 7:1 **7:3** [w] Rev 13:1
7:4 [x] Jer 4:7 [y] Eze 17:3

5“And there before me was a second
beast, which looked like a bear. It was
raised up on one of its sides, and it had
three ribs in its mouth between its teeth. It
was told, ‘Get up and eat your fill of flesh!’[z]
6“After that, I looked, and there before
me was another beast, one that looked like
a leopard.[a] And on its back it had four wings
like those of a bird. This beast had four
heads, and it was given authority to rule.
7“After that, in my vision at night I
looked, and there before me was a fourth
beast—terrifying and frightening and
very powerful. It had large iron[b] teeth;
it crushed and devoured its victims and
trampled underfoot whatever was left. It
was different from all the former beasts,
and it had ten horns.[c]
8“While I was thinking about the horns,
there before me was another horn, a little[d] one, which came up among them; and
three of the first horns were uprooted before it. This horn had eyes like the eyes of
a human being[e] and a mouth that spoke
boastfully.[f]
9“As I looked,

“thrones were set in place,
  and the Ancient of Days took his seat.
His clothing was as white as snow;
  the hair of his head was white like wool.[g]
His throne was flaming with fire,
  and its wheels[h] were all ablaze.
10 A river of fire[i] was flowing,
  coming out from before him.[j]
Thousands upon thousands attended him;
  ten thousand times ten thousand stood before him.
The court was seated,
  and the books[k] were opened.

11“Then I continued to watch because of
the boastful words the horn was speaking.
I kept looking until the beast was slain
and its body destroyed and thrown into
the blazing fire.[l] 12(The other beasts had
been stripped of their authority, but were
allowed to live for a period of time.)
13“In my vision at night I looked, and
there before me was one like a son of
man,[a][m] coming with the clouds of heaven.[n]
He approached the Ancient of Days and
was led into his presence. 14He was giv-
en authority,[o] glory and sovereign power;
all nations and peoples of every language
worshiped him.[p] His dominion is an everlasting dominion that will not pass away,
and his kingdom is one that will never be
destroyed.[q]

The Interpretation of the Dream

15“I, Daniel, was troubled in spirit, and
the visions that passed through my mind
disturbed me.[r] 16I approached one of those
standing there and asked him the meaning
of all this.

“So he told me and gave me the interpretation[s] of these things: 17‘The four great
beasts are four kings that will rise from
the earth. 18But the holy people of the Most
High will receive the kingdom and will
possess it forever—yes, for ever and ever.’[t]
19“Then I wanted to know the meaning of
the fourth beast, which was different from
all the others and most terrifying, with its
iron teeth and bronze claws—the beast
that crushed and devoured its victims and
trampled underfoot whatever was left. 20I
also wanted to know about the ten horns on
its head and about the other horn that came
up, before which three of them fell—the
horn that looked more imposing than the
others and that had eyes and a mouth that
spoke boastfully. 21As I watched, this horn
was waging war against the holy people
and defeating them,[u] 22until the Ancient of

a 13 The Aramaic phrase *bar enash* means *human being.* The phrase *son of man* is retained here because of its use in the New Testament as a title of Jesus, probably based largely on this verse.

7:5 *like a bear.* The bear seems to represent Babylon's successor, the Medo-Persian Empire (2:38–39). The three ribs may represent the three kingdoms that Medo-Persia devoured—Babylon, Libya, and Egypt.

7:6 *like a leopard.* The leopard is believed to represent Greece. The Greeks, under the leadership of Alexander the Great, rapidly conquered the known world. ***four heads.*** After Alexander's death, his empire was divided into four different parts (8:8–22)—Macedonia, Egypt, Syria, and Thracia.

7:7 *fourth beast.* The last of the beasts may represent Rome (2:40).

7:9 *Ancient of Days.* "Ancient of Days" is a reference to God the Father as certified by the submission of the "one like a son of man" (vv. 13–14) and His role in judgment (v. 22).

7:10 *and the books were opened.* The books record the names and deeds of those who will be judged (Rev. 20:12).

7:13 *one like a son of man.* The term "son of man" is an expression meaning "human," but clearly this "one like a son of man" was no ordinary human. Many expositors have identified this individual as the Messiah. Jesus Himself used this name to emphasize His humanity (Matt. 9:6; 10:23). ***with the clouds of heaven.*** John uses the same expression to speak of Jesus coming in judgment (Rev. 1:7).

7:14 *He was given authority.* Jesus will reign over all things (1 Cor. 15:27–28; Eph. 1:20–23; Phil. 2:9–11; Rev. 17:14; 19:10).

7:21 *this horn was waging war.* The little horn's militaristic character is seen also in 11:38–39 and

7:5 [z] Da 2:39 **7:6** [a] Rev 13:2 **7:7** [b] Da 2:40 [c] Rev 12:3 **7:8** [d] Da 8:9 [e] Rev 9:7 [f] Ps 12:3; Rev 13:5-6 **7:9** [g] Rev 1:14 [h] Eze 1:15; 10:6 **7:10** [i] Ps 50:3; 97:3; Isa 30:27 [j] Dt 33:2; Ps 68:17; Rev 5:11 [k] Rev 20:11-15 **7:11** [l] Rev 19:20 **7:13** [m] Mt 8:20*; Rev 1:13* [n] Mt 24:30; Rev 1:7 **7:14** [o] Mt 28:18 [p] Ps 72:11; 102:22; 1Co 15:27; Eph 1:22 [q] Da 2:44; Heb 12:28; Rev 11:15 **7:15** [r] Da 4:19 **7:16** [s] Da 8:16; 9:22; Zec 1:9 **7:18** [t] Isa 60:12-14; Rev 2:26; 20:4 **7:21** [u] Rev 13:7

Days came and pronounced judgment in favor of the holy people of the Most High, and the time came when they possessed the kingdom.

23"He gave me this explanation: 'The fourth beast is a fourth kingdom that will appear on earth. It will be different from all the other kingdoms and will devour the whole earth, trampling it down and crushing it.[v] 24The ten horns[w] are ten kings who will come from this kingdom. After them another king will arise, different from the earlier ones; he will subdue three kings. 25He will speak against the Most High[x] and oppress his holy people and try to change the set times[y] and the laws. The holy people will be delivered into his hands for a time, times and half a time.[a][z]

26" 'But the court will sit, and his power will be taken away and completely destroyed forever. 27Then the sovereignty, power and greatness of all the kingdoms under heaven will be handed over to the holy people of the Most High. His kingdom will be an everlasting[a] kingdom, and all rulers will worship[b] and obey him.'

28"This is the end of the matter. I, Daniel, was deeply troubled[c] by my thoughts, and my face turned pale, but I kept the matter to myself."

Daniel's Vision of a Ram and a Goat

8 In the third year of King Belshazzar's reign, I, Daniel, had a vision, after the one that had already appeared to me. 2In my vision I saw myself in the citadel of Susa[d] in the province of Elam;[e] in the vision I was beside the Ulai Canal. 3I looked up,[f] and there before me was a ram with two horns, standing beside the canal, and the horns were long. One of the horns was longer than the other but grew up later. 4I watched the ram as it charged toward the west and the north and the south. No animal could stand against it, and none could rescue from its power. It did as it pleased[g] and became great.

5As I was thinking about this, suddenly a goat with a prominent horn between its eyes came from the west, crossing the whole earth without touching the ground. 6It came toward the two-horned ram I had seen standing beside the canal and charged at it in great rage. 7I saw it attack the ram furiously, striking the ram and shattering its two horns. The ram was powerless to stand against it; the goat knocked it to the ground and trampled on it,[h] and none could rescue the ram from its power. 8The goat became very great, but at the height of its power the large horn was broken off,[i] and in its place four prominent horns grew up toward the four winds of heaven.[j]

9Out of one of them came another horn, which started small but grew in power to the south and to the east and toward the Beautiful Land.[k] 10It grew until it reached[l] the host of the heavens, and it threw some of the starry host down to the earth[m] and trampled[n] on them. 11It set itself up to be as great as the commander of the army of the LORD;[o] it took away the daily sacrifice[p] from the LORD, and his sanctuary was thrown down.[q] 12Because of rebellion, the LORD's people[b] and the daily sacrifice were given over to it. It prospered in everything it did, and truth was thrown to the ground.

---

[a] 25 Or *for a year, two years and half a year*
[b] 12 Or *rebellion, the armies*

---

particularly in Revelation 13:1–10. There, in the guise of a beast, this blasphemous enemy of the saints prevails for 42 months. The connection between Daniel's "little horn" and John's "beast coming out of the sea" is unmistakable.

7:24 ***The ten horns.*** Some perceive the fourth beast as representing Rome, and the ten horns as the fragments of the Roman Empire. Others see the fourth beast as a revived Roman Empire and the ten horns as kings of a future realm.

7:25 ***a time, times and half a time.*** If the expression "time" is taken to mean a year, and "times" as two years, the three and a half years would exactly equal the 42 months mentioned in the Book of Revelation (Rev. 13:1–10), half of the 70th "week" of years of 9:27. Some also believe that the expression does not indicate a specific number of years but instead a period of time that God in His mercy would shorten.

8:1 ***In the third year.*** After writing in Aramaic from 2:4–7:28, Daniel returns to writing in Hebrew.

8:3 ***a ram with two horns.*** The ram represents Medo-Persia (v. 20). The two horns symbolize the peoples of Media and Persia.

8:5 ***a goat.*** The goat represents Greece (v. 21). The notable horn symbolizes Alexander the Great (v. 21) who launched his attack against Persia in 334 B.C. Within two years, he had essentially subdued the Persian Empire. His conquest was so rapid that it seemed as if he never touched the ground.

8:8 ***the large horn was broken.*** Alexander the Great died at the height of his career, before he was 33 years old. After his death, his empire was divided among his four generals (11:4).

8:9 ***another horn.*** This horn is Antiochus Epiphanes, who ruled part of the Greek Empire from 175 to 164 B.C.

8:11 ***commander of the army.*** This is clearly God Himself. The "army" refers to God's people (12:3; Gen. 15:5). Antiochus is remembered in infamy by the Jews because he desecrated the temple by setting up a statue of Zeus and sacrificing a pig on the holy altar.

7:23 [v] Da 2:40 **7:24** [w] Rev 17:12 **7:25** [x] Isa 37:23; Da 11:36 [y] Da 2:21 [z] Da 8:24; 12:7; Rev 12:14
7:27 [a] Da 2:44; 4:34; Lk 1:33; Rev 11:15; 22:5 [b] Ps 22:27; 72:11; 86:9 **7:28** [c] Da 4:19 **8:2** [d] Est 1:2 [e] Ge 10:22
8:3 [f] Da 10:5 **8:4** [g] Da 11:3, 16 **8:7** [h] Da 7:7
8:8 [i] 2Ch 26:16-21; Da 5:20 [j] Da 7:2; Rev 7:1
8:9 [k] Da 11:16 **8:10** [l] Isa 14:13 [m] Rev 12:4 [n] Da 7:7
8:11 [o] Da 11:36-37 [p] Eze 46:13-14 [q] Da 11:31; 12:11

13Then I heard a holy one[r] speaking, and
another holy one said to him, "How long
will it take for the vision to be fulfilled[s]—
the vision concerning the daily sacrifice,
the rebellion that causes desolation, the
surrender of the sanctuary and the trampling underfoot[t] of the LORD's people?"
14He said to me, "It will take 2,300 evenings and mornings; then the sanctuary
will be reconsecrated."[u]

The Interpretation of the Vision

15While I, Daniel, was watching the vision[v] and trying to understand it, there before me stood one who looked like a man.[w]
16And I heard a man's voice from the Ulai
calling, "Gabriel,[x] tell this man the meaning of the vision."
17As he came near the place where I was
standing, I was terrified and fell prostrate.[y]
"Son of man,"[a] he said to me, "understand
that the vision concerns the time of the end."[z]
18While he was speaking to me, I was in
a deep sleep, with my face to the ground.[a]
Then he touched me and raised me to my
feet.[b]
19He said: "I am going to tell you what
will happen later in the time of wrath, because the vision concerns the appointed
time of the end.[b][c] 20The two-horned ram
that you saw represents the kings of Media
and Persia. 21The shaggy goat is the king
of Greece,[d] and the large horn between its
eyes is the first king.[e] 22The four horns that
replaced the one that was broken off represent four kingdoms that will emerge from
his nation but will not have the same power.
23"In the latter part of their reign, when
rebels have become completely wicked, a
fierce-looking king, a master of intrigue,
will arise. 24He will become very strong,
but not by his own power. He will cause
astounding devastation and will succeed
in whatever he does. He will destroy those
who are mighty, the holy people.[f] 25He will
cause deceit to prosper, and he will consider himself superior. When they feel secure,
he will destroy many and take his stand
against the Prince of princes.[g] Yet he will
be destroyed, but not by human power.[h]
26"The vision of the evenings and mornings that has been given you is true,[i] but
seal[j] up the vision, for it concerns the distant future."[k]
27I, Daniel, was worn out. I lay exhausted for several days. Then I got up and went
about the king's business.[l] I was appalled[m]
by the vision; it was beyond understanding.

Daniel's Prayer

9 In the first year of Darius[n] son of Xerxes[c] (a Mede by descent), who was made
ruler over the Babylonian[d] kingdom— 2in
the first year of his reign, I, Daniel, understood from the Scriptures, according
to the word of the LORD given to Jeremiah
the prophet, that the desolation of Jerusalem would last seventy[o] years. 3So I turned
to the Lord God and pleaded with him in
prayer and petition, in fasting, and in sackcloth and ashes.[p]
4I prayed to the LORD my God and confessed:

"Lord, the great and awesome God,[q]
who keeps his covenant of love[r] with
those who love him and keep his commandments, 5we have sinned and
done wrong.[s] We have been wicked
and have rebelled; we have turned
away[t] from your commands and laws.[u]

[a] 17 The Hebrew phrase *ben adam* means *human being*. The phrase *son of man* is retained as a form of address here because of its possible association with "Son of Man" in the New Testament.
[b] 19 Or *because the end will be at the appointed time* [c] 1 Hebrew *Ahasuerus* [d] 1 Or *Chaldean*

8:14 *2,300 evenings.* This was the amount of time between Antiochus' pollution of the temple and the Maccabees' cleansing of it.
8:16 *Gabriel.* This is the first mention of the angel Gabriel. This angel is mentioned by name three other times (9:21; Luke 1:19,26).
8:24 *not by his own power.* Like the antichrist (2 Thess. 2:9), Antiochus would be energized by Satan.
8:25 *destroyed, but not by human power.* According to the book of 2 Maccabees, Antiochus died of a painful disease.
9:2 *from the Scriptures.* By this time, Daniel himself had been in captivity for about 67 years, and he knew that the punishment was nearly over.
9:3–4 Prayer and Fasting—There are many examples in Scripture of people who pray to learn the will of God. There are also some examples of people who do not pray and find themselves in trouble (Josh. 9). Most Christians quickly learn that one of the most important ways we learn the will of God for our lives is through prayer. "If any of you lacks wisdom, you should ask God, who gives generously to all without finding fault, and it will be given to you" (James 1:5). See also Psalm 143:8–10 and James 4:2.

Other verses in the Bible link prayer with fasting. To fast is to abstain for a period of time from some important and necessary activity in our lives. The purpose of fasting is to be able to spend that time in prayer before God. Different kinds of fasting are possible. One may for a time refrain from sleep (2 Cor. 6:5; 11:27), marital sex (1 Cor. 7:1–5), or food (Matt. 4:1–2). There are also many examples of fasting in the Word: Moses in Deuteronomy 9:9, Elijah in 1 Kings 19:8, Daniel in Daniel 9:3, Ezra in Ezra 10:6, and Nehemiah in Nehemiah 1:4.

8:13 [r] Da 4:23 [s] Da 12:6 [t] Lk 21:24; Rev 11:2
8:14 [u] Da 12:11-12 **8:15** [v] ver 1 [w] Da 10:16-18
8:16 [x] Da 9:21; Lk 1:19 **8:17** [y] Eze 1:28; Da 2:46; Rev 1:17
[z] Hab 2:3 **8:18** [a] Da 10:9 [b] Eze 2:2; Da 10:16-18
8:19 [c] Hab 2:3 **8:21** [d] Da 10:20 [e] Da 11:3
8:24 [f] Da 7:25; 11:36 **8:25** [g] Da 11:36 [h] Da 2:34; 11:21
8:26 [i] Da 10:1 [j] Rev 22:10 [k] Da 10:14 **8:27** [l] Da 2:48
[m] Da 7:28 **9:1** [n] Da 5:31 **9:2** [o] 2Ch 36:21; Jer 29:10;
Zec 7:5 **9:3** [p] Ne 1:4; Jer 29:12 **9:4** [q] Dt 7:21 [r] Dt 7:9
9:5 [s] Ps 106:6 [t] Isa 53:6 [u] ver 11; La 1:20

6 We have not listened to your servants the prophets,[v] who spoke in your name to our kings, our princes and our ancestors, and to all the people of the land.

7 "Lord, you are righteous, but this day we are covered with shame[w]—the people of Judah and the inhabitants of Jerusalem and all Israel, both near and far, in all the countries where you have scattered[x] us because of our unfaithfulness to you.[y] 8 We and our kings, our princes and our ancestors are covered with shame, LORD, because we have sinned against you. 9 The Lord our God is merciful and forgiving,[z] even though we have rebelled against him;[a] 10 we have not obeyed the LORD our God or kept the laws he gave us through his servants the prophets.[b] 11 All Israel has transgressed your law and turned away, refusing to obey you.

"Therefore the curses and sworn judgments written in the Law of Moses, the servant of God, have been poured out on us, because we have sinned[c] against you. 12 You have fulfilled[d] the words spoken against us and against our rulers by bringing on us great disaster. Under the whole heaven nothing has ever been done like what has been done to Jerusalem.[e] 13 Just as it is written in the Law of Moses, all this disaster has come on us, yet we have not sought the favor of the LORD our God by turning from our sins and giving attention to your truth.[f] 14 The LORD did not hesitate to bring the disaster[g] on us, for the LORD our God is righteous in everything he does; yet we have not obeyed him.[h]

15 "Now, Lord our God, who brought your people out of Egypt with a mighty hand[i] and who made for yourself a name[j] that endures to this day, we have sinned, we have done wrong. 16 Lord, in keeping with all your righteous acts,[k] turn away your anger and your wrath from Jerusalem,[l] your city, your holy hill.[m] Our sins and the iniquities of our ancestors have made Jerusalem and your people an object of scorn[n] to all those around us.

17 "Now, our God, hear the prayers and petitions of your servant. For your sake, Lord, look with favor[o] on your desolate sanctuary. 18 Give ear, our God, and hear; open your eyes and see[p] the desolation of the city that bears your Name.[q] We do not make requests of you because we are righteous, but because of your great mercy. 19 Lord, listen! Lord, forgive![r] Lord, hear and act! For your sake, my God, do not delay, because your city and your people bear your Name."

The Seventy "Sevens"

20 While I was speaking and praying, confessing my sin and the sin of my people Israel and making my request to the LORD my God for his holy hill[s]— 21 while I was still in prayer, Gabriel,[t] the man I had seen in the earlier vision, came to me in swift flight about the time of the evening sacrifice.[u] 22 He instructed me and said to me, "Daniel, I have now come to give you insight and understanding. 23 As soon as you began to pray, a word went out, which I have come to tell you, for you are highly esteemed.[v] Therefore, consider the word and understand the vision:[w]

24 "Seventy 'sevens'[a] are decreed for your people and your holy city to finish[b] transgression, to put an end to sin, to atone[x] for wickedness, to bring in everlasting righteousness,[y] to seal up vision and prophecy and to anoint the Most Holy Place.[c]

25 "Know and understand this: From the time the word goes out to restore and rebuild[z] Jerusalem until the Anointed One,[d][a] the ruler, comes, there will be seven 'sevens,' and sixty-two 'sevens.' It will be rebuilt with streets and a trench, but in times of trouble. 26 After the sixty-two 'sevens,'

a 24 Or *'weeks'*; also in verses 25 and 26
b 24 Or *restrain*   *c* 24 Or *the most holy One*
d 25 Or *an anointed one*; also in verse 26

9:11 *the curses and sworn judgments.* Covenant documents typically contained statements concerning the penalties for covenant violation (Lev. 26:3–45; Deut. 27–28). The most feared and devastating curse of all had come to pass when the people were deported from the land.

9:21 *the time of the evening sacrifice.* The temple was in ruins, and regular daily sacrifices were impossible. Nevertheless, Daniel observed the ritual of worship by praying at the hour of the evening sacrifice. Daniel's prayer was his evening offering.

9:24 *Seventy 'sevens.'* The word "sevens" can also be translated "weeks." Many scholars agree that the "sevens" are periods of seven years.

9:25 *the time the word goes out to restore and rebuild Jerusalem.* This may refer to the decree of Cyrus in Ezra 1, the decree of Darius in Ezra 6, the decree of Artaxerxes in Ezra 7, or the decree of Artaxerxes in Nehemiah 2.

9:26 *sixty-two 'sevens.'* When the 7 'sevens' and

9:6 [v] 2Ch 36:16; Jer 44:5 **9:7** [w] Ps 44:15 [x] Dt 4:27; Am 9:9 [y] Jer 3:25 **9:9** [z] Ps 130:4 [a] Ne 9:17; Jer 14:7 **9:10** [b] 2Ki 17:13-15; 18:12 **9:11** [c] Isa 1:4-6; Jer 8:5-10 **9:12** [d] Isa 44:26; Zec 1:6 [e] Jer 44:2-6; Eze 5:9 **9:13** [f] Isa 9:13; Jer 2:30 **9:14** [g] Jer 44:27 [h] Ne 9:33 **9:15** [i] Jer 32:21 [j] Ne 9:10 **9:16** [k] Ps 31:1 [l] Jer 32:32 [m] Zec 8:3 [n] Eze 5:14 **9:17** [o] Nu 6:24-26; Ps 80:19 **9:18** [p] Ps 80:14 [q] Isa 37:17; Jer 7:10-12; 25:29 **9:19** [r] Ps 44:23 **9:20** [s] ver 3; Ps 145:18; Isa 58:9 **9:21** [t] Da 8:16; Lk 1:19 [u] Ex 29:39 **9:23** [v] Da 10:19; Lk 1:28 [w] Da 10:11-12; Mt 24:15 **9:24** [x] Isa 53:10 [y] Isa 56:1 **9:25** [z] Ezr 4:24 [a] Jn 4:25

the Anointed One will be put to death[b] and
will have nothing.[a] The people of the ruler
who will come will destroy the city and the
sanctuary. The end will come like a flood:[c]
War will continue until the end, and desolations have been decreed. 27He will confirm a covenant with many for one 'seven.'[b]
In the middle of the 'seven'[b] he will put an
end to sacrifice and offering. And at the
temple[c] he will set up an abomination that
causes desolation, until the end that is decreed[d] is poured out on him.[d]"[e]

Daniel's Vision of a Man

10 In the third year of Cyrus[e] king of
Persia, a revelation was given to
Daniel (who was called Belteshazzar).[f] Its
message was true[g] and it concerned a great
war.[f] The understanding of the message
came to him in a vision.

2At that time I, Daniel, mourned[h] for
three weeks. 3I ate no choice food; no meat
or wine touched my lips; and I used no lotions at all until the three weeks were over.

4On the twenty-fourth day of the first
month, as I was standing on the bank of
the great river, the Tigris,[i] 5I looked up and
there before me was a man dressed in linen,[j] with a belt of fine gold[k] from Uphaz
around his waist. 6His body was like topaz,
his face like lightning,[l] his eyes like flaming torches,[m] his arms and legs like the
gleam of burnished bronze,[n] and his voice
like the sound of a multitude.

7I, Daniel, was the only one who saw the
vision; those who were with me did not see
it,[o] but such terror overwhelmed them that
they fled and hid themselves. 8So I was left
alone,[p] gazing at this great vision; I had
no strength left,[q] my face turned deathly
pale and I was helpless.[r] 9Then I heard him
speaking, and as I listened to him, I fell into
a deep sleep, my face to the ground.[s]

10A hand touched me[t] and set me trembling on my hands and knees.[u] 11He said,
"Daniel, you who are highly esteemed,[v]
consider carefully the words I am about to
speak to you, and stand up,[w] for I have now
been sent to you." And when he said this to
me, I stood up trembling.

12Then he continued, "Do not be afraid,
Daniel. Since the first day that you set your
mind to gain understanding and to humble[x] yourself before your God, your words
were heard, and I have come in response to
them.[y] 13But the prince of the Persian kingdom resisted me twenty-one days. Then
Michael,[z] one of the chief princes, came to
help me, because I was detained there with
the king of Persia. 14Now I have come to
explain[a] to you what will happen to your
people in the future, for the vision concerns
a time yet to come.[b]"

15While he was saying this to me, I
bowed with my face toward the ground and
was speechless.[c] 16Then one who looked
like a man[g] touched my lips, and I opened
my mouth and began to speak.[d] I said to
the one standing before me, "I am overcome with anguish[e] because of the vision,

[a] 26 Or *death and will have no one*; or *death, but not for himself* [b] 27 Or *'week'* [c] 27 Septuagint and Theodotion; Hebrew *wing* [d] 27 Or *it* [e] 27 Or *And one who causes desolation will come upon the wing of the abominable temple, until the end that is decreed is poured out on the desolated city* [f] 1 Or *true and burdensome* [g] 16 Most manuscripts of the Masoretic Text; one manuscript of the Masoretic Text, Dead Sea Scrolls and Septuagint *Then something that looked like a human hand*

---

62 'sevens' (v. 25) are added together, they equal 483 years. If these years are added to the date of the decree of Artaxerxes in Nehemiah 2 (445 B.C.), with an adjustment to allow for a 360-day year, the end of the 69 weeks coincides with the date of the triumphal entry into Jerusalem just before the crucifixion. ***the ruler who will come.*** This seems to be a reference to the antichrist.

9:27 *In the middle of the 'seven.'* That is, 3–1/2 years later. These 3–1/2 years of the rule of the antichrist seem to correspond with the "time and times and the dividing of time" when the fourth beast rules (7:25) and with the 42-month rule of the beast from the sea (Rev. 13:1–10). ***abomination that causes desolation.*** Antiochus committed an abomination by setting up an altar to the god Zeus in the holy place in the temple in Jerusalem (11:31). The antichrist will also commit an abomination of desolation against the living God. Jesus' reference to "'the abomination that causes desolation,' spoken of though the prophet Daniel" (Matt. 24:15) occurred long after the desolation caused by Antiochus and indicates that this verse is describing the abomination of the antichrist and not that of Antiochus.

10:2 *three weeks.* This period of time refers to Daniel's observance of the Passover and the Festival of Unleavened Bread, which took place during the first month of the year (Ex. 12:1–20).

10:6 *his face like lightning.* The description of this man is very much like Ezekiel's description of the glory of God (Ezek. 1:4–28) and John's description of the risen Christ (Rev. 1:9–20).

10:13 *the prince of the Persian kingdom.* This prince cannot be a human ruler because the conflict referred to here is in the spiritual, heavenly realm, as the allusion to the angel Michael (also referred to as a prince) makes clear. This prince, therefore, must be understood as a satanic figure who was to supervise the affairs of Persia, inspiring its religious, social, and political structures to works of evil. The apostle Paul refers to "spiritual forces of evil in the heavenly realms" (Eph. 6:12). The prince of Persia apparently

9:26 [b] Isa 53:8 [c] Na 1:8 **9:27** [d] Isa 10:22 **10:1** [e] Da 1:21 [f] Da 1:7 [g] Da 8:26 **10:2** [h] Ezr 9:4 **10:4** [i] Ge 2:14 **10:5** [j] Eze 9:2; Rev 15:6 [k] Jer 10:9 **10:6** [l] Mt 17:2 [m] Rev 19:12 [n] Rev 1:15 **10:7** [o] 2Ki 6:17-20; Ac 9:7 **10:8** [p] Ge 32:24 [q] Da 8:27 [r] Hab 3:16 **10:9** [s] Da 8:18 **10:10** [t] Jer 1:9 [u] Rev 1:17 **10:11** [v] Da 9:23 [w] Eze 2:1 **10:12** [x] Da 9:3 [y] Da 9:20 **10:13** [z] ver 21; Da 12:1; Jude 1:9 **10:14** [a] Da 9:22 [b] Da 2:28; 8:26; Hab 2:3 **10:15** [c] Eze 24:27; Lk 1:20 **10:16** [d] Isa 6:7; Jer 1:9; Da 8:15-18 [e] Isa 21:3

my lord, and I feel very weak. 17How can I, your servant, talk with you, my lord? My strength is gone and I can hardly breathe."[f]

18Again the one who looked like a man touched[g] me and gave me strength. 19"Do not be afraid, you who are highly esteemed," he said. "Peace![h] Be strong now; be strong."[i]

When he spoke to me, I was strengthened and said, "Speak, my lord, since you have given me strength."[j]

20So he said, "Do you know why I have come to you? Soon I will return to fight against the prince of Persia, and when I go, the prince of Greece[k] will come; 21but first I will tell you what is written in the Book of Truth.[l] (No one supports me against them

11 except Michael,[m] your prince. 1And in the first year of Darius[n] the Mede, I took my stand to support and protect him.)

The Kings of the South and the North

2"Now then, I tell you the truth:[o] Three more kings will arise in Persia, and then a fourth, who will be far richer than all the others. When he has gained power by his wealth, he will stir up everyone against the kingdom of Greece.[p] 3Then a mighty king will arise, who will rule with great power and do as he pleases.[q] 4After he has arisen, his empire will be broken up and parceled out toward the four winds of heaven.[r] It will not go to his descendants, nor will it have the power he exercised, because his empire will be uprooted and given to others.

5"The king of the South will become strong, but one of his commanders will become even stronger than he and will rule his own kingdom with great power. 6After some years, they will become allies. The daughter of the king of the South will go to the king of the North to make an alliance, but she will not retain her power, and he and his power[a] will not last. In those days she will be betrayed, together with her royal escort and her father[b] and the one who supported her.

7"One from her family line will arise to take her place. He will attack the forces of the king of the North[s] and enter his fortress; he will fight against them and be victorious. 8He will also seize their gods,[t] their metal images and their valuable articles of silver and gold and carry them off to Egypt.[u] For some years he will leave the king of the North alone. 9Then the king of the North will invade the realm of the king of the South but will retreat to his own country. 10His sons will prepare for war and assemble a great army, which will sweep on like an irresistible flood[v] and carry the battle as far as his fortress.

11"Then the king of the South will march out in a rage and fight against the king of the North, who will raise a large army, but it will be defeated.[w] 12When the army is carried off, the king of the South will be filled with pride and will slaughter many thousands, yet he will not remain triumphant. 13For the king of the North will muster another army, larger than the first; and after several years, he will advance with a huge army fully equipped.

14"In those times many will rise against the king of the South. Those who are violent among your own people will rebel in fulfillment of the vision, but without success. 15Then the king of the North will come and build up siege ramps[x] and will capture a fortified city. The forces of the South will be powerless to resist; even their best troops will not have the strength to

[a] 6 Or *offspring* [b] 6 Or *child* (see Vulgate and Syriac)

sought to detain the angel so that Daniel would be prevented from hearing more of God's revelation (vv. 12–14). ***Michael.*** Michael seems to be one of the most powerful angels. He is mentioned three times in the Old Testament, all in the Book of Daniel (v. 21; 12:1), and twice in the New Testament (Jude 9; Rev. 12:7).

10:20 ***against the prince of Persia.*** Persia was under the ultimate dominion of an evil spirit from Satan (vv. 13–14), and so also was Greece. The succession of world powers follows the pattern of Daniel's second vision (8:20–22).

11:1 ***the first year of Darius.*** This is the same year as that of the revelation of the 70 weeks, 539 B.C.

11:2 ***Three more kings.*** Darius (under Cyrus) was followed by Cambyses (530–522 B.C.), Gaumata (522 B.C.), Darius I (522–486 B.C.), and Xerxes (486–465 B.C.)—who was the richest king of all, due to the extent of the empire's conquests and the severe taxation.

11:4 ***not go to his descendants.*** The "mighty king" of verse 3 fits with Alexander the Great, the first ruler of the Greek Empire. When Alexander died, his four generals carved up the Macedonian Empire. Antigonus ruled from southern Syria to central Asia; Cassander ruled over Macedonia; Ptolemy ruled in Egypt and southern Syria, including Palestine; Lysimachus ruled over Thrace.

11:5 ***The king of the South.*** Alexander's general Ptolemy I Soter was the first king of the southern kingdom—that is, Egypt.

11:6–15 ***After some years.*** The events described in these verses fit with the actual history of the divided Greek Empire. ***The daughter of the king.*** This refers to Berenice, the daughter of Ptolemy Philadelphus (285–246 B.C.) of Egypt. ***One from her family line.*** This is Berenice's brother, Ptolemy III Eurgetes (246–221 B.C.), who conquered Seleucus Callinicus (246–226 B.C.) of Syria (the king of the North). Seleucus did attempt a return attack on Egypt, but returned to Syria without accomplishing his goal. The kings of Egypt and Syria (the south and the north)

10:17 [f] Da 4:19 **10:18** [g] ver 16 **10:19** [h] Jdg 6:23; Isa 35:4 [i] Jos 1:9 [j] Isa 6:1-8 **10:20** [k] Da 8:21; 11:2 **10:21** [l] Da 11:2 [m] ver 13; Jude 1:9 **11:1** [n] Da 5:31 **11:2** [o] Da 10:21 [p] Da 10:20 **11:3** [q] Da 8:4, 21 **11:4** [r] Da 7:2; 8:22 **11:7** [s] ver 6 **11:8** [t] Isa 37:19; 46:1-2 [u] Jer 43:12 **11:10** [v] Isa 8:8; Jer 46:8; Da 9:26 **11:11** [w] Da 8:7-8 **11:15** [x] Eze 4:2

stand. 16The invader will do as he pleases;[y]
no one will be able to stand against him.[z]
He will establish himself in the Beautiful
Land and will have the power to destroy
it.[a] 17He will determine to come with the
might of his entire kingdom and will make
an alliance with the king of the South. And
he will give him a daughter in marriage
in order to overthrow the kingdom, but
his plans[a] will not succeed[b] or help him.
18Then he will turn his attention to the
coastlands[c] and will take many of them,
but a commander will put an end to his insolence and will turn his insolence back on
him.[d] 19After this, he will turn back toward
the fortresses of his own country but will
stumble and fall,[e] to be seen no more.[f]

20"His successor will send out a tax collector to maintain the royal splendor.[g] In a
few years, however, he will be destroyed,
yet not in anger or in battle.

21"He will be succeeded by a contemptible[h] person who has not been given the
honor of royalty.[i] He will invade the kingdom when its people feel secure, and he
will seize it through intrigue. 22Then an
overwhelming army will be swept away
before him; both it and a prince of the covenant will be destroyed.[j] 23After coming to
an agreement with him, he will act deceitfully,[k] and with only a few people he will
rise to power. 24When the richest provinces
feel secure, he will invade them and will
achieve what neither his fathers nor his
forefathers did. He will distribute plunder,
loot and wealth among his followers.[l] He
will plot the overthrow of fortresses—but
only for a time.

25"With a large army he will stir up his
strength and courage against the king of
the South. The king of the South will wage
war with a large and very powerful army,
but he will not be able to stand because of
the plots devised against him. 26Those who
eat from the king's provisions will try to
destroy him; his army will be swept away,
and many will fall in battle. 27The two
kings, with their hearts bent on evil,[m] will
sit at the same table and lie[n] to each other, but to no avail, because an end will still
come at the appointed time.[o] 28The king of
the North will return to his own country
with great wealth, but his heart will be set
against the holy covenant. He will take action against it and then return to his own
country.

29"At the appointed time he will invade
the South again, but this time the outcome
will be different from what it was before.
30Ships of the western coastlands[p] will oppose him, and he will lose heart. Then he
will turn back and vent his fury against
the holy covenant. He will return and show
favor to those who forsake the holy covenant.

31"His armed forces will rise up to desecrate the temple fortress and will abolish
the daily sacrifice. Then they will set up
the abomination that causes desolation.[q]
32With flattery he will corrupt those who
have violated the covenant, but the people
who know their God will firmly resist[r] him.

---

[a] 17 Or *but she*

---

continued to war against each other in the manner described in the prophecy. ***the king of the North.*** This is Antiochus II Theos (261–246 B.C.) of Syria. ***capture a fortified city.*** Antiochus of Syria defeated the fortified city of Sidon in 198 B.C.

11:17 ***a daughter.*** Antiochus III's daughter Cleopatra was given in marriage to Ptolemy V Epiphanes of Egypt in order to destroy or undermine Egypt, but Cleopatra sided with her husband over her father.

11:18–19 ***the coastlands ... his own country.*** Antiochus III undertook a vigorous campaign into Asia Minor and the Aegean region. The Roman Lucius Cornelius Scipio defeated Antiochus. Having lost all that he had gained, Antiochus returned to his own land, where he was defeated and killed while trying to plunder a temple.

11:21 ***a contemptible person.*** Antiochus IV Epiphanes seized the throne through treachery and later defiled the temple in Jerusalem (v. 31; 9:27).

11:29 ***he will invade the South again.*** After learning that Ptolemy VI and Ptolemy VII had formed a union against him, Antiochus returned to Egypt in 168 B.C., but he was driven out by the Romans.

11:31 ***abomination that causes desolation.*** Antiochus defiled the sanctuary by sacrificing a pig on the altar. He put a stop to the daily sacrifices, and he set up an image of Zeus In the holy place. Jesus said that a similar thing would happen just prior to His return (Matt. 24:15).

11:32 ***the people who know their God.*** The books of Maccabees record the story of Mattathias, the father of five sons, who refused to offer profane sacrifices and killed the king's agents. He and his sons then fled to the mountains and began the famous Maccabean revolt.

11:32 Know God Through His Word—The highest knowledge to which men and women can attain is personal knowledge of God (Jer. 9:24). One of the most valuable teachings of Scripture is that we can actually know God through His Word. To know God personally is to be saved and have eternal life (Job 17:3). We gain this knowledge primarily through interaction with His Word in four ways: First, we listen to and receive God's Word as the Holy Spirit interprets it and applies it to our hearts. Second, Scripture reveals God's nature and character. We know God through understanding of the works He has done, which are explained in Scripture. Third, our knowledge of God moves from intellectual to personal when we accept the invitation He has given us. Fourth, our personal knowledge of God grows as we rejoice in the love He shows us in Scripture and express joy in response to

11:16 [y] Da 8:4 [z] Jos 1:5; Da 8:7 [a] Da 8:9 **11:17** [b] Ps 20:4 **11:18** [c] Isa 66:19; Jer 25:22 [d] Hos 12:14 **11:19** [e] Ps 27:2 [f] Ps 37:36; Eze 26:21 **11:20** [g] Isa 60:17 **11:21** [h] Da 4:17 [i] Da 8:25 **11:22** [j] Da 8:10-11 **11:23** [k] Da 8:25 **11:24** [l] Ne 9:25 **11:27** [m] Ps 64:6 [n] Ps 12:2; Jer 9:5 [o] Hab 2:3 **11:30** [p] Ge 10:4 **11:31** [q] Da 8:11-13; 9:27; Mt 24:15*; Mk 13:14* **11:32** [r] Mic 5:7-9

33“Those who are wise will instruct[s]
many, though for a time they will fall by
the sword or be burned or captured or
plundered.[t] 34When they fall, they will receive a little help, and many who are not
sincere[u] will join them. 35Some of the wise
will stumble, so that they may be refined,[v]
purified and made spotless until the time
of the end, for it will still come at the appointed time.

The King Who Exalts Himself

36“The king will do as he pleases. He will
exalt and magnify himself above every god
and will say unheard-of things[w] against
the God of gods.[x] He will be successful until the time of wrath[y] is completed, for what
has been determined must take place. 37He
will show no regard for the gods of his ancestors or for the one desired by women,
nor will he regard any god, but will exalt
himself above them all. 38Instead of them,
he will honor a god of fortresses; a god unknown to his ancestors he will honor with
gold and silver, with precious stones and
costly gifts. 39He will attack the mightiest
fortresses with the help of a foreign god
and will greatly honor those who acknowledge him. He will make them rulers over
many people and will distribute the land
at a price.[a]

40“At the time of the end the king of the
South[z] will engage him in battle, and the
king of the North will storm[a] out against
him with chariots and cavalry and a great
fleet of ships. He will invade many countries and sweep through them like a flood.[b]
41He will also invade the Beautiful Land.
Many countries will fall, but Edom,[c] Moab[d]
and the leaders of Ammon will be delivered from his hand. 42He will extend his
power over many countries; Egypt will not
escape. 43He will gain control of the treasures of gold and silver and all the riches
of Egypt,[e] with the Libyans[f] and Cushites[b]
in submission. 44But reports from the east
and the north will alarm him, and he will
set out in a great rage to destroy and annihilate many. 45He will pitch his royal tents
between the seas at[c] the beautiful holy
mountain. Yet he will come to his end, and
no one will help him.

The End Times

12 “At that time Michael,[g] the great
prince who protects your people, will
arise. There will be a time of distress[h] such
as has not happened from the beginning
of nations until then. But at that time your
people—everyone whose name is found
written in the book[i]—will be delivered.[j]
2Multitudes who sleep in the dust of the
earth will awake: some to everlasting life,
others to shame and everlasting contempt.[k]
3Those who are wise[d][l] will shine[m] like the
brightness of the heavens, and those who
lead many to righteousness, like the stars
for ever and ever.[n] 4But you, Daniel, roll up
and seal[o] the words of the scroll until the
time of the end.[p] Many will go here and
there to increase knowledge.”

5Then I, Daniel, looked, and there before
me stood two others, one on this bank of
the river and one on the opposite bank.[q]
6One of them said to the man clothed in lin-
en,[r] who was above the waters of the river,
“How long will it be before these astonishing things are fulfilled?”[s]

7The man clothed in linen, who was
above the waters of the river, lifted his
right hand and his left hand toward heav-

---

[a] 39 Or *land for a reward* [b] 43 That is, people from the upper Nile region [c] 45 Or *the sea and* [d] 3 Or *who impart wisdom*

---

what He has done for us and given us. The Word leads to knowledge of all that is true about God. This knowledge of God then produces fellowship with Him.

11:35 *it will still come at the appointed time.* Clearly, the trouble and wickedness of Antiochus' reign was not the end. That is yet to come.

11:36 *The king.* Many ancient and modern interpreters have concluded that at this point a new person, the antichrist, is introduced. This king is distinguished from the king of the North (v. 40); therefore, he cannot be Antiochus Epiphanes. It appears that there is a gap of many years between verses 35 and 36, and this refers back to "the time of the end" which will come at the "appointed time" (v. 35).

11:38 *a god unknown to his ancestors.* This is probably a reference to self-worship (v. 37; 2 Thess. 2:4).

11:40 *time of the end.* This is the period just before the return of Christ (Matt. 24:14).

11:45 *no one will help him.* The end of the king is sealed at Christ's second coming (Rev. 19:11–21).

12:1 *written in the book.* The book of life is God's record of those who are justified by faith (Ex. 32:32; Ps. 69:28; Luke 10:20; Rev. 20:12).

12:2 *Multitudes who sleep ... will awake.* This passage appears to refer to a general resurrection, while other passages suggest that there is more than one (John 5:25). It is not unusual for prophecy in the Old Testament to present events separated by a considerable span of time as if they occurred in immediate relationship to each other (see, for example, Is. 61:1–2).

12:6 *How long.* This question refers to the duration of the trials, not the dates of the events.

12:7 *a time, times and half a time.* If a "time" is a year, this adds up to 3–1/2 years (7:25), which may refer to the period immediately preceding the second

11:33 [s] Mal 2:7 [t] Mt 24:9; Jn 16:2; Heb 11:32-38 **11:34** [u] Mt 7:15; Ro 16:18 **11:35** [v] Ps 78:38; Da 12:10; Zec 13:9; Jn 15:2 **11:36** [w] Rev 13:5-6 [x] Dt 10:17; Isa 14:13-14; Da 7:25; 8:11-12,25; 2Th 2:4 [y] Isa 10:25; 26:20 **11:40** [z] Isa 21:1 [a] Isa 5:28 [b] Eze 38:4 **11:41** [c] Isa 11:14 [d] Jer 48:47 **11:43** [e] Eze 30:4 [f] 2Ch 12:3; Na 3:9 **12:1** [g] Da 10:13 [h] Da 9:12; Mt 24:21; Mk 13:19; Rev 16:18 [i] Ex 32:32; Ps 56:8 [j] Jer 30:7 **12:2** [k] Isa 26:19; Mt 25:46; Jn 5:28-29 **12:3** [l] Da 11:33 [m] Mt 13:43; Jn 5:35 [n] 1Co 15:42 **12:4** [o] Isa 8:16 [p] ver 9, 13; Rev 22:10 **12:5** [q] Da 10:4 **12:6** [r] Eze 9:2 [s] Da 8:13

en, and I heard him swear by him who lives
forever,[t] saying, "It will be for a time, times
and half a time.[au] When the power of the
holy people[v] has been finally broken, all
these things will be completed.[w]"
8I heard, but I did not understand. So I
asked, "My lord, what will the outcome of
all this be?"
9He replied, "Go your way, Daniel, because the words are rolled up and sealed
until the time of the end.[x] 10Many will be
purified, made spotless and refined,[y] but
the wicked will continue to be wicked.[z]
None of the wicked will understand, but
those who are wise will understand.[a]
11"From the time that the daily sacrifice
is abolished and the abomination that causes desolation[b] is set up, there will be 1,290
days. 12Blessed is the one who waits[c] for
and reaches the end of the 1,335 days.[d]
13"As for you, go your way till the end.
You will rest,[e] and then at the end of the
days you will rise to receive your allotted
inheritance.[f]"

[a] 7 Or *a year, two years and half a year*

coming of Christ (7:27). Some believe that this expression is not meant to indicate anything more specific than a length of time.

12:11 ***1,290 days.*** Various interpretations have been suggested. One significant interpretation is that these days refer to the time following a point halfway through a seven-year period of tribulation prior to the coming of Christ (9:27).

12:12 ***1,335 days.*** The extra 45 days may be the amount of time that the last battles will take before the victory is completely established.

12:13 ***You will rest, and ... will rise to receive your allotted inheritance.*** Daniel died before these things came to pass, but at the end he will be among those resurrected (v. 2).

12:7 [t] Rev 10:5-6 [u] Da 7:25 [v] Da 8:24 [w] Lk 21:24; Rev 10:7 **12:9** [x] ver 4 **12:10** [y] Da 11:35 [z] Isa 32:7; Rev 22:11 [a] Hos 14:9 **12:11** [b] Da 8:11; 9:27; Mt 24:15*; Mk 13:14* **12:12** [c] Isa 30:18 [d] Da 8:14 **12:13** [e] Isa 57:2 [f] Ps 16:5; Rev 14:13

HOSEA

▶ **AUTHOR:** Few critics argue with the claim in 1:1 that Hosea is the author of this book. The author's place of birth is not given but his familiarity and obvious concern with the northern kingdom point to his living in Israel, rather than Judah. Hosea had a real compassion for his people. His personal suffering because of his wife, Gomer, gave him some understanding of God's grief over the people's sin, and this grief becomes the source of the unique tenderness and hope that characterizes Hosea's book.

▶ **TIME:** c. 755 – 710 B.C. ▶ **KEY VERSE:** Hos. 4:1

▶ **THEME:** Hosea was a contemporary of Isaiah, prophesying near the end of Israel's existence. It is clear from reading the text that Assyria was about to take over. In the second verse of Hosea, God tells Hosea to marry a prostitute named Gomer to provide a living illustration of God's faithfulness and Israel's unfaithfulness. By this, Hosea demonstrates that God loves us, as He did Israel, knowingly and in spite of all our propensities to reject His love for us.

---

1 The word of the LORD that came to Hosea son of Beeri during the reigns of Uzziah, Jotham, Ahaz and Hezekiah, kings of
Judah,[a] and during the reign of Jeroboam[b]
son of Jehoash[a] king of Israel:[c]

Hosea's Wife and Children

2When the LORD began to speak through
Hosea, the LORD said to him, "Go, marry
a promiscuous[d] woman and have children with her, for like an adulterous wife
this land is guilty of unfaithfulness[e] to the
LORD." 3So he married Gomer daughter of
Diblaim, and she conceived and bore him
a son.
4Then the LORD said to Hosea, "Call him
Jezreel,[f] because I will soon punish the
house of Jehu for the massacre at Jezreel,
and I will put an end to the kingdom of Israel. 5In that day I will break Israel's bow
in the Valley of Jezreel.[g]"
6Gomer[h] conceived again and gave birth
to a daughter. Then the LORD said to Hosea,
"Call her Lo-Ruhamah (which means "not
loved"), for I will no longer show love to Israel,[i] that I should at all forgive them. 7Yet
I will show love to Judah; and I will save
them—not by bow,[j] sword or battle, or by
horses and horsemen, but I, the LORD their
God,[k] will save them."
8After she had weaned Lo-Ruhamah,
Gomer had another son. 9Then the LORD
said, "Call him Lo-Ammi (which means
"not my people"), for you are not my people, and I am not your God.[b]
10"Yet the Israelites will be like the sand
on the seashore, which cannot be measured or counted.[l] In the place where it was
said to them, 'You are not my people,' they
will be called 'children of the living God.'[m]

[a] 1 Hebrew *Joash,* a variant of *Jehoash*
[b] 9 Or *your I AM*

1:2–3 ***promiscuous woman.*** Gomer may have been a common prostitute at the time Hosea married her, or perhaps she had participated in a ritual sexual act as part of a Baal cult. However, it is more likely that the descriptive phrase anticipates what Gomer would become following her marriage to Hosea. ***have children with her.*** This anticipates children born to a mother whose reputation and escapades would make their lineage suspect. Gomer's marital infidelity is a picture of Israel's idolatry and unfaithfulness to its covenant with God.
1:5 ***break Israel's bow.*** This phrase means to destroy an opponent's military strength (1 Sam. 2:4; Ps. 46:9; Jer. 49:35).
1:6 ***Lo-Ruhamah.*** This means "no mercy" or "not loved," foreshadowing the Lord's rejection of Israel.
1:9 ***Lo-Ammi.*** This means "not my people," threatening the termination of the Lord's covenant relationship with His people (Lev. 26:12).
1:10 ***like the sand on the seashore.*** The Lord would not reject His people forever. God would fulfill His promise to Abraham (Gen. 22:17; 32:12).

1:1 [a] Isa 1:1; Mic 1:1 [b] 2Ki 13:13 [c] Am 1:1 **1:2** [d] Jer 3:1; Hos 2:2, 5; 3:1 [e] Dt 31:16; Jer 3:14; Eze 23:3-21; Hos 5:3 **1:4** [f] 2Ki 10:1-14; Hos 2:22 **1:5** [g] 2Ki 15:29 **1:6** [h] ver 3 [i] Hos 2:4 **1:7** [j] Ps 44:6 [k] Zec 4:6 **1:10** [l] Ge 22:17; Jer 33:22 [m] ver 9; Ro 9:26*

11The people of Judah and the people of Israel will come together;[n] they will appoint one leader[o] and will come up out of the land,[p] for great will be the day of Jezreel.[a]

2 [b] "Say of your brothers, 'My people,' and of your sisters, 'My loved one.'[q]

Israel Punished and Restored

2"Rebuke your mother,[r] rebuke her,
for she is not my wife,
and I am not her husband.
Let her remove the adulterous[s] look
from her face
and the unfaithfulness from between
her breasts.
3Otherwise I will strip her naked
and make her as bare as on the day
she was born;[t]
I will make her like a desert,[u]
turn her into a parched land,
and slay her with thirst.
4I will not show my love to her
children,[v]
because they are the children of
adultery.
5Their mother has been unfaithful
and has conceived them in
disgrace.
She said, 'I will go after my lovers,[w]
who give me my food and my
water,
my wool and my linen, my olive oil
and my drink.'[x]
6Therefore I will block her path with
thornbushes;
I will wall her in so that she cannot
find her way.[y]
7She will chase after her lovers but not
catch them;
she will look for them but not find
them.[z]
Then she will say,
'I will go back to my husband as at
first,[a]
for then I was better off[b] than now.'
8She has not acknowledged[c] that I was
the one
who gave her the grain, the new wine
and oil,
who lavished on her the silver and
gold—
which they used for Baal.[d]
9"Therefore I will take away my grain[e]
when it ripens,
and my new wine[f] when it is ready.
I will take back my wool and my linen,
intended to cover her naked body.
10So now I will expose her lewdness
before the eyes of her lovers;
no one will take her out of my hands.[g]
11I will stop[h] all her celebrations:
her yearly festivals, her New Moons,
her Sabbath days—all her appointed
festivals.[i]
12I will ruin her vines[j] and her fig trees,
which she said were her pay from her
lovers;
I will make them a thicket,[k]
and wild animals will devour them.[l]
13I will punish her for the days
she burned incense to the Baals;[m]
she decked herself with rings and
jewelry,[n]
and went after her lovers,[o]
but me she forgot,[p]"
declares the LORD.

14"Therefore I am now going to allure
her;
I will lead her into the wilderness
and speak tenderly to her.
15There I will give her back her
vineyards,
and will make the Valley of Achor[c][q] a
door of hope.
There she will respond[d][r] as in the days
of her youth,[s]
as in the day she came up out of
Egypt.[t]

16"In that day," declares the LORD,
"you will call me 'my husband';
you will no longer call me 'my
master.[e]'

[a] *11* In Hebrew texts 1:10,11 is numbered 2:1,2.
[b] In Hebrew texts 2:1-23 is numbered 2:3-25.
[c] *15 Achor* means *trouble.* [d] *15* Or *sing*
[e] *16* Hebrew *baal*

2:2 *she is not my wife.* This may be a formal announcement of divorce or a realistic confession that the relationship between God and Israel had lost its vitality.
2:3 *make her like a desert.* This simile pictures the loss of fertility, an appropriate punishment for a nation that had sought fertility by worshiping another god.
2:6–7 *She will chase after her lovers.* This word draws attention to the strong passion the people of Israel felt for Baal. These verses anticipate the exile, when Israel would be separated from the idols of Baal.
2:12 *wild animals.* The Lord would break down the nation's defenses and turn them into overgrown thickets inhabited by wild beasts.
2:14 *I am now going to allure her.* Having separated Israel from her lovers, the Lord would seek to win her back by making romantic overtures and wooing her with tender words of love.
2:15 *Valley of Achor.* This meant "valley of trouble." It was a reminder of the sin of Achan and God's discipline of the nation of Israel for his sin (Josh. 7:24–26).

1:11 [n] Isa 11:12, 13 [o] Jer 23:5-8 [p] Eze 37:15-28
2:1 [q] ver 23 **2:2** [r] ver 5; Isa 50:1; Hos 1:2 [s] Eze 23:45
2:3 [t] Eze 16:4, 22 [u] Isa 32:13-14 **2:4** [v] Eze 8:18
2:5 [w] Jer 3:6 [x] Jer 44:17-18 **2:6** [y] Job 3:23; 19:8; La 3:9
2:7 [z] Hos 5:13 [a] Jer 2:2; 3:1 [b] Eze 16:8 **2:8** [c] Isa 1:3
[d] Eze 16:15-19; Hos 8:4 **2:9** [e] Hos 8:7 [f] Hos 9:2
2:10 [g] Eze 16:37 **2:11** [h] Jer 7:34 [i] Isa 1:14; Jer 16:9; Hos 3:4; Am 8:10 **2:12** [j] Isa 7:23; Jer 8:13 [k] Isa 5:6
[l] Hos 13:8 **2:13** [m] Hos 11:2 [n] Eze 16:17 [o] Hos 4:13
[p] Hos 4:6; 8:14; 13:6 **2:15** [q] Jos 7:24, 26 [r] Ex 15:1-18
[s] Jer 2:2 [t] Hos 12:9

17 I will remove the names of the Baals
from her lips;[u]
no longer will their names be
invoked.[v]
18 In that day I will make a covenant for
them
with the beasts of the field, the birds
in the sky
and the creatures that move along the
ground.[w]
Bow and sword and battle
I will abolish[x] from the land,
so that all may lie down in safety.[y]
19 I will betroth[z] you to me forever;
I will betroth you in[a] righteousness
and justice,[a]
in[a] love and compassion.
20 I will betroth you in[a] faithfulness,
and you will acknowledge[b] the LORD.

21 "In that day I will respond,"
declares the LORD—
"I will respond[c] to the skies,
and they will respond to the earth;
22 and the earth will respond to the grain,
the new wine and the olive oil,[d]
and they will respond to Jezreel.[b]
23 I will plant[e] her for myself in the land;
I will show my love to the one I called
'Not my loved one.[c][f]'
I will say to those called 'Not my
people,[d]' 'You are my people';[g]
and they will say, 'You are my
God.[h]'"

Hosea's Reconciliation With His Wife

3 The LORD said to me, "Go, show your
love to your wife again, though she is
loved by another man and is an adulteress.[i]
Love her as the LORD loves the Israelites,
though they turn to other gods and love the
sacred raisin cakes.[j]"
2 So I bought her for fifteen shekels[e] of
silver and about a homer and a lethek[f] of
barley. 3 Then I told her, "You are to live
with me many days; you must not be a
prostitute or be intimate with any man, and
I will behave the same way toward you."
4 For the Israelites will live many days
without king or prince,[k] without sacrifice[l]
or sacred stones, without ephod or household gods.[m] 5 Afterward the Israelites will
return and seek the LORD their God and
David their king.[n] They will come trembling to the LORD and to his blessings in
the last days.[o]

The Charge Against Israel

4 Hear the word of the LORD, you
Israelites,
because the LORD has a charge to
bring
against you who live in the land:
"There is no faithfulness, no love,
no acknowledgment[p] of God in the
land.
2 There is only cursing,[g] lying[q] and
murder,[r]
stealing[s] and adultery;
they break all bounds,
and bloodshed follows bloodshed.

[a] *19,20* Or *with* [b] *22* *Jezreel* means *God plants.* [c] *23* Hebrew *Lo-Ruhamah* (see 1:6) [d] *23* Hebrew *Lo-Ammi* (see 1:9) [e] *2* That is, about 6 ounces or about 170 grams [f] *2* A homer and a lethek possibly weighed about 430 pounds or about 195 kilograms. [g] *2* That is, to pronounce a curse on

2:19–20 *betroth.* Betrothal was a binding commitment, the last step before the wedding and consummation of the marriage.
3:1–2 *I bought her.* Gomer had become the property of another man. Hosea's purchase of Gomer symbolized God's great devotion, which moves Him to seek reconciliation even if it means subjecting Himself to humiliation (Phil. 2:8). One of the great truths presented in the Old Testament is God's undying love for Israel. From among all the ancient nations on Earth, He had chosen Israel.
3:1 The Extent of God's Love—People who think of the God of the Old Testament as a God of judgment and the God of the New Testament as a God of love should spend some time studying Hosea. In the book God instructs Hosea to marry a woman named Gomer who is consistently unfaithful. The Book of Hosea is a living parable about how far God will go to love Israel. While there is definitely judgment in Hosea, the consistent ongoing message is God will go to any extreme to demonstrate His love.

He is even willing to play the betrayed spouse in order to save us. He is willing to be an object of scorn and disrespect if that is what it takes to win us back to Him. God's own given law allows for the execution of both parties in an adulterous affair (Lev. 20:10). God cares deeply about this sin. He cares more deeply about His people. It is important to understand how much He takes the initiative. He does not wait passively for us to come to Him. He is faithful about the task of going after us. Even though there is every reason to reject and ignore us, God is right there working to win us in spite of the fact that we reject Him at every turn.
3:4 *sacred stones.* These were stone pillars used by the Canaanites in their worship of Baal and other gods (2 Kin. 3:2; 10:26–27; 17:10). ***ephod.*** This was a priestly garment.
4:1 *charge.* The Hebrew word refers to a formal complaint charging Israel with breaking the covenant. ***acknowledgment.*** This does not refer to intellectual awareness, but to recognition of God's authority as Israel's covenant Lord.
4:2 *cursing, lying and murder, stealing and adultery.* Five of the Ten Commandments are mentioned here.

2:17 [u] Ex 23:13; Ps 16:4 [v] Jos 23:7 **2:18** [w] Job 5:22 [x] Isa 2:4 [y] Jer 23:6; Eze 34:25 **2:19** [z] Isa 62:4 [a] Isa 1:27 **2:20** [b] Jer 31:34; Hos 6:6; 13:4 **2:21** [c] Isa 55:10; Zec 8:12 **2:22** [d] Jer 31:12; Joel 2:19 **2:23** [e] Jer 31:27 [f] Hos 1:6 [g] Hos 1:10 [h] Ro 9:25*; 1Pe 2:10 **3:1** [i] Hos 1:2 [j] 2Sa 6:19 **3:4** [k] Hos 13:11 [l] Da 11:31; Hos 2:11 [m] Jdg 17:5-6; Zec 10:2 **3:5** [n] Eze 34:23-24 [o] Jer 50:4-5 **4:1** [p] Jer 7:28 **4:2** [q] Hos 7:3; 10:4 [r] Hos 6:9 [s] Hos 7:1

3 Because of this the land dries up,[t]
and all who live in it waste away;[u]
the beasts of the field, the birds in the sky
and the fish in the sea are swept away.[v]

4 "But let no one bring a charge,
let no one accuse another,
for your people are like those
who bring charges against a priest.[w]
5 You stumble[x] day and night,
and the prophets stumble with you.
So I will destroy your mother[y]—
6 my people are destroyed from lack of knowledge.[z]

"Because you have rejected knowledge,
I also reject you as my priests;
because you have ignored the law[a] of your God,
I also will ignore your children.
7 The more priests there were,
the more they sinned against me;
they exchanged their glorious God[a][b]
for something disgraceful.[c]
8 They feed on the sins of my people
and relish their wickedness.[d]
9 And it will be: Like people, like priests.[e]
I will punish both of them for their ways
and repay them for their deeds.[f]

10 "They will eat but not have enough;[g]
they will engage in prostitution but not flourish,
because they have deserted[h] the LORD
to give themselves 11 to prostitution;[i]
old wine and new wine
take away their understanding.[j]
12 My people consult a wooden idol,[k]
and a diviner's rod speaks to them.[l]
A spirit of prostitution leads them astray;[m]
they are unfaithful to their God.
13 They sacrifice on the mountaintops
and burn offerings on the hills,
under oak,[n] poplar and terebinth,
where the shade is pleasant.[o]
Therefore your daughters turn to prostitution[p]
and your daughters-in-law to adultery.[q]

14 "I will not punish your daughters
when they turn to prostitution,
nor your daughters-in-law
when they commit adultery,
because the men themselves consort with harlots[r]
and sacrifice with shrine prostitutes—
a people without understanding will come to ruin!

15 "Though you, Israel, commit adultery,
do not let Judah become guilty.

"Do not go to Gilgal;[s]
do not go up to Beth Aven.[b]
And do not swear, 'As surely as the LORD lives!'
16 The Israelites are stubborn,
like a stubborn heifer.
How then can the LORD pasture them
like lambs[t] in a meadow?
17 Ephraim is joined to idols;
leave him alone!
18 Even when their drinks are gone,
they continue their prostitution;
their rulers dearly love shameful ways.
19 A whirlwind[u] will sweep them away,
and their sacrifices will bring them shame.[v]

Judgment Against Israel

5 "Hear this, you priests!
Pay attention, you Israelites!
Listen, royal house!
This judgment is against you:
You have been a snare[w] at Mizpah,
a net spread out on Tabor.
2 The rebels are knee-deep in slaughter.[x]
I will discipline all of them.[y]

---

[a] 7 Syriac (see also an ancient Hebrew scribal tradition); Masoretic Text *me; / I will exchange their glory* [b] 15 *Beth Aven* means *house of wickedness* (a derogatory name for Bethel, which means *house of God*).

4:5 – 6 *lack of knowledge.* The priests had failed to teach God's law to the people (Mal. 2:7). As a result, the priests would be the special object of God's judgment. He would terminate the priestly line.
4:7 – 8 *They feed on the sins of my people.* The priests greedily accepted the meat from the people's hypocritical and empty sacrifices (6:6; 8:11 – 13).
4:10 *prostitution.* This refers to religious prostitution associated with Baal worship, not to immorality in general. The Israelites worshiped Baal in order to have good crops and many children, but they still would not have enough to eat, nor would they multiply in number.
4:12 *diviner's rod.* This refers to wooden idols that Baal worshipers consulted for guidance.
4:15 *Gilgal.* This was an important religious center in the north, known in Hosea's time for its hypocritical religious practices (9:15; 12:11; Amos 4:4). ***Beth Aven.*** This means "house of iniquity," and is a sarcastic reference to the important religious center Bethel, which means "house of God" (Amos 5:5).
4:17 – 19 *Ephraim.* This tribe was one of the largest tribes of Israel. It is used here to represent the entire northern kingdom.

4:3 [t] Jer 4:28 [u] Isa 33:9 [v] Jer 4:25; Zep 1:3
4:4 [w] Dt 17:12; Eze 3:26 **4:5** [x] Eze 14:7 [y] Hos 2:2
4:6 [z] Hos 2:13; Mal 2:7-8 [a] Hos 8:1, 12 **4:7** [b] Hab 2:16
[c] Hos 10:1, 6; 13:6 **4:8** [d] Isa 56:11; Mic 3:11
4:9 [e] Isa 24:2 [f] Jer 5:31; Hos 8:13; 9:9, 15
4:10 [g] Lev 26:26; Mic 6:14 [h] Hos 7:14; 9:17 **4:11** [i] Hos 5:4
[j] Pr 20:1 **4:12** [k] Jer 2:27 [l] Hab 2:19 [m] Isa 44:20
4:13 [n] Isa 1:29 [o] Jer 3:6; Hos 11:2 [p] Jer 2:20; Am 7:17
[q] Hos 2:13 **4:14** [r] ver 11 **4:15** [s] Hos 9:15; 12:11; Am 4:4
4:16 [t] Isa 5:17; 7:25 **4:19** [u] Hos 12:1; 13:15 [v] Isa 1:29
5:1 [w] Hos 6:9; 9:8 **5:2** [x] Hos 4:2 [y] Hos 9:15

[3]I know all about Ephraim;
Israel is not hidden from me.
Ephraim, you have now turned to prostitution;
Israel is corrupt.[z]
[4]"Their deeds do not permit them
to return to their God.
A spirit of prostitution[a] is in their heart;
they do not acknowledge[b] the LORD.
[5]Israel's arrogance testifies[c] against them;
the Israelites, even Ephraim, stumble in their sin;
Judah also stumbles with them.
[6]When they go with their flocks and herds
to seek the LORD,[d]
they will not find him;
he has withdrawn[e] himself from them.
[7]They are unfaithful[f] to the LORD;
they give birth to illegitimate[g] children.
When they celebrate their New Moon feasts,
he will devour[ah] their fields.

[8]"Sound the trumpet in Gibeah,[i]
the horn in Ramah.[j]
Raise the battle cry in Beth Aven[b];[k]
lead on, Benjamin.
[9]Ephraim will be laid waste
on the day of reckoning.[l]
Among the tribes of Israel
I proclaim what is certain.[m]
[10]Judah's leaders are like those
who move boundary stones.[n]
I will pour out my wrath[o] on them
like a flood of water.
[11]Ephraim is oppressed,
trampled in judgment,
intent on pursuing idols.[cp]
[12]I am like a moth[q] to Ephraim,
like rot to the people of Judah.

[13]"When Ephraim saw his sickness,
and Judah his sores,
then Ephraim turned to Assyria,[r]
and sent to the great king for help.[s]
But he is not able to cure[t] you,
not able to heal your sores.[u]
[14]For I will be like a lion[v] to Ephraim,
like a great lion to Judah.
I will tear them to pieces and go away;
I will carry them off, with no one to rescue them.[w]
[15]Then I will return to my lair
until they have borne their guilt
and seek my face[x]—
in their misery[y]
they will earnestly seek me.[z]"

Israel Unrepentant

6 "Come, let us return to the LORD.
He has torn us to pieces[a]
but he will heal us;
he has injured us
but he will bind up our wounds.[b]
[2]After two days he will revive us;[c]
on the third day he will restore us,
that we may live in his presence.
[3]Let us acknowledge the LORD;
let us press on to acknowledge him.
As surely as the sun rises,
he will appear;
he will come to us like the winter rains,[d]
like the spring rains that water the earth.[e]"

[4]"What can I do with you, Ephraim?[f]
What can I do with you, Judah?
Your love is like the morning mist,
like the early dew that disappears.[g]
[5]Therefore I cut you in pieces with my prophets,
I killed you with the words of my mouth[h]—
then my judgments go forth like the sun.[di]

[a] 7 Or *Now their New Moon feasts / will devour them and* [b] 8 *Beth Aven* means *house of wickedness* (a derogatory name for Bethel, which means *house of God*). [c] 11 The meaning of the Hebrew for this word is uncertain. [d] 5 The meaning of the Hebrew for this line is uncertain.

5:4 ***spirit of prostitution.*** The people had an uncontrollable desire to worship other gods.
5:8–9 ***Sound the trumpet.*** This act signaled an emergency and mustered the fighting men to defend the land. The towns mentioned were north of Jerusalem, within or near the borders of Benjamin. The implication is that the enemy army had already swept through the north and was ready to invade Judah.
5:10 ***move boundary stones.*** Stones were used to mark the boundaries of property. A thief could steal a part of someone's land by moving one. The law warned that altering a boundary in this way would bring a special judgment from God (Deut. 19:14; 27:17; Prov. 22:28).
5:12 ***I am like a moth to Ephraim.*** As a moth slowly destroys clothing, so the Lord would destroy Israel (Job 13:28; Is. 50:9; 51:8). rot. Elsewhere this word refers to bone or to decay (Prov. 12:4; 14:30; Hab. 3:16).
5:14–15 ***like a lion.*** God would scatter His people as judgment for their treachery. But the purpose of the Lord's discipline was to drive the people to "earnestly" seek Him.
6:3 ***like the winter rains ... spring rains.*** Two periods of rain are mentioned here. The winterr rains came in the autumn and softened the ground for plowing and sowing. The spring rains came in the spring and caused the plants to grow.
6:5 ***judgments go forth like the sun.*** This comparison suggests that God's judgment, like bright

5:3 [z]Hos 6:10 **5:4** [a]Hos 4:11 [b]Hos 4:6 **5:5** [c]Hos 7:10 **5:6** [d]Mic 6:6-7 [e]Pr 1:28; Isa 1:15; Eze 8:6 **5:7** [f]Hos 6:7 [g]Hos 2:4 [h]Hos 2:11-12 **5:8** [i]Hos 9:9; 10:9 [j]Isa 10:29 [k]Hos 4:15 **5:9** [l]Isa 37:3; Hos 9:11-17 [m]Isa 46:10; Zec 1:6 **5:10** [n]Dt 19:14 [o]Eze 7:8 **5:11** [p]Hos 9:16; Mic 6:16 **5:12** [q]Isa 51:8 **5:13** [r]Hos 7:11; 8:9 [s]Hos 10:6 [t]Hos 14:3 [u]Jer 30:12 **5:14** [v]Am 3:4 [w]Mic 5:8 **5:15** [x]Hos 3:5 [y]Jer 2:27 [z]Isa 64:9 **6:1** [a]Hos 5:14 [b]Dt 32:39; Jer 30:17; Hos 14:4 **6:2** [c]Ps 30:5 **6:3** [d]Joel 2:23 [e]Ps 72:6 **6:4** [f]Hos 11:8 [g]Hos 7:1; 13:3 **6:5** [h]Jer 1:9-10; 23:29 [i]Heb 4:12

6 For I desire mercy, not sacrifice,[j]
and acknowledgment[k] of God rather
than burnt offerings.
7 As at Adam,[a] they have broken the
covenant;[l]
they were unfaithful[m] to me there.
8 Gilead is a city of evildoers,
stained with footprints of blood.
9 As marauders lie in ambush for a
victim,
so do bands of priests;
they murder on the road to Shechem,
carrying out their wicked schemes.[n]
10 I have seen a horrible[o] thing in Israel:
There Ephraim is given to
prostitution,
Israel is defiled.[p]
11 "Also for you, Judah,
a harvest[q] is appointed.

"Whenever I would restore the fortunes
of my people,
7 1 whenever I would heal Israel,
the sins of Ephraim are exposed
and the crimes of Samaria revealed.[r]
They practice deceit,[s]
thieves break into houses,[t]
bandits rob in the streets;
2 but they do not realize
that I remember[u] all their evil deeds.
Their sins engulf them;[v]
they are always before me.

3 "They delight the king with their
wickedness,
the princes with their lies.[w]
4 They are all adulterers,[x]
burning like an oven
whose fire the baker need not stir
from the kneading of the dough till it
rises.
5 On the day of the festival of our king
the princes become inflamed with
wine,[y]
and he joins hands with the mockers.
6 Their hearts are like an oven;[z]
they approach him with intrigue.
Their passion smolders all night;
in the morning it blazes like a
flaming fire.
7 All of them are hot as an oven;
they devour their rulers.
All their kings fall,
and none of them calls[a] on me.

8 "Ephraim mixes[b] with the nations;
Ephraim is a flat loaf not turned over.
9 Foreigners sap his strength,[c]
but he does not realize it.
His hair is sprinkled with gray,
but he does not notice.
10 Israel's arrogance testifies against
him,[d]
but despite all this
he does not return to the LORD his God
or search[e] for him.

11 "Ephraim is like a dove,[f]
easily deceived and senseless—
now calling to Egypt,
now turning to Assyria.[g]
12 When they go, I will throw my net[h] over
them;
I will pull them down like the birds in
the sky.
When I hear them flocking together,
I will catch them.
13 Woe[i] to them,
because they have strayed[j] from me!
Destruction to them,
because they have rebelled
against me!
I long to redeem them
but they speak about me[k] falsely.
14 They do not cry out to me from their
hearts[l]
but wail on their beds.

---

[a] 7 Or *Like Adam*; or *Like human beings*

---

sunlight, was obvious to all; or that, like a bolt of lightning or a blinding flash of light, it came swiftly.

6:11 *a harvest is appointed.* The comparison of God's judgment to a harvest indicates that the judgment was inevitable and implies that it would be thorough in its destruction.

7:4–7 *like an oven.* The background for these verses is the political turmoil of the northern kingdom. During a 20-year period (752–732 B.C.), four Israelite kings were assassinated (2 Kin. 15). The dangerous, uncontrollable perpetuators of these crimes are described here. These conspirators were like a large baker's oven that has been heating up for several hours while the bread dough rises. By morning the fire in the oven can be destructive.

7:8 *Ephraim mixes with the nations.* Instead of depending on the Lord for political stability, Israel formed alliances with surrounding nations. The destructive outcome of this policy is compared to a cake that has been placed over a fire and left unturned.

7:9–10 *hair is sprinkled with gray.* Israel did not recognize that its power was declining and its freedom was slipping away, like an aging man who is gradually overtaken by the signs of old age.

7:11–12 *Egypt ... Assyria.* Israel was caught between these two superpowers. It tried to maintain its independence by playing one power against the other, but this vacillating policy didn't work. Israel was like a silly dove, flitting about from place to place.

7:13 *Woe to them.* When prophets spoke this way, they were saying a funeral dirge for those under the sentence of God's judgment.

7:14 *grain and new wine.* God sent a drought on Israel, but instead of the people turning to Him in repentance, the idolatrous Israelites demonstrated their devotion to Baal. According to Canaanite religious beliefs, prolonged drought was a signal that

6:6 [j] Isa 1:11; Mt 9:13*; 12:7* [k] Hos 2:20 **6:7** [l] Hos 8:1 [m] Hos 5:7 **6:9** [n] Jer 7:9-10; Eze 22:9; Hos 7:1 **6:10** [o] Jer 5:30 [p] Hos 5:3 **6:11** [q] Jer 51:33; Joel 3:13 **7:1** [r] Hos 6:4 [s] ver 13 [t] Hos 4:2 **7:2** [u] Jer 14:10; Hos 8:13 [v] Jer 2:19 **7:3** [w] Hos 4:2; Mic 7:3 **7:4** [x] Jer 9:2 **7:5** [y] Isa 28:1,7 **7:6** [z] Ps 21:9 **7:7** [a] ver 16 **7:8** [b] ver 11; Ps 106:35; Hos 5:13 **7:9** [c] Isa 1:7; Hos 8:7 **7:10** [d] Hos 5:5 [e] Isa 9:13 **7:11** [f] Hos 11:11 [g] Hos 5:13; 12:1 **7:12** [h] Eze 12:13 **7:13** [i] Hos 9:12 [j] Jer 14:10; Eze 34:4-6; Hos 9:17 [k] ver 1; Mt 23:37 **7:14** [l] Jer 3:10

They slash themselves,[a] appealing to
their gods
for grain and new wine,[m]
but they turn away from me.[n]
15 I trained them and strengthened their
arms,
but they plot evil[o] against me.
16 They do not turn to the Most High;
they are like a faulty bow.[p]
Their leaders will fall by the sword
because of their insolent words.
For this they will be ridiculed[q]
in the land of Egypt.[r]

Israel to Reap the Whirlwind

8 "Put the trumpet to your lips!
An eagle[s] is over the house of the LORD
because the people have broken my
covenant
and rebelled against my law.[t]
2 Israel cries out to me,
'Our God, we acknowledge you!'
3 But Israel has rejected what is good;
an enemy will pursue him.
4 They set up kings without my consent;
they choose princes without my
approval.[u]
With their silver and gold
they make idols[v] for themselves
to their own destruction.
5 Samaria, throw out your calf-idol![w]
My anger burns against them.
How long will they be incapable of
purity?[x]
6 They are from Israel!
This calf—a metalworker has made it;
it is not God.
It will be broken in pieces,
that calf of Samaria.

7 "They sow the wind
and reap the whirlwind.[y]
The stalk has no head;
it will produce no flour.
Were it to yield grain,
foreigners would swallow it up.[z]
8 Israel is swallowed up;[a]
now she is among the nations
like something no one wants.[b]
9 For they have gone up to Assyria
like a wild donkey wandering alone.
Ephraim has sold herself to lovers.
10 Although they have sold themselves
among the nations,
I will now gather them together.[c]
They will begin to waste away[d]
under the oppression of the mighty
king.

11 "Though Ephraim built many altars for
sin offerings,
these have become altars for
sinning.[e]
12 I wrote for them the many things of my
law,
but they regarded them as something
foreign.
13 Though they offer sacrifices as gifts
to me,
and though they eat[f] the meat,
the LORD is not pleased with them.
Now he will remember[g] their
wickedness
and punish their sins:[h]
They will return to Egypt.[i]
14 Israel has forgotten[j] their Maker
and built palaces;
Judah has fortified many towns.
But I will send fire on their cities
that will consume their fortresses."[k]

Punishment for Israel

9 Do not rejoice, Israel;
do not be jubilant[l] like the other
nations.
For you have been unfaithful[m] to your
God;
you love the wages of a prostitute
at every threshing floor.

[a] *14* Some Hebrew manuscripts and Septuagint; most Hebrew manuscripts *They gather together*

the storm god Baal had been temporarily defeated by the god of death and was imprisoned by the underworld. Baal's worshipers would mourn his death in hopes that their tears might facilitate his resurrection and the restoration of crops.

8:1–3 ***An eagle.*** As a bird of prey would do, Assyria would invade Israel and take its people into captivity. ***we acknowledge you!*** Though Israel claimed to acknowledge the Lord's authority, it had violated His covenant and rejected the qualities the Lord regarded as good, such as justice, loyalty, and humility (Amos 5:14–15; Mic. 6:8).

8:4 ***They set up kings.*** This phrase alludes to the political turmoil surrounding the throne of the northern kingdom during the eighth century B.C., when four kings were assassinated during a 20-year period (7:4–7).

8:6 ***a metalworker has made it.*** Hosea reasoned that anything that is made with human hands cannot possibly qualify as a god.

8:9–10 ***a wild donkey.*** This comparison draws attention to Israel's free-spirited attitude and desire to live unrestrained by God's standards.

8:14 ***palaces . . . fortified many towns.*** True security comes from the Creator, but God's people trusted instead in their own efforts, symbolized by their important buildings.

9:1–2 ***threshing floor.*** Because of their association with the harvest, threshing floors were the site of agricultural festivals in which Israel offered up sacrifices to Baal. The Lord would take away the joy of the harvest by destroying the crops and leaving the threshing floors and wine vats empty.

7:14 [m] Am 2:8 [n] Hos 13:16 **7:15** [o] Na 1:9,11 **7:16** [p] Ps 78:9,57 [q] Eze 23:32 [r] Hos 9:3 **8:1** [s] Dt 28:49; Jer 4:13 [t] Hos 4:6; 6:7 **8:4** [u] Hos 13:10 [v] Hos 2:8 **8:5** [w] Hos 10:5 [x] Jer 13:27 **8:7** [y] Pr 22:8; Isa 66:15; Hos 10:12-13; Na 1:3 [z] Hos 2:9 **8:8** [a] Jer 51:34 [b] Jer 22:28 **8:10** [c] Eze 16:37; 22:20 [d] Jer 42:2 **8:11** [e] Hos 10:1; 12:11 **8:13** [f] Jer 7:21 [g] Hos 7:2 [h] Hos 4:9 [i] Hos 9:3,6 **8:14** [j] Dt 32:18; Hos 2:13 [k] Jer 17:27 **9:1** [l] Isa 22:12-13 [m] Hos 10:5

2 Threshing floors and winepresses will
not feed the people;
the new wine[n] will fail them.
3 They will not remain[o] in the LORD's
land;
Ephraim will return to Egypt[p]
and eat unclean food in Assyria.[q]
4 They will not pour out wine offerings to
the LORD,
nor will their sacrifices please[r] him.
Such sacrifices will be to them like the
bread of mourners;
all who eat them will be unclean.[s]
This food will be for themselves;
it will not come into the temple of the
LORD.

5 What will you do[t] on the day of your
appointed festivals,[u]
on the feast days of the LORD?
6 Even if they escape from destruction,
Egypt will gather them,
and Memphis[v] will bury them.
Their treasures of silver will be taken
over by briers,
and thorns[w] will overrun their tents.
7 The days of punishment[x] are coming,
the days of reckoning are at hand.
Let Israel know this.
Because your sins[y] are so many
and your hostility so great,
the prophet is considered a fool,[z]
the inspired person a maniac.
8 The prophet, along with my God,
is the watchman over Ephraim,[a]
yet snares[a] await him on all his paths,
and hostility in the house of
his God.
9 They have sunk deep into corruption,
as in the days of Gibeah.[b]
God will remember[c] their wickedness
and punish them for their sins.

10 "When I found Israel,
it was like finding grapes in the
desert;
when I saw your ancestors,
it was like seeing the early fruit on
the fig tree.
But when they came to Baal Peor,[d]
they consecrated themselves to that
shameful idol[e]
and became as vile as the thing they
loved.
11 Ephraim's glory will fly away like a
bird[f]—
no birth, no pregnancy, no
conception.[g]
12 Even if they rear children,
I will bereave them of every one.
Woe[h] to them
when I turn away from them![i]
13 I have seen Ephraim, like Tyre,
planted in a pleasant place.[j]
But Ephraim will bring out
their children to the slayer."

14 Give them, LORD—
what will you give them?
Give them wombs that miscarry
and breasts that are dry.[k]

15 "Because of all their wickedness in
Gilgal,[l]
I hated them there.
Because of their sinful deeds,[m]
I will drive them out of my house.
I will no longer love them;
all their leaders are rebellious.[n]
16 Ephraim[o] is blighted,
their root is withered,
they yield no fruit.[p]
Even if they bear children,
I will slay[q] their cherished offspring."

17 My God will reject them
because they have not obeyed[r] him;
they will be wanderers among the
nations.[s]

10 Israel was a spreading vine;[t]
he brought forth fruit for himself.
As his fruit increased,
he built more altars;[u]
as his land prospered,
he adorned his sacred stones.[v]

---

[a] 8 Or *The prophet is the watchman over Ephraim, / the people of my God*

9:3 *the LORD's land.* Israel had forgotten that their land belonged to the Lord. He alone decided who would or would not live in it (Lev. 25:23).
9:7 *the inspired person a maniac.* The word translated "maniac" is used in 1 Samuel 21:15 of David when he pretended to be insane before the Philistine king.
9:8 *watchman.* He would look for approaching armies and then warn the people so that they could secure the city and prepare for battle (Ezek. 33:6). The prophets were like watchmen because they were sent by God to warn the people of judgment and urge them to repent (Ezek. 3:17).
9:9 *as in the days of Gibeah.* The reference here is to the rape and murder of a young woman by men of Gibeah, an event that started a civil war (Judg. 19). Those who witnessed this violent deed remarked that it was the worst crime committed in Israel's history until that time. However, the sins of Hosea's generation rivaled the infamous Gibeah.
9:14 *wombs that miscarry.* Some women of Israel would be barren (v. 11); others would bear children, only to lose them to the invader's sword (vv. 12–13). Still others would conceive but miscarry.
10:1 *Israel was a spreading vine.* This refers to God's blessings upon the nation, which contrast with the nation's ingratitude and idolatry.

9:2 [n] Hos 2:9 **9:3** [o] Lev 25:23 [p] Hos 8:13 [q] Eze 4:13; Hos 7:11 **9:4** [r] Jer 6:20; Hos 8:13 [s] Hag 2:13-14 **9:5** [t] Isa 10:3; Jer 5:31 [u] Hos 2:11 **9:6** [v] Isa 19:13 [w] Isa 5:6; Hos 10:8 **9:7** [x] Isa 34:8; Jer 10:15; Mic 7:4 [y] Jer 16:18 [z] Isa 44:25; La 2:14; Eze 14:9-10 **9:8** [a] Hos 5:1 **9:9** [b] Jdg 19:16-30; Hos 5:8; 10:9 [c] Hos 8:13 **9:10** [d] Nu 25:1-5; Ps 106:28-29 [e] Jer 11:13; Hos 4:14 **9:11** [f] Hos 4:7; 10:5 [g] ver 14 **9:12** [h] Hos 7:13 [i] Dt 31:17 **9:13** [j] Eze 27:3 **9:14** [k] ver 11; Lk 23:29 **9:15** [l] Hos 4:15 [m] Hos 7:2 [n] Isa 1:23; Hos 4:9; 5:2 **9:16** [o] Hos 5:11 [p] Hos 8:7 [q] ver 12 **9:17** [r] Hos 4:10 [s] Dt 28:65; Hos 7:13 **10:1** [t] Eze 15:2 [u] 1Ki 14:23 [v] Hos 8:11; 12:11

[2]Their heart is deceitful,[w]
and now they must bear their guilt.[x]
The LORD will demolish their altars[y]
and destroy their sacred stones.[z]

[3]Then they will say, "We have no king
because we did not revere the LORD.
But even if we had a king,
what could he do for us?"
[4]They make many promises,
take false oaths[a]
and make agreements;[b]
therefore lawsuits spring up
like poisonous weeds in a plowed
field.
[5]The people who live in Samaria fear
for the calf-idol of Beth Aven.[a][c]
Its people will mourn over it,
and so will its idolatrous priests,[d]
those who had rejoiced over its
splendor,
because it is taken from them into
exile.[e]
[6]It will be carried to Assyria[f]
as tribute for the great king.[g]
Ephraim will be disgraced;[h]
Israel will be ashamed of its foreign
alliances.
[7]Samaria's king will be destroyed,[i]
swept away like a twig on the surface
of the waters.
[8]The high places of wickedness[b][j] will be
destroyed—
it is the sin of Israel.
Thorns[k] and thistles will grow up
and cover their altars.[l]
Then they will say to the mountains,
"Cover us!"
and to the hills, "Fall on us!"[m]

[9]"Since the days of Gibeah,[n] you have
sinned, Israel,
and there you have remained.[c]
Will not war again overtake
the evildoers in Gibeah?
[10]When I please, I will punish[o] them;
nations will be gathered against them
to put them in bonds for their double
sin.
[11]Ephraim is a trained heifer
that loves to thresh;
so I will put a yoke
on her fair neck.
I will drive Ephraim,
Judah must plow,
and Jacob must break up the ground.
[12]Sow righteousness[p] for yourselves,
reap the fruit of unfailing love,
and break up your unplowed ground;[q]
for it is time to seek[r] the LORD,
until he comes
and showers his righteousness[s] on
you.
[13]But you have planted wickedness,
you have reaped evil,[t]
you have eaten the fruit of deception.
Because you have depended on your
own strength
and on your many warriors,[u]
[14]the roar of battle will rise against your
people,
so that all your fortresses will be
devastated[v]—
as Shalman devastated Beth Arbel on
the day of battle,
when mothers were dashed to the
ground with their children.[w]
[15]So will it happen to you, Bethel,
because your wickedness is great.
When that day dawns,
the king of Israel will be completely
destroyed.[x]

God's Love for Israel

11 "When Israel was a child, I loved
him,
and out of Egypt I called my son.[y]
[2]But the more they were called,
the more they went away from me.[d]
They sacrificed to the Baals[z]
and they burned incense to images.[a]
[3]It was I who taught Ephraim to walk,
taking them by the arms;[b]
but they did not realize
it was I who healed[c] them.

[a] 5 *Beth Aven* means *house of wickedness* (a derogatory name for Bethel, which means *house of God*). [b] 8 Hebrew *aven,* a reference to Beth Aven (a derogatory name for Bethel); see verse 5. [c] 9 Or *there a stand was taken* [d] 2 Septuagint; Hebrew *them*

10:4 *lawsuits spring up like poisonous weeds in a plowed field.* In much the same way judgment would replace God's blessings.
10:11 *loves to thresh.* Israel preferred to be unrestrained, like an unmuzzled heifer at the threshing floor that can simply lean down and eat grain. ***Judah must plow.*** Israel's rebellious spirit necessitated harsh treatment, compared here to a farmer binding his calf to the yoke and forcing it to do hard labor. Threshing in this context refers to Israel's service to the Lord; plowing refers to the discipline that Israel had to acquire through judgment and exile.
10:12 *break up your unplowed ground.* Plowing and planting are necessary preliminary steps for growing a crop, which eventually sprouts when the rain falls in season. In the same way, repentance would set the stage for restored blessing, which God would eventually rain down on His people.
11:3 *I who taught Ephraim to walk.* Like a father teaching his child to walk, the Lord patiently gave the people of Israel direction and cared for them tenderly when they experienced pain or injury.

10:2 [w] 1Ki 18:21 [x] Hos 13:16 [y] ver 8 [z] Mic 5:13
10:4 [a] Hos 4:2 [b] Eze 17:19; Am 5:7 **10:5** [c] Hos 5:8 [d] 2Ki 23:5 [e] Hos 8:5; 9:1, 3, 11 **10:6** [f] Hos 11:5 [g] Hos 5:13 [h] Isa 30:3; Hos 4:7 **10:7** [i] Hos 13:11 **10:8** [j] 1Ki 12:28-30; Hos 4:13 [k] Hos 9:6 [l] ver 2; Isa 32:13 [m] Lk 23:30*; Rev 6:16
10:9 [n] Hos 5:8 **10:10** [o] Eze 5:13; Hos 4:9
10:12 [p] Pr 11:18 [q] Jer 4:3 [r] Hos 12:6 [s] Isa 45:8
10:13 [t] Job 4:8; Hos 7:3; 11:12; Gal 6:7-8 [u] Ps 33:16
10:14 [v] Isa 17:3 [w] Hos 13:16 **10:15** [x] ver 7
11:1 [y] Ex 4:22; Hos 12:9, 13; 13:4; Mt 2:15* **11:2** [z] Hos 2:13 [a] 2Ki 17:15; Isa 65:7; Jer 18:15 **11:3** [b] Dt 1:31; Hos 7:15 [c] Jer 30:17

4 I led them with cords of human
kindness,
with ties of love.[d]
To them I was like one who lifts
a little child to the cheek,
and I bent down to feed[e] them.
5 "Will they not return to Egypt[f]
and will not Assyria[g] rule over them
because they refuse to repent?
6 A sword[h] will flash in their cities;
it will devour their false prophets
and put an end to their plans.
7 My people are determined to turn
from me.[i]
Even though they call me God Most
High,
I will by no means exalt them.
8 "How can I give you up, Ephraim?[j]
How can I hand you over, Israel?
How can I treat you like Admah?
How can I make you like
Zeboyim?[k]
My heart is changed within me;
all my compassion is aroused.
9 I will not carry out my fierce anger,[l]
nor will I devastate[m] Ephraim
again.
For I am God, and not a man[n]—
the Holy One among you.
I will not come against their cities.
10 They will follow the LORD;
he will roar like a lion.
When he roars,
his children will come trembling
from the west.[o]
11 They will come from Egypt,
trembling like sparrows,
from Assyria,[p] fluttering like
doves.
I will settle them in their homes,"[q]
declares the LORD.

Israel's Sin

12 Ephraim has surrounded me with lies,[r]
Israel with deceit.
And Judah is unruly against God,
even against the faithful Holy One.[a]

12 [b] 1 Ephraim feeds on the wind;[s]
he pursues the east wind all
day
and multiplies lies and violence.
He makes a treaty with Assyria
and sends olive oil to Egypt.[t]
2 The LORD has a charge[u] to bring
against Judah;
he will punish Jacob[c] according to
his ways
and repay him according to his
deeds.[v]
3 In the womb he grasped his brother's
heel;[w]
as a man he struggled[x] with God.
4 He struggled with the angel and
overcame him;
he wept and begged for his favor.
He found him at Bethel[y]
and talked with him there—
5 the LORD God Almighty,
the LORD is his name![z]
6 But you must return to your God;
maintain love and justice,[a]
and wait for your God always.[b]

7 The merchant uses dishonest scales[c]
and loves to defraud.
8 Ephraim boasts,
"I am very rich; I have become
wealthy.[d]
With all my wealth they will not find
in me
any iniquity or sin."
9 "I have been the LORD your God
ever since you came out of Egypt;[e]
I will make you live in tents[f] again,
as in the days of your appointed
festivals.
10 I spoke to the prophets,
gave them many visions
and told parables[g] through them."[h]

---

[a] *12* In Hebrew texts this verse (11:12) is numbered 12:1. [b] In Hebrew texts 12:1-14 is numbered 12:2-15. [c] *2 Jacob* means *he grasps the heel*, a Hebrew idiom for *he takes advantage of* or *he deceives.*

11:4 *cords ... ties.* The Lord had placed restraints on Israel, but His regulations, rather than being overly strict or harsh, reflected His concern for the people's well-being. God did not drive them mercilessly but provided for their needs, like a farmer who periodically removes the yoke from an animal's neck so that it can eat.

11:6 *devour.* This is the same Hebrew word translated "fed" in verse 4. The people of Israel had rejected the gentle Master who fed them and provided for their needs. As a result, they would be devoured by the swords of the invading Assyrians.

11:9 *For I am God, and not a man.* When human beings get angry, they are often incapable of tempering their anger with compassion, but God's emotions operate in perfect balance.

12:1 *olive oil to Egypt.* Oil may have been used in a ritual ratifying a treaty or given as a sign of loyalty.

12:7 *dishonest scales.* In violation of the Old Testament law (Lev. 19:36), dishonest merchants sometimes rigged their scales so that they could give buyers less than what they thought they were purchasing (Prov. 11:1; 16:11).

12:9 *I will make you live in tents.* During the Festival of Tabernacles people lived in tents to commemorate the wilderness wandering (Lev. 23:33–43).

11:4 [d] Jer 31:2-3 [e] Ex 16:32; Ps 78:25 **11:5** [f] Hos 7:16 [g] Hos 10:6 **11:6** [h] Hos 13:16 **11:7** [i] Jer 3:6-7; 8:5 **11:8** [j] Hos 6:4 [k] Ge 14:8 **11:9** [l] Dt 13:17; Jer 30:11 [m] Mal 3:6 [n] Nu 23:19 **11:10** [o] Hos 6:1-3 **11:11** [p] Isa 11:11 [q] Eze 28:26 **11:12** [r] Hos 4:2 **12:1** [s] Eze 17:10 [t] 2Ki 17:4 **12:2** [u] Mic 6:2 [v] Hos 4:9 **12:3** [w] Ge 25:26 [x] Ge 32:24-29 **12:4** [y] Ge 28:12-15; 35:15 **12:5** [z] Ex 3:15 **12:6** [a] Mic 6:8 [b] Hos 6:1-3; 10:12; Mic 7:7 **12:7** [c] Am 8:5 **12:8** [d] Ps 62:10; Rev 3:17 **12:9** [e] Lev 23:43; Hos 11:1 [f] Ne 8:17 **12:10** [g] Eze 20:49 [h] 2Ki 17:13; Jer 7:25

[11]Is Gilead wicked?[i]
Its people are worthless!
Do they sacrifice bulls in Gilgal?[j]
Their altars will be like piles of stones
on a plowed field.[k]
[12]Jacob fled to the country of Aram[a];[l]
Israel served to get a wife,
and to pay for her he tended sheep.[m]
[13]The LORD used a prophet to bring Israel
up from Egypt,
by a prophet he cared for him.[n]
[14]But Ephraim has aroused his bitter
anger;
his Lord will leave on him the guilt of
his bloodshed[o]
and will repay him for his contempt.[p]

The LORD's Anger Against Israel

13 When Ephraim spoke, people
trembled;[q]
he was exalted[r] in Israel.
But he became guilty of Baal
worship[s] and died.
[2]Now they sin more and more;
they make idols for themselves from
their silver,[t]
cleverly fashioned images,
all of them the work of craftsmen.
It is said of these people,
"They offer human sacrifices!
They kiss[b] calf-idols![u]"
[3]Therefore they will be like the morning
mist,
like the early dew that disappears,[v]
like chaff[w] swirling from a threshing
floor,[x]
like smoke[y] escaping through a
window.

[4]"But I have been the LORD your God
ever since you came out of Egypt.[z]
You shall acknowledge no God but me,[a]
no Savior[b] except me.
[5]I cared for you in the wilderness,
in the land of burning heat.
[6]When I fed them, they were satisfied;
when they were satisfied, they
became proud;
then they forgot me.[c]
[7]So I will be like a lion to them,
like a leopard I will lurk by the path.
[8]Like a bear robbed of her cubs,[d]
I will attack them and rip them open;
like a lion I will devour them—
a wild animal will tear them apart.[e]

[9]"You are destroyed, Israel,
because you are against me,[f] against
your helper.[g]
[10]Where is your king,[h] that he may save
you?
Where are your rulers in all your
towns,
of whom you said,
'Give me a king and princes'?[i]
[11]So in my anger I gave you a king,
and in my wrath I took him away.[j]
[12]The guilt of Ephraim is stored up,
his sins are kept on record.[k]
[13]Pains as of a woman in childbirth[l] come
to him,
but he is a child without wisdom;
when the time arrives,
he doesn't have the sense to come out
of the womb.[m]

[14]"I will deliver this people from the
power of the grave;[n]
I will redeem them from death.
Where, O death, are your plagues?
Where, O grave, is your destruction?[o]

"I will have no compassion,
[15] even though he thrives[p] among his
brothers.
An east wind[q] from the LORD will come,
blowing in from the desert;
his spring will fail
and his well dry up.[r]
His storehouse will be plundered[s]
of all its treasures.
[16]The people of Samaria must bear their
guilt,[t]
because they have rebelled[u] against
their God.
They will fall by the sword;[v]
their little ones will be dashed[w] to the
ground,
their pregnant women[x] ripped open."[c]

---

[a] *12* That is, Northwest Mesopotamia [b] *2* Or *"Men who sacrifice / kiss* [c] *16* In Hebrew texts this verse (13:16) is numbered 14:1.

13:2 *kiss calf-idols!* This is a reference to the idolatrous practice of kissing images as a sign of homage (1 Kin. 19:18).

13:6–9 *I will be like a lion.* God provided for Israel's needs and richly blessed the people, like a shepherd leading his flock to lush pasturelands. In return, Israel forgot the Lord. The Lord's relationship with Israel would change drastically from caring Shepherd to ravaging Predator. Ironically and tragically, Israel's rebellion had turned its Helper into a Destroyer.

13:12 *stored up . . . kept on record.* God had kept a careful record of Israel's sins, to be revealed as evidence of guilt in the day of judgment.

13:13 *Pains as of a woman in childbirth.* This metaphor illustrates Israel's spiritual insensitivity. When the crucial time of judgment arrived, Israel would respond unwisely, resulting in death. The nation's failure to repent is compared to a baby that is not positioned properly during labor and jeopardizes the life of both mother and child.

12:11 [i] Hos 6:8 [j] Hos 4:15 [k] Hos 8:11 **12:12** [l] Ge 28:5 [m] Ge 29:18 **12:13** [n] Ex 13:3; Isa 63:11-14 **12:14** [o] Eze 18:13 [p] Da 11:18 **13:1** [q] Jdg 12:1 [r] Jdg 8:1 [s] Hos 11:2 **13:2** [t] Isa 46:6; Jer 10:4 [u] Isa 44:17-20 **13:3** [v] Hos 6:4 [w] Isa 17:13 [x] Da 2:35 [y] Ps 68:2 **13:4** [z] Hos 12:9 [a] Ex 20:3 [b] Isa 43:11; 45:21-22 **13:6** [c] Dt 32:12-15; Hos 2:13 **13:8** [d] 2Sa 17:8 [e] Ps 50:22 **13:9** [f] Jer 2:17-19 [g] Dt 33:29 **13:10** [h] 2Ki 17:4 [i] 1Sa 8:6; Hos 8:4 **13:11** [j] 1Ki 14:10; Hos 10:7 **13:12** [k] Dt 32:34 **13:13** [l] Isa 13:8; Mic 4:9-10 [m] Isa 66:9 **13:14** [n] Ps 49:15; Eze 37:12-13 [o] 1Co 15:55* **13:15** [p] Hos 10:1 [q] Eze 19:12 [r] Jer 51:36 [s] Jer 20:5 **13:16** [t] Hos 10:2 [u] Hos 7:14 [v] Hos 11:6 [w] 2Ki 8:12; Hos 10:14 [x] 2Ki 15:16; Isa 13:16

Repentance to Bring Blessing

14 [a] Return, Israel, to the LORD your
God.
Your sins have been your downfall![y]
2 Take words with you
and return to the LORD.
Say to him:
"Forgive all our sins
and receive us graciously,[z]
that we may offer the fruit of our
lips.[b][a]
3 Assyria cannot save us;
we will not mount warhorses.[b]
We will never again say 'Our gods'[c]
to what our own hands have made,
for in you the fatherless[d] find
compassion."

4 "I will heal[e] their waywardness
and love them freely,[f]
for my anger has turned away from
them.
5 I will be like the dew to Israel;
he will blossom like a lily.[g]
Like a cedar of Lebanon[h]
he will send down his roots;[i]
6 his young shoots will grow.
His splendor will be like an olive tree,[j]
his fragrance like a cedar of
Lebanon.[k]
7 People will dwell again in his
shade;[l]
they will flourish like the grain,
they will blossom like the vine—
Israel's fame will be like the wine[m] of
Lebanon.[n]
8 Ephraim, what more have I[c] to do with
idols?[o]
I will answer him and care for him.
I am like a flourishing juniper;
your fruitfulness comes from me."
9 Who is wise?[p] Let them realize these
things.
Who is discerning? Let them
understand.[q]
The ways of the LORD are right;[r]
the righteous walk[s] in them,
but the rebellious stumble in them.

---

[a] In Hebrew texts 14:1-9 is numbered 14:2-10.
[b] 2 Or *offer our lips as sacrifices of bulls*
[c] 8 Or Hebrew; Septuagint *What more has Ephraim*

14:1–3 *Forgive all our sins.* The final section of Hosea's prophecy begins with a call to repentance that includes a model prayer. The people of Israel were to pray for God's gracious forgiveness and renew their allegiance to Him by renouncing foreign alliances, their own military strength, and artificial gods.

14:4 *I will heal their waywardness.* The grief-stricken Hosea does not tell us whether a reconciliation took place between him and his adulterous wife Gomer. But there is no question concerning the outcome between God and faithless Israel. Several beautiful figures of speech are employed by Hosea to describe the results and effects of God's love for Israel.

14:9 *The ways of the LORD are right.* God's demands and principles are completely true. The wise person will choose to obey them, but the foolish person will ignore them and consequently stumble into judgment.

14:1 [y] Hos 5:5 **14:2** [z] Mic 7:18-19 [a] Heb 13:15
14:3 [b] Ps 33:17; Isa 31:1 [c] Hos 8:6 [d] Ps 10:14; 68:5
14:4 [e] Hos 6:1 [f] Zep 3:17 **14:5** [g] SS 2:1 [h] Isa 35:2
[i] Job 29:19 **14:6** [j] Ps 52:8; Jer 11:16 [k] SS 4:11
14:7 [l] Ps 91:1-4 [m] Hos 2:22 [n] Eze 17:23 **14:8** [o] ver 3
14:9 [p] Ps 107:43 [q] Pr 10:29; Isa 1:28 [r] Ps 111:7-8; Zep 3:5;
Ac 13:10 [s] Isa 26:7

JOEL

▶ **AUTHOR:** Although there are several other Joels in the Bible, the prophet Joel is known only from this book. It has been suggested that he lived not far from Jerusalem and some think that Joel was possibly a priest as well as a prophet on account of references to the priesthood throughout the book (Joel 1:13–14; 2:17).

▶ **TIME:** c. 835 B.C. ▶ **KEY VERSE:** Joel 2:11

▶ **THEME:** For the true agrarian society, crops are life itself. It is hard to imagine how devastating the natural disasters described in Joel are, and he uses these painful events as a megaphone to get the attention of the people. There is urgency in this call, because the day of the Lord is coming. This day will be a day of judgment or a day of blessing depending on where one stands with God.

1 The word of the LORD that came[a] to Joel[b] son of Pethuel.

An Invasion of Locusts

2 Hear this,[c] you elders;
listen, all who live in the land.[d]
Has anything like this ever happened in your days
or in the days of your ancestors?[e]
3 Tell it to your children,[f]
and let your children tell it to their children,
and their children to the next generation.
4 What the locust swarm has left
the great locusts have eaten;
what the great locusts have left
the young locusts have eaten;
what the young locusts have left
other locusts[a] have eaten.[g]

5 Wake up, you drunkards, and weep!
Wail, all you drinkers of wine;[h]
wail because of the new wine,
for it has been snatched from your lips.
6 A nation has invaded my land,
a mighty army without number;[i]
it has the teeth[j] of a lion,
the fangs of a lioness.
7 It has laid waste[k] my vines
and ruined my fig trees.[l]
It has stripped off their bark
and thrown it away,
leaving their branches white.
8 Mourn like a virgin in sackcloth[m]
grieving for the betrothed of her youth.
9 Grain offerings and drink offerings[n]
are cut off from the house of the LORD.
The priests are in mourning,
those who minister before the LORD.
10 The fields are ruined,
the ground is dried up;[o]
the grain is destroyed,
the new wine[p] is dried up,
the olive oil fails.

11 Despair, you farmers,[q]
wail, you vine growers;
grieve for the wheat and the barley,
because the harvest of the field is destroyed.[r]

[a] 4 The precise meaning of the four Hebrew words used here for locusts is uncertain.

1:2 ***happened in your days.*** The calamity of recent days was unprecedented in the memory of the people.
1:4 ***locust.*** Many interpreters have viewed these locusts as foreign armies that attacked Judah in successive waves—Assyria, Babylon, Greece, and Rome. Yet literal locust plagues were one of the judgments promised if the people disobeyed God and broke their covenant with Him (Deut. 28:38–42). Further, Joel's description of the damage done by the locusts compares with eyewitness reports. The impression given is one of overwhelming devastation.
1:9 ***Grain offerings and drink offerings.*** This phrase refers to the wine offerings that accompanied the priests' morning and evening sacrifices (Ex. 29:38–41). The devastation of the locust meant that no sacrifice could be offered.
1:10 ***The fields are ruined.*** The fields are ruined because the three principle crops they produced—grain, grapes, and olives—had been destroyed (Deut. 7:13; Ps. 104:15).

1:1 [a] Jer 1:2 [b] Ac 2:16 **1:2** [c] Hos 5:1 [d] Hos 4:1 [e] Joel 2:2 **1:3** [f] Ex 10:2; Ps 78:4 **1:4** [g] Dt 28:39; Na 3:15 **1:5** [h] Joel 3:3 **1:6** [i] Joel 2:2, 11, 25 [j] Rev 9:8 **1:7** [k] Isa 5:6 [l] Am 4:9 **1:8** [m] ver 13; Isa 22:12; Am 8:10 **1:9** [n] Hos 9:4; Joel 2:14, 17 **1:10** [o] Isa 24:4 [p] Hos 9:2 **1:11** [q] Jer 14:3-4; Am 5:16 [r] Isa 17:11

12 The vine is dried up
and the fig tree is withered;
the pomegranate, the palm and the
apple[a] tree—
all the trees of the field—are dried up.[s]
Surely the people's joy
is withered away.

A Call to Lamentation

13 Put on sackcloth,[t] you priests, and
mourn;
wail, you who minister[u] before the
altar.
Come, spend the night in sackcloth,
you who minister before my God;
for the grain offerings and drink
offerings[v]
are withheld from the house of your
God.
14 Declare a holy fast;[w]
call a sacred assembly.
Summon the elders
and all who live in the land
to the house of the LORD your God,
and cry out[x] to the LORD.

15 Alas for that[y] day!
For the day of the LORD[z] is near;
it will come like destruction from the
Almighty.[b]

16 Has not the food been cut off[a]
before our very eyes—
joy and gladness
from the house of our God?[b]
17 The seeds are shriveled
beneath the clods.[c][c]
The storehouses are in ruins,
the granaries have been broken
down,
for the grain has dried up.
18 How the cattle moan!
The herds mill about
because they have no pasture;
even the flocks of sheep are
suffering.

19 To you, LORD, I call,[d]
for fire[e] has devoured the pastures[f] in
the wilderness
and flames have burned up all the
trees of the field.
20 Even the wild animals pant for you;[g]
the streams of water have dried up[h]
and fire has devoured the pastures in
the wilderness.

An Army of Locusts

2 Blow the trumpet[i] in Zion;[j]
sound the alarm on my holy hill.

Let all who live in the land tremble,
for the day of the LORD[k] is coming.
It is close at hand[l]—
2 a day of darkness[m] and gloom,[n]
a day of clouds and blackness.
Like dawn spreading across the
mountains
a large and mighty army[o] comes,
such as never was in ancient times[p]
nor ever will be in ages to come.

3 Before them fire devours,
behind them a flame blazes.
Before them the land is like the garden
of Eden,[q]
behind them, a desert waste[r]—
nothing escapes them.
4 They have the appearance of horses;[s]
they gallop along like cavalry.
5 With a noise like that of chariots[t]
they leap over the mountaintops,
like a crackling fire[u] consuming stubble,
like a mighty army drawn up for
battle.

6 At the sight of them, nations are in
anguish;[v]
every face turns pale.[w]
7 They charge like warriors;
they scale walls like soldiers.
They all march in line,
not swerving[x] from their course.
8 They do not jostle each other;
each marches straight ahead.
They plunge through defenses
without breaking ranks.
9 They rush upon the city;
they run along the wall.
They climb into the houses;
like thieves they enter through the
windows.[y]

[a] 12 Or possibly *apricot* [b] 15 Hebrew *Shaddai*
[c] 17 The meaning of the Hebrew for this word is uncertain.

1:15 *the day of the LORD.* This phrase refers to a time of judgment and deliverance. Joel views the locust plague as a contemporary day of judgment that was serving as a token or forewarning of an even greater, future "day of the LORD."

1:17 *The seeds are shriveled.* This indicated further devastation in the land and an inability to replant the following year.

2:1 *at hand.* The Bible presents the day of the Lord as an imminent reality. It is not something that we are gradually moving toward; rather, it is ever ready to burst in on us. At any moment, the day that is "at hand" may become present.

2:2 *darkness and gloom.* This phrase is used as a figure for misery, distress, and judgment (Is. 8:22; 60:2; Jer. 13:16).

2:4 *the appearance of horses.* Joel compared the speed and strength of the invaders to galloping horses.

1:12 [s] Hag 2:19 **1:13** [t] Jer 4:8 [u] Joel 2:17 [v] ver 9 **1:14** [w] 2Ch 20:3 [x] Jnh 3:8 **1:15** [y] Jer 30:7 [z] Isa 13:6, 9; Joel 2:1, 11, 31 **1:16** [a] Isa 3:7 [b] Dt 12:7 **1:17** [c] Isa 17:10-11 **1:19** [d] Ps 50:15 [e] Am 7:4 [f] Jer 9:10 **1:20** [g] Ps 104:21 [h] 1Ki 17:7 **2:1** [i] Jer 4:5 [j] ver 15 [k] Joel 1:15; Zep 1:14-16 [l] Ob 1:15 **2:2** [m] Am 5:18 [n] Da 9:12 [o] Joel 1:6 [p] Joel 1:2 **2:3** [q] Ge 2:8 [r] Ps 105:34-35 **2:4** [s] Rev 9:7 **2:5** [t] Rev 9:9 [u] Isa 5:24; 30:30 **2:6** [v] Isa 13:8 [w] Na 2:10 **2:7** [x] Isa 5:27 **2:9** [y] Jer 9:21

10 Before them the earth shakes,[z]
the heavens tremble,
the sun and moon are darkened,[a]
and the stars no longer shine.[b]
11 The LORD[c] thunders
at the head of his army;
his forces are beyond number,
and mighty is the army that obeys his command.
The day of the LORD is great;[d]
it is dreadful.
Who can endure it?[e]

Rend Your Heart

12 "Even now," declares the LORD,
"return[f] to me with all your heart,
with fasting and weeping and mourning."

13 Rend your heart[g]
and not your garments.[h]
Return to the LORD your God,
for he is gracious and compassionate,
slow to anger and abounding in love,[i]
and he relents from sending calamity.[j]
14 Who knows? He may turn[k] and relent
and leave behind a blessing[l]—
grain offerings and drink offerings[m]
for the LORD your God.

15 Blow the trumpet[n] in Zion,
declare a holy fast,[o]
call a sacred assembly.[p]
16 Gather the people,
consecrate[q] the assembly;
bring together the elders,
gather the children,
those nursing at the breast.
Let the bridegroom[r] leave his room
and the bride her chamber.
17 Let the priests, who minister before the LORD,
weep between the portico and the altar.[s]
Let them say, "Spare your people, LORD.
Do not make your inheritance an object of scorn,[t]
a byword among the nations.
Why should they say among the peoples,
'Where is their God?[u]'"

The LORD's Answer

18 Then the LORD was jealous[v] for his land
and took pity on his people.

19 The LORD replied[a] to them:

"I am sending you grain, new wine and olive oil,[w]
enough to satisfy you fully;
never again will I make you
an object of scorn[x] to the nations.

20 "I will drive the northern horde[y] far from you,
pushing it into a parched and barren land;
its eastern ranks will drown in the Dead Sea
and its western ranks in the Mediterranean Sea.
And its stench[z] will go up;
its smell will rise."

Surely he has done great things!
21 Do not be afraid,[a] land of Judah;
be glad and rejoice.
Surely the LORD has done great things![b]
22 Do not be afraid, you wild animals,
for the pastures in the wilderness are becoming green.[c]
The trees are bearing their fruit;
the fig tree and the vine yield their riches.[d]

[a] *18,19* Or *LORD will be jealous . . . / and take pity . . . / 19The LORD will reply*

2:11 ***Who can endure it?*** Nothing will be able to withstand the wrath of God (Matt. 24:21 – 22).
2:13 ***Rend your heart.*** God is not satisfied with outward acts of repentance. Tearing one's garments was a customary way of expressing grief or remorse (Josh. 7:6; 1 Sam. 4:12). However, like all outward acts, the tearing of a garment could be done without true sorrow or repentance. God required more than mere external words or actions; He wanted a change of heart and sorrow over sin.
2:14 ***Who knows?*** These words suggest that even at the last moment, the Lord would withhold His wrath and display His grace if the people would truly repent. As a result, agriculture would be restored and productivity would return. There would be food and drink for the people and for offerings to the Lord.
2:16 ***bridegroom ... bride.*** According to Jewish tradition codified in the Mishnah, a couple could be excused from reciting daily prayers on their wedding day. But Joel excused no one from prayer at this time of spiritual emergency.
2:17 ***Why should they say among the peoples.*** This rhetorical question was designed to move God to intervene. Failure to come to Judah's aid might encourage the nations to make a mockery of Judah's God.
2:18 – 19 ***jealous for his land.*** The deep love of God for the land of Israel is coupled with His abiding love for the people. On every occasion in which God brought judgment on the land, there was the hope that one day His zeal for the land would lead to a renewal of blessing. In response to repentance, God would bring restoration and blessing.
2:22 ***the pastures ... are becoming green ... The trees are bearing their fruit.*** The renewal of agriculture would be a sign that God had renewed prosperity and peace to His land.

2:10 [z] Ps 18:7 [a] Mt 24:29 [b] Isa 13:10; Eze 32:8
2:11 [c] Joel 1:15 [d] Zep 1:14; Rev 18:8 [e] Eze 22:14
2:12 [f] Jer 4:1; Hos 12:6 **2:13** [g] Ps 34:18; Isa 57:15
[h] Job 1:20 [i] Ex 34:6 [j] Jer 18:8 **2:14** [k] Jer 26:3 [l] Hag 2:19
[m] Joel 1:13 **2:15** [n] Nu 10:2 [o] Jer 36:9 [p] Joel 1:14
2:16 [q] Ex 19:10,22 [r] Ps 19:5 **2:17** [s] Eze 8:16; Mt 23:35
[t] Dt 9:26-29; Ps 44:13 [u] Ps 42:3 **2:18** [v] Zec 1:14
2:19 [w] Jer 31:12 [x] Eze 34:29 **2:20** [y] Jer 1:14-15 [z] Isa 34:3
2:21 [a] Isa 54:4; Zep 3:16-17 [b] Ps 126:3 **2:22** [c] Ps 65:12
[d] Joel 1:18-20

23 Be glad, people of Zion,
rejoice[e] in the LORD your God,
for he has given you the autumn rains
because he is faithful.
He sends you abundant showers,
both autumn and spring rains,[f] as
before.
24 The threshing floors will be filled with
grain;
the vats will overflow[g] with new
wine[h] and oil.

25 "I will repay you for the years the
locusts have eaten—
the great locust and the young locust,
the other locusts and the locust
swarm[a]—
my great army that I sent among you.
26 You will have plenty to eat, until you
are full,[i]
and you will praise[j] the name of the
LORD your God,
who has worked wonders[k] for you;
never again will my people be shamed.
27 Then you will know that I am in Israel,
that I am the LORD[l] your God,
and that there is no other;
never again will my people be shamed.

The Day of the LORD

28 "And afterward,
I will pour out my Spirit[m] on all
people.
Your sons and daughters will prophesy,
your old men will dream dreams,
your young men will see visions.
29 Even on my servants,[n] both men and
women,
I will pour out my Spirit in those days.
30 I will show wonders in the heavens[o]
and on the earth,[p]
blood and fire and billows of smoke.
31 The sun will be turned to darkness[q]
and the moon to blood
before the coming of the great and
dreadful day of the LORD.[r]
32 And everyone who calls
on the name of the LORD will be
saved;[s]
for on Mount Zion[t] and in Jerusalem
there will be deliverance,[u]
as the LORD has said,
even among the survivors[v]
whom the LORD calls.[b]

The Nations Judged

3 [c] "In those days and at that time,
when I restore the fortunes[w] of Judah
and Jerusalem,
2 I will gather all nations
and bring them down to the Valley of
Jehoshaphat.[d]
There I will put them on trial[x]
for what they did to my inheritance,
my people Israel,
because they scattered my people
among the nations
and divided up my land.
3 They cast lots for my people
and traded boys for prostitutes;
they sold girls for wine[y] to
drink.

4 "Now what have you against me, Tyre
and Sidon[z] and all you regions of Philistia? Are you repaying me for something
I have done? If you are paying me back,
I will swiftly and speedily return on your
own heads what you have done.[a] 5 For you
took my silver and my gold and carried off
my finest treasures to your temples.[e][b] 6 You
sold the people of Judah and Jerusalem to
the Greeks, that you might send them far
from their homeland.
7 "See, I am going to rouse them out of the
places to which you sold them,[c] and I will
return on your own heads what you have
done. 8 I will sell your sons[d] and daughters
to the people of Judah,[e] and they will sell
them to the Sabeans, a nation far away."
The LORD has spoken.

9 Proclaim this among the nations:
Prepare for war![f]
Rouse the warriors![g]
Let all the fighting men draw near
and attack.

---

[a] *25* The precise meaning of the four Hebrew words used here for locusts is uncertain. [b] *32* In Hebrew texts 2:28-32 is numbered 3:1-5. [c] In Hebrew texts 3:1-21 is numbered 4:1-21. [d] *2* *Jehoshaphat* means *the LORD judges*; also in verse 12. [e] *5* Or *palaces*

2:28–32 ***I will pour out my Spirit on all people.*** Peter quotes this passage on the Day of Pentecost (Acts 2:17–21) to explain the miracle of speaking in tongues. There are three main viewpoints regarding how Peter uses Joel's prophecy: (1) Some interpreters see a complete fulfillment of Joel's prophecy in the experience of the first believers on the Day of Pentecost; (2) some interpreters believe that Peter was simply using Joel's prophecy as an illustration of what was happening. In effect, Peter was saying, "This is that same Holy Spirit which was spoken of by Joel"; (3) some others suggest that Joel's prophecy was partially fulfilled on the Day of Pentecost. The gift of the Holy Spirit was given, but the signs mentioned in verses 30–32 will be fulfilled later in connection with the return of Christ in great glory.

3:2 ***Valley of Jehoshaphat.*** The name Jehoshaphat means "the Lord judges." The location of this valley is not known. Perhaps this was merely a symbolic name for the location of the great battle in the end times.

2:23 [e] Ps 149:2; Isa 12:6; 41:16; Hab 3:18; Zec 10:7 [f] Lev 26:4 **2:24** [g] Lev 26:10; Mal 3:10 [h] Am 9:13 **2:26** [i] Lev 26:5 [j] Isa 62:9 [k] Ps 126:3; Isa 25:1 **2:27** [l] Joel 3:17 **2:28** [m] Eze 39:29 **2:29** [n] 1Co 12:13; Gal 3:28 **2:30** [o] Lk 21:11 [p] Mk 13:24-25 **2:31** [q] Mt 24:29 [r] Isa 13:9-10; Mal 4:1,5 **2:32** [s] Ac 2:17-21*; Ro 10:13* [t] Isa 46:13 [u] Ob 1:17 [v] Isa 11:11; Mic 4:7; Ro 9:27 **3:1** [w] Jer 16:15 **3:2** [x] Eze 36:5 **3:3** [y] Am 2:6 **3:4** [z] Mt 11:21 [a] Isa 34:8 **3:5** [b] 2Ch 21:16-17 **3:7** [c] Isa 43:5-6; Jer 23:8 **3:8** [d] Isa 60:14 [e] Isa 14:2 **3:9** [f] Isa 8:9 [g] Jer 46:4

10 Beat your plowshares into swords
and your pruning hooks[h] into spears.
Let the weakling[i] say,
"I am strong!"
11 Come quickly, all you nations from every side,
and assemble[j] there.

Bring down your warriors,[k] LORD!

12 "Let the nations be roused;
let them advance into the Valley of Jehoshaphat,
for there I will sit
to judge[l] all the nations on every side.
13 Swing the sickle,
for the harvest[m] is ripe.
Come, trample the grapes,
for the winepress[n] is full
and the vats overflow—
so great is their wickedness!"

14 Multitudes, multitudes
in the valley of decision!
For the day of the LORD[o] is near
in the valley of decision.
15 The sun and moon will be darkened,
and the stars no longer shine.
16 The LORD will roar from Zion
and thunder from Jerusalem;[p]
the earth and the heavens will tremble.[q]
But the LORD will be a refuge for his people,
a stronghold[r] for the people of Israel.

Blessings for God's People

17 "Then you will know that I, the LORD your God,[s]
dwell in Zion,[t] my holy hill.
Jerusalem will be holy;
never again will foreigners invade her.

18 "In that day the mountains will drip new wine,
and the hills will flow with milk;[u]
all the ravines of Judah will run with water.[v]
A fountain will flow out of the LORD's house[w]
and will water the valley of acacias.[a][x]
19 But Egypt will be desolate,
Edom a desert waste,
because of violence[y] done to the people of Judah,
in whose land they shed innocent blood.
20 Judah will be inhabited forever[z]
and Jerusalem through all generations.
21 Shall I leave their innocent blood unavenged?
No, I will not.[a]"

The LORD dwells in Zion!

[a] 18 Or *Valley of Shittim*

3:11 *nations ... warriors.* Joel saw two different armies assembling for battle (Mark 8:38; Rev. 19:14).
3:14 *the valley of decision.* This may be a symbolic name for the Valley of Jehoshaphat (v. 2), or it may refer to the option before the people to continue toward certain judgment or to turn to God in repentance (vv. 12–13).
3:18 *In that day.* These words indicate the prophetic future. Joel uses poetic imagery to describe the productivity of the land in the last days. The Valley of Acacias was the location of the last encampment before the Israelites entered Canaan (Num. 25:1; Josh. 3:1).

3:10 [h] Isa 2:4; Mic 4:3 [i] Zec 12:8 **3:11** [j] Eze 38:15-16; Zep 3:8 [k] Isa 13:3 **3:12** [l] Isa 2:4 **3:13** [m] Hos 6:11; Mt 13:39; Rev 14:15-19 [n] Rev 14:20 **3:14** [o] Isa 34:2-8; Joel 1:15 **3:16** [p] Am 1:2 [q] Eze 38:19 [r] Jer 16:19 **3:17** [s] Joel 2:27 [t] Isa 4:3 **3:18** [u] Ex 3:8 [v] Isa 30:25; 35:6 [w] Rev 22:1-2 [x] Eze 47:1; Am 9:13 **3:19** [y] Ob 1:10 **3:20** [z] Am 9:15 **3:21** [a] Eze 36:25

AMOS

▶ **AUTHOR:** The only Old Testament appearance of the name Amos is in this book. Amos's objective appraisal of Israel's spiritual condition was not well received, not least because he was just a farmer from Judah. The author said of his background, "I was neither a prophet nor the son of a prophet, but I was a shepherd, and I also took care of sycamore-fig trees." (7:14). He delivered his message in Bethel because it was the residence of the king of Israel and a center of idolatry.

▶ **TIME:** c. 760 – 753 B.C. ▶ **KEY VERSES:** Amos 3:1 – 2

▶ **THEME:** Amos was a contemporary of Isaiah and Hosea. The unusual aspect of his ministry is that he was a farmer and herdsman from Judah prophesying to the northern Israel. The issues he addresses are the usual prophetic concerns, but with a heavy emphasis on social justice. When injustice is rampant, expect God's judgment. No one is immune. In fact, the more God has given, the more God expects in response.

1 The words of Amos, one of the shepherds of Tekoa[a]—the vision he saw concerning Israel two years before the earthquake,[b] when Uzziah[c] was king of Judah
and Jeroboam[d] son of Jehoash[a] was king
of Israel.[e]
2He said:

"The LORD roars[f] from Zion
 and thunders from Jerusalem;[g]
the pastures of the shepherds dry up,
 and the top of Carmel[h] withers."[i]

Judgment on Israel's Neighbors

3This is what the LORD says:

"For three sins of Damascus,[j]
 even for four, I will not relent.[k]
Because she threshed Gilead
 with sledges having iron teeth,
4I will send fire[l] on the house of Hazael
 that will consume the fortresses[m] of
 Ben-Hadad.[n]
5I will break down the gate[o] of
 Damascus;
 I will destroy the king who is in[b] the
 Valley of Aven[c]
and the one who holds the scepter in
 Beth Eden.
 The people of Aram will go into exile
 to Kir,[p]"
 says the LORD.

6This is what the LORD says:

"For three sins of Gaza,[q]
 even for four, I will not relent.

[a] *1* Hebrew *Joash,* a variant of *Jehoash*
[b] *5* Or *the inhabitants of* [c] *5 Aven* means *wickedness.*

1:1 – 2:16 *The words of Amos.* The Lord sent Amos, a Judean, to Bethel to prophesy of coming judgment on Israel. But in Bethel, Amos faced a hostile audience. Israel's first king, Jeroboam I, had made the town a center of pagan worship. Because the temple in Jerusalem was in Judah and not in the nation of Israel, Jeroboam had encouraged the Israelites to worship at Bethel instead of Jerusalem. Thus the Israelites who gathered at Bethel would regard Amos, a Judean, with suspicion. Yet Amos bravely condemned there the sins of Israel's neighbors. He also points to the iniquity of Israel and Judah. They both had rejected the God who had covenanted with them.
1:1 *Tekoa.* This town was about ten miles south of Jerusalem, in a region well suited for raising sheep and goats.
1:3 *For three . . . even for four.* This stylistic device indicated the exhaustion of God's patience—the Syrians had continued to sin, again and again. This device is repeated as Amos speaks God's words against nation after sinful nation. ***Gilead.*** This was the region on the east side of the Jordan from the Yarmuk River to the Dead Sea.
1:4 *I will send fire . . . consume the fortresses.* Fire in an ancient city was a real threat. Cities were crowded with houses close together on very narrow streets; there was too little water to effectively fight them.
1:5 *the gate.* If the gate was broken, the city would lose its security and could be captured easily.
1:6 *Gaza.* This was one of the five principal cities of the Philistines.

1:1 [a] 2Sa 14:2 [b] Zec 14:5 [c] 2Ch 26:23 [d] 2Ki 14:23 [e] Hos 1:1 **1:2** [f] Isa 42:13 [g] Joel 3:16 [h] Am 9:3 [i] Jer 12:4 **1:3** [j] Isa 8:4; 17:1-3 [k] Am 2:6 **1:4** [l] Jer 49:27 [m] Jer 17:27 [n] 1Ki 20:1; 2Ki 6:24 **1:5** [o] Jer 51:30 [p] 2Ki 16:9 **1:6** [q] 1Sa 6:17; Zep 2:4

Because she took captive whole
communities
and sold them to Edom,[r]
7 I will send fire on the walls of Gaza
that will consume her fortresses.
8 I will destroy the king[a] of Ashdod[s]
and the one who holds the scepter in
Ashkelon.
I will turn my hand[t] against Ekron,
till the last of the Philistines[u] are
dead,"
says the Sovereign LORD.[v]

9 This is what the LORD says:

"For three sins of Tyre,[w]
even for four, I will not relent.
Because she sold whole communities of
captives to Edom,
disregarding a treaty of brotherhood,
10 I will send fire on the walls of Tyre
that will consume her fortresses.[x]"

11 This is what the LORD says:

"For three sins of Edom,[y]
even for four, I will not relent.
Because he pursued his brother with a
sword
and slaughtered the women of the
land,
because his anger raged continually
and his fury flamed unchecked,[z]
12 I will send fire on Teman[a]
that will consume the fortresses of
Bozrah."

13 This is what the LORD says:

"For three sins of Ammon,[b]
even for four, I will not relent.
Because he ripped open the pregnant
women[c] of Gilead
in order to extend his borders,
14 I will set fire to the walls of Rabbah[d]
that will consume her fortresses
amid war cries[e] on the day of battle,
amid violent winds on a stormy day.
15 Her king[b] will go into exile,
he and his officials together,"
says the LORD.

2 This is what the LORD says:

"For three sins of Moab,
even for four, I will not relent.
Because he burned to ashes
the bones of Edom's king,
2 I will send fire on Moab
that will consume the fortresses of
Kerioth.[c]
Moab will go down in great tumult
amid war cries and the blast of the
trumpet.
3 I will destroy her ruler[f]
and kill all her officials with him,"[g]
says the LORD.

4 This is what the LORD says:

"For three sins of Judah,[h]
even for four, I will not relent.
Because they have rejected the law[i] of
the LORD
and have not kept his decrees,[j]
because they have been led astray[k] by
false gods,[d][l]
the gods[e] their ancestors followed,[m]
5 I will send fire on Judah
that will consume the fortresses of
Jerusalem.[n]"

Judgment on Israel

6 This is what the LORD says:

"For three sins of Israel,
even for four, I will not relent.
They sell the innocent for silver,
and the needy for a pair of sandals.[o]
7 They trample on the heads of the poor
as on the dust of the ground
and deny justice to the oppressed.
Father and son use the same girl
and so profane my holy name.[p]
8 They lie down beside every altar
on garments taken in pledge.[q]
In the house of their god
they drink wine[r] taken as fines.

[a] 8 Or *inhabitants* [b] 15 Or / *Molek* [c] 2 Or *of her cities* [d] 4 Or *by lies* [e] 4 Or *lies*

1:11 *Edom.* This nation was located southeast of the Dead Sea. It controlled important caravan trade routes, and thus was deeply involved in commerce. Its citizens were descendants of Esau.

1:13 *Ammon.* The nation of Ammon was located east of Gilead on the edge of the desert. Its people were descended from one of the sons of Lot (Gen. 19:36–38).

2:1 *burned ... the bones.* This act was believed to desecrate the remains of a deceased person, a heinous act in ancient times and a great dishonor to the person's memory.

2:6 *sell the innocent for silver.* In His law, God had instructed the Israelites to work off their debts through indentured service—administered humanely and for a strictly limited time (Lev. 25:39–43; Deut. 15:12). By Amos' day, those in power in Israel were taking advantage of the courts to sell debtors as slaves, termed "the innocent" here because they were the innocent victims of the corruption of the courts. ***for a pair of sandals.*** This means for little or nothing.

2:7 *poor.* Those without power or influence should have been able to depend on the justice due them. Instead, justice was denied them. As a result, their lives were turned to poverty, oppression, and insecurity.

2:8 *garments taken in pledge.* Clothing taken as

1:6 [r] Ob 1:11 **1:8** [s] 2Ch 26:6 [t] Ps 81:14 [u] Eze 25:16 [v] Isa 14:28-32; Zep 2:4-7 **1:9** [w] 1Ki 5:1; 9:11-14; Isa 23:1-18; Jer 25:22; Joel 3:4; Mt 11:21 **1:10** [x] Zec 9:1-4 **1:11** [y] Nu 20:14-21; 2Ch 28:17; Jer 49:7-22 [z] Eze 25:12-14 **1:12** [a] Ob 1:9-10 **1:13** [b] Jer 49:1-6; Eze 21:28; 25:2-7 [c] Hos 13:16 **1:14** [d] Dt 3:11 [e] Am 2:2 **2:3** [f] Ps 2:10 [g] Isa 40:23 **2:4** [h] 2Ki 17:19; Hos 12:2 [i] Jer 6:19 [j] Eze 20:24 [k] Isa 9:16 [l] Isa 28:15 [m] 2Ki 22:13; Jer 16:12 **2:5** [n] Jer 17:27; Hos 8:14 **2:6** [o] Joel 3:3; Am 8:6 **2:7** [p] Am 5:11-12; 8:4 **2:8** [q] Ex 22:26 [r] Am 4:1; 6:6

9 "Yet I destroyed the Amorites[s] before them,
though they were tall as the cedars
and strong as the oaks.
I destroyed their fruit above
and their roots[t] below.
10 I brought you up out of Egypt[u]
and led you forty years in the wilderness[v]
to give you the land of the Amorites.[w]

11 "I also raised up prophets[x] from among your children
and Nazirites[y] from among your youths.
Is this not true, people of Israel?"
declares the LORD.
12 "But you made the Nazirites drink wine
and commanded the prophets not to prophesy.[z]

13 "Now then, I will crush you
as a cart crushes when loaded with grain.
14 The swift will not escape,
the strong[a] will not muster their strength,
and the warrior will not save his life.[b]
15 The archer[c] will not stand his ground,
the fleet-footed soldier will not get away,
and the horseman will not save his life.
16 Even the bravest warriors[d]
will flee naked on that day,"
declares the LORD.

Witnesses Summoned Against Israel

3 Hear this word, people of Israel, the
word the LORD has spoken against
you—against the whole family I brought
up out of Egypt:[e]

2 "You only have I chosen[f]
of all the families of the earth;
therefore I will punish you
for all your sins.[g]"

3 Do two walk together
unless they have agreed to do so?
4 Does a lion roar in the thicket
when it has no prey?[h]
Does it growl in its den
when it has caught nothing?
5 Does a bird swoop down to a trap on the ground
when no bait is there?
Does a trap spring up from the ground
if it has not caught anything?
6 When a trumpet sounds in a city,
do not the people tremble?
When disaster comes to a city,
has not the LORD caused it?[i]

7 Surely the Sovereign LORD does nothing
without revealing his plan[j]
to his servants the prophets.[k]

8 The lion has roared—
who will not fear?
The Sovereign LORD has spoken—
who can but prophesy?[l]

9 Proclaim to the fortresses of Ashdod
and to the fortresses of Egypt:
"Assemble yourselves on the mountains of Samaria;[m]
see the great unrest within her
and the oppression among her people."

---

security for a loan was supposed to be returned in the evening so that it could be used as bedding for the poor (Ex. 22:26–27). The powerful in Israel were spreading the clothes out as beds for themselves beside the altars, in a show of empty, merciless piety.

2:9 ***Yet I destroyed.*** This emphatic statement underscores the fact that God had been Israel's champion, and the nation's success had not been its own doing. ***the Amorites.*** This refers to the previous inhabitants of the land of Canaan.

3:1 ***the whole family I brought up.*** This phrase emphasizes the personal, intimate relationship that God had with Israel.

3:2 ***You only have I chosen.*** God's relationship with Israel was not only intimate, it was exclusive. God had been faithful to Israel, yet Israel had not been faithful to God. For this reason, the nation would be judged.

3:2 Selection of Israel—The selection of Israel as a special nation to God was part of God's plan (Rom. 11:2). Historically, the selection of Israel began with the Lord's promise to Abraham, "I will make you into a great nation" (Gen. 12:2). The name Israel actually comes from the new name which God gave to Abraham's grandson, Jacob, when they fought at the ford of Jabbok (Gen. 32:28). This fact explains why his descendants are often called the children of Israel.

The motivation for the Lord's choice of Israel as His select nation did not lay in any special attraction the nation possessed. Its people were, in fact, the least in number among all the nations (Deut. 7:6–8). Rather, the Lord chose them because of His love for them and because of His covenant with Abraham. This fact does not mean that God did not love other nations, because it was through Israel that He blessed all nations in Christ.

3:3–6 ***Do two walk together ... ?*** This series of rhetorical questions illustrates the seriousness, certainty, and righteousness of God's impending action against Israel. Each question is framed so as to require a resounding "no" as its answer.

2:9 [s] Nu 21:23-26; Jos 10:12 [t] Eze 17:9; Mal 4:1
2:10 [u] Ex 20:2; Am 3:1 [v] Dt 2:7 [w] Ex 3:8; Am 9:7
2:11 [x] Dt 18:18; Jer 7:25 [y] Nu 6:2-3; Jdg 13:5
2:12 [z] Isa 30:10; Jer 11:21; Am 7:12-13; Mic 2:6
2:14 [a] Jer 9:23 [b] Ps 33:16; Isa 30:16-17 **2:15** [c] Eze 39:3
2:16 [d] Jer 48:41 **3:1** [e] Am 2:10 **3:2** [f] Dt 7:6; Lk 12:47
[g] Jer 14:10 **3:4** [h] Ps 104:21; Hos 5:14 **3:6** [i] Isa 14:24-27; 45:7 **3:7** [j] Ge 18:17; Da 9:22; Jn 15:15; Rev 10:7
[k] Jer 23:22 **3:8** [l] Jer 20:9; Jnh 1:1-3; 3:1-3; Ac 4:20
3:9 [m] Am 4:1; 6:1

[10]"They do not know how to do right,[n]"
declares the LORD,
"who store up in their fortresses[o]
what they have plundered[p] and
looted."

[11]Therefore this is what the Sovereign
LORD says:

"An enemy will overrun your land,
pull down your strongholds
and plunder your fortresses.[q]"

[12]This is what the LORD says:

"As a shepherd rescues from the lion's[r]
mouth
only two leg bones or a piece of an
ear,
so will the Israelites living in Samaria
be rescued,
with only the head of a bed
and a piece of fabric[a] from a couch.[bs]"

[13]"Hear this and testify[t] against the descendants of Jacob," declares the Lord, the
LORD God Almighty.

[14]"On the day I punish Israel for her sins,
I will destroy the altars of Bethel;[u]
the horns of the altar will be cut off
and fall to the ground.
[15]I will tear down the winter house[v]
along with the summer house;[w]
the houses adorned with ivory[x] will be
destroyed
and the mansions will be
demolished,"
declares the LORD.

Israel Has Not Returned to God

4 Hear this word, you cows of Bashan[y]
on Mount Samaria,[z]
you women who oppress the poor and
crush the needy
and say to your husbands, "Bring us
some drinks![a]"

[2]The Sovereign LORD has sworn by his
holiness:
"The time will surely come
when you will be taken away[b] with
hooks,
the last of you with fishhooks.[c]
[3]You will each go straight out
through breaches in the wall,[c]
and you will be cast out toward
Harmon,[d]"
declares the LORD.

[4]"Go to Bethel and sin;
go to Gilgal[d] and sin yet more.
Bring your sacrifices every
morning,[e]
your tithes[f] every three years.[eg]
[5]Burn leavened bread[h] as a thank
offering
and brag about your freewill
offerings[i]—
boast about them, you Israelites,
for this is what you love to do,"
declares the Sovereign LORD.

[6]"I gave you empty stomachs in every
city
and lack of bread in every town,
yet you have not returned to me,"
declares the LORD.[j]

[7]"I also withheld rain from you
when the harvest was still three
months away.
I sent rain on one town,
but withheld it from another.[k]
One field had rain;
another had none and dried up.

---

[a] *12* The meaning of the Hebrew for this phrase is uncertain. [b] *12* Or *Israelites be rescued, / those who sit in Samaria / on the edge of their beds / and in Damascus on their couches.* [c] *2* Or *away in baskets, / the last of you in fish baskets* [d] *3* Masoretic Text; with a different word division of the Hebrew (see Septuagint) *out, you mountain of oppression* [e] *4* Or *days*

3:11 ***An enemy will overrun your land.*** This verse pictures a formal sentencing of Israel in the presence of the witnesses whom God had called (v. 9). Sapping Israel's strength was exactly what Assyria did in the years following Amos' prophecies, finally putting an end to the nation in 722 B.C.
3:12 ***As a shepherd rescues from the lion's mouth.*** The hired shepherd was responsible to the owner for the safety of the sheep. He had to make good any loss, unless he could prove it was unavoidable. A lion taking a sheep was an unavoidable loss, but the shepherd had to prove that the lion had taken it. A couple of small bones or a piece of an ear was sufficient; the owner would recognize the lion's work. As complete as the destruction of a sheep by a lion would be the destruction of Israel that God would bring.
3:15 ***the mansions will be demolished.*** The four houses mentioned here were all symbols of oppression. Many small inheritances had been stolen to form the large estates of the wealthy and powerful, where they built their opulent houses.
4:1 ***cows of Bashan.*** This phrase refers to the well-fed women of Samaria. Bashan, the region east and northeast of the Sea of Galilee, was a prime grassland area renowned for its cattle.
4:3 ***breaches in the wall.*** These were a symbol of the thoroughness of the destruction of the city and the homes that the people held so dear. In an undamaged city, the usual way in and out was the one main gate. But Samaria would be so ruined that the deportees would be driven straight through the breaches in the walls of their houses and their city.
4:6–11 ***you have not returned to me.*** This passage describes a series of five calamities that God had already sent upon the Israelites in an effort to drive them to repentance. A striking feature of this

3:10 [n] Jer 4:22; Am 5:7; 6:12 [o] Zep 1:9 [p] Hab 2:8
3:11 [q] Am 2:5; 6:14 **3:12** [r] 1Sa 17:34 [s] Am 6:4
3:13 [t] Eze 2:7 **3:14** [u] Am 5:5-6 **3:15** [v] Jer 36:22
[w] Jdg 3:20 [x] 1Ki 22:39 **4:1** [y] Ps 22:12; Eze 39:18 [z] Am 3:9
[a] Am 2:8; 5:11; 8:6 **4:2** [b] Am 6:8 **4:3** [c] Eze 12:5
4:4 [d] Hos 4:15 [e] Nu 28:3 [f] Dt 14:28 [g] Eze 20:39; Am 5:21-22 **4:5** [h] Lev 7:13 [i] Lev 22:18-21 **4:6** [j] Isa 3:1; Jer 5:3; Hag 2:17 **4:7** [k] Ex 9:4, 26; Dt 11:17; 2Ch 7:13

8 People staggered from town to town for
water[l]
but did not get enough to drink,
yet you have not returned[m] to me,"
declares the LORD.[n]

9 "Many times I struck your gardens and
vineyards,
destroying them with blight and
mildew.[o]
Locusts devoured your fig and olive
trees,[p]
yet you have not returned[q] to me,"
declares the LORD.

10 "I sent plagues[r] among you
as I did to Egypt.
I killed your young men with the sword,
along with your captured horses.
I filled your nostrils with the stench of
your camps,
yet you have not returned to me,"
declares the LORD.[s]

11 "I overthrew some of you
as I overthrew Sodom and
Gomorrah.[t]
You were like a burning stick snatched
from the fire,
yet you have not returned to me,"
declares the LORD.

12 "Therefore this is what I will do to you,
Israel,
and because I will do this to you,
Israel,
prepare to meet your God."

13 He who forms the mountains,[u]
who creates the wind,
and who reveals his thoughts[v] to
mankind,
who turns dawn to darkness,
and treads on the heights of the
earth[w]—
the LORD God Almighty is his name.[x]

A Lament and Call to Repentance

5 Hear this word, Israel, this lament[y] I
take up concerning you:

2 "Fallen is Virgin[z] Israel,
never to rise again,
deserted in her own land,
with no one to lift her up.[a]"

3 This is what the Sovereign LORD says
to Israel:

"Your city that marches out a thousand
strong
will have only a hundred left;
your town that marches out a hundred
strong
will have only ten left.[b]"

4 This is what the LORD says to Israel:

"Seek me and live;[c]
5 do not seek Bethel,
do not go to Gilgal,[d]
do not journey to Beersheba.[e]
For Gilgal will surely go into exile,
and Bethel will be reduced to
nothing.[a][f]"

6 Seek[g] the LORD and live,[h]
or he will sweep through the tribes of
Joseph like a fire;[i]
it will devour them,
and Bethel[j] will have no one to
quench it.

7 There are those who turn justice into
bitterness[k]
and cast righteousness to the ground.

8 He who made the Pleiades and Orion,[l]
who turns midnight into dawn[m]
and darkens day into night,[n]
who calls for the waters of the sea
and pours them out over the face of
the land—
the LORD is his name.[o]

[a] 5 Hebrew *aven*, a reference to Beth Aven (a derogatory name for Bethel); see Hosea 4:15.

narrative is God's emphatic claim that the Israelites had brought these disasters on themselves. They had repeatedly failed to understand the implications of the disasters.
4:10 *as I did to Egypt.* This fourth calamity suggests that God was reminding Israel of the ten plagues that preceded their exodus from Egypt; these included epidemic diseases and other disasters.
4:11 *like a burning stick snatched from the fire.* This refers to a stick snatched from a fire with one end already ablaze. Here it was a vivid metaphor for God's last-minute rescue of most of Israel from the fate He brought upon some of its cities and territories.
4:12 *prepare to meet your God.* Because Israel had not returned to God through these five calamities, it would have to meet God Himself. To be confronted—inescapably—by the God it had scorned and rejected would be a fate more terrible than Israel could imagine.
5:2 *Virgin Israel.* This term depicts the nation as a young maiden, cut off from her life before it had really begun. ***in her own land.*** This is a reminder that the land had been God's gift to Israel. By their faithlessness, the people had turned God's gift into the place of their death and burial.
5:6 *the tribes of Joseph.* This phrase refers to the whole nation.
5:8 *the Pleiades.* This refers to a cluster of stars within the constellation Taurus, one of the twelve signs of the Zodiac. One of Israel's idolatries was astral worship. Far from being deities, Amos asserted, the constellations also were God's creations. ***Orion.*** This is a reference to a prominent constellation in the southern sky in the shape of a hunter.

4:8 [l] Eze 4:16-17 [m] Jer 3:7 [n] Jer 14:4 **4:9** [o] Dt 28:22 [p] Joel 1:7 [q] Jer 3:10; Hag 2:17 **4:10** [r] Ex 9:3; Dt 28:27 [s] Isa 9:13 **4:11** [t] Ge 19:24; Jer 23:14 **4:13** [u] Ps 65:6 [v] Da 2:28 [w] Mic 1:3 [x] Isa 47:4; Am 5:8, 27; 9:6
5:1 [y] Eze 19:1 **5:2** [z] Jer 14:17 [a] Jer 50:32; Am 8:14
5:3 [b] Isa 6:13; Am 6:9 **5:4** [c] Isa 55:3; Jer 29:13
5:5 [d] 1Sa 11:14; Am 4:4 [e] Am 8:14 [f] 1Sa 7:16
5:6 [g] Isa 55:6 [h] ver 14 [i] Dt 4:24 [j] Am 3:14 **5:7** [k] Am 6:12
5:8 [l] Job 9:9 [m] Isa 42:16 [n] Ps 104:20; Am 8:9 [o] Ps 104:6-9; Am 4:13

9 With a blinding flash he destroys the stronghold
and brings the fortified city to ruin.[p]

10 There are those who hate the one who upholds justice in court[q]
and detest the one who tells the truth.[r]

11 You levy a straw tax on the poor[s]
and impose a tax on their grain.
Therefore, though you have built stone mansions,[t]
you will not live in them;
though you have planted lush vineyards,
you will not drink their wine.[u]
12 For I know how many are your offenses
and how great your sins.

There are those who oppress the innocent and take bribes
and deprive the poor of justice in the courts.[v]
13 Therefore the prudent keep quiet in such times,
for the times are evil.

14 Seek good, not evil,
that you may live.
Then the LORD God Almighty will be with you,
just as you say he is.
15 Hate evil,[w] love good;
maintain justice in the courts.
Perhaps the LORD God Almighty will have mercy[x]
on the remnant[y] of Joseph.

16 Therefore this is what the Lord, the LORD God Almighty, says:

"There will be wailing[z] in all the streets
and cries of anguish in every public square.
The farmers[a] will be summoned to weep
and the mourners to wail.
17 There will be wailing in all the vineyards,
for I will pass through[b] your midst,"
says the LORD.[c]

The Day of the LORD

18 Woe to you who long
for the day of the LORD![d]
Why do you long for the day of the LORD?
That day will be darkness,[e] not light.[f]
19 It will be as though a man fled from a lion
only to meet a bear,
as though he entered his house
and rested his hand on the wall
only to have a snake bite him.[g]
20 Will not the day of the LORD be darkness, not light—
pitch-dark, without a ray of brightness?[h]

21 "I hate, I despise your religious festivals;[i]
your assemblies[j] are a stench to me.

5:10 ***court.*** This was the location of the town's gate, where justice was to be upheld in all legal proceedings whether civil or criminal.

5:11 – 15 God's Justice—The Israelites in Amos' day had lost sight of God's commands to treat the poor compassionately. There is no record that Israel ever practiced the year of Jubilee (Lev. 25:11) that is part of Old Testament law for instance.

As many of the prophets did, Amos called on the Israelites to practice justice and see to it that the poor were not abused. He made it clear that the rich in his day were taking advantage of the poor. The justice system was ineffective because of rampant bribery. The prophets repeatedly made the point that the sacrifices were not enough. The sacrificial process needed to be connected with a response in behavior. God's justice demanded more than the sacrifices. It demanded obedience.

Amos teaches us to be observant about where this injustice is being practiced. He teaches us to look for movements, forces, or programs that can work against the accumulation of power and unjustly gained wealth.

One of the first things the Jerusalem church did when it formed was to put in place a system of some kind to care for the widows and orphans (Acts 6:1 – 4). Belief in God included an understanding of His desire for justice and the believer's need to act on it.

5:11 ***tax on their grain.*** To take grain taxes from the poor was to put them at risk of starvation if the harvest had not been bountiful. Yet the rich and powerful had sufficient resources to build luxurious houses for themselves. God promised that the rich would not enjoy their luxury stolen from the lifeblood of the poor and powerless.

5:12 ***your offenses.*** Israel's leaders did not sin incidentally or furtively; they sinned brazenly and habitually, as though God had never revealed Himself and His standards of justice and mercy.

5:18 ***the day of the LORD.*** The popular theology of Amos' time apparently looked forward to this day as the time of Israel's restoration to military, political, and economic greatness, perhaps to the greatness of the reigns of David and Solomon. Amos declared such hopes futile, even pitiable. What the people looked forward to as a day of light and triumph would rise upon them instead as a day of darkness and ruin.

5:19 ***bear . . . snake.*** These images evoke the terror that follows when a person escapes a terrible danger and is exhausted and relieved, only to find a worse danger so close at hand that it is inescapable.

5:21 – 23 ***festivals . . . assemblies.*** By stating He would no longer accept Israel's sacrifices or listen to them, God was rejecting Israel's worship as hypocritical, dishonest, and meaningless.

5:9 [p] Mic 5:11 **5:10** [q] Isa 29:21 [r] 1Ki 22:8 **5:11** [s] Am 8:6 [t] Am 3:15 [u] Mic 6:15 **5:12** [v] Isa 5:23; Am 2:6-7 **5:15** [w] Ps 97:10; Ro 12:9 [x] Joel 2:14 [y] Mic 5:7,8 **5:16** [z] Jer 9:17 [a] Joel 1:11 **5:17** [b] Ex 12:12 [c] Isa 16:10; Jer 48:33 **5:18** [d] Joel 1:15 [e] Joel 2:2 [f] Isa 5:19,30; Jer 30:7 **5:19** [g] Job 20:24; Isa 24:17-18; Jer 15:2-3; 48:44 **5:20** [h] Isa 13:10; Zep 1:15 **5:21** [i] Lev 26:31 [j] Isa 1:11-16

22 Even though you bring me burnt
offerings and grain offerings,
I will not accept them.
Though you bring choice fellowship
offerings,
I will have no regard for them.[k]
23 Away with the noise of your songs!
I will not listen to the music of your
harps.[l]
24 But let justice[m] roll on like a river,
righteousness like a never-failing
stream![n]
25 "Did you bring me sacrifices[o] and
offerings
forty years[p] in the wilderness, people
of Israel?
26 You have lifted up the shrine of your
king,
the pedestal of your idols,
the star of your god[a]—
which you made for yourselves.
27 Therefore I will send you into exile
beyond Damascus,"
says the LORD, whose name is God
Almighty.[q]

Woe to the Complacent

6 Woe to you[r] who are complacent in
Zion,
and to you who feel secure on Mount
Samaria,
you notable men of the foremost nation,
to whom the people of Israel come![s]
2 Go to Kalneh[t] and look at it;
go from there to great Hamath,[u]
and then go down to Gath[v] in
Philistia.
Are they better off than[w] your two
kingdoms?
Is their land larger than yours?
3 You put off the day of disaster
and bring near a reign of terror.[x]
4 You lie on beds adorned with ivory
and lounge on your couches.
You dine on choice lambs
and fattened calves.[y]
5 You strum away on your harps[z] like
David
and improvise on musical
instruments.[a]
6 You drink wine[b] by the bowlful
and use the finest lotions,
but you do not grieve[c] over the ruin of
Joseph.
7 Therefore you will be among the first to
go into exile;
your feasting and lounging will end.

The LORD Abhors the Pride of Israel

8 The Sovereign LORD has sworn by himself[d]—the LORD God Almighty declares:

"I abhor[e] the pride of Jacob[f]
and detest his fortresses;
I will deliver up[g] the city
and everything in it.[h]"

9 If ten[i] people are left in one house,
they too will die. 10 And if the relative who
comes to carry the bodies out of the house
to burn them[b][j] asks anyone who might be
hiding there, "Is anyone else with you?"
and he says, "No," then he will go on to say,
"Hush![k] We must not mention the name of
the LORD."

11 For the LORD has given the command,
and he will smash the great house[l]
into pieces
and the small house into bits.[m]
12 Do horses run on the rocky crags?
Does one plow the sea[c] with
oxen?
But you have turned justice into
poison[n]
and the fruit of righteousness into
bitterness[o]—
13 you who rejoice in the conquest of Lo
Debar[d]
and say, "Did we not take Karnaim[e]
by our own strength?[p]"
14 For the LORD God Almighty declares,
"I will stir up a nation[q] against you,
Israel,
that will oppress you all the way
from Lebo Hamath[r] to the valley of
the Arabah.[s]"

[a] 26 Or *lifted up Sakkuth your king / and Kaiwan your idols, / your star-gods*; Septuagint *lifted up the shrine of Molek / and the star of your god Rephan, / their idols* [b] 10 Or *to make a funeral fire in honor of the dead* [c] 12 With a different word division of the Hebrew; Masoretic Text *plow there* [d] 13 *Lo Debar* means *nothing.* [e] 13 *Karnaim* means *horns; horn* here symbolizes strength.

5:25 *Did you bring me.* This verse is a rhetorical question with "yes" as the expected answer.
6:3 *You put off the day of disaster.* This refers to those who insisted that Israel was too strong for destruction to fall upon the nation any time soon.
6:4–6 *lambs ... calves.* This passage describes the extravagant living indulged in by the rich and paid for with the wealth stolen from the poor. Meat was a luxury for most families of the ancient Middle East, consumed only on special occasions. Meat on a daily basis was the privilege only of the rich and powerful. The upper classes of Israel were so engrossed in their own privileges and luxuries that they cared nothing for the affliction of their fellow Israelites, though it was their transgressions that had caused it.

5:22 [k] Isa 66:3; Am 4:4; Mic 6:6-7 **5:23** [l] Am 6:5
5:24 [m] Jer 22:3 [n] Mic 6:8 **5:25** [o] Isa 43:23 [p] Dt 32:17
5:27 [q] Am 4:13; Ac 7:42-43* **6:1** [r] Lk 6:24 [s] Isa 32:9-11
6:2 [t] Ge 10:10 [u] 2Ki 18:34 [v] 2Ch 26:6 [w] Na 3:8
6:3 [x] Isa 56:12; Am 9:10 **6:4** [y] Eze 34:2-3; Am 3:12
6:5 [z] Isa 5:12; Am 5:23 [a] 1Ch 15:16 **6:6** [b] Am 2:8 [c] Eze 9:4
6:8 [d] Ge 22:16; Heb 6:13 [e] Lev 26:30 [f] Ps 47:4 [g] Am 4:2
[h] Dt 32:19 **6:9** [i] Am 5:3 **6:10** [j] 1Sa 31:12 [k] Am 8:3
6:11 [l] Am 3:15 [m] Isa 55:11 **6:12** [n] Hos 10:4 [o] Am 5:7
6:13 [p] Job 8:15; Isa 28:14-15 **6:14** [q] Jer 5:15 [r] 1Ki 8:65
[s] Am 3:11

Locusts, Fire and a Plumb Line

7 This is what the Sovereign LORD
showed me:[t] He was preparing swarms
of locusts[u] after the king's share had been
harvested and just as the late crops were
coming up. 2 When they had stripped the
land clean,[v] I cried out, "Sovereign LORD,
forgive! How can Jacob survive?[w] He is so
small![x]"

3 So the LORD relented.[y]

"This will not happen," the LORD said.[z]

4 This is what the Sovereign LORD
showed me: The Sovereign LORD was calling for judgment by fire;[a] it dried up the
great deep and devoured[b] the land. 5 Then I
cried out, "Sovereign LORD, I beg you, stop!
How can Jacob survive? He is so small![c]"

6 So the LORD relented.[d]

"This will not happen either," the Sovereign LORD said.

7 This is what he showed me: The Lord
was standing by a wall that had been built
true to plumb,[a] with a plumb line[b] in his
hand. 8 And the LORD asked me, "What do
you see,[e] Amos?[f]"

"A plumb line,[g]" I replied.

Then the Lord said, "Look, I am setting
a plumb line among my people Israel; I will
spare them no longer.[h]

9 "The high places of Isaac will be destroyed
and the sanctuaries[i] of Israel will be ruined;
with my sword I will rise against the house of Jeroboam.[j]"

Amos and Amaziah

10 Then Amaziah the priest of Bethel[k]
sent a message to Jeroboam[l] king of Israel:
"Amos is raising a conspiracy[m] against you
in the very heart of Israel. The land cannot
bear all his words.[n] 11 For this is what Amos
is saying:

"'Jeroboam will die by the sword,
and Israel will surely go into exile,
away from their native land.'"

12 Then Amaziah said to Amos, "Get out,
you seer! Go back to the land of Judah.
Earn your bread there and do your prophesying there.[o] 13 Don't prophesy anymore at
Bethel, because this is the king's sanctuary
and the temple of the kingdom.[p]"

14 Amos answered Amaziah, "I was neither a prophet[q] nor the son of a prophet,
but I was a shepherd, and I also took care
of sycamore-fig trees. 15 But the LORD took
me from tending the flock[r] and said to me,
'Go, prophesy to my people Israel.'[s] 16 Now
then, hear the word of the LORD. You say,

"'Do not prophesy against[t] Israel,
and stop preaching against the descendants of Isaac.'

17 "Therefore this is what the LORD says:

"'Your wife will become a prostitute[u] in the city,
and your sons and daughters will fall by the sword.
Your land will be measured and divided up,
and you yourself will die in a pagan[c] country.
And Israel will surely go into exile,
away from their native land.[v]'"

---

[a] 7 The meaning of the Hebrew for this phrase is uncertain. [b] 7 The meaning of the Hebrew for this phrase is uncertain; also in verse 8. [c] 17 Hebrew *an unclean*

7:1 ***the king's share.*** These words imply that the king took the first harvest of hay as a tax. Thus a swarm of locusts devouring the late crop would leave the people with nothing for themselves, inflicting a crippling economic blow.

7:2–3 ***How can Jacob survive?*** If God carried out the threatened punishment, Jacob (the nation of Israel) might be destroyed. One function of the prophet was to serve as intercessor for the people before God. Amos prayed that the vision decreed in heaven might be halted before it was accomplished on earth. The basis of Amos' petition lay in the true assessment of Israel's position. They were not large and strong, as they thought; rather they were small and weak. In response to Amos' intercession, and out of His own love for Israel, God stayed His decree.

7:7–9 ***a plumb line.*** This apparatus is a string with a weight tied to one end, used to establish a vertical line so that a wall can be built straight. ***What do you see.*** Unlike the first two visions of natural disasters, the visions of the plumb line and the basket of summer fruit were not self-explanatory. God asked Amos what he saw, then explained the vision's meaning. Also unlike the first two visions, God did not give Amos opportunity to intercede, nor did He relent. These judgments would be executed. ***the house of Jeroboam.*** This is a metaphor for the nation.

7:10–11 ***Amaziah.*** Amaziah was the priest in charge of the temple at Bethel, who informed the king about the prophet who was making threats against the king's house. Amaziah was reacting to Amos' third vision which ended with God's promise to bring the sword against the house of Jeroboam. Amaziah regarded Amos' words as a political threat, and reported them not as a prophecy from God, but as Amos' call to revolt.

7:14–17 ***nor the son of a prophet.*** Amos' answer to Amaziah came in two parts. First, he denied being a prophet by profession. He did not come from a family of prophets, nor had he been trained in prophecy.

7:1 [t] Am 8:1 [u] Joel 1:4 **7:2** [v] Ex 10:15 [w] Isa 37:4 [x] Eze 11:13 **7:3** [y] Dt 32:36; Jer 26:19; Jnh 3:10 [z] Hos 11:8 **7:4** [a] Isa 66:16 [b] Dt 32:22 **7:5** [c] ver 1-2; Joel 2:17 **7:6** [d] Jnh 3:10 **7:8** [e] Jer 1:11, 13 [f] Isa 28:17; La 2:8; Am 8:2 [g] 2Ki 21:13 [h] Jer 15:6; Eze 7:2-9 **7:9** [i] Lev 26:31 [j] 2Ki 15:9; Isa 63:18; Hos 10:8 **7:10** [k] 1Ki 12:32 [l] 2Ki 14:23 [m] Jer 38:4 [n] Jer 26:8-11 **7:12** [o] Mt 8:34 **7:13** [p] Am 2:12; Ac 4:18 **7:14** [q] 2Ki 2:5; 4:38 **7:15** [r] 2Sa 7:8 [s] Jer 7:1-2; Eze 2:3-4 **7:16** [t] Eze 20:46; Mic 2:6 **7:17** [u] Hos 4:13 [v] 2Ki 17:6; Eze 4:13; Hos 9:3

A Basket of Ripe Fruit

8 This is what the Sovereign LORD showed
me: a basket of ripe fruit. 2"What do you
see,[w] Amos?[x]" he asked.

"A basket of ripe fruit," I answered.

Then the LORD said to me, "The time is
ripe for my people Israel; I will spare them
no longer.[y]

3"In that day," declares the Sovereign
LORD, "the songs in the temple will turn to
wailing.[a][z] Many, many bodies—flung everywhere! Silence![a]"

4Hear this, you who trample the needy
and do away with the poor[b] of the
land,[c]

5saying,

"When will the New Moon be over
that we may sell grain,
and the Sabbath be ended
that we may market wheat?"—
skimping on the measure,
boosting the price
and cheating with dishonest scales,[d]
6buying the poor with silver
and the needy for a pair of sandals,
selling even the sweepings with the
wheat.[e]

7The LORD has sworn by himself, the
Pride of Jacob:[f] "I will never forget[g] anything they have done.

8"Will not the land tremble[h] for this,
and all who live in it mourn?
The whole land will rise like the Nile;
it will be stirred up and then sink
like the river of Egypt.[i]

9"In that day," declares the Sovereign
LORD,

"I will make the sun go down at noon
and darken the earth in broad
daylight.[j]
10I will turn your religious festivals into
mourning
and all your singing into weeping.
I will make all of you wear sackcloth[k]
and shave your heads.
I will make that time like mourning for
an only son[l]
and the end of it like a bitter day.[m]

11"The days are coming," declares the
Sovereign LORD,
"when I will send a famine through
the land—
not a famine of food or a thirst for water,
but a famine of hearing the words of
the LORD.[n]
12People will stagger from sea to sea
and wander from north to east,
searching for the word of the LORD,
but they will not find it.[o]

13"In that day

"the lovely young women and strong
young men
will faint because of thirst.[p]
14Those who swear by the sin of Samaria—
who say, 'As surely as your god lives,
Dan,'[q]
or, 'As surely as the god[b] of
Beersheba[r] lives'—
they will fall, never to rise again.[s]"

Israel to Be Destroyed

9 I saw the Lord standing by the altar,
and he said:

"Strike the tops of the pillars
so that the thresholds shake.
Bring them down on the heads[t] of all
the people;
those who are left I will kill with the
sword.
Not one will get away,
none will escape.
2Though they dig down to the depths
below,[u]
from there my hand will take them.
Though they climb up to the heavens
above,[v]
from there I will bring them down.[w]

[a] 3 Or *"the temple singers will wail* [b] 14 Hebrew *the way*

Amos made it clear that he had neither desired nor sought his prophetic task. ***Your wife will become a prostitute.*** The only way the spouse of an important official like Amaziah would be reduced to prostitution would be if all her family and all her resources were taken away and she were left to fend entirely for herself.

8:1–3 ***a basket of ripe fruit.*** The fruits that came at the end of the harvest in late summer included grapes, pomegranates, and figs. ***The time is ripe.*** Amos could not have discerned the meaning of this vision until God's pronouncement. Israel's wickedness was about to result in a harvest of judgment.

8:5 ***skimping on the measure.*** This was a way of cheating the customer of value received for price paid. ***price.*** Boosting the price was also a way of cheating.

8:12–13 ***sea to sea.*** This meant from the Dead Sea to the Mediterranean. ***lovely young women ... strong young men.*** This refers to those who are most vigorous to survive.

8:14 ***Dan ... Beersheba.*** This was a phrase that indicated the limits of the Israelite territory. In Amos's day, Beersheba was in the kingdom of Judah. Israel could swear oaths by the Lord, claiming they loyally worshiped Him from the extreme north to the extreme south of His land, but that would not relieve the famine of God's word.

9:2 ***depths below ... heavens.*** In this imagery, Israel's fugitives from God's judgment could escape

8:2 [w] Jer 24:3 [x] Am 7:8 [y] Eze 7:2-9 **8:3** [z] Am 5:16 [a] Am 5:23; 6:10 **8:4** [b] Pr 30:14 [c] Ps 14:4; Am 2:7 **8:5** [d] 2Ki 4:23; Ne 13:15-16; Hos 12:7; Mic 6:10-11 **8:6** [e] Am 2:6 **8:7** [f] Am 6:8 [g] Hos 8:13 **8:8** [h] Hos 4:3 [i] Ps 18:7; Jer 46:8; Am 9:5 **8:9** [j] Job 5:14; Isa 59:9-10; Jer 15:9; Am 5:8; Mic 3:6 **8:10** [k] Jer 48:37 [l] Jer 6:26; Zec 12:10 [m] Eze 7:18 **8:11** [n] 1Sa 3:1; 2Ch 15:3; Eze 7:26 **8:12** [o] Eze 20:3, 31 **8:13** [p] Isa 41:17; Hos 2:3 **8:14** [q] 1Ki 12:29 [r] Am 5:5 [s] Am 5:2 **9:1** [t] Ps 68:21 **9:2** [u] Ps 139:8 [v] Jer 51:53 [w] Ob 1:4

3 Though they hide themselves on the top
of Carmel,[x]
there I will hunt them down and seize
them.[y]
Though they hide from my eyes at the
bottom of the sea,
there I will command the serpent to
bite them.[z]
4 Though they are driven into exile by
their enemies,
there I will command the sword[a] to
slay them.

"I will keep my eye on them
for harm[b] and not for good."[c][d]

5 The Lord, the LORD Almighty—
he touches the earth and it melts,[e]
and all who live in it mourn;
the whole land rises like the Nile,
then sinks like the river of Egypt;[f]
6 he builds his lofty palace[a] in the
heavens
and sets its foundation[b] on the
earth;
he calls for the waters of the sea
and pours them out over the face of
the land—
the LORD is his name.[g]

7 "Are not you Israelites
the same to me as the Cushites[c]?"[h]
declares the LORD.
"Did I not bring Israel up from Egypt,
the Philistines from Caphtor[d][i]
and the Arameans from Kir?[j]

8 "Surely the eyes of the Sovereign LORD
are on the sinful kingdom.
I will destroy it
from the face of the earth.
Yet I will not totally destroy
the descendants of Jacob,"
declares the LORD.[k]
9 "For I will give the command,
and I will shake the people of Israel
among all the nations
as grain[l] is shaken in a sieve,[m]
and not a pebble will reach the
ground.
10 All the sinners among my people
will die by the sword,
all those who say,
'Disaster will not overtake or
meet us.'[n]

Israel's Restoration

11 "In that day

"I will restore David's fallen shelter—
I will repair its broken walls
and restore its ruins—
and will rebuild it as it used to be,[o]
12 so that they may possess the remnant of
Edom[p]
and all the nations that bear my
name,[e][q]"
declares the LORD,
who will do these things.[r]

13 "The days are coming," declares the
LORD,

"when the reaper will be overtaken by
the plowman[s]
and the planter by the one treading
grapes.
New wine will drip from the mountains
and flow from all the hills,[t]
14 and I will bring my people Israel back
from exile.[f]

"They will rebuild the ruined cities[u] and
live in them.
They will plant vineyards and drink
their wine;
they will make gardens and eat their
fruit.[v]
15 I will plant[w] Israel in their own land,
never again to be uprooted
from the land I have given them,"

says the LORD your God.[x]

---

[a] *6* The meaning of the Hebrew for this phrase is uncertain. [b] *6* The meaning of the Hebrew for this word is uncertain. [c] *7* That is, people from the upper Nile region [d] *7* That is, Crete
[e] *12* Hebrew; Septuagint *so that the remnant of people / and all the nations that bear my name may seek me* [f] *14* Or *will restore the fortunes of my people Israel*

---

neither up nor down; God would find them no matter where in the universe they fled.
9:3 ***top of Carmel.*** This peak represented the highest point on earth. Whether as high as that, or as low as the bottom of the sea, the earth would provide no escape.
9:8 ***the sinful kingdom.*** This is Israel. ***I will not totally destroy.*** This was a glimmer of hope in a long passage of judgment and doom. God's judgment would be thorough, but a remnant would survive.
9:9 ***as grain is shaken in a sieve.*** Sifting grain was the final operation in cleaning it before gathering it into storage. In winnowing, all the chaff was blown away; only pebbles and small clumps of mud remained with the grain. The sieve was constructed with holes that were sized so other debris were retained in the sieve.
9:13 ***the reaper will be overtaken by the plowman.*** For this to happen it would mean such an abundant harvest that it would last all summer and would not be gathered until the plowing had started again. Grapes were harvested from mid-summer to early fall. The grain crop was sown after the plowing in late fall.
9:15 ***plant Israel in their own land.*** God does not abandon His promises or His covenant, nor does He leave His people without hope. God's punishment is certain, but His restoration is just as certain. The word of hope for God's people of old is valid also for God's people of today.

9:3 [x] Am 1:2 [y] Ps 139:8-10 [z] Jer 16:16-17 **9:4** [a] Lev 26:33; Eze 5:12 [b] Jer 21:10 [c] Jer 39:16 [d] Jer 44:11 **9:5** [e] Ps 46:2; Mic 1:4 [f] Am 8:8 **9:6** [g] Ps 104:1-3,5-6,13; Am 5:8 **9:7** [h] Isa 20:4; 43:3 [i] Dt 2:23; Jer 47:4 [j] 2Ki 16:9; Isa 22:6; Am 1:5; 2:10 **9:8** [k] Jer 44:27 **9:9** [l] Lk 22:31 [m] Isa 30:28 **9:10** [n] Am 6:3 **9:11** [o] Ps 80:12 **9:12** [p] Nu 24:18 [q] Isa 43:7 [r] Ac 15:16-17* **9:13** [s] Lev 26:5 [t] Joel 3:18 **9:14** [u] Isa 61:4 [v] Jer 30:18; 31:28; Eze 28:25-26 **9:15** [w] Isa 60:21 [x] Jer 24:6; Eze 34:25-28; 37:12,25

OBADIAH

▶ **AUTHOR:** Obadiah was an obscure prophet who probably lived in the southern kingdom of Judah. It is assumed, however, that he was not a priest, since his father is not mentioned and nothing is given of his background. There are 13 Obadiahs in the Old Testament. Four of the better prospects for this Obadiah are: (1) the officer in Ahab's palace that hid God's prophets in a cave (1 Kin. 18:3); (2) one of the officials sent out by Jehoshaphat to teach the law in the cities of Judah (2 Chr. 17:7); (3) one of the overseers who took part in repairing the temple under Josiah (2 Chr. 34:12); or (4) a priest in the time of Nehemiah (Neh. 10:5).

▶ **TIME:** c. 840 B.C. ▶ **KEY VERSE:** Obad. 10

▶ **THEME:** Obadiah is a prophecy against Edom, the nation that descended from Esau. Edom included the area south and east of the Dead Sea. Throughout most of Old Testament history, if Edom is mentioned, it is in the context of some kind of skirmish. This friction started when the king of Edom refused to let the Israelites cross his territory as they journeyed towards the Promised Land in Numbers 20:14–21. When Israel and Judah were taken into exile, Edom stood by and watched. The purpose of Obadiah seems clear. He is out to encourage the Israelites in the context of captivity. God will rescue His people

Obadiah's Vision

1 The vision of Obadiah.

This is what the Sovereign LORD says about Edom[a]—

We have heard a message from the LORD:
An envoy[b] was sent to the nations to say,
"Rise, let us go against her for battle"[c]—
2 "See, I will make you small among the nations;
you will be utterly despised.
3 The pride[d] of your heart has deceived you,
you who live in the clefts of the rocks[a]
and make your home on the heights,
you who say to yourself,
'Who can bring me down to the ground?'[e]
4 Though you soar like the eagle
and make your nest[f] among the stars,
from there I will bring you down,"[g]
declares the LORD.[h]
5 "If thieves came to you,
if robbers in the night—
oh, what a disaster awaits you!—
would they not steal only as much as they wanted?
If grape pickers came to you,
would they not leave a few grapes?[i]
6 But how Esau will be ransacked,
his hidden treasures pillaged!
7 All your allies[j] will force you to the border;
your friends will deceive and overpower you;
those who eat your bread[k] will set a trap for you,[b]
but you will not detect it.

[a] 3 Or *of Sela* [b] 7 The meaning of the Hebrew for this clause is uncertain.

2 *I will make you small.* God would bring about a reversal of Edom's inflated self-importance.
3 *make your home on the heights.* Some of the mountain peaks of Edom reached over 6,000 feet. Jerusalem is about 2,300 feet above sea level. ***Who can bring me down to the ground?*** Edom's presumed physical safety led the Edomites to become haughty; this would be their downfall.
4 *soar like the eagle.* Edom's physical location became a metaphor of the proud and haughty spirit that the nation had displayed at the time of Judah's distress. Trusting in its high places and mountainous strongholds, Edom reckoned that no one could bring it to account for its actions.

1 [a] Isa 63:1-6; Jer 49:7-22; Eze 25:12-14; Am 1:11-12 [b] Isa 18:2 [c] Jer 6:4-5 **3** [d] Isa 16:6 [e] Isa 14:13-15; Rev 18:7 **4** [f] Hab 2:9 [g] Isa 14:13 [h] Job 20:6 **5** [i] Dt 24:21 **7** [j] Jer 30:14 [k] Ps 41:9

8 "In that day," declares the LORD,
"will I not destroy[l] the wise men of Edom,
those of understanding in the mountains of Esau?
9 Your warriors, Teman,[m] will be terrified,
and everyone in Esau's mountains
will be cut down in the slaughter.
10 Because of the violence[n] against your brother Jacob,[o]
you will be covered with shame;
you will be destroyed forever.[p]
11 On the day you stood aloof
while strangers carried off his wealth
and foreigners entered his gates
and cast lots[q] for Jerusalem,
you were like one of them.
12 You should not gloat over your brother
in the day of his misfortune,
nor rejoice[r] over the people of Judah
in the day of their destruction,[s]
nor boast so much
in the day of their trouble.[t]
13 You should not march through the gates of my people
in the day of their disaster,
nor gloat over them in their calamity[u]
in the day of their disaster,
nor seize their wealth
in the day of their disaster.
14 You should not wait at the crossroads
to cut down their fugitives,
nor hand over their survivors
in the day of their trouble.

15 "The day of the LORD is near[v]
for all nations.
As you have done, it will be done to you;
your deeds[w] will return upon your own head.
16 Just as you drank on my holy hill,
so all the nations will drink[x] continually;
they will drink and drink
and be as if they had never been.
17 But on Mount Zion will be deliverance;[y]
it will be holy,[z]
and Jacob will possess his inheritance.
18 Jacob will be a fire
and Joseph a flame;
Esau will be stubble,
and they will set him on fire and destroy[a] him.
There will be no survivors
from Esau."
The LORD has spoken.

19 People from the Negev will occupy
the mountains of Esau,
and people from the foothills will possess
the land of the Philistines.[b]
They will occupy the fields of Ephraim and Samaria,[c]
and Benjamin will possess Gilead.
20 This company of Israelite exiles who are in Canaan
will possess the land as far as Zarephath;[d]
the exiles from Jerusalem who are in Sepharad
will possess the towns of the Negev.[e]
21 Deliverers will go up on[a] Mount Zion
to govern the mountains of Esau.
And the kingdom will be the LORD's.[f]

---

[a] 21 Or *from*

---

8 *destroy the wise men of Edom.* The nation had a reputation for having many wise men among its citizens (Jer. 49:7).

9 *Teman.* This name comes from a son of Eliphaz, who was the firstborn son of Esau (Gen. 36:9–11).

11 *On the day.* This refers to the time of Judah's distress. ***strangers ... foreigners.*** These words are used to describe Judah's principal enemies, contrasted with the words of verse 10, "your brother." It was one thing for the Babylonians to attack Judah; for a nation like Edom to join the Babylonians against their own brothers was unthinkable.

13 *in their calamity.* This phrase is repeated three times in this verse. It refers to the day of God's judgment upon Judah, carried out by the hand of Nebuchadnezzar.

15 *The day of the LORD.* This is a technical term used by the prophets to indicate the day of God's judgment (Amos 5:18–20). Here the term likely refers to the time when God would judge all the nations, including Edom, that had participated in Judah's destruction.

18 *Jacob ... Joseph.* Together these signify a unified Israel. God intends to rejoin the kingdoms of Israel and Judah as one people again.

20 *Zarephath.* This was a Phoenician city 14 miles north of Tyre (1 Kin. 17:8–24). ***Sepharad.*** This was a city to which some Judeans were exiled. The restoration of Judah from exile, which these verses predict, was a sign to Judah and all nations that the God of Israel was not just a local God. He had not been defeated by the Babylonian god Marduk. The fact that He could allow His people to be carried into captivity in a foreign land and then bring them back to their own land was proof of His power and sovereignty over all the earth.

21 *Deliverers.* The Judeans who had been taken into captivity would come back as deliverers, and they would reign over the people of Edom. ***the kingdom will be the LORD's.*** These were Obadiah's last words against all human arrogance, pride, and rebellion. Edom had thought itself indestructible; but the Lord humbled that nation and restored the fallen Judah. Many people are tempted to consider themselves beyond the reach of God. But God will bring them low, just as He will lift those who humble themselves before Him. And one great day, He will establish His just rule over all.

1:1 *The word of the LORD.* This phrase affirms the

8 [l] Job 5:12; Isa 29:14 **9** [m] Ge 36:11, 34 **10** [n] Joel 3:19 [o] Ps 137:7; Am 1:11-12 [p] Eze 35:9 **11** [q] Na 3:10 **12** [r] Eze 35:15 [s] Pr 17:5 [t] Mic 4:11 **13** [u] Eze 35:5 **15** [v] Eze 30:3 [w] Jer 50:29; Hab 2:8 **16** [x] Jer 25:15; 49:12 **17** [y] Am 9:11-15 [z] Isa 4:3 **18** [a] Zec 12:6 **19** [b] Isa 11:14 [c] Jer 31:5 **20** [d] 1Ki 17:9-10 [e] Jer 33:13 **21** [f] Ps 22:28; Zec 14:9, 16; Rev 11:15

JONAH

▶ **AUTHOR:** Jonah was the "son of Amittai" and nothing more would be known about him were it not for a reference in 2 Kings 14:25 calling him a prophet in the reign of Jeroboam II of Israel. Jonah was a Galilean, contrary to the Pharisees' claim that "a prophet does not come out of Galilee" (John 7:52). One Jewish tradition says that Jonah was the son of the widow of Zarephath whom Elijah raised from the dead (1 Kin. 17:8–24).

▶ **TIME:** c. 760 B.C. ▶ **KEY VERSES:** Jon. 2:8–9

▶ **THEME:** The Book of Jonah directs us towards God's greatness and mercy. He will go to any lengths in order to assure that His message is heard. He makes it possible for people to repent and be redeemed no matter how decadent and far away from God they are. Jonah himself is a prime example of the power of storytelling, as he gives us an amazingly visual and memorable image of God's far reaching grace and His involvement in individual lives to accomplish His purposes.

Jonah Flees From the LORD

1 The word of the LORD came to Jonah[a] son of Amittai:[b] 2"Go to the great city of Nineveh[c] and preach against it, because its wickedness has come up before me."

3But Jonah ran[d] away from the LORD and headed for Tarshish. He went down to Joppa,[e] where he found a ship bound for that port. After paying the fare, he went aboard and sailed for Tarshish to flee from the LORD.

4Then the LORD sent a great wind on the sea, and such a violent storm arose that the ship threatened to break up.[f] 5All the sailors were afraid and each cried out to his own god. And they threw the cargo into the sea to lighten the ship.[g]

But Jonah had gone below deck, where he lay down and fell into a deep sleep. 6The captain went to him and said, "How can you sleep? Get up and call[h] on your god! Maybe he will take notice of us so that we will not perish."[i]

7Then the sailors said to each other, "Come, let us cast lots to find out who is responsible for this calamity."[j] They cast lots and the lot fell on Jonah. 8So they asked him, "Tell us, who is responsible for making all this trouble for us? What kind of work do you do? Where do you come from? What is your country? From what people are you?"

9He answered, "I am a Hebrew and I worship the LORD, the God of heaven,[k] who made the sea and the dry land.[l]"

10This terrified them and they asked, "What have you done?" (They knew he was running away from the LORD, because he had already told them so.)

11The sea was getting rougher and rougher. So they asked him, "What should we do to you to make the sea calm down for us?"

divine source of the message to Jonah (Jer. 1:4; Hos. 1:1; Joel 1:1; Mic. 1:1). The name "Jonah" means "Dove."

1:2 ***Nineveh.*** Nineveh is located on the Tigris River, the capital of ancient Assyria (2 Kin. 19:36) for about a century. It was over 500 miles from Jonah's home near Nazareth.

1:3 ***a ship bound for that port.*** The location of this port city is uncertain, but it could be Tartessus on the southeast coast of Spain. The city represents the most distant place known to the Israelites. Joppa was about 50 miles southwest of Jonah's hometown in the opposite direction from Nineveh.

1:4–5 ***the LORD sent a great wind.*** Throughout the Book of Jonah, the Lord shows Himself sovereign over every aspect of creation. In this case, the storm at sea was so ferocious that even the experienced mariners were afraid.

1:9 ***I am a Hebrew.*** With these words, Jonah identified himself with the people of the Lord's covenant (Gen. 14:13). ***I worship the LORD.*** Worship here indicates an ongoing activity of awe before the Lord, of piety in His presence, of obedience to His word, and of saving faith (Gen. 22:12; Ex. 20:20; Prov. 1:7). Yet Jonah's actions contradicted his words.

1:10 ***terrified.*** This is the same term for "worship" that Jonah used in his statement of piety (v. 9). But here the word means to be in terror; it refers to overwhelming dread (v. 16). God, the Creator of the universe, was after Jonah. And because God was after

1:1 [a] Mt 12:39-41 [b] 2Ki 14:25 **1:2** [c] Ge 10.11
1:3 [d] Ps 139:7 [e] Jos 19:46; Ac 9:36,43 **1:4** [f] Ps 107:23-26
1:5 [g] Ac 27:18-19 **1:6** [h] Jnh 3:8 [i] Ps 107:28
1:7 [j] Jos 7:10-18; 1Sa 14:42 **1:9** [k] Ac 17:24 [l] Ps 146:6

12"Pick me up and throw me into the
sea," he replied, "and it will become calm.
I know that it is my fault that this great
storm has come upon you."[m]
13Instead, the men did their best to row
back to land. But they could not, for the
sea grew even wilder than before.[n] 14Then
they cried out to the LORD, "Please, LORD,
do not let us die for taking this man's life.
Do not hold us accountable for killing an
innocent man,[o] for you, LORD, have done
as you pleased."[p] 15Then they took Jonah
and threw him overboard, and the raging
sea grew calm.[q] 16At this the men greatly
feared[r] the LORD, and they offered a sacrifice to the LORD and made vows to him.

Jonah's Prayer

17Now the LORD provided a huge fish
to swallow Jonah,[s] and Jonah was in the
belly of the fish three days and three nights.
2[a] 1From inside the fish Jonah prayed to
the LORD his God. 2He said:

"In my distress I called to the LORD,[t]
and he answered me.
From deep in the realm of the dead I
called for help,
and you listened to my cry.
3You hurled me into the depths,[u]
into the very heart of the seas,
and the currents swirled
about me;
all your waves and breakers
swept over me.[v]
4I said, 'I have been banished
from your sight;[w]
yet I will look again
toward your holy temple.'
5The engulfing waters threatened me,[b]
the deep surrounded me;
seaweed was wrapped around my
head.[x]
6To the roots of the mountains I sank
down;
the earth beneath barred me in
forever.
But you, LORD my God,
brought my life up from the pit.

7"When my life was ebbing away,
I remembered[y] you, LORD,
and my prayer[z] rose to you,
to your holy temple.[a]

8"Those who cling to worthless idols[b]
turn away from God's love for them.
9But I, with shouts of grateful praise,
will sacrifice[c] to you.
What I have vowed[d] I will make good.
I will say, 'Salvation[e] comes from the
LORD.'"

10And the LORD commanded the fish,
and it vomited Jonah onto dry land.

Jonah Goes to Nineveh

3 Then the word of the LORD came to Jonah[f] a second time: 2"Go to the great
city of Nineveh and proclaim to it the message I give you."
3Jonah obeyed the word of the LORD
and went to Nineveh. Now Nineveh was
a very large city; it took three days to go
through it. 4Jonah began by going a day's
journey into the city, proclaiming, "For-

---

[a] In Hebrew texts 2:1 is numbered 1:17, and 2:1-10 is numbered 2:2-11. [b] 5 Or *waters were at my throat*

Jonah, He was after the sailors as well. They had every right to be afraid (Gen. 12:18; Judg. 15:11).

1:14 ***they cried out to the LORD.*** Ironically, the pagan sailors prayed to the Lord on behalf of the Lord's rebellious prophet. Jonah needed God's grace as much as Nineveh did. ***as you pleased.*** The narrator skillfully uses the sailors' words to express one of the book's themes: the Lord is free to act as He wills.

1:17 ***the LORD provided a huge fish.*** God sent the fish — not a whale, as is commonly thought — to rescue Jonah from drowning, not to punish him (ch. 2). Three days and three nights may refer to one full day and portions of two more (Gen. 30:36; Ex. 3:18; 1 Sam. 30:12). Jesus Christ said that His death and resurrection were foreshadowed by Jonah's experience (Matt. 12:39 – 40; 16:4; Luke 11:29).

2:2 ***I called ... I called.*** These terms come from two different verbs. The first is a more general term meaning "to call aloud," with a wide range of usage in the Bible. The second is a term that means a "cry for help," particularly as a scream to God (Ps. 5:2; 18:6; 22:24; 88:13; 119:147).

2:4 ***I will look again toward your holy temple.*** The man who had run from God's presence was alone, yet he clung to the hope that God would not abandon him. The temple, the sanctuary in Jerusalem (Deut. 12:5 – 7; Ps. 48; 79:1; Heb. 9:24), was the symbol of God's presence.

2:6 ***the roots of the mountains.*** Jonah pictures himself so deep in the sea that it is as if he had found the deepest place possible. ***pit.*** This term, along with hell (v. 2), is used to describe the realm of the dead (Job 33:24; Ps. 30:9; 49:9).

2:9 ***I, with ... grateful praise, will sacrifice to you.*** This vow is common in the Psalms (Ps. 13:6; 142:7). ***What I have vowed I will make good.*** Jonah declares that he will keep his promise, a pledge both to sacrifice and to acknowledge God's help (Job 22:27; Ps. 50:14; 66:13; Rom. 6:13; 1 Pet. 2:5).

2:10 ***the LORD commanded the fish.*** The focus in the story of Jonah is on the Lord's sovereign control over creation to bring about His purpose.

3:1 – 2 ***the word of the LORD came to Jonah a second time.*** Jonah's new commission was essentially the same as the one he had received in 1:1.

1:12 [m] 2Sa 24:17; 1Ch 21:17 **1:13** [n] Pr 21:30
1:14 [o] Dt 21:8 [p] Ps 115:3 **1:15** [q] Ps 107:29; Lk 8:24
1:16 [r] Mk 4:41 **1:17** [s] Mt 12:40; 16:4; Lk 11:30
2:2 [t] Ps 18:6; 120:1 **2:3** [u] Ps 88:6 [v] Ps 42:7
2:4 [w] Ps 31:22 **2:5** [x] Ps 69:1-2 **2:7** [y] Ps 77:11-12
[z] 2Ch 30:27 [a] Ps 11:4; 18:6 **2:8** [b] 2Ki 17:15; Jer 10:8
2:9 [c] Ps 50:14, 23; Hos 14:2 [d] Ecc 5:4-5 [e] Ps 3:8
3:1 [f] Jnh 1:1

ty more days and Nineveh will be overthrown." 5The Ninevites believed God. A
fast was proclaimed, and all of them, from
the greatest to the least, put on sackcloth.[g]
6When Jonah's warning reached the
king of Nineveh, he rose from his throne,
took off his royal robes, covered himself
with sackcloth and sat down in the dust.[h]
7This is the proclamation he issued in Nineveh:

"By the decree of the king and his nobles:

Do not let people or animals, herds
or flocks, taste anything; do not let
them eat or drink.[i] 8But let people and
animals be covered with sackcloth.
Let everyone call[j] urgently on God. Let
them give up their evil ways and their
violence. 9Who knows?[k] God may yet
relent and with compassion turn[l] from
his fierce anger so that we will not perish."

10When God saw what they did and how
they turned from their evil ways, he relented[m] and did not bring on them the destruction[n] he had threatened.[o]

Jonah's Anger at the LORD's Compassion

4 But to Jonah this seemed very wrong,
and he became angry.[p] 2He prayed
to the LORD, "Isn't this what I said, LORD,
when I was still at home? That is what I
tried to forestall by fleeing to Tarshish. I
knew[q] that you are a gracious and compassionate God, slow to anger and abounding
in love,[r] a God who relents from sending
calamity.[s] 3Now, LORD, take away my life,[t]
for it is better for me to die[u] than to live."
4But the LORD replied, "Is it right for you
to be angry?"[v]
5Jonah had gone out and sat down at a
place east of the city. There he made himself a shelter, sat in its shade and waited to
see what would happen to the city. 6Then
the LORD God provided a leafy plant[a] and
made it grow up over Jonah to give shade
for his head to ease his discomfort, and
Jonah was very happy about the plant.
7But at dawn the next day God provided
a worm, which chewed the plant so that it
withered.[w] 8When the sun rose, God provided a scorching east wind, and the sun
blazed on Jonah's head so that he grew
faint. He wanted to die, and said, "It would
be better for me to die than to live."
9But God said to Jonah, "Is it right for
you to be angry about the plant?"
"It is," he said. "And I'm so angry I wish
I were dead."
10But the LORD said, "You have been concerned about this plant, though you did not
tend it or make it grow. It sprang up overnight and died overnight. 11And should
I not have concern[x] for the great city of
Nineveh,[y] in which there are more than
a hundred and twenty thousand people
who cannot tell their right hand from their
left—and also many animals?"

---

[a] 6 The precise identification of this plant is uncertain; also in verses 7, 9 and 10.

3:5 ***The Ninevites believed God.*** The term used for God here is the general term for deity. In contrast, the sailors in chapter 1 proclaimed faith in the Lord, using the personal, covenant name for God (1:16). The fact that the writer does not use the personal name for God here may suggest that the Ninevites had a short-lived or imperfect understanding of God's message. History bears this out. We have no historical record of a lasting period of belief in Nineveh. Eventually the city was destroyed in 612 B.C.
3:10 ***he relented.*** The Ninevites' repentance moved the Lord to extend grace and mercy to them.
4:1 ***to Jonah this seemed very wrong.*** Jonah's irritation stands in sharp contrast to the good news that the city would be spared God's judgment. ***became angry.*** In contrast to God, Jonah had no compassion on the people of Nineveh.
4:5 ***to see what would happen to the city.*** In his continuing stubbornness and lack of compassion, Jonah held out hope that God would judge Nineveh. This was God's chief complaint against him (Ps. 58).
4:7 ***God provided a worm.*** The Book of Jonah depicts the Lord as both sovereign and free to act in creation. God placed the worm in the plant to serve as His agent in Jonah's life.
4:9 ***right for you to be angry.*** Jonah's anger (v. 1) did not arise from a desire for justice, but from his own selfishness. He continued to justify his rebellious attitude. And again, God was merciful.
4:11 ***concern.*** The same word used to describe Jonah's feeling toward the plant in verse 10 is used for God's feeling toward the people of Nineveh. People are of more value than animals and animals of more value than plants, but the Lord has a concern that extends to all of His creation. The Lord's compassion comes from His character (v. 2; Joel 2:13–14).

3:5 [g] Da 9:3; Lk 11:32 **3:6** [h] Job 2:8, 13; Eze 27:30-31
3:7 [i] 2Ch 20:3 **3:8** [j] Ps 130:1; Jnh 1:6 **3:9** [k] 2Sa 12:22
[l] Joel 2:14 **3:10** [m] Am 7:6 [n] Jer 18:8 [o] Ex 32:14
4:1 [p] ver 4; Lk 15:28 **4:2** [q] Jer 20:7-8 [r] Ex 34:6; Ps 86:5, 15
[s] Joel 2:13 **4:3** [t] 1Ki 19:4 [u] Job 7:15 **4:4** [v] Mt 20:11-15
4:7 [w] Joel 1:12 **4:11** [x] Jnh 3:10 [y] Jnh 1:2; 3:2

MICAH

▶ **AUTHOR:** Micah was from Moresheth Gath (1:14) which was located about 25 miles southwest of Jerusalem, near Gath. Although Micah was not as politically aware as Isaiah or Daniel, he showed a profound concern for the suffering of the people and had a clear sense of his prophetic calling. A contemporary of Isaiah and Hosea, Micah may have been a farmer turned prophet like Amos.

▶ **TIME:** c. 735 – 710 B.C. ▶ **KEY VERSE:** Mic. 6:8

▶ **THEME:** Micah was from a town in southwestern Judah. His message was directed at both capital cities, Samaria and Jerusalem. He was probably around when the Assyrians destroyed Samaria in 722 B.C., and may have even lived through the siege of Jerusalem by Assyria. Micah's message comes out of unique visions from God. In effect he saw things that others couldn't, such as the prophecy of Bethlehem as the birthplace of Christ.

1 The word of the LORD that came to Micah of Moresheth[a] during the reigns of Jotham,[b] Ahaz[c] and Hezekiah, kings of Judah[d]—the vision[e] he saw concerning Samaria and Jerusalem.

2 Hear, you peoples, all of you,[f]
listen, earth[g] and all who live in it,
that the Sovereign LORD may bear witness[h] against you,
the Lord from his holy temple.[i]

Judgment Against Samaria and Jerusalem

3 Look! The LORD is coming from his dwelling[j] place;
he comes down and treads on the heights of the earth.[k]
4 The mountains melt[l] beneath him
and the valleys split apart,[m]
like wax before the fire,
like water rushing down a slope.
5 All this is because of Jacob's transgression,
because of the sins of the people of Israel.
What is Jacob's transgression?
Is it not Samaria?[n]
What is Judah's high place?
Is it not Jerusalem?
6 "Therefore I will make Samaria a heap of rubble,
a place for planting vineyards.
I will pour her stones[o] into the valley
and lay bare her foundations.[p]
7 All her idols[q] will be broken to pieces;
all her temple gifts will be burned with fire;
I will destroy all her images.[r]
Since she gathered her gifts from the wages of prostitutes,[s]
as the wages of prostitutes they will again be used."

1:1 ***Micah.*** The name means "Who is like the Lord?" The question presents a major biblical theme, the idea that God is incomparable (7:18; Deut. 4:32 – 40; Ps. 113:4 – 6). Micah's ministry centered on the Assyrian threat to Samaria, the capital of Israel, that was destroyed in 722 B.C. and Jerusalem, the capital of Judah.
1:3 ***The LORD is coming.*** This is the language of epiphany, the dramatic coming of God to earth, here in a solemn procession of judgment. In other texts the language of epiphany is used to describe God's dramatic acts of deliverance (Ps. 18:7 – 19).
1:5 ***Jacob's.*** The name is used to refer to the northern kingdom of Israel, whose transgression was centered in its capital Samaria. ***high place.*** Jerusalem, which was once "beautiful in elevation" (Ps. 48:2), was nothing more than another platform of pagan worship, like the "high places" of the Canaanites.
1:7 ***she gathered her gifts from the wages of prostitutes.*** Idolatry is often described in the Hebrew Bible as spiritual adultery (Jer. 3:1; Hos. 4:15). Israel is pictured here as a wife who is unfaithful to her husband. This is not just a metaphor, however; the worship system of Canaan was sexual in nature.

1:1 [a] Jer 26:18 [b] 1Ch 3:12 [c] 1Ch 3:13 [d] Hos 1:1 [e] Isa 1:1
1:2 [f] Ps 50:7 [g] Jer 6:19 [h] Ge 31:50; Dt 4:26; Isa 1:2 [i] Ps 11:4
1:3 [j] Isa 18:4 [k] Am 4:13 **1:4** [l] Ps 46:2,6 [m] Nu 16:31; Na 1:5 **1:5** [n] Am 8:14 **1:6** [o] Am 5:11 [p] Eze 13:14
1:7 [q] Eze 6:6 [r] Dt 9:21 [s] Dt 23:17-18

Weeping and Mourning

8 Because of this I will weep[t] and wail;
I will go about barefoot and naked.
I will howl like a jackal
and moan like an owl.
9 For Samaria's plague[u] is incurable;
it has spread to Judah.[v]
It has reached the very gate[w] of my people,
even to Jerusalem itself.
10 Tell it not in Gath[a];
weep not at all.
In Beth Ophrah[b]
roll in the dust.
11 Pass by naked[x] and in shame,
you who live in Shaphir.[c]
Those who live in Zaanan[d]
will not come out.
Beth Ezel is in mourning;
it no longer protects you.
12 Those who live in Maroth[e] writhe in pain,
waiting for relief,[y]
because disaster has come from the LORD,
even to the gate of Jerusalem.
13 You who live in Lachish,[z]
harness fast horses to the chariot.
You are where the sin of Daughter Zion began,
for the transgressions of Israel were found in you.
14 Therefore you will give parting gifts[a]
to Moresheth Gath.
The town of Akzib[f][b] will prove deceptive[c]
to the kings of Israel.
15 I will bring a conqueror against you
who live in Mareshah.[g][d]
The nobles of Israel
will flee to Adullam.[e]
16 Shave[f] your head in mourning
for the children in whom you delight;
make yourself as bald as the vulture,
for they will go from you into exile.

Human Plans and God's Plans

2 Woe to those who plan iniquity,
to those who plot evil on their beds![g]
At morning's light they carry it out
because it is in their power to do it.
2 They covet fields[h] and seize them,
and houses, and take them.
They defraud[i] people of their homes,
they rob them of their inheritance.

3 Therefore, the LORD says:

"I am planning disaster[j] against this people,
from which you cannot save yourselves.
You will no longer walk proudly,[k]
for it will be a time of calamity.
4 In that day people will ridicule you;
they will taunt you with this mournful song:
'We are utterly ruined;[l]
my people's possession is divided up.
He takes it from me!
He assigns our fields to traitors.'"

5 Therefore you will have no one in the assembly of the LORD
to divide the land[m] by lot.

False Prophets

6 "Do not prophesy," their prophets say.
"Do not prophesy about these things;
disgrace[n] will not overtake us.[o]"
7 You descendants of Jacob, should it be said,
"Does the LORD become[h] impatient?
Does he do such things?"

"Do not my words do good[p]
to the one whose ways are upright?[q]

---

[a] *10 Gath* sounds like the Hebrew for *tell.*
[b] *10 Beth Ophrah* means *house of dust.*
[c] *11 Shaphir* means *pleasant.* [d] *11 Zaanan* sounds like the Hebrew for *come out.*
[e] *12 Maroth* sounds like the Hebrew for *bitter.*
[f] *14 Akzib* means *deception.* [g] *15 Mareshah* sounds like the Hebrew for *conqueror.* [h] *7* Or *Is the Spirit of the LORD*

1:8 *barefoot and naked.* Micah's words describe mourning rites in which outer garments were laid aside in deep humility. The mourning person thought no longer about himself but only about the calamity that had overcome his senses.

1:10 *in Gath.* The reference here is to the lament of David in his mourning over the death of Saul and Jonathan (2 Sam. 1:20). Just as it was unseemly then to have the bad news of God's people profaned in a foreign city, so it would be in the present circumstance.

1:12 *Maroth.* This name means "bitterness." The name Jerusalem suggests "peace." Thus, the inhabitants of the "town of bitterness" would be sickened with dread, and the inhabitants of the "town of peace" would experience God's judgments.

1:16 *Shave your head.* This would have been the ultimate sign of mourning in a culture in which a man's hair was highly valued.

2:1–2 *plan iniquity . . . covet.* The ethical teaching of the prophets regularly included oracles of judgment against greed, theft, and oppression, actions of the powerful in attacking the weak. To covet is not just to have a passing thought; it is a determination to seize what is not one's own.

2:4 *He assigns our fields to traitors.* God would take the property rights from those who had seized them illegally and give them to people who were even more reprobate than they were.

2:5–6 *no one . . . to divide the land by lot.* Land-grabbers would no longer have a legitimate claim among God's people. God would dispossess

1:8 [t] Isa 15:3 **1:9** [u] Jer 46:11 [v] 2Ki 18:13 [w] Isa 3:26
1:11 [x] Eze 23:29 **1:12** [y] Jer 14:19 **1:13** [z] Jos 10:3
1:14 [a] 2Ki 16:8 [b] Jos 15:44 [c] Jer 15:18 **1:15** [d] Jos 15:44
[e] Jos 12:15 **1:16** [f] Job 1:20 **2:1** [g] Ps 36:4 **2:2** [h] Isa 5:8
[i] Jer 22:17 **2:3** [j] Jer 18:11; Am 3:1-2 [k] Isa 2:12
2:4 [l] Jer 4:13 **2:5** [m] Jos 18:4 **2:6** [n] Mic 6:16 [o] Am 2:12
2:7 [p] Ps 119:65 [q] Ps 15:2; 84:11

8 Lately my people have risen up
like an enemy.
You strip off the rich robe
from those who pass by without a care,
like men returning from battle.
9 You drive the women of my people
from their pleasant homes.[r]
You take away my blessing
from their children forever.
10 Get up, go away!
For this is not your resting place,[s]
because it is defiled,[t]
it is ruined, beyond all remedy.
11 If a liar and deceiver[u] comes and says,
'I will prophesy for you plenty of wine and beer,'
that would be just the prophet for this people![v]

Deliverance Promised

12 "I will surely gather all of you, Jacob;
I will surely bring together the remnant[w] of Israel.
I will bring them together like sheep in a pen,
like a flock in its pasture;
the place will throng with people.
13 The One who breaks open the way will go up before[x] them;
they will break through the gate and go out.
Their King will pass through before them,
the LORD at their head."

Leaders and Prophets Rebuked

3 Then I said,

"Listen, you leaders[y] of Jacob,
you rulers of Israel.
Should you not embrace justice,
2 you who hate good and love evil;
who tear the skin from my people
and the flesh from their bones;[z]
3 who eat my people's flesh,[a]
strip off their skin
and break their bones in pieces;[b]
who chop them up like meat for the pan,
like flesh for the pot?[c]"
4 Then they will cry out to the LORD,
but he will not answer them.[d]
At that time he will hide his face[e] from them
because of the evil they have done.

5 This is what the LORD says:

"As for the prophets
who lead my people astray,[f]
they proclaim 'peace'
if they have something to eat,
but prepare to wage war against anyone
who refuses to feed them.
6 Therefore night will come over you,
without visions,
and darkness, without divination.[g]
The sun will set for the prophets,[h]
and the day will go dark for them.
7 The seers will be ashamed[i]
and the diviners disgraced.[j]
They will all cover their faces
because there is no answer from God."
8 But as for me, I am filled with power,
with the Spirit of the LORD,
and with justice and might,
to declare to Jacob his transgression,
to Israel his sin.[k]

9 Hear this, you leaders of Jacob,
you rulers of Israel,
who despise justice
and distort all that is right;[l]
10 who build[m] Zion with bloodshed,[n]
and Jerusalem with wickedness.[o]
11 Her leaders judge for a bribe,
her priests teach for a price,
and her prophets tell fortunes for money.[p]
Yet they look for the LORD's support and say,
"Is not the LORD among us?
No disaster will come upon us."[q]

---

them even as they had dispossessed others. ***Do not prophesy.*** These words may have been a strong warning to Micah not to be like the lying prophets who counseled that all was well in the land.

2:12–13 ***gather . . . bring together . . . bring them together.*** The verbs are emphatic, demonstrating the certainty of God's determination to bring to pass His good pleasure on His people (Deut. 30:1–6). ***they will break through.*** This phrase speaks of regathering Israel from wherever the people may have been scattered.

3:1 ***Should you not embrace justice.*** The idea here is that one might not expect justice from pagan leaders in a faraway place. But the rulers of the people of God were expected to emphasize justice. Justice is one of the key concepts of the law (Deut. 10:18; 32:4; 33:21). Perverting justice was strongly prohibited by God (Deut. 16:19; 24:17), yet this was precisely what the leaders of Judah were doing. They had used their authority to destroy justice rather than to establish it among the people.

3:5–7 ***As for the prophets.*** This oracle was against false prophets who proclaimed peace, causing the people to be unprepared for trouble. These prophets would have neither true prophetic insight, nor help from the forbidden arts of divination. Finally, they would have nothing to say, for there would be no answer from God.

3:11 ***bribe . . . price . . . money.*** The wicked leaders and prophets of Israel "worked" only when they could gain something from it. Needless to say, if justice had to be paid for, it would not be justice. ***Is not the LORD***

2:9 [r] Jer 10:20 **2:10** [s] Dt 12:9 [t] Lev 18:25-29; Ps 106:38-39 **2:11** [u] Jer 5:31 [v] Isa 30:10 **2:12** [w] Mic 4:7; 5:7; 7:18 **2:13** [x] Isa 52:12 **3:1** [y] Jer 5:5 **3:2** [z] Ps 53:4; Eze 22:27 **3:3** [a] Ps 14:4 [b] Zep 3:3 [c] Eze 11:7 **3:4** [d] Ps 18:41; Isa 1:15 [e] Dt 31:17 **3:5** [f] Isa 3:12; 9:16 **3:6** [g] Isa 8:19-22 [h] Isa 29:10 **3:7** [i] Mic 7:16 [j] Isa 44:25 **3:8** [k] Isa 58:1 **3:9** [l] Ps 58:1-2; Isa 1:23 **3:10** [m] Jer 22:13 [n] Hab 2:12 [o] Eze 22:27 **3:11** [p] Isa 1:23; Jer 6:13; Hos 4:8, 18 [q] Jer 7:4

12 Therefore because of you,
Zion will be plowed like a field,
Jerusalem will become a heap of rubble,[r]
the temple hill a mound overgrown
with thickets.

The Mountain of the LORD

4 In the last days

the mountain[s] of the LORD's temple will
be established
as the highest of the mountains;
it will be exalted above the hills,[t]
and peoples will stream to it.[u]

2 Many nations will come and say,

"Come, let us go up to the mountain of
the LORD,[v]
to the temple of the God of Jacob.[w]
He will teach us his ways,[x]
so that we may walk in his paths."
The law will go out from Zion,
the word of the LORD from Jerusalem.
3 He will judge between many peoples
and will settle disputes for strong
nations far and wide.[y]
They will beat their swords into
plowshares
and their spears into pruning hooks.[z]
Nation will not take up sword against
nation,
nor will they train for war anymore.[a]
4 Everyone will sit under their own vine
and under their own fig tree,[b]
and no one will make them afraid,[c]
for the LORD Almighty has spoken.[d]
5 All the nations may walk
in the name of their gods,[e]
but we will walk in the name of the LORD
our God for ever and ever.[f]

The LORD's Plan

6 "In that day," declares the LORD,

"I will gather the lame;
I will assemble the exiles[g]
and those I have brought to grief.[h]
7 I will make the lame my remnant,[i]
those driven away a strong nation.
The LORD will rule over them in Mount
Zion
from that day and forever.[j]
8 As for you, watchtower of the flock,
stronghold[a] of Daughter Zion,
the former dominion will be restored[k] to
you;
kingship will come to Daughter
Jerusalem."

9 Why do you now cry aloud—
have you no king[b][l]?
Has your ruler[c] perished,
that pain seizes you like that of a
woman in labor?[m]
10 Writhe in agony, Daughter Zion,
like a woman in labor,
for now you must leave the city
to camp in the open field.
You will go to Babylon;[n]
there you will be rescued.
There the LORD will redeem[o] you
out of the hand of your enemies.

11 But now many nations
are gathered against you.
They say, "Let her be defiled,
let our eyes gloat[p] over Zion!"
12 But they do not know
the thoughts of the LORD;
they do not understand his plan,[q]
that he has gathered them like
sheaves to the threshing floor.
13 "Rise and thresh, Daughter Zion,
for I will give you horns of iron;
I will give you hooves of bronze,
and you will break to pieces many
nations."[r]
You will devote their ill-gotten gains to
the LORD,
their wealth to the Lord of all the
earth.

[a] 8 Or *hill* [b] 9 Or *King* [c] 9 Or *Ruler*

among us? Many people of Jerusalem believed that they would not be affected by God's judgment because God Himself dwelled in the holy temple in Jerusalem. They reasoned that, despite their evils, as long as God was in His temple they were safe—even from divine judgment. What people refused to believe was that God might leave His temple because of the sinfulness of the people (Ezek. 10).

4:1 *In the last days.* This is an indication of a prophecy of end times.

4:2 *we may walk in his paths.* Unlike the people of Micah's generation who were strangers to justice (3:1), the peoples of the coming kingdom will be obedient to God.

4:3 *swords ... spears.* All weapons of destruction will be recycled into tools of production. There will finally be an end to conflict. War will not even be a subject for study any more.

4:4 *vine ... fig tree.* Both are symbols of peace and prosperity (Zech. 3:10).

4:7 *remnant.* The majority of people in Israel did not live their lives in faith and dedication to the Lord. However, true faith never really died out in Israel, even in the worst of times.

4:9–10 *like that of a woman in labor.* The troubles of the present moment would lead finally to the birth of a deliverer. You will go ***to Babylon.*** This refers to the exile.

4:13 *Rise and thresh.* The nations would be gathered by the Lord like sheaves on the threshing floor (v. 12). This is a way of speaking of the final victory over all of Israel's foes.

3:12 [r] Jer 26:18 **4:1** [s] Zec 8:3 [t] Eze 17:22 [u] Ps 22:27; 86:9; Jer 3:17 **4:2** [v] Jer 31:6 [w] Zec 2:11; 14:16 [x] Ps 25:8-9; Isa 54:13 **4:3** [y] Isa 11:4 [z] Joel 3:10 [a] Isa 2:4 **4:4** [b] 1Ki 4:25 [c] Lev 26:6 [d] Isa 1:20; Zec 3:10 **4:5** [e] 2Ki 17:29 [f] Jos 24:14-15; Isa 26:8; Zec 10:12 **4:6** [g] Ps 147:2 [h] Eze 34:13, 16; 37:21; Zep 3:19 **4:7** [i] Mic 2:12 [j] Da 7:14; Lk 1:33; Rev 11:15 **4:8** [k] Isa 1:26 **4:9** [l] Jer 8:19 [m] Jer 30:6 **4:10** [n] 2Ki 20:18; Isa 43:14 [o] Isa 48:20 **4:11** [p] La 2:16; Ob 1:12 **4:12** [q] Isa 55:8; Ro 11:33-34 **4:13** [r] Da 2:44

A Promised Ruler From Bethlehem

5[a] Marshal your troops now, city of troops,
for a siege is laid against us.
They will strike Israel's ruler
on the cheek[s] with a rod.

2 "But you, Bethlehem[t] Ephrathah,[u]
though you are small among the clans[b] of Judah,
out of you will come for me
one who will be ruler over Israel,
whose origins are from of old,[v]
from ancient times."[w]

3 Therefore Israel will be abandoned
until the time when she who is in labor bears a son,
and the rest of his brothers return
to join the Israelites.

4 He will stand and shepherd his flock[x]
in the strength of the LORD,
in the majesty of the name of the LORD his God.
And they will live securely, for then his greatness[y]
will reach to the ends of the earth.

5 And he will be our peace[z]
when the Assyrians invade[a] our land
and march through our fortresses.
We will raise against them seven shepherds,
even eight commanders,[b]
6 who will rule[c] the land of Assyria with the sword,
the land of Nimrod[c] with drawn sword.[d][d]
He will deliver us from the Assyrians
when they invade our land
and march across our borders.[e]

7 The remnant[f] of Jacob will be
in the midst of many peoples
like dew from the LORD,
like showers on the grass,[g]
which do not wait for anyone
or depend on man.
8 The remnant of Jacob will be among the nations,
in the midst of many peoples,
like a lion among the beasts of the forest,[h]
like a young lion among flocks of sheep,
which mauls and mangles[i] as it goes,
and no one can rescue.[j]
9 Your hand will be lifted up[k] in triumph
over your enemies,
and all your foes will be destroyed.

10 "In that day," declares the LORD,

"I will destroy your horses from among you
and demolish your chariots.[l]
11 I will destroy the cities[m] of your land
and tear down all your strongholds.[n]
12 I will destroy your witchcraft
and you will no longer cast spells.[o]
13 I will destroy your idols
and your sacred stones from among you;
you will no longer bow down
to the work of your hands.[p]
14 I will uproot from among you your Asherah poles[e][q]
when I demolish your cities.
15 I will take vengeance[r] in anger and wrath
on the nations that have not obeyed me."

The LORD's Case Against Israel

6 Listen to what the LORD says:

"Stand up, plead my case before the mountains;[s]
let the hills hear what you have to say.

2 "Hear,[t] you mountains, the LORD's accusation;[u]
listen, you everlasting foundations of the earth.
For the LORD has a case against his people;
he is lodging a charge[v] against Israel.

---

[a] In Hebrew texts 5:1 is numbered 4:14, and 5:2-15 is numbered 5:1-14. [b] 2 Or *rulers* [c] 6 Or *crush* [d] 6 Or *Nimrod in its gates* [e] 14 That is, wooden symbols of the goddess Asherah

---

5:2 *Bethlehem.* This name means "House of Bread." ***Ephrathah.*** This locates the village in a known region in Judah (Gen. 35:16). This prophecy figures significantly in the New Testament story of the visit of the wise men to the Christ child (Matt. 2:1–12). ***origins.*** The birth of this Savior King would be unlike the birth of any other, because He was preexistent. He is "from ancient times."

5:3 *she who is in labor.* This probably refers to Zion (4:10). The metaphor refers to the deliverance in the end time of those who will be able to delight in the coming of God's kingdom (4:9—5:1).

5:7 *dew ... showers.* Jewish people are blessings from God on their neighbors.

5:10 *I will destroy.* It was God's intention to destroy the evils in Israel's society. Horses and chariots represent the pride of Israel's military power. Israel's tendency was to rely on its own military power rather than on the Lord.

6:1–2 *mountains ... hills.* These were among the witnesses to the covenant that God made with His people (Deut. 4:26; 32:1; Is. 1:2).

5:1 [s] La 3:30 **5:2** [t] Jn 7:42 [u] Ge 48:7 [v] Ps 102:25 [w] Mt 2:6* **5:4** [x] Isa 40:11; 49:9; Eze 34:11-15, 23; Mic 7:14 [y] Isa 52:13; Lk 1:32 **5:5** [z] Isa 9:6; Lk 2:14; Col 1:19-20 [a] Isa 8:7 [b] Isa 10:24-27 **5:6** [c] Ge 10:8 [d] Zep 2:13 [e] Na 2:11-13 **5:7** [f] Mic 2:12 [g] Isa 44:4 **5:8** [h] Ge 49:9 [i] Mic 4:13; Zec 10:5 [j] Ps 50:22; Hos 5:14 **5:9** [k] Ps 10:12 **5:10** [l] Hos 14:3; Zec 9:10 **5:11** [m] Isa 6:11 [n] Hos 10:14; Am 5:9 **5:12** [o] Dt 18:10-12; Isa 2:6; 8:19 **5:13** [p] Eze 6:9; Zec 13:2 **5:14** [q] Ex 34:13 **5:15** [r] Isa 65:12 **6:1** [s] Ps 50:1; Eze 6:2 **6:2** [t] Dt 32:1 [u] Hos 12:2 [v] Ps 50:7

3 "My people, what have I done to you?
How have I burdened[w] you?
Answer me.
4 I brought you up out of Egypt
and redeemed you from the land of slavery.[x]
I sent Moses[y] to lead you,
also Aaron[z] and Miriam.[a]
5 My people, remember
what Balak[b] king of Moab plotted
and what Balaam son of Beor answered.
Remember your journey from Shittim[c] to Gilgal,[d]
that you may know the righteous acts[e] of the LORD."

6 With what shall I come before the LORD
and bow down before the exalted God?
Shall I come before him with burnt offerings,
with calves a year old?[f]
7 Will the LORD be pleased with thousands of rams,[g]
with ten thousand rivers of olive oil?[h]
Shall I offer my firstborn[i] for my transgression,
the fruit of my body for the sin of my soul?[j]
8 He has shown you, O mortal, what is good.
And what does the LORD require of you?
To act justly[k] and to love mercy
and to walk humbly[a][l] with your God.[m]

Israel's Guilt and Punishment

9 Listen! The LORD is calling to the city—
and to fear your name is wisdom—
"Heed the rod and the One who appointed it.[b]
10 Am I still to forget your ill-gotten treasures, you wicked house,
and the short ephah,[c] which is accursed?[n]
11 Shall I acquit someone with dishonest scales,[o]
with a bag of false weights?
12 Your rich people are violent;[p]
your inhabitants are liars[q]
and their tongues speak deceitfully.[r]
13 Therefore, I have begun to destroy[s] you,
to ruin[d] you because of your sins.
14 You will eat but not be satisfied;[t]
your stomach will still be empty.[e]
You will store up but save nothing,[u]
because what you save[f] I will give to the sword.
15 You will plant but not harvest;[v]
you will press olives but not use the oil,
you will crush grapes but not drink the wine.[w]
16 You have observed the statutes of Omri[x]
and all the practices of Ahab's[y] house;
you have followed their traditions.[z]
Therefore I will give you over to ruin[a]
and your people to derision;
you will bear the scorn[b] of the nations.[g]"

Israel's Misery

7 What misery is mine!
I am like one who gathers summer fruit
at the gleaning of the vineyard;
there is no cluster of grapes to eat,
none of the early figs that I crave.
2 The faithful have been swept from the land;[c]
not one upright person remains.
Everyone lies in wait to shed blood;[d]
they hunt each other with nets.[e]
3 Both hands are skilled in doing evil;[f]
the ruler demands gifts,
the judge accepts bribes,
the powerful dictate what they desire—
they all conspire together.

---

[a] 8 Or *prudently* [b] 9 The meaning of the Hebrew for this line is uncertain. [c] 10 An ephah was a dry measure. [d] 13 Or *Therefore, I will make you ill and destroy you; / I will ruin* [e] 14 The meaning of the Hebrew for this word is uncertain. [f] 14 Or *You will press toward birth but not give birth, / and what you bring to birth* [g] 16 Septuagint; Hebrew *scorn due my people*

6:7 *Will the LORD be pleased.* The idea of bringing pleasure to God through sacrifice is found elsewhere in the Bible. God is pleased with those who do as He commands (Gen. 4:1–8).
6:8 *what does the LORD require of you?* This verse speaks of the underlying attitudes that must accompany all true worship. The idea here is that God seeks certain characteristics of true worship from His people. ***act justly . . . love mercy . . . walk humbly.*** These three phrases summarize biblical piety in true worship. The majority of the people of Israel had violated each of these standards repeatedly. ***with your God.*** It is the Lord who ultimately gives a person strength, courage, and ability to exercise the virtues of godly living.
7:1–2 *What misery is mine!* Micah was moved by the oracles of judgment that God delivered through him (1:8). There is not a cluster. For Micah, the harvest was over. There was nothing around him but undesirable fruit. ***The faithful have been swept from the land.*** The norms of society had broken down; everyone was out to destroy someone else.
7:3–4 *Both hands.* The people were pursuing evil with gusto. The leaders of the state were leading the

6:3 [w] Jer 2:5 **6:4** [x] Dt 7:8 [y] Ex 4:16 [z] Ps 77:20 [a] Ex 15:20 **6:5** [b] Nu 22:5-6 [c] Nu 25:1 [d] Jos 5:9-10 [e] Jdg 5:11; 1Sa 12:7 **6:6** [f] Ps 40:6-8; 51:16-17 **6:7** [g] Isa 40:16 [h] Ps 50:8-10 [i] Lev 18:21 [j] 2Ki 16:3 **6:8** [k] Isa 1:17; Jer 22:3 [l] Isa 57:15 [m] Dt 10:12-13; 1Sa 15:22; Hos 6:6 **6:10** [n] Eze 45:9-10; Am 3:10; 8:4-6 **6:11** [o] Lev 19:36; Hos 12:7 **6:12** [p] Isa 1:23 [q] Isa 3:8 [r] Jer 9:3 **6:13** [s] Isa 1:7; 6:11 **6:14** [t] Isa 9:20 [u] Isa 30:6 **6:15** [v] Dt 28:38; Jer 12:13 [w] Am 5:11; Zep 1:13 **6:16** [x] 1Ki 16:25 [y] 1Ki 16:29-33 [z] Jer 7:24 [a] Jer 25:9 [b] Jer 51:51 **7:2** [c] Ps 12:1 [d] Mic 3:10 [e] Jer 5:26 **7:3** [f] Pr 4:16

4 The best of them is like a brier,[g]
the most upright worse than a thorn hedge.
The day God visits you has come,
the day your watchmen sound the alarm.
Now is the time of your confusion.[h]
5 Do not trust a neighbor;
put no confidence in a friend.[i]
Even with the woman who lies in your embrace
guard the words of your lips.
6 For a son dishonors his father,
a daughter rises up against her mother,[j]
a daughter-in-law against her mother-in-law—
a man's enemies are the members of his own household.[k]

7 But as for me, I watch in hope[l] for the LORD,
I wait for God my Savior;
my God will hear[m] me.

Israel Will Rise

8 Do not gloat over me,[n] my enemy!
Though I have fallen, I will rise.[o]
Though I sit in darkness,
the LORD will be my light.[p]
9 Because I have sinned against him,
I will bear the LORD's wrath,[q]
until he pleads my case
and upholds my cause.
He will bring me out into the light;
I will see his righteousness.[r]
10 Then my enemy will see it
and will be covered with shame,[s]
she who said to me,
"Where is the LORD your God?"
My eyes will see her downfall;[t]
even now she will be trampled[u] underfoot
like mire in the streets.

11 The day for building your walls[v] will come,
the day for extending your boundaries.
12 In that day people will come to you
from Assyria and the cities of Egypt,
even from Egypt to the Euphrates
and from sea to sea
and from mountain to mountain.[w]
13 The earth will become desolate because of its inhabitants,
as the result of their deeds.[x]

Prayer and Praise

14 Shepherd[y] your people with your staff,[z]
the flock of your inheritance,
which lives by itself in a forest,
in fertile pasturelands.[a]
Let them feed in Bashan and Gilead[a]
as in days long ago.

15 "As in the days when you came out of Egypt,
I will show them my wonders.[b]"

16 Nations will see and be ashamed,[c]
deprived of all their power.
They will put their hands over their mouths
and their ears will become deaf.
17 They will lick dust like a snake,
like creatures that crawl on the ground.
They will come trembling out of their dens;
they will turn in fear[d] to the LORD our God
and will be afraid of you.
18 Who is a God like you,
who pardons sin[e] and forgives[f] the transgression
of the remnant[g] of his inheritance?[h]

[a] 14 Or *in the middle of Carmel*

---

way in evil (3:11). ***the day your watchman.*** This refers to the time when people needed to be alert for the approach of an enemy army. In this context, judgment was imminent.

7:7 *I watch in hope for the LORD.* While there would need to be a watchman for the coming of an enemy army, Micah was going to look for the advent of the Lord.

7:8–9 *I have sinned.* This is the confession of the people in saving faith.

7:11–12 *In that day.* These words call attention to a future day, the time of the end.

7:16–17 *Nations will see and be ashamed.* The response of the wicked nations to the renewed mercies of God on His people would be terror. The nations would be humiliated because they had taunted Israel in the day of its trouble (vv. 8–10).

7:18–20 God's Mercy—There is a significant passage on mercy or love like this in every book in the Old Testament. God wants His people to succeed and be prosperous. He wants the best for them. He is always eager to restore them. He protects, directs, sustains, and covenants with them. His steadfast love is characterized by faithfulness in spite of constant wandering in unfaithfulness.

In the New Testament, it is also easy to find passages in every book where someone is being judged. Usually it's the religious people who have set themselves up in God's place or those who have turned away from God when they should know better who are condemned.

The Old Testament predicts, leads toward, and sets the scene for the ultimate judgment of the New Testament. The entire Bible consistently points to the kind of creatures we are because of the fall and sin. Only God has the ultimate solution in Christ. God subjects Himself to that ultimate judgment for us so

7:4 [g] Eze 2:6 [h] Isa 22:5; Hos 9:7 **7:5** [i] Jer 9:4 **7:6** [j] Eze 22:7 [k] Mt 10:35-36* **7:7** [l] Ps 130:5; Isa 25:9 [m] Ps 4:3 **7:8** [n] Pr 24:17 [o] Ps 37:24; Am 9:11 [p] Isa 9:2 **7:9** [q] La 3:39-40 [r] Isa 46:13 **7:10** [s] Ps 35:26 [t] Isa 51:23 [u] Zec 10:5 **7:11** [v] Isa 54:11 **7:12** [w] Isa 19:23-25 **7:13** [x] Isa 3:10-11 **7:14** [y] Mic 5:4 [z] Ps 23:4 [a] Jer 50:19 **7:15** [b] Ex 3:20; Ps 78:12 **7:16** [c] Isa 26:11 **7:17** [d] Isa 25:3; 49:23; 59:19 **7:18** [e] Isa 43:25; Jer 50:20 [f] Ps 103:8-13 [g] Mic 2:12 [h] Ex 34:9

You do not stay angry[i] forever
but delight to show mercy.[j]
19 You will again have compassion on us;
you will tread our sins underfoot
and hurl all our iniquities[k] into the
depths of the sea.[l]
20 You will be faithful to
Jacob,
and show love to Abraham,
as you pledged on oath to our
ancestors[m]
in days long ago.

---

that all of His love for us may be realized. It's a mystery that we can solve only in our hearts by accepting and believing its implications.

Every day our prayer needs to be, "Lord, My sins are ever with me. I deserve your judgment. Thank you for the great mercy I've received through Jesus' death for me. That He died in my place must always be the primary reality in my life."

7:18 *Who is a God like you.* These words speak of the incomparability of God. There is nothing in all of creation to compare with God (Is. 40:25).

7:20 *as you pledged.* This last verse is reminiscent of God's promise to Abraham in Genesis 12; 15; 22 and His promises to Jacob in Genesis 32. The Lord had sworn to fulfill His promises to the patriarchs. He would not—could not—leave His promise unfulfilled (Ps. 89:33).

7:18 [i] Ps 103:9 [j] Jer 32:41 **7:19** [k] Isa 43:25 [l] Jer 31:34
7:20 [m] Dt 7:8; Lk 1:72

NAHUM

▸ **AUTHOR:** The only mention of Nahum in the Old Testament is found in 1:1 where he is called an Elkoshite. Scholars have been unable to determine the exact location of Elkosh and numerous theories exist, but due to his interest in the triumph of Judah (1:15; 2:2), some believe Nahum to be a prophet of the southern kingdom.

▸ **TIME:** c. 660 B.C. ▸ **KEY VERSES:** Nah. 1:7 – 8

▸ **THEME:** Nahum is unique in that it is a prophecy addressed completely to a nation other than Israel: Assyria and its capital Nineveh. While Nineveh may be powerful, her day of destruction is coming. Nineveh is not invincible. The message is that God's standards apply to all nations, not just Israel and Judah. They need to be prepared to live by those standards or face judgment.

1 A prophecy[a] concerning Nineveh.[b] The
book of the vision of Nahum the Elkoshite.

The LORD's Anger Against Nineveh

2 The LORD is a jealous[c] and avenging God;
the LORD takes vengeance[d] and is filled with wrath.
The LORD takes vengeance on his foes
and vents his wrath against his enemies.
3 The LORD is slow to anger[e] but great in power;
the LORD will not leave the guilty unpunished.[f]
His way is in the whirlwind and the storm,
and clouds[g] are the dust of his feet.
4 He rebukes the sea and dries it up;
he makes all the rivers run dry.
Bashan and Carmel[h] wither
and the blossoms of Lebanon fade.
5 The mountains quake[i] before him
and the hills melt away.[j]
The earth trembles at his presence,
the world and all who live in it.
6 Who can withstand his indignation?
Who can endure[k] his fierce anger?
His wrath is poured out like fire;[l]
the rocks are shattered[m] before him.

7 The LORD is good,[n]
a refuge in times of trouble.
He cares for[o] those who trust in him,
8 but with an overwhelming flood
he will make an end of Nineveh;
he will pursue his foes into the realm of darkness.

9 Whatever they plot against the LORD
he will bring[a] to an end;
trouble will not come a second time.
10 They will be entangled among thorns[p]
and drunk from their wine;
they will be consumed like dry stubble.[b][q]
11 From you, Nineveh, has one come forth
who plots evil against the LORD
and devises wicked plans.

[a] 9 Or *What do you foes plot against the LORD? / He will bring it* [b] 10 The meaning of the Hebrew for this verse is uncertain.

1:2 *The LORD is a jealous and avenging God.* The repetition of words and the use of parallel terms are typical devices in Hebrew poetry for intensifying and sharpening the poet's message.
1:3 *whirlwind ... storm ... clouds.* The peoples of the ancient Middle East worshiped nature gods, particularly deities associated with storms, clouds, and rainfall. In Canaan, this fixation on storms was centered in the worship of Baal and his consorts Anat and Asherah. The Scriptures testify that there are no gods but the Lord; it is He who rules and is above all creation.
1:8 *flood ... end ... darkness.* The judgment of the Lord will be inescapable. The word "flood" is both a poetic term for overwhelming devastation and a specific reference to the actual manner of Nineveh's fall. It is believed that the invaders of Nineveh entered the city through its flooded waterways (2:6).
1:11 *wicked.* "Wicked" is one of the harshest terms in biblical language, nearly a curse word. The term speaks of someone who is utterly worthless.

1:1 [a] Isa 13:1; 19:1; Jer 23:33-34 [b] Jnh 1:2; Na 2:8; Zep 2:13 **1:2** [c] Ex 20:5 [d] Dt 32:41; Ps 94:1 **1:3** [e] Ne 9:17 [f] Ex 34:7 [g] Ps 104:3 **1:4** [h] Isa 33:9 **1:5** [i] Ex 19:18 [j] Mic 1:4 **1:6** [k] Mal 3:2 [l] Jer 10:10 [m] 1Ki 19:11 **1:7** [n] Jer 33:11 [o] Ps 1:6 **1:10** [p] 2Sa 23:6 [q] Isa 5:24; Mal 4:1

12 This is what the LORD says:

"Although they have allies and are numerous,
they will be destroyed[r] and pass away.
Although I have afflicted you, Judah,
I will afflict you no more.[s]
13 Now I will break their yoke[t] from your neck
and tear your shackles away."

14 The LORD has given a command concerning you, Nineveh:
"You will have no descendants to bear your name.[u]
I will destroy the images[v] and idols
that are in the temple of your gods.
I will prepare your grave,[w]
for you are vile."

15 Look, there on the mountains,
the feet of one who brings good news,[x]
who proclaims peace![y]
Celebrate your festivals,[z] Judah,
and fulfill your vows.
No more will the wicked invade you;[a]
they will be completely destroyed.[a]

Nineveh to Fall

2 [b] An attacker[b] advances against you, Nineveh.
Guard the fortress,
watch the road,
brace yourselves,
marshal all your strength!

2 The LORD will restore[c] the splendor[d] of Jacob
like the splendor of Israel,
though destroyers have laid them waste
and have ruined their vines.

3 The shields of the soldiers are red;
the warriors are clad in scarlet.[e]
The metal on the chariots flashes
on the day they are made ready;
the spears of juniper are brandished.[c]
4 The chariots[f] storm through the streets,
rushing back and forth through the squares.
They look like flaming torches;
they dart about like lightning.

5 Nineveh summons her picked troops,
yet they stumble[g] on their way.
They dash to the city wall;
the protective shield is put in place.
6 The river gates[h] are thrown open
and the palace collapses.
7 It is decreed[d] that Nineveh
be exiled and carried away.
Her female slaves moan[i] like doves
and beat on their breasts.[j]
8 Nineveh is like a pool
whose water is draining away.
"Stop! Stop!" they cry,
but no one turns back.
9 Plunder the silver!
Plunder the gold!
The supply is endless,
the wealth from all its treasures!
10 She is pillaged, plundered, stripped!
Hearts melt, knees give way,
bodies tremble, every face grows pale.[k]

11 Where now is the lions' den,[l]
the place where they fed their young,
where the lion and lioness went,
and the cubs, with nothing to fear?
12 The lion killed[m] enough for his cubs
and strangled the prey for his mate,
filling his lairs with the kill
and his dens with the prey.

[a] 15 In Hebrew texts this verse (1:15) is numbered 2:1. [b] In Hebrew texts 2:1-13 is numbered 2:2-14. [c] 3 Hebrew; Septuagint and Syriac *ready; / the horsemen rush to and fro.* [d] 7 The meaning of the Hebrew for this word is uncertain.

1:14 ***you are vile.*** The only thing to be done with Nineveh was to dig a grave and bury it. The prophecy came true literally—the city was destroyed so completely that its very existence was questioned until its discovery by archaeologists in the nineteenth century (3:13–15).

2:1 ***Guard the fortress.*** These were sarcastic words to the people of Nineveh and its leaders, as if they would be able to protect themselves against the wrath of the Lord.

2:3–4 ***red ... scarlet ... flaming torches.*** These images speak of blood, violence, and warfare. Isaiah refers to the custom of the Assyrians of rolling their outer garments in blood before a battle (Is. 9:5) to strike terror in the hearts of their opponents. Here the tables would be turned. While others would have shields, chariots, and spears, the people of Nineveh would be bathed in blood—their own blood.

2:4 ***The chariots storm.*** The Assyrians used chariots as formidable war machines. The proficiency of the chariot drivers underlies the imagery of this verse. But, as in the case of the shields and spears of verse 3, the chariots of Nineveh would not prevail, no matter how fast they drove.

2:6 ***river gates.*** The destruction of Nineveh is believed to have taken place when the besiegers entered the city through its flooded waterways. The attack came at flood time, when rivers undermined the walls and defenses of the city. Archaeologists have found evidence of flood debris that may be associated with the destruction of the city. Thus, the words of Nahum were fulfilled exactly.

2:11–12 ***lions' den.*** Nineveh was the city of lions (v. 13). Yet, despite all the horrors that the lion of Nineveh had brought to other nations, it would no longer need to be feared by anyone. Although the Babylonians conquered the city, they were only God's instruments. Nineveh's greatest foe was God Himself.

1:12 [r] Isa 10:34 [s] Isa 54:6-8; La 3:31-32 **1:13** [t] Isa 9:4
1:14 [u] Isa 14:22 [v] Mic 5:13 [w] Eze 32:22-23
1:15 [x] Isa 40:9; Ro 10:15 [y] Isa 52:7 [z] Lev 23:2-4 [a] Isa 52:1
2:1 [b] Jer 51:20 **2:2** [c] Eze 37:23 [d] Isa 60:15
2:3 [e] Eze 23:14-15 **2:4** [f] Jer 4:13 **2:5** [g] Jer 46:12
2:6 [h] Na 3:13 **2:7** [i] Isa 59:11 [j] Isa 32:12 **2:10** [k] Isa 29:22
2:11 [l] Isa 5:29 **2:12** [m] Jer 51:34

13 "I am against[n] you,"
declares the LORD Almighty.
"I will burn up your chariots in smoke,[o]
and the sword will devour your young lions.
I will leave you no prey on the earth.
The voices of your messengers
will no longer be heard."

Woe to Nineveh

3 Woe to the city of blood,[p]
full of lies,
full of plunder,
never without victims!
2 The crack of whips,
the clatter of wheels,
galloping horses
and jolting chariots!
3 Charging cavalry,
flashing swords
and glittering spears!
Many casualties,
piles of dead,
bodies without number,
people stumbling over the corpses[q]—
4 all because of the wanton lust of a prostitute,
alluring, the mistress of sorceries,[r]
who enslaved nations by her prostitutions[s]
and peoples by her witchcraft.

5 "I am against[t] you," declares the LORD Almighty.
"I will lift your skirts[u] over your face.
I will show the nations your nakedness[v]
and the kingdoms your shame.
6 I will pelt you with filth,[w]
I will treat you with contempt[x]
and make you a spectacle.[y]
7 All who see you will flee from you and say,
'Nineveh[z] is in ruins—who will mourn for her?'[a]
Where can I find anyone to comfort[b] you?"

8 Are you better than[c] Thebes,[d]
situated on the Nile,[e]
with water around her?
The river was her defense,
the waters her wall.
9 Cush[a][f] and Egypt were her boundless strength;
Put[g] and Libya[h] were among her allies.
10 Yet she was taken captive[i]
and went into exile.
Her infants were dashed[j] to pieces
at every street corner.
Lots were cast for her nobles,
and all her great men were put in chains.
11 You too will become drunk;[k]
you will go into hiding[l]
and seek refuge from the enemy.

12 All your fortresses are like fig trees
with their first ripe fruit;
when they are shaken,
the figs[m] fall into the mouth of the eater.
13 Look at your troops—
they are all weaklings.[n]
The gates[o] of your land
are wide open to your enemies;
fire has consumed the bars of your gates.[p]

14 Draw water for the siege,[q]
strengthen your defenses![r]
Work the clay,
tread the mortar,
repair the brickwork!
15 There the fire will consume you;
the sword will cut you down—
they will devour you like a swarm of locusts.
Multiply like grasshoppers,
multiply like locusts![s]
16 You have increased the number of your merchants
till they are more numerous than the stars in the sky,
but like locusts they strip the land
and then fly away.

[a] 9 That is, the upper Nile region

3:4 *wanton lust of a prostitute.* Any worship of gods other than the God of Scriptures is an act of spiritual prostitution. Nineveh was so adept at pagan practices that the city earned the descriptive title, "the mistress of witchcrafts."

3:6–7 *I will pelt you with filth.* The Lord described the fate of Nineveh as comparable to a person on whom unspeakable filth was thrown. When Nineveh lay in ruins, no one would grieve for her. The nations would be glad that the city was gone.

3:8 *Thebes.* In Hebrew, Thebes is known as No Amon, derived from the Egyptian name meaning "city of the god Amon." The argument seems to suggest that, before its destruction, no one would have even dreamed of the fall of Thebes. But the destruction had happened—not long before the writing of the Book of Nahum. The city of Thebes was rebuilt only to be destroyed later during the Roman period (29 B.C.). Nineveh, however, would never be rebuilt.

3:11 *drunk ... hiding ... seek refuge.* Nineveh would be like a helpless drunk hoping for strength but finding nowhere to turn for it.

3:16–17 *when the sun appears.* The people of Nineveh would be like nocturnal insects that disappear at daylight.

2:13 [n] Jer 21:13; Na 3:5 [o] Ps 46:9 **3:1** [p] Eze 22:2; Mic 3:10 **3:3** [q] 2Ki 19:35; Isa 34:3 **3:4** [r] Isa 47:9 [s] Isa 23:17; Eze 16:25-29 **3:5** [t] Na 2:13 [u] Jer 13:22 [v] Isa 47:3 **3:6** [w] Job 9:31 [x] 1Sa 2:30; Jer 51:37 [y] Isa 14:16 **3:7** [z] Na 1:1 [a] Jer 15:5 [b] Isa 51:19 **3:8** [c] Am 6:2 [d] Jer 46:25 [e] Isa 19:6-9 **3:9** [f] 2Ch 12:3 [g] Eze 27:10 [h] Eze 30:5 **3:10** [i] Isa 20:4 [j] Isa 13:16; Hos 13:16 **3:11** [k] Isa 49:26 [l] Isa 2:10 **3:12** [m] Isa 28:4 **3:13** [n] Isa 19:16; Jer 50:37 [o] Na 2:6 [p] Isa 45:2 **3:14** [q] 2Ch 32:4 [r] Na 2:1 **3:15** [s] Joel 1:4

17 Your guards are like locusts,[t]
your officials like swarms of locusts
that settle in the walls on a cold day—
but when the sun appears they fly away,
and no one knows where.

18 King of Assyria, your shepherds[a] slumber;[u]
your nobles lie down to rest.[v]
Your people are scattered[w] on the mountains
with no one to gather them.

19 Nothing can heal you;[x]
your wound is fatal.
All who hear the news about you
clap their hands[y] at your fall,
for who has not felt
your endless cruelty?

[a] *18* That is, rulers

3:19 *All who hear.* Every nation and people that had suffered under the abusive power of Nineveh would shout and clap upon hearing of the city's destruction. There would be no mourning for Nineveh.

3:17 [t] Jer 51:27 **3:18** [u] Ps 76:5-6 [v] Isa 56:10 [w] 1Ki 22:17 **3:19** [x] Jer 30:13; Mic 1:9 [y] Job 27:23; La 2:15; Zep 2:15

HABAKKUK

▶ **AUTHOR:** In both the introduction to the book (1:1) and the closing psalm (3:1) the author identifies himself as Habakkuk the prophet. It is believed that he might have been a priest as he mentions in the closing psalm "For the director of music. On my stringed instruments" (3:19). Also, in the apocryphal book of Bel and the Dragon, Daniel is rescued a second time by the prophet Habakkuk.

▶ **TIME:** c. 607 B.C. ▶ **KEY VERSE:** Hab. 2:4

▶ **THEME:** This whole book of Habakkuk is really devoted to the question of "Lord, if you are all powerful, why is evil allowed to exist?" The events that seem to be precipitating this question are the victories of Babylon. God was using Babylon, a nation without God, to punish Israel, God's own people. The answers God gives us to this question in Habakkuk solidly point us in one direction, but ultimately the answers are in faith in Him alone.

1 The prophecy[a] that Habakkuk the prophet received.

Habakkuk's Complaint

2 How long, LORD, must I call for help,
but you do not listen?[b]
Or cry out to you, "Violence!"
but you do not save?[c]
3 Why do you make me look at injustice?
Why do you tolerate[d] wrongdoing?
Destruction and violence[e] are before me;
there is strife,[f] and conflict abounds.
4 Therefore the law[g] is paralyzed,
and justice never prevails.
The wicked hem in the righteous,
so that justice is perverted.[h]

The LORD's Answer

5 "Look at the nations and watch—
and be utterly amazed.[i]
For I am going to do something in your days
that you would not believe,
even if you were told.[j]
6 I am raising up the Babylonians,[a][k]
that ruthless and impetuous people,
who sweep across the whole earth
to seize dwellings not their own.[l]
7 They are a feared and dreaded people;[m]
they are a law to themselves
and promote their own honor.
8 Their horses are swifter[n] than leopards,
fiercer than wolves at dusk.
Their cavalry gallops headlong;
their horsemen come from afar.
They fly like an eagle swooping to devour;
9 they all come intent on violence.
Their hordes[b] advance like a desert wind
and gather prisoners[o] like sand.
10 They mock kings
and scoff at rulers.[p]
They laugh at all fortified cities;
by building earthen ramps they capture them.

[a] 6 Or *Chaldeans* [b] 9 The meaning of the Hebrew for this word is uncertain.

1:2 ***How long, LORD . . . ?*** This question is phrased as a formal complaint (Ps. 13:1–2).
1:4 ***the law is paralyzed.*** The revelation of God given at Mount Sinai had little impact on the hearts of people whose lives were focused on material success. These people had little interest in living by God's definition of what is fair and humane. ***wicked.*** God's chosen people committed and tolerated heinous acts through the corruption of the courts.
1:5 ***Look at the nations.*** The international scene during Habakkuk's lifetime was full of turmoil, with Assyria on the decline and Babylonia on the rise.
1:6 ***I am raising up.*** God controls the nations for His own purposes (Dan. 2:21), sometimes indirectly and at other times directly.
1:7 ***feared and dreaded.*** Far from being humane, the Babylonians prided themselves on their arrogant use of raw power.
1:9 ***gather prisoners like sand.*** The Babylonians resettled numerous conquered peoples with little regard for them as individuals.

1:1 [a] Na 1:1 **1:2** [b] Ps 13:1-2; 22:1-2 [c] Jer 14:9 **1:3** [d] ver 13 [e] Jer 20:8 [f] Ps 55:9 **1:4** [g] Ps 119:126 [h] Job 19:7; Isa 1:23; 5:20; Eze 9:9 **1:5** [i] Isa 29:9 [j] Ac 13:41* **1:6** [k] 2Ki 24:2 [l] Jer 13:20 **1:7** [m] Isa 18:7; Jer 39:5-9 **1:8** [n] Jer 4:13 **1:9** [o] Hab 2:5 **1:10** [p] 2Ch 36:6

[11]Then they sweep past like the wind[q]
and go on—
guilty people, whose own strength is their god."[r]

Habakkuk's Second Complaint

[12]LORD, are you not from everlasting?
My God, my Holy One,[s] you[a] will never die.
You, LORD, have appointed[t] them to execute judgment;
you, my Rock, have ordained them to punish.
[13]Your eyes are too pure to look on evil;
you cannot tolerate wrongdoing.[u]
Why then do you tolerate the treacherous?
Why are you silent while the wicked
swallow up those more righteous than themselves?
[14]You have made people like the fish in the sea,
like the sea creatures that have no ruler.
[15]The wicked foe pulls all of them up with hooks,[v]
he catches them in his net,[w]
he gathers them up in his dragnet;
and so he rejoices and is glad.
[16]Therefore he sacrifices to his net
and burns incense[x] to his dragnet,
for by his net he lives in luxury
and enjoys the choicest food.
[17]Is he to keep on emptying his net,
destroying nations without mercy?[y]

2 I will stand at my watch[z]
and station myself on the ramparts;[a]
I will look to see what he will say[b] to me,
and what answer I am to give to this complaint.[bc]

The LORD's Answer

[2]Then the LORD replied:

"Write[d] down the revelation
and make it plain on tablets
so that a herald[c] may run with it.
[3]For the revelation awaits an appointed time;
it speaks of the end[e]
and will not prove false.
Though it linger, wait[f] for it;
it[d] will certainly come
and will not delay.[g]

[4]"See, the enemy is puffed up;
his desires are not upright—
but the righteous person will live by his faithfulness[eh]—
[5]indeed, wine[i] betrays him;
he is arrogant and never at rest.
Because he is as greedy as the grave
and like death is never satisfied,[j]
he gathers to himself all the nations
and takes captive all the peoples.

[6]"Will not all of them taunt[k] him with ridicule and scorn, saying,

"'Woe to him who piles up stolen goods
and makes himself wealthy by extortion![l]
How long must this go on?'
[7]Will not your creditors suddenly arise?
Will they not wake up and make you tremble?
Then you will become their prey.[m]

---

[a] 12 An ancient Hebrew scribal tradition; Masoretic Text *we* [b] 1 Or *and what to answer when I am rebuked* [c] 2 Or *so that whoever reads it* [d] 3 Or *Though he linger, wait for him; / he* [e] 4 Or *faith*

1:12 ***are you not from everlasting?*** Habakkuk's point seems to be that God's holiness should have prohibited Him from using a "dirty" instrument such as Babylon to accomplish His purposes in judging and reproving His own people.
1:16 ***he sacrifices to his net.*** This phrase speaks of the contemptuous pride of the Babylonians in their devices of destruction.
2:1 ***I will stand ... on the ramparts.*** Habakkuk stationed himself as a watchman to look at the nations, as God had commanded him. ***what he will say to me.*** Habakkuk's faith is seen in his anticipation of a response from God. ***what answer I am to give to this complaint.*** This phrase indicates the prophet's submission to God.
2:3 ***an appointed time.*** This speaks of a determined time in God's eyes. ***Though it linger, wait for it.*** God knows His plan and the outworking of all things in accordance with His purposes. The godly are responsible to study and proclaim His revelation while awaiting its fulfillment. it will certainly come. The fulfillment of the vision would not take any longer than God had planned.
2:4 ***the righteous person will live by his faithfulness.*** True righteousness before God is linked to genuine faith in God. A proud person relies on self, power, position, and accomplishment; a righteous person relies on the Lord.
2:5 ***all the nations ... all the peoples.*** These peoples of the earth should have been gathered together before the Lord in holy worship (Ps. 117:1); instead, they became morsels for the rapacious appetite of Babylon.
2:6 ***Woe to him.*** A woe is an oracle of judgment consisting of two parts: a declaration of the wrong and a notice of impending judgment. The judgment usually applies the principle of the law of retribution.
2:7 ***they.*** This Hebrew term has the idea of "those who bite," suggesting sudden, hurtful attacks (Mic. 3:5).

1:11 [q] Jer 4:11-12 [r] Da 4:30 **1:12** [s] Isa 31:1 [t] Isa 10:6 **1:13** [u] La 3:34-36 **1:15** [v] Isa 19:8 [w] Jer 16:16 **1:16** [x] Jer 44:8 **1:17** [y] Isa 14:6; 19:8 **2:1** [z] Isa 21:8 [a] Ps 48:13 [b] Ps 85:8 [c] Ps 5:3 **2:2** [d] Rev 1:19 **2:3** [e] Da 8:17; 10:14 [f] Ps 27:14 [g] Eze 12:25; Heb 10:37-38 **2:4** [h] Ro 1:17*; Gal 3:11*; Heb 10:37-38* **2:5** [i] Pr 20:1 [j] Pr 27:20; 30:15-16 **2:6** [k] Isa 14:4 [l] Am 2:8 **2:7** [m] Pr 29:1

8 Because you have plundered many nations,
the peoples who are left will plunder you.[n]
For you have shed human blood;[o]
you have destroyed lands and cities
and everyone in them.

9 "Woe to him who builds[p] his house by unjust gain,
setting his nest on high
to escape the clutches of ruin!
10 You have plotted the ruin[q] of many peoples,
shaming[r] your own house and forfeiting your life.
11 The stones[s] of the wall will cry out,
and the beams of the woodwork will echo it.

12 "Woe to him who builds a city with bloodshed[t]
and establishes a town by injustice!
13 Has not the LORD Almighty determined
that the people's labor is only fuel for the fire,[u]
that the nations exhaust themselves for nothing?[v]
14 For the earth will be filled with the knowledge of the glory[w] of the LORD
as the waters cover the sea.[x]

15 "Woe to him who gives drink to his neighbors,
pouring it from the wineskin till they are drunk,
so that he can gaze on their naked bodies!
16 You will be filled with shame[y] instead of glory.
Now it is your turn! Drink and let your nakedness be exposed[a]![z]
The cup[a] from the LORD's right hand is coming around to you,
and disgrace will cover your glory.
17 The violence[b] you have done to Lebanon will overwhelm you,
and your destruction of animals will terrify you.[c]
For you have shed human blood;[d]
you have destroyed lands and cities
and everyone in them.

18 "Of what value is an idol[e] carved by a craftsman?
Or an image that teaches lies?
For the one who makes it trusts in his own creation;
he makes idols that cannot speak.[f]
19 Woe to him who says to wood, 'Come to life!'
Or to lifeless stone, 'Wake up!'[g]
Can it give guidance?
It is covered with gold and silver;[h]
there is no breath in it."

20 The LORD is in his holy temple;[i]
let all the earth be silent[j] before him.

Habakkuk's Prayer

3 A prayer of Habakkuk the prophet. On *shigionoth.*[b]

2 LORD, I have heard[k] of your fame;
I stand in awe[l] of your deeds, LORD.
Repeat[m] them in our day,
in our time make them known;
in wrath remember mercy.[n]

3 God came from Teman,
the Holy One from Mount Paran.[c]
His glory covered the heavens
and his praise filled the earth.[o]
4 His splendor was like the sunrise;
rays flashed from his hand,
where his power was hidden.

[a] *16* Masoretic Text; Dead Sea Scrolls, Aquila, Vulgate and Syriac (see also Septuagint) *and stagger* [b] *1* Probably a literary or musical term [c] *3* The Hebrew has *Selah* (a word of uncertain meaning) here and at the middle of verse 9 and at the end of verse 13.

2:11 *The stones of the wall will cry out, and the beams of the woodwork will echo it.* The whole structure of Israel's society called out for justice; every part reverberated with the need for righting wrongs.
2:14 *the glory of the LORD.* This speaks to the full manifestation of His person, significance, presence, and wonder. The true knowledge of God in the time of His kingdom on earth will be like the waters—all-embracing, inescapable, and fully enveloping.
2:16 *The cup from the LORD's right hand.* This represents the wrath of God (Is. 51:17,22; Rev. 14:10; 16:19).
2:18 *teaches lies.* Idolatry begins with deception, encourages deception, and calls for a commitment to deception (Is. 44:20).
2:20 *be silent before him.* The call to silence is not an invitation to worship, but a command to reflect on the terrible state of all who fall into the hands of the angry God (Zeph. 1:7).
3:2 *I have heard.* Habakkuk knew the stories of God's mighty acts as celebrated in song and in the feasts and festivals of Israel. These mighty acts included the exodus from Egypt, the miracles by the Red Sea, and the conquest of the land. ***Repeat ... in our time make them known.*** Habakkuk prayed for God's renewed involvement in Israel. The phrase "in our time" was a way of calling for a quick response.
3:4 *his power was hidden.* God reveals evidence of His power, but its totality and greatness remain hidden.

2:8 [n] Isa 33:1; Zec 2:8-9 [o] ver 17 **2:9** [p] Jer 22:13 **2:10** [q] Jer 26:19 [r] ver 16 **2:11** [s] Jos 24:27; Lk 19:40 **2:12** [t] Mic 3:10 **2:13** [u] Isa 50:11 [v] Isa 47:13 **2:14** [w] Nu 14:21 [x] Isa 11:9 **2:16** [y] ver 10 [z] La 4:21 [a] Isa 51:22 **2:17** [b] Jer 51:35 [c] Jer 50:15 [d] ver 8 **2:18** [e] Jer 5:21 [f] Ps 115:4-5; Jer 10:14 **2:19** [g] 1Ki 18:27 [h] Jer 10:4 **2:20** [i] Ps 11:4 [j] Isa 41:1 **3:2** [k] Ps 44:1 [l] Ps 119:120 [m] Ps 85:6 [n] Isa 54:8 **3:3** [o] Ps 48:10

5 Plague went before him;
pestilence followed his steps.
6 He stood, and shook the earth;
he looked, and made the nations
tremble.
The ancient mountains crumbled
and the age-old hills collapsed[p]—
but he marches on forever.
7 I saw the tents of Cushan in distress,
the dwellings of Midian[q] in
anguish.[r]

8 Were you angry with the rivers,[s] LORD?
Was your wrath against the streams?
Did you rage against the sea
when you rode your horses
and your chariots to victory?[t]
9 You uncovered your bow,
you called for many arrows.[u]
You split the earth with rivers;
10 the mountains saw you and writhed.
Torrents of water swept by;
the deep roared[v]
and lifted its waves[w] on high.

11 Sun and moon stood still[x] in the
heavens
at the glint of your flying arrows,[y]
at the lightning of your flashing
spear.
12 In wrath you strode through the earth
and in anger you threshed[z] the
nations.
13 You came out to deliver[a] your people,
to save your anointed one.
You crushed[b] the leader of the land of
wickedness,
you stripped him from head to foot.
14 With his own spear you pierced his
head
when his warriors stormed out to
scatter us,[c]
gloating as though about to devour
the wretched[d] who were in hiding.
15 You trampled the sea with your horses,
churning the great waters.[e]

16 I heard and my heart pounded,
my lips quivered at the sound;
decay crept into my bones,
and my legs trembled.
Yet I will wait patiently for the day of
calamity
to come on the nation invading us.
17 Though the fig tree does not bud
and there are no grapes on the vines,
though the olive crop fails
and the fields produce no food,[f]
though there are no sheep in the pen
and no cattle in the stalls,[g]
18 yet I will rejoice in the LORD,[h]
I will be joyful in God my Savior.

19 The Sovereign LORD is my strength;[i]
he makes my feet like the feet of a
deer,
he enables me to tread on the
heights.[j]

For the director of music. On my
stringed instruments.

3:8 ***rivers ... sea.*** The Lord had divided the Red Sea and the Jordan River for His people to cross (Ex. 14:26–15:5; Josh. 3:14–17). ***chariots to victory.*** The appearance of the Lord was for the purpose of bringing deliverance to His people.

3:16 ***I will wait patiently for the day of calamity.*** The prophet encouraged the godly not to be anxious in adversity.

3:17 God and Politics—Living in this physical, time-bound reality we see only a small portion of what God created. It is the bigger part of creation we need to be aware of and try to understand. We ultimately live beyond what we see and feel now. Life, as currently defined, is only that proverbial shadow of what it shall be. Our struggle is to have the vision to see beyond.

The same can be said for the political realities Habakkuk complains about. A season of failing crops isn't that much different than living a few years under the rule of an incompetent or cruel despot. It is tough and life can be severely affected, but the ultimate realities of how the world functions and how God relates to it remain unchanged.

God is a just God and will bring about justice. A period of injustice does not imply God has lost sight of what is going on or that He is losing His grip on the events of the world. He has different immediate purposes or works in a completely different timeframe. Despots usually don't last more than a generation. We had many in the twentieth century and most are gone, along with their whole empires.

3:19 ***my strength.*** God will strengthen those who trust in Him (Ps. 18:32,39). He will give those who live by faith the same confidence that a sure-footed deer has in climbing mountains.

3:6 [p] Ps 114:1-6 **3:7** [q] Jdg 7:24-25 [r] Ex 15:14 **3:8** [s] Ex 7:20 [t] Ps 68:17 **3:9** [u] Ps 7:12-13 **3:10** [v] Ps 98:7 [w] Ps 93:3 **3:11** [x] Jos 10:13 [y] Ps 18:14 **3:12** [z] Isa 41:15 **3:13** [a] Ps 20:6; 28:8 [b] Ps 68:21; 110:6 **3:14** [c] Jdg 7:22 [d] Ps 64:2-5 **3:15** [e] Ex 15:8; Ps 77:19 **3:17** [f] Joel 1:10-12, 18 [g] Jer 5:17 **3:18** [h] Isa 61:10; Php 4:4 **3:19** [i] Dt 33:29; Ps 46:1-5 [j] Dt 32:13; 2Sa 22:34; Ps 18:33

ZEPHANIAH

▶ **AUTHOR:** In the beginning of the book, Zephaniah traces his lineage back four generations to the godly King Hezekiah. This would make him the only prophet of royal descent. His use of the phrase "this place" in reference to Jerusalem indicates that he was probably an inhabitant of Judah's royal city (1:4).

▶ **TIME:** c. 630 B.C. ▶ **KEY VERSES:** Zeph. 1:14–15

▶ **THEME:** Contemporary with Jeremiah, Zephaniah was written during the reign of Josiah, one of the good kings of Judah. The book follows a fairly familiar pattern for the prophets. Judgment is pronounced on Judah as well as several surrounding nations. After the judgment of the first two chapters, the third declares a restoration process that sounds strongly encouraging.

1 The word of the LORD that came to Zephaniah son of Cushi, the son of Gedaliah, the son of Amariah, the son of Hezekiah, during the reign of Josiah[a] son of Amon king of Judah:

Judgment on the Whole Earth in the Day of the LORD

2 "I will sweep away everything
from the face of the earth,"[b]
declares the LORD.
3 "I will sweep away both man and beast;
I will sweep away the birds in the sky[c]
and the fish in the sea—
and the idols that cause the wicked to stumble."[a]
"When I destroy all mankind
on the face of the earth,"[d]
declares the LORD,
4 "I will stretch out my hand[e] against Judah
and against all who live in Jerusalem.
I will destroy every remnant of Baal worship in this place,[f]
the very names of the idolatrous priests[g]—
5 those who bow down on the roofs
to worship the starry host,
those who bow down and swear by the LORD
and who also swear by Molek,[b][h]
6 those who turn back from following[i] the LORD
and neither seek[j] the LORD nor
inquire[k] of him."

7 Be silent[l] before the Sovereign LORD,
for the day of the LORD[m] is near.
The LORD has prepared a sacrifice;[n]
he has consecrated those he has invited.
8 "On the day of the LORD's sacrifice
I will punish[o] the officials
and the king's sons[p]
and all those clad
in foreign clothes.

a 3 The meaning of the Hebrew for this line is uncertain. *b* 5 Hebrew *Malkam*

1:1 ***Zephaniah*** means "Hidden in the Lord," a name that relates to the principal message the prophet presented (2:3). The names of the prophets were often significantly associated with the message that God gave them to present to the people.
1:2–3 ***I will sweep away everything.*** The message of Zephaniah begins with a pronouncement of universal judgment (Gen. 6–8). These words not only introduce the particular judgment that would be pronounced upon Judah (v. 4), but they also speak of the final judgment that will usher in the kingdom of God on earth (Rev. 20:11–15).
1:4–6 ***I will destroy every remnant of Baal.*** Baal worship and its evils had led to the destruction of Israel and its capital Samaria in 722 B.C. Likewise Baal worship and its associations would lead to the destruction of Judah and its capital Jerusalem in 586 B.C.
1:7 ***Be silent.*** This prophetic call for silence was for solemn preparation for the horror of divine wrath (Hab. 2:20; Zech. 2:13). ***sacrifice.*** The people of God were expected to prepare sacrifices for the Lord as acts of contrition and celebration. But rebels, scofflaws, idolaters, and apostates would themselves become God's sacrifice.
1:8–9 ***foreign clothes.*** This suggests two things: (1) acts of greed and extortion against the populace, amassing funds for exotic clothing; (2) participation in foreign religious rites associated with exotic clothing.

1:1 [a] 2Ki 22:1; 2Ch 34:1-35:25 **1:2** [b] Ge 6:7 **1:3** [c] Jer 4:25 [d] Hos 4:3 **1:4** [e] Jer 6:12 [f] Mic 5:13 [g] Hos 10:5 **1:5** [h] Jer 5:7 **1:6** [i] Isa 1:4; Jer 2:13 [j] Isa 9:13 [k] Hos 7:7 **1:7** [l] Hab 2:20; Zec 2:13 [m] ver 14; Isa 13:6 [n] Isa 34:6; Jer 46:10 **1:8** [o] Isa 24:21 [p] Jer 39:6

9 On that day I will punish
all who avoid stepping on the
threshold,[a]
who fill the temple of their gods
with violence and deceit.[q]

10 "On that day,"
declares the LORD,
"a cry will go up from the Fish Gate,[r]
wailing from the New Quarter,
and a loud crash from the hills.
11 Wail,[s] you who live in the market
district[b];
all your merchants will be wiped out,
all who trade with[c] silver will be
destroyed.[t]
12 At that time I will search Jerusalem
with lamps
and punish those who are
complacent,[u]
who are like wine left on its dregs,[v]
who think, 'The LORD will do nothing,[w]
either good or bad.'
13 Their wealth will be plundered,[x]
their houses demolished.
Though they build houses,
they will not live in them;
though they plant vineyards,
they will not drink the wine."[y]

14 The great day of the LORD[z] is near[a]—
near and coming quickly.
The cry on the day of the LORD is bitter;
the Mighty Warrior shouts his battle
cry.
15 That day will be a day of wrath—
a day of distress and anguish,
a day of trouble and ruin,
a day of darkness and gloom,
a day of clouds and blackness[b]—
16 a day of trumpet and battle cry[c]
against the fortified cities
and against the corner towers.[d]

17 "I will bring such distress on all people
that they will grope about like those
who are blind,[e]
because they have sinned against the
LORD.
Their blood will be poured out[f] like dust
and their entrails like dung.[g]
18 Neither their silver nor their gold
will be able to save them
on the day of the LORD's wrath."[h]

In the fire of his jealousy
the whole earth will be consumed,[i]
for he will make a sudden end
of all who live on the earth.[j]

Judah and Jerusalem Judged Along With the Nations

Judah Summoned to Repent

2 Gather together,[k] gather yourselves
together,
you shameful[l] nation,
2 before the decree takes effect
and that day passes like windblown
chaff,[m]
before the LORD's fierce anger[n]
comes upon you,
before the day of the LORD's wrath
comes upon you.
3 Seek[o] the LORD, all you humble of the
land,
you who do what he commands.
Seek righteousness, seek humility;[p]
perhaps you will be sheltered[q]
on the day of the LORD's anger.

Philistia

4 Gaza[r] will be abandoned
and Ashkelon left in ruins.
At midday Ashdod will be emptied
and Ekron uprooted.
5 Woe to you who live by the sea,
you Kerethite[s] people;
the word of the LORD is against you,[t]
Canaan, land of the Philistines.
He says, "I will destroy you,
and none will be left."[u]
6 The land by the sea will become pastures
having wells for shepherds
and pens for flocks.[v]
7 That land will belong
to the remnant of the people of Judah;
there they will find pasture.

[a] 9 See 1 Samuel 5:5. [b] 11 Or *the Mortar* [c] 11 Or *in*

stepping on the threshold. This may refer to a pagan practice like the one mentioned in 1 Samuel 5:5. The priests of Dagon would not step on the doorway of the temple to Dagon because the hands and the head of Dagon had fallen there.
1:12–13 *The LORD will do nothing, either good or bad.* The complacency of the wicked people led them to believe that God is similarly complacent. Foolishly these people believed that the Lord would be inactive, neither blessing nor cursing, neither benefiting nor punishing His people.
1:17–18 *like those who are blind.* God's judgment would be so sudden and so overwhelming that the survivors would be in a state of shock, stumbling around in the dark.
2:1–3 *you will be sheltered.* The word "sheltered" is also translated "hidden." Zephaniah used a play on words with the meaning of his own name, "Hidden in the Lord." Even in the midst of the most calamitous of judgment scenes, the mercy and grace of the Lord is still available to a repentant people.
2:4–5 *Gaza . . . Ashkelon . . . Ashdod . . . Ekron.* The focus of the book moves from the description of divine judgment on Judah and Jerusalem to a description of divine judgment on the surrounding nations. The judgment begins with the nation to the west, Philistia and its major cities.

1:9 [q] Am 3:10 **1:10** [r] 2Ch 33:14 **1:11** [s] Jas 5:1 [t] Hos 9:6 **1:12** [u] Am 6:1 [v] Jer 48:11 [w] Eze 8:12 **1:13** [x] Jer 15:13 [y] Dt 28:30, 39; Am 5:11; Mic 6:15 **1:14** [z] ver 7; Joel 1:15 [a] Eze 7:7 **1:15** [b] Isa 22:5; Joel 2:2 **1:16** [c] Jer 4:19 [d] Isa 2:15 **1:17** [e] Isa 59:10 [f] Ps 79:3 [g] Jer 9:22 **1:18** [h] Eze 7:19 [i] ver 2-3; Zep 3:8 [j] Ge 6:7 **2:1** [k] 2Ch 20:4; Joel 1:14 [l] Jer 3:3; 6:15 **2:2** [m] Isa 17:13; Hos 13:3 [n] La 4:11 **2:3** [o] Am 5:6 [p] Ps 45:4; Am 5:14-15 [q] Ps 57:1 **2:4** [r] Am 1:6, 7-8; Zec 9:5-7 **2:5** [s] Eze 25:16 [t] Am 3:1 [u] Isa 14:30 **2:6** [v] Isa 5:17

In the evening they will lie down
in the houses of Ashkelon.
The LORD their God will care for them;
he will restore their fortunes.[a][w]

Moab and Ammon

8 "I have heard the insults[x] of Moab
and the taunts of the Ammonites,
who insulted[y] my people
and made threats against their land.
9 Therefore, as surely as I live,"
declares the LORD Almighty,
the God of Israel,
"surely Moab[z] will become like
Sodom,[a]
the Ammonites[b] like Gomorrah—
a place of weeds and salt pits,
a wasteland forever.
The remnant of my people will plunder[c]
them;
the survivors of my nation will
inherit their land.[d]"

10 This is what they will get in return for
their pride,[e]
for insulting[f] and mocking
the people of the LORD Almighty.
11 The LORD will be awesome[g] to them
when he destroys all the gods[h] of the
earth.
Distant nations will bow down to him,[i]
all of them in their own lands.

Cush

12 "You Cushites,[b][j] too,
will be slain by my sword.[k]"

Assyria

13 He will stretch out his hand against the
north
and destroy Assyria,
leaving Nineveh[l] utterly desolate
and dry as the desert.[m]
14 Flocks and herds will lie down there,
creatures of every kind.
The desert owl[n] and the screech owl
will roost on her columns.
Their hooting will echo through the
windows,
rubble will fill the doorways,
the beams of cedar will be
exposed.
15 This is the city of revelry[o]
that lived in safety.[p]
She said to herself,
"I am the one! And there is none
besides me."[q]
What a ruin she has become,
a lair for wild beasts!
All who pass by her scoff[r]
and shake their fists.

Jerusalem

3 Woe to the city of oppressors,[s]
rebellious and defiled![t]
2 She obeys[u] no one,
she accepts no correction.[v]
She does not trust in the LORD,
she does not draw near[w] to her God.
3 Her officials within her
are roaring lions;
her rulers are evening wolves,[x]
who leave nothing for the morning.
4 Her prophets are unprincipled;
they are treacherous people.[y]
Her priests profane the sanctuary
and do violence to the law.[z]
5 The LORD within her is righteous;
he does no wrong.[a]
Morning by morning he dispenses his
justice,
and every new day he does not fail,
yet the unrighteous know no shame.

Jerusalem Remains Unrepentant

6 "I have destroyed nations;
their strongholds are demolished.
I have left their streets deserted,
with no one passing through.
Their cities are laid waste;[b]
they are deserted and empty.
7 Of Jerusalem I thought,
'Surely you will fear me
and accept correction!'
Then her place of refuge[c] would not be
destroyed,
nor all my punishments come upon[d]
her.
But they were still eager
to act corruptly[c] in all they did.

---

[a] 7 Or *will bring back their captives* [b] 12 That is, people from the upper Nile region [c] 7 Or *her sanctuary* [d] 7 Or *all those I appointed over*

2:11 ***The LORD will be awesome to them.*** There may be a double meaning in these words. For the righteous people of Judah and Jerusalem, there would be a response of awe and wonder before God, who had responded to the prayer of His servant. But for the wicked there would be quite another response, one of terror and dread. ***Distant nations.*** Not only would there be a righteous remnant in Judah, there would also be people coming to God from the nations of the earth.
2:13–15 ***Their hooting will echo through the windows.*** The presence of birds in the ruins of Nineveh attests to the severity of the destruction announced on these people. ***city of revelry.*** The rejoicing here is ironic, seen as an act of the city's complacency. Soon the judgment of God would descend suddenly, and the region would be useful only for herding animals.

3:3–4 ***officials ... rulers ... prophets ... priests.*** God had designated these people to work for righteousness, but they were more wicked than the "regular" citizens of Jerusalem. These leaders were destroying and defrauding the weak, the needy, and the helpless.

2:7 [w] Ps 126:4; Jer 32:44 **2:8** [x] Jer 48:27 [y] Eze 25:3 **2:9** [z] Isa 15:1-16:14; Jer 48:1-47 [a] Dt 29:23 [b] Jer 49:1-6; Eze 25:1-7 [c] Isa 11:14 [d] Am 2:1-3 **2:10** [e] Isa 16:6 [f] Jer 48:27 **2:11** [g] Joel 2:11 [h] Zep 1:4 [i] Zep 3:9 **2:12** [j] Isa 18:1; 20:4 [k] Jer 46:10 **2:13** [l] Na 1:1 [m] Mic 5:6 **2:14** [n] Isa 14:23 **2:15** [o] Isa 32:9 [p] Isa 47:8 [q] Eze 28:2 [r] Na 3:19 **3:1** [s] Jer 6:6 [t] Eze 23:30 **3:2** [u] Jer 22:21 [v] Jer 7:28 [w] Ps 73:28; Jer 5:3 **3:3** [x] Eze 22:27 **3:4** [y] Jer 9:4 [z] Eze 22:26 **3:5** [a] Dt 32:4 **3:6** [b] Lev 26:31 **3:7** [c] Hos 9:9

8 Therefore wait[d] for me,"
declares the LORD,
"for the day I will stand up to testify.[a]
I have decided to assemble the nations,[e]
to gather the kingdoms
and to pour out my wrath on them—
all my fierce anger.
The whole world will be consumed[f]
by the fire of my jealous anger.

Restoration of Israel's Remnant

9 "Then I will purify the lips of the peoples,
that all of them may call[g] on the
name of the LORD
and serve[h] him shoulder to shoulder.
10 From beyond the rivers of Cush[b][i]
my worshipers, my scattered people,
will bring me offerings.[j]
11 On that day you, Jerusalem, will not be
put to shame[k]
for all the wrongs you have done
to me,
because I will remove from you
your arrogant boasters.
Never again will you be haughty
on my holy hill.
12 But I will leave within you
the meek[l] and humble.
The remnant of Israel
will trust[m] in the name of the LORD.
13 They[n] will do no wrong;[o]
they will tell no lies.[p]
A deceitful tongue
will not be found in their mouths.
They will eat and lie down[q]
and no one will make them afraid.[r]"
14 Sing, Daughter Zion;[s]
shout aloud,[t] Israel!
Be glad and rejoice with all your heart,
Daughter Jerusalem!
15 The LORD has taken away your
punishment,
he has turned back your enemy.
The LORD, the King of Israel, is with
you;[u]
never again will you fear[v] any harm.
16 On that day
they will say to Jerusalem,
"Do not fear, Zion;
do not let your hands hang limp.[w]
17 The LORD your God is with you,
the Mighty Warrior who saves.[x]
He will take great delight[y] in you;
in his love he will no longer rebuke
you,
but will rejoice over you with
singing."
18 "I will remove from you
all who mourn over the loss of your
appointed festivals,
which is a burden and reproach for
you.
19 At that time I will deal
with all who oppressed you.
I will rescue the lame;
I will gather the exiles.[z]
I will give them praise[a] and honor
in every land where they have
suffered shame.
20 At that time I will gather you;
at that time I will bring[b] you home.
I will give you honor[c] and praise
among all the peoples of the earth
when I restore your fortunes[c][d]
before your very eyes,"
says the LORD.

[a] 8 Septuagint and Syriac; Hebrew *will rise up to plunder* [b] *10* That is, the upper Nile region
[c] *20* Or *I bring back your captives*

3:8 *all my fierce anger.* God's response to the wickedness of Jerusalem was to declare His judgment. He would use other nations to punish the city for its rebellion.

3:8 God's Purpose in Judgment—What we don't properly understand is that judgment should lead us to a restoration or improvement in a relationship. We live with the tension of knowing God's judgment hangs over us while at the same time knowing that forgiveness is readily available to us too. Such is the message of Zephaniah.

Judgment implies a necessary purification process. You can't get the impurities out without first identifying their presence. We want to think of ourselves as pure without going through any process of purification. We want grace without judgment, but it doesn't work that way. Judgment reflects the true state of our being after the fall, namely that we are sinful and in need of grace. Often the only way to understand our reality is to go through a judgment process.

Once the judgment is accepted and the proper response is made, we fully experience God's grace. He deals with our enemies (v. 15). He quiets us with His love (v. 17). He removes our burdens (v. 18). God stands ready to gather us back to Himself (v. 19). He restores our fortunes (v. 20).

The commonly held thought that the writings of the Old Testament prophets are all gloom and doom is actually myth and misnomer. There's always hope and renewal in the prophetic message. There are always opportunities for repentance, forgiveness, and restoration. God's judgment is in fact good for us because the sin in our lives needs to be brought to light in order for us to be restored to full fellowship with God.

3:9–13 *purify the lips.* One day people will worship God in spirit and in truth (John 4:24). ***my worshipers.*** God's people would come from all nations to worship Him.

3:20 *I will give you honor and praise.* Ordinarily Scripture speaks of the praise that should be brought to God. Here we find the praise that God will bring to His people. ***says the LORD.*** This is a solemn vow of God to do what He has promised. Zephaniah begins and ends with the strong assertion that the Lord is speaking. The implication is clear: "Listen and live!"

3:8 [d] Ps 27:14 [e] Joel 3:2 [f] Zep 1:18 **3:9** [g] Zep 2:11 [h] Isa 19:18 **3:10** [i] Ps 68:31 [j] Isa 60:7 **3:11** [k] Joel 2:26-27 **3:12** [l] Isa 14:32 [m] Na 1:7 **3:13** [n] Isa 10:21; Mic 4:7 [o] Ps 119:3 [p] Rev 14:5 [q] Eze 34:15; Zep 2:7 [r] Eze 34:25-28 **3:14** [s] Zec 2:10 [t] Isa 12:6 **3:15** [u] Eze 37:26-28 [v] Isa 54:14 **3:16** [w] Job 4:3; Isa 35:3-4; Heb 12:12 **3:17** [x] Isa 63:1 [y] Isa 62:4 **3:19** [z] Eze 34:16; Mic 4:6 [a] Isa 60:18 **3:20** [b] Jer 29:14; Eze 37:12 [c] Isa 56:5; 66:22 [d] Joel 3:1

HAGGAI

▶ **AUTHOR:** The authorship of the book is virtually uncontested as Haggai's name is mentioned nine times. Haggai is known only from this book and two other references to him in Ezra 5:1 and 6:14. Haggai returned from Babylon with the remnant and may well have been one of the few people who could remember the former temple before its destruction. Haggai was therefore very instrumental in the rebuilding of the temple.

▶ **TIME:** c. 520 B.C. ▶ **KEY VERSES:** Hag. 1:7 – 8

▶ **THEME:** Haggai is the first of the postexilic prophets, addressing the immediate problem of the rebuilding of the temple. The people had returned about 20 years earlier, but apathy and opposition were keeping the work from being completed. Haggai's concern is that neglect of the temple is a symptom of a bigger problem. God has dropped out of the Israelites' sight as a priority. The people are more concerned with building their materialistic lifestyles than they are with their relationship with God.

A Call to Build the House of the LORD

1 In the second year of King Darius,[a] on
the first day of the sixth month, the
word of the LORD came through the prophet Haggai[b] to Zerubbabel[c] son of Shealtiel,
governor[d] of Judah, and to Joshua[e] son of
Jozadak,[a][f] the high priest:
2This is what the LORD Almighty says:
"These people say, 'The time has not yet
come to rebuild the LORD's house.'"
3Then the word of the LORD came
through the prophet Haggai:[g] 4"Is it a time
for you yourselves to be living in your paneled houses,[h] while this house remains a
ruin?[i]"
5Now this is what the LORD Almighty
says: "Give careful thought[j] to your ways.
6You have planted much, but harvested little.[k] You eat, but never have enough. You
drink, but never have your fill. You put on
clothes, but are not warm. You earn wages,[l] only to put them in a purse with holes
in it."
7This is what the LORD Almighty says:
"Give careful thought to your ways. 8Go
up into the mountains and bring down
timber and build my house, so that I may
take pleasure[m] in it and be honored," says
the LORD. 9"You expected much, but see, it
turned out to be little. What you brought
home, I blew away. Why?" declares the
LORD Almighty. "Because of my house,
which remains a ruin,[n] while each of you
is busy with your own house. 10Therefore,
because of you the heavens have withheld
their dew and the earth its crops.[o] 11I called
for a drought[p] on the fields and the mountains, on the grain, the new wine, the olive
oil and everything else the ground produces, on people and livestock, and on all the
labor of your hands.[q]"

[a] *1* Hebrew *Jehozadak*, a variant of *Jozadak*; also in verses 12 and 14

1:2 *The time has not yet come.* The people had decided that rebuilding the Lord's dwelling among His people was not important.
1:4 *your paneled houses.* Those who wanted to make their houses elaborate installed wood panels. The people of Haggai's time were making their homes elegant, rivaling royal residences and the holy temple itself. But they still did not feel that the "time was right" to begin working on the renewed temple. While this verse is not a blanket condemnation of elegant living among God's people, it certainly calls for a re-evaluation of priorities.
1:8 *that I may take pleasure in it.* God's joy in the temple is related to His pleasure in the people who would worship Him there. ***be honored.*** Clearly God does not need to receive more glory (Ps. 24:7 – 10); however, He gladly receives the adoration of His people.

1:1 [a] Ezr 4:24 [b] Ezr 5:1 [c] Mt 1:12-13 [d] Ezr 5:3 [e] Ezr 2:2 [f] 1Ch 6:15; Ezr 3:2 **1:3** [g] Ezr 5:1 **1:4** [h] 2Sa 7:2 [i] ver 9; Jer 33:12 **1:5** [j] La 3:40 **1:6** [k] Dt 28:38 [l] Hag 2:16; Zec 8:10 **1:8** [m] Ps 132:13-14 **1:9** [n] ver 4 **1:10** [o] Lev 26:19; Dt 28:23 **1:11** [p] Dt 28:22; 1Ki 17:1 [q] Hag 2:17

12Then Zerubbabel[r] son of Shealtiel,
Joshua son of Jozadak, the high priest, and
the whole remnant[s] of the people obeyed[t]
the voice of the LORD their God and the
message of the prophet Haggai, because
the LORD their God had sent him. And the
people feared[u] the LORD.
13Then Haggai, the LORD's messenger,
gave this message of the LORD to the people: "I am with[v] you," declares the LORD.
14So the LORD stirred up the spirit of Zerubbabel[w] son of Shealtiel, governor of Judah,
and the spirit of Joshua son of Jozadak, the
high priest, and the spirit of the whole remnant[x] of the people. They came and began
to work on the house of the LORD Almighty,
their God, 15on the twenty-fourth day of the
sixth month.[y]

The Promised Glory of the New House

2 In the second year of King Darius,
1on the twenty-first day of the seventh
month, the word of the LORD came through
the prophet Haggai: 2"Speak to Zerubbabel
son of Shealtiel, governor of Judah, to Joshua son of Jozadak,[a] the high priest, and
to the remnant of the people. Ask them,
3'Who of you is left who saw this house[z] in
its former glory? How does it look to you
now? Does it not seem to you like nothing?[a] 4But now be strong, Zerubbabel,'
declares the LORD. 'Be strong,[b] Joshua son
of Jozadak, the high priest. Be strong, all
you people of the land,' declares the LORD,
'and work. For I am with[c] you,' declares the
LORD Almighty. 5'This is what I covenanted with you when you came out of Egypt.[d]
And my Spirit[e] remains among you. Do not
fear.'
6"This is what the LORD Almighty says:
'In a little while[f] I will once more shake the
heavens and the earth,[g] the sea and the dry
land. 7I will shake all nations, and what is
desired by all nations will come, and I will
fill this house[h] with glory,' says the LORD
Almighty. 8'The silver is mine and the gold
is mine,' declares the LORD Almighty. 9'The
glory[i] of this present house will be greater
than the glory of the former house,' says
the LORD Almighty. 'And in this place I will
grant peace,' declares the LORD Almighty."

Blessings for a Defiled People

10On the twenty-fourth day of the ninth
month,[j] in the second year of Darius, the
word of the LORD came to the prophet Haggai: 11"This is what the LORD Almighty
says: 'Ask the priests[k] what the law says:
12If someone carries consecrated meat
in the fold of their garment, and that fold
touches some bread or stew, some wine,
olive oil or other food, does it become consecrated?[l]'"
The priests answered, "No."
13Then Haggai said, "If a person defiled
by contact with a dead body touches one of
these things, does it become defiled?"
"Yes," the priests replied, "it becomes defiled.[m]"
14Then Haggai said, "'So it is with this
people and this nation in my sight,' declares the LORD. 'Whatever they do and
whatever they offer[n] there is defiled.
15"'Now give careful thought[o] to this
from this day on[b]—consider how things
were before one stone was laid[p] on another in the LORD's temple.[q] 16When anyone came to a heap of twenty measures,
there were only ten. When anyone went
to a wine vat to draw fifty measures, there
were only twenty.[r] 17I struck all the work
of your hands[s] with blight,[t] mildew and
hail, yet you did not return to me,' declares
the LORD.[u] 18'From this day on, from this

[a] 2 Hebrew *Jehozadak*, a variant of *Jozadak*; also in verse 4 [b] 15 Or *to the days past*

1:13 *I am with you.* God's promise to Moses was, "I will be with you" (Ex. 3:12). God's promise to the people of Judah was that the name of the Coming One would be Immanuel, meaning "God with us" (Is. 7:14). Here God repeated the same message of comfort and encouragement.

2:3 *this house in its former glory.* The temple of Solomon was one of the wonders of the ancient world (1 Kin. 6). The older temple would have loomed large and magnificent, far outstripping the present structure. So even though the building was completed, there may have been the sense among some of the people that it was "as nothing."

2:6 *I will once more shake the heavens.* This is another way of speaking of the day of the Lord. The purpose of the day of the Lord is to prepare the earth for the glorious reign of Jesus Christ on earth (Matt. 24:29; Rev. 6:12–17).

2:9 *I will grant peace.* Peace includes good health, well-being, and an abundant life. The term speaks of everything being as it ought to be.

2:12 *does it become consecrated.* Since the role of the priest was to interpret God's law, it was reasonable that questions on holiness should be addressed to them. Haggai asked whether holiness could be transferred by contact. The answer was no.

2:13–14 *it becomes defiled.* The priests were asked if a religiously unclean person, someone who had touched a corpse, could contaminate someone else by touch. The answer was yes (Num. 19:11–13). The people had worked hard to rebuild the temple, only to be told that their worship would be unacceptable in the new temple. The existence of the temple

1:12 [r] ver 1 [s] ver 14; Isa 1:9; Hag 2:2 [t] Isa 50:10 [u] Dt 31:12
1:13 [v] Mt 28:20; Ro 8:31 **1:14** [w] Ezr 5:2 [x] ver 12
1:15 [y] ver 1 **2:3** [z] Ezr 3:12 [a] Zec 4:10 **2:4** [b] 1Ch 28:20; Zec 8:9; Eph 6:10 [c] 2Sa 5:10; Ac 7:9 **2:5** [d] Ex 29:46
[e] Ne 9:20; Isa 63:11 **2:6** [f] Isa 10:25 [g] Heb 12:26*
2:7 [h] Isa 60:7 **2:9** [i] Ps 85:9 **2:10** [j] ver 1
2:11 [k] Lev 10:10-11; Dt 17:8-11; Mal 2:7 **2:12** [l] Lev 6:27; Mt 23:19 **2:13** [m] Lev 22:4-6 **2:14** [n] Isa 1:13
2:15 [o] Hag 1:5 [p] Ezr 3:10 [q] Ezr 4:24 **2:16** [r] Hag 1:6
2:17 [s] Hag 1:11 [t] Dt 28:22; 1Ki 8:37; Am 4:9 [u] Am 4:6

twenty-fourth day of the ninth month, give
careful thought to the day when the foundation[v] of the LORD's temple was laid. Give
careful thought: 19 Is there yet any seed left
in the barn? Until now, the vine and the fig
tree, the pomegranate and the olive tree
have not borne fruit.
"'From this day on I will bless you.'"

Zerubbabel the LORD's Signet Ring

20 The word of the LORD came to Haggai
a second time on the twenty-fourth day
of the month: 21 "Tell Zerubbabel[w] governor of Judah that I am going to shake the
heavens and the earth. 22 I will overturn
royal thrones and shatter the power of the
foreign kingdoms.[x] I will overthrow chariots[y] and their drivers; horses and their
riders will fall, each by the sword of his
brother.[z]
23 "'On that day,' declares the LORD Almighty, 'I will take you, my servant[a] Zerubbabel son of Shealtiel,' declares the LORD,
'and I will make you like my signet ring,
for I have chosen you,' declares the LORD
Almighty."

---

itself guaranteed nothing. The hearts of the people had to be in harmony with the sacrifices being made.

2:23 ***signet ring.*** This was an item of great value in the ancient world. The owner used it much like we use our personal signature on checks or other important documents. God used this imagery to indicate that Zerubbabel was in His hand, that he was highly valued, and that he represented God's authority in his leadership of the people. Even though the people had been told they were still unclean in God's eyes (2:10–14), their leader Zerubbabel was encouraged to guide them through those spiritually trying times.

2:18 [v] Zec 8:9 **2:21** [w] Ezr 5:2 **2:22** [x] Da 2:44 [y] Mic 5:10 [z] Jdg 7:22 **2:23** [a] Isa 43:10

ZECHARIAH

▶ **AUTHOR:** The universal testimony of the Jewish and Christian tradition affirms Zechariah as the author of the entire book. Like Jeremiah and Ezekiel, he was of priestly lineage and was a young man when he was called to prophesy. According to Jewish tradition, Zechariah was a member of the Great Synagogue that collected and preserved the canon of revealed Scripture. He was born in Babylon and brought to Palestine by his grandfather when the Jewish exiles returned under Zerubbabel and Joshua the high priest.

▶ **TIME:** 520 – 470 B.C. ▶ **KEY VERSE:** Zech. 9:9

▶ **THEME:** Zechariah's writings were designed to encourage the Israelites and inspire energy, identity, and vision during the rebuilding of the temple. Like Isaiah, Daniel, and Ezekiel, his prophecies are characterized by visions of God and the future. In this context, many would describe the book to be apocalyptic with similarities to Revelation. Probably, more than any of the other books, Zechariah makes concrete predictions about Christ, which are fulfilled in the New Testament. He also makes some startling predictions about Israel in the end times that have already seen fulfillment.

A Call to Return to the LORD

1 In the eighth month of the second year
of Darius,[a] the word of the LORD came
to the prophet Zechariah[b] son of Berekiah,[c]
the son of Iddo:[d]
2"The LORD was very angry[e] with your
ancestors. 3Therefore tell the people: This
is what the LORD Almighty says: 'Return
to me,' declares the LORD Almighty, 'and I
will return to you,'[f] says the LORD Almighty.
4Do not be like your ancestors,[g] to whom the
earlier prophets proclaimed: This is what
the LORD Almighty says: 'Turn from your
evil ways[h] and your evil practices.' But they
would not listen or pay attention to me,[i] declares the LORD. 5Where are your ancestors
now? And the prophets, do they live forever? 6But did not my words and my decrees,
which I commanded my servants the prophets, overtake your ancestors?
"Then they repented and said, 'The LORD
Almighty has done to us what our ways
and practices deserve,[j] just as he determined to do.'"

The Man Among the Myrtle Trees

7On the twenty-fourth day of the eleventh month, the month of Shebat, in the
second year of Darius, the word of the
LORD came to the prophet Zechariah son
of Berekiah, the son of Iddo.
8During the night I had a vision, and
there before me was a man mounted on
a red[k] horse. He was standing among the
myrtle trees in a ravine. Behind him were
red, brown and white horses.[l]
9I asked, "What are these, my lord?"
The angel[m] who was talking with me answered, "I will show you what they are."
10Then the man standing among the myrtle trees explained, "They are the ones the
LORD has sent to go throughout the earth."[n]

1:1 ***Zechariah.*** The name means "Yahweh remembers," emphasizing God's faithfulness to His covenant promises and to His people.

1:3 ***Return to me.*** These words remind us of the depth of God's unconditional love. ***says the LORD Almighty.*** The personal name translated "Lord" speaks of God's gracious nature as He relates to His people (Ex. 3:14 – 16).

1:5 – 6 ***ancestors . . . prophets.*** The previous generation had been overtaken by God's judgment (Deut. 28:15 – 68).

1:7 — 6:15 ***the word of the LORD.*** This section contains a sequence of eight night visions concerning Israel's future, followed by the symbolic crowning of the high priest Joshua. Here Zechariah pursues the same end as Haggai, rebuilding the temple as the center of worship and world rule, and as a place of pilgrimage for the nations (8:20 – 23).

1:8 ***myrtle.*** This was an evergreen tree that was once very common in the vicinity of Jerusalem (Neh. 8:15).

1:1 [a] Ezr 4:24; 6:15 [b] Ezr 5:1 [c] Mt 23:35; Lk 11:51 [d] ver 7; Ne 12:4 **1:2** [e] 2Ch 36:16 **1:3** [f] Mal 3:7; Jas 4:8 **1:4** [g] 2Ch 36:15 [h] Ps 106:6 [i] 2Ch 24:19; Ps 78:8; Jer 6:17 **1:6** [j] Jer 12:14-17; La 2:17 **1:8** [k] Rev 6:4 [l] Zec 6:2-7 **1:9** [m] Zec 4:1, 4-5 **1:10** [n] Zec 6:5-8

11And they reported to the angel of the
LORD who was standing among the myrtle
trees, "We have gone throughout the earth
and found the whole world at rest and in
peace."[o]
12Then the angel of the LORD said, "LORD
Almighty, how long will you withhold mercy from Jerusalem and from the towns of
Judah, which you have been angry with
these seventy[p] years?" 13So the LORD spoke
kind and comforting words to the angel
who talked with me.[q]
14Then the angel who was speaking to
me said, "Proclaim this word: This is what
the LORD Almighty says: 'I am very jealous[r]
for Jerusalem and Zion, 15and I am very
angry with the nations that feel secure.[s] I
was only a little angry, but they went too
far with the punishment.'[t]
16"Therefore this is what the LORD says:
'I will return[u] to Jerusalem with mercy,
and there my house will be rebuilt. And the
measuring line[v] will be stretched out over
Jerusalem,' declares the LORD Almighty.
17"Proclaim further: This is what the
LORD Almighty says: 'My towns will again
overflow with prosperity, and the LORD
will again comfort[w] Zion and choose[x] Jerusalem.'"[y]

Four Horns and Four Craftsmen

18Then I looked up, and there before me
were four horns. 19I asked the angel who
was speaking to me, "What are these?"
He answered me, "These are the horns[z]
that scattered Judah, Israel and Jerusalem."
20Then the LORD showed me four craftsmen. 21I asked, "What are these coming
to do?"
He answered, "These are the horns that
scattered Judah so that no one could raise
their head, but the craftsmen have come to
terrify them and throw down these horns
of the nations who lifted up their horns[a]
against the land of Judah to scatter its
people."[ab]

A Man With a Measuring Line

2[b] Then I looked up, and there before me
was a man with a measuring line in
his hand. 2I asked, "Where are you going?"
He answered me, "To measure Jerusalem, to find out how wide and how long
it is."[c]
3While the angel who was speaking to
me was leaving, another angel came to
meet him 4and said to him: "Run, tell that
young man, 'Jerusalem will be a city without walls[d] because of the great number[e]
of people and animals in it. 5And I myself
will be a wall[f] of fire around it,' declares
the LORD, 'and I will be its glory[g] within.'
6"Come! Come! Flee from the land of the
north," declares the LORD, "for I have scattered you to the four winds of heaven,"[h] declares the LORD.
7"Come, Zion! Escape, you who live in
Daughter Babylon!"[i] 8For this is what the
LORD Almighty says: "After the Glorious
One has sent me against the nations that
have plundered you—for whoever touches you touches the apple of his eye[j]— 9I
will surely raise my hand against them so
that their slaves will plunder them.[ck] Then
you will know that the LORD Almighty has
sent me.[l]
10"Shout and be glad, Daughter Zion.[m]
For I am coming,[n] and I will live among
you,"[o] declares the LORD. 11"Many nations
will be joined with the LORD in that day and
will become my people. I will live among
you and you will know that the LORD Almighty has sent me to you. 12The LORD will
inherit[p] Judah as his portion in the holy
land and will again choose[q] Jerusalem.
13Be still[r] before the LORD, all mankind,
because he has roused himself from his
holy dwelling."

[a] *21* In Hebrew texts 1:18-21 is numbered 2:1-4.
[b] In Hebrew texts 2:1-13 is numbered 2:5-17.
[c] *8,9* Or *says after . . . eye: 9"I . . . plunder them."*

1:12–13 *angel of the LORD.* This may be a conversation between the pre-incarnate Jesus and the first Person of the Trinity, God the Father (Ps. 110:1–3). It is certainly an allusion to Jesus' role as Intercessor.

1:15 *I am very angry.* Here the anger of God was against the nations that He had used to punish His unrepentant people.

1:16 *line will be stretched.* A measuring line was used to make measurements in preparation for new construction. The stretching of the line was a promise that the work would begin and that the completion of the task would follow.

1:18 *four horns.* Animal horns were often used by poets and prophets as symbols of powerful nations and their kings (Dan. 7:7–8,24). The horns that persecuted Israel and Judah included Assyria, Babylon, Medo-Persia, and later Greece.

2:4–5 *a city without walls.* Jerusalem will have no need for defensive fortifications because God's presence will guarantee its safety and security. These words refer ultimately to the future Jerusalem under the rule of its glorious king (Zeph. 3:15–19).

2:8–9 *the apple of his eye.* This refers to the pupil, an endearing expression suggesting how enormously important the Hebrew people are to God because of His covenant with them. Just as we protect our eyes from even the smallest particles of dust, so God protects and cares for His people.

2:12 *the holy land.* Surprisingly, this phrase occurs in the Old Testament only here. The land is "holy" because of the presence of God among His believing people.

1:11 [o] Isa 14:7 **1:12** [p] Da 9:2 **1:13** [q] Zec 4:1 **1:14** [r] Joel 2:18; Zec 8:2 **1:15** [s] Jer 48:11 [t] Ps 123:3-4; Am 1:11 **1:16** [u] Zec 8:3 [v] Zec 2:1-2 **1:17** [w] Isa 51:3 [x] Isa 14:1 [y] Zec 2:12 **1:19** [z] Am 6:13 **1:21** [a] Ps 75:4 [b] Ps 75:10 **2:2** [c] Eze 40:3; Rev 21:15 **2:4** [d] Eze 38:11 [e] Isa 49:20; Jer 30:19; 33:22 **2:5** [f] Isa 26:1 [g] Rev 21:23 **2:6** [h] Eze 17:21 **2:7** [i] Isa 48:20 **2:8** [j] Dt 32:10 **2:9** [k] Isa 14:2 [l] Zec 4:9 **2:10** [m] Zep 3:14 [n] Zec 9:9 [o] Lev 26:12; Zec 8:3 **2:12** [p] Dt 32:9; Ps 33:12; Jer 10:16 [q] Zec 1:17 **2:13** [r] Hab 2:20

Clean Garments for the High Priest

3 Then he showed me Joshua[s] the high
priest standing before the angel of the
LORD, and Satan[a][t] standing at his right side
to accuse him. 2The LORD said to Satan,
"The LORD rebuke you,[u] Satan! The LORD,
who has chosen[v] Jerusalem, rebuke you! Is
not this man a burning stick snatched from
the fire?"[w]
3Now Joshua was dressed in filthy
clothes as he stood before the angel. 4The
angel said to those who were standing before him, "Take off his filthy clothes."
Then he said to Joshua, "See, I have tak-
en away your sin,[x] and I will put fine garments[y] on you."
5Then I said, "Put a clean turban[z] on his
head." So they put a clean turban on his
head and clothed him, while the angel of
the LORD stood by.
6The angel of the LORD gave this charge
to Joshua: 7"This is what the LORD Almighty says: 'If you will walk in obedience
to me and keep my requirements, then you
will govern my house[a] and have charge
of my courts, and I will give you a place
among these standing here.
8"'Listen, High Priest Joshua, you and
your associates seated before you, who are
men symbolic[b] of things to come: I am going to bring my servant, the Branch.[c] 9See,
the stone I have set in front of Joshua!
There are seven eyes[b] on that one stone,[d]
and I will engrave an inscription on it,' says
the LORD Almighty, 'and I will remove the
sin[e] of this land in a single day.
10"'In that day each of you will invite
your neighbor to sit under your vine and
fig tree,[f]' declares the LORD Almighty."

The Gold Lampstand and the Two Olive Trees

4 Then the angel who talked with me
returned and woke[g] me up, like someone awakened from sleep.[h] 2He asked me,
"What do you see?"[i]
I answered, "I see a solid gold lampstand[j]
with a bowl at the top and seven lamps[k] on
it, with seven channels to the lamps. 3Also
there are two olive trees[l] by it, one on the
right of the bowl and the other on its left."
4I asked the angel who talked with me,
"What are these, my lord?"
5He answered, "Do you not know what
these are?"
"No, my lord," I replied.[m]
6So he said to me, "This is the word of
the LORD to Zerubbabel:[n] 'Not by might nor
by power, but by my Spirit,'[o] says the LORD
Almighty.
7"What are you, mighty mountain? Before
Zerubbabel you will become level ground.[p]
Then he will bring out the capstone[q] to
shouts of 'God bless it! God bless it!'"
8Then the word of the LORD came to me:
9"The hands of Zerubbabel have laid the
foundation[r] of this temple; his hands will
also complete it.[s] Then you will know that
the LORD Almighty has sent me[t] to you.
10"Who dares despise the day of small
things,[u] since the seven eyes[v] of the LORD
that range throughout the earth will rejoice when they see the chosen capstone[c]
in the hand of Zerubbabel?"
11Then I asked the angel, "What are
these two olive trees[w] on the right and the
left of the lampstand?"
12Again I asked him, "What are these
two olive branches beside the two gold
pipes that pour out golden oil?"
13He replied, "Do you not know what
these are?"
"No, my lord," I said.
14So he said, "These are the two who
are anointed[x] to[d] serve the Lord of all the
earth."

---

[a] *1* Hebrew *satan* means *adversary.*
[b] *9* Or *facets* [c] *10* Or *the plumb line*
[d] *14* Or *two who bring oil and*

3:1 *Satan.* The Hebrew is literally "the Satan," meaning "the Accuser." The picture is not unlike that of Job 1, where Satan stands before the Lord making accusations against people who follow God.
3:3 *in filthy clothes.* The high priest represented the people before God (Ex. 28:29) and under no circumstances was he to become defiled or unclean (Ex. 28:2; Lev. 21:10 – 15). Joshua's garments were literally "befouled with excrement."
3:8 *the Branch.* Isaiah used this word and a similar one to describe the Messiah who will grow out of the root of the family of Jesse as a tender sprout shoots up from the ground (6:12; Is. 4:2; 11:1; 53:2). Joshua and his companions were "men wondered at" because the reinstitution of the priesthood made public God's continuing intention to fulfill His promises to His people.
4:2 – 3 *a solid gold lampstand.* This would remind people of the lampstand in the tabernacle and the temple.
4:6 *but by my Spirit.* The rebuilding of the temple, which had at last begun in earnest (Ezra 5:1 – 2; Hag. 1:14), would be accomplished not by human strength or resources, but by the power of God's Spirit.
4:7 *mighty mountain.* This was a figurative reference to the great obstacles the people faced in rebuilding the temple (Ezra 5:3 – 17). The setting of the "headstone" would mark the completion of the project. bless it. This may be understood as a prayer for God's favor, or as a cry of admiration over the grace and beauty of the newly built temple.
4:11 – 14 *two olive trees . . . two who are anointed.* These are identified as representatives of the religious

3:1 [s] Hag 1:1; Zec 6:11 [t] Ps 109:6 **3:2** [u] Jude 1:9 [v] Isa 14:1 [w] Am 4:11; Jude 1:23 **3:4** [x] Eze 36:25; Mic 7:18 [y] Isa 52:1; Rev 19:8 **3:5** [z] Ex 29:6 **3:7** [a] Dt 17:8-11; Eze 44:15-16 **3:8** [b] Eze 12:11 [c] Isa 4:2 **3:9** [d] Isa 28:16 [e] Jer 50:20 **3:10** [f] 1Ki 4:25; Mic 4:4 **4:1** [g] Da 8:18 [h] Jer 31:26 **4:2** [i] Jer 1:13 [j] Ex 25:31; Rev 1:12 [k] Rev 4:5 **4:3** [l] ver 11; Rev 11:4 **4:5** [m] Zec 1:9 **4:6** [n] Ezr 5:2 [o] Isa 11:2-4; Hos 1:7 **4:7** [p] Jer 51:25 [q] Ps 118:22 **4:9** [r] Ezr 3:11 [s] Ezr 3:8; 6:15; Zec 6:12 [t] Zec 2:9 **4:10** [u] Hag 2:3 [v] Zec 3:9; Rev 5:6 **4:11** [w] ver 3; Rev 11:4 **4:14** [x] Ex 29:7; 40:15; Da 9:24-26; Zec 3:1-7

The Flying Scroll

5 I looked again, and there before me was
a flying scroll.[y]
2He asked me, "What do you see?"
I answered, "I see a flying scroll, twenty
cubits long and ten cubits wide.[a]"
3And he said to me, "This is the curse[z]
that is going out over the whole land; for
according to what it says on one side, every thief[a] will be banished, and according
to what it says on the other, everyone who
swears falsely[b] will be banished. 4The
LORD Almighty declares, 'I will send it out,
and it will enter the house of the thief and
the house of anyone who swears falsely by
my name. It will remain in that house and
destroy it completely, both its timbers and
its stones.[c]'"

The Woman in a Basket

5Then the angel who was speaking to
me came forward and said to me, "Look
up and see what is appearing."
6I asked, "What is it?"
He replied, "It is a basket." And he added,
"This is the iniquity[b] of the people throughout the land."
7Then the cover of lead was raised, and
there in the basket sat a woman! 8He said,
"This is wickedness," and he pushed her
back into the basket and pushed its lead
cover down on it.[d]
9Then I looked up—and there before
me were two women, with the wind in
their wings! They had wings like those of
a stork,[e] and they lifted up the basket between heaven and earth.
10"Where are they taking the basket?" I
asked the angel who was speaking to me.
11He replied, "To the country of Babylonia[c][f] to build a house[g] for it. When the
house is ready, the basket will be set there
in its place."[h]

Four Chariots

6 I looked up again, and there before me
were four chariots[i] coming out from
between two mountains—mountains of
bronze. 2The first chariot had red horses,
the second black,[j] 3the third white,[k] and
the fourth dappled—all of them powerful.
4I asked the angel who was speaking to me,
"What are these, my lord?"
5The angel answered me, "These are
the four spirits[d][l] of heaven, going out from
standing in the presence of the Lord of
the whole world. 6The one with the black
horses is going toward the north country,
the one with the white horses toward the
west,[e] and the one with the dappled horses
toward the south."
7When the powerful horses went out,
they were straining to go throughout the
earth.[m] And he said, "Go throughout the
earth!" So they went throughout the earth.
8Then he called to me, "Look, those going toward the north country have given
my Spirit[f] rest[n] in the land of the north."

A Crown for Joshua

9The word of the LORD came to me:
10"Take silver and gold from the exiles
Heldai, Tobijah and Jedaiah, who have
arrived from Babylon.[o] Go the same day
to the house of Josiah son of Zephaniah.
11Take the silver and gold and make a
crown,[p] and set it on the head of the high
priest, Joshua[q] son of Jozadak.[g][r] 12Tell him
this is what the LORD Almighty says: 'Here
is the man whose name is the Branch,[s] and
he will branch out from his place and build
the temple of the LORD.[t] 13It is he who will
build the temple of the LORD, and he will be
clothed with majesty and will sit and rule
on his throne. And he[h] will be a priest[u] on
his throne. And there will be harmony between the two.' 14The crown will be given
to Heldai,[i] Tobijah, Jedaiah and Hen[j] son
of Zephaniah as a memorial in the temple

---

[a] 2 That is, about 30 feet long and 15 feet wide or about 9 meters long and 4.5 meters wide
[b] 6 Or *appearance*
[c] 11 Hebrew *Shinar*
[d] 5 Or *winds*
[e] 6 Or *horses after them*
[f] 8 Or *spirit*
[g] 11 Hebrew *Jehozadak*, a variant of *Jozadak*
[h] 13 Or *there*
[i] 14 Syriac; Hebrew *Helem*
[j] 14 Or *and the gracious one, the*

---

and political offices in Israel, or of priest and king. Many identify the two branches with the high priest Joshua and the governor Zerubbabel.

5:4 ***and destroy it.*** God's great love does not preclude the exercise of His judgment on those who violate His will. The judgment upon the disobedient would be certain and severe.

5:7–8 ***This is wickedness.*** The woman sitting inside the ephah (basket) is a personification of sin.

6:1 ***chariots.*** In ancient times two-wheeled and four-wheeled horse-drawn carts served as vehicles for transportation and for warfare. The war chariots usually had a crew of two or three men including a driver, an archer, and a defender who used a shield to protect the others.

6:5 ***four spirits of heaven.*** These spirits were probably angels.

6:11 ***make a crown.*** This crown was to be placed on the head of Joshua the high priest.

6:12 ***build the temple of the LORD.*** Since the restoration temple (the second temple) was already being built and would be complete by Zerubbabel (4:9), the temple referred to here may be the future temple of the messianic kingdom (Is. 2:2–4; Ezek. 40–42; Mic. 4:1–5; Hag. 2:7–9). The Messiah Himself will build it. The temple of Zerubbabel was a prophetic symbol of the temple that is still to come.

6:13 ***sit and rule ... be a priest.*** In the Messiah the two offices of king and priest will be united (John 1:49; Heb. 3:1).

5:1 [y] Eze 2:9; Rev 5:1 **5:3** [z] Isa 24:6; 43:28; Mal 3:9; 4:6 [a] Ex 20:15; Mal 3:8 [b] Isa 48:1 **5:4** [c] Lev 14:34-45; Hab 2:9-11; Mal 3:5 **5:8** [d] Mic 6:11 **5:9** [e] Lev 11:19 **5:11** [f] Ge 10:10 [g] Jer 29:5,28 [h] Da 1:2 **6:1** [i] ver 5 **6:2** [j] Rev 6:5 **6:3** [k] Rev 6:2 **6:5** [l] Eze 37:9; Mt 24:31; Rev 7:1 **6:7** [m] Zec 1:10 **6:8** [n] Eze 5:13; 24:13 **6:10** [o] Ezr 7:14-16; Jer 28:6 **6:11** [p] Ps 21:3 [q] Zec 3:1 [r] Ezr 3:2 **6:12** [s] Isa 4:2; Zec 3:8 [t] Ezr 3:8-10; Zec 4:6-9 **6:13** [u] Ps 110:4

of the LORD. 15Those who are far away will
come and help to build the temple of the
LORD,[v] and you will know that the LORD
Almighty has sent me to you.[w] This will
happen if you diligently obey[x] the LORD
your God."

Justice and Mercy, Not Fasting

7 In the fourth year of King Darius, the
word of the LORD came to Zechariah
on the fourth day of the ninth month, the
month of Kislev.[y] 2The people of Bethel
had sent Sharezer and Regem-Melek, together with their men, to entreat[z] the LORD
3by asking the priests of the house of the
LORD Almighty and the prophets, "Should
I mourn[a] and fast in the fifth[b] month, as I
have done for so many years?"
4Then the word of the LORD Almighty
came to me: 5"Ask all the people of the
land and the priests, 'When you fasted[c] and
mourned in the fifth and seventh months
for the past seventy years, was it really for
me that you fasted? 6And when you were
eating and drinking, were you not just
feasting for yourselves? 7Are these not the
words the LORD proclaimed through the
earlier prophets[d] when Jerusalem and its
surrounding towns were at rest[e] and prosperous, and the Negev and the western
foothills[f] were settled?' "
8And the word of the LORD came again
to Zechariah: 9"This is what the LORD Almighty said: 'Administer true justice;[g]
show mercy and compassion to one another. 10Do not oppress the widow or the fatherless, the foreigner[h] or the poor. Do not
plot evil against each other.'[i]
11"But they refused to pay attention;
stubbornly they turned their backs and
covered their ears.[j] 12They made their
hearts as hard as flint[k] and would not listen to the law or to the words that the LORD
Almighty had sent by his Spirit through
the earlier prophets.[l] So the LORD Almighty
was very angry.[m]
13" 'When I called, they did not listen;[n] so
when they called, I would not listen,'[o] says
the LORD Almighty.[p] 14'I scattered[q] them
with a whirlwind[r] among all the nations,
where they were strangers. The land they
left behind them was so desolate that no
one traveled through it. This is how they
made the pleasant land desolate.[s]' "

The LORD Promises to Bless Jerusalem

8 The word of the LORD Almighty came
to me.
2This is what the LORD Almighty says:
"I am very jealous for Zion; I am burning
with jealousy for her."
3This is what the LORD says: "I will return[t] to Zion and dwell in Jerusalem.[u] Then
Jerusalem will be called the Faithful City,
and the mountain of the LORD Almighty
will be called the Holy Mountain."
4This is what the LORD Almighty says:
"Once again men and women of ripe old
age will sit in the streets of Jerusalem,[v]
each of them with cane in hand because
of their age. 5The city streets will be filled
with boys and girls playing there.[w]"
6This is what the LORD Almighty says:
"It may seem marvelous to the remnant of
this people at that time,[x] but will it seem
marvelous to me?[y]" declares the LORD Almighty.
7This is what the LORD Almighty says: "I
will save my people from the countries of
the east and the west.[z] 8I will bring them
back[a] to live in Jerusalem; they will be my
people,[b] and I will be faithful and righteous
to them as their God."
9This is what the LORD Almighty says:
"Now hear these words, 'Let your hands
be strong[c] so that the temple may be built.'
This is also what the prophets[d] said who

7:3 ***the house of the LORD Almighty.*** This refers to the temple in Jerusalem.
7:5–6 ***was it really for me that you fasted?*** The rhetorical question was designed to confront the people and priests with the selfish motives of their self-righteous fasting. Biblical fasting is meant to be time taken from the normal routines of preparing and eating food to express humility and dependence on God during a time of prayer. There was only one required fast in the law of Moses, the fast on the Day of Atonement (Lev. 23:27).
7:9–10 ***Administer true justice.*** Judicial decisions must be made without partiality or bias. ***show mercy and compassion.*** Loving commitment and concern should guide our relationships with others. ***Do not oppress.*** No advantage is to be taken of the helpless and less fortunate. ***Do not plot evil against each other.*** Evil scheming against others is prohibited. Sacrifices and worship are of little interest to God if they are not accompanied by practical piety. Zechariah's four admonitions highlight the practical social concerns that many of the prophets emphasized (Is. 1:11–17; Hos. 6:6; Mic. 6:6–8).
8:1–3 ***Faithful City.*** This label will be valid only when the Messiah brings His righteous reign to that city. Then the land will be holy (2:12).
8:7–8 ***countries of the east and the west.*** These terms together represent all parts of the earth. ***my people . . . their God.*** This expression occurs in the descriptions of God's covenant relationship with His people (Ex. 19:5; 29:45; Lev. 26:12; Hos. 2:23). With these words, Zechariah anticipates a renewal of God's covenant with His people (Jer. 31:34).

6:15 [v] Isa 60:10 [w] Zec 2:9-11 [x] Isa 58:12; Jer 7:23; Zec 3:7 **7:1** [y] Ne 1:1 **7:2** [z] Jer 26:19; Zec 8:21 **7:3** [a] Zec 12:12-14 [b] Jer 52:12-14; Zec 8:19 **7:5** [c] Isa 58:5 **7:7** [d] Zec 1:4 [e] Jer 22:21 [f] Jer 17:26 **7:9** [g] Zec 8:16 **7:10** [h] Ex 22:21 [i] Ex 22:22; Isa 1:17 **7:11** [j] Jer 8:5; 11:10; 17:23 **7:12** [k] Jer 17:1; Eze 11:19 [l] Ne 9:29 [m] Da 9:12 **7:13** [n] Pr 1:24 [o] Isa 1:15; Jer 11:11; 14:12; Mic 3:4 [p] Pr 1:28 **7:14** [q] Dt 4:27; 28:64-67 [r] Jer 23:19 [s] Jer 44:6 **8:3** [t] Zec 1:16 [u] Zec 2:10 **8:4** [v] Isa 65:20 **8:5** [w] Jer 30:20; 31:13 **8:6** [x] Ps 118:23; 126:1-3 [y] Jer 32:17, 27 **8:7** [z] Ps 107:3; Isa 11:11; 43:5 **8:8** [a] Zec 10:10 [b] Eze 11:19-20; 36:28; Zec 2:11 **8:9** [c] Hag 2:4 [d] Ezr 5:1

were present when the foundation was laid
for the house of the LORD Almighty. 10Be-
fore that time there were no wages[e] for
people or hire for animals. No one could
go about their business safely because of
their enemies, since I had turned everyone
against their neighbor. 11But now I will not
deal with the remnant of this people as I did
in the past,"[f] declares the LORD Almighty.
12"The seed will grow well, the vine will
yield its fruit,[g] the ground will produce its
crops,[h] and the heavens will drop their
dew.[i] I will give all these things as an inheritance[j] to the remnant of this people.
13Just as you, Judah and Israel, have been
a curse[a][k] among the nations, so I will save
you, and you will be a blessing.[b][l] Do not be
afraid, but let your hands be strong."
14This is what the LORD Almighty says:
"Just as I had determined to bring disaster[m] on you and showed no pity when your
ancestors angered me," says the LORD Almighty, 15"so now I have determined to do
good[n] again to Jerusalem and Judah. Do
not be afraid. 16These are the things you
are to do: Speak the truth[o] to each other,
and render true and sound judgment in
your courts;[p] 17do not plot evil[q] against
each other, and do not love to swear falsely.[r] I hate all this," declares the LORD.
18The word of the LORD Almighty came
to me.
19This is what the LORD Almighty says:
"The fasts of the fourth,[s] fifth,[t] seventh[u]
and tenth[v] months will become joyful[w] and
glad occasions and happy festivals for Judah. Therefore love truth[x] and peace."
20This is what the LORD Almighty says:
"Many peoples and the inhabitants of
many cities will yet come, 21and the inhabitants of one city will go to another and
say, 'Let us go at once to entreat[y] the LORD
and seek the LORD Almighty. I myself am
going.' 22And many peoples and powerful
nations will come to Jerusalem to seek the
LORD Almighty and to entreat him."[z]
23This is what the LORD Almighty says:
"In those days ten people from all languages and nations will take firm hold of one
Jew by the hem of his robe and say, 'Let us
go with you, because we have heard that
God is with you.'"[a]

Judgment on Israel's Enemies

9 A prophecy:

The word of the LORD is against the
 land of Hadrak
 and will come to rest on
 Damascus[b]—
for the eyes of all people and all the
 tribes of Israel
 are on the LORD—[c]
2 and on Hamath[c] too, which borders
 on it,
 and on Tyre[d] and Sidon, though they
 are very skillful.
3 Tyre has built herself a stronghold;
 she has heaped up silver like dust,
 and gold like the dirt of the streets.[e]
4 But the Lord will take away her
 possessions
 and destroy her power on the sea,
 and she will be consumed by fire.[f]
5 Ashkelon will see it and fear;
 Gaza will writhe in agony,
 and Ekron too, for her hope will
 wither.
Gaza will lose her king
 and Ashkelon will be deserted.
6 A mongrel people will occupy Ashdod,
 and I will put an end to the pride of
 the Philistines.
7 I will take the blood from their mouths,
 the forbidden food from between
 their teeth.
Those who are left will belong to our
 God
 and become a clan in Judah,
 and Ekron will be like the Jebusites.

---

[a] *13* That is, your name has been used in cursing (see Jer. 29:22); or, you have been regarded as under a curse. [b] *13* Or *and your name will be used in blessings* (see Gen. 48:20); or *and you will be seen as blessed* [c] *1* Or *Damascus. / For the eye of the LORD is on all people, / as well as on the tribes of Israel,*

8:10 *no wages ... No one could go about their business safely.* Zechariah recounts the desperate situation in Judea before the work on the temple resumed in 520 B.C. (Hag. 1:1,6,10–11; 2:16–17).

8:11–13 *let your hands be strong.* In view of God's gracious purposes and future plans for His people, they were called to be diligent in their present efforts to serve Him with sincere hearts (1 Cor. 15:58).

8:16–17 *truth ... sound judgment.* Zechariah set forth the ethical obligations of a life of faith. He upheld these important values and condemned evil plans and false oaths.

8:20–23 *peoples ... will yet come.* Here Zechariah announces a great turning of the nations to God. During the Messianic Era, a multitude of people from many cities will go to Jerusalem to "seek the LORD." These Gentiles will be included among the people of God by faith (Eph. 2:13–19).

9:1 *prophecy.* This word suggests that a weighty judgment must be declared.

9:7 *blood from their mouths, the forbidden food from between their teeth.* These phrases refer to the cessation of unlawful and idolatrous practices (Lev. 17:14; Is. 65:4; 66:17).

8:10 [e] Hag 1:6 **8:11** [f] Isa 12:1 **8:12** [g] Joel 2:22 [h] Ps 67:6 [i] Ge 27:28 [j] Ob 1:17 **8:13** [k] Jer 42:18 [l] Ge 12:2 **8:14** [m] Jer 31:28; Eze 24:14 **8:15** [n] ver 13; Jer 29:11; Mic 7:18-20 **8:16** [o] Ps 15:2; Eph 4:25 [p] Zec 7:9 **8:17** [q] Pr 3:29 [r] Pr 6:16-19 **8:19** [s] Jer 39:2 [t] Jer 52:12 [u] 2Ki 25:25 [v] Jer 52:4 [w] Ps 30:11 [x] ver 16 **8:21** [y] Zec 7:2 **8:22** [z] Ps 117:1; Isa 60:3; Zec 2:11 **8:23** [a] Isa 45:14; 1Co 14:25 **9:1** [b] Isa 17:1 **9:2** [c] Jer 49:23 [d] Eze 28:1-19 **9:3** [e] Job 27:16; Eze 28:4 **9:4** [f] Isa 23:1; Eze 26:3-5; 28:18

8 But I will encamp at my temple
to guard it against marauding forces.
Never again will an oppressor overrun
my people,
for now I am keeping watch.[g]

The Coming of Zion's King

9 Rejoice greatly, Daughter Zion!
Shout, Daughter Jerusalem!
See, your king comes to you,
righteous and victorious,[h]
lowly and riding on a donkey,
on a colt, the foal of a donkey.[i]
10 I will take away the chariots from
Ephraim
and the warhorses from Jerusalem,
and the battle bow will be broken.[j]
He will proclaim peace to the nations.
His rule will extend from sea to sea
and from the River[a] to the ends of the
earth.[k]
11 As for you, because of the blood of my
covenant[l] with you,
I will free your prisoners[m] from the
waterless pit.
12 Return to your fortress,[n] you prisoners
of hope;
even now I announce that I will
restore twice as much to you.
13 I will bend Judah as I bend my bow
and fill it with Ephraim.[o]
I will rouse your sons, Zion,
against your sons, Greece,[p]
and make you like a warrior's
sword.[q]

The LORD Will Appear

14 Then the LORD will appear over them;[r]
his arrow will flash like lightning.[s]
The Sovereign LORD will sound the
trumpet;
he will march in the storms[t] of the
south,
15 and the LORD Almighty will shield[u]
them.
They will destroy
and overcome with slingstones.
They will drink and roar as with wine;
they will be full like a bowl
used for sprinkling[b] the corners[v] of
the altar.
16 The LORD their God will save his people
on that day
as a shepherd saves his flock.
They will sparkle in his land
like jewels in a crown.[w]
17 How attractive and beautiful they
will be!
Grain will make the young men
thrive,
and new wine the young women.

The LORD Will Care for Judah

10 Ask the LORD for rain in the
springtime;
it is the LORD who sends the
thunderstorms.
He gives showers of rain to all people,
and plants of the field to everyone.
2 The idols[x] speak deceitfully,
diviners see visions that lie;
they tell dreams that are false,
they give comfort in vain.
Therefore the people wander like
sheep
oppressed for lack of a shepherd.[y]

3 "My anger burns against the
shepherds,
and I will punish the leaders;[z]
for the LORD Almighty will care
for his flock, the people of Judah,
and make them like a proud horse in
battle.
4 From Judah will come the cornerstone,
from him the tent peg,[a]
from him the battle bow,[b]
from him every ruler.
5 Together they[c] will be like warriors in
battle
trampling their enemy into the mud
of the streets.[c]
They will fight because the LORD is
with them,
and they will put the enemy
horsemen to shame.[d]

6 "I will strengthen Judah
and save the tribes of Joseph.

[a] *10* That is, the Euphrates [b] *15* Or *bowl, / like*
[c] *4,5* Or *ruler, all of them together. / [5]They*

9:9 *lowly and riding on a donkey.* This prophecy was fulfilled on the day of the triumphal entry, when Jesus rode into Jerusalem on the colt of a donkey (Matt. 21:2–7). The donkey was the mount of princes (Judg. 5:10; 10:4) and kings (2 Sam. 16:1–2).

9:14 *storms of the south.* This description, patterned after God's appearance at Sinai (Ex. 19), reveals God's sovereignty and power to protect His own.

9:15 *They will drink.* The people will be filled with drink like sacrificial basins were filled with blood, and they will be filled with meat like the corners of a sacrificial altar (Ps. 110:6).

10:2 *lack of a shepherd.* The metaphor of *shepherd* was often used in the ancient Middle East to represent a king or ruler (Ezek. 34:6–8,23–24). Here the emphasis was on the lack of spiritual leadership.

10:3 *the people of Judah.* God will strengthen Judah so that she can overthrow the oppressors.

10:4–5 *tent peg.* A peg firmly in place suggests permanence and endurance (Is. 22:23). ***battle bow.*** This image pictures the strength necessary for military conquest (2 Kin. 13:17).

9:8 [g] Isa 52:1; 54:14 **9:9** [h] Isa 9:6-7; 43:3-11; Jer 23:5-6; Zep 3:14-15; Zec 2:10 [i] Mt 21:5*; Jn 12:15* **9:10** [j] Hos 1:7; 2:18; Mic 4:3; 5:10; Zec 10:4 [k] Ps 72:8 **9:11** [l] Ex 24:8 [m] Isa 42:7 **9:12** [n] Joel 3:16 **9:13** [o] Isa 49:2 [p] Joel 3:6 [q] Jer 51:20 **9:14** [r] Isa 31:5 [s] Ps 18:14; Hab 3:11 [t] Isa 21:1; 66:15 **9:15** [u] Isa 37.35; Zec 12:8 [v] Ex 27:2 **9:16** [w] Isa 62:3; Jer 31:11 **10:2** [x] Eze 21:21 [y] Eze 34:5; Hos 3:4; Mt 9:36 **10:3** [z] Jer 25:34 **10:4** [a] Isa 22:23 [b] Zec 9:10 **10:5** [c] 2Sa 22:43 [d] Am 2:15; Hag 2:22

I will restore them
because I have compassion on them.[e]
They will be as though
I had not rejected them,
for I am the LORD their God
and I will answer[f] them.
7 The Ephraimites will become like
warriors,
and their hearts will be glad as with
wine.[g]
Their children will see it and be joyful;
their hearts will rejoice in the LORD.
8 I will signal[h] for them
and gather them in.
Surely I will redeem them;
they will be as numerous[i] as before.
9 Though I scatter them among the
peoples,
yet in distant lands they will
remember me.[j]
They and their children will survive,
and they will return.
10 I will bring them back from Egypt
and gather them from Assyria.[k]
I will bring them to Gilead[l] and
Lebanon,
and there will not be room[m] enough
for them.
11 They will pass through the sea of
trouble;
the surging sea will be subdued
and all the depths of the Nile will
dry up.[n]
Assyria's pride[o] will be brought down
and Egypt's scepter[p] will pass away.
12 I will strengthen them in the LORD
and in his name they will live
securely,[q]"
declares the LORD.

11 Open your doors, Lebanon,[r]
so that fire may devour your cedars!
2 Wail, you juniper, for the cedar has
fallen;
the stately trees are ruined!
Wail, oaks of Bashan;
the dense forest[s] has been cut down!
3 Listen to the wail of the shepherds;
their rich pastures are destroyed!
Listen to the roar of the lions;
the lush thicket of the Jordan is
ruined![t]

Two Shepherds

4 This is what the LORD my God says:
"Shepherd the flock marked for slaughter.
5 Their buyers slaughter them and go unpunished. Those who sell them say, 'Praise
the LORD, I am rich!' Their own shepherds
do not spare them.[u] 6 For I will no longer
have pity on the people of the land," declares the LORD. "I will give everyone into
the hands of their neighbors[v] and their
king. They will devastate the land, and I
will not rescue anyone from their hands."[w]
7 So I shepherded the flock marked for
slaughter, particularly the oppressed of the
flock. Then I took two staffs and called one
Favor and the other Union, and I shepherded the flock. 8 In one month I got rid of the
three shepherds.
The flock detested me, and I grew weary
of them 9 and said, "I will not be your shepherd. Let the dying die, and the perishing
perish.[x] Let those who are left eat one another's flesh."
10 Then I took my staff called Favor[y] and
broke it, revoking[z] the covenant I had made
with all the nations. 11 It was revoked on
that day, and so the oppressed of the flock
who were watching me knew it was the
word of the LORD.
12 I told them, "If you think it best, give
me my pay; but if not, keep it." So they paid
me thirty pieces of silver.[a]
13 And the LORD said to me, "Throw it to
the potter"—the handsome price at which
they valued me! So I took the thirty pieces
of silver and threw them to the potter at the
house of the LORD.[b]

10:7 ***as with wine.*** What was promised to Judah in verse 5 is here promised to Ephraim. Wine is used here as a symbol of abundant joy (Ps. 104:15; Amos 9:13; John 2:1–11).
10:9 ***they will remember me.*** This phrase anticipates their turning to the Lord in repentance. ***will survive.*** This implies more than mere survival. God promises spiritual life and blessing to the repentant.
10:12 ***I will strengthen them.*** The regathering will be accomplished by God's power as He gives strength to His people. ***in his name they will live securely.*** In the last days, Israel will return to the land as a believing nation (v. 8; 12:10–13:1; Rom. 11:26).
11:7 ***Favor ... Union.*** These were the names of Zechariah's two staffs. The images suggest that he wanted the flock to enjoy God's favor and to experience national unity. According to Canaanite legend, the god Baal was given the two clubs named Driver and Chaser to battle the dark deities of the sea. It is appropriate that God's messenger Zechariah is given shepherd's staffs to guide the people, instead of clubs for fighting.
11:8 ***three shepherds.*** Some have suggested that the three shepherds represent classes of rulers in Israel: kings, priests, and prophets. Others suggest that they refer to the last three kings of Judah or to certain high priests of the Maccabean era.
11:12 ***thirty pieces of silver.*** Zechariah, taking the role of the messianic shepherd, requested his wages for service rendered. This amount was the price of a slave. It was also the price paid to Judas for betraying Jesus (Matt. 27:6–10).

10:6 [e] Zec 8:7-8 [f] Zec 13:9 **10:7** [g] Zec 9:15 **10:8** [h] Isa 5:26 [i] Jer 33:22; Eze 36:11 **10:9** [j] Eze 6:9 **10:10** [k] Isa 11:11 [l] Jer 50:19 [m] Isa 49:19 **10:11** [n] Isa 19:5-7; 51:10 [o] Zep 2:13 [p] Eze 30:13 **10:12** [q] Mic 4:5 **11:1** [r] Eze 31:3 **11:2** [s] Isa 32:19 **11:3** [t] Jer 2:15; 50:44 **11:5** [u] Jer 50:7; Eze 34:2-3 **11:6** [v] Zec 14:13 [w] Isa 9:19-21; Jer 13:14; Mic 5:8; 7:2-6 **11:9** [x] Jer 15:2; 43:11 **11:10** [y] ver 7 [z] Ps 89:39; Jer 14:21 **11:12** [a] Ex 21:32; Mt 26:15 **11:13** [b] Mt 27:9-10*; Ac 1:18-19

14Then I broke my second staff called Union, breaking the family bond between Judah and Israel.

15Then the LORD said to me, "Take again the equipment of a foolish shepherd. **16**For I am going to raise up a shepherd over the land who will not care for the lost, or seek the young, or heal the injured, or feed the healthy, but will eat the meat of the choice sheep, tearing off their hooves.

17"Woe to the worthless shepherd,[c]
who deserts the flock!
May the sword strike his arm[d] and his
right eye!
May his arm be completely withered,
his right eye totally blinded!"[e]

Jerusalem's Enemies to Be Destroyed

12 A prophecy: The word of the LORD concerning Israel.

The LORD, who stretches out the heavens,[f] who lays the foundation of the earth,[g] and who forms the human spirit within a person,[h] declares: **2**"I am going to make Jerusalem a cup[i] that sends all the surrounding peoples reeling.[j] Judah[k] will be besieged as well as Jerusalem. **3**On that day, when all the nations[l] of the earth are gathered against her, I will make Jerusalem an immovable rock[m] for all the nations. All who try to move it will injure[n] themselves. **4**On that day I will strike every horse with panic and its rider with madness," declares the LORD. "I will keep a watchful eye over Judah, but I will blind all the horses of the nations.[o] **5**Then the clans of Judah will say in their hearts, 'The people of Jerusalem are strong, because the LORD Almighty is their God.'

6"On that day I will make the clans of Judah like a firepot[p] in a woodpile, like a flaming torch among sheaves. They will consume[q] all the surrounding peoples right and left, but Jerusalem will remain intact in her place.

7"The LORD will save the dwellings of Judah first, so that the honor of the house of David and of Jerusalem's inhabitants may not be greater than that of Judah.[r] **8**On that day the LORD will shield[s] those who live in Jerusalem, so that the feeblest among them will be like David, and the house of David will be like God,[t] like the angel of the LORD going before[u] them. **9**On that day I will set out to destroy all the nations that attack Jerusalem.[v]

Mourning for the One They Pierced

10"And I will pour out on the house of David and the inhabitants of Jerusalem a spirit[a] of grace and supplication.[w] They will look on[b] me, the one they have pierced,[x] and they will mourn for him as one mourns for an only child, and grieve bitterly for him as one grieves for a firstborn son. **11**On that day the weeping in Jerusalem will be as great as the weeping of Hadad Rimmon in the plain of Megiddo.[y] **12**The land will mourn,[z] each clan by itself, with their wives by themselves: the clan of the house of David and their wives, the clan of the house of Nathan and their wives, **13**the clan of the house of Levi and their wives, the clan of Shimei and their wives, **14**and all the rest of the clans and their wives.

Cleansing From Sin

13 "On that day a fountain[a] will be opened to the house of David and the inhabitants of Jerusalem, to cleanse[b] them from sin and impurity.

2"On that day, I will banish the names of

[a] 10 Or *the Spirit* [b] 10 Or *to*

11:15–16 ***Take again the equipment of a foolish shepherd.*** This phrase means to behave like one. ***eat the meat of the choice sheep, tearing off their hooves.*** These phrases express the savagery of a foolish shepherd.

11:17 ***worthless shepherd.*** He will be judged. His "arm," which should have been used to protect the ship, will wither. His "right eye," which should have watched over the sheep, will be blinded.

12:1 ***A prophecy.*** As in 9:1, the burden is a weighty judgment that the prophet must discharge. ***heavens ... the earth ... the human spirit.*** Three phrases are used here in describing the greatness of God as Creator.

12:3 ***immovable rock.*** Jerusalem is compared to a heavy stone that brings injury to anyone who tries to remove it from its place.

12:6 ***Judah.*** Here, Judah is likened to (1) "a firepot" used to carry hot coals for the purpose of starting a fire, and (2) "a flaming torch" that could quickly ignite a field of cut grain.

12:10 ***spirit of grace.*** These words refer to the gracious working of the Holy Spirit that leads to conviction and repentance (John 16:8–11). ***supplication.*** The Spirit will stimulate an attitude of repentance and prayer for God's mercy. There are many significant ministries of the Holy Spirit in the period of the Hebrew kingdom.

12:12–14 ***the house of David ... the clan of the house of Levi and their wives.*** These words are quoted in the Talmud as an argument for separating men and women in worship. But the verse seems to indicate that each mourner will face his or her sorrow alone, without the comfort of companionship.

13:2 ***banish the names of the idols.*** In ancient times, a person's name reflected his or her reputation.

11:17 [c] Jer 23:1 [d] Eze 30:21-22 [e] Jer 23:1 **12:1** [f] Isa 42:5; Jer 51:15 [g] Ps 102:25; Heb 1:10 [h] Isa 57:16 **12:2** [i] Ps 75:8 [j] Isa 51:23 [k] Zec 14:14 **12:3** [l] Zec 14:2 [m] Da 2:34-35 [n] Mt 21:44 **12:4** [o] Ps 76:6 **12:6** [p] Isa 10:17-18; Zec 11:1 [q] Ob 1:18 **12:7** [r] Jer 30:18; Am 9:11 **12:8** [s] Joel 3:16; Zec 9:15 [t] Ps 82:6 [u] Mic 7:8 **12:9** [v] Zec 14:2-3 **12:10** [w] Isa 44:3; Eze 39:29; Joel 2:28-29 [x] Jn 19:34,37*; Rev 1:7 **12:11** [y] 2Ki 23:29 **12:12** [z] Mt 24:30; Rev 1:7 **13:1** [a] Jer 17:13 [b] Ps 51:2; Heb 9:14

the idols[c] from the land, and they will be remembered no more," declares the LORD Almighty. "I will remove both the prophets[d]
and the spirit of impurity from the land.
3And if anyone still prophesies, their father
and mother, to whom they were born, will
say to them, 'You must die, because you
have told lies in the LORD's name.' Then
their own parents will stab the one who
prophesies.[e]
4"On that day every prophet will be
ashamed[f] of their prophetic vision. They
will not put on a prophet's garment[g] of hair[h]
in order to deceive. 5Each will say, 'I am not
a prophet. I am a farmer; the land has been
my livelihood since my youth.[a]'[i] 6If someone asks, 'What are these wounds on your
body[b]?' they will answer, 'The wounds I was
given at the house of my friends.'

The Shepherd Struck, the Sheep Scattered

7"Awake, sword,[j] against my shepherd,[k]
against the man who is close to me!"
declares the LORD Almighty.
"Strike the shepherd,
and the sheep will be scattered,[l]
and I will turn my hand against the
little ones.
8In the whole land," declares the LORD,
"two-thirds will be struck down and
perish;
yet one-third will be left in it.[m]
9This third I will put into the fire;[n]
I will refine them like silver[o]
and test them like gold.
They will call[p] on my name
and I will answer[q] them;
I will say, 'They are my people,'[r]
and they will say, 'The LORD is our
God.[s]'"

The LORD Comes and Reigns

14 A day of the LORD[t] is coming, Jerusalem, when your possessions will
be plundered and divided up within your
very walls.
2I will gather all the nations to Jerusalem
to fight against it; the city will be captured,
the houses ransacked, and the women
raped. Half of the city will go into exile, but
the rest of the people will not be taken from
the city.[u] 3Then the LORD will go out and
fight[v] against those nations, as he fights on
a day of battle. 4On that day his feet will
stand on the Mount of Olives,[w] east of Jerusalem, and the Mount of Olives will be split
in two from east to west, forming a great
valley, with half of the mountain moving
north and half moving south. 5You will flee
by my mountain valley, for it will extend
to Azel. You will flee as you fled from the
earthquake[c][x] in the days of Uzziah king of
Judah. Then the LORD my God will come,[y]
and all the holy ones with him.[z]
6On that day there will be neither sunlight[a] nor cold, frosty darkness. 7It will be
a unique[b] day—a day known only to the
LORD—with no distinction between day
and night.[c] When evening comes, there
will be light.[d]
8On that day living water[e] will flow out
from Jerusalem, half of it east[f] to the Dead
Sea and half of it west to the Mediterranean Sea, in summer and in winter.
9The LORD will be king over the whole
earth.[g] On that day there will be one LORD,
and his name the only name.[h]

[a] 5 Or *farmer; a man sold me in my youth*
[b] 6 Or *wounds between your hands*
[c] 5 Or *5My mountain valley will be blocked and will extend to Azel. It will be blocked as it was blocked because of the earthquake*

Zechariah anticipated the complete removal of the reputation and acknowledgement of false gods.

13:4 ***garment of hair.*** This was the traditional clothing of a prophet. False prophets will deny that they are prophets for fear of punishment, and will refuse to wear one (2 Kin. 1:8; Matt. 3:4).

13:6 ***wounds on your body.*** This is probably a reference to the profession of an ecstatic prophet who slashed himself on the back or breast. Self-inflicted wounds were thought to gain the attention and blessing of the gods (1 Kin. 18:28). Under questioning, the man declares that the wounds were received from friends so that he will not be found out as a false prophet and be put to death (v. 3).

13:7 ***sword.*** The sword, an instrument of death, is likened to a warrior being roused for action. The Lord commands the sword to strike the Messiah. ***my shepherd.*** This clearly indicates that the death of Jesus was not accident, but was divinely determined.

13:9 ***refine them.*** The smelting pot uses intense heat to separate the dross from pure metal. ***test them.*** Once refined, precious metal must be analyzed to determine its value.

14:4 ***Mount of Olives.*** This is located east of Jerusalem and the Kidron valley: it is a north-south hill about 2,700 feet in elevation. The Messiah will return to the Mount of Olives, the very mountain from which He will have ascended after His time on earth. (Acts 1:10–11). On the day of Messiah's return, the mount will be split by a deep east-west valley.

14:8 ***living water.*** This term describes running water from a spring or river, in contrast to the stale and stagnant water of a cistern (Jer. 2:13). The water will flow from Jerusalem toward the eastern sea (the Dead Sea) and the western sea (the Mediterranean). In contrast with the seasonal streams that flow only during the rainy season, these streams will irrigate the land in both summer and winter.

13:2 [c] Ex 23:13; Eze 36:25; Hos 2:17 [d] 1Ki 22:22; Jer 23:14-15 **13:3** [e] Dt 13:6-11; 18:20; Jer 23:34; Eze 14:9 **13:4** [f] Jer 6:15; Mic 3:6-7 [g] Mt 3:4 [h] 2Ki 1:8; Isa 20:2 **13:5** [i] Am 7:14 **13:7** [j] Jer 47:6 [k] Isa 40:11; 53:4; Eze 37:24 [l] Mt 26:31*; Mk 14:27* **13:8** [m] Eze 5:2-4, 12 **13:9** [n] Mal 3:2 [o] Isa 48:10; 1Pe 1:6-7 [p] Ps 50:15 [q] Zec 10:6 [r] Jer 30:22 [s] Jer 29:12 **14:1** [t] Isa 13:9; Mal 4:1 **14:2** [u] Isa 13:6; Zec 13:8 **14:3** [v] Zec 9:14-15 **14:4** [w] Eze 11:23 **14:5** [x] Am 1:1 [y] Isa 29:6; 66:15-16 [z] Mt 16:27; 25:31 **14:6** [a] Isa 13:10; Jer 4:23 **14:7** [b] Jer 30:7 [c] Rev 21:23-25; 22:5 [d] Isa 30:26 **14:8** [e] Eze 47:1-12; Jn 7:38; Rev 22:1-2 [f] Joel 2:20 **14:9** [g] Dt 6:4; Isa 45:24; Rev 11:15 [h] Eph 4:5-6

10 The whole land, from Geba[i] to Rimmon, south of Jerusalem, will become like
the Arabah. But Jerusalem will be raised
up[j] high from the Benjamin Gate to the site
of the First Gate, to the Corner Gate, and
from the Tower of Hananel to the royal
winepresses, and will remain in its place.[k]
11 It will be inhabited; never again will it be
destroyed. Jerusalem will be secure.[l]

12 This is the plague with which the
LORD will strike all the nations that fought
against Jerusalem: Their flesh will rot
while they are still standing on their feet,
their eyes will rot in their sockets, and
their tongues will rot in their mouths.[m]
13 On that day people will be stricken by
the LORD with great panic. They will seize
each other by the hand and attack one another.[n] 14 Judah[o] too will fight at Jerusalem.
The wealth of all the surrounding nations
will be collected[p]—great quantities of gold
and silver and clothing. 15 A similar plague[q]
will strike the horses and mules, the camels and donkeys, and all the animals in
those camps.

16 Then the survivors from all the nations that have attacked Jerusalem will go
up year after year to worship the King, the
LORD Almighty, and to celebrate the Festival of Tabernacles.[r] 17 If any of the peoples of the earth do not go up to Jerusalem
to worship the King, the LORD Almighty,
they will have no rain.[s] 18 If the Egyptian
people do not go up and take part, they
will have no rain. The LORD[a] will bring on
them the plague he inflicts on the nations
that do not go up to celebrate the Festival
of Tabernacles.[t] 19 This will be the punishment of Egypt and the punishment of all
the nations that do not go up to celebrate
the Festival of Tabernacles.

20 On that day HOLY TO THE LORD will be
inscribed on the bells of the horses, and
the cooking pots[u] in the LORD's house will
be like the sacred bowls[v] in front of the altar. 21 Every pot in Jerusalem and Judah
will be holy[w] to the LORD Almighty, and all
who come to sacrifice will take some of the
pots and cook in them. And on that day[x]
there will no longer be a Canaanite[b][y] in the
house of the LORD Almighty.[z]

---

a 18 Or part, then the LORD *b 21 Or merchant*

14:11 *It will be inhabited ... secure.* This is a contrast to the time of Nehemiah when the population of Jerusalem was sparse (Neh. 7:4; 11:1). In the Lord's coming kingdom, the city will be inhabited and its citizens secure.

14:18–19 *Egyptian people.* In this passage, Egypt is used as an example of the nations that are unwilling to come to Jerusalem to worship King Messiah and celebrate the feast. It will be subject to divine judgment because it was a traditional enemy of Israel.

14:20–21 *HOLY TO THE LORD.* These words will be inscribed on the gold headband worn by the high priest (Ex. 28:36). Holiness will so permeate Messiah's kingdom that even the lowly cooking pots will be holy. The name "Canaanite" here refers to the merchants who frequented Jerusalem and the temple courts with their wares (Neh. 13:19–22; Matt. 21:12; John 2:14). None will profiteer in the worship of God in the coming age. God's search for true worshipers will be realized in the company of devoted, holy people.

14:10 [i] 1Ki 15:22 [j] Jer 30:18; Am 9:11 [k] Zec 12:6
14:11 [l] Eze 34:25-28 **14:12** [m] Lev 26:16; Dt 28:22
14:13 [n] Zec 11:6 **14:14** [o] Zec 12:2 [p] Isa 23:18
14:15 [q] ver 12 **14:16** [r] Isa 60:6-9 **14:17** [s] Jer 14:4; Am 4:7 **14:18** [t] ver 12 **14:20** [u] Eze 46:20 [v] Zec 9:15
14:21 [w] Ro 14:6-7; 1Co 10:31 [x] Ne 8:10 [y] Zec 9:8 [z] Eze 44:9

MALACHI

▶ **AUTHOR:** The only Old Testament mention of Malachi is in 1:1. Nothing else is known of Malachi, not even his father's name. But tradition holds that he too, like Zechariah, was a member of the Great Synagogue. He is generally accepted as the author of this book. It is likely that Malachi proclaimed his message when Nehemiah was absent from Judah between 432 B.C. and 425 B.C., almost a century after Haggai and Zechariah began to prophesy. Thus, because of its place in history and the Old Testament, Malachi is a transitional book. Its primary themes are consistent with rest of Old Testament, but it also serves as a precursor to the New Testament.

▶ **TIME:** c. 432–425 B.C. ▶ **KEY VERSE:** Mal. 2:17

▶ **THEME:** In Malachi, the days of political upheaval are past, and the country is living in an uneventful waiting period. The people are waiting for Messiah to bring the glorious restoration of their nation to the renewed prominence of the Davidic and Solomonic period. There is a sense the people are losing touch with God during this rather uneventful time. The old problem with idol worship is gone, but other problems have taken its place. Malachi's role is to call them back to a genuine enduring faith in God. His dominant admonition is for a personal relationship with the living God, who seeks men to walk with Him (2:6)

1 A prophecy:[a] The word[b] of the LORD to
Israel through Malachi.[a]

Israel Doubts God's Love

2"I have loved[c] you," says the LORD.
"But you ask, 'How have you loved us?'
"Was not Esau Jacob's brother?" declares the LORD. "Yet I have loved Jacob,[d]
3but Esau I have hated, and I have turned
his hill country into a wasteland[e] and left
his inheritance to the desert jackals.[f]"
4Edom may say, "Though we have been
crushed, we will rebuild[g] the ruins."
But this is what the LORD Almighty says:
"They may build, but I will demolish. They
will be called the Wicked Land, a people
always under the wrath of the LORD.[h] 5You
will see it with your own eyes and say,
'Great[i] is the LORD—even beyond the borders of Israel!'[j]

Breaking Covenant Through Blemished Sacrifices

6"A son honors his father, and a slave his
master. If I am a father, where is the honor
due me? If I am a master, where is the respect[k] due me?" says the LORD Almighty.[l]
"It is you priests who show contempt for
my name.
"But you ask, 'How have we shown contempt for your name?'
7"By offering defiled food[m] on my altar.
"But you ask, 'How have we defiled you?'
"By saying that the LORD's table is contemptible. 8When you offer blind animals
for sacrifice, is that not wrong? When you
sacrifice lame or diseased animals,[n] is
that not wrong? Try offering them to your

[a] 1 *Malachi* means *my messenger.*

1:1 *to Israel.* In the postexilic period, the use of the word Israel for the people of Judah expresses the hope that the Lord was in the process of reasserting the fullness of His original promises to His people. The name "Malachi" means "My Messenger."
1:3 *Esau I have hated.* The contrast between the words *love* and *hate* here and in verse 2 seems too strong. But on many occasions in the Old Testament, the verb *hate* has the basic meaning "not to choose." God's love for Jacob was expressed in His electing grace in extending His covenant to Jacob and to his descendants (Gen. 25:21–26; Is. 44:1–5). In His sovereign purpose, God set His love on the one and not the other. The term *hate* may carry the idea of indifference as well.
1:6 *A son honors his father.* Here the Lord uses truisms: A father and a master can expect honor from those beneath them, but God was not receiving the honor due Him. ***If I am a father.*** The image of God as Father is common in the New Testament, but less frequent in the Old Testament (Is. 63:16; 64:8).
1:8 *blind . . . lame or diseased.* The demands of the holy worship of God had been made clear in the law. Only the very best should be presented as an offering

1:1 [a] Na 1:1 [b] 1Pe 4:11 **1:2** [c] Dt 4:37 [d] Ro 9:13* **1:3** [e] Isa 34:10 [f] Eze 35:3-9 **1:4** [g] Isa 9:10 [h] Eze 25:12-14 **1:5** [i] Ps 35:27; Mic 5:4 [j] Am 1:11-12 **1:6** [k] Isa 1:2 [l] Job 5:17 **1:7** [m] ver 12; Lev 21:6 **1:8** [n] Lev 22:22; Dt 15:21

governor! Would he be pleased with you?
Would he accept you?" says the LORD Almighty.[o]
[9]"Now plead with God to be gracious to
us. With such offerings[p] from your hands,
will he accept you?"—says the LORD Almighty.
[10]"Oh, that one of you would shut the
temple doors, so that you would not light
useless fires on my altar! I am not pleased[q]
with you," says the LORD Almighty, "and I
will accept no offering[r] from your hands.
[11]My name will be great among the nations, from where the sun rises to where
it sets. In every place incense[s] and pure offerings will be brought to me, because my
name will be great among the nations,"
says the LORD Almighty.
[12]"But you profane it by saying, 'The
Lord's table is defiled,' and, 'Its food[t] is
contemptible.' [13]And you say, 'What a burden!'[u] and you sniff at it contemptuously,"
says the LORD Almighty.
"When you bring injured, lame or diseased animals and offer them as sacrifices, should I accept them from your hands?"
says the LORD. [14]"Cursed is the cheat who
has an acceptable male in his flock and
vows to give it, but then sacrifices a blemished animal[v] to the Lord. For I am a great
king,[w]" says the LORD Almighty, "and my
name is to be feared among the nations.

Additional Warning to the Priests

2 "And now, you priests, this warning is
for you.[x] [2]If you do not listen, and if you
do not resolve to honor my name," says the
LORD Almighty, "I will send a curse[y] on
you, and I will curse your blessings. Yes,
I have already cursed them, because you
have not resolved to honor me.
[3]"Because of you I will rebuke your descendants[a]; I will smear on your faces the
dung[z] from your festival sacrifices, and
you will be carried off with it.[a] [4]And you
will know that I have sent you this warning
so that my covenant with Levi[b] may continue," says the LORD Almighty. [5]"My covenant was with him, a covenant[c] of life and
peace,[d] and I gave them to him; this called
for reverence and he revered me and stood
in awe of my name. [6]True instruction[e] was
in his mouth and nothing false was found
on his lips. He walked with me in peace
and uprightness, and turned many from
sin.[f]
[7]"For the lips of a priest[g] ought to preserve knowledge, because he is the messenger[h] of the LORD Almighty and people
seek instruction from his mouth.[i] [8]But
you have turned from the way and by
your teaching have caused many to stumble;[j] you have violated the covenant with
Levi," says the LORD Almighty. [9]"So I have
caused you to be despised[k] and humiliated
before all the people, because you have not
followed my ways but have shown partiality in matters of the law."

Breaking Covenant Through Divorce

[10]Do we not all have one Father[b]?[l] Did
not one God create us? Why do we profane
the covenant[m] of our ancestors by being
unfaithful to one another?

[a] 3 Or *will blight your grain* [b] 10 Or *father*

to the Lord (Lev. 1:3); no one was to come with an offering that was blemished or unclean (Lev. 7:19–21).

1:11 *great among the nations.* God would one day receive praise from all the nations. Even the despised Gentiles would offer praise, while God's own people were profaning His holy name (Ps. 87; 117).

1:14 *I am a great king.* The reputation of the Lord among His people was to have been the means whereby all the nations would be drawn to worship Him as well.

2:2 *I will send a curse.* At the passage of the people into the Promised Land, the Levites spread before the people the blessings of obedience and the curses on disobedience (Deut. 27; 28). But the priests were not obeying the law that they were supposed to uphold. They would therefore receive the curses.

2:3 *dung.* This was the dung in the sacrificed animal that should have been removed when the animal was prepared for sacrifice to the Lord.

2:6 *True instruction.* The priests of the Old Testament period had a twofold responsibility: they were to represent the people in holy worship before the living God, and they were to teach and apply God's law to the people. ***in peace and uprightness.*** This refers to complete moral virtue in all things before the Lord.

2:7 *messenger.* In the Old Testaments, prophets were commonly called messengers. But apparently this is the only time in the Old Testament that priests are specifically called the messengers of the Lord (3:1).

2:10 God the Father of All—The Fatherhood of God applies in a general sense to everyone since all men and women are created by God in His image. God is the Father of the human race. Several Scriptures speak of God as "the Father of spirits" (Heb. 12:9; see Num. 16:22; Eccl. 12:7). Paul even agrees with a heathen poet that all men are God's offspring (Acts 17:28). James 3:9 says that men have been made in God's image.

God is also the Father of all as sustainer of life. Every person is an object of His fatherly care (Matt. 18:10) and a candidate for His Kingdom (Luke 18:16). Furthermore, God is not willing that any should perish (Matt. 18:14; 1 Tim. 2:4). Even when men and women reject God He still provides for them as He

1:8 [o] Isa 43:23 **1:9** [p] Lev 23:33-44 **1:10** [q] Hos 5:6 [r] Isa 1:11-14; Jer 14:12 **1:11** [s] Isa 60:6-7; Rev 8:3 **1:12** [t] ver 7 **1:13** [u] Isa 43:22-24 **1:14** [v] Lev 22:18-21 [w] 1Ti 6:15 **2:1** [x] ver 7 **2:2** [y] Dt 28:20 **2:3** [z] Ex 29:14 [a] 1Ki 14:10 **2:4** [b] Nu 3:12 **2:5** [c] Dt 33:9 [d] Nu 25:12 **2:6** [e] Dt 33:10 [f] Jer 23:22; Jas 5:19-20 **2:7** [g] Jer 18:18 [h] Nu 27:21 [i] Lev 10:11 **2:8** [j] Jer 18:15 **2:9** [k] 1Sa 2:30 **2:10** [l] 1Co 8:6 [m] Ex 19:5

11 Judah has been unfaithful. A detestable thing has been committed in Israel
and in Jerusalem: Judah has desecrated
the sanctuary the LORD loves by marrying[n] women who worship a foreign god.[o]
12 As for the man who does this, whoever he
may be, may the LORD remove[p] him from
the tents of Jacob[a]—even though he brings
an offering[q] to the LORD Almighty.
13 Another thing you do: You flood the
LORD's altar with tears. You weep and wail
because he no longer looks with favor[r] on
your offerings or accepts them with pleasure from your hands. 14 You ask, "Why?" It
is because the LORD is the witness between
you and the wife of your youth.[s] You have
been unfaithful to her, though she is your
partner, the wife of your marriage covenant.
15 Has not the one God made you?[t] You
belong to him in body and spirit. And what
does the one God seek? Godly offspring.[b][u]
So be on your guard, and do not be unfaithful to the wife of your youth.
16 "The man who hates and divorces his
wife,[v]" says the LORD, the God of Israel,
"does violence to the one he should protect,"[c] says the LORD Almighty.
So be on your guard, and do not be unfaithful.

Breaking Covenant Through Injustice

17 You have wearied[w] the LORD with your
words.
"How have we wearied him?" you ask.
By saying, "All who do evil are good in
the eyes of the LORD, and he is pleased with
them" or "Where is the God of justice?"

3 "I will send my messenger, who will
prepare the way before me.[x] Then suddenly the Lord you are seeking will come
to his temple; the messenger of the covenant, whom you desire, will come," says
the LORD Almighty.
2 But who can endure[y] the day of his coming? Who can stand when he appears? For
he will be like a refiner's fire[z] or a launderer's soap. 3 He will sit as a refiner and
purifier of silver;[a] he will purify[b] the Levites and refine them like gold and silver.

---

[a] 12 Or *12May the LORD remove from the tents of Jacob anyone who gives testimony in behalf of the man who does this* [b] 15 The meaning of the Hebrew for the first part of this verse is uncertain. [c] 16 Or *"I hate divorce," says the LORD, the God of Israel, "because the man who divorces his wife covers his garment with violence,"*

---

does believers with rain, fruitful seasons, food, and gladness (Matt. 5:45; Acts 14:17).

2:11 ***the sanctuary the LORD loves.*** The text presents the ideas of affection and revulsion which we usually think of in the verbs *to love* and *to hate*. Marriage is something God loves; divorce is something He hates (v. 16). The Lord's people had polluted something in which God takes great pleasure.

2:13 ***Another thing you do.*** The prophets at times spoke of the compounding sins of the people (Jer. 2:13). Here, tears seem to be judged as hypocritical acts of insincere repentance (Is. 1:10–15).

2:14 ***Why.*** The feigned surprise of the people fooled no one, certainly not the Lord. ***witness.*** There are some whose witness may be challenged, but the Lord is not among them (3:5). ***wife of your youth.*** These men had not only married pagan wives, but they had divorced their first wives to make room for their new ones.

2:15–16 God and Marriage—While couples make the marriage covenant with each other, God is a party in the relationship too. He owns us and makes us one, all at the same time. Going back to Genesis 2:24, He designed man and woman for each other; to be in relationship with each other, out of His wisdom for what was best for them. This design was the culminating action in the creation process. Out of it was to be the future of this race, this species that God created to rule with Him. Marriage is not just an institution for couples, but for society and God. In marriage we fulfill God's plan for the universe. God not only made the couple one, in a way He made Himself one with the couple too. It grieves Him when we cannot or will not follow through with our part of this covenant.

The best way to carry on the faith is through children of functioning covenant marriages. This only confirms what all the statistics are increasingly telling us. When divorce rates started soaring in the mid-twentieth century, many thought kids were resilient and handling the dissolution of their families well. Current studies, years later, indicate children of these divorces have significantly greater problems coping with life when compared with kids from intact families. While there is enormous complexity involved in a marriage relationship, nothing about it is more important in making it work than the commitment to maintain it.

2:15 ***You belong to him in body and in spirit.*** This somewhat difficult phrase most likely indicates the work of God in the life of the married couple. God has joined them and has worked on their behalf to strengthen them.

2:16 ***violence.*** To the Lord, attitudes of indifference to marriage vows and duties are the actions of a traitor.

2:17 ***You have wearied the LORD.*** God is wearied by people who do not submit to Him but who argue their points against His revelation. When justice comes, they will be sorry they asked (3:5).

3:1 ***messenger of the covenant.*** This is a messianic title, referring to the One who will initiate the New Covenant (Jer. 31:33–34; Matt. 26:28; Heb. 12:24). ***the messenger ... will come.*** As in Psalm 96:13, this dramatic wording indicates something that was just about to occur. However, it would be 400 years before these words would be fulfilled.

3:2 ***like a refiner's fire or a launderer's soap.*** These two images are vivid illustrations of the purifying process. The Savior King Himself will sift all people to prepare for His reign.

3:3 ***purify the Levites.*** Since the priests had come

2:11 [n] Ne 13:23 [o] Ezr 9:1; Jer 3:7-9 **2:12** [p] Eze 24:21 [q] Mal 1:10 **2:13** [r] Jer 14:12 **2:14** [s] Pr 5:18 **2:15** [t] Ge 2:24; Mt 19:4-6 [u] 1Co 7:14 **2:16** [v] Dt 24:1; Mt 5:31-32; 19:4-9 **2:17** [w] Isa 43:24 **3:1** [x] Isa 40:3; Mt 11:10*; Mk 1:2*; Lk 7:27* **3:2** [y] Eze 22:14; Rev 6:17 [z] Zec 13:9; Mt 3:10-12 **3:3** [a] Da 12:10 [b] Isa 1:25

Then the LORD will have men who will bring offerings in righteousness, 4and the offerings[c] of Judah and Jerusalem will be acceptable to the LORD, as in days gone by, as in former years.[d]

5"So I will come to put you on trial. I will be quick to testify against sorcerers, adulterers and perjurers,[e] against those who defraud laborers of their wages,[f] who oppress the widows[g] and the fatherless, and deprive the foreigners among you of justice, but do not fear me," says the LORD Almighty.

Breaking Covenant by Withholding Tithes

6"I the LORD do not change.[h] So you, the descendants of Jacob, are not destroyed. 7Ever since the time of your ancestors you have turned away[i] from my decrees and have not kept them. Return to me, and I will return to you,"[j] says the LORD Almighty.

"But you ask, 'How are we to return?'

8"Will a mere mortal rob God? Yet you rob me.

"But you ask, 'How are we robbing you?'

"In tithes[k] and offerings. 9You are under a curse—your whole nation—because you are robbing me. 10Bring the whole tithe into the storehouse,[l] that there may be food in my house. Test me in this," says the LORD Almighty, "and see if I will not throw open the floodgates[m] of heaven and pour out so much blessing that there will not be room enough to store it. 11I will prevent pests from devouring your crops, and the vines in your fields will not drop their fruit before it is ripe," says the LORD Almighty. 12"Then all the nations will call you blessed,[n] for yours will be a delightful land,"[o] says the LORD Almighty.

Israel Speaks Arrogantly Against God

13"You have spoken arrogantly[p] against me," says the LORD.

"Yet you ask, 'What have we said against you?'

14"You have said, 'It is futile[q] to serve God. What do we gain by carrying out his requirements and going about like mourners[r] before the LORD Almighty? 15But now we call the arrogant blessed. Certainly evildoers[s] prosper, and even when they put God to the test, they get away with it.'"

The Faithful Remnant

16Then those who feared the LORD talked with each other, and the LORD listened and heard.[t] A scroll[u] of remembrance was written in his presence concerning those who feared the LORD and honored his name.

17"On the day when I act," says the LORD Almighty, "they will be my treasured possession.[v] I will spare[w] them, just as a father has compassion and spares his son who serves him. 18And you will again see the distinction between the righteous[x] and the wicked, between those who serve God and those who do not.

Judgment and Covenant Renewal

4 [a] "Surely the day is coming;[y] it will burn like a furnace. All the arrogant and every evildoer will be stubble,[z] and the day that is coming will set them on fire," says the LORD Almighty. "Not a root or a branch will be left to them. 2But for you who revere my name, the sun of righteousness[a] will rise with healing[b] in its rays. And you will go out and frolic[c] like well-fed calves. 3Then you will trample[d] on the wicked; they will be ashes[e] under the soles of your

[a] In Hebrew texts 4:1-6 is numbered 3:19-24.

under such strong censure in this book (1:6–2:9), and since the prophet himself was likely a priest, these words would have had a special significance for him.

3:6 ***I the LORD do not change.*** We might expect these opening words to ensure the nation's doom. Instead, they give assurance of God's continuing mercy.

3:8 ***tithes.*** These were gifts to the Lord that the law required. There were three: two that were annual and one that came every three years. The tithe supported the priests and Levites, and also widows, orphans, and foreigners (Deut. 14:28–29).

3:12 ***all the nations.*** One of the ways in which other countries would be drawn to the worship of the Lord was by seeing how the people of Israel fared with the Lord as their God. ***a delightful land.*** The adjective indicates enjoyment, life that is genuinely pleasurable (1:10).

3:14 ***What do we gain.*** The people secretly entertained doubts about the value of following the Lord. In fact, they had not really carried out his requirements. The proper attitude is encouraged in Malachi 4:4.

3:16 ***A scroll of remembrance.*** God never forgets His promises. God teaches us to remember and value the good that people do (Phil. 4:8); He does the same as He commands us.

3:17 ***they will be my treasured possession.*** These words are exciting because we can sense in them the pride God has in His children.

3:18 ***those who serve God.*** Serving God means putting Him first, obeying His commands, and finding one's chief joy in life the advancement of the glory of His name.

4:2 ***with healing in its rays.*** The prophet compares the Savior to a bird whose comforting wings bring healing to the chicks that gather underneath (Ps. 91:1–4).

3:4 [c] 2Ch 7:12; Ps 51:19; Mal 1:11 [d] 2Ch 7:3 **3:5** [e] Jer 7:9 [f] Lev 19:13; Jas 5:4 [g] Ex 22:22 **3:6** [h] Nu 23:19; Jas 1:17 **3:7** [i] Jer 7:26; Ac 7:51 [j] Zec 1:3 **3:8** [k] Ne 13:10-12 **3:10** [l] Ne 13:12 [m] 2Ki 7:2 **3:12** [n] Isa 61:9 [o] Isa 62:4 **3:13** [p] Mal 2:17 **3:14** [q] Ps 73:13 [r] Isa 58:3 **3:15** [s] Jer 7:10 **3:16** [t] Ps 34:15 [u] Ps 56:8 **3:17** [v] Dt 7:6 [w] Ps 103:13; Isa 26:20 **3:18** [x] Ge 18:25 **4:1** [y] Joel 2:31 [z] Isa 5:24; Ob 1:18 **4:2** [a] Lk 1:78; Eph 5:14 [b] Isa 30:26 [c] Isa 35:6 **4:3** [d] Job 40:12 [e] Eze 28:18

feet on the day when I act," says the LORD
Almighty.
4 "Remember the law[f] of my servant Moses, the decrees and laws I gave him at Horeb for all Israel.
5 "See, I will send the prophet Elijah[g] to
you before that great and dreadful day of
the LORD comes.[h] 6 He will turn the hearts
of the parents to their children,[i] and the
hearts of the children to their parents; or
else I will come and strike[j] the land with
total destruction."[k]

4:5 *the prophet Elijah.* There are three ways in which this prophecy might be fulfilled: (1) John the Baptist, whom Malachi had already prophesied (3:1), was the first to fill the promise of the Elijah figure. John, like Elijah, was a minister of the Lord calling the people to repent and prepare for the coming of the Messiah (Matt. 11:14). (2) Elijah appeared in person along with Moses at the transfiguration (Matt. 17:1 – 8). (3) An Elijah-like figure will appear at the end times; he will call fire down from heaven just as Elijah did (1 Kin. 18:36; Rev. 11:1 – 7).

4:6 *parents to their children . . . children to their parents.* Malachi ends with a promise and a warning. As in every act of God announcing judgment, there is also an offer of His mercy (Jon. 4:2). ***total destruction.*** The term is one of the harshest in Scripture. The Hebrew word suggests complete annihilation. This is the term translated "accursed" in the account of the destruction of Jericho (Josh. 6).

4:4 [f] Ps 147:19 **4:5** [g] Mt 11:14; Lk 1:17 [h] Joel 2:31
4:6 [i] Lk 1:17 [j] Isa 11:4; Rev 19:15 [k] Zec 5:3

THE NEW TESTAMENT

The Words of Christ in Red

MATTHEW

▶ **AUTHOR:** The early church uniformly attributed this Gospel to Matthew, and no tradition to the contrary ever emerged. This book was known early and accepted quickly. Matthew occupied the unpopular post of tax collector in Capernaum for the Roman government, and as a result he was no doubt disliked by his Jewish countrymen. He was chosen as one of the twelve apostles, and the last appearance of his name in the Bible is in Acts 1:13. Matthew's life from that point on is veiled in tradition.

▶ **TIME:** c. 4 B.C. – A.D. 33 ▶ **KEY VERSES:** Matt. 16:16 – 19

▶ **THEME:** Matthew is typically described as the story of Jesus written by a Jew for Jewish people. In this context it contains the most references to Jewish culture and the Old Testament of the Gospels. The author's main purpose seems to be proving to his Jewish readers that Jesus is their Messiah. Matthew is also the fullest systematic account of Christ's teachings. These 5 "blocks" of teaching are one of the key differences with the other Gospels: Chapters 5 – 7, The Sermon on the Mount; chapter 10, The Mission Charge; chapter 13, The Parables of the Kingdom; chapter 18, The Church; chapters 23 – 25, Judgment and the End of the Age.

The Genealogy of Jesus the Messiah

1 This is the genealogy[a] of Jesus the Messiah[b] the son of David,[a] the son of Abraham:[b]

2 Abraham was the father of Isaac,[c]
Isaac the father of Jacob,[d]
Jacob the father of Judah and his brothers,[e]
3 Judah the father of Perez and Zerah, whose mother was Tamar,[f]
Perez the father of Hezron,
Hezron the father of Ram,
4 Ram the father of Amminadab,
Amminadab the father of Nahshon,
Nahshon the father of Salmon,
5 Salmon the father of Boaz, whose mother was Rahab,
Boaz the father of Obed, whose mother was Ruth,
Obed the father of Jesse,
6 and Jesse the father of King David.[g]

David was the father of Solomon, whose mother had been Uriah's wife,[h]
7 Solomon the father of Rehoboam,
Rehoboam the father of Abijah,
Abijah the father of Asa,
8 Asa the father of Jehoshaphat,
Jehoshaphat the father of Jehoram,
Jehoram the father of Uzziah,
9 Uzziah the father of Jotham,
Jotham the father of Ahaz,
Ahaz the father of Hezekiah,
10 Hezekiah the father of Manasseh,[i]
Manasseh the father of Amon,
Amon the father of Josiah,
11 and Josiah the father of Jeconiah[c] and his brothers at the time of the exile to Babylon.[j]

[a] *1* Or *is an account of the origin* [b] *1* Or *Jesus Christ. Messiah* (Hebrew) and *Christ* (Greek) both mean *Anointed One*; also in verse 18. [c] *11* That is, Jehoiachin; also in verse 12

1:1 ***genealogy.*** Jesus' genealogy is crucial to His claim to be the Messiah, as it traces the lineage of Joseph, His recognized father, back to Abraham through David. It shows that from a legal standpoint, Jesus is qualified to rule from the throne of David.
1:3 ***Tamar.*** The mention of women in a Jewish genealogy is unusual. But in addition to Mary, four women are listed in this catalogue of names: Tamar, who was involved in a scandal with Judah (Gen. 38); Rahab, the Canaanite harlot of Jericho (Josh. 2:1 – 21); Ruth, who was not an Israelite, but a Moabite (Ruth 1:4); and Bathsheba, the wife of Uriah, who committed adultery with David (2 Sam. 11:1:1 – 5). At the beginning of his Gospel, Matthew shows how God's grace forgives the darkest of sins and reaches beyond the nation of Israel to the world. He also points out that God can lift the lowest and place them in royal lineage.

1:1 [a] 2Sa 7:12-16; Isa 9:6, 7; 11:1; Jer 23:5, 6; Mt 9:27; Lk 1:32, 69; Ro 1:3; Rev 22:16 [b] Ge 22:18; Gal 3:16
1:2 [c] Ge 21:3, 12 [d] Ge 25:26 [e] Ge 29:35 **1:3** [f] Ge 38:27-30
1:6 [g] 1Sa 16:1; 17:12 [h] 2Sa 12:24 **1:10** [i] 2Ki 20:21
1:11 [j] 2Ki 24:14-16; Jer 27:20; Da 1:1, 2

12After the exile to Babylon:
Jeconiah was the father of Shealtiel,[k]
Shealtiel the father of Zerubbabel,[l]
13Zerubbabel the father of Abihud,
Abihud the father of Eliakim,
Eliakim the father of Azor,
14Azor the father of Zadok,
Zadok the father of Akim,
Akim the father of Elihud,
15Elihud the father of Eleazar,
Eleazar the father of Matthan,
Matthan the father of Jacob,
16and Jacob the father of Joseph, the
husband of Mary,[m] and Mary was
the mother of Jesus who is called
the Messiah.[n]

17Thus there were fourteen generations
in all from Abraham to David, fourteen
from David to the exile to Babylon, and
fourteen from the exile to the Messiah.

Joseph Accepts Jesus as His Son

18This is how the birth of Jesus the Messiah came about[a]: His mother Mary was
pledged to be married to Joseph, but before they came together, she was found to
be pregnant through the Holy Spirit.[o] 19Be-
cause Joseph her husband was faithful to
the law, and yet[b] did not want to expose
her to public disgrace, he had in mind to
divorce[p] her quietly.
20But after he had considered this, an angel of the Lord appeared to him in a dream
and said, "Joseph son of David, do not be
afraid to take Mary home as your wife, because what is conceived in her is from the
Holy Spirit. 21She will give birth to a son,
and you are to give him the name Jesus,[c][q]
because he will save his people from their
sins."[r]
22All this took place to fulfill what the
Lord had said through the prophet: 23"The
virgin will conceive and give birth to a son,
and they will call him Immanuel"[d][s] (which
means "God with us").
24When Joseph woke up, he did what the
angel of the Lord had commanded him and
took Mary home as his wife. 25But he did
not consummate their marriage until she
gave birth to a son. And he gave him the
name Jesus.[t]

The Magi Visit the Messiah

2 After Jesus was born in Bethlehem in
Judea,[u] during the time of King Herod,[v] Magi[e] from the east came to Jerusalem 2and asked, "Where is the one who has
been born king of the Jews?[w] We saw his
star[x] when it rose and have come to worship him."
3When King Herod heard this he was disturbed, and all Jerusalem with him. 4When
he had called together all the people's chief
priests and teachers of the law, he asked
them where the Messiah was to be born.
5"In Bethlehem[y] in Judea," they replied, "for
this is what the prophet has written:

6" 'But you, Bethlehem, in the land of
Judah,
are by no means least among the
rulers of Judah;
for out of you will come a ruler
who will shepherd my people
Israel.'[f]"[z]

7Then Herod called the Magi secretly
and found out from them the exact time the

---

[a] *18* Or *The origin of Jesus the Messiah was like this* [b] *19* Or *was a righteous man and*
[c] *21 Jesus* is the Greek form of *Joshua,* which means *the LORD saves.* [d] *23* Isaiah 7:14
[e] *1* Traditionally *wise men* [f] *6* Micah 5:2,4

1:16 *the husband of Mary.* Matthew was careful not to identify Jesus as the physical son of Joseph. ***called the Messiah.*** The words "Messiah" (from the Hebrew) and "Christ" (from the Greek) both mean "Anointed One."

1:17 *Abraham . . . to the Messiah.* The genealogy is broken down into three groups of names with 14 generations in each list. A basic covenant is set forth in each period: the Abrahamic covenant, the Davidic covenant, and the New Covenant.

1:18 *pledged to be married.* In Jewish culture, this covenant was made about a year before the marriage. Engagement was understood to be as binding as a marriage covenant, therefore a legal divorce was required to withdraw from the agreement.

1:23 *Immanuel.* The angel's message to Joseph indicated that Mary would fulfill the prophecy of Isaiah (Is. 7:14). "Jesus," the Greek form of "Joshua," means "salvation."

1:25 *did not consummate.* The clear implication is that Mary was a virgin only until the birth of Jesus. The brothers and sisters of Jesus (13:55–56) were probably younger siblings born to Joseph and Mary after Jesus' birth. Joseph could not have had children by a previous marriage, as some suppose, for then Jesus would not have been heir to the Davidic throne as the oldest son of Joseph.

2:1 *Magi from the east.* These "Magi," or wise men, would have been of the same class as the wise men of Babylon over whom Daniel was made ruler (Dan. 2:48). ***to Jerusalem.*** Contrary to popular belief, the events of chapter two probably took place some months after Jesus' birth. Herod murdered all the male children 2 years and under, going by the time the wise men said the star had appeared (and probably leaving a significant margin for error). In addition, it would have been strange for Mary and Joseph to offer the sacrifice of the poor (see Lev. 12:8; Luke 2:24) if the wise men had just given them rich gifts.

2:7 *Then Herod.* This is Herod the Great, who reigned over Palestine for over thirty years. A crafty ruler and lavish builder, Herod had a reign marked by cruelty and bloodshed.

1:12 [k] 1Ch 3:17 [l] 1Ch 3:19; Ezr 3:2 **1:16** [m] Lk 1:27 [n] Mt 27:17 **1:18** [o] Lk 1:35 **1:19** [p] Dt 24:1 **1:21** [q] Lk 1:31 [r] Lk 2:11; Ac 5:31; 13:23,28 **1:23** [s] Isa 7:14; 8:8,10 **1:25** [t] ver 21 **2:1** [u] Lk 2:4-7 [v] Lk 1:5 **2:2** [w] Jer 23:5; Mt 27:11; Mk 15:2; Jn 1:49; 18:33-37 [x] Nu 24:17 **2:5** [y] Jn 7:42 **2:6** [z] 2Sa 5:2; Mic 5:2

star had appeared. 8He sent them to Bethlehem and said, "Go and search carefully for
the child. As soon as you find him, report to
me, so that I too may go and worship him."
9After they had heard the king, they
went on their way, and the star they had
seen when it rose went ahead of them until
it stopped over the place where the child
was. 10When they saw the star, they were
overjoyed. 11On coming to the house, they
saw the child with his mother Mary, and
they bowed down and worshiped him.[a]
Then they opened their treasures and
presented him with gifts[b] of gold, frankincense and myrrh. 12And having been
warned[c] in a dream[d] not to go back to Herod, they returned to their country by another route.

The Escape to Egypt

13When they had gone, an angel[e] of the
Lord appeared to Joseph in a dream.[f] "Get
up," he said, "take the child and his mother and escape to Egypt. Stay there until I
tell you, for Herod is going to search for the
child to kill him."
14So he got up, took the child and his
mother during the night and left for Egypt,
15where he stayed until the death of Herod. And so was fulfilled what the Lord had
said through the prophet: "Out of Egypt I
called my son."[ag]
16When Herod realized that he had been
outwitted by the Magi, he was furious, and
he gave orders to kill all the boys in Bethlehem and its vicinity who were two years
old and under, in accordance with the time
he had learned from the Magi. 17Then what
was said through the prophet Jeremiah
was fulfilled:

18 "A voice is heard in Ramah,
weeping and great mourning,
Rachel weeping for her children
and refusing to be comforted,
because they are no more."[bh]

The Return to Nazareth

19After Herod died, an angel of the Lord
appeared in a dream[i] to Joseph in Egypt
20and said, "Get up, take the child and his
mother and go to the land of Israel, for
those who were trying to take the child's
life are dead."
21So he got up, took the child and his
mother and went to the land of Israel. 22But
when he heard that Archelaus was reigning in Judea in place of his father Herod,
he was afraid to go there. Having been
warned in a dream,[j] he withdrew to the district of Galilee,[k] 23and he went and lived in
a town called Nazareth.[l] So was fulfilled[m]
what was said through the prophets, that
he would be called a Nazarene.[n]

John the Baptist Prepares the Way

3 In those days John the Baptist[o] came,
preaching in the wilderness of Judea
2and saying, "Repent, for the kingdom of
heaven[p] has come near." 3This is he who
was spoken of through the prophet Isaiah:

"A voice of one calling in the
wilderness,
'Prepare the way for the Lord,
make straight paths for him.'"[cq]

4John's clothes were made of camel's
hair, and he had a leather belt around his
waist.[r] His food was locusts[s] and wild honey. 5People went out to him from Jerusalem
and all Judea and the whole region of the
Jordan. 6Confessing their sins, they were
baptized by him in the Jordan River.
7But when he saw many of the Pharisees
and Sadducees coming to where he was
baptizing, he said to them: "You brood of
vipers![t] Who warned you to flee from the
coming wrath?[u] 8Produce fruit in keeping
with repentance.[v] 9And do not think you
can say to yourselves, 'We have Abraham

[a] *15* Hosea 11:1 [b] *18* Jer. 31:15 [c] *3* Isaiah 40:3

2:15 ***was fulfilled.*** The prophecy quoted here, from Hosea 11:1, refers to the nation of Israel as God's son coming out of Egypt in the Exodus. Jesus is the genuine Son of God, and, as Israel's Messiah, is the true Israel (John 15:1); therefore He gives fuller meaning to the prophecy of Hosea.

2:18 ***Rachel weeping for her children.*** This prophecy comes from Jeremiah 31:15, in which Rachel, entombed near Bethlehem some 13 centuries before the Babylonian captivity, is seen weeping for her children as they are led away in 586 B.C. In the slaughter of the male infants at the time of Christ's birth, Rachel is again seen weeping for the violent loss of her sons.

2:23 ***Nazareth.*** Those who lived in Nazareth were looked down upon (John 1:46). Perhaps God chose this place for His Son to emphasize His humanness.

3:2 ***Repent.*** The Greek verb translated "repent" indicates a change of attitude. The basic idea is a recognition of sin and a reversal of thinking which changes one's life.

3:3 ***Prepare the way for the Lord.*** As roads were smoothed and straightened for the arrival of a king, so John was preparing a spiritual path for the Messiah. The quotation is from Isaiah 40:3.

3:7 ***Pharisees and Sadducees.*** The Pharisees and Sadducees were two prominent groups in Judaism at the time of Christ. The groups differed considerably in their beliefs. The Pharisees not only based their beliefs on the law of Moses, but also on a large body of oral tradition. They were devout and zealous, concerned with outward righteousness. The Sadducees

2:11 [a] Isa 60:3 [b] Ps 72:10 **2:12** [c] Heb 11:7 [d] ver 13, 19, 22; Mt 27:19 **2:13** [e] Ac 5:19 [f] ver 12, 19, 22 **2:15** [g] Ex 4:22, 23; Hos 11:1 **2:18** [h] Jer 31:15 **2:19** [i] ver 12, 13, 22 **2:22** [j] ver 12, 13, 19; Mt 27:19 [k] Lk 2:39 **2:23** [l] Lk 1:26; Jn 1:45, 46 [m] Mt 1:22 [n] Mk 1:24 **3:1** [o] Lk 1:13, 57-66; 3:2-19 **3:2** [p] Da 2:44; Mt 4:17; 6:10; Lk 11:20; 21:31; Jn 3:3, 5; Ac 1:3, 6 **3:3** [q] Isa 40:3; Mal 3:1; Lk 1:76; Jn 1:23 **3:4** [r] 2Ki 1:8 [s] Lev 11:22 **3:7** [t] Mt 12:34; 23:33 [u] Ro 1:18; 1Th 1:10 **3:8** [v] Ac 26:20

as our father.' I tell you that out of these
stones God can raise up children for Abraham. 10The ax is already at the root of the
trees, and every tree that does not produce
good fruit will be cut down and thrown
into the fire.[w]
11"I baptize you with[a] water for repentance. But after me comes one who is more
powerful than I, whose sandals I am not
worthy to carry. He will baptize you with[a]
the Holy Spirit[x] and fire.[y] 12His winnowing
fork is in his hand, and he will clear his
threshing floor, gathering his wheat into
the barn and burning up the chaff with unquenchable fire."[z]

The Baptism of Jesus

13Then Jesus came from Galilee to the
Jordan to be baptized by John.[a] 14But John
tried to deter him, saying, "I need to be baptized by you, and do you come to me?"
15Jesus replied, "Let it be so now; it is
proper for us to do this to fulfill all righteousness." Then John consented.
16As soon as Jesus was baptized, he went
up out of the water. At that moment heav-
en was opened, and he saw the Spirit of
God[b] descending like a dove and alighting
on him. 17And a voice from heaven[c] said,
"This is my Son,[d] whom I love; with him I
am well pleased."[e]

Jesus Is Tested in the Wilderness

4 Then Jesus was led by the Spirit into the
wilderness to be tempted[b] by the devil.
2After fasting forty days and forty nights,[f]
he was hungry. 3The tempter[g] came to him
and said, "If you are the Son of God,[h] tell
these stones to become bread."
4Jesus answered, "It is written: 'Man
shall not live on bread alone, but on every
word that comes from the mouth of God.'[c]"[i]
5Then the devil took him to the holy city[j]
and had him stand on the highest point
of the temple. 6"If you are the Son of God,"
he said, "throw yourself down. For it is written:

"'He will command his angels
concerning you,
and they will lift you up in their
hands,
so that you will not strike your foot
against a stone.'[d]"[k]

7Jesus answered him, "It is also written:
'Do not put the Lord your God to the test.'[e]"[l]
8Again, the devil took him to a very high
mountain and showed him all the kingdoms of the world and their splendor. 9"All
this I will give you," he said, "if you will
bow down and worship me."
10Jesus said to him, "Away from me, Satan![m] For it is written: 'Worship the Lord
your God, and serve him only.'[f]"[n]
11Then the devil left him, and angels
came and attended him.[o]

---

[a] *11* Or *in* [b] *1* The Greek for *tempted* can also mean *tested.* [c] *4* Deut. 8:3 [d] *6* Psalm 91:11,12 [e] *7* Deut. 6:16 [f] *10* Deut. 6:13

---

were associated with a priestly caste, and in doctrine they held primarily to the first five books of Moses. They did not believe in the resurrection of the dead, and did not adhere to all the detailed laws of the Pharisees. Formerly enemies, the two groups seemed to unite against a common enemy: the long awaited Messiah.

3:11 *baptize.* Sometimes fire has connotations of judgment in Scripture, but here the fire of God's Spirit represents the transforming power of His grace and love. The baptism of all Jesus' disciples with water is an outward sign of the inward work of the Holy Spirit. It is the symbol of obedience to the command to believe in Christ's saving work of grace on the cross.

3:15 *to fulfill all righteousness.* This phrase does not suggest that Jesus came for baptism because He had sinned; the Lord Jesus was without sin (2 Cor. 5:21; Heb. 4:15). His baptism probably served several purposes. By being baptized, He confirmed the ministry of John and fulfilled the Father's will.

3:17 God, the Father of Christ—Most Christians eventually wonder how God may be called the Father of Christ, and Christ the Son of God. First, one must recognize that God is spirit (John 4:24), and Christ was the Son of God before He assumed a human body in Bethlehem (John 3:16; Gal. 4:4). Passages which use terms implying physical origin must be taken in a figurative sense (Heb. 1:5). Second, the title expresses a sonship relationship, unique from that of His disciples (John 20:17). He was begotten of God unlike anyone else (John 1:14; 3:16). The Nicean council in the fourth century used the phrase "very God of very God; begotten, not made, being of one substance with the Father" to describe this unique relationship. Third, the title describes equality with God. When Jesus claimed to be "one" with the Father, He was speaking of a unity of "substance" with the Father and thus equality in all the attributes of deity (John 10:30). The Jews understood this claim, because they took up stones to stone Him, protesting that "you ... claim to be God" (John 10:33). Fourth, the title emphasizes Christ's role as the revealer of God. He alone possesses the knowledge of the Father (John 14:6–9; 1 John 1:2), and He is the sole mediator of that knowledge (1 Tim. 2:5). Therefore, no one can know the Father except through the Son (John 14:6).

4:1–4 *It is written.* Satan did not lead Jesus into the place of temptation, the Holy Spirit did. Perhaps part of the reason for this was to show us how to deal with temptation. Jesus quoted the Word of God, showing the power of Scripture in battling with the evil one.

4:10 *Satan.* Satan is not dispatched easily by anyone who merely says, "Away from me." The only way we can be victorious in temptation is through the blood and authority of Jesus Christ.

3:10 [w] Mt 7:19; Lk 13:6-9; Jn 15:2,6 **3:11** [x] Mk 1:8 [y] Isa 4:4; Ac 2:3,4 **3:12** [z] Mt 13:30 **3:13** [a] Mk 1:4 **3:16** [b] Isa 11:2; 42:1 **3:17** [c] Mt 17:5; Jn 12:28 [d] Ps 2:7; 2Pe 1:17,18 [e] Isa 42:1; Mt 12:18; 17:5; Mk 1:11; 9:7; Lk 9:35 **4:2** [f] Ex 34:28; 1Ki 19:8 **4:3** [g] 1Th 3:5 [h] Mt 3:17; Jn 5:25; Ac 9:20 **4:4** [i] Dt 8:3 **4:5** [j] Ne 11:1; Da 9:24; Mt 27:53 **4:6** [k] Ps 91:11,12 **4:7** [l] Dt 6:16 **4:10** [m] 1Ch 21:1 [n] Dt 6:13 **4:11** [o] Mt 26:53; Lk 22:43; Heb 1:14

Jesus Begins to Preach

12When Jesus heard that John had been
put in prison,[p] he withdrew to Galilee.[q]
13Leaving Nazareth, he went and lived in
Capernaum,[r] which was by the lake in the
area of Zebulun and Naphtali— 14to fulfill
what was said through the prophet Isaiah:

15"Land of Zebulun and land of Naphtali,
the Way of the Sea, beyond the
Jordan,
Galilee of the Gentiles—
16the people living in darkness
have seen a great light;
on those living in the land of the
shadow of death
a light has dawned."[a][s]

17From that time on Jesus began to
preach, "Repent, for the kingdom of heav-
en[t] has come near."

Jesus Calls His First Disciples

18As Jesus was walking beside the Sea
of Galilee,[u] he saw two brothers, Simon
called Peter[v] and his brother Andrew. They
were casting a net into the lake, for they
were fishermen. 19"Come, follow me,"[w]
Jesus said, "and I will send you out to fish
for people." 20At once they left their nets
and followed him.
21Going on from there, he saw two other brothers, James son of Zebedee and his
brother John.[x] They were in a boat with
their father Zebedee, preparing their nets.
Jesus called them, 22and immediately they
left the boat and their father and followed
him.

Jesus Heals the Sick

23Jesus went throughout Galilee,[y] teaching in their synagogues,[z] proclaiming the
good news[a] of the kingdom,[b] and healing
every disease and sickness among the people.[c] 24News about him spread all over Syria,[d] and people brought to him all who were
ill with various diseases, those suffering
severe pain, the demon-possessed,[e] those
having seizures,[f] and the paralyzed;[g] and
he healed them. 25Large crowds from Galilee, the Decapolis,[b] Jerusalem, Judea and
the region across the Jordan followed him.[h]

Introduction to the Sermon on the Mount

5 Now when Jesus saw the crowds, he
went up on a mountainside and sat
down. His disciples came to him, 2and he
began to teach them.

The Beatitudes

He said:

3"Blessed are the poor in spirit,
for theirs is the kingdom of heaven.[i]
4Blessed are those who mourn,
for they will be comforted.[j]
5Blessed are the meek,
for they will inherit the earth.[k]
6Blessed are those who hunger and
thirst for righteousness,
for they will be filled.[l]
7Blessed are the merciful,
for they will be shown mercy.
8Blessed are the pure in heart,[m]
for they will see God.[n]
9Blessed are the peacemakers,
for they will be called children of
God.[o]
10Blessed are those who are persecuted
because of righteousness,[p]
for theirs is the kingdom of heaven.

11"Blessed are you when people insult
you,[q] persecute you and falsely say all
kinds of evil against you because of me.
12Rejoice and be glad,[r] because great is
your reward in heaven, for in the same way
they persecuted the prophets who were before you.[s]

Salt and Light

13"You are the salt of the earth. But if the
salt loses its saltiness, how can it be made

---

[a] *16* Isaiah 9:1,2 [b] *25* That is, the Ten Cities

4:15–16 *great light.* The passage quoted here (Is. 9:1–2) foretells the reign of the Messiah in the coming kingdom.
4:18–20 *I will send you out to fish for people.* This allusion to Jeremiah 16:16 was used to call Peter and Andrew to a life of ministry.
4:23 *teaching ... proclaiming ... healing.* These words summarize Jesus' early ministry.
5:2 *he began to teach them.* The Sermon on the Mount wasn't given as the way of salvation for the lost, but as the way of life for the children of the kingdom. It was instruction for those who had responded to Jesus' invitation to repent.
5:3–12 The Beatitudes—In the Sermon on the Mount, Christ succinctly describes the basic character traits of those who will inherit the kingdom. The word *kingdom* usually implies someone who is on top, who rules and has authority over others. They are the privileged. In God's kingdom the people are not privileged because they are on top but because, by being on the bottom, they are in a better position to receive God's grace and favor. These characteristics are the reverse of what man generally values in the world. "Blessed" can also be translated as "Happy."

4:12 [p] Mt 14:3 [q] Mk 1:14 **4:13** [r] Mk 1:21; Lk 4:23,31; Jn 2:12; 4:46,47 **4:16** [s] Isa 9:1,2; Lk 2:32 **4:17** [t] Mt 3:2 **4:18** [u] Mt 15:29; Mk 7:31; Jn 6:1 [v] Mt 16:17,18 **4:19** [w] Mk 10:21,28,52 **4:21** [x] Mt 20:20 **4:23** [y] Mk 1:39; Lk 4:15,44 [z] Mt 9:35; 13:54; Mk 1:21; Lk 4:15; Jn 6:59 [a] Mk 1:14 [b] Mt 3:2; Ac 20:25 [c] Mt 8:16; 15:30; Ac 10:38 **4:24** [d] Lk 2:2 [e] Mt 8:16,28; 9:32; 15:22; Mk 1:32; 5:15,16,18 [f] Mt 17:15 [g] Mt 8:6; 9:2; Mk 2:3 **4:25** [h] Mk 3:7,8; Lk 6:17 **5:3** [i] ver 10,19; Mt 25:34 **5:4** [j] Isa 61:2,3; Rev 7:17 **5:5** [k] Ps 37:11; Ro 4:13 **5:6** [l] Isa 55:1,2 **5:8** [m] Ps 24:3,4 [n] Heb 12:14; Rev 22:4 **5:9** [o] ver 44,45; Ro 8:14 **5:10** [p] 1Pe 3:14 **5:11** [q] 1Pe 4:14 **5:12** [r] Ac 5:41; 1Pe 4:13,16 [s] Mt 23:31,37; Ac 7:52; 1Th 2:15

salty again? It is no longer good for anything, except to be thrown out and trampled underfoot.[t]

14 “You are the light of the world.[u] A town built on a hill cannot be hidden. 15 Neither do people light a lamp and put it under a bowl. Instead they put it on its stand, and it gives light to everyone in the house.[v] 16 In the same way, let your light shine before others, that they may see your good deeds and glorify[w] your Father in heaven.

The Fulfillment of the Law

17 “Do not think that I have come to abolish the Law or the Prophets; I have not come to abolish them but to fulfill them.[x] 18 For truly I tell you, until heaven and earth disappear, not the smallest letter, not the least stroke of a pen, will by any means disappear from the Law until everything is accomplished.[y] 19 Therefore anyone who sets aside one of the least of these commands[z] and teaches others accordingly will be called least in the kingdom of heaven, but whoever practices and teaches these commands will be called great in the kingdom of heaven. 20 For I tell you that unless your righteousness surpasses that of the Pharisees and the teachers of the law, you will certainly not enter the kingdom of heaven.

Murder

21 “You have heard that it was said to the people long ago, ‘You shall not murder,[a][a] and anyone who murders will be subject to judgment.’ 22 But I tell you that anyone who is angry with a brother or sister[b,c] will be subject to judgment.[b] Again, anyone who says to a brother or sister, ‘Raca,’[d] is answerable to the court.[c] And anyone who says, ‘You fool!’ will be in danger of the fire of hell.[d]

23 “Therefore, if you are offering your gift at the altar and there remember that your brother or sister has something against you, 24 leave your gift there in front of the altar. First go and be reconciled to them; then come and offer your gift.

25 “Settle matters quickly with your adversary who is taking you to court. Do it while you are still together on the way, or your adversary may hand you over to the judge, and the judge may hand you over to the officer, and you may be thrown into prison. 26 Truly I tell you, you will not get out until you have paid the last penny.

Adultery

27 “You have heard that it was said, ‘You shall not commit adultery.’[e][e] 28 But I tell you that anyone who looks at a woman lustfully has already committed adultery with her in his heart.[f] 29 If your right eye causes you to stumble,[g] gouge it out and throw it away. It is better for you to lose one part of your body than for your whole body to be thrown into hell. 30 And if your right hand causes you to stumble, cut it off and throw it away. It is better for you to lose one part of your body than for your whole body to go into hell.

Divorce

31 “It has been said, ‘Anyone who divorces his wife must give her a certificate of divorce.’[f][h] 32 But I tell you that anyone who divorces his wife, except for sexual immorality, makes her the victim of adultery, and anyone who marries a divorced woman commits adultery.[i]

Oaths

33 “Again, you have heard that it was said to the people long ago, ‘Do not break your oath,[j] but fulfill to the Lord the vows you have made.’[k] 34 But I tell you, do not swear an oath at all:[l] either by heaven, for it is God’s throne;[m] 35 or by the earth, for it is his footstool; or by Jerusalem, for it is the city of the Great King.[n] 36 And do not swear by your head, for you cannot make even one hair white or black. 37 All you need to say is simply ‘Yes’ or ‘No’;[o] anything beyond this comes from the evil one.[g][p]

---

[a] *21* Exodus 20:13 [b] *22* The Greek word for *brother or sister* (*adelphos*) refers here to a fellow disciple, whether man or woman; also in verse 23. [c] *22* Some manuscripts *brother or sister without cause* [d] *22* An Aramaic term of contempt [e] *27* Exodus 20:14 [f] *31* Deut. 24:1 [g] *37* Or *from evil*

The signs of being blessed aren’t power or material wealth. The sign of being blessed is receiving the benefits of God’s grace.

5:16 *let your light shine.* The believer does not have inherent light, rather, we have reflective light. As Christ followers, we must make sure that we do not allow anything to come between us and our Source of light.

5:27 *adultery.* Control of the heart and body begins with control of the eyes. Deeds of shame result from fantasies of shame. Jesus gives the sobering advice “if your right eye causes you to stumble, gouge it out and throw it away.” It should be clear here that Jesus is not advocating mutilating our bodies, but He is using a strong figure of speech to emphasize removing any temptation for evil, whatever the cost.

5:32 *sexual immorality.* This is a general term that includes premarital sex, extramarital infidelity, homosexuality, and bestiality.

5:13 [t] Mk 9:50; Lk 14:34, 35 **5:14** [u] Jn 8:12 **5:15** [v] Mk 4:21; Lk 8:16 **5:16** [w] Mt 9:8 **5:17** [x] Ro 3:31 **5:18** [y] Lk 16:17 **5:19** [z] Jas 2:10 **5:21** [a] Ex 20:13; Dt 5:17 **5:22** [b] 1Jn 3:15 [c] Mt 26:59 [d] Jas 3:6 **5:27** [e] Ex 20:14; Dt 5:18 **5:28** [f] Pr 6:25 **5:29** [g] Mt 18:6, 8, 9; Mk 9:42-47 **5:31** [h] Dt 24:1-4 **5:32** [i] Lk 16:18 **5:33** [j] Lev 19:12 [k] Nu 30:2; Dt 23:21; Mt 23:16-22 **5:34** [l] Jas 5:12 [m] Isa 66:1; Mt 23:22 **5:35** [n] Ps 48:2 **5:37** [o] Jas 5:12 [p] Mt 6:13; 13:19, 38; Jn 17:15; 2Th 3:3; 1Jn 2:13, 14; 3:12; 5:18, 19

Eye for Eye

38"You have heard that it was said, 'Eye
for eye, and tooth for tooth.'[a][q] 39But I tell
you, do not resist an evil person. If anyone slaps you on the right cheek, turn to
them the other cheek also.[r] 40And if anyone
wants to sue you and take your shirt, hand
over your coat as well. 41If anyone forces
you to go one mile, go with them two miles.
42Give to the one who asks you, and do not
turn away from the one who wants to borrow from you.[s]

Love for Enemies

43"You have heard that it was said, 'Love
your neighbor[b][t] and hate your enemy.'[u]
44But I tell you, love your enemies and pray
for those who persecute you,[v] 45that you
may be children[w] of your Father in heaven.
He causes his sun to rise on the evil and the
good, and sends rain on the righteous and
the unrighteous.[x] 46If you love those who
love you, what reward will you get?[y] Are not
even the tax collectors doing that? 47And if
you greet only your own people, what are
you doing more than others? Do not even
pagans do that? 48Be perfect, therefore, as
your heavenly Father is perfect.[z]

Giving to the Needy

6 "Be careful not to practice your righteousness in front of others to be seen
by them.[a] If you do, you will have no reward from your Father in heaven.

2"So when you give to the needy, do not
announce it with trumpets, as the hypocrites do in the synagogues and on the
streets, to be honored by others. Truly I
tell you, they have received their reward in
full. 3But when you give to the needy, do
not let your left hand know what your right
hand is doing, 4so that your giving may be
in secret. Then your Father, who sees what
is done in secret, will reward you.[b]

Prayer

5"And when you pray, do not be like the
hypocrites, for they love to pray standing[c]
in the synagogues and on the street corners to be seen by others. Truly I tell you,
they have received their reward in full.
6But when you pray, go into your room,
close the door and pray to your Father,[d]
who is unseen. Then your Father, who
sees what is done in secret, will reward
you. 7And when you pray, do not keep
on babbling[e] like pagans, for they think
they will be heard because of their many
words.[f] 8Do not be like them, for your Father knows what you need[g] before you ask
him.

9"This, then, is how you should pray:

"'Our Father in heaven,
hallowed be your name,
10 your kingdom[h] come,
your will be done,[i]
on earth as it is in heaven.
11 Give us today our daily bread.[j]
12 And forgive us our debts,
as we also have forgiven our
debtors.[k]
13 And lead us not into temptation,[c][l]
but deliver us from the evil one.[d]'[m]

14For if you forgive other people when they
sin against you, your heavenly Father will
also forgive you.[n] 15But if you do not forgive others their sins, your Father will not
forgive your sins.[o]

Fasting

16"When you fast, do not look somber[p] as
the hypocrites do, for they disfigure their
faces to show others they are fasting. Truly
I tell you, they have received their reward
in full. 17But when you fast, put oil on your
head and wash your face, 18so that it will
not be obvious to others that you are fasting, but only to your Father, who is unseen;
and your Father, who sees what is done in
secret, will reward you.[q]

---

[a] *38* Exodus 21:24; Lev. 24:20; Deut. 19:21
[b] *43* Lev. 19:18 [c] *13* The Greek for *temptation* can also mean *testing.* [d] *13* Or *from evil;* some late manuscripts *one, / for yours is the kingdom and the power and the glory forever. Amen.*

5:38 ***Eye for eye.*** This important Old Testament law (Ex. 21:24–25; Lev. 24:20; Deut. 19:21), known as the *lex talionis* (law of retaliation), covered what type of punishment should be meted out to transgressors. It limited the retribution the offender would have to bear, preventing the "head for eye, jaw for tooth" vengeance typical of humans.

5:41 ***forces.*** The Roman government could press anyone to carry a load as far as one mile.

5:45 ***children of your Father.*** In other words, "that you be like your heavenly Father who displays His love without discrimination."

5:48 ***Be perfect.*** God does not lower the standard to accommodate our sinfulness. Instead, he forgives us in our sin, makes us holy before him, and empowers us to live lives of repentance which lead to righteousness.

6:2 ***they have received their reward.*** The only reward the hypocrites will ever receive is to be honored by man.

6:9 ***This, then, is how you should pray.*** This does not mean to pray only these words, but to pray in this way, remembering the general topics of worship, request for both physical and spiritual needs, confession, and repentance of sins.

5:38 [q] Ex 21:24; Lev 24:20; Dt 19:21 **5:39** [r] Lk 6:29; Ro 12:17, 19; 1Co 6:7; 1Pe 3:9 **5:42** [s] Dt 15:8; Lk 6:30 **5:43** [t] Lev 19:18 [u] Dt 23:6 **5:44** [v] Lk 6:27, 28; 23:34; Ac 7:60; Ro 12:14; 1Co 4:12; 1Pe 2:23 **5:45** [w] ver 9 [x] Job 25:3 **5:46** [y] Lk 6:32 **5:48** [z] Lev 19:2; 1Pe 1:16 **6:1** [a] Mt 23:5 **6:4** [b] ver 6, 18; Col 3:23, 24 **6:5** [c] Mk 11:25; Lk 18:10-14 **6:6** [d] 2Ki 4:33 **6:7** [e] Ecc 5:2 [f] 1Ki 18:26-29 **6:8** [g] ver 32 **6:10** [h] Mt 3:2 [i] Mt 26:39 **6:11** [j] Pr 30:8 **6:12** [k] Mt 18:21-35 **6:13** [l] Jas 1:13 [m] Mt 5:37 **6:14** [n] Mt 18:21-35; Mk 11:25, 26; Eph 4:32; Col 3:13 **6:15** [o] Mt 18:35 **6:16** [p] Isa 58:5 **6:18** [q] ver 4, 6

Treasures in Heaven

19“Do not store up for yourselves treasures on earth,[r] where moths and vermin
destroy,[s] and where thieves break in and
steal. 20But store up for yourselves treasures in heaven,[t] where moths and vermin
do not destroy, and where thieves do not
break in and steal.[u] 21For where your treasure is, there your heart will be also.[v]
22“The eye is the lamp of the body. If
your eyes are healthy,[a] your whole body
will be full of light. 23But if your eyes are
unhealthy,[b] your whole body will be full
of darkness. If then the light within you is
darkness, how great is that darkness!
24“No one can serve two masters. Either
you will hate the one and love the other, or
you will be devoted to the one and despise
the other. You cannot serve both God and
money.[w]

Do Not Worry

25“Therefore I tell you, do not worry[x]
about your life, what you will eat or drink;
or about your body, what you will wear. Is
not life more than food, and the body more
than clothes? 26Look at the birds of the air;
they do not sow or reap or store away in
barns, and yet your heavenly Father feeds
them.[y] Are you not much more valuable
than they?[z] 27Can any one of you by worrying add a single hour to your life[c]?[a]
28“And why do you worry about clothes?
See how the flowers of the field grow. They
do not labor or spin. 29Yet I tell you that
not even Solomon in all his splendor[b] was
dressed like one of these. 30If that is how
God clothes the grass of the field, which
is here today and tomorrow is thrown
into the fire, will he not much more clothe
you—you of little faith?[c] 31So do not worry,
saying, ‘What shall we eat?’ or ‘What shall
we drink?’ or ‘What shall we wear?’ 32For
the pagans run after all these things, and
your heavenly Father knows that you need
them.[d] 33But seek first his kingdom and his
righteousness, and all these things will be
given to you as well.[e] 34Therefore do not
worry about tomorrow, for tomorrow will
worry about itself. Each day has enough
trouble of its own.

Judging Others

7 “Do not judge, or you too will be judged.[f]
2For in the same way you judge others,
you will be judged, and with the measure
you use, it will be measured to you.[g]
3“Why do you look at the speck of saw-
dust in your brother’s eye and pay no attention to the plank in your own eye? 4How
can you say to your brother, ‘Let me take
the speck out of your eye,’ when all the time
there is a plank in your own eye? 5You hypocrite, first take the plank out of your own
eye, and then you will see clearly to remove
the speck from your brother’s eye.
6“Do not give dogs what is sacred; do not
throw your pearls to pigs. If you do, they
may trample them under their feet, and
turn and tear you to pieces.

Ask, Seek, Knock

7“Ask and it will be given to you;[h] seek
and you will find; knock and the door will
be opened to you. 8For everyone who asks
receives; the one who seeks finds;[i] and
to the one who knocks, the door will be
opened.
9“Which of you, if your son asks for
bread, will give him a stone? 10Or if he asks
for a fish, will give him a snake? 11If you,
then, though you are evil, know how to
give good gifts to your children, how much
more will your Father in heaven give good
gifts to those who ask him! 12So in everything, do to others what you would have
them do to you,[j] for this sums up the Law
and the Prophets.[k]

The Narrow and Wide Gates

13“Enter through the narrow gate.[l] For
wide is the gate and broad is the road

---

[a] 22 The Greek for *healthy* here implies *generous*.
[b] 23 The Greek for *unhealthy* here implies *stingy*.
[c] 27 Or *single cubit to your height*

6:19 *Do not store up ... on earth.* In other words, don’t give priority to things that only last on earth, but instead put priority and energy into serving God.
6:24 Covetousness—God requires total allegiance and continuous subjection of our wills to Him. He asks for full commitment of our hearts and love for His service. We cannot serve God like that while under the influence of the god of money, urging us to make present, tangible, and worldly things the object of our thoughts and affections.
6:27 *add a single hour to your life.* Some translations say, “add one cubit,” a cubit was a unit of measure.” It seems that Jesus would bring a smile here; the mental picture either of growing taller, or of stretching time by worrying, helps us to see the futility of it.
7:1–2 *Do not judge.* The point of this verse is that a Christian must not judge or criticize in a way that they themselves would not want to be judged or criticized. Every judgment that a person makes becomes a basis for his or her own judgment (James 3:1–2).
7:6 *dogs ... pigs.* These insulting terms refer to people who are enemies of the gospel, as opposed to those who are merely unbelievers.

6:19 [r] Pr 23:4; Heb 13:5 [s] Jas 5:2,3 **6:20** [t] Mt 19:21; Lk 12:33; 18:22; 1Ti 6:19 [u] Lk 12:33 **6:21** [v] Lk 12:34 **6:24** [w] Lk 16:13 **6:25** [x] ver 27,28,31,34; Lk 10:41; 12:11, 22; Php 4:6; 1Pe 5:7 **6:26** [y] Job 38:41; Ps 147:9 [z] Mt 10:29-31 **6:27** [a] Ps 39:5 **6:29** [b] 1Ki 10:4-7 **6:30** [c] Mt 8:26; 14:31; 16:8 **6:32** [d] ver 8 **6:33** [e] Mt 19:29; Mk 10:29-30 **7:1** [f] Lk 6:37; Ro 14:4, 10, 13; 1Co 4:5; Jas 4:11, 12 **7:2** [g] Mk 4:24; Lk 6:38 **7:7** [h] Mt 21:22; Mk 11:24; Jn 14:13, 14; 15:7, 16; 16:23, 24; Jas 1:5-8; 4:2, 3; 1Jn 3:22; 5:14, 15 **7:8** [i] Pr 8:17; Jer 29:12, 13 **7:12** [j] Lk 6:31 [k] Ro 13:8-10; Gal 5:14 **7:13** [l] Lk 13:24

that leads to destruction, and many enter through it. 14But small is the gate and narrow the road that leads to life, and only a few find it.

True and False Prophets

15"Watch out for false prophets.[m] They come to you in sheep's clothing, but inwardly they are ferocious wolves.[n] 16By their fruit you will recognize them.[o] Do people pick grapes from thornbushes, or figs from thistles?[p] 17Likewise, every good tree bears good fruit, but a bad tree bears bad fruit. 18A good tree cannot bear bad fruit, and a bad tree cannot bear good fruit. 19Every tree that does not bear good fruit is cut down and thrown into the fire.[q] 20Thus, by their fruit you will recognize them.

True and False Disciples

21"Not everyone who says to me, 'Lord, Lord,'[r] will enter the kingdom of heaven, but only the one who does the will of my Father who is in heaven.[s] 22Many will say to me on that day,[t] 'Lord, Lord, did we not prophesy in your name and in your name drive out demons and in your name perform many miracles?'[u] 23Then I will tell them plainly, 'I never knew you. Away from me, you evildoers!'[v]

The Wise and Foolish Builders

24"Therefore everyone who hears these words of mine and puts them into practice[w] is like a wise man who built his house on the rock. 25The rain came down, the streams rose, and the winds blew and beat against that house; yet it did not fall, because it had its foundation on the rock. 26But everyone who hears these words of mine and does not put them into practice is like a foolish man who built his house on sand. 27The rain came down, the streams rose, and the winds blew and beat against that house, and it fell with a great crash."

28When Jesus had finished saying these things,[x] the crowds were amazed at his teaching,[y] 29because he taught as one who had authority, and not as their teachers of the law.

Jesus Heals a Man With Leprosy

8 When Jesus came down from the mountainside, large crowds followed him. 2A man with leprosy[a][z] came and knelt before him[a] and said, "Lord, if you are willing, you can make me clean."

3Jesus reached out his hand and touched the man. "I am willing," he said. "Be clean!" Immediately he was cleansed of his leprosy. 4Then Jesus said to him, "See that you don't tell anyone.[b] But go, show yourself to the priest and offer the gift Moses commanded,[c] as a testimony to them."

The Faith of the Centurion

5When Jesus had entered Capernaum, a centurion came to him, asking for help. 6"Lord," he said, "my servant lies at home paralyzed, suffering terribly."

7Jesus said to him, "Shall I come and heal him?"

8The centurion replied, "Lord, I do not deserve to have you come under my roof. But just say the word, and my servant will be healed.[d] 9For I myself am a man under authority, with soldiers under me. I tell this one, 'Go,' and he goes; and that one, 'Come,' and he comes. I say to my servant, 'Do this,' and he does it."

10When Jesus heard this, he was amazed and said to those following him, "Truly I tell you, I have not found anyone in Israel with such great faith.[e] 11I say to you that many will come from the east and the west,[f] and will take their places at the feast with Abraham, Isaac and Jacob in the kingdom of heaven.[g] 12But the subjects of the kingdom[h] will be thrown outside, into the darkness, where there will be weeping and gnashing of teeth."[i]

13Then Jesus said to the centurion, "Go! Let it be done just as you believed it would."[j] And his servant was healed at that moment.

Jesus Heals Many

14When Jesus came into Peter's house, he saw Peter's mother-in-law lying in bed with a fever. 15He touched her hand and the

---

[a] 2 The Greek word traditionally translated *leprosy* was used for various diseases affecting the skin.

7:15 *Watch out for false prophets.* Deuteronomy 13:1–11 and 18:20–22 provide information on discerning and responding to false prophets. The way to tell a false teacher from teachers of the truth is by their fruits. Fruit does not only refer to deeds, but also to doctrine (16:12; 1 John 4:1–3).

8:4 *show yourself to the priest.* This was no small undertaking. The sacrifice required was long and involved (Lev. 14:4–32). In obeying the law of Moses, the leper also would be a powerful testimony to the religious authorities in Jerusalem that the Messiah had arrived.

8:10 *I have not found anyone in Israel.* Jesus makes it clear that just being a physical descendant of Abraham does not guarantee entrance into His kingdom. The true children of Abraham are those who share his faith in God (Gal. 5:6–9).

7:15 [m] Jer 23:16; Mt 24:24; Mk 13:22; Lk 6:26; 2Pe 2:1; 1Jn 4:1; Rev 16:13 [n] Ac 20:29 **7:16** [o] Mt 12:33; Lk 6:44 [p] Jas 3:12 **7:19** [q] Mt 3:10 **7:21** [r] Hos 8:2; Mt 25:11 [s] Ro 2:13; Jas 1:22 **7:22** [t] Mt 10:15 [u] 1Co 13:1-3 **7:23** [v] Ps 6:8; Mt 25:12, 41; Lk 13:25-27 **7:24** [w] Jas 1:22-25 **7:28** [x] Mt 11:1; 13:53; 19:1; 26:1 [y] Mt 13:54; Mk 1:22; 6:2; Lk 4:32; Jn 7:46 **8:2** [z] Lk 5:12 [a] Mt 9:18; 15:25; 18:26; 20:20 **8:4** [b] Mt 9:30; Mk 5:43; 7:36; 8:30 [c] Lev 14:2-32 **8:8** [d] Ps 107:20 **8:10** [e] Mt 15:28 **8:11** [f] Ps 107:3; Isa 49:12; 59:19; Mal 1:11 [g] Lk 13:29 **8:12** [h] Mt 13:38 [i] Mt 13:42, 50; 22:13; 24:51; 25:30; Lk 13:28 **8:13** [j] Mt 9:22

fever left her, and she got up and began to wait on him.

16When evening came, many who were demon-possessed were brought to him, and he drove out the spirits with a word and healed all the sick.[k] 17This was to fulfill[l] what was spoken through the prophet Isaiah:

"He took up our infirmities
and bore our diseases."[a][m]

The Cost of Following Jesus

18When Jesus saw the crowd around him, he gave orders to cross to the other side of the lake.[n] 19Then a teacher of the law came to him and said, "Teacher, I will follow you wherever you go."

20Jesus replied, "Foxes have dens and birds have nests, but the Son of Man[o] has no place to lay his head."

21Another disciple said to him, "Lord, first let me go and bury my father."

22But Jesus told him, "Follow me,[p] and let the dead bury their own dead."

Jesus Calms the Storm

23Then he got into the boat and his disciples followed him. 24Suddenly a furious storm came up on the lake, so that the waves swept over the boat. But Jesus was sleeping. 25The disciples went and woke him, saying, "Lord, save us! We're going to drown!"

26He replied, "You of little faith,[q] why are you so afraid?" Then he got up and rebuked the winds and the waves, and it was completely calm.[r]

27The men were amazed and asked, "What kind of man is this? Even the winds and the waves obey him!"

Jesus Restores Two Demon-Possessed Men

28When he arrived at the other side in the region of the Gadarenes,[b] two demon-possessed[s] men coming from the tombs met him. They were so violent that no one could pass that way. 29"What do you want with us,[t] Son of God?" they shouted. "Have you come here to torture us before the appointed time?"[u]

30Some distance from them a large herd of pigs was feeding. 31The demons begged Jesus, "If you drive us out, send us into the herd of pigs."

32He said to them, "Go!" So they came out and went into the pigs, and the whole herd rushed down the steep bank into the lake and died in the water. 33Those tending the pigs ran off, went into the town and reported all this, including what had happened to the demon-possessed men. 34Then the whole town went out to meet Jesus. And when they saw him, they pleaded with him to leave their region.[v]

Jesus Forgives and Heals a Paralyzed Man

9 Jesus stepped into a boat, crossed over and came to his own town.[w] 2Some men brought to him a paralyzed man,[x] lying on a mat. When Jesus saw their faith,[y] he said to the man, "Take heart,[z] son; your sins are forgiven."[a]

3At this, some of the teachers of the law said to themselves, "This fellow is blaspheming!"[b]

4Knowing their thoughts,[c] Jesus said, "Why do you entertain evil thoughts in your hearts? 5Which is easier: to say, 'Your sins are forgiven,' or to say, 'Get up and walk'? 6But I want you to know that the Son of Man[d] has authority on earth to forgive sins." So he said to the paralyzed man, "Get up, take your mat and go home." 7Then the man got up and went home. 8When the crowd saw this, they were filled with awe; and they praised God,[e] who had given such authority to man.

The Calling of Matthew

9As Jesus went on from there, he saw a man named Matthew sitting at the tax collector's booth. "Follow me," he told him, and Matthew got up and followed him.

10While Jesus was having dinner at Matthew's house, many tax collectors and sinners came and ate with him and his disciples. 11When the Pharisees saw this, they asked his disciples, "Why does your teacher eat with tax collectors and sinners?"[f]

---

[a] *17* Isaiah 53:4 (see Septuagint) [b] *28* Some manuscripts *Gergesenes*; other manuscripts *Gerasenes*

8:17 *took our infirmities and bore our diseases.* This verse quotes Isaiah 53:4. Jesus healed because He had compassion on the people.

8:28–29 *demon-possessed.* We learn several things about demons in this passage. They recognize the deity of Christ, they are limited in their knowledge, they know they will ultimately be judged by Christ (25:41; James 2:19; 2 Pet. 2:4; Jude 6; Rev. 12:7–17), and they cannot act without the permission of higher authority.

9:2 *their faith.* This refers to the faith of the paralytic as well as that of the men who were carrying him.

9:10 *tax collectors.* Publicans were tax collectors who were often despised not only because they were seen as traitors, working for the hated Roman government, but also because they generally collected more than necessary and pocketed the difference.

8:16 [k] Mt 4:23,24 **8:17** [l] Mt 1:22 [m] Isa 53:4 **8:18** [n] Mk 4:35 **8:20** [o] Da 7:13; Mt 12:8,32,40; 16:13,27, 28; 17:9; 19:28; Mk 2:10; 8:31 **8:22** [p] Mt 4:19 **8:26** [q] Mt 6:30 [r] Ps 65:7; 89:9; 107:29 **8:28** [s] Mt 4:24 **8:29** [t] Jdg 11:12; 2Sa 16:10; 1Ki 17:18; Mk 1:24; Lk 4:34; Jn 2:4 [u] 2Pe 2:4 **8:34** [v] Lk 5:8; Ac 16:39 **9:1** [w] Mt 4:13 **9:2** [x] Mt 4:24 [y] ver 22 [z] Jn 16:33 [a] Lk 7:48 **9:3** [b] Mt 26:65; Jn 10:33 **9:4** [c] Ps 94:11; Mt 12:25; Lk 6:8; 9:47; 11:17 **9:6** [d] Mt 8:20 **9:8** [e] Mt 5:16; 15:31; Lk 7:16; 13:13; 17:15; 23:47; Jn 15:8; Ac 4:21; 11:18; 21:20 **9:11** [f] Mt 11:19; Lk 5:30; 15:2; Gal 2:15

12 On hearing this, Jesus said, "It is not the healthy who need a doctor, but the sick. 13 But go and learn what this means: 'I desire mercy, not sacrifice.'[a][g] For I have not come to call the righteous, but sinners."[h]

Jesus Questioned About Fasting

14 Then John's disciples came and asked him, "How is it that we and the Pharisees fast often,[i] but your disciples do not fast?"

15 Jesus answered, "How can the guests of the bridegroom mourn while he is with them?[j] The time will come when the bridegroom will be taken from them; then they will fast.[k]

16 "No one sews a patch of unshrunk cloth on an old garment, for the patch will pull away from the garment, making the tear worse. 17 Neither do people pour new wine into old wineskins. If they do, the skins will burst; the wine will run out and the wineskins will be ruined. No, they pour new wine into new wineskins, and both are preserved."

Jesus Raises a Dead Girl and Heals a Sick Woman

18 While he was saying this, a synagogue leader came and knelt before him[l] and said, "My daughter has just died. But come and put your hand on her,[m] and she will live." 19 Jesus got up and went with him, and so did his disciples.

20 Just then a woman who had been subject to bleeding for twelve years came up behind him and touched the edge of his cloak.[n] 21 She said to herself, "If I only touch his cloak, I will be healed."

22 Jesus turned and saw her. "Take heart, daughter," he said, "your faith has healed you."[o] And the woman was healed at that moment.[p]

23 When Jesus entered the synagogue leader's house and saw the noisy crowd and people playing pipes,[q] 24 he said, "Go away. The girl is not dead[r] but asleep."[s] But they laughed at him. 25 After the crowd had been put outside, he went in and took the girl by the hand, and she got up. 26 News of this spread through all that region.[t]

Jesus Heals the Blind and the Mute

27 As Jesus went on from there, two blind men followed him, calling out, "Have mercy on us, Son of David!"[u]

28 When he had gone indoors, the blind men came to him, and he asked them, "Do you believe that I am able to do this?"

"Yes, Lord," they replied.

29 Then he touched their eyes and said, "According to your faith let it be done to you";[v] 30 and their sight was restored. Jesus warned them sternly, "See that no one knows about this."[w] 31 But they went out and spread the news about him all over that region.[x]

32 While they were going out, a man who was demon-possessed[y] and could not talk[z] was brought to Jesus. 33 And when the demon was driven out, the man who had been mute spoke. The crowd was amazed and said, "Nothing like this has ever been seen in Israel."[a]

34 But the Pharisees said, "It is by the prince of demons that he drives out demons."[b]

The Workers Are Few

35 Jesus went through all the towns and villages, teaching in their synagogues, proclaiming the good news of the kingdom and healing every disease and sickness.[c] 36 When he saw the crowds, he had compassion on them,[d] because they were harassed and helpless, like sheep without a shepherd.[e] 37 Then he said to his disciples, "The harvest[f] is plentiful but the workers are few.[g] 38 Ask the Lord of the harvest, therefore, to send out workers into his harvest field."

Jesus Sends Out the Twelve

10 Jesus called his twelve disciples to him and gave them authority to drive out impure spirits[h] and to heal every disease and sickness.

2 These are the names of the twelve apostles: first, Simon (who is called Peter) and his brother Andrew; James son of Zebedee,

a 13 Hosea 6:6

9:12–13 *healthy.* Jesus refers ironically to the Pharisees as "the righteous." They were not righteous, that was only how they perceived themselves because of their pious and scrupulous law keeping (Phil. 3:6). But God is more interested in a person's loyal love than the observance of external rituals.

9:30 *See that no one knows about this.* Jesus may have wanted to discourage the masses from coming to Him for physical healing alone, because His primary purpose was spiritual healing.

9:37 *harvest.* The harvest marks the beginning of Christ sending his disciples out to testify, through their witness and miraculous works, of the arrival of the kingdom of God (10.7).The disciples are told to curse those who reject their message, but to bless those who accept it.

10:2 *the twelve.* The twelve are called disciples in verse 1; here they are called "apostles." The word "apostle" emphasizes delegated authority (1 Thess. 2:6).

9:13 [g] Hos 6:6; Mic 6:6-8; Mt 12:7 [h] 1Ti 1:15
9:14 [i] Lk 18:12 **9:15** [j] Jn 3:29 [k] Ac 13:2,3; 14:23
9:18 [l] Mt 8:2 [m] Mk 5:23 **9:20** [n] Mt 14:36; Mk 3:10
9:22 [o] Mk 10:52; Lk 7:50; 17:19; 18:42 [p] Mt 15:28
9:23 [q] 2Ch 35:25; Jer 9:17,18 **9:24** [r] Ac 20:10
[s] Jn 11:11-14 **9:26** [t] Mt 4:24 **9:27** [u] Mt 15:22; Mk 10:47; Lk 18:38-39 **9:29** [v] ver 22 **9:30** [w] Mt 8:4
9:31 [x] ver 26; Mk 7:36 **9:32** [y] Mt 4:24 [z] Mt 12:22-24
9:33 [a] Mk 2:12 **9:34** [b] Mt 12:24; Lk 11:15
9:35 [c] Mt 4:23 **9:36** [d] Mt 14:14 [e] Nu 27:17; Eze 34:5,6; Zec 10:2; Mk 6:34 **9:37** [f] Jn 4:35 [g] Lk 10:2
10:1 [h] Mk 3:13-15; Lk 9:1

and his brother John; 3Philip and Bartholomew; Thomas and Matthew the tax collector; James son of Alphaeus, and Thaddaeus; 4Simon the Zealot and Judas Iscariot, who betrayed him.[i]

5These twelve Jesus sent out with the following instructions: "Do not go among the Gentiles or enter any town of the Samaritans.[j] 6Go rather to the lost sheep of Israel.[k] 7As you go, proclaim this message: 'The kingdom of heaven[l] has come near.' 8Heal the sick, raise the dead, cleanse those who have leprosy,[a] drive out demons. Freely you have received; freely give.

9"Do not get any gold or silver or copper to take with you in your belts[m]— 10no bag for the journey or extra shirt or sandals or a staff, for the worker is worth his keep.[n] 11Whatever town or village you enter, search there for some worthy person and stay at their house until you leave. 12As you enter the home, give it your greeting.[o] 13If the home is deserving, let your peace rest on it; if it is not, let your peace return to you. 14If anyone will not welcome you or listen to your words, leave that home or town and shake the dust off your feet.[p] 15Truly I tell you, it will be more bearable for Sodom and Gomorrah[q] on the day of judgment[r] than for that town.[s]

16"I am sending you out like sheep among wolves.[t] Therefore be as shrewd as snakes and as innocent as doves.[u] 17Be on your guard; you will be handed over to the local councils[v] and be flogged in the synagogues.[w] 18On my account you will be brought before governors and kings[x] as witnesses to them and to the Gentiles. 19But when they arrest you, do not worry about what to say or how to say it.[y] At that time you will be given what to say, 20for it will not be you speaking, but the Spirit of your Father[z] speaking through you.

21"Brother will betray brother to death, and a father his child; children will rebel against their parents[a] and have them put to death. 22You will be hated by everyone because of me, but the one who stands firm to the end will be saved.[b] 23When you are persecuted in one place, flee to another. Truly I tell you, you will not finish going through the towns of Israel before the Son of Man comes.

24"The student is not above the teacher, nor a servant above his master.[c] 25It is enough for students to be like their teachers, and servants like their masters. If the head of the house has been called Beelzebul,[d] how much more the members of his household!

26"So do not be afraid of them, for there is nothing concealed that will not be disclosed, or hidden that will not be made known.[e] 27What I tell you in the dark, speak in the daylight; what is whispered in your ear, proclaim from the roofs. 28Do not be afraid of those who kill the body but cannot kill the soul. Rather, be afraid of the One[f] who can destroy both soul and body in hell. 29Are not two sparrows sold for a penny? Yet not one of them will fall to the ground outside your Father's care.[b] 30And even the very hairs of your head are all numbered.[g] 31So don't be afraid; you are worth more than many sparrows.[h]

32"Whoever acknowledges me before others,[i] I will also acknowledge before my Father in heaven. 33But whoever disowns me before others, I will disown before my Father in heaven.[j]

34"Do not suppose that I have come to bring peace to the earth. I did not come to bring peace, but a sword. 35For I have come to turn

"'a man against his father,
a daughter against her mother,
a daughter-in-law against her mother-in-law[k]—
36 a man's enemies will be the members of his own household.'[c][l]

37"Anyone who loves their father or mother more than me is not worthy of me; anyone who loves their son or daughter more than me is not worthy of me.[m] 38Whoever does not take up their cross and follow

[a] 8 The Greek word traditionally translated *leprosy* was used for various diseases affecting the skin.
[b] 29 Or *will*; or *knowledge*
[c] 36 Micah 7:6

10:15 *more bearable for Sodom and Gomorrah.* This verse, together with 11:22–24, could imply that there will be different degrees of judgment and torment for those who reject Christ.

10:18 *On my account.* God would use Jewish rejection and persecution of the messengers to bring the gospel message to the Gentiles.

10:25 Persecution—Believers must know that what the world has called our Lord, it will call us. The world has hated Jesus without cause, and they will hate those who bear His name in the same way.

10:32 *Whoever acknowledges.* Every act of our lives will be evaluated at the judgment seat of Christ (2 Cor. 5:10). To refuse to speak up for Christ because of intimidation or persecution will result in the believer's loss of reward and consequent loss of glory in the kingdom (Rom. 8:17; 2 Tim. 2:12).

10:38 *does not take up their cross.* "Taking up a cross" stands for commitment to the extent of being willing to die for something.

10:4 [i] Mt 26:14-16,25,47; Jn 13:2,26,27 **10:5** [j] 2Ki 17:24; Lk 9:52; Jn 4:4-26,39,40; Ac 8:5,25 **10:6** [k] Jer 50:6; Mt 15:24 **10:7** [l] Mt 3:2 **10:9** [m] Lk 22:35 **10:10** [n] 1Ti 5:18 **10:12** [o] 1Sa 25:6 **10:14** [p] Ne 5:13; Lk 10:11; Ac 13:51 **10:15** [q] 2Pe 2:6 [r] Mt 12:36; 2Pe 2:9; 1Jn 4:17 [s] Mt 11:22,24 **10:16** [t] Lk 10:3 [u] Ro 16:19 **10:17** [v] Mt 5:22 [w] Mt 23:34; Mk 13:9; Ac 5:40; 26:11 **10:18** [x] Ac 25:24-26 **10:19** [y] Ex 4:12 **10:20** [z] Ac 4:8 **10:21** [a] ver 35,36; Mic 7:6 **10:22** [b] Mt 24:13; Mk 13:13 **10:24** [c] Lk 6:40; Jn 13:16; 15:20 **10:25** [d] Mk 3:22 **10:26** [e] Mk 4:22; Lk 8:17 **10:28** [f] Isa 8:12,13; Heb 10:31 **10:30** [g] 1Sa 14:45; 2Sa 14:11; Lk 21:18; Ac 27:34 **10:31** [h] Mt 12:12 **10:32** [i] Ro 10:9 **10:33** [j] Mk 8:38; 2Ti 2:12 **10:35** [k] ver 21 **10:36** [l] Mic 7:6 **10:37** [m] Lk 14:26

me is not worthy of me.[n] 39 Whoever finds
their life will lose it, and whoever loses
their life for my sake will find it.[o]
40 "Anyone who welcomes you welcomes
me,[p] and anyone who welcomes me welcomes the one who sent me.[q] 41 Whoever
welcomes a prophet as a prophet will receive a prophet's reward, and whoever welcomes a righteous person as a righteous
person will receive a righteous person's
reward. 42 And if anyone gives even a cup
of cold water to one of these little ones who
is my disciple, truly I tell you, that person
will certainly not lose their reward."[r]

Jesus and John the Baptist

11 After Jesus had finished instructing
his twelve disciples,[s] he went on from
there to teach and preach in the towns of
Galilee.[a]
2 When John, who was in prison,[t] heard
about the deeds of the Messiah, he sent his
disciples 3 to ask him, "Are you the one who
is to come,[u] or should we expect someone
else?"
4 Jesus replied, "Go back and report to
John what you hear and see: 5 The blind
receive sight, the lame walk, those who
have leprosy[b] are cleansed, the deaf hear,
the dead are raised, and the good news is
proclaimed to the poor.[v] 6 Blessed is anyone
who does not stumble on account of me."[w]
7 As John's[x] disciples were leaving, Jesus
began to speak to the crowd about John:
"What did you go out into the wilderness
to see? A reed swayed by the wind? 8 If not,
what did you go out to see? A man dressed
in fine clothes? No, those who wear fine
clothes are in kings' palaces. 9 Then what
did you go out to see? A prophet?[y] Yes, I tell
you, and more than a prophet. 10 This is the
one about whom it is written:

"'I will send my messenger ahead of
you,
who will prepare your way before
you.'[c][z]

11 Truly I tell you, among those born of
women there has not risen anyone greater
than John the Baptist; yet whoever is least
in the kingdom of heaven is greater than
he. 12 From the days of John the Baptist until now, the kingdom of heaven has been
subjected to violence,[d] and violent people
have been raiding it. 13 For all the Prophets
and the Law prophesied until John. 14 And
if you are willing to accept it, he is the Elijah who was to come.[a] 15 Whoever has ears,
let them hear.[b]
16 "To what can I compare this generation? They are like children sitting in the
marketplaces and calling out to others:

17 "'We played the pipe for you,
and you did not dance;
we sang a dirge,
and you did not mourn.'

18 For John came neither eating[c] nor drinking,[d] and they say, 'He has a demon.' 19 The
Son of Man came eating and drinking, and
they say, 'Here is a glutton and a drunkard,
a friend of tax collectors and sinners.'[e] But
wisdom is proved right by her deeds."

Woe on Unrepentant Towns

20 Then Jesus began to denounce the
towns in which most of his miracles had
been performed, because they did not repent. 21 "Woe to you, Chorazin! Woe to you,
Bethsaida![f] For if the miracles that were
performed in you had been performed in
Tyre and Sidon,[g] they would have repented long ago in sackcloth and ashes.[h] 22 But
I tell you, it will be more bearable for Tyre
and Sidon on the day of judgment than for
you.[i] 23 And you, Capernaum,[j] will you be
lifted to the heavens? No, you will go down
to Hades.[e][k] For if the miracles that were
performed in you had been performed in
Sodom, it would have remained to this day.
24 But I tell you that it will be more bearable
for Sodom on the day of judgment than for
you."[l]

The Father Revealed in the Son

25 At that time Jesus said, "I praise you,
Father,[m] Lord of heaven and earth, because you have hidden these things from

---

[a] *1* Greek *in their towns* [b] *5* The Greek word traditionally translated *leprosy* was used for various diseases affecting the skin. [c] *10* Mal. 3:1 [d] *12* Or *been forcefully advancing* [e] *23* That is, the realm of the dead

---

11:3 *should we expect.* John probably expected the Messiah to immediately judge Israel and establish His kingdom (3:2–12). Jesus' failure to do what John anticipated may have planted seeds of doubt in John's mind about whether Jesus was the Messiah. But doubt that inquires and does not weaken faith is not evil. John went to the right person for answers, and Jesus reassured him by pointing out the fulfillment of prophecy.

11:12 *violent people have been raiding it.* This probably means that violent people forcibly oppose the kingdom with their hostility (23:13).

11:21 *Woe.* Jesus pronounced a direct judgment on Israel. They would be judged for seeing the Messiah and then rejecting Him.

11:23 *Capernaum.* Capernaum, which is on the north shore of the Sea of Galilee, was called "his own town" (9:1).

10:38 [n] Mt 16:24; Lk 14:27 **10:39** [o] Lk 17:33; Jn 12:25 **10:40** [p] Mt 18:5; Gal 4:14 [q] Lk 9:48; Jn 12:44; 13:20 **10:42** [r] Mt 25:40; Mk 9:41; Heb 6:10 **11:1** [s] Mt 7:28 **11:2** [t] Mt 14:3 **11:3** [u] Ps 118:26; Jn 11:27; Heb 10:37 **11:5** [v] Isa 35:4-6; 61:1; Lk 4:18, 19 **11:6** [w] Mt 13:21 **11:7** [x] Mt 3:1 **11:9** [y] Mt 21:26; Lk 1:76 **11:10** [z] Mal 3:1; Mk 1:2 **11:14** [a] Mal 4:5; Mt 17:10-13; Mk 9:11-13; Lk 1:17; Jn 1:21 **11:15** [b] Mt 13:9, 43; Mk 4:23; Lk 14:35; Rev 2:7 **11:18** [c] Mt 3:4 [d] Lk 1:15 **11:19** [e] Mt 9:11 **11:21** [f] Mk 6:45; Lk 9:10; Jn 12:21 [g] Mt 15:21; Lk 6:17; Ac 12:20 [h] Jnh 3:5-9 **11:22** [i] ver 24; Mt 10:15 **11:23** [j] Mt 4:13 [k] Isa 14:13-15 **11:24** [l] Mt 10:15 **11:25** [m] Lk 22:42; Jn 11:41

the wise and learned, and revealed them to little children.[n] 26Yes, Father, for this is what you were pleased to do.

27"All things have been committed to me[o] by my Father.[p] No one knows the Son except the Father, and no one knows the Father except the Son and those to whom the Son chooses to reveal him.[q]

28"Come to me,[r] all you who are weary and burdened, and I will give you rest. 29Take my yoke upon you and learn from me,[s] for I am gentle and humble in heart, and you will find rest for your souls.[t] 30For my yoke is easy and my burden is light."[u]

Jesus Is Lord of the Sabbath

12 At that time Jesus went through the grainfields on the Sabbath. His disciples were hungry and began to pick some heads of grain[v] and eat them. 2When the Pharisees saw this, they said to him, "Look! Your disciples are doing what is unlawful on the Sabbath."[w]

3He answered, "Haven't you read what David did when he and his companions were hungry?[x] 4He entered the house of God, and he and his companions ate the consecrated bread—which was not lawful for them to do, but only for the priests.[y] 5Or haven't you read in the Law that the priests on Sabbath duty in the temple desecrate the Sabbath[z] and yet are innocent? 6I tell you that something greater than the temple is here.[a] 7If you had known what these words mean, 'I desire mercy, not sacrifice,'[a][b] you would not have condemned the innocent. 8For the Son of Man[c] is Lord of the Sabbath."

9Going on from that place, he went into their synagogue, 10and a man with a shriveled hand was there. Looking for a reason to bring charges against Jesus, they asked him, "Is it lawful to heal on the Sabbath?"[d]

11He said to them, "If any of you has a sheep and it falls into a pit on the Sabbath, will you not take hold of it and lift it out?[e] 12How much more valuable is a person than a sheep![f] Therefore it is lawful to do good on the Sabbath."

13Then he said to the man, "Stretch out your hand." So he stretched it out and it was completely restored, just as sound as the other. 14But the Pharisees went out and plotted how they might kill Jesus.[g]

God's Chosen Servant

15Aware of this, Jesus withdrew from that place. A large crowd followed him, and he healed all who were ill.[h] 16He warned them not to tell others about him.[i] 17This was to fulfill what was spoken through the prophet Isaiah:

18 "Here is my servant whom I have chosen,
the one I love, in whom I delight;[j]
I will put my Spirit on him,
and he will proclaim justice to the nations.
19 He will not quarrel or cry out;
no one will hear his voice in the streets.
20 A bruised reed he will not break,
and a smoldering wick he will not snuff out,
till he has brought justice through to victory.
21 In his name the nations will put their hope."[b][k]

Jesus and Beelzebul

22Then they brought him a demon-possessed man who was blind and mute, and Jesus healed him, so that he could both talk and see.[l] 23All the people were astonished and said, "Could this be the Son of David?"[m]

24But when the Pharisees heard this, they said, "It is only by Beelzebul,[n] the prince of demons, that this fellow drives out demons."[o]

25Jesus knew their thoughts[p] and said to them, "Every kingdom divided against itself will be ruined, and every city or household divided against itself will not stand. 26If Satan[q] drives out Satan, he is divided against himself. How then can his kingdom stand? 27And if I drive out demons by Beelzebul, by whom do your people[r] drive them out? So then, they will be your judges. 28But if it is by the Spirit of God that I drive out demons, then the kingdom of God has come upon you.

---

a 7 Hosea 6:6 *b* *21* Isaiah 42:1-4

12:2 *is unlawful.* To desecrate the Sabbath was flagrant disobedience to the law of Moses (Num. 15:30–36). The Pharisees were trying to make Jesus into a lawbreaker and accuse Him of wrongdoing.

12:14 *how they might kill Jesus.* Because of Jesus' view of the Sabbath, the Pharisees concluded that He was trying to overthrow the entire Mosaic system, and therefore had to be destroyed. Their antagonism toward Jesus was growing.

12:17–21 *spoken through the prophet Isaiah.* This quotation of Isaiah 42:1–4 shows that the Messiah's gentleness was just as had been prophesied, and also that the Gentiles would be included in His blessing.

11:25 [n] 1Co 1:26-29 **11:27** [o] Mt 28:18 [p] Jn 3:35; 13:3; 17:2 [q] Jn 10:15 **11:28** [r] Jn 7:37 **11:29** [s] Jn 13:15; Php 2:5; 1Pe 2:21; 1Jn 2:6 [t] Jer 6:16 **11:30** [u] 1Jn 5:3 **12:1** [v] Dt 23:25 **12:2** [w] ver 10; Lk 13:14; 14:3; Jn 5:10; 7:23; 9:16 **12:3** [x] 1Sa 21:6 **12:4** [y] Lev 24:5,9 **12:5** [z] Nu 28:9, 10; Jn 7:22, 23 **12:6** [a] ver 41, 42 **12:7** [b] Hos 6:6; Mic 6:6-8; Mt 9:13 **12:8** [c] Mt 8:20 **12:10** [d] ver 2; Lk 13:14; 14:3; Jn 9:16 **12:11** [e] Lk 14:5 **12:12** [f] Mt 10:31 **12:14** [g] Mt 26:4; 27:1; Mk 3:6; Lk 6:11; Jn 5:18; 11:53 **12:15** [h] Mt 4:23 **12:16** [i] Mt 8:4 **12:18** [j] Mt 3:17 **12:21** [k] Isa 42:1-4 **12:22** [l] Mt 4:24; 9:32-33 **12:23** [m] Mt 9:27 **12:24** [n] Mk 3:22 [o] Mt 9:34 **12:25** [p] Mt 9:4 **12:26** [q] Mt 4:10 **12:27** [r] Ac 19:13

29"Or again, how can anyone enter a strong man's house and carry off his possessions unless he first ties up the strong man? Then he can plunder his house.

30"Whoever is not with me is against me, and whoever does not gather with me scatters.[s] 31And so I tell you, every kind of sin and slander can be forgiven, but blasphemy against the Spirit will not be forgiven.[t] 32Anyone who speaks a word against the Son of Man will be forgiven, but anyone who speaks against the Holy Spirit will not be forgiven, either in this age[u] or in the age to come.[v]

33"Make a tree good and its fruit will be good, or make a tree bad and its fruit will be bad, for a tree is recognized by its fruit.[w] 34You brood of vipers,[x] how can you who are evil say anything good? For the mouth speaks[y] what the heart is full of. 35A good man brings good things out of the good stored up in him, and an evil man brings evil things out of the evil stored up in him. 36But I tell you that everyone will have to give account on the day of judgment for every empty word they have spoken. 37For by your words you will be acquitted, and by your words you will be condemned."

The Sign of Jonah

38Then some of the Pharisees and teachers of the law said to him, "Teacher, we want to see a sign from you."[z]

39He answered, "A wicked and adulterous generation asks for a sign! But none will be given it except the sign of the prophet Jonah.[a] 40For as Jonah was three days and three nights in the belly of a huge fish,[b] so the Son of Man[c] will be three days and three nights in the heart of the earth.[d] 41The men of Nineveh[e] will stand up at the judgment with this generation and condemn it; for they repented at the preaching of Jonah,[f] and now something greater than Jonah is here. 42The Queen of the South will rise at the judgment with this generation and condemn it; for she came[g] from the ends of the earth to listen to Solomon's wisdom, and now something greater than Solomon is here.

43"When an impure spirit comes out of a person, it goes through arid places seeking rest and does not find it. 44Then it says, 'I will return to the house I left.' When it arrives, it finds the house unoccupied, swept clean and put in order. 45Then it goes and takes with it seven other spirits more wicked than itself, and they go in and live there. And the final condition of that person is worse than the first.[h] That is how it will be with this wicked generation."

Jesus' Mother and Brothers

46While Jesus was still talking to the crowd, his mother[i] and brothers[j] stood outside, wanting to speak to him. 47Someone told him, "Your mother and brothers are standing outside, wanting to speak to you."

48He replied to him, "Who is my mother, and who are my brothers?" 49Pointing to his disciples, he said, "Here are my mother and my brothers. 50For whoever does the will of my Father in heaven[k] is my brother and sister and mother."

The Parable of the Sower

13 That same day Jesus went out of the house[l] and sat by the lake. 2Such large crowds gathered around him that he got into a boat[m] and sat in it, while all the people stood on the shore. 3Then he told them many things in parables, saying: "A farmer went out to sow his seed. 4As he was scattering the seed, some fell along the path, and the birds came and ate it up. 5Some fell on rocky places, where it did not have much soil. It sprang up quickly, because the soil was shallow. 6But when the sun came up, the plants were scorched, and they withered because they had no root. 7Other seed fell among thorns, which grew up and choked the plants. 8Still other seed fell on good soil, where it produced a crop—a

---

12:31–32 *blasphemy.* The sin that shall not be forgiven is the stubborn refusal to heed the Holy Spirit's conviction and accept the salvation that Christ offers. Particularly in reference to the leaders of Israel, Jesus had offered them all the proof that could be expected, such as the ministry of John, the testimony of the Father, the prophecies of the Old Testament, His own testimony, and the substantiation of the Holy Spirit. Because the leaders rejected all proofs regarding Jesus as Messiah, nothing else would be given.

12:39 *the sign of the prophet Jonah.* The demand for signs was evidence of unbelief. The "sign of the prophet Jonah" is explained in verse 40 as the resurrection.

12:41–42 *The men of Nineveh ... The Queen of the South.* These terms represent Gentiles who come to faith because of the words of God's prophets and kings, lesser messengers than God's only Son.

12:43 *an impure spirit.* This analogy seems to be describing the moral reformation that took place in Israel as a result of the ministries of John the Baptist and Jesus. The reformation, however, was not genuine, and therefore Israel's unbelief and hardness of heart was worse than before. In the same way, a person who decides to try religion without being born again, and then decides "it's not for me," is worse off than if they had never tried, because their hearts are hardened to God's voice.

12:30 [s] Mk 9:40; Lk 11:23 **12:31** [t] Mk 3:28, 29; Lk 12:10 **12:32** [u] Titus 2:12 [v] Mk 10:30; Lk 20:34, 35; Eph 1:21; Heb 6:5 **12:33** [w] Mt 7:16, 17; Lk 6:43, 44 **12:34** [x] Mt 3:7; 23:33 [y] Mt 15:18; Lk 6:45 **12:38** [z] Mt 16:1; Mk 8:11, 12; Lk 11:16; Jn 2:18; 6:30; 1Co 1:22 **12:39** [a] Mt 16:4; Lk 11:29 **12:40** [b] Jnh 1:17 [c] Mt 8:20 [d] Mt 16:21 **12:41** [e] Jnh 1:2 [f] Jnh 3:5 **12:42** [g] 1Ki 10:1; 2Ch 9:1 **12:45** [h] 2Pe 2:20 **12:46** [i] Mt 1:18; 2:11, 13, 14, 20; Lk 1:43; 2:33, 34, 48, 51; Jn 2:1, 5; 19:25, 26 [j] Mt 13:55; Jn 2:12; 7:3, 5; Ac 1:14; 1Co 9:5; Gal 1:19 **12:50** [k] Jn 15:14 **13:1** [l] ver 36; Mt 9:28 **13:2** [m] Lk 5:3

hundred,[n] sixty or thirty times what was
sown. **9**Whoever has ears, let them hear."[o]
10The disciples came to him and asked,
"Why do you speak to the people in parables?"
11He replied, "Because the knowledge of
the secrets of the kingdom of heaven has
been given to you,[p] but not to them. **12**Whoever
has will be given more, and they will
have an abundance. Whoever does not
have, even what they have will be taken
from them.[q] **13**This is why I speak to them
in parables:

"Though seeing, they do not see;
though hearing, they do not hear or understand.[r]

14In them is fulfilled the prophecy of Isaiah:

"'You will be ever hearing but never understanding;
you will be ever seeing but never perceiving.
15For this people's heart has become calloused;
they hardly hear with their ears,
and they have closed their eyes.
Otherwise they might see with their eyes,
hear with their ears,
understand with their hearts
and turn, and I would heal them.'[a][s]

16But blessed are your eyes because they
see, and your ears because they hear.[t] **17**For
truly I tell you, many prophets and righteous
people longed to see what you see[u]
but did not see it, and to hear what you hear
but did not hear it.
18"Listen then to what the parable of
the sower means: **19**When anyone hears
the message about the kingdom[v] and does
not understand it, the evil one[w] comes and
snatches away what was sown in their
heart. This is the seed sown along the
path. **20**The seed falling on rocky ground
refers to someone who hears the word and
at once receives it with joy. **21**But since they
have no root, they last only a short time.
When trouble or persecution comes because
of the word, they quickly fall away.[x]
22The seed falling among the thorns refers
to someone who hears the word, but the
worries of this life and the deceitfulness
of wealth[y] choke the word, making it unfruitful.
23But the seed falling on good soil
refers to someone who hears the word and
understands it. This is the one who produces
a crop, yielding a hundred, sixty or
thirty times what was sown."[z]

The Parable of the Weeds

24Jesus told them another parable: "The
kingdom of heaven is like[a] a man who
sowed good seed in his field. **25**But while
everyone was sleeping, his enemy came
and sowed weeds among the wheat, and
went away. **26**When the wheat sprouted
and formed heads, then the weeds also appeared.
27"The owner's servants came to him
and said, 'Sir, didn't you sow good seed in
your field? Where then did the weeds come
from?'
28"'An enemy did this,' he replied.
"The servants asked him, 'Do you want
us to go and pull them up?'
29"'No,' he answered, 'because while you
are pulling the weeds, you may uproot the
wheat with them. **30**Let both grow together
until the harvest. At that time I will tell the
harvesters: First collect the weeds and tie
them in bundles to be burned; then gather
the wheat and bring it into my barn.'"[b]

The Parables of the Mustard Seed and the Yeast

31He told them another parable: "The
kingdom of heaven is like[c] a mustard seed,[d]
which a man took and planted in his field.
32Though it is the smallest of all seeds, yet
when it grows, it is the largest of garden
plants and becomes a tree, so that the birds
come and perch in its branches."[e]

---

a 15 Isaiah 6:9,10 (see Septuagint)

13:11 *has been given to you.* The purpose of this parable was to both reveal and conceal the truth. This hiding of the truth was a judgment for unbelief, as happened during Isaiah's ministry (Is. 6:9–10).

13:14–15 Spiritual Death—Genesis 3 teaches us that, through sin, man died spiritually. Here, Christ quotes from Isaiah 6 to detail the meaning of spiritual death: Our ability to perceive spiritual reality is absent. Key spiritual senses don't work as they were originally designed to work. We can't see the implications of spiritual events. We can't understand the meaning of spiritual words. It is as if our senses are dead. In order to have our spiritual senses restored, we need someone to heal us. Only Christ can provide the necessary healing to open our spiritual eyes and ears.

13:25 *his enemy came and sowed weeds.* These weeds closely resemble wheat but do not produce good food. They are indistinguishable from the real wheat until the fruit appears. Just like the weeds among the wheat, genuine believers and counterfeits will be allowed to remain together.

13:31 *like a mustard seed.* The parable of the mustard seed shows that the number of people who will inherit the kingdom will be very small at first, but it will grow to be completely out of proportion to its initial size.

13:8 [n] Ge 26:12 **13:9** [o] Mt 11:15 **13:11** [p] Mt 11:25; 16:17; 19:11; Jn 6:65; 1Co 2:10, 14; Col 1:27; 1Jn 2:20, 27 **13:12** [q] Mt 25:29; Lk 19:26 **13:13** [r] Dt 29:4; Jer 5:21; Eze 12:2 **13:15** [s] Isa 6:9, 10; Jn 12:40; Ac 28:26, 27; Ro 11:8 **13:16** [t] Mt 16:17 **13:17** [u] Jn 8:56; Heb 11:13; 1Pe 1:10-12 **13:19** [v] Mt 4:23 [w] Mt 5:37 **13:21** [x] Mt 11:6 **13:22** [y] Mt 19:23; 1Ti 6:9, 10, 17 **13:23** [z] ver 8 **13:24** [a] ver 31, 33, 45, 47; Mt 18:23; 20:1; 22:2; 25:1; Mk 4:26, 30 **13:30** [b] Mt 3:12 **13:31** [c] ver 24 [d] Mt 17:20; Lk 17:6 **13:32** [e] Ps 104:12; Eze 17:23; 31:6; Da 4:12

33He told them still another parable:
"The kingdom of heaven is like[f] yeast
that a woman took and mixed into about
sixty pounds[a] of flour[g] until it worked all
through the dough."[h]
34Jesus spoke all these things to the
crowd in parables; he did not say anything
to them without using a parable.[i] 35So was
fulfilled what was spoken through the
prophet:

"I will open my mouth in parables,
I will utter things hidden since the
creation of the world."[b][j]

The Parable of the Weeds Explained

36Then he left the crowd and went into
the house. His disciples came to him and
said, "Explain to us the parable[k] of the
weeds in the field."
37He answered, "The one who sowed the
good seed is the Son of Man.[l] 38The field is
the world, and the good seed stands for the
people of the kingdom. The weeds are the
people of the evil one,[m] 39and the enemy
who sows them is the devil. The harvest[n]
is the end of the age,[o] and the harvesters
are angels.[p]
40"As the weeds are pulled up and
burned in the fire, so it will be at the end
of the age. 41The Son of Man[q] will send out
his angels,[r] and they will weed out of his
kingdom everything that causes sin and
all who do evil. 42They will throw them
into the blazing furnace, where there will
be weeping and gnashing of teeth.[s] 43Then
the righteous will shine like the sun[t] in
the kingdom of their Father. Whoever has
ears, let them hear.[u]

The Parables of the Hidden Treasure and the Pearl

44"The kingdom of heaven is like[v] treasure hidden in a field. When a man found
it, he hid it again, and then in his joy went
and sold all he had and bought that field.[w]
45"Again, the kingdom of heaven is
like[x] a merchant looking for fine pearls.
46When he found one of great value, he
went away and sold everything he had
and bought it.

The Parable of the Net

47"Once again, the kingdom of heaven is
like[y] a net that was let down into the lake
and caught all kinds[z] of fish. 48When it was
full, the fishermen pulled it up on the shore.
Then they sat down and collected the good
fish in baskets, but threw the bad away.
49This is how it will be at the end of the
age. The angels will come and separate the
wicked from the righteous[a] 50and throw
them into the blazing furnace, where there
will be weeping and gnashing of teeth.[b]
51"Have you understood all these
things?" Jesus asked.
"Yes," they replied.
52He said to them, "Therefore every
teacher of the law who has become a disciple in the kingdom of heaven is like the
owner of a house who brings out of his
storeroom new treasures as well as old."

A Prophet Without Honor

53When Jesus had finished these parables,[c] he moved on from there. 54Coming
to his hometown, he began teaching the
people in their synagogue,[d] and they were
amazed.[e] "Where did this man get this wisdom and these miraculous powers?" they
asked. 55"Isn't this the carpenter's son?[f]
Isn't his mother's[g] name Mary, and aren't
his brothers James, Joseph, Simon and Judas? 56Aren't all his sisters with us? Where
then did this man get all these things?"
57And they took offense[h] at him.
But Jesus said to them, "A prophet is not
without honor except in his own town and
in his own home."[i]
58And he did not do many miracles there
because of their lack of faith.

[a] *33* Or about 27 kilograms [b] *35* Psalm 78:2

13:33 *like yeast.* Although leaven is sometimes used in Scripture to symbolize evil, here the kingdom of heaven is being compared to the dynamic character of yeast. When yeast is mixed with the dough, it expands from within, causing the dough to grow. Rather than being powered by outward armies or organizations, the kingdom of God will grow by the internal power of the Holy Spirit.

13:42 Hell—This verse describes the separation that comes between the righteous and the wicked at the end of the age. The place of their eternal dwelling is described as a "furnace of fire," perhaps because fire is one of man's most vivid concepts of suffering. Some think that there is no real, actual hell of fire, and that instead the wicked simply cease to exist, but this is difficult to support. The Scriptures consistently speak of hell as a real place of torment and anguish for all who do not receive the salvation that Jesus offers.

13:44 *like treasure.* The main point here is the immense value of the kingdom, which far outweighs any sacrifice or inconvenience one might encounter on earth.

13:47 *all kinds of fish.* The responsibility of the disciples would be to catch as many "fish" of every kind as possible. The work of judging or sorting out the false catch, however, is a job that disciples are neither called nor equipped to do. That work is assigned to angels at Christ's return.

13:33 [f] ver 24 [g] Ge 18:6 [h] Gal 5:9 **13:34** [i] Mk 4:33; Jn 16:25 **13:35** [j] Ps 78:2; Ro 16:25,26; 1Co 2:7; Eph 3:9; Col 1:26 **13:36** [k] Mt 15:15 **13:37** [l] Mt 8:20 **13:38** [m] Jn 8:44,45; 1Jn 3:10 **13:39** [n] Joel 3:13 [o] Mt 24:3; 28:20 [p] Rev 14:15 **13:41** [q] Mt 8:20 [r] Mt 24:31 **13:42** [s] ver 50; Mt 8:12 **13:43** [t] Da 12:3 [u] Mt 11:15 **13:44** [v] ver 24 [w] Isa 55:1; Php 3:7,8 **13:45** [x] ver 24 **13:47** [y] ver 24 [z] Mt 22:10 **13:49** [a] Mt 25:32 **13:50** [b] Mt 8:12 **13:53** [c] Mt 7:28 **13:54** [d] Mt 4:23 [e] Mt 7:28 **13:55** [f] Lk 3:23; Jn 6:42 [g] Mt 12:46 **13:57** [h] Jn 6:61 [i] Lk 4:24; Jn 4:44

John the Baptist Beheaded

14 At that time Herod[j] the tetrarch heard the reports about Jesus,[k] **2**and he said to his attendants, "This is John the Baptist;[l] he has risen from the dead! That is why miraculous powers are at work in him."

3Now Herod had arrested John and bound him and put him in prison[m] because of Herodias, his brother Philip's wife,[n] **4**for John had been saying to him: "It is not lawful for you to have her."[o] **5**Herod wanted to kill John, but he was afraid of the people, because they considered John a prophet.[p]

6On Herod's birthday the daughter of Herodias danced for the guests and pleased Herod so much **7**that he promised with an oath to give her whatever she asked. **8**Prompted by her mother, she said, "Give me here on a platter the head of John the Baptist." **9**The king was distressed, but because of his oaths and his dinner guests, he ordered that her request be granted **10**and had John beheaded[q] in the prison. **11**His head was brought in on a platter and given to the girl, who carried it to her mother. **12**John's disciples came and took his body and buried it.[r] Then they went and told Jesus.

Jesus Feeds the Five Thousand

13When Jesus heard what had happened, he withdrew by boat privately to a solitary place. Hearing of this, the crowds followed him on foot from the towns. **14**When Jesus landed and saw a large crowd, he had compassion on them[s] and healed their sick.[t]

15As evening approached, the disciples came to him and said, "This is a remote place, and it's already getting late. Send the crowds away, so they can go to the villages and buy themselves some food."

16Jesus replied, "They do not need to go away. You give them something to eat."

17"We have here only five loaves[u] of bread and two fish," they answered.

18"Bring them here to me," he said. **19**And he directed the people to sit down on the grass. Taking the five loaves and the two fish and looking up to heaven, he gave thanks and broke the loaves.[v] Then he gave them to the disciples, and the disciples gave them to the people. **20**They all ate and were satisfied, and the disciples picked up twelve basketfuls of broken pieces that were left over. **21**The number of those who ate was about five thousand men, besides women and children.

Jesus Walks on the Water

22Immediately Jesus made the disciples get into the boat and go on ahead of him to the other side, while he dismissed the crowd. **23**After he had dismissed them, he went up on a mountainside by himself to pray.[w] Later that night, he was there alone, **24**and the boat was already a considerable distance from land, buffeted by the waves because the wind was against it.

25Shortly before dawn Jesus went out to them, walking on the lake. **26**When the disciples saw him walking on the lake, they were terrified. "It's a ghost,"[x] they said, and cried out in fear.

27But Jesus immediately said to them: "Take courage![y] It is I. Don't be afraid."[z]

28"Lord, if it's you," Peter replied, "tell me to come to you on the water."

29"Come," he said.

Then Peter got down out of the boat, walked on the water and came toward Jesus. **30**But when he saw the wind, he was afraid and, beginning to sink, cried out, "Lord, save me!"

31Immediately Jesus reached out his hand and caught him. "You of little faith,"[a] he said, "why did you doubt?"

32And when they climbed into the boat, the wind died down. **33**Then those who were in the boat worshiped him, saying, "Truly you are the Son of God."[b]

34When they had crossed over, they landed at Gennesaret. **35**And when the men of that place recognized Jesus, they sent word to all the surrounding country. People brought all their sick to him **36**and begged him to let the sick just touch the edge of his cloak,[c] and all who touched it were healed.

That Which Defiles

15 Then some Pharisees and teachers of the law came to Jesus from Jerusalem and asked, **2**"Why do your disciples break the tradition of the elders? They don't wash their hands before they eat!"[d]

3Jesus replied, "And why do you break the command of God for the sake of your tradition? **4**For God said, 'Honor your fa-

---

14:3 ***because of Herodias.*** Herod had gone to Rome, where he met Herodias, the wife of his half brother Philip. After seducing Herodias, Herod divorced his own wife and married his sister-in-law. John had rebuked the king for his moral transgressions.

14:25 ***before dawn.*** This would be between 3:00 and 6:00 A.M.

15:2 ***the tradition of the elders.*** This was not the law of Moses, but oral tradition, based on interpretations of the law.

15:3 ***tradition.*** The scribes and Pharisees were placing their own views above the revelation of God, and yet claimed to be following Him.

14:1 [j] Mk 8:15; Lk 3:1, 19; 13:31; 23:7, 8; Ac 4:27; 12:1 [k] Lk 9:7-9 **14:2** [l] Mt 3:1 **14:3** [m] Mt 4:12; 11:2 [n] Lk 3:19, 20 **14:4** [o] Lev 18:16; 20:21 **14:5** [p] Mt 11:9 **14:10** [q] Mt 17:12 **14:12** [r] Ac 8:2 **14:14** [s] Mt 9:36 [t] Mt 4:23 **14:17** [u] Mt 16:9 **14:19** [v] 1Sa 9:13; Mt 26:26; Mk 8:6; Lk 24:30; Ac 2:42; 27:35; 1Ti 4:4 **14:23** [w] Lk 3:21 **14:26** [x] Lk 24:37 **14:27** [y] Mt 9:2; Ac 23:11 [z] Da 10:12; Mt 17:7; 28:10; Lk 1:13, 30; 2:10; Ac 18:9; 23:11; Rev 1:17 **14:31** [a] Mt 6:30 **14:33** [b] Ps 2:7; Mt 4:3 **14:36** [c] Mt 9:20 **15:2** [d] Lk 11:38

ther and mother'[a][e] and 'Anyone who
curses their father or mother is to be put
to death.'[b][f] 5But you say that if anyone declares that what might have been used to
help their father or mother is 'devoted to
God,' 6they are not to 'honor their father
or mother' with it. Thus you nullify the
word of God for the sake of your tradition.
7You hypocrites! Isaiah was right when he
prophesied about you:

8" 'These people honor me with their lips,
but their hearts are far from me.
9They worship me in vain;
their teachings are merely human
rules.[g]'[c][h]"

10Jesus called the crowd to him and said,
"Listen and understand. 11What goes into
someone's mouth does not defile them,[i] but
what comes out of their mouth, that is what
defiles them."[j]
12Then the disciples came to him and
asked, "Do you know that the Pharisees
were offended when they heard this?"
13He replied, "Every plant that my heavenly Father has not planted[k] will be pulled
up by the roots. 14Leave them; they are
blind guides.[d][l] If the blind lead the blind,
both will fall into a pit."[m]
15Peter said, "Explain the parable to us."[n]
16"Are you still so dull?"[o] Jesus asked
them. 17"Don't you see that whatever enters the mouth goes into the stomach and
then out of the body? 18But the things that
come out of a person's mouth come from
the heart,[p] and these defile them. 19For out
of the heart come evil thoughts—murder,
adultery, sexual immorality, theft, false
testimony, slander.[q] 20These are what defile a person;[r] but eating with unwashed
hands does not defile them."

The Faith of a Canaanite Woman

21Leaving that place, Jesus withdrew to
the region of Tyre and Sidon.[s] 22A Canaanite woman from that vicinity came to him,
crying out, "Lord, Son of David,[t] have mercy on me! My daughter is demon-possessed
and suffering terribly."[u]
23Jesus did not answer a word. So his
disciples came to him and urged him,
"Send her away, for she keeps crying out
after us."
24He answered, "I was sent only to the
lost sheep of Israel."[v]
25The woman came and knelt before
him.[w] "Lord, help me!" she said.
26He replied, "It is not right to take the
children's bread and toss it to the dogs."
27"Yes it is, Lord," she said. "Even the
dogs eat the crumbs that fall from their
master's table."
28Then Jesus said to her, "Woman, you
have great faith![x] Your request is granted." And her daughter was healed at that
moment.

Jesus Feeds the Four Thousand

29Jesus left there and went along the Sea
of Galilee. Then he went up on a mountainside and sat down. 30Great crowds came
to him, bringing the lame, the blind, the
crippled, the mute and many others, and
laid them at his feet; and he healed them.[y]
31The people were amazed when they saw
the mute speaking, the crippled made well,
the lame walking and the blind seeing.
And they praised the God of Israel.[z]
32Jesus called his disciples to him and
said, "I have compassion for these people;[a]
they have already been with me three days
and have nothing to eat. I do not want to
send them away hungry, or they may collapse on the way."
33His disciples answered, "Where could
we get enough bread in this remote place to
feed such a crowd?"
34"How many loaves do you have?" Jesus
asked.
"Seven," they replied, "and a few small
fish."
35He told the crowd to sit down on the
ground. 36Then he took the seven loaves
and the fish, and when he had given

---

a 4 Exodus 20:12; Deut. 5:16 *b* 4 Exodus 21:17; Lev. 20:9 *c* 9 Isaiah 29:13 *d* 14 Some manuscripts *blind guides of the blind*

15:7 *hypocrites.* The Pharisees had laid down many rigid and inflexible laws concerning diet, Sabbath day activities, ceremonial washings, and many other traditions. Not only did this reduce spiritual service to a harsh system of dos and don'ts, it also caused everyone, Pharisees included, to look for loopholes of escape from the burden of so many laws and rules. The ultimate outcome was religious hypocrisy. Christ came both to fulfill the law (5:17–18) and also to free us from its penalty (Gal. 3:13).

15:18 *come from the heart.* As we think in our hearts, or inner beings, so we are. The raw material of our actions is what we take into our minds and allow to settle in our hearts. David put it this way: " I have hidden your word in my heart that I might not sin against you" (Ps. 119:11). The other side is seen in Psalm 101:3 "I will not look with approval on anything that is vile." Paul says the believer must "take captive every thought to make it obedient to Christ" (2 Cor. 10:5).

15:22 *Lord, son of David, have mercy on me.* The woman was a Gentile who would have had no natural claim on the Jewish Messiah.

15:31 *praised the God of Israel.* The Gentiles believed and glorified Israel's God, while many in Israel remained blind to their Messiah.

15:4 [e] Ex 20:12; Dt 5:16; Eph 6:2 [f] Ex 21:17; Lev 20:9 **15:9** [g] Col 2:20-22 [h] Isa 29:13; Mal 2:2 **15:11** [i] Ac 10:14, 15 [j] ver 18 **15:13** [k] Isa 60:21; 61:3; Jn 15:2 **15:14** [l] Mt 23:16, 24; Ro 2:19 [m] Lk 6:39 **15:15** [n] Mt 13:36 **15:16** [o] Mt 16:9 **15:18** [p] Mt 12:34; Lk 6:45; Jas 3:6 **15:19** [q] Gal 5:19-21 **15:20** [r] Ro 14:14 **15:21** [s] Mt 11:21 **15:22** [t] Mt 9:27 [u] Mt 4:24 **15:24** [v] Mt 10:6, 23; Ro 15:8 **15:25** [w] Mt 8:2 **15:28** [x] Mt 9:22 **15:30** [y] Mt 4:23 **15:31** [z] Mt 9:8 **15:32** [a] Mt 9:36

thanks, he broke them[b] and gave them
to the disciples, and they in turn to the
people. 37They all ate and were satisfied.
Afterward the disciples picked up seven
basketfuls of broken pieces that were left
over.[c] 38The number of those who ate was
four thousand men, besides women and
children. 39After Jesus had sent the crowd
away, he got into the boat and went to the
vicinity of Magadan.

The Demand for a Sign

16 The Pharisees and Sadducees[d] came
to Jesus and tested him by asking him
to show them a sign from heaven.[e]
2He replied, "When evening comes, you
say, 'It will be fair weather, for the sky is
red,' 3and in the morning, 'Today it will be
stormy, for the sky is red and overcast.' You
know how to interpret the appearance of
the sky, but you cannot interpret the signs
of the times.[a][f] 4A wicked and adulterous
generation looks for a sign, but none will
be given it except the sign of Jonah."[g] Jesus
then left them and went away.

The Yeast of the Pharisees and Sadducees

5When they went across the lake, the
disciples forgot to take bread. 6"Be careful," Jesus said to them. "Be on your guard
against the yeast of the Pharisees and Sadducees."[h]
7They discussed this among themselves
and said, "It is because we didn't bring any
bread."
8Aware of their discussion, Jesus asked,
"You of little faith,[i] why are you talking
among yourselves about having no bread?
9Do you still not understand? Don't you remember the five loaves for the five thousand, and how many basketfuls you gathered?[j] 10Or the seven loaves for the four
thousand, and how many basketfuls you
gathered?[k] 11How is it you don't understand
that I was not talking to you about bread?
But be on your guard against the yeast of
the Pharisees and Sadducees." 12Then they
understood that he was not telling them to
guard against the yeast used in bread, but
against the teaching of the Pharisees and
Sadducees.[l]

Peter Declares That Jesus Is the Messiah

13When Jesus came to the region of
Caesarea Philippi, he asked his disciples,
"Who do people say the Son of Man is?"
14They replied, "Some say John the Baptist;[m] others say Elijah; and still others, Jeremiah or one of the prophets."[n]
15"But what about you?" he asked. "Who
do you say I am?"
16Simon Peter answered, "You are the
Messiah, the Son of the living God."[o]
17Jesus replied, "Blessed are you, Simon
son of Jonah, for this was not revealed to
you by flesh and blood,[p] but by my Father
in heaven. 18And I tell you that you are
Peter,[b][q] and on this rock I will build my
church,[r] and the gates of Hades[c] will not
overcome it. 19I will give you the keys[s] of
the kingdom of heaven; whatever you bind
on earth will be[d] bound in heaven, and
whatever you loose on earth will be[d] loosed
in heaven."[t] 20Then he ordered his disciples
not to tell anyone[u] that he was the Messiah.

Jesus Predicts His Death

21From that time on Jesus began to explain to his disciples that he must go to
Jerusalem and suffer many things[v] at the
hands of the elders, the chief priests and
the teachers of the law, and that he must
be killed and on the third day[w] be raised
to life.[x]
22Peter took him aside and began to rebuke him. "Never, Lord!" he said. "This
shall never happen to you!"
23Jesus turned and said to Peter, "Get behind me, Satan![y] You are a stumbling block
to me; you do not have in mind the concerns of God, but merely human concerns."
24Then Jesus said to his disciples, "Who-

[a] *2,3* Some early manuscripts do not have *When evening comes . . . of the times.* [b] *18* The Greek word for *Peter* means *rock.* [c] *18* That is, the realm of the dead [d] *19* Or *will have been*

16:11–12 *yeast.* In Scripture, leaven is often used as a symbol of evil. The doctrine of the Pharisees and Sadducees was hypocrisy and legalism, political opportunism, and spiritual hardness.

16:16 Church—Peter's confession "You are the Messiah, the Son of the living God" is the foundation on which the church is built. Never mind how small the apostolic band may be, the church is indestructible, and with unsurpassed power overcomes Satan and cannot be overcome. The power comes from God, the Creator of the universe, Owner and Master of the church. All the church has is derived from and dependent on the Almighty Son of God.

16:18 The Origin of the Church—The church was a mystery (not clearly revealed) in the Old Testament. Christ prophesied in these words spoken to Peter, "on this rock I will build my church." There is a play here on the word *rock,* which also happens to be Peter's name. Jesus said, "you are Peter"(masculine, *petros*) and "on this rock" (feminine, *petra*) "I will build My church." The Holy Spirit came upon the church on the Day of Pentecost in response to Peter's

15:36 [b] Mt 14:19 **15:37** [c] Mt 16:10 **16:1** [d] Ac 4:1 [e] Mt 12:38 **16:3** [f] Lk 12:54-56 **16:4** [g] Mt 12:39 **16:6** [h] Lk 12:1 **16:8** [i] Mt 6:30 **16:9** [j] Mt 14:17-21 **16:10** [k] Mt 15:34-38 **16:12** [l] Ac 4:1 **16:14** [m] Mt 3:1; 14:2 [n] Mk 6:15; Jn 1:21 **16:16** [o] Mt 4:3; Ps 42:2; Jn 11:27; Ac 14:15; 2Co 6:16; 1Th 1:9; 1Ti 3:15; Heb 10:31; 12:22 **16:17** [p] 1Co 15:50; Gal 1:16; Eph 6:12; Heb 2:14 **16:18** [q] Jn 1:42 [r] Eph 2:20 **16:19** [s] Isa 22:22; Rev 3:7 [t] Mt 18:18; Jn 20:23 **16:20** [u] Mk 8:30 **16:21** [v] Mk 10:34; Lk 17:25 [w] Jn 2:19 [x] Mt 17:22,23; 27:63; Mk 9:31; Lk 9:22; 18:31-33; 24:6,7 **16:23** [y] Mt 4:10

ever wants to be my disciple must deny
themselves and take up their cross and follow me.[z] 25For whoever wants to save their
life[a] will lose it, but whoever loses their life
for me will find it.[a] 26What good will it be
for someone to gain the whole world, yet
forfeit their soul? Or what can anyone give
in exchange for their soul? 27For the Son
of Man[b] is going to come[c] in his Father's
glory with his angels, and then he will reward each person according to what they
have done.[d]

28"Truly I tell you, some who are standing here will not taste death before they see
the Son of Man coming in his kingdom."

The Transfiguration

17 After six days Jesus took with him
Peter, James and John the brother of
James, and led them up a high mountain
by themselves. 2There he was transfigured before them. His face shone like the
sun, and his clothes became as white as
the light. 3Just then there appeared before
them Moses and Elijah, talking with Jesus.

4Peter said to Jesus, "Lord, it is good for
us to be here. If you wish, I will put up three
shelters—one for you, one for Moses and
one for Elijah."

5While he was still speaking, a bright
cloud covered them, and a voice from the
cloud said, "This is my Son, whom I love;
with him I am well pleased.[e] Listen to
him!"[f]

6When the disciples heard this, they fell
facedown to the ground, terrified. 7But
Jesus came and touched them. "Get up," he
said. "Don't be afraid."[g] 8When they looked
up, they saw no one except Jesus.

9As they were coming down the mountain, Jesus instructed them, "Don't tell anyone[h] what you have seen, until the Son of
Man[i] has been raised from the dead."[j]

10The disciples asked him, "Why then do
the teachers of the law say that Elijah must
come first?"

11Jesus replied, "To be sure, Elijah comes
and will restore all things.[k] 12But I tell you,
Elijah has already come,[l] and they did not
recognize him, but have done to him everything they wished.[m] In the same way
the Son of Man is going to suffer[n] at their
hands." 13Then the disciples understood
that he was talking to them about John the
Baptist.

Jesus Heals a Demon-Possessed Boy

14When they came to the crowd, a man
approached Jesus and knelt before him.
15"Lord, have mercy on my son," he said.
"He has seizures[o] and is suffering greatly.
He often falls into the fire or into the water.
16I brought him to your disciples, but they
could not heal him."

17"You unbelieving and perverse generation," Jesus replied, "how long shall I stay
with you? How long shall I put up with you?
Bring the boy here to me." 18Jesus rebuked
the demon, and it came out of the boy, and
he was healed at that moment.

19Then the disciples came to Jesus in private and asked, "Why couldn't we drive it
out?"

20He replied, "Because you have so little
faith. Truly I tell you, if you have faith[p] as
small as a mustard seed,[q] you can say to
this mountain, 'Move from here to there,'
and it will move.[r] Nothing will be impossible for you." [21][b]

Jesus Predicts His Death a Second Time

22When they came together in Galilee,
he said to them, "The Son of Man[s] is going to be delivered into the hands of men.
23They will kill him,[t] and on the third day[u]
he will be raised to life."[v] And the disciples
were filled with grief.

The Temple Tax

24After Jesus and his disciples arrived
in Capernaum, the collectors of the two-
drachma temple tax[w] came to Peter and

[a] *25* The Greek word means either *life* or *soul*; also in verse 26. [b] *21* Some manuscripts include here words similar to Mark 9:29.

---

sermon when "three thousand were added to their number" (Acts 2:41). This group, along with the original disciples, became "the church."

16:28 *not taste death.* In the transfiguration, Peter, James, and John saw a preview of the kingdom. Jesus was explaining that very soon those three disciples would see Him glorified as He will be in the kingdom.

17:3 *Moses and Elijah.* This amazing experience was not only to show the disciples that Jesus was God's Son, but also to show them that He supercedes the law and the prophets and that they were subordinate to Him. It also explained that what Jesus was doing was no mystery to the Old Testament. The Old Testament people had been long looking forward to the Messiah and His kingdom.

17:11–13 *Elijah.* Jesus indicates that the prophecies concerning Elijah had their fulfillment in John the Baptist, yet because the restoration is not complete, many conclude that the role of Elijah will be taken up by one of the two witnesses of Revelation 11:3–6.

17:24 *temple tax.* This was a tax given annually by every adult Jewish male over 20 years of age for maintaining the temple. It was based on Exodus 30:13, and amounted to two days' wages for a common laborer.

16:24 [z] Mt 10:38; Lk 14:27 **16:25** [a] Jn 12:25 **16:27** [b] Mt 8:20 [c] Ac 1:11 [d] Job 34:11; Ps 62:12; Jer 17:10; Ro 2:6; 2Co 5:10; Rev 22:12 **17:5** [e] Mt 3:17; 2Pe 1:17 [f] Ac 3:22,23 **17:7** [g] Mt 14:27 **17:9** [h] Mk 8:30 [i] Mt 8:20 [j] Mt 16:21 **17:11** [k] Mal 4:6; Lk 1:16,17 **17:12** [l] Mt 11:14 [m] Mt 14:3,10 [n] Mt 16:21 **17:15** [o] Mt 4:24 **17:20** [p] Mt 21:21 [q] Mt 13:31; Mk 11:23; Lk 17:6 [r] 1Co 13:2 **17:22** [s] Mt 8:20 **17:23** [t] Ac 2:23; 3:13 [u] Mt 16:21 [v] Mt 16:21 **17:24** [w] Ex 30:13

asked, “Doesn’t your teacher pay the temple tax?”

25“Yes, he does,” he replied.

When Peter came into the house, Jesus was the first to speak. “What do you think, Simon?” he asked. “From whom do the kings of the earth collect duty and taxes[x]—from their own children or from others?”

26“From others,” Peter answered.

“Then the children are exempt,” Jesus said to him. 27“But so that we may not cause offense,[y] go to the lake and throw out your line. Take the first fish you catch; open its mouth and you will find a four-drachma coin. Take it and give it to them for my tax and yours.”

The Greatest in the Kingdom of Heaven

18 At that time the disciples came to Jesus and asked, “Who, then, is the greatest in the kingdom of heaven?”

2He called a little child to him, and placed the child among them. 3And he said: “Truly I tell you, unless you change and become like little children,[z] you will never enter the kingdom of heaven.[a] 4Therefore, whoever takes the lowly position of this child is the greatest in the kingdom of heaven.[b] 5And whoever welcomes one such child in my name welcomes me.[c]

Causing to Stumble

6“If anyone causes one of these little ones—those who believe in me—to stumble, it would be better for them to have a large millstone hung around their neck and to be drowned in the depths of the sea.[d] 7Woe to the world because of the things that cause people to stumble! Such things must come, but woe to the person through whom they come![e] 8If your hand or your foot causes you to stumble,[f] cut it off and throw it away. It is better for you to enter life maimed or crippled than to have two hands or two feet and be thrown into eternal fire. 9And if your eye causes you to stumble,[g] gouge it out and throw it away. It is better for you to enter life with one eye than to have two eyes and be thrown into the fire of hell.[h]

The Parable of the Wandering Sheep

10“See that you do not despise one of these little ones. For I tell you that their angels[i] in heaven always see the face of my Father in heaven. [11][a]

12“What do you think? If a man owns a hundred sheep, and one of them wanders away, will he not leave the ninety-nine on the hills and go to look for the one that wandered off? 13And if he finds it, truly I tell you, he is happier about that one sheep than about the ninety-nine that did not wander off. 14In the same way your Father in heaven is not willing that any of these little ones should perish.

Dealing With Sin in the Church

15“If your brother or sister[b] sins,[c] go and point out their fault,[j] just between the two of you. If they listen to you, you have won them over. 16But if they will not listen, take one or two others along, so that ‘every matter may be established by the testimony of two or three witnesses.’[d][k] 17If they still refuse to listen, tell it to the church;[l] and if they refuse to listen even to the church, treat them as you would a pagan or a tax collector.[m]

18“Truly I tell you, whatever you bind on earth will be[e] bound in heaven, and whatever you loose on earth will be[e] loosed in heaven.[n]

19“Again, truly I tell you that if two of you on earth agree about anything they ask for, it will be done for them[o] by my Father in heaven. 20For where two or three gather in my name, there am I with them.”

The Parable of the Unmerciful Servant

21Then Peter came to Jesus and asked, “Lord, how many times shall I forgive my

---

[a] *11* Some manuscripts include here the words of Luke 19:10. [b] *15* The Greek word for *brother or sister* (*adelphos*) refers here to a fellow disciple, whether man or woman; also in verses 21 and 35. [c] *15* Some manuscripts *sins against you* [d] *16* Deut. 19:15 [e] *18* Or *will have been*

17:25 *others.* Most likely this means the king taxed the common people and not the imperial family.

18:3 *change.* Here to "change" means to turn around, to take a different course (Luke 22:32).

18:10 *their angels.* This verse seems to imply that angels watch over and serve His followers on earth (Heb. 1:14).

18:16 *two or three witnesses.* The principle of witnesses is taken from Deuteronomy 19:15. Evidently, in this case they are to witness that the offended brother is acting in good faith and the right spirit in attempting to work towards reconciliation. They would also be witnesses to any agreement.

18:17 *church.* Unfortunately "discipline" has sometimes been reduced to a merely negative concept. To be sure, discipline includes the notion of punishment and correction, but church discipline in this context clearly has the restoration of the offender in view. Severe measures may sometimes need to be taken with an erring brother or sister, but restoration and reconciliation should always be the goal.

17:25 [x] Mt 22:17-21; Ro 13:7 **17:27** [y] Jn 6:61
18:3 [z] Mt 19:14; 1Pe 2:2 [a] Mt 3:2 **18:4** [b] Mk 9:35
18:5 [c] Mt 10:40 **18:6** [d] Mk 9:42; Lk 17:2 **18:7** [e] Lk 17:1
18:8 [f] Mt 5:29; Mk 9:43,45 **18:9** [g] Mt 5:29 [h] Mt 5:22
18:10 [i] Ge 48:16; Ps 34:7; Ac 12:11, 15; Heb 1:14
18:15 [j] Lev 19:17; Lk 17:3; Gal 6:1; Jas 5:19, 20
18:16 [k] Nu 35:30; Dt 17:6; 19:15; Jn 8:17; 2Co 13:1; 1Ti 5:19; Heb 10:28 **18:17** [l] 1Co 6:1-6 [m] Ro 16:17; 2Th 3:6, 14
18:18 [n] Mt 16:19; Jn 20:23 **18:19** [o] Mt 7:7

brother or sister who sins against me?[p] Up
to seven times?"[q]
22 Jesus answered, "I tell you, not seven
times, but seventy-seven times.[a][r]
23 "Therefore, the kingdom of heaven is
like[s] a king who wanted to settle accounts[t]
with his servants. 24 As he began the settlement, a man who owed him ten thousand
bags of gold[b] was brought to him. 25 Since
he was not able to pay,[u] the master ordered
that he and his wife and his children and
all that he had be sold[v] to repay the debt.
26 "At this the servant fell on his knees before him.[w] 'Be patient with me,' he begged,
'and I will pay back everything.' 27 The servant's master took pity on him, canceled
the debt and let him go.
28 "But when that servant went out, he
found one of his fellow servants who owed
him a hundred silver coins.[c] He grabbed
him and began to choke him. 'Pay back
what you owe me!' he demanded.
29 "His fellow servant fell to his knees
and begged him, 'Be patient with me, and I
will pay it back.'
30 "But he refused. Instead, he went off
and had the man thrown into prison until he could pay the debt. 31 When the other servants saw what had happened, they
were outraged and went and told their
master everything that had happened.
32 "Then the master called the servant in.
'You wicked servant,' he said, 'I canceled
all that debt of yours because you begged
me to. 33 Shouldn't you have had mercy on
your fellow servant just as I had on you?'
34 In anger his master handed him over to
the jailers to be tortured, until he should
pay back all he owed.
35 "This is how my heavenly Father will
treat each of you unless you forgive your
brother or sister from your heart."[x]

Divorce

19 When Jesus had finished saying
these things,[y] he left Galilee and went
into the region of Judea to the other side of
the Jordan. 2 Large crowds followed him,
and he healed them[z] there.
3 Some Pharisees came to him to test
him. They asked, "Is it lawful for a man
to divorce his wife[a] for any and every reason?"
4 "Haven't you read," he replied, "that
at the beginning the Creator 'made them
male and female,'[d][b] 5 and said, 'For this
reason a man will leave his father and
mother and be united to his wife, and the
two will become one flesh'[e]?[c] 6 So they are
no longer two, but one flesh. Therefore
what God has joined together, let no one
separate."
7 "Why then," they asked, "did Moses
command that a man give his wife a certificate of divorce and send her away?"[d]
8 Jesus replied, "Moses permitted you to
divorce your wives because your hearts
were hard. But it was not this way from
the beginning. 9 I tell you that anyone who
divorces his wife, except for sexual immorality, and marries another woman commits adultery."[e]
10 The disciples said to him, "If this is the
situation between a husband and wife, it is
better not to marry."
11 Jesus replied, "Not everyone can accept this word, but only those to whom it
has been given.[f] 12 For there are eunuchs
who were born that way, and there are
eunuchs who have been made eunuchs by
others—and there are those who choose to
live like eunuchs for the sake of the kingdom of heaven. The one who can accept
this should accept it."

The Little Children and Jesus

13 Then people brought little children to
Jesus for him to place his hands on them[g]
and pray for them. But the disciples rebuked them.
14 Jesus said, "Let the little children come
to me, and do not hinder them, for the

[a] 22 Or *seventy times seven* [b] 24 Greek *ten thousand talents*; a talent was worth about 20 years of a day laborer's wages. [c] 28 Greek *a hundred denarii*; a denarius was the usual daily wage of a day laborer (see 20:2). [d] 4 Gen. 1:27 [e] 5 Gen. 2:24

18:22 *seventy-seven times.* Some translations say "seventy times seven." Whichever number is used, the point is the same: be ready to forgive over and over again, past counting. This verse does not only apply to forgiveness for seventy-seven times different sins. Sometimes, we may have to consciously decide to forgive and let go of an old hurt again and again, "seventy-seven times."

18:35 *forgive.* This verse is a serious warning (1 John 4:20).

19:9 *divorces his wife.* When the Pharisees asked Jesus if divorce could ever be considered lawful, He did not fall into their trap. He took them back to Genesis and God's original intent in marriage, one man and one woman for life (vv. 4–5; Gen. 1:27; 2:24). In spite of the "exception clause" one thing is surely clear: God hates divorce (Mal. 2:15–16). Marriage is a divine arrangement that is intended to be permanent and inviolable. Straying from God's path always has tragic consequences.

19:12 *eunuchs.* The term eunuch refers to a castrated man, whether by surgery, accident, or birth. In the ancient world, eunuchs were put in charge of harems, because they had the physical strength and endurance of a man, but would not be a sexual threat to the women of the harem.

18:21 [p] Mt 6:14 [q] Lk 17:4 **18:22** [r] Ge 4:24 **18:23** [s] Mt 13:24 [t] Mt 25:19 **18:25** [u] Lk 7:42 [v] Lev 25:39; 2Ki 4:1; Ne 5:5,8 **18:26** [w] Mt 8:2 **18:35** [x] Mt 6:14; Jas 2:13 **19:1** [y] Mt 7:28 **19:2** [z] Mt 4:23 **19:3** [a] Mt 5:31 **19:4** [b] Ge 1:27; 5:2 **19:5** [c] Ge 2:24; 1Co 6:16; Eph 5:31 **19:7** [d] Dt 24:1-4; Mt 5:31 **19:9** [e] Mt 5:32; Lk 16:18 **19:11** [f] Mt 13:11; 1Co 7:7-9, 17 **19:13** [g] Mk 5:23

kingdom of heaven belongs[h] to such as
these."[i] 15 When he had placed his hands
on them, he went on from there.

The Rich and the Kingdom of God

16 Just then a man came up to Jesus and
asked, "Teacher, what good thing must I do
to get eternal life[j]?"[k]

17 "Why do you ask me about what is
good?" Jesus replied. "There is only One
who is good. If you want to enter life, keep
the commandments."[l]

18 "Which ones?" he inquired.

Jesus replied, "'You shall not murder,
you shall not commit adultery,[m] you shall
not steal, you shall not give false testimony, 19 honor your father and mother,'[a][n] and
'love your neighbor as yourself.'[b]"[o]

20 "All these I have kept," the young man
said. "What do I still lack?"

21 Jesus answered, "If you want to be perfect,[p] go, sell your possessions and give to
the poor,[q] and you will have treasure in
heaven.[r] Then come, follow me."

22 When the young man heard this, he
went away sad, because he had great
wealth.

23 Then Jesus said to his disciples, "Truly I tell you, it is hard for someone who
is rich[s] to enter the kingdom of heaven.
24 Again I tell you, it is easier for a camel
to go through the eye of a needle than for
someone who is rich to enter the kingdom
of God."

25 When the disciples heard this, they
were greatly astonished and asked, "Who
then can be saved?"

26 Jesus looked at them and said, "With
man this is impossible, but with God all
things are possible."[t]

27 Peter answered him, "We have left everything to follow you![u] What then will
there be for us?"

28 Jesus said to them, "Truly I tell you, at
the renewal of all things, when the Son of
Man sits on his glorious throne,[v] you who
have followed me will also sit on twelve
thrones, judging the twelve tribes of Israel.[w] 29 And everyone who has left houses
or brothers or sisters or father or mother
or wife[c] or children or fields for my sake
will receive a hundred times as much and
will inherit eternal life.[x] 30 But many who
are first will be last, and many who are last
will be first.[y]

The Parable of the Workers in the Vineyard

20 "For the kingdom of heaven is like[z] a
landowner who went out early in the
morning to hire workers for his vineyard.[a]
2 He agreed to pay them a denarius[d] for the
day and sent them into his vineyard.

3 "About nine in the morning he went out
and saw others standing in the marketplace doing nothing. 4 He told them, 'You
also go and work in my vineyard, and I will
pay you whatever is right.' 5 So they went.

"He went out again about noon and
about three in the afternoon and did the
same thing. 6 About five in the afternoon
he went out and found still others standing around. He asked them, 'Why have
you been standing here all day long doing
nothing?'

7 "'Because no one has hired us,' they answered.

"He said to them, 'You also go and work
in my vineyard.'

8 "When evening came,[b] the owner of
the vineyard said to his foreman, 'Call the
workers and pay them their wages, beginning with the last ones hired and going on
to the first.'

9 "The workers who were hired about five
in the afternoon came and each received a
denarius. 10 So when those came who were
hired first, they expected to receive more.
But each one of them also received a denarius. 11 When they received it, they began to
grumble[c] against the landowner. 12 'These
who were hired last worked only one hour,'
they said, 'and you have made them equal
to us who have borne the burden of the
work and the heat[d] of the day.'

13 "But he answered one of them, 'I am
not being unfair to you, friend.[e] Didn't you
agree to work for a denarius? 14 Take your
pay and go. I want to give the one who was
hired last the same as I gave you. 15 Don't
I have the right to do what I want with my

---

[a] *19* Exodus 20:12-16; Deut. 5:16-20
[b] *19* Lev. 19:18 [c] *29* Some manuscripts do not have *or wife.* [d] *2* A denarius was the usual daily wage of a day laborer.

19:21 ***sell your possessions.*** This verse does not teach salvation by works (Rom. 3:23–24; Eph. 2:8–9). Rather, Jesus was proving that the rich young man could not have truly fulfilled all of the law of Moses. If he really loved his neighbor as the law required (Lev. 19:18), he would not have had any difficulty in giving away his wealth to the poor.

19:23–24 ***it is hard for someone who is rich to enter the kingdom.*** The point of this seems to be that fear of losing one's wealth can hold a person back to the extent that they will never become saved at all. One of the things that goes with being saved is saying, "God's way, not my way."

19:14 [h] Mt 25:34 [i] Mt 18:3; 1Pe 2:2 **19:16** [j] Mt 25:46 [k] Lk 10:25 **19:17** [l] Lev 18:5 **19:18** [m] Jas 2:11 **19:19** [n] Ex 20:12-16; Dt 5:16-20 [o] Lev 19:18; Mt 5:43 **19:21** [p] Mt 5:48 [q] Lk 12:33; Ac 2:45; 4:34-35 [r] Mt 6:20 **19:23** [s] Mt 13:22; 1Ti 6:9, 10 **19:26** [t] Ge 18:14; Job 42:2; Jer 32:17; Zec 8:6; Lk 1:37; 18:27; Ro 4:21 **19:27** [u] Mt 4:19 **19:28** [v] Mt 20:21; 25:31 [w] Lk 22:28-30; Rev 3:21; 4:4; 20:4 **19:29** [x] Mt 6:33; 25:46 **19:30** [y] Mt 20:16; Mk 10:31; Lk 13:30 **20:1** [z] Mt 13:24 [a] Mt 21:28, 33 **20:8** [b] Lev 19:13; Dt 24:15 **20:11** [c] Jnh 4:1 **20:12** [d] Jnh 4:8; Lk 12:55; Jas 1:11 **20:13** [e] Mt 22:12; 26:50

own money? Or are you envious because I am generous?'[f]

16"So the last will be first, and the first will be last."[g]

Jesus Predicts His Death a Third Time

17Now Jesus was going up to Jerusalem. On the way, he took the Twelve aside and said to them, 18"We are going up to Jerusalem,[h] and the Son of Man[i] will be delivered over to the chief priests and the teachers of the law.[j] They will condemn him to death 19and will hand him over to the Gentiles to be mocked and flogged[k] and crucified.[l] On the third day[m] he will be raised to life!"[n]

A Mother's Request

20Then the mother of Zebedee's sons[o] came to Jesus with her sons and, kneeling down,[p] asked a favor of him.

21"What is it you want?" he asked.

She said, "Grant that one of these two sons of mine may sit at your right and the other at your left in your kingdom."[q]

22"You don't know what you are asking," Jesus said to them. "Can you drink the cup[r] I am going to drink?"

"We can," they answered.

23Jesus said to them, "You will indeed drink from my cup,[s] but to sit at my right or left is not for me to grant. These places belong to those for whom they have been prepared by my Father."

24When the ten heard about this, they were indignant[t] with the two brothers. 25Jesus called them together and said, "You know that the rulers of the Gentiles lord it over them, and their high officials exercise authority over them. 26Not so with you. Instead, whoever wants to become great among you must be your servant,[u] 27and whoever wants to be first must be your slave— 28just as the Son of Man[v] did not come to be served, but to serve,[w] and to give his life as a ransom[x] for many."

Two Blind Men Receive Sight

29As Jesus and his disciples were leaving Jericho, a large crowd followed him. 30Two blind men were sitting by the roadside, and when they heard that Jesus was going by, they shouted, "Lord, Son of David,[y] have mercy on us!"

31The crowd rebuked them and told them to be quiet, but they shouted all the louder, "Lord, Son of David, have mercy on us!"

32Jesus stopped and called them. "What do you want me to do for you?" he asked.

33"Lord," they answered, "we want our sight."

34Jesus had compassion on them and touched their eyes. Immediately they received their sight and followed him.

Jesus Comes to Jerusalem as King

21 As they approached Jerusalem and came to Bethphage on the Mount of Olives,[z] Jesus sent two disciples, 2saying to them, "Go to the village ahead of you, and at once you will find a donkey tied there, with her colt by her. Untie them and bring them to me. 3If anyone says anything to you, say that the Lord needs them, and he will send them right away."

4This took place to fulfill what was spoken through the prophet:

5"Say to Daughter Zion,
'See, your king comes to you,
gentle and riding on a donkey,
and on a colt, the foal of a donkey.'"[a][a]

6The disciples went and did as Jesus had instructed them. 7They brought the donkey and the colt and placed their cloaks on them for Jesus to sit on. 8A very large crowd spread their cloaks[b] on the road, while others cut branches from the trees and spread them on the road. 9The crowds that went ahead of him and those that followed shouted,

"Hosanna[b] to the Son of David!"[c]

"Blessed is he who comes in the name of the Lord!"[c][d]

"Hosanna[b] in the highest heaven!"[e]

10When Jesus entered Jerusalem, the whole city was stirred and asked, "Who is this?"

---

[a] 5 Zech. 9:9 [b] 9 A Hebrew expression meaning "Save!" which became an exclamation of praise; also in verse 15 [c] 9 Psalm 118:25,26

20:16 *the last will be first.* The workers who were collected without an agreement represent the Gentiles who are made equal with the Jewish people when salvation became available to all through Jesus Christ (Rom. 11:15; Eph. 2:13 – 15; 3:6).

20:26 – 27 *whoever wants to become great.* The measure of greatness is not position, power, or prestige. It is service.

21:2 *a donkey tied.* This was prophesied in Zechariah 9:9.

21:9 *Hosanna.* Hosanna literally means "save now." The people were using it as an exclamation of joyous praise, but also they expected the Messiah to save them from the oppression of the Romans.

20:15 [f] Dt 15:9; Mk 7:22 **20:16** [g] Mt 19:30 **20:18** [h] Lk 9:51 [i] Mt 8:20 [j] Mt 16:21; 27:1, 2 **20:19** [k] Mt 16:21 [l] Ac 2:23 [m] Mt 16:21 [n] Mt 16:21 **20:20** [o] Mt 4:21 [p] Mt 8:2 **20:21** [q] Mt 19:28 **20:22** [r] Isa 51:17, 22; Jer 49:12; Mt 26:39, 42; Mk 14:36; Lk 22:42; Jn 18:11 **20:23** [s] Ac 12:2; Rev 1:9 **20:24** [t] Lk 22:24, 25 **20:26** [u] Mt 23:11; Mk 9:35 **20:28** [v] Mt 8:20 [w] Lk 22:27; Jn 13:13-16; 2Co 8:9; Php 2:7 [x] Isa 53:10; Mt 26:28; 1Ti 2:6; Titus 2:14; Heb 9:28; 1Pe 1:18, 19 **20:30** [y] Mt 9:27 **21:1** [z] Mt 24:3; 26:30; Mk 14:26; Lk 19:37; 21:37; 22:39; Jn 8:1; Ac 1:12 **21:5** [a] Isa 62:11; Zec 9:9 **21:8** [b] 2Ki 9:13 **21:9** [c] ver 15; Mt 9:27 [d] Ps 118:26; Mt 23:39 [e] Lk 2:14

11The crowds answered, "This is Jesus,
the prophet[f] from Nazareth in Galilee."

Jesus at the Temple

12Jesus entered the temple courts and
drove out all who were buying[g] and selling there. He overturned the tables of the
money changers[h] and the benches of those
selling doves.[i] 13"It is written," he said to
them, "'My house will be called a house of
prayer,'[a][j] but you are making it 'a den of
robbers.'[b][k]

14The blind and the lame came to him
at the temple, and he healed them.[l] 15But
when the chief priests and the teachers of
the law saw the wonderful things he did
and the children shouting in the temple
courts, "Hosanna to the Son of David,"[m]
they were indignant.[n]

16"Do you hear what these children are
saying?" they asked him.

"Yes," replied Jesus, "have you never
read,

"'From the lips of children and infants
you, Lord, have called forth your
praise'[c]?"[o]

17And he left them and went out of the
city to Bethany,[p] where he spent the night.

Jesus Curses a Fig Tree

18Early in the morning, as Jesus was on
his way back to the city, he was hungry.
19Seeing a fig tree by the road, he went up
to it but found nothing on it except leaves.
Then he said to it, "May you never bear
fruit again!" Immediately the tree withered.[q]

20When the disciples saw this, they were
amazed. "How did the fig tree wither so
quickly?" they asked.

21Jesus replied, "Truly I tell you, if you
have faith and do not doubt,[r] not only can
you do what was done to the fig tree, but
also you can say to this mountain, 'Go,
throw yourself into the sea,' and it will
be done. 22If you believe, you will receive
whatever you ask for[s] in prayer."

The Authority of Jesus Questioned

23Jesus entered the temple courts, and,
while he was teaching, the chief priests
and the elders of the people came to him.
"By what authority[t] are you doing these
things?" they asked. "And who gave you
this authority?"

24Jesus replied, "I will also ask you one
question. If you answer me, I will tell you
by what authority I am doing these things.
25John's baptism—where did it come from?
Was it from heaven, or of human origin?"

They discussed it among themselves and
said, "If we say, 'From heaven,' he will ask,
'Then why didn't you believe him?' 26But if
we say, 'Of human origin'—we are afraid
of the people, for they all hold that John
was a prophet."[u]

27So they answered Jesus, "We don't
know."

Then he said, "Neither will I tell you by
what authority I am doing these things.

The Parable of the Two Sons

28"What do you think? There was a man
who had two sons. He went to the first and
said, 'Son, go and work today in the vineyard.'[v]

29"'I will not,' he answered, but later he
changed his mind and went.

30"Then the father went to the other son
and said the same thing. He answered, 'I
will, sir,' but he did not go.

31"Which of the two did what his father
wanted?"

"The first," they answered.

Jesus said to them, "Truly I tell you, the
tax collectors[w] and the prostitutes[x] are entering the kingdom of God ahead of you.
32For John came to you to show you the
way of righteousness,[y] and you did not believe him, but the tax collectors[z] and the
prostitutes[a] did. And even after you saw
this, you did not repent[b] and believe him.

The Parable of the Tenants

33"Listen to another parable: There was
a landowner who planted[c] a vineyard. He
put a wall around it, dug a winepress in it
and built a watchtower.[d] Then he rented
the vineyard to some farmers and moved
to another place.[e] 34When the harvest time
approached, he sent his servants[f] to the
tenants to collect his fruit.

---

[a] *13* Isaiah 56:7 [b] *13* Jer. 7:11 [c] *16* Psalm 8:2 (see Septuagint)

21:19 ***Immediately.*** This does not necessarily mean instantly; it may have the idea of "very soon" as in Luke 19:11. (The account of this miracle in Mark 11:12–14,20–21 indicates some time passing.)

21:21 ***faith.*** Few if any besides our Savior will reach this kind of faith in its fullness. However, as each believer approaches such faith in prayer, his effort will be rewarded. Answers are always given, even to the feeblest prayers of faith.

21:33 ***planted a vineyard.*** The owner of the vineyard was God; the vinedressers were the people of Israel. The servants represent God's messengers, and the son is Jesus the Messiah.

21:11 [f] Lk 7:16,39; 24:19; Jn 1:21,25; 6:14; 7:40
21:12 [g] Dt 14:26 [h] Ex 30:13 [i] Lev 1:14 **21:13** [j] Isa 56:7 [k] Jer 7:11 **21:14** [l] Mt 4:23 **21:15** [m] ver 9; Mt 9:27 [n] Lk 19:39 **21:16** [o] Ps 8:2 **21:17** [p] Mt 26:6; Mk 11:1; Lk 24:50; Jn 11:1,18; 12:1 **21:19** [q] Isa 34:4; Jer 8:13
21:21 [r] Mt 17:20; Lk 17:6; 1Co 13:2; Jas 1:6
21:22 [s] Mt 7:7 **21:23** [t] Ac 4:7; 7:27 **21:26** [u] Mt 11:9; Mk 6:20 **21:28** [v] ver 33; Mt 20:1 **21:31** [w] Lk 7:29 [x] Lk 7:50 **21:32** [y] Mt 3:1-12 [z] Lk 3:12,13; 7:29 [a] Lk 7:36-50 [b] Lk 7:30 **21:33** [c] Ps 80:8 [d] Isa 5:1-7 [e] Mt 25:14,15 **21:34** [f] Mt 22:3

35“The tenants seized his servants;
they beat one, killed another, and stoned
a third.[g] 36Then he sent other servants[h] to
them, more than the first time, and the tenants treated them the same way. 37Last of
all, he sent his son to them. ‘They will respect my son,’ he said.
38“But when the tenants saw the son,
they said to each other, ‘This is the heir.[i]
Come, let’s kill him[j] and take his inheritance.’[k] 39So they took him and threw him
out of the vineyard and killed him.
40“Therefore, when the owner of the
vineyard comes, what will he do to those
tenants?”
41“He will bring those wretches to a
wretched end,”[l] they replied, “and he will
rent the vineyard to other tenants,[m] who
will give him his share of the crop at harvest time.”
42Jesus said to them, “Have you never
read in the Scriptures:

“ ‘The stone the builders rejected
has become the cornerstone;
the Lord has done this,
and it is marvelous in our eyes’[a]?[n]

43“Therefore I tell you that the kingdom
of God will be taken away from you[o] and
given to a people who will produce its fruit.
44Anyone who falls on this stone will be
broken to pieces; anyone on whom it falls
will be crushed.”[b][p]
45When the chief priests and the Pharisees heard Jesus’ parables, they knew he
was talking about them. 46They looked for
a way to arrest him, but they were afraid of
the crowd because the people held that he
was a prophet.[q]

The Parable of the Wedding Banquet

22 Jesus spoke to them again in parables, saying: 2“The kingdom of heav-
en is like[r] a king who prepared a wedding
banquet for his son. 3He sent his servants[s]
to those who had been invited to the banquet to tell them to come, but they refused
to come.
4“Then he sent some more servants[t] and
said, ‘Tell those who have been invited that
I have prepared my dinner: My oxen and
fattened cattle have been butchered, and
everything is ready. Come to the wedding
banquet.’
5“But they paid no attention and went
off—one to his field, another to his business. 6The rest seized his servants, mistreated them and killed them. 7The king
was enraged. He sent his army and destroyed those murderers[u] and burned their
city.
8“Then he said to his servants, ‘The
wedding banquet is ready, but those I invited did not deserve to come. 9So go to the
street corners[v] and invite to the banquet
anyone you find.’ 10So the servants went
out into the streets and gathered all the
people they could find, the bad as well as
the good,[w] and the wedding hall was filled
with guests.
11“But when the king came in to see
the guests, he noticed a man there who
was not wearing wedding clothes. 12He
asked, ‘How did you get in here without
wedding clothes, friend[x]?’ The man was
speechless.
13“Then the king told the attendants, ‘Tie
him hand and foot, and throw him outside,
into the darkness, where there will be
weeping and gnashing of teeth.’[y]
14“For many are invited, but few are chosen.”[z]

Paying the Imperial Tax to Caesar

15Then the Pharisees went out and laid
plans to trap him in his words. 16They sent
their disciples to him along with the Herodians.[a] “Teacher,” they said, “we know
that you are a man of integrity and that
you teach the way of God in accordance
with the truth. You aren’t swayed by others, because you pay no attention to who
they are. 17Tell us then, what is your opinion? Is it right to pay the imperial tax[c][b] to
Caesar or not?”
18But Jesus, knowing their evil intent,
said, “You hypocrites, why are you trying
to trap me? 19Show me the coin used for
paying the tax.” They brought him a denarius, 20and he asked them, “Whose image is
this? And whose inscription?”

---

a *42* Psalm 118:22,23 *b* *44* Some manuscripts do not have verse 44. *c* *17* A special tax levied on subject peoples, not on Roman citizens

---

21:42 ***cornerstone.*** The rejected stone was the Messiah, who became the head cornerstone, the one holding the whole building together (Ps. 118:22–23).
22:11 ***not wearing wedding clothes.*** Like the others, this visitor had been invited to the wedding, but he failed to prepare himself for it. In Revelation, the garment of fine linen worn by the bride of the Lamb is said to be the righteous deeds of the saints (Rev. 19:8). In this parable the garment may refer to the righteousness of Christ, graciously provided for us through His death. To refuse to put it on would mean a refusal of Christ’s sacrifice.
22:14 ***many are invited, but few are chosen.*** All Israel has been invited, but only a few will accept and follow Jesus. Not all those invited will be among the chosen of God, for not all will believe.

21:35 [g] 2Ch 24:21; Mt 23:34, 37; Heb 11:36, 37
21:36 [h] Mt 22:4 **21:38** [i] Heb 1:2 [j] Mt 12:14 [k] Ps 2:8
21:41 [l] Mt 8:11, 12 [m] Ac 13:46; 18:6; 28:28
21:42 [n] Ps 118:22, 23; Ac 4:11; 1Pe 2:7 **21:43** [o] Mt 8:12
21:44 [p] Lk 2:34 **21:46** [q] ver 11, 26 **22:2** [r] Mt 13:24
22:3 [s] Mt 21:34 **22:4** [t] Mt 21:36 **22:7** [u] Lk 19:27
22:9 [v] Eze 21:21 **22:10** [w] Mt 13:47, 48
22:12 [x] Mt 20:13; 26:50 **22:13** [y] Mt 8:12
22:14 [z] Rev 17:14 **22:16** [a] Mk 3:6 **22:17** [b] Mt 17:25

21"Caesar's," they replied.
Then he said to them, "So give back to
Caesar what is Caesar's,[c] and to God what
is God's."
22When they heard this, they were
amazed. So they left him and went away.[d]

Marriage at the Resurrection

23That same day the Sadducees,[e] who
say there is no resurrection,[f] came to him
with a question. 24"Teacher," they said,
"Moses told us that if a man dies without
having children, his brother must marry
the widow and raise up offspring for him.[g]
25Now there were seven brothers among
us. The first one married and died, and
since he had no children, he left his wife
to his brother. 26The same thing happened
to the second and third brother, right on
down to the seventh. 27Finally, the woman died. 28Now then, at the resurrection,
whose wife will she be of the seven, since
all of them were married to her?"
29Jesus replied, "You are in error because you do not know the Scriptures[h] or
the power of God. 30At the resurrection
people will neither marry nor be given in
marriage;[i] they will be like the angels in
heaven. 31But about the resurrection of the
dead—have you not read what God said to
you, 32'I am the God of Abraham, the God
of Isaac, and the God of Jacob'[a]?[j] He is not
the God of the dead but of the living."
33When the crowds heard this, they were
astonished at his teaching.[k]

The Greatest Commandment

34Hearing that Jesus had silenced the
Sadducees,[l] the Pharisees got together.
35One of them, an expert in the law,[m] tested
him with this question: 36"Teacher, which
is the greatest commandment in the Law?"
37Jesus replied: "'Love the Lord your
God with all your heart and with all your
soul and with all your mind.'[b][n] 38This is
the first and greatest commandment.
39And the second is like it: 'Love your
neighbor as yourself.'[c][o] 40All the Law
and the Prophets hang on these two commandments."[p]

Whose Son Is the Messiah?

41While the Pharisees were gathered
together, Jesus asked them, 42"What do
you think about the Messiah? Whose son
is he?"
"The son of David,"[q] they replied.
43He said to them, "How is it then that
David, speaking by the Spirit, calls him
'Lord'? For he says,

44"'The Lord said to my Lord:
"Sit at my right hand
until I put your enemies
under your feet."'[d][r]

45If then David calls him 'Lord,' how can he
be his son?" 46No one could say a word in
reply, and from that day on no one dared to
ask him any more questions.[s]

A Warning Against Hypocrisy

23 Then Jesus said to the crowds and to
his disciples: 2"The teachers of the
law[t] and the Pharisees sit in Moses' seat.
3So you must be careful to do everything
they tell you. But do not do what they do,
for they do not practice what they preach.
4They tie up heavy, cumbersome loads and
put them on other people's shoulders, but
they themselves are not willing to lift a finger to move them.[u]
5"Everything they do is done for peo-
ple to see:[v] They make their phylacteries[e][w]
wide and the tassels on their garments[x]
long; 6they love the place of honor at banquets and the most important seats in
the synagogues;[y] 7they love to be greeted
with respect in the marketplaces and to be
called 'Rabbi' by others.[z]
8"But you are not to be called 'Rabbi,'
for you have one Teacher, and you are all
brothers. 9And do not call anyone on earth

[a] *32* Exodus 3:6 [b] *37* Deut. 6:5 [c] *39* Lev. 19:18
[d] *44* Psalm 110:1 [e] *5* That is, boxes containing Scripture verses, worn on forehead and arm

22:21 *what is Caesar's.* When one subjects oneself to the state and accepts its protection and benefits, one is obligated to support it and obey its laws until it becomes sinful to do so (Rom. 13:1–7; 1 Pet. 2:13–17). But giving back to God what is His reaches far deeper than obedience to the state. Man has a duty to give himself to God, with all he is and all that he has.

22:42–45 *Messiah? Whose son is He?* The Old Testament foretold that the Messiah would come from David's royal line (2 Sam. 7:12–16; Ps. 89:3–4,34–36; Is. 9:7; 16:5; 55:3–4).

22:44 *The Lord said to my Lord.* The Hebrew text of Psalm 110:1 uses two different Hebrew words for "Lord." The first, translated "LORD," is the name Yahweh, the proper name of Israel's God. The second "Lord" means "master." David, the great king of Israel, calls one of his offspring "Lord" or "master." The implication is that Jesus, the Son of David, is divine.

23:5 *phylacteries.* Phylacteries were small boxes containing specific Scripture passages, in fulfillment of Deuteronomy 6:8 (Ex. 13:9,16; Prov. 3:3; 6:21; 7:3). They were worn on the forehead or arm. In order to be seen as especially righteous, some Pharisees wore conspicuously large phylacteries.

23:7 *Rabbi.* The title "rabbi" means "teacher."

22:21 [c] Ro 13:7 **22:22** [d] Mk 12:12 **22:23** [e] Ac 4:1 [f] Ac 23:8; 1Co 15:12 **22:24** [g] Dt 25:5,6 **22:29** [h] Jn 20:9 **22:30** [i] Mt 24:38 **22:32** [j] Ex 3:6; Ac 7:32 **22:33** [k] Mt 7:28 **22:34** [l] Ac 4:1 **22:35** [m] Lk 7:30; 10:25; 11:45; 14:3 **22:37** [n] Dt 6:5 **22:39** [o] Lev 19:18; Mt 5:43; 19:19; Gal 5:14 **22:40** [p] Mt 7:12 **22:42** [q] Mt 9:27 **22:44** [r] Ps 110:1; Ac 2:34,35; 1Co 15:25; Heb 1:13; 10:13 **22:46** [s] Mk 12:34; Lk 20:40 **23:2** [t] Ezr 7:6,25; Ne 8:4 **23:4** [u] Lk 11:46; Ac 15:10; Gal 6:13 **23:5** [v] Mt 6:1,2,5,16 [w] Ex 13:9; Dt 6:8 [x] Nu 15:38; Dt 22:12 **23:6** [y] Lk 11:43; 14:7; 20:46 **23:7** [z] ver 8; Mk 9:5; 10:51; Jn 1:38,49

'father,' for you have one Father,[a] and he is in heaven. 10Nor are you to be called instructors, for you have one Instructor, the Messiah. 11The greatest among you will be your servant.[b] 12For those who exalt themselves will be humbled, and those who humble themselves will be exalted.[c]

Seven Woes on the Teachers of the Law and the Pharisees

13"Woe to you, teachers of the law and Pharisees, you hypocrites![d] You shut the door of the kingdom of heaven in people's faces. You yourselves do not enter, nor will you let those enter who are trying to.[e] [14][a]

15"Woe to you, teachers of the law and Pharisees, you hypocrites! You travel over land and sea to win a single convert,[f] and when you have succeeded, you make them twice as much a child of hell[g] as you are.

16"Woe to you, blind guides![h] You say, 'If anyone swears by the temple, it means nothing; but anyone who swears by the gold of the temple is bound by that oath.'[i] 17You blind fools! Which is greater: the gold, or the temple that makes the gold sacred?[j] 18You also say, 'If anyone swears by the altar, it means nothing; but anyone who swears by the gift on the altar is bound by that oath.' 19You blind men! Which is greater: the gift, or the altar that makes the gift sacred?[k] 20Therefore, anyone who swears by the altar swears by it and by everything on it. 21And anyone who swears by the temple swears by it and by the one who dwells[l] in it. 22And anyone who swears by heaven swears by God's throne and by the one who sits on it.[m]

23"Woe to you, teachers of the law and Pharisees, you hypocrites! You give a tenth[n] of your spices—mint, dill and cumin. But you have neglected the more important matters of the law—justice, mercy and faithfulness.[o] You should have practiced the latter, without neglecting the former. 24You blind guides![p] You strain out a gnat but swallow a camel.

25"Woe to you, teachers of the law and Pharisees, you hypocrites! You clean the outside of the cup and dish,[q] but inside they are full of greed and self-indulgence.[r] 26Blind Pharisee! First clean the inside of the cup and dish, and then the outside also will be clean.

27"Woe to you, teachers of the law and Pharisees, you hypocrites! You are like whitewashed tombs,[s] which look beautiful on the outside but on the inside are full of the bones of the dead and everything unclean. 28In the same way, on the outside you appear to people as righteous but on the inside you are full of hypocrisy and wickedness.

29"Woe to you, teachers of the law and Pharisees, you hypocrites! You build tombs for the prophets[t] and decorate the graves of the righteous. 30And you say, 'If we had lived in the days of our ancestors, we would not have taken part with them in shedding the blood of the prophets.' 31So you testify against yourselves that you are the descendants of those who murdered the prophets.[u] 32Go ahead, then, and complete[v] what your ancestors started!

33"You snakes! You brood of vipers![w] How will you escape being condemned to hell?[x] 34Therefore I am sending you prophets and sages and teachers. Some of them you will kill and crucify;[y] others you will flog in your synagogues[z] and pursue from town to town.[a] 35And so upon you will come all the righteous blood that has been shed on earth, from the blood of righteous Abel[b] to the blood of Zechariah son of Berekiah,[c] whom you murdered between the temple and the altar.[d] 36Truly I tell you, all this will come on this generation.[e]

37"Jerusalem, Jerusalem, you who kill the prophets and stone those sent to you,[f] how often I have longed to gather your children together, as a hen gathers her chicks under her wings, and you were not willing. 38Look, your house is left to you desolate.[g] 39For I tell you, you will not see me again until you say, 'Blessed is he who comes in the name of the Lord.'[b][h]

---

a 14 Some manuscripts include here words similar to Mark 12:40 and Luke 20:47. *b 39* Psalm 118:26

23:10 *Nor are you to be called instructors.* This verse is a warning against the human tendency to replace a personal relationship with God with following an earthly leader. No matter how dynamic or even how godly such a leader is, as soon as people start looking to that person rather than to God, they have created an idol.

23:24 *swallow a camel.* The Pharisees would literally "strain out a gnat" in order not to violate Leviticus 11:41–43, but they swallowed "a camel" by neglecting mercy, justice, and faith.

23:25–26 *but inside.* The inside of the cup represents a person's character. Sometimes those who most loudly protest the sins of others are secretly guilty of those or worse sins themselves.

23:35 *Abel.* Abel was the first person murdered in the Old Testament (Gen. 4:8); Zechariah was the last. His death is recorded in 2 Chronicles 24:20–22, the last book of the Hebrew canon.

23:9 [a] Mal 1:6; Mt 7:11 **23:11** [b] Mt 20:26; Mk 9:35 **23:12** [c] Lk 14:11 **23:13** [d] ver 15,23,25,27,29 [e] Lk 11:52 **23:15** [f] Ac 2:11; 6:5; 13:43 [g] Mt 5:22 **23:16** [h] ver 24; Mt 15:14 [i] Mt 5:33-35 **23:17** [j] Ex 30:29 **23:19** [k] Ex 29:37 **23:21** [l] 1Ki 8:13; Ps 26:8 **23:22** [m] Ps 11:4; Mt 5:34 **23:23** [n] Lev 27:30 [o] Mic 6:8; Lk 11:42 **23:24** [p] ver 16 **23:25** [q] Mk 7:4 [r] Lk 11:39 **23:27** [s] Lk 11:44; Ac 23:3 **23:29** [t] Lk 11:47,48 **23:31** [u] Ac 7:51-52 **23:32** [v] 1Th 2:16 **23:33** [w] Mt 3:7; 12:34 [x] Mt 5:22 **23:34** [y] 2Ch 36:15, 16; Lk 11:49 [z] Mt 10:17 [a] Mt 10:23 **23:35** [b] Ge 4:8; Heb 11:4 [c] Zec 1:1 [d] 2Ch 24:21 **23:36** [e] Mt 10:23; 24:34 **23:37** [f] 2Ch 24:21; Mt 5:12 **23:38** [g] 1Ki 9:7,8; Jer 22:5 **23:39** [h] Ps 118:26; Mt 21:9

The Destruction of the Temple and Signs of the End Times

24 Jesus left the temple and was walking away when his disciples came up
to him to call his attention to its buildings.
2"Do you see all these things?" he asked.
"Truly I tell you, not one stone here will be
left on another;[i] every one will be thrown
down."
3As Jesus was sitting on the Mount of Olives,[j] the disciples came to him privately.
"Tell us," they said, "when will this happen,
and what will be the sign of your coming
and of the end of the age?"
4Jesus answered: "Watch out that no one
deceives you. 5For many will come in my
name, claiming, 'I am the Messiah,' and
will deceive many.[k] 6You will hear of wars
and rumors of wars, but see to it that you
are not alarmed. Such things must happen,
but the end is still to come. 7Nation will rise
against nation, and kingdom against kingdom.[l] There will be famines[m] and earthquakes in various places. 8All these are the
beginning of birth pains.
9"Then you will be handed over to be
persecuted[n] and put to death,[o] and you will
be hated by all nations because of me. 10At
that time many will turn away from the
faith and will betray and hate each other,
11and many false prophets[p] will appear
and deceive many people. 12Because of the
increase of wickedness, the love of most
will grow cold, 13but the one who stands
firm to the end will be saved.[q] 14And this
gospel of the kingdom[r] will be preached in
the whole world[s] as a testimony to all nations, and then the end will come.
15"So when you see standing in the holy
place[t] 'the abomination that causes desolation,'[a][u] spoken of through the prophet Daniel—let the reader understand—
16then let those who are in Judea flee to
the mountains. 17Let no one on the housetop[v] go down to take anything out of the
house. 18Let no one in the field go back to
get their cloak. 19How dreadful it will be in
those days for pregnant women and nursing mothers![w] 20Pray that your flight will
not take place in winter or on the Sabbath.
21For then there will be great distress, unequaled from the beginning of the world
until now—and never to be equaled again.[x]
22"If those days had not been cut short,
no one would survive, but for the sake of
the elect[y] those days will be shortened. 23At
that time if anyone says to you, 'Look, here
is the Messiah!' or, 'There he is!' do not
believe it.[z] 24For false messiahs and false
prophets will appear and perform great
signs and wonders[a] to deceive, if possible,
even the elect. 25See, I have told you ahead
of time.
26"So if anyone tells you, 'There he is, out

[a] *15* Daniel 9:27; 11:31; 12:11

24:1 *temple.* The first temple, built by Solomon, was destroyed by the Babylonians in 586 B.C. The second temple, built under the encouragement of Haggai and Zechariah, and the leadership of Zerubbabel and Joshua (Hag. 1:1), was completed after considerable delay in 516 B.C. This second temple was lavishly restored by Herod the Great, but not completed until A.D. 64. It stood completed for only six years before it was reduced to rubble by the Romans. The devastation in A.D. 70 was so complete that the precise location is still unknown today.
24:4 *Watch out that no one deceives you.* Jesus' warning about being deceived was especially appropriate for the disciples. The destruction of Jerusalem did not necessarily mean the nearness of the end of the age. This principle was a point of confusion for them (Luke 19:11–27; Acts 1:6–7).
24:6 *must happen.* This indicates a divine or logical necessity. Such things will happen because of the people's sin. False messiahs had existed before (Acts 5:36–38) and false preachers would come in the future (Acts 20:29; 2 Cor. 11:13–15). Verses 4–6 may describe the first part of Daniel's seventieth week (Dan. 9:25–27), but possibly they present a general picture of the present age.
24:7 *famines and earthquakes.* These disasters are more fully described in Revelation 6:1–8; 8:5–23; 9:13–21; 16:2–21).
24:10 Apostasy—Satan is a subtle adversary who works as an angel of light through false religious teachers (2 Cor. 11:14–15), and many will be misled. Apostasy is also the result of persecution. Jesus speaks of "temporary" faith, and says that a falling away often occurs when "trouble or persecution comes because of the word" (13:21). Perseverance in faith and in the accompanying results of faith are positive evidence of a genuine Christian profession.
24:15 *abomination that causes desolation.* This prophecy comes from Daniel, specifically Daniel 9:27; 11:31; 12:11. Many believe that Daniel 11:31 refers to Antiochus IV, who desecrated the temple by sacrificing a pig on its altar and setting up an idol to Zeus in it. His actions were certainly a prelude to what the ultimate "man of sin" will do. In A.D. 70, Titus destroyed Jerusalem, burned the temple, and set up an idol to mock the Jews. Significantly, Paul speaks of the Antichrist at the end times also setting himself up as a god (2 Thess. 2:3–4; Rev. 13:14–15).
24:16 *flee.* At the time of the war ending in the destruction of the temple in A.D. 70, many of the Christians did flee, hiding in the clefts of Petra. Some believe that the final fulfillment of this prophecy will occur in the future desecration of the temple (Dan. 9:27) and the subsequent setting up of an image of the "man of sin" in the Most Holy Place.
24:24 *signs and wonders.* Miracles by themselves do not prove that something is of God (7:21–23; 2 Thess. 2:9; Rev. 13:13–15). The teaching of those

24:2 [i] Lk 19:44 **24:3** [j] Mt 21:1 **24:5** [k] ver 11, 23, 24; 1Jn 2:18 **24:7** [l] Isa 19:2 [m] Ac 11:28 **24:9** [n] Mt 10:17 [o] Jn 16:2 **24:11** [p] Mt 7:15 **24:13** [q] Mt 10:22 **24:14** [r] Mt 4:23 [s] Lk 2:1; 4:5; Ac 11:28; 17:6; Ro 10:18; Col 1:6, 23; Rev 3:10; 16:14 **24:15** [t] Ac 6:13 [u] Da 9:27; 11:31; 12:11 **24:17** [v] 1Sa 9:25; Mt 10:27; Lk 12:3; Ac 10:9 **24:19** [w] Lk 23:29 **24:21** [x] Da 12:1; Joel 2:2 **24:22** [y] ver 24, 31 **24:23** [z] Lk 17:23; 21:8 **24:24** [a] 2Th 2:9-11; Rev 13:13

in the wilderness,' do not go out; or, 'Here he is, in the inner rooms,' do not believe it. 27 For as lightning[b] that comes from the east is visible even in the west, so will be the coming of the Son of Man.[c] 28 Wherever there is a carcass, there the vultures will gather.[d]

29 "Immediately after the distress of those days

"'the sun will be darkened,
  and the moon will not give its light;
the stars will fall from the sky,
  and the heavenly bodies will be
    shaken.'[ae]

30 "Then will appear the sign of the Son of Man in heaven. And then all the peoples of the earth[b] will mourn when they see the Son of Man coming on the clouds of heaven,[f] with power and great glory.[c] 31 And he will send his angels[g] with a loud trumpet call,[h] and they will gather his elect from the four winds, from one end of the heavens to the other.

32 "Now learn this lesson from the fig tree: As soon as its twigs get tender and its leaves come out, you know that summer is near. 33 Even so, when you see all these things, you know that it[d] is near, right at the door.[i] 34 Truly I tell you, this generation will certainly not pass away until all these things have happened.[j] 35 Heaven and earth will pass away, but my words will never pass away.[k]

The Day and Hour Unknown

36 "But about that day or hour no one knows, not even the angels in heaven, nor the Son,[e] but only the Father.[l] 37 As it was in the days of Noah,[m] so it will be at the coming of the Son of Man. 38 For in the days before the flood, people were eating and drinking, marrying and giving in marriage,[n] up to the day Noah entered the ark; 39 and they knew nothing about what would happen until the flood came and took them all away. That is how it will be at the coming of the Son of Man. 40 Two men will be in the field; one will be taken and the other left.[o] 41 Two women will be grinding with a hand mill; one will be taken and the other left.[p]

42 "Therefore keep watch, because you do not know on what day your Lord will come.[q] 43 But understand this: If the owner of the house had known at what time of night the thief was coming,[r] he would have kept watch and would not have let his house be broken into. 44 So you also must be ready,[s] because the Son of Man will come at an hour when you do not expect him.

45 "Who then is the faithful and wise servant,[t] whom the master has put in charge of the servants in his household to give them their food at the proper time? 46 It will be good for that servant whose master finds him doing so when he returns.[u] 47 Truly I tell you, he will put him in charge of all his possessions.[v] 48 But suppose that servant is wicked and says to himself, 'My master is staying away a long time,' 49 and he then begins to beat his fellow servants and to eat and drink with drunkards.[w] 50 The master of that servant will come on a day when he does not expect him and at an hour he is not aware of. 51 He will cut him to pieces and assign him a place with the hypocrites, where there will be weeping and gnashing of teeth.[x]

The Parable of the Ten Virgins

25 "At that time the kingdom of heaven will be like[y] ten virgins who took their lamps[z] and went out to meet the bridegroom.[a] 2 Five of them were foolish and five were wise.[b] 3 The foolish ones took their lamps but did not take any oil with them. 4 The wise ones, however, took oil in jars along with their lamps. 5 The bridegroom was a long time in coming, and they all became drowsy and fell asleep.[c]

6 "At midnight the cry rang out: 'Here's the bridegroom! Come out to meet him!'

---

[a] *29* Isaiah 13:10; 34:4 [b] *30* Or *the tribes of the land* [c] *30* See Daniel 7:13-14. [d] *33* Or *he*
[e] *36* Some manuscripts do not have *nor the Son.*

---

who perform signs and wonders must be tested against correct doctrine (Deut. 13:1 – 5; 1 John 4:1 – 3), and by the witness of God's Spirit (John 10:3 – 5,27).

24:29 *Immediately after.* This verse moves chronologically to the close of the tribulation, a period that will be marked by monumental cosmic disturbances (Is. 13:10; 34:4; Ezek. 32:7 – 8; Joel 2:30 – 31; 3:15; Hag. 2:6; Zech. 14:6; Rev. 6:12 – 14).

24:34 *this generation.* "Generation" may mean "race," indicating that Israel as a people will not cease to exist before God fulfills His promises to them. Another possibility is that the word describes a particular era in which people will see the end times. That is, the events will occur so rapidly that all will happen within one generation. Perhaps both interpretations are true.

24:36 *that day or hour no one knows.* Mark 13:32 indicates that even Jesus Himself did not know the exact time of His return. When the Lord Jesus was on earth, He voluntarily limited His use of His divine attributes (John 17:4 – 5; Phil. 2:5 – 8). Therefore He became hungry, thirsty, and tired. In this instance, Jesus surrendered the use of His divine omniscience.

24:27 [b] Lk 17:24 [c] Mt 8:20 **24:28** [d] Lk 17:37 **24:29** [e] Isa 13:10; 34:4; Eze 32:7; Joel 2:10,31; Zep 1:15; Rev 6:12, 13; 8:12 **24:30** [f] Da 7:13; Rev 1:7 **24:31** [g] Mt 13:41 [h] Isa 27:13; Zec 9:14; 1Co 15:52; 1Th 4:16; Rev 8:2; 10:7; 11:15 **24:33** [i] Jas 5:9 **24:34** [j] Mt 16:28; 23:36 **24:35** [k] Mt 5:18 **24:36** [l] Ac 1:7 **24:37** [m] Ge 6:5; 7:6-23 **24:38** [n] Mt 22:30 **24:40** [o] Lk 17:34 **24:41** [p] Lk 17:35 **24:42** [q] Mt 25:13; Lk 12:40 **24:43** [r] Lk 12:39 **24:44** [s] 1Th 5:6 **24:45** [t] Mt 25:21, 23 **24:46** [u] Rev 16:15 **24:47** [v] Mt 25:21, 23 **24:49** [w] Lk 21:34 **24:51** [x] Mt 8:12 **25:1** [y] Mt 13:24 [z] Lk 12:35-38; Ac 20:8; Rev 4:5 [a] Rev 19:7; 21:2 **25:2** [b] Mt 24:45 **25:5** [c] 1Th 5:6

7“Then all the virgins woke up and
trimmed their lamps. 8The foolish ones
said to the wise, ‘Give us some of your oil;
our lamps are going out.’[d]
9“ ‘No,’ they replied, ‘there may not be
enough for both us and you. Instead, go to
those who sell oil and buy some for yourselves.’
10“But while they were on their way to
buy the oil, the bridegroom arrived. The
virgins who were ready went in with him
to the wedding banquet.[e] And the door was
shut.
11“Later the others also came. ‘Lord,
Lord,’ they said, ‘open the door for us!’
12“But he replied, ‘Truly I tell you, I don’t
know you.’
13“Therefore keep watch, because you do
not know the day or the hour.[f]

The Parable of the Bags of Gold

14“Again, it will be like a man going on
a journey,[g] who called his servants and
entrusted his wealth to them. 15To one he
gave five bags of gold, to another two bags,
and to another one bag,[a] each according to
his ability.[h] Then he went on his journey.
16The man who had received five bags of
gold went at once and put his money to
work and gained five bags more. 17So also,
the one with two bags of gold gained two
more. 18But the man who had received one
bag went off, dug a hole in the ground and
hid his master’s money.
19“After a long time the master of those
servants returned and settled accounts
with them.[i] 20The man who had received
five bags of gold brought the other five.
‘Master,’ he said, ‘you entrusted me with
five bags of gold. See, I have gained five
more.’
21“His master replied, ‘Well done, good
and faithful servant! You have been faithful with a few things; I will put you in
charge of many things.[j] Come and share
your master’s happiness!’
22“The man with two bags of gold also
came. ‘Master,’ he said, ‘you entrusted me
with two bags of gold; see, I have gained
two more.’
23“His master replied, ‘Well done, good
and faithful servant! You have been faithful with a few things; I will put you in
charge of many things.[k] Come and share
your master’s happiness!’
24“Then the man who had received one
bag of gold came. ‘Master,’ he said, ‘I knew
that you are a hard man, harvesting where
you have not sown and gathering where
you have not scattered seed. 25So I was
afraid and went out and hid your gold in
the ground. See, here is what belongs to
you.’
26“His master replied, ‘You wicked, lazy
servant! So you knew that I harvest where
I have not sown and gather where I have
not scattered seed? 27Well then, you should
have put my money on deposit with the
bankers, so that when I returned I would
have received it back with interest.
28“ ‘So take the bag of gold from him and
give it to the one who has ten bags. 29For
whoever has will be given more, and they
will have an abundance. Whoever does
not have, even what they have will be tak-
en from them.[l] 30And throw that worthless
servant outside, into the darkness, where
there will be weeping and gnashing of
teeth.’[m]

The Sheep and the Goats

31“When the Son of Man comes[n] in his
glory, and all the angels with him, he will
sit on his glorious throne.[o] 32All the nations will be gathered before him, and he
will separate[p] the people one from another
as a shepherd separates the sheep from the
goats.[q] 33He will put the sheep on his right
and the goats on his left.
34“Then the King will say to those on his
right, ‘Come, you who are blessed by my
Father; take your inheritance, the kingdom[r] prepared for you since the creation
of the world.[s] 35For I was hungry and you
gave me something to eat, I was thirsty and
you gave me something to drink, I was a
stranger and you invited me in,[t] 36I needed

[a] 15 Greek *five talents . . . two talents . . . one talent*; also throughout this parable; a talent was worth about 20 years of a day laborer’s wage.

25:10 *the bridegroom arrived.* Christ’s return is often compared to a wedding (22:1 – 14; Rev. 19:7 – 8).
25:14 *entrusted his wealth to them.* The parable of the talents illustrates the faith required of God’s servants.
25:15 *bags of gold.* Sometimes translated “talents,” this was a large sum of money, about six thousand denarii.
25:23 *I will put you in charge of many things.* The first two servants received the same reward, based on their faithfulness, not on the size of their responsibilities. The smallest task in God’s work may receive a great reward if we are faithful in performing it (10:42).
25:32 – 40 Judgment — The Final Judgment will be according to the evidence, not according to what was professed but what was practiced. It will be not according to what was said, but what was done. These works cannot earn salvation, but they are works of love which reflect a life redeemed by the saving work of Christ through the Holy Spirit (Gal. 5:6). Love for God is demonstrated by love for man (1 John 4:20).

25:8 [d] Lk 12:35 **25:10** [e] Rev 19:9 **25:13** [f] Mt 24:42, 44; Mk 13:35; Lk 12:40 **25:14** [g] Mt 21:33; Lk 19:12 **25:15** [h] Mt 18:24, 25 **25:19** [i] Mt 18:23 **25:21** [j] ver 23; Mt 24:45, 47; Lk 16:10 **25:23** [k] ver 21 **25:29** [l] Mt 13:12; Mk 4:25; Lk 8:18; 19:26 **25:30** [m] Mt 8:12 **25:31** [n] Mt 16:27; Lk 17:30 [o] Mt 19:28 **25:32** [p] Mal 3:18 [q] Eze 34:17, 20 **25:34** [r] Mt 3:2; 5:3, 10, 19; 19:14; Ac 20:32; 1Co 15:50; Gal 5:21; Jas 2:5 [s] Heb 4:3; 9:26; Rev 13:8; 17:8 **25:35** [t] Job 31:32; Isa 58:7; Eze 18:7; Heb 13:2

clothes and you clothed me,[u] I was sick and
you looked after me,[v] I was in prison and
you came to visit me.’[w]
37“Then the righteous will answer him,
‘Lord, when did we see you hungry and
feed you, or thirsty and give you something
to drink? 38When did we see you a stranger
and invite you in, or needing clothes and
clothe you? 39When did we see you sick or
in prison and go to visit you?’
40“The King will reply, ‘Truly I tell you,
whatever you did for one of the least of
these brothers and sisters of mine, you did
for me.’[x]
41“Then he will say to those on his left,
‘Depart from me,[y] you who are cursed,
into the eternal fire[z] prepared for the devil and his angels.[a] 42For I was hungry and
you gave me nothing to eat, I was thirsty
and you gave me nothing to drink, 43I was
a stranger and you did not invite me in, I
needed clothes and you did not clothe me,
I was sick and in prison and you did not
look after me.’
44“They also will answer, ‘Lord, when
did we see you hungry or thirsty or a
stranger or needing clothes or sick or in
prison, and did not help you?’
45“He will reply, ‘Truly I tell you, whatever you did not do for one of the least of
these, you did not do for me.’[b]
46“Then they will go away to eternal punishment, but the righteous to eternal life.[c]”[d]

The Plot Against Jesus

26 When Jesus had finished saying all
these things,[e] he said to his disciples,
2“As you know, the Passover[f] is two days
away—and the Son of Man will be handed
over to be crucified.”
3Then the chief priests and the elders of
the people assembled[g] in the palace of the
high priest, whose name was Caiaphas,[h]
4and they schemed to arrest Jesus secretly
and kill him.[i] 5“But not during the festival,”
they said, “or there may be a riot[j] among
the people.”

Jesus Anointed at Bethany

6While Jesus was in Bethany[k] in the
home of Simon the Leper, 7a woman came
to him with an alabaster jar of very expensive perfume, which she poured on his
head as he was reclining at the table.
8When the disciples saw this, they were
indignant. “Why this waste?” they asked.
9“This perfume could have been sold at
a high price and the money given to the
poor.”
10Aware of this, Jesus said to them,
“Why are you bothering this woman? She
has done a beautiful thing to me. 11The
poor you will always have with you,[a][l] but
you will not always have me. 12When she
poured this perfume on my body, she did it
to prepare me for burial.[m] 13Truly I tell you,
wherever this gospel is preached throughout the world, what she has done will also
be told, in memory of her.”

Judas Agrees to Betray Jesus

14Then one of the Twelve—the one
called Judas Iscariot[n]—went to the chief
priests 15and asked, “What are you willing
to give me if I deliver him over to you?” So
they counted out for him thirty pieces of
silver.[o] 16From then on Judas watched for
an opportunity to hand him over.

The Last Supper

17On the first day of the Festival of Unleavened Bread,[p] the disciples came to
Jesus and asked, “Where do you want us
to make preparations for you to eat the
Passover?”
18He replied, “Go into the city to a certain man and tell him, ‘The Teacher says:
My appointed time[q] is near. I am going to
celebrate the Passover with my disciples
at your house.’ ” 19So the disciples did as
Jesus had directed them and prepared the
Passover.
20When evening came, Jesus was reclining at the table with the Twelve. 21And
while they were eating, he said, “Truly I tell
you, one of you will betray me.”[r]
22They were very sad and began to say to
him one after the other, “Surely you don’t
mean me, Lord?”
23Jesus replied, “The one who has dipped
his hand into the bowl with me will betray
me.[s] 24The Son of Man will go just as it is
written about him.[t] But woe to that man
who betrays the Son of Man! It would be
better for him if he had not been born.”

[a] *11* See Deut. 15:11.

26:14 *one of the Twelve.* The enormity of Judas’ sin is seen in these words: Jesus was betrayed by one of His own best friends.
26:15 *thirty pieces of silver.* Thirty pieces of silver was the price of a slave (Ex. 21:32). Zechariah prophesied this sum (Zech. 11:12–13).
26:21 *one of you will betray me.* This statement indicates the Lord’s omniscience. Repeatedly, Christ unveiled evidence of His deity to His disciples.

25:36 [u] Isa 58:7; Eze 18:7; Jas 2:15, 16 [v] Jas 1:27 [w] 2Ti 1:16 **25:40** [x] Pr 19:17; Mt 10:40, 42; Heb 6:10; 13:2 **25:41** [y] Mt 7:23 [z] Isa 66:24; Mt 3:12; 5:22; Mk 9:43, 48; Lk 3:17; Jude 7 [a] 2Pe 2:4 **25:45** [b] Pr 14:31; 17:5 **25:46** [c] Mt 19:29; Jn 3:15, 16, 36; 17:2, 3; Ro 2:7; Gal 6:8; 5:11, 13, 20 [d] Da 12:2; Jn 5:29; Ac 24:15; Ro 2:7, 8; Gal 6:8 **26:1** [e] Mt 7:28 **26:2** [f] Jn 11:55; 13:1 **26:3** [g] Ps 2:2 [h] ver 57; Jn 11:47-53; 18:13, 14, 24, 28 **26:4** [i] Mt 12:14 **26:5** [j] Mt 27:24 **26:6** [k] Mt 21:17 **26:11** [l] Dt 15:11 **26:12** [m] Jn 19:40 **26:14** [n] ver 25, 47; Mt 10:4 **26:15** [o] Ex 21:32; Zec 11:12 **26:17** [p] Ex 12:18-20 **26:18** [q] Jn 7:6, 8, 30; 12:23; 13:1; 17:1 **26:21** [r] Lk 22:21-23; Jn 13:21 **26:23** [s] Ps 41:9; Jn 13:18 **26:24** [t] Isa 53; Da 9:26; Mk 9:12; Lk 24:25-27, 46; Ac 17:2, 3; 26:22, 23

25Then Judas, the one who would betray
him, said, "Surely you don't mean me, Rabbi?"[u]
Jesus answered, "You have said so."
26While they were eating, Jesus took
bread, and when he had given thanks, he
broke it[v] and gave it to his disciples, saying,
"Take and eat; this is my body."
27Then he took a cup, and when he had
given thanks, he gave it to them, saying,
"Drink from it, all of you. 28This is my
blood of the[a] covenant,[w] which is poured
out for many for the forgiveness of sins.[x] 29I
tell you, I will not drink from this fruit of
the vine from now on until that day when I
drink it new with you[y] in my Father's kingdom."
30When they had sung a hymn, they
went out to the Mount of Olives.[z]

Jesus Predicts Peter's Denial

31Then Jesus told them, "This very night
you will all fall away on account of me,[a] for
it is written:

"'I will strike the shepherd,
and the sheep of the flock will be
scattered.'[b][b]

32But after I have risen, I will go ahead of
you into Galilee."[c]
33Peter replied, "Even if all fall away on
account of you, I never will."
34"Truly I tell you," Jesus answered, "this
very night, before the rooster crows, you
will disown me three times."[d]
35But Peter declared, "Even if I have to
die with you,[e] I will never disown you."
And all the other disciples said the same.

Gethsemane

36Then Jesus went with his disciples to
a place called Gethsemane, and he said to
them, "Sit here while I go over there and
pray." 37He took Peter and the two sons of
Zebedee[f] along with him, and he began to
be sorrowful and troubled. 38Then he said
to them, "My soul is overwhelmed with sorrow[g] to the point of death. Stay here and
keep watch with me."[h]
39Going a little farther, he fell with his
face to the ground and prayed, "My Father,
if it is possible, may this cup[i] be taken from
me. Yet not as I will, but as you will."[j]
40Then he returned to his disciples and
found them sleeping. "Couldn't you men
keep watch with me[k] for one hour?" he
asked Peter. 41"Watch and pray so that you
will not fall into temptation.[l] The spirit is
willing, but the flesh is weak."
42He went away a second time and
prayed, "My Father, if it is not possible for
this cup to be taken away unless I drink it,
may your will be done."
43When he came back, he again found
them sleeping, because their eyes were
heavy. 44So he left them and went away
once more and prayed the third time, saying the same thing.
45Then he returned to the disciples and
said to them, "Are you still sleeping and
resting? Look, the hour[m] has come, and
the Son of Man is delivered into the hands
of sinners. 46Rise! Let us go! Here comes
my betrayer!"

Jesus Arrested

47While he was still speaking, Judas,
one of the Twelve, arrived. With him was a
large crowd armed with swords and clubs,
sent from the chief priests and the elders
of the people. 48Now the betrayer had arranged a signal with them: "The one I kiss
is the man; arrest him." 49Going at once to
Jesus, Judas said, "Greetings, Rabbi!"[n] and
kissed him.
50Jesus replied, "Do what you came for,
friend."[c][o]
Then the men stepped forward, seized
Jesus and arrested him. 51With that, one of
Jesus' companions reached for his sword,[p]
drew it out and struck the servant of the
high priest, cutting off his ear.[q]
52"Put your sword back in its place,"
Jesus said to him, "for all who draw the
sword will die by the sword.[r] 53Do you
think I cannot call on my Father, and he
will at once put at my disposal more than

---

[a] *28* Some manuscripts *the new* [b] *31* Zech. 13:7
[c] *50* Or *"Why have you come, friend?"*

26:26–28 *my body . . . my blood.* The Lord Jesus, at this last meal with His disciples before He went to the cross, instituted this ordinance for His church throughout this age. It is called "the Lord's Supper" (1 Cor. 11:20). Using common everyday items, the bread and wine that could be found on any table, no matter how poor, He gave us a "remembrance" so that we would never forget that His broken body and shed blood bought salvation for us.

26:28 *my blood of the covenant.* This refers to the new covenant promised in the Old Testament (Jer. 31:31–34; 32:37–44; Ezek. 34:25–31; 37:26–28).

26:36 *Gethsemane.* The name "Gethsemane" means "oil press." This garden was east of Jerusalem on the Mount of Olives. In the place where olives were crushed and ground, the Anointed One was crushed.

26:51 *one of Jesus' companions.* John 18:10 informs us that the impetuous swordsman was Peter. This action was performed with one of the two swords that the disciples had (Luke 22:38).

26:53 *twelve legions of angels.* A legion in the

26:25 [u] Mt 23:7 **26:26** [v] Mt 14:19; 1Co 10:16
26:28 [w] Ex 24:6-8; Heb 9:20 [x] Mt 20:28; Mk 1:4
26:29 [y] Ac 10:41 **26:30** [z] Mt 21:1; Mk 14:26
26:31 [a] Mt 11:6 [b] Zec 13:7; Jn 16:32 **26:32** [c] Mt 28:7, 10, 16 **26:34** [d] ver 75; Jn 13:38 **26:35** [e] Jn 13:37
26:37 [f] Mt 4:21 **26:38** [g] Jn 12:27 [h] ver 40, 41
26:39 [i] Mt 20:22 [j] ver 42; Ps 40:6-8; Isa 50:5; Jn 5:30; 6:38
26:40 [k] ver 38 **26:41** [l] Mt 6:13 **26:45** [m] ver 18
26:49 [n] ver 25 **26:50** [o] Mt 20:13; 22:12
26:51 [p] Lk 22:36, 38 [q] Jn 18:10 **26:52** [r] Ge 9:6; Rev 13:10

twelve legions of angels?[s] 54But how then
would the Scriptures be fulfilled[t] that say
it must happen in this way?"
55In that hour Jesus said to the crowd,
"Am I leading a rebellion, that you have
come out with swords and clubs to capture
me? Every day I sat in the temple courts
teaching,[u] and you did not arrest me. 56But
this has all taken place that the writings of
the prophets might be fulfilled."[v] Then all
the disciples deserted him and fled.

Jesus Before the Sanhedrin

57Those who had arrested Jesus took
him to Caiaphas[w] the high priest, where
the teachers of the law and the elders had
assembled. 58But Peter followed him at a
distance, right up to the courtyard of the
high priest.[x] He entered and sat down with
the guards[y] to see the outcome.
59The chief priests and the whole Sanhedrin[z] were looking for false evidence
against Jesus so that they could put him to
death. 60But they did not find any, though
many false witnesses[a] came forward.
Finally two[b] came forward 61and declared, "This fellow said, 'I am able to destroy the temple of God and rebuild it in
three days.'"[c]
62Then the high priest stood up and said
to Jesus, "Are you not going to answer?
What is this testimony that these men are
bringing against you?" 63But Jesus remained silent.[d]
The high priest said to him, "I charge you
under oath[e] by the living God:[f] Tell us if you
are the Messiah, the Son of God."
64"You have said so," Jesus replied. "But I
say to all of you: From now on you will see
the Son of Man sitting at the right hand of
the Mighty One[g] and coming on the clouds
of heaven."[ah]
65Then the high priest tore his clothes[i]
and said, "He has spoken blasphemy! Why
do we need any more witnesses? Look, now
you have heard the blasphemy. 66What do
you think?"
"He is worthy of death,"[j] they answered.
67Then they spit in his face and struck
him with their fists.[k] Others slapped him
68and said, "Prophesy to us, Messiah. Who
hit you?"[l]

Peter Disowns Jesus

69Now Peter was sitting out in the courtyard, and a servant girl came to him.
"You also were with Jesus of Galilee," she
said.
70But he denied it before them all. "I don't
know what you're talking about," he said.
71Then he went out to the gateway, where
another servant girl saw him and said to
the people there, "This fellow was with
Jesus of Nazareth."
72He denied it again, with an oath: "I
don't know the man!"
73After a little while, those standing
there went up to Peter and said, "Surely
you are one of them; your accent gives you
away."
74Then he began to call down curses, and
he swore to them, "I don't know the man!"
Immediately a rooster crowed. 75Then
Peter remembered the word Jesus had
spoken: "Before the rooster crows, you will
disown me three times."[m] And he went outside and wept bitterly.

Judas Hangs Himself

27 Early in the morning, all the chief
priests and the elders of the people
made their plans how to have Jesus executed.[n] 2So they bound him, led him away
and handed him over[o] to Pilate the governor.[p]

[a] *64* See Psalm 110:1; Daniel 7:13.

Roman army was about six thousand men. When one considers the power of one angel (Ex. 32:23; 2 Sam. 24:15–17; 2 Kin. 19:35) the power of more than 72,000 angels is beyond comprehension. Jesus had all of heaven's power at His disposal, yet He refused to use it. His Father's will was for Him to go to the cross.

26:62 ***Are you not going to answer?*** In maintaining His silence, Jesus fulfilled the prophecy of Isaiah 53:7.

26:64 Second Coming—Throughout His ministry, Jesus had applied to Himself the Old Testament prophecies that were acknowledged as messianic by the Jewish teachers. Here, Jesus answers Caiaphas the high priest by combining two well-known messianic prophecies from Psalm 110:1 and Daniel 7:13. The first describes His enthronement and the other His second coming. The final word spoken by Christ to the Jews was about the certainty of His future return. About His first coming Jesus said, "For God did not send his Son into the world to condemn the world" (John 3:17). But the time will come when all the world will see Him enthroned at the right hand of God and given all power and majesty as the judge of the ages.

26:74 ***Immediately a rooster crowed.*** Some have detected a contradiction between this passage and the account in Mark 14:72. Others believe that seeing a contradiction is a forced reading of the text. Matthew, Luke, and John make the simple statement that a rooster would crow (Luke 22:61; John 18:27), whereas Mark, which is believed to be based on Peter's memories, would include more exact details.

27:2 ***Pilate.*** Pontius Pilate was governor of Judea, Samaria, and Idumea from A.D. 26 to 36. Because the Jews did not have authority to execute Jesus, they brought Him to Pilate.

26:53 [s] 2Ki 6:17; Da 7:10; Mt 4:11 **26:54** [t] ver 24
26:55 [u] Mk 12:35; Lk 21:37; Jn 7:14, 28; 18:20
26:56 [v] ver 24 **26:57** [w] ver 3 **26:58** [x] Jn 18:15
[y] Jn 7:32, 45, 46 **26:59** [z] Mt 5:22 **26:60** [a] Ps 27:12;
35:11; Ac 6:13 [b] Dt 19:15 **26:61** [c] Jn 2:19
26:63 [d] Mt 27:12, 14 [e] Lev 5:1 [f] Mt 16:16
26:64 [g] Ps 110:1 [h] Da 7:13; Rev 1:7 **26:65** [i] Mk 14:63
26:66 [j] Lev 24:16; Jn 19:7 **26:67** [k] Mt 16:21; 27:30
26:68 [l] Lk 22:63-65 **26:75** [m] ver 34; Jn 13:38
27:1 [n] Mt 12:14; Mk 15:1; Lk 22:66 **27:2** [o] Mt 20:19
[p] Mk 15:1; Lk 13:1; Ac 3:13; 1Ti 6:13

3 When Judas, who had betrayed him,[q]
saw that Jesus was condemned, he was
seized with remorse and returned the thirty pieces of silver[r] to the chief priests and
the elders. 4 "I have sinned," he said, "for I
have betrayed innocent blood."
"What is that to us?" they replied. "That's
your responsibility."[s]
5 So Judas threw the money into the
temple[t] and left. Then he went away and
hanged himself.[u]
6 The chief priests picked up the coins
and said, "It is against the law to put this
into the treasury, since it is blood money."
7 So they decided to use the money to buy
the potter's field as a burial place for foreigners. 8 That is why it has been called
the Field of Blood[v] to this day. 9 Then what
was spoken by Jeremiah the prophet was
fulfilled:[w] "They took the thirty pieces of
silver, the price set on him by the people of
Israel, 10 and they used them to buy the potter's field, as the Lord commanded me."[a][x]

Jesus Before Pilate

11 Meanwhile Jesus stood before the governor, and the governor asked him, "Are
you the king of the Jews?"[y]
"You have said so," Jesus replied.
12 When he was accused by the chief
priests and the elders, he gave no answer.[z]
13 Then Pilate asked him, "Don't you hear
the testimony they are bringing against
you?"[a] 14 But Jesus made no reply,[b] not even
to a single charge—to the great amazement of the governor.
15 Now it was the governor's custom at
the festival to release a prisoner[c] chosen by
the crowd. 16 At that time they had a well-
known prisoner whose name was Jesus[b]
Barabbas. 17 So when the crowd had gathered, Pilate asked them, "Which one do you
want me to release to you: Jesus Barabbas,
or Jesus who is called the Messiah?"[d] 18 For
he knew it was out of self-interest that they
had handed Jesus over to him.
19 While Pilate was sitting on the judge's
seat,[e] his wife sent him this message:
"Don't have anything to do with that innocent[f] man, for I have suffered a great deal
today in a dream[g] because of him."
20 But the chief priests and the elders persuaded the crowd to ask for Barabbas and
to have Jesus executed.[h]
21 "Which of the two do you want me to
release to you?" asked the governor.
"Barabbas," they answered.
22 "What shall I do, then, with Jesus who
is called the Messiah?"[i] Pilate asked.
They all answered, "Crucify him!"
23 "Why? What crime has he committed?" asked Pilate.
But they shouted all the louder, "Crucify him!"
24 When Pilate saw that he was getting
nowhere, but that instead an uproar[j] was
starting, he took water and washed his
hands[k] in front of the crowd. "I am innocent of this man's blood,"[l] he said. "It is
your responsibility!"[m]
25 All the people answered, "His blood is
on us and on our children!"[n]
26 Then he released Barabbas to them.
But he had Jesus flogged,[o] and handed him
over to be crucified.

The Soldiers Mock Jesus

27 Then the governor's soldiers took
Jesus into the Praetorium[p] and gathered
the whole company of soldiers around
him. 28 They stripped him and put a scarlet
robe on him,[q] 29 and then twisted together
a crown of thorns and set it on his head.
They put a staff in his right hand. Then
they knelt in front of him and mocked him.
"Hail, king of the Jews!" they said.[r] 30 They
spit on him, and took the staff and struck
him on the head again and again.[s] 31 After
they had mocked him, they took off the
robe and put his own clothes on him. Then
they led him away to crucify him.[t]

The Crucifixion of Jesus

32 As they were going out,[u] they met
a man from Cyrene,[v] named Simon,
and they forced him to carry the cross.[w]
33 They came to a place called Golgotha
(which means "the place of the skull").[x]

---

a 10 See Zech. 11:12,13; Jer. 19:1-13; 32:6-9.
b 16 Many manuscripts do not have *Jesus*; also in verse 17.

27:25 *His blood is on us and our children.* The sins of the fathers are visited on their children for those who hate God. But if anyone turns to Jesus and repents, He never fails to show His lovingkindness.

27:27 *the Praetorium.* This was the official residence of the governor when he was in Jerusalem.

27:31 *crucify.* Crucifixion, a practice probably adopted from Persia, was considered by the Romans to be the cruelest form of execution. This punishment was reserved for the worst criminals. The offender usually died after two or three days of agonizing suffering, enduring not only incomprehensible pain, but also hunger, thirst, and exposure. The offender's arms were nailed to a beam that was hoisted up and fixed to a post, to which his feet were nailed.

27:32 *named Simon.* Simon probably was (or later became) a follower of Christ; it is unlikely that he would be referred to by name if he were a stranger to the Christian community (Mark 15:21).

27:3 [q] Mt 10:4 [r] Mt 26:14, 15 **27:4** [s] ver 24
27:5 [t] Lk 1:9, 21 [u] Ac 1:18 **27:8** [v] Ac 1:19
27:9 [w] Mt 1:22 **27:10** [x] Zec 11:12, 13; Jer 32:6-9
27:11 [y] Mt 2:2 **27:12** [z] Mt 26:63; Mk 14:61; Jn 19:9
27:13 [a] Mt 26:62 **27:14** [b] Mk 14:61 **27:15** [c] Jn 18:39
27:17 [d] ver 22; Mt 1:16 **27:19** [e] Jn 19:13 [f] ver 24
[g] Ge 20:6; Nu 12:6; 1Ki 3:5; Job 33:14-16; Mt 1:20; 2:12, 13, 19, 22 **27:20** [h] Ac 3:14 **27:22** [i] Mt 1:16
27:24 [j] Mt 26:5 [k] Ps 26:6 [l] Dt 21:6-8 [m] ver 4
27:25 [n] Jos 2:19; Ac 5:28 **27:26** [o] Isa 53:5; Jn 19:1
27:27 [p] Jn 18:28, 33; 19:9 **27:28** [q] Jn 19:2
27:29 [r] Isa 53:3; Jn 19:2, 3 **27:30** [s] Mt 16:21; 26:67
27:31 [t] Isa 53:7 **27:32** [u] Heb 13:12 [v] Ac 2:10; 6:9; 11:20; 13:1 [w] Mk 15:21; Lk 23:26 **27:33** [x] Jn 19:17

34There they offered Jesus wine to drink,
mixed with gall;[y] but after tasting it, he
refused to drink it. 35When they had crucified him, they divided up his clothes by
casting lots.[z] 36And sitting down, they kept
watch[a] over him there. 37Above his head
they placed the written charge against
him: THIS IS JESUS, THE KING OF THE JEWS.
38Two rebels were crucified with him,[b]
one on his right and one on his left. 39Those
who passed by hurled insults at him, shaking their heads[c] 40and saying, "You who
are going to destroy the temple and build it
in three days,[d] save yourself![e] Come down
from the cross, if you are the Son of God!"[f]
41In the same way the chief priests, the
teachers of the law and the elders mocked
him. 42"He saved others," they said, "but he
can't save himself! He's the king of Israel![g]
Let him come down now from the cross,
and we will believe[h] in him. 43He trusts in
God. Let God rescue him[i] now if he wants
him, for he said, 'I am the Son of God.'" 44In
the same way the rebels who were crucified with him also heaped insults on him.

The Death of Jesus

45From noon until three in the afternoon
darkness[j] came over all the land. 46About
three in the afternoon Jesus cried out in a
loud voice, *"Eli, Eli,[a] lema sabachthani?"*
(which means "My God, my God, why have
you forsaken me?").[b] [k]
47When some of those standing there
heard this, they said, "He's calling Elijah."
48Immediately one of them ran and got a
sponge. He filled it with wine vinegar,[l] put
it on a staff, and offered it to Jesus to drink.
49The rest said, "Now leave him alone. Let's
see if Elijah comes to save him."
50And when Jesus had cried out again in
a loud voice, he gave up his spirit.[m]
51At that moment the curtain of the temple[n] was torn in two from top to bottom.
The earth shook, the rocks split[o] 52and the
tombs broke open. The bodies of many
holy people who had died were raised to
life. 53They came out of the tombs after
Jesus' resurrection and[c] went into the holy
city[p] and appeared to many people.
54When the centurion and those with
him who were guarding[q] Jesus saw the
earthquake and all that had happened,
they were terrified, and exclaimed, "Surely he was the Son of God!"[r]
55Many women were there, watching from a distance. They had followed
Jesus from Galilee to care for his needs.[s]
56Among them were Mary Magdalene,
Mary the mother of James and Joseph,[d]
and the mother of Zebedee's sons.[t]

The Burial of Jesus

57As evening approached, there came a
rich man from Arimathea, named Joseph,
who had himself become a disciple of
Jesus. 58Going to Pilate, he asked for Jesus'
body, and Pilate ordered that it be given
to him. 59Joseph took the body, wrapped
it in a clean linen cloth, 60and placed it in
his own new tomb[u] that he had cut out of
the rock. He rolled a big stone in front of
the entrance to the tomb and went away.
61Mary Magdalene and the other Mary
were sitting there opposite the tomb.

The Guard at the Tomb

62The next day, the one after Preparation Day, the chief priests and the Pharisees went to Pilate. 63"Sir," they said, "we

[a] 46 Some manuscripts *Eloi, Eloi* [b] 46 Psalm 22:1
[c] 53 Or *tombs, and after Jesus' resurrection they*
[d] 56 Greek *Joses,* a variant of *Joseph*

27:34 *wine ... mixed with gall.* It is believed that this mixture was meant to dull the victim's pain. The prophetic words of Psalm 69:21 were fulfilled here.

27:35 *casting lots.* The soldiers fulfilled the prophetic words of Psalm 22:18.

27:38 *Two rebels.* This is the fulfillment of Isaiah 53:12, He "was numbered with the transgressors." Psalm 22:6 predicted the insults that would be directed at the Messiah.

27:45 *darkness.* The darkness could not have been due to a natural cause, such as an eclipse of the sun, since the Passover occurred during a full moon. This was a supernatural occurrence.

27:46–50 Atonement—Because God cannot tolerate sin, as Jesus took upon Himself the sin of the whole human race, God had to turn away. Jesus felt this separation, and many believe it was as much for the dread of this as for the physical pain that Jesus wept in the garden. Jesus' cry to God is a quote from Psalm 22:1, a messianic verse that the Jews should have understood.

27:50 *cried out again in a loud voice.* The cry referred to here by Matthew was, "It is finished" (John 19:30). This was not a cry of exhaustion, but a cry of victory. The purpose for which Jesus came into the world had been accomplished. Redemption from sin had been purchased for all mankind.

27:51 *the curtain of the temple was torn in two from top to bottom.* The temple had two veils or curtains, one in front of the holy place and the other separating the holy place from the Most Holy Place. These curtains were heavy and very strong and thick. It was the second of these that was torn, demonstrating that through the death of Jesus, there was now open access to God. Jesus' blood covered our sins from God's sight.

27:57 *a rich man of Arimathea.* Joseph's actions fulfilled the prophecy of Isaiah, "He was assigned a grave with the wicked, and with the rich in his death" (Is. 53:9).

27:34 [y] ver 48; Ps 69:21 **27:35** [z] Ps 22:18 **27:36** [a] ver 54
27:38 [b] Isa 53:12 **27:39** [c] Ps 22:7; 109:25; La 2:15
27:40 [d] Mt 26:61; Jn 2:19 [e] ver 42 [f] Mt 4:3,6
27:42 [g] Jn 1:49; 12:13 [h] Jn 3:15 **27:43** [i] Ps 22:8
27:45 [j] Am 8:9 **27:46** [k] Ps 22:1 **27:48** [l] ver 34; Ps 69:21
27:50 [m] Jn 19:30 **27:51** [n] Ex 26:31-33; Heb 9:3,8 [o] ver 54
27:53 [p] Mt 4:5 **27:54** [q] ver 36 [r] Mt 4:3; 17:5
27:55 [s] Lk 8:2,3 **27:56** [t] Mk 15:47; Lk 24:10; Jn 19:25
27:60 [u] Mt 27:66; 28:2; Mk 16:4

remember that while he was still alive that
deceiver said, 'After three days I will rise
again.'[v] 64So give the order for the tomb to
be made secure until the third day. Otherwise, his disciples may come and steal the
body and tell the people that he has been
raised from the dead. This last deception
will be worse than the first."
65"Take a guard,"[w] Pilate answered.
"Go, make the tomb as secure as you know
how." 66So they went and made the tomb
secure by putting a seal[x] on the stone[y] and
posting the guard.[z]

Jesus Has Risen

28 After the Sabbath, at dawn on the
first day of the week, Mary Magdalene and the other Mary[a] went to look at
the tomb.
2There was a violent earthquake,[b] for an
angel[c] of the Lord came down from heav-
en and, going to the tomb, rolled back the
stone and sat on it. 3His appearance was
like lightning, and his clothes were white
as snow.[d] 4The guards were so afraid of
him that they shook and became like dead
men.
5The angel said to the women, "Do not be
afraid,[e] for I know that you are looking for
Jesus, who was crucified. 6He is not here;
he has risen, just as he said.[f] Come and see
the place where he lay. 7Then go quickly
and tell his disciples: 'He has risen from the
dead and is going ahead of you into Galilee.[g] There you will see him.' Now I have
told you."
8So the women hurried away from the
tomb, afraid yet filled with joy, and ran
to tell his disciples. 9Suddenly Jesus met
them.[h] "Greetings," he said. They came
to him, clasped his feet and worshiped
him. 10Then Jesus said to them, "Do not
be afraid. Go and tell my brothers[i] to go to
Galilee; there they will see me."

The Guards' Report

11While the women were on their way,
some of the guards[j] went into the city and
reported to the chief priests everything
that had happened. 12When the chief
priests had met with the elders and devised
a plan, they gave the soldiers a large sum
of money, 13telling them, "You are to say,
'His disciples came during the night and
stole him away while we were asleep.' 14If
this report gets to the governor,[k] we will
satisfy him and keep you out of trouble."
15So the soldiers took the money and did
as they were instructed. And this story has
been widely circulated among the Jews to
this very day.

The Great Commission

16Then the eleven disciples went to Galilee, to the mountain where Jesus had told
them to go.[l] 17When they saw him, they
worshiped him; but some doubted. 18Then
Jesus came to them and said, "All authority in heaven and on earth has been given
to me.[m] 19Therefore go and make disciples of all nations,[n] baptizing them in the
name of the Father and of the Son and of
the Holy Spirit,[o] 20and teaching[p] them to
obey everything I have commanded you.
And surely I am with you[q] always, to the
very end of the age."[r]

28:2 *rolled back the stone.* The tomb was not opened to allow Christ to come out; it was opened to allow others to go in and see for themselves that it was empty.

28:6 *he has risen, just as he said.* Jesus predicted His resurrection to His disciples, even though they did not understand Him (12:40; 16:21; 17:9,23; 26:32).

28:7 *go quickly and tell.* This is always the divine order: to tell others the good news that Jesus is alive (v. 19).

28:19 Why Share Our Faith—There are at least six compelling reasons for sharing our faith in Christ with those who have not experienced new life in Christ:

1. Because God has commanded us to do so (Acts 1:8).
2. Because it demonstrates our love for God. If we truly love Him we will keep His commandments (John 14:15).
3. Because all are lost without Christ (Rom. 3:10,23).
4. Because this is God's chosen method: He could use angels, but He only uses redeemed sinners to tell lost sinners about Christ (Rom. 10:14–17; 1 Tim. 1:15).
5. Because God desires to save all people (Acts 4:12; 1 Tim. 2:4; 2 Pet. 3:9).
6. Because faith grows best when each generation conscientiously strives to pass it on to the next.

28:20 *I am with you always.* Jesus is the true Immanuel, "God with us" (1:23; Heb. 13:5–6; Rev. 21:3).

27:63 [v] Mt 16:21 **27:65** [w] ver 66; Mt 28:11
27:66 [x] Da 6:17 [y] ver 60; Mt 28:2 [z] Mt 28:11
28:1 [a] Mt 27:56 **28:2** [b] Mt 27:51 [c] Jn 20:12
28:3 [d] Da 10:6; Mk 9:3; Jn 20:12 **28:5** [e] ver 10; Mt 14:27
28:6 [f] Mt 16:21 **28:7** [g] ver 10, 16; Mt 26:32
28:9 [h] Jn 20:14-18 **28:10** [i] Jn 20:17; Ro 8:29; Heb 2:11-13, 17 **28:11** [j] Mt 27:65, 66 **28:14** [k] Mt 27:2
28:16 [l] ver 7, 10; Mt 26:32 **28:18** [m] Da 7:13, 14; Lk 10:22; Jn 3:35; 17:2; 1Co 15:27; Eph 1:20-22; Php 2:9, 10
28:19 [n] Mk 16:15, 16; Lk 24:47; Ac 1:8; 14:21 [o] Ac 2:38; 8:16; Ro 6:3, 4 **28:20** [p] Ac 2:42 [q] Mt 18:20; Ac 18:10 [r] Mt 13:39

MARK

▶ **AUTHOR:** According to Acts 12:12, Mark's mother Mary had a large house that was used as a meeting place for believers in Jerusalem. Barnabas was Mark's cousin (Col. 4:10), but Peter may have been the person that led him to Christ (Peter called him "my son Mark" in 1 Pet. 5:13). It was this close association with Peter that lent apostolic authority to Mark's Gospel, since Peter was evidently Mark's primary source of information. It has been suggested that Mark was referring to himself in his account of a "young man" in Gethsemane (14:51). Since all the disciples had abandoned Jesus (14:50), this little incident may have been a firsthand account.

▶ **TIME:** c. A.D. 29–33 ▶ **KEY VERSES:** Mark 8:34–37

▶ **THEME:** Mark is the shortest and simplest of the Gospels. He doesn't seem to be telling the story in a way that appeals to a particular audience the way Matthew does. He also does not use the well-developed thematic structure that characterizes John. One of the most common terms in the book is one that is translated "immediately" or "at once." He uses this frequently as he moves from one anecdote to another. Mark's quickly paced Gospel is often confrontational, as he tells the story of the gospel as clearly as possible. He wants the reader to respond, and almost seems to be saying "here is the truth, believe it, and let's get on with following Jesus."

John the Baptist Prepares the Way

1 The beginning of the good news about
Jesus the Messiah,[a] the Son of God,[b][a]
2as it is written in Isaiah the prophet:

"I will send my messenger ahead of
you,
who will prepare your way"[c][b]—
3"a voice of one calling in the
wilderness,
'Prepare the way for the Lord,
make straight paths for him.'"[d][c]

4And so John the Baptist[d] appeared in the
wilderness, preaching a baptism of repentance[e] for the forgiveness of sins.[f] 5The
whole Judean countryside and all the people of Jerusalem went out to him. Confessing their sins, they were baptized by him
in the Jordan River. 6John wore clothing
made of camel's hair, with a leather belt
around his waist, and he ate locusts[g] and
wild honey. 7And this was his message:
"After me comes the one more powerful
than I, the straps of whose sandals I am
not worthy to stoop down and untie.[h] 8I
baptize you with[e] water, but he will baptize you with[e] the Holy Spirit."[i]

[a] *1* Or *Jesus Christ. Messiah* (Hebrew) and *Christ* (Greek) both mean *Anointed One.* [b] *1* Some manuscripts do not have *the Son of God.* [c] *2* Mal. 3:1 [d] *3* Isaiah 40:3 [e] *8* Or *in*

1:1 *The beginning of the good news about Jesus the Messiah.* Writing three decades after the resurrection of Christ, Mark starts his narrative with a simple declaration of the good news about God's Son, the Lord Jesus Christ. The *good news* refers to the basic story found in Christ's life, ministry, death and resurrection.

1:2–3 *as it is written.* Other than by quoting Jesus, Mark makes only one reference to the Old Testament.

1:4 *John ... preaching a baptism.* The mention of John without any introduction presupposes some knowledge of the Christian faith on the part of Mark's readers. ***the forgiveness of sins.*** This phrase does not mean that one is baptized in order to receive forgiveness of sins. The Greek preposition translated *of* in English probably means "with a view to," signifying that baptism looks to the forgiveness that God gives through the gift of repentance.

1:5 *were baptized by him.* John's baptizing was a recurring popular event that attracted large crowds. Mark vividly portrays the continuous stream of followers who flocked to John. As each person was baptized by John, he or she would admit to his or her individual sin and need for the Messiah.

1:7 *And this was his message.* The tense of these verbs indicates continuous action in past time. John's characteristic message was to promote expectancy and acceptance of the Lord Jesus Christ.

1:8 *I baptize you with water.* The water is a physical representation of the future life in the Spirit that people who followed the Messiah would have.

1:1 [a] Mt 4:3 **1:2** [b] Mal 3:1; Mt 11:10; Lk 7:27
1:3 [c] Isa 40:3; Jn 1:23 **1:4** [d] Mt 3:1 [e] Ac 13:24 [f] Lk 1:77
1:6 [g] Lev 11:22 **1:7** [h] Ac 13:25 **1:8** [i] Isa 44:3; Joel 2:28; Ac 1:5; 2:4; 11:16; 19:4-6

The Baptism and Testing of Jesus

9At that time Jesus came from Nazareth[j]
in Galilee and was baptized by John in
the Jordan. 10Just as Jesus was coming up
out of the water, he saw heaven being torn
open and the Spirit descending on him like
a dove.[k] 11And a voice came from heaven:
"You are my Son,[l] whom I love; with you I
am well pleased."

12At once the Spirit sent him out into the
wilderness, 13and he was in the wilderness
forty days, being tempted[a] by Satan.[m] He
was with the wild animals, and angels attended him.

Jesus Announces the Good News

14After John was put in prison, Jesus
went into Galilee,[n] proclaiming the good
news of God.[o] 15"The time has come,"[p] he
said. "The kingdom of God has come near.
Repent and believe the good news!"[q]

Jesus Calls His First Disciples

16As Jesus walked beside the Sea of Galilee, he saw Simon and his brother Andrew
casting a net into the lake, for they were
fishermen. 17"Come, follow me," Jesus said,
"and I will send you out to fish for people."
18At once they left their nets and followed
him.

19When he had gone a little farther, he
saw James son of Zebedee and his brother John in a boat, preparing their nets.
20Without delay he called them, and they
left their father Zebedee in the boat with
the hired men and followed him.

Jesus Drives Out an Impure Spirit

21They went to Capernaum, and when
the Sabbath came, Jesus went into the synagogue and began to teach.[r] 22The people
were amazed at his teaching, because he
taught them as one who had authority, not
as the teachers of the law.[s] 23Just then a man
in their synagogue who was possessed by
an impure spirit cried out, 24"What do you
want with us,[t] Jesus of Nazareth?[u] Have
you come to destroy us? I know who you
are—the Holy One of God!"[v]

25"Be quiet!" said Jesus sternly. "Come
out of him!"[w] 26The impure spirit shook the
man violently and came out of him with a
shriek.[x]

27The people were all so amazed[y] that
they asked each other, "What is this? A
new teaching—and with authority! He
even gives orders to impure spirits and
they obey him." 28News about him spread
quickly over the whole region[z] of Galilee.

Jesus Heals Many

29As soon as they left the synagogue,[a]
they went with James and John to the
home of Simon and Andrew. 30Simon's
mother-in-law was in bed with a fever, and
they immediately told Jesus about her. 31So
he went to her, took her hand and helped
her up.[b] The fever left her and she began to
wait on them.

32That evening after sunset the people
brought to Jesus all the sick and demon-possessed.[c] 33The whole town gathered at
the door, 34and Jesus healed many who had
various diseases.[d] He also drove out many
demons, but he would not let the demons
speak because they knew who he was.[e]

Jesus Prays in a Solitary Place

35Very early in the morning, while it
was still dark, Jesus got up, left the house
and went off to a solitary place, where he
prayed.[f] 36Simon and his companions went
to look for him, 37and when they found

---

[a] *13* The Greek for *tempted* can also mean *tested.*

1:9 *Jesus . . . was baptized by John.* Because He had no sins to repent of, Jesus' baptism was unique. It showed His identity with John's work and with the sinner for whom He would die. It also foreshadowed His own death, burial, and resurrection for sinners.
1:11 *a voice came from heaven.* Three times during Christ's earthly ministry a voice came from heaven. Here it was the Father's testimony to Christ's unique and divine Sonship. The other two confirming incidents were at the transfiguration (9:7) and on the day of Christ's triumphal entry into Jerusalem (John 12:28).
1:13 *angels attended him.* Mark is the only Gospel that mentions these angels.
1:15 *kingdom of God.* The kingdom was the subject of much Old Testament prophecy, and the theme was familiar to Jesus' listeners. ***Repent and believe.*** These are both acts of faith. When a person accepts the only true and worthy object of faith, that person readily turns from inferior substitutes.
1:19 *James . . . John.* The scenes of verses 16–20 are very colorful. Simon and Andrew are fishing when we encounter them. James and John are mending their nets. Such details indicate the testimony of an eyewitness, probably Peter.
1:21 *Capernaum.* This city is now in ruins, and sits beside the northern edge of the Sea of Galilee. It is mentioned 22 times in the Gospels. By contrast, only one recorded event during Christ's ministry occurred at Nazareth (Luke 4:16).
1:22 *the people were amazed at his teaching.* Christ's teaching differed from that of scribes and Pharisees because He did not lean on the wisdom of other teachers and rabbis. His authority came from Himself.
1:28 *News about him spread quickly over the whole region of Galilee.* Mark notes the extent of recognition this great miracle brought Jesus. He also creates suspense by contrasting the people who received Christ with the Pharisees and rulers who worked to bring about His death.
1:35 *where he prayed.* The verb tense indicates

1:9 [j] Mt 2:23 **1:10** [k] Jn 1:32 **1:11** [l] Mt 3:17 **1:13** [m] Mt 4:10 **1:14** [n] Mt 4:12 [o] Mt 4:23 **1:15** [p] Gal 4:4; Eph 1:10 [q] Ac 20:21 **1:21** [r] Mt 4:23; Mk 10:1 **1:22** [s] Mt 7:28, 29 **1:24** [t] Mt 8:29 [u] Mt 2:23; Lk 24:19; Ac 24:5 [v] Lk 1:35; Jn 6:69; Ac 3:14 **1:25** [w] ver 34 **1:26** [x] Mk 9:20 **1:27** [y] Mk 10:24, 32 **1:28** [z] Mt 9:26 **1:29** [a] ver 21, 23 **1:31** [b] Lk 7:14 **1:32** [c] Mt 4:24 **1:34** [d] Mt 4:23 [e] Mk 3:12; Ac 16:17, 18 **1:35** [f] Lk 3:21

him, they exclaimed: "Everyone is looking for you!"

[38]Jesus replied, "Let us go somewhere else—to the nearby villages—so I can preach there also. That is why I have come."[g] [39]So he traveled throughout Galilee, preaching in their synagogues[h] and driving out demons.[i]

Jesus Heals a Man With Leprosy

[40]A man with leprosy[a] came to him and begged him on his knees,[j] "If you are willing, you can make me clean."

[41]Jesus was indignant.[b] He reached out his hand and touched the man. "I am willing," he said. "Be clean!" [42]Immediately the leprosy left him and he was cleansed.

[43]Jesus sent him away at once with a strong warning: [44]"See that you don't tell this to anyone.[k] But go, show yourself to the priest[l] and offer the sacrifices that Moses commanded for your cleansing,[m] as a testimony to them." [45]Instead he went out and began to talk freely, spreading the news. As a result, Jesus could no longer enter a town openly but stayed outside in lonely places.[n] Yet the people still came to him from everywhere.[o]

Jesus Forgives and Heals a Paralyzed Man

2 A few days later, when Jesus again entered Capernaum, the people heard that he had come home. [2]They gathered in such large numbers[p] that there was no room left, not even outside the door, and he preached the word to them. [3]Some men came, bringing to him a paralyzed man,[q] carried by four of them. [4]Since they could not get him to Jesus because of the crowd, they made an opening in the roof above Jesus by digging through it and then lowered the mat the man was lying on. [5]When Jesus saw their faith, he said to the paralyzed man, "Son, your sins are forgiven."[r]

[6]Now some teachers of the law were sitting there, thinking to themselves, [7]"Why does this fellow talk like that? He's blaspheming! Who can forgive sins but God alone?"[s]

[8]Immediately Jesus knew in his spirit that this was what they were thinking in their hearts, and he said to them, "Why are you thinking these things? [9]Which is easier: to say to this paralyzed man, 'Your sins are forgiven,' or to say, 'Get up, take your mat and walk'? [10]But I want you to know that the Son of Man[t] has authority on earth to forgive sins." So he said to the man, [11]"I tell you, get up, take your mat and go home." [12]He got up, took his mat and walked out in full view of them all. This amazed everyone and they praised God,[u] saying, "We have never seen anything like this!"[v]

Jesus Calls Levi and Eats With Sinners

[13]Once again Jesus went out beside the lake. A large crowd came to him,[w] and he began to teach them. [14]As he walked along, he saw Levi son of Alphaeus sitting at the tax collector's booth. "Follow me,"[x] Jesus told him, and Levi got up and followed him.

[15]While Jesus was having dinner at Levi's house, many tax collectors and sinners were eating with him and his disciples, for there were many who followed him. [16]When the teachers of the law who were Pharisees[y] saw him eating with the sinners and tax collectors, they asked his disciples: "Why does he eat with tax collectors and sinners?"[z]

[17]On hearing this, Jesus said to them, "It is not the healthy who need a doctor, but the sick. I have not come to call the righteous, but sinners."[a]

Jesus Questioned About Fasting

[18]Now John's disciples and the Pharisees were fasting.[b] Some people came and

[a] *40* The Greek word traditionally translated *leprosy* was used for various diseases affecting the skin. [b] *41* Many manuscripts *Jesus was filled with compassion*

Jesus prayed continuously. Jesus' prayer life was successful because it was planned, private, and prolonged. He got up early enough, got far enough away, and stayed at it long enough.

1:44 *don't tell this to anyone.* Jesus' demand has several plausible explanations: (1) The report of Jesus' healing the man may have prejudiced the priest who needed to pronounce him clean; (2) Jesus did not want to be known primarily as a miracle worker, so He often commanded those who received His healing to remain quiet; and (3) the man's testimony would possibly have hastened the confrontation between Jesus and the religious leaders.

2:5 *saw their faith.* Not only did the four men have faith, but the paralytic himself had it too. When Jesus announced to him, "your sins are forgiven you," He was implicitly acknowledging the paralytic's trust that He was the Messiah.

2:6–7 *some teachers of the law.* Mark notes the opposition of the teachers of the law, who under their breath accused Jesus of blasphemy.

2:11 *get up, take your mat and go home.* By healing the paralytic, Jesus made His pronouncement of forgiveness far more credible.

2:13 *he began to teach them.* Jesus regularly taught the multitudes in retreat settings. This is indicated by the continuous tense of the verbs used here. They kept on coming and Jesus kept on teaching.

2:18 *fasting.* Jesus was not against fasting, if properly observed. He gave guidelines for fasting in the

1:38 [g] Isa 61:1 **1:39** [h] Mt 4:23 [i] Mt 4:24 **1:40** [j] Mk 10:17 **1:44** [k] Mt 8:4 [l] Lev 13:49 [m] Lev 14:1-32 **1:45** [n] Lk 5:15, 16 [o] Mk 2:13; Lk 5:17; Jn 6:2 **2:2** [p] ver 13; Mk 1:45 **2:3** [q] Mt 4:24 **2:5** [r] Lk 7:48 **2:7** [s] Isa 43:25 **2:10** [t] Mt 8:20 **2:12** [u] Mt 9:8 [v] Mt 9:33 **2:13** [w] Mk 1:45; Lk 5:15; Jn 6:2 **2:14** [x] Mt 4:19 **2:16** [y] Ac 23:9 [z] Mt 9:11 **2:17** [a] Lk 19:10; 1Ti 1:15 **2:18** [b] Mt 6:16-18; Ac 13:2

asked Jesus, "How is it that John's disciples
and the disciples of the Pharisees are fasting, but yours are not?"
19 Jesus answered, "How can the guests
of the bridegroom fast while he is with
them? They cannot, so long as they have
him with them. 20 But the time will come
when the bridegroom will be taken from
them,[c] and on that day they will fast.
21 "No one sews a patch of unshrunk
cloth on an old garment. Otherwise, the
new piece will pull away from the old,
making the tear worse. 22 And no one pours
new wine into old wineskins. Otherwise,
the wine will burst the skins, and both the
wine and the wineskins will be ruined. No,
they pour new wine into new wineskins."

Jesus Is Lord of the Sabbath

23 One Sabbath Jesus was going through
the grainfields, and as his disciples walked
along, they began to pick some heads of
grain.[d] 24 The Pharisees said to him, "Look,
why are they doing what is unlawful on the
Sabbath?"[e]
25 He answered, "Have you never read
what David did when he and his companions were hungry and in need? 26 In
the days of Abiathar the high priest,[f] he
entered the house of God and ate the consecrated bread, which is lawful only for
priests to eat.[g] And he also gave some to
his companions."[h]
27 Then he said to them, "The Sabbath
was made for man,[i] not man for the Sabbath.[j] 28 So the Son of Man[k] is Lord even of
the Sabbath."

Jesus Heals on the Sabbath

3 Another time Jesus went into the synagogue,[l] and a man with a shriveled
hand was there. 2 Some of them were looking for a reason to accuse Jesus, so they
watched him closely[m] to see if he would
heal him on the Sabbath.[n] 3 Jesus said to
the man with the shriveled hand, "Stand
up in front of everyone."
4 Then Jesus asked them, "Which is lawful on the Sabbath: to do good or to do evil,
to save life or to kill?" But they remained
silent.
5 He looked around at them in anger and,
deeply distressed at their stubborn hearts,
said to the man, "Stretch out your hand."
He stretched it out, and his hand was completely restored. 6 Then the Pharisees went
out and began to plot with the Herodians[o]
how they might kill Jesus.[p]

Crowds Follow Jesus

7 Jesus withdrew with his disciples to
the lake, and a large crowd from Galilee
followed.[q] 8 When they heard about all he
was doing, many people came to him from
Judea, Jerusalem, Idumea, and the regions
across the Jordan and around Tyre and Sidon.[r] 9 Because of the crowd he told his disciples to have a small boat ready for him, to
keep the people from crowding him. 10 For
he had healed many,[s] so that those with
diseases were pushing forward to touch
him.[t] 11 Whenever the impure spirits saw
him, they fell down before him and cried
out, "You are the Son of God."[u] 12 But he
gave them strict orders not to tell others
about him.[v]

Jesus Appoints the Twelve

13 Jesus went up on a mountainside and
called to him those he wanted, and they
came to him.[w] 14 He appointed twelve[a][x] that
they might be with him and that he might
send them out to preach 15 and to have au-

---

a 14 Some manuscripts *twelve—designating them apostles—*

Sermon on the Mount (Matt. 6:16–18). Here, the Pharisees' fasting, perhaps twice each week (Luke 18:12), is contrasted with Jesus feasting probably at Levi's house.

2:21–22 *No one sews . . . no one pours.* Mark records only four of Jesus' parables—two of which he includes here. The comparison implies that the newness of His message, and of the new covenant to follow, cannot fit into the old molds of Judaism. The Old Testament was preparation for the New Testament (Gal. 3:19–25).

2:24 *what is unlawful on the Sabbath.* The point to the Pharisees' accusation against Jesus and His disciples was that they had performed work on the Sabbath, but their charge was dubious. The act of plucking grain should not be confused with Sabbath work condemned by the law (Ex. 31:15). This incident is further proof of rising opposition to Jesus' ministry.

3:5 *He looked around at them in anger.* It is possible, as Paul exhorts, to be angry and not sin (Eph. 4:26). Jesus demonstrated this righteous anger. He was grieved with sin but did not sin Himself by retaliating or losing control of His emotions.

3:6 *Herodians.* The Pharisees were religious experts who should have led the people in righteousness. Instead they plotted Jesus' death with the Herodians, their bitter enemies. They were willing to set aside differences to destroy a common foe. The Herodians were Jews who supported Rome and the Herods in particular. Herod Antipas, a son of Herod the Great, ruled Galilee during the same time that Pilate served as Roman governor over Judea and Samaria.

3:11–12 *he gave them strict orders not to tell others about him.* Jesus rebuked the demons who proclaimed "Thou art the Son of God." This was not because the demons incorrectly identified Jesus, but because their testimony was untrustworthy.

2:20 [c] Lk 17:22 **2:23** [d] Dt 23:25 **2:24** [e] Mt 12:2
2:26 [f] 1Ch 24:6; 2Sa 8:17 [g] Lev 24:5-9 [h] 1Sa 21:1-6
2:27 [i] Ex 23:12; Dt 5:14 [j] Col 2:16 **2:28** [k] Mt 8:20
3:1 [l] Mt 4:23; Mk 1:21 **3:2** [m] Mt 12:10 [n] Lk 14:1
3:6 [o] Mt 22:16; Mk 12:13 [p] Mt 12:14 **3:7** [q] Mt 4:25
3:8 [r] Mt 11:21 **3:10** [s] Mt 4:23 [t] Mt 9:20 **3:11** [u] Mt 4:3; Mk 1:23, 24 **3:12** [v] Mt 8:4; Mk 1:24, 25, 34; Ac 16:17, 18
3:13 [w] Mt 5:1 **3:14** [x] Mk 6:30

thority to drive out demons.[y] 16These are
the twelve he appointed: Simon (to whom
he gave the name Peter),[z] 17James son of
Zebedee and his brother John (to them he
gave the name Boanerges, which means
"sons of thunder"), 18Andrew, Philip, Bartholomew, Matthew, Thomas, James son
of Alphaeus, Thaddaeus, Simon the Zealot 19and Judas Iscariot, who betrayed him.

Jesus Accused by His Family and by Teachers of the Law

20Then Jesus entered a house, and again
a crowd gathered,[a] so that he and his disciples were not even able to eat.[b] 21When his
family[a] heard about this, they went to take
charge of him, for they said, "He is out of
his mind."[c]

22And the teachers of the law who came
down from Jerusalem[d] said, "He is possessed by Beelzebul![e] By the prince of demons he is driving out demons."[f]

23So Jesus called them over to him and
began to speak to them in parables:[g] "How
can Satan[h] drive out Satan? 24If a kingdom
is divided against itself, that kingdom cannot stand. 25If a house is divided against
itself, that house cannot stand. 26And if Satan opposes himself and is divided, he cannot stand; his end has come. 27In fact, no
one can enter a strong man's house without first tying him up. Then he can plunder the strong man's house.[i] 28Truly I tell
you, people can be forgiven all their sins
and every slander they utter, 29but whoever blasphemes against the Holy Spirit
will never be forgiven; they are guilty of
an eternal sin."[j]

30He said this because they were saying,
"He has an impure spirit."

31Then Jesus' mother and brothers arrived.[k] Standing outside, they sent someone in to call him. 32A crowd was sitting
around him, and they told him, "Your
mother and brothers are outside looking
for you."

33"Who are my mother and my brothers?" he asked.

34Then he looked at those seated in a
circle around him and said, "Here are my
mother and my brothers! 35Whoever does
God's will is my brother and sister and
mother."

The Parable of the Sower

4 Again Jesus began to teach by the lake.[l]
The crowd that gathered around him
was so large that he got into a boat and sat
in it out on the lake, while all the people
were along the shore at the water's edge.
2He taught them many things by parables,[m] and in his teaching said: 3"Listen! A
farmer went out to sow his seed.[n] 4As he
was scattering the seed, some fell along
the path, and the birds came and ate it up.
5Some fell on rocky places, where it did not
have much soil. It sprang up quickly, because the soil was shallow. 6But when the
sun came up, the plants were scorched, and
they withered because they had no root.
7Other seed fell among thorns, which grew
up and choked the plants, so that they did
not bear grain. 8Still other seed fell on good
soil. It came up, grew and produced a crop,
some multiplying thirty, some sixty, some
a hundred times."[o]

9Then Jesus said, "Whoever has ears to
hear, let them hear."[p]

10When he was alone, the Twelve and
the others around him asked him about
the parables. 11He told them, "The secret
of the kingdom of God[q] has been given to

---

[a] 21 Or *his associates*

3:16–19 *gave the name Peter.* Jesus gave Peter a new name because it was the Jewish custom to rename someone who had experienced a life-changing event. This renaming of the disciples has similarities to the renaming of Abram (Gen. 17:3–5) and of Saul (Acts 9).

3:27 *strong man's house.* Whoever defeats Satan must be stronger than he. Jesus implies that He Himself has come to enter the house of the strong man, Satan, to seize his goods (1 John 3:8).

3:28–30 *whoever blasphemes against the Holy Spirit.* This person places himself or herself outside the redeeming grace of God. It is apparently not a single act of defiant behavior, but a continued state of opposition entered into willingly. The tense of "they were saying" indicates a continued action, not a one-time event. The words and works of Christ were spoken and performed by the power of the Holy Spirit. To attribute them to Satan is to call the work of heaven a work of hell. For such perverse belief there is no remedy. How someone can commit this sin today is a difficult question to answer, but those who persist in denigrating Christ by insulting His work or by attributing it to Satan may drive themselves past a point of no return (Matt. 12:31–32).

3:31 *Jesus' mother and brothers.* Opposition arose from Jesus' own immediate family. We are not told precisely what they wanted to say, but it likely involved a concern for Jesus' safety or reputation, since He was becoming widely known as a preaching prophet and a worker of miracles.

4:3–8 *A farmer went out to sow.* The point of the parable is that the condition of the soil determines the potential for growth. The principle is true for Christians and non-Christians alike. Those who have become complacent and lackadaisical are not likely to receive the Word with benefit (James 1:2–25).

4:11 *The secret of the kingdom of God has been given to you.* In Scripture, a mystery is a truth God has revealed or will reveal at the proper time (Rom. 16:25–26). Jesus apparently used parables for several reasons. First, they are interesting and grab the

3:15 [y] Mt 10:1 **3:16** [z] Jn 1:42 **3:20** [a] ver 7 [b] Mk 6:31 **3:21** [c] Jn 10:20; Ac 26:24 **3:22** [d] Mt 15:1 [e] Mt 10:25; 11:18; 12:24; Jn 7:20; 8:48,52; 10:20 [f] Mt 9:34 **3:23** [g] Mk 4:2 [h] Mt 4:10 **3:27** [i] Isa 49:24,25 **3:29** [j] Mt 12:31,32; Lk 12:10 **3:31** [k] ver 21 **4:1** [l] Mk 2:13; 3:7 **4:2** [m] ver 11; Mk 3:23 **4:3** [n] ver 26 **4:8** [o] Jn 15:5; Col 1:6 **4:9** [p] ver 23; Mt 11:15 **4:11** [q] Mt 3:2

you. But to those on the outside[r] everything is said in parables 12so that,

"'they may be ever seeing but never
perceiving,
and ever hearing but never
understanding;
otherwise they might turn and be
forgiven!'[a]"[s]

13Then Jesus said to them, "Don't you understand this parable? How then will you understand any parable? 14The farmer sows the word.[t] 15Some people are like seed along the path, where the word is sown. As soon as they hear it, Satan[u] comes and takes away the word that was sown in them. 16Others, like seed sown on rocky places, hear the word and at once receive it with joy. 17But since they have no root, they last only a short time. When trouble or persecution comes because of the word, they quickly fall away. 18Still others, like seed sown among thorns, hear the word; 19but the worries of this life, the deceitfulness of wealth[v] and the desires for other things come in and choke the word, making it unfruitful. 20Others, like seed sown on good soil, hear the word, accept it, and produce a crop—some thirty, some sixty, some a hundred times what was sown."

A Lamp on a Stand

21He said to them, "Do you bring in a lamp to put it under a bowl or a bed? Instead, don't you put it on its stand?[w] 22For whatever is hidden is meant to be disclosed, and whatever is concealed is meant to be brought out into the open.[x] 23If anyone has ears to hear, let them hear."[y]

24"Consider carefully what you hear," he continued. "With the measure you use, it will be measured to you—and even more.[z] 25Whoever has will be given more; whoever does not have, even what they have will be taken from them."[a]

The Parable of the Growing Seed

26He also said, "This is what the kingdom of God is like.[b] A man scatters seed on the ground. 27Night and day, whether he sleeps or gets up, the seed sprouts and grows, though he does not know how. 28All by itself the soil produces grain—first the stalk, then the head, then the full kernel in the head. 29As soon as the grain is ripe, he puts the sickle to it, because the harvest has come."[c]

The Parable of the Mustard Seed

30Again he said, "What shall we say the kingdom of God is like,[d] or what parable shall we use to describe it? 31It is like a mustard seed, which is the smallest of all seeds on earth. 32Yet when planted, it grows and becomes the largest of all garden plants, with such big branches that the birds can perch in its shade."

33With many similar parables Jesus spoke the word to them, as much as they could understand.[e] 34He did not say anything to them without using a parable.[f] But when he was alone with his own disciples, he explained everything.

Jesus Calms the Storm

35That day when evening came, he said to his disciples, "Let us go over to the other side." 36Leaving the crowd behind, they took him along, just as he was, in the boat.[g] There were also other boats with him. 37A furious squall came up, and the waves broke over the boat, so that it was nearly swamped. 38Jesus was in the stern, sleeping on a cushion. The disciples woke him and said to him, "Teacher, don't you care if we drown?"

39He got up, rebuked the wind and said to the waves, "Quiet! Be still!" Then the wind died down and it was completely calm.

a *12* Isaiah 6:9,10

---

listener's attention. Second, such stories are easily remembered. Third, they reveal truth to those who are ready spiritually to receive it. Fourth, they conceal truth from those who oppose Christ's message. Frequently Jesus' opponents failed to understand the lessons because of their own spiritual blindness (Matt. 21:45–46).

4:20 *hear the word, accept it, and produce a crop.* Only one soil produces fruit. Such a person recognizes God's call, determines to follow it, and experiences a profound transformation.

4:21–23 *a lamp.* These were small clay vessels that burned a wick set in olive oil. Like the lamp, Jesus' teachings reveal the motives of the human heart.

4:26–29 *the kingdom of God is like.* Plants develop in a complex, intricate process that humans still do not fully understand even two thousand years after Jesus spoke these words. Yet plants grow and bear fruit and seeds just the same. God's kingdom likewise is growing, although we do not understand all that is happening. This parable, which appears only in Mark's Gospel, presents God's kingdom in brief, from first sowing to final reaping.

4:35 *go over to the other side.* The Sea of Galilee is about eight miles wide and twelve miles long. Its unique geography produces a greatly varying climate. It is 700 feet below sea level with mountains that rise 3,000–4,000 feet around it. It is not unusual for sudden windstorms to appear during the evening hours. The warm tropical air from the lake's surface rises and meets the colder air from the nearby hills. The resulting turbulences and winds can be treacherous.

4:11 [r] 1Co 5:12, 13; Col 4:5; 1Th 4:12; 1Ti 3:7 **4:12** [s] Isa 6:9, 10; Mt 13:13-15 **4:14** [t] Mk 16:20; Lk 1:2; Ac 4:31; 8:4; 16:6; 17:11; Php 1:14 **4:15** [u] Mt 4:10 **4:19** [v] Mt 19:23; 1Ti 6:9, 10, 17; 1Jn 2:15-17 **4:21** [w] Mt 5:15 **4:22** [x] Jer 16:17; Mt 10:26; Lk 8:17; 12:2 **4:23** [y] ver 9; Mt 11:15 **4:24** [z] Mt 7:2; Lk 6:38 **4:25** [a] Mt 13:12; 25:29 **4:26** [b] Mt 13:24 **4:29** [c] Rev 14:15 **4:30** [d] Mt 13:24 **4:33** [e] Jn 16:12 **4:34** [f] Jn 16:25 **4:36** [g] ver 1; Mk 3:9; 5:2,21; 6:32,45

40He said to his disciples, "Why are you so afraid? Do you still have no faith?"[h]

41They were terrified and asked each other, "Who is this? Even the wind and the waves obey him!"

Jesus Restores a Demon-Possessed Man

5 They went across the lake to the region of the Gerasenes.[a] 2When Jesus got out of the boat,[i] a man with an impure spirit[j] came from the tombs to meet him. 3This man lived in the tombs, and no one could bind him anymore, not even with a chain. 4For he had often been chained hand and foot, but he tore the chains apart and broke the irons on his feet. No one was strong enough to subdue him. 5Night and day among the tombs and in the hills he would cry out and cut himself with stones.

6When he saw Jesus from a distance, he ran and fell on his knees in front of him. 7He shouted at the top of his voice, "What do you want with me,[k] Jesus, Son of the Most High God?[l] In God's name don't torture me!" 8For Jesus had said to him, "Come out of this man, you impure spirit!"

9Then Jesus asked him, "What is your name?"

"My name is Legion,"[m] he replied, "for we are many." 10And he begged Jesus again and again not to send them out of the area.

11A large herd of pigs was feeding on the nearby hillside. 12The demons begged Jesus, "Send us among the pigs; allow us to go into them." 13He gave them permission, and the impure spirits came out and went into the pigs. The herd, about two thousand in number, rushed down the steep bank into the lake and were drowned.

14Those tending the pigs ran off and reported this in the town and countryside, and the people went out to see what had happened. 15When they came to Jesus, they saw the man who had been possessed by the legion[n] of demons,[o] sitting there, dressed and in his right mind; and they were afraid. 16Those who had seen it told the people what had happened to the demon-possessed man—and told about the pigs as well. 17Then the people began to plead with Jesus to leave their region.

18As Jesus was getting into the boat, the man who had been demon-possessed begged to go with him. 19Jesus did not let him, but said, "Go home to your own people and tell them[p] how much the Lord has done for you, and how he has had mercy on you." 20So the man went away and began to tell in the Decapolis[b][q] how much Jesus had done for him. And all the people were amazed.

Jesus Raises a Dead Girl and Heals a Sick Woman

21When Jesus had again crossed over by boat to the other side of the lake,[r] a large crowd gathered around him while he was by the lake.[s] 22Then one of the synagogue leaders,[t] named Jairus, came, and when he saw Jesus, he fell at his feet. 23He pleaded earnestly with him, "My little daughter is dying. Please come and put your hands on[u] her so that she will be healed and live." 24So Jesus went with him.

A large crowd followed and pressed around him. 25And a woman was there who had been subject to bleeding[v] for twelve years. 26She had suffered a great deal under the care of many doctors and had spent all she had, yet instead of getting better she grew worse. 27When she heard about Jesus, she came up behind him in the crowd and touched his cloak, 28because she thought, "If I just touch his clothes,[w] I will be healed." 29Immediately her bleeding stopped and she felt in her body that she was freed from her suffering.[x]

30At once Jesus realized that power[y] had gone out from him. He turned around in

---

[a] *1* Some manuscripts *Gadarenes;* other manuscripts *Gergesenes* [b] *20* That is, the Ten Cities

---

4:41 ***Who is this.*** Mark uses the disciples' question to evoke a similar response in the minds of his readers. Mark relates the works and words of the one he calls "Jesus the Messiah, the Son of God" (1:1).

5:1 ***the region of the Gerasenes.*** This area is on the eastern shore of the Sea of Galilee. The form of the name varies (Matt. 8:28; Luke 8:26,37).

5:17–20 ***the people began to plead with Jesus to leave their region.*** Jesus was not well received in this region. His presence had cost financial loss to some, although it meant liberation to the demoniac. Jesus could have healed and saved in that region, but He was turned away by its fearful citizens. ***Decapolis.*** This literally means "ten cities." This largely Gentile, Greek-speaking area was an important strategic link in Rome's military defense.

5:22 ***one of the synagogue leaders.*** Jairus was a lay leader charged with supervising services at the synagogue.

5:26 ***suffered a great deal under the care of many doctors.*** Mark is not complimentary toward the physicians who had treated this woman.

5:29–30 ***Immediately.*** This word is used twice in this context. Both the woman and Jesus simultaneously knew what had happened. ***Who touched my clothes?*** Jesus turned when He was touched and confronted the woman before she disappeared. He wanted to correct any mistaken notion she may have had about her healing. It was not any magical quality of His clothing but His divine will that had made her well.

4:40 [h] Mt 14:31; Mk 16:14 **5:2** [i] Mk 4:1 [j] Mk 1:23 **5:7** [k] Mt 8:29 [l] Mt 4:3; Lk 1:32; 6:35; Ac 16:17; Heb 7:1 **5:9** [m] ver 15 **5:15** [n] ver 9 [o] ver 16, 18; Mt 4:24 **5:19** [p] Mt 8:4 **5:20** [q] Mt 4:25; Mk 7:31 **5:21** [r] Mt 9:1 [s] Mk 4:1 **5:22** [t] ver 35, 36, 38; Lk 13:14; Ac 13:15; 18:8, 17 **5:23** [u] Mt 19:13; Mk 6:5; 7:32; 8:23; 16:18; Lk 4:40; 13:13; Ac 6:6 **5:25** [v] Lev 15:25-30 **5:28** [w] Mt 9:20 **5:29** [x] ver 34 **5:30** [y] Lk 5:17; 6:19

the crowd and asked, “Who touched my clothes?”

31“You see the people crowding against you,” his disciples answered, “and yet you can ask, ‘Who touched me?’ ”

32But Jesus kept looking around to see who had done it. 33Then the woman, knowing what had happened to her, came and fell at his feet and, trembling with fear, told him the whole truth. 34He said to her, “Daughter, your faith has healed you.[z] Go in peace[a] and be freed from your suffering.”

35While Jesus was still speaking, some people came from the house of Jairus, the synagogue leader.[b] “Your daughter is dead,” they said. “Why bother the teacher anymore?”

36Overhearing[a] what they said, Jesus told him, “Don’t be afraid; just believe.”

37He did not let anyone follow him except Peter, James and John the brother of James.[c] 38When they came to the home of the synagogue leader,[d] Jesus saw a commotion, with people crying and wailing loudly. 39He went in and said to them, “Why all this commotion and wailing? The child is not dead but asleep.”[e] 40But they laughed at him.

After he put them all out, he took the child’s father and mother and the disciples who were with him, and went in where the child was. 41He took her by the hand[f] and said to her, *“Talitha koum!”* (which means “Little girl, I say to you, get up!”).[g] 42Immediately the girl stood up and began to walk around (she was twelve years old). At this they were completely astonished. 43He gave strict orders not to let anyone know about this,[h] and told them to give her something to eat.

A Prophet Without Honor

6 Jesus left there and went to his hometown,[i] accompanied by his disciples. 2When the Sabbath came,[j] he began to teach in the synagogue,[k] and many who heard him were amazed.[l]

“Where did this man get these things?” they asked. “What’s this wisdom that has been given him? What are these remarkable miracles he is performing? 3Isn’t this the carpenter? Isn’t this Mary’s son and the brother of James, Joseph,[b] Judas and Simon?[m] Aren’t his sisters here with us?” And they took offense at him.[n]

4Jesus said to them, “A prophet is not without honor except in his own town, among his relatives and in his own home.”[o] 5He could not do any miracles there, except lay his hands on[p] a few sick people and heal them. 6He was amazed at their lack of faith.

Jesus Sends Out the Twelve

Then Jesus went around teaching from village to village.[q] 7Calling the Twelve to him,[r] he began to send them out two by two[s] and gave them authority over impure spirits.[t]

8These were his instructions: “Take nothing for the journey except a staff—no bread, no bag, no money in your belts. 9Wear sandals but not an extra shirt. 10Whenever you enter a house, stay there until you leave that town. 11And if any place will not welcome you or listen to you, leave that place and shake the dust off your feet[u] as a testimony against them.”

12They went out and preached that people should repent.[v] 13They drove out many demons and anointed many sick people with oil[w] and healed them.

John the Baptist Beheaded

14King Herod heard about this, for Jesus’ name had become well known. Some were saying,[c] “John the Baptist[x] has been raised from the dead, and that is why miraculous powers are at work in him.”

15Others said, “He is Elijah.”[y]

And still others claimed, “He is a prophet,[z] like one of the prophets of long ago.”[a]

16But when Herod heard this, he said, “John, whom I beheaded, has been raised from the dead!”

17For Herod himself had given orders to

[a] 36 Or *Ignoring* [b] 3 Greek *Joses,* a variant of *Joseph* [c] 14 Some early manuscripts *He was saying*

5:33 *told him the whole truth.* Jesus’ kind manner and tender words must have eased the fear this woman had of being revealed. Naturally, the time that Jesus took to care for the woman must have worried the already tense disciples.

5:34 *Daughter.* Jesus used this tender word to address this woman, and He noted that her faith made the difference, for it was correctly placed in Him. Faith itself does not heal—it is the proper object of that faith, Jesus, who heals.

5:43 *He gave strict orders.* The command to keep the miracle a secret was a temporary measure, for certainly the girl’s appearance could not be hidden very long. Such orders would, however, allow Jesus to exit quietly. Jesus did not want to be known primarily as a miracle worker, lest people seek Him for the wrong reasons.

6:4 *A prophet is not without honor except in his own town.* This maxim is still repeated and is still true today. Perhaps others were jealous of Jesus’ popularity and huge following. Their envy even took the form of violence against Christ (Luke 4:29).

6:14 *King Herod.* This is Herod Antipas, one of the sons of Herod the Great, the king who tried to kill the baby Jesus (Matt. 2:1–18). After Herod the Great’s

5:34 [z] Mt 9:22 [a] Ac 15:33 **5:35** [b] ver 22 **5:37** [c] Mt 4:21 **5:38** [d] ver 22 **5:39** [e] Mt 9:24 **5:41** [f] Mk 1:31 [g] Lk 7:14; Ac 9:40 **5:43** [h] Mt 8:4 **6:1** [i] Mt 2:23 **6:2** [j] Mk 1:21 [k] Mt 4:23 [l] Mt 7:28 **6:3** [m] Mt 12:46 [n] Mt 11:6; Jn 6:61 **6:4** [o] Lk 4:24; Jn 4:44 **6:5** [p] Mk 5:23 **6:6** [q] Mt 9:35; Mk 1:39; Lk 13:22 **6:7** [r] Mk 3:13 [s] Dt 17:6; Lk 10:1 [t] Mt 10:1 **6:11** [u] Mt 10:14 **6:12** [v] Lk 9:6 **6:13** [w] Jas 5:14 **6:14** [x] Mt 3:1 **6:15** [y] Mal 4:5 [z] Mt 21:11 [a] Mt 16:14; Mk 8:28

have John arrested, and he had him bound and put in prison.[b] He did this because of Herodias, his brother Philip's wife, whom he had married. 18For John had been saying to Herod, "It is not lawful for you to have your brother's wife."[c] 19So Herodias nursed a grudge against John and wanted to kill him. But she was not able to, 20because Herod feared John and protected him, knowing him to be a righteous and holy man.[d] When Herod heard John, he was greatly puzzled[a]; yet he liked to listen to him.

21Finally the opportune time came. On his birthday Herod gave a banquet[e] for his high officials and military commanders and the leading men of Galilee.[f] 22When the daughter of[b] Herodias came in and danced, she pleased Herod and his dinner guests.

The king said to the girl, "Ask me for anything you want, and I'll give it to you." 23And he promised her with an oath, "Whatever you ask I will give you, up to half my kingdom."[g]

24She went out and said to her mother, "What shall I ask for?"

"The head of John the Baptist," she answered.

25At once the girl hurried in to the king with the request: "I want you to give me right now the head of John the Baptist on a platter."

26The king was greatly distressed, but because of his oaths and his dinner guests, he did not want to refuse her. 27So he immediately sent an executioner with orders to bring John's head. The man went, beheaded John in the prison, 28and brought back his head on a platter. He presented it to the girl, and she gave it to her mother. 29On hearing of this, John's disciples came and took his body and laid it in a tomb.

Jesus Feeds the Five Thousand

30The apostles[h] gathered around Jesus and reported to him all they had done and taught.[i] 31Then, because so many people were coming and going that they did not even have a chance to eat,[j] he said to them, "Come with me by yourselves to a quiet place and get some rest."

32So they went away by themselves in a boat[k] to a solitary place. 33But many who saw them leaving recognized them and ran on foot from all the towns and got there ahead of them. 34When Jesus landed and saw a large crowd, he had compassion on them, because they were like sheep without a shepherd.[l] So he began teaching them many things.

35By this time it was late in the day, so his disciples came to him. "This is a remote place," they said, "and it's already very late. 36Send the people away so that they can go to the surrounding countryside and villages and buy themselves something to eat."

37But he answered, "You give them something to eat."[m]

They said to him, "That would take more than half a year's wages[c]! Are we to go and spend that much on bread and give it to them to eat?"

38"How many loaves do you have?" he asked. "Go and see."

When they found out, they said, "Five—and two fish."[n]

39Then Jesus directed them to have all the people sit down in groups on the green grass. 40So they sat down in groups of hundreds and fifties. 41Taking the five loaves and the two fish and looking up to heaven, he gave thanks and broke the loaves.[o] Then he gave them to his disciples to distribute to the people. He also divided the two fish among them all. 42They all ate and were satisfied, 43and the disciples picked up twelve basketfuls of broken pieces of bread and fish. 44The number of the men who had eaten was five thousand.

---

[a] 20 Some early manuscripts *he did many things*
[b] 22 Some early manuscripts *When his daughter*
[c] 37 Greek *take two hundred denarii*

---

death in 4 B.C. his kingdom was divided between Archelaus, who received Judea and Samaria; Philip, who ruled Iturea and Trachonitis, north and east of Galilee; and Antipas, who controlled Galilee and Perea from 4 B.C. to A.D. 39. Jesus ministered largely in the territory ruled by Antipas.

6:18 ***not lawful.*** John's message to Herod was that his divorce was not lawful as grounds for remarriage. John's declaration could be based on Jesus' stern words about divorce (10:11 – 12) or on Leviticus 20:21, which prohibits a man from taking his brother's wife.

6:23 ***up to half my kingdom.*** This is an expression meaning a large amount but with some limits.

6:34 ***had compassion on them.*** The Gospels record several times that when Jesus saw a need He responded compassionately (1:41). That compassion led to action, despite an obvious lack of food in this instance.

6:36 – 37 ***Send the people away.*** The disciples sought to avoid responsibility for the hungry multitude.

6:39 – 40 ***in groups of hundreds and fifties.*** Details such as sitting on the green grass, which is possible only in late winter and early spring, and the fact that the groups were counted are indications that an eyewitness, probably Peter, recounted this story to Mark.

6:43 ***twelve basketfuls of broken pieces.*** These were small baskets commonly carried by travelers. It is possible to conclude that the leftovers gave each disciple enough food for his own use.

6:17 [b] Mt 4:12; 11:2; Lk 3:19,20 **6:18** [c] Lev 18:16; 20:21 **6:20** [d] Mt 11:9; 21:26 **6:21** [e] Est 1:3; 2:18 [f] Lk 3:1 **6:23** [g] Est 5:3,6; 7:2 **6:30** [h] Mt 10:2; Lk 9:10, 17.5, 22:14; 24:10; Ac 1:2,26 [i] Lk 9:10 **6:31** [j] Mk 3:20 **6:32** [k] ver 45; Mk 4:36 **6:34** [l] Mt 9:36 **6:37** [m] 2Ki 4:42-44 **6:38** [n] Mt 15:34; Mk 8:5 **6:41** [o] Mt 14:19

Jesus Walks on the Water

45Immediately Jesus made his disciples get into the boat[p] and go on ahead of
him to Bethsaida,[q] while he dismissed the
crowd. 46After leaving them, he went up on
a mountainside to pray.[r]
47Later that night, the boat was in the
middle of the lake, and he was alone on
land. 48He saw the disciples straining at the
oars, because the wind was against them.
Shortly before dawn he went out to them,
walking on the lake. He was about to pass
by them, 49but when they saw him walking
on the lake, they thought he was a ghost.[s]
They cried out, 50because they all saw him
and were terrified.
Immediately he spoke to them and said,
"Take courage! It is I. Don't be afraid."[t]
51Then he climbed into the boat[u] with
them, and the wind died down.[v] They were
completely amazed, 52for they had not
understood about the loaves; their hearts
were hardened.[w]
53When they had crossed over, they
landed at Gennesaret and anchored there.[x]
54As soon as they got out of the boat, people recognized Jesus. 55They ran throughout that whole region and carried the sick
on mats to wherever they heard he was.
56And wherever he went—into villages,
towns or countryside—they placed the sick
in the marketplaces. They begged him to
let them touch even the edge of his cloak,[y]
and all who touched it were healed.

That Which Defiles

7 The Pharisees and some of the teachers
of the law who had come from Jerusalem gathered around Jesus 2and saw some
of his disciples eating food with hands that
were defiled,[z] that is, unwashed. 3(The
Pharisees and all the Jews do not eat unless
they give their hands a ceremonial washing, holding to the tradition of the elders.[a]
4When they come from the marketplace
they do not eat unless they wash. And they
observe many other traditions, such as the
washing of cups, pitchers and kettles.[a])[b]
5So the Pharisees and teachers of the
law asked Jesus, "Why don't your disciples live according to the tradition of the
elders[c] instead of eating their food with defiled hands?"
6He replied, "Isaiah was right when he
prophesied about you hypocrites; as it is
written:

> "'These people honor me with their lips,
> but their hearts are far from me.
> 7They worship me in vain;
> their teachings are merely human
> rules.'[b][d]

8You have let go of the commands of God
and are holding on to human traditions."[e]
9And he continued, "You have a fine
way of setting aside the commands of God
in order to observe[c] your own traditions![f]
10For Moses said, 'Honor your father and
mother,'[d][g] and, 'Anyone who curses their
father or mother is to be put to death.'[e][h]
11But you say[i] that if anyone declares that
what might have been used to help their father or mother is Corban (that is, devoted
to God)— 12then you no longer let them do
anything for their father or mother. 13Thus
you nullify the word of God[j] by your tradition[k] that you have handed down. And you
do many things like that."
14Again Jesus called the crowd to him
and said, "Listen to me, everyone, and understand this. 15Nothing outside a person
can defile them by going into them. Rather,
it is what comes out of a person that defiles
them." [16][f]
17After he had left the crowd and entered
the house, his disciples asked him[l] about
this parable. 18"Are you so dull?" he asked.

---

[a] *4* Some early manuscripts *pitchers, kettles and dining couches* [b] *6,7* Isaiah 29:13 [c] *9* Some manuscripts *set up* [d] *10* Exodus 20:12; Deut. 5:16 [e] *10* Exodus 21:17; Lev. 20:9 [f] *16* Some manuscripts include here the words of 4:23.

6:51 ***he climbed into the boat with them.*** Three miracles are contained in this brief account (vv. 47–51): (1) In the darkness Jesus saw the disciples out in the storm miles away, (2) Jesus walked on the water, and (3) Jesus showed complete control over His creation when the wind ceased.
6:56 ***wherever he went—into villages, towns or countryside.*** Mark summarizes Jesus' healing ministry, noting how widespread it was.
7:3–4 ***The Pharisees.*** These two verses explain the tradition of handwashing and various kinds of ceremonial uncleanness. Mark's intended readers in Rome likely needed more background on the Jewish faith to understand this controversy.
7:5 ***the tradition of the elders.*** This phrase refers to a series of rules meant to bolster the ceremonial law of the Jews. Its authority was not supported by Scripture. The question indirectly challenged Jesus, for as the disciples' teacher He was judged responsible for their actions.
7:6–7 ***hypocrites.*** The term originally referred to actors who wore masks on stage as they played different characters. Thus the Pharisees were not genuinely religious; they were merely playing a part for all to see.
7:11–13 ***But you say.*** This shows the absolute contrast between God's will and man's empty tradition. ***Corban.*** This was evidently a pious-sounding evasion of the requirement of honoring one's parents by supporting them financially.

6:45 [p] ver 32 [q] Mt 11:21 **6:46** [r] Lk 3:21 **6:49** [s] Lk 24:37 **6:50** [t] Mt 14:27 **6:51** [u] ver 32 [v] Mk 4:39 **6:52** [w] Mk 8:17-21 **6:53** [x] Jn 6:24,25 **6:56** [y] Mt 9:20 **7:2** [z] Ac 10:14,28; 11:8; Ro 14:14 **7:3** [a] ver 5,8,9,13; Lk 11:38 **7:4** [b] Mt 23:25; Lk 11:39 **7:5** [c] ver 3; Gal 1:14; Col 2:8 **7:7** [d] Isa 29:13 **7:8** [e] ver 3 **7:9** [f] ver 3 **7:10** [g] Ex 20:12; Dt 5:16 [h] Ex 21:17; Lev 20:9 **7:11** [i] Mt 23:16,18 **7:13** [j] Heb 4:12 [k] ver 3 **7:17** [l] Mk 9:28

"Don't you see that nothing that enters a person from the outside can defile them? 19For it doesn't go into their heart but into their stomach, and then out of the body." (In saying this, Jesus declared all foods[m] clean.)[n]

20He went on: "What comes out of a person is what defiles them. 21For it is from within, out of a person's heart, that evil thoughts come—sexual immorality, theft, murder, 22adultery, greed,[o] malice, deceit, lewdness, envy, slander, arrogance and folly. 23All these evils come from inside and defile a person."

Jesus Honors a Syrophoenician Woman's Faith

24Jesus left that place and went to the vicinity of Tyre.[a][p] He entered a house and did not want anyone to know it; yet he could not keep his presence secret. 25In fact, as soon as she heard about him, a woman whose little daughter was possessed by an impure spirit[q] came and fell at his feet. 26The woman was a Greek, born in Syrian Phoenicia. She begged Jesus to drive the demon out of her daughter.

27"First let the children eat all they want," he told her, "for it is not right to take the children's bread and toss it to the dogs."

28"Lord," she replied, "even the dogs under the table eat the children's crumbs."

29Then he told her, "For such a reply, you may go; the demon has left your daughter."

30She went home and found her child lying on the bed, and the demon gone.

Jesus Heals a Deaf and Mute Man

31Then Jesus left the vicinity of Tyre[r] and went through Sidon, down to the Sea of Galilee[s] and into the region of the Decapolis.[b][t] 32There some people brought to him a man who was deaf and could hardly talk,[u] and they begged Jesus to place his hand on[v] him.

33After he took him aside, away from the crowd, Jesus put his fingers into the man's ears. Then he spit[w] and touched the man's tongue. 34He looked up to heaven[x] and with a deep sigh[y] said to him, "*Ephphatha!*" (which means "Be opened!"). 35At this, the man's ears were opened, his tongue was loosened and he began to speak plainly.[z]

36Jesus commanded them not to tell anyone.[a] But the more he did so, the more they kept talking about it. 37People were overwhelmed with amazement. "He has done everything well," they said. "He even makes the deaf hear and the mute speak."

Jesus Feeds the Four Thousand

8 During those days another large crowd gathered. Since they had nothing to eat, Jesus called his disciples to him and said, 2"I have compassion for these people;[b] they have already been with me three days and have nothing to eat. 3If I send them home hungry, they will collapse on the way, because some of them have come a long distance."

4His disciples answered, "But where in this remote place can anyone get enough bread to feed them?"

5"How many loaves do you have?" Jesus asked.

"Seven," they replied.

6He told the crowd to sit down on the ground. When he had taken the seven loaves and given thanks, he broke them and gave them to his disciples to distribute to the people, and they did so. 7They had a few small fish as well; he gave thanks for them also and told the disciples to distribute them.[c] 8The people ate and were satisfied. Afterward the disciples picked up seven basketfuls of broken pieces that were left over.[d] 9About four thousand were present. After he had sent them away, 10he got into the boat with his disciples and went to the region of Dalmanutha.

11The Pharisees came and began to question Jesus. To test him, they asked him

---

[a] 24 Many early manuscripts *Tyre and Sidon*
[b] 31 That is, the Ten Cities

7:24 ***the vicinity of Tyre.*** This city is the farthest Jesus traveled from Israel during his public ministry.
7:27 ***to the dogs.*** Jesus is not attempting to insult the woman by using this metaphor. In fact, He is testing her faith. Matthew records Jesus' reaction to her reply, "Woman, you have great faith" (Matt. 15:28).
7:28 ***she replied.*** The woman understood Jesus' test and persistently replied that even during the meal the dogs consume the children's crumbs that fall from the table.
7:32–35 ***who was deaf.*** The healing of this deaf man (who also had a speech impediment) is one of the two miracles recorded by Mark only. (The other is the healing of the blind man in 8:22–26.)
8:8 ***seven basketfuls.*** There was one basket for each original loaf. These baskets were much larger than the 12 small personal baskets mentioned in 6:43. It was the kind of larger basket that was used to lower Paul over the wall of Damascus (Acts 9:25).
8:10 ***Dalmanutha.*** This was probably on the western side of the Sea of Galilee, about three miles north of modern Tiberias and about five miles southwest of Capernaum. This is the only time it is mentioned in the New Testament.
8:11 ***The Pharisees came and began to question Jesus.*** The Pharisees' testing of Jesus was crafty and devious. Obviously these men did not heed the many signs and wonders that Jesus had already performed. John 20:30–31 indicates that the signs were meant to produce faith. It is doubtful that the Pharisees would

7:19 [m] Ro 14:1-12; Col 2:16; 1Ti 4:3-5 [n] Ac 10:15 **7:22** [o] Mt 20:15 **7:24** [p] Mt 11:21 **7:25** [q] Mt 4:24 **7:31** [r] ver 24; Mt 11:21 [s] Mt 4:18 [t] Mt 4:25; Mk 5:20 **7:32** [u] Mt 9:32; Lk 11:14 [v] Mk 5:23 **7:33** [w] Mk 8:23 **7:34** [x] Mk 6:41; Jn 11:41 [y] Mk 8:12 **7:35** [z] Isa 35:5,6 **7:36** [a] Mt 8:4 **8:2** [b] Mt 9:36 **8:7** [c] Mt 14:19 **8:8** [d] ver 20

for a sign from heaven.[e] 12He sighed deeply[f] and said, "Why does this generation ask for a sign? Truly I tell you, no sign will be given to it." 13Then he left them, got back into the boat and crossed to the other side.

The Yeast of the Pharisees and Herod

14The disciples had forgotten to bring bread, except for one loaf they had with them in the boat. 15"Be careful," Jesus warned them. "Watch out for the yeast[g] of the Pharisees[h] and that of Herod."[i]

16They discussed this with one another and said, "It is because we have no bread."

17Aware of their discussion, Jesus asked them: "Why are you talking about having no bread? Do you still not see or understand? Are your hearts hardened?[j] 18Do you have eyes but fail to see, and ears but fail to hear? And don't you remember? 19When I broke the five loaves for the five thousand, how many basketfuls of pieces did you pick up?"

"Twelve,"[k] they replied.

20"And when I broke the seven loaves for the four thousand, how many basketfuls of pieces did you pick up?"

They answered, "Seven."[l]

21He said to them, "Do you still not understand?"[m]

Jesus Heals a Blind Man at Bethsaida

22They came to Bethsaida,[n] and some people brought a blind man[o] and begged Jesus to touch him. 23He took the blind man by the hand and led him outside the village. When he had spit[p] on the man's eyes and put his hands on[q] him, Jesus asked, "Do you see anything?"

24He looked up and said, "I see people; they look like trees walking around."

25Once more Jesus put his hands on the man's eyes. Then his eyes were opened, his sight was restored, and he saw everything clearly. 26Jesus sent him home, saying, "Don't even go into[a] the village."

Peter Declares That Jesus Is the Messiah

27Jesus and his disciples went on to the villages around Caesarea Philippi. On the way he asked them, "Who do people say I am?"

28They replied, "Some say John the Baptist;[r] others say Elijah;[s] and still others, one of the prophets."

29"But what about you?" he asked. "Who do you say I am?"

Peter answered, "You are the Messiah."[t]

30Jesus warned them not to tell anyone about him.[u]

Jesus Predicts His Death

31He then began to teach them that the Son of Man[v] must suffer many things[w] and be rejected by the elders, the chief priests and the teachers of the law,[x] and that he must be killed[y] and after three days[z] rise again.[a] 32He spoke plainly[b] about this, and Peter took him aside and began to rebuke him.

33But when Jesus turned and looked at his disciples, he rebuked Peter. "Get behind me, Satan!"[c] he said. "You do not have in mind the concerns of God, but merely human concerns."

The Way of the Cross

34Then he called the crowd to him along with his disciples and said: "Whoever wants to be my disciple must deny themselves and take up their cross and follow me.[d] 35For whoever wants to save their life[b] will lose it, but whoever loses their life for

a *26* Some manuscripts *go and tell anyone in*
b *35* The Greek word means either *life* or *soul*; also in verses 36 and 37.

---

have changed their minds even if they had seen another miracle.

8:17–21 ***Do you still not see or understand?*** The disciples continued to show a lack of spiritual discernment despite the miracles they had witnessed. Jesus' rebuke was intended to make them recall what God had done for them.

8:27 ***Caesarea Philippi.*** This city is about 25 miles north of Bethsaida and the Sea of Galilee. It stands on the southern edge of Mount Hermon. One of the sources of the Jordan River springs forth from under a large rocky cliff that rises a hundred or more feet above the village. The name Philippi distinguishes this town from Caesarea by the sea.

8:29 ***Who do you say I am?*** Jesus emphatically asks His disciples for their understanding. ***you.*** Prominent in Jesus' question is the word "you." ***You are the Messiah.*** Peter answers for the group. Jesus wants His disciples to grasp firmly His true identity before He reveals to them the necessity of His coming death and resurrection. In Mark's Gospel, only the disciples come to understand who Jesus is.

8:30 ***not to tell anyone about him.*** Jesus' warning may seem strange. Its explanation lies in the fact that the Jews expected the Messiah to be a political liberator. Jesus' first coming was meant to accomplish another kind of liberation — release from sin. Hence Jesus was careful not to use the name Messiah publicly, for it was misunderstood by the Jewish people, their leaders, and the Roman authorities.

8:11 [e] Mt 12:38 **8:12** [f] Mk 7:34 **8:15** [g] 1Co 5:6-8 [h] Lk 12:1 [i] Mt 14:1; Mk 12:13 **8:17** [j] Isa 6:9, 10; Mk 6:52 **8:19** [k] Mt 14:20; Mk 6:41-44; Lk 9:17; Jn 6:13 **8:20** [l] ver 6-9; Mt 15:37 **8:21** [m] Mk 6:52 **8:22** [n] Mt 11:21 [o] Mk 10:46; Jn 9:1 **8:23** [p] Mk 7:33 [q] Mk 5:23 **8:28** [r] Mt 3:1 [s] Mal 4:5 **8:29** [t] Jn 6:69; 11:27 **8:30** [u] Mt 8:4; 16:20; 17:9; Mk 9:9; Lk 9:21 **8:31** [v] Mt 8:20 [w] Mt 16:21 [x] Mt 27:1, 2 [y] Ac 2:23; 3:13 [z] Mt 16:21 [a] Mt 16:21 **8:32** [b] Jn 18:20 **8:33** [c] Mt 4:10 **8:34** [d] Mt 10:38; Lk 14:27

me and for the gospel will save it.[e] 36What
good is it for someone to gain the whole
world, yet forfeit their soul? 37Or what can
anyone give in exchange for their soul? 38If
anyone is ashamed of me and my words
in this adulterous and sinful generation,
the Son of Man[f] will be ashamed of them[g]
when he comes[h] in his Father's glory with
the holy angels."

9 And he said to them, "Truly I tell you,
some who are standing here will not
taste death before they see that the kingdom of God has come[i] with power."[j]

The Transfiguration

2After six days Jesus took Peter, James
and John[k] with him and led them up a
high mountain, where they were all alone.
There he was transfigured before them.
3His clothes became dazzling white,[l] whiter than anyone in the world could bleach
them. 4And there appeared before them
Elijah and Moses, who were talking with
Jesus.

5Peter said to Jesus, "Rabbi,[m] it is good
for us to be here. Let us put up three shelters—one for you, one for Moses and one
for Elijah." 6(He did not know what to say,
they were so frightened.)

7Then a cloud appeared and covered
them, and a voice came from the cloud:[n]
"This is my Son, whom I love. Listen to
him!"[o]

8Suddenly, when they looked around,
they no longer saw anyone with them except Jesus.

9As they were coming down the mountain, Jesus gave them orders not to tell anyone[p] what they had seen until the Son of
Man[q] had risen from the dead. 10They kept
the matter to themselves, discussing what
"rising from the dead" meant.

11And they asked him, "Why do the
teachers of the law say that Elijah must
come first?"

12Jesus replied, "To be sure, Elijah does
come first, and restores all things. Why
then is it written that the Son of Man[r] must
suffer much[s] and be rejected?[t] 13But I tell
you, Elijah has come,[u] and they have done
to him everything they wished, just as it is
written about him."

Jesus Heals a Boy Possessed by an Impure Spirit

14When they came to the other disciples,
they saw a large crowd around them and
the teachers of the law arguing with them.
15As soon as all the people saw Jesus, they
were overwhelmed with wonder and ran to
greet him.

16"What are you arguing with them
about?" he asked.

17A man in the crowd answered, "Teacher, I brought you my son, who is possessed
by a spirit that has robbed him of speech.
18Whenever it seizes him, it throws him to
the ground. He foams at the mouth, gnashes his teeth and becomes rigid. I asked
your disciples to drive out the spirit, but
they could not."

19"You unbelieving generation," Jesus
replied, "how long shall I stay with you?
How long shall I put up with you? Bring
the boy to me."

20So they brought him. When the spirit saw Jesus, it immediately threw the
boy into a convulsion. He fell to the
ground and rolled around, foaming at the
mouth.[v]

21Jesus asked the boy's father, "How long
has he been like this?"

"From childhood," he answered. 22"It has
often thrown him into fire or water to kill
him. But if you can do anything, take pity
on us and help us."

23"'If you can'?" said Jesus. "Everything
is possible for one who believes."[w]

24Immediately the boy's father exclaimed, "I do believe; help me overcome
my unbelief!"

25When Jesus saw that a crowd was running to the scene,[x] he rebuked the impure
spirit. "You deaf and mute spirit," he said,
"I command you, come out of him and never enter him again."

26The spirit shrieked, convulsed him
violently and came out. The boy looked
so much like a corpse that many said,
"He's dead." 27But Jesus took him by the
hand and lifted him to his feet, and he
stood up.

28After Jesus had gone indoors, his disciples asked him privately,[y] "Why couldn't
we drive it out?"

8:38 *when he comes in his Father's glory.* This is the first glimpse of the fulfillment of all history (1 Cor. 15:24–28). Those who will reign with Christ invest their lives in that which will last (v. 35). Those who are willing to confess Him today will be rewarded before the Father in heaven (Matt. 5:10–12; 2 Tim. 2:11–13; Rev. 2:26–28).

9:4 *Elijah.* Elijah is mentioned in Malachi 4:5–6 in connection with the future coming of Christ. This is why people asked John the Baptist if he were Elijah (John 1:21). Moses was the lawgiver and liberator, while Elijah was the first of the great prophets. Their presence confirmed the reality that Jesus is the Messiah of Peter's confession.

9:24 *I do believe; help me overcome my unbelief!* These words express the dilemma that even those who believe can be nagged by doubt and hopelessness. This man took the correct course by appealing to Jesus for help.

8:35 [e] Jn 12:25 **8:38** [f] Mt 8:20 [g] Mt 10:33; Lk 12:9 [h] 1Th 2:19 **9:1** [i] Mk 13:30; Lk 22:18 [j] Mt 24:30; 25:31 **9:2** [k] Mt 4:21 **9:3** [l] Mt 28:3 **9:5** [m] Mt 23:7 **9:7** [n] Ex 24:16 [o] Mt 3:17 **9:9** [p] Mk 8:30 [q] Mt 8:20 **9:12** [r] Mt 8:20 [s] Mt 16:21 [t] Lk 23:11 **9:13** [u] Mt 11:14 **9:20** [v] Mk 1:26 **9:23** [w] Mt 21:21; Mk 11:23; Jn 11:40 **9:25** [x] ver 15 **9:28** [y] Mk 7:17

29He replied, "This kind can come out only by prayer.[a]"

Jesus Predicts His Death a Second Time

30They left that place and passed through Galilee. Jesus did not want anyone to know where they were, 31because he was teaching his disciples. He said to them, "The Son of Man[z] is going to be delivered into the hands of men. They will kill him,[a] and after three days[b] he will rise."[c] 32But they did not understand what he meant[d] and were afraid to ask him about it.

33They came to Capernaum.[e] When he was in the house,[f] he asked them, "What were you arguing about on the road?" 34But they kept quiet because on the way they had argued about who was the greatest.[g]

35Sitting down, Jesus called the Twelve and said, "Anyone who wants to be first must be the very last, and the servant of all."[h]

36He took a little child whom he placed among them. Taking the child in his arms,[i] he said to them, 37"Whoever welcomes one of these little children in my name welcomes me; and whoever welcomes me does not welcome me but the one who sent me."[j]

Whoever Is Not Against Us Is for Us

38"Teacher," said John, "we saw someone driving out demons in your name and we told him to stop, because he was not one of us."[k]

39"Do not stop him," Jesus said. "For no one who does a miracle in my name can in the next moment say anything bad about me, 40for whoever is not against us is for us.[l] 41Truly I tell you, anyone who gives you a cup of water in my name because you belong to the Messiah will certainly not lose their reward.[m]

Causing to Stumble

42"If anyone causes one of these little ones—those who believe in me—to stumble,[n] it would be better for them if a large millstone were hung around their neck and they were thrown into the sea.[o] 43If your hand causes you to stumble,[p] cut it off. It is better for you to enter life maimed than with two hands to go into hell,[q] where the fire never goes out.[r] [44][b] 45And if your foot causes you to stumble,[s] cut it off. It is better for you to enter life crippled than to have two feet and be thrown into hell.[t] [46][b] 47And if your eye causes you to stumble,[u] pluck it out. It is better for you to enter the kingdom of God with one eye than to have two eyes and be thrown into hell,[v] 48where

> " 'the worms that eat them do not die,
> and the fire is not quenched.'[c][w]

49Everyone will be salted[x] with fire.

50"Salt is good, but if it loses its saltiness, how can you make it salty again?[y] Have salt among yourselves,[z] and be at peace with each other."[a]

Divorce

10 Jesus then left that place and went into the region of Judea and across the Jordan.[b] Again crowds of people came to him, and as was his custom, he taught them.[c]

2Some Pharisees[d] came and tested him by asking, "Is it lawful for a man to divorce his wife?"

3"What did Moses command you?" he replied.

4They said, "Moses permitted a man to write a certificate of divorce and send her away."[e]

5"It was because your hearts were hard[f] that Moses wrote you this law," Jesus replied. 6"But at the beginning of creation God 'made them male and female.'[d][g] 7'For this reason a man will leave his father and mother and be united to his wife,[e] 8and the two will become one flesh.'[f][h] So they are no longer two, but one flesh. 9Therefore what God has joined together, let no one separate."

10When they were in the house again,

---

[a] *29* Some manuscripts *prayer and fasting*
[b] *44,46* Some manuscripts include here the words of verse 48.
[c] *48* Isaiah 66:24
[d] *6* Gen. 1:27
[e] *7* Some early manuscripts do not have *and be united to his wife.*
[f] *8* Gen. 2:24

9:40 ***for whoever is not against us is for us.*** Jesus is not endorsing all who claim to follow Him. Rather, this statement was meant to remind the disciples that God's work was not necessarily restricted to their small group.

9:49 ***Everyone will be salted with fire.*** This phrase may refer to the trials and judgments that all will face — believers with trials that purify faith, unbelievers with the eternal fire of God's judgment.

10:4 ***a certificate of divorce.*** This was a document signed before witnesses. Its intent was to limit frivolous divorces. In Jesus' day, the interpretation of this custom varied widely. The disciples of Hillel allowed divorce for almost any reason, but the followers of Shammai permitted divorce only for sexual impurity.

9:31 [z] Mt 8:20 [a] ver 12; Ac 2:23; 3:13 [b] Mt 16:21 [c] Mt 16:21 **9:32** [d] Lk 2:50; 9:45; 18:34; Jn 12:16 **9:33** [e] Mt 4:13 [f] Mk 1:29 **9:34** [g] Lk 22:24 **9:35** [h] Mt 18:4; 20:26; Mk 10:43; Lk 22:26 **9:36** [i] Mk 10:16 **9:37** [j] Mt 10:40 **9:38** [k] Nu 11:27-29 **9:40** [l] Mt 12:30; Lk 11:23 **9:41** [m] Mt 10:42 **9:42** [n] Mt 5:29 [o] Mt 18:6; Lk 17:2 **9:43** [p] Mt 5:29 [q] Mt 5:30; 18:8 [r] Mt 25:41 **9:45** [s] Mt 5:29 [t] Mt 18:8 **9:47** [u] Mt 5:29 [v] Mt 5:29; 18:9 **9:48** [w] Isa 66:24; Mt 25:41 **9:49** [x] Lev 2:13 **9:50** [y] Mt 5:13; Lk 14:34, 35 [z] Col 4:6 [a] Ro 12:18; 2Co 13:11; 1Th 5:13 **10:1** [b] Mk 1:5; Jn 10:40; 11:7 [c] Mt 4:23; Mk 2:13; 4:2; 6:6, 34 **10:2** [d] Mk 2:16 **10:4** [e] Dt 24:1-4; Mt 5:31 **10:5** [f] Ps 95:8; Heb 3:15 **10:6** [g] Ge 1:27; 5:2 **10:8** [h] Ge 2:24; 1Co 6:16

the disciples asked Jesus about this.
11 He answered, "Anyone who divorces his
wife and marries another woman commits
adultery against her.[i] 12 And if she divorces
her husband and marries another man, she
commits adultery."[j]

The Little Children and Jesus

13 People were bringing little children to
Jesus for him to place his hands on them,
but the disciples rebuked them. 14 When
Jesus saw this, he was indignant. He said
to them, "Let the little children come to me,
and do not hinder them, for the kingdom
of God belongs to such as these.[k] 15 Truly
I tell you, anyone who will not receive the
kingdom of God like a little child will never enter it."[l] 16 And he took the children in
his arms,[m] placed his hands on them and
blessed them.

The Rich and the Kingdom of God

17 As Jesus started on his way, a man ran
up to him and fell on his knees[n] before him.
"Good teacher," he asked, "what must I do
to inherit eternal life?"[o]
18 "Why do you call me good?" Jesus
answered. "No one is good—except God
alone. 19 You know the commandments:
'You shall not murder, you shall not commit adultery, you shall not steal, you shall
not give false testimony, you shall not defraud, honor your father and mother.'[a]"[p]
20 "Teacher," he declared, "all these I have
kept since I was a boy."
21 Jesus looked at him and loved him.
"One thing you lack," he said. "Go, sell everything you have and give to the poor,[q]
and you will have treasure in heaven.[r]
Then come, follow me."[s]
22 At this the man's face fell. He went
away sad, because he had great wealth.
23 Jesus looked around and said to his
disciples, "How hard it is for the rich[t] to
enter the kingdom of God!"
24 The disciples were amazed at his
words. But Jesus said again, "Children,
how hard it is[b] to enter the kingdom of
God![u] 25 It is easier for a camel to go through
the eye of a needle than for someone who is
rich to enter the kingdom of God."[v]
26 The disciples were even more amazed,
and said to each other, "Who then can be
saved?"
27 Jesus looked at them and said, "With
man this is impossible, but not with God;
all things are possible with God."[w]
28 Then Peter spoke up, "We have left everything to follow you!"[x]
29 "Truly I tell you," Jesus replied, "no one
who has left home or brothers or sisters or
mother or father or children or fields for
me and the gospel 30 will fail to receive a
hundred times as much[y] in this present
age: homes, brothers, sisters, mothers,
children and fields—along with persecutions—and in the age to come[z] eternal life.[a]
31 But many who are first will be last, and
the last first."[b]

Jesus Predicts His Death a Third Time

32 They were on their way up to Jerusalem, with Jesus leading the way, and the
disciples were astonished, while those who
followed were afraid. Again he took the
Twelve[c] aside and told them what was going to happen to him. 33 "We are going up to
Jerusalem,"[d] he said, "and the Son of Man[e]
will be delivered over to the chief priests
and the teachers of the law.[f] They will condemn him to death and will hand him over
to the Gentiles, 34 who will mock him and
spit on him, flog him[g] and kill him.[h] Three
days later[i] he will rise."[j]

The Request of James and John

35 Then James and John, the sons of
Zebedee, came to him. "Teacher," they
said, "we want you to do for us whatever
we ask."
36 "What do you want me to do for you?"
he asked.

---

[a] *19* Exodus 20:12-16; Deut. 5:16-20 [b] *24* Some manuscripts *is for those who trust in riches*

10:11 ***Anyone who divorces his wife.*** Mark includes no exception to Christ's prohibition of divorce, nor is any exception listed in Luke 16:18, Romans 7:1–2, or 1 Corinthians 7:10–11. Compare Matthew 5:32 where the exception is made.

10:18 ***No one is good—except God alone.*** This reply is a claim to deity, which Jesus asks the young ruler to recognize.

10:19 ***shall not.*** Jesus recounts the Seventh, Sixth, Eighth, Ninth, and Fifth Commandments. ***shall not defraud.*** Jesus inserts this phrase just before the Fifth Commandment. All of these commands concern the fair and ethical treatment of other people (Ex. 20:12–17).

10:25–27 ***It is easier.*** This comparison of a camel going through a needle is a literal one. In human terms, it is not just difficult, but totally impossible, for a rich man to be saved. But it is also impossible for anyone at all to be saved apart from God's grace and power. God provides the means of salvation, enlightens the sinner's understanding, and regenerates the believing soul.

10:30 ***in this present age.*** This is the time between Christ's first and second comings. Mark alone mentions that persecutions will follow as well—a point his Roman readers may have already known.

10:11 [i] Mt 5:32; Lk 16:18 **10:12** [j] Ro 7:3; 1Co 7:10, 11
10:14 [k] Mt 25:34 **10:15** [l] Mt 18:3 **10:16** [m] Mk 9:36
10:17 [n] Mk 1:40 [o] Lk 10:25; Ac 20:32 **10:19** [p] Ex 20:12-16; Dt 5:16-20 **10:21** [q] Ac 2:45 [r] Mt 6:20; Lk 12:33
[s] Mt 4:19 **10:23** [t] Ps 52:7; 62:10; 1Ti 6:9, 10, 17
10:24 [u] Mt 7:13, 14 **10:25** [v] Lk 12:16-20
10:27 [w] Mt 19:26 **10:28** [x] Mt 4:19 **10:30** [y] Mt 6:33
[z] Mt 12:32 [a] Mt 25:46 **10:31** [b] Mt 19:30
10:32 [c] Mk 3:16-19 **10:33** [d] Lk 9:51 [e] Mt 8:20 [f] Mt 27:1, 2
10:34 [g] Mt 16:21 [h] Ac 2:23; 3:13 [i] Mt 16:21 [j] Mt 16:21

37They replied, "Let one of us sit at your
right and the other at your left in your glory."[k]
38"You don't know what you are asking,"[l]
Jesus said. "Can you drink the cup[m] I drink
or be baptized with the baptism I am baptized with?"[n]
39"We can," they answered.
Jesus said to them, "You will drink the
cup I drink and be baptized with the baptism I am baptized with,[o] 40but to sit at my
right or left is not for me to grant. These
places belong to those for whom they have
been prepared."
41When the ten heard about this, they
became indignant with James and John.
42Jesus called them together and said, "You
know that those who are regarded as rulers of the Gentiles lord it over them, and
their high officials exercise authority over
them. 43Not so with you. Instead, whoever wants to become great among you must
be your servant,[p] 44and whoever wants to
be first must be slave of all. 45For even the
Son of Man did not come to be served, but
to serve,[q] and to give his life as a ransom
for many."[r]

Blind Bartimaeus Receives His Sight

46Then they came to Jericho. As Jesus
and his disciples, together with a large
crowd, were leaving the city, a blind man,
Bartimaeus (which means "son of Timae-
us"), was sitting by the roadside begging.
47When he heard that it was Jesus of Nazareth,[s] he began to shout, "Jesus, Son of
David,[t] have mercy on me!"
48Many rebuked him and told him to be
quiet, but he shouted all the more, "Son of
David, have mercy on me!"
49Jesus stopped and said, "Call him."
So they called to the blind man, "Cheer
up! On your feet! He's calling you."
50Throwing his cloak aside, he jumped to
his feet and came to Jesus.
51"What do you want me to do for you?"
Jesus asked him.
The blind man said, "Rabbi,[u] I want to
see."
52"Go," said Jesus, "your faith has healed
you."[v] Immediately he received his sight
and followed[w] Jesus along the road.

Jesus Comes to Jerusalem as King

11 As they approached Jerusalem and
came to Bethphage and Bethany[x] at
the Mount of Olives,[y] Jesus sent two of his
disciples, 2saying to them, "Go to the village ahead of you, and just as you enter it,
you will find a colt tied there, which no one
has ever ridden.[z] Untie it and bring it here.
3If anyone asks you, 'Why are you doing
this?' say, 'The Lord needs it and will send
it back here shortly.'"
4They went and found a colt outside in
the street, tied at a doorway.[a] As they untied it, 5some people standing there asked,
"What are you doing, untying that colt?"
6They answered as Jesus had told them
to, and the people let them go. 7When they
brought the colt to Jesus and threw their
cloaks over it, he sat on it. 8Many people
spread their cloaks on the road, while others spread branches they had cut in the
fields. 9Those who went ahead and those
who followed shouted,

"Hosanna![a]"

"Blessed is he who comes in the name
of the Lord!"[b][b]

---

[a] 9 A Hebrew expression meaning "Save!" which became an exclamation of praise; also in verse 10
[b] 9 Psalm 118:25,26

10:37 *at your right and the other at your left.* To be seated at a king's right hand was to take the position of the most prominence; the person seated at the left hand ranked just below that (Luke 22:24–30). Jesus had to remind the disciples again about the price of greatness in God's kingdom.

10:38 *drink the cup I drink . . . be baptized with the baptism.* These phrases are references to the suffering and death that awaited Jesus (14:36). Jesus wanted His disciples to understand the mocking, scourging, beating, and torture He would have to endure.

10:45 The Ministry of Christ—

1. *He is Savior.* Sinful men to be saved (1 Tim. 1:15); Christ's qualifications to be Savior (John 10:18–38); His humiliating death (John 19:18); bodily resurrection to guarantee our salvation (1 Cor. 15:13–22); and results of salvation (John 5:24). It is no wonder that, in light of these realities, Paul speaks of Christ as "our great God and Savior" (Titus 2:13).
2. *He is High Priest.* The high priest brought the people before God on the Day of Atonement (Lev. 16:32–33). Jesus is eminently qualified to be our High Priest: appointed by God (Heb. 5:5), eternal (Heb. 7:24–25), sinless (Heb. 7:26), His offering was final (Heb. 9:28), and His mediation is effective (Rom. 8:34; Heb. 7:25; 1 John 2:1). As the only qualified High Priest for men and women, Jesus Christ thus constitutes the only way to God (1 Tim. 2:5).
3. *He is King.* King implies sovereign authority and rule over all. This right belongs only to Jesus Christ who is called "Lord of lords and King of kings" (Rev. 17:14; 19:16). He is destined to rule as king and every knee must ultimately bow and acknowledge His authority (Phil. 2:10). Those who acknowledge Christ as King and Lord in this life will reign with Him; those who do not will be judged by Him (Rev. 20:11–15).

11:8–11 *Bethany.* Jesus retired there each night, perhaps staying in a friend's home. But in view of the

10:37 [k] Mt 19:28 **10:38** [l] Job 38:2 [m] Mt 20:22 [n] Lk 12:50
10:39 [o] Ac 12:2; Rev 1:9 **10:43** [p] Mk 9:35
10:45 [q] Mt 20:28 [r] Mt 20:28 **10:47** [s] Mk 1:24 [t] Mt 9:27
10:51 [u] Mt 23:7 **10:52** [v] Mt 9:22 [w] Mt 4:19
11:1 [x] Mt 21:17 [y] Mt 21:1 **11:2** [z] Nu 19:2; Dt 21:3; 1Sa 6:7
11:4 [a] Mk 14:16 **11:9** [b] Ps 118:25, 26; Mt 23:39

10 "Blessed is the coming kingdom of our
father David!"

"Hosanna in the highest heaven!"[c]

11 Jesus entered Jerusalem and went into the temple courts. He looked around at everything, but since it was already late, he went out to Bethany with the Twelve.[d]

Jesus Curses a Fig Tree and Clears the Temple Courts

12 The next day as they were leaving Bethany, Jesus was hungry. 13 Seeing in the distance a fig tree in leaf, he went to find out if it had any fruit. When he reached it, he found nothing but leaves, because it was not the season for figs.[e] 14 Then he said to the tree, "May no one ever eat fruit from you again." And his disciples heard him say it.

15 On reaching Jerusalem, Jesus entered the temple courts and began driving out those who were buying and selling there. He overturned the tables of the money changers and the benches of those selling doves, 16 and would not allow anyone to carry merchandise through the temple courts. 17 And as he taught them, he said, "Is it not written: 'My house will be called a house of prayer for all nations'[a]?[f] But you have made it 'a den of robbers.'[b]"[g]

18 The chief priests and the teachers of the law heard this and began looking for a way to kill him, for they feared him,[h] because the whole crowd was amazed at his teaching.[i]

19 When evening came, Jesus and his disciples[c] went out of the city.[j]

20 In the morning, as they went along, they saw the fig tree withered from the roots. 21 Peter remembered and said to Jesus, "Rabbi,[k] look! The fig tree you cursed has withered!"

22 "Have faith in God," Jesus answered. 23 "Truly[d] I tell you, if anyone says to this mountain, 'Go, throw yourself into the sea,' and does not doubt in their heart but believes that what they say will happen, it will be done for them.[l] 24 Therefore I tell you, whatever you ask for in prayer, believe that you have received it, and it will be yours.[m] 25 And when you stand praying, if you hold anything against anyone, forgive them, so that your Father in heaven may forgive you your sins."[n] [26][e]

The Authority of Jesus Questioned

27 They arrived again in Jerusalem, and while Jesus was walking in the temple courts, the chief priests, the teachers of the law and the elders came to him. 28 "By what authority are you doing these things?" they asked. "And who gave you authority to do this?"

29 Jesus replied, "I will ask you one question. Answer me, and I will tell you by what authority I am doing these things. 30 John's baptism—was it from heaven, or of human origin? Tell me!"

31 They discussed it among themselves and said, "If we say, 'From heaven,' he will ask, 'Then why didn't you believe him?' 32 But if we say, 'Of human origin' . . ." (They feared the people, for everyone held that John really was a prophet.)[o]

33 So they answered Jesus, "We don't know."

Jesus said, "Neither will I tell you by what authority I am doing these things."

The Parable of the Tenants

12 Jesus then began to speak to them in parables: "A man planted a vineyard.[p] He put a wall around it, dug a pit for the winepress and built a watchtower. Then he

---

[a] *17* Isaiah 56:7 [b] *17* Jer. 7:11 [c] *19* Some early manuscripts *came, Jesus* [d] *22,23* Some early manuscripts *"If you have faith in God," Jesus answered, 23"truly* [e] *26* Some manuscripts include here words similar to Matt. 6:15.

---

fact that Jesus appears to have had no breakfast the next day (v. 12), He and the Twelve may have camped outside this night.

11:13 ***not the season for figs.*** Passover always comes in March or April, and fig season is not until May or June. However, fig trees generally produce a number of buds in March, leaves in April and ripe fruit later on. Jesus was looking for the edible buds, the lack of which indicated that the tree would be fruitless that year.

11:17 ***den of robbers.*** Jesus was referring to the practice of cheating people, both Israelites and those of other nations, either through a crooked exchange of money or by selling inferior products.

11:21 ***The fig tree you cursed has withered!*** The passage emphasizes the power of true faith. Some have suggested that the fig tree represented Israel, which bore no fruit and would soon face the judgment of God.

11:29–30 ***Answer me.*** The intent of Jesus' question was to expose once again the insincerity of His detractors. ***John's baptism.*** This refers to the authority of John's baptism. ***from heaven.*** Was it ordained by God and worthy of obedience? ***of human origin.*** Or was it of human contrivance and void of any spiritual authority and reality?

12:1 ***Jesus then began to speak to them in parables.*** Parables usually get across a significant truth, but the details are not meant to correspond exactly with particular spiritual realities. In this parable, the owner of the vineyard represents God, but God Himself was never so mistaken as to assume they would respect His Son. God is omniscient, whereas the vineyard owner in the parable is not. This story illustrates the immense patience God had with Israel.

11:10 [c] Lk 2:14 **11:11** [d] Mt 21:12, 17 **11:13** [e] Lk 13:6-9 **11:17** [f] Isa 56:7 [g] Jer 7:11 **11:18** [h] Mt 21:46; Mk 12:12; Lk 20:19 [i] Mt 7:28 **11:19** [j] Lk 21:37 **11:21** [k] Mt 23:7 **11:23** [l] Mt 21:21 **11:24** [m] Mt 7:7 **11:25** [n] Mt 6:14 **11:32** [o] Mt 11:9 **12:1** [p] Isa 5:1-7

rented the vineyard to some farmers and
moved to another place. 2At harvest time
he sent a servant to the tenants to collect
from them some of the fruit of the vineyard. 3But they seized him, beat him and
sent him away empty-handed. 4Then he
sent another servant to them; they struck
this man on the head and treated him
shamefully. 5He sent still another, and that
one they killed. He sent many others; some
of them they beat, others they killed.

6"He had one left to send, a son, whom
he loved. He sent him last of all,[q] saying,
'They will respect my son.'

7"But the tenants said to one another,
'This is the heir. Come, let's kill him, and
the inheritance will be ours.' 8So they took
him and killed him, and threw him out of
the vineyard.

9"What then will the owner of the vineyard do? He will come and kill those tenants
and give the vineyard to others. 10Haven't
you read this passage of Scripture:

"'The stone the builders rejected
has become the cornerstone;[r]
11the Lord has done this,
and it is marvelous in our eyes'[a]?"[s]

12Then the chief priests, the teachers of
the law and the elders looked for a way to
arrest him because they knew he had spoken the parable against them. But they
were afraid of the crowd;[t] so they left him
and went away.[u]

Paying the Imperial Tax to Caesar

13Later they sent some of the Pharisees
and Herodians[v] to Jesus to catch him[w] in
his words. 14They came to him and said,
"Teacher, we know that you are a man of
integrity. You aren't swayed by others, because you pay no attention to who they are;
but you teach the way of God in accordance
with the truth. Is it right to pay the imperial
tax[b] to Caesar or not? 15Should we pay or
shouldn't we?"

But Jesus knew their hypocrisy. "Why
are you trying to trap me?" he asked.
"Bring me a denarius and let me look at
it." 16They brought the coin, and he asked
them, "Whose image is this? And whose
inscription?"

"Caesar's," they replied.

17Then Jesus said to them, "Give back to
Caesar what is Caesar's and to God what
is God's."[x]

And they were amazed at him.

Marriage at the Resurrection

18Then the Sadducees,[y] who say there is
no resurrection,[z] came to him with a question. 19"Teacher," they said, "Moses wrote
for us that if a man's brother dies and
leaves a wife but no children, the man must
marry the widow and raise up offspring for
his brother.[a] 20Now there were seven brothers. The first one married and died without leaving any children. 21The second
one married the widow, but he also died,
leaving no child. It was the same with the
third. 22In fact, none of the seven left any
children. Last of all, the woman died too.
23At the resurrection[c] whose wife will she
be, since the seven were married to her?"

24Jesus replied, "Are you not in error because you do not know the Scriptures[b] or
the power of God? 25When the dead rise,
they will neither marry nor be given in
marriage; they will be like the angels in
heaven.[c] 26Now about the dead rising—
have you not read in the Book of Moses, in
the account of the burning bush, how God
said to him, 'I am the God of Abraham, the
God of Isaac, and the God of Jacob'[d]?[d] 27He
is not the God of the dead, but of the living.
You are badly mistaken!"

The Greatest Commandment

28One of the teachers of the law[e] came
and heard them debating. Noticing that
Jesus had given them a good answer, he
asked him, "Of all the commandments,
which is the most important?"

---

a *11* Psalm 118:22,23 *b* *14* A special tax levied on subject peoples, not on Roman citizens
c *23* Some manuscripts *resurrection, when people rise from the dead,* *d* *26* Exodus 3:6

12:12 *looked for a way to arrest Him.* Only as the final points of the parable were made did these evil men realize that Jesus was speaking of them.
12:14 *you are a man of integrity. You aren't swayed by others.* This comment was intended as a compliment. The teachers recognized that Jesus was partial to no one. The question, however, was a lose-lose proposition: a *yes* answer would alienate Jews who opposed Rome, while a *no* answer could be taken as treason against the state.
12:18 *Sadducees.* These were an elite group of religious leaders who denied the existence of angels, the immortality of the soul, and the resurrection. They rejected the oral traditions and accepted only the validity of the Pentateuch, the first five books of the Old Testament.
12:19–22 *Moses wrote for us.* The custom of marrying the widow of one's brother was supported by Deuteronomy 25:5–6, but it was not absolutely binding (Deut. 25:7–10).
12:26–27 *I am the God of Abraham ... Isaac ... Jacob.* Jesus quotes from the law—the Book of Exodus—to make His point. God said I am the God of the three patriarchs mentioned, not "I was their God, but now they are dead." He still is their God because they are still alive. Their souls not only live after death, but their bodies will be raised anew as well.
12:28 *Of all the commandments, which is the most important?* At the beginning of answering

12:6 [q] Heb 1:1-3 **12:10** [r] Ac 4:11 **12:11** [s] Ps 118:22,23 **12:12** [t] Mk 11:18 [u] Mt 22:22 **12:13** [v] Mt 22:16; Mk 3:6 [w] Mt 12:10 **12:17** [x] Ro 13:7 **12:18** [y] Ac 4:1 [z] Ac 23:8; 1Co 15:12 **12:19** [a] Dt 25:5 **12:24** [b] 2Ti 3:15-17 **12:25** [c] 1Co 15:42,49,52 **12:26** [d] Ex 3:6 **12:28** [e] Lk 10:25-28; 20:39

29“The most important one,” answered
Jesus, “is this: ‘Hear, O Israel: The Lord
our God, the Lord is one.[a] 30Love the Lord
your God with all your heart and with all
your soul and with all your mind and with
all your strength.’[b][f] 31The second is this:
‘Love your neighbor as yourself.’[c][g] There
is no commandment greater than these.”
32“Well said, teacher,” the man replied.
“You are right in saying that God is one
and there is no other but him.[h] 33To love
him with all your heart, with all your understanding and with all your strength,
and to love your neighbor as yourself is
more important than all burnt offerings
and sacrifices.”[i]
34When Jesus saw that he had answered
wisely, he said to him, “You are not far from
the kingdom of God.”[j] And from then on no
one dared ask him any more questions.[k]

Whose Son Is the Messiah?

35While Jesus was teaching in the temple
courts,[l] he asked, “Why do the teachers of
the law say that the Messiah is the son of
David?[m] 36David himself, speaking by the
Holy Spirit,[n] declared:

“ ‘The Lord said to my Lord:
“Sit at my right hand
until I put your enemies
under your feet.” ’[d][o]

37David himself calls him ‘Lord.’ How then
can he be his son?”
The large crowd[p] listened to him with
delight.

Warning Against the Teachers of the Law

38As he taught, Jesus said, “Watch
out for the teachers of the law. They like
to walk around in flowing robes and be
greeted with respect in the marketplaces,
39and have the most important seats in the
synagogues and the places of honor at banquets.[q] 40They devour widows’ houses and
for a show make lengthy prayers. These
men will be punished most severely.”

The Widow’s Offering

41Jesus sat down opposite the place
where the offerings were put[r] and watched
the crowd putting their money into the
temple treasury. Many rich people threw
in large amounts. 42But a poor widow came
and put in two very small copper coins,
worth only a few cents.
43Calling his disciples to him, Jesus said,
“Truly I tell you, this poor widow has put
more into the treasury than all the others.
44They all gave out of their wealth; but she,
out of her poverty, put in everything—all
she had to live on.”[s]

The Destruction of the Temple and Signs of the End Times

13 As Jesus was leaving the temple, one
of his disciples said to him, “Look,
Teacher! What massive stones! What magnificent buildings!”
2“Do you see all these great buildings?”
replied Jesus. “Not one stone here will be
left on another; every one will be thrown
down.”[t]
3As Jesus was sitting on the Mount of
Olives[u] opposite the temple, Peter, James,
John[v] and Andrew asked him privately,
4“Tell us, when will these things happen?
And what will be the sign that they are all
about to be fulfilled?”

---

[a] *29* Or *The Lord our God is one Lord* [b] *30* Deut. 6:4,5 [c] *31* Lev. 19:18 [d] *36* Psalm 110:1

---

the question, “Which is the most important?,” Jesus quotes what is known in Judaism as the *Shema* (Deut. 6:4–5). The *Shema* is described by Jews as the most important words a Jew can know. These words should drive us to the cross. There, we understand His love for us and are constantly motivated to seek to love Him better because of what He has done. We can only be thankful at the comprehensiveness of His love. Even though we sin every day of our lives, He forgives. We just need to keep coming to Him for that forgiveness.

12:29 *Hear, O Israel.* This phrase from Deuteronomy 6:4 is commonly called the *Shema* (from a Hebrew word meaning “to hear”) and is repeated by Jews the world over, as expressing the essence of their faith in God.

12:35 *in the temple.* This does not refer to the sanctuary itself, where only the priests were allowed to minister. The temple environs included a number of porticos and courts. One was designated especially for women, another for men. Gentiles could view the temple from an outer area.

12:43–44 *this poor widow has put more into the treasury than all the others.* Jesus’ comparison of the percentages contributed by the rich and the poor reminds us that God measures not how much we give, but how much we retain. Those with greater income have an obligation to return a larger percentage of it to God’s work.

13:1–2 *What massive stones! What magnificent buildings!* The disciples’ excitement over the temple’s tremendous construction was a natural reaction to splendid and majestic architecture; each stone weighed several tons. Josephus described its magnificence. There was nothing like it in all the world. Begun by Herod the Great in 20 B.C., the temple was later completed by Herod’s descendants some time before A.D. 66. Its beautiful white marble stones with gold ornamentation reached 100 feet high. Surrounding it were colonnaded walkways, courtyards, and stairways that filled 20 acres of the most prominent landscape in all Jerusalem.

12:30 [f] Dt 6:4,5 **12:31** [g] Lev 19:18; Mt 5:43 **12:32** [h] Dt 4:35,39; Isa 45:6,14; 46:9 **12:33** [i] 1Sa 15:22; Hos 6:6; Mic 6:6-8; Heb 10:8 **12:34** [j] Mt 3:2 [k] Mt 22:46; Lk 20:40 **12:35** [l] Mt 26:55 [m] Mt 9:27 **12:36** [n] 2Sa 23:2 [o] Ps 110:1; Mt 22:44 **12:37** [p] Jn 12:9 **12:39** [q] Lk 11:43 **12:41** [r] 2Ki 12:9; Jn 8:20 **12:44** [s] 2Co 8:12 **13:2** [t] Lk 19:44 **13:3** [u] Mt 21:1 [v] Mt 4:21

5 Jesus said to them: "Watch out that no one deceives you.[w] 6 Many will come in my name, claiming, 'I am he,' and will deceive many. 7 When you hear of wars and rumors of wars, do not be alarmed. Such things must happen, but the end is still to come. 8 Nation will rise against nation, and kingdom against kingdom. There will be earthquakes in various places, and famines. These are the beginning of birth pains.

9 "You must be on your guard. You will be handed over to the local councils and flogged in the synagogues.[x] On account of me you will stand before governors and kings as witnesses to them. 10 And the gospel must first be preached to all nations. 11 Whenever you are arrested and brought to trial, do not worry beforehand about what to say. Just say whatever is given you at the time, for it is not you speaking, but the Holy Spirit.[y]

12 "Brother will betray brother to death, and a father his child. Children will rebel against their parents and have them put to death.[z] 13 Everyone will hate you because of me,[a] but the one who stands firm to the end will be saved.[b]

14 "When you see 'the abomination that causes desolation'[a][c] standing where it[b] does not belong—let the reader understand—then let those who are in Judea flee to the mountains. 15 Let no one on the housetop go down or enter the house to take anything out. 16 Let no one in the field go back to get their cloak. 17 How dreadful it will be in those days for pregnant women and nursing mothers![d] 18 Pray that this will not take place in winter, 19 because those will be days of distress unequaled from the beginning, when God created the world,[e] until now—and never to be equaled again.[f]

20 "If the Lord had not cut short those days, no one would survive. But for the sake of the elect, whom he has chosen, he has shortened them. 21 At that time if anyone says to you, 'Look, here is the Messiah!' or, 'Look, there he is!' do not believe it.[g] 22 For false messiahs and false prophets[h] will appear and perform signs and wonders[i] to deceive, if possible, even the elect. 23 So be on your guard;[j] I have told you everything ahead of time.

24 "But in those days, following that distress,

"'the sun will be darkened,
and the moon will not give its light;
25 the stars will fall from the sky,
and the heavenly bodies will be shaken.'[c][k]

26 "At that time people will see the Son of Man coming in clouds[l] with great power and glory. 27 And he will send his angels and gather his elect from the four winds, from the ends of the earth to the ends of the heavens.[m]

28 "Now learn this lesson from the fig tree: As soon as its twigs get tender and its leaves come out, you know that summer is near. 29 Even so, when you see these things happening, you know that it[b] is near, right at the door. 30 Truly I tell you, this generation[n] will certainly not pass away until all these things have happened.[o] 31 Heaven and earth will pass away, but my words will never pass away.[p]

The Day and Hour Unknown

32 "But about that day or hour no one knows, not even the angels in heaven, nor the Son, but only the Father.[q] 33 Be on guard! Be alert[d]![r] You do not know when that time will come. 34 It's like a man going away: He leaves his house and puts his ser-

[a] *14* Daniel 9:27; 11:31; 12:11 [b] *14,29* Or *he* [c] *25* Isaiah 13:10; 34:4 [d] *33* Some manuscripts *alert and pray*

13:11–12 *the Holy Spirit.* The promise given that the Holy Spirit will guide one's speech in the hour of trial applies first to the twelve and only secondarily to others who will experience persecution. But this promise does not assure escape from persecution or even freedom from being put to death.

13:13 *one who stands firm to the end shall be saved.* This is not referring to regeneration or justification but to physical deliverance from affliction (vv. 19–20). The ones who physically endure will be delivered into Christ's messianic kingdom.

13:14 *standing where it does not belong.* This phrase refers to the presence of an idol standing in the temple. Daniel's prediction primarily referred to placement of sacrifices to Zeus on the temple's altar by Antiochus Epiphanes. Some believe that the destruction of the Herodian temple in A.D. 70 fulfilled Jesus' prediction. Others still await its fulfillment in the blasphemous actions of the antichrist in the last days (2 Thess. 2:3–4).

13:28–29 *when you see these things happening.* Jesus likened the signs of His second coming to the sprouts of growth and leaves on a fig tree. Both point to the glories to come—the full flowering of the earth and return of Christ.

13:32 *But about that day or hour no one knows.* As one who was fully God and at the same time fully man, Jesus possessed all the attributes of deity, including omnipotence and omniscience. He knew what was in people's hearts (2:8), and He could still the waves (4:39). When Jesus became a man, however, He voluntarily placed certain knowledge in the hands of the Father. Of course today, glorified in heaven, Jesus now knows the day and hour of His return.

13:34–36 *like a man going away.* Jesus' parable of the absent master of the house is unique to Mark.

13:5 [w] ver 22; Jer 29:8; Eph 5:6; 2Th 2:3, 10-12; 1Ti 4:1; 2Ti 3:13; 1Jn 4:6 **13:9** [x] Mt 10:17 **13:11** [y] Mt 10:19, 20; Lk 12:11, 12 **13:12** [z] Mic 7:6; Mt 10:21; Lk 12:51-53 **13:13** [a] Jn 15:21 [b] Mt 10:22 **13:14** [c] Da 9:27; 11:31; 12:11 **13:17** [d] Lk 23:29 **13:19** [e] Mk 10:6 [f] Da 9:26; 12:1; Joel 2:2 **13:21** [g] Lk 17:23; 21:8 **13:22** [h] Mt 7:15 [i] Jn 4:48; 2Th 2:9, 10 **13:23** [j] 2Pe 3:17 **13:25** [k] Isa 13:10; 34:4; Mt 24:29 **13:26** [l] Da 7:13; Mt 16:27; Rev 1:7 **13:27** [m] Zec 2:6 **13:30** [n] Lk 17:25 [o] Mk 9:1 **13:31** [p] Mt 5:18 **13:32** [q] Ac 1:7; 1Th 5:1, 2 **13:33** [r] 1Th 5:6

vants[s] in charge, each with their assigned
task, and tells the one at the door to keep
watch.
35"Therefore keep watch because you do
not know when the owner of the house will
come back—whether in the evening, or at
midnight, or when the rooster crows, or at
dawn. 36If he comes suddenly, do not let
him find you sleeping. 37What I say to you,
I say to everyone: 'Watch!'"[t]

Jesus Anointed at Bethany

14 Now the Passover[u] and the Festival
of Unleavened Bread were only two
days away, and the chief priests and the
teachers of the law were scheming to arrest Jesus secretly and kill him.[v] 2"But not
during the festival," they said, "or the people may riot."
3While he was in Bethany,[w] reclining at
the table in the home of Simon the Leper, a
woman came with an alabaster jar of very
expensive perfume, made of pure nard.
She broke the jar and poured the perfume
on his head.[x]
4Some of those present were saying in-
dignantly to one another, "Why this waste
of perfume? 5It could have been sold for
more than a year's wages[a] and the money
given to the poor." And they rebuked her
harshly.
6"Leave her alone," said Jesus. "Why are
you bothering her? She has done a beautiful thing to me. 7The poor you will always
have with you,[b] and you can help them any
time you want.[y] But you will not always
have me. 8She did what she could. She
poured perfume on my body beforehand
to prepare for my burial.[z] 9Truly I tell you,
wherever the gospel is preached throughout the world,[a] what she has done will also
be told, in memory of her."
10Then Judas Iscariot, one of the Twelve,[b]
went to the chief priests to betray Jesus to
them.[c] 11They were delighted to hear this
and promised to give him money. So he
watched for an opportunity to hand him
over.

The Last Supper

12On the first day of the Festival of Unleavened Bread, when it was customary to
sacrifice the Passover lamb,[d] Jesus' disciples asked him, "Where do you want us to
go and make preparations for you to eat the
Passover?"
13So he sent two of his disciples, telling
them, "Go into the city, and a man carrying a jar of water will meet you. Follow
him. 14Say to the owner of the house he enters, 'The Teacher asks: Where is my guest
room, where I may eat the Passover with
my disciples?' 15He will show you a large
room upstairs,[e] furnished and ready. Make
preparations for us there."
16The disciples left, went into the city
and found things just as Jesus had told
them. So they prepared the Passover.
17When evening came, Jesus arrived
with the Twelve. 18While they were reclining at the table eating, he said, "Truly I tell
you, one of you will betray me—one who
is eating with me."
19They were saddened, and one by one
they said to him, "Surely you don't mean
me?"
20"It is one of the Twelve," he replied,
"one who dips bread into the bowl with me.[f]
21The Son of Man[g] will go just as it is written about him. But woe to that man who
betrays the Son of Man! It would be better
for him if he had not been born."
22While they were eating, Jesus took
bread, and when he had given thanks, he
broke it[h] and gave it to his disciples, saying,
"Take it; this is my body."
23Then he took a cup, and when he had
given thanks, he gave it to them, and they
all drank from it.[i]

[a] 5 Greek *than three hundred denarii* [b] 7 See Deut. 15:11.

The point of the parable is that the master could return at any time so all servants must be vigilant and watchful (Luke 19:11–27).

14:3 *alabaster.* Alabaster is a translucent stone still used to make ornamented jewelry boxes and other items of value. ***nard.*** Nard was a precious perfume imported from India, made from plants that grow in the high elevations of the Himalayas. This perfume is mentioned in the Song of Songs (1:12; 4:13–14).

14:7 *The poor you will always have with you.* Jesus' statement does not show callousness towards the poor (Deut. 15:7–11). His compassion for those overwhelmed by sickness and poverty appears frequently in the Gospels, and He encouraged others to meet their needs (10:21). But He also wanted people to give freely and of their own volition. No one can coerce a gift from another; no one should criticize another's gift; and no one can read the heart of a giver. A giver's motive is known only to God.

14:14–15 *a large room upstairs.* There is reason to suspect that the master of the house may have been Mark's father. Mark himself may have been the young man of verses 51 and 52. Acts 12:12 indicates that this house was later used as a gathering place for many believers who prayed together. Tradition has it that this was also the "upper room" of Acts 1:13 where over 100 believers met on Pentecost.

14:19 *Surely you don't mean me?* In Greek this is actually a negative question that implies a negative answer. The phrase means "It is not I, is it?" Matthew and John both identify the culprit as Judas, even though Mark does not (Matt. 26:25; John 13:26).

13:34 [s] Mt 25:14 **13:37** [t] Lk 12:35-40 **14:1** [u] Jn 11:55; 13:1 [v] Mt 12:14 **14:3** [w] Mt 21:17 [x] Lk 7:37-39 **14:7** [y] Dt 15:11 **14:8** [z] Jn 19:40 **14:9** [a] Mt 24:14; Mk 16:15 **14:10** [b] Mk 3:16-19 [c] Mt 10:4 **14:12** [d] Ex 12:1-11; Dt 16:1-4; 1Co 5:7 **14:15** [e] Ac 1:13 **14:20** [f] Jn 13:18-27 **14:21** [g] Mt 8:20 **14:22** [h] Mt 14:19 **14:23** [i] 1Co 10:16

24"This is my blood of the[a] covenant,[j]
which is poured out for many," he said to
them. 25"Truly I tell you, I will not drink
again from the fruit of the vine until that
day when I drink it new in the kingdom of
God."[k]
26When they had sung a hymn, they
went out to the Mount of Olives.[l]

Jesus Predicts Peter's Denial

27"You will all fall away," Jesus told
them, "for it is written:

"'I will strike the shepherd,
and the sheep will be scattered.'[b][m]

28But after I have risen, I will go ahead of
you into Galilee."[n]
29Peter declared, "Even if all fall away,
I will not."
30"Truly I tell you," Jesus answered,
"today—yes, tonight—before the rooster
crows twice[c] you yourself will disown me
three times."[o]
31But Peter insisted emphatically, "Even
if I have to die with you,[p] I will never disown you." And all the others said the same.

Gethsemane

32They went to a place called Gethsemane, and Jesus said to his disciples, "Sit here
while I pray." 33He took Peter, James and
John[q] along with him, and he began to be
deeply distressed and troubled. 34"My soul
is overwhelmed with sorrow to the point
of death,"[r] he said to them. "Stay here and
keep watch."
35Going a little farther, he fell to the
ground and prayed that if possible the
hour[s] might pass from him. 36"*Abba*,[d] Father,"[t] he said, "everything is possible for
you. Take this cup[u] from me. Yet not what
I will, but what you will."[v]
37Then he returned to his disciples and
found them sleeping. "Simon," he said to
Peter, "are you asleep? Couldn't you keep
watch for one hour? 38Watch and pray so
that you will not fall into temptation.[w] The
spirit is willing, but the flesh is weak."[x]
39Once more he went away and prayed
the same thing. 40When he came back, he
again found them sleeping, because their
eyes were heavy. They did not know what
to say to him.
41Returning the third time, he said to
them, "Are you still sleeping and resting?
Enough! The hour[y] has come. Look, the
Son of Man is delivered into the hands of
sinners. 42Rise! Let us go! Here comes my
betrayer!"

Jesus Arrested

43Just as he was speaking, Judas,[z] one
of the Twelve, appeared. With him was a
crowd armed with swords and clubs, sent
from the chief priests, the teachers of the
law, and the elders.
44Now the betrayer had arranged a
signal with them: "The one I kiss is the

[a] *24* Some manuscripts *the new* [b] *27* Zech. 13:7
[c] *30* Some early manuscripts do not have *twice*.
[d] *36* Aramaic for *father*

14:24 *This is my blood.* This means that the contents of this cup represented Jesus' blood that would be shed for our sins. The sprinkling of blood was required to institute the Mosaic covenant in Exodus 29:12 (Heb. 9:18–22). In the same way, Jesus' blood shed on the cross initiated the new covenant. His blood was shed for many. He died on the cross in the place of many sinners from every nation. He paid the price for all of their sins. All those who believe in Him will receive eternal life.

14:26 *When they had sung a hymn.* What they sang was no doubt from the Psalms. Frequently Psalms 113–118 were used in connection with the Passover.

14:30 *before the rooster crows twice.* Only Mark mentions Christ's prediction of Peter's denial. The incident would have remained vivid in Peter's mind when he related the story to Mark.

14:34 *My soul is overwhelmed with sorrow.* The crushing realization of having to bear the sin of the world and to lose, even temporarily, the fellowship of God the Father was nearly more than Jesus' soul could bear.

14:35 *the hour might pass from him.* This is a reference to the time Jesus would bear the punishment for the sin of the world in His own body, becoming, as it were, sin for all.

14:38 Temptation by the Flesh—*Flesh* in the Bible often means something other than the substance of the human body. It is used constantly to refer to the carnal, sinful principle within man that is opposed to God (Rom. 8:7). The actions produced by the flesh are given in detail in Galatians 5:19–21. Among these are all types of sexual immorality, impurity, hatred, anger, envy, and drunkenness. A person whose life is characterized by these sins cannot be a true Christian and is under the wrath of God (Gal. 5:21; Eph. 2:3). Though the flesh is not eradicated for the Christian, he does have the power to deny it (Rom. 7:15–25). He possesses a new nature empowered by the Holy Spirit. The solution to the urges of the flesh lies in acknowledging that the power of sin was nullified by Jesus' death (Rom. 6:11) and in living under the control of the Spirit's power (Gal. 5:16). The latter is a moment-by-moment dependence in faith on the Spirit's power. The believer must choose by an act of his will to benefit from the Spirit's enablement.

14:39–41 *Once more he went away.* The three apostles were exhorted to watch and pray several times, and no doubt truly desired to uphold their Lord in His deepest hour of need. Yet physical fatigue overcame spiritual alertness.

14:43 *With him was a crowd.* Judas came with a detachment of troops (John 18:3). It was one-tenth of a Roman legion or roughly 600 men.

14:24 [j] Mt 26:28 **14:25** [k] Mt 3:2 **14:26** [l] Mt 21:1 **14:27** [m] Zec 13:7 **14:28** [n] Mk 16:7 **14:30** [o] ver 66-72; Lk 22:34; Jn 13:38 **14:31** [p] Lk 22:33; Jn 13:37 **14:33** [q] Mt 4:21 **14:34** [r] Jn 12:27 **14:35** [s] ver 41; Mt 26:18 **14:36** [t] Ro 8:15; Gal 4:6 [u] Mt 20:22 [v] Mt 26:39 **14:38** [w] Mt 6:13 [x] Ro 7:22,23 **14:41** [y] ver 35; Mt 26:18 **14:43** [z] Mt 10:4

man; arrest him and lead him away under guard." [45]Going at once to Jesus, Judas said, "Rabbi!"[a] and kissed him. [46]The men seized Jesus and arrested him. [47]Then one of those standing near drew his sword and struck the servant of the high priest, cutting off his ear.

[48]"Am I leading a rebellion," said Jesus, "that you have come out with swords and clubs to capture me? [49]Every day I was with you, teaching in the temple courts,[b] and you did not arrest me. But the Scriptures must be fulfilled."[c] [50]Then everyone deserted him and fled.[d]

[51]A young man, wearing nothing but a linen garment, was following Jesus. When they seized him, [52]he fled naked, leaving his garment behind.

Jesus Before the Sanhedrin

[53]They took Jesus to the high priest, and all the chief priests, the elders and the teachers of the law came together. [54]Peter followed him at a distance, right into the courtyard of the high priest.[e] There he sat with the guards and warmed himself at the fire.[f]

[55]The chief priests and the whole Sanhedrin[g] were looking for evidence against Jesus so that they could put him to death, but they did not find any. [56]Many testified falsely against him, but their statements did not agree.

[57]Then some stood up and gave this false testimony against him: [58]"We heard him say, 'I will destroy this temple made with human hands and in three days will build another,[h] not made with hands.'" [59]Yet even then their testimony did not agree.

[60]Then the high priest stood up before them and asked Jesus, "Are you not going to answer? What is this testimony that these men are bringing against you?" [61]But Jesus remained silent and gave no answer.[i]

Again the high priest asked him, "Are you the Messiah, the Son of the Blessed One?"[j]

[62]"I am," said Jesus. "And you will see the Son of Man sitting at the right hand of the Mighty One and coming on the clouds of heaven."[k]

[63]The high priest tore his clothes.[l] "Why do we need any more witnesses?" he asked. [64]"You have heard the blasphemy. What do you think?"

They all condemned him as worthy of death.[m] [65]Then some began to spit at him; they blindfolded him, struck him with their fists, and said, "Prophesy!" And the guards took him and beat him.[n]

Peter Disowns Jesus

[66]While Peter was below in the courtyard,[o] one of the servant girls of the high priest came by. [67]When she saw Peter warming himself,[p] she looked closely at him.

"You also were with that Nazarene, Jesus,"[q] she said.

[68]But he denied it. "I don't know or understand what you're talking about,"[r] he said, and went out into the entryway.[a]

[69]When the servant girl saw him there, she said again to those standing around, "This fellow is one of them." [70]Again he denied it.[s]

After a little while, those standing near said to Peter, "Surely you are one of them, for you are a Galilean."[t]

[71]He began to call down curses, and he swore to them, "I don't know this man you're talking about."[u]

[72]Immediately the rooster crowed the second time.[b] Then Peter remembered the word Jesus had spoken to him: "Before the rooster crows twice[c] you will disown me three times."[v] And he broke down and wept.

Jesus Before Pilate

15 Very early in the morning, the chief priests, with the elders, the teachers of the law[w] and the whole Sanhedrin,[x] made their plans. So they bound Jesus,

[a] 68 Some early manuscripts *entryway and the rooster crowed* [b] 72 Some early manuscripts do not have *the second time.* [c] 72 Some early manuscripts do not have *twice.*

14:50–52 ***young man.*** Only Mark tells of this incident and many believe that this young man was Mark himself. How else would he have known this story, and why else should he have included it? If it was Mark, and if the Last Supper was at his home that evening, he could easily have risen from bed, pulled on a linen sheet, and followed the disciples.

14:61 ***remained silent.*** Jesus remained silent before Pilate and Herod Antipas. Finally they could find nothing substantial with which to charge Him. ***the Messiah, the Son of the Blessed.*** The trial was over, and Jesus stood falsely condemned for blasphemy, which in this context means laying claim to deity. Naturally, this is the boast of a liar or a lunatic—unless He is the Almighty God in human flesh, as Jesus was (Phil. 2:5–8; 1 John 1:1–3).

14:71–72 ***the rooster crowed.*** We are not told that Peter thought at all about Jesus' words. If he did, maybe he tried to conceal his identity more carefully, but to no avail. Each of the other Gospel writers tells us that the cock crowed immediately upon Peter's final denial (Matt. 26:74; Luke 22:60; John 18:27). This time he thought about it, and he wept.

15:1–3 ***made their plans.*** Rather than murdering Jesus privately, the Jewish politicians decided to seek

14:45 [a] Mt 23:7 **14:49** [b] Mt 26:55 [c] Isa 53:7-12; Mt 1:22 **14:50** [d] ver 27 **14:54** [e] Mt 26:3 [f] Jn 18:18 **14:55** [g] Mt 5:22 **14:58** [h] Mk 15:29; Jn 2:19 **14:61** [i] Isa 53:7; Mt 27:12, 14; Mk 15:5; Lk 23:9; Jn 19:9 [j] Mt 16:16; Jn 4:25, 26 **14:62** [k] Rev 1:7 **14:63** [l] Lev 10:6; 21:10; Nu 14:6; Ac 14:14 **14:64** [m] Lev 24:16 **14:65** [n] Mt 16:21 **14:66** [o] ver 54 **14:67** [p] ver 54 [q] Mk 1:24 **14:68** [r] ver 30, 72 **14:70** [s] ver 30, 68, 72 [t] Ac 2:7 **14:71** [u] ver 30, 72 **14:72** [v] ver 30, 68 **15:1** [w] Mt 27:1; Lk 22:66 [x] Mt 5:22

led him away and handed him over to Pilate.[y]
2“Are you the king of the Jews?”[z] asked
Pilate.
“You have said so,” Jesus replied.
3The chief priests accused him of many
things. 4So again Pilate asked him, “Aren’t
you going to answer? See how many things
they are accusing you of.”
5But Jesus still made no reply,[a] and Pilate
was amazed.
6Now it was the custom at the festival
to release a prisoner whom the people requested. 7A man called Barabbas was in
prison with the insurrectionists who had
committed murder in the uprising. 8The
crowd came up and asked Pilate to do for
them what he usually did.
9“Do you want me to release to you the
king of the Jews?”[b] asked Pilate, 10know-
ing it was out of self-interest that the chief
priests had handed Jesus over to him. 11But
the chief priests stirred up the crowd to
have Pilate release Barabbas[c] instead.
12“What shall I do, then, with the one
you call the king of the Jews?” Pilate asked
them.
13“Crucify him!” they shouted.
14“Why? What crime has he committed?” asked Pilate.
But they shouted all the louder, “Crucify him!”
15Wanting to satisfy the crowd, Pilate
released Barabbas to them. He had Jesus
flogged,[d] and handed him over to be crucified.

The Soldiers Mock Jesus

16The soldiers led Jesus away into the
palace[e] (that is, the Praetorium) and called
together the whole company of soldiers.
17They put a purple robe on him, then
twisted together a crown of thorns and set
it on him. 18And they began to call out to
him, “Hail, king of the Jews!”[f] 19Again and
again they struck him on the head with
a staff and spit on him. Falling on their
knees, they paid homage to him. 20And
when they had mocked him, they took off
the purple robe and put his own clothes on
him. Then they led him out[g] to crucify him.

The Crucifixion of Jesus

21A certain man from Cyrene,[h] Simon,
the father of Alexander and Rufus,[i] was
passing by on his way in from the country, and they forced him to carry the
cross.[j] 22They brought Jesus to the place
called Golgotha (which means “the place
of the skull”). 23Then they offered him wine
mixed with myrrh,[k] but he did not take it.
24And they crucified him. Dividing up his
clothes, they cast lots[l] to see what each
would get.
25It was nine in the morning when they
crucified him. 26The written notice of the
charge against him read: THE KING OF THE
JEWS.[m]
27They crucified two rebels with him,
one on his right and one on his left. [28][a]
29Those who passed by hurled insults at
him, shaking their heads[n] and saying, “So!
You who are going to destroy the temple
and build it in three days,[o] 30come down
from the cross and save yourself!” 31In the
same way the chief priests and the teachers
of the law mocked him[p] among themselves.
“He saved others,” they said, “but he can’t
save himself! 32Let this Messiah,[q] this king
of Israel,[r] come down now from the cross,
that we may see and believe.” Those crucified with him also heaped insults on him.

The Death of Jesus

33At noon, darkness came over the whole
land until three in the afternoon.[s] 34And at
three in the afternoon Jesus cried out in a
loud voice, *“Eloi, Eloi, lema sabachthani?”*
(which means “My God, my God, why have
you forsaken me?”).[b][t]
35When some of those standing near
heard this, they said, “Listen, he’s calling
Elijah.”
36Someone ran, filled a sponge with
wine vinegar,[u] put it on a staff, and offered

---

a *28* Some manuscripts include here words similar to Luke 22:37. *b* *34* Psalm 22:1

Pilate’s approval so they could execute the “blasphemer legally.” Their charges included many things but apparently centered on treason. Jesus claimed to be a king, thus defying Caesar (Luke 23:2). This crime was punishable in the Roman Empire by death. Pilate must have concluded that the charges against Jesus were groundless, for Mark tells us he desired to release Him.

15:15 ***flogged.*** This word, used only twice in the New Testament (Matt. 27:26 and here), actually describes a punishment more severe than flogging or beating. The prisoner was beaten with a whip fashioned of numerous strips of leather attached to a handle. To the leather strips were tied sharp pieces of bone and metal, which could rip and tear one’s skin to shreds.

15:22 ***Golgotha.*** This is an Aramaic word. The hill may have resembled the bony features of a skull or was called this because it was a place of death. The name Calvary comes from the Latin word for skull.

15:32 ***Let this Messiah.*** Jesus was mockingly called the Christ or Messiah by the chief priests and scribes. Their offer to believe in Christ if He would descend from the cross was not believable.

15:1 [y] Mt 27:2 **15:2** [z] ver 9, 12, 18, 26; Mt 2:2
15:5 [a] Mk 14:61 **15:9** [b] ver 2 **15:11** [c] Ac 3:14
15:15 [d] Isa 53:6 **15:16** [e] Jn 18:28, 33; 19:9 **15:18** [f] ver 2
15:20 [g] Heb 13:12 **15:21** [h] Mt 27:32 [i] Ro 16:13
[j] Mt 27:32; Lk 23:26 **15:23** [k] ver 36; Ps 69:21; Pr 31:6
15:24 [l] Ps 22:18 **15:26** [m] ver 2 **15:29** [n] Ps 22:7; 109:25
[o] Mk 14:58; Jn 2:19 **15:31** [p] Ps 22:7 **15:32** [q] Mk 14:61
[r] ver 2 **15:33** [s] Am 8:9 **15:34** [t] Ps 22:1
15:36 [u] ver 23; Ps 69:21

it to Jesus to drink. "Now leave him alone.
Let's see if Elijah comes to take him down,"
he said.
37 With a loud cry, Jesus breathed his
last.[v]
38 The curtain of the temple was torn in
two from top to bottom.[w] 39 And when the
centurion,[x] who stood there in front of
Jesus, saw how he died,[a] he said, "Surely
this man was the Son of God!"[y]
40 Some women were watching from a
distance.[z] Among them were Mary Magdalene, Mary the mother of James the
younger and of Joseph,[b] and Salome.[a] 41 In
Galilee these women had followed him and
cared for his needs. Many other women
who had come up with him to Jerusalem
were also there.[b]

The Burial of Jesus

42 It was Preparation Day (that is, the day
before the Sabbath).[c] So as evening approached, 43 Joseph of Arimathea, a prominent member of the Council,[d] who was
himself waiting for the kingdom of God,[e]
went boldly to Pilate and asked for Jesus'
body. 44 Pilate was surprised to hear that he
was already dead. Summoning the centurion, he asked him if Jesus had already died.
45 When he learned from the centurion[f]
that it was so, he gave the body to Joseph.
46 So Joseph bought some linen cloth, took
down the body, wrapped it in the linen, and
placed it in a tomb cut out of rock. Then he
rolled a stone against the entrance of the
tomb.[g] 47 Mary Magdalene and Mary the
mother of Joseph[h] saw where he was laid.

Jesus Has Risen

16 When the Sabbath was over, Mary
Magdalene, Mary the mother of
James, and Salome bought spices[i] so that
they might go to anoint Jesus' body. 2 Very
early on the first day of the week, just after sunrise, they were on their way to the
tomb 3 and they asked each other, "Who
will roll the stone away from the entrance
of the tomb?"[j]
4 But when they looked up, they saw that
the stone, which was very large, had been
rolled away. 5 As they entered the tomb,
they saw a young man dressed in a white
robe[k] sitting on the right side, and they
were alarmed.
6 "Don't be alarmed," he said. "You are
looking for Jesus the Nazarene,[l] who was
crucified. He has risen! He is not here. See
the place where they laid him. 7 But go, tell
his disciples and Peter, 'He is going ahead
of you into Galilee. There you will see
him,[m] just as he told you.'"[n]
8 Trembling and bewildered, the wom-
en went out and fled from the tomb. They
said nothing to anyone, because they were
afraid.[c]

[The earliest manuscripts and some other ancient witnesses do not have verses 9–20.]

9 When Jesus rose early on the first day of the
week, he appeared first to Mary Magdalene,[o]
out of whom he had driven seven demons. 10 She
went and told those who had been with him and
who were mourning and weeping. 11 When they
heard that Jesus was alive and that she had seen
him, they did not believe it.[p]
12 Afterward Jesus appeared in a different
form to two of them while they were walking

---

[a] 39 Some manuscripts *saw that he died with such a cry* [b] 40 Greek *Joses,* a variant of *Joseph;* also in verse 47 [c] 8 Some manuscripts have the following ending between verses 8 and 9, and one manuscript has it after verse 8 (omitting verses 9-20): *Then they quickly reported all these instructions to those around Peter. After this, Jesus himself also sent out through them from east to west the sacred and imperishable proclamation of eternal salvation. Amen.*

15:37 *With a loud cry, Jesus breathed his last.* Frequently, crucifixion produced a coma or unconsciousness prior to death, but Jesus was in control of all His faculties until the moment when He voluntarily gave up His life (John 10:17 – 18).

15:38 *The curtain of the temple.* The significance of this event is that access to God is now open to all. No longer through priests and the blood of bulls and goats do we approach God, but through the torn veil, which also symbolizes Jesus' broken and torn body (Heb. 10:20).

15:40 – 41 *Some women were watching from a distance.* These women were true disciples of Christ. They had ministered to Jesus' needs and would be the first witnesses of His resurrection. Mark does not name Jesus' mother here but includes other prominent women. Three Marys were present along with many other women and Salome. She was the mother of the disciples James and John (Matt. 27:56).

15:43 *Joseph of Arimathea.* He is identified as a prominent member of the Sanhedrin. To ask Pilate for the body of Jesus was not just a gesture of kindness. It was an act of bravery, which placed Joseph in opposition to the Sanhedrin and identified him as a follower of Jesus.

16:5 – 6 *a young man . . . sitting on the right side.* Mark does not identify the young man with the robe as an angel, but he is there to explain the mystery that confronts the women. ***He has risen!*** In the passive voice, this indicates that an act of God accomplished the raising up of Jesus.

16:9 – 20 *When Jesus rose.* The authenticity of these last twelve verses has been disputed. Those who doubt Mark's authorship of this passage point

15:37 [v] Jn 19:30 **15:38** [w] Heb 10:19, 20 **15:39** [x] ver 45 [y] Mk 1:1, 11; 9:7; Mt 4:3 **15:40** [z] Ps 38:11 [a] Mk 16:1; Lk 24:10; Jn 19:25 **15:41** [b] Mt 27:55, 56; Lk 8:2, 3 **15:42** [c] Mt 27:62; Jn 19:31 **15:43** [d] Mt 5:22 [e] Mt 3:2; Lk 2:25, 38 **15:45** [f] ver 39 **15:46** [g] Mk 16:3 **15:47** [h] ver 40 **16:1** [i] Lk 23:56; Jn 19:39, 40 **16:3** [j] Mk 15:46 **16:5** [k] Jn 20:12 **16:6** [l] Mk 1:24 **16:7** [m] Jn 21:1-23 [n] Mk 14:28 **16:9** [o] Jn 20:11-18 **16:11** [p] ver 13, 14; Lk 24:11

in the country.[q] 13 *These returned and reported*
it to the rest; but they did not believe them ei-
ther.
14 *Later Jesus appeared to the Eleven as they*
were eating; he rebuked them for their lack of
faith and their stubborn refusal to believe those
who had seen him after he had risen.[r]
15 *He said to them, "Go into all the world and*
preach the gospel to all creation.[s] 16 *Whoever*
believes and is baptized will be saved, but who-
ever does not believe will be condemned.[t] 17 *And*
these signs will accompany those who believe:
In my name they will drive out demons;[u] *they*
will speak in new tongues;[v] 18 *they will pick up*
snakes[w] *with their hands; and when they drink*
deadly poison, it will not hurt them at all; they
will place their hands on[x] *sick people, and they*
will get well."
19 *After the Lord Jesus had spoken to them,*
he was taken up into heaven[y] *and he sat at the*
right hand of God.[z] 20 *Then the disciples went*
out and preached everywhere, and the Lord
worked with them and confirmed his word by
the signs that accompanied it.

---

to two fourth-century manuscripts that omit these verses. Others believe that they should be included because even these two manuscripts leave space for all or some of these verses, indicating that their copyists knew of their existence. The difficulty is in knowing whether the space is for this longer version of Mark's ending or for one of the alternate endings found in the manuscripts. Important early church fathers endorsed this passage, and it does not seem likely that Mark would end his story on a note of fear (v. 8).

16:14 *to the Eleven.* After Judas' demise (Matt. 27:3–5; Acts 1:16–18), the disciples were known for a while as the Eleven. Jesus upbraided these disciples for not believing the accounts of eyewitnesses, but He pronounced a blessing on "those who have not seen and yet have believed" (John 20:29).

16:19 *he was taken up into heaven.* This was the final sign that Jesus was the Son of God.

16:12 [q] Lk 24:13-32 **16:14** [r] Lk 24:36-43 **16:15** [s] Mt 28:18-20; Lk 24:47, 48 **16:16** [t] Jn 3:16, 18, 36; Ac 16:31 **16:17** [u] Mk 9:38; Lk 10:17; Ac 5:16; 8:7; 16:18; 19:13-16 [v] Ac 2:4; 10:46; 19:6; 1Co 12:10, 28, 30 **16:18** [w] Lk 10:19; Ac 28:3-5 [x] Ac 6:6 **16:19** [y] Lk 24:50, 51; Jn 6:62; Ac 1:9-11; 1Ti 3:16 [z] Ps 110:1; Ro 8:34; Col 3:1; Heb 1:3; 12:2

LUKE

▶ **AUTHOR:** It is evident from the prologues to Luke and Acts (1:1 – 4; Acts 1:1 – 5) that both books were addressed to a man called Theophilus as a two-volume work. Acts begins with a summary of Luke and continues the story from where the Gospel of Luke concludes. Luke may have been a Hellenistic Jew, but it is more likely that he was a Gentile (this would make him the only Gentile contributor to the New Testament). It has been suggested that Luke may have been a Greek physician to a Roman family who at some point was set free and given Roman citizenship. Luke was not an eyewitness of the events in his Gospel, but he relied on the testimony of apostolic eyewitness and reliable written sources.

▶ **TIME:** c. 4 B.C. – A.D. 33 ▶ **KEY VERSE:** Luke 19:10

▶ **THEME:** The beginning of Luke makes reference to the fact that there was a great deal of oral tradition concerning Jesus circulating during the first century. The rapid growth of the church (over 3,000 on the Day of Pentecost alone) meant that there would have been potential for significant variety in stories about Jesus. Luke's stated agenda is reliability. Where Matthew goes to great lengths to tie Jesus' story to the history of the Jews, Luke is more interested in where the story fits in the history of the human race. Throughout the book, Christ reaches out to people from a variety of social strata, nationalities, and cultures. Luke sees Jesus as the Savior of the whole world.

Introduction

1 Many have undertaken to draw up an
account of the things that have been
fulfilled[a] among us, 2just as they were
handed down to us by those who from the
first[a] were eyewitnesses[b] and servants of
the word.[c] 3With this in mind, since I myself have carefully investigated everything
from the beginning, I too decided to write
an orderly account[d] for you, most excellent[e] Theophilus,[f] 4so that you may know
the certainty of the things you have been
taught.[g]

The Birth of John the Baptist Foretold

5In the time of Herod king of Judea[h]
there was a priest named Zechariah, who
belonged to the priestly division of Abijah;[i]
his wife Elizabeth was also a descendant
of Aaron. 6Both of them were righteous in
the sight of God, observing all the Lord's
commands and decrees blamelessly.[j] 7But
they were childless because Elizabeth was

[a] 1 Or *been surely believed*

1:1 *Many have undertaken to draw up an account.* Luke makes it clear that he was not the first to write a narrative of the ministry of Jesus.
1:2 *eyewitnesses.* These verses suggest that Luke was not an eyewitness to the events of Jesus' ministry, but that he had access to statements of those who were.
1:3 *orderly account.* Luke gave his narrative a basic structure. Not every part is in chronological sequence, but the broad sequence is Christ's ministry in Galilee, His travel to Jerusalem, and His struggles in Jerusalem. The order of events shows how Jesus gradually revealed Himself and how opposition to Him grew.
1:4 *the certainty.* Theophilus was likely a young Gentile believer. He not only needed to know the truth and accuracy of what the church taught, but he also needed to be reassured. He might well have been wondering what he as a Gentile was doing in a movement which was originally Jewish.
1:5 *Herod.* He was appointed by the Roman emperor and reigned over Judea, Samaria, Galilee, Perea, and Syria from 37 to 4 B.C.
1:7 *Elizabeth was not able to conceive.* Being childless was a grave disappointment in ancient Israel (1 Sam. 1). The Scriptures record a number of times when God blessed a barren woman by giving her a son (Gen. 18:11; 21:2).

1:2 [a] Mk 1:1; Jn 15:27; Ac 1:21,22 [b] Heb 2:3; 1Pe 5:1; 2Pe 1:16; 1Jn 1:1 [c] Mk 4:14 **1:3** [d] Ac 11:4 [e] Ac 24:3; 26:25 [f] Ac 1:1 **1:4** [g] Jn 20:31 **1:5** [h] Mt 2:1 [i] 1Ch 24:10 **1:6** [j] Ge 7:1; 1Ki 9:4

not able to conceive, and they were both
very old.
8Once when Zechariah's division was
on duty and he was serving as priest before God,[k] 9he was chosen by lot, according
to the custom of the priesthood, to go into
the temple of the Lord and burn incense.[l]
10And when the time for the burning of incense came, all the assembled worshipers
were praying outside.[m]
11Then an angel[n] of the Lord appeared to
him, standing at the right side of the altar
of incense.[o] 12When Zechariah saw him, he
was startled and was gripped with fear.[p]
13But the angel said to him: "Do not be
afraid,[q] Zechariah; your prayer has been
heard. Your wife Elizabeth will bear you
a son, and you are to call him John.[r] 14He
will be a joy and delight to you, and many
will rejoice because of his birth,[s] 15for he
will be great in the sight of the Lord. He
is never to take wine or other fermented
drink,[t] and he will be filled with the Holy
Spirit even before he is born.[u] 16He will
bring back many of the people of Israel to
the Lord their God. 17And he will go on before the Lord,[v] in the spirit and power of
Elijah,[w] to turn the hearts of the parents to
their children[x] and the disobedient to the
wisdom of the righteous—to make ready a
people prepared for the Lord."
18Zechariah asked the angel, "How can
I be sure of this? I am an old man and my
wife is well along in years."[y]
19The angel said to him, "I am Gabriel.[z]
I stand in the presence of God, and I have
been sent to speak to you and to tell you
this good news. 20And now you will be silent and not able to speak[a] until the day this
happens, because you did not believe my
words, which will come true at their appointed time."
21Meanwhile, the people were waiting for Zechariah and wondering why he
stayed so long in the temple. 22When he
came out, he could not speak to them. They
realized he had seen a vision in the temple,
for he kept making signs[b] to them but remained unable to speak.
23When his time of service was completed, he returned home. 24After this his wife
Elizabeth became pregnant and for five
months remained in seclusion. 25"The Lord
has done this for me," she said. "In these
days he has shown his favor and taken
away my disgrace[c] among the people."

The Birth of Jesus Foretold

26In the sixth month of Elizabeth's pregnancy, God sent the angel Gabriel[d] to
Nazareth,[e] a town in Galilee, 27to a virgin
pledged to be married to a man named Joseph,[f] a descendant of David. The virgin's
name was Mary. 28The angel went to her
and said, "Greetings, you who are highly
favored! The Lord is with you."
29Mary was greatly troubled at his
words and wondered what kind of greeting this might be. 30But the angel said to
her, "Do not be afraid,[g] Mary; you have
found favor with God. 31You will conceive
and give birth to a son, and you are to call
him Jesus.[h] 32He will be great and will be
called the Son of the Most High.[i] The Lord
God will give him the throne of his father
David, 33and he will reign over Jacob's descendants forever; his kingdom[j] will never
end."[k]
34"How will this be," Mary asked the angel, "since I am a virgin?"

1:8–9 *the custom of the priesthood.* Zacharias served for one week twice a year at the temple, one of perhaps 18,000 priests who served in a year.
1:13 *Do not be afraid.* Angels often calmed the fears of those to whom they appeared (v. 30; 2:10; Gen. 15:1; Dan. 10:12; Matt. 1:20; Acts 18:9; Rev. 1:17).
1:14 *joy and delight.* Joy is a major theme throughout the writings of Luke (vv. 44,47,58; 2:10; 10:20; 13:17; 15:5–7; Acts 5:41).
1:15 *never to take wine or other fermented drink.* As with Samuel and Samson, a vow was imposed on the child that indicated his special consecration to the Lord. ***filled with the Holy Spirit.*** Being filled with the Spirit means being directed by Him and obedient to Him (Eph. 5:18).
1:17 *in the spirit and power of Elijah.* John was the forerunner of the Messiah. This description recalls Matthew 3:1–6. John's ministry paralleled Elijah, for both prophets called Israel to repentance (1 Kin. 17:18).
1:19 *Gabriel.* Two angels are named in the Bible who function as messengers. Michael is the other one (Dan. 8:16; 9:21; 10:13,21; Jude 9; Rev. 12:7).
1:25 *my disgrace.* In ancient Israel barrenness was seen as a cause for shame. The "opening of the womb" indicated God's grace (Gen. 21:6; 30:23; 1 Sam. 1: 2). In this verse, Elizabeth praises the Lord for mercifully blessing her even as He moved His plan for all of human history forward.
1:32 *the Most High.* This phrase is another way or referring to the majesty of God. ***David.*** Jesus fulfilled God's promise to David concerning an unending dynasty.
1:34 *How will this be.* Mary did not ask for a sign, so this remark does not reflect unbelief. She accepts her role without question in verse 38, and thus is a model of faith, even though she does not fully understand everything. The work of God in Mary introduces something unknown before or after; the birth into the human race of One who is both God and man.

1:8 [k] 1Ch 24:19; 2Ch 8:14 **1:9** [l] Ex 30:7,8; 1Ch 23:13; 2Ch 29:11 **1:10** [m] Lev 16:17 **1:11** [n] Ac 5:19 [o] Ex 30:1-10 **1:12** [p] Jdg 6:22,23; 13:22 **1:13** [q] ver 30; Mt 14:27 [r] ver 60,63 **1:14** [s] ver 58 **1:15** [t] Nu 6:3; Jdg 13:4; Lk 7:33 [u] Jer 1:5; Gal 1:15 **1:17** [v] ver 76 [w] Mt 11:14 [x] Mal 4:5,6 **1:18** [y] ver 34; Ge 17:17 **1:19** [z] ver 26; Da 8:16; 9:21; Mt 18:10 **1:20** [a] Eze 3:26 **1:22** [b] ver 62 **1:25** [c] Ge 30:23; Isa 4:1 **1:26** [d] ver 19 [e] Mt 2:23 **1:27** [f] Mt 1:16,18,20; Lk 2:4 **1:30** [g] ver 13; Mt 14:27 **1:31** [h] Isa 7:14; Mt 1:21,25; Lk 2:21 **1:32** [i] ver 35,76; Mk 5:7 **1:33** [j] Mt 28:18 [k] Da 2:44; 7:14,27; Mic 4:7; Heb 1:8

35 The angel answered, "The Holy Spirit will come on you,[l] and the power of the
Most High[m] will overshadow you. So the
holy one[n] to be born will be called[a] the Son
of God.[o] 36 Even Elizabeth your relative is
going to have a child in her old age, and she
who was said to be unable to conceive is in
her sixth month. 37 For no word from God
will ever fail."[p]

38 "I am the Lord's servant," Mary answered. "May your word to me be fulfilled."
Then the angel left her.

Mary Visits Elizabeth

39 At that time Mary got ready and hurried to a town in the hill country of Judea,[q]
40 where she entered Zechariah's home
and greeted Elizabeth. 41 When Elizabeth
heard Mary's greeting, the baby leaped in
her womb, and Elizabeth was filled with
the Holy Spirit. 42 In a loud voice she exclaimed: "Blessed are you among wom-
en,[r] and blessed is the child you will bear!
43 But why am I so favored, that the mother
of my Lord should come to me? 44 As soon
as the sound of your greeting reached my
ears, the baby in my womb leaped for joy.
45 Blessed is she who has believed that the
Lord would fulfill his promises to her!"

Mary's Song

46 And Mary said:

"My soul glorifies the Lord[s]
47 and my spirit rejoices in God my
Savior,[t]
48 for he has been mindful
of the humble state of his servant.[u]
From now on all generations will call
me blessed,[v]
49 for the Mighty One has done great
things[w] for me—
holy is his name.[x]
50 His mercy extends to those who fear
him,
from generation to generation.[y]
51 He has performed mighty deeds with
his arm;[z]
he has scattered those who are proud
in their inmost thoughts.
52 He has brought down rulers from their
thrones
but has lifted up the humble.
53 He has filled the hungry with good
things[a]
but has sent the rich away
empty.
54 He has helped his servant Israel,
remembering to be merciful[b]
55 to Abraham and his descendants[c]
forever,
just as he promised our ancestors."

56 Mary stayed with Elizabeth for about
three months and then returned home.

The Birth of John the Baptist

57 When it was time for Elizabeth to have
her baby, she gave birth to a son. 58 Her
neighbors and relatives heard that the
Lord had shown her great mercy, and they
shared her joy.

59 On the eighth day they came to circumcise[d] the child, and they were going to
name him after his father Zechariah, 60 but
his mother spoke up and said, "No! He is to
be called John."[e]

61 They said to her, "There is no one
among your relatives who has that name."

62 Then they made signs[f] to his father, to
find out what he would like to name the
child. 63 He asked for a writing tablet, and
to everyone's astonishment he wrote, "His
name is John."[g] 64 Immediately his mouth
was opened and his tongue set free, and
he began to speak,[h] praising God. 65 All
the neighbors were filled with awe, and
throughout the hill country of Judea[i] people were talking about all these things.
66 Everyone who heard this wondered
about it, asking, "What then is this child
going to be?" For the Lord's hand was with
him.[j]

Zechariah's Song

67 His father Zechariah was filled with
the Holy Spirit and prophesied:[k]

[a] 35 Or *So the child to be born will be called holy,*

1:35 ***The Holy Spirit will come on you.*** This is a direct declaration of Jesus' divine conception. The child's conception means He is uniquely set apart.

1:38 ***servant.*** This term suggests humility before the Lord and a readiness for faithful and obedient service, which should characterize every believer. Paul uses the masculine form of this word to describe himself (Rom. 1:1).

1:46 ***My soul glorifies the Lord.*** The following hymn gets its name, the "Magnificat," from the Latin word for *magnifies*. Mary's hymn is a recital of what God had done for her and for others in the past.

1:48 ***all generations will call me blessed.*** Mary went from being a poor unknown Hebrew girl to the most honored woman in the history of the world.

1:50 ***mercy.*** This term expresses the Old Testament concept of God's loyal, gracious, faithful love (Ps. 103).

1:51–53 ***he has scattered those who are proud.*** Here Mary sings of events in the future as if they have already been completed. These verses portray a "reversal" in the end times, when those who have abused power will be judged and those who have suffered persecution will be exalted.

1:67 ***Zechariah was filled with the Holy Spirit and prophesied.*** The presence of the Holy Spirit

1:35 [l] Mt 1:18 [m] ver 32,76 [n] Mk 1:24 [o] Mt 4:3
1:37 [p] Mt 19:26 **1:39** [q] ver 65 **1:42** [r] Jdg 5:24
1:46 [s] Ps 34:2,3 **1:47** [t] 1Ti 1:1; 2:3 **1:48** [u] Ps 138:6
[v] Lk 11:27 **1:49** [w] Ps 71:19 [x] Ps 111:9 **1:50** [y] Ex 20:6;
Ps 103:17 **1:51** [z] Ps 98:1; Isa 40:10 **1:53** [a] Ps 107:9
1:54 [b] Ps 98:3 **1:55** [c] Ge 17:19; Ps 132:11; Gal 3:16
1:59 [d] Ge 17:12; Lev 12:3; Lk 2:21; Php 3:5 **1:60** [e] ver 13,
63 **1:62** [f] ver 22 **1:63** [g] ver 13,60 **1:64** [h] ver 20
1:65 [i] ver 39 **1:66** [j] Ge 39:2; Ac 11:21 **1:67** [k] Joel 2:28

68 "Praise be to the Lord, the God of
Israel,[l]
because he has come to his people
and redeemed them.[m]
69 He has raised up a horn[a][n] of salvation
for us
in the house of his servant David[o]
70 (as he said through his holy prophets of
long ago),[p]
71 salvation from our enemies
and from the hand of all who
hate us—
72 to show mercy to our ancestors[q]
and to remember his holy covenant,[r]
73 the oath he swore to our father
Abraham:[s]
74 to rescue us from the hand of our
enemies,
and to enable us to serve him[t] without
fear
75 in holiness and righteousness[u] before
him all our days.

76 And you, my child, will be called a
prophet[v] of the Most High;[w]
for you will go on before the Lord to
prepare the way for him,[x]
77 to give his people the knowledge of
salvation
through the forgiveness of their
sins,[y]
78 because of the tender mercy of our
God,
by which the rising sun[z] will come to
us from heaven
79 to shine on those living in darkness
and in the shadow of death,[a]
to guide our feet into the path of peace."

80 And the child grew and became strong
in spirit[b];[b] and he lived in the wilderness
until he appeared publicly to Israel.

The Birth of Jesus

2 In those days Caesar Augustus[c] issued
a decree that a census should be taken
of the entire Roman world.[d] 2 (This was the
first census that took place while[c] Quirinius was governor of Syria.)[e] 3 And everyone
went to their own town to register.
4 So Joseph also went up from the town of
Nazareth in Galilee to Judea, to Bethlehem[f]
the town of David, because he belonged to
the house and line of David. 5 He went there
to register with Mary, who was pledged
to be married to him and was expecting
a child. 6 While they were there, the time
came for the baby to be born, 7 and she gave
birth to her firstborn, a son. She wrapped
him in cloths and placed him in a manger,
because there was no guest room available
for them.
8 And there were shepherds living out in
the fields nearby, keeping watch over their
flocks at night. 9 An angel[g] of the Lord appeared to them, and the glory of the Lord
shone around them, and they were terrified. 10 But the angel said to them, "Do not
be afraid.[h] I bring you good news that will
cause great joy for all the people. 11 Today in
the town of David a Savior[i] has been born
to you; he is the Messiah,[j] the Lord. 12 This
will be a sign[k] to you: You will find a baby
wrapped in cloths and lying in a manger."
13 Suddenly a great company of the heavenly host appeared with the angel, praising
God and saying,

14 "Glory to God in the highest heaven,
and on earth peace[l] to those on whom
his favor rests."

[a] 69 *Horn* here symbolizes a strong king.
[b] 80 Or *in the Spirit* [c] 2 Or *This census took place before*

enabled Zacharias to announce God's promise. Zacharias's hymn is called the "Benedictus" from its first word in the Latin Vulgate translation. There are three types of prophecy in the Bible; foretelling future events, forth-telling the Word of God, and praising God. Zacharias's prophecy includes all three.

1:69 *horn of salvation.* The horn of an ox was considered a symbol of power in ancient Israel (Deut. 33:17; 1 Sam. 2:10; 2 Sam. 22:3; Ps. 75:4–5,10; 132:17; Ezek. 29:21).

1:77 *knowledge of salvation.* John's task was to prepare the people by informing them of their need to repent (3:1–14) and of the One who was coming (3:15–18).

1:78 *the rising sun will come to us.* This phrase is a reference to the coming of Messiah (Num. 24:17; Mal. 4:2).

2:1–2 *Augustus.* This was the Roman emperor from 31 B.C. to A.D. 14. ***Quirinius.*** Quirinius was the governor or administrator of a major census organized to facilitate the collection of taxes.

2:3–4 *to register.* The registration, following Jewish custom took place at a person's ancestral home (2 Sam. 24). The journey from Nazareth to Bethlehem was about 90 miles, at least a three-day trip.

2:9 *glory.* This word refers to evidence of God's majestic presence, later associated with Jesus (Acts 7:55). In this scene, the glory is the appearance of light in the midst of darkness.

2:11 *Savior . . . he is the Messiah, the Lord.* These three titles together summarize the saving work of Jesus and His sovereign position. What God was called in 1:47, Jesus is called here. The word Messiah means "Anointed." The word Lord was the title of a ruler.

2:14 *peace to those on whom his favor rests.* Peace is not for everyone, but for those who please God.

1:68 [l] Ps 72:18 [m] Ps 111:9; Lk 7:16 **1:69** [n] 1Sa 2:1, 10; Ps 18:2; 89:17; 132:17; Eze 29:21 [o] Mt 1:1 **1:70** [p] Jer 23:5 **1:72** [q] Mic 7:20 [r] Ps 105:8, 9; 106:45; Eze 16:60 **1:73** [s] Ge 22:16-18 **1:74** [t] Heb 9:14 **1:75** [u] Eph 4:24 **1:76** [v] Mt 11:9 [w] ver 32, 35 [x] ver 17; Mal 3:1 **1:77** [y] Jer 31:34; Mk 1:4 **1:78** [z] Mal 4:2 **1:79** [a] Isa 9:2; 59:9; Mt 4:16; Ac 26:18 **1:80** [b] Lk 2:40, 52 **2:1** [c] Mt 22:17; Lk 3:1 [d] Mt 24:14 **2:2** [e] Mt 4:24 **2:4** [f] Jn 7:42 **2:9** [g] Lk 1:11; Ac 5:19 **2:10** [h] Mt 14:27 **2:11** [i] Mt 1:21; Jn 4:42; Ac 5:31 [j] Mt 1:16; 16:16, 20; Jn 11:27; Ac 2:36 **2:12** [k] 1Sa 2:34; 2Ki 19:29; Isa 7:14 **2:14** [l] Lk 1:79; Ro 5:1; Eph 2:14, 17

15When the angels had left them and
gone into heaven, the shepherds said to
one another, "Let's go to Bethlehem and
see this thing that has happened, which
the Lord has told us about."
16So they hurried off and found Mary
and Joseph, and the baby, who was lying
in the manger. 17When they had seen him,
they spread the word concerning what
had been told them about this child, 18and
all who heard it were amazed at what the
shepherds said to them. 19But Mary treasured up all these things and pondered
them in her heart.[m] 20The shepherds returned, glorifying and praising God[n] for all
the things they had heard and seen, which
were just as they had been told.
21On the eighth day, when it was time to
circumcise the child,[o] he was named Jesus,
the name the angel had given him before
he was conceived.[p]

Jesus Presented in the Temple

22When the time came for the purification rites required by the Law of Moses,[q]
Joseph and Mary took him to Jerusalem to
present him to the Lord 23(as it is written in
the Law of the Lord, "Every firstborn male
is to be consecrated to the Lord"[a]),[r] 24and
to offer a sacrifice in keeping with what is
said in the Law of the Lord: "a pair of doves
or two young pigeons."[b][s]
25Now there was a man in Jerusalem
called Simeon, who was righteous and devout.[t] He was waiting for the consolation of
Israel,[u] and the Holy Spirit was on him. 26It
had been revealed to him by the Holy Spirit
that he would not die before he had seen
the Lord's Messiah. 27Moved by the Spirit,
he went into the temple courts. When the
parents brought in the child Jesus to do for
him what the custom of the Law required,[v]
28Simeon took him in his arms and praised
God, saying:

29"Sovereign Lord, as you have
promised,[w]
you may now dismiss[c] your servant
in peace.[x]
30For my eyes have seen your salvation,[y]
31 which you have prepared in the sight
of all nations:
32a light for revelation to the Gentiles,
and the glory of your people Israel."[z]

33The child's father and mother marveled at what was said about him. 34Then
Simeon blessed them and said to Mary, his
mother:[a] "This child is destined to cause
the falling[b] and rising of many in Israel,
and to be a sign that will be spoken against,
35so that the thoughts of many hearts will
be revealed. And a sword will pierce your
own soul too."
36There was also a prophet,[c] Anna, the
daughter of Penuel, of the tribe of Asher.
She was very old; she had lived with her
husband seven years after her marriage,
37and then was a widow until she was
eighty-four.[d][d] She never left the temple but
worshiped night and day, fasting and praying.[e] 38Coming up to them at that very moment, she gave thanks to God and spoke
about the child to all who were looking
forward to the redemption of Jerusalem.[f]
39When Joseph and Mary had done everything required by the Law of the Lord,
they returned to Galilee to their own town
of Nazareth.[g] 40And the child grew and
became strong; he was filled with wisdom,
and the grace of God was on him.[h]

The Boy Jesus at the Temple

41Every year Jesus' parents went to Jerusalem for the Festival of the Passover.[i]
42When he was twelve years old, they went
up to the festival, according to the custom.
43After the festival was over, while his parents were returning home, the boy Jesus
stayed behind in Jerusalem, but they were
unaware of it. 44Thinking he was in their
company, they traveled on for a day. Then
they began looking for him among their
relatives and friends. 45When they did not

[a] 23 Exodus 13:2,12 [b] 24 Lev. 12:8
[c] 29 Or *promised, / now dismiss* [d] 37 Or *then had been a widow for eighty-four years.*

2:21 *On the eighth day.* According to the law, a Jewish boy was to be circumcised on his eighth day (Gen. 17:12; Lev. 12:3).

2:25 *consolation of Israel.* Simeon was waiting for the comforter of Israel, a hope that parallels the hope of national deliverance expressed in the two hymns of chapter one. This deliverance would involve the work of Messiah, as verse 26 suggests.

2:32 *A light for revelation to the Gentiles.* This is the first explicit statement in Luke that includes both Jew and Gentile. Salvation is portrayed as light (1:79). It would be a revelation to Gentiles because they would be able to participate in God's blessing with a fullness that had not been revealed in the Old Testament (Eph. 2:11–3:7).

2:36 *There was also a prophet, Anna.* Anna's work as a prophetess in the temple court suggests that she addressed all who would listen to her, as did Miriam (Ex. 15:20), Deborah (Judg. 4:4), and Huldah (2 Kin. 22:14).

2:41 *Every year . . . went to Jerusalem.* The annual pilgrimage to Jerusalem was customary for many who lived outside the city. The laws commanded three pilgrimages for the men each year: Passover, Pentecost, and the Festival of Tabernacles (Ex. 23:14–17; Deut. 16:16).

2:19 [m] ver 51 **2:20** [n] Mt 9:8 **2:21** [o] Lk 1:59 [p] Lk 1:31
2:22 [q] Lev 12:2-8 **2:23** [r] Ex 13:2, 12, 15; Nu 3:13
2:24 [s] Lev 12:8 **2:25** [t] Lk 1:6 [u] ver 38; Isa 52:9; Lk 23:51
2:27 [v] ver 22 **2:29** [w] ver 26 [x] Ac 2:24 **2:30** [y] Isa 52:10; Lk 3:6 **2:32** [z] Isa 42:6; 49:6; Ac 13:47; 26:23
2:34 [a] Mt 12:46 [b] Isa 8:14; Mt 21:44; 1Co 1:23; 2Co 2:16; 1Pe 2:7,8 **2:36** [c] Ac 21:9 **2:37** [d] 1Ti 5:9 [e] Ac 13:3; 14:23; 1Ti 5:5 **2:38** [f] ver 25; Isa 40:2; Lk 1:68; 24:21
2:39 [g] ver 51; Mt 2:23 **2:40** [h] ver 52; Lk 1:80
2:41 [i] Ex 23:15; Dt 16:1-8

find him, they went back to Jerusalem to
look for him. 46 After three days they found
him in the temple courts, sitting among
the teachers, listening to them and asking them questions. 47 Everyone who heard
him was amazed[j] at his understanding and
his answers. 48 When his parents saw him,
they were astonished. His mother[k] said to
him, "Son, why have you treated us like
this? Your father[l] and I have been anxious-
ly searching for you."

49 "Why were you searching for me?" he
asked. "Didn't you know I had to be in my
Father's house?"[a][m] 50 But they did not understand what he was saying to them.[n]

51 Then he went down to Nazareth with
them[o] and was obedient to them. But his
mother treasured all these things in her
heart.[p] 52 And Jesus grew in wisdom and
stature, and in favor with God and man.[q]

John the Baptist Prepares the Way

3 In the fifteenth year of the reign of Tiberius Caesar—when Pontius Pilate[r]
was governor of Judea, Herod[s] tetrarch of
Galilee, his brother Philip tetrarch of Iturea and Traconitis, and Lysanias tetrarch
of Abilene— 2 during the high-priesthood
of Annas and Caiaphas,[t] the word of God
came to John[u] son of Zechariah[v] in the
wilderness. 3 He went into all the country
around the Jordan, preaching a baptism of
repentance for the forgiveness of sins.[w] 4 As
it is written in the book of the words of Isaiah the prophet:

"A voice of one calling in the
wilderness,
'Prepare the way for the Lord,
make straight paths for him.
5 Every valley shall be filled in,
every mountain and hill made low.
The crooked roads shall become
straight,
the rough ways smooth.
6 And all people will see God's
salvation.'"[b][x]

7 John said to the crowds coming out to
be baptized by him, "You brood of vipers![y]
Who warned you to flee from the coming
wrath?[z] 8 Produce fruit in keeping with repentance. And do not begin to say to yourselves, 'We have Abraham as our father.'[a]
For I tell you that out of these stones God
can raise up children for Abraham. 9 The
ax is already at the root of the trees, and
every tree that does not produce good fruit
will be cut down and thrown into the fire."[b]

10 "What should we do then?"[c] the crowd
asked.

11 John answered, "Anyone who has two
shirts should share with the one who has
none, and anyone who has food should do
the same."[d]

12 Even tax collectors came to be baptized.[e] "Teacher," they asked, "what should
we do?"

13 "Don't collect any more than you are
required to,"[f] he told them.

14 Then some soldiers asked him, "And
what should we do?"

He replied, "Don't extort money and
don't accuse people falsely[g]—be content
with your pay."

15 The people were waiting expectantly and were all wondering in their hearts
if John[h] might possibly be the Messiah.[i]
16 John answered them all, "I baptize you
with[c] water.[j] But one who is more powerful than I will come, the straps of whose

---

[a] 49 Or *be about my Father's business*
[b] 6 Isaiah 40:3-5 [c] 16 Or *in*

2:49 *I had to be in my Father's house.* This is the first indication in Luke's Gospel that Jesus knew He had a unique mission and a unique relationship to the Father.

3:1–2 *Tiberius Caesar ... Pontius Pilate ... Herod ... Annas ... Caiaphas.* The various rulers that Luke lists show the complexity of the historical and political situation in Israel during Jesus' day. A first century Israelite had to deal with the edicts of the Roman emperor, the regulations of the governor over Israel, and the judgments of the religious leaders of Israel.

3:4–6 *Prepare the way for the Lord.* This citation from Isaiah 40:3–5 declares the coming of God's deliverance. Luke cites the text more fully than Matthew or Mark. He carries the passage through to its mention of salvation being seen by all flesh (v. 6), thus highlighting that the gospel is for all people. The preparation for the arrival of a king typically meant that a road was prepared for his journey. This is what Isaiah compares to the arrival of God's salvation.

3:8 *Produce fruit.* John the Baptist warned that the fruits of repentance are necessary, not the claim of an ancestral connection to Abraham. External genealogical connections would not change one's attitude to God.

3:11 *two shirts.* One was an undergarment, and the other was an outer garment. A person did not need two when another person had none.

3:12 *tax collectors.* These men were Jewish agents employed by those who had purchased the right to collect taxes for the Roman state. Publicans often added interest to cover their own expenses and to pad their income. They were disliked both for their business practices and for their support of the occupying state.

3:16–17 *the Holy Spirit and fire.* These two facets of Christ's work relate to His first and second comings. As a result of Christ's work at His first coming,

2:47 [j] Mt 7:28 **2:48** [k] Mt 12:46 [l] Lk 3:23; 4:22
2:49 [m] Jn 2:16 **2:50** [n] Mk 9:32 **2:51** [o] ver 39; Mt 2:23
[p] ver 19 **2:52** [q] ver 40; 1Sa 2:26; Lk 1:80
3:1 [r] Mt 27:2 [s] Mt 14:1 **3:2** [t] Mt 26:3; Jn 18:13; Ac 4:6
[u] Mt 3:1 [v] Lk 1:13 **3:3** [w] ver 16; Mk 1:4 **3:6** [x] Ps 98:2;
Isa 40:3-5; 42:16; 52:10; Lk 2:30 **3:7** [y] Mt 12:34; 23:33
[z] Ro 1:18 **3:8** [a] Isa 51:2; Lk 19:9; Jn 8:33, 39; Ac 13:26;
Ro 4:1, 11, 12, 16, 17; Gal 3:7 **3:9** [b] Mt 3:10
3:10 [c] ver 12, 14; Ac 2:37; 16:30 **3:11** [d] Isa 58:7
3:12 [e] Lk 7:29 **3:13** [f] Lk 19:8 **3:14** [g] Ex 23:1; Lev 19:11
3:15 [h] Mt 3:1 [i] Jn 1:19, 20; Ac 13:25
3:16 [j] ver 3; Mk 1:4

sandals I am not worthy to untie. He will
baptize you with[a] the Holy Spirit and fire.[k]
17His winnowing fork[l] is in his hand to
clear his threshing floor and to gather the
wheat into his barn, but he will burn up
the chaff with unquenchable fire."[m] 18And
with many other words John exhorted the
people and proclaimed the good news to
them.

19But when John rebuked Herod[n] the tetrarch because of his marriage to Herodias, his brother's wife, and all the other evil
things he had done, 20Herod added this to
them all: He locked John up in prison.[o]

The Baptism and Genealogy of Jesus

21When all the people were being baptized, Jesus was baptized too. And as he
was praying,[p] heaven was opened 22and
the Holy Spirit descended on him[q] in bodily form like a dove. And a voice came from
heaven: "You are my Son,[r] whom I love;
with you I am well pleased."[s]

23Now Jesus himself was about thirty
years old when he began his ministry.[t]
He was the son, so it was thought, of Joseph,[u]

the son of Heli, 24the son of Matthat,
the son of Levi, the son of Melki,
the son of Jannai, the son of Joseph,
25the son of Mattathias, the son of Amos,
the son of Nahum, the son of Esli,
the son of Naggai, 26the son of Maath,
the son of Mattathias, the son of Sem-
ein,
the son of Josek, the son of Joda,
27the son of Joanan, the son of Rhesa,
the son of Zerubbabel,[v] the son of Shealtiel,
the son of Neri, 28the son of Melki,
the son of Addi, the son of Cosam,
the son of Elmadam, the son of Er,
29the son of Joshua, the son of Eliezer,
the son of Jorim, the son of Matthat,
the son of Levi, 30the son of Simeon,
the son of Judah, the son of Joseph,
the son of Jonam, the son of Eliakim,
31the son of Melea, the son of Menna,
the son of Mattatha, the son of Nathan,[w]
the son of David, 32the son of Jesse,
the son of Obed, the son of Boaz,
the son of Salmon,[b] the son of Nahshon,
33the son of Amminadab, the son of
Ram,[c]
the son of Hezron, the son of Perez,[x]
the son of Judah, 34the son of Jacob,
the son of Isaac, the son of Abraham,
the son of Terah, the son of Nahor,[y]
35the son of Serug, the son of Reu,
the son of Peleg, the son of Eber,
the son of Shelah, 36the son of Cainan,
the son of Arphaxad,[z] the son of Shem,
the son of Noah, the son of Lamech,[a]
37the son of Methuselah, the son of
Enoch,
the son of Jared, the son of Mahalalel,
the son of Kenan, 38the son of Enosh,
the son of Seth, the son of Adam,
the son of God.[b]

Jesus Is Tested in the Wilderness

4 Jesus, full of the Holy Spirit,[c] left the
Jordan[d] and was led by the Spirit[e] into
the wilderness, 2where for forty days[f] he
was tempted[d] by the devil. He ate nothing
during those days, and at the end of them
he was hungry.

3The devil said to him, "If you are the Son
of God, tell this stone to become bread."

[a] 16 Or *in* [b] 32 Some early manuscripts *Sala* [c] 33 Some manuscripts *Amminadab, the son of Admin, the son of Arni*; other manuscripts vary widely. [d] 2 The Greek for *tempted* can also mean *tested.*

believers are placed into one family (1 Cor. 12:13) and commended to the care of the Holy Spirit. When Christ comes a second time, He will come with the fire of judgment. ***winnowing fork.*** This tool was a wooden forklike shovel that lifted the grain in the air so that the wind could separate it from the chaff.

3:19–20 *all the other evil things he had done.* Herod had divorced his wife to marry his own niece Herodias, who already had been the wife of his brother Philip. Not only was the divorce a problem, so was marrying such a close relative (Lev. 18:16; 20:21).

3:22 *You are my Son, whom I love; with you I am well pleased.* This statement combines two ideas. The idea of God's Son comes from Psalm 2:7, a psalm about God's chosen King. The idea of pleasure comes from the image of the Servant in Isaiah 42:1. The fact that Jesus is both King and Servant is fundamental to Jesus' identity.

4:1–13 Temptation of Christ—Hebrews 2:18 makes the point that, because Christ was tempted, He is able to help those who are being tempted. We can see two examples of this quite plainly. The temptations are about security and power. In becoming man, Jesus gave up both (Phil. 2:5–11). Jesus didn't cling to any of what was by nature and identity rightfully His. In doing so, He had to trust fully in the Father for His life and very being. He can truly identify with our temptations. His experience wasn't just like ours are. No one ever gave up more power. No one of greater stature has ever been in such an insecure position. He can be there for us because He has been there before us.

4:3 *If you are the Son of God.* This is a conditional statement. In other words, Satan was saying: "Let's assume for the sake of argument that You are the Son of God." In fact, Satan was challenging Jesus' identity and authority.

3:16 [k] Jn 1:26,33; Ac 1:5; 11:16; 19:4 **3:17** [l] Isa 30:24 [m] Mt 13:30; 25:41 **3:19** [n] ver 1 **3:20** [o] Mt 14:3,4; Mk 6:17-18 **3:21** [p] Mt 14:23; Mk 1:35; 6:46; Lk 5:16; 6:12; 9:18,28; 11:1 **3:22** [q] Isa 42:1; Jn 1:32,33; Ac 10:38 [r] Mt 3:17 [s] Mt 3:17 **3:23** [t] Mt 4:17; Ac 1:1 [u] Lk 1:27 **3:27** [v] Mt 1:12 **3:31** [w] 2Sa 5:14; 1Ch 3:5 **3:33** [x] Ru 4:18-22; 1Ch 2:10-12 **3:34** [y] Ge 11:24,26 **3:36** [z] Ge 11:12 [a] Ge 5:28-32 **3:38** [b] Ge 5:1,2,6-9 **4:1** [c] ver 14,18 [d] Lk 3:3,21 [e] Lk 2:27 **4:2** [f] Ex 34:28; 1Ki 19:8

4Jesus answered, "It is written: 'Man
shall not live on bread alone.'[a]"[g]
5The devil led him up to a high place and
showed him in an instant all the kingdoms
of the world.[h] **6**And he said to him, "I will
give you all their authority and splendor; it
has been given to me,[i] and I can give it to
anyone I want to. **7**If you worship me, it will
all be yours."
8Jesus answered, "It is written: 'Worship
the Lord your God and serve him only.'[b]"[j]
9The devil led him to Jerusalem and had
him stand on the highest point of the temple. "If you are the Son of God," he said,
"throw yourself down from here. **10**For it
is written:

"'He will command his angels
concerning you
to guard you carefully;
11they will lift you up in their hands,
so that you will not strike your foot
against a stone.'[c]"[k]

12Jesus answered, "It is said: 'Do not put
the Lord your God to the test.'[d]"[l]
13When the devil had finished all this
tempting,[m] he left him[n] until an opportune
time.

Jesus Rejected at Nazareth

14Jesus returned to Galilee[o] in the power
of the Spirit, and news about him spread
through the whole countryside.[p] **15**He was
teaching in their synagogues,[q] and everyone praised him.
16He went to Nazareth,[r] where he had
been brought up, and on the Sabbath day
he went into the synagogue,[s] as was his
custom. He stood up to read, **17**and the
scroll of the prophet Isaiah was handed to
him. Unrolling it, he found the place where
it is written:

18"The Spirit of the Lord is on me,[t]
because he has anointed me
to proclaim good news to the poor.
He has sent me to proclaim freedom for
the prisoners
and recovery of sight for the blind,
to set the oppressed free,
19 to proclaim the year of the Lord's
favor."[e][u]

20Then he rolled up the scroll, gave it
back to the attendant and sat down.[v] The
eyes of everyone in the synagogue were
fastened on him. **21**He began by saying to
them, "Today this scripture is fulfilled in
your hearing."
22All spoke well of him and were
amazed at the gracious words that came
from his lips. "Isn't this Joseph's son?"
they asked.[w]
23Jesus said to them, "Surely you will
quote this proverb to me: 'Physician, heal
yourself!' And you will tell me, 'Do here in
your hometown[x] what we have heard that
you did in Capernaum.'"[y]
24"Truly I tell you," he continued, "no
prophet is accepted in his hometown.[z] **25**I
assure you that there were many widows
in Israel in Elijah's time, when the sky
was shut for three and a half years and
there was a severe famine throughout the
land.[a] **26**Yet Elijah was not sent to any of
them, but to a widow in Zarephath in the
region of Sidon.[b] **27**And there were many

---

[a] *4* Deut. 8:3 [b] *8* Deut. 6:13 [c] *11* Psalm 91:11,12
[d] *12* Deut. 6:16 [e] *19* Isaiah 61:1,2 (see Septuagint); Isaiah 58:6

4:4 *It is written.* Jesus responded to Satan's temptation by quoting Deuteronomy 8:3. Jesus refused to operate independently of God. The Spirit had led Him into the wilderness to prepare Him for His ministry, so eating at Satan's instruction would have shown a lack of dependence on the Father.
4:5 *all the kingdoms of the world.* This temptation was an attempt to offer Jesus power by the wrong means. Satan's method involved a detour around the cross, an inducement to "take the easy way" to power.
4:10–11 *He will command his angels concerning you to guard you.* Satan cited Psalm 91:11–12, reminding Jesus of God's promise of protection. However, the mere use of biblical words does not always reveal God's will, particularly if they are placed in the wrong context.
4:12 *Do not put the Lord your God to the test.* In response to Satan's third temptation, Jesus cited Deuteronomy 6:16. God is to be trusted, not tested. The Deuteronomy passage refers to Israel's attempt to test God at Meribah (Ex. 17:1–7). Jesus would not repeat the nation's error of unfaithfulness to God.
4:16–17 *stood up to read.* Most synagogue services had a reading from the Law and one from the Prophets, with an exposition that tied the texts together. Jesus expounded Isaiah 61.
4:18–19 *He has sent Me.* By citing Isaiah 61, Jesus was claiming to be a royal figure and to have a prophetic mission (v. 24). ***freedom for the prisoners.*** In the Old Testament, captivity refers to Israel's exile (1:68–74); here captivity refers to sin (1:77; 7:47; 24:47; Acts 2:38; 5:31; 10:43; 13:38; 26:18). ***to set the oppressed free.*** This was originally the call of Israel, but the nation had failed in its assignment (Is. 58:6). ***the year of the Lord's favor.*** This phrase is an allusion to the year of Jubilee when every 50th year all debt was forgiven and slaves were given their freedom (Lev. 25:10).
4:20 *he rolled up the scroll.* Jesus closed the book in the middle of the sentence. He did not continue because the next phrase—"the day of vengeance of our God"—was not being fulfilled then.

4:4 [g] Dt 8:3 **4:5** [h] Mt 24:14 **4:6** [i] Jn 12:31; 14:30; 1Jn 5:19 **4:8** [j] Dt 6:13 **4:11** [k] Ps 91:11, 12
4:12 [l] Dt 6:16 **4:13** [m] Heb 4:15 [n] Jn 14:30
4:14 [o] Mt 4:12 [p] Mt 9:26 **4:15** [q] Mt 4:23 **4:16** [r] Mt 2:23 [s] Mt 13:54 **4:18** [t] Jn 3:34 **4:19** [u] Lev 25:10; Isa 61:1, 2
4:20 [v] ver 17; Mt 26:55 **4:22** [w] Mt 13:54, 55; Jn 6:42; 7:15
4:23 [x] ver 16 [y] Mk 1:21-28; 2:1-12 **4:24** [z] Mt 13:57; Jn 4:44 **4:25** [a] 1Ki 17:1; 18:1; Jas 5:17, 18
4:26 [b] 1Ki 17:8-16; Mt 11:21

in Israel with leprosy[a] in the time of Elisha the prophet, yet not one of them was
cleansed—only Naaman the Syrian."[c]
28All the people in the synagogue were
furious when they heard this. **29**They got
up, drove him out of the town,[d] and took
him to the brow of the hill on which the
town was built, in order to throw him off
the cliff. **30**But he walked right through the
crowd and went on his way.[e]

Jesus Drives Out an Impure Spirit

31Then he went down to Capernaum,[f]
a town in Galilee, and on the Sabbath he
taught the people. **32**They were amazed at
his teaching,[g] because his words had authority.[h]
33In the synagogue there was a man possessed by a demon, an impure spirit. He
cried out at the top of his voice, **34**"Go away!
What do you want with us,[i] Jesus of Nazareth?[j] Have you come to destroy us? I know
who you are[k]—the Holy One of God!"[l]
35"Be quiet!" Jesus said sternly.[m] "Come
out of him!" Then the demon threw the
man down before them all and came out
without injuring him.
36All the people were amazed[n] and said
to each other, "What words these are! With
authority[o] and power he gives orders to impure spirits and they come out!" **37**And the
news about him spread throughout the surrounding area.[p]

Jesus Heals Many

38Jesus left the synagogue and went to
the home of Simon. Now Simon's mother-
in-law was suffering from a high fever, and
they asked Jesus to help her. **39**So he bent
over her and rebuked[q] the fever, and it left
her. She got up at once and began to wait
on them.
40At sunset, the people brought to Jesus
all who had various kinds of sickness, and
laying his hands on each one,[r] he healed
them.[s] **41**Moreover, demons came out of
many people, shouting, "You are the Son of
God!"[t] But he rebuked[u] them and would not
allow them to speak,[v] because they knew
he was the Messiah.
42At daybreak, Jesus went out to a solitary place. The people were looking for
him and when they came to where he was,
they tried to keep him from leaving them.
43But he said, "I must proclaim the good
news of the kingdom of God[w] to the other
towns also, because that is why I was sent."
44And he kept on preaching in the synagogues of Judea.[x]

Jesus Calls His First Disciples

5 One day as Jesus was standing by the
Lake of Gennesaret,[b] the people were
crowding around him and listening to the
word of God.[y] **2**He saw at the water's edge
two boats, left there by the fishermen, who
were washing their nets. **3**He got into one
of the boats, the one belonging to Simon,
and asked him to put out a little from shore.
Then he sat down and taught the people
from the boat.[z]
4When he had finished speaking, he said
to Simon, "Put out into deep water, and let
down the nets for a catch."[a]
5Simon answered, "Master,[b] we've
worked hard all night and haven't caught
anything.[c] But because you say so, I will let
down the nets."
6When they had done so, they caught
such a large number of fish that their nets
began to break.[d] **7**So they signaled their
partners in the other boat to come and help
them, and they came and filled both boats
so full that they began to sink.
8When Simon Peter saw this, he fell at
Jesus' knees and said, "Go away from me,
Lord; I am a sinful man!"[e] **9**For he and all
his companions were astonished at the
catch of fish they had taken, **10**and so were
James and John, the sons of Zebedee, Simon's partners.

---

[a] 27 The Greek word traditionally translated *leprosy* was used for various diseases affecting the skin. [b] 1 That is, the Sea of Galilee

---

4:34 *What do you want with us.* The demon knew that Jesus possessed divine authority, and he wanted nothing to do with Him.

4:35–36 *Be quiet!* This term in Aramaic was a technical term for calling evil into submission. Jesus' authority over evil forces is clear.

4:41 *You are the Son of God!* This confession, unique to the Gospel of Luke, shows the close connection Luke makes between Jesus' sonship and messiahship.

4:43 *kingdom of God.* In Luke, the kingdom is referred to thirty times and six times in Acts. Jesus announced the rule of God through His person, in dealing with sin (24:47), in distributing the Spirit as He mediates blessing from God's side (24:49), and in reigning with His followers according to the Old Testament promise (Ps. 2:7–12; Acts 3:18–22).

5:1 *Gennesaret.* This is another name for the Sea of Galilee or the Sea of Tiberias.

5:5 *because you say so, I will let down the nets.* This is Peter's statement of faith. The fisherman noted that he and his companions had just failed to make a catch at the best time for fishing, the evening. The circumstances were not good for a catch at the time of Jesus' command, but Peter chose to obey His word and let down his nets anyway.

4:27 [c] 2Ki 5:1-14 **4:29** [d] Nu 15:35; Ac 7:58; Heb 13:12 **4:30** [e] Jn 8:59; 10:39 **4:31** [f] ver 23; Mt 4:13 **4:32** [g] Mt 7:28 [h] ver 36; Mt 7:29 **4:34** [i] Mt 8:29 [j] Mk 1:24 [k] Jas 2:19 [l] ver 41; Mk 1:24 **4:35** [m] ver 39,41; Mt 8:26; Lk 8:24 **4:36** [n] Mt 7:28 [o] ver 32; Mt 7:29; Mt 10:1 **4:37** [p] ver 14; Mt 9:26 **4:39** [q] ver 35,41 **4:40** [r] Mk 5:23 [s] Mt 4:23 **4:41** [t] Mt 4:3 [u] ver 35 [v] Mt 8:4 **4:43** [w] Mt 3:2 **4:44** [x] Mt 4:23 **5:1** [y] Mk 4:14; Heb 4:12 **5:3** [z] Mt 13:2 **5:4** [a] Jn 21:6 **5:5** [b] Lk 8:24,45; 9:33,49; 17:13 [c] Jn 21:3 **5:6** [d] Jn 21:11 **5:8** [e] Ge 18:27; Job 42:6; Isa 6:5

Then Jesus said to Simon, "Don't be afraid;[f] from now on you will fish for people." 11So they pulled their boats up on shore, left everything and followed him.[g]

Jesus Heals a Man With Leprosy

12While Jesus was in one of the towns, a man came along who was covered with leprosy.[a][h] When he saw Jesus, he fell with his face to the ground and begged him, "Lord, if you are willing, you can make me clean."

13Jesus reached out his hand and touched the man. "I am willing," he said. "Be clean!" And immediately the leprosy left him.

14Then Jesus ordered him, "Don't tell anyone,[i] but go, show yourself to the priest and offer the sacrifices that Moses commanded[j] for your cleansing, as a testimony to them."

15Yet the news about him spread all the more,[k] so that crowds of people came to hear him and to be healed of their sicknesses. 16But Jesus often withdrew to lonely places and prayed.[l]

Jesus Forgives and Heals a Paralyzed Man

17One day Jesus was teaching, and Pharisees and teachers of the law[m] were sitting there. They had come from every village of Galilee and from Judea and Jerusalem. And the power of the Lord was with Jesus to heal the sick.[n] 18Some men came carrying a paralyzed man on a mat and tried to take him into the house to lay him before Jesus. 19When they could not find a way to do this because of the crowd, they went up on the roof and lowered him on his mat through the tiles into the middle of the crowd, right in front of Jesus.

20When Jesus saw their faith, he said, "Friend, your sins are forgiven."[o]

21The Pharisees and the teachers of the law began thinking to themselves, "Who is this fellow who speaks blasphemy? Who can forgive sins but God alone?"[p]

22Jesus knew what they were thinking and asked, "Why are you thinking these things in your hearts? 23Which is easier: to say, 'Your sins are forgiven,' or to say, 'Get up and walk'? 24But I want you to know that the Son of Man[q] has authority on earth to forgive sins." So he said to the paralyzed man, "I tell you, get up, take your mat and go home." 25Immediately he stood up in front of them, took what he had been lying on and went home praising God. 26Everyone was amazed and gave praise to God.[r] They were filled with awe and said, "We have seen remarkable things today."

Jesus Calls Levi and Eats With Sinners

27After this, Jesus went out and saw a tax collector by the name of Levi sitting at his tax booth. "Follow me,"[s] Jesus said to him, 28and Levi got up, left everything and followed him.[t]

29Then Levi held a great banquet for Jesus at his house, and a large crowd of tax collectors[u] and others were eating with them. 30But the Pharisees and the teachers of the law who belonged to their sect[v] complained to his disciples, "Why do you eat and drink with tax collectors and sinners?"[w]

31Jesus answered them, "It is not the healthy who need a doctor, but the sick. 32I have not come to call the righteous, but sinners to repentance."[x]

Jesus Questioned About Fasting

33They said to him, "John's disciples[y] often fast and pray, and so do the disciples of the Pharisees, but yours go on eating and drinking."

---

a 12 The Greek word traditionally translated *leprosy* was used for various diseases affecting the skin.

5:12 *leprosy.* This term was used broadly in the ancient world. It included psoriasis, lupus, and ringworm. Lepers were isolated from the rest of society (Lev. 13:45 – 46), but could be restored to the community when they recovered (Lev. 14).

5:14 *show yourself to the priest.* Jesus commanded that the regulation of Leviticus 14 be followed in silencing the healed leper. Jesus sought to avoid drawing excessive attention to His healing ministry.

5:21 *blasphemy.* The charge of the scribes and the Pharisees was that Jesus' claim dishonored God. This was a serious charge; the conviction of blasphemy would eventually lead to Jesus' death (22:70 – 71).

5:23 *Which is easier.* Jesus posed a riddle to His audience. From an external point of view, it would seem easier to declare sins forgiven than to actually heal a person. In reality, however, one has to possess more authority to forgive sin. Jesus linked the healing to what it represented, the forgiveness of sin. Jesus forgave the man's sins and healed him at the same time.

5:24 *Son of Man.* This is an Aramaic idiom that refers to a human being, meaning "someone" or "I." Jesus used this idiom as a title, taken from Daniel 7:13. In the Book of Daniel, the phrase "Son of Man" describes a figure who shares authority with the Ancient of Days.

5:29 *with them.* In ancient Israel the table was a place where spiritual points were taught and where fellowship occurred.

5:33 *fast.* The Pharisees fasted twice a week, on Mondays and Thursdays (18:12), as well as on the Day of Atonement (Lev. 16:29). They also fasted as an act of penitence (Is. 58:1 – 9) and to recall four times a year the destruction of Jerusalem (Zech. 7:3,5; 8:19). The goal of fasting was to dedicate oneself to prayer

5:10 [f] Mt 14:27 **5:11** [g] ver 28; Mt 4:19 **5:12** [h] Mt 8:2 **5:14** [i] Mt 8:4 [j] Lev 14:2-32 **5:15** [k] Mt 9:26 **5:16** [l] Mt 14:23; Lk 3:21 **5:17** [m] Mt 15:1; Lk 2:46 [n] Mk 5:30; Lk 6:19 **5:20** [o] Lk 7:48,49 **5:21** [p] Isa 43:25 **5:24** [q] Mt 8:20 **5:26** [r] Mt 9:8 **5:27** [s] Mt 4:19 **5:28** [t] ver 11; Mt 4:19 **5:29** [u] Lk 15:1 **5:30** [v] Ac 23:9 [w] Mt 9:11 **5:32** [x] Jn 3:17 **5:33** [y] Lk 7:18; Jn 1:35; 3:25,26

34 Jesus answered, "Can you make the
friends of the bridegroom[z] fast while he is
with them? 35 But the time will come when
the bridegroom will be taken from them;[a]
in those days they will fast."
36 He told them this parable: "No one
tears a piece out of a new garment to patch
an old one. Otherwise, they will have torn
the new garment, and the patch from the
new will not match the old. 37 And no one
pours new wine into old wineskins. Otherwise, the new wine will burst the skins; the
wine will run out and the wineskins will
be ruined. 38 No, new wine must be poured
into new wineskins. 39 And no one after
drinking old wine wants the new, for they
say, 'The old is better.'"

Jesus Is Lord of the Sabbath

6 One Sabbath Jesus was going through
the grainfields, and his disciples began
to pick some heads of grain, rub them in
their hands and eat the kernels.[b] 2 Some of
the Pharisees asked, "Why are you doing
what is unlawful on the Sabbath?"[c]
3 Jesus answered them, "Have you never read what David did when he and his
companions were hungry?[d] 4 He entered
the house of God, and taking the consecrated bread, he ate what is lawful only
for priests to eat.[e] And he also gave some
to his companions." 5 Then Jesus said to
them, "The Son of Man[f] is Lord of the Sabbath."
6 On another Sabbath[g] he went into the
synagogue and was teaching, and a man
was there whose right hand was shriveled.
7 The Pharisees and the teachers of the law
were looking for a reason to accuse Jesus,
so they watched him closely[h] to see if he
would heal on the Sabbath.[i] 8 But Jesus
knew what they were thinking[j] and said to
the man with the shriveled hand, "Get up
and stand in front of everyone." So he got
up and stood there.
9 Then Jesus said to them, "I ask you,
which is lawful on the Sabbath: to do good
or to do evil, to save life or to destroy it?"
10 He looked around at them all, and then
said to the man, "Stretch out your hand."
He did so, and his hand was completely restored. 11 But the Pharisees and the teachers of the law were furious[k] and began to
discuss with one another what they might
do to Jesus.

The Twelve Apostles

12 One of those days Jesus went out to a
mountainside to pray, and spent the night
praying to God.[l] 13 When morning came, he
called his disciples to him and chose twelve
of them, whom he also designated apostles:[m] 14 Simon (whom he named Peter),
his brother Andrew, James, John, Philip,
Bartholomew, 15 Matthew,[n] Thomas, James
son of Alphaeus, Simon who was called the
Zealot, 16 Judas son of James, and Judas Iscariot, who became a traitor.

Blessings and Woes

17 He went down with them and stood on
a level place. A large crowd of his disciples
was there and a great number of people
from all over Judea, from Jerusalem, and
from the coastal region around Tyre and Sidon,[o] 18 who had come to hear him and to be
healed of their diseases. Those troubled by
impure spirits were cured, 19 and the people
all tried to touch him,[p] because power was
coming from him and healing them all.[q]
20 Looking at his disciples, he said:

"Blessed are you who are poor,
for yours is the kingdom of God.[r]
21 Blessed are you who hunger now,
for you will be satisfied.[s]

---

and to focus on God. John led an ascetic life, which his followers also imitated (7:24 – 28; Matt. 11:1 – 19).
5:35 ***the time will come.*** The image of the removal of the bridegroom is the first hint in Jesus' ministry of His fast approaching death.
5:37 ***pours new wine into old wineskins.*** This would not work because as the new wine fermented, it would stretch the old skin and break it, ruining the wineskin and wasting the wine.
6:1 ***pick ... rub ... eat.*** According to Jewish tradition, the disciples were reaping, threshing, and preparing food, and so were violating the commandment not to work on the Sabbath. It is clear that at this point the Pharisees were watching Jesus carefully (v. 7).
6:3 – 4 ***consecrated bread.*** This was bread that was taken from the twelve loaves placed on a table in the holy place and changed once a week (Ex. 25:30; 39:36; Lev. 24:5 – 9). Jesus pointed out that if David and his men could violate the law to satisfy their hunger, His disciples could do the same.
6:5 ***Lord of the Sabbath.*** Regardless of the laws and customs that the Pharisees cited, Jesus has authority over the Sabbath. Jesus' claim of divine authority here is similar to His claim of authority to forgive sins in 5:21,24.
6:11 ***furious.*** The term here means irrational or mindless anger. The parallels in Matthew 12:14 and Mark 3:6 make it clear that the Pharisees started to plot against Jesus in earnest after this confrontation.
6:17 ***level place.*** This probably refers to a plateau on a mountain. The setting and the contents of the sermon that follows suggest that Luke is providing a shorter version of the Sermon on the Mount, omitting those portions that have to do with the law.
6:20 ***Blessed are you.*** Blessed means "happy," referring to the special joy and favor that comes upon those who experience God's grace.

5:34 [z] Jn 3:29 **5:35** [a] Lk 9:22; 17:22; Jn 16:5-7
6:1 [b] Dt 23:25 **6:2** [c] Mt 12:2 **6:3** [d] 1Sa 21:6
6:4 [e] Lev 24:5,9 **6:5** [f] Mt 8:20 **6:6** [g] ver 1
6:7 [h] Mt 12:10 [i] Mt 12:2 **6:8** [j] Mt 9:4 **6:11** [k] Jn 5:18
6:12 [l] Lk 3:21 **6:13** [m] Mk 6:30 **6:15** [n] Mt 9:9
6:17 [o] Mt 4:25; 11:21; Mk 3:7,8 **6:19** [p] Mt 9:20
[q] Mt 14:36; Mk 5:30; Lk 5:17 **6:20** [r] Mt 25:34
6:21 [s] Isa 55:1,2; Mt 5:6

Blessed are you who weep now,
for you will laugh.[t]
22 Blessed are you when people hate you,
when they exclude you[u] and insult
you[v]
and reject your name as evil,
because of the Son of Man.[w]

23"Rejoice in that day and leap for joy,[x]
because great is your reward in heaven.
For that is how their ancestors treated the
prophets.[y]

24"But woe to you who are rich,[z]
for you have already received your
comfort.[a]
25 Woe to you who are well fed now,
for you will go hungry.[b]
Woe to you who laugh now,
for you will mourn and weep.[c]
26 Woe to you when everyone speaks well
of you,
for that is how their ancestors treated
the false prophets.[d]

Love for Enemies

27"But to you who are listening I say:
Love your enemies, do good to those who
hate you,[e] 28bless those who curse you, pray
for those who mistreat you.[f] 29If someone
slaps you on one cheek, turn to them the
other also. If someone takes your coat, do
not withhold your shirt from them. 30Give
to everyone who asks you, and if anyone
takes what belongs to you, do not demand
it back.[g] 31Do to others as you would have
them do to you.[h]
32"If you love those who love you, what
credit is that to you?[i] Even sinners love
those who love them. 33And if you do good
to those who are good to you, what credit
is that to you? Even sinners do that. 34And
if you lend to those from whom you expect repayment, what credit is that to you?[j]
Even sinners lend to sinners, expecting to
be repaid in full. 35But love your enemies,
do good to them,[k] and lend to them without
expecting to get anything back. Then your
reward will be great, and you will be children[l] of the Most High,[m] because he is kind
to the ungrateful and wicked. 36Be merciful,[n] just as your Father[o] is merciful.

Judging Others

37"Do not judge, and you will not be
judged.[p] Do not condemn, and you will
not be condemned. Forgive, and you will
be forgiven.[q] 38Give, and it will be given
to you. A good measure, pressed down,
shaken together and running over, will be
poured into your lap.[r] For with the measure
you use, it will be measured to you."[s]
39He also told them this parable: "Can
the blind lead the blind? Will they not both
fall into a pit?[t] 40The student is not above
the teacher, but everyone who is fully
trained will be like their teacher.[u]
41"Why do you look at the speck of saw-
dust in your brother's eye and pay no attention to the plank in your own eye? 42How
can you say to your brother, 'Brother, let
me take the speck out of your eye,' when
you yourself fail to see the plank in your
own eye? You hypocrite, first take the
plank out of your eye, and then you will
see clearly to remove the speck from your
brother's eye.

A Tree and Its Fruit

43"No good tree bears bad fruit, nor does
a bad tree bear good fruit. 44Each tree is
recognized by its own fruit.[v] People do not
pick figs from thornbushes, or grapes from
briers. 45A good man brings good things
out of the good stored up in his heart, and
an evil man brings evil things out of the
evil stored up in his heart. For the mouth
speaks what the heart is full of.[w]

6:22 ***because of the Son of Man.*** Identification with Jesus usually leads to rejection and hardship, but the disciple who has left all to follow Jesus understands what placing Jesus first means. He or she also recognizes that God is aware of all suffering.

6:24 ***woe.*** A woe is a cry of pain that results from misfortune. Just as God presented blessings for obedience and curses for disobedience in Deuteronomy 28, Jesus presented blessings and woes to His disciples who were anticipating the kingdom. The same blessings and woes apply to believers today when their works are evaluated (1 Cor. 3:12 – 15; 2 Cor. 5:10; 1 John 2:28; Rev. 22:12).

6:27 – 28 ***Love your enemies.*** The threat of religious persecution was very real when Jesus presented His command for extraordinary love. The reference to a cursing enemy suggests a context of religious persecution.

6:30 ***do not demand it back.*** The commands of verses 29 and 30 are expressed in such absolute terms that they force the listener to reflect on them by contrasting them with the normal responses people would have to such injustices.

6:35 ***he is kind to the ungrateful and wicked.*** The practice of loving one's enemies is modeled by God Himself.

6:38 ***good measure.*** This illustration comes from the marketplace where grain was poured out, shaken down, and then filled to overflowing so the buyer received the full amount purchased. Such is the full measure that will be returned to one who has been generous.

6:21 [t] Isa 61:2, 3; Mt 5:4; Rev 7:17 **6:22** [u] Jn 9:22; 16:2 [v] Isa 51:7 [w] Jn 15:21 **6:23** [x] Mt 5:12 [y] Mt 5:12 **6:24** [z] Jas 5:1 [a] Lk 16:25 **6:25** [b] Isa 65:13 [c] Pr 14:13 **6:26** [d] Mt 7:15 **6:27** [e] ver 35; Mt 5:44; Ro 12:20 **6:28** [f] Mt 5:44 **6:30** [g] Dt 15:7, 8, 10; Pr 21:26 **6:31** [h] Mt 7:12 **6:32** [i] Mt 5:46 **6:34** [j] Mt 5:42 **6:35** [k] ver 27 [l] Ro 8:14 [m] Mk 5:7 **6:36** [n] Jas 2:13 [o] Mt 5:48; 6:1; Lk 11:2; 12:32; Ro 8:15; Eph 4:6; 1Pe 1:17; 1Jn 1:3; 3:1 **6:37** [p] Mt 7:1 [q] Mt 6:14 **6:38** [r] Ps 79:12; Isa 65:6, 7 [s] Mt 7:2; Mk 4:24 **6:39** [t] Mt 15:14 **6:40** [u] Mt 10:24; Jn 13:16 **6:44** [v] Mt 12:33 **6:45** [w] Pr 4:23; Mt 12:34, 35; Mk 7:20

The Wise and Foolish Builders

46“Why do you call me, ‘Lord, Lord,’[x] and do not do what I say?[y] 47As for everyone who comes to me and hears my words and puts them into practice,[z] I will show you what they are like. 48They are like a man building a house, who dug down deep and laid the foundation on rock. When a flood came, the torrent struck that house but could not shake it, because it was well built. 49But the one who hears my words and does not put them into practice is like a man who built a house on the ground without a foundation. The moment the torrent struck that house, it collapsed and its destruction was complete.”

The Faith of the Centurion

7 When Jesus had finished saying all this[a] to the people who were listening, he entered Capernaum. 2There a centurion’s servant, whom his master valued highly, was sick and about to die. 3The centurion heard of Jesus and sent some elders of the Jews to him, asking him to come and heal his servant. 4When they came to Jesus, they pleaded earnestly with him, “This man deserves to have you do this, 5because he loves our nation and has built our synagogue.” 6So Jesus went with them.

He was not far from the house when the centurion sent friends to say to him: “Lord, don’t trouble yourself, for I do not deserve to have you come under my roof. 7That is why I did not even consider myself worthy to come to you. But say the word, and my servant will be healed.[b] 8For I myself am a man under authority, with soldiers under me. I tell this one, ‘Go,’ and he goes; and that one, ‘Come,’ and he comes. I say to my servant, ‘Do this,’ and he does it.”

9When Jesus heard this, he was amazed at him, and turning to the crowd following him, he said, “I tell you, I have not found such great faith even in Israel.” 10Then the men who had been sent returned to the house and found the servant well.

Jesus Raises a Widow’s Son

11Soon afterward, Jesus went to a town called Nain, and his disciples and a large crowd went along with him. 12As he approached the town gate, a dead person was being carried out—the only son of his mother, and she was a widow. And a large crowd from the town was with her. 13When the Lord[c] saw her, his heart went out to her and he said, “Don’t cry.”

14Then he went up and touched the bier they were carrying him on, and the bearers stood still. He said, “Young man, I say to you, get up!”[d] 15The dead man sat up and began to talk, and Jesus gave him back to his mother.

16They were all filled with awe[e] and praised God.[f] “A great prophet[g] has appeared among us,” they said. “God has come to help his people.”[h] 17This news about Jesus spread throughout Judea and the surrounding country.[i]

Jesus and John the Baptist

18John’s[j] disciples[k] told him about all these things. Calling two of them, 19he sent them to the Lord to ask, “Are you the one who is to come, or should we expect someone else?”

20When the men came to Jesus, they said, “John the Baptist sent us to you to ask, ‘Are you the one who is to come, or should we expect someone else?’”

21At that very time Jesus cured many who had diseases, sicknesses[l] and evil spirits, and gave sight to many who were blind. 22So he replied to the messengers, “Go back and report to John what you have seen and heard: The blind receive sight, the lame walk, those who have leprosy[a] are cleansed, the deaf hear, the dead are raised, and the good news is proclaimed to the poor.[m] 23Blessed is anyone who does not stumble on account of me.”

24After John’s messengers left, Jesus began to speak to the crowd about John:

---

a 22 The Greek word traditionally translated *leprosy* was used for various diseases affecting the skin.

6:46 ***Lord, Lord.*** Jesus pointed out that those who called Him by this title of respect acknowledged submission to Him. However when these same people ignored His teaching, they were guilty of hypocrisy.

7:1 ***Capernaum.*** This city was on the northwest shore of the Sea of Galilee. It was an important town in northern Galilee with an economy centered on fishing and agriculture. Heavily Jewish, it was the center for Jesus’ Galilean ministry (4:31–44).

7:5 ***built our synagogue.*** The Roman government regarded synagogues as valuable because their moral emphasis helped maintain order.

7:9 ***not found … even in Israel.*** The Centurion’s example of faith came from outside the nation of Israel. This is one of only two cases where the Bible mentions that Jesus “was amazed” (Mark 6:6).

7:12 ***a dead person … carried out.*** This was a funeral procession. The cemetery was located outside the city gates. Funerals were normally held the day of death because keeping a body overnight rendered a house unclean.

7:24–26 ***Jesus began to speak to the crowd about John.*** The questions that Jesus asked were designed to emphasize that John the Baptist played a special role in God’s plan. The crowds did not go out

6:46 [x] Jn 13:13 [y] Mal 1:6; Mt 7:21 **6:47** [z] Lk 8:21; 11:28; Jas 1:22-25 **7:1** [a] Mt 7:28 **7:7** [b] Ps 107:20 **7:13** [c] ver 19; Lk 10:1; 13:15; 17:5; 22:61; 24:34; Jn 11:2 **7:14** [d] Mt 9:25; Mk 1:31; Lk 8:54; Jn 11:43; Ac 9:40 **7:16** [e] Lk 1:65 [f] Mt 9:8 [g] ver 39; Mt 21:11 [h] Lk 1:68 **7:17** [i] Mt 9:26 **7:18** [j] Mt 3:1 [k] Lk 5:33 **7:21** [l] Mt 4:23 **7:22** [m] Isa 29:18, 19; 35:5, 6; 61:1, 2; Lk 4:18

"What did you go out into the wilderness to
see? A reed swayed by the wind? 25If not,
what did you go out to see? A man dressed
in fine clothes? No, those who wear expensive clothes and indulge in luxury are in
palaces. 26But what did you go out to see?
A prophet?[n] Yes, I tell you, and more than
a prophet. 27This is the one about whom it
is written:

> "'I will send my messenger ahead of you,
> who will prepare your way before
> you.'[a][o]

28I tell you, among those born of women
there is no one greater than John; yet the
one who is least in the kingdom of God[p] is
greater than he."

29(All the people, even the tax collectors,
when they heard Jesus' words, acknowledged that God's way was right, because
they had been baptized by John.[q] 30But
the Pharisees and the experts in the law[r]
rejected God's purpose for themselves, because they had not been baptized by John.)

31Jesus went on to say, "To what, then,
can I compare the people of this generation? What are they like? 32They are like
children sitting in the marketplace and
calling out to each other:

> "'We played the pipe for you,
> and you did not dance;
> we sang a dirge,
> and you did not cry.'

33For John the Baptist came neither eating bread nor drinking wine,[s] and you say,
'He has a demon.' 34The Son of Man came
eating and drinking, and you say, 'Here is
a glutton and a drunkard, a friend of tax
collectors and sinners.'[t] 35But wisdom is
proved right by all her children."

Jesus Anointed by a Sinful Woman

36When one of the Pharisees invited
Jesus to have dinner with him, he went to
the Pharisee's house and reclined at the
table. 37A woman in that town who lived
a sinful life learned that Jesus was eating
at the Pharisee's house, so she came there
with an alabaster jar of perfume. 38As she
stood behind him at his feet weeping, she
began to wet his feet with her tears. Then
she wiped them with her hair, kissed them
and poured perfume on them.

39When the Pharisee who had invited
him saw this, he said to himself, "If this
man were a prophet,[u] he would know who
is touching him and what kind of woman
she is—that she is a sinner."

40Jesus answered him, "Simon, I have
something to tell you."

"Tell me, teacher," he said.

41"Two people owed money to a certain
moneylender. One owed him five hundred
denarii,[b] and the other fifty. 42Neither of
them had the money to pay him back, so
he forgave the debts of both. Now which of
them will love him more?"

43Simon replied, "I suppose the one who
had the bigger debt forgiven."

"You have judged correctly," Jesus said.

44Then he turned toward the woman and
said to Simon, "Do you see this woman? I
came into your house. You did not give me
any water for my feet,[v] but she wet my feet
with her tears and wiped them with her
hair. 45You did not give me a kiss,[w] but this
woman, from the time I entered, has not
stopped kissing my feet. 46You did not put
oil on my head,[x] but she has poured perfume on my feet. 47Therefore, I tell you,
her many sins have been forgiven—as her
great love has shown. But whoever has
been forgiven little loves little."

48Then Jesus said to her, "Your sins are
forgiven."[y]

49The other guests began to say among

---

[a] *27* Mal. 3:1 [b] *41* A denarius was the usual daily wage of a day laborer (see Matt. 20:2).

---

to the wilderness to see scenery or a man dressed in special clothes, but to see a prophet.

7:28 *the one who is least in the kingdom of God.* Jesus emphasizes the contrast between the old and new eras. John was the greatest prophet ever born. But the lowest person in the new era of God's kingdom is higher that the greatest prophet of the old era.

7:31–34 *To what, then, can I compare.* Jesus made a comparison between children playing a game in the marketplace and the present generation of Israel, referring especially to the Jewish religious leaders. The leaders were like the children in that they complained no matter what tune was played. John the Baptist refused to eat bread or drink wine, and the religious leaders dismissed him as demon-possessed. In contrast, Jesus, the Son of Man was accused of living loosely and associating with sinners. No matter what the style of God's messenger was, the religious leaders complained and rejected him.

7:36 *one of the Pharisees invited Jesus to have dinner with him.* This event is not the same as the one in Matthew 26:6–13; Mark 14:3–9; and John 12:1–8. The event described in those passages occurred in the house of a leper, a place where no Pharisee would ever have gone.

7:37 *alabaster jar.* This was made of soft stone to preserve the quality of the precious and expensive perfume. There is humility and devotion in the woman's act of service, as well as a great deal of courage, as she performed the deed in front of a crowd that knew her as a sinner.

7:44–46 *Do you see this woman?* Jesus contrasted the actions of the woman with the actions of the Pharisee Simon, implying that the woman knew more about forgiveness than Simon (v. 47).

7:26 [n] Mt 11:9 **7:27** [o] Mal 3:1; Mt 11:10; Mk 1:2 **7:28** [p] Mt 3:2 **7:29** [q] Mt 21:32; Mk 1:5; Lk 3:12 **7:30** [r] Mt 22:35 **7:33** [s] Lk 1:15 **7:34** [t] Lk 5:29, 30; 15:1, 2 **7:39** [u] ver 16; Mt 21:11 **7:44** [v] Ge 18:4; 19:2; 43:24; Jdg 19:21; Jn 13:4-14; 1Ti 5:10 **7:45** [w] Lk 22:47, 48; Ro 16:16 **7:46** [x] Ps 23:5; Ecc 9:8 **7:48** [y] Mt 9:2

themselves, "Who is this who even forgives sins?"

50Jesus said to the woman, "Your faith has saved you;[z] go in peace."[a]

The Parable of the Sower

8 After this, Jesus traveled about from one town and village to another, proclaiming the good news of the kingdom of God.[b] The Twelve were with him, **2**and also some women who had been cured of evil spirits and diseases: Mary (called Magdalene)[c] from whom seven demons had come out; **3**Joanna the wife of Chuza, the manager of Herod's[d] household; Susanna; and many others. These women were helping to support them out of their own means.

4While a large crowd was gathering and people were coming to Jesus from town after town, he told this parable: **5**"A farmer went out to sow his seed. As he was scattering the seed, some fell along the path; it was trampled on, and the birds ate it up. **6**Some fell on rocky ground, and when it came up, the plants withered because they had no moisture. **7**Other seed fell among thorns, which grew up with it and choked the plants. **8**Still other seed fell on good soil. It came up and yielded a crop, a hundred times more than was sown."

When he said this, he called out, "Whoever has ears to hear, let them hear."[e]

9His disciples asked him what this parable meant. **10**He said, "The knowledge of the secrets of the kingdom of God has been given to you,[f] but to others I speak in parables, so that,

> " 'though seeing, they may not see;
> though hearing, they may not
> understand.'[a][g]

11"This is the meaning of the parable: The seed is the word of God.[h] **12**Those along the path are the ones who hear, and then the devil comes and takes away the word from their hearts, so that they may not believe and be saved. **13**Those on the rocky ground are the ones who receive the word with joy when they hear it, but they have no root. They believe for a while, but in the time of testing they fall away.[i] **14**The seed that fell among thorns stands for those who hear, but as they go on their way they are choked by life's worries, riches[j] and pleasures, and they do not mature. **15**But the seed on good soil stands for those with a noble and good heart, who hear the word, retain it, and by persevering produce a crop.

A Lamp on a Stand

16"No one lights a lamp and hides it in a clay jar or puts it under a bed. Instead, they put it on a stand, so that those who come in can see the light.[k] **17**For there is nothing hidden that will not be disclosed, and nothing concealed that will not be known or brought out into the open.[l] **18**Therefore consider carefully how you listen. Whoever has will be given more; whoever does not have, even what they think they have will be taken from them."[m]

Jesus' Mother and Brothers

19Now Jesus' mother and brothers came to see him, but they were not able to get near him because of the crowd. **20**Someone told him, "Your mother and brothers[n] are standing outside, wanting to see you."

21He replied, "My mother and brothers are those who hear God's word and put it into practice."[o]

Jesus Calms the Storm

22One day Jesus said to his disciples, "Let us go over to the other side of the lake." So they got into a boat and set out. **23**As they sailed, he fell asleep. A squall came down on the lake, so that the boat was being swamped, and they were in great danger.

---

[a] *10* Isaiah 6:9

8:1–3 ***Mary (called Magdalene).*** Because she is introduced here, it is unlikely that she was the sinful woman of 7:36–50. ***Joanna.*** This is an example of how some women of means used their wealth to benefit the work of God.

8:10 ***kingdom ... parables.*** Jesus' parables both concealed and revealed truths. The disciples were privileged to learn the truths of parables. For other listeners, the parables served as judgments that concealed truth, as the reference to Isaiah 6:9 indicates. On occasion, a parable was understood by an outsider but was not accepted, thus still functioning as a message of judgment (20:9–19).

8:13 ***believe for a while ... fall away.*** Brief and superficial encounters with the Word of God will not stand times of testing. A person needs to meditate on the truths in Scripture and establish them as principles for living in order to withstand the trials and temptations that will inevitably come.

8:14 ***worries, riches and pleasures.*** According to this parable, these three are the great obstacles to spiritual fruitfulness. The concerns of life can squelch spiritual growth. This type of "soil" is viewed as tragically unsuccessful (2 Tim. 2:4; 4:10).

8:19–20 ***mother and brothers came to see him.*** Jesus' family was concerned about the direction of His ministry (Mark 3:31–35). Though some have suggested that the brothers here were sons of Joseph by a previous marriage or cousins of Jesus, most likely they were the sons of Joseph and Mary. Joseph's absence here may mean that he had died by this time.

8:23 ***A squall.*** The calming of the wind is the first of four miracles in verses 22–56 that demonstrate Jesus' authority over a variety of phenomena—nature,

7:50 [z] Mt 9:22; Mk 5:34; Lk 8:48 [a] Ac 15:33 **8:1** [b] Mt 4:23 **8:2** [c] Mt 27:55, 56 **8:3** [d] Mt 14:1 **8:8** [e] Mt 11:15 **8:10** [f] Mt 13:11 [g] Isa 6:9; Mt 13:13, 14 **8:11** [h] Heb 4:12 **8:13** [i] Mt 11:6 **8:14** [j] Mt 19:23; 1Ti 6:9, 10, 17 **8:16** [k] Mt 5:15; Mk 4:21; Lk 11:33 **8:17** [l] Mt 10:26; Mk 4:22; Lk 12:2 **8:18** [m] Mt 13:12; 25:29; Lk 19:26 **8:20** [n] Jn 7:5 **8:21** [o] Lk 6:47; 11:28; Jn 14:21

24 The disciples went and woke him, saying, "Master, Master,[p] we're going to drown!"

He got up and rebuked[q] the wind and the raging waters; the storm subsided, and all was calm.[r] 25 "Where is your faith?" he asked his disciples.

In fear and amazement they asked one another, "Who is this? He commands even the winds and the water, and they obey him."

Jesus Restores a Demon-Possessed Man

26 They sailed to the region of the Gerasenes,[a] which is across the lake from Galilee. 27 When Jesus stepped ashore, he was met by a demon-possessed man from the town. For a long time this man had not worn clothes or lived in a house, but had lived in the tombs. 28 When he saw Jesus, he cried out and fell at his feet, shouting at the top of his voice, "What do you want with me,[s] Jesus, Son of the Most High God?[t] I beg you, don't torture me!" 29 For Jesus had commanded the impure spirit to come out of the man. Many times it had seized him, and though he was chained hand and foot and kept under guard, he had broken his chains and had been driven by the demon into solitary places.

30 Jesus asked him, "What is your name?"

"Legion," he replied, because many demons had gone into him. 31 And they begged Jesus repeatedly not to order them to go into the Abyss.[u]

32 A large herd of pigs was feeding there on the hillside. The demons begged Jesus to let them go into the pigs, and he gave them permission. 33 When the demons came out of the man, they went into the pigs, and the herd rushed down the steep bank into the lake[v] and was drowned.

34 When those tending the pigs saw what had happened, they ran off and reported this in the town and countryside, 35 and the people went out to see what had happened. When they came to Jesus, they found the man from whom the demons had gone out, sitting at Jesus' feet,[w] dressed and in his right mind; and they were afraid. 36 Those who had seen it told the people how the demon-possessed[x] man had been cured. 37 Then all the people of the region of the Gerasenes asked Jesus to leave them,[y] because they were overcome with fear. So he got into the boat and left.

38 The man from whom the demons had gone out begged to go with him, but Jesus sent him away, saying, 39 "Return home and tell how much God has done for you." So the man went away and told all over town how much Jesus had done for him.

Jesus Raises a Dead Girl and Heals a Sick Woman

40 Now when Jesus returned, a crowd welcomed him, for they were all expecting him. 41 Then a man named Jairus, a synagogue leader,[z] came and fell at Jesus' feet, pleading with him to come to his house 42 because his only daughter, a girl of about twelve, was dying.

As Jesus was on his way, the crowds almost crushed him. 43 And a woman was there who had been subject to bleeding[a] for twelve years,[b] but no one could heal her. 44 She came up behind him and touched the edge of his cloak,[b] and immediately her bleeding stopped.

45 "Who touched me?" Jesus asked.

When they all denied it, Peter said, "Master,[c] the people are crowding and pressing against you."

46 But Jesus said, "Someone touched me;[d] I know that power has gone out from me."[e]

47 Then the woman, seeing that she could not go unnoticed, came trembling and fell at his feet. In the presence of all the people, she told why she had touched him and how she had been instantly healed. 48 Then he said to her, "Daughter, your faith has healed you.[f] Go in peace."[g]

49 While Jesus was still speaking, someone came from the house of Jairus, the synagogue leader.[h] "Your daughter is dead," he said. "Don't bother the teacher anymore."

---

a *26* Some manuscripts *Gadarenes*; other manuscripts *Gergesenes*; also in verse 37
b *43* Many manuscripts *years, and she had spent all she had on doctors*

---

demons, disease, and death. This miracle took place on the Sea of Galilee. Cool air rushing down the ravines and hills of the area collides with warm air from the Sea of Galilee, causing sudden and strong storms.

8:25 *Where is your faith?* Jesus' question was a rebuke of His disciples. Because God was aware of their situation, they could trust in His protection, for He was powerful enough to control the winds and waves.

8:28 *Son of the Most High God.* The demon's confession recalls the angel's announcement to Mary in 1:31–32 and the demonic confessions of 4:34,41.

8:30 *Legion.* This name reflects the fact that the man was possessed by multiple demons. A legion was a Roman military unit of about 6,000 soldiers.

8:31 *the Abyss.* This is an allusion to the underworld and the destruction of judgment (Rom. 10:7).

8:44 *her bleeding stopped.* This condition not only would have been embarrassing, it would have made the woman unclean (Lev. 15:25–31). It took great courage for her to seek out Jesus. Note that her action was not criticized, but commended (v. 48).

8:24 [p] Lk 5:5 [q] Lk 4:35,39,41 [r] Ps 107:29; Jnh 1:15 **8:28** [s] Mt 8:29 [t] Mk 5:7 **8:31** [u] Rev 9:1,2,11; 11:7; 17:8; 20:1,3 **8:33** [v] ver 22,23 **8:35** [w] Lk 10:39 **8:36** [x] Mt 4:24 **8:37** [y] Ac 16:39 **8:41** [z] ver 49; Mk 5:22 **8:43** [a] Lev 15:25-30 **8:44** [b] Mt 9:20 **8:45** [c] Lk 5:5 **8:46** [d] Mt 14:36; Mk 3:10 [e] Lk 5:17; 6:19 **8:48** [f] Mt 9:22 [g] Ac 15:33 **8:49** [h] ver 41

50Hearing this, Jesus said to Jairus,
"Don't be afraid; just believe, and she will
be healed."
51When he arrived at the house of Jairus,
he did not let anyone go in with him except
Peter, John and James,[i] and the child's father and mother. 52Meanwhile, all the people were wailing and mourning[j] for her.
"Stop wailing," Jesus said. "She is not dead
but asleep."[k]
53They laughed at him, knowing that she
was dead. 54But he took her by the hand
and said, "My child, get up!"[l] 55Her spirit
returned, and at once she stood up. Then
Jesus told them to give her something to
eat. 56Her parents were astonished, but he
ordered them not to tell anyone what had
happened.[m]

Jesus Sends Out the Twelve

9 When Jesus had called the Twelve together, he gave them power and authority to drive out all demons[n] and to cure diseases,[o] 2and he sent them out to proclaim
the kingdom of God[p] and to heal the sick.
3He told them: "Take nothing for the journey—no staff, no bag, no bread, no money, no extra shirt.[q] 4Whatever house you
enter, stay there until you leave that town.
5If people do not welcome you, leave their
town and shake the dust off your feet as a
testimony against them."[r] 6So they set out
and went from village to village, proclaiming the good news and healing people everywhere.
7Now Herod[s] the tetrarch heard about all
that was going on. And he was perplexed
because some were saying that John[t] had
been raised from the dead,[u] 8others that
Elijah had appeared,[v] and still others that
one of the prophets of long ago had come
back to life.[w] 9But Herod said, "I beheaded
John. Who, then, is this I hear such things
about?" And he tried to see him.[x]

Jesus Feeds the Five Thousand

10When the apostles[y] returned, they reported to Jesus what they had done. Then
he took them with him and they withdrew
by themselves to a town called Bethsaida,[z]
11but the crowds learned about it and followed him. He welcomed them and spoke
to them about the kingdom of God,[a] and
healed those who needed healing.
12Late in the afternoon the Twelve came
to him and said, "Send the crowd away so
they can go to the surrounding villages and
countryside and find food and lodging, because we are in a remote place here."
13He replied, "You give them something
to eat."
They answered, "We have only five
loaves of bread and two fish—unless we go
and buy food for all this crowd." 14(About
five thousand men were there.)
But he said to his disciples, "Have them
sit down in groups of about fifty each."
15The disciples did so, and everyone sat
down. 16Taking the five loaves and the
two fish and looking up to heaven, he gave
thanks and broke them.[b] Then he gave
them to the disciples to distribute to the
people. 17They all ate and were satisfied,
and the disciples picked up twelve basketfuls of broken pieces that were left over.

Peter Declares That Jesus Is the Messiah

18Once when Jesus was praying[c] in
private and his disciples were with him,
he asked them, "Who do the crowds say
I am?"
19They replied, "Some say John the Baptist;[d] others say Elijah; and still others, that
one of the prophets of long ago has come
back to life."[e]
20"But what about you?" he asked. "Who
do you say I am?"
Peter answered, "God's Messiah."[f]

Jesus Predicts His Death

21Jesus strictly warned them not to tell
this to anyone.[g] 22And he said, "The Son
of Man[h] must suffer many things[i] and be
rejected by the elders, the chief priests
and the teachers of the law,[j] and he must

8:52 *but asleep.* Sleeping was a common metaphor for death. Here it indicates that the girl's death was not permanent.

9:2 *to proclaim ... to heal the sick.* The entire nation of Israel needed to see the evidence of the kingdom of God and make a decision concerning the King. Jesus commissioned His disciples to spread the word about God's kingdom through preaching and healing.

9:11 *spoke ... healing.* Jesus had the same two-pronged ministry that the twelve disciples had: preaching and healing (v. 2). The topic of Jesus' preaching was always the kingdom of God.

9:13–17 *About five thousand men.* This is the only miracle of Jesus' ministry that appears in all four Gospels. The feeding of the 5,000 demonstrated Jesus' ability to provide.

9:20 *God's Messiah.* The emphasis here is on the messianic role of Jesus. He is the Promised One who was ushering in a new era. However, Jesus would soon reveal to the disciples that His messiahship would have elements of suffering that the disciples did not expect (vv. 22–23).

9:22 *must suffer ... be rejected ... be killed ... be raised.* This is the first of several predictions in Luke of Jesus' suffering and vindication (v. 44; 12:50;

8:51 [i] Mt 4:21 **8:52** [j] Lk 23:27 [k] Mt 9:24; Jn 11:11, 13
8:54 [l] Lk 7:14 **8:56** [m] Mt 8:4 **9:1** [n] Mt 10:1 [o] Mt 4:23; Lk 5:17 **9:2** [p] Mt 3:2 **9:3** [q] Lk 10:4; 22:35
9:5 [r] Mt 10:14 **9:7** [s] Mt 14:1 [t] Mt 3:1 [u] ver 19
9:8 [v] Mt 11:14 [w] ver 19; Jn 1:21 **9:9** [x] Lk 23:8
9:10 [y] Mk 6:30 [z] Mt 11:21 **9:11** [a] ver 2; Mt 3:2
9:16 [b] Mt 14:19 **9:18** [c] Lk 3:21 **9:19** [d] Mt 3:1 [e] ver 7,8
9:20 [f] Jn 1:49; 6:66-69; 11:27 **9:21** [g] Mt 16:20; Mk 8:30
9:22 [h] Mt 8:20 [i] Mt 16:21 [j] Mt 27:1,2

be killed[k] and on the third day[l] be raised
to life."[m]
23Then he said to them all: "Whoever
wants to be my disciple must deny themselves and take up their cross daily and follow me.[n] 24For whoever wants to save their
life will lose it, but whoever loses their life
for me will save it.[o] 25What good is it for
someone to gain the whole world, and yet
lose or forfeit their very self? 26Whoever
is ashamed of me and my words, the Son
of Man will be ashamed of them[p] when he
comes in his glory and in the glory of the
Father and of the holy angels.[q]
27"Truly I tell you, some who are standing here will not taste death before they see
the kingdom of God."

The Transfiguration

28About eight days after Jesus said this,
he took Peter, John and James[r] with him
and went up onto a mountain to pray.[s] 29As
he was praying, the appearance of his face
changed, and his clothes became as bright
as a flash of lightning. 30Two men, Moses
and Elijah, appeared in glorious splendor,
talking with Jesus. 31They spoke about his
departure,[a][t] which he was about to bring
to fulfillment at Jerusalem. 32Peter and his
companions were very sleepy,[u] but when
they became fully awake, they saw his
glory and the two men standing with him.
33As the men were leaving Jesus, Peter said
to him, "Master,[v] it is good for us to be here.
Let us put up three shelters—one for you,
one for Moses and one for Elijah." (He did
not know what he was saying.)
34While he was speaking, a cloud appeared and covered them, and they were
afraid as they entered the cloud. 35A voice
came from the cloud, saying, "This is my
Son, whom I have chosen;[w] listen to him."[x]
36When the voice had spoken, they found
that Jesus was alone. The disciples kept
this to themselves and did not tell anyone
at that time what they had seen.[y]

Jesus Heals a Demon-Possessed Boy

37The next day, when they came down
from the mountain, a large crowd met him.
38A man in the crowd called out, "Teacher, I
beg you to look at my son, for he is my only
child. 39A spirit seizes him and he suddenly screams; it throws him into convulsions
so that he foams at the mouth. It scarcely
ever leaves him and is destroying him. 40I
begged your disciples to drive it out, but
they could not."
41"You unbelieving and perverse generation,"[z] Jesus replied, "how long shall I stay
with you and put up with you? Bring your
son here."
42Even while the boy was coming, the
demon threw him to the ground in a convulsion. But Jesus rebuked the impure spirit, healed the boy and gave him back to his
father. 43And they were all amazed at the
greatness of God.

Jesus Predicts His Death a Second Time

While everyone was marveling at all that
Jesus did, he said to his disciples, 44"Listen
carefully to what I am about to tell you: The
Son of Man is going to be delivered into the
hands of men."[a] 45But they did not understand what this meant. It was hidden from
them, so that they did not grasp it,[b] and
they were afraid to ask him about it.
46An argument started among the disci-

---

[a] *31* Greek *exodos*

13:31–33; 17:25; 18:31–33). The disciples struggled to understand what Jesus was saying (v. 45; 18:34). They could not comprehend how Jesus' predictions fit into God's plan. Only after Jesus' resurrection and His explanation of the Scriptures to them did they begin to understand (24:25–27,44–49).

9:23 ***take up their cross daily.*** Although Jesus offered salvation as a free gift (John 1:12; 3:16–18), He also warned that following Him would entail suffering and hardship (Matt. 5:10–12; Rom. 8:17; 2 Thess. 1:5).

9:24–25 ***What good is it for someone to gain the whole world.*** It makes no sense to attempt to save our lives on earth only to lose everything when our lives quickly and inevitably pass away. The wise course is to invest our earthly resources—our time, talents, and wealth—in what is eternal.

9:31 ***spoke about his departure.*** This important allusion to the central Old Testament event of salvation is unique to Luke's account of the transfiguration. The comparison is made between Jesus' death and the journey to salvation that the nation of Israel experienced under Moses.

9:34 ***cloud.*** This is an allusion to the presence of God (Ex. 40:35).

9:41 ***unbelieving and perverse generation.*** This rebuke suggests that the disciples lacked the faith to cast out the spirit described in verses 38–40. There is also a hint of a competitive spirit among the disciples (v. 46).

9:45 ***they were afraid to ask.*** The indication here is that the disciples still had much to learn. Their fear shows that they understood something about what Jesus said, but they did not understand how and why Jesus could say such things about Himself, since He was the Messiah. The suffering of the Messiah was something the disciples did not yet understand. They would continue to be confused in their understanding of how such suffering fit into God's plan until Jesus' death and resurrection (24:25–26,43–49).

9:22 [k] Ac 2:23; 3:13 [l] Mt 16:21 [m] Mt 16:21
9:23 [n] Mt 10:38; Lk 14:27 **9:24** [o] Jn 12:25
9:26 [p] Mt 10:33; Lk 12:9; 2Ti 2:12 [q] Mt 16:27
9:28 [r] Mt 4:21 [s] Lk 3:21 **9:31** [t] 2Pe 1:15
9:32 [u] Mt 26:43 **9:33** [v] Lk 5:5 **9:35** [w] Isa 42:1 [x] Mt 3:17
9:36 [y] Mt 17:9 **9:41** [z] Dt 32:5 **9:44** [a] ver 22
9:45 [b] Mk 9:32

ples as to which of them would be the greatest.[c] 47 Jesus, knowing their thoughts,[d] took a little child and had him stand beside him. 48 Then he said to them, "Whoever welcomes this little child in my name welcomes me; and whoever welcomes me welcomes the one who sent me.[e] For it is the one who is least among you all who is the greatest."[f]

49 "Master,"[g] said John, "we saw someone driving out demons in your name and we tried to stop him, because he is not one of us."

50 "Do not stop him," Jesus said, "for whoever is not against you is for you."[h]

Samaritan Opposition

51 As the time approached for him to be taken up to heaven,[i] Jesus resolutely set out for Jerusalem.[j] 52 And he sent messengers on ahead, who went into a Samaritan[k] village to get things ready for him; 53 but the people there did not welcome him, because he was heading for Jerusalem. 54 When the disciples James and John[l] saw this, they asked, "Lord, do you want us to call fire down from heaven to destroy them[*a*]?"[m] 55 But Jesus turned and rebuked them. 56 Then he and his disciples went to another village.

The Cost of Following Jesus

57 As they were walking along the road,[n] a man said to him, "I will follow you wherever you go."

58 Jesus replied, "Foxes have dens and birds have nests, but the Son of Man[o] has no place to lay his head."

59 He said to another man, "Follow me."[p]

But he replied, "Lord, first let me go and bury my father."

60 Jesus said to him, "Let the dead bury their own dead, but you go and proclaim the kingdom of God."[q]

61 Still another said, "I will follow you, Lord; but first let me go back and say goodbye to my family."[r]

62 Jesus replied, "No one who puts a hand to the plow and looks back is fit for service in the kingdom of God."

Jesus Sends Out the Seventy-Two

10 After this the Lord[s] appointed seventy-two[*b*] others[t] and sent them two by two[u] ahead of him to every town and place where he was about to go.[v] 2 He told them, "The harvest is plentiful, but the workers are few. Ask the Lord of the harvest, therefore, to send out workers into his harvest field.[w] 3 Go! I am sending you out like lambs among wolves.[x] 4 Do not take a purse or bag or sandals; and do not greet anyone on the road.

5 "When you enter a house, first say, 'Peace to this house.' 6 If someone who promotes peace is there, your peace will rest on them; if not, it will return to you. 7 Stay there, eating and drinking whatever they give you, for the worker deserves his wages.[y] Do not move around from house to house.

8 "When you enter a town and are welcomed, eat what is offered to you.[z] 9 Heal the sick who are there and tell them, 'The kingdom of God[a] has come near to you.' 10 But when you enter a town and are not welcomed, go into its streets and say, 11 'Even the dust of your town we wipe from our feet as a warning to you.[b] Yet be sure of this: The kingdom of God has come near.'[c] 12 I tell you, it will be more bearable on that day for Sodom[d] than for that town.[e]

13 "Woe to you,[f] Chorazin! Woe to you, Bethsaida! For if the miracles that were performed in you had been performed in Tyre and Sidon, they would have repented long ago, sitting in sackcloth[g] and ashes.

a 54 Some manuscripts *them, just as Elijah did*
b 1 Some manuscripts *seventy*; also in verse 17

9:51 *Jesus resolutely set out for Jerusalem.* This is the first indication that Jesus' attention was turning toward His final suffering in Jerusalem (v. 53; 13:22; 17:11; 18:31; 19:11,28,41). Luke's Gospel uniquely emphasizes this journey to Jerusalem.

9:52 *Samaritan.* These people were the descendants of Jews who had married Gentiles after the fall of the northern kingdom, Israel. The Samaritans eventually developed their own religious rites which they practiced on Mount Gerizim instead of at the temple in Jerusalem. Though there was deep hostility between Jews and Samaritans, Jesus ministered to both groups.

9:54 *call fire down.* James and John wanted Jesus to bring judgment upon the Samaritan villages that refused to respond to His message, just as Elijah had done in 2 Kings 1:9–16. Their demand for judgment was antithetical to Jesus' loving response (v. 56).

9:59 *first let me go and bury my father.* This aspiring disciple placed family responsibilities ahead of following Jesus. The concerns of home were this man's stumbling block.

9:62 *fit for service in the kingdom.* This remark of Jesus demonstrates the seriousness of commitment to Him.

10:2 *The harvest is plentiful.* The picture of a great harvest suggests that a positive response awaited the laborers, even in the face of much rejection.

10:3 *lambs among wolves.* This image from Isaiah 40:11 was a popular one in Judaism.

10:13 *if the miracles ... had been performed.* Jesus' remark was meant to wake the people up to what their rejection of Him signified.

9:46 [c] Lk 22:24 **9:47** [d] Mt 9:4 **9:48** [e] Mt 10:40 [f] Mk 9:35 **9:49** [g] Lk 5:5 **9:50** [h] Mt 12:30; Lk 11:23 **9:51** [i] Mk 16:19 [j] Lk 13:22; 17:11; 18:31; 19:28 **9:52** [k] Mt 10:5 **9:54** [l] Mt 4:21 [m] 2Ki 1:10, 12 **9:57** [n] ver 51 **9:58** [o] Mt 8:20 **9:59** [p] Mt 4:19 **9:60** [q] Mt 3:2 **9:61** [r] 1Ki 19:20 **10:1** [s] Lk 7:13 [t] Lk 9:1, 2, 51, 52 [u] Mk 6:7 [v] Mt 10:1 **10:2** [w] Mt 9:37, 38; Jn 4:35 **10:3** [x] Mt 10:16 **10:7** [y] Mt 10:10; 1Co 9:14; 1Ti 5:18 **10:8** [z] 1Co 10:27 **10:9** [a] Mt 3:2; 10:7 **10:11** [b] Mt 10:14; Mk 6:11 [c] ver 9 **10:12** [d] Mt 10:15 [e] Mt 11:24 **10:13** [f] Lk 6:24-26 [g] Rev 11:3

14But it will be more bearable for Tyre and
Sidon at the judgment than for you. 15And
you, Capernaum,[h] will you be lifted to the
heavens? No, you will go down to Hades.[a]
16"Whoever listens to you listens to me;
whoever rejects you rejects me; but whoever rejects me rejects him who sent me."[i]
17The seventy-two[j] returned with joy and
said, "Lord, even the demons submit to us
in your name."[k]
18He replied, "I saw Satan[l] fall like lightning from heaven.[m] 19I have given you authority to trample on snakes[n] and scorpions and to overcome all the power of the
enemy; nothing will harm you. 20However,
do not rejoice that the spirits submit to you,
but rejoice that your names are written in
heaven."[o]
21At that time Jesus, full of joy through
the Holy Spirit, said, "I praise you, Father,
Lord of heaven and earth, because you
have hidden these things from the wise
and learned, and revealed them to little
children.[p] Yes, Father, for this is what you
were pleased to do.
22"All things have been committed to me
by my Father.[q] No one knows who the Son
is except the Father, and no one knows who
the Father is except the Son and those to
whom the Son chooses to reveal him."[r]
23Then he turned to his disciples and
said privately, "Blessed are the eyes that
see what you see. 24For I tell you that many
prophets and kings wanted to see what you
see but did not see it, and to hear what you
hear but did not hear it."[s]

The Parable of the Good Samaritan

25On one occasion an expert in the law
stood up to test Jesus. "Teacher," he asked,
"what must I do to inherit eternal life?"[t]
26"What is written in the Law?" he replied. "How do you read it?"
27He answered, " 'Love the Lord your
God with all your heart and with all your
soul and with all your strength and with
all your mind'[b];[u] and, 'Love your neighbor
as yourself.'[c]"[v]
28"You have answered correctly," Jesus
replied. "Do this and you will live."[w]
29But he wanted to justify himself,[x] so he
asked Jesus, "And who is my neighbor?"
30In reply Jesus said: "A man was going
down from Jerusalem to Jericho, when he
was attacked by robbers. They stripped
him of his clothes, beat him and went away,
leaving him half dead. 31A priest happened
to be going down the same road, and when
he saw the man, he passed by on the other
side.[y] 32So too, a Levite, when he came to
the place and saw him, passed by on the
other side. 33But a Samaritan,[z] as he traveled, came where the man was; and when
he saw him, he took pity on him. 34He went
to him and bandaged his wounds, pouring

[a] *15* That is, the realm of the dead [b] *27* Deut. 6:5
[c] *27* Lev. 19:18

10:16 *Whoever listens to you listens to me.* Hearing the messenger is the same as hearing the One who sent him. Authority resides not in the messenger, but in the person the messenger represents, the source of the message.
10:18 *I saw Satan.* This verse provides a commentary on what the disciples' healing ministry meant. The reversal of the effects of sin and death, which Satan introduced through his deception in Genesis 3 is portrayed graphically as Satan falling from heaven. Jesus' ministry and what grows out of it represents the defeat of Satan, sin, and death.
10:19–20 *I have given you authority.* This passage records the transmission of Jesus' power to His immediate circle of disciples. It should be noted that similar power was not given beyond that circle of disciples.
10:22 *All things have been committed to me.* This is Jesus' declaration of total authority as the Son of God (John 10:18; 17:2). Jesus declares His unique relationship with God the Father. The Lord reveals Himself only through Jesus. To know God, one must know His Son, Jesus.
10:25–26 *what must I do to inherit eternal life?* The question posed by the lawyer is really a challenge, since the verse speaks of the testing of Jesus. This is a similar, though probably distinct, event from Matthew 22:34–40 and Mark 12:28–34. To inherit something is to receive it. In other words, the man was asking, "What must I do to share in the reward at the resurrection of the righteous at the end?"
10:27 *Love the Lord ... your neighbor.* The lawyer responded to Jesus' question by quoting Deuteronomy 6:5, a text that was recited twice a day by every faithful Jew. This text summarized the central ethical standard of the law.
10:28 *Do this and you will live.* Jesus was not saying that righteousness is the result of works. Rather He was saying that love for and obedience to God will be a natural result of placing one's faith in the Lord.
10:29 *who is my neighbor?* This question was an attempt to limit the demands of the law by suggesting that some people are neighbors while others are not. The lawyer was looking for minimal obedience while Jesus was looking for absolute obedience.
10:30 *Jerusalem to Jericho.* This was a 17-mile journey on a road known to harbor many robbers.
10:31–33 *priest ... Levite ... Samaritan.* Part of the beauty of the story of the Good Samaritan is the reversal of stereotypes. The priest and Levite traditionally would have been the "good guys." The Samaritan would have been a "bad guy," a person who compromised in religious matters. However, the Samaritan knew how to treat his neighbor. The neighbor here was not someone the Samaritan knew or even someone of the same race, just someone in need.

10:15 [h] Mt 4:13 **10:16** [i] Mt 10:40; Jn 13:20 **10:17** [j] ver 1 [k] Mk 16:17 **10:18** [l] Mt 4:10 [m] Isa 14:12; Rev 9:1; 12:8, 9 **10:19** [n] Mk 16:18; Ac 28:3-5 **10:20** [o] Ex 32:32; Ps 69:28; Da 12:1; Php 4:3; Heb 12:23; Rev 13:8; 20:12; 21:27 **10:21** [p] 1Co 1:26-29 **10:22** [q] Mt 28:18 [r] Jn 1:18 **10:24** [s] 1Pe 1:10-12 **10:25** [t] Mt 19:16; Lk 18:18 **10:27** [u] Dt 6:5 [v] Lev 19:18; Mt 5:43 **10:28** [w] Lev 18:5; Ro 7:10 **10:29** [x] Lk 16:15 **10:31** [y] Lev 21:1-3 **10:33** [z] Mt 10:5

on oil and wine. Then he put the man on his own donkey, brought him to an inn and took care of him. 35The next day he took out two denarii[a] and gave them to the innkeeper. 'Look after him,' he said, 'and when I return, I will reimburse you for any extra expense you may have.'

36"Which of these three do you think was a neighbor to the man who fell into the hands of robbers?"

37The expert in the law replied, "The one who had mercy on him."

Jesus told him, "Go and do likewise."

At the Home of Martha and Mary

38As Jesus and his disciples were on their way, he came to a village where a woman named Martha[a] opened her home to him. 39She had a sister called Mary,[b] who sat at the Lord's feet[c] listening to what he said. 40But Martha was distracted by all the preparations that had to be made. She came to him and asked, "Lord, don't you care[d] that my sister has left me to do the work by myself? Tell her to help me!"

41"Martha, Martha," the Lord answered, "you are worried[e] and upset about many things, 42but few things are needed—or indeed only one.[b f] Mary has chosen what is better, and it will not be taken away from her."

Jesus' Teaching on Prayer

11 One day Jesus was praying[g] in a certain place. When he finished, one of his disciples said to him, "Lord,[h] teach us to pray, just as John taught his disciples."

2He said to them, "When you pray, say:

"'Father,[c]
hallowed be your name,
your kingdom[i] come.[d]
3Give us each day our daily bread.
4Forgive us our sins,
for we also forgive everyone who sins against us.[e j]
And lead us not into temptation.[f]'"[k]

5Then Jesus said to them, "Suppose you have a friend, and you go to him at midnight and say, 'Friend, lend me three loaves of bread; 6a friend of mine on a journey has come to me, and I have no food to offer him.' 7And suppose the one inside answers, 'Don't bother me. The door is already locked, and my children and I are in bed. I can't get up and give you anything.' 8I tell you, even though he will not get up and give you the bread because of friendship, yet because of your shameless audacity[g] he will surely get up and give you as much as you need.[l]

9"So I say to you: Ask and it will be given to you;[m] seek and you will find; knock and the door will be opened to you. 10For everyone who asks receives; the one who seeks finds; and to the one who knocks, the door will be opened.

11"Which of you fathers, if your son asks for[h] a fish, will give him a snake instead? 12Or if he asks for an egg, will give him a scorpion? 13If you then, though you are evil, know how to give good gifts to your children, how much more will your Father in heaven give the Holy Spirit to those who ask him!"

Jesus and Beelzebul

14Jesus was driving out a demon that was mute. When the demon left, the man who had been mute spoke, and the crowd was amazed.[n] 15But some of them said, "By Beelzebul,[o] the prince of demons, he is driving out demons."[p] 16Others tested him by asking for a sign from heaven.[q]

17Jesus knew their thoughts[r] and said to them: "Any kingdom divided against itself will be ruined, and a house divided against itself will fall. 18If Satan[s] is divided against

---

[a] 35 A denarius was the usual daily wage of a day laborer (see Matt. 20:2). [b] 42 Some manuscripts *but only one thing is needed* [c] 2 Some manuscripts *Our Father in heaven* [d] 2 Some manuscripts *come. May your will be done on earth as it is in heaven.* [e] 4 Greek *everyone who is indebted to us* [f] 4 Some manuscripts *temptation, but deliver us from the evil one* [g] 8 *Or yet to preserve his good name* [h] 11 Some manuscripts *for bread, will give him a stone? Or if he asks for*

10:36 *Which . . . was a neighbor.* The central issue is not determining who one's neighbor is, but being a good neighbor to all.

11:1 *Lord, teach us to pray.* The Lord's Prayer illustrates the variety of requests that one can and should make to God, as well as displaying the humble attitude that should accompany prayer. The use of the plural pronoun *us* throughout the prayer shows that it is not just the prayer of one person for his or her own personal needs, but a community prayer.

11:2 *your kingdom come.* The reference here is to God's program and promise. This is more affirmation than request, highlighting the petitioner's submission to God's will and the desire to see God's work come to pass.

11:4 *we also forgive.* The petitioner recognizes that if mercy is to be sought from God, then mercy must be shown to others. We need to adopt the same standard that we expect others to follow. ***lead us not into temptation.*** This remark is often misunderstood as suggesting that perhaps God can lead us into sin. The point is that if one is to avoid sin, one must follow where God leads. In short, the petitioner asks God for the spiritual protection necessary to avoid falling into sin.

11:17–18 *you claim that I drive out demons through Beelzebul.* The attribution of Jesus' miracles to Satan was not only blasphemous, it was

10:38 [a] Jn 11:1; 12:2 **10:39** [b] Jn 11:1; 12:3 [c] Lk 8:35 **10:40** [d] Mk 4:38 **10:41** [e] Mt 6:25-34; Lk 12:11,22 **10:42** [f] Ps 27:4 **11:1** [g] Lk 3:21 [h] Jn 13:13 **11:2** [i] Mt 3:2 **11:4** [j] Mt 18:35; Mk 11:25 [k] Mt 26:41; Jas 1:13 **11:8** [l] Lk 18:1-6 **11:9** [m] Mt 7:7 **11:14** [n] Mt 9:32,33 **11:15** [o] Mk 3:22 [p] Mt 9:34 **11:16** [q] Mt 12:38 **11:17** [r] Mt 9:4 **11:18** [s] Mt 4:10

himself, how can his kingdom stand? I say
this because you claim that I drive out demons by Beelzebul. **19**Now if I drive out demons by Beelzebul, by whom do your followers drive them out? So then, they will
be your judges. **20**But if I drive out demons
by the finger of God,[t] then the kingdom of
God[u] has come upon you.
21"When a strong man, fully armed,
guards his own house, his possessions are
safe. **22**But when someone stronger attacks
and overpowers him, he takes away the armor in which the man trusted and divides
up his plunder.
23"Whoever is not with me is against me,
and whoever does not gather with me scatters.[v]
24"When an impure spirit comes out of
a person, it goes through arid places seeking rest and does not find it. Then it says,
'I will return to the house I left.' **25**When it
arrives, it finds the house swept clean and
put in order. **26**Then it goes and takes sev-
en other spirits more wicked than itself,
and they go in and live there. And the final
condition of that person is worse than the
first."[w]
27As Jesus was saying these things, a
woman in the crowd called out, "Blessed is
the mother who gave you birth and nursed
you."[x]
28He replied, "Blessed rather are those
who hear the word of God[y] and obey it."[z]

The Sign of Jonah

29As the crowds increased, Jesus said,
"This is a wicked generation. It asks for
a sign,[a] but none will be given it except
the sign of Jonah.[b] **30**For as Jonah was a
sign to the Ninevites, so also will the Son
of Man be to this generation. **31**The Queen
of the South will rise at the judgment with
the people of this generation and condemn
them, for she came from the ends of the
earth to listen to Solomon's wisdom;[c] and
now something greater than Solomon is
here. **32**The men of Nineveh will stand up at
the judgment with this generation and condemn it, for they repented at the preaching
of Jonah;[d] and now something greater than
Jonah is here.

The Lamp of the Body

33"No one lights a lamp and puts it in a
place where it will be hidden, or under a
bowl. Instead they put it on its stand, so
that those who come in may see the light.[e]
34Your eye is the lamp of your body. When
your eyes are healthy,[a] your whole body
also is full of light. But when they are unhealthy,[b] your body also is full of darkness.
35See to it, then, that the light within you
is not darkness. **36**Therefore, if your whole
body is full of light, and no part of it dark,
it will be just as full of light as when a lamp
shines its light on you."

Woes on the Pharisees and the Experts in the Law

37When Jesus had finished speaking, a
Pharisee invited him to eat with him; so
he went in and reclined at the table.[f] **38**But
the Pharisee was surprised when he noticed that Jesus did not first wash before
the meal.[g]
39Then the Lord[h] said to him, "Now then,
you Pharisees clean the outside of the cup
and dish, but inside you are full of greed

---

[a] *34* The Greek for *healthy* here implies *generous.*
[b] *34* The Greek for *unhealthy* here implies *stingy.*

---

illogical. If Satan had cast out the demon (v. 14), he would have been destroying the result of his own work.

11:20 ***the finger of God.*** This phrase is an allusion to God's power, like that demonstrated in the exodus (Ex. 8:19; Deut. 9:10; Ps. 8:3). ***the kingdom of God has come upon you.*** Jesus' miracles represented the arrival of God's power and promise — in short, His rule. That rule comes in and through Jesus. The miracles of Jesus demonstrated God's victory over the forces of evil. The kingdom program, depicted as drawing near, will be consummated at the return of Jesus when this rule is manifested over every creature.

11:22 ***when someone stronger.*** Jesus portrays Himself as someone stronger than Satan who overruns Satan's house and gives the spoils of victory to those who are His (Eph. 4:8 – 9).

11:23 ***Whoever is not with Me.*** Jesus' ministry forces everyone to make a choice. Neutrality is not an option. Either Jesus comes from God or He does not. Not to align with Jesus is to be against Him.

11:26 ***the final condition.*** Jesus' point is that experiencing God's blessing and then ignoring it leaves one callous towards the work of God and exposed to the control of demonic forces.

11:29 ***the sign of Jonah.*** This refers to his prophetic call to repentance rather than to the resurrection foreshadowed by Jonah's return from the belly of the great fish.

11:36 ***your whole body is full of light.*** A person can become like light, a living picture of what God's Word teaches, by concentrating on the light of the truth.

11:39 ***clean the outside.*** These condemnations by Jesus are similar to those in Matthew 23. The Pharisees washed the outside of cups, making sure that the cups had not become unclean through contact with a dead insect (Lev. 11:31 – 38). Jesus pointed out that the Pharisees concerned themselves with outward appearances and ritual cleanness, while what was inside, what really counts, was full of selfishness and evil.

11:20 [t] Ex 8:19 [u] Mt 3:2 **11:23** [v] Mt 12:30; Mk 9:40; Lk 9:50 **11:26** [w] 2Pe 2:20 **11:27** [x] Lk 23:29 **11:28** [y] Heb 4:12 [z] Pr 8:32; Lk 6:47; 8:21; Jn 14:21 **11:29** [a] ver 16; Mt 12:38 [b] Jnh 1:17; Mt 16:4 **11:31** [c] 1Ki 10:1; 2Ch 9:1 **11:32** [d] Jnh 3:5 **11:33** [e] Mt 5:15; Mk 4:21; Lk 8:16 **11:37** [f] Lk 7:36; 14:1 **11:38** [g] Mk 7:3,4 **11:39** [h] Lk 7:13

and wickedness.[i] 40You foolish people![j] Did
not the one who made the outside make the
inside also? 41But now as for what is inside
you—be generous to the poor,[k] and everything will be clean for you.[l]
42"Woe to you Pharisees, because you
give God a tenth[m] of your mint, rue and
all other kinds of garden herbs, but you
neglect justice and the love of God.[n] You
should have practiced the latter without
leaving the former undone.[o]
43"Woe to you Pharisees, because you
love the most important seats in the synagogues and respectful greetings in the
marketplaces.[p]
44"Woe to you, because you are like un-
marked graves,[q] which people walk over
without knowing it."
45One of the experts in the law[r] answered
him, "Teacher, when you say these things,
you insult us also."
46Jesus replied, "And you experts in the
law, woe to you, because you load people
down with burdens they can hardly carry,
and you yourselves will not lift one finger
to help them.[s]
47"Woe to you, because you build tombs
for the prophets, and it was your ancestors
who killed them. 48So you testify that you
approve of what your ancestors did; they
killed the prophets, and you build their
tombs.[t] 49Because of this, God in his wisdom[u] said, 'I will send them prophets and
apostles, some of whom they will kill and
others they will persecute.'[v] 50Therefore
this generation will be held responsible
for the blood of all the prophets that has
been shed since the beginning of the world,
51from the blood of Abel[w] to the blood of
Zechariah,[x] who was killed between the
altar and the sanctuary. Yes, I tell you, this
generation will be held responsible for it
all.[y]
52"Woe to you experts in the law, because
you have taken away the key to knowledge.
You yourselves have not entered, and you
have hindered those who were entering."[z]
53When Jesus went outside, the Pharisees and the teachers of the law began to
oppose him fiercely and to besiege him
with questions, 54waiting to catch him in
something he might say.[a]

Warnings and Encouragements

12 Meanwhile, when a crowd of many
thousands had gathered, so that they
were trampling on one another, Jesus began to speak first to his disciples, saying:
"Be[a] on your guard against the yeast of
the Pharisees, which is hypocrisy.[b] 2There
is nothing concealed that will not be disclosed, or hidden that will not be made
known.[c] 3What you have said in the dark
will be heard in the daylight, and what
you have whispered in the ear in the inner
rooms will be proclaimed from the roofs.
4"I tell you, my friends,[d] do not be afraid
of those who kill the body and after that
can do no more. 5But I will show you
whom you should fear: Fear him who, after your body has been killed, has authority to throw you into hell. Yes, I tell you,
fear him.[e] 6Are not five sparrows sold for
two pennies? Yet not one of them is forgotten by God. 7Indeed, the very hairs of your

[a] *1* Or *speak to his disciples, saying: "First of all, be*

11:42 *give a tenth of your mint, rue and all other kinds of garden herbs.* Some Pharisees took the strictest interpretation and counted almost anything, including spices. However, they neglected two basic things that the prophets also had warned about: love and justice (Mic. 6:8; Zech. 7:8–10).

11:46 *burdens.* This term refers to a ship's cargo. The idea is that a heavy strain was being imposed on the people and yet, in the end, this burden did not bring them close to God. Here Jesus rebuked the tradition that had grown up around the law of Moses.

11:47–48 *you build tombs for the prophets.* Jesus made a biting, ironic comparison between the current generation of Israel and the generations of the past. Jesus was saying that the current generation finished the job of slaying the prophets that the previous generation had started. The building and care of tombs was supposed to be an act of honoring the prophets, but Jesus pointed out that something else was really going on.

11:52 *Woe to you experts in the law.* Jesus charged the lawyers with doing the opposite of what they claimed their calling to be. Rather than bringing people nearer to God, they had removed the possibility of their entering into that knowledge, and had prevented others from understanding it as well.

12:1–2 *yeast.* This represents the presence of corruption. Unleavened bread is what the Jews ate at Passover (Ex. 12:14–20). The corruption in view here is hypocrisy. Practicing hypocrisy is senseless because eventually all deeds—both good and evil—will be exposed.

12:4 *do not be afraid of those who kill the body.* This verse anticipates the presence of severe religious persecution in response to Jesus' remarks in Luke 11:39–54.

12:5 *Fear him.* Even in the context of physical persecution, the only One believers should fear is God, who sees how we live and judges us. Jesus was not guaranteeing physical preservation in this life, but was opening the prospect of deliverance in the next life.

12:6 *two pennies.* These were the smallest coins in circulation, worth about one-sixteenth of a basic day's wages.

11:39 [i] Mt 23:25, 26; Mk 7:20-23 **11:40** [j] Lk 12:20; 1Co 15:36 **11:41** [k] Lk 12:33 [l] Ac 10:15 **11:42** [m] Lk 18:12 [n] Dt 6:5; Mic 6:8 [o] Mt 23:23 **11:43** [p] Mt 23:6, 7; Mk 12:38-39; Lk 14:7; 20:46 **11:44** [q] Mt 23:27 **11:45** [r] Mt 22:35 **11:46** [s] Mt 23:4 **11:48** [t] Mt 23:29-32; Ac 7:51-53 **11:49** [u] 1Co 1:24, 30; Col 2:3 [v] Mt 23:34 **11:51** [w] Ge 4:8 [x] 2Ch 24:20, 21 [y] Mt 23:35, 36 **11:52** [z] Mt 23:13 **11:54** [a] Mt 12:10; Mk 12:13 **12:1** [b] Mt 16:6, 11, 12; Mk 8:15 **12:2** [c] Mk 4:22; Lk 8:17 **12:4** [d] Jn 15:14, 15 **12:5** [e] Heb 10:31

head are all numbered.[f] Don't be afraid; you are worth more than many sparrows.[g] 8"I tell you, whoever publicly acknowledges me before others, the Son of Man will also acknowledge before the angels of God.[h] 9But whoever disowns me before others will be disowned[i] before the angels of God. 10And everyone who speaks a word against the Son of Man[j] will be forgiven, but anyone who blasphemes against the Holy Spirit will not be forgiven.[k]

11"When you are brought before synagogues, rulers and authorities, do not worry about how you will defend yourselves or what you will say,[l] 12for the Holy Spirit will teach you at that time what you should say."[m]

The Parable of the Rich Fool

13Someone in the crowd said to him, "Teacher, tell my brother to divide the inheritance with me."

14Jesus replied, "Man, who appointed me a judge or an arbiter between you?" 15Then he said to them, "Watch out! Be on your guard against all kinds of greed; life does not consist in an abundance of possessions."[n]

16And he told them this parable: "The ground of a certain rich man yielded an abundant harvest. 17He thought to himself, 'What shall I do? I have no place to store my crops.'

18"Then he said, 'This is what I'll do. I will tear down my barns and build bigger ones, and there I will store my surplus grain. 19And I'll say to myself, "You have plenty of grain laid up for many years. Take life easy; eat, drink and be merry."'

20"But God said to him, 'You fool![o] This very night your life will be demanded from you.[p] Then who will get what you have prepared for yourself?'[q]

21"This is how it will be with whoever stores up things for themselves but is not rich toward God."[r]

Do Not Worry

22Then Jesus said to his disciples: "Therefore I tell you, do not worry about your life, what you will eat; or about your body, what you will wear. 23For life is more than food, and the body more than clothes. 24Consider the ravens: They do not sow or reap, they have no storeroom or barn; yet God feeds them.[s] And how much more valuable you are than birds! 25Who of you by worrying can add a single hour to your life[a]? 26Since you cannot do this very little thing, why do you worry about the rest?

27"Consider how the wild flowers grow. They do not labor or spin. Yet I tell you, not even Solomon in all his splendor[t] was dressed like one of these. 28If that is how God clothes the grass of the field, which is here today, and tomorrow is thrown into the fire, how much more will he clothe you—you of little faith![u] 29And do not set your heart on what you will eat or drink; do not worry about it. 30For the pagan world runs after all such things, and your Father[v] knows that you need them.[w] 31But seek his kingdom,[x] and these things will be given to you as well.[y]

32"Do not be afraid,[z] little flock, for your Father has been pleased to give you the kingdom.[a] 33Sell your possessions and give to the poor.[b] Provide purses for yourselves that will not wear out, a treasure in heaven[c] that will never fail, where no thief comes near and no moth destroys.[d] 34For where your treasure is, there your heart will be also.[e]

Watchfulness

35"Be dressed ready for service and keep your lamps burning, 36like servants waiting for their master to return from a wedding banquet, so that when he comes and knocks they can immediately open the door for him. 37It will be good for those

[a] 25 Or *single cubit to your height*

12:14 *who appointed me a judge.* Jesus refuses to enter into a dispute over money, which is clearly dividing a family. Such disputes over money destroy relationships, so Jesus tells a parable that explains the danger of focusing on wealth.

12:18 – 19 *This is what I'll do.* Including verse 17, the word "I" appears six times, showing the selfish focus this man has as a result of his fortune. His plan is to store his abundant resources for himself, as though the assets were his alone and should be hoarded. This focus on the self is what Jesus is condemning.

12:27 – 29 *God clothes the grass.* This illustration indicates that God cares enough to provide beauty for the parts of His creation that have a short life. Why should we worry if God takes such care of even the smallest blade of grass? The Lord knows our problems and will provide us with what we need.

12:33 *Sell your possessions.* In contrast to the world's hoarding of possessions, the disciple must be generous with what God gives. By serving God and others, you can invest in your eternal future. You cannot take possessions with you in the next life, but you can store up an eternal treasure by giving to others (Phil. 4:17).

12:34 *where your treasure is.* What people consider valuable is where their energy will be spent. Knowing God and investing in His purposes should be the treasure we seek.

12:7 [f] Mt 10:30 [g] Mt 12:12 **12:8** [h] Lk 15:10 **12:9** [i] Mk 8:38; 2Ti 2:12 **12:10** [j] Mt 8:20 [k] Mt 12:31, 32; Mk 3:28-29; 1Jn 5:16 **12:11** [l] Mt 10:17, 19; Mk 13:11; Lk 21:12, 14 **12:12** [m] Ex 4:12; Mt 10:20; Mk 13:11; Lk 21:15 **12:15** [n] Job 20:20; 31:24; Ps 62:10 **12:20** [o] Jer 17:11; Lk 11:40 [p] Job 27:8 [q] Ps 39:6; 49:10 **12:21** [r] ver 33 **12:24** [s] Job 38:41; Ps 147:9 **12:27** [t] 1Ki 10:4-7 **12:28** [u] Mt 6:30 **12:30** [v] Lk 6:36 [w] Mt 6:8 **12:31** [x] Mt 3:2 [y] Mt 19:29 **12:32** [z] Mt 14:27 [a] Mt 25:34 **12:33** [b] Mt 19:21; Ac 2:45 [c] Mt 6:20 [d] Jas 5:2 **12:34** [e] Mt 6:21

servants whose master finds them watching when he comes.[f] Truly I tell you, he will dress himself to serve, will have them recline at the table and will come and wait on them.[g] 38 It will be good for those servants whose master finds them ready, even if he comes in the middle of the night or toward daybreak. 39 But understand this: If the owner of the house had known at what hour the thief[h] was coming, he would not have let his house be broken into. 40 You also must be ready,[i] because the Son of Man will come at an hour when you do not expect him."

41 Peter asked, "Lord, are you telling this parable to us, or to everyone?"

42 The Lord[j] answered, "Who then is the faithful and wise manager, whom the master puts in charge of his servants to give them their food allowance at the proper time? 43 It will be good for that servant whom the master finds doing so when he returns. 44 Truly I tell you, he will put him in charge of all his possessions. 45 But suppose the servant says to himself, 'My master is taking a long time in coming,' and he then begins to beat the other servants, both men and women, and to eat and drink and get drunk. 46 The master of that servant will come on a day when he does not expect him and at an hour he is not aware of.[k] He will cut him to pieces and assign him a place with the unbelievers.

47 "The servant who knows the master's will and does not get ready or does not do what the master wants will be beaten with many blows.[l] 48 But the one who does not know and does things deserving punishment will be beaten with few blows.[m] From everyone who has been given much, much will be demanded; and from the one who has been entrusted with much, much more will be asked.

Not Peace but Division

49 "I have come to bring fire on the earth, and how I wish it were already kindled! 50 But I have a baptism[n] to undergo, and what constraint I am under until it is completed![o] 51 Do you think I came to bring peace on earth? No, I tell you, but division. 52 From now on there will be five in one family divided against each other, three against two and two against three. 53 They will be divided, father against son and son against father, mother against daughter and daughter against mother, mother-in-law against daughter-in-law and daughter-in-law against mother-in-law."[p]

Interpreting the Times

54 He said to the crowd: "When you see a cloud rising in the west, immediately you say, 'It's going to rain,' and it does.[q] 55 And when the south wind blows, you say, 'It's going to be hot,' and it is. 56 Hypocrites! You know how to interpret the appearance of the earth and the sky. How is it that you don't know how to interpret this present time?[r]

57 "Why don't you judge for yourselves what is right? 58 As you are going with your adversary to the magistrate, try hard to be reconciled on the way, or your adversary may drag you off to the judge, and the judge turn you over to the officer, and the officer throw you into prison.[s] 59 I tell you, you will not get out until you have paid the last penny."[t]

Repent or Perish

13 Now there were some present at that time who told Jesus about the Galileans whose blood Pilate[u] had mixed with their sacrifices. 2 Jesus answered, "Do you think that these Galileans were worse

---

12:38 *if he comes in the middle of the night or toward daybreak.* This verse speaks of a return at an unusually late hour. The exact time referred to depends on which system of time was used. In the Roman system the second and third watch would be 9 P.M. to 3 A.M. By the Jewish method it would be 10 P.M. to 6 A.M.

12:41 *to us, or to everyone.* Peter asked if Jesus' teaching was for the disciples only or for all people. Jesus did not answer the question directly. Instead He described a variety of categories of servants. Servants are those who belong to the Master and have their stewardship evaluated (19:11–27). Several responses, from faithfulness to blatant disobedience, are described in verses 42–48. The issue is who lives life in a way that looks for, and takes seriously, the return of Jesus (1 John 2:28).

12:45 *begins to beat the other servants.* This servant is depicted as consciously doing the opposite of caring for others, and of treating the Master's return as irrelevant.

12:46 *will cut him to pieces.* The image of being slain indicates the severity of this judgment, especially in contrast to the whippings of verses 47 and 48.

12:49 *I have come to bring fire on the earth.* Fire is an image associated with God's judgment (Jer. 5:14; 23:29). Jesus' coming brings judgment on those who refuse to accept Him and divides the believers from the faithless.

12:54–55 *a cloud rising in the west.* In Palestine, a western breeze meant moisture coming from the Mediterranean Sea. A south wind meant hot air coming from the desert.

12:56 *Hypocrites!* Jesus rebuked His audience for being able to discern the weather but not what God was doing through Him.

13:1 *Pilate.* Pilate was known for his insensitivity to the Jewish people early in his rule. The event probably occurred during the Festival of the Passover or

12:37 [f] Mt 24:42,46; 25:13 [g] Mt 20:28 **12:39** [h] Mt 6:19; 1Th 5:2; 2Pe 3:10; Rev 3:3; 16:15 **12:40** [i] Mk 13:33; Lk 21:36 **12:42** [j] Lk 7:13 **12:46** [k] ver 40 **12:47** [l] Dt 25:2 **12:48** [m] Lev 5:17; Nu 15:27-30 **12:50** [n] Mk 10:38 [o] Jn 19:30 **12:53** [p] Mic 7:6; Mt 10:21 **12:54** [q] Mt 16:2 **12:56** [r] Mt 16:3 **12:58** [s] Mt 5:25 **12:59** [t] Mt 5:26; Mk 12:42 **13:1** [u] Mt 27:2

sinners than all the other Galileans because they suffered this way?[v] 3I tell you,
no! But unless you repent, you too will all
perish. 4Or those eighteen who died when
the tower in Siloam[w] fell on them—do you
think they were more guilty than all the
others living in Jerusalem? 5I tell you, no!
But unless you repent,[x] you too will all perish."
6Then he told this parable: "A man had
a fig tree growing in his vineyard, and he
went to look for fruit on it but did not find
any.[y] 7So he said to the man who took care
of the vineyard, 'For three years now I've
been coming to look for fruit on this fig tree
and haven't found any. Cut it down![z] Why
should it use up the soil?'
8" 'Sir,' the man replied, 'leave it alone for
one more year, and I'll dig around it and
fertilize it. 9If it bears fruit next year, fine!
If not, then cut it down.' "

Jesus Heals a Crippled Woman on the Sabbath

10On a Sabbath Jesus was teaching in
one of the synagogues,[a] 11and a woman
was there who had been crippled by a spirit for eighteen years.[b] She was bent over
and could not straighten up at all. 12When
Jesus saw her, he called her forward and
said to her, "Woman, you are set free from
your infirmity." 13Then he put his hands on
her,[c] and immediately she straightened up
and praised God.
14Indignant because Jesus had healed on
the Sabbath,[d] the synagogue leader[e] said to
the people, "There are six days for work.[f]
So come and be healed on those days, not
on the Sabbath."
15The Lord answered him, "You hypocrites! Doesn't each of you on the Sabbath
untie your ox or donkey from the stall and
lead it out to give it water?[g] 16Then should
not this woman, a daughter of Abraham,[h]
whom Satan[i] has kept bound for eighteen
long years, be set free on the Sabbath day
from what bound her?"
17When he said this, all his opponents
were humiliated,[j] but the people were delighted with all the wonderful things he
was doing.

The Parables of the Mustard Seed and the Yeast

18Then Jesus asked, "What is the kingdom of God[k] like?[l] What shall I compare it
to? 19It is like a mustard seed, which a man
took and planted in his garden. It grew and
became a tree,[m] and the birds perched in
its branches."[n]
20Again he asked, "What shall I compare
the kingdom of God to? 21It is like yeast
that a woman took and mixed into about
sixty pounds[a] of flour until it worked all
through the dough."[o]

The Narrow Door

22Then Jesus went through the towns
and villages, teaching as he made his
way to Jerusalem.[p] 23Someone asked him,
"Lord, are only a few people going to be
saved?"
He said to them, 24"Make every effort to
enter through the narrow door,[q] because
many, I tell you, will try to enter and will
not be able to. 25Once the owner of the
house gets up and closes the door, you will
stand outside knocking and pleading, 'Sir,
open the door for us.'
"But he will answer, 'I don't know you or
where you come from.'[r]
26"Then you will say, 'We ate and drank
with you, and you taught in our streets.'
27"But he will reply, 'I don't know you or
where you come from. Away from me, all
you evildoers!'[s]

---

[a] *21* Or about 27 kilograms

Tabernacles, when Galileans most likely would have been at the temple.

13:5 *unless you repent.* The manner in which a person dies is not a measure of righteousness; what is important is not to die outside of God's grace and care. The way to avoid such a fate is to repent, to come to God through the care of the Physician Jesus (5:32).

13:6 *a fig tree.* This tree often represents God's blessing, or a people who have a special relationship with God (Mic. 7:1–2). The man in this parable represents God; the fig tree represents Israel.

13:7 *For three years.* A fig tree was often given some time to bear good fruit since its root structure was complex and took time to develop. Three years would have been enough for the tree to yield some fruit.

13:15 *hypocrites!* When the ruler of the synagogue became indignant regarding Jesus' healing on the Sabbath (vv. 10–14), Jesus pointed out that basic compassion was shown to animals on the Sabbath, so how much more compassion should be shown to a suffering woman (v. 16)?

13:18–19 *mustard.* A tree of the mustard family would grow to about twelve feet. The image of birds nesting in the trees is found frequently in the Old Testament (Ps. 104:12; Ezek. 17:22–24; Dan. 4:10–12).

13:26 *We ate and drank ... you taught.* The appeal here is by people who experience Jesus' presence. The passage primarily involves those Jews who witnessed Jesus' ministry. They were trying to gain entry into God's presence based simply on the fact that they had observed Jesus. Jesus refused them. Pointing out that it was not enough for them to have been close to Him. In order to have a relationship with God, one must embrace Jesus and come to know Him.

13:2 [v] Jn 9:2,3 **13:4** [w] Jn 9:7,11 **13:5** [x] Mt 3:2; Ac 2:38
13:6 [y] Isa 5:2; Jer 8:13; Mt 21:19 **13:7** [z] Mt 3:10
13:10 [a] Mt 4:23 **13:11** [b] ver 16 **13:13** [c] Mk 5:23
13:14 [d] Mt 12:2; Lk 14:3 [e] Mk 5:22 [f] Ex 20:9
13:15 [g] Lk 14:5 **13:16** [h] Lk 3:8; 19:9 [i] Mt 4:10
13:17 [j] Isa 66:5 **13:18** [k] Mt 3:2 [l] Mt 13:24
13:19 [m] Lk 17:6 [n] Mt 13:32 **13:21** [o] 1Co 5:6
13:22 [p] Lk 9:51 **13:24** [q] Mt 7:13 **13:25** [r] Mt 7:23; 25:10-12 **13:27** [s] Mt 7:23; 25:41

28"There will be weeping there, and
gnashing of teeth,[t] when you see Abraham, Isaac and Jacob and all the prophets
in the kingdom of God, but you yourselves
thrown out. 29People will come from east
and west[u] and north and south, and will
take their places at the feast in the kingdom of God. 30Indeed there are those who
are last who will be first, and first who will
be last."[v]

Jesus' Sorrow for Jerusalem

31At that time some Pharisees came to
Jesus and said to him, "Leave this place
and go somewhere else. Herod[w] wants to
kill you."

32He replied, "Go tell that fox, 'I will keep
on driving out demons and healing people
today and tomorrow, and on the third day
I will reach my goal.'[x] 33In any case, I must
press on today and tomorrow and the next
day—for surely no prophet[y] can die outside
Jerusalem!

34"Jerusalem, Jerusalem, you who kill
the prophets and stone those sent to you,
how often I have longed to gather your children together, as a hen gathers her chicks
under her wings,[z] and you were not willing. 35Look, your house is left to you desolate.[a] I tell you, you will not see me again
until you say, 'Blessed is he who comes in
the name of the Lord.'[a]"[b]

Jesus at a Pharisee's House

14 One Sabbath, when Jesus went to eat
in the house of a prominent Pharisee,[c]
he was being carefully watched.[d] 2There in
front of him was a man suffering from abnormal swelling of his body. 3Jesus asked
the Pharisees and experts in the law,[e] "Is
it lawful to heal on the Sabbath or not?"[f]
4But they remained silent. So taking hold
of the man, he healed him and sent him on
his way.

5Then he asked them, "If one of you has
a child[b] or an ox that falls into a well on
the Sabbath day, will you not immediately
pull it out?"[g] 6And they had nothing to say.

7When he noticed how the guests picked
the places of honor at the table,[h] he told
them this parable: 8"When someone invites
you to a wedding feast, do not take the place
of honor, for a person more distinguished
than you may have been invited. 9If so, the
host who invited both of you will come and
say to you, 'Give this person your seat.'
Then, humiliated, you will have to take the
least important place. 10But when you are
invited, take the lowest place, so that when
your host comes, he will say to you, 'Friend,
move up to a better place.' Then you will
be honored in the presence of all the other
guests. 11For all those who exalt themselves
will be humbled, and those who humble
themselves will be exalted."[i]

12Then Jesus said to his host, "When you
give a luncheon or dinner, do not invite
your friends, your brothers or sisters, your
relatives, or your rich neighbors; if you do,
they may invite you back and so you will
be repaid. 13But when you give a banquet,
invite the poor, the crippled, the lame, the
blind,[j] 14and you will be blessed. Although
they cannot repay you, you will be repaid
at the resurrection of the righteous."[k]

The Parable of the Great Banquet

15When one of those at the table with
him heard this, he said to Jesus, "Blessed
is the one who will eat at the feast[l] in the
kingdom of God."[m]

16Jesus replied: "A certain man was preparing a great banquet and invited many
guests. 17At the time of the banquet he sent
his servant to tell those who had been invited, 'Come, for everything is now ready.'

a 35 Psalm 118:26 *b* 5 Some manuscripts *donkey*

13:29 *east ... west ... north ... south.* People would come from all corners of the earth for entrance into God's kingdom. This passage alludes to the inclusion of Gentiles.

13:30 *there are those who are last who will be first.* There will be many surprises in God's kingdom. Those who are despised on earth—some Gentiles, for example—will be greatly honored in the kingdom. Conversely, those who are considered influential and powerful on earth—the Jewish religious leaders of Jesus' day, for example—will be excluded from the kingdom.

13:32 *Go tell that fox.* Herod is portrayed as more curious than hostile. The reference here is to Herod's cunning. Jesus' reply seems to take the Pharisees' warning at face value.

13:34 *Jerusalem, Jerusalem.* The double address indicates Jesus' deep sorrow (2 Sam. 18:33; Jer. 22:29). The city had executed many of God's messengers. Stephen makes a similar point about the nation of Israel in Acts 7:51–53.

13:35 *Blessed is he.* This is a citation of Psalm 118:26. The people of Israel would not see the Messiah again until they were ready to receive Him and recognize that He was sent from God. Psalm 118 reflects the greeting of a priest to a group entering the temple. Jesus used the language of this psalm to illustrate God's greeting to Him.

14:7 *picked the places of honor.* In ancient times the best seats at a meal were those next to the host.

14:17 *those who had been invited.* In the ancient world, invitations to a feast were sent out well in advance of the meal. Then on the day of the feast, servants would announce the start of the meal. This parable is similar to the one in Matthew 22:1–4, but was probably spoken on a different occasion.

13:28 [t] Mt 8:12 **13:29** [u] Mt 8:11 **13:30** [v] Mt 19:30 **13:31** [w] Mt 14:1 **13:32** [x] Heb 2:10 **13:33** [y] Mt 21:11 **13:34** [z] Mt 23:37 **13:35** [a] Jer 12:17; 22:5 [b] Ps 118:26; Mt 21:9; Lk 19:38 **14:1** [c] Lk 7:36; 11:37 [d] Mt 12:10 **14:3** [e] Mt 22:35 [f] Mt 12:2 **14:5** [g] Lk 13:15 **14:7** [h] Lk 11:43 **14:11** [i] Mt 23:12; Lk 18:14 **14:13** [j] ver 21 **14:14** [k] Ac 24:15 **14:15** [l] Isa 25:6; Mt 26:29; Lk 13:29; Rev 19:9 [m] Mt 3:2

18 "But they all alike began to make excuses. The first said, 'I have just bought a field, and I must go and see it. Please excuse me.'

19 "Another said, 'I have just bought five yoke of oxen, and I'm on my way to try them out. Please excuse me.'

20 "Still another said, 'I just got married, so I can't come.'

21 "The servant came back and reported this to his master. Then the owner of the house became angry and ordered his servant, 'Go out quickly into the streets and alleys of the town and bring in the poor, the crippled, the blind and the lame.'[n]

22 " 'Sir,' the servant said, 'what you ordered has been done, but there is still room.'

23 "Then the master told his servant, 'Go out to the roads and country lanes and compel them to come in, so that my house will be full. 24 I tell you, not one of those who were invited will get a taste of my banquet.' "[o]

The Cost of Being a Disciple

25 Large crowds were traveling with Jesus, and turning to them he said: 26 "If anyone comes to me and does not hate father and mother, wife and children, brothers and sisters—yes, even their own life—such a person cannot be my disciple.[p] 27 And whoever does not carry their cross and follow me cannot be my disciple.[q]

28 "Suppose one of you wants to build a tower. Won't you first sit down and estimate the cost to see if you have enough money to complete it? 29 For if you lay the foundation and are not able to finish it, everyone who sees it will ridicule you, 30 saying, 'This person began to build and wasn't able to finish.'

31 "Or suppose a king is about to go to war against another king. Won't he first sit down and consider whether he is able with ten thousand men to oppose the one coming against him with twenty thousand? 32 If he is not able, he will send a delegation while the other is still a long way off and will ask for terms of peace. 33 In the same way, those of you who do not give up everything you have cannot be my disciples.[r]

34 "Salt is good, but if it loses its saltiness, how can it be made salty again?[s] 35 It is fit neither for the soil nor for the manure pile; it is thrown out.[t]

"Whoever has ears to hear, let them hear."[u]

The Parable of the Lost Sheep

15 Now the tax collectors[v] and sinners were all gathering around to hear Jesus. 2 But the Pharisees and the teachers of the law muttered, "This man welcomes sinners and eats with them."[w]

3 Then Jesus told them this parable:[x] 4 "Suppose one of you has a hundred sheep and loses one of them. Doesn't he leave the ninety-nine in the open country and go after the lost sheep until he finds it?[y] 5 And when he finds it, he joyfully puts it on his shoulders 6 and goes home. Then he calls his friends and neighbors together and says, 'Rejoice with me; I have found my lost sheep.'[z] 7 I tell you that in the same way there will be more rejoicing in heaven over one sinner who repents than over ninety-nine righteous persons who do not need to repent.[a]

The Parable of the Lost Coin

8 "Or suppose a woman has ten silver coins[a] and loses one. Doesn't she light a lamp, sweep the house and search careful-

[a] 8 Greek *ten drachmas,* each worth about a day's wages

14:20 ***I just got married.*** While the Old Testament exempted a man from military duty because of marriage (Deut. 20:7; 24:5), marriage was not an excuse for avoiding social duties. The general point here is that the man regarded his own affairs as more important than the feast.
14:21 ***the poor, the crippled, the blind and the lame.*** This list matches that of verse 13. The crippled were excluded from full participation in Jewish worship (Lev. 21:17–23). The master's second invitation extended the scope of the offer to those who were rejected by society.
14:23 ***Go out to the roads.*** The master's second invitation extended beyond the city limits, encouraging even more people to come to the feast. This may picture the inclusion of Gentiles in God's salvation (Is. 49:6). The instruction to *compel* them to come in does not mean to force people in, but to urge them.
14:34 ***Salt is good.*** In the ancient world, salt was often used as a catalyst for burning fuel such as cattle dung. The salt of the time was impure and could lose its strength over time, becoming useless. Jesus' point is that the same is true of a "saltless" disciple.
15:1 ***tax collectors ... sinners.*** The three parables of chapter 15 explain why Jesus associated with the despised groups while the Pharisees and scribes did not. The parables in this chapter are found only in Luke.
15:4 ***a hundred sheep.*** This was a medium-sized flock. The average herd ran from 20 to 200 head, while a flock of 300 or more was considered large.
15:7 ***persons who do not need to repent.*** This phrase is a rhetorical way of describing the scribes and Pharisees. A similar description is found in 5:31, where it is said that some do not need a physician. The scribes and Pharisees believed that they did not need to repent because they were not lost.
15:8 ***ten silver coins.*** A drachma was a silver coin equal to a day's wage for a basic laborer. The woman needed a lamp because she lived in a windowless house. Her broom for sweeping would have been made of palm twigs.

14:21 [n] ver 13 **14:24** [o] Mt 21:43; Ac 13:46 **14:26** [p] Mt 10:37; Jn 12:25 **14:27** [q] Mt 10:38; Lk 9:23 **14:33** [r] Php 3:7,8 **14:34** [s] Mk 9:50 **14:35** [t] Mt 5:13 [u] Mt 11:15 **15:1** [v] Lk 5:29 **15:2** [w] Mt 9:11 **15:3** [x] Mt 13:3 **15:4** [y] Ps 23; 119:176; Jer 31:10; Eze 34:11-16; Lk 5:32; 19:10 **15:6** [z] ver 9 **15:7** [a] ver 10

ly until she finds it? 9And when she finds it,
she calls her friends and neighbors together and says, 'Rejoice with me; I have found
my lost coin.'[b] 10In the same way, I tell you,
there is rejoicing in the presence of the angels of God over one sinner who repents."[c]

The Parable of the Lost Son

11Jesus continued: "There was a man
who had two sons.[d] 12The younger one said
to his father, 'Father, give me my share of
the estate.'[e] So he divided his property[f] between them.
13"Not long after that, the younger son
got together all he had, set off for a distant
country and there squandered his wealth[g]
in wild living. 14After he had spent everything, there was a severe famine in that
whole country, and he began to be in need.
15So he went and hired himself out to a citizen of that country, who sent him to his
fields to feed pigs.[h] 16He longed to fill his
stomach with the pods that the pigs were
eating, but no one gave him anything.
17"When he came to his senses, he said,
'How many of my father's hired servants
have food to spare, and here I am starving
to death! 18I will set out and go back to my
father and say to him: Father, I have sinned[i]
against heaven and against you. 19I am no
longer worthy to be called your son; make
me like one of your hired servants.' 20So he
got up and went to his father.
"But while he was still a long way off, his
father saw him and was filled with compassion for him; he ran to his son, threw his
arms around him and kissed him.[j]
21"The son said to him, 'Father, I have
sinned against heaven and against you.[k] I
am no longer worthy to be called your son.'
22"But the father said to his servants,
'Quick! Bring the best robe[l] and put it on
him. Put a ring on his finger[m] and sandals on his feet. 23Bring the fattened calf
and kill it. Let's have a feast and celebrate.
24For this son of mine was dead and is alive
again;[n] he was lost and is found.' So they
began to celebrate.[o]
25"Meanwhile, the older son was in the
field. When he came near the house, he
heard music and dancing. 26So he called
one of the servants and asked him what
was going on. 27'Your brother has come,'
he replied, 'and your father has killed the
fattened calf because he has him back safe
and sound.'
28"The older brother became angry[p] and
refused to go in. So his father went out
and pleaded with him. 29But he answered
his father, 'Look! All these years I've
been slaving for you and never disobeyed
your orders. Yet you never gave me even
a young goat so I could celebrate with my
friends. 30But when this son of yours who
has squandered your property[q] with prostitutes[r] comes home, you kill the fattened
calf for him!'
31" 'My son,' the father said, 'you are always with me, and everything I have is
yours. 32But we had to celebrate and be
glad, because this brother of yours was
dead and is alive again; he was lost and is
found.' "[s]

The Parable of the Shrewd Manager

16 Jesus told his disciples: "There was
a rich man whose manager was accused of wasting his possessions.[t] 2So he
called him in and asked him, 'What is this
I hear about you? Give an account of your
management, because you cannot be manager any longer.'

15:15 ***to feed pigs.*** Feeding pigs was an insulting job for a Jewish person, since pigs were unclean according to the law of Moses.

15:20 ***his father saw him and was filled with compassion.*** Many scholars feel that the emphasis on the son in this parable causes people to miss the more important point, namely, the importance of the father's welcoming role. Still others think it could even be called the Parable of the Elder Brother. Interestingly, both brothers underestimate their father's love and grace. The younger brother is slow to realize the extent and permanence of his father's love. The elder brother has trouble understanding that the restored relationship with the younger son is vital to the life of the father. What makes the dramatic conversion possible is the younger son's knowledge that he will be accepted when he returns. While there are consequences to his behavior (his money is gone), he is welcomed to be a part of the family again. In many ways the welcome is even more than he could have hoped for. What is amazing about grace is that it is always more than we expect or deserve.

15:21 ***no longer worthy to be called your son.*** Despite his awareness of being accepted by his father, the son continued his confession of his sin. He then asked to become one of his father's servants. Similarly, a sinner realizes that he or she brings nothing to and deserves nothing from God, but must rely completely on God's mercy.

15:24 ***dead ... alive again ... lost ... found.*** The total transformation of the prodigal son is summarized in these two contrasts. Such a transformation is a reason to celebrate. It is also the reason Jesus chose to associate with the lost.

15:28 ***became angry.*** The elder brother's unhappiness over a fatted calf (v. 27) being killed to celebrate the return of his undisciplined brother illustrates the response of the Pharisees and scribes at the prospect of sinners becoming acceptable to God.

16:1 ***manager.*** This was a servant who supervised and administered an estate. The charge brought against this manager is incompetence.

15:9 [b] ver 6 **15:10** [c] ver 7 **15:11** [d] Mt 21:28 **15:12** [e] Dt 21:17 [f] ver 30 **15:13** [g] ver 30; Lk 16:1 **15:15** [h] Lev 11:7 **15:18** [i] Lev 26:40; Mt 3:2 **15:20** [j] Ge 45:14, 15, 46:29; Ac 20:37 **15:21** [k] Ps 51:4 **15:22** [l] Zec 3:4; Rev 6:11 [m] Ge 41:42 **15:24** [n] Eph 2:1, 5; 5:14; 1Ti 5:6 [o] ver 32 **15:28** [p] Jnh 4:1 **15:30** [q] ver 12, 13 [r] Pr 29:3 **15:32** [s] ver 24; Mal 3:17 **16:1** [t] Lk 15:13, 30

3“The manager said to himself, ‘What
shall I do now? My master is taking away
my job. I’m not strong enough to dig, and
I’m ashamed to beg— 4I know what I’ll do
so that, when I lose my job here, people will
welcome me into their houses.’
5“So he called in each one of his master’s
debtors. He asked the first, ‘How much do
you owe my master?’
6“‘Nine hundred gallons[a] of olive oil,’ he
replied.
“The manager told him, ‘Take your bill,
sit down quickly, and make it four hundred
and fifty.’
7“Then he asked the second, ‘And how
much do you owe?’
“‘A thousand bushels[b] of wheat,’ he replied.
“He told him, ‘Take your bill and make it
eight hundred.’
8“The master commended the dishonest
manager because he had acted shrewdly. For the people of this world[u] are more
shrewd[v] in dealing with their own kind
than are the people of the light.[w] 9I tell
you, use worldly wealth[x] to gain friends
for yourselves, so that when it is gone, you
will be welcomed into eternal dwellings.[y]
10“Whoever can be trusted with very
little can also be trusted with much,[z] and
whoever is dishonest with very little will
also be dishonest with much. 11So if you
have not been trustworthy in handling
worldly wealth,[a] who will trust you with
true riches? 12And if you have not been
trustworthy with someone else’s property,
who will give you property of your own?
13“No one can serve two masters. Either
you will hate the one and love the other, or
you will be devoted to the one and despise
the other. You cannot serve both God and
money.”[b]
14The Pharisees, who loved money,[c]
heard all this and were sneering at Jesus.[d]
15He said to them, “You are the ones who
justify yourselves[e] in the eyes of others, but
God knows your hearts.[f] What people value highly is detestable in God’s sight.

Additional Teachings

16“The Law and the Prophets were proclaimed until John.[g] Since that time, the
good news of the kingdom of God is being
preached,[h] and everyone is forcing their
way into it. 17It is easier for heaven and
earth to disappear than for the least stroke
of a pen to drop out of the Law.[i]
18“Anyone who divorces his wife and
marries another woman commits adultery,
and the man who marries a divorced woman commits adultery.[j]

The Rich Man and Lazarus

19“There was a rich man who was
dressed in purple and fine linen and lived
in luxury every day.[k] 20At his gate was laid
a beggar[l] named Lazarus, covered with
sores 21and longing to eat what fell from
the rich man’s table.[m] Even the dogs came
and licked his sores.
22“The time came when the beggar died
and the angels carried him to Abraham’s
side. The rich man also died and was buried. 23In Hades, where he was in torment,
he looked up and saw Abraham far away,
with Lazarus by his side. 24So he called to
him, ‘Father Abraham,[n] have pity on me
and send Lazarus to dip the tip of his finger in water and cool my tongue, because I
am in agony in this fire.’[o]
25“But Abraham replied, ‘Son, remember that in your lifetime you received your
good things, while Lazarus received bad
things,[p] but now he is comforted here and
you are in agony.[q] 26And besides all this,
between us and you a great chasm has
been set in place, so that those who want
to go from here to you cannot, nor can anyone cross over from there to us.’
27“He answered, ‘Then I beg you, father,
send Lazarus to my family, 28for I have five
brothers. Let him warn them,[r] so that they
will not also come to this place of torment.’

[a] 6 Or about 3,000 liters [b] 7 Or about 30 tons

16:8 ***The master commended the dishonest manager.*** The master recognized the foresight in the manager’s generosity. It is debatable whether the manager was dishonest and robbed the master by such reductions or was shrewd in using his authority to discount the goods (vv. 6–7). The fact that the master commended the manager may suggest that the master was not robbed and that the manager’s reduction was the result of either an adherence to the law or a lowering of the manager’s own commission.
16:9 ***worldly wealth.*** This is money and should be used generously to build works that last. Money is called unrighteous because it often manifests unrighteousness and selfishness in people (1 Tim. 6:6–10,17–19; James 1:9–11; 5:1–6).
16:19 ***dressed in purple.*** Purple clothes were extremely expensive because they were made with a special dye extracted from a kind of snail.
16:20–21 ***licked his sores.*** To have his sores licked by dogs threatened Lazarus with infection as well as ritual uncleanness, since dogs fed on garbage, including dead animals.
16:22 ***Abraham’s side.*** This was the blessed place of the dead. Angelic escorts for the dead were also known in Judaism. This verse indicates that the dead know their fate immediately.
16:24 ***I am in agony in this fire.*** The rich man desired relief from his suffering. The image of thirst for the experience of judgment is common (Is. 5:13; 65:13; Hos. 2:3).

16:8 [u] Ps 17:14 [v] Ps 18:26 [w] Jn 12:36; Eph 5:8; 1Th 5:5 **16:9** [x] ver 11, 13 [y] Mt 19:21; Lk 12:33 **16:10** [z] Mt 25:21, 23; Lk 19:17 **16:11** [a] ver 9, 13 **16:13** [b] ver 9, 11; Mt 6:24 **16:14** [c] 1Ti 3:3 [d] Lk 23:35 **16:15** [e] Lk 10:29 [f] 1Sa 16:7; Rev 2:23 **16:16** [g] Mt 11:12, 13 [h] Mt 4:23 **16:17** [i] Mt 5:18 **16:18** [j] Mt 5:31, 32; 19:9; Mk 10:11; Ro 7:2, 3; 1Co 7:10, 11 **16:19** [k] Eze 16:49 **16:20** [l] Ac 3:2 **16:21** [m] Mt 15:27 **16:24** [n] ver 30; Lk 3:8 [o] Mt 5:22 **16:25** [p] Ps 17:14 [q] Lk 6:21, 24, 25 **16:28** [r] Ac 2:40; 20:23; 1Th 4:6

29"Abraham replied, 'They have Moses[s] and the Prophets;[t] let them listen to them.'

30" 'No, father Abraham,'[u] he said, 'but if someone from the dead goes to them, they will repent.'

31"He said to him, 'If they do not listen to Moses and the Prophets, they will not be convinced even if someone rises from the dead.' "

Sin, Faith, Duty

17 Jesus said to his disciples: "Things that cause people to stumble[v] are bound to come, but woe to anyone through whom they come.[w] 2It would be better for them to be thrown into the sea with a millstone tied around their neck than to cause one of these little ones[x] to stumble.[y] 3So watch yourselves.

"If your brother or sister[a] sins against you, rebuke them;[z] and if they repent, forgive them.[a] 4Even if they sin against you seven times in a day and seven times come back to you saying 'I repent,' you must forgive them."[b]

5The apostles[c] said to the Lord,[d] "Increase our faith!"

6He replied, "If you have faith as small as a mustard seed,[e] you can say to this mulberry tree, 'Be uprooted and planted in the sea,' and it will obey you.[f]

7"Suppose one of you has a servant plowing or looking after the sheep. Will he say to the servant when he comes in from the field, 'Come along now and sit down to eat'? 8Won't he rather say, 'Prepare my supper, get yourself ready and wait on me[g] while I eat and drink; after that you may eat and drink'? 9Will he thank the servant because he did what he was told to do? 10So you also, when you have done everything you were told to do, should say, 'We are unworthy servants; we have only done our duty.' "[h]

Jesus Heals Ten Men With Leprosy

11Now on his way to Jerusalem,[i] Jesus traveled along the border between Samaria and Galilee.[j] 12As he was going into a village, ten men who had leprosy[b][k] met him. They stood at a distance[l] 13and called out in a loud voice, "Jesus, Master,[m] have pity on us!"

14When he saw them, he said, "Go, show yourselves to the priests."[n] And as they went, they were cleansed.

15One of them, when he saw he was healed, came back, praising God[o] in a loud voice. 16He threw himself at Jesus' feet and thanked him—and he was a Samaritan.[p]

17Jesus asked, "Were not all ten cleansed? Where are the other nine? 18Has no one returned to give praise to God except this foreigner?" 19Then he said to him, "Rise and go; your faith has made you well."[q]

The Coming of the Kingdom of God

20Once, on being asked by the Pharisees when the kingdom of God would come,[r] Jesus replied, "The coming of the kingdom of God is not something that can be observed, 21nor will people say, 'Here it is,' or 'There it is,'[s] because the kingdom of God is in your midst."[c]

22Then he said to his disciples, "The time is coming when you will long to see one of the days of the Son of Man,[t] but you will not see it.[u] 23People will tell you, 'There he is!' or 'Here he is!' Do not go running off after them.[v] 24For the Son of Man in his day[d] will be like the lightning,[w] which flashes and lights up the sky from one end

---

[a] *3* The Greek word for *brother or sister* (*adelphos*) refers here to a fellow disciple, whether man or woman. [b] *12* The Greek word traditionally translated *leprosy* was used for various diseases affecting the skin. [c] *21* Or *is within you*
[d] *24* Some manuscripts do not have *in his day.*

16:29 *They have Moses and the Prophets.* Abraham made it clear that the rich man's brothers should have known what to do, since they had the message of God in the ancient writings. The point here is that generosity with money and care for the poor were taught in the Old Testament (Deut. 14:28–29; Is. 3:14–15; Mic. 6:10–11).

17:1–2 *woe to anyone through whom they come.* Jesus warned that judgment awaits those who cause others to stumble. The severe form of the warning suggests that false teaching, or leading someone into apostasy, is in view here. ***a millstone.*** This was a heavy stone used in a grinding mill.

17:20 *kingdom of God.* In ancient Israel there was an expectation that the kingdom of God would come with cosmic signs (Joel 2:28–32). Jesus' concept of the kingdom of God, however, was broader than the time of the final consummation.

17:21 *in your midst.* This verse indicates that there was an aspect of kingdom promise involved in Jesus' first coming. The kingdom of God is among earthly kingdoms today; but one day the kingdom of God will swallow up all rival kingdoms (Rev. 11:15). In verses 22–37, Jesus makes it clear that the kingdom has two phases—one now and one to come. In the beginning of His kingdom on earth, God first prepares a King to rule; then He gathers a people for Him to rule over; then He gives the Ruler a realm in which to reign. The kingdom of God is not the same as the church, though the church is a part of the kingdom. The kingdom now is the presence of God alongside earthly kingdoms. One day, however, Jesus will rule over all, and He will share that rule with His people (Rev. 2:26–27; 5:9–10; 20:4–6).

16:29 [s] Lk 24:27,44; Jn 5:45-47; Ac 15:21 [t] Lk 4:17; Jn 1:45 **16:30** [u] ver 24; Lk 3:8 **17:1** [v] Mt 5:29 [w] Mt 18:7 **17:2** [x] Mk 10:24; Lk 10:21 [y] Mt 5:29 **17:3** [z] Mt 18:15 [a] Eph 4:32; Col 3:13 **17:4** [b] Mt 18:21,22 **17:5** [c] Mk 6:30 [d] Lk 7:13 **17:6** [e] Mt 13:31; 17:20; Lk 13:19 [f] Mt 21:21; Mk 9:23 **17:8** [g] Lk 12:37 **17:10** [h] 1Co 9:16 **17:11** [i] Lk 9:51 [j] Lk 9:51,52; Jn 4:3,4 **17:12** [k] Mt 8:2 [l] Lev 13:45,46 **17:13** [m] Lk 5:5 **17:14** [n] Lev 14:2; Mt 8:4 **17:15** [o] Mt 9:8 **17:16** [p] Mt 10:5 **17:19** [q] Mt 9:22 **17:20** [r] Mt 3:2 **17:21** [s] ver 23 **17:22** [t] Mt 8:20 [u] Mt 9:15; Lk 5:35 **17:23** [v] Mt 24:23; Mk 13:21; Lk 21:8 **17:24** [w] Mt 24:27

to the other. 25But first he must suffer many things[x] and be rejected[y] by this generation.[z]

26"Just as it was in the days of Noah,[a] so also will it be in the days of the Son of Man. 27People were eating, drinking, marrying and being given in marriage up to the day Noah entered the ark. Then the flood came and destroyed them all.

28"It was the same in the days of Lot.[b] People were eating and drinking, buying and selling, planting and building. 29But the day Lot left Sodom, fire and sulfur rained down from heaven and destroyed them all.

30"It will be just like this on the day the Son of Man is revealed.[c] 31On that day no one who is on the housetop, with possessions inside, should go down to get them. Likewise, no one in the field should go back for anything.[d] 32Remember Lot's wife![e] 33Whoever tries to keep their life will lose it, and whoever loses their life will preserve it.[f] 34I tell you, on that night two people will be in one bed; one will be taken and the other left. 35Two women will be grinding grain together; one will be taken and the other left."[g] [36][a]

37"Where, Lord?" they asked.

He replied, "Where there is a dead body, there the vultures will gather."[h]

The Parable of the Persistent Widow

18 Then Jesus told his disciples a parable to show them that they should always pray and not give up.[i] 2He said: "In a certain town there was a judge who neither feared God nor cared what people thought. 3And there was a widow in that town who kept coming to him with the plea, 'Grant me justice[j] against my adversary.'

4"For some time he refused. But finally he said to himself, 'Even though I don't fear God or care what people think, 5yet because this widow keeps bothering me, I will see that she gets justice, so that she won't eventually come and attack me!'"[k]

6And the Lord[l] said, "Listen to what the unjust judge says. 7And will not God bring about justice for his chosen ones, who cry out[m] to him day and night? Will he keep putting them off? 8I tell you, he will see that they get justice, and quickly. However, when the Son of Man[n] comes,[o] will he find faith on the earth?"

The Parable of the Pharisee and the Tax Collector

9To some who were confident of their own righteousness[p] and looked down on everyone else,[q] Jesus told this parable: 10"Two men went up to the temple to pray,[r] one a Pharisee and the other a tax collector. 11The Pharisee stood by himself[s] and prayed: 'God, I thank you that I am not like other people—robbers, evildoers, adulterers—or even like this tax collector. 12I fast[t] twice a week and give a tenth[u] of all I get.'

13"But the tax collector stood at a distance. He would not even look up to heaven, but beat his breast[v] and said, 'God, have mercy on me, a sinner.'[w]

14"I tell you that this man, rather than the other, went home justified before God. For all those who exalt themselves will be

[a] *36* Some manuscripts include here words similar to Matt. 24:40.

17:26 *in the days of Noah.* At that time people paid little attention to God and faced judgment as a result (Gen. 6:5–13). The same will be the case at Jesus' return.

17:32 *Lot's wife.* This woman represents those who are attached to earthly things, those whose hearts are still in this world. Like Lot's wife, such people will perish (Gen. 19:26).

17:34–37 *one will be taken.* This phrase suggests judgment such as when the soldiers took Jesus to crucify Him. Verse 37 makes it clear that those who are taken are taken to final judgment. The vultures will be gathered. When judgment comes, it will be final and terrible, with the stench of death and the presence of vultures everywhere. No one will need to look for the place of judgment; the presence of the birds will reveal where the carcasses are.

18:2 *a judge.* The Romans allowed the Jews to manage most of their own affairs. This judge did not fear God, and was therefore probably a secular judge, not a religious one. The dishonest judge represents corrupted power.

18:5 *this widow keeps bothering me.* The persistence of the widow is the lesson of the parable. God is a counterexample to the judge. God does not begrudge answering prayer. Jesus' point is that, if an insensitive judge will respond to the continual requests of a widow, God will certainly respond to the continual prayers of believers.

18:11–12 *God, I thank You.* The tone of the prayer reveals the Pharisee's problem. He uses the pronoun "I" four times in two verses. The Pharisee's attitude seems to be that God should be grateful to him for his commitment. The man obviously looked down on other people and was proud of his fasting and tithing.

18:13 *God, have mercy on me, a sinner.* This is an example of the humble spirit of repentance that Jesus commends. The tax collector knew that he could not say or bring anything to enhance his standing with God. He knew that only God's mercy and grace, and not his own works, could deliver him.

17:25 [x] Mt 16:21 [y] Lk 9:22; 18:32 [z] Mk 13:30; Lk 21:32 **17:26** [a] Ge 7:6-24 **17:28** [b] Ge 19:1-28 **17:30** [c] Mt 10:23; 16:27; 24:3, 27, 37, 39; 25:31; 1Co 1:7; 1Th 2:19; 2Th 1:7; 2:8; 2Pe 3:4; Rev 1:7 **17:31** [d] Mt 24:17, 18; Mk 13:15-16 **17:32** [e] Ge 19:26 **17:33** [f] Jn 12:25 **17:35** [g] Mt 24:41 **17:37** [h] Mt 24:28 **18:1** [i] Isa 40:31; Lk 11:5-8; Ac 1:14; Ro 12:12; Eph 6:18; Col 4:2; 1Th 5:17 **18:3** [j] Isa 1:17 **18:5** [k] Lk 11:8 **18:6** [l] Lk 7:13 **18:7** [m] Ex 22:23; Ps 88:1; Rev 6:10 **18:8** [n] Mt 8:20 [o] Mt 16:27 **18:9** [p] Lk 16:15 [q] Isa 65:5 **18:10** [r] Ac 3:1 **18:11** [s] Mt 6:5; Mk 11:25 **18:12** [t] Isa 58:3; Mt 9:14 [u] Mal 3:8; Lk 11:42 **18:13** [v] Isa 66:2; Jer 31:19; Lk 23:48 [w] Lk 5:32; 1Ti 1:15

humbled, and those who humble themselves will be exalted."[x]

The Little Children and Jesus

15People were also bringing babies to
Jesus for him to place his hands on them.
When the disciples saw this, they rebuked
them. 16But Jesus called the children to
him and said, "Let the little children come
to me, and do not hinder them, for the kingdom of God belongs to such as these. 17Tru-
ly I tell you, anyone who will not receive
the kingdom of God like a little child[y] will
never enter it."

The Rich and the Kingdom of God

18A certain ruler asked him, "Good
teacher, what must I do to inherit eternal
life?"[z]
19"Why do you call me good?" Jesus
answered. "No one is good—except God
alone. 20You know the commandments:
'You shall not commit adultery, you shall
not murder, you shall not steal, you shall
not give false testimony, honor your father
and mother.'[a]"[a]
21"All these I have kept since I was a
boy," he said.
22When Jesus heard this, he said to him,
"You still lack one thing. Sell everything
you have and give to the poor,[b] and you
will have treasure in heaven.[c] Then come,
follow me."
23When he heard this, he became very
sad, because he was very wealthy. 24Jesus
looked at him and said, "How hard it is for
the rich to enter the kingdom of God![d] 25In-
deed, it is easier for a camel to go through
the eye of a needle than for someone who is
rich to enter the kingdom of God."
26Those who heard this asked, "Who
then can be saved?"
27Jesus replied, "What is impossible with
man is possible with God."[e]
28Peter said to him, "We have left all we
had to follow you!"[f]
29"Truly I tell you," Jesus said to them,
"no one who has left home or wife or brothers or sisters or parents or children for the
sake of the kingdom of God 30will fail to receive many times as much in this age, and
in the age to come[g] eternal life."[h]

Jesus Predicts His Death a Third Time

31Jesus took the Twelve aside and told
them, "We are going up to Jerusalem,[i] and
everything that is written by the prophets[j] about the Son of Man[k] will be fulfilled.
32He will be delivered over to the Gentiles.[l]
They will mock him, insult him and spit on
him; 33they will flog him[m] and kill him.[n] On
the third day[o] he will rise again."[p]
34The disciples did not understand any
of this. Its meaning was hidden from them,
and they did not know what he was talking
about.[q]

A Blind Beggar Receives His Sight

35As Jesus approached Jericho,[r] a blind
man was sitting by the roadside begging.
36When he heard the crowd going by, he
asked what was happening. 37They told
him, "Jesus of Nazareth is passing by."[s]
38He called out, "Jesus, Son of David,[t]
have mercy[u] on me!"
39Those who led the way rebuked him
and told him to be quiet, but he shouted
all the more, "Son of David, have mercy
on me!"[v]
40Jesus stopped and ordered the man to
be brought to him. When he came near,
Jesus asked him, 41"What do you want me
to do for you?"
"Lord, I want to see," he replied.

[a] *20* Exodus 20:12-16; Deut. 5:16-20

18:16 *But Jesus called the children to him.* Jesus used the thoughtlessness of his disciples to make two points: (1) all people, even little children, are important to God; and (2) the kingdom of God consists of those who respond to Him with the trust that a little child gives to a parent.

18:22 *Sell everything you have and give to the poor.* This was a radical test of the ruler's concern for others (12:33–34). Jesus was determining whether the ruler's treasure (Matt. 6:19–21) lay with God or money (16:13). Jesus was not establishing a new requirement for being saved. He was examining the ruler's orientation to God by directly confronting him with the very thing that was hindering him—namely, his wealth.

18:24–25 *Indeed, it is easier for a camel to go through the eye of a needle.* Jesus used this figure of speech to emphasize the difficulty of turning from wealth to find salvation. Because many Jewish people believed that wealth was evidence of God's blessing, Jesus' statements would have been shocking to His audience.

18:34 *The disciples did not understand any of this.* The disciples may have understood something of what Jesus said, but they could not understand why God's Chosen One would have to face such suffering. For those who were expecting the Promised One to be an exalted figure who would deliver God's people, it would be very difficult to reconcile such an expectation with such terrible suffering.

18:38 *Son of David.* Note the irony in this verse. The blind man recognized who Jesus was more clearly than many people who were blessed with physical sight. The blind man's cry for mercy demonstrated his belief that Jesus had the power to heal him.

18:14 [x] Mt 23:12; Lk 14:11 **18:17** [y] Mt 11:25; 18:3 **18:18** [z] Lk 10:25 **18:20** [a] Ex 20:12-16; Dt 5:16-20; Ro 13:9 **18:22** [b] Ac 2:45 [c] Mt 6:20 **18:24** [d] Pr 11:28 **18:27** [e] Mt 19:26 **18:28** [f] Mt 4:19 **18:30** [g] Mt 12:32 [h] Mt 25:46 **18:31** [i] Lk 9:51 [j] Ps 22; Isa 53 [k] Mt 8:20 **18:32** [l] Lk 23:1 **18:33** [m] Mt 16:21 [n] Ac 2:23 [o] Mt 16:21 [p] Mt 16:21 **18:34** [q] Mk 9:32; Lk 9:45 **18:35** [r] Lk 19:1 **18:37** [s] Lk 19:4 **18:38** [t] ver 39; Mt 9:27 [u] Mt 17:15; Lk 18:13 **18:39** [v] ver 38

42 Jesus said to him, "Receive your sight; your faith has healed you."[w] 43 Immediately he received his sight and followed Jesus, praising God. When all the people saw it, they also praised God.[x]

Zacchaeus the Tax Collector

19 Jesus entered Jericho[y] and was passing through. 2 A man was there by the name of Zacchaeus; he was a chief tax collector and was wealthy. 3 He wanted to see who Jesus was, but because he was short he could not see over the crowd. 4 So he ran ahead and climbed a sycamore-fig[z] tree to see him, since Jesus was coming that way.[a]

5 When Jesus reached the spot, he looked up and said to him, "Zacchaeus, come down immediately. I must stay at your house today." 6 So he came down at once and welcomed him gladly.

7 All the people saw this and began to mutter, "He has gone to be the guest of a sinner."[b]

8 But Zacchaeus stood up and said to the Lord,[c] "Look, Lord! Here and now I give half of my possessions to the poor, and if I have cheated anybody out of anything,[d] I will pay back four times the amount."[e]

9 Jesus said to him, "Today salvation has come to this house, because this man, too, is a son of Abraham.[f] 10 For the Son of Man came to seek and to save the lost."[g]

The Parable of the Ten Minas

11 While they were listening to this, he went on to tell them a parable, because he was near Jerusalem and the people thought that the kingdom of God[h] was going to appear at once.[i] 12 He said: "A man of noble birth went to a distant country to have himself appointed king and then to return. 13 So he called ten of his servants[j] and gave them ten minas.[a] 'Put this money to work,' he said, 'until I come back.'

14 "But his subjects hated him and sent a delegation after him to say, 'We don't want this man to be our king.'

15 "He was made king, however, and returned home. Then he sent for the servants to whom he had given the money, in order to find out what they had gained with it.

16 "The first one came and said, 'Sir, your mina has earned ten more.'

17 " 'Well done, my good servant!'[k] his master replied. 'Because you have been trustworthy in a very small matter, take charge of ten cities.'[l]

18 "The second came and said, 'Sir, your mina has earned five more.'

19 "His master answered, 'You take charge of five cities.'

20 "Then another servant came and said, 'Sir, here is your mina; I have kept it laid away in a piece of cloth. 21 I was afraid of you, because you are a hard man. You take out what you did not put in and reap what you did not sow.'[m]

22 "His master replied, 'I will judge you by your own words,[n] you wicked servant! You knew, did you, that I am a hard man, taking out what I did not put in, and reaping what I did not sow?[o] 23 Why then didn't you put my money on deposit, so that when I came back, I could have collected it with interest?'

24 "Then he said to those standing by, 'Take his mina away from him and give it to the one who has ten minas.'

25 " 'Sir,' they said, 'he already has ten!'

26 "He replied, 'I tell you that to everyone who has, more will be given, but as for the one who has nothing, even what they have will be taken away.[p] 27 But those enemies of mine who did not want me to be king over them—bring them here and kill them in front of me.' "

Jesus Comes to Jerusalem as King

28 After Jesus had said this, he went on ahead, going up to Jerusalem.[q] 29 As he approached Bethphage and Bethany[r] at the hill called the Mount of Olives,[s] he sent two

---

[a] *13* A mina was about three months' wages.

19:2 *Zacchaeus.* This was the chief tax collector which meant he most likely bid for the right to collect taxes and then hired another tax collector to actually gather the money.

19:7 *All the people . . . began to mutter.* The crowd was not happy with Jesus' choice of who to honor with His fellowship. In the crowd's opinion, Zacchaeus was a sinner. Tax collectors often took for themselves a high percentage of what they demanded. They were hated and despised in ancient Israel.

19:11 *the people thought.* Evidently the disciples believed that Jesus' arrival in Jerusalem would signal the arrival of the kingdom of God. Jesus' parable in verses 12–27 was designed to dispel this misconception. Note that the disciples raised the same question in Acts 1:6.

19:13 *ten minas.* Each servant received one mina or about three months' wages for the average worker. The master, symbolizing Jesus Himself, wants to see fruit, or dividends from his investment. Did his servants put the money they received to good use?

19:20–23 *I was afraid of you.* The unfaithful servant's excuse for failure reflects a negative view of the nobleman. If the servant had really feared the master, he would have done something with the money. Even putting the money in the bank would have yielded interest.

18:42 [w] Mt 9:22 **18:43** [x] Mt 9:8; Lk 13:17 **19:1** [y] Lk 18:35 **19:4** [z] 1Ki 10:27; 1Ch 27:28; Isa 9:10 [a] Lk 18:37 **19:7** [b] Mt 9:11 **19:8** [c] Lk 7:13 [d] Lk 3:12, 13 [e] Ex 22:1; Lev 6:4, 5; Nu 5:7; 2Sa 12:6 **19:9** [f] Lk 3:8; 13:16; Ro 4:16; Gal 3:7 **19:10** [g] Eze 34:12, 16; Jn 3:17 **19:11** [h] Mt 3:2 [i] Lk 17:20; Ac 1:6 **19:13** [j] Mk 13:34 **19:17** [k] Pr 27:18 [l] Lk 16:10 **19:21** [m] Mt 25:24 **19:22** [n] 2Sa 1:16; Job 15:6 [o] Mt 25:26 **19:26** [p] Mt 13:12; 25:29; Lk 8:18 **19:28** [q] Mk 10:32; Lk 9:51 **19:29** [r] Mt 21:17 [s] Mt 21:1

of his disciples, saying to them, 30“Go to the
village ahead of you, and as you enter it,
you will find a colt tied there, which no one
has ever ridden. Untie it and bring it here.
31If anyone asks you, ‘Why are you untying
it?’ say, ‘The Lord needs it.’ ”
32Those who were sent ahead went and
found it just as he had told them.[t] 33As they
were untying the colt, its owners asked
them, “Why are you untying the colt?”
34They replied, “The Lord needs it.”
35They brought it to Jesus, threw their
cloaks on the colt and put Jesus on it. 36As
he went along, people spread their cloaks[u]
on the road.
37When he came near the place where
the road goes down the Mount of Olives,[v]
the whole crowd of disciples began joyfully
to praise God in loud voices for all the miracles they had seen:

38“Blessed is the king who comes in the
name of the Lord!”[a][w]

“Peace in heaven and glory in the
highest!”[x]

39Some of the Pharisees in the crowd
said to Jesus, “Teacher, rebuke your disciples!”[y]
40“I tell you,” he replied, “if they keep
quiet, the stones will cry out.”[z]
41As he approached Jerusalem and saw
the city, he wept over it[a] 42and said, “If you,
even you, had only known on this day what
would bring you peace—but now it is hidden from your eyes. 43The days will come
upon you when your enemies will build
an embankment against you and encircle
you and hem you in on every side.[b] 44They
will dash you to the ground, you and the
children within your walls.[c] They will not
leave one stone on another,[d] because you
did not recognize the time of God’s coming[e] to you.”

Jesus at the Temple

45When Jesus entered the temple courts,
he began to drive out those who were selling. 46“It is written,” he said to them, “ ‘My
house will be a house of prayer’[b];[f] but you
have made it ‘a den of robbers.’[c]”[g]
47Every day he was teaching at the temple.[h] But the chief priests, the teachers of
the law and the leaders among the people
were trying to kill him.[i] 48Yet they could
not find any way to do it, because all the
people hung on his words.

The Authority of Jesus Questioned

20 One day as Jesus was teaching the
people in the temple courts[j] and proclaiming the good news,[k] the chief priests
and the teachers of the law, together with
the elders, came up to him. 2“Tell us by
what authority you are doing these things,”
they said. “Who gave you this authority?”[l]
3He replied, “I will also ask you a question. Tell me: 4John’s baptism[m]—was it
from heaven, or of human origin?”
5They discussed it among themselves
and said, “If we say, ‘From heaven,’ he will
ask, ‘Why didn’t you believe him?’ 6But if
we say, ‘Of human origin,’ all the people[n]
will stone us, because they are persuaded
that John was a prophet.”[o]
7So they answered, “We don’t know
where it was from.”
8Jesus said, “Neither will I tell you by
what authority I am doing these things.”

---

[a] *38* Psalm 118:26 [b] *46* Isaiah 56:7
[c] *46* Jer. 7:11

19:31–34 ***The Lord needs it.*** Such borrowing of an animal was not as strange as it may appear. There was an ancient custom by which a political or religious leader could commandeer property for short-term use. Jesus was entering Jerusalem to celebrate the Passover and the Festival of Unleavened Bread, festivals that commemorated the great act of God’s deliverance of the nation. Such festivals were often celebrated at this time with the hope that God’s decisive deliverance would come.

19:41 ***wept over it.*** Jesus knew that so many of the people of Israel had rejected Him that the nation would suffer judgment, in the form of the terrible destruction that came on Jerusalem in A.D. 70.

19:43 ***build an embankment against you.*** This is a prediction of Rome’s successful siege of Jerusalem under Titus. The details reflect a divine judgment for covenant unfaithfulness, similar to the Babylonian destruction of Jerusalem in 586 B.C. (Is. 29:1–4; Jer. 6:6–21; Ezek. 4:1–3).

19:45 ***Jesus entered the temple.*** Jesus cleansed the temple in anger after seeing that the place of prayer had become an excuse for corrupt commerce. Merchants were selling sacrificial animals in the outer court of the temple (the court of the Gentiles) at exorbitant prices. Money changers were making an excessive profit exchanging currencies for the temple shekel. John records a temple cleansing in John 2:13–22, but it is not clear whether that event is the same as this one in Luke. Since John places the event early in Jesus’ ministry, Jesus might have cleansed the temple twice.

20:4 ***John’s baptism—was it from heaven, or of human origin?*** Here as throughout the Gospel of Luke, the ministries of John the Baptist and Jesus are linked. Jesus’ question presented the Pharisees with a dilemma. If they recognized John’s ministry as coming from heaven, they would be recognizing the same divine origin of Jesus’ similar “independent” Spirit directed ministry. But if the Pharisees denied that John was sent by God they risked angering the majority of the people, who believed that John’s ministry was divinely directed (vv. 5–6).

19:32 [t] Lk 22:13 **19:36** [u] 2Ki 9:13 **19:37** [v] Mt 21:1 **19:38** [w] Ps 118:26; Lk 13:35 [x] Lk 2:14 **19:39** [y] Mt 21:15, 16 **19:40** [z] Hab 2:11 **19:41** [a] Isa 22:4; Lk 13:34, 35 **19:43** [b] Isa 29:3; Jer 6:6; Eze 4:2; 26:8; Lk 21:20 **19:44** [c] Ps 137:9 [d] Mt 24:2; Mk 13:2; Lk 21:6 [e] 1Pe 2:12 **19:46** [f] Isa 56:7 [g] Jer 7:11 **19:47** [h] Mt 26:55 [i] Mt 12:14; Mk 11:18 **20:1** [j] Mt 26:55 [k] Lk 8:1 **20:2** [l] Jn 2:18; Ac 4:7; 7:27 **20:4** [m] Mk 1:4 **20:6** [n] Lk 7:29 [o] Mt 11:9

The Parable of the Tenants

9He went on to tell the people this parable: "A man planted a vineyard,[p] rented it
to some farmers and went away for a long
time.[q] 10At harvest time he sent a servant
to the tenants so they would give him some
of the fruit of the vineyard. But the tenants
beat him and sent him away empty-handed.
11He sent another servant, but that one also
they beat and treated shamefully and sent
away empty-handed. 12He sent still a third,
and they wounded him and threw him out.
13"Then the owner of the vineyard said,
'What shall I do? I will send my son, whom
I love;[r] perhaps they will respect him.'
14"But when the tenants saw him, they
talked the matter over. 'This is the heir,'
they said. 'Let's kill him, and the inheritance will be ours.' 15So they threw him
out of the vineyard and killed him.
"What then will the owner of the vineyard do to them? 16He will come and kill
those tenants[s] and give the vineyard to
others."
When the people heard this, they said,
"God forbid!"
17Jesus looked directly at them and
asked, "Then what is the meaning of that
which is written:

> "'The stone the builders rejected
> has become the cornerstone'[a]?[t]

18Everyone who falls on that stone will be
broken to pieces; anyone on whom it falls
will be crushed."[u]
19The teachers of the law and the chief
priests looked for a way to arrest him[v] immediately, because they knew he had spoken this parable against them. But they
were afraid of the people.[w]

Paying Taxes to Caesar

20Keeping a close watch on him, they
sent spies, who pretended to be sincere.
They hoped to catch Jesus in something he
said,[x] so that they might hand him over to
the power and authority of the governor.[y]
21So the spies questioned him: "Teacher,
we know that you speak and teach what
is right, and that you do not show partiality but teach the way of God in accordance
with the truth.[z] 22Is it right for us to pay
taxes to Caesar or not?"
23He saw through their duplicity and
said to them, 24"Show me a denarius.
Whose image and inscription are on it?"
"Caesar's," they replied.
25He said to them, "Then give back to
Caesar what is Caesar's,[a] and to God what
is God's."
26They were unable to trap him in what
he had said there in public. And astonished
by his answer, they became silent.

The Resurrection and Marriage

27Some of the Sadducees,[b] who say there
is no resurrection,[c] came to Jesus with a
question. 28"Teacher," they said, "Moses
wrote for us that if a man's brother dies and
leaves a wife but no children, the man must
marry the widow and raise up offspring for
his brother.[d] 29Now there were seven brothers. The first one married a woman and
died childless. 30The second 31and then the
third married her, and in the same way the
seven died, leaving no children. 32Finally,
the woman died too. 33Now then, at the resurrection whose wife will she be, since the
seven were married to her?"

---

[a] *17* Psalm 118:22

20:9 *A man planted a vineyard.* The imagery of the vineyard recalls the subject of Jesus' parable in 13:6–9. This parable is also found in Matthew 21:33–44 and Mark 12:1–12, with some slight variations of detail in each account.
20:14 *This is the heir.* The vinedressers hoped that with the son gone, the inheritance would fall to those who worked the property, a transfer that was possible in the ancient world. It should be noted that the details of this parable do not represent the thinking of those who crucified Jesus. The leaders of Israel thought they were stopping someone who was dangerous to Judaism, not that they were going to inherit Jesus' kingdom.
20:17 *The stone the builders rejected.* This passage, taken from Psalm 118:22, pictures the exaltation of the Righteous One, Jesus, after His rejection. Opposition will not stop God from making the One who is rejected the center of His work of salvation.
20:18 *Everyone who falls on that stone.* Jesus is the stone. Anyone who goes against the stone will be destroyed. Jesus' statement is similar to a late Jewish proverb: "If the stone falls on the pot, alas for the pot; if the pot falls on the stone, alas for the pot." The imagery for the stone is also found in 1 Peter 2:4–8.
20:22 *Is it right for us to pay taxes to Caesar.* This question concerned the poll tax to Rome, which was different from the taxes collected by the tax collectors. The poll tax was a citizenship tax paid directly to Rome, as an indication that Israel was subject to that Gentile nation. The Pharisees' query was a trick question. If Jesus answered yes, the people would be angry because He respected a foreign power. If He answered no, He could be charged with sedition.
20:24 *Whose image and inscription are on it?* Jesus' reply was clever. He had the Pharisees pull out a coin, indicating that they already recognized Roman sovereignty by using Roman coins themselves. A penny was a silver coin that had a picture of the emperor Tiberius on it.
20:27 *Sadducees.* The Sadducees, the Pharisees, and the Essenes were three major divisions in first-century Judaism. The Sadducees rejected the oral traditions that the Pharisees too stringently obeyed. Instead they based their teaching only on the first five books of the Old Testament. They also denied that there could be a resurrection.

20:9 [p] Isa 5:1-7 [q] Mt 25:14 **20:13** [r] Mt 3:17
20:16 [s] Lk 19:27 **20:17** [t] Ps 118:22; Ac 4:11
20:18 [u] Isa 8:14,15 **20:19** [v] Lk 19:47 [w] Mk 11:18
20:20 [x] Mt 12:10 [y] Mt 27:2 **20:21** [z] Jn 3:2
20:25 [a] Lk 23:2; Ro 13:7 **20:27** [b] Ac 4:1 [c] Ac 23:8;
1Co 15:12 **20:28** [d] Dt 25:5

34 Jesus replied, "The people of this age
marry and are given in marriage. 35 But
those who are considered worthy of taking part in the age to come[e] and in the resurrection from the dead will neither marry
nor be given in marriage, 36 and they can
no longer die; for they are like the angels.
They are God's children,[f] since they are
children of the resurrection. 37 But in the
account of the burning bush, even Moses
showed that the dead rise, for he calls the
Lord 'the God of Abraham, and the God of
Isaac, and the God of Jacob.'[a][g] 38 He is not
the God of the dead, but of the living, for to
him all are alive."

39 Some of the teachers of the law responded, "Well said, teacher!" 40 And no
one dared to ask him any more questions.[h]

Whose Son Is the Messiah?

41 Then Jesus said to them, "Why is it said
that the Messiah is the son of David?[i] 42 David himself declares in the Book of Psalms:

"'The Lord said to my Lord:
"Sit at my right hand
43 until I make your enemies
a footstool for your feet."'[b][j]

44 David calls him 'Lord.' How then can he
be his son?"

Warning Against the Teachers of the Law

45 While all the people were listening,
Jesus said to his disciples, 46 "Beware of
the teachers of the law. They like to walk
around in flowing robes and love to be
greeted with respect in the marketplaces
and have the most important seats in the
synagogues and the places of honor at banquets.[k] 47 They devour widows' houses and
for a show make lengthy prayers. These
men will be punished most severely."

The Widow's Offering

21 As Jesus looked up, he saw the rich
putting their gifts into the temple
treasury.[l] 2 He also saw a poor widow put
in two very small copper coins. 3 "Truly I
tell you," he said, "this poor widow has put
in more than all the others. 4 All these people gave their gifts out of their wealth; but
she out of her poverty put in all she had to
live on."[m]

The Destruction of the Temple and Signs of the End Times

5 Some of his disciples were remarking
about how the temple was adorned with
beautiful stones and with gifts dedicated
to God. But Jesus said, 6 "As for what you
see here, the time will come when not one
stone will be left on another;[n] every one of
them will be thrown down."

7 "Teacher," they asked, "when will these
things happen? And what will be the sign
that they are about to take place?"

8 He replied: "Watch out that you are not
deceived. For many will come in my name,
claiming, 'I am he,' and, 'The time is near.'
Do not follow them.[o] 9 When you hear of
wars and uprisings, do not be frightened.
These things must happen first, but the end
will not come right away."

10 Then he said to them: "Nation will rise
against nation, and kingdom against kingdom.[p] 11 There will be great earthquakes,
famines and pestilences in various places,
and fearful events and great signs from
heaven.[q]

12 "But before all this, they will seize you
and persecute you. They will hand you
over to synagogues and put you in prison,
and you will be brought before kings and

[a] 37 Exodus 3:6 [b] 43 Psalm 110:1

20:36 *they are like the angels.* The everlasting life of a resurrected person makes that person something like an angel. Paul explains further that in the resurrection we will be given resurrection bodies similar to Christ's (1 Cor. 15:25–58). This will be a new experience that will not necessarily parallel experiences on this earth, such as marriage.

20:41–42 *Why is it said that.* Here Jesus takes His turn at raising a theological issue. The dilemma He poses is how the Messiah could be called the Son of David, when David himself gave Him the title *Lord, my Lord*. This is a citation from Psalm 110:1. The Messiah was David's descendant and yet David gave Him the respect due to a superior, the reverse of what normally occurred in ancient times. Jesus was not denying the title *Son of David* to the Messiah, He was simply noting that the title *Lord*, meaning "Master," is more central. Even David one day will bow at the Messiah's feet and confess that He is Lord (Phil. 2:10).

21:2 *two very small copper coins.* These were the smallest currency available.

21:5 *gifts.* These were gift offerings for the decoration of the temple and included gold and silver-plated gates, grapevine clusters, and Babylonian linen tapestries which hung from the temple veil. Even Tacitus, the Roman historian, called it an "immensely opulent temple."

21:6 *not one stone will be left on another.* Jesus noted that the beautiful place of worship was temporary and would be destroyed. He was referring to the fall of Jerusalem in A.D. 70, which itself was a picture of the destruction of the last days.

21:8 *Watch out that you are not deceived.* The first century and early second century were times of great messianic fervor in Judaism, as the Israelites sought freedom from Roman rule. Many people claimed to be the Messiah. Jesus warned his disciples not to be fooled by such claims.

21:12 *synagogues and put you in prison ... kings and governors.* These references indicate

20:35 [e] Mt 12:32 **20:36** [f] Jn 1:12; 1Jn 3:1-2
20:37 [g] Ex 3:6 **20:40** [h] Mt 22:46; Mk 12:34
20:41 [i] Mt 1:1 **20:43** [j] Ps 110:1; Mt 22:44
20:46 [k] Lk 11:43 **21:1** [l] Mt 27:6; Jn 8:20
21:4 [m] 2Co 8:12 **21:6** [n] Lk 19:44 **21:8** [o] Lk 17:23
21:10 [p] 2Ch 15:6; Isa 19:2 **21:11** [q] Isa 29:6; Joel 2:30

governors, and all on account of my name. 13And so you will bear testimony to me.[r] 14But make up your mind not to worry beforehand how you will defend yourselves.[s] 15For I will give you[t] words and wisdom that none of your adversaries will be able to resist or contradict. 16You will be betrayed even by parents, brothers and sisters, relatives and friends,[u] and they will put some of you to death. 17Everyone will hate you because of me.[v] 18But not a hair of your head will perish.[w] 19Stand firm, and you will win life.[x]

20"When you see Jerusalem being surrounded by armies,[y] you will know that its desolation is near. 21Then let those who are in Judea flee to the mountains, let those in the city get out, and let those in the country not enter the city.[z] 22For this is the time of punishment[a] in fulfillment[b] of all that has been written. 23How dreadful it will be in those days for pregnant women and nursing mothers! There will be great distress in the land and wrath against this people. 24They will fall by the sword and will be taken as prisoners to all the nations. Jerusalem will be trampled[c] on by the Gentiles until the times of the Gentiles are fulfilled.

25"There will be signs in the sun, moon and stars. On the earth, nations will be in anguish and perplexity at the roaring and tossing of the sea.[d] 26People will faint from terror, apprehensive of what is coming on the world, for the heavenly bodies will be shaken.[e] 27At that time they will see the Son of Man[f] coming in a cloud[g] with power and great glory. 28When these things begin to take place, stand up and lift up your heads, because your redemption is drawing near."[h]

29He told them this parable: "Look at the fig tree and all the trees. 30When they sprout leaves, you can see for yourselves and know that summer is near. 31Even so, when you see these things happening, you know that the kingdom of God[i] is near.

32"Truly I tell you, this generation[j] will certainly not pass away until all these things have happened. 33Heaven and earth will pass away, but my words will never pass away.[k]

34"Be careful, or your hearts will be weighed down with carousing, drunkenness and the anxieties of life,[l] and that day will close on you suddenly[m] like a trap. 35For it will come on all those who live on the face of the whole earth. 36Be always on the watch, and pray[n] that you may be able to escape all that is about to happen, and that you may be able to stand before the Son of Man."

37Each day Jesus was teaching at the temple,[o] and each evening he went out[p] to spend the night on the hill called the Mount of Olives,[q] 38and all the people came early in the morning to hear him at the temple.[r]

Judas Agrees to Betray Jesus

22 Now the Festival of Unleavened Bread, called the Passover, was ap-

---

that all nations would share responsibility for the massacre of the disciples.

21:15 ***I will give you words and wisdom.*** Jesus promises the disciples that the Holy Spirit will assist them in giving testimony (12:11–12). The initial fulfillment of this promise is found in Acts 4:8–14; 7:54; and 26:24–30.

21:16 ***You will be betrayed.*** The persecution of the disciples would be painful and severe. Identifying with Jesus often means risking the rejection and denunciation of family, and in some cases martyrdom.

21:20 ***its desolation.*** This passage compared the desecration of the temple to what occurred in 167 B.C., when Antiochus Epiphanes erected an altar to Zeus in the temple. A similar desecration of the temple site occurred during the destruction of Jerusalem in A.D. 70.

21:22 ***time of punishment.*** Jerusalem had become an object of divine judgment because of its unfaithfulness. Jesus warned of this consequence throughout His ministry (13:9,34–35; 19:41–44). The premise for such judgment goes back to the curses of the Mosaic covenant and the Old Testament prophets' warnings of coming judgment (Deut. 28:49–57; 32:35; Jer. 6:1–8; 26:1–9; Hos. 9:7).

21:27 ***the Son of Man coming in a cloud.*** The reference here is to the authoritative return of Jesus. The allusion to the cloud and the figure comes from Daniel 7:13–14, with its picture of One who receives authority from the Ancient of Days. Jesus viewed this text in terms of an apocalyptic deliverance. The image of the cloud is important, since God is identified as riding the clouds in the Old Testament (Ex. 34:5; Ps. 104:3). The Son of Man has divine authority to judge the world.

21:29–30 ***When they sprout leaves.*** The tender buds that appear every spring on trees show that summer is approaching; the appearance of the signs Jesus describes will warn of the coming of the end times.

21:33 ***will never pass away.*** The disciples had the assurance that Jesus' promises concerning the end times were more certain than creation itself. God made an unconditional and unilateral covenant, and He will keep it (Gen. 12:1–3; 15:18–21; Ps. 89).

21:34 ***Be careful.*** Though the events of the end times may not come to pass for a long time, believers should continue to look for their arrival. The day of Jesus' return should not take us by surprise. We should live as if it is imminent.

22:1 ***the Festival of Unleavened Bread.*** This festival took place immediately following Passover (Ex. 12:1–20; Deut. 16:1–8). The two festivals were often considered as one. Passover commemorated

21:13 [r] Php 1:12 **21:14** [s] Lk 12:11 **21:15** [t] Lk 12:12 **21:16** [u] Lk 12:52, 53 **21:17** [v] Jn 15:21 **21:18** [w] Mt 10:30 **21:19** [x] Mt 10:22 **21:20** [y] Lk 19:43 **21:21** [z] Lk 17:31 **21:22** [a] Isa 63:4; Da 9:24-27; Hos 9:7 [b] Mt 1:22 **21:24** [c] Isa 5:5; 63:18; Da 8:13; Rev 11:2 **21:25** [d] 2Pe 3:10, 12 **21:26** [e] Mt 24:29 **21:27** [f] Mt 8:20 [g] Rev 1:7 **21:28** [h] Lk 18:7 **21:31** [i] Mt 3:2 **21:32** [j] Lk 11:50; 17:25 **21:33** [k] Mt 5:18 **21:34** [l] Mk 4:19 [m] Lk 12:40, 46; 1Th 5:2-7 **21:36** [n] Mt 26:41 **21:37** [o] Mt 26:55 [p] Mk 11:19 [q] Mt 21:1 **21:38** [r] Jn 8:2

proaching,[s] 2and the chief priests and the
teachers of the law were looking for some
way to get rid of Jesus,[t] for they were afraid
of the people. 3Then Satan[u] entered Judas,
called Iscariot,[v] one of the Twelve. 4And
Judas went to the chief priests and the officers of the temple guard[w] and discussed
with them how he might betray Jesus.
5They were delighted and agreed to give
him money.[x] 6He consented, and watched
for an opportunity to hand Jesus over to
them when no crowd was present.

The Last Supper

7Then came the day of Unleavened
Bread on which the Passover lamb had to
be sacrificed.[y] 8Jesus sent Peter and John,[z]
saying, "Go and make preparations for us
to eat the Passover."

9"Where do you want us to prepare for
it?" they asked.

10He replied, "As you enter the city, a
man carrying a jar of water will meet you.
Follow him to the house that he enters,
11and say to the owner of the house, 'The
Teacher asks: Where is the guest room,
where I may eat the Passover with my disciples?' 12He will show you a large room
upstairs, all furnished. Make preparations
there."

13They left and found things just as Jesus
had told them.[a] So they prepared the Passover.

14When the hour came, Jesus and his
apostles[b] reclined at the table.[c] 15And he
said to them, "I have eagerly desired to
eat this Passover with you before I suffer.[d]
16For I tell you, I will not eat it again until it
finds fulfillment in the kingdom of God."[e]

17After taking the cup, he gave thanks
and said, "Take this and divide it among
you. 18For I tell you I will not drink again
from the fruit of the vine until the kingdom
of God comes."

19And he took bread, gave thanks and
broke it,[f] and gave it to them, saying, "This
is my body given for you; do this in remembrance of me."

20In the same way, after the supper he
took the cup, saying, "This cup is the new
covenant[g] in my blood, which is poured out
for you.[a] 21But the hand of him who is going to betray me is with mine on the table.[h]
22The Son of Man[i] will go as it has been
decreed.[j] But woe to that man who betrays
him!" 23They began to question among
themselves which of them it might be who
would do this.

24A dispute also arose among them as to
which of them was considered to be greatest.[k] 25Jesus said to them, "The kings of the
Gentiles lord it over them; and those who
exercise authority over them call themselves Benefactors. 26But you are not to be
like that. Instead, the greatest among you
should be like the youngest,[l] and the one
who rules like the one who serves.[m] 27For
who is greater, the one who is at the table
or the one who serves? Is it not the one
who is at the table? But I am among you
as one who serves.[n] 28You are those who
have stood by me in my trials. 29And I con-
fer on you a kingdom,[o] just as my Father
conferred one on me, 30so that you may eat
and drink at my table in my kingdom[p] and
sit on thrones, judging the twelve tribes of
Israel.[q]

31"Simon, Simon, Satan has asked[r] to sift
all of you as wheat.[s] 32But I have prayed for
you,[t] Simon, that your faith may not fail.
And when you have turned back, strength-
en your brothers."[u]

33But he replied, "Lord, I am ready to go
with you to prison and to death."[v]

34Jesus answered, "I tell you, Peter,

[a] *19,20* Some manuscripts do not have *given for you . . . poured out for you.*

---

the night of the tenth plague in Egypt. The Festival of Unleavened Bread celebrated the exodus.

22:4 ***officers.*** These were Levites who were members of the temple guard. They were the ones who could make the arrest.

22:11 – 12 ***guest room.*** Such rooms were often made available to the thousands of pilgrims who came to Jerusalem for the celebration of Passover and the Festival of Unleavened Bread. Such a room would contain couches for guests at the festivals to recline for the meal. Access to the room was probably gained by stairs on the outside of the house.

22:19 ***my body . . . do this in remembrance.*** Jesus instituted a new meal which is not only a memorial of His death, but also a fellowship meal of unity. It is a proclamation and a symbol of the believer's anticipation of Jesus' return, when all God's promises will be fulfilled (1 Cor. 10:16 – 17; 11:23 – 26).

22:20 ***This cup is the new covenant.*** The wine of the Lord's Supper depicts the giving of life, a sacrifice of blood, which inaugurated the new covenant for those who respond to Jesus' offer of salvation (Heb. 8:8,13; 9:11 – 28).

22:30 ***eat and drink . . . sit on thrones, judging.*** This is a promise of future blessing and authority. The disciples were promised a seat at the banquet of victory and the right to help Jesus rule over Israel on His return (Matt. 19:28; 2 Tim. 2:12).

22:32 ***I have prayed for you . . . you have turned back.*** The Greek word for *you* here is singular, referring specifically to Peter. In effect, Jesus restored Peter even before his fall (vv. 54 – 62), and He instructed the disciple to shepherd the saints by strengthening them.

22:1 [s] Jn 11:55 **22:2** [t] Mt 12:14 **22:3** [u] Mt 4:10; Jn 13:2 [v] Mt 10:4 **22:4** [w] ver 52; Ac 4:1; 5:24 **22:5** [x] Zec 11:12 **22:7** [y] Ex 12:18-20; Dt 16:5-8; Mk 14:12 **22:8** [z] Ac 3:1, 11; 4:13, 19; 8:14 **22:13** [a] Lk 19:32 **22:14** [b] Mk 6:30 [c] Mt 26:20; Mk 14:17, 18 **22:15** [d] Mt 16:21 **22:16** [e] Lk 14:15; Rev 19:9 **22:19** [f] Mt 14:19 **22:20** [g] Ex 24:8; Isa 42:6; Jer 31:31-34; Zec 9:11; 2Co 3:6; Heb 8:6; 9:15 **22:21** [h] Ps 41:9 **22:22** [i] Mt 8:20 [j] Ac 2:23; 4:28 **22:24** [k] Mk 9:34; Lk 9:46 **22:26** [l] 1Pe 5:5 [m] Mk 9:35; Lk 9:48 **22:27** [n] Mt 20:28; Lk 12:37 **22:29** [o] Mt 25:34; 2Ti 2:12 **22:30** [p] Lk 14:15 [q] Mt 19:28 **22:31** [r] Job 1:6-12 [s] Am 9:9 **22:32** [t] Jn 17:9, 15; Ro 8:34 [u] Jn 21:15-17 **22:33** [v] Jn 11:16

before the rooster crows today, you will
deny three times that you know me."
35 Then Jesus asked them, "When I sent
you without purse, bag or sandals,[w] did you
lack anything?"
"Nothing," they answered.
36 He said to them, "But now if you have
a purse, take it, and also a bag; and if you
don't have a sword, sell your cloak and buy
one. 37 It is written: 'And he was numbered
with the transgressors'[a];[x] and I tell you that
this must be fulfilled in me. Yes, what is
written about me is reaching its fulfillment."
38 The disciples said, "See, Lord, here are
two swords."
"That's enough!" he replied.

Jesus Prays on the Mount of Olives

39 Jesus went out as usual[y] to the Mount
of Olives,[z] and his disciples followed him.
40 On reaching the place, he said to them,
"Pray that you will not fall into temptation."[a] 41 He withdrew about a stone's throw
beyond them, knelt down[b] and prayed,
42 "Father, if you are willing, take this cup[c]
from me; yet not my will, but yours be
done."[d] 43 An angel from heaven appeared
to him and strengthened him.[e] 44 And being
in anguish, he prayed more earnestly, and
his sweat was like drops of blood falling to
the ground.[b]
45 When he rose from prayer and went
back to the disciples, he found them asleep,
exhausted from sorrow. 46 "Why are you
sleeping?" he asked them. "Get up and pray
so that you will not fall into temptation."[f]

Jesus Arrested

47 While he was still speaking a crowd
came up, and the man who was called Judas, one of the Twelve, was leading them.
He approached Jesus to kiss him, 48 but
Jesus asked him, "Judas, are you betraying
the Son of Man with a kiss?"
49 When Jesus' followers saw what was
going to happen, they said, "Lord, should
we strike with our swords?"[g] 50 And one of
them struck the servant of the high priest,
cutting off his right ear.
51 But Jesus answered, "No more of this!"
And he touched the man's ear and healed
him.
52 Then Jesus said to the chief priests,
the officers of the temple guard,[h] and the
elders, who had come for him, "Am I leading a rebellion, that you have come with
swords and clubs? 53 Every day I was with
you in the temple courts,[i] and you did not
lay a hand on me. But this is your hour[j]—
when darkness reigns."[k]

Peter Disowns Jesus

54 Then seizing him, they led him away
and took him into the house of the high
priest.[l] Peter followed at a distance.[m] 55 And
when some there had kindled a fire in the
middle of the courtyard and had sat down
together, Peter sat down with them. 56 A
servant girl saw him seated there in the
firelight. She looked closely at him and
said, "This man was with him."
57 But he denied it. "Woman, I don't know
him," he said.
58 A little later someone else saw him and
said, "You also are one of them."
"Man, I am not!" Peter replied.
59 About an hour later another asserted,
"Certainly this fellow was with him, for he
is a Galilean."[n]
60 Peter replied, "Man, I don't know
what you're talking about!" Just as he was
speaking, the rooster crowed. 61 The Lord[o]
turned and looked straight at Peter. Then
Peter remembered the word the Lord had
spoken to him: "Before the rooster crows
today, you will disown me three times."[p]
62 And he went outside and wept bitterly.

The Guards Mock Jesus

63 The men who were guarding Jesus
began mocking and beating him. 64 They
blindfolded him and demanded, "Prophesy! Who hit you?" 65 And they said many
other insulting things to him.[q]

Jesus Before Pilate and Herod

66 At daybreak the council[r] of the elders
of the people, both the chief priests and

[a] 37 Isaiah 53:12 [b] *43,44* Many early manuscripts do not have verses 43 and 44.

22:37 ***what is written.*** Jesus cited Isaiah 53:12, which describes a righteous one who suffers as a criminal. Jesus noted that His death would fulfill Isaiah's prediction.

22:42 ***this cup.*** This is a figure of speech for wrath (Ps. 11:6; 75:7–8; Jer. 25:15–16; Ezek. 23:31–34).

22:43 ***strengthened him.*** God's answer to Jesus' prayer did not allow His Son to avoid suffering. However, God did provide angelic help for Jesus to face what was coming. Sometimes God answers prayer by eliminating trials; sometimes He answers by strengthening us in the midst of them.

22:52 ***a rebellion.*** The Greek term for *rebellion* was used of both highway bandits and revolutionaries. Jesus rebuked His captors for treating Him as though He were a dangerous lawbreaker.

22:59 ***for he is a Galilean.*** According to Mark 14:70, Peter's accent gave him away as being from the same region as Jesus.

22:66 ***the elders of the people ... met together.*** The description here is of a major morning trial that involved all the Jewish religious leaders, the entire council or Sanhedrin. This trial violated various

22:35 [w] Mt 10:9, 10; Lk 9:3; 10:4 **22:37** [x] Isa 53:12
22:39 [y] Lk 21:37 [z] Mt 21:1 **22:40** [a] Mt 6:13
22:41 [b] Lk 18:11 **22:42** [c] Mt 20:22 [d] Mt 26:39
22:43 [e] Mt 4:11; Mk 1:13 **22:46** [f] ver 40 **22:49** [g] ver 38
22:52 [h] ver 4 **22:53** [i] Mt 26:55 [j] Jn 12:27 [k] Mt 8:12;
Jn 1:5; 3:20 **22:54** [l] Mt 26:57; Mk 14:53 [m] Mt 26:58;
Mk 14:54; Jn 18:15 **22:59** [n] Lk 23:6 **22:61** [o] Lk 7:13
[p] ver 34 **22:65** [q] Mt 16:21 **22:66** [r] Mt 5:22

the teachers of the law, met together,[s] and
Jesus was led before them. 67"If you are the
Messiah," they said, "tell us."
Jesus answered, "If I tell you, you will
not believe me, 68and if I asked you, you
would not answer.[t] 69But from now on, the
Son of Man will be seated at the right hand
of the mighty God."[u]
70They all asked, "Are you then the Son
of God?"[v]
He replied, "You say that I am."[w]
71Then they said, "Why do we need any
more testimony? We have heard it from his
own lips."
23 Then the whole assembly rose and
led him off to Pilate.[x] 2And they began to accuse him, saying, "We have found
this man subverting our nation.[y] He opposes payment of taxes to Caesar[z] and claims
to be Messiah, a king."[a]
3So Pilate asked Jesus, "Are you the king
of the Jews?"
"You have said so," Jesus replied.
4Then Pilate announced to the chief
priests and the crowd, "I find no basis for a
charge against this man."[b]
5But they insisted, "He stirs up the people
all over Judea by his teaching. He started
in Galilee[c] and has come all the way here."
6On hearing this, Pilate asked if the man
was a Galilean.[d] 7When he learned that
Jesus was under Herod's jurisdiction, he
sent him to Herod,[e] who was also in Jerusalem at that time.
8When Herod saw Jesus, he was greatly pleased, because for a long time he had
been wanting to see him.[f] From what he
had heard about him, he hoped to see him
perform a sign of some sort. 9He plied him
with many questions, but Jesus gave him
no answer.[g] 10The chief priests and the
teachers of the law were standing there,
vehemently accusing him. 11Then Herod
and his soldiers ridiculed and mocked him.
Dressing him in an elegant robe,[h] they sent
him back to Pilate. 12That day Herod and
Pilate became friends[i]—before this they
had been enemies.
13Pilate called together the chief priests,
the rulers and the people, 14and said to
them, "You brought me this man as one
who was inciting the people to rebellion.
I have examined him in your presence
and have found no basis for your charges
against him.[j] 15Neither has Herod, for he
sent him back to us; as you can see, he has
done nothing to deserve death. 16There-
fore, I will punish him[k] and then release
him." [17][a]
18But the whole crowd shouted, "Away
with this man! Release Barabbas to us!"[l]
19(Barabbas had been thrown into prison
for an insurrection in the city, and for murder.)
20Wanting to release Jesus, Pilate appealed to them again. 21But they kept
shouting, "Crucify him! Crucify him!"
22For the third time he spoke to them:
"Why? What crime has this man committed? I have found in him no grounds for the
death penalty. Therefore I will have him
punished and then release him."[m]
23But with loud shouts they insistently
demanded that he be crucified, and their
shouts prevailed. 24So Pilate decided to
grant their demand. 25He released the man
who had been thrown into prison for insurrection and murder, the one they asked for,
and surrendered Jesus to their will.

---

a *17* Some manuscripts include here words similar to Matt. 27:15 and Mark 15:6.

Jewish legal rules given in later sources: meeting on the morning of a festival; meeting at Caiaphas's home; trying a defendant without defense; and reaching the verdict in one day instead of the two days that were required for capital cases.

22:69 *at the right hand of the mighty God.* Jesus' reply here alludes to the regal enthronement image of Psalm 110:1. This reply is what convicted Him. Apparently what offended Jesus' audience was His claim to sit in God's presence and to exercise divine authority. In effect, His answer to their question about being the Christ was more than they expected. It was not blasphemous to claim to be Messiah. What was blasphemous was the claim to be the Judge of Jewish people, with God's authority.

23:2 *began to accuse.* Three charges were lodged against Jesus: (1) subverting the nation, (2) forbidding payment of taxes to Rome, and (3) claiming to be the Christ. The first charge, which was a general complaint, involved disturbing the peace. The other two charges could have been construed as challenges to Rome. The second charge was a blatant lie (20:20–26). The third charge was true, but not in the threatening sense that the prosecutors suggested. A three-part Roman procedure was followed at the trial; charges, examination, and verdict.

23:5 *they insisted.* By mentioning the charge that Jesus stirred up the people, the leaders suggested that Pilate risked being found derelict in his duty if he let Jesus go.

23:7 *Herod's jurisdiction.* Herod was responsible for Galilee, so Pilate "passed the buck" for the ruling and showed political courtesy at the same time.

23:16 *punish him and then release him.* Pilate hoped that a public whipping might satisfy the crowd and tame Jesus, avoiding the need to resort to the death penalty.

23:18–19 *Away with this man!* The entire crowd is portrayed as wanting Jesus to die. Luke makes it clear that Jesus' death was not only instigated by Jewish officials but approved by the Jewish people.

22:66 [s] Mt 27:1; Mk 15:1 **22:68** [t] Lk 20:3-8 **22:69** [u] Mk 16:19 **22:70** [v] Mt 4:3 [w] Mt 27:11; Lk 23:3 **23:1** [x] Mt 27:2; Mk 15:1; Jn 18:28 **23:2** [y] ver 14 [z] Lk 20:22 [a] Jn 19:12 **23:4** [b] ver 14, 22, 41; Mt 27:23; Jn 18:38; 1Ti 6:13; 2Co 5:21 **23:5** [c] Mk 1:14 **23:6** [d] Lk 22:59 **23:7** [e] Mt 14:1; Lk 3:1 **23:8** [f] Lk 9:9 **23:9** [g] Mk 14:61 **23:11** [h] Mk 15:17-19; Jn 19:2, 3 **23:12** [i] Ac 4:27 **23:14** [j] ver 4 **23:16** [k] ver 22; Mt 27:26; Jn 19:1; Ac 16:37; 2Co 11:23, 24 **23:18** [l] Ac 3:13, 14 **23:22** [m] ver 16

The Crucifixion of Jesus

26 As the soldiers led him away, they seized Simon from Cyrene,[n] who was on his way in from the country, and put the cross on him and made him carry it behind Jesus.[o] 27 A large number of people followed him, including women who mourned and wailed[p] for him. 28 Jesus turned and said to them, "Daughters of Jerusalem, do not weep for me; weep for yourselves and for your children.[q] 29 For the time will come when you will say, 'Blessed are the childless women, the wombs that never bore and the breasts that never nursed!'[r] 30 Then

"'they will say to the mountains, "Fall on us!"
and to the hills, "Cover us!"'[a][s]

31 For if people do these things when the tree is green, what will happen when it is dry?"[t]

32 Two other men, both criminals, were also led out with him to be executed.[u] 33 When they came to the place called the Skull, they crucified him there, along with the criminals—one on his right, the other on his left. 34 Jesus said, "Father,[v] forgive them, for they do not know what they are doing."[b][w] And they divided up his clothes by casting lots.[x]

35 The people stood watching, and the rulers even sneered at him.[y] They said, "He saved others; let him save himself if he is God's Messiah, the Chosen One."[z]

36 The soldiers also came up and mocked him.[a] They offered him wine vinegar[b] 37 and said, "If you are the king of the Jews,[c] save yourself."

38 There was a written notice above him, which read: THIS IS THE KING OF THE JEWS.[d]

39 One of the criminals who hung there hurled insults at him: "Aren't you the Messiah? Save yourself and us!"[e]

40 But the other criminal rebuked him. "Don't you fear God," he said, "since you are under the same sentence? 41 We are punished justly, for we are getting what our deeds deserve. But this man has done nothing wrong."[f]

42 Then he said, "Jesus, remember me when you come into your kingdom.[c]"[g]

43 Jesus answered him, "Truly I tell you, today you will be with me in paradise."[h]

The Death of Jesus

44 It was now about noon, and darkness came over the whole land until three in the afternoon,[i] 45 for the sun stopped shining. And the curtain of the temple[j] was torn in two.[k] 46 Jesus called out with a loud voice,[l] "Father, into your hands I commit my spirit."[d][m] When he had said this, he breathed his last.[n]

47 The centurion, seeing what had happened, praised God[o] and said, "Surely this was a righteous man." 48 When all the people who had gathered to witness this sight saw what took place, they beat their breasts[p] and went away. 49 But all those who knew him, including the women who had followed him from Galilee,[q] stood at a distance,[r] watching these things.

The Burial of Jesus

50 Now there was a man named Joseph, a member of the Council, a good and upright man, 51 who had not consented to their decision and action. He came from the Judean town of Arimathea, and he himself was waiting for the kingdom of God.[s] 52 Going to Pilate, he asked for Jesus' body. 53 Then he took it down, wrapped it in linen cloth and placed it in a tomb cut in the rock, one in which no one had yet been laid.

---

[a] *30* Hosea 10:8 [b] *34* Some early manuscripts do not have this sentence. [c] *42* Some manuscripts *come with your kingly power* [d] *46* Psalm 31:5

23:26 *Simon from Cyrene* was recruited to carry Jesus' cross. He was from a leading city of Libya.

23:28 *do not weep for me.* Though He was dying, Jesus pointed out that their weeping should be for Jerusalem and its inhabitants, since judgment was going to fall on the city (19:41 – 44). Jerusalem here represents the entire nation of Israel.

23:31 *what will happen when it is dry?* The idea here seems to be "If this is what is done to a live tree, what will happen to the dead one?" In other words, "If Jesus, the living tree, has not been spared, how much more will dead wood not be spared." This is Jesus' final lament over the nation of Israel.

23:33 *the place called the Skull.* The name of the place in Aramaic is Golgotha, which means "skull." Calvary is the Latin name for Golgotha. Possibly the name referred to a geographical feature of the locale, something that resembled a skull.

23:36 *wine vinegar.* Wine vinegar was inexpensive and quenched thirst better than water. It was a drink of the poor.

23:44 *noon ... three in the afternoon.* During these three hours, signs of creation revealed that the hour was not one of light but of darkness (22:53).

23:47 *Surely this was a righteous man.* If Jesus was righteous and innocent, then He is who He claimed to be. Thus a second figure besides the thief on the cross had insight into Jesus' death.

23:52 *Jesus' body.* There is no doubt that Jesus died. Efforts to explain the resurrection as something like a return from a coma are more impossible than the idea of the resurrection itself.

23:26 [n] Mt 27:32 [o] Mk 15:21; Jn 19:17 **23:27** [p] Lk 8:52 **23:28** [q] Lk 19:41-44; 21:23,24 **23:29** [r] Mt 24:19 **23:30** [s] Isa 2:19; Hos 10:8; Rev 6:16 **23:31** [t] Eze 20:47 **23:32** [u] Isa 53:12; Mt 27:38; Mk 15:27; Jn 19:18 **23:34** [v] Mt 11:25 [w] Mt 5:44 [x] Ps 22:18 **23:35** [y] Ps 22:17 [z] Isa 42:1 **23:36** [a] Ps 22:7 [b] Ps 69:21; Mt 27:48 **23:37** [c] Lk 4:3,9 **23:38** [d] Mt 2:2 **23:39** [e] ver 35,37 **23:41** [f] ver 4 **23:42** [g] Mt 16:27 **23:43** [h] 2Co 12:3,4; Rev 2:7 **23:44** [i] Am 8:9 **23:45** [j] Ex 26:31-33; Heb 9:3,8 [k] Heb 10:19,20 **23:46** [l] Mt 27:50 [m] Ps 31:5; 1Pe 2:23 [n] Jn 19:30 **23:47** [o] Mt 9:8 **23:48** [p] Lk 18:13 **23:49** [q] Lk 8:2 [r] Ps 38:11 **23:51** [s] Lk 2:25,38

54 It was Preparation Day,[t] and the Sabbath
was about to begin.
55 The women who had come with Jesus
from Galilee[u] followed Joseph and saw
the tomb and how his body was laid in it.
56 Then they went home and prepared spices and perfumes.[v] But they rested on the
Sabbath in obedience to the commandment.[w]

Jesus Has Risen

24 On the first day of the week, very
early in the morning, the women
took the spices they had prepared[x] and
went to the tomb. 2 They found the stone
rolled away from the tomb, 3 but when they
entered, they did not find the body of the
Lord Jesus.[y] 4 While they were wondering
about this, suddenly two men in clothes
that gleamed like lightning[z] stood beside
them. 5 In their fright the women bowed
down with their faces to the ground, but
the men said to them, "Why do you look
for the living among the dead? 6 He is not
here; he has risen! Remember how he told
you, while he was still with you in Galilee:[a]
7 'The Son of Man[b] must be delivered over
to the hands of sinners, be crucified and on
the third day be raised again.' "[c] 8 Then they
remembered his words.[d]
9 When they came back from the tomb,
they told all these things to the Eleven and
to all the others. 10 It was Mary Magdalene,
Joanna, Mary the mother of James, and the
others with them[e] who told this to the apostles.[f] 11 But they did not believe[g] the women,
because their words seemed to them like
nonsense. 12 Peter, however, got up and ran
to the tomb. Bending over, he saw the strips
of linen lying by themselves,[h] and he went
away,[i] wondering to himself what had happened.

On the Road to Emmaus

13 Now that same day two of them were
going to a village called Emmaus, about
seven miles[a] from Jerusalem.[j] 14 They were
talking with each other about everything
that had happened. 15 As they talked and
discussed these things with each other,
Jesus himself came up and walked along
with them;[k] 16 but they were kept from recognizing him.[l]
17 He asked them, "What are you discussing together as you walk along?"
They stood still, their faces downcast.
18 One of them, named Cleopas,[m] asked
him, "Are you the only one visiting Jerusalem who does not know the things that
have happened there in these days?"
19 "What things?" he asked.
"About Jesus of Nazareth,"[n] they replied.
"He was a prophet,[o] powerful in word and
deed before God and all the people. 20 The
chief priests and our rulers[p] handed him
over to be sentenced to death, and they crucified him; 21 but we had hoped that he was
the one who was going to redeem Israel.[q]
And what is more, it is the third day[r] since
all this took place. 22 In addition, some of
our women amazed us.[s] They went to the
tomb early this morning 23 but didn't find
his body. They came and told us that they
had seen a vision of angels, who said he was
alive. 24 Then some of our companions went
to the tomb and found it just as the women
had said, but they did not see Jesus."[t]
25 He said to them, "How foolish you are,
and how slow to believe all that the prophets have spoken! 26 Did not the Messiah
have to suffer these things and then enter
his glory?"[u] 27 And beginning with Moses[v]
and all the Prophets,[w] he explained to them

[a] *13* Or about 11 kilometers

23:54 *Preparation day.* Jesus was buried late on Friday, on the day called Preparation when everything was made ready for the Sabbath, the day when no labor could take place.

24:2 *They found the stone rolled away.* Matthew 28:2 mentions that an earthquake moved the stone, which would have fit in a channel in front of the entrance to the tomb. Moving the stone would have been possible, though difficult, for a group of people. The earthquake settles the question of how the stone was moved.

24:11 *they did not believe the women.* Skepticism reigned among the disciples. It is clear that they did not expect a resurrection. The disciples thought the women's story was nonsense.

24:12 *Peter ... got up and ran.* Having already experienced a fulfilled prediction of the Lord (22:54–62), Peter hurried to the tomb to check out the women's story. It is hard to say whether Peter believed in the resurrection when he left the tomb. At that point he was probably more amazed than anything else.

24:19–21 *Jesus of Nazareth ... He was a prophet powerful in word and deed.* These disciples on the road to Emmaus regarded Jesus as the Revealer of God's way and the Doer of His work.

24:23 *he was alive.* The women reported that there was no body found in Jesus' tomb, and that angels had announced to them that Jesus lives. The fact that the men were still sad indicates that they did not believe the report.

24:25 *slow to believe.* Jesus, who at this time was still not known to the travelers, rebuked His companions and reminded them of the things that the prophets taught.

24:27 *And beginning with Moses.* Going from the books of Moses to the Prophets, Jesus provided an overview of God's plan in the Scriptures. This plan

23:54 [t] Mt 27:62 **23:55** [u] ver 49 **23:56** [v] Mk 16:1; Lk 24:1 [w] Ex 12:16; 20:10 **24:1** [x] Lk 23:56 **24:3** [y] ver 23, 24 **24:4** [z] Jn 20:12 **24:6** [a] Mt 17:22, 23; Mk 9:30-31; Lk 9:22; 24:44 **24:7** [b] Mt 8:20 [c] Mt 16:21 **24:8** [d] Jn 2:22 **24:10** [e] Lk 8:1-3 [f] Mk 6:30 **24:11** [g] Mk 16:11 **24:12** [h] Jn 20:3-7 [i] Jn 20:10 **24:13** [j] Mk 16:12 **24:15** [k] ver 36 **24:16** [l] Jn 20:14; 21:4 **24:18** [m] Jn 19:25 **24:19** [n] Mk 1:24 [o] Mt 21:11 **24:20** [p] Lk 23:13 **24:21** [q] Lk 1:68; 2:38; 21:28 [r] Mt 16:21 **24:22** [s] ver 1-10 **24:24** [t] ver 12 **24:26** [u] Heb 2:10; 1Pe 1:11 **24:27** [v] Ge 3:15; Nu 21:9; Dt 18:15 [w] Isa 7:14; 9:6; 40:10, 11; 53; Eze 34:23; Da 9:24; Mic 7:20; Mal 3:1

what was said in all the Scriptures concerning himself.[x]

28 As they approached the village to which they were going, Jesus continued on as if he were going farther. 29 But they urged him strongly, "Stay with us, for it is nearly evening; the day is almost over." So he went in to stay with them.

30 When he was at the table with them, he took bread, gave thanks, broke it[y] and began to give it to them. 31 Then their eyes were opened and they recognized him,[z] and he disappeared from their sight. 32 They asked each other, "Were not our hearts burning within us[a] while he talked with us on the road and opened the Scriptures[b] to us?"

33 They got up and returned at once to Jerusalem. There they found the Eleven and those with them, assembled together 34 and saying, "It is true! The Lord has risen and has appeared to Simon."[c] 35 Then the two told what had happened on the way, and how Jesus was recognized by them when he broke the bread.[d]

Jesus Appears to the Disciples

36 While they were still talking about this, Jesus himself stood among them and said to them, "Peace be with you."[e]

37 They were startled and frightened, thinking they saw a ghost.[f] 38 He said to them, "Why are you troubled, and why do doubts rise in your minds? 39 Look at my hands and my feet. It is I myself! Touch me and see;[g] a ghost does not have flesh and bones, as you see I have."

40 When he had said this, he showed them his hands and feet. 41 And while they still did not believe it because of joy and amazement, he asked them, "Do you have anything here to eat?" 42 They gave him a piece of broiled fish, 43 and he took it and ate it in their presence.[h]

44 He said to them, "This is what I told you while I was still with you:[i] Everything must be fulfilled[j] that is written about me in the Law of Moses,[k] the Prophets and the Psalms."[l]

45 Then he opened their minds so they could understand the Scriptures. 46 He told them, "This is what is written: The Messiah will suffer and rise from the dead on the third day, 47 and repentance for the forgiveness of sins will be preached in his name[m] to all nations,[n] beginning at Jerusalem. 48 You are witnesses[o] of these things. 49 I am going to send you what my Father has promised;[p] but stay in the city until you have been clothed with power from on high."

The Ascension of Jesus

50 When he had led them out to the vicinity of Bethany,[q] he lifted up his hands and blessed them. 51 While he was blessing them, he left them and was taken up into heaven.[r] 52 Then they worshiped him and returned to Jerusalem with great joy. 53 And they stayed continually at the temple,[s] praising God.

---

is present throughout the entire Old Testament (Acts 3:22 – 26; 10:43).

24:39 *flesh and bones.* Jesus pointed out that a raised body is not a disembodied spirit. The presence of his body indicates that Jesus had been raised and that He was not a hallucination. He was raised in the same physical body in which He had been put to death. The difference was that His resurrected body is not corruptible and not subject to death.

24:46 *The Messiah will suffer and rise from the dead.* Two parts of God's plan had been fulfilled. Jesus had been crucified and raised from the dead. Old Testament texts that predict these events are Psalm 22 and Psalm 118:22.

24:49 *what my Father has promised.* This is a reference to the baptism of the Holy Spirit at Pentecost (Acts 2:4). It was promised in Jeremiah 31:31 – 33, and in Joel 2:28. Peter called this coming of the Spirit "the beginning" (Acts 11:15) because the real fulfillment of God's promise of salvation would start in those people united by the Spirit to establish the church.

24:27 [x] Jn 1:45 **24:30** [y] Mt 14:19 **24:31** [z] ver 16 **24:32** [a] Ps 39:3 [b] ver 27,45 **24:34** [c] 1Co 15:5 **24:35** [d] ver 30,31 **24:36** [e] Jn 20:19,21,26; 14:27 **24:37** [f] Mk 6:49 **24:39** [g] Jn 20:27; 1Jn 1:1 **24:43** [h] Ac 10:41 **24:44** [i] Lk 9:45; 18:34 [j] Mt 16:21; Lk 9:22,44; 18:31-33; 22:37 [k] ver 27 [l] Ps 2; 16; 22; 69; 72; 110; 118 **24:47** [m] Ac 5:31; 10:43; 13:38 [n] Mt 28:19 **24:48** [o] Ac 1:8; 2:32; 5:32; 13:31; 1Pe 5:1 **24:49** [p] Jn 14:16; Ac 1:4 **24:50** [q] Mt 21:17 **24:51** [r] 2Ki 2:11 **24:53** [s] Ac 2:46

JOHN

▸ **AUTHOR:** Jesus nicknamed John and his brother, James, "sons of thunder" (Mark 3:17). John was evidently among the Galileans who followed John the Baptist until they were called to follow Jesus at the outset of His public ministry. These Galileans were later called to become full-time disciples of the Lord (Luke 5:1 – 11), and John was among the twelve men who were selected to be apostles (Luke 6:12 – 16). The author of this Gospel is identified only as the disciple "whom Jesus loved" (John 13:23; 19:26; 21:7), but attention to detail concerning geography and Jewish culture in the Gospel lend credibility to the author's claim to be an eyewitness. The strong testimony of the early church relates this eyewitness to the apostle John.

▸ **TIME:** c. A.D. 29 – 33 ▸ **KEY VERSES:** John 20:30 – 31

▸ **THEME:** John is a great book for new or young Christians because it intentionally helps the reader understand the significance of Jesus. What becomes increasingly clear as you read the Gospel of John is that Jesus does not fit the image of someone who is simply a nice moral teacher. Only a lunatic would make the claims he makes for himself unless he was who he said he was. John leaves no room for indecision. Like the many people Jesus encounters in the book, as you read, you must either reject him or accept him, and say in the end like Thomas: "My Lord and my God" (20:28). This Gospel is an incredibly powerful presentation of Jesus.

The Word Became Flesh

1 In the beginning was the Word,[a] and the
Word was with God,[b] and the Word was
God.[c] 2He was with God in the beginning.[d]
3Through him all things were made; without him nothing was made that has been
made.[e] 4In him was life,[f] and that life was
the light[g] of all mankind. 5The light shines
in the darkness, and the darkness has not
overcome[a] it.[h]
6There was a man sent from God whose
name was John.[i] 7He came as a witness
to testify[j] concerning that light, so that
through him all might believe.[k] 8He himself was not the light; he came only as a
witness to the light.
9The true light[l] that gives light to everyone[m] was coming into the world. 10He was
in the world, and though the world was
made through him,[n] the world did not recognize him. 11He came to that which was
his own, but his own did not receive him.

[a] 5 Or *understood*

1:1 ***In the beginning.*** Genesis 1:1 starts with the moment of creation and moves forward to the creation of humanity. John 1:1 starts with creation and contemplates eternity past. ***the Word was with God.*** This suggests a face-to-face relationship. In the ancient world, it was important that persons of equal station be on the same level when seated across from one another.
1:3 ***Through him all things were made.*** God the Father created the world (Gen. 1:1) through God the Son (Col. 1:16; Heb. 1:2). All creation was made through Him. Thus, He is the Creator God.
1:4 ***light of all mankind.*** This image conveys the concept of revelation. As the light, Jesus Christ reveals both sin and God to humans (Ps. 36:9). Later in this Gospel, Christ declares Himself to be both the life (11:25) and the light (8:12). Death and darkness flee when the life and light enter.
1:5 ***light shines in the darkness.*** Although Satan and his forces resist the light, they cannot thwart its power. In short, Jesus is life and light; those who accept Him are "sons of light" (12:35 – 36). As the creation of light was the beginning of the original creation, so, when believers receive the light, they become part of the new creation (2 Cor. 4:3 – 6).
1:7 ***as a witness.*** This phrase means "to testify" or "to declare." John uses the word translated *witness* 33 times as a verb and 14 times as a noun in his Gospel. The term is particularly important to his purpose, which is to record adequate witnesses to Jesus as the Messiah so that individuals might believe Him (20:30 – 31). ***believe.*** This word means "to trust." John uses this verb almost 100 times in his Gospel to express what must take place for a person to receive the gift of eternal life.
1:11 ***receive.*** This means "to receive with favor" and

1:1 [a] Rev 19:13 [b] Jn 17:5; 1Jn 1:2 [c] Php 2:6 **1:2** [d] Ge 1:1 **1:3** [e] 1Co 8:6; Col 1:16; Heb 1:2 **1:4** [f] Jn 5:26; 11:25; 14:6 [g] Jn 8:12 **1:5** [h] Jn 3:19 **1:6** [i] Mt 3:1 **1:7** [j] ver 15, 19, 32 [k] ver 12 **1:9** [l] 1Jn 2:8 [m] Isa 49:6 **1:10** [n] Heb 1:2

12Yet to all who did receive him, to those
who believed[o] in his name,[p] he gave the
right to become children of God[q]— 13chil-
dren born not of natural descent, nor of human decision or a husband's will, but born
of God.[r]
14The Word became flesh[s] and made his
dwelling among us. We have seen his glory, the glory of the one and only Son, who
came from the Father, full of grace and
truth.[t]
15(John testified[u] concerning him. He
cried out, saying, "This is the one I spoke
about when I said, 'He who comes after
me has surpassed me because he was
before me.' ")[v] 16Out of his fullness[w] we
have all received grace in place of grace
already given. 17For the law was given
through Moses;[x] grace and truth came
through Jesus Christ.[y] 18No one has ever
seen God,[z] but the one and only Son,
who is himself God and[aa] is in closest
relationship with the Father, has made
him known.

John the Baptist Denies Being the Messiah

19Now this was John's testimony when
the Jewish leaders[bb] in Jerusalem sent
priests and Levites to ask him who he was.
20He did not fail to confess, but confessed
freely, "I am not the Messiah."[c]
21They asked him, "Then who are you?
Are you Elijah?"[d]
He said, "I am not."
"Are you the Prophet?"[e]
He answered, "No."
22Finally they said, "Who are you?
Give us an answer to take back to those
who sent us. What do you say about yourself?"
23John replied in the words of Isaiah the
prophet, "I am the voice of one calling in
the wilderness,[f] 'Make straight the way for
the Lord.' "[cg]
24Now the Pharisees who had been sent
25questioned him, "Why then do you baptize if you are not the Messiah, nor Elijah,
nor the Prophet?"
26"I baptize with[d] water," John replied,
"but among you stands one you do not
know. 27He is the one who comes after me,[h]
the straps of whose sandals I am not worthy to untie."
28This all happened at Bethany on the
other side of the Jordan,[i] where John was
baptizing.

---

[a] *18* Some manuscripts *but the only Son, who*
[b] *19* The Greek term traditionally translated *the Jews* (*hoi Ioudaioi*) refers here and elsewhere in John's Gospel to those Jewish leaders who opposed Jesus; also in 5:10, 15, 16; 7:1, 11, 13; 9:22; 18:14, 28, 36; 19:7, 12, 31, 38; 20:19. [c] *23* Isaiah 40:3
[d] *26* Or *in*; also in verses 31 and 33 (twice)

---

implies "welcome." Instead of a welcome mat, Jesus had a door slammed in His face. The themes of rejection and reception (v. 12) introduced in the prologue (1:1–18) appear repeatedly throughout the Gospel of John.

1:12 ***he gave the right.*** This phrase refers to the legitimate entitlement to the position of children of God. By believing, undeserving sinners can become full members of God's family.

1:14 ***The Word became flesh.*** The Son of God who was from eternity became human, with limitations in time and space (Phil. 2:5–8). This is the doctrine of the incarnation: God became human. Nothing of the essential nature of deity was lost in this event; we might rephrase *became* as "took to Himself." John uses the word *flesh* to refer to the physical nature of humans, not to our sinful disposition. ***made his dwelling among us.*** The Greek word for *tent* or *dwelling* was also used in the Greek Old Testament for the tabernacle, where the presence of God dwelt. ***one and only.*** This means unique, one of a kind.

1:16 ***grace in place of grace.*** The background of this doubled term, as well as the use of the term in verse 17, is found in Exodus 32–34. Moses and the people had received grace, but they were in tremendous need of more grace (Ex. 33:13).

1:18 ***No one has ever seen God.*** God is Spirit (4:24) and is invisible (Col. 1:15; 1 Tim. 1:17) unless God chooses to reveal Himself. Humans cannot look at God and live (Ex. 33:20). However, the Son is in intimate relationship with the Father, face-to-face with God (1:1; 6:46; 1 John 1:2). God became visible to human eyes in the man Jesus. It is through seeing the Son that we see God.

1:19–20 ***the Jewish leaders.*** This refers to the Jewish leaders or the council (the Sanhedrin), who would be responsible for examining anyone thought to be a prophet, to see if the person was true or false.

1:23 ***Make straight.*** When a king traveled, roads were built so that the royal chariot would not have to travel over rough terrain or be stuck in the mud. Isaiah was saying that before God appeared to manifest His glory, a voice would be heard, inviting Israel to make straight the way by which God Himself would come.

1:24 ***the Pharisees.*** The Pharisees were an influential sect that numbered about 6,000. As strict interpreters of the law in Israel, they were extremely zealous for ritual and tradition.

1:27 ***the straps of whose sandals I am not worthy to untie.*** Undoing the shoe strap was the job of a slave. The Jewish Talmud says, "Everything that a servant will do for his master, a scholar shall perform for his teacher, except the menial task of loosing his sandal thong." Thus, John was saying that "Jesus Christ is the living Lord and I am the voice, His servant and slave. Actually, I'm not even worthy to be His slave."

1:12 [o] ver 7 [p] 1Jn 3:23 [q] Gal 3:26 **1:13** [r] Jn 3:6; Jas 1:18; 1Pe 1:23; 1Jn 3:9 **1:14** [s] Gal 4:4; Php 2:7,8; 1Ti 3:16; Heb 2:14 [t] Jn 14:6 **1:15** [u] ver 7 [v] ver 30; Mt 3:11 **1:16** [w] Eph 1:23; Col 1:19 **1:17** [x] Jn 7:19 [y] ver 14 **1:18** [z] Ex 33:20; Jn 6:46; Col 1:15; 1Ti 6:16 [a] Jn 3:16,18; 1Jn 4:9 **1:19** [b] Jn 2:18; 5:10,16; 6:41,52 **1:20** [c] Jn 3:28; Lk 3:15,16 **1:21** [d] Mt 11:14 [e] Dt 18:15 **1:23** [f] Mt 3:1 [g] Isa 40:3 **1:27** [h] ver 15,30 **1:28** [i] Jn 3:26; 10:40

John Testifies About Jesus

29The next day John saw Jesus coming
toward him and said, "Look, the Lamb of
God,[j] who takes away the sin of the world!
30This is the one I meant when I said, 'A
man who comes after me has surpassed
me because he was before me.'[k] 31I myself
did not know him, but the reason I came
baptizing with water was that he might be
revealed to Israel."
32Then John gave this testimony: "I saw
the Spirit come down from heaven as a
dove and remain on him.[l] 33And I myself
did not know him, but the one who sent me
to baptize with water[m] told me, 'The man
on whom you see the Spirit come down and
remain is the one who will baptize with the
Holy Spirit.'[n] 34I have seen and I testify that
this is God's Chosen One."[a][o]

John's Disciples Follow Jesus

35The next day John[p] was there again
with two of his disciples. 36When he saw
Jesus passing by, he said, "Look, the Lamb
of God!"[q]
37When the two disciples heard him
say this, they followed Jesus. 38Turning
around, Jesus saw them following and
asked, "What do you want?"
They said, "Rabbi"[r] (which means
"Teacher"), "where are you staying?"
39"Come," he replied, "and you will see."
So they went and saw where he was staying, and they spent that day with him. It
was about four in the afternoon.
40Andrew, Simon Peter's brother, was
one of the two who heard what John had
said and who had followed Jesus. 41The
first thing Andrew did was to find his
brother Simon and tell him, "We have
found the Messiah" (that is, the Christ).[s]
42And he brought him to Jesus.
Jesus looked at him and said, "You are
Simon son of John. You will be called[t]
Cephas" (which, when translated, is Peter[b]).[u]

Jesus Calls Philip and Nathanael

43The next day Jesus decided to leave
for Galilee. Finding Philip,[v] he said to him,
"Follow me."[w]
44Philip, like Andrew and Peter, was
from the town of Bethsaida.[x] 45Philip
found Nathanael[y] and told him, "We have
found the one Moses wrote about in the
Law,[z] and about whom the prophets also
wrote[a]—Jesus of Nazareth,[b] the son of Joseph."[c]
46"Nazareth! Can anything good come
from there?"[d] Nathanael asked.
"Come and see," said Philip.
47When Jesus saw Nathanael approaching, he said of him, "Here truly is an Israelite[e] in whom there is no deceit."[f]
48"How do you know me?" Nathanael
asked.
Jesus answered, "I saw you while you
were still under the fig tree before Philip
called you."
49Then Nathanael declared, "Rabbi,[g] you
are the Son of God;[h] you are the king of
Israel."[i]
50Jesus said, "You believe[c] because I told
you I saw you under the fig tree. You will
see greater things than that." 51He then
added, "Very truly I tell you,[d] you[d] will see
'heaven open,[j] and the angels of God ascending and descending[k] on'[e] the Son of
Man."[l]

Jesus Changes Water Into Wine

2 On the third day a wedding took place
at Cana in Galilee.[m] Jesus' mother[n] was

[a] *34* See Isaiah 42:1; many manuscripts *is the Son of God.* [b] *42 Cephas* (Aramaic) and *Peter* (Greek) both mean *rock.* [c] *50* Or *Do you believe . . . ?* [d] *51* The Greek is plural. [e] *51* Gen. 28:12

1:29 *the Lamb of God.* Jesus Christ is the Lamb that God would give as a sacrifice not only for Israel, but for the whole world (Is. 52:13 – 53:12).

1:33 *the one who will baptize with the Holy Spirit.* Seven times, the New Testament mentions this ministry of Jesus. Five are prophetic (Matt. 3:11; Mark 1:8; Luke 3:16; Acts 1:5); one is historical (Acts 11:16 – 18); one is doctrinal (1 Cor. 12:13).

1:42 *Cephas.* This is the Aramaic word for "rock" (Matt. 16:18).

1:45 *Nathanael.* This name is not mentioned in the Synoptic Gospels. But in every list of the apostles in Matthew, Mark, and Luke, the name Bartholomew is listed with Philip, as Nathanael is linked with Philip here. It is likely that Nathanael and Bartholomew were the same person.

1:46 *Nazareth.* Nathanael knew that the Old Testament prophets had predicted that the Messiah would be born in Bethlehem. Furthermore, Nazareth was an obscure village. Nathanael simply could not fathom that such a significant person as the Messiah could come from such an insignificant place as Nazareth.

1:48 – 49 *under the fig tree.* In the Old Testament, this expression often suggests being safe and at leisure (1 Kin. 4:25; Mic. 4:4; Zech. 3:10).

2:1 – 2 *Cana.* This city was about four and a half miles northwest of Nazareth. ***Jesus' mother was there, and Jesus and his disciples had also been invited to the wedding.*** This suggests that Jesus and His disciples were invited because of Mary. Her forwardness in asking Jesus to help when the wine ran out (v. 3) may indicate that she was in some way related to the family holding the wedding.

1:29 [j] ver 36; Isa 53:7; 1Pe 1:19; Rev 5:6 **1:30** [k] ver 15, 27 **1:32** [l] Mt 3:16; Mk 1:10 **1:33** [m] Mk 1:4 [n] Mt 3:11; Mk 1:8 **1:34** [o] ver 49; Mt 4:3 **1:35** [p] Mt 3:1 **1:36** [q] ver 29 **1:38** [r] ver 49; Mt 23:7 **1:41** [s] Jn 4:25 **1:42** [t] Ge 17:5, 15 [u] Mt 16:18 **1:43** [v] Mt 10:3; Jn 6:5-7; 12:21, 22; 14:8, 9 [w] Mt 4:19 **1:44** [x] Mt 11:21; Jn 12:21 **1:45** [y] Jn 21:2 [z] Lk 24:27 [a] Lk 24:27 [b] Mt 2:23; Mk 1:24 [c] Lk 3:23 **1:46** [d] Jn 7:41, 42, 52 **1:47** [e] Ro 9:4, 6 [f] Ps 32:2 **1:49** [g] ver 38; Mt 23:7 [h] ver 34; Mt 4:3 [i] Mt 2:2; 27:42; Jn 12:13 **1:51** [j] Mt 3:16 [k] Ge 28:12 [l] Mt 8:20 **2:1** [m] Jn 4:46; 21:2 [n] Mt 12:46

there, 2and Jesus and his disciples had also been invited to the wedding. 3When the wine was gone, Jesus' mother said to him, "They have no more wine."

4"Woman,[a][o] why do you involve me?"[p] Jesus replied. "My hour[q] has not yet come."

5His mother said to the servants, "Do whatever he tells you."[r]

6Nearby stood six stone water jars, the kind used by the Jews for ceremonial washing,[s] each holding from twenty to thirty gallons.[b]

7Jesus said to the servants, "Fill the jars with water"; so they filled them to the brim.

8Then he told them, "Now draw some out and take it to the master of the banquet."

They did so, 9and the master of the banquet tasted the water that had been turned into wine.[t] He did not realize where it had come from, though the servants who had drawn the water knew. Then he called the bridegroom aside 10and said, "Everyone brings out the choice wine first and then the cheaper wine after the guests have had too much to drink; but you have saved the best till now."

11What Jesus did here in Cana of Galilee was the first of the signs[u] through which he revealed his glory;[v] and his disciples believed in him.[w]

12After this he went down to Capernaum[x] with his mother and brothers[y] and his disciples. There they stayed for a few days.

Jesus Clears the Temple Courts

13When it was almost time for the Jewish Passover,[z] Jesus went up to Jerusalem.[a] 14In the temple courts he found people selling cattle, sheep and doves, and others sitting at tables exchanging money. 15So he made a whip out of cords, and drove all from the temple courts, both sheep and cattle; he scattered the coins of the money changers and overturned their tables. 16To those who sold doves he said, "Get these out of here! Stop turning my Father's house[b] into a market!" 17His disciples remembered that it is written: "Zeal for your house will consume me."[c][c]

18The Jews then responded to him, "What sign can you show us to prove your authority to do all this?"[d]

19Jesus answered them, "Destroy this temple, and I will raise it again in three days."[e]

20They replied, "It has taken forty-six years to build this temple, and you are going to raise it in three days?" 21But the temple he had spoken of was his body.[f] 22After he was raised from the dead, his disciples recalled what he had said.[g] Then they believed the scripture and the words that Jesus had spoken.

23Now while he was in Jerusalem at the Passover Festival,[h] many people saw the

---

[a] *4* The Greek for *Woman* does not denote any disrespect. [b] *6* Or from about 75 to about 115 liters [c] *17* Psalm 69:9

2:3 ***They have no more wine.*** Hospitality in the East was a sacred duty. A wedding feast often lasted for a week. To run out of wine at such an important event would have been humiliating for the bride and groom. The family of Jesus was not wealthy, and it is likely their relatives and acquaintances were not either. This may have been a "low-budget" wedding feast.

2:6 ***six stone water jars.*** Each jar held 20–30 gallons, for a total of 120–180 gallons of the finest wine (v. 10). ***by the Jews for ceremonial washing.*** Jewish tradition required several kinds of ceremonial washings. Strict Jews washed their hands before a meal, between courses, and after the meal. This "purifying" extended not only to washing hands, but also to washing cups and vessels (Mark 7:3–4).

2:11 ***the first of the signs.*** In the Gospel of John, the miracles of Jesus are called signs, indicating that they pointed to His messiahship. This sign signified Christ's glory—that is, His deity. When Jesus transformed water into wine, He demonstrated His power.

2:13 ***the Jewish Passover.*** Every male Jew was required to go to Jerusalem three times a year—for the Festival of Passover, the Festival of Weeks, and the Festival of Tabernacles (Ex. 23:14–19; Lev. 23). ***Jerusalem.*** The Synoptic Gospels concentrate on Jesus' Galilean ministry. John focuses on Jesus' ministry in Jerusalem.

2:14 ***In the temple courts he found people selling cattle, sheep and doves.*** The Synoptic Gospels place the cleansing of the temple at the conclusion of Jesus' ministry (Matt. 21:12–13), whereas John puts it at the beginning. Apparently, Jesus cleansed the temple two different times. The law of Moses required that any animal offered in sacrifice be unblemished and that every Jewish male over 19 years of age pay a temple tax (Lev. 1:3; Deut. 17:1). As a result, tax collectors and inspectors of sacrificial animals were present at the temple. However, these officials would not accept secular coins because they had an image of the Roman emperor. To put such coins into the temple treasury was thought to be an offense. Accordingly, merchants and moneychangers set up shop and charged high prices for changing currency and for sacrificial animals.

2:19 ***Destroy this temple.*** Jesus was not talking about the physical building; He was referring to His body, as John emphasizes in verse 21. Jesus was speaking of His death. ***I will raise it again.*** Note that Jesus did not say, "I will build it again." He was referring to His resurrection, three days after His death.

2:20 ***forty-six years.*** Herod the Great began restoring the temple in 20 B.C. The work was not finished at the time of this conversation. In fact, it was not completed until around A.D. 64 under Herod Agrippa.

2:23 ***many people … believed in his name.*** This was saving faith. John's purpose in recording Jesus'

2:4 [o] Jn 19:26 [p] Mt 8:29 [q] Mt 26:18; Jn 7:6 **2:5** [r] Ge 41:55 **2:6** [s] Mk 7:3,4; Jn 3:25 **2:9** [t] Jn 4:46 **2:11** [u] ver 23; Jn 3:2; 4:48; 6:2,14,26,30; 12:37; 20:30 [v] Jn 1:14 [w] Ex 14:31 **2:12** [x] Mt 4:13 [y] Mt 12:46 **2:13** [z] Jn 11:55 [a] Dt 16:1-6; Lk 2:41 **2:16** [b] Lk 2:49 **2:17** [c] Ps 69:9 **2:18** [d] Mt 12:38 **2:19** [e] Mt 26:61; 27:40; Mk 14:58; 15:29 **2:21** [f] 1Co 6:19 **2:22** [g] Lk 24:5-8; Jn 12:16; 14:26 **2:23** [h] ver 13

signs he was performing and believed in
his name.[a] 24But Jesus would not entrust
himself to them, for he knew all people.
25He did not need any testimony about
mankind, for he knew what was in each
person.[i]

Jesus Teaches Nicodemus

3 Now there was a Pharisee, a man
named Nicodemus[j] who was a member
of the Jewish ruling council.[k] 2He came to
Jesus at night and said, "Rabbi, we know
that you are a teacher who has come from
God. For no one could perform the signs[l]
you are doing if God were not with him."[m]
3Jesus replied, "Very truly I tell you, no
one can see the kingdom of God unless
they are born again.[b]"[n]
4"How can someone be born when they
are old?" Nicodemus asked. "Surely they
cannot enter a second time into their mother's womb to be born!"
5Jesus answered, "Very truly I tell you,
no one can enter the kingdom of God unless they are born of water and the Spirit.[o]
6Flesh gives birth to flesh, but the Spirit[c]
gives birth to spirit.[p] 7You should not be
surprised at my saying, 'You[d] must be born
again.' 8The wind blows wherever it pleases. You hear its sound, but you cannot tell
where it comes from or where it is going.
So it is with everyone born of the Spirit."[e]
9"How can this be?"[q] Nicodemus asked.
10"You are Israel's teacher,"[r] said Jesus,
"and do you not understand these things?
11Very truly I tell you, we speak of what
we know,[s] and we testify to what we have
seen, but still you people do not accept
our testimony.[t] 12I have spoken to you of
earthly things and you do not believe; how
then will you believe if I speak of heavenly
things? 13No one has ever gone into heav-
en[u] except the one who came from heav-
en[v]—the Son of Man.[f] 14Just as Moses
lifted up the snake in the wilderness,[w] so
the Son of Man must be lifted up,[g][x] 15that
everyone who believes[y] may have eternal
life in him."[h]
16For God so loved[z] the world that he
gave his one and only Son, that whoever
believes in him shall not perish but have
eternal life.[a] 17For God did not send his Son
into the world[b] to condemn the world, but
to save the world through him.[c] 18Who-
ever believes in him is not condemned,[d]
but whoever does not believe stands

---

[a] *23* Or *in him* [b] *3* The Greek for *again* also means *from above*; also in verse 7. [c] *6* Or *but spirit* [d] *7* The Greek is plural. [e] *8* The Greek for *Spirit* is the same as that for *wind.* [f] *13* Some manuscripts *Man, who is in heaven* [g] *14* The Greek for *lifted up* also means *exalted.* [h] *15* Some interpreters end the quotation with verse 21.

---

miracles was for people to believe and have eternal life (20:30–31).

2:24 *But Jesus would not entrust himself to them.* The word translated *entrust* is the same Greek word translated *believe* in verse 23. There is a play on words here. These individuals trusted Jesus, but Jesus did not entrust Himself to them.

3:2 *at night.* The fact that Nicodemus came to Jesus at night may reveal the timidity of his faith (12:42); however, his faith was developing (7:50–51; 19:39).

3:3 *unless they are born again.* Jesus was explaining to Nicodemus that there is more to having a right relationship with God than being physically born a Jew. The new birth is not physical; rather, it is spiritual (v. 6). It must come by the Spirit of God if it is a spiritual birth (v. 5).

3:5 *born of water and the Spirit.* There are several interpretations of this phrase. (1) Jesus was referring to water baptism (Acts 10:43–47). (2) Water is to be understood as a symbol for the Holy Spirit. (3) Water is to be understood as a symbol of the Word of God. (4) Jesus used the phrase "born of water" to refer to physical birth. He then used the contrasting phrase "of the Spirit" to refer to spiritual birth. (5) Jesus used the phrase "born of water" to refer to John the Baptist's baptism. (6) Jesus used the Old Testament imagery of "water" and "wind" to refer to the work of God from above (Is. 44:3–5).

3:8 *The wind.* Jesus used the wind as an illustration of the work of the Holy Spirit. The Greek word translated *Spirit* also means "wind." As the wind seemingly blows where it wills, so the Holy Spirit sovereignly works. Likewise, no one knows the origin or destination of the wind, but everyone knows it is there. The same is true of the Holy Spirit.

3:12 *heavenly things.* This refers to events like Christ's ascension (6:61–62) and the coming of the Holy Spirit (16:7).

3:14 *lifted up.* Every time these words occur in the Gospel of John, there is a reference to Jesus' death (8:28; 12:32,34). ***as Moses lifted up the snake in the wilderness.*** Those who looked at it lived (Num. 21:9). So it is with the Son of Man (1:51).

3:16 Belief—Belief involves understanding, knowing, living, and being committed to a relationship with God. How one does all that is so different from not doing it, it is like being born again to a new life. Nicodemus had a little knowledge. What Nicodemus failed to understand was the nature of spiritual reality. He was earthbound and didn't understand that Jesus and belief are God things. He could not get from where he was to where Jesus was on the road of his understanding. He needed to accept a new road, namely the one Jesus was walking, toward Him. Jesus draws us to that light, His light. We have to respond to it as Nicodemus did over time (John 7:50; 19:39). Belief involves internalizing these truths with our whole hearts and minds, being born again, letting all of ourselves be exposed to, and by, that light.

2:25 [i] Mt 9:4; Jn 6:61,64; 13:11 **3:1** [j] Jn 7:50; 19:39 [k] Lk 23:13 **3:2** [l] Jn 9:16,33 [m] Ac 2:22; 10:38 **3:3** [n] Jn 1:13; 1Pe 1:23 **3:5** [o] Titus 3:5 **3:6** [p] Jn 1:13; 1Co 15:50 **3:9** [q] Jn 6:52,60 **3:10** [r] Lk 2:46 **3:11** [s] Jn 1:18; 7:16,17 [t] ver 32 **3:13** [u] Pr 30:4; Ac 2:34; Eph 4:8-10 [v] Jn 6:38,42 **3:14** [w] Nu 21:8,9 [x] Jn 8:28; 12:32 **3:15** [y] ver 16,36 **3:16** [z] Ro 5:8; Eph 2:4; 1Jn 4:9,10 [a] ver 36; Jn 6:29,40; 11:25,26 **3:17** [b] Jn 6:29,57; 10:36; 11:42; 17:8,21; 20:21 [c] Jn 12:47; 1Jn 4:14 **3:18** [d] Jn 5:24

condemned already because they have not believed in the name of God's one and only Son.[e] 19This is the verdict: Light[f] has come into the world, but people loved darkness instead of light because their deeds were evil. 20Everyone who does evil hates the light, and will not come into the light for fear that their deeds will be exposed.[g] 21But whoever lives by the truth comes into the light, so that it may be seen plainly that what they have done has been done in the sight of God.

John Testifies Again About Jesus

22After this, Jesus and his disciples went out into the Judean countryside, where he spent some time with them, and baptized.[h] 23Now John also was baptizing at Aenon near Salim, because there was plenty of water, and people were coming and being baptized. 24(This was before John was put in prison.)[i] 25An argument developed between some of John's disciples and a certain Jew over the matter of ceremonial washing.[j] 26They came to John and said to him, "Rabbi,[k] that man who was with you on the other side of the Jordan—the one you testified[l] about—look, he is baptizing, and everyone is going to him."

27To this John replied, "A person can receive only what is given them from heaven. 28You yourselves can testify that I said, 'I am not the Messiah but am sent ahead of him.'[m] 29The bride belongs to the bridegroom.[n] The friend who attends the bridegroom waits and listens for him, and is full of joy when he hears the bridegroom's voice. That joy is mine, and it is now complete.[o] 30He must become greater; I must become less."[a]

31The one who comes from above[p] is above all; the one who is from the earth belongs to the earth, and speaks as one from the earth.[q] The one who comes from heaven is above all. 32He testifies to what he has seen and heard,[r] but no one accepts his testimony.[s] 33Whoever has accepted it has certified that God is truthful. 34For the one whom God has sent[t] speaks the words of God, for God[b] gives the Spirit[u] without limit. 35The Father loves the Son and has placed everything in his hands.[v] 36Whoever believes in the Son has eternal life,[w] but whoever rejects the Son will not see life, for God's wrath remains on them.

Jesus Talks With a Samaritan Woman

4 Now Jesus learned that the Pharisees had heard that he was gaining and baptizing more disciples than John[x]— 2although in fact it was not Jesus who baptized, but his disciples. 3So he left Judea[y] and went back once more to Galilee.

4Now he had to go through Samaria.

---

a *30* Some interpreters end the quotation with verse 36. *b* *34* Greek *he*

3:20 *Everyone who does evil hates the light.* People offer many excuses for not accepting Christ. Some cite the presence of hypocrites in the church. Others claim inability to believe some of the truths about Christ or the gospel. These are merely attempts to conceal a heart in rebellion against God. The ultimate reason people do not come to Christ is that they do not want to.

3:26 *they came to John.* John the Baptist's disciples were loyal to him. They were deeply concerned that one of his "disciples," Jesus, was competing with and surpassing him. In their astonishment, they exaggerated the predicament, saying, "all are coming to him." They were concerned that John was losing his audience to another preacher.

3:27 *John replied.* John the Baptist clarified the relationship between himself and Jesus. First, he talked about himself (vv. 27–29); then he talked about Jesus (vv. 30–36). John explained that he could not accept the position of supremacy that his disciples wanted to thrust upon him because he had not received it from heaven.

3:29 *The friend who attends the bridegroom.* John compared himself to this person who was generally appointed to arrange the preliminaries of the wedding, to manage the wedding, and to preside at the wedding feast.

3:31 *The one who comes from above.* This is a reference to Christ. ***one who is from the earth.*** This refers to John the Baptist. John emphasized his earthly origin and its limitations. John proclaimed divine truth on earth; Jesus, on the other hand, is from heaven and above all.

3:33 *has certified.* In a society where many could not read, seals were used to convey a clear message, even to the illiterate. A seal indicated ownership to all and expressed a person's personal guarantee. To receive Jesus' testimony is to certify that God is true regarding what He has sealed.

3:34 *God gives the Spirit without limit.* Unlike human teachers, Jesus was not given the Spirit in a limited way (Is. 11:1–2). All three Persons of the Trinity are referred to in this verse; God the Father sent Christ the Son, and gave Him the Holy Spirit without measure.

4:1 *Now Jesus learned.* This refers the reader back to 3:22–36. Christ's success in winning disciples had created jealousy among John's followers and provoked questions among the Pharisees. Since Jesus did not want to be drawn into a controversy over baptism at this stage of His ministry, He left Judea for Galilee (v. 3).

4:4 *he had to go through Samaria.* The shortest route from Judea in the south to Galilee in the north went through Samaria. The journey took three days if He wanted to travel the direct route. The Jews often avoided Samaria by going around it along the Jordan

3:18 [e] 1Jn 4:9 **3:19** [f] Jn 1:4; 8:12 **3:20** [g] Eph 5:11, 13 **3:22** [h] Jn 4:2 **3:24** [i] Mt 4:12; 14:3 **3:25** [j] Jn 2:6 **3:26** [k] Mt 23:7 [l] Jn 1:7 **3:28** [m] Jn 1:20, 23 **3:29** [n] Mt 9:15 [o] Jn 16:24; 17:13; Php 2:2; 1Jn 1:4; 2Jn 12 **3:31** [p] ver 13 [q] Jn 8:23; 1Jn 4:5 **3:32** [r] Jn 8:26; 15:15 [s] ver 11 **3:34** [t] ver 17 [u] Mt 12:18; Lk 4:18; Ac 10:38 **3:35** [v] Mt 28:18; Jn 5:20, 22; 17:2 **3:36** [w] ver 15; Jn 5:24; 6:47 **4:1** [x] Jn 3:22, 26 **4:3** [y] Jn 3:22

5So he came to a town in Samaria called
Sychar, near the plot of ground Jacob had
given to his son Joseph.[z] 6Jacob's well was
there, and Jesus, tired as he was from the
journey, sat down by the well. It was about
noon.
7When a Samaritan woman came to
draw water, Jesus said to her, "Will you
give me a drink?" 8(His disciples had gone
into the town[a] to buy food.)
9The Samaritan woman said to him,
"You are a Jew and I am a Samaritan[b]
woman. How can you ask me for a drink?"
(For Jews do not associate with Samaritans.[a])
10Jesus answered her, "If you knew the
gift of God and who it is that asks you for
a drink, you would have asked him and he
would have given you living water."[c]
11"Sir," the woman said, "you have nothing to draw with and the well is deep.
Where can you get this living water? 12Are
you greater than our father Jacob, who
gave us the well[d] and drank from it himself,
as did also his sons and his livestock?"
13Jesus answered, "Everyone who drinks
this water will be thirsty again, 14but whoever drinks the water I give them will never
thirst.[e] Indeed, the water I give them will
become in them a spring of water[f] welling
up to eternal life."[g]
15The woman said to him, "Sir, give me
this water so that I won't get thirsty[h] and
have to keep coming here to draw water."
16He told her, "Go, call your husband and
come back."
17"I have no husband," she replied.
Jesus said to her, "You are right when
you say you have no husband. 18The fact
is, you have had five husbands, and the
man you now have is not your husband.
What you have just said is quite true."
19"Sir," the woman said, "I can see that
you are a prophet.[i] 20Our ancestors worshiped on this mountain,[j] but you Jews
claim that the place where we must worship is in Jerusalem."[k]
21"Woman," Jesus replied, "believe me, a
time is coming[l] when you will worship the
Father neither on this mountain nor in Jerusalem.[m] 22You Samaritans worship what
you do not know;[n] we worship what we do
know, for salvation is from the Jews.[o] 23Yet
a time is coming and has now come[p] when
the true worshipers will worship the Father
in the Spirit[q] and in truth, for they are the
kind of worshipers the Father seeks. 24God
is spirit,[r] and his worshipers must worship
in the Spirit and in truth."
25The woman said, "I know that Messiah" (called Christ)[s] "is coming. When he
comes, he will explain everything to us."
26Then Jesus declared, "I, the one speaking to you—I am he."[t]

The Disciples Rejoin Jesus

27Just then his disciples returned[u] and
were surprised to find him talking with a
woman. But no one asked, "What do you
want?" or "Why are you talking with her?"
28Then, leaving her water jar, the woman went back to the town and said to the
people, 29"Come, see a man who told me
everything I ever did.[v] Could this be the
Messiah?"[w] 30They came out of the town
and made their way toward him.
31Meanwhile his disciples urged him,
"Rabbi,[x] eat something."
32But he said to them, "I have food to eat[y]
that you know nothing about."
33Then his disciples said to each other,
"Could someone have brought him food?"

[a] 9 Or *do not use dishes Samaritans have used*

River. The hatred between the Jews and Samaritans went back to the days of the exile. Samaria was the region between Judea and Galilee. When the northern kingdom was exiled to Assyria, King Sargon repopulated the area with captives from other lands. The intermarriage of these foreigners and the Jews who had been left complicated the ancestry of the Samaritans. The Jews hated the Samaritans and considered them to be no longer "pure" Jews.

4:14 ***a spring of water welling up to eternal life.*** Jesus desired a drink of water. He then directed the focus of discussion from physical water to spiritual water, pointing out the tremendous advantages of the second kind, which is obtained without cost or effort. This water satisfies completely and eternally.

4:16 ***Go, call your husband.*** Jesus mentioned the woman's husband in order to expose her sin (v. 18).

4:20 ***you Jews claim that the place . . . is in Jerusalem.*** The Jews insisted that the exclusive place of worship was Jerusalem. But the Samaritans had set up a rival worship site on Mount Gerizim, which according to their tradition was where Abraham went to sacrifice Isaac and where later on he met Melchizedek.

4:24 ***God is Spirit . . . must worship in the Spirit and in truth.*** God is not limited by time and space. When people are born of the Spirit, they can commune with God anywhere. *Spirit* is the opposite of what is material and earthly, for example, Mount Gerizim. Christ makes worship a matter of the heart. *Truth* is what is in harmony with the nature and will of God. The issue is not where a person worships, but how and whom.

4:29 ***everything I ever did.*** In her excitement, the woman exaggerated. She did not report what Jesus actually told her, but what He could have told her. Note the woman's spiritual journey. She first viewed Christ as a Jew (v. 9), then as a prophet (v. 19), and finally as the Messiah.

4:5 [z] Ge 33:19; 48:22; Jos 24:32 **4:8** [a] ver 5, 39 **4:9** [b] Mt 10:5; Lk 9:52, 53 **4:10** [c] Isa 44:3; Jer 2:13; Zec 14:8; Jn 7:37, 38; Rev 21:6; 22:1, 17 **4:12** [d] ver 6 **4:14** [e] Jn 6:35 [f] Jn 7:38 [g] Mt 25:46 **4:15** [h] Jn 6:34 **4:19** [i] Mt 21:11 **4:20** [j] Dt 11:29; Jos 8:33 [k] Lk 9:53 **4:21** [l] Jn 5:28; 16:2 [m] Mal 1:11; 1Ti 2:8 **4:22** [n] 2Ki 17:28-41 [o] Isa 2:3; Ro 3:1, 2; 9:4, 5 **4:23** [p] Jn 5:25; 16:32 [q] Php 3:3 **4:24** [r] Php 3:3 **4:25** [s] Mt 1:16 **4:26** [t] Jn 8:24; 9:35-37 **4:27** [u] ver 8 **4:29** [v] ver 17, 18 [w] Mt 12:23; Jn 7:26, 31 **4:31** [x] Mt 23:7 **4:32** [y] Job 23:12; Mt 4:4; Jn 6:27

34"My food," said Jesus, "is to do the will[z]
of him who sent me and to finish his work.[a]
35Don't you have a saying, 'It's still four
months until harvest'? I tell you, open your
eyes and look at the fields! They are ripe
for harvest.[b] **36**Even now the one who reaps
draws a wage and harvests[c] a crop for eternal life,[d] so that the sower and the reaper
may be glad together. **37**Thus the saying
'One sows and another reaps'[e] is true. **38**I
sent you to reap what you have not worked
for. Others have done the hard work, and
you have reaped the benefits of their labor."

Many Samaritans Believe

39Many of the Samaritans from that
town[f] believed in him because of the woman's testimony, "He told me everything I
ever did."[g] **40**So when the Samaritans came
to him, they urged him to stay with them,
and he stayed two days. **41**And because of
his words many more became believers.

42They said to the woman, "We no longer believe just because of what you said;
now we have heard for ourselves, and we
know that this man really is the Savior of
the world."[h]

Jesus Heals an Official's Son

43After the two days[i] he left for Galilee.
44(Now Jesus himself had pointed out that
a prophet has no honor in his own country.)[j] **45**When he arrived in Galilee, the Galileans welcomed him. They had seen all
that he had done in Jerusalem at the Passover Festival,[k] for they also had been there.

46Once more he visited Cana in Galilee,
where he had turned the water into wine.[l]
And there was a certain royal official
whose son lay sick at Capernaum. **47**When
this man heard that Jesus had arrived in
Galilee from Judea,[m] he went to him and
begged him to come and heal his son, who
was close to death.

48"Unless you people see signs and wonders,"[n] Jesus told him, "you will never believe."

49The royal official said, "Sir, come
down before my child dies."

50"Go," Jesus replied, "your son will live."
The man took Jesus at his word and departed. **51**While he was still on the way, his
servants met him with the news that his
boy was living. **52**When he inquired as to
the time when his son got better, they said
to him, "Yesterday, at one in the afternoon,
the fever left him."

53Then the father realized that this was
the exact time at which Jesus had said to
him, "Your son will live." So he and his
whole household[o] believed.

54This was the second sign[p] Jesus performed after coming from Judea to Galilee.

The Healing at the Pool

5 Some time later, Jesus went up to Jerusalem for one of the Jewish festivals.
2Now there is in Jerusalem near the Sheep
Gate[q] a pool, which in Aramaic[r] is called
Bethesda[a] and which is surrounded by five
covered colonnades. **3**Here a great number
of disabled people used to lie—the blind,
the lame, the paralyzed. **[4]**[b] **5**One who was
there had been an invalid for thirty-eight
years. **6**When Jesus saw him lying there
and learned that he had been in this condition for a long time, he asked him, "Do you
want to get well?"

7"Sir," the invalid replied, "I have no one
to help me into the pool when the water is
stirred. While I am trying to get in, someone else goes down ahead of me."

8Then Jesus said to him, "Get up! Pick up
your mat and walk."[s] **9**At once the man was
cured; he picked up his mat and walked.

The day on which this took place was a
Sabbath,[t] **10**and so the Jewish leaders[u] said
to the man who had been healed, "It is the
Sabbath; the law forbids you to carry your
mat."[v]

---

[a] 2 Some manuscripts *Bethzatha;* other manuscripts *Bethsaida* [b] 3,4 Some manuscripts include here, wholly or in part, *paralyzed—and they waited for the moving of the waters.* [4]*From time to time an angel of the Lord would come down and stir up the waters. The first one into the pool after each such disturbance would be cured of whatever disease they had.*

4:36 *draws a wage.* The reaper of a spiritual harvest receives wages—that is, fruit which brings joy. In this case, Jesus sowed by giving the message to the woman. The disciples were going to reap the harvest that He had sown.

4:42 *Savior of the world.* This title is used only here and in 1 John 4:14. The Jews of Jesus' day taught that to approach God, one first had to be a Jew. By including this incident in the Gospel, John demonstrates that Jesus is for all people of the world.

4:46 *a certain royal official.* This was probably someone who was in the service of the king. Herod Antipas was technically the "tetrarch" of Galilee, but he was referred to as a king.

5:2 *the Sheep Gate.* This was a gate in the wall of Jerusalem near the temple, through which sheep were brought for sacrifice.

5:8 *Pick up your mat and walk.* Carrying a bed on the Sabbath was considered a violation of the law of Moses (v. 10).

5:10 *the law forbids.* The law of Moses taught that the Sabbath must be different from other days. On it, neither people nor animals could work. The prophet Jeremiah had prohibited carrying burdens or working on the Sabbath (Jer. 17:21–22). Over the years, the

4:34 [z] Mt 26:39; Jn 6:38; 17:4; 19:30 [a] Jn 19:30 **4:35** [b] Mt 9:37; Lk 10:2 **4:36** [c] Ro 1:13 [d] Mt 25:46 **4:37** [e] Job 31:8; Mic 6:15 **4:39** [f] ver 5 [g] ver 29 **4:42** [h] Lk 2:11; 1Jn 4:14 **4:43** [i] ver 40 **4:44** [j] Mt 13:57; Lk 4:24 **4:45** [k] Jn 2:23 **4:46** [l] Jn 2:1-11 **4:47** [m] ver 3, 54 **4:48** [n] Da 4:2, 3; Jn 2:11; Ac 2:43; 14:3; Ro 15:19; 2Co 12:12; Heb 2:4 **4:53** [o] Ac 11:14 **4:54** [p] ver 48; Jn 2:11 **5:2** [q] Ne 3:1; 12:39 [r] Jn 19:13, 17, 20; 20:16; Ac 21:40; 22:2; 26:14 **5:8** [s] Mt 9:5, 6; Mk 2:11; Lk 5:24 **5:9** [t] Jn 9:14 **5:10** [u] ver 16 [v] Ne 13:15-22; Jer 17:21; Mt 12:2

11 But he replied, "The man who made
me well said to me, 'Pick up your mat and
walk.' "
12 So they asked him, "Who is this fellow
who told you to pick it up and walk?"
13 The man who was healed had no idea
who it was, for Jesus had slipped away into
the crowd that was there.
14 Later Jesus found him at the temple
and said to him, "See, you are well again.
Stop sinning[w] or something worse may
happen to you." 15 The man went away and
told the Jewish leaders[x] that it was Jesus
who had made him well.

The Authority of the Son

16 So, because Jesus was doing these
things on the Sabbath, the Jewish leaders
began to persecute him. 17 In his defense
Jesus said to them, "My Father is always
at his work[y] to this very day, and I too
am working." 18 For this reason they tried
all the more to kill him;[z] not only was he
breaking the Sabbath, but he was even
calling God his own Father, making himself equal with God.[a]
19 Jesus gave them this answer: "Very
truly I tell you, the Son can do nothing
by himself;[b] he can do only what he sees
his Father doing, because whatever the
Father does the Son also does. 20 For the
Father loves the Son[c] and shows him all
he does. Yes, and he will show him even
greater works than these,[d] so that you will
be amazed. 21 For just as the Father raises the dead and gives them life,[e] even so
the Son gives life[f] to whom he is pleased
to give it. 22 Moreover, the Father judges no
one, but has entrusted all judgment to the
Son,[g] 23 that all may honor the Son just as
they honor the Father. Whoever does not
honor the Son does not honor the Father,
who sent him.[h]
24 "Very truly I tell you, whoever hears
my word and believes him who sent me has
eternal life and will not be judged[i] but has
crossed over from death to life.[j] 25 Very truly I tell you, a time is coming and has now
come[k] when the dead will hear[l] the voice
of the Son of God and those who hear will
live. 26 For as the Father has life in himself,
so he has granted the Son also to have life
in himself. 27 And he has given him authority to judge[m] because he is the Son of Man.
28 "Do not be amazed at this, for a time is
coming[n] when all who are in their graves
will hear his voice 29 and come out—those
who have done what is good will rise to
live, and those who have done what is evil
will rise to be condemned.[o] 30 By myself
I can do nothing;[p] I judge only as I hear,
and my judgment is just,[q] for I seek not to
please myself but him who sent me.[r]

Testimonies About Jesus

31 "If I testify about myself, my testimony
is not true.[s] 32 There is another who testifies
in my favor,[t] and I know that his testimony
about me is true.
33 "You have sent to John and he has

Jewish leaders had amassed thousands of rules and regulations concerning the Sabbath. By Jesus' day, they had 39 different classifications of work. According to them, carrying furniture and even providing medical treatment on the Sabbath were forbidden. Jesus did not break the law. He violated the *traditions* of the Pharisees which had grown up around the law.

5:16 *the Jewish leaders began to persecute him.* This is the first recorded declaration of open hostility toward Jesus in the Gospel of John.

5:17 *My Father.* Jesus is the "one and only Son" (1:14,18; 3:16,18) — that is, the unique Son of God. Here He claims not only a unique relationship with God the Father, but also equality with God in nature. Since God continually does good works without allowing Himself to stop on the Sabbath, the Son does likewise, since He is equal with God. Certainly the Jewish leaders understood the implications of Jesus' claims (v. 18).

5:19 *the Son can do nothing by himself.* Action by the Son apart from the Father is impossible because of the unity of the Father and the Son (v. 17). ***whatever the Father does the Son also does.*** Here is a claim of deity and unity with the Father.

5:22 *judgment to the Son.* The Jews recognized that God alone had the right to judge humanity. In claiming that the Father committed all judgment to Him, Jesus again claimed equality with God.

5:24 Never-Ending Life — One of the primary features of the new life that we have in Christ is that it is an eternal or everlasting life. This truth completely changes how we look at our present lives and at the future. It needs to be seen as something we possess even now (John 10:28). We have entered into a new, personal relationship with God that gives us a spiritual vitality and fullness of life that we lacked before (John 17:3). It will be completely fulfilled in the future when we are bodily redeemed (Rom. 8:23). The greatness of this spiritual reality constitutes a wonderful incentive to vigorously proclaim the gospel to those who are still dead in *transgressions and sins* (Eph. 2:1).

5:26 *For.* This indicates that this verse explains the previous verse. Christ can give life because He Himself possesses life. He not only has a part in giving it, He is the source of it. This is another testimony to Jesus' deity because only God has life in Himself.

5:29 *will rise to live . . . will rise to be condemned.* Two separate resurrections are presented here in the fashion of the Old Testament prophets, who often grouped together events of the future without distinction of the time (Is. 61:2). Jesus was teaching the universality of resurrection, not the timing of it.

5:31 – 32 *my testimony is not true.* If Christ were the only one bearing witness of what He was claiming, His witness would not be accepted. According

5:14 [w] Mk 2:5; Jn 8:11 **5:15** [x] Jn 1:19 **5:17** [y] Jn 9:4; 14:10 **5:18** [z] Jn 7:1 [a] Jn 10:30,33; 19:7 **5:19** [b] ver 30; Jn 8:28 **5:20** [c] Jn 3:35 [d] Jn 14:12 **5:21** [e] Ro 4:17; 8:11 [f] Jn 11:25 **5:22** [g] ver 27; Jn 9:39; Ac 10:42; 17:31 **5:23** [h] Lk 10:16; 1Jn 2:23 **5:24** [i] Jn 3:18 [j] 1Jn 3:14 **5:25** [k] Jn 4:23 [l] Jn 8:43,47 **5:27** [m] ver 22; Ac 10:42; 17:31 **5:28** [n] Jn 4:21 **5:29** [o] Da 12:2; Mt 25:46 **5:30** [p] ver 19 [q] Jn 8:16 [r] Mt 26:39; Jn 4:34; 6:38 **5:31** [s] Jn 8:14 **5:32** [t] ver 37; Jn 8:18

testified[u] to the truth. 34Not that I accept
human testimony;[v] but I mention it that
you may be saved. 35John was a lamp that
burned and gave light,[w] and you chose for
a time to enjoy his light.
36"I have testimony weightier than that
of John.[x] For the works that the Father has
given me to finish—the very works that
I am doing[y]—testify that the Father has
sent me.[z] 37And the Father who sent me
has himself testified concerning me.[a] You
have never heard his voice nor seen his
form,[b] 38nor does his word dwell in you,[c]
for you do not believe the one he sent.[d]
39You study[*a*] the Scriptures[e] diligently because you think that in them you have eternal life. These are the very Scriptures that
testify about me,[f] 40yet you refuse to come
to me to have life.
41"I do not accept glory from human beings,[g] 42but I know you. I know that you do
not have the love of God in your hearts. 43I
have come in my Father's name, and you do
not accept me; but if someone else comes in
his own name, you will accept him. 44How
can you believe since you accept glory
from one another but do not seek the glory
that comes from the only God[*b*]?[h]
45"But do not think I will accuse you before the Father. Your accuser is Moses,[i] on
whom your hopes are set.[j] 46If you believed
Moses, you would believe me, for he wrote
about me.[k] 47But since you do not believe
what he wrote, how are you going to believe what I say?"[l]

Jesus Feeds the Five Thousand

6 Some time after this, Jesus crossed to
the far shore of the Sea of Galilee (that
is, the Sea of Tiberias), 2and a great crowd
of people followed him because they saw
the signs[m] he had performed by healing the
sick. 3Then Jesus went up on a mountainside[n] and sat down with his disciples. 4The
Jewish Passover Festival[o] was near.
5When Jesus looked up and saw a great
crowd coming toward him, he said to Philip,[p] "Where shall we buy bread for these
people to eat?" 6He asked this only to test
him, for he already had in mind what he
was going to do.
7Philip answered him, "It would take
more than half a year's wages[*c*] to buy
enough bread for each one to have a bite!"
8Another of his disciples, Andrew, Simon Peter's brother,[q] spoke up, 9"Here is a
boy with five small barley loaves and two
small fish, but how far will they go among
so many?"[r]
10Jesus said, "Have the people sit down."
There was plenty of grass in that place, and
they sat down (about five thousand men
were there). 11Jesus then took the loaves,
gave thanks,[s] and distributed to those who
were seated as much as they wanted. He
did the same with the fish.
12When they had all had enough to eat,
he said to his disciples, "Gather the pieces
that are left over. Let nothing be wasted."
13So they gathered them and filled twelve
baskets with the pieces of the five barley
loaves left over by those who had eaten.
14After the people saw the sign[t] Jesus
performed, they began to say, "Surely
this is the Prophet who is to come into the
world."[u] 15Jesus, knowing that they intended to come and make him king[v] by force,
withdrew again to a mountain by himself.[w]

a 39 Or *39Study*   *b* 44 Some early manuscripts *the Only One*   *c* 7 Greek *take two hundred denarii*

---

to Jewish legal practice, a person's testimony about himself was not accepted in court. So, in this case, Jesus offered another witness—John the Baptist (v. 33).

5:42 ***the love of God.*** This love is not love from God but love for God. Love from God is evidenced in Christ (3:16; Rom. 5:8). Since God loves us, we should love Him (Deut. 6:5; 1 John 4:19).

5:45 ***your hopes are set.*** Christ will not have to accuse the people on judgment day because the one in whom they place their trust, Moses, will. The people will be condemned by the very law they professed to keep.

5:46 ***for he wrote about me.*** Moses wrote about Christ in the promises to the patriarchs, in the history of the deliverance from Egypt, in the symbolic institutions of the law, and in the prediction of a Prophet like himself (Luke 24:25–26). If the people had believed Moses, they would have received Jesus gladly. Over 300 Old Testament prophecies were specifically fulfilled in the first coming of Christ.

6:1 ***Sea of Galilee (that is, the Sea of Tiberias).*** John's use of the name Tiberias is an indication that his Gospel was written for those outside of Palestine. The Jewish people called this body of water the Lake of Gennesaret. The Romans called it Tiberias, after the city built on its western shore by Herod Antipas and named for the Emperor Tiberius.

6:7 ***half a year's wages.*** One denarius was a day's wage for a laborer or field hand (Matt. 20:2). Two hundred denarii would have been almost a half a year's wages.

6:9 ***barley loaves.*** These were an inexpensive food of the common people and the poor.

6:10–11 ***(about five thousand men were there). Jesus ... distributed to those who were seated.*** This is the only miracle of Jesus that is recounted in all four Gospels.

6:15 ***make him king.*** Moses had not only miraculously provided food for the Israelites, he had also led them out of bondage in Egypt. Perhaps these men

5:33 [u] Jn 1:7 **5:34** [v] 1Jn 5:9 **5:35** [w] 2Pe 1:19
5:36 [x] 1Jn 5:9 [y] Jn 14:11; 15:24 [z] Jn 3:17; 10:25
5:37 [a] Jn 8:18 [b] Dt 4:12; 1Ti 1:17; Jn 1:18 **5:38** [c] 1Jn 2:14
[d] Jn 3:17 **5:39** [e] Ro 2:17, 18 [f] Lk 24:27, 44; Ac 13:27
5:41 [g] ver 44 **5:44** [h] Ro 2:29 **5:45** [i] Jn 9:28 [j] Ro 2:17
5:46 [k] Ge 3:15; Lk 24:27, 44; Ac 26:22 **5:47** [l] Lk 16:29, 31
6:2 [m] Jn 2:11 **6:3** [n] ver 15 **6:4** [o] Jn 2:13; 11:55
6:5 [p] Jn 1:43 **6:8** [q] Jn 1:40 **6:9** [r] 2Ki 4:43
6:11 [s] ver 23; Mt 14:19 **6:14** [t] Jn 2:11 [u] Dt 18:15, 18;
Mt 11:3; 21:11 **6:15** [v] Jn 18:36 [w] Mt 14:23; Mk 6:46

Jesus Walks on the Water

16When evening came, his disciples went down to the lake, 17where they got into a boat and set off across the lake for Capernaum. By now it was dark, and Jesus had not yet joined them. 18A strong wind was blowing and the waters grew rough. 19When they had rowed about three or four miles,[a] they saw Jesus approaching the boat, walking on the water;[x] and they were frightened. 20But he said to them, "It is I; don't be afraid."[y] 21Then they were willing to take him into the boat, and immediately the boat reached the shore where they were heading.

22The next day the crowd that had stayed on the opposite shore of the lake[z] realized that only one boat had been there, and that Jesus had not entered it with his disciples, but that they had gone away alone.[a] 23Then some boats from Tiberias[b] landed near the place where the people had eaten the bread after the Lord had given thanks.[c] 24Once the crowd realized that neither Jesus nor his disciples were there, they got into the boats and went to Capernaum in search of Jesus.

Jesus the Bread of Life

25When they found him on the other side of the lake, they asked him, "Rabbi,[d] when did you get here?"

26Jesus answered, "Very truly I tell you, you are looking for me,[e] not because you saw the signs[f] I performed but because you ate the loaves and had your fill. 27Do not work for food that spoils, but for food that endures[g] to eternal life,[h] which the Son of Man[i] will give you. For on him God the Father has placed his seal[j] of approval."

28Then they asked him, "What must we do to do the works God requires?"

29Jesus answered, "The work of God is this: to believe[k] in the one he has sent."[l]

30So they asked him, "What sign[m] then will you give that we may see it and believe you?[n] What will you do? 31Our ancestors ate the manna[o] in the wilderness; as it is written: 'He gave them bread from heaven to eat.'[b]"[p]

32Jesus said to them, "Very truly I tell you, it is not Moses who has given you the bread from heaven, but it is my Father who gives you the true bread from heaven. 33For the bread of God is the bread that comes down from heaven[q] and gives life to the world."

34"Sir," they said, "always give us this bread."[r]

35Then Jesus declared, "I am the bread of life.[s] Whoever comes to me will never go hungry, and whoever believes in me will never be thirsty.[t] 36But as I told you, you have seen me and still you do not believe. 37All those the Father gives me[u] will come to me, and whoever comes to me I will never drive away. 38For I have come down from heaven not to do my will but to do the will of him who sent me.[v] 39And this is the will of him who sent me, that I shall lose none of all those he has given me,[w] but raise them up at the last day.[x] 40For my Father's will is that everyone who looks to the Son and believes in him shall have eternal life,[y] and I will raise them up at the last day."

41At this the Jews there began to grumble about him because he said, "I am the bread that came down from heaven." 42They said, "Is this not Jesus, the son of Joseph,[z] whose father and mother we know?[a] How can he now say, 'I came down from heaven'?"[b]

43"Stop grumbling among yourselves," Jesus answered. 44"No one can come to me unless the Father who sent me draws them,[c] and I will raise them up at the last day. 45It is written in the Prophets: 'They will all be

a 19 Or about 5 or 6 kilometers *b 31* Exodus 16:4; Neh. 9:15; Psalm 78:24,25

---

felt that Jesus could lead them out of bondage to the Romans. Christ was at the zenith of His popularity, and the temptation to take the kingdom without the cross must have been great (Matt. 4:8–10).

6:19–21 *they saw Jesus ... walking on the water.* This miracle, the fifth sign recorded by John, pointed to Jesus' deity. Only God could walk on water, calm the sea, and supernaturally transport the disciples to their destination.

6:27 *Do not work.* The impression that one must work for eternal life is quickly corrected when Jesus adds "which the Son of Man will give you." The Son provides *life* as a gift (4:10).

6:31 *He gave them bread from heaven.* There was a tradition that said the Messiah would cause manna to fall from heaven as Moses did (Ex. 16:4,15). The people probably also saw this "miracle worker" as the perpetual provider of physical needs rather than spiritual ones.

6:32 *my Father.* The crowd misrepresented the truth, so Jesus corrected them. The manna had not come from Moses; it had been provided by God. Moreover, God still gives *true bread*—that is, eternal life (v. 33).

6:39–40 *the will of him who sent me.* This is twofold: (1) that all who come to the Son will be received and not lost; (2) that all who see and believe on the Son will have eternal life.

6:42 *the son of Joseph.* The religious leaders' proof that Jesus was not from heaven was that they knew His parents. To them, there was nothing supernatural about Jesus' origin.

6:19 [x] Job 9:8 **6:20** [y] Mt 14:27 **6:22** [z] ver 2 [a] ver 15-21 **6:23** [b] ver 1 [c] ver 11 **6:25** [d] Mt 23:7 **6:26** [e] ver 24 [f] ver 30; Jn 2:11 **6:27** [g] Isa 55:2 [h] ver 54; Mt 25:46; Jn 4:14 [i] Mt 8:20 [j] Ro 4:11; 1Co 9:2; 2Co 1:22; Eph 1:13; 4:30; 2Ti 2:19; Rev 7:3 **6:29** [k] 1Jn 3:23 [l] Jn 3:17 **6:30** [m] Jn 2:11 [n] Mt 12:38 **6:31** [o] Nu 11:7-9 [p] Ex 16:4, 15; Ne 9:15; Ps 78:24; 105:40 **6:33** [q] ver 50 **6:34** [r] Jn 4:15 **6:35** [s] ver 48, 51 [t] Jn 4:14 **6:37** [u] ver 39; Jn 17:2, 6, 9, 24 **6:38** [v] Jn 4:34; 5:30 **6:39** [w] Jn 10:28; 17:12; 18:9 [x] ver 40, 44, 54 **6:40** [y] Jn 3:15, 16 **6:42** [z] Lk 4:22 [a] Jn 7:27, 28 [b] ver 38, 62 **6:44** [c] ver 65; Jer 31:3; Jn 12:32

taught by God.'[a][d] Everyone who has heard the Father and learned from him comes to me. 46No one has seen the Father except the one who is from God;[e] only he has seen the Father. 47Very truly I tell you, the one who believes has eternal life. 48I am the bread of life.[f] 49Your ancestors ate the manna in the wilderness, yet they died.[g] 50But here is the bread that comes down from heaven,[h] which anyone may eat and not die. 51I am the living bread that came down from heaven. Whoever eats this bread will live forever. This bread is my flesh, which I will give for the life of the world."[i]

52Then the Jews began to argue sharply among themselves,[j] "How can this man give us his flesh to eat?"

53Jesus said to them, "Very truly I tell you, unless you eat the flesh of the Son of Man[k] and drink his blood, you have no life in you. 54Whoever eats my flesh and drinks my blood has eternal life, and I will raise them up at the last day.[l] 55For my flesh is real food and my blood is real drink. 56Whoever eats my flesh and drinks my blood remains in me, and I in them.[m] 57Just as the living Father sent me[n] and I live because of the Father, so the one who feeds on me will live because of me. 58This is the bread that came down from heaven. Your ancestors ate manna and died, but whoever feeds on this bread will live forever."[o] 59He said this while teaching in the synagogue in Capernaum.

Many Disciples Desert Jesus

60On hearing it, many of his disciples[p] said, "This is a hard teaching. Who can accept it?"

61Aware that his disciples were grumbling about this, Jesus said to them, "Does this offend you?[q] 62Then what if you see the Son of Man ascend to where he was before![r] 63The Spirit gives life;[s] the flesh counts for nothing. The words I have spoken to you—they are full of the Spirit[b] and life. 64Yet there are some of you who do not believe." For Jesus had known[t] from the beginning which of them did not believe and who would betray him. 65He went on to say, "This is why I told you that no one can come to me unless the Father has enabled them."[u]

66From this time many of his disciples[v] turned back and no longer followed him.

67"You do not want to leave too, do you?" Jesus asked the Twelve.[w]

68Simon Peter answered him,[x] "Lord, to whom shall we go? You have the words of eternal life. 69We have come to believe and to know that you are the Holy One of God."[y]

70Then Jesus replied, "Have I not chosen you,[z] the Twelve? Yet one of you is a devil!"[a] 71(He meant Judas, the son of Simon Iscariot, who, though one of the Twelve, was later to betray him.)

Jesus Goes to the Festival of Tabernacles

7 After this, Jesus went around in Galilee. He did not want[c] to go about in Judea because the Jewish leaders[b] there were looking for a way to kill him.[c] 2But when the Jewish Festival of Tabernacles[d] was near, 3Jesus' brothers[e] said to him, "Leave Galilee and go to Judea, so that your disciples there may see the works you do. 4No one who wants to become a public figure acts in secret. Since you are doing these things, show yourself to the world." 5For even his own brothers did not believe in him.[f]

6Therefore Jesus told them, "My time[g] is

---

a 45 Isaiah 54:13 *b* 63 Or *are Spirit*; or *are spirit*
c 1 Some manuscripts *not have authority*

6:47 *eternal life.* The believer, possessing both peace and purpose, can rejoice even in the midst of fiery trials, knowing that God Himself will arrange the outcome for His glory and the believer's good (Rom. 8:28).

6:48–49 *I am the bread of life.* Those who believe in Him have life (v. 47). The manna in the wilderness did not ultimately sustain life. Those who ate it eventually died because it could not provide eternal life.

6:53–58 *eat the flesh ... and drink his blood.* Jesus had made it abundantly clear in this context that eternal life is gained by believing (vv. 29,35,40,47). These verses teach that the benefits of Jesus' death must be appropriated, by faith, by each individual.

6:60 *This is a hard teaching.* It was hard for the Jewish learners to accept the idea of eating flesh and drinking blood. Jews were forbidden to even taste blood.

6:63 *The Spirit gives life.* Jesus was trying to get the religious leaders to see beyond the physical aspects of His teaching to the real issue—namely, that if they believed on Him they would have eternal life.

7:2 *Festival of Tabernacles.* This was one of the three great Jewish religious festivals (Passover and Pentecost were the other two). It was called the Festival of Tabernacles (Booths) because for seven days the people lived in makeshift shelters or lean-tos made of branches and leaves. The festival commemorated the days when the Israelites wandered in the wilderness and lived in tents (Lev. 23:40–43).

7:3–4 *Jesus' brothers.* Jesus' brothers argued, "If You are really working miracles and thus claiming to be the Messiah, do not hide in obscure Galilee. If you are doing miracles at all, then do them in Jerusalem at the Festival to convince the whole nation." These words were sarcastic, as verse 5 explains.

6:45 [d] Isa 54:13; Jer 31:33, 34; Heb 8:10, 11; 10:16 **6:46** [e] Jn 1:18; 5:37; 7:29 **6:48** [f] ver 35, 51 **6:49** [g] ver 31, 58 **6:50** [h] ver 33 **6:51** [i] Heb 10:10 **6:52** [j] Jn 7:43; 9:16; 10:19 **6:53** [k] Mt 8:20 **6:54** [l] ver 39 **6:56** [m] Jn 15:4-7; 1Jn 3:24; 4:15 **6:57** [n] Jn 3:17 **6:58** [o] ver 49-51; Jn 3:36 **6:60** [p] ver 66 **6:61** [q] Mt 11:6 **6:62** [r] Mk 16:19; Jn 3:13; 17:5 **6:63** [s] 2Co 3:6 **6:64** [t] Jn 2:25 **6:65** [u] ver 37, 44 **6:66** [v] ver 60 **6:67** [w] Mt 10:2 **6:68** [x] Mt 16:16 **6:69** [y] Mk 8:29; Lk 9:20 **6:70** [z] Jn 15:16, 19 [a] Jn 13:27 **7:1** [b] Jn 1:19 [c] Jn 5:18 **7:2** [d] Lev 23:34; Dt 16:16 **7:3** [e] Mt 12:46 **7:5** [f] Mk 3:21 **7:6** [g] Mt 26:18

not yet here; for you any time will do. 7The
world cannot hate you, but it hates me[h] because I testify that its works are evil.[i] 8You
go to the festival. I am not[a] going up to this
festival, because my time[j] has not yet fully
come." 9After he had said this, he stayed
in Galilee.
10However, after his brothers had left for
the festival, he went also, not publicly, but
in secret. 11Now at the festival the Jewish
leaders were watching for Jesus[k] and asking, "Where is he?"
12Among the crowds there was widespread whispering about him. Some said,
"He is a good man."
Others replied, "No, he deceives the people."[l] 13But no one would say anything publicly about him for fear of the leaders.[m]

Jesus Teaches at the Festival

14Not until halfway through the festival
did Jesus go up to the temple courts and
begin to teach.[n] 15The Jews[o] there were
amazed and asked, "How did this man
get such learning[p] without having been
taught?"[q]
16Jesus answered, "My teaching is not
my own. It comes from the one who sent
me.[r] 17Anyone who chooses to do the will
of God will find out[s] whether my teaching
comes from God or whether I speak on my
own. 18Whoever speaks on their own does
so to gain personal glory,[t] but he who seeks
the glory of the one who sent him is a man
of truth; there is nothing false about him.
19Has not Moses given you the law?[u] Yet
not one of you keeps the law. Why are you
trying to kill me?"[v]
20"You are demon-possessed,"[w] the
crowd answered. "Who is trying to kill
you?"
21Jesus said to them, "I did one miracle,
and you are all amazed. 22Yet, because
Moses gave you circumcision[x] (though
actually it did not come from Moses, but
from the patriarchs),[y] you circumcise a
boy on the Sabbath. 23Now if a boy can be
circumcised on the Sabbath so that the law
of Moses may not be broken, why are you
angry with me for healing a man's whole
body on the Sabbath? 24Stop judging by
mere appearances, but instead judge correctly."[z]

Division Over Who Jesus Is

25At that point some of the people of Jerusalem began to ask, "Isn't this the man
they are trying to kill? 26Here he is, speaking publicly, and they are not saying a
word to him. Have the authorities[a] really
concluded that he is the Messiah? 27But we
know where this man is from;[b] when the
Messiah comes, no one will know where
he is from."
28Then Jesus, still teaching in the temple courts,[c] cried out, "Yes, you know me,
and you know where I am from.[d] I am not
here on my own authority, but he who sent
me is true.[e] You do not know him, 29but I
know him[f] because I am from him and he
sent me."
30At this they tried to seize him, but
no one laid a hand on him,[g] because his
hour had not yet come. 31Still, many in the
crowd believed in him.[h] They said, "When
the Messiah comes, will he perform more
signs[i] than this man?"
32The Pharisees heard the crowd whispering such things about him. Then the
chief priests and the Pharisees sent temple
guards to arrest him.
33Jesus said, "I am with you for only a
short time,[j] and then I am going to the one
who sent me.[k] 34You will look for me, but
you will not find me; and where I am, you
cannot come."[l]
35The Jews said to one another, "Where
does this man intend to go that we cannot
find him? Will he go where our people live
scattered[m] among the Greeks,[n] and teach
the Greeks? 36What did he mean when he
said, 'You will look for me, but you will
not find me,' and 'Where I am, you cannot
come'?"
37On the last and greatest day of the
festival,[o] Jesus stood and said in a loud

[a] 8 Some manuscripts *not yet*

7:14 *halfway through the festival.* This would have been the fourth day of the seven-day festival. During the first half of the festival, Jesus remained in seclusion (v. 10). During the second half, He began to teach publicly. This is the first mention in the Gospel of John of Jesus teaching in the temple.

7:15 *without having been taught.* Jesus never attended a rabbinical school. Similar bewilderment was later expressed regarding Jesus' disciples (Acts 4:13).

7:28–29 *you know me, and you know where I am from.* Jesus reminded the leaders that they knew His origin. Their problem was that they did not know God, who sent Jesus. He explained to them that He knew God, was from God, and was sent by God.

7:32 *to arrest him.* The Jewish leaders decided earlier that they wanted to kill Christ (5:16), but this is the first real attempt on His life.

7:37–39 *greatest day of the festival.* On each day of the festival, the people came with palm branches and marched around the great altar. A priest took a golden pitcher filled with water from the pool of Siloam, carried it to the temple, and poured it on the altar as an offering to God. This dramatic ceremony

7:7 [h] Jn 15:18, 19 [i] Jn 3:19, 20 **7:8** [j] ver 6 **7:11** [k] Jn 11:56 **7:12** [l] ver 40, 43 **7:13** [m] Jn 9:22; 12:42; 19:38 **7:14** [n] ver 28; Mt 26:55 **7:15** [o] Jn 1:19 [p] Ac 26:24 [q] Mt 13:54 **7:16** [r] Jn 3:11; 14:24 **7:17** [s] Ps 25:14; Jn 8:43 **7:18** [t] Jn 5:41; 8:50, 54 **7:19** [u] Jn 1:17 [v] ver 1; Mt 12:14 **7:20** [w] Jn 8:48; 10:20 **7:22** [x] Lev 12:3 [y] Ge 17:10-14 **7:24** [z] Isa 11:3, 4; Jn 8:15 **7:26** [a] ver 48 **7:27** [b] Mt 13:55; Lk 4:22 **7:28** [c] ver 14 [d] Jn 8:14 [e] Jn 8:26, 42 **7:29** [f] Mt 11:27 **7:30** [g] ver 32, 44; Jn 10:39 **7:31** [h] Jn 8:30 [i] Jn 2:11 **7:33** [j] Jn 13:33; 16:16 [k] Jn 16:5, 10, 17, 28 **7:34** [l] Jn 8:21; 13:33 **7:35** [m] Jas 1:1 [n] Jn 12:20; 1Pe 1:1 **7:37** [o] Lev 23:36

voice, "Let anyone who is thirsty come
to me and drink.[p] 38Whoever believes in
me, as Scripture has said,[q] rivers of living water[r] will flow from within them."[a][s]
39By this he meant the Spirit,[t] whom those
who believed in him were later to receive.[u]
Up to that time the Spirit had not been
given, since Jesus had not yet been glorified.[v]
40On hearing his words, some of the people said, "Surely this man is the Prophet."[w]
41Others said, "He is the Messiah."
Still others asked, "How can the Messiah
come from Galilee?[x] 42Does not Scripture
say that the Messiah will come from David's descendants[y] and from Bethlehem,[z]
the town where David lived?" 43Thus the
people were divided[a] because of Jesus.
44Some wanted to seize him, but no one
laid a hand on him.[b]

Unbelief of the Jewish Leaders

45Finally the temple guards went back
to the chief priests and the Pharisees,
who asked them, "Why didn't you bring
him in?"
46"No one ever spoke the way this man
does,"[c] the guards replied.
47"You mean he has deceived you also?"[d]
the Pharisees retorted. 48"Have any of the
rulers or of the Pharisees believed in him?[e]
49No! But this mob that knows nothing of
the law—there is a curse on them."
50Nicodemus,[f] who had gone to Jesus
earlier and who was one of their own number, asked, 51"Does our law condemn a
man without first hearing him to find out
what he has been doing?"
52They replied, "Are you from Galilee,
too? Look into it, and you will find that a
prophet does not come out of Galilee."[g]

[The earliest manuscripts and many other ancient witnesses do not have John 7:53—8:11. A few manuscripts include these verses, wholly or in part, after John 7:36, John 21:25, Luke 21:38 or Luke 24:53.]

8 *53Then they all went home, 1but Jesus went*
to the Mount of Olives.[h]
2At dawn he appeared again in the temple
courts, where all the people gathered around
him, and he sat down to teach them.[i] *3The*
teachers of the law and the Pharisees brought
in a woman caught in adultery. They made
her stand before the group 4and said to Jesus,
"Teacher, this woman was caught in the act of
adultery. 5In the Law Moses commanded us
to stone such women.[j] *Now what do you say?"*
6They were using this question as a trap,[k] *in or-*
der to have a basis for accusing him.[l]
But Jesus bent down and started to write on
the ground with his finger. 7When they kept on
questioning him, he straightened up and said to
them, "Let any one of you who is without sin be
the first to throw a stone[m] *at her."*[n] *8Again he*
stooped down and wrote on the ground.
9At this, those who heard began to go away
one at a time, the older ones first, until only
Jesus was left, with the woman still standing
there. 10Jesus straightened up and asked her,
"Woman, where are they? Has no one con-
demned you?"

---

[a] *37,38* Or *me. And let anyone drink 38who believes in me." As Scripture has said, "Out of him* (or *them) will flow rivers of living water."*

---

was a memorial of the water that flowed from the rock when the Israelites traveled through the wilderness. On the last day of the feast, the people marched seven times around the altar in memory of the seven circuits around the walls of Jericho.

7:38 ***as Scripture has said.*** The reference is not to a single passage, but to the general emphasis of such passages as Deuteronomy 18:15, Isaiah 58:11, and Zechariah 14:8. In contrast to the small amount of water poured out each day during the festival, there will be a river of water coming out of those who believe in Christ. Not only will they be satisfied themselves, but they will also become a river so that others may drink and be satisfied (v. 39).

7:40–42 ***the Messiah will come from David's descendants.*** These people knew that the Messiah was to come from Bethlehem (Mic. 5:2). However, they did not know that Jesus had been born there. They thought He was from Galilee. They knew the Scripture, but they did not take the time to know the Messiah (5:39).

8:2 ***he sat down.*** Teachers in ancient Israel sat when they taught. Jesus assumed the position of an authoritative teacher.

8:3 ***a woman caught in adultery.*** The scribes and Pharisees were not interested in helping the woman, but in using her sinful circumstances to discredit Jesus (v. 6). His refusal to countenance the stoning of the woman does not bring Him into conflict with the law given to Moses, nor does He condone sin. The issue in the encounter was the accusers' blindness to their own sin.

8:4–5 ***commanded us to stone such women.*** Stoning was specified in certain cases of adultery (Deut. 22:23–24), though not all. (It is not clear why the authorities intended to punish the woman but not the man.) In the Greek text, the pronoun *you* is emphatic. The religious leaders were trying to trap Jesus into saying something that was contrary to the law.

8:6 ***as a trap.*** If Jesus had said not to stone her, He would have contradicted Jewish law. If He had said to stone her, He would have run counter to Roman law, which did not permit Jews to carry out their own executions (18:31). What Jesus wrote on the ground is a matter of conjecture.

7:37 [p] Isa 55:1; Rev 22:17 **7:38** [q] Isa 58:11 [r] Jn 4:10 [s] Jn 4:14 **7:39** [t] Joel 2:28; Ac 2:17,33 [u] Jn 20:22 [v] Jn 12:23; 13:31,32 **7:40** [w] Mt 21:11; Jn 1:21 **7:41** [x] ver 52; Jn 1:46 **7:42** [y] Mt 1:1 [z] Mic 5:2; Mt 2:5,6; Lk 2:4 **7:43** [a] Jn 9:16; 10:19 **7:44** [b] ver 30 **7:46** [c] Mt 7:28 **7:47** [d] ver 12 **7:48** [e] Jn 12:42 **7:50** [f] Jn 3:1; 19:39 **7:52** [g] ver 41 **8:1** [h] Mt 21:1 **8:2** [i] ver 20; Mt 26:55 **8:5** [j] Lev 20:10; Dt 22:22 **8:6** [k] Mt 22:15,18 [l] Mt 12:10 **8:7** [m] Dt 17:7 [n] Ro 2:1,22

11"No one, sir," she said.
*"Then neither do I condemn you,"[o] Jesus de-
clared. "Go now and leave your life of sin."[p]*

Dispute Over Jesus' Testimony

12When Jesus spoke again to the people,
he said, "I am[q] the light of the world.[r] Whoever follows me will never walk in darkness, but will have the light of life."[s]
13The Pharisees challenged him, "Here
you are, appearing as your own witness;
your testimony is not valid."[t]
14Jesus answered, "Even if I testify on
my own behalf, my testimony is valid, for
I know where I came from and where I am
going.[u] But you have no idea where I come
from[v] or where I am going. 15You judge by
human standards;[w] I pass judgment on no
one.[x] 16But if I do judge, my decisions are
true, because I am not alone. I stand with
the Father, who sent me.[y] 17In your own
Law it is written that the testimony of two
witnesses is true.[z] 18I am one who testifies
for myself; my other witness is the Father,
who sent me."[a]
19Then they asked him, "Where is your
father?"
"You do not know me or my Father,"[b]
Jesus replied. "If you knew me, you would
know my Father also."[c] 20He spoke these
words while teaching[d] in the temple courts
near the place where the offerings were
put.[e] Yet no one seized him, because his
hour had not yet come.[f]

Dispute Over Who Jesus Is

21Once more Jesus said to them, "I am
going away, and you will look for me, and
you will die[g] in your sin. Where I go, you
cannot come."[h]
22This made the Jews ask, "Will he kill
himself? Is that why he says, 'Where I go,
you cannot come'?"
23But he continued, "You are from below;
I am from above. You are of this world; I am
not of this world.[i] 24I told you that you would
die in your sins; if you do not believe that
I am he,[j] you will indeed die in your sins."
25"Who are you?" they asked.
"Just what I have been telling you from
the beginning," Jesus replied. 26"I have
much to say in judgment of you. But he who
sent me is trustworthy,[k] and what I have
heard from him I tell the world."[l]
27They did not understand that he was
telling them about his Father. 28So Jesus
said, "When you have lifted up[a] the Son of
Man,[m] then you will know that I am he and
that I do nothing on my own but speak just
what the Father has taught me. 29The one
who sent me is with me; he has not left me
alone,[n] for I always do what pleases him."[o]
30Even as he spoke, many believed in him.[p]

Dispute Over Whose Children Jesus' Opponents Are

31To the Jews who had believed him,
Jesus said, "If you hold to my teaching,[q]
you are really my disciples. 32Then you
will know the truth, and the truth will set
you free."[r]
33They answered him, "We are Abraham's descendants[s] and have never been
slaves of anyone. How can you say that we
shall be set free?"

---

a 28 The Greek for *lifted up* also means *exalted.*

8:13 *your testimony is not valid.* This phrase does not mean "false"; it means "not sufficient." The Pharisees challenged Jesus on legal grounds because no man on trial in a Jewish court was allowed to testify on his own behalf. Their point was that, if Jesus were the only one testifying as to who He claimed to be, it would not be enough to prove His case.

8:14 *my testimony is valid.* In 5:31 Jesus argued on the basis of legality and offered other witnesses. Sometimes, however, an individual is the only one who knows the facts about himself. Thus, self-disclosure is the only way to truth (7:29; 13:3).

8:15 *human standards.* This could mean either "according to appearance" or "by human standards." The religious leaders formed conclusions based on human standards and an imperfect, external, and superficial examination. Jesus did not judge according to human standards or outward appearances.

8:24 *I am he.* This was God's designation of Himself (Ex. 3:14). Jesus was claiming to be God. This assertion was not understood by the religious leaders at this time. Later, Jesus' claim to be the "I am" (v. 58) prompted the Jewish leaders to seek His life (v. 59).

8:31 God's Word Confirms—The Bible establishes the truth in our own hearts in several ways.

1. *It confirms our salvation.* In Jesus' own words in the Gospel of John: "Very truly I tell you, whoever hears my word and believes him who sent me has eternal life and will not be judged but has crossed over from death to life." (John 5:24). Compare John 3:16; 6:27,35,37,40; 10:27–29; Romans 8:1.
2. It confirms the hand of God in all of life's bitter *disappointments.* Romans 8:28 provides reassurance and comfort in these crucial situations: "And we know that in all things God works for the good of those who love him, who have been called according to his purpose."
3. *It confirms our forgiveness when we sin.* Repeatedly, the Bible assures us that all confessed sin is instantly and eternally forgiven (Ps. 32:5; 103:12; Is. 38:17).

8:33 *have never been slaves of anyone.* The Pharisees' objection is startling. In their past, the

8:11 [o] Jn 3:17 [p] Jn 5:14 **8:12** [q] Jn 6:35 [r] Jn 1:4; 12:35 [s] Pr 4:18; Mt 5:14 **8:13** [t] Jn 5:31 **8:14** [u] Jn 13:3; 16:28 [v] Jn 7:28; 9:29 **8:15** [w] Jn 7:24 [x] Jn 3:17 **8:16** [y] Jn 5:30 **8:17** [z] Dt 17:6; Mt 18:16 **8:18** [a] Jn 5:37 **8:19** [b] Jn 16:3 [c] Jn 14:7; 1Jn 2:23 **8:20** [d] Mt 26:55 [e] Mk 12:41 [f] Mt 26:18; Jn 7:30 **8:21** [g] Eze 3:18 [h] Jn 7:34; 13:33 **8:23** [i] Jn 3:31; 17:14 **8:24** [j] Jn 4:26; 13:19 **8:26** [k] Jn 7:28 [l] Jn 3:32; 15:15 **8:28** [m] Jn 3:14; 5:19; 12:32 **8:29** [n] ver 16; Jn 16:32 [o] Jn 4:34; 5:30; 6:38 **8:30** [p] Jn 7:31 **8:31** [q] Jn 15:7; 2Jn 9 **8:32** [r] Ro 8:2; Jas 2:12 **8:33** [s] ver 37,39; Mt 3:9

34 Jesus replied, "Very truly I tell you, everyone who sins is a slave to sin.[t] 35 Now a slave has no permanent place in the family, but a son belongs to it forever.[u] 36 So if the Son sets you free, you will be free indeed. 37 I know that you are Abraham's descendants. Yet you are looking for a way to kill me,[v] because you have no room for my word. 38 I am telling you what I have seen in the Father's presence,[w] and you are doing what you have heard from your father.[a]"

39 "Abraham is our father," they answered.

"If you were Abraham's children,"[x] said Jesus, "then you would[b] do what Abraham did. 40 As it is, you are looking for a way to kill me, a man who has told you the truth that I heard from God.[y] Abraham did not do such things. 41 You are doing the works of your own father."[z]

"We are not illegitimate children," they protested. "The only Father we have is God himself."[a]

42 Jesus said to them, "If God were your Father, you would love me,[b] for I have come here from God.[c] I have not come on my own;[d] God sent me.[e] 43 Why is my language not clear to you? Because you are unable to hear what I say. 44 You belong to your father, the devil,[f] and you want to carry out your father's desires.[g] He was a murderer from the beginning, not holding to the truth, for there is no truth in him. When he lies, he speaks his native language, for he is a liar and the father of lies.[h] 45 Yet because I tell the truth,[i] you do not believe me! 46 Can any of you prove me guilty of sin? If I am telling the truth, why don't you believe me? 47 Whoever belongs to God hears what God says.[j] The reason you do not hear is that you do not belong to God."

Jesus' Claims About Himself

48 The Jews answered him, "Aren't we right in saying that you are a Samaritan[k] and demon-possessed?"[l]

49 "I am not possessed by a demon," said Jesus, "but I honor my Father and you dishonor me. 50 I am not seeking glory for myself;[m] but there is one who seeks it, and he is the judge. 51 Very truly I tell you, whoever obeys my word will never see death."[n]

52 At this they exclaimed, "Now we know that you are demon-possessed! Abraham died and so did the prophets, yet you say that whoever obeys your word will never taste death. 53 Are you greater than our father Abraham?[o] He died, and so did the prophets. Who do you think you are?"

54 Jesus replied, "If I glorify myself,[p] my glory means nothing. My Father, whom you claim as your God, is the one who glorifies me.[q] 55 Though you do not know him,[r] I know him.[s] If I said I did not, I would be a liar like you, but I do know him and obey his word.[t] 56 Your father Abraham[u] rejoiced at the thought of seeing my day; he saw it[v] and was glad."

57 "You are not yet fifty years old," they said to him, "and you have seen Abraham!"

58 "Very truly I tell you," Jesus answered, "before Abraham was born,[w] I am!"[x] 59 At this, they picked up stones to stone him,[y] but Jesus hid himself,[z] slipping away from the temple grounds.

Jesus Heals a Man Born Blind

9 As he went along, he saw a man blind from birth. 2 His disciples asked him, "Rabbi,[a] who sinned,[b] this man[c] or his parents,[d] that he was born blind?"

3 "Neither this man nor his parents sinned," said Jesus, "but this happened so that the works of God might be displayed in him.[e] 4 As long as it is day,[f] we must do the works of him who sent me. Night is coming, when no one can work. 5 While I am in the world, I am the light of the world."[g]

---

[a] 38 Or *presence. Therefore do what you have heard from the Father.* [b] 39 Some early manuscripts *"If you are Abraham's children," said Jesus, "then*

Israelites had been in bondage to the Egyptians, the Assyrians, and the Babylonians. At the time they spoke, Israel was under the power of Rome.

8:39 ***Abraham is our father.*** The Pharisees believed that being a descendant of Abraham guaranteed them a place in heaven.

8:41 ***We are not illegitimate children.*** From ancient times, this has been interpreted as a sneer, as if to say, "We are not born of fornication, but You are." Apparently gossip followed Jesus, alleging that He had been conceived out of wedlock.

8:53 ***Are you greater than our father Abraham?*** Abraham and the prophets kept God's word and died. Jesus was claiming not that He would prevent physical death, but that He could give eternal life. To the Jewish leaders, this was proof that Jesus was demon-possessed.

8:58–59 ***I am.*** Jesus was not just claiming to have lived before Abraham; He was claiming eternal existence. He was claiming to be God Himself (Ex. 3:14). This time the Jewish leaders understood that Jesus was claiming to be God, so they took up stones to stone Him for blasphemy (Lev. 24:16).

9:1 ***a man blind from birth.*** Most likely he was a beggar. Beggars waited by the gates of the temple for gifts from worshipers. Therefore, it is likely that this scene took place near the temple.

9:2 ***who sinned.*** It was commonly supposed that sickness was a result of sin. It would follow that sin

8:34 [t] Ro 6:16; 2Pe 2:19 **8:35** [u] Gal 4:30 **8:37** [v] ver 39, 40 **8:38** [w] Jn 5:19,30; 14:10,24 **8:39** [x] ver 37; Ro 9:7; Gal 3:7 **8:40** [y] ver 26 **8:41** [z] ver 38,44 [a] Isa 63:16; 64:8 **8:42** [b] 1Jn 5:1 [c] Jn 16:27; 17:8 [d] Jn 7:28 [e] Jn 3:17 **8:44** [f] 1Jn 3:8 [g] ver 38,41 [h] Ge 3:4 **8:45** [i] Jn 18:37 **8:47** [j] Jn 18:37; 1Jn 4:6 **8:48** [k] Mt 10:5 [l] ver 52; Jn 7:20 **8:50** [m] ver 54; Jn 5:41 **8:51** [n] Jn 11:26 **8:53** [o] Jn 4:12 **8:54** [p] ver 50 [q] Jn 16:14; 17:1,5 **8:55** [r] ver 19 [s] Jn 7:28,29 [t] Jn 15:10 **8:56** [u] ver 37,39 [v] Mt 13:17; Heb 11:13 **8:58** [w] Jn 1:2; 17:5,24 [x] Ex 3:14 **8:59** [y] Lev 24:16; Jn 10:31; 11:8 [z] Jn 12:36 **9:2** [a] Mt 23:7 [b] ver 34; Lk 13:2; Ac 28:4 [c] Eze 18:20 [d] Ex 20:5; Job 21:19 **9:3** [e] Jn 11:4 **9:4** [f] Jn 11:9; 12:35 **9:5** [g] Jn 1:4; 8:12; 12:46

6After saying this, he spit[h] on the ground, made some mud with the saliva, and put it on the man's eyes. 7"Go," he told him, "wash in the Pool of Siloam"[i] (this word means "Sent"). So the man went and washed, and came home seeing.[j]

8His neighbors and those who had formerly seen him begging asked, "Isn't this the same man who used to sit and beg?"[k] 9Some claimed that he was.

Others said, "No, he only looks like him."

But he himself insisted, "I am the man."

10"How then were your eyes opened?" they asked.

11He replied, "The man they call Jesus made some mud and put it on my eyes. He told me to go to Siloam and wash. So I went and washed, and then I could see."[l]

12"Where is this man?" they asked him.

"I don't know," he said.

The Pharisees Investigate the Healing

13They brought to the Pharisees the man who had been blind. 14Now the day on which Jesus had made the mud and opened the man's eyes was a Sabbath.[m] 15Therefore the Pharisees also asked him how he had received his sight.[n] "He put mud on my eyes," the man replied, "and I washed, and now I see."

16Some of the Pharisees said, "This man is not from God, for he does not keep the Sabbath."[o]

But others asked, "How can a sinner perform such signs?" So they were divided.[p]

17Then they turned again to the blind man, "What have you to say about him? It was your eyes he opened."

The man replied, "He is a prophet."[q]

18They[r] still did not believe that he had been blind and had received his sight until they sent for the man's parents. 19"Is this your son?" they asked. "Is this the one you say was born blind? How is it that now he can see?"

20"We know he is our son," the parents answered, "and we know he was born blind. 21But how he can see now, or who opened his eyes, we don't know. Ask him. He is of age; he will speak for himself." 22His parents said this because they were afraid of the Jewish leaders,[s] who already had decided that anyone who acknowledged that Jesus was the Messiah would be put out[t] of the synagogue.[u] 23That was why his parents said, "He is of age; ask him."[v]

24A second time they summoned the man who had been blind. "Give glory to God by telling the truth,"[w] they said. "We know this man is a sinner."[x]

25He replied, "Whether he is a sinner or not, I don't know. One thing I do know. I was blind but now I see!"

26Then they asked him, "What did he do to you? How did he open your eyes?"

27He answered, "I have told you already[y] and you did not listen. Why do you want to hear it again? Do you want to become his disciples too?"

28Then they hurled insults at him and said, "You are this fellow's disciple! We are disciples of Moses![z] 29We know that God spoke to Moses, but as for this fellow, we don't even know where he comes from."[a]

30The man answered, "Now that is remarkable! You don't know where he comes from, yet he opened my eyes. 31We know that God does not listen to sinners. He listens to the godly person who does his will.[b] 32Nobody has ever heard of opening the eyes of a man born blind. 33If this man were not from God,[c] he could do nothing."

34To this they replied, "You were steeped in sin at birth;[d] how dare you lecture us!" And they threw him out.[e]

Spiritual Blindness

35Jesus heard that they had thrown him out, and when he found him, he said, "Do you believe in the Son of Man?"

36"Who is he, sir?" the man asked. "Tell me so that I may believe in him."[f]

37Jesus said, "You have now seen him; in fact, he is the one speaking with you."[g]

38Then the man said, "Lord, I believe," and he worshiped him.[h]

---

committed by a baby still in the womb or sin committed by parents could result in a baby being born with a disease. Jesus rejected both suggestions (v. 3).

9:7 *Pool of Siloam.* Hezekiah had a tunnel cut through solid rock to transport water from Gihon into the city of Jerusalem, to the pool of Siloam (2 Kin. 20:20; 2 Chr. 32:30). John emphasizes that the name Siloam means "Sent," because Jesus had just announced that He had been sent by God (v. 4).

9:22 *put out of the synagogue.* To take this action was a form of excommunication. The Jews had three types of excommunication: one lasting 30 days, during which the person could not come within six feet of anybody else; one for an indefinite time, during which the person was excluded from all fellowship and worship; and one that meant absolute expulsion forever. These judgments were very serious because no one could conduct business with a person who was excommunicated.

9:30–33 *remarkable.* There is no healing of a blind man recorded anywhere in the Old Testament.

9:38 *Lord, I believe.* Note the progression throughout this chapter of the healed man's understanding

9:6 [h] Mk 7:33; 8:23 **9:7** [i] ver 11; 2Ki 5:10; Lk 13:4 [j] Isa 35:5; Jn 11:37 **9:8** [k] Ac 3:2, 10 **9:11** [l] ver 7 **9:14** [m] Jn 5:9 **9:15** [n] ver 10 **9:16** [o] Mt 12:2 [p] Jn 6:52; 7:43; 10:19 **9:17** [q] Mt 21:11 **9:18** [r] Jn 1:19 **9:22** [s] Jn 7:13 [t] ver 34; Lk 6:22 [u] Jn 12:42; 16:2 **9:23** [v] ver 21 **9:24** [w] Jos 7:19 [x] ver 16 **9:27** [y] ver 15 **9:28** [z] Jn 5:45 **9:29** [a] Jn 8:14 **9:31** [b] Ge 18:23-32; Ps 34:15, 16; 66:18; 145:19, 20; Pr 15:29; Isa 1:15; 59:1, 2; Jn 15:7; Jas 5:16-18; 1Jn 5:14, 15 **9:33** [c] ver 16; Jn 3:2 **9:34** [d] ver 2 [e] ver 22, 35; Isa 66:5 **9:36** [f] Ro 10:14 **9:37** [g] Jn 4:26 **9:38** [h] Mt 28:9

39 Jesus said,[a] "For judgment[i] I have come
into this world,[j] so that the blind will see[k]
and those who see will become blind."[l]
40 Some Pharisees who were with him
heard him say this and asked, "What? Are
we blind too?"[m]
41 Jesus said, "If you were blind, you
would not be guilty of sin; but now that
you claim you can see, your guilt remains.[n]

The Good Shepherd and His Sheep

10 "Very truly I tell you Pharisees, anyone who does not enter the sheep pen
by the gate, but climbs in by some other way, is a thief and a robber. 2 The one
who enters by the gate is the shepherd of
the sheep.[o] 3 The gatekeeper opens the gate
for him, and the sheep listen to his voice.[p]
He calls his own sheep by name and leads
them out. 4 When he has brought out all his
own, he goes on ahead of them, and his
sheep follow him because they know his
voice. 5 But they will never follow a stranger; in fact, they will run away from him
because they do not recognize a stranger's
voice." 6 Jesus used this figure of speech,[q]
but the Pharisees did not understand what
he was telling them.
7 Therefore Jesus said again, "Very truly
I tell you, I am the gate for the sheep. 8 All
who have come before me[r] are thieves and
robbers, but the sheep have not listened
to them. 9 I am the gate; whoever enters
through me will be saved.[b] They will come
in and go out, and find pasture. 10 The thief
comes only to steal and kill and destroy;
I have come that they may have life, and
have it to the full.
11 "I am the good shepherd.[s] The good
shepherd lays down his life for the sheep.[t]
12 The hired hand is not the shepherd and
does not own the sheep. So when he sees
the wolf coming, he abandons the sheep
and runs away.[u] Then the wolf attacks the
flock and scatters it. 13 The man runs away
because he is a hired hand and cares nothing for the sheep.
14 "I am the good shepherd;[v] I know my
sheep[w] and my sheep know me— 15 just as
the Father knows me and I know the Father[x]—and I lay down my life for the sheep.
16 I have other sheep[y] that are not of this
sheep pen. I must bring them also. They
too will listen to my voice, and there shall
be one flock[z] and one shepherd.[a] 17 The reason my Father loves me is that I lay down
my life[b]—only to take it up again. 18 No one
takes it from me, but I lay it down of my
own accord.[c] I have authority to lay it down
and authority to take it up again. This command I received from my Father."[d]

[a] *38,39* Some early manuscripts do not have *Then the man said . . . 39Jesus said.* [b] *9* Or *kept safe*

---

of the person of Christ. First, he called Jesus "a man" (v. 11); then, "a prophet" (v. 17); and finally, he realized that Jesus is the Son of God (vv. 35–38).

10:1 *sheep pen.* A sheep pen was a walled enclosure or high fence made with stakes and having one door or gate; often the enclosure was a cave. ***some other way.*** The Pharisees had secured their power by illegitimate means.

10:3 *The gatekeeper.* The gatekeeper was the undershepherd. ***calls his own sheep by name.*** The naming of sheep was an ancient practice (Ps. 147:4; Is. 40:26).

10:7 *I am the gate.* In verses 1–5, Jesus is the shepherd; here, He is the door. Some shepherds lay down across the entry of the sheep pen at night to sleep. Wild beasts would be discouraged from entering, and sheep would not exit. Thus, the shepherd was also the door.

10:10 *have it to the full.* The thieves take life; the shepherd gives it. Abundant life includes salvation, nourishment, healing (v. 9), and much more. *Life* here refers to eternal life, God's life. It speaks not only of endlessness, but of quality of life. With Christ, life on earth can reach much higher quality, and then in heaven it will be complete and perfect.

10:11 The Ministry of Jesus—Jesus' most important teachings are: the kingdom of God (Matt. 5–7; 24–25); His divine authority over men (Matt. 7:28–29; Mark 2:10); His own role as God and Messiah demonstrated by miracles and signs; the significance of His death and resurrection (Matt. 16:21; Luke 24:26); the relationship which His disciples and subsequent believers are to share with Him (John 13–16); and the urgency of His commission to believers to make disciples (Matt. 28:19–20). The most significant events of His earthly life, His death, and resurrection, are central to the entire Christian faith (1 Cor. 15:14). The death of Christ was a humiliating physical death (John 19:18,33) that constituted a spiritual separation from God (Matt. 27:46). Within this moment there occurred the inexplicable mystery of the Father punishing the Son for the sins of the world (2 Cor. 5:21; 1 Pet. 3:18). The greatest crime of human history was in the plan of God (Acts 2:23) and became the basis of salvation for sinners (Is. 53:5). The resurrection of Christ demonstrated that His death, by which believing sinners are justified, was valid (1 Cor. 15:12–20). The historical evidence for the resurrection is plentiful: the many separate accounts of post-resurrection appearances, the empty tomb, and the transformed disciples. It is the power of the resurrection that empowers Christians today to live the Christian life (Eph. 1:19–20; Phil. 3:10).

10:16 *I have other sheep.* These were not Jews in heathen lands, but Gentiles. The Jewish people had asked if Jesus would go and teach the Gentiles (7:35). Jesus now declared that He had sheep among the despised heathen. ***one flock.*** This anticipates the salvation of the Gentiles and the formation of the church, in which converted Jews and Gentiles would form one spiritual body (Gal. 3:28; Eph. 2:16).

9:39 [i] Jn 5:22 [j] Jn 3:19 [k] Lk 4:18 [l] Mt 13:13
9:40 [m] Ro 2:19 **9:41** [n] Jn 15:22, 24 **10:2** [o] ver 11, 14
10:3 [p] ver 4, 5, 14, 16, 27 **10:6** [q] Jn 16:25
10:8 [r] Jer 23:1, 2 **10:11** [s] ver 14; Isa 40:11; Eze 34:11-16, 23; Heb 13:20; 1Pe 5:4; Rev 7:17 [t] Jn 15:13; 1Jn 3:16
10:12 [u] Zec 11:16, 17 **10:14** [v] ver 11 [w] ver 27
10:15 [x] Mt 11:27 **10:16** [y] Isa 56:8 [z] Jn 11:52; Eph 2:11-19 [a] Eze 37:24; 1Pe 2:25 **10:17** [b] ver 11, 15, 18
10:18 [c] Mt 26:53 [d] Jn 15:10; Php 2:8; Heb 5:8

19The Jews who heard these words were again divided.[e] 20Many of them said, "He is demon-possessed[f] and raving mad.[g] Why listen to him?"

21But others said, "These are not the sayings of a man possessed by a demon.[h] Can a demon open the eyes of the blind?"[i]

Further Conflict Over Jesus' Claims

22Then came the Festival of Dedication[a] at Jerusalem. It was winter, 23and Jesus was in the temple courts walking in Solomon's Colonnade.[j] 24The Jews[k] who were there gathered around him, saying, "How long will you keep us in suspense? If you are the Messiah, tell us plainly."[l]

25Jesus answered, "I did tell you,[m] but you do not believe. The works I do in my Father's name testify about me,[n] 26but you do not believe because you are not my sheep.[o] 27My sheep listen to my voice; I know them,[p] and they follow me.[q] 28I give them eternal life, and they shall never perish; no one will snatch them out of my hand.[r] 29My Father, who has given them to me,[s] is greater than all[b];[t] no one can snatch them out of my Father's hand. 30I and the Father are one."[u]

31Again his Jewish opponents picked up stones to stone him,[v] 32but Jesus said to them, "I have shown you many good works from the Father. For which of these do you stone me?"

33"We are not stoning you for any good work," they replied, "but for blasphemy, because you, a mere man, claim to be God."[w]

34Jesus answered them, "Is it not written in your Law,[x] 'I have said you are "gods"'[c]?[y] 35If he called them 'gods,' to whom the word of God came—and Scripture cannot be set aside— 36what about the one whom the Father set apart[z] as his very own[a] and sent into the world?[b] Why then do you accuse me of blasphemy because I said, 'I am God's Son'?[c] 37Do not believe me unless I do the works of my Father.[d] 38But if I do them, even though you do not believe me, believe the works, that you may know and understand that the Father is in me, and I in the Father."[e] 39Again they tried to seize him,[f] but he escaped their grasp.[g]

40Then Jesus went back across the Jordan[h] to the place where John had been baptizing in the early days. There he stayed, 41and many people came to him. They said, "Though John never performed a sign,[i] all that John said about this man was true."[j] 42And in that place many believed in Jesus.[k]

The Death of Lazarus

11 Now a man named Lazarus was sick. He was from Bethany,[l] the village of Mary and her sister Martha.[m] 2(This Mary, whose brother Lazarus now lay sick, was the same one who poured perfume on the Lord and wiped his feet with her hair.)[n] 3So the sisters sent word to Jesus, "Lord, the one you love[o] is sick."

4When he heard this, Jesus said, "This sickness will not end in death. No, it is for God's glory[p] so that God's Son may be glorified through it." 5Now Jesus loved Martha and her sister and Lazarus. 6So when he heard that Lazarus was sick, he stayed where he was two more days, 7and then he said to his disciples, "Let us go back to Judea."[q]

---

[a] 22 That is, Hanukkah [b] 29 Many early manuscripts *What my Father has given me is greater than all* [c] 34 Psalm 82:6

10:19–21 ***Many of them said ... others said.*** After Jesus' analogy of the good shepherd, the editorial comment by John is fitting. In the analogy, Jesus was the good shepherd whose sheep hear His voice, implying that there are sheep who do not hear His voice. John's comment indicates that some believe and others do not. This is the same division that occurred in 9:16.

10:22 ***the Festival of Dedication.*** This festival was celebrated for eight days. In 167 B.C. Antiochus Epiphanes desecrated the temple in Jerusalem, as prophesied in Daniel 11:31. The Maccabeans restored and purified the temple. In commemoration of the restoration, the Festival of Dedication was instituted. Today it is also known as the Festival of Lights or Hanukkah.

10:27–29 ***listen ... follow.*** The following of the sheep is a metaphor for faith. Other metaphors for faith in this Gospel include drinking water (4:14), eating bread (6:50–51), eating flesh, and drinking blood (6:54).

10:30 ***I and the Father are one.*** The Jewish opponents understood that Jesus was claiming to be God (vv. 31,33).

10:34 ***you are "gods."*** In the Old Testament, judges were called gods. They exercised godlike judicial sovereignty. Psalm 82:6, the verse quoted here, refers to judges who violate the law. Jesus' argument was that, if the divine name had been applied by God to mere men, there could be neither blasphemy nor folly in its application to the incarnate Son of God Himself.

11:1 ***Bethany.*** This was a small village on the southeast slope of the Mount of Olives. It was located about two miles from Jerusalem.

11:4 ***not end in death.*** This phrase means not having death as its final result.

11:6–8 ***he stayed ... two more days.*** God's purpose was to glorify His Son (v. 4) and to cause the disciples to grow (v. 15). Had Jesus immediately rushed to Lazarus' bedside and healed him, Lazarus would

10:19 [e] Jn 7:43; 9:16 **10:20** [f] Jn 7:20 [g] Mk 3:21 **10:21** [h] Mt 4:24 [i] Ex 4:11; Jn 9:32, 33 **10:23** [j] Ac 3:11; 5:12 **10:24** [k] Jn 1:19 [l] Jn 16:25, 29 **10:25** [m] Jn 8:58 [n] Jn 5:36 **10:26** [o] Jn 8:47 **10:27** [p] ver 14 [q] ver 4 **10:28** [r] Jn 6:39 **10:29** [s] Jn 17:2, 6, 24 [t] Jn 14:28 **10:30** [u] Jn 17:21-23 **10:31** [v] Jn 8:59 **10:33** [w] Lev 24:16; Jn 5:18 **10:34** [x] Jn 8:17; Ro 3:19 [y] Ps 82:6 **10:36** [z] Jer 1:5 [a] Jn 6:69 [b] Jn 3:17 [c] Jn 5:17, 18 **10:37** [d] ver 25; Jn 15:24 **10:38** [e] Jn 14:10, 11, 20; 17:21 **10:39** [f] Jn 7:30 [g] Lk 4:30; Jn 8:59 **10:40** [h] Jn 1:28 **10:41** [i] Jn 2:11; 3:30 [j] Jn 1:26, 27, 30, 34 **10:42** [k] Jn 7:31 **11:1** [l] Mt 21:17 [m] Lk 10:38 **11:2** [n] Mk 14:3; Lk 7:38; Jn 12:3 **11:3** [o] ver 5, 36 **11:4** [p] ver 40; Jn 9:3 **11:7** [q] Jn 10:40

8“But Rabbi,”[r] they said, “a short while
ago the Jews there tried to stone you,[s] and
yet you are going back?”
9Jesus answered, “Are there not twelve
hours of daylight? Anyone who walks in
the daytime will not stumble, for they see
by this world’s light.[t] 10It is when a person
walks at night that they stumble, for they
have no light.”
11After he had said this, he went on to
tell them, “Our friend[u] Lazarus has fall-
en asleep;[v] but I am going there to wake
him up.”
12His disciples replied, “Lord, if he
sleeps, he will get better.” 13Jesus had been
speaking of his death, but his disciples
thought he meant natural sleep.[w]
14So then he told them plainly, “Lazarus
is dead, 15and for your sake I am glad I was
not there, so that you may believe. But let
us go to him.”
16Then Thomas[x] (also known as Didymus[a]) said to the rest of the disciples, “Let
us also go, that we may die with him.”

Jesus Comforts the Sisters of Lazarus

17On his arrival, Jesus found that Lazarus
had already been in the tomb for four days.[y]
18Now Bethany[z] was less than two miles[b]
from Jerusalem, 19and many Jews had
come to Martha and Mary to comfort them
in the loss of their brother.[a] 20When Martha
heard that Jesus was coming, she went out
to meet him, but Mary stayed at home.[b]
21“Lord,” Martha said to Jesus, “if you
had been here, my brother would not have
died.[c] 22But I know that even now God will
give you whatever you ask.”[d]
23Jesus said to her, “Your brother will
rise again.”
24Martha answered, “I know he will rise
again in the resurrection[e] at the last day.”
25Jesus said to her, “I am the resurrection
and the life.[f] The one who believes in me
will live, even though they die; 26and whoever lives by believing in me will never die.
Do you believe this?”
27“Yes, Lord,” she replied, “I believe that
you are the Messiah,[g] the Son of God,[h] who
is to come into the world.”[i]
28After she had said this, she went back
and called her sister Mary aside. “The
Teacher[j] is here,” she said, “and is asking
for you.” 29When Mary heard this, she got
up quickly and went to him. 30Now Jesus
had not yet entered the village, but was still
at the place where Martha had met him.[k]
31When the Jews who had been with Mary
in the house, comforting her,[l] noticed how
quickly she got up and went out, they followed her, supposing she was going to the
tomb to mourn there.
32When Mary reached the place where
Jesus was and saw him, she fell at his feet
and said, “Lord, if you had been here, my
brother would not have died.”[m]
33When Jesus saw her weeping, and the
Jews who had come along with her also
weeping, he was deeply moved[n] in spirit and troubled.[o] 34“Where have you laid
him?” he asked.
“Come and see, Lord,” they replied.
35Jesus wept.[p]
36Then the Jews said, “See how he loved
him!”[q]
37But some of them said, “Could not he
who opened the eyes of the blind man[r] have
kept this man from dying?”[s]

Jesus Raises Lazarus From the Dead

38Jesus, once more deeply moved,[t] came
to the tomb. It was a cave with a stone laid
across the entrance.[u] 39“Take away the
stone,” he said.
“But, Lord,” said Martha, the sister of the
dead man, “by this time there is a bad odor,
for he has been there four days.”[v]
40Then Jesus said, “Did I not tell you
that if you believe,[w] you will see the glory
of God?”[x]
41So they took away the stone. Then
Jesus looked up[y] and said, “Father,[z] I thank
you that you have heard me. 42I knew that
you always hear me, but I said this for the
benefit of the people standing here,[a] that
they may believe that you sent me.”[b]
43When he had said this, Jesus called in
a loud voice, “Lazarus, come out!”[c] 44The

---

[a] *16 Thomas* (Aramaic) and *Didymus* (Greek) both mean *twin.* [b] *18* Or about 3 kilometers

---

not have died and Jesus would not have been able to manifest His glory by raising Lazarus.

11:16 ***Let us also go, that we may die with him.*** While the Lord saw their development in faith, Thomas saw their deaths. Yet, in his loyalty, he followed anyway.

11:33 ***troubled.*** This word means to be stirred up, disturbed. Jesus was moved by the mourning of Mary and indignant at the hypocritical lamentations of His enemies.

11:37 ***Could not he . . . have kept this man from dying.*** Some people misinterpreted Jesus' tears as powerlessness. They complained that He had healed others, but now was impotent.

11:43 ***Lazarus.*** Augustine once said that, if Jesus had not designated Lazarus by name, all the graves would have been emptied at His command (5:28). Raising Lazarus from the dead is the seventh sign of

11:8 [r] Mt 23:7 [s] Jn 8:59; 10:31 **11:9** [t] Jn 9:4; 12:35 **11:11** [u] ver 3 [v] Ac 7:60 **11:13** [w] Mt 9:24 **11:16** [x] Mt 10:3; Jn 14:5; 20:24-28; 21:2; Ac 1:13 **11:17** [y] ver 6, 39 **11:18** [z] ver 1 **11:19** [a] ver 31; Job 2:11 **11:20** [b] Lk 10:38-42 **11:21** [c] ver 32, 37 **11:22** [d] ver 41, 42; Jn 9:31 **11:24** [e] Da 12:2; Jn 5:28, 29; Ac 24:15 **11:25** [f] Jn 1:4 **11:27** [g] Lk 2:11 [h] Mt 16:16 [i] Jn 6:14 **11:28** [j] Mt 26:18; Jn 13:13 **11:30** [k] ver 20 **11:31** [l] ver 19 **11:32** [m] ver 21 **11:33** [n] ver 38 [o] Jn 12:27 **11:35** [p] Lk 19:41 **11:36** [q] ver 3 **11:37** [r] Jn 9:6, 7 [s] ver 21, 32 **11:38** [t] ver 33 [u] Mt 27:60; Lk 24:2; Jn 20:1 **11:39** [v] ver 17 **11:40** [w] ver 23-25 [x] ver 4 **11:41** [y] Jn 17:1 [z] Mt 11:25 **11:42** [a] Jn 12:30 [b] Jn 3:17 **11:43** [c] Lk 7:14

dead man came out, his hands and feet
wrapped with strips of linen,[d] and a cloth
around his face.[e]
Jesus said to them, "Take off the grave
clothes and let him go."

The Plot to Kill Jesus

45Therefore many of the Jews who had
come to visit Mary,[f] and had seen what
Jesus did,[g] believed in him.[h] 46But some of
them went to the Pharisees and told them
what Jesus had done. 47Then the chief
priests and the Pharisees[i] called a meeting[j]
of the Sanhedrin.[k]
"What are we accomplishing?" they
asked. "Here is this man performing many
signs.[l] 48If we let him go on like this, everyone will believe in him, and then the
Romans will come and take away both our
temple and our nation."
49Then one of them, named Caiaphas,[m]
who was high priest that year,[n] spoke up,
"You know nothing at all! 50You do not realize that it is better for you that one man
die for the people than that the whole nation perish."[o]
51He did not say this on his own, but as
high priest that year he prophesied that
Jesus would die for the Jewish nation, 52and
not only for that nation but also for the scattered children of God, to bring them together and make them one.[p] 53So from that day
on they plotted to take his life.[q]
54Therefore Jesus no longer moved
about publicly among the people of Judea.[r]
Instead he withdrew to a region near the
wilderness, to a village called Ephraim,
where he stayed with his disciples.
55When it was almost time for the Jewish
Passover,[s] many went up from the country
to Jerusalem for their ceremonial cleansing[t] before the Passover. 56They kept looking for Jesus,[u] and as they stood in the temple courts they asked one another, "What
do you think? Isn't he coming to the festival
at all?" 57But the chief priests and the Pharisees had given orders that anyone who
found out where Jesus was should report
it so that they might arrest him.

Jesus Anointed at Bethany

12 Six days before the Passover,[v] Jesus
came to Bethany,[w] where Lazarus
lived, whom Jesus had raised from the
dead. 2Here a dinner was given in Jesus'
honor. Martha served,[x] while Lazarus was
among those reclining at the table with
him. 3Then Mary took about a pint[a] of pure
nard, an expensive perfume;[y] she poured it
on Jesus' feet and wiped his feet with her
hair.[z] And the house was filled with the fragrance of the perfume.
4But one of his disciples, Judas Iscariot, who was later to betray him,[a] objected,
5"Why wasn't this perfume sold and the
money given to the poor? It was worth a
year's wages.[b]" 6He did not say this because
he cared about the poor but because he was
a thief; as keeper of the money bag,[b] he
used to help himself to what was put into it.
7"Leave her alone," Jesus replied. "It was
intended that she should save this perfume
for the day of my burial.[c] 8You will always
have the poor among you,[cd] but you will
not always have me."
9Meanwhile a large crowd of Jews found
out that Jesus was there and came, not only
because of him but also to see Lazarus,
whom he had raised from the dead.[e] 10So
the chief priests made plans to kill Lazarus as well, 11for on account of him[f] many

[a] 3 Or about 0.5 liter [b] 5 Greek *three hundred denarii* [c] 8 See Deut. 15:11.

Jesus' messiahship, the greatest miracle of all, giving life back to the dead.

11:49–52 *it is better.* In the opinion of Caiaphas, Jesus should die rather than plunge the nation into destruction. John adds that by virtue of his office Caiaphas pronounced a message of God unconsciously. Caiaphas was a prophet in spite of himself. John also saw in Caiaphas' words a prophecy that Jesus should die not only for Israel but for the Gentiles as well.

11:53 *they plotted to take his life.* Humanly speaking, the resurrection of Lazarus was a major factor that led to the plot by the Jewish religious leaders to kill Christ. At this point the council decided informally, if not formally, to put Jesus to death. It is ironic that these men believed they could put to death permanently One who could raise the dead.

12:1 *Six days before the Passover.* If the crucifixion took place on a Friday, this dinner occurred during the evening of the previous Saturday. Verse 12 seems to support this conclusion because the Jerusalem entry took place on Sunday.

12:3 *a pint of pure nard.* This was very expensive. Judas Iscariot said that this perfume cost a year's wages (v. 5) which amounts to about 300 denarii. One denarius was a laborer's wage for one day. ***poured it on Jesus' feet.*** Mary also anointed Jesus' head. The custom of that time was to anoint the heads of guests. Anointing Jesus' head was an act of honor; anointing His feet was a display of devotion.

12:10–11 *the chief priests made plans to kill Lazarus.* The chief priests were mostly Sadducees. They had an additional reason to kill Lazarus. He was a living refutation of their doctrine that there was no resurrection (11:57; Acts 23:8). Yet this was not a meeting of the Jewish council, nor was it a formal sentence of death. The ultimate motivation for wanting to kill Lazarus was that because of him many were believing in Jesus.

11:44 [d] Jn 19:40 [e] Jn 20:7 **11:45** [f] ver 19 [g] Jn 2:23 [h] Ex 14:31; Jn 7:31 **11:47** [i] ver 57 [j] Mt 26:3 [k] Mt 5:22 [l] Jn 2:11 **11:49** [m] Mt 26:3 [n] ver 51; Jn 18:13, 14 **11:50** [o] Jn 18:14 **11:52** [p] Isa 49:6; Jn 10:16 **11:53** [q] Mt 12:14 **11:54** [r] Jn 7:1 **11:55** [s] Ex 12:13, 23, 27; Mt 26:1, 2; Mk 14:1; Jn 13:1 [t] 2Ch 30:17, 18 **11:56** [u] Jn 7:11 **12:1** [v] Jn 11:55 [w] Mt 21:17 **12:2** [x] Lk 10:38-42 **12:3** [y] Mk 14:3 [z] Jn 11:2 **12:4** [a] Mt 10:4 **12:6** [b] Jn 13:29 **12:7** [c] Jn 19:40 **12:8** [d] Dt 15:11 **12:9** [e] Jn 11:43, 44 **12:11** [f] ver 17, 18; Jn 11:45

of the Jews were going over to Jesus and believing in him.[g]

Jesus Comes to Jerusalem as King

12The next day the great crowd that had come for the festival heard that Jesus was on his way to Jerusalem. 13They took palm branches and went out to meet him, shouting,

"Hosanna![*a*]"

"Blessed is he who comes in the name
of the Lord!"[*b*h]

"Blessed is the king of Israel!"[i]

14Jesus found a young donkey and sat on it, as it is written:

15"Do not be afraid, Daughter Zion;
see, your king is coming,
seated on a donkey's colt."[*c*j]

16At first his disciples did not understand all this.[k] Only after Jesus was glorified[l] did they realize that these things had been written about him and that these things had been done to him.

17Now the crowd that was with him[m] when he called Lazarus from the tomb and raised him from the dead continued to spread the word. 18Many people, because they had heard that he had performed this sign,[n] went out to meet him. 19So the Pharisees said to one another, "See, this is getting us nowhere. Look how the whole world has gone after him!"[o]

Jesus Predicts His Death

20Now there were some Greeks[p] among those who went up to worship at the festival. 21They came to Philip, who was from Bethsaida[q] in Galilee, with a request. "Sir," they said, "we would like to see Jesus." 22Philip went to tell Andrew; Andrew and Philip in turn told Jesus.

23Jesus replied, "The hour has come for the Son of Man to be glorified.[r] 24Very truly I tell you, unless a kernel of wheat falls to the ground and dies,[s] it remains only a single seed. But if it dies, it produces many seeds. 25Anyone who loves their life will lose it, while anyone who hates their life in this world will keep it[t] for eternal life. 26Whoever serves me must follow me; and where I am, my servant also will be.[u] My Father will honor the one who serves me.

27"Now my soul is troubled,[v] and what shall I say? 'Father,[w] save me from this hour'?[x] No, it was for this very reason I came to this hour. 28Father, glorify your name!"

Then a voice came from heaven,[y] "I have glorified it, and will glorify it again." 29The crowd that was there and heard it said it had thundered; others said an angel had spoken to him.

30Jesus said, "This voice was for your benefit,[z] not mine. 31Now is the time for judgment on this world;[a] now the prince of this world[b] will be driven out. 32And I, when I am lifted up[d] from the earth,[c] will draw all people to myself."[d] 33He said this to show the kind of death he was going to die.[e]

34The crowd spoke up, "We have heard from the Law that the Messiah will remain forever,[f] so how can you say, 'The Son of Man[g] must be lifted up'?[h] Who is this 'Son of Man'?"

35Then Jesus told them, "You are going to have the light[i] just a little while longer. Walk while you have the light,[j] before darkness overtakes you.[k] Whoever walks in the dark does not know where they are going. 36Believe in the light while you have the light, so that you may become children of light."[l] When he had finished speaking, Jesus left and hid himself from them.[m]

---

a *13* A Hebrew expression meaning "Save!" which became an exclamation of praise *b* *13* Psalm 118:25,26 *c* *15* Zech. 9:9 *d* *32* The Greek for *lifted up* also means *exalted.*

12:13–15 *the king of Israel.* Until this point, Jesus had discouraged expressions of support from the people (6:15; 7:1–8). Here, He allowed public enthusiasm. He entered Jerusalem on the back of a young donkey. This act fulfilled prophecy (Zech. 9:9) and as such was a symbolic proclamation that Jesus is the Messiah.

12:20 *to worship at the festival.* This verse indicates that these Greeks were Jewish proselytes. By recording this incident, perhaps John was hinting that the salvation rejected by many of the Jews was already passing to the Gentiles.

12:24 *unless a kernel of wheat ... dies.* When a seed dies, it produces fruit. Life comes by death. This principle is not only true in nature, but it is also true spiritually. Jesus was speaking first and foremost of Himself. He is the grain of wheat. His death would produce much fruit and would result in many living for God.

12:27 *Now my soul is troubled.* Jesus' agony over His impending death was not confined to Gethsemane, where He prayed for the cup to pass from Him (Matt. 26:39). He felt the agony and expressed it almost a week before Gethsemane.

12:35–36 *while you have the light.* Instead of answering the people's questions (v. 34), Jesus gave them a warning. Jesus is the light. He wanted the people to believe and abide in Him (v. 46).

12:11 [g] Jn 7:31 **12:13** [h] Ps 118:25,26 [i] Jn 1:49 **12:15** [j] Zec 9:9 **12:16** [k] Mk 9:32 [l] Jn 2:22; 7:39; 14:26 **12:17** [m] Jn 11:42 **12:18** [n] ver 11 **12:19** [o] Jn 11:47,48 **12:20** [p] Jn 7:35; Ac 11:20 **12:21** [q] Mt 11:21; Jn 1:44 **12:23** [r] Jn 13:32; 17:1 **12:24** [s] 1Co 15:36 **12:25** [t] Mt 10:39; Mk 8:35; Lk 14:26 **12:26** [u] Jn 14:3; 17:24; 2Co 5:8; 1Th 4:17 **12:27** [v] Mt 26:38,39; Jn 11:33,38; 13:21 [w] Mt 11:25 [x] ver 23 **12:28** [y] Mt 3:17 **12:30** [z] Jn 11:42 **12:31** [a] Jn 16:11 [b] Jn 14:30; 16:11; 2Co 4:4; Eph 2:2; 1Jn 4:4 **12:32** [c] ver 34; Jn 3:14; 8:28 [d] Jn 6:44 **12:33** [e] Jn 18:32 **12:34** [f] Ps 110:4; Isa 9:7; Eze 37:25; Da 7:14 [g] Mt 8:20 [h] Jn 3:14 **12:35** [i] ver 46 [j] Eph 5:8 [k] 1Jn 2:11 **12:36** [l] Lk 16:8 [m] Jn 8:59

Belief and Unbelief Among the Jews

37 Even after Jesus had performed so
many signs[n] in their presence, they still
would not believe in him. 38 This was to fulfill the word of Isaiah the prophet:

> "Lord, who has believed our message
> and to whom has the arm of the Lord
> been revealed?"[a][o]

39 For this reason they could not believe,
because, as Isaiah says elsewhere:

> 40 "He has blinded their eyes
> and hardened their hearts,
> so they can neither see with their eyes,
> nor understand with their hearts,
> nor turn—and I would heal them."[b][p]

41 Isaiah said this because he saw Jesus'
glory[q] and spoke about him.[r]
42 Yet at the same time many even among
the leaders believed in him.[s] But because of
the Pharisees[t] they would not openly acknowledge their faith for fear they would be
put out of the synagogue;[u] 43 for they loved
human praise more than praise from God.[v]
44 Then Jesus cried out, "Whoever believes in me does not believe in me only,
but in the one who sent me.[w] 45 The one who
looks at me is seeing the one who sent me.[x]
46 I have come into the world as a light,[y] so
that no one who believes in me should stay
in darkness.
47 "If anyone hears my words but does
not keep them, I do not judge that person.
For I did not come to judge the world, but
to save the world.[z] 48 There is a judge for the
one who rejects me and does not accept my
words; the very words I have spoken will
condemn them[a] at the last day. 49 For I did
not speak on my own, but the Father who
sent me commanded me[b] to say all that I
have spoken. 50 I know that his command
leads to eternal life. So whatever I say is
just what the Father has told me to say."

Jesus Washes His Disciples' Feet

13 It was just before the Passover Festival.[c] Jesus knew that the hour had
come[d] for him to leave this world and go
to the Father.[e] Having loved his own who
were in the world, he loved them to the end.
2 The evening meal was in progress,
and the devil had already prompted Judas, the son of Simon Iscariot, to betray
Jesus. 3 Jesus knew that the Father had put
all things under his power,[f] and that he
had come from God[g] and was returning
to God; 4 so he got up from the meal, took
off his outer clothing, and wrapped a towel around his waist. 5 After that, he poured
water into a basin and began to wash his
disciples' feet,[h] drying them with the towel
that was wrapped around him.
6 He came to Simon Peter, who said to
him, "Lord, are you going to wash my feet?"
7 Jesus replied, "You do not realize now
what I am doing, but later you will understand."[i]
8 "No," said Peter, "you shall never wash
my feet."
Jesus answered, "Unless I wash you, you
have no part with me."
9 "Then, Lord," Simon Peter replied, "not
just my feet but my hands and my head as
well!"
10 Jesus answered, "Those who have had
a bath need only to wash their feet; their
whole body is clean. And you are clean,[j]
though not every one of you." 11 For he knew
who was going to betray him, and that was
why he said not every one was clean.
12 When he had finished washing their
feet, he put on his clothes and returned to
his place. "Do you understand what I have
done for you?" he asked them. 13 "You call
me 'Teacher'[k] and 'Lord,'[l] and rightly so, for
that is what I am. 14 Now that I, your Lord
and Teacher, have washed your feet, you
also should wash one another's feet.[m] 15 I
have set you an example that you should do
as I have done for you.[n] 16 Very truly I tell
you, no servant is greater than his master,[o]
nor is a messenger greater than the one
who sent him. 17 Now that you know these
things, you will be blessed if you do them.[p]

---

[a] *38* Isaiah 53:1 [b] *40* Isaiah 6:10

12:42–43 ***Yet.*** This word marks a stark contrast between these believers and the unbelief spoken of in verses 37–41. These men were genuine believers. Their problem was that they feared the opinions of their fellow leaders. Such believers will be ashamed at Christ's return (1 John 2:28).

12:47 ***I do not judge that person.*** Christ will judge, but at His first coming He did not come to judge but to save (3:17).

13:1 ***to the end.*** This phrase means either "to the last" or "utterly and completely." What follows in verses 1–11 demonstrates Jesus' complete love. Jesus loved His disciples, even though He knew that one would betray Him, another would deny Him, and all would desert Him for a time.

13:8 ***no part with me.*** The washing was a symbol of spiritual cleansing (vv. 10–11). If Peter did not participate in the cleansing, he would not enjoy fellowship with Christ (1 John 1:9).

13:13 ***'Teacher' and 'Lord.'*** These were the ordinary titles of respect given to a rabbi.

12:37 [n] Jn 2:11 **12:38** [o] Isa 53:1; Ro 10:16 **12:40** [p] Isa 6:10; Mt 13:13, 15 **12:41** [q] Isa 6:1-4 [r] Lk 24:27 **12:42** [s] ver 11; Jn 7:48 [t] Jn 7:13 [u] Jn 9:22 **12:43** [v] Jn 5:44 **12:44** [w] Mt 10:40; Jn 5:24 **12:45** [x] Jn 14:9 **12:46** [y] Jn 1:4; 3:19; 8:12; 9:5 **12:47** [z] Jn 3:17 **12:48** [a] Jn 5:45 **12:49** [b] Jn 14:31 **13:1** [c] Jn 11:55 [d] Jn 12:23 [e] Jn 16:28 **13:3** [f] Mt 28:18 [g] Jn 8:42; 16:27, 28, 30 **13:5** [h] Lk 7:44 **13:7** [i] ver 12 **13:10** [j] Jn 15:3 **13:13** [k] Jn 11:28 [l] Lk 6:46; 1Co 12:3; Php 2:11 **13:14** [m] 1Pe 5:5 **13:15** [n] Mt 11:29 **13:16** [o] Mt 10:24; Lk 6:40; Jn 15:20 **13:17** [p] Mt 7:24, 25; Lk 11:28; Jas 1:25

Jesus Predicts His Betrayal

18“I am not referring to all of you;[q] I
know those I have chosen.[r] But this is to
fulfill this passage of Scripture: ‘He who
shared my bread[s] has turned[a][t] against
me.’[b][u]
19“I am telling you now before it happens, so that when it does happen you will
believe[v] that I am who I am.[w] 20Very truly I
tell you, whoever accepts anyone I send accepts me; and whoever accepts me accepts
the one who sent me.”[x]
21After he had said this, Jesus was troubled in spirit[y] and testified, “Very truly I tell
you, one of you is going to betray me.”[z]
22His disciples stared at one another, at
a loss to know which of them he meant.
23One of them, the disciple whom Jesus
loved,[a] was reclining next to him. 24Simon
Peter motioned to this disciple and said,
“Ask him which one he means.”
25Leaning back against Jesus, he asked
him, “Lord, who is it?”[b]
26Jesus answered, “It is the one to
whom I will give this piece of bread when
I have dipped it in the dish.” Then, dip-
ping the piece of bread, he gave it to Judas, the son of Simon Iscariot. 27As soon
as Judas took the bread, Satan entered into
him.[c]
So Jesus told him, “What you are about
to do, do quickly.” 28But no one at the meal
understood why Jesus said this to him.
29Since Judas had charge of the money,[d]
some thought Jesus was telling him to buy
what was needed for the festival, or to give
something to the poor. 30As soon as Judas
had taken the bread, he went out. And it
was night.[e]

Jesus Predicts Peter's Denial

31When he was gone, Jesus said, “Now
the Son of Man is glorified[f] and God is glorified in him.[g] 32If God is glorified in him,[c]
God will glorify the Son in himself,[h] and
will glorify him at once.
33“My children, I will be with you only a
little longer. You will look for me, and just
as I told the Jews, so I tell you now: Where
I am going, you cannot come.[i]
34“A new command[j] I give you: Love one
another.[k] As I have loved you, so you must
love one another.[l] 35By this everyone will
know that you are my disciples, if you love
one another.”[m]
36Simon Peter asked him, “Lord, where
are you going?”
Jesus replied, “Where I am going, you
cannot follow now,[n] but you will follow later.”[o]
37Peter asked, “Lord, why can't I follow
you now? I will lay down my life for you.”
38Then Jesus answered, “Will you really
lay down your life for me? Very truly I tell
you, before the rooster crows, you will disown me three times![p]

Jesus Comforts His Disciples

14 “Do not let your hearts be troubled.[q]
You believe in God[d]; believe also in
me. 2My Father's house has many rooms;
if that were not so, would I have told you
that I am going there[r] to prepare a place
for you? 3And if I go and prepare a place
for you, I will come back and take you to

[a] *18* Greek *has lifted up his heel* [b] *18* Psalm 41:9
[c] *32* Many early manuscripts do not have *If God is glorified in him.* [d] *1* Or *Believe in God*

13:18 *has turned against me.* Jesus quoted Psalm 41:9 to explain the action of Judas. In Psalm 41:9, this phrase, "has turned against me," is translated literally from the Hebrew as "has lifted up his heel." Lifting up one's heel was a gesture of insult or a preparation to kick. The blow had not yet been given. This was the attitude of Judas at that moment. He was eating with the disciples, but he was ready to strike.
13:23 *whom Jesus loved.* The disciple is never named in Scripture, but the tradition of the early church designates him as John, the author of this Gospel. ***reclining next to him.*** At this time people did not generally sit at a table to eat. They reclined on the left side of a low platform, resting on the left elbow and eating with the right hand, their feet extended outward. Reclining in such a way, a man's head was near the chest of the person on his left.
13:33 *My children.* This is an expression of tender affection used nowhere else in the Gospels. John did not forget the expression; he used it repeatedly in 1 John.
13:34 *Love one another.* One of the dominant themes in the apostle John's writings is love. God loves the whole world (3:16). Jesus repeatedly demonstrates His compassion for people in general and His love for His disciples in particular (10:11; 11:3; 13:1; 15:9).
13:35 *By this.* Unbelievers recognize Jesus' disciples not by their doctrinal distinctives, nor by dramatic miracles, nor even by their love for the lost. They recognize His disciples by their deeds of love for one another.
13:36 *Lord, where are you going?* This question Jesus had already addressed twice before, indicating that Peter completely missed the point of what Jesus said in verses 34 and 35.
13:37 I will lay down my life for you. Peter was ready to die for Jesus. Unfortunately, he was not ready, at this point, to live for Him. Later Peter would die for Christ (21:18 – 19). Church tradition states that Peter was crucified upside down, at his request, for he felt himself unworthy to be crucified like his Lord.
14:3 *I will come back and take you.* Peter may have failed Jesus (13:38), but Christ will not fail to

13:18 [q] ver 10 [r] Jn 15:16, 19 [s] Mt 26:23 [t] Jn 6:70 [u] Ps 41:9 **13:19** [v] Jn 14:29; 16:4 [w] Jn 8:24 **13:20** [x] Mt 10:40; Lk 10:16 **13:21** [y] Jn 12:27 [z] Mt 26:21 **13:23** [a] Jn 19:26; 20:2; 21:7, 20 **13:25** [b] Jn 21:20 **13:27** [c] Lk 22:3 **13:29** [d] Jn 12:6 **13:30** [e] Lk 22:53 **13:31** [f] Jn 7:39 [g] Jn 14:13; 17:4; 1Pe 4:11 **13:32** [h] Jn 17:1 **13:33** [i] Jn 7:33, 34 **13:34** [j] 1Jn 2:7-11; 3:11 [k] Lev 19:18; 1Th 4:9; 1Pe 1:22 [l] Jn 15:12; Eph 5:2; 1Jn 4:10, 11 **13:35** [m] 1Jn 3:14; 4:20 **13:36** [n] ver 33; Jn 14:2 [o] Jn 21:18, 19; 2Pe 1:14 **13:38** [p] Jn 18:27 **14:1** [q] ver 27 **14:2** [r] Jn 13:33, 36

be with me that you also may be where I am.[s] 4You know the way to the place where I am going."

Jesus the Way to the Father

5Thomas[t] said to him, "Lord, we don't know where you are going, so how can we know the way?"

6Jesus answered, "I am the way[u] and the truth and the life.[v] No one comes to the Father except through me. 7If you really know me, you will know[a] my Father as well.[w] From now on, you do know him and have seen him."

8Philip said, "Lord, show us the Father and that will be enough for us."

9Jesus answered: "Don't you know me, Philip, even after I have been among you such a long time? Anyone who has seen me has seen the Father.[x] How can you say, 'Show us the Father'? 10Don't you believe that I am in the Father, and that the Father is in me?[y] The words I say to you I do not speak on my own authority.[z] Rather, it is the Father, living in me, who is doing his work. 11Believe me when I say that I am in the Father and the Father is in me; or at least believe on the evidence of the works themselves.[a] 12Very truly I tell you, whoever believes[b] in me will do the works I have been doing,[c] and they will do even greater things than these, because I am going to the Father. 13And I will do whatever you ask[d] in my name, so that the Father may be glorified in the Son. 14You may ask me for anything in my name, and I will do it.

Jesus Promises the Holy Spirit

15"If you love me, keep my commands.[e] 16And I will ask the Father, and he will give you another advocate[f] to help you and be with you forever— 17the Spirit of truth.[g] The world cannot accept him,[h] because it neither sees him nor knows him. But you know him, for he lives with you and will be[b] in you. 18I will not leave you as orphans; I will come to you.[i] 19Before long, the world will not see me anymore, but you will see me.[j] Because I live, you also will live.[k] 20On that day you will realize that I am in my Father,[l] and you are in me, and I am in you. 21Whoever has my commands and keeps them is the one who loves me.[m] The one who loves me will be loved by my Father,[n] and I too will love them and show myself to them."

22Then Judas[o] (not Judas Iscariot) said, "But, Lord, why do you intend to show yourself to us and not to the world?"[p]

23Jesus replied, "Anyone who loves me will obey my teaching.[q] My Father will love them, and we will come to them and make our home with them.[r] 24Anyone who does not love me will not obey my teaching. These words you hear are not my own; they belong to the Father who sent me.[s]

25"All this I have spoken while still with you. 26But the Advocate,[t] the Holy Spirit, whom the Father will send in my name,[u] will teach you all things[v] and will remind you of everything I have said to you.[w] 27Peace I leave with you; my peace I give you.[x] I do not give to you as the world gives. Do not let your hearts be troubled and do not be afraid.

28"You heard me say, 'I am going away and I am coming back to you.'[y] If you loved me, you would be glad that I am going to the Father,[z] for the Father is greater than I.[a] 29I have told you now before it happens, so that when it does happen you will believe.[b]

[a] 7 Some manuscripts *If you really knew me, you would know* [b] 17 Some early manuscripts *and is*

---

return for Peter and for everyone else who has believed in Him (1 Thess. 4:16–17).

14:6 ***the way and the truth and the life.*** Through His death and resurrection, Jesus is the way to the Father. He is also the truth and the life. As truth, He is the revelation of God. As life, He is the source of our very beings.

14:12 ***greater things.*** Jesus had accomplished the greatest works possible, including raising the dead. How could He say that believers would do greater works? The answer is seen in the extent of what the apostles did. Jesus' work on earth was confined to Palestine; the apostles would preach everywhere and see the conversion of thousands. Peter's message at Pentecost brought more followers to Jesus than did Jesus' entire earthly ministry. The disciples were able to do this work because Christ would go to the Father and send the Holy Spirit to empower them.

14:17 ***the Spirit of truth.*** This is another name for the Holy Spirit because He is truth and guides us into all truth (1 Cor. 2:13; 2 Pet. 1:21).

14:18 ***orphans.*** He would not abandon them. He would come to them. There are three suggested interpretations as to when that statement would be fulfilled: (1) after the resurrection, (2) at Pentecost, in the person of the Holy Spirit, and (3) at the second coming.

14:23 ***Anyone who loves me will obey my teaching.*** In response to Judas' question (v. 22), Jesus explained that His manifestation to the disciples would be in response to their love and obedience. ***make our home with them.*** If a believer loves and obeys the Lord, he or she will experience fellowship with God.

14:24 ***Anyone who does not love me.*** If a person does not love Jesus, he or she will not obey Him. Disobedience is a serious matter, for Jesus' words are the words of God.

14:3 [s] Jn 12:26 **14:5** [t] Jn 11:16 **14:6** [u] Jn 10:9 [v] Jn 11:25 **14:7** [w] Jn 8:19 **14:9** [x] Jn 12:45; Col 1:15; Heb 1:3 **14:10** [y] Jn 10:38 [z] Jn 5:19 **14:11** [a] Jn 5:36; 10:38 **14:12** [b] Mt 21:21 [c] Lk 10:17 **14:13** [d] Mt 7:7 **14:15** [e] ver 21,23; Jn 15:10; 1Jn 5:3 **14:16** [f] Jn 15:26; 16:7 **14:17** [g] Jn 15:26; 16:13; 1Jn 4:6 [h] 1Co 2:14 **14:18** [i] ver 3, 28 **14:19** [j] Jn 7:33,34; 16:16 [k] Jn 6:57 **14:20** [l] Jn 10:38 **14:21** [m] 1Jn 5:3 [n] 1Jn 2:5 **14:22** [o] Lk 6:16; Ac 1:13 [p] Ac 10:41 **14:23** [q] ver 15 [r] 1Jn 2:24; Rev 3:20 **14:24** [s] Jn 7:16 **14:26** [t] Jn 15:26; 16:7 [u] Ac 2:33 [v] Jn 16:13; 1Jn 2:20,27 [w] Jn 2:22 **14:27** [x] Jn 16:33; Php 4:7; Col 3:15 **14:28** [y] ver 2-4, 18 [z] Jn 5:18 [a] Jn 10:29; Php 2:6 **14:29** [b] Jn 13:19; 16:4

30I will not say much more to you, for the prince of this world[c] is coming. He has no hold over me, 31but he comes so that the world may learn that I love the Father and do exactly what my Father has commanded me.[d]

"Come now; let us leave.

The Vine and the Branches

15 "I am the true vine,[e] and my Father is the gardener. 2He cuts off every branch in me that bears no fruit, while every branch that does bear fruit he prunes[a] so that it will be even more fruitful. 3You are already clean because of the word I have spoken to you.[f] 4Remain in me, as I also remain in you.[g] No branch can bear fruit by itself; it must remain in the vine. Neither can you bear fruit unless you remain in me.

5"I am the vine; you are the branches. If you remain in me and I in you, you will bear much fruit;[h] apart from me you can do nothing. 6If you do not remain in me, you are like a branch that is thrown away and withers; such branches are picked up, thrown into the fire and burned.[i] 7If you remain in me and my words remain in you, ask whatever you wish, and it will be done for you.[j] 8This is to my Father's glory,[k] that you bear much fruit, showing yourselves to be my disciples.[l]

9"As the Father has loved me,[m] so have I loved you. Now remain in my love. 10If you keep my commands,[n] you will remain in my love, just as I have kept my Father's commands and remain in his love. 11I have told you this so that my joy may be in you and that your joy may be complete.[o] 12My command is this: Love each other as I have loved you.[p] 13Greater love has no one than this: to lay down one's life for one's friends.[q] 14You are my friends[r] if you do what I command.[s] 15I no longer call you servants, because a servant does not know his master's business. Instead, I have called you friends, for everything that I learned from my Father I have made known to you.[t] 16You did not choose me, but I chose you and appointed you[u] so that you might go and bear fruit—fruit that will last—and so that whatever you ask in my name the Father will give you. 17This is my command: Love each other.[v]

The World Hates the Disciples

18"If the world hates you,[w] keep in mind that it hated me first. 19If you belonged to the world, it would love you as its own. As it is, you do not belong to the world, but I have chosen you[x] out of the world. That is why the world hates you.[y] 20Remember what I told you: 'A servant is not greater than his master.'[b][z] If they persecuted me, they will persecute you also.[a] If they obeyed my teaching, they will obey yours also. 21They will treat you this way because of my name,[b] for they do not know the one who sent me.[c] 22If I had not come and spoken to them, they would not be guilty of sin; but now they have no excuse for their sin.[d] 23Whoever hates me hates my Father as well. 24If I had not done among them the works no one else did,[e] they would not be guilty of sin. As it is, they have seen, and

---

[a] *2* The Greek for *he prunes* also means *he cleans.*
[b] *20* John 13:16

14:30 ***has no hold over me.*** These words indicate Jesus' sinlessness. Jesus' yielding to what was about to happen did not mean that Satan had any power over Him. Jesus would soon voluntarily yield to the death of the cross, in loving obedience to the Father (v. 31).

15:2 ***every branch in me.*** The emphasis of *in me* in this passage is on deep, abiding fellowship. Jesus' purpose was to move His disciples from servants to friends (vv. 13–15). This would involve a process of discipline in regard to His commandments. ***prunes.*** This word means "cleanses." Once the fruit is on the vine, the vinedresser cleanses the fruit of bugs and diseases. The spiritual counterpart is cleansing which is done through the Word (v. 3).

15:6 ***If you do not remain in me.*** Not remaining in Christ has serious consequences: (1) the person *is thrown away,* indicating the loss of fellowship; (2) the person *withers,* indicating a loss of vitality; (3) the person is *burned,* indicating a loss of reward.

15:8 ***This.*** Notice the striking parallel between this verse and 13:35. ***fruit.*** The love of 13:35 is pictured here. The text has come full circle in showing how strategic it is for disciples to love each other, as Christ's method of evangelizing the lost. Where there is good fruit, there are also seeds for propagation.

15:11 ***your joy may be complete.*** This phrase is an expression peculiar to John (3:29; 16:24; 17:13; 1 John 1:4; 2 John 12). It describes a believer's experience of Christ's love: complete joy.

15:14 ***if you do.*** Jesus is our model for love (v. 13). Intimacy with Him is the motive for loving as He loves. If believers obey His command to love, they enjoy the intimacy of His friendship. Not that friendship, unlike sonship, is a once-for-all gift, but develops as the result of obeying Jesus' command to love.

15:15 ***call you servants.*** Until this point, Jesus had called His disciples servants (12:26; 13:13–16). A servant does what he is told and sees what his master does, but does not necessarily know the meaning or purpose of it. ***friends.*** A friend knows what is happening because friends develop deep fellowship by communicating with one another.

15:22–23 ***not be guilty of sin ... no excuse for their sin.*** The world's hatred of Jesus was a sin against God, for He revealed the Father Himself to them.

14:30 [c] Jn 12:31 **14:31** [d] Jn 10:18; 12:49
15:1 [e] Isa 5:1-7 **15:3** [f] Jn 13:10; 17:17; Eph 5:26
15:4 [g] Jn 6:56; 1Jn 2:6 **15:5** [h] ver 16 **15:6** [i] ver 2
15:7 [j] Mt 7:7 **15:8** [k] Mt 5:16 [l] Jn 8:31 **15:9** [m] Jn 17:23, 24, 26 **15:10** [n] Jn 14:15 **15:11** [o] Jn 17:13
15:12 [p] Jn 13:34 **15:13** [q] Jn 10:11; Ro 5:7,8
15:14 [r] Lk 12:4 [s] Mt 12:50 **15:15** [t] Jn 8:26
15:16 [u] Jn 6:70; 13:18 **15:17** [v] ver 12 **15:18** [w] 1Jn 3:13
15:19 [x] ver 16 [y] Jn 17:14 **15:20** [z] Jn 13:16 [a] 2Ti 3:12
15:21 [b] Mt 10:22 [c] Jn 16:3 **15:22** [d] Jn 9:41; Ro 1:20
15:24 [e] Jn 5:36

yet they have hated both me and my Father.
25 But this is to fulfill what is written in their
Law: 'They hated me without reason.'[a][f]

The Work of the Holy Spirit

26 "When the Advocate[g] comes, whom
I will send to you from the Father[h]—the
Spirit of truth[i] who goes out from the Father—he will testify about me.[j] 27 And you
also must testify,[k] for you have been with
me from the beginning.[l]

16 "All this[m] I have told you so that you
will not fall away.[n] 2 They will put you
out of the synagogue;[o] in fact, the time is
coming when anyone who kills you will
think they are offering a service to God.[p]
3 They will do such things because they
have not known the Father or me.[q] 4 I have
told you this, so that when their time comes
you will remember[r] that I warned you about
them. I did not tell you this from the beginning because I was with you, 5 but now I
am going to him who sent me.[s] None of you
asks me, 'Where are you going?'[t] 6 Rather,
you are filled with grief because I have said
these things. 7 But very truly I tell you, it is
for your good that I am going away. Unless I go away, the Advocate[u] will not come
to you; but if I go, I will send him to you.[v]
8 When he comes, he will prove the world
to be in the wrong about sin and righteousness and judgment: 9 about sin,[w] because
people do not believe in me; 10 about righteousness,[x] because I am going to the Father, where you can see me no longer; 11 and
about judgment, because the prince of this
world[y] now stands condemned.
12 "I have much more to say to you, more
than you can now bear.[z] 13 But when he, the
Spirit of truth,[a] comes, he will guide you
into all the truth.[b] He will not speak on his
own; he will speak only what he hears, and
he will tell you what is yet to come. 14 He will
glorify me because it is from me that he will
receive what he will make known to you.
15 All that belongs to the Father is mine.[c]
That is why I said the Spirit will receive
from me what he will make known to you."

The Disciples' Grief Will Turn to Joy

16 Jesus went on to say, "In a little while[d]
you will see me no more, and then after a
little while you will see me."[e]
17 At this, some of his disciples said to one
another, "What does he mean by saying,
'In a little while you will see me no more,
and then after a little while you will see
me,'[f] and 'Because I am going to the Father'?"[g] 18 They kept asking, "What does
he mean by 'a little while'? We don't understand what he is saying."
19 Jesus saw that they wanted to ask him
about this, so he said to them, "Are you
asking one another what I meant when I

[a] 25 Psalms 35:19; 69:4

15:26–27 *he will testify.* As the disciples spoke, the Holy Spirit would bring inner conviction to unbelievers concerning Christ. This in turn would make the disciples witnesses for Jesus.

16:2 *They will put you out of the synagogue.* The persecution that the disciples would face included excommunication and even execution. Excommunication had economic as well as religious implications because much of the life of an ancient Jew revolved around the synagogue.

16:7 *it is for your good.* The disciples must have thought, "How can it be advantageous for us to be alone? The Romans hate us because they see us as disturbers of the peace. The Jewish leaders hate us because they see us as blasphemers." Jesus explained the benefits of His departure. When Jesus left, the believers would have (1) the provision of the Holy Spirit (vv. 7–15); (2) the potential of full joy (vv. 16–24); (3) the possibility of fuller knowledge (vv. 25–28); (4) the privilege of peace (vv. 29–33).

16:8 *prove.* The Holy Spirit would demonstrate the truth of Christ beyond the fear of contradiction. The Holy Spirit convicts unbelievers through believers who witness about Christ (15:26–27). Believers are the mouthpiece for God's voice.

16:11 *about judgment.* Satan, the ruler of the world, rules in the hearts of unregenerate people and blinds their minds (1 Cor. 2:6–8). Satan was judged at the cross, and the Holy Spirit would convince people of the judgment to come. Satan has been judged, so all who side with him will be judged with him.

16:12 *you.* Here, this refers to the apostles. Technically, what the Lord says about the ministry of the Holy Spirit in verses 12–15 applies primarily to the apostles. That ministry was threefold: (1) He would guide them into all truth (v. 13); (2) He would tell them of the future (v. 13); (3) He would help them glorify Christ (vv. 14–15). Jesus' words were fulfilled in the apostles' preaching and writings.

16:13 *Spirit of truth.* The phrase means that the Holy Spirit is the source of truth (14:17; 15:26). ***guide.*** The Holy Spirit would not compel or carry the disciples into truth. He would lead; their job was to follow.

16:14 *glorify me.* The Holy Spirit glorifies Christ by declaring Him or making Him known. It is the work of the Holy Spirit to throw light on Jesus Christ, who is the image of the invisible God. Christ is to be on center stage; that is the desire of both the Father and the Spirit. The apostles received truth from the Holy Spirit, truth about things to come, and truth about Christ. Then, under the guidance of the Holy Spirit, they wrote those truths in documents known today as the New Testament.

16:18 *a little while.* The biggest question weighing on the disciples' minds was the time factor. They simply did not understand the strange intervals marked by their separation from Jesus.

15:25 [f] Ps 35:19; 69:4 **15:26** [g] Jn 14:16 [h] Jn 14:26 [i] Jn 14:17 [j] 1Jn 5:7 **15:27** [k] Lk 24:48; 1Jn 1:2; 4:14 [l] Lk 1:2 **16:1** [m] Jn 15:18-27 [n] Mt 11:6 **16:2** [o] Jn 9:22 [p] Isa 66:5; Ac 26:9, 10; Rev 6:9 **16:3** [q] Jn 15:21; 17:25; 1Jn 3:1 **16:4** [r] Jn 13:19 **16:5** [s] Jn 7:33 [t] Jn 13:36; 14:5 **16:7** [u] Jn 14:16, 26; 15:26 [v] Jn 7:39 **16:9** [w] Jn 15:22 **16:10** [x] Ac 3:14; 7:52; 1Pe 3:18 **16:11** [y] Jn 12:31 **16:12** [z] Mk 4:33 **16:13** [a] Jn 14:17 [b] Jn 14:26 **16:15** [c] Jn 17:10 **16:16** [d] Jn 7:33 [e] Jn 14:18-24 **16:17** [f] ver 16 [g] ver 5

said, 'In a little while you will see me no
more, and then after a little while you will
see me'? 20 Very truly I tell you, you will
weep and mourn[h] while the world rejoices. You will grieve, but your grief will turn
to joy.[i] 21 A woman giving birth to a child
has pain[j] because her time has come; but
when her baby is born she forgets the anguish because of her joy that a child is born
into the world. 22 So with you: Now is your
time of grief,[k] but I will see you again[l] and
you will rejoice, and no one will take away
your joy. 23 In that day you will no longer
ask me anything. Very truly I tell you, my
Father will give you whatever you ask in
my name.[m] 24 Until now you have not asked
for anything in my name. Ask and you will
receive, and your joy will be complete.[n]
25 "Though I have been speaking figuratively,[o] a time is coming[p] when I will no longer use this kind of language but will tell
you plainly about my Father. 26 In that day
you will ask in my name.[q] I am not saying
that I will ask the Father on your behalf.
27 No, the Father himself loves you because
you have loved me[r] and have believed that
I came from God. 28 I came from the Father
and entered the world; now I am leaving
the world and going back to the Father."[s]
29 Then Jesus' disciples said, "Now you
are speaking clearly and without figures of
speech.[t] 30 Now we can see that you know
all things and that you do not even need
to have anyone ask you questions. This
makes us believe that you came from God."
31 "Do you now believe?" Jesus replied.
32 "A time is coming[u] and in fact has come
when you will be scattered,[v] each to your
own home. You will leave me all alone. Yet
I am not alone, for my Father is with me.[w]
33 "I have told you these things, so that in
me you may have peace.[x] In this world you
will have trouble.[y] But take heart! I have
overcome[z] the world."

Jesus Prays to Be Glorified

17 After Jesus said this, he looked toward heaven[a] and prayed:
"Father, the hour has come. Glorify
your Son, that your Son may glorify
you.[b] 2 For you granted him authority over all people that he might give
eternal life to all those you have giv-
en him.[c] 3 Now this is eternal life: that
they know you, the only true God, and
Jesus Christ, whom you have sent.[d] 4 I
have brought you glory[e] on earth by
finishing the work you gave me to do.[f]
5 And now, Father, glorify me in your
presence with the glory I had with
you[g] before the world began.[h]

Jesus Prays for His Disciples

6 "I have revealed you[a][i] to those
whom you gave me[j] out of the world.
They were yours; you gave them to
me and they have obeyed your word.
7 Now they know that everything you
have given me comes from you. 8 For
I gave them the words you gave me[k]
and they accepted them. They knew
with certainty that I came from you,[l]
and they believed that you sent me.[m]
9 I pray for them.[n] I am not praying for
the world, but for those you have given
me, for they are yours. 10 All I have is
yours, and all you have is mine.[o] And
glory has come to me through them.
11 I will remain in the world no longer,
but they are still in the world,[p] and I
am coming to you.[q] Holy Father, protect them by the power of[b] your name,
the name you gave me, so that they
may be one[r] as we are one.[s] 12 While

---

[a] 6 Greek *your name* [b] 11 Or *Father, keep them faithful to*

16:21 ***A woman giving birth to a child.*** Jesus used the example of a pregnant woman whose sorrow is transformed into joy in the birth of a child.
16:26 ***I will ask the Father on your behalf.*** Because Jesus provides forgiveness of sins through His death and now intercedes for all believers at the right hand of the Father (Heb. 7:25), we have direct access to the Father. We do not need the intercession of a priest, because Jesus acts as our High Priest before God.
16:31 ***Do you now believe?*** We continue in the Christian life the same way we begin, by believing in Jesus. The more we learn of Christ, the more we have to believe. The more we place our trust in Jesus, the more we receive. The more we receive, the more we can accomplish for His glory.
16:33 ***trouble.*** This is literally "pressure" and figuratively means "affliction" or "distress."
17:1 – 2 ***the hour has come.*** Throughout the Gospel of John, Jesus referred to the cross as His "hour" (2:4; 7:30; 8:20; 12:23; 13:1). The time for Him to die had arrived. ***Glorify your Son.*** Jesus was asking that His mission to the world would be made known through the cross. The reasons for this request are twofold: (1) that *your Son may glorify you.* In the cross, Jesus reveals the Father to the world, that is, His love and justice, and (2) that, through Jesus' death on the cross, God would provide forgiveness of sins and *give eternal life* to all those who believe in His Son.
17:3 ***that they know you.*** Eternal life consists of a growing knowledge of the only true God as opposed to false gods.
17:11 ***protect them by the power of your name.*** This verse reveals Jesus' sensitivity to the plight of His disciples brought on by His departure. He was

16:20 [h] Lk 23:27 [i] Jn 20:20 **16:21** [j] Isa 26:17; 1Th 5:3 **16:22** [k] ver 6 [l] ver 16 **16:23** [m] Mt 7:7; Jn 15:16 **16:24** [n] Jn 3:29; 15:11 **16:25** [o] Mt 13:34; Jn 10:6 [p] ver 2 **16:26** [q] ver 23,24 **16:27** [r] Jn 14:21,23 **16:28** [s] Jn 13:3 **16:29** [t] ver 25 **16:32** [u] ver 2,25 [v] Mt 26:31 [w] Jn 8:16,29 **16:33** [x] Jn 14:27 [y] Jn 15:18-21 [z] Ro 8:37; 1Jn 4:4 **17:1** [a] Jn 11:41 [b] Jn 12:23; 13:31,32 **17:2** [c] ver 6,9,24; Da 7:14; Jn 6:37,39 **17:3** [d] ver 8,18,21,23,25; Jn 3:17 **17:4** [e] Jn 13:31 [f] Jn 4:34 **17:5** [g] Php 2:6 [h] Jn 1:2 **17:6** [i] ver 26 [j] ver 2; Jn 6:37,39 **17:8** [k] ver 14,26 [l] Jn 16:27 [m] ver 3,18,21,23,25; Jn 3:17 **17:9** [n] Lk 22:32 **17:10** [o] Jn 16:15 **17:11** [p] Jn 13:1 [q] Jn 7:33 [r] ver 21-23 [s] Jn 10:30

I was with them, I protected them and
kept them safe by[a] that name you gave
me. None has been lost[t] except the one
doomed to destruction[u] so that Scripture would be fulfilled.
13“I am coming to you now, but I
say these things while I am still in the
world, so that they may have the full
measure of my joy[v] within them. 14I
have given them your word and the
world has hated them,[w] for they are
not of the world any more than I am
of the world.[x] 15My prayer is not that
you take them out of the world but that
you protect them from the evil one.[y]
16They are not of the world, even as
I am not of it.[z] 17Sanctify them by[b]
the truth; your word is truth.[a] 18As
you sent me into the world,[b] I have
sent them into the world.[c] 19For them I
sanctify myself, that they too may be
truly sanctified.

Jesus Prays for All Believers

20“My prayer is not for them alone.
I pray also for those who will believe
in me through their message, 21that all
of them may be one, Father, just as you
are in me and I am in you.[d] May they
also be in us so that the world may believe that you have sent me.[e] 22I have
given them the glory that you gave me,
that they may be one as we are one[f]—
23I in them and you in me—so that
they may be brought to complete unity. Then the world will know that you
sent me[g] and have loved them[h] even as
you have loved me.
24“Father, I want those you have giv-
en me to be with me where I am,[i] and
to see my glory,[j] the glory you have
given me because you loved me before
the creation of the world.[k]
25“Righteous Father, though the
world does not know you,[l] I know you,
and they know that you have sent me.[m]
26I have made you[c] known to them,[n]
and will continue to make you known
in order that the love you have for me
may be in them[o] and that I myself may
be in them.”

Jesus Arrested

18 When he had finished praying, Jesus
left with his disciples and crossed the
Kidron Valley.[p] On the other side there was
a garden,[q] and he and his disciples went
into it.[r]
2Now Judas, who betrayed him, knew
the place, because Jesus had often met
there with his disciples.[s] 3So Judas came
to the garden, guiding[t] a detachment of
soldiers and some officials from the chief
priests and the Pharisees.[u] They were carrying torches, lanterns and weapons.
4Jesus, knowing all that was going to
happen to him,[v] went out and asked them,
“Who is it you want?”[w]
5“Jesus of Nazareth,” they replied.
“I am he,” Jesus said. (And Judas the traitor was standing there with them.) 6When
Jesus said, “I am he,” they drew back and
fell to the ground.
7Again he asked them, “Who is it you
want?”[x]
“Jesus of Nazareth,” they said.
8Jesus answered, “I told you that I am
he. If you are looking for me, then let these
men go.” 9This happened so that the words

[a] 12 *Or kept them faithful to* [b] 17 *Or them to live in accordance with* [c] 26 *Greek your name*

going to the Father, but they would be left behind. Jesus asked the Father to keep them true to the revelation of God that Jesus had given to them while He was with them. The disciples would have a new union with the Father and Son through the future indwelling of the Holy Spirit.

17:14–16 *of the world.* This verse has profound implications for discipleship. Our desire should not be to isolate ourselves from the world, but to use Christ's Word and the Holy Spirit's power to serve Him while our life lasts. Yet, at the same time, we should not become like the world, succumbing to the evil influences of the world.

17:17 *Sanctify them.* This means "to set apart." There are two ways to understand this statement: (1) as separate for holiness, or (2) as set apart for service. According to the first view, Jesus was praying not only that the disciples should be kept from evil, but that they should advance in holiness.

17:21 *that all of them may be one.* The present tense of the verb "to be" indicates that Jesus was praying for the unity that takes place through the sanctification of believers. This is what Jesus was commanding in 13:34–35.

17:22 *the glory.* This is the revelation of Jesus Christ through His disciples and is the means to unity. Such unity begins with belief and correct thinking about Jesus and God the Father, that is, with doctrine. But correct belief must bear fruit—a life that demonstrates God's love and produces unity between all believers.

17:23 *I in them and you in me.* The mutual indwelling of the Father in the Son and the Son in the church is also the means to unity, the ultimate expression of God's love (13:35; Rom. 8:17).

18:1 *Kidron Valley.* This was a ravine that was between Jerusalem and the Mount of Olives.

18:3 *soldiers.* These were members of the temple police under the command of the Jewish council, the Sanhedrin.

17:12 [t] Jn 6:39 [u] Jn 6:70 **17:13** [v] Jn 3:29 **17:14** [w] Jn 15:19 [x] Jn 8:23 **17:15** [y] Mt 5:37 **17:16** [z] ver 14 **17:17** [a] Jn 15:3 **17:18** [b] ver 3, 8, 21, 23, 25 [c] Jn 20:21 **17:21** [d] Jn 10:38 [e] ver 3, 8, 18, 23, 25; Jn 3:17 **17:22** [f] Jn 14:20 **17:23** [g] Jn 3:17 [h] Jn 16:27 **17:24** [i] Jn 12:26 [j] Jn 1:14 [k] ver 5; Mt 25:34 **17:25** [l] Jn 15:21; 16:3 [m] ver 3, 8, 18, 21, 23; Jn 3:17; 7:29; 16:27 **17:26** [n] ver 6 [o] Jn 15:9 **18:1** [p] 2Sa 15:23 [q] ver 26 [r] Mt 26:36 **18:2** [s] Lk 21:37; 22:39 **18:3** [t] Ac 1:16 [u] ver 12 **18:4** [v] Jn 6:64; 13:1, 11 [w] ver 7 **18:7** [x] ver 4

he had spoken would be fulfilled: "I have
not lost one of those you gave me."[a][y]
10 Then Simon Peter, who had a sword,
drew it and struck the high priest's servant,
cutting off his right ear. (The servant's
name was Malchus.)
11 Jesus commanded Peter, "Put your
sword away! Shall I not drink the cup[z] the
Father has given me?"
12 Then the detachment of soldiers with
its commander and the Jewish officials[a]
arrested Jesus. They bound him 13 and
brought him first to Annas, who was the
father-in-law of Caiaphas,[b] the high priest
that year. 14 Caiaphas was the one who had
advised the Jewish leaders that it would be
good if one man died for the people.[c]

Peter's First Denial

15 Simon Peter and another disciple were
following Jesus. Because this disciple was
known to the high priest,[d] he went with
Jesus into the high priest's courtyard,[e]
16 but Peter had to wait outside at the door.
The other disciple, who was known to the
high priest, came back, spoke to the servant girl on duty there and brought Peter in.
17 "You aren't one of this man's disciples
too, are you?" she asked Peter.
He replied, "I am not."[f]
18 It was cold, and the servants and officials stood around a fire[g] they had made to
keep warm. Peter also was standing with
them, warming himself.[h]

The High Priest Questions Jesus

19 Meanwhile, the high priest questioned
Jesus about his disciples and his teaching.
20 "I have spoken openly to the world,"
Jesus replied. "I always taught in synagogues[i] or at the temple,[j] where all the Jews
come together. I said nothing in secret.[k]
21 Why question me? Ask those who heard
me. Surely they know what I said."
22 When Jesus said this, one of the officials[l] nearby slapped him in the face.[m] "Is
this the way you answer the high priest?"
he demanded.
23 "If I said something wrong," Jesus replied, "testify as to what is wrong. But if I
spoke the truth, why did you strike me?"[n]
24 Then Annas sent him bound to Caiaphas[o] the high priest.

Peter's Second and Third Denials

25 Meanwhile, Simon Peter was still
standing there warming himself.[p] So they
asked him, "You aren't one of his disciples
too, are you?"
He denied it, saying, "I am not."[q]
26 One of the high priest's servants, a relative of the man whose ear Peter had cut
off,[r] challenged him, "Didn't I see you with
him in the garden?"[s] 27 Again Peter denied
it, and at that moment a rooster began to
crow.[t]

Jesus Before Pilate

28 Then the Jewish leaders took Jesus
from Caiaphas to the palace of the Roman
governor.[u] By now it was early morning,
and to avoid ceremonial uncleanness they
did not enter the palace,[v] because they
wanted to be able to eat the Passover.[w]
29 So Pilate came out to them and asked,
"What charges are you bringing against
this man?"
30 "If he were not a criminal," they replied, "we would not have handed him over
to you."
31 Pilate said, "Take him yourselves and
judge him by your own law."
"But we have no right to execute any-

[a] 9 John 6:39

18:13 *Annas.* Annas was high priest from A.D. 7 to 14. He was deposed by the Romans. Then Caiaphas, Annas' son-in-law, was appointed to the position and served from A.D. 18 to 37. However, according to Jewish law the high priest was a lifetime position, so the Jews still considered Annas to be high priest. Therefore, they took Jesus to Annas first.

18:15 *another disciple.* Although this other disciple is never identified, the consensus is that he was John, the author of this Gospel.

18:21 *Ask those who heard me.* According to the law, the witnesses for the defense had to be called first. Jesus should not have been questioned until witnesses had testified.

18:27 *Again Peter denied it.* For the third time, Peter denied the Lord, as Jesus had said he would (13:38). In the upper room, Peter had boasted that he would remain true to the Lord to the end (13:37; Matt. 26:33,35). In the garden he surrendered to the desires of his body by sleeping three times when the Lord had commanded the disciples to stay up in prayer (Mark 14:34–42). Now he submitted to the pressure of the world and denied the Lord three times.

18:28 *the palace.* This was probably the Roman governor's official residence, the Fortress Antonia near the temple.

18:29–30 *What charges.* Pilate was not ignorant of the accusation. He was merely requesting that it be formally stated.

18:31 *we have no right to execute anyone.* The Romans did not allow the Jews to impose capital punishment. These Jewish leaders had no interest in a just trial; they simply wanted permission from Rome to have Jesus executed.

18:9 [y] Jn 17:12 **18:11** [z] Mt 20:22 **18:12** [a] ver 3
18:13 [b] ver 24; Mt 26:3 **18:14** [c] Jn 11:49-51
18:15 [d] Mt 26:3 [e] Mt 26:58; Mk 14:54; Lk 22:54
18:17 [f] ver 25 **18:18** [g] Jn 21:9 [h] Mk 14:54,67
18:20 [i] Mt 4:23 [j] Mt 26:55 [k] Jn 7:26 **18:22** [l] ver 3
[m] Mt 16:21; Jn 19:3 **18:23** [n] Mt 5:39; Ac 23:2-5
18:24 [o] ver 13; Mt 26:3 **18:25** [p] ver 18 [q] ver 17
18:26 [r] ver 10 [s] ver 1 **18:27** [t] Jn 13:38
18:28 [u] Mt 27:2; Mk 15:1; Lk 23:1 [v] ver 33; Jn 19:9
[w] Jn 11:55

one," they objected. 32 This took place to fulfill what Jesus had said about the kind of death he was going to die.[x]

33 Pilate then went back inside the palace,[y] summoned Jesus and asked him, "Are you the king of the Jews?"[z]

34 "Is that your own idea," Jesus asked, "or did others talk to you about me?"

35 "Am I a Jew?" Pilate replied. "Your own people and chief priests handed you over to me. What is it you have done?"

36 Jesus said, "My kingdom[a] is not of this world. If it were, my servants would fight to prevent my arrest by the Jewish leaders.[b] But now my kingdom is from another place."[c]

37 "You are a king, then!" said Pilate.

Jesus answered, "You say that I am a king. In fact, the reason I was born and came into the world is to testify to the truth.[d] Everyone on the side of truth listens to me."[e]

38 "What is truth?" retorted Pilate. With this he went out again to the Jews gathered there and said, "I find no basis for a charge against him.[f] 39 But it is your custom for me to release to you one prisoner at the time of the Passover. Do you want me to release 'the king of the Jews'?"

40 They shouted back, "No, not him! Give us Barabbas!" Now Barabbas had taken part in an uprising.[g]

Jesus Sentenced to Be Crucified

19 Then Pilate took Jesus and had him flogged.[h] 2 The soldiers twisted together a crown of thorns and put it on his head. They clothed him in a purple robe 3 and went up to him again and again, saying, "Hail, king of the Jews!"[i] And they slapped him in the face.[j]

4 Once more Pilate came out and said to the Jews gathered there, "Look, I am bringing him out[k] to you to let you know that I find no basis for a charge against him."[l] 5 When Jesus came out wearing the crown of thorns and the purple robe,[m] Pilate said to them, "Here is the man!"

6 As soon as the chief priests and their officials saw him, they shouted, "Crucify! Crucify!"

But Pilate answered, "You take him and crucify him.[n] As for me, I find no basis for a charge against him."[o]

7 The Jewish leaders insisted, "We have a law, and according to that law he must die,[p] because he claimed to be the Son of God."[q]

8 When Pilate heard this, he was even more afraid, 9 and he went back inside the palace.[r] "Where do you come from?" he asked Jesus, but Jesus gave him no answer.[s] 10 "Do you refuse to speak to me?" Pilate said. "Don't you realize I have power either to free you or to crucify you?"

11 Jesus answered, "You would have no power over me if it were not given to you from above.[t] Therefore the one who handed me over to you[u] is guilty of a greater sin."

12 From then on, Pilate tried to set Jesus free, but the Jewish leaders kept shouting, "If you let this man go, you are no friend of Caesar. Anyone who claims to be a king[v] opposes Caesar."

13 When Pilate heard this, he brought Jesus out and sat down on the judge's seat[w] at a place known as the Stone Pavement (which in Aramaic[x] is Gabbatha). 14 It was

---

18:34 ***Is that your own idea.*** In reply to Pilate, Jesus gave no violent protest of innocence, nor was He sullenly defiant. Jesus politely but directly asked whether Pilate was asking on his own initiative or whether the charge was secondhand. If Pilate's question originated with him, he was using *king* in the Roman sense of political ruler. If not, then *king* was being used in the Jewish sense of the messianic king. **18:38** ***What is truth?*** This question has been interpreted as (1) a cynical denial of the possibility of knowing truth; (2) a contemptuous jest at anything so impractical as abstract truth; and (3) a desire to know what no one had been able to tell him. ***no basis.*** This is a legal term meaning that there were no grounds for a criminal charge.

18:39 ***it is your custom.*** It appears that some in the crowd suggested that a prisoner should be released in honor of the Passover (Mark 15:8,11). Pilate jumped at the possible compromise. By promising to release Jesus on account of the custom rather than by proclaiming Him innocent, Pilate would avoid insulting the Jewish leaders, who had already pronounced Him guilty.

19:4 ***I am bringing him out to you.*** Perhaps Pilate was appealing to the people's compassion so that he could release Jesus.

19:7 ***We have a law.*** The Jewish leaders were telling Pilate, "If you are appealing to us, we say that, according to our law, He must die." As governor, Pilate was bound by Roman custom to respect Jewish law. ***he claimed to be the Son of God.*** The Jewish leaders were accusing Jesus of violating the laws against blasphemy (Lev. 24:16).

19:9 ***Jesus gave him no answer.*** Three times Pilate had publicly pronounced Jesus innocent (18:38; 19:4,6).

19:12 ***you are no friend of Caesar.*** The Jews shifted their focus from the religious charge (v. 7) to the political charge (18:33), which they backed up with an appeal to Caesar's own political interest. This new plea forced Pilate to choose between yielding to an indefinite sense of right or escaping the danger of an accusation from Rome.

18:32 [x] Mt 20:19; 26:2; Jn 3:14; 8:28; 12:32,33
18:33 [y] ver 28,29; Jn 19:9 [z] Lk 23:3; Mt 2:2
18:36 [a] Mt 3:2 [b] Mt 26:53 [c] Lk 17:21; Jn 6:15
18:37 [d] Jn 3:32 [e] Jn 8:47; 1Jn 4:6 **18:38** [f] Lk 23:4; Jn 19:4,6 **18:40** [g] Ac 3:14 **19:1** [h] Dt 25:3; Isa 50:6; 53:5; Mt 27:26 **19:3** [i] Mt 27:29 [j] Jn 18:22
19:4 [k] Jn 18:38 [l] ver 6; Lk 23:4 **19:5** [m] ver 2
19:6 [n] Ac 3:13 [o] ver 4; Lk 23:4 **19:7** [p] Lev 24:16 [q] Mt 26:63-66; Jn 5:18; 10:33 **19:9** [r] Jn 18:33 [s] Mk 14:61
19:11 [t] Ro 13:1 [u] Jn 18:28-30; Ac 3:13 **19:12** [v] Lk 23:2
19:13 [w] Mt 27:19 [x] Jn 5:2

the day of Preparation[y] of the Passover; it was about noon.[z]

"Here is your king,"[a] Pilate said to the Jews.

15But they shouted, "Take him away! Take him away! Crucify him!"

"Shall I crucify your king?" Pilate asked.

"We have no king but Caesar," the chief priests answered.

16Finally Pilate handed him over to them to be crucified.[b]

The Crucifixion of Jesus

So the soldiers took charge of Jesus. **17**Carrying his own cross,[c] he went out to the place of the Skull[d] (which in Aramaic[e] is called Golgotha). **18**There they crucified him, and with him two others[f]—one on each side and Jesus in the middle.

19Pilate had a notice prepared and fastened to the cross. It read: JESUS OF NAZARETH,[g] THE KING OF THE JEWS.[h] **20**Many of the Jews read this sign, for the place where Jesus was crucified was near the city,[i] and the sign was written in Aramaic, Latin and Greek. **21**The chief priests of the Jews protested to Pilate, "Do not write 'The King of the Jews,' but that this man claimed to be king of the Jews."[j]

22Pilate answered, "What I have written, I have written."

23When the soldiers crucified Jesus, they took his clothes, dividing them into four shares, one for each of them, with the undergarment remaining. This garment was seamless, woven in one piece from top to bottom.

24"Let's not tear it," they said to one another. "Let's decide by lot who will get it."

This happened that the scripture might be fulfilled[k] that said,

"They divided my clothes among them
and cast lots for my garment."[a][l]

So this is what the soldiers did.

25Near the cross[m] of Jesus stood his mother,[n] his mother's sister, Mary the wife of Clopas, and Mary Magdalene.[o] **26**When Jesus saw his mother[p] there, and the disciple whom he loved[q] standing nearby, he said to her, "Woman,[b] here is your son," **27**and to the disciple, "Here is your mother." From that time on, this disciple took her into his home.

The Death of Jesus

28Later, knowing that everything had now been finished,[r] and so that Scripture would be fulfilled,[s] Jesus said, "I am thirsty." **29**A jar of wine vinegar[t] was there, so they soaked a sponge in it, put the sponge on a stalk of the hyssop plant, and lifted it to Jesus' lips. **30**When he had received the drink, Jesus said, "It is finished."[u] With that, he bowed his head and gave up his spirit.

31Now it was the day of Preparation,[v] and the next day was to be a special Sabbath. Because the Jewish leaders did not want the bodies left on the crosses[w] during the Sabbath, they asked Pilate to have the legs broken and the bodies taken down. **32**The soldiers therefore came and broke the legs of the first man who had been crucified with Jesus, and then those of the other.[x] **33**But when they came to Jesus and found that he was already dead, they did not break his legs. **34**Instead, one of the soldiers pierced[y] Jesus' side with a spear, bringing

[a] *24* Psalm 22:18 [b] *26* The Greek for *Woman* does not denote any disrespect.

19:19 *had a noticed prepared.* It was a Roman custom to write the name of the condemned person and his crime on a plaque to be placed above his head at execution.

19:20 *written in Aramaic, Latin and Greek.* Multilingual inscriptions were common. The title was written in the local, common, and official languages of the day. Everyone could read the message in his or her own language.

19:23 *the soldiers.* According to Roman law, the garments of a condemned criminal belonged to the executioners. Jesus had two items of clothing. The cloak was a large, loose garment. The tunic was a close-fitting garment that went from the neck to the knees.

19:24 *cast lots.* The outer garment could be conveniently divided, but the inner garment could not. Thus, the soldiers divided the outer one and cast lots for the inner one. Unknowingly, the soldiers fulfilled David's prophecy in Psalm 22:18.

19:30 *It is finished.* Having fulfilled every command of the Father and every prophecy of Scripture, Jesus voluntarily died. This was not a cry of exhaustion, but of completion. Jesus had done what He had agreed to do.

19:31 *the day of Preparation.* This day was Friday, the day before the Sabbath Day. Bodies should not remain on the cross. It is ironic that in the midst of a deliberate judicial murder the Jews were scrupulous about keeping the ceremonial law. According to Jewish law (Deut. 21:23), it was necessary to remove the bodies of executed criminals before sunset. To avoid breaking the law, the Jews requested that the legs of the condemned be broken so that the men would die quickly and could be removed from their crosses. With his legs broken, a victim could no longer lift his body in order to breathe and would soon suffocate.

19:34 *one of the soldiers pierced Jesus' side.* After the soldier did this, blood and water came out, indicating that Jesus was already dead. Only blood would have flowed from a living body.

19:14 [y] Mt 27:62 [z] Mk 15:25 [a] ver 19,21 **19:16** [b] Mt 27:26; Mk 15:15; Lk 23:25 **19:17** [c] Ge 22:6; Lk 14:27; 23:26 [d] Lk 23:33 [e] Jn 5:2 **19:18** [f] Lk 23:32 **19:19** [g] Mk 1:24 [h] ver 14,21 **19:20** [i] Heb 13:12 **19:21** [j] ver 14 **19:24** [k] ver 28,36,37; Mt 1:22 [l] Ps 22:18 **19:25** [m] Mt 27:55,56; Mk 15:40,41; Lk 23:49 [n] Mt 12:46 [o] Lk 24:18 **19:26** [p] Mt 12:46 [q] Jn 13:23 **19:28** [r] ver 30; Jn 13:1 [s] ver 24,36,37 **19:29** [t] Ps 69:21 **19:30** [u] Lk 12:50; Jn 17:4 **19:31** [v] ver 14,42 [w] Dt 21:23; Jos 8:29; 10:26,27 **19:32** [x] ver 18 **19:34** [y] Zec 12:10

a sudden flow of blood and water.[z] 35The man who saw it[a] has given testimony, and his testimony is true.[b] He knows that he tells the truth, and he testifies so that you also may believe. 36These things happened so that the scripture would be fulfilled:[c] "Not one of his bones will be broken,"[ad] 37and, as another scripture says, "They will look on the one they have pierced."[be]

The Burial of Jesus

38Later, Joseph of Arimathea asked Pilate for the body of Jesus. Now Joseph was a disciple of Jesus, but secretly because he feared the Jewish leaders. With Pilate's permission, he came and took the body away. 39He was accompanied by Nicodemus,[f] the man who earlier had visited Jesus at night. Nicodemus brought a mixture of myrrh and aloes, about seventy-five pounds.[c] 40Taking Jesus' body, the two of them wrapped it, with the spices, in strips of linen.[g] This was in accordance with Jewish burial customs.[h] 41At the place where Jesus was crucified, there was a garden, and in the garden a new tomb, in which no one had ever been laid. 42Because it was the Jewish day of Preparation[i] and since the tomb was nearby,[j] they laid Jesus there.

The Empty Tomb

20 Early on the first day of the week, while it was still dark, Mary Magdalene[k] went to the tomb and saw that the stone had been removed from the entrance.[l] 2So she came running to Simon Peter and the other disciple, the one Jesus loved,[m] and said, "They have taken the Lord out of the tomb, and we don't know where they have put him!"[n]

3So Peter and the other disciple started for the tomb.[o] 4Both were running, but the other disciple outran Peter and reached the tomb first. 5He bent over and looked in[p] at the strips of linen[q] lying there but did not go in. 6Then Simon Peter came along behind him and went straight into the tomb. He saw the strips of linen lying there, 7as well as the cloth that had been wrapped around Jesus' head.[r] The cloth was still lying in its place, separate from the linen. 8Finally the other disciple, who had reached the tomb first,[s] also went inside. He saw and believed. 9(They still did not understand from Scripture[t] that Jesus had to rise from the dead.)[u] 10Then the disciples went back to where they were staying.

Jesus Appears to Mary Magdalene

11Now Mary stood outside the tomb crying. As she wept, she bent over to look into the tomb[v] 12and saw two angels in white,[w] seated where Jesus' body had been, one at the head and the other at the foot.

13They asked her, "Woman, why are you crying?"[x]

"They have taken my Lord away," she said, "and I don't know where they have put him."[y] 14At this, she turned around and saw Jesus standing there,[z] but she did not realize that it was Jesus.[a]

15He asked her, "Woman, why are you crying?[b] Who is it you are looking for?"

Thinking he was the gardener, she said, "Sir, if you have carried him away, tell me where you have put him, and I will get him."

16Jesus said to her, "Mary."

She turned toward him and cried out in Aramaic,[c] "Rabboni!"[d] (which means "Teacher").

17Jesus said, "Do not hold on to me, for I have not yet ascended to the Father. Go instead to my brothers[e] and tell them, 'I am ascending to my Father[f] and your Father, to my God and your God.'"

18Mary Magdalene[g] went to the disciples[h] with the news: "I have seen the Lord!" And she told them that he had said these things to her.

a 36 Exodus 12:46; Num. 9:12; Psalm 34:20
b 37 Zech. 12:10 *c* 39 Or about 34 kilograms

19:35 *The man who saw it.* John's words can be trusted because he is giving an eyewitness account, so that his readers will believe that Jesus is the Savior.
20:2 *They have taken the Lord.* Mary Magdalene jumped to the wrong conclusion.
20:5 *the strips of linen lying.* No one who came to steal the body would have taken the time to unwrap it and leave the clothes behind.
20:6 *saw the strips of linen.* The Greek term implies an intense stare, in contrast to the more casual look described in verse 5. Peter went into the tomb to get a good look. He carefully examined the place where Jesus' body had been.
20:9 *They still did not understand from Scripture.* The disciples believed because of what they saw in the tomb (v. 8), not because of what they knew from Old Testament passages describing the Savior's resurrection (Luke 24:25–27). Jesus had prophesied His death and resurrection in the disciples' presence, but the disciples had not understood what He was talking about.
20:17 *Do not hold on to me.* This means "to fasten oneself to" or "to cling." Mary had grabbed Christ and was holding on to Him as if she would never turn Him loose.

19:34 [z] 1Jn 5:6,8 **19:35** [a] Lk 24:48 [b] Jn 15:27; 21:24 **19:36** [c] ver 24,28,37; Mt 1:22 [d] Ex 12:46; Nu 9:12; Ps 34:20 **19:37** [e] Zec 12:10; Rev 1:7 **19:39** [f] Jn 3:1; 7:50 **19:40** [g] Lk 24:12; Jn 11:44; 20:5,7 [h] Mt 26:12 **19:42** [i] ver 14,31 [j] ver 20,41 **20:1** [k] ver 18; Jn 19:25 [l] Mt 27:60,66 **20:2** [m] Jn 13:23 [n] ver 13 **20:3** [o] Lk 24:12 **20:5** [p] ver 11 [q] Jn 19:40 **20:7** [r] Jn 11:44 **20:8** [s] ver 4 **20:9** [t] Mt 22:29; Jn 2:22 [u] Lk 24:26,46 **20:11** [v] ver 5 **20:12** [w] Mt 28:2,3; Mk 16:5; Lk 24:4; Ac 5:19 **20:13** [x] ver 15 [y] ver 2 **20:14** [z] Mt 28:9; Mk 16:9 [a] Lk 24:16; Jn 21:4 **20:15** [b] ver 13 **20:16** [c] Jn 5:2 [d] Mt 23:7 **20:17** [e] Mt 28:10 [f] Jn 7:33 **20:18** [g] ver 1 [h] Lk 24:10,22,23

Jesus Appears to His Disciples

19On the evening of that first day of the week, when the disciples were together, with the doors locked for fear of the Jewish leaders,[i] Jesus came and stood among them and said, "Peace[j] be with you!"[k] 20After he said this, he showed them his hands and side.[l] The disciples were overjoyed[m] when they saw the Lord.

21Again Jesus said, "Peace be with you![n] As the Father has sent me,[o] I am sending you."[p] 22And with that he breathed on them and said, "Receive the Holy Spirit.[q] 23If you forgive anyone's sins, their sins are forgiven; if you do not forgive them, they are not forgiven."[r]

Jesus Appears to Thomas

24Now Thomas[s] (also known as Didymus[a]), one of the Twelve, was not with the disciples when Jesus came. 25So the other disciples told him, "We have seen the Lord!"

But he said to them, "Unless I see the nail marks in his hands and put my finger where the nails were, and put my hand into his side,[t] I will not believe."[u]

26A week later his disciples were in the house again, and Thomas was with them. Though the doors were locked, Jesus came and stood among them and said, "Peace[v] be with you!"[w] 27Then he said to Thomas, "Put your finger here; see my hands. Reach out your hand and put it into my side. Stop doubting and believe."[x]

28Thomas said to him, "My Lord and my God!"

29Then Jesus told him, "Because you have seen me, you have believed;[y] blessed are those who have not seen and yet have believed."[z]

The Purpose of John's Gospel

30Jesus performed many other signs[a] in the presence of his disciples, which are not recorded in this book.[b] 31But these are written that you may believe[bc] that Jesus is the Messiah, the Son of God,[d] and that by believing you may have life in his name.[e]

Jesus and the Miraculous Catch of Fish

21 Afterward Jesus appeared again to his disciples,[f] by the Sea of Galilee.[cg] It happened this way: 2Simon Peter, Thomas[h] (also known as Didymus[a]), Nathanael[i] from Cana in Galilee,[j] the sons of Zebedee,[k] and two other disciples were together. 3"I'm going out to fish," Simon Peter told them, and they said, "We'll go with you." So they went out and got into the boat, but that night they caught nothing.[l]

4Early in the morning, Jesus stood on the shore, but the disciples did not realize that it was Jesus.[m]

5He called out to them, "Friends, haven't you any fish?"

"No," they answered.

6He said, "Throw your net on the right side of the boat and you will find some." When they did, they were unable to haul the net in because of the large number of fish.[n]

7Then the disciple whom Jesus loved[o] said to Peter, "It is the Lord!" As soon as Simon Peter heard him say, "It is the Lord," he wrapped his outer garment around him (for he had taken it off) and jumped into the water. 8The other disciples followed in the boat, towing the net full of fish, for they were not far from shore, about a hundred yards.[d] 9When they landed, they saw a fire[p] of burning coals there with fish on it,[q] and some bread.

10Jesus said to them, "Bring some of the fish you have just caught." 11So Simon Peter climbed back into the boat and dragged the net ashore. It was full of large fish, 153, but even with so many the net was not torn. 12Jesus said to them, "Come and have breakfast." None of the disciples dared ask him, "Who are you?" They knew it was the Lord. 13Jesus came, took the bread and gave it to them, and did the same with the

[a] *24,2 Thomas* (Aramaic) and *Didymus* (Greek) both mean *twin.* [b] *31 Or may continue to believe* [c] *1* Greek *Tiberias* [d] *8* Or *about 90 meters*

20:19 *Jesus came and stood among them.* Christ's appearance was miraculous because the doors were shut. Jesus, as God, could perform a variety of miracles without requiring a change in His humanity. Here Christ's body was a physical body, the same body in which He died and was buried. The difference is that His flesh had been changed to take on immortality and incorruptibility (1 Cor. 15:53).

20:31 *that you may believe.* John states the purpose of his book, which was to convince his readers that Jesus is the Christ, the Messiah who fulfilled God's promises to Israel. Jesus is the Son of God, God in the flesh. By believing these things, a person obtains eternal life (1:12).

21:4 *the disciples did not realize.* Perhaps the apostles did not recognize Jesus because they were preoccupied with their work, as Mary Magdalene had been with her sorrow (20:14). In addition, there was not much light at this time of day.

21:7 *Peter ... jumped into the water.* John was the first to recognize the Lord; Peter was the first to act.

20:19 [i] Jn 7:13 [j] Jn 14:27 [k] ver 21, 26; Lk 24:36-39
20:20 [l] Lk 24:39, 40; Jn 19:34 [m] Jn 16:20, 22
20:21 [n] ver 19 [o] Jn 3:17 [p] Mt 28:19; Jn 17:18
20:22 [q] Jn 7:39; Ac 2:38; 8:15-17; 19:2; Gal 3:2
20:23 [r] Mt 16:19; 18:18 **20:24** [s] Jn 11:16 **20:25** [t] ver 20 [u] Mk 16:11 **20:26** [v] Jn 14:27 [w] ver 21 **20:27** [x] ver 25; Lk 24:40 **20:29** [y] Jn 3:15 [z] 1Pe 1:8 **20:30** [a] Jn 2:11 [b] Jn 21:25 **20:31** [c] Jn 3:15; 19:35 [d] Mt 4:3 [e] Mt 25:46
21:1 [f] Jn 20:19, 26 [g] Jn 6:1 **21:2** [h] Jn 11:16 [i] Jn 1:45 [j] Jn 2:1 [k] Mt 4:21 **21:3** [l] Lk 5:5 **21:4** [m] Lk 24:16; Jn 20:14 **21:6** [n] Lk 5:4-7 **21:7** [o] Jn 13:23
21:9 [p] Jn 18:18 [q] ver 10, 13

fish.[r] 14 This was now the third time Jesus
appeared to his disciples[s] after he was
raised from the dead.

Jesus Reinstates Peter

15 When they had finished eating, Jesus
said to Simon Peter, "Simon son of John, do
you love me more than these?"
"Yes, Lord," he said, "you know that I
love you."[t]
Jesus said, "Feed my lambs."[u]
16 Again Jesus said, "Simon son of John,
do you love me?"
He answered, "Yes, Lord, you know that
I love you."
Jesus said, "Take care of my sheep."[v]
17 The third time he said to him, "Simon
son of John, do you love me?"
Peter was hurt because Jesus asked him
the third time, "Do you love me?"[w] He said,
"Lord, you know all things;[x] you know that
I love you."
Jesus said, "Feed my sheep.[y] 18 Very truly I tell you, when you were younger you
dressed yourself and went where you wanted; but when you are old you will stretch
out your hands, and someone else will
dress you and lead you where you do not
want to go." 19 Jesus said this to indicate the
kind of death[z] by which Peter would glorify God.[a] Then he said to him, "Follow me!"
20 Peter turned and saw that the disciple whom Jesus loved[b] was following
them. (This was the one who had leaned
back against Jesus at the supper and had
said, "Lord, who is going to betray you?")[c]
21 When Peter saw him, he asked, "Lord,
what about him?"
22 Jesus answered, "If I want him to remain alive until I return,[d] what is that to
you? You must follow me."[e] 23 Because of
this, the rumor spread among the believers[f]
that this disciple would not die. But Jesus
did not say that he would not die; he only
said, "If I want him to remain alive until I
return, what is that to you?"
24 This is the disciple who testifies to
these things[g] and who wrote them down.
We know that his testimony is true.[h]
25 Jesus did many other things as well.[i]
If every one of them were written down, I
suppose that even the whole world would
not have room for the books that would be
written.

21:17 ***you know that I love you.*** Peter denied the Lord at least three times. Here, he affirmed his love for the third time.
21:20–21 ***the disciple whom Jesus loved.*** This is commonly considered to be John, the author of this Gospel.
21:24 ***This is the disciple.*** This is basically John's signature to his Gospel.
21:25 ***Jesus did many other things as well.*** The Gospel of John is truthful (v. 24), but it is not exhaustive.

21:13 [r] ver 9 **21:14** [s] Jn 20:19, 26 **21:15** [t] Mt 26:33, 35; Jn 13:37 [u] Lk 12:32 **21:16** [v] Mt 2:6; Ac 20:28; 1Pe 5:2, 3 **21:17** [w] Jn 13:38 [x] Jn 16:30 [y] ver 16 **21:19** [z] Jn 12:33; 18:32 [a] 2Pe 1:14 **21:20** [b] ver 7; Jn 13:23 [c] Jn 13:25 **21:22** [d] Mt 16:27; 1Co 4:5; Rev 2:25 [e] ver 19 **21:23** [f] Ac 1:16 **21:24** [g] Jn 15:27 [h] Jn 19:35 **21:25** [i] Jn 20:30

ACTS

▸ **AUTHOR:** There are many "we" sections in Acts that imply the author was present for these events (16:10 – 17; 20:5 — 21:18; 27:1 — 28:16). These sections of Acts are the historical record of an eyewitness. For the remainder of this book, Luke no doubt followed the same careful investigative procedures that he used in writing his Gospel (Luke 1:1 – 4). As a close traveling companion of Paul, Luke had access to the principal eyewitness for chapters 13 – 18. It is also likely that he had opportunities to interview such key witnesses in Jerusalem as Peter and John for the information in chapters 13 – 28. Modern archeological discoveries have strikingly confirmed the trustworthiness and precision of Luke as an historian.

▸ **TIME:** C. A.D. 33 – 62 ▸ **KEY VERSES:** Acts 2:42 – 47

▸ **THEME:** Acts is the record of how the events surrounding Jesus' life and death and resurrection resulted in this worldwide movement called the church. The book is certainly not a comprehensive history. Acts is more like a photo album of snapshots. It is the record of an eyewitness who wrote about what he saw and what seemed to be the critical events in the beginnings of the church and its movement out of Jerusalem to the rest of the world. One could say that the Book of Acts is an elaboration on Acts 1:8: "But you will receive power when the Holy Spirit comes on you; and you will be my witnesses in Jerusalem, and in all Judea and Samaria, and to the ends of the earth."

Jesus Taken Up Into Heaven

1 In my former book,[a] Theophilus, I wrote
about all that Jesus began to do and to
teach[b] 2until the day he was taken up to
heaven,[c] after giving instructions[d] through
the Holy Spirit to the apostles[e] he had chosen.[f] 3After his suffering, he presented
himself to them and gave many convincing proofs that he was alive. He appeared
to them[g] over a period of forty days and
spoke about the kingdom of God. 4On one
occasion, while he was eating with them,
he gave them this command: "Do not leave
Jerusalem, but wait for the gift my Father
promised, which you have heard me speak
about.[h] 5For John baptized with[a] water, but
in a few days you will be baptized with[a] the
Holy Spirit."

6Then they gathered around him and
asked him, "Lord, are you at this time going to restore[i] the kingdom to Israel?"

7He said to them: "It is not for you to
know the times or dates the Father has set
by his own authority.[j] 8But you will receive
power when the Holy Spirit comes on you;[k]
and you will be my witnesses[l] in Jerusalem, and in all Judea and Samaria,[m] and to
the ends of the earth."[n]

[a] 5 Or *in*

1:3 *many convincing proofs.* This is the only time the Greek word *tekmerion* occurs, emphasizing the certainty of the resurrection.

1:5 Baptism — The promised Holy Spirit (Is. 32:15; Joel 2:28 – 32) is a gift to believers after the glorification of Jesus (John 7:39). John baptized for forgiveness of sins, but the outpouring of the Spirit resulted from Christ's victory and exaltation to God's right hand (2:33). Believers are sealed until redemption (Eph. 1:13), made one body, and filled with one Spirit (1 Cor. 12:13). The baptism of the Spirit is the immersion in the Spirit and uniting of believers into one body.

1:8 Living by Faith — God designed the Christian life to be one lived in the power of the Holy Spirit. Believers must appropriate daily, by faith, the power of the Holy Spirit to live as Christians (Rom. 8:4 – 5). This means that the believer trusts the Spirit to empower him in specific instances such as resisting temptation, being faithful, and sharing one's faith. There is no secret formula that makes the Spirit's power operational in our lives. Scripture tells us that the Spirit dwells and operates in us (1 Cor. 6:19). We have to learn by experience through interaction with God to understand how that dynamic works. First the disciples received the Holy Spirit. Then he gave them power and finally the disciples were told they would be Christ's witness to the very ends of the earth.

1:1 [a] Lk 1:1-4 [b] Lk 3:23 **1:2** [c] ver 9, 11; Mk 16:19 [d] Mt 28:19, 20 [e] Mk 6:30 [f] Jn 13:18 **1:3** [g] Mt 28:17; Lk 24:34, 36; Jn 20:19, 26; 21:1, 14; 1Co 15:5-7 **1:4** [h] Lk 24:49; Jn 14:16; Ac 2:33 **1:6** [i] Mt 17:11 **1:7** [j] Mt 24:36 **1:8** [k] Ac 2:1-4 [l] Lk 24:48 [m] Ac 8:1-25 [n] Mt 28:19

9After he said this, he was taken up[o] before their very eyes, and a cloud hid him
from their sight.
10They were looking intently up into the
sky as he was going, when suddenly two
men dressed in white[p] stood beside them.
11"Men of Galilee,"[q] they said, "why do you
stand here looking into the sky? This same
Jesus, who has been taken from you into
heaven, will come back[r] in the same way
you have seen him go into heaven."

Matthias Chosen to Replace Judas

12Then the apostles returned to Jerusalem[s] from the hill called the Mount of Olives,[t] a Sabbath day's walk[a] from the city.
13When they arrived, they went upstairs to
the room[u] where they were staying. Those
present were Peter, John, James and Andrew; Philip and Thomas, Bartholomew
and Matthew; James son of Alphaeus
and Simon the Zealot, and Judas son of
James.[v] 14They all joined together constantly in prayer,[w] along with the women[x]
and Mary the mother of Jesus, and with
his brothers.[y]
15In those days Peter stood up among
the believers (a group numbering about a
hundred and twenty) 16and said, "Brothers
and sisters,[b] the Scripture had to be fulfilled[z] in which the Holy Spirit spoke long
ago through David concerning Judas,[a]
who served as guide for those who arrested Jesus. 17He was one of our number[b] and
shared in our ministry."[c]
18(With the payment[d] he received for his
wickedness, Judas bought a field;[e] there
he fell headlong, his body burst open and
all his intestines spilled out. 19Everyone in
Jerusalem heard about this, so they called
that field in their language Akeldama, that
is, Field of Blood.)
20"For," said Peter, "it is written in the
Book of Psalms:

"'May his place be deserted;
let there be no one to dwell in it,'[c][f]

and,

"'May another take his place of
leadership.'[d][g]

21Therefore it is necessary to choose one of
the men who have been with us the whole
time the Lord Jesus was living among us,
22beginning from John's baptism[h] to the
time when Jesus was taken up from us. For
one of these must become a witness[i] with
us of his resurrection."
23So they nominated two men: Joseph
called Barsabbas (also known as Justus)
and Matthias. 24Then they prayed,[j] "Lord,
you know everyone's heart.[k] Show us
which of these two you have chosen 25to
take over this apostolic ministry, which
Judas left to go where he belongs." 26Then
they cast lots, and the lot fell to Matthias;
so he was added to the eleven apostles.[l]

The Holy Spirit Comes at Pentecost

2 When the day of Pentecost[m] came,
they were all together[n] in one place.
2Suddenly a sound like the blowing of a
violent wind came from heaven and filled
the whole house where they were sitting.[o]
3They saw what seemed to be tongues of
fire that separated and came to rest on
each of them. 4All of them were filled with
the Holy Spirit and began to speak in other
tongues[e][p] as the Spirit enabled them.
5Now there were staying in Jerusalem
God-fearing[q] Jews from every nation under heaven. 6When they heard this sound, a
crowd came together in bewilderment, because each one heard their own language
being spoken. 7Utterly amazed,[r] they
asked: "Aren't all these who are speaking Galileans?[s] 8Then how is it that each
of us hears them in our native language?
9Parthians, Medes and Elamites; residents of Mesopotamia, Judea and Cappadocia,[t] Pontus[u] and Asia,[f][v] 10Phrygia[w] and
Pamphylia,[x] Egypt and the parts of Libya
near Cyrene;[y] visitors from Rome 11(both
Jews and converts to Judaism); Cretans
and Arabs—we hear them declaring the
wonders of God in our own tongues!"
12Amazed and perplexed, they asked one
another, "What does this mean?"
13Some, however, made fun of them and
said, "They have had too much wine."[z]

---

[a] *12* That is, about 5/8 mile or about 1 kilometer
[b] *16* The Greek word for *brothers and sisters* (*adelphoi*) refers here to believers, both men and women, as part of God's family; also in 6:3; 11:29; 12:17; 16:40; 18:18, 27; 21:7, 17; 28:14, 15.
[c] *20* Psalm 69:25
[d] *20* Psalm 109:8
[e] *4* Or *languages*; also in verse 11
[f] *9* That is, the Roman province by that name

Effective witness requires that we first learn to rely on the Spirit to help us.

1:14 ***They all joined together.*** The disciples were like-minded; the people put aside personal positions and took on a common goal. True unity is an act of grace.

2:4 ***tongues.*** This means "diverse languages" and was essential to the rapid worldwide spread of the gospel. Those gathered for Pentecost came from around the known world and had various "mother tongues."

1:9 [o] ver 2 **1:10** [p] Lk 24:4; Jn 20:12 **1:11** [q] Ac 2:7 [r] Mt 16:27 **1:12** [s] Lk 24:52 [t] Mt 21:1 **1:13** [u] Ac 9:37; 20:8 [v] Mt 10:2-4; Mk 3:16-19; Lk 6:14-16 **1:14** [w] Ac 2:42; 6:4 [x] Lk 23:49,55 [y] Mt 12:46 **1:16** [z] ver 20 [a] Jn 13:18 **1:17** [b] Jn 6:70,71 [c] ver 25 **1:18** [d] Mt 26:14, 15 [e] Mt 27:3-10 **1:20** [f] Ps 69:25 [g] Ps 109:8 **1:22** [h] Mk 1:4 [i] ver 8 **1:24** [j] Ac 6:6; 14:23 [k] 1Sa 16:7; Jer 17:10; Ac 15:8; Rev 2:23 **1:26** [l] Ac 2:14 **2:1** [m] Lev 23:15, 16; Ac 20:16 [n] Ac 1:14 **2:2** [o] Ac 4:31 **2:4** [p] Mk 16:17; 1Co 12:10 **2:5** [q] Ac 8:2 **2:7** [r] ver 12 [s] Ac 1:11 **2:9** [t] 1Pe 1:1 [u] Ac 18:2 [v] Ac 16:6; Ro 16:5; 1Co 16:19; 2Co 1:8 **2:10** [w] Ac 16:6; 18:23 [x] Ac 13:13; 15:38 [y] Mt 27:32 **2:13** [z] 1Co 14:23

Peter Addresses the Crowd

14 Then Peter stood up with the Eleven,
raised his voice and addressed the crowd:
"Fellow Jews and all of you who live in Jerusalem, let me explain this to you; listen
carefully to what I say. 15 These people are
not drunk, as you suppose. It's only nine in
the morning![a] 16 No, this is what was spoken by the prophet Joel:

17 " 'In the last days, God says,
I will pour out my Spirit on all
people.[b]
Your sons and daughters will prophesy,[c]
your young men will see visions,
your old men will dream dreams.
18 Even on my servants, both men and
women,
I will pour out my Spirit in those
days,
and they will prophesy.[d]
19 I will show wonders in the heavens
above
and signs on the earth below,
blood and fire and billows of smoke.
20 The sun will be turned to darkness
and the moon to blood[e]
before the coming of the great and
glorious day of the Lord.
21 And everyone who calls
on the name of the Lord will be
saved.'[a][f]

22 "Fellow Israelites, listen to this: Jesus
of Nazareth was a man accredited by God
to you by miracles, wonders and signs,[g]
which God did among you through him,[h]
as you yourselves know. 23 This man was
handed over to you by God's deliberate
plan and foreknowledge;[i] and you, with the
help of wicked men,[b] put him to death by
nailing him to the cross.[j] 24 But God raised
him from the dead,[k] freeing him from the
agony of death, because it was impossible
for death to keep its hold on him.[l] 25 David
said about him:

" 'I saw the Lord always before me.
Because he is at my right hand,
I will not be shaken.
26 Therefore my heart is glad and my
tongue rejoices;
my body also will rest in hope,
27 because you will not abandon me to the
realm of the dead,
you will not let your holy one see
decay.[m]
28 You have made known to me the paths
of life;
you will fill me with joy in your
presence.'[c]

29 "Fellow Israelites, I can tell you confidently that the patriarch[n] David died and
was buried,[o] and his tomb is here[p] to this
day. 30 But he was a prophet and knew
that God had promised him on oath that
he would place one of his descendants on
his throne.[q] 31 Seeing what was to come, he
spoke of the resurrection of the Messiah,
that he was not abandoned to the realm of
the dead, nor did his body see decay.[r] 32 God
has raised this Jesus to life,[s] and we are all
witnesses[t] of it. 33 Exalted[u] to the right hand
of God,[v] he has received from the Father[w]
the promised Holy Spirit[x] and has poured
out[y] what you now see and hear. 34 For David did not ascend to heaven, and yet he
said,

" 'The Lord said to my Lord:
"Sit at my right hand
35 until I make your enemies
a footstool for your feet." '[d][z]

36 "Therefore let all Israel be assured of
this: God has made this Jesus, whom you
crucified, both Lord and Messiah."[a]
37 When the people heard this, they
were cut to the heart and said to Peter and
the other apostles, "Brothers, what shall
we do?"[b]
38 Peter replied, "Repent and be baptized,[c] every one of you, in the name of
Jesus Christ for the forgiveness of your
sins.[d] And you will receive the gift of the
Holy Spirit. 39 The promise is for you and
your children[e] and for all who are far off[f]—
for all whom the Lord our God will call."
40 With many other words he warned
them; and he pleaded with them, "Save
yourselves from this corrupt generation."[g]

---

[a] *21* Joel 2:28-32 [b] *23* Or *of those not having the law* (that is, Gentiles) [c] *28* Psalm 16:8-11 (see Septuagint) [d] *35* Psalm 110:1

2:17 *visions . . . dreams.* The Holy Spirit was poured out on the church at the beginning of this final age of Scripture.

2:37 Conviction of the Holy Spirit—Peter's preaching was extremely effective, for it came "with power, with the Holy Spirit and deep conviction" (1 Thess. 1:5). The result was they were "cut to the heart." Their response was, "Brothers, what shall we do?" The reality was that conviction by the Holy Spirit brought about a real search for an answer. Such a consciousness of sin is an indispensable prerequisite to conversion.

2:38 *Repent.* Peter called the Jews to turn their backs on their former lives and change. Faith involves an action of belief by those who accept Jesus.

2:15 [a] 1Th 5:7 **2:17** [b] Isa 44:3; Jn 7:37-39; Ac 10:45 [c] Ac 21:9 **2:18** [d] Ac 21:9-12 **2:20** [e] Mt 24:29 **2:21** [f] Ro 10:13 **2:22** [g] Jn 4:48; Ac 10:38 [h] Jn 3:2 **2:23** [i] Lk 22:22; Ac 3:18; 4:28 [j] Lk 24:20; Ac 3:13 **2:24** [k] ver 32; 1Co 6:14; 2Co 4:14; Eph 1:20; Col 2:12; Heb 13:20; 1Pe 1:21 [l] Jn 20:9 **2:27** [m] ver 31; Ac 13:35 **2:29** [n] Ac 7:8, 9 [o] 1Ki 2:10; Ac 13:36 [p] Ne 3:16 **2:30** [q] 2Sa 7:12; Ps 132:11 **2:31** [r] Ps 16:10 **2:32** [s] ver 24 [t] Ac 1:8 **2:33** [u] Php 2:9 [v] Mk 16:19 [w] Ac 1:4 [x] Jn 7:39; 14:26 [y] Ac 10:45 **2:35** [z] Ps 110:1; Mt 22:44 **2:36** [a] Lk 2:11 **2:37** [b] Lk 3:10, 12, 14 **2:38** [c] Ac 8:12, 16, 36, 38; 22:16 [d] Lk 24:47; Ac 3:19 **2:39** [e] Isa 44:3 [f] Ac 10:45; Eph 2:13 **2:40** [g] Dt 32:5

41Those who accepted his message were
baptized, and about three thousand were
added to their number that day.

The Fellowship of the Believers

42They devoted themselves to the apostles' teaching and to fellowship, to the
breaking of bread and to prayer.[h] 43Every-
one was filled with awe at the many wonders and signs performed by the apostles.[i]
44All the believers were together and had
everything in common.[j] 45They sold property and possessions to give to anyone who
had need.[k] 46Every day they continued to
meet together in the temple courts.[l] They
broke bread[m] in their homes and ate together with glad and sincere hearts, 47praising
God and enjoying the favor of all the people.[n] And the Lord added to their number[o]
daily those who were being saved.

Peter Heals a Lame Beggar

3 One day Peter and John[p] were going up
to the temple[q] at the time of prayer—at
three in the afternoon.[r] 2Now a man who
was lame from birth[s] was being carried to
the temple gate[t] called Beautiful, where he
was put every day to beg[u] from those going
into the temple courts. 3When he saw Peter and John about to enter, he asked them
for money. 4Peter looked straight at him, as
did John. Then Peter said, "Look at us!" 5So
the man gave them his attention, expecting
to get something from them.

6Then Peter said, "Silver or gold I do not
have, but what I do have I give you. In the
name of Jesus Christ of Nazareth,[v] walk."
7Taking him by the right hand, he helped
him up, and instantly the man's feet and
ankles became strong. 8He jumped to his
feet and began to walk. Then he went with
them into the temple courts, walking and
jumping,[w] and praising God. 9When all
the people[x] saw him walking and praising
God, 10they recognized him as the same
man who used to sit begging at the temple
gate called Beautiful,[y] and they were filled
with wonder and amazement at what had
happened to him.

Peter Speaks to the Onlookers

11While the man held on to Peter and
John,[z] all the people were astonished and
came running to them in the place called
Solomon's Colonnade.[a] 12When Peter saw
this, he said to them: "Fellow Israelites, why
does this surprise you? Why do you stare
at us as if by our own power or godliness
we had made this man walk? 13The God of
Abraham, Isaac and Jacob, the God of our
fathers,[b] has glorified his servant Jesus.
You handed him over to be killed, and you
disowned him before Pilate,[c] though he
had decided to let him go.[d] 14You disowned
the Holy[e] and Righteous One[f] and asked
that a murderer be released to you.[g] 15You
killed the author of life, but God raised him
from the dead.[h] We are witnesses of this.
16By faith in the name of Jesus, this man
whom you see and know was made strong.
It is Jesus' name and the faith that comes
through him that has completely healed
him, as you can all see.

17"Now, fellow Israelites, I know that you
acted in ignorance,[i] as did your leaders.[j]
18But this is how God fulfilled what he had
foretold[k] through all the prophets,[l] saying
that his Messiah would suffer.[m] 19Repent,
then, and turn to God, so that your sins
may be wiped out,[n] that times of refreshing may come from the Lord, 20and that
he may send the Messiah, who has been
appointed for you—even Jesus. 21Heaven
must receive him[o] until the time comes for
God to restore everything,[p] as he promised
long ago through his holy prophets.[q] 22For
Moses said, 'The Lord your God will raise
up for you a prophet like me from among
your own people; you must listen to everything he tells you.[r] 23Anyone who does not

---

2:42–47 Being in the Church—Converts were apparently immediately incorporated into the body of believers that became the church. Being involved in the Jerusalem church clearly must have changed the lives of these new believers dramatically. This was manifested in several ways: (1) they devoted themselves to new teaching; (2) they thought differently about all their possessions; (3) they became people of prayer; (4) they ate together and worshiped together with unified hearts. They weren't just saved from sin. They were saved to Christ and to this new body called the church, which of course is also His. We are called to be a part of one another's lives. We are to learn, share, pray, and worship together. As a body of believers, God expects us to have great concern for our fellow believers and to help one another mature.

3:7 *strong.* This account is told by a physician who describes instant healing. Before their eyes strength is given to muscles and bones. The man's feet could instantly hold his weight.

3:19 *Repent, then, and turn to God.* Peter challenges all to change their minds and change their courses. Not only is their sin addressed but their closed minds.

3:22 Messiah—Peter draws on the witness of the prophets who foretold the suffering of Christ. He quotes Moses, who spoke of a prophet like himself from among the Jews (Deut. 18:15–17). The crucified, risen, and ascended Jesus has fulfilled this role perfectly as God's anointed Servant sent to atone for

2:42 [h] Ac 1:14 **2:43** [i] Ac 5:12 **2:44** [j] Ac 4:32 **2:45** [k] Mt 19:21 **2:46** [l] Lk 24:53; Ac 5:21,42 [m] Ac 20:7 **2:47** [n] Ro 14:18 [o] ver 41; Ac 5:14 **3:1** [p] Lk 22:8 [q] Ac 2:46 [r] Ps 55:17 **3:2** [s] Ac 14:8 [t] Lk 16:20 [u] Jn 9:8 **3:6** [v] ver 16; Ac 4:10 **3:8** [w] Ac 14:10 **3:9** [x] Ac 4:16,21 **3:10** [y] ver 2 **3:11** [z] Lk 22:8 [a] Jn 10:23; Ac 5:12 **3:13** [b] Ac 5:30 [c] Mt 27:2 [d] Lk 23:4 **3:14** [e] Mk 1:24; Ac 4:27 [f] Ac 7:52 [g] Mk 15:11; Lk 23:18-25 **3:15** [h] Ac 2:24 **3:17** [i] Lk 23:34 [j] Ac 13:27 **3:18** [k] Ac 2:23 [l] Lk 24:27 [m] Ac 17:2,3; 26:22,23 **3:19** [n] Ac 2:38 **3:21** [o] Ac 1:11 [p] Mt 17:11 [q] Lk 1:70 **3:22** [r] Dt 18:15,18; Ac 7:37

listen to him will be completely cut off from
their people.'[a][s]
24"Indeed, beginning with Samuel, all
the prophets[t] who have spoken have foretold these days. 25And you are heirs[u] of
the prophets and of the covenant[v] God
made with your fathers. He said to Abraham, 'Through your offspring all peoples
on earth will be blessed.'[b][w] 26When God
raised up[x] his servant, he sent him first[y]
to you to bless you by turning each of you
from your wicked ways."

Peter and John Before the Sanhedrin

4 The priests and the captain of the temple guard[z] and the Sadducees[a] came up
to Peter and John while they were speaking to the people. 2They were greatly disturbed because the apostles were teaching
the people, proclaiming in Jesus the resurrection of the dead.[b] 3They seized Peter
and John and, because it was evening, they
put them in jail[c] until the next day. 4But
many who heard the message believed; so
the number of men who believed grew[d] to
about five thousand.
5The next day the rulers,[e] the elders and
the teachers of the law met in Jerusalem.
6Annas the high priest was there, and so
were Caiaphas,[f] John, Alexander and others of the high priest's family. 7They had
Peter and John brought before them and
began to question them: "By what power
or what name did you do this?"
8Then Peter, filled with the Holy Spirit,
said to them: "Rulers and elders of the people![g] 9If we are being called to account today for an act of kindness shown to a man
who was lame[h] and are being asked how
he was healed, 10then know this, you and
all the people of Israel: It is by the name of
Jesus Christ of Nazareth, whom you crucified but whom God raised from the dead,[i]
that this man stands before you healed.
11Jesus is

"'the stone you builders rejected,
which has become the cornerstone.'[c][j]

12Salvation is found in no one else, for
there is no other name under heaven given
to mankind by which we must be saved."[k]
13When they saw the courage of Peter and John[l] and realized that they were
unschooled, ordinary men,[m] they were
astonished and they took note that these
men had been with Jesus. 14But since they
could see the man who had been healed
standing there with them, there was nothing they could say. 15So they ordered them
to withdraw from the Sanhedrin[n] and then
conferred together. 16"What are we going
to do with these men?"[o] they asked. "Everyone living in Jerusalem knows they have
performed a notable sign,[p] and we cannot deny it. 17But to stop this thing from
spreading any further among the people,
we must warn them to speak no longer to
anyone in this name."
18Then they called them in again and
commanded them not to speak or teach at
all in the name of Jesus.[q] 19But Peter and
John replied, "Which is right in God's eyes:
to listen to you, or to him?[r] You be the judges! 20As for us, we cannot help speaking
about what we have seen and heard."
21After further threats they let them go.
They could not decide how to punish them,
because all the people[s] were praising God[t]
for what had happened. 22For the man who
was miraculously healed was over forty
years old.

The Believers Pray

23On their release, Peter and John went
back to their own people and reported all

---

[a] *23* Deut. 18:15,18,19 [b] *25* Gen. 22:18; 26:4
[c] *11* Psalm 118:22

---

humans. Jesus carried God's authority; the words of Jesus must be heeded since they give life to the dying sinner. A person greater than Moses has come to fulfill the prophets. Peter is proclaiming that Jesus is the deliberate fulfillment of God's promise for redemption.

4:1 *Saddicees.* The Sadducees were skeptics who rejected all of the Old Testament except the books of Moses, and who denied the resurrection from the dead. Peter's teaching about the resurrection challenged their beliefs and teaching.

4:5 *rulers, the elders and the teachers of the law.* The Sanhedrin, which consisted of 70 men plus the high priest, was the highest Jewish court. The group consisted of the wealthiest, most educated, and most powerful Jewish men in Israel.

4:8 The Filling of the Holy Spirit—This is the second description in the Book of Acts of someone being filled with the Holy Spirit (see v. 31; 2:4; 9:17; 13:9). The initial filling accompanies the baptism in the Spirit. This filling brought boldness for God's work. Jesus had promised His disciples that they would stand before kings and rulers and that the Spirit of God within them would implant in their minds exactly what to say to these leaders (Matt. 10:16–20).

4:19 *listen to you, or to him.* There is no authority apart from God. When human authority rejects God's authority, it becomes twisted and loses its right to demand compliance (5:29). God's people are responsible to obey the government because it has been set in place by God, but when government directs against God's will, the Author of authority has the higher claim on our allegiance. We must resist any command that is against God's will (Ex. 1; Dan. 3; Heb. 11:23).

3:23 [s] Dt 18:19 **3:24** [t] Lk 24:27 **3:25** [u] Ac 2:39 [v] Ro 9:4,5 [w] Ge 12:3; 22:18; 26:4; 28:14 **3:26** [x] ver 22; Ac 2:24 [y] Ac 13:46; Ro 1:16 **4:1** [z] Lk 22:4 [a] Mt 3:7 **4:2** [b] Ac 17:18 **4:3** [c] Ac 5:18 **4:4** [d] Ac 2:41 **4:5** [e] Lk 23:13 **4:6** [f] Mt 26:3; Lk 3:2 **4:8** [g] ver 5; Lk 23:13 **4:9** [h] Ac 3:6 **4:10** [i] Ac 2:24 **4:11** [j] Ps 118:22; Isa 28:16; Mt 21:42 **4:12** [k] Mt 1:21; Ac 10:43; 1Ti 2:5 **4:13** [l] Lk 22:8 [m] Mt 11:25 **4:15** [n] Mt 5:22 **4:16** [o] Jn 11:47 [p] Ac 3:6-10 **4:18** [q] Ac 5:40 **4:19** [r] Ac 5:29 **4:21** [s] Ac 5:26 [t] Mt 9:8

that the chief priests and the elders had said to them. 24 When they heard this, they raised their voices together in prayer to God. "Sovereign Lord," they said, "you made the heavens and the earth and the sea, and everything in them. 25 You spoke by the Holy Spirit through the mouth of your servant, our father David:[u]

"'Why do the nations rage
and the peoples plot in vain?
26 The kings of the earth rise up
and the rulers band together
against the Lord
and against his anointed one.[a][b][v]

27 Indeed Herod[w] and Pontius Pilate[x] met together with the Gentiles and the people of Israel in this city to conspire against your holy servant Jesus,[y] whom you anointed. 28 They did what your power and will had decided beforehand should happen.[z] 29 Now, Lord, consider their threats and enable your servants to speak your word with great boldness.[a] 30 Stretch out your hand to heal and perform signs and wonders[b] through the name of your holy servant Jesus."[c]

31 After they prayed, the place where they were meeting was shaken.[d] And they were all filled with the Holy Spirit and spoke the word of God boldly.[e]

The Believers Share Their Possessions

32 All the believers were one in heart and mind. No one claimed that any of their possessions was their own, but they shared everything they had.[f] 33 With great power the apostles continued to testify[g] to the resurrection[h] of the Lord Jesus. And God's grace was so powerfully at work in them all 34 that there were no needy persons among them. For from time to time those who owned land or houses sold them,[i] brought the money from the sales 35 and put it at the apostles' feet,[j] and it was distributed to anyone who had need.[k]

36 Joseph, a Levite from Cyprus, whom the apostles called Barnabas[l] (which means "son of encouragement"), 37 sold a field he owned and brought the money and put it at the apostles' feet.[m]

Ananias and Sapphira

5 Now a man named Ananias, together with his wife Sapphira, also sold a piece of property. 2 With his wife's full knowledge he kept back part of the money for himself, but brought the rest and put it at the apostles' feet.[n]

3 Then Peter said, "Ananias, how is it that Satan[o] has so filled your heart[p] that you have lied to the Holy Spirit[q] and have kept for yourself some of the money you received for the land? 4 Didn't it belong to you before it was sold? And after it was sold, wasn't the money at your disposal? What made you think of doing such a thing? You have not lied just to human beings but to God."

5 When Ananias heard this, he fell down and died.[r] And great fear[s] seized all who heard what had happened. 6 Then some young men came forward, wrapped up his body,[t] and carried him out and buried him.

7 About three hours later his wife came in, not knowing what had happened. 8 Peter asked her, "Tell me, is this the price you and Ananias got for the land?"

"Yes," she said, "that is the price."[u]

9 Peter said to her, "How could you conspire to test the Spirit of the Lord?[v] Listen! The feet of the men who buried your husband are at the door, and they will carry you out also."

10 At that moment she fell down at his feet and died.[w] Then the young men came in and, finding her dead, carried her out and buried her beside her husband. 11 Great fear[x] seized the whole church and all who heard about these events.

The Apostles Heal Many

12 The apostles performed many signs and wonders[y] among the people. And all the believers used to meet together[z] in Solomon's Colonnade.[a] 13 No one else dared join them, even though they were highly

[a] *26* That is, Messiah or Christ [b] *26* Psalm 2:1,2

5:3 Filled with Satan—Satan is the father of lies (John 8:44). When Ananias and Sapphira deliberately lied, they took upon themselves the moral character of the one who is behind all lies, the devil himself. A person who is listening to Satan begins to act like Satan; his or her thoughts and actions are "filled with Satan" rather than reflecting the filling and direction of the Holy Spirit. Satan or a demon cannot possess someone who is filled with the Holy Spirit, but by listening to Satan rather than the Holy Spirit a believer can behave like one who belongs to Satan rather than one who belongs to God.

5: Holy Spirit—This passage confirms the deity of the Holy Spirit. The Holy Spirit is the third Person of the triune Godhead. To lie to Him (v. 3) is to lie to God.

5:12 *signs and wonders.* These are miraculous occurrences that point to a warning, instruction, or encouragement from God. The signs and wonders which were done among the people at this time gave credibility to the apostles as messengers from God.

4:25 [u] Ac 1:16 **4:26** [v] Ps 2:1, 2; Da 9:25; Lk 4:18; Ac 10:38; Heb 1:9 **4:27** [w] Mt 14:1 [x] Mt 27:2; Lk 23:12 [y] ver 30 **4:28** [z] Ac 2:23 **4:29** [a] ver 13, 31; Ac 9:27; 14:3; Php 1:14 **4:30** [b] Jn 4:48 [c] ver 27 **4:31** [d] Ac 2:2 [e] ver 29 **4:32** [f] Ac 2:44 **4:33** [g] Lk 24:48 [h] Ac 1:22 **4:34** [i] Mt 19:21; Ac 2:45 **4:35** [j] ver 37; Ac 5:2 [k] Ac 2:45; 6:1 **4:36** [l] Ac 9:27; 1Co 9:6 **4:37** [m] ver 35; Ac 5:2 **5:2** [n] Ac 4:35, 37 **5:3** [o] Mt 4:10 [p] Jn 13:2, 27 [q] ver 9 **5:5** [r] ver 10 [s] ver 11 **5:6** [t] Jn 19:40 **5:8** [u] ver 2 **5:9** [v] ver 3 **5:10** [w] ver 5 **5:11** [x] ver 5; Ac 19:17 **5:12** [y] Ac 2:43 [z] Ac 4:32 [a] Ac 3:11

regarded by the people.[b] **14**Nevertheless, more and more men and women believed in the Lord and were added to their number. **15**As a result, people brought the sick into the streets and laid them on beds and mats so that at least Peter's shadow might fall on some of them as he passed by.[c] **16**Crowds gathered also from the towns around Jerusalem, bringing their sick and those tormented by impure spirits, and all of them were healed.[d]

The Apostles Persecuted

17Then the high priest and all his associates, who were members of the party[e] of the Sadducees,[f] were filled with jealousy. **18**They arrested the apostles and put them in the public jail.[g] **19**But during the night an angel[h] of the Lord opened the doors of the jail[i] and brought them out. **20**"Go, stand in the temple courts," he said, "and tell the people all about this new life."[j]

21At daybreak they entered the temple courts, as they had been told, and began to teach the people.

When the high priest and his associates[k] arrived, they called together the Sanhedrin[l]—the full assembly of the elders of Israel—and sent to the jail for the apostles. **22**But on arriving at the jail, the officers did not find them there. So they went back and reported, **23**"We found the jail securely locked, with the guards standing at the doors; but when we opened them, we found no one inside." **24**On hearing this report, the captain of the temple guard and the chief priests[m] were at a loss, wondering what this might lead to.

25Then someone came and said, "Look! The men you put in jail are standing in the temple courts teaching the people." **26**At that, the captain went with his officers and brought the apostles. They did not use force, because they feared that the people[n] would stone them.

27The apostles were brought in and made to appear before the Sanhedrin[o] to be questioned by the high priest. **28**"We gave you strict orders not to teach in this name,"[p] he said. "Yet you have filled Jerusalem with your teaching and are determined to make us guilty of this man's blood."[q]

29Peter and the other apostles replied: "We must obey God rather than human beings![r] **30**The God of our ancestors[s] raised Jesus from the dead[t]—whom you killed by hanging him on a cross.[u] **31**God exalted him to his own right hand[v] as Prince and Savior[w] that he might bring Israel to repentance and forgive their sins.[x] **32**We are witnesses of these things,[y] and so is the Holy Spirit,[z] whom God has given to those who obey him."

33When they heard this, they were furious[a] and wanted to put them to death. **34**But a Pharisee named Gamaliel,[b] a teacher of the law,[c] who was honored by all the people, stood up in the Sanhedrin and ordered that the men be put outside for a little while. **35**Then he addressed the Sanhedrin: "Men of Israel, consider carefully what you intend to do to these men. **36**Some time ago Theudas appeared, claiming to be somebody, and about four hundred men rallied to him. He was killed, all his followers were dispersed, and it all came to nothing. **37**After him, Judas the Galilean appeared in the days of the census[d] and led a band of people in revolt. He too was killed, and all his followers were scattered. **38**Therefore, in the present case I advise you: Leave these men alone! Let them go! For if their purpose or activity is of human origin, it will fail.[e] **39**But if it is from God, you will not be able to stop these men; you will only find yourselves fighting against God."[f]

40His speech persuaded them. They called the apostles in and had them flogged.[g] Then they ordered them not to speak in the name of Jesus, and let them go.

41The apostles left the Sanhedrin, rejoicing[h] because they had been counted worthy of suffering disgrace for the Name.[i] **42**Day after day, in the temple courts[j] and from house to house, they never stopped teaching and proclaiming the good news that Jesus is the Messiah.

The Choosing of the Seven

6 In those days when the number of disciples was increasing,[k] the Hellenistic Jews[a][l] among them complained against the

a 1 That is, Jews who had adopted the Greek language and culture

5:19 Angels—The word "angel" simply means "messenger." The phrase "angel of the Lord" is commonly used in the Old Testament to refer to spiritual messengers of God.

5:32 *witnesses of these things.* The witness of the believer is vitally related to the Holy Spirit. Jesus had said that the Holy Spirit would be a witness and that the apostles would be witnesses. The apostles were conscious that they were indwelt by the Holy Spirit of God, and that their witness depended upon this filling. There is a tremendous lesson here for every believer. No one can be a witness for Christ and a herald of the gospel by individual initiative. Empowerment must come from the Holy Spirit.

5:13 [b] Ac 2:47; 4:21 **5:15** [c] Ac 19:12 **5:16** [d] Mk 16:17 **5:17** [e] Ac 15:5 [f] Ac 4:1 **5:18** [g] Ac 4:3 **5:19** [h] Mt 1:20; Lk 1:11; Ac 8:26; 27:23 [i] Ac 16:26 **5:20** [j] Jn 6:63,68 **5:21** [k] Ac 4:5,6 [l] ver 27,34,41; Mt 5:22 **5:24** [m] Ac 4:1 **5:26** [n] Ac 4:21 **5:27** [o] Mt 5:22 **5:28** [p] Ac 4:18 [q] Mt 23:35; 27:25; Ac 2:23,36; 3:14,15; 7:52 **5:29** [r] Ac 4:19 **5:30** [s] Ac 3:13 [t] Ac 2:24 [u] Ac 10:39; 13:29; Gal 3:13; 1Pe 2:24 **5:31** [v] Ac 2:33 [w] Lk 2:11 [x] Mt 1:21; Lk 24:47; Ac 2:38 **5:32** [y] Lk 24:48 [z] Jn 15:26 **5:33** [a] Ac 2:37; 7:54 **5:34** [b] Ac 22:3 [c] Lk 2:46 **5:37** [d] Lk 2:1,2 **5:38** [e] Mt 15:13 **5:39** [f] Pr 21:30; Ac 7:51; 11:17 **5:40** [g] Mt 10:17 **5:41** [h] Mt 5:12 [i] Jn 15:21 **5:42** [j] Ac 2:46 **6:1** [k] Ac 2:41 [l] Ac 9:29

Hebraic Jews because their widows[m] were
being overlooked in the daily distribution
of food.[n] 2So the Twelve gathered all the
disciples together and said, "It would not
be right for us to neglect the ministry of
the word of God in order to wait on tables.
3Brothers and sisters,[o] choose seven men
from among you who are known to be full
of the Spirit and wisdom. We will turn this
responsibility over to them 4and will give
our attention to prayer[p] and the ministry
of the word."
5This proposal pleased the whole group.
They chose Stephen,[q] a man full of faith
and of the Holy Spirit;[r] also Philip,[s] Proc-
orus, Nicanor, Timon, Parmenas, and Nic-
olas from Antioch, a convert to Judaism.
6They presented these men to the apostles,
who prayed[t] and laid their hands on them.[u]
7So the word of God spread.[v] The number of disciples in Jerusalem increased rapidly, and a large number of priests became
obedient to the faith.

Stephen Seized

8Now Stephen, a man full of God's grace
and power, performed great wonders and
signs[w] among the people. 9Opposition
arose, however, from members of the Synagogue of the Freedmen (as it was called)—
Jews of Cyrene[x] and Alexandria as well as
the provinces of Cilicia[y] and Asia[z]—who
began to argue with Stephen. 10But they
could not stand up against the wisdom the
Spirit gave him as he spoke.[a]
11Then they secretly[b] persuaded some
men to say, "We have heard Stephen speak
blasphemous words against Moses and
against God."[c]
12So they stirred up the people and the
elders and the teachers of the law. They
seized Stephen and brought him before
the Sanhedrin.[d] 13They produced false
witnesses, who testified, "This fellow never
stops speaking against this holy place[e] and
against the law. 14For we have heard him
say that this Jesus of Nazareth will destroy
this place and change the customs Moses
handed down to us."[f]
15All who were sitting in the Sanhedrin[g]
looked intently at Stephen, and they saw
that his face was like the face of an angel.

Stephen's Speech to the Sanhedrin

7 Then the high priest asked Stephen,
"Are these charges true?"
2To this he replied: "Brothers and fathers,[h] listen to me! The God of glory[i] appeared to our father Abraham while he
was still in Mesopotamia, before he lived
in Harran.[j] 3'Leave your country and your
people,' God said, 'and go to the land I will
show you.'[a][k]
4"So he left the land of the Chaldeans
and settled in Harran. After the death of
his father, God sent him to this land where
you are now living.[l] 5He gave him no inheritance here, not even enough ground to set
his foot on. But God promised him that he
and his descendants after him would possess the land,[m] even though at that time
Abraham had no child. 6God spoke to him
in this way: 'For four hundred years your
descendants will be strangers in a country
not their own, and they will be enslaved
and mistreated.[n] 7But I will punish the nation they serve as slaves,' God said, 'and afterward they will come out of that country
and worship me in this place.'[b][o] 8Then he
gave Abraham the covenant of circumcision.[p] And Abraham became the father of
Isaac and circumcised him eight days after
his birth.[q] Later Isaac became the father of
Jacob,[r] and Jacob became the father of the
twelve patriarchs.[s]
9"Because the patriarchs were jealous
of Joseph,[t] they sold him as a slave into
Egypt.[u] But God was with him[v] 10and rescued him from all his troubles. He gave
Joseph wisdom and enabled him to gain
the goodwill of Pharaoh king of Egypt. So
Pharaoh made him ruler over Egypt and
all his palace.[w]

a 3 Gen. 12:1 *b* 7 Gen. 15:13,14

6:3 *full of the Spirit and wisdom.* The men's lives were consistent with their confession of faith. They knew the will of God and understood how to carry it out in their lives (Eph. 5:15 – 18). They could be trusted with responsibility and authority.

6:6 *laid their hands on them.* This was not done in order for the men to receive the Holy Spirit, because the seven men were already "full of the Holy Spirit" (vv. 3,5). Instead the apostles were conferring on these men the responsibility of carrying out the ministry. The laying on of hands was a meaningful tradition that dated back to the days of Moses (Num. 27:23); it identified people with the ministries to be performed.

6:8 *full of God's grace and power.* Stephen had the gifts, the boldness, and the brilliance to be a powerful witness; yet even his witness would be rejected by the religious leaders. Hearts are opened only by God, not by our gifts, boldness, or brilliance.

7:8 *circumcision.* This covenant and its outward symbol were given to Abraham that he might never forget God's promise to bless him. Abraham was saved by faith in God (Gen. 15:6); the symbol of circumcision was an outward sign of the inward reality of his faith. God's blessing was not based on the physical fact of circumcision but on genuine faith.

6:1 [m] Ac 9:39,41 [n] Ac 4:35 **6:3** [o] Ac 1:16 **6:4** [p] Ac 1:14
6:5 [q] ver 8; Ac 11:19 [r] Ac 11:24 [s] Ac 8:5-40; 21:8
6:6 [t] Ac 1:24; 8:17; 13:3; 2Ti 1:6 [u] Nu 8:10; Ac 9:17; 1Ti 4:14
6:7 [v] Ac 12:24; 19:20 **6:8** [w] Jn 4:48 **6:9** [x] Mt 27:32
[y] Ac 15:23,41; 22:3; 23:34 [z] Ac 2:9 **6:10** [a] Lk 21:15
6:11 [b] 1Ki 21:10 [c] Mt 26:59-61 **6:12** [d] Mt 5:22
6:13 [e] Ac 21:28 **6:14** [f] Ac 15:1; 21:21; 26:3; 28:17
6:15 [g] Mt 5:22 **7:2** [h] Ac 22:1 [i] Ps 29:3 [j] Ge 11:31; 15:7
7:3 [k] Ge 12:1 **7:4** [l] Ge 12:5 **7:5** [m] Ge 12:7; 17:8; 26:3
7:6 [n] Ex 12:40 **7:7** [o] Ex 3:12 **7:8** [p] Ge 17:9-14
[q] Ge 21:2-4 [r] Ge 25:26 [s] Ge 29:31-35; 30:5-13, 17-24;
35:16-18, 22-26 **7:9** [t] Ge 37:4, 11 [u] Ge 37:28; Ps 105:17
[v] Ge 39:2, 21, 23 **7:10** [w] Ge 41:37-43

11 "Then a famine struck all Egypt and Canaan, bringing great suffering, and our ancestors could not find food.[x] 12 When Jacob heard that there was grain in Egypt, he sent our forefathers on their first visit.[y] 13 On their second visit, Joseph told his brothers who he was,[z] and Pharaoh learned about Joseph's family. 14 After this, Joseph sent for his father Jacob and his whole family,[a] seventy-five in all.[b] 15 Then Jacob went down to Egypt, where he and our ancestors died.[c] 16 Their bodies were brought back to Shechem and placed in the tomb that Abraham had bought from the sons of Hamor at Shechem for a certain sum of money.[d]

17 "As the time drew near for God to fulfill his promise to Abraham, the number of our people in Egypt had greatly increased.[e] 18 Then 'a new king, to whom Joseph meant nothing, came to power in Egypt.'[a][f] 19 He dealt treacherously with our people and oppressed our ancestors by forcing them to throw out their newborn babies so that they would die.[g]

20 "At that time Moses was born, and he was no ordinary child.[b] For three months he was cared for by his family.[h] 21 When he was placed outside, Pharaoh's daughter took him and brought him up as her own son.[i] 22 Moses was educated in all the wisdom of the Egyptians[j] and was powerful in speech and action.

23 "When Moses was forty years old, he decided to visit his own people, the Israelites. 24 He saw one of them being mistreated by an Egyptian, so he went to his defense and avenged him by killing the Egyptian. 25 Moses thought that his own people would realize that God was using him to rescue them, but they did not. 26 The next day Moses came upon two Israelites who were fighting. He tried to reconcile them by saying, 'Men, you are brothers; why do you want to hurt each other?'

27 "But the man who was mistreating the other pushed Moses aside and said, 'Who made you ruler and judge over us? 28 Are you thinking of killing me as you killed the Egyptian yesterday?'[c] 29 When Moses heard this, he fled to Midian, where he settled as a foreigner and had two sons.[k]

30 "After forty years had passed, an angel appeared to Moses in the flames of a burning bush in the desert near Mount Sinai. 31 When he saw this, he was amazed at the sight. As he went over to get a closer look, he heard the Lord say:[l] 32 'I am the God of your fathers, the God of Abraham, Isaac and Jacob.'[d] Moses trembled with fear and did not dare to look.[m]

33 "Then the Lord said to him, 'Take off your sandals, for the place where you are standing is holy ground.[n] 34 I have indeed seen the oppression of my people in Egypt. I have heard their groaning and have come down to set them free. Now come, I will send you back to Egypt.'[e][o]

35 "This is the same Moses they had rejected with the words, 'Who made you ruler and judge?'[p] He was sent to be their ruler and deliverer by God himself, through the angel who appeared to him in the bush. 36 He led them out of Egypt[q] and performed wonders and signs in Egypt, at the Red Sea[r] and for forty years in the wilderness.

37 "This is the Moses who told the Israelites, 'God will raise up for you a prophet like me from your own people.'[f][s] 38 He was in the assembly in the wilderness, with the angel[t] who spoke to him on Mount Sinai, and with our ancestors;[u] and he received living words[v] to pass on to us.[w]

39 "But our ancestors refused to obey him. Instead, they rejected him and in their

---

a 18 Exodus 1:8 *b* 20 Or *was fair in the sight of God* *c* 28 Exodus 2:14 *d* 32 Exodus 3:6 *e* 34 Exodus 3:5,7,8,10 *f* 37 Deut. 18:15

7:16 *Shechem.* At the time of Stephen's defense, Shechem was the center of Samaritan life. Mount Gerizim, the Samaritan worship center, was located nearby. Stephen's point was not to speak against the temple in Jerusalem, but to point out that God had been speaking and moving in the lives of His people not only in Jerusalem or the temple. The most important address God made to His people was at Mount Sinai, which is nowhere near Jerusalem.

7:19 Persecution—Pharaoh enslaved and mistreated the Hebrews, and at the same time he feared their strength. It was his fear that led him to seek their destruction, persecuting them and destroying their children. It is easy to recognize the enormity and evil of the Egyptian persecution of the Jews as a race and a nation, but the ancient Egyptians are not the only ones guilty of such sin. Some of those claiming the name of Christ in recent times have been guilty of mistreating or even enslaving those of a different ethnic background. Feelings of racial superiority have no place in the heart of a Christian.

7:38 The Meaning of the Church—In modern English the word *church* is used five ways: (1) a building designated as a place of worship; (2) all who profess faith in Christ; (3) a denomination; (4) a single organized local church; and (5) the body of Christ, that is, the universal church. While all of these may be legitimate uses for modern English, the word *church* is used in the New Testament in only the last two senses—a local congregation or the Body of Christ, the universal church. At its root, the word *church* means a "called-out group." It is used for the nation of Israel (Acts 7:38), which was a group of people who were called out of the rest of the world to have a special national relationship to God. It is used for a local church (1 Thess. 1:1; Rev. 2:1) and for the universal church, the body of Christ

7:11 [x] Ge 41:54 **7:12** [y] Ge 42:1,2 **7:13** [z] Ge 45:1-4
7:14 [a] Ge 45:9,10 [b] Ge 46:26,27; Ex 1:5; Dt 10:22
7:15 [c] Ge 46:5-7; 49:33; Ex 1:6 **7:16** [d] Ge 23:16-20; 33:18, 19; 50:13; Jos 24:32 **7:17** [e] Ex 1:7; Ps 105:24
7:18 [f] Ex 1:8 **7:19** [g] Ex 1:10-22 **7:20** [h] Ex 2:2; Heb 11:23
7:21 [i] Ex 2:3-10 **7:22** [j] 1Ki 4:30; Isa 19:11
7:29 [k] Ex 2:11-15 **7:31** [l] Ex 3:1-4 **7:32** [m] Ex 3:6
7:33 [n] Ex 3:5; Jos 5:15 **7:34** [o] Ex 3:7-10 **7:35** [p] ver 27
7:36 [q] Ex 12:41; 33:1 [r] Ex 14:21 **7:37** [s] Dt 18:15, 18; Ac 3:22 **7:38** [t] ver 53 [u] Ex 19:17 [v] Dt 32:45-47; Heb 4:12 [w] Ro 3:2

hearts turned back to Egypt.[x] 40They told
Aaron, 'Make us gods who will go before
us. As for this fellow Moses who led us out
of Egypt—we don't know what has happened to him!'[ay] 41That was the time they
made an idol in the form of a calf. They
brought sacrifices to it and reveled in what
their own hands had made.[z] 42But God
turned away from them[a] and gave them
over to the worship of the sun, moon and
stars.[b] This agrees with what is written in
the book of the prophets:

"'Did you bring me sacrifices and
offerings
forty years in the wilderness, people
of Israel?
43 You have taken up the tabernacle of
Molek
and the star of your god Rephan,
the idols you made to worship.
Therefore I will send you into exile'[bc]
beyond Babylon.

44"Our ancestors had the tabernacle of
the covenant law[d] with them in the wilderness. It had been made as God directed Moses, according to the pattern he had seen.[e]
45After receiving the tabernacle, our ancestors under Joshua brought it with them
when they took the land from the nations
God drove out before them.[f] It remained in
the land until the time of David, 46who enjoyed God's favor and asked that he might
provide a dwelling place for the God of
Jacob.[cg] 47But it was Solomon who built a
house for him.

48"However, the Most High does not live
in houses made by human hands.[h] As the
prophet says:

49 "'Heaven is my throne,
and the earth is my footstool.[i]
What kind of house will you build
for me?
says the Lord.
Or where will my resting place be?
50 Has not my hand made all these
things?'[dj]

51"You stiff-necked people![k] Your hearts[l]
and ears are still uncircumcised. You are
just like your ancestors: You always resist
the Holy Spirit! 52Was there ever a prophet your ancestors did not persecute?[m] They
even killed those who predicted the coming of the Righteous One. And now you
have betrayed and murdered him[n]— 53you
who have received the law that was given
through angels[o] but have not obeyed it."

The Stoning of Stephen

54When the members of the Sanhedrin
heard this, they were furious[p] and gnashed
their teeth at him. 55But Stephen, full of the
Holy Spirit, looked up to heaven and saw
the glory of God, and Jesus standing at the
right hand of God.[q] 56"Look," he said, "I see
heaven open[r] and the Son of Man[s] standing
at the right hand of God."

57At this they covered their ears and,
yelling at the top of their voices, they all
rushed at him, 58dragged him out of the
city[t] and began to stone him.[u] Meanwhile,
the witnesses laid their coats[v] at the feet of
a young man named Saul.[w]

59While they were stoning him, Stephen
prayed, "Lord Jesus, receive my spirit."[x]
60Then he fell on his knees[y] and cried out,
"Lord, do not hold this sin against them."[z]
When he had said this, he fell asleep.

8 And Saul[a] approved of their killing him.

The Church Persecuted and Scattered

On that day a great persecution broke
out against the church in Jerusalem, and
all except the apostles were scattered[b]
throughout Judea and Samaria.[c] 2Godly

[a] 40 Exodus 32:1 [b] 43 Amos 5:25-27 (see Septuagint) [c] 46 Some early manuscripts *the house of Jacob* [d] 50 Isaiah 66:1,2

(Col. 1:18). The universal church comprises all believers from the Day of Pentecost until God completes His plan for the world. The local church is a local, visible, temporal manifestation of the universal church.

7:44 *tabernacle.* The ancient tabernacle had been the focus of the Israelites' national worship. Even after the miraculous deliverance from Egypt there was a tendency among the people to forget God. The tabernacle was a constant testimony of God's presence no matter where the people went. Paul tells us that we are the tabernacle, the temple of God (1 Cor. 3:16). We can never move beyond God's reach, for we carry His presence with us.

7:58 *dragged him out of the city.* Because Jewish law did not allow an execution within the walls of the holy city, the religious leaders took Stephen outside the city. Jerusalem is situated in a stony area and this made Stephen's hasty (and illegal) execution easy. His executioners had plenty of rocks at hand, they only had to bend over and pick them up (see John 10:31).

7:59–60 Death—Scripture affirms, and experience confirms, the universality of death. It comes to kings and commoners, saints and sinners alike. Christians die, as well as unbelievers. No one likes to think of dying violently, but Stephen's death shows that even this end can be met with courage and peace. In both life and death Stephen sought to imitate his Lord, and he departed without resentment, praying for the pardon of his foes.

7:39 [x] Nu 14:3,4 **7:40** [y] Ex 32:1,23 **7:41** [z] Ex 32:4-6; Ps 106:19,20; Rev 9:20 **7:42** [a] Jos 24:20; Isa 63:10 [b] Jer 19:13 **7:43** [c] Am 5:25-27 **7:44** [d] Ex 38:21 [e] Ex 25:8,9,40 **7:45** [f] Jos 3:14-17; 18:1; 23:9; 24:18; Ps 44:2 **7:46** [g] 2Sa 7:8-16; Ps 132:1-5 **7:48** [h] 1Ki 8:27; 2Ch 2:6 **7:49** [i] Mt 5:34,35 **7:50** [j] Isa 66:1,2 **7:51** [k] Ex 32:9; 33:3,5 [l] Lev 26:41; Dt 10:16; Jer 4:4; 9:26 **7:52** [m] 2Ch 36:16; Mt 5:12 [n] Ac 3:14; 1Th 2:15 **7:53** [o] ver 38; Gal 3:19; Heb 2:2 **7:54** [p] Ac 5:33 **7:55** [q] Mk 16:19 **7:56** [r] Mt 3:16 [s] Mt 8:20 **7:58** [t] Lk 4:29 [u] Lev 24:14,16; Dt 13:9 [v] Ac 22:20 [w] Ac 8:1 **7:59** [x] Ps 31:5; Lk 23:46 **7:60** [y] Ac 9:40 [z] Mt 5:44 **8:1** [a] Ac 7:58 [b] Ac 11:19 [c] Ac 9:31

men buried Stephen and mourned deeply
for him. 3But Saul[d] began to destroy the
church.[e] Going from house to house, he
dragged off both men and women and put
them in prison.

Philip in Samaria

4Those who had been scattered[f]
preached the word wherever they went.[g]
5Philip[h] went down to a city in Samaria
and proclaimed the Messiah there. 6When
the crowds heard Philip and saw the signs
he performed, they all paid close attention
to what he said. 7For with shrieks, impure
spirits came out of many,[i] and many who
were paralyzed or lame were healed.[j] 8So
there was great joy in that city.

Simon the Sorcerer

9Now for some time a man named Simon had practiced sorcery[k] in the city
and amazed all the people of Samaria. He
boasted that he was someone great,[l] 10and
all the people, both high and low, gave
him their attention and exclaimed, "This
man is rightly called the Great Power of
God."[m] 11They followed him because he
had amazed them for a long time with his
sorcery. 12But when they believed Philip as
he proclaimed the good news of the kingdom of God[n] and the name of Jesus Christ,
they were baptized,[o] both men and wom-
en. 13Simon himself believed and was baptized. And he followed Philip everywhere,
astonished by the great signs and miracles[p]
he saw.

14When the apostles in Jerusalem heard
that Samaria[q] had accepted the word of
God, they sent Peter and John[r] to Samaria.
15When they arrived, they prayed for the
new believers there that they might receive
the Holy Spirit,[s] 16because the Holy Spirit
had not yet come on any of them;[t] they had
simply been baptized in the name of the
Lord Jesus.[u] 17Then Peter and John placed
their hands on them,[v] and they received the
Holy Spirit.

18When Simon saw that the Spirit was
given at the laying on of the apostles'
hands, he offered them money 19and said,
"Give me also this ability so that everyone
on whom I lay my hands may receive the
Holy Spirit."

20Peter answered: "May your money
perish with you, because you thought you
could buy the gift of God with money![w]
21You have no part or share in this ministry, because your heart is not right[x] before God. 22Repent of this wickedness and
pray to the Lord in the hope that he may
forgive you for having such a thought in
your heart. 23For I see that you are full of
bitterness and captive to sin."

24Then Simon answered, "Pray to the
Lord for me[y] so that nothing you have said
may happen to me."

25After they had further proclaimed the
word of the Lord and testified about Jesus,
Peter and John returned to Jerusalem,
preaching the gospel in many Samaritan
villages.[z]

Philip and the Ethiopian

26Now an angel[a] of the Lord said to
Philip, "Go south to the road—the desert
road—that goes down from Jerusalem to
Gaza." 27So he started out, and on his way
he met an Ethiopian[ab] eunuch,[c] an important official in charge of all the treasury of
the Kandake (which means "queen of the
Ethiopians"). This man had gone to Jerusalem to worship,[d] 28and on his way home
was sitting in his chariot reading the Book

---

a *27 That is, from the southern Nile region*

8:5 *Samaria.* In the first century, the Jews and Samaritans despised one another. The Jews considered the Samaritans half-breeds and religious deviants. Following the fall of the northern kingdom of Israel in 722 B.C., Samaria had been resettled by colonists brought to the land by the Assyrians. These colonists intermarried with the remaining Jews, and the Samaritans of the New Testament era were descendants of these mixed marriages. Because of their mixed heritage and their rejection of the temple in Jerusalem and most of the Old Testament Scriptures (the Samaritans only accepted the five books of Moses), the Jews considered them to be unclean. The amazing work of the Holy Spirit in forming one fellowship out of Jewish and Samaritan believers indicates that there is no room for racial or ethnic division in His church (Gal. 3:26–28).

8:14–15 *that they might receive the Holy Spirit.* This episode clearly showed the Samaritans that salvation did come through the Jews, and that the Scriptures they had previously rejected were actually God's message. It also showed the Jewish believers that God had accepted the Samaritan believers fully into His family. The dependence of the Samaritans upon the Jews to receive the gift of the Holy Spirit was the healing sign that the two sides were to become one.

8:27 *had gone to Jerusalem to worship.* Many Gentiles in the first century had grown weary of the multiple gods and loose morals of their own cultures. In their search for something more, some of them came to Judaism. One who accepted Judaism, obeying all the law of Moses (including circumcision and baptism), was called a *proselyte.* Gentiles who did not become proselytes but did attend the Jewish synagogues to listen to the Scriptures were called *God-fearers.* We cannot be sure which category the Ethiopian eunuch fell into.

8:3 [d] Ac 7:58 [e] Ac 22:4, 19; 26:10, 11; 1Co 15:9; Gal 1:13, 23; Php 3:6; 1Ti 1:13 **8:4** [f] ver 1 [g] Ac 15:35 **8:5** [h] Ac 6:5 **8:7** [i] Mk 16:17 [j] Mt 4:24 **8:9** [k] Ac 13:6 [l] Ac 5:36 **8:10** [m] Ac 14:11; 28:6 **8:12** [n] Ac 1:3 [o] Ac 2:38 **8:13** [p] ver 6; Ac 19:11 **8:14** [q] ver 1 [r] Lk 22:8 **8:15** [s] Ac 2:38 **8:16** [t] Ac 19:2 [u] Mt 28:19; Ac 2:38 **8:17** [v] Ac 6:6 **8:20** [w] 2Ki 5:16; Da 5:17; Mt 10:8; Ac 2:38 **8:21** [x] Ps 78:37 **8:24** [y] Ex 8:8; Nu 21:7; 1Ki 13:6 **8:25** [z] ver 40 **8:26** [a] Ac 5:19 **8:27** [b] Ps 68:31; 87:4; Zep 3:10 [c] Isa 56:3-5 [d] 1Ki 8:41-43; Jn 12:20

of Isaiah the prophet. 29 The Spirit told[e]
Philip, "Go to that chariot and stay near it."
30 Then Philip ran up to the chariot and
heard the man reading Isaiah the prophet.
"Do you understand what you are reading?" Philip asked.
31 "How can I," he said, "unless someone
explains it to me?" So he invited Philip to
come up and sit with him.
32 This is the passage of Scripture the eunuch was reading:

"He was led like a sheep to the
slaughter,
and as a lamb before its shearer is
silent,
so he did not open his mouth.
33 In his humiliation he was deprived of
justice.
Who can speak of his descendants?
For his life was taken from the
earth."[a][f]

34 The eunuch asked Philip, "Tell me,
please, who is the prophet talking about,
himself or someone else?" 35 Then Philip
began[g] with that very passage of Scripture[h] and told him the good news about
Jesus.
36 As they traveled along the road, they
came to some water and the eunuch said,
"Look, here is water. What can stand in the
way of my being baptized?"[i] [37][b] 38 And he
gave orders to stop the chariot. Then both
Philip and the eunuch went down into the
water and Philip baptized him. 39 When
they came up out of the water, the Spirit of the Lord suddenly took Philip away,[j]
and the eunuch did not see him again, but
went on his way rejoicing. 40 Philip, however, appeared at Azotus and traveled about,
preaching the gospel in all the towns[k] until
he reached Caesarea.[l]

Saul's Conversion

9 Meanwhile, Saul was still breathing out
murderous threats against the Lord's
disciples.[m] He went to the high priest 2 and
asked him for letters to the synagogues in
Damascus, so that if he found any there
who belonged to the Way,[n] whether men or
women, he might take them as prisoners
to Jerusalem. 3 As he neared Damascus on
his journey, suddenly a light from heaven
flashed around him.[o] 4 He fell to the ground
and heard a voice say to him, "Saul, Saul,
why do you persecute me?"
5 "Who are you, Lord?" Saul asked.
"I am Jesus, whom you are persecuting," he replied. 6 "Now get up and go into
the city, and you will be told what you
must do."[p]
7 The men traveling with Saul stood
there speechless; they heard the sound[q]
but did not see anyone.[r] 8 Saul got up from
the ground, but when he opened his eyes
he could see nothing. So they led him by
the hand into Damascus. 9 For three days
he was blind, and did not eat or drink anything.
10 In Damascus there was a disciple
named Ananias. The Lord called to him in
a vision,[s] "Ananias!"
"Yes, Lord," he answered.
11 The Lord told him, "Go to the house of
Judas on Straight Street and ask for a man
from Tarsus[t] named Saul, for he is praying.
12 In a vision he has seen a man named Ananias come and place his hands on[u] him to
restore his sight."
13 "Lord," Ananias answered, "I have
heard many reports about this man and
all the harm he has done to your holy people[v] in Jerusalem.[w] 14 And he has come here
with authority from the chief priests[x] to arrest all who call on your name."
15 But the Lord said to Ananias, "Go!
This man is my chosen instrument[y] to proclaim my name to the Gentiles[z] and their
kings[a] and to the people of Israel. 16 I will

a 33 Isaiah 53:7,8 (see Septuagint) *b* 37 Some manuscripts include here *Philip said, "If you believe with all your heart, you may." The eunuch answered, "I believe that Jesus Christ is the Son of God."*

8:35 *told him the good news about Jesus.* First-century Jews did not speak much about a suffering Messiah. The Jewish people, facing the yoke of Roman rule, believed that the Messiah would come as the Lion of Judah, a delivering king, not a weak lamb. They believed and taught that the suffering One spoken of by Isaiah was the suffering nation of Israel. Philip's explanation of the passage gave a very different view, showing Jesus as the Messiah who came to suffer and die in order to redeem sinners.

9:2 *synagogues.* The early Jewish believers in Jesus were still attending the synagogues, gathering places where Jews came together to hear the Scriptures read and expounded upon. Part of Saul's mission was apparently to let the Damascus synagogues know beyond any doubt that the followers of "The Way" did not have the approval of the Sanhedrin.

9:4–5 Messiah—Apparently unimpressed by the witness of the dying Stephen (7:59), Saul needed a more serious, personal jolt to awaken his spiritual awareness. The light that blinded Saul prepared him to receive the True Light that came into the world to dispel the darkness of sin. This personal encounter with the risen Christ changed Saul from a fire-breathing persecutor into a dynamic preacher who was not ashamed to publicly claim the crucified Man from Galilee as his Lord and Savior.

8:29 [e] Ac 10:19; 11:12; 13:2; 20:23; 21:11 **8:33** [f] Isa 53:7,8 **8:35** [g] Mt 5:2 [h] Lk 24:27; Ac 17:2; 18:28; 28:23 **8:36** [i] Ac 10:47 **8:39** [j] 1Ki 18:12; 2Ki 2:16; Eze 3:12, 14; 8:3; 11:1, 24; 43:5; 2Co 12:2 **8:40** [k] ver 25 [l] Ac 10:1, 24; 12:19; 21:8, 16; 23:23, 33; 25:1, 4, 6, 13 **9:1** [m] Ac 8:3 **9:2** [n] Ac 19:9, 23; 22:4; 24:14, 22 **9:3** [o] 1Co 15:8 **9:6** [p] ver 16 **9:7** [q] Jn 12:29 [r] Da 10:7; Ac 22:9 **9:10** [s] Ac 10:3, 17, 19 **9:11** [t] ver 30; Ac 21:39; 22:3 **9:12** [u] Mk 5:23 **9:13** [v] ver 32; Ro 1:7; 16:2, 15 [w] Ac 8:3 **9:14** [x] ver 2, 21 **9:15** [y] Ac 13:2; Ro 1:1; Gal 1:15 [z] Ro 11:13; 15:15, 16; Gal 2:7, 8; Eph 3:7, 8 [a] Ac 25:22, 23; 26:1

show him how much he must suffer for my
name."[b]
17Then Ananias went to the house and
entered it. Placing his hands on[c] Saul, he
said, "Brother Saul, the Lord—Jesus, who
appeared to you on the road as you were
coming here—has sent me so that you may
see again and be filled with the Holy Spirit." 18Immediately, something like scales
fell from Saul's eyes, and he could see
again. He got up and was baptized, 19and
after taking some food, he regained his
strength.

Saul in Damascus and Jerusalem

Saul spent several days with the disciples[d] in Damascus.[e] 20At once he began to
preach in the synagogues[f] that Jesus is the
Son of God.[g] 21All those who heard him
were astonished and asked, "Isn't he the
man who raised havoc in Jerusalem among
those who call on this name?[h] And hasn't
he come here to take them as prisoners to
the chief priests?"[i] 22Yet Saul grew more
and more powerful and baffled the Jews
living in Damascus by proving that Jesus
is the Messiah.[j]
23After many days had gone by, there
was a conspiracy among the Jews to kill
him, 24but Saul learned of their plan.[k] Day
and night they kept close watch on the city
gates in order to kill him. 25But his followers took him by night and lowered him in
a basket through an opening in the wall.[l]
26When he came to Jerusalem,[m] he tried
to join the disciples, but they were all afraid
of him, not believing that he really was a
disciple. 27But Barnabas[n] took him and
brought him to the apostles. He told them
how Saul on his journey had seen the Lord
and that the Lord had spoken to him,[o] and
how in Damascus he had preached fearlessly in the name of Jesus.[p] 28So Saul
stayed with them and moved about freely
in Jerusalem, speaking boldly in the name
of the Lord. 29He talked and debated with
the Hellenistic Jews,[a][q] but they tried to kill
him.[r] 30When the believers[s] learned of this,
they took him down to Caesarea[t] and sent
him off to Tarsus.[u]
31Then the church throughout Judea,
Galilee and Samaria[v] enjoyed a time of
peace and was strengthened. Living in the
fear of the Lord and encouraged by the
Holy Spirit, it increased in numbers.

Aeneas and Dorcas

32As Peter traveled about the country, he
went to visit the Lord's people[w] who lived
in Lydda. 33There he found a man named
Aeneas, who was paralyzed and had been
bedridden for eight years. 34"Aeneas," Peter
said to him, "Jesus Christ heals you.[x] Get up
and roll up your mat." Immediately Aeneas
got up. 35All those who lived in Lydda and
Sharon[y] saw him and turned to the Lord.[z]
36In Joppa[a] there was a disciple named
Tabitha (in Greek her name is Dorcas); she
was always doing good[b] and helping the
poor. 37About that time she became sick and
died, and her body was washed and placed
in an upstairs room.[c] 38Lydda was near Joppa; so when the disciples[d] heard that Peter
was in Lydda, they sent two men to him and
urged him, "Please come at once!"
39Peter went with them, and when he arrived he was taken upstairs to the room.
All the widows[e] stood around him, crying and showing him the robes and other
clothing that Dorcas had made while she
was still with them.
40Peter sent them all out of the room;[f]
then he got down on his knees[g] and prayed.
Turning toward the dead woman, he said,
"Tabitha, get up." She opened her eyes, and
seeing Peter she sat up. 41He took her by
the hand and helped her to her feet. Then
he called for the believers, especially the
widows, and presented her to them alive.
42This became known all over Joppa, and
many people believed in the Lord. 43Peter
stayed in Joppa for some time with a tanner named Simon.[h]

Cornelius Calls for Peter

10 At Caesarea[i] there was a man named
Cornelius, a centurion in what was

[a] *29* That is, Jews who had adopted the Greek language and culture

9:17 ***Jesus, who appeared to you.*** Saul was not dreaming on the road to Damascus but instead had seen the resurrected Lord.
9:30 ***Tarsus.*** Saul's hometown was about three hundred miles north of Jerusalem and about ten miles inland from the Mediterranean Sea. Tarsus was a well known university city, surpassed in educational opportunities only by Athens and Alexandria.
9:31 ***peace.*** This peace was not due solely to Saul's conversion. Tiberius, the emperor of Rome, died around this time. He was replaced by Caligula, who wanted to erect a statue of himself in the temple at Jerusalem. The attention of the Jewish religious leaders was directed towards this new threat, and the emerging church was given a short season of respite.
10:1–11:18 The following two chapters mark an important turning point in the Book of Acts. Those who were scattered by persecution from Jerusalem had been preaching the gospel only to Jews (11:19).

9:16 [b] Ac 20:23; 21:11; 2Co 11:23-27 **9:17** [c] Ac 6:6
9:19 [d] Ac 11:26 [e] Ac 26:20 **9:20** [f] Ac 13:5, 14 [g] Mt 4:3
9:21 [h] Ac 8:3 [i] Gal 1:13, 23 **9:22** [j] Ac 18:5, 28
9:24 [k] Ac 20:3, 19 **9:25** [l] 1Sa 19:12; 2Co 11:32, 33
9:26 [m] Ac 22:17; 26:20; Gal 1:17, 18 **9:27** [n] Ac 4:36
[o] ver 3-6 [p] ver 20, 22 **9:29** [q] Ac 6:1 [r] 2Co 11:26
9:30 [s] Ac 1:16 [t] Ac 8:40 [u] ver 11 **9:31** [v] Ac 8:1
9:32 [w] ver 13 **9:34** [x] Ac 3:6, 16; 4:10 **9:35** [y] 1Ch 5:16; 27:29; Isa 33:9; 35:2; 65:10 [z] Ac 11:21 **9:36** [a] Jos 19:46; 2Ch 2:16; Ezr 3:7; Jnh 1:3; Ac 10:5 [b] 1Ti 2:10; Titus 3:8
9:37 [c] Ac 1:13 **9:38** [d] Ac 11:26 **9:39** [e] Ac 6:1
9:40 [f] Mt 9:25 [g] Lk 22:41; Ac 7:60 **9:43** [h] Ac 10:6
10:1 [i] Ac 8:40

known as the Italian Regiment. 2He and all his family were devout and God-fearing;[j] he gave generously to those in need and prayed to God regularly. 3One day at about three in the afternoon[k] he had a vision.[l] He distinctly saw an angel[m] of God, who came to him and said, "Cornelius!"

4Cornelius stared at him in fear. "What is it, Lord?" he asked.

The angel answered, "Your prayers and gifts to the poor have come up as a memorial offering[n] before God.[o] 5Now send men to Joppa[p] to bring back a man named Simon who is called Peter. 6He is staying with Simon the tanner,[q] whose house is by the sea."

7When the angel who spoke to him had gone, Cornelius called two of his servants and a devout soldier who was one of his attendants. 8He told them everything that had happened and sent them to Joppa.[r]

Peter's Vision

9About noon the following day as they were on their journey and approaching the city, Peter went up on the roof[s] to pray. 10He became hungry and wanted something to eat, and while the meal was being prepared, he fell into a trance.[t] 11He saw heaven opened and something like a large sheet being let down to earth by its four corners. 12It contained all kinds of four-footed animals, as well as reptiles and birds. 13Then a voice told him, "Get up, Peter. Kill and eat."

14"Surely not, Lord!"[u] Peter replied. "I have never eaten anything impure or unclean."[v]

15The voice spoke to him a second time, "Do not call anything impure that God has made clean."[w]

16This happened three times, and immediately the sheet was taken back to heaven.

17While Peter was wondering about the meaning of the vision, the men sent by Cornelius[x] found out where Simon's house was and stopped at the gate. 18They called out, asking if Simon who was known as Peter was staying there.

19While Peter was still thinking about the vision, the Spirit said[y] to him, "Simon, three[a] men are looking for you. 20So get up and go downstairs. Do not hesitate to go with them, for I have sent them."[z]

21Peter went down and said to the men, "I'm the one you're looking for. Why have you come?"

22The men replied, "We have come from Cornelius the centurion. He is a righteous and God-fearing man,[a] who is respected by all the Jewish people. A holy angel told him to ask you to come to his house so that he could hear what you have to say."[b] 23Then Peter invited the men into the house to be his guests.

Peter at Cornelius's House

The next day Peter started out with them, and some of the believers[c] from Joppa went along.[d] 24The following day he arrived in Caesarea.[e] Cornelius was expecting them and had called together his relatives and close friends. 25As Peter entered the house, Cornelius met him and fell at his feet in reverence. 26But Peter made him get up. "Stand up," he said, "I am only a man myself."[f]

27While talking with him, Peter went inside and found a large gathering of people. 28He said to them: "You are well aware that it is against our law for a Jew to associate with or visit a Gentile.[g] But God has shown me that I should not call anyone impure or unclean.[h] 29So when I was sent for, I came without raising any objection. May I ask why you sent for me?"

30Cornelius answered: "Three days ago I was in my house praying at this hour, at three in the afternoon. Suddenly a man in shining clothes stood before me 31and said, 'Cornelius, God has heard your prayer and remembered your gifts to the poor. 32Send to Joppa for Simon who is called Peter. He is a guest in the home of Simon the tanner, who lives by the sea.' 33So I sent for you immediately, and it was good of you to come. Now we are all here in the presence of God to listen to everything the Lord has commanded you to tell us."

34Then Peter began to speak: "I now realize how true it is that God does not show favoritism[i] 35but accepts from every nation the one who fears him and does what is right.[j] 36You know the message God sent

[a] *19* One early manuscript *two*; other manuscripts do not have the number.

At this point, they began to overcome their prejudices and carry the message of Christ to the Gentiles.
10:6 *Simon the tanner.* God cut away Peter's prejudices by having him stay for many days with one whose trade Peter likely considered repulsive. Since a tanner (one who makes leather) is constantly working with animals dead from various causes, he would spend much of his life ceremonially "unclean."
10:15 *Do not call anything impure that God has made clean.* Food may have been his first consideration, but Peter would soon understand the greater message. The vision was a sign from heaven that Jews were no longer to call Gentiles unclean.

10:2 [j] ver 22,35; Ac 13:16,26 **10:3** [k] Ac 3:1 [l] Ac 9:10 [m] Ac 5:19 **10:4** [n] Mt 26:13 [o] Rev 8:4 **10:5** [p] Ac 9:36 **10:6** [q] Ac 9:43 **10:8** [r] Ac 9:36 **10:9** [s] Mt 24:17 **10:10** [t] Ac 22:17 **10:14** [u] Ac 9:5 [v] Lev 11:4-8, 13-20; 20:25; Dt 14:3-20; Eze 4:14 **10:15** [w] Mt 15:11; Ro 14:14, 17,20; 1Co 10:25; 1Ti 4:3, 4; Titus 1:15 **10:17** [x] ver 7, 8 **10:19** [y] Ac 8:29 **10:20** [z] Ac 15:7-9 **10:22** [a] ver 2 [b] Ac 11:14 **10:23** [c] Ac 1:16 [d] ver 45; Ac 11:12 **10:24** [e] Ac 8:40 **10:26** [f] Ac 14:15; Rev 19:10 **10:28** [g] Jn 4:9; 18:28; Ac 11:3 [h] Ac 15:8, 9 **10:34** [i] Dt 10:17; 2Ch 19:7; Job 34:19; Ro 2:11; Gal 2:6; Eph 6:9; Col 3:25; 1Pe 1:17 **10:35** [j] Ac 15:9

to the people of Israel, announcing the good news[k] of peace[l] through Jesus Christ, who is Lord of all.[m] 37You know what has happened throughout the province of Judea, beginning in Galilee after the baptism that John preached— 38how God anointed[n] Jesus of Nazareth with the Holy Spirit and power, and how he went around doing good and healing[o] all who were under the power of the devil, because God was with him.[p]

39"We are witnesses[q] of everything he did in the country of the Jews and in Jerusalem. They killed him by hanging him on a cross,[r] 40but God raised him from the dead[s] on the third day and caused him to be seen. 41He was not seen by all the people,[t] but by witnesses whom God had already chosen—by us who ate[u] and drank with him after he rose from the dead. 42He commanded us to preach to the people[v] and to testify that he is the one whom God appointed as judge of the living and the dead.[w] 43All the prophets testify about him[x] that everyone[y] who believes in him receives forgiveness of sins through his name."

44While Peter was still speaking these words, the Holy Spirit came on[z] all who heard the message. 45The circumcised believers who had come with Peter[a] were astonished that the gift of the Holy Spirit had been poured out[b] even on Gentiles.[c] 46For they heard them speaking in tongues[a][d] and praising God.

Then Peter said, 47"Surely no one can stand in the way of their being baptized with water.[e] They have received the Holy Spirit just as we have."[f] 48So he ordered that they be baptized in the name of Jesus Christ.[g] Then they asked Peter to stay with them for a few days.

Peter Explains His Actions

11 The apostles and the believers[h] throughout Judea heard that the Gentiles also had received the word of God. 2So when Peter went up to Jerusalem, the circumcised believers[i] criticized him 3and said, "You went into the house of uncircumcised men and ate with them."[j]

4Starting from the beginning, Peter told them the whole story: 5"I was in the city of Joppa praying, and in a trance I saw a vision.[k] I saw something like a large sheet being let down from heaven by its four corners, and it came down to where I was. 6I looked into it and saw four-footed animals of the earth, wild beasts, reptiles and birds. 7Then I heard a voice telling me, 'Get up, Peter. Kill and eat.'

8"I replied, 'Surely not, Lord! Nothing impure or unclean has ever entered my mouth.'

9"The voice spoke from heaven a second time, 'Do not call anything impure that God has made clean.'[l] 10This happened three times, and then it was all pulled up to heaven again.

11"Right then three men who had been sent to me from Caesarea stopped at the house where I was staying. 12The Spirit told[m] me to have no hesitation about going with them.[n] These six brothers also went with me, and we entered the man's house. 13He told us how he had seen an angel appear in his house and say, 'Send to Joppa for Simon who is called Peter. 14He will bring you a message through which you and all your household[o] will be saved.'

15"As I began to speak, the Holy Spirit came on[p] them as he had come on us at the beginning.[q] 16Then I remembered what the Lord had said: 'John baptized with[b] water, but you will be baptized with[b] the Holy Spirit.'[r] 17So if God gave them the same gift he gave us[s] who believed in the Lord Jesus Christ, who was I to think that I could stand in God's way?"

18When they heard this, they had no further objections and praised God, saying, "So then, even to Gentiles God has granted repentance that leads to life."[t]

The Church in Antioch

19Now those who had been scattered by the persecution that broke out when Stephen was killed[u] traveled as far as Phoenicia, Cyprus and Antioch,[v] spreading the word only among Jews. 20Some of them, however, men from Cyprus[w] and Cyrene,[x] went to Antioch and began to speak

a 46 Or *other languages* *b* 16 Or *in*

10:44 *the Holy Spirit came on all who heard the message.* Following the plan laid out by Jesus before His ascension (1:8), the good news had reached the Jews, the Samaritans, and now the Gentiles. All were united by the same faith in the same Lord with the same gift of the Holy Spirit.

11:2 *the circumcised believers.* This term refers to Jewish believers in Jesus who taught that Gentiles had to become Jews (be circumcised and keep the law of Moses) in order to become Christians.

11:16 *baptized with the Holy Spirit.* This is found seven times in the New Testament (1:5; Matt. 3:11; Mark 1:8; Luke 3:16; John 1:33; 1 Cor. 12:13) and refers to an act by Christ for believers.

10:36 [k] Ac 13:32 [l] Lk 2:14 [m] Mt 28:18; Ro 10:12 **10:38** [n] Ac 4:26 [o] Mt 4:23 [p] Jn 3:2 **10:39** [q] Lk 24:48 [r] Ac 5:30 **10:40** [s] Ac 2:24 **10:41** [t] Jn 14:17,22 [u] Lk 24:43; Jn 21:13 **10:42** [v] Mt 28:19,20 [w] Jn 5:22; Ac 17:31; Ro 14:9; 2Co 5:10; 2Ti 4:1; 1Pe 4:5 **10:43** [x] Isa 53:11 [y] Ac 15:9 **10:44** [z] Ac 8:15, 16; 11:15; 15:8 **10:45** [a] ver 23 [b] Ac 2:33, 38 [c] Ac 11:18 **10:46** [d] Mk 16:17 **10:47** [e] Ac 8:36 [f] Ac 11:17 **10:48** [g] Ac 2:38; 8:16 **11:1** [h] Ac 1:16 **11:2** [i] Ac 10:45 **11:3** [j] Ac 10:25, 28; Gal 2:12 **11:5** [k] Ac 9:10; 10:9-32 **11:9** [l] Ac 10:15 **11:12** [m] Ac 8:29 [n] Ac 15:9; Ro 3:22 **11:14** [o] Jn 4:53; Ac 16:15, 31-34; 1Co 1:11, 16 **11:15** [p] Ac 10:44 [q] Ac 2:4 **11:16** [r] Mk 1:8; Ac 1:5 **11:17** [s] Ac 10:45, 47 **11:18** [t] Ro 10:12, 13; 2Co 7:10 **11:19** [u] Ac 8:1, 4 [v] ver 26, 27; Ac 13:1; 18:22; Gal 2:11 **11:20** [w] Ac 4:36 [x] Mt 27:32

to Greeks also, telling them the good news
about the Lord Jesus. 21The Lord's hand
was with them,[y] and a great number of people believed and turned to the Lord.[z]
22News of this reached the church in Jerusalem, and they sent Barnabas[a] to Antioch. 23When he arrived and saw what the
grace of God had done,[b] he was glad and
encouraged them all to remain true to the
Lord with all their hearts.[c] 24He was a good
man, full of the Holy Spirit and faith, and
a great number of people were brought to
the Lord.[d]
25Then Barnabas went to Tarsus[e] to
look for Saul, 26and when he found him,
he brought him to Antioch. So for a whole
year Barnabas and Saul met with the
church and taught great numbers of people. The disciples[f] were called Christians
first[g] at Antioch.
27During this time some prophets[h]
came down from Jerusalem to Antioch.
28One of them, named Agabus,[i] stood up
and through the Spirit predicted that a
severe famine would spread over the entire Roman world.[j] (This happened during
the reign of Claudius.)[k] 29The disciples,[l]
as each one was able, decided to provide
help[m] for the brothers and sisters[n] living in
Judea. 30This they did, sending their gift to
the elders[o] by Barnabas and Saul.[p]

Peter's Miraculous Escape From Prison

12 It was about this time that King Herod arrested some who belonged to
the church, intending to persecute them.
2He had James, the brother of John,[q] put to
death with the sword. 3When he saw that
this met with approval among the Jews,[r]
he proceeded to seize Peter also. This happened during the Festival of Unleavened
Bread.[s] 4After arresting him, he put him in
prison, handing him over to be guarded by
four squads of four soldiers each. Herod intended to bring him out for public trial after
the Passover.
5So Peter was kept in prison, but the
church was earnestly praying to God for
him.[t]
6The night before Herod was to bring
him to trial, Peter was sleeping between
two soldiers, bound with two chains,[u] and
sentries stood guard at the entrance. 7Sud-
denly an angel[v] of the Lord appeared and
a light shone in the cell. He struck Peter
on the side and woke him up. "Quick, get
up!" he said, and the chains fell off Peter's
wrists.[w]
8Then the angel said to him, "Put on
your clothes and sandals." And Peter did
so. "Wrap your cloak around you and follow me," the angel told him. 9Peter followed
him out of the prison, but he had no idea
that what the angel was doing was really
happening; he thought he was seeing a vision.[x] 10They passed the first and second
guards and came to the iron gate leading
to the city. It opened for them by itself,[y]
and they went through it. When they had
walked the length of one street, suddenly
the angel left him.
11Then Peter came to himself[z] and said,
"Now I know without a doubt that the Lord
has sent his angel and rescued me[a] from
Herod's clutches and from everything the
Jewish people were hoping would happen."
12When this had dawned on him, he
went to the house of Mary the mother of
John, also called Mark,[b] where many people had gathered and were praying.[c] 13Pe-
ter knocked at the outer entrance, and a
servant named Rhoda came to answer
the door.[d] 14When she recognized Peter's
voice, she was so overjoyed[e] she ran back

11:22–23 *Antioch.* Seleucus I founded the city of Antioch, naming it after his father. The city was cosmopolitan, attracting people of various cultures and ethnic backgrounds — including people from Persia, India, and even China. The gospel proclaimed in Antioch would have tremendous potential for reaching other areas of the world.

11:26 *called Christians.* Originally, the believers had called themselves "followers of The Way." Although the term "Christian" was apparently given to them by nonbelievers, they adopted it for themselves. Its essential meaning, "Christ-follower" is appropriate for those who have given their lives into the keeping of Jesus, the Messiah.

11:29–30 Benevolence — Christians must exercise responsibility and charity (love) towards all men, and especially to other believers (Gal. 6:10). The Christians at Antioch are an example of well implemented Christian giving. All gave in accordance with their means (2 Cor. 8:3). The gifts were placed in the charge of trustworthy Christians (2 Cor. 8:20–21), who could ensure a responsible delivery and administration of the gifts.

12:1–3 *King Herod.* This is Herod Agrippa I, the nephew of Herod Antipas who murdered John the Baptist, and the grandson of Herod the Great who had the children of Bethlehem put to death in his search for Jesus. Herod was not a Jew but an Edomite. The Jews resented the fact that a son of Edom was given the position of king of the Jews.

12:11 *rescued me from Herod's clutches.* Why was Peter's life spared while James' life was taken? The answer is the sovereign will of God. If we believe that God is good and wise, we can trust that what He allowed to happen was part of His wise plan for the good of all His people.

11:21 [y] Lk 1:66 [z] Ac 2:47 **11:22** [a] Ac 4:36
11:23 [b] Ac 13:43; 14:26; 20:24 [c] Ac 14:22 **11:24** [d] ver 21; Ac 5:14 **11:25** [e] Ac 9:11 **11:26** [f] Ac 6:1, 2; 13:52 [g] Ac 26:28; 1Pe 4:16 **11:27** [h] Ac 13:1; 15:32; 1Co 12:28, 29; Eph 4:11 **11:28** [i] Ac 21:10 [j] Mt 24:14 [k] Ac 18:2
11:29 [l] ver 26 [m] Ro 15:26; 2Co 9:2 [n] Ac 1:16
11:30 [o] Ac 14:23 [p] Ac 12:25 **12:2** [q] Mt 4:21
12:3 [r] Ac 24:27 [s] Ex 12:15; 23:15 **12:5** [t] Eph 6:18
12:6 [u] Ac 21:33 **12:7** [v] Ac 5:19 [w] Ac 16:26
12:9 [x] Ac 9:10 **12:10** [y] Ac 5:19; 16:26 **12:11** [z] Lk 15:17 [a] Ps 34:7; Da 3:28; 6:22; 2Co 1:10; 2Pe 2:9 **12:12** [b] ver 25; Ac 15:37, 39; Col 4:10; Phm 24; 1Pe 5:13 [c] ver 5
12:13 [d] Jn 18:16, 17 **12:14** [e] Lk 24:41

without opening it and exclaimed, “Peter
is at the door!”
15“You’re out of your mind,” they told her.
When she kept insisting that it was so, they
said, “It must be his angel.”[f]
16But Peter kept on knocking, and when
they opened the door and saw him, they
were astonished. 17Peter motioned with his
hand[g] for them to be quiet and described
how the Lord had brought him out of prison. “Tell James[h] and the other brothers and
sisters[i] about this,” he said, and then he left
for another place.
18In the morning, there was no small
commotion among the soldiers as to what
had become of Peter. 19After Herod had a
thorough search made for him and did not
find him, he cross-examined the guards
and ordered that they be executed.[j]

Herod’s Death

Then Herod went from Judea to Caesarea[k] and stayed there. 20He had been quarreling with the people of Tyre and Sidon;[l]
they now joined together and sought an
audience with him. After securing the support of Blastus, a trusted personal servant
of the king, they asked for peace, because
they depended on the king’s country for
their food supply.[m]
21On the appointed day Herod, wearing
his royal robes, sat on his throne and delivered a public address to the people. 22They
shouted, “This is the voice of a god, not
of a man.” 23Immediately, because Herod
did not give praise to God, an angel of the
Lord struck him down,[n] and he was eaten
by worms and died.
24But the word of God continued to
spread and flourish.[o]

Barnabas and Saul Sent Off

25When Barnabas[p] and Saul had finished their mission,[q] they returned from[a]
Jerusalem, taking with them John, also
13 called Mark.[r] 1Now in the church at
Antioch[s] there were prophets[t] and
teachers: Barnabas,[u] Simeon called Niger,
Lucius of Cyrene, Manaen (who had been
brought up with Herod[v] the tetrarch) and
Saul. 2While they were worshiping the
Lord and fasting, the Holy Spirit said,[w]
“Set apart for me Barnabas and Saul for
the work[x] to which I have called them.”[y]
3So after they had fasted and prayed, they
placed their hands on them[z] and sent them
off.[a]

On Cyprus

4The two of them, sent on their way by
the Holy Spirit,[b] went down to Seleucia and
sailed from there to Cyprus.[c] 5When they
arrived at Salamis, they proclaimed the
word of God in the Jewish synagogues.[d]
John[e] was with them as their helper.
6They traveled through the whole island until they came to Paphos. There they
met a Jewish sorcerer[f] and false prophet[g]
named Bar-Jesus, 7who was an attendant
of the proconsul,[h] Sergius Paulus. The proconsul, an intelligent man, sent for Barnabas and Saul because he wanted to hear
the word of God. 8But Elymas the sorcerer[i]
(for that is what his name means) opposed
them and tried to turn the proconsul[j] from
the faith.[k] 9Then Saul, who was also called
Paul, filled with the Holy Spirit,[l] looked
straight at Elymas and said, 10“You are a
child of the devil[m] and an enemy of everything that is right! You are full of all kinds
of deceit and trickery. Will you never stop
perverting the right ways of the Lord?[n]
11Now the hand of the Lord is against you.[o]
You are going to be blind for a time, not
even able to see the light of the sun.”
Immediately mist and darkness came
over him, and he groped about, seeking
someone to lead him by the hand. 12When
the proconsul[p] saw what had happened, he
believed, for he was amazed at the teaching about the Lord.

In Pisidian Antioch

13From Paphos,[q] Paul and his companions sailed to Perga in Pamphylia, where
John[r] left them to return to Jerusalem.

---

a 25 Some manuscripts *to*

12:22 *the voice of a god.* The Jewish historian Josephus also provides an account of this display, informing us that in an attempted appeasement of the king the people confessed that he was “more than mortal.”
13:2–4 Holy Spirit—God reveals His will to those who are sensitive to His leading. The believers in Antioch heard from the Lord as they were praying and fasting. Most often, God does not speak to us out of the blue. He speaks to us when we are listening. The Holy Spirit gave distinct direction to the listening, sensitive believers of the first century, and He leads believers in the same way today.
13:3 *placed their hands on them.* The laying on of hands was the church’s way of identifying with and affirming the mission to which God had called a particular person.
13:6–12 *Sergius Paulus.* Luke presents this man as the first Gentile ruler to believe the gospel. There is no evidence that Sergius Paulus was a God-fearer or had ever shown any interest in Judaism prior to this time. This pagan government official was amazed at the power of God and believed the truth.

12:15 [f] Mt 18:10 **12:17** [g] Ac 13:16; 19:33; 21:40 [h] Ac 15:13 [i] Ac 1:16 **12:19** [j] Ac 16:27 [k] Ac 8:40 **12:20** [l] Mt 11:21 [m] 1Ki 5:9, 11; Eze 27:17 **12:23** [n] 1Sa 25:38; 2Sa 24:16, 17 **12:24** [o] Ac 6:7; 19:20 **12:25** [p] Ac 4:36 [q] Ac 11:30 [r] ver 12 **13:1** [s] Ac 11:19 [t] Ac 11:27 [u] Ac 4:36; 11:22-26 [v] Mt 14:1 **13:2** [w] Ac 8:29 [x] Ac 14:26 [y] Ac 22:21 **13:3** [z] Ac 6:6 [a] Ac 14:26 **13:4** [b] ver 2, 3 [c] Ac 4:36 **13:5** [d] Ac 9:20 [e] Ac 12:12 **13:6** [f] Ac 8:9 [g] Mt 7:15 **13:7** [h] ver 8, 12; Ac 19:38 **13:8** [i] Ac 8:9 [j] ver 7 [k] Ac 6:7 **13:9** [l] Ac 4:8 **13:10** [m] Mt 13:38; Jn 8:44 [n] Hos 14:9 **13:11** [o] Ex 9:3; 1Sa 5:6, 7; Ps 32:4 **13:12** [p] ver 7 **13:13** [q] ver 6 [r] Ac 12:12

14 From Perga they went on to Pisidian
Antioch.[s] On the Sabbath[t] they entered
the synagogue[u] and sat down. 15 After the
reading from the Law[v] and the Prophets,
the leaders of the synagogue sent word
to them, saying, “Brothers, if you have a
word of exhortation for the people, please
speak.”

16 Standing up, Paul motioned with his
hand[w] and said: “Fellow Israelites and you
Gentiles who worship God, listen to me!
17 The God of the people of Israel chose our
ancestors; he made the people prosper during their stay in Egypt; with mighty power
he led them out of that country;[x] 18 for about
forty years he endured their conduct[a][y] in
the wilderness;[z] 19 and he overthrew seven
nations in Canaan,[a] giving their land to his
people[b] as their inheritance. 20 All this took
about 450 years.

“After this, God gave them judges[c] until the time of Samuel the prophet.[d] 21 Then
the people asked for a king,[e] and he gave
them Saul[f] son of Kish, of the tribe of Benjamin,[g] who ruled forty years. 22 After removing Saul,[h] he made David their king.[i]
God testified concerning him: ‘I have
found David son of Jesse, a man after my
own heart;[j] he will do everything I want
him to do.’

23 “From this man’s descendants[k] God
has brought to Israel the Savior[l] Jesus,[m]
as he promised.[n] 24 Before the coming of
Jesus, John preached repentance and baptism to all the people of Israel.[o] 25 As John
was completing his work,[p] he said: ‘Who
do you suppose I am? I am not the one you
are looking for.[q] But there is one coming
after me whose sandals I am not worthy
to untie.’[r]

26 “Fellow children of Abraham and you
God-fearing Gentiles, it is to us that this
message of salvation[s] has been sent. 27 The
people of Jerusalem and their rulers did
not recognize Jesus,[t] yet in condemning
him they fulfilled the words of the prophets[u] that are read every Sabbath. 28 Though
they found no proper ground for a death
sentence, they asked Pilate to have him
executed.[v] 29 When they had carried out
all that was written about him,[w] they took
him down from the cross[x] and laid him in
a tomb.[y] 30 But God raised him from the
dead,[z] 31 and for many days he was seen by
those who had traveled with him from Galilee to Jerusalem.[a] They are now his witnesses[b] to our people.

32 “We tell you the good news:[c] What God
promised our ancestors[d] 33 he has fulfilled
for us, their children, by raising up Jesus.
As it is written in the second Psalm:

“ ‘You are my son;
today I have become your father.’[b][e]

34 God raised him from the dead so that he
will never be subject to decay. As God has
said,

“ ‘I will give you the holy and sure
blessings promised to David.’[c][f]

35 So it is also stated elsewhere:

“ ‘You will not let your holy one see
decay.’[d][g]

36 “Now when David had served God’s
purpose in his own generation, he fell
asleep; he was buried with his ancestors[h]
and his body decayed. 37 But the one whom
God raised from the dead did not see decay.

38 “Therefore, my friends, I want you to
know that through Jesus the forgiveness of
sins is proclaimed to you.[i] 39 Through him
everyone who believes is set free from every sin, a justification you were not able to
obtain under the law of Moses.[j] 40 Take care
that what the prophets have said does not
happen to you:

41 “ ‘Look, you scoffers,
wonder and perish,
for I am going to do something in your
days
that you would never believe,
even if someone told you.’[e]”[k]

42 As Paul and Barnabas were leaving
the synagogue,[l] the people invited them
to speak further about these things on
the next Sabbath. 43 When the congregation was dismissed, many of the Jews
and devout converts to Judaism followed
Paul and Barnabas, who talked with them
and urged them to continue in the grace
of God.[m]

44 On the next Sabbath almost the whole
city gathered to hear the word of the Lord.

[a] *18* Some manuscripts *he cared for them*
[b] *33* Psalm 2:7 [c] *34* Isaiah 55:3 [d] *35* Psalm 16:10 (see Septuagint) [e] *41* Hab. 1:5

13:39 *everyone who believes is set free from every sin, a justification.* “Justified” is a technical legal term declaring that a person is acquitted and absolved. Because of Jesus’ death on the cross, our sin debt has been paid. Everyone who accepts this payment is justified before God, considered righteous through the blood of Christ.

13:14 [s] Ac 14:19,21 [t] Ac 16:13 [u] Ac 9:20 **13:15** [v] Ac 15:21 **13:16** [w] Ac 12:17 **13:17** [x] Ex 6:6,7; Dt 7:6-8 **13:18** [y] Dt 1:31 [z] Ac 7:36 **13:19** [a] Dt 7:1 [b] Jos 19:51

13:20 [c] Jdg 2:16 [d] 1Sa 3:19,20 **13:21** [e] 1Sa 8:5,19 [f] 1Sa 10:1 [g] 1Sa 9:1,2 **13:22** [h] 1Sa 15:23,26 [i] 1Sa 16:13; Ps 89:20 [j] 1Sa 13:14 **13:23** [k] Mt 1:1 [l] Lk 2:11 [m] Mt 1:21 [n] ver 32 **13:24** [o] Mk 1:4 **13:25** [p] Ac 20:24 [q] Jn 1:20 [r] Mt 3:11; Jn 1:27 **13:26** [s] Ac 4:12 **13:27** [t] Ac 3:17 [u] Lk 24:27 **13:28** [v] Mt 27:20-25; Ac 3:14 **13:29** [w] Lk 18:31 [x] Ac 5:30 [y] Lk 23:53 **13:30** [z] Mt 28:6; Ac 2:24 **13:31** [a] Mt 28:16 [b] Lk 24:48 **13:32** [c] Ac 5:42 [d] Ac 26:6; Ro 4:13 **13:33** [e] Ps 2:7 **13:34** [f] Isa 55:3 **13:35** [g] Ps 16:10; Ac 2:27 **13:36** [h] 1Ki 2:10; Ac 2:29 **13:38** [i] Lk 24:47; Ac 2:38 **13:39** [j] Ro 3:28 **13:41** [k] Hab 1:5 **13:42** [l] ver 14 **13:43** [m] Ac 11:23; 14:22

45When the Jews saw the crowds, they were filled with jealousy. They began to contradict what Paul was saying[n] and heaped abuse[o] on him.

46Then Paul and Barnabas answered them boldly: "We had to speak the word of God to you first.[p] Since you reject it and do not consider yourselves worthy of eternal life, we now turn to the Gentiles.[q] 47For this is what the Lord has commanded us:

"'I have made you[a] a light for the
    Gentiles,[r]
  that you[a] may bring salvation to the
    ends of the earth.'[b]"[s]

48When the Gentiles heard this, they were glad and honored the word of the Lord; and all who were appointed for eternal life believed.

49The word of the Lord spread through the whole region. 50But the Jewish leaders incited the God-fearing women of high standing and the leading men of the city. They stirred up persecution against Paul and Barnabas, and expelled them from their region.[t] 51So they shook the dust off their feet[u] as a warning to them and went to Iconium.[v] 52And the disciples were filled with joy and with the Holy Spirit.

In Iconium

14 At Iconium[w] Paul and Barnabas went as usual into the Jewish synagogue. There they spoke so effectively that a great number of Jews and Greeks believed. 2But the Jews who refused to believe stirred up the other Gentiles and poisoned their minds against the brothers. 3So Paul and Barnabas spent considerable time there, speaking boldly[x] for the Lord, who confirmed the message of his grace by enabling them to perform signs and wonders.[y] 4The people of the city were divided; some sided with the Jews, others with the apostles.[z] 5There was a plot afoot among both Gentiles and Jews, together with their leaders, to mistreat them and stone them.[a] 6But they found out about it and fled[b] to the Lycaonian cities of Lystra and Derbe and to the surrounding country, 7where they continued to preach[c] the gospel.[d]

In Lystra and Derbe

8In Lystra there sat a man who was lame. He had been that way from birth[e] and had never walked. 9He listened to Paul as he was speaking. Paul looked directly at him, saw that he had faith to be healed[f] 10and called out, "Stand up on your feet!" At that, the man jumped up and began to walk.[g]

11When the crowd saw what Paul had done, they shouted in the Lycaonian language, "The gods have come down to us in human form!"[h] 12Barnabas they called Zeus, and Paul they called Hermes because he was the chief speaker. 13The priest of Zeus, whose temple was just outside the city, brought bulls and wreaths to the city gates because he and the crowd wanted to offer sacrifices to them.

14But when the apostles Barnabas and Paul heard of this, they tore their clothes[i] and rushed out into the crowd, shouting: 15"Friends, why are you doing this? We too are only human,[j] like you. We are bringing you good news,[k] telling you to turn from these worthless things[l] to the living God,[m] who made the heavens and the earth[n] and the sea and everything in them.[o] 16In the past, he let[p] all nations go their own way.[q] 17Yet he has not left himself without testimony:[r] He has shown kindness by giving you rain from heaven and crops in their seasons;[s] he provides you with plenty of food and fills your hearts with joy." 18Even with these words, they had difficulty keeping the crowd from sacrificing to them.

19Then some Jews[t] came from Antioch and Iconium[u] and won the crowd over. They stoned Paul[v] and dragged him outside the city, thinking he was dead. 20But after

[a] 47 The Greek is singular. [b] 47 Isaiah 49:6

13:45 *the Jews.* When Luke refers to "the Jews," he is not speaking of all Jewish people, but rather of the Jewish religious establishment, which opposed the gospel.

13:52 Joy—The pursuit of happiness doesn't always lead to the possession of joy. Joy does not come from circumstances but from the presence of God. It is a fruit of the spirit, poured into a believer's life by the grace of God. The believers in this passage were not filled with joy because their lives were comfortable, or because they were wealthy or powerful, but because they saw God working and had His Holy Spirit in their lives.

14:11 *The gods have come down.* The Roman poet Ovid told of an ancient legend in which Zeus and Hermes came to the Phrygian hill country disguised as mortals seeking lodging. After being turned away from a thousand homes, they found refuge in the humble cottage of an elderly couple. In appreciation for the couple's hospitality, the gods transformed the cottage into a splendid temple and then destroyed all the houses of the inhospitable people. The people probably remembered this ancient legend, and wanted to make sure they did not make the same mistake their ancestors did.

13:45 [n] 1Th 2:16 [o] Ac 18:6; 1Pe 4:4; Jude 10
13:46 [p] ver 26; Ac 3:26 [q] Ac 18:6; 22:21; 28:28
13:47 [r] Lk 2:32 [s] Isa 49:6 **13:50** [t] 1Th 2:16
13:51 [u] Mt 10:14; Ac 18:6 [v] Ac 14:1, 19, 21; 2Ti 3:11
14:1 [w] Ac 13:51 **14:3** [x] Ac 4:29 [y] Jn 4:48; Heb 2:4
14:4 [z] Ac 17:4, 5 **14:5** [a] ver 19 **14:6** [b] Mt 10:23
14:7 [c] Ac 16:10 [d] ver 15, 21 **14:8** [e] Ac 3:2
14:9 [f] Mt 9:28, 29 **14:10** [g] Ac 3:8 **14:11** [h] Ac 8:10; 28:6
14:14 [i] Mk 14:63 **14:15** [j] Ac 10:26; Jas 5:17 [k] ver 7, 21; Ac 13:32 [l] 1Sa 12:21; 1Co 8:4; 1Th 1:9 [m] Mt 16:16 [n] Ge 1:1; Jer 14:22 [o] Ps 146:6; Rev 14:7 **14:16** [p] Ac 17:30
[q] Ps 81:12; Mic 4:5 **14:17** [r] Ac 17:27; Ro 1:20 [s] Dt 11:14; Job 5:10; Ps 65:10 **14:19** [t] Ac 13:45 [u] Ac 13:51
[v] 2Co 11:25; 2Ti 3:11

the disciples[w] had gathered around him, he got up and went back into the city. The next day he and Barnabas left for Derbe.

The Return to Antioch in Syria

21They preached the gospel in that city and won a large number of disciples. Then they returned to Lystra, Iconium[x] and Antioch, 22strengthening the disciples and encouraging them to remain true to the faith.[y] "We must go through many hardships[z] to enter the kingdom of God," they said. 23Paul and Barnabas appointed elders[a][a] for them in each church and, with prayer and fasting,[b] committed them to the Lord,[c] in whom they had put their trust. 24After going through Pisidia, they came into Pamphylia, 25and when they had preached the word in Perga, they went down to Attalia.

26From Attalia they sailed back to Antioch,[d] where they had been committed to the grace of God[e] for the work they had now completed.[f] 27On arriving there, they gathered the church together and reported all that God had done through them[g] and how he had opened a door[h] of faith to the Gentiles. 28And they stayed there a long time with the disciples.

The Council at Jerusalem

15 Certain people[i] came down from Judea to Antioch and were teaching the believers: "Unless you are circumcised,[j] according to the custom taught by Moses,[k] you cannot be saved." 2This brought Paul and Barnabas into sharp dispute and debate with them. So Paul and Barnabas were appointed, along with some other believers, to go up to Jerusalem[l] to see the apostles and elders[m] about this question. 3The church sent them on their way, and as they traveled through Phoenicia and Samaria, they told how the Gentiles had been converted.[n] This news made all the believers very glad. 4When they came to Jerusalem, they were welcomed by the church and the apostles and elders, to whom they reported everything God had done through them.[o]

5Then some of the believers who belonged to the party of the Pharisees stood up and said, "The Gentiles must be circumcised and required to keep the law of Moses."

6The apostles and elders met to consider this question. 7After much discussion, Peter got up and addressed them: "Brothers, you know that some time ago God made a choice among you that the Gentiles might hear from my lips the message of the gospel and believe. 8God, who knows the heart,[p] showed that he accepted them by giving the Holy Spirit to them,[q] just as he did to us. 9He did not discriminate between us and them,[r] for he purified their hearts by faith.[s] 10Now then, why do you try to test God by putting on the necks of Gentiles a yoke[t] that neither we nor our ancestors have been able to bear? 11No! We believe it is through the grace[u] of our Lord Jesus that we are saved, just as they are."

12The whole assembly became silent as they listened to Barnabas and Paul telling about the signs and wonders[v] God had done among the Gentiles through them.[w] 13When they finished, James[x] spoke up. "Brothers," he said, "listen to me. 14Simon[b] has described to us how God first intervened to choose a people for his name from the Gentiles. 15The words of the prophets are in agreement with this, as it is written:

16" 'After this I will return
  and rebuild David's fallen tent.
 Its ruins I will rebuild,
  and I will restore it,
17that the rest of mankind may seek the
   Lord,
  even all the Gentiles who bear my
   name,
 says the Lord, who does these
   things'[c][y]—
18 things known from long ago.[d]

19"It is my judgment, therefore, that we should not make it difficult for the Gentiles

---

[a] 23 Or *Barnabas ordained elders*; or *Barnabas had elders elected* [b] 14 Greek *Simeon*, a variant of *Simon*; that is, Peter [c] 17 Amos 9:11,12 (see Septuagint) [d] 17,18 Some manuscripts *things'— / 18the Lord's work is known to him from long ago*

14:23 *appointed elders.* The process outlined in 6:1–7 for selecting the seven men to serve the Jerusalem believers may provide a clue to the process used for selecting elders here. Both the assembly and the apostles were involved in the selection process.

15:11 *through the grace of our Lord Jesus that we are saved.* These are the last words of Peter in the Book of Acts. He leaves us with the eternal truth that we are saved through faith by grace alone. The emphasis in the narrative now moves from Peter to Paul, and his outreach to the Gentiles.

15:13 *James.* James was the leader of the church in Jerusalem until he was stoned to death at the insistence of the high priest in A.D. 62. It is believed that this James is the Lord's brother, the son of Mary and Joseph, who did not believe until the Lord appeared to him privately after the Resurrection (1 Cor. 15:7).

15:19–20 *abstain from food polluted by idols.* The Jerusalem council understood that it was not necessary for Gentiles to keep the whole of the law in order

14:20 [w] ver 22,28; Ac 11:26 **14:21** [x] Ac 13:51 **14:22** [y] Ac 11:23; 13:43 [z] Jn 16:33; 1Th 3:3; 2Ti 3:12 **14:23** [a] Ac 11:30; Titus 1:5 [b] Ac 13:3 [c] Ac 20:32 **14:26** [d] Ac 11:19 [e] Ac 15:40 [f] Ac 13:1,3 **14:27** [g] Ac 15:4, 12; 21:19 [h] 1Co 16:9; 2Co 2:12; Col 4:3; Rev 3:8 **15:1** [i] ver 24; Gal 2:12 [j] ver 5; Gal 5:2,3 [k] Ac 6:14 **15:2** [l] Gal 2:2 [m] Ac 11:30 **15:3** [n] Ac 14:27 **15:4** [o] ver 12; Ac 14:27 **15:8** [p] Ac 1:24 [q] Ac 10:44,47 **15:9** [r] Ac 10:28, 34; 11:12 [s] Ac 10:43 **15:10** [t] Mt 23:4; Gal 5:1 **15:11** [u] Ro 3:24; Eph 2:5-8 **15:12** [v] Jn 4:48 [w] Ac 14:27 **15:13** [x] Ac 12:17 **15:17** [y] Am 9:11,12

who are turning to God. 20 Instead we should write to them, telling them to abstain from food polluted by idols,[z] from sexual immorality,[a] from the meat of strangled animals and from blood.[b] 21 For the law of Moses has been preached in every city from the earliest times and is read in the synagogues on every Sabbath."[c]

The Council's Letter to Gentile Believers

22 Then the apostles and elders, with the whole church, decided to choose some of their own men and send them to Antioch with Paul and Barnabas. They chose Judas (called Barsabbas) and Silas,[d] men who were leaders among the believers. 23 With them they sent the following letter:

> The apostles and elders, your brothers,
>
> To the Gentile believers in Antioch,[e] Syria and Cilicia:[f]
>
> Greetings.[g]
>
> 24 We have heard that some went out from us without our authorization and disturbed you, troubling your minds by what they said.[h] 25 So we all agreed to choose some men and send them to you with our dear friends Barnabas and Paul— 26 men who have risked their lives[i] for the name of our Lord Jesus Christ. 27 Therefore we are sending Judas and Silas to confirm by word of mouth what we are writing. 28 It seemed good to the Holy Spirit[j] and to us not to burden you with anything beyond the following requirements: 29 You are to abstain from food sacrificed to idols, from blood, from the meat of strangled animals and from sexual immorality.[k] You will do well to avoid these things.
>
> Farewell.

30 So the men were sent off and went down to Antioch, where they gathered the church together and delivered the letter. 31 The people read it and were glad for its encouraging message. 32 Judas and Silas, who themselves were prophets, said much to encourage and strengthen the believers. 33 After spending some time there, they were sent off by the believers with the blessing of peace[l] to return to those who had sent them. [34][a] 35 But Paul and Barnabas remained in Antioch, where they and many others taught and preached[m] the word of the Lord.

Disagreement Between Paul and Barnabas

36 Some time later Paul said to Barnabas, "Let us go back and visit the believers in all the towns[n] where we preached the word of the Lord and see how they are doing." 37 Barnabas wanted to take John, also called Mark,[o] with them, 38 but Paul did not think it wise to take him, because he had deserted them[p] in Pamphylia and had not continued with them in the work. 39 They had such a sharp disagreement that they parted company. Barnabas took Mark and sailed for Cyprus, 40 but Paul chose Silas[q] and left, commended by the believers to the grace of the Lord.[r] 41 He went through Syria[s] and Cilicia,[t] strengthening the churches.[u]

Timothy Joins Paul and Silas

16 Paul came to Derbe and then to Lystra,[v] where a disciple named Timothy[w] lived, whose mother was Jewish and a believer but whose father was a Greek. 2 The believers[x] at Lystra and Iconium[y] spoke well of him. 3 Paul wanted to take him along on the journey, so he circum-

---

[a] *34* Some manuscripts include here *But Silas decided to remain there.*

---

to be believers in Jesus, but also recognized that they did not have the background of moral teaching the Jewish believers had. They needed both reassurance as to their acceptance as true Christians and teaching for a godly life. In looking at the present application of these requirements, it is important to remember that Acts is a transitional book, documenting the beginning of the Christian movement. Sexual purity and food regulations are both addressed more thoroughly elsewhere in the New Testament (1 Cor. 6–8).

15:20 Fornication—Illicit sexual relationships were not a matter of shame or sin among the Gentiles as they were among the Jews. In fact, many pagan religious practices included prostitution and sexual orgies. This made the need for teaching on sexual purity doubly urgent for the new Gentile believers. They would be constantly presented with temptation, not only for sexual sin but for returning to their old ways of worship. They needed to hear God's strict prohibition of such behavior.

15:39 ***that they parted company.*** Even though Paul and Barnabas had a heated disagreement, it is important to note that they did not bring their disagreement into the church fellowship, forcing others to take sides and causing more dissension. Instead, they simply parted ways, each continuing to faithfully serve the Lord. Later, the disagreement was apparently resolved, for Paul wrote to Timothy when he was imprisoned, asking for Mark to be sent to him, for "he is helpful to me in my ministry" (2 Tim. 4:11).

16:3 ***circumcised him.*** According to Jewish law, Timothy should have been circumcised and raised a

15:20 [z] 1Co 8:7-13; 10:14-28; Rev 2:14,20 [a] 1Co 10:7,8 [b] ver 29; Ge 9:4; Lev 3:17; Dt 12:16,23 **15:21** [c] Ac 13:15; 2Co 3:14,15 **15:22** [d] ver 27,32,40 **15:23** [e] ver 1 [f] ver 41 [g] Ac 23:25,26; Jas 1:1 **15:24** [h] ver 1; Gal 1:7; 5:10 **15:26** [i] Ac 9:23-25; 14:19 **15:28** [j] Ac 5:32 **15:29** [k] ver 20; Ac 21:25 **15:33** [l] Mk 5:34; Ac 16:36; 1Co 16:11 **15:35** [m] Ac 8:4 **15:36** [n] Ac 13:4,13,14,51; 14:1,6,24,25 **15:37** [o] Ac 12:12 **15:38** [p] Ac 13:13 **15:40** [q] ver 22 [r] Ac 11:23 **15:41** [s] ver 23 [t] Ac 6:9 [u] Ac 16:5 **16:1** [v] Ac 14:6 [w] Ac 17:14; 18:5; 19:22; Ro 16:21; 1Co 4:17; 2Co 1:1,19; 1Th 3:2,6; 1Ti 1:2,18; 2Ti 1:2,5,6 **16:2** [x] ver 40 [y] Ac 13:51

cised him because of the Jews who lived in that area, for they all knew that his father was a Greek.[z] [4]As they traveled from town to town, they delivered the decisions reached by the apostles and elders[a] in Jerusalem[b] for the people to obey.[c] [5]So the churches were strengthened[d] in the faith and grew daily in numbers.

Paul's Vision of the Man of Macedonia

[6]Paul and his companions traveled throughout the region of Phrygia[e] and Galatia,[f] having been kept by the Holy Spirit from preaching the word in the province of Asia.[g] [7]When they came to the border of Mysia, they tried to enter Bithynia, but the Spirit of Jesus[h] would not allow them to. [8]So they passed by Mysia and went down to Troas.[i] [9]During the night Paul had a vision[j] of a man of Macedonia[k] standing and begging him, "Come over to Macedonia and help us." [10]After Paul had seen the vision, we[l] got ready at once to leave for Macedonia, concluding that God had called us to preach the gospel[m] to them.

Lydia's Conversion in Philippi

[11]From Troas[n] we put out to sea and sailed straight for Samothrace, and the next day we went on to Neapolis. [12]From there we traveled to Philippi,[o] a Roman colony and the leading city of that district[a] of Macedonia.[p] And we stayed there several days.

[13]On the Sabbath[q] we went outside the city gate to the river, where we expected to find a place of prayer. We sat down and began to speak to the women who had gathered there. [14]One of those listening was a woman from the city of Thyatira[r] named Lydia, a dealer in purple cloth. She was a worshiper of God. The Lord opened her heart[s] to respond to Paul's message. [15]When she and the members of her household[t] were baptized, she invited us to her home. "If you consider me a believer in the Lord," she said, "come and stay at my house." And she persuaded us.

Paul and Silas in Prison

[16]Once when we were going to the place of prayer,[u] we were met by a female slave who had a spirit[v] by which she predicted the future. She earned a great deal of money for her owners by fortune-telling. [17]She followed Paul and the rest of us, shouting, "These men are servants of the Most High God,[w] who are telling you the way to be saved." [18]She kept this up for many days. Finally Paul became so annoyed that he turned around and said to the spirit, "In the name of Jesus Christ I command you to come out of her!" At that moment the spirit left her.[x]

[19]When her owners realized that their hope of making money[y] was gone, they seized Paul and Silas[z] and dragged[a] them into the marketplace to face the authorities. [20]They brought them before the magistrates and said, "These men are Jews, and are throwing our city into an uproar[b] [21]by advocating customs unlawful for us Romans[c] to accept or practice."[d]

[22]The crowd joined in the attack against Paul and Silas, and the magistrates ordered them to be stripped and beaten with rods.[e] [23]After they had been severely flogged, they were thrown into prison, and the jailer[f] was commanded to guard them carefully. [24]When he received these orders, he put them in the inner cell and fastened their feet in the stocks.[g]

[25]About midnight Paul and Silas were praying and singing hymns[h] to God, and the other prisoners were listening to them.

---

a 12 The text and meaning of the Greek for *the leading city of that district* are uncertain.

Jew, even with a Gentile father. For whatever reason, this had not happened, and the fact that he was an uncircumcised Jew would limit his effectiveness with Jewish Christians. The issue was not law but effectiveness.

16:12 *Philippi.* Named after the father of Alexander the Great, Philippi was a Roman colony loyal to the empire. The city itself was organized by the state of Rome and functioned as a military outpost. Because of its proximity to the sea as well as to one of the major roads to Europe, Philippi was a commercial center in Macedonia. Its influence throughout the region made it a good place to begin preaching the gospel of Jesus Christ.

16:13 *where we expected to find a place of prayer.* According to Jewish custom, a congregation consisted of ten households. If ten male household heads could be found in a city, a synagogue was formed. If not, a place of prayer was established. Philippi did not have a synagogue, but Paul was still able to find the God-fearers of the city.

16:25 Praise—Paul and Silas were praying and singing hymns of praise to God at midnight in spite of the fact that they had been arrested, stripped naked, and beaten, confined to an inner cell and clamped into an uncomfortable position. They could praise God because their joy was not based on circumstances but on a relationship. Jesus Christ and His love and grace are the same, no matter where you are or what is happening to you.

16:3 [z] Gal 2:3 **16:4** [a] Ac 11:30 [b] Ac 15:2 [c] Ac 15:28,29 **16:5** [d] Ac 9:31; 15:41 **16:6** [e] Ac 18:23 [f] Ac 18:23; Gal 1:2; 3:1 [g] Ac 2:9 **16:7** [h] Ro 8:9; Gal 4:6 **16:8** [i] ver 11; 2Co 2:12; 2Ti 4:13 **16:9** [j] Ac 9:10 [k] Ac 20:1,3 **16:10** [l] ver 10-17 [m] Ac 14:7 **16:11** [n] ver 8 **16:12** [o] Ac 20:6; Php 1:1; 1Th 2:2 [p] ver 9 **16:13** [q] Ac 13:14 **16:14** [r] Rev 1:11 [s] Lk 24:45 **16:15** [t] Ac 11:14 **16:16** [u] ver 13 [v] Dt 18:11; 1Sa 28:3,7 **16:17** [w] Mk 5:7 **16:18** [x] Mk 16:17 **16:19** [y] ver 16; Ac 19:25,26 [z] Ac 15:22 [a] Ac 8:3; 17:6; 21:30; Jas 2:6 **16:20** [b] Ac 17:6 **16:21** [c] ver 12 [d] Est 3:8 **16:22** [e] 2Co 11:25; 1Th 2:2 **16:23** [f] ver 27,36 **16:24** [g] Job 13:27; 33:11; Jer 20:2,3; 29:26 **16:25** [h] Eph 5:19

26 Suddenly there was such a violent earthquake that the foundations of the prison
were shaken.[i] At once all the prison doors
flew open,[j] and everyone's chains came
loose.[k] 27 The jailer woke up, and when
he saw the prison doors open, he drew
his sword and was about to kill himself
because he thought the prisoners had escaped.[l] 28 But Paul shouted, "Don't harm
yourself! We are all here!"

29 The jailer called for lights, rushed in
and fell trembling before Paul and Silas.
30 He then brought them out and asked,
"Sirs, what must I do to be saved?"[m]

31 They replied, "Believe in the Lord
Jesus, and you will be saved—you and
your household."[n] 32 Then they spoke the
word of the Lord to him and to all the
others in his house. 33 At that hour of the
night[o] the jailer took them and washed
their wounds; then immediately he and all
his household were baptized. 34 The jailer brought them into his house and set a
meal before them; he[p] was filled with joy
because he had come to believe in God—
he and his whole household.

35 When it was daylight, the magistrates
sent their officers to the jailer with the order: "Release those men." 36 The jailer[q] told
Paul, "The magistrates have ordered that
you and Silas be released. Now you can
leave. Go in peace."[r]

37 But Paul said to the officers: "They beat
us publicly without a trial, even though we
are Roman citizens,[s] and threw us into
prison. And now do they want to get rid of
us quietly? No! Let them come themselves
and escort us out."

38 The officers reported this to the magistrates, and when they heard that Paul
and Silas were Roman citizens, they were
alarmed.[t] 39 They came to appease them
and escorted them from the prison, requesting them to leave the city.[u] 40 After
Paul and Silas came out of the prison, they
went to Lydia's house,[v] where they met
with the brothers and sisters[w] and encouraged them. Then they left.

In Thessalonica

17 When Paul and his companions had
passed through Amphipolis and Apollonia, they came to Thessalonica,[x] where
there was a Jewish synagogue. 2 As was
his custom, Paul went into the synagogue,[y]
and on three Sabbath[z] days he reasoned
with them from the Scriptures,[a] 3 explaining and proving that the Messiah had to
suffer[b] and rise from the dead.[c] "This Jesus
I am proclaiming to you is the Messiah,"[d]
he said. 4 Some of the Jews were persuaded
and joined Paul and Silas,[e] as did a large
number of God-fearing Greeks and quite a
few prominent women.

5 But other Jews were jealous; so they
rounded up some bad characters from the
marketplace, formed a mob and started
a riot in the city.[f] They rushed to Jason's[g]
house in search of Paul and Silas in order
to bring them out to the crowd.[a] 6 But when
they did not find them, they dragged[h] Jason and some other believers before the
city officials, shouting: "These men who
have caused trouble all over the world[i]
have now come here,[j] 7 and Jason has welcomed them into his house. They are all defying Caesar's decrees, saying that there
is another king, one called Jesus."[k] 8 When
they heard this, the crowd and the city officials were thrown into turmoil. 9 Then they
made Jason[l] and the others post bond and
let them go.

---

[a] 5 Or *the assembly of the people*

16:31 It Begins with Faith—Paul and Silas's answer to the Philippian jailer's question is the essence of salvation; *Believe in the Lord Jesus, and you will be saved.* This verse raises two questions: What does it mean to believe, and what does it mean to be saved? Belief includes but is more than just an intellectual assent. Belief includes the idea of total trust, dependence, and submission of oneself to Christ as Lord (King, Master). To be saved is to be delivered. We are delivered from the very presence of sin and evil (Satan and hell) and will be delivered into the very presence of God (Christ and heaven). We receive this new life by faith—believing that we are sinful, that Jesus died for our sins, that His death was in our place, and that His payment for sin is fully acceptable in God's sight. Faith can be summarized in the acrostic:

Forsaking
All
I
Take
Him

16:33–34 Family—This man assumed spiritual leadership of his family by being the first to repent, to humble himself before God and ask for forgiveness and a change of life. By his example, the rest of his family was won. In the same way, every believing father has the responsibility to set the example of spiritual commitment, and to teach his family all he knows of following Christ.

16:37 *Roman citizens.* Paul was not simply seeking self-justification, he was protecting the infant church in Philippi. By forcing a public statement of their innocence, he minimized the possibility that the new believers would be regarded as "friends of criminals and troublemakers."

17:7 *defying Caesar's decrees.* In A.D. 49 the Roman emperor Caligula expelled all Jews from Rome due to riots ignited by a group of zealous Jews. Paul's accusers were trying to paint him as a revolutionary who was bringing sedition to Thessalonica.

16:26 [i] Ac 4:31 [j] Ac 12:10 [k] Ac 12:7 **16:27** [l] Ac 12:19 **16:30** [m] Ac 2:37 **16:31** [n] Ac 11:14 **16:33** [o] ver 25 **16:34** [p] Ac 11:14 **16:36** [q] ver 23, 27 [r] Ac 15:33 **16:37** [s] Ac 22:25-29 **16:38** [t] Ac 22:29 **16:39** [u] Mt 8:34 **16:40** [v] ver 14 [w] ver 2; Ac 1:16 **17:1** [x] ver 11, 13; Php 4:16; 1Th 1:1; 2Th 1:1; 2Ti 4:10 **17:2** [y] Ac 9:20 [z] Ac 13:14 [a] Ac 8:35 **17:3** [b] Lk 24:26; Ac 3:18 [c] Lk 24:46 [d] Ac 9:22; 18:28 **17:4** [e] Ac 15:22 **17:5** [f] ver 13; 1Th 2:16 [g] Ro 16:21 **17:6** [h] Ac 16:19 [i] Mt 24:14 [j] Ac 16:20 **17:7** [k] Lk 23:2; Jn 19:12 **17:9** [l] ver 5

In Berea

10As soon as it was night, the believers sent Paul and Silas away to Berea.[m] On arriving there, they went to the Jewish synagogue. **11**Now the Berean Jews were of more noble character than those in Thessalonica,[n] for they received the message with great eagerness and examined the Scriptures[o] every day to see if what Paul said was true. **12**As a result, many of them believed, as did also a number of prominent Greek women and many Greek men.

13But when the Jews in Thessalonica learned that Paul was preaching the word of God at Berea, some of them went there too, agitating the crowds and stirring them up. **14**The believers immediately sent Paul to the coast, but Silas[p] and Timothy[q] stayed at Berea. **15**Those who escorted Paul brought him to Athens[r] and then left with instructions for Silas and Timothy to join him as soon as possible.[s]

In Athens

16While Paul was waiting for them in Athens, he was greatly distressed to see that the city was full of idols. **17**So he reasoned in the synagogue[t] with both Jews and God-fearing Greeks, as well as in the marketplace day by day with those who happened to be there. **18**A group of Epicurean and Stoic philosophers began to debate with him. Some of them asked, "What is this babbler trying to say?" Others remarked, "He seems to be advocating foreign gods." They said this because Paul was preaching the good news about Jesus and the resurrection.[u] **19**Then they took him and brought him to a meeting of the Areopagus,[v] where they said to him, "May we know what this new teaching[w] is that you are presenting? **20**You are bringing some strange ideas to our ears, and we would like to know what they mean." **21**(All the Athenians and the foreigners who lived there spent their time doing nothing but talking about and listening to the latest ideas.)

22Paul then stood up in the meeting of the Areopagus and said: "People of Athens! I see that in every way you are very religious. **23**For as I walked around and looked carefully at your objects of worship, I even found an altar with this inscription: TO AN UNKNOWN GOD. So you are ignorant of the very thing you worship[x]—and this is what I am going to proclaim to you.

24"The God who made the world and everything in it[y] is the Lord of heaven and earth[z] and does not live in temples built by human hands.[a] **25**And he is not served by human hands, as if he needed anything. Rather, he himself gives everyone life and breath and everything else.[b] **26**From one man he made all the nations, that they should inhabit the whole earth; and he marked out their appointed times in history and the boundaries of their lands.[c] **27**God did this so that they would seek him and perhaps reach out for him and find him, though he is not far from any one of us.[d] **28**'For in him we live and move and have our being.'[a][e] As some of your own poets have said, 'We are his offspring.'[b]

29"Therefore since we are God's offspring, we should not think that the divine being is like gold or silver or stone—an image made by human design and skill.[f] **30**In the past God overlooked[g] such ignorance,[h] but now he commands all people everywhere to repent.[i] **31**For he has set a day when he will judge[j] the world with justice[k] by the man he has appointed.[l] He has given proof of this to everyone by raising him from the dead."[m]

32When they heard about the resurrection of the dead,[n] some of them sneered, but

a *28* From the Cretan philosopher Epimenides
b *28* From the Cilician Stoic philosopher Aratus

17:18 ***this babbler.*** This word is literally "seed picker." The philosophers were saying that Paul was like a gutter sparrow, picking up bits and scraps of knowledge without fully digesting or thinking about what he taught.

17:19 ***Areopagus.*** Just southwest of the Acropolis in Athens was a hill called the Hill of Ares (Mars, in Latin), the god of war. This was where court was held concerning questions of religion and morals. In Athens, the gospel message was examined by the supposed experts of philosophy and religion.

17:23 An Unknown God—In the sixth century B.C. it was said that a poet from Crete name Epimenides turned aside a horrible plague from the people of Athens by appealing to a god of whom the people had never heard. An altar was built to honor this god, and its inscription caught Paul's attention. Knowing that the Athenians had no background in the Old Testament Scriptures as did the Jews in the synagogues, Paul began his discourse with what they were already familiar with: their own legends and observation.

17:31 Resurrection—Christ has been raised from the dead not only for the purpose of returning to heaven and resuming His fellowship with the Father, a fellowship interrupted only by the alienation and abandonment at the cross; He has gone from His tomb to the right hand of His Father to intercede for us. And one day the mantle of Judge will be placed on Him, and everyone will stand before Him. The world has yet to see the last of Jesus Christ.

17:32 ***some of them sneered.*** Though they embraced the idea of the soul living on, the Greeks were

17:10 [m] ver 13; Ac 20:4 **17:11** [n] ver 1 [o] Lk 16:29; Jn 5:39 **17:14** [p] Ac 15:22 [q] Ac 16:1 **17:15** [r] ver 16, 21, 22; Ac 18:1; 1Th 3:1 [s] Ac 18:5 **17:17** [t] Ac 9:20 **17:18** [u] ver 31, 32; Ac 4:2 **17:19** [v] ver 22 [w] Mk 1:27 **17:23** [x] Jn 4:22 **17:24** [y] Isa 42:5; Ac 14:15 [z] Dt 10:14; Mt 11:25 [a] Ac 7:48 **17:25** [b] Ps 50:10-12; Isa 42:5 **17:26** [c] Dt 32:8; Job 12:23 **17:27** [d] Dt 4:7; Jer 23:23, 24; Ac 14:17 **17:28** [e] Job 12:10; Da 5:23 **17:29** [f] Isa 40:18-20; Ro 1:23 **17:30** [g] Ac 14:16; Ro 3:25 [h] ver 23; 1Pe 1:14 [i] Lk 24:47; Titus 2:11, 12 **17:31** [j] Mt 10:15 [k] Ps 9:8; 96:13; 98:9 [l] Ac 10:42 [m] Ac 2:24 **17:32** [n] ver 18, 31

others said, "We want to hear you again on
this subject." 33At that, Paul left the Council. 34Some of the people became followers
of Paul and believed. Among them was Di-
onysius, a member of the Areopagus,[o] also
a woman named Damaris, and a number
of others.

In Corinth

18 After this, Paul left Athens[p] and went
to Corinth.[q] 2There he met a Jew
named Aquila, a native of Pontus, who
had recently come from Italy with his wife
Priscilla,[r] because Claudius[s] had ordered
all Jews to leave Rome. Paul went to see
them, 3and because he was a tentmaker
as they were, he stayed and worked with
them.[t] 4Every Sabbath[u] he reasoned in the
synagogue, trying to persuade Jews and
Greeks.
5When Silas[v] and Timothy[w] came from
Macedonia,[x] Paul devoted himself exclusively to preaching, testifying to the Jews
that Jesus was the Messiah.[y] 6But when
they opposed Paul and became abusive,[z] he
shook out his clothes in protest and said to
them, "Your blood be on your own heads![a]
I am innocent of it.[b] From now on I will go
to the Gentiles."[c]
7Then Paul left the synagogue and went
next door to the house of Titius Justus, a
worshiper of God.[d] 8Crispus,[e] the synagogue leader,[f] and his entire household[g]
believed in the Lord; and many of the Corinthians who heard Paul believed and
were baptized.
9One night the Lord spoke to Paul in a vision: "Do not be afraid; keep on speaking,
do not be silent. 10For I am with you,[h] and
no one is going to attack and harm you, because I have many people in this city." 11So
Paul stayed in Corinth for a year and a half,
teaching them the word of God.
12While Gallio was proconsul of Achaia,[i]
the Jews of Corinth made a united attack
on Paul and brought him to the place of
judgment. 13"This man," they charged, "is
persuading the people to worship God in
ways contrary to the law."
14Just as Paul was about to speak, Gallio
said to them, "If you Jews were making a
complaint about some misdemeanor or serious crime, it would be reasonable for me
to listen to you. 15But since it involves questions about words and names and your
own law[j]—settle the matter yourselves.
I will not be a judge of such things." 16So
he drove them off. 17Then the crowd there
turned on Sosthenes[k] the synagogue leader
and beat him in front of the proconsul; and
Gallio showed no concern whatever.

Priscilla, Aquila and Apollos

18Paul stayed on in Corinth for some
time. Then he left the brothers and sisters[l] and sailed for Syria, accompanied by
Priscilla and Aquila. Before he sailed, he
had his hair cut off at Cenchreae[m] because
of a vow he had taken.[n] 19They arrived at
Ephesus,[o] where Paul left Priscilla and Aquila. He himself went into the synagogue
and reasoned with the Jews. 20When they
asked him to spend more time with them,
he declined. 21But as he left, he promised,
"I will come back if it is God's will."[p] Then
he set sail from Ephesus. 22When he landed
at Caesarea,[q] he went up to Jerusalem and
greeted the church and then went down to
Antioch.[r]
23After spending some time in Antioch,
Paul set out from there and traveled from
place to place throughout the region of Galatia[s] and Phrygia, strengthening all the
disciples.[t]
24Meanwhile a Jew named Apollos,[u] a
native of Alexandria, came to Ephesus. He
was a learned man, with a thorough knowledge of the Scriptures. 25He had been in-

---

repulsed by the idea of a bodily resurrection because they considered the body to be evil. This idea, known as *dualism,* was derived from the teachings of Socrates and Plato. It held that everything physical is evil and everything spiritual is good. Therefore, they believed the body and what is done with it is not important because it will be discarded at the end of life.

18:1 ***Corinth.*** Corinth was the political capital of Achaia. It was also a center for the worship of Aphrodite, the goddess of fertility, and it housed the major temple of Apollo. Because of the sensuous nature of the religious cult of Aphrodite, Corinth had a reputation for being a city of immorality. Beginning in the fifth century B.C., the Greeks used a word meaning "to act like a Corinthian" as a symbol for sexual immorality.

18:3 ***tentmaker.*** All young rabbinical students had to learn a trade. The province of Cilicia, from which Paul came, was noted for its cloth made from goats' hair. It is likely that Paul's skill involved making such cloth.

18:7 ***Justus.*** Most Romans had three names. This man's name was Titius Justus. Based on Paul's letter to the Corinthians, it is likely that Justus was the man called Gaius mentioned in 1 Corinthians 1:14.

18:18 ***had his hair cut off.*** Paul had his hair cut as part of a Nazirite vow he had made (see Num. 6:5). Such a vow had to be fulfilled in Jerusalem where the hair would be presented to God.

18:24 ***Apollos, a native of Alexandria.*** This Jew with a Greek name was from the second largest city in the Roman Empire. Alexandria was a seaport on the northern coast of Egypt. Founded by Alexander the Great, the city was very cosmopolitan. Egyptians, Romans, and Greeks all lived there; over one quarter

17:34 [o] ver 19,22 **18:1** [p] Ac 17:15 [q] Ac 19:1; 1Co 1:2; 2Co 1:1,23; 2Ti 4:20 **18:2** [r] Ro 16:3; 1Co 16:19; 2Ti 4:19 [s] Ac 11:28 **18:3** [t] Ac 20:34; 1Co 4:12; 1Th 2:9; 2Th 3:8 **18:4** [u] Ac 13:14 **18:5** [v] Ac 15:22 [w] Ac 16:1 [x] Ac 16:9; 17:14, 15 [y] ver 28; Ac 17:3 **18:6** [z] Ac 13:45 [a] 2Sa 1:16; Eze 18:13; 33:4 [b] Ac 20:26 [c] Ac 13:46 **18:7** [d] Ac 16:14 **18:8** [e] 1Co 1:14 [f] Mk 5:22 [g] Ac 11:14 **18:10** [h] Mt 28:20 **18:12** [i] ver 27 **18:15** [j] Ac 23:29; 25:11, 19 **18:17** [k] 1Co 1:1 **18:18** [l] Ac 1:16 [m] Ro 16:1 [n] Nu 6:2, 5, 18; Ac 21:24 **18:19** [o] ver 21, 24; 1Co 15:32 **18:21** [p] Ro 1:10; 1Co 4:19; Jas 4:15 **18:22** [q] Ac 8:40 [r] Ac 11:19 **18:23** [s] Ac 16:6 [t] Ac 14:22; 15:32, 41 **18:24** [u] Ac 19:1; 1Co 1:12; 3:5, 6, 22; 4:6; 16:12; Titus 3:13

structed in the way of the Lord, and he
spoke with great fervor[a][v] and taught about
Jesus accurately, though he knew only the
baptism of John.[w] 26He began to speak
boldly in the synagogue. When Priscilla
and Aquila heard him, they invited him to
their home and explained to him the way of
God more adequately.
27When Apollos wanted to go to Achaia,[x]
the brothers and sisters[y] encouraged him
and wrote to the disciples there to welcome
him. When he arrived, he was a great help
to those who by grace had believed. 28For
he vigorously refuted his Jewish opponents
in public debate, proving from the Scriptures[z] that Jesus was the Messiah.[a]

Paul in Ephesus

19 While Apollos was at Corinth,[b] Paul
took the road through the interior and
arrived at Ephesus.[c] There he found some
disciples 2and asked them, "Did you receive the Holy Spirit when[b] you believed?"
They answered, "No, we have not even
heard that there is a Holy Spirit."
3So Paul asked, "Then what baptism did
you receive?"
"John's baptism," they replied.
4Paul said, "John's baptism was a baptism of repentance. He told the people to
believe in the one coming after him, that
is, in Jesus."[d] 5On hearing this, they were
baptized in the name of the Lord Jesus.
6When Paul placed his hands on them,[e] the
Holy Spirit came on them,[f] and they spoke
in tongues[c][g] and prophesied. 7There were
about twelve men in all.
8Paul entered the synagogue[h] and spoke
boldly there for three months, arguing per-
suasively about the kingdom of God.[i] 9But
some of them[j] became obstinate; they refused to believe and publicly maligned the
Way.[k] So Paul left them. He took the disciples[l] with him and had discussions daily in
the lecture hall of Tyrannus. 10This went
on for two years,[m] so that all the Jews and
Greeks who lived in the province of Asia[n]
heard the word of the Lord.
11God did extraordinary miracles[o]
through Paul, 12so that even handkerchiefs
and aprons that had touched him were
taken to the sick, and their illnesses were
cured[p] and the evil spirits left them.
13Some Jews who went around driving
out evil spirits[q] tried to invoke the name
of the Lord Jesus over those who were demon-possessed. They would say, "In the
name of the Jesus[r] whom Paul preaches, I
command you to come out." 14Seven sons
of Sceva, a Jewish chief priest, were doing this. 15One day the evil spirit answered
them, "Jesus I know, and Paul I know
about, but who are you?" 16Then the man
who had the evil spirit jumped on them and
overpowered them all. He gave them such
a beating that they ran out of the house naked and bleeding.
17When this became known to the Jews
and Greeks living in Ephesus,[s] they were
all seized with fear,[t] and the name of the
Lord Jesus was held in high honor. 18Many
of those who believed now came and openly confessed what they had done. 19A number who had practiced sorcery brought
their scrolls together and burned them
publicly. When they calculated the value
of the scrolls, the total came to fifty thousand drachmas.[d] 20In this way the word of
the Lord spread widely and grew in power.[u]
21After all this had happened, Paul decided[e] to go to Jerusalem,[v] passing through
Macedonia[w] and Achaia.[x] "After I have been
there," he said, "I must visit Rome also."[y]

---

a 25 Or *with fervor in the Spirit* *b* 2 Or *after* *c* 6 Or *other languages* *d* 19 A drachma was a silver coin worth about a day's wages. *e* 21 Or *decided in the Spirit*

---

of the population was Jewish. The Greek translation of the Hebrew Scriptures had been produced in that city about 150 years before the birth of Jesus The city was famous for its great library and was considered the cultural and educational center of the world.

19:3 ***John's baptism.*** Baptism was a ritual used by the Jews as a picture of cleansing and purification. Gentiles who converted to Judaism would go through the rite of purification as their first act of worship. They would dip themselves in water as a sign of being cleansed from their old way of life. Before entering into the temple to worship, Jews would dip themselves in ritual bathing pools to show their desire for purification. John's baptism was a symbol of repentance from sin and a looking ahead to the coming of the Messiah.

19:6 ***placed his hands on them.*** The Holy Spirit was received without the laying on of hands in 10:44–48. By laying on his hands here, Paul was demonstrating his apostolic authority. He was also affirming the unity of the new church in Ephesus with the church in Jerusalem. Both were empowered by the Holy Spirit to speak in foreign tongues.

19:10 ***all … who lived in the province of Asia heard.*** From Ephesus, other churches were born in Asia Minor—in Colosse, Smyrna, Pergamos, Thyatira, Sardis, Philadelphia, and Laodicea. Paul and his students clearly did more than study. They must have actively evangelized as well.

19:13 ***the name of the Lord Jesus.*** The use of magical names in incantations was common in the ancient world. These practitioners had latched onto the name of Jesus to use as an incantation, but they discovered that it was not enough to know the name of Jesus; they needed to know Jesus personally.

18:25 [v] Ro 12:11 [w] Ac 19:3 **18:27** [x] ver 12 [y] ver 18 **18:28** [z] Ac 17:2 [a] ver 5; Ac 9:22 **19:1** [b] Ac 18:1 [c] Ac 18:19 **19:4** [d] Jn 1:7; Ac 13:24,25 **19:6** [e] Ac 6:6; 8:17 [f] Ac 2:4 [g] Mk 16:17; Ac 10:46 **19:8** [h] Ac 9:20 [i] Ac 1:3; 28:23 **19:9** [j] Ac 14:4 [k] ver 23; Ac 9:2 [l] ver 30; Ac 11:26 **19:10** [m] Ac 20:31 [n] ver 22,26,27 **19:11** [o] Ac 8:13 **19:12** [p] Ac 5:15 **19:13** [q] Mt 12:27 [r] Mk 9:38 **19:17** [s] Ac 18:19 [t] Ac 5:5,11 **19:20** [u] Ac 6:7; 12:24 **19:21** [v] Ac 20:16,22; Ro 15:25 [w] Ac 16:9 [x] Ac 18:12 [y] Ro 15:24,28

22He sent two of his helpers,[z] Timothy[a] and
Erastus,[b] to Macedonia, while he stayed in
the province of Asia[c] a little longer.

The Riot in Ephesus

23About that time there arose a great disturbance about the Way.[d] 24A silversmith
named Demetrius, who made silver shrines
of Artemis, brought in a lot of business for
the craftsmen there. 25He called them together, along with the workers in related
trades, and said: "You know, my friends,
that we receive a good income from this
business.[e] 26And you see and hear how this
fellow Paul has convinced and led astray
large numbers of people here in Ephesus[f]
and in practically the whole province of
Asia. He says that gods made by human
hands are no gods at all.[g] 27There is danger not only that our trade will lose its
good name, but also that the temple of the
great goddess Artemis will be discredited; and the goddess herself, who is worshiped throughout the province of Asia
and the world, will be robbed of her divine
majesty."

28When they heard this, they were furious and began shouting: "Great is Artemis
of the Ephesians!"[h] 29Soon the whole city
was in an uproar. The people seized Gaius[i] and Aristarchus,[j] Paul's traveling companions from Macedonia,[k] and all of them
rushed into the theater together. 30Paul
wanted to appear before the crowd, but the
disciples would not let him. 31Even some
of the officials of the province, friends of
Paul, sent him a message begging him not
to venture into the theater.

32The assembly was in confusion: Some
were shouting one thing, some another.[l]
Most of the people did not even know why
they were there. 33The Jews in the crowd
pushed Alexander to the front, and they
shouted instructions to him. He motioned[m]
for silence in order to make a defense before the people. 34But when they realized
he was a Jew, they all shouted in unison
for about two hours: "Great is Artemis of
the Ephesians!"

35The city clerk quieted the crowd and
said: "Fellow Ephesians,[n] doesn't all the
world know that the city of Ephesus is the
guardian of the temple of the great Artemis
and of her image, which fell from heaven?
36Therefore, since these facts are undeniable, you ought to calm down and not do
anything rash. 37You have brought these
men here, though they have neither robbed
temples[o] nor blasphemed our goddess. 38If,
then, Demetrius and his fellow craftsmen
have a grievance against anybody, the
courts are open and there are proconsuls.[p]
They can press charges. 39If there is anything further you want to bring up, it must
be settled in a legal assembly. 40As it is, we
are in danger of being charged with riot-
ing because of what happened today. In
that case we would not be able to account
for this commotion, since there is no reason for it." 41After he had said this, he dismissed the assembly.

Through Macedonia and Greece

20 When the uproar had ended, Paul
sent for the disciples[q] and, after encouraging them, said goodbye and set out
for Macedonia.[r] 2He traveled through that
area, speaking many words of encouragement to the people, and finally arrived in
Greece, 3where he stayed three months.
Because some Jews had plotted against
him[s] just as he was about to sail for Syria, he decided to go back through Macedonia.[t] 4He was accompanied by Sopater
son of Pyrrhus from Berea, Aristarchus[u]
and Secundus from Thessalonica,[v] Gaius[w]
from Derbe, Timothy[x] also, and Tychicus[y]
and Trophimus[z] from the province of Asia.
5These men went on ahead and waited for
us[a] at Troas.[b] 6But we sailed from Philippi[c]
after the Festival of Unleavened Bread, and
five days later joined the others at Troas,[d]
where we stayed seven days.

Eutychus Raised From the Dead at Troas

7On the first day of the week[e] we came
together to break bread. Paul spoke to the

19:29 *the theater.* This amphitheater seated 25,000 people.

19:40 *we are in danger.* The riot at Ephesus could have brought the discipline of Rome down upon the city. The Pax Romana, the peace that the Roman Empire brought to the Mediterranean world, was very important to Rome. The Romans would not tolerate any kind of uprising or rebellion. Ephesus risked losing its freedom and being ruled directly by the Roman army.

20:2 *encouragement.* This word has a full range of meanings, from rebuking to comforting. It includes instruction, appeal, affirmation, exhortation, warning, and correction.

20:7 The Lord's Supper—Although the phrase "to break bread" could mean an ordinary meal, it more likely refers to the observance of the Lord's Supper in obedience to Christ's command. The "breaking of bread" appears to be the primary purpose for the gathering, with Paul's sermon rising naturally in a group of people who had gathered to remember Christ.

19:22 [z] Ac 13:5 [a] Ac 16:1 [b] Ro 16:23; 2Ti 4:20 [c] ver 10, 26, 27 **19:23** [d] Ac 9:2 **19:25** [e] Ac 16:16, 19, 20 **19:26** [f] Ac 18:19 [g] Dt 4:28; Ps 115:4; Isa 44:10-20; Jer 10:3-5; Ac 17:29; 1Co 8:4; Rev 9:20 **19:28** [h] Ac 18:19 **19:29** [i] Ac 20:4; Ro 16:23; 1Co 1:14 [j] Ac 20:4; 27:2; Col 4:10; Phm 24 [k] Ac 16:9 **19:32** [l] Ac 21:34 **19:33** [m] Ac 12:17 **19:35** [n] Ac 18:19 **19:37** [o] Ro 2:22 **19:38** [p] Ac 13:7, 8, 12 **20:1** [q] Ac 11:26 [r] Ac 16:9 **20:3** [s] ver 19; Ac 9:23, 24; 23:12, 15, 30; 25:3; 2Co 11:26 [t] Ac 16:9 **20:4** [u] Ac 19:29 [v] Ac 17:1 [w] Ac 19:29 [x] Ac 16:1 [y] Eph 6:21; Col 4:7; 2Ti 4:12; Titus 3:12 [z] Ac 21:29; 2Ti 4:20 **20:5** [a] Ac 16:10 [b] Ac 16:8 **20:6** [c] Ac 16:12 [d] Ac 16:8 **20:7** [e] 1Co 16:2; Rev 1:10

people and, because he intended to leave
the next day, kept on talking until midnight. 8There were many lamps in the
upstairs room[f] where we were meeting.
9Seated in a window was a young man
named Eutychus, who was sinking into a
deep sleep as Paul talked on and on. When
he was sound asleep, he fell to the ground
from the third story and was picked up
dead. 10Paul went down, threw himself on
the young man[g] and put his arms around
him. "Don't be alarmed," he said. "He's
alive!"[h] 11Then he went upstairs again and
broke bread[i] and ate. After talking until daylight, he left. 12The people took the
young man home alive and were greatly
comforted.

Paul's Farewell to the Ephesian Elders

13We went on ahead to the ship and
sailed for Assos, where we were going to
take Paul aboard. He had made this arrangement because he was going there on
foot. 14When he met us at Assos, we took
him aboard and went on to Mitylene. 15The
next day we set sail from there and arrived
off Chios. The day after that we crossed
over to Samos, and on the following day
arrived at Miletus.[j] 16Paul had decided to
sail past Ephesus[k] to avoid spending time
in the province of Asia, for he was in a hurry to reach Jerusalem,[l] if possible, by the
day of Pentecost.[m]
17From Miletus, Paul sent to Ephesus for
the elders[n] of the church. 18When they arrived, he said to them: "You know how I
lived the whole time I was with you,[o] from
the first day I came into the province of
Asia. 19I served the Lord with great humility and with tears and in the midst of
severe testing by the plots of my Jewish
opponents.[p] 20You know that I have not
hesitated to preach anything[q] that would
be helpful to you but have taught you publicly and from house to house. 21I have declared to both Jews[r] and Greeks that they
must turn to God in repentance[s] and have
faith in our Lord Jesus.[t]
22"And now, compelled by the Spirit, I
am going to Jerusalem,[u] not knowing what
will happen to me there. 23I only know that
in every city the Holy Spirit warns me[v]
that prison and hardships are facing me.[w]
24However, I consider my life worth nothing to me;[x] my only aim is to finish the race
and complete the task[y] the Lord Jesus has
given me[z]—the task of testifying to the
good news of God's grace.
25"Now I know that none of you among
whom I have gone about preaching the
kingdom will ever see me again.[a] 26There-
fore, I declare to you today that I am innocent of the blood of any of you.[b] 27For I have
not hesitated to proclaim to you the whole
will of God.[c] 28Keep watch over yourselves
and all the flock of which the Holy Spirit has made you overseers.[d] Be shepherds
of the church of God,[a] which he bought
with his own blood.[b] 29I know that after I
leave, savage wolves[e] will come in among
you and will not spare the flock.[f] 30Even
from your own number men will arise and
distort the truth in order to draw away disciples[g] after them. 31So be on your guard!
Remember that for three years[h] I never
stopped warning each of you night and
day with tears.[i]
32"Now I commit you to God[j] and to the
word of his grace, which can build you up
and give you an inheritance[k] among all
those who are sanctified.[l] 33I have not coveted anyone's silver or gold or clothing.[m]
34You yourselves know that these hands of
mine have supplied my own needs and the
needs of my companions.[n] 35In everything
I did, I showed you that by this kind of hard
work we must help the weak, remembering
the words the Lord Jesus himself said: 'It is
more blessed to give than to receive.' "
36When Paul had finished speaking, he
knelt down with all of them and prayed.[o]

---

a 28 Many manuscripts *of the Lord* *b* 28 Or *with the blood of his own Son*

20:13–16 *going there on foot.* The distance between Troas and Assos was about thirty miles by sea, but Paul chose to go over land on foot.

20:17 *elders.* The words "elder" (literally, one who is older) and "overseer" (v. 28) appear to be used in the New Testament as interchangeable terms for the leaders of a particular fellowship.

20:22 *compelled by the spirit.* Some say that Paul was out of the will of God in going to Jerusalem after the warnings of bonds and afflictions. But there is no evidence that Paul was rebelling against God. On the contrary, Jesus Himself confirmed that the trip was part of His good and perfect will (23:11).

20:28 Church—The elders or overseers of God's flock must be men who are appointed not just by other men, but by the Holy Spirit of God. The leadership of the church is a solemn responsibility, and it should only be accepted by those who are convinced that they have been both called and equipped by the Holy Spirit to do this work. An elder has the responsibility to follow the example of our Chief Shepherd, Jesus Christ, as a servant leader.

20:35 *It is more blessed to give.* This saying of Jesus is not found in the Gospels, but it has been recorded here through Paul's knowledge of it.

20:8 [f] Ac 1:13 **20:10** [g] 1Ki 17:21; 2Ki 4:34 [h] Mt 9:23, 24 **20:11** [i] ver 7 **20:15** [j] ver 17; 2Ti 4:20 **20:16** [k] Ac 18:19 [l] Ac 19:21 [m] Ac 2:1; 1Co 16:8 **20:17** [n] Ac 11:30 **20:18** [o] Ac 18:19-21; 19:1-41 **20:19** [p] ver 3 **20:20** [q] ver 27 **20:21** [r] Ac 18:5 [s] Ac 2:38 [t] Ac 24:24; 26:18; Eph 1:15; Col 2:5; Phm 5 **20:22** [u] ver 16 **20:23** [v] Ac 21:4 [w] Ac 9:16 **20:24** [x] Ac 21:13 [y] 2Co 4:1 [z] Gal 1:1; Titus 1:3 **20:25** [a] ver 38 **20:26** [b] Ac 18:6 **20:27** [c] ver 20 **20:28** [d] 1Pe 5:2 **20:29** [e] Mt 7:15 [f] ver 28 **20:30** [g] Ac 11:26 **20:31** [h] Ac 19:10 [i] ver 19 **20:32** [j] Ac 14:23 [k] Eph 1:14; Col 1:12; 3:24; Heb 9:15; 1Pe 1:4 [l] Ac 26:18 **20:33** [m] 1Sa 12:3; 1Co 9:12; 2Co 7:2; 11:9; 12:14-17 **20:34** [n] Ac 18:3 **20:36** [o] Lk 22:41; Ac 21:5

37They all wept as they embraced him and
kissed him.[p] 38What grieved them most
was his statement that they would never
see his face again.[q] Then they accompanied him to the ship.

On to Jerusalem

21 After we[r] had torn ourselves away
from them, we put out to sea and
sailed straight to Kos. The next day we
went to Rhodes and from there to Patara.
2We found a ship crossing over to Phoenicia,[s] went on board and set sail. 3After
sighting Cyprus and passing to the south
of it, we sailed on to Syria. We landed at
Tyre, where our ship was to unload its cargo. 4We sought out the disciples[t] there and
stayed with them seven days. Through the
Spirit[u] they urged Paul not to go on to Jerusalem. 5When it was time to leave, we left
and continued on our way. All of them, including wives and children, accompanied
us out of the city, and there on the beach
we knelt to pray.[v] 6After saying goodbye to
each other, we went aboard the ship, and
they returned home.
7We continued our voyage from Tyre[w]
and landed at Ptolemais, where we greeted
the brothers and sisters[x] and stayed with
them for a day. 8Leaving the next day, we
reached Caesarea[y] and stayed at the house
of Philip[z] the evangelist,[a] one of the Sev-
en. 9He had four unmarried daughters who
prophesied.[b]
10After we had been there a number
of days, a prophet named Agabus[c] came
down from Judea. 11Coming over to us, he
took Paul's belt, tied his own hands and
feet with it and said, "The Holy Spirit says,
'In this way the Jewish leaders in Jerusalem will bind[d] the owner of this belt and
will hand him over to the Gentiles.'"[e]
12When we heard this, we and the people there pleaded with Paul not to go up to
Jerusalem. 13Then Paul answered, "Why
are you weeping and breaking my heart? I
am ready not only to be bound, but also to
die[f] in Jerusalem for the name of the Lord
Jesus."[g] 14When he would not be dissuad-
ed, we gave up and said, "The Lord's will
be done."
15After this, we started on our way up
to Jerusalem. 16Some of the disciples from
Caesarea[h] accompanied us and brought us
to the home of Mnason, where we were to
stay. He was a man from Cyprus[i] and one
of the early disciples.

Paul's Arrival at Jerusalem

17When we arrived at Jerusalem, the
brothers and sisters received us warmly.[j]
18The next day Paul and the rest of us went
to see James,[k] and all the elders[l] were present. 19Paul greeted them and reported in
detail what God had done among the Gentiles[m] through his ministry.[n]
20When they heard this, they praised
God. Then they said to Paul: "You see,
brother, how many thousands of Jews have
believed, and all of them are zealous[o] for
the law.[p] 21They have been informed that
you teach all the Jews who live among the
Gentiles to turn away from Moses,[q] telling them not to circumcise their children[r]
or live according to our customs.[s] 22What
shall we do? They will certainly hear that
you have come, 23so do what we tell you.
There are four men with us who have made
a vow.[t] 24Take these men, join in their purification rites[u] and pay their expenses,
so that they can have their heads shaved.[v]
Then everyone will know there is no truth
in these reports about you, but that you
yourself are living in obedience to the law.
25As for the Gentile believers, we have written to them our decision that they should
abstain from food sacrificed to idols, from
blood, from the meat of strangled animals
and from sexual immorality."[w]
26The next day Paul took the men and

21:2 *a ship crossing over to Phoenicia.* In the summer months, the wind of the Aegean Sea blows from the north, beginning very early in the morning. In the late afternoon the wind dies away. Sunset brings a dead calm, and later a gentle southerly breeze blows. If a ship was heading down the coast, it would typically anchor at evening and wait for the winds of the morning.

21:4 *Through the Spirit.* Because of this warning, many have thought that Paul's insistence in going to Jerusalem was disobedience to God's will. However, it is more likely that this was simply a warning to let him know what to expect in the future. Paul was obviously very sensitive to the Holy Spirit (16:6), and felt that he had received specific instructions to go to Jerusalem (20:22). Later Jesus Himself encouraged Paul concerning his decision to go (23:11).

21:10–14 *tied his own hands and feet.* The Holy Spirit did not forbid Paul to go to Jerusalem, but warned him of what it would cost him.

21:17 Fellowship—Fellowship means more than chatting over coffee and cookies, or sharing a potluck supper. Christian fellowship essentially means sharing one another's lives, participating in both the joy and sorrow of our brothers and sisters in Christ. Christian community extends beyond geography, class, color, and gender. As parts of one glorious whole, the body of Christ, believers rejoice in one another's joy, and reach out a helping hand for another's need.

21:25 *abstain from.* The spiritual unity of the body of believers is realized in its diversity, not in its conformity. From our diverse backgrounds and cultures we honor the same Lord.

20:37 [p] Lk 15:20 **20:38** [q] ver 25 **21:1** [r] Ac 16:10
21:2 [s] Ac 11:19 **21:4** [t] Ac 11:26 [u] ver 11; Ac 20:23
21:5 [v] Ac 20:36 **21:7** [w] Ac 12:20 [x] Ac 1:16
21:8 [y] Ac 8:40 [z] Ac 6:5; 8:5-40 [a] Eph 4:11; 2Ti 4:5
21:9 [b] Lk 2:36; Ac 2:17 **21:10** [c] Ac 11:28 **21:11** [d] ver 33
[e] 1Ki 22:11 **21:13** [f] Ac 20:24 [g] Ac 9:16 **21:16** [h] Ac 8:40
[i] ver 3,4 **21:17** [j] Ac 15:4 **21:18** [k] Ac 15:13 [l] Ac 11:30
21:19 [m] Ac 14:27 [n] Ac 1:17 **21:20** [o] Ac 22:3; Ro 10:2;
Gal 1:14 [p] Ac 15:1,5 **21:21** [q] ver 28 [r] Ac 15:19-21;
1Co 7:18, 19 [s] Ac 6:14 **21:23** [t] Ac 18:18 **21:24** [u] ver 26;
Ac 24:18 [v] Ac 18:18 **21:25** [w] Ac 15:20, 29

purified himself along with them. Then he
went to the temple to give notice of the date
when the days of purification would end
and the offering would be made for each
of them.[x]

Paul Arrested

27When the seven days were nearly over,
some Jews from the province of Asia saw
Paul at the temple. They stirred up the
whole crowd and seized him,[y] 28shouting,
"Fellow Israelites, help us! This is the man
who teaches everyone everywhere against
our people and our law and this place. And
besides, he has brought Greeks into the
temple and defiled this holy place."[z] 29(They
had previously seen Trophimus[a] the Ephesian[b] in the city with Paul and assumed that
Paul had brought him into the temple.)
30The whole city was aroused, and the
people came running from all directions.
Seizing Paul,[c] they dragged him[d] from the
temple, and immediately the gates were
shut. 31While they were trying to kill him,
news reached the commander of the Roman troops that the whole city of Jerusalem was in an uproar. 32He at once took
some officers and soldiers and ran down
to the crowd. When the rioters saw the
commander and his soldiers, they stopped
beating Paul.[e]
33The commander came up and arrested him and ordered him to be bound[f] with
two[g] chains.[h] Then he asked who he was
and what he had done. 34Some in the crowd
shouted one thing and some another,[i] and
since the commander could not get at the
truth because of the uproar, he ordered that
Paul be taken into the barracks.[j] 35When
Paul reached the steps,[k] the violence of
the mob was so great he had to be carried
by the soldiers. 36The crowd that followed
kept shouting, "Get rid of him!"[l]

Paul Speaks to the Crowd

37As the soldiers were about to take Paul
into the barracks,[m] he asked the commander, "May I say something to you?"
"Do you speak Greek?" he replied.
38"Aren't you the Egyptian who started a
revolt and led four thousand terrorists out
into the wilderness[n] some time ago?"[o]
39Paul answered, "I am a Jew, from Tarsus[p] in Cilicia,[q] a citizen of no ordinary
city. Please let me speak to the people."
40After receiving the commander's
permission, Paul stood on the steps and
motioned[r] to the crowd. When they were
all silent, he said to them in Aramaic[a];[s]

22 1"Brothers and fathers,[t] listen now to
my defense."
2When they heard him speak to them in
Aramaic,[u] they became very quiet.
Then Paul said: 3"I am a Jew,[v] born in
Tarsus[w] of Cilicia, but brought up in this
city. I studied under[x] Gamaliel[y] and was
thoroughly trained in the law of our ancestors.[z] I was just as zealous[a] for God as
any of you are today. 4I persecuted[b] the followers of this Way to their death, arresting
both men and women and throwing them
into prison,[c] 5as the high priest and all the
Council[d] can themselves testify. I even obtained letters from them to their associates[e] in Damascus,[f] and went there to bring
these people as prisoners to Jerusalem to
be punished.
6"About noon as I came near Damascus, suddenly a bright light from heaven
flashed around me.[g] 7I fell to the ground
and heard a voice say to me, 'Saul! Saul!
Why do you persecute me?'
8"'Who are you, Lord?' I asked.
"'I am Jesus of Nazareth, whom you are
persecuting,' he replied. 9My companions
saw the light,[h] but they did not understand
the voice[i] of him who was speaking to me.
10"'What shall I do, Lord?' I asked.
"'Get up,' the Lord said, 'and go into
Damascus. There you will be told all that
you have been assigned to do.'[j] 11My companions led me by the hand into Damascus, because the brilliance of the light had
blinded me.[k]
12"A man named Ananias came to see
me.[l] He was a devout observer of the law
and highly respected by all the Jews living
there.[m] 13He stood beside me and said,

[a] 40 Or possibly *Hebrew*; also in 22:2

21:28 *defiled this holy place.* The temple in New Testament times was surrounded by three courts. The innermost court was the court of Israel, where Jewish men could offer sacrifices. The second court was the court of Women where Jewish families could gather for prayer and worship. The outer court was the court of Gentiles, open to all who would worship God. The penalty for any Gentile who went beyond this court was death.

21:38 *Aren't you the Egyptian.* An assassin claiming to be a prophet had come to Jerusalem in A.D. 54, and led four thousand Jews up to the Mount of Olives, promising that at his word the walls of Jerusalem would fall and the Roman Empire would be destroyed. The uprising was crushed, leaving four hundred Jews dead and another two hundred as prisoners. The Egyptian escaped into the desert with some of his followers.

21:26 [x] Nu 6:13-20; Ac 24:18 **21:27** [y] Ac 24:18; 26:21
21:28 [z] Mt 24:15; Ac 24:5,6 **21:29** [a] Ac 20:4 [b] Ac 18:19
21:30 [c] Ac 26:21 [d] Ac 16:19 **21:32** [e] Ac 23:27
21:33 [f] ver 11 [g] Ac 12:6 [h] Ac 20:23; Eph 6:20; 2Ti 2:9
21:34 [i] Ac 19:32 [j] ver 37; Ac 23:10,16,32 **21:35** [k] ver 40
21:36 [l] Lk 23:18; Jn 19:15; Ac 22:22 **21:37** [m] ver 34
21:38 [n] Mt 24:26 [o] Ac 5:36 **21:39** [p] Ac 9:11 [q] Ac 22:3
21:40 [r] Ac 12:17 [s] Jn 5:2 **22:1** [t] Ac 7:2 **22:2** [u] Ac 21:40
22:3 [v] Ac 21:39 [w] Ac 9:11 [x] Lk 10:39 [y] Ac 5:34 [z] Ac 26:5
[a] Ac 21:20 **22:4** [b] Ac 8:3 [c] ver 19,20 **22:5** [d] Lk 22:66
[e] Ac 13:26 [f] Ac 9:2 **22:6** [g] Ac 9:3 **22:9** [h] Ac 26:13
[i] Ac 9:7 **22:10** [j] Ac 16:30 **22:11** [k] Ac 9:8
22:12 [l] Ac 9:17 [m] Ac 10:22

'Brother Saul, receive your sight!' And at
that very moment I was able to see him.
14“Then he said: 'The God of our ancestors[n] has chosen you to know his will and
to see[o] the Righteous One[p] and to hear
words from his mouth. 15You will be his
witness[q] to all people of what you have
seen and heard. 16And now what are you
waiting for? Get up, be baptized[r] and wash
your sins away,[s] calling on his name.'[t]
17“When I returned to Jerusalem[u] and
was praying at the temple, I fell into a
trance[v] 18and saw the Lord speaking to
me. 'Quick!' he said. 'Leave Jerusalem immediately, because the people here will not
accept your testimony about me.'
19“ 'Lord,' I replied, 'these people know
that I went from one synagogue to another
to imprison[w] and beat[x] those who believe in
you. 20And when the blood of your martyr[a]
Stephen was shed, I stood there giving my
approval and guarding the clothes of those
who were killing him.'[y]
21“Then the Lord said to me, 'Go; I will
send you far away to the Gentiles.' ”[z]

Paul the Roman Citizen

22The crowd listened to Paul until he
said this. Then they raised their voices and
shouted, “Rid the earth of him![a] He's not
fit to live!”[b]
23As they were shouting and throwing
off their cloaks[c] and flinging dust into the
air,[d] 24the commander ordered that Paul be
taken into the barracks.[e] He directed[f] that
he be flogged and interrogated in order
to find out why the people were shouting
at him like this. 25As they stretched him
out to flog him, Paul said to the centurion
standing there, “Is it legal for you to flog a
Roman citizen who hasn't even been found
guilty?”[g]
26When the centurion heard this, he went
to the commander and reported it. “What
are you going to do?” he asked. “This man
is a Roman citizen.”
27The commander went to Paul and
asked, “Tell me, are you a Roman citizen?”
“Yes, I am,” he answered.
28Then the commander said, “I had to
pay a lot of money for my citizenship.”
“But I was born a citizen,” Paul replied.
29Those who were about to interrogate
him withdrew immediately. The commander himself was alarmed when he realized that he had put Paul, a Roman citizen,[h] in chains.

Paul Before the Sanhedrin

30The commander wanted to find out exactly why Paul was being accused by the
Jews.[i] So the next day he released him[j] and
ordered the chief priests and all the members of the Sanhedrin[k] to assemble. Then
he brought Paul and had him stand before
them.
23 Paul looked straight at the Sanhedrin[l] and said, “My brothers,[m] I have
fulfilled my duty to God in all good conscience[n] to this day.” 2At this the high priest
Ananias[o] ordered those standing near
Paul to strike him on the mouth.[p] 3Then
Paul said to him, “God will strike you, you
whitewashed wall![q] You sit there to judge
me according to the law, yet you yourself
violate the law by commanding that I be
struck!”[r]
4Those who were standing near Paul
said, “How dare you insult God's high
priest!”
5Paul replied, “Brothers, I did not realize
that he was the high priest; for it is written:
'Do not speak evil about the ruler of your
people.'[b]”[s]
6Then Paul, knowing that some of them
were Sadducees and the others Pharisees,
called out in the Sanhedrin, “My brothers,[t]
I am a Pharisee,[u] descended from Pharisees. I stand on trial because of the hope

[a] 20 Or *witness* [b] 5 Exodus 22:28

22:16 *calling on his name.* Calling on the name of the Lord is what brings salvation, not the physical act of baptism (Rom. 10:9 – 13). Baptism is the public declaration of one's repentance and new life.

22:24 *flogged.* Soldiers commonly flogged prisoners with a leather whip, studded with pieces of metal or bone, fastened to a wooden handle. The victim was stretched out on the floor or bound to a pillar to be beaten. Flogging was a cruel torture, designed to maim or kill the victim.

22:28 *born a citizen.* Roman citizenship was originally limited to free Romans, but later it was offered to many others in the empire, either as a reward for outstanding service, or in exchange for a high price. Because Paul's father was a Roman citizen (how he became a citizen is unknown), Paul was born a citizen. Ultimately, God used Paul's Roman citizenship to spread the gospel to Rome.

23:1 Conscience—The human conscience is given as a tool, enabling us to tell right from wrong, and to evaluate our own actions. The problem is that the conscience of fallen humans is not a reliable guide. Because humans are not "basically good," an untrained conscience will not necessarily lead toward right. The conscience must be trained by good teaching. It can be rendered useless if it is seared or defiled, it can be deadened by constantly ignoring it. In order to provide useful guidance, the conscience must be recharged by the Holy Spirit. It must be kept clear by confession of sins, and refusing to accept violations.

22:14 [n] Ac 3:13 [o] 1Co 9:1; 15:8 [p] Ac 7:52 **22:15** [q] Ac 23:11; 26:16 **22:16** [r] Ac 2:38 [s] Heb 10:22 [t] Ro 10:13 **22:17** [u] Ac 9:26 [v] Ac 10:10 **22:19** [w] ver 4; Ac 8:3 [x] Mt 10:17 **22:20** [y] Ac 7:57-60; 8:1 **22:21** [z] Ac 9:15; 13:46 **22:22** [a] Ac 21:36 [b] Ac 25:24 **22:23** [c] Ac 7:58 [d] 2Sa 16:13 **22:24** [e] Ac 21:34 [f] ver 29 **22:25** [g] Ac 16:37 **22:29** [h] ver 24, 25; Ac 16:38 **22:30** [i] Ac 23:28 [j] Ac 21:33 [k] Mt 5:22 **23:1** [l] Ac 22:30 [m] Ac 22:5 [n] Ac 24:16; 1Co 4:4; 2Co 1:12; 2Ti 1:3; Heb 13:18 **23:2** [o] Ac 24:1 [p] Jn 18:22 **23:3** [q] Mt 23:27 [r] Lev 19:15; Dt 25:1, 2; Jn 7:51 **23:5** [s] Ex 22:28 **23:6** [t] Ac 22:5 [u] Ac 26:5; Php 3:5

of the resurrection of the dead."[v] 7When
he said this, a dispute broke out between
the Pharisees and the Sadducees, and the
assembly was divided. 8(The Sadducees
say that there is no resurrection,[w] and that
there are neither angels nor spirits, but the
Pharisees believe all these things.)

9There was a great uproar, and some of
the teachers of the law who were Pharisees[x] stood up and argued vigorously. "We
find nothing wrong with this man,"[y] they
said. "What if a spirit or an angel has spoken to him?"[z] 10The dispute became so violent that the commander was afraid Paul
would be torn to pieces by them. He ordered the troops to go down and take him
away from them by force and bring him
into the barracks.[a]

11The following night the Lord stood
near Paul and said, "Take courage![b] As
you have testified about me in Jerusalem,
so you must also testify in Rome."[c]

The Plot to Kill Paul

12The next morning some Jews formed
a conspiracy and bound themselves with
an oath not to eat or drink until they had
killed Paul.[d] 13More than forty men were
involved in this plot. 14They went to the
chief priests and the elders and said, "We
have taken a solemn oath not to eat anything until we have killed Paul.[e] 15Now
then, you and the Sanhedrin[f] petition the
commander to bring him before you on
the pretext of wanting more accurate information about his case. We are ready to
kill him before he gets here."

16But when the son of Paul's sister heard
of this plot, he went into the barracks[g] and
told Paul.

17Then Paul called one of the centurions
and said, "Take this young man to the commander; he has something to tell him." 18So
he took him to the commander.

The centurion said, "Paul, the prisoner,[h] sent for me and asked me to bring this
young man to you because he has something to tell you."

19The commander took the young man
by the hand, drew him aside and asked,
"What is it you want to tell me?"

20He said: "Some Jews have agreed to
ask you to bring Paul before the Sanhedrin[i]
tomorrow on the pretext of wanting more
accurate information about him.[j] 21Don't
give in to them, because more than forty[k] of
them are waiting in ambush for him. They
have taken an oath not to eat or drink until
they have killed him.[l] They are ready now,
waiting for your consent to their request."

22The commander dismissed the young
man with this warning: "Don't tell anyone
that you have reported this to me."

Paul Transferred to Caesarea

23Then he called two of his centurions
and ordered them, "Get ready a detachment of two hundred soldiers, seventy
horsemen and two hundred spearmen[a] to
go to Caesarea[m] at nine tonight.[n] 24Provide
horses for Paul so that he may be taken
safely to Governor Felix."[o]

25He wrote a letter as follows:

26Claudius Lysias,

To His Excellency,[p] Governor Felix:

Greetings.[q]

27This man was seized by the Jews
and they were about to kill him,[r] but
I came with my troops and rescued
him,[s] for I had learned that he is a Roman citizen.[t] 28I wanted to know why
they were accusing him, so I brought
him to their Sanhedrin.[u] 29I found that
the accusation had to do with questions about their law,[v] but there was
no charge against him[w] that deserved
death or imprisonment. 30When I was
informed[x] of a plot[y] to be carried out
against the man, I sent him to you at
once. I also ordered his accusers[z] to
present to you their case against him.

31So the soldiers, carrying out their orders, took Paul with them during the night
and brought him as far as Antipatris. 32The
next day they let the cavalry[a] go on with
him, while they returned to the barracks.[b]
33When the cavalry[c] arrived in Caesarea,[d]
they delivered the letter to the governor[e]
and handed Paul over to him. 34The governor read the letter and asked what province

[a] *23* The meaning of the Greek for this word is uncertain.

23:11 *testify in Rome.* Because of the earlier warnings of his friends (21:4,10–14), Paul may have begun to doubt his decision. The Lord gave Paul special encouragement at this time, that he was indeed doing just what God wanted him to do.

23:33 *the governor.* Antonius Felix governed Judea from A.D. 52 to 60. Felix had been a slave, but had gained the status of freedman under the emperor Claudius. Because Felix's brother was a friend of the emperor, Felix's political career blossomed, even though he was not popular among his peers. The writer Tacitus described him as "exercising the powers of a king with the character of a slave."

23:6 [v] Ac 24:15,21; 26:8 **23:8** [w] Mt 22:23
23:9 [x] Mk 2:16 [y] ver 29; Ac 25:25; 26:31 [z] Ac 22:7, 17, 18
23:10 [a] Ac 21:34 **23:11** [b] Ac 18:9 [c] Ac 19:21; 28:23
23:12 [d] ver 14, 21, 30; Ac 25:3 **23:14** [e] ver 12
23:15 [f] ver 1; Ac 22:30 **23:16** [g] ver 10; Ac 21:34
23:18 [h] Eph 3:1 **23:20** [i] ver 1 [j] ver 14, 15
23:21 [k] ver 13 [l] ver 12, 14 **23:23** [m] Ac 8:40 [n] ver 33
23:24 [o] ver 26, 33; Ac 24:1-3, 10; 25:14 **23:26** [p] Lk 1:3; Ac 24:3; 26:25 [q] Ac 15:23 **23:27** [r] Ac 21:32 [s] Ac 21:33 [t] Ac 22:25-29 **23:28** [u] Ac 22:30 **23:29** [v] Ac 18:15; 25:19 [w] ver 9; Ac 26:31 **23:30** [x] ver 20, 21 [y] Ac 20:3 [z] ver 35; Ac 24:19; 25:16 **23:32** [a] ver 23 [b] Ac 21:34
23:33 [c] ver 23, 24 [d] Ac 8:40 [e] ver 26

he was from. Learning that he was from
Cilicia,[f] [35]he said, "I will hear your case
when your accusers[g] get here." Then he
ordered that Paul be kept under guard[h] in
Herod's palace.

Paul's Trial Before Felix

24 Five days later the high priest Ananias[i] went down to Caesarea with some
of the elders and a lawyer named Tertullus, and they brought their charges[j] against
Paul before the governor.[k] [2]When Paul was
called in, Tertullus presented his case before Felix: "We have enjoyed a long period
of peace under you, and your foresight has
brought about reforms in this nation. [3]Ev-
erywhere and in every way, most excellent[l]
Felix, we acknowledge this with profound
gratitude. [4]But in order not to weary you
further, I would request that you be kind
enough to hear us briefly.

[5]"We have found this man to be a troublemaker, stirring up riots[m] among the
Jews[n] all over the world. He is a ringleader
of the Nazarene[o] sect[p] [6]and even tried to
desecrate the temple;[q] so we seized him.
[7][a] [8]By examining him yourself you will
be able to learn the truth about all these
charges we are bringing against him."

[9]The other Jews joined in the accusation,[r] asserting that these things were true.

[10]When the governor[s] motioned for him
to speak, Paul replied: "I know that for a
number of years you have been a judge
over this nation; so I gladly make my defense. [11]You can easily verify that no more
than twelve days[t] ago I went up to Jerusalem to worship. [12]My accusers did not find
me arguing with anyone at the temple,[u] or
stirring up a crowd[v] in the synagogues or
anywhere else in the city. [13]And they cannot prove to you the charges they are now
making against me.[w] [14]However, I admit
that I worship the God of our ancestors[x] as
a follower of the Way,[y] which they call a
sect.[z] I believe everything that is in accordance with the Law and that is written in
the Prophets,[a] [15]and I have the same hope
in God as these men themselves have, that
there will be a resurrection[b] of both the
righteous and the wicked.[c] [16]So I strive always to keep my conscience clear[d] before
God and man.

[17]"After an absence of several years, I
came to Jerusalem to bring my people gifts
for the poor[e] and to present offerings. [18]I
was ceremonially clean[f] when they found
me in the temple courts doing this. There
was no crowd with me, nor was I involved
in any disturbance.[g] [19]But there are some
Jews from the province of Asia, who ought
to be here before you and bring charges if
they have anything against me.[h] [20]Or these
who are here should state what crime they
found in me when I stood before the Sanhedrin— [21]unless it was this one thing I
shouted as I stood in their presence: 'It is
concerning the resurrection of the dead
that I am on trial before you today.'"[i]

[22]Then Felix, who was well acquainted
with the Way, adjourned the proceedings.
"When Lysias the commander comes," he
said, "I will decide your case." [23]He ordered
the centurion to keep Paul under guard[j] but
to give him some freedom[k] and permit his
friends to take care of his needs.[l]

[24]Several days later Felix came with his
wife Drusilla, who was Jewish. He sent for
Paul and listened to him as he spoke about
faith in Christ Jesus.[m] [25]As Paul talked
about righteousness, self-control[n] and the
judgment[o] to come, Felix was afraid and
said, "That's enough for now! You may
leave. When I find it convenient, I will send
for you." [26]At the same time he was hoping
that Paul would offer him a bribe, so he sent
for him frequently and talked with him.

[27]When two years had passed, Felix was
succeeded by Porcius Festus,[p] but because

---

[a] 6-8 Some manuscripts include here *him, and we would have judged him in accordance with our law. [7]But the commander Lysias came and took him from us with much violence, [8]ordering his accusers to come before you.*

24:14 *the Way.* Paul openly admitted that he was a follower of "the Way" (those who followed Jesus), but he contended that he still believed the Law and the Prophets. That is, he was a follower of Judaism, a religion which enjoyed the protection of Rome.

24:16 Conscience—There is a connection between Paul's belief in future judgment and his desire to maintain a clear conscience before God and man. The intensity of Paul's desire may be seen from the verb translated "strive," which occurs only here in the New Testament. Paul's desire to have a good conscience toward God and man reflects the summary of duties of the law of love toward God and neighbor. The conscience needs to be enlightened and purified by Scripture in regard to our responsibilities toward God and man.

24:22 *who was well acquainted with the Way.* Felix's wife Drusilla was Jewish, and part of the Herodian family. Felix had governed Judea and Samaria for six years. He had ample opportunity to understand both Judaism and "the Way" as he must have observed the workings of the early church in Jerusalem.

24:27 *When two years had passed.* Around A.D. 60, a riot broke out in Caesarea. Felix crushed it with such force that he was removed from office.

23:34 [f] Ac 6:9; 21:39 **23:35** [g] ver 30; Ac 24:19; 25:16 [h] Ac 24:27 **24:1** [i] Ac 23:2 [j] Ac 23:30,35 [k] Ac 23:24 **24:3** [l] Lk 1:3; Ac 23:26; 26:25 **24:5** [m] Ac 16:20; 17:6 [n] Ac 21:28 [o] Mk 1:24 [p] ver 14; Ac 26:5; 28:22 **24:6** [q] Ac 21:28 **24:9** [r] 1Th 2:16 **24:10** [s] Ac 23:24 **24:11** [t] Ac 21:27; ver 1 **24:12** [u] Ac 25:8; 28:17 [v] ver 18 **24:13** [w] Ac 25:7 **24:14** [x] Ac 3:13 [y] Ac 9:2 [z] ver 5 [a] Ac 26:6,22; 28:23 **24:15** [b] Ac 23:6; 28:20 [c] Da 12:2; Jn 5:28,29 **24:16** [d] Ac 23:1 **24:17** [e] Ac 11:29,30; Ro 15:25-28,31; 1Co 16:1-4,15; 2Co 8:1-4; Gal 2:10 **24:18** [f] Ac 21:26 [g] ver 12 **24:19** [h] Ac 23:30 **24:21** [i] Ac 23:6 **24:23** [j] Ac 23:35 [k] Ac 28:16 [l] Ac 23:16; 27:3 **24:24** [m] Ac 20:21 **24:25** [n] Gal 5:23; 2Pe 1:6 [o] Ac 10:42 **24:27** [p] Ac 25:1,4,9,14

Felix wanted to grant a favor to the Jews,[q] he left Paul in prison.[r]

Paul's Trial Before Festus

25 Three days after arriving in the province, Festus went up from Caesarea[s] to Jerusalem, 2where the chief priests and the Jewish leaders appeared before him and presented the charges against Paul.[t] 3They requested Festus, as a favor to them, to have Paul transferred to Jerusalem, for they were preparing an ambush to kill him along the way. 4Festus answered, "Paul is being held[u] at Caesarea, and I myself am going there soon. 5Let some of your leaders come with me, and if the man has done anything wrong, they can press charges against him there."

6After spending eight or ten days with them, Festus went down to Caesarea. The next day he convened the court[v] and ordered that Paul be brought before him. 7When Paul came in, the Jews who had come down from Jerusalem stood around him. They brought many serious charges against him,[w] but they could not prove them.[x]

8Then Paul made his defense: "I have done nothing wrong against the Jewish law or against the temple[y] or against Caesar."

9Festus, wishing to do the Jews a favor,[z] said to Paul, "Are you willing to go up to Jerusalem and stand trial before me there on these charges?"[a]

10Paul answered: "I am now standing before Caesar's court, where I ought to be tried. I have not done any wrong to the Jews, as you yourself know very well. 11If, however, I am guilty of doing anything deserving death, I do not refuse to die. But if the charges brought against me by these Jews are not true, no one has the right to hand me over to them. I appeal to Caesar!"[b]

12After Festus had conferred with his council, he declared: "You have appealed to Caesar. To Caesar you will go!"

Festus Consults King Agrippa

13A few days later King Agrippa and Bernice arrived at Caesarea[c] to pay their respects to Festus. 14Since they were spending many days there, Festus discussed Paul's case with the king. He said: "There is a man here whom Felix left as a prisoner.[d] 15When I went to Jerusalem, the chief priests and the elders of the Jews brought charges against him[e] and asked that he be condemned.

16"I told them that it is not the Roman custom to hand over anyone before they have faced their accusers and have had an opportunity to defend themselves against the charges.[f] 17When they came here with me, I did not delay the case, but convened the court the next day and ordered the man to be brought in.[g] 18When his accusers got up to speak, they did not charge him with any of the crimes I had expected. 19Instead, they had some points of dispute[h] with him about their own religion[i] and about a dead man named Jesus who Paul claimed was alive. 20I was at a loss how to investigate such matters; so I asked if he would be willing to go to Jerusalem and stand trial there on these charges.[j] 21But when Paul made his appeal to be held over for the Emperor's decision, I ordered him held until I could send him to Caesar."[k]

22Then Agrippa said to Festus, "I would like to hear this man myself."

He replied, "Tomorrow you will hear him."[l]

Paul Before Agrippa

23The next day Agrippa and Bernice[m] came with great pomp and entered the audience room with the high-ranking military officers and the prominent men of the city. At the command of Festus, Paul was brought in. 24Festus said: "King Agrippa, and all who are present with us, you see this man! The whole Jewish community[n] has petitioned me about him in Jerusalem and here in Caesarea, shouting that he ought not to live any longer.[o] 25I found he had done nothing deserving of death,[p] but because he made his appeal to the Emperor[q] I decided to send him to Rome. 26But I have nothing definite to write to His Majesty about him. Therefore I have brought him before all of you, and especially before you, King Agrippa, so that as a result of this investigation I may have something to write. 27For I think it is unreasonable to send a prisoner on to Rome without specifying the charges against him."

26 Then Agrippa said to Paul, "You have permission to speak for yourself."[r]

So Paul motioned with his hand and began his defense: 2"King Agrippa, I consider myself fortunate to stand before you today as I make my defense against all the

---

25:11 ***appeal to Caesar.*** If a Roman citizen thought he was not getting justice in a provincial court, he could appeal to the emperor himself. If the appeal was declared valid, all other proceedings in the lower courts ceased and the prisoner was sent to Rome for the disposition of his case.

24:27 [q] Ac 12:3; 25:9 [r] Ac 23:35; 25:14 **25:1** [s] Ac 8:40 **25:2** [t] ver 15; Ac 24:1 **25:4** [u] Ac 24:23 **25:6** [v] ver 17

25:7 [w] Mk 15:3; Lk 23:2, 10; Ac 24:5, 6 [x] Ac 24:13 **25:8** [y] Ac 6:13; 24:12; 28:17 **25:9** [z] Ac 24:27 [a] ver 20 **25:11** [b] ver 21, 25; Ac 26:32; 28:19 **25:13** [c] Ac 8:40 **25:14** [d] Ac 24:27 **25:15** [e] ver 2; Ac 24:1 **25:16** [f] ver 4, 5; Ac 23:30 **25:17** [g] ver 6, 10 **25:19** [h] Ac 18:15; 23:29 [i] Ac 17:22 **25:20** [j] ver 9 **25:21** [k] ver 11, 12 **25:22** [l] Ac 9:15 **25:23** [m] ver 13; Ac 26:30 **25:24** [n] ver 2, 3, 7 [o] Ac 22:22 **25:25** [p] Ac 23:9 [q] ver 11 **26:1** [r] Ac 9:15; 25:22

accusations of the Jews, 3and especially so
because you are well acquainted with all the
Jewish customs[s] and controversies.[t] Therefore, I beg you to listen to me patiently.
4"The Jewish people all know the way I
have lived ever since I was a child,[u] from
the beginning of my life in my own country, and also in Jerusalem. 5They have
known me for a long time[v] and can testify, if they are willing, that I conformed to
the strictest sect of our religion, living as
a Pharisee.[w] 6And now it is because of my
hope[x] in what God has promised our ancestors[y] that I am on trial today. 7This is
the promise our twelve tribes[z] are hoping
to see fulfilled as they earnestly serve God
day and night.[a] King Agrippa, it is because
of this hope that these Jews are accusing
me.[b] 8Why should any of you consider it
incredible that God raises the dead?[c]
9"I too was convinced[d] that I ought to do
all that was possible to oppose[e] the name of
Jesus of Nazareth.[f] 10And that is just what
I did in Jerusalem. On the authority of the
chief priests I put many of the Lord's people[g] in prison,[h] and when they were put to
death, I cast my vote against them.[i] 11Many
a time I went from one synagogue to another to have them punished,[j] and I tried to
force them to blaspheme. I was so obsessed
with persecuting them that I even hunted
them down in foreign cities.
12"On one of these journeys I was going
to Damascus with the authority and commission of the chief priests. 13About noon,
King Agrippa, as I was on the road, I saw
a light from heaven, brighter than the sun,
blazing around me and my companions.
14We all fell to the ground, and I heard a
voice[k] saying to me in Aramaic,[a] 'Saul,
Saul, why do you persecute me? It is hard
for you to kick against the goads.'
15"Then I asked, 'Who are you, Lord?'
"'I am Jesus, whom you are persecuting,'
the Lord replied. 16'Now get up and stand
on your feet.[l] I have appeared to you to appoint you as a servant and as a witness of
what you have seen and will see of me.[m]
17I will rescue you[n] from your own people
and from the Gentiles.[o] I am sending you
to them 18to open their eyes[p] and turn them
from darkness to light,[q] and from the power of Satan to God, so that they may receive
forgiveness of sins[r] and a place among
those who are sanctified by faith in me.'[s]
19"So then, King Agrippa, I was not disobedient to the vision from heaven. 20First
to those in Damascus,[t] then to those in Jerusalem[u] and in all Judea, and then to the
Gentiles,[v] I preached that they should repent[w] and turn to God and demonstrate
their repentance by their deeds.[x] 21That is
why some Jews seized me[y] in the temple
courts and tried to kill me.[z] 22But God has
helped me to this very day; so I stand here
and testify to small and great alike. I am
saying nothing beyond what the prophets
and Moses said would happen[a]— 23that the
Messiah would suffer and, as the first to rise
from the dead,[b] would bring the message of
light to his own people and to the Gentiles."[c]
24At this point Festus interrupted Paul's
defense. "You are out of your mind,[d] Paul!"
he shouted. "Your great learning[e] is driving you insane."
25"I am not insane, most excellent[f] Festus," Paul replied. "What I am saying is
true and reasonable. 26The king is familiar
with these things,[g] and I can speak freely
to him. I am convinced that none of this has
escaped his notice, because it was not done
in a corner. 27King Agrippa, do you believe
the prophets? I know you do."
28Then Agrippa said to Paul, "Do you
think that in such a short time you can persuade me to be a Christian?"[h]
29Paul replied, "Short time or long—I
pray to God that not only you but all who
are listening to me today may become what
I am, except for these chains."[i]

---

[a] 14 Or *Hebrew*

26:5 *living as a Pharisee.* Paul was not some stranger or foreigner trying to start a new religion. He was a Jew, and a member of the religious body which took God's law most seriously.

26:6–7 Hope—Paul faced a real paradox in his trial before Agrippa. He had been a faithful Pharisee, looking forward to the fulfillment of their common hope, the coming of the Messiah, and eventually the resurrection of the dead. Now that the Messiah had come, and Paul began proclaiming the truth of His atonement and resurrection, he was being persecuted by the very ones who had once shared his hope.

26:20 *that they should repent.* Repentance indicates a complete change in thinking, an "about face" of the mind and heart. Genuine repentance is evidenced by changed behavior.

26:22–23 Christ—Paul makes it clear that Jesus stood firmly in the tradition of the Hebrew Law and Prophets, and specifically identifies Him as the promised Messiah. The suffering and death of the Messiah were ordained by God and proclaimed by His prophets. The resurrection of Jesus provided evidence of the control God was exercising over the process of redemption. This triumphant event removed the purely local and national character of Christ's work, and gave His message of salvation worldwide dimensions, as had been prophesied (Is. 60:3; Mal. 1:11).

26:3 [s] ver 7; Ac 6:14 [t] Ac 25:19 **26:4** [u] Gal 1:13, 14; Php 3:5 **26:5** [v] Ac 22:3 [w] Ac 23:6; Php 3:5 **26:6** [x] Ac 23:6; 24:15; 28:20 [y] Ac 13:32; Ro 15:8 **26:7** [z] Jas 1:1 [a] 1Th 3:10; 1Ti 5:5 [b] ver 2 **26:8** [c] Ac 23:6 **26:9** [d] 1Ti 1:13 [e] Jn 16:2 [f] Jn 15:21 **26:10** [g] Ac 9:13 [h] Ac 8:3; 9:2, 14, 21 [i] Ac 22:20 **26:11** [j] Mt 10:17 **26:14** [k] Ac 9:7 **26:16** [l] Eze 2:1; Da 10:11 [m] Ac 22:14, 15 **26:17** [n] Jer 1:8, 19 [o] Ac 9:15 **26:18** [p] Isa 35:5 [q] Isa 42:7, 16; Eph 5:8; Col 1:13; 1Pe 2:9 [r] Lk 24:47; Ac 2:38 [s] Ac 20:21, 32 **26:20** [t] Ac 9:19-25 [u] Ac 9:26-29; 22:17-20 [v] Ac 9:15; 13:46 [w] Ac 3:19 [x] Mt 3:8; Lk 3:8 **26:21** [y] Ac 21:27, 30 [z] Ac 21:31 **26:22** [a] Lk 24:27, 44; Ac 10:43; 24:14 **26:23** [b] 1Co 15:20, 23; Col 1:18; Rev 1:5 [c] Lk 2:32 **26:24** [d] Jn 10:20; 1Co 4:10 [e] Jn 7:15 **26:25** [f] Ac 23:26 **26:26** [g] ver 3 **26:28** [h] Ac 11:26 **26:29** [i] Ac 21:33

30The king rose, and with him the governor and Bernice[j] and those sitting with
them. 31After they left the room, they began saying to one another, "This man is
not doing anything that deserves death or
imprisonment."[k]
32Agrippa said to Festus, "This man
could have been set free[l] if he had not appealed to Caesar."[m]

Paul Sails for Rome

27 When it was decided that we[n] would
sail for Italy,[o] Paul and some other
prisoners were handed over to a centurion
named Julius, who belonged to the Imperial Regiment.[p] 2We boarded a ship from
Adramyttium about to sail for ports along
the coast of the province of Asia,[q] and we
put out to sea. Aristarchus,[r] a Macedonian[s]
from Thessalonica,[t] was with us.
3The next day we landed at Sidon;[u] and
Julius, in kindness to Paul,[v] allowed him
to go to his friends so they might provide
for his needs.[w] 4From there we put out to
sea again and passed to the lee of Cyprus
because the winds were against us.[x] 5When
we had sailed across the open sea off the
coast of Cilicia[y] and Pamphylia, we landed at Myra in Lycia. 6There the centurion
found an Alexandrian ship[z] sailing for Italy[a] and put us on board. 7We made slow
headway for many days and had difficulty arriving off Cnidus. When the wind did
not allow us to hold our course,[b] we sailed
to the lee of Crete,[c] opposite Salmone. 8We
moved along the coast with difficulty and
came to a place called Fair Havens, near
the town of Lasea.
9Much time had been lost, and sailing
had already become dangerous because by
now it was after the Day of Atonement.[a][d]
So Paul warned them, 10"Men, I can see
that our voyage is going to be disastrous
and bring great loss to ship and cargo, and
to our own lives also."[e] 11But the centurion, instead of listening to what Paul said,
followed the advice of the pilot and of the
owner of the ship. 12Since the harbor was
unsuitable to winter in, the majority decided that we should sail on, hoping to reach
Phoenix and winter there. This was a harbor in Crete, facing both southwest and
northwest.

The Storm

13When a gentle south wind began to
blow, they saw their opportunity; so they
weighed anchor and sailed along the
shore of Crete. 14Before very long, a wind
of hurricane force,[f] called the Northeast-
er, swept down from the island. 15The ship
was caught by the storm and could not
head into the wind; so we gave way to it
and were driven along. 16As we passed to
the lee of a small island called Cauda, we
were hardly able to make the lifeboat secure, 17so the men hoisted it aboard. Then
they passed ropes under the ship itself to
hold it together. Because they were afraid
they would run aground[g] on the sandbars
of Syrtis, they lowered the sea anchor[b] and
let the ship be driven along. 18We took such
a violent battering from the storm that the
next day they began to throw the cargo
overboard.[h] 19On the third day, they threw
the ship's tackle overboard with their own
hands. 20When neither sun nor stars appeared for many days and the storm continued raging, we finally gave up all hope
of being saved.
21After they had gone a long time without food, Paul stood up before them and
said: "Men, you should have taken my advice[i] not to sail from Crete;[j] then you would
have spared yourselves this damage and
loss. 22But now I urge you to keep up your
courage,[k] because not one of you will be
lost; only the ship will be destroyed. 23Last
night an angel[l] of the God to whom I belong
and whom I serve[m] stood beside me[n] 24and
said, 'Do not be afraid, Paul. You must
stand trial before Caesar;[o] and God has
graciously given you the lives of all who
sail with you.'[p] 25So keep up your courage,[q]
men, for I have faith in God that it will happen just as he told me.[r] 26Nevertheless, we
must run aground[s] on some island."[t]

The Shipwreck

27On the fourteenth night we were still
being driven across the Adriatic[c] Sea,
when about midnight the sailors sensed
they were approaching land. 28They took
soundings and found that the water was
a hundred and twenty feet[d] deep. A short
time later they took soundings again and
found it was ninety feet[e] deep. 29Fearing
that we would be dashed against the rocks,
they dropped four anchors from the stern
and prayed for daylight. 30In an attempt to

[a] 9 That is, Yom Kippur [b] 17 Or *the sails*
[c] 27 In ancient times the name referred to an area extending well south of Italy. [d] 28 Or about 37 meters [e] 28 Or about 27 meters

27:4 *the winds were against us.* This happened just before the winter storms increased, and sailing became difficult. Paul was being sent to Rome by ship at the worst time of year for sailing.

26:30 [j] Ac 25:23 **26:31** [k] Ac 23:9 **26:32** [l] Ac 28:18 [m] Ac 25:11 **27:1** [n] Ac 16:10 [o] Ac 18:2; 25:12,25 [p] Ac 10:1 **27:2** [q] Ac 2:9 [r] Ac 19:29 [s] Ac 16:9 [t] Ac 17:1

27:3 [u] Mt 11:21 [v] ver 43 [w] Ac 24:23; 28:16 **27:4** [x] ver 7 **27:5** [y] Ac 6:9 **27:6** [z] Ac 28:11 [a] ver 1 **27:7** [b] ver 4 [c] ver 12,13,21 **27:9** [d] Lev 16:29-31; 23:27-29; Nu 29:7 **27:10** [e] ver 21 **27:14** [f] Mk 4:37 **27:17** [g] ver 26,39 **27:18** [h] ver 19,38; Jnh 1:5 **27:21** [i] ver 10 [j] ver 7 **27:22** [k] ver 25,36 **27:23** [l] Ac 5:19 [m] Ro 1:9 [n] Ac 18:9; 23:11; 2Ti 4:17 **27:24** [o] Ac 23:11 [p] ver 44 **27:25** [q] ver 22,36 [r] Ro 4:20,21 **27:26** [s] ver 17,39 [t] Ac 28:1

escape from the ship, the sailors let the lifeboat[u] down into the sea, pretending they were going to lower some anchors from the bow. 31Then Paul said to the centurion and the soldiers, "Unless these men stay with the ship, you cannot be saved."[v] 32So the soldiers cut the ropes that held the lifeboat and let it drift away.

33Just before dawn Paul urged them all to eat. "For the last fourteen days," he said, "you have been in constant suspense and have gone without food—you haven't eaten anything. 34Now I urge you to take some food. You need it to survive. Not one of you will lose a single hair from his head."[w] 35After he said this, he took some bread and gave thanks to God in front of them all. Then he broke it[x] and began to eat. 36They were all encouraged[y] and ate some food themselves. 37Altogether there were 276 of us on board. 38When they had eaten as much as they wanted, they lightened the ship by throwing the grain into the sea.[z]

39When daylight came, they did not recognize the land, but they saw a bay with a sandy beach,[a] where they decided to run the ship aground if they could. 40Cutting loose the anchors,[b] they left them in the sea and at the same time untied the ropes that held the rudders. Then they hoisted the foresail to the wind and made for the beach. 41But the ship struck a sandbar and ran aground. The bow stuck fast and would not move, and the stern was broken to pieces by the pounding of the surf.[c]

42The soldiers planned to kill the prisoners to prevent any of them from swimming away and escaping. 43But the centurion wanted to spare Paul's life[d] and kept them from carrying out their plan. He ordered those who could swim to jump overboard first and get to land. 44The rest were to get there on planks or on other pieces of the ship. In this way everyone reached land safely.[e]

Paul Ashore on Malta

28 Once safely on shore, we[f] found out that the island[g] was called Malta. 2The islanders showed us unusual kindness. They built a fire and welcomed us all because it was raining and cold. 3Paul gathered a pile of brushwood and, as he put it on the fire, a viper, driven out by the heat, fastened itself on his hand. 4When the islanders saw the snake hanging from his hand,[h] they said to each other, "This man must be a murderer; for though he escaped from the sea, the goddess Justice has not allowed him to live."[i] 5But Paul shook the snake off into the fire and suffered no ill effects.[j] 6The people expected him to swell up or suddenly fall dead; but after waiting a long time and seeing nothing unusual happen to him, they changed their minds and said he was a god.[k]

7There was an estate nearby that belonged to Publius, the chief official of the island. He welcomed us to his home and showed us generous hospitality for three days. 8His father was sick in bed, suffering from fever and dysentery. Paul went in to see him and, after prayer,[l] placed his hands on him and healed him.[m] 9When this had happened, the rest of the sick on the island came and were cured. 10They honored us in many ways; and when we were ready to sail, they furnished us with the supplies we needed.

Paul's Arrival at Rome

11After three months we put out to sea in a ship that had wintered in the island—it was an Alexandrian ship[n] with the figurehead of the twin gods Castor and Pollux. 12We put in at Syracuse and stayed there three days. 13From there we set sail and arrived at Rhegium. The next day the south wind came up, and on the following day we reached Puteoli. 14There we found some brothers and sisters[o] who invited us to spend a week with them. And so we came to Rome. 15The brothers and sisters[p] there had heard that we were coming, and they traveled as far as the Forum of Appius and the Three Taverns to meet us. At the sight of these people Paul thanked God and was encouraged. 16When we got to Rome, Paul was allowed to live by himself, with a soldier to guard him.[q]

Paul Preaches at Rome Under Guard

17Three days later he called together the local Jewish leaders.[r] When they had assembled, Paul said to them: "My brothers,[s] although I have done nothing against our people[t] or against the customs of our ancestors,[u] I was arrested in Jerusalem and handed over to the Romans. 18They examined me[v] and wanted to release me,[w] because I was not guilty of any crime deserving death.[x] 19The Jews objected, so I

28:8 ***suffering from fever.*** This fever was possibly Malta fever, which was common in Malta, Gibraltar, and other Mediterranean islands. The microorganism has since been traced to the milk of the Maltese goats. The fever usually lasted four months, but sometimes could last as long as two or three years.

28:17 ***local Jewish leaders.*** By this time, the decree of the emperor Claudius (18:2) had been allowed to lapse, and Jews had returned to Rome.

27:30 [u] ver 16 **27:31** [v] ver 24 **27:34** [w] Mt 10:30 **27:35** [x] Mt 14:19 **27:36** [y] ver 22,25 **27:38** [z] ver 18; Jnh 1:5 **27:39** [a] Ac 28:1 **27:40** [b] ver 29 **27:41** [c] 2Co 11:25 **27:43** [d] ver 3 **27:44** [e] ver 22,31 **28:1** [f] Ac 16:10 [g] Ac 27:26,39 **28:4** [h] Mk 16:18 [i] Lk 13:2,4 **28:5** [j] Lk 10:19 **28:6** [k] Ac 14:11 **28:8** [l] Jas 5:14,15 [m] Ac 9:40 **28:11** [n] Ac 27:6 **28:14** [o] Ac 1:16 **28:15** [p] Ac 1:16 **28:16** [q] Ac 24:23; 27:3 **28:17** [r] Ac 25:2 [s] Ac 22:5 [t] Ac 25:8 [u] Ac 6:14 **28:18** [v] Ac 22:24 [w] Ac 26:31,32 [x] Ac 23:9

was compelled to make an appeal to Caesar.[y] I certainly did not intend to bring any
charge against my own people. 20For this
reason I have asked to see you and talk
with you. It is because of the hope of Israel[z] that I am bound with this chain."[a]

21They replied, "We have not received
any letters from Judea concerning you,
and none of our people[b] who have come
from there has reported or said anything
bad about you. 22But we want to hear what
your views are, for we know that people
everywhere are talking against this sect."[c]

23They arranged to meet Paul on a certain day, and came in even larger numbers
to the place where he was staying. He witnessed to them from morning till evening,
explaining about the kingdom of God,[d]
and from the Law of Moses and from the
Prophets[e] he tried to persuade them about
Jesus.[f] 24Some were convinced by what he
said, but others would not believe.[g] 25They
disagreed among themselves and began to
leave after Paul had made this final statement: "The Holy Spirit spoke the truth to
your ancestors when he said through Isaiah the prophet:

26" 'Go to this people and say,
"You will be ever hearing but never
understanding;
you will be ever seeing but never
perceiving."
27For this people's heart has become
calloused;[h]
they hardly hear with their ears,
and they have closed their eyes.
Otherwise they might see with their
eyes,
hear with their ears,
understand with their hearts
and turn, and I would heal them.'[a][i]

28"Therefore I want you to know that
God's salvation[j] has been sent to the Gentiles,[k] and they will listen!" [29][b]

30For two whole years Paul stayed there
in his own rented house and welcomed all
who came to see him. 31He proclaimed the
kingdom of God[l] and taught about the Lord
Jesus Christ—with all boldness and without hindrance!

---

[a] 27 Isaiah 6:9,10 (see Septuagint) [b] 29 Some manuscripts include here *After he said this, the Jews left, arguing vigorously among themselves.*

28:20 Hope—The hope of Israel and the hope which Paul had found in Christ were not two different things. Wherever he went, he proclaimed Christ to the Jews as the fulfillment of their hope. That hope included not only the resurrection; it also included the Messiah and His kingdom. Paul is careful to emphasize that the hope which he now proclaims does not undermine the hope of Israel but rather is its divine fulfillment. His devotion to the hope of the fathers was the cause that brought about his imprisonment and put him in chains. His demeanor before these Jewish leaders in Rome must have been impressive. As he stood before these men whose influence could result in life or death for him, there was no quaking or fear. He had that hope which made him secure, whatever happened.

28:30 *two whole years.* Paul wrote four of the New Testament letters (Ephesians, Philippians, Colossians, and Philemon) during this period.

28:31 *proclaimed ... taught.* Apparently Paul's case had not been decided when Luke finished this book. It is thought that Paul was in fact released (there was really no case against him), and actually went to Spain as he desired (Rom. 15:24). Titus 1:5 implies that Paul ministered on the island of Crete (something not mentioned in Acts), and many believe that Paul resumed his missionary travel for a few more years before his final arrest, condemnation, and execution, sometime around A.D. 67.

28:19 [y] Ac 25:11 **28:20** [z] Ac 26:6, 7 [a] Ac 21:33 **28:21** [b] Ac 22:5 **28:22** [c] Ac 24:5, 14 **28:23** [d] Ac 19:8 [e] Ac 8:35 [f] Ac 17:3 **28:24** [g] Ac 14:4 **28:27** [h] Ps 119:70 [i] Isa 6:9, 10 **28:28** [j] Lk 2:30 [k] Ac 13:46 **28:31** [l] ver 23; Mt 4:23

ROMANS

▶ **AUTHOR:** All critical schools agree on the Pauline authorship of this foundational book. The vocabulary, style, logic, and theological development are consistent with Paul's other epistles. He wrote Romans in A.D. 57, near the end of his third missionary journey, evidently during his three-month stay in Greece (Acts 20:3–6), more specifically, in Corinth. The church in Rome was well-known (1:8), and it had been established for several years by the time of this letter. The believers were probably numerous, and evidently they met in several places (Rom. 16:1–16). The historian Tacitus even referred to the Christians who were persecuted there under Nero in A.D. 64 as an "immense multitude," as the gospel filled the gap left by the practically defunct polytheism of Roman religion.

▶ **TIME:** C. A.D. 57 ▶ **KEY VERSES:** Rom. 1:16–17

▶ **THEME:** Most scholars think that Paul probably wrote this letter from Corinth, shortly before going to Jerusalem with the relief funds for the believers there. At this point in his life and ministry, his theology has been fully developed through years of study and interaction with people as he preached the gospel. Romans systematically explains what Christ did, why He did it, and what has happened as a result. It speaks to what we are as humans and how God has interacted with us through Christ. It lays out God's plan for the world, clarifying what has happened and is still happening in biblical history. In this way, Paul forces us to deal with all the false versions of reality inspired by our fallen human nature as opposed to God's gracious, sustaining plan.

1 Paul, a servant of Christ Jesus, called
to be an apostle[a] and set apart[b] for the
gospel of God[c]— 2the gospel he promised
beforehand through his prophets in the
Holy Scriptures[d] 3regarding his Son, who
as to his earthly life[a][e] was a descendant
of David, 4and who through the Spirit of
holiness was appointed the Son of God
in power[b] by his resurrection from the
dead: Jesus Christ our Lord. 5Through
him we received grace and apostleship
to call all the Gentiles[f] to the obedience
that comes from[c] faith[g] for his name's
sake. 6And you also are among those
Gentiles who are called to belong to Jesus
Christ.[h]

7To all in Rome who are loved by God[i]
and called to be his holy people:

Grace and peace to you from God our Father and from the Lord Jesus Christ.[j]

Paul's Longing to Visit Rome

8First, I thank my God through Jesus
Christ for all of you,[k] because your faith
is being reported all over the world.[l] 9God,
whom I serve[m] in my spirit in preaching
the gospel of his Son, is my witness[n] how
constantly I remember you 10in my prayers
at all times; and I pray that now at last by
God's will the way may be opened for me
to come to you.[o]

11I long to see you[p] so that I may impart to you some spiritual gift to make you
strong— 12that is, that you and I may be
mutually encouraged by each other's faith.
13I do not want you to be unaware, brothers
and sisters,[d] that I planned many times to

a 3 Or *who according to the flesh* *b* 4 Or *was declared with power to be the Son of God* *c* 5 Or *that is* *d* 13 The Greek word for *brothers and sisters (adelphoi)* refers here to believers, both men and women, as part of God's family; also in 7:1, 4; 8:12, 29; 10:1; 11:25; 12:1; 15:14, 30; 16:14, 17.

1:1 [a] 1Co 1:1 [b] Ac 9:15 [c] 2Co 11:7 **1:2** [d] Gal 3:8 **1:3** [e] Jn 1:14 **1:5** [f] Ac 9:15 [g] Ac 6:7 **1:6** [h] Rev 17:14 **1:7** [i] Ro 8:39 [j] 1Co 1:3 **1:8** [k] 1Co 1:4 [l] Ro 16:19 **1:9** [m] 2Ti 1:3 [n] Php 1:8 **1:10** [o] Ro 15:32 **1:11** [p] Ro 15:23

1:1 ***servant.*** In this passage, servant means slave. Paul is talking about a slavery taken voluntarily out of love (see Ex. 21:1–6), unlike the forced slavery known to so many in the Roman Empire.
1:4 ***appointed.*** Jesus did not become the Son of God by the resurrection. Instead, the resurrection proved that Jesus was the Son of God.

come to you (but have been prevented from
doing so until now)[q] in order that I might
have a harvest among you, just as I have
had among the other Gentiles.
14I am obligated[r] both to Greeks and non-
Greeks, both to the wise and the foolish.
15That is why I am so eager to preach the
gospel also to you who are in Rome.[s]
16For I am not ashamed of the gospel,[t]
because it is the power of God[u] that brings
salvation to everyone who believes: first
to the Jew,[v] then to the Gentile.[w] 17For in
the gospel the righteousness of God is revealed[x]—a righteousness that is by faith
from first to last,[a] just as it is written: "The
righteous will live by faith."[b][y]

God's Wrath Against Sinful Humanity

18The wrath of God[z] is being revealed
from heaven against all the godlessness
and wickedness of people, who suppress
the truth by their wickedness, 19since what
may be known about God is plain to them,
because God has made it plain to them.[a]
20For since the creation of the world God's
invisible qualities—his eternal power and
divine nature—have been clearly seen, being understood from what has been made,[b]
so that people are without excuse.
21For although they knew God, they neither glorified him as God nor gave thanks
to him, but their thinking became futile
and their foolish hearts were darkened.[c]
22Although they claimed to be wise, they
became fools[d] 23and exchanged the glory
of the immortal God for images[e] made to
look like a mortal human being and birds
and animals and reptiles.
24Therefore God gave them over[f] in the
sinful desires of their hearts to sexual impurity for the degrading of their bodies
with one another.[g] 25They exchanged the
truth about God for a lie,[h] and worshiped
and served created things[i] rather than the
Creator—who is forever praised.[j] Amen.
26Because of this, God gave them over[k]
to shameful lusts.[l] Even their women exchanged natural sexual relations for unnatural ones.[m] 27In the same way the men
also abandoned natural relations with
women and were inflamed with lust for
one another. Men committed shameful acts
with other men, and received in themselves
the due penalty for their error.[n]
28Furthermore, just as they did not think
it worthwhile to retain the knowledge of
God, so God gave them over[o] to a depraved
mind, so that they do what ought not to be
done. 29They have become filled with every kind of wickedness, evil, greed and
depravity. They are full of envy, murder,
strife, deceit and malice. They are gossips,[p] 30slanderers, God-haters, insolent,
arrogant and boastful; they invent ways
of doing evil; they disobey their parents;[q]
31they have no understanding, no fidelity,
no love,[r] no mercy. 32Although they know
God's righteous decree that those who do
such things deserve death,[s] they not only
continue to do these very things but also
approve[t] of those who practice them.

[a] 17 Or *is from faith to faith* [b] 17 Hab. 2:4

1:14 *non-Greeks.* Paul is referring to the non-Greek Gentile populations, such as the northern European peoples, the Britons, the Gauls, and the Celts.

1:17 *faith from first to last.* Faith is at the beginning of the salvation process, and it is the goal as well. Paul had faith that God, through the Holy Spirit, could and would build true righteousness in him. For the believer this means prayerful self-examination, prayer to do better, and careful response to those inner nudges that say, "don't say that ... have pity ... encourage him ...," etc.

1:18–19 There Are No Excuses—Someone once said there were two points they understood about God: (1) "There is a God"; and (2) "I am not Him." Theologians use the term "general revelation" to describe the concept Paul is teaching here in Romans 1. God has revealed Himself through His creation so that everyone can understand that He exists and that He has created the world and man with a purpose. God created man with an inner sense that there is something bigger out there, something that transcends mankind. That something is God and He requires recognition. The created world points us to God, but we suppress that truth, preferring to put ourselves in the place of God, in effect saying, "There is no God but me." Paul further says that, because the revelation is so clear, we have no excuse for missing it, no legitimate reason for our blindness. People who do not see it are guilty of not acknowledging the most basic reality there is.

1:25 *lie.* This refers to the kind of wrong thinking that led to idol worship. This "lie" refuses to honor both God's law and His authority. When people stop knowing that God created the universe, that it is His, they adopt all kinds of wrong thinking about sin, society, morality, and especially, the role of God Himself.

1:27 *committed shameful.* Homosexuality is sin (Lev. 18:22), and the actions that are part of this lifestyle are called "shameful" by God. In this passage Paul explains that homosexual sin is the result of men having rejected God and exchanged what is natural for the unnatural. The problems from this way of living are themselves the "penalty" for this choice.

1:29–32 *become filled with every kind of wickedness.* These verses contain one of the most complete lists of sin in all of Scripture. This passage addresses not only the fact that God judges rightly that these sins are deserving of death, but it also addresses the idea that approving of these sins is something God judges.

1:13 [q] Ro 15:22,23 **1:14** [r] 1Co 9:16 **1:15** [s] Ro 15:20
1:16 [t] 2Ti 1:8 [u] 1Co 1:18 [v] Ac 3:26 [w] Ro 2:9,10
1:17 [x] Ro 3:21 [y] Hab 2:4; Gal 3:11; Heb 10:38
1:18 [z] Eph 5:6; Col 3:6 **1:19** [a] Ac 14:17 **1:20** [b] Ps 19:1-6
1:21 [c] Jer 2:5; Eph 4:17,18 **1:22** [d] 1Co 1:20,27
1:23 [e] Ps 106:20; Jer 2:11; Ac 17:29 **1:24** [f] Eph 4:19
[g] 1Pe 4:3 **1:25** [h] Isa 44:20 [i] Jer 10:14 [j] Ro 9:5
1:26 [k] ver 24,28 [l] 1Th 4:5 [m] Lev 18:22,23
1:27 [n] Lev 18:22; 20:13 **1:28** [o] ver 24,26
1:29 [p] 2Co 12:20 **1:30** [q] 2Ti 3:2 **1:31** [r] 2Ti 3:3
1:32 [s] Ro 6:23 [t] Ps 50:18; Lk 11:48; Ac 8:1; 22:20

God's Righteous Judgment

2 You, therefore, have no excuse,[u] you
who pass judgment on someone else,
for at whatever point you judge another,
you are condemning yourself, because
you who pass judgment do the same
things.[v] 2Now we know that God's judgment against those who do such things is
based on truth. 3So when you, a mere human being, pass judgment on them and yet
do the same things, do you think you will
escape God's judgment? 4Or do you show
contempt for the riches[w] of his kindness,[x]
forbearance[y] and patience,[z] not realizing
that God's kindness is intended to lead you
to repentance?[a]

5But because of your stubbornness and
your unrepentant heart, you are storing up
wrath against yourself for the day of God's
wrath, when his righteous judgment[b] will
be revealed. 6God "will repay each person
according to what they have done."[ac] 7To
those who by persistence in doing good
seek glory, honor[d] and immortality,[e] he
will give eternal life. 8But for those who
are self-seeking and who reject the truth
and follow evil,[f] there will be wrath and
anger. 9There will be trouble and distress
for every human being who does evil: first
for the Jew, then for the Gentile;[g] 10but glory, honor and peace for everyone who does
good: first for the Jew, then for the Gentile.[h]
11For God does not show favoritism.[i]

12All who sin apart from the law will also
perish apart from the law, and all who sin
under the law[j] will be judged by the law.
13For it is not those who hear the law who
are righteous in God's sight, but it is those
who obey[k] the law who will be declared
righteous. 14(Indeed, when Gentiles, who
do not have the law, do by nature things required by the law,[l] they are a law for themselves, even though they do not have the
law. 15They show that the requirements of
the law are written on their hearts, their
consciences also bearing witness, and
their thoughts sometimes accusing them
and at other times even defending them.)
16This will take place on the day when God
judges people's secrets[m] through Jesus
Christ,[n] as my gospel[o] declares.

The Jews and the Law

17Now you, if you call yourself a Jew; if
you rely on the law and boast in God;[p] 18if
you know his will and approve of what is
superior because you are instructed by the
law; 19if you are convinced that you are a
guide for the blind, a light for those who are
in the dark, 20an instructor of the foolish, a
teacher of little children, because you have
in the law the embodiment of knowledge
and truth— 21you, then, who teach others,
do you not teach yourself? You who preach
against stealing, do you steal?[q] 22You who
say that people should not commit adultery, do you commit adultery? You who abhor idols, do you rob temples?[r] 23You who
boast in the law,[s] do you dishonor God by
breaking the law? 24As it is written: "God's
name is blasphemed among the Gentiles
because of you."[bt]

25Circumcision has value if you observe
the law,[u] but if you break the law, you have
become as though you had not been circumcised.[v] 26So then, if those who are not
circumcised keep the law's requirements,[w]

a *6* Psalm 62:12; Prov. 24:12 *b* *24* Isaiah 52:5 (see Septuagint); Ezek. 36:20,22

2:1–4 *judge.* Paul points out in this passage that anyone who judges others condemns himself, for in this list of sins is something that everyone has been guilty of in one way or another. Paul asks if the judgers realize that it is God in His goodness who leads one to repentance, and that only God can judge rightly. Only He can judge the actions of the heart and person without condemning Himself, for only He is without sin.
2:4 *repentance.* Literally, this means "to change one's mind." In this context it means to reject one's sinful habits and turn to God.
2:7–8 *doing good ... eternal life.* According to these verses it might seem that "eternal life" can be gained by "doing good." But Romans clearly teaches justification by faith (3:22). The subject of this verse is judgment, not justification. Jesus said that "I tell you that everyone will have to give account on the day of judgment for every empty word they have spoken" (Matt. 12:36). Even Christians will see both the good and the evil that they have done. They are justified (considered righteous and therefore not punished for their sins because they have accepted Christ's death on their behalf) but they still have to see what they have done according to God's righteous judgment. Good works are a "foundation for the coming age [eternity]" (1 Tim. 6:17–19).
2:12 *apart from the law.* Gentiles, who did not receive the Mosaic law, were sometimes described by this term.
2:14 *do by nature things required by the law.* Gentiles who still do such things as honor their parents, respond in kindness, or live honestly, show that they do have the idea of a basic moral law and the concepts of right and wrong.
2:16 *secrets.* According to the gospel that Paul preached, God will judge not only people's actions, but their motives, or "secrets."
2:17–25 Self-Righteousness—Paul speaks of the lamentable disparity between the truth that the Jews knew, and their practice of the truth. Boasting about having God's law, while breaking the law in their lives, brings upon them the strongest condemnation, and establishes the truth that the law can only condemn.

2:1 [u] Ro 1:20 [v] 2Sa 12:5-7; Mt 7:1,2 **2:4** [w] Ro 9:23; Eph 1:7,18; 2:7 [x] Ro 11:22 [y] Ro 3:25 [z] Ex 34:6 [a] 2Pe 3:9 **2:5** [b] Jude 6 **2:6** [c] Ps 62:12; Mt 16:27 **2:7** [d] ver 10 [e] 1Co 15:53,54 **2:8** [f] 2Th 2:12 **2:9** [g] 1Pe 4:17 **2:10** [h] ver 9 **2:11** [i] Ac 10:34 **2:12** [j] Ro 3:19; 1Co 9:20,21 **2:13** [k] Jas 1:22,23,25 **2:14** [l] Ac 10:35 **2:16** [m] Ecc 12:14 [n] Ac 10:42 [o] Ro 16:25 **2:17** [p] ver 23; Mic 3:11; Ro 9:4 **2:21** [q] Mt 23:3,4 **2:22** [r] Ac 19:37 **2:23** [s] ver 17 **2:24** [t] Isa 52:5; Eze 36:22 **2:25** [u] Gal 5:3 [v] Jer 4:4 **2:26** [w] Ro 8:4

will they not be regarded as though they
were circumcised?[x] 27The one who is not
circumcised physically and yet obeys the
law will condemn you[y] who, even though
you have the[a] written code and circumcision, are a lawbreaker.
28A person is not a Jew who is one only
outwardly,[z] nor is circumcision merely outward and physical.[a] 29No, a person is a Jew
who is one inwardly; and circumcision is
circumcision of the heart, by the Spirit,[b]
not by the written code.[c] Such a person's
praise is not from other people, but from
God.[d]

God's Faithfulness

3 What advantage, then, is there in being
a Jew, or what value is there in circumcision? 2Much in every way! First of all, the
Jews have been entrusted with the very
words of God.[e]
3What if some were unfaithful?[f] Will
their unfaithfulness nullify God's faithfulness?[g] 4Not at all! Let God be true,[h]
and every human being a liar.[i] As it is
written:

"So that you may be proved right when
you speak
and prevail when you judge."[bj]

5But if our unrighteousness brings out
God's righteousness more clearly, what
shall we say? That God is unjust in bringing his wrath on us? (I am using a human
argument.)[k] 6Certainly not! If that were so,
how could God judge the world?[l] 7Someone
might argue, "If my falsehood enhances
God's truthfulness and so increases his
glory,[m] why am I still condemned as a sinner?" 8Why not say—as some slanderously claim that we say—"Let us do evil that
good may result"?[n] Their condemnation is
just!

No One Is Righteous

9What shall we conclude then? Do we
have any advantage? Not at all! For we
have already made the charge that Jews
and Gentiles alike are all under the power
of sin.[o] 10As it is written:

"There is no one righteous, not even
one;
11 there is no one who understands;
there is no one who seeks God.
12 All have turned away,
they have together become
worthless;
there is no one who does good,
not even one."[cp]
13 "Their throats are open graves;
their tongues practice deceit."[dq]
"The poison of vipers is on their lips."[er]
14 "Their mouths are full of cursing and
bitterness."[fs]
15 "Their feet are swift to shed blood;
16 ruin and misery mark their ways,
17 and the way of peace they do not
know."[g]
18 "There is no fear of God before their
eyes."[ht]

19Now we know that whatever the law
says,[u] it says to those who are under the
law,[v] so that every mouth may be silenced
and the whole world held accountable to
God. 20Therefore no one will be declared
righteous in God's sight by the works of the
law;[w] rather, through the law we become
conscious of our sin.[x]

Righteousness Through Faith

21But now apart from the law the righteousness of God[y] has been made known,
to which the Law and the Prophets testify.[z] 22This righteousness is given through
faith[a] in[i] Jesus Christ to all who believe.
There is no difference between Jew and
Gentile,[b] 23for all have sinned and fall

[a] 27 Or *who, by means of a* [b] 4 Psalm 51:4
[c] 12 Psalms 14:1-3; 53:1-3; Eccles. 7:20
[d] 13 Psalm 5:9 [e] 13 Psalm 140:3
[f] 14 Psalm 10:7 (see Septuagint)
[g] 17 Isaiah 59:7,8 [h] 18 Psalm 36:1
[i] 22 Or *through the faithfulness of*

2:29 *by the Spirit, not by the written code.* The internal circumcision of the heart is the work of the Holy Spirit. God condemns external observance if it is not the product of a righteous heart (Is. 1:10–18).
3:2 *words of God.* The entire Old Testament, the laws and the covenants that have been given by God Himself to the nation of Israel are the "words," or the things that God has spoken.
3:16 *ruin and misery.* In verses 10–18, Paul quotes without formal introduction a number of different verses from the Old Testament. In these passages it is shown that man not only does not seek God, but apart from Him they lack true goodness and will treat each other with violence, cursing, being quick to kill, and finding only "ruin and misery."
3:18 *fear of God.* This is an Old Testament expression for respect and reverence for God.
3:23 Universal Sin—We generally avoid the word *sin*. We want to call it something other than what it is because we don't like the implications of the word. We don't like being told we're rebels, that we're flawed and bent in our very natures, and that there is nothing we can do about it on our own (Gen. 3:6–7). We have this innate sense that we can overcome the problem with a little more effort or maturity. Even that innate sense is an illustration of the problem. The bold hard facts always point us back to Paul's conclusions; "we're sinners," period.

2:26 [x] 1Co 7:19 **2:27** [y] Mt 12:41,42 **2:28** [z] Mt 3:9; Jn 8:39; Ro 9:6,7 [a] Gal 6:15 **2:29** [b] Php 3:3; Col 2:11 [c] Ro 7:6 [d] Jn 5:44; 1Co 4:5; 2Co 10:18; 1Th 2:4; 1Pe 3:4 **3:2** [e] Dt 4:8; Ps 147:19 **3:3** [f] Heb 4:2 [g] 2Ti 2:13 **3:4** [h] Jn 3:33 [i] Ps 116:11 [j] Ps 51:4 **3:5** [k] Ro 6:19; Gal 3:15 **3:6** [l] Ge 18:25 **3:7** [m] ver 4 **3:8** [n] Ro 6:1 **3:9** [o] ver 19, 23; Gal 3:22 **3:12** [p] Ps 14:1-3 **3:13** [q] Ps 5:9 [r] Ps 140:3 **3:14** [s] Ps 10:7 **3:18** [t] Ps 36:1 **3:19** [u] Jn 10:34 [v] Ro 2:12 **3:20** [w] Ac 13:39; Gal 2:16 [x] Ro 7:7 **3:21** [y] Ro 1:17; 9:30 [z] Ac 10:43 **3:22** [a] Ro 9:30 [b] Ro 10:12; Gal 3:28; Col 3:11

short of the glory of God, 24 and all are justified freely by his grace[c] through the redemption[d] that came by Christ Jesus. 25 God presented Christ as a sacrifice of atonement,[a][e] through the shedding of his blood[f]—to be received by faith. He did this to demonstrate his righteousness, because in his forbearance he had left the sins committed beforehand unpunished[g]— 26 he did it to demonstrate his righteousness at the present time, so as to be just and the one who justifies those who have faith in Jesus.

27 Where, then, is boasting?[h] It is excluded. Because of what law? The law that requires works? No, because of the law that requires faith. 28 For we maintain that a person is justified by faith apart from the works of the law.[i] 29 Or is God the God of Jews only? Is he not the God of Gentiles too? Yes, of Gentiles too,[j] 30 since there is only one God, who will justify the circumcised by faith and the uncircumcised through that same faith.[k] 31 Do we, then, nullify the law by this faith? Not at all! Rather, we uphold the law.

Abraham Justified by Faith

4 What then shall we say that Abraham, our forefather according to the flesh, discovered in this matter? 2 If, in fact, Abraham was justified by works, he had something to boast about—but not before God.[l] 3 What does Scripture say? "Abraham believed God, and it was credited to him as righteousness."[b][m]

4 Now to the one who works, wages are not credited as a gift[n] but as an obligation. 5 However, to the one who does not work but trusts God who justifies the ungodly, their faith is credited as righteousness. 6 David says the same thing when he speaks of the blessedness of the one to whom God credits righteousness apart from works:

7 "Blessed are those
whose transgressions are forgiven,
whose sins are covered.
8 Blessed is the one
whose sin the Lord will never count
against them."[c][o]

9 Is this blessedness only for the circumcised, or also for the uncircumcised?[p] We have been saying that Abraham's faith was credited to him as righteousness.[q] 10 Under what circumstances was it credited? Was it after he was circumcised, or before? It was not after, but before! 11 And he received circumcision as a sign, a seal of the righteousness that he had by faith while he was still uncircumcised.[r] So then, he is the father[s] of all who believe[t] but have not been circumcised, in order that righteousness might be credited to them. 12 And he is then also the father of the circumcised who not only are circumcised but who also follow in the footsteps of the faith that our father Abraham had before he was circumcised.

13 It was not through the law that Abraham and his offspring received the promise[u] that he would be heir of the world,[v] but through the righteousness that comes by faith. 14 For if those who depend on the law are heirs, faith means nothing and the promise is worthless,[w] 15 because the law brings wrath.[x] And where there is no law there is no transgression.[y]

16 Therefore, the promise comes by faith, so that it may be by grace[z] and may be

---

[a] *25* The Greek for *sacrifice of atonement* refers to the atonement cover on the ark of the covenant (see Lev. 16:15,16). [b] *3* Gen. 15:6; also in verse 22
[c] *8* Psalm 32:1,2

3:24 *redemption.* Those who believe are *justified*, that is, declared righteous, freely, by God's grace or favor. Christ Jesus died to provide *redemption*, (or to "buy back," in the same way we "redeem" a promissory note). He died to pay the price required to ransom sinners. He transfers His righteousness to those who believe in Him, and on the basis of Christ's righteousness alone, believers can approach God's throne with praise.

3:25 *sacrifice of atonement.* By His death, Christ satisfied the justice of God. The phrase refers to appeasement. No man can ever appease God, for His wrath over sin and His judgment of sin are totally just. But God in His mercy provided that appeasement through Jesus Christ, who died on the cross to pay for the sins of the world and to open the way for sinners to come before our Holy God.

3:27 *law that requires faith.* The "law that requires faith" is a kind of play on words. Paul has been talking about the fact that the law does not give people a right relationship with God. The only "law" about having this relationship is that it must be by "faith," not by deeds, whether people are Jewish or Gentile. We can never earn our salvation.

3:31 *nullify the law.* In this passage the question of either nullifying the law or upholding the law means that if salvation is received by faith, it would seem like the law was of no value. But actually the fact that Christ came, which was promised through the whole Old Testament, and that He kept the law perfectly, establishes the law as being valid. Only after salvation can people keep the law at all, as Jesus explained in Matthew 22:40, for the law is summed up in loving God and loving our neighbor.

4:1 *according to the flesh.* Or "by his own labor."

4:16 *He is the father of us all.* God's promises to Abraham were not based on any performance or ritual, but on Abraham's belief, so Abraham is the "father" of all who believe.

3:24 [c] Ro 4:16; Eph 2:8 [d] Eph 1:7, 14; Col 1:14; Heb 9:12 **3:25** [e] 1Jn 4:10 [f] Heb 9:12, 14 [g] Ac 17:30 **3:27** [h] Ro 2:17, 23; 4:2; 1Co 1:29-31; Eph 2:9 **3:28** [i] ver 20, 21; Ac 13:39; Eph 2:9 **3:29** [j] Ro 9:24 **3:30** [k] Gal 3:8 **4:2** [l] 1Co 1:31 **4:3** [m] ver 5, 9, 22; Ge 15:6; Gal 3:6; Jas 2:23 **4:4** [n] Ro 11:6 **4:8** [o] Ps 32:1, 2; 2Co 5:19 **4:9** [p] Ro 3:30 [q] ver 3 **4:11** [r] Ge 17:10, 11 [s] ver 16, 17; Lk 19:9 [t] Ro 3:22 **4:13** [u] Gal 3:16, 29 [v] Ge 17:4-6 **4:14** [w] Gal 3:18 **4:15** [x] Ro 7:7-25; 1Co 15:56; 2Co 3:7; Gal 3:10; Ro 7:12 [y] Ro 3:20; 7:7 **4:16** [z] Ro 3:24

guaranteed[a] to all Abraham's offspring—not only to those who are of the law but also to those who have the faith of Abraham. He is the father of us all. 17 As it is written: "I have made you a father of many nations."[a][b] He is our father in the sight of God, in whom he believed—the God who gives life[c] to the dead and calls[d] into being things that were not.[e]

18 Against all hope, Abraham in hope believed and so became the father of many nations,[f] just as it had been said to him, "So shall your offspring be."[b][g] 19 Without weakening in his faith, he faced the fact that his body was as good as dead[h]—since he was about a hundred years old[i]—and that Sarah's womb was also dead.[j] 20 Yet he did not waver through unbelief regarding the promise of God, but was strengthened in his faith and gave glory to God,[k] 21 being fully persuaded that God had power to do what he had promised.[l] 22 This is why "it was credited to him as righteousness."[m] 23 The words "it was credited to him" were written not for him alone, 24 but also for us,[n] to whom God will credit righteousness—for us who believe in him[o] who raised Jesus our Lord from the dead.[p] 25 He was delivered over to death for our sins[q] and was raised to life for our justification.

Peace and Hope

5 Therefore, since we have been justified through faith,[r] we[c] have peace with God through our Lord Jesus Christ, 2 through whom we have gained access[s] by faith into this grace in which we now stand.[t] And we[d] boast in the hope[u] of the glory of God. 3 Not only so, but we[d] also glory in our sufferings,[v] because we know that suffering produces perseverance;[w] 4 perseverance, character; and character, hope. 5 And hope[x] does not put us to shame, because God's love has been poured out into our hearts through the Holy Spirit,[y] who has been given to us.

6 You see, at just the right time,[z] when we were still powerless, Christ died for the ungodly.[a] 7 Very rarely will anyone die for a righteous person, though for a good person someone might possibly dare to die. 8 But God demonstrates his own love for us in this: While we were still sinners, Christ died for us.[b]

9 Since we have now been justified by his blood,[c] how much more shall we be saved from God's wrath[d] through him! 10 For if, while we were God's enemies,[e] we were reconciled[f] to him through the death of his Son, how much more, having been reconciled, shall we be saved through his life![g] 11 Not only is this so, but we also boast in God through our Lord Jesus Christ, through whom we have now received reconciliation.

Death Through Adam, Life Through Christ

12 Therefore, just as sin entered the world through one man,[h] and death through sin,[i] and in this way death came to all people, because all sinned—

13 To be sure, sin was in the world before the law was given, but sin is not charged against anyone's account where there is no law.[j] 14 Nevertheless, death reigned from the time of Adam to the time of Moses, even over those who did not sin by breaking a command, as did Adam, who is a pattern of the one to come.[k]

15 But the gift is not like the trespass. For if the many died by the trespass of the one man,[l] how much more did God's grace and the gift that came by the grace of the one man, Jesus Christ,[m] overflow to the many! 16 Nor can the gift of God be compared with the result of one man's sin: The judgment followed one sin and brought condemnation, but the gift followed many trespasses and brought justification. 17 For

[a] *17* Gen. 17:5 [b] *18* Gen. 15:5 [c] *1* Many manuscripts *let us* [d] *2,3* Or *let us*

4:17 *gives life to the dead.* The description of God as one who "gives life to the dead" refers not only to God making Abraham and Sarah's dead reproductive systems alive, but also to the fact that God could and did resurrect Jesus. That is the kind of God He is; belief in the resurrection is central to Christianity, and also to our belief in our own eternal life through Christ.

5:1 Justification—God's gracious justification of the believer does not take place by stages or degrees. It is an instantaneous judicial "not guilty" declaration, based on the perfect obedience and the once-for-all sacrifice of Christ. The believer now has peace with God through Jesus Christ, full pardon of his sins, and the title to eternal life. The crowning gift is an abiding joy and peace in the Lord, which remains in spite of outside circumstances.

5:12 *one man.* The "one man" is Adam.

5:13 *charged.* "charged" means "to charge to one's account," as by an entry made into a ledger. In other words, sin was present in the world from Adam to Moses, but God did not keep an account of sins before the giving of the law because there was no law to obey or disobey. Those after Adam and before Moses did not sin like Adam because there were no prohibitions similar to the law of Moses. But they did sin, and the way we know this is that "death reigned." They all died.

4:16 [a] Ro 15:8 **4:17** [b] Ge 17:5 [c] Jn 5:21 [d] Isa 48:13 [e] 1Co 1:28 **4:18** [f] ver 17 [g] Ge 15:5 **4:19** [h] Heb 11:11, 12 [i] Ge 17:17 [j] Ge 18:11 **4:20** [k] Mt 9:8 **4:21** [l] Ge 18:14; Heb 11:19 **4:22** [m] ver 3 **4:24** [n] Ro 15:4; 1Co 9:10; 10:11 [o] Ro 10:9 [p] Ac 2:24 **4:25** [q] Isa 53:5, 6; Ro 5:6, 8 **5:1** [r] Ro 3:28 **5:2** [s] Eph 2:18 [t] 1Co 15:1 [u] Heb 3:6 **5:3** [v] Mt 5:12 [w] Jas 1:2, 3 **5:5** [x] Php 1:20 [y] Ac 2:33 **5:6** [z] Gal 4:4 [a] Ro 4:25 **5:8** [b] Jn 15:13; 1Pe 3:18 **5:9** [c] Ro 3:25 [d] Ro 1:18 **5:10** [e] Ro 11:28; Col 1:21 [f] 2Co 5:18, 19; Col 1:20, 22 [g] Ro 8:34 **5:12** [h] ver 15, 16, 17; 1Co 15:21, 22 [i] Ge 2:17; 3:19; Ro 6:23 **5:13** [j] Ro 4:15 **5:14** [k] 1Co 15:22, 45 **5:15** [l] ver 12, 18, 19 [m] Ac 15:11

if, by the trespass of the one man, death[n]
reigned through that one man, how much
more will those who receive God's abundant provision of grace and of the gift of
righteousness reign in life through the one
man, Jesus Christ!
18Consequently, just as one trespass resulted in condemnation for all people,[o] so
also one righteous act resulted in justification[p] and life for all people. 19For just
as through the disobedience of the one
man[q] the many were made sinners, so also
through the obedience[r] of the one man the
many will be made righteous.
20The law was brought in so that the
trespass might increase.[s] But where sin increased, grace increased all the more,[t] 21so
that, just as sin reigned in death,[u] so also
grace might reign through righteousness
to bring eternal life through Jesus Christ
our Lord.

Dead to Sin, Alive in Christ

6 What shall we say, then? Shall we go
on sinning so that grace may increase?[v]
2By no means! We are those who have died
to sin;[w] how can we live in it any longer?
3Or don't you know that all of us who were
baptized[x] into Christ Jesus were baptized
into his death? 4We were therefore buried
with him through baptism into death in order that, just as Christ was raised from the
dead[y] through the glory of the Father, we
too may live a new life.[z]
5For if we have been united with him
in a death like his, we will certainly also
be united with him in a resurrection like
his.[a] 6For we know that our old self[b] was
crucified with him[c] so that the body ruled
by sin[d] might be done away with,[a] that we
should no longer be slaves to sin— 7be-
cause anyone who has died has been set
free from sin.
8Now if we died with Christ, we believe
that we will also live with him. 9For we
know that since Christ was raised from the
dead,[e] he cannot die again; death no longer
has mastery over him.[f] 10The death he died,
he died to sin[g] once for all; but the life he
lives, he lives to God.
11In the same way, count yourselves dead
to sin[h] but alive to God in Christ Jesus.
12Therefore do not let sin reign in your
mortal body so that you obey its evil desires. 13Do not offer any part of yourself to
sin as an instrument of wickedness,[i] but
rather offer yourselves to God as those who
have been brought from death to life; and
offer every part of yourself to him as an instrument of righteousness.[j] 14For sin shall
no longer be your master, because you are
not under the law,[k] but under grace.[l]

Slaves to Righteousness

15What then? Shall we sin because we
are not under the law but under grace? By
no means! 16Don't you know that when you
offer yourselves to someone as obedient
slaves, you are slaves of the one you obey—
whether you are slaves to sin,[m] which leads
to death,[n] or to obedience, which leads to
righteousness? 17But thanks be to God[o]
that, though you used to be slaves to sin,
you have come to obey from your heart the
pattern of teaching[p] that has now claimed
your allegiance. 18You have been set free
from sin[q] and have become slaves to righteousness.
19I am using an example from everyday
life[r] because of your human limitations.
Just as you used to offer yourselves as
slaves to impurity and to ever-increasing
wickedness, so now offer yourselves as
slaves to righteousness[s] leading to holiness. 20When you were slaves to sin,[t] you
were free from the control of righteousness. 21What benefit did you reap at that
time from the things you are now ashamed
of? Those things result in death![u] 22But
now that you have been set free from sin[v]
and have become slaves of God,[w] the benefit you reap leads to holiness, and the result is eternal life. 23For the wages of sin is
death,[x] but the gift of God is eternal life[y] in[b]
Christ Jesus our Lord.

[a] 6 Or *be rendered powerless* [b] 23 Or *through*

5:19 *many will be made righteous.* Through the sanctifying work of the Holy Spirit, the believer who has been declared righteous by God is continually becoming more righteous in thought and action.
5:20 *where sin increased, grace increased.* Once the law had been revealed, the sin which was already there became much more obvious because it had been explicitly illustrated how wrong it was. But grace was even bigger than the sin. Sin can never exceed the grace provided by God, and it loses its threat when compared to the infinite grace of God.
6:6 *crucified with him.* Simply put, a believer is not the same person he or she was before conversion. A believer is a new creation in Christ (2 Cor. 5:17).
6:23 New Life: A Free Gift—This passage gets at the central point of the Christian gospel. When we are separated from God, sin directs our lives and there is a wage, a consequence, for that sin: death and permanent separation from God. In stark contrast, we do not earn a wage from God. His gifts are free and abundant—the gift of eternal life. There is nothing

5:17 [n] ver 12 **5:18** [o] ver 12 [p] Ro 4:25 **5:19** [q] ver 12 [r] Php 2:8 **5:20** [s] Ro 7:7,8; Gal 3:19 [t] 1Ti 1:13, 14 **5:21** [u] ver 12, 14 **6:1** [v] ver 15; Ro 3:5,8 **6:2** [w] Col 3:3, 5; 1Pe 2:24 **6:3** [x] Mt 28:19 **6:4** [y] Col 2:12 [z] Ro 7:6; Gal 6:15; Eph 4:22-24; Col 3:10 **6:5** [a] 2Co 4:10; Php 3:10, 11 **6:6** [b] Eph 4:22; Col 3:9 [c] Gal 2:20; Col 2:12, 20 [d] Ro 7:24 **6:9** [e] Ac 2:24 [f] Rev 1:18 **6:10** [g] ver 2 **6:11** [h] ver 2 **6:13** [i] ver 16, 19; Ro 7:5 [j] Ro 12:1; 1Pe 2:24 **6:14** [k] Gal 5:18 [l] Ro 3:24 **6:16** [m] Jn 8:34; 2Pe 2:19 [n] ver 23 **6:17** [o] Ro 1:8; 2Co 2:14 [p] 2Ti 1:13 **6:18** [q] ver 7, 22; Ro 8:2 **6:19** [r] Ro 3:5 [s] ver 13 **6:20** [t] ver 16 **6:21** [u] ver 23 **6:22** [v] ver 18 [w] 1Co 7:22; 1Pe 2:16 **6:23** [x] Ge 2:17; Ro 5:12; Gal 6:7,8; Jas 1:15 [y] Mt 25:46

Released From the Law, Bound to Christ

7 Do you not know, brothers and sisters[z]—for I am speaking to those who know the law—that the law has authority over someone only as long as that person lives? 2For example, by law a married woman is bound to her husband as long as he is alive, but if her husband dies, she is released from the law that binds her to him.[a] 3So then, if she has sexual relations with another man while her husband is still alive, she is called an adulteress. But if her husband dies, she is released from that law and is not an adulteress if she marries another man.

4So, my brothers and sisters, you also died to the law[b] through the body of Christ,[c] that you might belong to another, to him who was raised from the dead, in order that we might bear fruit for God. 5For when we were in the realm of the flesh,[a] the sinful passions aroused by the law[d] were at work in us,[e] so that we bore fruit for death. 6But now, by dying to what once bound us, we have been released from the law so that we serve in the new way of the Spirit, and not in the old way of the written code.[f]

The Law and Sin

7What shall we say, then? Is the law sinful? Certainly not! Nevertheless, I would not have known what sin was had it not been for the law.[g] For I would not have known what coveting really was if the law had not said, "You shall not covet."[b][h] 8But sin, seizing the opportunity afforded by the commandment,[i] produced in me every kind of coveting. For apart from the law, sin was dead.[j] 9Once I was alive apart from the law; but when the commandment came, sin sprang to life and I died. 10I found that the very commandment that was intended to bring life[k] actually brought death. 11For sin, seizing the opportunity afforded by the commandment, deceived me,[l] and through the commandment put me to death. 12So then, the law is holy, and the commandment is holy, righteous and good.[m]

13Did that which is good, then, become death to me? By no means! Nevertheless, in order that sin might be recognized as sin, it used what is good to bring about my death, so that through the commandment sin might become utterly sinful.

14We know that the law is spiritual; but I am unspiritual,[n] sold[o] as a slave to sin. 15I do not understand what I do. For what I want to do I do not do, but what I hate I do.[p] 16And if I do what I do not want to do, I agree that the law is good.[q] 17As it is, it is no longer I myself who do it, but it is sin living in me.[r] 18For I know that good itself does not dwell in me, that is, in my sinful nature.[c][s] For I have the desire to do what is good, but I cannot carry it out. 19For I do not do the good I want to do, but the evil I do not want to do—this I keep on doing.[t] 20Now if I do what I do not want to do, it is no longer I who do it, but it is sin living in me that does it.[u]

21So I find this law at work:[v] Although I want to do good, evil is right there with me. 22For in my inner being[w] I delight in God's law;[x] 23but I see another law at work in me, waging war[y] against the law of my mind and making me a prisoner of the law of sin at work within me. 24What a wretched man I am! Who will rescue me from this body that is subject to death?[z] 25Thanks be to God, who delivers me through Jesus Christ our Lord!

So then, I myself in my mind am a slave to God's law, but in my sinful nature[d] a slave to the law of sin.

---

[a] *5* In contexts like this, the Greek word for *flesh* (*sarx*) refers to the sinful state of human beings, often presented as a power in opposition to the Spirit. [b] *7* Exodus 20:17; Deut. 5:21 [c] *18* Or *my flesh* [d] *25* Or *in the flesh*

---

that one can do to earn this incredible gift. Eternal life is just that—eternal—it never ceases. All fear of death and its effects can end. Instead of being separated from God for all eternity, Christians will have union with Him. Jesus Christ accomplished all of this on the cross once and for all.

7:3 Adultery—In this passage Paul uses the marriage relationship as an illustration of the believer's relationship to the law and Christ. A wife cannot marry another without committing adultery, but if her husband is dead, she is free to marry another. In the same way, believers must count the law (reconciliation with God by works) dead, in order to "marry" Christ and have a new life. Believers cannot live by the law and by Grace, any more than a woman can have two husbands.

7:6 new way of the Spirit . . . old way of the written code. Believers have a new life in the Holy Spirit, not in trying to gain life by obeying ancient or old laws.

7:8 apart from the law, sin was dead. Sin can exist without the law, but without a standard of right and wrong, there can be no judgment of what is sin and what is not.

7:9 when the commandment came, sin sprang to life. Oddly enough, the very rules against certain behaviors arouse the desire to perform those evil acts.

7:13 become death to me. The problem is not the law; the problem is sin. Through the law, sin is shown for what it is, and realization that we are "dead" in sin. We cannot really "be good," even when we know what that is.

7:1 [z] Ro 1:13 **7:2** [a] 1Co 7:39 **7:4** [b] Ro 8:2; Gal 2:19 [c] Col 1:22 **7:5** [d] Ro 7:7-11 [e] Ro 6:13 **7:6** [f] Ro 2:29; 2Co 3:6 **7:7** [g] Ro 3:20; 4:15 [h] Ex 20:17; Dt 5:21 **7:8** [i] ver 11 [j] Ro 4:15; 1Co 15:56 **7:10** [k] Lev 18:5; Lk 10:26-28; Ro 10:5; Gal 3:12 **7:11** [l] Ge 3:13 **7:12** [m] 1Ti 1:8 **7:14** [n] 1Co 3:1 [o] 1Ki 21:20, 25; 2Ki 17:17 **7:15** [p] ver 19; Gal 5:17 **7:16** [q] ver 12 **7:17** [r] ver 20 **7:18** [s] ver 25 **7:19** [t] ver 15 **7:20** [u] ver 17 **7:21** [v] ver 23, 25 **7:22** [w] Eph 3:16 [x] Ps 1:2 **7:23** [y] Gal 5:17; Jas 4:1; 1Pe 2:11 **7:24** [z] Ro 6:6; 8:2

Life Through the Spirit

8 Therefore, there is now no condemnation[a] for those who are in Christ Jesus,[b] **2**because through Christ Jesus the law of the Spirit who gives life[c] has set you[a] free[d] from the law of sin[e] and death. **3**For what the law was powerless[f] to do because it was weakened by the flesh,[b] God did by sending his own Son in the likeness of sinful flesh[g] to be a sin offering.[ch] And so he condemned sin in the flesh, **4**in order that the righteous requirement of the law might be fully met in us, who do not live according to the flesh but according to the Spirit.[i]

5Those who live according to the flesh have their minds set on what the flesh desires;[j] but those who live in accordance with the Spirit have their minds set on what the Spirit desires.[k] **6**The mind governed by the flesh is death, but the mind governed by the Spirit is life[l] and peace. **7**The mind governed by the flesh is hostile to God;[m] it does not submit to God's law, nor can it do so. **8**Those who are in the realm of the flesh cannot please God.

9You, however, are not in the realm of the flesh but are in the realm of the Spirit, if indeed the Spirit of God lives in you.[n] And if anyone does not have the Spirit of Christ,[o] they do not belong to Christ. **10**But if Christ is in you,[p] then even though your body is subject to death because of sin, the Spirit gives life[d] because of righteousness. **11**And if the Spirit of him who raised Jesus from the dead[q] is living in you, he who raised Christ from the dead will also give life to your mortal bodies[r] because of[e] his Spirit who lives in you.

12Therefore, brothers and sisters, we have an obligation—but it is not to the flesh, to live according to it. **13**For if you live according to the flesh, you will die; but if by the Spirit you put to death the misdeeds of the body, you will live.[s]

14For those who are led by the Spirit of God[t] are the children of God.[u] **15**The Spirit you received does not make you slaves, so that you live in fear again;[v] rather, the Spirit you received brought about your adoption to sonship.[f] And by him we cry, "*Abba*,[g] Father."[w] **16**The Spirit himself testifies with our spirit[x] that we are God's children. **17**Now if we are children, then we are heirs[y]—heirs of God and co-heirs with Christ, if indeed we share in his sufferings in order that we may also share in his glory.[z]

Present Suffering and Future Glory

18I consider that our present sufferings are not worth comparing with the glory that will be revealed in us.[a] **19**For the creation waits in eager expectation for the children of God to be revealed. **20**For the creation was subjected to frustration, not by its own choice, but by the will of the one who subjected it,[b] in hope **21**that[h] the creation itself will be liberated from its bondage to decay[c] and brought into the freedom and glory of the children of God.

22We know that the whole creation has

---

a 2 The Greek is singular; some manuscripts *me*
b 3 In contexts like this, the Greek word for *flesh* (*sarx*) refers to the sinful state of human beings, often presented as a power in opposition to the Spirit; also in verses 4-13.
c 3 Or *flesh, for sin*
d 10 Or *you, your body is dead because of sin, yet your spirit is alive*
e 11 Some manuscripts *bodies through*
f 15 The Greek word for *adoption to sonship* is a term referring to the full legal standing of an adopted male heir in Roman culture; also in verse 23.
g 15 Aramaic for *father*
h 20,21 Or *subjected it in hope.* *21For*

8:1 Condemnation—God's justification ("not guilty"), once pronounced, is final. Christ's death blots out the sins of His people, and when His work is applied to the believer, there is no room for condemnation, for God's justice has removed all grounds for it forever. This does not mean that the believer does not still deal with overcoming sin on a regular basis, but through the work of the Holy Spirit, he can be free from the tyranny of sin, and for the love of Christ, live in a way that pleases his Savior.

8:3 *the law was powerless to do.* The law can point out sin, but it cannot do anything about sin itself.

8:4 *the righteous requirement of the law might be fully met in us.* The believer gains the righteous standard of the law—love—not by means of the law, but by being in Christ and walking "according to the Spirit."

8:15 God the Father—God is the Father of all who believe in Christ in a special sense not shared by unbelievers. God is called their Father, first of all, because they have a new standing before Him. While unbelievers are the offspring of God because He created them (Acts 17:28–29), they do not have the standing of sons or daughters. Their standing is rather as condemned sinners before God the Judge (John 3:18; Rev. 20:11). When a person believes in Christ as Savior, his estate is changed from condemnation to sonship. This new standing grants to all believers the legal right and spiritual privileges of divine sonship: "heirs of God and co-heirs with Christ" (Rom. 8:17). He gives them new life (John 3:3). This relationship then is a family one involving many of the same realities that exist between an earthly father and child: birth of the child (John 3:3); partaking of the father's nature (2 Pet. 1:4); the father's care for the child (Matt. 6:32–33; 7:9–11): and the father's discipline of the child (Heb. 12:6–8). Furthermore, this new Father-child relationship carries with it new brothers and sisters (Heb. 13:1). The one who believes in Christ as Savior enters into the Father-child relationship with God solely on the grounds of Christ's sonship (Rom. 8:17; Heb. 2:17).

8:1 [a] ver 34 [b] ver 39; Ro 16:3 **8:2** [c] 1Co 15:45 [d] Ro 6:18 [e] Ro 7:4 **8:3** [f] Ac 13:39; Heb 7:18 [g] Php 2:7 [h] Heb 2:14, 17 **8:4** [i] Gal 5:16 **8:5** [j] Gal 5:19-21 [k] Gal 5:22-25 **8:6** [l] Gal 6:8 **8:7** [m] Jas 4:4 **8:9** [n] 1Co 6:19; Gal 4:6 [o] Jn 14:17; 1Jn 4:13 **8:10** [p] Gal 2:20; Eph 3:17; Col 1:27 **8:11** [q] Ac 2:24 [r] Jn 5:21 **8:13** [s] Gal 6:8 **8:14** [t] Gal 5:18 [u] Jn 1:12; Rev 21:7 **8:15** [v] 2Ti 1:7; Heb 2:15 [w] Mk 14:36; Gal 4:5,6 **8:16** [x] Eph 1:13 **8:17** [y] Ac 20:32; Gal 4:7 [z] 1Pe 4:13 **8:18** [a] 2Co 4:17; 1Pe 4:13 **8:20** [b] Ge 3:17-19 **8:21** [c] Ac 3:21; 2Pe 3:13; Rev 21:1

been groaning[d] as in the pains of childbirth right up to the present time. 23Not only so, but we ourselves, who have the firstfruits of the Spirit,[e] groan[f] inwardly as we wait eagerly[g] for our adoption to sonship, the redemption of our bodies. 24For in this hope we were saved.[h] But hope that is seen is no hope at all. Who hopes for what they already have? 25But if we hope for what we do not yet have, we wait for it patiently.

26In the same way, the Spirit helps us in our weakness. We do not know what we ought to pray for, but the Spirit himself intercedes for us[i] through wordless groans. 27And he who searches our hearts[j] knows the mind of the Spirit, because the Spirit intercedes for God's people in accordance with the will of God.

28And we know that in all things God works for the good of those who love him, who[a] have been called[k] according to his purpose. 29For those God foreknew[l] he also predestined[m] to be conformed to the image of his Son,[n] that he might be the firstborn among many brothers and sisters. 30And those he predestined,[o] he also called; those he called, he also justified;[p] those he justified, he also glorified.[q]

More Than Conquerors

31What, then, shall we say in response to these things?[r] If God is for us, who can be against us?[s] 32He who did not spare his own Son,[t] but gave him up for us all—how will he not also, along with him, graciously give us all things? 33Who will bring any charge[u] against those whom God has chosen? It is God who justifies. 34Who then is the one who condemns? No one. Christ Jesus who died[v]—more than that, who was raised to life—is at the right hand of God[w] and is also interceding for us.[x] 35Who shall separate us from the love of Christ? Shall trouble or hardship or persecution or famine or nakedness or danger or sword?[y] 36As it is written:

"For your sake we face death all day long;
we are considered as sheep to be slaughtered."[bz]

37No, in all these things we are more than conquerors[a] through him who loved us.[b] 38For I am convinced that neither death nor life, neither angels nor demons,[c] neither the present nor the future, nor any powers,[c] 39neither height nor depth, nor anything else in all creation, will be able to separate us from the love of God[d] that is in Christ Jesus our Lord.

Paul's Anguish Over Israel

9 I speak the truth in Christ—I am not lying,[e] my conscience confirms[f] it through the Holy Spirit— 2I have great sorrow and unceasing anguish in my heart. 3For I could wish that I myself[g] were cursed[h] and cut off from Christ for the sake of my people, those of my own race,[i] 4the people of Israel. Theirs is the adoption to sonship;[j] theirs the divine glory, the covenants,[k] the receiving of the law,[l] the temple worship[m] and the promises.[n] 5Theirs are the patriarchs, and from them is traced the human ancestry of the Messiah,[o] who is God over all,[p] forever praised![dq] Amen.

God's Sovereign Choice

6It is not as though God's word had failed. For not all who are descended from Israel are Israel.[r] 7Nor because they are his

[a] 28 Or *that all things work together for good to those who love God, who;* or *that in all things God works together with those who love him to bring about what is good—with those who*
[b] 36 Psalm 44:22 [c] 38 Or *nor heavenly rulers*
[d] 5 Or *Messiah, who is over all. God be forever praised!* Or *Messiah. God who is over all be forever praised!*

8:38–39 The Ultimate Security—The first chapters of Romans contain the most complete and systematic presentation of the gospel in the Scriptures. This passage is the bottom-line statement. Nothing can separate us from the love of God that is in Christ. Sadly, too often we hear those words and aren't able to apply them to how we live on a day-to-day basis. Satan is known as a deceiver. He will always try to persuade us that God's love is less than what it is. No matter what the circumstances, no matter how much we mess up, no matter how many powerful forces there are that would try to damage our relationship with Him, God will be there for us with His love.

8:39 *will be able to separate us.* Christ created all things, "in heaven and on earth, visible and invisible," and He was "before all things, and in him all things hold together" (Col. 1:16–17). If God, who was from the beginning, is for us, no created thing can separate us from His love. Our security in Him is absolute.

9:1 Conscience—This word is used by Paul for the witness within a person which scrutinizes, examines, and renders a verdict on behavior. Paul is saying in the passage that his conscience verifies the truthfulness of his statement that he has great grief over the Jew's rejection of the gospel. The Holy Spirit is the revealer of truth to the soul, and only as the mind and heart are taught by Scripture and governed by the Holy Spirit is the voice of conscience a reliable guide in life.

9:6 *not all who are descended from Israel.* What about the Jewish people? They had the law, the

8:22 [d] Jer 12:4 **8:23** [e] 2Co 5:5 [f] 2Co 5:2,4 [g] Gal 5:5 **8:24** [h] 1Th 5:8 **8:26** [i] Eph 6:18 **8:27** [j] Rev 2:23 **8:28** [k] 1Co 1:9; 2Ti 1:9 **8:29** [l] Ro 11:2 [m] Eph 1:5,11 [n] 1Co 15:49; 2Co 3:18; Php 3:21; 1Jn 3:2 **8:30** [o] Eph 1:5,11 [p] 1Co 6:11 [q] Ro 9:23 **8:31** [r] Ro 4:1 [s] Ps 118:6 **8:32** [t] Jn 3:16; Ro 4:25; 5:8 **8:33** [u] Isa 50:8,9 **8:34** [v] Ro 5:6-8 [w] Mk 16:19 [x] Heb 7:25; 9:24; 1Jn 2:1 **8:35** [y] 1Co 4:11 **8:36** [z] Ps 44:22; 2Co 4:11 **8:37** [a] 1Co 15:57 [b] Gal 2:20; Rev 1:5; 3:9 **8:38** [c] Eph 1:21; 1Pe 3:22 **8:39** [d] Ro 5:8 **9:1** [e] 2Co 11:10; Gal 1:20; 1Ti 2:7 [f] Ro 1:9 **9:3** [g] Ex 32:32 [h] 1Co 12:3; 16:22 [i] Ro 11:14 **9:4** [j] Ex 4:22 [k] Ge 17:2; Ac 3:25; Eph 2:12 [l] Ps 147:19 [m] Heb 9:1 [n] Ac 13:32 **9:5** [o] Mt 1:1-16 [p] Jn 1:1 [q] Ro 1:25 **9:6** [r] Ro 2:28,29; Gal 6:16

descendants are they all Abraham's children. On the contrary, "It is through Isaac
that your offspring will be reckoned."[a][s] 8 In
other words, it is not the children by physical descent who are God's children,[t] but
it is the children of the promise who are
regarded as Abraham's offspring. 9 For this
was how the promise was stated: "At the
appointed time I will return, and Sarah will
have a son."[b][u]

10 Not only that, but Rebekah's children
were conceived at the same time by our
father Isaac.[v] 11 Yet, before the twins were
born or had done anything good or bad—
in order that God's purpose[w] in election
might stand: 12 not by works but by him
who calls—she was told, "The older will
serve the younger."[c][x] 13 Just as it is written:
"Jacob I loved, but Esau I hated."[d][y]

14 What then shall we say? Is God unjust?
Not at all![z] 15 For he says to Moses,

"I will have mercy on whom I have
mercy,
and I will have compassion on whom
I have compassion."[e][a]

16 It does not, therefore, depend on human
desire or effort, but on God's mercy.[b] 17 For
Scripture says to Pharaoh: "I raised you up
for this very purpose, that I might display
my power in you and that my name might
be proclaimed in all the earth."[f][c] 18 Therefore God has mercy on whom he wants
to have mercy, and he hardens whom he
wants to harden.[d]

19 One of you will say to me:[e] "Then why
does God still blame us? For who is able to
resist his will?"[f] 20 But who are you, a human being, to talk back to God? "Shall what
is formed say to the one who formed it,[g]
'Why did you make me like this?' "[g][h] 21 Does
not the potter have the right to make out of
the same lump of clay some pottery for special purposes and some for common use?[i]

22 What if God, although choosing to
show his wrath and make his power
known, bore with great patience[j] the objects of his wrath—prepared for destruction? 23 What if he did this to make the riches of his glory[k] known to the objects of his
mercy, whom he prepared in advance for
glory[l]— 24 even us, whom he also called,[m]
not only from the Jews but also from the
Gentiles?[n] 25 As he says in Hosea:

"I will call them 'my people' who are
not my people;
and I will call her 'my loved one' who
is not my loved one,"[h][o]

26 and,

"In the very place where it was said to
them,
'You are not my people,'
there they will be called 'children of
the living God.' "[i][p]

27 Isaiah cries out concerning Israel:

"Though the number of the Israelites be
like the sand by the sea,[q]
only the remnant will be saved.[r]
28 For the Lord will carry out
his sentence on earth with speed and
finality."[j][s]

29 It is just as Isaiah said previously:

"Unless the Lord Almighty[t]
had left us descendants,
we would have become like Sodom,
we would have been like
Gomorrah."[k][u]

Israel's Unbelief

30 What then shall we say? That the Gentiles, who did not pursue righteousness,
have obtained it, a righteousness that is by
faith;[v] 31 but the people of Israel, who pursued the law as the way of righteousness,[w]

---

[a] *7* Gen. 21:12 [b] *9* Gen. 18:10,14 [c] *12* Gen. 25:23 [d] *13* Mal. 1:2,3 [e] *15* Exodus 33:19 [f] *17* Exodus 9:16 [g] *20* Isaiah 29:16; 45:9 [h] *25* Hosea 2:23 [i] *26* Hosea 1:10 [j] *28* Isaiah 10:22,23 (see Septuagint) [k] *29* Isaiah 1:9

---

covenants, and the promises. God has not changed His mind about His chosen people. He always intended for them to understand His whole message, up to and including the Messiah (Christ), as Paul has just explained. But God has, throughout history, always worked with those who believed, not just according to bloodline.

9:15 ***I will have mercy.*** God does not "owe" any of us salvation. He has mercy on us in spite of the way we act, not because of the way we act.

9:20 ***to talk back to God.*** Herein lies the divine tension. The Lord says that He does not wish for any to perish, but for all to come to repentance (2 Pet. 3:9). But He also says that no one comes to Jesus unless the Father draws him (John 6:44). He has mercy on whom He desires, and He hardens whom He desires (v. 18). Paul insists on God's right to do as He pleases. Even though God both draws and hardens, He also says that who He is and His worthiness to be worshiped are made plain in creation, so man is without excuse (Rom. 1:18–21). The question is not, "Why are some saved and some condemned?" Everyone deserves condemnation and it is only by God's grace that anyone is saved. We can be sure that whatever God does, it will be righteous, and there is a bigger picture than we can understand from our finite point of view. The only real question is, "How can I be saved?"

9:7 [s] Ge 21:12; Heb 11:18 **9:8** [t] Ro 8:14 **9:9** [u] Ge 18:10, 14 **9:10** [v] Ge 25:21 **9:11** [w] Ro 8:28 **9:12** [x] Ge 25:23 **9:13** [y] Mal 1:2, 3 **9:14** [z] 2Ch 19:7 **9:15** [a] Ex 33:19 **9:16** [b] Eph 2:8 **9:17** [c] Ex 9:16 **9:18** [d] Ex 4:21 **9:19** [e] Ro 11:19 [f] 2Ch 20:6; Da 4:35 **9:20** [g] Isa 64:8 [h] Isa 29:16 **9:21** [i] 2Ti 2:20 **9:22** [j] Ro 2:4 **9:23** [k] Ro 2:4 [l] Ro 8:30 **9:24** [m] Ro 8:28 [n] Ro 3:29 **9:25** [o] Hos 2:23; 1Pe 2:10 **9:26** [p] Hos 1:10 **9:27** [q] Ge 22:17; Hos 1:10 [r] Ro 11:5 **9:28** [s] Isa 10:22, 23 **9:29** [t] Jas 5:4 [u] Isa 1:9; Dt 29:23; Isa 13:19; Jer 50:40 **9:30** [v] Ro 1:17; 10:6; Gal 2:16; Php 3:9; Heb 11:7 **9:31** [w] Isa 51:1; Ro 10:2, 3

have not attained their goal.[x] 32 Why not? Because they pursued it not by faith but as if it were by works. They stumbled over the stumbling stone.[y] 33 As it is written:

"See, I lay in Zion a stone that causes
people to stumble
and a rock that makes them fall,
and the one who believes in him will
never be put to shame."[az]

10 Brothers and sisters, my heart's desire and prayer to God for the Israelites is that they may be saved. 2 For I can testify about them that they are zealous[a] for God, but their zeal is not based on knowledge. 3 Since they did not know the righteousness of God and sought to establish their own, they did not submit to God's righteousness.[b] 4 Christ is the culmination of the law[c] so that there may be righteousness for everyone who believes.[d]

5 Moses writes this about the righteousness that is by the law: "The person who does these things will live by them."[be] 6 But the righteousness that is by faith[f] says: "Do not say in your heart, 'Who will ascend into heaven?'"[cg] (that is, to bring Christ down) 7 "or 'Who will descend into the deep?'"[d] (that is, to bring Christ up from the dead). 8 But what does it say? "The word is near you; it is in your mouth and in your heart,"[eh] that is, the message concerning faith that we proclaim: 9 If you declare[i] with your mouth, "Jesus is Lord," and believe in your heart that God raised him from the dead,[j] you will be saved. 10 For it is with your heart that you believe and are justified, and it is with your mouth that you profess your faith and are saved. 11 As Scripture says, "Anyone who believes in him will never be put to shame."[fk] 12 For there is no difference between Jew and Gentile[l]—the same Lord is Lord of all[m] and richly blesses all who call on him, 13 for, "Everyone who calls on the name of the Lord[n] will be saved."[go]

14 How, then, can they call on the one they have not believed in? And how can they believe in the one of whom they have not heard? And how can they hear without someone preaching to them? 15 And how can anyone preach unless they are sent? As it is written: "How beautiful are the feet of those who bring good news!"[hp]

16 But not all the Israelites accepted the good news. For Isaiah says, "Lord, who has believed our message?"[iq] 17 Consequently, faith comes from hearing the message,[r] and the message is heard through the word about Christ.[s] 18 But I ask: Did they not hear? Of course they did:

"Their voice has gone out into all the
earth,
their words to the ends of the world."[jt]

19 Again I ask: Did Israel not understand? First, Moses says,

"I will make you envious[u] by those who
are not a nation;
I will make you angry by a nation
that has no understanding."[kv]

20 And Isaiah boldly says,

"I was found by those who did not
seek me;
I revealed myself to those who did not
ask for me."[lw]

21 But concerning Israel he says,

"All day long I have held out my hands
to a disobedient and obstinate
people."[mx]

The Remnant of Israel

11 I ask then: Did God reject his people? By no means![y] I am an Israelite myself, a descendant of Abraham,[z] from the tribe of Benjamin.[a] 2 God did not reject his people, whom he foreknew.[b] Don't you know what Scripture says in the passage

---

a *33* Isaiah 8:14; 28:16 *b* *5* Lev. 18:5 *c* *6* Deut. 30:12 *d* *7* Deut. 30:13 *e* *8* Deut. 30:14 *f* *11* Isaiah 28:16 (see Septuagint) *g* *13* Joel 2:32 *h* *15* Isaiah 52:7 *i* *16* Isaiah 53:1 *j* *18* Psalm 19:4 *k* *19* Deut. 32:21 *l* *20* Isaiah 65:1 *m* *21* Isaiah 65:2

9:32 ***stumbled.*** Being committed to righteousness by works, Israel "stumbled" over the righteousness of faith offered in Christ, just as God had already seen they would and declared through the prophet Isaiah (v. 33).

10:3 Self-Righteousness—There are two things which hinder people from submitting themselves to God's plan of salvation. The first is ignorance of God's own righteous character, and the second is human pride. No one is ever a candidate for Christ's righteousness unless he sees himself as utterly devoid of all possibility of attaining it on his own merits.

10:4 ***Christ is the culmination of the law.*** Christ fulfilled all the requirements of the law, and He is also the opening to the only way of righteousness we can ever have.

10:8 ***The word is near you.*** Righteousness by faith is not far off and inaccessible, but it is as near as a person's mouth and heart.

10:11 ***Anyone.*** Paul emphasizes the universal offer of salvation.

11:1 ***Did God reject his people?*** Paul points out that he himself is an Israelite, and was chosen by God to be a believer and an apostle. As he develops this thought, Paul reminds us that there has always been a remnant of Israelites whom God has kept true to Himself.

9:31 [x] Gal 5:4 **9:32** [y] 1Pe 2:8 **9:33** [z] Isa 28:16; Ro 10:11 **10:2** [a] Ac 21:20 **10:3** [b] Ro 1:17 **10:4** [c] Gal 3:24; Ro 7:1-4 [d] Ro 3:22 **10:5** [e] Lev 18:5; Ne 9:29; Eze 20:11, 13, 21; Ro 7:10 **10:6** [f] Ro 9:30 [g] Dt 30:12 **10:8** [h] Dt 30:14 **10:9** [i] Mt 10:32; Lk 12:8 [j] Ac 2:24 **10:11** [k] Isa 28:16; Ro 9:33 **10:12** [l] Ro 3:22, 29 [m] Ac 10:36 **10:13** [n] Ac 2:21 [o] Joel 2:32 **10:15** [p] Isa 52:7; Na 1:15 **10:16** [q] Isa 53:1; Jn 12:38 **10:17** [r] Gal 3:2, 5 [s] Col 3:16 **10:18** [t] Ps 19:4; Mt 24:14; Col 1:6, 23; 1Th 1:8 **10:19** [u] Ro 11:11, 14 [v] Dt 32:21 **10:20** [w] Isa 65:1; Ro 9:30 **10:21** [x] Isa 65:2 **11:1** [y] 1Sa 12:22; Jer 31:37 [z] 2Co 11:22 [a] Php 3:5 **11:2** [b] Ro 8:29

about Elijah—how he appealed to God
against Israel: 3“Lord, they have killed
your prophets and torn down your altars;
I am the only one left, and they are trying
to kill me”[a]?[c] 4And what was God’s answer
to him? “I have reserved for myself seven
thousand who have not bowed the knee to
Baal.”[b][d] 5So too, at the present time there
is a remnant[e] chosen by grace. 6And if by
grace, then it cannot be based on works;[f]
if it were, grace would no longer be grace.
7What then? What the people of Israel
sought so earnestly they did not obtain.[g]
The elect among them did, but the others
were hardened,[h] 8as it is written:

“God gave them a spirit of stupor,
eyes that could not see
and ears that could not hear,[i]
to this very day.”[c][j]

9And David says:

“May their table become a snare and a
trap,
a stumbling block and a retribution
for them.
10May their eyes be darkened so they
cannot see,
and their backs be bent forever.”[d][k]

Ingrafted Branches

11Again I ask: Did they stumble so as to
fall beyond recovery? Not at all![l] Rather, because of their transgression, salvation has
come to the Gentiles[m] to make Israel envious.[n] 12But if their transgression means
riches for the world, and their loss means
riches for the Gentiles,[o] how much greater
riches will their full inclusion bring!
13I am talking to you Gentiles. Inas-
much as I am the apostle to the Gentiles,[p]
I take pride in my ministry 14in the hope
that I may somehow arouse my own people to envy[q] and save[r] some of them. 15For
if their rejection brought reconciliation[s] to
the world, what will their acceptance be
but life from the dead?[t] 16If the part of the
dough offered as firstfruits[u] is holy, then
the whole batch is holy; if the root is holy,
so are the branches.
17If some of the branches have been broken off,[v] and you, though a wild olive shoot,
have been grafted in among the others[w]
and now share in the nourishing sap from
the olive root, 18do not consider yourself to
be superior to those other branches. If you
do, consider this: You do not support the
root, but the root supports you.[x] 19You will
say then, “Branches were broken off so that
I could be grafted in.” 20Granted. But they
were broken off because of unbelief, and
you stand by faith.[y] Do not be arrogant,[z] but
tremble.[a] 21For if God did not spare the natural branches, he will not spare you either.
22Consider therefore the kindness[b] and
sternness of God: sternness to those who
fell, but kindness to you, provided that you
continue[c] in his kindness. Otherwise, you
also will be cut off.[d] 23And if they do not
persist in unbelief, they will be grafted
in, for God is able to graft them in again.[e]
24After all, if you were cut out of an olive
tree that is wild by nature, and contrary to
nature were grafted into a cultivated olive
tree, how much more readily will these, the
natural branches, be grafted into their own
olive tree!

All Israel Will Be Saved

25I do not want you to be ignorant[f] of this
mystery,[g] brothers and sisters, so that you
may not be conceited:[h] Israel has experienced a hardening[i] in part until the full
number of the Gentiles has come in,[j] 26and
in this way[e] all Israel will be saved. As it
is written:

“The deliverer will come from Zion;
he will turn godlessness away from
Jacob.
27And this is[f] my covenant with them
when I take away their sins.”[g][k]

28As far as the gospel is concerned, they
are enemies[l] for your sake; but as far as
election is concerned, they are loved on
account of the patriarchs,[m] 29for God’s
gifts and his call[n] are irrevocable.[o] 30Just
as you who were at one time disobedient[p]
to God have now received mercy as a result
of their disobedience, 31so they too have
now become disobedient in order that they
too may now[h] receive mercy as a result of

---

a *3* 1 Kings 19:10,14 *b* *4* 1 Kings 19:18
c *8* Deut. 29:4; Isaiah 29:10 *d* *10* Psalm 69:22,23
e *26* Or *and so* *f* *27* Or *will be*
g *27* Isaiah 59:20,21; 27:9 (see Septuagint);
Jer. 31:33,34 *h* *31* Some manuscripts do not have
now.

11:8–10 ***ears that could not hear.*** Paul quotes Isaiah and David to show that Israel’s spiritual indifference was a continual pattern.
11:25 ***mystery.*** The mystery is that Israel has been temporarily and partially hardened, but God has not rejected them.
11:26 ***all Israel.*** “All Israel” does not mean that every individual in the nation will turn to the Lord. It means that the nation as a whole will be saved, just as the nation as a whole (but not every individual in it) is now rejecting the Lord.

11:3 [c] 1Ki 19:10, 14 **11:4** [d] 1Ki 19:18 **11:5** [e] Ro 9:27 **11:6** [f] Ro 4:4 **11:7** [g] Ro 9:31 [h] ver 25; Ro 9:18 **11:8** [i] Mt 13:13-15 [j] Dt 29:4; Isa 29:10 **11:10** [k] Ps 69:22, 23 **11:11** [l] ver 1 [m] Ac 13:46 [n] Ro 10:19 **11:12** [o] ver 25 **11:13** [p] Ac 9:15 **11:14** [q] ver 11; Ro 10:19 [r] 1Co 1:21; 1Ti 2:4; Titus 3:5 **11:15** [s] Ro 5:10 [t] Lk 15:24, 32 **11:16** [u] Lev 23:10, 17; Nu 15:18-21 **11:17** [v] Jer 11:16; Jn 15:2 [w] Ac 2:39; Eph 2:11-13 **11:18** [x] Jn 4:22 **11:20** [y] 1Co 10:12; 2Co 1:24 [z] Ro 12:16; 1Ti 6:17 [a] 1Pe 1:17 **11:22** [b] Ro 2:4 [c] 1Co 15:2; Heb 3:6 [d] Jn 15:2 **11:23** [e] 2Co 3:16 **11:25** [f] Ro 1:13 [g] Ro 16:25 [h] Ro 12:16 [i] ver 7; Ro 9:18 [j] Lk 21:24 **11:27** [k] Isa 27:9; Heb 8:10, 12 **11:28** [l] Ro 5:10 [m] Dt 7:8; 10:15; Ro 9:5 **11:29** [n] Ro 8:28 [o] Heb 7:21 **11:30** [p] Eph 2:2

God's mercy to you. 32For God has bound
everyone over to disobedience[q] so that he
may have mercy on them all.

Doxology

33 Oh, the depth of the riches[r] of the
wisdom and[a] knowledge of
God![s]
How unsearchable his judgments,
and his paths beyond tracing out![t]
34 "Who has known the mind of the
Lord?
Or who has been his counselor?"[b][u]
35 "Who has ever given to God,
that God should repay them?"[c][v]
36 For from him and through him and for
him are all things.[w]
To him be the glory forever! Amen.[x]

A Living Sacrifice

12 Therefore, I urge you,[y] brothers and
sisters, in view of God's mercy, to offer your bodies as a living sacrifice,[z] holy
and pleasing to God—this is your true and
proper worship. 2Do not conform[a] to the
pattern of this world,[b] but be transformed
by the renewing of your mind.[c] Then you
will be able to test and approve what God's
will is[d]—his good, pleasing and perfect
will.

Humble Service in the Body of Christ

3For by the grace given me[e] I say to every
one of you: Do not think of yourself more
highly than you ought, but rather think of
yourself with sober judgment, in accordance with the faith God has distributed
to each of you. 4For just as each of us has
one body with many members, and these
members do not all have the same function,[f] 5so in Christ we, though many, form
one body,[g] and each member belongs to all
the others. 6We have different gifts,[h] according to the grace given to each of us. If
your gift is prophesying, then prophesy in
accordance with your[d] faith;[i] 7if it is serving, then serve; if it is teaching, then teach;[j]
8if it is to encourage, then give encouragement;[k] if it is giving, then give generously;[l]
if it is to lead,[e] do it diligently; if it is to show
mercy, do it cheerfully.

Love in Action

9Love must be sincere.[m] Hate what is
evil; cling to what is good. 10Be devoted to
one another in love.[n] Honor one another
above yourselves.[o] 11Never be lacking in
zeal, but keep your spiritual fervor,[p] serving the Lord. 12Be joyful in hope,[q] patient
in affliction,[r] faithful in prayer. 13Share
with the Lord's people who are in need.
Practice hospitality.[s]

14Bless those who persecute you;[t] bless
and do not curse. 15Rejoice with those who
rejoice; mourn with those who mourn.[u]
16Live in harmony with one another.[v] Do
not be proud, but be willing to associate
with people of low position.[f] Do not be
conceited.[w]

---

[a] 33 Or *riches and the wisdom and the*
[b] 34 Isaiah 40:13 [c] 35 Job 41:11 [d] 6 Or *the*
[e] 8 Or *to provide for others* [f] 16 Or *willing to do menial work*

12:1 *living sacrifice.* In the Old Testament sacrificial system, the "job" of the sacrificial lamb was ended with its death. An individual or household selected an animal according to the dictated forms, and it was sacrificed to cover sins. Since Christ became the final atonement for sin, we no longer need the old system. But Paul is calling believers to consider their whole life as a sacrifice dedicated to God and His purposes, a "living" sacrifice, both holy and single-minded.

12:2 Living Sacrifice—Confession of sin in itself is not enough to enable the believer to automatically walk in Christ. He or she must learn, by the constant, inward transformation of the Spirit, to yield their whole self to God (Rom. 6:13; James 4:7). This involves both the body (Rom. 12:1; 1 Cor. 6:20) and the mind (Rom. 12:2), since what is conceived in the mind is carried out by the body. One's whole being must be presented by a decisive act of the will to God for His service. Yielding leads not only to dedication but also can result in separation: "do not be conformed to this world" (Rom. 12:2). Finally, yielding includes being transformed by the renewing of our minds. Man's mind has been darkened by sin (8:7; Col. 1:21) and must be brought to the place where it thinks as God thinks (Eph. 4:23). Through our prayers (Phil. 4:6–7) and through meditating on the Word of God (Ps. 119:1), we are transformed by God. This transformation is an ongoing, lifelong process that is secured by Christ's work on the cross and finalized when the believer is reunited with Christ in glory (Phil. 1:6; 1 John 3:2).

12:4–5 Fellowship—A believer must not view himself exclusively as an individual, but must also see himself as part of the whole, as a member of "one body." Fellowship in the New Testament sense is not merely companionship, but a partnership, a responsibility to one another that is financial, practical, and spiritual.

12:6 *prophesying.* In its narrower sense, "prophesying" means the revealing of God's will in a particular situation (Acts 13:1–3).

12:9 *Love.* There are three words used for love in the New Testament: "self-sacrificial love," "brotherly love," and "kindly affection," the last of which is used in this verse. The greatest proof of the truth of the gospel message and of the reality of Jesus' love is the love believers show to each other.

11:32 [q] Ro 3:9 **11:33** [r] Ro 2:4 [s] Ps 92:5 [t] Job 11:7
11:34 [u] Isa 40:13, 14; Job 15:8; 36:22; 1Co 2:16
11:35 [v] Job 35:7 **11:36** [w] 1Co 8:6; Col 1:16; Heb 2:10
[x] Ro 16:27 **12:1** [y] Eph 4:1 [z] Ro 6:13, 16, 19; 1Pe 2:5
12:2 [a] 1Pe 1:14 [b] 1Jn 2:15 [c] Eph 4:23 [d] Eph 5:17
12:3 [e] Ro 15:15; Gal 2:9; Eph 4:7 **12:4** [f] 1Co 12:12-14; Eph 4:16 **12:5** [g] 1Co 10:17 **12:6** [h] 1Co 7:7; 12:4, 8-10
[i] 1Pe 4:10, 11 **12:7** [j] Eph 4:11 **12:8** [k] Ac 15:32
[l] 2Co 9:5-13 **12:9** [m] 1Ti 1:5 **12:10** [n] Heb 13:1 [o] Php 2:3
12:11 [p] Ac 18:25 **12:12** [q] Ro 5:2 [r] Heb 10:32, 36
12:13 [s] 1Ti 3:2 **12:14** [t] Mt 5:44 **12:15** [u] Job 30:25
12:16 [v] Ro 15:5 [w] Jer 45:5; Ro 11:25

17Do not repay anyone evil for evil.[x] Be
careful to do what is right in the eyes of
everyone.[y] 18If it is possible, as far as it depends on you, live at peace with everyone.[z]
19Do not take revenge,[a] my dear friends,
but leave room for God's wrath, for it is
written: "It is mine to avenge; I will repay,"[ab] says the Lord. 20On the contrary:

"If your enemy is hungry, feed him;
if he is thirsty, give him something to drink.
In doing this, you will heap burning
coals on his head."[bc]

21Do not be overcome by evil, but overcome
evil with good.

Submission to Governing Authorities

13 Let everyone be subject to the governing authorities,[d] for there is no
authority except that which God has established.[e] The authorities that exist have
been established by God. 2Consequently,
whoever rebels against the authority is rebelling against what God has instituted,
and those who do so will bring judgment
on themselves. 3For rulers hold no terror for
those who do right, but for those who do
wrong. Do you want to be free from fear of
the one in authority? Then do what is right
and you will be commended.[f] 4For the one
in authority is God's servant for your good.
But if you do wrong, be afraid, for rulers
do not bear the sword for no reason. They
are God's servants, agents of wrath to bring
punishment on the wrongdoer.[g] 5Therefore,
it is necessary to submit to the authorities,
not only because of possible punishment
but also as a matter of conscience.

6This is also why you pay taxes, for the
authorities are God's servants, who give
their full time to governing. 7Give to everyone what you owe them: If you owe taxes, pay taxes;[h] if revenue, then revenue; if
respect, then respect; if honor, then honor.

Love Fulfills the Law

8Let no debt remain outstanding, except
the continuing debt to love one another, for
whoever loves others has fulfilled the law.[i]
9The commandments, "You shall not commit adultery," "You shall not murder," "You
shall not steal," "You shall not covet,"[cj]
and whatever other command there may
be, are summed up in this one command:
"Love your neighbor as yourself."[dk] 10Love
does no harm to a neighbor. Therefore love
is the fulfillment of the law.[l]

The Day Is Near

11And do this, understanding the present
time: The hour has already come[m] for you
to wake up from your slumber,[n] because
our salvation is nearer now than when we
first believed. 12The night is nearly over;
the day is almost here.[o] So let us put aside
the deeds of darkness[p] and put on the armor[q] of light. 13Let us behave decently,
as in the daytime, not in carousing and
drunkenness, not in sexual immorality and
debauchery, not in dissension and jealousy.[r] 14Rather, clothe yourselves with the
Lord Jesus Christ,[s] and do not think about
how to gratify the desires of the flesh.[e]

The Weak and the Strong

14 Accept the one whose faith is weak,[t]
without quarreling over disputable
matters. 2One person's faith allows them
to eat anything, but another, whose faith
is weak, eats only vegetables. 3The one
who eats everything must not treat with
contempt[u] the one who does not, and the
one who does not eat everything must not
judge[v] the one who does, for God has accepted them. 4Who are you to judge someone else's servant?[w] To their own master,
servants stand or fall. And they will stand,
for the Lord is able to make them stand.

5One person considers one day more
sacred than another;[x] another considers
every day alike. Each of them should be
fully convinced in their own mind. 6Who-

---

a *19* Deut. 32:35 *b* *20* Prov. 25:21,22
c *9* Exodus 20:13-15,17; Deut. 5:17-19,21
d *9* Lev. 19:18 *e* *14* In contexts like this, the Greek word for *flesh* (*sarx*) refers to the sinful state of human beings, often presented as a power in opposition to the Spirit.

12:20 ***burning coals.*** Freed from vengeance, believers can give themselves to mercy, even toward their enemies. Such unexpected acts of mercy might even bring them to shame and repentance.
13:9 ***as yourself.*** This is not a command to love ourselves. It is a recognition that we do love ourselves, and a command to love others just as genuinely and sincerely.
13:10 ***love.*** "Love" excludes murder, adultery, stealing, and lying. Therefore when we love, we automatically fulfill the prohibitions of the law.
14:1 ***whose faith is weak.*** Those who are weak in the faith are not unbelievers, but they have not yet understood (or are not able to understand) some of the deeper thinking about the not so clearly defined situations that a Christian faces.
14:5 ***one day more sacred than another.*** This verse probably relates to the holy days of the Old Testament ceremonial law. The exhortation does not mean it is wrong to have strong convictions, but that

12:17 [x] Pr 20:22 [y] 2Co 8:21 **12:18** [z] Mk 9:50; Ro 14:19 **12:19** [a] Lev 19:18; Pr 20:22; 24:29 [b] Dt 32:35 **12:20** [c] Pr 25:21, 22; Mt 5:44; Lk 6:27 **13:1** [d] Titus 3:1; 1Pe 2:13, 14 [e] Da 2:21; Jn 19:11 **13:3** [f] 1Pe 2:14 **13:4** [g] 1Th 4:6 **13:7** [h] Mt 17:25; 22:17, 21; Lk 23:2 **13:8** [i] ver 10; Jn 13:34; Gal 5:14; Col 3:14 **13:9** [j] Ex 20:13-15, 17; Dt 5:17-19, 21 [k] Lev 19:18; Mt 19:19 **13:10** [l] ver 8; Mt 22:39, 40 **13:11** [m] 1Co 7:29-31; 10:11 [n] Eph 5:14; 1Th 5:5, 6 **13:12** [o] 1Jn 2:8 [p] Eph 5:11 [q] Eph 6:11, 13 **13:13** [r] Gal 5:20, 21 **13:14** [s] Gal 3:27; 5:16; Eph 4:24 **14:1** [t] Ro 15:1; 1Co 8:9-12 **14:3** [u] Lk 18:9 [v] Col 2:16 **14:4** [w] Jas 4:12 **14:5** [x] Gal 4:10

ever regards one day as special does so
to the Lord. Whoever eats meat does so
to the Lord, for they give thanks to God;[y]
and whoever abstains does so to the Lord
and gives thanks to God. **7**For none of us
lives for ourselves alone,[z] and none of us
dies for ourselves alone. **8**If we live, we live
for the Lord; and if we die, we die for the
Lord. So, whether we live or die, we belong
to the Lord.[a] **9**For this very reason, Christ
died and returned to life[b] so that he might
be the Lord of both the dead and the living.[c]
10You, then, why do you judge your
brother or sister[a]? Or why do you treat
them with contempt? For we will all stand
before God's judgment seat.[d] **11**It is written:

"'As surely as I live,' says the Lord,
'every knee will bow before me;
every tongue will acknowledge
God.'"[b][e]

12So then, each of us will give an account
of ourselves to God.[f]
13Therefore let us stop passing judgment[g] on one another. Instead, make up
your mind not to put any stumbling block
or obstacle in the way of a brother or sister.
14I am convinced, being fully persuaded in
the Lord Jesus, that nothing is unclean in
itself.[h] But if anyone regards something as
unclean, then for that person it is unclean.[i]
15If your brother or sister is distressed
because of what you eat, you are no longer acting in love.[j] Do not by your eating
destroy someone for whom Christ died.[k]
16Therefore do not let what you know is
good be spoken of as evil.[l] **17**For the kingdom of God is not a matter of eating and
drinking,[m] but of righteousness, peace and
joy in the Holy Spirit,[n] **18**because anyone
who serves Christ in this way is pleasing to
God and receives human approval.[o]
19Let us therefore make every effort to
do what leads to peace[p] and to mutual edification.[q] **20**Do not destroy the work of God
for the sake of food.[r] All food is clean, but it
is wrong for a person to eat anything that
causes someone else to stumble.[s] **21**It is better not to eat meat or drink wine or to do
anything else that will cause your brother
or sister to fall.[t]
22So whatever you believe about these
things keep between yourself and God.
Blessed is the one who does not condemn[u]
himself by what he approves. **23**But whoever has doubts[v] is condemned if they eat,
because their eating is not from faith; and
everything that does not come from faith
is sin.[c]

15 We who are strong ought to bear
with the failings of the weak[w] and
not to please ourselves. **2**Each of us should
please our neighbors for their good,[x] to
build them up.[y] **3**For even Christ did not
please himself[z] but, as it is written: "The
insults of those who insult you have fallen
on me."[d][a] **4**For everything that was written
in the past was written to teach us,[b] so that

---

[a] *10* The Greek word for *brother or sister* (*adelphos*) refers here to a believer, whether man or woman, as part of God's family; also in verses 13, 15 and 21. [b] *11* Isaiah 45:23 [c] *23* Some manuscripts place 16:25-27 here; others after 15:33. [d] *3* Psalm 69:9

---

all people must have their own convictions. Concerning "disputable matters," things that are not clearly defined as sin, we as Christians are supposed to think deeply about these things, and decide what we think best pleases the Lord. We are not supposed to live by default, doing what most others are doing, or being swayed by the strongest voice. We may find that we need to change our original conclusions, but we must do so thoughtfully, not impulsively. We must not condemn others who come to a different conclusion.

14:12 ***account of ourselves to God.*** We must give an account to God for these conclusions we have reached about how to live, and in light of that, we want to be sure that our conclusions do not cause someone else to stumble.

14:14 ***unclean.*** "Unclean" means common, and refers to the things prohibited by the Jewish ceremonial law. If anyone considers some activity to be wrong, then for him it is wrong to engage in that activity.

14:15 Selfishness—This chapter concerns weak and strong Christians and their attitudes toward each other in practical matters within the church. If a stronger brother fails to consider the scruples of the weaker brother, the stronger brother violates the obligations of love. He is selfishly putting his own desires above the real needs of one who is weak in faith.

14:16 ***good be spoken of as evil.*** Even if you have decided that eating certain foods is in accord with your understanding of what is pleasing to God, if it causes another believer to be grieved by the choice you have made, you should be eager to change. Your freedom should not look like license or gluttony. The kingdom of God is a lot more important than the things we eat and drink.

14:21 ***fall.*** A believer does not have to abandon his own convictions, but love should cause him to carefully observe how what he does affects others. It is a sin (v. 23) to do something that you are really convinced is wrong, even if others think it is all right. In light of this, if a believer is influencing another to violate his conscience, even if the believer is not violating his own conscience, he has caused the other brother to "fall," and that should not happen.

15:3 ***Christ.*** Jesus Christ is the ultimate model for the strong believer. He "did not consider equality with God something to be used to his own advantage; rather, he made himself nothing" (Phil. 2:5 – 7) so that He could clearly represent God and His cause.

14:6 [y] Mt 14:19; 1Co 10:30, 31; 1Ti 4:3, 4 **14:7** [z] 2Co 5:15; Gal 2:20 **14:8** [a] Php 1:20 **14:9** [b] Rev 1:18 [c] 2Co 5:15 **14:10** [d] 2Co 5:10 **14:11** [e] Isa 45:23; Php 2:10, 11 **14:12** [f] Mt 12:36; 1Pe 4:5 **14:13** [g] Mt 7:1 **14:14** [h] Ac 10:15 [i] 1Co 8:7 **14:15** [j] Eph 5:2 [k] 1Co 8:11 **14:16** [l] 1Co 10:30 **14:17** [m] 1Co 8:8 [n] Ro 15:13 **14:18** [o] 2Co 8:21 **14:19** [p] Ps 34:14; Ro 12:18; Heb 12:14 [q] Ro 15:2; 2Co 12:19 **14:20** [r] ver 15 [s] 1Co 8:9-12 **14:21** [t] 1Co 8:13 **14:22** [u] 1Jn 3:21 **14:23** [v] ver 5 **15:1** [w] Ro 14:1; Gal 6:1, 2; 1Th 5:14 **15:2** [x] 1Co 10:33 [y] Ro 14:19 **15:3** [z] 2Co 8:9 [a] Ps 69:9 **15:4** [b] Ro 4:23, 24

through the endurance taught in the Scriptures and the encouragement they provide
we might have hope.
5May the God who gives endurance and
encouragement give you the same attitude
of mind[c] toward each other that Christ
Jesus had, 6so that with one mind and one
voice you may glorify the God and Father[d]
of our Lord Jesus Christ.
7Accept one another,[e] then, just as Christ
accepted you, in order to bring praise to
God. 8For I tell you that Christ has become
a servant of the Jews[a][f] on behalf of God's
truth, so that the promises[g] made to the
patriarchs might be confirmed 9and, moreover, that the Gentiles[h] might glorify God[i]
for his mercy. As it is written:

> "Therefore I will praise you among the
> Gentiles;
> I will sing the praises of your name."[b][j]

10Again, it says,

> "Rejoice, you Gentiles, with his
> people."[c][k]

11And again,

> "Praise the Lord, all you Gentiles;
> let all the peoples extol him."[d][l]

12And again, Isaiah says,

> "The Root of Jesse[m] will spring up,
> one who will arise to rule over the
> nations;
> in him the Gentiles will hope."[e][n]

13May the God of hope fill you with all
joy and peace[o] as you trust in him, so that
you may overflow with hope by the power
of the Holy Spirit.[p]

Paul the Minister to the Gentiles

14I myself am convinced, my brothers
and sisters, that you yourselves are full of
goodness,[q] filled with knowledge[r] and competent to instruct one another. 15Yet I have
written you quite boldly on some points to
remind you of them again, because of the
grace God gave me[s] 16to be a minister of
Christ Jesus to the Gentiles.[t] He gave me
the priestly duty of proclaiming the gospel
of God,[u] so that the Gentiles might become
an offering[v] acceptable to God, sanctified
by the Holy Spirit.
17Therefore I glory in Christ Jesus[w] in
my service to God.[x] 18I will not venture
to speak of anything except what Christ
has accomplished through me in leading
the Gentiles[y] to obey God[z] by what I have
said and done— 19by the power of signs
and wonders,[a] through the power of the
Spirit of God.[b] So from Jerusalem[c] all the
way around to Illyricum, I have fully proclaimed the gospel of Christ. 20It has always been my ambition to preach the gospel where Christ was not known, so that
I would not be building on someone else's
foundation.[d] 21Rather, as it is written:

> "Those who were not told about him
> will see,
> and those who have not heard will
> understand."[f][e]

22This is why I have often been hindered
from coming to you.[f]

Paul's Plan to Visit Rome

23But now that there is no more place
for me to work in these regions, and since
I have been longing for many years to visit
you,[g] 24I plan to do so when I go to Spain.[h]
I hope to see you while passing through
and to have you assist me on my journey
there, after I have enjoyed your company
for a while. 25Now, however, I am on my
way to Jerusalem[i] in the service[j] of the
Lord's people there. 26For Macedonia[k] and
Achaia[l] were pleased to make a contribution for the poor among the Lord's people
in Jerusalem. 27They were pleased to do it,
and indeed they owe it to them. For if the
Gentiles have shared in the Jews' spiritual
blessings, they owe it to the Jews to share
with them their material blessings.[m] 28So
after I have completed this task and have

[a] *8* Greek *circumcision* [b] *9* 2 Samuel 22:50; Psalm 18:49 [c] *10* Deut. 32:43 [d] *11* Psalm 117:1
[e] *12* Isaiah 11:10 (see Septuagint)
[f] *21* Isaiah 52:15 (see Septuagint)

15:9 ***As it is written.*** Paul quotes from all three divisions of the Old Testament (the Law, the Prophets, and the Psalms) and from three great Jewish leaders (Moses, David, and Isaiah) to demonstrate that God's purpose was always to bless the Gentiles through Israel.

15:12 ***Root of Jesse.*** This is a title for the Messiah (Christ). Jesse was the father of David, and the Messiah was to be the Son of David. The Messiah is both the Origin and the Offspring of David.

15:25–26 Kindness—One of the New Testament commands is that Christians display kindness toward other believers (12:10). The Macedonian believers had just gathered a love offering for the needy saints in Jerusalem. Such kindness is a response to God's wonderful kindness to us. In fact, wanting to reach out to others is an evidence of our new birth, and as we bless others in this way, we will find ourselves receiving similar blessings of kindness (Luke 6:38).

15:28 ***Spain.*** No one knows for sure if Paul ever got to Spain, but he had it on his travel itinerary.

15:5 [c] Ro 12:16; 1Co 1:10 **15:6** [d] Rev 1:6 **15:7** [e] Ro 14:1 **15:8** [f] Mt 15:24; Ac 3:25, 26 [g] 2Co 1:20 **15:9** [h] Ro 3:29 [i] Mt 9:8 [j] 2Sa 22:50; Ps 18:49 **15:10** [k] Dt 32:43 **15:11** [l] Ps 117:1 **15:12** [m] Rev 5:5 [n] Isa 11:10; Mt 12:21 **15:13** [o] Ro 14:17 [p] ver 19; 1Co 2:4; 1Th 1:5 **15:14** [q] Eph 5:9 [r] 2Pe 1:12 **15:15** [s] Ro 12:3 **15:16** [t] Ac 9:15; Ro 11:13 [u] Ro 1:1 [v] Isa 66:20 **15:17** [w] Php 3:3 [x] Heb 2:17 **15:18** [y] Ac 15:12; 21:19; Ro 1:5 [z] Ro 16:26 **15:19** [a] Jn 4:48; Ac 19:11 [b] ver 13 [c] Ac 22:17-21 **15:20** [d] 2Co 10:15, 16 **15:21** [e] Isa 52:15 **15:22** [f] Ro 1:13 **15:23** [g] Ac 19:21; Ro 1:10, 11 **15:24** [h] ver 28 **15:25** [i] Ac 19:21 [j] Ac 24:17 **15:26** [k] Ac 16:9; 2Co 8:1 [l] Ac 18:12 **15:27** [m] 1Co 9:11

made sure that they have received this contribution, I will go to Spain and visit you on the way. 29I know that when I come to you,[n] I will come in the full measure of the blessing of Christ.
30I urge you, brothers and sisters, by our Lord Jesus Christ and by the love of the Spirit,[o] to join me in my struggle by praying to God for me.[p] 31Pray that I may be kept safe[q] from the unbelievers in Judea and that the contribution I take to Jerusalem may be favorably received by the Lord's people there, 32so that I may come to you[r] with joy, by God's will,[s] and in your company be refreshed.[t] 33The God of peace[u] be with you all. Amen.

Personal Greetings

16 I commend[v] to you our sister Phoebe, a deacon[a,b] of the church in Cenchreae.[w] 2I ask you to receive her in the Lord[x] in a way worthy of his people and to give her any help she may need from you, for she has been the benefactor of many people, including me.

3Greet Priscilla[c] and Aquila,[y] my co-workers in Christ Jesus.[z] 4They risked their lives for me. Not only I but all the churches of the Gentiles are grateful to them.
5Greet also the church that meets at their house.[a]
Greet my dear friend Epenetus, who was the first convert[b] to Christ in the province of Asia.
6Greet Mary, who worked very hard for you.
7Greet Andronicus and Junia, my fellow Jews[c] who have been in prison with me. They are outstanding among[d] the apostles, and they were in Christ before I was.
8Greet Ampliatus, my dear friend in the Lord.
9Greet Urbanus, our co-worker in Christ,[d] and my dear friend Stachys.
10Greet Apelles, whose fidelity to Christ has stood the test.
Greet those who belong to the household of Aristobulus.
11Greet Herodion, my fellow Jew.[e]
Greet those in the household of Narcissus who are in the Lord.
12Greet Tryphena and Tryphosa, those women who work hard in the Lord.
Greet my dear friend Persis, another woman who has worked very hard in the Lord.
13Greet Rufus, chosen in the Lord, and his mother, who has been a mother to me, too.
14Greet Asyncritus, Phlegon, Hermes, Patrobas, Hermas and the other brothers and sisters with them.
15Greet Philologus, Julia, Nereus and his sister, and Olympas and all the Lord's people[f] who are with them.[g]
16Greet one another with a holy kiss.[h]
All the churches of Christ send greetings.

17I urge you, brothers and sisters, to watch out for those who cause divisions and put obstacles in your way that are contrary to the teaching you have learned.[i] Keep away from them.[j] 18For such people are not serving our Lord Christ, but their own appetites.[k] By smooth talk and flattery they deceive[l] the minds of naive people. 19Everyone has heard[m] about your obedience, so I rejoice because of you; but I want you to be wise about what is good, and innocent about what is evil.[n]
20The God of peace[o] will soon crush[p] Satan under your feet.
The grace of our Lord Jesus be with you.[q]
21Timothy,[r] my co-worker, sends his greetings to you, as do Lucius,[s] Jason[t] and Sosipater, my fellow Jews.[u]
22I, Tertius, who wrote down this letter, greet you in the Lord.
23Gaius, whose hospitality I and the whole church here enjoy, sends you his greetings.
Erastus,[v] who is the city's director of

[a] *1* Or *servant* [b] *1* The word *deacon* refers here to a Christian designated to serve with the overseers/elders of the church in a variety of ways; similarly in Phil. 1:1 and 1 Tim. 3:8,12. [c] *3* Greek *Prisca*, a variant of *Priscilla* [d] *7* Or *are esteemed by*

15:29 ***when I come to you.*** Paul did get to Rome, but not in the time frame or way he had thought. God had a special plan for Paul. The Lord would give him the opportunity to testify of his faith in the emperor's court, but he would do so as a prisoner (Acts 28).

16:3–4 ***Priscilla and Aquila.*** This married couple is never mentioned separately, perhaps because they ministered so effectively together. Like Paul, they were tentmakers, and worked with him in Corinth and Ephesus. (Acts 18:1–3,18,26).

16:8–10 ***Ampliatus ... Urbanus ... Stachys ... Apelles.*** These were common slave names. ***Aristobulus.*** This was a familiar Greek name, and this man may have been the owner of the previously mentioned men, if they were indeed slaves.

16:23 ***Gaius.*** "Gaius" of Corinth (1 Cor. 1:14) not only gave Paul lodging, but offered his house as a meeting place for the church.

15:29 [n] Ro 1:10, 11 **15:30** [o] Gal 5:22 [p] 2Co 1:11; Col 4:12 **15:31** [q] 2Th 3:2 **15:32** [r] Ro 1:10, 13 [s] Ac 18:21 [t] 1Co 16:18 **15:33** [u] Ro 16:20; 2Co 13:11; Php 4:9; 1Th 5:23; Heb 13:20 **16:1** [v] 2Co 3:1 [w] Ac 18:18 **16:2** [x] Php 2:29 **16:3** [y] Ac 18:2 [z] ver 7, 9, 10 **16:5** [a] 1Co 16:19; Col 4:15; Phm 2 [b] 1Co 16:15 **16:7** [c] ver 11, 21 **16:9** [d] ver 3 **16:11** [e] ver 7, 21 **16:15** [f] ver 2 [g] ver 14 **16:16** [h] 1Co 16:20; 2Co 13:12; 1Th 5:26 **16:17** [i] Gal 1:8, 9; 1Ti 1:3; 6:3 [j] 2Th 3:6, 14; 2Jn 10 **16:18** [k] Php 3:19 [l] Col 2:4 **16:19** [m] Ro 1:8 [n] Mt 10:16; 1Co 14:20 **16:20** [o] Ro 15:33 [p] Ge 3:15 [q] 1Th 5:28 **16:21** [r] Ac 16:1 [s] Ac 13:1 [t] Ac 17:5 [u] ver 7, 11 **16:23** [v] Ac 19:22

public works, and our brother Quartus
send you their greetings. [24][a]

25Now to him who is able[w] to establish
you in accordance with my gospel,[x] the
message I proclaim about Jesus Christ,
in keeping with the revelation of the mystery[y] hidden for long ages past, 26but now
revealed and made known through the
prophetic writings by the command of the
eternal God, so that all the Gentiles might
come to the obedience that comes from[b]
faith— 27to the only wise God be glory forever through Jesus Christ! Amen.[z]

[a] 24 Some manuscripts include here *May the grace of our Lord Jesus Christ be with all of you. Amen.*
[b] 26 Or *that is*

16:25 *mystery.* Paul speaks of his message as a "mystery" (see 11:25) because God's complete plan of salvation was at first hidden but now was being revealed. Part of the mystery is that the church will consist of both Jews and Gentiles united in one body of Christ (Eph. 3:1 – 13).

16:25 [w] Eph 3:20 [x] Ro 2:16 [y] Eph 1:9; Col 1:26,27
16:27 [z] Ro 11:36

1 CORINTHIANS

▶ **AUTHOR:** Pauline authorship of 1 Corinthians is almost universally accepted. Instances of this widely held belief can be found as early as A.D. 95, when Clement of Rome wrote to the Corinthian church and cited this epistle in regard to the continuing problem of factions among themselves. Paul taught the Word of God in Corinth for eighteen months in A.D. 51 and 52, leaving Apollos to preach and teach in his absence. When Paul was in Ephesus during his third missionary journey, he became disturbed by reports of discord in the church of Corinth. First Corinthians is a record of Paul's initial response to these problems.

▶ **TIME:** c. A.D. 56 ▶ **KEY VERSE:** 1 Cor. 1:10

▶ **THEME:** The basic theme of this epistle is the application of Christian principles to carnality in the individual as well as in the church. Paul is responding to a letter he received from the Corinthians concerning five behavioral problems that are causing dissension in one way or another: (1) Divisions in the church; (2) a case of incest; (3) court cases between members; (4) the abuse of Christian "freedom"; and (5) the chaos occurring in connection with celebration of the Lord's Supper. Paul's ethical responses to the various behaviors of the Corinthian church are based on a theological understanding of what it means to be a part of the people of God in a complex multicultural, pagan environment.

1 Paul, called to be an apostle[a] of Christ
Jesus by the will of God,[b] and our brother Sosthenes,[c]

2To the church of God in Corinth,[d] to
those sanctified in Christ Jesus and called[e]
to be his holy people, together with all those
everywhere who call on the name of our
Lord Jesus Christ—their Lord and ours:

3Grace and peace to you from God our
Father and the Lord Jesus Christ.[f]

Thanksgiving

4I always thank my God for you[g] because
of his grace given you in Christ Jesus. 5For
in him you have been enriched[h] in every
way—with all kinds of speech and with
all knowledge[i]— 6God thus confirming
our testimony[j] about Christ among you.
7Therefore you do not lack any spiritual gift as you eagerly wait for our Lord
Jesus Christ to be revealed.[k] 8He will also
keep you firm to the end, so that you will
be blameless[l] on the day of our Lord Jesus
Christ. 9God is faithful,[m] who has called
you into fellowship with his Son, Jesus
Christ our Lord.[n]

A Church Divided Over Leaders

10I appeal to you, brothers and sisters,[a]
in the name of our Lord Jesus Christ,
that all of you agree with one another in
what you say and that there be no divisions among you, but that you be perfectly
united in mind and thought. 11My brothers

[a] *10* The Greek word for *brothers and sisters* (*adelphoi*) refers here to believers, both men and women, as part of God's family; also in verses 11 and 26; and in 2:1; 3:1; 4:6; 6:8; 7:24, 29; 10:1; 11:33; 12:1; 14:6, 20, 26, 39; 15:1, 6, 50, 58; 16:15, 20.

1:1 ***by the will of God.*** The Corinthian church greatly valued human wisdom. This misplaced emphasis had caused some in the church to challenge Paul's authority. They forgot that Jesus Christ Himself had called him to his ministry as an apostle of Christ.
1:2 ***sanctified in Christ Jesus.*** Holiness comes from our position in Christ, not from our own goodness. Jesus' death in payment for our sins makes a believer holy forever in God's eyes (Heb. 10:14). But in everyday living, sanctification involves small daily changes.
1:7 ***do not lack any spiritual gift.*** The Corinthians were richly blessed with spiritual gifts because God was giving them everything they needed to do His will (12:14–27).
1:10 ***united in mind.*** Christian unity is not uniformity of appearance, but unity of direction, and the bond of mutual love and esteem (Eph. 4:14–16).

1:1 [a] Ro 1:1; Eph 1:1 [b] 2Co 1:1 [c] Ac 18:17 **1:2** [d] Ac 18:1 [e] Ro 1:7 **1:3** [f] Ro 1:7 **1:4** [g] Ro 1:8 **1:5** [h] 2Co 9:11 [i] 2Co 8:7 **1:6** [j] Rev 1:2 **1:7** [k] Php 3:20; Titus 2:13; 2Pe 3:12 **1:8** [l] 1Th 3:13 **1:9** [m] Isa 49:7; 1Th 5:24 [n] 1Jn 1:3

and sisters, some from Chloe's household
have informed me that there are quarrels
among you. 12What I mean is this: One of
you says, "I follow Paul";[o] another, "I follow Apollos";[p] another, "I follow Cephas[a]";[q]
still another, "I follow Christ."
13Is Christ divided? Was Paul crucified
for you? Were you baptized in the name of
Paul?[r] 14I thank God that I did not baptize
any of you except Crispus[s] and Gaius,[t] 15so
no one can say that you were baptized in
my name. 16(Yes, I also baptized the household of Stephanas;[u] beyond that, I don't remember if I baptized anyone else.) 17For
Christ did not send me to baptize,[v] but to
preach the gospel—not with wisdom[w] and
eloquence, lest the cross of Christ be emptied of its power.

Christ Crucified Is God's Power and Wisdom

18For the message of the cross is foolishness to those who are perishing,[x] but to us
who are being saved it is the power of God.[y]
19For it is written:

"I will destroy the wisdom of the wise;
the intelligence of the intelligent I will
frustrate."[b][z]

20Where is the wise person?[a] Where is
the teacher of the law? Where is the philosopher of this age? Has not God made foolish[b] the wisdom of the world? 21For since
in the wisdom of God the world through
its wisdom did not know him, God was
pleased through the foolishness of what
was preached to save those who believe.
22Jews demand signs[c] and Greeks look for
wisdom, 23but we preach Christ crucified:
a stumbling block[d] to Jews and foolishness[e] to Gentiles, 24but to those whom God
has called,[f] both Jews and Greeks, Christ
the power of God and the wisdom of God.[g]
25For the foolishness[h] of God is wiser than
human wisdom, and the weakness[i] of God
is stronger than human strength.
26Brothers and sisters, think of what
you were when you were called. Not many
of you were wise by human standards; not
many were influential; not many were of
noble birth. 27But God chose[j] the foolish[k]
things of the world to shame the wise;
God chose the weak things of the world
to shame the strong. 28God chose the lowly things of this world and the despised
things—and the things that are not[l]—to
nullify the things that are, 29so that no
one may boast before him.[m] 30It is because
of him that you are in Christ Jesus, who
has become for us wisdom from God—
that is, our righteousness,[n] holiness and
redemption.[o] 31Therefore, as it is written: "Let the one who boasts boast in the
Lord."[c][p]

2 And so it was with me, brothers and sisters. When I came to you, I did not come
with eloquence or human wisdom[q] as I proclaimed to you the testimony about God.[d]
2For I resolved to know nothing while I was
with you except Jesus Christ and him crucified.[r] 3I came to you[s] in weakness with
great fear and trembling. 4My message and
my preaching were not with wise and persuasive words, but with a demonstration
of the Spirit's power,[t] 5so that your faith
might not rest on human wisdom, but on
God's power.[u]

God's Wisdom Revealed by the Spirit

6We do, however, speak a message of
wisdom among the mature,[v] but not the
wisdom of this age[w] or of the rulers of this
age, who are coming to nothing. 7No, we

a *12* That is, Peter *b* *19* Isaiah 29:14
c *31* Jer. 9:24 *d* *1* Some manuscripts *proclaimed to you God's mystery*

1:14 *Crispus and Gaius.* Crispus was the ruler of the synagogue in Corinth when Paul began to preach there (Acts 18:8). He was instrumental in the conversion of many other Christians. Gaius may be the same person who hosted Paul and the entire church (Rom. 16:23).
1:16 *Stephanas.* Stephanas was one of Paul's first converts in Achaia, the region of which Corinth was the capital. Paul praised him and his household for their devotion to the ministry and for their assistance (16:15). Stephanas was one of the couriers who took correspondence to and from Corinth.
1:17 *not . . . to baptize, but to preach the gospel.* Paul's primary ministry was not baptism, but preaching the truth. Baptism naturally follows conversion, but is secondary in importance.
1:20 *Where is the wise person?* All human efforts to find favor with God fall woefully short (Rom. 3:9 – 28). Only through faith in Christ can we be saved from our sins.
1:27 *the foolish things of the world.* God's plan of salvation does not conform to the world's priorities. Yet in reality, eternal salvation is more valuable than anything else.
1:28 *the lowly things . . . and the despised things.* Corinth had a large slave population, and many of these slaves became followers of Christ. Slaves were despised by the free-born and the well to do.
2:6 *the rulers of this age.* In some passages Paul uses the word "rulers" to refer to spiritual beings (Eph. 6:12; Col. 2:15); here it seems to be a reference to earthly rulers.
2:7 *mystery.* God's plan was kept hidden, known only to Him, until He chose to reveal it (Eph. 3:1 – 11). This is in contrast to the teachings of the Gnostics, a

1:12 [o] 1Co 3:4, 22 [p] Ac 18:24 [q] Jn 1:42 **1:13** [r] Mt 28:19
1:14 [s] Ac 18:8; Ro 16:23 [t] Ac 19:29 **1:16** [u] 1Co 16:15
1:17 [v] Jn 4:2 [w] 1Co 2:1, 4, 13 **1:18** [x] 2Co 2:15 [y] Ro 1:16
1:19 [z] Isa 29:14 **1:20** [a] Isa 19:11, 12 [b] Job 12:17; Ro 1:22
1:22 [c] Mt 12:38 **1:23** [d] Lk 2:34; Gal 5:11 [e] 1Co 2:14
1:24 [f] Ro 8:28 [g] ver 30; Col 2:3 **1:25** [h] ver 18 [i] 2Co 13:4
1:27 [j] Jas 2:5 [k] ver 20 **1:28** [l] Ro 4:17 **1:29** [m] Eph 2:9
1:30 [n] Jer 23:5, 6; 2Co 5:21 [o] Ro 3:24; Eph 1:7, 14
1:31 [p] Jer 9:23, 24; 2Co 10:17 **2:1** [q] 1Co 1:17
2:2 [r] Gal 6:14; 1Co 1:23 **2:3** [s] Ac 18:1-18 **2:4** [t] Ro 15:19
2:5 [u] 2Co 4:7; 6:7 **2:6** [v] Eph 4:13; Php 3:15; Heb 5:14
[w] 1Co 1:20

declare God's wisdom, a mystery that has
been hidden and that God destined for our
glory before time began. 8None of the rulers of this age understood it, for if they had,
they would not have crucified the Lord of
glory.[x] 9However, as it is written:

"What no eye has seen,
what no ear has heard,
and what no human mind has
conceived"[a]—
the things God has prepared for those
who love him—[y]

10these are the things God has revealed[z] to
us by his Spirit.[a]

The Spirit searches all things, even the
deep things of God. 11For who knows a
person's thoughts[b] except their own spirit[c] within them? In the same way no one
knows the thoughts of God except the Spirit of God. 12What we have received is not
the spirit[d] of the world,[e] but the Spirit who
is from God, so that we may understand
what God has freely given us. 13This is
what we speak, not in words taught us by
human wisdom[f] but in words taught by the
Spirit, explaining spiritual realities with
Spirit-taught words.[b] 14The person without
the Spirit does not accept the things that
come from the Spirit of God but considers
them foolishness,[g] and cannot understand
them because they are discerned only
through the Spirit. 15The person with the
Spirit makes judgments about all things,
but such a person is not subject to merely
human judgments, 16for,

"Who has known the mind of the
Lord
so as to instruct him?"[c][h]

But we have the mind of Christ.[i]

The Church and Its Leaders

3 Brothers and sisters, I could not address
you as people who live by the Spirit[j] but
as people who are still worldly[k]—mere infants[l] in Christ. 2I gave you milk, not solid
food,[m] for you were not yet ready for it.[n]
Indeed, you are still not ready. 3You are
still worldly. For since there is jealousy and
quarreling[o] among you, are you not worldly? Are you not acting like mere humans?
4For when one says, "I follow Paul," and another, "I follow Apollos,"[p] are you not mere
human beings?

5What, after all, is Apollos? And what is
Paul? Only servants, through whom you
came to believe—as the Lord has assigned
to each his task. 6I planted the seed,[q] Apollos watered it, but God has been making it
grow. 7So neither the one who plants nor
the one who waters is anything, but only
God, who makes things grow. 8The one
who plants and the one who waters have
one purpose, and they will each be rewarded according to their own labor.[r] 9For we
are co-workers in God's service;[s] you are
God's field,[t] God's building.[u]

10By the grace God has given me,[v] I laid
a foundation[w] as a wise builder, and someone else is building on it. But each one
should build with care. 11For no one can
lay any foundation other than the one already laid, which is Jesus Christ.[x] 12If anyone builds on this foundation using gold,
silver, costly stones, wood, hay or straw,
13their work will be shown for what it is,[y]
because the Day[z] will bring it to light. It
will be revealed with fire, and the fire will
test the quality of each person's work. 14If
what has been built survives, the builder
will receive a reward. 15If it is burned up,
the builder will suffer loss but yet will be
saved—even though only as one escaping
through the flames.[a]

16Don't you know that you yourselves
are God's temple[b] and that God's Spirit

---

a *9* Isaiah 64:4 *b* *13* Or *Spirit, interpreting spiritual truths to those who are spiritual*
c *16* Isaiah 40:13

---

group of false religious teachers who would infiltrate the early church (1 John 2:18–27). They claimed that there existed a body of secret knowledge that was only available to those initiated into an inner circle of spiritual teachers.

2:13 ***explaining spiritual realities with Spirit-taught words.*** This portion of text is difficult to translate and interpret. The Greek term translated "explaining" can also mean "combining." The two references to "spiritual" may mean explaining spiritual truths to spiritual persons, or else combining spiritual truths with spiritual words (2 Tim. 3:16; 2 Pet. 1:20–21).

3:2 ***I gave you milk.*** Paul did not expect the Corinthians to be mature when they first accepted Christ. Yet they should have grown in their faith—that is, become sanctified. The behavior of Christians should begin to line up with their righteous position in Christ.

3:3 ***You are still worldly.*** An immature Christian naturally lacks many Christian traits, but no one should expect this condition to last. Paul was surprised that the Corinthians had not yet grown into spiritual maturity or become able to distinguish between good and evil (Heb. 5:14).

3:13 ***the Day.*** This is the time when Christ will judge the merits of His servants' work (2 Cor. 5:10), not whether they receive forgiveness of sin. Likewise, the fire does not refer to the eternal fire of damnation (Rev. 20:10) but to the evaluation of believers' works (Rev. 22:12).

2:8 [x] Ac 7:2; Jas 2:1 **2:9** [y] Isa 64:4; 65:17
2:10 [z] Mt 13:11; Eph 3:3,5 [a] Jn 14:26 **2:11** [b] Jer 17:9
[c] Pr 20:27 **2:12** [d] Ro 8:15 [e] 1Co 1:20,27 **2:13** [f] 1Co 1:17
2:14 [g] 1Co 1:18 **2:16** [h] Isa 40:13 [i] Jn 15:15
3:1 [j] 1Co 2:15 [k] Ro 7:14; 1Co 2:14 [l] Heb 5:13
3:2 [m] Heb 5:12-14; 1Pe 2:2 [n] Jn 16:12 **3:3** [o] 1Co 1:11;
Gal 5:20 **3:4** [p] 1Co 1:12 **3:6** [q] Ac 18:4-11
3:8 [r] Ps 62:12 **3:9** [s] 2Co 6:1 [t] Isa 61:3 [u] Eph 2:20-22;
1Pe 2:5 **3:10** [v] Ro 12:3 [w] Ro 15:20 **3:11** [x] Isa 28:16;
Eph 2:20 **3:13** [y] 1Co 4:5 [z] 2Th 1:7-10 **3:15** [a] Jude 23
3:16 [b] 1Co 6:19; 2Co 6:16

dwells in your midst? 17If anyone destroys God's temple, God will destroy that person; for God's temple is sacred, and you together are that temple.

18Do not deceive yourselves. If any of you think you are wise[c] by the standards of this age, you should become "fools" so that you may become wise. 19For the wisdom of this world is foolishness[d] in God's sight. As it is written: "He catches the wise in their craftiness"[a];[e] 20and again, "The Lord knows that the thoughts of the wise are futile."[b][f] 21So then, no more boasting about human leaders![g] All things are yours,[h] 22whether Paul or Apollos or Cephas[c][i] or the world or life or death or the present or the future[j]—all are yours, 23and you are of Christ,[k] and Christ is of God.

The Nature of True Apostleship

4 This, then, is how you ought to regard us: as servants of Christ and as those entrusted[l] with the mysteries[m] God has revealed. 2Now it is required that those who have been given a trust must prove faithful. 3I care very little if I am judged by you or by any human court; indeed, I do not even judge myself. 4My conscience is clear, but that does not make me innocent.[n] It is the Lord who judges me. 5Therefore judge nothing[o] before the appointed time; wait until the Lord comes. He will bring to light what is hidden in darkness and will expose the motives of the heart. At that time each will receive their praise from God.[p]

6Now, brothers and sisters, I have applied these things to myself and Apollos for your benefit, so that you may learn from us the meaning of the saying, "Do not go beyond what is written."[q] Then you will not be puffed up in being a follower of one of us over against the other.[r] 7For who makes you different from anyone else? What do you have that you did not receive?[s] And if you did receive it, why do you boast as though you did not?

8Already you have all you want! Already you have become rich![t] You have begun to reign—and that without us! How I wish that you really had begun to reign so that we also might reign with you! 9For it seems to me that God has put us apostles on display at the end of the procession, like those condemned to die[u] in the arena. We have been made a spectacle[v] to the whole universe, to angels as well as to human beings. 10We are fools for Christ,[w] but you are so wise in Christ![x] We are weak, but you are strong![y] You are honored, we are dishonored! 11To this very hour we go hungry and thirsty, we are in rags, we are brutally treated, we are homeless.[z] 12We work hard with our own hands.[a] When we are cursed, we bless;[b] when we are persecuted, we endure it; 13when we are slandered, we answer kindly. We have become the scum of the earth, the garbage[c] of the world—right up to this moment.

Paul's Appeal and Warning

14I am writing this not to shame you but to warn you as my dear children.[d] 15Even if you had ten thousand guardians in Christ, you do not have many fathers, for in Christ Jesus I became your father through the gospel.[e] 16Therefore I urge you to imitate me.[f] 17For this reason I have sent to you Timothy, my son[g] whom I love, who is faithful in the Lord. He will remind you of my way of life in Christ Jesus, which agrees with what I teach everywhere in every church.[h]

18Some of you have become arrogant, as if I were not coming to you. 19But I will come to you very soon,[i] if the Lord is willing,[j] and then I will find out not only how these arrogant people are talking, but what power they have. 20For the kingdom of God is not a matter of talk but of power. 21What do you prefer? Shall I come to you with a rod of discipline,[k] or shall I come in love and with a gentle spirit?

Dealing With a Case of Incest

5 It is actually reported that there is sexual immorality among you, and of a kind that even pagans do not tolerate: A man is

[a] *19* Job 5:13 [b] *20* Psalm 94:11 [c] *22* That is, Peter

3:21 ***All things are yours.*** The Stoic literature of the time, which the Corinthians would have known, often spoke of the wise man as possessing everything. Everything God has done in the church, and in the entire universe, benefits all believers. There is no place for foolish boasting or competition among Christians.
4:5 ***judge nothing.*** While believers can benefit from the constructive evaluations of other believers, their ultimate Judge is the Lord Himself. We cannot know the whole picture, and we must be careful not to make premature evaluations of others.
4:6 ***puffed up.*** Greeks considered humility to be a fault, a characteristic of slaves. To the Christian, however, it exemplifies the attitude of Christ (Phil. 2:5–8).
4:10 ***fools for Christ.*** True strength is found in understanding our weakness and Christ's sufficiency (2 Cor. 12:7–10; Phil. 4:11–13).

5:1 ***sexual immorality.*** The sexual immorality of incest was forbidden by Old Testament law (Lev. 18:8; Deut. 22:30) and by Roman law. The phrase "his father's wife" probably indicates that the woman was

3:18 [c] Isa 5:21; 1Co 8:2 **3:19** [d] 1Co 1:20,27 [e] Job 5:13 **3:20** [f] Ps 94:11 **3:21** [g] 1Co 4:6 [h] Ro 8:32 **3:22** [i] 1Co 1:12 [j] Ro 8:38 **3:23** [k] 1Co 15:23; 2Co 10:7; Gal 3:29 **4:1** [l] 1Co 9:17; Titus 1:7 [m] Ro 16:25 **4:4** [n] Ro 2:13 **4:5** [o] Mt 7:1,2; Ro 2:1 [p] Ro 2:29 **4:6** [q] 1Co 1:19,31; 3:19,20 [r] 1Co 1:12 **4:7** [s] Jn 3:27; Ro 12:3,6 **4:8** [t] Rev 3:17,18 **4:9** [u] Ro 8:36 [v] Heb 10:33 **4:10** [w] 1Co 1:18; Ac 17:18 [x] 1Co 3:18 [y] 1Co 2:3 **4:11** [z] Ro 8:35; 2Co 11:23-27 **4:12** [a] Ac 18:3 [b] 1Pe 3:9 **4:13** [c] La 3:45 **4:14** [d] 1Th 2:11 **4:15** [e] 1Co 9:12,14,18,23 **4:16** [f] 1Co 11:1; Php 3:17; 1Th 1:6; 2Th 3:7,9 **4:17** [g] 1Ti 1:2 [h] 1Co 7:17 **4:19** [i] 2Co 1:15,16 [j] Ac 18:21 **4:21** [k] 2Co 1:23; 13:2,10

sleeping with his father's wife.[l] **2**And you
are proud! Shouldn't you rather have gone
into mourning[m] and have put out of your
fellowship the man who has been doing
this? **3**For my part, even though I am not
physically present, I am with you in spirit.[n] As one who is present with you in this
way, I have already passed judgment in the
name of our Lord Jesus[o] on the one who
has been doing this. **4**So when you are assembled and I am with you in spirit, and
the power of our Lord Jesus is present,
5hand this man over[p] to Satan for the destruction of the flesh,[a,b] so that his spirit
may be saved on the day of the Lord.

6Your boasting is not good.[q] Don't you
know that a little yeast[r] leavens the whole
batch of dough?[s] **7**Get rid of the old yeast, so
that you may be a new unleavened batch—
as you really are. For Christ, our Passover
lamb, has been sacrificed.[t] **8**Therefore let
us keep the Festival, not with the old bread
leavened with malice and wickedness, but
with the unleavened bread[u] of sincerity
and truth.

9I wrote to you in my letter not to associate[v] with sexually immoral people— **10**not
at all meaning the people of this world[w]
who are immoral, or the greedy and swindlers, or idolaters. In that case you would
have to leave this world. **11**But now I am
writing to you that you must not associate
with anyone who claims to be a brother or
sister[c] but is sexually immoral or greedy,
an idolater[x] or slanderer, a drunkard or
swindler. Do not even eat with such people.

12What business is it of mine to judge
those outside[y] the church? Are you not to
judge those inside?[z] **13**God will judge those
outside. "Expel the wicked person from
among you."[d,a]

Lawsuits Among Believers

6 If any of you has a dispute with another, do you dare to take it before the ungodly for judgment instead of before the
Lord's people?[b] **2**Or do you not know that
the Lord's people will judge the world?[c]
And if you are to judge the world, are you
not competent to judge trivial cases? **3**Do
you not know that we will judge angels?
How much more the things of this life!
4Therefore, if you have disputes about
such matters, do you ask for a ruling from
those whose way of life is scorned in the
church? **5**I say this to shame you.[d] Is it
possible that there is nobody among you
wise enough to judge a dispute between
believers?[e] **6**But instead, one brother takes
another to court—and this in front of unbelievers![f]

7The very fact that you have lawsuits
among you means you have been completely defeated already. Why not rather be
wronged? Why not rather be cheated?[g] **8**Instead, you yourselves cheat and do wrong,
and you do this to your brothers and sisters.[h] **9**Or do you not know that wrongdoers
will not inherit the kingdom of God?[i] Do
not be deceived:[j] Neither the sexually immoral nor idolaters nor adulterers nor men
who have sex with men[e] **10**nor thieves nor
the greedy nor drunkards nor slanderers
nor swindlers will inherit the kingdom of
God. **11**And that is what some of you were.[k]
But you were washed,[l] you were sanctified,[m] you were justified in the name of the
Lord Jesus Christ and by the Spirit of our
God.

---

a 5 In contexts like this, the Greek word for *flesh* (*sarx*) refers to the sinful state of human beings, often presented as a power in opposition to the Spirit. *b* 5 Or *of his body* *c* 11 The Greek word for *brother or sister* (*adelphos*) refers here to a believer, whether man or woman, as part of God's family; also in 8:11, 13. *d* 13 Deut. 13:5; 17:7; 19:19; 21:21; 22:21,24; 24:7 *e* 9 The words *men who have sex with men* translate two Greek words that refer to the passive and active participants in homosexual acts.

---

the offender's stepmother. Paul does not specify any discipline for the woman, which may indicate that she was not a believer.

5:2 *proud! Shouldn't you rather have gone into mourning.* The Corinthian Christians had a twisted view of grace that caused them to be proud of their tolerance of the sexual offender. They believed that, because God's grace is limitless, living in sin was no problem.

5:6 *a little yeast leavens.* The backdrop for this passage is the Passover (Ex. 12). In commemoration of their ancestors' hurried departure from Egypt, Jewish families would carefully remove all leaven (yeast) from their homes in preparation for the celebration of the Passover. In the New Testament, leaven is often used as a symbol of sin. Yeast spreads through a batch of dough, and unchallenged sin can soon contaminate the whole church. The sexual offender was guilty of sin, but the whole congregation was also guilty of ignoring the man's disobedience.

5:9 *my letter.* It is believed that this refers to an earlier letter which has not been preserved.

5:10 *of this world.* Christians are called to influence the world, not to run away from it (Matt. 5:13–16). They are agents of God to carry the light of Jesus Christ into a dark world (Phil. 2:14–16; 1 Pet. 2:11–12).

6:9 *kingdom of God.* This term seems to refer to a future time when God will rule the earth in righteousness (Matt. 6:10; Luke 11:2).

6:11 Changed Life—The greatest proof of the new birth is a changed life. The child of God now suddenly loves the following:

1. *He loves Jesus.* Before conversion the sinner might hold Christ in high esteem, but after conversion he loves the Savior (1 John 5:1–2).

5:1 [l] Lev 18:8; Dt 22:30 **5:2** [m] 2Co 7:7-11 **5:3** [n] Col 2:5 [o] 2Th 3:6 **5:5** [p] 1Ti 1:20 **5:6** [q] Jas 4:16 [r] Mt 16:6, 12 [s] Gal 5:9 **5:7** [t] Mk 14:12; 1Pe 1:19 **5:8** [u] Ex 12:14, 15; Dt 16:3 **5:9** [v] Eph 5:11; 2Th 3:6, 14 **5:10** [w] 1Co 10:27 **5:11** [x] 1Co 10:7, 14 **5:12** [y] Mk 4:11 [z] ver 3-5; 1Co 6:1-4 **5:13** [a] Dt 13:5 **6:1** [b] Mt 18:17 **6:2** [c] Mt 19:28; Lk 22:30 **6:5** [d] 1Co 4:14 [e] Ac 1:15 **6:6** [f] 2Co 6:14, 15 **6:7** [g] Mt 5:39, 40 **6:8** [h] 1Th 4:6 **6:9** [i] Gal 5:21 [j] 1Co 15:33; Jas 1:16 **6:11** [k] Eph 2:2 [l] Ac 22:16 [m] 1Co 1:2

Sexual Immorality

12"I have the right to do anything," you say—but not everything is beneficial.[n] "I have the right to do anything"—but I will not be mastered by anything. 13You say, "Food for the stomach and the stomach for food, and God will destroy them both."[o] The body, however, is not meant for sexual immorality but for the Lord, and the Lord for the body. 14By his power God raised the Lord from the dead, and he will raise us also.[p] 15Do you not know that your bodies are members of Christ himself?[q] Shall I then take the members of Christ and unite them with a prostitute? Never! 16Do you not know that he who unites himself with a prostitute is one with her in body? For it is said, "The two will become one flesh."[a][r] 17But whoever is united with the Lord is one with him in spirit.[b][s]

18Flee from sexual immorality.[t] All other sins a person commits are outside the body, but whoever sins sexually, sins against their own body.[u] 19Do you not know that your bodies are temples[v] of the Holy Spirit, who is in you, whom you have received from God? You are not your own;[w] 20you were bought at a price.[x] Therefore honor God with your bodies.

Concerning Married Life

7 Now for the matters you wrote about: "It is good for a man not to have sexual relations with a woman."[y] 2But since sexual immorality is occurring, each man should have sexual relations with his own wife, and each woman with her own husband. 3The husband should fulfill his marital duty to his wife,[z] and likewise the wife to her husband. 4The wife does not have authority over her own body but yields it to her husband. In the same way, the husband does not have authority over his own body but yields it to his wife. 5Do not deprive each other except perhaps by mutual consent and for a time,[a] so that you may devote yourselves to prayer. Then come together again so that Satan[b] will not tempt you[c] because of your lack of self-control. 6I say this as a concession, not as a command.[d] 7I

[a] *16* Gen. 2:24 [b] *17* Or *in the Spirit*

---

2. *He loves the Bible.* We should love God's Word as the psalmist did in Psalm 119. There he expresses his great love for God's Word 17 times.
3. *He loves other Christians.* "We know that we have passed from death to life, because we love each other. Anyone who does not love remains in death." (1 John 3:14).
4. *He loves his enemies.* (Matt. 5:43–45).
5. *He loves the souls of all people.* Like Paul, he too can cry out for the conversion of loved ones. "Brothers and sisters, my heart's desire and prayer to God for the Israelites is that they may be saved" (Rom. 10:1).
6. *He loves the pure life.* John says that if one loves the world, the love of the Father is not in him (1 John 2:15–17).
7. *He loves to talk to God.* "Speaking to one another with psalms, hymns, and songs from the Spirit. Sing and make music from your heart to the Lord" (Eph. 5:19).

6:13 *Food for the stomach and the stomach for food.* The stomach's purpose is to digest food, but it is not the purpose of the body to commit immorality. Furthermore, by design God put restrictions on both eating and sexual activity. Eating to the point of gluttony and having sex outside of marriage both violate God's intent and are sinful.

6:15 *your bodies are members of Christ.* Becoming a Christ follower is not just a "spiritual experience." Our bodies belong to Jesus as well as our souls, and nothing that we do with our bodies is apart from our relationship with Jesus Christ.

6:16 *one with her in body.* God designed sex as part of the intense "one flesh" bond between husband and wife, so sex is not a one-dimensional physical act. It involves soul, spirit, and emotions as well. Broken sexual relationships tear away at a person's very being in a way that nothing else does.

6:19 The Work of the Holy Spirit—The Holy Spirit is sometimes referred to as the *Paraclete.* The first part of that word, *para,* is a preposition that means "coming alongside." As the Spirit comes alongside of us, it ministers in the following ways:

1. *The Holy Spirit indwells Christians.* The Bible teaches that believers are indwelt and are the "temple of the Holy Spirit" (1 Cor. 6:19). The purpose of this indwelling ministry is to empower the newly created nature (2 Cor. 5:17; Eph. 3:16).
2. *The Holy Spirit fills believers.* We are admonished to "be filled with the Spirit" (Eph. 5:18). We are then to be subject to the control of the Spirit in contrast to being controlled by the lures of the world.
3. *The Holy Spirit sanctifies the believer* (Rom. 15:16; 2 Thess. 2:13).
4. *The Holy Spirit produces fruit in the life of the believer.* This fruit is described by Paul: "But the fruit of the Spirit is love, joy, peace, forbearance, kindness, goodness, faithfulness, gentleness and self-control" (Gal. 5:22–23).
5. *The Holy Spirit gives gifts to Christians* (Rom. 12:6–8; 1 Cor. 12:1–11; Eph. 4:7–12). These are abilities given to every Christian (1 Cor. 7:7; 1 Pet. 4:10). The purpose of these gifts is to glorify God (Rev. 4:11) and to edify the body of Christ (Eph. 4:12–13).
6. *The Holy Spirit teaches believers.* He will instruct us in all spiritual things as we read the Word of God (John 14:26) and abide in the Son of God (1 John 2:24–27).

6:20 *bought at a price.* With His death, Jesus Christ paid the cost to redeem us from our slavery to sin (Eph. 1:7; 1 Pet. 1:18–19).

7:6 *concession, not as a command.* The Corinthians seemed to be caught by two extreme false positions: the false concept that physical activity does

6:12 [n] 1Co 10:23 **6:13** [o] Col 2:22 **6:14** [p] Ro 6:5; Eph 1:19,20 **6:15** [q] Ro 12:5 **6:16** [r] Ge 2:24; Mt 19:5; Eph 5:31 **6:17** [s] Jn 17:21-23; Gal 2:20 **6:18** [t] 2Co 12:21; 1Th 4:3,4; Heb 13:4 [u] Ro 6:12 **6:19** [v] Jn 2:21 [w] Ro 14:7,8 **6:20** [x] Ac 20:28; 1Co 7:23; 1Pe 1:18, 19; Rev 5:9 **7:1** [y] ver 8,26 **7:3** [z] Ex 21: 10; 1Pe 3:7 **7:5** [a] Ex 19:15; 1Sa 21:4,5 [b] Mt 4:10 [c] 1Th 3:5 **7:6** [d] 2Co 8:8

wish that all of you were as I am.[e] But each of you has your own gift from God; one has this gift, another has that.[f]

8Now to the unmarried[a] and the widows I say: It is good for them to stay unmarried, as I do.[g] 9But if they cannot control themselves, they should marry,[h] for it is better to marry than to burn with passion.

10To the married I give this command (not I, but the Lord): A wife must not separate from her husband.[i] 11But if she does, she must remain unmarried or else be reconciled to her husband. And a husband must not divorce his wife.

12To the rest I say this (I, not the Lord):[j] If any brother has a wife who is not a believer and she is willing to live with him, he must not divorce her. 13And if a woman has a husband who is not a believer and he is willing to live with her, she must not divorce him. 14For the unbelieving husband has been sanctified through his wife, and the unbelieving wife has been sanctified through her believing husband. Otherwise your children would be unclean, but as it is, they are holy.[k]

15But if the unbeliever leaves, let it be so. The brother or the sister is not bound in such circumstances; God has called us to live in peace.[l] 16How do you know, wife, whether you will save[m] your husband?[n] Or, how do you know, husband, whether you will save your wife?

Concerning Change of Status

17Nevertheless, each person should live as a believer in whatever situation the Lord has assigned to them, just as God has called them.[o] This is the rule I lay down in all the churches.[p] 18Was a man already circumcised when he was called? He should not become uncircumcised. Was a man uncircumcised when he was called? He should not be circumcised.[q] 19Circumcision is nothing and uncircumcision is nothing.[r] Keeping God's commands is what counts. 20Each person should remain in the situation they were in when God called them.[s]

21Were you a slave when you were called? Don't let it trouble you—although if you can gain your freedom, do so. 22For the one who was a slave when called to faith in the Lord is the Lord's freed person;[t] similarly, the one who was free when called is Christ's slave.[u] 23You were bought at a price;[v] do not become slaves of human beings. 24Brothers and sisters, each person, as responsible to God, should remain in the situation they were in when God called them.[w]

Concerning the Unmarried

25Now about virgins: I have no command from the Lord,[x] but I give a judgment as one who by the Lord's mercy[y] is trustworthy. 26Because of the present crisis, I think that it is good for a man to remain as he is.[z] 27Are you pledged to a woman? Do not seek to be released. Are you free from such a commitment? Do not look for a wife. 28But if you do marry, you have not sinned; and if a virgin marries, she has not sinned. But those who marry will face many troubles in this life, and I want to spare you this.

29What I mean, brothers and sisters, is that the time is short.[a] From now on those who have wives should live as if they do not; 30those who mourn, as if they did not; those who are happy, as if they were not; those who buy something, as if it were not theirs to keep; 31those who use the things of the world, as if not engrossed in them. For this world in its present form is passing away.[b]

32I would like you to be free from concern. An unmarried man is concerned about the Lord's affairs[c]—how he can please the Lord. 33But a married man is concerned about the affairs of this world—how he can please his wife— 34and his interests are divided. An unmarried woman or virgin is concerned about the Lord's affairs: Her aim is to be devoted to the Lord in both body and spirit.[d] But a married woman is concerned about the affairs of this world—how she can please her husband. 35I am saying this for your own good, not to restrict you, but that you may live in a right way in undivided[e] devotion to the Lord.

36If anyone is worried that he might not be acting honorably toward the virgin he is engaged to, and if his passions are too

[a] 8 Or *widowers*

not affect the spirit, and the opposite incorrect idea that any kind of physical relationship is evil. Sexual relationships in marriage are good and God given, yet Paul also outlines the value of celibacy.

7:11 *remain unmarried.* This statement is consistent with Jesus' teaching (Mark 10:9–12).

7:16 *How do you know.* First Peter 3:1–6 reminds us that consistent obedience to God can make a skeptical spouse into a believing one, but there are no guarantees.

7:17 *live as a believer in whatever ... the Lord has assigned.* Social status is unimportant to God. He is interested in faithfulness.

7:27 *pledged to a woman ... released.* Considering the clear prohibition in verses 10–11, this verse is most likely referring to couples who are betrothed but not yet married.

7:7 [e] ver 8; 1Co 9:5 [f] Mt 19:11, 12; Ro 12:6; 1Co 12:4, 11 **7:8** [g] ver 1, 26 **7:9** [h] 1Ti 5:14 **7:10** [i] Mal 2:14-16; Mt 5:32; 19:3-9; Mk 10:11; Lk 16:18 **7:12** [j] ver 6, 10; 2Co 11:17 **7:14** [k] Mal 2:15 **7:15** [l] Ro 14:19; 1Co 14:33 **7:16** [m] Ro 11:14 [n] 1Pe 3:1 **7:17** [o] Ro 12:3 [p] 1Co 4:17; 14:33; 2Co 8:18; 11:28 **7:18** [q] Ac 15:1, 2 **7:19** [r] Ro 2:25-27; Gal 5:6; 6:15; Col 3:11 **7:20** [s] ver 24 **7:22** [t] Jn 8:32, 36; Phm 16 [u] Eph 6:6 **7:23** [v] 1Co 6:20 **7:24** [w] ver 20 **7:25** [x] ver 6; 2Co 8:8 [y] 2Co 4:1; 1Ti 1:13, 16 **7:26** [z] ver 1, 8 **7:29** [a] ver 31; Ro 13:11, 12 **7:31** [b] 1Jn 2:17 **7:32** [c] 1Ti 5:5 **7:34** [d] Lk 2:37 **7:35** [e] Ps 86:11

strong[a] and he feels he ought to marry, he
should do as he wants. He is not sinning.[f]
They should get married. 37But the man
who has settled the matter in his own mind,
who is under no compulsion but has control over his own will, and who has made
up his mind not to marry the virgin—this
man also does the right thing. 38So then, he
who marries the virgin does right,[g] but he
who does not marry her does better.[b]
39A woman is bound to her husband as
long as he lives.[h] But if her husband dies,
she is free to marry anyone she wishes, but
he must belong to the Lord.[i] 40In my judgment,[j] she is happier if she stays as she is—
and I think that I too have the Spirit of God.

Concerning Food Sacrificed to Idols

8 Now about food sacrificed to idols:[k] We
know that "We all possess knowledge."[l]
But knowledge puffs up while love builds
up. 2Those who think they know something[m] do not yet know as they ought to
know.[n] 3But whoever loves God is known
by God.[c][o]
4So then, about eating food sacrificed to
idols:[p] We know that "An idol is nothing at
all in the world"[q] and that "There is no God
but one."[r] 5For even if there are so-called
gods,[s] whether in heaven or on earth (as
indeed there are many "gods" and many
"lords"), 6yet for us there is but one God,
the Father,[t] from whom all things came[u]
and for whom we live; and there is but
one Lord,[v] Jesus Christ, through whom all
things came[w] and through whom we live.
7But not everyone possesses this knowledge. Some people are still so accustomed
to idols that when they eat sacrificial food
they think of it as having been sacrificed to
a god, and since their conscience is weak,[x]
it is defiled. 8But food does not bring us
near to God;[y] we are no worse if we do not
eat, and no better if we do.
9Be careful, however, that the exercise
of your rights does not become a stumbling block[z] to the weak.[a] 10For if someone
with a weak conscience sees you, with all
your knowledge, eating in an idol's temple, won't that person be emboldened to
eat what is sacrificed to idols? 11So this
weak brother or sister, for whom Christ
died, is destroyed[b] by your knowledge.
12When you sin against them[c] in this way
and wound their weak conscience, you sin
against Christ. 13Therefore, if what I eat
causes my brother or sister to fall into sin,
I will never eat meat again, so that I will not
cause them to fall.[d]

Paul's Rights as an Apostle

9 Am I not free? Am I not an apostle?[e]
Have I not seen Jesus our Lord?[f] Are
you not the result of my work in the Lord?[g]
2Even though I may not be an apostle to
others, surely I am to you! For you are the
seal[h] of my apostleship in the Lord.
3This is my defense to those who sit in
judgment on me. 4Don't we have the right
to food and drink?[i] 5Don't we have the right
to take a believing wife[j] along with us, as
do the other apostles and the Lord's brothers[k] and Cephas[d]? 6Or is it only I and Barnabas[l] who lack the right to not work for
a living?
7Who serves as a soldier at his own expense? Who plants a vineyard[m] and does
not eat its grapes? Who tends a flock and
does not drink the milk? 8Do I say this
merely on human authority? Doesn't the

[a] 36 Or *if she is getting beyond the usual age for marriage* [b] 36-38 Or [36]*If anyone thinks he is not treating his daughter properly, and if she is getting along in years* (or *if her passions are too strong*), *and he feels she ought to marry, he should do as he wants. He is not sinning. He should let her get married.* [37]*But the man who has settled the matter in his own mind, who is under no compulsion but has control over his own will, and who has made up his mind to keep the virgin unmarried—this man also does the right thing.* [38]*So then, he who gives his virgin in marriage does right, but he who does not give her in marriage does better.*
[c] 2,3 An early manuscript and another ancient witness *think they have knowledge do not yet know as they ought to know.* [3]*But whoever loves truly knows.* [d] 5 That is, Peter

7:40 *I think that I too have the Spirit of God.* The Holy Spirit enabled Paul to speak with apostolic authority and also with spiritual wisdom.
8:4 *There is no God but one.* The Corinthian believers who claimed to have knowledge readily admitted that an idol is nothing (Is. 37:19; Jer. 16:20; Gal. 4:8) and that there is only one God (Deut. 6:4). Therefore, since an idol is nothing, and since the whole world belongs to God, food which has been offered to idols is not contaminated (10:19,25–26).
8:7 *accustomed to idols.* Even though it is true that an idol is not a real god, a new believer leaving a life of idol worship is still accustomed to thinking of the idol as real. Because of this strong association, eating meat sacrificed to an idol might still feel like paying honor to the idol, and thus seem vile and contaminating. A person who still feels the pull of the old worship is right to flee from all remembrances of it (10:20–23).
8:12 *wound their weak conscience.* The believer is given responsibility for a weaker brother's conscience. It is sin to cause another to fall or to be wounded in the conscience. God is warning believers to stay away from questionable things.
9:1 *an apostle.* Paul could claim the title of apostle because he had seen the resurrected Lord (Acts 1:21–22), and the church in Corinth was his work in the Lord, a seal of his apostleship.

7:36 [f] ver 28 **7:38** [g] Heb 13:4 **7:39** [h] Ro 7:2,3 [i] 2Co 6:14 **7:40** [j] ver 25 **8:1** [k] Ac 15:20 [l] Ro 15:14 **8:2** [m] 1Co 3:18 [n] 1Co 13:8,9,12; 1Ti 6:4 **8:3** [o] Ro 8:29; Gal 4:9 **8:4** [p] ver 1,7,10 [q] 1Co 10:19 [r] Dt 6:4; Eph 4:6 **8:5** [s] 2Th 2:4 **8:6** [t] Mal 2:10 [u] Ro 11:36 [v] Eph 4:5 [w] Jn 1:3 **8:7** [x] Ro 14:14; 1Co 10:28 **8:8** [y] Ro 14:17 **8:9** [z] Gal 5:13 [a] Ro 14:1 **8:11** [b] Ro 14:15,20 **8:12** [c] Mt 18:6 **8:13** [d] Ro 14:21 **9:1** [e] 2Co 12:12 [f] 1Co 15:8 [g] 1Co 3:6; 4:15 **9:2** [h] 2Co 3:2,3 **9:4** [i] 1Th 2:6 **9:5** [j] 1Co 7:7,8 [k] Mt 12:46 **9:6** [l] Ac 4:36 **9:7** [m] Dt 20:6; Pr 27:18

Law say the same thing? 9 For it is written in the Law of Moses: "Do not muzzle an ox while it is treading out the grain."[a][n] Is it about oxen that God is concerned?[o] 10 Surely he says this for us, doesn't he? Yes, this was written for us,[p] because whoever plows and threshes should be able to do so in the hope of sharing in the harvest.[q] 11 If we have sown spiritual seed among you, is it too much if we reap a material harvest from you?[r] 12 If others have this right of support from you, shouldn't we have it all the more?

But we did not use this right.[s] On the contrary, we put up with anything rather than hinder[t] the gospel of Christ.

13 Don't you know that those who serve in the temple get their food from the temple, and that those who serve at the altar share in what is offered on the altar?[u] 14 In the same way, the Lord has commanded that those who preach the gospel should receive their living from the gospel.[v]

15 But I have not used any of these rights.[w] And I am not writing this in the hope that you will do such things for me, for I would rather die than allow anyone to deprive me of this boast.[x] 16 For when I preach the gospel, I cannot boast, since I am compelled to preach.[y] Woe to me if I do not preach the gospel! 17 If I preach voluntarily, I have a reward;[z] if not voluntarily, I am simply discharging the trust committed to me.[a] 18 What then is my reward? Just this: that in preaching the gospel I may offer it free of charge,[b] and so not make full use of my rights as a preacher of the gospel.

Paul's Use of His Freedom

19 Though I am free[c] and belong to no one, I have made myself a slave to everyone,[d] to win as many as possible.[e] 20 To the Jews I became like a Jew, to win the Jews.[f] To those under the law I became like one under the law (though I myself am not under the law), so as to win those under the law. 21 To those not having the law I became like one not having the law[g] (though I am not free from God's law but am under Christ's law), so as to win those not having the law. 22 To the weak I became weak, to win the weak. I have become all things to all people[h] so that by all possible means I might save some.[i] 23 I do all this for the sake of the gospel, that I may share in its blessings.

The Need for Self-Discipline

24 Do you not know that in a race all the runners run, but only one gets the prize? Run[j] in such a way as to get the prize. 25 Everyone who competes in the games goes into strict training. They do it to get a crown that will not last, but we do it to get a crown that will last forever.[k] 26 Therefore I do not run like someone running aimlessly; I do not fight like a boxer beating the air. 27 No, I strike a blow to my body[l] and make it my slave so that after I have preached to others, I myself will not be disqualified for the prize.

Warnings From Israel's History

10 For I do not want you to be ignorant of the fact, brothers and sisters, that our ancestors were all under the cloud[m] and that they all passed through the sea.[n] 2 They were all baptized into Moses in the cloud and in the sea. 3 They all ate the same spiritual food 4 and drank the same spiritual drink; for they drank from the spiritual rock[o] that accompanied them, and that rock was Christ. 5 Nevertheless, God was not pleased with most of them; their bodies were scattered in the wilderness.[p]

6 Now these things occurred as examples to keep us from setting our hearts on evil things as they did. 7 Do not be idolaters,[q] as some of them were; as it is written: "The people sat down to eat and drink and got

a 9 Deut. 25:4

9:14 *living from the gospel.* God commands that ministers of the gospel be supported. Even as the priests in Israel were supported for their work, New Testament ministers were to be provided for as well (1 Tim. 5:17–18).

9:20 *To the Jews I became like a Jew.* In order to relate to the Jews in Jerusalem, Paul made a Nazirite vow in the temple (Acts 21:23–24).

9:21 *under Christ's law.* Paul was not lawless; he was differentiating between the law of the Old Covenant and the broader law of Christ which includes great freedom and flexibility for the believer whose heart is obedient to Christ's will (11:1; Rom. 13:8; Gal. 6:2).

9:27 *will not be disqualified.* A careful distinction should be made between the *prize* and the *gift*. The free gift of justification cannot be the result of good works (Rom. 4:1–8). The prize or crown, however, is the reward for endurance and suffering for the cause of Christ (Phil. 1:29; 2 Tim. 2:12).

10:1 *under the cloud.* When the ancient Israelites were wandering in the wilderness, the pillar of cloud was the visible manifestation of God's presence with them.

10:6 *setting our hearts on evil things.* The first failure of the Israelites was that they were not satisfied with God's provision (Num. 11:4–34). It is not that the food they craved was evil in itself, but their lack of trust in God was sin.

10:7 *idolaters.* The Israelites had seen God's mighty hand work on their behalf, yet they still fell into idolatry and sexual immorality. Knowledge alone

9:9 [n] Dt 25:4; 1Ti 5:18 [o] Dt 22:1-4 **9:10** [p] Ro 4:23,24 [q] 2Ti 2:6 **9:11** [r] Ro 15:27 **9:12** [s] Ac 18:3 [t] 2Co 11:7-12 **9:13** [u] Lev 6:16,26; Dt 18:1 **9:14** [v] Mt 10:10; 1Ti 5:18 **9:15** [w] Ac 18:3 [x] 2Co 11:9,10 **9:16** [y] Ro 1:14; Ac 9:15 **9:17** [z] 1Co 3:8,14 [a] Gal 2:7; Col 1:25 **9:18** [b] 2Co 11:7; 12:13 **9:19** [c] ver 1 [d] Gal 5:13 [e] Mt 18:15; 1Pe 3:1 **9:20** [f] Ac 16:3; 21:20-26; Ro 11:14 **9:21** [g] Ro 2:12,14 **9:22** [h] 1Co 10:33 [i] Ro 11:14 **9:24** [j] Gal 2:2; 2Ti 4:7; Heb 12:1 **9:25** [k] Jas 1:12; Rev 2:10 **9:27** [l] Ro 8:13 **10:1** [m] Ex 13:21 [n] Ex 14:22,29 **10:4** [o] Ex 17:6; Nu 20:11; Ps 78:15 **10:5** [p] Nu 14:29; Heb 3:17 **10:7** [q] ver 14

up to indulge in revelry."[a][r] 8We should not
commit sexual immorality, as some of
them did—and in one day twenty-three
thousand of them died.[s] 9We should not test
Christ,[b] as some of them did—and were
killed by snakes.[t] 10And do not grumble,
as some of them did[u]—and were killed[v] by
the destroying angel.[w]
11These things happened to them as examples and were written down as warnings for us, on whom the culmination of
the ages has come.[x] 12So, if you think you
are standing firm,[y] be careful that you
don't fall! 13No temptation[c] has overtaken
you except what is common to mankind.
And God is faithful;[z] he will not let you be
tempted[c] beyond what you can bear.[a] But
when you are tempted,[c] he will also provide a way out so that you can endure it.

Idol Feasts and the Lord's Supper

14Therefore, my dear friends, flee from
idolatry. 15I speak to sensible people; judge
for yourselves what I say. 16Is not the cup
of thanksgiving for which we give thanks a
participation in the blood of Christ? And is
not the bread that we break a participation
in the body of Christ?[b] 17Because there is
one loaf, we, who are many, are one body,[c]
for we all share the one loaf.
18Consider the people of Israel: Do not
those who eat the sacrifices[d] participate in
the altar? 19Do I mean then that food sacrificed to an idol is anything, or that an idol
is anything?[e] 20No, but the sacrifices of
pagans are offered to demons,[f] not to God,
and I do not want you to be participants
with demons. 21You cannot drink the cup
of the Lord and the cup of demons too; you
cannot have a part in both the Lord's table and the table of demons.[g] 22Are we trying to arouse the Lord's jealousy?[h] Are we
stronger than he?[i]

The Believer's Freedom

23"I have the right to do anything," you
say—but not everything is beneficial.[j] "I
have the right to do anything"—but not everything is constructive. 24No one should
seek their own good, but the good of others.[k]
25Eat anything sold in the meat market
without raising questions of conscience,[l]
26for, "The earth is the Lord's, and everything in it."[d][m]
27If an unbeliever invites you to a meal
and you want to go, eat whatever is put before you[n] without raising questions of conscience. 28But if someone says to you, "This
has been offered in sacrifice," then do not
eat it, both for the sake of the one who told
you and for the sake of conscience.[o] 29I am
referring to the other person's conscience,
not yours. For why is my freedom[p] being
judged by another's conscience? 30If I take
part in the meal with thankfulness, why
am I denounced because of something I
thank God for?[q]
31So whether you eat or drink or whatever you do, do it all for the glory of God.[r]
32Do not cause anyone to stumble,[s] whether Jews, Greeks or the church of God[t]—
33even as I try to please everyone in every
way.[u] For I am not seeking my own good

---

[a] *7* Exodus 32:6 [b] *9* Some manuscripts *test the Lord* [c] *13* The Greek for *temptation* and *tempted* can also mean *testing* and *tested.* [d] *26* Psalm 24:1

---

does not protect against sin—obedience is a heart issue.

10:12 *be careful that you don't fall!* The Corinthians may have had the attitude that, since they were justified by God, nothing could happen to them. The discipline of God, however, is not to be taken lightly. No one can sin without consequences (Gal. 6:7–8).

10:14 *flee from idolatry.* This was not a simple thing to do in ancient Greek culture, where the worship of multiple gods was deeply ingrained. There were idols on street corners and in houses. Various civic societies paid homage to their favorite gods. Cities adopted certain gods as their special protectors. The pagan temples were frequented often, especially in Corinth with its temple prostitution. Most of the food in the marketplace had been offered in worship to different gods.

10:20 *offered to demons.* While the idols themselves are worthless, powerless, and certainly not gods, behind the statues and images is the very real evil and power of Satan and his demons. Anytime that worship is being directed at something that is not God, we can be sure that Satan is behind it.

10:22 *arouse the Lord's jealousy.* To participate in idolatrous activity is to deny that God is the only one worthy of worship.

10:23 *I have the right to do anything.* Though we have freedom, we also have a responsibility to help others in their Christian growth. Our first duty is to others, not to ourselves.

10:25 *Eat anything sold.* Paul himself did not ask whether meat was sacrificed in the temple, because pagan worship could not contaminate what God had made clean (Ps. 24:1; Acts 10:15).

10:28 *for the sake of conscience.* Believers do not need to fearfully ask whether the meat they are eating has been sacrificed to idols—it doesn't make any difference to the food itself. However, a Christian may give the impression to others, by eating sacrificed food, that he himself is also still involved in idol worship.

10:7 [r] Ex 32:4, 6, 19 **10:8** [s] Nu 25:1-9 **10:9** [t] Nu 21:5, 6
10:10 [u] Nu 16:41 [v] Nu 16:49 [w] Ex 12:23 **10:11** [x] Ro 13:11
10:12 [y] Ro 11:20 **10:13** [z] 1Co 1:9 [a] 2Pe 2:9
10:16 [b] Mt 26:26-28 **10:17** [c] Ro 12:5; 1Co 12:27
10:18 [d] Lev 7:6, 14, 15 **10:19** [e] 1Co 8:4
10:20 [f] Dt 32:17; Ps 106:37; Rev 9:20 **10:21** [g] 2Co 6:15, 16
10:22 [h] Dt 32:16, 21 [i] Ecc 6:10; Isa 45:9 **10:23** [j] 1Co 6:12
10:24 [k] ver 33; Ro 15:1, 2; 1Co 13:5; Php 2:4, 21
10:25 [l] Ac 10:15; 1Co 8:7 **10:26** [m] Ps 24:1
10:27 [n] Lk 10:7 **10:28** [o] 1Co 8:7, 10-12
10:29 [p] Ro 14:16; 1Co 9:1, 19 **10:30** [q] Ro 14:6
10:31 [r] Col 3:17; 1Pe 4:11 **10:32** [s] Ac 24:16 [t] Ac 20:28
10:33 [u] Ro 15:2; 1Co 9:22

but the good of many, so that they may be
11 saved.[v] 1 Follow my example,[w] as I follow the example of Christ.

On Covering the Head in Worship

2 I praise you[x] for remembering me in everything[y] and for holding to the traditions
just as I passed them on to you.[z] 3 But I want
you to realize that the head of every man
is Christ,[a] and the head of the woman is
man,[a][b] and the head of Christ is God.[c] 4 Every man who prays or prophesies with his
head covered dishonors his head. 5 But every woman who prays or prophesies[d] with
her head uncovered dishonors her head—
it is the same as having her head shaved.[e]
6 For if a woman does not cover her head,
she might as well have her hair cut off; but
if it is a disgrace for a woman to have her
hair cut off or her head shaved, then she
should cover her head.
7 A man ought not to cover his head,[b]
since he is the image[f] and glory of God; but
woman is the glory of man. 8 For man did
not come from woman, but woman from
man;[g] 9 neither was man created for woman, but woman for man.[h] 10 It is for this reason that a woman ought to have authority
over her own[c] head, because of the angels.
11 Nevertheless, in the Lord woman is not
independent of man, nor is man independent of woman. 12 For as woman came from
man, so also man is born of woman. But
everything comes from God.[i]
13 Judge for yourselves: Is it proper for a
woman to pray to God with her head uncovered? 14 Does not the very nature of
things teach you that if a man has long
hair, it is a disgrace to him, 15 but that if a
woman has long hair, it is her glory? For
long hair is given to her as a covering. 16 If
anyone wants to be contentious about this,
we have no other practice—nor do the
churches of God.[j]

Correcting an Abuse of the Lord's Supper

17 In the following directives I have no
praise for you,[k] for your meetings do more
harm than good. 18 In the first place, I hear
that when you come together as a church,
there are divisions[l] among you, and to
some extent I believe it. 19 No doubt there
have to be differences among you to show
which of you have God's approval.[m] 20 So
then, when you come together, it is not the
Lord's Supper you eat, 21 for when you are
eating, some of you go ahead with your
own private suppers.[n] As a result, one
person remains hungry and another gets

---

a 3 *Or of the wife is her husband* *b* 4-7 Or 4 *Every man who prays or prophesies with long hair dishonors his head.* 5 *But every woman who prays or prophesies with no covering of hair dishonors her head—she is just like one of the "shorn women."* 6 *If a woman has no covering, let her be for now with short hair; but since it is a disgrace for a woman to have her hair shorn or shaved, she should grow it again.* 7 *A man ought not to have long hair* *c* 10 *Or have a sign of authority on her*

11:3 ***the head.*** The term "head" primarily means "authority" when used in the context of human relationships, but it can also mean "source" or "origin." The relationship between men and women does not involve inferiority; in the parallel clause Christ is not inferior to God the Father. Just as Christ and God are equally divine, men and women are equal in God's image. But Jesus and God the Father have different roles in God's plan of salvation, and so also men and women are given different roles in life and in the church.

11:4 ***prays or prophesies.*** This may refer to intercessory prayer similar to that of Old Testament prophets (Gen. 20:7; 1 Sam. 12:23; Jer. 27:18), or Anna (Luke 2:36–38), or to the combination of tongues and prayer (14:13–16; Acts 2:4; 10:46). The term "prophesy" means to speak forth the words of God (14:3).

11:5 ***every woman who prays or prophesies.*** It is difficult from this passage alone to tell exactly what a woman's role is to be in the Christian assembly, but it appears that women did minister to other believers through prayer and prophecy (see also 1 Tim. 2:11–14). ***shaved.*** For a woman to have her head shaved was a sign of public disgrace.

11:9 ***woman for man.*** This does not mean that women are inferior to men; it refers only to the purposes of God for men and women in the created order, and the woman's God-given role of "helper" (Gen. 2:20).

11:10 ***authority.*** Some think that this might be a symbol of the woman's authority to prophesy in the new church age; others believe that it might refer to a symbol of the man's authority over the woman and her willingness to submit to God's order. ***because of the angels.*** Evidently God's angels are present at the meetings of the church and actually learn of God's work of grace through the lives and worship of God's people (Eph. 3:10).

11:11 ***nor . . . independent.*** Men and women need each other, and as creatures of God, both depend on Him. Neither man nor woman can have any claim to special status other than what God has purposed for them as their Creator.

11:19 ***God's approval.*** Paul is here being sarcastic, suggesting that some individuals within the church felt that they alone were truly approved of by the Lord, and trying to separate themselves from other believers whom they felt to be unapproved or less-approved by God than themselves. He condemns this attitude in these verses.

11:20 ***the Lord's Supper.*** The Lord's Supper was the centerpiece of early Christian worship. Gathered around one table, fellow believers met with the Lord and with each other in unity. Christ had expressed this type of humility and unity when He instituted the Supper (Matt. 26:26–30; Mark 14:22–26; Luke 22:14–23).

10:33 [v] Ro 11:14 **11:1** [w] 1Co 4:16 **11:2** [x] ver 17,22 [y] 1Co 4:17 [z] 1Co 15:2,3; 2Th 2:15 **11:3** [a] Eph 1:22 [b] Ge 3:16; Eph 5:23 [c] 1Co 3:23 **11:5** [d] Ac 21:9 [e] Dt 21:12 **11:7** [f] Ge 1:26; Jas 3:9 **11:8** [g] Ge 2:21-23; 1Ti 2:13 **11:9** [h] Ge 2:18 **11:12** [i] Ro 11:36 **11:16** [j] 1Co 7:17 **11:17** [k] ver 2,22 **11:18** [l] 1Co 1:10-12; 3:3 **11:19** [m] 1Jn 2:19 **11:21** [n] 2Pe 2:13; Jude 12

drunk. 22 Don't you have homes to eat and drink in? Or do you despise the church of God[o] by humiliating those who have nothing?[p] What shall I say to you? Shall I praise you?[q] Certainly not in this matter!

23 For I received from the Lord[r] what I also passed on to you:[s] The Lord Jesus, on the night he was betrayed, took bread, 24 and when he had given thanks, he broke it and said, "This is my body, which is for you; do this in remembrance of me." 25 In the same way, after supper he took the cup, saying, "This cup is the new covenant[t] in my blood;[u] do this, whenever you drink it, in remembrance of me." 26 For whenever you eat this bread and drink this cup, you proclaim the Lord's death until he comes.

27 So then, whoever eats the bread or drinks the cup of the Lord in an unworthy manner will be guilty of sinning against the body and blood of the Lord.[v] 28 Everyone ought to examine themselves[w] before they eat of the bread and drink from the cup. 29 For those who eat and drink without discerning the body of Christ eat and drink judgment on themselves. 30 That is why many among you are weak and sick, and a number of you have fallen asleep. 31 But if we were more discerning with regard to ourselves, we would not come under such judgment.[x] 32 Nevertheless, when we are judged in this way by the Lord, we are being disciplined[y] so that we will not be finally condemned with the world.

33 So then, my brothers and sisters, when you gather to eat, you should all eat together. 34 Anyone who is hungry[z] should eat something at home,[a] so that when you meet together it may not result in judgment.

And when I come[b] I will give further directions.

Concerning Spiritual Gifts

12 Now about the gifts of the Spirit,[c] brothers and sisters, I do not want you to be uninformed. 2 You know that when you were pagans,[d] somehow or other you were influenced and led astray to mute idols.[e] 3 Therefore I want you to know that no one who is speaking by the Spirit of God says, "Jesus be cursed,"[f] and no one can say, "Jesus is Lord,"[g] except by the Holy Spirit.[h]

4 There are different kinds of gifts, but the same Spirit[i] distributes them. 5 There are different kinds of service, but the same Lord. 6 There are different kinds of working, but in all of them and in everyone it is the same God[j] at work.

7 Now to each one the manifestation of the Spirit is given for the common good.[k] 8 To one there is given through the Spirit a message of wisdom,[l] to another a message of knowledge[m] by means of the same Spirit, 9 to another faith[n] by the same Spirit, to another gifts of healing[o] by that one Spirit, 10 to another miraculous powers,[p] to another prophecy, to another distinguishing between spirits,[q] to another speaking in different kinds of tongues,[a][r] and to still another the interpretation of tongues.[a] 11 All these are the work of one and the same Spirit,[s] and he distributes them to each one, just as he determines.

Unity and Diversity in the Body

12 Just as a body, though one, has many parts, but all its many parts form one body,[t] so it is with Christ.[u] 13 For we were all baptized by[b] one Spirit[v] so as to form one body—whether Jews or Gentiles, slave or free[w]—and we were all given the one Spirit to drink.[x] 14 Even so the body is not made up of one part but of many.

15 Now if the foot should say, "Because I am not a hand, I do not belong to the body," it would not for that reason stop being part

---

a 10 Or *languages;* also in verse 28 *b* 13 Or *with;* or *in*

11:26 *you proclaim the Lord's death till He comes.* The Lord's Supper looks back to Christ's death and forward to His second coming (Matt. 26:29; Mark 14:25; Luke 22:18).

11:30 *asleep.* The death of Christians is often referred to as "sleep" (15:18; 1 Thess. 4:15–16). In this passage, it refers to untimely death, a punishment suffered by some Christians who failed to examine themselves at the Lord's Supper (v. 28).

12:1–10 Using Spiritual Gifts—Spiritual gifts are discussed in detail in four passages of the New Testament: Romans 12:3–8; 1 Corinthians 12:1–10; Ephesians 4:11–12; and 1 Peter 4:10–11. These lists are not exhaustive but are to be regarded as representative of spiritual gifts. They are given by the Spirit of God to accomplish God's purpose in the world and for the edification of the church, the body of Christ. Every believer has been given spiritual gifts (Rom. 12:5–6; 1 Cor. 12:7; 1 Pet. 4:10). The gifts belong to God and are given for the believer to use for the glory of God (1 Pet. 4:11).

12:3 *cursed ... Lord.* A person speaking by the Holy Spirit will never curse Jesus; by the same token, no one can genuinely proclaim the lordship of Jesus without the enabling of the Spirit.

12:4 *gifts.* These gifts are spiritual capacities that God gives to individual Christians, through which He may strengthen His people.

12:13 *by one Spirit.* "By" here may also be translated "in," speaking of location. Christ places each new member of the body in the Holy Spirit for His care and safekeeping (2 Cor. 1:22).

11:22 [o] 1Co 10:32 [p] Jas 2:6 [q] ver 2, 17 **11:23** [r] Gal 1:12 [s] 1Co 15:3 **11:25** [t] Lk 22:20 [u] 1Co 10:16 **11:27** [v] Heb 10:29 **11:28** [w] 2Co 13:5 **11:31** [x] Ps 32:5; 1Jn 1:9 **11:32** [y] Ps 94:12; Heb 12:7-10; Rev 3:19 **11:34** [z] ver 21 [a] ver 22 [b] 1Co 4:19 **12:1** [c] Ro 1:11; 1Co 14:1, 37 **12:2** [d] Eph 2:11, 12; 1Pe 4:3 [e] Ps 115:5; Jer 10:5; Hab 2:18, 19; 1Th 1:9 **12:3** [f] Ro 9:3 [g] Jn 13:13 [h] 1Jn 4:2, 3 **12:4** [i] Ro 12:4-8; Eph 4:11; Heb 2:4 **12:6** [j] Eph 4:6 **12:7** [k] Eph 4:12 **12:8** [l] 1Co 2:6 [m] 2Co 8:7 **12:9** [n] Mt 17:19, 20; 2Co 4:13 [o] ver 28, 30 **12:10** [p] Gal 3:5 [q] 1Jn 4:1 [r] Mk 16:17 **12:11** [s] ver 4 **12:12** [t] Ro 12:5 [u] ver 27 **12:13** [v] Eph 2:18 [w] Gal 3:28; Col 3:11 [x] Jn 7:37-39

of the body. 16 And if the ear should say, "Because I am not an eye, I do not belong to the body," it would not for that reason stop being part of the body. 17 If the whole body were an eye, where would the sense of hearing be? If the whole body were an ear, where would the sense of smell be? 18 But in fact God has placed[y] the parts in the body, every one of them, just as he wanted them to be.[z] 19 If they were all one part, where would the body be? 20 As it is, there are many parts, but one body.[a]

21 The eye cannot say to the hand, "I don't need you!" And the head cannot say to the feet, "I don't need you!" 22 On the contrary, those parts of the body that seem to be weaker are indispensable, 23 and the parts that we think are less honorable we treat with special honor. And the parts that are unpresentable are treated with special modesty, 24 while our presentable parts need no special treatment. But God has put the body together, giving greater honor to the parts that lacked it, 25 so that there should be no division in the body, but that its parts should have equal concern for each other. 26 If one part suffers, every part suffers with it; if one part is honored, every part rejoices with it.

27 Now you are the body of Christ,[b] and each one of you is a part of it.[c] 28 And God has placed in the church[d] first of all apostles,[e] second prophets, third teachers, then miracles, then gifts of healing,[f] of helping, of guidance,[g] and of different kinds of tongues.[h] 29 Are all apostles? Are all prophets? Are all teachers? Do all work miracles? 30 Do all have gifts of healing? Do all speak in tongues[a]?[i] Do all interpret? 31 Now eagerly desire[j] the greater gifts.

Love Is Indispensable

And yet I will show you the most excellent way.

13 If I speak in the tongues[b][k] of men or of angels, but do not have love, I am only a resounding gong or a clanging cymbal. 2 If I have the gift of prophecy and can fathom all mysteries[l] and all knowledge, and if I have a faith[m] that can move mountains,[n] but do not have love, I am nothing. 3 If I give all I possess to the poor[o] and give over my body to hardship that I may boast,[c][p] but do not have love, I gain nothing.

4 Love is patient,[q] love is kind. It does not envy, it does not boast, it is not proud. 5 It does not dishonor others, it is not self-seeking,[r] it is not easily angered, it keeps no record of wrongs. 6 Love does not delight in evil[s] but rejoices with the truth.[t] 7 It always protects, always trusts, always hopes, always perseveres.

8 Love never fails. But where there are prophecies,[u] they will cease; where there are tongues,[v] they will be stilled; where there is knowledge, it will pass away. 9 For we know in part[w] and we prophesy in part, 10 but when completeness comes,[x] what is in part disappears. 11 When I was a child, I talked like a child, I thought like a child, I reasoned like a child. When I became a man, I put the ways of childhood behind me. 12 For now we see only a reflection as in a mirror; then we shall see face to face.[y] Now I know in part; then I shall know fully, even as I am fully known.[z]

13 And now these three remain: faith, hope and love.[a] But the greatest of these is love.[b]

[a] 30 Or *other languages* [b] 1 Or *languages*
[c] 3 Some manuscripts *body to the flames*

12:18 *God has placed the parts.* We should neither boast in what we do nor think too little of ourselves. Each one of us is important to God and has a mission to accomplish here on earth.

12:28 *apostles.* The term "apostle" or "sent one" refers generally to missionaries (15:7; Rom. 16:7; 2 Cor. 11:5; 12:11; Gal. 1:17–19). Other times the term is limited to the small group who witnessed the resurrected Christ and were given a special mission by Him as His representatives (9:1; 15:5,8).

12:31 *eagerly desire the greater gifts.* This phrase has generally been interpreted as Paul's exhortation to the Corinthians to seek after the more spiritually profitable gifts, yet it is possible that Paul is stating that the Corinthians were improperly desiring the gifts that would bring attention to themselves. In other words, he would be telling them that, although they desire this sort of gift, he wants to show them a more excellent way.

13:1–13 Love—The more one reads 1 Corinthians 13, the more one has to face the fact that we don't naturally have that kind of love in us. The only way to get it is to get it from God. Love comes from God (1 John 4:7). We're not very good at this kind of loving, and the only way we can be is through the empowering work of the Holy Spirit. It is tough because it means dependency on God for that which we cannot do by ourselves. It is tough because the objects of our love often act in unlovable ways or they reject our love when we give it. It is tough because we have to keep coming back with more love, even when it is rejected.

13:8 *Love never fails.* This uncompromising and bold affirmation introduces the contrast with the spiritual gifts which will not last. Paul wants the Corinthians to know that all the gifts would one day no longer be needed, but love.

13:10 *when completeness comes.* The Greek word for "perfect" means "end" or "completion." Most likely, this is a reference to the second coming of Christ and the completion of all things, but some have interpreted this as referring to the completion of the New Testament canon.

12:18 [y] ver 28 [z] ver 11 **12:20** [a] ver 12,14
12:27 [b] Eph 1:23; 4:12; Col 1:18,24 [c] Ro 12:5
12:28 [d] 1Co 10:32 [e] Eph 4:11 [f] ver 9 [g] Ro 12:6-8 [h] ver 10
12:30 [i] ver 10 **12:31** [j] 1Co 14:1,39 **13:1** [k] ver 8
13:2 [l] 1Co 14:2 [m] 1Co 12:9 [n] Mt 17:20; 21:21
13:3 [o] Mt 6:2 [p] Da 3:28 **13:4** [q] 1Th 5:14
13:5 [r] 1Co 10:24 **13:6** [s] 2Th 2:12 [t] 2Jn 4; 3Jn 3,4
13:8 [u] ver 2 [v] ver 1 **13:9** [w] ver 12; 1Co 8:2
13:10 [x] Php 3:12 **13:12** [y] Ge 32:30; 2Co 5:7; 1Jn 3:2
[z] 1Co 8:3 **13:13** [a] Gal 5:5,6 [b] 1Co 16:14

Intelligibility in Worship

14 Follow the way of love[c] and eagerly desire[d] gifts of the Spirit,[e] especially prophecy. 2For anyone who speaks in a tongue[a][f] does not speak to people but to God. Indeed, no one understands them; they utter mysteries[g] by the Spirit. 3But the one who prophesies speaks to people for their strengthening,[h] encouraging and comfort. 4Anyone who speaks in a tongue[i] edifies themselves, but the one who prophesies[j] edifies the church. 5I would like every one of you to speak in tongues,[b] but I would rather have you prophesy.[k] The one who prophesies is greater than the one who speaks in tongues,[b] unless someone interprets, so that the church may be edified.

6Now, brothers and sisters, if I come to you and speak in tongues, what good will I be to you, unless I bring you some revelation[l] or knowledge or prophecy or word of instruction?[m] 7Even in the case of lifeless things that make sounds, such as the pipe or harp, how will anyone know what tune is being played unless there is a distinction in the notes? 8Again, if the trumpet does not sound a clear call, who will get ready for battle?[n] 9So it is with you. Unless you speak intelligible words with your tongue, how will anyone know what you are saying? You will just be speaking into the air. 10Undoubtedly there are all sorts of languages in the world, yet none of them is without meaning. 11If then I do not grasp the meaning of what someone is saying, I am a foreigner to the speaker, and the speaker is a foreigner to me. 12So it is with you. Since you are eager for gifts of the Spirit, try to excel in those that build up the church.

13For this reason the one who speaks in a tongue should pray that they may interpret what they say. 14For if I pray in a tongue, my spirit prays, but my mind is unfruitful. 15So what shall I do? I will pray with my spirit, but I will also pray with my understanding; I will sing[o] with my spirit, but I will also sing with my understanding. 16Otherwise when you are praising God in the Spirit, how can someone else, who is now put in the position of an inquirer,[c] say "Amen"[p] to your thanksgiving,[q] since they do not know what you are saying? 17You are giving thanks well enough, but no one else is edified.

18I thank God that I speak in tongues more than all of you. 19But in the church I would rather speak five intelligible words to instruct others than ten thousand words in a tongue.

20Brothers and sisters, stop thinking like children.[r] In regard to evil be infants,[s] but in your thinking be adults. 21In the Law[t] it is written:

"With other tongues
  and through the lips of foreigners
I will speak to this people,
  but even then they will not listen
    to me,[u]
says the Lord."[d]

22Tongues, then, are a sign, not for believers but for unbelievers; prophecy,[v] however, is not for unbelievers but for believers. 23So if the whole church comes together and everyone speaks in tongues, and inquirers or unbelievers come in, will they not say that you are out of your mind?[w] 24But if an unbeliever or an inquirer comes in while everyone is prophesying, they are convicted of sin and are brought under judgment by all, 25as the secrets of their hearts are laid bare. So they will fall down and worship God, exclaiming, "God is really among you!"[x]

Good Order in Worship

26What then shall we say, brothers and sisters? When you come together, each of you[y] has a hymn,[z] or a word of instruction,[a] a revelation, a tongue or an interpretation. Everything must be done so that the church may be built up.[b] 27If anyone speaks in a tongue, two—or at the most three—should speak, one at a time, and someone must interpret. 28If there is no interpreter, the speaker should keep quiet in the church and speak to himself and to God.

29Two or three prophets should speak, and the others should weigh carefully what is said.[c] 30And if a revelation comes to someone who is sitting down, the first

---

[a] *2* Or *in another language;* also in verses 4, 13, 14, 19, 26 and 27 [b] *5* Or *in other languages;* also in verses 6, 18, 22, 23 and 39 [c] *16* The Greek word for *inquirer* is a technical term for someone not fully initiated into a religion; also in verses 23 and 24. [d] *21* Isaiah 28:11,12

14:3 *prophesies.* In this sense, prophecy incorporates all speaking gifts that edify the church (Rom. 12:6; 1 Pet. 4:11).

14:11 *I do not grasp the meaning.* Paul underlines the original purpose of all spiritual gifts: they must serve the church (vv. 13–14; 12:7). Tongues must convey meaning or else they fail to help those who listen.

14:16 *Amen.* The word "amen" means "truly" or "so be it" (John 3:5). Saying "amen" indicated agreement with what was being said (Deut. 27:14–26; Rev. 5:14).

14:29 *Two or three.* The meetings of the church should be characterized by orderliness and moderation. ***weigh carefully.*** No one, not even a person exercising a spiritual gift, is exempt from accountability to the church (6:5; 11:29–31).

14:1 [c] 1Co 16:14 [d] ver 39; 1Co 12:31 [e] 1Co 12:1 **14:2** [f] Mk 16:17 [g] 1Co 13:2 **14:3** [h] ver 4, 5, 12, 17, 26; Ro 14:19 **14:4** [i] Mk 16:17 [j] 1Co 13:2 **14:5** [k] Nu 11:29 **14:6** [l] ver 26; Eph 1:17 [m] Ro 6:17 **14:8** [n] Nu 10:9; Jer 4:19 **14:15** [o] Eph 5:19; Col 3:16 **14:16** [p] Dt 27:15-26; 1Ch 16:36; Ne 8:6; Ps 106:48; Rev 5:14; 7:12 [q] 1Co 11:24 **14:20** [r] Eph 4:14; Heb 5:12, 13; 1Pe 2:2 [s] Ro 16:19 **14:21** [t] Jn 10:34 [u] Isa 28:11, 12 **14:22** [v] ver 1 **14:23** [w] Ac 2:13 **14:25** [x] Isa 45:14; Zec 8:23 **14:26** [y] 1Co 12:7-10 [z] Eph 5:19 [a] ver 6 [b] Ro 14:19 **14:29** [c] 1Co 12:10

speaker should stop. 31 For you can all prophesy in turn so that everyone may be instructed and encouraged. 32 The spirits of prophets are subject to the control of prophets.[d] 33 For God is not a God of disorder[e] but of peace—as in all the congregations of the Lord's people.[f]

34 Women[a] should remain silent in the churches. They are not allowed to speak, but must be in submission,[g] as the law[h] says. 35 If they want to inquire about something, they should ask their own husbands at home; for it is disgraceful for a woman to speak in the church.[b]

36 Or did the word of God originate with you? Or are you the only people it has reached? 37 If anyone thinks they are a prophet[i] or otherwise gifted by the Spirit, let them acknowledge that what I am writing to you is the Lord's command.[j] 38 But if anyone ignores this, they will themselves be ignored.[c]

39 Therefore, my brothers and sisters, be eager[k] to prophesy, and do not forbid speaking in tongues. 40 But everything should be done in a fitting and orderly[l] way.

The Resurrection of Christ

15 Now, brothers and sisters, I want to remind you of the gospel[m] I preached to you, which you received and on which you have taken your stand. 2 By this gospel you are saved,[n] if you hold firmly[o] to the word I preached to you. Otherwise, you have believed in vain.

3 For what I received[p] I passed on to you[q] as of first importance[d]: that Christ died for our sins[r] according to the Scriptures,[s] 4 that he was buried, that he was raised[t] on the third day[u] according to the Scriptures,[v] 5 and that he appeared to Cephas,[e][w] and then to the Twelve.[x] 6 After that, he appeared to more than five hundred of the brothers and sisters at the same time, most of whom are still living, though some have fallen asleep. 7 Then he appeared to James, then to all the apostles,[y] 8 and last of all he appeared to me also,[z] as to one abnormally born.

9 For I am the least of the apostles[a] and do not even deserve to be called an apostle, because I persecuted[b] the church of God. 10 But by the grace of God I am what I am, and his grace to me[c] was not without effect. No, I worked harder than all of them[d]—yet not I, but the grace of God that was with me.[e] 11 Whether, then, it is I or they, this is what we preach, and this is what you believed.

The Resurrection of the Dead

12 But if it is preached that Christ has been raised from the dead, how can some of you say that there is no resurrection of the dead?[f] 13 If there is no resurrection of the dead, then not even Christ has

[a] 33,34 Or *peace. As in all the congregations of the Lord's people,* 34*women* [b] 34,35 In a few manuscripts these verses come after verse 40.
[c] 38 Some manuscripts *But anyone who is ignorant of this will be ignorant* [d] 3 Or *you at the first*
[e] 5 That is, Peter

14:32 *subject to the control of prophets.* Paul anticipated that some might excuse disorder by claiming that they could not prevent themselves from prophesying when God brought a revelation to them. He explained that the Holy Spirit does not overpower the person through whom He speaks.

14:34 *Women should remain silent.* This command is the subject of much debate, for it seems to contradict the fact that Paul spoke of women prophesying in 1 Corinthians 11:5. It has been suggested that Paul was addressing a particular problem in the Corinthian church, a group of women who were disruptive, but the prohibition is repeated at a different time to a different group of people (1 Tim. 2:11–12). This verse has also been interpreted as a prohibition on women interpreting prophecy, judging the prophets, or speaking in tongues. Others believe that women do prophesy and minister, but only to other women, or in a setting other than public church meetings, such as Priscilla and Aquila instructing Apollos (Acts 18:24–28).

14:40 *fitting and orderly.* This verse is the key to all church practice. In worship and teaching, as in all of life, believers should demonstrate self-control and consideration.

15:3–4 Gospel Message—Paul makes it clear here that evangelism should be centered on the gospel of Christ. The central point of the good news is Christ's death and resurrection. The four key points about that gospel are:

1. God's Word says all are sinners, condemned to hell (Is. 53:6; Rom. 3:10–11,23; 5:8,12; Rev. 20:15).
2. There is nothing a sinner can do on his own to save himself (Is. 64:6; Eph. 2:9).
3. Christ was born, crucified, and resurrected to save lost people from their sin (John 3:16; 1 Tim. 1:15).
4. To be saved, a sinner must believe God's Word and invite Christ into his or her heart by faith (John 5:24; Acts 16:31).

15:3 *according to the Scriptures.* Christ lived and died in accordance with the prophecies about Him in the Old Testament (Ps. 16:10; Is. 53:8–10).

15:8 *abnormally born.* This is probably Paul's comment on the unique way that he became an apostle. Unlike the other apostles, who had the benefit of an initial training period with Christ, Paul became an apostle abruptly, with no opportunity for earthly contact with Christ or His teaching.

15:9 *persecuted the church.* The story of Paul's persecuting and conversion is told in Acts 9; 22; Ephesians 3:8; 1 Timothy 1:15–16.

15:12 *no resurrection.* These opponents of Paul may have been denying the reality of Christ's resurrection. They may also have been teaching that

14:32 [d] 1Jn 4:1 **14:33** [e] ver 40 [f] Ac 9:13
14:34 [g] 1Ti 2:11,12 [h] Ge 3:16 **14:37** [i] 2Co 10:7 [j] 1Jn 4:6
14:39 [k] 1Co 12:31 **14:40** [l] ver 33 **15:1** [m] Ro 2:16
15:2 [n] Ro 1:16 [o] Ro 11:22 **15:3** [p] Gal 1:12 [q] 1Co 11:23
[r] Isa 53:5; 1Pe 2:24 [s] Lk 24:27; Ac 26:22,23 **15:4** [t] Ac 2:24
[u] Mt 16:21 [v] Ac 2:25,30,31 **15:5** [w] Lk 24:34 [x] Mk 16:14
15:7 [y] Lk 24:33,36,37; Ac 1:3,4 **15:8** [z] Ac 9:3-6,17; 1Co 9:1 **15:9** [a] Eph 3:8; 1Ti 1:15 [b] Ac 8:3
15:10 [c] Ro 12:3 [d] 2Co 11:23 [e] Php 2:13 **15:12** [f] Ac 17:32; 23:8; 2Ti 2:18

been raised. 14And if Christ has not been raised,[g] our preaching is useless and so is your faith. 15More than that, we are then found to be false witnesses about God, for we have testified about God that he raised Christ from the dead.[h] But he did not raise him if in fact the dead are not raised. 16For if the dead are not raised, then Christ has not been raised either. 17And if Christ has not been raised, your faith is futile; you are still in your sins.[i] 18Then those also who have fallen asleep in Christ are lost. 19If only for this life we have hope in Christ, we are of all people most to be pitied.[j]

20But Christ has indeed been raised from the dead,[k] the firstfruits[l] of those who have fallen asleep.[m] 21For since death came through a man,[n] the resurrection of the dead comes also through a man. 22For as in Adam all die, so in Christ all will be made alive.[o] 23But each in turn: Christ, the firstfruits;[p] then, when he comes,[q] those who belong to him. 24Then the end will come, when he hands over the kingdom[r] to God the Father after he has destroyed all dominion, authority and power.[s] 25For he must reign until he has put all his enemies under his feet.[t] 26The last enemy to be destroyed is death.[u] 27For he "has put everything under his feet."[a][v] Now when it says that "everything" has been put under him, it is clear that this does not include God himself, who put everything under Christ.[w] 28When he has done this, then the Son himself will be made subject to him who put everything under him,[x] so that God may be all in all.[y]

29Now if there is no resurrection, what will those do who are baptized for the dead? If the dead are not raised at all, why are people baptized for them? 30And as for us, why do we endanger ourselves every hour?[z] 31I face death every day[a]—yes, just as surely as I boast about you in Christ Jesus our Lord. 32If I fought wild beasts[b] in Ephesus[c] with no more than human hopes, what have I gained? If the dead are not raised,

"Let us eat and drink,
for tomorrow we die."[b][d]

33Do not be misled: "Bad company corrupts good character."[c] 34Come back to your senses as you ought, and stop sinning; for there are some who are ignorant of God—I say this to your shame.

The Resurrection Body

35But someone will ask,[e] "How are the dead raised? With what kind of body will they come?"[f] 36How foolish![g] What you sow does not come to life unless it dies.[h]

a 27 Psalm 8:6 *b* 32 Isaiah 22:13 *c* 33 From the Greek poet Menander

---

resurrection is only spiritual and not physical; or they may have been teaching that the resurrection had already happened (2 Tim. 2:18). Whatever the case, they contradicted the essential teaching that Christ had been physically raised from the dead and that all believers in Him will someday also be resurrected.

15:15 *false witnesses.* In verses 5–8 Paul listed several people, including himself, who had witnessed the resurrected Christ. To deny the resurrection was to call these people liars.

15:17 Resurrection—There are many biblical scholars these days who say that the resurrection was an invented story out of some kind of "faith" process. They relegate the critical event that defines Christianity to the imaginations of some well-meaning but deluded Palestinian peasants. Paul goes to great pains to put the resurrection in the realm of fact, not opinion or imagination. He talks about the eyewitness testimony of hundreds (v. 6). He references his own story of personal confrontation with Christ (v. 8). In the end he says that if the resurrection isn't a fact, then he is absolutely lost (v. 19). This sounds like a man who staked his entire life on an indisputable fact.

15:19 *pitied.* If Christ did not rise, then He is just another dead prophet with no power over sin or death, and the Christian's hope of eternal life is a lie.

15:20 *firstfruits.* The "firstfruits" is the first installment of a crop, which anticipates and guarantees the ultimate offering of the whole crop (16:15; Rom. 8:23). Because Christ rose from the dead, those who are asleep in Christ (1 Thess. 4:15–16) have a guarantee of their own resurrection.

15:21 *death came through a man.* The first man, Adam, transgressed God's law and brought sin and death into the world (Gen. 2:17; 3:19; Rom. 5:12–21); the second man, Jesus Christ, was the perfect sacrifice to take away sin and to bring life and resurrection to those who believe in Him (Rom. 5:15–21).

15:23 *each in turn.* The believers who have died will be the first to rise at Christ's coming and be reunited with their physical bodies. Following this is the removal of all living Christians from the earth (1 Thess. 4:13–18).

15:29 *baptized for the dead.* It may be that some of the Corinthians had for some reason been baptized on behalf of others who had died without baptism. Paul does not address whether this practice was right or wrong (although his use of "they" rather than "we" indicates that he did not participate), but makes the point that their own actions are inconsistent with their beliefs. There would be no point in doing anything for the dead if there is no resurrection.

15:30 *endanger.* If this life is all there is, it would make more sense to take the position of the Epicureans, seeking pleasure and avoiding pain.

15:32 *beasts in Ephesus.* This may be a figurative reference to Paul's enemies at Ephesus (Acts 19).

15:36 *unless it dies.* Difficulty understanding the nature of the resurrection should not cause a person to doubt its reality any more than not understanding

15:14 [g] 1Th 4:14 **15:15** [h] Ac 2:24 **15:17** [i] Ro 4:25 **15:19** [j] 1Co 4:9 **15:20** [k] 1Pe 1:3 [l] ver 23; Ac 26:23; Rev 1:5 [m] ver 6, 18 **15:21** [n] Ro 5:12 **15:22** [o] Ro 5:14-18 **15:23** [p] ver 20 [q] ver 52 **15:24** [r] Da 7:14, 27 [s] Ro 8:38 **15:25** [t] Ps 110:1; Mt 22:44 **15:26** [u] 2Ti 1:10; Rev 20:14; 21:4 **15:27** [v] Ps 8:6 [w] Mt 28:18 **15:28** [x] Php 3:21 [y] 1Co 3:23 **15:30** [z] 2Co 11:26 **15:31** [a] Ro 8:36 **15:32** [b] 2Co 1:8 [c] Ac 18:19 [d] Isa 22:13; Lk 12:19 **15:35** [e] Ro 9:19 [f] Eze 37:3 **15:36** [g] Lk 11:40 [h] Jn 12:24

37When you sow, you do not plant the
body that will be, but just a seed, perhaps
of wheat or of something else. 38But God
gives it a body as he has determined, and
to each kind of seed he gives its own body.[i]
39Not all flesh is the same: People have one
kind of flesh, animals have another, birds
another and fish another. 40There are also
heavenly bodies and there are earthly bodies; but the splendor of the heavenly bodies
is one kind, and the splendor of the earthly
bodies is another. 41The sun has one kind
of splendor, the moon another and the stars
another; and star differs from star in splendor.
42So will it be[j] with the resurrection of
the dead. The body that is sown is perishable, it is raised imperishable; 43it is sown
in dishonor, it is raised in glory;[k] it is sown
in weakness, it is raised in power; 44it is
sown a natural body, it is raised a spiritual body.[l]
If there is a natural body, there is also a
spiritual body. 45So it is written: "The first
man Adam became a living being"[a];[m] the
last Adam,[n] a life-giving spirit.[o] 46The spiritual did not come first, but the natural, and
after that the spiritual. 47The first man was
of the dust of the earth;[p] the second man is
of heaven.[q] 48As was the earthly man, so
are those who are of the earth; and as is
the heavenly man, so also are those who
are of heaven.[r] 49And just as we have borne
the image of the earthly man,[s] so shall we[b]
bear the image of the heavenly man.[t]
50I declare to you, brothers and sisters,
that flesh and blood[u] cannot inherit the
kingdom of God, nor does the perishable
inherit the imperishable. 51Listen, I tell
you a mystery:[v] We will not all sleep, but
we will all be changed[w]— 52in a flash, in
the twinkling of an eye, at the last trumpet. For the trumpet will sound,[x] the dead[y]
will be raised imperishable, and we will be
changed. 53For the perishable must clothe
itself with the imperishable,[z] and the mortal with immortality. 54When the perishable has been clothed with the imperishable, and the mortal with immortality, then
the saying that is written will come true:
"Death has been swallowed up in victory."[c][a]

55"Where, O death, is your victory?
Where, O death, is your sting?"[d][b]

56The sting of death is sin,[c] and the power
of sin is the law.[d] 57But thanks be to God![e]
He gives us the victory through our Lord
Jesus Christ.[f]
58Therefore, my dear brothers and sisters, stand firm. Let nothing move you.
Always give yourselves fully to the work
of the Lord,[g] because you know that your
labor in the Lord is not in vain.

The Collection for the Lord's People

16 Now about the collection[h] for the
Lord's people:[i] Do what I told the Galatian[j] churches to do. 2On the first day
of every week,[k] each one of you should
set aside a sum of money in keeping with
your income, saving it up, so that when I
come no collections will have to be made.[l]
3Then, when I arrive, I will give letters of
introduction to the men you approve[m] and
send them with your gift to Jerusalem. 4If it
seems advisable for me to go also, they will
accompany me.

Personal Requests

5After I go through Macedonia, I will
come to you[n]—for I will be going through
Macedonia.[o] 6Perhaps I will stay with you
for a while, or even spend the winter, so
that you can help me on my journey,[p] wherever I go. 7For I do not want to see you now
and make only a passing visit; I hope to
spend some time with you, if the Lord permits.[q] 8But I will stay on at Ephesus[r] until
Pentecost,[s] 9because a great door for effective work has opened to me,[t] and there are
many who oppose me.

---

[a] 45 Gen. 2:7 [b] 49 Some early manuscripts *so let us* [c] 54 Isaiah 25:8 [d] 55 Hosea 13:14

---

how a seed becomes a plant should cause disbelief in the coming harvest.

15:44 *natural body ... spiritual body.* The contrast is not between a material body and an immaterial body, but between a body subject to death and a body that is immortal.

15:54 *Death has been swallowed up in victory.* Satan's apparent victories in the garden of Eden (Gen. 3:13) and at the cross (Mark 15:22–24) were reversed by Jesus' death and resurrection (Col. 2:13–15).

15:58 *your labor ... is not in vain.* We are looking forward to eternal life because of the hope of the resurrection; everything we do on this earth matters for eternity.

16:2 *the first day of every week.* It appears that the custom of believers meeting on the first day of the week began early in Christian history. ***set aside.*** The Old Testament tithe was not adopted by the New Testament church, though certainly Christ practiced it. New Testament believers were encouraged to give liberally, but never a specified amount or percentage (Rom. 12:8). Considering the New Testament teachings on generosity and self-sacrifice, believers should probably expect to give much more than ten percent.

15:38 [i] Ge 1:11 **15:42** [j] Da 12:3; Mt 13:43
15:43 [k] Php 3:21; Col 3:4 **15:44** [l] ver 50
15:45 [m] Ge 2:7 [n] Ro 5:14 [o] Jn 5:21; Ro 8:2
15:47 [p] Ge 2:7; 3:19 [q] Jn 3:13,31 **15:48** [r] Php 3:20,21
15:49 [s] Ge 5:3 [t] Ro 8:29 **15:50** [u] Jn 3:3,5
15:51 [v] 1Co 13:2 [w] Php 3:21 **15:52** [x] Mt 24:31 [y] Jn 5:25
15:53 [z] 2Co 5:2,4 **15:54** [a] Isa 25:8; Rev 20:14
15:55 [b] Hos 13:14 **15:56** [c] Ro 5:12 [d] Ro 4:15
15:57 [e] 2Co 2:14 [f] Ro 8:37 **15:58** [g] 1Co 16:10
16:1 [h] Ac 24:17 [i] Ac 9:13 [j] Ac 16:6 **16:2** [k] Ac 20:7
[l] 2Co 9:4,5 **16:3** [m] 2Co 8:18,19 **16:5** [n] 1Co 4:19
[o] Ac 19:21 **16:6** [p] Ro 15:24 **16:7** [q] Ac 18:21
16:8 [r] Ac 18:19 [s] Ac 2:1 **16:9** [t] Ac 14:27

10When Timothy[u] comes, see to it that he
has nothing to fear while he is with you,
for he is carrying on the work of the Lord,[v]
just as I am. 11No one, then, should treat
him with contempt.[w] Send him on his way
in peace[x] so that he may return to me. I am
expecting him along with the brothers.
12Now about our brother Apollos:[y] I
strongly urged him to go to you with the
brothers. He was quite unwilling to go now,
but he will go when he has the opportunity.
13Be on your guard; stand firm[z] in the
faith; be courageous; be strong.[a] 14Do everything in love.[b]
15You know that the household of Stephanas[c] were the first converts[d] in Achaia,[e] and they have devoted themselves to
the service of the Lord's people. I urge
you, brothers and sisters, 16to submit[f] to
such people and to everyone who joins
in the work and labors at it. 17I was glad
when Stephanas, Fortunatus and Achaicus arrived, because they have supplied
what was lacking from you.[g] 18For they
refreshed[h] my spirit and yours also. Such
men deserve recognition.[i]

Final Greetings

19The churches in the province of Asia
send you greetings. Aquila and Priscilla[a][j] greet you warmly in the Lord, and so
does the church that meets at their house.[k]
20All the brothers and sisters here send you
greetings. Greet one another with a holy
kiss.[l]
21I, Paul, write this greeting in my own
hand.[m]
22If anyone does not love the Lord,[n] let
that person be cursed![o] Come, Lord[b]![p]
23The grace of the Lord Jesus be with
you.[q]
24My love to all of you in Christ Jesus.
Amen.[c]

---

a *19* Greek *Prisca,* a variant of *Priscilla* *b* *22* The Greek for *Come, Lord* reproduces an Aramaic expression (*Marana tha*) used by early Christians. *c* *24* Some manuscripts do not have *Amen.*

16:13 *be courageous.* This emphasizes courage as well as maturity. Paul's command to do everything with love serves as a balance to these strong exhortations.

16:17 *Stephanas, Fortunatus, and Achaicus.* These were probably the ones who confirmed the bad report brought by Chloe's household in 1 Corinthians 1:11.

16:19 *Aquila and Priscilla.* Aquila and Priscilla were tentmakers who had met Paul in Corinth. They followed him to Ephesus and made their house available for the meetings of the church (Rom. 16:3–5). They would have been known to many in the Corinthian church.

16:20 *holy kiss.* In the ancient world (as in many cultures still today), a kiss was a common form of friendly or affectionate greeting.

16:22 *cursed!* Paul does not condemn unbelievers, but rather unbelievers condemn themselves by ignoring the claims of the Creator on their lives.

16:10 [u] Ac 16:1 [v] 1Co 15:58 **16:11** [w] 1Ti 4:12 [x] Ac 15:33 **16:12** [y] Ac 18:24; 1Co 1:12 **16:13** [z] Gal 5:1; Php 1:27; 1Th 3:8; 2Th 2:15 [a] Eph 6:10 **16:14** [b] 1Co 14:1 **16:15** [c] 1Co 1:16 [d] Ro 16:5 [e] Ac 18:12 **16:16** [f] Heb 13:17 **16:17** [g] 2Co 11:9; Php 2:30 **16:18** [h] Phm 7 [i] Php 2:29 **16:19** [j] Ac 18:2 [k] Ro 16:5 **16:20** [l] Ro 16:16 **16:21** [m] Gal 6:11; Col 4:18 **16:22** [n] Eph 6:24 [o] Ro 9:3 [p] Rev 22:20 **16:23** [q] Ro 16:20

2 CORINTHIANS

▶ **AUTHOR:** External and internal evidence amply support the Pauline authorship of this letter. There is an interval of about a year between these two letters to the Corinthians. Since Paul's first letter, the Corinthian church had been swayed by false teachers who stirred the people against Paul. They claimed he was fickle, arrogant, unimpressive in appearance and speech, and unqualified to be an apostle of Jesus Christ. During this time Paul has paid them what must have been an unpleasant visit and then wrote them another letter, which we do not have (2:1 – 4). Paul wrote 2 Corinthians in A.D. 56 in Macedonia and sent the letter to the church with Titus and another brother (8:16).

▶ **TIME:** C. A.D. 56 ▶ **KEY VERSES:** 2 Cor. 4:5 – 6

▶ **THEME:** As Paul writes this letter, he is looking forward to yet another visit, and it appears that the Corinthians have listened to him and things are getting on the right track. But there are still some problems. The key issue seems to be Paul's leadership. He spends a good deal of the letter establishing his authority and the need to exercise it, which makes the letter intensely personal. In it we can see the depth of his relationship with the Corinthians, and we get an understanding of the hardships Paul went through for these people on his missionary journeys. Most importantly we see a faith that is so focused that Paul is ready to endure anything to see it spread.

1 Paul, an apostle of Christ Jesus by the
will of God,[a] and Timothy our brother,

To the church of God[b] in Corinth, together with all his holy people throughout
Achaia:[c]

2Grace and peace to you from God our
Father and the Lord Jesus Christ.[d]

Praise to the God of All Comfort

3Praise be to the God and Father of our
Lord Jesus Christ,[e] the Father of compassion and the God of all comfort, 4who
comforts us[f] in all our troubles, so that we
can comfort those in any trouble with the
comfort we ourselves receive from God.
5For just as we share abundantly in the
sufferings of Christ,[g] so also our comfort
abounds through Christ. 6If we are distressed, it is for your comfort and salvation;[h] if we are comforted, it is for your
comfort, which produces in you patient endurance of the same sufferings we suffer.
7And our hope for you is firm, because we
know that just as you share in our sufferings,[i] so also you share in our comfort.

8We do not want you to be uninformed,
brothers and sisters,[a] about the troubles we
experienced[j] in the province of Asia. We
were under great pressure, far beyond our
ability to endure, so that we despaired of
life itself. 9Indeed, we felt we had received
the sentence of death. But this happened
that we might not rely on ourselves but on
God,[k] who raises the dead. 10He has delivered us from such a deadly peril,[l] and he
will deliver us again. On him we have set
our hope that he will continue to deliver us,
11as you help us by your prayers.[m] Then
many will give thanks[n] on our behalf for

[a] 8 The Greek word for *brothers and sisters* (*adelphoi*) refers here to believers, both men and women, as part of God's family; also in 8:1; 13:11.

1:4 ***comforts us in all our troubles.*** God comforts us for our own encouragement and also to make us comforters of others. The comfort that God gives to us becomes a gift that we can give to others (7:6; Acts 9:10 – 19).

1:5 ***the sufferings of Christ.*** Jesus warned His disciples that they would experience the same kind of suffering that He did for the sake of the gospel (John 15:20).

1:8 ***Asia.*** This is the Roman province in western Asia Minor, present day Turkey. The trouble that Paul speaks of is likely the riots in Ephesus (Acts 19:23 – 41).

1:1 [a] 1Co 1:1; Eph 1:1; Col 1:1; 2Ti 1:1 [b] 1Co 10:32 [c] Ac 18:12
1:2 [d] Ro 1:7 **1:3** [e] Eph 1:3; 1Pe 1:3 **1:4** [f] 2Co 7:6, 7, 13
1:5 [g] 2Co 4:10; Col 1:24 **1:6** [h] 2Co 4:15 **1:7** [i] Ro 8:17
1:8 [j] 1Co 15:32 **1:9** [k] Jer 17:5, 7 **1:10** [l] Ro 15:31
1:11 [m] Ro 15:30; Php 1:19 [n] 2Co 4:15

the gracious favor granted us in answer to the prayers of many.

Paul's Change of Plans

12Now this is our boast: Our conscience[o] testifies that we have conducted ourselves in the world, and especially in our relations with you, with integrity[a] and godly sincerity.[p] We have done so, relying not on worldly wisdom[q] but on God's grace. 13For we do not write you anything you cannot read or understand. And I hope that, 14as you have understood us in part, you will come to understand fully that you can boast of us just as we will boast of you in the day of the Lord Jesus.[r]

15Because I was confident of this, I wanted to visit you[s] first so that you might benefit twice.[t] 16I wanted to visit you on my way[u] to Macedonia and to come back to you from Macedonia, and then to have you send me on my way to Judea. 17Was I fickle when I intended to do this? Or do I make my plans in a worldly manner[v] so that in the same breath I say both "Yes, yes" and "No, no"?

18But as surely as God is faithful,[w] our message to you is not "Yes" and "No." 19For the Son of God, Jesus Christ, who was preached among you by us—by me and Silas[b] and Timothy—was not "Yes" and "No," but in him it has always[x] been "Yes." 20For no matter how many promises[y] God has made, they are "Yes" in Christ. And so through him the "Amen"[z] is spoken by us to the glory of God. 21Now it is God who makes both us and you stand firm in Christ. He anointed[a] us, 22set his seal of ownership on us, and put his Spirit in our hearts as a deposit, guaranteeing what is to come.[b]

23I call God as my witness[c]—and I stake my life on it—that it was in order to spare you[d] that I did not return to Corinth. 24Not that we lord it over[e] your faith, but we work with you for your joy, because it is by faith[f]

2 you stand firm. 1So I made up my mind that I would not make another painful visit to you.[g] 2For if I grieve you,[h] who is left to make me glad but you whom I have grieved? 3I wrote as I did,[i] so that when I came I would not be distressed[j] by those who should have made me rejoice. I had confidence[k] in all of you, that you would all share my joy. 4For I wrote you[l] out of great distress and anguish of heart and with many tears, not to grieve you but to let you know the depth of my love for you.

Forgiveness for the Offender

5If anyone has caused grief,[m] he has not so much grieved me as he has grieved all of you to some extent—not to put it too severely. 6The punishment[n] inflicted on him by the majority is sufficient. 7Now instead, you ought to forgive and comfort him,[o] so that he will not be overwhelmed by excessive sorrow. 8I urge you, therefore, to reaffirm your love for him. 9Another reason I wrote you was to see if you would stand the test and be obedient in everything.[p] 10Anyone you forgive, I also forgive. And what I have forgiven—if there was anything to forgive—I have forgiven in the sight of Christ for your sake, 11in order that Satan[q] might not outwit us. For we are not unaware of his schemes.[r]

Ministers of the New Covenant

12Now when I went to Troas[s] to preach the gospel of Christ[t] and found that the Lord had opened a door[u] for me, 13I still had no peace of mind,[v] because I did not find my brother Titus[w] there. So I said goodbye to them and went on to Macedonia.

14But thanks be to God,[x] who always leads us as captives in Christ's triumphal procession and uses us to spread the

a 12 Many manuscripts *holiness* *b* 19 Greek *Silvanus*, a variant of *Silas*

1:12 *godly sincerity.* The Corinthians certainly were well acquainted with Paul's character, since he had spent 18 months with them (Acts 18:11).

1:19 *not "Yes" and "No."* Paul's preaching was not inconsistent or contradictory. Instead, his preaching reflected the truthfulness and faithfulness of God, because his teaching was based on the Scriptures and the teachings of Christ.

1:21 *anointed us.* God confirmed Paul and his fellow workers by anointing them, the special mark of service to God which was given to kings and priests in the Old Testament. This anointing probably refers to special empowerment by the Holy Spirit, similar to the anointing that John described in 1 John 2:20,27.

1:22 *set his seal . . . on us.* Sealing indicates ownership and security. The *sealing* and the *giving* of the Holy Spirit are also linked. The Holy Spirit is a guarantee, the down payment that there is more spiritual blessing to come and that the believer will receive eternal life.

2:5 *caused grief.* This is probably a reference to the incestuous man of 1 Corinthians 5.

2:7 *forgive and comfort him.* The purpose of church discipline is repentance and restoration. Forgiveness should always follow the correction, just as Christ instructed (Matt. 18:15–35).

2:12 *Troas.* Troas was a city on the Aegean coast, where Paul had received his call to preach the gospel in Macedonia (Acts 16:8).

1:12 [o] Ac 23:1 [p] 2Co 2:17 [q] 1Co 2:1, 4, 13 **1:14** [r] 1Co 1:8 **1:15** [s] 1Co 4:19 [t] Ro 1:11, 13; 15:29 **1:16** [u] 1Co 16:5-7 **1:17** [v] 2Co 10:2, 3 **1:18** [w] 1Co 1:9 **1:19** [x] Heb 13:8 **1:20** [y] Ro 15:8 [z] 1Co 14:16 **1:21** [a] 1Jn 2:20, 27 **1:22** [b] 2Co 5:5 **1:23** [c] Ro 1:9; Gal 1:20 [d] 1Co 4:21; 2Co 2:1, 3; 13:2, 10 **1:24** [e] 1Pe 5:3 [f] Ro 11:20; 1Co 15:1 **2:1** [g] 2Co 1:23 **2:2** [h] 2Co 7:8 **2:3** [i] 2Co 7:8, 12 [j] 2Co 12:21 [k] 2Co 8:22; Gal 5:10 **2:4** [l] 2Co 7:8, 12 **2:5** [m] 1Co 5:1, 2 **2:6** [n] 1Co 5:4, 5 **2:7** [o] Gal 6:1; Eph 4:32 **2:9** [p] 2Co 10:6 **2:11** [q] Mt 4:10 [r] Lk 22:31; 2Co 4:4; 1Pe 5:8, 9 **2:12** [s] Ac 16:8 [t] Ro 1:1 [u] Ac 14:27 **2:13** [v] 2Co 7:5 [w] 2Co 7:6, 13; 12:18 **2:14** [x] Ro 6:17

aroma[y] of the knowledge of him everywhere. 15For we are to God the pleasing
aroma of Christ among those who are being saved and those who are perishing.[z]
16To the one we are an aroma that brings
death;[a] to the other, an aroma that brings
life. And who is equal to such a task?[b] 17Un-
like so many, we do not peddle the word of
God for profit.[c] On the contrary, in Christ
we speak before God with sincerity,[d] as
those sent from God.[e]

3 Are we beginning to commend ourselves[f] again? Or do we need, like some
people, letters of recommendation[g] to you
or from you? 2You yourselves are our letter, written on our hearts, known and read
by everyone.[h] 3You show that you are a letter from Christ, the result of our ministry,
written not with ink but with the Spirit of
the living God, not on tablets of stone[i] but
on tablets of human hearts.[j]

4Such confidence[k] we have through
Christ before God. 5Not that we are competent in ourselves to claim anything for
ourselves, but our competence comes from
God.[l] 6He has made us competent as ministers of a new covenant[m]—not of the letter
but of the Spirit; for the letter kills, but the
Spirit gives life.[n]

The Greater Glory of the New Covenant

7Now if the ministry that brought death,
which was engraved in letters on stone,
came with glory, so that the Israelites
could not look steadily at the face of Moses because of its glory,[o] transitory though
it was, 8will not the ministry of the Spirit be even more glorious? 9If the ministry
that brought condemnation[p] was glorious,
how much more glorious is the ministry
that brings righteousness![q] 10For what was
glorious has no glory now in comparison
with the surpassing glory. 11And if what
was transitory came with glory, how much
greater is the glory of that which lasts!

12Therefore, since we have such a hope,
we are very bold.[r] 13We are not like Moses, who would put a veil over his face[s]
to prevent the Israelites from seeing the
end of what was passing away. 14But their
minds were made dull,[t] for to this day the
same veil remains when the old covenant[u]
is read.[v] It has not been removed, because
only in Christ is it taken away. 15Even to
this day when Moses is read, a veil covers
their hearts. 16But whenever anyone turns
to the Lord,[w] the veil is taken away.[x] 17Now
the Lord is the Spirit,[y] and where the Spirit
of the Lord is, there is freedom.[z] 18And we
all, who with unveiled faces contemplate[a][a]
the Lord's glory,[b] are being transformed
into his image[c] with ever-increasing glory, which comes from the Lord, who is the
Spirit.

Present Weakness and Resurrection Life

4 Therefore, since through God's mercy[d]
we have this ministry, we do not lose
heart. 2Rather, we have renounced secret
and shameful ways;[e] we do not use deception, nor do we distort the word of God.[f]
On the contrary, by setting forth the truth
plainly we commend ourselves to everyone's conscience[g] in the sight of God. 3And
even if our gospel[h] is veiled,[i] it is veiled to
those who are perishing.[j] 4The god[k] of this
age has blinded[l] the minds of unbelievers,

---

a 18 Or *reflect*

2:16 *an aroma that brings death.* The gospel message gives life to those who choose to accept it, but it represents death and judgment to those who reject it.

3:2 *You yourselves are our letter.* Paul sometimes did use letters of recommendation (8:22; Rom. 16:1; 1 Cor. 16:10; Col. 4:10), but he did not need one for the Corinthians. They already knew him personally and had personally benefited from his ministry. Paul's love for the Corinthians was known to all who were acquainted with him. One of the qualifications for ministry is love for people, both God's people and the lost.

3:6 *not of the letter.* The "letter" is the old covenant of law. The "letter" kills because no one can be perfect enough to keep the whole law all the time, and the penalty for breaking it is death.

3:7 *ministry that brought death.* Though the law itself is holy (Rom. 7:12), the ministration, or ministry, of the law is the ministry of death because the law defines and convicts of sin but offers no salvation.

3:9 *ministry that brings righteousness.* God declares righteous those who believe in His Son, and then the Holy Spirit empowers the believer to live righteously. This first work of God is called justification, and the second is called sanctification.

3:11 *which lasts.* The new covenant supersedes the old covenant established at Mount Sinai between God and the nation of Israel.

3:18 *the Lords's glory ... glory.* As believers behold the glory of God in the Word of God, the Spirit of God changes their hearts and actions to make them more and more like Jesus Christ.

4:2 *distort the word of God.* Apparently Paul had been accused of being crafty (12:16) and of being deceitful in the way that he preached. In fact, his ministry was based on the truthfulness of the word of God.

4:4 *The god of this age has blinded.* Because of Satan's deception, sometimes what the world thinks is obviously true is painfully wrong (Prov. 14:12).

2:14 [y] Eph 5:2; Php 4:18 **2:15** [z] 1Co 1:18 **2:16** [a] Lk 2:34 [b] 2Co 3:5,6 **2:17** [c] 2Co 4:2 [d] 1Co 5:8 [e] 2Co 1:12
3:1 [f] 2Co 5:12; 12:11 [g] Ac 18:27 **3:2** [h] 1Co 9:2
3:3 [i] Ex 24:12 [j] Pr 3:3; Jer 31:33; Eze 11:19 **3:4** [k] Eph 3:12
3:5 [l] 1Co 15:10 **3:6** [m] Lk 22:20 [n] Jn 6:63
3:7 [o] Ex 34:29-35 **3:9** [p] ver 7 [q] Ro 1:17; 3:21,22
3:12 [r] Eph 6:19 **3:13** [s] ver 7; Ex 34:33 **3:14** [t] Ro 11:7,8 [u] Ac 13:15 [v] ver 6 **3:16** [w] Ro 11:23 [x] Ex 34:34
3:17 [y] Isa 61:1,2 [z] Jn 8:32 **3:18** [a] 1Co 13:12 [b] 2Co 4:4,6 [c] Ro 8:29 **4:1** [d] 1Co 7:25 **4:2** [e] 1Co 4:5 [f] 2Co 2:17
[g] 2Co 5:11 **4:3** [h] 2Co 2:12 [i] 2Co 3:14 [j] 1Co 1:18
4:4 [k] Jn 12:31 [l] 2Co 3:14

so that they cannot see the light of the gospel that displays the glory of Christ, who is
the image of God. 5For what we preach is
not ourselves,[m] but Jesus Christ as Lord,
and ourselves as your servants[n] for Jesus'
sake. 6For God, who said, "Let light shine
out of darkness,"[a][o] made his light shine
in our hearts[p] to give us the light of the
knowledge of God's glory displayed in the
face of Christ.
7But we have this treasure in jars of clay[q]
to show that this all-surpassing power is
from God[r] and not from us. 8We are hard
pressed on every side,[s] but not crushed;
perplexed, but not in despair; 9persecuted,[t]
but not abandoned;[u] struck down, but not
destroyed.[v] 10We always carry around in
our body the death of Jesus, so that the life
of Jesus may also be revealed in our body.[w]
11For we who are alive are always being
given over to death for Jesus' sake,[x] so that
his life may also be revealed in our mortal
body. 12So then, death is at work in us, but
life is at work in you.[y]
13It is written: "I believed; therefore I
have spoken."[b][z] Since we have that same
spirit of[c] faith, we also believe and therefore speak, 14because we know that the one
who raised the Lord Jesus from the dead
will also raise us with Jesus[a] and present
us with you to himself.[b] 15All this is for your
benefit, so that the grace that is reaching
more and more people may cause thanksgiving[c] to overflow to the glory of God.
16Therefore we do not lose heart. Though
outwardly we are wasting away, yet inwardly[d] we are being renewed[e] day by day.
17For our light and momentary troubles are
achieving for us an eternal glory that far
outweighs them all.[f] 18So we fix our eyes
not on what is seen, but on what is unseen,[g]
since what is seen is temporary, but what is
unseen is eternal.

Awaiting the New Body

5 For we know that if the earthly[h] tent[i]
we live in is destroyed, we have a building from God, an eternal house in heaven,
not built by human hands. 2Meanwhile we
groan,[j] longing to be clothed instead with
our heavenly dwelling,[k] 3because when we
are clothed, we will not be found naked.
4For while we are in this tent, we groan
and are burdened, because we do not wish
to be unclothed but to be clothed instead
with our heavenly dwelling,[l] so that what
is mortal may be swallowed up by life.
5Now the one who has fashioned us for
this very purpose is God, who has given us
the Spirit as a deposit, guaranteeing what
is to come.[m]
6Therefore we are always confident
and know that as long as we are at home
in the body we are away from the Lord.
7For we live by faith, not by sight.[n] 8We
are confident, I say, and would prefer to be
away from the body and at home with the
Lord.[o] 9So we make it our goal to please
him,[p] whether we are at home in the body
or away from it. 10For we must all appear
before the judgment seat of Christ, so that
each of us may receive what is due us[q] for
the things done while in the body, whether
good or bad.

The Ministry of Reconciliation

11Since, then, we know what it is to fear
the Lord,[r] we try to persuade others. What

a 6 Gen. 1:3 *b 13* Psalm 116:10 (see Septuagint)
c 13 Or *Spirit-given*

image of God. Jesus Christ is God's Son, and He perfectly reveals God the Father to us. Human beings have been created in the image of God, but through sin they have fallen from a perfect relationship with God. Jesus Christ is restoring believers to what they were originally created to be (3:18; Gen. 1:26).

4:8 *but not crushed.* As believers we will face trials, but we must remember that God controls trials and uses them to strengthen His people. God's glory is manifested through broken vessels, through people who endure troubles by relying on His power.

4:9 *struck down.* This literally happened (Acts 14:19). In Lystra a crowd stoned Paul, leaving him for dead. But the Lord spared his life so that he could continue to preach the gospel and testify to God's deliverance.

4:12 *life is at work in you.* Had Paul not been willing to risk death to bring the gospel to Corinth, the Corinthians would not have received eternal life.

4:17 *achieving for us.* Afflictions produce glory, but the glory is far greater than the affliction (Mark 10:30).

5:2 *we groan.* Along with the rest of creation, our spirits cry out for what we were meant to be (Rom. 8:22–23).

5:5 *guaranteeing.* The Holy Spirit's work in believers' lives can be compared to a down payment, or earnest money (1:22). The presence of the Holy Spirit assures believers that God has purchased them. They are no longer slaves to sin, but are now His children.

5:8 *at home with the Lord.* This is one of the passages indicating where believers will go after death; they will be with Jesus in heaven (Luke 23:43; Phil. 1:23).

5:9 *we make it our goal.* Pleasing the Lord should always be our first concern in this life, since it is the only thing which will carry over into the next life.

5:10 *each of us may receive what is due us.* The believer will either be approved or ashamed (5:3; Luke 19:11–26; 1 Cor. 3:14–15; 9:27; 1 John 2:28; 2 John 7–8).

5:11 *fear the Lord.* This is the fear of standing before the Lord and having one's life exposed and

4:5 [m] 1Co 1:13 [n] 1Co 9:19 **4:6** [o] Ge 1:3 [p] 2Pe 1:19
4:7 [q] Job 4:19; 2Co 5:1 [r] 1Co 2:5 **4:8** [s] 2Co 7:5
4:9 [t] Jn 15:20 [u] Heb 13:5 [v] Ps 37:24 **4:10** [w] Ro 6:5
4:11 [x] Ro 8:36 **4:12** [y] 2Co 13:9 **4:13** [z] Ps 116:10
4:14 [a] 1Th 4:14 [b] Eph 5:27 **4:15** [c] 2Co 1:11
4:16 [d] Ro 7:22 [e] Col 3:10 **4:17** [f] Ro 8:18; 1Pe 1:6,7
4:18 [g] Ro 8:24; Heb 11:1 **5:1** [h] 1Co 15:47 [i] 2Pe 1:13,14
5:2 [j] ver 4; Ro 8:23 [k] 1Co 15:53,54 **5:4** [l] 1Co 15:53,54
5:5 [m] Ro 8:23; 2Co 1:22 **5:7** [n] 1Co 13:12 **5:8** [o] Php 1:23
5:9 [p] Ro 14:18 **5:10** [q] Mt 16:27; Ro 14:10; Eph 6:8
5:11 [r] Heb 10:31; Jude 23

we are is plain to God, and I hope it is also
plain to your conscience.[s] 12We are not trying to commend ourselves to you again,[t]
but are giving you an opportunity to take
pride in us,[u] so that you can answer those
who take pride in what is seen rather than
in what is in the heart. 13If we are "out of
our mind,"[v] as some say, it is for God; if we
are in our right mind, it is for you. 14For
Christ's love compels us, because we are
convinced that one died for all, and therefore all died.[w] 15And he died for all, that
those who live should no longer live for
themselves[x] but for him who died for them
and was raised again.

16So from now on we regard no one from
a worldly[y] point of view. Though we once
regarded Christ in this way, we do so no
longer. 17Therefore, if anyone is in Christ,
the new creation[z] has come:[a] The old has
gone, the new is here![a] 18All this is from
God, who reconciled us to himself through
Christ[b] and gave us the ministry of reconciliation: 19that God was reconciling the
world to himself in Christ, not counting
people's sins against them.[c] And he has
committed to us the message of reconciliation. 20We are therefore Christ's ambassadors,[d] as though God were making
his appeal through us. We implore you
on Christ's behalf: Be reconciled to God.
21God made him who had no sin[e] to be sin[b]
for us, so that in him we might become the
righteousness of God.[f]

6 As God's co-workers[g] we urge you not
to receive God's grace in vain. 2For he
says,

> "In the time of my favor I heard you,
> and in the day of salvation I helped
> you."[ch]

I tell you, now is the time of God's favor,
now is the day of salvation.

Paul's Hardships

3We put no stumbling block in anyone's
path,[i] so that our ministry will not be discredited. 4Rather, as servants of God we
commend ourselves in every way: in great
endurance; in troubles, hardships and dis-
tresses; 5in beatings, imprisonments[j] and
riots; in hard work, sleepless nights and
hunger;[k] 6in purity, understanding, patience and kindness; in the Holy Spirit[l]
and in sincere love; 7in truthful speech[m]
and in the power of God; with weapons of
righteousness[n] in the right hand and in the
left; 8through glory and dishonor,[o] bad report and good report; genuine, yet regarded as impostors;[p] 9known, yet regarded
as unknown; dying,[q] and yet we live on;[r]
beaten, and yet not killed; 10sorrowful, yet
always rejoicing;[s] poor, yet making many
rich;[t] having nothing, and yet possessing
everything.[u]

---

[a] 17 Or *Christ, that person is a new creation.*
[b] 21 Or *be a sin offering* [c] 2 Isaiah 49:8

---

evaluated. The reality of giving an account to the Lord motivated Paul to persuade people, in this context meaning to convince the Corinthians of his sincerity and integrity.

5:14 *Christ's love.* This phrase can mean either Christ's love for us or our love for Christ.

5:15 *for him.* Believers are united with Jesus both in His death and in His resurrection, and therefore they participate in the new creation. That is, they receive the benefits of being restored by Christ to what God had originally created them to be (Gen. 1:26; 1 Cor. 15:45–49).

5:17 Our New Nature—The term "new nature" refers to the spiritual transformation that occurs within people when they believe in Christ as Savior. New does not mean renewed, renovated, reformed, or rehabilitated. It means completely and distinctly new, with a new family, a new set of values, new motivations, and a whole new life. The old man is still present in the new life and expresses himself in sinful deeds such as lying (Eph. 4:22; Col. 3:9). The new man, to be visible, must be *put on,* as one would put on a new suit of clothes (Col. 3:10). In other words, the new nature must be cultivated or nurtured by spiritual decisiveness to grow in Christ. We must not revert to putting on the old suit of the former life; rather, we must continue to grow in this new life (Eph. 5:8).

5:18 *ministry of reconciliation.* Reconciliation is the change of relation from enmity to peace. We who have been reconciled to God through Christ have the privilege of telling others that they can be reconciled to Him as well.

5:19 *reconciling the world to himself.* God could change His relationship toward us because our sins have been imputed (charged) to Christ instead of to us. If we believe in Jesus, God counts Jesus' righteousness as our righteousness (v. 21).

5:20 *ambassadors.* Ambassadors are representatives of the sovereign who sends them, the "stand in" for their own ruler in a foreign country. Christians have been called by their King to serve as ambassadors in a world that is in rebellion against Him, with the responsibility to bring a message of peace and of reconciliation.

6:1 *in vain.* Believers who live for themselves may have received the grace of God, but they will miss out on a heavenly reward for their service to Him. Paul encourages those who have been saved to work out or develop their salvation (Phil. 2:12). The Corinthians were failing at this very point. They were saved and stuck, so to speak.

6:4 *in great endurance.* Believers must not expect that it will be easy or comfortable to be a disciple, but it will be more deeply fulfilling than anything else could be.

5:11 [s] 2Co 4:2 **5:12** [t] 2Co 3:1 [u] 2Co 1:14
5:13 [v] 2Co 11:1, 16, 17 **5:14** [w] Gal 2:20 **5:15** [x] Ro 14:7-9
5:16 [y] 2Co 11:18 **5:17** [z] Gal 6:15 [a] Isa 65:17; Rev 21:4, 5
5:18 [b] Ro 5:10; Col 1:20 **5:19** [c] Ro 4:8 **5:20** [d] 2Co 6:1; Eph 6:20 **5:21** [e] Heb 4:15; 1Pe 2:22, 24; 1Jn 3:5 [f] Ro 1:17
6:1 [g] 1Co 3:9; 2Co 5:20 **6:2** [h] Isa 49:8 **6:3** [i] Ro 14:13, 20; 1Co 9:12; 10:32 **6:5** [j] 2Co 11:23-25 [k] 1Co 4:11
6:6 [l] 1Th 1:5 **6:7** [m] 2Co 4:2 [n] 2Co 10:4; Eph 6:10-18
6:8 [o] 1Co 4:10 [p] Mt 27:63 **6:9** [q] Ro 8:36 [r] 2Co 1:8-10; 4:10, 11 **6:10** [s] 2Co 7:4 [t] 2Co 8:9 [u] Ro 8:32; 1Co 3:21

11We have spoken freely to you, Corinthians, and opened wide our hearts to you.[v]
12We are not withholding our affection
from you, but you are withholding yours
from us. **13**As a fair exchange—I speak as
to my children[w]—open wide your hearts
also.

Warning Against Idolatry

14Do not be yoked together[x] with unbelievers. For what do righteousness and
wickedness have in common? Or what
fellowship can light have with darkness?[y]
15What harmony is there between Christ
and Belial[a]? Or what does a believer[z] have
in common with an unbeliever? **16**What
agreement is there between the temple of
God and idols? For we are the temple[a] of
the living God. As God has said:

"I will live with them
and walk among them,
and I will be their God,
and they will be my people."[b][b]

17Therefore,

"Come out from them[c]
and be separate,
says the Lord.
Touch no unclean thing,
and I will receive you."[c][d]

18And,

"I will be a Father to you,
and you will be my sons and
daughters,[e]
says the Lord Almighty."[d]

7 Therefore, since we have these promises,[f] dear friends, let us purify ourselves
from everything that contaminates body
and spirit, perfecting holiness out of reverence for God.

Paul's Joy Over the Church's Repentance

2Make room for us in your hearts.[g] We
have wronged no one, we have corrupted
no one, we have exploited no one. **3**I do not
say this to condemn you; I have said before
that you have such a place in our hearts[h]
that we would live or die with you. **4**I have
spoken to you with great frankness; I take
great pride in you. I am greatly encouraged;
in all our troubles my joy knows no bounds.[i]
5For when we came into Macedonia,[j] we
had no rest, but we were harassed at every
turn[k]—conflicts on the outside, fears within.[l] **6**But God, who comforts the downcast,[m]
comforted us by the coming of Titus,[n] **7**and
not only by his coming but also by the comfort you had given him. He told us about
your longing for me, your deep sorrow,
your ardent concern for me, so that my joy
was greater than ever.

8Even if I caused you sorrow by my letter,[o] I do not regret it. Though I did regret
it—I see that my letter hurt you, but only
for a little while— **9**yet now I am happy, not
because you were made sorry, but because
your sorrow led you to repentance. For you
became sorrowful as God intended and so
were not harmed in any way by us. **10**Godly sorrow brings repentance that leads to
salvation[p] and leaves no regret, but worldly sorrow brings death. **11**See what this
godly sorrow has produced in you: what
earnestness, what eagerness to clear yourselves, what indignation, what alarm, what
longing, what concern,[q] what readiness to
see justice done. At every point you have
proved yourselves to be innocent in this
matter. **12**So even though I wrote to you,[r] it
was neither on account of the one who did
the wrong[s] nor on account of the injured
party, but rather that before God you could
see for yourselves how devoted to us you
are. **13**By all this we are encouraged.

In addition to our own encouragement,
we were especially delighted to see how
happy Titus[t] was, because his spirit has

[a] *15* Greek *Beliar,* a variant of *Belial*
[b] *16* Lev. 26:12; Jer. 32:38; Ezek. 37:27
[c] *17* Isaiah 52:11; Ezek. 20:34,41
[d] *18* 2 Samuel 7:14; 7:8

6:14 *Do not be yoked together with unbelievers.* This verse has most often been applied to the subject of marriage, warning believers not to bind themselves for life to one who does not love the Lord.
6:15 *Belial.* This term for Satan occurs only here in the New Testament. It refers to one who is vile and wicked and who causes destruction.
6:16 *we are the temple.* This reference to Leviticus 26:11–12 and Ezekiel 37:27 reminds believers of their relationship with God. Since the Holy Spirit is living in them, they are God's new dwelling place (1 Cor. 6:19).
6:17 *be separate.* Paul was not encouraging isolation from unbelievers (1 Cor. 9:5–13) but discouraging compromise with their sinful values and practices. He was urging them (and us) to maintain integrity in the world just as Christ did (John 15:14–16; Phil. 2:14–16).
7:1 *perfecting holiness.* This means dedicating ourselves to Christ and living righteously (Heb. 6:1).
7:3 *you have such a place in our hearts.* Paul was not throwing his weight around or trying to be controlling. He loved the Corinthians and wanted the very best for them.
7:10 *brings repentance.* A person can be sorry that he or she was caught in sin, or sorry to have to bear the consequences, without repenting of sin. True sorrow leads to a change of heart and a turning to God. Repentance means changing direction, and results in spiritual deliverance.

6:11 [v] 2Co 7:3 **6:13** [w] 1Co 4:14 **6:14** [x] 1Co 5:9, 10 [y] Eph 5:7, 11; 1Jn 1:6 **6:15** [z] Ac 5:14 **6:16** [a] 1Co 3:16 [b] Lev 26:12; Jer 32:38; Eze 37:27 **6:17** [c] Rev 18:4 [d] Isa 52:11 **6:18** [e] Isa 43:6 **7:1** [f] 2Co 6:17, 18 **7:2** [g] 2Co 6:12, 13 **7:3** [h] 2Co 6:11, 12 **7:4** [i] 2Co 6:10 **7:5** [j] 2Co 2:13 [k] 2Co 4:8 [l] Dt 32:25 **7:6** [m] 2Co 1:3, 4 [n] ver 13; 2Co 2:13 **7:8** [o] 2Co 2:2, 4 **7:10** [p] Ac 11:18 **7:11** [q] ver 7 **7:12** [r] ver 8; 2Co 2:3, 9 [s] 1Co 5:1, 2 **7:13** [t] ver 6; 2Co 2:13

been refreshed by all of you. **14**I had boasted to him about you,[u] and you have not
embarrassed me. But just as everything
we said to you was true, so our boasting
about you to Titus[v] has proved to be true as
well. **15**And his affection for you is all the
greater when he remembers that you were
all obedient,[w] receiving him with fear and
trembling.[x] **16**I am glad I can have complete
confidence in you.[y]

The Collection for the Lord's People

8 And now, brothers and sisters, we want
you to know about the grace that God
has given the Macedonian[z] churches. **2**In
the midst of a very severe trial, their overflowing joy and their extreme poverty
welled up in rich generosity. **3**For I testify
that they gave as much as they were able,[a]
and even beyond their ability. Entirely on
their own, **4**they urgently pleaded with us
for the privilege of sharing in this service[b]
to the Lord's people.[c] **5**And they exceeded
our expectations: They gave themselves
first of all to the Lord, and then by the will
of God also to us. **6**So we urged[d] Titus,[e]
just as he had earlier made a beginning, to
bring also to completion[f] this act of grace
on your part. **7**But since you excel in everything[g]—in faith, in speech, in knowledge,[h]
in complete earnestness and in the love we
have kindled in you[a]—see that you also excel in this grace of giving.

8I am not commanding you,[i] but I want to
test the sincerity of your love by comparing
it with the earnestness of others. **9**For you
know the grace of our Lord Jesus Christ,[j]
that though he was rich, yet for your sake
he became poor,[k] so that you through his
poverty might become rich.

10And here is my judgment[l] about what
is best for you in this matter. Last year you
were the first not only to give but also to
have the desire to do so.[m] **11**Now finish the
work, so that your eager willingness[n] to
do it may be matched by your completion
of it, according to your means. **12**For if the
willingness is there, the gift is acceptable
according to what one has,[o] not according
to what one does not have.

13Our desire is not that others might be
relieved while you are hard pressed, but
that there might be equality. **14**At the present time your plenty will supply what they
need,[p] so that in turn their plenty will supply what you need. The goal is equality, **15**as
it is written: "The one who gathered much
did not have too much, and the one who
gathered little did not have too little."[b][q]

Titus Sent to Receive the Collection

16Thanks be to God,[r] who put into the
heart[s] of Titus[t] the same concern I have for
you. **17**For Titus not only welcomed our appeal, but he is coming to you with much enthusiasm and on his own initiative.[u] **18**And
we are sending along with him the brother[v]
who is praised by all the churches[w] for his
service to the gospel.[x] **19**What is more, he
was chosen by the churches to accompany
us[y] as we carry the offering, which we administer in order to honor the Lord himself
and to show our eagerness to help.[z] **20**We
want to avoid any criticism of the way we
administer this liberal gift. **21**For we are taking pains to do what is right, not only in the
eyes of the Lord but also in the eyes of man.[a]

22In addition, we are sending with them
our brother who has often proved to us in
many ways that he is zealous, and now
even more so because of his great confidence in you. **23**As for Titus, he is my partner[b] and co-worker[c] among you; as for our
brothers,[d] they are representatives of the
churches and an honor to Christ. **24**Therefore show these men the proof of your love
and the reason for our pride in you,[e] so that
the churches can see it.

9 There is no need[f] for me to write to you
about this service to the Lord's people.[g] **2**For I know your eagerness to help,
and I have been boasting[h] about it to the
Macedonians, telling them that since last
year[i] you in Achaia[j] were ready to give; and
your enthusiasm has stirred most of them
to action. **3**But I am sending the brothers in
order that our boasting about you in this
matter should not prove hollow, but that
you may be ready, as I said you would be.[k]
4For if any Macedonians[l] come with me
and find you unprepared, we—not to say

[a] *7* Some manuscripts *and in your love for us*
[b] *15* Exodus 16:18

8:1 ***Macedonian.*** Macedonia corresponds to the northern part of present day Greece. Paul had established churches in the Macedonian cities of Philippi, Thessalonica, and Berea.
8:8 ***test the sincerity of your love.*** Generosity is the natural result of sincere love.
8:9 ***you ... might become rich.*** Jesus offers forgiveness, justification, regeneration, eternal life, and glorification. He purchased us from slavery to sin, giving us the position of children of God with free access to His presence.
8:10 ***what is best.*** Giving in this life is an investment for eternity (Matt. 6:19–21).
9:4 ***Macedonians.*** Paul was in Macedonia when he wrote this letter (2:13; 7:5). When he made his visit to Corinth he would no doubt bring traveling companions from Macedonia.

7:14 [u] ver 4 [v] ver 6 **7:15** [w] 2Co 2:9 [x] Php 2:12
7:16 [y] 2Co 2:3 **8:1** [z] Ac 16:9 **8:3** [a] 1Co 16:2
8:4 [b] Ac 24:17 [c] Ro 15:25; 2Co 9:1 **8:6** [d] ver 17; 2Co 12:18
[e] ver 16, 23 [f] ver 10, 11 **8:7** [g] 2Co 9:8 [h] 1Co 1:5
8:8 [i] 1Co 7:6 **8:9** [j] 2Co 13:14 [k] Mt 20:28; Php 2:6-8
8:10 [l] 1Co 7:25, 40 [m] 1Co 16:2, 3; 2Co 9:2 **8:11** [n] 2Co 9:2
8:12 [o] Mk 12:43, 44; Lk 21:3 **8:14** [p] 2Co 9:12
8:15 [q] Ex 16:18 **8:16** [r] 2Co 2:14 [s] Rev 17:17 [t] 2Co 2:13
8:17 [u] ver 6 **8:18** [v] 2Co 12:18 [w] 1Co 7:17 [x] 2Co 2:12
8:19 [y] 1Co 16:3, 4 [z] ver 11, 12 **8:21** [a] Ro 12:17; 14:18
8:23 [b] Phm 17 [c] Php 2:25 [d] ver 18, 22 **8:24** [e] 2Co 7:4, 14;
9:2 **9:1** [f] 1Th 4:9 [g] 2Co 8:4 **9:2** [h] 2Co 7:4, 14 [i] 2Co 8:10
[j] Ac 18:12 **9:3** [k] 1Co 16:2 **9:4** [l] Ro 15:26

anything about you—would be ashamed of having been so confident. 5So I thought it necessary to urge the brothers to visit you in advance and finish the arrangements for the generous gift you had promised. Then it will be ready as a generous gift,[m] not as one grudgingly given.[n]

Generosity Encouraged

6Remember this: Whoever sows sparingly will also reap sparingly, and whoever sows generously will also reap generously.[o] 7Each of you should give what you have decided in your heart to give,[p] not reluctantly or under compulsion,[q] for God loves a cheerful giver.[r] 8And God is able[s] to bless you abundantly, so that in all things at all times, having all that you need,[t] you will abound in every good work. 9As it is written:

> "They have freely scattered their gifts
> to the poor;
> their righteousness endures
> forever."[a][u]

10Now he who supplies seed to the sower and bread for food[v] will also supply and increase your store of seed and will enlarge the harvest of your righteousness.[w] 11You will be enriched[x] in every way so that you can be generous on every occasion, and through us your generosity will result in thanksgiving to God.[y]

12This service that you perform is not only supplying the needs[z] of the Lord's people but is also overflowing in many expressions of thanks to God.[a] 13Because of the service[b] by which you have proved yourselves, others will praise God[c] for the obedience that accompanies your confession of the gospel of Christ,[d] and for your generosity in sharing with them and with everyone else. 14And in their prayers for you their hearts will go out to you, because of the surpassing grace God has given you. 15Thanks be to God[e] for his indescribable gift![f]

Paul's Defense of His Ministry

10 By the humility and gentleness[g] of Christ, I appeal to you—I, Paul,[h] who am "timid" when face to face with you, but "bold" toward you when away! 2I beg you that when I come I may not have to be as bold[i] as I expect to be toward some people who think that we live by the standards of this world. 3For though we live in the world, we do not wage war as the world does. 4The weapons we fight with[j] are not the weapons of the world. On the contrary, they have divine power[k] to demolish strongholds.[l] 5We demolish arguments and every pretension that sets itself up against the knowledge of God,[m] and we take captive every thought to make it obedient[n] to Christ. 6And we will be ready to punish every act of disobedience, once your obedience is complete.[o]

7You are judging by appearances.[b][p] If anyone is confident that they belong to Christ,[q] they should consider again that we belong to Christ just as much as they do.[r] 8So even if I boast somewhat freely about the authority the Lord gave us for building you up rather than tearing you down,[s] I will not be ashamed of it. 9I do not want to seem to be trying to frighten you with my letters. 10For some say, "His letters are weighty and forceful, but in person he is unimpressive[t] and his speaking amounts to nothing."[u] 11Such people should realize that what we are in our letters when we are absent, we will be in our actions when we are present.

12We do not dare to classify or compare

---

[a] 9 Psalm 112:9 [b] 7 Or *Look at the obvious facts*

9:6–8 Giving—There is no better indicator of growth in the new life than in the area of giving. This passage and others deal with several aspects of giving:

1. Giving should be done generously, even extravagantly (2 Cor. 9:6).
2. Giving should be done cheerfully (2 Cor. 9:7).
3. Giving should be regular (1 Cor. 16:2).
4. Giving should be systematic (1 Cor. 16:2).
5. Giving should be proportionate (2 Cor. 8:3).

God is more concerned with the motive that lies the giving than the gift itself. The person who fails to honor God with his giving actually robs God (Mal. 3:8), not because it impoverishes God but because it denies the God-ordained means for the support of His work and His ministers. For the child of God who honors God with his giving, God promises abundant blessing (Mal. 3:10; Luke 6:38) and the provision of his every need (Phil. 4:19).

9:6 *reap sparingly.* The law of the harvest is referred to repeatedly in Scripture (Prov. 11:24–25; 19:17; Luke 6:38; Gal. 6:7). If you do not plant, you will have no harvest.

9:8 *God is able.* God sees to it that the generous giver will not suffer want. Instead, God generously provides for those who give so that they can continue to do so.

9:15 *indescribable gift.* Our gifts can never compare with God's sacrifice for us.

10:4 *we fight with.* The world is hostile to Christ and His followers because the world is following Satan. The life of a believer is not one of ease but a constant spiritual battle.

10:8 *building you up.* Paul's exhortation was aimed at correcting abuses, not the tearing down of the church.

9:5 [m] Php 4:17 [n] 2Co 12:17,18 **9:6** [o] Pr 11:24,25; 22:9; Gal 6:7,9 **9:7** [p] Ex 25:2; 2Co 8:12 [q] Dt 15:10 [r] Ro 12:8 **9:8** [s] Eph 3:20 [t] Php 4:19 **9:9** [u] Ps 112:9 **9:10** [v] Isa 55:10 [w] Hos 10:12 **9:11** [x] 1Co 1:5 [y] 2Co 1:11 **9:12** [z] 2Co 8:14 [a] 2Co 1:11 **9:13** [b] 2Co 8:4 [c] Mt 9:8 [d] 2Co 2:12 **9:15** [e] 2Co 2:14 [f] Ro 5:15,16 **10:1** [g] Mt 11:29 [h] Gal 5:2 **10:2** [i] 1Co 4:21; 2Co 13:2,10 **10:4** [j] 2Co 6:7 [k] 1Co 2:5 [l] Jer 1:10; 2Co 13:10 **10:5** [m] Isa 2:11,12; 1Co 1:19 [n] 2Co 9:13 **10:6** [o] 2Co 2:9; 7:15 **10:7** [p] Jn 7:24 [q] 1Co 1:12; 3:23; 14:37 [r] 2Co 11:23 **10:8** [s] 2Co 13:10 **10:10** [t] 1Co 2:3; Gal 4:13,14 [u] 1Co 1:17

ourselves with some who commend themselves.[v] When they measure themselves by themselves and compare themselves with themselves, they are not wise. 13We, however, will not boast beyond proper limits, but will confine our boasting to the sphere of service God himself has assigned to us,[w] a sphere that also includes you. 14We are not going too far in our boasting, as would be the case if we had not come to you, for we did get as far as you[x] with the gospel of Christ.[y] 15Neither do we go beyond our limits by boasting of work done by others.[z] Our hope is that, as your faith continues to grow,[a] our sphere of activity among you will greatly expand, 16so that we can preach the gospel in the regions beyond you.[b] For we do not want to boast about work already done in someone else's territory. 17But, "Let the one who boasts boast in the Lord."[ac] 18For it is not the one who commends himself[d] who is approved, but the one whom the Lord commends.[e]

Paul and the False Apostles

11 I hope you will put up with[f] me in a little foolishness.[g] Yes, please put up with me! 2I am jealous for you with a godly jealousy. I promised you to one husband,[h] to Christ, so that I might present you[i] as a pure virgin to him. 3But I am afraid that just as Eve was deceived by the serpent's cunning,[j] your minds may somehow be led astray from your sincere and pure devotion to Christ. 4For if someone comes to you and preaches a Jesus other than the Jesus we preached,[k] or if you receive a different spirit[l] from the Spirit you received, or a different gospel[m] from the one you accepted, you put up with it easily enough.

5I do not think I am in the least inferior to those "super-apostles."[bn] 6I may indeed be untrained as a speaker,[o] but I do have knowledge.[p] We have made this perfectly clear to you in every way. 7Was it a sin[q] for me to lower myself in order to elevate you by preaching the gospel of God to you free of charge?[r] 8I robbed other churches by receiving support from them[s] so as to serve you. 9And when I was with you and needed something, I was not a burden to anyone, for the brothers who came from Macedonia supplied what I needed. I have kept myself from being a burden to you[t] in any way, and will continue to do so. 10As surely as the truth of Christ is in me,[u] nobody in the regions of Achaia[v] will stop this boasting[w] of mine. 11Why? Because I do not love you? God knows I do![x]

12And I will keep on doing what I am doing in order to cut the ground from under those who want an opportunity to be considered equal with us in the things they boast about. 13For such people are false apostles,[y] deceitful[z] workers, masquerading as apostles of Christ.[a] 14And no wonder, for Satan himself masquerades as an angel of light. 15It is not surprising, then, if his servants also masquerade as servants of righteousness. Their end will be what their actions deserve.[b]

Paul Boasts About His Sufferings

16I repeat: Let no one take me for a fool.[c] But if you do, then tolerate me just as you would a fool, so that I may do a little boasting. 17In this self-confident boasting I am not talking as the Lord would,[d] but as a fool. 18Since many are boasting in the way the world does, I too will boast.[e] 19You gladly put up with fools since you are so wise![f] 20In fact, you even put up with anyone who enslaves you[g] or exploits you or takes advantage of you or puts on airs or slaps you in the face. 21To my shame I admit that we were too weak[h] for that!

Whatever anyone else dares to boast

a 17 Jer. 9:24 *b* 5 Or *to the most eminent apostles*

10:16 *regions beyond you.* Paul states in Romans that his ambition was to preach the gospel in Spain (Rom. 15:24).

11:2 *jealous.* Usually jealousy has a negative connotation to us — we confuse jealousy with envy or spite. The word has the same root as "zealous," and it can mean a sincere and energetic protection of the rights or purity of a person or place.

11:6 *untrained as a speaker.* Paul may have lacked gifts as a professional speaker, but he did not lack knowledge since he had received direct revelation from the Lord (Gal. 1:11 – 12).

11:7 *free of charge.* Professional philosophers and teachers in Greek society charged for teaching.

11:14 *masquerades as an angel of light.* Don't make the mistake of believing that evil always appears grotesque, ugly, or repulsive. Satan's main tool is deception and he is quite capable of making evil appear beautiful.

11:17 *I am not talking as the Lord would.* This kind of boasting was not characteristic of the Lord. Jesus Christ was an example of humility (Phil. 2:5 – 11).

11:18 *in the way the world does.* The false apostles measured themselves by their own standards rather than by God's.

11:21 *too weak.* Paul's critics had accused him of being weak (10:10). He sarcastically said that he was too weak to rule the Corinthians harshly as the false apostles had done.

10:12 [v] 2Co 3:1 **10:13** [w] ver 15, 16 **10:14** [x] 1Co 3:6 [y] 2Co 2:12 **10:15** [z] Ro 15:20 [a] 2Th 1:3 **10:16** [b] Ac 19:21 **10:17** [c] Jer 9:24; 1Co 1:31 **10:18** [d] ver 12 [e] Ro 2:29; 1Co 4:5 **11:1** [f] ver 4, 19, 20; Mt 17:17 [g] ver 16, 17, 21; 2Co 5:13 **11:2** [h] Hos 2:19; Eph 5:26, 27 [i] 2Co 4:14 **11:3** [j] Ge 3:1-6, 13; Jn 8:44; 1Ti 2:14; Rev 12:9 **11:4** [k] 1Co 3:11 [l] Ro 8:15 [m] Gal 1:6-9 **11:5** [n] 2Co 12:11; Gal 2:6 **11:6** [o] 1Co 1:17 [p] Eph 3:4 **11:7** [q] 2Co 12:13 [r] 1Co 9:18 **11:8** [s] Php 4:15, 18 **11:9** [t] 2Co 12:13, 14, 16 **11:10** [u] Ro 9:1 [v] Ac 18:12 [w] 1Co 9:15 **11:11** [x] 2Co 12:15 **11:13** [y] 2Pe 2:1 [z] Titus 1:10 [a] Rev 2:2 **11:15** [b] Php 3:19 **11:16** [c] ver 1 **11:17** [d] 1Co 7:12, 25 **11:18** [e] Php 3:3, 4 **11:19** [f] 1Co 4:10 **11:20** [g] Gal 2:4 **11:21** [h] 2Co 10:1, 10

about—I am speaking as a fool—I also
dare to boast about.[i] 22Are they Hebrews?
So am I.[j] Are they Israelites? So am I.[k] Are
they Abraham's descendants? So am I.
23Are they servants of Christ? (I am out
of my mind to talk like this.) I am more.
I have worked much harder,[l] been in prison more frequently,[m] been flogged more
severely, and been exposed to death again
and again. 24Five times I received from the
Jews the forty lashes[n] minus one. 25Three
times I was beaten with rods,[o] once I was
pelted with stones,[p] three times I was shipwrecked, I spent a night and a day in the
open sea, 26I have been constantly on the
move. I have been in danger from rivers,
in danger from bandits, in danger from my
fellow Jews,[q] in danger from Gentiles; in
danger in the city,[r] in danger in the country, in danger at sea; and in danger from
false believers.[s] 27I have labored and toiled
and have often gone without sleep; I have
known hunger and thirst and have often
gone without food;[t] I have been cold and
naked. 28Besides everything else, I face
daily the pressure of my concern for all
the churches. 29Who is weak, and I do not
feel weak? Who is led into sin, and I do not
inwardly burn?

30If I must boast, I will boast of the things
that show my weakness.[u] 31The God and
Father of the Lord Jesus, who is to be
praised forever,[v] knows that I am not lying.
32In Damascus the governor under King
Aretas had the city of the Damascenes
guarded in order to arrest me.[w] 33But I was
lowered in a basket from a window in the
wall and slipped through his hands.[x]

Paul's Vision and His Thorn

12 I must go on boasting.[y] Although
there is nothing to be gained, I will
go on to visions and revelations[z] from the
Lord. 2I know a man in Christ who fourteen years ago was caught up[a] to the third
heaven.[b] Whether it was in the body or out
of the body I do not know—God knows.[c]
3And I know that this man—whether in
the body or apart from the body I do not
know, but God knows— 4was caught up to
paradise[d] and heard inexpressible things,
things that no one is permitted to tell. 5I will
boast about a man like that, but I will not
boast about myself, except about my weaknesses. 6Even if I should choose to boast, I
would not be a fool,[e] because I would be
speaking the truth. But I refrain, so no one
will think more of me than is warranted by
what I do or say, 7or because of these sur-
passingly great revelations. Therefore, in
order to keep me from becoming conceited,
I was given a thorn in my flesh,[f] a messenger of Satan, to torment me. 8Three times I
pleaded with the Lord to take it away from
me.[g] 9But he said to me, "My grace is sufficient for you, for my power[h] is made perfect
in weakness." Therefore I will boast all the
more gladly about my weaknesses, so that
Christ's power may rest on me. 10That is
why, for Christ's sake, I delight in weaknesses, in insults, in hardships,[i] in persecutions,[j] in difficulties. For when I am weak,
then I am strong.[k]

Paul's Concern for the Corinthians

11I have made a fool of myself,[l] but you
drove me to it. I ought to have been commended by you, for I am not in the least
inferior to the "super-apostles,"[a][m] even
though I am nothing.[n] 12I persevered in
demonstrating among you the marks of a
true apostle, including signs, wonders and
miracles.[o] 13How were you inferior to the
other churches, except that I was never a
burden to you?[p] Forgive me this wrong![q]
14Now I am ready to visit you for the

[a] 11 Or *the most eminent apostles*

11:23 ***out of my mind.*** Paul acknowledged the silliness of such bragging. He knew that only God had made his preaching and service effective. Paul's credentials were superior to those of the false teachers on every point of experience and background, but even so his ministry had authority only because he received it from God.
12:1 ***visions and revelations.*** This boasting may have been to counter similar claims by the false teachers.
12:2 ***fourteen years.*** Paul wrote 2 Corinthians in A.D. 56; 14 years earlier would have been A.D. 42, probably when he was in Antioch (Acts 11:26). ***third heaven.*** It was common to speak of three "heavens:" The first is the atmosphere where the birds fly; the second is the place of the sun, moon, and stars; the third is where God dwells.
12:7 ***thorn in my flesh.*** Most commentators interpret Paul's thorn as a physical ailment, and many suggest that it was eye trouble on the basis of Galatians 4:15. It is also possible that "flesh" is a reference to the fallen human nature, in which case the thorn could be a temptation, or it could refer to persecution or opposition. ***messenger of Satan.*** God permitted Satan to afflict Paul as He did Job (Job 1–2).
12:11 ***drove me.*** Only the fact that the Corinthians had listened to the silly slander against Paul had made him waste time on boasting.
12:12 ***marks of a true apostle.*** God has often used miracles as supernatural evidences of His authority in a new work (Acts 14:3).
12:14 ***the third time.*** It is not clear whether Paul had already made two previous visits to Corinth, or

11:21 [i] Php 3:4 **11:22** [j] Php 3:5 [k] Ro 9:4
11:23 [l] 1Co 15:10 [m] Ac 16:23; 2Co 6:4,5 **11:24** [n] Dt 25:3
11:25 [o] Ac 16:22 [p] Ac 14:19 **11:26** [q] Ac 9:23; 14:5
[r] Ac 21:31 [s] Gal 2:4 **11:27** [t] 1Co 4:11, 12; 2Co 6:5
11:30 [u] 1Co 2:3 **11:31** [v] Ro 9:5 **11:32** [w] Ac 9:24
11:33 [x] Ac 9:25 **12:1** [y] 2Co 11:16, 30 [z] ver 7
12:2 [a] Ac 8:39 [b] Eph 4:10 [c] 2Co 11:11 **12:4** [d] Lk 23:43;
Rev 2:7 **12:6** [e] 2Co 11:16 **12:7** [f] Nu 33:55
12:8 [g] Mt 26:39,44 **12:9** [h] Php 4:13 **12:10** [i] 2Co 6:4
[j] Ro 5:3; 2Th 1:4 [k] 2Co 13:4 **12:11** [l] 2Co 11:1 [m] 2Co 11:5
[n] 1Co 15:9, 10 **12:12** [o] Jn 4:48 **12:13** [p] 1Co 9:12, 18
[q] 2Co 11:7

third time,[r] and I will not be a burden to
you, because what I want is not your possessions but you. After all, children should
not have to save up for their parents,[s] but
parents for their children.[t] 15So I will very
gladly spend for you everything I have and
expend myself as well.[u] If I love you more,
will you love me less? 16Be that as it may, I
have not been a burden to you.[v] Yet, crafty
fellow that I am, I caught you by trickery!
17Did I exploit you through any of the men
I sent to you? 18I urged[w] Titus to go to you
and I sent our brother[x] with him. Titus did
not exploit you, did he? Did we not walk
in the same footsteps by the same Spirit?

19Have you been thinking all along that
we have been defending ourselves to you?
We have been speaking in the sight of God[y]
as those in Christ; and everything we do,
dear friends, is for your strengthening.[z]
20For I am afraid that when I come[a] I may
not find you as I want you to be, and you
may not find me as you want me to be.[b] I
fear that there may be discord,[c] jealousy,
fits of rage, selfish ambition,[d] slander, gossip,[e] arrogance and disorder.[f] 21I am afraid
that when I come again my God will humble me before you, and I will be grieved[g]
over many who have sinned earlier[h] and
have not repented of the impurity, sexual
sin and debauchery in which they have indulged.

Final Warnings

13 This will be my third visit to you.[i] "Every matter must be established by the
testimony of two or three witnesses."[a][j] 2I
already gave you a warning when I was
with you the second time. I now repeat it
while absent: On my return I will not spare[k]
those who sinned earlier[l] or any of the others, 3since you are demanding proof that
Christ is speaking through me.[m] He is not
weak in dealing with you, but is powerful
among you. 4For to be sure, he was crucified in weakness,[n] yet he lives by God's
power.[o] Likewise, we are weak[p] in him, yet
by God's power we will live with him in our
dealing with you.

5Examine yourselves[q] to see whether you
are in the faith; test yourselves.[r] Do you not
realize that Christ Jesus is in you[s]—unless,
of course, you fail the test? 6And I trust that
you will discover that we have not failed
the test. 7Now we pray to God that you will
not do anything wrong—not so that people
will see that we have stood the test but so
that you will do what is right even though
we may seem to have failed. 8For we cannot
do anything against the truth, but only for
the truth. 9We are glad whenever we are
weak but you are strong; and our prayer
is that you may be fully restored.[t] 10This
is why I write these things when I am absent, that when I come I may not have to be
harsh in my use of authority—the authority the Lord gave me for building you up,
not for tearing you down.[u]

Final Greetings

11Finally, brothers and sisters,[v] rejoice!
Strive for full restoration, encourage one
another, be of one mind, live in peace.[w] And
the God of love and peace[x] will be with you.
12Greet one another with a holy kiss.[y]
13All God's people here send their greetings.[z]

14May the grace of the Lord Jesus
Christ,[a] and the love of God,[b] and the fellowship of the Holy Spirit[c] be with you all.

---

[a] *1* Deut. 19:15

---

whether this refers to the third attempt to visit. We know that he had tried to come and had been prevented at least once (1:15–16,23; 2:1–4).

13:4 ***in weakness.*** Christ appeared to be weak when He was crucified, but He was raised by the power of God; similarly, Paul was weak, but by the power of God he would live with Christ in strength toward them.

13:5 ***Examine yourselves.*** Paul did not doubt that they were true believers (1:1,24; 7:1; 8:1; 12:14). He wanted them to ask themselves whether they were walking according to the gospel that they professed. He wanted them to apply the same standard to themselves that they were applying to him.

13:9 ***restored.*** The Greek word for "restored" was used to describe the setting of bones and the reconciliation of alienated friends.

13:14 ***the fellowship of the Holy Spirit.*** At the end of his letter, Paul identifies the solution to many of the Corinthians' problems. The Holy Spirit, who dwelled in each of them, could empower them to live righteously. Furthermore, the Spirit could reconcile them to each other. They could love and encourage each other instead of fighting each other (12:20). They needed God's grace, not selfishness; God's love, not anger; and communion, not conflict.

12:14 [r] 2Co 13:1 [s] 1Co 4:14, 15 [t] Pr 19:14 **12:15** [u] Php 2:17; 1Th 2:8 **12:16** [v] 2Co 11:9 **12:18** [w] 2Co 8:6, 16 [x] 2Co 8:18 **12:19** [y] Ro 9:1 [z] 2Co 10:8 **12:20** [a] 2Co 2:1-4 [b] 1Co 4:21 [c] 1Co 1:11; 3:3 [d] Gal 5:20 [e] Ro 1:29 [f] 1Co 14:33 **12:21** [g] 2Co 2:1, 4 [h] 2Co 13:2 **13:1** [i] 2Co 12:14 [j] Dt 19:15; Mt 18:16 **13:2** [k] 2Co 1:23 [l] 2Co 12:21 **13:3** [m] Mt 10:20; 1Co 5:4 **13:4** [n] Php 2:7, 8; 1Pe 3:18 [o] Ro 1:4; 6:4 [p] ver 9 **13:5** [q] 1Co 11:28 [r] Jn 6:6 [s] Ro 8:10 **13:9** [t] ver 11 **13:10** [u] 2Co 10:8 **13:11** [v] 1Th 4:1; 2Th 3:1 [w] Mk 9:50 [x] Ro 15:33; Eph 6:23 **13:12** [y] Ro 16:16 **13:13** [z] Php 4:22 **13:14** [a] Ro 16:20; 2Co 8:9 [b] Ro 5:5; Jude 21 [c] Php 2:1

GALATIANS

▶ **AUTHOR:** The Pauline authorship and the unity of this epistle are virtually unchallenged. The first verse clearly identifies the author as, "Paul, an apostle" as does 5:2, "I, Paul, tell you." In fact, Paul actually wrote, or at least finished, Galatians by his own hand (6:11) instead of dictating it to a secretary, as was his usual practice. There is some controversy as to whether Paul was writing to the northern Galatians or the southern Galatians. If the former theory is correct, this epistle was written sometime during Paul's third missionary journey in A.D. 53–56. If the latter theory is correct, this epistle was written before the Jerusalem Council (Acts 15) in A.D. 49, right after the first missionary journey. Regardless of the timing of its writing, Galatians affords us a clear glimpse into the ministry and theology of Paul as a Jewish Christian.

▶ **TIME:** c. A.D. 49–53 ▶ **KEY VERSES:** Gal. 2:20–21

▶ **THEME:** The big question for the church in its first generation was "Did a person have to become a Jew before they could be a Christian?" There were many Jews who thought this was the case. Three things happened to move the church away from this perspective: Peter's vision as recorded in Acts 10; the decision of the Jerusalem Council in Acts 15 that Gentiles didn't need to adopt all the Jewish customs; and Paul's received revelation that he was to deliver to the Gentiles. Even with all this evidence, there were still some Jews who followed Paul around and attempted to teach Jewish regulations to his newly planted churches. Paul was furious at these events and used this letter to set the record straight. Christ brought freedom and died for people of all cultures, an idea that was a new paradigm for many of the Jews who were stuck in a "God loves us most" mode. Paul goes to great lengths to review with the Galatians what he had taught them and where this teaching had come from.

---

1 Paul, an apostle—sent not from men
nor by a man, but by Jesus Christ[a] and
God the Father, who raised him from the
dead[b]— 2and all the brothers and sisters[a]
with me,[c]

To the churches in Galatia:[d]

3Grace and peace to you from God our
Father and the Lord Jesus Christ,[e] 4who
gave himself for our sins[f] to rescue us from
the present evil age, according to the will
of our God and Father,[g] 5to whom be glory
for ever and ever. Amen.[h]

No Other Gospel

6I am astonished that you are so quickly
deserting the one who called[i] you to live in
the grace of Christ and are turning to a different gospel[j]— 7which is really no gospel
at all. Evidently some people are throwing
you into confusion[k] and are trying to per-

[a] 2 The Greek word for *brothers and sisters* (*adelphoi*) refers here to believers, both men and women, as part of God's family; also in verse 11; and in 3:15; 4:12, 28, 31; 5:11, 13; 6:1, 18.

1:1 ***an apostle.*** Paul calls himself this title to assert his divinely given authority to speak to the problem confronting the Galatian churches. ***by Jesus Christ and God the Father.*** Paul makes reference to his unique call to be an apostle (vv. 15–16) which came to him at the same time as his salvation on the road to Damascus (Acts 26:12–18).
1:2 ***To the churches in Galatia.*** Galatians is a circular letter, intended for several churches.
1:3 ***Grace and peace to you.*** These words are a variation from the standard greeting of ancient letters in Paul's time. Paul adds the Greek word for the traditional Hebrew greeting, "peace."
1:4 ***rescue us from the present evil age.*** This passage is similar to Colossians 1:13, which states, "For he has rescued us from the dominion of darkness and brought us into the kingdom of the Son he loves." Both passages develop this truth based on Christ's redemptive work (Col. 1:14), implying that the word "rescue" refers to sanctification in the face of temptations of this present age.
1:6–7 ***astonished.*** Use of this word reveals Paul's ongoing shock at the Galatians' defection from the

1:1 [a] Ac 9:15 [b] Ac 2:24 **1:2** [c] Php 4:21 [d] Ac 16:6; 1Co 16:1 **1:3** [e] Ro 1:7 **1:4** [f] Mt 20:28; Ro 4:25; Gal 2:20 [g] Php 4:20 **1:5** [h] Ro 11:36 **1:6** [i] Gal 5:8 [j] 2Co 11:4 **1:7** [k] Ac 15:24; Gal 5:10

vert the gospel of Christ. 8But even if we
or an angel from heaven should preach a
gospel other than the one we preached to
you,[l] let them be under God's curse![m] 9As
we have already said, so now I say again: If
anybody is preaching to you a gospel other
than what you accepted,[n] let them be under
God's curse!
10Am I now trying to win the approval
of human beings, or of God? Or am I trying to please people?[o] If I were still trying
to please people, I would not be a servant
of Christ.

Paul Called by God

11I want you to know, brothers and sisters,[p] that the gospel I preached is not of human origin. 12I did not receive it from any
man,[q] nor was I taught it; rather, I received
it by revelation[r] from Jesus Christ.
13For you have heard of my previous
way of life in Judaism,[s] how intensely I
persecuted the church of God and tried
to destroy it.[t] 14I was advancing in Judaism beyond many of my own age among
my people and was extremely zealous for
the traditions of my fathers.[u] 15But when
God, who set me apart from my mother's
womb[v] and called me[w] by his grace, was
pleased 16to reveal his Son in me so that I
might preach him among the Gentiles,[x] my
immediate response was not to consult any
human being.[y] 17I did not go up to Jerusalem to see those who were apostles before
I was, but I went into Arabia. Later I returned to Damascus.
18Then after three years,[z] I went up to
Jerusalem[a] to get acquainted with Cephas[a]
and stayed with him fifteen days. 19I saw
none of the other apostles—only James,[b]
the Lord's brother. 20I assure you before
God that what I am writing you is no lie.[c]
21Then I went to Syria and Cilicia.[d] 22I
was personally unknown to the churches
of Judea[e] that are in Christ. 23They only
heard the report: "The man who formerly persecuted us is now preaching the
faith[f] he once tried to destroy." 24And they
praised God[g] because of me.

Paul Accepted by the Apostles

2 Then after fourteen years, I went up
again to Jerusalem,[h] this time with
Barnabas. I took Titus along also. 2I went
in response to a revelation and, meeting
privately with those esteemed as leaders, I
presented to them the gospel that I preach
among the Gentiles.[i] I wanted to be sure I
was not running and had not been running
my race[j] in vain. 3Yet not even Titus,[k] who
was with me, was compelled to be circumcised, even though he was a Greek.[l] 4This
matter arose because some false believers[m] had infiltrated our ranks to spy on[n]
the freedom[o] we have in Christ Jesus and
to make us slaves. 5We did not give in to
them for a moment, so that the truth of the
gospel[p] might be preserved for you.
6As for those who were held in high esteem[q]—whatever they were makes no difference to me; God does not show favoritism[r]—they added nothing to my message.

a *18* That is, Peter

---

gospel of God's undeserved grace. The Galatians had unwittingly fallen for a different message.

1:8–9 ***If anybody.*** Paul's concern for the purity of the gospel message is revealed by his assertion that he would condemn to destruction anyone who taught a false gospel.

1:10 ***please people.*** This was neither Paul's motivation nor the source of his authority (v. 1). Paul continually sought the approval of God. He did not base his decisions on the opinions of other people. Instead he single-mindedly aimed at pleasing God (Phil. 3:14).

1:13–14 ***Judaism.*** This refers to the Jewish way of life, which was based partly on the Old Testament and partly on additional traditions (Matt. 15:2).

1:15–17 ***set me apart . . . called me by his grace.*** Paul related that God had chosen him to be an apostle (v. 1) before his birth, not unlike Jeremiah's call to be a prophet (Jer. 1:5). Paul, like the Judaizers in Galatia, had previously tried to earn his salvation by works (v. 14). He needed no human validation because of the way he had received his message.

1:19 ***James, the Lord's brother.*** This reference indicates that the "apostles" were not always restricted to the Twelve.

2:1 ***fourteen years.*** This timeframe may refer to twelve full years plus fractions of the first and last years (1:18). The span could date from Paul's previous visit to Jerusalem, but more likely from his conversion.

2:3 ***Titus.*** One of Paul's companions was a kind of "test-case" Gentile. ***circumcised.*** This term introduces a central topic of the Jewish false teachers, one which Paul addresses repeatedly in Galatians (5:2–3,6). Unlike Timothy, whom Paul had circumcised because Timothy's mother was Jewish, Titus was not circumcised. Circumcising him would have been a sign to all other Gentiles that following Jewish law was required for a person to become a Christian. As Paul explains in this letter, circumcising Titus would be a rejection of the good news that salvation is God's gift to those who believe in His Son.

2:4 ***false believers.*** This phrase apparently indicates that, although these people passed themselves off convincingly as Christians, there was reason to view their profession as a sham. These pseudo-Christians did not announce their purpose, which was to curtail Christian liberty (5:1,13).

2:6 ***those who were held in high esteem.*** While Paul recognized the leadership roles of James, Peter, and John, he pointed out that they were in no way superior to him in their understanding of the gospel.

1:8 [l] 2Co 11:4 [m] Ro 9:3 **1:9** [n] Ro 16:17 **1:10** [o] Ro 2:29; 1Th 2:4 **1:11** [p] 1Co 15:1 **1:12** [q] ver 1 [r] ver 16 **1:13** [s] Ac 26:4,5 [t] Ac 8:3 **1:14** [u] Mt 15:2 **1:15** [v] Isa 49:1,5; Jer 1:5 [w] Ac 9:15 **1:16** [x] Gal 2:9 [y] Mt 16:17 **1:18** [z] Ac 9:22,23 [a] Ac 9:26,27 **1:19** [b] Mt 13:55 **1:20** [c] Ro 9:1 **1:21** [d] Ac 6:9 **1:22** [e] 1Th 2:14 **1:23** [f] Ac 6:7 **1:24** [g] Mt 9:8 **2:1** [h] Ac 15:2 **2:2** [i] Ac 15:4,12 [j] 1Co 9:24; Php 2:16 **2:3** [k] 2Co 2:13 [l] Ac 16:3; 1Co 9:21 **2:4** [m] 2Co 11:26 [n] Jude 4 [o] Ac 15:1; Gal 5:1,13 **2:5** [p] ver 14 **2:6** [q] Gal 6:3 [r] Ac 10:34

7On the contrary, they recognized that I had been entrusted with the task[s] of preaching the gospel to the uncircumcised,[a][t] just as Peter[u] had been to the circumcised.[b] 8For God, who was at work in Peter as an apostle[v] to the circumcised, was also at work in me as an apostle to the Gentiles. 9James, Cephas[c][w] and John, those esteemed as pillars,[x] gave me and Barnabas[y] the right hand of fellowship when they recognized the grace given to me.[z] They agreed that we should go to the Gentiles, and they to the circumcised. 10All they asked was that we should continue to remember the poor,[a] the very thing I had been eager to do all along.

Paul Opposes Cephas

11When Cephas[b] came to Antioch,[c] I opposed him to his face, because he stood condemned. 12For before certain men came from James, he used to eat with the Gentiles.[d] But when they arrived, he began to draw back and separate himself from the Gentiles because he was afraid of those who belonged to the circumcision group.[e] 13The other Jews joined him in his hypocrisy, so that by their hypocrisy even Barnabas[f] was led astray.

14When I saw that they were not acting in line with the truth of the gospel,[g] I said to Cephas[h] in front of them all, "You are a Jew, yet you live like a Gentile and not like a Jew.[i] How is it, then, that you force Gentiles to follow Jewish customs?

15"We who are Jews by birth[j] and not sinful Gentiles[k] 16know that a person is not justified by the works of the law, but by faith in Jesus Christ.[l] So we, too, have put our faith in Christ Jesus that we may be justified by faith in[d] Christ and not by the works of the law, because by the works of the law no one will be justified.

17"But if, in seeking to be justified in Christ, we Jews find ourselves also among the sinners,[m] doesn't that mean that Christ promotes sin? Absolutely not![n] 18If I rebuild what I destroyed, then I really would be a lawbreaker.

19"For through the law I died to the law[o] so that I might live for God.[p] 20I have been crucified with Christ[q] and I no longer live, but Christ lives in me.[r] The life I now live in the body, I live by faith in the Son of God,[s] who loved me[t] and gave himself for me.[u] 21I do not set aside the grace of God, for if righteousness could be gained through the law,[v] Christ died for nothing!"[e]

Faith or Works of the Law

3 You foolish Galatians! Who has bewitched you?[w] Before your very eyes Jesus Christ was clearly portrayed as crucified.[x] 2I would like to learn just one thing from you: Did you receive the Spirit by the works of the law, or by believing what you heard?[y] 3Are you so foolish? After beginning by means of the Spirit, are you now trying to finish by means of the flesh?[f] 4Have you experienced[g] so much in

---

[a] *7* That is, Gentiles [b] *7* That is, Jews; also in verses 8 and 9 [c] *9* That is, Peter; also in verses 11 and 14 [d] *16* Or *but through the faithfulness of . . . justified on the basis of the faithfulness of* [e] *21* Some interpreters end the quotation after verse 14. [f] *3* In contexts like this, the Greek word for *flesh* (*sarx*) refers to the sinful state of human beings, often presented as a power in opposition to the Spirit. [g] *4* Or *suffered*

2:7–10 ***uncircumcised ... circumcised.*** There were not two different gospels. Rather, the primary scope of Paul's apostolic ministry was to the Gentiles (Rom. 11:13), while Peter's apostleship was, first and foremost, targeted toward the Jews. ***remember the poor.*** Almost certainly, this is a reference to the poor among the church in Judea (Acts 11:29–30).

2:11–12 ***Antioch.*** This city was the largest of the Roman province of Syria. It became a center for missionary outreach to other Gentile cities in Asia Minor and Macedonia (Acts 13:1–3).

2:14 ***they were not acting in line with the truth.*** Peter's hypocritical example implied that Gentiles had to behave like Jews in order to receive God's grace. It had already been decided (vv. 1–5) that it was not proper to compel Gentiles to live as Jews, because salvation was through faith alone.

2:15–17 ***We who are Jews by birth.*** Paul is not denying that those who are Jews by birth are sinners, as are all Gentiles (Rom. 3:23). Rather he is implying that Jews enjoy spiritual privileges (Rom. 9:4–5) that should make them more knowledgeable about how to be justified before God (3:6; Gen. 15:6). The Jews should have been aware that no person can be declared righteous or justified by obedience to the law of Moses (3:10–21).

2:17–19 ***doesn't that mean that Christ promotes sin?*** Paul strongly rejects the erroneous conclusion that being justified by faith in Christ actually made Jews sinners. Those who attempt to be justified through "the works of the law" are "cursed" (3:10). If anyone attempts to reassert the "works of the law" as having any part in the justification before God, the law itself convicts that person. The law itself is not sinful; its purpose is to convince individuals of their personal, spiritual deadness in sin outside of faith in Christ (Rom. 7:7–13).

3:1 ***You foolish Galatians!*** This phrase does not indicate lack of intelligence, but lack of wisdom. Paul wonders whether something like an evil spell had prevented the Galatians from recalling the gospel of the crucified Christ.

3:3 ***After beginning by means of the Spirit . . . by means of the flesh.*** The Galatians were mistakenly trying to achieve perfection through their own efforts, especially through circumcision.

2:7 [s] 1Th 2:4; 1Ti 1:11 [t] Ac 9:15 [u] ver 9, 11, 14
2:8 [v] Ac 1:25 **2:9** [w] ver 7, 11, 14 [x] 1Ti 3:15 [y] Ac 4:36 [z] Ro 12:3 **2:10** [a] Ac 24:17 **2:11** [b] ver 7, 9, 14 [c] Ac 11:19
2:12 [d] Ac 11:3 [e] Ac 11:2 **2:13** [f] ver 1; Ac 4:36
2:14 [g] ver 5 [h] ver 7, 9, 11 [i] Ac 10:28 **2:15** [j] Php 3:4, 5 [k] 1Sa 15:18 **2:16** [l] Ac 13:39; Ro 9:30 **2:17** [m] ver 15 [n] Gal 3:21 **2:19** [o] Ro 7:4 [p] Ro 6:10, 11, 14; 2Co 5:15
2:20 [q] Ro 6:6 [r] 1Pe 4:2 [s] Mt 4:3 [t] Ro 8:37 [u] Gal 1:4
2:21 [v] Gal 3:21 **3:1** [w] Gal 5:7 [x] 1Co 1:23 **3:2** [y] Ro 10:17

vain—if it really was in vain? 5So again I
ask, does God give you his Spirit and work
miracles[z] among you by the works of the
law, or by your believing what you heard?
6So also Abraham "believed God, and it
was credited to him as righteousness."[aa]
7Understand, then, that those who have
faith[b] are children of Abraham. 8Scripture
foresaw that God would justify the Gentiles by faith, and announced the gospel in
advance to Abraham: "All nations will be
blessed through you."[bc] 9So those who rely
on faith[d] are blessed along with Abraham,
the man of faith.
10For all who rely on the works of the law
are under a curse, as it is written: "Cursed
is everyone who does not continue to do everything written in the Book of the Law."[ce]
11Clearly no one who relies on the law is
justified before God, because "the righteous will live by faith."[df] 12The law is not
based on faith; on the contrary, it says,
"The person who does these things will
live by them."[eg] 13Christ redeemed us from
the curse of the law[h] by becoming a curse
for us, for it is written: "Cursed is everyone
who is hung on a pole."[fi] 14He redeemed us
in order that the blessing given to Abraham might come to the Gentiles through
Christ Jesus,[j] so that by faith we might receive the promise of the Spirit.[k]

The Law and the Promise

15Brothers and sisters, let me take an example from everyday life. Just as no one
can set aside or add to a human covenant
that has been duly established, so it is in
this case. 16The promises were spoken to
Abraham and to his seed.[l] Scripture does
not say "and to seeds," meaning many people, but "and to your seed,"[g] meaning one
person, who is Christ. 17What I mean is
this: The law, introduced 430 years[m] later,
does not set aside the covenant previously
established by God and thus do away with
the promise. 18For if the inheritance depends on the law, then it no longer depends
on the promise;[n] but God in his grace gave
it to Abraham through a promise.
19Why, then, was the law given at all? It
was added because of transgressions[o] until the Seed[p] to whom the promise referred
had come. The law was given through
angels[q] and entrusted to a mediator.[r] 20A
mediator,[s] however, implies more than one
party; but God is one.
21Is the law, therefore, opposed to the
promises of God? Absolutely not![t] For if
a law had been given that could impart
life, then righteousness would certainly
have come by the law.[u] 22But Scripture has
locked up everything under the control of
sin,[v] so that what was promised, being giv-
en through faith in Jesus Christ, might be
given to those who believe.

Children of God

23Before the coming of this faith,[h] we
were held in custody[w] under the law, locked
up until the faith that was to come would
be revealed. 24So the law was our guardian

[a] *6* Gen. 15:6 [b] *8* Gen. 12:3; 18:18; 22:18
[c] *10* Deut. 27:26 [d] *11* Hab. 2:4 [e] *12* Lev. 18:5
[f] *13* Deut. 21:23 [g] *16* Gen. 12:7; 13:15; 24:7
[h] *22,23* Or *through the faithfulness of Jesus . . .*
23Before faith came

3:6 *believed God.* There are several reasons for Paul's reference to Abraham's faith as an example: (1) Abraham was the father of the Jewish nation (Gen. 12:1–3); (2) Abraham is the clearest example of justification in the Old Testament; (3) the Judaizers almost certainly were pointing back to Abraham, probably in connection with circumcision (2:3; 5:2–3). The example of Abraham's faith is also developed in Romans 4 and Hebrews 11.
3:7 *who have faith.* These are the spiritual sons of Abraham, even if they are not Jews. They are part of God's people.
3:8–9 *Scripture.* Here, Scripture is personified as a preacher who foretells that Abraham and his example of faith (Gen. 15:6) would become a life-changing blessing to all nations (Gen. 12:3; Matt. 28:19) as the gospel spread. All who have faith, as Abraham did, join in his "blessed" status.
3:10 *Cursed is everyone.* The quotation from Deuteronomy 27:26 says that those who do not keep the whole law are cursed, proving that all are cursed who follow the law, because all fall short of the law's standards (Rom. 1:17; 3:10,18,23).
3:13 *the curse of the law.* Paul knew that many of his readers would perceive that they were actually under the curse of the law. For them, as for us, it is incredibly comforting to know that Christ became that curse for us on the cross (Deut. 21:23).
3:16 *to Abraham and to his Seed.* Jesus Christ is the fulfillment of the covenant (v. 15) God made with Abraham. Although in one sense all Jews are the physical seed of Abraham, Christ is the final focus of God's promises, the ultimate Seed.
3:19–20 *Why, then, was the law given at all?* The purpose of the law of Moses was not to justify man in God's eyes (2:16). Rather, the law was added after God's promise to Abraham to clarify the issue of sin until Christ, the seed, came.
3:21–22 *Is the law, therefore, opposed to the promises of God?* The relationship of the law and the promises is one of need and fulfillment. The law was not designed by God to give eternal life and righteousness. Rather, the law showed humanity's need for the promise of life through faith in Jesus Christ (v. 9; 2:16).
3:23–25 *locked up … guardian.* Paul gives two different illustrations concerning the function of the law until Christ came (4:4–5). The law acted as a jailor

3:5 [z] 1Co 12:10 **3:6** [a] Ge 15:6; Ro 4:3 **3:7** [b] ver 9
3:8 [c] Ge 12:3; Ac 3:25 **3:9** [d] ver 7; Ro 4:16
3:10 [e] Dt 27:26; Jer 11:3 **3:11** [f] Hab 2:4; Gal 2:16; Heb 10:38 **3:12** [g] Lev 18:5; Ro 10:5 **3:13** [h] Gal 4:5
[i] Dt 21:23; Ac 5:30 **3:14** [j] Ro 4:9, 16 [k] ver 2; Joel 2:28; Ac 2:33 **3:16** [l] Lk 1:55; Ro 4:13, 16 **3:17** [m] Ge 15:13, 14; Ex 12:40 **3:18** [n] Ro 4:14 **3:19** [o] Ro 5:20 [p] ver 16
[q] Ac 7:53 [r] Ex 20:19 **3:20** [s] Heb 8:6; 9:15; 12:24
3:21 [t] Gal 2:17 [u] Gal 2:21 **3:22** [v] Ro 3:9-19; 11:32
3:23 [w] Ro 11:32

until Christ came[x] that we might be justified by faith.[y] 25Now that this faith has
come, we are no longer under a guardian.
26So in Christ Jesus you are all children
of God[z] through faith, 27for all of you who
were baptized into Christ[a] have clothed
yourselves with Christ.[b] 28There is neither
Jew nor Gentile, neither slave nor free,[c] nor
is there male and female, for you are all one
in Christ Jesus.[d] 29If you belong to Christ,[e]
then you are Abraham's seed, and heirs according to the promise.[f]

4 What I am saying is that as long as an
heir is underage, he is no different from
a slave, although he owns the whole estate.
2The heir is subject to guardians and trustees until the time set by his father. 3So also,
when we were underage, we were in slavery[g] under the elemental spiritual forces[a]
of the world.[h] 4But when the set time had
fully come,[i] God sent his Son, born of a
woman,[j] born under the law,[k] 5to redeem
those under the law, that we might receive
adoption[l] to sonship.[b] 6Because you are his
sons, God sent the Spirit of his Son into our
hearts,[m] the Spirit who calls out, "*Abba*,[c]
Father."[n] 7So you are no longer a slave, but
God's child; and since you are his child,
God has made you also an heir.[o]

Paul's Concern for the Galatians

8Formerly, when you did not know God,[p]
you were slaves to those who by nature are
not gods.[q] 9But now that you know God—or
rather are known by God[r]—how is it that
you are turning back to those weak and
miserable forces[d]? Do you wish to be enslaved[s] by them all over again?[t] 10You are
observing special days and months and
seasons and years![u] 11I fear for you, that
somehow I have wasted my efforts on you.[v]
12I plead with you, brothers and sisters,[w]
become like me, for I became like you. You
did me no wrong. 13As you know, it was because of an illness[x] that I first preached the
gospel to you, 14and even though my illness
was a trial to you, you did not treat me with
contempt or scorn. Instead, you welcomed
me as if I were an angel of God, as if I were
Christ Jesus himself.[y] 15Where, then, is
your blessing of me now? I can testify that,
if you could have done so, you would have
torn out your eyes and given them to me.
16Have I now become your enemy by telling you the truth?[z]
17Those people are zealous to win you
over, but for no good. What they want is
to alienate you from us, so that you may
have zeal for them. 18It is fine to be zealous,
provided the purpose is good, and to be so
always, not just when I am with you.[a] 19My
dear children,[b] for whom I am again in the
pains of childbirth until Christ is formed
in you,[c] 20how I wish I could be with you
now and change my tone, because I am
perplexed about you!

[a] 3 Or *under the basic principles* [b] 5 The Greek word for *adoption to sonship* is a legal term referring to the full legal standing of an adopted male heir in Roman culture. [c] 6 Aramaic for *Father* [d] 9 Or *principles*

---

to hold humankind in custody until faith in Christ was revealed. But the law also served as a guardian. A guardian in ancient Greek culture would accompany the children in his care, instructing and disciplining them when necessary. The law was like a guardian because it both corrected and instructed the Israelites in God's ways until Christ was revealed and such an overseer was no longer needed (4:1–2).

3:28 *There is neither Jew nor Gentile.* The context of this verse is justification by faith in Christ Jesus. Racial, social, and gender distinctions that so easily divide in no way hinder a person from coming to Christ in order to receive His mercy. All people equally can become God's heirs and recipients of His eternal promises (4:5–7).

4:1–2 *until the time set by his father.* In ancient society a child had to wait until the proper time before he could inherit what was his. Paul uses this idea to explain why God delayed Jesus Christ's coming, leaving people with His law as a guide (3:23–25).

4:4–5 *born under the law.* This means Christ was subject to the Jewish law (Matt. 5:17–19), further establishing His identification with all people who are subject to the law. ***redeem.*** This verb was used in the context of buying from a slave market. It describes Christ's supreme and final payment for the sins of humanity. His death on the cross frees those who believe in Him from the curse of the law and slavery to sin. This decisive payment and resulting freedom clear the way for Christians to become God's sons.

4:6 *God sent the Spirit.* Just as "God sent his Son" when "the time had fully come" in world history (v. 4), so God has also sent the Spirit at just the right time for every person who believes in Christ.

4:9 *how is it that you are turning back.* The Galatians had come to know God through faith in Jesus Christ (John 17:2–3). He had adopted them as His own sons, but they were turning back to the law that had once enslaved them.

4:12 *I plead with you.* To get beyond the present dilemma, Paul appeals to the Galatians to follow his example (1 Cor. 11:1). He had abandoned the ceremonial rules and regulations connected with Judaism so that he could freely preach the gospel of Christ to Jew and Gentile alike in the cities of Galatia. They too should not hinder the gospel of Christ with laws and regulations.

4:17–18 *What they want is to alienate you.* Paul was strongly implying that the false teachers in Galatia were making the same mistake he had made prior to his conversion. Their zeal for the law was blinding them to the freedom and truth to be found in Jesus Christ.

4:19 *My dear children.* Paul calls the Galatians

3:24 [x] Ro 10:4 [y] Gal 2:16 **3:26** [z] Ro 8:14
3:27 [a] Mt 28:19; Ro 6:3 [b] Ro 13:14 **3:28** [c] Col 3:11
[d] Jn 10:16; 17:11; Eph 2:14, 15 **3:29** [e] 1Co 3:23 [f] ver 16
4:3 [g] Gal 2:4 [h] Col 2:8, 20 **4:4** [i] Mk 1:15; Eph 1:10 [j] Jn 1:14
[k] Lk 2:27 **4:5** [l] Jn 1:12 **4:6** [m] Ro 5:5 [n] Ro 8:15, 16
4:7 [o] Ro 8:17 **4:8** [p] 1Co 1:21; Eph 2:12; 1Th 4:5
[q] 2Ch 13:9; Isa 37:19 **4:9** [r] 1Co 8:3 [s] ver 3 [t] Col 2:20
4:10 [u] Ro 14:5 **4:11** [v] 1Th 3:5 **4:12** [w] Gal 6:18
4:13 [x] 1Co 2:3 **4:14** [y] Mt 10:40 **4:16** [z] Am 5:10
4:18 [a] ver 13, 14 **4:19** [b] 1Co 4:15 [c] Eph 4:13

Hagar and Sarah

21Tell me, you who want to be under the
law, are you not aware of what the law
says? 22For it is written that Abraham had
two sons, one by the slave woman[d] and the
other by the free woman.[e] 23His son by the
slave woman was born according to the
flesh,[f] but his son by the free woman was
born as the result of a divine promise.[g]
24These things are being taken figuratively: The women represent two covenants. One covenant is from Mount Sinai
and bears children who are to be slaves:
This is Hagar. 25Now Hagar stands for
Mount Sinai in Arabia and corresponds to
the present city of Jerusalem, because she
is in slavery with her children. 26But the
Jerusalem that is above[h] is free, and she is
our mother. 27For it is written:

"Be glad, barren woman,
  you who never bore a child;
shout for joy and cry aloud,
  you who were never in labor;
because more are the children of the
    desolate woman
  than of her who has a husband."[a][i]

28Now you, brothers and sisters, like
Isaac, are children of promise. 29At that
time the son born according to the flesh[j]
persecuted the son born by the power of
the Spirit.[k] It is the same now. 30But what
does Scripture say? "Get rid of the slave
woman and her son, for the slave woman's
son will never share in the inheritance
with the free woman's son."[b][l] 31There-
fore, brothers and sisters, we are not children of the slave woman, but of the free
woman.

Freedom in Christ

5 It is for freedom that Christ has set us
free.[m] Stand firm,[n] then, and do not let
yourselves be burdened again by a yoke of
slavery.[o]
2Mark my words! I, Paul, tell you that if
you let yourselves be circumcised,[p] Christ
will be of no value to you at all. 3Again I
declare to every man who lets himself be
circumcised that he is obligated to obey the
whole law.[q] 4You who are trying to be justified by the law have been alienated from
Christ; you have fallen away from grace.[r]
5For through the Spirit we eagerly await by
faith the righteousness for which we hope.[s]
6For in Christ Jesus neither circumcision
nor uncircumcision has any value.[t] The
only thing that counts is faith expressing
itself through love.[u]
7You were running a good race.[v] Who
cut in on you[w] to keep you from obeying
the truth? 8That kind of persuasion does
not come from the one who calls you.[x]
9"A little yeast works through the whole
batch of dough."[y] 10I am confident[z] in the
Lord that you will take no other view.[a] The

a *27* Isaiah 54:1 *b* *30* Gen. 21:10

---

children because of their lack of spiritual growth and depth. The apostle also portrays himself as the Galatians' "spiritual mother." He was feeling the labor pains of their birth all over again because they had fallen into serious error.

4:21 – 22 *slave woman . . . free woman.* To clinch his argument about the bondage of the law and freedom found in Christ, Paul uses as examples the two sons of Abraham, Ishmael and Isaac. Ishmael was born of a slave woman, Hagar, and Isaac was born of Sarah, a free woman (Gen. 16:15; 21:2). Paul counters the Jewish false teachers' zeal for the law with an argument based on the Law, the Pentateuch. He uses allegory to prove his point because it was a rhetorical technique the false teachers used. In other words, Paul was demonstrating that he could argue from the law just as well as they could, but to prove that the law of Moses pointed to the Messiah, Jesus Christ.

4:26 *Jerusalem that is above.* This phrase represents the Jewish hope of heaven finally coming to earth (Rev. 21 – 22). Paul was strongly implying that the question at hand was not allegiance to Jerusalem, but allegiance to which Jerusalem — the new or the old? Would the Galatians follow the shortsighted present Jerusalem and its legalism or the liberty of the heavenly Jerusalem?

4:28 – 30 *Now you, brothers and sisters, like Isaac, are children of promise.* This portion of Paul's allegory is based on Genesis 21:9 – 10. Isaac was continually persecuted by his older half-brother Ishmael. Eventually, Ishmael and his mother Hagar were expelled because Ishmael had no standing in God's eyes as an heir of Abraham. In creating a parallel between the story from Genesis and the Galatians' situation, Paul points out that (1) the persecution by the Jewish legalists of his day was not unexpected, and (2) it would not go on indefinitely because the legalists would soon be cast out.

4:31 – 5:1 *Therefore.* This phrase represents the conclusion of the previous section, while "then" signals that Paul is going to apply this spiritual truth to the lives of the Galatian believers.

5:2 – 3 *if you let yourselves be circumcised.* The legalistic Jewish teachers in Galatia were urging believers to be circumcised (6:12 – 13). Paul points out that circumcision would change the entire orientation of salvation away from God's grace to one's own actions. One who is circumcised in an attempt to gain God's acceptance is obligated to keep the whole law, which history has abundantly demonstrated no one can do (Rom. 3:10 – 18).

5:5 *eagerly await by faith the righteousness.* We can be assured that we will be declared righteous before the Lord on that last day because we have a foretaste of that righteousness from the Spirit who lives within us (2 Cor. 5:5).

5:9 – 10 *yeast.* This symbolizes the intruders,

4:22 [d] Ge 16:15 [e] Ge 21:2 **4:23** [f] Ro 9:7,8 [g] Ge 18:10-14; Heb 11:11 **4:26** [h] Heb 12:22; Rev 3:12 **4:27** [i] Isa 54:1 **4:29** [j] ver 23 [k] Ge 21:9 **4:30** [l] Ge 21:10 **5:1** [m] Jn 8:32 [n] 1Co 16:13 [o] Ac 15:10; Gal 2:4 **5:2** [p] Ac 15:1 **5:3** [q] Gal 3:10 **5:4** [r] Heb 12:15; 2Pe 3:17 **5:5** [s] Ro 8:23, 24 **5:6** [t] 1Co 7:19 [u] 1Th 1:3 **5:7** [v] 1Co 9:24 [w] Gal 3:1 **5:8** [x] Ro 8:28; Gal 1:6 **5:9** [y] 1Co 5:6 **5:10** [z] 2Co 2:3 [a] Php 3:15

one who is throwing you into confusion,[b] whoever that may be, will have to pay the penalty. 11 Brothers and sisters, if I am still preaching circumcision, why am I still being persecuted?[c] In that case the offense[d] of the cross has been abolished. 12 As for those agitators,[e] I wish they would go the whole way and emasculate themselves!

Life by the Spirit

13 You, my brothers and sisters, were called to be free. But do not use your freedom to indulge the flesh[a];[f] rather, serve one another[g] humbly in love. 14 For the entire law is fulfilled in keeping this one command: "Love your neighbor as yourself."[b][h] 15 If you bite and devour each other, watch out or you will be destroyed by each other.

16 So I say, walk by the Spirit,[i] and you will not gratify the desires of the flesh.[j] 17 For the flesh desires what is contrary to the Spirit, and the Spirit what is contrary to the flesh.[k] They are in conflict with each other, so that you are not to do whatever[c] you want.[l] 18 But if you are led by the Spirit, you are not under the law.[m]

19 The acts of the flesh are obvious: sexual immorality,[n] impurity and debauchery; 20 idolatry and witchcraft; hatred, discord, jealousy, fits of rage, selfish ambition, dissensions, factions 21 and envy; drunkenness, orgies, and the like.[o] I warn you, as I did before, that those who live like this will not inherit the kingdom of God.

22 But the fruit[p] of the Spirit is love,[q] joy, peace, forbearance, kindness, goodness, faithfulness, 23 gentleness and self-control.[r] Against such things there is no law. 24 Those who belong to Christ Jesus have crucified the flesh[s] with its passions and desires.[t] 25 Since we live by the Spirit, let us keep in step with the Spirit. 26 Let us not become conceited,[u] provoking and envying each other.

---

[a] *13* In contexts like this, the Greek word for *flesh* (*sarx*) refers to the sinful state of human beings, often presented as a power in opposition to the Spirit; also in verses 16, 17, 19 and 24; and in 6:8.
[b] *14* Lev. 19:18 [c] *17* Or *you do not do what*

---

with their false doctrine and its sinister influence. They were taking the gospel of free forgiveness away from the Galatians. The one who causes such harm will experience God's judgment (2 Cor. 5:10).

5:11 ***the offense of the cross.*** The cross is offensive to people because it proclaims God's unmerited grace and leaves no place for people's good works.

5:13 ***freedom.*** Christian liberty is the freedom to serve one another in love (vv. 5–6). As we grow in our knowledge of the Word of God, understand and apply its meaning, we should increasingly be involved in serving God and our fellow believers. The Spirit of God has given us spiritual gifts, but those gifts are worthless unless they are used in the service of God and His church. Paul often uses the figure of the human body to show the importance of each part serving the others (Rom. 12:4–5; 1 Cor. 12:12–31). While some parts of the body have more prominent places of service than others, all are equally important. To maintain strength, health, and vitality, every part of the body must function and serve all the other parts of the body. This is also true of the spiritual or new life. We will grow in the new life, become strong, and maintain good spiritual health as we use the talents and abilities that God has given us to meet the needs of the other parts of the body.

5:14 ***the entire law.*** The Christian does not live under the law of Moses, but instead under "the law of Christ" (6:2). Living in Christ empowers us to love others, which is the fulfillment of the law (Matt. 22:36–40).

5:16 ***walk by the Spirit.*** The only consistent way to overcome the sinful desires of our human nature (the flesh) is to live step-by-step in the power of the Holy Spirit as He works through our spirit.

5:17 ***the flesh desires what is contrary to the Spirit.*** The potential of the flesh energized by Satan in the life of the Christian should not be underestimated. Given free rein, the flesh will direct our choices, making us do what we know we should not do. This inner conflict between the flesh and the Spirit is very real. Although the precise meaning of "flesh" is unclear, Paul's intent is plain. The desires of our flesh are at odds with what the Holy Spirit desires for us: to be free from sin.

5:19–21 The Human Condition—The last part of Galatians 5 contrasts *acts of the flesh* with *fruit of the Spirit.* The acts of the flesh here are represented by those kinds of activities that are characteristic of our old natures. Without God, our lives are dominated by these more obvious sins and less obvious sinful attitudes. It is our sinful nature to be this way. Those who operate with these sins as a regular part of their lives, with no sense of guilt, demonstrate their need for salvation. It is the role of the Spirit to change these sinful behaviors. Paul points out that, if changes are not occurring, then there is a need for the Spirit that comes with the gift of salvation.

5:22–24 The New Nature—While the deeds of the flesh portray a disintegrating life, the fruit of the Spirit describes a life where things are working harmoniously. It points to qualities of personality and to behaviors that make us function as better people. It points to what God wants to see in us and should see in us as we mature in the faith.

5:22 ***fruit of the Spirit.*** This analogy is reminiscent of Jesus' teaching on the vine, branches, and fruitful harvest.

5:24 ***have crucified the flesh.*** Those who have mastered these sinful desires are those who have kept their focus on God (Jer. 9:23–24; Dan. 11:32; John 17:3; Heb. 12:1–3).

5:10 [b] Gal 1:7 **5:11** [c] Gal 4:29; 6:12 [d] 1Co 1:23 **5:12** [e] ver 10 **5:13** [f] 1Co 8:9; 1Pe 2:16 [g] 1Co 9:19; Eph 5:21 **5:14** [h] Lev 19:18; Mt 22:39 **5:16** [i] Ro 8:2, 4-6, 9, 14 [j] ver 24 **5:17** [k] Ro 8:5-8 [l] Ro 7:15-23 **5:18** [m] Ro 6:14; 1Ti 1:9 **5:19** [n] 1Co 6:18 **5:21** [o] Ro 13:13 **5:22** [p] Mt 7:16-20; Eph 5:9 [q] Col 3:12-15 **5:23** [r] Ac 24:25 **5:24** [s] Ro 6:6 [t] ver 16, 17 **5:26** [u] Php 2:3

Doing Good to All

6 Brothers and sisters, if someone is caught in a sin, you who live by the Spirit[v] should restore that person gently. But watch yourselves, or you also may be tempted. 2Carry each other's burdens, and in this way you will fulfill the law of Christ.[w] 3If anyone thinks they are something[x] when they are not, they deceive themselves. 4Each one should test their own actions. Then they can take pride in themselves alone, without comparing themselves to someone else, 5for each one should carry their own load. 6Nevertheless, the one who receives instruction in the word should share all good things with their instructor.[y]

7Do not be deceived:[z] God cannot be mocked. A man reaps what he sows.[a] 8Whoever sows to please their flesh, from the flesh will reap destruction;[b] whoever sows to please the Spirit, from the Spirit will reap eternal life.[c] 9Let us not become weary in doing good,[d] for at the proper time we will reap a harvest if we do not give up.[e] 10Therefore, as we have opportunity, let us do good[f] to all people, especially to those who belong to the family[g] of believers.

Not Circumcision but the New Creation

11See what large letters I use as I write to you with my own hand![h]

12Those who want to impress people by means of the flesh are trying to compel you to be circumcised.[i] The only reason they do this is to avoid being persecuted[j] for the cross of Christ. 13Not even those who are circumcised keep the law,[k] yet they want you to be circumcised that they may boast about your circumcision in the flesh.[l] 14May I never boast except in the cross of our Lord Jesus Christ, through which[a] the world has been crucified to me, and I to the world.[m] 15Neither circumcision nor uncircumcision means anything;[n] what counts is the new creation.[o] 16Peace and mercy to all who follow this rule—to[b] the Israel of God.

17From now on, let no one cause me trouble, for I bear on my body the marks[p] of Jesus.

18The grace of our Lord Jesus Christ[q] be with your spirit,[r] brothers and sisters. Amen.

---

[a] 14 Or *whom* [b] 16 Or *rule and to*

6:1 *restore that person gently.* A believer devastated by sin needs to be approached gently by fellow believers.

6:2 *the law of Christ.* This phrase is probably referring to the summation of the law: "Love your neighbor" (5:14; Matt. 22:39; John 13:34–35). Bearing the burdens of one another is precisely what Christ expects of all believers. The Greek word for *burdens* refers to something beyond the normal capacity to carry, as opposed to a "load" (v. 5), which is what a person could be expected to carry.

6:7–8 *Whoever sows to please their flesh.* The principle of sowing and reaping was known to everyone in a largely agricultural society. It would be foolish for Christians to think that they could escape the harvest of destruction and judgment if they persist in sin. ***destruction.*** This is a term used for a field in which the produce is too rotten to harvest (Heb. 6:8). ***whoever sows to please the Spirit, from the Spirit will reap eternal life.*** This does not mean that eternal life is earned by works. Rather, Paul is saying that eternal life is the glorious end of those who follow the guidance of the Spirit (Rom. 6:22). Jesus said that He came so that we might have life and have it more abundantly (John 10:10). In this life, through the indwelling of the Spirit, Christians are developing a capacity to experience Christ to the fullest in the life to come.

6:9 *doing good.* The apostle has argued at length that such works cannot justify (2:16) or sanctify (3:3) anyone. However, good works are, in fact, an important fruit of the life of faith (5:5) that God has planned for each believer (Eph. 2:8–10).

6:12 *impress.* The Judaizers were trying to appear spiritual by becoming circumcised and demanding that others become circumcised (5:2–12). By teaching that all Christians should become circumcised, the Judaizers were trying to make Christianity into a sect of Judaism. This would have two advantages. First, they could counter the persecution that they suffered from the zealous Jews. Second, they could include themselves with an officially sanctioned religion of the Roman Empire, Judaism.

6:13 *Not even those ... keep the law.* The Judaizers knew that they were unable to keep the entire law even though they were required to do so. They still attempted to persuade the Galatians to be circumcised so that they could boast about having them as their followers.

6:16 *the Israel of God.* This probably refers to the remnant of believing Jews (Rom. 11:1–2,7). They are Abraham's spiritual descendants (3:6–9) because they believe in God and rely on His grace.

6:17 *I bear on my body.* Paul's scars branded him as a slave for Christ (Rom. 1:1). Such marks far outweighed the "mark" of circumcision so valued by the false teachers in Galatia (vv. 12–15).

6:1 [v] 1Co 2:15 **6:2** [w] Ro 15:1; Jas 2:8 **6:3** [x] Ro 12:3; 1Co 8:2 **6:6** [y] 1Co 9:11, 14 **6:7** [z] 1Co 6:9 [a] 2Co 9:6 **6:8** [b] Job 4:8; Hos 8:7 [c] Jas 3:18 **6:9** [d] 1Co 15:58 [e] Rev 2:10 **6:10** [f] Pr 3:27 [g] Eph 2:19 **6:11** [h] 1Co 16:21 **6:12** [i] Ac 15:1 [j] Gal 5:11 **6:13** [k] Ro 2:25 [l] Php 3:3 **6:14** [m] Ro 6:2, 6 **6:15** [n] 1Co 7:19 [o] 2Co 5:17 **6:17** [p] Isa 44:5; 2Co 1:5 **6:18** [q] Ro 16:20 [r] 2Ti 4:22

EPHESIANS

▶ **AUTHOR:** All internal and external evidence strongly supports the Pauline authorship of Ephesians. In recent years, however, critics have turned to internal grounds to challenge this unanimous ancient tradition. It has been argued that the vocabulary and style are different from other Pauline epistles, but this overlooks Paul's flexibility under different circumstances (as in Romans and 2 Corinthians). The theology of Ephesians in some ways reflects a later development, but this must be attributed to Paul's own growth and meditation on the church as the body of Christ. Ephesians was written during his first Roman imprisonment in A.D. 60–62, perhaps around the same time as Philippians, Colossians, and Philemon.

▶ **TIME:** c. A.D. 60–61 ▶ **KEY VERSES:** Eph. 4:1–3

▶ **THEME:** Ephesians is like a grand landscape whose subject is the whole world. Paul paints a richly textured picture of God's plan to bless the world through Christ. God is bringing light to darkness, healing to brokenness and reconciliation to the separated. Central to this teaching is the role of the church in the world and the gifts God has given it. God will bring about these things through the church. Once we understand and believe all that God has done and is doing, it is our responsibility to obey and live in light of His actions. Paul gives us much more than the theory in Ephesians. He makes critical connections between big picture theology and the practical implications for living the day-to-day Christian life.

1 Paul, an apostle[a] of Christ Jesus by the
will of God,[b]

To God's holy people in Ephesus,[a] the
faithful[c] in Christ Jesus:

2 Grace and peace to you from God our
Father and the Lord Jesus Christ.[d]

Praise for Spiritual Blessings in Christ

3 Praise be to the God and Father of our
Lord Jesus Christ,[e] who has blessed us in
the heavenly realms[f] with every spiritual blessing in Christ. 4 For he chose us in
him before the creation of the world to be
holy and blameless[g] in his sight. In love[h]
5 he[b] predestined[i] us for adoption to sonship[c] through Jesus Christ, in accordance
with his pleasure[j] and will— 6 to the praise
of his glorious grace, which he has freely
given us in the One he loves.[k] 7 In him we
have redemption[l] through his blood, the
forgiveness of sins, in accordance with the
riches of God's grace 8 that he lavished on
us. With all wisdom and understanding,

[a] *1* Some early manuscripts do not have *in Ephesus.* [b] *4,5* Or *sight in love.* [5]*He* [c] *5* The Greek word for *adoption to sonship* is a legal term referring to the full legal standing of an adopted male heir in Roman culture.

1:1–2 *Grace and peace to you.* The salutations in the New Testament epistles follow the form of the typical first-century letter. The writer is mentioned first and the recipient next, followed by a blessing or best wishes for good health. The difference here lies in the content of the blessing: pagan letters mentioned nonexistent gods and goddesses such as Diana or Apollo; the apostles call upon the one true God and His Son Jesus Christ to bless their readers. ***holy people.*** In the New Testament all believers are set apart by God in Christ.

1:3 *every spiritual blessing.* God does not guarantee health, wealth, and prosperity to the New Testament believer. The blessings of Christianity are largely spiritual.

1:4–5 *love.* In this instance the Greek *agape* is used. That love is a love that is by choice or one's will, not just a sentimental feeling. ***he predestined us.*** Predestination is not a cold-hearted determinism or set fate, but rather a loving choice on God's part.

1:6 *One he loves.* This title is messianic, referring to God's Son, Jesus.

1:7 *redemption.* The word means "buy back" or "ransom." In ancient times, one could buy back a person who was sold into slavery. In the same way, Christ through His death bought us from our slavery to sin.

1:1 [a] 1Co 1:1 [b] 2Co 1:1 [c] Col 1:2 **1:2** [d] Ro 1:7
1:3 [e] 2Co 1:3 [f] Eph 2:6; 3:10; 6:12 **1:4** [g] Eph 5:27; Col 1:22
[h] Eph 4:2, 15, 16 **1:5** [i] Ro 8:29, 30 [j] 1Co 1:21
1:6 [k] Mt 3:17 **1:7** [l] Ro 3:24

9he[a] made known to us the mystery[m] of
his will according to his good pleasure,
which he purposed in Christ, 10to be put
into effect when the times reach their fulfillment[n]—to bring unity to all things in
heaven and on earth under Christ.[o]
11In him we were also chosen,[b] having
been predestined according to the plan of
him who works out everything in conformity with the purpose[p] of his will, 12in order that we, who were the first to put our
hope in Christ, might be for the praise of
his glory.[q] 13And you also were included
in Christ when you heard the message of
truth,[r] the gospel of your salvation. When
you believed, you were marked in him with
a seal,[s] the promised Holy Spirit, 14who is a
deposit guaranteeing our inheritance[t] until
the redemption of those who are God's possession—to the praise of his glory.

Thanksgiving and Prayer

15For this reason, ever since I heard about
your faith in the Lord Jesus and your love
for all God's people,[u] 16I have not stopped
giving thanks for you,[v] remembering you
in my prayers. 17I keep asking that the God
of our Lord Jesus Christ, the glorious Father,[w] may give you the Spirit[c] of wisdom[x]
and revelation, so that you may know him
better. 18I pray that the eyes of your heart
may be enlightened[y] in order that you may
know the hope to which he has called you,
the riches of his glorious inheritance in his
holy people, 19and his incomparably great
power for us who believe. That power[z] is the
same as the mighty strength[a] 20he exerted
when he raised Christ from the dead[b] and
seated him at his right hand in the heavenly
realms, 21far above all rule and authority,
power and dominion, and every name[c] that
is invoked, not only in the present age but
also in the one to come. 22And God placed
all things under his feet[d] and appointed him
to be head[e] over everything for the church,
23which is his body, the fullness of him who
fills everything in every way.

Made Alive in Christ

2 As for you, you were dead in your transgressions and sins,[f] 2in which you used
to live[g] when you followed the ways of this
world and of the ruler of the kingdom of the
air,[h] the spirit who is now at work in those
who are disobedient.[i] 3All of us also lived
among them at one time, gratifying the
cravings of our flesh[d][j] and following its desires and thoughts. Like the rest, we were
by nature deserving of wrath. 4But because
of his great love for us, God, who is rich
in mercy, 5made us alive with Christ even
when we were dead in transgressions[k]—it
is by grace you have been saved.[l] 6And God
raised us up with Christ and seated us with
him[m] in the heavenly realms[n] in Christ
Jesus, 7in order that in the coming ages he
might show the incomparable riches of his
grace, expressed in his kindness[o] to us in
Christ Jesus. 8For it is by grace you have
been saved,[p] through faith—and this is not

---

[a] 8,9 Or *us with all wisdom and understanding. 9And he* [b] 11 Or *were made heirs* [c] 17 Or *a spirit* [d] 3 In contexts like this, the Greek word for *flesh* (*sarx*) refers to the sinful state of human beings, often presented as a power in opposition to the Spirit.

---

his blood. The blood of Christ is the means by which our redemption comes. The Old Testament and the New both clearly teach that there is no forgiveness without the shedding of blood.

1:9 ***the mystery.*** This is not a puzzle to solve, or knowledge only for the few and the initiated, as in the mystery religions of Paul's day. In Paul's use, the word *mystery* refers to an aspect of God's will that was once hidden or obscure, but now was being revealed by God (Rom. 11:25).

1:14 ***guaranteeing our inheritance.*** The Greek word for *guarantee* can also be used to indicate an engagement ring. As Christ is the bridegroom and the church is the bride, so the Holy Spirit is the down payment, the earnest money in the long-awaited marriage of the two (Rev. 19:7). ***possession.*** The Old Testament described the nation of Israel as God's special treasure, one He had purchased by His mighty acts of deliverance during the exodus (Ex. 19:5). Here Paul describes Christians as a possession, bought with the blood of Christ.

1:18–19 ***the eyes of your heart.*** This phrase refers to spiritual understanding. To describe this, Paul uses words that picture eyes that have been brightened with divine illumination.

1:21 ***not only in the present age but also in the one to come.*** The Jews of Christ's time understood the end times to be divided into two time periods, the age in which they were living and the coming age. The Messiah, called "the Coming One," would rule in the age which is to come.

2:2 ***you used to live.*** Believers are saved out of their rebellion to God and are empowered to live a life characterized by good works (v. 10). ***ruler of the kingdom of the air.*** This is a reference to Satan.

2:4–7 ***we were dead in transgressions.*** Because of Adam's sin, the entire human race is spiritually dead. Only God can grant new life and save us from this predicament. Out of His mercy, God gave His Son for us while we were yet His enemies. He loved us long before we loved Him (1 John 4:9–10).

2:8–10 ***you have been saved, through faith.*** The grace of God is the source of salvation; faith is the channel, not the cause. God alone saves. Salvation never originates in the efforts of people; it always arises out of the lovingkindness of God. ***the gift of God.*** We cannot do anything to earn our salvation.

1:9 [m] Ro 16:25 **1:10** [n] Gal 4:4 [o] Col 1:20 **1:11** [p] Eph 3:11; Heb 6:17 **1:12** [q] ver 6, 14 **1:13** [r] Col 1:5 [s] Eph 4:30 **1:14** [t] Ac 20:32 **1:15** [u] Col 1:4 **1:16** [v] Ro 1:8 **1:17** [w] Jn 20:17 [x] Col 1:9 **1:18** [y] Ac 26:18; 2Co 4:6 **1:19** [z] Col 1:29 [a] Eph 6:10 **1:20** [b] Ac 2:24 **1:21** [c] Php 2:9, 10 **1:22** [d] Mt 28:18 [e] Eph 4:15; 5:23 **2:1** [f] ver 5; Col 2:13 **2:2** [g] Col 3:7 [h] Jn 12:31; Eph 6:12 [i] Eph 5:6 **2:3** [j] Gal 5:16 **2:5** [k] ver 1 [l] ver 8; Ac 15:11 **2:6** [m] Eph 1:20 [n] Eph 1:3 **2:7** [o] Titus 3:4 **2:8** [p] ver 5

from yourselves, it is the gift of God— 9not
by works,[q] so that no one can boast.[r] 10For
we are God's handiwork, created[s] in Christ
Jesus to do good works,[t] which God prepared in advance for us to do.

Jew and Gentile Reconciled Through Christ

11Therefore, remember that formerly
you who are Gentiles by birth and called
"uncircumcised" by those who call themselves "the circumcision" (which is done in
the body by human hands)[u]— 12remember
that at that time you were separate from
Christ, excluded from citizenship in Israel and foreigners to the covenants of the
promise,[v] without hope[w] and without God
in the world. 13But now in Christ Jesus you
who once were far away have been brought
near[x] by the blood of Christ.[y]

14For he himself is our peace, who has
made the two groups one[z] and has destroyed the barrier, the dividing wall of
hostility, 15by setting aside in his flesh[a]
the law with its commands and regulations.[b] His purpose was to create in himself one[c] new humanity out of the two,
thus making peace, 16and in one body to
reconcile both of them to God through
the cross,[d] by which he put to death their
hostility. 17He came and preached peace
to you who were far away and peace to
those who were near.[e] 18For through him
we both have access[f] to the Father[g] by one
Spirit.[h]

19Consequently, you are no longer foreigners and strangers,[i] but fellow citizens[j]
with God's people and also members of his
household,[k] 20built on the foundation[l] of the
apostles and prophets, with Christ Jesus
himself as the chief cornerstone.[m] 21In him
the whole building is joined together and
rises to become a holy temple[n] in the Lord.
22And in him you too are being built together to become a dwelling in which God
lives by his Spirit.

God's Marvelous Plan for the Gentiles

3 For this reason I, Paul, the prisoner[o] of
Christ Jesus for the sake of you Gentiles—

2Surely you have heard about the administration of God's grace that was given to
me[p] for you, 3that is, the mystery[q] made
known to me by revelation,[r] as I have already written briefly. 4In reading this, then,
you will be able to understand my insight[s]
into the mystery of Christ, 5which was not
made known to people in other generations
as it has now been revealed by the Spirit
to God's holy apostles and prophets.[t] 6This
mystery is that through the gospel the Gentiles are heirs[u] together with Israel, members together of one body,[v] and sharers together in the promise in Christ Jesus.

7I became a servant of this gospel[w] by
the gift of God's grace given me through
the working of his power.[x] 8Although I am
less than the least of all the Lord's people,[y]
this grace was given me: to preach to the
Gentiles the boundless riches of Christ,
9and to make plain to everyone the administration of this mystery,[z] which for ages
past was kept hidden in God, who created all things. 10His intent was that now,
through the church, the manifold wisdom
of God[a] should be made known[b] to the rulers and authorities[c] in the heavenly realms,
11according to his eternal purpose that he
accomplished in Christ Jesus our Lord.
12In him and through faith in him we may
approach God[d] with freedom and confidence.[e] 13I ask you, therefore, not to be discouraged because of my sufferings for you,
which are your glory.

A Prayer for the Ephesians

14For this reason I kneel[f] before the Father, 15from whom every family[a] in heaven
and on earth derives its name. 16I pray that

[a] 15 The Greek for *family* (*patria*) is derived from the Greek for *father* (*pater*).

2:14 *the dividing wall of hostility.* This was vividly portrayed by an actual partition in the temple area, with a sign warning that any Gentile going beyond the Court of the Gentiles would receive swift and sudden death.
2:15 *one new humanity.* In the early days of Christianity, the church was largely made up of Jews. But, under the direction of God's Spirit, the believers witnessed to Gentiles (Acts 10), who then soon outnumbered the Jewish members. As the two groups learned to work together, they became something completely new.
2:20 *the apostles and prophets.* The early church was established on the teaching and preaching of the apostles. They were the foundation of the church.
2:21 *joined together.* This idea pictures the process in Roman construction whereby laborers would turn huge rocks around until they fit each other perfectly.
3:5–6 *the Gentiles are heirs.* In Old Testament times people had only partial knowledge of God and His works. While Genesis pointed to the fact that God's grace would come to the Gentiles (Gen. 12:3), no one understood that they would also be fully equal with the Jews.
3:10 *manifold wisdom.* God's ways are not only "mysterious," but also varied. Angels are also learning about God's wisdom as they watch His grace working in us (1 Cor. 11:10).

2:9 [q] 2Ti 1:9 [r] 1Co 1:29 **2:10** [s] Eph 4:24 [t] Titus 2:14
2:11 [u] Col 2:11 **2:12** [v] Gal 3:17 [w] 1Th 4:13
2:13 [x] ver 17; Ac 2:39 [y] Col 1:20 **2:14** [z] 1Co 12:13
2:15 [a] Col 1:21,22 [b] Col 2:14 [c] Gal 3:28 **2:16** [d] Col 1:20, 22 **2:17** [e] Ps 148:14; Isa 57:19 **2:18** [f] Eph 3:12
[g] Col 1:12 [h] 1Co 12:13 **2:19** [i] ver 12 [j] Php 3:20 [k] Gal 6:10
2:20 [l] Mt 16:18; Rev 21:14 [m] 1Pe 2:4-8 **2:21** [n] 1Co 3:16, 17 **3:1** [o] Ac 23:18; Eph 4:1 **3:2** [p] Col 1:25
3:3 [q] Ro 16:25 [r] 1Co 2:10 **3:4** [s] 2Co 11:6 **3:5** [t] Ro 16:26
3:6 [u] Gal 3:29 [v] Eph 2:15, 16 **3:7** [w] 1Co 3:5 [x] Eph 1:19
3:8 [y] 1Co 15:9 **3:9** [z] Ro 16:25 **3:10** [a] 1Co 2:7
[b] 1Pe 1:12 [c] Eph 1:21 **3:12** [d] Eph 2:18 [e] Heb 4:16
3:14 [f] Php 2:10

out of his glorious riches he may strengthen
you with power[g] through his Spirit in your
inner being,[h] 17so that Christ may dwell
in your hearts[i] through faith. And I pray
that you, being rooted[j] and established in
love, 18may have power, together with all
the Lord's holy people, to grasp how wide
and long and high and deep[k] is the love of
Christ, 19and to know this love that surpasses knowledge—that you may be filled[l]
to the measure of all the fullness of God.[m]
20Now to him who is able[n] to do immeasurably more than all we ask or imagine,
according to his power that is at work within us, 21to him be glory in the church and
in Christ Jesus throughout all generations,
for ever and ever! Amen.[o]

Unity and Maturity in the Body of Christ

4 As a prisoner[p] for the Lord, then, I urge
you to live a life worthy[q] of the calling
you have received. 2Be completely humble
and gentle; be patient, bearing with one another[r] in love.[s] 3Make every effort to keep
the unity[t] of the Spirit through the bond of
peace. 4There is one body and one Spirit,[u]
just as you were called to one hope when
you were called; 5one Lord, one faith, one
baptism; 6one God and Father of all, who is
over all and through all and in all.[v]
7But to each one of us[w] grace has been
given[x] as Christ apportioned it. 8This is
why it[a] says:

"When he ascended on high,
he took many captives[y]
and gave gifts to his people."[b][z]

9(What does "he ascended" mean except
that he also descended to the lower, earthly regions[c]? 10He who descended is the

[a] 8 Or *God* [b] 8 Psalm 68:18 [c] 9 Or *the depths of the earth*

3:17 ***Christ may dwell in your hearts.*** Christ actually resides or makes His home in the believer's heart.

3:21 The Purpose of the Church—The ultimate purpose of the church is to bring honor and glory to Jesus Christ. It does this as it fulfills its three purposes related to God's plan for the world.

Worship—As the church worships, it continually declares to believers and the world God's view of reality. God is the world's Creator and Sustainer. Through Jesus Christ, God has redeemed the world and provided a way of salvation for people who rebel against Him.

Evangelism—The Great Commission in Matthew 28 clearly points to evangelism as a primary purpose for the church. "Teaching" implies that there is more to evangelism than simply declaring the good news. Evangelism should lead to discipleship, which involves the work of helping the new believer reach full maturity in Christ. This happens much as a parent raises children, nurturing them in every way possible so that they can grow. Christ makes baptism an important element in this process. In baptism, one indicates that he has been identified with Christ in His death, burial, and resurrection and that he wishes to be identified with the church.

Edification—Ephesians 4:12 points to the fact that the saints need to be built up (that is equipped) to fully do the work of the church, namely the ministry of Christ to the world. This involves making believers aware of everything they have in Christ and how the Spirit's gifts enable them to serve the body of Christ effectively.

4:1 ***then ... live a life worthy of the calling you have received.*** The second half of Ephesians, like that of a number of Paul's epistles, emphasizes the behavior that should result from the doctrines or beliefs taught in the first half.

4:2 ***Be completely humble and gentle; be patient.*** These are the attitudes that Jesus demonstrated when He was on earth (Phil. 2:5–8). These attitudes do not come naturally, but must be cultivated by the determination to place others above ourselves. Only the Spirit can empower us to treat people this way consistently.

4:3 The Person of the Holy Spirit—Many people make the serious error of thinking of the Holy Spirit as only some kind of vague principle or an influence. On the contrary, the Holy Spirit is as much a person (individual existence of a conscious being) as the Father and the Son.

1. *The personality of the Holy Spirit.* The Bible speaks of the mind (Rom. 8:27) and will (1 Cor. 2:11) of the Spirit. He is often described as speaking directly to men in the Book of Acts. During Paul's second missionary journey, the apostle was forbidden by the Spirit to visit a certain mission field (Acts 16:6–7) and then was instructed to proceed toward another field of service (Acts 16:10). It was God's Spirit who spoke directly to Christian leaders in the Antioch church, commanding them to send Paul and Barnabas on their first missionary journey (Acts 13:2).
2. *The deity of the Holy Spirit.* He is not only a distinct being, but He is also God. As is God the Father, He too is everywhere at once (Ps. 139:7). As the Son is eternal, the Holy Spirit has also existed forever (Heb. 9:14). He is often referred to as God in the Bible (Acts 5:3–4). Finally, the Holy Spirit is equal with the Father and Son. This is seen during the baptism of Christ (Matt. 3:16–17) and is mentioned by Jesus Himself just prior to His ascension from the Mount of Olives (Matt. 28:19–20).

4:7 ***grace has been given as Christ apportioned it.*** Like Peter (1 Pet. 4:10), Paul taught that all Christians have a spiritual gift or gifts. The gifts are given sovereignly by the ascended Christ in order to build up the church (1 Cor. 12:11). Thus the body of Christ is to function like a machine in which every part is essential for getting a job done. But, unlike a machine, the body of Christ should maintain itself and build every one of its members up so that they can do good works (1 Cor. 12:7).

4:8 ***When he ascended on high.*** Paul quotes Psalms 68:18 to picture the ascended Messiah triumphant over Satan and his hosts, distributing spiritual gifts to His people.

3:16 [g] Col 1:11 [h] Ro 7:22 **3:17** [i] Jn 14:23 [j] Col 1:23 **3:18** [k] Job 11:8,9 **3:19** [l] Col 2:10 [m] Eph 1:23 **3:20** [n] Ro 16:25 **3:21** [o] Ro 11:36 **4:1** [p] Eph 3:1 [q] Php 1:27; Col 1:10 **4:2** [r] Col 3:12, 13 [s] Eph 1:4 **4:3** [t] Col 3:14 **4:4** [u] 1Co 12:13 **4:6** [v] Ro 11:36 **4:7** [w] 1Co 12:7,11 [x] Ro 12:3 **4:8** [y] Col 2:15 [z] Ps 68:18

very one who ascended higher than all the heavens, in order to fill the whole universe.) 11So Christ himself gave the apostles,[a] the prophets, the evangelists,[b] the pastors and teachers, 12to equip his people for works of service, so that the body of Christ[c] may be built up 13until we all reach unity[d] in the faith and in the knowledge of the Son of God and become mature,[e] attaining to the whole measure of the fullness of Christ.

14Then we will no longer be infants,[f] tossed back and forth by the waves,[g] and blown here and there by every wind of teaching and by the cunning and craftiness of people in their deceitful scheming.[h] 15Instead, speaking the truth in love, we will grow to become in every respect the mature body of him who is the head,[i] that is, Christ. 16From him the whole body, joined and held together by every supporting ligament, grows[j] and builds itself up in love, as each part does its work.

Instructions for Christian Living

17So I tell you this, and insist on it in the Lord, that you must no longer live as the Gentiles do, in the futility of their thinking.[k] 18They are darkened in their understanding[l] and separated from the life of God[m] because of the ignorance that is in them due to the hardening of their hearts.[n] 19Having lost all sensitivity,[o] they have given themselves over[p] to sensuality[q] so as to indulge in every kind of impurity, and they are full of greed.

20That, however, is not the way of life you learned 21when you heard about Christ and were taught in him in accordance with the truth that is in Jesus. 22You were taught, with regard to your former way of life, to put off[r] your old self,[s] which is being corrupted by its deceitful desires; 23to be made new in the attitude of your minds;[t] 24and to put on the new self,[u] created to be like God in true righteousness and holiness.[v]

25Therefore each of you must put off falsehood and speak truthfully[w] to your neighbor, for we are all members of one body.[x] 26"In your anger do not sin"[a]: Do not let the sun go down while you are still angry, 27and do not give the devil a foothold. 28Anyone who has been stealing must steal no longer, but must work,[y] doing something useful with their own hands,[z] that they may have something to share with those in need.[a]

29Do not let any unwholesome talk come out of your mouths,[b] but only what is helpful for building others up according to their needs, that it may benefit those who listen. 30And do not grieve the Holy Spirit of God,[c] with whom you were sealed for the day of redemption.[d] 31Get rid of all bitterness, rage and anger, brawling and slander, along with every form of malice.[e] 32Be kind and compassionate to one another, forgiving each other, just as in Christ God

5 forgave you.[f] 1Follow God's example,[g] therefore, as dearly loved children 2and walk in the way of love, just as Christ loved us and gave himself up for us[h] as a fragrant offering and sacrifice to God.[i]

3But among you there must not be even a hint of sexual immorality, or of any kind of impurity, or of greed,[j] because these are improper for God's holy people. 4Nor should there be obscenity, foolish talk or coarse joking, which are out of place, but rather thanksgiving.[k] 5For of this you can be sure: No immoral, impure or greedy person—such a person is an idolater[l]—has any inheritance in the kingdom of Christ and of God.[b][m] 6Let no one deceive you with empty words, for because of such things

[a] *26* Psalm 4:4 (see Septuagint) [b] *5* Or *kingdom of the Messiah and God*

4:11 *apostles ... prophets ... evangelists ... pastors and teachers.* Apostles, meaning "envoys" or "ambassadors," in its strict sense refers to those who saw Christ in resurrected form and were specially chosen by Christ to tell others about Him from their eyewitness accounts. Prophets delivered direct revelations from God. They foretold God's actions in the future and they proclaimed what God had already said in the Scriptures. Evangelists play a major role in bringing people into the body of Christ. Pastors function as shepherds. They feed, nurture, care for, and protect the members of the body. The Greek ties in teacher with pastor.

4:12–13 *equip his people for works of service, so that the body of Christ may be built up.* Three stages of growth are presented here. Leaders are responsible to equip. The well-equipped saints do the work of the ministry, and the result is that the body is built up. The final goal is maturity, truth, and love.

4:16 *the whole body ... every supporting ligament.* There are no insignificant parts in the body (1 Cor. 12:14–27). Anything that builds up believers and the church can be said to be edifying.

4:22–24 *put off your old self.* Paul compares the Christian life to stripping off the dirty clothes of a sinful past and putting on the snowy white robes of Christ's righteousness.

4:30 *the Holy Spirit of God.* We should never push away, ignore, or reject the Holy Spirit. If we would remember that the One who lives in us is God's own Spirit, we would be much more selective about what we think, read, watch, say, and do.

5:1 *Follow God's example.* Believers are to follow the example of God's actions. He loved us when we were still His enemies.

4:11 [a] 1Co 12:28 [b] Ac 21:8 **4:12** [c] 1Co 12:27 **4:13** [d] ver 3, 5 [e] Col 1:28 **4:14** [f] 1Co 14:20 [g] Jas 1:6 [h] Eph 6:11 **4:15** [i] Eph 1:22 **4:16** [j] Col 2:19 **4:17** [k] Ro 1:21 **4:18** [l] Ro 1:21 [m] Eph 2:12 [n] 2Co 3:14 **4:19** [o] 1Ti 4:2 [p] Ro 1:24 [q] Col 3:5 **4:22** [r] 1Pe 2:1 [s] Ro 6:6 **4:23** [t] Col 3:10 **4:24** [u] Ro 6:4 [v] Eph 2:10 **4:25** [w] Zec 8:16 [x] Ro 12:5 **4:28** [y] Ac 20:35 [z] 1Th 4:11 [a] Lk 3:11 **4:29** [b] Col 3:8 **4:30** [c] 1Th 5:19 [d] Ro 8:23 **4:31** [e] Col 3:8 **4:32** [f] Mt 6:14, 15 **5:1** [g] Lk 6:36 **5:2** [h] Gal 1:4 [i] 2Co 2:15; Heb 7:27 **5:3** [j] Col 3:5 **5:4** [k] ver 20 **5:5** [l] Col 3:5 [m] 1Co 6:9

God's wrath[n] comes on those who are disobedient. [7]Therefore do not be partners
with them.
[8]For you were once[o] darkness, but now
you are light in the Lord. Live as children
of light[p] [9](for the fruit[q] of the light consists in all goodness, righteousness and
truth) [10]and find out what pleases the
Lord. [11]Have nothing to do with the fruitless deeds of darkness, but rather expose
them. [12]It is shameful even to mention what
the disobedient do in secret. [13]But everything exposed by the light[r] becomes visible—and everything that is illuminated
becomes a light. [14]This is why it is said:

"Wake up, sleeper,[s]
rise from the dead,[t]
and Christ will shine on you."[u]

[15]Be very careful, then, how you live—
not as unwise but as wise, [16]making the
most of every opportunity,[v] because the
days are evil.[w] [17]Therefore do not be foolish, but understand what the Lord's will is.[x]
[18]Do not get drunk on wine,[y] which leads
to debauchery. Instead, be filled with the
Spirit,[z] [19]speaking to one another with
psalms, hymns, and songs from the Spirit.[a] Sing and make music from your heart
to the Lord, [20]always giving thanks[b] to God
the Father for everything, in the name of
our Lord Jesus Christ.

Instructions for Christian Households

[21]Submit to one another[c] out of reverence
for Christ.
[22]Wives, submit yourselves to your own
husbands[d] as you do to the Lord.[e] [23]For the
husband is the head of the wife as Christ is
the head of the church,[f] his body, of which
he is the Savior. [24]Now as the church submits to Christ, so also wives should submit
to their husbands in everything.
[25]Husbands, love your wives,[g] just as
Christ loved the church and gave himself
up for her[h] [26]to make her holy, cleansing[a]
her by the washing[i] with water through the

[a] 26 Or *having cleansed*

5:12 *in secret.* This verse effectively bans Christians from indulging in the modern preoccupation with examining the lurid details of evils such as the occult and other perverted practices.
5:16 *making the most of every opportunity.* This means taking advantage of opportunities for service. Paul exhorts us to use as much time as is possible for advancing Christ's purposes in this world.
5:18 *drunk on wine.* Just as a person who is drunk is under the control of alcohol, so a Spirit-filled believer is controlled by the Spirit. ***filled.*** Filling is a step beyond the sealing of the Holy Spirit (1:13). Sealing is an action God took at the point of our new birth. The tense of the Greek word translated *filled* indicates that filling is a moment-by-moment repeatable action. To be filled with the Spirit is to be controlled by the Spirit and is therefore crucial to successfully living the Christian life. The imperative says that the believer is to be filled with the presence of the Spirit so that he comes to know God in all His fullness, living in relationship with Him. Out of this relationship, the believer is able to manifest Christlike character. The certainty of being filled with the Spirit may be confirmed by the believer's faith and life. The believer must, of course, believe God's Word that meeting the conditions will result in the filling. The Spirit-filled person will exhibit the Christlike character described in Galatians 5:22–23 as the fruit of the Spirit. Included in that list are all the vibrant, attractive qualities desired by all Christians. Any Christian may be transformed by the filling of the Spirit and possess these qualities.
5:19 *Sing and make music.* Most believe that these words refer to three larger categories: (1) the 150 psalms in the Psalter, (2) hymns or compositions addressed directly to God, and (3) spiritual songs, hymns about the Christian experience.
5:21–22 *Submit.* Verse 21 completes the thought of the previous verses (vv. 18–20), which address how being filled with the Spirit manifests itself in the believer's life. It also introduces the next section (5:22–6:4), about how members of a Christian family should relate to each other. The Greek word for *submit* does not refer to being under the absolute control of another but to voluntarily place oneself under the authority of another.
5:22–24 *Wives, submit.* Just as Christ is not inferior to the Father, but is the second Person in the Trinity, so wives are equal to their own husbands. Yet, in a marriage relationship, a husband and wife have different roles. A wife's voluntary submission arises out of her own submission to Christ.
5:25 *Husbands, love.* Paul does not emphasize the husband's authority; instead, he calls on husbands to love self-sacrificially. Husbands are to emulate Christ's love, the kind of love that is willing to lay down one's life for another. as ***Christ loved the church.*** The relationship between Christ and the church was initiated by Christ, who loved the church and gave Himself for it. The details of that relationship are described with seven images:

1. *The Shepherd and the sheep* emphasizes both the warm leadership and protection of Christ and the helplessness and dependency of believers (John 10:1–18).
2. *The vine and the branches* points out the necessity for Christians to depend on Christ's sustaining strength for growth (John 15:1–8).
3. *Christ as high priest* and *the church as a kingdom of priests* stress the joyful worship, fellowship, and service which the church can render to God through Christ (Heb. 5:1–10; 7:1; 8:6; 1 Pet. 2:5–9).
4. *The cornerstone and building stones* (Matt. 21:42) accents the foundational value of Christ to everything the church is and does, as well as Christ's value to the unity of believers. Love

5:6 [n] Ro 1:18 **5:8** [o] Eph 2:2 [p] Lk 16:8 **5:9** [q] Gal 5:22 **5:13** [r] Jn 3:20,21 **5:14** [s] Ro 13:11 [t] Jn 5:25 [u] Isa 60:1 **5:16** [v] Col 4:5 [w] Eph 6:13 **5:17** [x] Ro 12:2; 1Th 4:3 **5:18** [y] Pr 20:1 [z] Lk 1:15 **5:19** [a] Ac 16:25; Col 3:16 **5:20** [b] Ps 34:1 **5:21** [c] Gal 5:13 **5:22** [d] Ge 3:16; 1Pe 3:1,5,6 [e] Eph 6:5 **5:23** [f] 1Co 11:3; Eph 1:22 **5:25** [g] Col 3:19 [h] ver 2 **5:26** [i] Ac 22:16

word, 27and to present her to himself as a radiant church, without stain or wrinkle or any other blemish, but holy and blameless.[j] 28In this same way, husbands ought to love their wives[k] as their own bodies. He who loves his wife loves himself. 29After all, no one ever hated their own body, but they feed and care for their body, just as Christ does the church— 30for we are members of his body.[l] 31"For this reason a man will leave his father and mother and be united to his wife, and the two will become one flesh."[a][m] 32This is a profound mystery—but I am talking about Christ and the church. 33However, each one of you also must love his wife[n] as he loves himself, and the wife must respect her husband.

6 Children, obey your parents in the Lord, for this is right.[o] 2"Honor your father and mother"—which is the first commandment with a promise— 3"so that it may go well with you and that you may enjoy long life on the earth."[b][p]

4Fathers,[c] do not exasperate your children;[q] instead, bring them up in the training and instruction of the Lord.[r]

5Slaves, obey your earthly masters with respect[s] and fear, and with sincerity of heart,[t] just as you would obey Christ.[u] 6Obey them not only to win their favor when their eye is on you, but as slaves of Christ, doing the will of God from your heart. 7Serve wholeheartedly, as if you were serving the Lord, not people,[v] 8because you know that the Lord will reward each one for whatever good they do,[w] whether they are slave or free.

9And masters, treat your slaves in the same way. Do not threaten them, since you know that he who is both their Master and yours[x] is in heaven, and there is no favoritism with him.

The Armor of God

10Finally, be strong in the Lord[y] and in his mighty power.[z] 11Put on the full armor of God,[a] so that you can take your stand against the devil's schemes. 12For our struggle is not against flesh and blood, but against the rulers, against the authorities,[b] against the powers[c] of this dark world and against the spiritual forces of evil in the heavenly realms.[d] 13Therefore put on the

[a] *31* Gen. 2:24 [b] *3* Deut. 5:16 [c] *4* Or *Parents*

is to be the mortar which solidly holds the living stones together (1 Cor. 3:9; 13:1–13; Eph. 2:19–22; 1 Pet. 2:5).

5. *The head and many-membered body,* the church is a vibrant organism, not merely an organization; it draws its vitality and direction from Christ, the Head, and each believer has a unique and necessary place in its growth (1 Cor. 12:12–13,27: Eph. 4:4).
6. *The last Adam and new creation* presents Christ as the initiator of a new creation of believers as Adam was of the old creation (1 Cor. 15:22,45; 2 Cor. 5:17).
7. *The bridegroom and bride* beautifully emphasizes the intimate fellowship and co-ownership existing between Christ and the church (Eph. 5:25–33; Rev. 19:7–8; 21:9).

5:31 *the two will become one flesh.* Paul quotes Genesis 2:24, which teaches that the special union between husband and wife supersedes the original family ties.

5:32 *This is a profound mystery.* A sacred secret revealed is that Christian marriage parallels the union that exists spiritually between Christ and His bride, the church.

6:1–4 *Children, obey ... Fathers, do not exasperate.* This paragraph has the beautiful balance we expect to find in God's Word: children are to obey their parents, and parents are to treat their children in such a way that the children will want to obey.

6:4 Parenting—The father is the parent responsible for setting the pattern for the child's obedience in the family. The father's responsibility is set forth in two ways: First, what the father is *not to do*—"do not exasperate your children." He is not to overdiscipline them or rule the household in such a way that the child can only react in a rage. Second, what the father *is to do*—"bring them up in the training and instruction of the Lord." "Bring them up" involves three ideas:

a. It is a continuous job. As long as the child is a dependent, the father is to be responsible for providing for the child so that he becomes what God wants him to be.
b. It is a loving job. To "bring up" means literally to nourish tenderly; children should be objects of tender, loving care.
c. It is a job that involves nurture and admonition. The child needs to be nurtured physically and spiritually. He also needs corrective discipline that will be effective in bringing about obedience to the Word of God (Prov. 13:24; 19:18; 29:15–17).

6:5 *Slaves, obey.* Slaves made up a large percentage of the population of the Roman Empire. These people were considered mere property and could be abused and even killed by their masters with no resulting investigation by the state. In the church, wealthy slave owners and their slaves broke bread together at the Lord's Table as equals.

6:6 *not only to win their favor.* Servants and employees should serve faithfully even when no one is looking. After all, God sees all that we do.

6:11 *the full armor of God.* This equipment is the believer's protection against evil and the devil. Paul presented the extended metaphor of the battle dress roughly according to the order in which the various pieces were put on.

6:12 *For our struggle is not against.* The real battle is not with human cultists, false religionists, atheists, agnostics, and pseudo-Christians, but with the demonic beings working through them.

5:27 [j] Eph 1:4; Col 1:22 **5:28** [k] ver 25 **5:30** [l] 1Co 12:27 **5:31** [m] Ge 2:24; Mt 19:5; 1Co 6:16 **5:33** [n] ver 25 **6:1** [o] Col 3:20 **6:3** [p] Ex 20:12 **6:4** [q] Col 3:21 [r] Ge 18:19; Dt 6:7 **6:5** [s] 1Ti 6:1 [t] Col 3:22 [u] Eph 5:22 **6:7** [v] Col 3:23 **6:8** [w] Col 3:24 **6:9** [x] Job 31:13,14 **6:10** [y] 1Co 16:13 [z] Eph 1:19 **6:11** [a] Ro 13:12 **6:12** [b] Eph 1:21 [c] Ro 8:38 [d] Eph 1:3

full armor of God, so that when the day of
evil comes, you may be able to stand your
ground, and after you have done everything, to stand. 14Stand firm then, with the
belt of truth buckled around your waist,[e]
with the breastplate of righteousness in
place,[f] 15and with your feet fitted with the
readiness that comes from the gospel of
peace.[g] 16In addition to all this, take up
the shield of faith,[h] with which you can extinguish all the flaming arrows of the evil
one. 17Take the helmet of salvation[i] and the
sword of the Spirit, which is the word of
God.[j]

18And pray in the Spirit on all occasions[k]
with all kinds of prayers and requests.[l]
With this in mind, be alert and always
keep on praying for all the Lord's people.
19Pray also for me,[m] that whenever I speak,
words may be given me so that I will fearlessly[n] make known the mystery of the
gospel, 20for which I am an ambassador[o]
in chains.[p] Pray that I may declare it fearlessly, as I should.

Final Greetings

21Tychicus,[q] the dear brother and faithful servant in the Lord, will tell you everything, so that you also may know how I am
and what I am doing. 22I am sending him
to you for this very purpose, that you may
know how we are,[r] and that he may encourage you.

23Peace[s] to the brothers and sisters,[a] and
love with faith from God the Father and
the Lord Jesus Christ. 24Grace to all who
love our Lord Jesus Christ with an undying love.[b]

[a] 23 The Greek word for *brothers and sisters* (*adelphoi*) refers here to believers, both men and women, as part of God's family. [b] 24 Or *Grace and immortality to all who love our Lord Jesus Christ.*

6:14 *truth.* This is a reference to integrity, a life of practical truthfulness and honesty. ***breastplate.*** In Roman times this went completely around the body and was made of hard leather or metal. ***righteousness.*** This is not the righteousness of Christ, which all believers possess, but the practical, righteous character and deeds of the believer.

6:15 *that comes from the gospel of peace.* This may mean either that the gospel is the firm foundation on which Christians are to stand or that the Christian soldier should be ready to go out to defend and spread the gospel.

6:16 *shield of faith.* The Christian's shield offers protection against all forms of evil. Flaming arrows could not penetrate the fireproof shield of the ancient Roman soldier, nor can the assaults of Satan penetrate to the believer who places his or her faith in God.

6:17 *the sword of the Spirit.* This is the only offensive weapon in the believer's armor. This weapon is not necessarily the Bible as a whole, but the specific word that needs to be spoken in a specific situation.

6:21–24 *that you also may know how I am and what I am doing.* The last verses of Ephesians reveal Paul's appreciation of the ministry of others, especially the ministry of Tychicus (Col. 4:7). The fact that this letter does not conclude with personal greetings, as Paul's other letters do, may indicate that this was a circular letter, one intended for a number of churches around Ephesus.

6:14 [e] Isa 11:5 [f] Isa 59:17 **6:15** [g] Isa 52:7 **6:16** [h] 1Jn 5:4 **6:17** [i] Isa 59:17 [j] Heb 4:12 **6:18** [k] Lk 18:1 [l] Mt 26:41; Php 1:4 **6:19** [m] 1Th 5:25 [n] Ac 4:29; 2Co 3:12 **6:20** [o] 2Co 5:20 [p] Ac 21:33 **6:21** [q] Ac 20:4 **6:22** [r] Col 4:7-9 **6:23** [s] Gal 6:16; 1Pe 5:14

PHILIPPIANS

▸ **AUTHOR:** The external and internal evidence for the Pauline authorship of Philippians is very strong, and there is scarcely any doubt that anyone but Paul wrote it. Paul's "Macedonian call" in Troas during his second missionary journey led to his ministry in Philippi with the conversion of Lydia and others. Internal evidence suggests that the epistle was written from Rome (1:3; 4:22), although some commentators argue for Caesarea or Ephesus. It seems that during the writing of this letter Paul's life was at stake, and he was evidently awaiting the verdict of the imperial court (2:20–26).

▸ **TIME:** c. A.D. 62 ▸ **KEY VERSES:** Phil. 4:4–7

▸ **THEME:** Even though Paul probably wrote this letter while imprisoned in Rome, the letter is often called the Epistle of Joy. It gives us valuable insight into key areas of the Christian life by helping understand how we should identify with Christ in a variety of circumstances. We gain some insight into what Christian relationships should look like and what the content of our prayers for each other should be. Philippians also provides great insight in setting spiritual direction and determining practical priorities. Christians desiring to mature in the Lord will return to study it often.

1 Paul and Timothy,[a] servants of Christ
Jesus,

To all God's holy people[b] in Christ Jesus
at Philippi,[c] together with the overseers[d]
and deacons[a]:[e]

2Grace and peace to you from God our
Father and the Lord Jesus Christ.[f]

Thanksgiving and Prayer

3I thank my God every time I remember
you.[g] 4In all my prayers for all of you, I always pray[h] with joy 5because of your partnership[i] in the gospel from the first day[j] until now, 6being confident of this, that he who
began a good work in you will carry it on to
completion until the day of Christ Jesus.[k]

7It is right[l] for me to feel this way about
all of you, since I have you in my heart[m]
and, whether I am in chains[n] or defending[o]
and confirming the gospel, all of you share

[a] *1* The word *deacons* refers here to Christians designated to serve with the overseers/elders of the church in a variety of ways; similarly in Romans 16:1 and 1 Tim. 3:8,12.

1:1–11 ***To all God's holy people.*** This term means "saints" (those who are separated to God) and refers to all the believers in Philippi. ***overseers.*** This refers to those who watch over the spiritual welfare of the local church. ***deacons.*** This is a reference to those who serve the congregation in special service capacities. They were charged with handling the physical and material concerns of the church (Acts 6:1–7). In the first few verses, Paul reveals his great love for the Philippians. He thinks of them often (vv. 3–6), he is concerned about them (vv. 7–8), and he regularly prays for them (vv. 9–11).
1:3 ***I thank.*** The tense of the Greek verb indicates that Paul was continually thankful to God for the Philippian Christians. ***every time I remember you.*** Every time God brought them to his mind, Paul gave thanks.
1:4 ***joy.*** This is the first of five uses of the Greek word for *joy* in the letter (v. 25; 2:2,29; 4:1). Paul also uses the Greek word for *rejoice* eight times in this letter (v. 18; 2:17–18, 28 ("glad"); 3:1; 4:4).
1:5 ***partnership.*** This term is a commercial term for a joint-partnership in a business venture in which all parties actively participate to ensure the success of the business. In the Christian community, the word expresses intimacy with Christ (1 Cor. 1:9).
1:6 ***until.*** This word can also be translated "as far as." It expresses progress toward a goal and indicates that a time is coming when God will completely finish His work among the Philippian Christians.
1:7 ***right.*** This word conveys a sense of moral uprightness and is often translated throughout the New Testament as "righteous." In this context, the word indicates that Paul's thoughts regarding the Philippians were in perfect accord with God's will. ***confirming.*** Used only here and in Hebrews 6:16 in the New Testament, this word is a legal and commercial term meaning "a validating guarantee."

1:1 [a] Ac 16:1; 2Co 1:1 [b] Ac 9:13 [c] Ac 16:12 [d] 1Ti 3:1 [e] 1Ti 3:8
1:2 [f] Ro 1:7 **1:3** [g] Ro 1:8 **1:4** [h] Ro 1:10 **1:5** [i] Ac 2:42; Php 4:15 [j] Ac 16:12-40 **1:6** [k] ver 10; 1Co 1:8
1:7 [l] 2Pe 1:13 [m] 2Co 7:3 [n] ver 13,14,17; Ac 21:33 [o] ver 16

in God's grace with me. 8God can testify[p] how I long for all of you with the affection of Christ Jesus.

9And this is my prayer: that your love[q] may abound more and more in knowledge and depth of insight, 10so that you may be able to discern what is best and may be pure and blameless for the day of Christ,[r] 11filled with the fruit of righteousness[s] that comes through Jesus Christ—to the glory and praise of God.

Paul's Chains Advance the Gospel

12Now I want you to know, brothers and sisters,[a] that what has happened to me has actually served to advance the gospel. 13As a result, it has become clear throughout the whole palace guard[b] and to everyone else that I am in chains[t] for Christ. 14And because of my chains,[u] most of the brothers and sisters have become confident in the Lord and dare all the more to proclaim the gospel without fear.

15It is true that some preach Christ out of envy and rivalry, but others out of goodwill. 16The latter do so out of love, knowing that I am put here for the defense of the gospel.[v] 17The former preach Christ out of selfish ambition,[w] not sincerely, supposing that they can stir up trouble for me while I am in chains.[x] 18But what does it matter? The important thing is that in every way, whether from false motives or true, Christ is preached. And because of this I rejoice.

Yes, and I will continue to rejoice, 19for I know that through your prayers[y] and God's provision of the Spirit of Jesus Christ[z] what has happened to me will turn out for my deliverance.[c] 20I eagerly expect[a] and hope that I will in no way be ashamed, but will have sufficient courage[b] so that now as always Christ will be exalted in my body,[c] whether by life or by death.[d] 21For to me, to live is Christ[e] and to die is gain. 22If I am to go on living in the body, this will mean fruitful labor for me. Yet what shall I choose? I do not know! 23I am torn between the two: I desire to depart[f] and be with Christ,[g] which is better by far; 24but it is more necessary for you that I remain in the body. 25Convinced of this, I know that I will remain, and I will continue with all of you for your progress and joy in the faith, 26so that through my being with you again your boasting in Christ Jesus will abound on account of me.

---

[a] *12* The Greek word for *brothers and sisters* (*adelphoi*) refers here to believers, both men and women, as part of God's family; also in verse 14; and in 3:1, 13, 17; 4:1, 8, 21. [b] *13* Or *whole palace* [c] *19* Or *vindication*; or *salvation*

1:8 *the affection of Christ Jesus.* The word translated "affection" literally means the internal organs, regarded by the first century reader as the center of the deepest feelings. Whereas the heart is the seat of reflection, Paul now speaks of his deep feelings for the believers. His feelings for the Philippians were like those of Jesus Christ, who loved them and died for them.
1:9 *love.* The kind of love that Paul sought for the believers is the highest form of Christian love, based on a lasting, unconditional commitment, not on an unstable emotion. ***knowledge.*** The first of two terms on which a directed love is built, knowledge suggests an intimate understanding based on a relationship with a person. Here the focus of this knowledge is God. ***depth of insight.*** Found only here in the New Testament, the Greek word means moral or ethical understanding based on both the intellect and the senses.
1:10 *that you may be able to discern.* This verb is used in ancient literature for the testing of gold to determine its purity and for trying oxen to assess their usefulness for the task at hand.
1:12 *advance.* This phrase could suggest a pioneer beating or cutting a path through a densely forested area. Paul's imprisonment was a strategic advance in the kingdom of God because it was clearing the way for the gospel to penetrate the ranks of the Roman military.
1:13 *palace guard.* This is a reference to the Praetorian Guard, a force consisting of several thousand highly trained, elite soldiers of the Roman Empire who were headquartered at Rome. For the one to two years that Paul had been under house arrest in Rome, different soldiers had taken turns guarding him. Although Paul could not go to the world to preach, in this way God brought the world to Paul. In an ironic twist, they were the captives and Paul was free to preach.
1:18 *from false motives or true.* Whether the preaching was done for false motives or pure, whether for appearance's sake or for the sake of what was right, Paul was pleased that the gospel was being spread.
1:19 *deliverance.* In the New Testament this word is used for physical healing, rescue from danger or death, justification, sanctification, and glorification.
1:20 *be exalted.* Paul was committed to ensuring that Christ would be made even more conspicuous in his own life than ever. He was not relying on himself to magnify Christ but looked to the Holy Spirit (v. 19) to magnify Christ in him (John 16:14).
1:21 *Christ ... gain.* Paul would experience gain in his own death because He would be with Christ (v. 23). In fact, Paul may have been expressing his confidence that his imprisonment had furthered the gospel; God would also use his death to further His kingdom.
1:22 *what shall I choose? I do not know.* Paul was in a dilemma because he clearly saw the advantages of both life and death, for the Christian life meant an opportunity to minister to people like the Philippians (v. 24), while death meant being with Christ his Savior.
1:25 *your progress.* Paul was not satisfied that the Philippian Christians should simply be saved, but that they should advance to maturity in Christ.

1:8 [p] Ro 1:9 **1:9** [q] 1Th 3:12 **1:10** [r] ver 6; 1Co 1:8 **1:11** [s] Jas 3:18 **1:13** [t] ver 7, 14, 17 **1:14** [u] ver 7, 13, 17 **1:16** [v] ver 7, 12 **1:17** [w] Php 2:3 [x] ver 7, 13, 14 **1:19** [y] 2Co 1:11 [z] Ac 16:7 **1:20** [a] Ro 8:19 [b] ver 14 [c] 1Co 6:20 [d] Ro 14:8 **1:21** [e] Gal 2:20 **1:23** [f] 2Ti 4:6 [g] Jn 12:26; 2Co 5:8

Life Worthy of the Gospel

27 Whatever happens, conduct yourselves in a manner worthy[h] of the gospel of
Christ. Then, whether I come and see you
or only hear about you in my absence, I will
know that you stand firm[i] in the one Spirit,[a] striving together[j] as one for the faith of
the gospel 28 without being frightened in
any way by those who oppose you. This is
a sign to them that they will be destroyed,
but that you will be saved—and that by
God. 29 For it has been granted to you[k] on
behalf of Christ not only to believe in him,
but also to suffer[l] for him, 30 since you are
going through the same struggle[m] you
saw[n] I had, and now hear[o] that I still have.

Imitating Christ's Humility

2 Therefore if you have any encouragement from being united with Christ, if
any comfort from his love, if any common
sharing in the Spirit,[p] if any tenderness
and compassion,[q] 2 then make my joy complete[r] by being like-minded,[s] having the
same love, being one[t] in spirit and of one
mind. 3 Do nothing out of selfish ambition
or vain conceit.[u] Rather, in humility value
others above yourselves,[v] 4 not looking to
your own interests but each of you to the
interests of the others.
5 In your relationships with one another,
have the same mindset as Christ Jesus:[w]

6 Who, being in very nature[b] God,[x]
did not consider equality with God[y]
something to be used to his own
advantage;
7 rather, he made himself nothing
by taking the very nature[c] of a
servant,[z]
being made in human likeness.[a]
8 And being found in appearance as a man,
he humbled himself
by becoming obedient to death[b]—
even death on a cross!
9 Therefore God exalted him[c] to the
highest place
and gave him the name that is above
every name,[d]
10 that at the name of Jesus every knee
should bow,[e]
in heaven and on earth and under the
earth,[f]

---

[a] 27 Or *in one spirit* [b] 6 Or *in the form of*
[c] 7 Or *the form*

1:27 *conduct yourselves.* The word used could refer to discharging the obligations of a citizen. Because Philippi held the privileged status of a Roman colony, its citizens understood the responsibilities associated with citizenship. Paul here commanded them to shift their perspective from the earthly realm to the heavenly one. They should live in this world as citizens of another world, the heavenly kingdom. Their conduct should reveal their heavenly citizenship.

1:28 *frightened.* This word is a strong term that is used for the terror of a panicked horse. The Philippians are not to be terror-stricken in the face of their enemies.

1:29 *to suffer for him.* Suffering matures us as Christians in the present (James 1:2–4) and enables us to be glorified with Christ in the future (Rom. 8:17).

2:1 *if . . . if . . . if.* The conditional clauses in this verse indicate certainties, not "maybes." Each *if* here expresses the idea of "since," and each following clause may be considered to be true.

2:2 *being like-minded.* In this verse the apostle sets forth a fourfold appeal that expresses one major idea—namely, the unity of the church. Paul is strongly emphasizing the unity that should exist between believers and how they must single-mindedly strive together to advance the gospel of Jesus Christ.

2:3 *value others above yourselves.* This verb indicates a thorough analysis of the facts in order to reach a correct conclusion about the matter. In other words, each Philippian Christian was to properly assess himself or herself. Such an assessment would lead to valuing others.

2:5 *In your relationships.* Thinking and being like Christ are requirements not only for an individual but also for the corporate body of believers. Together, we need to think and act like one being, like the Person of Jesus Christ. ***have the same mindset.*** All godly action begins with the "renewing of the mind." Right thinking produces right actions. Our actions are the fruit of our deepest thoughts.

2:6 *did not consider . . . something to be used to his own advantage.* Because Christ was God, He did not look on sharing God's nature as something to come, as if He did not already possess it, or as a thing to be retained, as though He might lose it.

2:7 *made himself nothing.* Christ did this by taking on the form of a servant. In doing this, He did not empty Himself of any part of His essence as God. Instead, He gave up His privileges as God and took upon Himself existence as a man. While remaining completely God, He became completely human. ***nature.*** Jesus added to His divine essence (v. 6) a servant's essence, that is, the essential characteristics of a human being seeking to fulfill the will of another. Paul does not say that Christ exchanged the form of God for the form of a servant, involving a loss of deity or the attributes of deity. Rather, in the incarnation, Christ continued in the very nature of God but added to Himself the nature of a servant.

2:8 *He humbled himself.* Jesus willingly took the role of a servant; no one forced Him to do it. ***obedient.*** Although He never sinned and did not deserve to die, He chose to die so that the sins of the world could be charged to His account. Subsequently, He could credit His righteousness to the account of all who believe in Him (2 Cor. 5:21; Gal. 1:4). ***even death on a cross.*** Paul describes the depths of Christ's humiliation by reminding his readers that Christ died by the cruelest form of capital punishment, crucifixion. The Jews viewed death on a cross as a curse from God (Deut. 21:23; Gal. 3:13).

1:27 [h] Eph 4:1 [i] 1Co 16:13 [j] Jude 3 **1:29** [k] Mt 5:11, 12 [l] Ac 14:22 **1:30** [m] Col 2:1; 1Th 2:2 [n] Ac 16:19-40 [o] ver 13 **2:1** [p] 2Co 13:14 [q] Col 3:12 **2:2** [r] Jn 3:29 [s] Php 4:2 [t] Ro 12:16 **2:3** [u] Gal 5:26 [v] Ro 12:10; 1Pe 5:5 **2:5** [w] Mt 11:29 **2:6** [x] Jn 1:1 [y] Jn 5:18 **2:7** [z] Mt 20:28 [a] Jn 1:14; Heb 2:17 **2:8** [b] Mt 26:39; Jn 10:18; Heb 5:8 **2:9** [c] Ac 2:33; Heb 2:9 [d] Eph 1:20, 21 **2:10** [e] Ro 14:11 [f] Mt 28:18

11 and every tongue acknowledge that
Jesus Christ is Lord,[g]
to the glory of God the Father.

Do Everything Without Grumbling

12 Therefore, my dear friends, as you
have always obeyed—not only in my presence, but now much more in my absence—
continue to work out your salvation with
fear and trembling,[h] 13 for it is God who
works in you[i] to will and to act in order to
fulfill his good purpose.
14 Do everything without grumbling[j] or
arguing, 15 so that you may become blameless and pure, "children of God[k] without
fault in a warped and crooked generation."[a][l] Then you will shine among them
like stars in the sky 16 as you hold firmly
to the word of life. And then I will be able
to boast on the day of Christ that I did not
run or labor in vain.[m] 17 But even if I am
being poured out like a drink offering[n]
on the sacrifice[o] and service coming from
your faith, I am glad and rejoice with all
of you. 18 So you too should be glad and rejoice with me.

Timothy and Epaphroditus

19 I hope in the Lord Jesus to send Timothy to you soon,[p] that I also may be cheered
when I receive news about you. 20 I have no
one else like him,[q] who will show genuine
concern for your welfare. 21 For everyone
looks out for their own interests,[r] not those
of Jesus Christ. 22 But you know that Timothy has proved himself, because as a son
with his father[s] he has served with me in
the work of the gospel. 23 I hope, therefore,
to send him as soon as I see how things go
with me.[t] 24 And I am confident[u] in the Lord
that I myself will come soon.
25 But I think it is necessary to send back
to you Epaphroditus, my brother, co-worker[v] and fellow soldier,[w] who is also your
messenger, whom you sent to take care of
my needs.[x] 26 For he longs for all of you[y] and
is distressed because you heard he was ill.
27 Indeed he was ill, and almost died. But
God had mercy on him, and not on him
only but also on me, to spare me sorrow
upon sorrow. 28 Therefore I am all the more
eager to send him, so that when you see
him again you may be glad and I may have
less anxiety. 29 So then, welcome him in the
Lord with great joy, and honor people like
him,[z] 30 because he almost died for the work
of Christ. He risked his life to make up for
the help you yourselves could not give me.[a]

No Confidence in the Flesh

3 Further, my brothers and sisters, rejoice
in the Lord! It is no trouble for me to
write the same things to you again, and it
is a safeguard for you. 2 Watch out for those
dogs,[b] those evildoers, those mutilators of
the flesh. 3 For it is we who are the circumcision,[c] we who serve God by his Spirit,
who boast in Christ Jesus, and who put no
confidence in the flesh— 4 though I myself
have reasons for such confidence.

---

a *15* Deut. 32:5

2:11 ***acknowledge.*** The term Paul uses is a strong, intensive verb, which means "agree with" or "say the same thing." Essentially Paul is saying that everyone will unanimously affirm what God the Father has already stated (Is. 45:23): that Jesus Christ is Lord.
2:12 ***work out.*** The Greek term speaks of the present deliverance of the Philippians. The word translated *work out* is used by a first century author to speak of digging silver out of silver mines. Thus, salvation can be compared to a huge gift that needs to be unwrapped for one's thorough enjoyment. Note that Paul is encouraging the Philippians to develop and *work out* their salvation, but not to work *for* their salvation.
2:15 ***a warped and crooked generation.*** Paul describes the world as being the opposite of Christian. On the one hand, the world is turned away from the truth, while on the other hand, it exerts a corrupting influence that is opposed to the truth.
2:17 ***poured out.*** Paul was probably saying that he was presently being offered as a living sacrifice on behalf of the faith of the Philippians. ***sacrifice.*** This means primarily the act of offering something to God.
2:19 ***Timothy.*** He had accompanied Paul on his second missionary journey, during which time they had established the church at Philippi. Timothy was apparently well loved by the Philippians, and he in turn exhibited a great concern for them.
2:22 ***as a son with his father.*** In New Testament times a son who served his father did so to learn the family trade. Serving in this way meant learning all about the business and being willing to obey the teacher in order to become as skillful as possible in the work.
2:25 ***Epaphroditus.*** He was a Philippian Christian sent by the church in Philippi to take a gift to Paul and to assist Paul in his ministry.
2:27 ***ill, and almost died.*** Paul was making certain that the Philippians understood the effort that Epaphroditus had made for the cause of Christ. His condition had been far worse than perhaps they had imagined. Paul viewed Epaphroditus's healing as God's direct intervention.
3:2 ***for those dogs.*** In New Testament times, dogs were hated scavengers. The term came to be used for all who had morally impure minds. ***those mutilators.*** Paul here points sarcastically and specifically to those who desire to reinstate Jewish religious practices as necessary for salvation. He chooses a term that literally means "to cut." By doing so, he suggests that these people do not even understand the truth about the Old Testament practice of circumcision.
3:3 ***the circumcision.*** Paul defines this as a matter of the heart and not of the flesh. He reveals three aspects: (1) worshiping God in the Spirit; (2) rejoicing in

2:11 [g] Jn 13:13 **2:12** [h] 2Co 7:15 **2:13** [i] Ezr 1:5
2:14 [j] 1Co 10:10; 1Pe 4:9 **2:15** [k] Mt 5:45,48; Eph 5:1
[l] Ac 2:40 **2:16** [m] 1Th 2:19 **2:17** [n] 2Ti 4:6 [o] Ro 15:16
2:19 [p] ver 23 **2:20** [q] 1Co 16:10 **2:21** [r] 1Co 10:24; 13:5
2:22 [s] 1Co 4:17; 1Ti 1:2 **2:23** [t] ver 19 **2:24** [u] Php 1:25
2:25 [v] Php 4:3 [w] Phm 2 [x] Php 4:18 **2:26** [y] Php 1:8
2:29 [z] 1Co 16:18; 1Ti 5:17 **2:30** [a] 1Co 16:17
3:2 [b] Ps 22:16,20 **3:3** [c] Ro 2:28,29; Gal 6:15; Col 2:11

If someone else thinks they have reasons to put confidence in the flesh, I have more: 5circumcised[d] on the eighth day, of the people of Israel,[e] of the tribe of Benjamin,[f] a Hebrew of Hebrews; in regard to the law, a Pharisee;[g] 6as for zeal, persecuting the church;[h] as for righteousness based on the law,[i] faultless.

7But whatever were gains to me I now consider loss[j] for the sake of Christ. 8What is more, I consider everything a loss because of the surpassing worth of knowing[k] Christ Jesus my Lord, for whose sake I have lost all things. I consider them garbage, that I may gain Christ 9and be found in him, not having a righteousness of my own that comes from the law,[l] but that which is through faith in[a] Christ—the righteousness that comes from God on the basis of faith.[m] 10I want to know Christ—yes, to know the power of his resurrection and participation in his sufferings,[n] becoming like him in his death,[o] 11and so, somehow, attaining to the resurrection[p] from the dead.

12Not that I have already obtained all this, or have already arrived at my goal,[q] but I press on to take hold[r] of that for which Christ Jesus took hold of me.[s] 13Brothers and sisters, I do not consider myself yet to have taken hold of it. But one thing I do: Forgetting what is behind[t] and straining toward what is ahead, 14I press on[u] toward the goal to win the prize for which God has called[v] me heavenward in Christ Jesus.

Following Paul's Example

15All of us, then, who are mature[w] should take such a view of things.[x] And if on some point you think differently, that too God will make clear to you. 16Only let us live up to what we have already attained.

17Join together in following my example,[y] brothers and sisters, and just as you have us as a model, keep your eyes on those who live as we do. 18For, as I have often told you before and now tell you again even with tears,[z] many live as enemies of the cross of Christ.[a] 19Their destiny is destruction, their god is their stomach,[b] and their glory is in their shame.[c] Their mind is set on earthly things.[d] 20But our citizenship[e] is in heaven.[f] And we eagerly await a Savior from there, the Lord Jesus Christ,[g] 21who, by the power[h] that enables him to bring everything under his control, will transform our lowly bodies[i] so that they will be like his glorious body.[j]

[a] 9 Or *through the faithfulness of*

Christ; and (3) placing no confidence in any human honor or accomplishment as a means to reach God.

3:5 *eighth day.* Paul's parents obeyed God's law and had Paul circumcised on the appropriate day after his birth (Lev. 12:2–3). ***tribe of Benjamin.*** This tribe was highly regarded because it had produced the first king of Israel and had remained loyal to David. ***Hebrew of Hebrews.*** This description of Paul may indicate that (1) both his parents were Jews, (2) he was a model Jew, or (3) he was educated completely as a Jew. ***Pharisee.*** They rigorously followed and defended the letter of the Jewish law.

3:7 *loss.* This word indicates that which is damaged or of no further use (v. 8). Those things that Paul thought to be important became unimportant after confronting the resurrected Messiah.

3:8 *loss.* This word means anything that is detestable or worthless. All things of this world are dung compared to Christ. Even our righteousness is like filthy rags (Is. 64:6).

3:10 *power of his resurrection.* Paul does not say the power "in" His resurrection, which would specify the power of the one-time event of His resurrection. Rather, Paul seeks the ongoing power that is the day-to-day experience of being in Christ. ***Participation in his sufferings.*** Paul sees the value of participating in the persecutions or struggles that naturally accompany one who is in partnership with Christ and His sufferings. ***becoming like him in his death.*** Paul desires to imitate Christ—even in His death. In other words, Paul wants to be completely obedient to God the Father, just as Jesus was obedient to His Father's will (Luke 22:42).

3:12 *already arrived at my goal.* The Greek term means mature or complete, finished. It does not specifically mean a moral or sinless perfection. Paul is not speaking of moral perfection or righteousness but of reaching the state of completion as a Christian. ***take hold.*** This phrase adds the idea of overtaking by surprise to the sense of seizing some object. Paul urgently wants to "grab hold of" God as God had laid hold of him.

3:13 *Forgetting.* Paul was indicating that it is an ongoing process. He might even be implying that he wanted to forget everything so that he would not rest on his past successes in Christ, but continue to labor for the Lord.

3:16 *let us live.* Paul commands the Philippians to conduct themselves as soldiers who "march in line" together, organized each in his proper position.

3:17 *example.* The word indicates an exact representation of the original. The example of Paul's life is so evident that one can readily see it and use it as a pattern for living.

3:19 *glory is in their shame.* The things in which they take pride actually are the things that will bring "disgrace" or "humiliation" to them, things of which they should have been ashamed.

3:20 *citizenship is in heaven.* Here Paul presents a direct contrast to the earthly focus of enemies of the cross in v. 19. The eager desire of Christians is not earthly things, but a heavenly Person, the Savior.

3:21 *like his glorious body.* Our bodies now are weak and susceptible to sin, disease, and death. But God will change our bodies to resemble Christ's glorious resurrection body.

3:5 [d] Lk 1:59 [e] 2Co 11:22 [f] Ro 11:1 [g] Ac 23:6 **3:6** [h] Ac 8:3 [i] Ro 10:5 **3:7** [j] Mt 13:44; Lk 14:33 **3:8** [k] Eph 4:13; 2Pe 1:2 **3:9** [l] Ro 10:5 [m] Ro 9:30 **3:10** [n] Ro 8:17 [o] Ro 6:3-5 **3:11** [p] Rev 20:5,6 **3:12** [q] 1Co 13:10 [r] 1Ti 6:12 [s] Ac 9:5,6 **3:13** [t] Lk 9:62 **3:14** [u] Heb 6:1 [v] Ro 8:28 **3:15** [w] 1Co 2:6 [x] Gal 5:10 **3:17** [y] 1Co 4:16; 1Pe 5:3 **3:18** [z] Ac 20:31 [a] Gal 6:12 **3:19** [b] Ro 16:18 [c] Ro 6:21 [d] Ro 8:5,6 **3:20** [e] Eph 2:19 [f] Col 3:1 [g] 1Co 1:7 **3:21** [h] Eph 1:19 [i] 1Co 15:43-53 [j] Col 3:4

Closing Appeal for Steadfastness and Unity

4 Therefore, my brothers and sisters, you whom I love and long for,[k] my joy and crown, stand firm[l] in the Lord in this way, dear friends!

2I plead with Euodia and I plead with Syntyche to be of the same mind[m] in the Lord. **3**Yes, and I ask you, my true companion, help these women since they have contended at my side in the cause of the gospel, along with Clement and the rest of my co-workers, whose names are in the book of life.

Final Exhortations

4Rejoice in the Lord always. I will say it again: Rejoice![n] **5**Let your gentleness be evident to all. The Lord is near.[o] **6**Do not be anxious about anything,[p] but in every situation, by prayer and petition, with thanksgiving, present your requests to God.[q] **7**And the peace of God,[r] which transcends all understanding, will guard your hearts and your minds in Christ Jesus.

8Finally, brothers and sisters, whatever is true, whatever is noble, whatever is right, whatever is pure, whatever is lovely, whatever is admirable—if anything is excellent or praiseworthy—think about such things. **9**Whatever you have learned or received or heard from me, or seen in me—put it into practice.[s] And the God of peace[t] will be with you.

Thanks for Their Gifts

10I rejoiced greatly in the Lord that at last you renewed your concern for me.[u] Indeed, you were concerned, but you had no opportunity to show it. **11**I am not saying this because I am in need, for I have learned to be content[v] whatever the circumstances. **12**I know what it is to be in need, and I know what it is to have plenty. I have learned the secret of being content in any and every situation, whether well fed or hungry,[w] whether living in plenty or in want.[x] **13**I can do all this through him who gives me strength.[y]

14Yet it was good of you to share[z] in my troubles. **15**Moreover, as you Philippians know, in the early days[a] of your acquaintance with the gospel, when I set out from Macedonia, not one church shared with me in the matter of giving and receiving, except you only;[b] **16**for even when I was in Thessalonica,[c] you sent me aid more than once when I was in need.[d] **17**Not that I desire your gifts; what I desire is that more be credited to your account.[e] **18**I have received full payment and have more than enough. I am amply supplied, now that I have received from Epaphroditus[f] the gifts you sent. They are a fragrant[g] offering, an acceptable sacrifice, pleasing to God. **19**And my God will meet all your needs[h] according to the riches of his glory[i] in Christ Jesus.

20To our God and Father[j] be glory for ever and ever. Amen.[k]

Final Greetings

21Greet all God's people in Christ Jesus. The brothers and sisters who are with me[l] send greetings. **22**All God's people[m] here send you greetings, especially those who belong to Caesar's household.

23The grace of the Lord Jesus Christ[n] be with your spirit. Amen.[a]

---

[a] *23* Some manuscripts do not have *Amen.*

4:2 *Euodia . . . Syntyche.* What is written here is all that is known about the two women and their dispute. Paul does not take sides in the argument, but instead encourages them to be reconciled.

4:4 *Rejoice in the Lord.* The joy of Christians is not based on agreeable circumstances; instead, it is based on their relationship to God. Christians will face trouble in this world, but they should rejoice in the trials they face because they know God is using those situations to improve their character.

4:6 *be anxious about anything.* Paul prohibits the Philippians from worrying about their own problems. Instead, they are to commit their problems to God in prayer, trusting that He will provide deliverance.

4:7 *will guard.* Paul's choice of a military term "guard" implies that the mind is in a battle zone and needs to be protected by a "military guard" since the purpose of such a guard in a wartime situation is either to prevent a hostile invasion or to keep the inhabitants of a besieged city from escaping.

4:9 *learned.* This verb conveys not only the concept of "increasing in intellectual knowledge," but also the idea of "learning by habitual practice." In some areas of their Christian development, the Philippians had been excellent disciples of Paul, practicing what he had taught.

4:11 *content.* The word literally means "self-sufficient." In Stoic philosophy this Greek word described a person who dispassionately accepted whatever circumstances brought. For the Greeks, this contentment came from personal sufficiency. But for Paul, true sufficiency is found in the strength of Christ.

4:17 *account.* Paul uses business terminology. The Philippians' gift was producing spiritual profit, just as money deposited in a bank account accrues interest. But Paul was not as concerned with their gift as with the development in the Philippians of the spiritual ability to give.

4:20 *Amen.* The Jewish practice of closing prayers with the word *amen* carried over to the Christian church as well. When found at the end of a sentence, as it is here, the word can be translated "so be it" or "may it be fulfilled." At the beginning of a sentence, it means "surely," "truly," or "most assuredly."

4:1 [k] Php 1:8 [l] 1Co 16:13; Php 1:27 **4:2** [m] Php 2:2 **4:4** [n] Ro 12:12; Php 3:1 **4:5** [o] Heb 10:37; Jas 5:8,9 **4:6** [p] Mt 6:25-34 [q] Eph 6:18 **4:7** [r] Isa 26:3; Jn 14:27; Col 3:15 **4:9** [s] Php 3:17 [t] Ro 15:33 **4:10** [u] 2Co 11:9 **4:11** [v] 1Ti 6:6,8 **4:12** [w] 1Co 4:11 [x] 2Co 11:9 **4:13** [y] 2Co 12:9 **4:14** [z] Php 1:7 **4:15** [a] Php 1:5 [b] 2Co 11:8,9 **4:16** [c] Ac 17:1 [d] 1Th 2:9 **4:17** [e] 1Co 9:11,12 **4:18** [f] Php 2:25 [g] 2Co 2:14 **4:19** [h] Ps 23:1; 2Co 9:8 [i] Ro 2:4 **4:20** [j] Gal 1:4 [k] Ro 11:36 **4:21** [l] Gal 1:2 **4:22** [m] Ac 9:13 **4:23** [n] Ro 16:20

COLOSSIANS

▶ **AUTHOR:** The external testimony to the Pauline authorship of Colossians is ancient and consistent, and the internal evidence is also very good. It not only claims to be written by Paul (1:1,23; 4:18), but the personal details and close parallels with Ephesians and Philemon make the case even stronger. It is evident from 1:4–8 and 2:1 that Paul had never visited the church at Colosse, which was founded by Epaphras. On his third missionary journey, Paul devoted almost three years to an Asian ministry centered in Ephesus (Acts 19:10; 20:31), and Epaphras probably came to Christ during this time. He then carried the gospel to cities like Colosse in the Lycus valley. Epaphras visited Paul in prison (4:12) and his report concerning the church in Colosse prompted this epistle.

▶ **TIME:** c. A.D. 60–61 ▶ **KEY VERSES:** Col. 2:9–10

▶ **THEME:** The problem of the Colossian church was similar to what we experience in many churches today. This is often called syncretism, the tendency to regard other philosophies and religions as equally valid as Christianity. The people in Colosse wanted to believe Christian truth, but they also wanted to hang on to their old beliefs as well by blending them with the gospel. Paul's purpose in this letter is to settle for once and for all the issue of Christ's centrality and supremacy. He writes to restore Jesus, the Messiah, to the center of these believers' lives. Here we can see Paul's unwavering confidence in the incomparability of Christ, as it has completely shaped his views on all of life. He writes to introduce the Colossians to this same vision.

---

1 Paul, an apostle[a] of Christ Jesus by the
will of God,[b] and Timothy our brother,
2 To God's holy people in Colossae, the
faithful brothers and sisters[a] in Christ:

Grace[c] and peace to you from God our
Father.[bd]

Thanksgiving and Prayer

3 We always thank God,[e] the Father of
our Lord Jesus Christ, when we pray for
you, 4 because we have heard of your faith
in Christ Jesus and of the love[f] you have
for all God's people[g]— 5 the faith and love
that spring from the hope[h] stored up for
you in heaven[i] and about which you have
already heard in the true message of the
gospel 6 that has come to you. In the same
way, the gospel is bearing fruit[j] and growing
throughout the whole world[k]—just as
it has been doing among you since the day
you heard it and truly understood God's
grace. 7 You learned it from Epaphras,[l] our
dear fellow servant,[c] who is a faithful minister[m]
of Christ on our[d] behalf, 8 and who
also told us of your love in the Spirit.[n]
9 For this reason, since the day we heard
about you,[o] we have not stopped praying

[a] 2 The Greek word for *brothers and sisters* (*adelphoi*) refers here to believers, both men and women, as part of God's family; also in 4:15. [b] 2 Some manuscripts *Father and the Lord Jesus Christ* [c] 7 Or *slave* [d] 7 Some manuscripts *your*

1:1 ***an apostle.*** Paul calls himself an apostle, a word whose root means "to send." The Greek word was first used for a cargo ship or fleet, but later denoted a commander of a fleet. The New Testament employs the word to signify an approved spokesman sent as a personal representative.
1:2 ***holy people.*** The essence of "holiness" is being set apart to God. All believers are saints, not because they are perfect, but because they belong to God. ***in Christ.*** This is a favorite expression of the apostle Paul, used some 80 times in his letters.
1:4–8 ***faith ... love ... hope.*** Paul often uses these three terms together (Rom. 5:2–5; 1 Cor. 13:13; 1 Thess. 1:3; 5:8). Faith is in Christ. Love flows from faith and proves the genuineness of one's faith (James 2:14–26). Hope refers to the result of faith, the treasure laid up in heaven.
1:9 ***all the wisdom and understanding.*** *Wisdom* is the practical outworking of knowledge (James

1:1 [a] 1Co 1:1 [b] 2Co 1:1 **1:2** [c] Col 4:18 [d] Ro 1:7 **1:3** [e] Ro 1:8 **1:4** [f] Gal 5:6 [g] Eph 1:15 **1:5** [h] 1Th 5:8; Titus 1:2 [i] 1Pe 1:4 **1:6** [j] Jn 15:16 [k] Ro 10:18 **1:7** [l] Phm 23 [m] Col 4:7 **1:8** [n] Ro 15:30 **1:9** [o] Eph 1:15

for you. We continually ask God to fill you
with the knowledge of his will[p] through all
the wisdom and understanding that the
Spirit gives,[a][q] 10so that you may live a life
worthy[r] of the Lord and please him in every way: bearing fruit in every good work,
growing in the knowledge of God, 11being
strengthened with all power[s] according to
his glorious might so that you may have
great endurance and patience,[t] 12and giving joyful thanks to the Father,[u] who has
qualified you[b] to share in the inheritance[v]
of his holy people in the kingdom of light.
13For he has rescued us from the dominion
of darkness[w] and brought us into the kingdom[x] of the Son he loves,[y] 14in whom we
have redemption,[z] the forgiveness of sins.[a]

The Supremacy of the Son of God

15The Son is the image[b] of the invisible
God,[c] the firstborn over all creation. 16For
in him all things were created:[d] things in
heaven and on earth, visible and invisible,
whether thrones or powers or rulers or
authorities;[e] all things have been created
through him and for him.[f] 17He is before all
things,[g] and in him all things hold together. 18And he is the head[h] of the body, the
church; he is the beginning and the firstborn from among the dead,[i] so that in everything he might have the supremacy. 19For
God was pleased[j] to have all his fullness[k]
dwell in him, 20and through him to reconcile[l] to himself all things, whether things
on earth or things in heaven,[m] by making
peace through his blood,[n] shed on the cross.
21Once you were alienated from God
and were enemies[o] in your minds[p] because
of[c] your evil behavior. 22But now he has
reconciled you by Christ's physical body[q]
through death to present you holy in his
sight, without blemish and free from accusation[r]— 23if you continue in your faith,
established[s] and firm, and do not move

[a] 9 Or *all spiritual wisdom and understanding*
[b] 12 Some manuscripts *us*
[c] 21 Or *minds, as shown by*

3:17), and that knowledge cannot be separated from the *spiritual understanding* that comes through the discernment given by the Holy Spirit.

1:10 *life worthy of the Lord.* Paul wanted the Colossians to live in a manner that adequately reflected what God had done for them and was doing in them. Being "worthy of God" is a phrase that occurs in ancient pagan inscriptions throughout Asia. It pictures someone's life being weighed on scales to determine its worth.

1:12 *qualified you.* This means to be able or qualified for a task. Believers can never be qualified on their own; instead, God must make them sufficient through Jesus Christ. The tense of the verb points to "qualifying" as an act in the past rather than a process.

1:13 *rescued . . . brought.* God has liberated believers from the dominion of darkness. The apostle uses the common symbolism of light and darkness for good and evil, for God's kingdom and Satan's kingdom, that is found throughout the New Testament. The kingdom from which believers have been rescued is the kingdom of darkness.

1:14 *redemption.* The Greek word points naturally to the payment of a price or ransom for the release of a slave. They are freed from bondage to sin by forgiveness through the blood of Jesus (Eph. 1:7).

1:15 *firstborn over all creation.* Verses 15–20 are thought to be an early Christian hymn celebrating the supremacy of Christ. *Firstborn* could denote a priority in time or in rank. The word does not describe Christ as the first being created in time because the hymn proclaims that all things were "created through him" and that "he is before all things." Being firstborn referred more to rank and privilege than to order of birth.

1:16 *all things have been created through him and for him.* Not only did Jesus create all things, everything was created for His purposes (Heb. 1:2, where Christ is said to be the "heir of all things").

1:18 *head of the body.* No one should underestimate the significance of the church, for it is in fact Christ's body. The sovereign Creator of the universe, as Head of the church, provides leadership and oversight over it.

1:19 *fullness.* The opponents of Paul, and later the Greek Gnostics, seem to have used this word as a technical term for the sphere between heaven and earth where a hierarchy of angels lived. The Gnostics viewed Christ as one of many spirits existing in this hierarchy between God and all people. However, Paul used the term *fullness* to refer to the complete embodiment of God.

1:20–22 Jesus Pays the Price—Salvation is a free gift, but it is not a cheap one. It costs us nothing, but it cost God dearly—it cost Jesus His life. In physically dying on the cross, Jesus sacrificed Himself and satisfied the debt that we had incurred through sin, so that it is possible for God and man to be reconciled. As Jesus hung on the cross, He cried, "My God, My God, why have you forsaken me?" (Matt. 27:46). Jesus was separated from God the Father so that we do not have to be. This is the heart of the atonement (becoming *at one* with God). The marvel of it all is that He did this while we were His enemies: "But God demonstrates his own love for us in this: While we were still sinners, Christ died for us" (Rom. 5:8).

1:20–21 *to reconcile to himself all things.* This phrase shows the significance of Christ's work on the cross. It does not mean that all people will be saved, since many passages clearly say that unbelievers will suffer eternal separation from God (Matt. 25:46).

1:22 *holy . . . without blemish and free from accusation.* We who were once enemies of God and alienated by our own wicked works will one day be presented as above reproach on account of Christ's death for us.

1:23 *if you continue in your faith.* The perseverance of the Colossians was proof of the reconciling

1:9 [p] Eph 5:17 [q] Eph 1:17 **1:10** [r] Eph 4:1
1:11 [s] Eph 3:16 [t] Eph 4:2 **1:12** [u] Eph 5:20 [v] Ac 20:32
1:13 [w] Ac 26:18 [x] Eph 6:12; 2Pe 1:11 [y] Mt 3:17
1:14 [z] Ro 3:24 [a] Eph 1:7 **1:15** [b] 2Co 4:4 [c] Jn 1:18
1:16 [d] Jn 1:3 [e] Eph 1:20,21 [f] Ro 11:36 **1:17** [g] Jn 1:2
1:18 [h] Eph 1:22 [i] Ac 26:23; Rev 1:5 **1:19** [j] Eph 1:5
[k] Jn 1:16 **1:20** [l] 2Co 5:18 [m] Eph 1:10 [n] Eph 2:13
1:21 [o] Ro 5:10 [p] Eph 2:3 **1:22** [q] Ro 7:4
[r] Eph 5:27 **1:23** [s] Eph 3:17

from the hope[t] held out in the gospel. This is the gospel that you heard and that has been proclaimed to every creature under heaven,[u] and of which I, Paul, have become a servant.[v]

Paul's Labor for the Church

24Now I rejoice in what I am suffering for you, and I fill up in my flesh what is still lacking in regard to Christ's afflictions,[w] for the sake of his body, which is the church. 25I have become its servant[x] by the commission God gave me[y] to present to you the word of God in its fullness— 26the mystery[z] that has been kept hidden for ages and generations, but is now disclosed to the Lord's people. 27To them God has chosen to make known[a] among the Gentiles the glorious riches of this mystery, which is Christ in you, the hope of glory.

28He is the one we proclaim, admonishing[b] and teaching everyone with all wisdom,[c] so that we may present everyone fully mature[d] in Christ. 29To this end I strenuously[e] contend[f] with all the energy Christ so powerfully works in me.[g]

2 I want you to know how hard I am contending[h] for you and for those at Laodicea,[i] and for all who have not met me personally. 2My goal is that they may be encouraged in heart[j] and united in love, so that they may have the full riches of complete understanding, in order that they may know the mystery of God, namely, Christ, 3in whom are hidden all the treasures of wisdom and knowledge.[k] 4I tell you this so that no one may deceive you by fine-sounding arguments.[l] 5For though I am absent from you in body, I am present with you in spirit[m] and delight to see how disciplined[n] you are and how firm[o] your faith in Christ is.

Spiritual Fullness in Christ

6So then, just as you received Christ Jesus as Lord,[p] continue to live your lives in him, 7rooted[q] and built up in him, strengthened in the faith as you were taught, and overflowing with thankfulness.

8See to it that no one takes you captive through hollow and deceptive philosophy,[r] which depends on human tradition and the elemental spiritual forces[a] of this world[s] rather than on Christ.

9For in Christ all the fullness of the Deity lives in bodily form, 10and in Christ you have been brought to fullness. He is the head[t] over every power and authority. 11In him you were also circumcised[u] with a circumcision not performed by human hands. Your whole self ruled by the flesh[b][v] was put off when you were circumcised by[c] Christ, 12having been buried with him in baptism, in which you were also raised with him[w] through your faith in the working of God, who raised him from the dead.[x]

---

[a] *8* Or *the basic principles;* also in verse 20
[b] *11* In contexts like this, the Greek word for *flesh* (*sarx*) refers to the sinful state of human beings, often presented as a power in opposition to the Spirit; also in verse 13.
[c] *11* Or *put off in the circumcision of*

---

work of Christ on their behalf. ***every creature under heaven.*** Paul uses this exaggeration to illustrate the rapid spread of the gospel. Compare Acts 17:6 where the apostles are said to have turned the world upside down, even though their ministry, up to that point, had been limited to a small portion of the eastern Mediterranean region.

1:24 ***what I am suffering for you.*** Paul is making the point that a Christian will endure the sufferings that Christ would be enduring if He were still in the world (2 Cor. 1:5; 4:11).

1:26–27 ***mystery.*** In Greek pagan religions, a mystery was a secret teaching reserved for a few spiritual teachers who had been initiated into an inner circle. Paul uses the word to refer to knowledge that had been "hidden for ages and generations" but was now being revealed by God. The mystery is that Christ now lives within Gentile believers.

2:1 ***Laodicea.*** It was a sister city of Colosse about 11 miles away. The two churches were to share their letters from Paul.

2:2–3 ***may know of the mystery of God.*** Paul reminds the Colossians that true knowledge will be acknowledged by bringing people together in Christian love in the church. The Gnostics thought only certain "knowledgeable" people could join their elite group; Paul teaches that every believer has access to complete wisdom found in Christ.

2:4 ***fine-sounding arguments.*** Some texts translate this "philosophy." This verse has been used at times to teach that Christians should not study or read philosophy. This is not Paul's meaning. Paul himself was adept at philosophy, evidenced by his interaction with the Stoic and Epicurean philosophers in Athens (Acts 17:1–34). Paul was warning the believers not to be taken in by any philosophy that does not conform to a proper knowledge of Christ. The false teachers at Colosse had combined worldly philosophies with the gospel.

2:9 ***all the fullness of the Deity lives in bodily form.*** In this verse Paul clearly proclaims the incarnation, the fact that God became a man bodily. This contradicts the Gnostic idea of the inherent evil of physical bodies and the claim that Jesus is merely a spirit.

2:10 ***you have been brought to fullness.*** Paul emphasizes the sufficiency of Christ in order to refute the Gnostics and the Judaizers who respectively believed that special knowledge or works were necessary to make a Christian complete.

2:12–13 ***buried with him in baptism.*** Baptism is the symbol of the believer's association with Christ's death on the cross. Water baptism itself does not

1:23 [t] ver 5 [u] Ro 10:18 [v] ver 25; 1Co 3:5 **1:24** [w] 2Co 1:5 **1:25** [x] ver 23 [y] Eph 3:2 **1:26** [z] Ro 16:25 **1:27** [a] Mt 13:11 **1:28** [b] Col 3:16 [c] 1Co 2:6,7 [d] Eph 5:27 **1:29** [e] 1Co 15:10 [f] Col 2:1 [g] Eph 1:19 **2:1** [h] Col 1:29; 4:12 [i] Rev 1:11 **2:2** [j] Col 4:8 **2:3** [k] Ro 11:33; 1Co 1:24,30 **2:4** [l] Ro 16:18 **2:5** [m] 1Th 2:17 [n] 1Co 14:40 [o] 1Pe 5:9 **2:6** [p] Col 1:10 **2:7** [q] Eph 3:17 **2:8** [r] 1Ti 6:20 [s] Gal 4:3 **2:10** [t] Eph 1:22 **2:11** [u] Ro 2:29; Php 3:3 [v] Gal 5:24 **2:12** [w] Ro 6:5 [x] Ac 2:24

13When you were dead in your sins[y] and
in the uncircumcision of your flesh, God
made you[a] alive with Christ. He forgave us
all our sins, 14having canceled the charge
of our legal indebtedness,[z] which stood
against us and condemned us; he has tak-
en it away, nailing it to the cross.[a] 15And
having disarmed the powers and authorities,[b] he made a public spectacle of them,
triumphing over them[c] by the cross.[b]

Freedom From Human Rules

16Therefore do not let anyone judge you[d]
by what you eat or drink,[e] or with regard
to a religious festival,[f] a New Moon celebration[g] or a Sabbath day.[h] 17These are a
shadow of the things that were to come;[i]
the reality, however, is found in Christ.
18Do not let anyone who delights in false
humility[j] and the worship of angels dis-
qualify you.[k] Such a person also goes into
great detail about what they have seen;
they are puffed up with idle notions by
their unspiritual mind. 19They have lost
connection with the head,[l] from whom the
whole body, supported and held together
by its ligaments and sinews, grows as God
causes it to grow.[m]
20Since you died with Christ to the elemental spiritual forces of this world,[n] why,
as though you still belonged to the world,
do you submit to its rules:[o] 21"Do not handle! Do not taste! Do not touch!"? 22These
rules, which have to do with things that are
all destined to perish[p] with use, are based
on merely human commands and teachings.[q] 23Such regulations indeed have an
appearance of wisdom, with their self-im-
posed worship, their false humility and
their harsh treatment of the body, but they
lack any value in restraining sensual indulgence.

Living as Those Made Alive in Christ

3 Since, then, you have been raised with
Christ, set your hearts on things above,
where Christ is, seated at the right hand
of God. 2Set your minds on things above,
not on earthly things.[r] 3For you died,[s] and
your life is now hidden with Christ in God.
4When Christ, who is your[c] life, appears,[t]
then you also will appear with him in
glory.[u]
5Put to death, therefore, whatever belongs to your earthly nature: sexual immorality, impurity, lust, evil desires and
greed,[v] which is idolatry.[w] 6Because of
these, the wrath of God[x] is coming.[d] 7You
used to walk in these ways, in the life you
once lived.[y] 8But now you must also rid
yourselves[z] of all such things as these:
anger, rage, malice, slander,[a] and filthy
language from your lips.[b] 9Do not lie to
each other,[c] since you have taken off your
old self with its practices 10and have put
on the new self, which is being renewed[d]
in knowledge in the image of its Creator.[e]
11Here there is no Gentile or Jew,[f] circumcised or uncircumcised,[g] barbarian, Scythian, slave or free,[h] but Christ is all,[i] and is
in all.
12Therefore, as God's chosen people,
holy and dearly loved, clothe yourselves

[a] *13* Some manuscripts *us* [b] *15* Or *them in him* [c] *4* Some manuscripts *our* [d] *6* Some early manuscripts *coming on those who are disobedient*

---

bring forgiveness of sins, but Paul uses the rite to help explain the work of the Spirit. The early church would never have understood the idea of an unbaptized Christian.

2:15 ***powers and authorities.*** These words allude to Satan and the fallen angels. Paul is describing Christ's victory on the cross over the powers that opposed Him and that were against God's faithful people. To describe this victory, Paul uses the spectacle of the military triumph, when prisoners of war were stripped and paraded before the populace behind the conquering general.

2:16–19 ***false humility.*** People who do not champion salvation in Christ alone often appear to be humble. But their search for a new spiritual experience or advocacy of some work as necessary for salvation is actually human pride. They do not want to submit to God's plan of salvation.

2:20–23 ***submit to its rules.*** Since believers have been released from ritualistic observances, why should they let others bind them down again (Rom. 6:3–14)? No human work can be added to the merit of Christ's death. His work on the cross is the only acceptable work in God's eyes.

3:1–4 ***Set your minds on things above.*** The false teachers were instructing the Colossians to concentrate on temporal observances; in contrast, Paul instructs them to concentrate on the eternal realities of heaven. The Greek verb for *set* emphasizes an ongoing decision. Christians must continually discipline themselves to focus on eternal realities instead of the temporal realities of this earth.

3:9–10 ***old self ... new self.*** These two terms do not refer to the Christian's fleshly and spiritual natures. Instead, Paul describes our former unredeemed life as the old man and our life as God's child as the new man. The new man has the image of the new creation in Christ, just as the old man bears the image of our fallen nature. The old man is under an old master, Satan, while the new man has a new master, the Spirit of God living within.

3:11 ***barbarian.*** In the Roman Empire a person who did not speak Greek was despised. ***Scythian.*** An uncultured person who came from the area around the Black Sea.

2:13 [y] Eph 2:1,5 **2:14** [z] Eph 2:15 [a] 1Pe 2:24
2:15 [b] Eph 6:12 [c] Lk 10:18 **2:16** [d] Ro 14:3,4 [e] Ro 14:17
[f] Ro 14:5 [g] 1Ch 23:31 [h] Gal 4:10 **2:17** [i] Heb 8:5
2:18 [j] ver 23 [k] Php 3:14 **2:19** [l] Eph 1:22 [m] Eph 4:16
2:20 [n] Gal 4:3,9 [o] ver 14,16
2:22 [p] 1Co 6:13 [q] Isa 29:13; Mt 15:9; Titus 1:14
3:2 [r] Php 3:19,20 **3:3** [s] Ro 6:2; 2Co 5:14 **3:4** [t] 1Co 1:7
[u] 1Pe 1:13; 1Jn 3:2 **3:5** [v] Eph 5:3 [w] Eph 5:5
3:6 [x] Ro 1:18 **3:7** [y] Eph 2:2 **3:8** [z] Eph 4:22 [a] Eph 4:31
[b] Eph 4:29 **3:9** [c] Eph 4:22,25 **3:10** [d] Ro 12:2; Eph 4:23
[e] Eph 2:10 **3:11** [f] Ro 10:12 [g] 1Co 7:19 [h] Gal 3:28
[i] Eph 1:23

with compassion, kindness, humility,[j]
gentleness and patience.[k] 13Bear with each
other[l] and forgive one another if any of
you has a grievance against someone. Forgive as the Lord forgave you.[m] 14And over
all these virtues put on love,[n] which binds
them all together in perfect unity.[o]
15Let the peace of Christ[p] rule in your
hearts, since as members of one body you
were called to peace. And be thankful.
16Let the message of Christ[q] dwell among
you richly as you teach and admonish one
another with all wisdom[r] through psalms,
hymns, and songs from the Spirit, singing to God with gratitude in your hearts.[s]
17And whatever you do,[t] whether in word
or deed, do it all in the name of the Lord
Jesus, giving thanks[u] to God the Father
through him.

Instructions for Christian Households

18Wives, submit yourselves to your husbands,[v] as is fitting in the Lord.
19Husbands, love your wives and do not
be harsh with them.
20Children, obey your parents in everything, for this pleases the Lord.
21Fathers,[a] do not embitter your children, or they will become discouraged.
22Slaves, obey your earthly masters in
everything; and do it, not only when their
eye is on you and to curry their favor, but
with sincerity of heart and reverence for
the Lord. 23Whatever you do, work at it
with all your heart, as working for the
Lord, not for human masters, 24since you
know that you will receive an inheritance[w]
from the Lord as a reward. It is the Lord
Christ you are serving. 25Anyone who does
wrong will be repaid for their wrongs, and
there is no favoritism.[x]

4 Masters, provide your slaves with what
is right and fair, because you know that
you also have a Master in heaven.

Further Instructions

2Devote yourselves to prayer,[y] being
watchful and thankful. 3And pray for us,
too, that God may open a door[z] for our message, so that we may proclaim the mystery
of Christ, for which I am in chains.[a] 4Pray
that I may proclaim it clearly, as I should.
5Be wise[b] in the way you act toward outsiders;[c] make the most of every opportunity.[d] 6Let your conversation be always full
of grace,[e] seasoned with salt,[f] so that you
may know how to answer everyone.[g]

Final Greetings

7Tychicus[h] will tell you all the news
about me. He is a dear brother, a faithful
minister and fellow servant[b][i] in the Lord.
8I am sending him to you for the express
purpose that you may know about our[c]
circumstances and that he may encourage
your hearts.[j] 9He is coming with Onesimus,[k] our faithful and dear brother, who is
one of you. They will tell you everything
that is happening here.
10My fellow prisoner Aristarchus[l] sends
you his greetings, as does Mark, the cousin
of Barnabas.[m] (You have received instructions about him; if he comes to you, welcome him.) 11Jesus, who is called Justus,
also sends greetings. These are the only
Jews[d] among my co-workers for the kingdom of God, and they have proved a comfort to me. 12Epaphras,[n] who is one of you
and a servant of Christ Jesus, sends greetings. He is always wrestling in prayer for
you,[o] that you may stand firm in all the will
of God, mature[p] and fully assured. 13I vouch
for him that he is working hard for you
and for those at Laodicea[q] and Hierapolis.
14Our dear friend Luke,[r] the doctor, and Demas[s] send greetings. 15Give my greetings

[a] 21 Or *Parents* [b] 7 Or *slave*; also in verse 12
[c] 8 Some manuscripts *that he may know about your* [d] 11 Greek *only ones of the circumcision group*

3:18–23 *submit.* See notes on Ephesians 5:19–31.
3:22–25 *receive an inheritance from the Lord.* The strong motivation to serve someone well is found in the future reward that Christ gives to those who are faithful in this service. We normally think we receive eternal rewards for spiritual practices like reading the Bible, prayer, or evangelism. Here, Paul asserts that all work done to the honor of Christ will bring an eternal reward (1:22–23; 2:18).
4:5 *Be wise in the way you act toward outsiders.* Early Christians were often viewed with suspicion, distrust, and disdain. They were considered atheists because they would not worship the gods of Rome and Greece. Many labeled them as unpatriotic because they would not burn incense before the image of the emperor. Some even accused the early Christians of participating in orgies because of their talk of "love feasts" (Jude 12). Others harbored suspicions that Christians were really cannibals who ate and drank the blood and body of the Lord. With such misrepresentations of Christian belief and practice running rampant, it was very important for misunderstandings to be dispelled by the virtuous and impeccable lives of Christian believers.
4:9 *Onesimus.* This slave of Philemon probably accompanied Tychicus to Colosse. Paul's letter to Philemon would have been carried along with the letter to the Colossians. It dealt with a personal situation between Onesimus and his master.
4:10–15 *Mark.* This is the author of the Gospel of Mark.

3:12 [j] Php 2:3 [k] 2Co 6:6; Gal 5:22,23 **3:13** [l] Eph 4:2 [m] Eph 4:32 **3:14** [n] 1Co 13:1-13 [o] Eph 4:3 **3:15** [p] Jn 14:27 **3:16** [q] Ro 10:17 [r] Col 1:28 [s] Eph 5:19 **3:17** [t] 1Co 10:31 [u] Eph 5:20 **3:18** [v] Eph 5:22 **3:24** [w] Ac 20:32 **3:25** [x] Ac 10:34 **4:2** [y] Lk 18:1 **4:3** [z] Ac 14:27 [a] Eph 6:19,20 **4:5** [b] Eph 5:15 [c] Mk 4:11 [d] Eph 5:16 **4:6** [e] Eph 4:29 [f] Mk 9:50 [g] 1Pe 3:15 **4:7** [h] Ac 20:4 [i] Eph 6:21,22 **4:8** [j] Eph 6:21,22 **4:9** [k] Phm 10 **4:10** [l] Ac 19:29 [m] Ac 4:36 **4:12** [n] Col 1:7; Phm 23 [o] Ro 15:30 [p] 1Co 2:6 **4:13** [q] Col 2:1 **4:14** [r] 2Ti 4:11; Phm 24

to the brothers and sisters at Laodicea, and
to Nympha and the church in her house.[t]
16 After this letter has been read to you,
see that it is also read[u] in the church of the
Laodiceans and that you in turn read the
letter from Laodicea.

17 Tell Archippus:[v] "See to it that you
complete the ministry you have received
in the Lord."[w]
18 I, Paul, write this greeting in my own
hand.[x] Remember[y] my chains. Grace be
with you.[z]

4:18 ***this greeting in my own hand.*** The apostle dictated his letters to a secretary, but it was his custom to give a greeting in his own handwriting at the end (2 Thess. 2:1; 3:17). This served to personalize and authenticate the letter.

4:14 [s] 2Ti 4:10 **4:15** [t] Ro 16:5 **4:16** [u] 2Th 3:14 **4:17** [v] Phm 2 [w] 2Ti 4:5 **4:18** [x] 1Co 16:21 [y] Heb 13:3 [z] 1Ti 6:21; 2Ti 4:22; Titus 3:15; Heb 13:25

1 THESSALONIANS

▶ **AUTHOR:** First Thessalonians went unchallenged as a Pauline epistle until the nineteenth century, when radical critics claimed that its lack of doctrinal content made its authenticity suspect. But this is a weak objection on two counts: (1) the proportion of doctrinal teaching in Paul's epistles varies widely, and (2) 4:13–5:11 is a foundational passage for New Testament eschatology (future events). Paul had quickly grounded the Thessalonians in Christian doctrine, and the only problematic issue when this epistle was written concerned the matter of Christ's return. Paul planted the Thessalonian church on his second missionary journey, and wrote this epistle as a response to a good report regarding the church from Timothy in A.D. 51.

▶ **TIME:** c. A.D. 51 ▶ **KEY VERSES:** 1 Thess. 3:12–13

▶ **THEME:** In that Paul's time in Thessalonica was cut short, Paul used these letters to clarify some of his teaching. After a review of the basics, the primary issues covered in 1 Thessalonians are what happens when people die and the timing of the second coming of Christ. In that there were so many people around at that time that had seen Jesus, the promise of His return was met with anxious expectation. We tend to be blasé about it because we have watched so many predictions concerning the end times come and go, but this book will help us to sharpen and renew our expectations.

---

1 Paul, Silas[a] and Timothy,[a]

To the church of the Thessalonians[b] in God the Father and the Lord Jesus Christ:

Grace and peace to you.[c]

Thanksgiving for the Thessalonians' Faith

2We always thank God for all of you[d]
and continually mention you in our
prayers. 3We remember before our God
and Father your work produced by faith,[e]
your labor prompted by love, and your
endurance inspired by hope in our Lord
Jesus Christ.
4For we know, brothers and sisters[b]
loved by God, that he has chosen you, 5because our gospel[f] came to you not simply
with words but also with power, with the
Holy Spirit and deep conviction. You know
how we lived among you for your sake.

[a] *1* Greek *Silvanus*, a variant of *Silas* [b] *4* The Greek word for *brothers and sisters* (*adelphoi*) refers here to believers, both men and women, as part of God's family; also in 2:1, 9, 14, 17; 3:7; 4:1, 10, 13; 5:1, 4, 12, 14, 25, 27.

1:1 ***Silas.*** After Paul had separated from Barnabas (Acts 15:36–40), Silas became Paul's traveling companion on the second missionary journey, and he may have served as Paul's secretary. He was a leader of the Jerusalem church (Acts 15:22–23), and he accompanied Paul and Barnabas to Antioch to deliver the decree of the Jerusalem council (Acts 15:22–23). He and Paul suffered a beating at Philippi (Acts 16:22–24), and he had helped found the church at Thessalonica (Acts 17:1–4). ***Timothy.*** Timothy was also with Paul on the second missionary journey. Paul considered him like a son and loved him dearly (Acts 16:3; 1 Tim. 1:2). This letter is a response to Timothy's report from the church in Thessalonica. ***To the church.*** The Greek word *ekklçsia* was a familiar term meaning any gathering or assembly. In its New Testament usage this word calls to mind the relationship of believers in Thessalonica as a body.

1:3 ***endurance inspired by hope.*** The believers at Thessalonica fixed their hope solidly on the return of Jesus Christ (v. 10). Notice that each of the virtues has Christ as its object. Jesus is constantly the focus. This is a good standard for evaluating any Christian service.

1:5 ***our gospel.*** Paul had preached the gospel to them clearly when he was with them. For three weeks he had "reasoned with them from the Scriptures, explaining and proving that the Messiah had to suffer and rise from the dead. 'This Jesus I am proclaiming to you is the Messiah,' he said" (Acts 17:2–3). This message was far different from the messianic expectations that Paul knew from his own training as a Pharisee. The Jews of that day were not looking for a suffering savior but a conquering champion.

1:5 Sharing Our Faith—In order to share our faith successfully, we must keep the following rules in mind:

1:1 [a] Ac 16:1; 2Th 1:1 [b] Ac 17:1 [c] Ro 1:7 **1:2** [d] Ro 1:8 **1:3** [e] 2Th 1:11 **1:5** [f] 2Th 2:14

6You became imitators of us[g] and of the Lord, for you welcomed the message in the midst of severe suffering[h] with the joy given by the Holy Spirit.[i] 7And so you became a model to all the believers in Macedonia and Achaia. 8The Lord's message rang out from you not only in Macedonia and Achaia—your faith in God has become known everywhere.[j] Therefore we do not need to say anything about it, 9for they themselves report what kind of reception you gave us. They tell how you turned to God from idols[k] to serve the living and true God, 10and to wait for his Son from heaven, whom he raised from the dead[l]—Jesus, who rescues us from the coming wrath.[m]

Paul's Ministry in Thessalonica

2 You know, brothers and sisters, that our visit to you[n] was not without results. 2We had previously suffered[o] and been treated outrageously in Philippi, as you know, but with the help of our God we dared to tell you his gospel in the face of strong opposition. 3For the appeal we make does not spring from error or impure motives,[p] nor are we trying to trick you. 4On the contrary, we speak as those approved by God to be entrusted with the gospel.[q] We are not trying to please people[r] but God, who tests our hearts. 5You know we never used flattery, nor did we put on a mask to cover up greed[s]—God is our witness.[t] 6We were not looking for praise from people, not from you or anyone else, even though as apostles[u] of Christ we could have asserted our authority. 7Instead, we were like young children[a] among you.

Just as a nursing mother cares for her children,[v] 8so we cared for you. Because we loved you so much, we were delighted to share with you not only the gospel of God but our lives as well.[w] 9Surely you remember, brothers and sisters, our toil and hardship; we worked[x] night and day in order not to be a burden to anyone[y] while we preached the gospel of God to you. 10You are witnesses,[z] and so is God, of how holy,[a] righteous and blameless we were among you who believed. 11For you know that we dealt with each of you as a father deals with his own children,[b] 12encouraging, comforting and urging you to live lives worthy[c] of God, who calls you into his kingdom and glory.

13And we also thank God continually[d] because, when you received the word of God,[e] which you heard from us, you accepted it not as a human word, but as it actually is, the word of God, which is indeed at work in you who believe. 14For you, brothers and sisters, became imitators of God's churches in Judea,[f] which are in Christ Jesus: You suffered from your own people[g] the same things those churches suffered from the Jews 15who killed the Lord Jesus[h] and the prophets[i] and also drove us out. They displease God and are hostile to everyone 16in their effort to keep us from speaking to the Gentiles[j] so that they may be saved. In this way they always heap up their sins to the limit.[k] The wrath of God has come upon them at last.[b]

---

[a] 7 Some manuscripts *were gentle* [b] 16 Or *them fully*

First, we must be clean vessels. God reminds Isaiah the prophet of this: "Come out from it and be pure, you who carry the articles of the LORD's house." (Is. 52:11). David prays for forgiveness and cleansing, and a willing spirit. He states, "Then I will teach transgressors your ways, so that sinners shall turn back to you" (Ps. 51:13).

We must be able to clearly give out the simple facts of the gospel without getting bogged down with profound theological concepts. Philip the evangelist demonstrated how to do this when he dealt with the Ethiopian eunuch in the desert. "Then Philip began with that very passage of Scripture and told him the good news about Jesus" (Acts 8:35).

We must avoid arguments and stick to the basic issues of man's sin and Christ's sacrifice.

We must use the Word of God. Paul's tremendous success as an evangelist can be linked directly to his constant use of God's Word (Acts 17:2; 18:28; 2 Tim. 2:15; 3:14–17).

We must depend upon the Spirit of God (John 3:15; Acts 6:10; 1 Cor. 2:4).

1:6 *imitators of us and of the Lord.* As we focus on Jesus we will reflect His image to others (2 Cor. 3:18).

1:8 *rang out.* Since Thessalonica was a port city on the much-traveled Egnatian Way, those who saw the virtuous life and persistent faith of the Thessalonican Christians would spread the word throughout the entire region.

1:10 *rescues us from the coming wrath.* Because Christ endured God's wrath at Calvary, all who are in Christ will escape that wrath. They have nothing to fear.

2:2 *in Philippi.* Paul and Silas were beaten and put in the stocks in Philippi (Acts 16:22–24).

2:5 *flattery.* Far from flattering, Paul preached boldly that everyone was a sinner who needed to be saved by the grace of God.

2:9 *toil.* This word indicates strenuous work that produces weariness. Paul made tents to provide for his financial needs (Acts 18:3), showing that his ministry was motivated by an unselfish desire to promote the well-being of others rather than to advance his own needs.

2:13 *actually is.* Gentile Christians in Thessalonica could contrast the pure Word of God, with its transforming effect, with the immoral pagan religions, which only perverted people even more. Likewise, Jewish believers could contrast the love and grace of God in the gospel to the legalism and pride often produced by the Jewish religion.

2:16 *always heap up their sins to the limit.* The

1:6 [g] 1Co 4:16 [h] Ac 17:5-10 [i] Ac 13:52 **1:8** [j] Ro 1:8; 10:18
1:9 [k] 1Co 12:2; Gal 4:8 **1:10** [l] Ac 2:24 [m] Ro 5:9
2:1 [n] 1Th 1:5,9 **2:2** [o] Ac 16:22; Php 1:30 **2:3** [p] 2Co 2:17
2:4 [q] Gal 2:7 [r] Gal 1:10 **2:5** [s] Ac 20:33 [t] Ro 1:9
2:6 [u] 1Co 9:1,2 **2:7** [v] ver 11 **2:8** [w] 2Co 12:15; 1Jn 3:16
2:9 [x] Ac 18:3 [y] 2Th 3:8 **2:10** [z] 1Th 1:5 [a] 2Co 1:12
2:11 [b] ver 7; 1Co 4:14 **2:12** [c] Eph 4:1 **2:13** [d] 1Th 1:2
[e] Heb 4:12 **2:14** [f] Gal 1:22 [g] Ac 17:5; 2Th 1:4
2:15 [h] Ac 2:23 [i] Mt 5:12 **2:16** [j] Ac 13:45,50 [k] Mt 23:32

Paul's Longing to See the Thessalonians

17But, brothers and sisters, when we were orphaned by being separated from you for a short time (in person, not in thought),[l] out of our intense longing we made every effort to see you.[m] 18For we wanted to come to you—certainly I, Paul, did, again and again—but Satan[n] blocked our way.[o] 19For what is our hope, our joy, or the crown[p] in which we will glory[q] in the presence of our Lord Jesus when he comes?[r] Is it not you? 20Indeed, you are our glory[s] and joy.

3 So when we could stand it no longer,[t] we thought it best to be left by ourselves in Athens.[u] 2We sent Timothy, who is our brother and co-worker in God's service in spreading the gospel of Christ, to strengthen and encourage you in your faith, 3so that no one would be unsettled by these trials. For you know quite well that we are destined for them.[v] 4In fact, when we were with you, we kept telling you that we would be persecuted. And it turned out that way, as you well know.[w] 5For this reason, when I could stand it no longer,[x] I sent to find out about your faith. I was afraid that in some way the tempter[y] had tempted you and that our labors might have been in vain.[z]

Timothy's Encouraging Report

6But Timothy has just now come to us from you[a] and has brought good news about your faith and love.[b] He has told us that you always have pleasant memories of us and that you long to see us, just as we also long to see you. 7Therefore, brothers and sisters, in all our distress and persecution we were encouraged about you because of your faith. 8For now we really live, since you are standing firm[c] in the Lord. 9How can we thank God enough for you[d] in return for all the joy we have in the presence of our God because of you? 10Night and day we pray[e] most earnestly that we may see you again[f] and supply what is lacking in your faith.

11Now may our God and Father himself and our Lord Jesus clear the way for us to come to you. 12May the Lord make your love increase and overflow for each other[g] and for everyone else, just as ours does for you. 13May he strengthen your hearts so that you will be blameless[h] and holy in the presence of our God and Father when our Lord Jesus comes[i] with all his holy ones.

Living to Please God

4 As for other matters, brothers and sisters,[j] we instructed you how to live in order to please God,[k] as in fact you are living. Now we ask you and urge you in the Lord Jesus to do this more and more. 2For you know what instructions we gave you by the authority of the Lord Jesus.

3It is God's will that you should be sanctified: that you should avoid sexual immorality;[l] 4that each of you should learn to control your own body[a][m] in a way that is holy and honorable, 5not in passionate lust[n] like the pagans,[o] who do not know God; 6and that in this matter no one should wrong or take advantage of a brother or sister.[b][p] The Lord will punish all those who commit such sins,[q] as we told you and warned you before. 7For God did not call us to be impure, but to live a holy life.[r] 8Therefore, anyone who rejects this instruction does not reject a human being but God, the very God who gives you his Holy Spirit.[s]

---

[a] 4 Or *learn to live with your own wife;* or *learn to acquire a wife* [b] 6 The Greek word for *brother or sister* (*adelphos*) refers here to a believer, whether man or woman, as part of God's family.

---

implication is that God will allow a nation, group, or individual to go only so far in sin before He brings judgment upon them (Gen. 15:16).

2:18 *Satan blocked our way.* Satan has a vested interest in hindering the spread of the gospel, and we may be sure that when we are engaged in the Lord's work, we will experience spiritual attacks and opposition of various kinds.

3:1 *Athens.* When forced to leave Thessalonica, Paul and Silas went to Berea, the next city west of Thessalonica. The Thessalonian Jews who had opposed Paul learned that he was at Berea, and went there also to stir up opposition. Paul's friends then escorted him south to Athens (Acts 17:13 – 15).

3:3 *unsettled by these trials.* The Bible teaches that those who live godly lives should expect persecution (2 Tim. 3:12). In fact, Christ warned His disciples that they would experience the same type of rejection He had experienced (John 15:18 – 21). But such suffering should not make us depressed. Instead we should rejoice that we are allied with His name (Matt. 5:10 – 12).

3:12 *increase and overflow for each other.* Christ had told His disciples that His followers would be identified by their love for one another (John 13:35).

3:13 *all his holy ones.* The word holy ones means "saints" or "those set apart." It can be used to apply to believers, or to holy angels. Angels will participate in the second coming (4:16; Jude 14; Rev. 19:14).

4:1 *how to live.* The Christian life not only begins with faith, but it continues as a daily walk of faith. Christians are not to live like unsaved Gentiles (Eph. 4:17), instead they are to walk worthy of their calling from God (Eph. 4:1). John exhorts Christians to walk in the light, that is, in the revealed will of God (1 John 1:7).

4:3 *avoid sexual immorality.* A major problem for the early church was maintaining sexual purity (1 Cor. 5:1, 9 – 11). Pagan religions often included sexual orgies as part of their rites of worship, and temple

2:17 [l] 1Co 5:3; Col 2:5 [m] 1Th 3:10 **2:18** [n] Mt 4:10 [o] Ro 1:13; 15:22 **2:19** [p] Php 4:1 [q] 2Co 1:14 [r] Mt 16:27; 1Th 3:13 **2:20** [s] 2Co 1:14 **3:1** [t] ver 5 [u] Ac 17:15 **3:3** [v] Ac 9:16; 14:22 **3:4** [w] 1Th 2:14 **3:5** [x] ver 1 [y] Mt 4:3 [z] Gal 2:2; Php 2:16 **3:6** [a] Ac 18:5 [b] 1Th 1:3 **3:8** [c] 1Co 16:13 **3:9** [d] 1Th 1:2 **3:10** [e] 2Ti 1:3 [f] 1Th 2:17 **3:12** [g] 1Th 4:9, 10 **3:13** [h] 1Co 1:8 [i] 1Th 2:19 **4:1** [j] 2Co 13:11 [k] 2Co 5:9 **4:3** [l] 1Co 6:18 **4:4** [m] 1Co 7:2, 9 **4:5** [n] Ro 1:26 [o] Eph 4:17 **4:6** [p] 1Co 6:8 [q] Heb 13:4 **4:7** [r] Lev 11:44; 1Pe 1:15 **4:8** [s] Ro 5:5; Gal 4:6

9Now about your love for one another[t] we do not need to write to you,[u] for you yourselves have been taught by God to love each other.[v] 10And in fact, you do love all of God's family throughout Macedonia.[w] Yet we urge you, brothers and sisters, to do so more and more,[x] 11and to make it your ambition to lead a quiet life: You should mind your own business and work with your hands,[y] just as we told you, 12so that your daily life may win the respect of outsiders[z] and so that you will not be dependent on anybody.

Believers Who Have Died

13Brothers and sisters, we do not want you to be uninformed about those who sleep in death, so that you do not grieve like the rest of mankind, who have no hope.[a] 14For we believe that Jesus died and rose again, and so we believe that God will bring with Jesus those who have fallen asleep in him.[b] 15According to the Lord's word, we tell you that we who are still alive, who are left until the coming of the Lord, will certainly not precede those who have fallen asleep.[c] 16For the Lord himself will come down from heaven, with a loud command, with the voice of the archangel and with the trumpet call of God,[d] and the dead in Christ will rise first.[e] 17After that, we who are still alive and are left[f] will be caught up together with them in the clouds[g] to meet the Lord in the air. And so we will be with the Lord[h] forever. 18Therefore encourage one another with these words.

The Day of the Lord

5 Now, brothers and sisters, about times and dates[i] we do not need to write to you,[j] 2for you know very well that the day of the Lord[k] will come like a thief in the night.[l] 3While people are saying, "Peace and safety," destruction will come on them suddenly, as labor pains on a pregnant woman, and they will not escape.

4But you, brothers and sisters, are not in darkness[m] so that this day should surprise you like a thief. 5You are all children of the light and children of the day. We do not belong to the night or to the darkness. 6So then, let us not be like others, who are asleep,[n] but let us be awake and sober. 7For those who sleep, sleep at night, and those who get drunk, get drunk at night.[o] 8But since we belong to the day, let us be sober, putting on faith and love as a breastplate,[p] and the hope of salvation[q] as a helmet.[r] 9For God did not appoint us to suffer wrath but to receive salvation through our Lord Jesus Christ.[s] 10He died for us so that, whether

---

prostitutes were dedicated to various gods. In contrast, Christianity taught that the body is God's temple (1 Cor. 6:18–20). The body should be honored as created by God and should be sanctified in keeping with its holy purpose.

4:10 ***do so more and more.*** These believers already had a good record of loving one another, but Paul desired that love to increase. This was the commandment of Jesus (John 13:34–35; 15:12,17) and is an important basis of evangelism. In a world that is filled with self-serving individuals, the genuine love of Christians should attract others to the faith.

4:11 ***ambition to lead a quiet life.*** This does not refer to a lack of activity but rather to an inner quietness and peace befitting the Christian faith (2 Thess. 3:12; 1 Tim. 2:11). ***work with your hands.*** Usually people who are busy running other people's affairs do not run their own affairs well. A Christian's house should be in order as a testimony to others.

4:14 ***those who have fallen asleep in him.*** Some believe this phrase indicates that departed Christians are unconscious until the second coming. But the Bible indicates that to be absent from our present body is to be present with the Lord Jesus (5:10; 2 Cor. 5:8; Phil. 1:23).

4:16 ***come down from heaven, with a loud command.*** Accompanying the descent of Christ from heaven will be the voice of an archangel, perhaps Michael, who is portrayed as the leader of the army of God (Dan. 10:13,21; Jude 9; Rev. 12:7–9). The only other angel named in Scripture is Gabriel, who is given a prominent role as a messenger of God (Dan. 8:16; 9:21; Luke 1:19,26). ***the dead in Christ will rise.*** Clearly this will be a physical resurrection in which bodily existence will be restored, as confirmed in 1 Corinthians 15:51–53. The resurrected bodies of Christians will be like the body of Christ (1 John 3:2), incorruptible and immortal, and yet they will be bodies of flesh and bone (Luke 24:39–40; John 20:20,25,27).

4:17 ***caught up.*** The English word *rapture* comes from the Latin for "caught up."

5:2 ***the day of the Lord.*** This expression was familiar to those who knew the Hebrew Scriptures. The day of the Lord in the Old Testament was characterized by two phases: God's judgment against sinful people and God's eternal reign over His people. God's judgment will be a time of darkness and an expression of His wrath (Joel 2:1–2; Amos 5:18–20; Zeph. 1:14–15). His reign will also be a time of blessing (Is. 2:1–3; 11;1–9; 30:23–26; Zech. 14:1,7–11,20–21; Matt. 19:28; Acts 3:19–21).

5:4 ***not in darkness.*** Though the day of the Lord will overtake the unsaved world unexpectedly, it will not overtake Christians, because they will be looking forward to and expecting it. The fact that Christ could come at any moment should motivate unbelievers to accept His forgiveness, and believers to live daily for Him.

5:8 ***sober.*** A sober life is not only free from drunkenness, but awake to spiritual realities.

5:9 ***did not appoint us to suffer wrath.*** There will be wrath at the day of the Lord, but it will be God's wrath on the unbelieving world that has spurned and mocked Christ (Rev. 6:12–17).

4:9 [t] Ro 12:10 [u] 1Th 5:1 [v] Jn 13:34 **4:10** [w] 1Th 1:7 [x] 1Th 3:12 **4:11** [y] Eph 4:28; 2Th 3:10-12 **4:12** [z] Mk 4:11 **4:13** [a] Eph 2:12 **4:14** [b] 1Co 15:18 **4:15** [c] 1Co 15:52 **4:16** [d] Mt 24:31 [e] 1Co 15:23; 2Th 2:1 **4:17** [f] 1Co 15:52 [g] Ac 1:9; Rev 11:12 [h] Jn 12:26 **5:1** [i] Ac 1:7 [j] 1Th 4:9 **5:2** [k] 1Co 1:8 [l] 2Pe 3:10 **5:4** [m] Ac 26:18; 1Jn 2:8 **5:6** [n] Ro 13:11 **5:7** [o] Ac 2:15; 2Pe 2:13 **5:8** [p] Eph 6:14 [q] Ro 8:24 [r] Eph 6:17 **5:9** [s] 2Th 2:13, 14

we are awake or asleep, we may live together with him.[t] 11Therefore encourage
one another and build each other up, just
as in fact you are doing.

Final Instructions

12Now we ask you, brothers and sisters, to acknowledge those who work hard
among you, who care for you in the Lord[u]
and who admonish you. 13Hold them in
the highest regard in love because of their
work. Live in peace with each other.[v] 14And
we urge you, brothers and sisters, warn
those who are idle[w] and disruptive, encourage the disheartened, help the weak,[x]
be patient with everyone. 15Make sure that
nobody pays back wrong for wrong,[y] but
always strive to do what is good for each
other[z] and for everyone else.

16Rejoice always,[a] 17pray continually,
18give thanks in all circumstances; for this
is God's will for you in Christ Jesus.
19Do not quench the Spirit.[b] 20Do not
treat prophecies[c] with contempt 21but test
them all;[d] hold on to what is good, 22reject
every kind of evil.
23May God himself, the God of peace,[e]
sanctify you through and through. May
your whole spirit, soul and body be kept
blameless at the coming of our Lord Jesus
Christ. 24The one who calls you is faithful,[f]
and he will do it.

25Brothers and sisters, pray for us.[g]
26Greet all God's people with a holy kiss.[h]
27I charge you before the Lord to have this
letter read to all the brothers and sisters.[i]
28The grace of our Lord Jesus Christ be
with you.[j]

5:12 *Now we ask you.* Significantly, Paul combines prophecy with practical teachings for the Christian life. God never intended prophecy to just be a field for academic debate, but to be a truth that would provide believers hope and direction in their lives.
5:16 *Rejoice always.* Regardless of difficult circumstances, a Christian always has grounds for rejoicing. The Lord is a sovereign Ruler and will accomplish His purpose. Christian joy is not based on circumstances, but on a growing awareness of God and the certain future of eternal life with Christ (Rev. 21:1 – 7).
5:17 *pray continually.* To pray without ceasing seems impossible, but a person can develop an attitude and habit of constant prayer. No matter what else is going on, we should be aware of God's presence with us, and turn to Him with every thought and action.
5:23 *spirit, soul and body.* Every part of the Christian life should bear evidence that we are set apart as holy to God.
5:26 *a holy kiss.* A kiss was a customary greeting among friends (as it still is in some cultures), something like our modern handshake.

5:10 [t] 2Co 5:15 **5:12** [u] 1Ti 5:17; Heb 13:17 **5:13** [v] Mk 9:50 **5:14** [w] 2Th 3:6, 7, 11 [x] Ro 14:1 **5:15** [y] 1Pe 3:9 [z] Gal 6:10; Eph 4:32 **5:16** [a] Php 4:4 **5:19** [b] Eph 4:30 **5:20** [c] 1Co 14:1-40 **5:21** [d] 1Co 14:29; 1Jn 4:1 **5:23** [e] Ro 15:33 **5:24** [f] 1Co 1:9 **5:25** [g] Eph 6:19 **5:26** [h] Ro 16:16 **5:27** [i] Col 4:16 **5:28** [j] Ro 16:20

2 THESSALONIANS

▸ **AUTHOR:** The external attestation to the authenticity of 2 Thessalonians as a Pauline epistle is even stronger than that for 1 Thessalonians. Internally the vocabulary, style, and doctrinal content support the claims in 1:1 and 3:17 that it was written by Paul. This letter was probably written a few months after 1 Thessalonians, while Paul was still in Corinth with Silas and Timothy (1:1; Acts 18:5).

▸ **TIME:** C. A.D. 51 ▸ **KEY VERSES:** 2 Thess. 2:2 – 3

▸ **THEME:** This letter to the Thessalonians appears to have been written fairly soon after the first one. He provides some further clarification on some of the same issues he addressed in the first letter. There appears to still be some confusion about the events of the end times, which he clarifies. He also wisely encourages the believers in the basics he has taught them in his role as a caring pastor.

1 Paul, Silas[a] and Timothy,[a]

To the church of the Thessalonians in
God our Father and the Lord Jesus Christ:

2 Grace and peace to you from God the
Father and the Lord Jesus Christ.[b]

Thanksgiving and Prayer

3 We ought always to thank God for
you, brothers and sisters,[*b*] and rightly so,
because your faith is growing more and
more, and the love all of you have for one
another is increasing.[c] 4 Therefore, among
God's churches we boast[d] about your perseverance and faith[e] in all the persecutions
and trials you are enduring.[f]

5 All this is evidence[g] that God's judgment is right, and as a result you will be
counted worthy of the kingdom of God, for
which you are suffering. 6 God is just: He
will pay back trouble to those who trouble you[h] 7 and give relief to you who are
troubled, and to us as well. This will happen when the Lord Jesus is revealed from
heaven in blazing fire with his powerful
angels.[i] 8 He will punish those who do not
know God[j] and do not obey the gospel of
our Lord Jesus.[k] 9 They will be punished
with everlasting destruction[l] and shut out
from the presence of the Lord and from the
glory of his might[m] 10 on the day[n] he comes
to be glorified[o] in his holy people and to
be marveled at among all those who have
believed. This includes you, because you
believed our testimony to you.[p]

11 With this in mind, we constantly
pray for you, that our God may make you
worthy[q] of his calling, and that by his

[*a*] *1* Greek *Silvanus,* a variant of *Silas* [*b*] *3* The Greek word for *brothers and sisters (adelphoi)* refers here to believers, both men and women, as part of God's family; also in 2:1, 13, 15; 3:1, 6, 13.

1:1 ***Silas and Timothy.*** Silas had been Paul's traveling companion ever since the start of the second missionary journey. He had participated in the founding of the church at Thessalonica (Acts 17:1 – 4). Timothy also accompanied Paul on his second missionary journey. His report from the Thessalonian church had been the occasion for writing 1 Thessalonians (1 Thess. 3:6 – 8). ***To the church.*** The Greek word *ekklçsia* means "gathering" or "assembly."

1:5 ***counted worthy of the kingdom of God.*** If believers handle their persecutions properly, they will be counted worthy of great reward in the coming kingdom of God (Matt. 5:12; 1 Pet. 2:19 – 20). Christians are called to endure suffering in this world, for they will receive a far greater reward in the next (2 Tim. 2:12).

1:7 – 8 ***when the Lord Jesus is revealed.*** Presently the Lord Jesus is enthroned in glory at the right hand of the Father (John 17:5). Stephen saw this glory before he was martyred (Acts 7:55 – 56), but one day, and it may be soon, "every eye will see him" (Rev. 1:7). ***in blazing fire.*** Some believe that this is the fulfillment of John the Baptist's prophecy of the One who would "baptize with ... fire" (Matt. 3:11 – 12; Luke 3:16 – 17).

1:8 ***do not know . . . do not obey.*** Those who do not know are the unbelieving Gentiles, those who do not obey are the unbelieving Jews who knew about God and rejected His Son (Rom. 10:1,16).

1:1 [a] Ac 16:1; 1Th 1:1 **1:2** [b] Ro 1:7 **1:3** [c] 1Th 3:12
1:4 [d] 2Co 7.14 [e] 1Th 1:3 [f] 1Th 2:14 **1:5** [g] Php 1:28
1:6 [h] Col 3:25; Rev 6:10 **1:7** [i] 1Th 4:16; Jude 14
1:8 [j] Gal 4:8 [k] Ro 2:8 **1:9** [l] Php 3:19; 2Pe 3:7 [m] 2Th 2:8
1:10 [n] 1Co 3:13 [o] Jn 17:10 [p] 1Co 1:6 **1:11** [q] ver 5

power he may bring to fruition your every
desire for goodness and your every deed
prompted by faith.[r] 12We pray this so that
the name of our Lord Jesus may be glorified in you,[s] and you in him, according to
the grace of our God and the Lord Jesus
Christ.[a]

The Man of Lawlessness

2 Concerning the coming of our Lord
Jesus Christ and our being gathered to
him,[t] we ask you, brothers and sisters, 2not
to become easily unsettled or alarmed by
the teaching allegedly from us—whether by a prophecy or by word of mouth or
by letter[u]—asserting that the day of the
Lord[v] has already come. 3Don't let anyone
deceive you[w] in any way, for that day will
not come until the rebellion occurs and the
man of lawlessness[b] is revealed,[x] the man
doomed to destruction. 4He will oppose
and will exalt himself over everything that
is called God[y] or is worshiped, so that he
sets himself up in God's temple, proclaiming himself to be God.[z]
5Don't you remember that when I was
with you I used to tell you these things?
6And now you know what is holding him
back, so that he may be revealed at the
proper time. 7For the secret power of lawlessness is already at work; but the one
who now holds it back will continue to do
so till he is taken out of the way. 8And then
the lawless one will be revealed, whom the
Lord Jesus will overthrow with the breath
of his mouth[a] and destroy by the splendor
of his coming. 9The coming of the lawless
one will be in accordance with how Satan
works. He will use all sorts of displays of
power through signs and wonders[b] that
serve the lie, 10and all the ways that wickedness deceives those who are perishing.[c]
They perish because they refused to love
the truth and so be saved. 11For this reason
God sends them[d] a powerful delusion so
that they will believe the lie 12and so that all
will be condemned who have not believed
the truth but have delighted in wickedness.[e]

Stand Firm

13But we ought always to thank God for
you, brothers and sisters loved by the Lord,
because God chose you as firstfruits[c][f] to be
saved[g] through the sanctifying work of the
Spirit[h] and through belief in the truth. 14He
called you to this through our gospel, that
you might share in the glory of our Lord
Jesus Christ.
15So then, brothers and sisters, stand
firm[i] and hold fast to the teachings[d] we
passed on to you,[j] whether by word of
mouth or by letter.
16May our Lord Jesus Christ himself and

---

[a] 12 Or *God and Lord, Jesus Christ* [b] 3 Some manuscripts *sin* [c] 13 Some manuscripts *because from the beginning God chose you* [d] 15 Or *traditions*

1:12 *glorified in you.* Christ will be glorified not only among, but also in the saints, for believers reflect His glory.

2:1 *Concerning the coming.* After writing 1 Thessalonians, Paul had received word that the believers in Thessalonica were being misled by false teachers who were confusing the believers with erroneous ideas about the second coming. ***gathered to him.*** This will be the first time that the whole church, including every believer, will be gathered before the Lord to worship Him. The phrase seems to refer to the event described in 1 Thessalonians 4:17, where Paul speaks of meeting the Lord in the air.

2:2 *the day of the Lord has already come.* The false teaching was that the day of the Lord (1 Thess. 5:2–4) had already come, bringing with it the tribulations they were experiencing. Thus, some Thessalonian believers thought that they had missed the second coming.

2:3 *rebellion.* The Greek word translated "rebellion" is the word commonly used to describe a military rebellion. In the Scriptures, the word is used for rebellion against God. Some have therefore interpreted this verse to refer to a general defection from the truth, perhaps even by those professing to be the church. This rebellions apostasy would prepare the way for the antichrist. ***the man of lawlessness.*** Paul does not use the title "antichrist" for this man, but his description parallels John's description of the antichrist (1 John 2:18; Rev. 13). The man of lawlessness will lead the world into rebellion against God (v. 10), perform wonders through Satan's power (v. 9), and finally will present himself as a god to be worshiped (v. 4).

2:4 *he sets himself up in God's temple.* This is the ultimate fulfillment of the "abomination of desolation" spoken of by Daniel (Dan. 7:23; 9:26; 11:31,36–37; 12:11) and Jesus (Matt. 24:15; Mark 13:14).

2:7 *is already at work.* The evil and deception that the man of sin embodies already exist in this world (1 John 2:18). Anyone who opposes Christ and His church and seeks to deceive others into worshiping false gods is against Christ (antichrist). ***taken out of the way.*** Many believe that this verse refers to the rapture of the church (1 Thess. 4:16–17), and the cessation of the Holy Spirit working through believers to restrain the power of sin in this world. There are a variety of other interpretations for the identity of the restrainer, including the Roman state, or the principle of law and government embodied in the state.

2:8 *whom the Lord Jesus will overthrow ... and destroy.* Although the man of lawlessness will be revealed as extremely powerful (Rev. 13:7), he will be destroyed by Christ and cast into the lake of fire when the Lord comes (Rev. 19:19–20).

2:14 *share in the glory.* The Thessalonians have already been saved (v. 13), and called, but they must respond to God's work in them. Through the power of the Holy Spirit (v. 13), believers on this earth prepare

1:11 [r] 1Th 1:3 **1:12** [s] Php 2:9-11 **2:1** [t] Mk 13:27; 1Th 4:15-17 **2:2** [u] 2Th 3:17 [v] 1Co 1:8 **2:3** [w] Eph 5:6-8 [x] Da 7:25; 8:25; 11:36; Rev 13:5,6 **2:4** [y] 1Co 8:5 [z] Isa 14:13, 14; Eze 28:2 **2:8** [a] Isa 11:4; Rev 19:15 **2:9** [b] Mt 24:24; Jn 4:48 **2:10** [c] 1Co 1:18 **2:11** [d] Ro 1:28 **2:12** [e] Ro 1:32 **2:13** [f] Eph 1:4 [g] 1Th 5:9 [h] 1Pe 1:2 **2:15** [i] 1Co 16:13 [j] 1Co 11:2

God our Father, who loved us[k] and by his grace gave us eternal encouragement and good hope, 17encourage[l] your hearts and strengthen[m] you in every good deed and word.

Request for Prayer

3 As for other matters, brothers and sisters,[n] pray for us[o] that the message of the Lord[p] may spread rapidly and be honored, just as it was with you. 2And pray that we may be delivered from wicked and evil people,[q] for not everyone has faith. 3But the Lord is faithful,[r] and he will strengthen you and protect you from the evil one.[s] 4We have confidence[t] in the Lord that you are doing and will continue to do the things we command. 5May the Lord direct your hearts[u] into God's love and Christ's perseverance.

Warning Against Idleness

6In the name of the Lord Jesus Christ,[v] we command you, brothers and sisters, to keep away from[w] every believer who is idle and disruptive[x] and does not live according to the teaching[a] you received from us.[y] 7For you yourselves know how you ought to follow our example.[z] We were not idle when we were with you, 8nor did we eat anyone's food without paying for it. On the contrary, we worked[a] night and day, laboring and toiling so that we would not be a burden to any of you. 9We did this, not because we do not have the right to such help,[b] but in order to offer ourselves as a model for you to imitate.[c] 10For even when we were with you,[d] we gave you this rule: "The one who is unwilling to work[e] shall not eat."

11We hear that some among you are idle and disruptive. They are not busy; they are busybodies.[f] 12Such people we command and urge in the Lord Jesus Christ[g] to settle down and earn the food they eat.[h] 13And as for you, brothers and sisters, never tire of doing what is good.[i]

14Take special note of anyone who does not obey our instruction in this letter. Do not associate with them,[j] in order that they may feel ashamed. 15Yet do not regard them as an enemy, but warn them as you would a fellow believer.[k]

Final Greetings

16Now may the Lord of peace[l] himself give you peace at all times and in every way. The Lord be with all of you.[m]

17I, Paul, write this greeting in my own hand,[n] which is the distinguishing mark in all my letters. This is how I write.

18The grace of our Lord Jesus Christ be with you all.[o]

---

[a] 6 Or *tradition*

---

for a future with Christ by living in a holy manner (1:10; 1 Thess. 4:1–2).

2:17 *encourage your hearts and strengthen.* It is interesting to note that Paul uses the singular form of these verbs, with the plural subject of "Jesus Christ and God our Father," supporting the trinity and equality of God (1 Thess. 3:11).

3:2 *wicked and evil people.* These may have been the unbelieving Jews in Corinth who were persecuting Paul at the time he wrote this letter (Acts 18:12–13). Justice in this world may never come for Christians, but they can certainly pray for deliverance from the wicked.

3:5 *direct your hearts.* The heart, the seat of a person's will and emotions, is the place where spiritual renewal begins. There God plants love and patience, traits that will produce a harvest of good works.

3:6 *command.* This is not just a friendly suggestion, but a binding order with the authority of Jesus Christ. ***keep away.*** Among other things, this would include not participating with the person in love feasts and the Lord's Supper (Matt. 18:15–17; 1 Cor. 5:9–12).

3:9 *not because we do not have the right.* It is right for the church to financially support those who do the Lord's work (Luke 10:7; 1 Cor. 9:6–14; Gal. 6:6; 1 Tim. 5:17–18).

3:11 *not busy.* Some Thessalonians, apparently using the impending return of the Lord as an excuse, had refused to work and were expecting others in the church to feed them. In his previous letter, Paul had already exhorted them to work (1 Thess. 4:11–12). Since they had not heeded, the time had come to take further steps. While believers must always act with gentleness and love toward one another, it is wrong to enable another person to continue in sin.

3:12 *settle down and earn the food they eat.* The cure for gossips and busybodies is hard work. There is much truth in the saying "Satan finds work for idle hands."

3:15 *a fellow believer.* The disobedient one is not an enemy, but one who needs compassionate correction.

3:18 *our Lord Jesus Christ.* Not only is Jesus our ultimate hope, it is He who lovingly strengthens us to endure trials.

2:16 [k] Jn 3:16 **2:17** [l] 1Th 3:2 [m] 2Th 3:3 **3:1** [n] 1Th 4:1 [o] 1Th 5:25 [p] 1Th 1:8 **3:2** [q] Ro 15:31 **3:3** [r] 1Co 1:9 [s] Mt 5:37 **3:4** [t] 2Co 2:3 **3:5** [u] 1Ch 29:18 **3:6** [v] 1Co 5:4 [w] Ro 16:17 [x] ver 7, 11 [y] 1Co 11:2 **3:7** [z] 1Co 4:16 **3:8** [a] Ac 18:3; Eph 4:28 **3:9** [b] 1Co 9:4-14 [c] ver 7 **3:10** [d] 1Th 3:4 [e] 1Th 4:11 **3:11** [f] ver 6, 7; 1Ti 5:13 **3:12** [g] 1Th 4:1 [h] 1Th 4:11; Eph 4:28 **3:13** [i] Gal 6:9 **3:14** [j] ver 6 **3:15** [k] Gal 6:1; 1Th 5:14 **3:16** [l] Ro 15:33 [m] Ru 2:4 **3:17** [n] 1Co 16:21 **3:18** [o] Ro 16:20

1 TIMOTHY

▶ **AUTHOR:** The external evidence solidly supports the position that Paul wrote the letters to Timothy and Titus. Only Romans and 1 Corinthians have better attestation among the Pauline Epistles. Pauline authorship of the Pastoral Epistles requires Paul's release from his Roman imprisonment (Acts 28), the continuation of his missionary endeavors, and his imprisonment for a second time in Rome. Unfortunately, the order of events can only be reconstructed from hints, because there is no concurrent history paralleling Acts to chronicle the last years of the apostle. It is most probable that Paul wrote 1 Timothy from Macedonia in A.D. 62 or 63 while Timothy was serving as his representative in Ephesus.

▶ **TIME:** c. A.D. 62–63 ▶ **KEY VERSES:** 1 Tim. 3:15–16

▶ **THEME:** The letters to Timothy and Titus are generally called "the Pastoral Epistles." They are pastoral in tone and in the subject matter they address. While covering much of the apostolic instruction on the life and doctrine of the church, they also provide some guidelines on how Christians in the church should relate to society. One of the overriding concerns of the books is that truth be valued and guarded. Too often today, truth is subjective and culturally conditioned to the point where people don't even have problems believing mutually contradictory ideas. Paul speaks of the value of truth in his own apostolic role, and he stands against false teachers who would distort the truth for their own ends.

1 Paul, an apostle of Christ Jesus by the command of God[a] our Savior and of Christ Jesus our hope,[b]

2To Timothy[c] my true son[d] in the faith:

Grace, mercy and peace from God the Father and Christ Jesus our Lord.

Timothy Charged to Oppose False Teachers

3As I urged you when I went into Macedonia, stay there in Ephesus[e] so that you may command certain people not to teach false doctrines[f] any longer **4**or to devote themselves to myths[g] and endless genealogies. Such things promote controversial speculations[h] rather than advancing God's work—which is by faith. **5**The goal of this command is love, which comes from a pure heart[i] and a good conscience and a sincere faith.[j] **6**Some have departed from these and have turned to meaningless talk. **7**They want to be teachers of the law, but they do not know what they are talking about or what they so confidently affirm.

8We know that the law is good[k] if one uses it properly. **9**We also know that the law is made not for the righteous but for lawbreakers and rebels,[l] the ungodly and sinful, the unholy and irreligious, for those who kill their fathers or mothers, for murderers, **10**for the sexually immoral, for those practicing homosexuality, for slave traders and liars and perjurers—and for

1:1 ***apostle of Christ Jesus.*** The Greek word for "apostle" means "sent one." Paul was an ambassador sent by Christ (Acts 9).
1:2 ***Timothy.*** Timothy was a young believer from Lystra who traveled with Paul during his second and third missionary journeys.
1:3 ***that you may command.*** Paul's request that Timothy stay in Ephesus to minister to the believers there demonstrates Paul's confidence in the young man.
1:4 ***myths and endless genealogies.*** The errors that Paul left Timothy to correct in Ephesus appear to have been primarily Jewish in nature. The Jews tended to place a lot of importance on the genealogies and also on allegorical interpretations of the law.
1:6 ***meaningless talk.*** Gossip, speculation, and criticism should not come from the lips of believers.
1:8 ***law.*** The proper function of the law is to make sinners aware of their sinfulness (Rom. 3:20).
1:10 ***perjurers.*** The term "perjure" is more significant than simply "lie," as it deals with false promises.

1:1 [a] Titus 1:3 [b] Col 1:27 **1:2** [c] Ac 16:1 [d] 2Ti 1:2; Titus 1:4 **1:3** [e] Ac 18:19 [f] Gal 1:6,7 **1:4** [g] 1Ti 4:7; Titus 1:14 [h] 1Ti 6:4 **1:5** [i] 2Ti 2:22 [j] 2Ti 1:5 **1:8** [k] Ro 7:12 **1:9** [l] Gal 3:19

whatever else is contrary to the sound doctrine[m] 11that conforms to the gospel concerning the glory of the blessed God, which
he entrusted to me.[n]

The Lord's Grace to Paul

12I thank Christ Jesus our Lord, who has
given me strength,[o] that he considered me
trustworthy, appointing me to his service.
13Even though I was once a blasphemer
and a persecutor[p] and a violent man, I was
shown mercy because I acted in ignorance
and unbelief.[q] 14The grace of our Lord was
poured out on me abundantly,[r] along with
the faith and love that are in Christ Jesus.[s]
15Here is a trustworthy saying[t] that deserves full acceptance: Christ Jesus came
into the world to save sinners—of whom I
am the worst. 16But for that very reason I
was shown mercy[u] so that in me, the worst
of sinners, Christ Jesus might display his
immense patience as an example for those
who would believe in him and receive eternal life. 17Now to the King[v] eternal, immortal, invisible,[w] the only God, be honor and
glory for ever and ever. Amen.[x]

The Charge to Timothy Renewed

18Timothy, my son, I am giving you this
command in keeping with the prophecies
once made about you,[y] so that by recalling
them you may fight the battle well,[z] 19hold-
ing on to faith and a good conscience,
which some have rejected and so have suffered shipwreck with regard to the faith.[a]
20Among them are Hymenaeus[b] and Alexander,[c] whom I have handed over to Satan[d]
to be taught not to blaspheme.

Instructions on Worship

2 I urge, then, first of all, that petitions,
prayers, intercession and thanksgiving
be made for all people— 2for kings and all
those in authority,[e] that we may live peaceful and quiet lives in all godliness and holiness. 3This is good, and pleases God our
Savior, 4who wants[f] all people[g] to be saved
and to come to a knowledge of the truth.[h]
5For there is one God[i] and one mediator[j] between God and mankind, the man Christ
Jesus, 6who gave himself as a ransom for
all people. This has now been witnessed to[k]
at the proper time.[l] 7And for this purpose I
was appointed a herald and an apostle—I

To swear an oath and then not carry through is a serious thing indeed.

1:13 ***I was shown mercy.*** Paul found mercy and forgiveness even after his intense persecution of the church. God surely offers salvation to all people (2:4).

1:14 ***grace.*** Grace is God's undeserved, unearned, freely given favor.

1:15–16 Believing Jesus—Jesus came to earth to save sinners. Paul knew this firsthand. When he became a Christian, Paul realized the extent of his sin in terms of both his past sins and his current tendencies. But he also knew exactly where he stood in Christ as a believer. The mercy of God can only be acquired through belief. Paul reminds Timothy here of God's perfect patience and mercy and urges others to come to faith and receive the benefit of new and everlasting life, as he has. Eternal life can only begin with belief. It is an active choice of the individual. We must believe that Jesus is the saving Christ or reject Him. Paul says, *I was shown mercy so that in me … Christ Jesus might display his immense patience as an example for those who would believe in him and receive eternal life.* If you have never believed in Jesus, take this opportunity to tell God how you feel. Believe in Jesus as Savior and begin on the path of a new life.

1:16 ***believe in him.*** As stated over 185 times in the New Testament, the sole condition for salvation is belief, having faith or trust in Jesus Christ. The gospel (or "good news") is that Jesus Christ, God's Son, gave up His heavenly kingdom for a time to become a human. As a man, He died for our sins, was buried, and rose on the third day. All who place their trust in Jesus will be saved from the coming judgment and from the present power of sin. To add any other condition to faith for salvation is to make it dependent on our own works (Rom. 11:6; Gal. 2:16).

1:20 ***handed over to Satan.*** Paul did not have some sort of authority over these men to have them "delivered" in the sense that they would now belong to Satan. Rather, Paul had stopped trying to exhort them, or show them the way they should go. They would not listen, so Paul had to say, "so be it, go your own way."

2:4 ***wants all people to be saved.*** God desires that all men would be saved, although this does not mean that He will force this to happen. Only those who believe in Christ will receive salvation (Rom. 1:16–17; 3:21–26; 5:17). Christ died for the sins of the entire world, but only those who believe will receive the benefits of His sacrifice. ***to come to a knowledge of the truth.*** God not only wants our salvation (justification), He also wants us to grow in truth (sanctification) so that we will not be led astray by false teachers.

2:5 ***one God.*** This is the central truth of the Hebrew Scriptures. The only living God desires that all should be saved. He is the only one to whom our prayers should be addressed. ***mediator.*** This is a concept that came from the ceremonial worship in the Old Testament. In the tabernacle and later in the temple, the priests mediated between God and Israel by offering sacrifices to atone for the sins of the people. In their position of mediator, the priests were the only ones eligible to enter into the holy place, the place where God had made His presence known. When Jesus came, He came as the Mediator between man and God. Through Him we can be eligible to enter into God's holy presence.

2:6 ***ransom.*** The Greek word translated "ransom" is found only here in the New Testament. It specifically refers to a ransom paid for a slave.

2:7 ***a true and faithful teacher.*** Paul was called not

1:10 [m] 2Ti 4:3; Titus 1:9 **1:11** [n] Gal 2:7 **1:12** [o] Php 4:13
1:13 [p] Ac 8:3 [q] Ac 26:9 **1:14** [r] Ro 5:20 [s] 2Ti 1:13
1:15 [t] 1Ti 3:1; 2Ti 2:11; Titus 3:8 **1:16** [u] ver 13
1:17 [v] Rev 15:3 [w] Col 1:15 [x] Ro 11:36 **1:18** [y] 1Ti 4:14
[z] 2Ti 2:3 **1:19** [a] 1Ti 6:21 **1:20** [b] 2Ti 2:17 [c] 2Ti 4:14
[d] 1Co 5:5 **2:2** [e] Ezr 6:10; Ro 13:1 **2:4** [f] Eze 18:23, 32
[g] Titus 2:11 [h] 2Ti 2:25 **2:5** [i] Ro 3:29, 30 [j] Gal 3:20
2:6 [k] 1Co 1:6 [l] 1Ti 6:15

am telling the truth, I am not lying—and a
true and faithful teacher[m] of the Gentiles.[n]
8Therefore I want the men everywhere
to pray, lifting up holy hands[o] without anger or disputing. 9I also want the women to
dress modestly, with decency and propriety,
adorning themselves, not with elaborate
hairstyles or gold or pearls or expensive
clothes,[p] 10but with good deeds, appropriate for women who profess to worship God.
11A woman[a] should learn in quietness
and full submission.[q] 12I do not permit a
woman to teach or to assume authority
over a man;[b] she must be quiet. 13For Adam
was formed first, then Eve.[r] 14And Adam
was not the one deceived; it was the woman
who was deceived and became a sinner.[s]
15But women[c] will be saved through childbearing—if they continue in faith, love[t]
and holiness with propriety.

Qualifications for Overseers and Deacons

3 Here is a trustworthy saying:[u] Whoever
aspires to be an overseer[v] desires a noble task. 2Now the overseer is to be above
reproach,[w] faithful to his wife, temperate,
self-controlled, respectable, hospitable,[x]
able to teach,[y] 3not given to drunkenness,
not violent but gentle, not quarrelsome,[z]
not a lover of money.[a] 4He must manage his
own family well and see that his children
obey him, and he must do so in a manner
worthy of full[d] respect.[b] 5(If anyone does
not know how to manage his own family,
how can he take care of God's church?)[c]
6He must not be a recent convert, or he

[a] 11 Or *wife*; also in verse 12 [b] 12 Or *over her husband* [c] 15 Greek *she* [d] 4 Or *him with proper*

only to preach the gospel to the Gentiles, but also to guide their growth in truth.

2:8 *men.* The Greek word translated "men" in this verse refers specifically to males as distinguished from females. Some believe that this verse means specifically public worship, while others believe it refers to life in general. ***lifting up holy hands.*** This is a Hebrew way of praying (1 Kin. 8:22; Ps. 141:2). "Holy" means morally and spiritually clean.

2:9 *dress modestly.* Modesty means more than just covering up enough. It means not flaunting one's wealth, or one's jewels, or one's name brands, as well as not flaunting one's body. ***propriety.*** This word means reverence and respect, shrinking away from what is inappropriate.

2:10 *good deeds.* A Christian woman's beauty should be found in her godly character and her love for the Lord as demonstrated in all types of good works.

2:11 *in quietness and full submission.* These verses are not easy to understand, and there are many differences of opinion as to their meaning. The Scripture here does actually say just what it looks like: that women must be silent and submissive. It is universally accepted that this is referring to times of public worship, although the Bible makes it clear that a woman must submit to her husband (Eph. 5:22; Col. 3:18), but the concept of submission also applies to all believers. Philippians 4:5 says, "Let your gentleness be evident to all. The Lord is near." Being submissive means not being unruly or argumentative. There are times when it is proper for a woman to teach, pray, or prophesy (1 Cor. 11), but apparently this is not supposed to happen in public worship.

2:12 *to teach or to assume authority.* It seems best to understand this passage as saying that women may exercise their spiritual gifts in a variety of ministries in the local assembly, as long as those gifts are exercised under the appropriate leadership of men. We have problems understanding the roles of men and women in the church. Often we want to ignore the subject altogether and say that men and women are entirely equal, the alternative being that men become despotic and tyrannical, while women become spiritually weak with no teaching and no opportunity to use their God-given gifts. Men and women are equal in God's eyes in terms of their value as people and eligibility for spiritual growth and relationship with God, but He created this difference in roles. Many tend to feel that this role difference is because of the fall, but God did create men and women to be different. The mess and confusion we have with our God-given positions is the result of the fall.

2:14 *Adam was not the one deceived.* This seems to point to the fact that Adam sinned with his eyes open; he knew what he was doing. Eve sinned because she was deceived. Paul's arguments from creation and the fall seem to indicate that the prohibitions in verses 9–12 are permanent, not cultural.

2:15 *will be saved through childbearing.* This is a very difficult verse to understand and there is much disagreement about what it means. We know that it does not mean "saved" in terms of receiving eternal life, because the Bible elsewhere makes it very clear we are saved by faith alone (John 3:15–18; Rom. 1:16–17; 3:23–26). Some think that it has to do with daily sanctification and the woman's special task of bearing children. Others say it is referring to being delivered from the desire to dominate by recognizing one's appropriate place in God's creation order. Still others believe that it refers specifically to the birth of Jesus Christ, the seed born of woman prophesied in Genesis 3:15.

3:1 *overseer.* This means a person who oversees a congregation. The words "overseer" and "elder" are used interchangeably for the same office (Titus 1:5–7). ***noble.*** The idea is not that an overseer is sinless, but that he displays mature consistent Christian conduct that gives no reason for anyone to accuse him of anything.

3:2 *faithful to his wife.* This phrase is also subject to much disagreement. Many feel that it means "a one-woman kind of man," indicating a lifestyle of fidelity. Others feel that it is more specific, and prohibits a divorced and remarried man from the elder position. Certainly it is an exclusion of any one who is sexually immoral or a polygamist.

3:3 *violent.* An overseer is not to be a quarrelsome man.

2:7 [m] 2Ti 1:11 [n] Ac 9:15; Eph 3:7,8 **2:8** [o] Ps 134:2; Lk 24:50 **2:9** [p] 1Pe 3:3 **2:11** [q] 1Co 14:34 **2:13** [r] Ge 2:7,22; 1Co 11:8 **2:14** [s] Ge 3:1-6,13; 2Co 11:3 **2:15** [t] 1Ti 1:14 **3:1** [u] 1Ti 1:15 [v] Ac 20:28 **3:2** [w] Titus 1:6-8 [x] Ro 12:13 [y] 2Ti 2:24 **3:3** [z] 2Ti 2:24 [a] Heb 13:5; 1Pe 5:2 **3:4** [b] Titus 1:6 **3:5** [c] 1Co 10:32

may become conceited[d] and fall under the
same judgment as the devil. 7He must also
have a good reputation with outsiders, so
that he will not fall into disgrace and into
the devil's trap.[e]
8In the same way, deacons[a][f] are to be
worthy of respect, sincere, not indulging
in much wine,[g] and not pursuing dishonest gain. 9They must keep hold of the deep
truths of the faith with a clear conscience.[h]
10They must first be tested; and then if
there is nothing against them, let them
serve as deacons.
11In the same way, the women[b] are to be
worthy of respect, not malicious talkers[i]
but temperate and trustworthy in everything.
12A deacon must be faithful to his wife
and must manage his children and his
household well.[j] 13Those who have served
well gain an excellent standing and great
assurance in their faith in Christ Jesus.

Reasons for Paul's Instructions

14Although I hope to come to you soon, I
am writing you these instructions so that,
15if I am delayed, you will know how people ought to conduct themselves in God's
household, which is the church[k] of the
living God, the pillar and foundation of
the truth. 16Beyond all question, the mystery[l] from which true godliness springs is
great:

He appeared in the flesh,[m]
was vindicated by the Spirit,[c]
was seen by angels,
was preached among the nations,[n]
was believed on in the world,
was taken up in glory.[o]

4 The Spirit[p] clearly says that in later
times[q] some will abandon the faith and
follow deceiving spirits[r] and things taught
by demons. 2Such teachings come through
hypocritical liars, whose consciences have
been seared as with a hot iron.[s] 3They forbid people to marry[t] and order them to abstain from certain foods,[u] which God created[v] to be received with thanksgiving[w] by
those who believe and who know the truth.
4For everything God created is good,[x] and
nothing is to be rejected if it is received
with thanksgiving, 5because it is consecrated by the word of God and prayer.
6If you point these things out to the
brothers and sisters,[d] you will be a good
minister of Christ Jesus, nourished on the
truths of the faith[y] and of the good teaching that you have followed. 7Have nothing

[a] *8* The word *deacons* refers here to Christians designated to serve with the overseers/elders of the church in a variety of ways; similarly in verse 12; and in Romans 16:1 and Phil. 1:1. [b] *11* Possibly deacons' wives or women who are deacons
[c] *16* Or *vindicated in spirit* [d] *6* The Greek word for *brothers and sisters* (*adelphoi*) refers here to believers, both men and women, as part of God's family.

3:7 *good reputation.* An overseer must have a good reputation in the community. A non-Christian should not be able to reproach or insult an elder because of his behavior. The elder's good testimony avoids the traps of Satan.
3:8 *deacons.* Deacons fill a second leadership position in the local assembly. The Greek word for deacon means "servant." ***sincere.*** This speaks specifically of the dangers of gossip, especially changing sides or changing a story to fit the audience.
3:9 *deep truths of the faith.* The mystery of the faith is the coming of God in the flesh (v. 16). The Son of God becoming a human in order to serve humanity (Mark 10:43 – 45) is the embodiment of service.
3:11 *the women.* Some believe here that Paul is speaking of another office in the local body, that of "deaconess," godly women who serve under the leadership of the elders. Others, however, believe that this verse refers to the wives of the deacons, and not to an office. It could be assumed that both are true, and that the deacon and his wife are supposed to work together as a team, serving the church. The original language leaves the verse open to interpretation, since the Greek uses one word to mean both woman and wife.
3:15 *pillar and foundation of the truth.* Misconduct and disorder in the local church weaken the support of God's truth in the world. We as believers have a tremendous responsibility to keep the name of our Lord without spot or criticism from the nonbelieving world.
3:16 *appeared in the flesh.* This refers to Christ's incarnation, the fact that Jesus became man (John 1:14). ***vindicated by the Spirit.*** This is the work of the Holy Spirit in Jesus' ministry and resurrection (Matt. 3:15 – 17; John 16:7 – 10; Rom. 1:4). ***seen by angels.*** This refers to the angelic witness of Christ's ministry and resurrection. ***preached among the nations.*** This refers to the preaching of Christ to the Gentiles (Col. 1:23). ***believed on in the world.*** This is the response of individuals to God's plan of salvation (Col. 1:18 – 25). ***taken up in glory.*** Christ ascended to heaven and is seated at God's right hand there (Acts 1:9; Heb. 1:3 – 4).
4:1 *The Spirit clearly says.* When Paul speaks of the Holy Spirit's words here, he may be referring to various prophecies inspired by the Holy Spirit concerning defection from God's truth (Dan. 7:25; 8:23; Matt. 24:4 – 12), or also he may have been referring to a revelation the Spirit had given him.
4:5 *consecrated.* Consecrated means "set apart," or "made holy." Paul is saying that God has set apart all the good things He created, from marriage to the food we eat. Nothing is less in accord with God than to begin forbidding the good things He made for us.
4:7 *old wives' tales.* This is not to say that such fables are appropriate for old women either. Paul is merely using the term "old wives' tales" to describe

3:6 [d] 1Ti 6:4 **3:7** [e] 2Ti 2:26 **3:8** [f] Php 1:1 [g] Titus 2:3 **3:9** [h] 1Ti 1:19 **3:11** [i] 2Ti 3:3; Titus 2:3 **3:12** [j] ver 4 **3:15** [k] ver 5; Eph 2:21 **3:16** [l] Ro 16:25 [m] Jn 1:14 [n] Col 1:23 [o] Mk 16:19 **4:1** [p] Jn 16:13 [q] 2Ti 3:1 [r] 2Th 2:3 **4:2** [s] Eph 4:19 **4:3** [t] Heb 13:4 [u] Col 2:16 [v] Ge 1:29 [w] Ro 14:6 **4:4** [x] Ro 14:14-18 **4:6** [y] 1Ti 1:10

to do with godless myths and old wives'
tales;[z] rather, train yourself to be godly.
8For physical training is of some value, but
godliness has value for all things,[a] holding
promise for both the present life[b] and the
life to come. 9This is a trustworthy saying[c]
that deserves full acceptance. 10That is
why we labor and strive, because we have
put our hope in the living God, who is the
Savior of all people, and especially of those
who believe.

11Command and teach these things.[d]
12Don't let anyone look down on you because you are young, but set an example[e]
for the believers in speech, in conduct, in
love, in faith[f] and in purity. 13Until I come,
devote yourself to the public reading of
Scripture, to preaching and to teaching.
14Do not neglect your gift, which was giv-
en you through prophecy[g] when the body
of elders laid their hands on you.[h]

15Be diligent in these matters; give yourself wholly to them, so that everyone may
see your progress. 16Watch your life and
doctrine closely. Persevere in them, because if you do, you will save both yourself
and your hearers.

Widows, Elders and Slaves

5 Do not rebuke an older man[i] harshly,[j]
but exhort him as if he were your father. Treat younger men[k] as brothers, 2old-
er women as mothers, and younger women
as sisters, with absolute purity.

3Give proper recognition to those widows who are really in need.[l] 4But if a widow has children or grandchildren, these
should learn first of all to put their religion
into practice by caring for their own family
and so repaying their parents and grand-
parents,[m] for this is pleasing to God.[n] 5The
widow who is really in need[o] and left all
alone puts her hope in God[p] and continues
night and day to pray[q] and to ask God for
help. 6But the widow who lives for pleasure
is dead even while she lives.[r] 7Give the people these instructions,[s] so that no one may
be open to blame. 8Anyone who does not
provide for their relatives, and especially
for their own household, has denied[t] the
faith and is worse than an unbeliever.

9No widow may be put on the list of widows unless she is over sixty, has been faithful to her husband, 10and is well known
for her good deeds,[u] such as bringing up
children, showing hospitality, washing the
feet[v] of the Lord's people, helping those in
trouble[w] and devoting herself to all kinds
of good deeds.

11As for younger widows, do not put
them on such a list. For when their sensual desires overcome their dedication to
Christ, they want to marry. 12Thus they
bring judgment on themselves, because
they have broken their first pledge. 13Be-
sides, they get into the habit of being idle
and going about from house to house. And
not only do they become idlers, but also
busybodies[x] who talk nonsense, saying
things they ought not to. 14So I counsel
younger widows to marry,[y] to have children, to manage their homes and to give
the enemy no opportunity for slander.[z]
15Some have in fact already turned away
to follow Satan.[a]

16If any woman who is a believer has

---

the superstitions and thoughtless beliefs that were prevalent.

4:8 ***of some value.*** This contrasts the short-term value of physical exercise with the long-term benefits of godliness for all things.

4:10 ***Savior of all people.*** This describes God as the One who gives life, breath and existence to all.

4:12 ***set an example.*** Timothy, in spite of youth, was to set an example in five areas: "in speech," meaning his words were to reflect the love of Christ; "in conduct," or behavior; "in love," which is the love of God; "in faith," meaning trust in God; "in purity," both in thought and action. These are qualities every believer should strive after, practice, and desire.

4:16 ***save both yourself.*** This is not a reference to justification by works, but to sanctification, which is the Christian's daily walk of faith (Mark 8:34–38; John 12:25–26). Timothy's example and hard work in teaching would serve to help others with their walk also.

5:2 ***absolute purity.*** Believing men must respect the purity of a young woman as the purity of a sister.

5:3 ***really in need.*** This refers to a woman who when widowed is left with no family at all, as opposed to those widows who still have living children or other relations.

5:4 ***put their religion into practice by caring for their own family.*** Piety is respect, reverence, or obligation. Honoring our parents includes caring for them physically and financially as they grow older.

5:8 ***does not provide for their relatives.*** A believer is to provide for his family and this seems to include any of his relatives that need help. Failure to do this denies the faith he has said to believe in and smirches the name of Christianity.

5:9 ***put on the list.*** Many believe the list referred to here was a list of widows whom the church was to assist. Some have maintained that this was an official order of widows. These women were to pray for the church and practice works of charity (vv. 5,10).

5:13–14 ***idle ... busybodies.*** An old saying tells us "Idle hands are the devil's workshop." Do not allow yourself to become so idle that you begin to gossip. As odd as it may sound, it will happen. Employ yourself with the tasks God has set before you. Look around. There are lots of things we as believers should be doing.

4:7 [z] 2Ti 2:16 **4:8** [a] 1Ti 6:6 [b] Ps 37:9, 11; Mk 10:29, 30 **4:9** [c] 1Ti 1:15 **4:11** [d] 1Ti 5:7; 6:2 **4:12** [e] Titus 2:7; 1Pe 5:3 [f] 1Ti 1:14 **4:14** [g] 1Ti 1:18 [h] Ac 6:6; 2Ti 1:6 **5:1** [i] Titus 2:2 [j] Lev 19:32 [k] Titus 2:6 **5:3** [l] ver 5, 16 **5:4** [m] Eph 6:1, 2 [n] 1Ti 2:3 **5:5** [o] ver 3, 16 [p] 1Co 7:34; 1Pe 3:5 [q] Lk 2:37 **5:6** [r] Lk 15:24 **5:7** [s] 1Ti 4:11 **5:8** [t] 2Pe 2:1; Jude 4; Titus 1:16 **5:10** [u] Ac 9:36; 1Ti 6:18; 1Pe 2:12 [v] Lk 7:44 [w] ver 16 **5:13** [x] 2Th 3:11 **5:14** [y] 1Co 7:9 [z] 1Ti 6:1 **5:15** [a] Mt 4:10

widows in her care, she should continue to help them and not let the church be burdened with them, so that the church can help those widows who are really in need.[b]

17The elders[c] who direct the affairs of the church well are worthy of double honor,[d] especially those whose work is preaching and teaching. 18For Scripture says, "Do not muzzle an ox while it is treading out the grain,"[a][e] and "The worker deserves his wages."[b][f] 19Do not entertain an accusation against an elder[g] unless it is brought by two or three witnesses.[h] 20But those elders who are sinning you are to reprove[i] before everyone, so that the others may take warning.[j] 21I charge you, in the sight of God and Christ Jesus[k] and the elect angels, to keep these instructions without partiality, and to do nothing out of favoritism.

22Do not be hasty in the laying on of hands,[l] and do not share in the sins of others.[m] Keep yourself pure.

23Stop drinking only water, and use a little wine[n] because of your stomach and your frequent illnesses.

24The sins of some are obvious, reaching the place of judgment ahead of them; the sins of others trail behind them. 25In the same way, good deeds are obvious, and even those that are not obvious cannot remain hidden forever.

6 All who are under the yoke of slavery should consider their masters worthy of full respect,[o] so that God's name and our teaching may not be slandered.[p] 2Those who have believing masters should not show them disrespect just because they are fellow believers.[q] Instead, they should serve them even better because their masters are dear to them as fellow believers and are devoted to the welfare[c] of their slaves.

False Teachers and the Love of Money

These are the things you are to teach and insist on.[r] 3If anyone teaches otherwise[s] and does not agree to the sound instruction[t] of our Lord Jesus Christ and to godly teaching, 4they are conceited and understand nothing. They have an unhealthy interest in controversies and quarrels about words[u] that result in envy, strife, malicious talk, evil suspicions 5and constant friction between people of corrupt mind, who have been robbed of the truth[v] and who think that godliness is a means to financial gain.

6But godliness with contentment[w] is great gain.[x] 7For we brought nothing into the world, and we can take nothing out of it.[y] 8But if we have food and clothing, we will be content with that.[z] 9Those who want to get rich[a] fall into temptation and a trap[b] and into many foolish and harmful desires that plunge people into ruin and destruction. 10For the love of money[c] is a root of all kinds of evil. Some people, eager for money, have wandered from the faith[d] and pierced themselves with many griefs.

---

[a] *18* Deut. 25:4 [b] *18* Luke 10:7 [c] *2* Or *and benefit from the service*

5:18 *Scripture says.* Paul quotes two passages: Deuteronomy 25:4 and Luke 10:7. The quotation from Luke is especially interesting as it shows that Paul considered the Gospels to be Scripture as well as the Old Testament.

5:19 *an accusation against an elder.* Charges against elders are to be factual, not based on a single opinion or rumor.

5:20 *those elders who are sinning.* This seems to refer to elders who fail in their leadership, whether in the church, in their social relationships, or in their home life. Public rebuke is to serve as a warning to other believers. Sin is a serious matter, especially for those who are in leadership, setting an example for others (1 Pet. 4:14).

5:22 *hasty.* This verse is believed to be warning against too quickly restoring a leader who has fallen. Correction in love and restoration to fellowship should occur as soon as possible, but restoration to leadership should not be made without time and biblical evaluation. Not only does this apply to former leaders, it is a caution not to share responsibility for someone else's sins by restoring or appointing someone who is not qualified.

5:25 *obvious cannot remain hidden.* Unnoticed good works always come to light, if not in this life, at the judgment seat, but even sins hidden from men cannot be concealed from God.

6:1 *yoke of slavery.* This serves as an example of how believers should act in the workplace. We are Christians, who are to represent our faith, and Christ Himself. If we do this badly, we minimize not only our faith, but the power and testimony of Christ.

6:2 *These are the things.* "These are the things" is probably best understood as the content of the entire letter to Timothy.

6:9 *Those who want to get rich.* Inside of every man there is a "God-shaped void." Many unbelievers try to fill this inner longing with wealth and possessions. Greed drives people to temptation and foolish and harmful desires. This is not an ailment of unbelievers only. Many believers also try to gain material things rather than the imperishable things of righteousness, godliness, faith, love, perseverance, and gentleness (v. 11). These are the things we should pursue with all of our being.

6:10 *love of money.* Money in and of itself is not a problem, but the love of money is. Christians can be so blinded by greed that they no longer see the need

5:16 [b] ver 3-5 **5:17** [c] Ac 11:30 [d] Php 2:29; 1Th 5:12 **5:18** [e] Dt 25:4; 1Co 9:7-9 [f] Lk 10:7; Lev 19:13; Dt 24:14, 15; Mt 10:10; 1Co 9:14 **5:19** [g] Ac 11:30 [h] Mt 18:16 **5:20** [i] 2Ti 4:2; Titus 1:13 [j] Dt 13:11 **5:21** [k] 1Ti 6:13; 2Ti 4:1 **5:22** [l] Ac 6:6 [m] Eph 5:11 **5:23** [n] 1Ti 3:8 **6:1** [o] Eph 6:5; Titus 2:9; 1Pe 2:18 [p] Titus 2:5, 8 **6:2** [q] Phm 16 [r] 1Ti 4:11 **6:3** [s] 1Ti 1:3 [t] 1Ti 1:10 **6:4** [u] 2Ti 2:14 **6:5** [v] Titus 1:15 **6:6** [w] Php 4:11; Heb 13:5 [x] 1Ti 4:8 **6:7** [y] Job 1:21; Ecc 5:15 **6:8** [z] Heb 13:5 **6:9** [a] Pr 15:27 [b] 1Ti 3:7 **6:10** [c] 1Ti 3:3 [d] Jas 5:19

Final Charge to Timothy

11But you, man of God,[e] flee from all this,
and pursue righteousness, godliness, faith,
love,[f] endurance and gentleness. 12Fight the
good fight[g] of the faith. Take hold of[h] the
eternal life to which you were called when
you made your good confession in the presence of many witnesses. 13In the sight of
God, who gives life to everything, and of
Christ Jesus, who while testifying before
Pontius Pilate[i] made the good confession, I
charge you[j] 14to keep this command without spot or blame until the appearing of our
Lord Jesus Christ, 15which God will bring
about in his own time—God, the blessed[k]
and only Ruler,[l] the King of kings and Lord
of lords,[m] 16who alone is immortal[n] and
who lives in unapproachable light, whom
no one has seen or can see.[o] To him be hon-
or and might forever. Amen.

17Command those who are rich in this
present world not to be arrogant nor to put
their hope in wealth,[p] which is so uncertain, but to put their hope in God,[q] who
richly provides us with everything for our
enjoyment.[r] 18Command them to do good,
to be rich in good deeds,[s] and to be generous and willing to share.[t] 19In this way
they will lay up treasure for themselves[u]
as a firm foundation for the coming age,
so that they may take hold of the life that
is truly life.

20Timothy, guard what has been entrusted[v] to your care. Turn away from godless
chatter[w] and the opposing ideas of what
is falsely called knowledge, 21which some
have professed and in so doing have departed from the faith.[x]

Grace be with you all.[y]

---

for holy living. A life focused on material things brings only pain.

6:12 ***Take hold of the eternal life.*** Use the hope of everlasting life with the Savior as your lifeline, your comfort, and your guide.

6:14 ***appearing of our Lord Jesus Christ.*** The imminent return of Christ should be a motive for godly living (1 John 2:28).

6:16 ***immortal.*** This may also be translated "without death." The glorified Christ can never die.

6:20 ***falsely called knowledge.*** Gnosticism (from the Greek word for knowledge) is a heresy that teaches that salvation comes through secret knowledge of spiritual mysteries.

6:21 ***Grace be with you all.*** The Greek word for "you" here is plural, including the whole church. God's grace to us as sinners is indeed amazing.

6:11 [e] 2Ti 3:17 [f] 2Ti 2:22 **6:12** [g] 1Co 9:25,26; 1Ti 1:18 [h] Php 3:12 **6:13** [i] Jn 18:33-37 [j] 1Ti 5:21 **6:15** [k] 1Ti 1:11 [l] 1Ti 1:17 [m] Rev 17:14; 19:16 **6:16** [n] 1Ti 1:17 [o] Jn 1:18 **6:17** [p] Lk 12:20,21 [q] 1Ti 4:10 [r] Ac 14:17 **6:18** [s] 1Ti 5:10 [t] Ro 12:8, 13 **6:19** [u] Mt 6:20 **6:20** [v] 2Ti 1:12, 14 [w] 2Ti 2:16 **6:21** [x] 2Ti 2:18 [y] Col 4:18

2 TIMOTHY

▶ **AUTHOR:** Fearing for their own lives, the Asian believers failed to support Paul after this second Roman imprisonment and his first defense before the Imperial Court (1:15; 4:16). Now he was in a cold Roman cell (4:13) without hope of acquittal in spite of the success of his initial defense. Under these conditions, Paul wrote this epistle in the fall of A.D. 67, hoping that Timothy would be able to visit him before the approaching winter (4:21).

▶ **TIME:** c. A.D. 66–67 ▶ **KEY VERSES:** 2 Tim. 3:14–17

▶ **THEME:** This is likely the last of Paul's writings that we have. He writes this letter from a prison cell where he is being kept like a common criminal. He knows that his work on earth is nearing its conclusion, and these are then his last words of counsel to his trusted companion in ministry. One can sense his weariness, but also his strongly held conviction about what is necessary for the continued growth of the church. One can also clearly see the hope that sustains him as he looks forward to going home to Christ.

1 Paul, an apostle of Christ Jesus by the
will of God,[a] in keeping with the promise of life that is in Christ Jesus,[b]

2To Timothy,[c] my dear son:[d]

Grace, mercy and peace from God the
Father and Christ Jesus our Lord.

Thanksgiving

3I thank God,[e] whom I serve, as my ancestors did, with a clear conscience, as
night and day I constantly remember you
in my prayers.[f] 4Recalling your tears,[g] I
long to see you,[h] so that I may be filled with
joy. 5I am reminded of your sincere faith,[i]
which first lived in your grandmother Lois
and in your mother Eunice[j] and, I am persuaded, now lives in you also.

Appeal for Loyalty to Paul and the Gospel

6For this reason I remind you to fan
into flame the gift of God, which is in you
through the laying on of my hands.[k] 7For
the Spirit God gave us does not make us
timid,[l] but gives us power, love and self-
discipline. 8So do not be ashamed[m] of the
testimony about our Lord or of me his prisoner.[n] Rather, join with me in suffering for
the gospel,[o] by the power of God. 9He has
saved us and called[p] us to a holy life—not
because of anything we have done but
because of his own purpose and grace.
This grace was given us in Christ Jesus
before the beginning of time, 10but it has
now been revealed[q] through the appearing of our Savior, Christ Jesus, who has
destroyed death[r] and has brought life and

1:1 ***the promise of life.*** This message of life stands in ironic contrast to the fact that Paul was writing from a Roman prison, facing his execution.
1:3 ***my ancestors.*** Paul's forefathers were the patriarchs of the faith: Abraham, Isaac, and Jacob. Paul had great love for Israel (Rom. 9:1–5). The reason that he connects himself to Israel's forefathers may be to demonstrate that he is not advocating a new religion but one of which the godly of the past are also a part.
1:5 ***Lois . . . Eunice.*** The prayers, witness, and faith of his godly mother and grandmother were central factors in the spiritual development of Timothy (1 Tim. 2:15).
1:8 ***do not be ashamed of the testimony.*** *Testimony* is the witness of the Lord; the Greek term is the source of the English word *martyr.* Church tradition says that most of the apostles died as martyrs.
1:9 ***not because of anything we have done.*** It is impossible for people to earn their way into heaven. Salvation is by grace, the unearned and undeserved favor of God.
1:10 ***destroyed death.*** Knowing that leaving our earthly bodies simply means that we will live forever with the Lord effectively robs death of its dread. The same gospel that offers us the forgiveness of sins and draws us to holy living also announces life and immortality. Believing the gospel, we begin to live in the power of an endless life (1 John 5:11–13,20).

1:1 [a] 2Co 1:1 [b] Eph 3:6; 1Ti 6:19 **1:2** [c] Ac 16:1 [d] 1Ti 1:2
1:3 [e] Ro 1:8 [f] Ro 1:10 **1:4** [g] Ac 20:37 [h] 2Ti 4:9
1:5 [i] 1Ti 1:5 [j] Ac 16:1 **1:6** [k] 1Ti 4:14 **1:7** [l] Ro 8:15
1:8 [m] Mk 8:38; Ro 1:16 [n] Eph 3:1 [o] 2Ti 2:3,9; 4:5
1:9 [p] Ro 8:28 **1:10** [q] Eph 1:9 [r] 1Co 15:26,54

immortality to light through the gospel.
11And of this gospel I was appointed a herald and an apostle and a teacher.[s] 12That is
why I am suffering as I am. Yet this is no
cause for shame, because I know whom I
have believed, and am convinced that he is
able to guard[t] what I have entrusted to him
until that day.[u]
13What you heard from me, keep[v] as the
pattern of sound teaching, with faith and
love in Christ Jesus.[w] 14Guard the good deposit that was entrusted to you—guard it
with the help of the Holy Spirit who lives
in us.[x]

Examples of Disloyalty and Loyalty

15You know that everyone in the province of Asia has deserted me,[y] including
Phygelus and Hermogenes.
16May the Lord show mercy to the household of Onesiphorus,[z] because he often refreshed me and was not ashamed of my
chains. 17On the contrary, when he was
in Rome, he searched hard for me until he
found me. 18May the Lord grant that he
will find mercy from the Lord on that day!
You know very well in how many ways he
helped me[a] in Ephesus.

The Appeal Renewed

2 You then, my son, be strong[b] in the grace
that is in Christ Jesus. 2And the things
you have heard me say[c] in the presence of
many witnesses[d] entrust to reliable people
who will also be qualified to teach others.
3Join with me in suffering, like a good soldier[e] of Christ Jesus. 4No one serving as
a soldier gets entangled in civilian affairs,
but rather tries to please his commanding
officer. 5Similarly, anyone who competes
as an athlete does not receive the victor's
crown[f] except by competing according to
the rules. 6The hardworking farmer should
be the first to receive a share of the crops.
7Reflect on what I am saying, for the Lord
will give you insight into all this.
8Remember Jesus Christ, raised from
the dead,[g] descended from David.[h] This
is my gospel,[i] 9for which I am suffering[j]
even to the point of being chained like a
criminal. But God's word is not chained.
10Therefore I endure everything[k] for the
sake of the elect, that they too may obtain
the salvation that is in Christ Jesus, with
eternal glory.[l]
11Here is a trustworthy saying:

If we died with him,
  we will also live with him;[m]
12 if we endure,
  we will also reign with him.[n]
If we disown him,
  he will also disown us;[o]
13 if we are faithless,
  he remains faithful,[p]
  for he cannot disown himself.

Dealing With False Teachers

14Keep reminding God's people of these
things. Warn them before God against
quarreling about words;[q] it is of no value,
and only ruins those who listen. 15Do your
best to present yourself to God as one approved, a worker who does not need to be
ashamed and who correctly handles the
word of truth.[r] 16Avoid godless chatter,[s] because those who indulge in it will become
more and more ungodly. 17Their teaching
will spread like gangrene. Among them
are Hymenaeus[t] and Philetus, 18who have
departed from the truth. They say that the
resurrection has already taken place, and
they destroy the faith of some.[u] 19Neverthe-

1:12 ***what I have entrusted.*** It is certain that God will keep our "deposit" safe. Paul was preparing for imminent death, but in spite of this he was hopeful. He had spent his time, resources, and even his life on proclaiming the gospel, and this investment in Christ's kingdom would bring him an abundant reward in eternity (Luke 19:15; 1 Cor. 3:10–15; Rev. 11:15,18).

1:14 ***the good deposit.*** This is the truth of the kingdom of heaven (Matt. 13:44–45; 1 Tim. 6:20).

2:1 ***strong in the grace that is in Christ Jesus.*** The emphasis is on the strength of Christ, not on Timothy's own power. If we trust in ourselves, we are doomed to fail.

2:2 ***entrust to reliable people.*** Since the time of Christ, there has been an endless chain of Christian discipleship (Matt. 28:18–20).

2:8 ***descended from David.*** Jesus is the fulfillment of all the promises that God gave to David (2 Sam. 7:11–16).

2:11 ***if we died ... we will also live.*** Believers are united with Christ in His death and resurrection (Rom. 6:3–11).

2:12 ***if we endure.*** Persevering in our faith, even in the face of hardship or persecution, will result in a reward when Christ returns (Luke 19:11–27; Rom. 8:17; Rev. 3:21).

2:13 ***faithless.*** This word describes an immature believer who lives for self and not for the Savior (1 Cor. 3:1–3,15). ***he remains faithful.*** For Christ to abandon us would be contrary to His faithful nature (John 10:27–30; Heb. 10:23; 13:5).

2:15 ***Do your best.*** The position of teaching God's word is a position of great responsibility, not to be taken lightly (James 3:1).

2:18 ***already taken place.*** This was probably an early form of Gnosticism, a body of teaching which emphasized the "spiritual," and considered the physical world and the human body unreal and unimportant.

1:11 [s] 1Ti 2:7 **1:12** [t] 1Ti 6:20 [u] ver 18 **1:13** [v] Titus 1:9 [w] 1Ti 1:14 **1:14** [x] Ro 8:9 **1:15** [y] 2Ti 4:10,11,16 **1:16** [z] 2Ti 4:19 **1:18** [a] Heb 6:10 **2:1** [b] Eph 6:10 **2:2** [c] 2Ti 1:13 [d] 1Ti 6:12 **2:3** [e] 1Ti 1:18 **2:5** [f] 1Co 9:25 **2:8** [g] Ac 2:24 [h] Mt 1:1 [i] Ro 2:16 **2:9** [j] Ac 9:16 **2:10** [k] Col 1:24 [l] 2Co 4:17 **2:11** [m] Ro 6:2-11 **2:12** [n] Ro 8:17; 1Pe 4:13 [o] Mt 10:33 **2:13** [p] Nu 23:19; Ro 3:3 **2:14** [q] 1Ti 6:4 **2:15** [r] Eph 1:13; Jas 1:18 **2:16** [s] Titus 3:9 **2:17** [t] 1Ti 1:20 **2:18** [u] 1Ti 1:19

less, God's solid foundation stands firm,[v] sealed with this inscription: "The Lord knows those who are his,"[w] and, "Everyone who confesses the name of the Lord[x] must turn away from wickedness."

20 In a large house there are articles not only of gold and silver, but also of wood and clay; some are for special purposes and some for common use.[y] 21 Those who cleanse themselves from the latter will be instruments for special purposes, made holy, useful to the Master and prepared to do any good work.[z]

22 Flee the evil desires of youth and pursue righteousness, faith, love[a] and peace, along with those who call on the Lord out of a pure heart.[b] 23 Don't have anything to do with foolish and stupid arguments, because you know they produce quarrels. 24 And the Lord's servant must not be quarrelsome but must be kind to everyone, able to teach, not resentful.[c] 25 Opponents must be gently instructed, in the hope that God will grant them repentance leading them to a knowledge of the truth,[d] 26 and that they will come to their senses and escape from the trap of the devil,[e] who has taken them captive to do his will.

3 But mark this: There will be terrible times in the last days.[f] 2 People will be lovers of themselves, lovers of money,[g] boastful, proud,[h] abusive, disobedient to their parents,[i] ungrateful, unholy, 3 without love, unforgiving, slanderous, without self-control, brutal, not lovers of the good, 4 treacherous, rash, conceited,[j] lovers of pleasure rather than lovers of God— 5 having a form of godliness but denying its power. Have nothing to do with such people.

6 They are the kind who worm their way[k] into homes and gain control over gullible women, who are loaded down with sins and are swayed by all kinds of evil desires, 7 always learning but never able to come to a knowledge of the truth. 8 Just as Jannes and Jambres opposed Moses,[l] so also these teachers oppose[m] the truth. They are men of depraved minds,[n] who, as far as the faith is concerned, are rejected. 9 But they will not get very far because, as in the case of those men,[o] their folly will be clear to everyone.

A Final Charge to Timothy

10 You, however, know all about my teaching,[p] my way of life, my purpose, faith, patience, love, endurance, 11 persecutions, sufferings—what kinds of things happened to me in Antioch,[q] Iconium and Lystra, the persecutions I endured.[r] Yet the Lord rescued me from all of them.[s] 12 In fact, everyone who wants to live a godly life in Christ Jesus will be persecuted,[t] 13 while evildoers and impostors will go from bad to worse,[u] deceiving and being deceived. 14 But as for you, continue in what you have learned and have become convinced of, because you know those from whom you learned it,[v] 15 and how from infancy[w] you have known the Holy Scriptures,[x] which are able to make you wise[y] for salvation through faith in Christ Jesus. 16 All Scripture is God-breathed[z] and is useful for teaching,[a] rebuking, correcting and training in righteousness, 17 so that the servant of God[ab] may be thoroughly equipped for every good work.[c]

---

[a] 17 Or *that you, a man of God,*

2:21 ***Master.*** This is a strong term for God's authority over the lives of believers, regardless of their level of spiritual maturity.

2:22 ***Flee ... pursue.*** When we run toward righteousness, we are running away from sin. The two are completely opposite, and a person cannot follow both at once.

2:25 ***gently instructed.*** The aim of instruction is repentance or a change of thinking, not self-justification or the pleasure of argument.

2:26 ***come to their senses.*** False teaching has an intoxicating effect that dulls the mind to God's truth.

3:5 ***a form of godliness.*** This is an outward appearance of reverence for God. Denying its power describes religious activity that is not connected to a living relationship with Jesus Christ. This kind of religion provokes God's anger (Is. 1:10–18; Matt. 23:25–28).

3:8 ***Jannes and Jambres.*** They are not named in the Old Testament, but according to Jewish tradition, Jannes and Jambres were two of the Egyptian magicians who opposed Moses (Ex. 7:11).

3:12 ***will be persecuted.*** God does not promise deliverance *from* persecution, but deliverance *through* it. Persecution is one of the means that God uses to bring about our growth and sanctification (2:12; Matt. 5:10–12; Rev. 2:10).

3:16 ***God-breathed.*** Scripture was freely produced by human writers, but the original Author is God Himself. God "breathed out" the Scriptures so that they are not only human words, but simultaneously and ultimately the very utterances of God. Thus, Scripture is true in all that it affirms and is completely authoritative (1 Pet. 1:20–21). The Bible not only "contains God's words," it *is* God's Word. Therefore the Scriptures are fully consistent and inerrant, authoritative and trustworthy.

3:17 ***every good work.*** Paul emphasizes the essential link between knowing God's Word and applying it to one's daily life. Right doctrine should produce right practice.

2:19 [v] Isa 28:16 [w] Jn 10:14 [x] 1Co 1:2 **2:20** [y] Ro 9:21 **2:21** [z] 2Ti 3:17 **2:22** [a] 1Ti 1:14; 6:11 [b] 1Ti 1:5 **2:24** [c] 1Ti 3:2, 3 **2:25** [d] 1Ti 2:4 **2:26** [e] 1Ti 3:7 **3:1** [f] 1Ti 4:1 **3:2** [g] 1Ti 3:3 [h] Ro 1:30 [i] Ro 1:30 **3:4** [j] 1Ti 3:6 **3:6** [k] Jude 4 **3:8** [l] Ex 7:11 [m] Ac 13:8 [n] 1Ti 6:5 **3:9** [o] Ex 7:12 **3:10** [p] 1Ti 4:6 **3:11** [q] Ac 13:14, 50 [r] 2Co 11:23-27 [s] Ps 34:19 **3:12** [t] Ac 14:22 **3:13** [u] 2Ti 2:16 **3:14** [v] 2Ti 1:13 **3:15** [w] 2Ti 1:5 [x] Jn 5:39 [y] Ps 119:98, 99 **3:16** [z] 2Pe 1:20, 21 [a] Ro 4:23, 24 **3:17** [b] 1Ti 6:11 [c] 2Ti 2:21

4 In the presence of God and of Christ Jesus, who will judge the living and the dead,[d] and in view of his appearing and his kingdom, I give you this charge:[e] 2Preach[f] the word;[g] be prepared in season and out of season; correct, rebuke[h] and encourage—with great patience and careful instruction. 3For the time will come when people will not put up with sound doctrine.[i] Instead, to suit their own desires, they will gather around them a great number of teachers to say what their itching ears want to hear. 4They will turn their ears away from the truth and turn aside to myths.[j] 5But you, keep your head in all situations, endure hardship,[k] do the work of an evangelist,[l] discharge all the duties of your ministry.

6For I am already being poured out like a drink offering,[m] and the time for my departure is near.[n] 7I have fought the good fight,[o] I have finished the race,[p] I have kept the faith. 8Now there is in store for me[q] the crown of righteousness, which the Lord, the righteous Judge, will award to me on that day[r]—and not only to me, but also to all who have longed for his appearing.

Personal Remarks

9Do your best to come to me quickly, 10for Demas,[s] because he loved this world,[t] has deserted me and has gone to Thessalonica. Crescens has gone to Galatia,[u] and Titus to Dalmatia. 11Only Luke[v] is with me.[w] Get Mark[x] and bring him with you, because he is helpful to me in my ministry. 12I sent Tychicus[y] to Ephesus. 13When you come, bring the cloak that I left with Carpus at Troas, and my scrolls, especially the parchments.

14Alexander[z] the metalworker did me a great deal of harm. The Lord will repay him for what he has done.[a] 15You too should be on your guard against him, because he strongly opposed our message.

16At my first defense, no one came to my support, but everyone deserted me. May it not be held against them.[b] 17But the Lord stood at my side[c] and gave me strength, so that through me the message might be fully proclaimed and all the Gentiles might hear it.[d] And I was delivered from the lion's mouth. 18The Lord will rescue me from every evil attack[e] and will bring me safely to his heavenly kingdom. To him be glory for ever and ever. Amen.[f]

Final Greetings

19Greet Priscilla[a] and Aquila[g] and the household of Onesiphorus. 20Erastus[h] stayed in Corinth, and I left Trophimus[i] sick in Miletus. 21Do your best to get here before winter.[j] Eubulus greets you, and so do Pudens, Linus, Claudia and all the brothers and sisters.[b]

22The Lord be with your spirit.[k] Grace be with you all.[l]

---

a 19 Greek *Prisca,* a variant of *Priscilla* *b* 21 The Greek word for *brothers and sisters* (*adelphoi*) refers here to believers, both men and women, as part of God's family.

4:2 *great patience.* Patience and correct doctrine are two necessary components of an effective ministry. True spiritual growth occurs over a period of time, through consistent teaching and application of God's Word.

4:6 *drink offering.* An offering performed by pouring wine out on the ground or altar (Num. 28:11–31). Paul's life was already being poured out in service to Christ.

4:7 *fought the good fight.* Paul did not make these comments until the end of his race, when he was about to die. He did not presume or rely on His past service. Instead, he persevered, struggled, and served God until the end (1 Cor. 9:24–27).

4:8 *longed for his appearing.* These are the believers who have lived faithfully in the hope of His return (Titus 2:11–15; 1 John 2:28).

4:11 *Mark.* Mark's desertion of Paul in Pamphylia on his first missionary journey had led to the separation of Paul and Barnabas at the beginning of Paul's second missionary journey (Acts 15:36–40). Later Paul and Mark were reconciled, and Mark served Paul in the ministry (Col. 4:10). It is believed that Mark later wrote the Gospel of Mark.

4:12 *Tychicus.* Tychicus was Paul's faithful coworker (Acts 20:4; Eph. 6:21; Col. 4:7).

4:14 *Alexander.* This may be the person named in 1 Timothy 1:20 or Acts 19:33, who caused harm to Paul's ministry in Ephesus.

4:19 *Priscilla and Aquila.* Paul had met Priscilla and Aquila in Corinth on his second missionary journey (Acts 18:1–3), and they had assisted in God's work in Ephesus (Acts 18:18–19).

4:20 *Trophimus.* Trophimus, a member of the church of Ephesus (Acts 21:29), had traveled with Paul to Jerusalem (Acts 20:4).

4:1 [d] Ac 10:42 [e] 1Ti 5:21 **4:2** [f] 1Ti 4:13 [g] Gal 6:6 [h] 1Ti 5:20; Titus 1:13; 2:15 **4:3** [i] 1Ti 1:10 **4:4** [j] 1Ti 1:4 **4:5** [k] 2Ti 1:8 [l] Ac 21:8 **4:6** [m] Php 2:17 [n] Php 1:23 **4:7** [o] 1Ti 1:18 [p] 1Co 9:24 **4:8** [q] Col 1:5 [r] 2Ti 1:12 **4:10** [s] Col 4:14 [t] 1Jn 2:15 [u] Ac 16:6 **4:11** [v] Col 4:14 [w] 2Ti 1:15 [x] Ac 12:12 **4:12** [y] Ac 20:4 **4:14** [z] Ac 19:33 [a] Ro 12:19 **4:16** [b] Ac 7:60 **4:17** [c] Ac 23:11 [d] Ac 9:15 **4:18** [e] Ps 121:7 [f] Ro 11:36 **4:19** [g] Ac 18:2 **4:20** [h] Ac 19:22 [i] Ac 20:4 **4:21** [j] ver 9 **4:22** [k] Gal 6:18; Phm 25 [l] Col 4:18

TITUS

▸ **AUTHOR:** Titus was one of Paul's Gentile converts. He probably worked with Paul during his time at Ephesus on his third missionary journey. Later he also worked in Corinth and this letter indicates that Paul is commissioning him to work on the island of Crete. Paul wrote this letter about A.D. 63, perhaps from Corinth, taking advantage of the journey of Zenas and Apollos (3:13), whose destination would take them by way of Crete.

▸ **TIME:** c. A.D. 63 ▸ **KEY VERSE:** Titus 3:8

▸ **THEME:** Paul's instructions to Titus are similar to those he gives to Timothy. He gives him instructions about the leadership and organization of the church and guidance in dealing with the opposition of those who would contradict his teaching. His tone is that of a seasoned leader passing on the essential instructions to a valued disciple.

---

1 Paul, a servant of God[a] and an apostle of
Jesus Christ to further the faith of God's
elect and their knowledge of the truth[b] that
leads to godliness— 2in the hope of eternal
life,[c] which God, who does not lie, promised before the beginning of time,[d] 3and
which now at his appointed season[e] he has
brought to light[f] through the preaching entrusted to me[g] by the command of God our
Savior,[h]

4To Titus,[i] my true son in our common
faith:

Grace and peace from God the Father
and Christ Jesus our Savior.

Appointing Elders Who Love What Is Good

5The reason I left you in Crete[j] was that
you might put in order what was left unfinished and appoint[a] elders[k] in every
town, as I directed you. 6An elder must
be blameless,[l] faithful to his wife, a man
whose children believe[b] and are not open
to the charge of being wild and disobedient. 7Since an overseer[m] manages God's
household,[n] he must be blameless—
not overbearing, not quick-tempered,
not given to drunkenness, not violent,

[a] 5 Or *ordain* [b] 6 Or *children are trustworthy*

1:2 We Can Trust God—Often Christians will doubt our position with God simply because we do not *feel* saved. We don't understand that the basis for our standing is the promise of God and not emotional feelings. One helpful way to see these promises is in relation to the Trinity:

1. *The promise and work of the Father.* He has promised to graciously accept in Christ all repenting sinners (Eph. 1:6 and Col. 3:3). This means a Christian has the right to be in heaven someday, for he is in Christ. God guarantees us that He will work out all things for our ultimate good (Rom. 8:28).
2. *The promise and work of the Son.* He has promised us eternal life (John 5:24) and abundant life (John 10:10). This promise covers not only our final destiny in heaven, but also our present Christian service here on earth. He is, in fact, right now praying for us and ministering to us at His Father's right hand (Heb. 8:1; 9:24).
3. *The promise and work of the Holy Spirit.* The Holy Spirit is said to indwell the believer (John 14:16). In addition, He places all believing sinners into the body of Christ, thus assuring us of union with God's family (1 Cor. 12:13).

1:3 *preaching.* Paul places the emphasis on the message, not on the messenger. Christ is the center of our faith, not any one preacher (1 Cor. 9:16; 2 Cor. 4:5).
1:5 *appoint elders.* The Greek words for "elder" and "overseer" seem to have been used interchangeably by Paul (v. 7). "Elder" perhaps speaks more of the office and its authority, while "overseer" may speak more of the person's function and the ministry of oversight (Acts 20:17).
1:6 *faithful to his wife.* The exact application of this phrase is debated; some believe that it merely forbids polygamy, while others believe that it also prohibits a man who is divorced and remarried. It is clearly emphasizing the importance of marital faithfulness (Matt. 19:5). ***children believe.*** The man must have a good relationship with his wife, and he should also have children who demonstrate faithfulness to God. If a man has children who reject the ways of God, or who are out of control, this reflects on the father's ability to lead others outside his home.

1:1 [a] Ro 1:1 [b] 1Ti 2:4 **1:2** [c] 2Ti 1:1 [d] 2Ti 1:9 **1:3** [e] 1Ti 2:6 [f] 2Ti 1:10 [g] 1Ti 1:11 [h] Lk 1:47 **1:4** [i] 2Co 2:13 **1:5** [j] Ac 27:7 [k] Ac 11:30 **1:6** [l] 1Ti 3:2 **1:7** [m] 1Ti 3:1 [n] 1Co 4:1

not pursuing dishonest gain.[o] 8Rather, he
must be hospitable,[p] one who loves what is
good,[q] who is self-controlled, upright, holy
and disciplined. 9He must hold firmly[r] to
the trustworthy message as it has been
taught, so that he can encourage others
by sound doctrine[s] and refute those who
oppose it.

Rebuking Those Who Fail to Do Good

10For there are many rebellious people,
full of meaningless talk[t] and deception, especially those of the circumcision group.[u]
11They must be silenced, because they are
disrupting whole households[v] by teaching things they ought not to teach—and
that for the sake of dishonest gain. 12One
of Crete's own prophets[w] has said it: "Cretans[x] are always liars, evil brutes, lazy
gluttons."[a] 13This saying is true. Therefore
rebuke[y] them sharply, so that they will be
sound in the faith[z] 14and will pay no attention to Jewish myths[a] or to the merely
human commands[b] of those who reject the
truth. 15To the pure, all things are pure, but
to those who are corrupted and do not believe, nothing is pure.[c] In fact, both their
minds and consciences are corrupted.
16They claim to know God, but by their actions they deny him.[d] They are detestable,
disobedient and unfit for doing anything
good.

Doing Good for the Sake of the Gospel

2 You, however, must teach what is appropriate to sound doctrine.[e] 2Teach
the older men to be temperate, worthy of
respect, self-controlled, and sound in faith,[f]
in love and in endurance.

3Likewise, teach the older women to
be reverent in the way they live, not to be
slanderers or addicted to much wine,[g] but
to teach what is good. 4Then they can urge
the younger women to love their husbands
and children, 5to be self-controlled and
pure, to be busy at home, to be kind, and
to be subject to their husbands,[h] so that no
one will malign the word of God.[i]

6Similarly, encourage the young men[j] to
be self-controlled. 7In everything set them
an example[k] by doing what is good. In
your teaching show integrity, seriousness
8and soundness of speech that cannot be
condemned, so that those who oppose you
may be ashamed because they have nothing bad to say about us.[l]

9Teach slaves to be subject to their masters in everything,[m] to try to please them,
not to talk back to them, 10and not to steal
from them, but to show that they can be
fully trusted, so that in every way they will
make the teaching about God our Savior
attractive.[n]

11For the grace of God has appeared that

a *12* From the Cretan philosopher Epimenides

1:9 *refute.* The word *refute* here means to rebuke in such a way as to produce repentance and confession of sin (John 16:8). A rebuke can have the positive results of producing change in a person's life.
1:10 *those of the circumcision.* Apparently there were Jewish Christians in the churches of Crete who were limiting the Christian freedom of Gentile Christians by requiring an adherence to Jewish laws (Gal. 3).
1:12 *Cretans are always liars.* Paul is quoting the Cretan poet Epimenides, who wrote these words around 600 B.C. The Cretans were so much regarded as liars in the Mediterranean world that the expression "to Cretinize" meant "to lie."
1:14 *Jewish myths.* These were probably legends about Old Testament figures, like some that survive to this day in non-biblical writings.
1:15 *To the pure . . . to those who are corrupted.* Paul highlights the mistaken asceticism of the Cretan false teachers. They had identified certain foods and practices as defiled when in reality it was their minds that were defiled and unbelieving. On the other hand, to the pure, all things are pure. The Cretan believers had placed their trust in Christ, focusing their minds on Him, and therefore they would be empowered by God's Spirit to lead pure lives. Jesus taught the same principle in Matthew 15:11. Physical objects or external practices do not defile a person, but a mind focused on evil thoroughly corrupts.
2:1 *sound doctrine.* "Sound" means "healthy." Right thinking is the raw material for right actions (Ps. 119:11; Prov. 23:7; Rom. 12:2; James 1:13–15). Our actions will naturally reveal the direction of our thoughts.
2:2 *older men.* Maturity is not determined simply by age or even by how much a person knows; it is determined by how skilled a person is in applying the truth to life and in distinguishing good from evil (Heb. 5:13–14).
2:4 *love their husbands . . . children.* This is not just romantic or emotional love, but the commitment of a woman to the welfare of her husband and children.
2:5 *subject to their husbands.* Women are not under the authority of men in general, but rather the authority of their own husbands (Eph. 5:21). ***no one will malign the word of God.*** The older women are to teach the younger women so that their actions will glorify God, build His kingdom, and strengthen the family. Failure to follow Paul's instructions will result in the word of God being maligned in the pagan community.
2:6 *young men.* Young men are to pursue the character qualities that older men should possess already.
2:7 *example by doing what is good.* More people will learn from our daily actions than from what we say.
2:11 *appeared.* Christ came the first time in grace to save men from their sins; the second time He will come in glory to reign (v. 13).

1:7 [o] 1Ti 3:3,8 **1:8** [p] 1Ti 3:2 [q] 2Ti 3:3 **1:9** [r] 1Ti 1:19 [s] 1Ti 1:10 **1:10** [t] 1Ti 1:6 [u] Ac 11:2 **1:11** [v] 2Ti 3:6 **1:12** [w] Ac 17:28 [x] Ac 2:11 **1:13** [y] 2Co 13:10 [z] Titus 2:2 **1:14** [a] 1Ti 1:4 [b] Col 2:22 **1:15** [c] Ro 14:14,23 **1:16** [d] 1Jn 2:4 **2:1** [e] 1Ti 1:10 **2:2** [f] Titus 1:13 **2:3** [g] 1Ti 3:8 **2:5** [h] Eph 5:22 [i] 1Ti 6:1 **2:6** [j] 1Ti 5:1 **2:7** [k] 1Ti 4:12 **2:8** [l] 1Pe 2:12 **2:9** [m] Eph 6:5 **2:10** [n] Mt 5:16

offers salvation to all people.[o] 12It teaches
us to say "No" to ungodliness and worldly
passions,[p] and to live self-controlled, upright and godly lives[q] in this present age,
13while we wait for the blessed hope—the
appearing of the glory of our great God and
Savior, Jesus Christ,[r] 14who gave himself
for us to redeem us from all wickedness
and to purify for himself a people that are
his very own,[s] eager to do what is good.[t]
15These, then, are the things you should
teach. Encourage and rebuke with all authority. Do not let anyone despise you.

Saved in Order to Do Good

3 Remind the people to be subject to rulers and authorities,[u] to be obedient, to
be ready to do whatever is good,[v] 2to slander no one,[w] to be peaceable and considerate, and always to be gentle toward everyone.
3At one time we too were foolish, disobedient, deceived and enslaved by all
kinds of passions and pleasures. We lived
in malice and envy, being hated and hating one another. 4But when the kindness[x]
and love of God our Savior appeared,[y] 5he
saved us, not because of righteous things
we had done,[z] but because of his mercy. He
saved us through the washing of rebirth
and renewal[a] by the Holy Spirit, 6whom
he poured out on us[b] generously through
Jesus Christ our Savior, 7so that, having
been justified by his grace,[c] we might become heirs[d] having the hope[e] of eternal
life.[f] 8This is a trustworthy saying.[g] And
I want you to stress these things, so that
those who have trusted in God may be
careful to devote themselves to doing what
is good.[h] These things are excellent and
profitable for everyone.
9But avoid foolish controversies and genealogies and arguments and quarrels[i]
about the law, because these are unprofitable and useless. 10Warn a divisive person once, and then warn them a second
time. After that, have nothing to do with
them.[j] 11You may be sure that such people
are warped and sinful; they are self-con-
demned.

Final Remarks

12As soon as I send Artemas or Tychicus[k] to you, do your best to come to me at
Nicopolis, because I have decided to winter
there.[l] 13Do everything you can to help Zenas the lawyer and Apollos[m] on their way
and see that they have everything they
need. 14Our people must learn to devote
themselves to doing what is good,[n] in order to provide for urgent needs and not live
unproductive lives.
15Everyone with me sends you greetings.
Greet those who love us in the faith.[o]
Grace be with you all.[p]

2:13 ***wait for the blessed hope.*** Paul reminded Timothy that there is a special crown awaiting all who "have longed for his appearing" (2 Tim. 4:8). ***great God and Savior, Jesus Christ.*** This is one of the strongest statements of the deity of Christ in the New Testament.

2:14 ***redeem.*** "Redeem" means "to purchase." With His death on the cross, Christ paid the price to release us from the bondage of sin (Rom. 6:6–7,17,20; Eph. 1:7). God's purpose in redeeming us is not only to save us from hell; He also wants to free us from sin so that we can produce good works that glorify Him (Eph. 2:8–10).

3:1 ***Remind the people.*** The Cretans notoriously lacked the virtue of good citizenship (1:12). Disobedience permeated the Cretan's lifestyle, both in the church (v. 10) and in government. Believers who got along with civil authorities and who lived peacefully with their neighbors would reflect positively on their faith and would glorify God.

3:5 ***not because of righteous things.*** Paul has been exhorting Titus to emphasize good works in his ministry with the Cretans, and he wants to make it clear that such good works have no value in saving a person. It is solely on the basis of God's mercy that we are delivered from the penalty of our sin. ***washing of rebirth.*** This phrase refers to the work of the Holy Spirit, in whom we are "born again" (John 3:3,6), given a new nature and cleansed from old sin. ***renewal by the Holy Spirit.*** There are two works performed by the Holy Spirit in preparing nonbelievers to become Christians. (1) *The Holy Spirit convicts.* Mankind's sin and righteousness are exposed by the Holy Spirit (John 16:8). Two examples of such conviction are Felix, a Roman governor who "trembled" under conviction (Acts 24:25), and King Agrippa, who was almost persuaded in Acts 26:28. (2) *The Holy Spirit regenerates.* When a repenting sinner accepts Christ as Savior, he is given a new nature by the Holy Spirit (2 Cor. 5:17). Jesus carefully explained this ministry of the Holy Spirit to Nicodemus (John 3:3–7).

3:7 ***we might become heirs.*** God justifies believers so that they might become co-heirs with Jesus Christ in His coming reign (Rom. 8:17; 2 Tim. 2:12).

3:10 ***Warn a divisive person.*** A sinner must always be given ample opportunity to repent, but if he insists on continuing in sin, the church is required to let him go (Matt. 18:15–17; 2 Thess. 3:14–15).

3:12 ***Tychicus.*** Tychicus, one of Paul's assistants, is also mentioned in Acts 20:4; Ephesians 6:21; Colossians 4:7; 2 Timothy 4:12.

3:13 ***Apollos.*** Apollos was a fellow worker of Paul's (1 Cor. 16:12), an Alexandrian who had been taught by Priscilla and Aquila and who had eloquently preached the gospel at Ephesus and Corinth (Acts 18:24–19:1).

3:14 ***not live unproductive lives.*** Justification is a free gift from God, but we will be rewarded according to what we do on this earth (Rev. 22:12). It would be tragedy to stand ashamed at Christ's return (1 John 2:28).

2:11 [o] 1Ti 2:4 **2:12** [p] Titus 3:3 [q] 2Ti 3:12 **2:13** [r] 2Pe 1:1
2:14 [s] Ex 19:5 [t] Eph 2:10 **3:1** [u] Ro 13:1 [v] 2Ti 2:21
3:2 [w] Eph 4:31; 2Ti 2:24 **3:4** [x] Eph 2:7 [y] Titus 2:11
3:5 [z] Eph 2:9 [a] Ro 12:2 **3:6** [b] Ro 5:5 **3:7** [c] Ro 3:24
[d] Ro 8:17 [e] Ro 8:24 [f] Titus 1:2 **3:8** [g] 1Ti 1:15 [h] Titus 2:14
3:9 [i] 1Ti 1:4; 2Ti 2:14 **3:10** [j] Ro 16:17 **3:12** [k] Ac 20:4
[l] 2Ti 4:9,21 **3:13** [m] Ac 18:24 **3:14** [n] ver 8
3:15 [o] 1Ti 1:2 [p] Col 4:18

PHILEMON

▶ **AUTHOR:** Though some critics deny its authenticity, the general consensus of scholarship recognizes Philemon as Paul's work. There could have been no doctrinal motive for its forgery, and it is supported externally by consistent tradition and internally by no less than three references to Paul (Philem. 1,9,19).

▶ **TIME:** C. A.D. 60–61 ▶ **KEY VERSES:** Philem. 16–17

▶ **THEME:** Paul wrote this letter to a slave owner in the church at Colosse. Apparently, Onesimus, the slave of Philemon had stolen from him and had run away, an act punishable by death under Roman law. Onesimus had since met Paul and become a Christian. Paul's letter is a personal appeal in an effort to help them reconcile and renew their relationship.

---

1 Paul, a prisoner[a] of Christ Jesus, and
Timothy our brother,[b]

To Philemon our dear friend and fellow
worker[c]— 2 also to Apphia our sister and
Archippus[d] our fellow soldier[e]—and to the
church that meets in your home:[f]

3 Grace and peace to you[a] from God our
Father and the Lord Jesus Christ.

Thanksgiving and Prayer

4 I always thank my God[g] as I remember
you in my prayers, 5 because I hear about
your love for all his holy people[h] and your
faith in the Lord Jesus. 6 I pray that your partnership with us in the faith may be effective
in deepening your understanding of every
good thing we share for the sake of Christ.
7 Your love has given me great joy and encouragement,[i] because you, brother, have
refreshed[j] the hearts of the Lord's people.

Paul's Plea for Onesimus

8 Therefore, although in Christ I could be
bold and order you to do what you ought to
do, 9 yet I prefer to appeal to you on the basis of love. It is as none other than Paul—an
old man and now also a prisoner[k] of Christ
Jesus— 10 that I appeal to you for my son[l]
Onesimus,[b][m] who became my son while I
was in chains. 11 Formerly he was useless
to you, but now he has become useful both
to you and to me.
12 I am sending him—who is my very
heart—back to you. 13 I would have liked
to keep him with me so that he could take
your place in helping me while I am in
chains for the gospel. 14 But I did not want
to do anything without your consent, so
that any favor you do would not seem
forced[n] but would be voluntary. 15 Perhaps
the reason he was separated from you for
a little while was that you might have him
back forever— 16 no longer as a slave, but
better than a slave, as a dear brother.[o] He
is very dear to me but even dearer to you,

a 3 The Greek is plural; also in verses 22 and 25; elsewhere in this letter "you" is singular.
b 10 *Onesimus* means *useful.*

1–2 *To Philemon ... and to the church.* Paul addresses the letter to Philemon and the Colossian church, but this intensely personal epistle uses the singular "I" and "you," demonstrating that the letter is Paul's personal plea to Philemon. It was written at the same time as the letter to the Colossians, and doubtless carried by the same messenger.
2 *Apphia ... Archippus.* Apphia may have been the wife of Philemon; Archippus may have been Philemon's son, or perhaps an elder in the Colossian church (Col. 4:17).
6 *faith may be effective.* Working faith is a sharing faith; it is the acknowledgment of what Christ has done in the believer's life (Eph. 3:17–19).
9 *Paul—an old man.* The apostle is either speaking of his old age, or of the office of an elder.
11 *useless ... useful.* Paul uses an interesting play on words here. Having mentioned Onesimus, whose name means "useful," the apostle describes him as someone who was formerly useless, but who has become useful through the work of Christ in his life.
14 *not ... forced.* Service for Christ is never forced. Paul has given Philemon several good reasons to forgive Onesimus, but here he returns to the foundation of his argument: Philemon's actions must proceed from his own love (v. 9).

1 [a] ver 9,23; Eph 3:1 [b] 2Co 1:1 [c] Php 2:25 **2** [d] Col 4:17 [e] Php 2:25 [f] Ro 16:5 **4** [g] Ro 1:8 **5** [h] Eph 1:15; Col 1:4 **7** [i] 2Co 7:4,13 [j] ver 20 **9** [k] ver 1,23 **10** [l] 1Co 4:15 [m] Col 4:9 **14** [n] 2Co 9:7; 1Pe 5:2 **16** [o] Mt 23:8; 1Ti 6:2

both as a fellow man and as a brother in
the Lord.
17So if you consider me a partner,[p] welcome him as you would welcome me. 18If
he has done you any wrong or owes you
anything, charge it to me. 19I, Paul, am
writing this with my own hand. I will pay
it back—not to mention that you owe me
your very self. 20I do wish, brother, that
I may have some benefit from you in the
Lord; refresh[q] my heart in Christ. 21Con-
fident[r] of your obedience, I write to you,
knowing that you will do even more than
I ask.
22And one thing more: Prepare a guest
room for me, because I hope to be[s] restored
to you in answer to your prayers.[t]

23Epaphras,[u] my fellow prisoner in
Christ Jesus, sends you greetings. 24And so
do Mark,[v] Aristarchus,[w] Demas[x] and Luke,
my fellow workers.
25The grace of the Lord Jesus Christ be
with your spirit.[y]

---

18 ***any wrong.*** Onesimus had probably stolen something from Philemon when he left. ***owes you anything.*** This accounting imagery reminds us of the theological truth that our sins were charged over to Christ even though He had not earned them. Forgiveness is costly (Is. 53:6).
19 ***my own hand.*** Paul wrote this personal letter himself, and therefore it could be considered a legal document obligating him to pay the damages that Onesimus had caused.
22 ***Prepare a guest room.*** It is believed that Paul wrote this letter during his imprisonment in Rome (Acts 28), and that he was released shortly afterwards. He was probably not at liberty for very long, but it is possible that he was able to visit Colosse before his second imprisonment and execution.
23–24 ***Epaphras ... Mark, Aristarchus, Demas and Luke.*** These five co-workers are also mentioned in Colossians 4:10–14.

17 [p] 2Co 8:23 **20** [q] ver 7 **21** [r] 2Co 2:3
22 [s] Php 1:25; 2:24 [t] 2Co 1:11 **23** [u] Col 1:7
24 [v] Ac 12:12 [w] Ac 19:29 [x] Col 4:14 **25** [y] 2Ti 4:22

HEBREWS

▶ **AUTHOR:** The origin of Hebrews is unknown. Uncertainty plagues not only its authorship, but also its date and its readership. Hebrews 13:18 – 24 tells us that this book was not anonymous to the original readers; they evidently knew the author. For some reason however, early church tradition is divided over the identity of the author. Part of the church attributed it to Paul, others preferred Barnabas, Luke, or Clement, and some chose anonymity. Some aspects of the language style and theology of Hebrews are very similar to Paul's epistles. However, significant stylistic differences have led the majority of biblical scholars to reject Pauline authorship of this book.

▶ **TIME:** c. A.D. 64 – 68 ▶ **KEY VERSES:** Heb. 4:14 – 16

▶ **THEME:** Hebrews was written for a group of Jewish Christians who were thinking about returning to their original faith. The author goes to great lengths to convince them to stay with their new faith. Point by point he goes through a whole series of arguments showing how Judaism was a foreshadowing of Christ. Everything promising about Old Testament Judaism is fulfilled in Christ. The new way is the superior way, as Christ and the faith that he established supersedes what has gone before. Understanding Jewish faith and practice, and the role of Moses and Aaron in biblical history is a prerequisite to understanding Hebrews.

God's Final Word: His Son

1 In the past God spoke[a] to our ancestors
through the prophets[b] at many times
and in various ways,[c] 2but in these last days
he has spoken to us by his Son, whom he
appointed heir[d] of all things, and through
whom[e] also he made the universe. 3The
Son is the radiance of God's glory[f] and the
exact representation of his being, sustaining all things[g] by his powerful word. After
he had provided purification for sins,[h] he
sat down at the right hand of the Majesty in
heaven.[i] 4So he became as much superior
to the angels as the name he has inherited
is superior to theirs.[j]

The Son Superior to Angels

5For to which of the angels did God ever
say,

"You are my Son;
today I have become your Father"*[a]*?[k]

Or again,

"I will be his Father,
and he will be my Son"*[b]*?[l]

6And again, when God brings his firstborn
into the world,[m] he says,

"Let all God's angels worship him."[c][n]

[a] 5 Psalm 2:7 *[b]* 5 2 Samuel 7:14; 1 Chron. 17:13
[c] 6 Deut. 32:43 (see Dead Sea Scrolls and Septuagint)

1:2 *by his Son.* This could be rephrased as "in such a person as a Son." The emphasis rests on the character of the revelation. It is a revelation of the Son, a revelation not so much in what He has said as in who He is and what He has done.
1:3 *radiance of God's glory.* The author of Hebrews is emphasizing that this is not a reflected brightness like the light of the moon. Instead, this is an inherent brightness like a ray from the sun. Jesus' glorious brightness comes from being essentially divine. ***exact representation.*** In Greek literature the word was used for stamping a coin from the die. ***sustaining.*** This means to "bear" or "carry," referring to movement and progress toward a final end. The Son not only created the universe by His powerful word, but also maintains and directs its course. He is the Governor of the universe. ***sat down.*** This suggests the formal act of assuming the office of High Priest and implies a contrast to the Levitical priest, who never finished his work and sat down (10:11 – 13).
1:5 *Today I have become your Father.* This probably refers to the day Christ sat down at the Father's right hand after He accomplished His work as the Messiah.
1:6 *When God brings his firstborn.* "Firstborn" refers to rank, meaning one who ranks above all others (Ps. 89:27).

1:1 [a] Jn 9:29; Heb 2:2,3 [b] Ac 2:30 [c] Nu 12:6,8 **1:2** [d] Ps 2:8 [e] Jn 1:3 **1:3** [f] Jn 1:14 [g] Col 1:17 [h] Heb 7:27 [i] Mk 16:19 **1:4** [j] Eph 1:21; Php 2:9,10 **1:5** [k] Ps 2:7 [l] 2Sa 7:14 **1:6** [m] Heb 10:5 [n] Dt 32:43 (LXX and DSS); Ps 97:7

[7]In speaking of the angels he says,

"He makes his angels spirits,
and his servants flames of fire."[a][o]

[8]But about the Son he says,

"Your throne, O God, will last for ever
and ever;
a scepter of justice will be the scepter
of your kingdom.
[9]You have loved righteousness and hated
wickedness;
therefore God, your God, has set you
above your companions[p]
by anointing you with the oil[q] of
joy."[b]

[10]He also says,

"In the beginning, Lord, you laid the
foundations of the earth,
and the heavens are the work of your
hands.
[11]They will perish, but you remain;
they will all wear out like a garment.[r]
[12]You will roll them up like a robe;
like a garment they will be changed.
But you remain the same,[s]
and your years will never end."[c][t]

[13]To which of the angels did God ever say,

"Sit at my right hand
until I make your enemies
a footstool[u] for your feet"[d]?[v]

[14]Are not all angels ministering spirits[w]
sent to serve those who will inherit salvation?[x]

Warning to Pay Attention

2 We must pay the most careful attention, therefore, to what we have heard,
so that we do not drift away. [2]For since
the message spoken[y] through angels[z] was
binding, and every violation and disobedience received its just punishment,[a] [3]how
shall we escape if we ignore so great a
salvation?[b] This salvation, which was first
announced by the Lord,[c] was confirmed to
us by those who heard him.[d] [4]God also testified to it by signs, wonders and various
miracles,[e] and by gifts of the Holy Spirit[f]
distributed according to his will.[g]

Jesus Made Fully Human

[5]It is not to angels that he has subjected the world to come, about which we are
speaking. [6]But there is a place where someone has testified:

"What is mankind that you are mindful
of them,
a son of man that you care for him?[h]
[7]You made them a little[e] lower than the
angels;
you crowned them with glory and
honor
[8] and put everything under their feet."[f,g][i]

In putting everything under them,[h] God
left nothing that is not subject to them.[h] Yet
at present we do not see everything subject to them.[h] [9]But we do see Jesus, who
was made lower than the angels for a little
while, now crowned with glory and hon-
or[j] because he suffered death,[k] so that by
the grace of God he might taste death for
everyone.[l]

---

[a] 7 Psalm 104:4 [b] 9 Psalm 45:6,7 [c] 12 Psalm 102:25-27 [d] 13 Psalm 110:1 [e] 7 Or *them for a little while* [f] 6-8 Psalm 8:4-6 [g] 7,8 Or *[7]You made him a little lower than the angels;/ you crowned him with glory and honor/ [8]and put everything under his feet."* [h] 8 Or *him*

1:7 *servants.* The Son is superior to angels because He is the Sovereign who is worshiped, while the angels are *servants,* that is, servants of God. The author of Hebrews quotes Psalm 104 because that psalm places angels in a long list of created objects which God sovereignly controls.
1:9 *companions.* This term comes from a word that means "close associates" or "partners." The concept of believers being partners with Christ is key in Hebrews (3:1,14; 6:4; 12:8) The term refers to those who will be participants with Christ in His reign.
1:10 – 12 *Lord, you.* The context of Psalm 102 here indicates that the Lord is the One who would appear in the future to Israel and the nations (Ps. 102:12 – 16).
1:14 *those who will inherit salvation.* Salvation here is not justification because it is in the future, not in the past. The reference is to believers who inherit the kingdom or rule in God's kingdom as a reward for their service to the Son (9:28; Col. 3:24).
2:1 *drift away.* The author's audience was marked by immaturity and spiritual sluggishness (5:11 – 12). The author warned them not to be carried away by the popular opinions that surrounded them. Instead, they were to hold fast to Christ's words because they were the words of God.
2:3 *how shall we escape.* If the people who heard the message delivered through angels were justly punished when they disobeyed the law, how can believers expect to escape punishment when they neglect the even greater message delivered through the greater Messenger, the Son?
2:4 *signs, wonders.* This phrase refers to the miracles performed by the Holy Spirit through the Lord and His apostles in fulfillment of the ancient promises regarding the coming of the Messiah (Acts 2:22,43; 4:30; 5:12; 6:8; 14:3; 15:12; 1 Cor. 12:12).
2:6 – 8 *and put everything under their feet.* Since the Son's humanity might appear to be an obstacle to the claim of His superiority, the author of Hebrews cites Psalm 8, a lyrical reflection on Genesis 1, to prove that God has placed humanity over all created things, which includes the angelic world.

1:7 [o] Ps 104:4 **1:9** [p] Php 2:9 [q] Isa 61:1,3 **1:11** [r] Isa 34:4 **1:12** [s] Heb 13:8 [t] Ps 102:25-27 **1:13** [u] Jos 10:24; Heb 10:13 [v] Ps 110:1 **1:14** [w] Ps 103:20 [x] Heb 5:9 **2:2** [y] Heb 1:1 [z] Dt 33:2; Ac 7:53 [a] Heb 10:28 **2:3** [b] Heb 10:29 [c] Heb 1:2 [d] Lk 1:2 **2:4** [e] Jn 4:48 [f] 1Co 12:4 [g] Eph 1:5 **2:6** [h] Job 7:17 **2:8** [i] Ps 8:4-6; 1Co 15:25 **2:9** [j] Ac 2:33; 3:13; Php 2:9 [k] Php 2:7-9 [l] Jn 3:16; 2Co 5:15

10 In bringing many sons and daughters
to glory, it was fitting that God, for whom
and through whom everything exists,[m]
should make the pioneer of their salvation
perfect through what he suffered.[n] 11 Both
the one who makes people holy and those
who are made holy[o] are of the same family.
So Jesus is not ashamed to call them brothers and sisters.[ap] 12 He says,

> "I will declare your name to my
> brothers and sisters;
> in the assembly I will sing your
> praises."[bq]

13 And again,

> "I will put my trust in him."[cr]

And again he says,

> "Here am I, and the children God has
> given me."[ds]

14 Since the children have flesh and
blood, he too shared in their humanity[t] so
that by his death he might break the power[u] of him who holds the power of death—
that is, the devil[v]— 15 and free those who
all their lives were held in slavery by their
fear[w] of death. 16 For surely it is not angels
he helps, but Abraham's descendants. 17 For
this reason he had to be made like them,[ex]
fully human in every way, in order that he
might become a merciful[y] and faithful high
priest[z] in service to God,[a] and that he might
make atonement for the sins of the people.
18 Because he himself suffered when he was
tempted, he is able to help those who are
being tempted.[b]

Jesus Greater Than Moses

3 Therefore, holy brothers and sisters,[c]
who share in the heavenly calling,
fix your thoughts on Jesus, whom we acknowledge[d] as our apostle and high priest.[e]
2 He was faithful to the one who appointed him, just as Moses was faithful in all
God's house.[f] 3 Jesus has been found worthy of greater honor than Moses, just as the
builder of a house has greater honor than
the house itself. 4 For every house is built by
someone, but God is the builder of everything. 5 "Moses was faithful as a servant[g]
in all God's house,"[fh] bearing witness to
what would be spoken by God in the future. 6 But Christ is faithful as the Son[i] over
God's house. And we are his house,[j] if indeed we hold firmly[k] to our confidence and
the hope[l] in which we glory.

---

[a] *11* The Greek word for *brothers and sisters* (*adelphoi*) refers here to believers, both men and women, as part of God's family; also in verse 12; and in 3:1, 12; 10:19; 13:22. [b] *12* Psalm 22:22 [c] *13* Isaiah 8:17 [d] *13* Isaiah 8:18 [e] *17* Or *like his brothers* [f] *5* Num. 12:7

2:10 ***pioneer of their salvation.*** The Greek word here means "leader" or "originator." The word describes a pioneer or pathfinder. Jesus' endurance of sufferings on this earth makes Him our leader. He not only endured them but also triumphed over sin, death, and Satan through them.
2:12 ***to my brothers and sisters.*** Psalm 22 is quoted here. In it, the Messiah refers to "my brothers and sisters," identifying Himself with all those who place their faith in God.
2:14–16 ***he might break ... free those who all their lives were held in slavery.*** Having established the unity between the Son and believer, the author concludes that there are two purposes of this close identification. The Son became human so that He could destroy the devil and release those who were in bondage to sin.
2:16 ***Abraham's descendants.*** The author may have used the expression because the recipients of this letter were primarily Jewish believers. The author is pointing out that Christ came to the aid of Abraham's sons, not the angelic hosts.
2:17 ***in service to God.*** Jesus participated in our nature and in our sufferings on earth so that He could be a sympathetic Mediator between God and humanity. He understands our weaknesses and intercedes for us in the presence of God the Father. ***make atonement.*** This term refers to the satisfaction of the claims of a holy and righteous God against sinners who have broken His law. Christ appeased God's righteous wrath by dying on the cross in our place (Rom. 3:21–26). Although completely sinless, Christ voluntarily submitted to the penalty of sin, His agonizing death on the cross. This voluntary sacrifice of Himself for our welfare satisfied the justice and holiness of God. The benefits of His sacrifice are applied to all who place their faith in Him.
2:18 ***he himself suffered when he was tempted.*** Christ's suffering included temptation. He experienced the lure of sin, but He never surrendered Himself to it. He knows what it is like to be tempted, so He knows how to assist those who are being tempted.
3:2 ***in all God's house.*** This phrase is taken from Numbers 12:7. "House" refers to the tabernacle, the center of Israelite worship. Moses had faithfully obeyed God's instructions concerning the tabernacle. In the same way, Jesus had been obedient to the mission the Father had given Him. Through obedience, God established a new house of God, the church.
3:3–4 ***worthy of greater honor than Moses.*** The implication is that the covenant established through Jesus' death is more glorious than the covenant established at Mount Sinai.
3:5 ***as a servant.*** The author of Hebrews continues the comparison between Moses and Jesus. While Moses was faithful as a servant, Christ's faithfulness was greater because it was performed by a Son. ***what would be spoken ... in the future.*** Moses' work pointed forward to Christ (9:10; 10:3). The regulations of the law of Moses pointed out both the sin of humanity and the need for a perfect sacrifice to reconcile people to their holy Creator.

2:10 [m] Ro 11:36 [n] Lk 24:26; Heb 7:28 **2:11** [o] Heb 10:10 [p] Mt 28:10; Jn 20:17 **2:12** [q] Ps 22:22 **2:13** [r] Isa 8:17 [s] Isa 8:18; Jn 10:29 **2:14** [t] Jn 1:14 [u] 1Co 15:54-57; 2Ti 1:10 [v] 1Jn 3:8 **2:15** [w] 2Ti 1:7 **2:17** [x] Php 2:7 [y] Heb 5:2 [z] Heb 4:14, 15; 7:26, 28 [a] Heb 5:1 **2:18** [b] Heb 4:15 **3:1** [c] Heb 2:11 [d] Heb 4:14 [e] Heb 2:17 **3:2** [f] Nu 12:7 **3:5** [g] Ex 14:31 [h] ver 2; Nu 12:7 **3:6** [i] Heb 1:2 [j] 1Co 3:16 [k] Ro 11:22 [l] Ro 5:2

Warning Against Unbelief

7So, as the Holy Spirit says:[m]

"Today, if you hear his voice,
8 do not harden your hearts
as you did in the rebellion,
during the time of testing in the
wilderness,
9 where your ancestors tested and
tried me,
though for forty years they saw what
I did.[n]
10 That is why I was angry with that
generation;
I said, 'Their hearts are always going
astray,
and they have not known my ways.'
11 So I declared on oath in my anger,
'They shall never enter my rest.'[o]"[a][p]

12See to it, brothers and sisters, that none
of you has a sinful, unbelieving heart that
turns away from the living God. 13But encourage one another daily,[q] as long as it is
called "Today," so that none of you may be
hardened by sin's deceitfulness.[r] 14We have
come to share in Christ, if indeed we hold[s]
our original conviction firmly to the very
end. 15As has just been said:

"Today, if you hear his voice,
do not harden your hearts
as you did in the rebellion."[b][t]

16Who were they who heard and rebelled? Were they not all those Moses
led out of Egypt?[u] 17And with whom was
he angry for forty years? Was it not with
those who sinned, whose bodies perished
in the wilderness?[v] 18And to whom did God
swear that they would never enter his rest[w]
if not to those who disobeyed?[x] 19So we see
that they were not able to enter, because of
their unbelief.[y]

A Sabbath-Rest for the People of God

4 Therefore, since the promise of entering his rest still stands, let us be careful that none of you be found to have fall-
en short of it.[z] 2For we also have had the
good news proclaimed to us, just as they
did; but the message they heard was of no
value to them, because they did not share
the faith of those who obeyed.[c][a] 3Now we
who have believed enter that rest, just as
God has said,

"So I declared on oath in my anger,
'They shall never enter my rest.'"[d][b]

And yet his works have been finished since
the creation of the world. 4For somewhere
he has spoken about the seventh day in
these words: "On the seventh day God rested from all his works."[e][c] 5And again in the
passage above he says, "They shall never
enter my rest."[d]

6Therefore since it still remains for some
to enter that rest, and since those who formerly had the good news proclaimed to
them did not go in because of their disobedience,[e] 7God again set a certain day,
calling it "Today." This he did when a long
time later he spoke through David, as in
the passage already quoted:

"Today, if you hear his voice,
do not harden your hearts."[b][f]

8For if Joshua had given them rest,[g] God
would not have spoken[h] later about another day. 9There remains, then, a Sabbath-
rest for the people of God; 10for anyone

---

a *11* Psalm 95:7-11 *b* *15,7* Psalm 95:7,8
c 2 Some manuscripts *because those who heard did not combine it with faith* *d* *3* Psalm 95:11; also in verse 5 *e* *4* Gen. 2:2

3:7–11 *do not harden your hearts.* The author of Hebrews quotes Psalm 95:7–11 to warn the Jewish Christians about hardening their hearts to God and the salvation He offers. Moses' generation had refused to trust in God to provide for their needs in the wilderness (Ex. 17:1–7), and the readers of this letter were also in danger. ***my rest.*** This is a key concept in Hebrews. In the Old Testament, the conquest of the Promised Land and the cessation of fighting in the land was viewed as a form of rest (Deut. 3:20; 12:9; 25:19; Josh. 11:23; 21:44; 22:4). In the New Testament, "rest" speaks of the believer's eternal home and the joy that he or she will experience in Jesus' presence (4:1).

3:12–13 *unbelieving heart.* In essence, unbelief is a stubborn refusal to trust in the truthfulness of His word. It is a grave sin because it leads us away from God.

3:14 *come to share in Christ.* This is the same word translated *companions* in 1:9. Believers will be partners with Christ in His future kingdom (Rev. 2:26–27).

3:15–19 *with whom was he angry.* The Jewish Christians to whom this letter was addressed were in danger of following in their ancestors' footsteps. They were tempted to doubt the words of Jesus. With the rhetorical questions in these verses, the author of Hebrews was encouraging them to place their faith firmly in Christ.

4:2 *the good news proclaimed.* This is the translation of a single Greek word meaning "the good news was announced."

4:4 *God rested.* The theme of rest has its beginning in God's own rest after creation. The fact that Genesis makes no mention of the evening of the seventh day of creation provides a basis for some Jewish commentators to conclude that the rest of God lasts throughout all history.

4:9 *Sabbath-rest.* The word used here is different from the word used in verses 1,3,5,10–11; 3:11,18. Jews commonly taught that the Sabbath foreshadowed the world to come, and they spoke of "a day of which shall be all Sabbath."

3:7 [m] Heb 9:8 **3:9** [n] Ac 7:36 **3:11** [o] Heb 4:3,5 [p] Ps 95:7-11 **3:13** [q] Heb 10:24,25 [r] Eph 4:22 **3:14** [s] ver 6 **3:15** [t] ver 7,8; Ps 95:7,8 **3:16** [u] Nu 14:2 **3:17** [v] Nu 14:29; Ps 106:26 **3:18** [w] Nu 14:20-23 [x] Heb 4:6 **3:19** [y] Jn 3:36 **4:1** [z] Heb 12:15 **4:2** [a] 1Th 2:13 **4:3** [b] Ps 95:11; Heb 3:11 **4:4** [c] Ge 2:2,3; Ex 20:11 **4:5** [d] Ps 95:11 **4:6** [e] Heb 3:18 **4:7** [f] Ps 95:7,8; Heb 3:7,8, 15 **4:8** [g] Jos 22:4 [h] Heb 1:1

who enters God's rest also rests from their
works,[a] just as God did from his.[i] 11 Let us,
therefore, make every effort to enter that
rest, so that no one will perish by following
their example of disobedience.[j]
12 For the word of God[k] is alive and active.[l] Sharper than any double-edged
sword,[m] it penetrates even to dividing soul
and spirit, joints and marrow; it judges
the thoughts and attitudes of the heart.[n]
13 Nothing in all creation is hidden from
God's sight.[o] Everything is uncovered and
laid bare before the eyes of him to whom
we must give account.

Jesus the Great High Priest

14 Therefore, since we have a great high
priest who has ascended into heaven,[b][p]
Jesus the Son of God, let us hold firmly to
the faith we profess.[q] 15 For we do not have
a high priest who is unable to empathize
with our weaknesses, but we have one who
has been tempted in every way, just as we
are[r]—yet he did not sin.[s] 16 Let us then approach God's throne of grace with confidence, so that we may receive mercy and
find grace to help us in our time of need.

5 Every high priest is selected from
among the people and is appointed to
represent the people in matters related to
God, to offer gifts and sacrifices[t] for sins.[u]
2 He is able to deal gently with those who
are ignorant and are going astray,[v] since
he himself is subject to weakness.[w] 3 This
is why he has to offer sacrifices for his own
sins, as well as for the sins of the people.[x]
4 And no one takes this honor on himself,
but he receives it when called by God, just
as Aaron was.[y]

5 In the same way, Christ did not take
on himself the glory[z] of becoming a high
priest. But God said[a] to him,

> "You are my Son;
> today I have become your
> Father."[c][b]

6 And he says in another place,

> "You are a priest forever,
> in the order of Melchizedek."[d][c]

7 During the days of Jesus' life on earth,
he offered up prayers and petitions with
fervent cries and tears[d] to the one who
could save him from death, and he was
heard because of his reverent submission.[e]
8 Son though he was, he learned obedience
from what he suffered[f] 9 and, once made
perfect,[g] he became the source of eternal
salvation for all who obey him 10 and was
designated by God to be high priest[h] in the
order of Melchizedek.[i]

Warning Against Falling Away

11 We have much to say about this, but it is
hard to make it clear to you because you no
longer try to understand. 12 In fact, though
by this time you ought to be teachers, you
need someone to teach you the elementary
truths[j] of God's word all over again. You
need milk, not solid food![k] 13 Anyone who
lives on milk, being still an infant,[l] is not
acquainted with the teaching about righteousness. 14 But solid food is for the mature,[m] who by constant use have trained
themselves to distinguish good from evil.[n]

---

[a] *10* Or *labor* [b] *14* Greek *has gone through the heavens* [c] *5* Psalm 2:7 [d] *6* Psalm 110:4

4:11 ***make every effort to enter that rest.*** The rest is not automatic. Determined diligence is required. The danger is that believers today, like the Israelites of the past, will not stand, but will fall in disobedience.
4:13 ***laid bare before the eyes.*** This phrase suggests complete exposure and defenselessness before God.
4:15 ***empathize.*** This word means "to suffer with" and expresses the feeling of one who has entered into suffering.
4:16 ***Let us then approach.*** This command strongly contrasts with God's command at Mt Sinai: "go not up into the mount, or touch the border of it" (Ex. 19:12). Because of Christ's priestly work, believers can approach God's presence. ***confidence.*** This word carries with it the idea of "fearlessness" or "courageousness." Believers should boldly approach God in prayer because He is our gracious High Priest who sits at God's right hand interceding for us.
5:1–4 ***high priest.*** He represents the people and thus must identify with their human nature. But he also represents God to the people and thus must be called by God to his office.
5:2 ***ignorant and are going astray.*** This phrase describes those who unintentionally sin (Num. 15:30–36).
5:8 ***he learned obedience.*** Jesus experienced all of what a person goes through on this earth. He knows how difficult it is to obey God completely, just as He understands the attraction of temptation (2:18).
5:9 ***once made perfect.*** This phrase does not suggest that Jesus had not been perfect before. It means that He successfully carried out God's plan for Him. He endured suffering and temptation so that He could truly function as our High Priest, understanding our weaknesses and interceding before God for us.
5:12 ***elementary truths.*** The phrase refers to the letters of the alphabet in writing or to addition and subtraction tables in arithmetic. They are principles out of which everything else develops.
5:13 ***not acquainted with the teaching about righteousness.*** The readers of this letter did not necessarily lack information concerning righteousness; they lacked experience in practicing the information they had.

4:10 [i] ver 4 **4:11** [j] Heb 3:18 **4:12** [k] 1Pe 1:23 [l] Jer 23:29 [m] Eph 6:17; Rev 1:16 [n] 1Co 14:24,25 **4:13** [o] Ps 33:13-15 **4:14** [p] Heb 6:20 [q] Heb 3:1 **4:15** [r] Heb 2:18 [s] 2Co 5:21 **5:1** [t] Heb 8:3 [u] Heb 7:27 **5:2** [v] Heb 2:18 [w] Heb 7:28 **5:3** [x] Heb 7:27; 9:7 **5:4** [y] Ex 28:1 **5:5** [z] Jn 8:54 [a] Heb 1:1 [b] Ps 2:7 **5:6** [c] Ps 110:4; Heb 7:17,21 **5:7** [d] Mt 27:46,50 [e] Mk 14:36 **5:8** [f] Php 2:8 **5:9** [g] Heb 2:10 **5:10** [h] ver 5 [i] ver 6 **5:12** [j] Heb 6:1 [k] 1Co 3:2; 1Pe 2:2 **5:13** [l] 1Co 14:20 **5:14** [m] 1Co 2:6 [n] Isa 7:15

6 Therefore let us move beyond[o] the elementary teachings[p] about Christ and
be taken forward to maturity, not laying
again the foundation of repentance from
acts that lead to death,[a][q] and of faith in
God, 2instruction about cleansing rites,[b][r]
the laying on of hands,[s] the resurrection of
the dead,[t] and eternal judgment. 3And God
permitting,[u] we will do so.
4It is impossible for those who have once
been enlightened,[v] who have tasted the
heavenly gift,[w] who have shared in the
Holy Spirit,[x] 5who have tasted the goodness of the word of God and the powers
of the coming age 6and who have fallen[c]
away, to be brought back to repentance.[y]
To their loss they are crucifying the Son of
God all over again and subjecting him to
public disgrace. 7Land that drinks in the
rain often falling on it and that produces a
crop useful to those for whom it is farmed
receives the blessing of God. 8But land that
produces thorns and thistles is worthless
and is in danger of being cursed.[z] In the
end it will be burned.
9Even though we speak like this, dear
friends,[a] we are convinced of better things
in your case—the things that have to do
with salvation. 10God is not unjust; he will
not forget your work and the love you have
shown him as you have helped his people
and continue to help them.[b] 11We want
each of you to show this same diligence
to the very end, so that what you hope[c] for
may be fully realized. 12We do not want
you to become lazy, but to imitate[d] those
who through faith and patience[e] inherit
what has been promised.[f]

The Certainty of God's Promise

13When God made his promise to Abraham, since there was no one greater for
him to swear by, he swore by himself,[g]
14saying, "I will surely bless you and give
you many descendants."[d][h] 15And so after
waiting patiently, Abraham received what
was promised.[i]
16People swear by someone greater than
themselves, and the oath confirms what is
said and puts an end to all argument.[j] 17Be-
cause God wanted to make the unchanging[k] nature of his purpose very clear to the
heirs of what was promised,[l] he confirmed
it with an oath. 18God did this so that, by
two unchangeable things in which it is impossible for God to lie,[m] we who have fled
to take hold of the hope[n] set before us may
be greatly encouraged. 19We have this
hope as an anchor for the soul, firm and
secure. It enters the inner sanctuary behind the curtain,[o] 20where our forerunner,
Jesus, has entered on our behalf.[p] He has
become a high priest[q] forever, in the order
of Melchizedek.[r]

---

a 1 Or *from useless rituals* *b* 2 Or *about baptisms* *c* 6 Or *age,* 6*if they fall*
d 14 Gen. 22:17

6:1 *repentance from acts that lead to death.* This phrase refers to a change of mind about the demands of the law of Moses (9:14). Even though the law was good (1 Tim. 1:8), it was weak because of the weakness of our sinful nature (Rom. 8:3). What is needed for salvation is not lifeless works that cannot save, but faith directed toward God.
6:2 *laying on of hands.* This action was used to impart the Holy Spirit (Acts 8:17–18; 19:6). It was also used for ordination of the ministry (Acts 6:6; 13:3). This practice is also found in the Old Testament in commissioning someone to a public office (Num. 27:18,23; Deut. 34:9) or in the context of presenting a sacrificial offering to the Lord (Lev. 1:4; 3:2; 4:4; 8:14; 16:21). ***eternal judgment.*** This refers to the belief that everyone will be judged by the great Judge.
6:4–6 *and who have fallen away.* This difficult passage has been interpreted in various ways. Some insist that the author is speaking of nominal Christians who heard the truth and appeared to believe in Christ but were not sincere in their faith. Others view these verses as a hypothetical argument. In other words, the author is using this hypothetical case to warn the spiritually immature. These two positions are supported by passages that speak of God's consistency in His work, that nothing can separate us from His love (John 6:39–40; 10:27–29; Rom. 8:28–30). But another group of commentators insists that the author is speaking of genuine Christians who renounce Christ. They point out that those who "tasted the heavenly gift" fall away. Passages such as 2 Corinthians 11:1–4; 2 Timothy 2:17–18; 1 John 2:21–25 are in support of this position. Whatever way one interprets this passage, it is clear that the author of Hebrews has given us a clear warning not to renounce Christ or spurn His offer of salvation.
6:6 *brought back.* This word means "restore." In other words, it is impossible for continuous effort on the part of anyone in the Christian community to restore an apostate back to fellowship with God. Continuing Christian immaturity is dangerous.
6:13–15 *Abraham.* Here is an example of faith and patience in God's promise (v. 12). He waited 25 years from the time the promise was first made until Isaac, the promised son, was born (Gen. 12:3–4; 15:4; 18:10; 21:5).
6:18 *two unchangeable things.* These things are God's Word and God's oath. Since God does not lie and since He is all-powerful, He will fulfill all His promises.
6:20 *forerunner.* This word was used in the second century A.D. for the smaller boats sent into the harbor by larger ships unable to enter due to the buffeting of the weather. These smaller boats carried the anchor through the breakers inside the harbor and dropped it there, securing the larger ship. *Forerunner* also

6:1 [o] Php 3:12-14 [p] Heb 5:12 [q] Heb 9:14 **6:2** [r] Jn 3:25 [s] Ac 6:6 [t] Ac 17:18,32 **6:3** [u] Ac 18:21 **6:4** [v] Heb 10:32 [w] Eph 2:8 [x] Gal 3:2 **6:6** [y] 2Pe 2:21; 1Jn 5:16 **6:8** [z] Ge 3:17, 18; Isa 5:6 **6:9** [a] 1Co 10:14 **6:10** [b] Mt 10:40, 42; 25:40; 1Th 1:3 **6:11** [c] Heb 3:6 **6:12** [d] Heb 13:7 [e] 2Th 1:4; Jas 1:3; Rev 13:10 [f] Heb 10:36 **6:13** [g] Ge 22:16; Lk 1:73 **6:14** [h] Ge 22:17 **6:15** [i] Ge 21:5 **6:16** [j] Ex 22:11 **6:17** [k] Ps 110:4 [l] Heb 11:9 **6:18** [m] Nu 23:19; Titus 1:2 [n] Heb 3:6 **6:19** [o] Lev 16:2; Heb 9:2,3,7 **6:20** [p] Heb 4:14 [q] Heb 2:17 [r] Heb 5:6

Melchizedek the Priest

7 This Melchizedek was king of Salem and priest of God Most High.[s] He met Abraham returning from the defeat of the kings and blessed him,[t] 2and Abraham gave him a tenth of everything. First, the name Melchizedek means "king of righteousness"; then also, "king of Salem" means "king of peace." 3Without father or mother, without genealogy,[u] without beginning of days or end of life, resembling the Son of God,[v] he remains a priest forever.

4Just think how great he was: Even the patriarch[w] Abraham gave him a tenth of the plunder![x] 5Now the law requires the descendants of Levi who become priests to collect a tenth from the people[y]—that is, from their fellow Israelites—even though they also are descended from Abraham. 6This man, however, did not trace his descent from Levi, yet he collected a tenth from Abraham and blessed[z] him who had the promises.[a] 7And without doubt the lesser is blessed by the greater. 8In the one case, the tenth is collected by people who die; but in the other case, by him who is declared to be living.[b] 9One might even say that Levi, who collects the tenth, paid the tenth through Abraham, 10because when Melchizedek met Abraham, Levi was still in the body of his ancestor.

Jesus Like Melchizedek

11If perfection could have been attained through the Levitical priesthood—and indeed the law given to the people[c] established that priesthood—why was there still need for another priest to come,[d] one in the order of Melchizedek,[e] not in the order of Aaron? 12For when the priesthood is changed, the law must be changed also. 13He of whom these things are said belonged to a different tribe,[f] and no one from that tribe has ever served at the altar.[g] 14For it is clear that our Lord descended from Judah,[h] and in regard to that tribe Moses said nothing about priests. 15And what we have said is even more clear if another priest like Melchizedek appears, 16one who has become a priest not on the basis of a regulation as to his ancestry but on the basis of the power of an indestructible life. 17For it is declared:

"You are a priest forever,
  in the order of Melchizedek."[a][i]

18The former regulation is set aside because it was weak and useless[j] 19(for the law made nothing perfect),[k] and a better hope is introduced, by which we draw near to God.[l]

20And it was not without an oath! Others became priests without any oath, 21but he became a priest with an oath when God said to him:

"The Lord has sworn
  and will not change his mind:[m]
  'You are a priest forever.'"[a][n]

22Because of this oath, Jesus has become the guarantor of a better covenant.[o]

23Now there have been many of those priests, since death prevented them from continuing in office; 24but because Jesus lives forever, he has a permanent priesthood.[p] 25Therefore he is able to save completely[b] those who come to God[q] through him, because he always lives to intercede for them.[r]

---

a *17,21* Psalm 110:4 *b* *25* Or *forever*

---

presupposes that others will follow. Thus, Jesus is like a runner boat that has taken our anchor into port and secured it there.

7:1 *Melchizedek.* The name means "king of righteousness." ***Salem.*** This means "peace." The ideal king rules in righteousness, which assures peace (Is. 32:17).

7:3 *Without father or mother, without genealogy.* Genesis, a book with many genealogies, has none for Melchizedek. The author is not saying that Melchizedek was born without a father and mother, only that there is no record of his birth in the genealogies of Genesis. This description of Melchizedek prefigures the eternal priesthood of Jesus. Like Melchizedek, Jesus is both a Priest and a King belonging to a righteous priesthood that is independent of Aaron's.

7:4 *patriarch.* In the Greek text this word is emphatic. The greatness of Abraham, the one who possessed the promises of God (v. 6), underscores the even greater rank of Melchizedek, the priest of righteousness.

7:8–10 *the tenth is collected by people who die.* Melchizedek was not only superior to Abraham, but he was also superior to the Levitical priesthood in two ways: first, the Levitical priests were mortal. In contrast, Melchizedek seems to be immortal. At least, the Old Testament does not record his death. Second, in a sense, Levi paid tithes to Melchizedek through Abraham's gift. Because he was descended from Abraham, he is counted as having paid tithes to Melchizedek.

7:12 *changed.* This word means removal (12:27). If the Melchizedek priesthood removed the Levitical priesthood, then the Mosaic law is also removed. In short, the believer is not under the law but instead relies on the righteousness of Christ (Rom. 6:14; Gal. 3:24–25).

7:15–18 *on the basis of the power of an indestructable life.* This point is proved by Psalm 110:4, quoted in verse 17. Jesus is a different kind of priest, another indication that the law has been changed. There has been a *disannulling,* a putting away, of the law.

7:25 *he is able to save.* Christ is able to save because He is fully God and fully human (2:18; 4:15).

7:1 [s] Mk 5:7 [t] Ge 14:18-20 **7:3** [u] ver 6 [v] Mt 4:3
7:4 [w] Ac 2:29 [x] Ge 14:20 **7:5** [y] Nu 18:21, 26
7:6 [z] Ge 14:19, 20 [a] Ro 4:13 **7:8** [b] Heb 5:6; 6:20
7:11 [c] ver 18, 19; Heb 8:7 [d] Heb 10:1 [e] ver 17
7:13 [f] ver 11 [g] ver 14 **7:14** [h] Isa 11:1; Mt 1:3; Lk 3:33
7:17 [i] Ps 110:4; ver 21; Heb 5:6 **7:18** [j] Ro 8:3
7:19 [k] Ac 13:39; Ro 3:20; Heb 9:9 [l] Heb 4:16
7:21 [m] 1Sa 15:29 [n] Ps 110:4 **7:22** [o] Heb 8:6
7:24 [p] ver 28 **7:25** [q] ver 19 [r] Ro 8:34

26Such a high priest truly meets our
need—one who is holy, blameless, pure,
set apart from sinners,[s] exalted above the
heavens.[t] 27Unlike the other high priests,
he does not need to offer sacrifices[u] day
after day, first for his own sins,[v] and then
for the sins of the people. He sacrificed for
their sins once for all[w] when he offered himself.[x] 28For the law appoints as high priests
men in all their weakness;[y] but the oath,
which came after the law, appointed the
Son,[z] who has been made perfect[a] forever.

The High Priest of a New Covenant

8 Now the main point of what we are
saying is this: We do have such a high
priest,[b] who sat down at the right hand of
the throne of the Majesty in heaven, 2and
who serves in the sanctuary, the true tabernacle[c] set up by the Lord, not by a mere
human being.

3Every high priest is appointed to offer
both gifts and sacrifices,[d] and so it was
necessary for this one also to have something to offer.[e] 4If he were on earth, he
would not be a priest, for there are already
priests who offer the gifts prescribed by
the law.[f] 5They serve at a sanctuary that is
a copy[g] and shadow[h] of what is in heaven.
This is why Moses was warned[i] when he
was about to build the tabernacle: "See to
it that you make everything according to
the pattern shown you on the mountain."[a][j]
6But in fact the ministry Jesus has received
is as superior to theirs as the covenant[k] of
which he is mediator[l] is superior to the old
one, since the new covenant is established
on better promises.

7For if there had been nothing wrong
with that first covenant, no place would
have been sought for another.[m] 8But God
found fault with the people and said[b]:

"The days are coming, declares the Lord,
when I will make a new covenant[n]
with the people of Israel
and with the people of Judah.
9It will not be like the covenant
I made with their ancestors[o]
when I took them by the hand
to lead them out of Egypt,
because they did not remain faithful to my covenant,
and I turned away from them,
declares the Lord.
10This is the covenant I will establish
with the people of Israel
after that time, declares the Lord.
I will put my laws in their minds
and write them on their hearts.[p]
I will be their God,
and they will be my people.[q]
11No longer will they teach their neighbor,
or say to one another, 'Know the Lord,'
because they will all know me,[r]
from the least of them to the greatest.
12For I will forgive their wickedness
and will remember their sins no more.[s]"[c][t]

13By calling this covenant "new," he has
made the first one obsolete;[u] and what is
obsolete and outdated will soon disappear.

---

[a] 5 Exodus 25:40 [b] 8 Some manuscripts may be translated *fault and said to the people.* [c] 12 Jer. 31:31-34

Since this verse speaks to Jesus' present intercession for us, the word "save" in this verse speaks of our sanctification, the continuing process by which we are freed from the power of sin. This continuing process of salvation will eventually be completed in our glorification, when we are saved from the presence of sin.

7:26–28 ***Unlike the other high priests, he does not need to offer sacrifices day after day.*** The high priest offered an annual sacrifice on the Day of Atonement for the atonement of the people's sins (9:7; 10:1), but the priests also offered sacrifices every day before the Lord (Ex. 29:36). In contrast Jesus offered Himself once, a perfect, sinless sacrifice for the sins of all. Since Jesus is perfect, He did not have to offer sacrifices for His own sins.

8:2 ***sanctuary.*** This word refers to the heavenly reality represented by the Most Holy Place (9:2,8,24;10:19; 13:11). The reality is the presence of God. Our High Priest serves there and desires to bring us there (10:19).

8:8 ***a new covenant.*** This covenant is the "better covenant" of verse 6. This covenant was made with Israel and Judah, yet the church enjoys the spiritual blessings of this covenant now. The Abrahamic covenant was made with Abraham and his physical descendants (Gen. 17:7). Yet the Abrahamic covenant also contained spiritual promise (Gen. 12:3) in which the church participates (Rom. 11:11–27; Gal. 3:13–14). The new covenant in fact is a fulfillment of the spiritual redemption promise in the Abrahamic and Davidic covenants (Matt. 26:26–29; Luke 22:20).

8:10–12 ***after that time, declares the Lord.*** There are four provisions of the new covenant: (1) God's law will be written on believers' minds and hearts. (2) Believers will have a relationship with God fulfilling the promise of Leviticus 26:12 (2 Cor. 6:16). (3) All will know God. No longer will Pharisees and scribes have to teach the intricacies of the law to the people. (4) God will forgive the sins of believers and remember them no more. The continual sacrifice of animals for the atonement of sin will cease.

8:13 ***obsolete and outdated.*** At the time the author of Hebrews wrote these words, the ceremonies of the Mosaic covenant were still being conducted in the temple in Jerusalem. In A.D. 70 the Roman general Titus destroyed the temple, fulfilling these words.

7:26 [s] 2Co 5:21 [t] Heb 4:14 **7:27** [u] Heb 5:1 [v] Heb 5:3 [w] Heb 9:12, 26, 28 [x] Eph 5:2; Heb 9:14, 28 **7:28** [y] Heb 5:2 [z] Heb 1:2 [a] Heb 2:10 **8:1** [b] Heb 2:17 **8:2** [c] Heb 9:11, 24 **8:3** [d] Heb 5:1 [e] Heb 9:14 **8:4** [f] Heb 5:1 **8:5** [g] Heb 9:23 [h] Col 2:17; Heb 10:1 [i] Heb 11:7; 12:25 [j] Ex 25:40 **8:6** [k] Lk 22:20 [l] Heb 7:22 **8:7** [m] Heb 7:11, 18 **8:8** [n] Jer 31:31 **8:9** [o] Ex 19:5, 6 **8:10** [p] 2Co 3:3; Heb 10:16 [q] Zec 8:8 **8:11** [r] Isa 54:13; Jn 6:45 **8:12** [s] Heb 10:17 [t] Ro 11:27 **8:13** [u] 2Co 5:17

Worship in the Earthly Tabernacle

9 Now the first covenant had regulations for worship and also an earthly sanctuary.[v] **2**A tabernacle[w] was set up. In its first room were the lampstand[x] and the table[y] with its consecrated bread;[z] this was called the Holy Place. **3**Behind the second curtain was a room called the Most Holy Place,[a] **4**which had the golden altar of incense[b] and the gold-covered ark of the covenant.[c] This ark contained the gold jar of manna,[d] Aaron's staff that had budded,[e] and the stone tablets of the covenant. **5**Above the ark were the cherubim of the Glory,[f] overshadowing the atonement cover. But we cannot discuss these things in detail now.

6When everything had been arranged like this, the priests entered regularly[g] into the outer room to carry on their ministry. **7**But only the high priest entered[h] the inner room, and that only once a year,[i] and never without blood, which he offered for himself[j] and for the sins the people had committed in ignorance. **8**The Holy Spirit was showing[k] by this that the way[l] into the Most Holy Place had not yet been disclosed as long as the first tabernacle was still functioning. **9**This is an illustration for the present time, indicating that the gifts and sacrifices being offered[m] were not able to clear the conscience of the worshiper. **10**They are only a matter of food[n] and drink[o] and various ceremonial washings—external regulations[p] applying until the time of the new order.

The Blood of Christ

11But when Christ came as high priest[q] of the good things that are now already here,[a][r] he went through the greater and more perfect tabernacle[s] that is not made with human hands, that is to say, is not a part of this creation. **12**He did not enter by means of the blood of goats and calves;[t] but he entered the Most Holy Place[u] once for all[v] by his own blood, thus obtaining[b] eternal redemption. **13**The blood of goats and bulls and the ashes of a heifer[w] sprinkled on those who are ceremonially unclean sanctify them so that they are outwardly clean. **14**How much more, then, will the blood of Christ, who through the eternal Spirit[x] offered himself unblemished to God, cleanse our consciences[y] from acts that lead to death,[c][z] so that we may serve the living God!

15For this reason Christ is the mediator[a] of a new covenant, that those who are called may receive the promised eternal inheritance—now that he has died as a ransom to set them free from the sins committed under the first covenant.[b]

16In the case of a will,[d] it is necessary to prove the death of the one who made it, **17**because a will is in force only when somebody has died; it never takes effect while the one who made it is living. **18**This is why even the first covenant was not put into effect without blood.[c] **19**When Moses had proclaimed every command of the law to all the people, he took the blood of calves, together with water, scarlet wool and branches of hyssop, and sprinkled the scroll and all the people.[d] **20**He said, "This is the blood of the covenant, which God has commanded you to keep."[e][e] **21**In the same way, he sprinkled with the blood both the tabernacle and everything used in its ceremonies. **22**In fact, the law requires that nearly everything be cleansed with blood,[f] and without the shedding of blood there is no forgiveness.[g]

---

a 11 Some early manuscripts *are to come*
b 12 Or *blood, having obtained* *c* 14 Or *from useless rituals* *d* 16 Same Greek word as *covenant*; also in verse 17 *e* 20 Exodus 24:8

9:2–5 *A tabernacle was set up.* These verses simply describe the furniture of the tabernacle. The tabernacle courtyard contained an altar for animal sacrifice and a laver for ceremonial washings. The tabernacle was divided into two rooms by a veil. The first part was the sanctuary or holy place, housing the lampstand, the table for the showbread, and the altar of incense. The second room was the Most Holy Place, containing the ark of the covenant, in which were stored the symbols of the Mosaic covenant.

9:7–8 *once a year.* In the provisions of the Mosaic covenant, access to God was limited. The fact that the high priest had such little access himself indicates the striking failure of the Mosaic covenant to bring believers into the presence of God.

9:9 *were not able to clear the conscience of the worshiper.* The Mosaic covenant covered sins of ignorance (v. 7), but not premeditated sins or the sinful nature of all people (Ps. 51). In other words, the old system was lacking. It did not completely reconcile the people to God.

9:12 *by his own blood.* Christ obtained eternal redemption. His sacrifice never has to be repeated because it is perfect.

9:13 *ashes of a heifer.* These were mixed with water and were used to cleanse a person who had become ceremonially defiled by touching a corpse (Num. 19:11–13). The author of Hebrews points out that these ceremonies could purify only a person's exterior, not a person's heart.

9:14 *the eternal Spirit.* All three persons of the Trinity are involved in cleansing. The defilement is internal, not external (v. 13). Christ's death has the power to purify a person's mind and soul.

9:15 *ransom.* Christ paid the price to free us from our own sin. His death substitutes for our death, the penalty of our sins. Like the Israelites, believers receive an inheritance, but our inheritance is eternal (v. 14).

9:1 [v] Ex 25:8 **9:2** [w] Ex 25:8, 9 [x] Ex 25:31-39 [y] Ex 25:23-29 [z] Lev 24:5-8 **9:3** [a] Ex 26:31-33 **9:4** [b] Ex 30:1-5 [c] Ex 25:10-22 [d] Ex 16:32, 33 [e] Nu 17:10 **9:5** [f] Ex 25:17-19 **9:6** [g] Nu 28:3 **9:7** [h] Lev 16:11-19 [i] Lev 16:34 [j] Heb 5:2, 3 **9:8** [k] Heb 3:7 [l] Jn 14:6; Heb 10:19, 20 **9:9** [m] Heb 5:1 **9:10** [n] Lev 11:2-23 [o] Col 2:16 [p] Heb 7:16 **9:11** [q] Heb 2:17 [r] Heb 10:1 [s] Heb 8:2 **9:12** [t] Heb 10:4 [u] ver 24 [v] Heb 7:27 **9:13** [w] Nu 19:9, 17, 18 **9:14** [x] 1Pe 3:18 [y] Titus 2:14; Heb 10:2, 22 [z] Heb 6:1 **9:15** [a] 1Ti 2:5 [b] Heb 7:22 **9:18** [c] Ex 24:6-8 **9:19** [d] Ex 24:6-8 **9:20** [e] Ex 24:8; Mt 26:28 **9:22** [f] Lev 8:15 [g] Lev 17:11

23 It was necessary, then, for the copies[h]
of the heavenly things to be purified with
these sacrifices, but the heavenly things
themselves with better sacrifices than
these. 24 For Christ did not enter a sanctuary made with human hands that was only
a copy of the true one;[i] he entered heaven
itself, now to appear for us in God's presence. 25 Nor did he enter heaven to offer
himself again and again, the way the high
priest enters the Most Holy Place[j] every
year with blood that is not his own.[k] 26 Otherwise Christ would have had to suffer
many times since the creation of the world.[l]
But he has appeared once for all[m] at the
culmination of the ages to do away with sin
by the sacrifice of himself. 27 Just as people
are destined to die once,[n] and after that to
face judgment,[o] 28 so Christ was sacrificed
once to take away the sins of many; and
he will appear a second time,[p] not to bear
sin,[q] but to bring salvation to those who are
waiting for him.[r]

Christ's Sacrifice Once for All

10 The law is only a shadow[s] of the good
things[t] that are coming—not the realities themselves.[u] For this reason it can
never, by the same sacrifices repeated
endlessly year after year, make perfect[v]
those who draw near to worship. 2 Otherwise, would they not have stopped being
offered? For the worshipers would have
been cleansed once for all, and would no
longer have felt guilty for their sins. 3 But
those sacrifices are an annual reminder of
sins.[w] 4 It is impossible for the blood of bulls
and goats[x] to take away sins.
5 Therefore, when Christ came into the
world,[y] he said:

"Sacrifice and offering you did not desire,
but a body you prepared for me;[z]
6 with burnt offerings and sin offerings
you were not pleased.
7 Then I said, 'Here I am—it is written
about me in the scroll[a]—
I have come to do your will, my God.'"[ab]

8 First he said, "Sacrifices and offerings,
burnt offerings and sin offerings you did
not desire, nor were you pleased with
them"[c]—though they were offered in accordance with the law. 9 Then he said,
"Here I am, I have come to do your will."[d]
He sets aside the first to establish the second. 10 And by that will, we have been made
holy[e] through the sacrifice of the body[f] of
Jesus Christ once for all.[g]
11 Day after day every priest stands and
performs his religious duties; again and
again he offers the same sacrifices,[h] which
can never take away sins.[i] 12 But when this
priest had offered for all time one sacrifice
for sins, he sat down at the right hand of
God, 13 and since that time he waits for his
enemies to be made his footstool.[j] 14 For by
one sacrifice he has made perfect[k] forever
those who are being made holy.
15 The Holy Spirit also testifies[l] to us
about this. First he says:

16 "This is the covenant I will make with
them
after that time, says the Lord.
I will put my laws in their hearts,
and I will write them on their
minds."[bm]

17 Then he adds:

"Their sins and lawless acts
I will remember no more."[cn]

18 And where these have been forgiven, sacrifice for sin is no longer necessary.

---

[a] 7 Psalm 40:6-8 (see Septuagint) [b] 16 Jer. 31:33
[c] 17 Jer. 31:34

9:24 *Christ did not enter a sanctuary made with human hands.* Christ's sacrifice was better than sacrifices made under the Mosaic covenant because Christ did not enter a man-made sanctuary, which was a copy; instead, He entered the true sanctuary, which is in heaven—the very presence of God.

9:26 *But he has appeared once.* Christ's sacrifice was better than the sacrifices made under the Mosaic covenant because He did not offer an annual sacrifice of animals but offered Himself once for all time.

10:1–4 *not the realities themselves.* The sacrifices of the Mosaic covenant prefigured Christ's ultimate sacrifice of Himself. Therefore, these imperfect sacrifices of mere animals could not completely purify the person who offered them. If they had been able to, these sacrifices would have ceased. Instead of thoroughly atoning for the sins of the people, the annual sacrifice on the Day of Atonement was a visible reminder of the people's sins.

10:5–7 *to do your will.* The Old Testament prophets had warned the Israelites that sacrifices alone would not please God. He desired obedience as well (Ps. 51:16–17; Is. 1:13–17; Mark 12:33). This messianic psalm indicates that Jesus' obedience to God the Father was one of the reasons His sacrifice was better than the Old Testament sacrifices.

10:8–9 *He sets aside the first to establish the second.* The author is explaining Psalm 40. The verb translated "sets aside" means "abolishes." The imperfect sacrifices were abolished so that the perfect Sacrifice could impart true life.

10:11–12 *sat down.* Sitting indicates that His work of atonement is finished. His final words on the cross, "It is finished," declare this spiritual reality (John 19:30).

10:16–18 *I will remember no more.* This phrase does not mean to forget, but not to hold sin against us any longer.

9:23 [h] Heb 8:5 **9:24** [i] Heb 8:2 **9:25** [j] Heb 10:19 [k] ver 7,8 **9:26** [l] Heb 4:3 [m] Heb 7:27 **9:27** [n] Ge 3:19 [o] 2Co 5:10 **9:28** [p] Titus 2:13 [q] 1Pe 2:24 [r] 1Co 1:7 **10:1** [s] Heb 8:5 [t] Heb 9:11 [u] Heb 9:23 [v] Heb 7:19 **10:3** [w] Heb 9:7 **10:4** [x] Heb 9:12, 13 **10:5** [y] Heb 1:6 [z] 1Pe 2:24 **10:7** [a] Jer 36:2 [b] Ps 40:6-8 **10:8** [c] ver 5,6; Mk 12:33 **10:9** [d] ver 7 **10:10** [e] Jn 17:19 [f] Heb 2:14; 1Pe 2:24 [g] Heb 7:27 **10:11** [h] Heb 5:1 [i] ver 1,4 **10:13** [j] Heb 1:13 **10:14** [k] ver 1 **10:15** [l] Heb 3:7 **10:16** [m] Jer 31:33; Heb 8:10 **10:17** [n] Heb 8:12

A Call to Persevere in Faith

19Therefore, brothers and sisters, since
we have confidence to enter the Most Holy
Place[o] by the blood of Jesus, 20by a new
and living way[p] opened for us through
the curtain,[q] that is, his body, 21and since
we have a great priest[r] over the house of
God, 22let us draw near to God[s] with a sincere heart and with the full assurance that
faith brings, having our hearts sprinkled
to cleanse us from a guilty conscience[t] and
having our bodies washed with pure water.
23Let us hold unswervingly to the hope[u] we
profess, for he who promised is faithful.[v]
24And let us consider how we may spur one
another on toward love and good deeds,
25not giving up meeting together,[w] as some
are in the habit of doing, but encouraging
one another[x]—and all the more as you see
the Day approaching.

26If we deliberately keep on sinning[y]
after we have received the knowledge of
the truth, no sacrifice for sins is left, 27but
only a fearful expectation of judgment
and of raging fire[z] that will consume the
enemies of God. 28Anyone who rejected
the law of Moses died without mercy on
the testimony of two or three witnesses.[a] 29How much more severely do you
think someone deserves to be punished
who has trampled the Son of God underfoot,[b] who has treated as an unholy thing
the blood of the covenant[c] that sanctified
them, and who has insulted the Spirit[d] of
grace?[e] 30For we know him who said, "It is
mine to avenge; I will repay,"[af] and again,
"The Lord will judge his people."[bg] 31It is a
dreadful thing to fall into the hands of the
living God.[h]

32Remember those earlier days after
you had received the light,[i] when you endured in a great conflict full of suffering.[j]
33Sometimes you were publicly exposed to
insult and persecution;[k] at other times you
stood side by side with those who were so
treated.[l] 34You suffered along with those
in prison[m] and joyfully accepted the confiscation of your property, because you
knew that you yourselves had better and
lasting possessions.[n] 35So do not throw
away your confidence; it will be richly rewarded.

36You need to persevere[o] so that when
you have done the will of God, you will receive what he has promised. 37For,

> "In just a little while,
> he who is coming[p] will come
> and will not delay."[cq]

38And,

> "But my righteous[d] one will live by
> faith.[r]
> And I take no pleasure
> in the one who shrinks
> back."[e]

39But we do not belong to those who shrink
back and are destroyed, but to those who
have faith and are saved.

---

[a] *30* Deut. 32:35 [b] *30* Deut. 32:36; Psalm 135:14 [c] *37* Isaiah 26:20; Hab. 2:3 [d] *38* Some early manuscripts *But the righteous* [e] *38* Hab. 2:4 (see Septuagint)

10:19 ***Therefore.*** The author has spent five chapters explaining the superiority of Christ's priesthood to the Levitical priesthood and the superiority of the new covenant to the Mosaic covenant. Unlike the Israelites, who approached God at Mount Sinai with fear and trembling (Ex. 20:18–21), believers can approach God with boldness (3:6; 4:16; 10:35) because we possess Christ's righteousness and not our own.

10:20 ***his body.*** The Old Testament high priest passed through a veil to get to the Most Holy Place. Now, believers enter God's presence through Christ's flesh, meaning His sacrificial death.

10:22 ***our hearts sprinkled ... our bodies washed.*** Our consciences can be cleansed through the blood of Christ (9:14). Just as the high priest washed before entering the Most Holy Place (Lev. 16:3–4), so believers are cleansed before they come before the Holy One.

10:24–25 ***spur one another on toward love and good deeds.*** The Greek word translated "spur" means "convulse." In this context the word speaks forcefully of the tremendous impact believers can have on each other. That is why the author exhorts the Hebrews to gather together. Evidently, some believers had stopped attending the worship services of the church, perhaps because they feared persecution.

10:26 ***deliberately keep on sinning.*** The reference here is not to an occasional act of sin (which can be confessed and forgiven) but to a conscious rejection of God. The Old Testament speaks in Numbers 15:30–31 of committing willful sin. A person who sinned presumptuously was to be cut off from the people. To sin deliberately after receiving the knowledge of the truth is apostasy. If a Christian rejects God's provision for his or her salvation, there is no other remedy for sins, since forgiveness for sins can only be found in Christ's perfect sacrifice.

10:29 ***Spirit of grace.*** This is a reference to the Holy Spirit, the agent of God's gracious gift of salvation. A believer who commits these offenses will be judged with a punishment worse than physical death.

10:35 ***do not throw away your confidence.*** For the recipients of Hebrews to return to the safety of Judaism would mean a loss of eternal reward at the judgment seat of Christ.

10:19 [o] Eph 2:18; Heb 9:8, 12, 25 **10:20** [p] Heb 9:8 [q] Heb 9:3 **10:21** [r] Heb 2:17 **10:22** [s] Heb 7:19 [t] Eze 36:25; Heb 9:14 **10:23** [u] Heb 3:6 [v] 1Co 1:9 **10:25** [w] Ac 2:42 [x] Heb 3:13 **10:26** [y] Nu 15:30; 2Pe 2:20 **10:27** [z] Isa 26:11; 2Th 1:7; Heb 9:27 **10:28** [a] Dt 17:6, 7; Heb 2:2 **10:29** [b] Heb 6:6 [c] Mt 26:28 [d] Eph 4:30; Heb 6:4 [e] Heb 2:3 **10:30** [f] Dt 32:35; Ro 12:19 [g] Dt 32:36 **10:31** [h] Mt 16:16 **10:32** [i] Heb 6:4 [j] Php 1:29, 30 **10:33** [k] 1Co 4:9 [l] Php 4:14; 1Th 2:14 **10:34** [m] Heb 13:3 [n] Heb 11:16 **10:36** [o] Lk 21:19; Heb 12:1 **10:37** [p] Mt 11:3 [q] Rev 22:20 **10:38** [r] Ro 1:17; Gal 3:11

Faith in Action

11 Now faith is confidence in what we
hope for and assurance about what
we do not see.[s] 2This is what the ancients
were commended for.[t]
3By faith we understand that the universe was formed at God's command,[u] so
that what is seen was not made out of what
was visible.
4By faith Abel brought God a better offering than Cain did. By faith he was commended as righteous, when God spoke well
of his offerings.[v] And by faith Abel still
speaks, even though he is dead.[w]
5By faith Enoch was taken from this life,
so that he did not experience death: "He
could not be found, because God had tak-
en him away."[a][x] For before he was taken, he
was commended as one who pleased God.
6And without faith it is impossible to please
God, because anyone who comes to him[y]
must believe that he exists and that he rewards those who earnestly seek him.
7By faith Noah, when warned about
things not yet seen, in holy fear built an
ark[z] to save his family.[a] By his faith he
condemned the world and became heir of
the righteousness that is in keeping with
faith.
8By faith Abraham, when called to go to
a place he would later receive as his inheritance,[b] obeyed and went,[c] even though he
did not know where he was going. 9By faith
he made his home in the promised land[d]
like a stranger in a foreign country; he lived
in tents,[e] as did Isaac and Jacob, who were
heirs with him of the same promise.[f] 10For
he was looking forward to the city[g] with
foundations,[h] whose architect and builder is God. 11And by faith even Sarah, who
was past childbearing age,[i] was enabled to
bear children[j] because she[b] considered him
faithful who had made the promise. 12And
so from this one man, and he as good as
dead,[k] came descendants as numerous as
the stars in the sky and as countless as the
sand on the seashore.[l]
13All these people were still living by
faith when they died. They did not receive
the things promised;[m] they only saw them
and welcomed them from a distance,[n] admitting that they were foreigners and
strangers on earth.[o] 14People who say
such things show that they are looking for
a country of their own. 15If they had been
thinking of the country they had left, they
would have had opportunity to return.[p]
16Instead, they were longing for a better
country—a heavenly one.[q] Therefore God
is not ashamed[r] to be called their God,[s] for
he has prepared a city[t] for them.
17By faith Abraham, when God tested him, offered Isaac as a sacrifice.[u] He
who had embraced the promises was
about to sacrifice his one and only son,
18even though God had said to him, "It is
through Isaac that your offspring will be
reckoned."[c][v] 19Abraham reasoned that
God could even raise the dead,[w] and so in
a manner of speaking he did receive Isaac
back from death.
20By faith Isaac blessed Jacob and Esau
in regard to their future.[x]
21By faith Jacob, when he was dying,
blessed each of Joseph's sons,[y] and worshiped as he leaned on the top of his staff.
22By faith Joseph, when his end was
near, spoke about the exodus of the Israelites from Egypt and gave instructions concerning the burial of his bones.[z]

---

[a] 5 Gen. 5:24 [b] 11 Or *By faith Abraham, even though he was too old to have children—and Sarah herself was not able to conceive—was enabled to become a father because he*
[c] 18 Gen. 21:12

11:1 *Now faith is.* This verse is not a definition of faith, but a description of what faith does. ***confidence.*** This means "essence" or "reality." Faith treats things hoped for as reality. ***assurance.*** This means "proof." Faith itself proves that what is unseen is real, such as the believer's rewards at the return of Christ (2 Cor. 4:18).

11:4 *a better offering than Cain.* Evidently, Cain offered his sacrifice without faith (Gen. 4). ***still speaks.*** Abel still speaks to us because his righteous deeds have been recorded in Scripture.

11:6 *comes.* This word is used repeatedly in Hebrews to refer to the privilege of drawing near to God (4:16; 7:25; 10:1,22). Here, the author of Hebrews explains that faith is mandatory for those who approach Him. ***rewards.*** God rewards not only those who seek Him, but also those who do good works in the Holy Spirit's power (Rev. 22:12).

11:8 *did not know where he was going.* Abraham placed his trust in God. Faith means obediently stepping into the unknown (v. 1). Abraham did this, and God considered him righteous because of it (Gen. 15:6; Rom. 4:1–12).

11:15 *opportunity to return.* The patriarchs and Sarah did not return to Ur, even though they could have if they had wanted to. The recipients of Hebrews were to follow the patriarchs' example and refuse to return to the religion of their ancestors, a religious system that no longer provided atonement for sin (8:7–13).

11:17–19 *Abraham ... tested.* Abraham believed that God could raise Isaac from the dead (Gen. 22:5), if necessary. The incident is figurative of what God has done for us. Isaac was as good as dead, but God provided a ram to sacrifice in his place (Gen. 22:9–14).

11:1 [s] Ro 8:24; 2Co 4:18 **11:2** [t] ver 4,39 **11:3** [u] Ge 1; Jn 1:3; 2Pe 3:5 **11:4** [v] Ge 4:4; 1Jn 3:12 [w] Heb 12:24 **11:5** [x] Ge 5:21-24 **11:6** [y] Heb 7:19 **11:7** [z] Ge 6:13-22 [a] 1Pe 3:20 **11:8** [b] Ge 12:7 [c] Ge 12:1-4; Ac 7:2-4 **11:9** [d] Ac 7:5 [e] Ge 12:8; 18:1,9 [f] Heb 6:17 **11:10** [g] Heb 12:22; 13:14 [h] Rev 21:2, 14 **11:11** [i] Ge 17:17-19; 18:11-14 [j] Ge 21:2 **11:12** [k] Ro 4:19 [l] Ge 22:17 **11:13** [m] ver 39 [n] Mt 13:17 [o] Ge 23:4; Ps 39:12; 1Pe 1:17 **11:15** [p] Ge 24:6-8 **11:16** [q] 2Ti 4:18 [r] Mk 8:38 [s] Ex 3:6, 15 [t] Heb 13:14 **11:17** [u] Ge 22:1-10; Jas 2:21 **11:18** [v] Ge 21:12; Ro 9:7 **11:19** [w] Ro 4:21 **11:20** [x] Ge 27:27-29,39,40 **11:21** [y] Ge 48:1,8-22 **11:22** [z] Ge 50:24,25; Ex 13:19

23By faith Moses' parents hid him for three months after he was born,[a] because they saw he was no ordinary child, and they were not afraid of the king's edict.[b]

24By faith Moses, when he had grown up, refused to be known as the son of Pharaoh's daughter.[c] 25He chose to be mistreated[d] along with the people of God rather than to enjoy the fleeting pleasures of sin. 26He regarded disgrace[e] for the sake of Christ as of greater value than the treasures of Egypt, because he was looking ahead to his reward.[f] 27By faith he left Egypt,[g] not fearing the king's anger; he persevered because he saw him who is invisible. 28By faith he kept the Passover and the application of blood, so that the destroyer of the firstborn would not touch the firstborn of Israel.[h]

29By faith the people passed through the Red Sea as on dry land; but when the Egyptians tried to do so, they were drowned.[i]

30By faith the walls of Jericho fell, after the army had marched around them for seven days.[j]

31By faith the prostitute Rahab, because she welcomed the spies, was not killed with those who were disobedient.[ak]

32And what more shall I say? I do not have time to tell about Gideon, Barak,[l] Samson and Jephthah, about David[m] and Samuel[n] and the prophets, 33who through faith conquered kingdoms,[o] administered justice, and gained what was promised; who shut the mouths of lions,[p] 34quenched the fury of the flames, and escaped the edge of the sword; whose weakness was turned to strength;[q] and who became powerful in battle and routed foreign armies.[r] 35Women received back their dead, raised to life again.[s] There were others who were tortured, refusing to be released so that they might gain an even better resurrection. 36Some faced jeers and flogging,[t] and even chains and imprisonment.[u] 37They were put to death by stoning;[bv] they were sawed in two; they were killed by the sword.[w] They went about in sheepskins and goatskins,[x] destitute, persecuted and mistreated— 38the world was not worthy of them. They wandered in deserts and mountains, living in caves[y] and in holes in the ground.

39These were all commended[z] for their faith, yet none of them received what had been promised,[a] 40since God had planned something better for us so that only together with us would they be made perfect.

12 Therefore, since we are surrounded by such a great cloud of witnesses, let us throw off everything that hinders and the sin that so easily entangles. And let us run[b] with perseverance[c] the race marked out for us, 2fixing our eyes on Jesus, the pioneer and perfecter of faith. For the joy set before him he endured the cross,[d] scorning its shame,[e] and sat down at the right hand of the throne of God. 3Consider him who endured such opposition from sinners, so that you will not grow weary[f] and lose heart.

God Disciplines His Children

4In your struggle against sin, you have not yet resisted to the point of shedding your blood.[g] 5And have you completely forgotten this word of encouragement that addresses you as a father addresses his son? It says,

"My son, do not make light of the Lord's
discipline,

---

[a] *31* Or *unbelieving* [b] *37* Some early manuscripts *stoning; they were put to the test;*

11:26 *disgrace for the sake of Christ.* This phrase refers to the earthly disgrace Christ received. Like Christ, Moses chose to suffer the indignities associated with God's people, instead of embracing the worldly pleasures of Pharaoh's court.

11:28 *application of blood.* God told Moses to sprinkle blood on the doorposts. Moses believed God's word and heeded His warning, and, as a result, the firstborn of every Israelite family was saved (Ex. 12:1–13).

11:35 *Women received back their dead.* This is probably a reference to the raising of the son of the widow of Zarephath (1 Kin. 17:17–24) and of the Shunammite woman (2 Kin. 4:32–37). But the author of Hebrews also points out that not all who had faith won victories, at least not in the same hour. ***tortured.*** This is usually understood to be an allusion to the heroic martyrs of Maccabean times, who were well-known.

11:40 *made perfect.* This phrase means "made complete." This completion, the realization of all of God's promises in Christ's coming kingdom, awaits all believers.

12:1 *cloud of witnesses.* This refers to the people of faith mentioned in chapter 11. They are not actually spectators watching us; they are witnesses testifying to the truth of the faith (11:2,4–6).

12:2 *perfecter.* Christ has done everything necessary for us to endure in our faith. He is our example and model. ***the joy set before him.*** His attention was not on the agonies of the cross, but on the crown, not on the suffering, but on the reward.

12:3 *Consider.* This thought involves the idea of comparison, as an accountant would compare the various columns of a balance sheet. Believers should compare their sufferings to the torture Christ endured on their behalf (v. 4).

11:23 [a] Ex 2:2 [b] Ex 1:16,22 **11:24** [c] Ex 2:10,11 **11:25** [d] ver 37 **11:26** [e] Heb 13:13 [f] Heb 10:35 **11:27** [g] Ex 12:50,51 **11:28** [h] Ex 12:21-23 **11:29** [i] Ex 14:21-31 **11:30** [j] Jos 6:12-20 **11:31** [k] Jos 2:1, 9-14; 6:22-25; Jas 2:25 **11:32** [l] Jdg 4-5 [m] 1Sa 16:1,13 [n] 1Sa 1:20 **11:33** [o] 2Sa 7:11; 8:1-3 [p] Da 6:22 **11:34** [q] 2Ki 20:7 [r] Jdg 15:8 **11:35** [s] 1Ki 17:22,23 **11:36** [t] Jer 20:2 [u] Ge 39:20 **11:37** [v] 2Ch 24:21 [w] 1Ki 19:10 [x] 2Ki 1:8 **11:38** [y] 1Ki 18:4 **11:39** [z] ver 2,4 [a] ver 13 **12:1** [b] 1Co 9:24 [c] Heb 10:36 **12:2** [d] Php 2:8,9 [e] Heb 13:13 **12:3** [f] Gal 6:9 **12:4** [g] Heb 10:32-34

and do not lose heart when he
rebukes you,
6because the Lord disciplines the one he
loves,[h]
and he chastens everyone he accepts
as his son."[a][i]

7Endure hardship as discipline; God is
treating you as his children.[j] For what children are not disciplined by their father?
8If you are not disciplined—and everyone
undergoes discipline[k]—then you are not
legitimate, not true sons and daughters at
all. 9Moreover, we have all had human fathers who disciplined us and we respected them for it. How much more should we
submit to the Father of spirits[l] and live![m]
10They disciplined us for a little while as
they thought best; but God disciplines us
for our good, in order that we may share in
his holiness.[n] 11No discipline seems pleasant at the time, but painful. Later on, however, it produces a harvest of righteousness and peace[o] for those who have been
trained by it.

12Therefore, strengthen your feeble arms
and weak knees.[p] 13"Make level paths for
your feet,"[b][q] so that the lame may not be
disabled, but rather healed.[r]

Warning and Encouragement

14Make every effort to live in peace with
everyone[s] and to be holy;[t] without holiness
no one will see the Lord.[u] 15See to it that
no one falls short of the grace of God[v] and
that no bitter root grows up to cause trouble and defile many. 16See that no one is
sexually immoral, or is godless like Esau,
who for a single meal sold his inheritance
rights as the oldest son.[w] 17Afterward, as
you know, when he wanted to inherit this
blessing, he was rejected. Even though he
sought the blessing with tears,[x] he could
not change what he had done.

The Mountain of Fear and the Mountain of Joy

18You have not come to a mountain that
can be touched and that is burning with
fire; to darkness, gloom and storm;[y] 19to a
trumpet blast[z] or to such a voice speaking
words that those who heard it begged that
no further word be spoken to them,[a] 20be-
cause they could not bear what was commanded: "If even an animal touches the
mountain, it must be stoned to death."[c][b]
21The sight was so terrifying that Moses
said, "I am trembling with fear."[d]

22But you have come to Mount Zion, to
the city[c] of the living God, the heavenly
Jerusalem.[d] You have come to thousands
upon thousands of angels in joyful assembly, 23to the church of the firstborn, whose
names are written in heaven.[e] You have
come to God, the Judge of all,[f] to the spirits
of the righteous made perfect,[g] 24to Jesus
the mediator of a new covenant, and to the
sprinkled blood that speaks a better word
than the blood of Abel.[h]

25See to it that you do not refuse him who
speaks. If they did not escape when they refused him who warned[i] them on earth, how
much less will we, if we turn away from
him who warns us from heaven?[j] 26At that
time his voice shook the earth,[k] but now
he has promised, "Once more I will shake
not only the earth but also the heavens."[e][l]
27The words "once more" indicate the removing of what can be shaken[m]—that is,
created things—so that what cannot be
shaken may remain.

28Therefore, since we are receiving a
kingdom that cannot be shaken,[n] let us be
thankful, and so worship God acceptably
with reverence and awe,[o] 29for our "God is
a consuming fire."[f][p]

---

[a] *5,6* Prov. 3:11,12 (see Septuagint) [b] *13* Prov. 4:26 [c] *20* Exodus 19:12,13 [d] *21* See Deut. 9:19. [e] *26* Haggai 2:6 [f] *29* Deut. 4:24

12:8 ***then you are not legitimate, not true sons and daughters.*** In Roman society an illegitimate son was one who had no inheritance rights.

12:11 ***a harvest of righteousness and peace.*** This phrase suggests that the result of God's discipline is peace and righteousness.

12:18–24 ***You have not come to a mountain.*** In these verses, the author of Hebrews contrasts the Mosaic covenant with the new covenant by contrasting two mountains: Mount Sinai and Mount Zion. At Mount Sinai, the Israelites received the law from God with fear and trembling, for God displayed at that time His awesome power (Ex. 19:10–20:26). In contrast, Christian believers have come to a heavenly Jerusalem on Mount Zion through Jesus' blood. This mountain is a celebration of the Holy One, attended by angels, believers, and righteous people. The author makes the contrast between the two covenants vivid and then once again exhorts his readers not to reject Christ's offer of salvation (vv. 25–29).

12:23 ***spirits of the righteous made perfect.*** This phrase refers to all believers who have died. They are just because they have been justified or made righteous and perfect because they are now "complete" in heaven.

12:25 ***him who warns us from heaven.*** This is a reference to Christ, who spoke on earth and is now in heaven.

12:29 ***God is a consuming fire.*** The author concludes his lengthy warning to those who are tempted to abandon the faith (2:1–12:29) with a vivid description of God's judgment (Deut. 4:24). The Lord will judge His people (10:27,30).

12:6 [h] Ps 94:12; Rev 3:19 [i] Pr 3:11,12 **12:7** [j] Dt 8:5
12:8 [k] 1Pe 5:9 **12:9** [l] Nu 16:22 [m] Isa 38:16
12:10 [n] 2Pe 1:4 **12:11** [o] Isa 32:17; Jas 3:17,18
12:12 [p] Isa 35:3 **12:13** [q] Pr 4:26 [r] Gal 6:1
12:14 [s] Ro 14:19 [t] Ro 6:22 [u] Mt 5:8 **12:15** [v] Gal 5:4; Heb 3:12 **12:16** [w] Ge 25:29-34 **12:17** [x] Ge 27:30-40
12:18 [y] Ex 19:12-22; Dt 4:11 **12:19** [z] Ex 20:18 [a] Ex 20:19; Dt 5:5,25 **12:20** [b] Ex 19:12,13 **12:22** [c] Heb 11:10 [d] Gal 4:26 **12:23** [e] Lk 10:20 [f] Ps 94:2 [g] Php 3:12
12:24 [h] Ge 4:10; Heb 11:4 **12:25** [i] Heb 8:5; 11:7 [j] Heb 2:2, 3 **12:26** [k] Ex 19:18 [l] Hag 2:6 **12:27** [m] 1Co 7:31; 2Pe 3:10 **12:28** [n] Da 2:44 [o] Heb 13:15 **12:29** [p] Dt 4:24

Concluding Exhortations

13 Keep on loving one another as brothers and sisters.[q] 2Do not forget to
show hospitality to strangers,[r] for by so
doing some people have shown hospitality
to angels without knowing it.[s] 3Continue to
remember those in prison[t] as if you were
together with them in prison, and those
who are mistreated as if you yourselves
were suffering.
4Marriage should be honored by all, and
the marriage bed kept pure, for God will
judge the adulterer and all the sexually immoral.[u] 5Keep your lives free from the love
of money and be content with what you
have,[v] because God has said,

"Never will I leave you;
never will I forsake you."[a][w]

6So we say with confidence,

"The Lord is my helper; I will not be
afraid.
What can mere mortals do
to me?"[b]

7Remember your leaders,[x] who spoke the
word of God to you. Consider the outcome
of their way of life and imitate[y] their faith.
8Jesus Christ is the same yesterday and today and forever.[z]
9Do not be carried away by all kinds of
strange teachings.[a] It is good for our hearts
to be strengthened[b] by grace, not by eating
ceremonial foods,[c] which is of no benefit to
those who do so. 10We have an altar from
which those who minister at the tabernacle
have no right to eat.[d]
11The high priest carries the blood of
animals into the Most Holy Place as a sin
offering, but the bodies are burned outside
the camp.[e] 12And so Jesus also suffered
outside the city gate[f] to make the people
holy through his own blood. 13Let us, then,
go to him outside the camp, bearing the
disgrace he bore.[g] 14For here we do not
have an enduring city, but we are looking
for the city that is to come.[h]
15Through Jesus, therefore, let us continually offer to God a sacrifice[i] of praise—
the fruit of lips[j] that openly profess his
name. 16And do not forget to do good and
to share with others,[k] for with such sacrifices[l] God is pleased.
17Have confidence in your leaders and
submit to their authority, because they
keep watch over you[m] as those who must
give an account. Do this so that their work
will be a joy, not a burden, for that would
be of no benefit to you.
18Pray for us.[n] We are sure that we have
a clear conscience[o] and desire to live honorably in every way. 19I particularly urge
you to pray so that I may be restored to you
soon.[p]

a 5 Deut. 31:6 *b* 6 Psalm 118:6,7

13:2 *shown hospitality to angels.* This is a reference to men in the Old Testament who encounter heavenly beings. These men included Abraham (Gen. 18), Lot (Gen. 19), and Gideon (Judg. 6). The idea is that, when you practice hospitality, you may be helping a messenger of God without realizing it.
13:5 *Never will I leave you; never will I forsake you.* This quotation is one of the emphatic statements in the New Testament. In Greek it contains two double negatives, similar to saying in English, "I will never, ever, ever forsake you." Jesus uses the same technique to express the certainty of eternal life for believers (John 10:28).
13:9 *strange teachings.* This implies ideas foreign to the gospel message. Many of the ideas which the author was confronting were Jewish in origin—pertaining to ritual observances, sacrificial feasts, and various laws identifying what was clean and unclean.
13:11 *burned outside the camp.* The believer has a sacrifice, Jesus Christ. He atoned for the sins of humanity with His death on the cross. But, unlike the high priests from the Old Testament, believers receive their sustenance from Christ in a symbolic way, by believing in Him (John 6:41–58).
13:15–16 *sacrifice of praise.* Although the Old Testament sacrifices are now obsolete (8:13), believers are to offer spiritual sacrifices which include their praise, their possessions, and even their lives (Rom. 12:1–2).
13:15 Worship—Since worship encompasses thought, feeling, and deed, there are many expressions of it. Worship especially includes praise and thanksgiving which may be expressed privately or publicly, whether by grateful declarations (Heb. 13:15) or by joyful singing (Ps. 100:2; Eph. 5:19; Col. 3:16). Portions of early Christian hymns of worship have been preserved in the New Testament (Phil. 2:5–11; 1 Tim. 3:16; 2 Tim. 2:11–13). One very important expression of worship for the church is remembering the death of Christ through the Lord's Supper (1 Cor. 11:26). The Lord's Supper was instituted by Christ Himself (Matt. 26:26–28) and judged by Paul to be taken very seriously (1 Cor. 11:28–32). Since worship means giving something to God, the cheerful giving of money to God's work is certainly an act of worship (2 Cor. 9:7). The exercise of one of the spiritual gifts in ministry to the body of Christ constitutes worship as service (1 Cor. 12) as does faithfully occupying a church office (Eph. 4:11; 1 Tim. 3:1–13; Titus 1:5–9). In fact, presenting ourselves (mind and body) to God to serve in any context is described as an act of worship in Romans 12:1. In this manner our whole lives become acts of worship.

13:1 [q] Ro 12:10; 1Pe 1:22 **13:2** [r] Mt 25:35 [s] Ge 18:1-33
13:3 [t] Mt 25:36; Col 4:18 **13:4** [u] 1Co 6:9
13:5 [v] Php 4:11 [w] Dt 31:6,8; Jos 1:5 **13:7** [x] ver 17,24
[y] Heb 6:12 **13:8** [z] Heb 1:12 **13:9** [a] Eph 4:14 [b] Col 2:7
[c] Col 2:16 **13:10** [d] 1Co 9:13; 10:18 **13:11** [e] Ex 29:14;
Lev 16:27 **13:12** [f] Jn 19:17 **13:13** [g] Heb 11:26
13:14 [h] Php 3:20; Heb 12:22 **13:15** [i] 1Pe 2:5 [j] Hos 14:2
13:16 [k] Ro 12:13 [l] Php 4:18 **13:17** [m] Isa 62:6; Ac 20:28
13:18 [n] 1Th 5:25 [o] Ac 23:1 **13:19** [p] Phm 22

Benediction and Final Greetings

20Now may the God of peace,[q] who
through the blood of the eternal covenant[r]
brought back from the dead[s] our Lord
Jesus, that great Shepherd of the sheep,[t]
21equip you with everything good for doing his will, and may he work in us[u] what
is pleasing to him,[v] through Jesus Christ, to
whom be glory for ever and ever. Amen.[w]
22Brothers and sisters, I urge you to bear
with my word of exhortation, for in fact I
have written to you quite briefly.[x]
23I want you to know that our brother
Timothy[y] has been released. If he arrives
soon, I will come with him to see you.
24Greet all your leaders[z] and all the
Lord's people. Those from Italy[a] send you
their greetings.
25Grace be with you all.[b]

13:20 ***great Shepherd of the sheep.*** Having laid down His life for them (John 10:15) and now continuing to make intercession for them (7:25), this is another description of Jesus' ministry.
13:22 ***word of exhortation.*** This phrase refers to the whole epistle to the Hebrews. It is an exhortation not to depart from the living God (3:12), but to go on to maturity (6:1) and endure in the faith to the end (3:6,14).
13:24 ***Those from Italy.*** This phrase may refer to people living in Italy, or else to people from there who were now living elsewhere. Because of its ambiguity, this phrase does not reveal the location of the author or of the recipients.

13:20 [q] Ro 15:33 [r] Isa 55:3; Eze 37:26; Zec 9:11 [s] Ac 2:24 [t] Jn 10:11 **13:21** [u] Php 2:13 [v] 1Jn 3:22 [w] Ro 11:36 **13:22** [x] 1Pe 5:12 **13:23** [y] Ac 16:1 **13:24** [z] ver 7, 17 [a] Ac 18:2 **13:25** [b] Col 4:18

JAMES

▶ **AUTHOR:** Four men are named James in the New Testament, one of which is the Lord's brother (Matt. 13:55; Mark 6:3; Gal. 1:19). Tradition points to this prominent figure as the author of the epistle, and this best fits the evidence of Scripture. The brevity and limited doctrinal emphasis of James kept it from wide circulation, and by the time it became known in the church as a whole, there was uncertainty about the identity of the James in 1:1. Growing recognition that it was written by the Lord's brother led to its acceptance as a canonical book.

▶ **TIME:** c. A.D. 46–49 ▶ **KEY VERSES:** James 1:19–22

▶ **THEME:** James is for the practical person. While most of Paul's epistles have a theological and practical section, there isn't much theoretical or systematic theology in this book. The subject matters covered in James are the issues we face daily if not hourly. How do we respond to trials and temptation? What are we doing with our money? Do we keep our tongues under control? Are we acting on our faith? What are we doing with our prayer lives? The main point of all these questions James raises is that saving faith needs to result in changed behavior.

---

1 James,[a] a servant of God[b] and of the
Lord Jesus Christ,

To the twelve tribes[c] scattered[d] among
the nations:

Greetings.

Trials and Temptations

2Consider it pure joy, my brothers and
sisters,[a] whenever you face trials of many
kinds,[e] 3because you know that the testing
of your faith produces perseverance. 4Let
perseverance finish its work so that you
may be mature and complete, not lacking
anything. 5If any of you lacks wisdom, you
should ask God,[f] who gives generously to
all without finding fault, and it will be giv-
en to you.[g] 6But when you ask, you must believe and not doubt,[h] because the one who
doubts is like a wave of the sea, blown and
tossed by the wind. 7That person should
not expect to receive anything from the
Lord. 8Such a person is double-minded[i]
and unstable in all they do.

9Believers in humble circumstances
ought to take pride in their high position.
10But the rich should take pride in their
humiliation—since they will pass away
like a wild flower.[j] 11For the sun rises with
scorching heat and withers[k] the plant; its
blossom falls and its beauty is destroyed.[l]
In the same way, the rich will fade away
even while they go about their business.

---

[a] 2 The Greek word for *brothers and sisters* (*adelphoi*) refers here to believers, both men and women, as part of God's family; also in verses 16 and 19; and in 2:1, 5, 14; 3:10, 12; 4:11; 5:7, 9, 10, 12, 19.

1:1 *To the twelve tribes.* This salutation probably means the letter is for Jewish Christians living outside of Palestine. The letter was not intended for one specific church but was to be passed around among various local assemblies.

1:2 *trials.* These are outward circumstances—conflicts, sufferings, and troubles—encountered by all believers. Trials are not pleasant and may be extremely grievous, but believers are to consider them as opportunities for rejoicing. Troubles and difficulties are a tool which refines and purifies our faith, producing patience and endurance.

1:3 *testing of your faith.* The word that is translated into this phrase occurs only here and in 1 Peter 1:7. The term was used for coins that were genuine and not debased. The aim of trying is not to destroy or afflict, but to purge and refine. "Patience" here transcends the idea of bearing affliction; it includes the idea of standing fast under pressure, with a staying power that turns adversities into opportunities.

1:5 *wisdom.* The starting point for wisdom is a genuine reverence for the Almighty (Ps. 111:10; Prov. 9:10) and a steadfast confidence that God controls all circumstances, guiding them to His good purposes (Rom. 8:28).

1:8 *double-minded.* This person is literally one with "two souls." If one part of a person is set on God and the other is set on this world (Matt. 6:24), there will be constant conflict within.

1:1 [a] Ac 15:13 [b] Titus 1:1 [c] Ac 26:7 [d] Dt 32:26; Jn 7:35; 1Pe 1:1 **1:2** [e] Mt 5:12; 1Pe 1:6 **1:5** [f] 1Ki 3:9, 10; Pr 2:3-6 [g] Mt 7:7 **1:6** [h] Mk 11:24 **1:8** [i] Jas 4:8 **1:10** [j] 1Co 7:31; 1Pe 1:24 **1:11** [k] Ps 102:4, 11 [l] Isa 40:6-8

12Blessed is the one who perseveres under trial because, having stood the test, that
person will receive the crown of life[m] that the
Lord has promised to those who love him.[n]
13When tempted, no one should say,
"God is tempting me." For God cannot be
tempted by evil, nor does he tempt anyone;
14but each person is tempted when they are
dragged away by their own evil desire and
enticed. 15Then, after desire has conceived,
it gives birth to sin;[o] and sin, when it is full-
grown, gives birth to death.[p]
16Don't be deceived,[q] my dear brothers
and sisters.[r] 17Every good and perfect gift
is from above,[s] coming down from the Father of the heavenly lights, who does not
change[t] like shifting shadows. 18He chose
to give us birth[u] through the word of truth,
that we might be a kind of firstfruits[v] of all
he created.

Listening and Doing

19My dear brothers and sisters, take note
of this: Everyone should be quick to listen,
slow to speak[w] and slow to become angry,
20because human anger does not produce
the righteousness that God desires. 21There-
fore, get rid of[x] all moral filth and the evil
that is so prevalent and humbly accept the
word planted in you,[y] which can save you.
22Do not merely listen to the word, and
so deceive yourselves. Do what it says.
23Anyone who listens to the word but does
not do what it says is like someone who
looks at his face in a mirror 24and, after
looking at himself, goes away and immediately forgets what he looks like. 25But whoever looks intently into the perfect law that
gives freedom,[z] and continues in it—not
forgetting what they have heard, but doing
it—they will be blessed in what they do.[a]
26Those who consider themselves religious and yet do not keep a tight rein on
their tongues[b] deceive themselves, and
their religion is worthless. 27Religion that
God our Father accepts as pure and faultless is this: to look after[c] orphans and widows[d] in their distress and to keep oneself
from being polluted by the world.[e]

Favoritism Forbidden

2 My brothers and sisters, believers in
our glorious[f] Lord Jesus Christ must not
show favoritism.[g] 2Suppose a man comes
into your meeting wearing a gold ring and
fine clothes, and a poor man in filthy old
clothes also comes in. 3If you show special
attention to the man wearing fine clothes
and say, "Here's a good seat for you," but
say to the poor man, "You stand there" or
"Sit on the floor by my feet," 4have you not
discriminated among yourselves and become judges[h] with evil thoughts?
5Listen, my dear brothers and sisters:[i]
Has not God chosen those who are poor in
the eyes of the world[j] to be rich in faith[k] and
to inherit the kingdom he promised those
who love him?[l] 6But you have dishonored
the poor.[m] Is it not the rich who are exploiting you? Are they not the ones who are
dragging you into court?[n] 7Are they not the
ones who are blaspheming the noble name
of him to whom you belong?
8If you really keep the royal law found
in Scripture, "Love your neighbor as yourself,"[a][o] you are doing right. 9But if you
show favoritism,[p] you sin and are convicted by the law as lawbreakers.[q] 10For whoever keeps the whole law and yet stumbles

[a] 8 Lev. 19:18

1:12 ***will receive the crown of life.*** The Bible describes the believer's reward (2 Cor. 5:10; Rev. 22:12) under various vivid images, such as precious metals (1 Cor. 3:8–14), garments (Rev. 3:5,18; 19:7–8), and crowns (1 Cor. 9:25; Rev. 2:10; 3:11).
1:13 ***nor does he tempt anyone.*** Enticement to sin does not come from God. God will never deliberately lead a person to commit sin because that would not only go against His nature, but it would also be opposed to His purpose of molding His creation into His holy image. Yet, God does sometimes place His people in adverse circumstances for the purpose of building godly character (Gen. 22:1,12).
1:19 ***quick to listen, slow to speak and slow to become angry.*** These three exhortations reveal the outline of this letter (1:21—2:26 for "quick to listen"; 3:1–18 for "slow to speak"; 4:1—5:18 for "slow to become angry").
1:21 ***humbly accept the word planted in you.*** The believer should have a teachable spirit—without resisting, disputing, or questioning. Receiving God's Word this way will save the believer's soul.
1:22 ***Do not merely listen to the word, and so deceive yourselves. Do what it says.*** Believers who hear the Word of God (v. 19) must receive it with a teachable spirit (v. 21), applying it to their daily lives. To hear and not obey is to be deceived.
1:25 ***the perfect law that gives freedom.*** Loving God and loving one's neighbor sum up the law (Rom. 13:8–10). But it is Christ's love (Eph. 3:17–19) which frees us from our sins to truly love others (John 8:36–38; Gal. 5:13).
1:27 ***orphans and widows.*** These people were among the most unprotected and needy classes in ancient societies (Ezek. 22:7). Pure religion does not merely give material goods for the relief of the distressed; it also oversees their care (Acts 6:1–7).
2:5 ***inherit the kingdom.*** This inheritance means more than entering the kingdom; it also involves ruling with Christ (1 Cor. 6:9; Gal. 5:21; 2 Tim. 2:12).
2:9 ***if you show favoritism, you sin.*** James alludes to Leviticus 19:15, which prohibits favoritism to either the poor or the rich.
2:10 ***guilty of breaking all of it.*** God does not

1:12 [m] 1Co 9:25 [n] Jas 2:5 **1:15** [o] Job 15:35; Ps 7:14 [p] Ro 6:23 **1:16** [q] 1Co 6:9 [r] ver 19 **1:17** [s] Jn 3:27 [t] Nu 23:19; Mal 3:6 **1:18** [u] Jn 1:13 [v] Eph 1:12; Rev 14:4 **1:19** [w] Pr 10:19 **1:21** [x] Eph 4:22 [y] Eph 1:13 **1:25** [z] Jas 2:12 [a] Jn 13:17 **1:26** [b] Ps 34:13; 1Pe 3:10 **1:27** [c] Mt 25:36 [d] Isa 1:17,23 [e] Ro 12:2 **2:1** [f] 1Co 2:8 [g] Lev 19:15 **2:4** [h] Jn 7:24 **2:5** [i] Jas 1:16,19 [j] 1Co 1:26-28 [k] Lk 12:21 [l] Jas 1:12 **2:6** [m] 1Co 11:22 [n] Ac 8:3 **2:8** [o] Lev 19:18 **2:9** [p] ver 1 [q] Dt 1:17

at just one point is guilty of breaking all of
it.[r] 11For he who said, "You shall not commit adultery,"[a][s] also said, "You shall not
murder."[b][t] If you do not commit adultery
but do commit murder, you have become
a lawbreaker.
12Speak and act as those who are going
to be judged by the law that gives freedom,[u]
13because judgment without mercy will be
shown to anyone who has not been merciful.[v] Mercy triumphs over judgment.

Faith and Deeds

14What good is it, my brothers and sisters, if someone claims to have faith but
has no deeds?[w] Can such faith save them?
15Suppose a brother or a sister is without
clothes and daily food.[x] 16If one of you says
to them, "Go in peace; keep warm and well
fed," but does nothing about their physical
needs, what good is it?[y] 17In the same way,
faith by itself, if it is not accompanied by
action, is dead.
18But someone will say, "You have faith;
I have deeds."

Show me your faith without deeds,[z] and I
will show you my faith by my deeds.[a] 19You
believe that there is one God.[b] Good! Even
the demons believe that[c]—and shudder.
20You foolish person, do you want evidence that faith without deeds is useless[c]?[d]
21Was not our father Abraham considered
righteous for what he did when he offered
his son Isaac on the altar?[e] 22You see that
his faith and his actions were working together,[f] and his faith was made complete
by what he did.[g] 23And the scripture was
fulfilled that says, "Abraham believed God,
and it was credited to him as righteousness,"[d][h] and he was called God's friend.[i]
24You see that a person is considered righteous by what they do and not by faith alone.
25In the same way, was not even Rahab
the prostitute considered righteous for
what she did when she gave lodging to the
spies and sent them off in a different direction?[j] 26As the body without the spirit is
dead, so faith without deeds is dead.[k]

Taming the Tongue

3 Not many of you should become teachers, my fellow believers, because you
know that we who teach will be judged
more strictly. 2We all stumble[l] in many
ways. Anyone who is never at fault in what
they say[m] is perfect,[n] able to keep their
whole body in check.[o]
3When we put bits into the mouths of
horses to make them obey us, we can turn
the whole animal.[p] 4Or take ships as an example. Although they are so large and are
driven by strong winds, they are steered
by a very small rudder wherever the pilot wants to go. 5Likewise, the tongue is a
small part of the body, but it makes great
boasts.[q] Consider what a great forest is set
on fire by a small spark. 6The tongue also
is a fire,[r] a world of evil among the parts of
the body. It corrupts the whole body,[s] sets
the whole course of one's life on fire, and is
itself set on fire by hell.
7All kinds of animals, birds, reptiles and
sea creatures are being tamed and have
been tamed by mankind, 8but no human
being can tame the tongue. It is a restless
evil, full of deadly poison.[t]
9With the tongue we praise our Lord

[a] *11* Exodus 20:14; Deut. 5:18 [b] *11* Exodus 20:13; Deut. 5:17 [c] *20* Some early manuscripts *dead* [d] *23* Gen. 15:6

---

allow selective obedience. We cannot choose to obey the parts of the law that are to our own liking and disregard the rest. Some of the Pharisees were guilty of this. They carefully observed some of the requirements of the law, such as keeping the Sabbath, and ignored others, such as honoring their parents (Matt. 15:1–7). Sin is a violation of the perfect righteousness of God, who is the Lawgiver. James is saying that the whole divine law has to be accepted as an expression of God's will for His people. The violation of even one Commandment separates an individual from God and His purposes.

2:14 ***What good is it.*** James is implying in this verse that faith in Christ will demonstrate itself in love for others (John 13:34–35).

2:19 ***Even the demons believe that—and shudder.*** While they believe, the demons do not love Him (Matt. 8:29). Their kind of belief does not lead to love, submission, and obedience; instead, it leads to hatred, rebellion, and disobedience.

2:21 ***righteous.*** James is using the word *righteous* to mean "proved." We prove to others our genuine faith in Christ through our works. But the justification that comes through faith is before God, and we do not "prove" ourselves to Him; instead, God declares us righteous through our association with Christ, the One who died for our sins (Rom. 3:28).

2:22 ***faith ... actions.*** These two should be together; there is a close relationship between the two. Faith produces right action; and right action makes faith perfect, meaning "mature" or "complete."

3:1 ***will be judged more strictly.*** James does not give the warning of condemnation to others without applying it to himself.

3:7–8 ***no human being can tame the tongue.*** The instincts of animals can be subdued through conditioning and punishment, but the sinful nature that inspires evil words is beyond our control. Only the work of the Holy Spirit within us can bring this destructive force under control.

3:9 ***we praise our Lord and Father.*** James is pointing out the inconsistency of blessing God while cursing people who are created in His image.

2:10 [r] Mt 5:19; Gal 3:10 **2:11** [s] Ex 20:14; Dt 5:18 [t] Ex 20:13; Dt 5:17 **2:12** [u] Jas 1:25 **2:13** [v] Mt 5:7; 18:32-35 **2:14** [w] Mt 7:26; Jas 1:22-25 **2:15** [x] Mt 25:35, 36 **2:16** [y] 1Jn 3:17, 18 **2:18** [z] Ro 3:28 [a] Jas 3:13 **2:19** [b] Dt 6:4 [c] Mt 8:29; Lk 4:34 **2:20** [d] ver 17, 26 **2:21** [e] Ge 22:9, 12 **2:22** [f] Heb 11:17 [g] 1Th 1:3 **2:23** [h] Ge 15:6; Ro 4:3 [i] 2Ch 20:7; Isa 41:8 **2:25** [j] Heb 11:31 **2:26** [k] ver 17, 20 **3:2** [l] 1Ki 8:46; Jas 2:10 [m] 1Pe 3:10 [n] Mt 12:37 [o] Jas 1:26 **3:3** [p] Ps 32:9 **3:5** [q] Ps 12:3, 4 **3:6** [r] Pr 16:27 [s] Mt 15:11, 18, 19 **3:8** [t] Ps 140:3; Ro 3:13

and Father, and with it we curse human beings, who have been made in God's likeness.[u] 10Out of the same mouth come praise and cursing. My brothers and sisters, this should not be. 11Can both fresh water and salt water flow from the same spring? 12My brothers and sisters, can a fig tree bear olives, or a grapevine bear figs?[v] Neither can a salt spring produce fresh water.

Two Kinds of Wisdom

13Who is wise and understanding among you? Let them show it[w] by their good life, by deeds done in the humility that comes from wisdom. 14But if you harbor bitter envy and selfish ambition[x] in your hearts, do not boast about it or deny the truth.[y] 15Such "wisdom" does not come down from heaven[z] but is earthly, unspiritual, demonic.[a] 16For where you have envy and selfish ambition, there you find disorder and every evil practice.

17But the wisdom that comes from heaven[b] is first of all pure; then peace-loving, considerate, submissive, full of mercy[c] and good fruit, impartial and sincere.[d] 18Peacemakers who sow in peace reap a harvest of righteousness.[e]

Submit Yourselves to God

4 What causes fights and quarrels[f] among you? Don't they come from your desires that battle[g] within you? 2You desire but do not have, so you kill. You covet but you cannot get what you want, so you quarrel and fight. You do not have because you do not ask God. 3When you ask, you do not receive,[h] because you ask with wrong motives,[i] that you may spend what you get on your pleasures.

4You adulterous people,[a] don't you know that friendship with the world[j] means enmity against God?[k] Therefore, anyone who chooses to be a friend of the world becomes an enemy of God.[l] 5Or do you think Scripture says without reason that he jealously longs for the spirit he has caused to dwell in us[b]? 6But he gives us more grace. That is why Scripture says:

"God opposes the proud
but shows favor to the humble."[c][m]

7Submit yourselves, then, to God. Resist the devil,[n] and he will flee from you. 8Come near to God and he will come near to you.[o] Wash your hands,[p] you sinners, and purify your hearts, you double-minded.[q] 9Grieve, mourn and wail. Change your laughter to mourning and your joy to gloom.[r] 10Humble yourselves before the Lord, and he will lift you up.

11Brothers and sisters, do not slander one another.[s] Anyone who speaks against a brother or sister[d] or judges them[t] speaks against the law and judges it. When you judge the law, you are not keeping it,[u] but sitting in judgment on it. 12There is only one Lawgiver and Judge, the one who is able to save and destroy.[v] But you—who are you to judge your neighbor?[w]

---

a *4* An allusion to covenant unfaithfulness; see Hosea 3:1. *b* *5* Or *that the spirit he caused to dwell in us envies intensely;* or *that the Spirit he caused to dwell in us longs jealously* *c* *6* Prov. 3:34 *d* *11* The Greek word for *brother or sister (adelphos)* refers here to a believer, whether man or woman, as part of God's family.

3:16 *envy and selfish ambition.* On the other hand, God brings harmony and wisdom (1 Cor. 14:33). It is likely that the Jewish Christians to whom James was writing were going through turmoil because of sinful acts like the ones mentioned here. James wanted his readers to set aside their petty attitudes and seek reconciliation.

4:1 *fights and quarrels.* The source of problems is the conflict between desires for pleasure and the desire for God's will, an attitude the Holy Spirit has placed within us.

4:3 *you ask with wrong motives.* Some might have protested James's admonition (vv. 1–2) by claiming that they had not received an answer to their prayers (Matt. 7:7). James responds by suggesting that they were praying for the wrong things. Instead of praying for their sinful desires, they should have been praying for God's good will for them.

4:4 *anyone who chooses.* This verse does not speak of God's attitude toward the believer, but of the believer's attitude toward God. The difference between the world and God is so vast that, as we move toward the world, we alienate ourselves from God. In the world, sin is considered acceptable and pleasurable. Ultimately the world has lost its awareness of sin, and thus sin has become habitual.

4:6 *God opposes the proud.* James quotes from Proverbs 3:34 to prove his point. Those who submit to divine wisdom will receive the necessary grace from God to put into practice the kind of life James describes (3:13–18). On the other hand, those who elevate themselves will face a formidable foe (v. 4). God Himself will fight against their plans, because they are not on His side.

4:9 *Grieve, mourn and wail.* When a believer who has fallen into sin responds to God's call for repentance, he or she should place laughter and joy aside to reflect on the sin with genuine sorrow (2 Cor. 7:9–10). In this verse, laughter seems to refer to the loud revelry of pleasure-loving people. They immerse themselves in a celebration of their sins in an effort to forget God's judgment. A Christian should never laugh at sin. However, Christian sorrow leads to repentance; repentance leads to forgiveness; and forgiveness leads to true joy over one's reconciliation with God (Ps. 32:1; 126:2; Prov. 15:13).

3:9 [u] Ge 1:26,27; 1Co 11:7 **3:12** [v] Mt 7:16 **3:13** [w] Jas 2:18 **3:14** [x] ver 16 [y] Jas 5:19 **3:15** [z] Jas 1:17 [a] 1Ti 4:1 **3:17** [b] 1Co 2:6 [c] Lk 6:36 [d] Ro 12:9 **3:18** [e] Pr 11:18; Isa 32:17 **4:1** [f] Titus 3:9 [g] Ro 7:23 **4:3** [h] Ps 18:41 [i] 1Jn 3:22; 5:14 **4:4** [j] Jas 1:27 [k] 1Jn 2:15 [l] Jn 15:19 **4:6** [m] Ps 138:6; Pr 3:34; Mt 23:12 **4:7** [n] Eph 4:27; 1Pe 5:6-9 **4:8** [o] 2Ch 15:2 [p] Isa 1:16 [q] Jas 1:8 **4:9** [r] Lk 6:25 **4:11** [s] 1Pe 2:1 [t] Mt 7:1 [u] Jas 1:22 **4:12** [v] Mt 10:28 [w] Ro 14:4

Boasting About Tomorrow

13Now listen, you who say, "Today or
tomorrow we will go to this or that city,
spend a year there, carry on business and
make money."[x] 14Why, you do not even
know what will happen tomorrow. What is
your life? You are a mist that appears for a
little while and then vanishes.[y] 15Instead,
you ought to say, "If it is the Lord's will,[z] we
will live and do this or that." 16As it is, you
boast in your arrogant schemes. All such
boasting is evil.[a] 17If anyone, then, knows
the good they ought to do and doesn't do it,
it is sin for them.[b]

Warning to Rich Oppressors

5 Now listen, you rich people,[c] weep and
wail because of the misery that is coming on you. 2Your wealth has rotted, and
moths have eaten your clothes.[d] 3Your gold
and silver are corroded. Their corrosion
will testify against you and eat your flesh
like fire. You have hoarded wealth in the
last days.[e] 4Look! The wages you failed to
pay the workers[f] who mowed your fields
are crying out against you. The cries[g] of
the harvesters have reached the ears of the
Lord Almighty.[h] 5You have lived on earth
in luxury and self-indulgence. You have fattened yourselves[i] in the day of slaughter.[a][j]
6You have condemned and murdered the
innocent one,[k] who was not opposing you.

Patience in Suffering

7Be patient, then, brothers and sisters,
until the Lord's coming. See how the farmer waits for the land to yield its valuable
crop, patiently waiting for the autumn
and spring rains.[l] 8You too, be patient and
stand firm, because the Lord's coming is
near.[m] 9Don't grumble against one another,
brothers and sisters,[n] or you will be judged.
The Judge[o] is standing at the door![p]

10Brothers and sisters, as an example of
patience in the face of suffering, take the
prophets[q] who spoke in the name of the
Lord. 11As you know, we count as blessed[r]
those who have persevered. You have
heard of Job's perseverance[s] and have seen
what the Lord finally brought about.[t] The
Lord is full of compassion and mercy.[u]

12Above all, my brothers and sisters, do
not swear—not by heaven or by earth or
by anything else. All you need to say is a
simple "Yes" or "No." Otherwise you will
be condemned.[v]

The Prayer of Faith

13Is anyone among you in trouble? Let
them pray.[w] Is anyone happy? Let them
sing songs of praise.[x] 14Is anyone among
you sick? Let them call the elders of the
church to pray over them and anoint them
with oil[y] in the name of the Lord. 15And the
prayer offered in faith will make the sick
person well; the Lord will raise them up.
If they have sinned, they will be forgiven.
16Therefore confess your sins[z] to each other and pray for each other so that you may
be healed.[a] The prayer of a righteous person is powerful and effective.[b]

17Elijah was a human being, even as
we are.[c] He prayed earnestly that it would
not rain, and it did not rain on the land for
three and a half years.[d] 18Again he prayed,
and the heavens gave rain, and the earth
produced its crops.[e]

19My brothers and sisters, if one of you
should wander from the truth[f] and someone should bring that person back,[g] 20re-
member this: Whoever turns a sinner from
the error of their way will save[h] them from
death and cover over a multitude of sins.[i]

---

[a] 5 Or *yourselves as in a day of feasting*

4:13 ***we will go . . . and make money.*** The problem here is not the plan or the concept of planning; it is leaving God out of the plan (v. 15).
5:2–3 ***your clothes.*** In the ancient world, food, costly clothing, and precious metals were conspicuous signs of wealth. James pronounces judgment and destruction on all three.
5:12–13 ***do not swear.*** James is not forbidding a believer from taking an oath in court or invoking God as witness to some significant statement (1 Thess. 2:5). Instead, he is prohibiting the ancient practice of appealing to a variety of different objects to confirm the veracity of one's statement. This practice was extremely close to idolatry, for it implied that such objects contained spirits. The warning in these verses can serve as a reminder to us to watch what we say. We should not use God's name in a reckless manner, and we should be careful to speak the truth.
5:14 ***anoint them with oil.*** This may refer to medicinal treatment (Luke 10:34). Yet, in this passage, it most likely refers to the healing power of the Holy Spirit, for verse 15 speaks of prayer saving the person. In either case, there is no indication that calling the elders excludes the use of a physician or medicine.
5:15 ***the prayer offered in faith.*** Whether a believer is healed through medicine or through miraculous means, all healing is ultimately from the Lord. That is why prayers should be consistently offered for the sick.
5:16 ***prayer . . . is powerful and effective.*** The prayer of righteous people is effective when it is used. Among other things, God uses prayer to release his people from sin, to heal them according to his will (v. 15), and to encourage them in times of great trouble (v. 13).

4:13 [x] Pr 27:1 **4:14** [y] Job 7:7; Ps 102:3 **4:15** [z] Ac 18:21 **4:16** [a] 1Co 5:6 **4:17** [b] Lk 12:47; Jn 9:41 **5:1** [c] Lk 6:24 **5:2** [d] Job 13:28; Mt 6:19,20 **5:3** [e] ver 7,8 **5:4** [f] Lev 19:13 [g] Dt 24:15 [h] Ro 9:29 **5:5** [i] Am 6:1 [j] Jer 12:3; 25:34 **5:6** [k] Heb 10:38 **5:7** [l] Dt 11:14; Jer 5:24 **5:8** [m] Ro 13:11; 1Pe 4:7 **5:9** [n] Jas 4:11 [o] 1Co 4:5; 1Pe 4:5 [p] Mt 24:33 **5:10** [q] Mt 5:12 **5:11** [r] Mt 5:10 [s] Job 1:21,22; 2:10 [t] Job 42:10,12-17 [u] Nu 14:18 **5:12** [v] Mt 5:34-37 **5:13** [w] Ps 50:15 [x] Col 3:16 **5:14** [y] Mk 6:13 **5:16** [z] Mt 3:6 [a] 1Pe 2:24 [b] Jn 9:31 **5:17** [c] Ac 14:15 [d] 1Ki 17:1; Lk 4:25 **5:18** [e] 1Ki 18:41-45 **5:19** [f] Jas 3:14 [g] Mt 18:15 **5:20** [h] Ro 11:14 [i] 1Pe 4:8

1 PETER

▸ **AUTHOR:** The early church universally acknowledged the authenticity and authority of 1 Peter. It is likely that Peter used Silvanus as his scribe (5:12). This epistle was addressed to Christians throughout Asia Minor, indicating the spread of the gospel in regions not evangelized when Acts was written. It was written from Babylon (5:13), but scholars are divided as to whether this refers literally to Babylon in Mesopotamia or symbolically to Rome. It is probably the latter as tradition consistently indicates that Peter spent the last few years of his life in Rome.

▸ **TIME:** c. A.D. 63–34 ▸ **KEY VERSES:** 1 Pet. 4:12–13

▸ **THEME:** First Peter was probably written to the Roman provinces of Turkey at the beginning of Nero's persecutions of Christians. Its primary message is one of comfort, hope, and encouragement. He asks the readers to hold fast to the faith in the midst of the coming persecution. In these letters we get a picture of a mature Peter who has incorporated Christ's crucifixion and death and resurrection into his thinking about suffering. He fully understands, and even looks forward to, the glory that is to come after the sufferings of this life.

1 Peter, an apostle of Jesus Christ,[a]

To God's elect,[b] exiles scattered throughout the provinces of Pontus, Galatia, Cappadocia, Asia and Bithynia,[c] 2who have
been chosen according to the foreknowledge[d] of God the Father, through the sanctifying work of the Spirit,[e] to be obedient to
Jesus Christ and sprinkled with his blood:[f]

Grace and peace be yours in abundance.

Praise to God for a Living Hope

3Praise be to the God and Father of our
Lord Jesus Christ![g] In his great mercy[h] he
has given us new birth into a living hope
through the resurrection of Jesus Christ
from the dead,[i] 4and into an inheritance
that can never perish, spoil or fade. This
inheritance is kept in heaven for you,[j] 5who
through faith are shielded by God's power[k] until the coming of the salvation that
is ready to be revealed in the last time. 6In
all this you greatly rejoice,[l] though now for
a little while[m] you may have had to suffer
grief in all kinds of trials.[n] 7These have
come so that the proven genuineness[o] of
your faith—of greater worth than gold,
which perishes even though refined by
fire[p]—may result in praise, glory and hon-
or when Jesus Christ is revealed.[q] 8Though
you have not seen him, you love him; and

1:1 ***exiles.*** This term conveys the idea of being dispersed, much like the Jewish exiles of the Old Testament who were not living in their homeland but in Babylon.
1:2 ***sanctifying work of the Spirit.*** Sanctification is the ongoing process whereby the Holy Spirit works in believers, making their lives holy, separated from their old ways and to God in order to be more like him. ***sprinkled with his blood.*** This concept, the second reason why God chooses us, draws our attention to three situations in the Old Testament when the Israelites were sprinkled with the blood of animals: (1) Moses' sprinkling of blood on the Israelites at Mount Sinai to symbolize their initiation into the covenant (Ex. 24:5–8); (2) the sprinkling of Aaron and his sons to be the priests of Israel (Ex. 29:19–21); and (3) the sprinkling of the blood performed by priest over healed lepers to symbolize their cleansing (Lev. 14:1–9). Any of these three cases could be the one that Peter has in mind here.
1:3 ***In his great mercy.*** Our salvation is grounded in God's mercy, His act of compassion toward us despite our condition of sinfulness. ***has given us new birth.*** God has given believers a new, spiritual life that enables us to live in an entirely different dimension than the one our physical birth allowed.
1:4 ***inheritance.*** The Greek word here suggests both a present and a future reality. God has already determined what we will one day experience in its totality. ***kept.*** God has set aside in heaven a wonderful inheritance that is waiting for us even now.
1:7 ***that the proven genuineness of your faith.*** As the purity of gold is brought forth by intense heat,

1:1 [a] 2Pe 1:1 [b] Mt 24:22 [c] Ac 16:7 **1:2** [d] Ro 8:29 [e] 2Th 2:13 [f] Heb 10:22; 12:24 **1:3** [g] 2Co 1:3; Eph 1:3 [h] Titus 3:5; Jas 1:18 [i] 1Co 15:20 **1:4** [j] Col 1:5 **1:5** [k] Jn 10:28 **1:6** [l] Ro 5:2 [m] 1Pe 5:10 [n] Jas 1:2 **1:7** [o] Jas 1:3 [p] Job 23:10; Ps 66:10; Pr 17:3 [q] Ro 2:7

even though you do not see him now, you
believe in him[r] and are filled with an inexpressible and glorious joy, 9for you are
receiving the end result of your faith, the
salvation of your souls.[s]
10Concerning this salvation, the prophets, who spoke[t] of the grace that was to
come to you, searched intently and with
the greatest care,[u] 11trying to find out the
time and circumstances to which the Spirit of Christ[v] in them was pointing when he
predicted the sufferings of the Messiah
and the glories that would follow. 12It was
revealed to them that they were not serving themselves but you, when they spoke
of the things that have now been told you
by those who have preached the gospel to
you[w] by the Holy Spirit sent from heaven.
Even angels long to look into these things.

Be Holy

13Therefore, with minds that are alert
and fully sober, set your hope on the grace
to be brought to you when Jesus Christ is
revealed at his coming. 14As obedient children, do not conform[x] to the evil desires
you had when you lived in ignorance.[y]
15But just as he who called you is holy, so
be holy in all you do;[z] 16for it is written: "Be
holy, because I am holy."[a][a]
17Since you call on a Father who judges
each person's work impartially,[b] live out
your time as foreigners here in reverent
fear.[c] 18For you know that it was not with
perishable things such as silver or gold
that you were redeemed[d] from the empty
way of life handed down to you from your
ancestors, 19but with the precious blood
of Christ, a lamb[e] without blemish or defect.[f] 20He was chosen before the creation
of the world,[g] but was revealed in these last
times[h] for your sake. 21Through him you
believe in God,[i] who raised him from the
dead and glorified him, and so your faith
and hope are in God.
22Now that you have purified[j] yourselves
by obeying the truth so that you have sincere love for each other, love one another
deeply,[k] from the heart.[b] 23For you have
been born again,[l] not of perishable seed,
but of imperishable, through the living and
enduring word of God.[m] 24For,

"All people are like grass,
and all their glory is like the flowers
of the field;
the grass withers and the flowers
fall,
25 but the word of the Lord endures
forever."[c][n]

And this is the word that was preached to
you.

2 Therefore, rid yourselves[o] of all malice and all deceit, hypocrisy, envy, and
slander[p] of every kind. 2Like newborn
babies, crave pure spiritual milk,[q] so that
by it you may grow up[r] in your salvation,
3now that you have tasted that the Lord is
good.[s]

---

a 16 Lev. 11:44,45; 19:2 *b* 22 Some early manuscripts *from a pure heart* *c* 25 Isaiah 40:6-8 (see Septuagint)

---

so the reality and purity of our faith are revealed as a result of the fiery trials we face. Ultimately the testing of our faith not only demonstrates our final salvation but also develops our capacity to bring glory to the Lord Jesus Christ when He comes into His kingdom and we reign with Him (Rom. 8:17; 2 Tim. 2:12; Rev. 5:9–12).

1:10 ***the prophets.*** Peter indicates that the Old Testament prophets knew of the gracious salvation we would one day receive and, as a result, studied it carefully and intensively.

1:12 ***by the Holy Spirit.*** Although humans may preach God's message of salvation, ultimately the Holy Spirit is the One who proclaims these great truths. Even the angels are amazed at what a wonderful salvation God has enacted on our behalf (Eph. 3:10).

1:13 ***with minds that are alert.*** Just as people in biblical times would gather up their long robes and tie them around their waists so that they could move quickly and freely, we need to do whatever it takes to focus our thoughts on those things that allow us to serve God successfully, all the while eliminating any thoughts that would trip us up (Heb. 12:1). ***and fully sober.*** Peter's concern here is primarily using mentally or spiritually sound judgment. ***set your hope on.*** We need to exhibit confidence that God will accomplish all that He promised He would do (v. 3; Rom. 8:24–25).

1:17 ***in reverent fear.*** For Christians, this phrase should be understood as something between terror and reverential awe. We need to remember that God is both our merciful Savior (vv. 3,18–21) and our holy Judge (vv. 15–17).

1:19 ***a lamb.*** Peter describes Christ as the ultimate sacrificial Lamb, who is offered in our place to pay the price for our sins. The analogy here may be a reference either to the Passover lamb (Ex. 12:3–6) or to the many lambs without blemish that were offered as part of the Old Testament sacrificial system (Lev. 23:12; Num. 6:14; 28:3).

1:20 ***chosen.*** God has known (v. 2) the One who would bring salvation, even as He has known those to whom that salvation is offered and secured (Rom. 11:2). ***but was revealed.*** This phrase contrasts with the first half of the verse. What was known only to God before the creation of the world is now made known to us.

1:22 ***purified yourselves.*** We accomplish the purification of our souls by obedience to God's truth.

2:2 ***you may grow up.*** The purpose of studying God's truth is not only to learn more, but to become mature in the faith.

1:8 [r] Jn 20:29 **1:9** [s] Ro 6:22 **1:10** [t] Mt 26:24 [u] Mt 13:17 **1:11** [v] 2Pe 1:21 **1:12** [w] ver 25 **1:14** [x] Ro 12:2 [y] Eph 4:18 **1:15** [z] 2Co 7:1; 1Th 4:7 **1:16** [a] Lev 11:44,45 **1:17** [b] Ac 10:34 [c] Heb 12:28 **1:18** [d] Mt 20:28; 1Co 6:20 **1:19** [e] Jn 1:29 [f] Ex 12:5 **1:20** [g] Eph 1:4 [h] Heb 9:26 **1:21** [i] Ro 4:24 **1:22** [j] Jas 4:8 [k] Jn 13:34; Heb 13:1 **1:23** [l] Jn 1:13 [m] Heb 4:12 **1:25** [n] Isa 40:6-8 **2:1** [o] Eph 4:22 [p] Jas 4:11 **2:2** [q] 1Co 3:2 [r] Eph 4:15, 16 **2:3** [s] Heb 6:5

The Living Stone and a Chosen People

4As you come to him, the living Stone[t]—
rejected by humans but chosen by God
and precious to him— 5you also, like living stones, are being built[u] into a spiritual house[av] to be a holy priesthood,[w] offering spiritual sacrifices acceptable to God
through Jesus Christ.[x] 6For in Scripture it
says:

> "See, I lay a stone in Zion,
> a chosen and precious cornerstone,[y]
> and the one who trusts in him
> will never be put to shame."[bz]

7Now to you who believe, this stone is precious. But to those who do not believe,[a]

> "The stone the builders rejected
> has become the cornerstone,"[cb]

8and,

> "A stone that causes people to stumble
> and a rock that makes them fall."[dc]

They stumble because they disobey the
message—which is also what they were
destined for.[d]
9But you are a chosen people,[e] a royal
priesthood, a holy nation,[f] God's special
possession, that you may declare the praises of him who called you out of darkness
into his wonderful light.[g] 10Once you were
not a people, but now you are the people of
God;[h] once you had not received mercy, but
now you have received mercy.

Living Godly Lives in a Pagan Society

11Dear friends, I urge you, as foreigners
and exiles, to abstain from sinful desires,[i]
which wage war against your soul.[j] 12Live
such good lives among the pagans that,
though they accuse you of doing wrong,
they may see your good deeds[k] and glorify
God[l] on the day he visits us.
13Submit yourselves for the Lord's sake
to every human authority:[m] whether to the
emperor, as the supreme authority, 14or to
governors, who are sent by him to punish
those who do wrong[n] and to commend those
who do right.[o] 15For it is God's will[p] that by
doing good you should silence the ignorant
talk of foolish people.[q] 16Live as free people,[r] but do not use your freedom as a cover-up for evil; live as God's slaves.[s] 17Show
proper respect to everyone, love the family
of believers,[t] fear God, honor the emperor.[u]
18Slaves, in reverent fear of God submit yourselves to your masters,[v] not only
to those who are good and considerate,[w]
but also to those who are harsh. 19For it is

---

[a] 5 Or *into a temple of the Spirit* [b] 6 Isaiah 28:16
[c] 7 Psalm 118:22 [d] 8 Isaiah 8:14

2:4 *living Stone.* This phrase anticipates the Old Testament quotations in verses 6–8. Jesus, as a living stone, is superior to the Old Testament temple.
2:5 *stones.* Christians are part of God's great spiritual building project. Referenced here are stones that are shaped and ready for use in construction, as opposed to natural rock. ***a holy priesthood.*** Unlike the Old Testament priesthood, in which only those who were born into a certain tribe could be priests, all who are reborn into God's family, that is, all believers, are priests who have the privilege and responsibility of offering spiritual sacrifices to God (Rom. 12:1–2; Heb. 13:15–16).
2:6 *a chosen and precious cornerstone.* Jesus is the foundation stone from which the placement of all other living stones in the spiritual house (v. 5) is determined (Is. 28:16). In ancient buildings, the cornerstone was first situated on the foundation and then all of the other stones were aligned to it. Thus as part of the house of God, we need to keep our focus on our Cornerstone (Heb. 12:2).
2:9 *a chosen people.* God has not left to chance who will be part of a unique body of people, a group who will serve Him. ***a royal priesthood.*** Believers are transformed not only internally (v. 5), which describes us as being made into a "holy priesthood" but also externally. We are a priesthood that functions in a ruling capacity, as kings. ***a holy nation.*** Believers are a unified group of people who are set apart for God's use. ***special possession.*** God protects those whom He has adopted into His family.
2:11 *foreigners and exiles.* With these words, Peter reminds believers (1:1) that this earth is not our home. We are foreigners here, traveling to our eternal home, heaven.
2:12 *day he visits us.* This term probably refers to the final day of judgment when all people, believers and unbelievers alike, will fall on their knees and acknowledge who Jesus Christ is and what He has done through His people.
2:13 *every human authority.* This phrase suggests that the submission of Christians is not to be exercised solely in relation to civil authorities (v. 14), but to all kinds of rules that Christians encounter (2:18; 3:1).
2:13 Our Responsibility to Human Government—As children of God, our responsibility to human government is threefold:

1. We are to recognize and accept that the powers that be are ordained by God (Rom. 13:1). This truth even applies to governments that are anti-Christian. If a given law is clearly anti-scriptural, the believer is required to obey God rather than man (Dan. 3; 6; Acts 4:18–20).
2. We are to pay our taxes to human government (Matt. 17:24; 22:21; Rom. 13:7).
3. We are to pray for the leaders in human government (1 Tim. 2:1–3).

2:16 *as a cover-up for evil.* This may be understood either as an excuse made up before the fact, or after the fact.
2:18 *in reverent fear of God submit yourselves.* Workers are to take their responsibilities seriously, even when serving the worst of bosses.

2:4 [t] ver 7 **2:5** [u] 1Co 3:9 [v] 1Ti 3:15 [w] Isa 61:6 [x] Php 4:18; Heb 13:15 **2:6** [y] Eph 2:20 [z] Isa 28:16 **2:7** [a] 2Co 2:16 [b] Ps 118:22 **2:8** [c] Isa 8:14; 1Co 1:23 [d] Ro 9:22 **2:9** [e] Dt 10:15 [f] Isa 62:12 [g] Ac 26:18 **2:10** [h] Hos 1:9,10 **2:11** [i] Gal 5:16 [j] Jas 4:1 **2:12** [k] Php 2:15; 1Pe 3:16 [l] Mt 5:16; 9:8 **2:13** [m] Ro 13:1 **2:14** [n] Ro 13:4 [o] Ro 13:3 **2:15** [p] 1Pe 3:17 [q] ver 12 **2:16** [r] Jn 8:32 [s] Ro 6:22 **2:17** [t] Ro 12:10 [u] Ro 13:7 **2:18** [v] Eph 6:5 [w] Jas 3:17

commendable if someone bears up under
the pain of unjust suffering because they
are conscious of God.[x] 20But how is it to
your credit if you receive a beating for doing wrong and endure it? But if you suffer
for doing good and you endure it, this is
commendable before God.[y] 21To this[z] you
were called, because Christ suffered for
you, leaving you an example,[a] that you
should follow in his steps.

22“He committed no sin,
and no deceit was found in his
mouth.”[a][b]

23When they hurled their insults at him, he
did not retaliate; when he suffered, he made
no threats.[c] Instead, he entrusted himself[d]
to him who judges justly. 24“He himself
bore our sins”[e] in his body on the cross, so
that we might die to sins[f] and live for righteousness; “by his wounds you have been
healed.”[g] 25For “you were like sheep going
astray,”[b][h] but now you have returned to the
Shepherd[i] and Overseer of your souls.

3 Wives, in the same way submit yourselves[j] to your own husbands[k] so that, if
any of them do not believe the word, they
may be won over[l] without words by the behavior of their wives, 2when they see the
purity and reverence of your lives. 3Your
beauty should not come from outward
adornment, such as elaborate hairstyles
and the wearing of gold jewelry or fine
clothes.[m] 4Rather, it should be that of your
inner self,[n] the unfading beauty of a gentle
and quiet spirit, which is of great worth in
God’s sight. 5For this is the way the holy
women of the past who put their hope in
God[o] used to adorn themselves. They submitted themselves to their own husbands,
6like Sarah, who obeyed Abraham and
called him her lord.[p] You are her daughters if you do what is right and do not give
way to fear.
7Husbands,[q] in the same way be considerate as you live with your wives, and treat
them with respect as the weaker partner
and as heirs with you of the gracious gift
of life, so that nothing will hinder your
prayers.

Suffering for Doing Good

8Finally, all of you, be like-minded, be
sympathetic, love one another,[r] be compassionate and humble.[s] 9Do not repay
evil with evil[t] or insult with insult.[u] On the
contrary, repay evil with blessing, because
to this[v] you were called so that you may inherit a blessing.[w] 10For,

“Whoever would love life
and see good days
must keep their tongue from evil
and their lips from deceitful speech.
11They must turn from evil and do
good;
they must seek peace and pursue it.
12For the eyes of the Lord are on the
righteous
and his ears are attentive to their
prayer,
but the face of the Lord is against those
who do evil.”[c][x]

13Who is going to harm you if you are
eager to do good?[y] 14But even if you should

---

[a] *22* Isaiah 53:9 [b] *24,25* Isaiah 53:4,5,6 (see Septuagint) [c] *12* Psalm 34:12-16

2:20 *how is it to your credit.* There is no advantage to believers for successfully enduring a deserved punishment for wrongdoing, yet there is great value when we honor God with our actions when we are unfairly condemned by others (3:17). ***endure it.*** Patience and perseverance in the face of suffering pleases God.
2:24 *He himself bore our sins.* The Greek wording emphasizes Jesus’ personal involvement in the act of paying the price for our sins. ***die to sins and live for righteousness.*** The purpose of Christ’s bearing our sins is that we might live to please Him.
2:25 *Overseer.* No one else is qualified to be the one Shepherd and Overseer of our souls—only Christ is. For this reason the New Testament regularly describes the church and its congregations as having more than one leader (Titus 1:5).
3:1 *without words.* A godly wife does not preach to her non-Christian husband with words but with the Christlike beauty of her daily life. The goal is to see that husband become a Christian.
3:3 *outward.* Christians are to spend more time developing their inner character than attempting to make themselves look beautiful on the outside (1 Sam. 16). Peter is not condemning women who wear jewelry. He is emphasizing the importance of a woman’s character.
3:4 *gentle and quiet spirit.* Peter encourages Christian wives to exhibit attitudes that do not demand personal rights, attitudes that are not harsh and grating but are soothing and tranquil.
3:6 *called him her lord.* Sarah was not worshiping Abraham; she was showing him respect.
3:7 *treat them with respect.* A Christian husband should be intimately aware of his wife’s needs, her strengths and weaknesses, and her goals and desires. He should know as much about her as possible in order to respond in the best way to her.
3:9 *evil with evil.* Peter encourages Christians to act like the Lord Jesus. He endured suffering and ridicule in silence, entrusting His just cause to the ultimate Judge.
3:12 *eyes . . . ears.* Peter uses this imagery to remind his readers that God knows everything about believers, especially their suffering, and that He listens and responds to their cries for help (Heb. 4:12–16).

2:19 [x] 1Pe 3:14, 17 **2:20** [y] 1Pe 3:17 **2:21** [z] Ac 14:22 [a] Mt 16:24 **2:22** [b] Isa 53:9 **2:23** [c] Isa 53:7 [d] Lk 23:46 **2:24** [e] Heb 9:28 [f] Ro 6:2 [g] Isa 53:5; Heb 12:13; Jas 5:16 **2:25** [h] Isa 53:6 [i] Jn 10:11 **3:1** [j] 1Pe 2:18 [k] Eph 5:22 [l] 1Co 7:16; 9:19 **3:3** [m] Isa 3:18-23; 1Ti 2:9 **3:4** [n] Ro 7:22 **3:5** [o] 1Ti 5:5 **3:6** [p] Ge 18:12 **3:7** [q] Eph 5:25-33 **3:8** [r] Ro 12:10 [s] 1Pe 5:5 **3:9** [t] Ro 12:17 [u] 1Pe 2:23 [v] 1Pe 2:21 [w] Heb 6:14 **3:12** [x] Ps 34:12-16 **3:13** [y] Pr 16:7

suffer for what is right, you are blessed.[z]
"Do not fear their threats[a]; do not be frightened."[b][a] 15But in your hearts revere Christ
as Lord. Always be prepared to give an answer[b] to everyone who asks you to give the
reason for the hope that you have. But do
this with gentleness and respect, 16keep-
ing a clear conscience,[c] so that those who
speak maliciously against your good behavior in Christ may be ashamed of their
slander.[d] 17For it is better, if it is God's will,[e]
to suffer for doing good[f] than for doing evil.
18For Christ also suffered once for sins,[g] the
righteous for the unrighteous, to bring you
to God. He was put to death in the body[h]
but made alive in the Spirit.[i] 19After being
made alive,[c] he went and made proclamation to the imprisoned spirits[j]— 20to those
who were disobedient long ago when God
waited patiently in the days of Noah while
the ark was being built.[k] In it only a few
people, eight in all, were saved[l] through
water, 21and this water symbolizes baptism
that now saves you[m] also—not the removal of dirt from the body but the pledge of a
clear conscience toward God.[d] It saves you
by the resurrection of Jesus Christ,[n] 22who
has gone into heaven and is at God's right
hand[o]—with angels, authorities and powers in submission to him.[p]

Living for God

4 Therefore, since Christ suffered in his
body, arm yourselves also with the
same attitude, because whoever suffers in
the body is done with sin. 2As a result, they
do not live the rest of their earthly lives for
evil human desires,[q] but rather for the will
of God. 3For you have spent enough time
in the past[r] doing what pagans choose to
do—living in debauchery, lust, drunkenness, orgies, carousing and detestable
idolatry. 4They are surprised that you do
not join them in their reckless, wild living,
and they heap abuse on you.[s] 5But they will
have to give account to him who is ready to
judge the living and the dead.[t] 6For this is
the reason the gospel was preached even
to those who are now dead,[u] so that they
might be judged according to human standards in regard to the body, but live according to God in regard to the spirit.
7The end of all things is near.[v] Therefore be alert and of sober mind so that you
may pray. 8Above all, love each other deeply,[w] because love covers over a multitude
of sins.[x] 9Offer hospitality to one another

[a] 14 Or *fear what they fear* [b] 14 Isaiah 8:12
[c] 18,19 Or *but made alive in the spirit, 19in which also* [d] 21 Or *but an appeal to God for a clear conscience*

3:15 *in your hearts revere Christ as Lord.* Believers should acknowledge the eternal holiness of Christ by revering Him as the Lord of the universe who is in control of all things. ***to give an answer.*** Peter assumes that the Christian faith will be falsely accused. He therefore encourages Christians to have rational answers to respond to those false accusations.

3:17 *For it is better.* Peter is not encouraging believers to seek out situations in which they will experience suffering. Instead, he is saying that believers should make certain that when they suffer, it is the result of having been faithful to God rather than because they have done evil (2:19).

3:19–20 *imprisoned spirits.* The Greek term translated *spirits* can refer to human spirits, angels, or demons. There are three main interpretations: (1) Some interpret these verses as describing Jesus as going to the place where fallen angels are incarcerated and declaring His final victory over evil in His work on the cross; (2) others hold that *spirits* refers to human spirits; thus Christ preached to human beings who had died in Noah's day and were in the realm of the dead (hell or hades); and (3) another major interpretation understands this passage as describing Christ preaching through Noah to the unbelievers of his day.

4:1 *is done with sin.* Those who serve God faithfully in the midst of suffering take on a different attitude toward sin than what they previously held. Sin no longer holds the same grip on them.

4:3 *detestable idolatry.* The idea here is that some forms of idolatry may have been detestable even to the civil authorities. Of course, all types of idolatry are hateful to God.

4:5 *will have to give account.* Although unbelievers think they are free to do as they please, they are greatly mistaken. There are consequences to what they do. One day they will stand defenseless before God and give an account of all of their wickedness (Rev. 20:11–15).

4:6 *to those who are now dead.* There are four main interpretations of Peter's meaning here: (1) Some see a connection between the gospel preached in this verse and the proclamation of Christ in 3:19–20; accordingly, they understand this verse to be about Christ offering salvation to those who lived in pre-Christian times; (2) another group of commentators also connects this preaching to 3:19–20, but holds that this verse is speaking of Christ preaching the gospel only to the righteous people of Old Testament times; (3) Peter was speaking of the gospel which was preached to believers who are now dead; and (4) Peter is referring to the spiritually dead; the gospel was being preached to them so that they could come alive spiritually.

4:8 *love covers over a multitude of sins.* Peter is not suggesting that one Christian's love atones for another Christian's sins. Rather, by introducing this proverb from the Old Testament (Prov. 10:12), he is reminding us that love does not stir up sins. We can demonstrate our love for our fellow believers by truly forgiving them and not talking openly about their past sins.

4:9 *Offer hospitality.* In New Testament times,

3:14 [z] 1Pe 2:19,20; 4:15,16 [a] Isa 8:12,13 **3:15** [b] Col 4:6
3:16 [c] Heb 13:18 [d] 1Pe 2:12,15 **3:17** [e] 1Pe 2:15 [f] 1Pe 2:20
3:18 [g] 1Pe 2:21 [h] Col 1:22; 1Pe 4:1 [i] 1Pe 4:6
3:19 [j] 1Pe 4:6 **3:20** [k] Ge 6:3,5,13,14 [l] Heb 11:7
3:21 [m] Titus 3:5 [n] 1Pe 1:3 **3:22** [o] Mk 16:19 [p] Ro 8:38
4:2 [q] Ro 6:2 **4:3** [r] Eph 2:2 **4:4** [s] 1Pe 3:16
4:5 [t] Ac 10:42; 2Ti 4:1 **4:6** [u] 1Pe 3:19 **4:7** [v] Ro 13:11
4:8 [w] 1Pe 1:22 [x] Pr 10:12

without grumbling.[y] 10Each of you should
use whatever gift you have received to
serve others,[z] as faithful[a] stewards of
God's grace in its various forms. 11If anyone speaks, they should do so as one who
speaks the very words of God. If anyone
serves, they should do so with the strength
God provides,[b] so that in all things God
may be praised[c] through Jesus Christ. To
him be the glory and the power for ever
and ever. Amen.

Suffering for Being a Christian

12Dear friends, do not be surprised at
the fiery ordeal that has come on you[d] to
test you, as though something strange
were happening to you. 13But rejoice inas-
much as you participate in the sufferings of
Christ, so that you may be overjoyed when
his glory is revealed.[e] 14If you are insulted because of the name of Christ, you are
blessed,[f] for the Spirit of glory and of God
rests on you. 15If you suffer, it should not
be as a murderer or thief or any other kind
of criminal, or even as a meddler. 16How-
ever, if you suffer as a Christian, do not be
ashamed, but praise God that you bear that
name.[g] 17For it is time for judgment to begin with God's household;[h] and if it begins
with us, what will the outcome be for those
who do not obey the gospel of God?[i] 18And,

> "If it is hard for the righteous to be
> saved,
> what will become of the ungodly and
> the sinner?"[a][j]

19So then, those who suffer according
to God's will should commit themselves to
their faithful Creator and continue to do
good.

To the Elders and the Flock

5 To the elders among you, I appeal as a
fellow elder[k] and a witness[l] of Christ's
sufferings who also will share in the glory to be revealed:[m] 2Be shepherds of God's
flock[n] that is under your care, watching
over them—not because you must, but because you are willing, as God wants you to
be; not pursuing dishonest gain,[o] but eager
to serve; 3not lording it over[p] those entrusted to you, but being examples[q] to the flock.
4And when the Chief Shepherd appears,
you will receive the crown of glory[r] that
will never fade away.
5In the same way, you who are younger,
submit yourselves[s] to your elders. All of
you, clothe yourselves with humility toward one another, because,

> "God opposes the proud
> but shows favor to the
> humble."[b][t]

6Humble yourselves, therefore, under
God's mighty hand, that he may lift you up
in due time.[u] 7Cast all your anxiety on him[v]
because he cares for you.[w]
8Be alert and of sober mind. Your enemy the devil prowls around[x] like a roaring
lion looking for someone to devour. 9Resist
him,[y] standing firm in the faith,[z] because
you know that the family of believers
throughout the world is undergoing the
same kind of sufferings.[a]

---

a 18 Prov. 11:31 (see Septuagint) *b* 5 Prov. 3:34

---

hospitality typically meant housing and feeding travelers for two to three days with no expectation of payment in return.

4:10 ***Each of you should use whatever gift.*** Every believer is gifted to serve. ***stewards.*** These are managers or trustees who will be held accountable for using their gift in the best interest of the One who gave it to them.

4:12 ***do not be surprised.*** Apparently Peter's readers were astonished that they had to suffer as Christians, especially to the extent that they were suffering. ***fiery ordeal.*** The Greek word translated here was also used to speak of the intense fire that burned away impurities in metals.

4:17 ***for judgment to begin.*** Judgment does not always imply condemnation in Scripture. When used in relation to Christians, it consistently refers to the evaluation of a believer's works for the purpose of reward (1 Cor. 3:10–15).

5:1 ***share.*** This term speaks of partaking in Christ's reign in the coming kingdom (Rom. 8:17; Rev. 2:26–28; 5:9–10). Peter considers himself to be already participating partly in the glory that one day he will experience fully.

5:2 ***shepherds of God's flock.*** An ancient Israelite shepherd would go before his sheep to lead them; he would not drive the sheep in front of him. Church leaders should lead the people of God in the same way; feeding, protecting, and guiding them (John 21:15–17). Christian leaders should also remember that they have been given responsibility for tending a flock that belongs to God, not to themselves. ***not pursuing dishonest gain.*** Christian leaders need to make certain that their work is not motivated by money, but by a passion for the good of those believers put in their charge (1 Tim. 3:3,8; Titus 1:11).

5:3 ***not lording it over those entrusted to you.*** Echoing a command that Peter heard directly from Jesus during His earthly ministry, Peter reminds all Christian leaders that they need to perform the role of servants, not masters, to those whom God has assigned to their care (Matt. 20:25–28; Mark 10:42–45).

5:8 ***Your enemy.*** Satan is our avowed enemy. He never ceases from being hostile toward us; he is constantly accusing us before God (Job 1:9–2:7; Zech. 3:1; Luke 22:31; Rev. 12:10). ***like a roaring lion.*** Satan

4:9 [y] Php 2:14 **4:10** [z] Ro 12:6,7 [a] 1Co 4:2
4:11 [b] Eph 6:10 [c] 1Co 10:31 **4:12** [d] 1Pe 1:6,7
4:13 [e] Ro 8:17 **4:14** [f] Mt 5:11 **4:16** [g] Ac 5:41
4:17 [h] Jer 25:29 [i] 2Th 1:8 **4:18** [j] Pr 11:31; Lk 23:31
5:1 [k] Ac 11:30 [l] Lk 24:48 [m] 1Pe 1:5,7; Rev 1:9
5:2 [n] Jn 21:16 [o] 1Ti 3:3 **5:3** [p] Eze 34:4 [q] Php 3:17
5:4 [r] 1Co 9:25 **5:5** [s] Eph 5:21 [t] Pr 3:34; Jas 4:6
5:6 [u] Jas 4:10 **5:7** [v] Ps 37:5; Mt 6:25 [w] Heb 13:5
5:8 [x] Job 1:7 **5:9** [y] Jas 4:7 [z] Col 2:5 [a] Ac 14:22

[10]And the God of all grace, who called you to his eternal glory[b] in Christ, after you have suffered a little while, will himself restore you and make you strong,[c] firm and steadfast. [11]To him be the power for ever and ever. Amen.[d]

Final Greetings

[12]With the help of Silas,[a][e] whom I regard as a faithful brother, I have written to you briefly,[f] encouraging you and testifying that this is the true grace of God. Stand fast in it.

[13]She who is in Babylon, chosen together with you, sends you her greetings, and so does my son Mark.[g] [14]Greet one another with a kiss of love.[h]

Peace[i] to all of you who are in Christ.

[a] 12 Greek *Silvanus*, a variant of *Silas*

is both cunning and cruel. He attacks when least expected and desires to destroy completely those whom he attacks.

5:10 *make you strong, firm and steadfast.* As a consequence of our facing the attacks of our enemy, God will build in us a firm foundation that makes us steadfast and immovable.

5:11 *power for ever and ever.* God is in control of all things both in this world and throughout eternity.

5:10 [b] 2Co 4:17 [c] 2Th 2:17 **5:11** [d] Ro 11:36
5:12 [e] 2Co 1:19 [f] Heb 13:22 **5:13** [g] Ac 12:12
5:14 [h] Ro 16:16 [i] Eph 6:23

2 PETER

▶ **AUTHOR:** No other book in the New Testament poses as many problems of authenticity as does 2 Peter. But in spite of the external and internal problems, the traditional position of Petrine authorship overcomes more difficulties than any other option. This epistle was written just before the apostle's death (1:14), probably from Rome.

▶ **TIME:** c. A.D. 64–66 ▶ **KEY VERSES:** 2 Pet. 1:20–21

▶ **THEME:** While 1 Peter deals with suffering and persecution caused by people outside the church, 2 Peter deals more with the need for the true spiritual knowledge and maturity in the face of false teachers who would distort the faith from inside the church. He gives his readers insight into the thinking of the false teachers and encourages opposition to them. He also urges watchfulness for Christ's return through all the events at the end of the age.

1 Simon Peter, a servant[a] and apostle of Jesus Christ,[b]

To those who through the righteousness[c] of our God and Savior Jesus Christ[d] have received a faith as precious as ours:

2Grace and peace be yours in abundance through the knowledge of God and of Jesus our Lord.[e]

Confirming One's Calling and Election

3His divine power[f] has given us everything we need for a godly life through our knowledge of him who called us[g] by his own glory and goodness. 4Through these
he has given us his very great and precious promises,[h] so that through them you may participate in the divine nature,[i] having escaped the corruption in the world caused by evil desires.[j]
5For this very reason, make every effort to add to your faith goodness; and to goodness, knowledge;[k] 6and to knowledge, self-control;[l] and to self-control, perseverance; and to perseverance, godliness;[m] 7and to godliness, mutual affection; and to mutual affection, love.[n] 8For if you possess these qualities in increasing measure, they will keep you from being ineffective and unproductive[o] in your knowledge of our Lord Jesus Christ. 9But whoever does not have

1:1 *apostle.* With this term Peter identifies himself as an authorized spokesman for the truth that Christ proclaimed. In verses 1–4 Peter describes the resources his readers have that will make growth in grace and knowledge possible. His apostleship is the first of these resources. ***a faith as precious as ours.*** Anyone who has faith in Jesus has the same access to God as any other believer. This access is the second great resource that Peter's readers possess.
1:2 *the knowledge of God.* The Greek word translated *knowledge* is a key word in this letter. It describes a special kind of knowledge, a kind that is complete. Since our knowledge of Jesus grows as we mature in the faith, we will experience His grace and peace on many different occasions in our Christian walk.
1:3 *divine power.* This power is identified as the "power of resurrection" (Phil. 3:10; 4:13). This power is the third resource for godly living that Peter lists in this letter. ***by his own glory and goodness.*** These words suggest the qualities of Jesus that attract believers to Him. The glory that John saw in Jesus (John 1:14) was His authority and power.
1:4 *his very great and precious promises.* This phrase refers to the numerous offers of divine provision found in Scripture. These promises offer us the glory and virtue of Christ as the basis for our growing participation in the divine nature. We have Christ within us, as He promised (John 14:23), to enable us to become increasingly Christlike (2 Cor. 3:18).
1:5 *goodness.* This term is the same word used in verse 3 in reference to Christ's character. We cannot produce goodness ourselves; but we can choose to obey the promptings of the Holy Spirit who lives in us.
1:6 *perseverance.* A person who exercises self-control will not easily succumb to discouragement or the temptation to quit. Viewing all circumstances as coming from the hand of a loving Father who is in control of all things is the secret of perseverance.
1:9 *blind.* This kind of person is one who looks only

1:1 [a] Ro 1:1 [b] 1Pe 1:1 [c] Ro 3:21-26 [d] Titus 2:13 **1:2** [e] Php 3:8 **1:3** [f] 1Pe 1:5 [g] 1Th 2:12 **1:4** [h] 2Co 7:1 [i] Eph 4:24; Heb 12:10; 1Jn 3:2 [j] 2Pe 2:18-20 **1:5** [k] Col 2:3 **1:6** [l] Ac 24:25 [m] ver 3 **1:7** [n] 1Th 3:12 **1:8** [o] Jn 15:2; Titus 3:14

them is nearsighted and blind,[p] forgetting
that they have been cleansed from their
past sins.[q]
10Therefore, my brothers and sisters,[a]
make every effort to confirm your calling
and election. For if you do these things, you
will never stumble,[r] 11and you will receive
a rich welcome into the eternal kingdom of
our Lord and Savior Jesus Christ.

Prophecy of Scripture

12So I will always remind you of these
things,[s] even though you know them and
are firmly established in the truth you now
have. 13I think it is right to refresh your
memory as long as I live in the tent of this
body,[t] 14because I know that I will soon put
it aside,[u] as our Lord Jesus Christ has made
clear to me.[v] 15And I will make every effort
to see that after my departure[w] you will always be able to remember these things.
16For we did not follow cleverly devised
stories when we told you about the coming of our Lord Jesus Christ in power, but
we were eyewitnesses of his majesty.[x] 17He
received honor and glory from God the Father when the voice came to him from the
Majestic Glory, saying, "This is my Son,
whom I love; with him I am well pleased."[b][y]
18We ourselves heard this voice that came
from heaven when we were with him on
the sacred mountain.[z]
19We also have the prophetic message
as something completely reliable, and you
will do well to pay attention to it, as to a
light[a] shining in a dark place, until the day
dawns and the morning star[b] rises in your
hearts. 20Above all, you must understand
that no prophecy of Scripture came about
by the prophet's own interpretation of
things. 21For prophecy never had its origin
in the human will, but prophets, though human, spoke from God[c] as they were carried
along by the Holy Spirit.[d]

False Teachers and Their Destruction

2 But there were also false prophets[e]
among the people, just as there will be
false teachers among you.[f] They will secretly introduce destructive heresies, even
denying the sovereign Lord[g] who bought
them[h]—bringing swift destruction on
themselves. 2Many will follow their depraved conduct and will bring the way of
truth into disrepute. 3In their greed these
teachers will exploit you[i] with fabricated
stories. Their condemnation has long been
hanging over them, and their destruction
has not been sleeping.
4For if God did not spare angels when
they sinned, but sent them to hell,[c] putting them in chains of darkness[d] to be held

[a] 10 The Greek word for *brothers and sisters* (*adelphoi*) refers here to believers, both men and women, as part of God's family. [b] 17 Matt. 17:5; Mark 9:7; Luke 9:35 [c] 4 Greek *Tartarus*
[d] 4 Some manuscripts *in gloomy dungeons*

---

at earthly and material values—what is close at hand—and does not see the eternal spiritual realities. Concerned only with this present life, such a person becomes blind to the things of God, forgetting the wonderful sense of cleansing that comes from turning oneself over to Christ.

1:11 *rich welcome into the eternal kingdom.* Peter distinguishes between a just-barely-made-it entrance into the eternal kingdom and a richly abundant one. The Scripture indicates that fruitful and faithful living here will be rewarded by greater privileges and rewards in glory (Rev. 22:12).

1:15 *after my departure ... to remember.* Several early church fathers took these words to be Peter's promise to leave behind a testimony of the truth for his readers, which they considered to be the Gospel of Mark.

1:16 *cleverly devised stories.* Peter countered the false teacher's faith claims with an eyewitness account. Peter himself had actually seen the power and the coming of the Lord Jesus Christ. These are the twin themes of this letter; the power of Jesus available for holy living and the coming of Jesus as the glorious hope of each believer.

1:19 *the prophetic message ... reliable.* As strong as an eyewitness account (vv. 16–18) may be, there is an even stronger confirmation that Jesus is who He said He was. The written Scriptures are even more trustworthy than the personal experience of the apostle Peter.

1:20 *by the prophets own interpretation.* Although some have taken this phrase to mean that no individual Christian has the right to interpret prophecy for himself or herself, the context and the Greek word for *interpretation* indicates another meaning for the verse. The Greek word for *interpretation* can also mean "origin." In the context of verse 21, it is clear that Peter is speaking of Scripture's "origin" from God Himself and not the credentials of the one who interprets it. There is no private source for the Bible; the prophets did not supply their own solutions or explanations to the mysteries of life. Rather, God spoke through them; He alone is responsible for what is written in Scripture.

2:1 *destructive heresies.* Peter is addressing here the ethical implication of false teaching. The Greek word translated *destructive* means "shameful" or "deliberately immoral." The false teachers gloried in the privileges of Christianity but treated its moral demands with indifference.

2:3 *condemnation ... destruction.* Peter turns from the description of the false teachers to a description of their fate. Verses 4–8 provide examples of judgment of false teachers of the past.

2:4 *angels when they sinned.* There are two main interpretations of this passage, depending on one's understanding of Genesis 6:1–6. Some think that

1:9 [p] 1Jn 2:11 [q] Eph 5:26 **1:10** [r] 2Pe 3:17
1:12 [s] Php 3:1; 1Jn 2:21 **1:13** [t] 2Co 5:1,4 **1:14** [u] 2Ti 4:6
[v] Jn 21:18, 19 **1:15** [w] Lk 9:31 **1:16** [x] Mt 17:1-8
1:17 [y] Mt 3:17 **1:18** [z] Mt 17:6 **1:19** [a] Ps 119:105
[b] Rev 22:16 **1:21** [c] 2Ti 3:16 [d] 2Sa 23:2; Ac 1:16; 1Pe 1:11
2:1 [e] Dt 13:1-3 [f] 1Ti 4:1 [g] Jude 4 [h] 1Co 6:20
2:3 [i] 2Co 2:17; 1Th 2:5

for judgment;[j] 5if he did not spare the ancient world[k] when he brought the flood on its ungodly people, but protected Noah, a preacher of righteousness, and seven others;[l] 6if he condemned the cities of Sodom and Gomorrah by burning them to ashes,[m] and made them an example[n] of what is going to happen to the ungodly; 7and if he rescued Lot,[o] a righteous man, who was distressed by the depraved conduct of the lawless[p] 8(for that righteous man, living among them day after day, was tormented in his righteous soul by the lawless deeds he saw and heard)— 9if this is so, then the Lord knows how to rescue the godly from trials[q] and to hold the unrighteous for punishment on the day of judgment. 10This is especially true of those who follow the corrupt desire[r] of the flesh[a] and despise authority.

Bold and arrogant, they are not afraid to heap abuse on celestial beings;[s] 11yet even angels, although they are stronger and more powerful, do not heap abuse on such beings when bringing judgment on them from[b] the Lord.[t] 12But these people blaspheme in matters they do not understand. They are like unreasoning animals, creatures of instinct, born only to be caught and destroyed, and like animals they too will perish.[u]

13They will be paid back with harm for the harm they have done. Their idea of pleasure is to carouse in broad daylight.[v] They are blots and blemishes, reveling in their pleasures while they feast with you.[c][w] 14With eyes full of adultery, they never stop sinning; they seduce[x] the unstable; they are experts in greed[y]—an accursed brood![z] 15They have left the straight way and wandered off to follow the way of Balaam[a] son of Bezer,[d] who loved the wages of wickedness. 16But he was rebuked for his wrongdoing by a donkey—an animal without speech—who spoke with a human voice and restrained the prophet's madness.[b]

17These people are springs without water[c] and mists driven by a storm. Blackest darkness is reserved for them.[d] 18For they mouth empty, boastful words[e] and, by appealing to the lustful desires of the flesh, they entice people who are just escaping from those who live in error. 19They promise them freedom, while they themselves are slaves of depravity—for "people are slaves to whatever has mastered them."[f] 20If they have escaped the corruption of the world by knowing[g] our Lord and Savior Jesus Christ and are again entangled in it and are overcome, they are worse off at the end than they were at the beginning.[h]

---

[a] *10* In contexts like this, the Greek word for *flesh* (*sarx*) refers to the sinful state of human beings, often presented as a power in opposition to the Spirit; also in verse 18. [b] *11* Many manuscripts *beings in the presence of* [c] *13* Some manuscripts *in their love feasts* [d] *15* Greek *Bosor*

Peter is referring to "sons of God" in Genesis 6:2. According to this interpretation, the "sons of God" were angels who rebelled against God and their role in creation. They began to engage in forbidden practices with the daughters of men. Their conduct was met with immediate judgment. A second group of commentators balk at the suggestion of sexual relations between angels and women. They consider this verse to simply be a reference to those angels who fell with Satan.
2:5 ***did not spare the ancient world.*** Peter's second example of God's judgment is the flood (3:6). ***preacher of righteousness.*** This is a reference to Noah because his righteous life put to shame the immoral lives of his neighbors. Noah's building of the ark would certainly have given him the opportunity to explain the coming judgment and to invite people to repent and believe in God. But the entreaties fell on deaf ears, just as the truth of Christ's atonement fell on the deaf ears of the false teachers of Peter's day. Such indifference and unbelief brought the ungodly of Noah's world to certain destruction.
2:6 ***Sodom and Gomorrah.*** These cities are Peter's third example of God's judgment. Genesis 19 makes it clear that sexual perversion was the primary cause of their destruction.
2:9–10 ***Bold and arrogant.*** These words describe the character and methods of false teachers. Their actions are characterized by boldness; they recklessly defy both God and man. Behind their presumption is a commitment to their own desires.
2:12 ***like unreasoning animals.*** False teachers are compared to animals in their behavior because they act in ignorance of the realities of death and judgment. Like animals they also react only to present circumstances, without giving thought to the consequences of their actions.
2:13 ***carouse in broad daylight.*** Even pagan societies thought it strange and unnatural to hold drunken riots in the daylight. However, the false teachers had no qualms about practicing their erroneous concept of Christian liberty in clear daylight.
2:14 ***eyes full of adultery.*** They could not cease from sin because their fantasizing had become habitual. As a consequence, they convinced unstable souls in the church that adultery was acceptable Christian behavior and lured them into sexual immorality.
2:15–16 ***follow the way of Balaam.*** The account of Balaam in Numbers 22–24 is used here, as well as in Jude 11 and Revelation 2:14, to depict the danger of forsaking the right way and going astray.
2:17 ***springs ... mists.*** Peter accuses the heretical teachers of awakening false expectations, like wells that contain no water or storm clouds that darken but produce no rain.
2:20 ***they have escaped.*** The subject of this phrase is the heretical teachers who are called "servants of corruption" in verse 19. This verse seems to indicate that the teachers had formerly turned from the

2:4 [j] Jude 6; Rev 20:1,2 **2:5** [k] 2Pe 3:6 [l] Heb 11:7; 1Pe 3:20 **2:6** [m] Ge 19:24,25 [n] Nu 26:10; Jude 7 **2:7** [o] Ge 19:16 [p] 2Pe 3:17 **2:9** [q] 1Co 10:13 **2:10** [r] 2Pe 3:3 [s] Jude 8 **2:11** [t] Jude 9 **2:12** [u] Jude 10 **2:13** [v] Ro 13:13 [w] 1Co 11:20,21; Jude 12 **2:14** [x] ver 18 [y] ver 3 [z] Eph 2:3 **2:15** [a] Nu 22:4-20; Jude 11 **2:16** [b] Nu 22:21-30 **2:17** [c] Jude 12 [d] Jude 13 **2:18** [e] Jude 16 **2:19** [f] Jn 8:34; Ro 6:16 **2:20** [g] 2Pe 1:2 [h] Mt 12:45

21It would have been better for them not to have known the way of righteousness, than to have known it and then to turn their backs on the sacred command that was passed on to them.[i] 22Of them the proverbs are true: "A dog returns to its vomit,"[aj] and, "A sow that is washed returns to her wallowing in the mud."

The Day of the Lord

3 Dear friends, this is now my second letter to you. I have written both of them as reminders[k] to stimulate you to wholesome thinking. 2I want you to recall the words spoken in the past by the holy prophets and the command given by our Lord and Savior through your apostles.

3Above all, you must understand that in the last days[l] scoffers will come, scoffing and following their own evil desires.[m] 4They will say, "Where is this 'coming' he promised?[n] Ever since our ancestors died, everything goes on as it has since the beginning of creation."[o] 5But they deliberately forget that long ago by God's word[p] the heavens came into being and the earth was formed out of water and by water.[q] 6By these waters also the world of that time was deluged and destroyed.[r] 7By the same word the present heavens and earth are reserved for fire,[s] being kept for the day of judgment and destruction of the ungodly.

8But do not forget this one thing, dear friends: With the Lord a day is like a thousand years, and a thousand years are like a day.[t] 9The Lord is not slow in keeping his promise,[u] as some understand slowness. Instead he is patient[v] with you, not wanting anyone to perish, but everyone to come to repentance.[w]

10But the day of the Lord will come like a thief.[x] The heavens will disappear with a roar; the elements will be destroyed by fire, and the earth and everything done in it will be laid bare.[by]

11Since everything will be destroyed in this way, what kind of people ought you to be? You ought to live holy and godly lives 12as you look forward[z] to the day of God and speed its coming.[ca] That day will bring about the destruction of the heavens by fire, and the elements will melt in the heat.[b] 13But in keeping with his promise we are looking forward to a new heaven and a new earth,[c] where righteousness dwells.

14So then, dear friends, since you are looking forward to this, make every effort to be found spotless, blameless[d] and at peace with him. 15Bear in mind that our Lord's patience[e] means salvation,[f] just as our dear brother Paul also wrote you with the wisdom that God gave him.[g] 16He writes the same way in all his letters, speaking in them of these matters. His letters contain some things that are hard to understand, which ignorant and unstable[h] people distort, as they do the other Scriptures,[i] to their own destruction.

17Therefore, dear friends, since you have been forewarned, be on your guard[j] so that you may not be carried away by the error[k] of the lawless and fall from your secure position.[l] 18But grow in the grace and knowledge of our Lord and Savior Jesus Christ.[m] To him be glory both now and forever! Amen.

---

[a] 22 Prov. 26:11 [b] 10 Some manuscripts *be burned up* [c] 12 Or *as you wait eagerly for the day of God to come*

---

pollution of the world through a full and experiential knowledge of Christ. Now, however, they have fallen again into immorality, even becoming teachers of sinful lifestyles. ***they are worse off at the end than they were at the beginning.*** This phrase is almost certainly taken from Jesus' words in Matthew 12:45 and probably reflects Peter's memory of that occasion.

2:22 *Of them the proverbs are true.* Jews considered dogs and pigs among the lowest of animals, so Peter chooses these animals to describe people who have known the truth but have turned away from it.

3:2 *words spoken in the past.* The only way Peter's readers could recognize the errors of the heretical teachers was to compare their teaching with the teaching of the holy prophets and apostles. As Peter had already reminded his readers in 1:21, "holy men" spoke words given to them by the Holy Spirit, which were therefore utterly reliable.

3:4 *ancestors died.* This refers to the Old Testament patriarchs. ***everything goes on.*** The basis for denying the supernatural reappearance of Jesus is that nothing of that nature has occurred in the past.

3:8 *a thousand years.* God will surely accomplish His purposes and promises, even though it may appear that He is slow in doing so. His timing is always perfect.

3:10 *day of the Lord.* This phrase describes the end-time events, the second coming (Dan. 9:24 – 27; 1 Thess. 5:2; 2 Thess. 2:1 – 12). Peter's description requires the unlimited power of God in dissolving the very elements of the universe, from which He will create a new heaven and a new earth (v. 13; Rev. 21:22).

3:11 *what kind of people.* The primary purpose of prophetic teaching is not to satisfy our curiosity but to motivate us to change our lives. Rather than work for things that will ultimately be destroyed, we should work for things that are eternal.

3:16 *ignorant and unstable people distort.* *Untaught* refers to one whose mind is untrained and undisciplined in habits of thought. *Unstable* refers to one whose conduct is not properly established.

2:21 [i] Heb 6:4-6 **2:22** [j] Pr 26:11 **3:1** [k] 2Pe 1:13
3:3 [l] 1Ti 4:1 [m] 2Pe 2:10; Jude 18 **3:4** [n] Isa 5:19; Eze 12:22; Mt 24:48 [o] Mk 10:6 **3:5** [p] Ge 1:6, 9; Heb 11:3 [q] Ps 24:2
3:6 [r] Ge 7:21, 22 **3:7** [s] ver 10, 12; 2Th 1:7 **3:8** [t] Ps 90:4
3:9 [u] Hab 2:3; Heb 10:37 [v] Ro 2:4 [w] 1Ti 2:4
3:10 [x] Lk 12:39; 1Th 5:2 [y] Mt 24:35; Rev 21:1
3:12 [z] 1Co 1:7 [a] Ps 50:3 [b] ver 10 **3:13** [c] Isa 65:17; 66:22; Rev 21:1 **3:14** [d] 1Th 3:13 **3:15** [e] Ro 2:4 [f] ver 9 [g] Eph 3:3 **3:16** [h] 2Pe 2:14 [i] ver 2 **3:17** [j] 1Co 10:12 [k] 2Pe 2:18 [l] Rev 2:5 **3:18** [m] 2Pe 1:11

1 JOHN

▸ **AUTHOR:** First John was universally accepted without dispute as authoritative by the early church. The internal evidence supports this tradition because the "we" (apostles), "you" (readers), and "they" (false teachers) phraseology places the writer in the sphere of apostolic eyewitness (1:1–3; 4:14). John's name was well known to the readers, and it was unnecessary for him to mention it. The style and vocabulary of 1 John are so similar to those of the Fourth Gospel that most scholars acknowledge these books to be by the same hand. First John was probably written in Ephesus after the Gospel of John, but the date cannot be fixed with certainty.

▸ **TIME:** c. A.D. 89–95 ▸ **KEY VERSES:** 1 John 1:3–4

▸ **THEME:** Shortly after the church began, people like the Gnostics continually tried to recast the gospel in their own terms. Gnosticism made a distinction between the material or carnal, which was evil to them, and the spiritual, which was pure. John writes as one who was acquainted with Jesus personally, physically, and spiritually. He wants the reader to take the Christ he knew at face value. John wants his readers to believe the truth of his experience of Jesus and not the philosophical speculation of the Gnostics. In these letters we see the same themes as in John's Gospel — light and darkness, truth and falsehood, life and death, love and hate. John weaves these themes together with a straightforward skill and fatherly care.

The Incarnation of the Word of Life

1 That which was from the beginning,[a]
which we have heard, which we have
seen with our eyes,[b] which we have looked
at and our hands have touched[c]—this we
proclaim concerning the Word of life. 2The
life appeared;[d] we have seen it and testify to it, and we proclaim to you the eternal
life, which was with the Father and has appeared to us. 3We proclaim to you what we
have seen and heard, so that you also may
have fellowship with us. And our fellowship is with the Father and with his Son,
Jesus Christ.[e] 4We write this[f] to make our[a]
joy complete.[g]

Light and Darkness, Sin and Forgiveness

5This is the message we have heard[h]
from him and declare to you: God is light;
in him there is no darkness at all. 6If we
claim to have fellowship with him and yet
walk in the darkness,[i] we lie and do not live
out the truth.[j] 7But if we walk in the light,
as he is in the light, we have fellowship
with one another, and the blood of Jesus,
his Son, purifies us from all[b] sin.[k]
8If we claim to be without sin,[l] we de-

[a] 4 Some manuscripts *your* [b] 7 Or *every*

1:1–4 ***the Word of life.*** These verses emphasize the personal experience of the apostles with the incarnate Word. The memory of Jesus Christ burned in the mind of John as he reflected on the three and one-half years that he and the other disciples were with the Lord. Now he wanted to be sure that the churches under his care enjoyed fellowship with the resurrected Lord and other disciples.

1:2 ***life appeared.*** The life was not hidden or obscured so that few, if any, could find it. Rather, this life was made known openly and had its origin in God the Father. God had provided truth about Himself in nature and through the prophets of old, but the revelation in His Son (Heb. 1:1–2) is God's finest and clearest presentation of Himself.

1:3 ***have fellowship.*** The idea of this word carries both the thought of a positive relationship that people share and participation in a common interest or goal.

1:5 ***God is light.*** This is God's nature, in His essential being, just as He is Spirit (John 4:24) and love (4:8). Light refers to God's moral character. ***no darkness at all.*** God is holy, untouched by any evil or sin. Because God is light, those who desire fellowship with Him must also be pure.

1:6 ***fellowship with him and yet walk in the darkness.*** To walk in darkness means to live contrary to the moral character of God, to live a sinful life. To claim fellowship with God without living a moral life or practicing the truth is to live a lie, since God cannot compromise His holiness to accommodate sin.

1:8–9 ***If we claim to be without sin.*** To confess

1:1 [a] Jn 1:2 [b] Jn 1:14; 2Pe 1:16 [c] Jn 20:27 **1:2** [d] Jn 1:1-4; 1Ti 3:16 **1:3** [e] 1Co 1:9 **1:4** [f] 1Jn 2:1 [g] Jn 3:29 **1:5** [h] 1Jn 3:11 **1:6** [i] 2Co 6:14 [j] Jn 3:19-21 **1:7** [k] Heb 9:14; Rev 1:5 **1:8** [l] Pr 20:9; Jas 3:2

ceive ourselves and the truth is not in us.[m]
9If we confess our sins, he is faithful and
just and will forgive us our sins[n] and purify
us from all unrighteousness. 10If we claim
we have not sinned, we make him out to be
a liar[o] and his word is not in us.[p]

2 My dear children,[q] I write this to you
so that you will not sin. But if anybody
does sin, we have an advocate[r] with the
Father—Jesus Christ, the Righteous One.
2He is the atoning sacrifice for our sins,[s]
and not only for ours but also for the sins
of the whole world.

Love and Hatred for Fellow Believers

3We know that we have come to know
him if we keep his commands.[t] 4Whoever
says, "I know him," but does not do what
he commands is a liar, and the truth is not
in that person.[u] 5But if anyone obeys his
word,[v] love for God[a] is truly made complete
in them.[w] This is how we know we are in
him: 6Whoever claims to live in him must
live as Jesus did.[x]
7Dear friends, I am not writing you a
new command but an old one, which you
have had since the beginning.[y] This old
command is the message you have heard.
8Yet I am writing you a new command;[z] its
truth is seen in him and in you, because the
darkness is passing[a] and the true light[b] is
already shining.[c]
9Anyone who claims to be in the light but
hates a brother or sister[b] is still in the darkness. 10Anyone who loves their brother and
sister[c] lives in the light,[d] and there is nothing
in them to make them stumble. 11But anyone
who hates a brother or sister is in the darkness and walks around in the darkness.
They do not know where they are going,
because the darkness has blinded them.[e]

Reasons for Writing

12 I am writing to you, dear children,
because your sins have been forgiven
on account of his name.
13 I am writing to you, fathers,
because you know him who is from
the beginning.
I am writing to you, young men,
because you have overcome the evil one.[f]

14 I write to you, dear children,
because you know the Father.
I write to you, fathers,
because you know him who is from
the beginning.
I write to you, young men,
because you are strong,[g]
and the word of God lives in you,[h]
and you have overcome the evil one.[i]

---

[a] 5 Or *word, God's love* [b] 9 The Greek word for *brother or sister* (*adelphos*) refers here to a believer, whether man or woman, as part of God's family; also in verse 11; and in 3:15, 17; 4:20; 5:16. [c] 10 The Greek word for *brother and sister* (*adelphos*) refers here to a believer, whether man or woman, as part of God's family; also in 3:10; 4:20, 21.

---

is to agree with God, to admit that we are sinners in need of His mercy. If a believer confesses his or her specific sins to God, He will cleanse all unrighteousness from that person. Forgiveness and cleansing are guaranteed because God is faithful to His promises. Those promises are legitimated because God is just. God can maintain His perfect character and yet forgive us because of the perfect and righteous sacrifice of Jesus, His own Son (2:2).

1:10 *his word is not in us.* A person who denies committing sinful acts does not have the Word of God changing his or her life.

2:1 *My dear children ... that you will not sin.* John's statements about sin (1:8–10) were designed to make believers aware of sin's ever-present danger and to put them on guard against it. According to Greek grammar, the *if* before *anybody does sin* carries the added sense of "and it is assumed that we all do." This statement is not an encouragement to sin but a warning to all Christians to be on guard against sinful tendencies.

2:2 *atoning sacrifice.* This act brings about the merciful removal of guilt through divine forgiveness. In the Greek Old Testament, the Greek term for atoning sacrifice was used for the sacrificial mercy seat on which the high priest placed the blood of the Israelites' sacrifices (Ex. 25:17–22). This practice indicates that God's righteous wrath had to be appeased somehow. God sent His Son and satisfied His own wrath with Jesus' sacrifice on the cross. Our sins made it necessary for Jesus to suffer the agonies of the crucifixion; but God demonstrated His love and justice by providing His own Son.

2:3 *we have come to know him.* The New Testament speaks of knowing God in two senses. One who has trusted Christ knows Him (John 17:3), that is to say, has met Him. One who has previously met the Lord can also come to know Him intimately (Phil. 3:10). In this verse John is talking about knowing the Lord intimately.

2:6 *live in him.* Abiding is habitual obedience. It has the idea of settling down in Christ or resting in Him. It is evidenced by a life modeled after Christ. ***must live as Jesus.*** The admonition to live by the teaching of Jesus reveals that this conformity comes from us. The Christian, as a child of God, ought to obey God because of a sincere desire to do so. It should be a joy to follow in the footsteps of the One who died for us.

2:8 *new command.* This refers to love (v. 10). It may be that John is simply repeating the statement of Christ in John 13:34. The command to love reached its truest and fullest expression in the life of Christ. He demonstrated what true love is by coming into our world and giving His life for us.

2:11 *anyone who hates a brother or sister.* Hating one's brother opposes the teaching of Christ to love one another. The idea that one could hate a brother and yet claim fellowship with God shows the utter darkness that has blinded the Christian to the truth.

1:8 [m] 1Jn 2:4 **1:9** [n] Ps 32:5; 51:2 **1:10** [o] 1Jn 5:10 [p] 1Jn 2:14 **2:1** [q] ver 12, 13, 28 [r] Ro 8:34; Heb 7:25 **2:2** [s] Ro 3:25 **2:3** [t] Jn 14:15 **2:4** [u] 1Jn 1:6, 8 **2:5** [v] Jn 14:21, 23 [w] 1Jn 4:12 **2:6** [x] Mt 11:29; 1Pe 2:21 **2:7** [y] 1Jn 3:11, 23; 2Jn 5, 6 **2:8** [z] Jn 13:34 [a] Ro 13:12 [b] Jn 1:9 [c] Eph 5:8; 1Th 5:5 **2:10** [d] 1Jn 3:14 **2:11** [e] Jn 12:35 **2:13** [f] ver 14 **2:14** [g] Eph 6:10 [h] Jn 5:38; 1Jn 1:10 [i] ver 13

On Not Loving the World

[15]Do not love the world or anything in the world.[j] If anyone loves the world, love for the Father[a] is not in them.[k] [16]For everything in the world—the lust of the flesh,[l] the lust of the eyes,[m] and the pride of life—comes not from the Father but from the world. [17]The world and its desires pass away,[n] but whoever does the will of God lives forever.

Warnings Against Denying the Son

[18]Dear children, this is the last hour; and as you have heard that the antichrist is coming,[o] even now many antichrists have come.[p] This is how we know it is the last hour. [19]They went out from us,[q] but they did not really belong to us. For if they had belonged to us, they would have remained with us; but their going showed that none of them belonged to us.[r]

[20]But you have an anointing[s] from the Holy One,[t] and all of you know the truth.[b][u] [21]I do not write to you because you do not know the truth, but because you do know it[v] and because no lie comes from the truth. [22]Who is the liar? It is whoever denies that Jesus is the Christ. Such a person is the antichrist—denying the Father and the Son.[w] [23]No one who denies the Son has the Father; whoever acknowledges the Son has the Father also.[x]

[24]As for you, see that what you have heard from the beginning remains in you. If it does, you also will remain in the Son and in the Father.[y] [25]And this is what he promised us—eternal life.

[26]I am writing these things to you about those who are trying to lead you astray.[z] [27]As for you, the anointing[a] you received from him remains in you, and you do not need anyone to teach you. But as his anointing teaches you about all things and as that anointing is real, not counterfeit—just as it has taught you, remain in him.

God's Children and Sin

[28]And now, dear children,[b] continue in him, so that when he appears[c] we may be confident[d] and unashamed before him at his coming.[e]

[29]If you know that he is righteous,[f] you know that everyone who does what is right has been born of him.

3 See what great love[g] the Father has lavished on us, that we should be called children of God![h] And that is what we are! The reason the world does not know us is that it did not know him.[i] [2]Dear friends, now we are children of God, and what we will be has not yet been made known. But we know that when Christ appears,[c] we shall be like him,[j] for we shall see him as

[a] 15 Or *world, the Father's love* [b] 20 Some manuscripts *and you know all things* [c] 2 Or *when it is made known*

2:15 *Do not love the world.* These words may be rephrased as "stop loving the world." John's readers were acting in a way that was inconsistent with the relationship with Christ. "World" here is the morally evil system opposed to all that God is and holds dear. In this sense, the "world" is the satanic system opposing Christ's kingdom on this earth (v. 16; 3:1; 4:4; 5:19; John 12:31; Eph. 6:11–12; James 4:4).
2:16 *lust of the flesh ... lust of the eyes ... pride of life.* The world is characterized by these three lusts, which have been interpreted as corresponding to the three different ways Eve was tempted in the garden (Gen. 3:6), or the three different temptations Jesus experienced (Luke 4:1–12). However, the correspondences are not close enough to make it certain that John was alluding to either of these. Instead, John was probably making a short list of the different ways believers could be lured away from a loving God. *The lust of the flesh* refers to desires of sinful sensual pleasure. *The lust of the eyes* refers to covetousness or materialism. *The pride of life* refers to being proud about one's position in this world.
2:17 *pass away.* John highlights the brevity of life. To be consumed with this life is to be unprepared for the next.
2:18 *antichrists.* This word is a combination of two Greek words: *anti*, meaning "instead of" or "against"; and *christos*, meaning "anointed one." *Antichrists* most likely means those who seek to take the place of Christ.
2:20 *anointing.* This is a reference to either the Holy Spirit or to Scripture. This unction, or anointing, is the protection that believers have against the false teachers. The true Anointed One, Jesus, also has representatives who are anointed. One of the main heresies the first century church faced was Gnosticism, whose followers claimed to have secret knowledge of the truth that led to salvation. Here John was opposing this teaching by asserting that all believers knew the truth.
2:22–23 *that Jesus is the Christ.* In John's epistles, denying that Jesus came in the flesh is to deny His status as the Anointed One. A person cannot worship God while denying Jesus' full deity and full humanity.
2:28 *unashamed before him at his coming.* Shame is the result of not having had a lifestyle of obedience when Christ returns. John tells his readers to live in Christ, so that they can be unashamed.
3:1 *what great love.* John stands in amazement of God's love. But the greater amazement and appreciation is for the fact that God's love is expressed to human beings and that Christians are included in His family.
3:2 We Have a New Family—One of the primary benefits of becoming a Christian is that we also become part of Christ's family. The Bible refers to this change as being *born again* (John 3:3). When an individual places his faith in Christ as Savior, he is born again into a new, spiritual, familial relationship with

2:15 [j] Ro 12:2 [k] Jas 4:4 **2:16** [l] Ro 13:14 [m] Pr 27:20 **2:17** [n] 1Co 7:31 **2:18** [o] ver 22; 1Jn 4:3; 2Jn 7 [p] 1Jn 4:1 **2:19** [q] Ac 20:30 [r] 1Co 11:19 **2:20** [s] 2Co 1:21 [t] Mk 1:24 [u] Jn 14:26 **2:21** [v] 2Pe 1:12; Jude 5 **2:22** [w] 2Jn 7 **2:23** [x] Jn 8:19; 1Jn 4:15 **2:24** [y] Jn 14:23 **2:26** [z] 2Jn 7 **2:27** [a] ver 20 **2:28** [b] ver 1 [c] 1Jn 3:2 [d] 1Jn 4:17 [e] 1Th 2:19 **2:29** [f] 1Jn 3:7 **3:1** [g] Jn 3:16 [h] Jn 1:12 [i] Jn 16:3 **3:2** [j] Ro 8:29; 2Pe 1:4

he is.[k] 3All who have this hope in him purify themselves,[l] just as he is pure.
4Everyone who sins breaks the law; in
fact, sin is lawlessness.[m] 5But you know
that he appeared so that he might take
away our sins. And in him is no sin.[n] 6No
one who lives in him keeps on sinning.[o] No
one who continues to sin has either seen
him[p] or known him.[q]
7Dear children,[r] do not let anyone lead
you astray.[s] The one who does what is right
is righteous, just as he is righteous.[t] 8The
one who does what is sinful is of the devil,[u]
because the devil has been sinning from
the beginning. The reason the Son of God
appeared was to destroy the devil's work.
9No one who is born of God[v] will continue to sin,[w] because God's seed[x] remains in
them; they cannot go on sinning, because
they have been born of God. 10This is how
we know who the children of God are and
who the children of the devil are: Anyone
who does not do what is right is not God's
child, nor is anyone who does not love[y]
their brother and sister.

More on Love and Hatred

11For this is the message you heard[z] from
the beginning: We should love one another.[a] 12Do not be like Cain, who belonged
to the evil one and murdered his brother.[b]
And why did he murder him? Because his
own actions were evil and his brother's
were righteous. 13Do not be surprised, my
brothers and sisters,[a] if the world hates
you.[c] 14We know that we have passed from
death to life,[d] because we love each other. Anyone who does not love remains in
death.[e] 15Anyone who hates a brother or
sister is a murderer,[f] and you know that no
murderer has eternal life residing in him.[g]
16This is how we know what love is: Jesus
Christ laid down his life for us. And we
ought to lay down our lives for our brothers and sisters.[h] 17If anyone has material
possessions and sees a brother or sister in
need but has no pity on them,[i] how can the
love of God be in that person?[j] 18Dear children,[k] let us not love with words or speech
but with actions and in truth.[l]
19This is how we know that we belong to
the truth and how we set our hearts at rest
in his presence: 20If our hearts condemn
us, we know that God is greater than our
hearts, and he knows everything. 21Dear
friends, if our hearts do not condemn us,
we have confidence before God[m] 22and receive from him anything we ask,[n] because
we keep his commands and do what pleases him.[o] 23And this is his command: to believe[p] in the name of his Son, Jesus Christ,
and to love one another as he commanded
us.[q] 24The one who keeps God's commands
lives in him,[r] and he in them. And this is
how we know that he lives in us: We know
it by the Spirit he gave us.[s]

---

[a] *13* The Greek word for *brothers and sisters* (*adelphoi*) refers here to believers, both men and women, as part of God's family; also in verse 16.

God (Gal. 3:26). He gains God as Father (Eph. 4:6) and other Christians as brothers and sisters (Heb. 3:1). God also adopts us when we become His children (Eph. 1:5). This image implies a dramatic transformation of status from slave to son (Gal. 4:1–5). One is no longer in bondage to the master but becomes a free son possessing all the rights and privileges of sonship. One of these benefits is the right to call God *Abba*, an affectionate term meaning "Father" (Rom. 8:15). A marvelous relationship is possible when one becomes a part of the family of God. As in any family, there are also responsibilities. The Christian must exhibit the family character and grow into spiritual maturity.

3:3 ***All who have this hope.*** Knowing that Christ is morally pure helps a person pursue purity even more.

3:4 ***sins.*** This verse is not referring to occasional sin but a consistent lifestyle of sin. ***lawlessness.*** This is active rebellion against the law.

3:5–6 ***No one who lives in him keeps on sinning.*** Habitually sinful conduct indicates an absence of fellowship with Christ. Thus, if we claim to be a Christian but sin is our way of life, our status as children of God can legitimately be questioned.

3:8 ***destroy the devil's work.*** A person who sins is of the devil in the sense that he is participating in the devil's activity (2:19). Thus John is indicating that it is possible for believers to do that which is of the devil (Mark 8:31–33; James 3:6).

3:10 ***children of the devil.*** Believers who sin are not expressing their nature as children of God; instead, they are following the devil's pattern.

3:14 ***have passed from death to life.*** The tense of the verb "have passed" indicates that something experienced in the past has continuing and abiding results in the present. Thus John is saying that Christians, who have experienced Christ's salvation in the past, should demonstrate their salvation by loving their fellow believers in the present.

3:18 ***love with words or speech.*** This phrase means to speak loving words but to stop short of doing anything to prove that love. The opposite of loving in word is loving *with actions and in truth.*

3:20 ***our hearts condemn us.*** Our hearts condemn us when we recognize that we do not measure up to the standard of love and feel insecure in approaching God. Our conscience may not acknowledge the loving deeds we have done in the power of the Holy Spirit, but God does, and He is superior to our heart. Unlike our conscience, God takes everything into account, including Christ's atoning work for us. God is more compassionate and understanding toward us than we sometimes are toward ourselves.

3:24 We Have a Witness — Some of the benefits of being a believer are best described as being spiritual

3:2 [k] 2Co 3:18 **3:3** [l] 2Co 7:1; 2Pe 3:13,14 **3:4** [m] 1Jn 5:17
3:5 [n] 2Co 5:21 **3:6** [o] ver 9 [p] 3Jn 11 [q] 1Jn 2:4
3:7 [r] 1Jn 2:1 [s] 1Jn 2:26 [t] 1Jn 2:29 **3:8** [u] Jn 8:44
3:9 [v] Jn 1:13 [w] 1Jn 5:18 [x] 1Pe 1:23 **3:10** [y] 1Jn 4:8
3:11 [z] 1Jn 1:5 [a] Jn 13:34,35; 2Jn 5 **3:12** [b] Ge 4:8
3:13 [c] Jn 15:18,19; 17:14 **3:14** [d] Jn 5:24 [e] 1Jn 2:9
3:15 [f] Mt 5:21,22; Jn 8:44 [g] Gal 5:20,21 **3:16** [h] Jn 15:13
3:17 [i] Dt 15:7,8 [j] 1Jn 4:20 **3:18** [k] 1Jn 2:1 [l] Eze 33:31; Ro 12:9 **3:21** [m] 1Jn 5:14 **3:22** [n] Mt 7:7 [o] Jn 8:29
3:23 [p] Jn 6:29 [q] Jn 13:34 **3:24** [r] 1Jn 2:6 [s] 1Jn 4:13

On Denying the Incarnation

4 Dear friends, do not believe every spirit, but test the spirits to see whether they
are from God, because many false prophets
have gone out into the world.[t] 2This is how
you can recognize the Spirit of God: Every
spirit that acknowledges that Jesus Christ
has come in the flesh[u] is from God,[v] 3but every spirit that does not acknowledge Jesus
is not from God. This is the spirit of the
antichrist,[w] which you have heard is coming and even now is already in the world.
4You, dear children, are from God and
have overcome them, because the one who
is in you[x] is greater than the one who is in
the world.[y] 5They are from the world[z] and
therefore speak from the viewpoint of the
world, and the world listens to them. 6We
are from God, and whoever knows God
listens to us; but whoever is not from God
does not listen to us.[a] This is how we recognize the Spirit[a] of truth[b] and the spirit
of falsehood.

God's Love and Ours

7Dear friends, let us love one another,[c]
for love comes from God. Everyone who
loves has been born of God and knows
God.[d] 8Whoever does not love does not
know God, because God is love.[e] 9This is
how God showed his love among us: He
sent his one and only Son into the world
that we might live through him.[f] 10This
is love: not that we loved God, but that he
loved us[g] and sent his Son as an atoning
sacrifice for our sins.[h] 11Dear friends, since
God so loved us,[i] we also ought to love one
another. 12No one has ever seen God;[j] but
if we love one another, God lives in us and
his love is made complete in us.[k]
13This is how we know that we live in
him and he in us: He has given us of his
Spirit.[l] 14And we have seen and testify[m]
that the Father has sent his Son to be the
Savior of the world.[n] 15If anyone acknowledges that Jesus is the Son of God,[o] God
lives in them and they in God. 16And so we
know and rely on the love God has for us.
God is love.[p] Whoever lives in love lives
in God, and God in them.[q] 17This is how
love is made complete[r] among us so that
we will have confidence on the day of
judgment: In this world we are like Jesus.
18There is no fear in love. But perfect love
drives out fear,[s] because fear has to do with
punishment. The one who fears is not made
perfect in love.
19We love because he first loved us.[t]
20Whoever claims to love God yet hates
a brother or sister[u] is a liar.[v] For whoever
does not love their brother and sister,
whom they have seen,[w] cannot love God,
whom they have not seen.[x] 21And he has
given us this command: Anyone who loves
God must also love their brother and sister.[y]

Faith in the Incarnate Son of God

5 Everyone who believes that Jesus is the
Christ[z] is born of God,[a] and everyone
who loves the father loves his child as well.[b]

[a] 6 Or *spirit*

---

or even mystical. The whole idea of abiding in Christ while He abides in us is one of those concepts. Abide is best understood as "remain with." God doesn't come and go in our lives. He carries on a permanent relationship with us because He is always there for us and in us. We sense His presence primarily through the work of the Holy Spirit, whose role it is to stand beside us and comfort us. It happens in our hearts and minds and is largely invisible. Yet, it is also what most accurately describes the most important aspect of our day-to-day life as Christians. As we abide in Christ, He nourishes us spiritually the same way a vine gives nourishment to its branches (John 15:16).

4:1 *false prophets.* These persons obey evil spirits. A true prophet is one who receives direct revelation from God. A false prophet claims to have received direct revelation from God but in fact promotes erroneous ideas.

4:2 *Christ has come in the flesh.* This test seems to be aimed at Docetists. They taught that Christ did not have a physical body. The test may also be aimed at the followers of Cerinthus who claimed that Jesus and "the Christ" were two separate beings, one physical and the other spiritual. In this letter, John is careful to use the name and the title of Jesus Christ together to clearly express the complete union of the two titles in one person.

4:4 *one who is in the world.* This phrase refers to the devil.

4:8 *does not know God.* The knowledge of God here refers to an intimate, experiential knowledge (v. 6; 2:3) of God, rather than just information about God. John never says that those who do not love are not born of God (v. 7). Yet it is impossible to know God intimately without loving others, for God is love. Anyone in whom God dwells reflects His character. To claim to know God while failing to love others is to make a false claim (1:6).

4:13 *that we live in him and he in us.* Mutual abiding refers to the fellowship we have with God as a result of our salvation. The evidence that God abides in us and we in Him is the experience of the Holy Spirit dwelling in us. In the remainder of this passage, John explains how a believer can know that the Spirit is working in his or her life.

4:15 *If anyone acknowledges.* To be a Christian, a person must believe that Jesus is the Son of God.

5:1 *born of God.* This condition happens when one believes or trusts in Jesus Christ. Only correct, sincere belief produces spiritual birth. This birth is reflected in love for others who also have been born into the family of God (2:3–11).

4:1 [t] 2Pe 2:1; 1Jn 2:18 **4:2** [u] Jn 1:14; 1Jn 2:23 [v] 1Co 12:3 **4:3** [w] 1Jn 2:22; 2Jn 7 **4:4** [x] Ro 8:31 [y] Jn 12:31 **4:5** [z] Jn 15:19 **4:6** [a] Jn 8:47 [b] Jn 14:17 **4:7** [c] 1Jn 3:11 [d] 1Jn 2:4 **4:8** [e] ver 7, 16 **4:9** [f] Jn 3:16, 17; 1Jn 5:11 **4:10** [g] Ro 5:8, 10 [h] 1Jn 2:2 **4:11** [i] Jn 3:16 **4:12** [j] Jn 1:18; 1Ti 6:16 [k] 1Jn 2:5 **4:13** [l] 1Jn 3:24 **4:14** [m] Jn 15:27 [n] Jn 3:17 **4:15** [o] Ro 10:9 **4:16** [p] ver 8 [q] 1Jn 3:24 **4:17** [r] 1Jn 2:5 **4:18** [s] Ro 8:15 **4:19** [t] ver 10 **4:20** [u] 1Jn 2:9 [v] 1Jn 2:4 [w] 1Jn 3:17 [x] ver 12 **4:21** [y] Mt 5:43 **5:1** [z] 1Jn 2:22 [a] Jn 1:13; 1Jn 2:23 [b] Jn 8:42

2This is how we know that we love the children of God: by loving God and carrying
out his commands. 3In fact, this is love for
God: to keep his commands.[c] And his commands are not burdensome,[d] 4for everyone
born of God overcomes[e] the world. This is
the victory that has overcome the world,
even our faith. 5Who is it that overcomes
the world? Only the one who believes that
Jesus is the Son of God.

6This is the one who came by water and
blood[f]—Jesus Christ. He did not come by
water only, but by water and blood. And
it is the Spirit who testifies, because the
Spirit is the truth.[g] 7For there are three[h]
that testify: 8the[a] Spirit, the water and the
blood; and the three are in agreement. 9We
accept human testimony,[i] but God's testimony is greater because it is the testimony of God,[j] which he has given about his
Son. 10Whoever believes in the Son of God
accepts this testimony.[k] Whoever does not
believe God has made him out to be a liar,[l]
because they have not believed the testimony God has given about his Son. 11And this
is the testimony: God has given us eternal
life, and this life is in his Son.[m] 12Whoever
has the Son has life; whoever does not have
the Son of God does not have life.[n]

Concluding Affirmations

13I write these things to you who believe in the name of the Son of God[o] so
that you may know that you have eternal
life.[p] 14This is the confidence[q] we have in
approaching God: that if we ask anything
according to his will, he hears us.[r] 15And
if we know that he hears us—whatever
we ask—we know[s] that we have what we
asked of him.

16If you see any brother or sister commit
a sin that does not lead to death, you should
pray and God will give them life.[t] I refer
to those whose sin does not lead to death.
There is a sin that leads to death.[u] I am not
saying that you should pray about that.[v]
17All wrongdoing is sin,[w] and there is sin
that does not lead to death.[x]

18We know that anyone born of God does
not continue to sin; the One who was born
of God keeps them safe, and the evil one
cannot harm them.[y] 19We know that we are
children of God,[z] and that the whole world
is under the control of the evil one.[a] 20We
know also that the Son of God has come
and has given us understanding,[b] so that
we may know him who is true.[c] And we are
in him who is true by being in his Son Jesus
Christ. He is the true God and eternal life.[d]

21Dear children, keep yourselves from
idols.[e]

---

[a] 7,8 Late manuscripts of the Vulgate *testify in heaven: the Father, the Word and the Holy Spirit, and these three are one.* 8*And there are three that testify on earth: the* (not found in any Greek manuscript before the fourteenth century)

5:6 *by water and blood.* This phrase has been interpreted at least four ways: (1) as Jesus' baptism and death; (2) as His incarnation; (3) as the water and blood that flowed from His side on the cross; and (4) as the baptism of the believer and the Lord's Supper. Most scholars favor the first interpretation. John is correcting the false teacher, Cerinthus, who claimed that the Spirit came on Jesus at His baptism but left Him before His death (4:2–3).

5:11 *this is the testimony.* God's witness or testimony is that He has given us eternal life in his Son. Eternal life is not a wage to be earned, but a gift to be received from God (Rom. 6:23).

5:14–15 *according to his will.* The key to knowing that God hears is to pray this way.

5:16–17 *There is a sin that leads to death.* This phrase may refer to blaspheming the Holy Spirit, rejecting Christ as Savior, rejecting the humanity or deity of Jesus, a specific sin such as murder (3:12,15), or a life of habitual sin. Whatever it is, the sin seems to be a flagrant violation of the sanctity of the Christian community (Acts 5:1–11; 1 Cor. 5:5; 11:30). In other words, John is encouraging us to help fellow believers who are straying; we can be the tools God uses to restore an erring brother or sister to the true fellowship.

5:18–20 *We know.* This phrase introduces three concluding absolute truths. The general idea of this concluding section is that a proper relationship with God results in confidence of our position in Christ with a hostile world.

5:21 *idols.* This term may refer to literal idols, foods sacrificed to idols, false ideas in contrast to God's truth, or doctrines of false teachers. John has just reminded his readers of the true God (v. 20). It is appropriate that he closes by exhorting them to stay away from false gods.

5:3 [c] Jn 14:15; 2Jn 6 [d] Mt 11:30 **5:4** [e] Jn 16:33 **5:6** [f] Jn 19:34 [g] Jn 14:17 **5:7** [h] Mt 18:16 **5:9** [i] Jn 5:34 [j] Mt 3:16, 17; Jn 8:17, 18 **5:10** [k] Ro 8:16; Gal 4:6 [l] Jn 3:33 **5:11** [m] Jn 1:4; 1Jn 2:25 **5:12** [n] Jn 3:15, 16, 36 **5:13** [o] 1Jn 3:23 [p] Jn 20:31; 1Jn 1:1, 2 **5:14** [q] 1Jn 3:21 [r] Mt 7:7 **5:15** [s] ver 18, 19, 20 **5:16** [t] Jas 5:15 [u] Heb 6:4-6; 10:26 [v] Jer 7:16 **5:17** [w] 1Jn 3:4 [x] 1Jn 2:1 **5:18** [y] Jn 14:30 **5:19** [z] 1Jn 4:6 [a] Gal 1:4 **5:20** [b] Lk 24:45 [c] Jn 17:3 [d] ver 11 **5:21** [e] 1Co 10:14; 1Th 1:9

2 JOHN

▶ **AUTHOR:** Second John was not widely circulated at first because of its brevity and subject matter. Its strong resemblance to the tone and style of 1 John and the Fourth Gospel support the early tradition that John was the author of this epistle sometime after A.D. 90.

▶ **TIME:** c. A.D. 89–95 ▶ **KEY VERSES:** 2 John 9–10

▶ **THEME:** The addressee of 2 John is a woman in a local church that apparently had a strong friendship with John. The apostle writes to warn her about showing hospitality to false teachers. He cautions her against unwittingly aiding these teachers who were sowing seeds of heresy and hurting the church.

---

1 The elder,[a]

To the lady chosen by God[b] and to her
children, whom I love in the truth—and not
I only, but also all who know the truth[c]—
2 because of the truth,[d] which lives in us[e]
and will be with us forever:

3 Grace, mercy and peace from God the
Father and from Jesus Christ,[f] the Father's
Son, will be with us in truth and love.

4 It has given me great joy to find some of
your children walking in the truth,[g] just as
the Father commanded us. **5** And now, dear
lady, I am not writing you a new command
but one we have had from the beginning.[h]
I ask that we love one another. **6** And this is
love:[i] that we walk in obedience to his commands. As you have heard from the beginning, his command is that you walk in love.
7 I say this because many deceivers, who
do not acknowledge Jesus Christ[j] as coming in the flesh, have gone out into the
world.[k] Any such person is the deceiver
and the antichrist.[l] **8** Watch out that you
do not lose what we[a] have worked for, but
that you may be rewarded fully.[m] **9** Anyone
who runs ahead and does not continue in
the teaching of Christ does not have God;
whoever continues in the teaching has both
the Father and the Son.[n] **10** If anyone comes
to you and does not bring this teaching,
do not take them into your house or welcome them.[o] **11** Anyone who welcomes them
shares[p] in their wicked work.
12 I have much to write to you, but I do not
want to use paper and ink. Instead, I hope
to visit you and talk with you face to face,[q]
so that our joy may be complete.

13 The children of your sister, who is chosen by God,[r] send their greetings.

---

a 8 Some manuscripts *you*

---

1 ***The elder.*** This is probably the apostle John. The title can refer either to an old man, an older person deserving respect, or a church leader. ***the lady chosen by God*** may be a specific person, or the phrase may be a figurative description of the local church.
4 ***walking in the truth.*** This phrase means having an authentic relationship with God. Our walk with the Lord, if genuine, must be based upon His word.
6 ***his commands.*** God's love is the basis of His desire for our obedience, and it is the reason He has revealed His will in His word. We prove our obedience to Christ by demonstrating love toward one another. Love is an unlimited resource readily available to us, and it is tremendously effective in furthering the work of Christ.
7 ***coming in the flesh.*** These words refer to the Incarnation, the fact that Jesus is the God-man. The humanity of Jesus provides a test by which false teachers can be identified. The Gnostic heresy, against which John wrote in 1 and 2 John, included a denial of the physical body of Christ. People who deny the physical reality of Jesus are not Christians, but antichrists.
8 ***Watch out.*** Being seduced by false teachers is one way that Christians can lose their reward at the judgment. With this is mind, John writes that the reason to guard against deceivers is our own desire not to lose our reward at the judgment seat of Christ.
9 ***who runs ahead and does not continue.*** Departure from Christ into doctrinal error indicates that a person does not have God.
10 ***this teaching.*** Jesus is completely human and completely divine. A Christian should not only refuse to receive false teachers in the sense of supporting them while they visit the community, a Christian should also avoid appearing to endorse their teachings. The proper response to deceivers is to reject them as unbelievers. This shows how seriously we should take the Scriptures and how careful we should be in evaluating the teachings of everyone.

1 [a] 3Jn 1 [b] Ro 16:13 [c] Jn 8:32 **2** [d] 2Pe 1:12 [e] 1Jn 1:8
3 [f] Ro 1:7 **4** [g] 3Jn 3, 4 **5** [h] 1Jn 2:7; 3:11 **6** [i] 1Jn 2:5
7 [j] 1Jn 2:22; 4:2, 3 [k] 1Jn 4:1 [l] 1Jn 2:18 **8** [m] 1Co 3:8
9 [n] 1Jn 2:23 **10** [o] Ro 16:17 **11** [p] 1Ti 5:22
12 [q] 3Jn 13, 14 **13** [r] ver 1

3 JOHN

▶ **AUTHOR:** Much like 2 John, this letter had a very limited circulation in the early church, but was accepted as authoritative on account of its apostolic authorship. Its style and vocabulary strongly resemble that of John's Gospel and other epistles.

▶ **TIME:** C. A.D. 89–95 ▶ **KEY VERSE:** 3 John 11

▶ **THEME:** Third John has two main purposes. The first is to commend Gaius for being hospitable to itinerant missionaries. The second is to advise Gaius about Diotrephes, a man in the church who refuses to help the same kind of missionaries and who even gossips about them.

1The elder,[a]

To my dear friend Gaius, whom I love in
the truth.

2Dear friend, I pray that you may enjoy
good health and that all may go well with
you, even as your soul is getting along well.
3It gave me great joy when some believers[b]
came and testified about your faithfulness
to the truth, telling how you continue to
walk in it.[c] 4I have no greater joy than to
hear that my children[d] are walking in the
truth.
5Dear friend, you are faithful in what
you are doing for the brothers and sisters,[a]
even though they are strangers to you.[e]
6They have told the church about your love.
Please send them on their way in a manner
that honors God. 7It was for the sake of the
Name[f] that they went out, receiving no help
from the pagans.[g] 8We ought therefore to
show hospitality to such people so that we
may work together for the truth.
9I wrote to the church, but Diotrephes,
who loves to be first, will not welcome us.
10So when I come,[h] I will call attention to
what he is doing, spreading malicious nonsense about us. Not satisfied with that, he
even refuses to welcome other believers.[i]
He also stops those who want to do so and
puts them out of the church.[j]
11Dear friend, do not imitate what is evil
but what is good.[k] Anyone who does what
is good is from God.[l] Anyone who does
what is evil has not seen God.[m] 12Deme-
trius is well spoken of by everyone[n]—and
even by the truth itself. We also speak well
of him, and you know that our testimony
is true.[o]
13I have much to write you, but I do not
want to do so with pen and ink. 14I hope to
see you soon, and we will talk face to face.[p]

15Peace to you. The friends here send
their greetings. Greet the friends there by
name.[q]

[a] 5 The Greek word for *brothers and sisters* (*adelphoi*) refers here to believers, both men and women, as part of God's family.

2 *may enjoy good health and that all may go well with you.* John's greeting may imply that Gaius was physically weak though spiritually strong. Most likely John is simply following the pattern of greetings common to Greek letters.

4 *my children.* This is a description Paul uses of those he has led to saving faith in Christ (1 Cor. 4:14–17) and may indicate that Gaius was one of John's converts. It may also be a term John uses to describe those under his pastoral care as reflected in 1 John 2:1,12,18; 3:7,18; 4:4; 5:21.

5–12 *you are faithful in what you are doing.* In these verses, John affirms Gaius' responsibility to assist Demetrius despite the opposition of Diotrephes and his expulsion of those who receive traveling missionaries.

11 *has not seen God.* Our sin is a result of a faulty vision of God. Therefore, the Scriptures encourage us to look at Christ (2 Cor. 3:18; 4:16–18; Heb. 12:2–3), for the day when we see Him perfectly will be the day that we will be like Him (1 John 3:2–3).

12 *by the truth itself.* Demetrius' life measured up to the teaching of Scripture and Christ's commands. His conduct matched his theology.

1 [a] 2Jn 1 **3** [b] ver 5,10 [c] 2Jn 4 **4** [d] 1Co 4:15; 1Jn 2:1 **5** [e] Ro 12:13; Heb 13:2 **7** [f] Jn 15:21 [g] Ac 20:33,35 **10** [h] 2Jn 12 [i] ver 5 [j] Jn 9:22,34 **11** [k] Ps 37:27 [l] 1Jn 2:29 [m] 1Jn 3:6,9,10 **12** [n] 1Ti 3:7 [o] Jn 21:24 **14** [p] 2Jn 12 [q] Jn 10:3

JUDE

▶ **AUTHOR:** In spite of its limited subject matter and size, Jude was accepted as authentic and quoted by early church fathers. It is unlikely that the author is the apostle Jude (Luke 6:16), but rather Jude the brother of Jesus and James (called Judas in Matt. 13:55 and Mark 6:3). Because of the silence of the New Testament and tradition concerning Jude's later years, we cannot know where or when this epistle was written.

▶ **TIME:** c. A.D. 66–80 ▶ **KEY VERSE:** Jude 3

▶ **THEME:** Jude's letter is hard-hitting, short, and right to the point. False teachers are on the loose in the church and Jude wants to make sure his readers understand the destructive implications of their teaching. He urges Christians to resist these false teachers and to defend the faith and the body of truth received from the apostles that they have come to know and believe. He finishes by reminding them of the hope they have in knowing Christ is coming again.

1 Jude,[a] a servant of Jesus Christ and a
brother of James,

To those who have been called,[b] who are
loved in God the Father and kept for[a] Jesus
Christ:[c]

2 Mercy, peace and love be yours in abundance.[d]

The Sin and Doom of Ungodly People

3 Dear friends, although I was very eager to write to you about the salvation we
share,[e] I felt compelled to write and urge
you to contend[f] for the faith that was once
for all entrusted to God's holy people. 4 For
certain individuals whose condemnation
was written about[b] long ago have secretly
slipped in among you.[g] They are ungodly
people, who pervert the grace of our God
into a license for immorality and deny
Jesus Christ our only Sovereign and Lord.[h]
5 Though you already know all this, I
want to remind you that the Lord[c] at one
time delivered his people out of Egypt, but
later destroyed those who did not believe.[i]
6 And the angels who did not keep their positions of authority but abandoned their
proper dwelling—these he has kept in
darkness, bound with everlasting chains
for judgment on the great Day.[j] 7 In a similar way, Sodom and Gomorrah and the
surrounding towns[k] gave themselves up to
sexual immorality and perversion. They
serve as an example of those who suffer
the punishment of eternal fire.[l]
8 In the very same way, on the strength of

[a] *1* Or *by*; or *in* [b] *4* Or *individuals who were marked out for condemnation* [c] *5* Some early manuscripts *Jesus*

2 *peace.* This is the state of a person who rests in God completely for salvation and protection.
3 *salvation we share.* Jude intended to write a more general doctrinal letter, but the present crisis demanded this short, pointed attack on doctrinal error.
4 *pervert the grace of our God into a license for immorality.* The teaching of grace can be dangerous when perverted by false teachers or carnal people who believe that because they have been saved by grace they may live as they please (Rom. 6:1–2).
5 *destroyed those who did not believe.* The Israelites of the exodus had a magnificent beginning in Egypt but a disastrous ending in the wilderness. The false believers who had infiltrated God's people would be judged, just like the false believers who rejected God in the wilderness (Num. 25:1–9).
6 *angels.* These are not holy angels of God. Instead these angels could be those who had previously fallen with Satan. Some think that these angels are "the sons of God" of Genesis 6:2, who took on human form and married women before the flood.
8 *reject authority.* The false teachers even despised those who were placed in positions of authority in local congregations. They not only preferred error to truth but also demeaned and rejected those who taught the truth.

1 [a] Mt 13:55; Ac 1:13 [b] Ro 1:6,7 [c] Jn 17:12 **2** [d] 2Pe 1:2
3 [e] Titus 1:4 [f] 1Ti 6:12 **4** [g] Gal 2:4 [h] Titus 1:16; 2Pe 2:1
5 [i] Nu 14:29; Ps 106:26 **6** [j] 2Pe 2:4,9 **7** [k] Dt 29:23
[l] 2Pe 2:6

their dreams these ungodly people pollute
their own bodies, reject authority and heap
abuse on celestial beings.[m] 9But even the
archangel Michael,[n] when he was disputing with the devil about the body of Moses,
did not himself dare to condemn him for
slander but said, "The Lord rebuke you!"[a][o]
10Yet these people slander whatever they
do not understand, and the very things
they do understand by instinct—as irrational animals do—will destroy them.[p]

11Woe to them! They have taken the way
of Cain;[q] they have rushed for profit into
Balaam's error;[r] they have been destroyed
in Korah's rebellion.[s]

12These people are blemishes at your
love feasts,[t] eating with you without the
slightest qualm—shepherds who feed
only themselves. They are clouds without
rain,[u] blown along by the wind;[v] autumn
trees, without fruit and uprooted[w]—twice
dead. 13They are wild waves of the sea,[x]
foaming up their shame;[y] wandering stars,
for whom blackest darkness has been reserved forever.[z]

14Enoch,[a] the seventh from Adam,
prophesied about them: "See, the Lord is
coming with thousands upon thousands of
his holy ones[b] 15to judge[c] everyone, and to
convict all of them of all the ungodly acts
they have committed in their ungodliness,
and of all the defiant words ungodly sinners have spoken against him."[b][d] 16These
people are grumblers and faultfinders;
they follow their own evil desires; they
boast[e] about themselves and flatter others
for their own advantage.

A Call to Persevere

17But, dear friends, remember what the
apostles of our Lord Jesus Christ foretold.[f]
18They said to you, "In the last times[g] there
will be scoffers who will follow their own
ungodly desires."[h] 19These are the people
who divide you, who follow mere natural
instincts and do not have the Spirit.[i]

20But you, dear friends, by building
yourselves up[j] in your most holy faith and
praying in the Holy Spirit,[k] 21keep yourselves in God's love as you wait[l] for the
mercy of our Lord Jesus Christ to bring
you to eternal life.

22Be merciful to those who doubt; 23save
others by snatching them from the fire;[m] to
others show mercy, mixed with fear—hating even the clothing stained by corrupted
flesh.[c][n]

Doxology

24To him who is able[o] to keep you from
stumbling and to present you before his
glorious presence[p] without fault[q] and with
great joy— 25to the only God[r] our Savior
be glory, majesty, power and authority,
through Jesus Christ our Lord, before all
ages, now and forevermore![s] Amen.[t]

---

[a] 9 Jude is alluding to the Jewish *Testament of Moses* (approximately the first century A.D.).
[b] *14,15* From the Jewish *First Book of Enoch* (approximately the first century B.C.)
[c] *22,23* The Greek manuscripts of these verses vary at several points.

---

9 *disputing ... about the body of Moses.* Jude's description here is probably taken from an apocryphal book called *The Assumption of Moses*, written in the first century A.D. There is no record in the Bible itself of the archangel's encounter with Satan, or a detailed account of Moses' body.

11 *They have taken the way of Cain.* The heretics are compared to three Old Testament failures. Cain did not place his faith in the Lord. The "way of Cain" is the way of pride and self-righteousness (Gen. 4:3–8; Heb. 11:4; 1 John 3:12). ***Balaam's error.*** He was the epitome of the sin of greed (Num. 31:16). ***Korah's rebellion.*** This was the Levite Korah (Num. 16:1–3; 31–35) who resented the prominent positions of Moses and Aaron as God's representatives. The Lord brought judgment on him and his followers for rebelling against those He had place in authority.

13 *wild waves ... foaming ... wandering stars.* These godless people put on a great show but lacked any substance. They boasted of liberty but placed the people of God in bondage to sin (2 Pet. 2:19). After they had done their evil deeds and made their profits, they, like wandering stars, moved on to other places to exploit God's people again.

15 *ungodly.* This word is repeated four times, making the verse one of the most striking in the letter. In view of the wicked nature of evil persons, how could the church allow them to stay in their midst?

18 *there will be scoffers.* One of the main tactics that the false teachers used to gain credibility was to tear down godly leaders.

22–23 *to others show mercy.* We have certain obligations to other believers. First, we need to show compassion to those in any kind of spiritual or physical need. Second, we need to use discernment in helping our brothers and sisters in the church. Some will require tender care and patience to help them grow in Christ. With others we may need to use drastic action to rescue them from the temptations of sin. ***hating even the clothing stained by corrupted flesh.*** This is a metaphor for staying wary of sin—as Paul says, "watch yourselves or you also may be tempted" (Gal. 6:1).

24 *without fault.* This is a Greek word used for sacrificial animals that had no blemish and thus were fit to be offered to God. Only God can save us, cleanse us from our sins, and present us to Himself as faultless, for God is the Author and Finisher of our faith (Heb. 12:2).

8 [m] 2Pe 2:10 **9** [n] Da 10:13, 21 [o] Zec 3:2 **10** [p] 2Pe 2:12 **11** [q] Ge 4:3-8; 1Jn 3:12 [r] 2Pe 2:15 [s] Nu 16:1-3, 31-35 **12** [t] 2Pe 2:13; 1Co 11:20-22 [u] Pr 25:14; 2Pe 2:17 [v] Eph 4:14 [w] Mt 15:13 **13** [x] Isa 57:20 [y] Php 3:19 [z] 2Pe 2:17 **14** [a] Ge 5:18, 21-24 [b] Dt 33:2; Da 7:10 **15** [c] 2Pe 2:6-9 [d] 1Ti 1:9 **16** [e] 2Pe 2:18 **17** [f] 2Pe 3:2 **18** [g] 1Ti 4:1 [h] 2Pe 2:1 **19** [i] 1Co 2:14, 15 **20** [j] Col 2:7 [k] Eph 6:18 **21** [l] Titus 2:13; 2Pe 3:12 **23** [m] Am 4:11; Zec 3:2-5 [n] Rev 3:4 **24** [o] Ro 16:25 [p] 2Co 4:14 [q] Col 1:22 **25** [r] Jn 5:44; 1Ti 1:17 [s] Heb 13:8 [t] Ro 11:36

REVELATION

▶ **AUTHOR:** The style, symmetry, and plan of Revelation show that it was written by one author, four times named "John" (Rev. 1:1,4,9; 22:8). Because of its contents and its address to seven churches, Revelation quickly circulated and became widely known and accepted in the early church. From the beginning, Revelation was considered an authentic work of the apostle John, the same John who wrote the Gospel and Epistles. Revelation was written at a time when Roman hostility to Christianity was erupting into overt persecution. It is likely that John wrote this book in A.D. 95 or 96 when the severe persecution of Christians began under the emperor Domitian.

▶ **TIME:** c. A.D. 95 – 96 ▶ **KEY VERSES:** Rev. 19:11 – 15

▶ **THEME:** John wrote this book late in his life while in exile on the island of Patmos off the coast of Asia. It is safe to say that no book of the Bible has generated more theories of interpretation over the last two millennia. In this context probably one of the best approaches to interpreting and understanding Revelation is to concentrate on the major themes such as worship. When the reader does that, one finds great comfort and assurance in the book. Many scholars think the purpose of the book is to provide comfort in the midst of persecution and difficult times, as the form of the book is in the tradition of Jewish apocalyptic literature that is designed to communicate hope through symbolic imagery.

Prologue

1 The revelation from Jesus Christ, which
God gave him to show his servants what
must soon take place. He made it known
by sending his angel[a] to his servant John,
2who testifies to everything he saw—that
is, the word of God and the testimony of
Jesus Christ.[b] 3Blessed is the one who
reads aloud the words of this prophecy,
and blessed are those who hear it and take
to heart what is written in it,[c] because the
time is near.

Greetings and Doxology

4John,

To the seven churches in the province of Asia:

Grace and peace to you from him who
is, and who was, and who is to come, and
from the seven spirits[ad] before his throne,
5and from Jesus Christ, who is the faithful
witness,[e] the firstborn from the dead,[f] and
the ruler of the kings of the earth.[g]

To him who loves us and has freed us
from our sins by his blood, 6and has made
us to be a kingdom and priests[h] to serve
his God and Father—to him be glory and
power for ever and ever! Amen.[i]

7"Look, he is coming with the
clouds,"[bj]
and "every eye will see him,

a 4 That is, the sevenfold Spirit *b* 7 Daniel 7:13

1:1 *revelation.* The word "revelation," which means "unveiling," or "disclosure," indicates that this book is a type of literature known as *apocalyptic literature,* or literature which reveals hidden things. ***from Jesus Christ.*** This revelation is both from Jesus Christ and about Him. ***John.*** John is the human writer, and Jesus is the divine Author.

1:3 *Blessed.* The word "blessed" means "spiritually happy." Even though some of the words of this book speak of terrifying and solemn times, it is a blessing to know how thoroughly the Lord holds all time and all times in His hands. Those who take time to read and try to understand this book will find themselves blessed by the hope of heaven and by the nearness of our Lord and Savior.

1:4 *the seven churches.* The seven churches are in the Roman province of Asia, which today is southwestern Turkey. The churches fit within a square 50 miles on each side, and their names are given in order going clockwise from the southwest.

1:5 *firstborn from the dead.* This phrase refers to the resurrection of Christ, the first to come back from the dead. This is the basis of the hope of resurrection held by Christians (1 Cor. 15:20 – 24).

1:7 *coming with the clouds . . . every eye.* "Coming

1:1 [a] Rev 22:16 **1:2** [b] 1Co 1:6; Rev 12:17 **1:3** [c] Lk 11:28 **1:4** [d] Rev 3:1; 4:5 **1:5** [e] Rev 3:14 [f] Col 1:18 [g] Rev 17:14 **1:6** [h] 1Pe 2:5 [i] Ro 11:36 **1:7** [j] Da 7:13

even those who pierced him”;
and all peoples on earth “will mourn[k]
because of him.”[a]
So shall it be! Amen.

8“I am the Alpha and the Omega,”[l] says
the Lord God, “who is, and who was, and
who is to come, the Almighty.”[m]

John’s Vision of Christ

9I, John, your brother and companion
in the suffering[n] and kingdom and patient
endurance[o] that are ours in Jesus, was on
the island of Patmos because of the word
of God and the testimony of Jesus. 10On
the Lord’s Day I was in the Spirit,[p] and I
heard behind me a loud voice like a trumpet,[q] 11which said: “Write on a scroll what
you see and send it to the seven churches:[r]
to Ephesus, Smyrna, Pergamum, Thyatira,
Sardis,[s] Philadelphia and Laodicea.”

12I turned around to see the voice that
was speaking to me. And when I turned
I saw seven golden lampstands,[t] 13and
among the lampstands was someone like
a son of man,[b][u] dressed in a robe reaching down to his feet and with a golden sash
around his chest.[v] 14The hair on his head
was white like wool, as white as snow, and
his eyes were like blazing fire.[w] 15His feet
were like bronze glowing in a furnace,[x]
and his voice was like the sound of rushing
waters.[y] 16In his right hand he held seven
stars,[z] and coming out of his mouth was a
sharp, double-edged sword.[a] His face was
like the sun shining in all its brilliance.

17When I saw him, I fell at his feet[b] as
though dead. Then he placed his right hand
on me and said: “Do not be afraid. I am the
First and the Last.[c] 18I am the Living One;
I was dead,[d] and now look, I am alive for
ever and ever![e] And I hold the keys of death
and Hades.[f]

19“Write, therefore, what you have seen,
what is now and what will take place later.
20The mystery of the seven stars that you
saw in my right hand and of the seven gold-
en lampstands[g] is this: The seven stars are
the angels[c] of the seven churches,[h] and the
seven lampstands are the seven churches.[i]

To the Church in Ephesus

2 “To the angel[d] of the church in Ephesus write:

These are the words of him who
holds the seven stars in his right hand[j]
and walks among the seven golden
lampstands.[k] 2I know your deeds,[l]
your hard work and your perseverance. I know that you cannot tolerate
wicked people, that you have tested[m]
those who claim to be apostles but are
not, and have found them false.[n] 3You
have persevered and have endured
hardships for my name,[o] and have not
grown weary.

4Yet I hold this against you: You
have forsaken the love you had at
first.[p] 5Consider how far you have
fallen! Repent[q] and do the things you

[a] *7* Zech. 12:10 [b] *13* See Daniel 7:13. [c] *20* Or *messengers* [d] *1* Or *messenger*; also in verses 8, 12 and 18

---

with the clouds” recalls Daniel’s vision of the Son of Man (Dan. 7:13; Matt. 24:30) and the ascension of Christ (Acts 1:11). “Every eye” indicates that Christ will be universally visible at His second coming.

1:8 *the Alpha and the Omega.* The Lord’s description of Himself as the first and last letters of the Greek alphabet means that He is the beginning and the end of all creation.

1:9 *suffering.* The apostle Paul said there would be many hardships (Acts 14:22), and John identifies both the suffering of others and his own exile on Patmos as part of this.. The great tribulation is the time when the wrath of God is poured out on the earth (Mark 13:14 – 23); that time is explained in greater detail in this book.

1:12 *seven golden lampstands.* The seven lampstands represent the seven churches.

1:13 *someone like a son of man.* The term “son of man” echoes Daniel 7:13. Comparisons of these two passages, along with Jesus’ common use of the name “son of man” for Himself, indicate that Christ is the subject of verses 12 – 18.

1:14 *white.* The white appearance is parallel to the description of the “Ancient of Days” in Daniel 7:9, and of Christ on the mount of transfiguration (Matt. 17:2). The similarity of descriptions demonstrates the purity and eternality of both God the Father and God the Son. Overcoming believers will also “be dressed in white” (3:5; 19:8) in Christ’s presence, symbolizing purity.

1:16 *sharp, double-edged sword.* The sword coming out of Christ’s mouth is symbolic of the judging power of the Word of God (Is. 49:2; Heb. 4:12).

1:18 *keys of death and Hades.* Christ has authority over those who have died physically and over their present resting place, which will be emptied and destroyed at the time of the great white throne judgment (20:11 – 15). Hades is the place where the dead rest.

1:20 *angels.* Angels are created spirit beings who minister to believers (Heb. 1:14).

2:1 *Ephesus.* Ephesus was the most important city in Asia Minor when Revelation was written. It was the center of the worship of Artemis (or Diana; Acts 19:28), a goddess of fertility. It was a strategic commercial center and a great seaport.

2:5 *Consider.* A generation earlier the same church was commended for love (Eph. 1:15; 6:24).

1:7 [k] Zec 12:10 **1:8** [l] Rev 21:6 [m] Rev 4:8 **1:9** [n] Php 4:14 [o] 2Ti 2:12 **1:10** [p] Rev 4:2 [q] Rev 4:1 **1:11** [r] ver 4, 20 [s] Rev 3:1 **1:12** [t] Ex 25:31-40; Zec 4:2 **1:13** [u] Eze 1:26; Da 7:13; 10:16 [v] Da 10:5; Rev 15:6 **1:14** [w] Da 7:9; 10:6; Rev 19:12 **1:15** [x] Da 10:6 [y] Eze 43:2; Rev 14:2 **1:16** [z] Rev 2:1; 3:1 [a] Isa 49:2; Heb 4:12; Rev 2:12, 16 **1:17** [b] Eze 1:28; Da 8:17, 18 [c] Isa 41:4; 44:6; 48:12; Rev 22:13 **1:18** [d] Ro 6:9 [e] Rev 4:9, 10 [f] Rev 20:1 **1:20** [g] Zec 4:2 [h] ver 4, 11 [i] Mt 5:14, 15 **2:1** [j] Rev 1:16 [k] Rev 1:12, 13 **2:2** [l] Rev 3:1, 8, 15 [m] 1Jn 4:1 [n] 2Co 11:13 **2:3** [o] Jn 15:21 **2:4** [p] Mt 24:12

did at first. If you do not repent, I will come to you and remove your lampstand[r] from its place. 6But you have this in your favor: You hate the practices of the Nicolaitans,[s] which I also hate.

7Whoever has ears, let them hear[t] what the Spirit says to the churches. To the one who is victorious, I will give the right to eat from the tree of life,[u] which is in the paradise[v] of God.

To the Church in Smyrna

8"To the angel of the church in Smyrna[w] write:

These are the words of him who is the First and the Last,[x] who died and came to life again.[y] 9I know your afflictions and your poverty—yet you are rich![z] I know about the slander of those who say they are Jews and are not,[a] but are a synagogue of Satan.[b] 10Do not be afraid of what you are about to suffer. I tell you, the devil will put some of you in prison to test you,[c] and you will suffer persecution for ten days.[d] Be faithful,[e] even to the point of death, and I will give you life as your victor's crown.

11Whoever has ears, let them hear what the Spirit says to the churches. The one who is victorious will not be hurt at all by the second death.[f]

To the Church in Pergamum

12"To the angel of the church in Pergamum[g] write:

These are the words of him who has the sharp, double-edged sword.[h] 13I know where you live—where Satan has his throne. Yet you remain true to my name. You did not renounce your faith in me,[i] not even in the days of Antipas, my faithful witness, who was put to death in your city—where Satan lives.[j]

14Nevertheless, I have a few things against you:[k] There are some among you who hold to the teaching of Balaam,[l] who taught Balak to entice the Israelites to sin so that they ate food sacrificed to idols and committed sexual immorality.[m] 15Likewise, you also have those who hold to the teaching of the Nicolaitans.[n] 16Repent therefore! Otherwise, I will soon come to you and will fight against them with the sword of my mouth.[o]

17Whoever has ears, let them hear what the Spirit says to the churches. To the one who is victorious, I will give some of the hidden manna.[p] I will also give that person a white stone with a new name[q] written on it, known only to the one who receives it.[r]

To the Church in Thyatira

18"To the angel of the church in Thyatira[s] write:

These are the words of the Son of God, whose eyes are like blazing fire and whose feet are like burnished bronze.[t] 19I know your deeds,[u] your love and faith, your service and perseverance, and that you are now doing more than you did at first.

2:6 ***Nicolaitans.*** The Nicolaitans were a heretical group that troubled the churches at Ephesus and Pergamos (v. 15). Apparently their teaching and practice were immoral, perhaps even idolatrous (v. 14).
2:7 ***paradise.*** Jesus told the believing thief on the cross that he would be with Jesus in paradise (Luke 23:42). Paul uses the term interchangeably with "the third heaven" (2 Cor. 12:2,4).
2:8 ***Smyrna.*** Smyrna was an important seaport 35 miles north of Ephesus. The presence of a Roman imperial cult and a large Jewish population made life difficult for believers in Smyrna. However, the churches of Smyrna and Philadelphia are the only two of the seven not rebuked by Christ in some way.
2:10 ***life as your victor's crown.*** The Greek crown or garland of green leaves was given to winners in athletic events. James 1:12 also promises the crown of life to believers who persevere under trial.
2:11 ***second death.*** The second death refers to the experience of eternal death in the lake of fire (20:14–15). No believer will suffer the second death.
2:12 ***Pergamum.*** Pergamum was the ancient capital of the province of Asia. It was said to be the place where parchment was first used. Pergamum means "citadel" in Greek. It was located 50 miles north of Smyrna and was situated on a high hill dominating the valley below. ***double-edged sword.*** The double-edged sword is the powerful word of the Lord (1:16; Heb. 4:12).
2:13 ***where Satan has his throne.*** This implies that Satan's authority and power were honored either openly or in effect. ***Antipas.*** Antipas (not Herod Antipas) had already suffered martyrdom, thus receiving the promised "victor's crown."
2:14 ***teaching of Balaam.*** The background for this teaching is in the Old Testament (Num. 22:1–25:31). Balak hired Balaam to turn the hearts of Israel away from the Lord. Apparently seduction similar to that which Balaam instigated was taking place at the church at Pergamum, especially in relation to idols and sexual immorality (Acts 15:20).
2:18 ***Thyatira.*** Thyatira was a city with a large military detachment about 30 miles southeast of Pergamum. Recognized for its wool and dye industries, the city was also noted for its trade guilds. ***eyes are like blazing fire ... feet are like burnished bronze.*** This is essentially the same wording as Daniel 10:6.

2:5 [q] ver 16,22 [r] Rev 1:20 **2:6** [s] ver 15 **2:7** [t] Mt 11:15; Rev 3:6, 13, 22 [u] Ge 2:9; Rev 22:2, 14, 19 [v] Lk 23:43 **2:8** [w] Rev 1:11 [x] Rev 1:17 [y] Rev 1:18 **2:9** [z] Jas 2:5 [a] Rev 3:9 [b] Mt 4:10 **2:10** [c] Rev 3:10 [d] Da 1:12, 14 [e] ver 13 **2:11** [f] Rev 20:6, 14; 21:8 **2:12** [g] Rev 1:11 [h] Rev 1:16 **2:13** [i] Rev 14:12 [j] ver 9, 24 **2:14** [k] ver 20 [l] 2Pe 2:15 [m] 1Co 6:13 **2:15** [n] ver 6 **2:16** [o] 2Th 2:8; Rev 1:16 **2:17** [p] Jn 6:49, 50 [q] Isa 62:2 [r] Rev 19:12 **2:18** [s] Rev 1:11 [t] Rev 1:14, 15 **2:19** [u] ver 2

20Nevertheless, I have this against
you: You tolerate that woman Jezebel,[v] who calls herself a prophet. By
her teaching she misleads my servants
into sexual immorality and the eating
of food sacrificed to idols. 21I have giv-
en her time[w] to repent of her immorality, but she is unwilling.[x] 22So I will
cast her on a bed of suffering, and I
will make those who commit adultery[y]
with her suffer intensely, unless they
repent of her ways. 23I will strike her
children dead. Then all the churches
will know that I am he who searches
hearts and minds,[z] and I will repay
each of you according to your deeds.
24Now I say to the rest of you in
Thyatira, to you who do not hold to
her teaching and have not learned
Satan's so-called deep secrets, 'I will
not impose any other burden on you,[a]
25except to hold on to what you have[b]
until I come.'
26To the one who is victorious and
does my will to the end, I will give authority over the nations[c]— 27that one
'will rule them with an iron scepter[d]
and will dash them to pieces like pottery'[a][e]—just as I have received authority from my Father. 28I will also give
that one the morning star.[f] 29Whoever
has ears, let them hear[g] what the Spirit
says to the churches.

To the Church in Sardis

3 "To the angel[b] of the church in Sardis
write:

These are the words of him who
holds the seven spirits[c][h] of God and the
seven stars.[i] I know your deeds;[j] you
have a reputation of being alive, but
you are dead.[k] 2Wake up! Strengthen
what remains and is about to die, for
I have found your deeds unfinished
in the sight of my God. 3Remember,
therefore, what you have received and
heard; hold it fast, and repent.[l] But if
you do not wake up, I will come like a
thief,[m] and you will not know at what
time I will come to you.
4Yet you have a few people in Sardis who have not soiled their clothes.[n]
They will walk with me, dressed in
white,[o] for they are worthy. 5The one
who is victorious will, like them, be
dressed in white. I will never blot out
the name of that person from the book
of life,[p] but will acknowledge that
name before my Father[q] and his angels. 6Whoever has ears, let them hear[r]
what the Spirit says to the churches.

To the Church in Philadelphia

7"To the angel of the church in Philadelphia[s] write:

These are the words of him who is
holy and true,[t] who holds the key of
David.[u] What he opens no one can
shut, and what he shuts no one can
open. 8I know your deeds. See, I have
placed before you an open door[v] that
no one can shut. I know that you have
little strength, yet you have kept my
word and have not denied my name.[w]
9I will make those who are of the synagogue of Satan,[x] who claim to be Jews
though they are not, but are liars—I
will make them come and fall down at
your feet[y] and acknowledge that I have
loved you.[z] 10Since you have kept my

a 27 Psalm 2:9 *b* *1* Or *messenger*; also in verses 7 and 14 *c* *1* That is, the sevenfold Spirit

2:24 ***Satan's so-called deep secrets.*** The deep things may be secrets known by those initiated into the things of the devil. When the apostle Paul addressed the subject of walking in the Light (the revelation of Christ), he not only said not to participate in the unfruitful deeds of darkness, but he went on to say that it is disgraceful even to speak of those things done in secret (Eph. 5:11–12).

2:28 ***the morning star.*** The morning star is Christ Himself in 22:16. For the believer, Christ's presence is the light in the dark and difficult times. The morning star (the planet Venus, which can be seen in the sky just before sunrise) is the harbinger of day; it is easy to see how the return of Christ could be paralleled with the morning star. When Satan is referred to as the morning star, that is thought to be a description of what Satan was like before he rebelled (Is. 14:12).

3:1 ***Sardis.*** Sardis, located 30 miles southeast of Thyatira, had been the capital of Lydia. The worship of the Roman Caesar and Artemis, goddess of fertility, were active here.

3:3 ***like a thief.*** Christ's warning that He will come as unexpectedly as a thief echoes His repeated emphasis in Matthew 24:36–25:13 (see also 16:15).

3:5 ***book of life.*** The book of life is the list of the redeemed (20:11–15; Ex. 32:32–33).

3:7 ***Philadelphia.*** Philadelphia, which means "brotherly love" in Greek, was a small city located about 40 miles southeast of Sardis. Its location, vineyards, and wine production made it wealthy and commercially important. ***key of David.*** This key represents the authority of the One who opens and shuts the door in the Davidic kingdom (Is. 22:22), a prerogative that is Christ's as the rightful "son of David" (Matt. 1:1).

3:8 ***an open door that no one can shut.*** The door, in this context, seems to be entrance into heaven and "the new Jerusalem" (v. 12; chs. 21–22).

3:10 ***keep you from the hour of trial.*** Christ's promise to keep the believers from the hour of trial is often considered a promise that He will remove

2:20 [v] 1Ki 16:31; 21:25; 2Ki 9:7 **2:21** [w] Ro 2:4 [x] Rev 9:20 **2:22** [y] Rev 17:2; 18:9 **2:23** [z] 1Sa 16:7; Jer 11:20; Ac 1:24; Ro 8:27 **2:24** [a] Ac 15:28 **2:25** [b] Rev 3:11 **2:26** [c] Ps 2:8; Rev 3:21 **2:27** [d] Rev 12:5 [e] Isa 30:14; Jer 19:11 **2:28** [f] Rev 22:16 **2:29** [g] ver 7 **3:1** [h] Rev 1:4 [i] Rev 1:16 [j] Rev 2:2 [k] 1Ti 5:6 **3:3** [l] Rev 2:5 [m] 2Pe 3:10 **3:4** [n] Jude 23 [o] Rev 4:4; 6:11; 7:9, 13, 14 **3:5** [p] Rev 20:12 [q] Mt 10:32 **3:6** [r] Rev 2:7 **3:7** [s] Rev 1:11 [t] 1Jn 5:20 [u] Isa 22:22; Mt 16:19 **3:8** [v] Ac 14:27 [w] Rev 2:13 **3:9** [x] Rev 2:9 [y] Isa 49:23 [z] Isa 43:4

command to endure patiently, I will
also keep you[a] from the hour of trial
that is going to come on the whole world
to test[b] the inhabitants of the earth.[c]
11I am coming soon. Hold on to what
you have,[d] so that no one will take
your crown.[e] 12The one who is victorious I will make a pillar[f] in the temple of my God. Never again will they
leave it. I will write on them the name
of my God[g] and the name of the city of
my God, the new Jerusalem,[h] which is
coming down out of heaven from my
God; and I will also write on them my
new name. 13Whoever has ears, let
them hear what the Spirit says to the
churches.

To the Church in Laodicea

14"To the angel of the church in Laodicea
write:

These are the words of the Amen,
the faithful and true witness, the ruler
of God's creation.[i] 15I know your deeds,
that you are neither cold nor hot.[j] I
wish you were either one or the other!
16So, because you are lukewarm—neither hot nor cold—I am about to spit
you out of my mouth. 17You say, 'I am
rich; I have acquired wealth and do not
need a thing.'[k] But you do not realize
that you are wretched, pitiful, poor,
blind and naked. 18I counsel you to buy
from me gold refined in the fire, so you
can become rich; and white clothes to
wear, so you can cover your shameful
nakedness;[l] and salve to put on your
eyes, so you can see.

19Those whom I love I rebuke and
discipline.[m] So be earnest and repent.[n]
20Here I am! I stand at the door[o] and
knock. If anyone hears my voice and
opens the door,[p] I will come in[q] and eat
with that person, and they with me.

21To the one who is victorious, I will
give the right to sit with me on my
throne,[r] just as I was victorious[s] and
sat down with my Father on his throne.
22Whoever has ears, let them hear[t]
what the Spirit says to the churches."

The Throne in Heaven

4 After this I looked, and there before me
was a door standing open in heaven.
And the voice I had first heard speaking
to me like a trumpet[u] said, "Come up here,[v]
and I will show you what must take place
after this."[w] 2At once I was in the Spirit,[x]
and there before me was a throne in heav-
en[y] with someone sitting on it. 3And the
one who sat there had the appearance of
jasper and ruby. A rainbow[z] that shone
like an emerald encircled the throne. 4Sur-
rounding the throne were twenty-four
other thrones, and seated on them were
twenty-four elders.[a] They were dressed
in white[b] and had crowns of gold on their
heads. 5From the throne came flashes of
lightning, rumblings and peals of thunder.[c] In front of the throne, seven lamps[d]
were blazing. These are the seven spirits[a][e]
of God. 6Also in front of the throne there
was what looked like a sea of glass,[f] clear
as crystal.

In the center, around the throne, were
four living creatures,[g] and they were covered with eyes, in front and in back. 7The
first living creature was like a lion, the
second was like an ox, the third had a face
like a man, the fourth was like a flying
eagle.[h] 8Each of the four living creatures
had six wings[i] and was covered with eyes
all around, even under its wings. Day and
night they never stop saying:

"'Holy, holy, holy
is the Lord God Almighty,'[b][j]
who was, and is, and is to come."[k]

9Whenever the living creatures give glory, honor and thanks to him who sits on
the throne[l] and who lives for ever and ever,
10the twenty-four elders[m] fall down before
him[n] who sits on the throne[o] and worship

[a] 5 That is, the sevenfold Spirit [b] 8 Isaiah 6:3

them before the period of unparalleled tribulation (1 Thess. 4:16–18). Others believe that this means that believers will not be removed, but will be protected during the trial. The "hour of trial" is another way of referring to the unparalleled judgment of the "great tribulation" (7:14) predicted in Daniel 12:1 and Matthew 24:21.

3:14 ***Laodicea.*** Laodicea was 45 miles southeast of Philadelphia and 90 miles east of Ephesus. It was a wealthy city with thriving banks, a textile industry, and a medical school. The city was also known for its sparse water supply. All of these characteristics are played upon in Christ's message to the church.

4:4 ***dressed in white ... crowns.*** The white robes point to those who are confirmed in righteousness. The crowns are for those who possess ruling authority, and possibly also indicate that the elders have already been judged and rewarded.

4:6 ***four living creatures.*** These creatures are remarkably similar to the cherubim (angels) that Ezekiel saw close to God's throne (Ezek. 1:4–10).

4:7 ***lion ... ox ... man ... eagle.*** This description recalls the four cherubim in Ezekiel 1:4–10.

4:10 ***lay their crowns before the throne.*** This act symbolizes the willing surrender of their authority in light of the worthiness of God as Creator. Because

3:10 [a] 2Pe 2:9 [b] Rev 2:10 [c] Rev 6:10; 17:8 **3:11** [d] Rev 2:25 [e] Rev 2:10 **3:12** [f] Gal 2:9 [g] Rev 14:1; 22:4 [h] Rev 21:2, 10 **3:14** [i] Col 1:16, 18 **3:15** [j] Ro 12:11 **3:17** [k] Hos 12:8; 1Co 4:8 **3:18** [l] Rev 16:15 **3:19** [m] Pr 3:12; Heb 12:5, 6 [n] Rev 2:5 **3:20** [o] Mt 24:33 [p] Lk 12:36 [q] Jn 14:23 **3:21** [r] Mt 19:28 [s] Rev 5:5 **3:22** [t] Rev 2:7 **4:1** [u] Rev 1:10 [v] Rev 11:12 [w] Rev 1:19 **4:2** [x] Rev 1:10 [y] Isa 6:1; Eze 1:26-28; Da 7:9 **4:3** [z] Eze 1:28 **4:4** [a] Rev 11:16 [b] Rev 3:4, 5 **4:5** [c] Rev 8:5; 16:18 [d] Zec 4:2 [e] Rev 1:4 **4:6** [f] Rev 15:2 [g] Eze 1:5 **4:7** [h] Eze 1:10; 10:14 **4:8** [i] Isa 6:2 [j] Isa 6:3; Rev 1:8 [k] Rev 1:4 **4:9** [l] Ps 47:8 **4:10** [m] ver 4 [n] Rev 5:8, 14 [o] ver 2

him who lives for ever and ever. They lay
their crowns before the throne and say:

11 "You are worthy, our Lord and God,
to receive glory and honor and
power,[p]
for you created all things,
and by your will they were created
and have their being."[q]

The Scroll and the Lamb

5 Then I saw in the right hand of him who
sat on the throne[r] a scroll with writing
on both sides[s] and sealed[t] with seven seals.
2 And I saw a mighty angel proclaiming in
a loud voice, "Who is worthy to break the
seals and open the scroll?" 3 But no one in
heaven or on earth or under the earth could
open the scroll or even look inside it. 4 I wept
and wept because no one was found who
was worthy to open the scroll or look inside.
5 Then one of the elders said to me, "Do not
weep! See, the Lion[u] of the tribe of Judah,
the Root of David,[v] has triumphed. He is
able to open the scroll and its seven seals."
6 Then I saw a Lamb,[w] looking as if it had
been slain, standing at the center of the
throne, encircled by the four living creatures and the elders. The Lamb had seven
horns and seven eyes,[x] which are the seven
spirits[a] of God sent out into all the earth.
7 He went and took the scroll from the right
hand of him who sat on the throne.[y] 8 And
when he had taken it, the four living creatures and the twenty-four elders fell down
before the Lamb. Each one had a harp[z] and
they were holding golden bowls full of incense, which are the prayers[a] of God's people. 9 And they sang a new song, saying:[b]

"You are worthy[c] to take the scroll
and to open its seals,
because you were slain,
and with your blood[d] you purchased[e]
for God
persons from every tribe and
language and people and nation.
10 You have made them to be a kingdom
and priests[f] to serve our God,
and they will reign[b] on the earth."

11 Then I looked and heard the voice of
many angels, numbering thousands upon
thousands, and ten thousand times ten
thousand.[g] They encircled the throne and
the living creatures and the elders. 12 In a
loud voice they were saying:

"Worthy is the Lamb, who was
slain,
to receive power and wealth and
wisdom and strength
and honor and glory and praise!"[h]

13 Then I heard every creature in heaven
and on earth and under the earth[i] and on
the sea, and all that is in them, saying:

"To him who sits on the throne and to
the Lamb[j]
be praise and honor and glory and
power,
for ever and ever!"[k]

14 The four living creatures said, "Amen,"[l]
and the elders fell down and worshiped.[m]

The Seals

6 I watched as the Lamb[n] opened the first
of the seven seals.[o] Then I heard one of
the four living creatures[p] say in a voice like
thunder,[q] "Come!" 2 I looked, and there before me was a white horse![r] Its rider held
a bow, and he was given a crown,[s] and he
rode out as a conqueror bent on conquest.[t]
3 When the Lamb opened the second
seal, I heard the second living creature[u]
say, "Come!" 4 Then another horse came
out, a fiery red one.[v] Its rider was given
power to take peace from the earth[w] and
to make people kill each other. To him was
given a large sword.
5 When the Lamb opened the third seal,
I heard the third living creature[x] say,
"Come!" I looked, and there before me was
a black horse![y] Its rider was holding a pair
of scales in his hand. 6 Then I heard what
sounded like a voice among the four living
creatures,[z] saying, "Two pounds[c] of wheat
for a day's wages,[d] and six pounds[e] of barley for a day's wages,[d] and do not damage[a]
the oil and the wine!"

[a] *6* That is, the sevenfold Spirit [b] *10* Some manuscripts *they reign* [c] *6* Or about 1 kilogram [d] *6* Greek *a denarius* [e] *6* Or about 3 kilograms

no one but God can create, He alone should be worshiped and recognized as sovereign.

5:1 *a scroll.* The scroll apparently contains the judgments and redemption seen in later chapters. It may also be the book that was sealed in Daniel 12:4. There appears to be an allusion to the scroll the Lord handed Ezekiel 2:9–10. ***sealed with seven seals.*** A scroll cannot be unrolled until the seals have all been opened.

5:5 *Lion of the tribe of Judah, the Root of David.* Both of these titles are messianic titles (Gen. 49:8–10, Is. 11:1,10).

5:7 *took the scroll.* The Lamb taking the book from the Father demonstrates that judgment and authority over the earth is committed to the Son (Dan. 7:13–14). The scroll may be the same one that was sealed in Daniel 12:9.

6:2 *white horse . . . a conqueror.* Because the first rider is on a white horse and is conquering, some take it to be Christ (19:11). If so, His full conquest is considerably delayed (19:11—20:6). Another view is that this is a spirit of conquest and delusion (Matt. 23:3–6). The bow suggests that the rider is a warrior. The crown suggests that he is a ruler.

4:11 [p] Rev 5:12 [q] Rev 10:6 **5:1** [r] ver 7, 13 [s] Eze 2:9, 10 [t] Isa 29:11; Da 12:4 **5:5** [u] Ge 49:9 [v] Isa 11:1, 10; Ro 15:12; Rev 22:16 **5:6** [w] Jn 1:29 [x] Zec 4:10 **5:7** [y] ver 1 **5:8** [z] Rev 14:2 [a] Ps 141:2 **5:9** [b] Ps 40:3 [c] Rev 4:11 [d] Heb 9:12 [e] 1Co 6:20 **5:10** [f] 1Pe 2:5 **5:11** [g] Da 7:10; Heb 12:22 **5:12** [h] Rev 4:11 **5:13** [i] ver 3; Php 2:10 [j] Rev 6:16 [k] 1Ch 29:11 **5:14** [l] Rev 4:9 [m] Rev 4:10; 19:4 **6:1** [n] Rev 5:6 [o] Rev 5:1 [p] Rev 4:6, 7 [q] Rev 14:2; 19:6 **6:2** [r] Zec 6:3; Rev 19:11 [s] Zec 6:11; Rev 14:14 [t] Ps 45:4 **6:3** [u] Rev 4:7 **6:4** [v] Zec 6:2 [w] Mt 10:34 **6:5** [x] Rev 4:7 [y] Zec 6:2 **6:6** [z] Rev 4:6, 7 [a] Rev 9:4

7 When the Lamb opened the fourth seal,
I heard the voice of the fourth living creature[b] say, "Come!" 8 I looked, and there
before me was a pale horse![c] Its rider was
named Death, and Hades[d] was following
close behind him. They were given power
over a fourth of the earth to kill by sword,
famine and plague, and by the wild beasts
of the earth.[e]
9 When he opened the fifth seal, I saw under the altar[f] the souls of those who had
been slain[g] because of the word of God and
the testimony they had maintained. 10 They
called out in a loud voice, "How long,[h] Sovereign Lord, holy and true,[i] until you judge
the inhabitants of the earth and avenge our
blood?"[j] 11 Then each of them was given a
white robe,[k] and they were told to wait a
little longer, until the full number of their
fellow servants, their brothers and sisters,[a]
were killed just as they had been.[l]
12 I watched as he opened the sixth seal.
There was a great earthquake.[m] The sun
turned black[n] like sackcloth made of goat
hair, the whole moon turned blood red,
13 and the stars in the sky fell to earth,[o] as
figs drop from a fig tree[p] when shaken by a
strong wind. 14 The heavens receded like a
scroll being rolled up, and every mountain
and island was removed from its place.[q]
15 Then the kings of the earth, the princes, the generals, the rich, the mighty, and
everyone else, both slave and free, hid in
caves and among the rocks of the mountains.[r] 16 They called to the mountains and
the rocks, "Fall on us[s] and hide us[b] from
the face of him who sits on the throne and
from the wrath of the Lamb! 17 For the great
day[t] of their[c] wrath has come, and who can
withstand it?"[u]

144,000 Sealed

7 After this I saw four angels standing at
the four corners of the earth, holding
back the four winds[v] of the earth to prevent
any wind from blowing on the land or on
the sea or on any tree. 2 Then I saw another
angel coming up from the east, having the
seal of the living God. He called out in a
loud voice to the four angels who had been
given power to harm the land and the sea:
3 "Do not harm[w] the land or the sea or the
trees until we put a seal on the foreheads[x]
of the servants of our God." 4 Then I heard
the number[y] of those who were sealed:
144,000[z] from all the tribes of Israel.

5 From the tribe of Judah 12,000 were
sealed,
from the tribe of Reuben 12,000,
from the tribe of Gad 12,000,
6 from the tribe of Asher 12,000,
from the tribe of Naphtali 12,000,
from the tribe of Manasseh 12,000,
7 from the tribe of Simeon 12,000,
from the tribe of Levi 12,000,
from the tribe of Issachar 12,000,
8 from the tribe of Zebulun 12,000,
from the tribe of Joseph 12,000,
from the tribe of Benjamin 12,000.

---

[a] *11* The Greek word for *brothers and sisters* (*adelphoi*) refers here to believers, both men and women, as part of God's family; also in 12:10; 19:10.
[b] *16* See Hosea 10:8.
[c] *17* Some manuscripts *his*

6:8 *pale.* The color of the pale horse is the color of a corpse. It is fitting that this pale horse is ridden by a figure named "Death." This fourth judgment is the inevitable consequence of the first three. ***sword . . . famine . . . plague.*** These trials are the same means that God used to bring the nation of Israel to repentance (1 Kin. 8:33–39; 1 Chr. 21:12), and in Revelation a godly remnant does arise as a result of these judgments (7:3–8).

6:9 *under the altar.* Sacrificial blood was poured beside the base of the altar in the temple (Ex. 29:12).

6:12–13 *sun . . . moon . . . stars.* The effects of the great earthquake on the sun, moon, and stars are worded similarly to Matthew 24:29, placing these events in proximity to the coming of the Son of Man (Matt. 24:30).

6:14 *receded . . . rolled up.* When the sky is rolled back, the people on earth can see "him who sits on the throne" (v. 16). They will suddenly see that God is not far away or nonexistent and they will have to be accountable to Him.

6:17 *who can withstand it?* This rhetorical question is answered in the surrounding context. The unbelievers, no matter how strong, cannot stand. Those who are protected by the Lord are enabled to stand, whether on earth (7:1–8) or in God's presence in heaven (7:9–17).

7:3 *seal.* The seal was a mark of ownership or authority. In ancient times a seal was fixed to a document by pressing a carved stamp or signet into a lump of clay or wax at the point where the document was opened and closed.

7:4 *144,000.* Those sealed are all the children of Israel, fulfilling the promise that when the "full number of the Gentiles has come in" all Israel will be saved (Rom. 11:25–27).

7:5–8 *Judah.* Judah is placed first in this list of the Israelite tribes because Christ, the Messiah, is the "Lion of the tribe of Judah" (5:5; Gen. 49:8–10). ***Reuben.*** Reuben is next as Jacob's firstborn (Gen. 49:3–4). Dan and Ephraim are omitted, perhaps because of their gross idolatry during the period of the judges, demonstrated by the incident in the territory of Dan (Judg. 18). ***Joseph.*** Joseph and his son Manasseh are both included, bringing the number of tribes to twelve.

6:7 [b] Rev 4:7 **6:8** [c] Zec 6:3 [d] Hos 13:14 [e] Jer 15:2,3; Eze 5:12,17 **6:9** [f] Rev 14:18; 16:7 [g] Rev 20:4 **6:10** [h] Zec 1:12 [i] Rev 3:7 [j] Rev 19:2 **6:11** [k] Rev 3:4 [l] Heb 11:40 **6:12** [m] Rev 16:18 [n] Mt 24:29 **6:13** [o] Mt 24:29; Rev 8:10; 9:1 [p] Isa 34:4 **6:14** [q] Jer 4:24; Rev 16:20 **6:15** [r] Isa 2:10,19,21 **6:16** [s] Hos 10:8; Lk 23:30 **6:17** [t] Zep 1:14,15; Rev 16:14 [u] Ps 76:7 **7:1** [v] Da 7:2 **7:3** [w] Rev 6:6 [x] Eze 9:4; Rev 22:4 **7:4** [y] Rev 9:16 [z] Rev 14:1,3

The Great Multitude in White Robes

9 After this I looked, and there before me
was a great multitude that no one could
count, from every nation, tribe, people and
language,[a] standing before the throne[b] and
before the Lamb. They were wearing white
robes and were holding palm branches in
their hands. 10 And they cried out in a loud
voice:

> "Salvation belongs to our God,[c]
> who sits on the throne,
> and to the Lamb."

11 All the angels were standing around the
throne and around the elders[d] and the four
living creatures.[e] They fell down on their
faces[f] before the throne and worshiped
God, 12 saying:

> "Amen!
> Praise and glory
> and wisdom and thanks and honor
> and power and strength
> be to our God for ever and ever.
> Amen!"[g]

13 Then one of the elders asked me,
"These in white robes—who are they, and
where did they come from?"
14 I answered, "Sir, you know."
And he said, "These are they who have
come out of the great tribulation; they have
washed their robes[h] and made them white
in the blood of the Lamb.[i] 15 Therefore,

> "they are before the throne of God[j]
> and serve him[k] day and night in his temple;[l]
> and he who sits on the throne
> will shelter them with his presence.[m]
> 16 'Never again will they hunger;
> never again will they thirst.
> The sun will not beat down on them,'*[a]*
> nor any scorching heat.[n]
> 17 For the Lamb at the center of the throne
> will be their shepherd;[o]
> 'he will lead them to springs of living water.'*[a]*
> 'And God will wipe away every tear
> from their eyes.'*[b]*[p]

The Seventh Seal and the Golden Censer

8 When he opened the seventh seal,[q]
there was silence in heaven for about
half an hour.
2 And I saw the seven angels[r] who stand
before God, and seven trumpets were given to them.
3 Another angel,[s] who had a golden censer, came and stood at the altar. He was
given much incense to offer, with the
prayers of all God's people,[t] on the golden
altar[u] in front of the throne. 4 The smoke
of the incense, together with the prayers of
God's people, went up before God[v] from the
angel's hand. 5 Then the angel took the censer, filled it with fire from the altar,[w] and
hurled it on the earth; and there came peals
of thunder,[x] rumblings, flashes of lightning
and an earthquake.[y]

The Trumpets

6 Then the seven angels who had the seven trumpets[z] prepared to sound them.
7 The first angel sounded his trumpet,
and there came hail and fire[a] mixed with
blood, and it was hurled down on the earth.
A third[b] of the earth was burned up, a third
of the trees were burned up, and all the
green grass was burned up.[c]
8 The second angel sounded his trumpet,
and something like a huge mountain,[d] all
ablaze, was thrown into the sea. A third[e] of
the sea turned into blood,[f] 9 a third[g] of the
living creatures in the sea died, and a third
of the ships were destroyed.
10 The third angel sounded his trumpet,
and a great star, blazing like a torch, fell
from the sky[h] on a third of the rivers and
on the springs of water[i]— 11 the name of the
star is Wormwood.[c] A third[j] of the waters
turned bitter, and many people died from
the waters that had become bitter.[k]
12 The fourth angel sounded his trumpet,

a *16,17* Isaiah 49:10 *b* *17* Isaiah 25:8
c *11* Wormwood is a bitter substance.

7:14 *great tribulation.* This vast multitude has come out of the great tribulation, referring to "the hour of trial that is going to come on the whole world" (3:10). In view of the great loss of life during this time period, martyrdom is most likely the means of their escape. Tribulation was already being experienced by the church in John's day (2:10; Acts 14:22). However, the great tribulation, predicted in Daniel 12:1, will be of an intensity "unequaled from the beginning of the world until now—and never to be equaled again" (Matt. 24:21).

8:1 *seventh seal.* When the seventh seal is broken, the book can finally be opened.

8:7 *hail ... fire ... blood.* This blend of destruction and horror sounds like a combination of the first and seventh plagues of God upon Egypt (Ex. 7:19–20; 9:22–25).

8:11 *Wormwood.* Wormwood is a plant found in the Middle East, known for its bitter taste. Here and elsewhere (Lam. 3:19) the term is figurative for bitterness. Normally wormwood is not poisonous, but the plague of the third trumpet involves effects far more potent than the taste of this bitter plant: many men die from the water.

7:9 [a] Rev 5:9 [b] ver 15 **7:10** [c] Ps 3:8; Rev 12:10; 19:1 **7:11** [d] Rev 4:4 [e] Rev 4:6 [f] Rev 4:10 **7:12** [g] Rev 5:12-14 **7:14** [h] Rev 22:14 [i] Heb 9:14; 1Jn 1:7 **7:15** [j] ver 9 [k] Rev 22:3 [l] Rev 11:19 [m] Isa 4:5,6; Rev 21:3 **7:16** [n] Isa 49:10 **7:17** [o] Ps 23:1; Jn 10:11 [p] Isa 25:8; Rev 21:4 **8:1** [q] Rev 6:1 **8:2** [r] ver 6-13; Rev 9:1, 13; 11:15 **8:3** [s] Rev 7:2 [t] Rev 5:8 [u] Ex 30:1-6; Heb 9:4; Rev 9:13 **8:4** [v] Ps 141:2 **8:5** [w] Lev 16:12, 13 [x] Rev 4:5 [y] Rev 6:12 **8:6** [z] ver 2 **8:7** [a] Eze 38:22 [b] ver 7-12; Rev 9:15, 18; 12:4 [c] Rev 9:4 **8:8** [d] Jer 51:25 [e] ver 7 [f] Rev 16:3 **8:9** [g] ver 7 **8:10** [h] Isa 14:12; Rev 6:13; 9:1 [i] Rev 14:7; 16:4 **8:11** [j] ver 7 [k] Jer 9:15; 23:15

and a third of the sun was struck, a third of
the moon, and a third of the stars, so that a
third[l] of them turned dark.[m] A third of the
day was without light, and also a third of
the night.
13 As I watched, I heard an eagle that was
flying in midair[n] call out in a loud voice:
"Woe! Woe! Woe[o] to the inhabitants of the
earth, because of the trumpet blasts about
to be sounded by the other three angels!"
9 The fifth angel sounded his trumpet,
and I saw a star that had fallen from the
sky to the earth.[p] The star was given the
key to the shaft of the Abyss.[q] 2 When he
opened the Abyss, smoke rose from it like
the smoke from a gigantic furnace.[r] The
sun and sky were darkened[s] by the smoke
from the Abyss. 3 And out of the smoke locusts[t] came down on the earth and were
given power like that of scorpions[u] of the
earth. 4 They were told not to harm[v] the
grass of the earth or any plant or tree,[w]
but only those people who did not have the
seal of God on their foreheads.[x] 5 They were
not allowed to kill them but only to torture
them for five months.[y] And the agony they
suffered was like that of the sting of a scorpion[z] when it strikes. 6 During those days
people will seek death but will not find it;
they will long to die, but death will elude
them.[a]
7 The locusts looked like horses prepared
for battle.[b] On their heads they wore something like crowns of gold, and their faces
resembled human faces.[c] 8 Their hair was
like women's hair, and their teeth were like
lions' teeth.[d] 9 They had breastplates like
breastplates of iron, and the sound of their
wings was like the thundering of many
horses and chariots rushing into battle.[e]
10 They had tails with stingers, like scorpions, and in their tails they had power to
torment people for five months.[f] 11 They had
as king over them the angel of the Abyss,[g]
whose name in Hebrew is Abaddon and in
Greek is Apollyon (that is, Destroyer).
12 The first woe is past; two other woes
are yet to come.[h]
13 The sixth angel sounded his trumpet,
and I heard a voice coming from the four
horns[i] of the golden altar that is before
God.[j] 14 It said to the sixth angel who had
the trumpet, "Release the four angels who
are bound at the great river Euphrates."[k]
15 And the four angels who had been kept
ready for this very hour and day and month
and year were released to kill a third of
mankind.[l] 16 The number of the mounted
troops was twice ten thousand times ten
thousand. I heard their number.[m]
17 The horses and riders I saw in my vision looked like this: Their breastplates
were fiery red, dark blue, and yellow as
sulfur. The heads of the horses resembled
the heads of lions, and out of their mouths[n]
came fire, smoke and sulfur.[o] 18 A third of
mankind was killed[p] by the three plagues
of fire, smoke and sulfur[q] that came out of
their mouths. 19 The power of the horses
was in their mouths and in their tails; for
their tails were like snakes, having heads
with which they inflict injury.
20 The rest of mankind who were not
killed by these plagues still did not repent
of the work of their hands;[r] they did not
stop worshiping demons,[s] and idols of gold,
silver, bronze, stone and wood—idols that
cannot see or hear or walk.[t] 21 Nor did they
repent[u] of their murders, their magic arts,[v]
their sexual immorality[w] or their thefts.

8:13 ***Woe! Woe! Woe.*** The "woes" refer to the impact of the three remaining trumpet judgments on the unbelieving inhabitants of the earth. The first woe is the fifth trumpet (9:12); the second woe is the sixth trumpet (11:14). The third woe comes quickly and may be the same as the seventh trumpet (11:15–19), although that is not stated. If not, the final woe may be focused on Babylon, the great harlot, because of the climactic use of "woe" in 18:10, 16, and 19.

9:1 ***star that had fallen from the sky.*** The star may be a demon (v. 11), Satan himself (12:9), or an angel serving God (20:1). ***Abyss.*** The Abyss is the interim jail for some demons (Luke 8:31). It is also the place of origin of the beast (11:7; 17:8). Furthermore, it will be the place where Satan will be imprisoned during Christ's reign (20:2–3).

9:3 ***locusts.*** Locusts, or grasshoppers, were greatly feared in agricultural societies because they devoured crops. In Exodus 10:12–15, a plague of locusts wiped out what was left of Egypt's crops. Joel 1:2 tells of an invasion of locusts that the Lord used to judge unrepentant Judah, which was a foreshadowing of the day of the Lord. ***scorpions.*** Scorpions sting with their tails, causing great pain and even death (v. 10).

9:11 ***angel of the Abyss.*** The angel of the Abyss is demonic and controls the demonic locusts (3:10). If this angel serves God, this is another instance where the activity of Satan or his demons is under the Lord's sovereign control (2 Cor. 12:7,9).

9:14 ***great river Euphrates.*** This river is the eastern boundary of the land promised to Abraham for his descendants (Gen. 15:18), as well as the geographic area from which powerful enemies like Assyria and Babylon came to invade Israel (Is. 8:5–8). It may represent the seat of Satan's former victory (in the Garden of Eden).

9:18 ***A third of mankind.*** A third of mankind could number in the billions. Coupled with the former destruction of one-fourth of humanity (6:8), over one-half of the world's population will have been killed.

8:12 [l] ver 7 [m] Ex 10:21-23; Rev 6:12, 13 **8:13** [n] Rev 14:6; 19:17 [o] Rev 9:12; 11:14 **9:1** [p] Rev 8:10 [q] ver 2, 11; Lk 8:31 **9:2** [r] Ge 19:28; Ex 19:18 [s] Joel 2:2, 10 **9:3** [t] Ex 10:12-15 [u] ver 5, 10 **9:4** [v] Rev 6:6 [w] Rev 8:7 [x] Rev 7:2, 3 **9:5** [y] ver 10 [z] ver 3 **9:6** [a] Job 3:21; Jer 8:3; Rev 6:16 **9:7** [b] Joel 2:4 [c] Da 7:8 **9:8** [d] Joel 1:6 **9:9** [e] Joel 2:5 **9:10** [f] ver 3, 5, 19 **9:11** [g] ver 1, 2 **9:12** [h] Rev 8:13 **9:13** [i] Ex 30:1-3 [j] Rev 8:3 **9:14** [k] Rev 16:12 **9:15** [l] ver 18 **9:16** [m] Rev 5:11; 7:4 **9:17** [n] Rev 11:5 [o] ver 18 **9:18** [p] ver 15 [q] ver 17 **9:20** [r] Dt 31:29 [s] 1Co 10:20 [t] Ps 115:4-7; 135:15-17; Da 5:23 **9:21** [u] Rev 2:21 [v] Rev 18:23 [w] Rev 17:2, 5

The Angel and the Little Scroll

10 Then I saw another mighty angel[x]
coming down from heaven. He was
robed in a cloud, with a rainbow above his
head; his face was like the sun,[y] and his
legs were like fiery pillars.[z] 2He was holding a little scroll, which lay open in his
hand. He planted his right foot on the sea
and his left foot on the land, 3and he gave
a loud shout like the roar of a lion. When
he shouted, the voices of the seven thunders[a] spoke. 4And when the seven thunders
spoke, I was about to write; but I heard a
voice from heaven say, "Seal up what the
seven thunders have said and do not write
it down."[b]
5Then the angel I had seen standing on
the sea and on the land raised his right
hand to heaven.[c] 6And he swore by him
who lives for ever and ever, who created
the heavens and all that is in them, the
earth and all that is in it, and the sea and
all that is in it,[d] and said, "There will be no
more delay![e] 7But in the days when the seventh angel is about to sound his trumpet,
the mystery[f] of God will be accomplished,
just as he announced to his servants the
prophets."
8Then the voice that I had heard from
heaven[g] spoke to me once more: "Go, take
the scroll that lies open in the hand of the
angel who is standing on the sea and on
the land."
9So I went to the angel and asked him
to give me the little scroll. He said to me,
"Take it and eat it. It will turn your stomach sour, but 'in your mouth it will be as
sweet as honey.'[a][h] 10I took the little scroll
from the angel's hand and ate it. It tasted
as sweet as honey in my mouth, but when
I had eaten it, my stomach turned sour.
11Then I was told, "You must prophesy[i]
again about many peoples, nations, languages and kings."

The Two Witnesses

11 I was given a reed like a measuring
rod[j] and was told, "Go and measure
the temple of God and the altar, with its
worshipers. 2But exclude the outer court;[k]
do not measure it, because it has been giv-
en to the Gentiles.[l] They will trample on
the holy city[m] for 42 months.[n] 3And I will
appoint my two witnesses,[o] and they will
prophesy for 1,260 days, clothed in sackcloth."[p] 4They are "the two olive trees"[q]
and the two lampstands, and "they stand
before the Lord of the earth."[b][r] 5If anyone
tries to harm them, fire comes from their
mouths and devours their enemies.[s] This
is how anyone who wants to harm them
must die.[t] 6They have power to shut up the
heavens so that it will not rain during the
time they are prophesying; and they have
power to turn the waters into blood[u] and to
strike the earth with every kind of plague
as often as they want.
7Now when they have finished their testimony, the beast[v] that comes up from the
Abyss will attack them,[w] and overpower

a 9 Ezek. 3:3 *b* 4 See Zech. 4:3,11,14.

10:1 *mighty angel.* This mighty angel could be the same "mighty angel" of 5:2 or the angel who "had great authority" in 18:1. It is unlikely that this is Michael, who is referred to by name elsewhere (12:7; Dan. 12:1) or Christ, since He is never called an angel in the New Testament. Furthermore, unlike Christ, this angel comes to earth before the time of tribulation is over.
10:2 *little scroll.* The little scroll is not the same as the book that was unsealed in 6:1 – 8:1. It is more like the scroll eaten by Ezekiel (Ezek. 2:9 – 3:3), although this scroll caused John's stomach to turn sour (vv. 9 – 10), not just his spirit (Ezek. 3:14).
10:10 *sweet ... sour.* The Word of God is always sweet, but the soberness of the judgments and what this will mean to the "peoples, nations, languages and kings," to whom John must prophesy is enough to turn John's stomach. It is a terrible thing to contemplate the fate of those who refuse to repent (9:21).
11:1 *reed like a measuring rod.* John's measuring rod is much like that used by Ezekiel (Ezek. 40:3 – 5) in his vision of measuring the temple.
11:3 *two witnesses.* The two unnamed witnesses are strikingly similar to Elijah (vv. 5 – 6; 1 Kin. 17; Mal. 4:5) and Moses (v. 6; Ex. 7 – 11), who appeared together with Christ on the Mount of Transfiguration (Luke 9:29 – 32). ***1,260.*** 42 months (v. 2) is the same length of time as 1,260 days (12:6). Almost certainly "a time, times and half a time" (12:14) is also a period of three and a half years made up of 42 thirty-day months. These expressions draw from the prophecies in Daniel (Dan. 12:6 – 7,11 – 12). ***sackcloth.*** Sackcloth is a sign of mourning.
11:4 *two olive trees ... two lampstands.* The witnesses are described as olive trees and lampstands, linking them to the vision in Zechariah 4 of "the two who are anointed to serve the Lord of all the earth" (Zech. 4:14). The passage in Zechariah refers to Zerubbabel and Joshua the priest. But the overarching principle for these and all other witnesses for the Lord is that their testimony to the truth is "Not by might nor by power, but by my Spirit" (Zech. 4:6).
11:6 *will not rain ... waters ... blood ... plague.* The power to prevent rain identifies the witnesses with Elijah (James 5:17), and turning the water into blood and striking the earth with plague is reminiscent of Moses in Egypt (Ex. 7:11 – 21).
11:7 *Abyss.* The beast, who emerges as the satanically empowered world ruler (13; 17), comes from the bottomless pit, as did the demonic locust plague of the fifth trumpet (9:1 – 10).

10:1 [x] Rev 5:2 [y] Mt 17:2; Rev 1:16 [z] Rev 1:15
10:3 [a] Rev 4:5 **10:4** [b] Da 8:26; 12:4,9; Rev 22:10
10:5 [c] Da 12:7 **10:6** [d] Rev 4:11; 14:7 [e] Rev 16:17
10:7 [f] Ro 16:25 **10:8** [g] ver 4 **10:9** [h] Jer 15:16; Eze 2:8-3:3 **10:11** [i] Eze 37:4,9 **11:1** [j] Eze 40:3; Rev 21:15 **11:2** [k] Eze 40:17,20 [l] Lk 21:24 [m] Rev 21:2 [n] Da 7:25; Rev 13:5 **11:3** [o] Rev 1:5 [p] Ge 37:34
11:4 [q] Ps 52:8; Jer 11:16; Zec 4:3,11 [r] Zec 4:14
11:5 [s] 2Ki 1:10; Jer 5:14 [t] Nu 16:29,35 **11:6** [u] Ex 7:17,19
11:7 [v] Rev 13:1-4 [w] Da 7:21

and kill them. 8Their bodies will lie in the
public square of the great city—which is
figuratively called Sodom[x] and Egypt—
where also their Lord was crucified.[y] 9For
three and a half days some from every people, tribe, language and nation will gaze on
their bodies and refuse them burial.[z] 10The
inhabitants of the earth[a] will gloat over
them and will celebrate by sending each
other gifts,[b] because these two prophets
had tormented those who live on the earth.
11But after the three and a half days the
breath[a] of life from God entered them,[c]
and they stood on their feet, and terror
struck those who saw them. 12Then they
heard a loud voice from heaven saying to
them, "Come up here."[d] And they went up
to heaven in a cloud,[e] while their enemies
looked on.
13At that very hour there was a severe
earthquake[f] and a tenth of the city collapsed. Seven thousand people were killed
in the earthquake, and the survivors were
terrified and gave glory[g] to the God of
heaven.[h]
14The second woe has passed; the third
woe is coming soon.[i]

The Seventh Trumpet

15The seventh angel sounded his trumpet,[j] and there were loud voices[k] in heaven,
which said:

"The kingdom of the world has become
the kingdom of our Lord and of his
Messiah,[l]
and he will reign for ever and
ever."[m]

16And the twenty-four elders,[n] who were
seated on their thrones before God, fell on
their faces and worshiped God, 17saying:

"We give thanks to you, Lord God
Almighty,[o]
the One who is and who was,
because you have taken your great
power
and have begun to reign.[p]
18The nations were angry,[q]
and your wrath has come.
The time has come for judging the dead,
and for rewarding your servants the
prophets[r]
and your people who revere your name,
both great and small[s]—
and for destroying those who destroy
the earth."

19Then God's temple[t] in heaven was
opened, and within his temple was seen
the ark of his covenant. And there came
flashes of lightning, rumblings, peals of
thunder, an earthquake and a severe hailstorm.[u]

The Woman and the Dragon

12 A great sign appeared in heaven: a
woman clothed with the sun, with
the moon under her feet and a crown of
twelve stars on her head. 2She was pregnant and cried out in pain[v] as she was
about to give birth. 3Then another sign appeared in heaven: an enormous red dragon
with seven heads and ten horns[w] and sev-
en crowns[x] on its heads. 4Its tail swept a

[a] *11* Or *Spirit* (see Ezek. 37:5,14)

11:8 *great city.* The great city in Revelation is often Babylon (14:8), which possibly represents Rome (1 Pet. 5:13). But the further description "where also their Lord was crucified" seems to refer to Jerusalem. ***Sodom and Egypt.*** Sodom is the prototype for the moral degeneration of this great city (Gen. 19) and Egypt was the prototype for its rampant idolatry.
11:14 *second woe.* The second woe includes the sixth trumpet (9:12–21) and a second interlude (10:1–11:13). ***third woe.*** The third woe is apparently the seventh trumpet (vv. 15–19), since it "is coming soon" and 8:13 relates the woes to the last three blasts of the trumpet. The final woe may extend further since the word "woe" recurs in 12:12.
11:17–18 *We give thanks to you.* The 24 elders (4:10–11; 5:8–10) praise God's power and wrath, and the corresponding distribution of reward and judgment. This stanza of heavenly thanksgiving seems to reflect on the fulfillment of the great messianic prophecy in Psalm 2.
11:19 *ark of his covenant.* The ark of the covenant made by Moses disappeared at the time of the Babylonian captivity (2 Chr. 36:18–19). The ark represented God's presence, leadership, and protection of Israel (Num. 10:33–36; Josh. 3:3,15–17).
12:1 *woman clothed with the sun.* The woman is the nation Israel. To Israel belongs the covenant and the promises. If Satan can make even one of those promises fail, he will have "won." This is why the dragon stands over the woman in such a predatory manner (v. 4).
12:3 *enormous red dragon.* The sign of the dragon is interpreted in verse 9 as Satan, who first appeared in Scripture as the serpent in the garden of Eden (Gen. 3). The imagery is in keeping with Old Testament and extrabiblical usage (Is. 27:1). ***seven heads ... ten horns ... seven crowns.*** The dragon with the seven heads and ten horns refers to Satan and the empire over which he rules during the course of time. The seven heads, ten horns, and seven crowns refer to Satan's brilliance, power, and glory as "god of this age" (2 Cor. 4:4). This description is almost identical to that of the beast from the sea in 13:1.
12:4 *a third of the stars.* This image may refer to the rebellion of a third of the angelic host following Satan. ***devour her child.*** The attempt of the dragon to devour the newborn Christ Child reveals that the

11:8 [x] Isa 1:9 [y] Heb 13:12 **11:9** [z] Ps 79:2,3
11:10 [a] Rev 3:10 [b] Est 9:19,22 **11:11** [c] Eze 37:5,9,10,14
11:12 [d] Rev 4:1 [e] 2Ki 2:11; Ac 1:9 **11:13** [f] Rev 6:12
[g] Rev 14:7 [h] Rev 16:11 **11:14** [i] Rev 8:13
11:15 [j] Rev 10:7 [k] Rev 16:17; 19:1 [l] Rev 12:10 [m] Da 2:44; 7:14,27 **11:16** [n] Rev 4:4 **11:17** [o] Rev 1:8 [p] Rev 19:6
11:18 [q] Ps 2:1 [r] Rev 10:7 [s] Rev 19:5 **11:19** [t] Rev 15:5,8
[u] Rev 16:21 **12:2** [v] Gal 4:19 **12:3** [w] Da 7:7,20; Rev 13:1
[x] Rev 19:12

third[y] of the stars out of the sky and flung
them to the earth.[z] The dragon stood in
front of the woman who was about to give
birth, so that it might devour her child[a] the
moment he was born. 5She gave birth to a
son, a male child, who "will rule all the nations with an iron scepter."[ab] And her child
was snatched up to God and to his throne.
6The woman fled into the wilderness to a
place prepared for her by God, where she
might be taken care of for 1,260 days.[c]

7Then war broke out in heaven. Michael
and his angels fought against the dragon,[d]
and the dragon and his angels fought back.
8But he was not strong enough, and they
lost their place in heaven. 9The great dragon was hurled down—that ancient serpent[e] called the devil,[f] or Satan, who leads
the whole world astray.[g] He was hurled to
the earth,[h] and his angels with him.

10Then I heard a loud voice in heaven[i]
say:

"Now have come the salvation and the power
and the kingdom of our God,
and the authority of his Messiah.
For the accuser of our brothers and sisters,[j]
who accuses them before our God day and night,
has been hurled down.
11 They triumphed over him
by the blood of the Lamb[k]
and by the word of their testimony;[l]
they did not love their lives so much
as to shrink from death.[m]
12 Therefore rejoice, you heavens[n]
and you who dwell in them!
But woe[o] to the earth and the sea,[p]
because the devil has gone down to you!
He is filled with fury,
because he knows that his time is short."

13When the dragon[q] saw that he had
been hurled to the earth, he pursued the
woman who had given birth to the male
child.[r] 14The woman was given the two
wings of a great eagle,[s] so that she might
fly to the place prepared for her in the wilderness, where she would be taken care of
for a time, times and half a time,[t] out of the
serpent's reach. 15Then from his mouth the
serpent spewed water like a river, to overtake the woman and sweep her away with
the torrent. 16But the earth helped the woman by opening its mouth and swallowing
the river that the dragon had spewed out of
his mouth. 17Then the dragon was enraged
at the woman and went off to wage war[u]
against the rest of her offspring[v]—those
who keep God's commands[w] and hold fast
their testimony about Jesus.[x]

The Beast out of the Sea

13 The dragon[b] stood on the shore of the
sea. And I saw a beast coming out of
the sea.[y] It had ten horns and seven heads,[z]
with ten crowns on its horns, and on each
head a blasphemous name.[a] 2The beast I

a 5 Psalm 2:9 *b* 1 Some manuscripts *And I*

strategy of Herod to kill the baby Jesus (Matt. 2:3–16) was satanically inspired.

12:5 *male child, who will rule.* The male child who will rule with a rod of iron is the messianic figure of Psalms 2:8–9; however, there is no earthly rule over all nations at this point. From the perspective of this heavenly scene, the Child-ruler is soon caught up to the throne of God, apparently referring to the ascension of Christ (Acts 1:9).

12:6 *1,260 days.* The detailed way in which this same length of time is expressed ("a time, times and half a time," v. 14), suggests half of a literal seven-year tribulation period (Dan. 9:27).

12:7–8 *Michael.* Michael is an archangel (Jude 9). According to Daniel 12:1, he is a special guardian angel for the nation of Israel. Apparently he commands an army of angels. Michael and the heavenly forces are victorious, making heaven off-limits to Satan and his demons. (In Job 1 and 1 Kings 22:22 it is clear that at one time Satan did have access to heaven.)

12:9 *to the earth.* The devil's expulsion from heaven to the earth means that this world becomes his base of operations, and that his anger is vented toward the remaining inhabitants of the earth (v. 12). It is likely that the end times will be the greatest period of spiritual warfare (Eph. 6:10–18) in history.

12:11 *blood of the Lamb . . . word of their testimony . . . did not love their lives.* The heavenly defeat of Satan (vv. 7–9) is followed by reference to his earthly setbacks, including the crucifixion of Christ, the verbal witness of believers, and the martyrdom of some of the believers. The fact that these witnesses were willing to die for their testimony showed that they knew that Christ had defeated death.

12:14 *a time.* A "time" probably equals one year, so the period of protection here is three and a half years, which corresponds to the length of the two witnesses' testimony in 11:3. It is also equivalent to the period of the beast's authority ("forty-two months" in 13:5), which includes his ability to "wage war against God's holy people and to conquer them" (13:7; Ps. 122:7; Dan. 7:25).

12:17 *the rest of her offspring.* The rest of the children are believers in Christ.

13:1 *a blasphemous name.* The blasphemous name may be the common claim of ancient Roman emperors to be divine, or blasphemy against the name of the true God (vv. 5–6) as Daniel predicted of the willful king during the tribulation period (Dan. 11:36).

13:1–2 *beast.* The parallel to the four beasts (especially the fourth) in Daniel 7, and the explanation

12:4 [y] Rev 8:7 [z] Da 8:10 [a] Mt 2:16 **12:5** [b] Ps 2:9; Rev 2:27
12:6 [c] Rev 11:2 **12:7** [d] ver 3 **12:9** [e] Ge 3:1-7 [f] Mt 25:41
[g] Rev 20:3, 8, 10 [h] Lk 10:18; Jn 12:31 **12:10** [i] Rev 11:15
[j] Job 1:9-11; Zec 3:1 **12:11** [k] Rev 7:14 [l] Rev 6:9 [m] Lk 14:26
12:12 [n] Ps 96:11; Isa 49:13; Rev 18:20 [o] Rev 8:13 [p] Rev 10:6
12:13 [q] ver 3 [r] ver 5 **12:14** [s] Ex 19:4 [t] Da 7:25
12:17 [u] Rev 11:7 [v] Ge 3:15 [w] Rev 14:12 [x] Rev 1:2
13:1 [y] Da 7:1-6; Rev 15:2 [z] Rev 12:3 [a] Da 11:36; Rev 17:3

saw resembled a leopard,[b] but had feet like
those of a bear[c] and a mouth like that of a
lion.[d] The dragon gave the beast his power
and his throne and great authority.[e] **3**One of
the heads of the beast seemed to have had a
fatal wound, but the fatal wound had been
healed.[f] The whole world was filled with
wonder[g] and followed the beast. **4**People
worshiped the dragon because he had giv-
en authority to the beast, and they also worshiped the beast and asked, "Who is like[h]
the beast? Who can wage war against it?"
5The beast was given a mouth to utter
proud words and blasphemies[i] and to exercise its authority for forty-two months.[j] **6**It
opened its mouth to blaspheme God, and
to slander his name and his dwelling place
and those who live in heaven.[k] **7**It was given
power to wage war[l] against God's holy people and to conquer them. And it was giv-
en authority over every tribe, people, language and nation.[m] **8**All inhabitants of the
earth[n] will worship the beast—all whose
names have not been written in the Lamb's
book of life,[o] the Lamb who was slain from
the creation of the world.[a][p]
9Whoever has ears, let them hear.[q]

10"If anyone is to go into captivity,
into captivity they will go.
If anyone is to be killed[b] with the
sword,
with the sword they will be killed."[c][r]

This calls for patient endurance and faithfulness[s] on the part of God's people.[t]

The Beast out of the Earth

11Then I saw a second beast, coming out
of the earth. It had two horns like a lamb,
but it spoke like a dragon. **12**It exercised
all the authority[u] of the first beast on its
behalf,[v] and made the earth and its inhabitants worship the first beast,[w] whose fatal wound had been healed.[x] **13**And it performed great signs,[y] even causing fire to
come down from heaven[z] to the earth in full
view of the people. **14**Because of the signs[a]
it was given power to perform on behalf of
the first beast, it deceived[b] the inhabitants
of the earth. It ordered them to set up an image in honor of the beast who was wounded by the sword and yet lived. **15**The second
beast was given power to give breath to the
image of the first beast, so that the image
could speak and cause all who refused to
worship the image to be killed.[c] **16**It also
forced all people, great and small,[d] rich
and poor, free and slave, to receive a mark
on their right hands or on their foreheads,[e]
17so that they could not buy or sell unless
they had the mark,[f] which is the name
of the beast or the number of its name.[g]
18This calls for wisdom.[h] Let the person
who has insight calculate the number of
the beast, for it is the number of a man.[d][i]
That number is 666.

[a] 8 Or *written from the creation of the world in the book of life belonging to the Lamb who was slain* [b] 10 Some manuscripts *anyone kills* [c] 10 Jer. 15:2 [d] 18 Or *is humanity's number*

of the beast given in 17:8–11 make it seem that the beast symbolizes both a revived Roman Empire, which exercises universal authority, and a specific ruler, whom John calls the antichrist (1 John 2:18).

13:3 ***fatal wound.*** The apparently fatal wound that was healed is a satanic attempt to mimic the wounds of Christ from His crucifixion, which Christ still carries after the resurrection. This is part of the fulfillment of the prophecy of the "power through signs and wonders that serve the lie, and all the ways that wickedness deceives" that accompany the "lawless one" (2 Thess. 2:8–12).

13:4 ***worshiped the dragon . . . and . . . the beast.*** Any false worship or idolatry is ultimately demonic and satanic (1 Cor. 10:20–22).

13:5 ***forty-two months.*** Forty-two months is the duration of the beast's worldwide supremacy, in keeping with the prophecy of Daniel 7:25.

13:9 ***Whoever has ears, let them hear.*** This phrase is used frequently in the Bible. It seems to imply that what has just been said has a wider context, or a significant present application. The statement is not just for future reference. Therefore, widespread spiritual delusion and blasphemy, as well as persecution and martyrdom, should not surprise believers at any point in history.

13:11 ***a second beast.*** This beast's actions described in verses 12–17 make it virtually certain that he is the false prophet spoken of in 16:13; 19:20; 20:10. The two beasts may symbolize the intermingling of religious power and of secular, political power during the Roman period and during the last days. ***lamb.*** This is the only place in Revelation where "lamb" does not refer to Christ. The lamb with two horns is an emblem of Jewish worship and religious authority.

13:12–15 ***great signs.*** Calling fire from heaven and giving speech to the image of the first beast are persuasive signs of power. These signs are similar to those performed by the two witnesses (11:5–6). The performance of great signs and the power of Satan is part of the mass deception prophesied by Paul in 2 Thessalonians 2:8–12.

13:16 ***to receive a mark.*** The mark is some sort of identifiable proof of ownership and loyalty, an evil counterfeit of the seal on the foreheads of the servants of God (7:3; 14:1).

13:18 ***Let the person who has insight calculate . . . 666.*** No one knows exactly what this means. It is the number of the beast, and the number of a man, so the beast is merely a man, not a god. We can be sure that this "man's number" will someday be understood in relation to the number 666, and that when the people who are living at the time of

13:2 [b] Da 7:6 [c] Da 7:5 [d] Da 7:4 [e] Rev 16:10 **13:3** [f] ver 12, 14 [g] Rev 17:8 **13:4** [h] Ex 15:11 **13:5** [i] Da 7:8, 11, 20, 25; 11:36; 2Th 2:4 [j] Rev 11:2 **13:6** [k] Rev 12:12 **13:7** [l] Da 7:21; Rev 11:7 [m] Rev 5:9 **13:8** [n] Rev 3:10 [o] Rev 3:5; 20:12 [p] Mt 25:34 **13:9** [q] Rev 2:7 **13:10** [r] Jer 15:2; 43:11 [s] Heb 6:12 [t] Rev 14:12 **13:12** [u] ver 4 [v] ver 14 [w] Rev 14:9, 11 [x] ver 3 **13:13** [y] Mt 24:24 [z] 1Ki 18:38; Rev 20:9 **13:14** [a] 2Th 2:9, 10 [b] Rev 12:9 **13:15** [c] Da 3:3-6 **13:16** [d] Rev 19:5 [e] Rev 14:9 **13:17** [f] Rev 14:9 [g] Rev 14:11; 15:2 **13:18** [h] Rev 17:9 [i] Rev 15:2; 21:17

The Lamb and the 144,000

14 Then I looked, and there before me
was the Lamb,[j] standing on Mount
Zion,[k] and with him 144,000[l] who had his
name and his Father's name[m] written on
their foreheads. 2And I heard a sound from
heaven like the roar of rushing waters[n]
and like a loud peal of thunder. The sound
I heard was like that of harpists playing
their harps.[o] 3And they sang a new song[p]
before the throne and before the four living creatures and the elders. No one could
learn the song except the 144,000[q] who had
been redeemed from the earth. 4These are
those who did not defile themselves with
women, for they remained virgins.[r] They
follow the Lamb wherever he goes. They
were purchased from among mankind[s]
and offered as firstfruits[t] to God and the
Lamb. 5No lie was found in their mouths;[u]
they are blameless.[v]

The Three Angels

6Then I saw another angel flying in midair,[w] and he had the eternal gospel to proclaim to those who live on the earth[x]—to
every nation, tribe, language and people.[y] 7He said in a loud voice, "Fear God[z]
and give him glory,[a] because the hour of
his judgment has come. Worship him who
made the heavens, the earth, the sea and
the springs of water."[b]
8A second angel followed and said,
"'Fallen! Fallen is Babylon the Great,'[a][c]
which made all the nations drink the mad-
dening wine of her adulteries."[d]
9A third angel followed them and said in
a loud voice: "If anyone worships the beast
and its image[e] and receives its mark on
their forehead or on their hand, 10they, too,
will drink the wine of God's fury,[f] which
has been poured full strength into the cup
of his wrath.[g] They will be tormented with
burning sulfur in the presence of the holy
angels and of the Lamb. 11And the smoke
of their torment will rise for ever and ever.[h]
There will be no rest day or night for those
who worship the beast and its image, or for
anyone who receives the mark of its name."
12This calls for patient endurance on the
part of the people of God[i] who keep his
commands and remain faithful to Jesus.
13Then I heard a voice from heaven say,
"Write this: Blessed are the dead who die in
the Lord[j] from now on."
"Yes," says the Spirit, "they will rest
from their labor, for their deeds will follow
them."

Harvesting the Earth and Trampling the Winepress

14I looked, and there before me was a
white cloud, and seated on the cloud was
one like a son of man[b][k] with a crown[l] of
gold on his head and a sharp sickle in his
hand. 15Then another angel came out of
the temple and called in a loud voice to him
who was sitting on the cloud, "Take your
sickle[m] and reap, because the time to reap
has come, for the harvest[n] of the earth is
ripe." 16So he who was seated on the cloud
swung his sickle over the earth, and the
earth was harvested.
17Another angel came out of the temple
in heaven, and he too had a sharp sickle.
18Still another angel, who had charge of
the fire, came from the altar and called in a
loud voice to him who had the sharp sickle,
"Take your sharp sickle and gather the clusters of grapes from the earth's vine, because
its grapes are ripe." 19The angel swung his
sickle on the earth, gathered its grapes
and threw them into the great winepress
of God's wrath.[o] 20They were trampled in
the winepress[p] outside the city,[q] and blood
flowed out of the press, rising as high as the
horses' bridles for a distance of 1,600 stadia.[c]

a 8 Isaiah 21:9 *b* 14 See Daniel 7:13. *c* 20 That is, about 180 miles or about 300 kilometers

the fulfillment of the prophecies in this book need to understand this clearly, the Lord will make it plain. In the meantime, the warning is enough for all that will hear.

14:5 *they are blameless.* This statement is not a reference to sinless perfection, but it is stating that they are considered pure before God. They have been sealed by God because of their belief in Christ (v. 1; 7:4).

14:6 – 7 *angel ... eternal gospel.* The angel who preaches the gospel to "every nation, tribe, language and people" helps to fulfill God's promise that the gospel "will be preached in the whole world as a testimony to all nations" (Matt. 24:14) before Christ returns. The word "gospel," which literally means "good news," is used in Revelation only once. Even at this late stage in God's judgment He continues to offer everlasting life to the world (John 3:16). The gospel message at this point beseeches unbelievers to fear God and give glory to Him, and to escape the hour of His judgment.

14:8 *Babylon.* Babylon is first mentioned in Revelation here, and it becomes the focus of God's judgment in the following sections (chs. 16 – 18).

14:13 *Blessed.* "Blessed" signals the second of seven beatitudes in Revelation (1:3; 16:15; 19:9; 20:6; 22:7,14). Six of the seven are clustered in the latter third of the book, perhaps as promises to encourage exemplary Christian response in the extremely difficult circumstances of the end times.

14:16 *swung his sickle.* The power of the Son of Man (Jesus Christ) is shown in that, with one swing

14:1 [j] Rev 5:6 [k] Ps 2:6 [l] Rev 7:4 [m] Rev 3:12
14:2 [n] Rev 1:15 [o] Rev 5:8 **14:3** [p] Rev 5:9 [q] ver 1
14:4 [r] 2Co 11:2; Rev 3:4 [s] Rev 5:9 [t] Jas 1:18
14:5 [u] Ps 32:2; Zep 3:13 [v] Eph 5:27 **14:6** [w] Rev 8:13 [x] Rev 3:10 [y] Rev 13:7 **14:7** [z] Rev 15:4 [a] Rev 11:13 [b] Rev 8:10 **14:8** [c] Isa 21:9; Jer 51:8 [d] Rev 17:2, 4; 18:3, 9
14:9 [e] Rev 13:14 **14:10** [f] Isa 51:17; Jer 25:15 [g] Rev 18:6
14:11 [h] Isa 34:10; Rev 19:3 **14:12** [i] Rev 13:10
14:13 [j] 1Co 15:18; 1Th 4:16 **14:14** [k] Da 7:13; Rev 1:13 [l] Rev 6:2 **14:15** [m] Joel 3:13 [n] Jer 51:33
14:19 [o] Rev 19:15 **14:20** [p] Isa 63:3 [q] Heb 13:12; Rev 11:8

Seven Angels With Seven Plagues

15 I saw in heaven another great and marvelous sign:[r] seven angels[s] with the seven last plagues[t]—last, because with them God's wrath is completed.
2And I saw what looked like a sea of glass[u] glowing with fire and, standing beside the sea, those who had been victorious over the beast and its image[v] and over the number of its name. They held harps given them by God
3and sang the song of God's servant Moses[w] and of the Lamb:

"Great and marvelous are your deeds,[x]
Lord God Almighty.
Just and true are your ways,[y]
King of the nations.[a]
4Who will not fear you, Lord,[z]
and bring glory to your name?
For you alone are holy.
All nations will come
and worship before you,[a]
for your righteous acts have been revealed."[b]

5After this I looked, and I saw in heaven the temple[b]—that is, the tabernacle of the covenant law[c]—and it was opened.
6Out of the temple[d] came the seven angels with the seven plagues.[e] They were dressed in clean, shining linen and wore golden sashes around their chests.[f]
7Then one of the four living creatures[g] gave to the seven angels seven golden bowls filled with the wrath of God, who lives for ever and ever.
8And the temple was filled with smoke[h] from the glory of God and from his power, and no one could enter the temple[i] until the seven plagues of the seven angels were completed.

The Seven Bowls of God's Wrath

16 Then I heard a loud voice from the temple saying to the seven angels,[j] "Go, pour out the seven bowls of God's wrath on the earth."
2The first angel went and poured out his bowl on the land,[k] and ugly, festering sores[l] broke out on the people who had the mark of the beast and worshiped its image.[m]
3The second angel poured out his bowl on the sea, and it turned into blood like that of a dead person, and every living thing in the sea died.[n]
4The third angel poured out his bowl on the rivers and springs of water,[o] and they became blood.[p]
5Then I heard the angel in charge of the waters say:

"You are just in these judgments,[q]
O Holy One,[r]
you who are and who were;[s]
6for they have shed the blood of your holy people and your prophets,
and you have given them blood to drink[t] as they deserve."

7And I heard the altar[u] respond:

"Yes, Lord God Almighty,
true and just are your judgments."[v]

8The fourth angel[w] poured out his bowl on the sun, and the sun was allowed to scorch people with fire.[x]
9They were seared by the intense heat and they cursed the name of God,[y] who had control over these plagues, but they refused to repent[z] and glorify him.[a]

---

[a] 3 Some manuscripts *ages* [b] 3,4 Phrases in this song are drawn from Psalm 111:2,3; Deut. 32:4; Jer. 10:7; Psalms 86:9; 98:2.

---

of His sickle, the harvest of the earth is reaped. This pictures the events of chapters 16–19 as parts of one rapid succession of judgment, which is experienced by the inhabitants of the entire world.

15:1 *another great and marvelous sign.* The previous sign was about the woman clothed with the sun (12:1). This sign is "great and marvelous" because it deals with the seven last plagues sent by the Lord. The plagues, the "bowls of God's wrath" (16:1), are much stronger and more widespread than the trumpet judgments in 8:2–11:19. The wrath of God is complete with the seven last plagues (15:1–19:5). They are immediately followed by the second coming and the marriage supper of the Lamb (19:6–21).

15:3 *song of ... Moses.* The song of Moses is a reference to Exodus 15:1–18 in which Israel celebrated its deliverance from Pharaoh's army (Ex. 14). This song was sung by Jews in their Sabbath gatherings, as well as by early Christians at Easter. ***and of the Lamb.*** The song of the Lamb celebrates the finished work of God, when all of His righteous acts have been revealed, from creation to atonement to judgment.

16:6 *holy people.* These holy people are those who are set apart because of their relationship with Jesus Christ. ***prophets.*** The prophets are God's spokesmen. Probably this passage is referring both to the holy people and prophets (11:3–18) who have been killed and persecuted during the tribulation as well as those from past history. Jesus referred to the pattern of killing prophets (Matt. 23:35) when He spoke to the Pharisees of the coming judgment.

16:8 *fourth ... bowl.* The fourth bowl and the fourth trumpet both affect the sun, but in the bowl judgment the sun's heat is intensified instead of diminished.

16:9–10 *refused to repent.* They cannot argue against the existence or power of God, but even so they will not repent and give glory to God. The good news of Christ is still in effect even just before His return (19:11–21), though it is apparently rejected by all unbelievers who are still alive.

15:1 [r] Rev 12:1,3 [s] Rev 16:1 [t] Lev 26:21 **15:2** [u] Rev 4:6 [v] Rev 13:14 **15:3** [w] Ex 15:1; Dt 32:4 [x] Ps 111:2 [y] Ps 145:17 **15:4** [z] Jer 10:7 [a] Isa 66:23 **15:5** [b] Rev 11:19 [c] Nu 1:50 **15:6** [d] Rev 14:15 [e] ver 1 [f] Rev 1:13 **15:7** [g] Rev 4:6 **15:8** [h] Isa 6:4 [i] Ex 40:34,35; 1Ki 8:10,11; 2Ch 5:13,14 **16:1** [j] Rev 15:1 **16:2** [k] Rev 8:7 [l] Ex 9:9-11 [m] Rev 13:15-17 **16:3** [n] Ex 7:17-21; Rev 8:8,9 **16:4** [o] Rev 8:10 [p] Ex 7:17-21 **16:5** [q] Rev 15:3 [r] Rev 15:4 [s] Rev 1:4 **16:6** [t] Isa 49:26; Rev 17:6 **16:7** [u] Rev 6:9 [v] Rev 15:3; 19:2 **16:8** [w] Rev 8:12 [x] Rev 14:18 **16:9** [y] ver 11,21 [z] Rev 2:21 [a] Rev 11:13

10The fifth angel poured out his bowl
on the throne of the beast,[b] and its kingdom was plunged into darkness.[c] People gnawed their tongues in agony 11and
cursed[d] the God of heaven[e] because of their
pains and their sores,[f] but they refused to
repent of what they had done.[g]
12The sixth angel poured out his bowl
on the great river Euphrates,[h] and its water was dried up to prepare the way for the
kings from the East.[i] 13Then I saw three
impure spirits that looked like frogs; they
came out of the mouth of the dragon,[j] out
of the mouth of the beast[k] and out of the
mouth of the false prophet.[l] 14They are demonic spirits[m] that perform signs, and they
go out to the kings of the whole world, to
gather them for the battle[n] on the great day
of God Almighty.

15"Look, I come like a thief! Blessed is
the one who stays awake[o] and remains
clothed, so as not to go naked and be
shamefully exposed."

16Then they gathered the kings together to
the place that in Hebrew[p] is called Armageddon.[q]
17The seventh angel poured out his bowl
into the air,[r] and out of the temple[s] came a
loud voice[t] from the throne, saying, "It is
done!"[u] 18Then there came flashes of lightning, rumblings, peals of thunder[v] and a
severe earthquake.[w] No earthquake like it
has ever occurred since mankind has been
on earth,[x] so tremendous was the quake.
19The great city[y] split into three parts, and
the cities of the nations collapsed. God remembered[z] Babylon the Great[a] and gave
her the cup filled with the wine of the fury
of his wrath.[b] 20Every island fled away and
the mountains could not be found.[c] 21From
the sky huge hailstones,[d] each weighing
about a hundred pounds,[a] fell on people.
And they cursed God on account of the
plague of hail,[e] because the plague was so
terrible.

Babylon, the Prostitute on the Beast

17 One of the seven angels[f] who had the
seven bowls[g] came and said to me,
"Come, I will show you the punishment[h]
of the great prostitute,[i] who sits by many
waters.[j] 2With her the kings of the earth
committed adultery, and the inhabitants of
the earth were intoxicated with the wine of
her adulteries."[k]
3Then the angel carried me away in
the Spirit into a wilderness.[l] There I saw
a woman sitting on a scarlet beast that
was covered with blasphemous names[m]
and had seven heads and ten horns.[n] 4The
woman was dressed in purple and scarlet, and was glittering with gold, precious
stones and pearls.[o] She held a golden cup[p]
in her hand, filled with abominable things
and the filth of her adulteries. 5The name
written on her forehead was a mystery:

BABYLON THE GREAT[q]
THE MOTHER OF PROSTITUTES
AND OF THE ABOMINATIONS OF THE EARTH.

6I saw that the woman was drunk with the
blood of God's holy people,[r] the blood of
those who bore testimony to Jesus.

---

[a] *21* Or about 45 kilograms

16:12 ***sixth ... bowl.*** The sixth bowl involves the Euphrates River, as does the sixth trumpet (9:14). Both judgments deal with demonically inspired military forces. The army of two hundred million (9:16) will kill a third of all humankind (9:18); the army of verses 12–14 will do battle against God (19:19–21).
16:13–14 ***impure spirits ... go out to the kings.*** The kings of the earth recoil in fear before the judgment of the Lamb (6:15–16), yet because of the deceptive words of the demons, they are willing to wage war against God. The difference seems to be their confidence in the power of the beast, since they reason, "Who can wage war against it?" (13:4). ***great day of God.*** The battle of that great day takes place at Armageddon (Mount of Megiddo) (v. 16; 19:17–21).
16:15 ***Blessed.*** This is the third of seven beatitudes in Revelation (see note on 14:13). Jesus warned believers to be vigilant because of the unexpected timing of His return (Matt. 24:43–44). The warning to watch is a reminder of the parable of the ten virgins (Matt. 25:1–13): "Therefore keep watch, because you do not know the day or the hour."
16:17 ***It is done!*** The seventh bowl is the climax of all of Revelation's judgments. This is God's final act of judgment before Christ comes.
16:19 ***Babylon.*** Babylon may refer to the rebuilt ancient city, or it may be a symbolic name for Rome (17:9). It may also be a way of referring to any proud human society that attempts to exist apart from God. Babylon's classic manifestations of rebellion against God are the Tower of Babel (Gen. 11:1–9) and the Babylonian Empire under Nebuchadnezzar (Dan. 4:30).
17:1 ***punishment of the great prostitute.*** Babylon is called "the prostitute" in verses 1,5,16, and 19:2. Her habitual immorality was introduced in 14:8, as was her imminent and well-deserved judgment. Both the kings of the earth and the inhabitants of the earth are seduced into committing spiritual adultery with Babylon. The indication is that she made them drunk with power, material possessions, false worship, and pride. The wine of Babylon's immorality (14:8) is judged forcefully and finally by God in the "wine of the fury of his wrath" (16:19).

16:10 [b] Rev 13:2 [c] Rev 9:2 **16:11** [d] ver 9,21 [e] Rev 11:13 [f] ver 2 [g] Rev 2:21 **16:12** [h] Rev 9:14 [i] Isa 41:2 **16:13** [j] Rev 12:3 [k] Rev 13:1 [l] Rev 19:20 **16:14** [m] 1Ti 4:1 [n] Rev 17:14 **16:15** [o] Lk 12:37 **16:16** [p] Rev 9:11 [q] 2Ki 23:29,30 **16:17** [r] Eph 2:2 [s] Rev 14:15 [t] Rev 11:15 [u] Rev 21:6 **16:18** [v] Rev 4:5 [w] Rev 6:12 [x] Da 12:1 **16:19** [y] Rev 17:18 [z] Rev 18:5 [a] Rev 14:8 [b] Rev 14:10 **16:20** [c] Rev 6:14 **16:21** [d] Rev 11:19 [e] Ex 9:23-25 **17:1** [f] Rev 15:1 [g] Rev 21:9 [h] Rev 16:19 [i] Rev 19:2 [j] Jer 51:13 **17:2** [k] Rev 14:8; 18:3 **17:3** [l] Rev 12:6,14 [m] Rev 13:1 [n] Rev 12:3 **17:4** [o] Rev 18:16 [p] Jer 51:7; Rev 18:6 **17:5** [q] Rev 14:8 **17:6** [r] Rev 18:24

When I saw her, I was greatly astonished. 7Then the angel said to me: “Why
are you astonished? I will explain to you
the mystery[s] of the woman and of the beast
she rides, which has the seven heads and
ten horns.[t] 8The beast, which you saw,
once was, now is not, and yet will come
up out of the Abyss and go to its destruction.[u] The inhabitants of the earth[v] whose
names have not been written in the book
of life[w] from the creation of the world will
be astonished[x] when they see the beast,
because it once was, now is not, and yet
will come.
9“This calls for a mind with wisdom.[y]
The seven heads are seven hills on which
the woman sits. 10They are also seven
kings. Five have fallen, one is, the other
has not yet come; but when he does come,
he must remain for only a little while. 11The
beast who once was, and now is not,[z] is an
eighth king. He belongs to the seven and is
going to his destruction.
12“The ten horns[a] you saw are ten kings
who have not yet received a kingdom, but
who for one hour[b] will receive authority as
kings along with the beast. 13They have one
purpose and will give their power and authority to the beast.[c] 14They will wage war[d]
against the Lamb, but the Lamb will triumph over them because he is Lord of lords
and King of kings[e]—and with him will be
his called, chosen[f] and faithful followers.”
15Then the angel said to me, “The waters[g] you saw, where the prostitute sits, are
peoples, multitudes, nations and languages.[h] 16The beast and the ten horns you saw
will hate the prostitute. They will bring her
to ruin[i] and leave her naked;[j] they will eat
her flesh[k] and burn her with fire.[l] 17For God
has put it into their hearts to accomplish
his purpose by agreeing to hand over to
the beast their royal authority, until God’s
words are fulfilled.[m] 18The woman you saw
is the great city[n] that rules over the kings
of the earth.”

Lament Over Fallen Babylon

18 After this I saw another angel[o] coming down from heaven.[p] He had great
authority, and the earth was illuminated
by his splendor.[q] 2With a mighty voice he
shouted:

> “ ‘Fallen! Fallen is Babylon the
> Great!’[a][r]
> She has become a dwelling for
> demons
> and a haunt for every impure
> spirit,
> a haunt for every unclean bird,
> a haunt for every unclean and
> detestable animal.[s]
> 3For all the nations have drunk
> the maddening wine of her
> adulteries.[t]
> The kings of the earth committed
> adultery with her,[u]
> and the merchants of the earth
> grew rich[v] from her excessive
> luxuries.”[w]

a 2 Isaiah 21:9

17:9 *seven hills.* Most interpreters understand this as a reference to the seven hills along the Tiber River, a well-known designation of the city of Rome.
17:10 *Five have fallen.* The five that have fallen would be past kingdoms, perhaps Egypt, Assyria, Babylon, Medo-Persia, and Greece. ***one is.*** The Roman Empire was the current power at the time of this writing. ***not yet come.*** People speculate that the future kingdom may be a revived Roman Empire.
17:11 *an eighth king ... belongs to the seven.* The beast is related to the seventh king, but also has a separate identity. It seems that the eighth world empire may be some form of a revived Roman Empire over which the antichrist establishes the imperial authority of a dictator. He will overcome three horns, or nations (Dan. 7:20), and will claim universal authority.
17:12 *one hour.* The time frame for these events may coincide with 16:14, in which the preparations for the battle at Armageddon are described.
17:14 *wage war against the Lamb.* The Lamb (Christ) will easily overcome the ten kings at His second coming (19:19–21). The beast and his forces are allowed by God to “wage war against God’s holy people and to conquer them” (13:7). Many of those whom the beast defeated and even killed are now numbered in the conquering army of the Lamb. The Lord’s army is composed of the called, chosen, and faithful, probably the heavenly soldiers of 19:14.
17:16–17 *ten horns ... will hate the prostitute.* Since this description is similar to God’s judgment on Babylon in 18:8, it seems that the Lord uses the forces of the beast as His instrument of judgment on the kingdom of antichrist (ch. 18) before they themselves are destroyed (19:19–21). With the advent of the beast as a supreme ruler given to self-deification (Dan. 11:36; Matt. 24:15; 2 Thess. 2), Satan has originated an entirely new order. This order is so radically different from the great harlot (vv. 1–6) that the beast, or perhaps the political aspect of Babylon, turns upon and destroys the religious aspect of Babylon.
17:18 *the great city.* The woman in John’s vision is the great city Babylon (16:19), yet she is also the ancient “mother of prostitutes” (v. 5). The satanic influence of this city over the world’s leaders has continued from Babel through Babylon to Rome (vv. 9–10), its classic manifestation in the first century A.D.

17:7 [s] ver 5 [t] ver 3 **17:8** [u] Rev 13:10 [v] Rev 3:10 [w] Rev 13:8 [x] Rev 13:3 **17:9** [y] Rev 13:18 **17:11** [z] ver 8 **17:12** [a] Rev 12:3 [b] Rev 18:10, 17, 19 **17:13** [c] ver 17 **17:14** [d] Rev 16:14 [e] 1Ti 6:15; Rev 19:16 [f] Mt 22:14 **17:15** [g] Isa 8:7 [h] Rev 13:7 **17:16** [i] Rev 18:17, 19 [j] Eze 16:37, 39 [k] Rev 19:18 [l] Rev 18:8 **17:17** [m] Rev 10:7 **17:18** [n] Rev 16:19 **18:1** [o] Rev 17:1 [p] Rev 10:1 [q] Eze 43:2 **18:2** [r] Rev 14:8 [s] Isa 13:21, 22; Jer 50:39 **18:3** [t] Rev 14:8 [u] Rev 17:2 [v] Eze 27:9-25 [w] ver 7, 9

Warning to Escape Babylon's Judgment

4Then I heard another voice from heav-
en say:

"'Come out of her, my people,'[a][x]
so that you will not share in her sins,
so that you will not receive any of her plagues;
5for her sins are piled up to heaven,[y]
and God has remembered[z] her crimes.
6Give back to her as she has given;
pay her back[a] double for what she has done.
Pour her a double portion from her own cup.[b]
7Give her as much torment and grief
as the glory and luxury she gave herself.[c]
In her heart she boasts,
'I sit enthroned as queen.
I am not a widow;[b]
I will never mourn.'[d]
8Therefore in one day[e] her plagues will overtake her:
death, mourning and famine.
She will be consumed by fire,[f]
for mighty is the Lord God who judges her.

Threefold Woe Over Babylon's Fall

9"When the kings of the earth who committed adultery with her[g] and shared her
luxury see the smoke of her burning,[h] they
will weep and mourn over her.[i] 10Terrified
at her torment, they will stand far off[j] and
cry:

"'Woe! Woe to you, great city,[k]
you mighty city of Babylon!
In one hour[l] your doom has come!'

11"The merchants[m] of the earth will
weep and mourn over her because no one
buys their cargoes anymore[n]— 12cargoes
of gold, silver, precious stones and pearls;
fine linen, purple, silk and scarlet cloth;
every sort of citron wood, and articles of
every kind made of ivory, costly wood,
bronze, iron and marble;[o] 13cargoes of cinnamon and spice, of incense, myrrh and
frankincense, of wine and olive oil, of fine
flour and wheat; cattle and sheep; horses
and carriages; and human beings sold as
slaves.[p]
14"They will say, 'The fruit you longed
for is gone from you. All your luxury and
splendor have vanished, never to be recovered.' 15The merchants who sold these
things and gained their wealth from her[q]
will stand far off, terrified at her torment.
They will weep and mourn[r] 16and cry out:

"'Woe! Woe to you, great city,
dressed in fine linen, purple and scarlet,
and glittering with gold, precious stones and pearls![s]
17In one hour[t] such great wealth has been brought to ruin!'[u]

"Every sea captain, and all who travel by
ship, the sailors, and all who earn their living from the sea,[v] will stand far off. 18When
they see the smoke of her burning, they
will exclaim, 'Was there ever a city like
this great city?'[w] 19They will throw dust on
their heads,[x] and with weeping and mourning cry out:

"'Woe! Woe to you, great city,
where all who had ships on the sea
became rich through her wealth!
In one hour she has been brought to ruin!'[y]
20"Rejoice over her, you heavens![z]
Rejoice, you people of God!
Rejoice, apostles and prophets!
For God has judged her
with the judgment she imposed on you."[a]

The Finality of Babylon's Doom

21Then a mighty angel[b] picked up a boul-
der the size of a large millstone and threw
it into the sea,[c] and said:

"With such violence
the great city of Babylon will be thrown down,
never to be found again.

a 4 Jer. 51:45 *b* 7 See Isaiah 47:7,8.

18:4 *Come out.* The command echoes Isaiah 52:11 and especially Jeremiah 51:45, prophecies proclaimed at a time when the Babylonian Empire was ripe for judgment.

18:9–19 *weep and mourn over her.* This section is framed like an ancient lament and is especially similar in content to Ezekiel's lament over the destruction of Tyre (Ezek. 27).

18:20 *Rejoice ... you heavens ... people of God ... apostles and prophets.* This call to rejoice is a compressed introduction to the longer praise hymn in 19:1–5. Judgment for killing God's prophets is mentioned in 16:6, but this is the only place in Revelation other than 21:14 where Christ's apostles are mentioned. If specific apostles are in mind here, Peter and Paul's deaths at the hands of the state in Rome probably apply. If Babylon is the symbol of all the enemies of God and His people, and not just the Babylonian

18:4 [x] Isa 48:20; Jer 50:8; 2Co 6:17 **18:5** [y] Jer 51:9 [z] Rev 16:19 **18:6** [a] Ps 137:8; Jer 50:15,29 [b] Rev 14:10; 16:19 **18:7** [c] Eze 28:2-8 [d] Isa 47:7,8; Zep 2:15 **18:8** [e] ver 10; Isa 47:9; Jer 50:31,32 [f] Rev 17:16 **18:9** [g] Rev 17:2,4 [h] ver 18; Rev 19:3 [i] Eze 26:17,18 **18:10** [j] ver 15,17 [k] ver 16,19 [l] Rev 17:12 **18:11** [m] Eze 27:27 [n] ver 3 **18:12** [o] Rev 17:4 **18:13** [p] Eze 27:13; 1Ti 1:10 **18:15** [q] ver 3 [r] Eze 27:31 **18:16** [s] Rev 17:4 **18:17** [t] ver 10 [u] Rev 17:16 [v] Eze 27:28-30 **18:18** [w] Eze 27:32; Rev 13:4 **18:19** [x] Jos 7:6; Eze 27:30 [y] Rev 17:16 **18:20** [z] Jer 51:48; Rev 12:12 [a] Rev 19:2 **18:21** [b] Rev 5:2 [c] Jer 51:63

22 The music of harpists and musicians,
pipers and trumpeters,
will never be heard in you again.[d]
No worker of any trade
will ever be found in you again.
The sound of a millstone
will never be heard in you again.[e]
23 The light of a lamp
will never shine in you again.
The voice of bridegroom and bride
will never be heard in you again.[f]
Your merchants were the world's
important people.[g]
By your magic spell[h] all the nations
were led astray.
24 In her was found the blood of
prophets and of God's holy
people,[i]
of all who have been slaughtered on
the earth."[j]

Threefold Hallelujah Over Babylon's Fall

19 After this I heard what sounded like
the roar of a great multitude[k] in heav-
en shouting:

"Hallelujah!
Salvation[l] and glory and power[m] belong
to our God,
2 for true and just are his judgments.
He has condemned the great
prostitute
who corrupted the earth by her
adulteries.
He has avenged on her the blood of his
servants."[n]

3 And again they shouted:

"Hallelujah!
The smoke from her goes up for ever
and ever."[o]

4 The twenty-four elders[p] and the four
living creatures[q] fell down[r] and worshiped
God, who was seated on the throne. And
they cried:

"Amen, Hallelujah!"

5 Then a voice came from the throne, saying:

"Praise our God,
all you his servants,[s]
you who fear him,
both great and small!"[t]

6 Then I heard what sounded like a great
multitude,[u] like the roar of rushing waters
and like loud peals of thunder, shouting:

"Hallelujah!
For our Lord God Almighty reigns.
7 Let us rejoice and be glad
and give him glory!
For the wedding of the Lamb[v] has
come,
and his bride[w] has made herself ready.
8 Fine linen, bright and clean,
was given her to wear."
(Fine linen stands for the righteous acts[x] of
God's holy people.)

9 Then the angel said to me,[y] "Write this:[z]
Blessed are those who are invited to the
wedding supper of the Lamb!"[a] And he
added, "These are the true words of God."[b]
10 At this I fell at his feet to worship him.[c]
But he said to me, "Don't do that! I am a fellow servant with you and with your brothers and sisters who hold to the testimony of
Jesus. Worship God![d] For it is the Spirit of
prophecy who bears testimony to Jesus."[e]

The Heavenly Warrior Defeats the Beast

11 I saw heaven standing open and there
before me was a white horse, whose rider[f] is called Faithful and True.[g] With justice he judges and wages war.[h] 12 His eyes
are like blazing fire,[i] and on his head are
many crowns.[j] He has a name written on
him that no one knows but he himself.[k]
13 He is dressed in a robe dipped in blood,[l]
and his name is the Word of God.[m] 14 The
armies of heaven were following him, riding on white horses and dressed in fine
linen,[n] white and clean. 15 Coming out of
his mouth is a sharp sword[o] with which
to strike down[p] the nations. "He will rule
them with an iron scepter."[a][q] He treads the
winepress[r] of the fury of the wrath of God
Almighty. 16 On his robe and on his thigh
he has this name written:[s]

KING OF KINGS AND LORD OF LORDS.[t]

---

a 15 Psalm 2:9

---

or Roman manifestations, even the killing of James in Acts 12:1–2 is being avenged here.
19:9 ***Blessed.*** This is the fourth of the seven beatitudes in Revelation (see note on 14:13). ***wedding supper.*** The wedding supper of John's day would begin on the evening of the wedding, but the celebration might continue for days. The wedding supper here is a time of joyous feasting to be enjoyed by the saints.
19:15 ***sharp sword.*** The sharp sword that comes out of Christ's mouth is the double-edged sword spoken of in 1:16. ***iron scepter.*** Christ will rule with an iron scepter in fulfillment of the messianic prophecies in Psalms 2:8–9 and Isaiah 11:4.

18:22 [d] Isa 24:8; Eze 26:13 [e] Jer 25:10 **18:23** [f] Jer 7:34; 16:9; 25:10 [g] Isa 23:8 [h] Na 3:4 **18:24** [i] Rev 16:6; 17:6 [j] Jer 51:49 **19:1** [k] Rev 11:15 [l] Rev 7:10 [m] Rev 4:11 **19:2** [n] Dt 32:43; Rev 6:10 **19:3** [o] Isa 34:10; Rev 14:11 **19:4** [p] Rev 4:4 [q] Rev 4:6 [r] Rev 5:14 **19:5** [s] Ps 134:1 [t] Rev 11:18; 20:12 **19:6** [u] Rev 11:15 **19:7** [v] Mt 22:2; 25:10; Eph 5:32 [w] Rev 21:2,9 **19:8** [x] Rev 15:4 **19:9** [y] ver 10 [z] Rev 1:19 [a] Lk 14:15 [b] Rev 21:5; 22:6 **19:10** [c] Rev 22:8 [d] Ac 10:25,26; Rev 22:9 [e] Rev 12:17 **19:11** [f] Rev 6:2 [g] Rev 3:14 [h] Isa 11:4 **19:12** [i] Rev 1:14 [j] Rev 6:2 [k] Rev 2:17 **19:13** [l] Isa 63:2,3 [m] Jn 1:1 **19:14** [n] ver 8 **19:15** [o] Rev 1:16 [p] Isa 11:4; 2Th 2:8 [q] Ps 2:9; Rev 2:27 [r] Rev 14:20 **19:16** [s] ver 12 [t] Rev 17:14

17And I saw an angel standing in the sun,
who cried in a loud voice to all the birds[u]
flying in midair,[v] "Come,[w] gather together
for the great supper of God, 18so that you
may eat the flesh of kings, generals, and
the mighty, of horses and their riders, and
the flesh of all people,[x] free and slave, great
and small."

19Then I saw the beast and the kings of
the earth[y] and their armies gathered together to wage war against the rider on
the horse and his army. 20But the beast
was captured, and with it the false prophet[z] who had performed the signs on its
behalf.[a] With these signs he had deluded
those who had received the mark of the
beast and worshiped its image. The two of
them were thrown alive into the fiery lake[b]
of burning sulfur.[c] 21The rest were killed
with the sword[d] coming out of the mouth
of the rider on the horse,[e] and all the birds[f]
gorged themselves on their flesh.

The Thousand Years

20 And I saw an angel coming down
out of heaven,[g] having the key[h] to
the Abyss and holding in his hand a great
chain. 2He seized the dragon, that ancient
serpent, who is the devil, or Satan,[i] and
bound him for a thousand years.[j] 3He threw
him into the Abyss, and locked and sealed[k]
it over him, to keep him from deceiving the
nations[l] anymore until the thousand years
were ended. After that, he must be set free
for a short time.

4I saw thrones[m] on which were seated
those who had been given authority to
judge. And I saw the souls of those who
had been beheaded[n] because of their testimony about Jesus and because of the
word of God. They[a] had not worshiped the
beast[o] or its image and had not received its
mark on their foreheads or their hands.[p]
They came to life and reigned with Christ
a thousand years. 5(The rest of the dead did
not come to life until the thousand years
were ended.) This is the first resurrection.[q]
6Blessed[r] and holy are those who share in
the first resurrection. The second death[s]
has no power over them, but they will be
priests[t] of God and of Christ and will reign
with him[u] for a thousand years.

The Judgment of Satan

7When the thousand years are over,[v]
Satan will be released from his prison
8and will go out to deceive the nations[w]
in the four corners of the earth—Gog and

---

[a] 4 Or *God; I also saw those who*

19:20–21 ***beast ... false prophet ... thrown alive into the fiery lake.*** This lake of fire is the eternal destiny of all unbelievers (20:10,14–15). They are apparently the first to suffer the torment of the lake. The rest of the beast's allies are killed by the word from the mouth of the victorious Christ. Apparently all those who now suffer death go to Hades (Matt. 16:18), to which Jesus has the keys (1:8), until death and Hades are emptied and cast into the lake of fire (20:13–15).

20:1 ***angel.*** The angel here may be the same one who had the key to the bottomless pit in 9:1–2.

20:2–3 ***Abyss ... locked and sealed it ... until the thousand years were ended.*** The abyss, or bottomless pit, is presently the place of imprisonment of some demons (Luke 8:31) and will be the place from which the beast ascends (17:8). Thus, it is fitting that the devil will be held there for a thousand years. The dragon of 12:3,9, known as Satan, was in control of the serpent in the garden of Eden (Gen. 3). God has a plan for Satan. He will be shut up in the abyss for a thousand years and then will be briefly released to deceive the nations one final time (vv. 7–9) before being cast into the lake of fire (v. 10). ***must be set free.*** This phrase indicates that Satan will not escape from the pit but instead will be allowed to go forth from the pit to fulfill God's plan.

20:4 ***thrones ... reigned.*** This may be a partial fulfillment of Daniel 7:18,27. The aspect of judgment in ruling is referred to in 1 Corinthians 6:2–4. At the onset of the kingdom, authority is officially transferred from angels to men (Heb. 2:5,8). Christ, as the second Adam, fulfills God's original purpose for the earth. A new world order is established with the overcoming saints of the church age ruling together with Christ in His kingdom (Rom. 8:17). Incredible as it may seem, with a perfect Ruler who is totally just, totally kind, and totally wise, there will still be men who will rebel (vv. 7–9).

20:5 ***did not come to life.*** The resurrection of the dead will not encompass all people at the same time (Dan. 12:2; John 5:29). This passage indicates that there will be a first resurrection of dead believers before the thousand years of Christ's reign (1 Cor. 15:23,52) and a final resurrection after the millennium is finished, before the great white throne judgment (vv. 11–13). It is generally considered that this is the time of resurrection of the Old Testament saints as well as those martyred in the great tribulation.

20:6 ***Blessed.*** This is the fifth of the seven beatitudes in Revelation (see note on 14:13). All look forward to life with Christ beyond the first resurrection (v. 5). Resurrection is assured for all believers. But the blessedness mentioned here belongs more precisely to those martyrs who will have a part as rulers with Christ in the first resurrection. ***second death.*** The second death is the everlasting death of torment in the lake of fire for unbelievers who face the great white throne judgment (vv. 11–15). John has previously stated that the one who overcomes will not be hurt by the second death (2:11).

20:8 ***Gog and Magog.*** Gog and Magog was a common rabbinical title for the nations in rebellion against the Lord, and the names recall the prophesied

19:17 [u] ver 21 [v] Rev 8:13 [w] Eze 39:17
19:18 [x] Eze 39:18-20 **19:19** [y] Rev 16:14, 16
19:20 [z] Rev 16:13 [a] Rev 13:12 [b] Da 7:11; Rev 20:10, 14, 15; 21:8 [c] Rev 14:10 **19:21** [d] ver 15 [e] ver 11, 19 [f] ver 17
20:1 [g] Rev 10:1 [h] Rev 1:18 **20:2** [i] Rev 12:9 [j] 2Pe 2:4
20:3 [k] Da 6:17 [l] Rev 12:9 **20:4** [m] Da 7:9 [n] Rev 6:9 [o] Rev 13:12 [p] Rev 13:16 **20:5** [q] Lk 14:14; Php 3:11
20:6 [r] Rev 14:13 [s] Rev 2:11 [t] Rev 1:6 [u] ver 4 **20:7** [v] ver 2
20:8 [w] ver 3, 10

Magog[x]—and to gather them for battle.[y] In
number they are like the sand on the seashore.[z] 9They marched across the breadth
of the earth and surrounded[a] the camp of
God's people, the city he loves. But fire
came down from heaven[b] and devoured
them. 10And the devil, who deceived them,[c]
was thrown into the lake of burning sulfur,
where the beast and the false prophet had
been thrown. They will be tormented day
and night for ever and ever.[d]

The Judgment of the Dead

11Then I saw a great white throne[e] and
him who was seated on it. The earth and
the heavens fled from his presence, and
there was no place for them. 12And I saw
the dead, great and small, standing before
the throne, and books were opened.[f] Another book was opened, which is the book
of life.[g] The dead were judged according
to what they had done[h] as recorded in the
books. 13The sea gave up the dead that
were in it, and death and Hades[i] gave up
the dead[j] that were in them, and each person was judged according to what they
had done. 14Then death[k] and Hades were
thrown into the lake of fire. The lake of fire
is the second death. 15Anyone whose name
was not found written in the book of life[l]
was thrown into the lake of fire.

A New Heaven and a New Earth

21 Then I saw "a new heaven and a new
earth,"[am] for the first heaven and the
first earth had passed away, and there was
no longer any sea. 2I saw the Holy City, the
new Jerusalem, coming down out of heaven
from God,[n] prepared as a bride beautifully dressed for her husband. 3And I heard a
loud voice from the throne saying, "Look!
God's dwelling place is now among the people, and he will dwell with them. They will
be his people, and God himself will be with
them and be their God.[o] 4'He will wipe every
tear from their eyes.[p] There will be no more
death'[bq] or mourning or crying or pain,[r] for
the old order of things has passed away."

5He who was seated on the throne[s] said,
"I am making everything new!" Then he
said, "Write this down, for these words are
trustworthy and true."[t]

---

[a] *1* Isaiah 65:17 [b] *4* Isaiah 25:8

---

invasion of Israel in Ezekiel 38:18. Some hold that the battle of verses 8–9 is the one spoken of in Ezekiel, but there are major differences as well as similarities in the two passages.

20:9 *the city he loves.* The beloved city may symbolically refer to the home of God's people. However, the new Jerusalem is commonly called "the city of my God" (3:12) and "the Holy City" (21:2). The city here may be the renewed earthly Jerusalem, ready to give way to the everlasting sinless glory of the new Jerusalem (21:1–22:5).

20:11 *great white throne.* The great white throne is a picture of God's holy rule and judgment. The One occupying the throne may be God the Father (1 Cor. 15:24–28) or both the Father and the Lamb (Christ), as in the new Jerusalem (22:1–3). ***The earth and the heavens fled.*** There is no place for this sin-polluted creation in the new heaven and new earth (21:1–22:5). The earth and all of its works will be burned up (2 Pet. 3:10–13).

20:12 *the dead.* The dead, called "the rest of the dead" (v. 5), are raised and made to stand before God's throne of judgment. ***books.*** The books are thought to refer to the record of all works done in this life. Since all have sinned and fall short of God's standard (Rom. 3:23), the opening of these books will certainly lead to eternal sentences in the lake of fire. ***book of life.*** The book of life is God's register of those who have believed in Jesus (17:8). Although no one can be judged acceptable based on works (Eph. 2:8–9) many will be saved by God's grace received by faith in Jesus Christ.

20:14 *death and Hades.* Death and Hades refers not only to dying, but to existence beyond the grave (1:18; 6:8). If one considers "death" as a place, it would be the place where the body lies, and Hades would be the place for the soul. The picture here is of all human bodies being given up to God's judgment. While unbelieving humanity is judged according to its works, death and Hades, the Lord's final enemy (1 Cor. 15:26), is also destroyed by being cast into the lake of fire. ***second death.*** The second death is spiritual and eternal, the just punishment of the wicked. The first death is physical dying. Both are included in the overall meaning of the death that came upon the human race because of Adam and Eve's sin (Gen. 2:16–17; 3:1–19; Rom. 5:12).

20:15 *not found written in the book of life.* Only those who have accepted Jesus Christ as their Savior will be found in the book. The rejection of the eternal gospel results in eternal condemnation (14:6–7).

21:1 *new.* "New" here suggest freshness, not just a second beginning. This is the fulfillment of the prophecies of Isaiah 65:17; 66:22 and 2 Peter 3:13. Significantly, this eternal renewal has already begun in the life of the believer because, using the same term, Paul says, "if anyone is in Christ, the new creation has come" (2 Cor. 5:17). ***passed away . . . no longer any sea.*** The present heaven and earth, including the sea, were burned up in the great white throne judgment (20:11–13). There will be a continuation of some features of the present creation in the new heaven and new earth, yet the drastic difference in the new eternal state is obvious from the fact that there will be no more sea, which was a major part of the original creation (Gen. 1:6–10).

21:2 *bride.* Christ's bride (v. 9) is the new Jerusalem, the redeemed inhabitants of the holy city (vv. 3–7,24–27).

20:8 [x] Eze 38:2; 39:1 [y] Rev 16:14 [z] Heb 11:12
20:9 [a] Eze 38:9, 16 [b] Eze 38:22; 39:6 **20:10** [c] Rev 19:20
[d] Rev 14:10, 11 **20:11** [e] Rev 4:2 **20:12** [f] Da 7:10
[g] Rev 3:5 [h] Jer 17:10; Mt 16:27; Rev 2:23 **20:13** [i] Rev 6:8
[j] Isa 26:19 **20:14** [k] 1Co 15:26 **20:15** [l] ver 12
21:1 [m] Isa 65:17; 2Pe 3:13 **21:2** [n] Heb 11:10; 12:22;
Rev 3:12 **21:3** [o] 2Co 6:16 **21:4** [p] Rev 7:17 [q] 1Co 15:26;
Rev 20:14 [r] Isa 35:10; 65:19 **21:5** [s] Rev 4:9; 20:11
[t] Rev 19:9

6 He said to me: "It is done.[u] I am the Alpha and the Omega,[v] the Beginning and the End. To the thirsty I will give water without cost from the spring of the water of life.[w] 7 Those who are victorious will inherit all this, and I will be their God and they will be my children. 8 But the cowardly, the unbelieving, the vile, the murderers, the sexually immoral, those who practice magic arts, the idolaters and all liars[x]—they will be consigned to the fiery lake of burning sulfur. This is the second death."[y]

The New Jerusalem, the Bride of the Lamb

9 One of the seven angels who had the seven bowls full of the seven last plagues[z] came and said to me, "Come, I will show you the bride,[a] the wife of the Lamb." 10 And he carried me away[b] in the Spirit[c] to a mountain great and high, and showed me the Holy City, Jerusalem, coming down out of heaven from God. 11 It shone with the glory of God,[d] and its brilliance was like that of a very precious jewel, like a jasper, clear as crystal.[e] 12 It had a great, high wall with twelve gates, and with twelve angels at the gates. On the gates were written the names of the twelve tribes of Israel.[f] 13 There were three gates on the east, three on the north, three on the south and three on the west. 14 The wall of the city had twelve foundations, and on them were the names of the twelve apostles of the Lamb.

15 The angel who talked with me had a measuring rod[g] of gold to measure the city, its gates and its walls. 16 The city was laid out like a square, as long as it was wide. He measured the city with the rod and found it to be 12,000 stadia[a] in length, and as wide and high as it is long. 17 The angel measured the wall using human measurement, and it was 144 cubits[b] thick.[c] 18 The wall was made of jasper,[h] and the city of pure gold, as pure as glass.[i] 19 The foundations of the city walls were decorated with every kind of precious stone.[j] The first foundation was jasper, the second sapphire, the third agate, the fourth emerald, 20 the fifth onyx, the sixth ruby,[k] the seventh chrysolite, the eighth beryl, the ninth topaz, the tenth turquoise, the eleventh jacinth, and the twelfth amethyst.[d] 21 The twelve gates were twelve pearls, each gate made of a single pearl. The great street of the city was of gold, as pure as transparent glass.[l]

22 I did not see a temple[m] in the city, because the Lord God Almighty[n] and the Lamb[o] are its temple. 23 The city does not need the sun or the moon to shine on it, for the glory of God gives it light,[p] and the Lamb is its lamp. 24 The nations will walk by its light, and the kings of the earth will bring their splendor into it.[q] 25 On no day will its gates ever be shut,[r] for there will be no night there.[s] 26 The glory and honor of the nations will be brought into it. 27 Nothing impure will ever enter it, nor will anyone who does what is shameful or deceitful,[t] but only those whose names are written in the Lamb's book of life.

Eden Restored

22 Then the angel showed me the river of the water of life, as clear as crystal,[u] flowing[v] from the throne of God and of the Lamb 2 down the middle of the great

---

a *16* That is, about 1,400 miles or about 2,200 kilometers *b* *17* That is, about 200 feet or about 65 meters *c* *17* Or *high* *d* *20* The precise identification of some of these precious stones is uncertain.

21:6 *It is done.* For the third time, it is done. The first statement of "finishing" was on the cross (John 19:30), the second was at the end of God's wrath (16:17), and the third is when there is no more death, a new heaven and a new earth.

21:6 *water of life.* The water of life may be recalling Jesus' references to living water in John 4:14 and 7:38, in connection with eternal life and life in the Holy Spirit. This water is further described in 22:1. A similar offer of God's grace to him who spiritually thirsts is repeated in 22:17.

21:12 *twelve gates ... twelve tribes.* The description of the high wall and the twelve gates echoes Ezekiel 48:30–35. It is a glorious picture of the place that Israel holds in the New Jerusalem when the New Covenant with Israel is at last fulfilled.

21:14 *twelve foundations ... apostles.* This picture calls to mind Paul's imagery of the apostles as the foundation of the house of God in Ephesians 2:20.

21:19–20 *every kind of precious stone.* The exact color of some of the stones is uncertain, but it is probable that jasper is colorless, sapphire is blue, chalcedony is green or greenish-blue, emerald is bright green, sardonyx has layers of red and white, sardius is blood red, chrysolite is yellow, beryl is blue or blue-green, topaz is golden, and amethyst is purple or violet.

22:2 *tree of life.* The tree of life in the original creation was in the middle of the Garden of Eden (Gen. 2:9), from which all of humanity was excluded after sin entered the world (Gen. 3:22–24). Ezekiel's apocalyptic vision included trees bearing fruit every month with medicinal leaves (Ezek. 47:12). Since only one tree of life is mentioned here, even though it is on both sides of the river, it is probably meant as a parallel to Genesis 2, implying that a new, better, and everlasting Eden has come.

21:6 [u] Rev 16:17 [v] Rev 1:8; 22:13 [w] Jn 4:10 **21:8** [x] 1Co 6:9 [y] Rev 2:11 **21:9** [z] Rev 15:1,6,7 [a] Rev 19:7 **21:10** [b] Rev 17:3 [c] Rev 1:10 **21:11** [d] Rev 15:8; 22:5 [e] Rev 4:6 **21:12** [f] Eze 48:30-34 **21:15** [g] Rev 11:1 **21:18** [h] ver 11 [i] ver 21 **21:19** [j] Isa 54:11, 12 **21:20** [k] Rev 4:3 **21:21** [l] ver 18 **21:22** [m] Jn 4:21,23 [n] Rev 1:8 [o] Rev 5:6 **21:23** [p] Isa 24:23; 60:19, 20; Rev 22:5 **21:24** [q] Isa 60:3,5 **21:25** [r] Isa 60:11 [s] Zec 14:7; Rev 22:5 **21:27** [t] Isa 52:1; Joel 3:17; Rev 22:14, 15 **22:1** [u] Rev 4:6 [v] Eze 47:1; Zec 14:8

street of the city. On each side of the river
stood the tree of life,[w] bearing twelve crops
of fruit, yielding its fruit every month. And
the leaves of the tree are for the healing of
the nations.[x] 3 No longer will there be any
curse.[y] The throne of God and of the Lamb
will be in the city, and his servants will
serve him.[z] 4 They will see his face,[a] and his
name will be on their foreheads.[b] 5 There
will be no more night.[c] They will not need
the light of a lamp or the light of the sun,
for the Lord God will give them light.[d] And
they will reign for ever and ever.[e]

John and the Angel

6 The angel said to me,[f] "These words are
trustworthy and true.[g] The Lord, the God
who inspires the prophets,[h] sent his angel[i]
to show his servants the things that must
soon take place."

7 "Look, I am coming soon![j] Blessed[k] is
the one who keeps the words of the prophecy written in this scroll."

8 I, John, am the one who heard and saw
these things.[l] And when I had heard and
seen them, I fell down to worship at the
feet[m] of the angel who had been showing
them to me. 9 But he said to me, "Don't do
that! I am a fellow servant with you and
with your fellow prophets and with all
who keep the words of this scroll.[n] Worship God!"[o]

10 Then he told me, "Do not seal up[p] the
words of the prophecy of this scroll, because the time is near.[q] 11 Let the one who
does wrong continue to do wrong; let the
vile person continue to be vile; let the one
who does right continue to do right; and let
the holy person continue to be holy."[r]

Epilogue: Invitation and Warning

12 "Look, I am coming soon![s] My reward
is with me,[t] and I will give to each person
according to what they have done. 13 I am
the Alpha and the Omega,[u] the First and
the Last,[v] the Beginning and the End.[w]

14 "Blessed are those who wash their
robes, that they may have the right to the
tree of life[x] and may go through the gates[y]
into the city.[z] 15 Outside[a] are the dogs,[b]
those who practice magic arts, the sexually immoral, the murderers, the idolaters and everyone who loves and practices
falsehood.

16 "I, Jesus,[c] have sent my angel to give
you[a] this testimony for the churches.[d] I am
the Root[e] and the Offspring of David, and
the bright Morning Star."[f]

17 The Spirit[g] and the bride say, "Come!"
And let the one who hears say, "Come!" Let
the one who is thirsty come; and let the one
who wishes take the free gift of the water
of life.

---

a 16 The Greek is plural.

22:3 *no longer will there be any curse.* The affliction of sin, especially on the human race and creation (Gen. 3:14–19), will be erased. As God had fellowship with Adam and Eve before their fall into sin (Gen. 3:8), so the Lord will again be with His servants eternally. In turn, His servants will worship and serve Him (Rom. 12:1).

22:4 *see his face.* The believer's hope today is to see the Lord face to face (1 Cor. 13:12), something neither Moses nor any other human was previously allowed to do (Ex. 33:20).

22:7 *Blessed.* "Blessed," begins the sixth of seven beatitudes in Revelation (see note on 14:13). And indeed, those who pay attention to this book will be blessed. The Lord has shown the things that must come to pass, the things that His servants must pay attention to, the ultimate fate of unbelievers, and a beautiful glimpse of eternity, which leaves all believers with an eagerness for the return of the Lord.

22:11 *wrong ... vile ... right ... holy.* This verse, on the surface, seems to be a statement that believers and unbelievers will live out their lives true to their nature until the final judgment (20:12–15). However, because this book is to be read before the events it foretells take place, it is almost certainly an implied, indirect evangelistic appeal based on the continuing offer of the gospel (v. 17; 14:6–7).

22:12–13 *My reward is with me.* The rewarding of each believer according to his or her works is taught in 2 Corinthians 5:10. Christ's rewards are meant to provide a powerful incentive for an obedient life. Little wonder that the apostle Paul rigorously disciplined himself so that he would not be disqualified from the prize (1 Cor. 9:24–27; Phil. 3:10–14). The judgment seat of Christ can be a time of great regret (1 Cor. 3:5–10), or it can be an occasion of supreme joy (2 Cor. 5:9–11). After Christ comes again, He will give rewards to His own. This can be counted on because Christ is in control of all history and all eternity.

22:14 *Blessed.* This is the last of the seven beatitudes in Revelation (see note on 14:13). This beatitude is speaking of those justified by faith who express that faith in obedience (Eph. 2:8–10).

22:15 *dogs.* According to the context of Deuteronomy 23:18 a "dog" is a male prostitute.

22:16 *the Root and the Offspring of David.* Jesus is both the Source and Son of David, echoing the words of Isaiah 11:1,10. Jesus is both greater than David and the rightful heir to the throne of David.

22:17 *Come!* This book, so full of the pictures of the fulfillment of God's righteous judgment, still closes with the sweet and compelling invitation to come to Christ. This is one of the reasons it is "blessed" to read this book.

22:2 [w] Rev 2:7 [x] Eze 47:12 **22:3** [y] Zec 14:11
22:3 [z] Rev 7:15 **22:4** [a] Mt 5:8 [b] Rev 14:1
22:5 [c] Rev 21:25 [d] Rev 21:23 [e] Da 7:27; Rev 20:4
22:6 [f] Rev 1:1 [g] Rev 19:9; 21:5 [h] Heb 12:9 [i] ver 16
22:7 [j] Rev 3:11 [k] Rev 1:3 **22:8** [l] Rev 1:1 [m] Rev 19:10
22:9 [n] ver 10, 18, 19 [o] Rev 19:10 **22:10** [p] Da 8:26; Rev 10:4 [q] Rev 1:3 **22:11** [r] Eze 3:27; Da 12:10
22:12 [s] ver 7, 20 [t] Isa 40:10 **22:13** [u] Rev 1:8 [v] Rev 1:17 [w] Rev 21:6 **22:14** [x] Rev 2:7 [y] Rev 21:12 [z] Rev 21:27
22:15 [a] 1Co 6:9, 10; Gal 5:19-21; Col 3:5,6 [b] Php 3:2
22:16 [c] Rev 1:1 [d] Rev 1:4 [e] Rev 5:5 [f] 2Pe 1:19; Rev 2:28
22:17 [g] Rev 2:7

18I warn everyone who hears the words
of the prophecy of this scroll: If anyone
adds anything to them,[h] God will add to
that person the plagues described in this
scroll.[i] 19And if anyone takes words away[j]
from this scroll of prophecy, God will take
away from that person any share in the
tree of life and in the Holy City, which are
described in this scroll.
20He who testifies to these things[k] says,
"Yes, I am coming soon."

Amen. Come, Lord Jesus.[l]
21The grace of the Lord Jesus be with
God's people.[m] Amen.

22:18–19 *adds ... takes words away.* The Book of Revelation was intended to be heard and obeyed (v. 7; 1:3), not tampered with. The person who either adds to or takes away from its contents will receive from God the strictest punishment, a punishment with eternal consequences.

22:20 *I am coming soon.* The fact that Jesus is coming quickly within the scope of God's overall plan for this creation is a repeated theme in Revelation (vv. 7–12; 3:11). John adds the hope of all believers to the declaration of Christ with his prayer, "Come, Lord Jesus."

22:21 *grace.* The grace of our Lord Jesus Christ begins and concludes the Book of Revelation (1:4), implying that the message of grace and the free gift of eternal life in Christ (Eph. 2:8–9), not merely the message of judgment upon unbelievers, can be found in this book.

22:18 [h] Dt 4:2; Pr 30:6 [i] Rev 15:6-16:21 **22:19** [j] Dt 4:2
22:20 [k] Rev 1:2 [l] 1Co 16:22 **22:21** [m] Ro 16:20

Table of Weights and Measures

	Biblical Unit	Approximate American Equivalent	Approximate Metric Equivalent
Weights	talent (60 minas)	75 pounds	34 kilograms
	mina (50 shekels)	1 $^1/_4$ pounds	560 grams
	shekel (2 bekas)	$^2/_5$ ounce	11.5 grams
	pim ($^2/_3$ shekel)	$^1/_4$ ounce	7.8 grams
	beka (10 gerahs)	$^1/_5$ ounce	5.7 grams
	gerah	$^1/_{50}$ ounce	0.6 gram
	daric	$^1/_3$ ounce	8.4 grams
Length	cubit	18 inches	45 centimeters
	span	9 inches	23 centimeters
	handbreadth	3 inches	7.5 centimeters
	stadion (pl. stadia)	600 feet	183 meters
Capacity			
Dry Measure	cor [homer] (10 ephahs)	6 bushels	220 liters
	lethek (5 ephahs)	3 bushels	110 liters
	ephah (10 omers)	$^3/_5$ bushel	22 liters
	seah ($^1/_3$ ephah)	7 quarts	7.5 liters
	omer ($^1/_{10}$ ephah)	2 quarts	2 liters
	cab ($^1/_{18}$ ephah)	1 quart	1 liter
Liquid Measure	bath (1 ephah)	6 gallons	22 liters
	hin ($^1/_6$ bath)	1 gallon	3.8 liters
	log ($^1/_{72}$ bath)	$^1/_3$ quart	0.3 liter

The figures of the table are calculated on the basis of a shekel equaling 11.5 grams, a cubit equaling 18 inches and an ephah equaling 22 liters. The quart referred to is either a dry quart (slightly larger than a liter) or a liquid quart (slightly smaller than a liter), whichever is applicable. The ton referred to in the footnotes is the American ton of 2,000 pounds. These weights are calculated relative to the particular commodity involved. Accordingly, the same measure of capacity in the text may be converted into different weights in the footnotes.

This table is based upon the best available information, but it is not intended to be mathematically precise; like the measurement equivalents in the footnotes, it merely gives approximate amounts and distances. Weights and measures differed somewhat at various times and places in the ancient world. There is uncertainty particularly about the ephah and the bath; further discoveries may shed more light on these units of capacity.

Theological Notes Index by Location

Theological Notes Index by Title

Concordance

The NIV Concordance, created by John R. Kohlenberger III, has been developed specifically for use with the New International Version (NIV). Like all concordances, it is a special index that contains an alphabetical listing of words used in the Bible text.

This concordance contains 2,474 word entries, with more than 10,000 Scripture references. Each word entry is followed by significant Scripture references in which that particular word is found, as well as by a brief excerpt from the surrounding context. In the context, the entry word is abbreviated by its first letter in bold print. Other forms of the entry word and related words indexed in this concordance are in parentheses.

This concordance also contains 155 biographical entries for significant people in the Bible. The descriptive phrases replace the brief context surrounding each occurrence of the name. In those instances where more than one Bible character has the same name, that name is placed under one block entry, and each person is given a number (1), (2), etc.

Two entries are marked with an asterisk (*). LORD* and LORD'S* list occurrences of the proper name of God, *Yahweh,* spelled "Lord" and "Lord's" in the NIV. These entries are distinguished from LORD and LORD's, which list occurrences of the title "Lord" and "Lord's."

This concordance is a valuable tool for Bible study. While one of its key purposes is to help the reader find forgotten references to familiar verses, it can also be used to do word studies and to locate and trace biblical themes. Whenever you find a significant context, be sure to read at least the whole verse in the NIV to discover its fuller meaning in its larger context.

AARON

Priesthood of (Ex 28:1; Nu 17; Heb 5:1–4; 7), garments (Ex 28; 39), consecration (Ex 29), ordination (Lev 8).

Spokesman for Moses (Ex 4:14–16, 27–31; 7:1–2). Supported Moses' hands in battle (Ex 17:8–13). Built golden calf (Ex 32; Dt 9:20). Talked against Moses (Nu 12). Priesthood opposed (Nu 16); staff budded (Nu 17). Forbidden to enter land (Nu 20:1–12). Death (Nu 20:22–29; 33:38–39).

ABANDON

Dt 4: 31 he will not **a** or destroy you
1Ti 4: 1 in later times some will **a** the faith

ABBA

Ro 8: 15 And by him we cry, "***A***, Father."
Gal 4: 6 the Spirit who calls out, "***A***,

ABEL

Second son of Adam (Ge 4:2). Offered proper sacrifice (Ge 4:4; Heb 11:4). Murdered by Cain (Ge 4:8; Mt 23:35; Lk 11:51; 1Jn 3:12).

ABIGAIL

Wife of Nabal (1Sa 25:30); pled for his life with David (1Sa 25:14–35). Became David's wife (1Sa 25:36–42).

ABIJAH

Son of Rehoboam; king of Judah (1Ki 14:31—15:8; 2Ch 12:16—14:1).

ABILITY (ABLE)

Ezr 2: 69 According to their **a** they gave
2Co 1: 8 far beyond our **a** to endure,
8: 3 were able, and even beyond their **a**.

ABIMELEK

1. King of Gerar who took Abraham's wife Sarah, believing her to be his sister (Ge 20). Later made a covenant with Abraham (Ge 21:22–33).

2. King of Gerar who took Isaac's wife Rebekah, believing her to be his sister (Ge 26:1–11). Later made a covenant with Isaac (Ge 26:12–31).

ABLE (ABILITY ENABLE ENABLED ENABLES)

Eze 7: 19 gold will not be **a** to deliver them
Da 3: 17 the God we serve is **a** to deliver us
Ro 8: 39 will be **a** to separate us
Ro 14: 4 the Lord is **a** to make them stand.
16: 25 to him who is **a** to establish you
2Co 9: 8 God is **a** to bless you abundantly,
Eph 3: 20 him who is **a** to do immeasurably
2Ti 1: 12 that he is **a** to guard what I have
3: 15 which are **a** to make you wise
Heb 7: 25 he is **a** to save completely
Jude : 24 To him who is **a** to keep you
Rev 5: 5 He is **a** to open the scroll and its

ABOLISH

Mt 5: 17 think that I have come to **a** the Law

ABOMINATION

Da 11: 31 set up the **a** that causes desolation.

ABOUND (ABOUNDING ABOUNDS)

2Co 9: 8 you will **a** in every good work.
Php 1: 9 your love may **a** more and more

ABOUNDING (ABOUND)

Ex 34: 6 to anger, **a** in love and faithfulness,
Ps 86: 5 **a** in love to all who call to you.

ABOUNDS (ABOUND)

2Co 1: 5 also our comfort **a** through Christ.

ABRAHAM

Covenant relation with the Lord (Ge 12:1–3; 13:14–17; 15; 17; 22:15–18; Ex 2:24; Ne 9:8; Ps 105; Mic 7:20; Lk 1:68–75; Ro 4; Heb 6:13–15).

Called from Ur, via Harran, to Canaan (Ge 12:1; Ac 7:2–4; Heb 11:8–10). Moved to Egypt, nearly lost Sarah to Pharoah (Ge 12:10–20). Divided the land with Lot (Ge 13). Saved Lot from four kings (Ge 14:1–16); blessed by Melchizedek (Ge 14:17–20; Heb 7:1–20). Declared righteous by faith (Ge 15:6; Ro 4:3; Gal 3:6–9). Fathered Ishmael by Hagar (Ge 16).

Name changed from Abram (Ge 17:5; Ne 9:7). Circumcised (Ge 17; Ro 4:9–12). Entertained three visitors (Ge 18); promised a son by Sarah (Ge 18:9–15; 17:16). Moved to Gerar; nearly lost Sarah to Abimelek (Ge 20). Fathered Isaac by Sarah (Ge 21:1–7; Ac 7:8; Heb 11.11–12); sent away Hagar and Ishmael (Ge 21:8–21; Gal 4:22–30). Tested by offering Isaac (Ge 22; Heb 11:17–19; Jas 2:21–24). Sarah died; bought field of Ephron for burial (Ge 23). Secured wife for Isaac (Ge 24). Death (Ge 25:7–11).

ABSALOM

Son of David by Maakah (2Sa 3:3; 1Ch 3:2). Killed Amnon for rape of his sister Tamar; banished by David (2Sa 13). Returned to Jerusalem; received by David (2Sa 14). Rebelled against David; seized kingdom (2Sa 15–17). Killed (2Sa 18).

ABSTAIN (ABSTAINS)
1Pe 2: 11 and exiles, to **a** from sinful desires,

ABSTAINS (ABSTAIN)
Ro 14: 6 and whoever **a** does so to the Lord

ABUNDANCE (ABUNDANT)
Lk 12: 15 not consist in an **a** of possessions."
Jude : 2 peace and love be yours in **a**.

ABUNDANT (ABUNDANCE)
Dt 28: 11 will grant you **a** prosperity—
Ps 145: 7 They celebrate your **a** goodness
Pr 28: 19 work their land will have **a** food,
Ro 5: 17 who receive God's **a** provision

ABUSE
2Pe 2: 11 do not heap **a** on such beings

ACCEPT (ACCEPTED ACCEPTS)
Ex 23: 8 "Do not **a** a bribe, for a bribe
Pr 10: 8 The wise in heart **a** commands,
19: 20 Listen to advice and **a** discipline,
Ro 15: 7 **A** one another, then, just as Christ
Jas 1: 21 humbly **a** the word planted in you,

ACCEPTED (ACCEPT)
Lk 4: 24 "no prophet is **a** in his hometown.

ACCEPTS (ACCEPT)
Ps 6: 9 the LORD **a** my prayer.
Jn 13: 20 whoever **a** anyone I send **a** me;

ACCOMPANY
Mk 16: 17 *these signs will **a** those who believe:*

ACCOMPLISH
Isa 55: 11 but will **a** what I desire and achieve

ACCORD
Nu 24: 13 not do anything of my own **a**,
Jn 10: 18 me, but I lay it down of my own **a**.

ACCOUNT (ACCOUNTABLE)
Mt 12: 36 will have to give **a** on the day
Ro 14: 12 of us will give an **a** of ourselves
Heb 4: 13 of him to whom we must give **a**.

ACCOUNTABLE (ACCOUNT)
Eze 33: 6 I will hold the watchman **a** for
Ro 3: 19 and the whole world held **a** to God.

ACCUSATION (ACCUSE)
1Ti 5: 19 not entertain an **a** against an elder

ACCUSE (ACCUSATION)
Pr 3: 30 Do not **a** anyone for no reason—
Lk 3: 14 money and don't **a** people falsely—

ACHAN

Sin at Jericho caused defeat at Ai; stoned (Jos 7; 22:20; 1Ch 2:7).

ACHE
Pr 14: 13 Even in laughter the heart may **a**,

ACKNOWLEDGE
Mt 10: 32 also **a** before my Father in heaven.
1Th 5: 12 **a** those who work hard among you,
Php 2: 11 every tongue **a** that Jesus Christ is
1Jn 4: 3 spirit that does not **a** Jesus is not

ACQUIT
Ex 23: 7 to death, for I will not **a** the guilty.

ACTION (ACTIONS ACTIVE ACTS)
Jas 2: 17 if it is not accompanied by **a**,

ACTIONS (ACTION)
Gal 6: 4 Each one should test their own **a**.
Titus 1: 16 God, but by their **a** they deny him.

ACTIVE (ACTION)
Heb 4: 12 For the word of God is alive and **a**.

ACTS (ACTION)
Ps 145: 12 people may know of your mighty **a**
150: 2 Praise him for his **a** of power;
Isa 64: 6 all our righteous **a** are like filthy

ADAM

First man (Ge 1:26—2:25; Ro 5:14; 1Ti 2:13). Sin of (Ge 3; Hos 6:7; Ro 5:12–21). Children of (Ge 4:1—5:5). Death of (Ge 5:5; Ro 5:12–21; 1Co 15:22).

ADD
Dt 12: 32 do not **a** to it or take away from it.
Pr 30: 6 Do not **a** to his words, or he will
Lk 12: 25 by worrying can **a** a single hour
Rev 22: 18 them, God will **a** to that person

ADMIRABLE
Php 4: 8 whatever is lovely, whatever is **a**—

ADMONISH
Col 3: 16 and **a** one another with all wisdom

ADOPTION
Ro 8: 23 wait eagerly for our **a** to sonship,
Eph 1: 5 he predestined us for **a** to sonship

ADORE
SS 1: 4 How right they are to **a** you!

ADORNMENT (ADORNS)
1Pe 3: 3 should not come from outward **a**,

ADORNS (ADORNMENT)
Ps 93: 5 holiness **a** your house for endless

ADULTERY
Ex 20: 14 "You shall not commit **a**.
Mt 5: 27 was said, 'You shall not commit **a**.'
5: 28 lustfully has already committed **a**
5: 32 a divorced woman commits **a**.
15: 19 murder, **a**, sexual immorality, theft,

ADULTS
1Co 14: 20 but in your thinking be **a**.

ADVANCED
Job 32: 7 **a** years should teach wisdom.'

ADVANTAGE
Ex 22: 22 "Do not take **a** of the widow
Dt 24: 14 Do not take **a** of a hired worker
1Th 4: 6 should wrong or take **a** of a brother

ADVERSITY
Pr 17: 17 a brother is born for a time of **a**.

ADVICE
1Ki 12: 8 Rehoboam rejected the **a** the elders
12: 14 he followed the **a** of the young men
Pr 12: 5 but the **a** of the wicked is deceitful.
12: 15 to them, but the wise listen to **a**.
19: 20 Listen to **a** and accept discipline,
20: 18 Plans are established by seeking **a**;

ADVOCATE
Jn 14: 16 he will give you another **a** to help
14: 26 But the **A**, the Holy Spirit,
1Jn 2: 1 sin, we have an **a** with the Father—

AFFECTION
2Pe 1: 7 and to godliness, mutual **a**; and to mutual **a**, love.

AFFLICTION
Ro 12: 12 patient in **a**, faithful in prayer.

AFRAID (FEAR)
Ge 26: 24 Do not be **a**, for I am with you;
Ex 3: 6 because he was **a** to look at God.
Ps 27: 1 of my life—of whom shall I be **a**?
56: 3 When I am **a**, I put my trust in
Pr 3: 24 you lie down, you will not be **a**;
Jer 1: 8 Do not be **a** of them, for I am
Mt 8: 26 of little faith, why are you so **a**?"
10: 28 Do not be **a** of those who kill
10: 31 So don't be **a**; you are worth more
Mk 5: 36 said, Jesus told him, "Don't be **a**;
Jn 14: 27 hearts be troubled and do not be **a**.
Heb 13: 6 Lord is my helper; I will not be **a**.

AGED
Job 12: 12 Is not wisdom found among the **a**?
Pr 17: 6 children are a crown to the **a**,

AGREE
Mt 18: 19 earth **a** about anything they ask for,
Ro 7: 16 want to do, I **a** that the law is good.

AHAB

Son of Omri; king of Israel (1Ki 16:28—22:40), husband of Jezebel (1Ki 16:31). Promoted Baal worship (1Ki 16:31–33); opposed by Elijah (1Ki 17:1; 18; 21), a prophet (1Ki 20:35–43), Micaiah (1Ki 22:1–28). Defeated Ben-Hadad (1Ki 20). Killed for failing to kill Ben-Hadad and for murder of Naboth (1Ki 20:35—21:40).

AHAZ

Son of Jotham; king of Judah, (2Ki 16; 2Ch 28; Isa 7).

AHAZIAH

1. Son of Ahab; king of Israel (1Ki 22:51–2Ki 1:18; 2Ch 20:35–37).
2. Son of Jehoram; king of Judah (2Ki 8:25–29; 9:14–29), also called Jehoahaz (2Ch 21:17—22:9; 25:23).

AIM
1Co 7: 34 Her **a** is to be devoted to the Lord

AIR
1Co 9: 26 not fight like a boxer beating the **a**.
Eph 2: 2 the ruler of the kingdom of the **a**,
1Th 4: 17 clouds to meet the Lord in the **a**.

ALABASTER
Mt 26: 7 him with an **a** jar of very expensive

ALERT
Jos 8: 4 far from it. All of you be on the **a**.
Mk 13: 33 Be **a**! You do not know
Eph 6: 18 be **a** and always keep on praying
1Pe 1: 13 with minds that are **a** and fully

ALIENATED
Gal 5: 4 the law have been **a** from Christ;

ALIVE (LIVE)
Ac 1: 3 convincing proofs that he was **a**.
Ro 6: 11 to sin but **a** to God in Christ Jesus.
1Co 15: 22 die, so in Christ all will be made **a**.
Heb 4: 12 the word of God is **a** and active.

ALMIGHTY (MIGHT)
Ge 17: 1 to him and said, "I am God **A**;
Job 11: 7 Can you probe the limits of the **A**?
33: 4 the breath of the **A** gives me life.
Ps 91: 1 will rest in the shadow of the **A**.
Isa 6: 3 "Holy, holy, holy is the LORD **A**;

ALTAR
Ge 22: 9 Abraham built an **a** there
Ex 27: 1 "Build an **a** of acacia wood,
1Ki 18: 30 he repaired the **a** of the LORD,
2Ch 4: 1 a bronze **a** twenty cubits long,
4: 19 the golden **a**; the tables

ALWAYS
Ps 16: 8 I keep my eyes **a** on the LORD.
26: 3 for I have **a** been mindful of your
51: 3 and my sin is **a** before me.
Mt 26: 11 The poor you will **a** have with you,
28: 20 And surely I am with you **a**,
1Co 13: 7 It **a** protects, **a** trusts, **a** hopes,
Php 4: 4 Rejoice in the Lord **a**. I will say it
1Pe 3: 15 **A** be prepared to give an answer

AMAZIAH
Son of Joash; king of Judah (2Ki 14; 2Ch 25).

AMBASSADORS
2Co 5: 20 We are therefore Christ's **a**,

AMBITION
Ro 15: 20 It has always been my **a** to preach
1Th 4: 11 make it your **a** to lead a quiet life:

AMON
Son of Manasseh; king of Judah (2Ki 21:18–26; 1Ch 3:14; 2Ch 33:21–25).

ANANIAS
1. Husband of Sapphira; died for lying to God (Ac 5:1–11).
2. Disciple who baptized Saul (Ac 9:10–19).
3. High priest at Paul's arrest (Ac 22:30—24:1).

ANCESTORS
Heb 1: 1 spoke to our **a** through the prophets

ANCHOR
Heb 6: 19 We have this hope as an **a**

ANCIENT
Da 7: 9 and the **A** of Days took his seat.

ANDREW
Apostle; brother of Simon Peter (Mt 4:18; 10:2; Mk 1:16–18, 29; 3:18; 13:3; Lk 6:14; Jn 1:35–44; 6:8–9; 12:22; Ac 1:13).

ANGEL (ANGELS ARCHANGEL)
Ps 34: 7 The **a** of the LORD encamps
Ac 6: 15 his face was like the face of an **a**.
2Co 11: 14 Satan himself masquerades as an **a**
Gal 1: 8 or an **a** from heaven should preach

ANGELS (ANGEL)
Ps 8: 5 a little lower than the **a**
91: 11 command his **a** concerning you
Mt 18: 10 that their **a** in heaven always see
25: 41 fire prepared for the devil and his **a**.
Lk 20: 36 for they are like the **a**.
1Co 6: 3 you not know that we will judge **a**?
Heb 1: 4 the **a** as the name he has inherited
1: 14 Are not all **a** ministering spirits
2: 7 them a little lower than the **a**;
13: 2 hospitality to **a** without knowing it.
1Pe 1: 12 Even **a** long to look into these
2Pe 2: 4 if God did not spare **a** when they

ANGER (ANGERED ANGRY)
Ex 32: 10 that my **a** may burn against them
34: 6 slow to **a**, abounding in love
Dt 29: 28 In furious **a** and in great wrath
2Ki 22: 13 Great is the LORD's **a** that burns
Ps 30: 5 For his **a** lasts only a moment,
Pr 15: 1 wrath, but a harsh word stirs up **a**.

ANGERED (ANGER)
Pr 22: 24 do not associate with one easily **a**,
1Co 13: 5 it is not easily **a**, it keeps no record

ANGRY (ANGER)
Ps 2: 12 he will be **a** and your way will lead
Pr 29: 22 An **a** person stirs up conflict,
Jas 1: 19 to speak and slow to become **a**,

ANOINT
Ps 23: 5 You **a** my head with oil;
Jas 5: 14 **a** them with oil in the name

ANOTHER
1Pe 3: 8 love one **a**, be compassionate

ANT
Pr 6: 6 Go to the **a**, you sluggard;

ANTICHRIST
1Jn 2: 18 have heard that the **a** is coming,
2Jn : 7 person is the deceiver and the **a**.

ANTIOCH
Ac 11: 26 were called Christians first at **A**.

ANXIETY (ANXIOUS)
Pr 12: 25 **A** weighs down the heart,
1Pe 5: 7 Cast all your **a** on him because he

ANXIOUS (ANXIETY)
Php 4: 6 Do not be **a** about anything,

APOLLOS
Christian from Alexandria, learned in the Scriptures; instructed by Aquila and Priscilla (Ac 18:24–28). Ministered at Corinth (Ac 19:1; 1Co 1:12; 3; Titus 3:13).

APOSTLES
See also Andrew, Bartholomew, James, John, Judas, Matthew, Nathanael, Paul, Peter, Philip, Simon, Thaddaeus, Thomas.
Ac 1: 26 so he was added to the eleven **a**.
2: 43 and signs performed by the **a**.
1Co 12: 28 placed in the church first of all **a**,
15: 9 For I am the least of the **a** and do
2Co 11: 13 For such people are false **a**,
Eph 2: 20 built on the foundation of the **a**

APPEAR (APPEARANCE APPEARING)
Mk 13: 22 false prophets will **a** and perform
2Co 5: 10 we must all **a** before the judgment
Col 3: 4 you also will **a** with him in glory.
Heb 9: 24 now to **a** for us in God's presence.
9: 28 and he will **a** a second time,

APPEARANCE (APPEAR)
1Sa 16: 7 People look at the outward **a**,

APPEARING (APPEAR)
2Ti 4: 8 to all who have longed for his **a**.
Titus 2: 13 the **a** of the glory of our great God

APPLY
Pr 22: 17 **a** your heart to what I teach,
23: 12 **A** your heart to instruction and

APPROACH
Eph 3: 12 we may **a** God with freedom
Heb 4: 16 then **a** God's throne of grace

APPROVED
2Ti 2: 15 to present yourself to God as one **a**,

AQUILA
Husband of Priscilla; co-worker with Paul, instructor of Apollos (Ac 18; Ro 16:3; 1Co 16:19; 2Ti 4:19).

ARARAT
Ge 8: 4 to rest on the mountains of **A**.

ARCHANGEL (ANGEL)
1Th 4: 16 with the voice of the **a**
Jude : 9 But even the **a** Michael, when he

ARCHITECT
Heb 11: 10 whose **a** and builder is God.

ARGUING
Php 2: 14 everything without grumbling or **a**,

ARK
Ge 6: 14 So make yourself an **a** of cypress
Dt 10: 5 put the tablets in the **a** I had made,
2Ch 35: 3 "Put the sacred **a** in the temple
Heb 9: 4 This **a** contained the gold jar

ARM (ARMY)
Nu 11: 23 "Is the LORD's **a** too short?
1Pe 4: 1 **a** yourselves also with the same

ARMAGEDDON
Rev 16: 16 place that in Hebrew is called **A**.

ARMOR (ARMY)
1Ki 20: 11 his **a** should not boast like one who

Eph 6: 11 Put on the full **a** of God, so that
6: 13 Therefore put on the full **a** of God,

ARMS (ARMY)
Dt 33: 27 underneath are the everlasting **a**.
Ps 18: 32 It is God who **a** me with strength
Pr 31: 20 She opens her **a** to the poor
Isa 40: 11 He gathers the lambs in his **a**
Mk 10: 16 And he took the children in his **a**,

ARMY (ARM ARMOR ARMS)
Ps 33: 16 king is saved by the size of his **a**;
Rev 19: 19 the rider on the horse and his **a**.

AROMA
2Co 2: 15 the pleasing **a** of Christ among
2: 16 one we are an **a** that brings death;
2: 16 to the other, an **a** that brings life.

ARRAYED
Ps 110: 3 **A** in holy splendor, your young
Isa 61: 10 **a** me in a robe of his righteousness,

ARROGANT
Ro 11: 20 Do not be **a**, but tremble.

ARROWS
Eph 6: 16 can extinguish all the flaming **a**

ASA
King of Judah (1Ki 15:8–24; 1Ch 3:10; 2Ch 14–16).

ASCENDED
Eph 4: 8 "When he **a** on high, he took many

ASCRIBE
1Ch 16: 28 **A** to the LORD, all you families
16: 28 **a** to the LORD glory and strength.
Job 36: 3 I will **a** justice to my Maker.
Ps 29: 2 **A** to the LORD the glory due his

ASHAMED (SHAME)
Lk 9: 26 Whoever is **a** of me and my words, the Son of Man will be **a** of them
Ro 1: 16 For I am not **a** of the gospel,
2Ti 1: 8 So do not be **a** of the testimony
2: 15 worker who does not need to be **a**

ASSIGNED
Mk 13: 34 each with their **a** task, and tells
1Co 3: 5 as the Lord has **a** to each his task.
7: 17 whatever situation the Lord has **a**

ASSOCIATE
Pr 22: 24 do not **a** with one easily angered,
Ro 12: 16 be willing to **a** with people of low
1Co 5: 11 you must not **a** with anyone who
2Th 3: 14 Do not **a** with them, in order

ASSURANCE
Heb 10: 22 and with the full **a** that faith brings,

ASTRAY
Pr 10: 17 ignores correction leads others **a**.
Isa 53: 6 have gone **a**, each of us has turned
Jer 50: 6 their shepherds have led them **a**
1Pe 2: 25 For "you were like sheep going **a**,"
1Jn 3: 7 do not let anyone lead you **a**.

ATHALIAH
Evil queen of Judah (2Ki 11; 2Ch 23).

ATHLETE
2Ti 2: 5 competes as an **a** does not receive

ATONEMENT
Ex 25: 17 "Make an **a** cover of pure gold—
30: 10 Once a year Aaron shall make **a**
Lev 17: 11 blood that makes **a** for one's life.
23: 27 this seventh month is the Day of **A**.
Nu 25: 13 God and made **a** for the Israelites."
Ro 3: 25 presented Christ as a sacrifice of **a**,
Heb 2: 17 that he might make **a** for the sins

ATTENTION
Pr 4: 1 pay **a** and gain understanding.
5: 1 My son, pay **a** to my wisdom,
22: 17 Pay **a** and turn your ear
Titus 1: 14 and will pay no **a** to Jewish myths

ATTITUDE (ATTITUDES)
Eph 4: 23 made new in the **a** of your minds;
1Pe 4: 1 yourselves also with the same **a**,

ATTITUDES (ATTITUDE)
Heb 4: 12 the thoughts and **a** of the heart.

ATTRACTIVE
Titus 2: 10 teaching about God our Savior **a**.

AUTHORITIES (AUTHORITY)
Ro 13: 5 it is necessary to submit to the **a**,
13: 6 for the **a** are God's servants,
Titus 3: 1 to be subject to rulers and **a**,
1Pe 3: 22 **a** and powers in submission to him.

AUTHORITY (AUTHORITIES)
Mt 7: 29 he taught as one who had **a**,
9: 6 the Son of Man has **a** on earth
28: 18 "All **a** in heaven and on earth has
Ro 13: 1 for there is no **a** except
13: 2 rebels against the **a** is rebelling
1Co 11: 10 ought to have **a** over her own head,
1Ti 2: 2 for kings and all those in **a**, that we
2: 12 to teach or to assume **a** over a man;
Heb 13: 17 your leaders and submit to their **a**,

AVENGE (VENGEANCE)
Dt 32: 35 It is mine to **a**; I will repay.

AVOID
Pr 20: 3 It is to one's honor to **a** strife,
20: 19 so **a** anyone who talks too much.
1Th 4: 3 you should **a** sexual immorality;
2Ti 2: 16 **A** godless chatter, because those
Titus 3: 9 But **a** foolish controversies

AWAKE
Ps 17: 15 when I **a**, I will be satisfied
1Th 5: 6 asleep, but let us be **a** and sober.

AWE (AWESOME)
Job 25: 2 "Dominion and **a** belong to God;
Ps 119:120 of you; I stand in **a** of your laws.
Isa 29: 23 will stand in **a** of the God of Israel.
Jer 33: 9 they will be in **a** and will tremble
Hab 3: 2 I stand in **a** of your deeds, LORD.
Mal 2: 5 me and stood in **a** of my name.
Mt 9: 8 saw this, they were filled with **a**;
Lk 7: 16 They were all filled with **a**
Ac 2: 43 Everyone was filled with **a**
Heb 12: 28 acceptably with reverence and **a**,

AWESOME (AWE)
Ge 28: 17 and said, "How **a** is this place!
Ex 15: 11 majestic in holiness, **a** in glory,
Dt 7: 21 is among you, is a great and **a** God.
10: 17 God, mighty and **a**, who shows no
28: 58 revere this glorious and **a** name—
Jdg 13: 6 looked like an angel of God, very **a**.
Ne 1: 5 the great and **a** God, who keeps his
9: 32 God, mighty and **a**, who keeps his
Job 10: 16 again display your **a** power against
37: 22 God comes in **a** majesty.
Ps 45: 4 your right hand achieve **a** deeds.
47: 2 For the LORD Most High is **a**,
66: 5 has done, his **a** deeds for mankind!
68: 35 You, God, are **a** in your sanctuary;
89: 7 he is more **a** than all who surround
99: 3 praise your great and **a** name—
111: 9 holy and **a** is his name.
145: 6 tell of the power of your **a** works—
Da 9: 4 the great and **a** God, who keeps his

BAAL
1Ki 18: 25 Elijah said to the prophets of **B**,

BAASHA
King of Israel (1Ki 15:16—16:7; 2Ch 16:1–6).

BABIES (BABY)
Lk 18: 15 bringing **b** to Jesus for him to place
1Pe 2: 2 Like newborn **b**, crave pure

BABY (BABIES)
Isa 49: 15 "Can a mother forget the **b** at her
Lk 1: 44 the **b** in my womb leaped for joy.
2: 12 You will find a **b** wrapped in cloths
Jn 16: 21 **b** is born she forgets the anguish

BABYLON
Ps 137: 1 By the rivers of **B** we sat and wept

BACKSLIDING
Jer 3: 22 I will cure you of **b**."
Eze 37: 23 save them from all their sinful **b**,

BAGS
Mt 25: 15 To one he gave five **b** of gold, to another two **b**, and to another one

BALAAM
Prophet who attempted to curse Israel (Nu 22–24; Dt 23:4–5; 2Pe 2:15; Jude 11). Killed (Nu 31:8; Jos 13:22).

BALM
Jer 8: 22 Is there no **b** in Gilead? Is there no

BANISH
Jer 25: 10 will **b** from them the sounds of joy

BANQUET
SS 2: 4 Let him lead me to the **b** hall,
Lk 14: 13 But when you give a **b**,

BAPTIZE (BAPTIZED)
Mt 3: 11 "I **b** you with water for repentance.

Mt 3: 11 He will **b** you with the Holy Spirit
Mk 1: 8 I **b** you with water, but he will **b**
1Co 1: 17 For Christ did not send me to **b**,

BAPTIZED (BAPTIZE)
Mt 3: 6 they were **b** by him in the Jordan
Mk 1: 9 and was **b** by John in the Jordan.
10: 38 be **b** with the baptism I am **b** with?"
16: 16 *believes and is* ***b*** *will be saved,*
Jn 4: 2 in fact it was not Jesus who **b**,
Ac 1: 5 For John **b** with water, but in a few

BARABBAS
Mt 27: 17 release to you: Jesus **B**, or Jesus

BARBS
Nu 33: 55 remain will become **b** in your eyes

BARE
Heb 4: 13 and laid **b** before the eyes of him

BARNABAS
Disciple, originally Joseph (Ac 4:36), prophet (Ac 13:1), apostle (Ac 14:14). Brought Paul to apostles (Ac 9:27), Antioch (Ac 11:22–29; Gal 2:1–13), on the first missionary journey (Ac 13–14). Together at Jerusalem Council, they separated over John Mark (Ac 15). Later co-workers (1Co 9:6; Col 4:10).

BARTHOLOMEW
Apostle (Mt 10:3; Mk 3:18; Lk 6:14; Ac 1:13). Possibly also known as Nathanael (Jn 1:45–49; 21:2).

BATH
Jn 13: 10 who have had a **b** need only

BATHSHEBA
Wife of Uriah who committed adultery with and became wife of David (2Sa 11), mother of Solomon (2Sa 12:24; 1Ki 1–2; 1Ch 3:5).

BATTLE
2Ch 20: 15 For the **b** is not yours, but God's.
Ps 24: 8 mighty, the LORD mighty in **b**.
Ecc 9: 11 to the swift or the **b** to the strong,

BEAR (BEARING BIRTH BIRTHRIGHT BORE BORN FIRSTBORN NEWBORN)
Ge 4: 13 punishment is more than I can **b**.
Ps 38: 4 me like a burden too heavy to **b**.
Isa 53: 11 many, and he will **b** their iniquities.
Da 7: 5 beast, which looked like a **b**.
Mt 7: 18 A good tree cannot **b** bad fruit,
Jn 15: 2 branch that does **b** fruit he prunes
15: 16 so that you might go and **b** fruit—
Ro 15: 1 We who are strong ought to **b**
1Co 10: 13 tempted beyond what you can **b**.
Col 3: 13 **B** with each other and forgive one

BEARING (BEAR)
Eph 4: 2 patient, **b** with one another in love.
Col 1: 10 **b** fruit in every good work,

BEAST
Rev 13: 18 calculate the number of the **b**, for it

BEAT (BEATING)
Isa 2: 4 They will **b** their swords
Joel 3: 10 **B** your plowshares into swords

BEATING (BEAT)
1Co 9: 26 I do not fight like a boxer **b** the air.
1Pe 2: 20 if you receive a **b** for doing wrong

BEAUTIFUL (BEAUTY)
Ge 6: 2 the daughters of humans were **b**,
12: 11 "I know what a **b** woman you are.
12: 14 saw that Sarai was a very **b** woman.
24: 16 The woman was very **b**, a virgin;
26: 7 of Rebekah, because she is **b**."
29: 17 had a lovely figure and was **b**.
Pr 11: 22 snout is a **b** woman who shows no
Ecc 3: 11 He has made everything **b** in its
Isa 4: 2 the Branch of the LORD will be **b**
52: 7 How **b** on the mountains are the
Eze 20: 6 and honey, the most **b** of all lands.
Zec 9: 17 How attractive and **b** they will be!
Mt 23: 27 which look **b** on the outside
26: 10 She has done a **b** thing to me.
Ro 10: 15 "How **b** are the feet of those who

BEAUTY (BEAUTIFUL)
Ps 27: 4 to gaze on the **b** of the LORD
45: 11 the king be enthralled by your **b**;
Pr 31: 30 is deceptive, and **b** is fleeting;
Isa 33: 17 Your eyes will see the king in his **b**
53: 2 He had no **b** or majesty to attract
61: 3 them a crown of **b** instead of ashes,
Eze 28. 12 full of wisdom and perfect in **b**.
1Pe 3: 4 unfading **b** of a gentle and quiet

BED
Heb 13: 4 and the marriage **b** kept pure,

BEELZEBUL
Lk 11: 15 said, "By **B**, the prince of demons,

BEER
Pr 20: 1 Wine is a mocker and **b** a brawler;

BEERSHEBA
Jdg 20: 1 all Israel from Dan to **B**

BEGINNING
Ge 1: 1 In the **b** God created the heavens
Ps 102: 25 In the **b** you laid the foundations
111: 10 of the LORD is the **b** of wisdom;
Pr 1: 7 the LORD is the **b** of knowledge,
4: 7 The **b** of wisdom is this:
Jn 1: 1 In the **b** was the Word,
1Jn 1: 1 That which was from the **b**,
Rev 21: 6 and the Omega, the **B** and the End.

BEHAVE (BEHAVIOR)
Ro 13: 13 us **b** decently, as in the daytime,

BEHAVIOR (BEHAVE)
Pr 1: 3 receiving instruction in prudent **b**,

BELIEVE (BELIEVED BELIEVER BELIEVERS BELIEVES BELIEVING)
Pr 14: 15 The simple **b** anything,
Mt 18: 6 those who **b** in me—
21: 22 If you **b**, you will receive whatever
Mk 1: 15 Repent and **b** the good news!"
9: 24 the boy's father exclaimed, "I do **b**;
16: 17 *accompany those who* ***b:***
Lk 8: 50 just **b**, and she will be healed."
24: 25 how slow to **b** all that the prophets
Jn 1: 7 so that through him all might **b**.
3: 18 does not **b** stands condemned
6: 29 to **b** in the one he has sent."
10: 38 even though you do not **b** me,
11: 27 "I **b** that you are the Messiah,
14: 1 You **b** in God; **b** also in me.
14: 11 **B** me when I say that I am
16: 30 This makes us **b** that you came
16: 31 "Do you now **b**?" Jesus replied.
17: 21 the world may **b** that you have sent
20: 27 into my side. Stop doubting and **b**."
20: 31 may **b** that Jesus is the Messiah,
Ac 16: 31 They replied, "**B** in the Lord Jesus,
24: 14 I **b** everything that is in accordance
Ro 3: 22 faith in Jesus Christ to all who **b**.
4: 11 he is the father of all who **b**
10: 9 **b** in your heart that God raised
10: 14 how can they **b** in the one of whom
1Th 4: 14 For we **b** that Jesus died and rose
2Th 2: 11 delusion so that they will **b** the lie
1Ti 4: 10 and especially of those who **b**.
Titus 1: 6 a man whose children **b** and are
Heb 11: 6 comes to him must **b** that he exists
Jas 2: 19 You **b** that there is one God. Good! Even the demons **b** that—
1Jn 4: 1 Dear friends, do not **b** every spirit,

BELIEVED (BELIEVE)
Ge 15: 6 Abram **b** the LORD, and he
Jnh 3: 5 The Ninevites **b** God. A fast was
Jn 1: 12 to those who **b** in his name,
2: 22 Then they **b** the scripture
3: 18 already because they have not **b**
20: 8 also went inside. He saw and **b**.
20: 29 who have not seen and yet have **b**."
Ac 13: 48 were appointed for eternal life **b**.
Ro 4: 3 "Abraham **b** God, and it was
10: 14 call on the one they have not **b** in?
1Co 15: 2 Otherwise, you have **b** in vain.
Gal 3: 6 So also Abraham "**b** God, and it
2Ti 1: 12 because I know whom I have **b**,
Jas 2: 23 that says, "Abraham **b** God, and it

BELIEVER (BELIEVE)
1Co 7: 12 brother has a wife who is not a **b**
2Co 6: 15 what does a **b** have in common

BELIEVERS (BELIEVE)
Ac 4: 32 All the **b** were one in heart
5: 12 all the **b** used to meet together
1Co 6: 5 to judge a dispute between **b**?
1Ti 4: 12 set an example for the **b** in speech,
1Pe 2: 17 love the family of **b**, fear God,

BELIEVES (BELIEVE)
Mk 9: 23 is possible for one who **b**."
11: 23 **b** that what they say will happen,
16: 16 *Whoever* ***b*** *and is baptized*
Jn 3: 16 whoever **b** in him shall not perish
3: 36 Whoever **b** in the Son has eternal
5: 24 **b** him who sent me has eternal life
6: 35 and whoever **b** in me will never be

Jn 6: 40 and **b** in him shall have eternal life,
6: 47 you, the one who **b** has eternal life.
7: 38 Whoever **b** in me, as Scripture has
Ro 1: 16 salvation to everyone who **b**:
9: 33 the one who **b** in him will never be
10: 4 righteousness for everyone who **b**.
1Jn 5: 1 Everyone who **b** that Jesus is
5: 5 Only the one who **b** that Jesus is

BELIEVING (BELIEVE)
Jn 11: 26 whoever lives by **b** in me will never
20: 31 by **b** you may have life in his name.

BELONG (BELONGS)
Dt 29: 29 The secret things **b** to the LORD
Job 25: 2 "Dominion and awe **b** to God;
Ps 47: 9 for the kings of the earth **b** to God;
95: 4 and the mountain peaks **b** to him.
Jn 8: 44 You **b** to your father, the devil,
15: 19 As it is, you do not **b** to the world,
Ro 1: 6 those Gentiles who are called to **b**
7: 4 that you might **b** to another, to him
14: 8 we live or die, we **b** to the Lord.
Gal 5: 24 Those who **b** to Christ Jesus have
1Th 5: 8 But since we **b** to the day, let us be

BELONGS (BELONG)
Job 41: 11 Everything under heaven **b** to me.
Ps 111: 10 To him **b** eternal praise.
Eze 18: 4 For everyone **b** to me, the parent as
Jn 8: 47 Whoever **b** to God hears what God
Ro 12: 5 each member **b** to all the others.

BELOVED (LOVE)
Dt 33: 12 "Let the **b** of the LORD rest
SS 2: 16 My **b** is mine and I am his;
7: 10 I belong to my **b**, and his desire is

BELT
Isa 11: 5 Righteousness will be his **b**
Eph 6: 14 the **b** of truth buckled around your

BENEFICIAL (BENEFIT)
1Co 10: 23 but not everything is **b**.

BENEFIT (BENEFICIAL BENEFITS)
Ro 6: 22 the **b** you reap leads to holiness,
2Co 4: 15 All this is for your **b**,

BENEFITS (BENEFIT)
Ps 103: 2 my soul, and forget not all his **b**—
Jn 4: 38 and you have reaped the **b** of their

BENJAMIN
Twelfth son of Jacob by Rachel (Ge 35:16–24; 46:19–21; 1Ch 2:2). Jacob refused to send him to Egypt, but relented (Ge 42–45).

BEREAN
Ac 17: 11 the **B** Jews were of more noble

BESTOWS
Ps 84: 11 the LORD **b** favor and honor;

BETHLEHEM
Mt 2: 1 After Jesus was born in **B** in Judea,

BETRAY
Pr 25: 9 do not **b** another's confidence,

BIND (BINDS)
Dt 6: 8 and **b** them on your foreheads.
Pr 6: 21 **B** them always on your heart;
Isa 61: 1 He has sent me to **b**
Mt 16: 19 whatever you **b** on earth will be

BINDS (BIND)
Ps 147: 3 and **b** up their wounds.
Isa 30: 26 when the LORD **b** up the bruises

BIRDS
Mt 8: 20 "Foxes have dens and **b** have nests,

BIRTH (BEAR)
Ps 58: 3 Even from **b** the wicked go astray;
Mt 1: 18 This is how the **b** of Jesus
1Pe 1: 3 great mercy he has given us new **b**

BIRTHRIGHT (BEAR)
Ge 25: 34 up and left. So Esau despised his **b**.

BLAMELESS
Ge 17: 1 walk before me faithfully and be **b**.
Job 1: 1 This man was **b** and upright;
Ps 84: 11 from those whose walk is **b**.
119: 1 are those whose ways are **b**,
Pr 19: 1 poor whose walk is **b** than a fool
1Co 1: 8 so that you will be **b** on the day
Eph 5: 27 any other blemish, but holy and **b**.
Php 2: 15 that you may become **b** and pure,
1Th 3: 13 your hearts so that you will be **b**
5: 23 body be kept **b** at the coming of
Titus 1: 6 An elder must be **b**, faithful to his
Heb 7: 26 one who is holy, **b**, pure, set apart
2Pe 3: 14 spotless, **b** and at peace with him.

BLASPHEMES
Mk 3: 29 whoever **b** against the Holy Spirit

BLEMISH
1Pe 1: 19 Christ, a lamb without **b** or defect.

BLESS (BLESSED BLESSING BLESSINGS)
Ge 12: 3 I will **b** those who **b** you,
Ro 12: 14 **B** those who persecute you;

BLESSED (BLESS)
Ge 1: 22 God **b** them and said, "Be fruitful
2: 3 Then God **b** the seventh day
22: 18 all nations on earth will be **b**,
Ps 1: 1 **B** is the one who does not walk
2: 12 **B** are all who take refuge in him.
33: 12 **B** is the nation whose God is
41: 1 **B** are those who have regard
84: 5 **B** are those whose strength is
106: 3 **B** are those who act justly,
112: 1 **B** are those who fear the LORD,
118: 26 **B** is he who comes in the name
Pr 29: 18 **b** is the one who heeds wisdom's
31: 28 Her children arise and call her **b**;
Mt 5: 3 "**B** are the poor in spirit, for theirs
5: 4 **B** are those who mourn, for they
5: 5 **B** are the meek, for they will
5: 6 **B** are those who hunger and thirst
5: 7 **B** are the merciful, for they will
5: 8 **B** are the pure in heart, for they
5: 9 **B** are the peacemakers, for they
5: 10 **B** are those who are persecuted
5: 11 "**B** are you when people insult you,
Lk 1: 48 on all generations will call me **b**,
Jn 12: 13 "**B** is he who comes in the name
Ac 20: 35 'It is more **b** to give than
Titus 2: 13 while we wait for the **b** hope—
Jas 1: 12 **B** is the one who perseveres under
Rev 1: 3 **B** is the one who reads aloud
22: 14 "**B** are those who wash their robes,

BLESSING (BLESS)
Eze 34: 26 there will be showers of **b**.

BLESSINGS (BLESS)
Pr 10: 6 **B** crown the head of the righteous,

BLIND
Mt 15: 14 If the **b** lead the **b**, both will fall
23: 16 "Woe to you, **b** guides! You say,
Jn 9: 25 I do know. I was **b** but now I see!"

BLOOD
Ge 9: 6 "Whoever sheds human **b**, by humans shall their **b** be shed;
Ex 12: 13 The **b** will be a sign for you
24: 8 "This is the **b** of the covenant
Lev 17: 11 For the life of a creature is in the **b**,
17: 11 it is the **b** that makes atonement
Ps 72: 14 for precious is their **b** in his sight.
Pr 6: 17 hands that shed innocent **b**,
Mt 26: 28 This is my **b** of the covenant,
Ro 3: 25 through the shedding of his **b**—
5: 9 have now been justified by his **b**,
1Co 11: 25 cup is the new covenant in my **b**;
Eph 1: 7 we have redemption through his **b**,
2: 13 brought near by the **b** of Christ.
Col 1: 20 by making peace through his **b**,
Heb 9: 12 once for all by his own **b**,
9: 22 everything be cleansed with **b**,
1Pe 1: 19 but with the precious **b** of Christ,
1Jn 1: 7 and the **b** of Jesus, his Son,
Rev 1: 5 has freed us from our sins by his **b**,
5: 9 with your **b** you purchased for God
7: 14 them white in the **b** of the Lamb.
12: 11 over him by the **b** of the Lamb

BLOT (BLOTS)
Ex 32: 32 **b** me out of the book you have
Ps 51: 1 to your great compassion **b** out my
Rev 3: 5 I will never **b** out the name

BLOTS (BLOT)
Isa 43: 25 "I, even I, am he who **b** out your

BLOWN
Eph 4: 14 and **b** here and there by every wind
Jas 1: 6 the sea, **b** and tossed by the wind.

BOAST
1Ki 20: 11 his armor should not **b** like one
Ps 44: 8 In God we make our **b** all day long,
Pr 27: 1 Do not **b** about tomorrow, for you
1Co 1: 31 "Let the one who boasts **b**
Gal 6: 14 May I never **b** except in the cross
Eph 2: 9 not by works, so that no one can **b**.

BOAZ
Wealthy Bethlehemite who showed favor to Ruth (Ru 2), married her (Ru 4). Ancestor of David (Ru 4:18–22; 1Ch 2:12–15), Jesus (Mt 1:5–16; Lk 3:23–32).

BODIES (BODY)
Ro 12: 1 to offer your **b** as a living sacrifice,
1Co 6: 15 not know that your **b** are members
6: 19 not know that your **b** are temples
Eph 5: 28 to love their wives as their own **b**.

BODY (BODIES)
Zec 13: 6 are these wounds on your **b**?'
Mt 10: 28 can destroy both soul and **b** in hell.
10: 28 be afraid of those who kill the **b**
26: 26 "Take and eat; this is my **b**."
Jn 13: 10 their whole **b** is clean.
1Co 11: 24 "This is my **b**, which is for you;
12: 12 Just as a **b**, though one, has many
Eph 5: 30 for we are members of his **b**.

BOLD (BOLDNESS)
Pr 21: 29 The wicked put up a **b** front,
28: 1 but the righteous are as **b** as a lion.

BOLDNESS (BOLD)
Ac 4: 29 to speak your word with great **b**.

BONDAGE
Ezr 9: 9 God has not forsaken us in our **b**.

BOOK (BOOKS)
Jos 1: 8 Keep this **B** of the Law always
Ne 8: 8 They read from the **B** of the Law
Jn 20: 30 which are not recorded in this **b**.
Php 4: 3 whose names are in the **b** of life.
Rev 21: 27 are written in the Lamb's **b** of life.

BOOKS (BOOK)
Ecc 12: 12 Of making many **b** there is no end,

BORE (BEAR)
Isa 53: 4 up our pain and **b** our suffering,

BORN (BEAR)
Isa 9: 6 For to us a child is **b**, to us a son is
Jn 3: 7 my saying, 'You must be **b** again.'
1Pe 1: 23 For you have been **b** again,
1Jn 4: 7 Everyone who loves has been **b**
5: 1 that Jesus is the Christ is **b** of God,

BORROWER
Pr 22: 7 and the **b** is slave to the lender.

BOUGHT
Ac 20: 28 which he **b** with his own blood.
1Co 6: 20 you were **b** at a price.
7: 23 You were **b** at a price;
2Pe 2: 1 the sovereign Lord who **b** them—

BOUNDLESS
Eph 3: 8 the Gentiles the **b** riches of Christ,

BOW
Ps 95: 6 Come, let us **b** down in worship,
Isa 45: 23 Before me every knee will **b**;
Ro 14: 11 Lord, 'every knee will **b** before me;
Php 2: 10 name of Jesus every knee should **b**,

BRANCH (BRANCHES)
Isa 4: 2 that day the **B** of the LORD will be
Jer 33: 15 I will make a righteous **B** sprout

BRANCHES (BRANCH)
Jn 15: 5 "I am the vine; you are the **b**.

BRAVE
2Sa 2: 7 then, be strong and **b**, for Saul your

BREAD
Dt 8: 3 that man does not live on **b** alone
Pr 30: 8 riches, but give me only my daily **b**.
Isa 55: 2 spend money on what is not **b**,
Mt 4: 4 'Man shall not live on **b** alone,
6: 11 Give us today our daily **b**.
Jn 6: 35 Jesus declared, "I am the **b** of life.
21: 13 took the **b** and gave it to them,
1Co 11: 23 the night he was betrayed, took **b**,

BREAK (BREAKING BROKEN)
Nu 30: 2 he must not **b** his word but must
Jdg 2: 1 'I will never **b** my covenant
Ps 2: 9 You will **b** them with a rod of iron;
Isa 42: 3 A bruised reed he will not **b**,
Mt 12: 20 A bruised reed he will not **b**,

BREAKING (BREAK)
Jas 2: 10 just one point is guilty of **b** all of it.

BREASTPIECE (BREASTPLATE)
Ex 28: 15 "Fashion a **b** for making decisions

BREASTPLATE (BREASTPIECE)
Isa 59: 17 He put on righteousness as his **b**,
Eph 6: 14 the **b** of righteousness in place,
1Th 5: 8 putting on faith and love as a **b**,

BREATHED (GOD-BREATHED)
Ge 2: 7 **b** into his nostrils the breath of life,
Jn 20: 22 with that he **b** on them and said,

BRIBE
Ex 23: 8 "Do not accept a **b**, for a **b** blinds
Pr 6: 35 he will refuse a **b**, however great it

BRIDE
Rev 19: 7 and his **b** has made herself ready.

BRIGHTER (BRIGHTNESS)
Pr 4: 18 shining ever **b** till the full light

BRIGHTNESS (BRIGHTER)
2Sa 22: 13 Out of the **b** of his presence bolts
Da 12: 3 who are wise will shine like the **b**

BROAD
Mt 7: 13 gate and **b** is the road that leads

BROKEN (BREAK)
Ps 51: 17 My sacrifice, O God, is a **b** spirit;
Ecc 4: 12 of three strands is not quickly **b**.

BROKENHEARTED (HEART)
Ps 34: 18 The LORD is close to the **b**
109: 16 the poor and the needy and the **b**.
147: 3 He heals the **b** and binds up their
Isa 61: 1 He has sent me to bind up the **b**,

BROTHER (BROTHER'S BROTHERS)
Pr 17: 17 a **b** is born for a time of adversity.
18: 24 a friend who sticks closer than a **b**.
Mt 18: 15 "If your **b** or sister sins,
Mk 3: 35 Whoever does God's will is my **b**
Lk 17: 3 "If your **b** or sister sins against you,
1Co 8: 13 if what I eat causes my **b** or sister
1Jn 2: 10 who loves their **b** and sister

BROTHER'S (BROTHER)
Ge 4: 9 "Am I my **b** keeper?"

BROTHERS (BROTHER)
Mt 25: 40 did for one of the least of these **b**
Mk 10: 29 "no one who has left home or **b**
Heb 13: 1 Keep on loving one another as **b**

BUILD (BUILDING BUILDS BUILT)
Mt 16: 18 on this rock I will **b** my church,
Ac 20: 32 which can **b** you up and give you
1Co 3: 10 But each one should **b** with care.
14: 12 excel in those that **b** up the church.
1Th 5: 11 one another and **b** each other up,

BUILDING (BUILD)
1Co 3: 9 you are God's field, God's **b**.
2Co 10: 8 authority the Lord gave us for **b**
Eph 4: 29 only what is helpful for **b** others

BUILDS (BUILD)
Ps 127: 1 Unless the LORD **b** the house,
1Co 8: 1 puffs up while love **b** up.

BUILT (BUILD)
Mt 7: 24 is like a wise man who **b** his house
1Co 14: 26 so that the church may be **b** up.
Eph 2: 20 **b** on the foundation of the apostles
4: 12 that the body of Christ may be **b**

BURDEN (BURDENED BURDENS)
Ps 38: 4 overwhelmed me like a **b** too heavy
Mt 11: 30 my yoke is easy and my **b** is light."

BURDENED (BURDEN)
Gal 5: 1 do not let yourselves be **b** again

BURDENS (BURDEN)
Ps 68: 19 our Savior, who daily bears our **b**.
Gal 6: 2 Carry each other's **b**, and in this

BURIED
Ro 6: 4 We were therefore **b** with him
1Co 15: 4 that he was **b**, that he was raised

BURNING
Lev 6: 9 the fire must be kept **b** on the altar.
Ro 12: 20 you will heap **b** coals on his head."

BUSINESS
Da 8: 27 got up and went about the king's **b**.
1Th 4: 11 You should mind your own **b**

BUSY
1Ki 20: 40 While your servant was **b** here
2Th 3: 11 are not **b**; they are busybodies.
Titus 2: 5 pure, to be **b** at home, to be kind,

CAESAR
Mt 22: 21 give back to **C** what is Caesar's,

CHEEK
Mt 5: 39 turn to them the other **c** also.

CHEERFUL (CHEERS)
Pr 15: 13 A happy heart makes the face **c**,
15: 15 the **c** heart has a continual feast.
17: 22 A **c** heart is good medicine,
2Co 9: 7 for God loves a **c** giver.

CHEERS (CHEERFUL)
Pr 12: 25 the heart, but a kind word **c** it up.

CHILD (CHILDHOOD CHILDLESS CHILDREN)
Pr 22: 15 Folly is bound up in the heart of a **c**,
23: 13 not withhold discipline from a **c**;
29: 15 but a **c** left undisciplined disgraces
Isa 9: 6 For to us a **c** is born, to us a son is
11: 6 and a little **c** will lead them.
66: 13 As a mother comforts her **c**, so will
Mt 18: 2 He called a little **c** to him,
Lk 1: 42 and blessed is the **c** you will bear!
1: 80 And the **c** grew and became strong
1Co 13: 11 When I was a **c**, I talked like a **c**,
1Jn 5: 1 loves the father loves his **c** as well.

CHILDHOOD (CHILD)
1Co 13: 11 I put the ways of **c** behind me.

CHILDLESS (CHILD)
Ps 113: 9 settles the **c** woman in her home

CHILDREN (CHILD)
Dt 4: 9 Teach them to your **c** and to their **c**
11: 19 Teach them to your **c**,
Ps 8: 2 Through the praise of **c** and infants
Pr 13: 24 spares the rod hates their **c**,
17: 6 parents are the pride of their **c**.
20: 11 Even small **c** are known by their
22: 6 Start **c** off on the way they should
29: 17 Discipline your **c**, and they will
31: 28 Her **c** arise and call her blessed;
Mt 7: 11 how to give good gifts to your **c**,
11: 25 and revealed them to little **c**.
18: 3 change and become like little **c**,
19: 14 said, "Let the little **c** come to me,
21: 16 "'From the lips of **c** and infants
Mk 9: 37 these little **c** in my name welcomes
10: 14 them, "Let the little **c** come to me,
10: 16 And he took the **c** in his arms,
13: 12 **C** will rebel against their parents
Lk 10: 21 and revealed them to little **c**.
18: 16 said, "Let the little **c** come to me,
Jn 12: 36 so that you may become **c** of light."
Ro 8: 16 with our spirit that we are God's **c**.
2Co 12: 14 **c** should not have to save for
Eph 6: 1 **C**, obey your parents in the Lord,
6: 4 Fathers, do not exasperate your **c**;
Col 3: 20 **C**, obey your parents in everything,
3: 21 do not embitter your **c**, or they will
1Ti 3: 4 well and see that his **c** obey him,
3: 12 and must manage his **c** and his
5: 10 such as bringing up **c**,
Heb 12: 7 God is treating you as his **c**.
1Jn 3: 1 that we should be called **c** of God!

CHOOSE (CHOOSES CHOSE CHOSEN)
Dt 30: 19 Now **c** life, so that you and your
Jos 24: 15 **c** for yourselves this day whom you
Pr 8: 10 **C** my instruction instead of silver,
Jn 15: 16 You did not **c** me, but I chose you
Ac 15: 14 God first intervened to **c** a people

CHOOSES (CHOOSE)
Jn 7: 17 who **c** to do the will of God

CHOSE (CHOOSE)
Ge 13: 11 Lot **c** for himself the whole plain
Ps 33: 12 the people he **c** for his inheritance.
Jn 15: 16 but I **c** you and appointed you so
1Co 1: 27 But God **c** the foolish things
Eph 1: 4 For he **c** us in him before
2Th 2: 13 because God **c** you as firstfruits

CHOSEN (CHOOSE)
Isa 41: 8 whom I have **c**, you descendants
Mt 22: 14 many are invited, but few are **c**."
Lk 10: 42 Mary has **c** what is better, and it
23: 35 if he is God's Messiah, the **C** One."
Jn 15: 19 but I have **c** you out of the world.
1Pe 1: 20 He was **c** before the creation
2: 9 But you are a **c** people, a royal

CHRIST (CHRIST'S CHRISTIAN MESSIAH)
Jn 1: 41 found the Messiah" (that is, the **C**).
Ro 3: 22 faith in Jesus **C** to all who believe.
5: 6 powerless, **C** died for the ungodly.
5: 8 we were still sinners, **C** died for us.
5: 17 life through the one man, Jesus **C**!
Ro 6: 4 just as **C** was raised from the dead
8: 1 for those who are in **C** Jesus,
8: 9 does not have the Spirit of **C**, they do not belong to **C**.
8: 35 separate us from the love of **C**?
10: 4 **C** is the culmination of the law so
14: 9 **C** died and returned to life so that
15: 3 even **C** did not please himself but,
1Co 1: 23 but we preach **C** crucified:
2: 2 while I was with you except Jesus **C**
3: 11 one already laid, which is Jesus **C**.
5: 7 For **C**, our Passover lamb, has been
8: 6 Jesus **C**, through whom all things
10: 4 them, and that rock was **C**.
10: 9 We should not test **C**, as some
11: 1 as I follow the example of **C**.
11: 3 that the head of every man is **C**,
11: 3 and the head of **C** is God.
12: 27 Now you are the body of **C**,
15: 3 that **C** died for our sins according
15: 14 And if **C** has not been raised,
15: 22 die, so in **C** all will be made alive.
15: 57 victory through our Lord Jesus **C**.
2Co 3: 3 show that you are a letter from **C**,
4: 5 but Jesus **C** as Lord, and ourselves
5: 10 before the judgment seat of **C**,
5: 17 if anyone is in **C**, the new creation
11: 2 to **C**, so that I might present you as
Gal 2: 20 I have been crucified with **C**
3: 13 **C** redeemed us from the curse
6: 14 in the cross of our Lord Jesus **C**,
Eph 1: 3 and Father of our Lord Jesus **C**,
3: 8 Gentiles the boundless riches of **C**,
4: 13 whole measure of the fullness of **C**.
5: 2 just as **C** loved us and gave himself
5: 23 head of the wife as **C** is the head
5: 25 just as **C** loved the church and gave
Php 1: 21 to live is **C** and to die is gain.
1: 27 manner worthy of the gospel of **C**.
4: 19 to the riches of his glory in **C** Jesus.
Col 1: 27 which is **C** in you, the hope
1: 28 present everyone fully mature in **C**.
2: 6 as you received **C** Jesus as Lord,
2: 17 the reality, however, is found in **C**.
3: 15 Let the peace of **C** rule in your
2Th 2: 1 the coming of our Lord Jesus **C**
1Ti 1: 15 **C** Jesus came into the world to save
2: 5 and mankind, the man **C** Jesus,
2Ti 2: 3 like a good soldier of **C** Jesus.
3: 15 salvation through faith in **C** Jesus.
Titus 2: 13 our great God and Savior, Jesus **C**,
Heb 3: 14 We have come to share in **C**,
9: 14 will the blood of **C**, who through
9: 15 For this reason **C** is the mediator
9: 28 so **C** was sacrificed once to take
10: 10 of the body of Jesus **C** once for all.
13: 8 Jesus **C** is the same yesterday
1Pe 1: 19 but with the precious blood of **C**,
2: 21 called, because **C** suffered for you,
3: 18 For **C** also suffered once for sins,
4: 14 insulted because of the name of **C**,
1Jn 2: 22 whoever denies that Jesus is the **C**.
3: 16 Jesus **C** laid down his life for us.
5: 1 who believes that Jesus is the **C**
Rev 20: 4 reigned with **C** a thousand years.

CHRISTIAN (CHRIST)
1Pe 4: 16 if you suffer as a **C**, do not be

CHRIST'S (CHRIST)
2Co 5: 14 For **C** love compels us, because we
5: 20 We are therefore **C** ambassadors,
12: 9 so that **C** power may rest on me.

CHURCH
Mt 16: 18 and on this rock I will build my **c**,
18: 17 if they refuse to listen even to the **c**,
Ac 20: 28 Be shepherds of the **c** of God,
1Co 5: 12 mine to judge those outside the **c**?
14: 4 one who prophesies edifies the **c**.
14: 12 excel in those that build up the **c**.
14: 26 done so that the **c** may be built up.
Eph 5: 23 wife as Christ is the head of the **c**,
Col 1: 24 the sake of his body, which is the **c**.

CIRCUMCISED
Ge 17: 10 Every male among you shall be **c**.
Gal 2: 8 in Peter as an apostle to the **c**,

CIRCUMSTANCES
Php 4: 11 to be content whatever the **c**.
1Th 5: 18 give thanks in all **c**; for this is God's

CITIZENS (CITIZENSHIP)
Eph 2: 19 but fellow **c** with God's people

COMMENDS (COMMEND)
2Co 10: 18 but the one whom the Lord **c**.

COMMIT (COMMITS COMMITTED)
Ex 20: 14 "You shall not **c** adultery.
Ps 37: 5 **C** your way to the LORD;
Mt 5: 27 was said, 'You shall not **c** adultery.'
Lk 23: 46 into your hands I **c** my spirit."
Ac 20: 32 "Now I **c** you to God
1Co 10: 8 We should not **c** sexual immorality,
1Pe 4: 19 to God's will should **c** themselves

COMMITS (COMMIT)
Pr 6: 32 a man who **c** adultery has no sense;
29: 22 hot-tempered person **c** many sins.
Mt 19: 9 marries another woman **c** adultery."

COMMITTED (COMMIT)
Nu 5: 7 must confess the sin they have **c**.
1Ki 8: 61 may your hearts be fully **c**
2Ch 16: 9 those whose hearts are fully **c**
Mt 5: 28 lustfully has already **c** adultery
2Co 5: 19 And he has **c** to us the message
1Pe 2: 22 "He **c** no sin, and no deceit was

COMMON
Pr 22: 2 Rich and poor have this in **c**:
1Co 10: 13 has overtaken you except what is **c**
2Co 6: 14 and wickedness have in **c**?

COMPANION
Pr 13: 20 for a **c** of fools suffers harm.
28: 7 a **c** of gluttons disgraces his father.
29: 3 but a **c** of prostitutes squanders his

COMPANY
Pr 24: 1 the wicked, do not desire their **c**;
Jer 15: 17 I never sat in the **c** of revelers,
1Co 15: 33 "Bad **c** corrupts good character."

COMPARED (COMPARING)
Eze 31: 2 "'Who can be **c** with you

COMPARING (COMPARED)
Ro 8: 18 present sufferings are not worth **c**
2Co 8: 8 of your love by **c** it
Gal 6: 4 without **c** themselves to someone

COMPASSION (COMPASSIONATE COMPASSIONS)
Ex 33: 19 I will have **c** on whom I will have **c**.
Ne 9: 19 your great **c** you did not abandon
9: 28 in your **c** you delivered them time
Ps 51: 1 to your great **c** blot out my
103: 4 pit and crowns you with love and **c**,
103: 13 As a father has **c** on his children,
145: 9 he has **c** on all he has made.
Isa 49: 13 will have **c** on his afflicted ones.
49: 15 and have no **c** on the child she has
Hos 2: 19 and justice, in love and **c**.
11: 8 all my **c** is aroused.
Jnh 3: 9 with **c** turn from his fierce anger so
Mt 9: 36 saw the crowds, he had **c** on them,
Mk 8: 2 "I have **c** for these people;
Ro 9: 15 I will have **c** on whom I have **c**."
Col 3: 12 clothe yourselves with **c**, kindness,
Jas 5: 11 The Lord is full of **c** and mercy.

COMPASSIONATE (COMPASSION)
Ne 9: 17 gracious and **c**, slow to anger
Ps 103: 8 The LORD is **c** and gracious,
112: 4 for those who are gracious and **c**
Eph 4: 32 Be kind and **c** to one another,
1Pe 3: 8 love one another, be **c** and humble.

COMPASSIONS (COMPASSION)
La 3: 22 not consumed, for his **c** never fail.

COMPEL (COMPELLED COMPELS)
Lk 14: 23 lanes and **c** them to come in,

COMPELLED (COMPEL)
Ac 20: 22 "And now, **c** by the Spirit, I am
1Co 9: 16 boast, since I am **c** to preach.

COMPELS (COMPEL)
2Co 5: 14 For Christ's love **c** us, because we

COMPETENCE (COMPETENT)
2Co 3: 5 but our **c** comes from God.

COMPETENT (COMPETENCE)
Ro 15: 14 and **c** to instruct one another.
1Co 6: 2 are you not **c** to judge trivial cases?
2Co 3: 5 Not that we are **c** in ourselves
3: 6 He has made us **c** as ministers

COMPETES
1Co 9: 25 Everyone who **c** in the games goes
2Ti 2: 5 anyone who **c** as an athlete does

COMPLACENT
Am 6: 1 Woe to you who are **c** in Zion,

COMPLETE
Jn 15: 11 in you and that your joy may be **c**.
16: 24 will receive, and your joy will be **c**.
17: 23 they may be brought to **c** unity.
Ac 20: 24 **c** the task the Lord Jesus has given
Php 2: 2 then make my joy **c** by being
Col 4: 17 it that you **c** the ministry you have
Jas 1: 4 so that you may be mature and **c**,
2: 22 faith was made **c** by what he did.

CONCEAL (CONCEALED CONCEALS)
Ps 40: 10 I do not **c** your love and your
Pr 25: 2 It is the glory of God to **c** a matter;

CONCEALED (CONCEAL)
Jer 16: 17 me, nor is their sin **c** from my eyes.
Mt 10: 26 for there is nothing **c** that will not
Mk 4: 22 whatever is **c** is meant to be

CONCEALS (CONCEAL)
Pr 28: 13 Whoever **c** their sins does not

CONCEITED
Gal 5: 26 Let us not become **c**,
1Ti 6: 4 they are **c** and understand nothing.

CONCEIVE (CONCEIVED)
Isa 7: 14 The virgin will **c** and give birth
Mt 1: 23 "The virgin will **c** and give birth

CONCEIVED (CONCEIVE)
Mt 1: 20 because what is **c** in her is
1Co 2: 9 and what no human mind has **c**"—

CONCERN (CONCERNED)
Eze 36: 21 I had **c** for my holy name,
1Co 7: 32 I would like you to be free from **c**.
12: 25 that its parts should have equal **c**
2Co 11: 28 of my **c** for all the churches.

CONCERNED (CONCERN)
Jnh 4: 10 "You have been **c** about this plant,
1Co 7: 32 An unmarried man is **c**

CONDEMN (CONDEMNATION CONDEMNED CONDEMNING CONDEMNS)
Job 40: 8 you **c** me to justify yourself?
Isa 50: 9 Who will **c** me? They will all wear
Lk 6: 37 Do not **c**, and you will not be
Jn 3: 17 Son into the world to **c** the world,
12: 48 words I have spoken will **c** them
Ro 2: 27 yet obeys the law will **c** you who,
1Jn 3: 20 If our hearts **c** us, we know that

CONDEMNATION (CONDEMN)
Ro 5: 18 just as one trespass resulted in **c**
8: 1 there is now no **c** for those who are
2Co 3: 9 that brought **c** was glorious,

CONDEMNED (CONDEMN)
Ps 34: 22 who takes refuge in him will be **c**.
Mt 12: 37 and by your words you will be **c**."
23: 33 How will you escape being **c**
Jn 3: 18 Whoever believes in him is not **c**,
16: 11 prince of this world now stands **c**.
Ro 14: 23 whoever has doubts is **c** if they eat,
1Co 11: 32 that we will not be finally **c**
Heb 11: 7 By his faith he **c** the world

CONDEMNING (CONDEMN)
Pr 17: 15 the guilty and **c** the innocent—
Ro 2: 1 you are **c** yourself, because you

CONDEMNS (CONDEMN)
Pr 14: 34 exalts a nation, but sin **c** any people
Ro 8: 34 Who then is the one who **c**?

CONDUCT
Pr 20: 11 is their **c** really pure and upright?
21: 8 but the **c** of the innocent is upright.
Ecc 6: 8 how to **c** themselves before others?
Jer 4: 18 "Your own **c** and actions have
17: 10 each person according to their **c**,
Eze 7: 3 I will judge you according to your **c**
1Ti 3: 15 how people ought to **c** themselves

CONFESS (CONFESSION)
Lev 16: 21 and **c** over it all the wickedness
26: 40 if they will **c** their sins and the sins
Nu 5: 7 **c** the sin they have committed.
Ps 38: 18 I **c** my iniquity; I am troubled by
Jas 5: 16 Therefore **c** your sins to each other
1Jn 1: 9 If we **c** our sins, he is faithful

CONFESSION (CONFESS)
2Co 9: 13 accompanies your **c** of the gospel

CONFIDENCE
Ps 71: 5 LORD, my **c** since my youth.
Pr 11: 13 A gossip betrays a **c**,
25: 9 to court, do not betray another's **c**,

Pr 31: 11 Her husband has full **c** in her
Isa 32: 17 will be quietness and **c** forever.
Jer 17: 7 in the LORD, whose **c** is in him.
Php 3: 3 and who put no **c** in the flesh—
Heb 4: 16 God's throne of grace with **c**,
10: 19 since we have **c** to enter the Most
10: 35 So do not throw away your **c**;
11: 1 Now faith is **c** in what we hope
13: 17 Have **c** in your leaders and submit
1Jn 5: 14 This is the **c** we have

CONFIRM
2Pe 1: 10 make every effort to **c** your calling

CONFLICT
Pr 6: 14 his heart—he always stirs up **c**.
6: 19 a person who stirs up **c**
10: 12 Hatred stirs up **c**, but love covers
15: 18 A hot-tempered person stirs up **c**,
16: 28 A perverse person stirs up **c**,
28: 25 The greedy stir up **c**,
29: 22 An angry person stirs up **c**,

CONFORM (CONFORMED)
Ro 12: 2 not **c** to the pattern of this world,
1Pe 1: 14 do not **c** to the evil desires you had

CONFORMED (CONFORM)
Ro 8: 29 predestined to be **c** to the image

CONQUERORS
Ro 8: 37 are more than **c** through him who

CONSCIENCE (CONSCIENCES)
Ro 13: 5 but also as a matter of **c**.
1Co 8: 7 a god, and since their **c** is weak,
8: 12 this way and wound their weak **c**,
10: 25 without raising questions of **c**,
10: 29 being judged by another's **c**?
Heb 10: 22 to cleanse us from a guilty **c**
1Pe 3: 16 keeping a clear **c**, so that those who

CONSCIENCES (CONSCIENCE)
Ro 2: 15 hearts, their **c** also bearing witness,
1Ti 4: 2 whose **c** have been seared as
Titus 1: 15 their minds and **c** are corrupted.
Heb 9: 14 cleanse our **c** from acts that lead

CONSCIOUS
Ro 3: 20 through the law we become **c** of
1Pe 2: 19 unjust suffering because they are **c**

CONSECRATE (CONSECRATED)
Ex 13: 2 "**C** to me every firstborn male.
Lev 20: 7 " '**C** yourselves and be holy,

CONSECRATED (CONSECRATE)
Ex 29: 43 and the place will be **c** by my glory.
1Ti 4: 5 because it is **c** by the word of God

CONSIDER (CONSIDERATE CONSIDERED CONSIDERS)
1Sa 12: 24 **c** what great things he has done
Job 37: 14 stop and **c** God's wonders.
Ps 8: 3 When I **c** your heavens, the work
143: 5 and **c** what your hands have done.
Lk 12: 24 **C** the ravens: They do not sow
12: 27 "**C** how the wild flowers grow.
Php 3: 8 I **c** everything a loss because
Heb 10: 24 And let us **c** how we may spur one
Jas 1: 2 **C** it pure joy, my brothers
1: 26 Those who **c** themselves religious

CONSIDERATE (CONSIDER)
Titus 3: 2 to be peaceable and **c**, and always
Jas 3: 17 then peace-loving, **c**, submissive,
1Pe 2: 18 only to those who are good and **c**,
3: 7 the same way be **c** as you live

CONSIDERED (CONSIDER)
Job 1: 8 "Have you **c** my servant Job?
2: 3 "Have you **c** my servant Job?
Ps 44: 22 we are **c** as sheep to be slaughtered.
Isa 53: 4 yet we **c** him punished by God,
Ro 8: 36 all day long; we are **c** as sheep to be

CONSIDERS (CONSIDER)
Pr 31: 16 She **c** a field and buys it; out of her
Ro 14: 5 One person **c** one day more sacred

CONSIST
Lk 12: 15 life does not **c** in an abundance

CONSOLATION
Ps 94: 19 within me, your **c** brought me joy.

CONSTRUCTIVE
1Co 10: 23 but not everything is **c**.

CONSUME (CONSUMING)
Jn 2: 17 "Zeal for your house will **c** me."

CONSUMING (CONSUME)
Dt 4: 24 For the LORD your God is a **c** fire,
Heb 12: 29 for our "God is a **c** fire."

CONTAIN
1Ki 8: 27 the highest heaven, cannot **c** you.
2Pe 3: 16 His letters **c** some things that are

CONTAMINATES
2Co 7: 1 from everything that **c** body

CONTEMPLATE
2Co 3: 18 unveiled faces **c** the Lord's glory,

CONTEMPT
Pr 14: 31 oppresses the poor shows **c** for
17: 5 Whoever mocks the poor shows **c**
18: 3 so does **c**, and with shame comes
Da 12: 2 others to shame and everlasting **c**.
Ro 2: 4 do you show **c** for the riches of his
Gal 4: 14 did not treat me with **c** or scorn.
1Th 5: 20 Do not treat prophecies with **c**

CONTEND
Jude : 3 urge you to **c** for the faith that was

CONTENT (CONTENTMENT)
Pr 13: 25 The righteous eat to their hearts' **c**,
Php 4: 11 to be **c** whatever the circumstances.
4: 12 learned the secret of being **c** in any
1Ti 6: 8 clothing, we will be **c** with that.
Heb 13: 5 and be **c** with what you have,

CONTENTMENT (CONTENT)
1Ti 6: 6 But godliness with **c** is great gain.

CONTINUAL (CONTINUE)
Pr 15: 15 but the cheerful heart has a **c** feast.

CONTINUE (CONTINUAL)
Php 2: 12 **c** to work out your salvation
2Ti 3: 14 **c** in what you have learned and
1Jn 5: 18 born of God does not **c** to sin;
Rev 22: 11 let the one who does right **c** to do
22: 11 let the holy person **c** to be holy."

CONTRITE
Ps 51: 17 a broken and **c** heart you, God,
Isa 57: 15 and to revive the heart of the **c**.
66: 2 who are humble and **c** in spirit,

CONTROL (CONTROLLED SELF-CONTROL SELF-CONTROLLED)
1Co 7: 9 But if they cannot **c** themselves,
7: 37 but has **c** over his own will,
1Th 4: 4 should learn to **c** your own body

CONTROLLED (CONTROL)
Ps 32: 9 understanding but must be **c** by bit

CONTROVERSIES
Titus 3: 9 But avoid foolish **c** and genealogies

CONVERSATION
Col 4: 6 Let your **c** be always full of grace,

CONVERT
1Ti 3: 6 He must not be a recent **c**, or he

CONVICTION
Heb 3: 14 we hold our original **c** firmly

CONVINCED (CONVINCING)
Ro 8: 38 I am **c** that neither death nor life,
2Ti 1: 12 am **c** that he is able to guard what I
3: 14 have learned and have become **c** of,

CONVINCING (CONVINCED)
Ac 1: 3 and gave many **c** proofs that he was

CORNELIUS
Roman to whom Peter preached; first Gentile Christian (Ac 10).

CORNERSTONE (STONE)
Ps 118: 22 builders rejected has become the **c**;
Isa 28: 16 a precious **c** for a sure foundation;
Eph 2: 20 Christ Jesus himself as the chief **c**.
1Pe 2: 6 a chosen and precious **c**,
2: 7 rejected has become the **c**,"

CORRECT (CORRECTING CORRECTION CORRECTS)
2Ti 4: 2 **c**, rebuke and encourage—

CORRECTING (CORRECT)
2Ti 3: 16 **c** and training in righteousness,

CORRECTION (CORRECT)
Pr 10: 17 but whoever ignores **c** leads others
12: 1 but whoever hates **c** is stupid.
15: 5 whoever heeds **c** shows prudence.
15: 10 the one who hates **c** will die.

CORRECTS (CORRECT)
Job 5: 17 "Blessed is the one whom God **c**;
Pr 9: 7 Whoever **c** a mocker invites insults

CORRUPT (CORRUPTS)
Ge 6: 11 Now the earth was **c** in God's sight

CORRUPTS (CORRUPT)
Ecc 7: 7 into a fool, and a bribe **c** the heart.
1Co 15: 33 "Bad company **c** good character."
Jas 3: 6 It **c** the whole body, sets the whole

COST
Pr 4: 7 Though it **c** all you have,
Isa 55: 1 milk without money and without **c**.
Rev 21: 6 thirsty I will give water without **c**

COUNSEL (COUNSELOR)
1Ki 22: 5 "First seek the **c** of the LORD."
Pr 15: 22 Plans fail for lack of **c**,
Rev 3: 18 I **c** you to buy from me gold

COUNSELOR (COUNSEL)
Isa 9: 6 And he will be called Wonderful **C**,

COUNT (COUNTING COUNTS)
Ro 4: 8 Lord will never **c** against them."
6: 11 **c** yourselves dead to sin but alive

COUNTING (COUNT)
2Co 5: 19 not **c** people's sins against them.

COUNTRY
Jn 4: 44 prophet has no honor in his own **c**.

COUNTS (COUNT)
Jn 6: 63 the flesh **c** for nothing.
1Co 7: 19 God's commands is what **c**.
Gal 5: 6 **c** is faith expressing itself through

COURAGE (COURAGEOUS)
Ac 23: 11 stood near Paul and said, "Take **c**!

COURAGEOUS (COURAGE)
Dt 31: 6 Be strong and **c**. Do not be afraid
Jos 1: 6 Be strong and **c**, because you will
1Co 16: 13 firm in the faith; be **c**; be strong.

COURSE
Ps 19: 5 a champion rejoicing to run his **c**.
Pr 15: 21 understanding keeps a straight **c**.

COURTS
Ps 84: 10 your **c** than a thousand elsewhere;
100: 4 thanksgiving and his **c** with praise;

COVENANT (COVENANTS)
Ge 9: 9 "I now establish my **c** with you
Ex 19: 5 if you obey me fully and keep my **c**,
1Ch 16: 15 He remembers his **c** forever,
Job 31: 1 "I made a **c** with my eyes not
Jer 31: 31 I will make a new **c** with the people
1Co 11: 25 "This cup is the new **c** in my blood;
Gal 4: 24 One **c** is from Mount Sinai
Heb 9: 15 Christ is the mediator of a new **c**,

COVENANTS (COVENANT)
Ro 9: 4 the **c**, the receiving of the law,
Gal 4: 24 The women represent two **c**.

COVER (COVER-UP COVERED COVERS)
Ps 91: 4 He will **c** you with his feathers,
Jas 5: 20 and **c** over a multitude of sins.

COVERED (COVER)
Ps 32: 1 are forgiven, whose sins are **c**.
Isa 6: 2 With two wings they **c** their faces,
Ro 4: 7 are forgiven, whose sins are **c**.
1Co 11: 4 with his head **c** dishonors his head.

COVERS (COVER)
Pr 10: 12 conflict, but love **c** over all wrongs.
1Pe 4: 8 because love **c** over a multitude

COVER-UP (COVER)
1Pe 2: 16 do not use your freedom as a **c**

COVET
Ex 20: 17 "You shall not **c** your neighbor's
Ro 13: 9 "You shall not **c**," and whatever

COWARDLY
Rev 21: 8 But the **c**, the unbelieving, the vile,

CRAFTINESS (CRAFTY)
1Co 3: 19 "He catches the wise in their **c**";

CRAFTY (CRAFTINESS)
Ge 3: 1 the serpent was more **c** than any
2Co 12: 16 Yet, **c** fellow that I am, I caught you

CRAVE
Pr 23: 3 Do not **c** his delicacies, for that
1Pe 2: 2 babies, **c** pure spiritual milk,

CREATE (CREATED CREATION CREATOR)
Ps 51: 10 **C** in me a pure heart, O God,
Isa 45: 18 he did not **c** it to be empty

CREATED (CREATE)
Ge 1: 1 In the beginning God **c** the heavens
1: 21 So God **c** the great creatures
1: 27 So God **c** mankind in his own
1: 27 male and female he **c** them.
Ps 148: 5 for at his command they were **c**,
Ro 1: 25 and served **c** things rather than
1Co 11: 9 neither was man **c** for woman,
Col 1: 16 For in him all things were **c**:
1Ti 4: 4 For everything God **c** is good,
Rev 10: 6 who **c** the heavens and all that is

CREATION (CREATE)
Mk 16: 15 *preach the gospel to all **c**.*
Jn 17: 24 because you loved me before the **c**
Ro 8: 19 For the **c** waits in eager expectation
8: 39 nor anything else in all **c**, will be
2Co 5: 17 is in Christ, the new **c** has come:
Col 1: 15 God, the firstborn over all **c**.
1Pe 1: 20 He was chosen before the **c**
Rev 13: 8 was slain from the **c** of the world.

CREATOR (CREATE)
Ge 14: 22 Most High, **C** of heaven and earth,
Isa 42: 5 LORD says—the **C** of the heavens,
Ro 1: 25 created things rather than the **C**—

CREATURE (CREATURES)
Lev 17: 11 For the life of a **c** is in the blood,

CREATURES (CREATURE)
Ge 6: 19 into the ark two of all living **c**,
Ps 104: 24 the earth is full of your **c**.

CREDIT (CREDITED)
Ro 4: 24 whom God will **c** righteousness—
1Pe 2: 20 it to your **c** if you receive a beating

CREDITED (CREDIT)
Ge 15: 6 and he **c** it to him as righteousness.
Ro 4: 5 their faith is **c** as righteousness.
Gal 3: 6 it was **c** to him as righteousness."
Jas 2: 23 it was **c** to him as righteousness,"

CRIED (CRY)
Ps 18: 6 I **c** to my God for help.

CRIMSON
Isa 1: 18 though they are red as **c**, they shall

CRIPPLED
Mk 9: 45 to enter life **c** than to have two feet

CRITICISM
2Co 8: 20 want to avoid any **c** of the way we

CROOKED
Pr 10: 9 whoever takes **c** paths will be
Php 2: 15 fault in a warped and **c** generation."

CROSS
Mt 10: 38 Whoever does not take up their **c**
Lk 9: 23 take up their **c** daily and follow me.
Ac 2: 23 to death by nailing him to the **c**.
1Co 1: 17 lest the **c** of Christ be emptied of
Gal 6: 14 in the **c** of our Lord Jesus Christ,
Php 2: 8 even death on a **c**!
Col 1: 20 through his blood, shed on the **c**.
2: 14 taken it away, nailing it to the **c**.
2: 15 triumphing over them by the **c**.
Heb 12: 2 joy set before him he endured the **c**,

CROWD
Ex 23: 2 pervert justice by siding with the **c**,

CROWN (CROWNED CROWNS)
Pr 4: 9 and present you with a glorious **c**."
10: 6 Blessings **c** the head
12: 4 noble character is her husband's **c**,
17: 6 Children's children are a **c**
Isa 61: 3 on them a **c** of beauty instead
Zec 9: 16 in his land like jewels in a **c**.
Mt 27: 29 then twisted together a **c** of thorns
1Co 9: 25 to get a **c** that will last forever.
2Ti 4: 8 store for me the **c** of righteousness,
Rev 2: 10 will give you life as your victor's **c**.

CROWNED (CROWN)
Ps 8: 5 the angels and **c** them with glory
Pr 14: 18 the prudent are **c** with knowledge.
Heb 2: 7 you **c** them with glory and honor

CROWNS (CROWN)
Rev 4: 10 They lay their **c** before the throne
19: 12 fire, and on his head are many **c**.

CRUCIFIED (CRUCIFY)
Mt 20: 19 to be mocked and flogged and **c**.
27: 38 Two rebels were **c** with him,
Lk 24: 7 be **c** and on the third day be raised
Jn 19: 18 they **c** him, and with him two

Ac 2: 36 Jesus, whom you **c**, both Lord
Ro 6: 6 that our old self was **c** with him so
1Co 1: 23 but we preach Christ **c**:
2: 2 you except Jesus Christ and him **c**.
Gal 2: 20 I have been **c** with Christ and I no
5: 24 Christ Jesus have **c** the flesh with

CRUCIFY (CRUCIFIED CRUCIFYING)
Mt 27: 22 They all answered, "**C** him!"
27: 31 Then they led him away to **c** him.

CRUCIFYING (CRUCIFY)
Heb 6: 6 their loss they are **c** the Son of God

CRUSH (CRUSHED)
Ge 3: 15 he will **c** your head, and you will
Isa 53: 10 it was the LORD's will to **c** him
Ro 16: 20 peace will soon **c** Satan under your

CRUSHED (CRUSH)
Ps 34: 18 and saves those who are **c** in spirit.
Isa 53: 5 he was **c** for our iniquities;
2Co 4: 8 pressed on every side, but not **c**;

CRY (CRIED)
Ps 34: 15 and his ears are attentive to their **c**;
40: 1 he turned to me and heard my **c**.
130: 1 Out of the depths I **c** to you,

CULMINATION
Ro 10: 4 Christ is the **c** of the law so

CUP
Ps 23: 5 my head with oil; my **c** overflows.
Mt 10: 42 anyone gives even a **c** of cold water
23: 25 You clean the outside of the **c**
26: 39 may this **c** be taken from me.
1Co 11: 25 "This **c** is the new covenant in my

CURSE (CURSED)
Dt 11: 26 you today a blessing and a **c**—
21: 23 is hung on a pole is under God's **c**.
Lk 6: 28 bless those who **c** you,
Gal 1: 8 to you, let them be under God's **c**!
3: 13 redeemed us from the **c** of the law by becoming a **c** for us,
Rev 22: 3 No longer will there be any **c**.

CURSED (CURSE)
Ge 3: 17 "**C** is the ground because of you;
Dt 27: 15 "**C** is anyone who makes an idol—
27: 16 "**C** is anyone who dishonors their
27: 17 "**C** is anyone who moves their
27: 18 "**C** is anyone who leads the blind
27: 19 "**C** is anyone who withholds justice
27: 20 "**C** is anyone who sleeps with his
27: 21 "**C** is anyone who has sexual
27: 22 "**C** is anyone who sleeps with his
27: 23 "**C** is anyone who sleeps with his
27: 24 "**C** is anyone who kills their
27: 25 "**C** is anyone who accepts a bribe
27: 26 "**C** is anyone who does not uphold
Ro 9: 3 I could wish that I myself were **c**
Gal 3: 10 "**C** is everyone who does not

CURTAIN
Ex 26: 33 Hang the **c** from the clasps
26: 33 The **c** will separate the Holy Place
Lk 23: 45 the **c** of the temple was torn in two.
Heb 10: 20 way opened for us through the **c**,

CYMBAL
1Co 13: 1 a resounding gong or a clanging **c**.

DANCE (DANCING)
Ecc 3: 4 a time to mourn and a time to **d**,
Mt 11: 17 the pipe for you, and you did not **d**;

DANCING (DANCE)
Ps 30: 11 You turned my wailing into **d**;
149: 3 Let them praise his name with **d**

DANGER
Pr 27: 12 The prudent see **d** and take refuge,
Ro 8: 35 or nakedness or **d** or sword?

DANIEL
Hebrew exile to Babylon, name changed to Belteshazzar (Da 1:6–7). Refused to eat unclean food (Da 1:8–21). Interpreted Nebuchadnezzar's dreams (Da 2; 4), writing on the wall (Da 5). Thrown into lions' den (Da 6). Visions of (Da 7–12)

DARK (DARKEST DARKNESS)
Ro 2: 19 a light for those who are in the **d**,
2Pe 1: 19 it, as to a light shining in a **d** place,

DARKEST (DARK)
Ps 23: 4 though I walk through the **d** valley,

DARKNESS (DARK)
Ge 1: 4 he separated the light from the **d**.
2Sa 22: 29 the LORD turns my **d** into light.
Job 34: 22 utter **d**, where evildoers can hide.
Jn 3: 19 but people loved **d** instead of light
2Co 6: 14 fellowship can light have with **d**?
Eph 5: 8 For you were once **d**, but now you
1Pe 2: 9 out of **d** into his wonderful light.
1Jn 1: 5 in him there is no **d** at all.
2: 9 a brother or sister is still in the **d**.

DAUGHTERS
Joel 2: 28 Your sons and **d** will prophesy,

DAVID
Son of Jesse (Ru 4:17–22; 1Ch 2:13–15), ancestor of Jesus (Mt 1:1–17; Lk 3:31).
Anointed king by Samuel (1Sa 16:1–13). Musician to Saul (1Sa 16:14–23; 18:10). Killed Goliath (1Sa 17). Relation with Jonathan (1Sa 18:1–4; 19–20; 23:16–18; 2Sa 1). Disfavor of Saul (1Sa 18:6—23:29). Spared Saul's life (1Sa 24; 26). Among Philistines (1Sa 21:10–14; 27–30). Lament for Saul and Jonathan (2Sa 1).
Anointed king of Judah (2Sa 2:1–11); of Israel (2Sa 5:1–4; 1Ch 11:1–3). Promised eternal dynasty (2Sa 7; 1Ch 17; Ps 132). Adultery with Bathsheba (2Sa 11–12). Absalom's revolt (2Sa 14–18). Last words (2Sa 23:1–7). Death (1Ki 2:10–12; 1Ch 29:28).

DAWN
Ps 37: 6 righteous reward shine like the **d**,

DAY (DAYS)
Ge 1: 5 God called the light "**d**,"
Ex 20: 8 "Remember the Sabbath **d**
Lev 23: 28 because it is the **D** of Atonement,
Nu 14: 14 them in a pillar of cloud by **d**
Jos 1: 8 meditate on it **d** and night,
Ps 84: 10 Better is one **d** in your courts than
96: 2 proclaim his salvation **d** after **d**.
118: 24 The LORD has done it this very **d**;
Pr 27: 1 do not know what a **d** may bring.
Joel 2: 31 great and dreadful **d** of the LORD.
Ob : 15 "The **d** of the LORD is near for all
Lk 11: 3 Give us each **d** our daily bread.
Ac 17: 11 examined the Scriptures every **d**
2Co 4: 16 we are being renewed **d** by **d**.
1Th 5: 2 the **d** of the Lord will come like
2Pe 3: 8 With the Lord a **d** is like a thousand

DAYS (DAY)
Dt 17: 19 he is to read it all the **d** of his life so
Ps 23: 6 love will follow me all the **d** of my
90: 10 Our **d** may come to seventy years,
Ecc 12: 1 Creator in the **d** of your youth,
Joel 2: 29 I will pour out my Spirit in those **d**.
Mic 4: 1 In the last **d** the mountain
Heb 1: 2 in these last **d** he has spoken to us
2Pe 3: 3 that in the last **d** scoffers will come,

DEACONS
1Ti 3: 8 way, **d** are to be worthy of respect,

DEAD (DIE)
Dt 18: 11 or spiritist or who consults the **d**.
Mt 28: 7 'He has risen from the **d** and is
Ro 6: 11 count yourselves **d** to sin but alive
Eph 2: 1 you were **d** in your transgressions
1Th 4: 16 and the **d** in Christ will rise first.
Jas 2: 17 is not accompanied by action, is **d**.
2: 26 so faith without deeds is **d**.

DEATH (DIE)
Nu 35: 16 the murderer is to be put to **d**.
Ps 116: 15 of the LORD is the **d** of his faithful
Pr 8: 36 all who hate me love **d**."
14: 12 right, but in the end it leads to **d**.
Ecc 7: 2 for **d** is the destiny of everyone;
Isa 25: 8 he will swallow up **d** forever.
53: 12 he poured out his life unto **d**,
Jn 5: 24 but has crossed over from **d** to life.
Ro 5: 12 **d** through sin, and in this way **d**
6: 23 For the wages of sin is **d**,
8: 13 Spirit you put to **d** the misdeeds
1Co 15: 21 For since **d** came through a man,
15: 31 I face **d** every day—yes, just as
15: 55 "Where, O **d**, is your victory?
1Pe 3: 18 He was put to **d** in the body
Rev 1: 18 I hold the keys of **d** and Hades.
20: 6 The second **d** has no power over
20: 14 The lake of fire is the second **d**.
21: 4 There will be no more **d**'

DEBAUCHERY
Ro 13: 13 not in sexual immorality and **d**,
Eph 5: 18 drunk on wine, which leads to **d**.

DEBORAH
Prophetess who led Israel to victory over Canaanites (Jdg 4–5).

DEBT (DEBTORS DEBTS)
Ro 13: 8 except the continuing **d** to love

DEBTORS (DEBT)
Mt 6: 12 as we also have forgiven our **d**.

DEBTS (DEBT)
Dt 15: 1 seven years you must cancel **d**.
Mt 6: 12 And forgive us our **d**, as we

DECAY
Ps 16: 10 will you let your faithful one see **d**.
Ac 2: 27 will not let your holy one see **d**.

DECEIT (DECEIVE)
Mk 7: 22 greed, malice, **d**, lewdness, envy,
1Pe 2: 1 yourselves of all malice and all **d**,
2: 22 and no **d** was found in his mouth."

DECEITFUL (DECEIVE)
Jer 17: 9 The heart is **d** above all things
2Co 11: 13 are false apostles, **d** workers,

DECEITFULNESS (DECEIVE)
Mk 4: 19 the **d** of wealth and the desires
Heb 3: 13 of you may be hardened by sin's **d**.

DECEIVE (DECEIT DECEITFUL DECEITFULNESS DECEIVED DECEPTIVE)
Lev 19: 11 " 'Do not **d** one another.
Pr 14: 5 An honest witness does not **d**,
Mt 24: 5 am the Messiah,' and will **d** many.
Ro 16: 18 flattery they **d** the minds of naive
1Co 3: 18 Do not **d** yourselves. If any of you
Gal 6: 3 they are not, they **d** themselves.
Eph 5: 6 no one **d** you with empty words,
Jas 1: 22 to the word, and so **d** yourselves.
Jas 1: 26 rein on their tongues **d** themselves,
1Jn 1: 8 we **d** ourselves and the truth is not

DECEIVED (DECEIVE)
Ge 3: 13 said, "The serpent **d** me, and I ate."
Gal 6: 7 Do not be **d**: God cannot be
1Ti 2: 14 And Adam was not the one **d**; it was the woman who was **d**
2Ti 3: 13 to worse, deceiving and being **d**.
Jas 1: 16 Don't be **d**, my dear brothers

DECENCY
1Ti 2: 9 modestly, with **d** and propriety,

DECEPTIVE (DECEIVE)
Pr 31: 30 Charm is **d**, and beauty is fleeting;
Col 2: 8 through hollow and **d** philosophy,

DECLARE (DECLARED DECLARING)
1Ch 16: 24 **D** his glory among the nations,
Ps 19: 1 The heavens **d** the glory of God;
96: 3 **D** his glory among the nations,
Isa 42: 9 taken place, and new things I **d**;
Ro 10: 9 If you **d** with your mouth, "Jesus is

DECLARED (DECLARE)
Mk 7: 19 saying this, Jesus **d** all foods clean.)
Ro 2: 13 the law who will be **d** righteous.
3: 20 no one will be **d** righteous

DECLARING (DECLARE)
Ps 71: 8 **d** your splendor all day long.
Ac 2: 11 hear them **d** the wonders of God

DECREED (DECREES)
La 3: 37 it happen if the Lord has not **d** it?
Lk 22: 22 Son of Man will go as it has been **d**.

DECREES (DECREED)
Lev 10: 11 Israelites all the **d** the LORD has
Ps 119:112 on keeping your **d** to the very end.

DEDICATE (DEDICATION)
Pr 20: 25 It is a trap to **d** something rashly

DEDICATION (DEDICATE)
1Ti 5: 11 sensual desires overcome their **d**

DEED (DEEDS)
Col 3: 17 whether in word or **d**, do it all

DEEDS (DEED)
1Sa 2: 3 knows, and by him **d** are weighed.
Ps 65: 5 us with awesome and righteous **d**,
66: 3 to God, "How awesome are your **d**!
78: 4 next generation the praiseworthy **d**
86: 10 you are great and do marvelous **d**;
92: 4 For you make me glad by your **d**,
111: 3 Glorious and majestic are his **d**,
Hab 3: 2 I stand in awe of your **d**, LORD.
Mt 5: 16 that they may see your good **d**
11: 19 wisdom is proved right by her **d**."
Ac 26: 20 their repentance by their **d**.
Jas 2: 14 claims to have faith but has no **d**?
2: 20 that faith without **d** is useless?
1Pe 2: 12 they may see your good **d**

DEEP (DEPTH)
1Co 2: 10 things, even the **d** things of God.
1Ti 3: 9 must keep hold of the **d** truths

DEER
Ps 42: 1 As the **d** pants for streams of water,

DEFEND (DEFENSE)
Ps 74: 22 Rise up, O God, and **d** your cause;
Pr 31: 9 **d** the rights of the poor and needy.
Jer 50: 34 He will vigorously **d** their cause so

DEFENSE (DEFEND)
Ps 35: 23 Awake, and rise to my **d**!
Php 1: 16 put here for the **d** of the gospel.

DEFERRED
Pr 13: 12 Hope **d** makes the heart sick,

DEFILE (DEFILED)
Da 1: 8 Daniel resolved not to **d** himself

DEFILED (DEFILE)
Isa 24: 5 The earth is **d** by its people;

DEFRAUD
Lev 19: 13 " 'Do not **d** or rob your neighbor.

DEITY
Col 2: 9 Christ all the fullness of the **D** lives

DELIGHT (DELIGHTS)
1Sa 15: 22 "Does the LORD **d** in burnt
Ps 1: 2 but whose **d** is in the law
16: 3 noble ones in whom is all my **d**."
35: 9 the LORD and **d** in his salvation.
37: 4 Take **d** in the LORD, and he will
43: 4 of God, to God, my joy and my **d**.
51: 16 You do not **d** in sacrifice,
119: 77 I may live, for your law is my **d**.
Isa 42: 1 my chosen one in whom I **d**;
55: 2 you will **d** in the richest of fare.
61: 10 I **d** greatly in the LORD;
Jer 9: 24 earth, for in these I **d**,"
15: 16 they were my joy and my heart's **d**,
Mic 7: 18 angry forever but **d** to show mercy.
Zep 3: 17 He will take great **d** in you;
Mt 12: 18 the one I love, in whom I **d**;
1Co 13: 6 Love does not **d** in evil but rejoices
2Co 12: 10 for Christ's sake, I **d** in weaknesses,

DELIGHTS (DELIGHT)
Ps 22: 8 deliver him, since he **d** in him."
35: 27 who **d** in the well-being of his
36: 8 them drink from your river of **d**.
Pr 3: 12 he loves, as a father the son he **d** in.
12: 22 **d** in people who are trustworthy.
29: 17 will bring you the **d** you desire.

DELILAH
Woman who betrayed Samson (Jdg 16:4–22).

DELIVER (DELIVERANCE DELIVERED DELIVERER DELIVERS)
Ps 72: 12 he will **d** the needy who cry out,
79: 9 **d** us and forgive our sins for your
Da 3: 17 the God we serve is able to **d** us
Mt 6: 13 but **d** us from the evil one.'
2Co 1: 10 that he will continue to **d** us,

DELIVERANCE (DELIVER)
Ps 3: 8 From the LORD comes **d**.
32: 7 and surround me with songs of **d**.
33: 17 A horse is a vain hope for **d**;

DELIVERED (DELIVER)
Ps 34: 4 he **d** me from all my fears.
Ro 4: 25 He was **d** over to death for our sins

DELIVERER (DELIVER)
Ps 18: 2 is my rock, my fortress and my **d**;
40: 17 You are my help and my **d**;
140: 7 my strong **d**, you shield my head
144: 2 stronghold and my **d**, my shield,

DELIVERS (DELIVER)
Ps 34: 17 he **d** them from all their troubles.
34: 19 the LORD **d** him from them all;
37: 40 The LORD helps them and **d** them;

DEMANDED
Lk 12: 20 This very night your life will be **d**
12: 48 been given much, much will be **d**;

DEMONS
Mt 12: 27 And if I drive out **d** by Beelzebul,
Mk 5: 15 been possessed by the legion of **d**,
Ro 8: 38 life, neither angels nor **d**,
Jas 2: 19 Good! Even the **d** believe that—

DEMONSTRATE (DEMONSTRATES)
Ac 26: 20 **d** their repentance by their deeds.
Ro 3: 26 he did it to **d** his righteousness

DEMONSTRATES (DEMONSTRATE)
Ro 5: 8 God **d** his own love for us in this:

DEN
Da 6: 16 and threw him into the lions' **d**.
Mt 21: 13 but you are making it 'a **d**

DENARIUS
Mk 12: 15 "Bring me a **d** and let me look

DENIED (DENY)
1Ti 5: 8 has **d** the faith and is worse than

DENIES (DENY)
1Jn 2: 23 No one who **d** the Son has

DENY (DENIED DENIES DENYING)
Ex 23: 6 "Do not **d** justice to your poor
Job 27: 5 till I die, I will not **d** my integrity.
La 3: 35 **d** people their rights before the
Lk 9: 23 be my disciple must **d** themselves
Titus 1: 16 but by their actions they **d** him.

DENYING (DENY)
Eze 22: 29 the foreigner, **d** them justice.
2Ti 3: 5 a form of godliness but **d** its power.
2Pe 2: 1 even **d** the sovereign Lord who

DEPART (DEPARTED)
Ge 49: 10 The scepter will not **d** from Judah,
Job 1: 21 mother's womb, and naked I will **d**.
Mt 25: 41 to those on his left, '**D** from me,
Php 1: 23 I desire to **d** and be with Christ,

DEPARTED (DEPART)
1Sa 4: 21 "The Glory has **d** from Israel"—
Ps 119:102 I have not **d** from your laws,

DEPOSIT
2Co 1: 22 put his Spirit in our hearts as a **d**,
5: 5 who has given us the Spirit as a **d**,
Eph 1: 14 who is a **d** guaranteeing our
2Ti 1: 14 Guard the good **d** that was entrusted

DEPRAVED (DEPRAVITY)
Ro 1: 28 God gave them over to a **d** mind,
2Pe 2: 7 was distressed by the **d** conduct

DEPRAVITY (DEPRAVED)
Ro 1: 29 of wickedness, evil, greed and **d**.

DEPRIVE
Dt 24: 17 Do not **d** the foreigner
Pr 18: 5 and so **d** the innocent of justice.
Isa 10: 2 to **d** the poor of their rights
29: 21 with false testimony **d** the innocent
1Co 7: 5 Do not **d** each other except

DEPTH (DEEP)
Ro 8: 39 neither height nor **d**, nor anything
11: 33 the **d** of the riches of the wisdom

DESERTED (DESERTS)
Mt 26: 56 all the disciples **d** him and fled.
2Ti 1: 15 in the province of Asia has **d** me,

DESERTING (DESERTS)
Gal 1: 6 you are so quickly **d** the one who

DESERTS (DESERTED DESERTING)
Zec 11: 17 shepherd, who **d** the flock!

DESERVE (DESERVES)
Ps 103: 10 he does not treat us as our sins **d**
Jer 21: 14 I will punish you as your deeds **d**,
Mt 22: 8 those I invited did not **d** to come.
Ro 1: 32 those who do such things **d** death,

DESERVES (DESERVE)
Lk 10: 7 for the worker **d** his wages.
1Ti 5: 18 and "The worker **d** his wages."

DESIRABLE (DESIRE)
Pr 22: 1 name is more **d** than great riches;

DESIRE (DESIRABLE DESIRES)
Ge 3: 16 Your **d** will be for your husband,
Dt 5: 21 You shall not set your **d** on your
Ps 40: 6 and offering you did not **d**—
40: 8 I **d** to do your will, my God;
73: 25 earth has nothing I **d** besides you.
Pr 3: 15 nothing you **d** can compare
10: 24 what the righteous **d** will be
11: 23 The **d** of the righteous ends only
19: 2 **D** without knowledge is not good
Isa 26: 8 and renown are the **d** of our hearts.
53: 2 appearance that we should **d** him.
55: 11 but will accomplish what I **d**
Hos 6: 6 For I **d** mercy, not sacrifice,
Mt 9: 13 'I **d** mercy, not sacrifice.'
Ro 7: 18 For I have the **d** to do what is good,
1Co 12: 31 Now eagerly **d** the greater gifts.
14: 1 and eagerly **d** gifts of the Spirit,
Php 1: 23 I **d** to depart and be with Christ,
Heb 13: 18 **d** to live honorably in every way.
Jas 1: 15 after **d** has conceived, it gives birth

DESIRES (DESIRE)
Ge 4: 7 it **d** to have you, but you must rule
1Ch 29: 18 keep these **d** and thoughts
Ps 34: 12 life and **d** to see many good days,
37: 4 will give you the **d** of your heart.
103: 5 who satisfies your **d** with good
145: 19 He fulfills the **d** of those who fear
Pr 11: 6 the unfaithful are trapped by evil **d**.
19: 22 What a person **d** is unfailing love;
Mk 4: 19 and the **d** for other things come
Ro 8: 5 minds set on what the Spirit **d**.
13: 14 how to gratify the **d** of the flesh.
Gal 5: 16 and you will not gratify the **d**
5: 17 For the flesh **d** what is contrary
1Ti 3: 1 to be an overseer **d** a noble task.
6: 9 harmful **d** that plunge people
2Ti 2: 22 Flee the evil **d** of youth and pursue
Jas 1: 20 the righteousness that God **d**.
4: 1 from your **d** that battle within you?
1Pe 2: 11 to abstain from sinful **d**,
1Jn 2: 17 The world and its **d** pass away,

DESOLATE
Isa 54: 1 the children of the **d** woman than

DESPAIR
Isa 61: 3 of praise instead of a spirit of **d**.
2Co 4: 8 perplexed, but not in **d**;

DESPISE (DESPISED DESPISES)
Job 42: 6 Therefore I **d** myself and repent
Pr 1: 7 fools **d** wisdom and instruction.
3: 11 do not **d** the LORD's discipline,
14: 21 It is a sin to **d** one's neighbor,
15: 32 disregard discipline **d** themselves,
23: 22 do not **d** your mother when she is
Zec 4: 10 "Who dares **d** the day of small
Lk 16: 13 devoted to the one and **d** the other.
Titus 2: 15 Do not let anyone **d** you.

DESPISED (DESPISE)
Ge 25: 34 and left. So Esau **d** his birthright.
Isa 53: 3 He was **d** and rejected by mankind,
1Co 1: 28 of this world and the **d** things—

DESPISES (DESPISE)
Pr 15: 20 but a foolish man **d** his mother.

DESTINED (DESTINY)
Lk 2: 34 "This child is **d** to cause the falling

DESTINY (DESTINED PREDESTINED)
Ps 73: 17 then I understood their final **d**.
Ecc 7: 2 for death is the **d** of everyone;

DESTITUTE
Pr 31: 8 for the rights of all who are **d**.
Heb 11: 37 in sheepskins and goatskins, **d**,

DESTROY (DESTROYED DESTROYS DESTRUCTION)
Pr 1: 32 complacency of fools will **d** them;
11: 9 the godless **d** their neighbors,
Mt 10: 28 of the One who can **d** both soul

DESTROYED (DESTROY)
Job 19: 26 And after my skin has been **d**,
1Co 8: 11 is **d** by your knowledge.
15: 26 The last enemy to be **d** is death.
2Co 5: 1 if the earthly tent we live in is **d**,
Heb 10: 39 those who shrink back and are **d**,
2Pe 3: 10 the elements will be **d** by fire,

DESTROYS (DESTROY)
Pr 6: 32 whoever does so **d** himself.
18: 9 his work is brother to one who **d**.
28: 24 wrong," is partner to one who **d**.
Ecc 9: 18 but one sinner **d** much good.
1Co 3: 17 If anyone **d** God's temple, God will

DESTRUCTION (DESTROY)
Ps 1: 6 the way of the wicked leads to **d**.
Pr 16: 18 Pride goes before **d**, a haughty
Hos 13: 14 Where, O grave, is your **d**?
Mt 7: 13 broad is the road that leads to **d**,
Gal 6: 8 flesh, from the flesh will reap **d**;
2Th 1: 9 will be punished with everlasting **d**
1Ti 6: 9 that plunge people into ruin and **d**.
2Pe 2: 1 bringing swift **d** on themselves.
3: 16 other Scriptures, to their own **d**.

DETERMINED (DETERMINES)
Job 14: 5 A person's days are **d**;
Isa 14: 26 This is the plan **d** for the whole
Da 11: 36 what has been **d** must take place.

DETERMINES (DETERMINED)
Ps 147: 4 He **d** the number of the stars
1Co 12: 11 them to each one, just as he **d**.

DETESTABLE (DETESTS)
Pr 21: 27 The sacrifice of the wicked is **d**—
28: 9 even their prayers are **d**.
Isa 1: 13 Your incense is **d** to me.
Lk 16: 15 What people value highly is **d**
Titus 1: 16 They are **d**, disobedient and unfit

DETESTS (DETESTABLE)
Dt 22: 5 the LORD your God **d** anyone who
23: 18 the LORD your God **d** them both.
25: 16 the LORD your God **d** anyone who
Pr 11: 1 The LORD **d** dishonest scales,
12: 22 The LORD **d** lying lips, but he
15: 8 The LORD **d** the sacrifice
15: 9 The LORD **d** the way
15: 26 The LORD **d** the thoughts
16: 5 The LORD **d** all the proud
17: 15 the LORD **d** them both.
20: 23 The LORD **d** differing weights,

DEVIL (DEVIL'S)
Mt 13: 39 the enemy who sows them is the **d**.
25: 41 the eternal fire prepared for the **d**
Lk 4: 2 forty days he was tempted by the **d**.
8: 12 then the **d** comes and takes away
Eph 4: 27 and do not give the **d** a foothold.
2Ti 2: 26 and escape from the trap of the **d**,
Jas 4: 7 Resist the **d**, and he will flee
1Pe 5: 8 Your enemy the **d** prowls around
1Jn 3: 8 who does what is sinful is of the **d**,
Rev 12: 9 that ancient serpent called the **d**,

DEVIL'S (DEVIL)
Eph 6: 11 your stand against the **d** schemes.
1Ti 3: 7 into disgrace and into the **d** trap.
1Jn 3: 8 was to destroy the **d** work.

DEVISED
2Pe 1: 16 we did not follow cleverly **d** stories

DEVOTE (DEVOTED DEVOTING DEVOTION DEVOUT)
Job 11: 13 "Yet if you **d** your heart to him
Jer 30: 21 who is he who will **d** himself to be
Col 4: 2 **D** yourselves to prayer,
1Ti 4: 13 **d** yourself to the public reading
Titus 3: 8 may be careful to **d** themselves

DEVOTED (DEVOTE)
Ezr 7: 10 For Ezra had **d** himself to the study
Ac 2: 42 They **d** themselves to the apostles'
Ro 12: 10 Be **d** to one another in love.
1Co 7: 34 Her aim is to be **d** to the Lord

DEVOTING (DEVOTE)
1Ti 5: 10 **d** herself to all kinds of good deeds.

DEVOTION (DEVOTE)
1Ch 28: 9 serve him with wholehearted **d**
1Co 7: 35 way in undivided **d** to the Lord.
2Co 11: 3 your sincere and pure **d** to Christ.

DEVOUR
2Sa 2: 26 to Joab, "Must the sword **d** forever?
Mk 12: 40 They **d** widows' houses
1Pe 5: 8 lion looking for someone to **d**.

DEVOUT (DEVOTE)
Lk 2: 25 Simeon, who was righteous and **d**.

DIE (DEAD DEATH DIED DIES)
Ge 2: 17 eat from it you will certainly **d**."
Ex 11: 5 Every firstborn son in Egypt will **d**,
Ru 1: 17 Where you **d** I will **d**, and there I
2Ki 14: 6 each will **d** for their own sin."
Pr 5: 23 For lack of discipline they will **d**,
10: 21 many, but fools **d** for lack of sense.
11: 7 placed in mortals **d** with them;
15: 10 one who hates correction will **d**.
23: 13 them with the rod, they will not **d**.
Ecc 3: 2 a time to be born and a time to **d**,
Isa 66: 24 the worms that eat them will not **d**,
Eze 3: 18 wicked person will **d** for their sin,
18: 4 one who sins is the one who will **d**.
33: 8 wicked person will **d** for their sin,
Mt 26: 52 all who draw the sword will **d**
Jn 11: 25 in me will live, even though they **d**;
11: 26 by believing in me will never **d**.
Ro 5: 7 Very rarely will anyone **d**
14: 8 and if we **d**, we **d** for the Lord.
1Co 15: 22 For as in Adam all **d**, so in Christ
Php 1: 21 to live is Christ and to **d** is gain.
Heb 9: 27 as people are destined to **d** once,
Rev 14: 13 Blessed are the dead who **d**

DIED (DIE)
Ro 5: 6 Christ **d** for the ungodly.
6: 2 We are those who have **d** to sin;
6: 8 Now if we **d** with Christ, we believe
14: 15 someone for whom Christ **d**.
1Co 8: 11 for whom Christ **d**, is destroyed
15: 3 that Christ **d** for our sins according
2Co 5: 14 one **d** for all, and therefore all **d**.
Col 3: 3 For you **d**, and your life is now
1Th 5: 10 He **d** for us so that, whether we are
2Ti 2: 11 If we **d** with him, we will also live
Heb 9: 15 that he has **d** as a ransom to set
Rev 2: 8 Last, who **d** and came to life again.

DIES (DIE)
Job 14: 14 If someone **d**, will they live again?
1Co 15: 36 does not come to life unless it **d**.

DIFFERENCE (DIFFERENT)
Ro 10: 12 For there is no **d** between Jew

DIFFERENT (DIFFERENCE)
1Co 12: 4 There are **d** kinds of gifts,
2Co 11: 4 or a **d** gospel from the one you

DIGNITY
Pr 31: 25 She is clothed with strength and **d**;

DIGS
Pr 26: 27 Whoever **d** a pit will fall into it;

DILIGENCE (DILIGENT)
Heb 6: 11 show this same **d** to the very end,

DILIGENT (DILIGENCE)
Pr 21: 5 The plans of the **d** lead to profit as
1Ti 4: 15 Be **d** in these matters;

DIRECT (DIRECTS)
Ps 119: 35 **D** me in the path of your
119:133 **D** my footsteps according to your
Jer 10: 23 it is not for them to **d** their steps.
2Th 3: 5 May the Lord **d** your hearts

DIRECTS (DIRECT)
Ps 42: 8 By day the LORD **d** his love,
Isa 48: 17 who **d** you in the way you should

DIRGE
Mt 11: 17 we sang a **d**, and you did not

DISAPPEAR
Mt 5: 18 until heaven and earth **d**,
Lk 16: 17 earth to **d** than for the least stroke

DISASTER
Ps 57: 1 your wings until the **d** has passed.
Pr 3: 25 Have no fear of sudden **d**
17: 5 whoever gloats over **d** will not go
Isa 45: 7 I bring prosperity and create **d**;
Eze 7: 5 Unheard-of **d**! See, it comes!

DISCERN (DISCERNING)
Ps 19: 12 But who can **d** their own errors?
139: 3 You **d** my going out and my lying
Php 1: 10 you may be able to **d** what is best

DISCERNING (DISCERN)
Pr 14: 6 knowledge comes easily to the **d**.
15: 14 The **d** heart seeks knowledge,
17: 10 A rebuke impresses a **d** person
17: 24 A **d** person keeps wisdom in view,
17: 28 and **d** if they hold their tongues.
19: 25 rebuke the **d**, and they will gain
28: 11 and **d** sees how deluded they are.

DISCIPLE (DISCIPLES)
Mt 10: 42 of these little ones who is my **d**,
Lk 14: 27 and follow me cannot be my **d**.

DISCIPLES (DISCIPLE)
Mt 28: 19 go and make **d** of all nations,
Jn 8: 31 my teaching, you are really my **d**.
13: 35 will know that you are my **d**, if you
Ac 11: 26 The **d** were called Christians first

DISCIPLINE (DISCIPLINED DISCIPLINES)
Ps 38: 1 your anger or **d** me in your wrath.
39: 11 rebuke and **d** anyone for their sin,
94: 12 Blessed is the one you **d**, LORD,
Pr 3: 11 do not despise the LORD's **d**,
5: 12 You will say, "How I hated **d**!
5: 23 For lack of **d** they will die,
10: 17 Whoever heeds **d** shows the way
12: 1 Whoever loves **d** loves knowledge,
13: 18 Whoever disregards **d** comes
13: 24 their children is careful to **d** them.
15: 5 A fool spurns a parent's **d**,
15: 32 disregard **d** despise themselves,
19: 18 **D** your children, for in that there is
19: 20 Listen to advice and accept **d**,

Pr 22: 15 the rod of **d** will drive it far away.
23: 13 Do not withhold **d** from a child;
29: 17 **D** your children, and they will give
Heb 12: 5 do not make light of the Lord's **d**,
12: 7 Endure hardship as **d**;
12: 11 No **d** seems pleasant at the time,
Rev 3: 19 Those whom I love I rebuke and **d**.

DISCIPLINED (DISCIPLINE)
Jer 31: 18 'You **d** me like an unruly calf,
1Co 11: 32 we are being **d** so that we will not
Col 2: 5 delight to see how **d** you are
Titus 1: 8 upright, holy and **d**.
Heb 12: 7 For what children are not **d** by

DISCIPLINES (DISCIPLINE)
Dt 8: 5 so the LORD your God **d** you.
Pr 3: 12 because the LORD **d** those he
Heb 12: 6 the Lord **d** the one he loves,
12: 10 but God **d** us for our good,

DISCLOSED
Lk 8: 17 nothing hidden that will not be **d**,

DISCOURAGED
Jos 1: 9 do not be **d**, for the LORD your
10: 25 "Do not be afraid; do not be **d**.
1Ch 28: 20 Do not be afraid or **d**,
Isa 42: 4 or be **d** till he establishes justice
Col 3: 21 children, or they will become **d**.

DISCREDITED
2Co 6: 3 so that our ministry will not be **d**.

DISCRETION
1Ch 22: 12 May the LORD give you **d**
Pr 1: 4 knowledge and **d** to the young—
2: 11 **D** will protect you,
5: 2 that you may maintain **d** and your
8: 12 I possess knowledge and **d**.
11: 22 beautiful woman who shows no **d**.

DISCRIMINATED
Jas 2: 4 have you not **d** among yourselves

DISFIGURED
Isa 52: 14 his appearance was so **d** beyond

DISGRACE (DISGRACEFUL DISGRACES)
Pr 11: 2 then comes **d**, but with humility
19: 26 is a child who brings shame and **d**.
Ac 5: 41 worthy of suffering **d** for the Name.
Heb 13: 13 the camp, bearing the **d** he bore.

DISGRACEFUL (DISGRACE)
Pr 10: 5 sleeps during harvest is a **d** son.
17: 2 servant will rule over a **d** son

DISGRACES (DISGRACE)
Pr 28: 7 companion of gluttons **d** his father.
29: 15 left undisciplined **d** its mother.

DISGUISE
Pr 26: 24 Enemies **d** themselves with their

DISHONEST
Pr 11: 1 The LORD detests **d** scales,
29: 27 The righteous detest the **d**;
Lk 16: 10 whoever is **d** with very little will
1Ti 3: 8 wine, and not pursuing **d** gain.

DISHONOR (DISHONORS)
Lev 18: 7 " 'Do not **d** your father by having
Pr 30: 9 and so **d** the name of my God.
1Co 13: 5 It does not **d** others, it is not
15: 43 it is sown in **d**, it is raised in glory;

DISHONORS (DISHONOR)
Dt 27: 16 is anyone who **d** their father

DISMAYED
Isa 41: 10 do not be **d**, for I am your God.

DISOBEDIENCE (DISOBEY)
Ro 5: 19 as through the **d** of the one man
11: 32 has bound everyone over to **d** so
Heb 2: 2 and **d** received its just punishment,
4: 6 did not go in because of their **d**,
4: 11 by following their example of **d**.

DISOBEDIENT (DISOBEY)
2Ti 3: 2 proud, abusive, **d** to their parents,
Titus 1: 6 to the charge of being wild and **d**.
1: 16 **d** and unfit for doing anything

DISOBEY (DISOBEDIENCE DISOBEDIENT)
Dt 11: 28 the curse if you **d** the commands
2Ch 24: 20 'Why do you **d** the LORD's
Ro 1: 30 of doing evil; they **d** their parents;

DISORDER
1Co 14: 33 For God is not a God of **d**
2Co 12: 20 slander, gossip, arrogance and **d**.
Jas 3: 16 there you find **d** and every evil

DISOWN
Pr 30: 9 I may have too much and **d** you
Mt 10: 33 will **d** before my Father in heaven.
26: 35 to die with you, I will never **d** you."
2Ti 2: 12 If we **d** him, he will also **d** us;

DISPLAY (DISPLAYS)
Eze 39: 21 "I will **d** my glory among
1Ti 1: 16 Christ Jesus might **d** his immense

DISPLAYS (DISPLAY)
Isa 44: 23 Jacob, he **d** his glory in Israel.

DISPUTE (DISPUTES)
Pr 17: 14 the matter before a **d** breaks out.
1Co 6: 1 If any of you has a **d** with another,

DISPUTES (DISPUTE)
Pr 18: 18 Casting the lot settles **d** and keeps

DISQUALIFIED
1Co 9: 27 I myself will not be **d** for the prize.

DISREGARD
Pr 15: 32 Those who **d** discipline despise

DISREPUTE
2Pe 2: 2 will bring the way of truth into **d**.

DISSENSION
Ro 13: 13 debauchery, not in **d** and jealousy.

DISTINGUISH
1Ki 3: 9 and to **d** between right and wrong.
Heb 5: 14 have trained themselves to **d** good

DISTORT
2Co 4: 2 nor do we **d** the word of God.
2Pe 3: 16 ignorant and unstable people **d**,

DISTRESS (DISTRESSED)
Ps 18: 6 In my **d** I called to the LORD;
Jnh 2: 2 "In my **d** I called to the LORD,
Jas 1: 27 and widows in their **d** and to keep

DISTRESSED (DISTRESS)
Ro 14: 15 sister is **d** because of what you eat,

DIVIDED (DIVISION)
Mt 12: 25 "Every kingdom **d** against itself
Lk 23: 34 **d** up his clothes by casting lots.
1Co 1: 13 Is Christ **d**? Was Paul crucified

DIVINATION
Lev 19: 26 " 'Do not practice **d** or seek

DIVINE
Ro 1: 20 his eternal power and **d** nature—
2Co 10: 4 they have **d** power to demolish
2Pe 1: 4 may participate in the **d** nature,

DIVISION (DIVIDED DIVISIONS DIVISIVE)
Lk 12: 51 peace on earth? No, I tell you, but **d**.
1Co 12: 25 there should be no **d** in the body,

DIVISIONS (DIVISION)
Ro 16: 17 to watch out for those who cause **d**
1Co 1: 10 and that there be no **d** among you,
11: 18 as a church, there are **d** among you,

DIVISIVE (DIVISION)
Titus 3: 10 Warn a **d** person once,

DIVORCE (DIVORCES)
Mt 19: 3 for a man to **d** his wife for any
1Co 7: 11 a husband must not **d** his wife.

DIVORCES (DIVORCE)
Mal 2: 16 man who hates and **d** his wife,"

DOCTOR
Mt 9: 12 "It is not the healthy who need a **d**,

DOCTRINE
1Ti 4: 16 Watch your life and **d** closely.
Titus 2: 1 what is appropriate to sound **d**.

DOMINION
Ps 22: 28 for **d** belongs to the LORD and he

DOOR
Ps 141: 3 keep watch over the **d** of my lips.
Mt 6: 6 close the **d** and pray to your Father,
7: 7 and the **d** will be opened to you.
Rev 3: 20 I stand at the **d** and knock.

DOORKEEPER
Ps 84: 10 I would rather be a **d** in the house

DOUBLE-EDGED
Heb 4: 12 Sharper than any **d** sword,
Rev 1: 16 of his mouth was a sharp, **d** sword.
2: 12 of him who has the sharp, **d** sword.

DOUBLE-MINDED (MIND)
Ps 119:113 I hate **d** people, but I love your law.
Jas 1: 8 Such a person is **d** and unstable

DOUBT
Mt 14: 31 faith," he said, "why did you **d**?"
21: 21 if you have faith and do not **d**,
Mk 11: 23 and does not **d** in their heart
Jas 1: 6 you must believe and not **d**,
Jude : 22 Be merciful to those who **d**;

DOWNCAST
Ps 42: 5 Why, my soul, are you **d**?
2Co 7: 6 who comforts the **d**, comforted us

DRAW (DRAWING DRAWS)
Mt 26: 52 "for all who **d** the sword will die
Jn 12: 32 earth, will **d** all people to myself."
Heb 10: 22 let us **d** near to God with a sincere

DRAWING (DRAW)
Lk 21: 28 your redemption is **d** near."

DRAWS (DRAW)
Jn 6: 44 the Father who sent me **d** them,

DREADFUL
Heb 10: 31 It is a **d** thing to fall into the hands

DRESS
1Ti 2: 9 want the women to **d** modestly,

DRINK (DRUNK DRUNKARDS DRUNKENNESS)
Pr 5: 15 **D** water from your own cistern,
Lk 12: 19 eat, **d** and be merry." '
Jn 7: 37 who is thirsty come to me and **d**.
1Co 12: 13 were all given the one Spirit to **d**.

DRIVES
1Jn 4: 18 But perfect love **d** out fear,

DROP
Pr 17: 14 so **d** the matter before a dispute
Isa 40: 15 Surely the nations are like a **d**

DRUNK (DRINK)
Eph 5: 18 Do not get **d** on wine, which leads

DRUNKARDS (DRINK)
Pr 23: 21 for **d** and gluttons become poor,
1Co 6: 10 the greedy nor **d** nor slanderers

DRUNKENNESS (DRINK)
Lk 21: 34 **d** and the anxieties of life,
Ro 13: 13 not in carousing and **d**,
Gal 5: 21 and envy; **d**, orgies, and the like.
1Pe 4: 3 living in debauchery, lust, **d**, orgies,

DRY
Isa 53: 2 and like a root out of **d** ground.
Eze 37: 4 bones and say to them, '**D** bones,

DUST
Ge 2: 7 a man from the **d** of the ground
Ps 103: 14 he remembers that we are **d**.
Ecc 3: 20 come from **d**, and to **d** all return.

DUTY
Ecc 12: 13 for this is the **d** of all mankind.
Ac 23: 1 I have fulfilled my **d** to God in all
1Co 7: 3 husband should fulfill his marital **d**

DWELL (DWELLING DWELLS)
1Ki 8: 27 "But will God really **d** on earth?
Ps 23: 6 I will **d** in the house of the LORD
Isa 43: 18 do not **d** on the past.
Eph 3: 17 Christ may **d** in your hearts
Col 1: 19 to have all his fullness **d** in him,
3: 16 of Christ **d** among you richly

DWELLING (DWELL)
Eph 2: 22 built together to become a **d**

DWELLS (DWELL)
1Co 3: 16 that God's Spirit **d** in your midst?

EAGER
Pr 31: 13 and flax and works with **e** hands.
1Pe 5: 2 dishonest gain, but **e** to serve;

EAGLE'S (EAGLES)
Ps 103: 5 your youth is renewed like the **e**.

EAGLES (EAGLE'S)
Isa 40: 31 They will soar on wings like **e**;

EAR (EARS)
1Co 2: 9 eye has seen, what no **e** has heard,
12: 16 And if the **e** should say, "Because I

EARS (EAR)
Job 42: 5 My **e** had heard of you but now my
Ps 34: 15 and his **e** are attentive to their cry;
Pr 21: 13 Whoever shuts their **e** to the cry
2Ti 4: 3 to say what their itching **e** want

EARTH (EARTHLY)
Ge 1: 1 God created the heavens and the **e**.
Ps 24: 1 The **e** is the LORD's,
Ps 108: 5 let your glory be over all the **e**.
Isa 6: 3 the whole **e** is full of his glory."
51: 6 the **e** will wear out like a garment
55: 9 the heavens are higher than the **e**,
66: 1 throne, and the **e** is my footstool.
Jer 23: 24 "Do not I fill heaven and **e**?"
Hab 2: 20 let all the **e** be silent before him.
Mt 6: 10 will be done, on **e** as it is in heaven.
16: 19 you bind on **e** will be bound
24: 35 Heaven and **e** will pass away,
28: 18 and on **e** has been given to me.
Lk 2: 14 on **e** peace to those on whom his
1Co 10: 26 for, "The **e** is the Lord's,
Php 2: 10 heaven and on **e** and under the **e**,
2Pe 3: 13 to a new heaven and a new **e**,

EARTHLY (EARTH)
Php 3: 19 Their mind is set on **e** things.
Col 3: 2 on things above, not on **e** things.

EAST
Ps 103: 12 as far as the **e** is from the west,

EASY
Mt 11: 30 For my yoke is **e** and my burden is

EAT (EATING)
Ge 2: 17 you must not **e** from the tree
Isa 55: 1 have no money, come, buy and **e**!
65: 25 the lion will **e** straw like the ox,
Mt 26: 26 his disciples, saying, "Take and **e**;
Ro 14: 2 faith allows them to **e** anything,
1Co 8: 13 if what I **e** causes my brother
10: 31 So whether you **e** or drink
2Th 3: 10 is unwilling to work shall not **e**."

EATING (EAT)
Ro 14: 17 kingdom of God is not a matter of **e**

EDICT
Heb 11: 23 they were not afraid of the king's **e**.

EDIFIES
1Co 14: 4 speaks in a tongue **e** themselves,

EFFECT
Isa 32: 17 its **e** will be quietness
Heb 9: 18 was not put into **e** without blood.

EFFORT
Lk 13: 24 "Make every **e** to enter through
Ro 9: 16 depend on human desire or **e**,
14: 19 Let us therefore make every **e** to do
Eph 4: 3 Make every **e** to keep the unity
Heb 4: 11 make every **e** to enter that rest,
12: 14 Make every **e** to live in peace
2Pe 1: 5 make every **e** to add to your faith
3: 14 make every **e** to be found spotless,

ELAH
Son of Baasha; king of Israel (1Ki 16:6–14).

ELDERLY (ELDERS)
Lev 19: 32 show respect for the **e** and revere

ELDERS (ELDERLY)
1Ti 5: 17 The **e** who direct the affairs

ELECTION
Ro 9: 11 God's purpose in **e** might stand:
2Pe 1: 10 to confirm your calling and **e**.

ELI
High priest in youth of Samuel (1Sa 1–4). Blessed Hannah (1Sa 1:12–18); raised Samuel (1Sa 2:11–26).

ELIJAH
Prophet; predicted famine in Israel (1Ki 17:1; Jas 5:17). Fed by ravens (1Ki 17:2–6). Raised Sidonian widow's son (1Ki 17:7–24). Defeated prophets of Baal at Carmel (1Ki 18:16–46). Ran from Jezebel (1Ki 19:1–9). Prophesied death of Azariah (2Ki 1). Succeeded by Elisha (1Ki 19:19–21; 2Ki 2:1–18). Taken to heaven in whirlwind (2Ki 2:11–12).

Return prophesied (Mal 4:5–6); equated with John the Baptist (Mt 17:9–13; Mk 9:9–13; Lk 1:17). Appeared with Moses in transfiguration of Jesus (Mt 17:1–8; Mk 9:1–8).

ELISHA
Prophet; successor of Elijah (1Ki 19:16–21); inherited his cloak (2Ki 2:1–18). Miracles of (2Ki 2–6).

ELIZABETH
Mother of John the Baptist, relative of Mary (Lk 1:5–58).

EMBITTER
Col 3: 21 Fathers, do not **e** your children,

EMPEROR
1Pe 2: 17 of believers, fear God, honor the **e**.

EMPTY
Mt 12: 36 for every **e** word they have spoken.

Eph 5: 6 no one deceive you with **e** words,
1Pe 1: 18 you were redeemed from the **e** way

ENABLE (ABLE)
Lk 1: 74 to **e** us to serve him without fear
Ac 4: 29 **e** your servants to speak your word

ENABLED (ABLE)
Lev 26: 13 **e** you to walk with heads held high.
Jn 6: 65 me unless the Father has **e** them."

ENABLES (ABLE)
Php 3: 21 by the power that **e** him to bring

ENCAMPS
Ps 34: 7 the LORD **e** around those who fear

ENCOURAGE (ENCOURAGEMENT ENCOURAGING)
Ps 10: 17 you **e** them, and you listen to their
Ac 15: 32 said much to **e** and strengthen
Ro 12: 8 if it is to **e**, then give
1Th 4: 18 Therefore **e** one another with these
2Ti 4: 2 correct, rebuke and **e**—
Titus 2: 6 Similarly, **e** the young men to be
Heb 3: 13 But **e** one another daily, as long as

ENCOURAGEMENT (ENCOURAGE)
Ac 4: 36 (which means "son of **e**"),
Ro 15: 4 the **e** they provide we might have
15: 5 **e** give you the same attitude of
Heb 12: 5 completely forgotten this word of **e**

ENCOURAGING (ENCOURAGE)
1Co 14: 3 their strengthening, **e** and comfort.
Heb 10: 25 habit of doing, but **e** one another—

END
Ps 119: 33 that I may follow it to the **e**.
Pr 14: 12 right, but in the **e** it leads to death.
19: 20 the **e** you will be counted among
23: 32 In the **e** it bites like a snake
Ecc 12: 12 making many books there is no **e**,
Mt 10: 22 stands firm to the **e** will be saved.
Lk 21: 9 but the **e** will not come right away."
1Co 15: 24 Then the **e** will come, when he

ENDURANCE (ENDURE)
Ro 15: 4 so that through the **e** taught
15: 5 May the God who gives **e**
2Co 1: 6 you patient **e** of the same sufferings
Col 1: 11 might so that you may have great **e**
1Ti 6: 11 faith, love, **e** and gentleness.
Titus 2: 2 and sound in faith, in love and in **e**.

ENDURE (ENDURANCE ENDURES)
Ps 72: 17 May his name **e** forever;
Pr 12: 19 Truthful lips **e** forever, but a lying
27: 24 for riches do not **e** forever,
Ecc 3: 14 everything God does will **e** forever;
Mal 3: 2 who can **e** the day of his coming?
2Ti 2: 12 if we **e**, we will also reign with him.
Heb 12: 7 **E** hardship as discipline;
Rev 3: 10 kept my command to **e** patiently,

ENDURES (ENDURE)
Ps 112: 9 poor, their righteousness **e** forever;
136: 1 *His love **e** forever.*
Da 9: 15 yourself a name that **e** to this day,
1Pe 1: 25 but the word of the Lord **e** forever."

ENEMIES (ENEMY)
Ps 23: 5 before me in the presence of my **e**.
Mic 7: 6 a man's **e** are the members of his
Mt 5: 44 love your **e** and pray for those who
Lk 20: 43 until I make your **e** a footstool

ENEMY (ENEMIES ENMITY)
Pr 24: 17 Do not gloat when your **e** falls;
25: 21 If your **e** is hungry, give him food
27: 6 trusted, but an **e** multiplies kisses.
1Co 15: 26 The last **e** to be destroyed is death.
1Ti 5: 14 and to give the **e** no opportunity
Jas 4: 4 of the world becomes an **e** of God.

ENJOY (JOY)
Dt 6: 2 and so that you may **e** long life.
Eph 6: 3 and that you may **e** long life
Heb 11: 25 than to **e** the fleeting pleasures

ENJOYMENT (JOY)
Ecc 4: 8 why am I depriving myself of **e**?"
1Ti 6: 17 us with everything for our **e**.

ENLIGHTENED (LIGHT)
Eph 1: 18 eyes of your heart may be **e** in
Heb 6: 4 for those who have once been **e**,

ENMITY (ENEMY)
Ge 3: 15 I will put **e** between you

ENOCH
Walked with God and taken by him (Ge 5:18–24; Heb 11:5). Prophet (Jude 14).

ENTANGLED (ENTANGLES)
2Ti 2: 4 soldier gets **e** in civilian affairs,
2Pe 2: 20 Jesus Christ and are again **e** in it

ENTANGLES (ENTANGLED)
Heb 12: 1 hinders and the sin that so easily **e**.

ENTER (ENTERED ENTERS)
Ps 100: 4 **E** his gates with thanksgiving
Mt 5: 20 will certainly not **e** the kingdom
7: 13 "**E** through the narrow gate.
18: 8 It is better for you to **e** life maimed
Mk 10: 15 like a little child will never **e** it."
10: 23 the rich to **e** the kingdom of God!"

ENTERED (ENTER)
Ro 5: 12 just as sin **e** the world through one
Heb 9: 12 he **e** the Most Holy Place once

ENTERS (ENTER)
Mk 7: 18 that nothing that **e** a person
Jn 10: 2 The one who **e** by the gate is

ENTERTAIN
1Ti 5: 19 Do not **e** an accusation against

ENTHRALLED
Ps 45: 11 Let the king be **e** by your beauty;

ENTHRONED (THRONE)
1Sa 4: 4 who is **e** between the cherubim.
Ps 2: 4 The One **e** in heaven laughs;
102: 12 But you, LORD, sit **e** forever;
Isa 40: 22 He sits **e** above the circle

ENTICE
Pr 1: 10 if sinful men **e** you, do not give
2Pe 2: 18 they **e** people who are just escaping

ENTIRE
Gal 5: 14 For the **e** law is fulfilled in keeping

ENTRUSTED (TRUST)
1Ti 6: 20 guard what has been **e** to your care.
2Ti 1: 12 to guard what I have **e** to him until
1: 14 good deposit that was **e** to you—
Jude : 3 once for all **e** to God's holy people.

ENVY
Pr 3: 31 Do not **e** the violent or choose any
14: 30 to the body, but **e** rots the bones.
1Co 13: 4 It does not **e**, it does not boast,

EPHRAIM
1. Second son of Joseph (Ge 41:52; 46:20). Blessed as firstborn by Jacob (Ge 48).
2. Synonymous with Northern Kingdom (Isa 7:17; Hos 5).

EQUAL
Isa 40: 25 Or who is my **e**?" says the Holy
Jn 5: 18 Father, making himself **e** with God.
1Co 12: 25 its parts should have **e** concern

EQUIP (EQUIPPED)
Eph 4: 12 to **e** his people for works of service,
Heb 13: 21 **e** you with everything good

EQUIPPED (EQUIP)
2Ti 3: 17 God may be thoroughly **e** for every

ERROR
Jas 5: 20 the **e** of their way will save them

ESAU
Firstborn of Isaac, twin of Jacob (Ge 25:21–26). Also called Edom (Ge 25:30). Sold Jacob his birthright (Ge 25:29–34); lost blessing (Ge 27). Reconciled to Jacob (Gen 33).

ESCAPE (ESCAPING)
Ro 2: 3 think you will **e** God's judgment?
Heb 2: 3 how shall we **e** if we ignore so great

ESCAPING (ESCAPE)
1Co 3: 15 only as one **e** through the flames.

ESTABLISH (ESTABLISHED ESTABLISHES)
Ge 6: 18 But I will **e** my covenant with you,
1Ch 28: 7 I will **e** his kingdom forever if he is
Ro 10: 3 of God and sought to **e** their own,

ESTABLISHED (ESTABLISH)
Ps 8: 2 infants you have **e** a stronghold

ESTABLISHES (ESTABLISH)
Pr 16: 9 course, but the LORD **e** their steps.

ESTEEM (ESTEEMED)
Isa 53: 3 and we held him in low **e**.

ESTEEMED (ESTEEM)
Pr 22: 1 to be **e** is better than silver or gold.

ESTHER
Jewess who lived in Persia; cousin of Mordecai (Est 2:7). Chosen queen of Xerxes (Est 2:8–18). Foiled Haman's plan to exterminate the Jews (Est 3–4; 7–9).

ETERNAL (ETERNITY)
Ps 16: 11 with **e** pleasures at your right hand.
111: 10 To him belongs **e** praise.
119: 89 Your word, LORD, is **e**;
Isa 26: 4 the LORD himself, is the Rock **e**.
Mt 19: 16 good thing must I do to get **e** life?"
25: 41 the **e** fire prepared for the devil
25: 46 but the righteous to **e** life."
Jn 3: 15 who believes may have **e** life
3: 16 him shall not perish but have **e** life.
3: 36 believes in the Son has **e** life,
4: 14 of water welling up to **e** life."
5: 24 believes him who sent me has **e** life
6: 47 the one who believes has **e** life.
6: 68 You have the words of **e** life.
10: 28 I give them **e** life, and they shall
17: 3 Now this is **e** life: that they know
Ro 1: 20 his **e** power and divine nature—
6: 23 of God is **e** life in Christ Jesus our
2Co 4: 17 for us an **e** glory that far outweighs
4: 18 temporary, but what is unseen is **e**.
1Ti 1: 16 believe in him and receive **e** life.
1: 17 Now to the King **e**, immortal,
Heb 9: 12 thus obtaining **e** redemption.
1Jn 5: 11 God has given us **e** life, and this life
5: 13 you may know that you have **e** life.

ETERNITY (ETERNAL)
Ps 93: 2 you are from all **e**.
Ecc 3: 11 has also set **e** in the human heart;

ETHIOPIAN
Jer 13: 23 Can an **E** change his skin

EUNUCHS
Mt 19: 12 choose to live like **e** for the sake

EVANGELIST (EVANGELISTS)
2Ti 4: 5 do the work of an **e**, discharge all

EVANGELISTS (EVANGELIST)
Eph 4: 11 the **e**, the pastors and teachers,

EVE
2Co 11: 3 afraid that just as **E** was deceived
1Ti 2: 13 For Adam was formed first, then **E**.

EVEN-TEMPERED
Pr 17: 27 whoever has understanding is **e**.

EVER (EVERLASTING FOREVER)
Ex 15: 18 "The LORD reigns for **e** and **e**."
Dt 8: 19 you **e** forget the LORD your God
Ps 5: 11 you be glad; let them **e** sing for joy.
10: 16 The LORD is King for **e** and **e**;
25: 3 one who hopes in you will **e** be put
45: 6 throne, O God, will last for **e** and **e**;
52: 8 I trust in God's unfailing love for **e**
89: 33 nor will I **e** betray my faithfulness.
145: 1 I will praise your name for **e** and **e**.
Pr 4: 18 shining **e** brighter till the full light
5: 19 may you **e** be intoxicated with her
Isa 66: 8 Who has **e** heard of such things?
Jer 31: 36 "will Israel **e** cease being a nation
Da 7: 18 possess it forever—yes, for **e** and **e**.'
12: 3 like the stars for **e** and **e**.
Mk 4: 12 " 'they may be **e** seeing but never
Jn 1: 18 No one has **e** seen God, but
Rev 1: 18 now look, I am alive for **e** and **e**!
22: 5 And they will reign for **e** and **e**.

EVER-INCREASING (INCREASE)
Ro 6: 19 to impurity and to **e** wickedness,
2Co 3: 18 into his image with **e** glory,

EVERLASTING (EVER)
Dt 33: 27 and underneath are the **e** arms.
Ne 9: 5 your God, who is from **e** to **e**."
Ps 90: 2 world, from **e** to **e** you are God.
139: 24 in me, and lead me in the way **e**.
Isa 9: 6 Mighty God, **E** Father,
33: 14 of us can dwell with **e** burning?"
35: 10 **e** joy will crown their heads.
45: 17 by the LORD with an **e** salvation;
54: 8 **e** kindness I will have compassion
55: 3 I will make an **e** covenant with you,
63: 12 them, to gain for himself **e** renown,
Jer 31: 3 "I have loved you with an **e** love;
Da 9: 24 to bring in **e** righteousness, to seal
12: 2 some to **e** life, others to shame and **e** contempt.
2Th 1: 9 will be punished with **e** destruction
Jude : 6 bound with **e** chains for judgment

EVER-PRESENT
Ps 46: 1 and strength, an **e** help in trouble.

EVIDENCE (EVIDENT)
Jn 14: 11 on the **e** of the works themselves.

EVIDENT (EVIDENCE)
Php 4: 5 Let your gentleness be **e** to all.

EVIL (EVILDOER EVILDOERS)
Ge 2: 9 of the knowledge of good and **e**.
Job 1: 1 he feared God and shunned **e**.
1: 8 a man who fears God and shuns **e**."
34: 10 Far be it from God to do **e**,
Ps 23: 4 will fear no **e**, for you are with me;
34: 14 Turn from **e** and do good;
51: 4 and done what is **e** in your sight;
97: 10 those who love the LORD hate **e**,
101: 4 have nothing to do with what is **e**.
Pr 8: 13 To fear the LORD is to hate **e**;
11: 27 **e** comes to one who searches for it.
Isa 5: 20 who call **e** good and good **e**,
13: 11 I will punish the world for its **e**,
Hab 1: 13 Your eyes are too pure to look on **e**;
Mt 5: 45 He causes his sun to rise on the **e**
6: 13 but deliver us from the **e** one.'
7: 11 you are **e**, know how to give
12: 35 an **e** man brings **e** things out of the **e**
Jn 17: 15 you protect them from the **e** one.
Ro 2: 9 for every human being who does **e**:
12: 9 Hate what is **e**; cling to what is
12: 17 Do not repay anyone **e** for **e**.
16: 19 and innocent about what is **e**.
1Co 13: 6 Love does not delight in **e**
14: 20 In regard to **e** be infants, but in
Eph 6: 16 all the flaming arrows of the **e** one.
1Th 5: 22 reject every kind of **e**.
1Ti 6: 10 of money is a root of all kinds of **e**.
2Ti 2: 22 Flee the **e** desires of youth
Jas 1: 13 For God cannot be tempted by **e**,
1Pe 2: 16 your freedom as a cover-up for **e**;
3: 9 Do not repay **e** with **e** or insult
3: 9 the contrary, repay **e** with blessing,

EVILDOER (EVIL)
Pr 24: 20 for the **e** has no future hope,

EVILDOERS (EVIL)
Pr 24: 19 Do not fret because of **e** or be

EXACT
Heb 1: 3 the **e** representation of his being,

EXALT (EXALTED EXALTS)
Ps 30: 1 I will **e** you, LORD, for you lifted
34: 3 let us **e** his name together.
118: 28 you are my God, and I will **e** you.
Isa 24: 15 **e** the name of the LORD, the God
Mt 23: 12 For those who **e** themselves will be

EXALTED (EXALT)
2Sa 22: 47 **E** be my God, the Rock, my Savior!
1Ch 29: 11 you are **e** as head over all.
Ne 9: 5 and may it be **e** above all blessing
Ps 21: 13 Be **e** in your strength, LORD;
46: 10 I will be **e** among the nations,
57: 5 Be **e**, O God, above the heavens;
97: 9 you are **e** far above all gods.
99: 2 he is **e** over all the nations.
108: 5 Be **e**, O God, above the heavens;
148: 13 the LORD, for his name alone is **e**;
Isa 6: 1 high and **e**, seated on a throne;
12: 4 and proclaim that his name is **e**.
33: 5 The LORD is **e**, for he dwells
Eze 21: 26 The lowly will be **e** and the **e** will
Mt 23: 12 who humble themselves will be **e**.
Php 1: 20 now as always Christ will be **e**
2: 9 Therefore God **e** him to the highest

EXALTS (EXALT)
Ps 75: 7 He brings one down, he **e** another.
Pr 14: 34 Righteousness **e** a nation, but sin

EXAMINE (EXAMINED)
Ps 26: 2 try me, **e** my heart and my mind;
Jer 17: 10 search the heart and **e** the mind,
La 3: 40 Let us **e** our ways and test them,
1Co 11: 28 to **e** themselves before they eat
2Co 13: 5 **E** yourselves to see whether you

EXAMINED (EXAMINE)
Ac 17: 11 **e** the Scriptures every day to see

EXAMPLE (EXAMPLES)
Jn 13: 15 I have set you an **e** that you should
1Co 11: 1 Follow my **e**, as I follow the **e**
1Ti 4: 12 set an **e** for the believers in speech,
Titus 2: 7 everything set them an **e** by doing
1Pe 2: 21 leaving you an **e**, that you should

EXAMPLES (EXAMPLE)
1Co 10: 6 Now these things occurred as **e**
10: 11 things happened to them as **e**
1Pe 5: 3 to you, but being **e** to the flock.

1Th 5: 8 be sober, putting on **f** and love as
1Ti 2: 15 if they continue in **f**,
4: 1 later times some will abandon the **f**
5: 8 has denied the **f** and is worse than
6: 12 Fight the good fight of the **f**.
2Ti 3: 15 salvation through **f** in Christ Jesus.
4: 7 finished the race, I have kept the **f**.
Phm : 6 with us in the **f** may be effective
Heb 10: 38 my righteous one will live by **f**.
11: 1 Now **f** is confidence in what we
11: 3 By **f** we understand that the
11: 5 By **f** Enoch was taken from this
11: 6 without **f** it is impossible to please
11: 7 By **f** Noah, when warned
11: 7 By his **f** he condemned the world
11: 8 By **f** Abraham, when called to go
11: 17 By **f** Abraham, when God tested
11: 20 By **f** Isaac blessed Jacob and Esau
11: 21 By **f** Jacob, when he was dying,
11: 22 By **f** Joseph, when his end was
11: 24 By **f** Moses, when he had grown
11: 31 By **f** the prostitute Rahab,
12: 2 Jesus, the pioneer and perfecter of **f**.
Jas 2: 14 Can such **f** save them?
2: 17 In the same way, **f** by itself, if it is
2: 26 is dead, so **f** without deeds is dead.
2Pe 1: 5 effort to add to your **f** goodness;
1Jn 5: 4 overcome the world, even our **f**.
Jude : 3 contend for the **f** that was once

FAITHFUL (FAITH)
Nu 12: 7 he is **f** in all my house.
Dt 7: 9 he is the **f** God, keeping his
32: 4 A **f** God who does no wrong,
2Sa 22: 26 "To the **f** you show yourself **f**,
Ps 16: 10 will you let your **f** one see decay.
25: 10 and **f** toward those who keep
31: 23 Love the LORD, all his **f** people!
33: 4 right and true; he is **f** in all he does.
37: 28 just and will not forsake his **f** ones.
97: 10 for he guards the lives of his **f** ones
116: 15 is the death of his **f** servants.
145: 13 all he promises and **f** in all he does.
145: 17 in all his ways and **f** in all he does.
146: 6 he remains **f** forever.
Pr 31: 26 and **f** instruction is on her tongue.
Mt 25: 21 'Well done, good and **f** servant!
25: 21 You have been **f** with a few things;
Ro 12: 12 patient in affliction, **f** in prayer.
1Co 4: 2 been given a trust must prove **f**.
10: 13 And God is **f**; he will not let you be
1Th 5: 24 The one who calls you is **f**, and he
1Ti 3: 2 to be above reproach, **f** to his wife,
2Ti 2: 13 he remains **f**, for he cannot disown
Heb 3: 6 Christ is **f** as the Son over God's
10: 23 profess, for he who promised is **f**.
1Pe 4: 10 as **f** stewards of God's grace in its
4: 19 themselves to their **f** Creator
1Jn 1: 9 he is **f** and just and will forgive us
Rev 1: 5 who is the **f** witness, the firstborn
2: 10 Be **f**, even to the point of death,
19: 11 whose rider is called **F** and True.

FAITHFULLY (FAITH)
Dt 11: 13 So if you **f** obey the commands
1Sa 12: 24 and serve him **f** with all your heart;
1Ki 2: 4 if they walk **f** before me with all

FAITHFULNESS (FAITH)
Ps 51: 6 you desired **f** even in the womb;
57: 10 your **f** reaches to the skies.
85: 10 Love and **f** meet together;
86: 15 to anger, abounding in love and **f**.
89: 1 make your **f** known through all
89: 14 love and **f** go before you.
91: 4 his **f** will be your shield
117: 2 the **f** of the LORD endures forever.
119: 75 and that in **f** you have afflicted me.
Pr 3: 3 Let love and **f** never leave you;
Isa 11: 5 and **f** the sash around his waist.
La 3: 23 new every morning; great is your **f**.
Hab 2: 4 righteous person will live by his **f**—
Ro 3: 3 their unfaithfulness nullify God's **f**?
Gal 5: 22 forbearance, kindness, goodness, **f**,

FAITHLESS (FAITH)
Ps 119:158 I look on the **f** with loathing,
Jer 3: 22 "Return, **f** people; I will cure you
2Ti 2: 13 if we are **f**, he remains faithful,

FALL (FALLEN FALLS)
Ps 37: 24 he will not **f**, for the LORD
69: 9 of those who insult you **f** on me.
Pr 11: 28 who trust in their riches will **f**,
Lk 11: 17 a house divided against itself will **f**.
Jn 16: 1 you so that you will not **f** away.
Ro 3: 23 and **f** short of the glory of God,
14: 4 own master, servants stand or **f**.

FALLEN (FALL)
2Sa 1: 19 How the mighty have **f**!
Isa 14: 12 How you have **f** from heaven,
1Co 15: 20 of those who have **f** asleep.
Gal 5: 4 you have **f** away from grace.
1Th 4: 15 precede those who have **f** asleep.
Heb 6: 6 and who have **f** away, to be brought

FALLS (FALL)
Pr 24: 17 Do not gloat when your enemy **f**;
Jn 12: 24 a kernel of wheat **f** to the ground

FALSE (FALSEHOOD FALSELY)
Ex 20: 16 shall not give **f** testimony against
23: 1 "Do not spread **f** reports.
Pr 13: 5 The righteous hate what is **f**,
19: 5 A **f** witness will not go unpunished,
Mt 7: 15 "Watch out for **f** prophets.
19: 18 steal, you shall not give **f** testimony,
24: 11 and many **f** prophets will appear
Php 1: 18 whether from **f** motives or true,
1Ti 1: 3 not to teach **f** doctrines any longer
2Pe 2: 1 there will be **f** teachers among you.

FALSEHOOD (FALSE)
Ps 119:163 and detest **f** but I love your law.
Pr 30: 8 Keep **f** and lies far from me;
Eph 4: 25 each of you must put off **f**

FALSELY (FALSE)
Lev 19: 12 " 'Do not swear **f** by my name
Lk 3: 14 money and don't accuse people **f**—
1Ti 6: 20 ideas of what is **f** called knowledge,

FALTER
Pr 24: 10 If you **f** in a time of trouble,
Isa 42: 4 he will not **f** or be discouraged till

FAMILIES (FAMILY)
Ps 68: 6 God sets the lonely in **f**, he leads

FAMILY (FAMILIES)
Pr 31: 15 she provides food for her **f**
Lk 9: 61 go back and say goodbye to my **f**."
12: 52 in one **f** divided against each other,
1Ti 3: 4 He must manage his own **f** well
3: 5 know how to manage his own **f**,
5: 4 practice by caring for their own **f**

FAMINE
Ge 41: 30 seven years of **f** will follow them.
Am 8: 11 I will send a **f** through the land—
Ro 8: 35 or persecution or **f** or nakedness

FAN
2Ti 1: 6 this reason I remind you to **f**

FAST
Dt 13: 4 serve him and hold **f** to him.
Jos 22: 5 to hold **f** to him and to serve him
23: 8 to hold **f** to the LORD your God,
Ps 119: 31 I hold **f** to your statutes, LORD;
139: 10 me, your right hand will hold me **f**.
Mt 6: 16 "When you **f**, do not look somber
1Pe 5: 12 the true grace of God. Stand **f** in it.

FATHER (FATHER'S FATHERLESS FATHERS)
Ge 2: 24 That is why a man leaves his **f**
17: 4 You will be the **f** of many nations.
Ex 20: 12 "Honor your **f** and your mother,
21: 15 "Anyone who attacks their **f**
21: 17 "Anyone who curses their **f**
Lev 18: 7 " 'Do not dishonor your **f**
19: 3 must respect your mother and **f**,
Dt 5: 16 "Honor your **f** and your mother,
21: 18 son who does not obey his **f**
Ps 27: 10 Though my **f** and mother forsake
68: 5 A **f** to the fatherless, a defender
Pr 10: 1 A wise son brings joy to his **f**,
23: 22 Listen to your **f**, who gave you life,
23: 24 The **f** of a righteous child has great
28: 7 of gluttons disgraces his **f**.
29: 3 loves wisdom brings joy to his **f**,
Isa 9: 6 Everlasting **F**, Prince of Peace.
Mt 6: 9 " 'Our **F** in heaven, hallowed be
10: 37 "Anyone who loves their **f**
15: 4 said, 'Honor your **f** and mother'
19: 5 this reason a man will leave his **f**
Lk 12: 53 **f** against son and son against **f**,
23: 34 Jesus said, "**F**, forgive them,
Jn 6: 44 unless the **F** who sent me draws
6: 46 from God; only he has seen the **F**.
8: 44 You belong to your **f**, the devil,

Jn 10: 30 I and the **F** are one."
14: 6 comes to the **F** except through me.
14: 9 who has seen me has seen the **F**.
Ro 4: 11 he is the **f** of all who believe
2Co 6: 18 And, "I will be a **F** to you, and you
Eph 6: 2 "Honor your **f** and mother"—
Heb 12: 7 are not disciplined by their **f**?

FATHER'S (FATHER)
Pr 13: 1 wise son heeds his **f** instruction,
19: 13 A foolish child is a **f** ruin,
Lk 2: 49 know I had to be in my **F** house?"
Jn 2: 16 Stop turning my **F** house
10: 29 can snatch them out of my **F** hand.
14: 2 My **F** house has many rooms;

FATHERLESS (FATHER)
Dt 10: 18 He defends the cause of the **f**
24: 17 the foreigner or the **f** of justice,
24: 19 the foreigner, the **f** and the widow,
Ps 68: 5 A father to the **f**, a defender
Pr 23: 10 or encroach on the fields of the **f**,

FATHERS (FATHER)
Lk 11: 11 "Which of you **f**, if your son asks
Eph 6: 4 **F**, do not exasperate your children;
Col 3: 21 **F**, do not embitter your children,

FATHOM
Job 11: 7 "Can you **f** the mysteries of God?
Ps 145: 3 his greatness no one can **f**.
Ecc 3: 11 no one can **f** what God has done
Isa 40: 28 his understanding no one can **f**.
1Co 13: 2 of prophecy and can **f** all mysteries

FAULT (FAULTS)
Mt 18: 15 sins, go and point out their **f**,
Php 2: 15 of God without **f** in a warped
Jas 1: 5 generously to all without finding **f**,
Jude : 24 his glorious presence without **f**

FAULTFINDERS
Jude : 16 These people are grumblers and **f**;

FAULTS (FAULT)
Ps 19: 12 Forgive my hidden **f**.

FAVORITISM
Ex 23: 3 do not show **f** to a poor person
Lev 19: 15 to the poor or **f** to the great,
Ac 10: 34 true it is that God does not show **f**
Ro 2: 11 For God does not show **f**.
Gal 2: 6 God does not show **f**—
Eph 6: 9 heaven, and there is no **f** with him.
Col 3: 25 for their wrongs, and there is no **f**.
1Ti 5: 21 and to do nothing out of **f**.
Jas 2: 1 Lord Jesus Christ must not show **f**.
2: 9 But if you show **f**, you sin and are

FEAR (AFRAID FEARS)
Dt 6: 13 **F** the LORD your God, serve him
10: 12 you but to **f** the LORD your God,
31: 12 learn to **f** the LORD your God
Ps 19: 9 The **f** of the LORD is pure,
23: 4 the darkest valley, I will **f** no evil,
27: 1 and my salvation—whom shall I **f**?
91: 5 You will not **f** the terror of night,
111: 10 The **f** of the LORD is
Pr 8: 13 To **f** the LORD is to hate evil;
9: 10 The **f** of the LORD is
10: 27 The **f** of the LORD adds length
14: 27 The **f** of the LORD is a fountain
15: 33 instruction is to **f** the LORD,
16: 6 through the **f** of the LORD evil is
19: 23 The **f** of the LORD leads to life;
29: 25 **F** of man will prove to be a snare,
Ecc 5: 7 Therefore **f** God.
Isa 11: 3 will delight in the **f** of the LORD.
41: 10 So do not **f**, for I am with you;
Lk 12: 5 will show you whom you should **f**:
Php 2: 12 to work out your salvation with **f**
1Jn 4: 18 There is no **f** in love. But perfect love drives out **f**,

FEARS (FEAR)
Job 1: 8 a man who **f** God and shuns evil."
Ps 34: 4 he delivered me from all my **f**.
Pr 31: 30 a woman who **f** the LORD is to be
1Jn 4: 18 The one who **f** is not made perfect

FEED
Jn 21: 15 Jesus said, "**F** my lambs."
21: 17 Jesus said, "**F** my sheep.
Ro 12: 20 "If your enemy is hungry, **f** him;
Jude : 12 shepherds who **f** only themselves.

FEET (FOOT)
Ps 8: 6 you put everything under their **f**:
22: 16 they pierce my hands and my **f**.
40: 2 he set my **f** on a rock and gave me
110: 1 enemies a footstool for your **f**."
119:105 Your word is a lamp to my **f**
Ro 10: 15 "How beautiful are the **f** of those
1Co 12: 21 And the head cannot say to the **f**,
15: 25 has put all his enemies under his **f**.
Heb 12: 13 "Make level paths for your **f**,"

FELLOWSHIP
2Co 6: 14 **f** can light have with darkness?
13: 14 the **f** of the Holy Spirit be with you
1Jn 1: 6 If we claim to have **f** with him
1: 7 light, we have **f** with one another,

FEMALE
Ge 1: 27 male and **f** he created them.
Gal 3: 28 nor is there male and **f**, for you are

FERVOR
Ro 12: 11 but keep your spiritual **f**,

FIDELITY
Ro 1: 31 no understanding, no **f**, no love,

FIELD (FIELDS)
Mt 6: 28 See how the flowers of the **f** grow.
13: 38 The **f** is the world, and the good
1Co 3: 9 you are God's **f**, God's building.

FIELDS (FIELD)
Lk 2: 8 shepherds living out in the **f**
Jn 4: 35 open your eyes and look at the **f**!

FIERY (FIRE)
1Pe 4: 12 do not be surprised at the **f** ordeal

FIG (FIGS)
Ge 3: 7 so they sewed **f** leaves together

FIGHT (FOUGHT)
Ex 14: 14 The LORD will **f** for you;
Dt 1: 30 is going before you, will **f** for you,
3: 22 the LORD your God himself will **f**
Ne 4: 20 Our God will **f** for us!"
Ps 35: 1 **f** against those who **f** against me.
Jn 18: 36 my servants would **f** to prevent my
1Co 9: 26 I do not **f** like a boxer beating
2Co 10: 4 The weapons we **f** with are not
1Ti 1: 18 them you may **f** the battle well,
6: 12 **F** the good **f** of the faith.
2Ti 4: 7 I have fought the good **f**, I have

FIGS (FIG)
Lk 6: 44 People do not pick **f**

FILL (FILLED FILLS FULL FULLNESS FULLY)
Ge 1: 28 **f** the earth and subdue it.
Ps 16: 11 you will **f** me with joy in your
81: 10 wide your mouth and I will **f** it.
Pr 28: 19 chase fantasies will have their **f**
Hag 2: 7 and I will **f** this house with glory,'
Jn 6: 26 you ate the loaves and had your **f**.
Ac 2: 28 you will **f** me with joy in your
Ro 15: 13 May the God of hope **f** you with all

FILLED (FILL)
Ps 72: 19 may the whole earth be **f** with his
119: 64 The earth is **f** with your love,
Isa 11: 9 for the earth will be **f**
Eze 43: 5 glory of the LORD **f** the temple.
Hab 2: 14 For the earth will be **f**
Lk 1: 15 he will be **f** with the Holy Spirit
1: 41 Elizabeth was **f** with the Holy Spirit.
Jn 12: 3 the house was **f** with the fragrance
Ac 2: 4 of them were **f** with the Holy Spirit
4: 8 Then Peter, **f** with the Holy Spirit,
9: 17 and be **f** with the Holy Spirit."
13: 9 called Paul, **f** with the Holy Spirit,
Eph 5: 18 Instead, be **f** with the Spirit,
Php 1: 11 **f** with the fruit of righteousness

FILLS (FILL)
Nu 14: 21 of the LORD **f** the whole earth,
Ps 107: 9 and **f** the hungry with good things.
Eph 1: 23 him who **f** everything in every way.

FILTHY
Isa 64: 6 all our righteous acts are like **f** rags;
Col 3: 8 and **f** language from your lips.

FIND (FINDS FOUND)
Nu 32: 23 be sure that your sin will **f** you out.
Dt 4: 29 you will **f** him if you seek him
1Sa 23: 16 and helped him **f** strength in God.
Ps 91: 4 under his wings you will **f** refuge;
112: 1 LORD, who **f** great delight in his
Pr 14: 22 those who plan what is good **f** love
31: 10 wife of noble character who can **f**?
Jer 6: 16 and you will **f** rest for your souls.
Mt 7: 7 seek and you will **f**;

Mt 11: 29 and you will **f** rest for your souls.
16: 25 loses their life for me will **f** it.
Lk 18: 8 will he **f** faith on the earth?"
Jn 10: 9 come in and go out, and **f** pasture.

FINDS (FIND)
Ps 62: 1 Truly my soul **f** rest in God;
119:162 promise like one who **f** great spoil.
Pr 18: 22 He who **f** a wife **f** what is good
Mt 7: 8 the one who seeks **f**; and to the one
10: 39 Whoever **f** their life will lose it,
Lk 12: 37 whose master **f** them watching
15: 4 go after the lost sheep until he **f** it?

FINISH (FINISHED)
Jn 4: 34 him who sent me and to **f** his work.
5: 36 that the Father has given me to **f**—
Ac 20: 24 my only aim is to **f** the race
2Co 8: 11 Now **f** the work, so that your eager
Gal 3: 3 are you now trying to **f** by means
Jas 1: 4 Let perseverance **f** its work so

FINISHED (FINISH)
Ge 2: 2 seventh day God had **f** the work he
Jn 19: 30 the drink, Jesus said, "It is **f**."
2Ti 4: 7 the good fight, I have **f** the race,

FIRE (FIERY)
Ex 13: 21 in a pillar of **f** to give them light,
Lev 6: 12 The **f** on the altar must be kept
Isa 30: 27 and his tongue is a consuming **f**.
Jer 23: 29 "Is not my word like **f**,"
Mt 3: 11 you with the Holy Spirit and **f**.
5: 22 will be in danger of the **f** of hell.
25: 41 the eternal **f** prepared for the devil
Mk 9: 43 hell, where the **f** never goes out.
Ac 2: 3 to be tongues of **f** that separated
1Co 3: 13 It will be revealed with **f**, and the **f**
Heb 12: 29 for our "God is a consuming **f**."
Jas 3: 5 what a great forest is set on **f**
2Pe 3: 10 the elements will be destroyed by **f**,
Jude : 23 by snatching them from the **f**;
Rev 20: 14 **f**. The lake of **f** is the second death.

FIRM
Ex 14: 13 Stand **f** and you will see
2Ch 20: 17 stand **f** and see the deliverance
Ps 33: 11 plans of the LORD stand **f** forever,
37: 23 The LORD makes **f** the steps
40: 2 and gave me a **f** place to stand.
89: 2 that your love stands **f** forever,
119: 89 it stands **f** in the heavens.
Zec 8: 23 nations will take **f** hold of one Jew
Mk 13: 13 the one who stands **f** to the end
1Co 16: 13 on your guard; stand **f** in the faith;
2Co 1: 24 because it is by faith you stand **f**.
Eph 6: 14 Stand **f** then, with the belt of truth
Col 4: 12 that you may stand **f** in all the will
2Th 2: 15 stand **f** and hold fast to the teachings
2Ti 2: 19 God's solid foundation stands **f**,
Heb 6: 19 anchor for the soul, **f** and secure.
1Pe 5: 9 Resist him, standing **f** in the faith,

FIRST
Isa 44: 6 I am the **f** and I am the last;
48: 12 I am the **f** and I am the last.
Mt 5: 24 **F** go and be reconciled to them;
6: 33 But seek **f** his kingdom and his
7: 5 **f** take the plank out of your own
20: 27 wants to be **f** must be your slave—
22: 38 This is the **f** and greatest
23: 26 **F** clean the inside of the cup
Mk 13: 10 the gospel must **f** be preached to all
Ac 11: 26 disciples were called Christians **f**
Ro 1: 16 **f** to the Jew, then to the Gentile.
1Co 12: 28 in the church **f** of all apostles,
2Co 8: 5 They gave themselves **f** of all
1Ti 2: 13 For Adam was formed **f**, then Eve.
Jas 3: 17 comes from heaven is **f** of all pure;
1Jn 4: 19 We love because he **f** loved us.
3Jn : 9 who loves to be **f**, will not welcome
Rev 1: 17 I am the **F** and the Last.
2: 4 have forsaken the love you had at **f**.

FIRSTBORN (BEAR)
Ex 11: 5 Every **f** son in Egypt will die,

FIRSTFRUITS
Ex 23: 19 "Bring the best of the **f** of your soil

FISH
Mk 1: 17 I will send you out to **f** for people."
Lk 5: 10 from now on you will **f** for people."

FITTING
Ps 33: 1 it is **f** for the upright to praise him.
147: 1 how pleasant and **f** to praise him!
Pr 19: 10 It is not **f** for a fool to live
26: 1 in harvest, honor is not **f** for a fool.
1Co 14: 40 everything should be done in a **f**
Col 3: 18 your husbands, as is **f** in the Lord.
Heb 2: 10 to glory, it was **f** that God,

FIX (FIXING)
Dt 11: 18 **F** these words of mine in your
Pr 4: 25 **f** your gaze directly before you.
2Co 4: 18 So we **f** our eyes not on what is
Heb 3: 1 calling, **f** your thoughts on Jesus,

FIXING (FIX)
Heb 12: 2 **f** our eyes on Jesus, the pioneer

FLAME (FLAMES FLAMING)
2Ti 1: 6 you to fan into **f** the gift of God,

FLAMES (FLAME)
1Co 3: 15 only as one escaping through the **f**.

FLAMING (FLAME)
Eph 6: 16 you can extinguish all the **f** arrows

FLASH
1Co 15: 52 in a **f**, in the twinkling of an eye,

FLATTER (FLATTERING FLATTERY)
Ps 12: 2 they **f** with their lips but harbor
Job 32: 21 no partiality, nor will I **f** anyone;
Jude : 16 **f** others for their own advantage.

FLATTERING (FLATTER)
Ps 12: 3 May the LORD silence all **f** lips
Pr 26: 28 it hurts, and a **f** mouth works ruin.

FLATTERY (FLATTER)
Ro 16: 18 **f** they deceive the minds of naive
1Th 2: 5 You know we never used **f**, nor did

FLAWLESS
2Sa 22: 31 The LORD's word is **f**;
Job 11: 4 'My beliefs are **f** and I am pure
Ps 12: 6 And the words of the LORD are **f**,
18: 30 The LORD's word is **f**;
Pr 30: 5 "Every word of God is **f**; he is
SS 5: 2 my darling, my dove, my **f** one.

FLEE
Ps 139: 7 Where can I **f** from your presence?
1Co 6: 18 **F** from sexual immorality.
10: 14 my dear friends, **f** from idolatry.
1Ti 6: 11 man of God, **f** from all this,
2Ti 2: 22 **F** the evil desires of youth
Jas 4: 7 the devil, and he will **f** from you.

FLEETING
Ps 89: 47 Remember how **f** is my life.
Pr 31: 30 is deceptive, and beauty is **f**;

FLESH
Ge 2: 23 bone of my bones and **f** of my **f**;
2: 24 to his wife, and they become one **f**.
Job 19: 26 yet in my **f** I will see God;
Eze 11: 19 of stone and give them a heart of **f**.
36: 26 of stone and give you a heart of **f**.
Mt 26: 41 spirit is willing, but the **f** is weak."
Mk 10: 8 and the two will become one **f**.'
Jn 1: 14 The Word became **f** and made his
6: 51 bread is my **f**, which I will give
Ro 8: 4 do not live according to the **f** but
8: 8 realm of the **f** cannot please God.
1Co 6: 16 said, "The two will become one **f**."
Gal 3: 3 trying to finish by means of the **f**?
5: 19 The acts of the **f** are obvious:
5: 24 crucified the **f** with its passions
Eph 5: 31 and the two will become one **f**."
6: 12 For our struggle is not against **f**

FLOCK (FLOCKS)
Isa 40: 11 He tends his **f** like a shepherd:
Eze 34: 2 not shepherds take care of the **f**?
Zec 11: 17 shepherd, who deserts the **f**!
Mt 26: 31 the sheep of the **f** will be scattered.'
Ac 20: 28 all the **f** of which the Holy Spirit
1Pe 5: 2 of God's **f** that is under your care,

FLOCKS (FLOCK)
Lk 2: 8 keeping watch over their **f** at night.

FLOG
Ac 22: 25 **f** a Roman citizen who hasn't even

FLOODGATES
Mal 3: 10 will not throw open the **f** of heaven

FLOURISHING
Ps 52: 8 am like an olive tree **f** in the house

FLOW (FLOWING)
Nu 13: 27 and it does **f** with milk and honey!
Jn 7: 38 of living water will **f** from within

FRANKINCENSE
Mt 2: 11 him with gifts of gold, **f** and myrrh.

FREE (FREED FREEDOM FREELY)
Ps 146: 7 The LORD sets prisoners **f**,
Jn 8: 32 truth, and the truth will set you **f**."
Ro 6: 18 You have been set **f** from sin
Gal 3: 28 neither slave nor **f**, nor is there
1Pe 2: 16 Live as **f** people, but do not use

FREED (FREE)
Rev 1: 5 has **f** us from our sins by his blood,

FREEDOM (FREE)
Ro 8: 21 brought into the **f** and glory
2Co 3: 17 the Spirit of the Lord is, there is **f**.
Gal 5: 13 But do not use your **f** to indulge
1Pe 2: 16 do not use your **f** as

FREELY (FREE)
Isa 55: 7 to our God, for he will **f** pardon.
Mt 10: 8 **F** you have received; **f** give.
Ro 3: 24 and all are justified **f** by his grace
Eph 1: 6 which he has **f** given us in the One

FRIEND (FRIENDS)
Ex 33: 11 face to face, as one speaks to a **f**.
Pr 17: 17 A **f** loves at all times, and a brother
18: 24 there is a **f** who sticks closer than
27: 6 Wounds from a **f** can be trusted,
27: 10 Do not forsake your **f** or a **f** of your
Jas 4: 4 to be a **f** of the world becomes

FRIENDS (FRIEND)
Pr 16: 28 and a gossip separates close **f**.
18: 24 who has unreliable **f** soon comes
Zec 13: 6 I was given at the house of my **f**.'
Jn 15: 13 to lay down one's life for one's **f**.

FRUIT (FRUITFUL)
Ps 1: 3 which yields its **f** in season
Pr 11: 30 The **f** of the righteous is a tree
Mt 7: 16 By their **f** you will recognize them.
Jn 15: 2 branch that does bear **f** he prunes
Gal 5: 22 But the **f** of the Spirit is love, joy,
Rev 22: 2 bearing twelve crops of **f**, yielding its **f** every month.

FRUITFUL (FRUIT)
Ge 1: 22 "Be **f** and increase in number
Ps 128: 3 wife will be like a **f** vine within
Jn 15: 2 so that it will be even more **f**.

FULFILL (FULFILLED FULFILLMENT)
Ps 116: 14 I will **f** my vows to the LORD
Mt 5: 17 to abolish them but to **f** them.
1Co 7: 3 The husband should **f** his marital

FULFILLED (FULFILL)
Pr 13: 19 A longing **f** is sweet to the soul,
Mk 14: 49 But the Scriptures must be **f**."
Ro 13: 8 whoever loves others has **f** the law.

FULFILLMENT (FULFILL)
Ro 13: 10 Therefore love is the **f** of the law.

FULL (FILL)
Ps 127: 5 Blessed is the man whose quiver is **f**
Pr 31: 11 Her husband has **f** confidence in her
Isa 6: 3 the whole earth is **f** of his glory."
Lk 6: 45 speaks what the heart is **f** of.
Jn 10: 10 may have life, and have it to the **f**.
Ac 6: 3 who are known to be **f** of the Spirit

FULLNESS (FILL)
Col 1: 19 to have all his **f** dwell in him,
2: 9 in Christ all the **f** of the Deity lives

FULLY (FILL)
1Ki 8: 61 may your hearts be **f** committed
2Ch 16: 9 whose hearts are **f** committed
Ps 119: 4 precepts that are to be **f** obeyed.
119:138 righteous; they are **f** trustworthy.
1Co 15: 58 Always give yourselves **f**

FUTURE
Ps 37: 37 a **f** awaits those who seek peace.
Pr 23: 18 There is surely a **f** hope for you,
Ro 8: 38 neither the present nor the **f**,

GABRIEL
Angel who interpreted Daniel's visions (Da 8:16–26; 9:20–27); announced births of John (Lk 1:11–20), Jesus (Lk 1:26–38).

GAIN (GAINED)
Ps 60: 12 With God we will **g** the victory,
Mk 8: 36 for someone to **g** the whole world,
1Co 13: 3 but do not have love, I **g** nothing.
Php 1: 21 me, to live is Christ and to die is **g**.
3: 8 them garbage, that I may **g** Christ
1Ti 6: 6 with contentment is great **g**.
1Pe 5: 2 not pursuing dishonest **g**, but eager

GAINED (GAIN)
Ro 5: 2 through whom we have **g** access

GALILEE
Isa 9: 1 in the future he will honor **G**

GALL
Mt 27: 34 Jesus wine to drink, mixed with **g**;

GAP
Eze 22: 30 stand before me in the **g** on behalf

GARBAGE
Php 3: 8 I consider them **g**, that I may gain

GARDENER
Jn 15: 1 true vine, and my Father is the **g**.

GARMENT (GARMENTS)
Ps 102: 26 they will all wear out like a **g**.
Mt 9: 16 the patch will pull away from the **g**,
Jn 19: 23 This **g** was seamless, woven in one
19: 24 them and cast lots for my **g**."

GARMENTS (GARMENT)
Ge 3: 21 The LORD God made **g** of skin
Isa 61: 10 For he has clothed me with **g**
63: 1 with his **g** stained crimson?

GATE (GATES)
Mt 7: 13 "Enter through the narrow **g**.
Jn 10: 9 I am the **g**; whoever enters through

GATES (GATE)
Ps 100: 4 Enter his **g** with thanksgiving
Mt 16: 18 the **g** of Hades will not overcome

GATHER (GATHERS)
Zec 14: 2 I will **g** all the nations to Jerusalem
Mt 12: 30 and whoever does not **g** with me
23: 37 longed to **g** your children together,

GATHERS (GATHER)
Isa 40: 11 He **g** the lambs in his arms
Mt 23: 37 as a hen **g** her chicks under her

GAVE (GIVE)
Ezr 2: 69 their ability they **g** to the treasury
Job 1: 21 The LORD **g** and the LORD has
Jn 3: 16 so loved the world that he **g** his
2Co 8: 5 They **g** themselves first of all
Gal 2: 20 loved me and **g** himself for me.
1Ti 2: 6 who **g** himself as a ransom for all

GAZE
Ps 27: 4 to **g** on the beauty of the LORD
Pr 4: 25 fix your **g** directly before you.

GENEALOGIES
1Ti 1: 4 themselves to myths and endless **g**.

GENERATIONS
Ps 22: 30 **g** will be told about the Lord.
102: 12 renown endures through all **g**.
145: 13 dominion endures through all **g**.
Lk 1: 48 now on all **g** will call me blessed,
Eph 3: 5 other **g** as it has now been revealed

GENEROUS
Ps 112: 5 Good will come to those who are **g**
Pr 22: 9 The **g** will themselves be blessed,
2Co 9: 5 Then it will be ready as a **g** gift,
1Ti 6: 18 and to be **g** and willing to share.

GENTILE (GENTILES)
Ro 1: 16 first to the Jew, then to the **G**.
10: 12 no difference between Jew and **G**—

GENTILES (GENTILE)
Isa 42: 6 for the people and a light for the **G**,
Ro 3: 9 **G** alike are all under the power
11: 13 as I am the apostle to the **G**, I take
1Co 1: 23 block to Jews and foolishness to **G**,

GENTLE (GENTLENESS)
Pr 15: 1 A **g** answer turns away wrath,
Mt 11: 29 for I am **g** and humble in heart,
21: 5 to you, **g** and riding on a donkey,
1Co 4: 21 I come in love and with a **g** spirit?
1Pe 3: 4 unfading beauty of a **g** and quiet

GENTLENESS (GENTLE)
2Co 10: 1 By the humility and **g** of Christ,
Gal 5: 23 **g** and self-control.
Php 4: 5 Let your **g** be evident to all.
Col 3: 12 kindness, humility, **g** and patience.
1Ti 6: 11 faith, love, endurance and **g**
1Pe 3: 15 But do this with **g** and respect,

GETHSEMANE
Mt 26: 36 his disciples to a place called **G**,

GIDEON
Judge, also called Jerub-Baal; freed Israel from Midianites (Jdg 6–8; Heb 11:32). Given sign of fleece (Jdg 6:36–40).

GIFT (GIFTS)
Pr 21: 14 A **g** given in secret soothes anger,
Mt 5: 23 you are offering your **g** at the altar
Ac 2: 38 you will receive the **g** of the Holy
Ro 6: 23 the **g** of God is eternal life in Christ
1Co 7: 7 of you has your own **g** from God;
2Co 8: 12 the **g** is acceptable according
9: 15 be to God for his indescribable **g**!
Eph 2: 8 yourselves, it is the **g** of God—
1Ti 4: 14 Do not neglect your **g**, which was
2Ti 1: 6 you to fan into flame the **g** of God,
Jas 1: 17 good and perfect **g** is from above,
1Pe 4: 10 should use whatever **g** you have

GIFTS (GIFT)
Ro 11: 29 for God's **g** and his call are
12: 6 We have different **g**,
1Co 12: 4 There are different kinds of **g**,
12: 31 Now eagerly desire the greater **g**.
14: 1 and eagerly desire **g** of the Spirit,
14: 12 Since you are eager for **g**

GILEAD
Jer 8: 22 Is there no balm in **G**? Is there no

GIVE (GAVE GIVEN GIVER GIVES GIVING)
Nu 6: 26 toward you and **g** you peace." '
1Sa 1: 11 forget your servant but **g** her a son,
1: 11 I will **g** him to the LORD for all
2Ch 15: 7 be strong and do not **g** up, for your
Pr 21: 26 the righteous **g** without sparing.
23: 26 **g** me your heart and let your eyes
28: 27 Those who **g** to the poor will lack
30: 8 but **g** me only my daily bread.
Eze 36: 26 I will **g** you a new heart and put
Mt 6: 11 **G** us today our daily bread.
10: 8 Freely you have received; freely **g**.
22: 21 them, "So **g** back to Caesar what is
Mk 8: 37 what can anyone **g** in exchange
Lk 6: 38 **G**, and it will be given to you.
11: 13 Father in heaven **g** the Holy Spirit
Jn 10: 28 I **g** them eternal life, and they shall
13: 34 "A new command I **g** you:
Ac 20: 35 'It is more blessed to **g** than
Ro 12: 8 encourage, then **g** encouragement;
12: 8 if it is giving, then **g** generously;
13: 7 **G** to everyone what you owe them:
14: 12 then, each of us will **g** an account
2Co 9: 7 should **g** what you have decided
Rev 14: 7 voice, "Fear God and **g** him glory,

GIVEN (GIVE)
Nu 8: 16 Israelites who are to be **g** wholly
Ps 115: 16 but the earth he has **g** to mankind.
Isa 9: 6 a son is **g**, and the government
Mt 6: 33 all these things will be **g** to you as
7: 7 "Ask and it will be **g** to you;
Lk 22: 19 saying, "This is my body **g** for you;
Jn 3: 27 can receive only what is **g** them
Ro 5: 5 Holy Spirit, who has been **g** to us.
1Co 4: 2 those who have been **g** a trust must
12: 13 and we were all **g** the one Spirit
Eph 4: 7 of us grace has been **g** as Christ

GIVER (GIVE)
Pr 18: 16 ushers the **g** into the presence
2Co 9: 7 for God loves a cheerful **g**.

GIVES (GIVE)
Ps 119:130 unfolding of your words **g** light;
Pr 14: 30 A heart at peace **g** life to the body,
15: 30 good news **g** health to the bones.
Isa 40: 29 He **g** strength to the weary
Mt 10: 42 anyone **g** even a cup of cold water
Jn 6: 63 The Spirit **g** life; the flesh counts
1Co 15: 57 He **g** us the victory through our
2Co 3: 6 the letter kills, but the Spirit **g** life.

GIVING (GIVE)
Ne 8: 8 **g** the meaning so that the people
Ps 19: 8 LORD are right, **g** joy to the heart.
Mt 6: 4 so that your **g** may be in secret.
2Co 8: 7 you also excel in this grace of **g**.

GLAD (GLADNESS)
Ps 31: 7 I will be **g** and rejoice in your love,
46: 4 whose streams make **g** the city
97: 1 LORD reigns, let the earth be **g**;
118: 24 let us rejoice today and be **g**.
Zec 2: 10 "Shout and be **g**, Daughter Zion.
Mt 5: 12 Rejoice and be **g**, because great is

GLADNESS (GLAD)
Ps 45: 15 Led in with joy and **g**, they enter
51: 8 Let me hear joy and **g**;
100: 2 Worship the LORD with **g**;
Jer 31: 13 I will turn their mourning into **g**;

GLORIFIED (GLORY)
Jn 13: 31 "Now the Son of Man is **g** and God is **g** in him.
Ro 8: 30 those he justified, he also **g**.
2Th 1: 10 he comes to be **g** in his holy people

GLORIFY (GLORY)
Ps 34: 3 **G** the LORD with me; let us exalt
86: 12 I will **g** your name forever.
Mt 5: 16 deeds and **g** your Father in heaven.
Jn 13: 32 God will **g** the Son in himself,
17: 1 **G** your Son, that your Son may **g**

GLORIOUS (GLORY)
Ps 45: 13 All **g** is the princess within her
111: 3 **G** and majestic are his deeds,
145: 5 They speak of the **g** splendor
Isa 4: 2 the LORD will be beautiful and **g**,
12: 5 LORD, for he has done **g** things;
42: 21 to make his law great and **g**.
63: 15 from your lofty throne, holy and **g**.
Mt 19: 28 Son of Man sits on his **g** throne,
Lk 9: 30 and Elijah, appeared in **g** splendor,
Ac 2: 20 of the great and **g** day of the Lord.
2Co 3: 8 of the Spirit be even more **g**?
Php 3: 21 so that they will be like his **g** body.
Jude : 24 you before his **g** presence without

GLORY (GLORIFIED GLORIFY GLORIOUS)
Ex 15: 11 awesome in **g**, working wonders?
33: 18 said, "Now show me your **g**."
1Sa 4: 21 "The **G** has departed from Israel"
1Ch 16: 24 Declare his **g** among the nations,
16: 28 ascribe to the LORD **g**
29: 11 power and the **g** and the majesty
Ps 8: 5 crowned them with **g** and honor.
19: 1 The heavens declare the **g** of God;
24: 7 that the King of **g** may come in.
29: 1 beings, ascribe to the LORD **g**
34: 2 I will **g** in the LORD;
72: 19 the whole earth be filled with his **g**.
96: 3 Declare his **g** among the nations,
Pr 19: 11 is to one's **g** to overlook an offense.
25: 2 It is the **g** of God to conceal
25: 2 a matter is the **g** of kings.
Isa 6: 3 the whole earth is full of his **g**."
42: 8 I will not yield my **g** to another
48: 11 I will not yield my **g** to another.
Eze 43: 2 and I saw the **g** of the God of Israel
Mt 24: 30 of heaven, with power and great **g**.
25: 31 the Son of Man comes in his **g**,
Mk 8: 38 in his Father's **g** with the holy
13: 26 in clouds with great power and **g**.
Lk 2: 9 and the **g** of the Lord shone around
2: 14 "**G** to God in the highest heaven,
Jn 1: 14 have seen his **g**, the **g** of the one
17: 5 your presence with the **g** I had
17: 24 and to see my **g**, the **g** you have
Ac 7: 2 God of **g** appeared to our father
Ro 1: 23 exchanged the **g** of the immortal
3: 23 and fall short of the **g** of God,
8: 18 with the **g** that will be revealed
9: 4 theirs the divine **g**, the covenants,
1Co 10: 31 you do, do it all for the **g** of God.
11: 7 since he is the image and **g** of God;
11: 7 but woman is the **g** of man.
15: 43 sown in dishonor, it is raised in **g**;
2Co 3: 10 what was glorious has no **g** now
3: 18 faces contemplate the Lord's **g**,
4: 17 us an eternal **g** that far outweighs
Php 4: 19 the riches of his **g** in Christ Jesus.
Col 1: 27 is Christ in you, the hope of **g**.
3: 4 you also will appear with him in **g**.
1Ti 3: 16 on in the world, was taken up in **g**.
Titus 2: 13 appearing of the **g** of our great God
Heb 1: 3 The Son is the radiance of God's **g**
2: 7 crowned them with **g** and honor
1Pe 1: 24 all their **g** is like the flowers
Rev 4: 11 to receive **g** and honor and power,
21: 23 for the **g** of God gives it light,

GLUTTONS
Titus 1: 12 always liars, evil brutes, lazy **g**."

GNASHING
Mt 8: 12 will be weeping and **g** of teeth."

GNAT
Mt 23: 24 You strain out a **g** but swallow

GOAL
2Co 5: 9 So we make it our **g** to please him,
Php 3: 14 on toward the **g** to win the prize

GOAT (GOATS SCAPEGOAT)
Isa 11: 6 leopard will lie down with the **g**,

GOATS (GOAT)
Nu 7: 17 five male **g** and five male lambs

GOD (GOD'S GODLINESS GODLY GODS)
Ge 1: 1 beginning **G** created the heavens
1: 2 of **G** was hovering over the waters.
1: 26 Then **G** said, "Let us make
1: 27 So **G** created mankind in his own
1: 31 **G** saw all that he had made, and it
2: 3 Then **G** blessed the seventh day
2: 22 the LORD **G** made a woman
3: 21 The LORD **G** made garments
3: 23 So the LORD **G** banished him
5: 22 walked faithfully with **G** 300 years
6: 2 sons of **G** saw that the daughters
9: 16 everlasting covenant between **G**
17: 1 to him and said, "I am **G** Almighty;
21: 33 name of the LORD, the Eternal **G**.
22: 8 "**G** himself will provide the lamb
28: 12 the angels of **G** were ascending
32: 28 because you have struggled with **G**
32: 30 "It is because I saw **G** face to face,
35: 10 **G** said to him, "Your name is
41: 51 said, "It is because **G** has made me
50: 20 me, but **G** intended it for good
Ex 2: 24 **G** heard their groaning and he
3: 6 he said, "I am the **G** of your father,
3: 6 because he was afraid to look at **G**.
6: 7 know that I am the LORD your **G**,
8: 10 is no one like the LORD our **G**.
13: 18 So **G** led the people around
15: 2 He is my **G**, and I will praise him,
17: 9 with the staff of **G** in my hands."
19: 3 Then Moses went up to **G**,
20: 2 "I am the LORD your **G**,
20: 5 the LORD your **G**, am a jealous **G**,
20: 19 But do not have **G** speak to us
22: 28 "Do not blaspheme **G** or curse
31: 18 stone inscribed by the finger of **G**.
34: 6 the compassionate and gracious **G**,
34: 14 name is Jealous, is a jealous **G**.
Lev 18: 21 not profane the name of your **G**.
19: 2 I, the LORD your **G**, am holy.
26: 12 walk among you and be your **G**,
Nu 22: 38 I must speak only what **G** puts
23: 19 **G** is not human, that he should lie,
Dt 1: 17 anyone, for judgment belongs to **G**.
3: 22 the LORD your **G** himself will
3: 24 For what **g** is there in heaven
4: 24 **G** is a consuming fire, a jealous **G**.
4: 31 the LORD your **G** is a merciful **G**;
4: 39 day that the LORD is **G** in heaven
5: 11 the name of the LORD your **G**,
5: 14 is a sabbath to the LORD your **G**.
5: 26 voice of the living **G** speaking
6: 4 The LORD our **G**, the LORD is
6: 5 Love the LORD your **G** with all
6: 13 Fear the LORD your **G**, serve him
6: 16 Do not put the LORD your **G**
7: 9 is **G**; he is the faithful **G**,
7: 12 the LORD your **G** will keep his
7: 21 is a great and awesome **G**.
8: 5 the LORD your **G** disciplines you.
10: 12 what does the LORD your **G** ask you but to fear the LORD your **G**,
10: 14 To the LORD your **G** belong
10: 17 For the LORD your **G** is **G** of gods
11: 13 to love the LORD your **G**
13: 3 The LORD your **G** is testing you
13: 4 It is the LORD your **G** you must
15: 6 the LORD your **G** will bless you
19: 9 to love the LORD your **G**
25: 16 the LORD your **G** detests anyone
29: 29 things belong to the LORD our **G**,
30: 2 return to the LORD your **G**
30: 16 today to love the LORD your **G**,
30: 20 you may love the LORD your **G**,
31: 6 the LORD your **G** goes with you;
32: 3 Oh, praise the greatness of our **G**!
32: 4 A faithful **G** who does no wrong,
33: 27 The eternal **G** is your refuge,
Jos 1: 9 the LORD your **G** will be with you
14: 8 the LORD my **G** wholeheartedly,
22: 5 to love the LORD your **G**, to walk
22: 34 that the LORD is **G**.
23: 11 careful to love the LORD your **G**.
Jos 23: 14 the LORD your **G** gave you has
Jdg 16: 28 Please, **G**, strengthen me just once
Ru 1: 16 be my people and your **G** my **G**.
1Sa 2: 2 there is no Rock like our **G**.
2: 3 for the LORD is a **G** who knows,
2: 25 **G** may mediate for the offender;
10: 26 men whose hearts **G** had touched.
12: 12 the LORD your **G** was your king.
17: 26 defy the armies of the living **G**?"
17: 46 know that there is a **G** in Israel.
30: 6 found strength in the LORD his **G**.
2Sa 14: 14 But that is not what **G** desires;
22: 3 my **G** is my rock, in whom I take
22: 31 "As for **G**, his way is perfect:
1Ki 4: 29 **G** gave Solomon wisdom and very
8: 23 there is no **G** like you in heaven
8: 27 "But will **G** really dwell on earth?
8: 61 committed to the LORD our **G**,
18: 21 If the LORD is **G**, follow him;
18: 37 are **G**, and that you are turning
20: 28 think the LORD is a **g** the hills
2Ki 19: 15 you alone are **G** over all
1Ch 16: 35 Cry out, "Save us, **G** our Savior;
28: 2 for the footstool of our **G**, and I
28: 9 acknowledge the **G** of your father,
29: 10 LORD, the **G** of our father Israel,
29: 17 my **G**, that you test the heart and
2Ch 2: 4 for the Name of the LORD my **G**
5: 14 the LORD filled the temple of **G**.
6: 18 will **G** really dwell on earth
18: 13 can tell him only what my **G** says."
20: 6 you not the **G** who is in heaven?
25: 8 for **G** has the power to help
30: 9 for the LORD your **G** is gracious
33: 12 the favor of the LORD his **G**
Ezr 8: 22 "The gracious hand of our **G** is
9: 6 my **G**, to lift up my face to you,
9: 13 our **G**, you have punished us less
Ne 1: 5 the great and awesome **G**,
8: 8 from the Book of the Law of **G**,
9: 17 But you are a forgiving **G**,
9: 32 "Now therefore, our **G**, the great **G**,
Job 1: 1 he feared **G** and shunned evil.
2: 10 Shall we accept good from **G**,
4: 17 mortal be more righteous than **G**?
5: 17 is the one whom **G** corrects;
11: 7 you fathom the mysteries of **G**?
19: 26 yet in my flesh I will see **G**;
22: 13 Yet you say, 'What does **G** know?
25: 4 a mortal be righteous before **G**?
33: 14 For **G** does speak—now one way,
34: 12 unthinkable that **G** would do wrong,
36: 26 How great is **G**—
37: 22 **G** comes in awesome majesty.
Ps 18: 2 my **G** is my rock, in whom I take
18: 28 my **G** turns my darkness into light.
19: 1 The heavens declare the glory of **G**;
22: 1 My **G**, my **G**, why have you
29: 3 the **G** of glory thunders, the LORD
31: 14 I say, "You are my **G**."
40: 3 mouth, a hymn of praise to our **G**.
40: 8 I desire to do your will, my **G**;
42: 2 My soul thirsts for **G**, for the living
42: 2 When can I go and meet with **G**?
42: 11 Put your hope in **G**, for I will yet
45: 6 O **G**, will last for ever and ever;
46: 1 **G** is our refuge and strength,
46: 10 "Be still, and know that I am **G**;
47: 7 For **G** is the King of all the earth;
50: 3 Our **G** comes and will not be silent
51: 1 O **G**, according to your unfailing
51: 10 O **G**, and renew a steadfast spirit
51: 17 sacrifice, O **G**, is a broken spirit;
62: 7 and my honor depend on **G**;
65: 5 and righteous deeds, **G** our Savior,
66: 1 Shout for joy to **G**, all the earth!
66: 16 Come and hear, all you who fear **G**;
68: 6 **G** sets the lonely in families,
71: 17 my youth, **G**, you have taught
71: 19 Who is like you, **G**?
71: 22 harp for your faithfulness, my **G**;
73: 26 but **G** is the strength of my heart
77: 13 What **g** is as great as our **G**?
78: 19 They spoke against **G**;
81: 1 Sing for joy to **G** our strength;
84: 2 my flesh cry out for the living **G**.
84: 10 the house of my **G** than dwell
86: 12 you, Lord my **G**, with all my heart,
89: 7 of the holy ones **G** is greatly feared;
90: 2 to everlasting you are **G**.
91: 2 fortress, my **G**, in whom I trust."

Ps 95: 7 for he is our **G** and we are
100: 3 Know that the LORD is **G**. It is he
108: 1 My heart, O **G**, is steadfast;
113: 5 Who is like the LORD our **G**,
139: 23 Search me, **G**, and know my heart;
Pr 3: 4 a good name in the sight of **G**
25: 2 It is the glory of **G** to conceal
30: 5 "Every word of **G** is flawless;
Ecc 3: 11 can fathom what **G** has done
11: 5 cannot understand the work of **G**,
12: 13 of the matter: Fear **G** and keep his
Isa 9: 6 Mighty **G**, Everlasting Father,
37: 16 you alone are **G** over all
40: 3 in the desert a highway for our **G**.
40: 8 the word of our **G** endures forever."
40: 28 The LORD is the everlasting **G**,
41: 10 not be dismayed, for I am your **G**.
44: 6 apart from me there is no **G**.
52: 7 who say to Zion, "Your **G** reigns!"
55: 7 and to our **G**, for he will freely
57: 21 says my **G**, "for the wicked."
59: 2 have separated you from your **G**;
61: 10 my soul rejoices in my **G**.
62: 5 so will your **G** rejoice over you.
Jer 23: 23 "Am I only a **G** nearby,"
31: 33 I will be their **G**, and they will be
32: 27 the LORD, the **G** of all mankind.
Eze 28: 13 You were in Eden, the garden of **G**;
Da 3: 17 the **G** we serve is able to deliver us
9: 4 the great and awesome **G**,
Hos 12: 6 But you must return to your **G**;
Joel 2: 13 Return to the LORD your **G**, for he
Am 4: 12 Israel, prepare to meet your **G**."
Mic 6: 8 and to walk humbly with your **G**.
Na 1: 2 is a jealous and avenging **G**;
Zec 14: 5 Then the LORD my **G** will come,
Mal 3: 8 "Will a mere mortal rob **G**?
Mt 1: 23 (which means "**G** with us").
5: 8 pure in heart, for they will see **G**.
6: 24 You cannot serve both **G**
19: 6 Therefore what **G** has joined
19: 26 but with **G** all things are possible."
22: 21 Caesar's, and to **G** what is God's."
22: 37 "'Love the Lord your **G** with all
27: 46 (which means "My **G**, my **G**,
Mk 12: 29 The Lord our **G**, the Lord is one.
16: 19 *at the right hand of* **G**.
Lk 1: 37 For no word from **G** will ever fail."
1: 47 my spirit rejoices in **G** my Savior,
10: 9 'The kingdom of **G** has come near
10: 27 "'Love the Lord your **G** with all
18: 19 "No one is good—except **G** alone.
Jn 1: 1 and the Word was with **G**, and the Word was **G**.
1: 18 No one has ever seen **G**, but
1: 18 who is himself **G** and is in closest
3: 16 For **G** so loved the world that he
4: 24 **G** is spirit, and his worshipers must
7: 17 to do the will of **G** will find
14: 1 You believe in **G**;
20: 28 said to him, "My Lord and my **G**!"
Ac 2: 24 But **G** raised him from the dead,
5: 4 lied just to human beings but to **G**."
5: 29 "We must obey **G** rather than
7: 55 to heaven and saw the glory of **G**,
17: 23 inscription: TO AN UNKNOWN **G**.
20: 27 to you the whole will of **G**.
20: 32 "Now I commit you to **G**
Ro 1: 17 righteousness of **G** is revealed—
2: 11 For **G** does not show favoritism.
3: 4 Let **G** be true, and every human
3: 23 and fall short of the glory of **G**,
4: 24 **G** will credit righteousness—
5: 8 **G** demonstrates his own love for us
6: 23 the gift of **G** is eternal life in Christ
8: 28 in all things **G** works for the good
11: 22 the kindness and sternness of **G**:
14: 12 give an account of ourselves to **G**.
1Co 1: 20 not **G** made foolish the wisdom
2: 9 the things **G** has prepared for those
3: 6 it, but **G** has been making it grow.
6: 20 Therefore honor **G** with your
7: 24 they were in when **G** called them.
8: 8 food does not bring us near to **G**;
10: 13 **G** is faithful; he will not let you
10: 31 you do, do it all for the glory of **G**.
14: 33 For **G** is not a **G** of disorder
15: 28 him, so that **G** may be all in all.
2Co 1: 9 not rely on ourselves but on **G**,
2: 14 But thanks be to **G**, who always
3: 5 our competence comes from **G**.
4: 7 this all-surpassing power is from **G**
2Co 5: 19 that **G** was reconciling the world
5: 21 become the righteousness of **G**.
6: 16 we are the temple of the living **G**.
9: 7 for **G** loves a cheerful giver.
9: 8 **G** is able to bless you abundantly,
Gal 2: 6 **G** does not show favoritism—
6: 7 **G** cannot be mocked.
Eph 2: 10 **G** prepared in advance for us
4: 6 one **G** and Father of all, who is
Php 2: 6 being in very nature **G**, did not consider equality with **G**
4: 19 And my **G** will meet all your needs
1Th 2: 4 not trying to please people but **G**,
4: 7 For **G** did not call us to be impure,
4: 9 yourselves have been taught by **G**
5: 9 For **G** did not appoint us to suffer
1Ti 2: 5 there is one **G** and one mediator
4: 4 For everything **G** created is good,
5: 4 for this is pleasing to **G**.
Titus 2: 13 of the glory of our great **G**
Heb 1: 1 the past **G** spoke to our ancestors
4: 12 For the word of **G** is alive
6: 10 **G** is not unjust; he will not forget
10: 31 fall into the hands of the living **G**.
11: 6 faith it is impossible to please **G**,
12: 10 but **G** disciplines us for our good,
12: 29 for our "**G** is a consuming fire."
13: 15 us continually offer to **G** a sacrifice
Jas 1: 13 For **G** cannot be tempted by evil,
2: 19 You believe that there is one **G**.
2: 23 "Abraham believed **G**, and it was
4: 4 the world becomes an enemy of **G**.
4: 8 Come near to **G** and he will come
1Pe 4: 11 who speaks the very words of **G**.
2Pe 1: 21 from **G** as they were carried along
1Jn 1: 5 him and declare to you: **G** is light;
2: 5 love for **G** is truly made complete
3: 20 that **G** is greater than our hearts,
4: 7 another, for love comes from **G**.
4: 7 has been born of **G** and knows **G**.
4: 9 This is how **G** showed his love
4: 11 Dear friends, since **G** so loved us,
4: 12 No one has ever seen **G**; but if we
4: 16 Whoever lives in love lives in **G**,
Rev 4: 8 holy is the Lord **G** Almighty,'
7: 17 **G** will wipe away every tear
19: 6 For our Lord **G** Almighty reigns.

GOD-BREATHED (BREATHED)
2Ti 3: 16 All Scripture is **G** and is useful

GODLINESS (GOD)
1Ti 2: 2 quiet lives in all **g** and holiness.
4: 8 value, but **g** has value for all things,
6: 6 **g** with contentment is great gain.
6: 11 and pursue righteousness, **g**, faith,

GODLY (GOD)
2Co 7: 10 **G** sorrow brings repentance
11: 2 jealous for you with a **g** jealousy.
2Ti 3: 12 live a **g** life in Christ Jesus will be
2Pe 3: 11 You ought to live holy and **g** lives

GOD'S (GOD)
2Ch 20: 15 For the battle is not yours, but **G**.
Job 37: 14 stop and consider **G** wonders.
Ps 52: 8 I trust in **G** unfailing love for ever
69: 30 I will praise **G** name in song
Mk 3: 35 Whoever does **G** will is my brother
Jn 10: 36 because I said, 'I am **G** Son'?
Ro 2: 3 think you will escape **G** judgment?
2: 4 that **G** kindness is intended
3: 3 nullify **G** faithfulness?
7: 22 my inner being I delight in **G** law;
9: 16 desire or effort, but on **G** mercy.
11: 29 for **G** gifts and his call are
12: 2 test and approve what **G** will is—
13: 6 for the authorities are **G** servants,
1Co 7: 19 Keeping **G** commands is what
2Co 6: 2 now is the time of **G** favor, now is
Eph 1: 7 with the riches of **G** grace
5: 1 Follow **G** example, therefore,
1Th 4: 3 It is **G** will that you should be
5: 18 for this is **G** will for you in Christ
1Ti 6: 1 so that **G** name and our teaching
2Ti 2: 19 **G** solid foundation stands firm,
Titus 1: 7 an overseer manages **G** household,
Heb 1: 3 The Son is the radiance of **G** glory
9: 24 to appear for us in **G** presence.
11: 3 was formed at **G** command,
1Pe 2: 15 For it is **G** will that by doing good
3: 4 which is of great worth in **G** sight.

GODS (GOD)
Ex 20: 3 shall have no other **g** before me.
Ac 19: 26 by human hands are no **g** at all.

GOLD
Job 23: 10 tested me, I will come forth as **g**.
Ps 19: 10 precious than **g**, than much pure **g**;
119:127 love your commands more than **g**,
Pr 22: 1 esteemed is better than silver or **g**.

GOLGOTHA
Jn 19: 17 (which in Aramaic is called **G**).

GOLIATH
Philistine giant killed by David (1Sa 17; 21:9).

GOOD
Ge 1: 4 God saw that the light was **g**,
1: 31 he had made, and it was very **g**.
2: 18 "It is not **g** for the man to be alone.
50: 20 God intended it for **g**
Job 2: 10 Shall we accept **g** from God,
Ps 14: 1 there is no one who does **g**.
34: 8 Taste and see that the LORD is **g**;
37: 3 Trust in the LORD and do **g**;
84: 11 no **g** thing does he withhold
86: 5 are forgiving and **g**,
103: 5 your desires with **g** things so
119: 68 You are **g**, and what you do is **g**;
133: 1 How **g** and pleasant it is
147: 1 How **g** it is to sing praises to our
Pr 3: 4 and a **g** name in the sight of God
11: 27 Whoever seeks **g** finds favor,
13: 21 are rewarded with **g** things.
17: 22 A cheerful heart is **g** medicine,
18: 22 He who finds a wife finds what is **g**
22: 1 A **g** name is more desirable than
31: 12 She brings him **g**, not harm,
Isa 5: 20 Woe to those who call evil **g** and **g**
52: 7 the feet of those who bring **g** news,
Jer 6: 16 ask where the **g** way is, and walk
Mic 6: 8 shown you, O mortal, what is **g**.
Mt 5: 45 sun to rise on the evil and the **g**,
7: 17 Likewise, every **g** tree bears **g** fruit,
12: 35 A **g** man brings **g** things out of the **g**
19: 17 "There is only One who is **g**.
25: 21 'Well done, **g** and faithful servant!
Mk 3: 4 to do **g** or to do evil, to save life
8: 36 What **g** is it for someone to gain
Lk 6: 27 do **g** to those who hate you,
Jn 10: 11 "I am the **g** shepherd. The **g**
Ro 8: 28 for the **g** of those who love him,
10: 15 feet of those who bring **g** news!"
12: 9 Hate what is evil; cling to what is **g**.
1Co 10: 24 their own **g**, but the **g** of others.
15: 33 company corrupts **g** character."
2Co 9: 8 you will abound in every **g** work.
Gal 6: 9 us not become weary in doing **g**,
6: 10 let us do **g** to all people,
Eph 2: 10 in Christ Jesus to do **g** works,
Php 1: 6 he who began a **g** work in you will
1Th 5: 21 test them all; hold on to what is **g**,
2Th 3: 13 never tire of doing what is **g**.
1Ti 3: 7 have a **g** reputation with outsiders,
4: 4 For everything God created is **g**,
6: 12 Fight the **g** fight of the faith.
6: 18 do **g**, to be rich in **g** deeds,
2Ti 3: 17 equipped for every **g** work.
4: 7 I have fought the **g** fight, I have
Heb 12: 10 but God disciplines us for our **g**,
1Pe 2: 3 you have tasted that the Lord is **g**.
2: 12 Live such **g** lives among the pagans

GOSPEL
Ro 1: 16 For I am not ashamed of the **g**,
15: 16 duty of proclaiming the **g** of God,
1Co 1: 17 to baptize, but to preach the **g**—
9: 16 Woe to me if I do not preach the **g**!
15: 1 to remind you of the **g** I preached
Gal 1: 7 trying to pervert the **g** of Christ.
Php 1: 27 a manner worthy of the **g** of Christ.
1: 27 as one for the faith of the **g**

GOSSIP
Pr 11: 13 A **g** betrays a confidence,
16: 28 and a **g** separates close friends.
18: 8 of a **g** are like choice morsels;
26: 20 without a **g** a quarrel dies down.
2Co 12: 20 slander, **g**, arrogance and disorder.

GOVERNED
Ro 8: 6 the mind **g** by the Spirit is life

GRACE (GRACIOUS)
Ps 45: 2 lips have been anointed with **g**,
Jn 1: 17 **g** and truth came through Jesus
Ac 20: 32 to God and to the word of his **g**,
Ro 3: 24 by his **g** through the redemption
5: 15 that came by the **g** of the one man,
5: 17 God's abundant provision of **g**
5: 20 increased, **g** increased all the more,
6: 14 are not under the law, but under **g**.
11: 6 if it were, **g** would no longer be **g**.
2Co 6: 1 you not to receive God's **g** in vain.
8: 9 you know the **g** of our Lord Jesus
12: 9 to me, "My **g** is sufficient for you,
Gal 2: 21 I do not set aside the **g** of God,
5: 4 you have fallen away from **g**.
Eph 1: 7 with the riches of God's **g**
2: 5 it is by **g** you have been saved.
2: 7 the incomparable riches of his **g**,
2: 8 For it is by **g** you have been saved,
Php 1: 7 all of you share in God's **g** with me.
Col 4: 6 conversation be always full of **g**,
2Th 2: 16 **g** gave us eternal encouragement
2Ti 2: 1 be strong in the **g** that is in Christ
Titus 2: 11 For the **g** of God has appeared
3: 7 having been justified by his **g**,
Heb 2: 9 the **g** of God he might taste death
4: 16 approach God's throne of **g**
4: 16 **g** to help us in our time of need.
Jas 4: 6 But he gives us more **g**. That is why
2Pe 3: 18 grow in the **g** and knowledge of

GRACIOUS (GRACE)
Nu 6: 25 face shine on you and be **g** to you;
Isa 30: 18 the LORD longs to be **g** to you;

GRAIN
Ecc 11: 1 Ship your **g** across the sea;
1Co 9: 9 an ox while it is treading out the **g**."

GRANTED
Php 1: 29 For it has been **g** to you on behalf

GRASS
Ps 103: 15 The life of mortals is like **g**,
1Pe 1: 24 the **g** withers and the flowers fall,

GRAVE (GRAVES)
Pr 7: 27 Her house is a highway to the **g**,
Hos 13: 14 Where, O **g**, is your destruction?

GRAVES (GRAVE)
Jn 5: 28 are in their **g** will hear his voice
Ro 3: 13 "Their throats are open **g**;

GREAT (GREATER GREATEST GREATNESS)
Ge 12: 2 "I will make you into a **g** nation,
Dt 10: 17 gods and Lord of lords, the **g** God,
2Sa 22: 36 your help has made me **g**.
Ps 19: 11 in keeping them there is **g** reward.
89: 1 sing of the LORD's **g** love forever;
103: 11 so **g** is his love for those who fear
108: 4 For **g** is your love, higher than
119:165 **G** peace have those who love your
145: 3 **G** is the LORD and most worthy
Pr 23: 24 father of a righteous child has **g** joy
Isa 42: 21 his righteousness to make his law **g**
La 3: 23 **g** is your faithfulness.
Mk 10: 43 become **g** among you must be your
Lk 21: 27 in a cloud with power and **g** glory.
1Ti 6: 6 with contentment is **g** gain.
Titus 2: 13 appearing of the glory of our **g** God
Heb 2: 3 if we ignore so **g** a salvation?
1Jn 3: 1 See what **g** love the Father has

GREATER (GREAT)
Mk 12: 31 is no commandment **g** than these."
Jn 1: 50 You will see **g** things than that."
15: 13 **G** love has no one than this:
1Co 12: 31 Now eagerly desire the **g** gifts.
Heb 11: 26 as of **g** value than the treasures
1Jn 3: 20 that God is **g** than our hearts,
4: 4 is in you is **g** than the one who is

GREATEST (GREAT)
Mt 22: 38 is the first and **g** commandment.
Lk 9: 48 least among you all who is the **g**."
1Co 13: 13 But the **g** of these is love.

GREATNESS (GREAT)
Ps 145: 3 his **g** no one can fathom.
150: 2 praise him for his surpassing **g**.
Isa 9: 7 the **g** of his government and peace
63: 1 forward in the **g** of his strength?

GREED (GREEDY)
Lk 12: 15 guard against all kinds of **g**;
Ro 1: 29 wickedness, evil, **g** and depravity.
Eph 5: 3 or of **g**, because these are improper
Col 3: 5 desires and **g**, which is idolatry.
2Pe 2: 14 they are experts in **g**—

GREEDY (GREED)
Pr 15: 27 The **g** bring ruin to their
1Co 6: 10 thieves nor the **g** nor drunkards
Eph 5: 5 No immoral, impure or **g** person—

GREEN
Ps 23: 2 makes me lie down in **g** pastures,

GREW (GROW)
Lk 2: 52 And Jesus **g** in wisdom and stature,
Ac 16: 5 in the faith and **g** daily in numbers.

GRIEF (GRIEVE)
Ps 10: 14 you consider their **g** and take it
Pr 14: 13 ache, and rejoicing may end in **g**.
La 3: 32 Though he brings **g**, he will show
Jn 16: 20 grieve, but your **g** will turn to joy.
1Pe 1: 6 have had to suffer **g** in all kinds

GRIEVE (GRIEF)
Eph 4: 30 do not **g** the Holy Spirit of God,
1Th 4: 13 so that you do not **g** like the rest

GROUND
Ge 3: 17 it,' "Cursed is the **g** because of you;
Ex 3: 5 where you are standing is holy **g**."
Eph 6: 13 you may be able to stand your **g**,

GROW (GREW)
Pr 13: 11 money little by little makes it **g**.
1Co 3: 6 it, but God has been making it **g**.
2Pe 3: 18 But **g** in the grace and knowledge

GRUMBLE (GRUMBLING)
1Co 10: 10 do not **g**, as some of them did—
Jas 5: 9 Don't **g** against one another,

GRUMBLING (GRUMBLE)
Jn 6: 43 "Stop **g** among yourselves,"
1Pe 4: 9 hospitality to one another without **g**.

GUARANTEEING (GUARANTOR)
2Co 1: 22 as a deposit, **g** what is to come.
Eph 1: 14 is a deposit **g** our inheritance until

GUARANTOR (GUARANTEEING)
Heb 7: 22 Jesus has become the **g** of a better

GUARD (GUARDIAN, GUARDIAN-REDEEMER)
Ps 141: 3 Set a **g** over my mouth, LORD;
Pr 4: 23 Above all else, **g** your heart,
13: 3 Those who **g** their lips preserve
21: 23 Those who **g** their mouths and
Isa 52: 12 God of Israel will be your rear **g**.
Mk 13: 33 Be on **g**! Be alert! You do not know
1Co 16: 13 Be on your **g**; stand firm
Php 4: 7 will **g** your hearts and your minds
1Ti 6: 20 **g** what has been entrusted to your

GUARDIAN (GUARD)
Gal 3: 25 come, we are no longer under a **g**.

GUARDIAN-REDEEMER (GUARD)
Ru 3: 9 since you are a **g** of our family."

GUIDE
Ex 13: 21 of cloud to **g** them on their way
15: 13 In your strength you will **g** them
Ne 9: 19 cloud did not fail to **g** them on
Ps 25: 5 **G** me in your truth and teach me,
48: 14 he will be our **g** even to the end.
67: 4 and **g** the nations of the earth.
73: 24 You **g** me with your counsel,
139: 10 even there your hand will **g** me,
Pr 6: 22 When you walk, they will **g** you;
Isa 58: 11 The LORD will **g** you always;
Jn 16: 13 he will **g** you into all the truth.

GUILTY
Ex 34: 7 does not leave the **g** unpunished;
Jn 8: 46 Can any of you prove me **g** of sin?
Heb 10: 22 to cleanse us from a **g** conscience
Jas 2: 10 at just one point is **g** of breaking all

HADES
Mt 16: 18 the gates of **H** will not overcome it.
Lk 16: 23 In **H**, where he was in torment,

HAGAR
Servant of Sarah, wife of Abraham, mother of Ishmael (Ge 16:1–6; 25:12). Driven away by Sarah while pregnant (Ge 16:5–16); after birth of Isaac (Ge 21:9–21; Gal 4:21–31).

HAGGAI
Post-exilic prophet who encouraged rebuilding of the temple (Ezr 5:1; 6:14; Hag 1–2).

HAIR (HAIRS)
Lk 21: 18 not a **h** of your head will perish.
1Co 11: 6 for a woman to have her **h** cut off

HAIRS (HAIR)
Mt 10: 30 even the very **h** of your head are all

HALLELUJAH
Rev 19: 1, multitude in heaven shouting: "**H**!

HALLOWED (HOLY)
Mt 6: 9 Father in heaven, **h** be your name,

HAND (HANDIWORK HANDS)
Ps 16: 8 With him at my right **h**, I will not
37: 24 the LORD upholds him with his **h**.
139: 10 even there your **h** will guide me,
Ecc 9: 10 Whatever your **h** finds to do, do it
Mt 6: 3 not let your left **h** know what your right **h** is doing,
Jn 10: 28 one will snatch them out of my **h**.
1Co 12: 15 say, "Because I am not a **h**, I do not

HANDIWORK (HAND WORK)
Eph 2: 10 For we are God's **h**,

HANDS (HAND)
Ps 22: 16 they pierce my **h** and my feet.
24: 4 one who has clean **h** and a pure
31: 5 Into your **h** I commit my spirit;
31: 15 My times are in your **h**;
Pr 10: 4 but diligent **h** bring wealth.
31: 20 and extends her **h** to the needy.
Isa 55: 12 trees of the field will clap their **h**.
65: 2 out my **h** to an obstinate people,
Lk 23: 46 into your **h** I commit my spirit."
1Th 4: 11 business and work with your **h**,
1Ti 2: 8 lifting up holy **h** without anger
5: 22 not be hasty in the laying on of **h**,

HANNAH
Wife of Elkanah, mother of Samuel (1Sa 1). Prayer at dedication of Samuel (1Sa 2:1–10). Blessed (1Sa 2:18–21).

HAPPY
Ps 68: 3 may they be **h** and joyful.
Pr 15: 13 A **h** heart makes the face cheerful,
Ecc 3: 12 better for people than to be **h**
Jas 5: 13 Is anyone **h**? Let them sing songs

HARD (HARDEN HARDSHIP)
Ge 18: 14 Is anything too **h** for the LORD?
Ps 118: 5 When **h** pressed, I cried
Mt 19: 23 it is **h** for someone who is rich
1Co 4: 12 We work **h** with our own hands.
1Th 5: 12 those who work **h** among you,

HARDEN (HARD)
Ro 9: 18 he hardens whom he wants to **h**.
Heb 3: 8 do not **h** your hearts as you did

HARDHEARTED (HEART)
Dt 15: 7 do not be **h** or tightfisted toward

HARDSHIP (HARD)
Ro 8: 35 Shall trouble or **h** or persecution
2Ti 4: 5 endure **h**, do the work
Heb 12: 7 Endure **h** as discipline;

HARM
Ps 121: 6 the sun will not **h** you by day,
Pr 3: 29 not plot **h** against your neighbor,
31: 12 good, not **h**, all the days of her life.
Ro 13: 10 Love does no **h** to a neighbor.
1Jn 5: 18 and the evil one cannot **h** them.

HARMONY
Ro 12: 16 Live in **h** with one another.
2Co 6: 15 What **h** is there between Christ

HARVEST
Mt 9: 37 "The **h** is plentiful but the workers
Jn 4: 35 at the fields! They are ripe for **h**.
Gal 6: 9 at the proper time we will reap a **h**
Heb 12: 11 it produces a **h** of righteousness

HASTE (HASTY)
Pr 21: 5 lead to profit as surely as **h** leads
29: 20 you see someone who speaks in **h**?

HASTY (HASTE)
Pr 19: 2 how much more will **h** feet miss
Ecc 5: 2 do not be **h** in your heart to utter
1Ti 5: 22 Do not be **h** in the laying

HATE (HATED HATES HATRED)
Lev 19: 17 "'Do not **h** a fellow Israelite
Ps 5: 5 You **h** all who do wrong;
45: 7 righteousness and **h** wickedness;
97: 10 those who love the LORD **h** evil,
139: 21 Do I not **h** those who **h** you,
Pr 8: 13 To fear the LORD is to **h** evil; I **h**
Am 5: 15 **H** evil, love good;
Mt 5: 43 your neighbor and **h** your enemy.'
Lk 6: 27 do good to those who **h** you,
Ro 12: 9 **H** what is evil; cling to what is

HATED (HATE)
Mt 10: 22 be **h** by everyone because of me,

Ro 9: 13 “Jacob I loved, but Esau I **h**.”
Eph 5: 29 all, no one ever **h** their own body,
Heb 1: 9 righteousness and **h** wickedness;

HATES (HATE)
Pr 6: 16 There are six things the LORD **h**,
13: 24 spares the rod **h** their children,
Mal 2: 16 “The man who **h** and divorces his
Jn 3: 20 Everyone who does evil **h** the light,
1Jn 2: 9 to be in the light but **h** a brother

HATRED (HATE)
Pr 10: 12 **H** stirs up conflict, but love covers

HAUGHTY
Pr 16: 18 destruction, a **h** spirit before a fall.

HAY
1Co 3: 12 costly stones, wood, **h** or straw,

HEAD (HEADS HOTHEADED)
Ge 3: 15 he will crush your **h**, and you will
Ps 23: 5 You anoint my **h** with oil;
Pr 25: 22 will heap burning coals on his **h**,
Isa 59: 17 the helmet of salvation on his **h**;
Mt 8: 20 of Man has no place to lay his **h**.”
Ro 12: 20 will heap burning coals on his **h**.”
1Co 11: 3 the **h** of every man is Christ, and the **h** of the woman is man, and the **h** of Christ is God.
12: 21 And the **h** cannot say to the feet,
Eph 5: 23 the husband is the **h** of the wife as Christ is the **h**
2Ti 4: 5 keep your **h** in all situations,
Rev 19: 12 fire, and on his **h** are many crowns.

HEADS (HEAD)
Lev 26: 13 you to walk with **h** held high.
Isa 35: 10 everlasting joy will crown their **h**.

HEAL (HEALED HEALING HEALS)
2Ch 7: 14 their sin and will **h** their land.
Ps 41: 4 **h** me, for I have sinned against
Mt 10: 8 **H** the sick, raise the dead,
Lk 4: 23 ‘Physician, **h** yourself!’
5: 17 Lord was with Jesus to **h** the sick.

HEALED (HEAL)
Isa 53: 5 him, and by his wounds we are **h**.
Mt 9: 22 he said, “your faith has **h** you.”
14: 36 and all who touched it were **h**.
Ac 4: 10 that this man stands before you **h**.
14: 9 saw that he had faith to be **h**
Jas 5: 16 each other so that you may be **h**.
1Pe 2: 24 “by his wounds you have been **h**.”

HEALING (HEAL)
Eze 47: 12 for food and their leaves for **h**.”
Mal 4: 2 righteousness will rise with **h** in its
1Co 12: 9 to another gifts of **h** by that one
12: 30 Do all have gifts of **h**? Do all speak
Rev 22: 2 the tree are for the **h** of the nations.

HEALS (HEAL)
Ex 15: 26 for I am the LORD, who **h** you.”
Ps 103: 3 your sins and **h** all your diseases,
147: 3 He **h** the brokenhearted and binds

HEALTH (HEALTHY)
Pr 3: 8 This will bring **h** to your body
15: 30 good news gives **h** to the bones.

HEALTHY (HEALTH)
Mk 2: 17 “It is not the **h** who need a doctor,

HEAR (HEARD HEARING HEARS)
Dt 6: 4 **H**, O Israel: The LORD our God,
31: 13 law, must **h** it and learn to fear
2Ch 7: 14 then I will **h** from heaven,
Ps 94: 9 he who fashioned the ear not **h**?
Isa 29: 18 day the deaf will **h** the words
65: 24 they are still speaking I will **h**.
Mt 11: 15 Whoever has ears, let them **h**.
Jn 8: 47 The reason you do not **h** is that
2Ti 4: 3 what their itching ears want to **h**.

HEARD (HEAR)
Job 42: 5 My ears had **h** of you but now my
Isa 66: 8 Who has ever **h** of such things?
Mt 5: 21 “You have **h** that it was said
5: 27 “You have **h** that it was said,
5: 33 you have **h** that it was said
5: 38 “You have **h** that it was said,
5: 43 “You have **h** that it was said,
1Co 2: 9 what no ear has **h**, and what no
1Th 2: 13 which you **h** from us, you accepted
2Ti 1: 13 What you **h** from me, keep as
Jas 1: 25 not forgetting what they have **h**,

HEARING (HEAR)
Ro 10: 17 faith comes from **h** the message,

HEARS (HEAR)
Jn 5: 24 whoever **h** my word and believes
1Jn 5: 14 according to his will, he **h** us.
Rev 3: 20 If anyone **h** my voice and opens

HEART (BROKENHEARTED HARDHEARTED HEARTS WHOLEHEARTEDLY)
Ex 25: 2 everyone whose **h** prompts them
Lev 19: 17 not hate a fellow Israelite in your **h**.
Dt 4: 29 him if you seek him with all your **h**
6: 5 LORD your God with all your **h**
10: 12 LORD your God with all your **h**
15: 10 and do so without a grudging **h**;
30: 6 you may love him with all your **h**
30: 10 LORD your God with all your **h**
Jos 22: 5 and to serve him with all your **h**
1Sa 13: 14 sought out a man after his own **h**
16: 7 but the LORD looks at the **h**.”
2Ki 23: 3 and decrees with all his **h** and
1Ch 28: 9 for the LORD searches every **h**
2Ch 7: 16 eyes and my **h** will always be there.
Job 22: 22 and lay up his words in your **h**.
37: 1 “At this my **h** pounds and leaps
Ps 14: 1 says in his **h**, “There is no God.”
19: 14 this meditation of my **h** be pleasing
37: 4 will give you the desires of your **h**.
45: 1 My **h** is stirred by a noble theme as
51: 10 Create in me a pure **h**, O God,
51: 17 a broken and contrite **h** you, God,
66: 18 If I had cherished sin in my **h**,
86: 11 give me an undivided **h**, that I may
119: 11 in my **h** that I might not sin against
139: 23 Search me, God, and know my **h**;
Pr 3: 5 Trust in the LORD with all your **h**
4: 21 sight, keep them within your **h**;
4: 23 guard your **h**, for everything you
7: 3 write them on the tablet of your **h**.
13: 12 Hope deferred makes the **h** sick,
14: 13 Even in laughter the **h** may ache,
15: 30 eyes brings joy to the **h**, and good
17: 22 A cheerful **h** is good medicine,
24: 17 stumble, do not let your **h** rejoice,
27: 19 the face, so one’s life reflects the **h**.
Ecc 3: 11 also set eternity in the human **h**;
8: 5 the wise **h** will know the proper
SS 4: 9 You have stolen my **h**, my sister,
Isa 40: 11 and carries them close to his **h**;
57: 15 and to revive the **h** of the contrite.
Jer 17: 9 The **h** is deceitful above all things
29: 13 when you seek me with all your **h**.
Eze 36: 26 I will give you a new **h** and put
Mt 5: 8 Blessed are the pure in **h**, for they
6: 21 treasure is, there your **h** will be
12: 34 mouth speaks what the **h** is full of.
22: 37 the Lord your God with all your **h**
Lk 6: 45 mouth speaks what the **h** is full of.
Ro 2: 29 is circumcision of the **h**,
10: 10 it is with your **h** that you believe
Eph 5: 19 music from your **h** to the Lord,
6: 6 doing the will of God from your **h**.
Col 3: 23 you do, work at it with all your **h**,
1Pe 1: 22 one another deeply, from the **h**.

HEARTS (HEART)
Dt 11: 18 Fix these words of mine in your **h**
1Ki 8: 39 do, since you know their **h** (for you
8: 61 may your **h** be fully committed
Ps 62: 8 pour out your **h** to him, for God is
Jer 31: 33 their minds and write it on their **h**.
Lk 16: 15 of others, but God knows your **h**.
24: 32 “Were not our **h** burning within us
Jn 14: 1 “Do not let your **h** be troubled.
Ac 15: 9 for he purified their **h** by faith.
Ro 2: 15 of the law are written on their **h**,
1Co 14: 25 the secrets of their **h** are laid bare.
2Co 3: 2 written on our **h**, known and read
3: 3 of stone but on tablets of human **h**.
4: 6 shine in our **h** to give us the light
Eph 3: 17 may dwell in your **h** through faith.
Col 3: 1 Christ, set your **h** on things above,
Heb 3: 8 do not harden your **h** as you did
10: 16 I will put my laws in their **h**, and I
1Jn 3: 20 that God is greater than our **h**,

HEAT
2Pe 3: 12 and the elements will melt in the **h**.

HEAVEN (HEAVENLY HEAVENS)
Ge 14: 19 Most High, Creator of **h** and earth.
1Ki 8: 27 even the highest **h**, cannot contain
2Ki 2: 1 take Elijah up to **h** in a whirlwind,
2Ch 7: 14 then I will hear from **h**, and I will
Isa 14: 12 How you have fallen from **h**,

Isa 66: 1 "**H** is my throne, and the earth is
Da 7: 13 man, coming with the clouds of **h**.
Mt 6: 9 "'Our Father in **h**, hallowed be
6: 20 up for yourselves treasures in **h**,
16: 19 you the keys of the kingdom of **h**;
16: 19 bind on earth will be bound in **h**,
19: 23 is rich to enter the kingdom of **h**.
24: 35 **H** and earth will pass away, but my
26: 64 and coming on the clouds of **h**."
28: 18 "All authority in **h** and on earth has
Mk 16: 19 *was taken up into* **h**
Lk 15: 7 **h** over one sinner who repents
18: 22 and you will have treasure in **h**.
Ro 10: 6 heart, 'Who will ascend into **h**?'"
2Co 5: 1 an eternal house in **h**, not built
12: 2 ago was caught up to the third **h**.
Php 2: 10 in **h** and on earth and under
3: 20 But our citizenship is in **h**.
1Th 1: 10 and to wait for his Son from **h**,
Heb 8: 5 a copy and shadow of what is in **h**.
9: 24 he entered **h** itself, now to appear
2Pe 3: 13 we are looking forward to a new **h**
Rev 21: 1 I saw "a new **h** and a new earth,"

HEAVENLY (HEAVEN)
2Co 5: 2 clothed instead with our **h** dwelling,
Eph 1: 3 who has blessed us in the **h** realms
1: 20 at his right hand in the **h** realms,
2Ti 4: 18 bring me safely to his **h** kingdom.
Heb 12: 22 of the living God, the **h** Jerusalem.

HEAVENS (HEAVEN)
Ge 1: 1 In the beginning God created the **h**
1Ki 8: 27 The **h**, even the highest heaven,
2Ch 2: 6 since the **h**, even the highest **h**,
Ps 8: 3 When I consider your **h**, the work
19: 1 The **h** declare the glory of God;
102: 25 the **h** are the work of your hands.
108: 4 is your love, higher than the **h**;
119: 89 it stands firm in the **h**.
139: 8 If I go up to the **h**, you are there;
Isa 51: 6 the **h** will vanish like smoke,
55: 9 "As the **h** are higher than the earth,
65: 17 will create new **h** and a new earth.
Joel 2: 30 I will show wonders in the **h**
Eph 4: 10 ascended higher than all the **h**,
2Pe 3: 10 The **h** will disappear with a roar;

HEBREW
Ge 14: 13 and reported this to Abram the **H**.

HEEDS
Pr 13: 1 A wise son **h** his father's
13: 18 whoever **h** correction is honored.
15: 5 but whoever **h** correction shows
15: 32 but the one who **h** correction gains

HEEL
Ge 3: 15 head, and you will strike his **h**."

HEIRS (INHERIT)
Ro 8: 17 **h** of God and co-heirs with Christ,
Gal 3: 29 and **h** according to the promise.
Eph 3: 6 gospel the Gentiles are **h** together
1Pe 3: 7 as **h** with you of the gracious gift

HELL
Mt 5: 22 will be in danger of the fire of **h**.
2Pe 2: 4 but sent them to **h**, putting them

HELMET
Isa 59: 17 and the **h** of salvation on his head;
Eph 6: 17 Take the **h** of salvation
1Th 5: 8 and the hope of salvation as a **h**.

HELP (HELPED HELPER HELPING HELPS)
2Sa 22: 36 You make your saving **h** my shield;
Ps 18: 6 I cried to my God for **h**.
30: 2 called to you for **h**, and you healed
46: 1 an ever-present **h** in trouble.
70: 4 long for your saving **h** always say,
79: 9 **H** us, God our Savior, for the glory
121: 1 where does my **h** come from?
Isa 41: 10 I will strengthen you and **h** you;
Jnh 2: 2 the realm of the dead I called for **h**,
Mk 9: 24 **h** me overcome my unbelief!"
Ac 16: 9 over to Macedonia and **h** us."

HELPED (HELP)
1Sa 7: 12 "Thus far the LORD has **h** us."

HELPER (HELP)
Ge 2: 18 I will make a **h** suitable for him."
Ps 10: 14 you are the **h** of the fatherless.
Heb 13: 6 confidence, "The Lord is my **h**;

HELPING (HELP)
Ac 9: 36 always doing good and **h** the poor.

1Co 12: 28 gifts of healing, of **h**, of guidance,
1Ti 5: 10 **h** those in trouble and devoting

HELPS (HELP)
Ro 8: 26 the Spirit **h** us in our weakness.

HEN
Mt 23: 37 as a **h** gathers her chicks under her

HERITAGE (INHERIT)
Ps 127: 3 Children are a **h** from the LORD,

HEROD
1. King of Judea who tried to kill Jesus (Mt 2; Lk 1:5).
2. Son of 1. Tetrarch of Galilee who arrested and beheaded John the Baptist (Mt 14:1–12; Mk 6:14–29; Lk 3:1, 19–20; 9:7–9); tried Jesus (Lk 23:6–15).
3. Grandson of 1. King of Judea who killed James (Ac 12:2); arrested Peter (Ac 12:3–19). Death (Ac 12:19–23).

HERODIAS
Wife of Herod the Tetrarch who persuaded her daughter to ask for John the Baptist's head (Mt 14:1–12; Mk 6:14–29).

HEZEKIAH
King of Judah. Restored the temple and worship (2Ch 29–31). Sought the LORD for help against Assyria (2Ki 18–19; 2Ch 32:1–23; Isa 36–37). Illness healed (2Ki 20:1–11; 2Ch 32:24–26; Isa 38). Judged for showing Babylonians his treasures (2Ki 20:12–21; 2Ch 32:31; Isa 39).

HID (HIDE)
Ge 3: 8 they **h** from the LORD God among
Ex 2: 2 child, she **h** him for three months.
Jos 6: 17 because she **h** the spies we sent.
Heb 11: 23 faith Moses' parents **h** him for

HIDDEN (HIDE)
Ps 19: 12 Forgive my **h** faults.
119: 11 I have **h** your word in my heart
Pr 2: 4 and search for it as for **h** treasure,
Isa 59: 2 your sins have **h** his face from you,
Mt 5: 14 A town built on a hill cannot be **h**.
13: 44 heaven is like treasure **h** in a field.
Col 1: 26 that has been kept **h** for ages
2: 3 in whom are **h** all the treasures
3: 3 and your life is now **h** with Christ

HIDE (HID HIDDEN)
Ps 17: 8 **h** me in the shadow of your wings
143: 9 LORD, for I **h** myself in you.

HIGH
Isa 57: 15 "I live in a **h** and holy place,

HILL (HILLS)
Mt 5: 14 town built on a **h** cannot be hidden.

HILLS (HILL)
Ps 50: 10 and the cattle on a thousand **h**.

HINDER (HINDERS)
1Sa 14: 6 Nothing can **h** the LORD
Mt 19: 14 do not **h** them, for the kingdom
1Co 9: 12 anything rather than **h** the gospel
1Pe 3: 7 so that nothing will **h** your prayers.

HINDERS (HINDER)
Heb 12: 1 let us throw off everything that **h**

HINT
Eph 5: 3 you there must not be even a **h**

HOLD
Ex 20: 7 LORD will not **h** anyone guiltless
Lev 19: 13 "'Do not **h** back the wages
Jos 22: 5 to **h** fast to him and to serve him
Ps 73: 23 you **h** me by my right hand.
Pr 4: 4 "Take **h** of my words with all your
Isa 54: 2 tent curtains wide, do not **h** back;
Mk 11: 25 if you **h** anything against anyone,
Php 2: 16 as you **h** firmly to the word of life.
3: 12 which Christ Jesus took **h** of me.
Col 1: 17 and in him all things **h** together.
1Th 5: 21 test them all; **h** on to what is good,
1Ti 6: 12 Take **h** of the eternal life
Heb 10: 23 Let us **h** unswervingly to the hope

HOLINESS (HOLY)
Ex 15: 11 majestic in **h**, awesome in glory,
Ps 29: 2 the LORD in the splendor of his **h**.
96: 9 the LORD in the splendor of his **h**;
Ro 6: 19 to righteousness leading to **h**.
2Co 7: 1 perfecting **h** out of reverence
Eph 4: 24 God in true righteousness and **h**.
Heb 12: 10 in order that we may share in his **h**.
12: 14 without **h** no one will see the Lord.

HOLY (HALLOWED HOLINESS)
Ex 19: 6 kingdom of priests and a **h** nation.'
20: 8 the Sabbath day by keeping it **h**.

Mt 12: 25 or **h** divided against itself will not
1Ti 3: 12 manage his children and his **h** well.
3: 15 to conduct themselves in God's **h**,

HOUSEHOLDS (HOUSE)
Pr 15: 27 The greedy bring ruin to their **h**,

HUMAN (HUMANITY)
Ge 9: 6 "Whoever sheds **h** blood,
1Sa 15: 29 for he is not a **h** being, that he
Ac 5: 29 obey God rather than **h** beings!
2Pe 1: 21 never had its origin in the **h** will,

HUMANITY (HUMAN)
Heb 2: 14 he too shared in their **h** so

HUMBLE (HUMBLED HUMILIATE HUMILIATING HUMILITY)
2Ch 7: 14 will **h** themselves and pray and
Ps 25: 9 He guides the **h** in what is right
Pr 3: 34 favor to the **h** and oppressed.
Isa 66: 2 those who are **h** and contrite
Mt 11: 29 for I am gentle and **h** in heart,
Eph 4: 2 Be completely **h** and gentle;
Jas 4: 10 **H** yourselves before the Lord,
1Pe 5: 6 **H** yourselves, therefore,

HUMBLED (HUMBLE)
Mt 23: 12 who exalt themselves will be **h**,
Php 2: 8 he **h** himself by becoming obedient

HUMILIATE (HUMBLE)
Pr 25: 7 for him to **h** you before his nobles.

HUMILIATING (HUMBLE)
1Co 11: 22 God by **h** those who have nothing?

HUMILITY (HUMBLE)
Pr 11: 2 but with **h** comes wisdom.
15: 33 LORD, and **h** comes before honor.
2Co 10: 1 the **h** and gentleness of Christ,
Php 2: 3 in **h** value others above yourselves,
1Pe 5: 5 with **h** toward one another,

HUNGRY
Ps 107: 9 and fills the **h** with good things.
146: 7 oppressed and gives food to the **h**.
Pr 25: 21 If your enemy is **h**, give him food
Eze 18: 7 his food to the **h** and provides
Mt 25: 35 For I was **h** and you gave me
Lk 1: 53 has filled the **h** with good things
Jn 6: 35 comes to me will never go **h**,
Ro 12: 20 "If your enemy is **h**, feed him;

HURT (HURTS)
Ecc 8: 9 lords it over others to his own **h**.
Mk 16: 18 *it will not* **h** *them*
Rev 2: 11 one who is victorious will not be **h**

HURTS (HURT)
Ps 15: 4 who keeps an oath even when it **h**,
Pr 26: 28 A lying tongue hates those it **h**,

HUSBAND (HUSBAND'S HUSBANDS)
1Co 7: 3 The **h** should fulfill his marital
7: 3 and likewise the wife to her **h**.
7: 4 her own body but yields it to her **h**.
7: 4 the **h** does not have authority over
7: 10 wife must not separate from her **h**.
7: 11 And a **h** must not divorce his wife.
7: 13 And if a woman has a **h** who is not
7: 39 But if her **h** dies, she is free
2Co 11: 2 I promised you to one **h**, to Christ,
Eph 5: 23 For the **h** is the head of the wife as
5: 33 and the wife must respect her **h**.

HUSBAND'S (HUSBAND)
Pr 12: 4 of noble character is her **h** crown,

HUSBANDS (HUSBAND)
Eph 5: 22 yourselves to your own **h** as you do
5: 25 **H**, love your wives, just as Christ
Titus 2: 4 the younger women to love their **h**
1Pe 3: 1 yourselves to your own **h** so that,
3: 7 **H**, in the same way be considerate

HYMN
1Co 14: 26 each of you has a **h**, or a word

HYPOCRISY (HYPOCRITE HYPOCRITES)
Mt 23: 28 on the inside you are full of **h**
1Pe 2: 1 of all malice and all deceit, **h**, envy,

HYPOCRITE (HYPOCRISY)
Mt 7: 5 You **h**, first take the plank

HYPOCRITES (HYPOCRISY)
Ps 26: 4 deceitful, nor do I associate with **h**.
Mt 6: 5 do not be like the **h**, for they love

HYSSOP
Ps 51: 7 Cleanse me with **h**, and I will be

IDLE (IDLENESS)
1Th 5: 14 those who are **i** and disruptive,
2Th 3: 6 away from every believer who is **i**
1Ti 5: 13 they get into the habit of being **i**

IDLENESS (IDLE)
Pr 31: 27 and does not eat the bread of **i**.

IDOL (IDOLATRY IDOLS)
Isa 44: 17 From the rest he makes a god, his **i**;
1Co 8: 4 We know that "An **i** is nothing

IDOLATRY (IDOL)
Col 3: 5 evil desires and greed, which is **i**.

IDOLS (IDOL)
1Co 8: 1 Now about food sacrificed to **i**:

IGNORANT (IGNORE)
1Co 15: 34 there are some who are **i** of God—
Heb 5: 2 to deal gently with those who are **i**
1Pe 2: 15 good you should silence the **i** talk
2Pe 3: 16 **i** and unstable people distort,

IGNORE (IGNORANT IGNORES)
Dt 22: 1 not **i** it but be sure to take it back
Ps 9: 12 he does not **i** the cries
Heb 2: 3 escape if we **i** so great a salvation?

IGNORES (IGNORE)
Pr 10: 17 whoever **i** correction leads others

ILLUMINATED
Rev 18: 1 and the earth was **i** by his splendor.

IMAGE
Ge 1: 26 "Let us make mankind in our **i**,
1: 27 God created mankind in his own **i**, in the **i** of God he created them;
Ro 8: 29 to be conformed to the **i** of his Son,
1Co 11: 7 since he is the **i** and glory of God;
2Co 3: 18 into his **i** with ever-increasing glory,
Col 1: 15 The Son is the **i** of the invisible
3: 10 in knowledge in the **i** of its Creator.

IMAGINE
Eph 3: 20 more than all we ask or **i**,

IMITATE (IMITATORS)
1Co 4: 16 Therefore I urge you to **i** me.
Heb 6: 12 but to **i** those who through faith
13: 7 of their way of life and **i** their faith.
3Jn : 11 do not **i** what is evil but what is

IMITATORS (IMITATE)
1Th 1: 6 You became **i** of us and of the Lord,
2: 14 became **i** of God's churches

IMMANUEL
Isa 7: 14 birth to a son, and will call him **I**.
Mt 1: 23 they will call him **I**" (which means

IMMORAL (IMMORALITY)
1Co 5: 9 to associate with sexually **i** people
5: 10 the people of this world who are **i**,
5: 11 or sister but is sexually **i** or greedy,
6: 9 Neither the sexually **i** nor idolaters
Eph 5: 5 No **i**, impure or greedy person—
Heb 12: 16 See that no one is sexually **i**, or is
13: 4 the adulterer and all the sexually **i**.
Rev 21: 8 the sexually **i**, those who practice
22: 15 arts, the sexually **i**, the murderers,

IMMORALITY (IMMORAL)
Mt 5: 32 except for sexual **i**, makes her
19: 9 except for sexual **i**, and marries
1Co 6: 13 is not meant for sexual **i**
6: 18 Flee from sexual **i**. All other sins
10: 8 We should not commit sexual **i**,
Gal 5: 19 sexual **i**, impurity and debauchery;
Eph 5: 3 must not be even a hint of sexual **i**,
1Th 4: 3 that you should avoid sexual **i**;
Jude : 4 grace of our God into a license for **i**

IMMORTAL (IMMORTALITY)
Ro 1: 23 exchanged the glory of the **i** God
1Ti 1: 17 Now to the King eternal, **i**,
6: 16 who alone is **i** and who lives

IMMORTALITY (IMMORTAL)
Ro 2: 7 and **i**, he will give eternal life.
1Co 15: 53 and the mortal with **i**.
2Ti 1: 10 and **i** to light through the gospel.

IMPERISHABLE
1Pe 1: 23 seed, but of **i**, through the living

IMPORTANCE (IMPORTANT)
1Co 15: 3 I passed on to you as of first **i**:

IMPORTANT (IMPORTANCE)
Mt 23: 23 have neglected the more **i** matters
Mk 12: 29 "The most **i** one," answered Jesus,

Mk 12: 33 as yourself is more **i** than all burnt
Php 1: 18 The **i** thing is that in every way,

IMPOSSIBLE
Mt 17: 20 Nothing will be **i** for you."
Lk 18: 27 "What is **i** with man is possible
Heb 6: 18 in which it is **i** for God to lie,
11: 6 without faith it is **i** to please God,

IMPROPER
Eph 5: 3 because these are **i** for God's holy

IMPURE (IMPURITY)
Ac 10: 15 "Do not call anything **i** that God
Eph 5: 5 No immoral, **i** or greedy person—
1Th 4: 7 For God did not call us to be **i**,
Rev 21: 27 Nothing **i** will ever enter it,

IMPURITY (IMPURE)
Ro 1: 24 hearts to sexual **i** for the degrading
Eph 5: 3 or of any kind of **i**, or of greed,

INCENSE
Ex 40: 5 Place the gold altar of **i** in front
Ps 141: 2 my prayer be set before you like **i**;

INCOME
Ecc 5: 10 is never satisfied with their **i**.
1Co 16: 2 of money in keeping with your **i**,

INCOMPARABLE
Eph 2: 7 ages he might show the **i** riches

INCREASE (EVER-INCREASING INCREASED INCREASING)
Ge 1: 22 "Be fruitful and **i** in number and
Ps 62: 10 though your riches **i**, do not set
Lk 17: 5 said to the Lord, "**I** our faith!"
1Th 3: 12 May the Lord make your love **i**

INCREASED (INCREASE)
Ac 6: 7 of disciples in Jerusalem **i** rapidly,
Ro 5: 20 where sin **i**, grace **i** all the more,

INCREASING (INCREASE)
Ac 6: 1 the number of disciples was **i**,
2Th 1: 3 all of you have for one another is **i**.
2Pe 1: 8 these qualities in **i** measure,

INDEPENDENT
1Co 11: 11 in the Lord woman is not **i** of man, nor is man **i** of woman.

INDESCRIBABLE
2Co 9: 15 Thanks be to God for his **i** gift!

INDISPENSABLE
1Co 12: 22 body that seem to be weaker are **i**,

INEFFECTIVE
2Pe 1: 8 they will keep you from being **i**

INEXPRESSIBLE
2Co 12: 4 up to paradise and heard **i** things,
1Pe 1: 8 are filled with an **i** and glorious joy,

INFANTS
Mt 21: 16 the lips of children and **i** you, Lord,
1Co 14: 20 In regard to evil be **i**, but in your

INHERIT (CO-HEIRS HEIRS HERITAGE INHERITANCE)
Ps 37: 11 the meek will **i** the land and enjoy
37: 29 The righteous will **i** the land
Mt 5: 5 the meek, for they will **i** the earth.
Mk 10: 17 "what must I do to **i** eternal life?"
1Co 15: 50 cannot **i** the kingdom of God,

INHERITANCE (INHERIT)
Dt 4: 20 to be the people of his **i**, as you
Pr 13: 22 A good person leaves an **i** for their
Eph 1: 14 deposit guaranteeing our **i** until
5: 5 has any **i** in the kingdom of Christ
Heb 9: 15 receive the promised eternal **i**—
1Pe 1: 4 This **i** is kept in heaven for you,

INIQUITIES (INIQUITY)
Ps 78: 38 he forgave their **i** and did not
103: 10 or repay us according to our **i**.
Isa 59: 2 your **i** have separated you from
Mic 7: 19 hurl all our **i** into the depths

INIQUITY (INIQUITIES)
Ps 51: 2 Wash away all my **i** and cleanse me
Isa 53: 6 has laid on him the **i** of us all.

INJUSTICE
2Ch 19: 7 the LORD our God there is no **i**

INNOCENT
Pr 17: 26 a fine on the **i** is not good,
Mt 10: 16 shrewd as snakes and as **i** as doves.
27: 4 said, "for I have betrayed **i** blood."
1Co 4: 4 clear, but that does not make me **i**.

INSCRIPTION
Mt 22: 20 image is this? And whose **i**?"

INSOLENT
Ro 1: 30 **i**, arrogant and boastful;

INSTITUTED
Ro 13: 2 is rebelling against what God has **i**,

INSTRUCT (INSTRUCTED INSTRUCTION)
Ps 32: 8 I will **i** you and teach you
Pr 9: 9 **I** the wise and they will be wiser
Ro 15: 14 and competent to **i** one another.

INSTRUCTED (INSTRUCT)
2Ti 2: 25 Opponents must be gently **i**,

INSTRUCTION (INSTRUCT)
Pr 1: 3 for receiving **i** in prudent behavior,
1: 7 but fools despise wisdom and **i**.
1: 8 your father's **i** and do not forsake
4: 1 Listen, my sons, to a father's **i**;
4: 13 Hold on to **i**, do not let it go;
6: 23 correction and **i** are the way to life,
8: 10 Choose my **i** instead of silver,
8: 33 Listen to my **i** and be wise;
13: 1 A wise son heeds his father's **i**,
13: 13 Whoever scorns **i** will pay for it,
16: 20 Whoever gives heed to **i** prospers,
16: 21 and gracious words promote **i**.
23: 12 Apply your heart to **i** and your ears
23: 23 wisdom, **i** and insight as well.
Isa 8: 20 Consult God's **i** and the testimony
1Co 14: 6 or prophecy or word of **i**?
14: 26 hymn, or a word of **i**, a revelation,
Eph 6: 4 in the training and **i** of the Lord.
1Th 4: 8 who rejects this **i** does not reject
2Th 3: 14 anyone who does not obey our **i**
1Ti 6: 3 sound **i** of our Lord Jesus Christ
2Ti 4: 2 with great patience and careful **i**.

INSULT (INSULTS)
Pr 12: 16 but the prudent overlook an **i**.
Mt 5: 11 are you when people **i** you,
Lk 6: 22 when they exclude you and **i** you
1Pe 3: 9 not repay evil with evil or **i** with **i**.

INSULTS (INSULT)
Pr 9: 7 corrects a mocker invites **i**;

INTEGRITY
1Ki 9: 4 walk before me faithfully with **i**
Job 2: 3 And he still maintains his **i**,
27: 5 till I die, I will not deny my **i**.
Pr 10: 9 Whoever walks in **i** walks securely,
11: 3 The **i** of the upright guides them,
29: 10 The bloodthirsty hate a person of **i**
Titus 2: 7 In your teaching show **i**,

INTELLIGENCE
Isa 29: 14 the **i** of the intelligent will vanish."
1Co 1: 19 the **i** of the intelligent I will

INTELLIGIBLE
1Co 14: 19 I would rather speak five **i** words

INTERCEDE (INTERCEDES INTERCESSION)
Heb 7: 25 him, because he always lives to **i**

INTERCEDES (INTERCEDE)
Ro 8: 26 the Spirit himself **i** for us through

INTERCESSION (INTERCEDE)
Isa 53: 12 and made **i** for the transgressors.
1Ti 2: 1 **i** and thanksgiving be made for all

INTEREST
Ne 5: 10 But let us stop charging **i**!

INTERESTS
1Co 7: 34 and his **i** are divided.
Php 2: 4 not looking to your own **i** but each of you to the **i** of the others.
2: 21 everyone looks out for their own **i**,

INTERMARRY (MARRY)
Dt 7: 3 Do not **i** with them. Do not give

INVESTIGATED
Lk 1: 3 I myself have carefully **i** everything

INVISIBLE
Ro 1: 20 of the world God's **i** qualities—
Col 1: 15 The Son is the image of the **i** God,
1Ti 1: 17 eternal, immortal, **i**, the only God,

INVITE (INVITED INVITES)
Lk 14: 13 you give a banquet, **i** the poor,

INVITED (INVITE)
Mt 22: 14 "For many are **i**, but few are
25: 35 I was a stranger and you **i** me in,

INVITES (INVITE)
1Co 10: 27 If an unbeliever **i** you to a meal

IRON
1Ti 4: 2 have been seared as with a hot **i**.
Rev 2: 27 'will rule them with an **i** scepter

IRREVOCABLE
Ro 11: 29 for God's gifts and his call are **i**.

ISAAC
Son of Abraham by Sarah (Ge 17:19; 21:1–7; 1Ch 1:28). Offered up by Abraham (Ge 22; Heb 11:17–19). Rebekah taken as wife (Ge 24). Fathered Esau and Jacob (Ge 25:19–26; 1Ch 1:34). Tricked into blessing Jacob (Ge 27). Father of Israel (Ex 3:6; Dt 29:13; Ro 9:10).

ISAIAH
Prophet to Judah (Isa 1:1). Called by the LORD (Isa 6).

ISHMAEL
Son of Abraham by Hagar (Ge 16; 1Ch 1:28). Blessed, but not son of covenant (Ge 17:18–21; Gal 4:21–31). Sent away by Sarah (Ge 21:8–21).

ISRAEL (ISRAELITES)
1. Name given to Jacob (see JACOB).
2. Corporate name of Jacob's descendants; often specifically Northern Kingdom.
Dt 6: 4 Hear, O **I**: The LORD our God,
1Sa 4: 21 "The Glory has departed from **I**"—
Isa 27: 6 **I** will bud and blossom and fill all
Jer 31: 10 'He who scattered **I** will gather
Eze 39: 23 that the people of **I** went into exile
Mk 12: 29 'Hear, O **I**: The Lord our God,
Lk 22: 30 judging the twelve tribes of **I**.
Ro 9: 6 all who are descended from **I** are **I**.
11: 26 and in this way all **I** will be saved.
Eph 3: 6 Gentiles are heirs together with **I**,

ISRAELITES (ISRAEL)
Ex 14: 22 the **I** went through the sea on dry
16: 35 The **I** ate manna forty years,
Hos 1: 10 "Yet the **I** will be like the sand
Ro 9: 27 number of the **I** be like the sand

ITCHING
2Ti 4: 3 say what their **i** ears want to hear.

JACOB
Second son of Isaac, twin of Esau (Ge 25:21–26; 1Ch 1:34). Bought Esau's birthright (Ge 25:29–34); tricked Isaac into blessing him (Ge 27:1–37). Abrahamic covenant perpetuated through (Ge 28:13–15; Mal 1:2). Vision at Bethel (Ge 28:10–22). Wives and children (Ge 29:1—30:24; 35:16–26; 1Ch 2–9). Wrestled with God; name changed to Israel (Ge 32:22–32). Sent sons to Egypt during famine (Ge 42–43). Settled in Egypt (Ge 46). Blessed Ephraim and Manasseh (Ge 48). Blessed sons (Ge 49:1–28; Heb 11:21). Death (Ge 49:29–33). Burial (Ge 50:1–14).

JAMES
1. Apostle; brother of John (Mt 4:21–22; 10:2; Mk 3:17; Lk 5:1–10). At transfiguration (Mt 17:1–13; Mk 9:1–13; Lk 9:28–36). Killed by Herod (Ac 12:2).
2. Apostle; son of Alphaeus (Mt 10:3; Mk 3:18; Lk 6:15).
3. Brother of Jesus (Mt 13:55; Mk 6:3; Lk 24:10; Gal 1:19) and Judas (Jude 1). With believers before Pentecost (Ac 1:13). Leader of church at Jerusalem (Ac 12:17; 15; 21:18; Gal 2:9, 12). Author of epistle (Jas 1:1).

JAPHETH
Son of Noah (Ge 5:32; 1Ch 1:4–5). Blessed (Ge 9:18–28).

JARS
2Co 4: 7 we have this treasure in **j** of clay

JEALOUS (JEALOUSY)
Ex 20: 5 am a **j** God, punishing the children
34: 14 whose name is **J**, is a **j** God.
Dt 4: 24 God is a consuming fire, a **j** God.
Joel 2: 18 Then the LORD was **j** for his land
Zec 1: 14 I am very **j** for Jerusalem and Zion,
2Co 11: 2 am **j** for you with a godly jealousy.

JEALOUSY (JEALOUS)
1Co 3: 3 For since there is **j** and quarreling
2Co 11: 2 I am jealous for you with a godly **j**.
Gal 5: 20 hatred, discord, **j**, fits of rage,

JEHOAHAZ
1. Son of Jehu; king of Israel (2Ki 13:1–9).
2. Son of Josiah; king of Judah (2Ki 23:31–34; 2Ch 36:1–4).

JEHOASH
Son of Jehoahaz; king of Israel (2Ki 13–14; 2Ch 25).

JEHOIACHIN
Son of Jehoiakim; king of Judah exiled by Nebuchadnezzar (2Ki 24:8–17; 2Ch 36:8–10; Jer 22:24–30; 24:1). Raised from prisoner status (2Ki 25:27–30; Jer 52:31–34).

JEHOIAKIM
Son of Josiah; king of Judah (2Ki 23:34—24:6; 2Ch 36:4–8; Jer 22:18–23; 36).

JEHORAM
Son of Jehoshaphat; king of Judah (2Ki 8:16–24).

JEHOSHAPHAT
Son of Asa; king of Judah (1Ki 22:41–50; 2Ki 3; 2Ch 17–20).

JEHU
King of Israel (1Ki 19:16–19; 2Ki 9–10).

JEPHTHAH
Judge from Gilead who delivered Israel from Ammon (Jdg 10:6—12:7). Made rash vow concerning his daughter (Jdg 11:30–40).

JEREMIAH
Prophet to Judah (Jer 1:1–3). Called by the LORD (Jer 1). Put in stocks (Jer 20:1–3). Threatened for prophesying (Jer 11:18–23; 26). Opposed by Hananiah (Jer 28). Scroll burned (Jer 36). Imprisoned (Jer 37). Thrown into cistern (Jer 38). Forced to Egypt with those fleeing Babylonians (Jer 43).

JEROBOAM
1. Official of Solomon; rebelled to become first king of Israel (1Ki 11:26–40; 12:1–20; 2Ch 10). Idolatry (1Ki 12:25–33); judgment for (1Ki 13–14; 2Ch 13).
2. Son of Jehoash; king of Israel (1Ki 14:23–29).

JERUSALEM
2Ki 23: 27 and I will reject **J**, the city I chose,
2Ch 6: 6 now I have chosen **J** for my Name
Ne 2: 17 let us rebuild the wall of **J**,
Ps 122: 6 Pray for the peace of **J**:
125: 2 As the mountains surround **J**,
137: 5 If I forget you, **J**, may my right
Isa 40: 9 You who bring good news to **J**,
65: 18 for I will create **J** to be a delight
Joel 3: 17 **J** will be holy; never again will
Zep 3: 16 On that day they will say to **J**,
Zec 2: 4 man, '**J** will be a city without walls
8: 8 I will bring them back to live in **J**;
14: 8 living water will flow out from **J**,
Mt 23: 37 "**J**, **J**, you who kill the prophets
Lk 13: 34 "**J**, **J**, you who kill the prophets
21: 24 **J** will be trampled
Jn 4: 20 where we must worship is in **J**."
Ac 1: 8 and you will be my witnesses in **J**,
Gal 4: 25 to the present city of **J**,
Rev 21: 2 the new **J**, coming down

JESUS
LIFE: Genealogy (Mt 1:1–17; Lk 3:21–37). Birth announced (Mt 1:18–25; Lk 1:26–45). Birth (Mt 2:1–12; Lk 2:1–40). Escape to Egypt (Mt 2:13–23). As a boy in the temple (Lk 2:41–52). Baptism (Mt 3:13–17; Mk 1:9–11; Lk 3:21–22; Jn 1:32–34). Temptation (Mt 4:1–11; Mk 1:12–13; Lk 4:1–13). Ministry in Galilee (Mt 4:12—18:35; Mk 1:14—9:50; Lk 4:14—13:9; Jn 1:35—2:11; 4; 6), Transfiguration (Mt 17:1–8; Mk 9:2–8; Lk 9:28–36), on the way to Jerusalem (Mt 19–20; Mk 10; Lk 13:10—19:27), in Jerusalem (Mt 21–25; Mk 11–13; Lk 19:28—21:38; Jn 2:12—3:36; 5; 7–12). Last supper (Mt 26:17–35; Mk 14:12–31; Lk 22:1–38; Jn 13–17). Arrest and trial (Mt 26:36—27:31; Mk 14:43—15:20; Lk 22:39—23:25; Jn 18:1—19:16). Crucifixion (Mt 27:32–66; Mk 15:21–47; Lk 23:26–55; Jn 19:28–42). Resurrection and appearances (Mt 28; Mk 16; Lk 24; Jn 20–21; Ac 1:1–11; 7:56; 9:3–6; 1Co 15:1–8; Rev 1:1–20).

MIRACLES. Healings: official's son (Jn 4:43–54), demoniac in Capernaum (Mk 1:23–26; Lk 4:33–35), Peter's mother-in-law (Mt 8:14–17; Mk 1:29–31; Lk 4:38–39), leper (Mt 8:2–4; Mk 1:40–45; Lk 5:12–16), paralytic (Mt 9:1–8; Mk 2:1–12; Lk 5:17–26), cripple (Jn 5:1–9), shriveled hand (Mt 12:10–13; Mk 3:1–5; Lk 6:6–11), centurion's servant (Mt 8:5–13; Lk 7:1–10), widow's son raised (Lk 7:11–17), demoniac (Mt 12:22–23; Lk 11:14), Gadarene demoniacs (Mt 8:28–34; Mk 5:1–20; Lk 8:26–39), woman's bleeding and Jairus' daughter (Mt 9:18–26; Mk 5:21–43; Lk 8:40–56), blind man (Mt 9:27–31), mute man (Mt 9:32–33), Canaanite woman's daughter (Mt 15:21–28; Mk 7:24–30), deaf man (Mk 7:31–37), blind man (Mk 8:22–26), demoniac boy (Mt 17:14–18; Mk 9:14–29; Lk 9:37–43), ten lepers (Lk 17:11–19), man born blind (Jn 9:1–7), Lazarus raised (Jn 11), crippled woman (Lk 13:11–17), man with dropsy (Lk 14:1–6), two blind men (Mt 20:29–34; Mk 10:46–52; Lk 18:35–43), Malchus' ear (Lk 22:50–51). Other Miracles: water to wine (Jn 2:1–11), catch of fish (Lk 5:1–11), storm stilled (Mt 8:23–27; Mk 4:37–41; Lk 8:22–25), 5,000 fed (Mt 14:15–21; Mk 6:35–44; Lk 9:10–17; Jn 6:1–14), walking on water (Mt 14:25–33; Mk 6:48–52; Jn 6:15–21), 4,000 fed (Mt 15:32–39; Mk 8:1–9), money from fish (Mt 17:24–27), fig tree cursed (Mt 21:18–22; Mk 11:12–14), catch of fish (Jn 21:1–14).

MAJOR TEACHING: Sermon on the Mount (Mt 5–7; Lk 6:17–49), to Nicodemus (Jn 3), to Samaritan woman (Jn 4), Bread of Life (Jn 6:22–59), at Feast of Tabernacles (Jn 7–8), woes to Pharisees (Mt

23; Lk 11:37–54), Good Shepherd (Jn 10:1–18), Olivet Discourse (Mt 24–25; Mk 13; Lk 21:5–36), Upper Room Discourse (Jn 13–16).

PARABLES: Sower (Mt 13:3–23; Mk 4:3–25; Lk 8:5–18), seed's growth (Mk 4:26–29), wheat and weeds (Mt 13:24–30, 36–43), mustard seed (Mt 13:31–32; Mk 4:30–32), yeast (Mt 13:33; Lk 13:20–21), hidden treasure (Mt 13:44), valuable pearl (Mt 13:45–46), net (Mt 13:47–51), house owner (Mt 13:52), good Samaritan (Lk 10:25–37), unmerciful servant (Mt 18:15–35), lost sheep (Mt 18:10–14; Lk 15:4–7), lost coin (Lk 15:8–10), prodigal son (Lk 15:11–32), dishonest manager (Lk 16:1–13), rich man and Lazarus (Lk 16:19–31), persistent widow (Lk 18:1–8), Pharisee and tax collector (Lk 18:9–14), payment of workers (Mt 20:1–16), tenants and the vineyard (Mt 21:28–46; Mk 12:1–12; Lk 20:9–19), wedding banquet (Mt 22:1–14), faithful servant (Mt 24:45–51), ten virgins (Mt 25:1–13), talents (Mt 25:1–30; Lk 19:12–27).

DISCIPLES see APOSTLES. Call of (Jn 1:35–51; Mt 4:18–22; 9:9; Mk 1:16–20; 2:13–14; Lk 5:1–11, 27–28). Named Apostles (Mk 3:13–19; Lk 6:12–16). Twelve sent out (Mt 10; Mk 6:7–11; Lk 9:1–5). Seventy sent out (Lk 10:1–24). Defection of (Jn 6:60–71; Mt 26:56; Mk 14:50–52). Final commission (Mt 28:16–20; Jn 21:15–23; Ac 1:3–8).

Ac 2: 32 God has raised this **J** to life, and we
9: 5 Saul asked. "I am **J**, whom you are
15: 11 of our Lord **J** that we are saved,
16: 31 "Believe in the Lord **J**, and you will
Ro 3: 24 redemption that came by Christ **J**.
5: 17 life through the one man, **J** Christ!
8: 1 for those who are in Christ **J**,
1Co 2: 2 I was with you except **J** Christ
8: 6 and there is but one Lord, **J** Christ,
12: 3 and no one can say, "**J** is Lord,"
2Co 4: 5 but **J** Christ as Lord, and ourselves
Gal 2: 16 of the law, but by faith in **J** Christ.
3: 28 for you are all one in Christ **J**.
5: 6 in Christ **J** neither circumcision
Eph 2: 10 in Christ **J** to do good works,
2: 20 with Christ **J** himself as the chief
Php 1: 6 until the day of Christ **J**.
2: 5 have the same mindset as Christ **J**:
2: 10 name of **J** every knee should bow,
Col 3: 17 do it all in the name of the Lord **J**,
2Th 2: 1 the coming of our Lord **J** Christ
1Ti 1: 15 **J** came into the world to save
2Ti 3: 12 life in Christ **J** will be persecuted,
Titus 2: 13 our great God and Savior, **J** Christ,
Heb 2: 9 But we do see **J**, who was made
3: 1 fix your thoughts on **J**, whom we
4: 14 into heaven, **J** the Son of God,
7: 22 **J** has become the guarantor
7: 24 but because **J** lives forever, he has
12: 2 fixing our eyes on **J**, the pioneer
2Pe 1: 16 of our Lord **J** Christ in power,
1Jn 1: 7 and the blood of **J**, his Son,
2: 1 **J** Christ, the Righteous One.
2: 6 to live in him must live as **J** did.
4: 15 acknowledges that **J** is the Son
Rev 22: 20 Amen. Come, Lord **J**.

JEW (JEWS JUDAISM)
Zec 8: 23 take firm hold of one **J** by the hem
Ro 1: 16 first to the **J**, then to the Gentile.
10: 12 there is no difference between **J**
1Co 9: 20 To the Jews I became like a **J**,
Gal 3: 28 There is neither **J** nor Gentile,

JEWELRY (JEWELS)
1Pe 3: 3 wearing of gold **j** or fine clothes.

JEWELS (JEWELRY)
Isa 61: 10 as a bride adorns herself with her **j**.
Zec 9: 16 in his land like **j** in a crown.

JEWS (JEW)
Mt 2: 2 who has been born king of the **J**?
27: 11 him, "Are you the king of the **J**?"
Jn 4: 22 know, for salvation is from the **J**.
Ro 3: 29 Or is God the God of **J** only?
1Co 1: 22 **J** demand signs and Greeks look
9: 20 To the **J** I became like a Jew, to win
12: 13 whether **J** or Gentiles,
Rev 3: 9 claim to be **J** though they are not,

JEZEBEL

Sidonian wife of Ahab (1Ki 16:31). Promoted Baal worship (1Ki 16:32–33). Killed prophets of the LORD (1Ki 18:4, 13). Opposed Elijah (1Ki 19:1–2). Had Naboth killed (1Ki 21). Death prophesied (1Ki 21:17–24). Killed by Jehu (2Ki 9:30–37).

JOASH

Son of Ahaziah; king of Judah. Sheltered from Athaliah by Jehoiada (2Ki 11; 2Ch 22:10—23:21). Repaired temple (2Ki 12; 2Ch 24).

JOB

Wealthy man from Uz; feared God (Job 1:1–5). Righteousness tested by disaster (Job 1:6–22), personal affliction (Job 2). Maintained innocence in debate with three friends (Job 3–31), Elihu (Job 32–37). Rebuked by the LORD (Job 38–41). Vindicated and restored to greater stature by the LORD (Job 42). Example of righteousness (Eze 14:14, 20).

JOHN

1. Son of Zechariah and Elizabeth (Lk 1). Called the Baptist (Mt 3:1–12; Mk 1:2–8). Witness to Jesus (Mt 3:11–12; Mk 1:7–8; Lk 3:15–18; Jn 1:6–35; 3:27–30; 5:33–36). Doubts about Jesus (Mt 11:2–6; Lk 7:18–23). Arrest (Mt 4:12; Mk 1:14). Execution (Mt 14:1–12; Mk 6:14–29; Lk 9:7–9). Ministry compared to Elijah (Mt 11:7–19; Mk 9:11–13; Lk 7:24–35).

2. Apostle; brother of James (Mt 4:21–22; 10:2; Mk 3:17; Lk 5:1–10). At transfiguration (Mt 17:1–13; Mk 9:1–13; Lk 9:28–36). Desire to be greatest (Mk 10:35–45). Leader of church at Jerusalem (Ac 4:1–3; Gal 2:9). Elder who wrote epistles (2Jn 1; 3Jn 1). Prophet who wrote Revelation (Rev 1:1; 22:8).

3. Cousin of Barnabas, co-worker with Paul, (Ac 12:12—13:13; 15:37), see MARK.

JOIN (JOINED)
Pr 23: 20 not **j** those who drink too much
24: 21 do not **j** with rebellious officials,
Ro 15: 30 to **j** me in my struggle by praying
2Ti 1: 8 **j** with me in suffering
2Ti 2: 3 **J** with me in suffering, like a good

JOINED (JOIN)
Mt 19: 6 Therefore what God has **j** together,
Mk 10: 9 Therefore what God has **j** together,
Eph 2: 21 the whole building is **j** together
4: 16 body, **j** and held together by every

JOINTS
Heb 4: 12 soul and spirit, **j** and marrow;

JOKING
Eph 5: 4 foolish talk or coarse **j**, which are

JONAH

Prophet in days of Jeroboam II (2Ki 14:25). Called to Nineveh; fled to Tarshish (Jnh 1:1–3). Cause of storm; thrown into sea (Jnh 1:4–16). Swallowed by fish (Jnh 1:17). Prayer (Jnh 2). Preached to Nineveh (Jnh 3). Attitude reproved by the LORD (Jnh 4). Sign of (Mt 12:39–41; Lk 11:29–32).

JONATHAN

Son of Saul (1Sa 13:16; 1Ch 8:33). Valiant warrior (1Sa 13–14). Relation to David (1Sa 18:1–4; 19–20; 23:16–18). Killed at Gilboa (1Sa 31). Mourned by David (2Sa 1).

JORAM

Son of Ahab; king of Israel (2Ki 3; 8–9; 2Ch 22).

JORDAN
Nu 34: 12 boundary will go down along the **J**
Jos 4: 22 'Israel crossed the **J** on dry ground.'
Mt 3: 6 baptized by him in the **J** River.

JOSEPH

1. Son of Jacob by Rachel (Ge 30:24; 1Ch 2:2). Favored by Jacob, hated by brothers (Ge 37:3–4). Dreams (Ge 37:5–11). Sold by brothers (Ge 37:12–36). Served Potiphar; imprisoned by false accusation (Ge 39). Interpreted dreams of Pharaoh's servants (Ge 40), of Pharaoh (Ge 41:4–40). Made greatest in Egypt (Ge 41:41–57). Sold grain to brothers (Ge 42–45). Brought Jacob and sons to Egypt (Ge 46–47). Sons Ephraim and Manasseh blessed (Ge 48). Blessed (Ge 49:22–26; Dt 33:13–17). Death (Ge 50:22–26; Ex 13:19; Heb 11:22). 12,000 from (Rev 7:8).

2. Husband of Mary, mother of Jesus (Mt 1:16–24; 2:13–19; Lk 1:27; 2; Jn 1:45).

3. Disciple from Arimathea, who gave his tomb for Jesus' burial (Mt 27:57–61; Mk 15:43–47; Lk 23:50–53).

4. Original name of Barnabas (Ac 4:36).

JOSHUA

1. Son of Nun; name changed from Hoshea (Nu 13:8, 16; 1Ch 7:27). Fought Amalekites under Moses (Ex 17:9–14). Servant of Moses on Sinai (Ex 24:13; 32:17). Spied Canaan (Nu 13). With Caleb, allowed to enter land (Nu 14:6, 30). Succeeded Moses (Dt 1:38; 31:1–8; 34:9).

Charged Israel to conquer Canaan (Jos 1). Crossed Jordan (Jos 3–4). Circumcised sons of wilderness wanderings (Jos 5). Conquered Jericho (Jos 6), Ai (Jos 7–8), five kings at Gibeon (Jos 10:1–28), southern Canaan (Jos 10:29–43), northern Canaan (Jos 11–12). Defeated at Ai (Jos 7). Deceived by Gibeonites (Jos 9). Renewed covenant (Jos 8:30–35; 24:1–27). Divided land among tribes (Jos 13–22). Last words (Jos 23). Death (Jos 24:28–31).

2. High priest during rebuilding of temple (Hag 1–2; Zec 3:1–9; 6:11).

JOSIAH

Son of Amon; king of Judah (2Ki 22–23; 2Ch 34–35).

JOTHAM

Son of Azariah (Uzziah); king of Judah (2Ki 15:32–38; 2Ch 26:21—27:9).

JOY (ENJOY ENJOYMENT JOYFUL OVERJOYED REJOICE REJOICES REJOICING)
Dt 16: 15 hands, and your **j** will be complete.
1Ch 16: 27 and **j** are in his dwelling place.
Ne 8: 10 for the **j** of the LORD is your
Est 9: 22 their sorrow was turned into **j**
Job 38: 7 and all the angels shouted for **j**?
Ps 4: 7 Fill my heart with **j** when their
21: 6 glad with the **j** of your presence.
30: 11 sackcloth and clothed me with **j**,
43: 4 God, to God, my **j** and my delight.
51: 12 to me the **j** of your salvation
66: 1 Shout for **j** to God, all the earth!
96: 12 all the trees of the forest sing for **j**.
107: 22 tell of his works with songs of **j**.
119:111 forever; they are the **j** of my heart.
Pr 10: 1 A wise son brings **j** to his father,
10: 28 The prospect of the righteous is **j**,
12: 20 those who promote peace have **j**.
15: 30 in a messenger's eyes brings **j**
Isa 35: 10 everlasting **j** will crown their heads
51: 11 Gladness and **j** will overtake them,
55: 12 You will go out in **j** and be led
Lk 1: 44 the baby in my womb leaped for **j**.
2: 10 will cause great **j** for all the people.
Jn 15: 11 and that your **j** may be complete.
16: 20 grieve, but your grief will turn to **j**.
2Co 8: 2 trial, their overflowing **j** and their
Php 2: 2 then make my **j** complete by being
4: 1 love and long for, my **j** and crown,
1Th 2: 19 our **j**, or the crown in which we
Phm : 7 Your love has given me great **j**
Heb 12: 2 the **j** set before him he endured
Jas 1: 2 Consider it pure **j**, my brothers
1Pe 1: 8 an inexpressible and glorious **j**,
2Jn : 4 It has given me great **j** to find some
3Jn : 4 I have no greater **j** than to hear

JOYFUL (JOY)
Ps 100: 2 come before him with **j** songs.
Pr 23: 25 may she who gave you birth be **j**!
Hab 3: 18 I will be **j** in God my Savior.

JUDAH
1. Son of Jacob by Leah (Ge 29:35; 35:23; 1Ch 2:1). Tribe of blessed as ruling tribe (Ge 49:8–12; Dt 33:7).
2. Name used for people and land of Southern Kingdom.

Jer 13: 19 All **J** will be carried into exile,
Zec 10: 4 From **J** will come the cornerstone,
Heb 7: 14 that our Lord descended from **J**,

JUDAISM (JEW)
Gal 1: 13 of my previous way of life in **J**,

JUDAS
1. Apostle (Lk 6:16; Jn 14:22; Ac 1:13). Probably also called Thaddaeus (Mt 10:3; Mk 3:18).
2. Brother of James and Jesus (Mt 13:55; Mk 6:3), also called Jude (Jude 1).
3. Apostle, also called Iscariot, who betrayed Jesus (Mt 10:4; 26:14–56; Mk 3:19; 14:10–50; Lk 6:16; 22:3–53; Jn 6:71; 12:4; 13:2–30; 18:2–11). Suicide of (Mt 27:3–5; Ac 1:16–25).

JUDGE (JUDGED JUDGES JUDGING JUDGMENT)
Ge 18: 25 Will not the **J** of all the earth do
1Ch 16: 33 LORD, for he comes to **j** the earth.
Joel 3: 12 there I will sit to **j** all the nations
Mt 7: 1 "Do not **j**, or you too will be
Jn 7: 24 but instead **j** correctly."
12: 47 For I did not come to **j** the world,
Ac 17: 31 set a day when he will **j** the world
1Co 4: 3 indeed, I do not even **j** myself.
6: 2 the Lord's people will **j** the world?
2Ti 4: 1 who will **j** the living and the dead,
4: 8 the righteous **J**, will award to me
Jas 4: 12 who are you to **j** your neighbor?
Rev 20: 4 who had been given authority to **j**.

JUDGED (JUDGE)
Mt 7: 1 "Do not judge, or you too will be **j**.
Jn 5: 24 will not be **j** but has crossed over
Jas 3: 1 who teach will be **j** more strictly.
Rev 20: 12 The dead were **j** according to what

JUDGES (JUDGE)
Jdg 2: 16 Then the LORD raised up **j**,
Ps 9: 8 and **j** the peoples with equity.
58: 11 there is a God who **j** the earth."
Ro 2: 16 God **j** people's secrets through Jesus
Heb 4: 12 it **j** the thoughts and attitudes
Rev 19: 11 With justice he **j** and wages war.

JUDGING (JUDGE)
Mt 19: 28 **j** the twelve tribes of Israel.
Jn 7: 24 Stop **j** by mere appearances,
2Co 10: 7 You are **j** by appearances.

JUDGMENT (JUDGE)
Dt 1: 17 of anyone, for **j** belongs to God.
Ps 1: 5 the wicked will not stand in the **j**,
119: 66 Teach me knowledge and good **j**,
Ecc 12: 14 God will bring every deed into **j**,
Isa 66: 16 his sword the LORD will execute **j**
Mt 5: 21 who murders will be subject to **j**.'
10: 15 Gomorrah on the day of **j** than
12: 36 the day of **j** for every empty word
Jn 5: 22 but has entrusted all **j** to the Son,
16: 8 about sin and righteousness and **j**:
Ro 14: 10 will all stand before God's **j** seat.
14: 13 Therefore let us stop passing **j**
1Co 11: 29 eat and drink **j** on themselves.
11: 31 we would not come under such **j**.
2Co 5: 10 we must all appear before the **j** seat
Heb 9: 27 to die once, and after that to face **j**,
10: 27 only a fearful expectation of **j**
1Pe 4: 17 For it is time for **j** to begin
Jude : 6 everlasting chains for **j** on the great

JUST (JUSTICE JUSTIFICATION JUSTIFIED JUSTIFY JUSTLY)
Dt 32: 4 are perfect, and all his ways are **j**.
Ps 37: 28 For the LORD loves the **j** and will
111: 7 of his hands are faithful and **j**;
Pr 1: 3 doing what is right and **j** and fair;
2: 8 for he guards the course of the **j**
Da 4: 37 does is right and all his ways are **j**.
Ro 3: 26 time, so as to be **j** and the one who
Heb 2: 2 received its **j** punishment,
1Jn 1: 9 he is faithful and **j** and will forgive
Rev 16: 7 true and **j** are your judgments."

JUSTICE (JUST)
Ex 23: 2 do not pervert **j** by siding
23: 6 "Do not deny **j** to your poor people
Job 37: 23 in his **j** and great righteousness,
Ps 9: 16 LORD is known by his acts of **j**;
11: 7 the LORD is righteous, he loves **j**;
45: 6 a scepter of **j** will be the scepter
101: 1 I will sing of your love and **j**;
Pr 21: 15 When **j** is done, it brings joy
29: 4 By **j** a king gives a country stability,
29: 26 is from the LORD that one gets **j**.
Isa 9: 7 and upholding it with **j**
28: 17 I will make **j** the measuring line
30: 18 For the LORD is a God of **j**.
42: 1 and he will bring **j** to the nations.
42: 4 be discouraged till he establishes **j**
56: 1 "Maintain **j** and do what is right,
61: 8 "For I, the LORD, love **j**;
Eze 34: 16 I will shepherd the flock with **j**.
Am 5: 15 maintain **j** in the courts.
5: 24 But let **j** roll on like a river,
Zec 7: 9 'Administer true **j**; show mercy
Lk 11: 42 you neglect **j** and the love of God.

JUSTIFICATION (JUST)
Ac 13: 39 sin, a **j** you were not able to obtain
Ro 4: 25 sins and was raised to life for our **j**.
5: 18 one righteous act resulted in **j**

JUSTIFIED (JUST)
Ro 3: 24 all are **j** freely by his grace through
3: 28 that a person is **j** by faith apart
5: 1 since we have been **j** through faith,
5: 9 Since we have now been **j** by his
8: 30 he called, he also **j**; those he **j**,
1Co 6: 11 you were **j** in the name of the Lord
Gal 2: 16 that a person is not **j** by the works
3: 11 relies on the law is **j** before God,
3: 24 came that we might be **j** by faith.

JUSTIFY (JUST)
Gal 3: 8 that God would **j** the Gentiles

JUSTLY (JUST)
Ps 106: 3 Blessed are those who act **j**,
Mic 6: 8 To act **j** and to love mercy

KEEP (KEEPER KEEPING KEEPS KEPT)
Ge 31: 49 "May the LORD **k** watch between
Ex 20: 6 love me and **k** my commandments.
Nu 6: 24 LORD bless you and **k** you;
Ps 18: 28 You, LORD, **k** my lamp burning;
19: 13 **K** your servant also from willful
121: 7 The LORD will **k** you from all
141: 3 **k** watch over the door of my lips.
Pr 4: 24 **K** your mouth free of perversity;
17: 28 are thought wise if they **k** silent,
Isa 26: 3 You will **k** in perfect peace those
Am 5: 13 Therefore the prudent **k** quiet
Mt 10: 10 staff, for the worker is worth his **k**.
Lk 12: 35 service and **k** your lamps burning,
Gal 5: 25 let us **k** in step with the Spirit.

Eph 4: 3 Make every effort to **k** the unity
1Ti 5: 22 the sins of others. **K** yourself pure.
2Ti 4: 5 you, **k** your head in all situations,
Heb 13: 5 **K** your lives free from the love
Jas 1: 26 and yet do not **k** a tight rein on
2: 8 If you really **k** the royal law found
1Jn 5: 3 love for God: to **k** his commands.
Jude : 24 To him who is able to **k** you

KEEPER (KEEP)
Ge 4: 9 "Am I my brother's **k**?"

KEEPING (KEEP)
Ex 20: 8 the Sabbath day by **k** it holy.
Ps 19: 11 in **k** them there is great reward.
Mt 3: 8 Produce fruit in **k** with repentance.
Lk 2: 8 **k** watch over their flocks at night.
1Co 7: 19 **K** God's commands is what counts.
2Pe 3: 9 Lord is not slow in **k** his promise,

KEEPS (KEEP)
1Co 13: 5 angered, it **k** no record of wrongs.
Jas 2: 10 For whoever **k** the whole law

KEPT (KEEP)
Ps 130: 3 LORD, **k** a record of sins, Lord,
2Ti 4: 7 finished the race, I have **k** the faith.
1Pe 1: 4 This inheritance is **k** in heaven

KEYS
Mt 16: 19 will give you the **k** of the kingdom

KILL (KILLS)
Mt 17: 23 will **k** him, and on the third day

KILLS (KILL)
Lev 24: 21 whoever **k** a human being is to be
2Co 3: 6 for the letter **k**, but the Spirit gives

KIND (KINDNESS KINDS)
Ge 1: 24 animals, each according to its **k**."
2Ch 10: 7 "If you will be **k** to these people
Pr 11: 17 Those who are **k** benefit themselves,
12: 25 the heart, but a **k** word cheers it up.
14: 21 blessed is the one who is **k**
14: 31 whoever is **k** to the needy honors
19: 17 Whoever is **k** to the poor lends
Da 4: 27 by being **k** to the oppressed.
Lk 6: 35 because he is **k** to the ungrateful
1Co 13: 4 Love is patient, love is **k**.
15: 35 what **k** of body will they come?"
Eph 4: 32 Be **k** and compassionate to one
2Ti 2: 24 but must be **k** to everyone,
Titus 2: 5 to be **k**, and to be subject to their

KINDNESS (KIND)
Ac 14: 17 He has shown **k** by giving you rain
Ro 11: 22 but **k** to you, provided that you continue in his **k**.
Gal 5: 22 peace, forbearance, **k**, goodness,
Eph 2: 7 expressed in his **k** to us in Christ

KINDS (KIND)
1Co 12: 4 There are different **k** of gifts,
1Ti 6: 10 of money is a root of all **k** of evil.

KING (KINGDOM KINGS)

1. Kings of Judah and Israel: see Saul, David, Solomon.

2. Kings of Judah: see Rehoboam, Abijah, Asa, Jehoshaphat, Jehoram, Ahaziah, Athaliah (Queen), Joash, Amaziah, Uzziah, Jotham, Ahaz, Hezekiah, Manasseh, Amon, Josiah, Jehoahaz, Jehoiakim, Jehoiachin, Zedekiah.

3. Kings of Israel: see Jeroboam I, Nadab, Baasha, Elah, Zimri, Tibni, Omri, Ahab, Ahaziah, Joram, Jehu, Jehoahaz, Jehoash, Jeroboam II, Zechariah, Shallum, Menahem, Pekah, Pekahiah, Hoshea.

Jdg 17: 6 In those days Israel had no **k**;
1Sa 12: 12 'No, we want a **k** to rule over us'—
12: 12 the LORD your God was your **k**.
Ps 24: 7 that the **K** of glory may come in.
Isa 32: 1 a **k** will reign in righteousness
Zec 9: 9 See, your **k** comes to you,
1Ti 6: 15 the **K** of kings and Lord of lords,
Rev 19: 16 thigh he has this name written: K

KINGDOM (KING)
Ex 19: 6 you will be for me a **k** of priests
1Ch 29: 11 Yours, LORD, is the **k**;
Ps 45: 6 justice will be the scepter of your **k**.
Da 4: 3 His **k** is an eternal **k**;
Mt 3: 2 for the **k** of heaven has come near."
5: 3 spirit, for theirs is the **k** of heaven.
6: 10 your **k** come, your will be done,
6: 33 But seek first his **k** and his
7: 21 Lord,' will enter the **k** of heaven,
11: 11 the **k** of heaven is greater than he.
13: 24 "The **k** of heaven is like a man who
13: 31 "The **k** of heaven is like a mustard
Mt 13: 33 "The **k** of heaven is like yeast
13: 44 "The **k** of heaven is like treasure
13: 45 the **k** of heaven is like a merchant
13: 47 the **k** of heaven is like a net that
16: 19 you the keys of the **k** of heaven;
18: 23 the **k** of heaven is like a king who
19: 24 who is rich to enter the **k** of God."
24: 7 rise against nation, and **k** against **k**.
24: 14 gospel of the **k** will be preached
25: 34 the **k** prepared for you since
Mk 9: 47 you to enter the **k** of God with one
10: 14 for the **k** of God belongs to such as
10: 23 for the rich to enter the **k** of God!"
Lk 10: 9 'The **k** of God has come near
12: 31 But seek his **k**, and these things
17: 21 is,' because the **k** of God is in your
Jn 3: 5 one can enter the **k** of God unless
18: 36 said, "My **k** is not of this world.
1Co 6: 9 wrongdoers will not inherit the **k**
15: 24 when he hands over the **k** to God
Rev 1: 6 has made us to be a **k** and priests
11: 15 "The **k** of the world has become

KINGS (KING)
Ps 2: 2 The **k** of the earth rise
72: 11 May all **k** bow down to him and all
Da 7: 24 ten horns are ten **k** who will come
1Ti 2: 2 for **k** and all those in authority,
Rev 1: 5 and the ruler of the **k** of the earth.

KISS
Ps 2: 12 **K** his son, or he will be angry
Pr 24: 26 An honest answer is like a **k**
Lk 22: 48 the Son of Man with a **k**?"

KNEE (KNEES)
Isa 45: 23 Before me every **k** will bow;
Ro 14: 11 Lord, 'every **k** will bow before me;
Php 2: 10 name of Jesus every **k** should bow,

KNEES (KNEE)
Isa 35: 3 hands, steady the **k** that give way;
Heb 12: 12 your feeble arms and weak **k**.

KNEW (KNOW)
Job 23: 3 If only I **k** where to find him;
Jnh 4: 2 I **k** that you are a gracious
Mt 7: 23 tell them plainly, 'I never **k** you.

KNOCK
Mt 7: 7 **k** and the door will be opened
Rev 3: 20 I stand at the door and **k**.

KNOW (FOREKNEW KNEW KNOWING KNOWLEDGE KNOWN KNOWS)
Dt 18: 21 "How can we **k** when a message
Job 19: 25 I **k** that my redeemer lives,
42: 3 things too wonderful for me to **k**.
Ps 46: 10 says, "Be still, and **k** that I am God;
73: 11 Does the Most High **k** anything?"
139: 1 LORD, and you **k** me.
139: 23 Search me, God, and **k** my heart;
Pr 27: 1 you do not **k** what a day may bring.
Jer 24: 7 I will give them a heart to **k** me,
31: 34 because they will all **k** me,
Mt 6: 3 let your left hand **k** what your right
24: 42 because you do not **k** on what day
Lk 1: 4 so that you may **k** the certainty
Jn 3: 11 you, we speak of what we **k**, and we
4: 22 worship what you do not **k**;
9: 25 One thing I do **k**. I was blind
10: 14 I **k** my sheep and my sheep **k** me—
17: 3 that they **k** you, the only true God,
21: 24 We **k** that his testimony is true.
Ac 1: 7 "It is not for you to **k** the times
Ro 6: 6 we **k** that our old self was crucified
7: 18 I **k** that good itself does not dwell
8: 28 we **k** that in all things God works
1Co 2: 2 I resolved to **k** nothing while I was
6: 15 Do you not **k** that your bodies are
6: 19 Do you not **k** that your bodies are
8: 2 do not yet **k** as they ought to **k**.
13: 12 Now I **k** in part; then I shall **k** fully,
15: 58 because you **k** that your labor
Php 3: 10 I want to **k** Christ—yes, to **k**
2Ti 1: 12 because I **k** whom I have believed,
Jas 4: 14 do not even **k** what will happen
1Jn 2: 4 Whoever says, "I **k** him," but does
3: 14 We **k** that we have passed
3: 16 This is how we **k** what love is:
5: 2 This is how we **k** that we love
5: 13 may **k** that you have eternal life.

KNOWING (KNOW)
Ge 3: 5 will be like God, **k** good and evil."
Php 3: 8 worth of **k** Christ Jesus my Lord,

KNOWLEDGE (KNOW)
Ge 2: 9 the tree of the **k** of good and evil.
Job 42: 3 that obscures my plans without **k**?'
Ps 19: 2 night after night they reveal **k**.
139: 6 Such **k** is too wonderful for me,
Pr 1: 7 of the LORD is the beginning of **k**,
10: 14 The wise store up **k**, but the mouth
12: 1 Whoever loves discipline loves **k**,
13: 16 All who are prudent act with **k**,
19: 2 Desire without **k** is not good—
Isa 11: 9 the **k** of the LORD as the waters
Hab 2: 14 will be filled with the **k** of the glory
Ro 11: 33 riches of the wisdom and **k** of God!
1Co 8: 1 But **k** puffs up while love builds up.
8: 11 Christ died, is destroyed by your **k**.
13: 2 can fathom all mysteries and all **k**,
2Co 2: 14 aroma of the **k** of him everywhere.
4: 6 of the **k** of God's glory displayed
Eph 3: 19 know this love that surpasses **k**—
Col 2: 3 all the treasures of wisdom and **k**.
1Ti 6: 20 ideas of what is falsely called **k**,
2Pe 3: 18 grow in the grace and **k** of our Lord

KNOWN (KNOW)
Ps 16: 11 You make **k** to me the path of life;
105: 1 make **k** among the nations what he
Isa 46: 10 I make **k** the end
Mt 10: 26 or hidden that will not be made **k**.
Ro 1: 19 since what may be **k** about God is
11: 34 "Who has **k** the mind of the Lord?
15: 20 the gospel where Christ was not **k**,
2Co 3: 2 our hearts, **k** and read by everyone.
2Pe 2: 21 than to have **k** it and then to turn

KNOWS (KNOW)
1Sa 2: 3 for the LORD is a God who **k**,
Job 23: 10 But he **k** the way that I take;
Ps 44: 21 since he **k** the secrets of the heart?
94: 11 The LORD **k** all human plans; he **k**
Ecc 8: 7 Since no one **k** the future, who can
Mt 6: 8 your Father **k** what you need
24: 36 about that day or hour no one **k**,
Ro 8: 27 searches our hearts **k** the mind
2Ti 2: 19 "The Lord **k** those who are his,"

LABAN
Brother of Rebekah (Ge 24:29–51), father of Rachel and Leah (Ge 29–31).

LABOR
Ex 20: 9 Six days you shall **l** and do all your
Isa 55: 2 your **l** on what does not satisfy?
Mt 6: 28 They do not **l** or spin.
1Co 3: 8 rewarded according to their own **l**.
15: 58 know that your **l** in the Lord is not

LACK (LACKING LACKS)
Pr 15: 22 Plans fail for **l** of counsel,
Col 2: 23 but they **l** any value in restraining

LACKING (LACK)
Ro 12: 11 Never be **l** in zeal, but keep your
Jas 1: 4 and complete, not **l** anything.

LACKS (LACK)
Jas 1: 5 If any of you **l** wisdom, you should

LAID (LAY)
Isa 53: 6 and the LORD has **l** on him
1Co 3: 11 other than the one already **l**,
1Jn 3: 16 Jesus Christ **l** down his life for us.

LAKE
Rev 19: 20 into the fiery **l** of burning sulfur.
20: 14 The **l** of fire is the second death.

LAMB (LAMB'S LAMBS)
Ge 22: 8 "God himself will provide the **l**
Ex 12: 21 and slaughter the Passover **l**.
Isa 11: 6 The wolf will live with the **l**,
53: 7 he was led like a **l** to the slaughter,
Jn 1: 29 "Look, the **L** of God, who takes
1Co 5: 7 our Passover **l**, has been sacrificed.
1Pe 1: 19 a **l** without blemish or defect.
Rev 5: 6 Then I saw a **L**, looking as if it had
5: 12 "Worthy is the **L**, who was slain,
14: 4 as firstfruits to God and the **L**.

LAMB'S (LAMB)
Rev 21: 27 names are written in the **L** book

LAMBS (LAMB)
Lk 10: 3 you out like **l** among wolves.
Jn 21: 15 Jesus said, "Feed my **l**."

LAMENT
2Sa 1: 17 took up this **l** concerning Saul

LAMP (LAMPS)
2Sa 22: 29 You, LORD, are my **l**;
Ps 18: 28 You, LORD, keep my **l** burning;
119:105 Your word is a **l** to my feet
Pr 31: 18 and her **l** does not go out at night.
Lk 8: 16 "No one lights a **l** and hides it
Rev 21: 23 gives it light, and the Lamb is its **l**.

LAMPS (LAMP)
Mt 25: 1 be like ten virgins who took their **l**
Lk 12: 35 service and keep your **l** burning,

LAND
Ge 1: 10 God called the dry ground "**l**,"
1: 11 said, "Let the **l** produce vegetation:
12: 7 your offspring I will give this **l**."
Ex 3: 8 a **l** flowing with milk and honey—
Nu 35: 33 Bloodshed pollutes the **l**,
Dt 34: 1 LORD showed him the whole **l**—
Jos 13: 2 "This is the **l** that remains:
14: 4 Levites received no share of the **l**
2Ch 7: 14 their sin and will heal their **l**.
7: 20 then I will uproot Israel from my **l**,
Eze 36: 24 bring you back into your own **l**.

LANGUAGE
Ge 11: 1 Now the whole world had one **l**
Jn 8: 44 speaks his native **l**, for he is a liar
Ac 2: 6 heard their own **l** being spoken.
Col 3: 8 slander, and filthy **l** from your lips.
Rev 5: 9 God persons from every tribe and **l**

LAST (LASTING LASTS LATTER)
2Sa 23: 1 These are the **l** words of David:
Isa 44: 6 I am the first and I am the **l**;
Mt 19: 30 But many who are first will be **l**,
Mk 10: 31 will be **l**, and the **l** first."
Jn 15: 16 fruit that will **l**—and so
Ro 1: 17 that is by faith from first to **l**,
2Ti 3: 1 will be terrible times in the **l** days.
2Pe 3: 3 in the **l** days scoffers will come,
Rev 1: 17 I am the First and the **L**.
22: 13 the First and the **L**, the Beginning

LASTING (LAST)
Ex 12: 14 to the LORD—a **l** ordinance.
Lev 24: 8 of the Israelites, as a **l** covenant.
Nu 25: 13 have a covenant of a **l** priesthood,
Heb 10: 34 had better and **l** possessions.

LASTS (LAST)
Ps 30: 5 For his anger **l** only a moment,
2Co 3: 11 greater is the glory of that which **l**!

LATTER (LAST)
Job 42: 12 The LORD blessed the **l** part

LAUGH (LAUGHS)
Ecc 3: 4 a time to weep and a time to **l**,

LAUGHS (LAUGH)
Ps 2: 4 The One enthroned in heaven **l**;
37: 13 but the Lord **l** at the wicked, for he

LAVISHED
Eph 1: 8 that he **l** on us. With all wisdom
1Jn 3: 1 See what great love the Father has **l**

LAW (LAWS)
Dt 31: 11 you shall read this **l** before them
31: 26 "Take this Book of the **L** and place
Jos 1: 8 Keep this Book of the **L** always
Ne 8: 8 from the Book of the **L** of God,
Ps 1: 2 delight is in the **l** of the LORD,
19: 7 The **l** of the LORD is perfect,
119: 18 may see wonderful things in your **l**.
119: 72 The **l** from your mouth is more
119: 97 Oh, how I love your **l**! I meditate
119:165 peace have those who love your **l**,
Jer 31: 33 "I will put my **l** in their minds
Mt 5: 17 that I have come to abolish the **L**
7: 12 you, for this sums up the **L**
22: 40 All the **L** and the Prophets hang
Lk 16: 17 stroke of a pen to drop out of the **L**.
Jn 1: 17 For the **l** was given through Moses;
Ro 2: 12 All who sin apart from the **l** will
2: 15 requirements of the **l** are written
5: 13 account where there is no **l**.
5: 20 The **l** was brought in so
6: 14 because you are not under the **l**,
7: 6 we have been released from the **l** so
7: 12 So then, the **l** is holy,
8: 3 For what the **l** was powerless to do
10: 4 Christ is the culmination of the **l**
13: 10 love is the fulfillment of the **l**.
Gal 3: 13 curse of the **l** by becoming a curse
3: 24 So the **l** was our guardian until

Gal 5: 3 he is obligated to obey the whole **l**.
5: 4 by the **l** have been alienated
5: 14 For the entire **l** is fulfilled
Heb 7: 19 (for the **l** made nothing perfect),
10: 1 The **l** is only a shadow of the good
Jas 1: 25 the perfect **l** that gives freedom,
2: 10 For whoever keeps the whole **l**

LAWLESSNESS
2Th 2: 3 occurs and the man of **l** is revealed,
2: 7 the secret power of **l** is already
1Jn 3: 4 sins breaks the law; in fact, sin is **l**.

LAWS (LAW)
Lev 25: 18 and be careful to obey my **l**,
Ps 119: 30 I have set my heart on your **l**.
119:120 fear of you; I stand in awe of your **l**.
Heb 8: 10 I will put my **l** in their minds
10: 16 I will put my **l** in their hearts, and I

LAY (LAID LAYING)
Job 22: 22 and **l** up his words in your heart.
Isa 28: 16 "See, I **l** a stone in Zion, a tested
Mt 8: 20 of Man has no place to **l** his head."
Jn 10: 15 and I **l** down my life for the sheep.
15: 13 to **l** down one's life for one's
1Co 3: 11 no one can **l** any foundation other
1Jn 3: 16 we ought to **l** down our lives for
Rev 4: 10 They **l** their crowns before

LAYING (LAY)
1Ti 5: 22 not be hasty in the **l** on of hands,
Heb 6: 1 not **l** again the foundation

LAZARUS
1. Poor man in Jesus' parable (Lk 16:19–31).
2. Brother of Mary and Martha whom Jesus raised from the dead (Jn 11:1—12:19).

LAZY
Pr 10: 4 **L** hands make for poverty,
Heb 6: 12 We do not want you to become **l**,

LEAD (LEADERS LEADS LED)
Ex 15: 13 love you will **l** the people you have
Ps 27: 11 **l** me in a straight path because
61: 2 **l** me to the rock that is higher than I.
139: 24 and **l** me in the way everlasting.
143: 10 may your good Spirit **l** me on level
Ecc 5: 6 Do not let your mouth **l** you
Isa 11: 6 and a little child will **l** them.
Da 12: 3 those who **l** many to righteousness,
Mt 6: 13 And **l** us not into temptation,
1Jn 3: 7 do not let anyone **l** you astray.

LEADERS (LEAD)
Heb 13: 7 Remember your **l**, who spoke
13: 17 Have confidence in your **l**

LEADS (LEAD)
Ps 23: 2 he **l** me beside quiet waters,
Pr 19: 23 The fear of the LORD **l** to life;
Isa 40: 11 he gently **l** those that have young.
Mt 7: 13 gate and broad is the road that **l**
Jn 10: 3 sheep by name and **l** them out.
Ro 14: 19 every effort to do what **l** to peace
2Co 2: 14 God, who always **l** us as captives

LEAH
Wife of Jacob (Ge 29:16–30); bore six sons and one daughter (Ge 29:31—30:21; 34:1; 35:23).

LEAN
Pr 3: 5 **l** not on your own understanding;

LEARN (LEARNED LEARNING)
Isa 1: 17 **L** to do right; seek justice.
Mt 11: 29 my yoke upon you and **l** from me,

LEARNED (LEARN)
Php 4: 11 I have **l** to be content whatever
2Ti 3: 14 know those from whom you **l** it,

LEARNING (LEARN)
Pr 1: 5 the wise listen and add to their **l**,
2Ti 3: 7 always **l** but never able to come

LED (LEAD)
Isa 53: 7 he was **l** like a lamb
Am 2: 10 **l** you forty years in the wilderness
Ro 8: 14 For those who are **l** by the Spirit

LEFT
Jos 1: 7 turn from it to the right or to the **l**,
Pr 4: 27 Do not turn to the right or the **l**;
Mt 6: 3 do not let your **l** hand know what
25: 33 on his right and the goats on his **l**.

LEGION
Mk 5: 9 "My name is **L**," he replied,

LEND (LENDS)
Dt 15: 8 freely **l** them whatever they need.
Ps 37: 26 are always generous and **l** freely;
Lk 6: 34 Even sinners **l** to sinners,

LENDS (LEND)
Pr 19: 17 kind to the poor **l** to the LORD,

LENGTH (LONG)
Pr 10: 27 fear of the LORD adds **l** to life,

LEPROSY
2Ki 7: 3 Now there were four men with **l**

LETTER (LETTERS)
Mt 5: 18 not the smallest **l**, not the least
2Co 3: 2 You yourselves are our **l**,
3: 6 not of the **l** but of the Spirit; for the **l** kills,
2Th 3: 14 not obey our instruction in this **l**.

LETTERS (LETTER)
2Co 3: 7 which was engraved in **l** on stone,
10: 10 "His **l** are weighty and forceful,
2Pe 3: 16 He writes the same way in all his **l**,

LEVEL
Ps 143: 10 good Spirit lead me on **l** ground.
Isa 26: 7 The path of the righteous is **l**;
Heb 12: 13 "Make **l** paths for your feet,"

LEVI (LEVITES)
1. Son of Jacob by Leah (Ge 29:34; 46:11; 1Ch 2:1). Tribe of blessed (Ge 49:5–7; Dt 33:8–11), chosen as priests (Nu 3–4), numbered (Nu 3:39; 26:62), allotted cities, but not land (Nu 18; 35; Dt 10:9; Jos 13:14; 21), land (Eze 48:8–22), 12,000 from (Rev 7:7).
2. See MATTHEW.

LEVITES (LEVI)
Nu 1: 53 The **L** are to be responsible
8: 6 "Take the **L** from among all
18: 21 "I give to the **L** all the tithes

LEWDNESS
Mk 7: 22 malice, deceit, **l**, envy, slander,

LIAR (LIE)
Pr 19: 22 better to be poor than a **l**.
Jn 8: 44 for he is a **l** and the father of lies.
Ro 3: 4 be true, and every human being a **l**.

LIBERATED
Ro 8: 21 the creation itself will be **l** from its

LIE (LIAR LIED LIES LYING)
Lev 19: 11 "'Do not **l**. "'Do not deceive
Nu 23: 19 that he should **l**, not a human
Dt 6: 7 when you **l** down and when you
Ps 23: 2 He makes me **l** down in green
Isa 11: 6 the leopard will **l** down
Eze 34: 14 There they will **l** down in good
Ro 1: 25 the truth about God for a **l**,
Col 3: 9 Do not **l** to each other, since you
Heb 6: 18 which it is impossible for God to **l**,

LIED (LIE)
Ac 5: 4 You have not **l** just to human

LIES (LIE)
Ps 34: 13 evil and your lips from telling **l**.
Jn 8: 44 for he is a liar and the father of **l**.

LIFE (LIVE)
Ge 2: 7 into his nostrils the breath of **l**,
2: 9 of the garden were the tree of **l**
9: 11 Never again will all **l** be destroyed
Ex 21: 23 injury, you are to take **l** for **l**,
Lev 17: 14 because the **l** of every creature is its
24: 18 must make restitution—**l** for **l**.
Dt 30: 19 Now choose **l**, so that you and your
Ps 16: 11 make known to me the path of **l**;
23: 6 will follow me all the days of my **l**,
34: 12 Whoever of you loves **l** and desires
39: 4 let me know how fleeting my **l** is.
49: 7 one can redeem the **l** of another
104: 33 I will sing to the LORD all my **l**;
Pr 6: 23 and instruction are the way to **l**,
7: 23 little knowing it will cost him his **l**.
8: 35 For those who find me find **l**
11: 30 fruit of the righteous is a tree of **l**,
21: 21 righteousness and love finds **l**,
Eze 37: 5 enter you, and you will come to **l**.
Da 12: 2 some to everlasting **l**,
Mt 6: 25 do not worry about your **l**,
7: 14 and narrow the road that leads to **l**,
10: 39 whoever loses their **l** for my sake
16: 25 wants to save their **l** will lose it,
20: 28 to give his **l** as a ransom for many."
Mk 10: 45 to give his **l** as a ransom for many."
Lk 12: 15 **l** does not consist in an abundance

Lk 12: 22 do not worry about your **l**,
14: 26 yes, even their own **l**—
Jn 1: 4 In him was **l**, and that **l** was the light
3: 15 who believes may have eternal **l**
3: 36 believes in the Son has eternal **l**,
4: 14 of water welling up to eternal **l**."
5: 24 has crossed over from death to **l**.
6: 35 Jesus declared, "I am the bread of **l**.
6: 47 the one who believes has eternal **l**.
6: 68 You have the words of eternal **l**.
10: 10 I have come that they may have **l**,
10: 15 and I lay down my **l** for the sheep.
10: 28 I give them eternal **l**, and they shall
11: 25 "I am the resurrection and the **l**.
14: 6 am the way and the truth and the **l**.
15: 13 lay down one's **l** for one's friends.
20: 31 by believing you may have **l** in his
Ac 13: 48 appointed for eternal **l** believed.
Ro 4: 25 was raised to **l** for our justification.
6: 13 have been brought from death to **l**;
6: 23 God is eternal **l** in Christ Jesus our
8: 38 convinced that neither death nor **l**,
1Co 15: 19 If only for this **l** we have hope
2Co 3: 6 the letter kills, but the Spirit gives **l**.
Gal 2: 20 The **l** I now live in the body, I live
Eph 4: 1 to live a **l** worthy of the calling you
Php 2: 16 as you hold firmly to the word of **l**.
Col 1: 10 you may live a **l** worthy of the Lord
1Th 4: 12 your daily **l** may win the respect
1Ti 4: 8 the present **l** and the **l** to come.
4: 16 Watch your **l** and doctrine closely.
6: 19 take hold of the **l** that is truly **l**.
2Ti 3: 12 live a godly **l** in Christ Jesus will be
Jas 1: 12 person will receive the crown of **l**
3: 13 Let them show it by their good **l**,
1Pe 3: 10 "Whoever would love **l** and see
2Pe 1: 3 a godly **l** through our knowledge
1Jn 3: 14 we have passed from death to **l**,
5: 11 God has given us eternal **l**, and this **l**
Rev 13: 8 written in the Lamb's book of **l**,
20: 12 was opened, which is the book of **l**.
21: 27 are written in the Lamb's book of **l**.
22: 2 side of the river stood the tree of **l**,

LIFT (LIFTED LIFTING)
Ps 121: 1 I **l** up my eyes to the mountains—
134: 2 **L** up your hands in the sanctuary
La 3: 41 Let us **l** up our hearts and our hands

LIFTED (LIFT)
Ps 40: 2 He **l** me out of the slimy pit,
Jn 3: 14 so the Son of Man must be **l** up,
12: 32 I, when I am **l** up from the earth,

LIFTING (LIFT)
1Ti 2: 8 **l** up holy hands without anger

LIGHT (ENLIGHTENED)
Ge 1: 3 "Let there be **l**," and there was **l**.
2Sa 22: 29 LORD turns my darkness into **l**.
Job 38: 19 "What is the way to the abode of **l**?
Ps 4: 6 Let the **l** of your face shine on us.
19: 8 are radiant, giving **l** to the eyes.
27: 1 The LORD is my **l** and my
56: 13 walk before God in the **l** of life.
76: 4 You are radiant with **l**,
104: 2 The LORD wraps himself in **l** as
119:105 lamp to my feet and a **l** for my path.
119:130 unfolding of your words gives **l**;
Isa 2: 5 let us walk in the **l** of the LORD.
9: 2 in darkness have seen a great **l**;
49: 6 also make you a **l** for the Gentiles,
Mt 4: 16 shadow of death a **l** has dawned."
5: 16 way, let your **l** shine before others,
11: 30 yoke is easy and my burden is **l**."
Jn 3: 19 **L** has come into the world,
8: 12 he said, "I am the **l** of the world.
2Co 4: 6 made his **l** shine in our hearts
6: 14 Or what fellowship can **l** have
11: 14 masquerades as an angel of **l**.
1Ti 6: 16 and who lives in unapproachable **l**,
1Pe 2: 9 of darkness into his wonderful **l**.
1Jn 1: 5 God is **l**; in him there is no darkness
1: 7 But if we walk in the **l**, as he is
Rev 21: 23 for the glory of God gives it **l**,

LIGHTNING
Da 10: 6 his face like **l**, his eyes like flaming
Mt 24: 27 For as **l** that comes from the east is
28: 3 His appearance was like **l**, and his

LIKENESS
Ge 1: 26 in our **l**, so that they may rule over
Ps 17: 15 will be satisfied with seeing your **l**.
Isa 52: 14 his form marred beyond human **l**
Ro 8: 3 his own Son in the **l** of sinful flesh
Php 2: 7 a servant, being made in human **l**.
Jas 3: 9 who have been made in God's **l**.

LION
Isa 11: 7 and the **l** will eat straw like the ox.
1Pe 5: 8 around like a roaring **l** looking
Rev 5: 5 See, the **L** of the tribe of Judah,

LIPS
Ps 34: 1 his praise will always be on my **l**.
119:171 May my **l** overflow with praise,
Pr 13: 3 who guard their **l** preserve their
27: 2 an outsider, and not your own **l**.
Isa 6: 5 For I am a man of unclean **l**, and I
Mt 21: 16 read, "'From the **l** of children
Col 3: 8 and filthy language from your **l**.

LISTEN (LISTENING)
Dt 30: 20 LORD your God, **l** to his voice,
Pr 1: 5 let the wise **l** and add to their
12: 15 to them, but the wise **l** to advice.
Jn 10: 27 My sheep **l** to my voice;
Jas 1: 19 Everyone should be quick to **l**,
1: 22 Do not merely **l** to the word,

LISTENING (LISTEN)
1Sa 3: 9 LORD, for your servant is **l**.'"
Pr 18: 13 To answer before **l**—that is folly

LIVE (ALIVE LIFE LIVES LIVING)
Ex 20: 12 that you may **l** long in the land
33: 20 face, for no one may see me and **l**."
Dt 8: 3 that man does not **l** on bread alone
Job 14: 14 If someone dies, will they **l** again?
Ps 119:175 Let me **l** that I may praise you,
Isa 55: 3 come to me; listen, that you may **l**.
Eze 37: 3 "Son of man, can these bones **l**?"
Hab 2: 4 the righteous person will **l** by his
Mt 4: 4 'Man shall not **l** on bread alone,
Ac 17: 24 not **l** in temples built by human
17: 28 'For in him we **l** and move and
Ro 1: 17 "The righteous will **l** by faith."
2Co 5: 7 For we **l** by faith, not by sight.
Gal 2: 20 The life I now **l** in the body,
5: 25 Since we **l** by the Spirit, let us keep
Php 1: 21 me, to **l** is Christ and to die is gain.
1Th 5: 13 **L** in peace with each other.
2Ti 3: 12 who wants to **l** a godly life
Heb 12: 14 Make every effort to **l** in peace
1Pe 1: 17 **l** out your time as foreigners here

LIVES (LIVE)
Job 19: 25 I know that my redeemer **l**,
Pr 11: 30 and the one who is wise saves **l**.
Isa 57: 15 he who **l** forever, whose name is
Da 3: 28 to give up their **l** rather than serve
Jn 14: 17 he **l** with you and will be in you.
Gal 2: 20 I no longer live, but Christ **l** in me.
Heb 13: 5 Keep your **l** free from the love
2Pe 3: 11 You ought to live holy and godly **l**
1Jn 3: 16 to lay down our **l** for our brothers
4: 16 Whoever **l** in love **l** in God,

LIVING (LIVE)
Ge 2: 7 life, and the man became a **l** being.
Jer 2: 13 the spring of **l** water, and have dug
Mt 22: 32 the God of the dead but of the **l**."
Jn 7: 38 said, rivers of **l** water will flow
Ro 12: 1 to offer your bodies as a **l** sacrifice,
Heb 10: 31 to fall into the hands of the **l** God.
Rev 1: 18 I am the **L** One; I was dead,

LOAD
Gal 6: 5 each one should carry their own **l**.

LOCUSTS
Mt 3: 4 His food was **l** and wild honey.

LOFTY
Ps 139: 6 for me, too **l** for me to attain.

LONELY
Ps 68: 6 God sets the **l** in families, he leads

LONG (LENGTH LONGED LONGING LONGS)
1Ki 18: 21 "How **l** will you waver between
Jn 9: 4 As **l** as it is day, we must do
Eph 3: 18 to grasp how wide and **l** and high
1Pe 1: 12 Even angels **l** to look into these

LONGED (LONG)
Mt 13: 17 righteous people **l** to see what you
23: 37 how often I have **l** to gather your
2Ti 4: 8 to all who have **l** for his appearing.

LONGING (LONG)
Pr 13: 19 A **l** fulfilled is sweet to the soul,
2Co 5: 2 **l** to be clothed instead with our

Ps 89: 5 heavens praise your wonders, **L**,
95: 1 Come, let us sing for joy to the **L**;
96: 1 Sing to the **L** a new song;
98: 4 Shout for joy to the **L**, all the earth,
100: 1 Shout for joy to the **L**, all the earth.
103: 1 Praise the **L**, my soul; all my
103: 8 The **L** is compassionate
104: 1 Praise the **L**, my soul. **L** my God,
107: 8 to the **L** for his unfailing love
110: 1 The **L** says to my lord: "Sit at my
113: 4 The **L** is exalted over all the nations
115: 1 Not to us, **L**, not to us but to your
116: 15 the sight of the **L** is the death of his
118: 1 Give thanks to the **L**, for he is good;
118: 24 The **L** has done it this very day;
121: 2 My help comes from the **L**,
121: 5 The **L** watches over you—the **L** is
125: 2 so the **L** surrounds his people both
127: 1 Unless the **L** builds the house,
127: 3 Children are a heritage from the **L**,
130: 3 If you, **L**, kept a record of sins,
135: 6 The **L** does whatever pleases him,
136: 1 Give thanks to the **L**, for he is good.
139: 1 You have searched me, **L**, and you
144: 3 **L**, what are human beings that you
145: 3 Great is the **L** and most worthy
145: 18 The **L** is near to all who call on him,
Pr 1: 7 The fear of the **L** is the beginning
3: 5 Trust in the **L** with all your heart
3: 9 Honor the **L** with your wealth,
3: 12 because the **L** disciplines those he
3: 19 By wisdom the **L** laid the earth's
5: 21 your ways are in full view of the **L**,
6: 16 There are six things the **L** hates,
10: 27 The fear of the **L** adds length to life,
11: 1 The **L** detests dishonest scales,
12: 22 The **L** detests lying lips, but he
14: 26 Whoever fears the **L** has a secure
15: 3 The eyes of the **L** are everywhere,
16: 2 but motives are weighed by the **L**.
16: 4 The **L** works out everything to its
16: 9 but the **L** establishes their steps.
16: 33 but its every decision is from the **L**.
18: 10 name of the **L** is a fortified tower;
18: 22 and receives favor from the **L**.
19: 14 but a prudent wife is from the **L**.
19: 17 is kind to the poor lends to the **L**,
21: 3 acceptable to the **L** than sacrifice.
21: 30 plan that can succeed against the **L**.
21: 31 battle, but victory rests with the **L**.
22: 2 The **L** is the Maker of them all.
24: 18 or the **L** will see and disapprove
31: 30 a woman who fears the **L** is to be
Isa 6: 3 holy, holy is the **L** Almighty;
11: 2 The Spirit of the **L** will rest on him
11: 9 of the **L** as the waters cover the sea.
12: 2 The **L**, the **L** himself, is my strength
24: 1 the **L** is going to lay waste the earth
25: 8 The Sovereign **L** will wipe away
29: 15 to hide their plans from the **L**,
33: 6 the fear of the **L** is the key to this
35: 10 those the **L** has rescued will return.
40: 5 For the mouth of the **L** has spoken.
40: 7 because the breath of the **L** blows
40: 10 the Sovereign **L** comes with power,
40: 28 The **L** is the everlasting God,
40: 31 in the **L** will renew their strength.
42: 8 "I am the **L**; that is my name!
43: 11 I am the **L**, and apart from me
44: 24 I am the **L**, the Maker of all things,
45: 5 I am the **L**, and there is no other;
45: 21 Was it not I, the **L**? And there is no
51: 11 Those the **L** has rescued will return
53: 6 the **L** has laid on him the iniquity
53: 10 the will of the **L** will prosper in his
55: 6 Seek the **L** while he may be found;
58: 8 of the **L** will be your rear guard.
58: 11 The **L** will guide you always;
59: 1 the arm of the **L** is not too short
61: 3 a planting of the **L** for the display
61: 10 I delight greatly in the **L**;
Jer 1: 9 Then the **L** reached out his hand
9: 24 in these I delight," declares the **L**.
16: 19 **L**, my strength and my fortress,
17: 7 is the one who trusts in the **L**,
La 3: 40 and let us return to the **L**.
Eze 1: 28 of the likeness of the glory of the **L**.
Hos 1: 7 but I, the **L** their God, will save
3: 5 return and seek the **L** their God
6: 1 "Come, let us return to the **L**.
Joel 2: 1 for the day of the **L** is coming.
2: 11 The day of the **L** is great;
3: 14 day of the **L** is near in the valley
Am 5: 18 you who long for the day of the **L**!
Jnh 1: 3 But Jonah ran away from the **L**
Mic 4: 2 the word of the **L** from Jerusalem.
6: 8 what does the **L** require of you?
Na 1: 2 The **L** is a jealous and avenging
1: 3 The **L** is slow to anger but great
Hab 2: 14 of the **L** as the waters cover the sea.
2: 20 The **L** is in his holy temple;
Zep 3: 17 The **L** your God is with you,
Zec 1: 17 and the **L** will again comfort Zion
9: 16 The **L** their God will save his people
14: 5 Then the **L** my God will come,
14: 9 On that day there will be one **L**,
Mal 4: 5 and dreadful day of the **L** comes.

LORD'S* (LORD*; this is the proper name of God, *Yahweh*, spelled "LORD's" in the NIV)
Ex 34: 34 he entered the **L** presence to speak
Nu 14: 41 you disobeying the **L** command?
Dt 6: 18 is right and good in the **L** sight,
32: 9 For the **L** portion is his people,
Jos 21: 45 all the **L** good promises to Israel
Ps 24: 1 The earth is the **L**,
32: 10 the **L** unfailing love surrounds
89: 1 I will sing of the **L** great love
103: 17 the **L** love is with those who fear
Pr 3: 11 do not despise the **L** discipline,
Isa 24: 14 west they acclaim the **L** majesty.
62: 3 a crown of splendor in the **L** hand,
Jer 48: 10 who is lax in doing the **L** work!
La 3: 22 Because of the **L** great love we are
Mic 4: 1 the mountain of the **L** temple will

LOSE (LOSES LOSS LOST)
1Sa 17: 32 "Let no one **l** heart on account
Mt 10: 39 Whoever finds their life will **l** it,
Lk 9: 25 and yet **l** or forfeit their very self?
Jn 6: 39 that I shall **l** none of all those
Heb 12: 3 will not grow weary and **l** heart.
12: 5 not **l** heart when he rebukes you,

LOSES (LOSE)
Mt 5: 13 But if the salt **l** its saltiness,
Lk 15: 4 a hundred sheep and **l** one of them.
15: 8 has ten silver coins and **l** one.

LOSS (LOSE)
Ro 11: 12 their **l** means riches for the Gentiles,
1Co 3: 15 the builder will suffer **l** but yet will
Php 3: 8 I consider everything a **l** because

LOST (LOSE)
Ps 73: 2 I had nearly **l** my foothold.
Jer 50: 6 "My people have been **l** sheep;
Eze 34: 4 the strays or searched for the **l**.
34: 16 I will search for the **l** and bring
Lk 15: 4 go after the **l** sheep until he finds
15: 6 I have found my **l** sheep.'
15: 9 I have found my **l** coin.'
15: 24 he was **l** and is found.'
19: 10 came to seek and to save the **l**."
Php 3: 8 for whose sake I have **l** all things.

LOT (LOTS)
Nephew of Abraham (Ge 11:27; 12:5). Chose to live in Sodom (Ge 13). Rescued from four kings (Ge 14). Rescued from Sodom (Ge 19:1–29; 2Pe 2:7). Fathered Moab and Ammon by his daughters (Ge 19:30–38).

Est 3: 7 the **l**) was cast in the presence
9: 24 the **l**) for their ruin and destruction.
Pr 16: 33 The **l** is cast into the lap, but its
18: 18 Casting the **l** settles disputes
Ecc 3: 22 their work, because that is their **l**.
Ac 1: 26 cast lots, and the **l** fell to Matthias;

LOTS (LOT)
Ps 22: 18 them and cast **l** for my garment.
Mt 27: 35 divided up his clothes by casting **l**.

LOVE (BELOVED LOVED LOVELY LOVER LOVERS LOVES LOVING)
Ge 22: 2 son, your only son, whom you **l**—
Ex 15: 13 In your unfailing **l** you will lead
20: 6 showing **l** to a thousand generations
34: 6 abounding in **l** and faithfulness,
Lev 19: 18 but **l** your neighbor as yourself.
19: 34 **L** them as yourself, for you were
Nu 14: 18 abounding in **l** and forgiving sin
Dt 5: 10 showing **l** to a thousand generations
6: 5 **L** the LORD your God with all
7: 13 He will **l** you and bless you
10: 12 to **l** him, to serve the LORD your
11: 13 to **l** the LORD your God

Dt 13: 6 or the wife you **l**, or your closest
30: 6 you may **l** him with all your heart
Jos 22: 5 to **l** the LORD your God, to walk
1Ki 3: 3 Solomon showed his **l**
8: 23 you who keep your covenant of **l**
2Ch 5: 13 his **l** endures forever."
Ne 1: 5 covenant of **l** with those who **l** him
Ps 18: 1 I **l** you, LORD, my strength.
23: 6 **l** will follow me all the days of my
25: 6 your great mercy and **l**, for they are
31: 16 save me in your unfailing **l**.
32: 10 LORD's unfailing **l** surrounds
33: 5 the earth is full of his unfailing **l**.
33: 18 whose hope is in his unfailing **l**,
36: 5 Your **l**, LORD,
36: 7 How priceless is your unfailing **l**,
45: 7 You **l** righteousness and hate
51: 1 God, according to your unfailing **l**;
57: 10 For great is your **l**,
63: 3 Because your **l** is better than life,
66: 20 prayer or withheld his **l** from me!
77: 8 his unfailing **l** vanished forever?
85: 7 Show us your unfailing **l**, LORD,
85: 10 **L** and faithfulness meet together;
86: 13 For great is your **l** toward me;
89: 1 sing of the LORD's great **l** forever;
89: 33 but I will not take my **l** from him,
92: 2 proclaiming your **l** in the morning
94: 18 slipping," your unfailing **l**, LORD,
100: 5 is good and his **l** endures forever;
101: 1 I will sing of your **l** and justice;
103: 4 crowns you with **l** and compassion,
103: 8 slow to anger, abounding in **l**.
103: 11 so great is his **l** for those who fear
107: 8 to the LORD for his unfailing **l**
108: 4 For great is your **l**, higher than
116: 1 I **l** the LORD, for he heard my
118: 1 he is good; his **l** endures forever.
119: 47 your commands because I **l** them.
119: 64 The earth is filled with your **l**,
119: 76 May your unfailing **l** be my
119: 97 Oh, how I **l** your law! I meditate
119:119 dross; therefore I **l** your statutes.
119:124 your servant according to your **l**
119:132 do to those who **l** your name.
119:159 See how I **l** your precepts;
119:163 detest falsehood but I **l** your law.
119:165 peace have those who **l** your law,
122: 6 "May those who **l** you be secure.
130: 7 for with the LORD is unfailing **l**
136: 1 *His **l** endures forever.*
143: 8 bring me word of your unfailing **l**,
145: 8 slow to anger and rich in **l**.
145: 20 LORD watches over all who **l** him,
147: 11 put their hope in his unfailing **l**.
Pr 3: 3 Let **l** and faithfulness never leave
4: 6 **l** her, and she will watch over you.
5: 19 you ever be intoxicated with her **l**.
8: 17 I **l** those who **l** me, and those who
9: 8 rebuke the wise and they will **l** you.
10: 12 but **l** covers over all wrongs.
14: 22 those who plan what is good find **l**
15: 17 with **l** than a fattened calf
17: 9 Whoever would foster **l** covers
19: 22 a person desires is unfailing **l**;
20: 6 Many claim to have unfailing **l**,
20: 13 Do not **l** sleep or you will grow
20: 28 **L** and faithfulness keep a king safe;
21: 21 righteousness and **l** finds life,
27: 5 is open rebuke than hidden **l**.
Ecc 9: 6 Their **l**, their hate and their
9: 9 whom you **l**, all the days of this
SS 2: 4 and let his banner over me be **l**.
8: 6 for **l** is as strong as death,
8: 7 Many waters cannot quench **l**;
Isa 5: 1 sing for the one I **l** a song about his
16: 5 In **l** a throne will be established;
38: 17 In your **l** you kept me from the pit
54: 10 yet my unfailing **l** for you will not
55: 3 my faithful **l** promised to David.
61: 8 "For I, the LORD, **l** justice;
63: 9 In his **l** and mercy he redeemed
Jer 5: 31 and my people **l** it this way.
31: 3 loved you with an everlasting **l**;
32: 18 You show **l** to thousands but bring
33: 11 his **l** endures forever."
La 3: 22 of the LORD's great **l** we are not
3: 32 so great is his unfailing **l**.
Eze 33: 32 more than one who sings **l** songs
Da 9: 4 covenant of **l** with those who **l** him
Hos 2: 19 and justice, in **l** and compassion.
Hos 3: 1 **L** her as the LORD loves
11: 4 of human kindness, with ties of **l**.
12: 6 maintain **l** and justice, and wait
Joel 2: 13 slow to anger and abounding in **l**,
Am 5: 15 Hate evil, **l** good; maintain justice
Mic 3: 2 you who hate good and **l** evil;
6: 8 to **l** mercy and to walk humbly
Zep 3: 17 his **l** he will no longer rebuke you,
Zec 8: 19 Therefore **l** truth and peace."
Mt 3: 17 said, "This is my Son, whom I **l**;
5: 44 **l** your enemies and pray for those
6: 24 will hate the one and **l** the other,
17: 5 said, "This is my Son, whom I **l**;
19: 19 '**l** your neighbor as yourself.' "
22: 37 " '**L** the Lord your God with all
Lk 6: 32 "If you **l** those who **l** you,
7: 42 which of them will **l** him more?"
20: 13 I will send my son, whom I **l**;
Jn 13: 34 command I give you: **L** one another.
13: 35 my disciples, if you **l** one another."
14: 15 "If you **l** me, keep my commands.
15: 13 Greater **l** has no one than this:
15: 17 This is my command: **L** each other.
21: 15 do you **l** me more than these?"
Ro 5: 5 because God's **l** has been poured
5: 8 God demonstrates his own **l** for us
8: 28 for the good of those who **l** him,
8: 35 separate us from the **l** of Christ?
8: 39 separate us from the **l** of God that
12: 9 **L** must be sincere. Hate what is
12: 10 Be devoted to one another in **l**.
13: 8 continuing debt to **l** one another,
13: 9 "**L** your neighbor as yourself."
13: 10 Therefore **l** is the fulfillment
1Co 2: 9 prepared for those who **l** him—
8: 1 puffs up while **l** builds up.
13: 1 but do not have **l**, I am only
13: 2 but do not have **l**, I am nothing.
13: 3 but do not have **l**, I gain nothing.
13: 4 **L** is patient, **l** is kind. It does not
13: 6 **L** does not delight in evil
13: 8 **L** never fails. But where there are
13: 13 these three remain: faith, hope and **l**. But the greatest of these is **l**.
14: 1 Follow the way of **l** and eagerly
16: 14 Do everything in **l**.
2Co 5: 14 For Christ's **l** compels us,
8: 8 sincerity of your **l** by comparing it
8: 24 show these men the proof of your **l**
Gal 5: 6 is faith expressing itself through **l**.
5: 13 serve one another humbly in **l**.
5: 22 But the fruit of the Spirit is **l**, joy,
Eph 1: 4 holy and blameless in his sight. In **l**
2: 4 But because of his great **l** for us,
3: 17 being rooted and established in **l**,
3: 18 high and deep is the **l** of Christ,
3: 19 and to know this **l** that surpasses
4: 2 bearing with one another in **l**.
4: 15 speaking the truth in **l**, we will
5: 2 and walk in the way of **l**, just as
5: 25 Husbands, **l** your wives, just as
5: 28 to **l** their wives as their own bodies.
5: 33 must **l** his wife as he loves himself,
Php 1: 9 that your **l** may abound more
2: 2 having the same **l**, being one
Col 1: 5 **l** that spring from the hope stored
2: 2 in heart and united in **l**,
3: 14 And over all these virtues put on **l**,
3: 19 **l** your wives and do not be harsh
1Th 1: 3 your labor prompted by **l**, and your
4: 9 been taught by God to **l** each other.
5: 8 on faith and **l** as a breastplate,
2Th 3: 5 Lord direct your hearts into God's **l**
1Ti 1: 5 The goal of this command is **l**,
2: 15 faith, **l** and holiness with propriety.
4: 12 conduct, in **l**, in faith and in purity.
6: 10 For the **l** of money is a root of all
6: 11 faith, **l**, endurance and gentleness.
2Ti 1: 7 us power, **l** and self-discipline.
2: 22 faith, **l** and peace, along with those
3: 10 faith, patience, **l**, endurance,
Titus 2: 4 women to **l** their husbands
Phm : 9 to appeal to you on the basis of **l**.
Heb 6: 10 the **l** you have shown him as you
10: 24 may spur one another on toward **l**
13: 5 your lives free from the **l** of money
Jas 1: 12 has promised to those who **l** him.
2: 5 he promised those who **l** him?
2: 8 "**L** your neighbor as yourself,"
1Pe 1: 22 you have sincere **l** for each other,
2: 17 everyone, **l** the family of believers,

Ps 93: 1 Lord reigns, he is robed in **m**;
145: 5 the glorious splendor of your **m**—
Isa 53: 2 beauty or **m** to attract us to him,
Eze 31: 2 can be compared with you in **m**?
2Pe 1: 16 but we were eyewitnesses of his **m**.
Jude : 25 only God our Savior be glory, **m**,

MAKE (MADE MAKER MAKES MAKING)
Ge 1: 26 "Let us **m** mankind in our image,
2: 18 I will **m** a helper suitable for him."
12: 2 "I will **m** you into a great nation,
Ex 22: 3 steals must certainly **m** restitution,
Nu 6: 25 the Lord **m** his face shine on you
Ps 108: 1 sing and **m** music with all my soul.
Isa 14: 14 I will **m** myself like the Most
29: 16 formed it, "You did not **m** me"?
Jer 31: 31 "when I will **m** a new covenant
Mt 3: 3 Lord, **m** straight paths for him.'"
28: 19 go and **m** disciples of all nations,
Lk 13: 24 "**M** every effort to enter through
Ro 14: 19 Let us therefore **m** every effort to
2Co 5: 9 So we **m** it our goal to please him,
Eph 4: 3 **M** every effort to keep the unity
Col 4: 5 **m** the most of every opportunity.
1Th 4: 11 **m** it your ambition to lead a quiet
Heb 4: 11 **m** every effort to enter that rest,
12: 14 **M** every effort to live in peace
2Pe 1: 5 **m** every effort to add to your faith
3: 14 **m** every effort to be found spotless,

MAKER (MAKE)
Job 4: 17 man be more pure than his **M**?
36: 3 I will ascribe justice to my **M**.
Ps 95: 6 us kneel before the Lord our **M**;
Pr 22: 2 The Lord is the **M** of them all.
Isa 45: 9 to those who quarrel with their **M**,
54: 5 For your **M** is your husband—
Jer 10: 16 these, for he is the **M** of all things,

MAKES (MAKE)
1Co 3: 7 but only God, who **m** things grow.

MAKING (MAKE)
Ps 19: 7 are trustworthy, **m** wise the simple.
Ecc 12: 12 Of **m** many books there is no end,
Jn 5: 18 Father, **m** himself equal with God.
Eph 5: 16 **m** the most of every opportunity,

MALE
Ge 1: 27 **m** and female he created them.
Gal 3: 28 nor free, nor is there **m** and female,

MALICE (MALICIOUS)
Ro 1: 29 envy, murder, strife, deceit and **m**.
Col 3: 8 anger, rage, **m**, slander, and filthy
1Pe 2: 1 rid yourselves of all **m** and all

MALICIOUS (MALICE)
1Ti 3: 11 not **m** talkers but temperate
6: 4 envy, strife, **m** talk, evil suspicions

MAN (MANKIND MEN WOMAN WOMEN)
Ge 2: 7 the Lord God formed a **m**
2: 18 not good for the **m** to be alone.
2: 23 for she was taken out of **m**."
Dt 8: 3 **m** does not live on bread alone
1Sa 13: 14 sought out a **m** after his own heart
Ps 127: 5 Blessed is the **m** whose quiver is
Pr 30: 19 way of a **m** with a young woman.
Isa 53: 3 by mankind, a **m** of suffering,
Mt 19: 5 this reason a **m** will leave his father
Lk 4: 4 '**M** shall not live on bread alone.'"
Ro 5: 12 entered the world through one **m**,
1Co 7: 2 **m** should have sexual relations
11: 3 that the head of every **m** is Christ,
11: 3 and the head of the woman is **m**,
13: 11 When I became a **m**, I put the ways
Php 2: 8 being found in appearance as a **m**,
1Ti 2: 5 and mankind, the **m** Christ Jesus,
2: 12 or to assume authority over a **m**;

MANAGE
Jer 12: 5 how will you **m** in the thickets
1Ti 3: 4 He must **m** his own family well
3: 12 to his wife and must **m** his children
5: 14 to **m** their homes and to give

MANASSEH
1. Firstborn of Joseph (Ge 41:51; 46:20). Blessed (Ge 48).
2. Son of Hezekiah; king of Judah (2Ki 21:1–18; 2Ch 33:1–20).

MANGER
Lk 2: 12 in cloths and lying in a **m**."

MANKIND (MAN)
Ge 1: 26 "Let us make **m** in our image,

MANNA
Ex 16: 31 people of Israel called the bread **m**.
Dt 8: 16 He gave you **m** to eat
Jn 6: 49 Your ancestors ate the **m**
Rev 2: 17 I will give some of the hidden **m**.

MANNER
1Co 11: 27 in an unworthy **m** will be guilty
Php 1: 27 conduct yourselves in a **m** worthy

MARITAL (MARRY)
Ex 21: 10 of her food, clothing and **m** rights.
1Co 7: 3 husband should fulfill his **m** duty

MARK (MARKS)
Cousin of Barnabas (Col 4:10; 2Ti 4:11; Phm 24; 1Pe 5:13), see JOHN.

Ge 4: 15 the Lord put a **m** on Cain so
Rev 13: 16 to receive a **m** on their right hands

MARKS (MARK)
Jn 20: 25 "Unless I see the nail **m** in his
Gal 6: 17 I bear on my body the **m** of Jesus.

MARRED
Isa 52: 14 and his form **m** beyond human

MARRIAGE (MARRY)
Mt 22: 30 neither marry nor be given in **m**;
24: 38 marrying and giving in **m**,
Heb 13: 4 **M** should be honored by all,

MARRIED (MARRY)
Ro 7: 2 by law a **m** woman is bound to her
1Co 7: 33 But a **m** man is concerned
7: 36 is not sinning. They should get **m**.

MARRIES (MARRY)
Mt 5: 32 anyone who **m** a divorced woman
19: 9 and **m** another woman commits
Lk 16: 18 the man who **m** a divorced woman

MARRY (INTERMARRY MARITAL MARRIAGE MARRIED MARRIES)
Mt 22: 30 people will neither **m** nor be given
1Co 7: 9 they should **m**, for it is better to **m**
1Ti 5: 14 So I counsel younger widows to **m**,

MARTHA
Sister of Mary and Lazarus (Lk 10:38–42; Jn 11; 12:2).

MARVELED
Lk 2: 33 mother **m** at what was said

MARY
1. Mother of Jesus (Mt 1:16–25; Lk 1:27–56; 2:1–40). With Jesus at temple (Lk 2:41–52), at the wedding in Cana (Jn 2:1–5), questioning his sanity (Mk 3:21), at the cross (Jn 19:25–27). Among disciples after Ascension (Ac 1:14).
2. Magdalene; former demoniac (Lk 8:2). Helped support Jesus' ministry (Lk 8:1–3). At the cross (Mt 27:56; Mk 15:40; Jn 19:25), burial (Mt 27:61; Mk 15:47). Saw angel after resurrection (Mt 28:1–10; Mk 16:1–9; Lk 24:1–12); also Jesus (Jn 20:1–18).
3. Sister of Martha and Lazarus (Jn 11). Washed Jesus' feet (Jn 12:1–8).

MASQUERADES
2Co 11: 14 for Satan himself **m** as an angel

MASTER (MASTERED MASTERS)
Mt 10: 24 teacher, nor a servant above his **m**.
24: 46 servant whose **m** finds him doing
25: 21 "His **m** replied, 'Well done,
Ro 6: 14 For sin shall no longer be your **m**,
14: 4 To their own **m**, servants stand
2Ti 2: 21 useful to the **M** and prepared to do

MASTERED (MASTER)
1Co 6: 12 but I will not be **m** by anything.
2Pe 2: 19 are slaves to whatever has **m** them."

MASTERS (MASTER)
Mt 6: 24 "No one can serve two **m**.
Eph 6: 5 obey your earthly **m** with respect
6: 9 **m**, treat your slaves in the same
Titus 2: 9 be subject to their **m** in everything,

MATTHEW
Apostle; former tax collector (Mt 9:9–13; 10:3; Mk 3:18; Lk 6:15; Ac 1:13). Also called Levi (Mk 2:14–17; Lk 5:27–32).

MATURE (MATURITY)
Eph 4: 13 of the Son of God and become **m**,
Php 3: 15 who are **m** should take such a view
Heb 5: 14 But solid food is for the **m**,
Jas 1: 4 its work so that you may be **m**

MATURITY (MATURE)
Heb 6: 1 Christ and be taken forward to **m**,

MEAL
1Co 10: 27 If an unbeliever invites you to a **m**
Heb 12: 16 single **m** sold his inheritance rights

MULTITUDES (MULTITUDE)
Joel 3: 14 **M, m** in the valley of decision!

MURDER (MURDERER MURDERERS)
Ex 20: 13 "You shall not **m**.
Mt 15: 19 **m**, adultery, sexual immorality,
Ro 13: 9 "You shall not **m**," "You shall not
Jas 2: 11 commit adultery but do commit **m**,

MURDERER (MURDER)
Nu 35: 16 a **m**; the **m** is to be put to death.
Jn 8: 44 He was a **m** from the beginning,
1Jn 3: 15 hates a brother or sister is a **m**,

MURDERERS (MURDER)
1Ti 1: 9 kill their fathers or mothers, for **m**,
Rev 21: 8 vile, the **m**, the sexually immoral,

MUSIC
Ps 27: 6 sing and make **m** to the LORD.
95: 2 and extol him with **m** and song.
98: 4 burst into jubilant song with **m**;
108: 1 sing and make **m** with all my soul.
Eph 5: 19 make **m** from your heart to the Lord,

MUSTARD
Mt 13: 31 kingdom of heaven is like a **m** seed,
17: 20 you have faith as small as a **m** seed,

MUZZLE
Dt 25: 4 Do not **m** an ox while it is treading
Ps 39: 1 I will put a **m** on my mouth while
1Co 9: 9 Do not **m** an ox while it is treading

MYRRH
Mt 2: 11 gifts of gold, frankincense and **m**.
Mk 15: 23 offered him wine mixed with **m**,

MYSTERY
Ro 16: 25 the revelation of the **m** hidden
1Co 15: 51 Listen, I tell you a **m**: We will not
Eph 5: 32 This is a profound **m**—but I am
Col 1: 26 the **m** that has been kept hidden
1Ti 3: 16 the **m** from which true godliness

MYTHS
1Ti 4: 7 Have nothing to do with godless **m**

NADAB
Son of Jeroboam I; king of Israel (1Ki 15:25–32).

NAIL (NAILING)
Jn 20: 25 "Unless I see the **n** marks in his

NAILING (NAIL)
Ac 2: 23 him to death by **n** him to the cross.
Col 2: 14 has taken it away, **n** it to the cross.

NAKED
Ge 2: 25 Adam and his wife were both **n**,
Job 1: 21 womb, and **n** I will depart.
Isa 58: 7 you see the **n**, to clothe them,
2Co 5: 3 are clothed, we will not be found **n**.

NAME
Ex 3: 15 "This is my **n** forever, the **n** you
20: 7 "You shall not misuse the **n**
Dt 5: 11 "You shall not misuse the **n**
28: 58 this glorious and awesome **n**—
1Ki 5: 5 will build the temple for my **N**.'
2Ch 7: 14 people, who are called by my **n**,
Ps 34: 3 let us exalt his **n** together.
103: 1 my inmost being, praise his holy **n**.
147: 4 the stars and calls them each by **n**.
Pr 22: 1 A good **n** is more desirable than
30: 4 What is his **n**, and what is the **n**
Isa 40: 26 and calls forth each of them by **n**.
57: 15 who lives forever, whose **n** is holy:
Jer 14: 7 LORD, for the sake of your **n**.
Da 12: 1 everyone whose **n** is found written
Joel 2: 32 the **n** of the LORD will be saved;
Zec 14: 9 one LORD, and his **n** the only **n**.
Mt 1: 21 you are to give him the **n** Jesus,
6: 9 in heaven, hallowed be your **n**,
18: 20 where two or three gather in my **n**,
Jn 10: 3 He calls his own sheep by **n**
16: 24 not asked for anything in my **n**.
Ac 4: 12 is no other **n** under heaven given
Ro 10: 13 on the **n** of the Lord will be saved."
Php 2: 9 the **n** that is above every **n**,
Col 3: 17 do it all in the **n** of the Lord Jesus,
Heb 1: 4 the angels as the **n** he has inherited
Rev 20: 15 whose **n** was not found written

NAOMI
Mother-in-law of Ruth (Ru 1). Advised Ruth to seek marriage with Boaz (Ru 2–4).

NARROW
Mt 7: 13 "Enter through the **n** gate.

NATHANAEL
Apostle (Jn 1:45–49; 21:2). Probably also called Bartholomew (Mt 10:3).

NATION (NATIONS)
Ge 12: 2 "I will make you into a great **n**,
Ps 33: 12 Blessed is the **n** whose God is
Pr 14: 34 Righteousness exalts a **n**, but sin
Isa 65: 1 a **n** that did not call on my name,
1Pe 2: 9 a holy **n**, God's special possession,
Rev 7: 9 could count, from every **n**, tribe,

NATIONS (NATION)
Ge 17: 4 You will be the father of many **n**.
18: 18 and all **n** on earth will be blessed
Ex 19: 5 of all **n** you will be my treasured
Ne 1: 8 I will scatter you among the **n**,
Ps 96: 3 Declare his glory among the **n**,
Isa 40: 15 Surely the **n** are like a drop
Eze 36: 23 has been profaned among the **n**,
Hag 2: 7 what is desired by all **n** will come,
Zec 8: 23 **n** will take firm hold of one Jew
14: 2 I will gather all the **n** to Jerusalem
Mt 28: 19 go and make disciples of all **n**,
Rev 21: 24 The **n** will walk by its light,

NATURAL (NATURE)
1Co 15: 44 it is sown a **n** body, it is raised

NATURE (NATURAL)
Php 2: 6 Who, being in very **n** God, did not

NAZARENE
Mt 2: 23 that he would be called a **N**.

NAZIRITE
Jdg 13: 7 because the boy will be a **N** of God

NECESSARY
Ro 13: 5 it is **n** to submit to the authorities,

NEED (NEEDS NEEDY)
Mt 6: 8 knows what you **n** before you ask
Ro 12: 13 the Lord's people who are in **n**.
1Co 12: 21 say to the hand, "I don't **n** you!"
1Jn 3: 17 sister in **n** but has no pity on them,

NEEDLE
Mt 19: 24 to go through the eye of a **n** than

NEEDS (NEED)
Isa 58: 11 he will satisfy your **n**
Php 4: 19 God will meet all your **n** according

NEEDY (NEED)
Pr 14: 21 is the one who is kind to the **n**.
14: 31 is kind to the **n** honors God.
31: 20 and extends her hands to the **n**.
Mt 6: 2 "So when you give to the **n**, do not

NEGLECT (NEGLECTED)
Ne 10: 39 "We will not **n** the house of our
Ps 119: 16 I will not **n** your word.
Ac 6: 2 for us to **n** the ministry of the word
1Ti 4: 14 not **n** your gift, which was given

NEGLECTED (NEGLECT)
Mt 23: 23 But you have **n** the more important

NEHEMIAH
Cupbearer of Artaxerxes (Ne 2:1); governor of Israel (Ne 8:9). Returned to Jerusalem to rebuild walls (Ne 2–6). With Ezra, reestablished worship (Ne 8). Prayer confessing nation's sin (Ne 9). Dedicated wall (Ne 12).

NEIGHBOR (NEIGHBOR'S)
Ex 20: 16 give false testimony against your **n**.
Lev 19: 18 people, but love your **n** as yourself.
Pr 27: 10 better a **n** nearby than a relative far
Mt 19: 19 and 'love your **n** as yourself.' "
Lk 10: 29 asked Jesus, "And who is my **n**?"
Ro 13: 10 Love does no harm to a **n**.

NEIGHBOR'S (NEIGHBOR)
Ex 20: 17 "You shall not covet your **n** house.
Dt 5: 21 "You shall not covet your **n** wife.
19: 14 not move your **n** boundary stone
Pr 25: 17 Seldom set foot in your **n** house—

NEW
Ps 40: 3 He put a **n** song in my mouth,
Ecc 1: 9 there is nothing **n** under the sun.
Isa 65: 17 I will create **n** heavens and a **n**
Jer 31: 31 I will make a **n** covenant
Eze 36: 26 I will give you a **n** heart and put a **n** spirit in you;
Mt 9: 17 they pour **n** wine into **n** wineskins,
Lk 22: 20 "This cup is the **n** covenant in my
2Co 5: 17 in Christ, the **n** creation has come:
Eph 4: 24 and to put on the **n** self,
2Pe 3: 13 to a **n** heaven and a **n** earth,
1Jn 2: 8 Yet I am writing you a **n** command;

NEWBORN (BEAR)
1Pe 2: 2 Like **n** babies, crave pure spiritual

NEWS
Isa 52: 7 the feet of those who bring good **n**,
Mk 1: 15 Repent and believe the good **n**!"
Lk 2: 10 I bring you good **n** that will cause
Ac 5: 42 proclaiming the good **n** that Jesus
17: 18 Paul was preaching the good **n**
Ro 10: 15 feet of those who bring good **n**!"

NICODEMUS
Pharisee who visited Jesus at night (Jn 3). Argued fair treatment of Jesus (Jn 7:50–52). With Joseph, prepared Jesus for burial (Jn 19:38–42).

NIGHT
Job 35: 10 Maker, who gives songs in the **n**,
Ps 1: 2 meditates on his law day and **n**.
91: 5 You will not fear the terror of **n**,
Jn 3: 2 He came to Jesus at **n** and said,
1Th 5: 2 Lord will come like a thief in the **n**.
5: 5 We do not belong to the **n**
Rev 21: 25 shut, for there will be no **n** there.

NOAH
Righteous man (Eze 14:14, 20) called to build ark (Ge 6–8; Heb 11:7; 1Pe 3:20; 2Pe 2:5). God's covenant with (Ge 9:1–17). Drunkenness of (Ge 9:18–23). Blessed sons, cursed Canaan (Ge 9:24–27).

NOBLE
Ru 3: 11 you are a woman of **n** character.
Ps 45: 1 by a **n** theme as I recite my verses
Pr 12: 4 **n** character is her husband's crown,
31: 10 wife of **n** character who can find?
31: 29 "Many women do **n** things, but
Isa 32: 8 But the **n** make **n** plans, and by **n**
Lk 8: 15 good soil stands for those with a **n**
Php 4: 8 whatever is **n**, whatever is right,

NOTHING
Ne 9: 21 they lacked **n**, their clothes did not
Jer 32: 17 **N** is too hard for you.
Jn 15: 5 apart from me you can do **n**.

NULLIFY
Ro 3: 31 we, then, **n** the law by this faith?

OATH
Dt 7: 8 and kept the **o** he swore to your

OBEDIENCE (OBEY)
2Ch 31: 21 of God's temple and in **o** to the law
Ro 1: 5 all the Gentiles to the **o** that comes
6: 16 to death, or to **o**, which leads
2Jn : 6 that we walk in **o** to his commands.

OBEDIENT (OBEY)
Lk 2: 51 with them and was **o** to them.
Php 2: 8 himself by becoming **o** to death—
1Pe 1: 14 As **o** children, do not conform

OBEY (OBEDIENCE OBEDIENT OBEYED)
Ex 12: 24 "**O** these instructions as a lasting
Dt 6: 3 be careful to **o** so that it may go
13: 4 Keep his commands and **o** him;
21: 18 son who does not **o** his father
30: 2 God and **o** him with all your heart
32: 46 to **o** carefully all the words
1Sa 15: 22 To **o** is better than sacrifice,
Ps 119: 34 your law and **o** it with all my heart.
Mt 28: 20 to **o** everything I have commanded
Jn 14: 23 who loves me will **o** my teaching.
Ac 5: 29 must **o** God rather than human
Ro 6: 16 you are slaves of the one you **o**—
Gal 5: 3 he is obligated to **o** the whole law.
Eph 6: 1 **o** your parents in the Lord, for this
6: 5 heart, just as you would **o** Christ.
Col 3: 20 **o** your parents in everything,
1Ti 3: 4 and see that his children **o** him,

OBEYED (OBEY)
Ps 119: 4 precepts that are to be fully **o**.
Jnh 3: 3 Jonah **o** the word of the LORD
Jn 17: 6 to me and they have **o** your word.
Heb 11: 8 as his inheritance, **o** and went,
1Pe 3: 6 who **o** Abraham and called him

OBLIGATED
Ro 1: 14 I am **o** both to Greeks
Gal 5: 3 that he is **o** to obey the whole law.

OBSCENITY
Eph 5: 4 Nor should there be **o**, foolish talk

OBSOLETE
Heb 8: 13 "new," he has made the first one **o**;

OBTAINED
Ro 9: 30 not pursue righteousness, have **o** it,
Php 3: 12 Not that I have already **o** all this,

OFFENSE (OFFENSIVE)
Pr 17: 9 would foster love covers over an **o**,
19: 11 it is to one's glory to overlook an **o**.

OFFENSIVE (OFFENSE)
Ps 139: 24 See if there is any **o** way in me,

OFFER (OFFERED OFFERING OFFERINGS)
Ro 12: 1 **o** your bodies as a living sacrifice,
Heb 13: 15 let us continually **o** to God

OFFERED (OFFER)
Heb 7: 27 sins once for all when he **o** himself.

OFFERING (OFFER)
Ge 22: 8 provide the lamb for the burnt **o**,
Ps 40: 6 Sacrifice and **o** you did not desire
Isa 53: 10 the LORD makes his life an **o**
Mt 5: 23 if you are **o** your gift at the altar
Eph 5: 2 himself up for us as a fragrant **o**
Heb 10: 5 "Sacrifice and **o** you did not desire,

OFFERINGS (OFFER)
Mal 3: 8 we robbing you?' "In tithes and **o**.
Mk 12: 33 is more important than all burnt **o**

OFFICER
2Ti 2: 4 tries to please his commanding **o**.

OFFSPRING
Ge 3: 15 and between your **o** and hers;
12: 7 "To your **o** I will give this land."

OIL
Ps 23: 5 You anoint my head with **o**;
Isa 61: 3 the **o** of joy instead of mourning,
Heb 1: 9 by anointing you with the **o** of joy."

OLIVE (OLIVES)
Zec 4: 3 Also there are two **o** trees by it,
Ro 11: 17 though a wild **o** shoot, have been
Rev 11: 4 They are "the two **o** trees"

OLIVES (OLIVE)
Jas 3: 12 can a fig tree bear **o**, or a grapevine

OMEGA
Rev 1: 8 "I am the Alpha and the **O**,"

OMRI
King of Israel (1Ki 16:21–26).

OPINIONS
1Ki 18: 21 will you waver between two **o**?
Pr 18: 2 but delight in airing their own **o**.

OPPORTUNITY
Ro 7: 11 sin, seizing the **o** afforded
Gal 6: 10 as we have **o**, let us do good to all
Eph 5: 16 making the most of every **o**,
Col 4: 5 make the most of every **o**.
1Ti 5: 14 to give the enemy no **o** for slander.

OPPOSES
Jas 4: 6 "God **o** the proud but shows favor
1Pe 5: 5 "God **o** the proud but shows favor

OPPRESS (OPPRESSED)
Ex 22: 21 "Do not mistreat or **o** a foreigner,
Zec 7: 10 Do not **o** the widow

OPPRESSED (OPPRESS)
Ps 9: 9 The LORD is a refuge for the **o**,
Isa 53: 7 He was **o** and afflicted, yet he did
Zec 10: 2 the people wander like sheep **o**

ORDERLY
1Co 14: 40 be done in a fitting and **o** way.

ORGIES
Gal 5: 21 drunkenness, **o**, and the like.
1Pe 4: 3 lust, drunkenness, **o**,

ORIGIN
2Pe 1: 21 For prophecy never had its **o**

ORPHANS
Jn 14: 18 I will not leave you as **o**;
Jas 1: 27 to look after **o** and widows in their

OUTCOME
Heb 13: 7 Consider the **o** of their way of life
1Pe 4: 17 what will the **o** be for those who do

OUTSIDERS
Col 4: 5 wise in the way you act toward **o**;
1Th 4: 12 daily life may win the respect of **o**
1Ti 3: 7 also have a good reputation with **o**,

OUTSTANDING
SS 5: 10 and ruddy, **o** among ten thousand.
Ro 13: 8 Let no debt remain **o**,

OUTSTRETCHED
Ex 6: 6 I will redeem you with an **o** arm
Jer 27: 5 power and **o** arm I made the earth
Eze 20: 33 with a mighty hand and an **o** arm

OUTWEIGHS
2Co 4: 17 an eternal glory that far **o** them all.

OVERCOME (OVERCOMES)
Mt 16: 18 and the gates of Hades will not **o** it.
Mk 9: 24 help me **o** my unbelief!"
Jn 16: 33 But take heart! I have **o** the world."
Ro 12: 21 Do not be **o** by evil, but **o** evil
1Jn 5: 4 is the victory that has **o** the world,

OVERCOMES (OVERCOME)
1Jn 5: 4 everyone born of God **o** the world.
5: 5 Who is it that **o** the world?

OVERFLOW (OVERFLOWS)
Ps 119:171 May my lips **o** with praise, for you
Ro 15: 13 so that you may **o** with hope
2Co 4: 15 may cause thanksgiving to **o**
1Th 3: 12 love increase and **o** for each other

OVERFLOWS (OVERFLOW)
Ps 23: 5 anoint my head with oil; my cup **o**.

OVERJOYED (JOY)
Da 6: 23 The king was **o** and gave orders
Mt 2: 10 they saw the star, they were **o**.
Jn 20: 20 disciples were **o** when they saw
Ac 12: 14 she was so **o** she ran back without
1Pe 4: 13 that you may be **o** when his glory

OVERSEER (OVERSEERS)
1Ti 3: 1 to be an **o** desires a noble task.
3: 2 Now the **o** is to be above reproach,
Titus 1: 7 Since an **o** manages God's

OVERSEERS (OVERSEER)
Ac 20: 28 the Holy Spirit has made you **o**.
Php 1: 1 together with the **o** and deacons:

OVERWHELMED
Ps 38: 4 My guilt has **o** me like a burden
65: 3 When we were **o** by sins,
Mt 26: 38 "My soul is **o** with sorrow
Mk 7: 37 People were **o** with amazement.

OWE
Ro 13: 7 Give to everyone what you **o** them:
Phm : 19 that you **o** me your very self.

OX
Dt 25: 4 Do not muzzle an **o** while it is
Isa 11: 7 the lion will eat straw like the **o**.
1Co 9: 9 "Do not muzzle an **o** while it is

PAGANS
Mt 5: 47 Do not even **p** do that?
1Pe 2: 12 such good lives among the **p** that,

PAIN (PAINFUL PAINS)
Job 33: 19 on a bed of **p** with constant distress
Jn 16: 21 to a child has **p** because her time

PAINFUL (PAIN)
Ge 3: 17 through **p** toil you will eat food
Heb 12: 11 seems pleasant at the time, but **p**.

PAINS (PAIN)
Ge 3: 16 "I will make your **p** in childbearing

PALMS
Isa 49: 16 engraved you on the **p** of my hands

PANTS
Ps 42: 1 As the deer **p** for streams of water, so my soul **p** for you,

PARADISE
Lk 23: 43 today you will be with me in **p**."
2Co 12: 4 was caught up to **p** and heard
Rev 2: 7 tree of life, which is in the **p** of God.

PARALYZED
Mk 2: 3 bringing to him a **p** man,

PARDON (PARDONS)
Isa 55: 7 and to our God, for he will freely **p**.

PARDONS (PARDON)
Mic 7: 18 like you, who **p** sin and forgives

PARENT (PARENT'S PARENTS)
Pr 17: 21 is no joy for the **p** of a godless fool.

PARENT'S (PARENT)
15: 5 A fool spurns a **p** discipline,

PARENTS (PARENT)
Ex 20: 5 for the sin of the **p** to the third
Pr 17: 6 **p** are the pride of their children.
Lk 18: 29 sisters or **p** or children for the sake
21: 16 You will be betrayed even by **p**,
Ro 1: 30 of doing evil; they disobey their **p**;
2Co 12: 14 not have to save up for their **p**,
Eph 6: 1 Children, obey your **p** in the Lord,
Col 3: 20 obey your **p** in everything,
2Ti 3: 2 disobedient to their **p**, ungrateful,

PARTIALITY
Dt 10: 17 who shows no **p** and accepts no
2Ch 19: 7 our God there is no injustice or **p**
Lk 20: 21 that you do not show **p** but teach

PARTICIPATION
1Co 10: 16 bread that we break a **p** in the body

PASS
Ex 12: 13 I see the blood, I will **p** over you.
La 1: 12 nothing to you, all you who **p** by?
Lk 21: 33 but my words will never **p** away.
1Co 13: 8 there is knowledge, it will **p** away.

PASSION (PASSIONS)
1Co 7: 9 to marry than to burn with **p**.

PASSIONS (PASSION)
Gal 5: 24 have crucified the flesh with its **p**
Titus 2: 12 to ungodliness and worldly **p**,

PASSOVER
Ex 12: 11 Eat it in haste; it is the LORD's **P**.
Dt 16: 1 celebrate the **P** of the LORD your
1Co 5: 7 For Christ, our **P** lamb, has been

PAST
Isa 43: 18 do not dwell on the **p**.
Ro 15: 4 was written in the **p** was written
Heb 1: 1 the **p** God spoke to our ancestors

PASTORS
Eph 4: 11 the evangelists, the **p** and teachers,

PASTURE (PASTURES)
Ps 37: 3 dwell in the land and enjoy safe **p**.
100: 3 are his people, the sheep of his **p**.
Jer 50: 7 their verdant **p**, the LORD,
Eze 34: 13 I will **p** them on the mountains
Jn 10: 9 come in and go out, and find **p**.

PASTURES (PASTURE)
Ps 23: 2 He makes me lie down in green **p**,

PATCH
Mt 9: 16 No one sews a **p** of unshrunk cloth

PATH (PATHS)
Ps 27: 11 me in a straight **p** because of my
119: 9 person stay on the **p** of purity?
119:105 to my feet and a light for my **p**.
Pr 15: 19 the **p** of the upright is a highway.
15: 24 The **p** of life leads upward
Isa 26: 7 The **p** of the righteous is level;
Lk 1: 79 guide our feet into the **p** of peace."
2Co 6: 3 no stumbling block in anyone's **p**,

PATHS (PATH)
Ps 23: 3 He guides me along the right **p**
25: 4 ways, LORD, teach me your **p**.
Pr 3: 6 and he will make your **p** straight.
Ro 11: 33 and his **p** beyond tracing out!
Heb 12: 13 "Make level **p** for your feet,"

PATIENCE (PATIENT)
Pr 19: 11 A person's wisdom yields **p**; it is
2Co 6: 6 understanding, **p** and kindness;
Col 1: 11 may have great endurance and **p**,
3: 12 humility, gentleness and **p**.

PATIENT (PATIENCE PATIENTLY)
Pr 15: 18 the one who is **p** calms a quarrel.
Ro 12: 12 Be joyful in hope, **p** in affliction,
1Co 13: 4 Love is **p**, love is kind. It does not
Eph 4: 2 be **p**, bearing with one another
1Th 5: 14 help the weak, be **p** with everyone.

PATIENTLY (PATIENT)
Ps 40: 1 I waited **p** for the LORD;
Ro 8: 25 we do not yet have, we wait for it **p**.

PATTERN
Ro 5: 14 who is a **p** of the one to come.
12: 2 not conform to the **p** of this world,
2Ti 1: 13 keep as the **p** of sound teaching,

PAUL
Also called Saul (Ac 13:9). Pharisee from Tarsus (Ac 9:11; Php 3:5). Apostle (Gal 1). At stoning of Stephen (Ac 8:1). Persecuted Church (Ac 9:1–2; Gal 1:13). Vision of Jesus on road to Damascus (Ac 9:4–9; 26:12–18). In Arabia (Gal 1:17). Preached in Damascus; escaped death through the wall in a basket (Ac 9:19–25). In Jerusalem; sent back to Tarsus (Ac 9:26–30).

Brought to Antioch by Barnabas (Ac 11:22–26). First missionary journey to Cyprus and Galatia (Ac 13–14). Stoned at Lystra (Ac 14:19–20). At Jerusalem council (Ac 15). Split with Barnabas over Mark (Ac 15:36–41).

Second missionary journey with Silas (Ac 16–20). Called to Macedonia (Ac 16:6–10). Freed from prison in Philippi (Ac 16:16–

40). In Thessalonica (Ac 17:1–9). Speech in Athens (Ac 17:16–33). In Corinth (Ac 18). In Ephesus (Ac 19). Return to Jerusalem (Ac 20). Farewell to Ephesian elders (Ac 20:13–38). Arrival in Jerusalem (Ac 21:1–26). Arrested (Ac 21:27–36). Addressed crowds (Ac 22), Sanhedrin (Ac 23:1–11). Transferred to Caesarea (Ac 23:12–35). Trial before Felix (Ac 24), Festus (Ac 25:1–12). Before Agrippa (Ac 25:13—26:32). Voyage to Rome; shipwreck (Ac 27). Arrival in Rome (Ac 28).

PAY (REPAID REPAY)
Lev 26: 43 They will **p** for their sins because
Pr 22: 17 **P** attention and turn your ear
Mt 22: 17 Is it right to **p** the imperial tax
Ro 13: 6 This is also why you **p** taxes,
2Pe 1: 19 you will do well to **p** attention to it,

PEACE (PEACEMAKERS)
Nu 6: 26 toward you and give you **p**."'
Ps 34: 14 and do good; seek **p** and pursue it.
85: 10 righteousness and **p** kiss each
119:165 Great **p** have those who love your
122: 6 Pray for the **p** of Jerusalem:
Pr 14: 30 A heart at **p** gives life to the body,
17: 1 Better a dry crust with **p** and quiet
Isa 9: 6 Everlasting Father, Prince of **P**.
26: 3 in perfect **p** those whose minds are
48: 22 "There is no **p**," says the LORD,
Zec 9: 10 He will proclaim **p** to the nations.
Mt 10: 34 I did not come to bring **p**,
Lk 2: 14 and on earth **p** to those on whom
Jn 14: 27 **P** I leave with you; my **p** I give you.
16: 33 so that in me you may have **p**.
Ro 5: 1 we have **p** with God through our
1Co 7: 15 God has called us to live in **p**.
14: 33 is not a God of disorder but of **p**—
Gal 5: 22 Spirit is love, joy, **p**, forbearance,
Eph 2: 14 For he himself is our **p**, who has
Php 4: 7 the **p** of God, which transcends
Col 1: 20 by making **p** through his blood,
3: 15 Let the **p** of Christ rule in your
1Th 5: 3 people are saying, "**P** and safety,"
2Th 3: 16 the Lord of **p** himself give you **p**
2Ti 2: 22 love and **p**, along with those who
1Pe 3: 11 they must seek **p** and pursue it.
Rev 6: 4 power to take **p** from the earth

PEACEMAKERS (PEACE)
Mt 5: 9 Blessed are the **p**, for they will be
Jas 3: 18 **P** who sow in peace reap a harvest

PEARL (PEARLS)
Rev 21: 21 each gate made of a single **p**.

PEARLS (PEARL)
Mt 7: 6 do not throw your **p** to pigs.
13: 45 like a merchant looking for fine **p**.
1Ti 2: 9 or gold or **p** or expensive clothes,
Rev 21: 21 The twelve gates were twelve **p**,

PEKAH
King of Israel (2Ki 15:25–31; Isa 7:1).

PEKAHIAH
Son of Menahem; king of Israel (2Ki 15:22–26).

PEN
Mt 5: 18 not the least stroke of a **p**,

PENTECOST
Ac 2: 1 When the day of **P** came, they were

PEOPLE (PEOPLES)
Dt 32: 9 For the LORD's portion is his **p**,
Ru 1: 16 Your **p** will be my **p** and your God
2Ch 7: 14 if my **p**, who are called by my
Ps 133: 1 it is when God's **p** live together
Jer 24: 7 They will be my **p**, and I will be
Zec 2: 11 in that day and will become my **p**.
Mt 4: 19 I will send you out to fish for **p**."
Lk 2: 10 will cause great joy for all the **p**.
Jn 12: 32 earth, will draw all **p** to myself."
Ac 15: 14 to choose a **p** for his name
Ro 5: 12 and in this way death came to all **p**,
8: 27 for God's **p** in accordance
1Co 9: 22 I have become all things to all **p** so
2Co 6: 16 their God, and they will be my **p**."
Eph 1: 18 glorious inheritance in his holy **p**,
6: 18 keep on praying for all the Lord's **p**.
1Ti 2: 4 who wants all **p** to be saved
2Ti 2: 2 entrust to reliable **p** who will also
Titus 2: 14 himself a **p** that are his very own,
Heb 9: 27 Just as **p** are destined to die once,
1Pe 2: 9 But you are a chosen **p**, a royal
Rev 5: 8 which are the prayers of God's **p**.
19: 8 the righteous acts of God's holy **p**.)
21: 3 They will be his **p**, and God

PEOPLES (PEOPLE)
Da 7: 14 **p** of every language worshiped him
Mic 4: 1 the hills, and **p** will stream to it.

PERCEIVING
Isa 6: 9 be ever seeing, but never **p**.'

PERFECT (PERFECTER PERFECTION)
SS 6: 9 but my dove, my **p** one, is unique,
Isa 26: 3 in **p** peace those whose minds are
Mt 5: 48 Be **p**, therefore, as your heavenly Father is **p**.
Ro 12: 2 his good, pleasing and **p** will.
2Co 12: 9 my power is made **p** in weakness."
Col 3: 14 binds them all together in **p** unity.
Heb 9: 11 more **p** tabernacle that is not made
10: 14 he has made **p** forever those who
Jas 1: 17 good and **p** gift is from above,
1: 25 looks intently into the **p** law
3: 2 never at fault in what they say is **p**,
1Jn 4: 18 But **p** love drives out fear,

PERFECTER (PERFECT)
Heb 12: 2 on Jesus, the pioneer and **p** of faith.

PERFECTION (PERFECT)
Ps 119: 96 To all **p** I see a limit, but your
Heb 7: 11 If **p** could have been attained

PERFORMS
Ps 77: 14 You are the God who **p** miracles;

PERISH (PERISHABLE)
Ps 102: 26 They will **p**, but you remain;
Lk 13: 3 you repent, you too will all **p**.
Jn 10: 28 eternal life, and they shall never **p**;
Col 2: 22 that are all destined to **p** with use,
Heb 1: 11 They will **p**, but you remain;
2Pe 3: 9 you, not wanting anyone to **p**,

PERISHABLE (PERISH)
1Co 15: 42 The body that is sown is **p**, it is

PERJURERS
1Ti 1: 10 for slave traders and liars and **p**—

PERMIT
1Ti 2: 12 I do not **p** a woman to teach

PERSECUTE (PERSECUTED PERSECUTION)
Mt 5: 11 **p** you and falsely say all kinds
Jn 15: 20 persecuted me, they will **p** you
Ac 9: 4 "Saul, Saul, why do you **p** me?"
Ro 12: 14 Bless those who **p** you; bless and

PERSECUTED (PERSECUTE)
1Co 4: 12 when we are **p**, we endure it;
2Ti 3: 12 godly life in Christ Jesus will be **p**,

PERSECUTION (PERSECUTE)
Ro 8: 35 trouble or hardship or **p** or famine

PERSEVERANCE (PERSEVERE)
Ro 5: 3 we know that suffering produces **p**;
5: 4 **p**, character; and character, hope.
Heb 12: 1 let us run with **p** the race marked
Jas 1: 3 testing of your faith produces **p**.
2Pe 1: 6 and to self-control, **p**; and to **p**,

PERSEVERE (PERSEVERANCE PERSEVERED PERSEVERES)
1Ti 4: 16 **P** in them, because if you do,
Heb 10: 36 You need to **p** so that when you

PERSEVERED (PERSEVERE)
Heb 11: 27 he **p** because he saw him who is
Jas 5: 11 count as blessed those who have **p**.
Rev 2: 3 You have **p** and have endured

PERSEVERES (PERSEVERE)
1Co 13: 7 trusts, always hopes, always **p**.
Jas 1: 12 one who **p** under trial because,

PERSUADE
2Co 5: 11 to fear the Lord, we try to **p** others.

PERVERSION (PERVERT)
Lev 18: 23 sexual relations with it; that is a **p**.
Jude : 7 up to sexual immorality and **p**.

PERVERT (PERVERSION)
Gal 1: 7 are trying to **p** the gospel of Christ.

PESTILENCE
Ps 91: 6 the **p** that stalks in the darkness,

PETER
Apostle, brother of Andrew, also called Simon (Mt 10:2; Mk 3:16; Lk 6:14; Ac 1:13), and Cephas (Jn 1:42). Confession of Christ (Mt 16:13–20; Mk 8:27–30; Lk 9:18–27). At transfiguration (Mt 17:1–8; Mk 9:2–8; Lk 9:28–36; 2Pe 1:16–18). Caught fish with coin (Mt 17:24–27). Denial of Jesus predicted (Mt 26:31–35; Mk 14:27–31; Lk 22:31–34; Jn 13:31–38). Denied Jesus (Mt 26:69–75; Mk 14:66–72; Lk 22:54–62; Jn 18:15–27). Commissioned by Jesus to shepherd his flock (Jn 21:15–23).

Speech at Pentecost (Ac 2). Healed beggar (Ac 3:1–10). Speech at temple (Ac 3:11–26), before Sanhedrin (Ac 4:1–22). In Samaria (Ac 8:14–25). Sent by vision to Cornelius (Ac 10). Announced salvation of Gentiles in Jerusalem (Ac 11; 15). Freed from prison (Ac 12). Inconsistency at Antioch (Gal 2:11–21). At Jerusalem Council (Ac 15).

PHARISEES
Mt 5: 20 surpasses that of the **P**

PHILIP
1. Apostle (Mt 10:3; Mk 3:18; Lk 6:14; Jn 1:43–48; 14:8; Ac 1:13).
2. Deacon (Ac 6:1–7); evangelist in Samaria (Ac 8:4–25), to Ethiopian (Ac 8:26–40).

PHILOSOPHY
Col 2: 8 through hollow and deceptive **p**,

PHYLACTERIES
Mt 23: 5 They make their **p** wide

PHYSICAL
1Ti 4: 8 For **p** training is of some value,
Jas 2: 16 does nothing about their **p** needs,

PIECES
Ge 15: 17 and passed between the **p**.
Jer 34: 18 two and then walked between its **p**.

PIERCE (PIERCED)
Ps 22: 16 they **p** my hands and my feet.

PIERCED (PIERCE)
Isa 53: 5 he was **p** for our transgressions,
Zec 12: 10 the one they have **p**, and they will
Jn 19: 37 will look on the one they have **p**."

PIGS
Mt 7: 6 do not throw your pearls to **p**.

PILATE
Governor of Judea. Questioned Jesus (Mt 27:1–26; Mk 15:15; Lk 22:66—23:25; Jn 18:28—19:16); sent him to Herod (Lk 23:6–12); consented to his crucifixion when crowds chose Barabbas (Mt 27:15–26; Mk 15:6–15; Lk 23:13–25; Jn 19:1–10).

PILLAR
Ge 19: 26 back, and she became a **p** of salt.
Ex 13: 21 by night in a **p** of fire to give them
1Ti 3: 15 the **p** and foundation of the truth.

PIT
Ps 40: 2 He lifted me out of the slimy **p**,
103: 4 who redeems your life from the **p**
Mt 15: 14 the blind, both will fall into a **p**."

PITIED
1Co 15: 19 we are of all people most to be **p**.

PLAGUE
2Ch 6: 28 famine or **p** comes to the land,

PLAIN
Ro 1: 19 God has made it **p** to them.

PLAN (PLANNED PLANS)
Pr 14: 22 those who **p** what is good find love
Eph 1: 11 to the **p** of him who works

PLANK
Mt 7: 3 attention to the **p** in your own eye?
Lk 6: 41 attention to the **p** in your own eye?

PLANNED (PLAN)
Ps 40: 5 have done, the things you **p** for us.
Isa 46: 11 what I have **p**, that I will do.
Heb 11: 40 since God had **p** something better

PLANS (PLAN)
Ps 20: 4 heart and make all your **p** succeed.
33: 11 But the **p** of the LORD stand firm
Pr 20: 18 **P** are established by seeking advice;
Isa 32: 8 But the noble make noble **p**,

PLANTED (PLANTS)
Ps 1: 3 person is like a tree **p** by streams
Mt 15: 13 Father has not **p** will be pulled
1Co 3: 6 I **p** the seed, Apollos watered it,

PLANTS (PLANTED)
1Co 3: 7 neither the one who **p** nor the one
9: 7 Who **p** a vineyard and does not eat

PLATTER
Mk 6: 25 head of John the Baptist on a **p**."

PLAYED
Lk 7: 32 "'We **p** the pipe for you, and you
1Co 14: 7 what tune is being **p** unless there is

PLEADED
2Co 12: 8 Three times I **p** with the Lord

PLEASANT (PLEASE)
Ps 16: 6 lines have fallen for me in **p** places;
133: 1 and **p** it is when God's people live
147: 1 how **p** and fitting to praise him!
Heb 12: 11 No discipline seems **p** at the time,

PLEASE (PLEASANT PLEASED PLEASES PLEASING PLEASURE PLEASURES)
Pr 20: 23 and dishonest scales do not **p** him.
Jer 6: 20 your sacrifices do not **p** me."
Jn 5: 30 for I seek not to **p** myself but him
Ro 8: 8 realm of the flesh cannot **p** God.
15: 2 Each of us should **p** our neighbors
1Co 7: 32 how he can **p** the Lord.
10: 33 even as I try to **p** everyone in every
2Co 5: 9 So we make it our goal to **p** him,
Gal 1: 10 If I were still trying to **p** people,
1Th 4: 1 you how to live in order to **p** God,
2Ti 2: 4 tries to **p** his commanding officer.
Heb 11: 6 faith it is impossible to **p** God,

PLEASED (PLEASE)
Mt 3: 17 with him I am well **p**."
1Co 1: 21 God was **p** through the foolishness
Col 1: 19 God was **p** to have all his fullness
Heb 11: 5 commended as one who **p** God.
2Pe 1: 17 with him I am well **p**."

PLEASES (PLEASE)
Ps 135: 6 The LORD does whatever **p** him,
Pr 15: 8 the prayer of the upright **p** him.
Jn 3: 8 The wind blows wherever it **p**.
8: 29 alone, for I always do what **p** him."
Col 3: 20 in everything, for this **p** the Lord.
1Ti 2: 3 is good, and **p** God our Savior,
1Jn 3: 22 his commands and do what **p** him.

PLEASING (PLEASE)
Ps 104: 34 May my meditation be **p** to him,
Ro 12: 1 living sacrifice, holy and **p** to God
Php 4: 18 an acceptable sacrifice, **p** to God.
Heb 13: 21 he work in us what is **p** to him,

PLEASURE (PLEASE)
Ps 147: 10 His **p** is not in the strength
Pr 21: 17 loves **p** will become poor;
Eze 18: 32 For I take no **p** in the death
Eph 1: 5 in accordance with his **p** and will—
1: 9 of his will according to his good **p**,
2Ti 3: 4 lovers of **p** rather than lovers

PLEASURES (PLEASE)
Ps 16: 11 with eternal **p** at your right hand.
Heb 11: 25 than to enjoy the fleeting **p** of sin.
2Pe 2: 13 reveling in their **p** while they feast

PLENTIFUL
Mt 9: 37 "The harvest is **p** but the workers

PLOW (PLOWSHARES)
Lk 9: 62 "No one who puts a hand to the **p**

PLOWSHARES (PLOW)
Isa 2: 4 They will beat their swords into **p**
Joel 3: 10 Beat your **p** into swords and your

PLUNDER
Ex 3: 22 And so you will **p** the Egyptians."

POINT
Jas 2: 10 yet stumbles at just one **p** is guilty

POISON
Mk 16: 18 *and when they drink deadly* **p**,
Jas 3: 8 It is a restless evil, full of deadly **p**.

POLLUTE (POLLUTED)
Nu 35: 33 "'Do not **p** the land where you
Jude : 8 these ungodly people **p** their own

POLLUTED (POLLUTE)
Ezr 9: 11 is a land **p** by the corruption
Pr 25: 26 a **p** well are the righteous who give
Ac 15: 20 to abstain from food **p** by idols,
Jas 1: 27 oneself from being **p** by the world.

PONDER
Ps 64: 9 of God and **p** what he has done.
119: 95 me, but I will **p** your statutes.

POOR (POVERTY)
Dt 15: 4 need be no **p** people among you,
15: 11 There will always be **p** people
Ps 34: 6 This **p** man called, and the LORD
82: 3 uphold the cause of the **p**
112: 9 freely scattered their gifts to the **p**,
Pr 13: 7 another pretends to be **p**, yet has
14: 31 oppresses the **p** shows contempt
19: 1 Better the **p** whose walk is
19: 17 Whoever is kind to the **p** lends
22: 2 Rich and **p** have this in common:
22: 9 they share their food with the **p**.
28: 6 Better the **p** whose walk is

Pr 31: 20 She opens her arms to the **p**
Isa 61: 1 to proclaim good news to the **p**.
Mt 5: 3 "Blessed are the **p** in spirit,
11: 5 good news is proclaimed to the **p**.
19: 21 your possessions and give to the **p**,
26: 11 The **p** you will always have
Mk 12: 42 a **p** widow came and put in two
Ac 10: 4 and gifts to the **p** have come up as
1Co 13: 3 If I give all I possess to the **p**
2Co 8: 9 yet for your sake he became **p**,
Jas 2: 2 and a **p** man in filthy old clothes

PORTION
Dt 32: 9 For the LORD's **p** is his people,
2Ki 2: 9 "Let me inherit a double **p** of your
La 3: 24 to myself, "The LORD is my **p**;

POSSESS (POSSESSING POSSESSION POSSESSIONS)
Nu 33: 53 for I have given you the land to **p**.

POSSESSING (POSSESS)
2Co 6: 10 nothing, and yet **p** everything.

POSSESSION (POSSESS)
Ge 15: 7 give you this land to take **p** of it."
Nu 13: 30 go up and take **p** of the land,
Eph 1: 14 of those who are God's **p**—

POSSESSIONS (POSSESS)
Lk 12: 15 not consist in an abundance of **p**."
2Co 12: 14 because what I want is not your **p**
1Jn 3: 17 If anyone has material **p** and sees

POSSIBLE
Mt 19: 26 but with God all things are **p**."
Mk 9: 23 "Everything is **p** for one who
10: 27 all things are **p** with God."
Ro 12: 18 If it is **p**, as far as it depends on you
1Co 9: 22 by all **p** means I might save some.

POT (POTSHERDS POTTER POTTERY)
2Ki 4: 40 of God, there is death in the **p**!"
Jer 18: 4 the potter formed it into another **p**,

POTSHERDS (POT)
Isa 45: 9 but **p** among the **p** on the ground.

POTTER (POT)
Isa 29: 16 Can the pot say to the **p**,
45: 9 Does the clay say to the **p**,
64: 8 We are the clay, you are the **p**;
Jer 18: 6 do with you, Israel, as this **p** does?"
Ro 9: 21 Does not the **p** have the right

POTTERY (POT)
Ro 9: 21 of clay some **p** for special purposes

POUR (POURED)
Ps 62: 8 **p** out your hearts to him, for God
Joel 2: 28 I will **p** out my Spirit on all people.
Mal 3: 10 **p** out so much blessing that there
Ac 2: 17 I will **p** out my Spirit on all people.

POURED (POUR)
Ac 10: 45 the Holy Spirit had been **p** out
Ro 5: 5 because God's love has been **p**

POVERTY (POOR)
Pr 14: 23 but mere talk leads only to **p**.
21: 5 profit as surely as haste leads to **p**.
30: 8 give me neither **p** nor riches,
Mk 12: 44 she, out of her **p**, put in everything
2Co 8: 2 their extreme **p** welled up in rich
8: 9 you through his **p** might become

POWER (POWERFUL POWERS)
1Ch 29: 11 greatness and the **p** and the glory
2Ch 32: 7 for there is a greater **p** with us than
Job 36: 22 "God is exalted in his **p**. Who is
Ps 63: 2 and beheld your **p** and your glory.
68: 34 Proclaim the **p** of God,
147: 5 Great is our Lord and mighty in **p**;
Pr 24: 5 The wise prevail through great **p**,
Isa 40: 10 Sovereign LORD comes with **p**,
Zec 4: 6 'Not by might nor by **p**, but by my
Mt 22: 29 the Scriptures or the **p** of God.
24: 30 of heaven, with **p** and great glory.
Ac 1: 8 you will receive **p** when the Holy
4: 33 With great **p** the apostles
10: 38 with the Holy Spirit and **p**,
Ro 1: 16 because it is the **p** of God
1Co 1: 18 us who are being saved it is the **p**
15: 56 is sin, and the **p** of sin is the law.
2Co 12: 9 so that Christ's **p** may rest on me.
Eph 1: 19 his incomparably great **p** for us
Php 3: 10 to know the **p** of his resurrection
Col 1: 11 strengthened with all **p** according
2Ti 1: 7 us timid, but gives us **p**,
Heb 7: 16 of the **p** of an indestructible life.
Rev 4: 11 to receive glory and honor and **p**,
19: 1 glory and **p** belong to our God,
20: 6 second death has no **p** over them,

POWERFUL (POWER)
Ps 29: 4 The voice of the LORD is **p**;
Lk 24: 19 **p** in word and deed before God
2Th 1: 7 in blazing fire with his **p** angels.
Heb 1: 3 sustaining all things by his **p** word.
Jas 5: 16 prayer of a righteous person is **p**

POWERLESS
Ro 5: 6 when we were still **p**, Christ died
8: 3 what the law was **p** to do because it

POWERS (POWER)
Ro 8: 38 present nor the future, nor any **p**,
1Co 12: 10 to another miraculous **p**,
Col 1: 16 whether thrones or **p** or rulers
2: 15 And having disarmed the **p**

PRACTICE
Lev 19: 26 " 'Do not **p** divination or seek
Mt 23: 3 for they do not **p** what they preach.
Lk 8: 21 hear God's word and put it into **p**."
Ro 12: 13 who are in need. **P** hospitality.
1Ti 5: 4 put their religion into **p** by caring

PRAISE (PRAISED PRAISES PRAISING)
Ex 15: 2 and I will **p** him, my father's God,
Dt 32: 3 Oh, **p** the greatness of our God!
Ru 4: 14 "**P** be to the LORD, who this day
2Sa 22: 47 **P** be to my Rock!
1Ch 16: 25 the LORD and most worthy of **p**;
2Ch 20: 21 to **p** him for the splendor of his
Ps 8: 2 Through the **p** of children
33: 1 it is fitting for the upright to **p** him.
34: 1 his **p** will always be on my lips.
40: 3 mouth, a hymn of **p** to our God.
48: 1 and most worthy of **p**, in the city
68: 19 **P** be to the Lord, to God our Savior,
89: 5 The heavens **p** your wonders,
100: 4 give thanks to him and **p** his name.
105: 2 Sing to him, sing **p** to him;
106: 1 **P** the LORD. Give thanks
119:175 Let me live that I may **p** you,
139: 14 I **p** you because I am fearfully
145: 21 Let every creature **p** his holy name
146: 1 **P** the LORD. **P** the LORD, my soul.
150: 2 **p** him for his surpassing greatness.
150: 6 Let everything that has breath **p** the LORD. **P** the LORD.
Pr 27: 2 Let someone else **p** you, and not
27: 21 but people are tested by their **p**.
31: 31 let her works bring her **p** at the city
Mt 21: 16 Lord, have called forth your **p**'?"
Jn 12: 43 they loved human **p** more than **p** from God.
Eph 1: 6 to the **p** of his glorious grace,
1: 12 might be for the **p** of his glory.
1: 14 to the **p** of his glory.
Heb 13: 15 offer to God a sacrifice of **p**—
Jas 5: 13 Let them sing songs of **p**.

PRAISED (PRAISE)
1Ch 29: 10 David **p** the LORD in the presence
Ne 8: 6 Ezra **p** the LORD, the great God;
Da 2: 19 Then Daniel **p** the God of heaven
Ro 9: 5 who is God over all, forever **p**!
1Pe 4: 11 God may be **p** through Jesus Christ

PRAISES (PRAISE)
2Sa 22: 50 I will sing the **p** of your name.
Ps 47: 6 Sing **p** to God, sing **p**; sing **p**
147: 1 good it is to sing **p** to our God,
Pr 31: 28 her husband also, and he **p** her:

PRAISING (PRAISE)
Ac 10: 46 speaking in tongues and **p** God.
1Co 14: 16 when you are **p** God in the Spirit,

PRAY (PRAYED PRAYER PRAYERS PRAYING)
Dt 4: 7 our God is near us whenever we **p**
1Sa 12: 23 the LORD by failing to **p** for you.
2Ch 7: 14 will humble themselves and **p**
Job 42: 8 My servant Job will **p** for you,
Ps 122: 6 **P** for the peace of Jerusalem:
Mt 5: 44 and **p** for those who persecute you,
6: 5 for they love to **p** standing
6: 9 "This, then, is how you should **p**:
26: 36 here while I go over there and **p**."
Lk 6: 28 you, **p** for those who mistreat you.
18: 1 them that they should always **p**
22: 40 them, "**P** that you will not fall
Ro 8: 26 not know what we ought to **p** for,
1Co 14: 13 in a tongue should **p** that they may
1Th 5: 17 **p** continually,
Jas 5: 13 Let them **p**. Is anyone happy?
5: 16 **p** for each other so that you may be

Pr 17: 14 Starting a **q** is like breaching a dam
17: 19 Whoever loves a **q** loves sin;

QUARRELSOME (QUARREL)
Pr 19: 13 **q** wife is like the constant dripping
1Ti 3: 3 gentle, not **q**, not a lover of money.
2Ti 2: 24 the Lord's servant must not be **q**

QUENCH
1Th 5: 19 Do not **q** the Spirit.

QUICK-TEMPERED
Titus 1: 7 not **q**, not given to drunkenness,

QUIET (QUIETNESS)
Ps 23: 2 he leads me beside **q** waters,
Lk 19: 40 "if they keep **q**, the stones will cry
1Ti 2: 2 peaceful and **q** lives in all godliness
1Pe 3: 4 beauty of a gentle and **q** spirit,

QUIETNESS (QUIET)
Isa 30: 15 in **q** and trust is your strength,
32: 17 its effect will be **q** and confidence
1Ti 2: 11 woman should learn in **q** and full

QUIVER
Ps 127: 5 Blessed is the man whose **q** is full

RACE
Ecc 9: 11 The **r** is not to the swift or
1Co 9: 24 that in a **r** all the runners run,
2Ti 4: 7 I have finished the **r**, I have kept
Heb 12: 1 with perseverance the **r** marked

RACHEL
Daughter of Laban (Ge 29:16); wife of Jacob (Ge 29:28); bore two sons (Ge 30:22–24; 35:16–24; 46:19).

RADIANCE (RADIANT)
Heb 1: 3 The Son is the **r** of God's glory

RADIANT (RADIANCE)
Ex 34: 29 that his face was **r** because he had
Ps 34: 5 Those who look to him are **r**;
SS 5: 10 My beloved is **r** and ruddy,
Isa 60: 5 Then you will look and be **r**,
Eph 5: 27 her to himself as a **r** church,

RAIN (RAINBOW)
Mt 5: 45 and sends **r** on the righteous

RAINBOW (RAIN)
Ge 9: 13 I have set my **r** in the clouds, and it

RAISED (RISE)
Ro 4: 25 was **r** to life for our justification.
10: 9 your heart that God **r** him
1Co 15: 4 he was **r** on the third day according

RAN (RUN)
Jnh 1: 3 But Jonah **r** away from the LORD

RANSOM
Mt 20: 28 to give his life as a **r** for many."
Heb 9: 15 he has died as a **r** to set them free

RAVENS
1Ki 17: 6 The **r** brought him bread and meat
Lk 12: 24 Consider the **r**: They do not sow

READ (READS)
Jos 8: 34 Joshua **r** all the words of the law—
Ne 8: 8 understood what was being **r**.
2Co 3: 2 hearts, known and **r** by everyone.

READS (READ)
Rev 1: 3 is the one who **r** aloud the words

REAL (REALITY)
Jn 6: 55 For my flesh is **r** food and my blood is **r** drink.

REALITY (REAL)
Col 2: 17 the **r**, however, is found in Christ.

REAP (REAPS)
Job 4: 8 evil and those who sow trouble **r** it.
2Co 9: 6 generously will also **r** generously.

REAPS (REAP)
Gal 6: 7 A man **r** what he sows.

REASON
1Pe 3: 15 asks you to give the **r** for the hope

REBEKAH
Sister of Laban, secured as bride for Isaac (Ge 24). Mother of Esau and Jacob (Ge 25:19–26). Taken by Abimelek as sister of Isaac; returned (Ge 26:1–11). Encouraged Jacob to trick Isaac out of blessing (Ge 27:1–17).

REBEL
Mt 10: 21 children will **r** against their parents

REBUKE (REBUKING)
Pr 9: 8 **r** the wise and they will love you.
27: 5 Better is open **r** than hidden love.
Lk 17: 3 or sister sins against you, **r** them;
2Ti 4: 2 correct, **r** and encourage—
Rev 3: 19 Those whom I love I **r**

REBUKING (REBUKE)
2Ti 3: 16 and is useful for teaching, **r**,

RECEIVE (RECEIVED RECEIVES)
Ac 1: 8 you will **r** power when the Holy
20: 35 more blessed to give than to **r**.' "
2Co 6: 17 no unclean thing, and I will **r** you."
Rev 4: 11 to **r** glory and honor and power,

RECEIVED (RECEIVE)
Mt 6: 2 they have **r** their reward in full.
10: 8 Freely you have **r**; freely give.
1Co 11: 23 For I **r** from the Lord what I
Col 2: 6 just as you **r** Christ Jesus as Lord,
1Pe 4: 10 should use whatever gift you have **r**

RECEIVES (RECEIVE)
Mt 7: 8 For everyone who asks **r**;
Ac 10: 43 who believes in him **r** forgiveness

RECKONING
Isa 10: 3 What will you do on the day of **r**,

RECOGNIZE (RECOGNIZED)
Mt 7: 16 By their fruit you will **r** them.

RECOGNIZED (RECOGNIZE)
Mt 12: 33 be bad, for a tree is **r** by its fruit.
Ro 7: 13 in order that sin might be **r** as sin,

RECOMPENSE
Isa 40: 10 him, and his **r** accompanies him.

RECONCILE (RECONCILED RECONCILIATION)
Eph 2: 16 and in one body to **r** both of them

RECONCILED (RECONCILE)
Mt 5: 24 First go and be **r** to them;
Ro 5: 10 were **r** to him through the death
2Co 5: 18 who **r** us to himself through Christ

RECONCILIATION (RECONCILE)
Ro 5: 11 whom we have now received **r**.
11: 15 For if their rejection brought **r**
2Co 5: 18 and gave us the ministry of **r**:
5: 19 committed to us the message of **r**.

RECORD
Ps 130: 3 you, LORD, kept a **r** of sins, Lord,

RED
Isa 1: 18 though they are **r** as crimson,

REDEEM (REDEEMED REDEEMER REDEMPTION)
2Sa 7: 23 out to **r** as a people for himself,
Ps 49: 7 No one can **r** the life of another
Gal 4: 5 to **r** those under the law, that we

REDEEMED (REDEEM)
Gal 3: 13 Christ **r** us from the curse of the law
1Pe 1: 18 you were **r** from the empty way

REDEEMER (REDEEM)
Job 19: 25 I know that my **r** lives,

REDEMPTION (REDEEM)
Ps 130: 7 love and with him is full **r**.
Lk 21: 28 because your **r** is drawing near."
Ro 8: 23 to sonship, the **r** of our bodies.
Eph 1: 7 we have **r** through his blood,
Col 1: 14 in whom we have **r**, the forgiveness
Heb 9: 12 blood, thus obtaining eternal **r**.

REFUGE
Nu 35: 11 some towns to be your cities of **r**,
Dt 33: 27 The eternal God is your **r**,
Ru 2: 12 wings you have come to take **r**."
Ps 46: 1 God is our **r** and strength,
91: 2 "He is my **r** and my fortress,

REHOBOAM
Son of Solomon (1Ki 11:43; 1Ch 3:10). Harsh treatment of subjects caused divided kingdom (1Ki 12:1–24; 14:21–31; 2Ch 10–12).

REIGN (REIGNS)
Ro 6: 12 not let sin **r** in your mortal body
1Co 15: 25 he must **r** until he has put all his
2Ti 2: 12 if we endure, we will also **r** with
Rev 20: 6 **r** with him for a thousand years.

REIGNS (REIGN)
Ex 15: 18 "The LORD **r** for ever and ever."

REJECTED (REJECTS)
Ps 118: 22 stone the builders **r** has become
Isa 53: 3 was despised and **r** by mankind,
1Ti 4: 4 nothing is to be **r** if it is received
1Pe 2: 4 **r** by humans but chosen by God
2: 7 stone the builders **r** has become

REJECTS (REJECTED)
Lk 10: 16 whoever **r** me **r** him who sent me."
Jn 3: 36 whoever **r** the Son will not see life,

REJOICE (JOY)
Ps 66: 6 come, let us **r** in him.
118: 24 let us **r** today and be glad.
Pr 5: 18 you **r** in the wife of your youth.
Lk 10: 20 but **r** that your names are written
15: 6 together and says, '**R** with me;
Ro 12: 15 **R** with those who **r**;
Php 4: 4 **R** in the Lord always. I will say it again: **R**!

REJOICES (JOY)
Isa 61: 10 my soul **r** in my God.
Lk 1: 47 and my spirit **r** in God my Savior,
1Co 12: 26 is honored, every part **r** with it.
13: 6 delight in evil but **r** with the truth.

REJOICING (JOY)
Ps 30: 5 night, but **r** comes in the morning.
Lk 15: 7 the same way there will be more **r**
Ac 5: 41 **r** because they had been counted

RELIABLE
2Ti 2: 2 entrust to **r** people who will also be

RELIGION
1Ti 5: 4 of all to put their **r** into practice
Jas 1: 27 **R** that God our Father accepts as

REMAIN (REMAINS)
Nu 33: 55 you allow to **r** will become barbs
Jn 15: 7 If you **r** in me and my words **r**
Ro 13: 8 Let no debt **r** outstanding,
1Co 13: 13 And now these three **r**:

REMAINS (REMAIN)
Ps 146: 6 he **r** faithful forever.
2Ti 2: 13 if we are faithless, he **r** faithful,
Heb 7: 3 Son of God, he **r** a priest forever.

REMEMBER (REMEMBERS REMEMBRANCE)
Ex 20: 8 "**R** the Sabbath day by keeping it
1Ch 16: 12 **R** the wonders he has done,
Ecc 12: 1 **R** your Creator in the days of your
Jer 31: 34 and will **r** their sins no more."
Gal 2: 10 we should continue to **r** the poor,
Php 1: 3 I thank my God every time I **r** you.
Heb 8: 12 and will **r** their sins no more."

REMEMBERS (REMEMBER)
Ps 103: 14 are formed, he **r** that we are dust.
111: 5 he **r** his covenant forever.
Isa 43: 25 own sake, and **r** your sins no more.

REMEMBRANCE (REMEMBER)
1Co 11: 24 is for you; do this in **r** of me."

REMIND
Jn 14: 26 will **r** you of everything I have said

REMOVED
Ps 30: 11 you **r** my sackcloth and clothed me
103: 12 so far has he **r** our transgressions
Jn 20: 1 that the stone had been **r**

RENEW (RENEWED RENEWING)
Ps 51: 10 and **r** a steadfast spirit within me.
Isa 40: 31 in the LORD will **r** their strength.

RENEWED (RENEW)
Ps 103: 5 that your youth is **r** like the eagle's.
2Co 4: 16 yet inwardly we are being **r** day

RENEWING (RENEW)
Ro 12: 2 transformed by the **r** of your mind.

RENOUNCE (RENOUNCES)
Da 4: 27 **R** your sins by doing what is right,

RENOUNCES (RENOUNCE)
Pr 28: 13 confesses and **r** them finds mercy.

RENOWN
Isa 63: 12 to gain for himself everlasting **r**,
Jer 32: 20 have gained the **r** that is still yours.

REPAID (PAY)
Lk 14: 14 you will be **r** at the resurrection
Col 3: 25 Anyone who does wrong will be **r**

REPAY (PAY)
Dt 32: 35 It is mine to avenge; I will **r**.
Ru 2: 12 May the LORD **r** you for what you
Ro 12: 19 I will **r**," says the Lord.
1Pe 3: 9 the contrary, **r** evil with blessing,

REPENT (REPENTANCE REPENTS)
Job 42: 6 I despise myself and **r** in dust
Jer 15: 19 "If you **r**, I will restore you that you
Mt 4: 17 time on Jesus began to preach, "**R**,
Lk 13: 3 But unless you **r**, you too will all
17: 3 and if they **r**, forgive them.
Ac 2: 38 Peter replied, "**R** and be baptized,
17: 30 all people everywhere to **r**.

REPENTANCE (REPENT)
Lk 3: 8 Produce fruit in keeping with **r**.
5: 32 call the righteous, but sinners to **r**."
Ac 26: 20 demonstrate their **r** by their deeds.
2Co 7: 10 Godly sorrow brings **r** that leads

REPENTS (REPENT)
Lk 15: 10 of God over one sinner who **r**."

REPROACH
1Ti 3: 2 Now the overseer is to be above **r**,

REPUTATION
1Ti 3: 7 also have a good **r** with outsiders,

REQUESTS
Ps 20: 5 May the LORD grant all your **r**.
Php 4: 6 present your **r** to God.

REQUIRE
Mic 6: 8 what does the LORD **r** of you?

RESCUE (RESCUES)
Da 6: 20 been able to **r** you from the lions?"
2Pe 2: 9 the Lord knows how to **r** the godly

RESCUES (RESCUE)
1Th 1: 10 who **r** us from the coming wrath.

RESIST
Jas 4: 7 **R** the devil, and he will flee
1Pe 5: 9 **R** him, standing firm in the faith,

RESOLVED
Da 1: 8 Daniel **r** not to defile himself
1Co 2: 2 For I **r** to know nothing while I

RESPECT (RESPECTABLE)
Lev 19: 3 of you must **r** your mother
19: 32 show **r** for the elderly and revere
Mal 1: 6 a master, where is the **r** due me?"
1Th 4: 12 that your daily life may win the **r**
1Ti 3: 4 do so in a manner worthy of full **r**.
1Pe 2: 17 Show proper **r** to everyone,
3: 7 them with **r** as the weaker partner

RESPECTABLE (RESPECT)
1Ti 3: 2 self-controlled, **r**, hospitable,

REST
Ex 31: 15 seventh day is a day of sabbath **r**,
Ps 91: 1 the Most High will **r** in the shadow
Jer 6: 16 and you will find **r** for your souls.
Mt 11: 28 burdened, and I will give you **r**.

RESTITUTION
Ex 22: 3 who steals must certainly make **r**,
Lev 6: 5 must make **r** in full, add a fifth

RESTORE
Ps 51: 12 **R** to me the joy of your salvation
Gal 6: 1 by the Spirit should **r** that person

RESURRECTION
Mt 22: 30 the **r** people will neither marry nor
Lk 14: 14 be repaid at the **r** of the righteous."
Jn 11: 25 said to her, "I am the **r** and the life.
Ro 1: 4 in power by his **r** from the dead:
1Co 15: 12 say that there is no **r** of the dead?
Php 3: 10 yes, to know the power of his **r**
Rev 20: 5 This is the first **r**.

RETRIBUTION
Jer 51: 56 For the LORD is a God of **r**;

RETURN
2Ch 30: 9 If you **r** to the LORD, then your
Ne 1: 9 but if you **r** to me and obey my
Isa 55: 11 It will not **r** to me empty, but will
Hos 6: 1 "Come, let us **r** to the LORD.
Joel 2: 12 "**r** to me with all your heart,

REVEALED (REVELATION)
Dt 29: 29 but the things **r** belong to us
Isa 40: 5 the glory of the LORD will be **r**,
Mt 11: 25 and **r** them to little children.
Ro 1: 17 the righteousness of God is **r**—
8: 18 with the glory that will be **r** in us.

REVELATION (REVEALED)
Gal 1: 12 I received it by **r** from Jesus Christ.
Rev 1: 1 The **r** from Jesus Christ,

REVENGE (VENGEANCE)
Lev 19: 18 "'Do not seek **r** or bear a grudge
Ro 12: 19 Do not take **r**, my dear friends,

REVERE (REVERENCE)
Ps 33: 8 all the people of the world **r** him.

RULES (RULE)
Ps 103: 19 heaven, and his kingdom **r** over all.
Lk 22: 26 and the one who **r** like the one who
2Ti 2: 5 by competing according to the **r**.

RUMORS
Mt 24: 6 You will hear of wars and **r** of wars,

RUN (RAN)
Isa 40: 31 they will **r** and not grow weary,
1Co 9: 24 **R** in such a way as to get the prize.
Heb 12: 1 let us **r** with perseverance the race

RUTH

Moabitess; widow who went to Bethlehem with mother-in-law Naomi (Ru 1). Gleaned in field of Boaz; shown favor (Ru 2). Proposed marriage to Boaz (Ru 3). Married (Ru 4:1–12); bore Obed, ancestor of David (Ru 4:13–22), Jesus (Mt 1:5).

SABBATH
Ex 20: 8 "Remember the **S** day by keeping it
Dt 5: 12 "Observe the **S** day by keeping it
Col 2: 16 New Moon celebration or a **S** day.

SACKCLOTH
Mt 11: 21 would have repented long ago in **s**

SACRED
Mt 7: 6 "Do not give dogs what is **s**;
1Co 3: 17 for God's temple is **s**, and you

SACRIFICE (SACRIFICED)
Ge 22: 2 **S** him there as a burnt offering
Ex 12: 27 'It is the Passover **s** to the LORD,
1Sa 15: 22 To obey is better than **s**,
Ps 51: 17 My **s**, O God, is a broken spirit;
Hos 6: 6 not **s**, and acknowledgment of God
Mt 9: 13 'I desire mercy, not **s**.'
Ro 12: 1 to offer your bodies as a living **s**,
Heb 9: 26 away with sin by the **s** of himself.
13: 15 offer to God a **s** of praise—
1Jn 2: 2 He is the atoning **s** for our sins,

SACRIFICED (SACRIFICE)
1Co 5: 7 our Passover lamb, has been **s**.
8: 1 Now about food **s** to idols:
Heb 9: 28 so Christ was **s** once to take away

SADDUCEES
Mk 12: 18 Then the **S**, who say there is no

SAFE (SAVE)
Ps 37: 3 in the land and enjoy **s** pasture.
Pr 18: 10 the righteous run to it and are **s**.

SAFETY (SAVE)
Ps 4: 8 alone, LORD, make me dwell in **s**.
1Th 5: 3 "Peace and **s**," destruction will

SAINTS See FAITHFUL, [GOD'S] PEOPLE

SAKE
Ps 44: 22 your **s** we face death all day long;
Php 3: 7 consider loss for the **s** of Christ.
Heb 11: 26 disgrace for the **s** of Christ as

SALT
Ge 19: 26 back, and she became a pillar of **s**.
Mt 5: 13 "You are the **s** of the earth.

SALVATION (SAVE)
Ex 15: 2 he has become my **s**.
1Ch 16: 23 proclaim his **s** day after day.
Ps 27: 1 The LORD is my light and my **s**—
51: 12 Restore to me the joy of your **s**
62: 2 Truly he is my rock and my **s**;
85: 9 Surely his **s** is near those who fear
96: 2 proclaim his **s** day after day.
Isa 25: 9 let us rejoice and be glad in his **s**."
45: 17 the LORD with an everlasting **s**;
51: 6 But my **s** will last forever,
59: 17 and the helmet of **s** on his head;
61: 10 has clothed me with garments of **s**
Jnh 2: 9 '**S** comes from the LORD.'"
Lk 2: 30 For my eyes have seen your **s**,
Jn 4: 22 we do know, for **s** is from the Jews.
Ac 4: 12 **S** is found in no one else, for there
13: 47 that you may bring **s** to the ends
Ro 11: 11 **s** has come to the Gentiles to make
2Co 7: 10 brings repentance that leads to **s**
Eph 6: 17 Take the helmet of **s** and the sword
Php 2: 12 to work out your **s** with fear
1Th 5: 8 and the hope of **s** as a helmet.
2Ti 3: 15 make you wise for **s** through faith
Heb 2: 3 we escape if we ignore so great a **s**?
6: 9 the things that have to do with **s**.
1Pe 1: 10 Concerning this **s**, the prophets,
2: 2 by it you may grow up in your **s**,

SAMARITAN
Lk 10: 33 But a **S**, as he traveled, came where

SAMSON

Danite judge. Birth promised (Jdg 13). Married to Philistine (Jdg 14). Vengeance on Philistines (Jdg 15). Betrayed by Delilah (Jdg 16:1–22). Death (Jdg 16:23–31). Feats of strength: killed lion (Jdg 14:6), 30 Philistines (Jdg 14:19), 1,000 Philistines with jawbone (Jdg 15:13–17), carried off gates of Gaza (Jdg 16:3), pushed down temple of Dagon (Jdg 16:25–30).

SAMUEL

Ephraimite judge and prophet (Heb 11:32). Birth prayed for (1Sa 1:10–18). Dedicated to temple by Hannah (1Sa 1:21–28). Raised by Eli (1Sa 2:11, 18–26). Called as prophet (1Sa 3). Led Israel to victory over Philistines (1Sa 7). Asked by Israel for a king (1Sa 8). Anointed Saul as king (1Sa 9–10). Farewell speech (1Sa 12). Rebuked Saul for sacrifice (1Sa 13). Announced rejection of Saul (1Sa 15). Anointed David as king (1Sa 16). Protected David from Saul (1Sa 19:18–24). Death (1Sa 25:1). Returned from dead to condemn Saul (1Sa 28).

SANCTIFIED (SANCTIFY)
Ac 20: 32 among all those who are **s**.
Ro 15: 16 to God, **s** by the Holy Spirit.
1Co 6: 11 you were **s**, you were justified
7: 14 husband has been **s** through his
Heb 10: 29 blood of the covenant that **s** them,

SANCTIFY (SANCTIFIED SANCTIFYING)
1Th 5: 23 peace, **s** you through and through.

SANCTIFYING (SANCTIFY)
2Th 2: 13 be saved through the **s** work

SANCTUARY
Ex 25: 8 "Then have them make a **s** for me,

SAND
Ge 22: 17 sky and as the **s** on the seashore.
Mt 7: 26 man who built his house on **s**.

SANDALS
Ex 3: 5 "Take off your **s**, for the place
Jos 5: 15 "Take off your **s**, for the place

SANG (SING)
Job 38: 7 while the morning stars **s** together
Rev 5: 9 And they **s** a new song, saying:

SARAH

Wife of Abraham, originally named Sarai; barren (Ge 11:29–31; 1Pe 3:6). Taken by Pharaoh as Abraham's sister; returned (Ge 12:10–20). Gave Hagar to Abraham; sent her away in pregnancy (Ge 16). Name changed; Isaac promised (Ge 17:15–21; 18:10–15; Heb 11:11). Taken by Abimelek as Abraham's sister; returned (Ge 20). Isaac born; Hagar and Ishmael sent away (Ge 21:1–21; Gal 4:21–31). Death (Ge 23).

SATAN
Job 1: 6 and **S** also came with them.
Zec 3: 2 to **S**, "The LORD rebuke you, **S**!
Mk 4: 15 **S** comes and takes away the word
2Co 11: 14 **S** himself masquerades as an angel
12: 7 a messenger of **S**, to torment me.
Rev 12: 9 or **S**, who leads the whole world
20: 2 **S**, and bound him for a thousand
20: 7 **S** will be released from his prison

SATISFIED (SATISFY)
Isa 53: 11 he will see the light of life and be **s**;

SATISFIES (SATISFY)
Ps 103: 5 **s** your desires with good things

SATISFY (SATISFIED SATISFIES)
Isa 55: 2 and your labor on what does not **s**?

SAUL

1. Benjamite; anointed by Samuel as first king of Israel (1Sa 9–10). Defeated Ammonites (1Sa 11). Rebuked for offering sacrifice (1Sa 13:1–15). Defeated Philistines (1Sa 14). Rejected as king for failing to annihilate Amalekites (1Sa 15). Soothed from evil spirit by David (1Sa 16:14–23). Sent David against Goliath (1Sa 17). Jealousy and attempted murder of David (1Sa 18:1–11). Gave David Michal as wife (1Sa 18:12–30). Second attempt to kill David (1Sa 19). Anger at Jonathan (1Sa 20:26–34). Pursued David: killed priests at Nob (1Sa 22), went to Keilah and Ziph (1Sa 23), life spared by David at En Gedi (1Sa 24) and in his tent (1Sa 26). Rebuked by Samuel's spirit for consulting witch at Endor (1Sa 28). Wounded by Philistines; took his own life (1Sa 31; 1Ch 10).

2. See PAUL

SAVE (SAFE SAFETY SALVATION SAVED SAVIOR)
Isa 63: 1 proclaiming victory, mighty to **s**."
Mt 1: 21 because he will **s** his people
16: 25 wants to **s** their life will lose it,
Lk 19: 10 came to seek and to **s** the lost."
Jn 3: 17 but to **s** the world through him.
1Ti 1: 15 came into the world to **s** sinners—
Jas 5: 20 of their way will **s** them from death

SAVED (SAVE)
Ps 34: 6 he **s** him out of all his troubles.
Isa 45: 22 "Turn to me and be **s**, all you ends
Joel 2: 32 the name of the LORD will be **s**;
Mk 13: 13 stands firm to the end will be **s**.
16: 16 *believes and is baptized will be* **s**,
Jn 10: 9 enters through me will be **s**.
Ac 4: 12 mankind by which we must be **s**."
16: 30 "Sirs, what must I do to be **s**?"
Ro 9: 27 the sea, only the remnant will be **s**.
10: 9 him from the dead, you will be **s**.
1Co 3: 15 will suffer loss but yet will be **s**—
15: 2 By this gospel you are **s**, if you hold
Eph 2: 5 it is by grace you have been **s**.
2: 8 For it is by grace you have been **s**,
1Ti 2: 4 who wants all people to be **s**

SAVIOR (SAVE)
Ps 89: 26 Father, my God, the Rock my **S**.'
Isa 43: 11 and apart from me there is no **s**.
Hos 13: 4 no God but me, no **S** except me.
Lk 1: 47 and my spirit rejoices in God my **S**,
2: 11 town of David a **S** has been born
Jn 4: 42 that this man really is the **S**
Eph 5: 23 his body, of which he is the **S**.
1Ti 4: 10 God, who is the **S** of all people,
Titus 2: 10 about God our **S** attractive.
2: 13 the glory of our great God and **S**,
3: 4 and love of God our **S** appeared,
1Jn 4: 14 his Son to be the **S** of the world.
Jude : 25 to the only God our **S** be glory,

SCALES
Lev 19: 36 Use honest **s** and honest weights,
Da 5: 27 You have been weighed on the **s**

SCAPEGOAT (GOAT)
Lev 16: 10 it into the wilderness as a **s**.

SCARLET
Isa 1: 18 "Though your sins are like **s**,

SCATTERED
Jer 31: 10 'He who **s** Israel will gather them
Ac 8: 4 who had been **s** preached the word

SCEPTER
Rev 19: 15 "He will rule them with an iron **s**."

SCHEMES
2Co 2: 11 For we are not unaware of his **s**.
Eph 6: 11 your stand against the devil's **s**.

SCOFFERS
2Pe 3: 3 that in the last days **s** will come,

SCORPION
Rev 9: 5 of the sting of a **s** when it strikes.

SCRIPTURE (SCRIPTURES)
Jn 10: 35 and **S** cannot be set aside—
1Ti 4: 13 yourself to the public reading of **S**,
2Ti 3: 16 All **S** is God-breathed and is useful
2Pe 1: 20 that no prophecy of **S** came

SCRIPTURES (SCRIPTURE)
Lk 24: 27 in all the **S** concerning himself.
Jn 5: 39 You study the **S** diligently because
Ac 17: 11 examined the **S** every day to see

SCROLL
Eze 3: 1 eat what is before you, eat this **s**;

SEA
Ex 14: 16 the Israelites can go through the **s**
Isa 57: 20 the wicked are like the tossing **s**,
Mic 7: 19 iniquities into the depths of the **s**.
Jas 1: 6 who doubts is like a wave of the **s**,
Rev 13: 1 I saw a beast coming out of the **s**.

SEAL (SEALS)
Jn 6: 27 God the Father has placed his **s**
2Co 1: 22 set his **s** of ownership on us,
Eph 1: 13 you were marked in him with a **s**,

SEALS (SEAL)
Rev 5: 2 "Who is worthy to break the **s**
6: 1 opened the first of the seven **s**.

SEARCH (SEARCHED SEARCHES SEARCHING)
Ps 4: 4 beds, **s** your hearts and be silent.
139: 23 **S** me, God, and know my heart;
Pr 2: 4 and **s** for it as for hidden treasure,
Jer 17: 10 "I the LORD **s** the heart
Eze 34: 16 I will **s** for the lost and bring back
Lk 15: 8 and **s** carefully until she finds it?

SEARCHED (SEARCH)
Ps 139: 1 You have **s** me, LORD, and you

SEARCHES (SEARCH)
Ro 8: 27 who **s** our hearts knows the mind
1Co 2: 10 The Spirit **s** all things, even the

SEARCHING (SEARCH)
Am 8: 12 east, **s** for the word of the LORD,

SEARED
1Ti 4: 2 whose consciences have been **s** as

SEASON
2Ti 4: 2 be prepared in **s** and out of **s**;

SEAT (SEATED SEATS)
Da 7: 9 and the Ancient of Days took his **s**.
2Co 5: 10 all appear before the judgment **s**

SEATED (SEAT)
Ps 47: 8 God is **s** on his holy throne.
Isa 6: 1 high and exalted, **s** on a throne;
Col 3: 1 Christ is, **s** at the right hand of God.

SEATS (SEAT)
Lk 11: 43 you love the most important **s**

SECRET (SECRETS)
Dt 29: 29 The **s** things belong to the LORD
Jdg 16: 6 "Tell me the **s** of your great
Ps 90: 8 you, our **s** sins in the light of your
Pr 11: 13 but a trustworthy person keeps a **s**.
Mt 6: 4 so that your giving may be in **s**.
2Co 4: 2 we have renounced **s** and shameful
Php 4: 12 have learned the **s** of being content

SECRETS (SECRET)
Ps 44: 21 since he knows the **s** of the heart?
1Co 14: 25 as the **s** of their hearts are laid bare.

SECURE (SECURITY)
Ps 112: 8 Their hearts are **s**, they will have
Heb 6: 19 an anchor for the soul, firm and **s**.

SECURITY (SECURE)
Job 31: 24 or said to pure gold, 'You are my **s**,'

SEED (SEEDS)
Lk 8: 11 The **s** is the word of God.
1Co 3: 6 I planted the **s**, Apollos watered it,
2Co 9: 10 he who supplies **s** to the sower
Gal 3: 29 you are Abraham's **s**, and heirs
1Pe 1: 23 again, not of perishable **s**,

SEEDS (SEED)
Jn 12: 24 But if it dies, it produces many **s**.
Gal 3: 16 Scripture does not say "and to **s**,"

SEEK (SEEKS SELF-SEEKING)
Dt 4: 29 you will find him if you **s** him
1Ch 28: 9 If you **s** him, he will be found
2Ch 7: 14 pray and **s** my face and turn
Ps 119: 10 I **s** you with all my heart; do not let
Isa 55: 6 **S** the LORD while he may be
65: 1 found by those who did not **s** me.
Mt 6: 33 But **s** first his kingdom and his
Lk 19: 10 For the Son of Man came to **s**
Ro 10: 20 found by those who did not **s** me;
1Co 7: 27 Do not **s** to be released.

SEEKS (SEEK)
Jn 4: 23 the kind of worshipers the Father **s**.

SEER
1Sa 9: 9 of today used to be called a **s**.)

SELF-CONTROL (CONTROL)
1Co 7: 5 tempt you because of your lack of **s**.
Gal 5: 23 gentleness and **s**.
2Pe 1: 6 and to knowledge, **s**; and to **s**,

SELF-CONTROLLED (CONTROL)
1Ti 3: 2 his wife, temperate, **s**, respectable,
Titus 1: 8 what is good, who is **s**, upright,
2: 2 worthy of respect, **s**, and sound
2: 5 to be **s** and pure, to be busy
2: 6 encourage the young men to be **s**.
2: 12 to live **s**, upright and godly lives

SELF-INDULGENCE
Mt 23: 25 inside they are full of greed and **s**.

SELFISH
Ps 119: 36 statutes and not toward **s** gain.
Pr 18: 1 unfriendly person pursues **s** ends
Gal 5: 20 fits of rage, **s** ambition, dissensions,
Php 1: 17 preach Christ out of **s** ambition,
2: 3 Do nothing out of **s** ambition
Jas 3: 14 envy and **s** ambition in your hearts,
3: 16 you have envy and **s** ambition,

SELF-SEEKING (SEEK)
1Co 13: 5 it is not **s**, it is not easily angered,

SEND (SENDING SENT)
Isa 6: 8 And I said, "Here am I. **S** me!"
Mt 9: 38 to **s** out workers into his harvest
Jn 16: 7 but if I go, I will **s** him to you.

SENDING (SEND)
Jn 20: 21 the Father has sent me, I am **s** you."

SENSES
Lk 15: 17 "When he came to his **s**, he said,
1Co 15: 34 Come back to your **s** as you ought,
2Ti 2: 26 that they will come to their **s**

SENSUAL
Col 2: 23 value in restraining **s** indulgence.

SENT (SEND)
Isa 55: 11 achieve the purpose for which I **s** it.
Mt 10: 40 me welcomes the one who **s** me.
Jn 4: 34 "is to do the will of him who **s** me
Ro 10: 15 anyone preach unless they are **s**?
1Jn 4: 10 **s** his Son as an atoning sacrifice

SEPARATE (SEPARATED SEPARATES)
Mt 19: 6 has joined together, let no one **s**."
Ro 8: 35 Who shall **s** us from the love
1Co 7: 10 A wife must not **s** from her
2Co 6: 17 "Come out from them and be **s**,

SEPARATED (SEPARATE)
Isa 59: 2 your iniquities have **s** you from

SEPARATES (SEPARATE)
Pr 16: 28 and a gossip **s** close friends.

SERPENT
Ge 3: 1 Now the **s** was more crafty than
Rev 12: 9 that ancient **s** called the devil,

SERVANT (SERVANTS)
1Sa 3: 10 "Speak, for your **s** is listening."
Mt 20: 26 great among you must be your **s**,
25: 21 'Well done, good and faithful **s**!
Php 2: 7 by taking the very nature of a **s**,
2Ti 2: 24 And the Lord's **s** must not be

SERVANTS (SERVANT)
Lk 17: 10 do, should say, 'We are unworthy **s**;
Jn 15: 15 I no longer call you **s**,

SERVE (SERVICE SERVING)
Dt 10: 12 to **s** the LORD your God with all
Jos 22: 5 and to **s** him with all your heart
24: 15 household, we will **s** the LORD."
Mt 4: 10 Lord your God, and **s** him only.'"
6: 24 "No one can **s** two masters.
6: 24 You cannot **s** both God and money.
20: 28 but to **s**, and to give his life as
Eph 6: 7 **S** wholeheartedly, as if you were

SERVICE (SERVE)
1Co 12: 5 There are different kinds of **s**,
Eph 4: 12 to equip his people for works of **s**,

SERVING (SERVE)
Ro 12: 11 your spiritual fervor, **s** the Lord.
Eph 6: 7 as if you were **s** the Lord,
Col 3: 24 It is the Lord Christ you are **s**.
2Ti 2: 4 No one **s** as a soldier gets entangled

SEVEN (SEVENTH)
Ge 7: 2 Take with you **s** pairs of every kind
Jos 6: 4 march around the city **s** times,
1Ki 19: 18 Yet I reserve **s** thousand in Israel—
Pr 6: 16 hates, **s** that are detestable to him:
24: 16 though the righteous fall **s** times,
Isa 4: 1 that day **s** women will take hold
Da 9: 25 comes, there will be **s** 'sevens,'
Mt 18: 21 sins against me? Up to **s** times?"
Lk 11: 26 takes **s** other spirits more wicked
Ro 11: 4 myself **s** thousand who have not
Rev 1: 4 To the **s** churches in the province
1: 4 from the **s** spirits before his throne,
6: 1 Lamb opened the first of the **s** seals.
8: 2 I saw the **s** angels who stand before
8: 2 and **s** trumpets were given to them.
10: 4 And when the **s** thunders spoke,
15: 7 to the **s** angels **s** golden bowls filled

SEVENTH (SEVEN)
Ge 2: 2 so on the **s** day he rested from all
Ex 23: 12 but on the **s** day do not work,

SEX (SEXUAL SEXUALLY)
1Co 6: 9 nor men who have **s** with men

SEXUAL (SEX)
Mt 5: 32 except for **s** immorality, makes her
19: 9 except for **s** immorality,
1Co 6: 13 is not meant for **s** immorality
6: 18 Flee from **s** immorality.
7: 1 a man not to have **s** relations
10: 8 should not commit **s** immorality,
Eph 5: 3 not be even a hint of **s** immorality,
1Th 4: 3 you should avoid **s** immorality;

SEXUALLY (SEX)
1Co 5: 9 associate with **s** immoral people—
6: 18 but whoever sins **s**, sins against

SHADOW
Ps 36: 7 take refuge in the **s** of your wings.
Heb 10: 1 The law is only a **s** of the good

SHALLUM
King of Israel (2Ki 15:10–16).

SHAME (ASHAMED)
Ps 22: 5 they trusted and were not put to **s**.
34: 5 faces are never covered with **s**.
Pr 13: 18 discipline comes to poverty and **s**,
Heb 12: 2 scorning its **s**, and sat down

SHARE (SHARED)
Ge 21: 10 that woman's son will never **s**
Lk 3: 11 who has two shirts should **s**
Gal 4: 30 the slave woman's son will never **s**
6: 6 the word should **s** all good things
Eph 4: 28 they may have something to **s**
1Ti 6: 18 to be generous and willing to **s**.
Heb 12: 10 order that we may **s** in his holiness.
13: 16 to do good and to **s** with others,

SHARED (SHARE)
Heb 2: 14 he too **s** in their humanity so

SHARON
SS 2: 1 I am a rose of **S**, a lily

SHARPER
Heb 4: 12 **S** than any double-edged sword,

SHED (SHEDDING)
Ge 9: 6 by humans shall their blood be **s**;
Col 1: 20 through his blood, **s** on the cross.

SHEDDING (SHED)
Heb 9: 22 without the **s** of blood there is no

SHEEP
Ps 100: 3 are his people, the **s** of his pasture.
119:176 I have strayed like a lost **s**.
Isa 53: 6 We all, like **s**, have gone astray,
Jer 50: 6 "My people have been lost **s**;
Eze 34: 11 I myself will search for my **s**
Mt 9: 36 helpless, like **s** without a shepherd.
Jn 10: 3 He calls his own **s** by name
10: 15 and I lay down my life for the **s**.
10: 27 My **s** listen to my voice;
21: 17 Jesus said, "Feed my **s**.
1Pe 2: 25 For "you were like **s** going astray,"

SHELTER
Ps 61: 4 take refuge in the **s** of your wings.
91: 1 in the **s** of the Most High will rest

SHEM
Son of Noah (Ge 5:32; 6:10). Blessed (Ge 9:26). Descendants (Ge 10:21–31; 11:10–32).

SHEPHERD (SHEPHERDS)
Ps 23: 1 The LORD is my **s**, I lack nothing.
Isa 40: 11 He tends his flock like a **s**:
Jer 31: 10 will watch over his flock like a **s**.'
Eze 34: 12 a **s** looks after his scattered flock
Zec 11: 17 "Woe to the worthless **s**,
Mt 9: 36 and helpless, like sheep without a **s**.
Jn 10: 11 "I am the good **s**. The good **s** lays
10: 16 there shall be one flock and one **s**.
1Pe 5: 4 And when the Chief **S** appears,

SHEPHERDS (SHEPHERD)
Jer 23: 1 "Woe to the **s** who are destroying
Lk 2: 8 there were **s** living out in the fields
Ac 20: 28 Be **s** of the church of God,
1Pe 5: 2 Be **s** of God's flock that is under

SHIELD
Ps 28: 7 LORD is my strength and my **s**;
Eph 6: 16 take up the **s** of faith,

SHINE (SHONE)
Ps 4: 6 Let the light of your face **s** on us.
80: 1 between the cherubim, **s** forth
Isa 60: 1 "Arise, **s**, for your light has come,
Da 12: 3 are wise will **s** like the brightness
Mt 5: 16 let your light **s** before others,
13: 43 the righteous will **s** like the sun
2Co 4: 6 made his light **s** in our hearts
Eph 5: 14 the dead, and Christ will **s** on you."

SHIPWRECK (SHIPWRECKED)
1Ti 1: 19 so have suffered **s** with regard

SHIPWRECKED (SHIPWRECK)
2Co 11: 25 three times I was **s**, I spent a night

SHONE (SHINE)
Mt 17: 2 His face **s** like the sun, and his
Lk 2: 9 glory of the Lord **s** around them,
Rev 21: 11 It **s** with the glory of God, and its

SHORT
Isa 59: 1 of the LORD is not too **s** to save,
Ro 3: 23 and fall **s** of the glory of God,

SHOULDERS
Isa 9: 6 the government will be on his **s**.
Lk 15: 5 finds it, he joyfully puts it on his **s**

SHOWED
1Jn 4: 9 This is how God **s** his love among

SHREWD
Mt 10: 16 Therefore be as **s** as snakes and as

SHUN
Job 28: 28 and to **s** evil is understanding."
Pr 3: 7 fear the LORD and **s** evil.

SICK
Pr 13: 12 Hope deferred makes the heart **s**,
Mt 9: 12 who need a doctor, but the **s**.
25: 36 I was **s** and you looked after me,
Jas 5: 14 Is anyone among you **s**?

SICKLE
Joel 3: 13 Swing the **s**, for the harvest is ripe.

SIDE
Ps 91: 7 A thousand may fall at your **s**,
124: 1 the LORD had not been on our **s**—
2Ti 4: 17 Lord stood at my **s** and gave me

SIGHT
Ps 90: 4 years in your **s** are like a day
116: 15 in the **s** of the LORD is the death
2Co 5: 7 For we live by faith, not by **s**.
1Pe 3: 4 which is of great worth in God's **s**.

SIGN (SIGNS)
Isa 7: 14 the Lord himself will give you a **s**:

SIGNS (SIGN)
Mt 24: 24 and perform great **s** and wonders
Mk 16: 17 *these **s** will accompany those who*
Jn 3: 2 could perform the **s** you are doing
9: 16 can a sinner perform such **s**?"
20: 30 Jesus performed many other **s**
1Co 1: 22 Jews demand **s** and Greeks look

SILENT
Pr 17: 28 are thought wise if they keep **s**,
Isa 53: 7 as a sheep before its shearers is **s**,
Hab 2: 20 let all the earth be **s** before him.
1Co 14: 34 Women should remain **s**

SILVER
Pr 25: 11 of **s** is a ruling rightly given.
Hag 2: 8 'The **s** is mine and the gold is
1Co 3: 12 on this foundation using gold, **s**,

SIMON
1. See PETER.
2. Apostle, called the Zealot (Mt 10:4; Mk 3:18; Lk 6:15; Ac 1:13).
3. Samaritan sorcerer (Ac 8:9–24).

SIN (SINFUL SINNED SINNER SINNERS SINNING SINS)
Nu 5: 7 and must confess the **s** they have
32: 23 sure that your **s** will find you out.
Dt 24: 16 each will die for their own **s**.
1Ki 8: 46 there is no one who does not **s**—
2Ch 7: 14 I will forgive their **s** and will heal
Ps 4: 4 Tremble and do not **s**; when you
32: 2 is the one whose **s** the LORD does
32: 5 And you forgave the guilt of my **s**.
51: 2 iniquity and cleanse me from my **s**.
66: 18 If I had cherished **s** in my heart,
119: 11 that I might not **s** against you.
119:133 to your word; let no **s** rule over me.
Isa 6: 7 taken away and your **s** atoned for."
Mic 7: 18 you, who pardons **s** and forgives
Jn 1: 29 who takes away the **s** of the world!
8: 34 everyone who sins is a slave to **s**.
Ro 5: 12 just as **s** entered the world through
5: 20 But where **s** increased,
6: 11 count yourselves dead to **s** but alive
6: 23 For the wages of **s** is death,
14: 23 that does not come from faith is **s**.
2Co 5: 21 God made him who had no **s** to be **s**
Gal 6: 1 if someone is caught in a **s**,
Heb 9: 26 to do away with **s** by the sacrifice
11: 25 to enjoy the fleeting pleasures of **s**.
12: 1 and the **s** that so easily entangles.
1Pe 2: 22 "He committed no **s**, and no deceit
1Jn 1: 8 If we claim to be without **s**,
3: 4 in fact, **s** is lawlessness.
3: 5 away our sins. And in him is no **s**.
3: 9 is born of God will continue to **s**,
5: 18 born of God does not continue to **s**;

SINCERE
Ro 12: 9 Love must be **s**. Hate what is evil;
Heb 10: 22 us draw near to God with a **s** heart

SINFUL (SIN)
Ps 51: 5 Surely I was **s** at birth,
Ro 7: 5 the **s** passions aroused by the law
1Pe 2: 11 to abstain from **s** desires,

SINFUL NATURE See FLESH

SING (SANG SINGING SONG SONGS)
Ps 30: 4 **S** the praises of the LORD, you his
47: 6 **S** praises to God, **s** praises; **s** praises
59: 16 in the morning I will **s** of your love
89: 1 I will **s** of the LORD's great love
101: 1 I will **s** of your love and justice;
Eph 5: 19 **S** and make music from your heart

SINGING (SING)
Ps 63: 5 **s** lips my mouth will praise you.
Ac 16: 25 were praying and **s** hymns to God,

SINNED (SIN)
2Sa 12: 13 "I have **s** against the LORD."
Job 1: 5 "Perhaps my children have **s**
Ps 51: 4 have I **s** and done what is evil
Da 9: 5 we have **s** and done wrong.
Mic 7: 9 Because I have **s** against him, I will
Lk 15: 18 I have **s** against heaven and against
Ro 3: 23 for all have **s** and fall short
1Jn 1: 10 If we claim we have not **s**, we make

SINNER (SIN)
Ecc 9: 18 war, but one **s** destroys much good.
Lk 15: 7 heaven over one **s** who repents
18: 13 said, 'God, have mercy on me, a **s**.'
Jas 5: 20 Whoever turns a **s** from the error
1Pe 4: 18 become of the ungodly and the **s**?"

SINNERS (SIN)
Ps 1: 1 stand in the way that **s** take or sit
Pr 23: 17 Do not let your heart envy **s**,
Mt 9: 13 come to call the righteous, but **s**."
Ro 5: 8 While we were still **s**, Christ died
1Ti 1: 15 came into the world to save **s**—

SINNING (SIN)
Ex 20: 20 be with you to keep you from **s**."
1Co 15: 34 senses as you ought, and stop **s**;
Heb 10: 26 If we deliberately keep on **s** after
1Jn 3: 6 one who lives in him keeps on **s**.
3: 9 they cannot go on **s**, because they

SINS (SIN)
Ezr 9: 6 because our **s** are higher than our
Ps 19: 13 your servant also from willful **s**;
32: 1 are forgiven, whose **s** are covered.
103: 3 who forgives all your **s** and heals
130: 3 LORD, kept a record of **s**, Lord,
Pr 28: 13 Whoever conceals their **s** does not
Isa 1: 18 "Though your **s** are like scarlet,
43: 25 and remembers your **s** no more.
59: 2 your **s** have hidden his face
Eze 18: 4 The one who **s** is the one who will
Mt 1: 21 will save his people from their **s**."
18: 15 "If your brother or sister **s**,
Lk 11: 4 Forgive us our **s**, for we also forgive everyone who **s** against us.
17: 3 your brother or sister **s** against you,
Ac 22: 16 be baptized and wash your **s** away,
1Co 15: 3 Christ died for our **s** according
Eph 2: 1 dead in your transgressions and **s**,
Col 2: 13 He forgave us all our **s**,
Heb 1: 3 he had provided purification for **s**,
7: 27 He sacrificed for their **s** once for all
8: 12 will remember their **s** no more."
10: 12 for all time one sacrifice for **s**,
Jas 5: 16 Therefore confess your **s** to each
5: 20 and cover over a multitude of **s**.
1Pe 2: 24 so that we might die to **s** and live
3: 18 For Christ also suffered once for **s**,
1Jn 1: 9 If we confess our **s**, he is faithful
1: 9 will forgive us our **s** and purify us
Rev 1: 5 freed us from our **s** by his blood,

SITS
Ps 99: 1 he **s** enthroned between
Isa 40: 22 He **s** enthroned above the circle
Mt 19: 28 Son of Man **s** on his glorious throne,
Rev 4: 9 thanks to him who **s** on the throne

SKIN
Job 19: 20 escaped only by the **s** of my teeth.

SOVEREIGN
Da 4: 25 Most High is **s** over all kingdoms

SOW (SOWS)
Job 4: 8 and those who **s** trouble reap it.
Mt 6: 26 they do not **s** or reap or store away
2Pe 2: 22 "A **s** that is washed returns to her

SOWS (SOW)
2Co 9: 6 and whoever **s** generously will

SPARE (SPARES)
Ro 8: 32 He who did not **s** his own Son,
11: 21 God did not **s** the natural branches,

SPARES (SPARE)
Pr 13: 24 Whoever **s** the rod hates their

SPEARS
Isa 2: 4 and their **s** into pruning hooks.
Joel 3: 10 and your pruning hooks into **s**.
Mic 4: 3 and their **s** into pruning hooks.

SPECTACLE
1Co 4: 9 have been made a **s** to the whole
Col 2: 15 he made a public **s** of them,

SPIN
Mt 6: 28 They do not labor or **s**.

SPIRIT (SPIRITS SPIRITUAL)
Ge 1: 2 the **S** of God was hovering over
6: 3 said, "My **S** will not contend
2Ki 2: 9 inherit a double portion of your **s**,"
Job 33: 4 The **S** of God has made me;
Ps 31: 5 Into your hands I commit my **s**;
51: 10 and renew a steadfast **s** within me.
51: 11 or take your Holy **S** from me.
51: 17 My sacrifice, O God, is a broken **s**;
139: 7 Where can I go from your **S**?
Isa 57: 15 to revive the **s** of the lowly
63: 10 rebelled and grieved his Holy **S**.
Eze 11: 19 heart and put a new **s** in them;
36: 26 a new heart and put a new **s** in you;
Joel 2: 28 I will pour out my **S** on all people.
Zec 4: 6 but by my **S**,' says the LORD
Mt 1: 18 to be pregnant through the Holy **S**.
3: 11 He will baptize you with the Holy **S**
3: 16 he saw the **S** of God descending
4: 1 led by the **S** into the wilderness
5: 3 "Blessed are the poor in **s**, for
26: 41 The **s** is willing, but the flesh is
28: 19 and of the Son and of the Holy **S**,
Lk 1: 80 child grew and became strong in **s**;
11: 13 in heaven give the Holy **S** to those
Jn 4: 24 God is **s**, and his worshipers must worship in the **S**
7: 39 that time the **S** had not been given,
14: 26 the Holy **S**, whom the Father will
16: 13 But when he, the **S** of truth, comes,
20: 22 and said, "Receive the Holy **S**.
Ac 1: 5 will be baptized with the Holy **S**."
2: 4 tongues as the **S** enabled them.
2: 38 will receive the gift of the Holy **S**.
6: 3 who are known to be full of the **S**
19: 2 "Did you receive the Holy **S**
Ro 8: 9 if indeed the **S** of God lives in you.
8: 26 the **S** helps us in our weakness.
1Co 2: 10 God has revealed to us by his **S**.
2: 10 The **S** searches all things,
2: 14 without the **S** does not accept
3: 1 as people who live by the **S** but as
6: 19 bodies are temples of the Holy **S**,
12: 1 Now about the gifts of the **S**,
12: 13 we were all baptized by one **S**
12: 13 and we were all given the one **S**
14: 1 and eagerly desire gifts of the **S**,
2Co 3: 6 the letter kills, but the **S** gives life.
5: 5 who has given us the **S** as a deposit,
Gal 5: 16 say, walk by the **S**, and you will not
5: 22 But the fruit of the **S** is love, joy,
5: 25 Since we live by the **S**, let us keep
Gal 6: 1 who live by the **S** should restore
Eph 1: 13 with a seal, the promised Holy **S**,
4: 30 do not grieve the Holy **S** of God,
5: 18 Instead, be filled with the **S**,
5: 19 hymns, and songs from the **S**.
6: 17 of salvation and the sword of the **S**,
1Th 5: 19 Do not quench the **S**.
2Th 2: 13 the sanctifying work of the **S**
Heb 4: 12 even to dividing soul and **s**,
1Pe 3: 4 beauty of a gentle and quiet **s**,
2Pe 1: 21 were carried along by the Holy **S**.
1Jn 4: 1 do not believe every **s**, but test

SPIRITS (SPIRIT)
1Co 12: 10 another distinguishing between **s**,
14: 32 The **s** of prophets are subject
1Jn 4: 1 but test the **s** to see whether they

SPIRITUAL (SPIRIT)
Ro 12: 11 but keep your **s** fervor,
1Co 2: 13 the Spirit, explaining **s** realities
15: 44 a natural body, it is raised a **s** body.
Eph 1: 3 realms with every **s** blessing
6: 12 against the **s** forces of evil
1Pe 2: 2 crave pure **s** milk, so that by it you
2: 5 offering **s** sacrifices acceptable

SPLENDOR
1Ch 16: 29 the LORD in the **s** of his holiness.
29: 11 glory and the majesty and the **s**,
Job 37: 22 of the north he comes in golden **s**;
Ps 29: 2 the LORD in the **s** of his holiness.
45: 3 clothe yourself with **s** and majesty.
96: 6 **S** and majesty are before him;
96: 9 the LORD in the **s** of his holiness;
104: 1 you are clothed with **s** and majesty.
145: 5 of the glorious **s** of your majesty—
Isa 61: 3 the LORD for the display of his **s**.
63: 1 robed in **s**, striding forward
Lk 9: 30 Elijah, appeared in glorious **s**,
2Th 2: 8 and destroy by the **s** of his coming.

SPOIL
Ps 119:162 promise like one who finds great **s**.

SPOTLESS
2Pe 3: 14 make every effort to be found **s**,

SPREAD (SPREADING)
Ac 12: 24 the word of God continued to **s**
19: 20 way the word of the Lord **s** widely

SPREADING (SPREAD)
1Th 3: 2 in God's service in **s** the gospel

SPRING
Jer 2: 13 forsaken me, the **s** of living water,
Jn 4: 14 in them a **s** of water welling
Jas 3: 12 can a salt **s** produce fresh water.

SPUR
Heb 10: 24 how we may **s** one another

SPURNS
Pr 15: 5 A fool **s** a parent's discipline,

STAFF
Ps 23: 4 your rod and your **s**, they comfort

STAKES
Isa 54: 2 your cords, strengthen your **s**.

STAND (STANDING STANDS)
Ex 14: 13 **S** firm and you will see
2Ch 20: 17 **s** firm and see the deliverance
Ps 1: 5 Therefore the wicked will not **s**
40: 2 rock and gave me a firm place to **s**.
119:120 fear of you; I **s** in awe of your laws.
Eze 22: 30 **s** before me in the gap on behalf
Zec 14: 4 day his feet will **s** on the Mount
Mt 12: 25 divided against itself will not **s**.
Ro 14: 10 we will all **s** before God's judgment
1Co 15: 58 dear brothers and sisters, **s** firm.
Eph 6: 14 **S** firm then, with the belt of truth
2Th 2: 15 firm and hold fast to the teachings
Jas 5: 8 be patient and **s** firm,
Rev 3: 20 I **s** at the door and knock.

STANDING (STAND)
Ex 3: 5 where you are **s** is holy ground."
Jos 5: 15 the place where you are **s** is holy."
1Pe 5: 9 Resist him, **s** firm in the faith,

STANDS (STAND)
Ps 89: 2 that your love **s** firm forever,
119: 89 it **s** firm in the heavens.
2Ti 2: 19 God's solid foundation **s** firm,

STAR (STARS)
Nu 24: 17 A **s** will come out of Jacob;
Rev 22: 16 David, and the bright Morning **S**."

STARS (STAR)
Da 12: 3 like the **s** for ever and ever.
Php 2: 15 you will shine among them like **s**

STEADFAST
Ps 51: 10 and renew a **s** spirit within me.
Isa 26: 3 peace those whose minds are **s**,
1Pe 5: 10 and make you strong, firm and **s**.

STEAL
Ex 20: 15 "You shall not **s**.
Mt 19: 18 you shall not **s**, you shall not give
Eph 4: 28 has been stealing must **s** no longer,

STEP (STEPS)
Gal 5: 25 let us keep in **s** with the Spirit.

STEPS (STEP)
Pr 16: 9 but the LORD establishes their **s**.
Jer 10: 23 it is not for them to direct their **s**.
1Pe 2: 21 that you should follow in his **s**.

STICKS
Pr 18: 24 there is a friend who **s** closer than

STIFF-NECKED
Ex 34: 9 Although this is a **s** people,

STILL
Ps 46: 10 "Be **s**, and know that I am God;
Zec 2: 13 Be **s** before the LORD,

STIRS
Pr 6: 19 a person who **s** up conflict
10: 12 Hatred **s** up conflict, but love
15: 1 wrath, but a harsh word **s** up anger.
29: 22 An angry person **s** up conflict,

STONE (CORNERSTONE MILLSTONE)
1Sa 17: 50 the Philistine with a sling and a **s**;
Isa 8: 14 and Judah he will be a **s** that causes
Eze 11: 19 remove from them their heart of **s**
Mk 16: 3 "Who will roll the **s** away
Lk 4: 3 God, tell this **s** to become bread."
Jn 8: 7 *the first to throw a **s** at her."*
2Co 3: 3 not on tablets of **s** but on tablets

STORE
Pr 10: 14 The wise **s** up knowledge,
Mt 6: 19 "Do not **s** up for yourselves

STOREHOUSE (HOUSE)
Mal 3: 10 Bring the whole tithe into the **s**,

STRAIGHT
Pr 3: 6 and he will make your paths **s**.
4: 25 Let your eyes look **s** ahead;
15: 21 understanding keeps a **s** course.
Jn 1: 23 'Make **s** the way for the Lord.'"

STRAIN
Mt 23: 24 You **s** out a gnat but swallow

STRANGER
Mt 25: 35 I was a **s** and you invited me in,
Jn 10: 5 But they will never follow a **s**;

STRAPS
Mk 1: 7 **s** of whose sandals I am not worthy

STREAMS
Ps 1: 3 person is like a tree planted by **s**
46: 4 a river whose **s** make glad the city
Ecc 1: 7 All **s** flow into the sea, yet the sea is

STRENGTH (STRONG)
Ex 15: 2 "The LORD is my **s** and my
Dt 6: 5 all your soul and with all your **s**.
2Sa 22: 33 It is God who arms me with **s**
Ne 8: 10 the joy of the LORD is your **s**."
Ps 28: 7 The LORD is my **s** and my shield;
46: 1 God is our refuge and **s**,
96: 7 ascribe to the LORD glory and **s**.
118: 14 The LORD is my **s** and my
147: 10 pleasure is not in the **s** of the horse,
Isa 40: 31 in the LORD will renew their **s**.
Mk 12: 30 all your mind and with all your **s**.'
1Co 1: 25 of God is stronger than human **s**.
Php 4: 13 this through him who gives me **s**.
1Pe 4: 11 do so with the **s** God provides,

STRENGTHEN (STRONG)
2Ch 16: 9 to **s** those whose hearts are fully
Ps 119: 28 **s** me according to your word.
Isa 35: 3 **S** the feeble hands, steady the
41: 10 I will **s** you and help you;
Eph 3: 16 of his glorious riches he may **s** you
2Th 2: 17 and **s** you in every good deed
Heb 12: 12 **s** your feeble arms and weak knees.

STRIFE
Pr 20: 3 It is to one's honor to avoid **s**,
22: 10 out the mocker, and out goes **s**;

STRIKE
Ge 3: 15 your head, and you will **s** his heel."
Zec 13: 7 "**S** the shepherd, and the sheep will
Mt 26: 31 "'I will **s** the shepherd,

STRONG (STRENGTH STRENGTHEN)
Dt 31: 6 Be **s** and courageous. Do not be
1Ki 2: 2 "So be **s**, act like a man,
Pr 31: 17 her arms are **s** for her tasks.
SS 8: 6 for love is as **s** as death, its jealousy
Lk 2: 40 And the child grew and became **s**;
Ro 15: 1 We who are **s** ought to bear
1Co 1: 27 things of the world to shame the **s**.
16: 13 in the faith; be courageous; be **s**.
2Co 12: 10 For when I am weak, then I am **s**.
Eph 6: 10 be **s** in the Lord and in his mighty

STRUGGLE
Ro 15: 30 join me in my **s** by praying to God
Eph 6: 12 For our **s** is not against flesh
Heb 12: 4 In your **s** against sin, you have not

STUDY
Ezr 7: 10 Ezra had devoted himself to the **s**
Ecc 12: 12 end, and much **s** wearies the body.
Jn 5: 39 You **s** the Scriptures diligently

STUMBLE (STUMBLING)
Ps 37: 24 though he may **s**, he will not fall,
119:165 law, and nothing can make them **s**.
Isa 8: 14 be a stone that causes people to **s**
Jer 31: 9 a level path where they will not **s**,
Eze 7: 19 for it has caused them to **s** into sin.
1Co 10: 32 Do not cause anyone to **s**,
1Pe 2: 8 "A stone that causes people to **s**

STUMBLING (STUMBLE)
Ro 14: 13 your mind not to put any **s** block
1Co 8: 9 rights does not become a **s** block
2Co 6: 3 We put no **s** block in anyone's path,

SUBDUE
Ge 1: 28 fill the earth and **s** it.

SUBJECT (SUBJECTED)
1Co 14: 32 of prophets are **s** to the control
15: 28 the Son himself will be made **s**
Titus 2: 5 and to be **s** to their husbands,
2: 9 slaves to be **s** to their masters
3: 1 Remind the people to be **s** to rulers

SUBJECTED (SUBJECT)
Ro 8: 20 the creation was **s** to frustration,

SUBMISSION (SUBMIT)
1Co 14: 34 but must be in **s**, as the law says.
1Ti 2: 11 learn in quietness and full **s**.

SUBMISSIVE (SUBMIT)
Jas 3: 17 considerate, **s**, full of mercy

SUBMIT (SUBMISSION SUBMISSIVE SUBMITS)
Ro 13: 5 necessary to **s** to the authorities,
1Co 16: 16 to **s** to such people and to everyone
Eph 5: 21 **S** to one another out of reverence
Col 3: 18 **s** yourselves to your husbands, as is
Heb 12: 9 How much more should we **s**
13: 17 leaders and **s** to their authority,
Jas 4: 7 **S** yourselves, then, to God.
1Pe 2: 18 reverent fear of God **s** yourselves

SUBMITS (SUBMIT)
Eph 5: 24 Now as the church **s** to Christ,

SUCCESSFUL
Jos 1: 7 that you may be **s** wherever you go.
2Ki 18: 7 he was **s** in whatever he undertook.
2Ch 20: 20 in his prophets and you will be **s**."

SUFFER (SUFFERED SUFFERING SUFFERINGS SUFFERS)
Isa 53: 10 to crush him and cause him to **s**,
Mk 8: 31 Son of Man must **s** many things
Lk 24: 26 the Messiah have to **s** these things
24: 46 The Messiah will **s** and rise
Php 1: 29 believe in him, but also to **s** for him,
1Pe 4: 16 if you **s** as a Christian, do not be

SUFFERED (SUFFER)
Heb 2: 9 and honor because he **s** death,
2: 18 Because he himself **s** when he was
1Pe 2: 21 called, because Christ **s** for you,

SUFFERING (SUFFER)
Isa 53: 3 a man of **s**, and familiar with pain.
Ac 5: 41 been counted worthy of **s** disgrace
2Ti 1: 8 join with me in **s** for the gospel,

SUFFERINGS (SUFFER)
Ro 8: 17 if indeed we share in his **s** in order
8: 18 that our present **s** are not worth
2Co 1: 5 share abundantly in the **s** of Christ,
Php 3: 10 and participation in his **s**,

SUFFERS (SUFFER)
Pr 13: 20 for a companion of fools **s** harm.
1Co 12: 26 If one part **s**, every part **s** with it;

SUFFICIENT
2Co 12: 9 said to me, "My grace is **s** for you,

SUITABLE
Ge 2: 18 I will make a helper **s** for him."

SUN
Ecc 1: 9 there is nothing new under the **s**.

Mal 4: 2 the **s** of righteousness will rise
Mt 5: 45 He causes his **s** to rise on the evil
17: 2 His face shone like the **s**, and his
Rev 1: 16 His face was like the **s** shining in
21: 23 The city does not need the **s**

SUPERIOR
Heb 1: 4 as the name he has inherited is **s**
8: 6 he is mediator is **s** to the old one,

SUPREMACY
Col 1: 18 in everything he might have the **s**.

SURE
Nu 32: 23 you may be **s** that your sin will find
Dt 6: 17 Be **s** to keep the commands
14: 22 Be **s** to set aside a tenth of all
Isa 28: 16 cornerstone for a **s** foundation;

SURPASS (SURPASSES SURPASSING)
Pr 31: 29 noble things, but you **s** them all."

SURPASSES (SURPASS)
Mt 5: 20 that unless your righteousness **s**
Eph 3: 19 to know this love that **s** knowledge

SURPASSING (SURPASS)
Ps 150: 2 praise him for his **s** greatness.
2Co 3: 10 in comparison with the **s** glory.
9: 14 of the **s** grace God has given you.
Php 3: 8 a loss because of the **s** worth

SURROUNDED
Heb 12: 1 since we are **s** by such a great cloud

SUSPENDS
Job 26: 7 he **s** the earth over nothing.

SUSTAINING (SUSTAINS)
Heb 1: 3 **s** all things by his powerful word.

SUSTAINS (SUSTAINING)
Ps 18: 35 shield, and your right hand **s** me;
146: 9 the foreigner and **s** the fatherless
147: 6 The LORD **s** the humble but casts
Isa 50: 4 to know the word that **s** the weary.

SWALLOWED
1Co 15: 54 "Death has been **s** up in victory."
2Co 5: 4 so that what is mortal may be **s**

SWEAR
Mt 5: 34 I tell you, do not **s** an oath at all:

SWORD (SWORDS)
Ps 45: 3 Gird your **s** on your side,
Mt 10: 34 not come to bring peace, but a **s**.
26: 52 all who draw the **s** will die by the **s**.
Lk 2: 35 a **s** will pierce your own soul too."
Ro 13: 4 for rulers do not bear the **s** for no
Eph 6: 17 of salvation and the **s** of the Spirit,
Heb 4: 12 Sharper than any double-edged **s**,
Rev 1: 16 was a sharp, double-edged **s**.

SWORDS (SWORD)
Pr 12: 18 words of the reckless pierce like **s**,
Isa 2: 4 They will beat their **s**
Joel 3: 10 Beat your plowshares into **s**

SYMPATHETIC
1Pe 3: 8 be **s**, love one another,

SYNAGOGUE
Lk 4: 16 the Sabbath day he went into the **s**,
Ac 17: 2 Paul went into the **s**, and on three

TABERNACLE
Ex 40: 34 the glory of the LORD filled the **t**.

TABLE (TABLES)
Ps 23: 5 You prepare a **t** before me

TABLES (TABLE)
Ac 6: 2 word of God in order to wait on **t**.

TABLET (TABLETS)
Pr 3: 3 write them on the **t** of your heart.
7: 3 write them on the **t** of your heart.

TABLETS (TABLET)
Ex 31: 18 Sinai, he gave him the two **t**
Dt 10: 5 put the **t** in the ark I had made,
2Co 3: 3 not on **t** of stone but on **t** of human

TAKE (TAKEN TAKES TAKING TOOK)
Dt 12: 32 do not add to it or **t** away from it.
31: 26 "**T** this Book of the Law and place
Job 23: 10 But he knows the way that I **t**;
Ps 49: 17 for they will **t** nothing with them
51: 11 or **t** your Holy Spirit from me.
Mt 10: 38 Whoever does not **t** up their cross
11: 29 **T** my yoke upon you and learn
16: 24 deny themselves and **t** up their cross

TAKEN (TAKE)
Lev 6: 4 they have stolen or **t** by extortion,
Isa 6: 7 your guilt is **t** away and your sin
Mt 24: 40 one will be **t** and the other left.
Mk 16: 19 *them, he was **t** up into heaven*
1Ti 3: 16 on in the world, was **t** up in glory.

TAKES (TAKE)
1Ki 20: 11 not boast like one who **t** it off.'"
Jn 1: 29 who **t** away the sin of the world!
Rev 22: 19 if anyone **t** words away from this

TAKING (TAKE)
Php 2: 7 nothing by **t** the very nature

TALENT See BAGS

TAME
Jas 3: 8 no human being can **t** the tongue.

TASK
Mk 13: 34 each with their assigned **t**, and tells
Ac 20: 24 complete the **t** the Lord Jesus has
1Co 3: 5 the Lord has assigned to each his **t**.
2Co 2: 16 And who is equal to such a **t**?

TASTE (TASTED)
Ps 34: 8 **T** and see that the LORD is good;
Col 2: 21 Do not **t**! Do not touch!"?
Heb 2: 9 God he might **t** death for everyone.

TASTED (TASTE)
1Pe 2: 3 you have **t** that the Lord is good.

TAUGHT (TEACH)
Mt 7: 29 because he **t** as one who had
1Co 2: 13 but in words **t** by the Spirit,
Gal 1: 12 it from any man, nor was I **t** it;

TAX (TAXES)
Mt 22: 17 to pay the imperial **t** to Caesar

TAXES (TAX)
Ro 13: 7 you owe them: If you owe **t**, pay **t**;

TEACH (TAUGHT TEACHER TEACHERS TEACHES TEACHING)
Ex 33: 13 **t** me your ways so I may know you
Dt 4: 9 **T** them to your children and to
8: 3 to **t** you that man does not live
11: 19 **T** them to your children,
1Sa 12: 23 I will **t** you the way that is good
Ps 32: 8 **t** you in the way you should go;
51: 13 I will **t** transgressors your ways,
90: 12 **T** us to number our days, that we
143: 10 **T** me to do your will, for you are
Jer 31: 34 longer will they **t** their neighbor,
Lk 11: 1 "Lord, **t** us to pray, just as John
Jn 14: 26 will **t** you all things and will
1Ti 2: 12 I do not permit a woman to **t**
3: 2 respectable, hospitable, able to **t**,
Titus 2: 1 **t** what is appropriate to sound
Heb 8: 11 longer will they **t** their neighbor,
Jas 3: 1 that we who **t** will be judged more
1Jn 2: 27 you do not need anyone to **t** you.

TEACHER (TEACH)
Mt 10: 24 "The student is not above the **t**,
23: 8 for you have one **T**, and you are
Jn 13: 14 your Lord and **T**, have washed

TEACHERS (TEACH)
1Co 12: 28 prophets, third **t**, then miracles,
Eph 4: 11 the evangelists, the pastors and **t**,
Heb 5: 12 by this time you ought to be **t**,

TEACHES (TEACH)
1Ti 6: 3 If anyone **t** otherwise and does not

TEACHING (TEACH)
Pr 1: 8 and do not forsake your mother's **t**.
Mt 28: 20 **t** them to obey everything I have
Jn 7: 17 out whether my **t** comes from God
14: 23 who loves me will obey my **t**.
1Ti 4: 13 of Scripture, to preaching and to **t**.
2Ti 3: 16 is God-breathed and is useful for **t**,
Titus 2: 7 In your **t** show integrity,

TEAR (TEARS)
Rev 7: 17 God will wipe away every **t**

TEARS (TEAR)
Ps 126: 5 Those who sow with **t** will reap
Php 3: 18 and now tell you again even with **t**,

TEETH (TOOTH)
Mt 8: 12 will be weeping and gnashing of **t**."

TEMPERATE
1Ti 3: 2 reproach, faithful to his wife, **t**,
3: 11 not malicious talkers but **t**
Titus 2: 2 Teach the older men to be **t**,

TEMPEST
Ps 55: 8 shelter, far from the **t** and storm."

TEMPLE (TEMPLES)
1Ki 8: 27 How much less this **t** I have built!
Hab 2: 20 The LORD is in his holy **t**;
1Co 3: 16 that you yourselves are God's **t**
2Co 6: 16 For we are the **t** of the living God.

TEMPLES (TEMPLE)
Ac 17: 24 does not live in **t** built by human
1Co 6: 19 your bodies are **t** of the Holy Spirit,

TEMPT (TEMPTATION TEMPTED)
1Co 7: 5 Satan will not **t** you because of

TEMPTATION (TEMPT)
Mt 6: 13 lead us not into **t**, but deliver us
26: 41 pray so that you will not fall into **t**.
1Co 10: 13 No **t** has overtaken you except

TEMPTED (TEMPT)
Mt 4: 1 the wilderness to be **t** by the devil.
1Co 10: 13 not let you be **t** beyond what you
Heb 2: 18 he himself suffered when he was **t**,
2: 18 able to help those who are being **t**.
4: 15 but we have one who has been **t**
Jas 1: 13 For God cannot be **t** by evil,

TEN (TENTH TITHE TITHES)
Ex 34: 28 the **T** Commandments.
Ps 91: 7 side, **t** thousand at your right hand,
Mt 25: 28 give it to the one who has **t** bags.
Lk 15: 8 suppose a woman has **t** silver coins

TENTH (TEN)
Dt 14: 22 Be sure to set aside a **t** of all

TERRIBLE (TERROR)
2Ti 3: 1 There will be **t** times in the last

TERROR (TERRIBLE)
Ps 91: 5 You will not fear the **t** of night,
Lk 21: 26 People will faint from **t**,
Ro 13: 3 rulers hold no **t** for those who do

TEST (TESTED TESTS)
Dt 6: 16 your God to the **t** as you did
Ps 139: 23 **t** me and know my anxious
Ro 12: 2 you will be able to **t** and approve
1Co 3: 13 the fire will **t** the quality of each
1Jn 4: 1 **t** the spirits to see whether they are

TESTED (TEST)
Ge 22: 1 Some time later God **t** Abraham.
Job 23: 10 when he has **t** me, I will come forth
Pr 27: 21 but people are **t** by their praise.
1Ti 3: 10 They must first be **t**;

TESTIFY (TESTIMONY)
Jn 5: 39 These are the very Scriptures that **t**

TESTIMONY (TESTIFY)
Isa 8: 20 instruction and the **t** of warning.
Lk 18: 20 you shall not give false **t**,
2Ti 1: 8 be ashamed of the **t** about our Lord

TESTS (TEST)
Pr 17: 3 for gold, but the LORD **t** the heart.
1Th 2: 4 people but God, who **t** our hearts.

THADDAEUS
Apostle (Mt 10:3; Mk 3:18); probably also known as Judas son of James (Lk 6:16; Ac 1:13).

THANKFUL (THANKS)
Heb 12: 28 let us be **t**, and so worship God

THANKS (THANKFUL THANKSGIVING)
Ne 12: 31 assigned two large choirs to give **t**.
Ps 100: 4 give **t** to him and praise his name.
1Co 15: 57 But **t** be to God! He gives us
2Co 2: 14 But **t** be to God, who always leads
9: 15 **T** be to God for his indescribable
1Th 5: 18 give **t** in all circumstances;

THANKSGIVING (THANKS)
Ps 95: 2 Let us come before him with **t**
100: 4 Enter his gates with **t** and his
Php 4: 6 **t**, present your requests to God.
1Ti 4: 3 to be received with **t** by those who

THIEF (THIEVES)
1Th 5: 2 of the Lord will come like a **t**
Rev 16: 15 "Look, I come like a **t**!

THIEVES (THIEF)
1Co 6: 10 nor **t** nor the greedy nor drunkards

THINK (THOUGHT THOUGHTS)
Ro 12: 3 Do not **t** of yourself more highly
Php 4: 8 **t** about such things.

THIRST (THIRSTY)
Ps 69: 21 food and gave me vinegar for my **t**.
Mt 5: 6 hunger and **t** for righteousness,
Jn 4: 14 the water I give them will never **t**.

THIRSTY (THIRST)
Isa 55: 1 all you who are **t**,
Jn 7: 37 "Let anyone who is **t** come to me
Rev 22: 17 Let the one who is **t** come;

THOMAS
Apostle (Mt 10:3; Mk 3:18; Lk 6:15; Jn 11:16; 14:5; 21:2; Ac 1:13). Doubted resurrection (Jn 20:24–28).

THORN (THORNS)
2Co 12: 7 I was given a **t** in my flesh,

THORNS (THORN)
Nu 33: 55 in your eyes and **t** in your sides.
Mt 27: 29 twisted together a crown of **t** and
Heb 6: 8 land that produces **t** and thistles is

THOUGHT (THINK)
Pr 14: 15 the prudent give **t** to their steps.
1Co 13: 11 I talked like a child, I **t** like a child,

THOUGHTS (THINK)
Ps 139: 23 test me and know my anxious **t**.
Isa 55: 8 "For my **t** are not your **t**, neither
Heb 4: 12 it judges the **t** and attitudes

THREE
Ecc 4: 12 of **t** strands is not quickly broken.
Mt 12: 40 the Son of Man will be **t** days and **t** nights in the heart of the earth.
18: 20 where two or **t** gather in my name,
27: 63 said, 'After **t** days I will rise again.'
1Co 13: 13 And now these **t** remain:
14: 27 or at the most **t**—should speak,
2Co 13: 1 testimony of two or **t** witnesses."

THRESHING
2Sa 24: 18 altar to the LORD on the **t** floor

THRONE (ENTHRONED)
2Sa 7: 16 your **t** will be established
Ps 45: 6 Your **t**, O God, will last for ever
47: 8 God is seated on his holy **t**.
Isa 6: 1 high and exalted, seated on a **t**;
66: 1 "Heaven is my **t**, and the earth is
Heb 4: 16 then approach God's **t** of grace
12: 2 at the right hand of the **t** of God.
Rev 4: 10 They lay their crowns before the **t**
20: 11 I saw a great white **t** and him who
22: 3 The **t** of God and of the Lamb will

THROW
Jn 8: 7 *the first to* **t** *a stone at her."*
Heb 10: 35 So do not **t** away your confidence;
12: 1 let us **t** off everything that hinders

THWART
Isa 14: 27 has purposed, and who can **t** him?

TIBNI
King of Israel (1Ki 16:21–22).

TIME (TIMES)
Est 4: 14 royal position for such a **t** as this?"
Da 7: 25 be delivered into his hands for a **t**, times and half a **t**.
Hos 10: 12 for it is **t** to seek the LORD,
Ro 9: 9 "At the appointed **t** I will return,
Heb 9: 28 and he will appear a second **t**,
10: 12 had offered for all **t** one sacrifice
1Pe 4: 17 For it is **t** for judgment to begin

TIMES (TIME)
Ps 9: 9 a stronghold in **t** of trouble.
31: 15 My **t** are in your hands;
62: 8 Trust in him at all **t**, you people;
Pr 17: 17 A friend loves at all **t**,
Am 5: 13 in such **t**, for the **t** are evil.
Mt 18: 21 sins against me? Up to seven **t**?"
Ac 1: 7 "It is not for you to know the **t**
Rev 12: 14 care of for a time, **t** and half a time,

TIMID
2Ti 1: 7 God gave us does not make us **t**,

TIMOTHY
Believer from Lystra (Ac 16:1). Joined Paul on second missionary journey (Ac 16–20). Sent to settle problems at Corinth (1Co 4:17; 16:10). Led church at Ephesus (1Ti 1:3). Co-writer with Paul (1Th 1:1; 2Th 1:1; Phm 1).

TIRE (TIRED)
2Th 3: 13 never **t** of doing what is good.

TIRED (TIRE)
Ex 17: 12 When Moses' hands grew **t**,
Isa 40: 28 He will not grow **t** or weary,

VOMIT
Pr 26: 11 As a dog returns to its **v**, so fools
2Pe 2: 22 "A dog returns to its **v**," and,

VOW
Nu 30: 2 a man makes a **v** to the LORD

WAGES
Lk 10: 7 you, for the worker deserves his **w**.
Ro 4: 4 **w** are not credited as a gift but as
6: 23 the **w** of sin is death, but the gift

WAILING
Ps 30: 11 You turned my **w** into dancing;

WAIST
2Ki 1: 8 had a leather belt around his **w**."
Mt 3: 4 he had a leather belt around his **w**.

WAIT (WAITED WAITS)
Ps 27: 14 **W** for the LORD; be strong
130: 5 I **w** for the LORD, my whole being
Isa 30: 18 Blessed are all who **w** for him!
Ac 1: 4 **w** for the gift my Father promised,
Ro 8: 23 groan inwardly as we **w** eagerly
1Th 1: 10 and to **w** for his Son from heaven,
Titus 2: 13 while we **w** for the blessed hope—

WAITED (WAIT)
Ps 40: 1 I **w** patiently for the LORD;

WAITS (WAIT)
Ro 8: 19 the creation **w** in eager expectation

WALK (WALKED)
Dt 11: 19 and when you **w** along the road,
Ps 1: 1 Blessed is the one who does not **w**
23: 4 though I **w** through the darkest
89: 15 **w** in the light of your presence,
Isa 2: 5 let us **w** in the light of the LORD.
30: 21 saying, "This is the way; **w** in it."
40: 31 weary, they will **w** and not be faint.
Jer 6: 16 and **w** in it, and you will find rest
Da 4: 37 those who **w** in pride he is able
Am 3: 3 Do two **w** together unless they
Mic 6: 8 and to **w** humbly with your God.
Mk 2: 9 say, 'Get up, take your mat and **w**'?
Jn 8: 12 Whoever follows me will never **w**
1Jn 1: 7 But if we **w** in the light, as he is
2Jn : 6 his command is that you **w** in love.

WALKED (WALK)
Ge 5: 24 Enoch **w** faithfully with God;
Jos 14: 9 which your feet have **w** will be
Mt 14: 29 **w** on the water and came toward

WALL
Jos 6: 20 gave a loud shout, the **w** collapsed;
Ne 2: 17 let us rebuild the **w** of Jerusalem,
Rev 21: 12 a great, high **w** with twelve gates,

WALLOWING
2Pe 2: 22 returns to her **w** in the mud."

WANT (WANTED WANTING WANTS)
1Sa 8: 19 they said. "We **w** a king over us.
Lk 19: 14 say, 'We don't **w** this man to be our
Ro 7: 15 For what I **w** to do I do not do,
Php 3: 10 I **w** to know Christ—yes, to know

WANTED (WANT)
1Co 12: 18 of them, just as he **w** them to be.

WANTING (WANT)
Da 5: 27 weighed on the scales and found **w**.
2Pe 3: 9 with you, not **w** anyone to perish,

WANTS (WANT)
Mt 20: 26 whoever **w** to become great among
Mk 8: 35 For whoever **w** to save their life
Ro 9: 18 on whom he **w** to have mercy,
9: 18 he hardens whom he **w** to harden.
1Ti 2: 4 who **w** all people to be saved

WAR (WARS)
Isa 2: 4 nor will they train for **w** anymore.
Da 9: 26 **W** will continue until the end,
2Co 10: 3 we do not wage **w** as the world
Rev 19: 11 justice he judges and wages **w**.

WARN (WARNED WARNINGS)
Eze 3: 19 if you do **w** the wicked person
33: 9 if you do **w** the wicked person

WARNED (WARN)
Ps 19: 11 By them your servant is **w**;

WARNINGS (WARN)
1Co 10: 11 and were written down as **w** for us,

WARS (WAR)
Ps 46: 9 He makes **w** cease to the ends
Mt 24: 6 will hear of **w** and rumors of **w**,

WASH (WASHED WASHING)
Ps 51: 7 **w** me, and I will be whiter than
Jn 13: 5 and began to **w** his disciples' feet,
Ac 22: 16 be baptized and **w** your sins away,
Rev 22: 14 are those who **w** their robes,

WASHED (WASH)
1Co 6: 11 But you were **w**, you were
Rev 7: 14 they have **w** their robes and made

WASHING (WASH)
Eph 5: 26 the **w** with water through the word,
Titus 3: 5 saved us through the **w** of rebirth

WATCH (WATCHES WATCHING WATCHMAN)
Ge 31: 49 the LORD keep **w** between you
Jer 31: 10 them and will **w** over his flock like
Mt 24: 42 "Therefore keep **w**, because you do
26: 41 "**W** and pray so that you will not
Lk 2: 8 keeping **w** over their flocks at night
1Ti 4: 16 **W** your life and doctrine closely.

WATCHES (WATCH)
Ps 1: 6 For the LORD **w** over the way
121: 3 he who **w** over you will not

WATCHING (WATCH)
Lk 12: 37 servants whose master finds them **w**

WATCHMAN (WATCH)
Eze 3: 17 I have made you a **w** for the people

WATER (WATERED WATERS)
Ps 1: 3 like a tree planted by streams of **w**,
22: 14 I am poured out like **w**, and all my
Pr 25: 21 if he is thirsty, give him **w** to drink.
Isa 49: 10 and lead them beside springs of **w**.
Jer 2: 13 broken cisterns that cannot hold **w**.
Zec 14: 8 On that day living **w** will flow
Mk 9: 41 anyone who gives you a cup of **w**
Jn 4: 10 he would have given you living **w**."
7: 38 rivers of living **w** will flow
Eph 5: 26 washing with **w** through the word,
1Pe 3: 21 this **w** symbolizes baptism that
Rev 21: 6 thirsty I will give **w** without cost

WATERED (WATER)
1Co 3: 6 I planted the seed, Apollos **w** it,

WATERS (WATER)
Ps 23: 2 he leads me beside quiet **w**,
Isa 58: 11 like a spring whose **w** never fail.
1Co 3: 7 nor the one who **w** is anything,

WAVE (WAVES)
Jas 1: 6 the one who doubts is like a **w**

WAVES (WAVE)
Isa 57: 20 whose **w** cast up mire and mud.
Mt 8: 27 the winds and the **w** obey him!"
Eph 4: 14 tossed back and forth by the **w**,

WAY (WAYS)
Dt 1: 33 to show you the **w** you should go.
2Sa 22: 31 "As for God, his **w** is perfect:
Job 23: 10 But he knows the **w** that I take;
Ps 1: 1 stand in the **w** that sinners take
37: 5 Commit your **w** to the LORD;
139: 24 and lead me in the **w** everlasting.
Pr 14: 12 is a **w** that appears to be right,
22: 6 off on the **w** they should go,
Isa 30: 21 behind you, saying, "This is the **w**;
53: 6 of us has turned to our own **w**;
Mt 3: 3 'Prepare the **w** for the Lord,
Jn 14: 6 "I am the **w** and the truth
1Co 10: 13 provide a **w** out so that you can
12: 31 will show you the most excellent **w**.
Heb 4: 15 who has been tempted in every **w**,
9: 8 the **w** into the Most Holy Place had
10: 20 living **w** opened for us through

WAYS (WAY)
Ex 33: 13 teach me your **w** so I may know
Ps 25: 10 All the **w** of the LORD are loving
51: 13 I will teach transgressors your **w**,
Pr 3: 6 in all your **w** submit to him, and he
16: 17 who guard their **w** preserve their
Isa 55: 7 Let the wicked forsake their **w**
55: 8 neither are your **w** my **w**,"
Jas 3: 2 We all stumble in many **w**.

WEAK (WEAKER WEAKNESS)
Mt 26: 41 spirit is willing, but the flesh is **w**."
Ro 14: 1 Accept the one whose faith is **w**,
1Co 1: 27 chose the **w** things of the world
8: 9 a stumbling block to the **w**.
9: 22 To the **w** I became **w**, to win the **w**.
2Co 12: 10 For when I am **w**, then I am strong.
Heb 12: 12 your feeble arms and **w** knees.

WEAKER (WEAK)
1Co 12: 22 seem to be **w** are indispensable,
1Pe 3: 7 them with respect as the **w** partner

WEAKNESS (WEAK)
Ro 8: 26 way, the Spirit helps us in our **w**.
1Co 1: 25 **w** of God is stronger than human
2Co 12: 9 my power is made perfect in **w**."
Heb 5: 2 since he himself is subject to **w**.

WEALTH
Pr 3: 9 Honor the LORD with your **w**,
Mk 10: 22 away sad, because he had great **w**.
Lk 15: 13 and there squandered his **w** in wild

WEAPONS
2Co 10: 4 The **w** we fight with are not the **w**

WEARIES (WEARY)
Ecc 12: 12 and much study **w** the body.

WEARY (WEARIES)
Isa 40: 31 they will run and not grow **w**,
Mt 11: 28 all you who are **w** and burdened,
Gal 6: 9 not become **w** in doing good,

WEDDING
Mt 22: 11 who was not wearing **w** clothes.
Rev 19: 7 For the **w** of the Lamb has come,

WEEP (WEEPING WEPT)
Ecc 3: 4 a time to **w** and a time to laugh,
Lk 6: 21 Blessed are you who **w** now, for

WEEPING (WEEP)
Ps 30: 5 **w** may stay for the night,
126: 6 Those who go out **w**, carrying seed
Mt 8: 12 where there will be **w** and gnashing

WELCOMES
Mt 18: 5 **w** one such child in my name **w** me.
2Jn : 11 Anyone who **w** them shares in

WELL
Lk 17: 19 your faith has made you **w**."
Jas 5: 15 faith will make the sick person **w**;

WEPT (WEEP)
Ps 137: 1 and **w** when we remembered Zion.
Jn 11: 35 Jesus **w**.

WEST
Ps 103: 12 as far as the east is from the **w**,

WHIRLWIND (WIND)
2Ki 2: 1 to take Elijah up to heaven in a **w**,
Hos 8: 7 They sow the wind and reap the **w**.
Na 1: 3 His way is in the **w** and the storm,

WHITE (WHITER)
Isa 1: 18 scarlet, they shall be as **w** as snow;
Da 7: 9 His clothing was as **w** as snow;
Rev 1: 14 hair on his head was **w** like wool,
3: 4 dressed in **w**, for they are worthy.
20: 11 I saw a great **w** throne and him

WHITER (WHITE)
Ps 51: 7 wash me, and I will be **w** than snow.

WHOLE
Mt 16: 26 for someone to gain the **w** world,
24: 14 in the **w** world as a testimony to all
Jn 13: 10 their **w** body is clean.
21: 25 even the **w** world would not have
Ac 20: 27 proclaim to you the **w** will of God.
Ro 3: 19 and the **w** world held accountable
8: 22 the **w** creation has been groaning
Gal 5: 3 he is obligated to obey the **w** law.
Eph 4: 13 attaining to the **w** measure
Jas 2: 10 For whoever keeps the **w** law
1Jn 2: 2 but also for the sins of the **w** world.

WHOLEHEARTEDLY (HEART)
Dt 1: 36 he followed the LORD **w**."
Eph 6: 7 Serve **w**, as if you were serving

WICKED (WICKEDNESS)
Ps 1: 1 does not walk in step with the **w**
1: 5 Therefore the **w** will not stand
73: 3 when I saw the prosperity of the **w**.
Pr 10: 20 the heart of the **w** is of little value.
11: 21 The **w** will not go unpunished,
Isa 53: 9 was assigned a grave with the **w**,
55: 7 Let the **w** forsake their ways
57: 20 But the **w** are like the tossing sea,
Eze 3: 18 that **w** person will die for their sin,
18: 23 any pleasure in the death of the **w**?
33: 14 And if I say to a **w** person,

WICKEDNESS (WICKED)
Eze 28: 15 you were created till **w** was found

WIDE
Isa 54: 2 stretch your tent curtains **w**, do not
Mt 7: 13 For **w** is the gate and broad is
Eph 3: 18 to grasp how **w** and long and high

WIDOW (WIDOWS)
Dt 10: 18 cause of the fatherless and the **w**,
Lk 21: 2 saw a poor **w** put in two very small

WIDOWS (WIDOW)
Jas 1: 27 orphans and **w** in their distress

WIFE (WIVES)
Ge 2: 24 and mother and is united to his **w**,
24: 67 So she became his **w**, and he loved
Ex 20: 17 shall not covet your neighbor's **w**,
Dt 5: 21 shall not covet your neighbor's **w**.
Pr 5: 18 you rejoice in the **w** of your youth.
12: 4 A **w** of noble character is her
18: 22 who finds a **w** finds what is good
19: 13 quarrelsome **w** is like the constant
31: 10 A **w** of noble character who can
Mt 19: 3 for a man to divorce his **w** for any
1Co 7: 2 sexual relations with his own **w**,
7: 33 how he can please his **w**—
Eph 5: 23 head of the **w** as Christ is the head
5: 33 must love his **w** as he loves himself,
5: 33 the **w** must respect her husband.
1Ti 3: 2 faithful to his **w**, temperate,
Rev 21: 9 you the bride, the **w** of the Lamb."

WILD
Lk 15: 13 squandered his wealth in **w** living.
Ro 11: 17 and you, though a **w** olive shoot,

WILL (WILLING WILLINGNESS)
Ps 40: 8 I desire to do your **w**, my God;
143: 10 Teach me to do your **w**, for you are
Isa 53: 10 Yet it was the LORD's **w** to crush
Mt 6: 10 kingdom come, your **w** be done,
26: 39 Yet not as I **w**, but as you **w**."
Jn 7: 17 chooses to do the **w** of God **w** find
Ac 20: 27 to you the whole **w** of God.
Ro 12: 2 test and approve what God's **w** is—
1Co 7: 37 but has control over his own **w**,
Eph 5: 17 understand what the Lord's **w** is.
Php 2: 13 for it is God who works in you to **w**
1Th 4: 3 It is God's **w** that you should be
5: 18 for this is God's **w** for you in Christ
Heb 9: 16 In the case of a **w**, it is necessary
10: 7 I have come to do your **w**,
Jas 4: 15 "If it is the Lord's **w**, we **w** live
1Jn 5: 14 ask anything according to his **w**,
Rev 4: 11 by your **w** they were created

WILLING (WILL)
Ps 51: 12 salvation and grant me a **w** spirit,
Da 3: 28 were **w** to give up their lives rather
Mt 18: 14 Father in heaven is not **w** that any
23: 37 her wings, and you were not **w**.
26: 41 The spirit is **w**, but the flesh is

WILLINGNESS (WILL)
2Co 8: 12 For if the **w** is there, the gift is

WIN
Php 3: 14 on toward the goal to **w** the prize
1Th 4: 12 your daily life may **w** the respect

WIND (WHIRLWIND)
Jas 1: 6 the sea, blown and tossed by the **w**.

WINE
Pr 20: 1 **W** is a mocker and beer a brawler;
Isa 55: 1 buy **w** and milk without money
Mt 9: 17 Neither do people pour new **w**
Lk 23: 36 They offered him **w** vinegar
Ro 14: 21 drink **w** or to do anything else
Eph 5: 18 Do not get drunk on **w**, which

WINESKINS
Mt 9: 17 people pour new wine into old **w**.

WINGS
Ru 2: 12 under whose **w** you have come
Ps 17: 8 hide me in the shadow of your **w**
Isa 40: 31 They will soar on **w** like eagles;
Lk 13: 34 gathers her chicks under her **w**,

WIPE
Rev 7: 17 God will **w** away every tear

WISDOM (WISE)
1Ki 4: 29 God gave Solomon **w** and very
Ps 111: 10 the LORD is the beginning of **w**;
Pr 31: 26 She speaks with **w**, and faithful
Jer 10: 12 he founded the world by his **w**
Mt 11: 19 **w** is proved right by her deeds."
Lk 2: 52 And Jesus grew in **w** and stature,

Ro 11: 33 the depth of the riches of the **w**
Col 2: 3 are hidden all the treasures of **w**
Jas 1: 5 If any of you lacks **w**, you should

WISE (WISDOM WISER)
1Ki 3: 12 I will give you a **w** and discerning
Job 5: 13 He catches the **w** in their craftiness,
Ps 19: 7 trustworthy, making **w** the simple.
Pr 3: 7 Do not be **w** in your own eyes;
9: 8 rebuke the **w** and they will love
10: 1 A **w** son brings joy to his father,
11: 30 and the one who is **w** saves lives.
13: 20 Walk with the **w** and become **w**,
17: 28 Even fools are thought **w** if they
Da 12: 3 Those who are **w** will shine like
Mt 11: 25 hidden these things from the **w**
1Co 1: 27 things of the world to shame the **w**;
2Ti 3: 15 make you **w** for salvation through

WISER (WISE)
1Co 1: 25 of God is **w** than human wisdom,

WITHER (WITHERS)
Ps 1: 3 and whose leaf does not **w**—

WITHERS (WITHER)
Isa 40: 7 The grass **w** and the flowers fall,
1Pe 1: 24 the grass **w** and the flowers fall,

WITHHOLD
Ps 84: 11 no good thing does he **w** from
Pr 23: 13 Do not **w** discipline from a child;

WITNESS (WITNESSES)
Jn 1: 8 he came only as a **w** to the light.

WITNESSES (WITNESS)
Dt 19: 15 by the testimony of two or three **w**.
Ac 1: 8 and you will be my **w** in Jerusalem,

WIVES (WIFE)
Eph 5: 22 **W**, submit yourselves to your own
5: 25 love your **w**, just as Christ loved
1Pe 3: 1 **W**, in the same way submit

WOE
Isa 6: 5 "**W** to me!" I cried. "I am ruined!

WOLF
Isa 65: 25 The **w** and the lamb will feed

WOMAN (MAN)
Ge 2: 22 the LORD God made a **w**
3: 15 put enmity between you and the **w**,
Lev 20: 13 with a man as one does with a **w**,
Dt 22: 5 A **w** must not wear men's clothing,
Ru 3: 11 that you are a **w** of noble character.
Pr 31: 30 a **w** who fears the LORD is to be
Mt 5: 28 a **w** lustfully has already committed
Jn 8: 3 *brought in a **w** caught*
Ro 7: 2 by law a married **w** is bound to her
1Co 11: 3 and the head of the **w** is man,
11: 13 Is it proper for a **w** to pray to God
1Ti 2: 11 A **w** should learn in quietness

WOMB
Job 1: 21 I came from my mother's **w**,
Jer 1: 5 I formed you in the **w** I knew you,
Lk 1: 44 the baby in my **w** leaped for joy.

WOMEN (MAN)
Lk 1: 42 "Blessed are you among **w**,
1Co 14: 34 **W** should remain silent
1Ti 2: 9 I also want the **w** to dress modestly,
Titus 2: 3 teach the older **w** to be reverent
1Pe 3: 5 the way the holy **w** of the past

WONDERFUL (WONDERS)
Job 42: 3 things too **w** for me to know.
Ps 119: 18 that I may see **w** things in your law.
119: 27 I may meditate on your **w** deeds.
119:129 statutes are **w**; therefore I obey
139: 6 Such knowledge is too **w** for me,
Isa 9: 6 he will be called **W** Counselor,
1Pe 2: 9 out of darkness into his **w** light.

WONDERS (WONDERFUL)
Job 37: 14 stop and consider God's **w**.
Ps 17: 7 Show me the **w** of your great love,
31: 21 for he showed me the **w** of his love
Joel 2: 30 I will show **w** in the heavens
Ac 2: 19 I will show **w** in *the heavens*

WOOD
Isa 44: 19 Shall I bow down to a block of **w**?"
1Co 3: 12 costly stones, **w**, hay or straw,

WORD (WORDS)
Dt 8: 3 but on every **w** that comes
2Sa 22: 31 The LORD's **w** is flawless;
Ps 119: 9 By living according to your **w**.
119: 11 I have hidden your **w** in my heart
119:105 Your **w** is a lamp to my feet
Pr 12: 25 the heart, but a kind **w** cheers it up.
30: 5 "Every **w** of God is flawless; he is
Isa 55: 11 so is my **w** that goes out from my
Jn 1: 1 In the beginning was the **W**, and the **W** was with God, and the **W** was God.
1: 14 The **W** became flesh and made his
2Co 2: 17 we do not peddle the **w** of God
4: 2 nor do we distort the **w** of God.
Eph 6: 17 of the Spirit, which is the **w** of God.
Php 2: 16 as you hold firmly to the **w** of life.
2Ti 2: 15 and who correctly handles the **w**
Heb 4: 12 the **w** of God is alive and active.
Jas 1: 22 Do not merely listen to the **w**,

WORDS (WORD)
Dt 11: 18 Fix these **w** of mine in your hearts
Ps 119:103 How sweet are your **w** to my taste,
119:130 unfolding of your **w** gives light;
119:160 All your **w** are true; all your
Pr 30: 6 Do not add to his **w**, or he will
Jer 15: 16 When your **w** came, I ate them;
Mt 24: 35 but my **w** will never pass away.
Jn 6: 68 You have the **w** of eternal life.
15: 7 in me and my **w** remain in you,
1Co 14: 19 rather speak five intelligible **w**
Rev 22: 19 if anyone takes **w** away from this

WORK (HANDIWORK WORKER WORKERS WORKING WORKS)
Ex 23: 12 but on the seventh day do not **w**,
Nu 8: 11 be ready to do the **w** of the LORD.
Dt 5: 14 On it you shall not do any **w**,
Jer 48: 10 who is lax in doing the LORD's **w**!
Jn 6: 27 Do not **w** for food that spoils,
9: 4 is coming, when no one can **w**.
1Co 3: 13 test the quality of each person's **w**.
Php 1: 6 he who began a good **w** in you will
2: 12 continue to **w** out your salvation
Col 3: 23 you do, **w** at it with all your heart,
1Th 5: 12 those who **w** hard among you,
2Th 3: 10 is unwilling to **w** shall not eat."
2Ti 3: 17 equipped for every good **w**.
Heb 6: 10 he will not forget your **w**

WORKER (WORK)
Lk 10: 7 for the **w** deserves his wages.
1Ti 5: 18 and "The **w** deserves his wages."
2Ti 2: 15 a **w** who does not need to be

WORKERS (WORK)
Mt 9: 37 is plentiful but the **w** are few.
1Co 3: 9 For we are **c** in God's service;

WORKING (WORK)
Col 3: 23 all your heart, as **w** for the Lord,

WORKS (WORK)
Pr 31: 31 her **w** bring her praise at the city
Ro 8: 28 in all things God **w** for the good
Eph 2: 9 not by **w**, so that no one can boast.
4: 12 to equip his people for **w** of service,

WORLD (WORLDLY)
Ps 50: 12 for the **w** is mine, and all that is
Isa 13: 11 I will punish the **w** for its evil,
Mt 5: 14 "You are the light of the **w**.
16: 26 for someone to gain the whole **w**,
Mk 16: 15 *"Go into all the **w** and preach*
Jn 1: 29 who takes away the sin of the **w**!
3: 16 God so loved the **w** that he gave his
8: 12 he said, "I am the light of the **w**.
15: 19 but I have chosen you out of the **w**. That is why the **w** hates you.
16: 33 I have overcome the **w**."
18: 36 said, "My kingdom is not of this **w**.
Ro 3: 19 and the whole **w** held accountable
1Co 3: 19 the wisdom of this **w** is foolishness
2Co 5: 19 that God was reconciling the **w**
10: 3 For though we live in the **w**, we do
1Ti 6: 7 For we brought nothing into the **w**,
1Jn 2: 2 but also for the sins of the whole **w**.
2: 15 not love the **w** or anything in the **w**.
Rev 13: 8 slain from the creation of the **w**.

WORLDLY (WORLD)
Titus 2: 12 to ungodliness and **w** passions,

WORMS
Mk 9: 48 where "'the **w** that eat them do

WORRY (WORRYING)
Mt 6: 25 I tell you, do not **w** about your life,
10: 19 do not **w** about what to say or how

WORRYING (WORRY)
Mt 6: 27 you by **w** add a single hour to your

WORSHIP
1Ch 16: 29 **W** the LORD in the splendor of his
Ps 95: 6 let us bow down in **w**, let us kneel
Mt 2: 2 it rose and have come to **w** him."
Jn 4: 24 his worshipers must **w** in the Spirit
Ro 12: 1 this is your true and proper **w**.

WORTH (WORTHY)
Job 28: 13 No mortal comprehends its **w**;
Pr 31: 10 She is **w** far more than rubies.
Mt 10: 31 you are **w** more than many
Ro 8: 18 sufferings are not **w** comparing
1Pe 1: 7 of greater **w** than gold,
3: 4 which is of great **w** in God's sight.

WORTHLESS
Pr 11: 4 Wealth is **w** in the day of wrath,
Jas 1: 26 themselves, and their religion is **w**.

WORTHY (WORTH)
1Ch 16: 25 is the LORD and most **w** of praise;
Eph 4: 1 live a life **w** of the calling you have
Php 1: 27 in a manner **w** of the gospel
Rev 5: 2 "Who is **w** to break the seals

WOUNDS
Pr 27: 6 **W** from a friend can be trusted,
Isa 53: 5 and by his **w** we are healed.
Zec 13: 6 'What are these **w** on your body?'
1Pe 2: 24 "by his **w** you have been healed."

WRATH
2Ch 36: 16 at his prophets until the **w**
Ps 2: 5 anger and terrifies them in his **w**,
76: 10 Surely your **w** against mankind
Pr 15: 1 A gentle answer turns away **w**,
Jer 25: 15 cup filled with the wine of my **w**
Ro 1: 18 The **w** of God is being revealed
5: 9 saved from God's **w** through him!
1Th 5: 9 God did not appoint us to suffer **w**
Rev 6: 16 and from the **w** of the Lamb!

WRESTLED
Ge 32: 24 a man **w** with him till daybreak.

WRITE (WRITING WRITTEN)
Dt 6: 9 **W** them on the doorframes of your
Pr 7: 3 **w** them on the tablet of your heart.
Heb 8: 10 minds and **w** them on their hearts.

WRITING (WRITE)
1Co 14: 37 what I am **w** to you is the Lord's

WRITTEN (WRITE)
Jos 1: 8 be careful to do everything **w** in it.
Da 12: 1 everyone whose name is found **w**
Lk 10: 20 that your names are **w** in heaven."
Jn 20: 31 these are **w** that you may believe
1Co 4: 6 "Do not go beyond what is **w**."
2Co 3: 3 **w** not with ink but with the Spirit
Heb 12: 23 whose names are **w** in heaven.

WRONG (WRONGDOING WRONGED WRONGS)
Ex 23: 2 not follow the crowd in doing **w**.
Nu 5: 7 restitution for the **w** they have
Job 34: 12 unthinkable that God would do **w**,
1Th 5: 15 that nobody pays back **w** for **w**,

WRONGDOING (WRONG)
Job 1: 22 not sin by charging God with **w**.

WRONGED (WRONG)
1Co 6: 7 Why not rather be **w**?

WRONGS (WRONG)
Pr 10: 12 conflict, but love covers over all **w**.
1Co 13: 5 angered, it keeps no record of **w**.

YEARS
Ps 90: 4 A thousand **y** in your sight are like
90: 10 Our days may come to seventy **y**,
2Pe 3: 8 the Lord a day is like a thousand **y**,
Rev 20: 2 and bound him for a thousand **y**.

YESTERDAY
Heb 13: 8 Jesus Christ is the same **y** and today

YOKE (YOKED)
Mt 11: 29 Take my **y** upon you and learn

YOKED (YOKE)
2Co 6: 14 Do not be **y** together

YOUNG (YOUTH)
Ps 119: 9 can a **y** person stay on the path
1Ti 4: 12 down on you because you are **y**,

YOUTH (YOUNG)
Ps 103: 5 your **y** is renewed like the eagle's.
Ecc 12: 1 your Creator in the days of your **y**,
2Ti 2: 22 Flee the evil desires of **y** and

ZEAL
Jn 2: 17 **Z** for your house will consume me.
Ro 12: 11 Never be lacking in **z**, but keep

ZECHARIAH
1. Son of Jeroboam II; king of Israel (2Ki 15:8–12).
2. Post-exilic prophet who encouraged rebuilding of temple (Ezr 5:1; 6:14; Zec 1:1).
3. Father of John the Baptist (Lk 1:13; 3:2).

ZEDEKIAH
Mattaniah, son of Josiah (1Ch 3:15), made king of Judah by Nebuchadnezzar (2Ki 24:17—25:7; 2Ch 36:10–14; Jer 37–39; 52:1–11).

ZERUBBABEL
Descendant of David (1Ch 3:19; Mt 1:3). Led return from exile (Ezr 2–3; Ne 7:7; Hag 1–2; Zec 4).

ZIMRI
King of Israel (1Ki 16:9–20).

ZION
Ps 137: 3 "Sing us one of the songs of **Z**!"
Jer 50: 5 They will ask the way to **Z** and
Ro 9: 33 I lay in **Z** a stone that causes people
11: 26 "The deliverer will come from **Z**;

WORLD OF THE PATRIARCHS

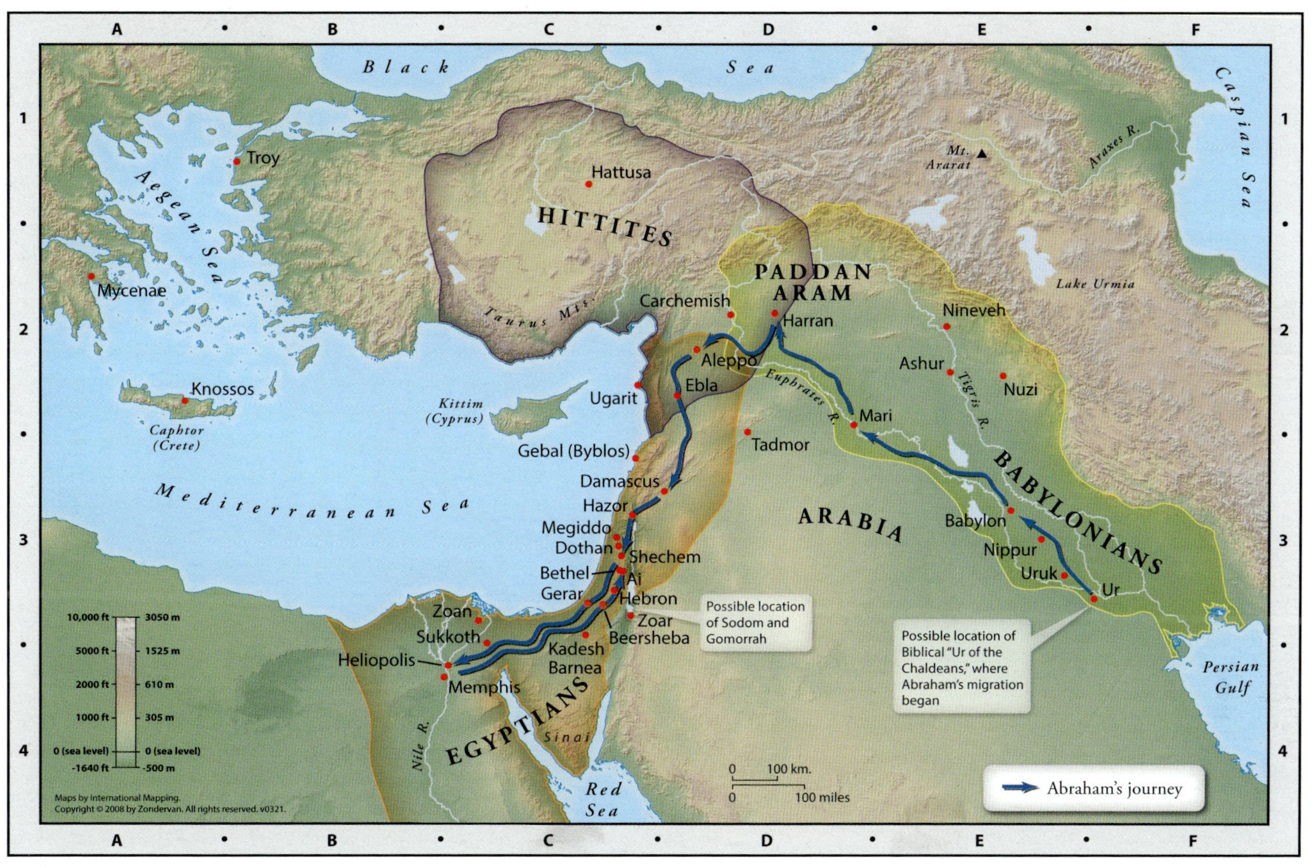

EXODUS AND CONQUEST OF CANAAN

LAND OF THE TWELVE TRIBES

KINGDOM OF DAVID AND SOLOMON

JESUS' MINISTRY

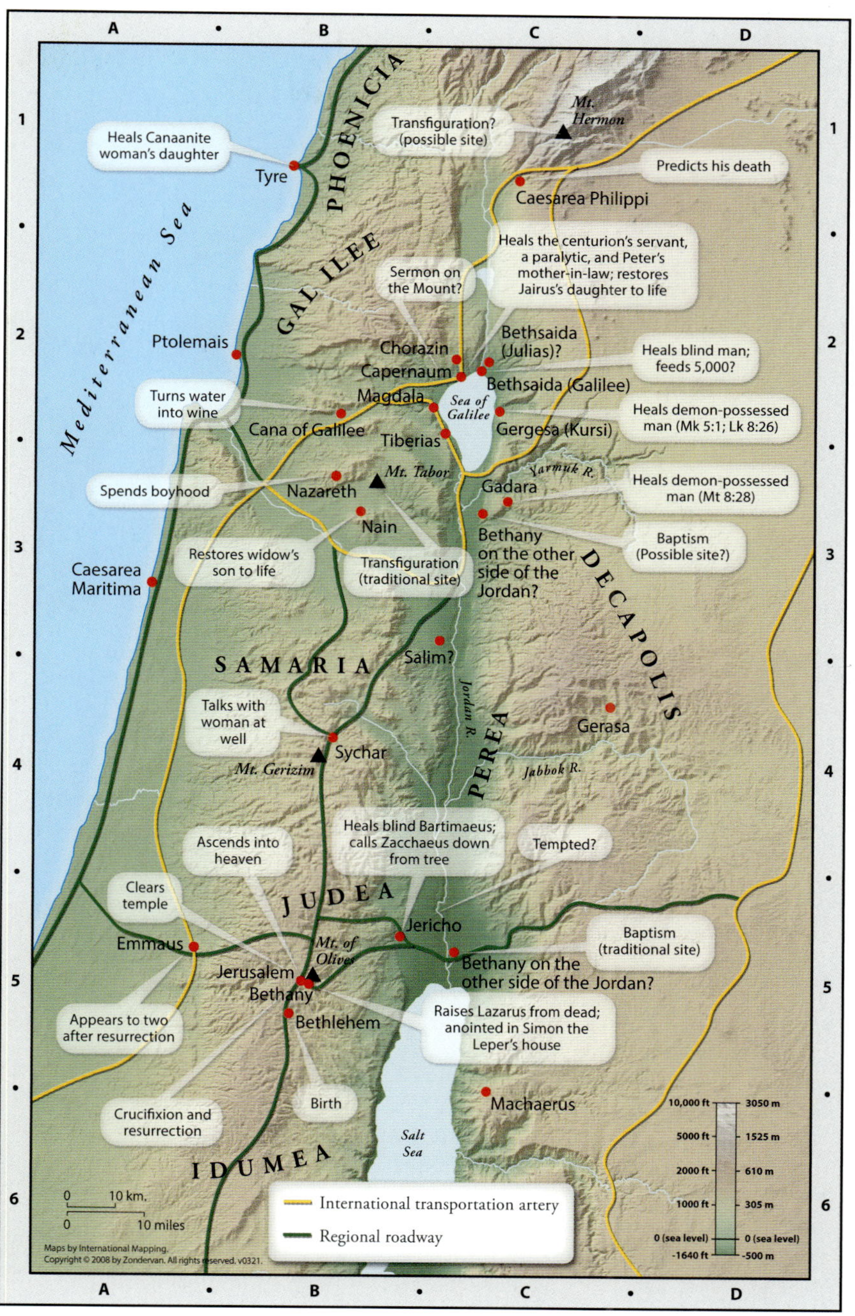

PAUL'S MISSIONARY JOURNEYS

DACIA
MOESIA
THRACE
Black Sea
BITHYNIA & PONTUS
GALATIA
CAPPADOCIA
ASIA
MYSIA
LYDIA
LYCAONIA
PISIDIA
PAMPHYLIA
LYCIA
CILICIA
COMMAGENE
SYRIA
PHOENICIA
ABILENE
JUDEA
ARABIA
EGYPT
ENAICA
Mediterranean Sea
Aegean Sea
Philippi
Neapolis
Samothrace
Apollonia?
Troas
Assos
Mitylene
Chios
Pergamum
Thyatira
Sardis
Smyrna
Ephesus
Philadelphia
Laodicea
Colossae
Samos
Miletus
Patmos
Cos
Cnidus
Rhodes
Patara
Myra
Attalia
Perga
Antioch (Pisidian)
Iconium
Lystra
Derbe
Tarsus
Issus
Seleucia Pieria
Aleppo
Antioch (Syrian)
Euphrates R.
Cyprus
Salamis
Paphos
Sidon
Tyre
Ptolemais
Damascus
Caesarea Maritima
Jordan R.
Jerusalem
Salt Sea
Nile R.
Red Sea
Delphi
Athens
Corinth
Cenchreae
Sparta
Mt. Olympus
Crete
Phoenix
Salmone
Lasea
Cauda
Fair Havens
10,000 ft
5000 ft
2000 ft
1000 ft
0 (sea level)
-1640 ft
3050 m
1525 m
610 m
305 m
0 (sea level)
-500 m
0
200 km.
0
200 miles
5
6
7
8
A
B
C
D
E
F

JERUSALEM IN THE TIME OF JESUS

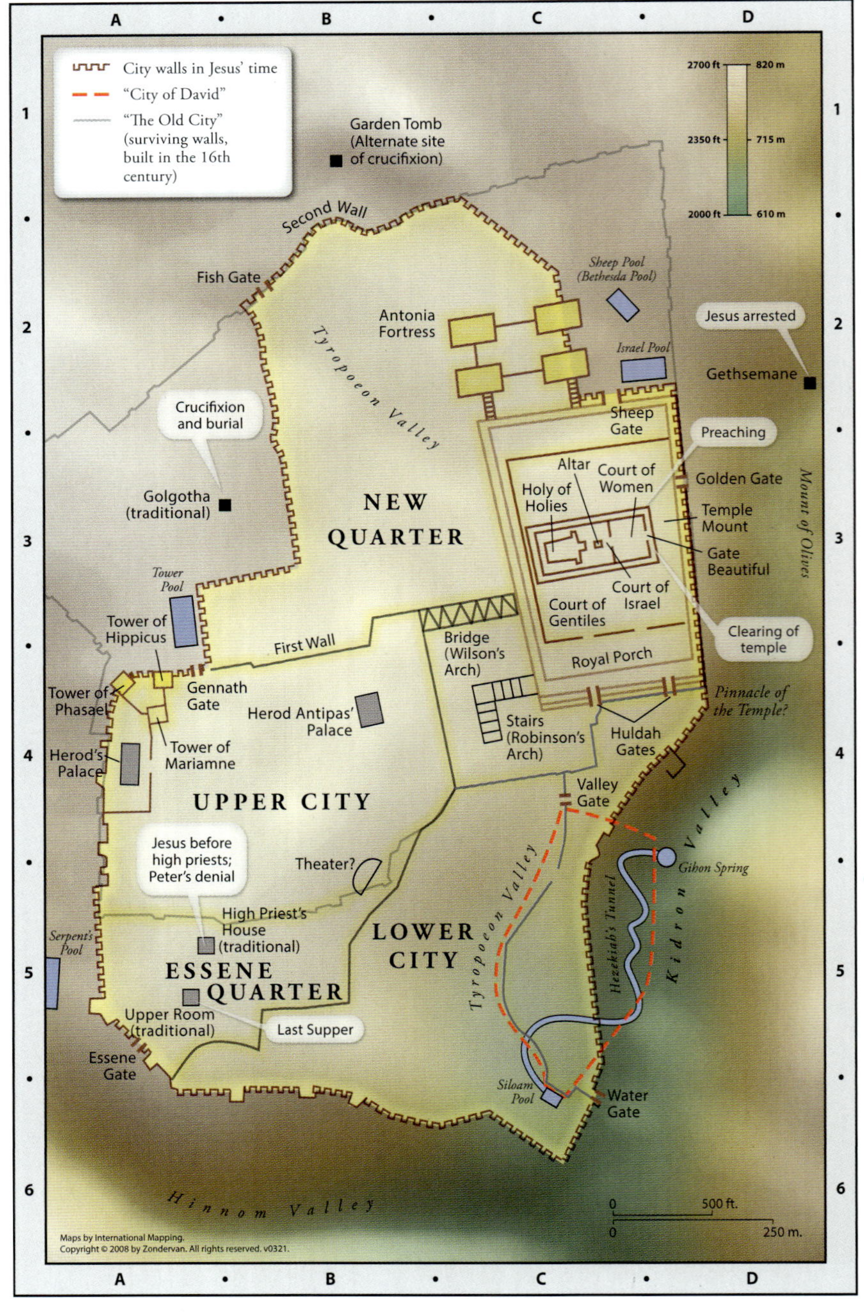